2005 County and City Extra

13th Edition

2005 County and City Extra
Annual Metro, City, and County Data Book
13th Edition

Editors
Deirdre A. Gaquin
Katherine A. DeBrandt

BERNAN PRESS
Lanham, MD

© 2005 Bernan Press, an imprint of Bernan Associates, a division of The Kraus Organization Limited.

No part of this publication may be reproduced, stored in a retrieval system, or transmitted, in any form or by any means, electronic, mechanical, photocopying, recording, or otherwise, without the prior written permission of the copyright holder. Bernan Press does not claim copyright in U.S. government information.

First edition 1992. 13th edition 2005.

ISBN: 1-886222-17-7

ISSN: 1059-9096

Composed and printed by Automated Graphic Systems, Inc., White Plains, MD, on acid-free paper that meets the American National Standards Institute Z39-48 standard.

2005   2004   4 3 2 1

BERNAN PRESS
4611-F Assembly Drive
Lanham, MD 20706
800-274-4447
email: info@bernan.com
www.bernanpress.com

Contents

ABOUT THE EDITORS

Deirdre A. Gaquin has been a data use consultant to private organizations, government agencies, and universities for over 20 years. Prior to that, she was Director of Data Access Services at Data Use & Access Laboratories, a pioneer in private sector distribution of federal statistical data. A former President of the Association of Public Data Users, Ms. Gaquin has served on numerous boards, panels, and task forces concerned with federal statistical data and has worked on four decennial censuses. She holds a Master of Urban Planning (MUP) degree from Hunter College. Ms. Gaquin is also an editor of Bernan Press' *The Who, What, and Where of America: Understanding the Census Results*; *Places, Towns and Townships*; and *The Almanac of American Education*.

Katherine A. DeBrandt is a senior data analyst with Bernan Press. She received her B.A. in political science from Colgate University. She is also a co-editor of *The Who, What, and Where of America: Understanding the Census Results*; *The Almanac of American Education*; and *Social Change in America: The Historical Handbook,* all published by Bernan Press.

ACKNOWLEDGEMENTS

County and City Extra: Annual Metro, City, and County Data Book is part of Bernan Press' *County and City Extra* series. The editors of *County and City Extra* extend their appreciation to Courtenay Slater and the late George Hall, the originators of this publication. Their initial contributions continue to enrich the *County and City Extra* series.

We are extremely grateful to Kara Prezocki, Bernan Press' production team leader, for managing the production aspects of this volume as well as for preparing the graphics and cover design. Production assistant Rebecca Zayas capably assisted Kara in coordinating this project. We also appreciate the assistance of staff editor Jacalyn Houston, who copy edited this volume. With support from Director of Publishing Tamera Wells-Lee; Automated Graphics Systems; and International Mapping Associates, Kara, Rebecca, and Jacalyn assisted the editors tremendously with finalizing this special edition.

As always, we are especially grateful to the many federal agency personnel who assisted us in obtaining the data, provided excellent resources on their Web sites, and patiently answered our questions.

INTRODUCTION

County and City Extra is an annual publication providing the most up-to-date statistical information available for every state, county, metropolitan area, congressional district, and for all cities in the United States with a 2000 population of 25,000 or more. Data for places including towns and cities under 25,000 population are published in a separate companion Bernan Press volume, *Places, Towns and Townships.* These two volumes are designed to meet the needs of libraries, businesses, and other organizations or individuals who desire convenient and timely sources of the most frequently sought information about geographic entities within the United States. Annual updating of *County and City Extra* ensures its stature as a reliable and authoritative source for statistical information.

County and City Extra and *Places, Towns and Townships* are large volumes, but not big enough to accommodate the wealth of information from the 2000 census. Two additional volumes in the *County and City Extra* series provide detailed data from the 2000 census. *County and City Extra—Special Decennial Census Edition* includes basic population and housing information from the complete count date. *The Who, What, and Where of America—Understanding the Census Results* includes social and economic details from the long form of the 2000 census.

New and Updated Information for the 2005 Edition

Data from the 2002 Census of Governments, which covers three major subject fields: government organization, public employment, and government finances, are included in this edition of *County and City Extra.* 2002 Census of Agriculture data are included for each county or county equivalent, state, and the nation. Both censuses are taken every five years, and update data last collected in 1997.

Table E (Congressional Districts) includes 2000 census data for the newly drawn congressional districts, as well as the representatives for the 109th Congress.

Table C (Metropolitan Areas) includes a completely new set of Metropolitan Areas, defined in 2003 by the Office of Management and Budget using new standards and data from the 2000 census. More details about the new Metropolitan Areas can be found in Appendix A.

The Census Bureau is phasing in a new survey, the American Community Survey (ACS), that is scheduled to replace the long form in future censuses. ACS data for all states are available for 2003 and are included in Table A (States).

In addition to the 2000 census and the ACS, updated data in this edition include 2003 population estimates for states, counties, metropolitan areas, and cities. Civilian labor force, crimes known to police, residential construction, and federal funds data have all been updated for states, counties, metropolitan areas, and cities. Vital statistics (births and deaths), income and poverty, personal income, and employment and payroll have been updated for states, counties, and metropolitan areas.

Although some of the state data are also included in Table B (States and Counties), the separate state data table offers several important features:

- Additional data not available at the county level can be found. Examples include population projections, health insurance coverage, number of immigrants, personal tax payments, information on health service firms not subject to federal tax, and exports by state of origin.

- Additional detail that exceeds the space limitations for counties can be found for states. Examples are age of householder, the more detailed information on employment in retail trade and services, and the expanded presentation of federal grants and payments to individuals by type.

- State totals can be found more quickly and compared more readily.

In addition to the new data and special features, users will find in this volume not only a careful selection of the most frequently used data from the 2000 census, but also the latest available data for population estimates, education, vital statistics, employment and unemployment, production by industry, health resources, crime, the distribution of federal funds, city government finances, weather statistics, and many other topics.

Subjects Covered and Volume Organization

Immediately following this introduction (pages **xiii–xv**) is a chart summarizing the **subjects covered** in each of the five tables in this volume. The **colored map portfolio** begins on page **xvii**.

The main body of this volume contains five basic parts. Each part includes a table that is preceded by highlights and rankings, as well as the complete column heading for the table. **Part A**, which begins on page **1**, contains data for states. **Part B**, beginning on page **51**, contains information for states and counties, while **Part C**, beginning on page **733**, contains similar information for metropolitan areas. The county geography codes include *county typology* codes from the Economic Research Service of the Department of Agriculture. These codes characterize counties by size of the largest place as well as other criteria for nonmetropolitan counties (see Appendix A for the definition of each code). Statistics for cities with a 2000 population of 25,000 or more can be found in **Part D**, which begins on page **895**. **Part E**, beginning on page **1151**, contains data for congressional districts of the 109th Congress. A contents page preceding each of tables B through E lists the page number where the data for a given geographic area begin. Counties and cities are listed alphabetically by state. Metropolitan areas are listed alphabetically, except that Metropolitan Divisions are listed alphabetically within the Metropolitan Statistical Area of which they are components. Congressional districts are listed in numeric order within state.

The Appendices include definitions of geographic concepts (**Appendix A**), sources and definitions of each data item included in this volume (**Appendix F**), a listing of metropolitan areas with their component counties delineated as of December 2003 listed alphabetically (**Appendix B**), a listing of Metropolitan and Micropolitan Areas and their component counties as of June 2003, with populations (**Appendix C**), a list of cities by county (**Appendix E**), and maps showing Congressional districts, counties, and selected places within each state (**Appendix D**).

Symbols and Terms

The following symbols are used in this volume:

D   Indicates that a figure has been withheld to avoid disclosure of information pertaining to a specific organization or individual, or because it does not meet statistical standards for publication.

NA   Indicates that data are not available.

X   Indicates that data are not applicable or meaningful for this geographic unit.

Figures that are less than half of the unit of measure shown appear in this volume as zero.

Sources

The great majority of the data in this volume have been obtained from federal government sources. A few items are obtained from private sources that are widely recognized as reliable basic sources of those particular data items. Complete source notes for each item are included in **Appendix F**, beginning on page F-1. Data included in this volume meet the publication standards established by the Census Bureau and the other federal statistical agencies from which they were obtained. Every effort has been made to select data that are accurate, meaningful, and useful. All data from censuses, surveys, and administrative records are subject to error arising from factors such as sampling variability, reporting errors, incomplete coverage, nonresponse, imputations, and processing error. Responsibility of the editors and publisher of this volume is limited to reasonable care in the reproduction and presentation of data obtained from sources believed to be reliable.

SUBJECTS COVERED, BY GEOGRAPHY TYPE

State data begin on page 24
County data begin on page 72
Metropolitan area data begin on page 796
City data begin on page 910
Congressional District data begin on page 1160

	Column Number				
Subject	Table A: States	Table B: States and Counties	Table C: Metropolitan Areas	Table D: Cities	Table E: Congressional Districts
Land area in 2000	1	1	1	1	1
Population:					
Total in 1980	29				
Total in 1990	30	20	20	22	
Total in 2000	31	21	21	23	2
Total in 2003	2	2	2	2	
Rank in 2003	3	3	3	3	
Per square kilometer	4	4	4	4	3
Race and Hispanic or Latino origin in 2000	40-45			5-11	4-10
Race and Hispanic or Latino origin in 2003	5-9	5-9	5-9		
Immigrants in 2003	28				
Foreign-born population in 2000	46				
Age distribution 2000	44-52			12-21	12-20
Age distribution 2003	10-18	10-18	10-18		
Percent female	19,53	19	19	25	21
Median age	20				
Population change 1980–1990	31				
Population change 1990–2000	33	22	22	6	
Population change 2000–2003	34	23	23	8	
Components of population change	35-39	24-26	24-26		
Households:					
Number in 2000	57	27	27	26	22
Number in 2003	21				
Change	22,58	28	28	27	
Persons per household	23,59	29	29	28	23
Age of householder	24-27				
Female-family householder	60	30	30	29	24
One-person household	61	31	31	30	25
Vital Statistics:					
Births, birth rate	62-63	32-33	32-33		
Deaths, death rate	64,66	34,36	34,36		
Age-adjusted death rate	67				
Infant deaths, infant death rate	65,68	35,37	35,37		
Health:					
Physicians	69-70	38-39	38-39		
Hospitals	71-73	40-42	40-42		
Persons in group quarters				31-34	26-28
Persons in nursing homes				33	27
Medicare enrollees	74	43	43		
Persons lacking health insurance	99				
Children lacking health insurance	100				
Crime:					
Serious	75-76	44-45	44-45	35-36	
Violent	77	46	46	37	
Property	78	47	47	38	

SUBJECTS COVERED, BY GEOGRAPHY TYPE — Continued

State data begin on page 24
County data begin on page 72
Metropolitan area data begin on page 796
City data begin on page 910
Congressional District data begin on page 1160

Subject	Column Number				
	Table A: States	Table B: States and Counties	Table C: Metropolitan Areas	Table D: Cities	Table E: Congressional Districts
Education:					
Enrollment	79-80	48-49	48-49	39-40	29-30
Attainment	81-84	50-51	50-51	41-42	31-32
Local government expenditures	85-86	52-53	52-53		
Income and Personal Taxes					
Per capita and personal income, 2003	87-92,101-104	54-58,62-65	54-57,62-65	43-46	33-35
Poverty	93-95	59	59	47-49	36-37
Children in poverty	97	60-61	60-61		
Seniors in poverty	98				
Personal income by type	105-113	66-74	66-74		
Personal tax payments	115				
Disposable personal income	116-117				
Earnings by industry	118-126	75-83	75-83		
Gross state product	127				
Transfer payments by type	108-113	69-74	69-74		
Social Security recipients	142-143	84-85	84-85		
Supplemental Security Income recipients	144	86	86		
Construction and Housing:					
Housing units in 2000	132,134				38-43
Housing units in 2003	127,129	87,89	87,89	50,52-60	
Percent change in housing units	128,133	88	88	51	
Percent owner-occupied	130,135	90	90	57	40
Median or mean value, owner costs	131,136-138	91-93	91-93		41-43
Median or mean gross rent, rent/income ratio	139-140	94-95	94-95		44-45
Substandard units	141	96	96		46
Value of new residential construction	283-286	133-134	133-134	69-71	
Labor Force and Employment:					
Civilian labor force, change in labor force	148-150	97-98	97-98	61-62	47
Unemployment, unemployment rate	151-152	99-100	99-100	63-64	48-49
Employment in selected occupations	145-147	101-103	101-103	65-67	50-52
Employment disabled persons				68	53
Nonfarm establishments		104	104		
Earnings and employment in manufacturing	155-157				
Employment by industry	153-154,158-163	105-110	105-110		
Payroll		111-112	111-112		
Agriculture:					
Farms	164-166	113-115	113-115		
Farm operators	167	116	116		
Acreage	168-172	117-121	117-121		
Value of land and buildings	173-174	122-123	122-123		
Value of machinery and equipment	175	124	124		
Value of agricultural sales	176-181	125-130	125-130		
Government payments		131,132	131,132		
Land and Water:					
Land owned by the federal government	182				
Developed land	183				
Water use	184				

SUBJECTS COVERED, BY GEOGRAPHY TYPE — Continued

State data begin on page 24
County data begin on page 72
Metropolitan area data begin on page 796
City data begin on page 910
Congressional District data begin on page 1160

Subject	Column Number				
	Table A: States	Table B: States and Counties	Table C: Metropolitan Areas	Table D: Cities	Table E: Congressional Districts
Manufacturing:	185-194 273-274	151-154	151-154	88-91	
Construction:	195-198 271-272				
Wholesale Trade:	199-202 275-276	135-138	135-138	72-75	
Retail Trade:	203-210 277-278	139-142	139-142	76-79	
Transportation and Warehousing:	211-214				
Finance and Insurance:	215-218 279-280				
Real Estate and Rental and Leasing:	217-222 279-280	143-146	143-146	80-83	
Information:	223-230				
Utilities:	231-234				
Professional, Scientific, and Technical Services:	235-242 281-282	147-150	147-150	84-87	
Arts, Entertainment, and Recreation:	243-246			96-99	
Health Care and Social Assistance:	247-258 281-282	159-162	159-162	100-103	
Accommodation and Food Services:	259-263	155-158	155-158	92-95	
Other Services:	264-270 281-282	163-166	163-166	104-107	
Export of goods produced	287-289				
Federal Funds and Grants:					
Payments to individuals	294-300	168-170	168-170	115-116	
Total, salaries and wages	290-291	167,171	167,171		
Procurement contract awards	292-293	172-173	172-173	108-109	
Grants by purpose	301-307	174-177	174-177	110-114	
Government Finances:					
Revenue	308-315	178-179	178-179	117-119	
Taxes	312-315	180-182	180-182	120-123	
Expenditures	316-324	183-189	183-189	124-136	
Debt outstanding	325-326	190-191	190-191	137-139	
Government Employment:					
Federal civilian and military	327-328	192-193	192-193		
State and/or local	329	194	194	140	
Election results	330-332	195-197	195-197		
Climate				141-147	

Population Change
2000–2003

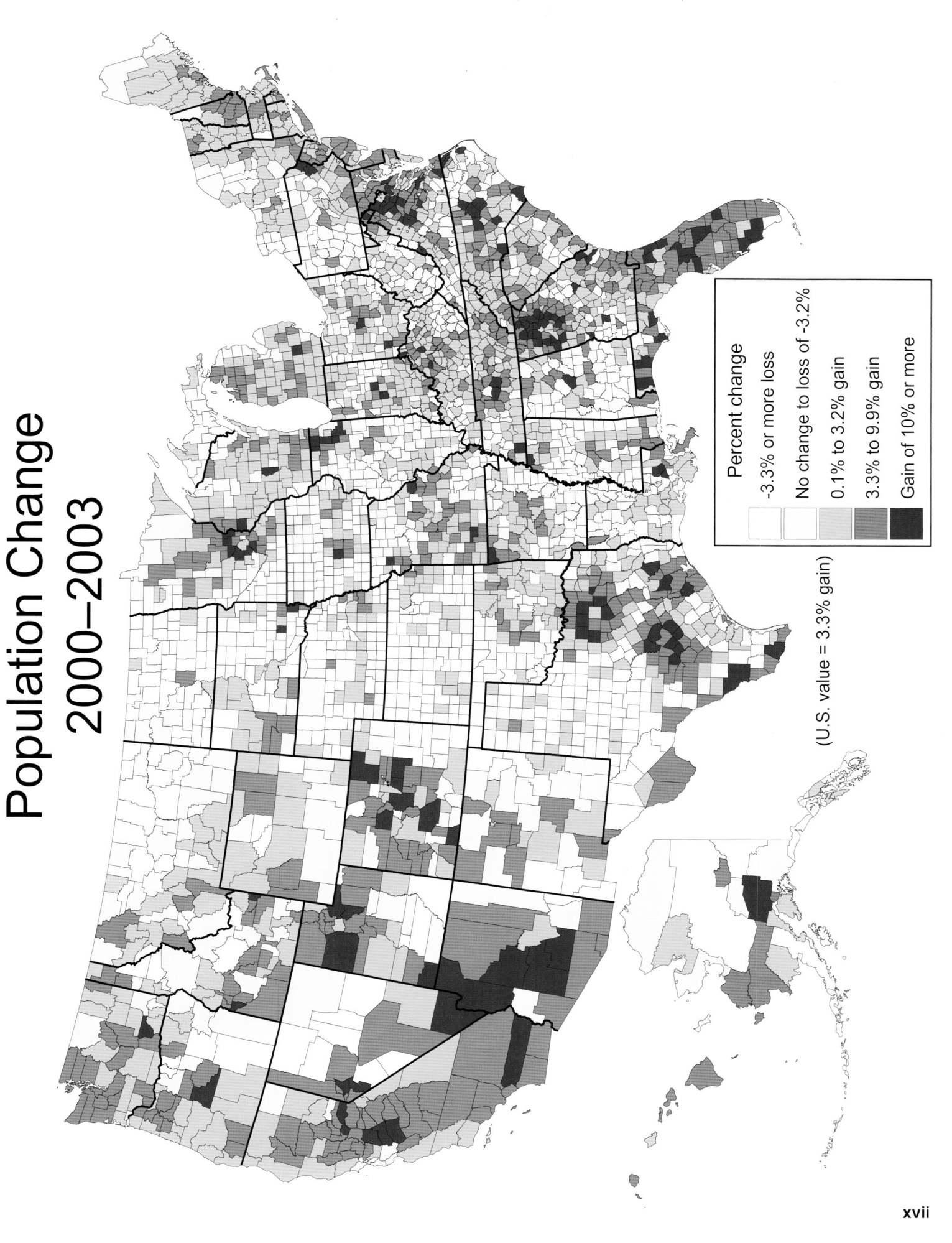

Percent change

	-3.3% or more loss
	No change to loss of -3.2%
	0.1% to 3.2% gain
	3.3% to 9.9% gain
	Gain of 10% or more

(U.S. value = 3.3% gain)

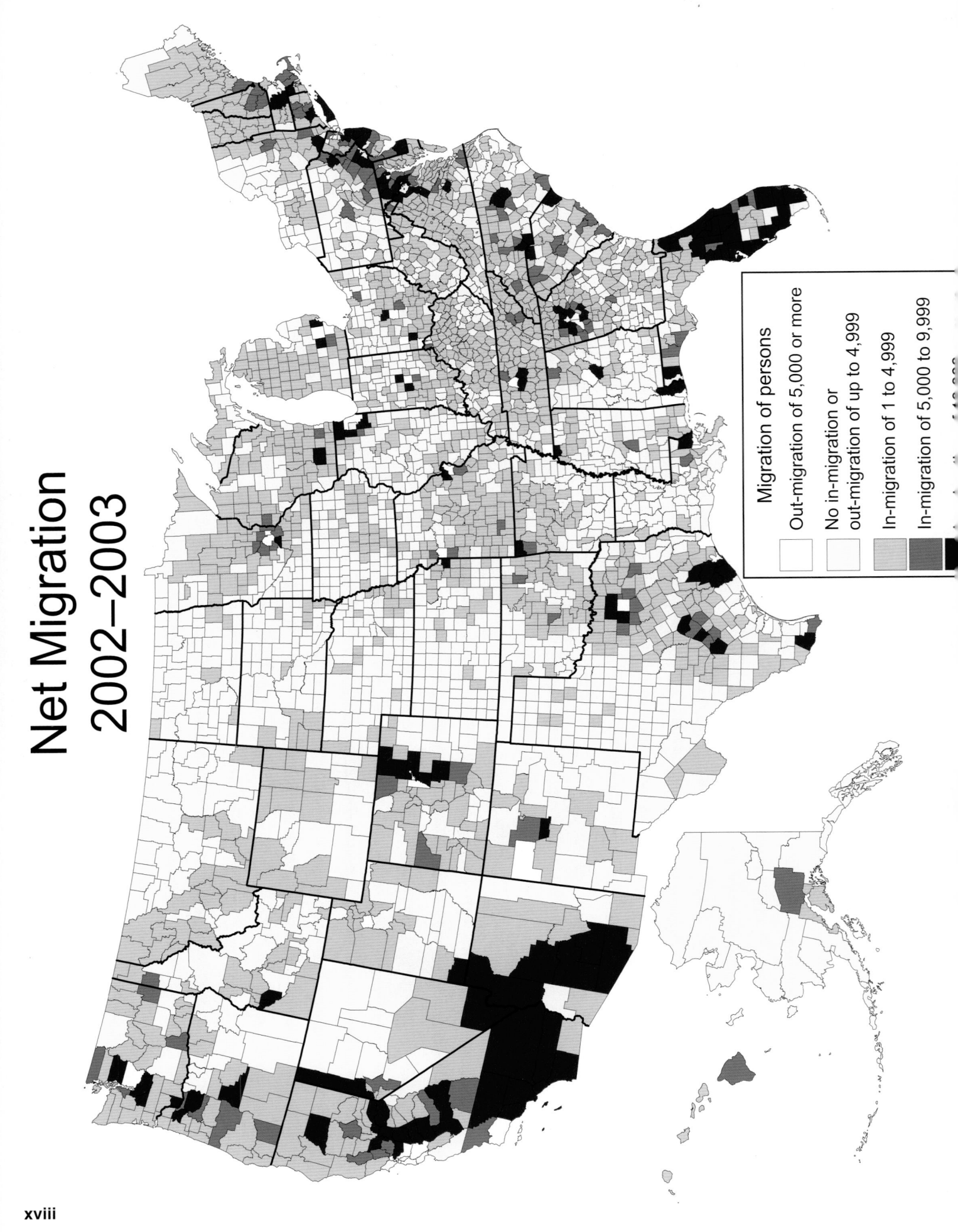

Net Migration
2002–2003

Migration of persons

Out-migration of 5,000 or more

No in-migration or
out-migration of up to 4,999

In-migration of 1 to 4,999

In-migration of 5,000 to 9,999

xviii

White, Not Hispanic or Latino, Population 2003

Percent White, not Hispanic or Latino

- Less than 50.0%
- 50.0% to 68.9%
- 69.0% to 84.9%
- 85.0% to 94.9%
- 95.0% or more

(U.S. value = 69.0%)

Black, Not Hispanic or Latino, Population 2003

Percent Black,
not Hispanic or Latino

Less than 1.0%

1.0% to 4.9%

5.0% to 12.6%

12.7% to 49.9%

(U.S. value = 12.7%)

xx

Hispanic or Latino Population 2003

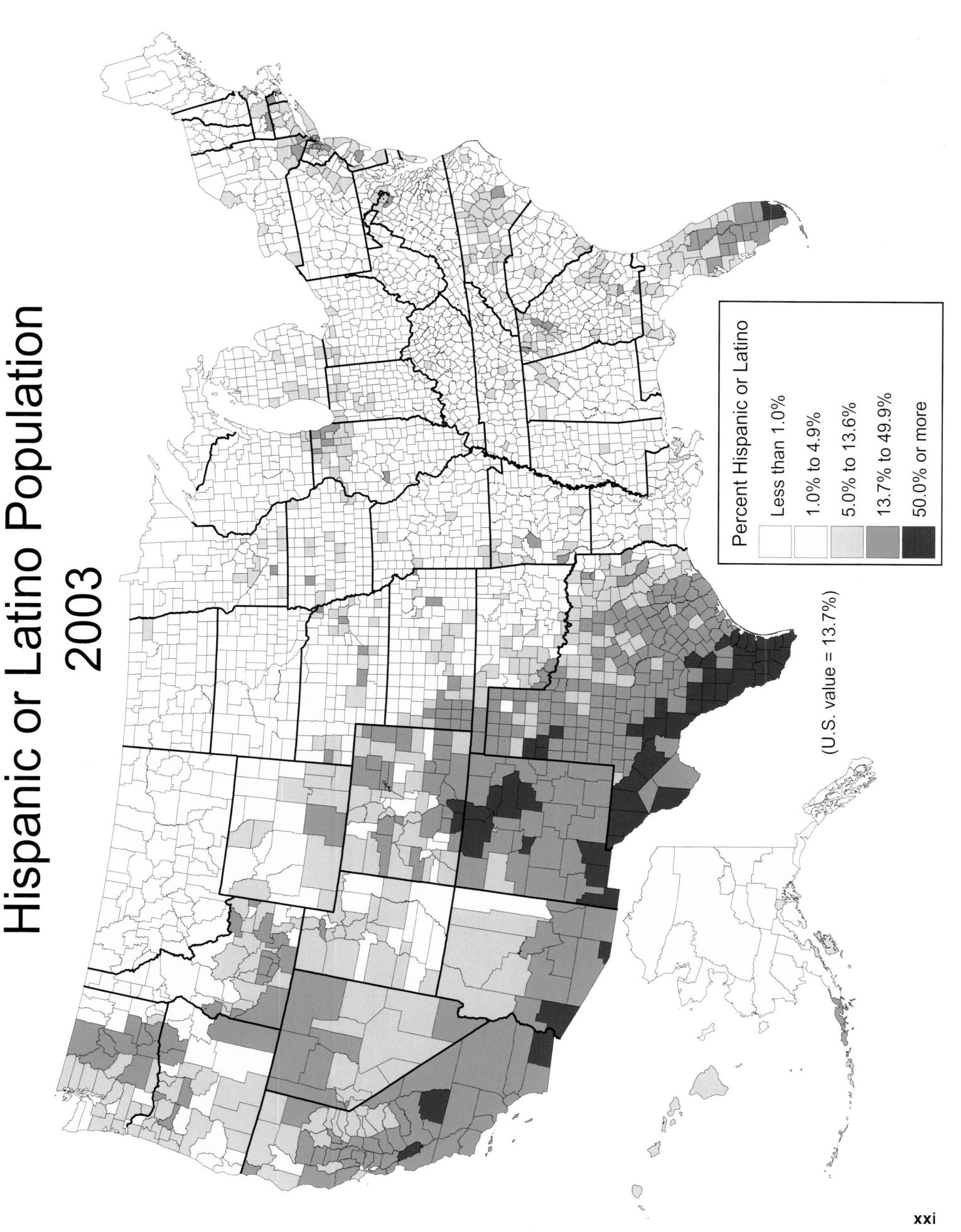

Percent Hispanic or Latino

Less than 1.0%
1.0% to 4.9%
5.0% to 13.6%
13.7% to 49.9%
50.0% or more

(U.S. value = 13.7%)

Population Under 18 Years Old

2003

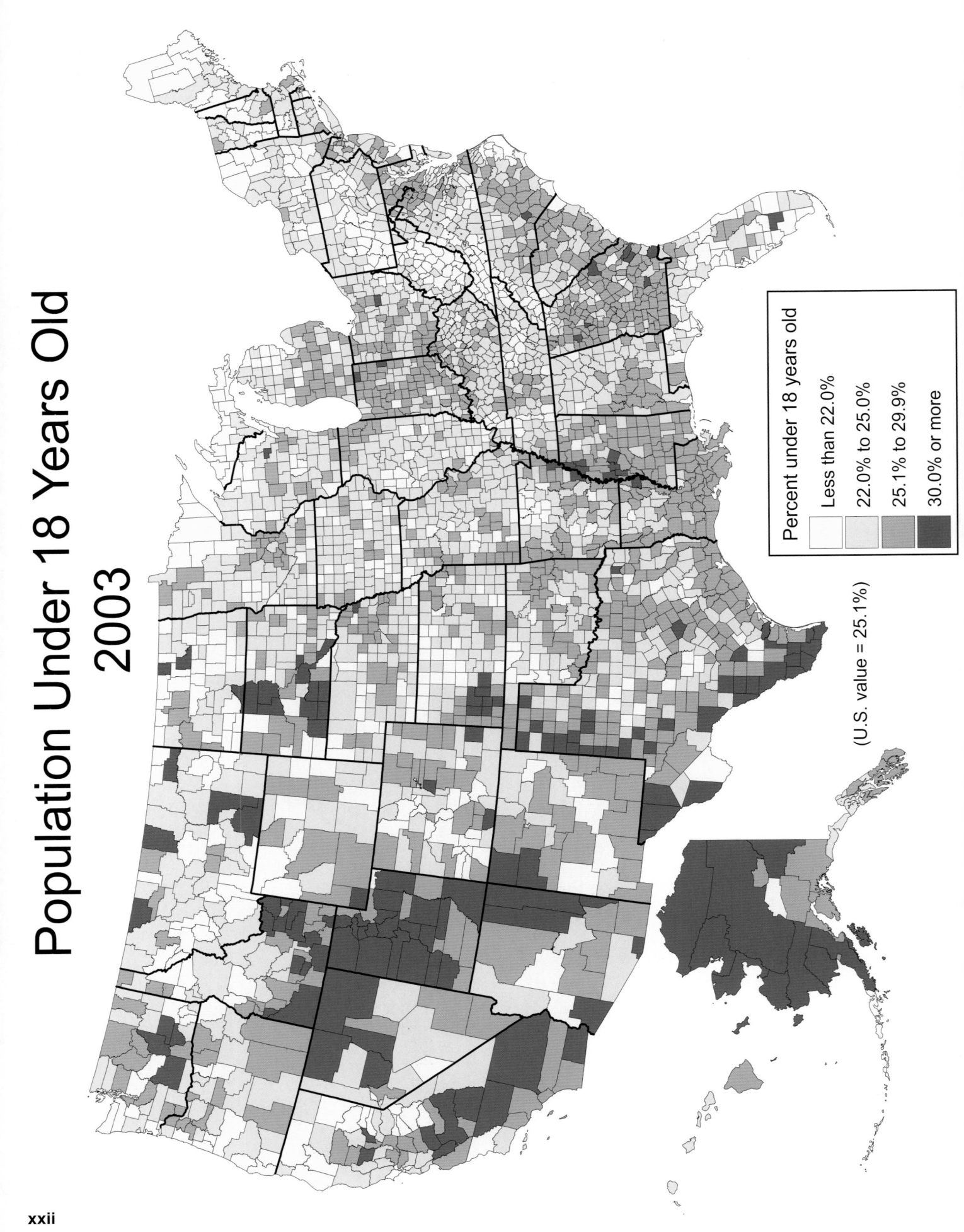

Percent under 18 years old

- Less than 22.0%
- 22.0% to 25.0%
- 25.1% to 29.9%
- 30.0% or more

(U.S. value = 25.1%)

Population 65 Years Old and Over

2003

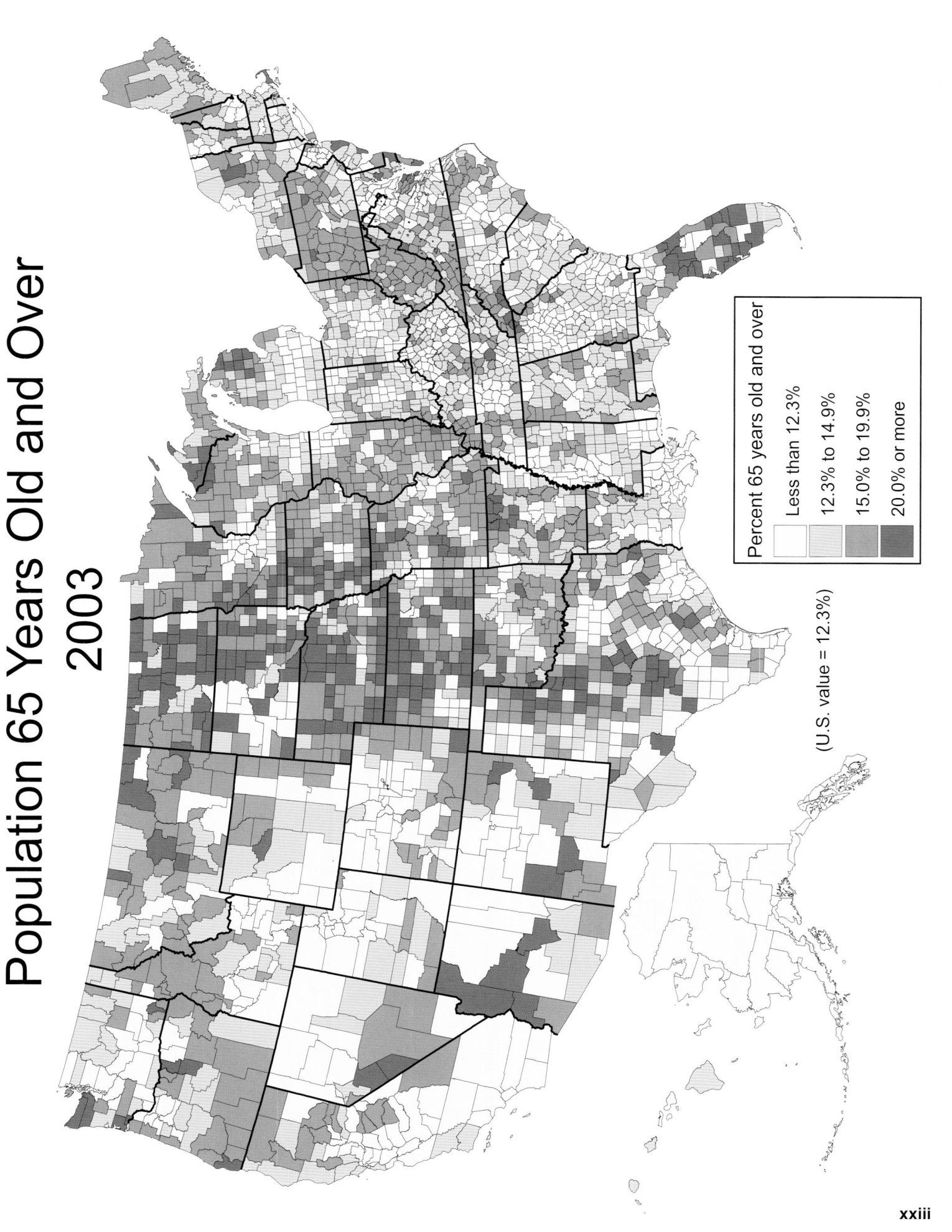

Percent 65 years old and over

- Less than 12.3%
- 12.3% to 14.9%
- 15.0% to 19.9%
- 20.0% or more

(U.S. value = 12.3%)

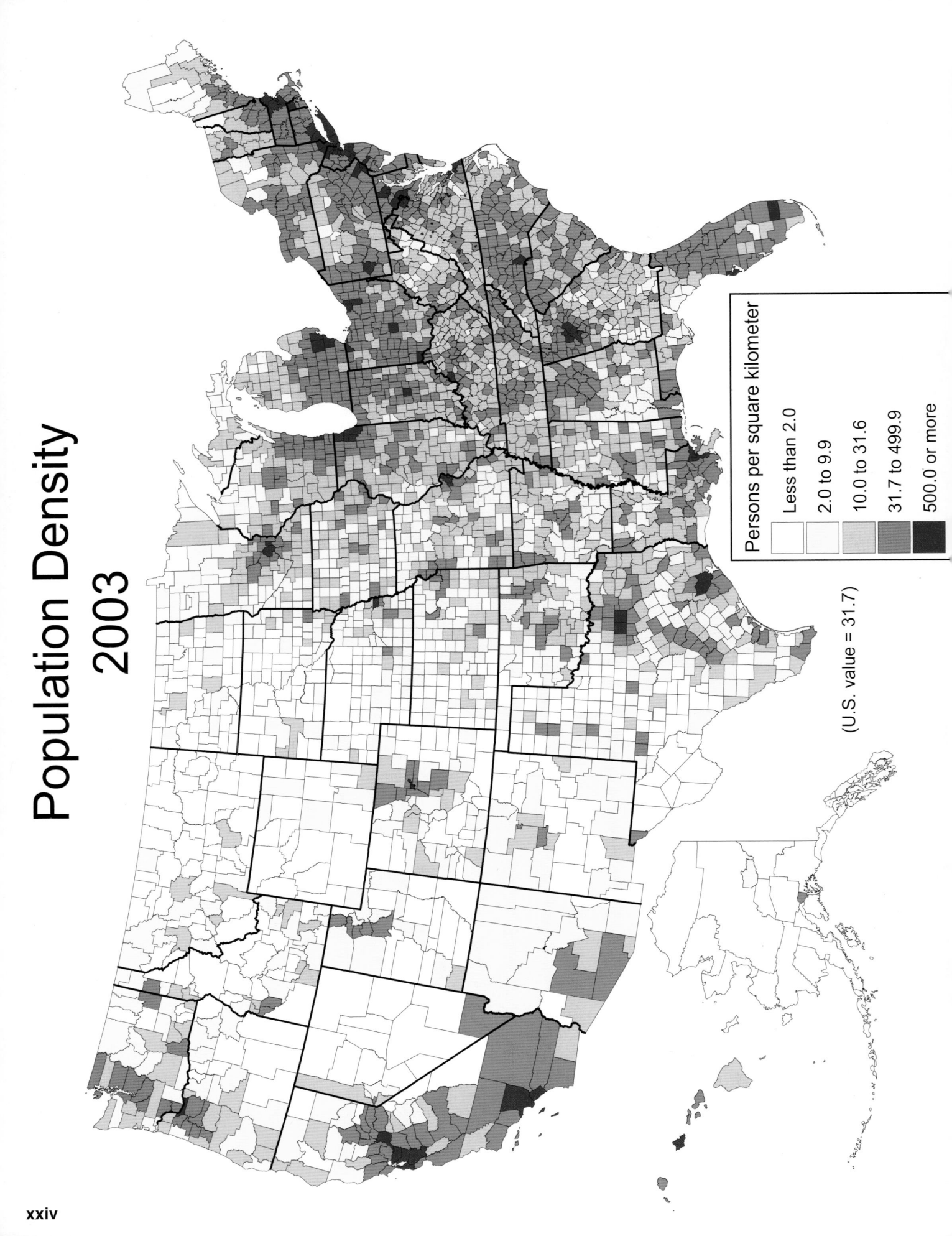

Population Density
2003

Persons per square kilometer

	Less than 2.0
	2.0 to 9.9
	10.0 to 31.6
	31.7 to 499.9
	500.0 or more

(U.S. value = 31.7)

Educational Expenditures per Student
2001

(U.S. value = $7,426)

Expenditures per student

	Expenditures per student
	Less than $6,000
	$6,000 to $7,425
	$7,426 to $8,999
	$9,000 or more

Population with a High School Diploma or Less
2000

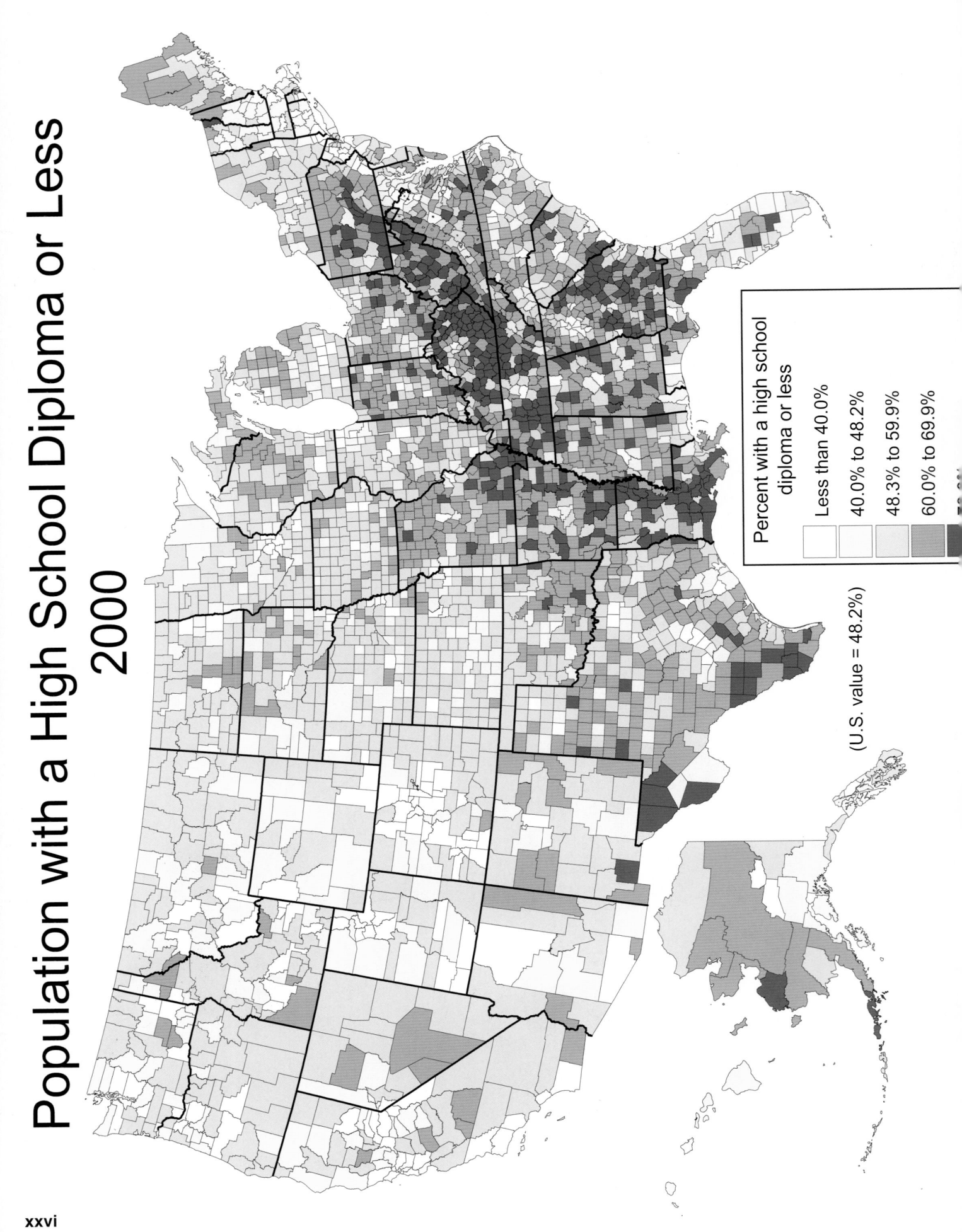

Percent with a high school
diploma or less

Less than 40.0%
40.0% to 48.2%
48.3% to 59.9%
60.0% to 69.9%

(U.S. value = 48.2%)

Population with a Bachelor's Degree or More
2000

Percent with a bachelor's degree or more

Less than 10.0%
10.0% to 13.9%
14.0% to 18.9%
19.0% to 24.3%
24.4% or more

(U.S. value = 24.4%)

Note: Persons 25 years old and over.

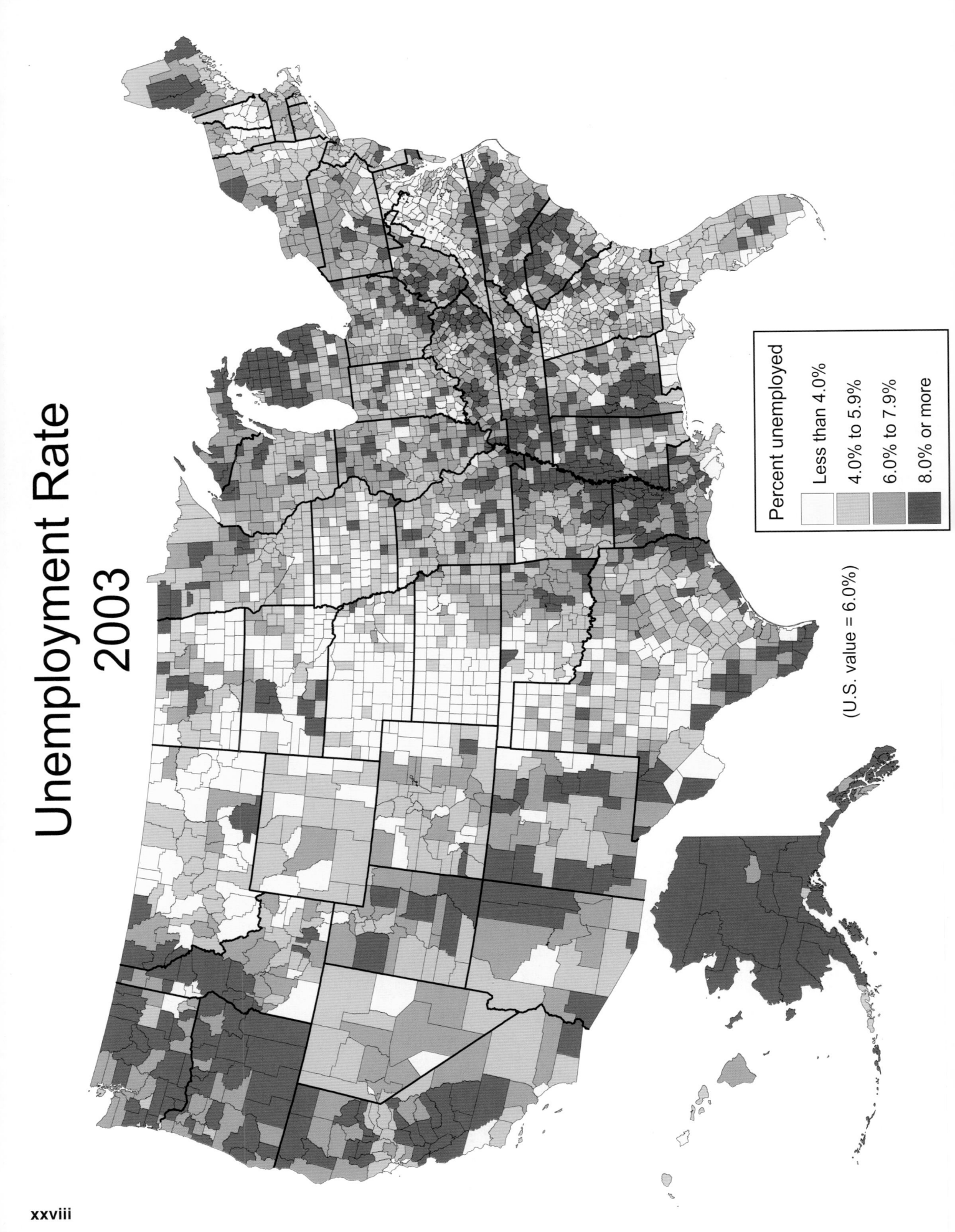

Unemployment Rate 2003

Percent unemployed

Less than 4.0%
4.0% to 5.9%
6.0% to 7.9%
8.0% or more

(U.S. value = 6.0%)

Land in Farms
2002

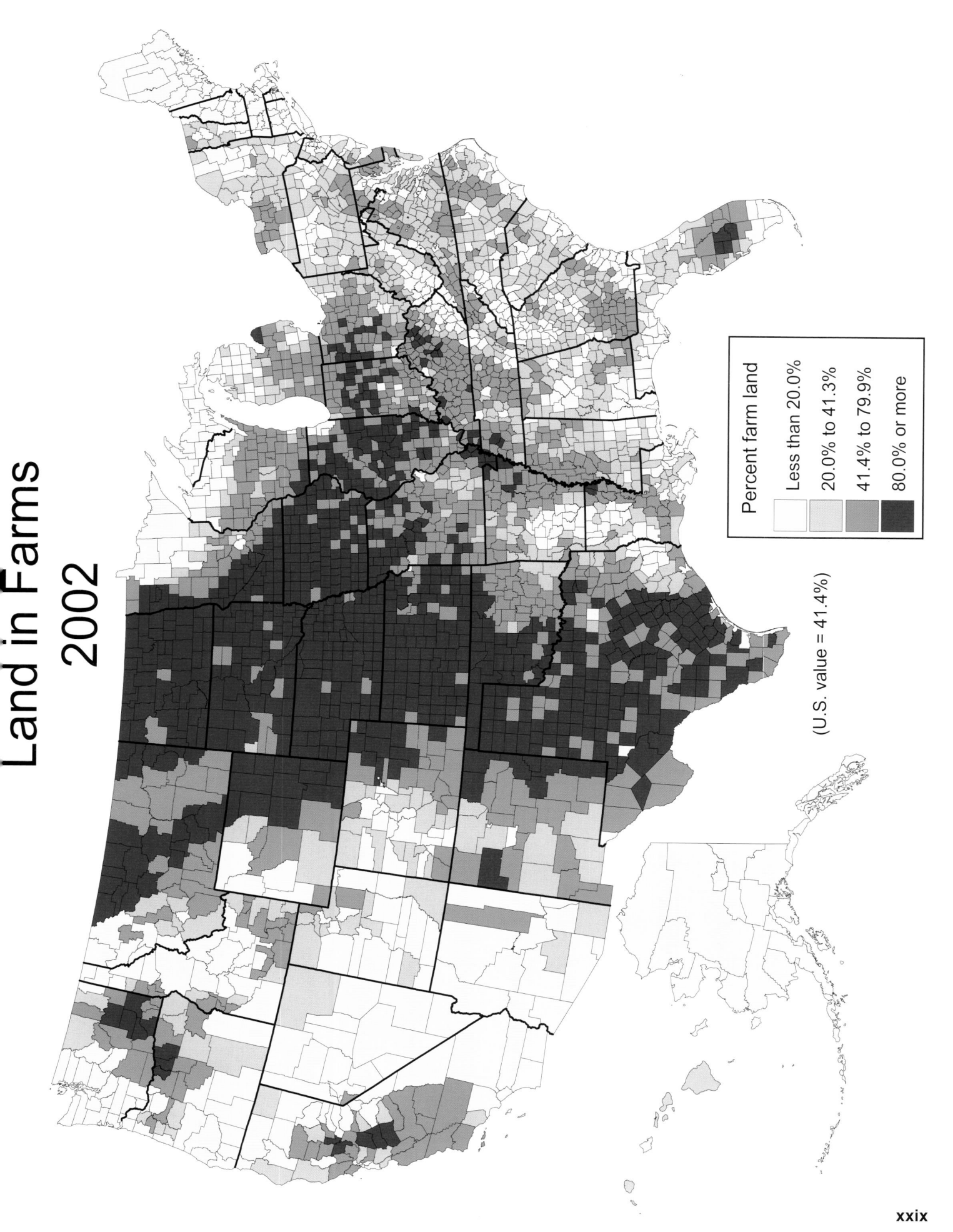

Percent farm land

Less than 20.0%
20.0% to 41.3%
41.4% to 79.9%
80.0% or more

(U.S. value = 41.4%)

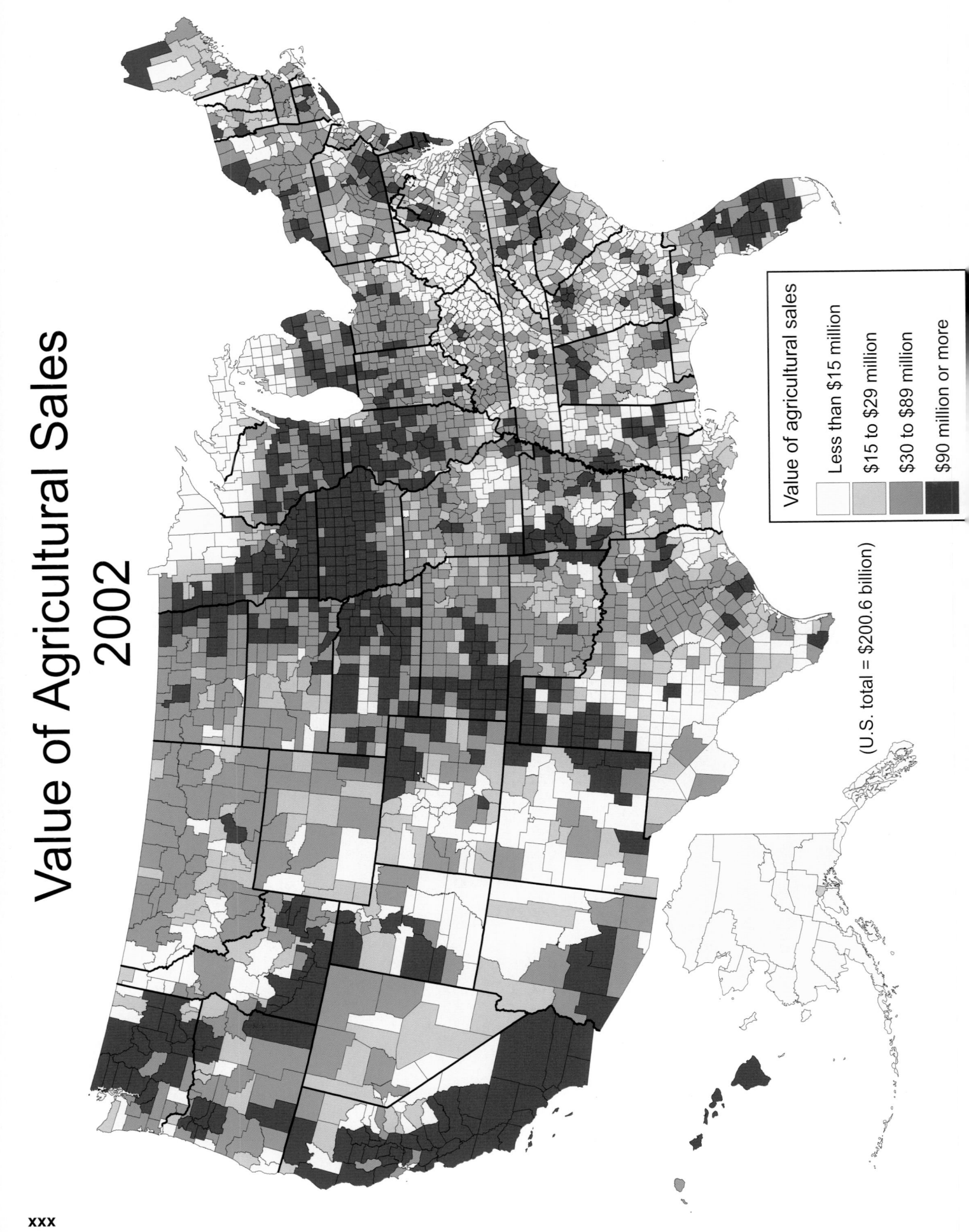

Value of Agricultural Sales
2002

Value of agricultural sales

- Less than $15 million
- $15 to $29 million
- $30 to $89 million
- $90 million or more

(U.S. total = $200.6 billion)

Farm Subsidies 2002

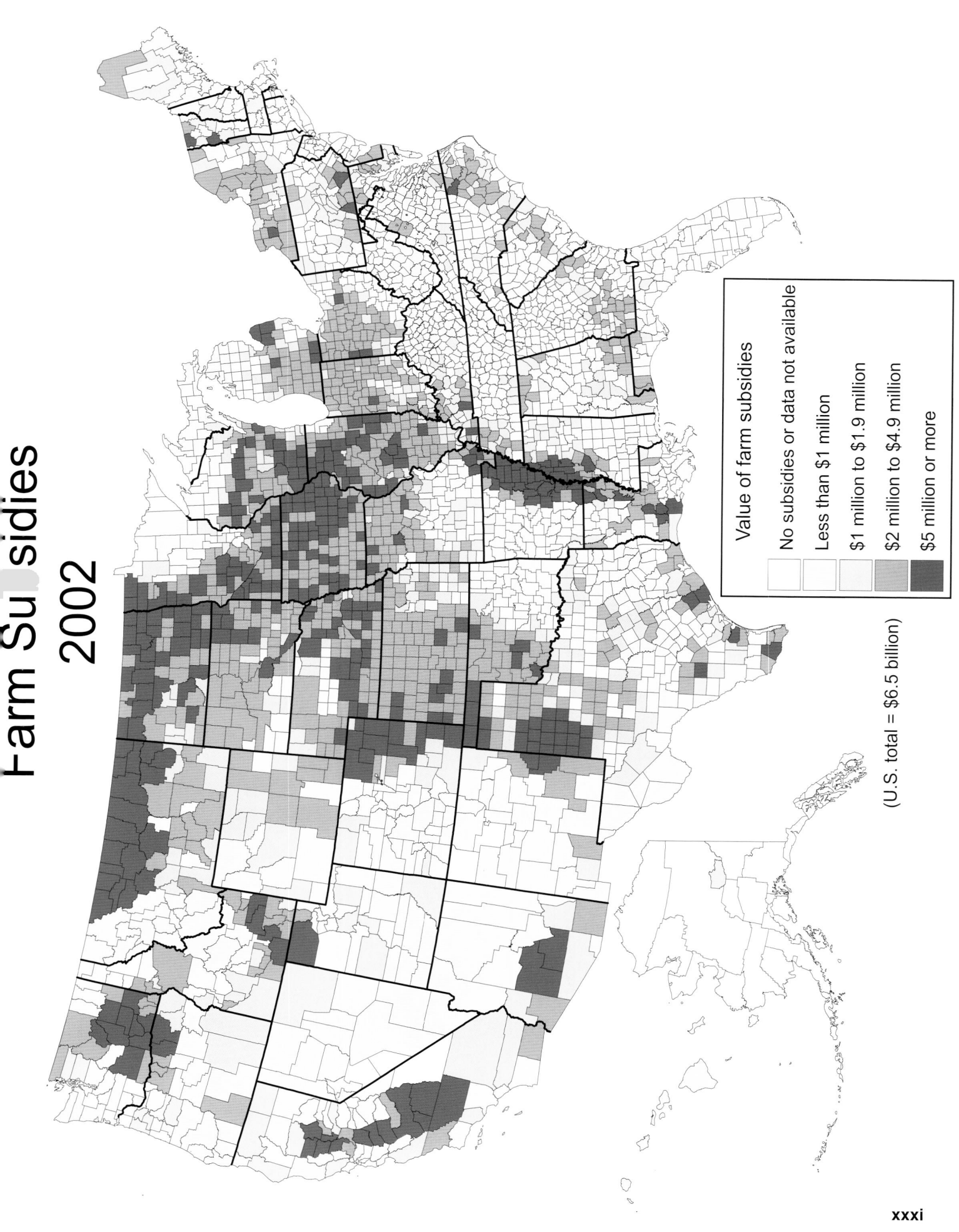

Value of farm subsidies

No subsidies or data not available

Less than $1 million

$1 million to $1.9 million

$2 million to $4.9 million

$5 million or more

(U.S. total = $6.5 billion)

Margin of Victory in Presidential Election

2004

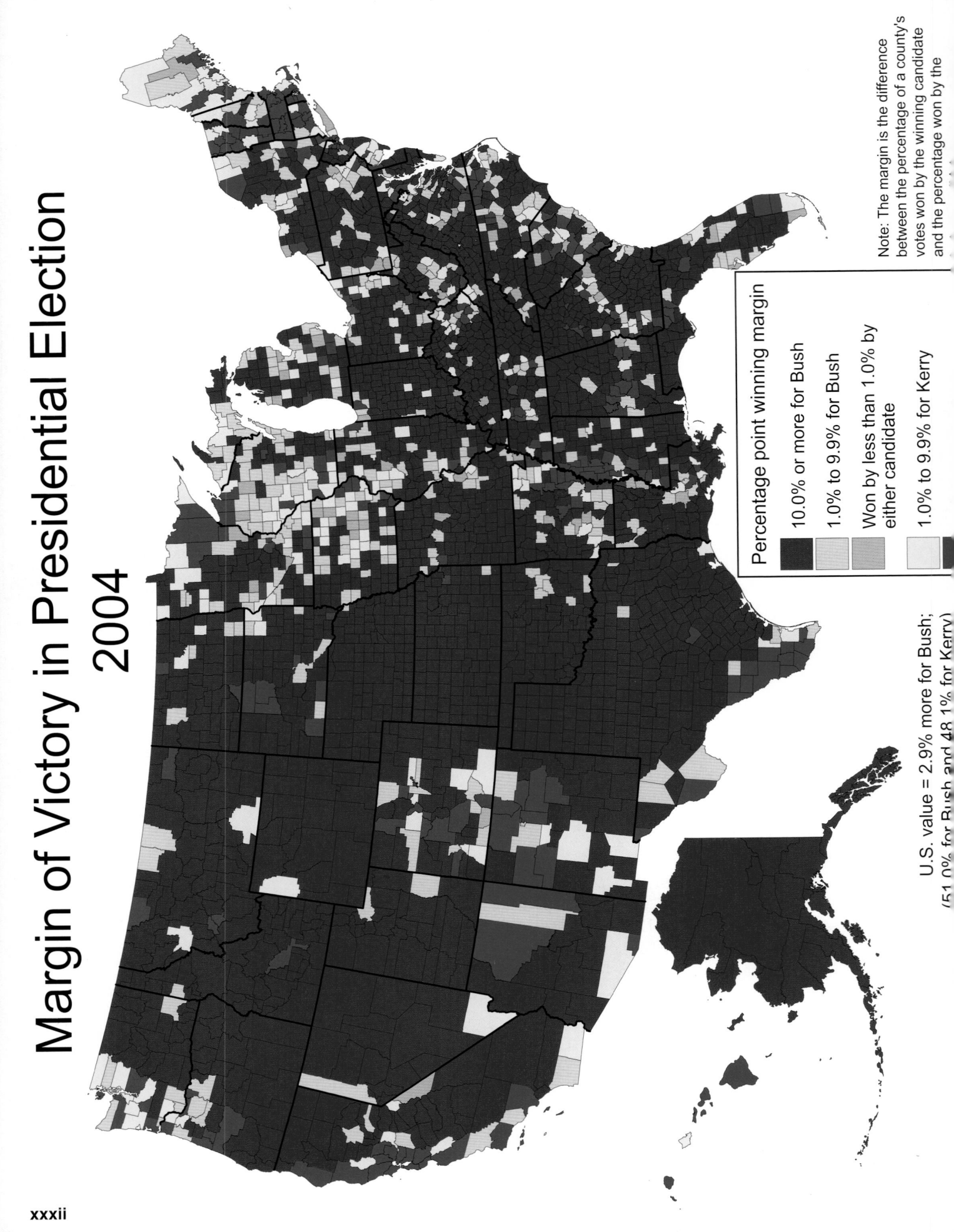

Percentage point winning margin

- 10.0% or more for Bush
- 1.0% to 9.9% for Bush
- Won by less than 1.0% by either candidate
- 1.0% to 9.9% for Kerry

Note: The margin is the difference between the percentage of a county's votes won by the winning candidate and the percentage won by the

U.S. value = 2.9% more for Bush; (51.0% for Bush and 48.1% for Kerry)

PART A:

States

(For explanation of symbols, see page xii)

Table A Highlights and Rankings

There is no simple relationship between population size and land area for most of the geographic entities for which data are presented here. At the state level, for example, population in 2003 ranged from a high of 35.5 million for California; that is more than 70 times the low of 501,000 for Wyoming. (The median population for states—with half having a larger and half a smaller populace—is about 4.1 million people.) While California is also one of our largest states in land area (ranking third), Alaska is by far the largest state in area, more than twice the size of Texas, even though its population rank is close to the bottom (47th). Texas is the second largest state in both land area and total population. At the other end of the geographic size spectrum are many of the New England states (with Rhode Island the smallest), as well as Delaware and Hawaii. As a consequence of the differing area size and population rank, New Jersey is the most densely settled state, with about 450 persons per square kilometer of land, while Alaska is the least densely settled, with under one person (0.4) per square kilometer. California, which is the state with the largest population and third largest land area, ranks 13th in terms of population density (with about 88 persons per square kilometer).

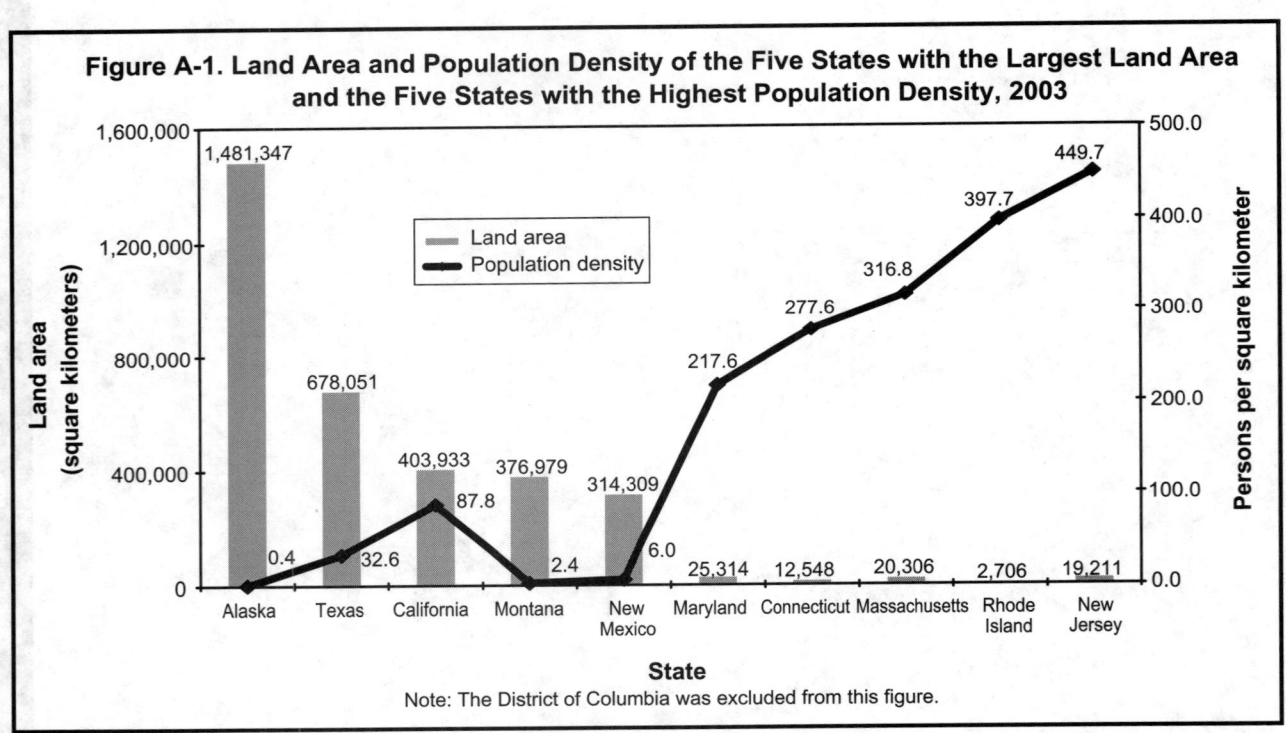

Figure A-1. Land Area and Population Density of the Five States with the Largest Land Area and the Five States with the Highest Population Density, 2003

Note: The District of Columbia was excluded from this figure.

2

States and the District of Columbia
Selected Rankings

Population, 2003			Total land area, 2000				Population density, 2003			
Population rank	State	Population [col 2]	Population rank	Land area rank	State	Land area (square kilometers) [col 1]	Population rank	Density rank	State	Density (per square kilometer) [col 4]
X	United States	290 809 777	X	X	United States	9 161 924	X	X	United States	31.7
1	California	35 484 453	47	1	Alaska	1 481 347	50	1	District of Columbia	3 543.3
2	Texas	22 118 509	2	2	Texas	678 051	10	2	New Jersey	449.7
3	New York	19 190 115	1	3	California	403 933	43	3	Rhode Island	397.7
4	Florida	17 019 068	44	4	Montana	376 979	13	4	Massachusetts	316.8
5	Illinois	12 653 544	36	5	New Mexico	314 309	29	5	Connecticut	277.6
6	Pennsylvania	12 365 455	18	6	Arizona	294 312	19	6	Maryland	217.6
7	Ohio	11 435 798	35	7	Nevada	284 448	45	7	Delaware	161.6
8	Michigan	10 079 985	22	8	Colorado	268 627	3	8	New York	156.9
9	Georgia	8 684 715	51	9	Wyoming	251 489	4	9	Florida	121.9
10	New Jersey	8 638 396	27	10	Oregon	248 631	7	10	Ohio	107.8
11	North Carolina	8 407 248	39	11	Idaho	214 314	6	11	Pennsylvania	106.5
12	Virginia	7 386 330	34	12	Utah	212 751	5	12	Illinois	87.9
13	Massachusetts	6 433 422	33	13	Kansas	211 900	1	13	California	87.8
14	Indiana	6 195 643	21	14	Minnesota	206 189	42	14	Hawaii	75.6
15	Washington	6 131 445	38	15	Nebraska	199 099	12	15	Virginia	72.0
16	Tennessee	5 841 748	46	16	South Dakota	196 540	8	16	Michigan	68.5
17	Missouri	5 704 484	48	17	North Dakota	178 647	14	17	Indiana	66.7
18	Arizona	5 580 811	17	18	Missouri	178 414	11	18	North Carolina	66.6
19	Maryland	5 508 909	28	19	Oklahoma	177 847	9	19	Georgia	57.9
20	Wisconsin	5 472 299	15	20	Washington	172 348	41	20	New Hampshire	55.4
21	Minnesota	5 059 375	9	21	Georgia	149 976	16	21	Tennessee	54.7
22	Colorado	4 550 688	8	22	Michigan	147 121	25	22	South Carolina	53.2
23	Alabama	4 500 752	30	23	Iowa	144 701	26	23	Kentucky	40.0
24	Louisiana	4 496 334	5	24	Illinois	143 961	24	24	Louisiana	39.9
25	South Carolina	4 147 152	20	25	Wisconsin	140 663	20	25	Wisconsin	38.9
26	Kentucky	4 117 827	4	26	Florida	139 670	15	26	Washington	35.6
27	Oregon	3 559 596	32	27	Arkansas	134 856	23	27	Alabama	34.2
28	Oklahoma	3 511 532	23	28	Alabama	131 426	2	28	Texas	32.6
29	Connecticut	3 483 372	11	29	North Carolina	126 161	17	29	Missouri	32.0
30	Iowa	2 944 062	3	30	New York	122 283	37	30	West Virginia	29.0
31	Mississippi	2 881 281	31	31	Mississippi	121 488	49	31	Vermont	25.8
32	Arkansas	2 725 714	6	32	Pennsylvania	116 074	21	32	Minnesota	24.5
33	Kansas	2 723 507	24	33	Louisiana	112 825	31	33	Mississippi	23.7
34	Utah	2 351 467	16	34	Tennessee	106 752	30	34	Iowa	20.3
35	Nevada	2 241 154	7	35	Ohio	106 056	32	35	Arkansas	20.2
36	New Mexico	1 874 614	26	36	Kentucky	102 896	28	36	Oklahoma	19.7
37	West Virginia	1 810 354	12	37	Virginia	102 548	18	37	Arizona	19.0
38	Nebraska	1 739 291	14	38	Indiana	92 895	22	38	Colorado	16.9
39	Idaho	1 366 332	40	39	Maine	79 931	40	39	Maine	16.3
40	Maine	1 305 728	25	40	South Carolina	77 983	27	40	Oregon	14.3
41	New Hampshire	1 287 687	37	41	West Virginia	62 361	33	41	Kansas	12.9
42	Hawaii	1 257 608	19	42	Maryland	25 314	34	42	Utah	11.1
43	Rhode Island	1 076 164	49	43	Vermont	23 956	38	43	Nebraska	8.7
44	Montana	917 621	41	44	New Hampshire	23 227	35	44	Nevada	7.9
45	Delaware	817 491	13	45	Massachusetts	20 306	39	45	Idaho	6.4
46	South Dakota	764 309	10	46	New Jersey	19 211	36	46	New Mexico	6.0
47	Alaska	648 818	42	47	Hawaii	16 635	46	47	South Dakota	3.9
48	North Dakota	633 837	29	48	Connecticut	12 548	48	48	North Dakota	3.5
49	Vermont	619 107	45	49	Delaware	5 060	44	49	Montana	2.4
50	District of Columbia	563 384	43	50	Rhode Island	2 706	51	50	Wyoming	2.0
51	Wyoming	501 242	50	51	District of Columbia	159	47	51	Alaska	0.4

States and the District of Columbia
Selected Rankings

Percent White, not Hispanic or Latino, alone or in combination, 2003				Percent Black, not Hispanic or Latino, alone or in combination, 2003				Percent Hispanic or Latino,[1] 2003			
Population rank	White rank	State	Percent White [col 5]	Population rank	Black rank	State	Percent Black [col 6]	Population rank	Hispanic or Latino rank	State	Percent Hispanic or Latino [col 9]
X	X	United States	69.0	X	X	United States	12.7	X	X	United States	13.7
40	1	Maine	97.2	50	1	District of Columbia	58.6	36	1	New Mexico	43.2
49	2	Vermont	97.0	31	2	Mississippi	37.0	1	2	California	34.3
41	3	New Hampshire	95.5	24	3	Louisiana	33.0	2	3	Texas	34.2
37	4	West Virginia	95.2	25	4	South Carolina	30.2	18	4	Arizona	27.8
30	5	Iowa	92.7	9	5	Georgia	28.8	35	5	Nevada	21.9
48	6	North Dakota	92.2	19	6	Maryland	28.4	22	6	Colorado	18.6
44	7	Montana	90.5	23	7	Alabama	26.6	4	6	Florida	18.6
26	8	Kentucky	89.6	11	8	North Carolina	22.0	3	8	New York	16.3
51	9	Wyoming	89.5	12	9	Virginia	20.3	10	9	New Jersey	14.5
46	10	South Dakota	88.6	45	10	Delaware	19.7	5	10	Illinois	13.6
39	11	Idaho	88.4	16	11	Tennessee	17.0	29	11	Connecticut	10.1
21	11	Minnesota	88.4	32	12	Arkansas	16.4	34	12	Utah	9.9
20	13	Wisconsin	87.4	3	13	New York	16.0	43	13	Rhode Island	9.5
38	14	Nebraska	87.3	4	14	Florida	15.6	50	14	District of Columbia	9.4
14	15	Indiana	86.2	5	15	Illinois	15.3	27	15	Oregon	9.2
34	16	Utah	85.4	8	16	Michigan	14.8	39	16	Idaho	8.7
7	17	Ohio	84.7	10	17	New Jersey	13.8	15	17	Washington	8.3
17	18	Missouri	84.4	7	18	Ohio	12.1	33	18	Kansas	7.8
27	19	Oregon	84.3	17	19	Missouri	11.9	42	19	Hawaii	7.6
6	20	Pennsylvania	84.2	2	20	Texas	11.4	13	20	Massachusetts	7.4
33	21	Kansas	83.4	6	21	Pennsylvania	10.4	51	21	Wyoming	6.8
43	22	Rhode Island	82.4	29	22	Connecticut	9.7	9	22	Georgia	6.2
13	23	Massachusetts	82.1	14	23	Indiana	8.9	38	23	Nebraska	6.1
15	24	Washington	80.3	28	24	Oklahoma	8.4	28	24	Oklahoma	5.7
8	25	Michigan	79.5	26	25	Kentucky	7.9	11	25	North Carolina	5.6
16	26	Tennessee	79.3	35	26	Nevada	7.1	45	26	Delaware	5.3
32	27	Arkansas	78.6	1	27	California	6.9	12	26	Virginia	5.3
29	28	Connecticut	77.5	33	28	Kansas	6.4	19	28	Maryland	4.8
28	29	Oklahoma	76.9	13	29	Massachusetts	6.2	47	29	Alaska	4.6
22	30	Colorado	74.2	20	29	Wisconsin	6.2	14	30	Indiana	3.9
45	31	Delaware	72.8	43	31	Rhode Island	5.3	20	30	Wisconsin	3.9
47	32	Alaska	71.1	38	32	Nebraska	4.5	32	32	Arkansas	3.7
12	33	Virginia	70.4	47	33	Alaska	4.4	8	33	Michigan	3.5
23	34	Alabama	70.3	21	33	Minnesota	4.4	6	34	Pennsylvania	3.4
11	35	North Carolina	69.8	22	35	Colorado	4.3	21	35	Minnesota	3.3
5	36	Illinois	67.3	15	36	Washington	4.1	30	36	Iowa	3.1
25	37	South Carolina	65.9	37	37	West Virginia	3.6	25	37	South Carolina	2.8
35	38	Nevada	65.3	18	38	Arizona	3.3	24	38	Louisiana	2.6
10	38	New Jersey	65.3	42	39	Hawaii	3.1	16	39	Tennessee	2.5
4	40	Florida	63.9	30	40	Iowa	2.6	17	40	Missouri	2.3
9	41	Georgia	62.6	36	41	New Mexico	2.1	44	41	Montana	2.1
24	41	Louisiana	62.6	27	41	Oregon	2.1	23	42	Alabama	2.0
19	41	Maryland	62.6	41	43	New Hampshire	1.1	7	42	Ohio	2.0
18	44	Arizona	62.4	46	43	South Dakota	1.1	41	44	New Hampshire	1.8
3	45	New York	61.3	34	43	Utah	1.1	26	45	Kentucky	1.7
31	46	Mississippi	60.4	51	43	Wyoming	1.1	31	46	Mississippi	1.5
2	47	Texas	51.3	48	47	North Dakota	1.0	46	46	South Dakota	1.5
1	48	California	46.8	40	48	Maine	0.8	48	48	North Dakota	1.3
36	49	New Mexico	44.6	49	48	Vermont	0.8	49	49	Vermont	0.9
42	50	Hawaii	35.3	39	50	Idaho	0.7	40	50	Maine	0.8
50	51	District of Columbia	29.2	44	51	Montana	0.6	37	51	West Virginia	0.7

1. Hispanic or Latino persons may be of any race.

4

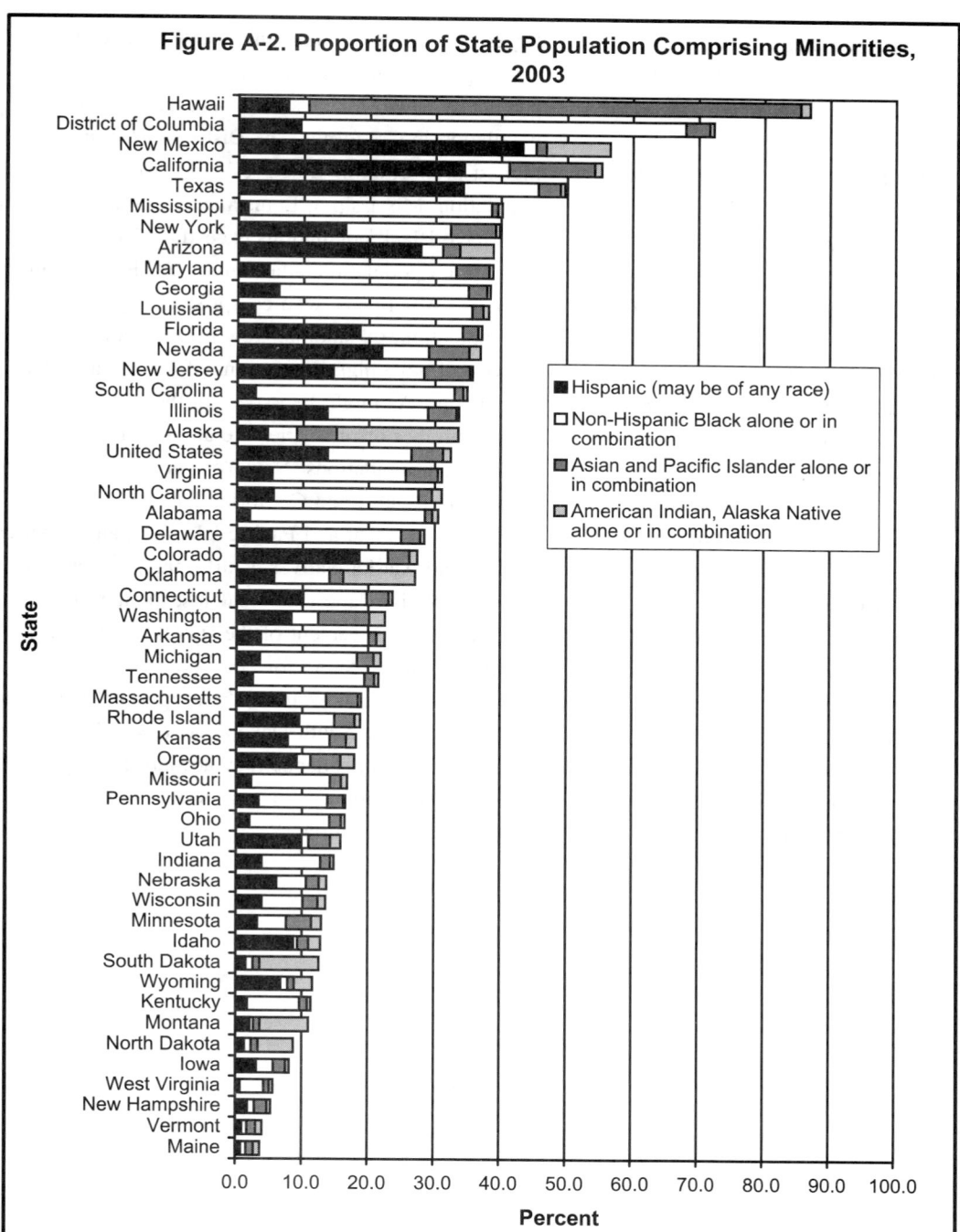

Figure A-2. Proportion of State Population Comprising Minorities, 2003

Legend:
- ■ Hispanic (may be of any race)
- ☐ Non-Hispanic Black alone or in combination
- ▦ Asian and Pacific Islander alone or in combination
- ▨ American Indian, Alaska Native alone or in combination

X-axis: Percent (0.0 to 100.0)
Y-axis: State

The population of the United States as a whole increased by 3.3 percent between 2000 and 2003, with 19 states exceeding this rate and the remainder growing more slowly. States with the fastest population growth in the new decade are concentrated in the West, with the three fastest growing states located in that region. Heading the list is Nevada, whose population increased by 12.2 percent in only 3 years. In 2003, Georgia overtook New Jersey to become the ninth largest state in the nation. This is the first change in the top 10 since 1998, when Illinois's population grew larger than that of Pennsylvania. While most states gained population since 2000, North Dakota and the District of Columbia registered small losses.

Many minority groups have had above average growth rates over the past decade. There are currently three states, and the District of Columbia where the minority population outnumber non-Hispanic Whites. And in Texas, minorities make up just less than 50 percent of the population. Nationally, 69 percent of the U.S. population is non-Hispanic White, but the racial and ethnic compositions of the states vary widely. In Hawaii, the state with the highest proportion of minorities, Asians and Pacific Islanders alone or in combination are the largest race group, comprising nearly three-quarters of the state's population. Hispanics make up more than 43 percent of New Mexico's residents, and 34 percent of the population in California. The District of Columbia has the highest proportion of Black residents, well over half the population. Mississippi, Louisiana, and South Carolina each have Black populations exceeding 30 percent of the state's total population. Alaska has the highest proportion of Native Americans, who comprise nearly 20 percent of the population. Oklahoma, New Mexico, and South Dakota all have high proportions of American Indian populations. As might be expected, the states with the largest number of minorities are among the states with the higher total populations. New York is home to more than 12 million Blacks, and California has the largest number of Hispanics, Asian and Pacific Islanders, and American Indians and Alaska Natives. California has more than half a million Native American residents, though they comprise just 1.9 percent of the state's population. Oklahoma ranks second for both the total number of Native Americans as well for the proportion of the state's population. While South Dakota has fewer than 70,000 Native American residents, they account for 9 percent of the state's population, which is the fourth highest proportion in the nation.

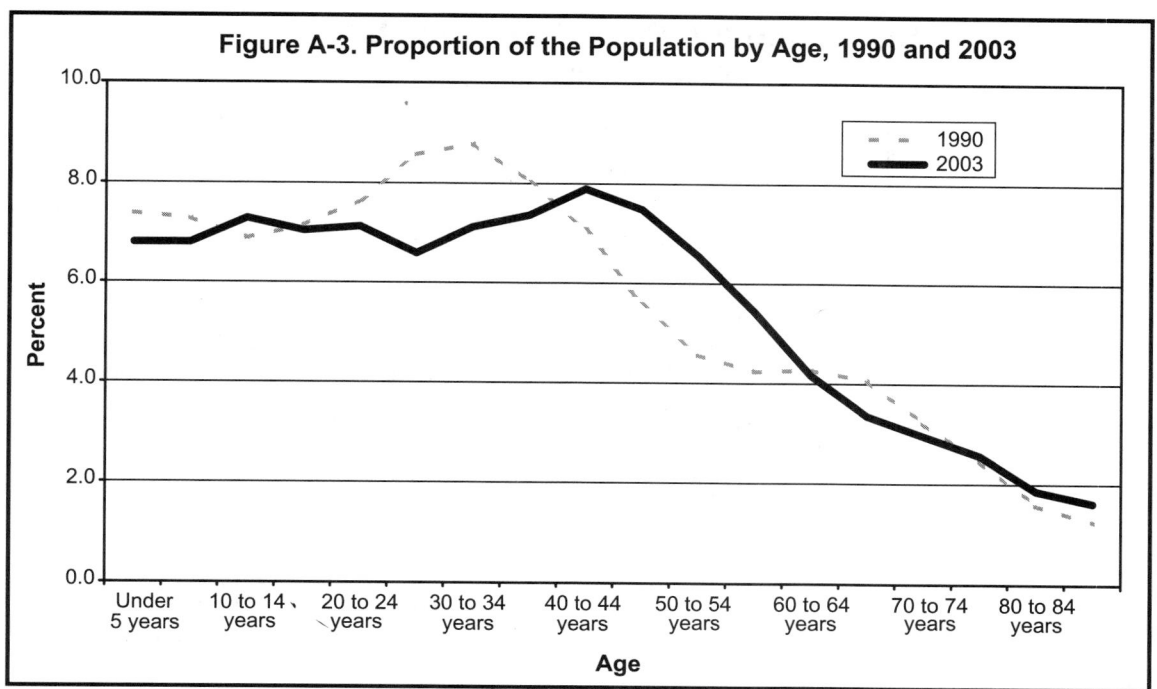

Figure A-3. Proportion of the Population by Age, 1990 and 2003

The U.S. median age has increased from 32.9 years in 1990 to 35.9 years in 2003. This is primarily a result of an aging Baby Boomer population, which is evident in the growth of the proportion of the population between 45 and 54 years. The median age by state ranges from 40.2 years in Maine to 27.5 years in Utah. Utah has the highest proportion of residents under 18 years old. Nearly 45 percent of the state's population is younger than 24 years old. The District of Columbia has just 19.2 percent of its population under 18 years of age, which is also among the lowest when compared with the 75 largest cities. West Virginia and Maine have the lowest proportions of young people among the 50 states.

The population age 65 years and over ranges from just over 6 percent in Alaska to about 17 percent in Florida. The District of Columbia, Colorado, Vermont, and Alaska all have proportions of the working-age population (between 18 and 64 years) exceeding 64.5 percent. In Utah, Florida, and Arizona, 60 percent or less of the population is working age. Alaska and Nevada have the lowest proportions of female residents, and are among just nine states where males outnumber females.

Natural growth is the difference between the number of births and the number of deaths. Alaska had the fewest births between 2000 and 2003. West Virginia is the only state to have more deaths than births. The net migration of over 4,000 people prevented the state from having a

population loss from 2000 to 2003. California, the largest state in the nation, had nearly one million more births than deaths, and 600,000 new residents through net migration. This gave California the largest numeric increase in population. Texas and Florida are the only other states with more than one million new residents since 2000. North Dakota and the District of Columbia are the only places with fewer residents in 2003 than in 2000, which is primarily the result of a high number of out-migrants.

Utah has the highest birth rate in the nation, with 21.2 births per 1,000 population. Texas ranks second with a birth rate of 17.1. The U.S. average is 13.9. Vermont and Maine have the lowest birth rates with 10.4 and 10.5, respectively. Alaska has the lowest crude death rate with 4.7 deaths per 1,000 population. However, Alaska has a relatively young population, 40 percent of which is under 24 years old, and when the death rate is adjusted for age, it increases to a more average rate of 7.9. West Virginia and Pennsylvania have the highest crude death rates in the nation. Both states have more than 15 percent of their populations over 65 years old. Florida is the only state with a higher proportion of senior citizens. However, Florida has a higher proportion of people under 18 years of age, which helps give the state a crude death rate below the top five. When Florida's death rate is age-adjusted, it drops to among the lowest 15 in the nation. Mississippi, the District of Columbia, Alabama, and Louisiana have the highest age-adjusted death rates in the nation.

States and the District of Columbia
Selected Rankings

Percent population change, 2000–2003				Percent under 18 years old, 2003				Percent 65 years old and over, 2003			
Population rank	Percent change rank	State	Percent change [col 34]	Population rank	Under 18 years old rank	State	Percent under 18 years old [col 10 and 11]	Population rank	65 years old and over rank	State	Percent 65 years old and over [col 17 and 18]
X	X	United States	3.3	X	X	United States	25.1	X	X	United States	12.4
35	1	Nevada	12.2	34	1	Utah	31.6	4	1	Florida	17.1
18	2	Arizona	8.8	47	2	Alaska	29.2	6	2	Pennsylvania	15.3
4	3	Florida	6.5	2	3	Texas	28.2	37	2	West Virginia	15.3
9	4	Georgia	6.1	18	4	Arizona	27.2	48	4	North Dakota	14.8
2	4	Texas	6.1	39	4	Idaho	27.2	30	5	Iowa	14.7
22	6	Colorado	5.8	36	6	New Mexico	26.8	40	6	Maine	14.4
39	7	Idaho	5.6	1	7	California	26.6	46	7	South Dakota	14.2
34	8	Utah	5.3	9	8	Georgia	26.5	43	8	Rhode Island	14.1
1	9	California	4.8	31	9	Mississippi	26.4	32	9	Arkansas	13.9
11	10	North Carolina	4.4	24	10	Louisiana	26.2	44	10	Montana	13.7
45	11	Delaware	4.3	35	11	Nevada	25.9	29	11	Connecticut	13.5
12	11	Virginia	4.3	14	12	Indiana	25.8	42	12	Hawaii	13.4
41	13	New Hampshire	4.2	46	13	South Dakota	25.6	17	12	Missouri	13.4
19	14	Maryland	4.0	5	14	Illinois	25.5	38	12	Nebraska	13.4
27	14	Oregon	4.0	33	14	Kansas	25.5	13	15	Massachusetts	13.3
15	14	Washington	4.0	22	16	Colorado	25.3	7	15	Ohio	13.3
42	17	Hawaii	3.8	38	16	Nebraska	25.3	23	17	Alabama	13.2
47	18	Alaska	3.5	8	18	Michigan	25.2	45	18	Delaware	13.1
25	19	South Carolina	3.4	28	19	Oklahoma	25.1	28	18	Oklahoma	13.1
36	20	New Mexico	3.1	32	20	Arkansas	25.0	10	20	New Jersey	13.0
21	21	Minnesota	2.8	19	20	Maryland	25.0	3	20	New York	13.0
10	22	New Jersey	2.7	11	22	North Carolina	24.8	20	20	Wisconsin	13.0
43	22	Rhode Island	2.7	10	23	New Jersey	24.7	33	23	Kansas	12.9
16	22	Tennessee	2.7	25	23	South Carolina	24.7	49	23	Vermont	12.9
40	25	Maine	2.4	23	25	Alabama	24.6	18	25	Arizona	12.8
29	26	Connecticut	2.3	21	25	Minnesota	24.6	27	26	Oregon	12.7
32	27	Arkansas	2.0	17	25	Missouri	24.6	26	27	Kentucky	12.4
17	27	Missouri	2.0	7	25	Ohio	24.6	16	27	Tennessee	12.4
20	27	Wisconsin	2.0	15	29	Washington	24.5	14	29	Indiana	12.3
5	30	Illinois	1.9	12	30	Virginia	24.4	8	29	Michigan	12.3
14	30	Indiana	1.9	20	30	Wisconsin	24.4	25	29	South Carolina	12.3
26	30	Kentucky	1.9	45	32	Delaware	24.3	31	32	Mississippi	12.2
28	33	Oklahoma	1.8	26	33	Kentucky	24.2	50	33	District of Columbia	12.1
44	34	Montana	1.7	51	33	Wyoming	24.2	11	33	North Carolina	12.1
49	34	Vermont	1.7	29	35	Connecticut	24.0	21	35	Minnesota	12.0
38	36	Nebraska	1.6	27	36	Oregon	23.9	36	35	New Mexico	12.0
51	37	Wyoming	1.5	16	36	Tennessee	23.9	5	37	Illinois	11.9
8	38	Michigan	1.4	41	38	New Hampshire	23.8	41	37	New Hampshire	11.9
33	39	Kansas	1.3	42	39	Hawaii	23.7	51	37	Wyoming	11.9
13	39	Massachusetts	1.3	30	40	Iowa	23.6	24	40	Louisiana	11.7
31	39	Mississippi	1.3	3	40	New York	23.6	39	41	Idaho	11.4
46	39	South Dakota	1.3	44	42	Montana	23.5	19	41	Maryland	11.4
23	43	Alabama	1.2	4	43	Florida	23.1	12	43	Virginia	11.3
3	44	New York	1.1	13	43	Massachusetts	23.1	35	44	Nevada	11.2
7	45	Ohio	0.7	48	43	North Dakota	23.1	15	44	Washington	11.2
6	45	Pennsylvania	0.7	6	46	Pennsylvania	22.9	1	46	California	10.6
30	47	Iowa	0.6	43	47	Rhode Island	22.7	2	47	Texas	9.8
24	47	Louisiana	0.6	49	48	Vermont	22.2	22	48	Colorado	9.7
37	49	West Virginia	0.1	40	49	Maine	21.9	9	49	Georgia	9.5
48	50	North Dakota	-1.3	37	50	West Virginia	21.6	34	50	Utah	8.6
50	51	District of Columbia	-1.5	50	51	District of Columbia	19.3	47	51	Alaska	6.2

States and the District of Columbia
Selected Rankings

	Number of immigrants, 2003				Birth rate, 2002				Infant death rate, 2002		
Popu- lation rank	Immi- grant rank	State	Number of immigrants [col 28]	Popu- lation rank	Birth rate rank	State	Birth rate (per 1,000 population) [col 63]	Popu- lation rank	Infant death rank	State	Infant death rate (per 1,000 live births) [col 68]
X	X	United States	705 827	X	X	United States	13.9	X	X	United States	7.0
1	1	California...............	176 375	34	1	Utah	21.2	50	1	District of Columbia	11.3
3	2	New York	89 661	2	2	Texas	17.1	24	2	Louisiana...............	10.3
82	3	Texas	53 592	18	3	Arizona..................	16.1	31	2	Mississippi...............	10.3
4	4	Florida....................	52 969	9	4	Georgia..................	15.6	16	4	Tennessee	9.4
10	5	New Jersey	40 818	39	4	Idaho.....................	15.6	25	5	South Carolina..............	9.3
5	6	Illinois.................	32 488	47	6	Alaska	15.4	23	6	Alabama...............	9.1
13	7	Massachusetts...............	20 184	22	7	Colorado	15.2	37	6	West Virginia............	9.1
12	8	Virginia..................	19 781	1	8	California.................	15.1	9	8	Georgia................	8.9
15	9	Washington	18 017	35	9	Nevada	15.0	45	9	Delaware...............	8.7
19	10	Maryland.................	17 813	36	9	New Mexico	15.0	17	10	Missouri................	8.5
6	11	Pennsylvania	14 638	38	11	Nebraska.................	14.7	32	11	Arkansas	8.3
8	12	Michigan	13 546	33	12	Kansas...................	14.5	11	12	North Carolina	8.2
18	13	Arizona	11 001	24	12	Louisiana................	14.5	8	13	Michigan	8.1
9	14	Georgia	10 805	31	12	Mississippi...............	14.5	28	13	Oklahoma	8.1
22	15	Colorado	10 713	28	15	Oklahoma	14.4	7	15	Ohio	7.9
7	16	Ohio	9 805	5	16	Illinois................	14.3	14	16	Indiana	7.7
11	17	North Carolina	9 479	11	17	North Carolina	14.1	6	17	Pennsylvania	7.6
21	18	Minnesota	8 435	46	17	South Dakota	14.1	4	18	Florida..................	7.5
29	19	Connecticut...............	8 296	42	19	Hawaii	14.0	19	18	Maryland	7.5
27	20	Oregon	6 968	32	20	Arkansas	13.8	44	18	Montana	7.5
35	21	Nevada	6 369	14	20	Indiana	13.8	5	21	Illinois	7.4
17	22	Missouri	6 179	45	22	Delaware	13.7	12	21	Virginia	7.4
14	23	Indiana	5 255	12	22	Virginia..................	13.7	42	23	Hawaii	7.3
42	24	Hawaii	4 907	21	24	Minnesota	13.6	26	24	Kentucky	7.2
20	25	Wisconsin	4 378	19	25	Maryland	13.4	33	25	Kansas	7.1
33	26	Kansas	3 811	10	25	New Jersey	13.4	38	26	Nebraska...............	7.0
30	27	Iowa	3 425	16	25	Tennessee	13.4	43	26	Rhode Island.............	7.0
16	28	Tennessee	3 373	26	28	Kentucky	13.3	20	28	Wisconsin...............	6.9
34	29	Utah	3 174	17	28	Missouri................	13.3	51	29	Wyoming	6.7
26	30	Kentucky	3 047	25	28	South Carolina	13.3	29	30	Connecticut..............	6.5
38	31	Nebraska	2 836	23	31	Alabama	13.1	46	30	South Dakota	6.5
50	32	District of Columbia	2 497	50	31	District of Columbia	13.1	18	32	Arizona................	6.4
43	33	Rhode Island	2 495	3	31	New York	13.1	2	32	Texas	6.4
28	34	Oklahoma	2 394	51	31	Wyoming	13.1	36	34	New Mexico	6.3
36	35	New Mexico	2 342	7	35	Ohio	13.0	48	34	North Dakota	6.3
24	36	Louisiana	2 221	15	35	Washington	13.0	22	36	Colorado	6.1
25	37	South Carolina.............	1 946	8	37	Michigan	12.9	39	36	Idaho	6.1
32	38	Arkansas	1 911	30	38	Iowa	12.8	35	38	Nevada	6.0
41	39	New Hampshire	1 873	27	38	Oregon	12.8	3	38	New York	6.0
23	40	Alabama	1 693	20	40	Wisconsin................	12.6	27	40	Oregon	5.8
39	41	Idaho.....................	1 692	13	41	Massachusetts	12.5	15	40	Washington	5.8
45	42	Delaware	1 490	4	42	Florida..................	12.3	10	42	New Jersey	5.7
47	43	Alaska	1 196	48	43	North Dakota..............	12.2	34	43	Utah	5.6
40	44	Maine	999	29	44	Connecticut	12.1	47	44	Alaska	5.5
31	45	Mississippi	730	44	44	Montana	12.1	1	44	California	5.5
49	46	Vermont	554	43	44	Rhode Island..............	12.1	21	46	Minnesota	5.4
46	47	South Dakota	488	6	47	Pennsylvania	11.6	30	47	Iowa	5.3
37	48	West Virginia	485	37	48	West Virginia	11.5	41	48	New Hampshire	5.0
44	49	Montana	456	41	49	New Hampshire	11.3	13	49	Massachusetts	4.9
48	50	North Dakota	332	40	50	Maine	10.5	40	50	Maine	4.4
51	51	Wyoming.................	259	49	51	Vermont	10.4	49	50	Vermont	4.4

States and the District of Columbia
Selected Rankings

Population rank	Percent high school graduates rank	State	Percent high school graduates [col 83]	Population rank	Percent college graduates rank	State	Percent college graduates [col 84]	Population rank	Median income rank	State	Median income (dollars) [col 91]
X	X	United States	84.5	X	X	United States	27.2	X	X	United States	43 527
41	1	New Hampshire	92.1	50	1	District of Columbia	46.4	10	1	New Jersey	55 221
21	2	Minnesota	91.6	13	2	Massachusetts	37.6	19	2	Maryland	55 213
51	3	Wyoming	90.9	19	3	Maryland	37.2	41	3	New Hampshire	55 166
38	4	Nebraska	90.8	22	4	Colorado	36.0	47	4	Alaska	55 143
47	5	Alaska	90.6	12	5	Virginia	34.2	29	5	Connecticut	55 004
44	6	Montana	90.1	41	6	New Hampshire	34.0	21	6	Minnesota	54 480
30	7	Iowa	89.7	29	7	Connecticut	33.5	12	7	Virginia	52 587
48	7	North Dakota	89.7	10	8	New Jersey	33.4	13	8	Massachusetts	52 084
34	9	Utah	89.4	21	9	Minnesota	32.7	45	9	Delaware	50 451
15	10	Washington	89.1	49	10	Vermont	31.3	22	10	Colorado	50 224
49	11	Vermont	88.9	33	11	Kansas	31.0	42	11	Hawaii	49 839
22	12	Colorado	88.7	1	12	California	29.8	34	12	Utah	49 143
45	12	Delaware	88.7	3	13	New York	29.6	1	13	California	48 979
46	12	South Dakota	88.7	15	14	Washington	28.8	20	14	Wisconsin	46 782
33	15	Kansas	88.6	34	15	Utah	28.4	35	15	Nevada	46 118
20	15	Wisconsin	88.6	45	16	Delaware	28.1	15	16	Washington	45 960
42	17	Hawaii	88.5	5	16	Illinois	28.1	5	17	Illinois	45 607
17	18	Missouri	88.3	43	18	Rhode Island	27.6	43	18	Rhode Island	45 205
39	19	Idaho	88.2	42	19	Hawaii	27.0	8	19	Michigan	45 176
12	20	Virginia	87.8	38	20	Nebraska	26.8	38	20	Nebraska	44 35
19	21	Maryland	87.6	17	21	Missouri	26.6	6	21	Pennsylvania	43 869
8	21	Michigan	87.6	27	22	Oregon	26.4	33	22	Kansas	43 622
29	23	Connecticut	87.5	18	23	Arizona	26.0	9	23	Georgia	43 535
7	24	Ohio	87.2	4	24	Florida	25.8	7	23	Ohio	43 535
13	25	Massachusetts	87.1	48	25	North Dakota	25.2	17	25	Missouri	43 492
27	26	Oregon	86.9	9	26	Georgia	25.0	49	26	Vermont	43 212
40	27	Maine	86.6	7	26	Ohio	25.0	3	27	New York	43 160
14	28	Indiana	86.4	44	28	Montana	24.9	50	28	District of Columbia	42 597
10	29	New Jersey	86.2	6	29	Pennsylvania	24.8	27	29	Oregon	42 429
50	30	District of Columbia	86.0	2	30	Texas	24.7	14	30	Indiana	42 124
6	30	Pennsylvania	86.0	30	31	Iowa	24.6	18	31	Arizona	42 062
5	32	Illinois	85.9	28	32	Oklahoma	24.3	30	32	Iowa	41 985
28	33	Oklahoma	85.7	20	33	Wisconsin	24.1	51	33	Wyoming	41 501
35	34	Nevada	85.6	47	34	Alaska	24.0	2	34	Texas	40 934
9	35	Georgia	85.1	46	35	South Dakota	23.9	39	35	Idaho	40 230
4	36	Florida	84.7	11	36	North Carolina	23.8	46	36	South Dakota	39 829
3	37	New York	84.2	40	37	Maine	23.7	25	37	South Carolina	38 791
18	38	Arizona	83.8	36	37	New Mexico	23.7	4	38	Florida	38 572
26	39	Kentucky	82.8	16	39	Tennessee	23.5	48	39	North Dakota	38 212
36	40	New Mexico	81.7	8	40	Michigan	23.3	26	40	Kentucky	38 161
11	41	North Carolina	81.4	23	41	Alabama	22.7	11	41	North Carolina	38 096
31	42	Mississippi	81.2	39	42	Idaho	22.5	40	42	Maine	37 619
1	43	California	81.1	24	43	Louisiana	22.3	16	43	Tennessee	37 529
43	44	Rhode Island	81.0	25	43	South Carolina	22.3	23	44	Alabama	37 419
16	44	Tennessee	81.0	14	45	Indiana	22.2	28	45	Oklahoma	36 733
32	46	Arkansas	80.9	26	46	Kentucky	21.3	36	46	New Mexico	35 265
25	47	South Carolina	80.8	35	47	Nevada	21.2	44	47	Montana	34 375
23	48	Alabama	79.9	51	48	Wyoming	20.7	24	48	Louisiana	34 307
24	49	Louisiana	79.8	31	49	Mississippi	19.3	32	49	Arkansas	33 259
37	50	West Virginia	78.7	32	50	Arkansas	17.4	31	50	Mississippi	31 887
2	51	Texas	77.2	37	51	West Virginia	15.3	37	51	West Virginia	31 210

1. Persons 25 years old and over.

Nearly 85 percent of the nation's population 25 years old and over are high school graduates. Six states have high school attainment levels exceeding 90 percent. States in the Midwest and the West tend to have above average high school attainment rates. States in the South tend to have below average rates. Texas, West Virginia, Louisiana, and Alabama have rates below 80 percent. States with above average high school attainment levels do not necessarily have high proportions of college graduates. Nationally, 27.2 percent of the population hold bachelor's degrees. Even when compared with other large cities, the District of Columbia has among the 10 highest proportions of college graduates. Of the 50 states, Massachusetts, Maryland, and Colorado top the list with more than 36 percent of their populations holding bachelor's degrees. States in the Northeast tend to have above average college attainment levels, while states in the South have below average rates.

The United States labor force grew by 1.1 percent between 2002 and 2003, which is an improvement after two years of growth of less than 1 percent. Rhode Island has the highest labor force growth in the nation, and is one of four states with growth exceeding 3 percent. While no states had experienced declining labor forces in the late 1990s, nine states have shrinking labor forces from 2002 to 2003. The District of Columbia and Illinois each has a decrease in labor force size for the third consecutive year. The District's population has decreased during this period, but Illinois continues to have population growth, increasing by more than 200,000 people since 2000. Both Illinois and the District of Columbia have among the 10 highest unemployment rates for 2003. South Dakota has the lowest unemployment rate with 3.6 percent, followed by North Dakota and Nebraska, each with 4.0 percent. North Dakota's population has decreased over the past three years, and South Dakota and Nebraska have among the lowest population growth rates. All three states have a lower than average proportion of their populations between the ages of 25 and 44 years old. Oregon and Alaska have the highest unemployment rates in the nation, both 8 percent or higher.

States and the District of Columbia
Selected Rankings

Unemployment rate, 2003				Per capita state taxes, 2002				Exports of goods by state of origin, 2003			
Popu-lation rank	Unem-ployment rate rank	State	Unem-ployment rate [col 152]	Popu-lation rank	Taxes rank	State	State taxes per capita (dollars) [col 314]	Popu-lation rank	Exports rank	State	Exports (millions of dollars) [col 287]
X	X	United States	6.0	X	X	United States	X	X	X	United States	724 006
27	1	Oregon	8.2	42	2	Hawaii	2 756	2	1	Texas	98 846
47	2	Alaska	8.0	45	3	Delaware	2 697	1	2	California	93 995
15	3	Washington	7.5	21	4	Minnesota	2 632	3	3	New York	39 181
8	4	Michigan	7.3	29	5	Connecticut	2 611	15	4	Washington	34 173
50	5	District of Columbia	7.0	49	6	Vermont	2 465	8	5	Michigan	32 941
25	6	South Carolina	6.8	13	7	Massachusetts	2 308	7	6	Ohio	29 764
2	6	Texas	6.8	3	8	New York	2 261	5	7	Illinois	26 473
1	8	California	6.7	1	9	California	2 221	4	8	Florida	24 953
5	8	Illinois	6.7	51	10	Wyoming	2 193	13	9	Massachusetts	18 663
24	10	Louisiana	6.6	8	11	Michigan	2 177	24	10	Louisiana	18 390
11	11	North Carolina	6.5	20	12	Wisconsin	2 172	10	11	New Jersey	16 818
36	12	New Mexico	6.4	10	13	New Jersey	2 137	14	12	Indiana	16 402
31	13	Mississippi	6.3	15	14	Washington	2 082	6	13	Pennsylvania	16 299
3	13	New York	6.3	40	15	Maine	2 028	9	14	Georgia	16 286
32	15	Arkansas	6.2	43	16	Rhode Island	1 992	11	15	North Carolina	16 199
26	15	Kentucky	6.2	19	17	Maryland	1 985	18	16	Arizona	13 323
7	17	Ohio	6.1	37	18	West Virginia	1 968	16	17	Tennessee	12 612
37	17	West Virginia	6.1	36	19	New Mexico	1 959	25	18	South Carolina	11 773
22	19	Colorado	6.0	26	20	Kentucky	1 950	20	19	Wisconsin	11 510
10	20	New Jersey	5.9	32	21	Arkansas	1 931	21	20	Minnesota	11 266
23	21	Alabama	5.8	11	22	North Carolina	1 871	12	21	Virginia	10 853
13	21	Massachusetts	5.8	35	23	Nevada	1 821	26	22	Kentucky	10 734
16	21	Tennessee	5.8	6	24	Pennsylvania	1 795	27	23	Oregon	10 357
28	24	Oklahoma	5.7	5	25	Illinois	1 786	23	24	Alabama	8 340
18	25	Arizona	5.6	33	26	Kansas	1 773	29	25	Connecticut	8 136
17	25	Missouri	5.6	7	27	Ohio	1 764	17	26	Missouri	7 234
6	25	Pennsylvania	5.6	48	28	North Dakota	1 762	22	27	Colorado	6 109
34	25	Utah	5.6	12	29	Virginia	1 754	30	28	Iowa	5 236
20	25	Wisconsin	5.6	28	30	Oklahoma	1 734	19	29	Maryland	4 941
29	30	Connecticut	5.5	38	31	Nebraska	1 732	33	30	Kansas	4 553
39	31	Idaho	5.4	30	32	Iowa	1 705	34	31	Utah	4 115
33	31	Kansas	5.4	47	33	Alaska	1 700	32	32	Arkansas	2 962
43	33	Rhode Island	5.3	34	34	Utah	1 693	47	33	Alaska	2 739
35	34	Nevada	5.2	39	35	Idaho	1 691	38	34	Nebraska	2 724
4	35	Florida	5.1	14	36	Indiana	1 657	28	35	Oklahoma	2 660
14	35	Indiana	5.1	31	37	Mississippi	1 649	49	36	Vermont	2 627
40	35	Maine	5.1	24	38	Louisiana	1 644	31	37	Mississippi	2 558
21	38	Minnesota	5.0	9	39	Georgia	1 612	37	38	West Virginia	2 380
9	39	Georgia	4.7	44	40	Montana	1 585	36	39	New Mexico	2 326
44	39	Montana	4.7	18	41	Arizona	1 558	40	40	Maine	2 188
49	41	Vermont	4.6	17	42	Missouri	1 539	39	41	Idaho	2 096
30	42	Iowa	4.5	22	43	Colorado	1 538	35	42	Nevada	2 033
19	42	Maryland	4.5	4	44	Florida	1 519	41	43	New Hampshire	1 931
45	44	Delaware	4.4	41	45	New Hampshire	1 489	45	44	Delaware	1 886
51	44	Wyoming	4.4	25	46	South Carolina	1 483	43	45	Rhode Island	1 178
42	46	Hawaii	4.3	27	47	Oregon	1 467	48	46	North Dakota	854
41	46	New Hampshire	4.3	23	48	Alabama	1 453	50	47	District of Columbia	809
12	48	Virginia	4.1	16	49	Tennessee	1 347	46	48	South Dakota	672
38	49	Nebraska	4.0	2	50	Texas	1 319	51	49	Wyoming	582
48	49	North Dakota	4.0	46	51	South Dakota	1 285	42	50	Hawaii	368
46	51	South Dakota	3.6	50	X	District of Columbia	X	44	51	Montana	361

The poverty threshold for an individual is $9,393. New Mexico, Arkansas, and West Virginia have the highest proportion of persons living in poverty, each exceeding 17 percent. The threshold for a four-person household with two children is $18,660. The number of children living in poverty increased from 2002 to 2003. Among children under 18 years old, 17.6 percent are living in poverty, compared with 16.7 percent in 2002. The proportion of children living in poverty exceeds that of people 18 to 64 years old and people over age 65 years.

More than 30 percent of children in the District of Columbia live in poverty. New Mexico, Arkansas, West Virginia, and Louisiana each have one-quarter of their residents under 18 years old living in poverty. New Hampshire has the lowest proportion of people in poverty. New Hampshire also has the third highest median household income in the nation, exceeding $55,000. West Virginia, Mississippi, and Arkansas have median household incomes below $34,000. The Northeast has the highest median household income, and the South has the lowest.

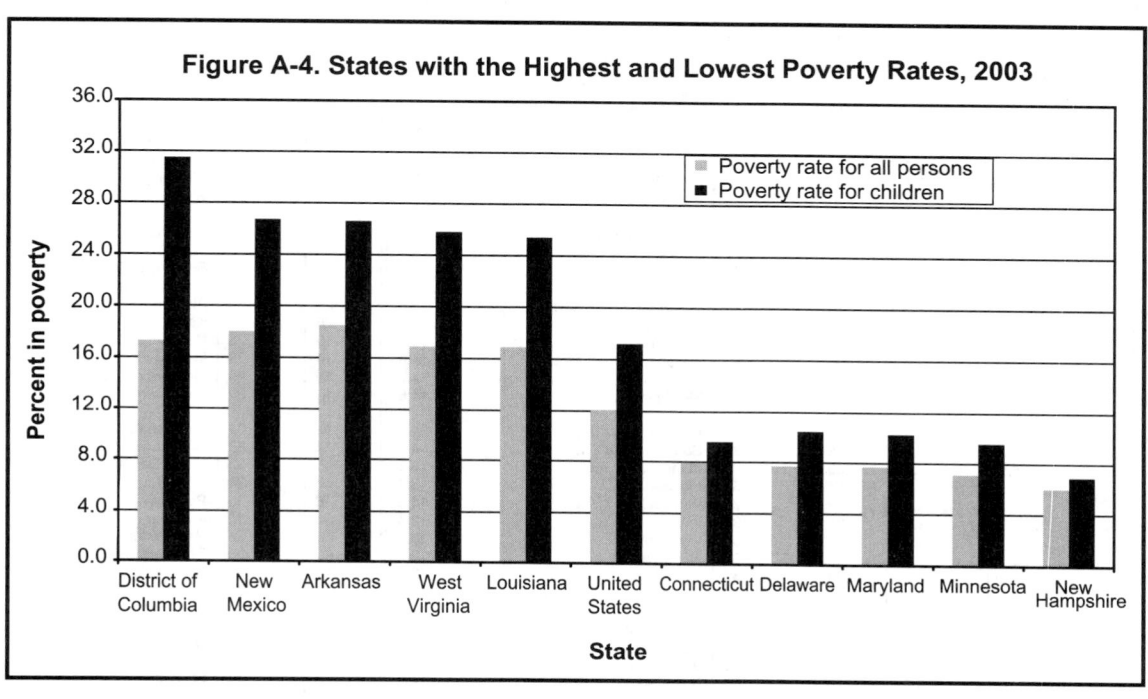

Figure A-4. States with the Highest and Lowest Poverty Rates, 2003

States and the District of Columbia
Selected Rankings

Percent of persons below the poverty level, 2003

Population rank	Poverty rate rank	State	Poverty rate [col 96]
X	X	United States	12.5
36	1	New Mexico	18.1
32	2	Arkansas	17.8
37	3	West Virginia	17.4
24	4	Louisiana	17.0
2	4	Texas	17.0
50	6	District of Columbia	16.8
31	7	Mississippi	16.0
11	8	North Carolina	15.7
44	9	Montana	15.1
23	10	Alabama	15.0
26	11	Kentucky	14.4
3	12	New York	14.3
16	13	Tennessee	14.0
18	14	Arizona	13.5
1	15	California	13.1
28	16	Oklahoma	12.8
4	17	Florida	12.7
25	17	South Carolina	12.7
46	17	South Dakota	12.7
5	20	Illinois	12.6
15	20	Washington	12.6
27	22	Oregon	12.5
9	23	Georgia	11.9
40	24	Maine	11.6
43	25	Rhode Island	11.5
8	26	Michigan	11.4
35	27	Nevada	10.9
7	27	Ohio	10.9
33	29	Kansas	10.8
17	30	Missouri	10.7
6	31	Pennsylvania	10.5
13	32	Massachusetts	10.3
39	33	Idaho	10.2
12	34	Virginia	10.0
14	35	Indiana	9.9
38	36	Nebraska	9.8
20	36	Wisconsin	9.8
51	36	Wyoming	9.8
22	39	Colorado	9.7
48	39	North Dakota	9.7
47	41	Alaska	9.6
42	42	Hawaii	9.3
34	43	Utah	9.1
30	44	Iowa	8.9
19	45	Maryland	8.6
10	45	New Jersey	8.6
49	47	Vermont	8.5
29	48	Connecticut	8.1
21	49	Minnesota	7.4
45	50	Delaware	7.3
41	51	New Hampshire	5.8

Percent of children under 18 years old below the poverty level, 2003

Population rank	Poverty rate of children under 18 rank	State	Poverty rate of children under 18 [col 97]
X	X	United States	17.6
50	1	District of Columbia	31.5
36	2	New Mexico	26.9
32	3	Arkansas	26.8
37	4	West Virginia	26.7
24	5	Louisiana	25.5
2	6	Texas	24.0
31	7	Mississippi	23.1
11	7	North Carolina	23.1
23	9	Alabama	22.3
44	10	Montana	20.2
27	11	Oregon	20.1
3	12	New York	19.9
4	13	Florida	19.2
18	14	Arizona	19.1
15	14	Washington	19.1
16	16	Tennessee	18.7
1	17	California	18.5
26	18	Kentucky	18.1
9	19	Georgia	17.7
5	20	Illinois	17.4
25	20	South Carolina	17.4
43	22	Rhode Island	17.1
28	23	Oklahoma	17.0
7	24	Ohio	16.5
40	25	Maine	15.6
6	26	Pennsylvania	15.5
20	27	Wisconsin	15.4
35	28	Nevada	14.8
17	29	Missouri	14.7
8	30	Michigan	14.6
33	31	Kansas	14.5
46	32	South Dakota	14.0
39	33	Idaho	13.8
14	34	Indiana	13.7
12	35	Virginia	13.5
30	36	Iowa	13.4
51	37	Wyoming	13.1
48	38	North Dakota	12.7
34	39	Utah	12.4
42	40	Hawaii	12.0
13	40	Massachusetts	12.0
22	42	Colorado	11.9
47	43	Alaska	11.2
10	43	New Jersey	11.2
45	45	Delaware	11.0
38	45	Nebraska	11.0
49	47	Vermont	10.9
19	48	Maryland	10.6
29	49	Connecticut	10.1
21	50	Minnesota	9.7
41	51	New Hampshire	7.2

Percent of persons lacking health insurance, 2003

Population rank	Percent lacking health insurance rank	State	Percent lacking health insurance [col 99]
X	X	United States	15.6
2	1	Texas	24.6
36	2	New Mexico	22.1
24	3	Louisiana	20.6
28	4	Oklahoma	20.4
44	5	Montana	19.4
47	6	Alaska	18.9
35	6	Nevada	18.9
39	8	Idaho	18.6
1	9	California	18.4
4	10	Florida	18.2
31	11	Mississippi	17.9
32	12	Arkansas	17.4
11	13	North Carolina	17.3
22	14	Colorado	17.2
27	14	Oregon	17.2
18	16	Arizona	17.0
37	17	West Virginia	16.6
9	18	Georgia	16.4
51	19	Wyoming	15.9
15	20	Washington	15.5
3	21	New York	15.1
5	22	Illinois	14.4
25	22	South Carolina	14.4
50	24	District of Columbia	14.3
23	25	Alabama	14.2
26	26	Kentucky	14.0
10	26	New Jersey	14.0
14	28	Indiana	13.9
19	28	Maryland	13.9
16	30	Tennessee	13.2
12	31	Virginia	13.0
34	32	Utah	12.7
46	33	South Dakota	12.2
7	34	Ohio	12.1
6	35	Pennsylvania	11.4
30	36	Iowa	11.3
38	36	Nebraska	11.3
45	38	Delaware	11.1
33	39	Kansas	11.0
17	39	Missouri	11.0
8	41	Michigan	10.9
48	41	North Dakota	10.9
20	41	Wisconsin	10.9
13	44	Massachusetts	10.7
29	45	Connecticut	10.4
40	45	Maine	10.4
41	47	New Hampshire	10.3
43	48	Rhode Island	10.2
42	49	Hawaii	10.1
49	50	Vermont	9.5
21	51	Minnesota	8.7

States and the District of Columbia
Selected Rankings

	Defense contracts, 2003				Value of agricultural products sold, 2002				Violent crime rate, 2003 (violent crimes known to police)		
Population rank	Defense contracts rank	State	Defense contracts (millions of dollars) [col 292]	Population rank	Value of sales rank	State	Value of sales (millions of dollars) [col 176]	Population rank	Crime rate rank	State	Crime rate (per 100,000 population) [col 77]
X	X	United States	200 183	X	X	United States	2 006 464	X	X	United States	475
1	1	California	26 079	1	1	California	257 372	50	1	District of Columbia	1 608
2	2	Texas	20 821	2	2	Texas	141 347	25	2	South Carolina	794
12	3	Virginia	19 493	30	3	Iowa	122 736	4	3	Florida	730
4	4	Florida	7 999	38	4	Nebraska	97 037	19	4	Maryland	704
29	5	Connecticut	7 895	33	5	Kansas	87 462	16	5	Tennessee	688
18	6	Arizona	7 564	21	6	Minnesota	85 756	36	6	New Mexico	665
19	7	Maryland	7 171	5	7	Illinois	76 762	45	7	Delaware	658
13	8	Massachusetts	6 365	11	8	North Carolina	69 617	24	8	Louisiana	646
17	9	Missouri	6 244	4	9	Florida	62 423	35	9	Nevada	614
6	10	Pennsylvania	5 607	20	10	Wisconsin	56 233	47	10	Alaska	593
23	11	Alabama	5 510	15	11	Washington	53 307	1	11	California	579
7	12	Ohio	4 271	17	12	Missouri	49 833	5	12	Illinois	557
3	13	New York	4 253	32	13	Arkansas	49 504	2	13	Texas	553
10	14	New Jersey	3 873	9	14	Georgia	49 118	18	14	Arizona	513
9	15	Georgia	3 324	14	15	Indiana	47 832	8	15	Michigan	511
26	16	Kentucky	3 223	22	16	Colorado	45 252	28	16	Oklahoma	506
15	17	Washington	3 196	28	17	Oklahoma	44 564	17	17	Missouri	473
14	18	Indiana	2 567	7	18	Ohio	42 635	13	18	Massachusetts	469
5	19	Illinois	2 514	6	19	Pennsylvania	42 570	3	19	New York	465
8	20	Michigan	2 494	39	20	Idaho	39 083	32	20	Arkansas	456
22	21	Colorado	2 471	46	21	South Dakota	38 346	11	21	North Carolina	455
16	22	Tennessee	2 161	8	22	Michigan	37 724	9	22	Georgia	454
31	23	Mississippi	2 126	23	23	Alabama	32 649	23	23	Alabama	430
11	24	North Carolina	1 988	48	24	North Dakota	32 334	6	24	Pennsylvania	398
24	25	Louisiana	1 951	27	25	Oregon	31 955	33	25	Kansas	396
34	26	Utah	1 871	3	26	New York	31 178	10	26	New Jersey	366
50	27	District of Columbia	1 753	31	27	Mississippi	31 163	44	27	Montana	365
42	28	Hawaii	1 750	26	28	Kentucky	30 801	14	28	Indiana	353
21	29	Minnesota	1 542	18	29	Arizona	23 954	15	29	Washington	347
25	30	South Carolina	1 487	12	30	Virginia	23 609	22	30	Colorado	345
28	31	Oklahoma	1 471	16	31	Tennessee	21 998	7	31	Ohio	333
20	32	Wisconsin	1 244	44	32	Montana	18 821	31	32	Mississippi	326
47	33	Alaska	1 237	24	33	Louisiana	18 158	29	33	Connecticut	308
33	34	Kansas	1 219	36	34	New Mexico	17 000	27	34	Oregon	296
40	35	Maine	1 176	25	35	South Carolina	14 898	38	35	Nebraska	289
36	36	New Mexico	955	19	36	Maryland	12 933	43	36	Rhode Island	286
30	37	Iowa	658	34	37	Utah	11 159	12	37	Virginia	276
32	38	Arkansas	578	51	38	Wyoming	8 639	30	38	Iowa	272
41	39	New Hampshire	531	10	39	New Jersey	7 499	42	39	Hawaii	270
43	40	Rhode Island	499	45	40	Delaware	6 189	21	40	Minnesota	263
27	41	Oregon	474	42	41	Hawaii	5 334	51	41	Wyoming	262
49	42	Vermont	455	37	42	West Virginia	4 828	26	42	Kentucky	262
35	43	Nevada	387	49	43	Vermont	4 731	37	43	West Virginia	258
38	44	Nebraska	312	29	44	Connecticut	4 706	34	44	Utah	249
48	45	North Dakota	262	40	45	Maine	4 636	39	45	Idaho	243
39	46	Idaho	207	35	46	Nevada	4 470	20	46	Wisconsin	221
46	47	South Dakota	196	13	47	Massachusetts	3 843	46	47	South Dakota	173
44	48	Montana	190	41	48	New Hampshire	1 448	41	48	New Hampshire	149
37	49	West Virginia	185	43	49	Rhode Island	555	49	49	Vermont	110
45	50	Delaware	164	47	50	Alaska	461	40	50	Maine	109
51	51	Wyoming	072	50	X	District of Columbia	X	48	51	North Dakota	78

COLUMN HEADINGS FOR STATES

Table A. States — **Land Area and Population**

STATE code	STATE	Land area,[1] 2000 (sq km)	Population and population characteristics, 2003			Race alone or in combination, not Hispanic or Latino (percent)				Percent Hispanic or Latino[2]	Age (percent)			
			Population											
			Total persons	Rank	Per square kilometer	White	Black	American Indian, Alaska Native	Asian and Pacific Islander	Percent Hispanic or Latino[2]	Under 5 years	5 to 17 years	18 to 24 years	25 to 34 years
		1	2	3	4	5	6	7	8	9	10	11	12	13

1. Dry land or land partially or temporarily covered by water.   2. Hispanic or Latino persons may be of any race.

Table A. States — **Population and Households**

STATE	Population and population characteristics, 2003 (cont'd)							Households, 2003						
	Age (percent) (cont'd)										Age of householder (percent)			
	35 to 44 years	45 to 54 years	55 to 64 years	65 to 74 years	75 years and over	Percent female	Median age	Number	Percent change, 2000–2003	Persons per household	Under 25 years	25 to 44 years	45 to 64 years	65 years and over
	14	15	16	17	18	19	20	21	22	23	24	25	26	27

Table A. States — **Immigration and Population Change**

STATE	Immigrants admitted to legal status, 2003	Population, 1980–2000			Population change, 1990–2003								
		Census counts			Percent change			Components of change, 2000–2003					
											Migration		
		1980	1990	2000	1980–1990	1990–2000	2000–2003	Births	Deaths	Net migration	Inter-national	Net internal
	28	29	30	31	32	33	34	35	36	37	38	39

Table A. States — **Population Characteristics, 2000**

STATE	Population characteristics, 2000 (percent)																
	Race							Age									
	White alone	Black alone	American Indian, Alaska Native alone	Asian and Pacific Islander alone	Some other race or two or more races	Hispanic or Latino[1]	Foreign born	Under 5 years	5 to 17 years	18 to 24 years	25 to 34 years	35 to 44 years	45 to 54 years	55 to 64 years	65 to 74 years	75 years and over	Female
	40	41	42	43	44	45	46	47	48	49	50	51	52	53	54	55	56

1. Hispanic or Latino persons may be of any race.

COLUMN HEADINGS FOR STATES

Table A. States — Households 2000, Vital Statistics, and Health Resources

STATE	Households, 2000					Births, 2002		Deaths, 2002					Physicians, 2000	
				Percent				Number		Rate				
										Total				
	Number	Percent change, 1990–2000	Persons per household	Female family householder[1]	One person	Total	Rate[2]	Total	Infant[3]	Crude[2]	Age-adjusted	Infant[4]	Number	Rate[5]
	57	58	59	60	61	62	63	64	65	66	67	68	69	70

1. No spouse present. 2. Per 1,000 resident population. 3. Deaths of infants under 1 year old. 4. Deaths of infants under 1 year old per 1,000 live births.
5. Per 100,000 resident population as of April 1 of the year shown.

Table A. States — Health Resources, Crime, and Education

| STATE | Hospitals, 1998 | | | | Serious crimes known to police,[2] 2003 | | | | Elementary and secondary school enrollment, 2001–2002 | | Educational attainment[4] (percent) | | | |
| | | Beds | | | Total | Rate[3] | | | | | 2000 | | 2003 | |
	Total	Number	Rate[1]	Medicare enrollees, 2003	Number	Rate[3]	Violent	Property	Total	Percent private	High school graduate or more	Bachelor's degree or more	High school graduate or more	Bachelor's degree or more
	71	72	73	74	75	76	77	78	79	80	81	82	83	84

1. Per 100,000 resident population as of July 1 of the year shown. 2. Data for serious crimes have not been adjusted for underreporting; this may affect comparability between geographic areas
and over time. 3. Per 100,000 population estimated by the FBI. 4. Persons 25 years old and over.

Table A. States — Education Expenditures, Money Income, Poverty, and Health Insurance

STATE	Local government expenditures for education, 2001–2002		Money income						Percent below poverty level						Percent lacking health insurance, 2003	
			1999						1999			2003				
			Households				Median household income average, 2001–2003 (dollars)	Median income of family of four, 2002	Persons							
			Median income													
	Total current expenditures (mil dol)	Current expenditures per student (dollars)	Per capita[1] income (dollars)	Dollars	Percent change, 1989–1999 (constant 1999 dollars)	Percent with income of $100,000 or more			Total	Percent change in rate, 1989–1999	Families	Persons	Children under 18 years	Persons over 65 years	Persons	Children under 18 years
	85	86	87	88	89	90	91	92	93	94	95	96	97	98	99	100

1. Based on population enumerated as of April 1, 2000.

Table A. States — Personal Income

STATE	Personal income, 2003												
			Per capita[1]		Sources of personal income (mil dol)								
									Transfer payments				
										Government payments to individuals			
	Total (mil dol)	Percent change, 2002–2003	Dollars	Rank	Wages and salaries[2]	Proprietors' income	Dividends, interest, and rent	Total	Total	Social Security	Medical payments	Income maintenance	Unemployment insurance
	101	102	103	104	105	106	107	108	109	110	111	112	113

1. Based on the resident population estimated as of July 1 of the year shown. 2. Includes other labor income.

COLUMN HEADINGS FOR STATES

Table A. States — **Personal Income and Earnings**

STATE	Personal tax payments, 2003 (mil dol)	Disposable personal income, 2003		Earnings, 2003									Gross state product, 2001 (mil dol)
						Percent by selected industries							
						Goods-related[2]		Service-related and other[3]					
		Total (mil dol)	Per capita[1] (dollars)	Total (mil dol)	Farm	Total	Manu-facturing	Total	Retail trade	Finance, insurance, and real estate	Services	Government	
	114	115	116	117	118	119	120	121	122	123	124	125	126

1. Based on the resident population estimated as of July 1 of the year shown. 2. Includes mining, construction, and manufacturing. 3. Includes private sector earnings in agricultural services, forestry, and fisheries; transportation and public utilities; wholesale and retail trade; finance, insurance, and real estate; and services.

Table A. States — **Housing**

STATE	Housing units, 2003					Housing units, 2000									
			Occupied units					Occupied units							
									Owner-occupied				Renter-occupied		
											Median owner cost as a percent of income				
	Total	Percent change, 2000–2003	Total	Percent owner-occupied	Median value of units with mortgage[1] (dollars)	Total	Percent change, 1990–2000	Total	Percent	Median value[1] (dollars)	With a mortgage	Without a mort-gage[2]	Median rent[3] (dollars)	Median rent as a per-cent of income	Sub-standard units[4] (percent)
	127	128	129	130	131	132	133	134	135	136	137	138	139	140	141

1. Specified owner-occupied units. 2. Median monthly owner costs is often in the minimum category—9.9 percent or less, which is indicated as 9.9 percent. 3. Specified renter-occupied units. 4. Over-crowded or lacking complete plumbing facilities.

Table A. States — **Social Security, Employment, and Labor Force**

STATE	Social Security beneficiaries, December 2003		Supple-mental Security Income recipients, December 2003	Civilian employment and selected occupations,[2] March 2000			Civilian labor force annual average, 2003				
					Percent					Unemployed	
	Number	Rate[1]		Total	Profes-sional, managerial, and technical	Precision production, craft, and repair	Total	Percent change, 2002–2003	Employed	Total	Rate[3]
	142	143	144	145	146	147	148	149	150	151	152

1. Per 1,000 resident population estimated as of July 1 of the year shown. 2. Persons 16 years old and over. 3. Percent of civilian labor force.

Table A. States — **Nonfarm Employment and Earnings**

STATE	Private nonfarm employment and earnings, 2003										
	Employment		Manufacturing			Employment (1,000)					
				Average earnings of production workers							
	Total (1,000)	Percent change, 2002–2003	Employ-ment (1,000)	Hourly	Weekly	Con-struction	Trans-portation and public utilities	Whole-sale trade	Retail trade	Financial activities	Services[1]
	153	154	155	156	157	158	159	160	161	162	163

1. Includes professional and business services, educational and health services, leisure and hospitality, and other services.

COLUMN HEADINGS FOR STATES

Table A. States — **Agriculture**

STATE	Agriculture, 2002										
	Farms				Land in farms					Value of land and buildings (dollars)	
		Percent with —		Farm operators whose principal occupation is farming (percent)				Acres			
	Number	Less than 50 acres	500 acres and over		Acreage (1,000)	Percent change, 1997–2002	Average size of farm	Total irrigated (1,000)	Total cropland (1,000)	Average per farm	Average per acre
	164	165	166	167	168	169	170	171	172	173	174

Table A. States — **Agriculture, Land, and Water**

STATE	Agriculture, 2002 (cont'd)							Land, 1997		
	Value of machinery and equipment average per farm (dollars)	Value of products sold				Percent of farms with sales of —		Owned by federal government (percent)	Developed (percent)	Water consumption, 2000 (mil gal per day)
		Total (mil dol)	Average per farm (dollars)	Percent from —						
				Crops	Livestock and poultry products	$10,000 or more	$100,000 or more			
	175	176	177	178	179	180	181	182	183	184

Table A. States — **Manufactures and Construction**

STATE	Manufactures, 2001										Construction, 1997			
	All employees			Production workers				Value added by manufacture (mil dol)	Value of shipments (mil dol)	Total capital expenditures (mil dol)	Establishments	Value (mil dol)	Paid employees	Annual payroll (mil dol)
	Number (1,000)	Percent change, 2000–2001	Annual payroll (mil dol)	Number (1,000)	Work hours (millions)	Wages								
						Total (mil dol)	Average per worker (dollars)							
	185	186	187	188	189	190	191	192	193	194	195	196	197	198

Table A. States — **Wholesale Trade and Retail Trade**

STATE	Wholesale trade, 1997				Retail trade,[1] 1997								
	Number of establishments	Number of employees	Sales (mil dol)	Annual payroll (mil dol)	Number of establishments	Number of employees						Sales (mil dol)	Annual payroll (mil dol)
						Total	Motor vehicle and parts dealers	Food and beverage stores	Clothing and clothing accessory stores	General merchandise stores			
	199	200	201	202	203	204	205	206	207	208		209	210

1. Establishments with payroll.

19

COLUMN HEADINGS FOR STATES

Table A. States — Transportation and Warehousing, Finance and Insurance, and Real Estate

STATE	Transportation and warehousing, 1997				Finance and insurance, 1997				Real estate and rental and leasing, 1997			
	Number of establish-ments	Number of employees	Receipts (mil dol)	Annual payroll (mil dol)	Number of establish-ments	Number of employees	Receipts (mil dol)	Annual payroll (mil dol)	Number of establish-ments	Number of employees	Receipts (mil dol)	Annual payroll (mil dol)
	211	212	213	214	215	216	217	218	219	220	221	222

Table A. States — Information and Utilities

STATE	Information, 1997								Utilities, 1997			
	Number of establish-ments	Number of employees					Receipts (mil dol)	Annual payroll (mil dol)	Number of establish-ments	Number of employees	Receipts (mil dol)	Annual payroll (mil dol)
		Total	Publishing	Motion picture and sound recording	Broadcast and telecommuni-cations	Information and data processing services						
	223	224	225	226	227	228	229	230	231	232	233	234

Table A. States — Professional Services and Arts, Entertainment, and Recreation

STATE	Professional, scientific, and technical services,[1] 1997								Arts, entertainment, and recreation,[1] 1997			
	Number of establish-ments	Number of employees					Receipts (mil dol)	Annual payroll (mil dol)	Number of establish-ments	Number of employees	Receipts (mil dol)	Annual payroll (mil dol)
		Total	Legal services	Accounting and related services	Architectural, engineering, and related services	Computer systems design and related services						
	235	236	237	238	239	240	241	242	243	244	245	246

1. Firms subject to federal tax.

Table A. States — Health Care and Social Assistance

STATE	Health care and social assistance, 1997											
	Subject to federal tax						Tax exempt					
	Number of establish-ments	Number of employees			Receipts (mil dol)	Annual payroll (mil dol)	Number of establish-ments	Number of employees			Receipts (mil dol)	Annual payroll (mil dol)
		Total	Ambulatory health care services	Hospitals				Total	Ambulatory health care services	Hospitals		
	247	248	249	250	251	252	253	254	255	256	257	258

COLUMN HEADINGS FOR STATES

Table A. States — **Accommodation and Food Services and Other Services**

STATE	Accommodation and food services, 1997					Other services, 1997						
	Number of employees						Number of employees					
	Number of establishments	Total	Food services and drinking places	Receipts (mil dol)	Annual payroll (mil dol)	Number of establishments[1]	Total[1]	Repair and maintenance[1]	Personal and laundry services[1]	Religious, civic, and similar services[2]	Receipts[1] (mil dol)	Annual payroll[1] (mil dol)
	259	260	261	262	263	264	265	266	267	268	269	270

1. Firms subject to federal tax.   2. Firms not subject to federal tax; not included in totals.

Table A. States — **Economic Census by SIC Code**

STATE	Construction		Manufacturing		Wholesale trade		Retail trade		Finance, insurance, and real estate		Service industries, subject to federal tax	
	Paid employees, 1997	Percent change, 1992–1997	Paid employees, 1997	Percent change, 1992–1997	Paid employees, 1997	Percent change, 1992–1997	Paid employees, 1997	Percent change, 1992–1997	Paid employees, 1997	Percent change, 1992–1997	Paid employees, 1997	Percent change, 1992–1997
	271	272	273	274	275	276	277	278	279	280	281	282

Table A. States — **Residential Construction, Exports, and Federal Funds**

STATE	Value of residential construction authorized by building permits, 2003				Exports of goods by state of origin, 2003 (mil dol)			Federal funds and grants, 2002–2003 (mil dol)			
										Procurement contract awards	
	New construction ($1,000)	Number of housing units	Percent single family	Manufactured housing units put in place, 2003 (1,000)	Total	Manufactured	Non-manufactured	Total	Salaries and wages	Defense	Other
	283	284	285	286	287	288	289	290	291	292	293

Table A. States — **Federal Funds**

STATE	Federal funds and grants, 2002–2003 (mil dol) (cont'd)											
	Direct payments for individuals						Grants					
	Total	Social Security and government retirement	Medicare	Food stamps	Supplemental Security Income	Educational assistance	Housing assistance	Total[1]	Medicaid and other health-related	Nutrition and family welfare	Education	Housing and community development	Homeland security	Energy and environment
	294	295	296	297	298	299	300	301	302	303	304	305	306	307

1. Includes program categories not shown separately.

21

COLUMN HEADINGS FOR STATES

Table A. States — **State Government Finances**

STATE	State government finances, 2001–2002											
	General revenue (mil dol)									General expenditures (mil dol)		
	From federal government			From own sources								Direct general expenditures	
					Taxes		Taxes per capita[1] (dollars)					
	Total	Total	Per capita[1] (dollars)	Total	Total	Sales and gross receipts	Total	Sales and gross receipts	Total	To local governments	Total	Per capita[1] (dollars)
	308	309	310	311	312	313	314	315	316	317	318	319

1. Based on the resident population as of July 1 at the start of the fiscal year shown.

Table A. States — **State Government Finances, Government Employment, and Elections**

STATE	State government finances, 2001–2002 (cont'd)							Government employment, 2003			Presidential election, 2004 (percent of vote cast)		
	General expenditures (mil dol) (cont'd)					Debt outstanding							
	By selected function (mil dol)												
	Education	Health and hospitals	Highways	Public safety	Public welfare	Total (mil dol)	Per capita[1]	Federal civilian	Federal military	State and local	Democratic	Republican	All other
	320	321	322	323	324	325	326	327	328	329	330	331	332

1. Based on the resident population as of July 1 at the start of the fiscal year shown.

Table A. States — Land Area and Population

			Population and population characteristics, 2003										
			Population			Race alone or in combination, not Hispanic or Latino (percent)					Age (percent)			
STATE code	STATE	Land area,[1] 2000 (sq km)	Total persons	Rank	Per square kilometer	White	Black	American Indian, Alaska Native	Asian and Pacific Islander	Percent Hispanic or Latino[2]	Under 5 years	5 to 17 years	18 to 24 years	25 to 34 years
		1	2	3	4	5	6	7	8	9	10	11	12	13
00	UNITED STATES	9 161 924	290 809 777	X	31.7	69.0	12.7	1.2	4.8	13.7	6.8	18.3	9.9	13.7
01	ALABAMA	131 426	4 500 752	23	34.2	70.3	26.6	0.9	1.1	2.0	6.6	18.0	10.1	13.2
02	ALASKA	1 481 347	648 818	47	0.4	71.1	4.4	18.5	6.0	4.6	7.5	21.7	10.7	12.7
04	ARIZONA	294 312	5 580 811	18	19.0	62.4	3.3	5.1	2.6	27.8	7.8	19.4	9.9	14.4
05	ARKANSAS	134 856	2 725 714	32	20.2	78.6	16.4	1.3	1.2	3.7	6.8	18.2	10.1	13.0
06	CALIFORNIA	403 933	35 484 453	1	87.8	46.8	6.9	1.1	13.0	34.3	7.2	19.4	10.1	14.9
08	COLORADO	268 627	4 550 688	22	16.9	74.2	4.3	1.2	3.2	18.6	7.2	18.1	10.0	15.7
09	CONNECTICUT	12 548	3 483 372	29	277.6	77.5	9.7	0.6	3.3	10.1	6.1	17.9	8.7	12.0
10	DELAWARE	5 060	817 491	45	161.6	72.8	19.7	0.6	2.9	5.3	6.6	17.7	10.0	13.1
11	DISTRICT OF COLUMBIA	159	563 384	50	3 543.3	29.2	58.6	0.7	3.6	9.4	6.0	13.3	11.4	19.4
12	FLORIDA	139 670	17 019 068	4	121.9	63.9	15.6	0.6	2.4	18.6	6.2	16.9	8.8	12.4
13	GEORGIA	149 976	8 684 715	9	57.9	62.6	28.8	0.6	2.8	6.2	7.6	18.9	10.2	15.5
15	HAWAII	16 635	1 257 608	42	75.6	35.3	3.1	1.5	74.8	7.6	6.8	16.9	10.0	13.1
16	IDAHO	214 314	1 366 332	39	6.4	88.4	0.7	1.9	1.6	8.7	7.4	19.8	11.2	13.1
17	ILLINOIS	143 961	12 653 544	5	87.9	67.3	15.3	0.4	4.3	13.6	7.0	18.5	9.9	14.3
18	INDIANA	92 895	6 195 643	14	66.7	86.2	8.9	0.6	1.5	3.9	6.9	18.9	10.2	13.2
19	IOWA	144 701	2 944 062	30	20.3	92.7	2.6	0.6	1.9	3.1	6.2	17.4	10.8	12.3
20	KANSAS	211 900	2 723 507	33	12.9	83.4	6.4	1.5	2.5	7.8	6.9	18.6	10.9	12.9
21	KENTUCKY	102 896	4 117 827	26	40.0	89.6	7.9	0.6	1.2	1.7	6.6	17.6	10.0	13.7
22	LOUISIANA	112 825	4 496 334	24	39.9	62.6	33.0	0.9	1.7	2.6	7.2	19.0	11.1	13.2
23	MAINE	79 931	1 305 728	40	16.3	97.2	0.8	1.0	1.1	0.8	5.1	16.8	9.3	11.2
24	MARYLAND	25 314	5 508 909	19	217.6	62.6	28.4	0.6	5.0	4.8	6.6	18.4	9.2	13.1
25	MASSACHUSETTS	20 306	6 433 422	13	316.8	82.1	6.2	0.5	4.9	7.4	6.2	16.9	9.3	13.8
26	MICHIGAN	147 121	10 079 985	8	68.5	79.5	14.8	1.1	2.5	3.5	6.4	18.8	9.8	13.0
27	MINNESOTA	206 189	5 059 375	21	24.5	88.4	4.4	1.5	3.8	3.3	6.4	18.2	10.3	13.3
28	MISSISSIPPI	121 488	2 881 281	31	23.7	60.4	37.0	0.7	1.0	1.5	7.3	19.1	11.2	13.3
29	MISSOURI	178 414	5 704 484	17	32.0	84.4	11.9	1.0	1.7	2.3	6.5	18.1	10.1	12.9
30	MONTANA	376 979	917 621	44	2.4	90.5	0.6	7.4	1.0	2.1	5.8	17.7	10.5	11.3
31	NEBRASKA	199 099	1 739 291	38	8.7	87.3	4.5	1.2	1.9	6.1	6.9	18.4	10.8	13.0
32	NEVADA	284 448	2 241 154	35	7.9	65.3	7.1	1.7	6.2	21.9	7.3	18.6	8.9	15.3
33	NEW HAMPSHIRE	23 227	1 287 687	41	55.4	95.5	1.1	0.6	1.9	1.8	5.7	18.1	9.3	11.6
34	NEW JERSEY	19 211	8 638 396	10	449.7	65.3	13.8	0.4	7.0	14.5	6.6	18.1	8.4	12.9
35	NEW MEXICO	314 309	1 874 614	36	6.0	44.6	2.1	9.7	1.5	43.2	7.1	19.7	10.6	12.3
36	NEW YORK	122 283	19 190 115	3	156.9	61.3	16.0	0.6	6.9	16.3	6.3	17.3	9.5	13.9
37	NORTH CAROLINA	126 161	8 407 248	11	66.6	69.8	22.0	1.5	2.0	5.6	7.0	17.8	9.8	14.6
38	NORTH DAKOTA	178 647	633 837	48	3.5	92.2	1.0	5.4	1.0	1.3	5.8	17.3	12.0	12.2
39	OHIO	106 056	11 435 798	7	107.8	84.7	12.1	0.6	1.7	2.0	6.5	18.1	9.8	12.8
40	OKLAHOMA	177 847	3 511 532	28	19.7	76.9	8.4	10.9	2.1	5.7	7.0	18.1	10.9	13.1
41	OREGON	248 631	3 559 596	27	14.3	84.3	2.1	2.2	4.5	9.2	6.3	17.6	9.8	14.1
42	PENNSYLVANIA	116 074	12 365 455	6	106.5	84.2	10.4	0.4	2.4	3.4	5.7	17.2	9.5	11.9
44	RHODE ISLAND	2 706	1 076 164	43	397.7	82.4	5.3	0.9	3.1	9.5	5.7	17.0	10.6	12.7
45	SOUTH CAROLINA	77 983	4 147 152	25	53.2	65.9	30.2	0.6	1.3	2.8	6.7	18.0	10.3	13.5
46	SOUTH DAKOTA	196 540	764 309	46	3.9	88.6	1.1	9.0	1.0	1.5	6.8	18.8	11.1	11.8
47	TENNESSEE	106 752	5 841 748	16	54.7	79.3	17.0	0.6	1.5	2.5	6.6	17.3	9.8	14.0
48	TEXAS	678 051	22 118 509	2	32.6	51.3	11.4	0.7	3.4	34.2	8.2	20.0	10.6	14.8
49	UTAH	212 751	2 351 467	34	11.1	85.4	1.1	1.6	3.3	9.9	9.8	21.8	13.3	16.2
50	VERMONT	23 956	619 107	49	25.8	97.0	0.8	1.0	1.3	0.9	5.0	17.2	10.3	11.4
51	VIRGINIA	102 548	7 386 330	12	72.0	70.4	20.3	0.7	4.8	5.3	6.7	17.7	10.0	13.8
53	WASHINGTON	172 348	6 131 445	15	35.6	80.3	4.1	2.4	7.8	8.3	6.4	18.1	10.1	13.9
54	WEST VIRGINIA	62 361	1 810 354	37	29.0	95.2	3.6	0.6	0.8	0.7	5.6	16.0	9.6	12.4
55	WISCONSIN	140 663	5 472 299	20	38.9	87.4	6.2	1.2	2.2	3.9	6.2	18.2	10.3	12.5
56	WYOMING	251 489	501 242	51	2.0	89.5	1.1	2.8	1.0	6.8	6.2	18.0	11.1	11.9

1. Dry land or land partially or temporarily covered by water.　　2. Hispanic or Latino persons may be of any race.

Table A. States — **Population and Households**

STATE	35 to 44 years	45 to 54 years	55 to 64 years	65 to 74 years	75 years and over	Percent female	Median age	Number	Percent change, 2000–2003	Persons per house-hold	Under 25 years	25 to 44 years	45 to 64 years	65 years and over
	14	15	16	17	18	19	20	21	22	23	24	25	26	27
UNITED STATES	15.3	14.0	9.6	6.3	6.0	50.8	35.9	108 419 506	2.8	2.52	5.6	38.6	35.6	20.2
ALABAMA	14.5	14.1	10.2	7.1	6.1	51.6	36.6	1 743 476	0.4	2.75	6.4	36.5	35.9	21.3
ALASKA	16.1	16.3	8.8	3.8	2.4	48.3	33.2	229 408	3.5	2.67	6.9	40.7	41.8	10.7
ARIZONA	14.1	12.4	9.2	6.8	6.0	50.0	33.9	2 048 918	7.8	2.46	7.3	38.5	33.0	21.2
ARKANSAS	14.1	13.5	10.4	7.3	6.6	51.1	36.5	1 075 918	3.2	2.92	7.1	36.0	34.4	22.6
CALIFORNIA	15.7	13.5	8.7	5.4	5.2	50.1	34.0	11 856 538	3.1	2.44	5.3	41.3	35.4	18.0
COLORADO	15.8	14.6	8.9	5.2	4.5	49.6	34.3	1 821 318	9.8	2.55	6.7	42.2	35.2	15.9
CONNECTICUT	16.5	15.0	10.4	6.3	7.2	51.4	38.5	1 323 339	1.7	2.61	3.3	38.2	37.4	21.1
DELAWARE	15.5	13.9	10.1	7.0	6.1	51.3	36.8	303 790	1.7	2.14	5.1	39.0	34.8	21.1
DISTRICT OF COLUMBIA	15.0	13.2	9.8	6.1	6.0	52.8	35.0	246 669	-0.7	2.50	5.2	44.3	31.8	18.7
FLORIDA	14.8	13.5	10.5	8.6	8.5	51.0	39.1	6 637 845	4.7	2.68	5.1	34.8	33.9	26.2
GEORGIA	16.0	13.4	8.9	5.2	4.3	50.6	33.6	3 152 672	4.9	2.91	5.8	43.9	34.4	16.0
HAWAII	14.7	14.7	10.5	6.6	6.8	49.9	37.5	419 441	4.0	2.65	4.6	33.6	39.6	22.2
IDAHO	13.9	13.8	9.3	5.9	5.5	49.9	33.8	503 145	7.1	2.67	7.6	36.6	36.9	18.9
ILLINOIS	15.2	13.9	9.3	5.9	6.0	50.9	35.2	4 624 605	0.7	2.56	4.8	40.2	35.2	19.8
INDIANA	14.8	14.1	9.5	6.2	6.1	50.8	35.5	2 350 535	0.6	2.45	6.4	38.5	35.3	19.8
IOWA	14.3	14.5	9.8	6.9	7.8	50.8	37.7	1 158 018	0.8	2.50	7.1	35.1	35.0	22.8
KANSAS	14.4	14.1	9.2	6.2	6.7	50.4	35.5	1 058 600	2.0	2.49	8.4	37.3	33.7	20.6
KENTUCKY	15.1	14.4	10.2	6.6	5.8	51.0	36.6	1 607 214	1.0	2.61	6.2	38.0	35.5	20.3
LOUISIANA	14.5	13.9	9.4	6.2	5.5	51.5	34.6	1 672 717	1.0	2.37	6.9	38.1	35.3	19.7
MAINE	15.9	16.1	11.2	7.3	7.1	51.2	40.2	535 091	3.3	2.62	5.2	35.3	38.0	21.6
MARYLAND	16.5	14.8	10.0	5.9	5.5	51.6	36.8	2 048 134	3.4	2.55	4.3	39.6	37.6	18.5
MASSACHUSETTS	16.3	14.4	9.8	6.3	7.0	51.7	37.5	2 435 941	-0.3	2.53	3.4	39.8	35.7	21.2
MICHIGAN	15.3	14.7	9.8	6.2	6.1	50.9	36.4	3 884 081	2.6	2.45	5.8	37.5	36.3	20.4
MINNESOTA	15.9	14.6	9.2	5.8	6.2	50.4	36.2	2 011 984	6.2	2.64	6.0	39.7	34.9	19.3
MISSISSIPPI	14.1	13.4	9.5	6.5	5.7	51.5	34.3	1 055 591	0.9	2.42	6.1	37.7	35.4	20.9
MISSOURI	14.9	14.1	10.0	6.8	6.6	51.2	36.7	2 284 663	4.1	2.44	7.1	37.2	34.7	21.1
MONTANA	14.1	16.1	10.9	7.0	6.7	50.1	39.0	365 680	2.0	2.50	7.2	32.1	38.9	21.8
NEBRASKA	14.3	14.1	9.2	6.5	6.9	50.6	35.7	675 472	1.4	2.65	7.5	36.6	34.7	21.1
NEVADA	15.3	13.3	10.0	6.6	4.6	49.0	34.9	833 679	11.0	2.54	6.2	40.6	35.5	17.8
NEW HAMPSHIRE	17.1	15.9	10.4	6.1	5.8	50.7	38.5	492 948	3.9	2.70	4.6	37.0	39.6	18.8
NEW JERSEY	16.6	14.5	10.0	6.4	6.6	51.3	37.6	3 122 552	1.9	2.63	2.5	38.5	37.7	21.3
NEW MEXICO	14.2	14.2	9.9	6.5	5.5	50.8	35.3	698 088	3.0	2.61	6.5	36.9	36.3	20.3
NEW YORK	15.8	14.2	10.0	6.5	6.5	51.7	37.0	7 118 706	0.9	2.49	3.7	38.5	36.8	21.0
NORTH CAROLINA	15.2	13.7	9.8	6.5	5.6	50.9	35.5	3 270 705	4.4	2.39	6.2	39.9	34.4	19.5
NORTH DAKOTA	13.7	14.7	9.4	6.9	7.9	50.0	37.3	254 464	-1.0	2.49	8.7	34.5	34.0	22.8
OHIO	14.9	14.7	9.9	6.7	6.6	51.3	37.1	4 480 461	0.8	2.53	5.6	36.7	36.5	21.2
OKLAHOMA	14.1	13.8	10.0	6.9	6.2	50.7	35.8	1 341 376	-0.1	2.47	7.7	35.4	35.9	21.0
OREGON	14.4	15.0	10.2	6.2	6.5	50.3	36.7	1 409 401	5.7	2.48	7.0	36.5	36.6	20.0
PENNSYLVANIA	15.0	14.9	10.3	7.3	8.0	51.6	39.0	4 801 049	0.5	2.52	4.3	35.0	36.4	24.4
RHODE ISLAND	15.7	14.5	9.8	6.4	7.7	51.8	37.8	411 579	0.8	2.56	5.0	37.0	35.8	22.2
SOUTH CAROLINA	14.7	14.1	10.4	6.7	5.6	51.3	36.1	1 567 798	2.2	2.46	6.6	37.8	35.7	19.9
SOUTH DAKOTA	14.0	14.1	9.1	6.8	7.4	50.3	36.3	299 280	3.1	2.48	9.1	34.9	33.8	22.2
TENNESSEE	15.2	14.3	10.3	6.7	5.7	51.2	36.7	2 295 640	2.8	2.82	6.2	37.3	36.6	19.8
TEXAS	15.0	13.1	8.4	5.3	4.5	50.2	32.6	7 634 767	3.3	2.61	7.1	41.8	34.2	17.0
UTAH	12.3	11.1	6.9	4.5	4.1	49.8	27.5	752 030	7.2	3.07	9.6	43.2	30.8	16.4
VERMONT	15.6	16.4	11.1	6.6	6.3	50.9	39.3	242 047	0.6	2.47	5.3	34.7	39.9	20.0
VIRGINIA	16.0	14.5	10.1	6.0	5.3	50.8	36.3	2 790 262	3.4	2.56	5.4	39.3	36.7	18.7
WASHINGTON	15.6	15.0	9.8	5.6	5.6	50.1	36.1	2 382 320	4.9	2.51	6.2	39.9	36.1	17.9
WEST VIRGINIA	14.0	15.6	11.4	8.0	7.3	51.2	39.8	731 690	-0.7	2.41	5.8	32.6	37.7	24.0
WISCONSIN	15.5	14.7	9.6	6.4	6.6	50.5	37.0	2 159 083	3.6	2.46	7.0	37.6	34.9	20.5
WYOMING	14.0	16.2	10.6	6.4	5.5	49.7	37.4	198 778	2.7	2.45	7.6	34.1	39.1	19.2

Table A. States — **Immigration and Population Change**

STATE	Immigrants admitted to legal status, 2003	Census counts 1980	1990	2000	Percent change 1980–1990	1990–2000	2000–2003	Births	Deaths	Net migration	International	Net internal
	28	29	30	31	32	33	34	35	36	37	38	39
UNITED STATES	705 827	226 542 204	248 790 925	281 421 906	9.8	13.1	3.3	13 085 539	7 889 270	4 190 277	4 190 277	X
ALABAMA	1 693	3 894 025	4 040 389	4 447 100	3.8	10.1	1.2	198 297	149 646	6 723	16 549	-9 826
ALASKA	1 196	401 851	550 043	626 932	36.9	14.0	3.5	32 190	10 102	-117	3 620	-3 737
ARIZONA	11 001	2 716 546	3 665 339	5 130 632	34.9	40.0	8.8	278 744	136 492	306 247	111 543	194 704
ARKANSAS	1 911	2 286 357	2 350 624	2 673 400	2.8	13.7	2.0	122 012	92 026	22 760	14 210	8 550
CALIFORNIA	176 375	23 667 765	29 811 427	33 871 648	26.0	13.6	4.8	1 701 252	756 758	660 643	937 831	- 277 188
COLORADO	10 713	2 889 735	3 294 473	4 301 261	14.0	30.6	5.8	217 234	93 256	122 281	74 258	48 023
CONNECTICUT	8 296	3 107 564	3 287 116	3 405 565	5.8	3.6	2.3	137 197	97 971	41 354	50 574	-9 220
DELAWARE	1 490	594 338	666 168	783 600	12.1	17.6	4.3	35 263	23 141	22 308	7 386	14 922
DISTRICT OF COLUMBIA	2 497	638 432	606 900	572 059	-4.9	-5.7	-1.5	25 698	19 520	-14 898	13 622	-28 520
FLORIDA	52 969	9 746 961	12 938 071	15 982 378	32.7	23.5	6.5	675 642	543 406	889 862	349 333	540 529
GEORGIA	10 805	5 462 982	6 478 149	8 186 453	18.6	26.4	6.1	438 289	212 673	267 059	127 050	140 009
HAWAII	4 907	964 691	1 108 229	1 211 537	14.9	9.3	3.8	59 044	29 180	16 797	19 338	-2 541
IDAHO	1 692	944 127	1 006 734	1 293 953	6.6	28.5	5.6	66 337	32 085	36 648	9 479	27 169
ILLINOIS	32 488	11 427 409	11 430 602	12 419 293	0.0	8.6	1.9	598 234	347 071	-20 773	217 631	- 238 404
INDIANA	5 255	5 490 214	5 544 156	6 080 485	1.0	9.7	1.9	277 808	181 651	21 305	36 229	-14 924
IOWA	3 425	2 913 808	2 776 831	2 926 324	-4.7	5.4	0.6	121 048	91 168	-10 393	19 335	-29 728
KANSAS	3 811	2 364 236	2 477 588	2 688 418	4.8	8.5	1.3	125 734	80 523	-10 108	25 497	-35 605
KENTUCKY	3 047	3 660 324	3 686 892	4 041 769	0.7	9.6	1.9	177 581	130 520	30 493	17 753	12 740
LOUISIANA	2 221	4 206 116	4 221 826	4 468 976	0.4	5.9	0.6	219 361	135 991	-55 144	12 630	-67 774
MAINE	999	1 125 043	1 227 928	1 274 923	9.1	3.8	2.4	43 434	40 920	28 848	3 126	25 722
MARYLAND	17 813	4 216 933	4 780 753	5 296 486	13.4	10.8	4.0	241 352	144 272	111 121	72 453	38 668
MASSACHUSETTS	20 184	5 737 093	6 016 425	6 349 097	4.9	5.5	1.3	265 871	185 556	5 832	108 737	- 102 905
MICHIGAN	13 546	9 262 044	9 295 287	9 938 444	0.4	6.9	1.4	428 261	285 979	3 918	82 169	-78 251
MINNESOTA	8 435	4 075 970	4 375 665	4 919 479	7.4	12.4	2.8	216 100	122 759	46 271	47 425	-1 154
MISSISSIPPI	730	2 520 770	2 575 475	2 844 658	2.2	10.5	1.3	141 826	92 710	-11 761	6 410	-18 171
MISSOURI	6 179	4 916 766	5 116 901	5 595 211	4.1	9.3	2.0	245 375	180 689	45 116	28 149	16 967
MONTANA	456	786 690	799 065	902 195	1.6	12.9	1.7	35 234	27 673	7 907	1 343	6 564
NEBRASKA	2 836	1 569 825	1 578 417	1 711 263	0.5	8.4	1.6	80 474	50 477	-979	14 878	-15 857
NEVADA	6 369	800 508	1 201 675	1 998 257	50.1	66.3	12.2	102 521	53 711	190 642	43 954	146 688
NEW HAMPSHIRE	1 873	920 610	1 109 252	1 235 786	20.5	11.4	4.2	47 194	32 188	37 082	7 454	29 628
NEW JERSEY	40 818	7 365 011	7 747 750	8 414 350	5.2	8.6	2.7	370 057	240 899	99 345	192 044	-92 699
NEW MEXICO	2 342	1 303 302	1 515 069	1 819 046	16.2	20.1	3.1	87 305	45 302	13 805	18 188	-4 383
NEW YORK	89 661	17 558 165	17 990 778	18 976 457	2.5	5.5	1.1	835 326	515 916	- 108 872	442 800	- 551 672
NORTH CAROLINA	9 479	5 880 095	6 632 448	8 049 313	12.8	21.4	4.4	386 343	235 328	210 546	102 905	107 641
NORTH DAKOTA	332	652 717	638 800	642 200	-2.1	0.5	-1.3	24 648	19 620	-13 288	2 374	-15 662
OHIO	9 805	10 797 603	10 847 115	11 353 140	0.5	4.7	0.7	493 802	354 822	-53 041	50 359	- 103 400
OKLAHOMA	2 394	3 025 487	3 145 576	3 450 654	4.0	9.7	1.8	162 253	115 649	15 639	24 310	-8 671
OREGON	6 968	2 633 156	2 842 337	3 421 399	7.9	20.4	4.0	145 101	100 483	95 743	47 963	47 780
PENNSYLVANIA	14 638	11 864 720	11 882 842	12 281 054	0.2	3.4	0.7	464 646	424 782	52 463	68 935	-16 472
RHODE ISLAND	2 495	947 154	1 003 464	1 048 319	5.9	4.5	2.7	40 114	31 964	20 573	12 549	8 024
SOUTH CAROLINA	1 946	3 120 729	3 486 310	4 012 012	11.7	15.1	3.4	182 193	122 447	77 775	23 056	54 719
SOUTH DAKOTA	488	690 768	696 004	754 844	0.8	8.5	1.3	33 914	22 917	-1 114	2 492	-3 606
TENNESSEE	3 373	4 591 023	4 877 203	5 689 283	6.2	16.7	2.7	255 980	181 364	79 587	32 816	46 771
TEXAS	53 592	14 225 513	16 986 335	20 851 820	19.4	22.8	6.1	1 190 484	475 020	546 729	439 765	106 964
UTAH	3 174	1 461 037	1 722 850	2 233 169	17.9	29.6	5.3	154 257	42 133	3 623	33 271	-29 648
VERMONT	554	511 456	562 758	608 827	10.0	8.2	1.7	20 066	16 774	7 514	2 890	4 624
VIRGINIA	19 781	5 346 797	6 189 197	7 078 515	15.8	14.4	4.3	321 528	184 285	168 252	90 536	77 716
WASHINGTON	18 017	4 132 353	4 866 669	5 894 121	17.8	21.1	4.0	255 338	144 509	128 164	88 929	39 235
WEST VIRGINIA	485	1 950 186	1 793 477	1 808 344	-8.0	0.8	0.1	66 283	68 098	4 504	2 098	2 406
WISCONSIN	4 378	4 705 642	4 891 954	5 363 675	4.0	9.6	2.0	220 988	153 446	44 586	30 643	13 943
WYOMING	259	469 557	453 589	493 782	-3.4	8.9	1.5	20 306	13 398	700	1 388	-688

Table A. States — Population Characteristics, 2000

	Population characteristics, 2000 (percent)																
STATE	Race							Age									
	White alone	Black alone	American Indian, Alaska Native alone	Asian and Pacific Islander alone	Some other race or two or more races	Hispanic or Latino[1]	Foreign born	Under 5 years	5 to 17 years	18 to 24 years	25 to 34 years	35 to 44 years	45 to 54 years	55 to 64 years	65 to 74 years	75 years and over	Female
	40	41	42	43	44	45	46	47	48	49	50	51	52	53	54	55	56
UNITED STATES	69.1	12.1	0.7	3.7	1.8	12.5	11.1	6.8	18.9	9.7	14.2	16.0	13.4	8.6	6.5	5.9	50.9
ALABAMA	70.3	25.9	0.5	0.7	0.9	1.7	2.0	6.7	18.6	9.9	13.6	15.4	13.5	9.3	7.1	5.9	51.7
ALASKA	67.6	3.4	15.4	4.5	5.1	4.1	5.9	7.6	22.8	9.1	14.3	18.2	15.1	7.1	3.6	2.1	48.3
ARIZONA	63.8	2.9	4.5	1.9	1.6	25.3	12.8	7.5	19.2	10.0	14.5	15.0	12.2	8.6	7.1	5.9	50.1
ARKANSAS	78.6	15.6	0.6	0.8	1.2	3.2	2.8	6.8	18.7	9.8	13.2	14.9	13.1	9.6	7.4	6.6	51.2
CALIFORNIA	46.7	6.4	0.5	11.1	2.9	32.4	26.2	7.3	20.0	9.9	15.4	16.2	12.8	7.7	5.6	5.0	50.2
COLORADO	74.5	3.7	0.7	2.3	1.8	17.1	8.6	6.9	18.7	10.0	15.4	17.1	14.3	7.9	5.3	4.4	49.6
CONNECTICUT	77.5	8.7	0.2	2.4	1.8	9.4	10.9	6.6	18.2	8.0	13.3	17.1	14.1	9.1	6.8	7.0	51.6
DELAWARE	72.5	18.9	0.3	2.1	1.4	4.8	5.7	6.6	18.3	9.6	13.9	16.3	13.3	9.1	7.2	5.8	51.4
DISTRICT OF COLUMBIA ..	27.8	59.4	0.2	2.7	2.0	7.9	12.9	5.7	14.4	12.7	17.8	15.3	13.2	8.7	6.3	5.9	52.9
FLORIDA	65.4	14.2	0.3	1.7	1.7	16.8	16.7	5.9	16.9	8.3	13.0	15.5	12.9	9.8	9.1	8.5	51.2
GEORGIA	62.6	28.5	0.2	2.1	1.2	5.3	7.1	7.3	19.2	10.2	15.9	16.5	13.2	8.1	5.4	4.3	50.8
HAWAII	22.9	1.7	0.2	49.7	18.2	7.2	17.5	6.5	18.0	9.5	14.1	15.8	14.1	8.8	7.0	6.2	49.8
IDAHO	88.0	0.4	1.2	1.0	1.5	7.9	5.0	7.5	21.0	10.7	13.1	14.9	13.2	8.3	5.9	5.4	49.9
ILLINOIS	67.8	14.9	0.1	3.4	1.3	12.3	12.3	7.1	19.1	9.8	14.6	16.0	13.1	8.4	6.2	5.9	51.0
INDIANA	85.8	8.3	0.2	1.0	1.1	3.5	3.1	7.0	18.9	10.1	13.7	15.8	13.4	8.7	6.5	5.9	51.0
IOWA	92.6	2.1	0.3	1.3	0.9	2.8	3.1	6.4	18.6	10.2	12.4	15.2	13.4	8.8	7.2	7.7	50.9
KANSAS	83.1	5.6	0.8	1.8	1.7	7.0	5.0	7.0	19.5	10.3	13.1	15.6	13.2	8.2	6.5	6.7	50.6
KENTUCKY	89.3	7.3	0.2	0.8	1.0	1.5	2.0	6.6	18.0	9.9	14.1	15.9	13.8	9.2	6.8	5.7	51.1
LOUISIANA	62.5	32.3	0.5	1.2	1.0	2.4	2.6	7.1	20.2	10.6	13.5	15.5	13.1	8.5	6.3	5.2	51.6
MAINE	96.5	0.5	0.5	0.7	1.0	0.7	2.9	5.5	18.1	8.1	12.4	16.7	15.1	9.7	7.5	6.8	51.3
MARYLAND	62.1	27.7	0.3	4.0	1.7	4.3	9.8	6.7	18.9	8.5	14.1	17.3	14.3	8.9	6.1	5.2	51.7
MASSACHUSETTS	81.9	5.0	0.2	3.8	2.4	6.8	12.2	6.3	17.4	9.1	14.6	16.7	13.8	8.6	6.7	6.8	51.8
MICHIGAN	78.6	14.1	0.5	1.8	1.8	3.3	5.3	6.8	19.4	9.4	13.7	16.1	13.8	8.7	6.5	5.8	51.0
MINNESOTA	88.2	3.4	1.1	2.9	1.5	2.9	5.3	6.7	19.5	9.6	13.7	16.8	13.5	8.2	6.0	6.1	50.5
MISSISSIPPI	60.7	36.2	0.4	0.7	0.7	1.4	1.4	7.2	20.1	10.9	13.4	15.0	12.7	8.6	6.5	5.5	51.7
MISSOURI	83.8	11.2	0.4	1.1	1.4	2.1	2.7	6.6	18.9	9.6	13.2	15.9	13.3	9.1	7.0	6.5	51.4
MONTANA	89.5	0.3	6.0	0.6	1.6	2.0	1.8	6.1	19.4	9.5	11.4	15.7	15.0	9.4	6.9	6.5	50.2
NEBRASKA	87.3	3.9	0.8	1.3	1.1	5.5	4.4	6.8	19.5	10.2	13.0	15.4	13.2	8.3	6.8	6.8	50.7
NEVADA	65.2	6.6	1.1	4.8	2.6	19.7	15.8	7.3	18.3	9.0	15.3	16.1	13.5	9.5	6.6	4.4	49.1
NEW HAMPSHIRE	95.1	0.7	0.2	1.3	1.0	1.7	4.4	6.1	18.9	8.4	13.0	17.9	14.9	8.9	6.3	5.6	50.8
NEW JERSEY	66.0	13.0	0.1	5.7	1.8	13.3	17.5	6.7	18.1	8.0	14.1	17.1	13.8	9.0	6.8	6.4	51.5
NEW MEXICO	44.7	1.7	8.9	1.1	1.6	42.1	8.2	7.2	20.8	9.8	12.9	15.5	13.5	8.7	6.5	5.2	50.8
NEW YORK	62.0	14.8	0.3	5.5	2.3	15.1	20.4	6.5	18.2	9.3	14.5	16.2	13.5	8.9	6.7	6.2	51.8
NORTH CAROLINA..........	70.2	21.4	1.2	1.4	1.1	4.7	5.3	6.7	17.7	10.0	15.1	16.0	13.5	9.0	6.6	5.4	51.0
NORTH DAKOTA	91.7	0.6	4.8	0.6	1.1	1.2	1.9	6.1	18.9	11.4	12.0	15.3	13.3	8.3	7.1	7.6	50.1
OHIO	84.0	11.4	0.2	1.2	1.3	1.9	3.0	6.6	18.8	9.3	13.4	15.9	13.8	8.9	7.0	6.3	51.4
OKLAHOMA	74.1	7.5	7.7	1.4	4.1	5.2	3.8	6.8	19.0	10.3	13.1	15.2	13.1	9.2	7.0	6.2	50.9
OREGON	83.5	1.6	1.2	3.1	2.6	8.0	8.5	6.5	18.2	9.6	13.8	15.4	14.8	8.9	6.4	6.4	50.4
PENNSYLVANIA	84.1	9.8	0.1	1.8	1.0	3.2	4.1	5.9	17.9	8.9	12.7	15.9	13.9	9.2	7.9	7.7	51.7
RHODE ISLAND	81.9	4.0	0.4	2.3	2.8	8.7	11.4	6.1	17.5	10.2	13.4	16.2	13.5	8.5	7.0	7.5	52.0
SOUTH CAROLINA...........	66.1	29.4	0.3	0.9	0.9	2.4	2.9	6.6	18.6	10.2	14.0	15.6	13.7	9.3	6.7	5.4	51.4
SOUTH DAKOTA	88.0	0.6	8.1	0.6	1.2	1.4	1.8	6.8	20.1	10.3	12.1	15.3	12.9	8.3	7.0	7.3	50.4
TENNESSEE	79.2	16.3	0.2	1.0	1.0	2.2	2.8	6.6	18.0	9.6	14.3	15.9	13.8	9.4	6.7	5.6	51.3
TEXAS	52.4	11.3	0.3	2.7	1.2	32.0	13.9	7.8	20.4	10.5	15.2	15.9	12.5	7.7	5.5	4.5	50.4
UTAH	85.3	0.7	1.2	2.3	1.5	9.0	7.1	9.4	22.8	14.2	14.6	13.4	10.6	6.4	4.5	4.0	49.9
VERMONT	96.2	0.5	0.4	0.9	1.2	0.9	3.8	5.6	18.6	9.3	12.2	16.7	15.4	9.3	6.7	6.0	51.0
VIRGINIA	70.2	19.4	0.3	3.7	1.8	4.7	8.1	6.5	18.0	9.6	14.6	17.0	14.1	8.9	6.1	5.1	51.0
WASHINGTON	78.9	3.1	1.4	5.8	3.2	7.5	10.4	6.7	19.0	9.5	14.3	16.5	14.4	8.4	5.7	5.5	50.2
WEST VIRGINIA	94.6	3.1	0.2	0.5	0.9	0.7	1.1	5.6	16.6	9.5	12.7	15.1	15.0	10.2	8.2	7.1	51.4
WISCONSIN	87.3	5.6	0.8	1.7	1.0	3.6	3.6	6.4	19.1	9.7	13.2	16.3	13.7	8.5	6.6	6.5	50.6
WYOMING	88.9	0.7	2.1	0.6	1.3	6.4	2.3	6.3	19.8	10.1	12.1	16.0	15.0	9.0	6.3	5.3	49.7

1. Hispanic or Latino persons may be of any race.

STATE	Households, 2000					Births, 2002		Deaths, 2002					Physicians, 2000	
				Percent				Number		Rate				
										Total				
	Number	Percent change, 1990–2000	Persons per house-hold	Female family house-holder[1]	One person	Total	Rate[2]	Total	Infant[3]	Crude[2]	Age-adjusted	Infant[4]	Number	Rate[5]
	57	58	59	60	61	62	63	64	65	66	67	68	69	70
UNITED STATES	105 480 101	14.7	2.59	12.2	25.8	4 021 726	13.9	2 443 387	28 034	8.5	8.5	7.0	587 994	209
ALABAMA	1 737 080	15.3	2.49	14.2	26.1	58 967	13.1	46 069	539	10.3	10.0	9.1	7 605	171
ALASKA	221 600	17.3	2.74	10.8	23.5	9 938	15.4	3 030	55	4.7	7.9	5.5	1 087	173
ARIZONA	1 901 327	38.9	2.64	11.1	24.8	87 837	16.1	42 816	559	7.8	8.0	6.4	9 612	187
ARKANSAS	1 042 696	17.0	2.49	12.1	25.6	37 437	13.8	28 513	312	10.5	9.6	8.3	4 267	160
CALIFORNIA	11 502 870	10.8	2.87	12.6	23.5	529 357	15.1	234 565	2 889	6.7	7.6	5.5	75 739	224
COLORADO	1 658 238	29.3	2.53	9.6	26.3	68 418	15.2	29 210	415	6.5	7.9	6.1	9 342	217
CONNECTICUT	1 301 670	5.8	2.53	12.1	26.4	42 001	12.1	30 122	274	8.7	7.6	6.5	10 162	298
DELAWARE	298 736	20.7	2.54	13.1	25.0	11 090	13.7	6 861	96	8.5	8.4	8.7	1 677	214
DISTRICT OF COLUMBIA	248 338	-0.5	2.16	18.9	43.8	7 498	13.1	5 851	85	10.2	10.2	11.3	4 093	715
FLORIDA	6 337 929	23.4	2.46	12.0	26.6	205 579	12.3	167 814	1 548	10.0	7.9	7.5	33 929	212
GEORGIA	3 006 369	27.0	2.65	14.5	23.6	133 300	15.6	65 449	1 192	7.6	9.5	8.9	17 317	212
HAWAII	403 240	13.2	2.92	12.4	21.9	17 477	14.0	8 801	127	7.1	6.6	7.3	3 138	259
IDAHO	469 645	30.2	2.69	8.7	22.4	20 970	15.6	9 923	128	7.4	7.9	6.1	1 831	142
ILLINOIS	4 591 779	9.3	2.63	12.3	26.8	180 622	14.3	106 667	1 339	8.5	8.6	7.4	25 778	208
INDIANA	2 336 306	13.1	2.53	11.1	25.9	85 081	13.8	55 396	657	9.0	9.0	7.7	10 572	174
IOWA	1 149 276	8.0	2.46	8.6	27.2	37 559	12.8	27 978	199	9.5	7.7	5.3	5 236	179
KANSAS	1 037 891	9.9	2.51	9.3	27.0	39 412	14.5	25 021	281	9.2	8.4	7.1	4 801	179
KENTUCKY	1 590 647	15.3	2.47	11.8	26.0	54 233	13.3	40 697	392	9.9	9.9	7.2	7 010	173
LOUISIANA	1 656 053	10.5	2.62	16.6	25.3	64 872	14.7	41 984	665	9.4	10.0	10.3	9 061	203
MAINE	518 200	11.4	2.39	9.5	27.0	13 559	10.5	12 694	59	9.8	8.5	4.4	2 816	221
MARYLAND	1 980 859	13.3	2.61	14.1	25.0	73 323	13.4	43 970	551	8.1	8.6	7.5	16 561	313
MASSACHUSETTS	2 443 580	8.7	2.51	11.9	28.0	80 645	12.5	56 928	395	8.9	7.9	4.9	20 757	327
MICHIGAN	3 785 661	10.7	2.56	12.5	26.2	129 967	12.9	87 795	1 057	8.7	8.8	8.1	21 114	212
MINNESOTA	1 895 127	15.0	2.52	8.9	26.9	68 025	13.6	38 510	364	7.7	7.5	5.4	10 124	206
MISSISSIPPI	1 046 434	14.8	2.63	17.3	24.6	41 518	14.5	28 853	428	10.0	10.4	10.3	4 116	145
MISSOURI	2 194 594	11.9	2.48	11.6	27.3	75 251	13.3	55 940	637	9.9	9.2	8.5	11 883	212
MONTANA	358 667	17.1	2.45	8.9	27.4	11 049	12.1	8 506	83	9.4	8.5	7.5	1 646	182
NEBRASKA	666 184	10.6	2.49	9.1	27.6	25 383	14.7	15 738	178	9.1	8.1	7.0	3 091	181
NEVADA	751 165	61.1	2.62	11.1	24.9	32 571	15.0	16 927	197	7.8	9.2	6.0	2 983	149
NEW HAMPSHIRE	474 606	15.4	2.53	9.1	24.4	14 442	11.3	9 853	72	7.7	7.8	5.0	2 603	211
NEW JERSEY	3 064 645	9.7	2.68	12.6	24.5	114 751	13.4	74 009	655	8.6	8.1	5.7	20 834	248
NEW MEXICO	677 971	24.9	2.63	13.2	25.4	27 753	15.0	14 344	174	7.7	8.2	6.3	3 602	198
NEW YORK	7 056 860	6.3	2.61	14.7	28.1	251 415	13.1	158 118	1 519	8.3	7.8	6.0	58 453	308
NORTH CAROLINA	3 132 013	24.4	2.49	12.5	25.4	117 335	14.1	72 027	959	8.7	9.1	8.2	16 441	204
NORTH DAKOTA	257 152	6.8	2.41	7.8	29.3	7 757	12.2	5 892	49	9.3	7.5	6.3	1 355	211
OHIO	4 445 773	8.8	2.49	12.1	27.3	148 720	13.0	109 766	1 180	9.6	9.1	7.9	23 939	211
OKLAHOMA	1 342 293	11.3	2.49	11.4	26.7	50 387	14.4	35 502	410	10.2	9.7	8.1	5 448	158
OREGON	1 333 723	20.9	2.51	9.8	26.1	45 192	12.8	31 119	260	8.8	8.3	5.8	7 338	214
PENNSYLVANIA	4 777 003	6.3	2.48	11.6	27.7	142 850	11.6	130 223	1 091	10.6	8.6	7.6	31 671	258
RHODE ISLAND	408 424	8.1	2.47	12.9	28.6	12 894	12.1	10 246	90	9.6	8.1	7.0	2 859	273
SOUTH CAROLINA	1 533 854	21.9	2.53	14.8	25.0	54 570	13.3	37 736	507	9.2	9.5	9.3	6 704	167
SOUTH DAKOTA	290 245	12.0	2.50	9.0	27.6	10 698	14.1	6 898	70	9.1	7.7	6.5	1 307	173
TENNESSEE	2 232 905	20.5	2.48	12.9	25.8	77 482	13.4	56 606	727	9.8	9.8	9.4	11 281	198
TEXAS	7 393 354	21.8	2.74	12.7	23.7	372 450	17.1	155 524	2 368	7.1	8.7	6.4	35 952	172
UTAH	701 281	30.5	3.13	9.4	17.8	49 182	21.2	13 116	273	5.7	7.8	5.6	3 665	164
VERMONT	240 634	14.2	2.44	9.3	26.2	6 387	10.4	5 075	28	8.2	7.8	4.4	1 535	252
VIRGINIA	2 699 173	17.8	2.54	11.9	25.1	99 672	13.7	57 196	741	7.8	8.6	7.4	14 280	202
WASHINGTON	2 271 398	21.3	2.53	9.9	26.2	79 028	13.0	45 338	456	7.5	7.9	5.8	16 660	283
WEST VIRGINIA	736 481	7.0	2.40	10.7	27.1	20 712	11.5	21 016	188	11.7	9.9	9.1	3 593	199
WISCONSIN	2 084 544	14.4	2.50	9.6	26.8	68 560	12.6	46 981	472	8.6	8.0	6.9	10 763	201
WYOMING	193 608	14.7	2.48	8.7	26.3	6 550	13.1	4 174	44	8.4	8.6	6.7	762	154

1. No spouse present. 2. Per 1,000 resident population. 3. Deaths of infants under 1 year old. 4. Deaths of infants under 1 year old per 1,000 live births.
5. Per 100,000 resident population as of April 1 of the year shown.

Table A. States — **Health Resources, Crime, and Education**

STATE	Hospitals, 1998 Total	Beds Number	Beds Rate[1]	Medicare enrollees, 2003	Serious crimes known to police,[2] 2003 Total Number	Total Rate[3]	Rate[3] Violent	Rate[3] Property	Elementary and secondary school enrollment, 2001–2002 Total	Percent private	Educational attainment[4] (percent) 2000 High school graduate or more	2000 Bachelor's degree or more	2003 High school graduate or more	2003 Bachelor's degree or more
	71	72	73	74	75	76	77	78	79	80	81	82	83	84
UNITED STATES..................	5 214	895 681	331	40 172 605	11 816 782	4 063	475	3 588	53 029 387	10.1	84.1	25.6	84.5	27.2
ALABAMA	110	17 785	409	719 246	201 572	4 479	430	4 049	813 928	9.4	77.5	20.4	79.9	22.7
ALASKA	16	1 324	216	47 749	28 130	4 336	593	3 742	141 105	4.8	90.4	28.1	90.6	24.0
ARIZONA	61	10 161	218	728 885	342 973	6 146	513	5 632	966 540	4.6	85.1	24.6	83.8	26.0
ARKANSAS..........................	80	10 107	398	452 676	111 141	4 078	456	3 621	479 095	6.1	81.7	18.4	80.9	17.4
CALIFORNIA........................	444	90 767	278	4 078 426	1 420 637	4 004	579	3 424	6 904 112	9.5	81.2	27.5	81.1	29.8
COLORADO.........................	68	9 438	238	493 454	195 046	4 286	345	3 941	796 595	6.8	89.7	34.6	88.7	36.0
CONNECTICUT	35	7 782	238	522 403	101 537	2 915	308	2 607	641 375	11.1	88.2	31.6	87.5	33.5
DELAWARE..........................	9	1 990	268	119 302	33 046	4 042	658	3 384	141 920	18.6	86.1	24.0	88.7	28.1
DISTRICT OF COLUMBIA ...	10	4 322	826	73 794	41 738	7 408	1 608	5 800	95 435	21.0	83.2	38.3	86.0	46.4
FLORIDA..............................	214	51 241	344	2 920 971	881 976	5 182	730	4 452	2 803 571	10.8	84.0	22.8	84.7	25.8
GEORGIA	157	24 637	322	973 794	408 923	4 709	454	4 255	1 587 863	7.4	82.6	23.1	85.1	25.0
HAWAII	19	3 166	265	174 633	69 267	5 508	270	5 238	224 745	17.9	87.4	26.3	88.5	27.0
IDAHO.................................	43	3 271	266	177 700	43 058	3 151	243	2 909	256 812	4.0	86.2	20.0	88.2	22.5
ILLINOIS.............................	206	40 475	336	1 661 454	486 049	3 841	557	3 284	2 364 681	12.4	85.5	27.1	85.9	28.1
INDIANA..............................	117	19 596	332	877 954	229 890	3 711	353	3 358	1 107 390	10.0	84.6	17.1	86.4	22.2
IOWA..................................	120	13 473	471	482 340	95 198	3 234	272	2 961	533 579	8.9	89.7	25.5	89.7	24.6
KANSAS..............................	132	11 383	433	394 206	119 548	4 389	396	3 994	511 232	8.0	88.1	27.3	88.6	31.0
KENTUCKY..........................	105	16 966	431	648 400	121 195	2 943	262	2 682	727 182	10.0	78.7	20.5	82.8	21.3
LOUISIANA	133	18 314	419	620 196	224 631	4 996	646	4 350	868 594	15.8	80.8	22.5	79.8	22.3
MAINE.................................	40	4 371	351	226 696	33 500	2 566	109	2 457	224 365	8.4	89.3	24.1	86.6	23.7
MARYLAND	48	13 611	265	674 448	248 196	4 505	704	3 801	1 014 501	15.2	85.7	32.3	87.6	37.2
MASSACHUSETTS	90	20 369	331	965 943	194 214	3 019	469	2 550	1 113 950	12.6	85.1	32.7	87.1	37.6
MICHIGAN	167	31 719	323	1 444 987	381 880	3 788	511	3 277	1 907 694	9.3	86.2	23.0	87.6	23.3
MINNESOTA	142	17 140	363	676 156	170 979	3 379	263	3 117	952 564	10.6	90.8	31.2	91.6	32.7
MISSISSIPPI	104	12 563	456	436 677	116 575	4 046	326	3 720	546 072	9.6	80.3	18.7	81.2	19.3
MISSOURI	134	21 768	400	884 449	255 972	4 487	473	4 015	1 034 118	12.0	86.6	26.2	88.3	26.6
MONTANA	54	4 084	464	142 457	31 779	3 463	365	3 098	161 888	6.1	89.6	23.8	90.1	24.9
NEBRASKA	89	7 870	473	257 171	69 578	4 000	289	3 711	328 232	13.1	90.4	24.6	90.8	26.8
NEVADA	23	3 716	213	273 724	109 874	4 903	614	4 288	373 437	4.5	82.8	19.3	85.6	21.2
NEW HAMPSHIRE	26	3 179	268	179 564	28 364	2 203	149	2 054	231 597	10.7	88.1	30.1	92.1	34.0
NEW JERSEY......................	94	30 258	373	1 219 935	251 398	2 910	366	2 544	1 559 843	14.0	87.3	30.1	86.2	33.4
NEW MEXICO......................	36	4 015	231	250 113	89 771	4 789	665	4 124	343 897	6.9	82.2	23.6	81.7	23.7
NEW YORK..........................	235	73 682	405	2 763 299	520 713	2 713	465	2 248	3 364 650	14.6	82.5	28.7	84.2	29.6
NORTH CAROLINA.............	121	21 735	288	1 205 466	397 906	4 733	455	4 278	1 418 582	7.3	79.2	23.2	81.4	23.8
NORTH DAKOTA	46	4 304	674	103 220	13 779	2 174	78	2 096	112 829	6.0	85.5	22.6	89.7	25.2
OHIO..................................	188	39 924	356	1 727 096	454 420	3 974	333	3 641	2 087 412	12.3	87.0	24.6	87.2	25.0
OKLAHOMA	110	11 495	343	521 286	168 966	4 812	506	4 306	652 718	4.7	86.1	22.5	85.7	24.3
OREGON	62	7 352	224	513 253	180 750	5 078	296	4 782	596 928	7.6	88.1	27.2	86.9	26.4
PENNSYLVANIA	214	46 466	387	2 110 470	349 857	2 829	398	2 431	2 153 098	15.4	85.7	24.3	86.0	24.8
RHODE ISLAND	10	2 814	285	172 474	35 305	3 281	286	2 995	184 171	14.2	81.3	26.4	81.0	27.6
SOUTH CAROLINA.............	64	11 249	293	606 323	218 579	5 271	794	4 477	750 015	7.9	83.0	19.0	80.8	22.3
SOUTH DAKOTA	51	4 195	568	121 777	16 624	2 175	173	2 002	138 492	7.9	91.8	25.7	88.7	23.9
TENNESSEE	135	21 953	404	871 938	296 010	5 067	688	4 379	1 017 129	9.1	79.9	22.0	81.0	23.5
TEXAS	406	55 695	282	2 390 053	1 138 623	5 148	553	4 595	4 405 121	5.5	79.2	23.9	77.2	24.7
UTAH	39	4 269	203	220 221	105 207	4 474	249	4 226	501 491	3.4	90.7	26.4	89.4	28.4
VERMONT	15	1 566	265	92 724	14 303	2 310	110	2 200	114 237	11.4	90.0	28.8	88.9	31.3
VIRGINIA	92	18 211	268	946 470	220 106	2 980	276	2 704	1 273 084	8.6	86.6	31.9	87.8	34.2
WASHINGTON	92	12 093	213	775 358	312 820	5 102	347	4 755	1 091 389	7.5	91.8	28.6	89.1	28.8
WEST VIRGINIA..................	56	8 397	464	347 459	47 375	2 617	258	2 359	298 622	5.3	77.1	15.3	78.7	15.3
WISCONSIN	126	17 111	328	803 678	169 842	3 104	221	2 883	1 021 173	13.9	86.7	23.8	88.6	24.1
WYOMING...........................	26	2 309	480	68 590	17 962	3 583	262	3 321	90 337	2.4	90.0	20.6	90.9	20.7

1. Per 100,000 resident population as of July 1 of the year shown. 2. Data for serious crimes have not been adjusted for underreporting; this may affect comparability between geographic areas and over time. 3. Per 100,000 population estimated by the FBI. 4. Persons 25 years old and over.

Table A. States — Education Expenditures, Money Income, Poverty, and Health Insurance

STATE	Local government expenditures for education, 2001–2002		Money income						Percent below poverty level						Percent lacking health insurance, 2003	
			1999				Median household income average, 2001–2003 (dollars)	Median income of family of four, 2002	1999			2003				
			Households						Persons							
			Median income													
	Total current expenditures (mil dol)	Current expenditures per student (dollars)	Per capita[1] income (dollars)	Dollars	Percent change, 1989–1999 (constant 1999 dollars)	Percent with income of $100,000 or more			Total	Percent change in rate, 1989–1999	Families	Persons	Children under 18 years	Persons over 65 years	Persons	Children under 18 years
	85	86	87	88	89	90	91	92	93	94	95	96	97	98	99	100
UNITED STATES	368 499	7 734	21 587	41 994	4.0	12.3	43 527	62 732	12.4	-5.3	9.2	12.5	17.6	10.2	15.6	11.4
ALABAMA	4 444	6 029	18 189	34 135	7.7	7.6	37 419	53 754	16.1	-12.0	12.5	15.0	22.3	8.4	14.2	8.7
ALASKA	1 285	9 563	22 660	51 571	-7.3	16.1	55 143	69 868	6.4	-28.9	6.7	9.6	11.2	NA	18.9	12.3
ARIZONA	5 500	5 964	20 275	40 558	9.6	10.8	42 062	56 857	13.9	-11.5	9.9	13.5	19.1	5.5	17.0	14.6
ARKANSAS	2 823	6 276	16 904	32 182	13.3	6.0	33 259	49 551	15.8	-17.3	12.0	17.8	26.8	17.1	17.4	10.5
CALIFORNIA	46 266	7 434	22 711	47 493	-1.3	17.3	48 979	65 766	14.2	13.6	10.6	13.1	18.5	8.5	18.4	12.5
COLORADO	5 151	6 941	24 049	47 203	16.6	14.2	50 224	68 089	9.3	-20.5	6.2	9.7	11.9	9.4	17.2	13.7
CONNECTICUT	6 031	10 577	28 766	53 935	-3.8	20.2	55 004	81 891	7.9	16.2	5.6	8.1	10.1	5.7	10.4	8.3
DELAWARE	1 073	9 284	23 305	47 381	1.1	14.0	50 451	69 469	9.2	5.7	6.5	7.3	11.0	4.4	11.1	8.5
DISTRICT OF COLUMBIA	912	12 102	28 659	40 127	-2.8	16.4	42 597	55 692	20.2	19.5	16.7	16.8	31.5	NA	14.3	11.4
FLORIDA	15 536	6 213	21 557	38 819	5.1	10.4	38 572	57 473	12.5	-1.6	9.0	12.7	19.2	9.7	18.2	15.5
GEORGIA	10 853	7 380	21 154	42 433	8.8	12.3	43 535	60 676	13.0	-11.6	9.9	11.9	17.7	9.6	16.4	13.7
HAWAII	1 348	7 306	21 525	49 820	-4.5	16.6	49 839	67 564	10.7	28.9	7.6	9.3	12.0	10.1	10.1	7.4
IDAHO	1 482	6 011	17 841	37 572	10.7	7.3	40 230	54 279	11.8	-11.3	8.3	10.2	13.8	4.0	18.6	13.7
ILLINOIS	16 481	7 956	23 104	46 590	7.5	14.4	45 607	69 168	10.7	-10.1	7.8	12.6	17.4	9.4	14.4	10.0
INDIANA	7 705	7 734	20 397	41 567	7.4	9.2	42 124	63 022	9.5	-11.2	6.7	9.9	13.7	6.9	13.9	9.0
IOWA	3 566	7 338	19 674	39 469	12.0	7.3	41 985	61 238	9.1	-20.9	6.0	8.9	13.4	7.4	11.3	8.6
KANSAS	3 451	7 339	20 506	40 624	10.8	9.3	43 622	61 926	9.9	-13.9	6.7	10.8	14.5	9.1	11.0	6.4
KENTUCKY	4 269	6 523	18 093	33 672	11.2	7.2	38 161	54 030	15.8	-16.8	12.7	14.4	18.1	10.0	14.0	10.5
LOUISIANA	4 803	6 567	16 912	32 566	10.4	7.4	34 307	52 299	19.6	-16.9	15.8	17.0	25.5	11.9	20.6	15.2
MAINE	1 813	8 818	19 533	37 240	-0.5	7.1	37 619	58 802	10.9	0.9	7.8	11.6	15.6	10.0	10.4	6.0
MARYLAND	7 481	8 692	25 614	52 868	-0.1	18.1	55 213	77 938	8.5	2.4	6.1	8.6	10.6	9.5	13.9	8.1
MASSACHUSETTS	9 957	10 232	25 952	50 502	1.7	17.7	52 084	78 312	9.3	4.5	6.7	10.3	12.0	16.0	10.7	7.9
MICHIGAN	14 975	8 653	22 168	44 667	7.2	12.7	45 176	67 995	10.5	-19.8	7.4	11.4	14.6	6.9	10.9	5.8
MINNESOTA	6 587	7 736	23 198	47 111	13.4	12.6	54 480	72 379	7.9	-22.5	5.1	7.4	9.7	9.2	8.7	6.2
MISSISSIPPI	2 642	5 354	15 853	31 330	15.8	6.0	31 887	47 847	19.9	-21.0	16.0	16.0	23.1	11.7	17.9	12.1
MISSOURI	6 492	7 135	19 936	37 934	7.1	8.8	43 492	59 764	11.7	-12.0	8.6	10.7	14.7	8.9	11.0	7.3
MONTANA	1 073	7 062	17 151	33 024	6.9	5.6	34 375	51 791	14.6	-9.3	10.5	15.1	20.2	11.2	19.4	17.7
NEBRASKA	2 207	7 741	19 613	39 250	12.3	8.1	44 357	60 129	9.7	-12.6	6.7	9.8	11.0	10.8	11.3	7.0
NEVADA	2 169	6 079	21 989	44 581	7.0	11.3	46 118	59 588	10.5	2.9	7.5	10.9	14.8	8.8	18.9	17.4
NEW HAMPSHIRE	1 641	7 935	23 844	49 467	1.3	13.8	55 166	72 369	6.5	1.6	4.3	5.8	7.2	5.4	10.3	5.5
NEW JERSEY	15 823	11 793	27 006	55 146	0.3	21.3	55 221	82 406	8.5	11.8	6.3	8.6	11.2	9.6	14.0	11.0
NEW MEXICO	2 204	6 882	17 261	34 133	5.5	7.6	35 265	48 422	18.4	-10.7	14.5	18.1	26.9	9.3	22.1	13.2
NEW YORK	32 219	11 218	23 389	43 393	-2.0	15.3	43 160	65 461	14.6	12.3	11.5	14.3	19.9	14.2	15.1	9.4
NORTH CAROLINA	8 551	6 501	20 307	39 184	9.4	9.4	38 096	58 227	12.3	-5.4	9.0	15.7	23.1	14.0	17.3	11.9
NORTH DAKOTA	711	6 709	17 769	34 604	11.0	5.7	38 212	57 070	11.9	-17.4	8.3	9.7	12.7	7.9	10.9	7.5
OHIO	14 774	8 069	21 003	40 956	6.2	9.8	43 535	63 934	10.6	-15.2	7.8	10.9	16.5	8.0	12.1	8.3
OKLAHOMA	3 876	6 229	17 646	33 400	5.4	6.6	36 733	51 377	14.7	-12.0	11.2	12.8	17.0	11.8	20.4	17.9
OREGON	4 215	7 642	20 940	40 916	11.8	10.0	42 429	60 262	11.6	-6.5	7.9	12.5	20.1	5.4	17.2	13.5
PENNSYLVANIA	15 551	8 537	20 880	40 106	2.7	10.3	43 869	64 310	11.0	-0.9	7.8	10.5	15.5	9.4	11.4	8.4
RHODE ISLAND	1 533	9 703	21 688	42 090	-2.7	11.5	45 205	67 646	11.9	24.0	8.9	11.5	17.1	10.9	10.2	5.2
SOUTH CAROLINA	4 745	7 017	18 795	37 082	5.1	8.1	38 791	56 110	14.1	-8.4	10.7	12.7	17.4	12.7	14.4	8.9
SOUTH DAKOTA	819	6 424	17 562	35 282	16.7	5.9	39 829	55 359	13.2	-17.0	9.3	12.7	14.0	8.9	12.2	8.4
TENNESSEE	5 511	5 959	19 393	36 360	9.1	8.3	37 529	55 605	13.5	-14.0	10.3	14.0	18.7	12.5	13.2	10.3
TEXAS	28 191	6 771	19 617	39 927	10.0	11.5	40 934	56 278	15.4	-14.9	12.0	17.0	24.0	17.3	24.6	20.0
UTAH	2 375	4 900	18 185	45 726	15.5	11.2	49 143	59 864	9.4	-17.5	6.5	9.1	12.4	4.1	12.7	9.0
VERMONT	992	9 806	20 625	40 856	2.1	8.7	43 212	62 331	9.4	-5.1	6.3	8.5	10.9	7.0	9.5	3.9
VIRGINIA	8 719	7 496	23 975	46 677	4.2	15.1	52 587	66 889	9.6	-5.9	7.0	10.0	13.5	10.4	13.0	8.9
WASHINGTON	7 104	7 039	22 973	45 776	9.3	12.6	45 960	66 531	10.6	-2.8	7.3	12.6	19.1	10.0	15.5	8.4
WEST VIRGINIA	2 219	7 844	16 477	29 696	6.3	5.0	31 210	47 550	17.9	-9.1	13.9	17.4	26.7	8.4	16.6	8.4
WISCONSIN	7 592	8 634	21 271	43 791	10.7	9.4	46 782	66 988	8.7	-18.7	5.6	9.8	15.4	8.2	10.9	7.7
WYOMING	762	8 645	19 134	37 892	4.1	6.7	41 501	57 148	11.4	-4.2	8.0	9.8	13.1	NA	15.9	12.5

1. Based on population enumerated as of April 1, 2000.

Table A. States — Personal Income

STATE	Personal income, 2003												
			Per capita[1]		Sources of personal income (mil dol)								
								Transfer payments					
									Government payments to individuals				
	Total (mil dol)	Percent change, 2002–2003	Dollars	Rank	Wages and salaries[2]	Proprietors' income	Dividends, interest, and rent	Total	Total	Social Security	Medical payments	Income mainte-nance	Unemploy-ment insurance
	101	102	103	104	105	106	107	108	109	110	111	112	113
UNITED STATES	9 148 680	3.2	31 459	X	6 271 507	839 126	1 475 401	1 335 323	1 275 144	463 320	548 986	130 464	53 512
ALABAMA	118 260	4.1	26 276	42	77 863	9 229	18 159	21 598	20 686	8 244	8 287	2 435	412
ALASKA	21 576	3.2	33 254	14	15 809	2 191	3 140	3 267	3 159	575	1 244	330	166
ARIZONA	150 295	4.6	26 931	39	101 543	13 130	24 491	23 249	22 201	8 687	9 222	2 078	511
ARKANSAS	66 224	4.3	24 296	50	42 645	6 298	10 190	13 187	12 585	4 953	4 986	1 358	406
CALIFORNIA	1 185 302	3.1	33 403	11	805 116	133 798	194 091	153 570	146 095	43 886	63 463	20 733	7 281
COLORADO	157 043	2.2	34 510	8	107 326	20 612	25 835	15 135	14 266	5 511	5 734	1 311	710
CONNECTICUT	150 801	2.0	43 292	2	99 663	16 564	24 543	17 333	16 656	6 422	7 420	1 287	927
DELAWARE	27 240	4.0	33 321	12	21 401	2 175	4 363	3 839	3 647	1 519	1 526	282	160
DISTRICT OF COLUMBIA	26 651	2.0	47 305	1	54 237	3 332	3 970	3 383	3 295	632	1 821	512	116
FLORIDA	510 090	3.6	29 972	25	313 515	31 200	118 186	84 413	80 907	33 326	34 919	6 772	1 622
GEORGIA	254 104	3.0	29 259	28	181 508	23 804	38 050	32 618	30 607	11 322	12 683	3 694	1 038
HAWAII	38 470	4.7	30 589	22	27 973	2 605	6 258	4 838	4 637	1 939	1 685	591	167
IDAHO	34 954	2.9	25 583	46	21 897	4 159	6 032	5 201	4 950	2 061	1 794	390	251
ILLINOIS	420 156	1.9	33 205	15	296 547	33 220	72 664	54 101	51 310	19 755	21 102	5 224	3 020
INDIANA	178 415	3.8	28 797	33	124 229	12 365	27 590	25 827	24 482	10 776	9 447	2 161	960
IOWA	83 604	2.1	28 398	36	55 972	6 744	14 598	12 766	12 100	5 494	4 684	840	467
KANSAS	80 466	2.8	29 545	27	54 297	7 220	13 431	11 359	10 729	4 564	4 133	808	525
KENTUCKY	108 515	4.3	26 352	41	74 608	7 928	16 593	19 927	18 975	7 247	7 587	2 236	644
LOUISIANA	117 074	3.4	26 038	44	76 139	10 858	16 714	21 865	20 742	6 808	9 583	2 896	400
MAINE	37 781	4.1	28 935	31	23 901	2 977	6 100	7 004	6 745	2 429	3 118	610	165
MARYLAND	206 166	3.8	37 424	5	130 601	13 959	32 535	22 783	21 582	7 718	10 061	1 815	752
MASSACHUSETTS	253 528	1.5	39 408	4	183 308	20 462	41 937	33 881	32 641	10 814	15 713	2 515	2 362
MICHIGAN	314 460	4.1	31 196	20	224 866	24 302	44 749	46 874	45 063	18 249	18 097	4 641	2 563
MINNESOTA	172 217	3.3	34 039	9	127 076	11 740	29 397	21 514	20 370	7 713	8 907	1 580	1 030
MISSISSIPPI	67 258	4.6	23 343	51	41 155	5 575	9 550	14 422	13 813	4 828	6 034	1 906	269
MISSOURI	165 967	3.1	29 094	29	116 099	13 035	27 604	27 301	26 164	10 216	11 411	2 383	775
MONTANA	23 651	5.0	25 775	45	14 386	2 709	4 682	3 894	3 698	1 584	1 260	334	103
NEBRASKA	52 755	5.8	30 331	24	35 693	5 814	9 413	7 306	6 968	2 849	2 850	575	169
NEVADA	70 567	6.1	31 487	19	49 292	5 922	13 208	8 091	7 698	3 350	2 893	630	390
NEW HAMPSHIRE	44 686	2.8	34 703	7	28 491	3 999	6 785	5 059	4 800	2 186	1 914	290	154
NEW JERSEY	345 557	2.3	40 002	3	224 145	29 041	53 405	42 912	41 142	15 233	18 354	2 663	2 677
NEW MEXICO	47 807	4.4	25 502	47	30 949	4 133	7 771	8 387	7 967	2 709	3 435	945	180
NEW YORK	696 531	2.4	36 296	6	490 805	71 238	106 934	121 567	117 428	32 208	62 713	12 684	3 945
NORTH CAROLINA	237 931	3.1	28 301	37	166 452	17 601	38 404	37 300	35 699	13 961	14 477	4 000	1 413
NORTH DAKOTA	18 078	7.7	28 521	35	12 035	2 431	3 150	2 717	2 597	1 082	1 004	189	59
OHIO	342 533	3.2	29 953	26	239 139	23 237	52 575	55 887	53 097	19 868	22 071	4 961	1 790
OKLAHOMA	93 290	3.6	26 567	40	56 802	12 305	14 631	15 785	15 103	5 948	5 887	1 554	397
OREGON	102 538	2.1	28 806	32	70 181	9 036	18 893	15 948	15 282	6 096	5 255	1 371	1 303
PENNSYLVANIA	392 058	3.1	31 706	18	259 718	31 881	61 660	69 053	66 401	24 937	29 259	5 064	3 608
RHODE ISLAND	34 369	3.7	31 937	17	22 161	2 483	5 440	6 038	5 828	1 945	2 687	532	261
SOUTH CAROLINA	108 398	3.7	26 138	43	72 753	7 377	16 787	19 125	18 196	7 095	7 246	2 131	570
SOUTH DAKOTA	21 629	6.7	28 299	38	13 195	2 931	4 326	3 124	2 993	1 283	1 181	236	39
TENNESSEE	166 867	4.4	28 565	34	113 177	19 604	21 291	28 423	27 346	10 104	12 052	3 060	773
TEXAS	643 129	3.1	29 076	30	443 115	88 525	83 420	81 863	77 784	27 089	33 521	9 526	3 001
UTAH	59 327	2.8	25 230	48	43 291	5 809	8 722	6 770	6 334	2 564	2 286	529	289
VERMONT	18 904	3.6	30 534	23	12 190	1 615	3 431	3 006	2 848	1 068	1 247	275	120
VIRGINIA	248 554	3.8	33 651	10	179 739	17 274	38 611	26 520	25 062	10 766	9 359	2 291	791
WASHINGTON	203 956	2.8	33 264	13	141 366	17 954	33 410	27 826	26 475	9 311	9 683	2 183	2 285
WEST VIRGINIA	44 665	3.1	24 672	49	26 741	2 952	6 387	11 919	11 567	4 015	4 110	1 071	256
WISCONSIN	168 128	3.1	30 723	21	116 686	11 842	27 651	23 437	22 412	9 569	8 856	1 829	1 179
WYOMING	16 157	4.9	32 235	16	9 713	1 929	3 638	2 114	2 011	810	724	154	61

1. Based on the resident population estimated as of July 1 of the year shown. 2. Includes other labor income.

Table A. States — Personal Income and Earnings

STATE	Personal tax payments, 2003 (mil dol)	Disposable personal income, 2003		Earnings, 2003									Gross state product, 2001 (mil dol)
		Total (mil dol)	Per capita[1] (dollars)	Total (mil dol)	Farm	Goods-related[2]		Service-related and other[3]				Government	
						Total	Manu-facturing	Total	Retail trade	Finance, insurance, and real estate	Services		
	114	115	116	117	118	119	120	121	122	123	124	125	126
UNITED STATES	1 000 467	8 148 213	28 019	7 110 633	0.7	20.3	13.4	62.7	6.8	9.9	29.2	16.3	10 137 190
ALABAMA	10 524	107 736	23 937	87 092	1.3	24.8	17.8	53.8	7.6	6.7	27.3	20.1	121 490
ALASKA	1 935	19 641	30 272	18 000	0.1	18.1	3.8	50.1	6.9	4.7	25.0	31.8	28 581
ARIZONA	14 545	135 750	24 324	114 672	0.7	19.7	10.7	62.5	8.3	10.3	31.8	17.0	160 687
ARKANSAS	5 978	60 246	22 103	48 943	3.1	24.0	18.2	55.7	7.0	5.5	27.3	17.1	67 913
CALIFORNIA	140 016	1 045 286	29 458	938 914	0.9	18.8	12.4	64.5	6.9	10.1	33.0	15.7	1 359 265
COLORADO	17 364	139 679	30 694	127 937	0.6	18.3	8.5	65.5	6.4	10.5	31.5	15.6	173 772
CONNECTICUT	22 705	128 096	36 774	116 227	0.2	19.8	14.4	68.0	6.5	17.3	33.3	12.1	166 165
DELAWARE	3 189	24 051	29 420	23 576	0.5	18.1	12.0	67.5	6.6	16.5	34.6	13.9	40 509
DISTRICT OF COLUMBIA	3 472	23 179	41 143	57 569	0.0	1.9	0.4	56.8	1.0	5.4	42.2	41.4	64 459
FLORIDA	49 053	461 037	27 089	344 716	0.5	13.4	6.5	69.8	8.3	10.0	38.0	16.3	491 488
GEORGIA	27 030	227 074	26 146	205 313	1.1	17.9	11.9	64.0	6.7	8.6	29.9	17.0	299 874
HAWAII	3 928	34 542	27 466	30 578	0.7	9.4	2.6	58.5	6.9	6.2	35.1	31.4	43 710
IDAHO	3 203	31 752	23 239	26 057	3.8	21.5	13.2	56.0	8.4	6.1	29.8	18.8	36 905
ILLINOIS	46 467	373 690	29 532	329 767	0.4	20.6	14.1	65.4	5.9	11.6	33.4	13.6	475 541
INDIANA	18 057	160 358	25 882	136 594	0.6	34.5	27.8	51.6	6.7	6.6	26.8	13.3	189 919
IOWA	7 868	75 737	25 725	62 716	2.3	25.5	19.2	55.7	7.7	9.5	25.2	16.5	90 942
KANSAS	8 015	72 451	26 602	61 517	1.3	23.4	16.7	56.9	6.9	7.5	26.2	18.3	87 196
KENTUCKY	11 321	97 194	23 603	82 536	0.8	27.0	19.5	53.5	7.2	6.0	27.1	18.8	120 266
LOUISIANA	10 082	106 993	23 796	86 997	0.7	23.5	11.9	56.5	7.1	6.3	30.3	19.3	148 697
MAINE	3 880	33 901	25 963	26 878	0.3	20.3	13.5	60.8	9.2	7.9	32.3	18.6	37 449
MARYLAND	26 252	179 915	32 659	144 559	0.2	14.7	7.2	62.4	6.7	9.2	35.2	22.8	195 007
MASSACHUSETTS	34 225	219 303	34 088	203 769	0.1	18.5	12.6	69.9	5.9	13.0	39.0	11.5	287 802
MICHIGAN	32 376	282 084	27 985	249 169	0.2	30.6	24.9	56.0	6.3	7.5	31.7	13.2	320 470
MINNESOTA	20 613	151 604	29 965	138 817	0.8	22.3	15.7	63.4	6.4	10.4	32.4	13.6	188 050
MISSISSIPPI	5 180	62 078	21 545	46 730	2.0	23.2	16.8	51.8	8.0	5.2	26.9	23.0	67 125
MISSOURI	16 960	149 007	26 121	129 134	0.6	21.4	14.5	62.5	7.1	7.9	33.2	15.5	181 493
MONTANA	2 219	21 432	23 356	17 095	1.3	16.3	6.0	59.9	9.2	8.3	29.5	22.5	22 635
NEBRASKA	5 091	47 663	27 404	41 507	5.2	18.4	11.9	59.1	6.9	8.3	27.8	17.3	56 967
NEVADA	7 048	63 519	28 342	55 214	0.2	16.9	4.7	68.3	7.7	9.2	41.4	14.7	79 220
NEW HAMPSHIRE	4 515	40 172	31 197	32 490	0.1	23.4	16.3	64.6	10.2	9.4	32.7	11.9	47 183
NEW JERSEY	43 497	302 060	34 967	253 185	0.1	16.5	11.2	69.1	7.1	11.3	34.4	14.3	365 388
NEW MEXICO	4 252	43 555	23 234	35 082	1.8	16.0	6.2	53.8	7.9	5.6	31.0	28.4	55 426
NEW YORK	98 021	598 509	31 188	562 043	0.1	12.0	7.6	73.3	5.2	18.8	35.4	14.6	826 488
NORTH CAROLINA	25 179	212 752	25 306	184 053	0.8	24.2	17.8	55.8	7.0	7.9	28.8	19.2	275 615
NORTH DAKOTA	1 441	16 637	26 248	14 466	7.2	15.9	8.3	55.1	7.5	6.3	26.1	21.8	19 005
OHIO	37 784	304 748	26 649	262 376	0.3	26.9	21.2	57.9	7.0	7.9	31.2	14.9	373 798
OKLAHOMA	8 866	84 424	24 042	69 107	1.7	24.8	15.0	52.3	7.3	6.2	26.3	21.2	93 855
OREGON	11 735	90 803	25 509	79 216	1.2	21.8	15.4	60.2	7.4	7.6	30.3	16.8	120 055
PENNSYLVANIA	42 538	349 520	28 266	291 599	0.4	22.1	15.7	64.4	7.0	9.1	35.1	13.2	408 373
RHODE ISLAND	3 886	30 483	28 325	24 644	0.1	19.0	13.0	63.7	6.9	9.5	36.3	17.3	36 939
SOUTH CAROLINA	10 028	98 370	23 720	80 130	0.7	26.0	18.8	53.0	8.1	6.9	27.2	20.4	115 204
SOUTH DAKOTA	1 613	20 016	26 188	16 126	6.6	17.2	10.7	57.3	8.2	9.1	28.7	18.8	24 251
TENNESSEE	12 712	154 155	26 389	132 782	0.1	24.2	18.1	62.0	8.0	8.2	31.8	13.7	182 515
TEXAS	55 185	587 944	26 582	531 640	0.7	23.2	12.8	60.8	6.8	9.5	28.3	15.4	763 874
UTAH	5 708	53 618	22 802	49 100	0.5	20.8	12.4	59.7	7.9	8.2	30.9	18.9	70 409
VERMONT	1 887	17 017	27 486	13 805	0.9	23.8	16.6	58.3	8.7	6.5	32.2	17.0	19 149
VIRGINIA	29 887	218 667	29 604	197 012	0.2	15.4	8.7	60.8	6.1	8.3	34.4	23.6	273 070
WASHINGTON	18 861	185 095	30 188	159 321	0.9	18.7	12.1	61.4	6.9	8.0	29.3	18.9	222 950
WEST VIRGINIA	3 893	40 772	22 521	29 693	-0.1	24.1	12.9	53.8	7.8	4.8	29.5	22.2	42 368
WISCONSIN	18 760	149 368	27 295	128 528	0.9	29.4	23.0	55.2	6.8	8.0	28.5	14.5	177 354
WYOMING	1 626	14 531	28 991	11 642	1.7	27.4	5.0	47.3	7.1	6.0	22.5	23.6	20 418

1. Based on the resident population estimated as of July 1 of the year shown.   2. Includes mining, construction, and manufacturing.   3. Includes private sector earnings in agricultural services, forestry, and fisheries; transportation and public utilities; wholesale and retail trade; finance, insurance, and real estate; and services.

Table A. States — **Housing**

STATE	Housing units, 2003 — Total	Percent change, 2000–2003	Occupied units — Total	Percent owner-occupied	Median value of units with mortgage[1] (dollars)	Housing units, 2000 — Total	Percent change, 1990–2000	Owner-occupied — Total	Owner-occupied — Percent	Owner-occupied — Median value[1] (dollars)	Median owner cost as a percent of income — With a mortgage	Median owner cost as a percent of income — Without a mortgage[2]	Renter-occupied — Median rent[3] (dollars)	Renter-occupied — Median rent as a percent of income	Sub-standard units[4] (percent)
	127	128	129	130	131	132	133	134	135	136	137	138	139	140	141
UNITED STATES..................	120 879 390	4.3	108 419 506	66.2	147 275	115 904 641	13.3	105 480 101	66.2	119 600	21.7	10.5	602	25.5	6.3
ALABAMA..........................	2 031 595	3.5	1 743 476	72.5	96 106	1 963 711	17.6	1 737 080	72.5	85 100	19.8	9.9	447	24.8	3.5
ALASKA..............................	267 987	2.7	229 408	62.5	174 146	260 978	12.2	221 600	62.5	144 200	22.3	9.9	720	24.8	13.0
ARIZONA............................	2 392 746	9.3	2 048 918	68.0	146 124	2 189 189	31.9	1 901 327	68.0	121 300	22.1	9.9	619	26.6	9.3
ARKANSAS	1 214 302	3.5	1 075 918	69.4	83 699	1 173 043	17.2	1 042 696	69.4	72 800	19.4	9.9	453	24.4	4.4
CALIFORNIA	12 656 882	3.6	11 856 538	56.9	334 426	12 214 549	9.2	11 502 870	56.9	211 500	25.3	9.9	747	27.7	15.6
COLORADO........................	1 973 622	9.1	1 821 318	67.3	210 398	1 808 037	22.4	1 658 238	67.3	166 600	22.6	9.9	671	26.4	4.9
CONNECTICUT	1 410 459	1.8	1 323 339	66.8	226 202	1 385 975	4.9	1 301 670	66.8	166 900	22.4	13.1	681	25.4	3.2
DELAWARE	357 480	4.2	303 790	72.3	165 739	343 072	18.3	298 736	72.3	130 400	20.8	9.9	639	24.3	3.1
DISTRICT OF COLUMBIA	272 394	-0.9	246 669	40.8	248 171	274 845	-1.3	248 338	40.8	157 200	22.2	9.9	618	24.8	9.5
FLORIDA	7 788 543	6.6	6 637 845	70.1	144 507	7 302 947	19.7	6 337 929	70.1	105 500	22.8	10.5	641	27.5	6.8
GEORGIA...........................	3 576 427	9.0	3 152 672	67.5	140 734	3 281 737	24.4	3 006 369	67.5	111 200	20.8	9.9	613	24.9	5.3
HAWAII..............................	475 972	3.4	419 441	56.5	324 661	460 542	18.1	403 240	56.5	272 700	26.3	9.9	779	27.2	16.1
IDAHO...............................	564 474	6.9	503 145	72.4	118 174	527 824	27.7	469 645	72.4	106 300	21.5	9.9	515	25.3	5.4
ILLINOIS	5 030 728	3.0	4 624 605	67.3	160 551	4 885 615	8.4	4 591 779	67.3	130 800	21.7	11.1	605	24.4	5.3
INDIANA............................	2 651 165	4.7	2 350 535	71.4	106 840	2 532 319	12.7	2 336 306	71.4	94 300	19.3	9.9	521	23.9	2.7
IOWA.................................	1 269 685	3.0	1 158 018	72.3	91 427	1 232 511	7.8	1 149 276	72.3	82 500	19.1	9.9	470	23.2	2.3
KANSAS	1 170 718	3.5	1 058 600	69.2	100 257	1 131 200	8.3	1 037 891	69.2	83 500	19.3	9.9	498	23.4	3.4
KENTUCKY	1 814 575	3.6	1 607 214	70.8	104 103	1 750 927	16.2	1 590 647	70.8	86 700	19.6	9.9	445	24.0	2.9
LOUISIANA	1 896 748	2.7	1 672 717	67.9	99 215	1 847 181	7.6	1 656 053	67.9	85 000	19.6	9.9	466	25.8	5.8
MAINE...............................	671 089	2.9	535 091	71.6	134 846	651 901	11.0	518 200	71.6	98 700	21.4	12.1	497	25.3	2.1
MARYLAND........................	2 219 423	3.5	2 048 134	67.7	186 139	2 145 283	13.4	1 980 859	67.7	146 000	22.2	9.9	689	24.7	4.0
MASSACHUSETTS..............	2 660 847	1.5	2 435 941	61.7	309 736	2 621 989	6.0	2 443 580	61.7	185 700	21.9	12.4	684	25.5	3.4
MICHIGAN.........................	4 383 456	3.5	3 884 081	73.8	141 413	4 234 279	10.0	3 785 661	73.8	115 600	19.6	9.9	546	24.4	3.4
MINNESOTA	2 167 054	4.9	2 011 984	74.6	169 778	2 065 946	11.8	1 895 127	74.6	122 400	20.0	9.9	566	24.7	3.3
MISSISSIPPI	1 206 630	3.8	1 055 591	72.3	85 142	1 161 953	15.0	1 046 434	72.3	71 400	20.4	9.9	439	25.0	5.7
MISSOURI..........................	2 532 960	3.7	2 284 663	70.3	108 625	2 442 017	11.0	2 194 594	70.3	89 900	19.5	9.9	484	24.0	2.9
MONTANA	419 726	1.7	365 680	69.1	118 887	412 633	14.3	358 667	69.1	99 500	22.2	10.4	447	25.3	3.8
NEBRASKA.........................	746 397	3.3	675 472	67.4	100 539	722 668	9.4	666 184	67.4	88 000	19.7	10.5	491	23.0	3.0
NEVADA............................	935 934	13.1	833 679	60.9	170 333	827 457	59.5	751 165	60.9	142 000	23.8	9.9	699	26.5	8.9
NEW HAMPSHIRE...............	569 016	4.0	492 948	69.7	208 403	547 024	8.6	474 606	69.7	133 300	22.3	13.6	646	24.2	2.1
NEW JERSEY.......................	3 398 272	2.7	3 122 552	65.6	245 573	3 310 275	7.6	3 064 645	65.6	170 800	23.7	15.3	751	25.5	5.4
NEW MEXICO......................	816 436	4.6	698 088	70.0	118 764	780 579	23.5	677 971	70.0	108 100	22.2	9.9	503	26.6	8.7
NEW YORK.........................	7 802 245	1.6	7 118 706	53.0	198 883	7 679 307	6.3	7 056 860	53.0	148 700	23.2	13.6	672	26.8	8.4
NORTH CAROLINA..............	3 779 034	7.3	3 270 705	69.4	125 428	3 523 944	25.0	3 132 013	69.4	108 300	21.3	9.9	548	24.3	4.0
NORTH DAKOTA.................	296 959	2.5	254 464	66.6	81 796	289 677	4.8	257 152	66.6	74 400	19.4	10.2	412	22.3	2.5
OHIO.................................	4 918 787	2.8	4 480 461	69.1	118 956	4 783 051	9.4	4 445 773	69.1	103 700	20.6	10.6	515	24.2	2.1
OKLAHOMA.......................	1 552 599	2.5	1 341 376	68.4	85 502	1 514 400	7.7	1 342 293	68.4	70 700	19.2	9.9	456	24.3	4.2
OREGON............................	1 515 354	4.3	1 409 401	64.3	171 039	1 452 709	21.7	1 333 723	64.3	152 100	23.2	10.5	620	26.9	5.3
PENNSYLVANIA..................	5 365 486	2.2	4 801 049	71.3	110 020	5 249 750	6.3	4 777 003	71.3	97 000	21.6	12.2	531	25.0	2.4
RHODE ISLAND..................	445 783	1.4	411 579	60.0	205 244	439 837	6.1	408 424	60.0	133 000	22.7	13.4	553	25.7	3.3
SOUTH CAROLINA..............	1 854 624	5.8	1 567 798	72.2	121 290	1 753 670	23.1	1 533 854	72.2	94 900	20.5	9.9	510	24.4	3.8
SOUTH DAKOTA.................	337 100	4.3	299 280	68.2	96 977	323 208	10.5	290 245	68.2	79 600	19.7	10.5	426	22.9	3.6
TENNESSEE	2 552 506	4.6	2 295 640	69.9	110 000	2 439 443	20.4	2 232 905	69.9	93 000	21.1	9.9	505	24.8	3.3
TEXAS	8 658 290	6.1	7 634 767	63.8	99 139	8 157 575	16.4	7 393 354	63.8	82 500	20.1	10.9	574	24.4	10.0
UTAH.................................	826 551	7.5	752 030	71.5	156 657	768 594	28.4	701 281	71.5	146 100	22.9	9.9	597	24.9	6.3
VERMONT..........................	302 106	2.6	242 047	70.6	138 457	294 382	8.5	240 634	70.6	111 500	22.4	13.9	553	26.2	2.0
VIRGINIA...........................	3 058 766	5.3	2 790 262	68.1	162 080	2 904 192	16.3	2 699 173	68.1	125 400	21.4	9.9	650	24.5	3.9
WASHINGTON	2 567 328	4.7	2 382 320	64.6	200 235	2 451 075	20.6	2 271 398	64.6	168 300	23.8	10.4	663	26.5	5.5
WEST VIRGINIA..................	854 817	1.2	731 690	75.2	85 709	844 623	8.1	736 481	75.2	72 800	19.5	9.9	401	25.8	2.3
WISCONSIN	2 417 364	4.1	2 159 083	68.4	131 908	2 321 144	12.9	2 084 544	68.4	112 200	20.9	11.2	540	23.4	2.8
WYOMING..........................	229 949	2.7	198 778	70.0	116 360	223 854	10.1	193 608	70.0	96 600	19.7	9.9	437	22.5	3.2

1. Specified owner-occupied units.   2. Median monthly owner costs is often in the minimum category—9.9 percent or less, which is indicated as 9.9 percent.   3. Specified renter-occupied units.   4. Over-crowded or lacking complete plumbing facilities.

Table A. States — Social Security, Employment, and Labor Force

STATE	Social Security beneficiaries, December 2003		Supplemental Security Income recipients, December 2003	Civilian employment and selected occupations,[2] March 2000			Civilian labor force annual average, 2003				
					Percent					Unemployed	
	Number	Rate[1]		Total	Professional, managerial, and technical	Precision production, craft, and repair	Total	Percent change, 2002–2003	Employed	Total	Rate[3]
	142	143	144	145	146	147	148	149	150	151	152
UNITED STATES	47 038 391	162	6 902 364	135 073 000	33.4	11.0	146 178 717	0.9	137 736 000	8 750 005	6.0
ALABAMA	867 601	193	163 772	2 033 192	30.9	12.1	2 147 321	2.5	2 022 659	124 662	5.8
ALASKA	60 860	94	10 651	301 792	35.8	12.0	331 675	2.5	305 114	26 561	8.0
ARIZONA	863 874	155	91 853	2 306 594	32.6	11.4	2 690 294	0.9	2 539 359	150 935	5.6
ARKANSAS	543 727	199	86 563	1 163 865	28.1	11.5	1 264 519	-1.3	1 186 387	78 132	6.2
CALIFORNIA	4 363 657	123	1 161 467	16 435 173	35.4	10.2	17 460 005	0.5	16 282 683	1 177 322	6.7
COLORADO	557 253	122	54 054	2 209 598	38.8	11.1	2 477 874	1.7	2 328 182	149 692	6.0
CONNECTICUT	582 877	167	51 170	1 661 290	39.3	9.9	1 803 108	0.6	1 703 961	99 147	5.5
DELAWARE	141 488	173	12 968	404 114	35.6	10.2	417 256	-0.6	398 966	18 290	4.4
DISTRICT OF COLUMBIA	72 209	128	20 393	259 744	51.0	4.9	302 286	-0.3	281 190	21 096	7.0
FLORIDA	3 330 425	196	410 027	7 308 900	31.5	11.3	8 164 237	0.9	7 743 804	420 433	5.1
GEORGIA	1 168 095	135	199 991	3 966 348	31.2	12.5	4 414 014	3.1	4 206 823	207 191	4.7
HAWAII	194 019	154	21 757	577 443	29.3	8.1	618 310	1.9	591 798	26 512	4.3
IDAHO	211 528	155	20 279	648 392	28.3	12.0	692 543	1.0	655 103	37 440	5.4
ILLINOIS	1 867 671	148	255 262	6 005 978	32.4	10.6	6 330 059	-0.6	5 907 796	422 263	6.7
INDIANA	1 032 417	167	94 027	2 970 497	29.0	13.0	3 187 734	0.6	3 024 367	163 367	5.1
IOWA	546 065	185	41 890	1 534 836	30.9	11.6	1 612 328	-3.0	1 540 105	72 223	4.5
KANSAS	443 706	163	37 813	1 322 160	32.1	11.0	1 434 070	1.7	1 356 771	77 299	5.4
KENTUCKY	768 861	187	178 852	1 859 668	30.2	10.5	1 956 384	1.2	1 835 909	120 475	6.2
LOUISIANA	731 511	163	167 800	1 927 933	32.3	12.1	2 037 050	1.9	1 903 519	133 531	6.6
MAINE	262 533	201	31 438	656 764	29.7	12.9	693 083	1.9	658 068	35 015	5.1
MARYLAND	751 359	136	90 983	2 721 724	40.3	9.0	2 904 139	0.3	2 773 312	130 827	4.5
MASSACHUSETTS	1 061 851	165	167 883	3 163 104	40.5	10.0	3 415 518	-1.5	3 217 207	198 311	5.8
MICHIGAN	1 699 384	169	216 629	4 900 723	32.5	11.4	5 042 094	0.8	4 673 973	368 121	7.3
MINNESOTA	765 228	151	69 020	2 710 298	35.4	11.2	2 923 083	0.3	2 777 684	145 399	5.0
MISSISSIPPI	533 375	185	126 282	1 224 651	27.3	13.1	1 312 127	1.6	1 228 992	83 135	6.3
MISSOURI	1 033 886	181	115 131	2 830 403	34.3	10.9	3 020 592	1.3	2 850 466	170 126	5.6
MONTANA	163 659	178	14 365	443 904	28.0	11.0	474 910	2.5	452 416	22 494	4.7
NEBRASKA	287 891	166	21 876	899 429	29.6	10.1	976 034	2.1	936 664	39 370	4.0
NEVADA	327 319	146	30 983	968 759	27.6	11.5	1 141 351	1.1	1 081 912	59 439	5.2
NEW HAMPSHIRE	211 499	164	12 762	664 293	36.8	12.2	718 885	1.8	688 151	30 734	4.3
NEW JERSEY	1 363 838	158	149 376	4 003 801	36.3	9.5	4 375 020	0.5	4 118 037	256 983	5.9
NEW MEXICO	294 669	157	50 212	797 978	33.5	11.7	896 867	2.5	839 667	57 200	6.4
NEW YORK	3 035 697	158	623 774	8 402 431	34.4	9.1	9 315 319	-0.3	8 726 360	588 959	6.3
NORTH CAROLINA	1 436 124	171	194 611	3 773 489	30.3	13.1	4 229 772	1.5	3 956 946	272 826	6.5
NORTH DAKOTA	114 047	180	8 101	329 218	28.9	10.3	346 471	0.8	332 725	13 746	4.0
OHIO	1 932 026	169	243 679	5 605 933	33.4	11.4	5 915 176	1.2	5 551 791	363 385	6.1
OKLAHOMA	613 515	175	75 262	1 601 921	29.9	12.1	1 696 060	0.1	1 600 026	96 034	5.7
OREGON	591 461	166	57 506	1 679 869	34.3	10.5	1 858 879	1.0	1 706 728	152 151	8.2
PENNSYLVANIA	2 386 426	193	310 485	5 785 679	33.9	10.5	6 170 013	-1.8	5 826 129	343 884	5.6
RHODE ISLAND	192 662	179	29 143	479 830	36.8	9.9	572 956	3.6	542 798	30 158	5.3
SOUTH CAROLINA	735 084	177	105 693	1 843 393	31.5	13.1	2 002 520	3.0	1 866 223	136 297	6.8
SOUTH DAKOTA	137 880	180	12 574	391 625	29.9	9.7	424 876	1.4	409 606	15 270	3.6
TENNESSEE	1 041 360	178	161 361	2 691 676	32.6	11.4	2 909 445	-0.6	2 740 491	168 954	5.8
TEXAS	2 792 148	126	455 232	9 955 270	32.3	11.7	10 910 344	2.1	10 172 828	737 516	6.8
UTAH	256 551	109	21 394	1 066 661	35.4	11.7	1 184 385	1.7	1 117 732	66 653	5.6
VERMONT	108 248	175	12 819	322 674	34.2	11.5	350 684	0.6	334 671	16 013	4.6
VIRGINIA	1 093 695	148	133 731	3 548 047	39.0	10.6	3 773 263	1.1	3 619 741	153 522	4.1
WASHINGTON	890 466	145	109 056	2 804 086	35.1	10.6	3 139 877	1.0	2 902 912	236 965	7.5
WEST VIRGINIA	405 444	224	75 257	792 367	29.4	12.1	787 286	-2.0	739 076	48 210	6.1
WISCONSIN	928 505	170	88 750	2 854 473	28.8	12.3	3 078 254	1.8	2 904 721	173 533	5.6
WYOMING	78 745	157	5 665	260 596	29.1	14.0	278 367	3.1	266 163	12 204	4.4

1. Per 1,000 resident population estimated as of July 1 of the year shown.   2. Persons 16 years old and over.   3. Percent of civilian labor force.

Table A. States — Nonfarm Employment and Earnings

	Private nonfarm employment and earnings, 2003										
	Employment		Manufacturing			Employment (1,000)					
				Average earnings of production workers							
STATE	Total (1,000)	Percent change, 2002–2003	Employ- ment (1,000)	Hourly	Weekly	Con- struction	Trans- portation and public utilities	Whole- sale trade	Retail trade	Financial activities	Services[1]
	153	154	155	156	157	158	159	160	161	162	163
UNITED STATES	108 356	-0.4	14 525.0	15.74	636	6 722.0	4 757.5	5 605.6	14 911.5	7 974.0	50 092.0
ALABAMA	1 516	-0.8	293.7	13.56	556	98.9	65.7	76.7	228.8	96.6	610.7
ALASKA	218	1.7	11.7	12.16	520	16.7	20.8	6.1	34.1	14.4	97.1
ARIZONA	1 896	1.1	174.0	14.38	581	176.6	76.6	93.1	275.1	159.3	883.7
ARKANSAS	946	-0.5	206.2	13.55	537	50.7	65.9	44.6	129.2	50.2	372.0
CALIFORNIA	11 984	-0.2	1 544.9	15.05	597	788.8	480.7	651.4	1 589.9	886.8	5 547.8
COLORADO	1 794	-1.8	156.2	16.89	682	149.8	72.8	92.2	239.0	154.2	831.3
CONNECTICUT	1 397	-1.3	199.5	17.74	734	61.3	48.5	65.4	191.1	143.4	647.3
DELAWARE	356	-0.4	35.7	16.90	681	24.2	12.3	14.2	51.6	45.5	165.3
DISTRICT OF COLUMBIA	433	0.2	2.6	NA	NA	13.0	6.3	4.5	17.1	31.0	334.3
FLORIDA	6 230	1.5	388.8	14.09	578	445.9	228.8	313.2	920.4	484.3	3 269.4
GEORGIA	3 227	-0.5	451.6	14.08	560	195.4	174.0	205.4	443.4	216.7	1 402.0
HAWAII	448	2.1	14.9	12.90	480	NA	26.8	16.8	64.4	28.3	258.7
IDAHO	459	0.6	62.0	13.72	567	36.5	18.7	24.4	72.4	26.9	205.2
ILLINOIS	4 962	-1.2	717.5	15.20	617	276.5	254.7	304.8	627.3	403.0	2 233.5
INDIANA	2 474	-0.4	572.8	17.84	751	144.8	120.9	117.9	333.8	141.1	994.8
IOWA	1 196	-0.7	220.0	15.70	655	64.7	57.3	65.1	180.7	95.4	476.7
KANSAS	1 062	-2.1	172.0	15.83	640	62.7	52.4	58.6	150.6	69.9	442.1
KENTUCKY	1 471	-0.2	266.3	16.02	668	83.3	86.9	72.9	211.0	86.1	615.5
LOUISIANA	1 526	0.2	155.8	16.86	744	119.0	82.1	75.7	223.2	101.1	692.7
MAINE	503	-0.2	63.8	16.28	651	30.4	16.6	20.9	85.5	35.0	236.7
MARYLAND	2 020	0.2	147.6	15.75	622	NA	75.2	91.0	295.8	155.9	1 035.5
MASSACHUSETTS	2 770	-1.9	326.2	16.53	671	137.2	84.9	134.7	352.9	223.7	1 416.8
MICHIGAN	3 731	-1.6	727.2	21.28	896	190.0	125.1	173.6	516.6	218.9	1 700.4
MINNESOTA	2 249	0.0	344.3	15.43	620	125.2	92.1	127.8	301.7	176.0	1 013.3
MISSISSIPPI	873	-1.2	178.3	12.88	514	51.3	45.3	35.1	138.7	46.2	354.6
MISSOURI	2 249	-0.9	312.8	18.21	738	133.6	104.0	118.4	310.3	162.6	1 035.5
MONTANA	315	1.1	18.9	14.02	538	23.1	15.4	15.4	53.6	20.3	154.2
NEBRASKA	744	-0.4	102.1	14.86	618	45.9	46.4	40.7	107.1	61.9	317.1
NEVADA	953	3.4	43.7	14.63	571	100.0	41.5	34.3	119.4	58.6	530.6
NEW HAMPSHIRE	527	-0.6	80.1	14.85	594	28.8	15.7	26.8	96.2	37.2	229.2
NEW JERSEY	3 356	-0.4	351.7	15.46	634	159.3	177.3	232.2	468.8	277.1	1 585.7
NEW MEXICO	580	0.9	36.3	13.19	520	47.0	22.8	22.1	90.7	33.9	297.3
NEW YORK	6 918	-0.7	614.6	16.78	671	319.4	263.3	352.7	856.7	697.1	3 531.4
NORTH CAROLINA	3 159	-1.2	604.3	13.66	544	211.8	124.8	163.6	432.5	191.5	1 346.9
NORTH DAKOTA	257	0.7	23.4	14.04	562	15.9	13.0	18.0	40.9	18.4	116.6
OHIO	4 590	-1.2	844.2	18.00	738	229.8	182.4	235.0	627.7	312.0	2 049.4
OKLAHOMA	1 159	-2.3	143.0	14.13	555	62.9	53.3	54.6	169.3	83.3	531.4
OREGON	1 294	-0.4	195.9	15.20	597	77.2	55.7	74.5	184.0	98.3	565.3
PENNSYLVANIA	4 859	-0.9	715.5	14.98	599	245.1	225.7	226.8	662.0	337.9	2 304.8
RHODE ISLAND	417	0.9	58.9	12.88	506	20.8	11.3	16.4	53.1	33.6	212.1
SOUTH CAROLINA	1 484	0.3	277.1	14.19	586	112.4	61.0	63.0	223.0	91.4	623.7
SOUTH DAKOTA	304	0.2	37.7	13.13	559	19.4	11.6	16.7	48.4	27.5	134.9
TENNESSEE	2 255	0.1	414.1	13.56	540	115.5	139.4	127.8	313.0	139.3	950.3
TEXAS	7 725	-0.9	900.9	13.94	577	551.3	384.8	458.4	1 084.5	585.4	3 378.6
UTAH	877	-0.2	112.1	14.90	592	67.3	43.6	40.2	129.7	64.8	382.3
VERMONT	247	-0.7	37.6	14.54	582	15.3	8.5	10.3	39.2	13.2	115.3
VIRGINIA	2 862	0.1	304.9	15.88	648	217.8	118.4	113.3	402.8	187.3	1 406.0
WASHINGTON	2 138	0.0	266.5	18.03	712	156.1	87.9	115.7	306.8	152.8	951.2
WEST VIRGINIA	584	-1.1	64.7	16.05	663	32.5	25.1	22.7	87.6	31.0	285.9
WISCONSIN	2 367	0.0	506.4	16.12	650	123.5	106.2	113.0	319.0	157.7	987.8
WYOMING	187	0.6	9.3	16.74	673	19.5	11.7	7.0	29.8	10.2	76.5

1. Includes professional and business services, educational and health services, leisure and hospitality, and other services.

Table A. States — **Agriculture**

STATE	Farms — Number	Farms — Percent with Less than 50 acres	Farms — Percent with 500 acres and over	Farm operators whose principal occupation is farming (percent)	Land in farms — Acreage (1,000)	Land in farms — Percent change, 1997–2002	Acres — Average size of farm	Acres — Total irrigated (1,000)	Acres — Total cropland (1,000)	Value of land and buildings (dollars) — Average per farm	Value of land and buildings (dollars) — Average per acre
	164	165	166	167	168	169	170	171	172	173	174
UNITED STATES	2 128 982	34.9	15.9	57.5	938 279	0.7	441	55 311	434 165	537 833	1 213
ALABAMA	45 126	37.1	8.3	53.1	8 904	2.3	197	109	3 733	335 217	1 698
ALASKA	609	42.0	16.1	60.8	901	2.2	1 479	3	98	543 213	367
ARIZONA	7 294	58.0	17.6	58.9	26 587	-1.1	3 645	932	1 262	1 456 759	398
ARKANSAS	47 483	27.3	14.5	57.7	14 503	1.0	305	4 150	9 576	447 104	1 469
CALIFORNIA	79 631	61.7	10.5	61.7	27 589	-0.4	346	8 709	10 994	1 206 822	3 526
COLORADO	31 369	32.8	29.0	58.4	31 093	-5.0	991	2 591	11 531	757 613	756
CONNECTICUT	4 191	62.3	2.8	49.6	357	-0.5	85	10	171	840 302	9 491
DELAWARE	2 391	52.3	11.0	69.4	540	-7.4	226	97	457	980 323	4 054
DISTRICT OF COLUMBIA	X	X	X	X	X	X	X	X	X	X	X
FLORIDA	44 081	64.9	6.8	52.2	10 415	-0.4	236	1 815	3 715	665 376	2 836
GEORGIA	49 311	39.2	9.9	50.9	10 744	0.7	218	871	4 677	457 427	2 112
HAWAII	5 398	88.0	3.1	57.9	1 300	-10.6	241	69	211	842 875	3 507
IDAHO	25 017	49.2	18.0	55.4	11 767	-0.5	470	3 289	6 153	613 303	1 270
ILLINOIS	73 027	26.9	24.0	64.1	27 311	0.4	374	391	24 171	913 251	2 425
INDIANA	60 296	39.9	13.8	55.7	15 059	-0.3	250	313	12 909	637 645	2 567
IOWA	90 655	23.3	22.7	68.3	31 729	1.8	350	142	27 153	707 730	2 005
KANSAS	64 414	17.4	34.6	63.1	47 228	2.4	733	2 678	29 542	505 999	687
KENTUCKY	86 541	34.8	5.6	54.2	13 844	3.7	160	37	8 412	294 056	1 824
LOUISIANA	27 413	41.2	13.9	54.0	7 831	-0.6	286	939	5 072	444 007	1 534
MAINE	7 196	38.6	8.0	47.4	1 370	11.5	190	20	537	322 690	1 637
MARYLAND	12 198	47.8	7.8	57.2	2 078	-3.7	170	81	1 487	694 061	4 084
MASSACHUSETTS	6 075	60.0	2.7	54.0	519	0.1	85	24	208	755 254	9 234
MICHIGAN	53 315	41.1	9.0	54.5	10 143	2.7	190	456	7 984	509 299	2 667
MINNESOTA	80 839	24.9	19.0	62.9	27 512	5.5	340	455	22 729	517 132	1 513
MISSISSIPPI	42 186	30.0	9.9	48.8	11 098	8.8	263	1 176	5 823	370 689	1 381
MISSOURI	106 797	23.1	14.0	57.2	29 946	3.7	280	1 033	18 885	424 347	1 508
MONTANA	27 870	23.3	46.4	63.5	59 612	1.7	2 139	1 976	18 316	835 250	386
NEBRASKA	49 355	14.8	41.6	73.0	45 903	0.8	930	7 625	22 521	723 863	776
NEVADA	2 989	46.7	24.2	58.7	6 331	-1.2	2 118	747	940	953 619	446
NEW HAMPSHIRE	3 363	45.9	5.2	48.6	445	6.7	132	2	129	400 943	3 131
NEW JERSEY	9 924	70.5	3.5	52.3	806	-3.4	81	97	548	741 808	9 245
NEW MEXICO	15 170	44.7	28.8	55.9	44 810	-2.2	2 954	845	2 575	698 908	234
NEW YORK	37 255	30.4	9.4	60.8	7 661	5.3	206	75	4 841	345 504	1 708
NORTH CAROLINA	53 930	45.6	7.2	58.7	9 079	-0.5	264	264	5 472	518 719	3 088
NORTH DAKOTA	30 619	6.7	56.8	70.7	39 295	-0.2	1 283	203	26 506	517 448	404
OHIO	77 797	39.5	9.0	55.9	14 583	3.3	187	41	11 424	509 307	2 732
OKLAHOMA	83 300	24.2	18.0	55.3	33 662	1.3	404	518	14 843	285 730	699
OREGON	40 033	62.5	10.2	53.9	17 080	-2.2	427	1 908	5 417	508 882	1 202
PENNSYLVANIA	58 105	37.8	4.2	56.7	7 745	7.5	133	43	5 121	452 874	3 419
RHODE ISLAND	858	59.8	1.3	51.5	61	10.2	71	4	24	658 290	9 225
SOUTH CAROLINA	24 541	41.7	8.3	46.4	4 846	5.2	197	96	2 270	410 897	2 067
SOUTH DAKOTA	31 736	13.6	49.0	72.6	43 785	-1.3	1 380	401	20 318	618 651	442
TENNESSEE	87 595	43.6	4.3	50.3	11 682	4.8	133	61	6 993	325 783	2 405
TEXAS	228 926	32.6	18.0	53.6	129 878	-1.1	567	5 075	38 658	439 066	768
UTAH	15 282	54.8	14.0	48.7	11 731	-2.5	768	1 091	2 067	586 310	756
VERMONT	6 571	33.7	8.4	53.1	1 245	-1.4	189	2	568	386 695	2 051
VIRGINIA	47 606	35.9	7.5	53.6	8 625	4.6	181	99	4 194	490 064	2 675
WASHINGTON	35 939	57.5	12.8	58.5	15 318	0.9	426	1 823	8 038	623 333	1 486
WEST VIRGINIA	20 812	27.3	6.3	50.5	3 585	3.6	172	2	1 173	231 999	1 315
WISCONSIN	77 131	27.6	8.2	59.4	15 742	5.3	204	386	10 729	464 127	2 272
WYOMING	9 422	21.4	44.5	61.1	34 403	0.9	3 651	1 542	2 990	1 080 945	290

Table A. States — **Agriculture, Land, and Water**

STATE	Value of machinery and equipment average per farm (dollars)	Value of products sold — Total (mil dol)	Value of products sold — Average per farm (dollars)	Percent from — Crops	Percent from — Livestock and poultry products	Percent of farms with sales of — $10,000 or more	Percent of farms with sales of — $100,000 or more	Land, 1997 — Owned by federal government (percent)	Land, 1997 — Developed (percent)	Water consumption, 2000 (mil gal per day)
	175	176	177	178	179	180	181	182	183	184
UNITED STATES.................	66 570	200 646	94 245	47.4	52.6	40.7	14.6	20.7	5.1	404 769
ALABAMA	42 705	3 265	72 352	18.1	81.9	28.9	10.4	3.0	6.7	9 990
ALASKA	71 790	46	75 768	44.5	55.5	40.6	11.7	NA	NA	305
ARIZONA	88 651	2 395	328 413	66.3	33.7	35.7	16.3	41.7	2.0	6 730
ARKANSAS	65 299	4 950	104 256	32.7	67.3	39.7	17.9	9.1	4.1	10 900
CALIFORNIA........................	81 933	25 737	323 205	74.4	25.6	54.0	24.6	45.9	5.4	51 200
COLORADO.........................	87 871	4 525	144 257	26.9	73.1	39.6	12.5	35.7	2.5	12 600
CONNECTICUT....................	51 214	471	112 297	69.6	30.4	32.7	10.5	0.5	27.4	4 150
DELAWARE	113 755	619	258 826	24.3	75.7	63.2	42.8	2.0	14.7	1 320
DISTRICT OF COLUMBIA ...	X	X	X	X	X	X	X	NA	NA	10
FLORIDA.............................	39 884	6 242	141 609	80.8	19.2	36.6	11.6	10.1	14	20 100
GEORGIA	51 847	4 912	99 608	32.2	67.8	30.7	12.7	5.6	10.5	6 500
HAWAII	35 568	533	98 819	83.5	16.5	43.7	9.0	8.7	4.3	641
IDAHO	91 746	3 908	156 224	45.7	54.3	37.2	15.6	62.7	1.4	19 500
ILLINOIS	102 242	7 676	105 115	76.5	23.5	58.6	26.7	1.4	8.8	13 700
INDIANA	80 240	4 783	79 328	62.6	37.4	46.0	17.2	2.0	9.8	10 100
IOWA.................................	100 422	12 274	135 388	49.5	50.5	64.6	30.2	0.5	4.7	3 360
KANSAS.............................	95 124	8 746	135 782	27.7	72.3	51.7	17.1	1.0	3.7	6 610
KENTUCKY.........................	41 458	3 080	35 591	36.0	64.0	32.7	5.9	4.6	6.7	4 160
LOUISIANA.........................	64 379	1 816	66 239	58.7	41.3	33.5	12.5	4.2	5.2	10 400
MAINE...............................	54 316	464	64 425	48.0	52.0	29.2	9.4	1.0	3.4	799
MARYLAND	74 528	1 293	106 026	34.8	65.2	39.5	17.2	2.1	15.7	7 910
MASSACHUSETTS	50 243	384	63 262	72.1	27.9	36.4	11.4	1.8	27.7	4 660
MICHIGAN	73 910	3 772	70 757	62.6	37.4	37.8	12.2	8.8	9.5	10 000
MINNESOTA.......................	86 369	8 576	106 083	53.2	46.8	51.8	22.9	6.2	4.0	3 870
MISSISSIPPI.......................	51 839	3 116	73 870	32.9	67.1	25.9	10.3	5.8	4.8	2 960
MISSOURI	49 940	4 983	46 661	40.0	60.0	41.0	8.8	4.3	5.6	8 230
MONTANA	83 976	1 882	67 532	39.0	61.0	49.6	18.0	28.8	1.1	8 290
NEBRASKA.........................	111 776	9 704	196 609	34.9	65.1	69.5	32.0	1.3	2.4	12 300
NEVADA.............................	110 619	447	149 545	35.3	64.7	44.6	19.4	84.6	0.5	2 810
NEW HAMPSHIRE	40 868	145	43 067	57.4	42.6	26.2	7.5	12.8	9.9	1 210
NEW JERSEY......................	53 954	750	75 561	87.7	12.3	29.0	10.7	2.8	34.1	5 560
NEW MEXICO	58 262	1 700	112 065	23.4	76.6	31.7	10.5	34.0	1.5	3 260
NEW YORK	96 252	3 118	83 689	36.4	63.6	44.1	17.3	0.7	10.2	12 100
NORTH CAROLINA.............	63 902	6 962	129 087	28.9	71.1	36.3	16.3	7.4	11.4	11 400
NORTH DAKOTA	124 298	3 233	105 600	76.1	23.9	61.5	28.8	3.9	2.2	1 140
OHIO	68 119	4 264	54 804	54.1	45.9	40.0	11.4	1.4	13.7	11 100
OKLAHOMA........................	42 155	4 456	53 498	18.4	81.6	37.2	7.7	2.6	4.3	2 020
OREGON............................	63 462	3 195	79 822	68.7	31.3	30.9	10.5	50.3	2.0	6 930
PENNSYLVANIA..................	59 995	4 257	73 263	31.0	69.0	39.1	16.5	2.5	13.7	9 950
RHODE ISLAND	57 882	56	64 740	84.9	15.1	42.3	13.1	0.4	24.7	429
SOUTH CAROLINA.............	53 108	1 490	60 705	39.8	60.2	21.6	6.8	5.2	10.5	7 170
SOUTH DAKOTA.................	107 376	3 835	120 829	41.1	58.9	68.1	30.5	6.3	1.9	528
TENNESSEE	45 263	2 200	25 113	48.8	51.2	22.5	4.4	4.6	8.8	10 800
TEXAS	40 553	14 135	61 744	26.4	73.6	28.5	6.4	1.7	5.0	29 600
UTAH	62 600	1 116	73 020	23.1	76.9	33.6	10.4	63.1	1.2	4 970
VERMONT	66 094	473	71 993	15.1	84.9	39.4	17.8	6.4	5.2	447
VIRGINIA	43 303	2 361	49 593	30.4	69.6	32.7	8.2	9.8	9.7	8 830
WASHINGTON	80 212	5 331	148 327	67.2	32.8	40.6	18.4	27.1	4.7	5 310
WEST VIRGINIA..................	26 188	483	23 199	14.4	85.6	17.5	3.3	7.8	5.6	5 150
WISCONSIN	72 300	5 623	72 906	30.1	69.9	46.0	18.1	5.1	6.7	7 590
WYOMING	74 757	864	91 688	15.9	84.1	53.2	19.2	45.9	1.0	5 170

Table A. States — Manufactures and Construction

STATE	Manufactures, 2001										Construction, 1997			
	All employees			Production workers										
						Wages								
	Number (1,000)	Percent change, 2000–2001	Annual payroll (mil dol)	Number (1,000)	Work hours (millions)	Total (mil dol)	Average per worker (dollars)	Value added by manu- facture (mil dol)	Value of ship- ments (mil dol)	Total capital expenditures (mil dol)	Estab- lishments	Value (mil dol)	Paid employees	Annual payroll (mil dol)
	185	186	187	188	189	190	191	192	193	194	195	196	197	198
UNITED STATES	15 879.5	-4.6	593 051	11 235	22 347	342 990	30 528	1 853 929	3 970 500	143 652	656 448	845 544	5 664 853	174 185
ALABAMA	315.1	-6.0	9 890	247	487	6 708	27 138	27 844	67 172	2 819	9 586	12 567	95 218	2 476
ALASKA	12.6	1.6	409	10	21	297	29 267	1 182	3 987	97	2 034	2 406	14 114	565
ARIZONA	186.4	-7.2	7 367	115	222	3 146	27 445	28 430	42 168	2 593	11 058	18 866	131 871	3 621
ARKANSAS	227.0	-3.5	6 363	185	363	4 538	24 578	19 868	46 530	1 410	5 457	5 143	42 033	983
CALIFORNIA	1 792.2	-2.6	72 189	1 148	2 276	33 383	29 090	219 584	414 762	19 629	60 162	93 145	561 338	19 148
COLORADO	163.1	-2.5	6 541	108	212	3 317	30 669	17 799	35 627	2 084	14 681	19 442	125 228	3 808
CONNECTICUT	229.8	-3.3	10 557	137	271	4 807	35 032	27 595	47 055	1 783	9 057	9 729	63 935	2 247
DELAWARE	38.0	-6.7	1 458	28	55	928	32 634	6 621	16 664	353	2 294	3 052	20 421	633
DISTRICT OF COLUMBIA	1.8	-39.8	90	1	2	51	37 716	93	178	22	310	1 437	6 356	240
FLORIDA	401.3	-5.0	13 591	268	530	6 757	25 201	39 974	76 541	2 506	36 608	50 174	324 844	8 803
GEORGIA	484.0	-5.7	15 721	372	752	10 281	27 655	57 578	127 624	3 409	17 896	28 171	163 981	4 688
HAWAII	14.4	-2.0	447	9	17	225	24 809	907	3 196	157	2 335	3 902	21 791	845
IDAHO	63.9	1.6	2 126	48	93	1 424	29 923	3 670	15 076	1 158	5 360	5 365	40 535	1 131
ILLINOIS	811.3	-6.3	31 498	559	1 130	17 577	31 416	94 124	196 449	6 357	27 953	39 447	240 092	8 885
INDIANA	597.7	-6.3	23 155	449	901	15 195	33 868	72 122	154 264	5 273	16 000	19 228	140 520	4 345
IOWA	235.9	-4.4	8 221	177	351	5 221	29 545	29 636	65 428	1 804	7 941	7 941	62 146	1 734
KANSAS	193.8	-0.9	7 093	140	290	4 366	31 184	21 008	53 031	1 178	7 115	8 762	61 915	1 756
KENTUCKY	276.3	-5.5	10 002	214	432	6 734	31 450	31 722	84 180	3 500	8 878	9 754	76 876	2 001
LOUISIANA	156.9	-3.2	6 335	116	239	4 191	36 160	22 545	85 488	3 260	7 812	11 331	107 773	3 033
MAINE	77.7	-2.7	2 832	58	112	1 822	31 603	7 880	15 066	1 333	4 249	2 812	25 157	662
MARYLAND	162.4	-2.7	6 917	104	204	3 324	32 010	18 757	36 038	3 615	14 525	20 881	141 469	4 368
MASSACHUSETTS	376.7	-2.3	16 623	227	452	7 535	33 235	44 447	79 851	6 981	14 959	20 413	107 813	3 869
MICHIGAN	749.5	-7.2	33 028	564	1 142	22 179	39 340	86 262	209 003	2 579	25 399	30 400	187 135	6 281
MINNESOTA	376.7	-3.5	14 519	249	487	7 709	30 934	38 545	82 304	1 169	12 993	18 125	103 200	3 604
MISSISSIPPI	197.8	-8.0	5 559	158	309	3 838	24 252	15 573	38 560	2 835	4 824	5 978	47 695	1 155
MISSOURI	346.6	-3.9	12 226	252	496	7 432	29 462	40 284	89 682	191	15 020	18 772	130 555	3 978
MONTANA	20.4	-4.9	619	15	28	417	27 841	2 091	5 423	698	3 452	2 209	18 096	446
NEBRASKA	105.0	-4.9	3 348	83	176	2 282	27 515	11 962	31 133	249	5 198	5 389	40 363	1 148
NEVADA	40.4	1.3	1 518	28	55	791	28 646	3 844	7 581	855	4 436	11 697	70 168	2 313
NEW HAMPSHIRE	96.7	-4.4	3 795	67	128	2 218	33 067	8 621	16 975	3 644	3 684	3 279	22 690	678
NEW JERSEY	379.5	-2.0	15 534	253	513	8 167	32 221	50 754	98 230	631	22 102	24 513	143 627	5 190
NEW MEXICO	32.7	-9.5	1 147	23	46	735	31 361	6 632	11 464	5 075	4 673	4 746	39 671	1 027
NEW YORK	707.2	-4.0	26 380	482	950	14 217	29 487	78 484	146 455	5 208	36 806	43 891	275 501	9 670
NORTH CAROLINA	693.7	-6.7	21 436	532	1 034	13 622	25 620	91 184	167 124	2 770	23 990	26 506	198 367	5 178
NORTH DAKOTA	23.4	-2.2	726	17	32	439	26 232	2 669	6 517	234	2 034	1 802	15 782	408
OHIO	923.5	-6.0	36 190	682	1 366	23 431	34 351	107 440	241 902	7 364	26 047	33 175	224 302	7 068
OKLAHOMA	161.7	-6.1	5 350	118	230	3 341	28 377	18 059	40 063	1 496	6 751	6 502	50 556	1 256
OREGON	199.2	-3.0	7 200	142	280	4 369	30 675	22 027	43 271	2 900	11 740	12 948	80 041	2 649
PENNSYLVANIA	768.7	-3.2	28 512	545	1 087	16 896	31 029	87 984	178 613	6 025	27 563	33 423	230 026	7 276
RHODE ISLAND	70.0	-5.0	2 396	46	95	1 260	27 202	5 877	10 958	351	3 060	3 690	17 070	552
SOUTH CAROLINA	312.4	-6.0	10 694	241	482	6 951	28 895	35 017	78 738	2 770	10 430	10 800	86 200	2 114
SOUTH DAKOTA	39.6	-5.4	1 115	29	58	729	24 776	4 558	11 093	195	2 418	1 721	14 488	355
TENNESSEE	441.4	-5.6	14 531	335	651	9 387	28 017	46 349	104 109	4 621	11 417	17 064	119 458	3 360
TEXAS	950.4	-4.4	35 377	648	1 303	19 410	29 964	120 086	321 361	11 247	35 315	59 457	426 765	12 398
UTAH	121.8	-2.1	4 174	82	162	2 341	28 461	11 783	25 908	1 281	7 288	8 418	55 801	1 578
VERMONT	45.8	4.9	1 740	30	60	849	28 252	5 078	8 926	715	2 474	1 667	13 101	331
VIRGINIA	327.4	-6.9	11 268	246	487	7 076	28 772	53 043	92 874	2 703	19 537	22 797	179 909	4 837
WASHINGTON	309.2	-4.7	12 603	195	389	6 922	35 566	38 193	89 280	2 173	19 867	21 433	138 194	4 529
WEST VIRGINIA	67.7	-2.6	2 519	50	103	1 643	32 576	7 202	16 201	571	4 506	3 022	31 312	757
WISCONSIN	544.3	-4.9	19 817	397	769	12 302	31 021	59 585	126 542	3 710	14 976	16 628	115 488	3 864
WYOMING	9.0	-12.2	305	7	14	213	30 956	1 358	3 835	84	2 177	1 522	13 867	345

STATE	Wholesale trade, 1997				Retail trade,[1] 1997							
						Number of employees						
	Number of establishments	Number of employees	Sales (mil dol)	Annual payroll (mil dol)	Number of establishments	Total	Motor vehicle and parts dealers	Food and beverage stores	Clothing and clothing accessory stores	General merchandise stores	Sales (mil dol)	Annual payroll (mil dol)
	199	200	201	202	203	204	205	206	207	208	209	210
UNITED STATES	453 470	5 796 557	4 059 657.8	214 915.4	1 118 446	13 991 004	1 718 963	2 893 074	1 280 153	2 507 540	2 460 963.0	237 201.0
ALABAMA	6 315	79 229	40 986.3	2 394.7	20 163	231 665	28 935	47 883	20 397	47 697	36 623.3	3 381.7
ALASKA	784	6 860	2 989.8	256.8	2 866	32 502	3 965	7 622	2 463	6 912	6 251.4	670.5
ARIZONA	6 689	80 155	45 899.1	2 748.9	16 283	232 050	34 688	43 818	17 411	38 525	43 960.9	4 223.9
ARKANSAS	3 619	41 385	27 515.4	1 136.6	12 600	132 335	16 255	25 232	9 307	31 801	21 643.7	1 904.4
CALIFORNIA	57 841	757 294	548 864.5	29 875.0	106 357	1 354 797	174 669	268 874	144 936	215 325	263 118.3	26 362.7
COLORADO	7 383	88 364	60 310.4	3 282.0	18 299	225 647	28 164	41 242	19 259	37 873	40 536.0	4 163.3
CONNECTICUT	5 283	77 716	76 167.9	3 595.3	14 574	186 935	20 876	43 270	19 413	24 650	34 938.9	3 634.3
DELAWARE	906	13 509	12 585.5	619.5	3 736	47 116	6 082	9 605	4 082	8 412	8 237.0	798.7
DISTRICT OF COLUMBIA	348	5 008	3 918.6	223.0	2 075	19 608	482	5 572	3 469	1 452	2 788.8	351.5
FLORIDA	31 214	296 139	187 079.9	9 678.2	66 643	841 814	107 767	196 921	80 667	143 248	151 191.2	14 169.5
GEORGIA	13 978	191 087	163 782.6	7 519.7	33 073	420 676	52 692	92 982	38 596	74 468	72 212.5	6 943.6
HAWAII	1 872	18 532	7 147.5	576.0	5 088	64 218	5 739	12 269	11 409	12 586	11 317.8	1 161.8
IDAHO	1 980	22 828	10 127.8	628.0	5 848	63 732	9 894	10 998	3 936	11 112	11 649.6	1 079.7
ILLINOIS	21 951	325 752	275 968.4	13 324.5	44 568	610 790	69 604	109 745	60 545	113 502	108 002.2	10 596.0
INDIANA	8 896	112 705	66 350.1	3 737.8	24 954	337 867	40 300	59 909	23 949	73 621	57 241.7	5 273.8
IOWA	5 399	63 596	35 453.7	1 820.1	14 695	175 694	22 099	37 582	12 451	30 028	26 723.8	2 633.4
KANSAS	5 085	59 954	42 209.9	1 946.8	12 271	140 412	17 846	28 684	10 423	27 776	22 571.9	2 191.1
KENTUCKY	5 051	69 309	37 242.9	2 071.2	17 369	212 189	26 010	43 623	14 324	44 452	33 332.7	3 128.1
LOUISIANA	6 390	76 350	46 972.3	2 375.2	17 863	224 412	28 561	47 341	18 327	46 951	35 807.9	3 307.9
MAINE	1 726	19 932	7 305.6	616.2	7 074	72 897	8 930	16 636	5 547	11 281	12 737.1	1 164.2
MARYLAND	6 283	92 458	54 906.7	3 656.3	19 798	274 260	33 636	61 969	27 846	45 060	46 428.2	4 914.0
MASSACHUSETTS	9 993	146 827	112 792.4	6 484.8	26 209	335 736	34 301	86 377	36 560	45 293	58 578.0	5 894.8
MICHIGAN	13 936	189 057	158 757.3	7 629.6	39 564	529 441	64 429	96 770	44 447	116 058	93 706.1	8 922.3
MINNESOTA	9 348	131 787	99 444.5	5 024.0	20 883	282 282	31 889	54 634	20 926	50 297	48 077.7	4 525.7
MISSISSIPPI	3 173	36 520	18 445.2	1 012.1	12 791	138 372	16 921	30 128	10 476	32 314	20 774.5	1 935.3
MISSOURI	9 522	125 929	91 411.9	4 639.8	24 181	297 556	39 365	51 029	22 005	62 480	51 269.9	4 945.0
MONTANA	1 574	14 356	7 596.8	371.6	5 042	48 337	7 261	8 733	2 780	8 231	7 779.1	746.5
NEBRASKA	3 157	41 002	38 015.4	1 170.2	8 295	102 684	11 353	20 126	7 016	18 531	16 529.3	1 554.6
NEVADA	2 253	27 251	12 806.9	918.5	6 222	89 452	11 430	16 587	8 165	15 910	18 220.8	1 798.2
NEW HAMPSHIRE	2 033	22 631	11 371.1	875.0	6 645	84 170	10 384	18 316	7 444	14 470	15 890.1	1 428.2
NEW JERSEY	17 812	266 944	227 309.0	11 886.1	34 837	420 724	44 951	109 004	50 706	56 016	79 914.9	7 926.0
NEW MEXICO	2 182	21 344	7 397.6	601.1	7 421	86 300	11 470	14 352	6 777	15 779	14 984.5	1 455.5
NEW YORK	37 499	414 249	319 697.6	17 185.8	75 241	805 208	72 275	190 395	102 985	118 379	139 303.9	14 329.8
NORTH CAROLINA	12 284	157 774	98 080.1	5 574.1	35 563	416 287	54 750	83 706	38 088	74 486	72 356.8	6 697.4
NORTH DAKOTA	1 604	16 992	8 618.4	454.4	3 569	40 685	6 193	7 505	2 345	7 559	6 702.1	616.1
OHIO	17 322	254 226	160 415.6	9 192.2	44 521	630 098	75 633	125 217	46 151	129 491	102 938.8	9 924.5
OKLAHOMA	5 191	59 641	32 132.3	1 756.1	14 352	161 613	23 418	28 420	11 438	35 788	27 065.6	2 406.9
OREGON	5 943	74 790	53 679.1	2 578.7	14 467	178 349	25 422	33 345	14 650	33 171	33 396.8	3 308.8
PENNSYLVANIA	17 138	237 567	159 354.2	8 588.2	50 208	650 144	79 521	152 042	56 354	105 437	109 948.5	10 561.9
RHODE ISLAND	1 590	18 762	7 602.7	635.2	4 169	45 747	4 725	11 885	4 011	6 974	7 505.8	752.2
SOUTH CAROLINA	5 035	58 910	34 179.8	1 866.8	18 481	209 256	24 983	46 596	21 374	37 949	33 634.3	3 107.2
SOUTH DAKOTA	1 402	15 509	7 874.2	389.8	4 311	45 867	5 866	9 253	2 861	7 759	11 707.1	689.6
TENNESSEE	8 234	120 228	82 626.4	3 975.4	24 808	304 452	38 615	58 824	27 531	64 223	50 813.2	4 810.3
TEXAS	33 346	425 750	323 111.7	15 504.9	74 105	950 848	129 773	183 970	86 657	190 380	182 516.1	16 197.1
UTAH	3 277	44 312	21 271.9	1 420.4	7 656	114 474	14 590	20 592	9 189	21 022	19 964.6	1 856.9
VERMONT	941	10 987	4 731.4	330.6	4 093	36 306	4 453	9 342	2 727	3 420	5 898.6	603.3
VIRGINIA	7 868	106 365	61 046.7	3 784.4	29 032	379 039	47 195	73 141	36 212	65 241	62 569.9	6 202.6
WASHINGTON	10 039	118 810	75 397.8	4 376.0	22 841	283 653	37 408	55 974	24 915	46 693	52 472.9	5 385.9
WEST VIRGINIA	1 956	23 805	10 290.4	681.1	8 082	90 087	11 622	18 509	5 572	18 530	14 057.9	1 309.3
WISCONSIN	8 025	110 309	57 192.9	3 764.9	21 717	305 255	37 641	61 524	19 470	54 081	50 520.5	4 826.2
WYOMING	800	5 761	2 547.1	161.9	2 939	26 934	3 928	5 001	1 564	4 846	4 530.5	426.7

1. Establishments with payroll.

Table A. States — Transportation and Warehousing, Finance and Insurance, and Real Estate

STATE	Transportation and warehousing, 1997				Finance and insurance, 1997				Real estate and rental and leasing, 1997			
	Number of establish-ments	Number of employees	Receipts (mil dol)	Annual payroll (mil dol)	Number of establish-ments	Number of employees	Receipts (mil dol)	Annual payroll (mil dol)	Number of establish-ments	Number of employees	Receipts (mil dol)	Annual payroll (mil dol)
	211	212	213	214	215	216	217	218	219	220	221	222
UNITED STATES...............	178 025	2 920 777	318 245.0	82 346.2	395 203	5 835 214	2 197 808	264 551.4	288 273	1 702 420	240 917.6	41 590.7
ALABAMA..........................	3 024	44 692	4 285.3	1 151.6	5 640	70 679	NA	2 323.1	3 664	20 629	2 130.3	396.7
ALASKA............................	940	13 562	3 346.9	576.6	666	6 728	NA	253.7	716	4 014	543.2	98.3
ARIZONA...........................	2 257	45 233	4 086.2	1 107.2	6 568	84 970	NA	3 007.9	5 450	32 529	4 110.1	747.4
ARKANSAS........................	2 330	39 917	3 804.4	1 093.4	3 478	32 597	NA	1 000.8	2 269	9 761	1 001.6	163.2
CALIFORNIA.......................	16 056	317 832	36 610.2	9 344.2	40 503	618 971	NA	29 660.2	37 243	243 168	37 937.4	6 563.7
COLORADO........................	2 411	38 399	3 626.9	1 017.5	7 400	86 239	NA	3 473.2	6 663	38 224	4 853.5	883.8
CONNECTICUT	1 568	28 540	3 266.1	859.0	5 550	117 684	NA	6 533.0	3 372	20 635	3 522.8	609.3
DELAWARE........................	585	7 258	594.1	179.6	1 619	44 780	NA	1 942.1	1 101	5 243	5 006.5	118.3
DISTRICT OF COLUMBIA ...	215	3 356	567.1	91.3	908	16 481	NA	1 318.7	934	7 725	1 354.2	275.4
FLORIDA............................	9 768	157 343	19 852.1	4 429.8	24 785	317 250	NA	11 928.3	20 388	118 086	15 360.4	2 652.2
GEORGIA..........................	4 733	85 109	8 306.3	2 359.4	11 668	153 755	NA	6 005.3	7 794	47 669	6 912.9	1 308.8
HAWAII.............................	686	16 684	1 249.3	427.7	1 573	21 757	NA	775.1	1 753	12 446	1 824.1	311.9
IDAHO..............................	1 233	10 633	948.0	237.8	1 919	14 583	NA	454.9	1 236	4 870	450.3	73.9
ILLINOIS............................	8 559	153 788	16 521.6	4 377.2	20 195	334 241	NA	16 014.5	11 411	73 819	12 830.0	2 101.4
INDIANA...........................	4 389	77 568	8 991.9	2 177.4	8 946	108 304	NA	3 727.5	5 427	28 948	3 269.1	572.6
IOWA...............................	3 100	36 220	3 914.1	948.5	5 238	72 895	NA	2 509.3	2 518	12 619	1 457.5	249.0
KANSAS...........................	2 332	32 051	3 220.1	870.2	4 973	53 304	NA	1 827.0	2 602	13 005	1 525.8	259.6
KENTUCKY........................	2 919	49 545	6 288.7	1 447.9	5 373	60 241	NA	1 860.0	3 227	16 284	1 961.6	314.3
LOUISIANA........................	3 715	64 767	7 889.9	1 875.5	6 968	66 707	NA	2 143.8	4 151	28 571	3 342.1	642.2
MAINE..............................	1 232	9 199	934.6	223.5	1 657	22 213	NA	805.5	1 343	5 929	601.7	114.2
MARYLAND	3 136	46 415	4 023.3	1 259.6	7 064	103 894	NA	4 436.6	5 065	39 502	4 764.7	971.3
MASSACHUSETTS	3 283	53 297	4 704.3	1 391.8	8 875	212 188	NA	11 427.7	5 834	41 233	5 925.4	1 214.1
MICHIGAN.........................	4 733	77 977	9 249.2	2 493.8	12 249	181 898	NA	6 598.9	8 302	50 941	6 492.7	1 126.2
MINNESOTA......................	3 810	53 811	5 662.8	1 375.1	7 999	124 827	NA	5 390.5	5 051	30 172	3 886.4	687.2
MISSISSIPPI......................	2 201	24 411	2 475.5	657.3	4 059	33 400	NA	979.8	2 125	8 354	794.2	132.1
MISSOURI	4 874	69 082	7 681.6	1 725.1	8 738	122 082	NA	4 474.4	5 500	31 301	3 991.1	698.1
MONTANA.........................	967	8 758	948.9	196.2	1 553	12 581	NA	366.8	1 186	4 265	353.4	58.1
NEBRASKA........................	1 874	24 848	3 475.1	700.7	3 369	50 003	NA	1 576.2	1 587	8 240	891.1	160.8
NEVADA...........................	830	18 368	1 410.5	419.0	2 799	27 162	NA	916.4	2 460	16 890	2 276.5	381.5
NEW HAMPSHIRE	733	13 714	933.3	332.7	1 646	23 143	NA	871.2	1 399	6 639	719.4	151.1
NEW JERSEY......................	6 632	131 171	14 404.7	4 053.0	10 567	208 318	NA	10 519.9	8 292	47 558	8 881.9	1 376.5
NEW MEXICO.....................	1 009	11 841	1 392.3	293.6	2 453	22 936	NA	662.3	1 887	8 844	893.9	165.2
NEW YORK.........................	10 485	178 698	17 635.2	4 848.9	24 691	611 857	NA	52 522.2	27 214	145 326	27 770.1	4 447.8
NORTH CAROLINA..............	5 077	77 841	6 625.9	2 123.9	10 831	142 234	NA	5 276.5	7 346	39 349	5 026.0	900.6
NORTH DAKOTA.................	913	8 297	862.5	191.5	1 364	11 790	NA	336.0	657	3 325	287.0	46.3
OHIO...............................	6 709	117 984	11 722.3	3 531.0	16 208	251 657	NA	9 008.4	9 692	62 628	7 243.7	1 334.6
OKLAHOMA.......................	2 112	30 145	4 590.4	868.8	5 587	54 064	NA	1 697.8	3 344	15 354	1 576.0	284.5
OREGON...........................	2 610	38 544	3 771.3	1 163.5	5 172	63 386	NA	2 317.2	4 556	23 058	2 704.0	470.9
PENNSYLVANIA..................	6 379	126 839	11 540.6	3 400.0	16 601	287 143	NA	11 173.6	8 684	57 519	7 668.6	1 360.5
RHODE ISLAND..................	546	5 947	587.2	145.0	1 250	22 920	NA	812.9	922	4 649	573.4	105.4
SOUTH CAROLINA..............	2 126	35 301	3 303.1	913.0	5 596	57 283	NA	1 801.0	3 541	18 760	2 012.6	377.1
SOUTH DAKOTA.................	957	7 361	887.1	162.0	1 612	18 869	NA	508.3	719	2 951	245.7	45.1
TENNESSEE	3 945	73 973	7 083.4	2 244.3	8 345	102 124	NA	3 650.4	4 999	29 626	3 732.0	667.3
TEXAS..............................	12 800	209 782	28 532.9	6 137.1	28 074	352 019	NA	13 833.6	20 753	128 915	15 957.4	3 119.2
UTAH...............................	1 167	29 028	2 854.2	799.9	3 167	39 603	NA	1 228.8	2 169	12 318	1 342.6	236.0
VERMONT	512	4 856	390.5	111.8	897	9 228	NA	328.3	701	2 362	240.6	42.2
VIRGINIA	4 482	60 884	6 338.2	1 666.9	9 549	135 689	NA	5 064.4	6 717	43 976	5 749.2	1 028.4
WASHINGTON	3 984	61 576	7 289.5	1 933.2	8 332	91 844	NA	3 697.3	7 544	41 899	5 352.8	935.3
WEST VIRGINIA..................	1 439	14 526	1 979.3	419.9	2 115	21 144	NA	555.3	1 449	5 812	665.0	100.8
WISCONSIN.......................	5 068	69 166	7 028.7	1 868.2	8 062	129 664	NA	4 785.4	4 598	23 924	2 637.5	464.1
WYOMING.........................	580	4 640	557.5	123.9	782	5 885	NA	169.7	717	2 463	220.8	39.5

Table A. States — **Information and Utilities**

STATE	Information, 1997								Utilities, 1997			
	Number of establish-ments	Number of employees					Receipts (mil dol)	Annual payroll (mil dol)	Number of establish-ments	Number of employees	Receipts (mil dol)	Annual payroll (mil dol)
		Total	Publishing	Motion picture and sound recording	Broadcast and telecommuni-cations	Information and data processing services						
	223	224	225	226	227	228	229	230	231	232	233	234
UNITED STATES	114 475	3 066 167	1 006 214	275 981	1 434 455	349 517	623 213.9	129 481.6	15 513	702 703	411 713.3	36 594.7
ALABAMA	1 430	35 476	8 863	1 302	22 528	2 783	6 477.5	1 320.1	455	14 286	6 607.8	798.7
ALASKA	353	5 209	1 247	352	3 439	171	1 038.6	203.1	85	1 670	598.4	102.6
ARIZONA	1 731	42 238	12 643	3 370	22 499	3 726	7 209.4	1 487.1	235	10 546	5 840.3	595.4
ARKANSAS	904	20 101	7 233	1 225	9 405	2 238	3 326.6	583.9	359	7 711	3 423.2	352.7
CALIFORNIA	16 302	450 511	154 837	98 151	163 482	34 041	108 719.1	22 868.5	894	52 662	27 017.6	3 090.5
COLORADO	2 653	76 024	21 109	3 881	43 139	7 895	12 743.0	3 306.3	317	9 771	5 205.7	467.7
CONNECTICUT	1 561	48 173	16 027	1 989	20 893	9 264	9 054.2	2 136.8	145	11 161	5 253.3	666.4
DELAWARE	275	8 701	1 571	316	5 093	1 721	1 652.6	310.0	27	D	D	D
DISTRICT OF COLUMBIA	632	23 787	9 456	1 396	9 880	3 055	6 351.0	1 363.0	33	D	D	D
FLORIDA	5 883	145 025	40 014	10 952	78 187	15 872	27 830.2	5 522.4	524	27 652	12 879.4	1 385.8
GEORGIA	3 163	100 656	24 347	4 781	61 056	10 472	18 939.2	4 176.5	498	21 420	10 729.9	1 053.0
HAWAII	458	8 996	2 066	1 496	5 100	334	1 464.2	318.7	43	3 216	1 261.2	153.9
IDAHO	526	9 017	3 229	697	4 540	551	1 313.6	257.5	169	3 216	1 261.2	153.9
ILLINOIS	4 994	129 204	50 296	10 037	58 436	10 435	26 496.6	5 488.0	390	33 717	15 364.5	1 989.6
INDIANA	2 032	43 961	16 597	3 273	19 353	4 738	8 130.9	1 406.6	418	18 511	9 070.3	867.6
IOWA	1 502	34 363	13 479	1 732	12 653	6 499	5 433.0	1 016.2	280	8 353	3 422.2	363.0
KANSAS	1 357	32 258	11 785	1 934	16 778	1 761	7 324.2	1 161.9	248	7 811	3 697.9	378.3
KENTUCKY	1 261	29 098	9 516	1 820	12 739	5 023	5 056.1	814.7	328	11 367	8 236.0	505.2
LOUISIANA	1 285	27 271	5 876	2 013	18 008	1 374	4 621.7	907.8	516	12 641	6 797.8	609.4
MAINE	647	9 693	3 503	438	4 753	999	1 303.0	297.4	105	3 766	1 687.8	170.7
MARYLAND	2 026	56 781	16 507	3 213	28 435	8 626	10 618.5	2 302.1	106	11 295	5 065.0	645.7
MASSACHUSETTS	3 282	113 698	57 901	4 921	36 815	14 061	20 548.9	5 395.7	222	15 931	12 081.6	942.2
MICHIGAN	3 273	90 178	26 353	6 184	34 788	22 853	18 878.4	3 362.4	385	25 464	15 044.2	1 486.1
MINNESOTA	2 430	58 855	23 652	4 308	24 185	6 710	9 660.3	2 111.5	240	13 205	4 441.1	675.6
MISSISSIPPI	880	14 259	3 257	683	9 693	626	2 480.8	466.6	617	8 307	3 085.6	340.4
MISSOURI	2 254	75 706	25 662	4 143	38 152	7 749	12 112.4	2 743.6	342	16 685	6 172.1	838.1
MONTANA	568	7 077	2 036	693	3 610	738	1 061.7	177.5	215	3 296	949.3	160.1
NEBRASKA	841	28 950	8 099	1 120	9 413	10 318	4 242.2	984.4	141	D	D	D
NEVADA	660	10 750	2 978	1 203	6 201	368	2 110.9	376.3	86	D	D	D
NEW HAMPSHIRE	669	11 602	6 004	644	4 217	737	1 839.2	483.7	104	3 222	1 484.7	179.5
NEW JERSEY	3 384	131 970	38 059	6 283	78 402	9 226	21 004.9	6 833.3	294	21 147	11 626.2	1 254.4
NEW MEXICO	767	11 265	3 772	1 341	5 696	456	1 905.1	320.2	206	5 868	2 168.7	251.1
NEW YORK	9 454	287 054	99 892	27 891	119 678	39 593	83 185.9	14 837.6	371	59 255	23 107.7	3 019.2
NORTH CAROLINA	2 584	60 047	17 572	4 116	34 127	4 232	11 337.2	2 126.3	390	23 765	9 018.2	1 218.8
NORTH DAKOTA	382	7 710	2 627	332	3 357	1 394	921.6	206.8	129	3 303	1 158.0	154.9
OHIO	3 518	102 414	36 336	8 488	45 595	11 995	18 139.8	3 746.8	533	31 560	16 893.4	1 533.3
OKLAHOMA	1 338	28 871	6 708	1 730	17 353	3 080	5 281.8	926.9	362	9 128	5 170.3	401.9
OREGON	1 631	31 382	13 357	2 618	13 793	1 614	5 839.9	1 181.0	226	7 402	4 568.6	424.6
PENNSYLVANIA	4 168	118 315	44 615	6 468	53 020	14 212	21 854.5	4 272.8	606	38 952	39 604.0	2 080.8
RHODE ISLAND	359	10 611	3 773	444	4 014	2 380	1 441.0	363.7	27	1 963	1 038.7	99.6
SOUTH CAROLINA	1 099	25 054	7 287	1 485	13 414	2 868	4 714.5	845.3	267	12 209	4 353.9	600.1
SOUTH DAKOTA	466	6 243	2 058	421	3 673	91	916.1	155.5	137	2 153	619.7	84.0
TENNESSEE	2 101	45 015	14 213	4 366	23 518	2 918	7 949.7	1 511.9	162	3 771	1 815.0	155.0
TEXAS	7 520	210 654	49 949	15 791	114 361	30 553	40 363.2	8 605.6	1 816	57 717	74 102.3	2 817.5
UTAH	971	24 253	8 758	2 204	10 024	3 267	3 567.7	807.9	152	5 580	3 882.5	293.8
VERMONT	483	6 667	2 829	362	2 751	725	1 724.1	188.7	53	1 838	831.7	93.7
VIRGINIA	2 945	90 346	23 602	4 740	47 411	14 593	20 400.4	4 347.3	291	17 251	10 386.6	916.7
WASHINGTON	2 546	61 830	23 439	4 563	29 996	3 832	14 571.3	3 102.5	339	6 245	3 217.9	291.2
WEST VIRGINIA	605	11 862	3 135	490	7 649	588	1 773.5	305.8	240	7 767	3 263.4	353.8
WISCONSIN	2 009	43 546	16 920	3 227	17 343	6 056	7 733.9	1 362.9	253	13 762	5 486.6	716.3
WYOMING	313	3 440	1 170	354	1 810	106	549.9	82.6	132	2 767	1 012.4	137.9

STATE	Professional, scientific, and technical services,[1] 1997								Arts, entertainment, and recreation,[1] 1997			
	Number of establishments	Number of employees					Receipts (mil dol)	Annual payroll (mil dol)	Number of establishments	Number of employees	Receipts (mil dol)	Annual payroll (mil dol)
		Total	Legal services	Accounting and related services	Architectural, engineering, and related services	Computer systems design and related services						
	235	236	237	238	239	240	241	242	243	244	245	246
UNITED STATES	615 305	5 212 745	1 012 092	966 533	1 038 317	764 659	579 542.1	225 376.1	79 637	1 207 943	85 129.4	26 115.0
ALABAMA	7 076	54 413	12 773	8 097	14 353	7 904	5 295.6	2 051.4	791	9 381	435.7	105.0
ALASKA	1 437	7 892	2 030	1 146	3 027	418	945.9	370.8	320	3 055	168.3	34.9
ARIZONA	10 163	75 789	14 064	15 992	17 543	9 195	6 669.4	2 724.7	1 071	24 416	2 033.3	475.1
ARKANSAS	4 125	23 094	5 608	5 165	4 303	3 010	1 825.8	719.6	594	5 343	228.7	56.8
CALIFORNIA	78 635	805 856	124 890	242 857	129 826	101 494	89 555.7	35 258.6	12 015	182 004	15 913.8	6 296.6
COLORADO	14 315	103 008	15 384	12 498	23 939	27 261	12 887.7	4 625.1	1 494	30 541	1 909.6	625.0
CONNECTICUT	9 393	71 058	14 748	10 537	10 930	9 377	9 115.8	3 700.1	1 046	27 236	2 526.8	589.2
DELAWARE	1 717	12 382	3 859	1 753	2 548	1 609	1 430.4	553.4	216	4 074	240.1	62.0
DISTRICT OF COLUMBIA	3 760	61 123	28 841	5 430	3 785	4 188	10 365.2	3 935.5	171	1 564	161.9	56.1
FLORIDA	42 403	276 263	67 822	54 881	52 415	31 272	27 231.1	10 803.5	4 763	103 980	7 871.5	1 972.9
GEORGIA	17 810	138 198	23 148	26 704	24 718	27 116	15 266.4	5 908.8	1 653	23 437	1 533.7	408.9
HAWAII	2 480	15 743	4 325	3 155	3 735	906	1 574.0	606.5	386	6 925	409.6	116.6
IDAHO	2 364	19 669	3 386	2 308	10 225	1 009	2 046.1	756.2	457	4 425	174.1	45.2
ILLINOIS	30 378	274 714	51 486	44 700	40 670	41 999	33 855.1	13 105.4	3 097	46 972	3 640.3	1 040.6
INDIANA	9 795	69 393	14 161	15 664	14 409	8 216	5 974.2	2 207.5	1 500	24 903	1 918.3	516.1
IOWA	4 670	31 115	7 332	6 347	4 220	2 876	2 435.6	887.9	875	14 169	919.8	220.3
KANSAS	5 345	39 534	6 737	8 086	10 169	4 736	3 559.3	1 396.0	652	7 618	374.5	91.0
KENTUCKY	6 189	41 991	10 036	8 445	8 708	4 604	3 820.3	1 260.1	906	10 580	550.2	126.3
LOUISIANA	9 077	63 642	18 467	13 162	18 537	3 040	5 754.6	2 159.0	1 016	22 828	1 958.1	412.9
MAINE	2 552	13 747	3 918	2 633	3 654	742	1 215.6	474.8	524	5 456	254.4	64.0
MARYLAND	14 115	146 814	17 537	17 492	36 646	36 640	15 940.2	6 483.8	1 460	19 398	1 412.4	494.8
MASSACHUSETTS	18 086	177 345	28 887	21 727	38 025	32 595	22 744.1	9 261.4	1 781	22 598	1 578.5	518.6
MICHIGAN	18 614	162 971	27 677	28 444	42 085	19 296	16 231.7	6 882.9	2 693	34 161	2 202.8	664.6
MINNESOTA	12 391	96 677	18 445	13 690	15 041	19 384	10 447.9	4 091.3	1 593	27 958	1 469.7	477.9
MISSISSIPPI	3 627	21 671	6 814	4 702	5 444	1 046	1 761.6	662.1	483	21 239	1 394.0	371.7
MISSOURI	10 601	93 792	18 383	16 493	18 076	15 307	9 953.3	3 643.6	1 493	29 484	1 803.9	684.2
MONTANA	2 082	10 735	2 700	2 075	2 710	763	769.4	297.7	639	5 638	306.5	62.2
NEBRASKA	3 076	25 720	4 336	4 767	4 318	3 546	2 273.4	838.0	517	5 957	258.6	58.1
NEVADA	4 171	28 963	6 396	4 064	8 395	1 590	2 974.4	1 171.1	811	23 960	1 667.5	465.8
NEW HAMPSHIRE	3 341	18 268	4 469	4 008	3 214	2 685	1 626.6	713.1	460	6 545	365.0	99.6
NEW JERSEY	25 849	220 238	39 180	36 932	31 200	50 602	25 943.8	10 441.0	2 393	27 187	1 981.2	602.2
NEW MEXICO	3 702	31 535	5 450	3 477	7 147	2 078	3 243.4	1 307.3	440	8 679	520.4	115.4
NEW YORK	45 619	416 892	109 483	78 021	47 439	41 878	57 475.0	21 773.1	7 311	77 057	7 029.0	2 284.6
NORTH CAROLINA	14 351	101 610	17 536	18 315	21 380	14 218	9 760.9	3 693.5	2 090	23 481	1 632.6	470.5
NORTH DAKOTA	1 077	7 076	1 609	1 349	1 340	1 322	418.0	175.7	248	3 154	164.3	32.6
OHIO	21 182	182 805	33 925	29 820	37 298	26 134	18 294.7	6 948.0	2 902	37 210	2 308.6	706.6
OKLAHOMA	7 009	40 633	10 986	7 642	8 958	4 167	3 543.0	1 323.7	746	8 904	531.4	110.3
OREGON	8 117	52 514	10 464	10 662	10 806	6 861	4 734.6	1 925.0	968	16 098	875.8	260.6
PENNSYLVANIA	23 184	235 025	46 483	33 381	58 166	35 029	26 240.3	10 448.3	2 883	40 892	2 439.3	810.6
RHODE ISLAND	2 349	14 866	3 522	3 414	3 149	1 633	1 418.1	541.5	307	3 877	234.8	58.1
SOUTH CAROLINA	6 576	47 679	11 256	8 301	16 571	3 517	6 820.9	1 850.5	1 325	18 499	1 107.1	251.9
SOUTH DAKOTA	1 282	6 228	1 673	1 419	1 050	878	450.4	161.7	432	4 647	299.2	60.2
TENNESSEE	8 812	72 225	12 572	11 830	17 174	6 827	6 911.8	2 686.6	1 755	18 263	1 228.7	394.3
TEXAS	42 492	351 422	70 228	53 143	92 449	50 071	42 044.1	15 906.7	3 894	65 218	3 743.8	1 143.4
UTAH	4 282	36 468	5 861	6 511	8 211	6 730	3 306.1	1 303.1	480	9 444	412.4	137.7
VERMONT	1 622	7 792	1 988	1 051	1 596	1 302	719.1	279.0	293	5 450	226.9	61.4
VIRGINIA	17 539	212 632	21 082	19 896	52 792	66 065	24 151.7	9 729.8	1 613	26 624	1 397.9	392.9
WASHINGTON	13 411	101 848	19 122	14 797	26 137	13 232	10 564.8	4 247.3	1 680	27 971	1 620.1	544.6
WEST VIRGINIA	2 517	15 714	4 814	3 353	3 532	799	1 166.9	395.2	408	4 996	273.3	56.6
WISCONSIN	9 281	70 689	14 887	14 876	14 616	7 321	6 398.9	2 542.3	1 730	22 339	1 327.5	384.3
WYOMING	1 264	5 274	1 312	1 321	1 638	171	388.8	146.9	262	2 108	93.3	23.3

1. Firms subject to federal tax.

Table A. States — Health Care and Social Assistance

STATE	Health care and social assistance, 1997										
	Subject to federal tax					Tax exempt					
	Number of establishments	Number of employees			Receipts (mil dol)	Annual payroll (mil dol)	Number of establishments	Number of employees			Receipts (mil dol)	Annual payroll (mil dol)
		Total	Ambulatory health care services	Hospitals				Total	Ambulatory health care services	Hospitals		
	247	248	249	250	251	252	253	254	255	256	257	258
UNITED STATES	531 069	6 231 768	3 744 279	511 584	418 602.2	182 256.3	114 784	7 329 811	669 335	4 421 454	466 451.8	195 949.4
ALABAMA	7 121	104 492	55 516	16 915	7 116.7	3 104.8	1 375	93 858	8 567	68 868	6 075.5	2 463.9
ALASKA	1 143	8 156	6 222	790	758.1	309.4	427	18 858	1 444	10 400	1 283.2	583.6
ARIZONA	9 155	97 091	58 340	7 344	6 687.9	2 893.3	1 366	89 141	9 554	52 682	6 153.3	2 370.6
ARKANSAS	4 571	59 960	28 478	8 079	3 655.1	1 609.7	1 205	67 065	5 348	41 630	3 642.0	1 429.1
CALIFORNIA	69 857	664 539	422 929	59 673	51 968.0	20 619.3	10 715	586 414	49 193	357 559	48 778.8	17 749.8
COLORADO	8 611	85 370	54 140	3 412	5 790.8	2 538.1	1 709	91 319	9 636	54 858	5 866.8	2 392.0
CONNECTICUT	7 515	100 363	60 395	D	6 849.7	3 199.3	1 828	113 366	12 823	60 723	7 058.3	3 296.7
DELAWARE	1 465	15 980	10 043	D	1 131.6	526.4	365	23 991	2 276	14 149	1 500.3	662.3
DISTRICT OF COLUMBIA	1 464	13 692	8 294	904	1 054.8	476.7	655	45 837	1 645	30 712	3 826.3	1 651.4
FLORIDA	35 568	447 117	254 419	81 958	32 559.1	13 610.7	4 170	294 240	28 422	178 820	19 415.1	7 800.2
GEORGIA	13 960	173 768	96 547	18 587	12 065.1	5 158.0	2 028	161 127	14 284	116 039	11 646.5	4 477.7
HAWAII	2 360	18 221	13 828	D	1 646.3	730.8	581	29 344	3 172	17 876	2 329.1	886.9
IDAHO	2 551	26 365	15 393	2 197	1 548.3	680.1	519	22 760	797	15 906	1 287.2	547.3
ILLINOIS	21 122	248 667	150 878	12 907	16 870.2	7 441.8	4 920	355 013	20 457	221 511	22 905.3	9 350.5
INDIANA	10 236	132 416	77 163	5 945	8 132.3	3 675.3	2 565	167 894	11 713	106 580	9 910.6	4 061.4
IOWA	4 876	56 374	32 156	D	3 183.2	1 540.6	2 319	117 658	6 652	64 543	5 582.4	2 425.5
KANSAS	4 793	66 613	38 032	D	4 116.1	1 771.8	1 621	81 767	3 963	46 923	4 082.2	1 817.1
KENTUCKY	6 805	94 720	48 595	11 593	5 936.2	2 620.3	1 579	100 156	8 609	64 953	6 026.7	2 386.4
LOUISIANA	8 580	129 773	69 375	24 000	7 967.6	3 341.5	1 506	110 849	2 121	80 152	6 477.3	2 625.8
MAINE	2 727	28 944	14 464	D	1 608.4	766.3	1 074	47 404	6 469	23 258	2 641.0	1 119.8
MARYLAND	10 841	116 241	76 315	2 859	8 060.7	3 538.0	2 181	144 008	8 363	87 288	9 405.0	3 816.7
MASSACHUSETTS	11 887	182 902	102 893	8 984	11 361.4	5 310.5	4 537	266 968	37 592	139 988	16 091.6	7 410.6
MICHIGAN	18 943	186 954	128 354	1 638	11 811.5	5 696.8	4 684	301 078	27 857	189 458.5	19 458.5	8 309.7
MINNESOTA	8 033	106 839	66 962	D	5 864.5	2 946.0	2 929	191 473	32 851	83 648	10 965.0	4 893.3
MISSISSIPPI	4 139	55 529	29 916	7 299	3 632.3	1 547.0	847	68 886	3 245	54 786	4 249.0	1 660.9
MISSOURI	10 213	131 485	69 052	10 901	7 885.5	3 596.7	2 580	184 143	11 577	119 145	10 535.6	4 410.5
MONTANA	2 034	15 673	9 118	D	928.6	412.6	691	29 526	3 450	16 885	1 440.4	619.1
NEBRASKA	3 057	34 763	19 225	D	2 027.7	970.3	914	55 235	1 641	35 363	3 074.8	1 263.6
NEVADA	3 226	39 476	23 312	8 604	3 406.5	1 358.9	361	17 185	931	11 538	1 261.6	506.9
NEW HAMPSHIRE	2 373	28 889	15 341	2 228	1 734.1	836.3	834	37 674	8 075	18 197	2 246.2	878.2
NEW JERSEY	18 905	172 723	120 922	1 122	13 702.4	5 900.2	2 742	227 434	21 103	148 173	14 828.8	6 842.7
NEW MEXICO	2 923	32 824	21 144	3 138	2 057.3	864.3	778	43 501	4 479	25 609	2 412.3	1 089.3
NEW YORK	36 054	358 075	259 094	10 262	26 008.3	10 970.9	9 880	768 835	105 062	407 706	48 759.5	23 372.8
NORTH CAROLINA	12 582	173 770	94 102	8 741	10 708.8	4 859.6	2 794	187 651	13 552	129 016	12 400.3	5 006.8
NORTH DAKOTA	1 013	13 181	8 237	D	904.1	386.4	539	33 578	909	16 585	1 463.7	668.9
OHIO	20 399	261 520	156 386	2 579	15 440.1	7 477.0	4 779	352 454	26 617	214 539	21 423.5	9 093.7
OKLAHOMA	6 991	91 803	47 776	8 847	5 061.4	2 244.0	1 463	76 949	4 052	51 711	4 283.6	1 758.5
OREGON	7 328	68 285	42 060	1 410	4 431.4	1 899.6	1 788	82 517	7 491	45 158	4 869.2	2 097.6
PENNSYLVANIA	24 888	262 603	174 984	6 961	17 633.5	7 994.9	6 624	453 579	37 043	260 036	27 620.1	11 860.5
RHODE ISLAND	2 074	25 368	13 270	D	1 459.3	647.4	606	38 409	4 861	20 710	2 443.0	1 132.3
SOUTH CAROLINA	6 261	78 888	40 632	13 530	5 318.5	2 361.3	1 271	75 881	3 537	53 077	4 729.9	1 922.6
SOUTH DAKOTA	1 314	14 080	8 732	167	881.6	414.3	623	33 920	1 156	19 717	1 646.8	753.3
TENNESSEE	10 113	155 667	84 719	22 103	10 753.0	4 659.9	2 180	129 028	11 485	86 739	8 459.9	3 429.5
TEXAS	37 974	557 007	324 347	89 469	35 620.9	14 725.4	5 546	334 563	24 434	223 849	21 137.9	8 357.4
UTAH	3 851	46 989	27 659	5 700	2 988.8	1 226.7	521	33 973	1 583	23 515	2 070.3	859.6
VERMONT	1 262	11 481	6 146	D	631.6	273.9	592	20 697	4 672	9 772	1 129.0	496.6
VIRGINIA	12 014	150 797	89 453	17 193	9 859.6	4 417.9	2 143	135 917	7 245	87 411	8 975.6	3 539.8
WASHINGTON	12 310	122 813	73 402	2 089	7 797.7	3 390.2	2 575	140 792	21 340	78 274	8 982.2	4 039.8
WEST VIRGINIA	3 266	40 085	21 188	5 172	2 575.0	1 056.9	973	55 653	6 667	33 425	3 250.1	1 350.2
WISCONSIN	9 315	114 562	69 466	587	6 917.4	3 447.3	2 932	175 152	18 639	93 326	9 654.7	4 089.4
WYOMING	1 006	7 875	4 865	555	493.6	210.3	350	15 091	681	8 210	695.9	320.6

Table A. States — Accommodation and Food Services and Other Services

STATE	Accommodation and food services, 1997					Other services, 1997						
	Number of employees			Receipts (mil dol)	Annual payroll (mil dol)	Number of establishments[1]	Number of employees				Receipts[1] (mil dol)	Annual payroll[1] (mil dol)
	Number of establishments	Total	Food services and drinking places				Total[1]	Repair and maintenance[1]	Personal and laundry services[1]	Religious, civic, and similar services[2]		
	259	260	261	262	263	264	265	266	267	268	269	270
UNITED STATES	545 060	9 451 056	7 754 462	350 389.1	97 003.9	420 950	2 493 574	1 276 389	1 217 185	762 604	163 033.3	48 452.6
ALABAMA	6 955	134 719	120 455	3 881.8	1 059.6	6 329	37 061	19 092	17 969	5 480	2 241.7	659.3
ALASKA	1 763	20 587	15 108	1 065.5	301.5	852	4 364	2 489	1 875	2 127	331.0	93.4
ARIZONA	9 089	184 323	143 326	6 633.0	1 823.2	6 494	43 669	24 677	18 992	9 381	2 794.0	829.6
ARKANSAS	4 663	73 397	63 326	2 179.7	589.9	3 553	18 809	9 759	9 050	3 308	1 113.9	310.5
CALIFORNIA	62 532	1 052 715	866 573	42 261.1	11 437.2	44 642	282 762	158 338	124 424	71 943	20 521.5	5 852.2
COLORADO	10 064	195 126	152 323	6 705.5	1 937.4	6 793	39 363	21 585	17 778	13 958	2 571.1	770.0
CONNECTICUT	6 903	96 556	85 802	3 746.6	1 062.8	6 121	34 089	15 534	18 555	11 215	2 370.2	727.8
DELAWARE	1 605	26 969	24 532	1 009.0	280.8	1 198	7 006	3 349	3 657	3 096	420.5	140.7
DISTRICT OF COLUMBIA	1 700	42 650	27 281	2 263.5	701.4	978	6 218	951	5 267	36 416	404.8	111.1
FLORIDA	28 999	608 834	462 266	24 165.3	6 239.5	26 121	146 360	72 673	73 687	47 246	9 123.6	2 665.7
GEORGIA	13 829	274 322	229 132	9 689.9	2 695.1	11 482	69 422	35 701	33 721	13 418	4 580.7	1 407.5
HAWAII	3 081	88 083	47 978	5 007.9	1 507.5	1 476	10 375	3 941	6 434	7 096	683.2	206.4
IDAHO	2 978	42 067	33 222	1 232.5	345.7	1 858	9 461	5 979	2 562	2 562	550.6	151.7
ILLINOIS	23 984	397 300	345 271	14 826.8	4 018.7	18 806	118 317	61 653	56 664	47 363	8 296.8	2 503.0
INDIANA	11 705	215 710	192 910	6 646.3	1 865.3	9 243	60 711	32 426	28 285	15 556	3 701.4	1 127.8
IOWA	6 830	99 148	85 641	2 762.8	769.5	5 234	24 383	12 589	11 794	8 008	1 486.5	411.3
KANSAS	5 677	91 173	81 206	2 685.7	757.1	4 604	24 081	12 846	11 235	7 737	1 548.4	452.9
KENTUCKY	6 546	129 442	113 557	4 056.1	1 140.6	5 383	31 164	15 971	15 193	5 534	1 870.3	551.4
LOUISIANA	7 151	147 016	118 902	5 259.9	1 408.9	5 998	39 764	23 348	16 416	6 418	2 595.2	767.2
MAINE	3 714	39 624	32 211	1 509.3	428.8	1 923	8 820	4 687	4 133	3 201	612.3	169.6
MARYLAND	9 049	161 273	142 027	5 972.5	1 644.7	7 871	55 241	26 167	29 074	18 724	3 561.3	1 129.2
MASSACHUSETTS	14 800	227 476	198 069	9 269.9	2 575.6	10 806	61 557	28 744	32 813	18 807	4 359.8	1 338.6
MICHIGAN	18 958	320 014	287 623	10 158.7	2 835.8	14 705	93 792	50 987	42 805	22 180	6 159.1	1 893.8
MINNESOTA	9 982	179 487	149 584	5 934.2	1 688.8	7 614	55 723	27 703	28 020	21 512	3 394.6	1 103.6
MISSISSIPPI	4 050	84 834	61 742	3 064.8	814.5	3 491	17 449	9 171	8 278	3 701	1 057.1	299.6
MISSOURI	11 150	203 849	169 646	6 780.8	1 933.3	9 427	52 060	26 216	25 844	14 434	3 203.3	963.1
MONTANA	3 278	38 533	30 120	1 198.9	325.4	1 612	6 986	4 518	2 468	2 278	449.1	117.0
NEBRASKA	4 070	61 048	53 127	1 726.6	488.2	3 288	16 940	9 770	7 170	6 500	1 039.2	297.1
NEVADA	3 632	241 672	51 613	15 322.7	4 665.3	2 175	16 185	8 124	8 061	3 033	1 061.7	328.0
NEW HAMPSHIRE	3 029	43 942	36 251	1 543.5	449.8	2 159	11 379	5 720	5 659	3 271	794.5	236.6
NEW JERSEY	16 974	251 872	180 343	13 407.4	3 608.2	15 077	78 644	35 774	42 870	18 414	5 434.8	1 665.1
NEW MEXICO	3 825	67 134	52 969	2 144.9	599.1	2 318	13 448	7 651	5 797	3 814	759.1	227.2
NEW YORK	38 045	473 327	399 485	21 671.1	6 101.1	30 104	146 365	59 977	86 388	76 173	10 014.6	2 858.7
NORTH CAROLINA	14 579	262 848	229 210	8 625.0	2 393.2	11 483	64 802	33 418	31 384	14 644	4 060.6	1 204.0
NORTH DAKOTA	1 827	26 330	21 495	684.9	189.0	1 281	6 294	3 074	3 220	3 410	364.3	101.3
OHIO	22 631	401 206	365 806	12 411.0	3 444.2	17 314	116 165	58 331	57 834	29 986	7 087.5	2 165.7
OKLAHOMA	6 534	105 934	95 639	3 151.3	856.8	4 572	26 308	13 465	12 843	5 709	1 599.4	458.5
OREGON	8 363	124 425	105 930	4 385.7	1 236.6	4 794	28 185	16 554	11 631	7 463	1 897.5	561.9
PENNSYLVANIA	24 465	365 158	317 321	12 227.2	3 364.1	19 754	107 502	51 109	56 393	36 273	7 085.7	2 049.0
RHODE ISLAND	2 617	34 162	31 264	1 220.9	340.6	1 949	8 602	4 142	4 460	3 325	546.2	167.8
SOUTH CAROLINA	7 775	150 621	126 533	4 835.8	1 313.8	5 672	32 166	17 395	14 771	7 364	1 901.0	563.8
SOUTH DAKOTA	2 258	30 131	23 609	888.0	234.4	1 356	5 828	3 296	2 532	2 670	344.7	90.7
TENNESSEE	9 604	197 881	166 252	6 790.2	1 880.3	7 767	49 204	22 362	26 842	11 871	2 996.7	918.7
TEXAS	34 160	638 333	552 066	22 698.8	6 175.4	29 162	197 113	107 946	89 167	38 747	12 477.7	3 785.0
UTAH	3 780	74 390	58 884	2 309.0	648.8	2 728	17 612	10 403	7 209	3 284	1 090.5	312.6
VERMONT	1 932	27 088	18 000	910.2	277.2	1 171	4 490	2 263	2 227	2 859	304.7	76.4
VIRGINIA	12 343	233 639	192 645	8 281.2	2 320.7	11 301	68 807	33 111	35 696	27 818	4 397.2	1 360.3
WASHINGTON	13 105	194 955	169 685	6 995.1	1 962.9	8 771	49 756	27 517	22 239	14 138	3 492.0	1 033.0
WEST VIRGINIA	3 290	51 529	43 149	1 633.2	462.3	2 512	14 805	7 551	7 254	3 308	867.4	255.9
WISCONSIN	13 252	190 411	163 318	5 641.0	1 548.5	8 648	49 101	23 608	25 493	14 402	2 991.3	886.4
WYOMING	1 751	24 950	17 192	808.9	219.0	980	4 866	2 734	2 132	1 429	422.8	94.8

1. Firms subject to federal tax.   2. Firms not subject to federal tax; not included in totals.

STATE	Construction Paid employees, 1997	Construction Percent change, 1992–1997	Manufacturing Paid employees, 1997	Manufacturing Percent change, 1992–1997	Wholesale trade Paid employees, 1997	Wholesale trade Percent change, 1992–1997	Retail trade Paid employees, 1997	Retail trade Percent change, 1992–1997	Finance, insurance, and real estate Paid employees, 1997	Finance, insurance, and real estate Percent change, 1992–1997	Service industries, subject to federal tax Paid employees, 1997	Service industries, subject to federal tax Percent change, 1992–1997
	271	272	273	274	275	276	277	278	279	280	281	282
UNITED STATES..................	5 567 052	19.3	17 557 008	3.6	6 509 333	12.4	21 165 862	15.0	7 314 321	12.4	25 278 399	31.0
ALABAMA	94 525	20.8	364 887	0.0	90 151	12.6	342 835	27.1	86 105	18.7	319 408	28.6
ALASKA	13 911	7.3	13 402	-13.4	D	D	46 235	17.1	9 842	8.0	38 822	21.7
ARIZONA..............................	129 315	49.1	199 959	18.9	93 586	36.0	363 999	26.3	110 539	25.7	488 055	63.1
ARKANSAS...........................	D	D	239 244	7.5	48 274	10.0	189 643	24.7	40 995	14.1	174 209	30.5
CALIFORNIA.........................	548 028	7.2	1 867 099	1.1	D	D	D	D	820 011	6.7	3 285 881	24.2
COLORADO...........................	122 733	46.5	186 156	7.0	101 918	21.3	366 950	29.5	119 331	20.6	457 757	43.5
CONNECTICUT	D	D	262 959	-9.3	D	D	264 497	9.8	137 061	-8.9	348 287	27.8
DELAWARE	20 070	13.5	41 969	-3.7	15 805	-1.7	69 887	16.1	52 071	35.5	70 912	30.9
DISTRICT OF COLUMBIA ...	D	D	11 906	0.4	D	D	D	D	26 621	-6.5	130 661	8.3
FLORIDA...............................	D	D	463 791	2.3	333 153	18.6	1 274 403	15.6	D	D	1 745 657	37.0
GEORGIA	160 111	29.2	552 706	6.1	214 242	19.4	630 376	23.8	190 856	15.4	755 082	50.5
HAWAII	20 985	-35.2	16 412	-17.8	20 809	-10.7	110 892	0.4	35 201	-5.4	120 784	2.4
IDAHO	40 060	80.3	71 274	14.9	27 231	9.4	93 090	25.9	18 741	6.3	88 434	39.2
ILLINOIS...............................	D	D	915 860	4.6	357 606	7.7	931 248	10.1	401 132	6.5	1 150 231	27.5
INDIANA...............................	D	D	637 736	7.6	129 290	11.7	516 853	16.9	D	D	455 626	28.5
IOWA....................................	D	D	244 994	10.4	75 462	8.8	250 724	10.9	82 571	16.9	210 117	29.3
KANSAS...............................	61 345	28.0	203 303	11.9	68 008	10.1	214 819	15.6	64 496	8.7	220 599	36.2
KENTUCKY	76 131	19.4	296 956	11.7	80 672	14.8	315 734	20.9	71 664	14.7	279 646	32.7
LOUISIANA	106 314	15.7	173 489	0.5	87 291	7.4	333 931	15.6	81 495	8.3	391 385	32.0
MAINE..................................	24 902	16.1	88 327	-2.1	23 360	6.8	102 614	14.0	26 289	9.9	87 636	28.8
MARYLAND	139 269	3.8	174 740	-3.4	105 973	5.4	404 802	10.4	140 830	6.7	557 370	33.2
MASSACHUSETTS	D	D	441 770	-0.7	161 894	14.4	522 783	11.3	247 872	14.4	703 699	29.0
MICHIGAN	D	D	850 368	8.6	213 537	15.3	796 730	12.7	226 680	18.8	819 080	33.4
MINNESOTA.........................	D	D	399 756	15.3	147 559	19.8	419 310	12.7	152 750	22.4	468 166	34.1
MISSISSIPPI........................	47 242	36.7	234 764	-0.1	43 026	7.7	194 483	28.8	39 365	6.6	179 905	66.2
MISSOURI............................	129 183	33.1	391 945	4.6	144 328	11.3	451 894	15.4	149 584	14.3	478 052	28.0
MONTANA............................	17 987	34.5	22 526	5.1	17 417	6.2	75 840	17.8	D	D	33 381	13.8
NEBRASKA..........................	40 127	33.3	111 098	16.4	48 010	2.0	149 478	13.1	57 400	18.3	64 191	9.6
NEVADA	68 283	66.4	39 954	48.8	32 203	47.5	137 171	38.2	40 038	41.1	20 265	23.0
NEW HAMPSHIRE	22 371	30.4	102 193	14.4	26 379	28.9	117 518	21.0	28 719	-0.5	42 407	16.7
NEW JERSEY.......................	140 900	7.2	432 049	-9.7	287 964	9.6	585 436	12.1	251 453	10.3	257 500	5.1
NEW MEXICO	38 990	26.2	42 254	9.4	26 259	16.2	135 164	20.3	30 150	16.8	49 430	15.1
NEW YORK	271 483	5.5	860 233	-10.0	450 559	3.9	1 181 372	8.5	771 470	4.8	900 533	3.4
NORTH CAROLINA	195 189	34.1	789 476	1.0	178 604	18.2	628 124	23.7	170 949	30.1	607 654	43.0
NORTH DAKOTA	15 693	33.0	23 218	26.8	20 321	10.1	59 130	14.3	14 314	16.6	46 358	42.3
OHIO	221 240	16.2	1 009 620	5.5	D	D	971 264	15.9	303 312	22.0	950 157	25.3
OKLAHOMA.........................	49 861	14.1	168 926	10.2	D	D	251 502	19.0	67 101	13.2	259 359	32.1
OREGON..............................	78 985	48.4	226 715	12.6	D	D	274 347	21.0	83 852	29.1	275 689	41.1
PENNSYLVANIA...................	226 488	6.1	857 041	-0.8	269 103	5.8	940 957	9.2	342 807	13.8	978 912	22.8
RHODE ISLAND	16 820	20.3	78 452	-7.2	20 487	4.9	75 777	12.6	26 944	-2.1	84 785	31.6
SOUTH CAROLINA	83 661	20.1	353 858	-0.3	67 606	19.3	328 850	24.6	73 899	18.6	325 235	39.6
SOUTH DAKOTA..................	14 229	10.9	48 306	38.2	19 329	18.1	66 008	14.8	D	D	48 237	40.0
TENNESSEE	118 094	31.6	495 760	2.2	135 432	17.3	457 976	24.4	123 091	21.6	487 855	34.6
TEXAS	420 823	25.4	985 731	11.0	D	D	1 464 183	19.0	452 103	13.6	1 968 608	37.6
UTAH	54 881	57.0	122 200	20.2	50 823	28.3	167 441	32.6	48 569	34.2	207 939	50.1
VERMONT	12 967	9.2	44 648	0.8	D	D	52 529	14.5	D	D	46 922	26.4
VIRGINIA	176 432	22.8	387 576	0.4	125 191	8.1	555 088	17.0	173 123	13.0	716 667	36.3
WASHINGTON	D	D	347 549	5.4	134 842	10.1	D	D	127 681	10.9	461 505	30.0
WEST VIRGINIA..................	30 892	23.7	76 772	1.5	27 352	11.8	129 956	16.0	D	D	106 642	27.1
WISCONSIN	114 490	18.3	575 318	12.2	128 690	9.4	453 927	12.1	152 563	14.9	416 814	31.6
WYOMING	13 703	25.2	9 763	8.8	D	D	D	D	D	D	33 771	27.6

Table A. States — **Residential Construction, Exports, and Federal Funds**

STATE	Value of residential construction authorized by building permits, 2003				Exports of goods by state of origin, 2003 (mil dol)			Federal funds and grants, 2002–2003 (mil dol)		Procurement contract awards	
	New construction ($1,000)	Number of housing units	Percent single family	Manufactured housing units put in place, 2003 (1,000)	Total	Manufactured	Non-manufactured	Total	Salaries and wages	Defense	Other
	283	284	285	286	287	288	289	290	291	292	293
UNITED STATES	249 693 105	1 889 214	77.3	137.7	724 006	577 763	73 924	2 043 951	209 328	200 183	125 965
ALABAMA	2 463 568	22 256	79.4	3.9	8 340	7 350	784	36 871	3 224	5 510	1 557
ALASKA	560 200	3 531	49.3	D	2 739	600	2 112	7 944	1 617	1 237	443
ARIZONA	10 518 958	74 996	87.8	5.0	13 323	11 098	579	37 801	3 335	7 564	993
ARKANSAS	1 541 009	14 839	67.9	2.7	2 962	2 606	142	18 340	1 339	578	286
CALIFORNIA	31 778 214	191 948	72.9	8.1	93 995	69 154	8 917	219 706	20 611	26 079	10 971
COLORADO	6 258 256	39 569	85.5	1.7	6 109	4 907	142	28 874	4 329	2 471	2 671
CONNECTICUT	1 664 859	10 435	78.4	D	8 136	7 362	357	28 595	1 516	7 895	589
DELAWARE	790 664	7 760	87.0	1.0	1 886	1 646	49	5 061	489	164	81
DISTRICT OF COLUMBIA	95 696	1 427	10.7	X	809	698	60	34 750	14 760	1 753	9 623
FLORIDA	28 351 596	213 567	73.4	10.9	24 953	20 647	1 350	113 341	9 746	7 999	2 900
GEORGIA	10 837 216	96 704	83.4	5.0	16 286	13 844	1 276	51 910	8 015	3 324	1 919
HAWAII	1 316 090	7 284	85.3	D	368	250	75	11 269	2 864	1 750	228
IDAHO	1 942 662	15 091	83.5	0.9	2 096	1 788	150	8 654	834	207	1 324
ILLINOIS	9 105 577	62 211	72.9	2.4	26 473	23 269	1 053	73 020	6 553	2 514	3 215
INDIANA	5 392 722	39 421	80.9	3.1	16 402	15 006	244	35 525	2 338	2 567	735
IOWA	2 062 916	16 082	73.6	0.7	5 236	4 734	333	17 550	1 129	658	451
KANSAS	1 895 406	15 049	76.4	0.9	4 553	3 910	398	18 208	2 108	1 219	801
KENTUCKY	2 346 693	20 404	85.4	4.8	10 734	9 047	664	31 153	3 112	3 223	1 896
LOUISIANA	2 595 720	22 220	83.2	5.1	18 390	8 651	9 542	31 646	2 648	1 951	1 243
MAINE	1 066 671	7 933	92.1	1.3	2 188	1 632	446	9 966	888	1 176	136
MARYLAND	3 723 627	29 914	78.2	0.6	4 941	4 132	336	57 646	10 331	7 171	9 045
MASSACHUSETTS	3 141 366	20 257	64.4	0.5	18 663	16 534	798	51 265	3 446	6 365	1 993
MICHIGAN	7 052 549	53 913	83.0	4.7	32 941	29 946	1 300	57 870	3 418	2 494	1 390
MINNESOTA	6 269 475	42 046	77.8	2.5	11 266	9 842	771	27 580	2 120	1 542	864
MISSISSIPPI	1 268 335	12 010	84.4	3.3	2 558	2 232	201	21 741	1 970	2 126	499
MISSOURI	3 596 524	29 309	77.6	3.4	7 234	6 723	242	43 874	3 832	6 244	1 748
MONTANA	411 698	3 767	62.1	0.6	361	232	81	7 092	845	190	307
NEBRASKA	1 250 209	10 339	83.7	0.3	2 724	2 154	468	11 000	1 192	312	296
NEVADA	4 879 197	43 366	76.3	0.9	2 033	1 625	77	11 637	1 222	387	1 086
NEW HAMPSHIRE	1 207 854	8 641	76.2	0.8	1 931	1 589	157	7 349	571	531	207
NEW JERSEY	3 781 901	32 984	67.2	0.8	16 818	13 118	1 291	53 679	4 159	3 873	1 588
NEW MEXICO	1 703 302	13 759	86.2	1.7	2 326	2 138	79	18 736	1 926	955	4 864
NEW YORK	6 193 971	49 708	48.7	3.2	39 181	27 268	3 548	137 898	8 535	4 253	3 505
NORTH CAROLINA	10 267 977	79 226	84.4	8.1	16 199	13 984	843	51 766	6 541	1 988	1 806
NORTH DAKOTA	397 521	3 721	63.0	0.4	854	616	221	5 726	717	262	135
OHIO	7 502 920	53 041	80.5	3.9	29 764	27 426	972	69 902	5 362	4 271	2 276
OKLAHOMA	1 861 185	14 968	85.0	2.5	2 660	2 421	111	25 254	3 353	1 471	1 017
OREGON	3 770 948	25 015	71.5	2.6	10 357	8 117	1 539	21 253	1 781	474	724
PENNSYLVANIA	6 051 793	47 356	81.4	3.9	16 299	14 134	766	90 350	6 363	5 607	2 530
RHODE ISLAND	338 012	2 286	85.2	D	1 178	898	149	8 036	817	499	160
SOUTH CAROLINA	4 616 026	38 191	82.6	4.9	11 773	10 943	215	28 038	2 863	1 487	2 128
SOUTH DAKOTA	540 686	4 986	81.4	0.6	672	581	62	6 202	673	196	185
TENNESSEE	4 478 748	37 530	85.8	5.8	12 612	9 856	1 501	42 602	3 357	2 161	5 361
TEXAS	19 551 763	177 194	75.7	11.7	98 846	78 546	4 923	140 451	13 939	20 821	9 002
UTAH	3 081 981	22 525	81.8	0.5	4 115	3 872	146	13 500	2 047	1 871	794
VERMONT	405 980	2 843	85.5	0.3	2 627	1 650	73	4 443	360	455	111
VIRGINIA	6 876 972	55 936	82.7	3.3	10 853	8 759	1 603	82 454	14 756	19 493	11 346
WASHINGTON	6 346 021	42 825	77.3	2.8	34 173	28 427	4 688	43 368	5 758	3 196	3 433
WEST VIRGINIA	645 988	5 133	90.9	2.6	2 380	2 003	280	14 226	1 289	185	480
WISCONSIN	5 504 609	40 884	70.3	2.3	11 510	10 181	677	30 237	1 785	1 244	764
WYOMING	389 272	2 814	80.5	0.7	582	500	69	4 226	510	72	274

Table A. States — **Federal Funds**

STATE	Federal funds and grants, 2002–2003 (mil dol) (cont'd)													
	Direct payments for individuals							Grants						
	Total	Social Security and government retirement	Medicare	Food stamps	Supple- mental Security Income	Educational assistance	Housing assistance	Total[1]	Medicaid and other health- related	Nutrition and family welfare	Education	Housing and community devel- opment	Homeland security	Energy and environ- ment
	294	295	296	297	298	299	300	301	302	303	304	305	306	307
UNITED STATES................	1 073 383	597 853	272 466	21 337	32 491	14 938	4 191	435 095	208 825	61 371	36 927	31 457	6 619	5 638
ALABAMA	19 930	11 476	4 833	466	756	271	120	6 649	3 252	770	597	363	124	86
ALASKA........................	1 625	996	212	66	44	13	12	3 022	1 103	242	307	127	17	107
ARIZONA......................	18 675	11 557	4 178	498	465	335	26	7 235	3 688	1 042	777	367	9	70
ARKANSAS....................	11 596	6 662	2 637	304	376	165	30	4 541	2 172	507	374	217	87	26
CALIFORNIA..................	110 716	56 329	31 692	1 808	4 907	1 612	190	51 329	23 534	10 635	4 556	4 038	87	537
COLORADO	13 389	8 115	2 768	203	259	208	16	6 014	2 034	708	450	430	27	108
CONNECTICUT	13 218	7 288	3 946	165	262	100	76	5 376	2 623	696	389	573	21	81
DELAWARE	3 146	1 881	698	48	64	113	11	1 181	476	145	115	84	12	28
DISTRICT OF COLUMBIA ...	4 304	1 826	771	90	108	55	64	4 310	1 416	291	316	767	10	114
FLORIDA.......................	75 233	43 198	22 774	988	1 993	708	116	17 463	8 388	2 576	1 704	1 202	63	158
GEORGIA	28 092	15 756	6 215	782	909	360	123	10 561	5 051	1 594	1 031	740	29	120
HAWAII	4 516	2 905	874	156	109	36	15	1 911	657	279	236	159	4	34
IDAHO..........................	4 431	2 769	789	77	96	84	2	1 858	743	215	176	77	9	65
ILLINOIS.......................	45 018	23 397	11 992	1 053	1 389	592	292	15 720	7 013	2 604	1 462	1 627	59	228
INDIANA.......................	22 572	12 920	5 374	484	474	433	45	7 313	3 629	942	627	505	61	119
IOWA...........................	11 434	6 590	2 559	149	190	188	7	3 877	1 839	520	339	225	26	17
KANSAS........................	10 665	6 015	2 476	140	181	131	17	3 415	1 422	483	395	194	29	50
KENTUCKY....................	16 288	9 305	3 788	486	863	234	52	6 634	3 246	848	567	403	93	64
LOUISIANA	17 983	8 759	5 253	685	800	277	83	7 820	4 071	1 008	694	459	260	82
MAINE	5 156	3 260	1 114	124	143	73	10	2 610	1 429	292	181	177	14	47
MARYLAND	22 467	12 831	5 056	257	475	180	89	8 632	4 438	964	583	616	70	130
MASSACHUSETTS	26 133	13 033	8 141	254	760	421	127	13 328	7 347	1 276	817	1 607	54	244
MICHIGAN	37 598	20 917	10 193	783	1 126	420	69	12 970	6 174	2 317	1 193	839	41	226
MINNESOTA	16 141	9 284	3 538	227	343	253	67	6 914	3 363	1 062	542	530	57	129
MISSISSIPPI	11 827	6 354	2 803	335	569	239	32	5 318	2 763	689	474	261	87	81
MISSOURI	23 396	12 964	5 853	568	545	299	63	8 655	4 617	1 033	684	609	64	107
MONTANA	3 812	2 247	698	69	68	62	4	1 938	653	219	217	86	15	38
NEBRASKA....................	6 688	3 854	1 297	89	102	85	12	2 512	1 066	347	237	135	15	38
NEVADA	6 988	4 562	1 352	113	146	50	18	1 955	765	265	207	152	13	74
NEW HAMPSHIRE	4 174	2 776	898	40	62	56	9	1 865	801	177	133	149	21	45
NEW JERSEY.................	32 578	17 678	9 338	339	710	287	216	11 481	5 007	1 408	893	1 255	49	125
NEW MEXICO	6 669	4 151	1 191	184	237	117	14	4 322	1 887	502	520	149	11	118
NEW YORK....................	74 030	37 462	21 968	1 677	3 043	1 309	1 045	47 575	26 019	5 893	2 773	3 612	3 864	273
NORTH CAROLINA	29 818	17 961	6 230	645	844	402	109	11 613	6 238	1 546	987	605	145	110
NORTH DAKOTA	3 074	1 414	559	37	33	49	2	1 537	417	161	158	65	10	28
OHIO...........................	42 305	24 062	11 383	880	1 285	510	206	15 687	7 841	2 615	1 269	1 253	130	223
OKLAHOMA	14 277	8 422	3 366	362	351	208	29	5 136	2 260	784	570	347	51	70
OREGON	13 171	7 740	2 604	381	285	170	22	5 103	2 364	694	445	303	40	78
PENNSYLVANIA	57 228	30 528	16 803	785	1 544	726	277	18 624	9 647	2 513	1 272	1 425	81	148
RHODE ISLAND	4 326	2 403	1 183	69	132	71	25	2 234	1 119	249	147	249	11	38
SOUTH CAROLINA	15 592	9 627	3 125	443	479	230	35	5 969	3 128	662	564	306	24	63
SOUTH DAKOTA	3 450	1 753	604	51	56	114	5	1 698	469	176	182	94	15	29
TENNESSEE	22 666	13 004	5 658	722	740	298	105	9 057	5 307	995	659	458	103	86
TEXAS	68 266	37 151	16 283	1 881	1 998	1 097	131	28 423	12 679	3 982	3 109	1 626	368	372
UTAH	5 943	3 787	1 040	102	105	181	7	2 845	1 130	393	293	118	19	58
VERMONT	2 186	1 305	460	38	53	47	4	1 331	615	162	116	86	6	32
VIRGINIA......................	28 973	18 937	5 067	366	616	494	75	7 886	3 057	984	813	565	74	143
WASHINGTON	22 100	13 019	4 173	394	568	243	44	8 881	4 200	1 258	715	574	56	159
WEST VIRGINIA	8 711	5 288	2 077	216	375	104	17	3 562	1 665	425	283	176	47	72
WISCONSIN	18 900	11 194	4 239	233	424	203	25	7 544	3 725	1 099	636	438	30	129
WYOMING	1 754	1 125	345	24	26	27	2	1 616	279	120	119	34	8	31

1. Includes program categories not shown separately.

Table A. States — **State Government Finances**

STATE	State government finances, 2001–2002											
	General revenue (mil dol)								General expenditures (mil dol)			
	From federal government			From own sources							Direct general expenditures	
					Taxes		Taxes per capita[1] (dollars)			To local govern-ments		
	Total	Total	Per capita[1] (dollars)	Total	Total	Sales and gross receipts	Total	Sales and gross receipts	Total		Total	Per capita[1] (dollars)
	308	309	310	311	312	313	314	315	316	317	318	319
UNITED STATES	X	X	X	X	X	X	X	X	X	X	X	X
ALABAMA	15 986	6 275	1 401	9 711	6 510	3 383	1 453	755	17 996	4 096	13 901	3 104
ALASKA	5 423	1 556	2 428	3 866	1 090	142	1 700	222	7 402	1 056	6 347	9 902
ARIZONA	15 860	5 260	967	10 600	8 477	5 352	1 558	984	18 119	6 969	11 150	2 049
ARKANSAS	10 533	3 429	1 267	7 104	5 226	2 649	1 931	979	11 521	3 071	8 450	3 123
CALIFORNIA	141 481	43 861	1 253	97 620	77 755	30 702	2 221	877	184 928	74 687	110 240	3 150
COLORADO	13 875	3 866	859	10 009	6 923	2 835	1 538	630	16 823	4 295	12 528	2 783
CONNECTICUT	15 382	3 769	1 090	11 613	9 033	4 516	2 611	1 306	20 117	3 735	16 382	4 736
DELAWARE	4 633	922	1 144	3 711	2 174	323	2 697	401	4 646	823	3 823	4 744
DISTRICT OF COLUMBIA	X	X	X	X	X	X	X	X	X	X	X	X
FLORIDA	46 995	13 141	787	33 854	25 352	19 456	1 519	1 166	51 834	14 054	37 780	2 263
GEORGIA	26 114	8 611	1 008	17 503	13 772	6 018	1 612	704	30 053	8 645	21 408	2 506
HAWAII	6 042	1 367	1 102	4 675	3 421	2 118	2 756	1 707	7 446	130	7 315	5 895
IDAHO	4 375	1 330	991	3 045	2 271	1 116	1 691	831	5 234	1 407	3 827	2 850
ILLINOIS	40 340	11 435	909	28 905	22 475	11 256	1 786	894	49 131	13 091	36 040	2 864
INDIANA	20 011	6 028	979	13 983	10 201	5 425	1 657	881	22 205	6 557	15 648	2 542
IOWA	11 026	3 445	1 173	7 581	5 006	2 538	1 705	865	12 721	3 326	9 394	3 200
KANSAS	9 179	2 992	1 103	6 187	4 808	2 432	1 773	897	10 592	2 971	7 620	2 810
KENTUCKY	15 810	5 121	1 252	10 689	7 975	3 741	1 950	915	18 407	3 560	14 847	3 630
LOUISIANA	17 659	6 049	1 351	11 610	7 357	4 192	1 644	936	18 319	4 168	14 151	3 162
MAINE	5 600	1 830	1 413	3 770	2 627	1 237	2 028	955	6 265	1 010	5 255	4 058
MARYLAND	19 909	5 453	1 000	14 456	10 821	4 699	1 985	862	23 317	5 236	18 082	3 317
MASSACHUSETTS	26 476	5 431	846	21 045	14 823	5 211	2 308	811	32 848	6 284	26 564	4 136
MICHIGAN	40 886	11 507	1 146	29 379	21 864	10 069	2 177	1 003	49 184	19 067	30 117	2 999
MINNESOTA	21 910	5 427	1 080	16 483	13 224	5 767	2 632	1 148	26 693	8 271	18 421	3 666
MISSISSIPPI	11 044	4 535	1 582	6 509	4 729	3 183	1 649	1 110	12 742	3 457	9 286	3 239
MISSOURI	18 654	6 819	1 203	11 835	8 729	4 140	1 539	730	20 841	5 073	15 768	2 781
MONTANA	3 721	1 427	1 568	2 294	1 443	371	1 585	407	4 265	911	3 354	3 686
NEBRASKA	5 987	1 823	1 055	4 164	2 993	1 505	1 732	871	6 537	1 820	4 717	2 730
NEVADA	6 167	1 338	618	4 829	3 945	3 338	1 821	1 540	7 348	2 433	4 915	2 268
NEW HAMPSHIRE	4 391	1 389	1 091	3 001	1 897	605	1 489	475	4 823	1 179	3 644	2 860
NEW JERSEY	33 897	8 677	1 012	25 220	18 329	8 777	2 137	1 024	41 988	9 320	32 667	3 810
NEW MEXICO	8 478	2 855	1 541	5 623	3 628	1 823	1 959	984	10 084	2 768	7 316	3 950
NEW YORK	92 897	37 730	1 972	55 167	43 262	13 121	2 261	686	119 199	38 982	80 217	4 192
NORTH CAROLINA	29 972	10 202	1 228	19 771	15 537	6 565	1 871	790	33 124	9 451	23 673	2 850
NORTH DAKOTA	2 868	1 043	1 645	1 825	1 117	620	1 762	978	3 020	586	2 435	3 840
OHIO	40 232	12 654	1 109	27 578	20 130	9 328	1 764	818	52 594	15 052	37 542	3 291
OKLAHOMA	12 761	4 120	1 181	8 641	6 053	2 273	1 734	651	14 727	3 377	11 350	3 252
OREGON	14 305	5 710	1 622	8 594	5 164	650	1 467	185	18 029	4 213	13 816	3 925
PENNSYLVANIA	46 544	13 734	1 114	32 811	22 136	10 948	1 795	888	55 171	12 788	42 383	3 438
RHODE ISLAND	4 836	1 720	1 610	3 116	2 128	1 161	1 992	1 087	5 767	749	5 018	4 698
SOUTH CAROLINA	14 477	5 434	1 324	9 042	6 088	3 158	1 483	769	20 009	4 241	15 768	3 842
SOUTH DAKOTA	2 604	1 063	1 399	1 541	977	777	1 285	1 023	2 772	506	2 265	2 981
TENNESSEE	17 620	7 316	1 264	10 303	7 798	6 046	1 347	1 044	20 029	4 478	15 551	2 686
TEXAS	62 181	21 385	984	40 796	28 662	23 577	1 319	1 085	70 274	16 681	53 594	2 466
UTAH	8 623	2 279	983	6 345	3 925	2 023	1 693	872	10 107	2 171	7 936	3 422
VERMONT	3 229	1 087	1 764	2 142	1 518	570	2 465	925	3 512	919	2 593	4 209
VIRGINIA	24 843	5 531	759	19 312	12 781	4 782	1 754	656	28 044	8 369	19 675	2 700
WASHINGTON	22 775	6 348	1 046	16 427	12 629	9 950	2 082	1 640	30 378	6 806	23 572	3 885
WEST VIRGINIA	8 053	2 899	1 606	5 153	3 552	1 921	1 968	1 064	9 409	1 454	7 956	4 408
WISCONSIN	22 874	7 031	1 292	15 843	11 814	5 428	2 172	998	26 749	9 523	17 226	3 167
WYOMING	2 768	1 169	2 343	1 599	1 094	544	2 193	1 090	2 948	975	1 974	3 955

1. Based on the resident population as of July 1 at the start of the fiscal year shown.

State Government Finances, Government Employment, and Elections

STATE	State government finances, 2001–2002 (cont'd) General expenditures (mil dol) (cont'd) By selected function (mil dol)					Debt outstanding		Government employment, 2003			Presidential election, 2004 (percent of vote cast)		
	Education	Health and hospitals	Highways	Public safety	Public welfare	Total (mil dol)	Per capita¹	Federal civilian	Federal military	State and local	Demo-cratic	Repub-lican	All other
	320	321	322	323	324	325	326	327	328	329	330	331	332
UNITED STATES	X	X	X	X	X	X	X	2 755 000	1 992 000	18 719 000	48.1	51.0	0.9
ALABAMA	6 811	1 837	1 256	460	4 110	6 405	1 430	49 160	32 042	303 882	36.8	62.5	0.7
ALASKA	1 567	193	687	252	1 151	5 308	8 281	16 712	23 414	61 511	35.0	62.0	3.0
ARIZONA	6 327	730	1 680	901	3 437	4 348	799	49 207	33 488	332 201	44.5	54.9	0.6
ARKANSAS	4 375	723	1 079	356	2 578	3 002	1 109	20 548	14 896	173 364	44.5	54.3	1.1
CALIFORNIA	53 610	14 071	7 899	6 973	42 965	71 263	2 036	249 140	231 874	2 184 184	54.6	44.3	1.1
COLORADO	5 798	939	1 421	838	3 132	5 419	1 204	52 215	39 749	309 044	46.6	52.2	1.2
CONNECTICUT	4 786	1 947	851	802	3 599	20 784	6 009	20 141	15 383	222 895	54.3	44.0	1.7
DELAWARE	1 434	329	370	316	660	4 038	5 010	5 226	8 207	53 270	53.3	45.8	0.9
DISTRICT OF COLUMBIA	X	X	X	X	X	X	X	192 109	24 023	38 777	89.5	9.3	1.2
FLORIDA	15 643	2 848	4 826	2 625	11 879	20 266	1 214	123 406	104 361	915 825	47.1	52.1	0.8
GEORGIA	12 155	1 443	2 005	1 544	6 525	8 243	965	92 095	95 758	541 756	41.4	58.1	0.6
HAWAII	2 257	638	236	167	1 126	5 656	4 558	30 880	54 298	87 347	54.0	45.3	0.7
IDAHO	1 830	158	500	218	1 003	2 545	1 895	13 321	9 518	99 383	30.4	68.5	1.2
ILLINOIS	14 098	3 496	3 656	1 751	10 940	34 761	2 762	89 916	47 977	754 418	54.7	44.7	0.6
INDIANA	7 931	826	1 570	841	5 125	9 456	1 536	36 275	18 246	382 034	39.2	60.1	0.8
IOWA	4 577	958	1 360	375	2 617	3 713	1 265	18 632	12 295	224 376	49.2	50.1	0.8
KANSAS	3 988	608	1 131	390	1 986	2 288	844	25 470	24 801	231 885	36.5	62.2	1.4
KENTUCKY	5 853	1 023	1 731	625	4 796	9 039	2 210	36 501	44 853	261 727	39.7	59.5	0.8
LOUISIANA	6 047	1 934	1 053	878	3 407	9 233	2 063	34 279	40 517	340 256	42.2	56.8	1.1
MAINE	1 505	413	462	166	1 802	4 321	3 337	13 752	8 896	87 715	53.1	45.0	1.9
MARYLAND	6 892	1 743	1 643	1 447	4 626	12 309	2 258	155 770	47 815	324 373	55.7	43.3	1.0
MASSACHUSETTS	6 553	2 421	2 744	1 434	5 988	45 216	7 041	51 292	18 510	370 593	62.1	37.0	0.9
MICHIGAN	19 133	4 570	2 717	2 027	9 524	21 947	2 185	54 839	19 246	618 071	51.2	47.8	1.0
MINNESOTA	8 820	699	1 666	620	6 741	6 408	1 275	33 480	17 162	353 324	51.1	47.6	1.2
MISSISSIPPI	3 922	933	969	340	3 413	4 160	1 451	25 221	34 118	220 167	39.6	59.6	0.8
MISSOURI	6 717	1 375	1 871	832	5 497	12 693	2 239	57 613	33 280	378 694	46.1	53.4	0.6
MONTANA	1 289	304	453	150	660	2 752	3 024	13 700	8 075	69 064	38.6	59.1	2.4
NEBRASKA	2 191	535	526	243	1 661	2 215	1 282	16 296	14 434	135 309	32.1	66.6	1.3
NEVADA	2 523	318	568	290	1 040	3 668	1 693	16 419	12 986	115 668	47.9	50.5	1.6
NEW HAMPSHIRE	1 530	193	377	116	975	5 397	4 236	7 815	3 270	80 391	50.3	49.0	0.7
NEW JERSEY	10 244	2 262	2 257	1 541	6 703	32 093	3 743	61 768	22 840	542 148	52.7	46.5	0.9
NEW MEXICO	3 514	739	938	330	2 028	4 493	2 426	29 116	16 966	165 726	48.9	50.0	1.1
NEW YORK	25 562	8 838	3 295	3 116	34 598	89 856	4 696	131 910	49 369	1 306 202	57.8	40.5	1.8
NORTH CAROLINA	11 956	2 219	2 629	1 260	6 846	11 128	1 340	60 097	124 018	586 657	43.5	56.1	0.4
NORTH DAKOTA	943	95	377	52	627	1 673	2 639	9 853	12 500	57 254	35.5	62.9	1.6
OHIO	15 626	3 128	3 139	1 697	11 504	20 009	1 754	77 709	32 536	731 410	48.7	50.8	0.5
OKLAHOMA	5 269	618	1 263	613	3 202	6 477	1 856	45 020	38 250	246 713	34.4	65.6	0.0
OREGON	5 208	1 771	817	788	3 856	7 668	2 178	29 952	11 572	230 901	51.5	47.6	1.0
PENNSYLVANIA	13 775	4 151	4 566	2 428	15 118	20 983	1 702	105 201	37 911	661 133	50.8	48.6	0.6
RHODE ISLAND	1 344	295	260	205	1 690	5 856	5 483	9 961	8 195	58 907	59.5	38.9	1.6
SOUTH CAROLINA	5 656	1 626	1 349	645	4 373	10 116	2 465	27 624	53 338	295 519	40.8	58.0	1.1
SOUTH DAKOTA	799	125	420	97	593	2 308	3 036	11 079	7 532	59 773	38.4	59.9	1.6
TENNESSEE	6 095	1 237	1 534	661	6 896	3 628	627	50 063	21 842	358 726	42.5	56.8	0.7
TEXAS	25 763	5 057	5 219	3 553	15 271	24 008	1 104	176 109	165 397	1 449 311	38.3	61.2	0.5
UTAH	4 327	733	856	372	1 581	4 729	2 039	34 840	16 102	160 655	26.4	71.1	2.5
VERMONT	1 340	82	296	131	766	2 284	3 707	6 117	3 950	44 208	59.1	38.9	2.0
VIRGINIA	9 848	2 445	2 823	1 790	4 200	13 785	1 892	160 370	173 350	496 733	45.3	54.0	0.7
WASHINGTON	10 298	2 313	1 795	976	6 174	13 552	2 234	68 657	73 479	445 219	53.0	45.5	1.4
WEST VIRGINIA	2 495	311	986	218	2 136	4 537	2 514	21 452	7 815	118 656	43.2	56.1	0.7
WISCONSIN	8 299	1 295	1 717	1 068	5 515	14 870	2 733	29 190	15 703	378 369	49.8	49.4	0.9
WYOMING	866	139	357	109	374	1 298	2 601	7 482	5 843	53 276	29.1	69.0	1.9

1. Based on the resident population as of July 1 at the start of the fiscal year shown.

States and Counties

(For explanation of symbols, see page xii)

Page

TABLE B Highlights and Rankings

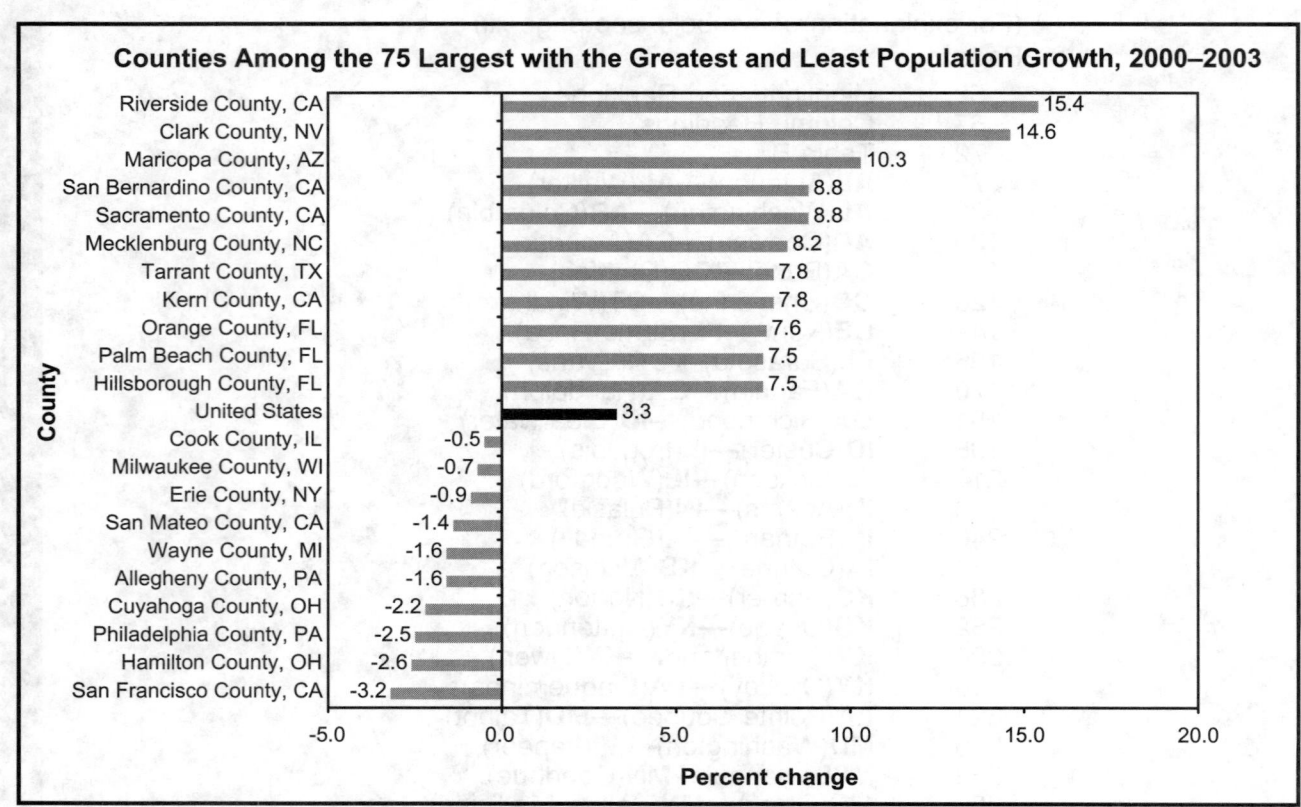

Counties Among the 75 Largest with the Greatest and Least Population Growth, 2000–2003

County	Percent change
Riverside County, CA	15.4
Clark County, NV	14.6
Maricopa County, AZ	10.3
San Bernardino County, CA	8.8
Sacramento County, CA	8.8
Mecklenburg County, NC	8.2
Tarrant County, TX	7.8
Kern County, CA	7.8
Orange County, FL	7.6
Palm Beach County, FL	7.5
Hillsborough County, FL	7.5
United States	3.3
Cook County, IL	-0.5
Milwaukee County, WI	-0.7
Erie County, NY	-0.9
San Mateo County, CA	-1.4
Wayne County, MI	-1.6
Allegheny County, PA	-1.6
Cuyahoga County, OH	-2.2
Philadelphia County, PA	-2.5
Hamilton County, OH	-2.6
San Francisco County, CA	-3.2

Many of the fastest growing counties are in the suburbs of large metropolitan areas. Loudoun County, VA (near Washington, DC), Douglas County, CO (near Denver), Rockwall County, TX (near Dallas), Forsyth County, GA (near Atlanta) had population growth exceeding 25 percent since 2000. Chattahoochee County, GA is the only county among the top five not near a major metropolitan area. Of the 75 largest counties, three of the top five counties are located in California. About 1,300 counties lost population or experienced no growth in the first 3 years of the twenty-first century. Many of these were small counties, but large counties also suffered losses. Philadelphia County, PA, Cuyahoga County, OH (Cleveland), Cook County, IL (Chicago) and Suffolk County, MA (Boston) experienced population loss since 2000.

Within states, the number and physical size of counties varies considerably; Delaware has three counties while Texas has over 250 counties. For the approximately 3,140 counties (and county equivalents—see Appendix A) in the United States, populations in 2003 ranged from nearly 10 million in Los Angeles County, CA, to 62 in Loving County, TX. Another particularly large county in terms of population is Cook County, IL (over 5 million population), encompassing Chicago and its suburbs. Harris County,

TX, (containing Houston) and Maricopa County, AZ (containing Phoenix) both have over 3 million people. There are 37 counties with a population of 1,000,000 or more, which combined contain about one-fourth of the U.S. population. About half of the U.S. population live in the 150 largest counties, those with a population of about 400,000 or more. At the other extreme, there are 32 counties with fewer than 1,000 people. The median county population size is about 25,000.

In terms of land area, counties range from the nearly 378,000 square kilometers of Yukon-Koyukuk census area, AK to New York County, NY with 59 square kilometers, Arlington County, VA with 67 and Bristol County, RI with 64 square kilometers.[1] Counties tend to be larger in the western United States (most of the largest 50 are in that region). The median land area for all U.S. counties was about 1,600 square kilometers in 2000.

While New York County (Manhattan) may have one of the smallest land areas, it has by far the highest population density among U.S. counties, with over 26,500 persons per square kilometer. No other county approached that density (although three other New York City boroughs

---

[1] Several independent cities in Virginia, which are treated as counties for tabulation purposes, were excluded here.

are among the top-five counties in population density). San Francisco has the highest density outside New York City, with Chicago (Cook County, IL), Philadelphia, and Milwaukee also among the top 10. The median county only has about 17 persons per square kilometer, with only 108 counties having more than 500 persons per square kilometer. Los Angeles, the nation's largest county in terms of population, has a population density of 938 persons per square kilometer, ranking 20th among all U.S. counties.

Proportionally large year-to-year labor force changes are not unusual for counties with small populations, but no county's labor force grew more than 25 percent between 2002 and 2003. Among the 75 largest counties, only San Bernardino County, CA had growth of 3 percent or more. Twenty-seven of the largest counties exceeded the national average growth of 0.9 percent. Santa Clara County, CA and San Francisco County, CA were the only large counties with labor forces decreasing by more than 3 percent. Among all the counties, the labor force decreased in about 1,000 counties, with seven small counties losing 10 percent or more.

Nearly 1,400 counties have unemployment rates above the national average of 6 percent. Six counties have unemployment rates greater than 20 percent, including two counties in Texas and two in Alaska. Of the 10 counties with the highest unemployment rates, only Yuma County, AZ and Imperial County, CA have populations over 100,000. About 30 counties have unemployment rates less than 2 percent.

75 Largest Counties by 2003 Population
Selected Rankings

Total population, 2003			Land area, 2000				Population density, 2003			
Population rank	County	Population [col 2]	Population rank	Land area rank	County	Land area (square kilometers) [col 1]	Population rank	Density rank	County	Density (per square kilometer) [col 4]
1	Los Angeles County, CA	9 871 506	12	1	San Bernardino County, CA	51 936	18	1	New York County, NY	26 522.0
2	Cook County, IL	5 351 552	4	2	Maricopa County, AZ	23 836	7	2	Kings County, NY	13 511.1
3	Harris County, TX	3 596 086	50	3	Pima County, AZ	23 792	26	3	Bronx County, NY	12 506.4
4	Maricopa County, AZ	3 389 260	72	4	Kern County, CA	21 085	10	4	Queens County, NY	7 863.9
5	Orange County, CA	2 957 766	17	5	Clark County, NV	20 488	68	5	San Francisco County, CA	6 212.2
6	San Diego County, CA	2 930 886	13	6	Riverside County, CA	18 667	20	6	Philadelphia County, PA	4 226.7
7	Kings County, NY	2 472 523	54	7	Fresno County, CA	15 443	61	7	Essex County, NJ	2 435.2
8	Miami-Dade County, FL	2 341 167	6	8	San Diego County, CA	10 878	2	8	Cook County, IL	2 185.2
9	Dallas County, TX	2 284 096	1	9	Los Angeles County, CA	10 518	27	9	Nassau County, NY	1 802.8
10	Queens County, NY	2 225 486	14	10	King County, WA	5 506	41	10	Milwaukee County, WI	1 490.8
11	Wayne County, MI	2 028 778	30	11	Palm Beach County, FL	5 113	49	11	Bergen County, NJ	1 478.7
12	San Bernardino County, CA	1 859 678	8	12	Miami-Dade County, FL	5 040	5	12	Orange County, CA	1 446.3
13	Riverside County, CA	1 782 650	62	13	Ventura County, CA	4 779	42	13	Pinellas County, FL	1 277.4
14	King County, WA	1 761 411	3	14	Harris County, TX	4 478	11	14	Wayne County, MI	1 275.2
15	Broward County, FL	1 731 347	69	15	Pierce County, WA	4 348	25	15	Cuyahoga County, OH	1 149.0
16	Santa Clara County, CA	1 678 421	65	16	Worcester County, MA	3 919	43	16	Du Page County, IL	1 070.8
17	Clark County, NV	1 576 541	16	17	Santa Clara County, CA	3 343	9	17	Dallas County, TX	1 002.7
18	New York County, NY	1 564 798	22	18	Bexar County, TX	3 229	37	18	Fairfax County, VA	977.9
19	Tarrant County, TX	1 559 148	15	19	Broward County, FL	3 122	63	19	Middlesex County, NJ	973.8
20	Philadelphia County, PA	1 479 339	34	20	Hillsborough County, FL	2 722	1	20	Los Angeles County, CA	938.5
21	Middlesex County, MA	1 471 724	39	21	Erie County, NY	2 704	52	21	Marion County, IN	841.4
22	Bexar County, TX	1 471 644	73	22	El Paso County, TX	2 624	40	22	Westchester County, NY	838.8
23	Suffolk County, NY	1 468 037	53	23	Travis County, TX	2 562	3	23	Harris County, TX	803.1
24	Alameda County, CA	1 461 030	28	24	Sacramento County, CA	2 501	57	24	Hamilton County, OH	780.5
25	Cuyahoga County, OH	1 363 888	2	25	Cook County, IL	2 449	33	25	Franklin County, OH	778.9
26	Bronx County, NY	1 363 198	23	26	Suffolk County, NY	2 363	32	26	Hennepin County, MN	777.4
27	Nassau County, NY	1 339 463	38	27	Orange County, FL	2 350	35	27	St. Louis County, MO	770.4
28	Sacramento County, CA	1 330 711	9	28	Dallas County, TX	2 278	24	28	Alameda County, CA	764.9
29	Allegheny County, PA	1 261 303	31	29	Oakland County, MI	2 260	45	29	Montgomery County, MD	716.2
30	Palm Beach County, FL	1 216 282	19	30	Tarrant County, TX	2 236	74	30	Jefferson County, KY	701.1
31	Oakland County, MI	1 207 869	21	31	Middlesex County, MA	2 133	19	31	Tarrant County, TX	697.3
32	Hennepin County, MN	1 121 035	5	32	Orange County, CA	2 045	21	32	Middlesex County, MA	690.0
33	Franklin County, OH	1 088 944	59	33	Duval County, FL	2 004	56	33	Prince George's County, MD	667.2
34	Hillsborough County, FL	1 073 407	46	34	Shelby County, TN	1 954	29	34	Allegheny County, PA	667.0
35	St. Louis County, MO	1 013 123	24	35	Alameda County, CA	1 910	60	35	Macomb County, MI	654.3
36	Contra Costa County, CA	1 001 136	44	35	Salt Lake County, UT	1 910	23	36	Suffolk County, NY	621.3
37	Fairfax County, VA	1 000 405	51	37	Hartford County, CT	1 905	66	37	Montgomery County, PA	616.1
38	Orange County, FL	964 865	29	38	Allegheny County, PA	1 891	75	38	San Mateo County, CA	599.7
39	Erie County, NY	941 293	36	39	Contra Costa County, CA	1 865	58	39	Fulton County, GA	597.8
40	Westchester County, NY	940 302	71	40	Monroe County, NY	1 708	47	40	Honolulu County, HI	581.3
41	Milwaukee County, WI	933 221	48	41	Fairfield County, CT	1 621	70	41	Essex County, MA	568.9
42	Pinellas County, FL	926 146	11	42	Wayne County, MI	1 591	48	42	Fairfield County, CT	554.7
43	Du Page County, IL	925 188	55	43	New Haven County, CT	1 569	15	43	Broward County, FL	554.6
44	Salt Lake County, UT	924 247	47	44	Honolulu County, HI	1 553	67	44	Mecklenburg County, NC	552.0
45	Montgomery County, MD	918 881	64	45	Baltimore County, MD	1 550	36	45	Contra Costa County, CA	536.8
46	Shelby County, TN	906 178	32	46	Hennepin County, MN	1 442	55	46	New Haven County, CT	536.6
47	Honolulu County, HI	902 709	33	47	Franklin County, OH	1 398	31	47	Oakland County, MI	534.5
48	Fairfield County, CT	899 152	58	48	Fulton County, GA	1 369	28	48	Sacramento County, CA	532.1
49	Bergen County, NJ	897 569	67	49	Mecklenburg County, NC	1 363	16	49	Santa Clara County, CA	502.1
50	Pima County, AZ	892 798	35	50	St. Louis County, MO	1 315	64	50	Baltimore County, MD	501.4
51	Hartford County, CT	871 457	70	51	Essex County, MA	1 297	44	51	Salt Lake County, UT	483.9
52	Marion County, IN	863 251	45	52	Montgomery County, MD	1 283	8	52	Miami-Dade County, FL	464.5
53	Travis County, TX	857 204	56	53	Prince George's County, MD	1 257	46	53	Shelby County, TN	463.8
54	Fresno County, CA	850 325	66	54	Montgomery County, PA	1 251	51	54	Hartford County, CT	457.5
55	New Haven County, CT	841 873	60	55	Macomb County, MI	1 244	22	55	Bexar County, TX	455.8
56	Prince George's County, MD	838 716	25	56	Cuyahoga County, OH	1 187	71	56	Monroe County, NY	431.3
57	Hamilton County, OH	823 472	75	57	San Mateo County, CA	1 163	38	57	Orange County, FL	410.6
58	Fulton County, GA	818 322	40	58	Westchester County, NY	1 121	59	58	Duval County, FL	407.9
59	Duval County, FL	817 480	57	59	Hamilton County, OH	1 055	34	59	Hillsborough County, FL	394.3
60	Macomb County, MI	813 948	52	60	Marion County, IN	1 026	39	60	Erie County, NY	348.1
61	Essex County, NJ	796 313	37	61	Fairfax County, VA	1 023	53	61	Travis County, TX	334.6
62	Ventura County, CA	791 130	74	62	Jefferson County, KY	997	14	62	King County, WA	319.9
63	Middlesex County, NJ	780 995	43	63	Du Page County, IL	864	6	63	San Diego County, CA	269.4
64	Baltimore County, MD	777 184	63	64	Middlesex County, NJ	802	73	64	El Paso County, TX	268.8
65	Worcester County, MA	776 610	27	65	Nassau County, NY	743	30	65	Palm Beach County, FL	237.9
66	Montgomery County, PA	770 747	42	66	Pinellas County, FL	725	65	66	Worcester County, MA	198.2
67	Mecklenburg County, NC	752 366	41	67	Milwaukee County, WI	626	69	67	Pierce County, WA	170.4
68	San Francisco County, CA	751 682	49	68	Bergen County, NJ	607	62	68	Ventura County, CA	165.5
69	Pierce County, WA	740 957	20	69	Philadelphia County, PA	350	4	69	Maricopa County, AZ	142.2
70	Essex County, MA	737 848	61	70	Essex County, NJ	327	13	70	Riverside County, CA	95.5
71	Monroe County, NY	736 738	10	71	Queens County, NY	283	17	71	Clark County, NV	76.9
72	Kern County, CA	713 087	7	72	Kings County, NY	183	54	72	Fresno County, CA	55.1
73	El Paso County, TX	705 436	68	73	San Francisco County, CA	121	50	73	Pima County, AZ	37.5
74	Jefferson County, KY	699 017	26	74	Bronx County, NY	109	12	74	San Bernardino County, CA	35.8
75	San Mateo County, CA	697 456	18	75	New York County, NY	59	72	75	Kern County, CA	33.8

75 Largest Counties by 2003 Population
Selected Rankings

Percent population change, 2000–2003				Percent White, not Hispanic or Latino, 2003				Percent Black, not Hispanic or Latino, 2003			
Population rank	Percent change rank	County	Percent change [col 23]	Population rank	White rank	County	Percent White [col 5]	Population rank	Black rank	County	Percent Black [col 6]
13	1	Riverside County, CA	15.4	60	1	Macomb County, MI	91.0	56	1	Prince George's County, MD	64.9
17	2	Clark County, NV	14.6	65	2	Worcester County, MA	86.1	46	2	Shelby County, TN	50.9
4	3	Maricopa County, AZ	10.3	66	3	Montgomery County, PA	85.0	20	3	Philadelphia County, PA	44.4
28	4	Sacramento County, CA	8.8	29	4	Allegheny County, PA	84.2	58	4	Fulton County, GA	43.2
12	4	San Bernardino County, CA	8.8	21	5	Middlesex County, MA	83.7	11	5	Wayne County, MI	42.8
67	6	Mecklenburg County, NC	8.2	42	6	Pinellas County, FL	81.9	61	6	Essex County, NJ	42.0
72	7	Kern County, CA	7.8	70	7	Essex County, MA	81.6	7	7	Kings County, NY	35.9
19	7	Tarrant County, TX	7.8	31	8	Oakland County, MI	81.0	26	8	Bronx County, NY	32.0
38	9	Orange County, FL	7.6	44	9	Salt Lake County, UT	80.5	59	9	Duval County, FL	30.0
34	10	Hillsborough County, FL	7.5	39	10	Erie County, NY	80.3	67	10	Mecklenburg County, NC	29.6
30	10	Palm Beach County, FL	7.5	32	11	Hennepin County, MN	78.9	25	11	Cuyahoga County, OH	28.6
15	12	Broward County, FL	6.7	69	12	Pierce County, WA	78.8	41	12	Milwaukee County, WI	26.5
54	13	Fresno County, CA	6.4	23	13	Suffolk County, NY	76.7	2	13	Cook County, IL	26.3
50	14	Pima County, AZ	5.8	71	14	Monroe County, NY	76.4	52	14	Marion County, IN	25.9
22	15	Bexar County, TX	5.7	43	15	Du Page County, IL	76.1	57	15	Hamilton County, OH	24.6
3	15	Harris County, TX	5.7	74	15	Jefferson County, KY	76.1	15	16	Broward County, FL	24.1
69	15	Pierce County, WA	5.7	35	17	St. Louis County, MO	74.7	64	17	Baltimore County, MD	22.4
36	18	Contra Costa County, CA	5.5	55	18	New Haven County, CT	74.2	35	18	St. Louis County, MO	21.2
53	18	Travis County, TX	5.5	33	19	Franklin County, OH	74.1	9	19	Dallas County, TX	20.6
45	20	Montgomery County, MD	5.2	14	19	King County, WA	74.1	10	19	Queens County, NY	20.6
59	21	Duval County, FL	5.0	48	21	Fairfield County, CT	73.0	74	21	Jefferson County, KY	20.3
62	21	Ventura County, CA	5.0	51	22	Hartford County, CT	72.7	38	21	Orange County, FL	20.3
56	23	Prince George's County, MD	4.6	57	23	Hamilton County, OH	72.6	33	23	Franklin County, OH	20.0
6	24	San Diego County, CA	4.2	64	24	Baltimore County, MD	72.2	8	24	Miami-Dade County, FL	19.5
63	25	Middlesex County, NJ	4.1	27	25	Nassau County, NY	71.1	3	25	Harris County, TX	18.2
8	26	Miami-Dade County, FL	3.9	49	26	Bergen County, NJ	70.2	34	26	Hillsborough County, FL	16.0
5	26	Orange County, CA	3.9	52	27	Marion County, IN	68.2	30	27	Palm Beach County, FL	15.7
73	28	El Paso County, TX	3.8	30	28	Palm Beach County, FL	67.6	18	28	New York County, NY	15.4
1	29	Los Angeles County, CA	3.7	25	29	Cuyahoga County, OH	66.0	71	29	Monroe County, NY	15.0
23	30	Suffolk County, NY	3.4	4	30	Maricopa County, AZ	64.1	45	29	Montgomery County, MD	15.0
65	30	Worcester County, MA	3.4	37	31	Fairfax County, VA	64.0	24	31	Alameda County, CA	14.8
60	32	Macomb County, MI	3.3	59	32	Duval County, FL	62.4	40	32	Westchester County, NY	14.7
37	33	Fairfax County, VA	3.2	40	33	Westchester County, NY	62.2	39	33	Erie County, NY	13.9
64	34	Baltimore County, MD	3.0	34	34	Hillsborough County, FL	61.3	19	34	Tarrant County, TX	13.5
47	34	Honolulu County, HI	3.0	41	35	Milwaukee County, WI	60.7	29	35	Allegheny County, PA	13.2
9	36	Dallas County, TX	2.9	17	36	Clark County, NV	60.3	51	36	Hartford County, CT	12.4
44	36	Salt Lake County, UT	2.9	45	37	Montgomery County, MD	60.1	55	37	New Haven County, CT	12.1
66	38	Montgomery County, PA	2.8	50	37	Pima County, AZ	60.1	31	38	Oakland County, MI	11.5
26	39	Bronx County, NY	2.3	19	39	Tarrant County, TX	59.9	27	39	Nassau County, NY	11.3
43	39	Du Page County, IL	2.3	63	40	Middlesex County, NJ	58.9	28	40	Sacramento County, CA	11.2
55	41	New Haven County, CT	2.2	67	41	Mecklenburg County, NC	58.8	32	41	Hennepin County, MN	10.7
70	42	Essex County, MA	2.0	28	42	Sacramento County, CA	58.5	48	42	Fairfield County, CT	10.5
48	43	Fairfield County, CT	1.9	36	43	Contra Costa County, CA	57.8	42	43	Pinellas County, FL	10.1
33	43	Franklin County, OH	1.9	62	44	Ventura County, CA	56.5	36	44	Contra Costa County, CA	9.9
18	45	New York County, NY	1.8	6	45	San Diego County, CA	55.5	1	45	Los Angeles County, CA	9.7
40	45	Westchester County, NY	1.8	53	46	Travis County, TX	55.3	12	45	San Bernardino County, CA	9.7
51	47	Hartford County, CT	1.7	38	47	Orange County, FL	54.6	63	47	Middlesex County, NJ	9.5
49	48	Bergen County, NJ	1.5	15	48	Broward County, FL	53.1	17	48	Clark County, NV	9.3
14	49	King County, WA	1.4	11	49	Wayne County, MI	51.0	37	49	Fairfax County, VA	9.0
24	50	Alameda County, CA	1.2	5	50	Orange County, CA	50.9	53	50	Travis County, TX	8.9
31	51	Oakland County, MI	1.1	75	51	San Mateo County, CA	50.7	69	51	Pierce County, WA	8.6
46	52	Shelby County, TN	1.0	13	52	Riverside County, CA	49.9	66	52	Montgomery County, PA	8.1
74	53	Jefferson County, KY	0.8	72	53	Kern County, CA	48.4	68	53	San Francisco County, CA	7.8
42	54	Pinellas County, FL	0.5	2	54	Cook County, IL	47.0	23	53	Suffolk County, NY	7.8
32	55	Hennepin County, MN	0.4	18	54	New York County, NY	47.0	22	55	Bexar County, TX	6.9
21	55	Middlesex County, MA	0.4	58	56	Fulton County, GA	46.7	14	56	King County, WA	6.7
27	55	Nassau County, NY	0.4	68	57	San Francisco County, CA	45.5	13	57	Riverside County, CA	6.6
61	58	Essex County, NJ	0.3	46	58	Shelby County, TN	44.3	72	58	Kern County, CA	6.1
58	58	Fulton County, GA	0.3	16	59	Santa Clara County, CA	43.8	6	58	San Diego County, CA	6.1
7	58	Kings County, NY	0.3	12	60	San Bernardino County, CA	42.5	49	60	Bergen County, NJ	5.6
52	58	Marion County, IN	0.3	24	61	Alameda County, CA	41.6	54	61	Fresno County, CA	5.5
71	62	Monroe County, NY	0.2	20	61	Philadelphia County, PA	41.6	60	62	Macomb County, MI	4.5
10	63	Queens County, NY	-0.2	9	63	Dallas County, TX	40.7	4	63	Maricopa County, AZ	4.1
16	63	Santa Clara County, CA	-0.2	3	64	Harris County, TX	40.3	21	64	Middlesex County, MA	4.0
35	65	St. Louis County, MO	-0.3	54	65	Fresno County, CA	39.5	47	65	Honolulu County, HI	3.9
2	66	Cook County, IL	-0.5	61	66	Essex County, NJ	37.4	43	66	Du Page County, IL	3.8
41	67	Milwaukee County, WI	-0.7	7	67	Kings County, NY	35.2	75	67	San Mateo County, CA	3.5
39	68	Erie County, NY	-0.9	22	68	Bexar County, TX	34.9	65	68	Worcester County, MA	3.3
75	69	San Mateo County, CA	-1.4	10	69	Queens County, NY	32.2	50	69	Pima County, AZ	3.2
29	70	Allegheny County, PA	-1.6	1	70	Los Angeles County, CA	31.3	16	70	Santa Clara County, CA	2.9
11	70	Wayne County, MI	-1.6	47	71	Honolulu County, HI	31.2	70	71	Essex County, MA	2.8
25	72	Cuyahoga County, OH	-2.2	56	72	Prince George's County, MD	22.9	73	72	El Paso County, TX	2.3
20	73	Philadelphia County, PA	-2.5	8	73	Miami-Dade County, FL	18.8	62	73	Ventura County, CA	2.1
57	74	Hamilton County, OH	-2.6	73	74	El Paso County, TX	15.4	5	74	Orange County, CA	1.8
68	75	San Francisco County, CA	-3.2	26	75	Bronx County, NY	13.6	44	75	Salt Lake County, UT	1.4

75 Largest Counties by 2003 Population
Selected Rankings

Percent American Indian, Alaska Native, 2003				Percent Asian and Pacific Islander, 2003				Percent Hispanic or Latino, 2003			
Population rank	American Indian, Alaska Native rank	County	Percent American Indian, Alaska Native [col 7]	Population rank	Asian and Pacific Islander rank	County	Percent Asian and Pacific Islander [col 8]	Population rank	Hispanic or Latino rank	County	Percent Hispanic or Latino [col 9]
50	1	Pima County, AZ	3.3	47	1	Honolulu County, HI	77.7	73	1	El Paso County, TX	81.3
69	2	Pierce County, WA	2.6	68	2	San Francisco County, CA	34.1	8	2	Miami-Dade County, FL	60.5
4	3	Maricopa County, AZ	2.0	16	3	Santa Clara County, CA	30.4	22	3	Bexar County, TX	56.5
28	4	Sacramento County, CA	1.9	24	4	Alameda County, CA	25.7	26	4	Bronx County, NY	51.3
14	5	King County, WA	1.7	75	5	San Mateo County, CA	25.4	1	5	Los Angeles County, CA	46.3
72	6	Kern County, CA	1.5	10	6	Queens County, NY	21.6	54	6	Fresno County, CA	46.0
32	7	Hennepin County, MN	1.4	63	7	Middlesex County, NJ	17.1	12	7	San Bernardino County, CA	42.6
54	8	Fresno County, CA	1.3	37	8	Fairfax County, VA	16.4	72	8	Kern County, CA	41.5
47	8	Honolulu County, HI	1.3	5	9	Orange County, CA	16.3	13	9	Riverside County, CA	39.1
17	10	Clark County, NV	1.2	28	10	Sacramento County, CA	14.8	3	10	Harris County, TX	36.0
36	10	Contra Costa County, CA	1.2	14	11	King County, WA	14.5	62	11	Ventura County, CA	35.3
13	10	Riverside County, CA	1.2	36	12	Contra Costa County, CA	14.2	9	12	Dallas County, TX	34.3
12	10	San Bernardino County, CA	1.2	45	13	Montgomery County, MD	13.8	5	13	Orange County, CA	32.1
24	14	Alameda County, CA	1.1	1	14	Los Angeles County, CA	13.5	50	14	Pima County, AZ	31.9
41	14	Milwaukee County, WI	1.1	49	15	Bergen County, NJ	12.8	53	15	Travis County, TX	30.9
44	14	Salt Lake County, UT	1.1	6	16	San Diego County, CA	11.2	6	16	San Diego County, CA	28.7
6	14	San Diego County, CA	1.1	18	17	New York County, NY	11.0	4	17	Maricopa County, AZ	28.0
39	18	Erie County, NY	0.9	43	18	Du Page County, IL	10.1	18	18	New York County, NY	27.4
56	18	Prince George's County, MD	0.9	7	19	Kings County, NY	9.3	10	19	Queens County, NY	26.2
10	18	Queens County, NY	0.9	54	20	Fresno County, CA	9.2	16	20	Santa Clara County, CA	24.5
19	18	Tarrant County, TX	0.9	69	21	Pierce County, WA	8.4	17	21	Clark County, NV	24.4
62	18	Ventura County, CA	0.9	21	22	Middlesex County, MA	8.2	19	22	Tarrant County, TX	22.5
11	18	Wayne County, MI	0.9	17	23	Clark County, NV	7.2	75	23	San Mateo County, CA	22.3
33	24	Franklin County, OH	0.8	62	24	Ventura County, CA	6.9	2	24	Cook County, IL	21.5
60	24	Macomb County, MI	0.8	27	25	Nassau County, NY	6.5	38	25	Orange County, FL	21.2
68	24	San Francisco County, CA	0.8	32	26	Hennepin County, MN	6.0	7	26	Kings County, NY	20.3
9	27	Dallas County, TX	0.7	12	26	San Bernardino County, CA	6.0	24	27	Alameda County, CA	20.2
59	27	Duval County, FL	0.7	2	28	Cook County, IL	5.8	15	27	Broward County, FL	20.2
34	27	Hillsborough County, FL	0.7	3	28	Harris County, TX	5.8	34	27	Hillsborough County, FL	20.2
31	27	Oakland County, MI	0.7	40	28	Westchester County, NY	5.8	36	30	Contra Costa County, CA	20.1
5	27	Orange County, CA	0.7	31	31	Oakland County, MI	5.6	40	31	Westchester County, NY	17.9
42	27	Pinellas County, FL	0.7	20	31	Philadelphia County, PA	5.6	28	32	Sacramento County, CA	17.7
16	27	Santa Clara County, CA	0.7	53	33	Travis County, TX	5.5	61	33	Essex County, NJ	16.8
53	27	Travis County, TX	0.7	66	34	Montgomery County, PA	5.3	63	34	Middlesex County, NJ	15.3
64	35	Baltimore County, MD	0.6	13	35	Riverside County, CA	5.1	30	35	Palm Beach County, FL	14.9
26	35	Bronx County, NY	0.6	44	36	Salt Lake County, UT	5.0	68	36	San Francisco County, CA	14.0
57	35	Hamilton County, OH	0.6	38	37	Orange County, FL	4.7	44	37	Salt Lake County, UT	13.4
74	35	Jefferson County, KY	0.6	9	38	Dallas County, TX	4.6	70	38	Essex County, MA	13.2
1	35	Los Angeles County, CA	0.6	19	38	Tarrant County, TX	4.6	48	39	Fairfield County, CT	12.9
52	35	Marion County, IN	0.6	61	40	Essex County, NJ	4.4	23	40	Suffolk County, NY	12.5
67	35	Mecklenburg County, NC	0.6	33	40	Franklin County, OH	4.4	37	41	Fairfax County, VA	12.3
71	35	Monroe County, NY	0.6	56	40	Prince George's County, MD	4.4	45	41	Montgomery County, MD	12.3
45	35	Montgomery County, MD	0.6	48	43	Fairfield County, CT	4.2	51	43	Hartford County, CT	12.2
55	35	New Haven County, CT	0.6	72	44	Kern County, CA	4.1	49	44	Bergen County, NJ	12.1
38	35	Orange County, FL	0.6	67	44	Mecklenburg County, NC	4.1	27	45	Nassau County, NY	11.7
20	35	Philadelphia County, PA	0.6	64	46	Baltimore County, MD	4.0	55	46	New Haven County, CT	11.1
75	35	San Mateo County, CA	0.6	58	46	Fulton County, GA	4.0	43	47	Du Page County, IL	10.7
22	48	Bexar County, TX	0.5	59	48	Duval County, FL	3.9	41	48	Milwaukee County, WI	9.8
25	48	Cuyahoga County, OH	0.5	65	49	Worcester County, MA	3.7	20	49	Philadelphia County, PA	9.1
61	48	Essex County, NJ	0.5	26	50	Bronx County, NY	3.6	56	50	Prince George's County, MD	8.5
37	48	Fairfax County, VA	0.5	23	51	Suffolk County, NY	3.5	67	51	Mecklenburg County, NC	8.0
58	48	Fulton County, GA	0.5	15	52	Broward County, FL	3.4	65	52	Worcester County, MA	7.3
3	48	Harris County, TX	0.5	41	52	Milwaukee County, WI	3.4	47	53	Honolulu County, HI	6.8
51	48	Hartford County, CT	0.5	51	54	Hartford County, CT	3.3	58	54	Fulton County, GA	6.7
7	48	Kings County, NY	0.5	35	54	St. Louis County, MO	3.3	14	55	King County, WA	6.3
18	48	New York County, NY	0.5	60	56	Macomb County, MI	3.2	69	55	Pierce County, WA	6.3
46	48	Shelby County, TN	0.5	71	56	Monroe County, NY	3.2	71	57	Monroe County, NY	6.1
35	48	St. Louis County, MO	0.5	55	56	New Haven County, CT	3.2	42	58	Pinellas County, FL	5.6
23	48	Suffolk County, NY	0.5	70	59	Essex County, MA	3.1	32	59	Hennepin County, MN	4.9
65	48	Worcester County, MA	0.5	34	59	Hillsborough County, FL	3.1	52	60	Marion County, IN	4.8
29	61	Allegheny County, PA	0.4	4	59	Maricopa County, AZ	3.1	21	60	Middlesex County, MA	4.8
15	61	Broward County, FL	0.4	50	62	Pima County, AZ	2.9	59	62	Duval County, FL	4.5
2	61	Cook County, IL	0.4	42	62	Pinellas County, FL	2.9	11	63	Wayne County, MI	4.2
43	61	Du Page County, IL	0.4	25	64	Cuyahoga County, OH	2.6	39	64	Erie County, NY	3.7
73	61	El Paso County, TX	0.4	11	64	Wayne County, MI	2.6	25	65	Cuyahoga County, OH	3.5
70	61	Essex County, MA	0.4	29	66	Allegheny County, PA	2.4	46	66	Shelby County, TN	2.9
21	61	Middlesex County, MA	0.4	30	67	Palm Beach County, FL	2.3	33	67	Franklin County, OH	2.7
63	61	Middlesex County, NJ	0.4	46	67	Shelby County, TN	2.3	31	68	Oakland County, MI	2.6
66	61	Montgomery County, PA	0.4	57	69	Hamilton County, OH	2.2	66	69	Montgomery County, PA	2.2
30	61	Palm Beach County, FL	0.4	22	70	Bexar County, TX	2.1	74	70	Jefferson County, KY	2.1
40	61	Westchester County, NY	0.4	39	70	Erie County, NY	2.1	64	71	Baltimore County, MD	2.0
49	72	Bergen County, NJ	0.3	74	70	Jefferson County, KY	2.1	60	72	Macomb County, MI	1.8
48	72	Fairfield County, CT	0.3	52	73	Marion County, IN	2.0	35	73	St. Louis County, MO	1.2
27	72	Nassau County, NY	0.3	8	74	Miami-Dade County, FL	1.7	57	74	Hamilton County, OH	1.2
8	75	Miami-Dade County, FL	0.2	73	75	El Paso County, TX	1.1	29	75	Allegheny County, PA	0.9

75 Largest Counties by 2003 Population

Selected Rankings

Percent under 18 years old, 2003				Percent 65 years old and over, 2003				Percent female-headed family households, 2003			
Population rank	Under 18 years old rank	County	Percent under 18 years old [cols 10 and 11]	Population rank	65 years old and over rank	County	Percent 65 years old and over [cols 17 and 18]	Population rank	Female households rank	County	Percent female households [col 30]
73	1	El Paso County, TX	32.0	30	1	Palm Beach County, FL	21.9	26	1	Bronx County, NY	30.4
12	2	San Bernardino County, CA	30.8	42	2	Pinellas County, FL	21.5	7	2	Kings County, NY	22.3
54	3	Fresno County, CA	30.4	29	3	Allegheny County, PA	17.5	20	2	Philadelphia County, PA	22.3
72	3	Kern County, CA	30.4	39	4	Erie County, NY	15.8	11	4	Wayne County, MI	20.6
44	5	Salt Lake County, UT	30.2	25	5	Cuyahoga County, OH	15.5	61	5	Essex County, NJ	20.4
26	6	Bronx County, NY	29.2	49	6	Bergen County, NJ	15.0	46	6	Shelby County, TN	20.1
3	6	Harris County, TX	29.2	27	6	Nassau County, NY	15.0	56	7	Prince George's County, MD	19.6
9	8	Dallas County, TX	28.7	15	8	Broward County, FL	14.7	73	8	El Paso County, TX	18.0
13	9	Riverside County, CA	28.5	66	8	Montgomery County, PA	14.7	8	9	Miami-Dade County, FL	17.2
22	10	Bexar County, TX	28.4	64	10	Baltimore County, MD	14.4	58	10	Fulton County, GA	16.5
19	10	Tarrant County, TX	28.4	51	11	Hartford County, CT	14.3	41	11	Milwaukee County, WI	16.3
4	12	Maricopa County, AZ	27.9	68	12	San Francisco County, CA	14.2	10	12	Queens County, NY	16.0
11	13	Wayne County, MI	27.8	35	13	St. Louis County, MO	14.1	25	13	Cuyahoga County, OH	15.7
46	14	Shelby County, TN	27.5	55	14	New Haven County, CT	14.0	2	14	Cook County, IL	15.6
1	15	Los Angeles County, CA	27.3	50	15	Pima County, AZ	13.9	59	14	Duval County, FL	15.6
62	16	Ventura County, CA	27.2	20	16	Philadelphia County, PA	13.8	22	16	Bexar County, TX	15.5
52	17	Marion County, IN	26.9	40	16	Westchester County, NY	13.8	54	17	Fresno County, CA	15.2
28	17	Sacramento County, CA	26.9	70	18	Essex County, MA	13.6	52	18	Marion County, IN	14.9
59	19	Duval County, FL	26.8	57	18	Hamilton County, OH	13.6	12	19	San Bernardino County, CA	14.8
61	20	Essex County, NJ	26.5	47	20	Honolulu County, HI	13.5	74	20	Jefferson County, KY	14.7
41	20	Milwaukee County, WI	26.5	74	21	Jefferson County, KY	13.4	1	20	Los Angeles County, CA	14.7
5	20	Orange County, CA	26.5	60	21	Macomb County, MI	13.4	72	22	Kern County, CA	14.5
56	20	Prince George's County, MD	26.5	8	21	Miami-Dade County, FL	13.4	57	23	Hamilton County, OH	14.3
17	24	Clark County, NV	26.2	71	24	Monroe County, NY	13.1	9	24	Dallas County, TX	14.1
69	24	Pierce County, WA	26.2	48	25	Fairfield County, CT	13.0	28	24	Sacramento County, CA	14.1
7	26	Kings County, NY	26.0	10	26	Queens County, NY	12.8	39	26	Erie County, NY	13.7
67	26	Mecklenburg County, NC	26.0	21	27	Middlesex County, MA	12.7	3	26	Harris County, TX	13.7
38	26	Orange County, FL	26.0	75	27	San Mateo County, CA	12.7	38	26	Orange County, FL	13.7
2	29	Cook County, IL	25.9	41	29	Milwaukee County, WI	12.5	55	29	New Haven County, CT	13.6
43	29	Du Page County, IL	25.9	65	29	Worcester County, MA	12.5	51	30	Hartford County, CT	13.5
36	31	Contra Costa County, CA	25.7	18	31	New York County, NY	12.3	71	31	Monroe County, NY	13.4
34	31	Hillsborough County, FL	25.7	63	32	Middlesex County, NJ	11.9	34	32	Hillsborough County, FL	13.2
37	33	Fairfax County, VA	25.6	23	32	Suffolk County, NY	11.9	24	33	Alameda County, CA	13.0
6	33	San Diego County, CA	25.6	11	32	Wayne County, MI	11.9	33	33	Franklin County, OH	13.0
48	35	Fairfield County, CT	25.3	7	35	Kings County, NY	11.7	64	35	Baltimore County, MD	12.8
33	35	Franklin County, OH	25.3	2	36	Cook County, IL	11.6	35	36	St. Louis County, MO	12.7
20	37	Philadelphia County, PA	25.2	61	36	Essex County, NJ	11.6	18	37	New York County, NY	12.6
58	38	Fulton County, GA	25.1	13	36	Riverside County, CA	11.6	15	38	Broward County, FL	12.5
57	38	Hamilton County, OH	25.1	34	39	Hillsborough County, FL	11.5	29	39	Allegheny County, PA	12.4
45	38	Montgomery County, MD	25.1	31	40	Oakland County, MI	11.3	70	39	Essex County, MA	12.4
70	41	Essex County, MA	24.9	45	41	Montgomery County, MD	11.2	67	39	Mecklenburg County, NC	12.4
50	41	Pima County, AZ	24.9	36	42	Contra Costa County, CA	11.1	47	42	Honolulu County, HI	12.3
23	43	Suffolk County, NY	24.8	4	43	Maricopa County, AZ	11.0	19	43	Tarrant County, TX	12.2
16	44	Santa Clara County, CA	24.7	52	43	Marion County, IN	11.0	40	43	Westchester County, NY	12.2
53	44	Travis County, TX	24.7	32	45	Hennepin County, MN	10.9	13	45	Riverside County, CA	12.0
65	44	Worcester County, MA	24.7	6	45	San Diego County, CA	10.9	17	46	Clark County, NV	11.8
8	47	Miami-Dade County, FL	24.6	28	47	Sacramento County, CA	10.7	69	46	Pierce County, WA	11.8
24	48	Alameda County, CA	24.5	14	48	King County, WA	10.4	50	46	Pima County, AZ	11.8
25	48	Cuyahoga County, OH	24.5	17	49	Clark County, NV	10.3	6	49	San Diego County, CA	11.6
31	48	Oakland County, MI	24.5	62	49	Ventura County, CA	10.3	36	50	Contra Costa County, CA	11.5
40	51	Westchester County, NY	24.4	24	51	Alameda County, CA	10.2	48	50	Fairfield County, CT	11.5
15	52	Broward County, FL	24.3	22	51	Bexar County, TX	10.2	65	52	Worcester County, MA	11.4
74	52	Jefferson County, KY	24.3	59	53	Duval County, FL	10.1	27	53	Nassau County, NY	10.9
35	52	St. Louis County, MO	24.3	26	54	Bronx County, NY	10.0	62	53	Ventura County, CA	10.9
71	55	Monroe County, NY	24.1	5	54	Orange County, CA	10.0	63	55	Middlesex County, NJ	10.8
51	56	Hartford County, CT	23.9	69	54	Pierce County, WA	10.0	23	55	Suffolk County, NY	10.8
63	57	Middlesex County, NJ	23.8	43	57	Du Page County, IL	9.9	4	57	Maricopa County, AZ	10.7
55	57	New Haven County, CT	23.8	73	57	El Paso County, TX	9.9	5	57	Orange County, CA	10.7
32	59	Hennepin County, MN	23.7	16	57	Santa Clara County, CA	9.9	45	59	Montgomery County, MD	10.5
60	60	Macomb County, MI	23.6	1	60	Los Angeles County, CA	9.8	42	59	Pinellas County, FL	10.5
66	61	Montgomery County, PA	23.5	46	60	Shelby County, TN	9.8	44	61	Salt Lake County, UT	10.4
27	61	Nassau County, NY	23.5	33	62	Franklin County, OH	9.6	53	61	Travis County, TX	10.4
64	63	Baltimore County, MD	23.0	54	62	Fresno County, CA	9.6	60	63	Macomb County, MI	10.1
47	63	Honolulu County, HI	23.0	38	62	Orange County, FL	9.6	75	63	San Mateo County, CA	10.1
49	65	Bergen County, NJ	22.9	72	65	Kern County, CA	9.0	16	65	Santa Clara County, CA	10.0
75	65	San Mateo County, CA	22.9	37	66	Fairfax County, VA	8.3	32	66	Hennepin County, MN	9.9
39	67	Erie County, NY	22.8	67	66	Mecklenburg County, NC	8.3	21	66	Middlesex County, MA	9.9
21	68	Middlesex County, MA	22.4	44	68	Salt Lake County, UT	8.1	49	68	Bergen County, NJ	9.7
10	69	Queens County, NY	22.3	12	68	San Bernardino County, CA	8.1	30	68	Palm Beach County, FL	9.7
14	70	King County, WA	21.7	19	68	Tarrant County, TX	8.1	31	70	Oakland County, MI	9.5
30	70	Palm Beach County, FL	21.7	9	71	Dallas County, TX	8.0	14	71	King County, WA	9.0
29	72	Allegheny County, PA	21.4	58	71	Fulton County, GA	8.0	68	72	San Francisco County, CA	8.9
42	73	Pinellas County, FL	19.9	56	73	Prince George's County, MD	7.9	66	73	Montgomery County, PA	8.8
18	74	New York County, NY	17.7	3	74	Harris County, TX	7.3	37	74	Fairfax County, VA	8.6
68	75	San Francisco County, CA	14.6	53	75	Travis County, TX	6.6	43	75	Du Page County, IL	7.9

75 Largest Counties by 2003 Population
Selected Rankings

Birth rate, average 1999–2001				Infant death rate, average 1999–2001				Percent college graduates (bachelor's degree or more), 2000			
Population rank	Birth rate rank	County	Birth rate (per 1,000 population) [col 33]	Population rank	Infant death rank	County	Infant death rate (per 1,000 live births) [col 37]	Population rank	Percent college graduate rank	County	Percent college grads [col 51]
73	1	El Paso County, TX	20.7	46	1	Shelby County, TN	12.7	37	1	Fairfax County, VA	54.8
44	2	Salt Lake County, UT	20.0	20	2	Philadelphia County, PA	11.1	45	2	Montgomery County, MD	54.6
9	3	Dallas County, TX	18.8	56	2	Prince George's County, MD	11.1	18	3	New York County, NY	49.4
3	4	Harris County, TX	18.3	59	4	Duval County, FL	10.4	68	4	San Francisco County, CA	45.0
54	5	Fresno County, CA	17.7	57	4	Hamilton County, OH	10.4	21	5	Middlesex County, MA	43.6
19	6	Tarrant County, TX	17.5	11	6	Wayne County, MI	10.3	43	6	Du Page County, IL	41.6
72	7	Kern County, CA	17.4	61	7	Essex County, NJ	9.8	58	7	Fulton County, GA	41.4
4	7	Maricopa County, AZ	17.4	41	7	Milwaukee County, WI	9.8	40	8	Westchester County, NY	40.9
53	9	Travis County, TX	17.3	2	9	Cook County, IL	9.7	53	9	Travis County, TX	40.6
26	10	Bronx County, NY	17.1	25	10	Cuyahoga County, OH	9.5	16	10	Santa Clara County, CA	40.5
22	11	Bexar County, TX	17.0	52	10	Marion County, IN	9.5	14	11	King County, WA	40.0
58	12	Fulton County, GA	16.8	33	12	Franklin County, OH	8.5	48	12	Fairfield County, CT	39.9
52	12	Marion County, IN	16.8	34	13	Hillsborough County, FL	8.3	32	13	Hennepin County, MN	39.1
12	14	San Bernardino County, CA	16.7	29	14	Allegheny County, PA	8.1	75	14	San Mateo County, CA	39.0
67	15	Mecklenburg County, NC	16.5	58	14	Fulton County, GA	8.1	66	15	Montgomery County, PA	38.6
1	16	Los Angeles County, CA	16.3	64	16	Baltimore County, MD	8.0	49	16	Bergen County, NJ	38.2
46	16	Shelby County, TN	16.3	39	16	Erie County, NY	8.0	31	16	Oakland County, MI	38.2
7	18	Kings County, NY	16.2	42	16	Pinellas County, FL	8.0	67	18	Mecklenburg County, NC	37.1
5	18	Orange County, CA	16.2	67	19	Mecklenburg County, NC	7.6	27	19	Nassau County, NY	35.4
16	20	Santa Clara County, CA	16.0	38	19	Orange County, FL	7.6	35	19	St. Louis County, MO	35.4
17	21	Clark County, NV	15.9	35	19	St. Louis County, MO	7.6	36	21	Contra Costa County, CA	35.0
33	21	Franklin County, OH	15.9	51	22	Hartford County, CT	7.5	24	22	Alameda County, CA	34.9
2	23	Cook County, IL	15.8	12	22	San Bernardino County, CA	7.5	63	23	Middlesex County, NJ	33.0
41	23	Milwaukee County, WI	15.8	47	24	Honolulu County, HI	7.4	33	24	Franklin County, OH	31.8
13	23	Riverside County, CA	15.8	19	25	Tarrant County, TX	7.2	70	25	Essex County, MA	31.3
59	26	Duval County, FL	15.6	71	26	Monroe County, NY	7.1	71	26	Monroe County, NY	31.2
6	27	San Diego County, CA	15.5	72	27	Kern County, CA	7.0	5	27	Orange County, CA	30.8
61	28	Essex County, NJ	15.4	74	28	Jefferson County, KY	6.9	64	28	Baltimore County, MD	30.6
38	28	Orange County, FL	15.4	26	29	Bronx County, NY	6.8	51	29	Hartford County, CT	29.6
62	30	Ventura County, CA	15.2	4	29	Maricopa County, AZ	6.8	6	30	San Diego County, CA	29.5
56	31	Prince George's County, MD	15.0	7	31	Kings County, NY	6.7	57	31	Hamilton County, OH	29.2
11	31	Wayne County, MI	15.0	60	31	Macomb County, MI	6.7	29	32	Allegheny County, PA	28.3
24	33	Alameda County, CA	14.9	55	33	New Haven County, CT	6.6	2	33	Cook County, IL	28.0
43	33	Du Page County, IL	14.9	30	33	Palm Beach County, FL	6.6	47	34	Honolulu County, HI	27.9
45	35	Montgomery County, MD	14.8	15	35	Broward County, FL	6.5	30	35	Palm Beach County, FL	27.6
28	35	Sacramento County, CA	14.8	69	35	Pierce County, WA	6.5	55	36	New Haven County, CT	27.6
37	37	Fairfax County, VA	14.6	17	37	Clark County, NV	6.4	61	37	Essex County, NJ	27.5
32	37	Hennepin County, MN	14.6	43	37	Du Page County, IL	6.4	23	37	Suffolk County, NY	27.5
34	37	Hillsborough County, FL	14.6	50	39	Pima County, AZ	6.3	44	39	Salt Lake County, UT	27.4
75	40	San Mateo County, CA	14.5	54	40	Fresno County, CA	6.2	56	40	Prince George's County, MD	27.2
57	41	Hamilton County, OH	14.4	9	41	Dallas County, TX	6.1	9	41	Dallas County, TX	27.0
50	41	Pima County, AZ	14.4	28	41	Sacramento County, CA	6.1	3	42	Harris County, TX	26.9
74	43	Jefferson County, KY	14.3	31	43	Oakland County, MI	6.0	62	42	Ventura County, CA	26.9
20	43	Philadelphia County, PA	14.3	13	43	Riverside County, CA	6.0	65	42	Worcester County, MA	26.9
69	43	Pierce County, WA	14.3	22	45	Bexar County, TX	5.9	50	45	Pima County, AZ	26.6
8	46	Miami-Dade County, FL	14.2	63	46	Middlesex County, NJ	5.8	19	46	Tarrant County, TX	26.6
10	46	Queens County, NY	14.2	32	47	Hennepin County, MN	5.7	38	47	Orange County, FL	26.1
47	48	Honolulu County, HI	14.1	66	47	Montgomery County, PA	5.7	4	48	Maricopa County, AZ	25.9
23	48	Suffolk County, NY	14.1	18	47	New York County, NY	5.7	52	49	Marion County, IN	25.4
48	50	Fairfield County, CT	14.0	8	50	Miami-Dade County, FL	5.6	46	50	Shelby County, TN	25.3
63	51	Middlesex County, NJ	13.7	10	50	Queens County, NY	5.6	25	51	Cuyahoga County, OH	25.1
40	51	Westchester County, NY	13.7	6	50	San Diego County, CA	5.6	34	51	Hillsborough County, FL	25.1
36	53	Contra Costa County, CA	13.6	3	53	Harris County, TX	5.5	1	53	Los Angeles County, CA	24.9
15	54	Broward County, FL	13.4	65	53	Worcester County, MA	5.5	74	54	Jefferson County, KY	24.8
31	54	Oakland County, MI	13.4	24	55	Alameda County, CA	5.4	28	54	Sacramento County, CA	24.8
25	56	Cuyahoga County, OH	13.3	27	56	Nassau County, NY	5.3	15	56	Broward County, FL	24.5
70	56	Essex County, MA	13.3	44	56	Salt Lake County, UT	5.3	39	56	Erie County, NY	24.5
65	56	Worcester County, MA	13.3	1	58	Los Angeles County, CA	5.2	10	58	Queens County, NY	24.3
21	59	Middlesex County, MA	13.0	49	59	Bergen County, NJ	5.0	41	59	Milwaukee County, WI	23.6
18	59	New York County, NY	13.0	45	59	Montgomery County, MD	5.0	42	60	Pinellas County, FL	22.9
51	61	Hartford County, CT	12.9	23	59	Suffolk County, NY	5.0	22	61	Bexar County, TX	22.6
60	62	Macomb County, MI	12.8	53	59	Travis County, TX	5.0	59	62	Duval County, FL	21.9
14	63	King County, WA	12.7	70	63	Essex County, MA	4.9	7	63	Kings County, NY	21.8
71	64	Monroe County, NY	12.6	48	63	Fairfield County, CT	4.9	8	64	Miami-Dade County, FL	21.6
27	64	Nassau County, NY	12.6	14	63	King County, WA	4.9	69	65	Pierce County, WA	20.6
66	66	Montgomery County, PA	12.5	73	66	El Paso County, TX	4.8	20	66	Philadelphia County, PA	17.9
55	67	New Haven County, CT	12.4	62	66	Ventura County, CA	4.8	60	67	Macomb County, MI	17.6
35	67	St. Louis County, MO	12.4	36	68	Contra Costa County, CA	4.7	54	68	Fresno County, CA	17.5
49	69	Bergen County, NJ	12.1	37	69	Fairfax County, VA	4.6	17	69	Clark County, NV	17.3
30	70	Palm Beach County, FL	11.8	5	69	Orange County, CA	4.6	11	70	Wayne County, MI	17.2
39	71	Erie County, NY	11.7	40	69	Westchester County, NY	4.6	73	71	El Paso County, TX	16.6
64	72	Baltimore County, MD	11.6	16	72	Santa Clara County, CA	4.5	13	71	Riverside County, CA	16.6
29	73	Allegheny County, PA	11.1	75	73	San Mateo County, CA	4.3	12	73	San Bernardino County, CA	15.9
68	74	San Francisco County, CA	10.7	21	74	Middlesex County, MA	4.2	26	74	Bronx County, NY	14.6
42	75	Pinellas County, FL	10.2	68	75	San Francisco County, CA	3.9	72	75	Kern County, CA	13.5

75 Largest Counties by 2003 Population
Selected Rankings

Expenditures per student, 2000–2001				Per capita personal income, 2002				Median household income, 1999			
Popu-lation rank	Expendi-tures rank	County	Expenditures per student (dollars) [col 53]	Popu-lation rank	Per capita income rank	County	Per capita income (dollars) [col 64]	Popu-lation rank	Median income rank	County	Median income (dollars) [col 55]
40	1	Westchester County, NY	13 915	18	1	New York County, NY	84 591	37	1	Fairfax County, VA	81 050
27	2	Nassau County, NY	13 601	48	2	Fairfield County, CT	59 727	16	2	Santa Clara County, CA	74 335
61	3	Essex County, NJ	12 888	40	3	Westchester County, NY	55 522	27	3	Nassau County, NY	72 030
23	4	Suffolk County, NY	12 592	68	4	San Francisco County, CA	54 639	45	4	Montgomery County, MD	71 551
49	5	Bergen County, NJ	11 743	75	5	San Mateo County, CA	53 315	75	5	San Mateo County, CA	70 819
26	6	Bronx County, NY	11 112	49	6	Bergen County, NJ	52 867	43	6	Du Page County, IL	67 887
7	6	Kings County, NY	11 112	37	7	Fairfax County, VA	52 199	23	7	Suffolk County, NY	65 288
18	6	New York County, NY	11 112	45	8	Montgomery County, MD	51 750	48	8	Fairfield County, CT	65 249
10	6	Queens County, NY	11 112	27	9	Nassau County, NY	49 543	49	9	Bergen County, NJ	65 241
63	10	Middlesex County, NJ	10 859	58	10	Fulton County, GA	47 478	36	10	Contra Costa County, CA	63 675
71	11	Monroe County, NY	10 684	66	11	Montgomery County, PA	47 461	40	11	Westchester County, NY	63 582
39	12	Erie County, NY	10 572	31	12	Oakland County, MI	47 394	31	12	Oakland County, MI	61 907
48	13	Fairfield County, CT	10 318	21	13	Middlesex County, MA	46 499	63	13	Middlesex County, NJ	61 446
66	14	Montgomery County, PA	10 254	16	13	Santa Clara County, CA	46 499	66	14	Montgomery County, PA	60 829
21	15	Middlesex County, MA	10 131	43	15	Du Page County, IL	45 214	21	15	Middlesex County, MA	60 821
51	16	Hartford County, CT	9 883	36	16	Contra Costa County, CA	44 326	62	16	Ventura County, CA	59 666
55	17	New Haven County, CT	9 757	32	17	Hennepin County, MN	44 302	5	17	Orange County, CA	58 820
45	18	Montgomery County, MD	9 543	14	18	King County, WA	44 135	24	18	Alameda County, CA	55 946
58	19	Fulton County, GA	9 303	30	19	Palm Beach County, FL	44 120	56	19	Prince George's County, MD	55 256
29	20	Allegheny County, PA	9 086	35	20	St. Louis County, MO	41 126	68	20	San Francisco County, CA	55 221
31	21	Oakland County, MI	9 068	51	21	Hartford County, CT	38 579	14	21	King County, WA	53 157
41	22	Milwaukee County, WI	9 049	67	22	Mecklenburg County, NC	38 556	60	22	Macomb County, MI	52 102
37	23	Fairfax County, VA	9 038	5	23	Orange County, CA	38 367	47	23	Honolulu County, HI	51 914
25	24	Cuyahoga County, OH	9 006	61	24	Essex County, NJ	38 312	32	24	Hennepin County, MN	51 711
70	25	Essex County, MA	8 941	70	25	Essex County, MA	38 309	70	25	Essex County, MA	51 576
32	26	Hennepin County, MN	8 894	64	26	Baltimore County, MD	38 159	51	26	Hartford County, CT	50 756
11	27	Wayne County, MI	8 684	24	27	Alameda County, CA	37 945	64	27	Baltimore County, MD	50 667
65	28	Worcester County, MA	8 610	23	28	Suffolk County, NY	37 650	67	28	Mecklenburg County, NC	50 579
60	29	Macomb County, MI	8 231	63	29	Middlesex County, NJ	37 449	35	29	St. Louis County, MO	50 532
2	30	Cook County, IL	8 226	3	30	Harris County, TX	36 825	55	30	New Haven County, CT	48 834
35	31	St. Louis County, MO	8 210	29	31	Allegheny County, PA	36 500	44	31	Salt Lake County, UT	48 373
33	32	Franklin County, OH	8 172	9	32	Dallas County, TX	36 289	65	32	Worcester County, MA	47 874
43	33	Du Page County, IL	8 163	57	33	Hamilton County, OH	35 883	58	33	Fulton County, GA	47 321
57	34	Hamilton County, OH	8 117	53	34	Travis County, TX	35 492	6	34	San Diego County, CA	47 067
52	35	Marion County, IN	8 113	55	35	New Haven County, CT	35 339	18	35	New York County, NY	47 030
64	36	Baltimore County, MD	8 051	2	36	Cook County, IL	35 224	53	36	Travis County, TX	46 761
68	37	San Francisco County, CA	8 035	6	37	San Diego County, CA	34 872	19	37	Tarrant County, TX	46 179
75	38	San Mateo County, CA	7 728	62	38	Ventura County, CA	34 572	2	38	Cook County, IL	45 922
56	39	Prince George's County, MD	7 625	74	39	Jefferson County, KY	33 466	4	39	Maricopa County, AZ	45 358
28	40	Sacramento County, CA	7 302	25	40	Cuyahoga County, OH	33 382	69	40	Pierce County, WA	45 204
16	41	Santa Clara County, CA	7 232	65	41	Worcester County, MA	33 229	30	41	Palm Beach County, FL	45 062
54	42	Fresno County, CA	7 181	42	42	Pinellas County, FL	33 167	61	42	Essex County, NJ	44 944
24	43	Alameda County, CA	7 152	33	43	Franklin County, OH	32 947	71	43	Monroe County, NY	44 891
6	44	San Diego County, CA	7 141	46	44	Shelby County, TN	32 914	17	44	Clark County, NV	44 616
74	45	Jefferson County, KY	7 079	60	45	Macomb County, MI	32 571	28	45	Sacramento County, CA	43 816
1	46	Los Angeles County, CA	7 063	71	46	Monroe County, NY	32 506	9	46	Dallas County, TX	43 324
53	47	Travis County, TX	7 049	52	47	Marion County, IN	32 129	13	47	Riverside County, CA	42 887
72	48	Kern County, CA	7 012	15	48	Broward County, FL	31 785	33	48	Franklin County, OH	42 734
67	49	Mecklenburg County, NC	7 010	47	49	Honolulu County, HI	31 707	3	49	Harris County, TX	42 598
14	50	King County, WA	6 738	19	50	Tarrant County, TX	31 307	10	50	Queens County, NY	42 439
22	51	Bexar County, TX	6 685	1	51	Los Angeles County, CA	30 804	1	51	Los Angeles County, CA	42 189
36	52	Contra Costa County, CA	6 625	56	52	Prince George's County, MD	30 489	12	52	San Bernardino County, CA	42 066
47	53	Honolulu County, HI	6 599	41	53	Milwaukee County, WI	30 456	15	53	Broward County, FL	41 691
13	54	Riverside County, CA	6 575	28	54	Sacramento County, CA	29 631	38	54	Orange County, FL	41 311
20	55	Philadelphia County, PA	6 571	59	55	Duval County, FL	29 624	57	55	Hamilton County, OH	40 964
8	56	Miami-Dade County, FL	6 552	34	56	Hillsborough County, FL	29 602	11	56	Wayne County, MI	40 776
69	57	Pierce County, WA	6 545	17	57	Clark County, NV	29 396	59	57	Duval County, FL	40 703
12	58	San Bernardino County, CA	6 523	69	58	Pierce County, WA	29 221	34	58	Hillsborough County, FL	40 663
3	59	Harris County, TX	6 504	39	59	Erie County, NY	29 208	52	59	Marion County, IN	40 421
5	60	Orange County, CA	6 421	4	60	Maricopa County, AZ	29 020	46	60	Shelby County, TN	39 593
62	61	Ventura County, CA	6 340	10	61	Queens County, NY	28 877	74	61	Jefferson County, KY	39 457
9	62	Dallas County, TX	6 307	44	62	Salt Lake County, UT	28 539	25	62	Cuyahoga County, OH	39 168
73	63	El Paso County, TX	6 302	22	63	Bexar County, TX	27 910	39	63	Erie County, NY	38 567
30	64	Palm Beach County, FL	6 266	38	64	Orange County, FL	27 695	29	64	Allegheny County, PA	38 329
42	65	Pinellas County, FL	6 150	11	65	Wayne County, MI	27 684	22	65	Bexar County, TX	38 328
19	66	Tarrant County, TX	6 138	8	66	Miami-Dade County, FL	26 780	41	66	Milwaukee County, WI	38 100
34	67	Hillsborough County, FL	6 055	20	67	Philadelphia County, PA	26 369	42	67	Pinellas County, FL	37 111
46	68	Shelby County, TN	5 953	50	68	Pima County, AZ	25 278	50	68	Pima County, AZ	36 758
15	69	Broward County, FL	5 853	7	69	Kings County, NY	25 138	8	69	Miami-Dade County, FL	35 966
38	70	Orange County, FL	5 721	13	70	Riverside County, CA	24 814	72	70	Kern County, CA	35 446
59	71	Duval County, FL	5 665	54	71	Fresno County, CA	23 492	54	71	Fresno County, CA	34 725
17	72	Clark County, NV	5 525	12	72	San Bernardino County, CA	23 379	7	72	Kings County, NY	32 135
50	73	Pima County, AZ	5 491	72	73	Kern County, CA	22 635	73	73	El Paso County, TX	31 051
4	74	Maricopa County, AZ	5 178	26	74	Bronx County, NY	20 950	20	74	Philadelphia County, PA	30 746
44	75	Salt Lake County, UT	4 543	73	75	El Paso County, TX	20 129	26	75	Bronx County, NY	27 611

75 Largest Counties by 2003 Population
Selected Rankings

Percent of persons below the poverty level, 1999				Percent of families with children below the poverty level, 1999				Median value of owner-occupied housing units, 2000			
Popu-lation rank	Poverty rate rank	County	Poverty rate [col 58]	Popu-lation rank	Poverty rate for families with children rank	County	Poverty rate for families with children [col 61]	Popu-lation rank	Median value rank	County	Median value in 2000 (dollars) [col 91]
26	1	Bronx County, NY	30.7	26	1	Bronx County, NY	36.5	18	1	New York County, NY	1 000 001 [1]
7	2	Kings County, NY	25.1	7	2	Kings County, NY	29.1	75	2	San Mateo County, CA	469 200
73	3	El Paso County, TX	23.8	18	3	New York County, NY	26.8	16	3	Santa Clara County, CA	446 400
54	4	Fresno County, CA	22.9	73	4	El Paso County, TX	26.6	68	4	San Francisco County, CA	396 400
20	4	Philadelphia County, PA	22.9	20	5	Philadelphia County, PA	26.0	40	5	Westchester County, NY	325 800
72	6	Kern County, CA	20.8	54	6	Fresno County, CA	24.8	47	6	Honolulu County, HI	309 000
18	7	New York County, NY	20.0	72	7	Kern County, CA	22.9	24	7	Alameda County, CA	303 100
8	8	Miami-Dade County, FL	18.0	1	8	Los Angeles County, CA	19.9	48	8	Fairfield County, CT	288 500
1	9	Los Angeles County, CA	17.9	8	9	Miami-Dade County, FL	19.3	5	9	Orange County, CA	270 000
11	10	Wayne County, MI	16.4	41	10	Milwaukee County, WI	18.5	36	10	Contra Costa County, CA	267 800
46	11	Shelby County, TN	16.0	11	10	Wayne County, MI	18.5	49	11	Bergen County, NJ	250 300
22	12	Bexar County, TX	15.9	46	12	Shelby County, TN	18.3	62	12	Ventura County, CA	248 700
12	13	San Bernardino County, CA	15.8	58	13	Fulton County, GA	18.2	21	13	Middlesex County, MA	247 900
58	14	Fulton County, GA	15.7	22	14	Bexar County, TX	18.0	27	14	Nassau County, NY	242 300
61	15	Essex County, NJ	15.6	61	15	Essex County, NJ	17.9	14	15	King County, WA	236 900
41	16	Milwaukee County, WI	15.3	12	16	San Bernardino County, CA	16.8	37	16	Fairfax County, VA	233 300
3	17	Harris County, TX	15.0	10	17	Queens County, NY	16.5	6	17	San Diego County, CA	227 200
50	18	Pima County, AZ	14.7	50	18	Pima County, AZ	16.4	7	18	Kings County, NY	224 100
10	19	Queens County, NY	14.6	3	19	Harris County, TX	16.3	45	19	Montgomery County, MD	221 800
13	20	Riverside County, CA	14.2	25	20	Cuyahoga County, OH	16.2	70	20	Essex County, MA	220 000
28	21	Sacramento County, CA	14.1	2	21	Cook County, IL	15.4	10	21	Queens County, NY	212 600
2	22	Cook County, IL	13.5	28	21	Sacramento County, CA	15.4	1	22	Los Angeles County, CA	209 300
9	23	Dallas County, TX	13.4	74	23	Jefferson County, KY	15.3	61	23	Essex County, NJ	208 400
25	24	Cuyahoga County, OH	13.1	39	24	Erie County, NY	15.2	43	24	Du Page County, IL	195 000
34	25	Hillsborough County, FL	12.5	13	25	Riverside County, CA	15.1	26	25	Bronx County, NY	190 400
53	25	Travis County, TX	12.5	9	26	Dallas County, TX	14.8	23	26	Suffolk County, NY	185 200
74	27	Jefferson County, KY	12.4	57	27	Hamilton County, OH	13.8	31	27	Oakland County, MI	181 200
6	27	San Diego County, CA	12.4	34	28	Hillsborough County, FL	13.7	58	28	Fulton County, GA	180 700
39	29	Erie County, NY	12.2	59	29	Duval County, FL	13.5	63	29	Middlesex County, NJ	168 500
38	30	Orange County, FL	12.1	6	30	San Diego County, CA	13.3	66	30	Montgomery County, PA	160 700
59	31	Duval County, FL	11.9	29	31	Allegheny County, PA	13.1	2	31	Cook County, IL	157 700
57	32	Hamilton County, OH	11.8	52	31	Marion County, IN	13.1	44	32	Salt Lake County, UT	157 000
4	33	Maricopa County, AZ	11.7	71	31	Monroe County, NY	13.1	55	33	New Haven County, CT	151 900
33	34	Franklin County, OH	11.6	38	34	Orange County, FL	13.0	69	34	Pierce County, WA	149 600
15	35	Broward County, FL	11.5	15	35	Broward County, FL	12.6	51	35	Hartford County, CT	147 300
52	36	Marion County, IN	11.4	4	36	Maricopa County, AZ	12.3	13	36	Riverside County, CA	146 500
68	37	San Francisco County, CA	11.3	33	37	Franklin County, OH	12.1	65	37	Worcester County, MA	146 000
29	38	Allegheny County, PA	11.2	17	38	Clark County, NV	11.8	56	38	Prince George's County, MD	145 600
71	38	Monroe County, NY	11.2	68	38	San Francisco County, CA	11.8	28	39	Sacramento County, CA	144 200
24	40	Alameda County, CA	11.0	30	40	Palm Beach County, FL	11.5	32	40	Hennepin County, MN	143 400
17	41	Clark County, NV	10.8	69	41	Pierce County, WA	11.3	67	41	Mecklenburg County, NC	141 800
19	42	Tarrant County, TX	10.6	19	41	Tarrant County, TX	11.3	17	42	Clark County, NV	139 500
69	43	Pierce County, WA	10.5	42	43	Pinellas County, FL	11.2	60	43	Macomb County, MI	139 200
5	44	Orange County, CA	10.3	55	44	New Haven County, CT	11.0	30	44	Palm Beach County, FL	135 200
42	45	Pinellas County, FL	10.0	53	44	Travis County, TX	11.0	53	45	Travis County, TX	134 700
47	46	Honolulu County, HI	9.9	24	46	Alameda County, CA	10.9	12	46	San Bernardino County, CA	131 500
30	46	Palm Beach County, FL	9.9	51	46	Hartford County, CT	10.9	4	47	Maricopa County, AZ	129 200
55	48	New Haven County, CT	9.5	47	48	Honolulu County, HI	10.3	15	48	Broward County, FL	128 600
51	49	Hartford County, CT	9.3	70	49	Essex County, MA	10.1	64	49	Baltimore County, MD	127 300
67	50	Mecklenburg County, NC	9.2	5	49	Orange County, CA	10.1	8	50	Miami-Dade County, FL	124 000
62	50	Ventura County, CA	9.2	65	51	Worcester County, MA	9.9	35	51	St. Louis County, MO	116 600
65	50	Worcester County, MA	9.2	40	52	Westchester County, NY	9.4	33	52	Franklin County, OH	116 200
70	53	Essex County, MA	8.9	67	53	Mecklenburg County, NC	9.3	50	53	Pima County, AZ	114 600
40	54	Westchester County, NY	8.8	62	54	Ventura County, CA	9.1	25	54	Cuyahoga County, OH	113 800
14	55	King County, WA	8.4	32	55	Hennepin County, MN	8.0	57	55	Hamilton County, OH	111 400
32	56	Hennepin County, MN	8.3	14	55	King County, WA	8.0	38	56	Orange County, FL	107 500
44	57	Salt Lake County, UT	8.0	44	55	Salt Lake County, UT	8.0	54	57	Fresno County, CA	104 900
56	58	Prince George's County, MD	7.7	36	58	Contra Costa County, CA	7.9	41	58	Milwaukee County, WI	103 200
36	59	Contra Costa County, CA	7.6	35	58	St. Louis County, MO	7.9	74	59	Jefferson County, KY	103 000
16	60	Santa Clara County, CA	7.5	48	60	Fairfield County, CT	7.2	11	60	Wayne County, MI	99 400
48	61	Fairfield County, CT	6.9	56	60	Prince George's County, MD	7.2	52	61	Marion County, IN	99 000
35	61	St. Louis County, MO	6.9	16	62	Santa Clara County, CA	6.8	71	62	Monroe County, NY	98 700
63	63	Middlesex County, NJ	6.6	64	63	Baltimore County, MD	6.5	34	63	Hillsborough County, FL	97 700
64	64	Baltimore County, MD	6.5	60	64	Macomb County, MI	6.3	42	64	Pinellas County, FL	96 500
21	64	Middlesex County, MA	6.5	21	64	Middlesex County, MA	6.3	72	65	Kern County, CA	93 300
23	66	Suffolk County, NY	6.0	63	66	Middlesex County, NJ	6.0	9	66	Dallas County, TX	92 700
75	67	San Mateo County, CA	5.8	23	67	Suffolk County, NY	5.7	46	67	Shelby County, TN	92 200
60	68	Macomb County, MI	5.6	31	68	Oakland County, MI	5.5	39	68	Erie County, NY	90 800
31	69	Oakland County, MI	5.5	45	69	Montgomery County, MD	5.0	19	69	Tarrant County, TX	90 300
45	70	Montgomery County, MD	5.4	27	70	Nassau County, NY	4.9	59	70	Duval County, FL	89 600
27	71	Nassau County, NY	5.2	75	70	San Mateo County, CA	4.9	3	71	Harris County, TX	87 000
49	72	Bergen County, NJ	5.0	49	72	Bergen County, NJ	4.6	29	72	Allegheny County, PA	84 200
37	73	Fairfax County, VA	4.5	37	73	Fairfax County, VA	4.3	22	73	Bexar County, TX	74 100
66	74	Montgomery County, PA	4.4	66	74	Montgomery County, PA	4.1	73	74	El Paso County, TX	69 600
43	75	Du Page County, IL	3.6	43	75	Du Page County, IL	3.5	20	75	Philadelphia County, PA	59 700

1. $1,000,001 is the top code symbolizing a median value over one million dollars.

75 Largest Counties by 2003 Population
Selected Rankings

	Median gross rent of renter-occupied housing units, 2000				Unemployment rate, 2003				Manufacturing employment as a percent of total nonfarm employment, 2001		
Population rank	Median rate rank	County	Median rent (dollars) [col 94]	Population rank	Unemployment rate rank	County	Unemployment rate [col 100]	Population rank	Manufacturing rank	County	Percent employed in manufacturing [col 107/col 105]
16	1	Santa Clara County, CA	1 185	54	1	Fresno County, CA	14.2	60	1	Macomb County, MI	26.5
75	2	San Mateo County, CA	1 144	72	2	Kern County, CA	12.3	70	2	Essex County, MA	19.6
37	3	Fairfax County, VA	998	26	3	Bronx County, NY	10.4	16	3	Santa Clara County, CA	19.3
27	4	Nassau County, NY	964	73	4	El Paso County, TX	9.7	71	4	Monroe County, NY	18.4
23	5	Suffolk County, NY	945	7	5	Kings County, NY	9.2	65	5	Worcester County, MA	17.5
68	6	San Francisco County, CA	928	11	6	Wayne County, MI	9.0	11	6	Wayne County, MI	15.8
5	7	Orange County, CA	923	18	7	New York County, NY	8.2	73	7	El Paso County, TX	15.5
45	8	Montgomery County, MD	914	16	7	Santa Clara County, CA	8.2	55	8	New Haven County, CT	15.4
36	9	Contra Costa County, CA	898	9	9	Dallas County, TX	7.9	5	9	Orange County, CA	15.4
62	10	Ventura County, CA	892	69	10	Pierce County, WA	7.8	41	10	Milwaukee County, WI	15.3
49	11	Bergen County, NJ	872	20	11	Philadelphia County, PA	7.6	1	11	Los Angeles County, CA	15.2
24	12	Alameda County, CA	852	2	12	Cook County, IL	7.3	12	12	San Bernardino County, CA	14.9
63	13	Middlesex County, NJ	845	61	12	Essex County, NJ	7.3	39	13	Erie County, NY	14.6
40	14	Westchester County, NY	839	8	14	Miami-Dade County, FL	7.2	62	14	Ventura County, CA	14.3
48	15	Fairfield County, CT	838	41	15	Milwaukee County, WI	7.1	24	15	Alameda County, CA	14.3
43	16	Du Page County, IL	837	3	16	Harris County, TX	7.0	25	16	Cuyahoga County, OH	13.9
21	17	Middlesex County, MA	835	1	16	Los Angeles County, CA	7.0	51	17	Hartford County, CT	13.8
47	18	Honolulu County, HI	802	10	18	Queens County, NY	6.9	19	18	Tarrant County, TX	13.6
18	19	New York County, NY	796	24	19	Alameda County, CA	6.8	21	19	Middlesex County, MA	13.6
10	20	Queens County, NY	775	25	19	Cuyahoga County, OH	6.8	57	20	Hamilton County, OH	13.4
6	21	San Diego County, CA	761	70	19	Essex County, MA	6.8	13	21	Riverside County, CA	13.2
14	22	King County, WA	758	14	19	King County, WA	6.8	74	22	Jefferson County, KY	12.9
15	23	Broward County, FL	757	68	19	San Francisco County, CA	6.8	2	23	Cook County, IL	12.9
66	23	Montgomery County, PA	757	65	24	Worcester County, MA	6.7	48	24	Fairfield County, CT	12.6
30	25	Palm Beach County, FL	739	60	25	Macomb County, MI	6.6	14	25	King County, WA	12.6
56	26	Prince George's County, MD	737	19	26	Tarrant County, TX	6.5	63	26	Middlesex County, NJ	12.5
53	27	Travis County, TX	727	46	27	Shelby County, TN	6.4	53	27	Travis County, TX	12.2
17	28	Clark County, NV	716	51	28	Hartford County, CT	6.2	23	28	Suffolk County, NY	12.1
58	29	Fulton County, GA	709	39	29	Erie County, NY	6.1	66	29	Montgomery County, PA	11.9
31	30	Oakland County, MI	707	13	29	Riverside County, CA	6.1	54	30	Fresno County, CA	11.8
1	31	Los Angeles County, CA	704	74	31	Jefferson County, KY	6.0	32	31	Hennepin County, MN	11.6
38	32	Orange County, FL	699	55	31	New Haven County, CT	6.0	52	32	Marion County, IN	11.6
67	33	Mecklenburg County, NC	693	53	33	Travis County, TX	5.9	43	33	Du Page County, IL	11.2
61	34	Essex County, NJ	675	58	34	Fulton County, GA	5.8	50	34	Pima County, AZ	11.1
7	35	Kings County, NY	672	67	34	Mecklenburg County, NC	5.8	44	35	Salt Lake County, UT	11.1
64	36	Baltimore County, MD	670	12	34	San Bernardino County, CA	5.8	6	36	San Diego County, CA	11.1
4	37	Maricopa County, AZ	666	22	37	Bexar County, TX	5.7	9	37	Dallas County, TX	10.9
55	37	New Haven County, CT	666	59	37	Duval County, FL	5.7	49	38	Bergen County, NJ	10.6
70	39	Essex County, MA	665	44	37	Salt Lake County, UT	5.7	4	39	Maricopa County, AZ	10.3
13	40	Riverside County, CA	660	71	40	Monroe County, NY	5.6	69	40	Pierce County, WA	10.2
28	41	Sacramento County, CA	659	30	40	Palm Beach County, FL	5.6	31	41	Oakland County, MI	10.0
32	42	Hennepin County, MN	654	28	40	Sacramento County, CA	5.6	61	42	Essex County, NJ	9.9
2	43	Cook County, IL	648	15	43	Broward County, FL	5.5	35	43	St. Louis County, MO	9.9
12	43	San Bernardino County, CA	648	36	43	Contra Costa County, CA	5.5	42	44	Pinellas County, FL	9.8
9	45	Dallas County, TX	647	52	45	Marion County, IN	5.4	3	45	Harris County, TX	9.3
8	45	Miami-Dade County, FL	647	63	45	Middlesex County, NJ	5.4	64	46	Baltimore County, MD	9.2
51	47	Hartford County, CT	645	17	47	Clark County, NV	5.3	10	47	Queens County, NY	8.9
44	48	Salt Lake County, UT	638	62	47	Ventura County, CA	5.3	7	48	Kings County, NY	8.9
69	49	Pierce County, WA	624	43	49	Du Page County, IL	5.2	72	49	Kern County, CA	8.3
34	50	Hillsborough County, FL	623	31	49	Oakland County, MI	5.2	33	50	Franklin County, OH	8.1
26	51	Bronx County, NY	620	29	51	Allegheny County, PA	5.1	75	51	San Mateo County, CA	7.9
42	52	Pinellas County, FL	616	57	51	Hamilton County, OH	5.1	29	52	Allegheny County, PA	7.6
71	53	Monroe County, NY	612	21	51	Middlesex County, MA	5.1	46	53	Shelby County, TN	7.3
19	53	Tarrant County, TX	612	75	51	San Mateo County, CA	5.1	67	54	Mecklenburg County, NC	7.2
59	55	Duval County, FL	604	35	51	St. Louis County, MO	5.1	59	55	Duval County, FL	6.9
60	56	Macomb County, MI	603	64	56	Baltimore County, MD	4.9	8	56	Miami-Dade County, FL	6.6
35	57	St. Louis County, MO	601	49	56	Bergen County, NJ	4.9	22	57	Bexar County, TX	6.6
33	58	Franklin County, OH	595	33	56	Franklin County, OH	4.9	20	58	Philadelphia County, PA	6.5
3	59	Harris County, TX	590	4	56	Maricopa County, AZ	4.9	27	59	Nassau County, NY	6.4
65	60	Worcester County, MA	580	38	56	Orange County, FL	4.9	28	60	Sacramento County, CA	6.2
20	61	Philadelphia County, PA	569	48	61	Fairfield County, CT	4.8	30	61	Palm Beach County, FL	6.0
52	62	Marion County, IN	567	32	62	Hennepin County, MN	4.7	34	62	Hillsborough County, FL	6.0
46	63	Shelby County, TN	566	56	62	Prince George's County, MD	4.7	36	63	Contra Costa County, CA	5.8
22	64	Bexar County, TX	556	66	64	Montgomery County, PA	4.4	38	64	Orange County, FL	5.8
41	65	Milwaukee County, WI	555	42	64	Pinellas County, FL	4.4	15	65	Broward County, FL	5.6
50	66	Pima County, AZ	544	23	64	Suffolk County, NY	4.4	26	66	Bronx County, NY	5.0
25	67	Cuyahoga County, OH	541	50	67	Pima County, AZ	4.3	40	67	Westchester County, NY	4.4
54	68	Fresno County, CA	534	6	67	San Diego County, CA	4.3	56	68	Prince George's County, MD	4.2
11	69	Wayne County, MI	530	34	69	Hillsborough County, FL	4.1	58	69	Fulton County, GA	4.2
72	70	Kern County, CA	518	40	70	Westchester County, NY	4.0	47	70	Honolulu County, HI	3.6
29	71	Allegheny County, PA	516	47	71	Honolulu County, HI	3.9	68	71	San Francisco County, CA	3.4
39	71	Erie County, NY	516	27	71	Nassau County, NY	3.9	45	72	Montgomery County, MD	3.1
74	73	Jefferson County, KY	494	5	73	Orange County, CA	3.8	17	73	Clark County, NV	2.9
57	74	Hamilton County, OH	485	45	74	Montgomery County, MD	2.6	18	74	New York County, NY	2.8
73	75	El Paso County, TX	468	37	75	Fairfax County, VA	2.5	37	75	Fairfax County, VA	2.3

75 Largest Counties by 2003 Population
Selected Rankings

Employment in professional, scientific, and technical services as a percent of total nonfarm employment, 2001				Finance and insurance employment as a percent of total nonfarm employment, 2001				Per capita local government taxes, 2002			
Population rank	Services rank	County	Percent employed in services [col 110/col 105]	Population rank	Finance and insurance rank	County	Percent employed in finance and insurance [col 109/col 105]	Population rank	Local taxes rank	County	Local per capita taxes (dollars) [col 181]
37	1	Fairfax County, VA	25.6	18	1	New York County, NY	17.2	27	1	Nassau County, NY	3 431
45	2	Montgomery County, MD	16.6	51	2	Hartford County, CT	14.2	40	2	Westchester County, NY	3 094
68	3	San Francisco County, CA	14.5	67	3	Mecklenburg County, NC	14.1	26	3	Bronx County, NY	2 750
16	4	Santa Clara County, CA	14.1	59	4	Duval County, FL	12.6	7	3	Kings County, NY	2 750
18	5	New York County, NY	13.6	68	5	San Francisco County, CA	11.7	18	3	New York County, NY	2 750
21	6	Middlesex County, MA	12.7	66	6	Montgomery County, PA	11.3	10	3	Queens County, NY	2 750
63	7	Middlesex County, NJ	12.6	20	7	Philadelphia County, PA	9.7	23	7	Suffolk County, NY	2 721
58	8	Fulton County, GA	11.5	33	8	Franklin County, OH	9.7	45	8	Montgomery County, MD	2 669
75	9	San Mateo County, CA	11.3	48	9	Fairfield County, CT	9.2	68	9	San Francisco County, CA	2 634
1	10	Los Angeles County, CA	11.1	32	10	Hennepin County, MN	8.9	58	10	Fulton County, GA	2 330
20	11	Philadelphia County, PA	10.5	28	11	Sacramento County, CA	8.5	49	11	Bergen County, NJ	2 312
31	12	Oakland County, MI	10.3	36	12	Contra Costa County, CA	8.5	48	12	Fairfield County, CT	2 213
56	13	Prince George's County, MD	10.2	41	13	Milwaukee County, WI	8.4	25	13	Cuyahoga County, OH	2 142
6	14	San Diego County, CA	9.3	34	14	Hillsborough County, FL	8.2	16	14	Santa Clara County, CA	2 078
53	15	Travis County, TX	9.3	58	15	Fulton County, GA	8.0	53	15	Travis County, TX	2 025
34	16	Hillsborough County, FL	9.1	27	16	Nassau County, NY	7.9	9	16	Dallas County, TX	2 000
2	17	Cook County, IL	8.5	2	17	Cook County, IL	7.5	33	17	Franklin County, OH	1 979
14	18	King County, WA	8.4	25	18	Cuyahoga County, OH	7.3	37	18	Fairfax County, VA	1 969
48	19	Fairfield County, CT	8.3	4	19	Maricopa County, AZ	7.0	43	19	Du Page County, IL	1 918
36	20	Contra Costa County, CA	8.3	64	20	Baltimore County, MD	7.0	57	20	Hamilton County, OH	1 902
29	21	Allegheny County, PA	8.1	62	21	Ventura County, CA	7.0	2	21	Cook County, IL	1 863
43	22	Du Page County, IL	8.1	29	22	Allegheny County, PA	7.0	63	22	Middlesex County, NJ	1 800
32	23	Hennepin County, MN	8.0	22	23	Bexar County, TX	6.9	75	23	San Mateo County, CA	1 793
61	24	Essex County, NJ	7.9	74	24	Jefferson County, KY	6.8	20	24	Philadelphia County, PA	1 772
27	25	Nassau County, NY	7.9	44	25	Salt Lake County, UT	6.7	30	25	Palm Beach County, FL	1 761
66	26	Montgomery County, PA	7.8	9	26	Dallas County, TX	6.6	3	26	Harris County, TX	1 722
9	27	Dallas County, TX	7.8	5	27	Orange County, CA	6.4	51	27	Hartford County, CT	1 714
5	28	Orange County, CA	7.6	35	28	St. Louis County, MO	6.3	66	28	Montgomery County, PA	1 713
3	29	Harris County, TX	7.6	61	29	Essex County, NJ	6.2	14	29	King County, WA	1 701
24	30	Alameda County, CA	7.5	42	30	Pinellas County, FL	6.1	71	30	Monroe County, NY	1 681
64	31	Baltimore County, MD	7.1	52	31	Marion County, IN	6.0	61	31	Essex County, NJ	1 670
23	32	Suffolk County, NY	6.9	39	32	Erie County, NY	6.0	24	32	Alameda County, CA	1 655
44	33	Salt Lake County, UT	6.9	57	33	Hamilton County, OH	5.9	21	33	Middlesex County, MA	1 622
67	34	Mecklenburg County, NC	6.9	15	34	Broward County, FL	5.9	19	34	Tarrant County, TX	1 604
57	35	Hamilton County, OH	6.9	31	35	Oakland County, MI	5.8	29	35	Allegheny County, PA	1 593
25	36	Cuyahoga County, OH	6.8	49	36	Bergen County, NJ	5.7	55	36	New Haven County, CT	1 587
4	37	Maricopa County, AZ	6.7	65	37	Worcester County, MA	5.7	64	37	Baltimore County, MD	1 579
40	38	Westchester County, NY	6.6	8	38	Miami-Dade County, FL	5.6	35	38	St. Louis County, MO	1 511
35	39	St. Louis County, MO	6.6	30	39	Palm Beach County, FL	5.5	39	39	Erie County, NY	1 484
28	40	Sacramento County, CA	6.5	43	40	Du Page County, IL	5.4	67	40	Mecklenburg County, NC	1 476
33	41	Franklin County, OH	6.5	45	41	Montgomery County, MD	5.4	46	41	Shelby County, TN	1 446
49	42	Bergen County, NJ	6.5	40	42	Westchester County, NY	5.1	52	42	Marion County, IN	1 440
8	43	Miami-Dade County, FL	6.4	19	43	Tarrant County, TX	5.1	32	43	Hennepin County, MN	1 439
62	44	Ventura County, CA	6.4	37	44	Fairfax County, VA	5.0	38	44	Orange County, FL	1 397
30	45	Palm Beach County, FL	6.2	47	45	Honolulu County, HI	5.0	15	45	Broward County, FL	1 333
15	46	Broward County, FL	6.2	14	46	King County, WA	4.9	41	46	Milwaukee County, WI	1 300
51	47	Hartford County, CT	6.2	63	47	Middlesex County, NJ	4.9	70	47	Essex County, MA	1 295
38	48	Orange County, FL	6.0	54	48	Fresno County, CA	4.8	31	48	Oakland County, MI	1 287
22	49	Bexar County, TX	5.9	75	49	San Mateo County, CA	4.7	5	49	Orange County, CA	1 272
42	50	Pinellas County, FL	5.7	53	50	Travis County, TX	4.7	8	50	Miami-Dade County, FL	1 271
71	51	Monroe County, NY	5.7	1	51	Los Angeles County, CA	4.7	56	51	Prince George's County, MD	1 265
72	52	Kern County, CA	5.5	3	52	Harris County, TX	4.7	65	52	Worcester County, MA	1 255
52	53	Marion County, IN	5.4	23	53	Suffolk County, NY	4.6	36	53	Contra Costa County, CA	1 250
50	54	Pima County, AZ	5.4	38	54	Orange County, FL	4.6	1	54	Los Angeles County, CA	1 222
70	55	Essex County, MA	5.3	55	55	New Haven County, CT	4.5	42	55	Pinellas County, FL	1 202
47	56	Honolulu County, HI	5.2	46	56	Shelby County, TN	4.4	4	56	Maricopa County, AZ	1 184
41	57	Milwaukee County, WI	5.1	11	57	Wayne County, MI	4.4	17	57	Clark County, NV	1 163
39	58	Erie County, NY	5.1	6	58	San Diego County, CA	4.4	62	58	Ventura County, CA	1 155
55	59	New Haven County, CT	4.9	69	59	Pierce County, WA	4.2	22	59	Bexar County, TX	1 143
19	60	Tarrant County, TX	4.9	72	60	Kern County, CA	4.1	34	60	Hillsborough County, FL	1 137
59	61	Duval County, FL	4.8	70	61	Essex County, MA	3.9	6	61	San Diego County, CA	1 134
60	62	Macomb County, MI	4.7	56	62	Prince George's County, MD	3.8	74	62	Jefferson County, KY	1 100
11	63	Wayne County, MI	4.7	17	63	Clark County, NV	3.7	11	62	Wayne County, MI	1 100
17	64	Clark County, NV	4.6	7	64	Kings County, NY	3.6	59	64	Duval County, FL	1 090
74	65	Jefferson County, KY	4.6	71	65	Monroe County, NY	3.6	50	65	Pima County, AZ	1 069
65	66	Worcester County, MA	4.3	73	66	El Paso County, TX	3.5	44	66	Salt Lake County, UT	1 056
46	67	Shelby County, TN	4.2	24	67	Alameda County, CA	3.5	69	67	Pierce County, WA	989
54	68	Fresno County, CA	4.2	12	68	San Bernardino County, CA	3.3	28	68	Sacramento County, CA	943
69	69	Pierce County, WA	3.6	21	69	Middlesex County, MA	3.1	13	69	Riverside County, CA	942
73	70	El Paso County, TX	3.6	50	70	Pima County, AZ	3.0	73	70	El Paso County, TX	917
7	71	Kings County, NY	3.3	10	71	Queens County, NY	2.6	60	71	Macomb County, MI	861
13	72	Riverside County, CA	2.9	13	72	Riverside County, CA	2.5	72	72	Kern County, CA	835
12	73	San Bernardino County, CA	2.8	60	73	Macomb County, MI	2.1	54	73	Fresno County, CA	761
10	74	Queens County, NY	2.6	16	74	Santa Clara County, CA	2.1	12	74	San Bernardino County, CA	749
26	75	Bronx County, NY	2.1	26	75	Bronx County, NY	1.4	47	75	Honolulu County, HI	596

75 Largest Counties by 2003 Population
Selected Rankings

Violent crime rate, 2000 (violent crimes known to police)

Population rank	Crime rate rank	County	Violent crime rate (per 100,000 population) [col 46]
58	1	Fulton County, GA	1 356
20	2	Philadelphia County, PA	1 316
46	3	Shelby County, TN	1 216
11	4	Wayne County, MI	1 176
34	5	Hillsborough County, FL	1 122
8	6	Miami-Dade County, FL	1 116
67	7	Mecklenburg County, NC	1 091
38	8	Orange County, FL	1 039
56	9	Prince George's County, MD	1 026
61	10	Essex County, NJ	967
3	11	Harris County, TX	912
59	12	Duval County, FL	902
1	12	Los Angeles County, CA	902
52	14	Marion County, IN	894
9	15	Dallas County, TX	862
64	16	Baltimore County, MD	844
42	17	Pinellas County, FL	824
26	18	Bronx County, NY	790
7	18	Kings County, NY	790
18	18	New York County, NY	790
10	18	Queens County, NY	790
68	22	San Francisco County, CA	758
30	23	Palm Beach County, FL	747
22	24	Bexar County, TX	727
17	25	Clark County, NV	726
33	26	Franklin County, OH	696
41	27	Milwaukee County, WI	664
24	28	Alameda County, CA	646
57	29	Hamilton County, OH	640
28	29	Sacramento County, CA	640
50	31	Pima County, AZ	631
54	32	Fresno County, CA	616
73	33	El Paso County, TX	606
74	34	Jefferson County, KY	595
13	35	Riverside County, CA	594
4	36	Maricopa County, AZ	565
12	37	San Bernardino County, CA	563
25	38	Cuyahoga County, OH	556
69	39	Pierce County, WA	555
15	40	Broward County, FL	545
19	41	Tarrant County, TX	534
29	42	Allegheny County, PA	523
72	43	Kern County, CA	491
39	44	Erie County, NY	482
6	45	San Diego County, CA	481
32	46	Hennepin County, MN	479
65	47	Worcester County, MA	453
36	48	Contra Costa County, CA	433
53	49	Travis County, TX	428
70	50	Essex County, MA	398
14	51	King County, WA	396
55	52	New Haven County, CT	383
51	53	Hartford County, CT	359
16	54	Santa Clara County, CA	357
44	55	Salt Lake County, UT	351
31	56	Oakland County, MI	316
48	57	Fairfield County, CT	312
60	58	Macomb County, MI	310
71	58	Monroe County, NY	310
35	60	St. Louis County, MO	297
47	61	Honolulu County, HI	289
75	62	San Mateo County, CA	284
40	63	Westchester County, NY	281
5	64	Orange County, CA	278
62	65	Ventura County, CA	259
45	66	Montgomery County, MD	234
63	67	Middlesex County, NJ	230
21	68	Middlesex County, MA	221
23	69	Suffolk County, NY	218
27	70	Nassau County, NY	198
66	71	Montgomery County, PA	197
49	72	Bergen County, NJ	120
37	73	Fairfax County, VA	59
2	74	Cook County, IL	NA
43	74	Du Page County, IL	NA

Military as a percent of all federal employment, 2002

Population rank	Military rank	County	Percent federal employment military [col 193/col 192 + 193]
6	1	San Diego County, CA	74.9
69	2	Pierce County, WA	73.0
47	3	Honolulu County, HI	64.9
12	4	San Bernardino County, CA	64.1
59	5	Duval County, FL	61.8
22	6	Bexar County, TX	59.7
73	7	El Paso County, TX	59.1
17	8	Clark County, NV	51.0
62	9	Ventura County, CA	50.2
50	10	Pima County, AZ	47.4
66	11	Montgomery County, PA	42.7
34	12	Hillsborough County, FL	40.0
65	13	Worcester County, MA	39.8
4	14	Maricopa County, AZ	39.3
35	15	St. Louis County, MO	34.0
72	16	Kern County, CA	33.9
7	17	Kings County, NY	33.6
44	18	Salt Lake County, UT	32.4
30	19	Palm Beach County, FL	31.4
31	20	Oakland County, MI	30.8
27	21	Nassau County, NY	30.7
5	22	Orange County, CA	30.5
70	23	Essex County, MA	30.0
48	24	Fairfield County, CT	30.0
49	25	Bergen County, NJ	29.6
15	26	Broward County, FL	29.1
42	27	Pinellas County, FL	29.0
13	27	Riverside County, CA	28.8
71	29	Monroe County, NY	27.6
21	30	Middlesex County, MA	27.6
32	31	Hennepin County, MN	26.4
63	32	Middlesex County, NJ	26.4
43	33	Du Page County, IL	26.3
75	34	San Mateo County, CA	25.2
8	35	Miami-Dade County, FL	25.1
3	36	Harris County, TX	24.9
56	37	Prince George's County, MD	24.3
1	38	Los Angeles County, CA	24.0
14	39	King County, WA	23.9
41	40	Milwaukee County, WI	23.6
28	41	Sacramento County, CA	23.6
19	42	Tarrant County, TX	23.5
24	43	Alameda County, CA	23.4
46	44	Shelby County, TN	23.3
67	45	Mecklenburg County, NC	21.9
29	46	Allegheny County, PA	21.6
16	47	Santa Clara County, CA	21.3
55	48	New Haven County, CT	21.1
60	49	Macomb County, MI	20.9
33	50	Franklin County, OH	20.8
10	51	Queens County, NY	20.7
38	52	Orange County, FL	20.6
51	53	Hartford County, CT	20.4
52	54	Marion County, IN	20.3
40	55	Westchester County, NY	19.7
36	56	Contra Costa County, CA	19.6
11	57	Wayne County, MI	19.6
25	58	Cuyahoga County, OH	19.1
2	59	Cook County, IL	18.6
9	60	Dallas County, TX	18.3
57	61	Hamilton County, OH	16.8
53	62	Travis County, TX	16.5
39	63	Erie County, NY	16.1
26	64	Bronx County, NY	15.5
37	65	Fairfax County, VA	14.8
58	66	Fulton County, GA	14.8
23	67	Suffolk County, NY	14.5
45	68	Montgomery County, MD	12.5
61	69	Essex County, NJ	11.9
74	70	Jefferson County, KY	11.8
20	71	Philadelphia County, PA	11.8
54	72	Fresno County, CA	11.1
64	73	Baltimore County, MD	11.0
18	74	New York County, NY	7.6
68	75	San Francisco County, CA	7.1

Percentage of votes for George W. Bush, 2004

Population rank	Vote for Bush rank	County	Percent of votes for Bush [col 196]
72	1	Kern County, CA	66.9
19	2	Tarrant County, TX	62.5
44	3	Salt Lake County, UT	59.7
5	4	Orange County, CA	59.6
54	5	Fresno County, CA	57.9
13	6	Riverside County, CA	57.8
59	7	Duval County, FL	57.7
4	8	Maricopa County, AZ	56.9
12	9	San Bernardino County, CA	55.7
22	10	Bexar County, TX	54.9
3	10	Harris County, TX	54.9
43	12	Du Page County, IL	54.3
34	13	Hillsborough County, FL	53.0
57	14	Hamilton County, OH	52.8
6	15	San Diego County, CA	52.2
62	16	Ventura County, CA	50.7
17	17	Clark County, NV	50.5
9	18	Dallas County, TX	50.4
60	19	Macomb County, MI	50.2
38	20	Orange County, FL	49.6
42	20	Pinellas County, FL	49.6
31	22	Oakland County, MI	49.3
28	23	Sacramento County, CA	48.9
74	24	Jefferson County, KY	48.8
52	25	Marion County, IN	48.7
23	25	Suffolk County, NY	48.7
47	27	Honolulu County, HI	48.3
69	28	Pierce County, WA	48.2
71	29	Monroe County, NY	48.0
67	30	Mecklenburg County, NC	47.9
49	31	Bergen County, NJ	47.7
48	32	Fairfield County, CT	47.3
64	33	Baltimore County, MD	47.1
50	34	Pima County, AZ	47.0
37	35	Fairfax County, VA	46.6
27	35	Nassau County, NY	46.6
8	37	Miami-Dade County, FL	45.9
33	38	Franklin County, OH	45.7
35	39	St. Louis County, MO	45.1
66	40	Montgomery County, PA	44.0
55	41	New Haven County, CT	43.9
73	42	El Paso County, TX	43.3
63	43	Middlesex County, NJ	42.9
65	44	Worcester County, MA	42.6
53	45	Travis County, TX	42.2
29	46	Allegheny County, PA	42.1
46	47	Shelby County, TN	42.0
39	48	Erie County, NY	41.5
70	49	Essex County, MA	40.7
40	50	Westchester County, NY	40.6
32	51	Hennepin County, MN	39.5
51	52	Hartford County, CT	39.4
58	53	Fulton County, GA	39.2
30	54	Palm Beach County, FL	39.0
41	55	Milwaukee County, WI	37.4
36	56	Contra Costa County, CA	36.7
1	57	Los Angeles County, CA	35.9
21	58	Middlesex County, MA	34.7
16	58	Santa Clara County, CA	34.7
15	60	Broward County, FL	34.5
14	61	King County, WA	34.1
45	62	Montgomery County, MD	33.2
25	63	Cuyahoga County, OH	33.1
11	64	Wayne County, MI	29.9
2	65	Cook County, IL	29.4
61	65	Essex County, NJ	29.4
75	65	San Mateo County, CA	29.4
10	68	Queens County, NY	28.0
7	69	Kings County, NY	24.8
24	70	Alameda County, CA	24.4
20	71	Philadelphia County, PA	19.3
56	72	Prince George's County, MD	17.5
26	73	Bronx County, NY	16.7
18	74	New York County, NY	16.6
68	75	San Francisco County, CA	15.4

All Counties
Selected Rankings

Defense contracts, 2002–2003				Non-defense contracts, 2002–2003				Federal grants, 2002–2003			
Population rank	Defense contracts rank	County	Defense contracts (millions of dollars) [col 172]	Population rank	Non-defense contracts rank	County	Non-defense contracts (millions of dollars) [col 173]	Population rank	Grants rank	County	Grants (millions of dollars) [col 174 + 175 + 176 + 177]
1	1	Los Angeles County, CA	10 431	101	1	District of Columbia	9 623	1	1	Los Angeles, CA	14 158
19	2	Tarrant County, TX	9 968	3	2	Harris County, TX	4 480	28	2	Sacramento, CA	8 268
37	3	Fairfax County, VA	6 555	45	3	Montgomery County, MD	4 411	2	3	Cook, IL	8 009
179	4	St. Louis city, MO	4 907	37	4	Fairfax County, VA	3 773	195	4	Albany, NY	6 938
6	5	San Diego County, CA	4 698	1	5	Los Angeles County, CA	3 696	78	5	Suffolk, MA	5 341
4	6	Maricopa County, AZ	4 277	705	6	Anderson County, TN	2 421	20	6	Philadelphia, PA	4 835
203	7	Madison County, AL	4 040	304	7	Arlington County, VA	2 415	8	7	Miami-Dade, FL	4 326
16	8	Santa Clara County, CA	3 786	98	8	Bernalillo County, NM	2 401	101	8	District of Columbia	4 310
51	9	Hartford County, CT	3 445	365	9	Benton County, WA	2 391	53	9	Travis, TX	4 281
21	10	Middlesex County, MA	3 181	24	10	Alameda County, CA	2 307	92	10	Baltimore city, MD	3 838
50	11	Pima County, AZ	2 782	56	11	Prince George's County, MD	2 300	6	11	San Diego, CA	3 791
223	12	New London County, CT	2 350	1 870	12	Los Alamos County, NM	1 994	11	12	Wayne, MI	3 669
304	13	Arlington County, VA	2 348	2	13	Cook County, IL	1 993	33	13	Franklin, OH	3 377
74	14	Jefferson County, KY	2 199	391	14	Aiken County, SC	1 598	4	14	Maricopa, AZ	3 372
5	15	Orange County, CA	2 137	1 703	15	Fairfax City, VA	1 350	3	15	Harris, TX	3 299
38	16	Orange County, FL	2 026	9	16	Dallas County, TX	1 270	58	16	Fulton, GA	3 052
22	17	Bexar County, TX	1 931	766	17	McCracken County, KY	1 188	14	17	King, WA	2 942
247	18	Norfolk City, VA	1 856	58	18	Fulton County, GA	1 172	24	18	Alameda, CA	2 575
14	19	King County, WA	1 810	22	19	Bexar County, TX	1 080	21	19	Middlesex, MA	2 557
3	20	Harris County, TX	1 786	110	20	Jefferson County, CO	1 079	232	20	Dauphin, PA	2 521
20	20	Philadelphia County, PA	1 786	21	21	Middlesex County, MA	1 061	245	21	Leon, FL	2 520
101	22	District of Columbia	1 753	118	22	Brevard County, FL	1 016	29	22	Allegheny, PA	2 484
47	23	Honolulu County, HI	1 625	92	23	Baltimore city, MD	996	68	23	San Francisco, CA	2 422
70	24	Essex County, MA	1 581	617	24	Bonneville County, ID	982	25	24	Cuyahoga, OH	2 311
48	25	Fairfield County, CT	1 574	17	25	Clark County, NV	943	61	25	Essex, NJ	2 073
60	26	Macomb County, MI	1 532	16	26	Santa Clara County, CA	935	16	26	Santa Clara, CA	2 070
105	27	El Paso County, CO	1 518	83	27	Jackson County, MO	791	52	27	Wake, NC	2 069
9	28	Dallas County, TX	1 513	29	28	Allegheny County, PA	715	76	28	Marion, IN	2 054
264	29	Loudoun County, VA	1 430	68	29	San Francisco County, CA	676	208	29	Ingham, MI	2 027
1 703	30	Fairfax City, VA	1 408	203	30	Madison County, AL	671	300	30	Sangamon, IL	2 024
421	31	Jackson County, MS	1 359	6	31	San Diego County, CA	638	9	31	Dallas, TX	1 982
118	32	Brevard County, FL	1 316	5	32	Orange County, CA	635	102	32	Denver, CO	1 967
438	33	Alexandria City, VA	1 298	129	33	Orleans County, LA	626	51	33	Hartford, CT	1 938
45	34	Montgomery County, MD	1 263	761	34	Lynchburg City, VA	623	100	34	Davidson, TN	1 921
57	35	Hamilton County, OH	1 258	80	35	Oklahoma County, OK	620	22	35	Bexar, TX	1 880
141	36	Burlington County, NJ	1 243	57	36	Hamilton County, OH	615	140	36	Dane, WI	1 829
581	37	St. Mary's County, MD	1 239	23	37	Suffolk County, NY	615	41	36	Milwaukee, WI	1 829
116	38	Anne Arundel County, MD	1 160	11	38	Wayne County, MI	568	5	38	Orange, CA	1 823
46	39	Shelby County, TN	1 137	4	39	Maricopa County, AZ	551	172	39	Mercer, NJ	1 811
86	40	Cobb County, GA	1 133	67	40	Mecklenburg County, NC	537	32	40	Hennepin, MN	1 785
231	41	Davis County, UT	1 105	270	41	Frederick County, MD	515	87	41	Providence, RI	1 708
2	42	Cook County, IL	1 068	192	42	Hamilton County, TN	508	364	42	Rensselaer, NY	1 657
129	43	Orleans County, LA	1 047	438	43	Alexandria City, VA	506	39	43	Erie, NY	1 624
32	44	Hennepin County, MN	1 036	102	44	Denver County, CO	490	117	44	Ramsey, MN	1 586
56	45	Prince George's County, MD	1 034	20	45	Philadelphia County, PA	489	12	45	San Bernardino, CA	1 554
29	46	Allegheny County, PA	1 016	46	46	Shelby County, TN	472	148	46	East Baton Rouge, LA	1 548
52	47	Marion County, IN	999	502	47	Washington County, TN	462	23	47	Suffolk, NY	1 528
91	48	Monmouth County, NJ	948	14	48	King County, WA	453	46	48	Shelby, TN	1 521
320	49	Okaloosa County, FL	931	25	49	Cuyahoga County, OH	450	55	49	New Haven, CT	1 520
59	50	Duval County, FL	847	2 401	50	Falls Church City, VA	405	295	50	Richmond City, VA	1 513
1 227	51	Sagadahoc County, ME	752	32	51	Hennepin County, MN	403	44	51	Salt Lake, UT	1 455
80	52	Oklahoma County, OK	740	1 035	52	Box Elder County, UT	401	179	52	St. Louis city, MO	1 433
28	53	Sacramento County, CA	738	480	53	Potter County, TX	385	47	53	Honolulu, HI	1 416
42	54	Pinellas County, FL	713	390	54	Hampton City, VA	383	346	54	Brazos, TX	1 414
92	55	Baltimore city, MD	696	711	55	Leavenworth County, KS	375	57	55	Hamilton, OH	1 391
132	56	Sedgwick County, KS	686	179	56	St. Louis city, MO	360	79	56	Multnomah, OR	1 352
85	57	Norfolk County, MA	659	156	57	Knox County, TN	359	80	57	Oklahoma, OK	1 301
215	58	Anchorage County, AK	643	137	58	Kane County, IL	337	262	58	Thurston, WA	1 299
73	58	El Paso County, TX	643	211	59	Boulder County, CO	332	40	59	Westchester, NY	1 291
104	60	Montgomery County, OH	628	79	60	Multnomah County, OR	331	129	60	Orleans, LA	1 286
221	61	St. Joseph County, IN	620	100	61	Davidson County, TN	316	27	61	Nassau, NY	1 276
150	62	Santa Barbara County, CA	616	249	62	Durham County, NC	313	13	62	Riverside, CA	1 258
349	63	Winnebago County, WI	614	116	63	Anne Arundel County, MD	307	45	63	Montgomery, MD	1 236
62	64	Ventura County, CA	608	78	64	Suffolk County, MA	303	63	64	Middlesex, NJ	1 218
184	65	Charleston County, SC	605	230	65	St. Clair County, IL	299	50	65	Pima, AZ	1 213
650	66	Hunt County, TX	605	387	66	Schenectady County, NY	288	71	66	Monroe, NY	1 206
23	67	Suffolk County, NY	595	8	67	Miami-Dade County, FL	282	59	67	Duval, FL	1 195
34	68	Hillsborough County, FL	590	194	68	Williamson County, TX	274	94	68	Hudson, NJ	1 144
240	69	Bell County, TX	580	38	69	Orange County, FL	267	169	69	Pulaski, AR	1 144
58	70	Fulton County, GA	558	39	70	Erie County, NY	265	54	70	Fresno, CA	1 139
193	71	Cumberland County, NC	555	33	71	Franklin County, OH	264	239	71	Hinds, MS	1 123
27	72	Nassau County, NY	542	28	72	Sacramento County, CA	263	84	72	Jefferson, AL	1 078
1 569	73	Austin County, TX	538	52	73	Marion County, IN	244	700	73	Cole, MO	1 076
373	74	Greene County, OH	537	64	74	Baltimore County, MD	240	261	74	Montgomery, AL	1 072
2 401	75	Falls Church City, VA	524	104	75	Montgomery County, OH	237	180	75	Richland, SC	1 031

75 Counties with Highest Agricultural Sales, 2002
Selected Rankings

Value of agricultural sales, 2002			Average agricultural sales per farm, 2002				Number of farms, 2002			
Value of sales rank	County	Value of sales (millions of dollars) [col 125]	Value of sales rank	Average sales rank	County	Average sales per farm (dollars) [col 126]	Value of sales rank	Number of farms rank	County	Number of farms [col 113]
1	Fresno County, CA	2 759	35	1	Haskell County, KS	2 124 121	1	1	Fresno County, CA	6 281
2	Tulare County, CA	2 339	9	2	Imperial County, CA	1 942 791	2	2	Tulare County, CA	5 738
3	Monterey County, CA	2 190	3	3	Monterey County, CA	1 801 086	17	3	Lancaster County, PA	5 293
4	Kern County, CA	2 059	38	4	Hartley County, TX	1 767 886	12	4	San Diego County, CA	5 255
5	Merced County, CA	1 409	16	5	Yuma County, AZ	1 511 051	63	5	Clackamas County, OR	4 676
6	Stanislaus County, CA	1 229	51	6	Hansford County, TX	1 265 144	6	6	Stanislaus County, CA	4 267
7	San Joaquin County, CA	1 222	15	7	Deaf Smith County, TX	1 197 464	7	7	San Joaquin County, CA	4 026
8	Weld County, CO	1 128	29	8	Castro County, TX	1 107 742	14	8	Yakima County, WA	3 730
9	Imperial County, CA	1 043	71	9	Moore County, TX	1 098 815	32	9	Sonoma County, CA	3 447
10	Ventura County, CA	1 019	65	10	Grant County, KS	1 041 153	40	10	Marion County, OR	3 203
11	Riverside County, CA	1 008	62	11	Scott County, KS	1 025 687	11	11	Riverside County, CA	3 186
12	San Diego County, CA	951	34	12	Finney County, KS	1 005 611	58	12	Stearns County, MN	3 152
13	Grant County, WA	882	68	13	Wichita County, KS	964 600	8	13	Weld County, CO	3 121
14	Yakima County, WA	844	4	14	Kern County, CA	958 875	45	14	Hillsborough County, FL	2 969
15	Deaf Smith County, TX	842	73	15	Sherman County, TX	916 366	5	15	Merced County, CA	2 964
16	Yuma County, AZ	802	28	16	Parmer County, TX	915 015	68	16	Washington County, AR	2 800
17	Lancaster County, PA	798	50	17	Dallam County, TX	897 376	53	17	Benton County, AR	2 376
18	Kings County, CA	793	48	18	Hendry County, FL	824 149	44	18	San Luis Obispo County, CA	2 322
19	Palm Beach County, FL	760	74	19	Elmore County, ID	804 545	10	19	Ventura County, CA	2 318
20	Maricopa County, AZ	740	54	20	Gray County, KS	752 205	61	20	Cullman County, AL	2 301
21	Santa Barbara County, CA	717	59	21	Phelps County, NE	726 127	31	21	Miami-Dade County, FL	2 244
22	Duplin County, NC	715	18	22	Kings County, CA	687 228	4	22	Kern County, CA	2 147
23	Madera County, CA	710	19	23	Palm Beach County, FL	684 565	20	23	Maricopa County, AZ	2 110
24	Sampson County, NC	676	25	24	Texas County, OK	661 186	38	24	Rockingham County, VA	2 043
25	Texas County, OK	663	30	25	Cuming County, NE	642 698	47	25	Chester County, PA	1 918
26	San Bernardino County, CA	618	33	26	Yuma County, CO	628 108	13	26	Grant County, WA	1 801
27	Sioux County, IA	617	42	27	Pinal County, AZ	618 280	23	27	Madera County, CA	1 780
28	Parmer County, TX	604	22	28	Duplin County, NC	601 057	70	28	Darke County, OH	1 764
29	Castro County, TX	593	37	29	Morgan County, CO	588 650	27	29	Sioux County, IA	1 673
30	Cuming County, NE	581	24	30	Sampson County, NC	573 592	41	30	Napa County, CA	1 456
31	Miami-Dade County, FL	578	46	31	Cassia County, ID	552 789	21	31	Santa Barbara County, CA	1 444
32	Sonoma County, CA	572	55	32	Gooding County, ID	531 928	26	32	San Bernardino County, CA	1 386
33	Yuma County, CO	543	49	33	Dawson County, NE	517 176	43	33	Benton County, WA	1 313
34	Finney County, KS	488	72	34	Swisher County, TX	512 610	36	34	Sussex County, DE	1 312
35	Haskell County, KS	482	21	35	Santa Barbara County, CA	496 715	75	35	Twin Falls County, ID	1 297
36	Sussex County, DE	463	13	36	Grant County, WA	489 592	3	36	Monterey County, CA	1 216
37	Morgan County, CO	448	52	37	Santa Cruz County, CA	479 975	22	37	Duplin County, NC	1 190
38	Hartley County, TX	447	5	38	Merced County, CA	475 457	24	38	Sampson County, NC	1 178
38	Rockingham County, VA	447	26	39	San Bernardino County, CA	445 776	65	39	Renville County, MN	1 164
40	Marion County, OR	431	64	40	Wayne County, NC	440 063	18	40	Kings County, CA	1 154
41	Napa County, CA	429	10	41	Ventura County, CA	439 544	19	41	Palm Beach County, FL	1 110
42	Pinal County, AZ	425	1	42	Fresno County, CA	439 328	67	42	Yolo County, CA	1 060
43	Benton County, WA	401	2	43	Tulare County, CA	407 560	25	43	Texas County, OK	1 002
44	San Luis Obispo County, CA	396	23	44	Madera County, CA	399 120	56	44	Franklin County, WA	943
45	Hillsborough County, FL	392	60	45	Walla Walla County, WA	381 004	56	45	Logan County, CO	930
46	Cassia County, ID	383	56	46	Logan County, CO	376 402	30	46	Cuming County, NE	904
47	Chester County, PA	377	56	47	Franklin County, WA	371 668	60	47	Walla Walla County, WA	890
48	Hendry County, FL	376	27	48	Sioux County, IA	368 711	33	48	Yuma County, CO	864
49	Dawson County, NE	371	8	49	Weld County, CO	361 376	37	49	Morgan County, CO	761
50	Dallam County, TX	370	36	50	Sussex County, DE	352 769	52	50	Santa Cruz County, CA	754
51	Hansford County, TX	367	20	51	Maricopa County, AZ	350 797	64	51	Wayne County, NC	722
52	Santa Cruz County, CA	362	11	52	Riverside County, CA	316 470	49	52	Dawson County, NE	718
53	Benton County, AR	361	43	53	Benton County, WA	305 080	15	53	Deaf Smith County, TX	703
54	Gray County, KS	354	7	54	San Joaquin County, CA	303 640	46	54	Cassia County, ID	692
55	Gooding County, ID	353	67	55	Yolo County, CA	297 605	42	55	Pinal County, AZ	687
56	Franklin County, WA	350	41	56	Napa County, CA	294 651	55	56	Gooding County, ID	663
56	Logan County, CO	350	6	57	Stanislaus County, CA	287 932	28	57	Parmer County, TX	660
58	Stearns County, MN	344	65	58	Renville County, MN	272 348	72	58	Swisher County, TX	578
59	Phelps County, NE	341	31	59	Miami-Dade County, FL	257 576	9	59	Imperial County, CA	537
60	Walla Walla County, WA	339	14	60	Yakima County, WA	226 239	29	60	Castro County, TX	535
61	Cullman County, AL	337	75	61	Twin Falls County, ID	225 021	16	61	Yuma County, AZ	531
62	Scott County, KS	335	38	62	Rockingham County, VA	218 631	34	62	Finney County, KS	485
63	Clackamas County, OR	332	47	63	Chester County, PA	196 440	54	63	Gray County, KS	470
64	Wayne County, NC	318	12	64	San Diego County, CA	180 925	59	63	Phelps County, NE	470
65	Grant County, KS	317	70	65	Darke County, OH	172 452	48	65	Hendry County, FL	456
65	Renville County, MN	317	44	66	San Luis Obispo County, CA	170 712	50	66	Dallam County, TX	412
67	Yolo County, CA	315	32	67	Sonoma County, CA	165 857	74	67	Elmore County, ID	364
68	Washington County, AR	314	53	68	Benton County, AR	151 908	62	68	Scott County, KS	327
68	Wichita County, KS	314	17	69	Lancaster County, PA	150 831	68	69	Wichita County, KS	326
70	Darke County, OH	304	61	70	Cullman County, AL	146 658	73	70	Sherman County, TX	322
71	Moore County, TX	303	40	71	Marion County, OR	134 457	65	71	Grant County, KS	304
72	Swisher County, TX	296	45	72	Hillsborough County, FL	132 176	51	72	Hansford County, TX	290
73	Sherman County, TX	295	68	73	Washington County, AR	112 012	71	73	Moore County, TX	276
74	Elmore County, ID	293	58	74	Stearns County, MN	109 029	38	74	Hartley County, TX	253
75	Twin Falls County, ID	292	63	75	Clackamas County, OR	71 002	35	75	Haskell County, KS	227

75 Counties with Highest Agricultural Sales, 2002
Selected Rankings

Average size of farm, 1997				Average value of land and buildings per farm, 2002				Average value of land and buildings per acre, 2002			
Value of sales rank	Size of farm rank	County	Average size of farm (acres) [col 119]	Value of sales rank	Value of land and buildings per farm rank	County	Average value per farm (dollars) [col 122]	Value of sales rank	Value of land and buildings per acre rank	County	Average value per acre (dollars) [col 123]
38	1	Hartley County, TX	3 120	48	1	Hendry County, FL	4 518 569	41	1	Napa County, CA	19 350
50	2	Dallam County, TX	2 146	3	2	Monterey County, CA	3 222 212	32	2	Sonoma County, CA	11 058
51	3	Hansford County, TX	2 045	9	3	Imperial County, CA	2 931 721	47	3	Chester County, PA	10 358
71	4	Moore County, TX	1 991	41	4	Napa County, CA	2 734 325	31	4	Miami-Dade County, FL	9 726
35	5	Haskell County, KS	1 788	4	5	Kern County, CA	2 213 516	63	5	Clackamas County, OR	9 600
73	6	Sherman County, TX	1 696	42	6	Pinal County, AZ	2 080 379	52	6	Santa Cruz County, CA	9 335
42	7	Pinal County, AZ	1 691	18	7	Kings County, CA	2 012 543	10	7	Ventura County, CA	8 839
34	8	Finney County, KS	1 653	16	8	Yuma County, AZ	1 998 970	17	8	Lancaster County, PA	7 955
33	9	Yuma County, CO	1 567	21	9	Santa Barbara County, CA	1 893 146	12	9	San Diego County, CA	7 635
62	10	Scott County, KS	1 515	32	10	Sonoma County, CA	1 710 715	7	10	San Joaquin County, CA	6 673
68	11	Wichita County, KS	1 444	19	11	Palm Beach County, FL	1 623 283	6	11	Stanislaus County, CA	6 068
15	12	Deaf Smith County, TX	1 372	67	12	Yolo County, CA	1 531 470	45	12	Hillsborough County, FL	5 410
4	13	Kern County, CA	1 272	44	13	San Luis Obispo County, CA	1 523 567	40	13	Marion County, OR	5 107
48	14	Hendry County, FL	1 211	10	14	Ventura County, CA	1 441 670	11	14	Riverside County, CA	4 830
56	15	Logan County, CO	1 195	5	15	Merced County, CA	1 363 034	16	15	Yuma County, AZ	4 544
25	16	Texas County, OK	1 179	35	16	Haskell County, KS	1 316 845	38	16	Rockingham County, VA	4 043
46	17	Cassia County, ID	1 076	50	17	Dallam County, TX	1 232 703	36	17	Sussex County, DE	3 951
54	18	Gray County, KS	1 066	23	18	Madera County, CA	1 209 723	2	18	Tulare County, CA	3 949
29	19	Castro County, TX	1 053	7	19	San Joaquin County, CA	1 203 010	48	19	Hendry County, FL	3 846
3	20	Monterey County, CA	1 037	52	20	Santa Cruz County, CA	1 179 533	5	20	Merced County, CA	3 826
37	21	Morgan County, CO	996	38	21	Hartley County, TX	1 170 274	21	21	Santa Barbara County, CA	3 684
65	22	Grant County, KS	993	59	22	Phelps County, NE	1 159 506	67	22	Yolo County, CA	3 645
72	23	Swisher County, TX	980	71	23	Moore County, TX	1 121 030	18	23	Kings County, CA	3 643
9	24	Imperial County, CA	957	13	24	Grant County, WA	1 115 289	1	24	Fresno County, CA	3 612
74	25	Elmore County, ID	951	1	25	Fresno County, CA	1 101 948	19	25	Palm Beach County, FL	3 348
28	26	Parmer County, TX	873	11	26	Riverside County, CA	1 089 879	3	26	Monterey County, CA	3 248
49	27	Dawson County, NE	867	46	27	Cassia County, ID	1 087 864	70	27	Darke County, OH	3 170
60	28	Walla Walla County, WA	787	6	28	Stanislaus County, CA	1 062 751	61	28	Cullman County, AL	3 167
59	29	Phelps County, NE	779	65	29	Renville County, MN	1 053 600	64	29	Wayne County, NC	3 162
56	30	Franklin County, WA	705	60	30	Walla Walla County, WA	989 427	23	30	Madera County, CA	3 120
13	31	Grant County, WA	596	56	31	Franklin County, WA	962 716	24	31	Sampson County, NC	3 084
8	32	Weld County, CO	581	2	32	Tulare County, CA	948 550	53	32	Benton County, AR	3 031
65	33	Renville County, MN	570	34	33	Finney County, KS	946 701	20	33	Maricopa County, AZ	3 026
44	34	San Luis Obispo County, CA	568	36	34	Sussex County, DE	926 312	9	34	Imperial County, CA	2 976
18	35	Kings County, CA	559	73	35	Sherman County, TX	919 130	22	35	Duplin County, NC	2 959
21	36	Santa Barbara County, CA	524	20	36	Maricopa County, AZ	898 974	68	36	Washington County, AR	2 779
67	37	Yolo County, CA	519	47	37	Chester County, PA	889 836	44	37	San Luis Obispo County, CA	2 676
19	38	Palm Beach County, FL	483	33	38	Yuma County, CO	852 401	27	38	Sioux County, IA	2 655
43	39	Benton County, WA	463	62	39	Scott County, KS	836 477	55	39	Gooding County, ID	2 535
14	40	Yakima County, WA	450	49	40	Dawson County, NE	830 919	26	40	San Bernardino County, CA	2 144
16	41	Yuma County, AZ	435	54	41	Gray County, KS	827 769	75	41	Twin Falls County, ID	1 946
30	42	Cuming County, NE	405	37	42	Morgan County, CO	810 693	13	42	Grant County, WA	1 923
23	43	Madera County, CA	383	55	43	Gooding County, ID	795 709	65	43	Renville County, MN	1 889
26	44	San Bernardino County, CA	371	24	44	Sampson County, NC	784 955	4	44	Kern County, CA	1 816
75	45	Twin Falls County, ID	340	43	45	Benton County, WA	782 342	43	45	Benton County, WA	1 701
5	46	Merced County, CA	339	27	46	Sioux County, IA	776 515	58	46	Stearns County, MN	1 579
1	47	Fresno County, CA	307	8	47	Weld County, CO	759 282	30	47	Cuming County, NE	1 571
27	48	Sioux County, IA	302	51	48	Hansford County, TX	759 133	59	48	Phelps County, NE	1 479
20	49	Maricopa County, AZ	297	12	49	San Diego County, CA	740 112	56	49	Franklin County, WA	1 448
55	50	Gooding County, ID	294	64	50	Wayne County, NC	722 503	8	50	Weld County, CO	1 379
24	51	Sampson County, NC	253	26	51	San Bernardino County, CA	708 212	60	51	Walla Walla County, WA	1 330
2	52	Tulare County, CA	243	74	52	Elmore County, ID	676 926	14	52	Yakima County, WA	1 271
64	53	Wayne County, NC	237	68	53	Wichita County, KS	673 525	42	53	Pinal County, AZ	1 230
58	54	Stearns County, MN	216	65	54	Grant County, KS	666 523	49	54	Dawson County, NE	1 014
36	54	Sussex County, DE	216	29	55	Castro County, TX	661 867	46	55	Cassia County, ID	986
7	56	San Joaquin County, CA	202	30	56	Cuming County, NE	658 526	37	56	Morgan County, CO	801
22	57	Duplin County, NC	197	15	57	Deaf Smith County, TX	644 463	54	57	Gray County, KS	791
70	58	Darke County, OH	192	56	58	Logan County, CO	643 347	35	58	Haskell County, KS	744
6	59	Stanislaus County, CA	185	70	59	Darke County, OH	617 607	74	59	Elmore County, ID	719
32	60	Sonoma County, CA	182	75	60	Twin Falls County, ID	614 239	29	60	Castro County, TX	665
11	61	Riverside County, CA	180	17	61	Lancaster County, PA	610 359	65	61	Grant County, KS	664
41	62	Napa County, CA	163	25	62	Texas County, OK	605 676	34	62	Finney County, KS	616
10	63	Ventura County, CA	143	14	63	Yakima County, WA	577 843	50	63	Dallam County, TX	601
53	64	Benton County, AR	132	22	64	Duplin County, NC	564 942	28	64	Parmer County, TX	599
68	65	Washington County, AR	131	31	65	Miami-Dade County, FL	545 496	71	65	Moore County, TX	574
38	66	Rockingham County, VA	122	28	66	Parmer County, TX	525 201	33	66	Yuma County, CO	573
40	67	Marion County, OR	106	40	67	Marion County, OR	510 810	56	67	Logan County, CO	560
61	68	Cullman County, AL	101	38	68	Rockingham County, VA	498 534	73	67	Sherman County, TX	560
45	69	Hillsborough County, FL	96	72	69	Swisher County, TX	458 818	62	69	Scott County, KS	555
52	70	Santa Cruz County, CA	89	45	70	Hillsborough County, FL	454 871	25	70	Texas County, OK	519
47	71	Chester County, PA	88	63	71	Clackamas County, OR	418 469	68	71	Wichita County, KS	503
17	72	Lancaster County, PA	78	53	72	Benton County, AR	386 606	72	72	Swisher County, TX	460
12	72	San Diego County, CA	78	68	73	Washington County, AR	363 663	15	73	Deaf Smith County, TX	440
63	74	Clackamas County, OR	46	58	74	Stearns County, MN	358 266	38	74	Hartley County, TX	376
31	75	Miami-Dade County, FL	40	61	75	Cullman County, AL	290 950	51	75	Hansford County, TX	369

COLUMN HEADINGS FOR STATES AND COUNTIES

Table B. States and Counties — **Land Area and Population**

STATE/ County code	CBSA code[1]	County Type[2]	STATE County	Land area,[3] (sq km) 2000	Population and population characteristics, 2003														
								Race alone or in combination, not Hispanic or Latino (percent)					Age (percent)						
					Total persons	Rank	Per square kilometer	White	Black	Am. Indian, Alaska Native	Asian and Pacific Islander	Percent Hispanic or Latino[4]	Under 5 years	5 to 17 years	18 to 24 years	25 to 34 years	35 to 44 years	45 to 54 years
					1	2	3	4	5	6	7	8	9	10	11	12	13	14	15

1. CBSA = Core Based Statistical Area. See Appendix A for explanation. See Appendix B for list of metropolitan areas with component counties. Service of USDA Rural-Urban Continuum Codes. See Appendix A for definition. 3. Dry land or land partially or temporarily covered by water. 2. County type code from the Economic Research 4. Hispanic or Latino persons may be of any race.

Table B. States and Counties — **Population and Households**

STATE County	Population, 2003 (cont'd)				Population — change and components of change, 1990–2003							Households, 2000				
	Age (percent) (cont'd)				Total persons		Percent change		Components of change, 2000–2003						Percent	
	55 to 64 years	65 to 74 years	75 years and over	Percent female	1990	2000	1990–2000	2000–2003	Births	Deaths	Net migration	Number	Percent change, 1990–2000	Persons per house-hold	Female family house-holder[1]	One person
	16	17	18	19	20	21	22	23	24	25	26	27	28	29	30	31

1. No spouse present.

Table B. States and Counties — **Vital Statistics, Health Resources, and Crime**

STATE County	Births, average 1999–2001		Deaths, average 1999–2001				Physicians,[4] 2000		Hospitals,[4] 1998			Medicare enrollees, 2003	Serious crimes known to police,[6] 2002	
			Number		Rate					Beds			Total	
	Total	Rate[1]	Total	Infant[2]	Total[1]	Infant[3]	Number	Rate[5]	Number	Number	Rate[5]		Number	Rate[7]
	32	33	34	35	36	37	38	39	40	41	42	43	44	45

1. Per 1,000 estimated resident population. 2. Deaths of infants under 1 year old. 3. Deaths of infants under 1 year old per 1,000 live births. 4. Data subject to copyright. 5. Per 100,000 resident population as of July 1 of the year shown. 6. Data for serious crimes have not been adjusted for underreporting; this may affect comparability between geographic areas and over time. 7. Per 100,000 population estimated by the FBI.

Table B. States and Counties — **Crime, Education, Money Income, and Poverty**

STATE County	Serious crimes known to police,[1] 2002 (cont'd)		Education							Money income, 1999				Percent below poverty level, 1999			
	Rate[2]		School enrollment and attainment, 2000				Local government expenditures,[5] 2000–2001			Households							
			Enrollment[3]		Attainment[4] (percent)				Per capita income[6] (dollars)	Median income		Percent with income of $100,000 or more				
	Violent	Property	Total	Percent private	High school grad-uate or less	Bach-elor's degree or more	Total current expendi-tures (mil dol)	Current expendi-tures per student (dollars)		Dollars	Percent change, 1989–1999 (constant 1999 dollars)		Persons	House-holds	Families	Families with children
	46	47	48	49	50	51	52	53	54	55	56	57	58	59	60	61

1. Data for serious crimes have not been adjusted for underreporting; this may affect comparability between geographic areas and over time. 2. Per 100,000 population estimated by the FBI. 3. All persons 3 years old and over enrolled in nursery school through college. 4. Persons 25 years old and over. 5. Elementary and secondary education expenditures. 6. Based on population enumerated as of April 1, 2000.

COLUMN HEADINGS FOR STATES AND COUNTIES

Table B. States and Counties — **Personal Income**

STATE County	Personal income, 2002							Transfer payments					
			Per capita[1]						Government payments to individuals				
	Total (mil dol)	Percent change, 2001–2002	Dollars	Rank	Wages and salaries[2] (mil dol)	Proprietor's income (mil dol)	Dividends, interest, and rent (mil dol)	Total (mil dol)	Total (mil dol)	Social Security (mil dol)	Medical payments (mil dol)	Income maintenance (mil dol)	Unemployment insurance (mil dol)
	62	63	64	65	66	67	68	69	70	71	72	73	74

1. Based on the resident population estimated as of July 1 of the year shown.   2. Includes other labor income.

Table B. States and Counties — **Earnings, Social Security, and Housing**

STATE County	Earnings, 2002									Social Security beneficiaries, December 2003		Supplemental Security Income recipients, December 2003	Housing units, 2003	
			Percent by selected industries											
			Goods-related[1]		Service-related and health									
	Total (mil dol)	Farm	Total	Manu-facturing	Information and professional and technical services	Retail trade	Finance, insurance, and real estate	Health services	Govern-ment	Number	Rate[2]		Total	Percent change, 2000–2003
	75	76	77	78	79	80	81	82	83	84	85	86	87	88

1. Covers mining, construction, and manufacturing.   2. Per 1,000 resident population estimated as of July 1 of the year shown.

Table B. States and Counties — **Housing, Labor Force, and Employment**

STATE County	Housing units, 2000								Civilian labor force, 2003				Civilian employment,[6] 2000		
		Occupied units									Unemployment			Percent	
			Owner-occupied				Renter-occupied								
				Median owner cost as a percent of income											Production, transportation, and material moving occupations
	Total	Percent	Median value[1]	With a mortgage	Without a mortgage[2]	Median rent[3]	Median rent as a percent of income	Sub-standard units[4] (percent)	Total	Percent change, 2002–2003	Total	Rate[5]	Total	Management, professional and related occupations	
	89	90	91	92	93	94	95	96	97	98	99	100	101	102	103

1. Specified owner-occupied units.   2. Median monthly owner costs is often in the minimum category—9.9 percent or less, which is indicated as 9.9 percent.   3. Specified renter-occupied units.   4. Overcrowded or lacking complete plumbing facilities.   5. Percent of civilian labor force.   6. Persons 16 years old and over.

Table B. States and Counties — **Nonfarm Employment and Agriculture**

STATE County	Private nonfarm establishments, employment and payroll, 2001								Agriculture, 2002			
		Employment						Annual payroll		Farms		
											Percent with—	
	Number of establish-ments	Total	Health care and social assistance	Manufac-turing	Retail trade	Finance and insurance	Professional, scientific, and technical services	Total (mil dol)	Average per employee (dollars)	Number	Less than 50 acres	500 acres and over	Farm operators whose principal occupation is farming (percent)
	104	105	106	107	108	109	110	111	112	113	114	115	116

COLUMN HEADINGS FOR STATES AND COUNTIES

Table B. States and Counties — **Agriculture**

STATE County	Agriculture, 2002 (cont'd)															
	Land in farms					Value of land and buildings (dollars)			Value of products sold				Percent of farms with sales of —		Government payments	
		Acres						Value of machinery and equipment average per farm (dollars)			Percent from —					
	Acreage (1,000)	Percent change, 1997–2002	Average size of farm	Total irrigated (1,000)	Total cropland (1,000)	Average per farm	Average per acre		Total (mil dol)	Average per farm (dollars)	Crops	Live-stock and poultry products	$10,000 or more	$100,000 or more	Total ($1,000)	Percent of farms
	117	118	119	120	121	122	123	124	125	126	127	128	129	130	131	132

Table B. States and Counties — **Residential Construction, Wholesale Trade, Retail Trade, and Real Estate**

STATE County	Value of residential construction authorized by building permits, 2003		Wholesale trade, 1997				Retail trade,[1] 1997				Real estate and rental and leasing, 1997			
	New construction ($1,000)	Number of housing units	Number of establish-ments	Number of employees	Sales (mil dol)	Annual payroll (mil dol)	Number of establish-ments	Number of employees	Sales (mil dol)	Annual payroll (mil dol)	Number of establish-ments	Number of employees	Receipts (mil dol)	Annual payroll (mil dol)
	133	134	135	136	137	138	139	140	141	142	143	144	145	146

1. Establishments with payroll.

Table B. States and Counties — **Professional Services, Manufacturing, and Accommodation and Foodservices**

STATE County	Professional, scientific, and technical services,[1] 1997				Manufacturing, 1997				Accommodation and foodservices, 1997			
	Number of establish-ments	Number of employees	Receipts (mil dol)	Annual payroll (mil dol)	Number of establish-ments	Number of employees	Receipts (mil dol)	Annual payroll (mil dol)	Number of establish-ments	Number of employees	Sales (mil dol)	Annual payroll (mil dol)
	147	148	149	150	151	152	153	154	155	156	157	158

1. Firms subject to federal tax.

Table B. States and Counties — **Health Care and Social Assistance, Other Services, and Federal Funds**

STATE County	Health care and social assistance,[1] 1997				Other services,[1] 1997				Federal funds and grants, 2002–2003			
									Expenditures (mil dol)			
										Direct payments for individuals[2]		
	Number of establish-ments	Number of employees	Receipts (mil dol)	Annual payroll (mil dol)	Number of establish-ments	Number of employees	Receipts (mil dol)	Annual payroll (mil dol)	Total	Social Security and government retirement	Medicare	Food stamps and Supplemental Security Income
	159	160	161	162	163	164	165	166	167	168	169	170

1. Firms subject to federal tax.   2. State totals may include programs not allocated by county.

69

COLUMN HEADINGS FOR STATES AND COUNTIES

Table B. States and Counties — **Federal Funds and Local Government Finances**

	Federal funds and grants, 2002–2003 (cont'd)							Local government finances, 2002				
	Expenditures (mil dol) (cont'd)							General revenue				
	Procurement contract awards			Grants[1]						Taxes		
											Per capita[2] (dollars)	
STATE County	Salaries and wages	Defense	Other	Medicaid and other health-related	Nutrition and family welfare	Education	Other	Total (mil dol)	Intergovern-mental (mil dol)	Total (mil dol)	Total	Property
	171	172	173	174	175	176	177	178	179	180	181	182

1. State totals may include programs not allocated by county.   2. Based on the resident population estimated as of July 1 of the year shown.

Table B. States and Counties — **Local Government Finances, Government Employment, and Elections**

	Local government finances, 2002 (cont'd)									Government employment, 2002			Presidential election, 2004		
	Direct general expenditure							Debt outstanding					Percent of vote cast —		
			Percent of total for —												
STATE County	Total (mil dol)	Per capita[1] (dollars)	Educa-tion	Health and hospitals	Police protec-tion	Public welfare	High-ways	Total (mil dol)	Per capita[1] (dollars)	Federal civilian	Federal military	State and local	Demo-cratic	Republi-can	All other
	183	184	185	186	187	188	189	190	191	192	193	194	195	196	197

1. Based on the resident population estimated as of July 1 of the year shown.

70

Table B. States and Counties — **Land Area and Population**

STATE/ County code	CBSA code[1]	County Type[2]	STATE County	Land area,[3] (sq km) 2000	Total persons	Rank	Per square kilometer	White	Black	Am. Indian, Alaska Native	Asian and Pacific Islander	Percent Hispanic or Latino[4]	Under 5 years	5 to 17 years	18 to 24 years	25 to 34 years	35 to 44 years	45 to 54 years
				1	2	3	4	5	6	7	8	9	10	11	12	13	14	15
00 000	...	X	UNITED STATES	9 161 924	290 809 777	X	31.7	69.0	12.7	1.2	4.8	13.7	6.8	18.3	9.9	13.7	15.3	14.0
01 000	...	X	ALABAMA	131 426	4 500 752	X	34.2	70.3	26.6	0.9	1.1	2.0	6.6	18.0	10.1	13.2	14.5	14.1
01 001	33860	2	Autauga	1 544	46 491	988	30.1	80.5	17.2	0.9	0.9	1.3	6.7	20.4	9.5	12.6	16.7	13.1
01 003	19300	4	Baldwin	4 135	151 831	371	36.7	87.3	10.1	1.0	0.5	2.0	6.0	17.4	9.0	11.8	14.4	13.7
01 005	...	6	Barbour	2 292	28 816	1 436	12.6	49.9	47.0	0.6	0.4	2.5	6.7	17.9	10.4	13.7	15.3	13.8
01 007	13820	1	Bibb	1 614	21 206	1 743	13.1	75.8	22.7	0.5	0.1	1.3	6.8	18.0	9.4	14.6	15.6	13.3
01 009	13820	1	Blount	1 672	54 136	888	32.4	92.3	1.3	0.9	0.3	5.9	6.3	18.2	9.1	13.4	14.6	13.6
01 011	...	6	Bullock	1 619	11 339	2 345	7.0	23.3	71.6	0.5	0.3	4.6	6.7	18.2	10.9	14.2	14.8	13.5
01 013	...	6	Butler	2 012	20 693	1 764	10.3	57.5	41.4	0.2	0.2	0.8	6.8	18.8	10.2	10.5	13.5	14.4
01 015	11500	3	Calhoun	1 576	112 012	495	71.1	77.7	19.6	0.8	0.9	1.8	6.5	16.8	10.4	12.5	14.2	14.5
01 017	46740	6	Chambers	1 547	35 751	1 251	23.1	60.1	38.8	0.3	0.2	0.9	6.0	18.0	9.0	12.8	13.9	14.0
01 019	...	8	Cherokee	1 433	24 429	1 603	17.0	93.1	5.7	0.7	0.3	0.8	5.8	16.1	8.0	12.4	14.1	14.6
01 021	13820	1	Chilton	1 797	40 878	1 112	22.7	85.6	10.7	0.6	0.3	3.3	6.3	18.4	9.4	13.7	14.5	13.6
01 023	...	9	Choctaw	2 366	15 284	2 076	6.5	54.8	44.5	0.2	0.1	0.7	6.6	18.3	9.0	11.2	14.1	14.6
01 025	...	7	Clarke	3 207	27 487	1 485	8.6	55.7	43.4	0.3	0.2	0.6	7.4	19.8	9.4	11.9	14.5	13.2
01 027	...	9	Clay	1 567	14 182	2 152	9.1	82.0	15.8	0.9	0.1	1.8	6.1	16.8	8.9	12.0	14.6	13.8
01 029	...	8	Cleburne	1 451	14 675	2 120	10.1	94.1	3.9	0.7	0.1	1.6	5.9	17.5	9.3	12.6	14.9	14.3
01 031	21460	6	Coffee	1 759	44 625	1 032	25.4	76.5	19.0	1.7	1.5	2.7	5.9	17.7	9.2	12.9	14.3	14.0
01 033	22520	3	Colbert	1 540	54 531	880	35.4	81.1	17.1	0.9	0.4	1.2	5.9	17.1	8.7	12.2	14.5	14.5
01 035	...	9	Conecuh	2 204	13 588	2 193	6.2	55.0	43.9	0.3	0.1	0.8	6.3	18.6	9.1	10.9	14.0	14.5
01 037	...	8	Coosa	1 690	11 500	2 334	6.8	65.8	32.4	0.6	0.1	1.4	5.3	17.7	8.8	11.8	15.3	14.8
01 039	...	7	Covington	2 678	36 940	1 213	13.8	85.7	12.8	0.9	0.3	0.8	5.7	17.0	9.1	10.9	14.0	13.9
01 041	...	8	Crenshaw	1 579	13 578	2 194	8.6	74.2	24.8	0.6	0.1	0.6	6.0	17.8	9.1	11.6	14.0	14.3
01 043	18980	6	Cullman	1 913	78 270	667	40.9	95.7	1.0	1.0	0.3	2.7	6.2	17.2	9.5	12.8	14.6	13.9
01 045	21460	4	Dale	1 453	49 298	947	33.9	74.2	21.0	1.3	2.0	3.3	7.6	18.8	9.7	14.7	14.7	13.0
01 047	42820	4	Dallas	2 540	44 977	1 025	17.7	33.2	65.8	0.1	0.5	0.6	8.0	20.1	10.4	10.9	13.9	13.4
01 049	...	6	De Kalb	2 015	66 469	756	33.0	89.7	1.7	1.7	0.2	7.6	6.9	17.5	9.4	13.7	14.4	13.4
01 051	33860	2	Elmore	1 609	70 691	715	43.9	76.7	21.3	1.0	0.6	1.4	6.6	18.1	10.3	14.4	16.1	13.6
01 053	...	6	Escambia	2 454	38 179	1 180	15.6	64.3	31.7	3.6	0.4	0.9	6.2	17.2	10.2	13.3	15.1	14.0
01 055	23460	3	Etowah	1 385	103 035	528	74.4	82.6	14.9	0.7	0.5	2.0	6.2	17.1	9.1	12.6	13.8	14.4
01 057	...	6	Fayette	1 626	18 241	1 894	11.2	86.9	11.9	0.4	0.2	0.8	5.7	17.0	9.4	11.9	14.0	14.5
01 059	...	6	Franklin	1 646	30 802	1 388	18.7	86.1	4.4	0.7	0.3	9.1	6.5	17.5	9.3	13.0	14.2	13.3
01 061	20020	3	Geneva	1 493	25 490	1 551	17.1	86.8	10.5	1.1	0.2	1.9	5.8	17.0	8.6	11.5	14.1	14.2
01 063	46220	3	Greene	1 673	9 900	2 453	5.9	19.2	80.0	0.1	0.2	0.6	7.4	20.3	10.3	10.1	13.5	14.8
01 065	46220	3	Hale	1 667	18 299	1 888	11.0	39.5	59.5	0.2	0.2	0.9	7.2	19.8	10.6	13.2	14.8	13.1
01 067	20020	3	Henry	1 455	16 437	2 001	11.3	64.7	33.5	0.4	0.1	1.8	6.2	17.0	9.4	11.6	13.1	14.7
01 069	20020	3	Houston	1 503	91 409	589	60.8	72.1	25.8	0.8	0.8	1.4	6.8	18.4	9.0	12.5	14.8	13.9
01 071	42460	6	Jackson	2 794	53 801	891	19.3	92.9	3.8	3.3	0.3	1.4	6.0	17.4	8.8	13.1	14.6	14.6
01 073	13820	1	Jefferson	2 882	658 141	84	228.4	56.1	40.9	0.5	1.4	1.9	6.7	17.7	9.3	13.8	15.0	14.7
01 075	...	9	Lamar	1 567	15 146	2 090	9.7	86.5	12.0	0.2	0.1	1.4	5.4	16.8	9.3	12.1	14.9	14.1
01 077	22520	3	Lauderdale	1 734	86 968	618	50.2	88.7	9.8	0.6	0.5	1.1	5.7	16.5	10.3	12.4	14.4	14.3
01 079	19460	3	Lawrence	1 796	34 594	1 289	19.3	80.8	12.8	8.0	0.1	1.2	6.1	18.5	9.0	13.1	16.0	14.1
01 081	12220	3	Lee	1 577	119 561	472	75.8	73.3	23.4	0.5	2.2	1.5	5.7	16.6	18.8	16.1	13.0	11.2
01 083	26620	2	Limestone	1 471	68 245	763	46.4	83.1	13.3	0.8	0.5	3.0	6.3	17.8	9.3	14.0	16.6	14.0
01 085	33860	2	Lowndes	1 859	13 374	2 207	7.2	26.9	72.3	0.2	0.2	0.6	7.7	20.9	10.5	11.2	14.7	13.2
01 087	46260	6	Macon	1 581	23 449	1 641	14.8	14.3	84.5	0.4	0.6	0.7	5.9	18.3	16.8	11.5	11.3	12.9
01 089	26620	2	Madison	2 085	289 662	203	138.9	71.6	23.8	1.6	2.9	2.0	6.4	18.4	9.9	13.0	16.7	13.8
01 091	...	7	Marengo	2 531	22 341	1 689	8.8	46.6	51.8	0.1	0.3	1.4	7.0	20.4	9.4	10.9	13.8	13.6
01 093	...	8	Marion	1 920	30 182	1 399	15.7	94.5	3.8	0.5	0.2	1.4	5.6	16.1	8.5	12.3	14.8	14.0
01 095	10700	4	Marshall	1 469	83 698	638	57.0	90.2	1.8	0.9	0.5	7.4	6.8	17.8	9.2	13.1	14.8	13.3
01 097	33660	2	Mobile	3 194	399 747	151	125.2	62.0	34.6	1.1	2.0	1.2	7.3	19.6	10.1	13.0	14.6	13.7
01 099	...	7	Monroe	2 657	23 871	1 619	9.0	57.5	40.7	1.2	0.3	0.8	7.2	19.8	9.8	11.7	13.9	13.9
01 101	33860	2	Montgomery	2 045	221 980	261	108.5	46.3	51.3	0.5	1.6	1.3	7.4	18.4	11.3	14.3	14.7	13.6
01 103	19460	3	Morgan	1 508	112 610	493	74.7	83.1	11.9	1.2	0.7	4.1	6.5	18.1	8.9	12.6	15.9	14.4
01 105	...	8	Perry	1 863	11 705	2 313	6.3	30.2	68.7	0.1	0.2	1.1	8.3	21.1	12.7	10.6	12.1	11.7
01 107	...	8	Pickens	2 283	20 544	1 773	9.0	56.4	42.9	0.2	0.2	0.8	7.2	19.1	9.7	11.2	14.0	13.5
01 109	45980	6	Pike	1 738	29 276	1 428	16.8	59.9	37.8	1.6	0.7	1.4	6.9	17.2	14.5	13.0	12.7	12.4
01 111	...	6	Randolph	1 505	22 273	1 692	14.8	76.3	22.4	0.3	0.3	1.0	6.3	18.1	9.3	12.3	14.0	13.7
01 113	17980	2	Russell	1 661	48 986	956	29.5	54.6	42.6	0.7	0.9	2.0	6.7	19.1	9.5	13.6	14.7	13.5
01 115	13820	1	St. Clair	1 641	68 659	731	41.8	90.4	8.0	0.9	0.3	1.2	6.1	18.1	9.0	13.4	15.6	14.1
01 117	13820	1	Shelby	2 058	159 445	347	77.5	87.5	8.4	0.5	1.6	2.6	7.4	18.5	9.0	14.7	16.4	14.7
01 119	...	8	Sumter	2 344	14 182	2 152	6.1	24.4	74.5	0.2	0.3	1.1	6.4	21.1	12.3	12.0	12.4	13.2
01 121	45180	4	Talladega	1 915	79 928	652	41.7	66.9	31.8	0.5	0.5	1.1	6.7	17.9	9.7	12.9	14.7	14.6
01 123	...	6	Tallapoosa	1 859	40 764	1 116	21.9	72.8	26.1	0.5	0.3	0.7	6.1	17.3	8.4	11.5	14.2	14.7
01 125	46220	3	Tuscaloosa	3 430	166 446	340	48.5	67.4	30.3	0.6	1.2	1.4	6.5	16.6	14.5	14.6	13.3	13.6
01 127	13820	1	Walker	2 057	70 181	721	34.1	92.2	6.4	0.6	0.3	1.1	6.2	16.8	8.9	12.7	14.5	14.5

Population and population characteristics, 2003. Race alone or in combination, not Hispanic or Latino (percent). Age (percent).

1. CBSA = Core Based Statistical Area. See Appendix A for explanation. See Appendix B for list of metropolitan areas with component counties. 2. County type code from the Economic Research Service of USDA Rural-Urban Continuum Codes. See Appendix A for definition. 3. Dry land or land partially or temporarily covered by water. 4. Hispanic or Latino persons may be of any race.

Table B. States and Counties — Population and Households

STATE County	Population, 2003 (cont'd) Age (percent) (cont'd)				Population — change and components of change, 1990–2003							Households, 2000				
					Total persons		Percent change		Components of change, 2000–2003						Percent	
	55 to 64 years	65 to 74 years	75 years and over	Percent female	1990	2000	1990–2000	2000–2003	Births	Deaths	Net migration	Number	Percent change, 1990–2000	Persons per household	Female family householder[1]	One person
	16	17	18	19	20	21	22	23	24	25	26	27	28	29	30	31
UNITED STATES............	9.6	6.3	6.0	50.8	248 790 925	281 421 906	13.1	3.3	13 085 539	7 889 270	4 190 277	105 480 101	14.7	2.59	12.2	25.8
ALABAMA	10.2	7.1	6.1	51.6	4 040 389	4 447 100	10.1	1.2	198 297	149 646	6 723	1 737 080	15.3	2.49	14.2	26.1
Autauga..........................	9.6	6.2	4.0	51.3	34 222	43 671	27.6	6.5	2 018	1 194	1 976	16 003	35.3	2.71	13.1	19.9
Baldwin...........................	10.8	8.6	6.9	50.9	98 280	140 415	42.9	8.1	5 965	4 697	10 080	55 336	49.4	2.50	10.2	23.3
Barbour...........................	9.5	6.8	6.3	47.7	25 417	29 038	14.2	-0.8	1 362	1 079	-473	10 409	12.9	2.53	19.1	26.5
Bibb................................	10.0	6.5	5.2	48.5	16 598	20 826	25.5	1.8	927	693	1 043	7 421	29.2	2.64	12.7	22.1
Blount.............................	10.7	7.2	5.5	50.0	39 248	51 024	30.0	6.1	2 132	1 549	2 501	19 265	31.6	2.62	7.9	20.8
Bullock...........................	8.7	6.0	7.1	47.1	11 042	11 714	6.1	-3.2	551	490	-353	3 986	5.3	2.56	28.2	28.9
Butler.............................	10.3	7.8	8.4	52.9	21 892	21 399	-2.3	-3.3	982	973	-708	8 398	5.8	2.52	18.2	27.5
Calhoun..........................	10.3	8.0	6.2	52.0	116 032	112 249	-3.3	-0.2	4 999	4 557	-627	45 307	5.4	2.42	13.4	26.9
Chambers........................	10.7	8.1	8.0	52.4	36 876	36 583	-0.8	-2.3	1 424	1 559	-669	14 522	5.3	2.48	17.4	27.0
Cherokee.........................	12.6	9.4	6.6	50.9	19 543	23 988	22.7	1.8	889	843	410	9 719	30.2	2.43	9.2	23.9
Chilton............................	10.5	7.0	5.5	50.4	32 458	39 593	22.0	3.2	1 672	1 289	925	15 287	26.2	2.57	10.5	22.9
Choctaw..........................	12.2	7.9	7.1	52.9	16 018	15 922	-0.6	-4.0	676	530	-759	6 363	10.7	2.48	16.0	26.5
Clarke.............................	10.4	7.5	6.2	52.7	27 240	27 867	2.3	-1.4	1 393	1 020	-745	10 578	11.3	2.60	15.7	25.5
Clay................................	11.3	8.5	8.2	50.9	13 252	14 254	7.6	-0.5	575	584	-46	5 765	15.2	2.43	10.5	26.7
Cleburne.........................	11.4	7.8	5.7	49.8	12 730	14 123	10.9	3.9	572	454	436	5 590	17.0	2.51	8.7	23.0
Coffee.............................	10.5	7.8	6.5	51.1	40 240	43 615	8.4	2.3	1 637	1 374	757	17 421	14.2	2.46	12.1	24.9
Colbert............................	11.5	8.2	7.4	52.1	51 666	54 984	6.4	-0.8	2 007	1 975	-406	22 461	11.8	2.42	12.1	26.1
Conecuh..........................	11.4	8.2	7.7	52.9	14 054	14 089	0.2	-3.6	594	512	-579	5 792	10.1	2.42	16.2	30.1
Coosa.............................	11.2	8.6	6.8	50.1	11 063	12 202	10.3	-5.8	376	396	-349	4 682	16.6	2.52	13.5	24.3
Covington........................	11.3	9.3	8.8	52.1	36 478	37 631	3.2	-1.8	1 413	1 661	-412	15 640	8.3	2.37	11.3	28.6
Crenshaw........................	10.8	8.4	8.5	52.6	13 635	13 665	0.2	-0.6	549	619	-5	5 577	6.0	2.42	15.4	28.2
Cullman..........................	10.9	7.8	6.7	50.6	67 613	77 483	14.6	1.0	3 105	2 918	680	30 706	19.9	2.49	8.7	24.0
Dale................................	9.3	7.0	5.2	50.3	49 633	49 129	-1.0	0.3	2 464	1 456	-819	18 878	7.4	2.51	13.6	24.3
Dallas.............................	9.7	7.2	6.7	54.4	48 130	46 365	-3.7	-3.0	2 565	1 798	-2 153	17 841	4.7	2.57	25.4	27.8
De Kalb...........................	10.3	7.4	6.2	50.9	54 651	64 452	17.9	3.1	3 019	2 133	1 141	25 113	19.8	2.53	9.9	23.8
Elmore............................	9.1	5.9	4.7	49.2	49 210	65 874	33.9	7.3	3 074	1 666	3 345	22 737	37.5	2.66	12.0	20.0
Escambia........................	10.5	7.4	6.5	49.0	35 518	38 440	8.2	-0.7	1 659	1 420	-454	14 297	10.8	2.48	15.1	26.4
Etowah...........................	10.7	8.1	7.8	52.0	99 840	103 459	3.6	-0.4	4 228	4 326	-248	41 615	7.6	2.44	13.1	26.3
Fayette............................	11.8	8.3	7.9	51.4	17 962	18 495	3.0	-1.4	674	744	-162	7 493	9.2	2.42	10.6	26.6
Franklin...........................	10.8	8.4	6.9	50.6	27 814	31 223	12.3	-1.3	1 374	1 201	-605	12 259	13.0	2.51	10.4	24.5
Geneva............................	12.0	8.8	8.0	51.4	23 647	25 764	9.0	-1.1	968	1 040	-195	10 477	13.5	2.43	11.0	26.3
Greene............................	9.1	7.3	7.3	53.0	10 153	9 974	-1.8	-0.7	512	331	-244	3 931	11.9	2.52	27.1	30.8
Hale................................	8.6	6.3	6.3	49.5	15 498	17 185	10.9	6.5	868	686	-151	6 415	18.9	2.63	22.0	26.4
Henry..............................	11.4	8.4	8.0	52.3	15 374	16 310	6.1	0.8	692	688	140	6 525	13.1	2.47	14.7	25.3
Houston...........................	9.9	7.3	6.4	52.4	81 331	88 787	9.2	3.0	4 100	2 956	1 579	35 834	16.2	2.45	14.1	26.4
Jackson...........................	11.8	7.9	6.0	51.1	47 796	53 926	12.8	-0.2	2 120	1 905	-281	21 615	20.0	2.47	10.5	24.3
Jefferson	9.1	6.8	6.8	52.7	651 520	662 047	1.6	-0.6	30 295	23 921	-10 007	263 265	4.7	2.45	17.2	28.7
Lamar.............................	11.8	8.8	7.8	51.6	15 715	15 904	1.2	-4.8	552	711	-601	6 468	7.7	2.43	10.9	25.4
Lauderdale	10.8	8.2	7.2	52.1	79 661	87 966	10.4	-1.1	3 207	3 008	-1 118	36 088	16.8	2.39	10.8	26.4
Lawrence.........................	11.1	7.0	5.3	51.0	31 513	34 803	10.4	-0.6	1 417	1 161	-436	13 538	18.7	2.55	11.2	22.6
Lee.................................	7.2	4.6	3.5	50.8	87 146	115 092	32.1	3.9	4 267	2 651	2 947	45 702	38.1	2.42	11.8	27.8
Limestone.......................	9.9	6.5	4.8	49.0	54 135	65 676	21.3	3.9	2 861	1 838	1 563	24 688	25.4	2.55	10.4	23.4
Lowndes.........................	9.3	7.1	5.5	53.1	12 658	13 473	6.4	-0.7	721	495	-319	4 909	21.0	2.73	25.7	24.6
Macon	9.1	6.8	7.4	54.1	24 928	24 105	-3.3	-2.7	922	963	-612	8 950	5.5	2.44	25.8	33.0
Madison..........................	9.5	6.6	4.6	51.1	238 912	276 700	15.8	4.7	11 754	7 225	8 571	109 955	20.6	2.45	11.8	27.2
Marengo..........................	10.5	7.7	6.9	52.7	23 084	22 539	-2.4	-0.9	1 101	845	-442	8 767	7.5	2.55	19.4	26.5
Marion............................	12.4	8.9	7.7	50.4	29 830	31 214	4.6	-3.3	1 082	1 196	-911	12 697	10.2	2.39	9.5	26.5
Marshall..........................	10.6	7.8	6.2	51.1	70 832	82 231	16.1	1.8	3 797	3 049	792	32 547	17.2	2.50	10.7	24.6
Mobile.............................	9.4	6.4	5.7	52.1	378 643	399 843	5.6	0.0	19 685	13 007	-6 638	150 179	9.7	2.61	17.7	24.8
Monroe...........................	10.1	7.3	6.8	52.4	23 968	24 324	1.5	-1.9	1 139	823	-766	9 383	11.5	2.57	16.1	25.7
Montgomery.....................	8.5	6.2	5.7	52.3	209 085	223 510	6.9	-0.7	11 497	6 748	-6 257	86 068	11.5	2.46	18.6	29.5
Morgan...........................	10.4	7.0	5.6	50.9	100 043	111 064	11.0	1.4	4 749	3 347	225	43 602	15.4	2.51	11.2	24.8
Perry..............................	9.5	7.6	6.9	53.9	12 759	11 861	-7.0	-1.3	692	533	-312	4 333	3.1	2.63	25.1	27.9
Pickens...........................	10.3	8.6	7.3	53.2	20 699	20 949	1.2	-1.9	1 025	857	-553	8 086	6.8	2.56	18.2	26.4
Pike................................	9.8	6.8	6.0	52.6	27 595	29 605	7.3	-1.1	1 397	1 109	-709	11 933	15.7	2.38	16.8	29.8
Randolph.........................	10.6	8.4	7.7	51.5	19 881	22 380	12.6	-0.5	890	924	-52	8 642	14.4	2.52	12.2	25.6
Russell............................	9.5	7.6	5.9	52.4	46 860	49 756	6.2	-1.5	2 095	1 865	-977	19 741	12.8	2.49	18.9	28.0
St. Clair..........................	10.6	6.9	4.8	49.4	49 811	64 742	30.0	6.1	2 702	1 891	3 074	24 143	36.7	2.60	10.0	20.8
Shelby.............................	8.8	5.0	3.4	50.7	99 363	143 293	44.2	11.3	7 693	3 004	11 253	54 631	51.8	2.59	8.1	21.7
Sumter............................	8.0	6.5	7.8	54.4	16 174	14 798	-8.5	-4.2	614	485	-749	5 708	2.9	2.55	23.5	31.2
Talladega.........................	10.5	7.3	6.0	51.4	74 109	80 321	8.4	-0.5	3 609	2 943	-973	30 674	16.0	2.50	15.2	25.9
Tallapoosa.......................	11.8	8.7	7.9	52.1	38 826	41 475	6.8	-1.7	1 676	1 891	-798	16 656	13.3	2.44	14.3	26.5
Tuscaloosa......................	8.4	6.1	5.1	51.8	150 500	164 875	9.6	1.0	7 373	4 979	-696	64 517	16.6	2.42	14.0	28.4
Walker............................	11.5	8.3	6.9	51.7	67 670	70 713	4.5	-0.8	2 942	2 904	-496	28 364	11.0	2.46	11.9	25.3

1. No spouse present.

Table B. States and Counties — **Vital Statistics, Health Resources, and Crime**

STATE County	Births, average 1999–2001 Total	Rate[1]	Deaths, average 1999–2001 Number Total	Number Infant[2]	Rate Total[1]	Rate Infant[3]	Physicians,[4] 2000 Number	Rate[5]	Hospitals,[4] 1998 Number	Beds Number	Beds Rate[5]	Medicare enrollees, 2003	Serious crimes known to police,[6] 2002 Total Number	Rate[7]
	32	33	34	35	36	37	38	39	40	41	42	43	44	45
UNITED STATES............	4 014 721	14.2	2 403 725	27 847	8.5	6.9	587 994	209	5 214	895 681	331	40 172 605	11 877 218	4 119
ALABAMA	61 958	13.9	45 061	590	10.1	9.5	7 605	171	110	17 785	409	719 246	200 331	4 465
Autauga................	605	13.8	360	3	8.2	D	47	108	0	0	0	5 971	NA	NA
Baldwin................	1 829	13.0	1 348	15	9.6	8.0	186	132	3	235	177	26 474	3 342	2 848
Barbour................	389	13.4	309	2	10.7	D	20	69	1	52	193	4 380	NA	NA
Bibb.....................	303	14.4	207	3	9.8	D	15	72	1	138	729	3 364	311	1 480
Blount..................	654	12.8	455	7	8.9	10.2	18	35	1	56	121	6 319	912	1 859
Bullock.................	161	13.8	144	3	12.4	D	7	60	1	62	548	1 937	NA	NA
Butler..................	302	14.1	288	2	13.5	D	12	56	2	91	419	4 102	863	4 351
Calhoun................	1 555	13.8	1 328	15	11.8	9.4	175	156	3	366	313	21 741	6 614	5 840
Chambers..............	462	12.6	491	4	13.4	D	37	101	1	168	458	6 970	1 059	3 833
Cherokee..............	283	11.8	265	2	11.1	D	16	67	1	45	206	3 940	NA	NA
Chilton.................	528	13.4	402	7	10.2	12.6	22	56	1	25	68	5 834	1 054	2 998
Choctaw...............	210	13.2	167	2	10.5	D	5	31	0	0	0	2 948	58	361
Clarke..................	428	15.4	301	3	10.8	D	27	97	3	107	375	5 000	713	2 711
Clay.....................	176	12.4	179	2	12.6	D	5	35	1	116	830	2 808	185	1 287
Cleburne...............	186	13.2	142	1	10.0	D	4	28	0	0	0	2 498	325	2 281
Coffee..................	546	12.5	423	2	9.7	D	51	117	2	229	540	7 465	1 240	2 857
Colbert.................	658	12.0	609	6	11.1	D	88	160	2	280	529	10 528	1 901	3 481
Conecuh...............	187	13.3	180	3	12.8	D	10	71	1	44	315	2 672	228	1 674
Coosa..................	124	10.2	123	3	10.1	D	1	8	0	0	0	2 183	NA	NA
Covington..............	448	11.9	501	3	13.3	D	36	96	3	177	473	7 984	1 331	3 528
Crenshaw..............	174	12.7	181	1	13.2	D	8	59	1	55	403	2 840	NA	NA
Cullman................	992	12.8	858	8	11.1	7.7	81	105	2	215	287	13 529	3 137	4 172
Dale....................	761	15.5	441	6	9.0	D	52	106	1	79	162	10 123	NA	NA
Dallas..................	785	16.9	549	7	11.8	8.5	94	203	2	259	554	8 726	3 865	8 263
De Kalb................	934	14.4	656	8	10.1	8.2	29	45	1	103	176	10 762	NA	NA
Elmore..................	950	14.4	551	7	8.3	7.7	29	44	2	138	223	9 959	1 523	2 720
Escambia..............	508	13.2	437	6	11.4	D	30	78	2	142	386	6 540	1 303	3 360
Etowah.................	1 329	12.8	1 294	12	12.5	9.3	185	179	2	538	517	19 773	5 421	5 194
Fayette.................	218	11.8	225	1	12.2	D	15	81	1	153	844	3 275	205	1 497
Franklin................	438	14.0	378	4	12.1	D	29	93	2	133	448	6 191	NA	NA
Geneva.................	308	12.0	313	4	12.2	D	10	39	1	169	678	5 291	528	2 208
Greene.................	153	15.3	110	2	11.0	D	6	60	1	72	729	1 748	NA	NA
Hale.....................	267	15.6	207	3	12.1	D	9	52	1	30	179	3 183	306	2 098
Henry...................	205	12.6	199	2	12.2	D	7	43	0	0	0	3 214	443	2 787
Houston................	1 297	14.6	881	9	9.9	6.7	267	301	2	639	744	12 317	3 467	4 094
Jackson................	662	12.3	551	5	10.2	D	48	89	2	191	372	9 722	1 464	2 767
Jefferson..............	9 373	14.1	7 278	116	11.0	12.4	2 568	388	13	4 650	705	111 509	35 685	5 747
Lamar..................	182	11.5	203	2	12.8	D	3	19	0	0	0	3 350	93	670
Lauderdale............	1 019	11.6	894	6	10.2	D	139	158	2	627	744	16 302	2 288	2 588
Lawrence..............	435	12.5	354	3	10.2	D	12	34	1	51	152	4 600	434	1 258
Lee......................	1 407	12.2	759	14	6.6	9.7	138	120	1	289	288	11 506	6 584	5 670
Limestone.............	883	13.4	545	5	8.3	D	51	78	1	101	162	8 802	1 222	1 844
Lowndes...............	215	16.0	135	2	10.1	D	2	15	0	0	0	1 833	315	2 524
Macon..................	291	12.1	283	4	11.7	D	39	162	0	0	0	3 643	1 791	7 365
Madison................	3 730	13.4	2 135	29	7.7	7.7	494	179	3	859	309	37 859	13 415	4 814
Marengo...............	335	14.9	260	5	11.6	D	13	58	1	99	423	3 678	757	3 408
Marion.................	364	11.7	378	4	12.2	D	28	90	2	189	610	5 903	484	1 540
Marshall...............	1 208	14.7	918	11	11.1	9.4	75	91	2	192	239	15 769	3 238	3 903
Mobile..................	6 156	15.4	3 919	64	9.8	10.4	925	231	6	1 762	441	59 320	24 377	6 400
Monroe.................	353	14.5	258	3	10.6	D	14	58	1	65	271	3 924	635	2 588
Montgomery	3 519	15.7	2 046	30	9.2	8.5	501	224	5	1 208	555	31 873	18 981	8 418
Morgan.................	1 537	13.8	1 026	13	9.2	8.2	146	131	3	446	408	18 130	4 743	4 318
Perry...................	199	16.8	155	2	13.1	D	8	67	1	76	600	2 025	NA	NA
Pickens................	300	14.3	256	2	12.2	D	14	67	1	56	266	4 076	232	1 098
Pike....................	426	14.4	322	5	10.9	D	23	78	1	65	227	5 097	1 179	4 286
Randolph...............	297	13.3	274	2	12.3	D	20	89	2	90	452	4 226	544	2 409
Russell.................	711	14.3	578	10	11.6	13.6	38	76	1	120	238	8 650	1 386	2 761
St. Clair...............	852	13.1	579	9	8.9	10.6	24	37	1	72	116	8 567	NA	NA
Shelby.................	2 306	16.0	879	17	6.1	7.4	136	95	1	164	117	13 296	2 109	1 638
Sumter.................	205	13.9	161	3	10.9	D	7	47	1	33	209	2 520	NA	NA
Talladega..............	1 122	14.0	878	10	10.9	8.6	71	88	2	237	309	14 335	NA	NA
Tallapoosa............	533	12.9	540	4	13.0	D	46	111	2	103	254	7 557	1 716	4 214
Tuscaloosa............	2 285	13.8	1 476	30	8.9	13.3	316	192	2	680	423	23 273	9 330	5 609
Walker.................	931	13.2	920	9	13.0	10.0	52	74	1	267	376	14 871	1 687	3 154

1. Per 1,000 estimated resident population. 2. Deaths of infants under 1 year old. 3. Deaths of infants under 1 year old per 1,000 live births. 4. Data subject to copyright. 5. Per 100,000 resident population as of July 1 of the year shown. 6. Data for serious crimes have not been adjusted for underreporting; this may affect comparability between geographic areas and over time. 7. Per 100,000 population estimated by the FBI.

Table B. States and Counties — Crime, Education, Money Income, and Poverty

STATE County	Serious crimes known to police,[1] 2002 (cont'd) Rate[2] Violent	Property	Education — School enrollment and attainment, 2000 — Enrollment[3] Total	Percent private	Attainment[4] (percent) High school graduate or less	Bachelor's degree or more	Local government expenditures,[5] 2000–2001 Total current expenditures (mil dol)	Current expenditures per student (dollars)	Money income, 1999 Per capita income[6] (dollars)	Households — Median income Dollars	Percent change, 1989–1999 (constant 1999 dollars)	Percent with income of $100,000 or more	Percent below poverty level, 1999 Persons	House- holds	Families	Families with children
	46	47	48	49	50	51	52	53	54	55	56	57	58	59	60	61
UNITED STATES............	495	3 624	76 632 927	16.4	48.2	24.4	345 291.9	7 426	21 587	41 994	4.0	12.3	12.4	11.8	9.2	13.6
ALABAMA	444	4 021	1 155 504	13.9	55.1	19.0	4 328.5	5 941	18 189	34 135	7.7	7.6	16.1	16.7	12.5	18.2
Autauga..........................	NA	NA	11 887	16.6	55.1	18.0	43.8	5 077	18 518	42 013	10.4	7.6	10.9	11.5	8.2	10.8
Baldwin...........................	251	2 597	32 637	16.1	47.6	23.1	133.5	5 893	20 826	40 250	16.5	9.5	10.1	10.3	7.6	11.5
Barbour...........................	NA	NA	6 889	11.3	67.8	10.9	27.4	5 860	13 316	25 101	-3.6	5.0	26.8	26.8	21.6	32.0
Bibb................................	262	1 218	4 908	12.7	72.5	7.1	20.0	5 619	14 105	31 420	18.3	3.5	20.6	19.4	14.9	24.4
Blount.............................	67	1 792	11 833	9.5	65.6	9.6	43.9	5 154	16 325	35 241	17.2	5.0	11.7	13.6	8.6	12.1
Bullock...........................	NA	NA	2 884	14.4	74.8	7.7	11.8	5 938	10 163	20 605	4.0	2.6	33.5	33.6	29.8	41.2
Butler.............................	398	3 952	5 453	15.4	66.7	10.4	21.5	5 910	15 715	24 791	14.9	4.8	24.6	24.7	20.4	26.6
Calhoun..........................	689	5 152	27 855	9.5	58.3	15.2	104.4	5 744	17 367	31 768	-0.7	5.9	16.1	16.9	12.4	19.5
Chambers........................	619	3 214	8 386	14.2	67.9	9.5	31.4	5 642	15 147	29 667	3.9	3.3	17.0	18.7	14.3	19.9
Cherokee.........................	NA	NA	4 661	6.4	71.3	9.7	23.1	5 905	15 543	30 874	7.5	3.6	15.6	16.4	11.8	18.1
Chilton...........................	1 112	1 886	9 022	8.9	69.6	9.9	37.6	5 546	15 303	32 588	12.2	4.0	15.7	16.4	12.6	16.2
Choctaw..........................	12	349	3 792	21.8	69.8	9.6	14.3	6 312	14 635	24 749	7.6	4.9	24.5	24.9	20.7	29.7
Clarke.............................	361	2 350	6 977	14.5	66.8	12.1	30.7	5 822	14 581	27 388	6.9	5.0	22.6	22.5	18.1	24.0
Clay................................	97	1 189	3 083	7.9	71.8	7.8	13.5	5 554	13 785	27 885	7.8	2.0	17.1	18.9	12.9	18.7
Cleburne.........................	84	2 197	3 139	7.6	72.9	9.2	14.2	5 570	14 762	30 820	8.4	3.5	13.9	16.4	10.9	15.4
Coffee............................	237	2 620	11 041	8.2	53.1	19.3	48.5	6 054	18 321	33 664	4.8	6.6	14.7	14.5	11.3	18.7
Colbert...........................	143	3 338	12 414	8.3	60.6	14.1	55.3	6 476	17 533	31 954	6.3	5.8	14.0	15.4	11.1	16.4
Conecuh.........................	264	1 410	3 355	13.0	70.4	9.2	12.6	5 970	12 964	22 111	2.9	3.6	26.6	28.7	21.7	29.5
Coosa.............................	NA	NA	2 688	8.8	72.6	8.0	9.6	5 546	14 875	29 873	9.6	3.5	14.9	16.6	11.8	16.6
Covington........................	374	3 155	8 418	4.2	64.5	12.2	36.7	5 668	15 365	26 336	6.6	4.3	18.4	19.6	14.1	20.5
Crenshaw........................	NA	NA	3 118	10.0	68.9	11.2	13.1	5 497	14 565	26 054	17.8	3.7	22.1	23.4	18.6	25.1
Cullman..........................	165	4 007	18 082	7.4	61.6	11.9	66.8	5 466	16 992	32 256	10.8	5.5	13.0	14.5	9.5	12.6
Dale................................	NA	NA	12 680	9.3	51.4	14.0	42.1	5 733	16 010	31 998	-1.1	3.9	15.1	16.1	12.6	17.6
Dallas.............................	977	7 286	13 032	15.1	63.2	13.9	51.8	5 741	13 638	23 370	5.5	4.2	31.1	31.0	27.2	38.3
De Kalb...........................	NA	NA	14 045	5.6	70.2	8.3	61.1	5 848	15 818	30 137	11.4	4.3	15.4	17.0	11.7	15.6
Elmore............................	168	2 552	16 377	14.7	56.2	16.6	63.9	5 367	17 650	41 243	16.5	8.2	10.2	10.7	7.4	11.2
Escambia........................	557	2 803	8 744	9.0	66.2	10.6	39.1	6 322	14 396	28 319	14.1	4.8	20.9	19.9	15.2	21.3
Etowah...........................	771	4 423	23 661	11.1	58.2	13.4	90.8	5 742	16 783	31 170	4.0	5.6	15.7	16.2	12.3	18.9
Fayette...........................	387	1 110	4 234	5.4	68.9	9.2	15.7	5 640	14 439	28 539	7.0	2.7	17.3	19.1	13.1	17.8
Franklin..........................	NA	NA	6 948	5.3	68.4	9.7	32.4	5 861	14 814	27 177	13.0	3.9	18.9	21.1	15.2	22.0
Geneva...........................	309	1 899	5 693	6.5	66.4	8.7	23.0	5 562	14 620	26 448	-1.7	3.6	19.6	20.4	15.9	23.7
Greene............................	NA	NA	2 616	9.4	70.1	10.5	12.4	7 122	13 686	19 819	23.0	3.3	34.3	34.6	29.9	39.9
Hale................................	562	1 536	4 564	8.7	70.7	8.1	19.3	5 837	12 661	25 807	32.4	3.3	26.9	28.3	22.2	29.2
Henry..............................	390	2 397	3 715	9.5	62.4	14.1	16.2	5 806	15 681	30 353	2.1	4.8	19.1	20.0	14.5	22.8
Houston..........................	267	3 828	22 033	15.7	53.8	18.4	88.3	5 943	18 759	34 431	3.3	8.0	15.0	15.8	11.8	18.2
Jackson..........................	206	2 561	11 505	5.1	67.8	10.4	55.9	6 238	16 000	32 020	8.8	4.6	13.7	15.5	10.3	13.9
Jefferson........................	698	5 049	174 793	16.0	47.0	24.6	693.9	6 335	20 892	36 868	6.1	10.1	14.8	14.7	11.6	17.0
Lamar.............................	72	598	3 521	4.7	72.5	7.8	15.5	5 792	14 435	28 059	1.3	2.7	16.1	18.3	13.3	18.3
Lauderdale......................	230	2 358	22 201	11.4	57.8	18.5	82.2	6 257	18 626	33 354	4.8	7.1	14.4	15.5	10.5	16.0
Lawrence.........................	81	1 177	8 031	8.3	73.8	7.5	37.4	6 113	16 515	31 549	9.1	5.8	15.3	17.6	13.1	15.2
Lee.................................	583	5 087	45 855	8.7	45.3	27.9	107.8	6 012	17 158	30 952	8.5	7.2	21.8	25.2	11.1	14.1
Limestone.......................	100	1 745	16 015	10.7	58.0	16.9	68.3	6 347	17 782	37 405	3.6	8.0	12.3	13.2	9.8	14.2
Lowndes..........................	401	2 123	3 714	12.0	69.1	11.0	17.2	6 556	12 457	23 050	10.1	4.2	31.4	33.2	26.6	37.1
Macon.............................	567	6 797	8 743	34.4	55.0	18.8	22.7	5 845	13 714	21 180	0.8	3.9	32.8	32.0	26.8	38.1
Madison..........................	426	4 388	78 591	17.4	36.5	34.3	275.8	6 198	23 091	44 704	0.7	13.3	10.5	10.8	8.1	12.2
Marengo..........................	500	2 908	5 926	10.7	65.4	12.1	28.1	5 969	15 308	27 025	7.8	5.9	25.9	26.7	22.2	29.9
Marion............................	124	1 416	6 373	7.7	69.7	8.0	28.1	5 515	15 321	27 475	10.8	4.0	15.6	17.7	12.0	16.8
Marshall..........................	284	3 619	18 171	6.3	61.1	13.9	89.0	5 984	17 089	32 167	11.6	6.4	14.7	16.4	11.7	16.8
Mobile............................	597	5 803	110 152	21.3	55.2	18.6	351.1	5 404	17 178	33 710	9.1	6.7	18.5	18.3	15.6	22.8
Monroe...........................	587	2 001	6 146	13.3	66.5	11.8	25.4	5 726	14 862	29 093	2.4	4.4	21.3	22.9	18.2	24.9
Montgomery....................	705	7 713	65 349	20.8	44.1	28.5	190.5	5 728	19 358	35 962	0.8	9.7	17.3	15.7	13.5	20.1
Morgan...........................	239	4 080	26 429	10.8	54.0	18.4	127.8	6 598	19 223	37 803	-0.8	8.6	12.3	13.1	9.7	14.3
Perry...............................	NA	NA	3 389	10.4	68.0	10.0	13.4	5 833	10 948	20 200	9.2	3.1	35.4	33.4	31.2	43.4
Pickens...........................	90	1 008	5 436	10.1	68.1	9.8	22.4	6 039	13 746	26 254	9.3	3.7	24.9	24.5	20.1	29.7
Pike................................	251	4 035	9 104	13.4	60.9	18.4	27.6	6 144	14 904	25 551	9.9	4.7	23.1	24.8	18.5	25.7
Randolph.........................	301	2 108	5 262	8.8	70.1	10.0	20.4	5 437	14 147	28 675	9.8	3.5	17.0	17.8	12.6	19.5
Russell............................	281	2 480	12 521	10.3	66.5	9.7	52.2	5 930	14 015	27 492	-2.5	2.5	19.9	20.7	16.8	22.9
St. Clair..........................	NA	NA	15 126	12.8	63.3	11.1	56.0	5 117	17 960	37 285	15.1	7.1	12.1	12.6	9.6	12.6
Shelby............................	167	1 471	37 311	21.2	36.2	36.8	129.0	6 409	27 176	55 440	12.0	19.4	6.3	6.8	4.6	6.3
Sumter............................	NA	NA	4 704	10.6	66.4	12.4	18.3	6 571	11 491	18 911	9.9	2.2	38.7	38.2	32.9	42.5
Talladega........................	NA	NA	19 125	10.2	64.8	11.2	78.8	5 975	15 704	31 628	10.1	5.2	17.6	18.5	13.9	19.7
Tallapoosa......................	476	3 738	9 775	5.8	62.9	14.1	40.8	5 871	16 909	30 745	3.9	6.2	16.6	17.1	13.5	20.4
Tuscaloosa......................	525	5 084	52 373	10.6	49.6	24.0	152.3	6 040	18 998	34 436	11.2	7.8	17.0	18.8	11.3	16.2
Walker............................	144	3 010	15 536	9.6	67.5	9.1	66.3	6 140	15 546	29 076	5.8	4.7	16.5	18.1	13.2	18.5

1. Data for serious crimes have not been adjusted for underreporting; this may affect comparability between geographic areas and over time.   2. Per 100,000 population estimated by the FBI.   3. All persons 3 years old and over enrolled in nursery school through college.   4. Persons 25 years old and over.   5. Elementary and secondary education expenditures.   6. Based on population enumerated as of April 1, 2000.

STATE County	Personal income, 2002												
			Per capita[1]						Transfer payments				
										Government payments to individuals			
	Total (mil dol)	Percent change, 2001–2002	Dollars	Rank	Wages and salaries[2] (mil dol)	Proprietor's income (mil dol)	Dividends, interest, and rent (mil dol)	Total (mil dol)	Total (mil dol)	Social Security (mil dol)	Medical payments (mil dol)	Income maintenance (mil dol)	Unemployment insurance (mil dol)
	62	63	64	65	66	67	68	69	70	71	72	73	74
UNITED STATES	8 900 007	2.3	30 906	X	6 007 587	800 354	1 550 330	1 291 729	1 220 858	446 559	526 310	121 884	53 974
ALABAMA	114 428	3.1	25 548	X	73 978	9 060	19 035	20 622	19 560	7 889	7 791	2 227	422
Autauga	1 128	3.0	24 736	1 202	377	89	154	165	154	67	56	18	3
Baldwin	4 037	4.0	27 224	665	1 593	295	901	647	612	305	223	39	10
Barbour	595	0.9	20 524	2 423	360	70	102	137	130	47	56	20	3
Bibb	395	4.5	18 800	2 782	129	21	52	97	92	35	39	11	2
Blount	1 123	1.4	21 169	2 245	282	84	155	201	188	86	73	16	5
Bullock	201	4.5	17 790	2 919	96	22	29	61	58	16	27	12	1
Butler	458	3.5	22 018	2 011	212	50	69	121	116	41	51	16	3
Calhoun	2 618	5.0	23 504	1 567	1 737	141	458	578	552	215	221	59	10
Chambers	800	2.3	22 141	1 973	434	55	109	186	177	75	69	22	4
Cherokee	497	3.7	20 431	2 451	150	36	83	113	107	48	43	10	1
Chilton	857	3.4	21 185	2 241	263	53	114	169	159	67	64	17	4
Choctaw	319	3.0	20 634	2 389	210	20	54	85	82	33	34	11	2
Clarke	581	2.1	21 101	2 269	315	37	100	146	139	53	57	21	4
Clay	291	2.8	20 436	2 448	142	25	45	74	71	29	31	6	1
Cleburne	288	0.9	19 748	2 604	103	32	37	61	58	26	23	6	1
Coffee	1 156	3.6	26 265	839	414	102	222	212	201	78	84	18	3
Colbert	1 191	1.0	21 808	2 063	839	71	199	290	277	124	99	22	10
Conecuh	283	2.1	20 554	2 419	136	28	38	83	79	28	32	12	2
Coosa	228	4.0	19 661	2 618	63	7	32	56	53	24	18	7	2
Covington	841	2.9	22 731	1 808	420	101	142	210	201	80	86	21	4
Crenshaw	330	0.0	24 287	1 315	98	71	46	74	71	26	31	9	1
Cullman	1 812	0.5	23 262	1 641	883	205	273	362	344	146	144	24	8
Dale	1 070	5.2	21 696	2 090	1 107	65	147	229	218	74	94	26	4
Dallas	933	0.8	20 589	2 406	563	45	153	283	272	82	110	59	7
De Kalb	1 450	1.5	22 068	1 999	819	179	199	291	276	115	117	27	5
Elmore	1 648	4.3	23 846	1 457	477	102	215	274	258	104	105	26	4
Escambia	735	0.2	19 107	2 740	442	60	116	187	178	73	68	22	5
Etowah	2 365	3.2	22 999	1 723	1 249	145	357	561	537	229	221	51	9
Fayette	380	0.1	20 752	2 355	183	20	70	93	89	39	34	10	2
Franklin	662	-0.1	21 463	2 159	316	72	105	164	156	61	70	14	7
Geneva	579	1.3	22 711	1 817	155	76	79	138	132	53	56	14	2
Greene	187	3.3	18 862	2 774	67	13	27	55	53	17	22	12	1
Hale	325	4.6	17 806	2 917	108	30	44	93	89	27	40	16	2
Henry	372	5.0	22 778	1 789	158	36	60	85	81	32	34	10	2
Houston	2 407	4.0	26 728	748	1 717	132	453	410	389	161	147	46	7
Jackson	1 174	1.5	21 802	2 067	597	72	178	246	233	100	94	22	7
Jefferson	21 777	3.7	33 057	184	18 311	2 719	4 015	3 168	3 011	1 238	1 193	332	58
Lamar	312	0.0	20 266	2 485	160	19	50	84	80	33	34	8	2
Lauderdale	2 035	0.1	23 372	1 603	925	131	414	420	399	186	146	33	14
Lawrence	715	-3.3	20 570	2 412	253	53	88	140	132	59	49	14	4
Lee	2 530	3.8	21 445	2 168	1 457	149	416	357	329	140	115	39	7
Limestone	1 590	2.1	23 546	1 550	988	116	228	251	234	102	84	22	6
Lowndes	245	0.7	18 219	2 868	109	20	32	67	64	20	26	14	2
Macon	396	2.3	16 728	3 009	205	15	47	119	113	33	45	22	1
Madison	8 633	4.1	30 239	331	8 132	410	1 541	965	897	383	328	87	22
Marengo	529	3.7	23 598	1 535	283	47	89	121	115	44	47	18	2
Marion	601	3.5	19 813	2 584	353	45	96	152	145	61	61	13	4
Marshall	2 011	2.1	24 172	1 350	1 088	132	308	386	366	150	156	35	8
Mobile	9 033	1.9	22 620	1 843	6 591	598	1 400	1 908	1 813	681	740	241	44
Monroe	491	-0.6	20 494	2 435	349	28	74	117	111	43	44	15	3
Montgomery	6 643	4.7	29 813	364	5 831	544	1 286	1 022	971	341	368	150	17
Morgan	2 927	1.1	26 227	850	1 886	208	470	488	462	199	196	37	13
Perry	209	3.5	17 849	2 914	72	10	29	77	74	21	32	16	2
Pickens	409	0.1	19 604	2 629	128	28	62	122	117	41	51	17	2
Pike	691	3.3	23 662	1 512	385	91	97	161	154	48	63	22	3
Randolph	432	1.7	19 177	2 719	166	29	69	115	110	44	42	11	2
Russell	1 034	1.7	20 978	2 304	437	41	122	244	232	86	85	33	6
St. Clair	1 540	3.6	22 873	1 758	462	68	201	259	243	111	90	23	5
Shelby	5 353	4.2	34 819	147	2 184	257	739	433	396	205	138	24	7
Sumter	255	4.4	17 892	2 911	128	16	35	83	80	23	31	18	2
Talladega	1 776	8.0	22 134	1 980	1 082	91	223	410	391	156	160	51	10
Tallapoosa	930	2.0	22 656	1 835	484	51	165	223	213	89	85	24	5
Tuscaloosa	4 360	3.5	26 339	823	3 109	309	710	763	723	274	307	77	11
Walker	1 606	3.8	22 766	1 796	586	97	241	427	410	159	175	37	6

1. Based on the resident population estimated as of July 1 of the year shown.　2. Includes other labor income.

Table B. States and Counties — Earnings, Social Security, and Housing

STATE County	Earnings, 2002									Social Security beneficiaries, December 2003		Supplemental Security Income recipients, December 2003	Housing units, 2003	
	Total (mil dol)	Farm	Goods-related[1]		Service-related and health				Govern-ment	Number	Rate[2]		Total	Percent change, 2000–2003
			Total	Manu-facturing	Infor-mation and profes-sional and technical services	Retail trade	Finance, insur-ance, and real estate	Health services						
	75	76	77	78	79	80	81	82	83	84	85	86	87	88
UNITED STATES............	6 807 941	0.6	20.2	13.2	13.1	6.9	10.0	9.2	16.2	47 038 391	162	6 902 364	120 879 390	4.3
ALABAMA	83 038	1.2	24.9	17.5	9.9	7.7	6.4	9.4	19.9	867 601	193	163 772	2 031 595	3.5
Autauga............................	466	1.2	D	23.8	4.1	11.4	7.1	4.4	15.9	7 695	166	1 288	18 702	5.9
Baldwin............................	1 888	1.5	21.1	11.0	6.3	12.7	9.3	9.0	16.5	32 420	214	2 818	80 856	8.8
Barbour............................	430	9.3	34.8	31.4	D	6.4	3.3	6.2	16.4	5 755	200	1 630	12 722	2.1
Bibb.................................	150	1.6	D	9.7	3.8	7.9	3.0	D	30.5	4 190	198	924	8 540	2.3
Blount..............................	366	7.2	D	14.5	6.1	11.1	5.0	D	18.3	9 735	180	1 193	21 763	2.9
Bullock............................	117	14.9	D	D	D	7.1	2.9	7.4	24.4	2 125	187	931	4 753	0.6
Butler..............................	263	8.4	26.5	19.8	3.3	11.8	2.6	10.7	14.2	4 990	241	1 291	10 224	2.7
Calhoun...........................	1 878	0.5	D	19.3	6.1	8.4	3.1	8.4	29.8	25 045	224	4 658	52 609	2.5
Chambers.........................	489	0.7	43.9	38.2	D	8.9	1.8	D	11.0	8 050	225	1 429	16 386	0.8
Cherokee..........................	186	8.7	D	20.4	3.3	10.8	4.7	5.2	21.8	5 430	222	727	14 351	2.3
Chilton.............................	315	3.7	D	15.4	D	13.3	4.8	D	18.8	7 635	187	1 272	18 176	3.0
Choctaw...........................	229	1.3	D	59.7	D	5.1	1.6	D	8.8	3 795	248	964	8 017	2.3
Clarke..............................	352	0.2	D	28.4	2.6	11.0	4.5	D	20.2	6 145	224	1 713	12 880	2.0
Clay.................................	167	3.8	46.4	43.4	1.5	5.2	2.5	4.1	20.2	3 475	245	521	6 715	1.6
Cleburne..........................	135	9.6	D	27.5	1.2	7.5	1.5	1.4	20.7	3 165	216	481	6 354	2.7
Coffee..............................	516	9.1	20.5	16.3	6.8	11.6	4.3	11.4	17.7	9 115	204	1 455	20 413	2.9
Colbert.............................	910	0.7	28.2	19.9	D	9.4	3.4	6.7	31.3	12 995	238	1 887	25 601	2.5
Conecuh...........................	165	4.1	14.2	12.2	2.1	4.8	1.3	D	19.2	3 360	247	854	7 382	1.6
Coosa..............................	70	3.3	D	43.0	D	4.1	D	4.2	22.0	2 805	244	519	6 251	1.8
Covington.........................	521	6.1	D	23.6	4.1	9.4	3.3	D	14.8	9 395	254	1 669	18 801	1.2
Crenshaw.........................	169	25.5	8.3	3.3	2.2	6.8	2.6	D	13.2	3 270	241	734	6 774	2.0
Cullman...........................	1 089	5.5	D	18.9	D	9.9	4.3	13.7	12.4	16 515	211	2 455	36 062	2.4
Dale.................................	1 172	2.0	D	24.9	1.8	2.8	1.1	1.8	51.3	8 950	182	1 922	22 232	2.1
Dallas..............................	608	1.5	34.9	30.0	D	9.2	3.0	12.3	17.5	10 120	225	4 867	20 724	1.3
De Kalb............................	998	6.4	D	43.8	D	7.9	2.9	5.7	10.3	13 575	204	2 224	28 728	2.4
Elmore.............................	579	0.0	30.8	18.3	5.7	9.2	3.6	D	23.2	11 780	167	1 975	27 044	5.1
Escambia..........................	502	1.3	34.2	27.5	D	9.2	4.7	D	21.0	8 240	216	1 466	16 819	1.7
Etowah.............................	1 393	1.2	D	19.1	4.6	8.8	5.1	18.5	14.7	24 265	236	4 422	47 038	2.3
Fayette............................	203	0.3	42.5	25.2	D	8.3	2.4	D	22.3	4 515	248	767	8 651	2.1
Franklin...........................	388	9.6	D	32.1	D	5.9	3.2	D	19.9	6 945	225	1 158	13 998	1.8
Geneva............................	232	19.7	19.1	10.2	D	8.8	3.9	4.1	20.5	6 300	247	1 176	12 326	1.7
Greene.............................	81	10.0	18.6	14.9	1.2	5.1	D	D	27.5	2 205	223	929	5 232	2.2
Hale.................................	138	12.4	29.0	25.8	3.0	5.5	2.6	D	24.6	3 415	187	1 219	8 013	3.3
Henry..............................	194	10.7	D	24.7	D	5.3	3.0	D	14.2	3 840	234	746	8 186	1.9
Houston...........................	1 849	1.6	18.9	13.0	5.5	10.6	6.1	15.5	16.3	18 180	199	3 651	41 297	4.4
Jackson............................	669	2.9	40.6	36.1	D	8.1	2.9	D	24.5	11 090	206	1 784	24 772	2.5
Jefferson..........................	21 030	0.0	17.3	8.5	14.8	7.0	11.2	13.0	13.8	124 085	189	22 934	294 718	2.3
Lamar..............................	180	0.0	45.2	41.3	2.3	5.4	3.1	8.0	13.3	3 835	253	642	7 644	1.7
Lauderdale........................	1 056	0.4	D	14.4	5.7	11.5	6.1	11.3	23.9	19 435	223	2 787	41 233	2.0
Lawrence..........................	306	6.6	D	35.8	2.9	7.2	2.0	D	18.4	6 775	196	1 211	15 398	2.6
Lee..................................	1 607	0.4	22.1	15.7	D	9.6	4.6	7.0	34.5	15 080	126	2 804	54 096	7.5
Limestone.........................	1 103	1.7	39.6	35.3	9.6	6.6	2.5	D	25.3	11 665	171	1 735	27 856	3.6
Lowndes...........................	129	7.6	D	37.6	D	6.1	3.6	2.9	17.5	2 640	197	930	5 867	1.1
Macon..............................	220	2.1	D	0.7	D	4.6	1.5	D	48.9	4 255	181	1 291	10 857	2.2
Madison...........................	8 543	0.0	D	20.5	20.1	6.1	3.4	5.9	27.2	42 415	146	5 879	124 786	3.7
Marengo...........................	331	1.5	35.8	32.7	2.8	6.7	4.6	4.0	18.1	5 120	229	1 535	10 305	1.8
Marion.............................	397	2.1	42.0	39.3	5.8	7.1	3.4	9.4	14.1	7 065	234	1 027	14 793	2.6
Marshall...........................	1 221	3.8	D	32.6	4.4	10.4	4.1	4.7	16.6	17 350	207	3 031	37 250	2.5
Mobile.............................	7 189	0.4	21.4	12.7	9.8	8.2	6.2	11.0	17.3	72 950	182	13 910	171 249	3.7
Monroe............................	377	0.7	D	41.5	2.3	5.8	2.2	D	14.2	4 990	209	1 078	11 613	2.4
Montgomery	6 375	0.2	13.9	7.5	11.7	6.0	8.7	9.8	31.1	37 465	169	9 494	97 782	2.5
Morgan............................	2 095	0.9	44.9	36.0	3.9	7.4	4.6	7.4	13.9	21 135	188	3 161	48 809	3.0
Perry...............................	82	7.0	D	D	D	6.7	3.0	8.1	27.1	2 835	242	1 250	5 517	2.1
Pickens............................	156	5.0	D	19.4	D	7.9	4.9	D	22.2	4 970	242	1 423	9 713	2.0
Pike.................................	476	9.9	21.2	14.7	2.3	7.9	5.6	7.3	19.7	5 830	199	1 694	14 360	2.7
Randolph..........................	194	3.9	D	30.5	3.2	9.1	3.3	D	23.1	5 095	229	836	10 447	1.6
Russell............................	478	1.3	D	32.7	3.7	9.6	3.7	6.0	18.7	9 855	201	2 069	23 873	4.6
St. Clair............................	530	0.4	D	19.8	D	10.2	3.8	6.5	18.3	12 190	178	1 510	28 743	5.3
Shelby.............................	2 441	0.2	28.8	17.3	11.2	8.1	6.6	6.6	9.4	20 455	128	1 538	66 167	11.6
Sumter.............................	144	5.6	18.3	14.8	D	7.3	2.7	D	31.7	3 010	212	1 212	7 088	1.9
Talladega..........................	1 173	0.3	D	41.9	2.9	6.7	2.7	D	17.0	17 630	221	4 135	35 368	2.6
Tallapoosa........................	535	0.2	D	31.1	4.6	7.8	4.0	D	14.5	9 835	241	1 845	20 837	1.6
Tuscaloosa........................	3 417	0.1	34.5	21.2	5.2	7.3	3.8	7.5	24.5	29 380	177	6 025	75 305	5.4
Walker.............................	683	0.2	15.5	6.5	6.7	13.8	5.6	D	17.6	17 090	244	3 230	33 085	2.1

1. Covers mining, construction, and manufacturing.   2. Per 1,000 resident population estimated as of July 1 of the year shown.

Table B. States and Counties — Housing, Labor Force, and Employment

STATE County	Housing units, 2000								Civilian labor force, 2003				Civilian employment,[6] 2000		
	Occupied units							Sub-stand-ard units[4] (percent)		Percent change, 2002–2003	Unemployment			Percent	
	Owner-occupied			Median owner cost as a percent of income		Renter-occupied									
				With a mortgage	Without a mortgage[2]	Median rent[3]	Median rent as a percent of income							Management, professional and related occupations	Production, transportation, and material moving occupations
	Total	Percent	Median value[1]						Total		Total	Rate[5]	Total		
	89	90	91	92	93	94	95	96	97	98	99	100	101	102	103
UNITED STATES	105 480 101	66.2	119 600	21.7	10.5	602	25.5	6.3	146 178 717	0.9	8 750 005	6.0	129 721 512	33.6	14.6
ALABAMA	1 737 080	72.5	85 100	19.8	9.9	447	24.8	3.5	2 147 321	2.5	124 662	5.8	1 920 189	29.5	19.0
Autauga	16 003	80.8	94 800	19.4	9.9	537	22.6	3.2	22 954	3.1	1 030	4.5	19 595	27.1	18.0
Baldwin	55 336	79.6	122 500	20.8	9.9	566	24.5	2.8	75 772	2.6	3 248	4.3	62 938	29.5	13.7
Barbour	10 409	73.2	68 600	20.4	10.2	333	25.1	5.6	13 437	1.2	801	6.0	10 193	23.3	29.1
Bibb	7 421	80.2	74 600	19.2	9.9	348	22.9	4.4	7 302	1.4	528	7.2	7 967	22.1	26.4
Blount	19 265	83.5	86 800	19.6	10.3	385	21.7	3.8	26 397	0.6	950	3.6	22 701	23.6	21.8
Bullock	3 986	74.4	56 600	29.6	11.6	324	35.1	8.3	4 637	6.3	557	12.0	3 441	18.0	31.0
Butler	8 398	76.2	57 700	20.5	12.3	328	26.1	4.3	9 487	3.6	980	10.3	8 006	20.9	25.9
Calhoun	45 307	72.5	71 600	19.0	9.9	413	24.6	2.4	53 527	3.6	2 914	5.4	47 856	25.5	23.2
Chambers	14 522	75.7	58 900	18.3	10.7	374	24.0	3.3	15 329	-2.4	1 097	7.2	15 695	19.6	31.7
Cherokee	9 719	81.7	76 100	19.9	10.2	362	22.2	2.6	11 110	7.0	475	4.3	10 180	19.0	32.8
Chilton	15 287	82.2	81 800	20.6	9.9	385	23.6	2.7	18 439	1.7	854	4.6	17 437	22.0	20.0
Choctaw	6 363	86.3	60 500	18.4	10.5	284	23.4	5.2	4 959	0.8	628	12.7	5 469	21.9	25.9
Clarke	10 578	81.1	67 900	18.0	10.1	343	19.5	4.4	12 712	2.7	1 020	8.0	10 343	23.9	25.3
Clay	5 765	77.2	62 200	19.9	9.9	272	19.5	3.2	6 550	3.1	477	7.3	5 930	19.4	35.1
Cleburne	5 590	80.4	71 300	20.9	9.9	378	21.4	2.4	6 726	-1.5	384	5.7	6 188	21.3	28.8
Coffee	17 421	71.4	76 600	18.8	9.9	415	22.3	3.4	20 065	5.7	882	4.4	17 905	29.9	19.5
Colbert	22 461	75.7	72 300	20.0	10.4	414	25.4	2.1	24 176	-0.7	1 904	7.9	23 093	24.0	23.3
Conecuh	5 792	81.1	58 600	20.5	12.3	289	27.9	2.6	5 667	3.1	474	8.4	4 863	19.4	28.1
Coosa	4 682	84.8	59 500	21.0	9.9	295	22.0	3.8	5 270	-0.2	431	8.2	4 841	16.3	34.3
Covington	15 640	77.7	56 700	19.5	11.0	340	23.5	2.9	16 727	4.3	1 265	7.6	15 304	26.3	21.8
Crenshaw	5 577	76.6	51 300	19.1	10.6	279	20.9	4.9	5 041	5.8	409	8.1	5 463	22.4	24.3
Cullman	30 706	78.1	85 000	21.6	9.9	398	22.3	2.7	40 433	3.3	2 155	5.3	35 092	24.5	25.2
Dale	18 878	64.2	69 000	18.7	9.9	398	22.6	3.6	20 875	2.6	980	4.7	18 803	24.0	17.9
Dallas	17 841	65.7	64 100	19.9	10.3	350	27.4	5.9	18 344	-0.6	2 371	12.9	15 391	24.6	23.9
De Kalb	25 113	78.7	67 200	20.0	10.8	370	21.7	4.3	33 928	2.3	1 727	5.1	29 280	19.7	37.3
Elmore	22 737	81.4	98 000	19.5	9.9	486	22.5	2.9	32 141	3.4	1 436	4.5	27 970	29.1	16.6
Escambia	14 297	77.1	66 700	19.1	9.9	351	22.3	4.0	15 480	-0.7	1 315	8.5	14 598	22.6	25.4
Etowah	41 615	74.4	71 200	19.7	9.9	395	23.1	2.1	47 192	0.1	2 863	6.1	43 426	25.3	23.2
Fayette	7 493	77.2	64 100	20.0	9.9	283	22.2	2.9	7 512	2.4	536	7.1	7 391	20.7	30.4
Franklin	12 259	74.3	62 800	20.6	10.0	335	22.9	3.7	15 320	0.2	1 501	9.8	13 089	20.0	34.8
Geneva	10 477	80.6	55 900	20.2	9.9	319	24.3	2.5	9 817	6.5	546	5.6	10 809	22.2	22.8
Greene	3 931	75.6	57 000	24.6	13.2	235	23.5	8.7	2 862	-0.9	338	11.8	3 109	20.8	25.7
Hale	6 415	80.2	66 300	19.7	9.9	295	25.8	7.3	6 897	1.7	738	10.7	5 842	19.6	27.4
Henry	6 525	80.9	69 100	19.8	11.2	336	24.6	5.4	6 361	0.5	403	6.3	6 780	24.9	23.2
Houston	35 834	69.5	82 000	17.9	9.9	413	22.7	3.0	46 609	3.3	2 038	4.4	40 355	29.5	17.0
Jackson	21 615	77.9	72 400	19.3	9.9	370	22.4	2.8	25 535	3.9	2 066	8.1	24 982	21.7	31.9
Jefferson	263 265	66.5	90 700	20.2	9.9	500	24.5	3.2	332 533	2.3	16 795	5.1	297 123	34.0	12.7
Lamar	6 468	76.9	55 200	21.3	9.9	282	22.7	2.3	6 235	-4.2	647	10.4	6 547	19.8	34.3
Lauderdale	36 088	73.2	85 000	19.8	9.9	420	27.0	1.8	39 159	-1.5	3 111	7.9	38 923	26.2	21.5
Lawrence	13 538	83.1	75 000	20.5	11.0	361	23.7	3.4	16 012	-0.4	1 100	6.9	14 784	18.1	29.6
Lee	45 702	62.1	104 100	19.8	9.9	449	35.1	3.2	53 530	4.1	2 108	3.9	52 980	33.9	15.4
Limestone	24 688	77.3	86 400	18.9	9.9	392	21.9	3.4	32 689	4.9	1 780	5.4	29 709	27.0	24.0
Lowndes	4 909	83.4	55 500	22.6	12.7	298	27.0	7.9	4 396	0.6	577	13.1	4 443	23.4	26.9
Macon	8 950	67.3	64 200	22.3	11.7	352	29.4	7.3	6 832	-4.4	486	7.1	8 133	29.6	15.3
Madison	109 955	69.9	103 300	18.6	9.9	503	23.6	2.3	151 487	4.9	6 509	4.3	134 916	43.3	12.8
Marengo	8 767	79.2	65 900	18.7	9.9	305	23.2	7.2	11 290	2.6	555	4.9	8 031	23.0	27.8
Marion	12 697	77.9	63 500	20.3	9.9	328	21.7	2.4	13 703	5.7	930	6.8	12 868	19.9	32.1
Marshall	32 547	74.7	80 900	20.7	9.9	406	23.4	3.2	39 130	2.1	2 138	5.5	36 609	25.1	25.1
Mobile	150 179	68.9	80 500	20.1	9.9	476	26.8	4.9	197 415	3.0	13 809	7.0	164 654	29.0	16.2
Monroe	9 383	80.4	66 900	18.6	9.9	351	25.4	5.1	8 783	-1.9	884	10.1	9 155	21.5	30.2
Montgomery	86 068	64.0	87 700	20.0	9.9	526	26.4	4.6	111 457	3.4	5 989	5.4	95 811	36.6	11.6
Morgan	43 602	73.1	88 600	19.2	9.9	429	23.2	3.4	55 287	0.2	3 843	7.0	50 604	27.1	24.4
Perry	4 333	73.8	47 600	22.4	11.7	341	31.3	9.0	4 049	2.9	445	11.0	3 480	23.3	33.4
Pickens	8 086	79.2	66 000	20.2	10.4	245	23.5	6.0	7 781	-0.4	727	9.3	7 644	22.9	26.1
Pike	11 933	67.2	71 400	20.6	9.9	334	26.1	4.0	14 130	7.9	836	5.9	12 684	24.8	18.3
Randolph	8 642	79.1	63 800	20.8	9.9	312	20.7	4.7	9 438	3.9	774	8.2	9 124	20.2	32.3
Russell	19 741	62.4	71 500	21.0	11.1	428	24.2	4.7	25 370	3.8	1 985	7.8	19 902	22.6	22.5
St. Clair	24 143	83.7	99 800	20.5	9.9	482	20.9	3.4	32 726	2.0	1 452	4.4	28 213	25.0	19.3
Shelby	54 631	80.9	146 700	19.7	9.9	635	22.4	2.0	85 632	2.0	2 140	2.5	74 604	42.9	8.9
Sumter	5 708	72.3	54 000	22.5	10.9	298	27.3	8.6	5 006	2.7	588	11.7	4 624	22.5	25.2
Talladega	30 674	76.4	72 200	20.3	9.9	351	23.6	3.5	35 451	2.7	3 307	9.3	31 894	24.3	25.6
Tallapoosa	16 656	76.3	73 600	20.7	9.9	358	24.7	2.8	19 622	0.4	1 281	6.5	17 232	23.7	25.0
Tuscaloosa	64 517	63.5	106 600	20.4	9.9	487	29.2	3.4	85 298	2.2	3 154	3.7	74 397	32.0	16.7
Walker	28 364	80.0	66 700	20.0	10.0	368	24.9	2.5	28 240	3.2	1 865	6.6	27 911	22.4	21.7

1. Specified owner-occupied units.   2. Median monthly owner costs is often in the minimum category—9.9 percent or less, which is indicated as 9.9 percent.   3. Specified renter-occupied units.   4. Overcrowded or lacking complete plumbing facilities.   5. Percent of civilian labor force.   6. Persons 16 years old and over.

STATE County	Private nonfarm establishments, employment and payroll, 2001								Agriculture, 2002			
		Employment					Annual payroll		Farms			
										Percent with—		
	Number of establish- ments	Total	Health care and social assistance	Manufac- turing	Retail trade	Finance and insurance	Professional, scientific, and technical services	Total (mil dol)	Average per employee (dollars)	Number	Less than 50 acres	500 acres and over	Farm operators whose principal occu- pation is farming (percent)
	104	105	106	107	108	109	110	111	112	113	114	115	116
UNITED STATES............	7 095 302	115 061 184	14 534 726	15 950 424	14 890 289	6 248 400	7 156 579	3 989 086	34 669	2 128 982	34.9	15.9	57.5
ALABAMA	99 261	1 620 952	208 130	312 352	227 367	72 319	76 061	45 162	27 861	45 126	37.1	8.3	53.1
Autauga..........	795	9 189	714	1 943	2 239	230	248	220	23 919	373	26.8	12.9	51.2
Baldwin..........	3 910	43 734	5 408	5 975	8 620	1 138	1 545	946	21 636	1 062	48.2	8.1	50.7
Barbour..........	575	10 516	796	4 854	1 206	300	128	238	22 651	531	17.7	18.5	42.9
Bibb..............	330	3 294	391	710	534	105	64	69	20 892	187	26.7	15.0	50.3
Blount...........	720	8 131	871	2 501	1 270	284	269	180	22 077	1 248	40.1	2.9	52.7
Bullock..........	136	2 122	312	D	266	67	D	43	20 043	273	17.6	33.3	49.1
Butler...........	488	5 311	609	1 165	904	174	77	111	20 868	425	25.9	5.6	48.2
Calhoun..........	2 555	39 752	5 583	9 911	6 472	982	1 189	925	23 265	673	45.8	2.4	54.1
Chambers.........	623	10 850	1 232	4 653	1 474	187	118	271	24 945	306	23.9	17.3	46.4
Cherokee.........	354	3 290	233	1 028	718	146	D	67	20 513	546	32.1	9.0	50.0
Chilton..........	745	6 903	719	1 346	1 723	268	97	142	20 562	667	35.8	4.3	52.9
Choctaw..........	311	3 643	210	D	420	85	74	139	38 269	244	27.5	12.3	45.1
Clarke...........	705	7 473	867	1 907	1 577	393	108	179	23 998	284	25.4	8.8	49.3
Clay.............	227	4 394	602	2 509	433	75	38	87	19 760	427	21.1	6.6	53.9
Cleburne.........	186	2 317	184	1 031	250	45	37	49	21 251	326	31.0	3.1	60.4
Coffee...........	940	11 400	1 652	3 011	2 252	558	547	236	20 683	854	28.7	10.5	54.6
Colbert..........	1 316	18 709	1 821	4 539	2 777	525	259	434	23 171	584	32.9	8.9	47.8
Conecuh..........	238	3 710	352	931	252	62	20	87	23 385	369	25.5	10.3	53.7
Coosa............	116	1 270	D	803	117	D	D	31	24 239	228	26.8	6.1	58.8
Covington........	889	11 013	1 474	2 765	1 973	313	292	250	22 735	1 013	24.8	8.2	48.1
Crenshaw.........	244	2 716	376	574	332	64	D	57	20 949	570	22.6	10.9	53.2
Cullman..........	1 677	22 526	2 790	5 933	3 409	648	491	537	23 845	2 301	48.5	2.7	58.9
Dale.............	825	9 823	1 248	1 136	1 447	329	275	258	26 265	459	23.5	14.8	53.6
Dallas...........	913	14 933	2 191	5 633	2 207	411	213	346	23 167	490	23.3	24.7	52.7
De Kalb..........	1 208	21 910	1 733	12 338	2 189	510	617	498	22 721	2 177	46.6	3.2	56.8
Elmore...........	1 052	10 225	1 057	2 220	1 971	318	293	205	20 012	633	38.7	6.8	53.7
Escambia	828	11 144	1 204	2 311	1 703	493	185	252	22 585	444	47.1	10.4	59.9
Etowah	2 133	32 845	5 386	6 397	4 821	957	552	770	23 444	974	52.1	2.3	50.0
Fayette..........	352	5 345	880	2 063	681	92	35	125	23 342	365	17.5	8.5	53.2
Franklin.........	589	8 920	792	4 634	945	382	60	192	21 508	929	30.7	5.3	55.7
Geneva...........	527	4 020	835	817	764	193	85	77	19 090	998	28.6	10.1	54.9
Greene...........	135	1 413	176	461	196	41	21	29	20 388	349	24.6	23.5	55.9
Hale.............	230	2 950	461	1 340	376	80	D	63	21 380	433	19.6	18.9	58.0
Henry............	327	4 157	359	1 641	457	96	92	90	21 634	346	20.2	22.3	56.1
Houston..........	2 772	45 434	7 890	7 561	7 589	1 099	1 158	1 212	26 676	700	34.3	13.9	53.1
Jackson..........	907	13 810	1 276	6 686	2 045	397	183	332	24 055	1 375	40.4	7.1	53.7
Jefferson	17 397	356 034	50 970	34 876	42 817	28 194	19 012	11 884	33 378	463	58.3	2.4	47.7
Lamar............	293	4 321	340	1 921	413	152	D	127	29 466	463	33.0	6.9	40.8
Lauderdale.......	2 043	30 869	5 241	6 309	5 400	959	904	643	20 837	1 485	45.8	4.7	47.5
Lawrence.........	405	4 872	524	1 866	745	152	43	151	31 044	1 597	44.1	4.6	49.2
Lee..............	2 016	32 564	4 964	6 217	5 205	810	698	704	21 633	336	34.8	10.7	60.1
Limestone........	1 118	17 031	1 734	6 772	2 657	379	382	517	30 349	1 235	44.5	7.0	54.3
Lowndes..........	144	2 229	116	1 228	304	57	30	86	38 623	420	28.6	23.3	60.0
Macon	232	6 304	2 102	D	417	85	85	151	24 027	368	25.8	19.3	41.8
Madison..........	7 175	130 045	14 705	23 489	17 132	3 229	20 064	4 281	32 918	1 117	46.6	6.2	52.6
Marengo..........	499	6 381	694	2 240	963	289	81	167	26 135	508	21.9	18.9	53.9
Marion...........	724	8 964	1 173	4 004	1 122	359	102	201	22 433	756	28.3	4.4	50.1
Marshall.........	1 937	32 889	2 942	12 348	5 171	813	483	683	20 777	1 686	53.4	2.5	53.1
Mobile...........	9 227	152 459	21 491	18 956	21 088	4 979	7 919	4 254	27 904	740	56.8	6.8	53.5
Monroe...........	432	7 978	627	2 429	941	161	64	225	28 209	443	31.4	14.0	55.8
Montgomery	6 019	110 410	14 680	11 125	15 513	7 956	6 428	3 031	27 456	703	33.3	16.2	51.9
Morgan	2 741	46 206	5 009	13 816	6 342	1 895	1 101	1 228	26 569	1 308	47.6	2.6	50.1
Perry............	165	1 784	156	542	276	63	D	33	18 409	376	21.8	18.1	61.7
Pickens..........	341	2 950	681	610	622	173	53	61	20 729	493	26.2	9.9	51.5
Pike.............	647	9 181	933	1 937	1 628	341	272	208	22 705	612	21.9	17.6	52.1
Randolph.........	382	5 065	640	2 202	767	153	74	91	18 051	610	25.9	6.6	60.3
Russell..........	875	10 241	1 041	2 250	1 883	336	164	263	25 691	245	32.7	19.2	60.8
St. Clair........	1 128	12 169	1 322	3 239	1 477	381	271	306	25 125	667	42.7	3.7	54.6
Shelby...........	3 815	59 016	3 782	5 955	7 416	4 604	4 663	2 057	34 853	486	46.7	4.7	50.8
Sumter...........	239	2 805	274	387	454	68	37	60	21 560	443	26.0	21.9	56.4
Talladega........	1 343	21 078	2 465	7 052	3 196	605	286	543	25 765	584	26.5	9.1	53.8
Tallapoosa.......	805	18 837	2 150	3 818	1 702	367	185	530	28 146	377	26.5	6.1	48.3
Tuscaloosa.......	3 920	68 658	11 070	12 158	9 978	1 601	2 313	1 901	27 686	547	36.4	8.4	58.5
Walker...........	1 392	14 796	2 512	1 450	3 745	664	474	350	23 657	543	47.3	5.2	54.5

Table B. States and Counties — **Agriculture**

STATE County	Land in farms Acreage (1,000)	Percent change, 1997–2002	Acres Average size of farm	Total irrigated (1,000)	Total cropland (1,000)	Value of land and buildings (dollars) Average per farm	Average per acre	Value of machinery and equipment average per farm (dollars)	Value of products sold Total (mil dol)	Average per farm (dollars)	Percent from — Crops	Live-stock and poultry products	Percent of farms with sales of — $10,000 or more	$100,000 or more	Government payments Total ($1,000)	Percent of farms
	117	118	119	120	121	122	123	124	125	126	127	128	129	130	131	132
UNITED STATES	938 279	0.7	441	55 311	434 165	537 833	1 213	66 570	200 646	94 245	47.4	52.6	40.7	14.6	6 545 678	33.2
ALABAMA	8 904	2.3	197	109	3 733	335 217	1 698	42 705	3 265	72 352	18.1	81.9	28.9	10.4	77 930	28.5
Autauga	118	12.4	318	1	52	580 986	1 879	67 378	19	49 871	43.7	56.3	33.2	7.5	962	32.7
Baldwin	181	9.0	171	11	108	403 492	2 502	65 796	86	80 697	82.9	17.1	31.5	8.9	2 279	25.4
Barbour	191	24.0	359	5	67	423 927	1 197	64 643	61	114 056	24.7	75.3	31.8	11.1	2 274	54.4
Bibb	45	-4.3	240	0	15	401 324	1 712	34 839	2	8 907	25.0	75.0	23.0	0.5	93	23.5
Blount	143	2.9	115	1	63	275 002	2 556	37 480	114	91 532	6.3	93.7	33.0	14.4	302	15.1
Bullock	146	-13.6	536	1	30	834 658	1 432	57 499	29	105 292	70.0	30.0	31.9	8.1	713	36.6
Butler	83	-14.4	196	0	28	345 623	1 547	38 514	58	135 529	2.9	97.1	25.6	10.4	470	27.8
Calhoun	75	-2.6	111	2	33	273 823	2 598	33 520	43	63 975	18.2	81.8	23.3	6.5	362	17.5
Chambers	93	-1.1	303	0	25	302 338	994	27 990	6	18 293	22.3	77.7	26.8	4.6	195	23.2
Cherokee	121	-1.6	222	2	63	299 140	1 542	51 735	34	62 124	42.4	57.6	30.6	7.5	2 135	39.0
Chilton	98	-1.0	147	1	40	294 636	1 796	34 426	13	19 651	68.8	31.2	25.6	3.7	229	14.7
Choctaw	55	-15.4	226	D	14	276 601	1 283	33 045	6	24 874	6.4	93.7	18.4	3.3	160	23.0
Clarke	57	-6.6	201	0	15	245 352	1 303	25 579	2	6 469	25.9	74.1	16.9	0.0	65	19.4
Clay	84	12.0	198	0	24	292 694	1 390	35 182	23	53 401	2.2	97.8	34.4	8.0	206	22.0
Cleburne	44	-13.7	136	D	14	287 413	1 921	38 841	52	159 449	2.6	97.4	42.6	22.1	173	21.8
Coffee	197	5.3	231	5	92	324 492	1 201	61 834	134	156 919	9.1	90.9	38.2	18.7	3 320	48.4
Colbert	132	13.8	226	2	69	311 005	1 380	52 054	35	59 251	32.2	67.8	25.2	7.9	1 750	33.6
Conecuh	82	-6.8	222	0	25	300 904	1 109	27 257	5	14 069	26.6	73.3	24.9	2.4	722	48.2
Coosa	39	-7.1	173	0	11	236 190	1 350	31 669	1	6 465	D	D	23.2	0.0	24	14.9
Covington	202	12.2	199	2	82	325 278	1 616	45 680	68	66 644	18.8	81.2	30.6	11.7	2 899	46.3
Crenshaw	130	0.8	229	D	41	284 903	1 330	40 279	74	130 084	2.1	97.9	30.4	16.3	1 746	47.5
Cullman	231	13.8	101	0	113	290 950	3 167	44 425	337	146 658	2.9	97.1	39.5	25.1	1 075	17.8
Dale	139	6.1	304	4	62	431 396	1 422	52 422	45	97 090	18.8	81.2	34.6	14.4	1 678	46.8
Dallas	236	-5.2	481	2	83	606 590	1 173	73 214	26	52 622	33.7	66.3	32.0	8.6	1 946	37.8
De Kalb	237	5.8	109	1	127	257 090	2 392	38 531	268	123 254	3.8	96.2	32.1	18.0	1 076	27.0
Elmore	104	-16.1	165	1	45	331 666	1 968	39 635	12	18 957	57.0	43.0	22.1	4.3	1 412	17.1
Escambia	94	8.0	213	1	55	265 217	1 426	51 667	9	21 021	62.3	37.7	24.5	5.0	1 699	36.3
Etowah	90	-5.3	93	0	45	252 802	2 856	31 743	48	49 003	5.5	94.5	21.5	8.4	587	15.0
Fayette	75	19.0	206	D	29	217 007	1 108	38 338	12	33 250	12.5	87.5	24.1	4.7	277	29.6
Franklin	146	14.1	157	0	57	209 952	1 415	28 613	107	115 601	1.9	98.2	30.9	15.5	495	26.2
Geneva	227	9.7	228	9	115	325 516	1 513	48 930	103	103 092	17.4	82.6	37.9	14.8	4 870	59.6
Greene	128	4.1	367	0	34	384 843	1 102	60 518	20	56 473	1.8	98.2	31.5	7.4	586	38.1
Hale	161	1.9	371	0	41	484 526	1 164	76 519	44	102 465	3.6	96.4	34.6	15.7	558	33.7
Henry	151	-1.9	436	4	85	538 386	1 199	79 339	26	75 617	53.6	46.4	47.7	15.6	2 630	47.1
Houston	188	-5.1	269	9	118	371 301	1 342	66 914	40	56 553	61.4	38.6	39.7	11.6	4 393	51.1
Jackson	229	3.6	167	0	123	290 284	2 197	34 858	70	51 141	14.6	85.4	25.7	8.0	1 693	28.9
Jefferson	42	2.4	91	1	17	236 830	2 607	27 980	14	31 182	12.2	87.8	17.3	1.9	49	8.2
Lamar	87	22.5	187	D	24	197 504	1 161	28 035	5	11 073	20.2	79.8	15.1	1.5	364	34.3
Lauderdale	208	-1.9	140	1	117	224 293	1 807	31 918	28	18 943	40.6	59.4	20.4	3.7	2 193	26.7
Lawrence	234	14.1	147	2	138	265 057	1 716	39 575	90	56 053	18.7	81.3	21.2	8.1	4 478	38.9
Lee	74	-2.6	220	1	22	373 440	2 280	39 870	29	86 130	D	D	26.2	3.6	302	25.0
Limestone	226	-11.0	183	9	142	400 417	2 212	53 466	52	42 338	57.6	42.4	24.5	7.5	2 919	35.2
Lowndes	197	13.9	468	3	56	590 690	1 144	55 333	42	98 861	15.0	85.0	35.0	10.0	1 394	25.2
Macon	129	1.6	351	3	40	482 249	1 315	42 247	9	25 573	73.2	26.8	24.2	3.5	817	29.6
Madison	198	-5.7	178	4	141	391 014	2 161	43 477	38	33 693	70.4	29.6	24.9	6.9	2 989	25.5
Marengo	189	-4.5	372	0	65	364 141	1 001	39 545	15	28 725	11.6	88.4	27.6	4.7	934	30.1
Marion	119	21.4	158	0	43	223 982	1 484	41 764	45	59 085	3.3	96.7	24.1	9.1	312	29.0
Marshall	161	10.3	95	0	78	242 494	2 725	34 643	186	110 464	2.2	97.8	29.0	12.9	675	24.8
Mobile	101	-16.5	136	2	52	454 768	3 361	43 995	75	101 446	87.1	12.9	38.6	11.1	1 366	13.0
Monroe	120	-11.1	271	1	53	333 132	1 367	63 740	10	22 879	39.8	60.2	30.9	3.2	1 961	43.1
Montgomery	213	-11.6	303	1	86	657 216	1 948	38 116	36	51 004	25.5	74.5	34.3	6.4	975	22.2
Morgan	149	-6.3	114	1	74	280 136	2 812	27 426	79	60 717	6.1	93.9	24.5	8.2	930	19.3
Perry	165	13.8	439	0	53	480 459	955	40 944	18	47 531	9.4	90.6	31.1	8.2	1 242	38.3
Pickens	143	16.3	289	1	37	416 378	1 252	45 105	74	149 922	2.6	97.4	36.9	19.1	564	24.3
Pike	187	7.5	306	2	61	426 954	1 423	49 582	66	107 100	8.9	91.1	36.9	15.8	2 086	45.8
Randolph	110	1.9	180	0	32	303 999	1 898	39 709	52	85 771	1.9	98.1	30.8	12.5	188	20.0
Russell	105	9.4	430	3	28	596 334	1 304	35 899	8	34 170	82.1	17.9	30.6	4.5	668	33.9
St. Clair	83	7.8	124	2	32	353 889	2 364	40 003	47	70 144	14.9	85.1	24.0	9.3	121	9.7
Shelby	64	-5.9	132	2	31	439 060	2 795	32 621	13	26 937	70.5	29.5	19.8	2.9	500	12.1
Sumter	177	1.1	399	3	45	395 776	1 018	31 530	13	29 451	6.1	93.9	30.0	5.2	933	39.5
Talladega	109	-0.9	187	2	53	467 402	2 567	50 981	27	45 719	20.1	79.9	28.6	7.5	621	23.5
Tallapoosa	78	0.0	207	D	21	273 674	1 448	32 071	5	13 747	27.3	72.6	18.3	2.4	134	13.0
Tuscaloosa	103	3.0	188	1	37	388 447	1 972	41 327	21	37 501	30.4	69.6	21.8	5.7	696	17.7
Walker	75	36.4	138	0	27	247 760	1 731	24 863	51	93 742	2.3	97.7	21.4	10.9	78	10.7

Table B. States and Counties — Residential Construction, Wholesale Trade, Retail Trade, and Real Estate

STATE County	Value of residential construction authorized by building permits, 2003		Wholesale trade, 1997				Retail trade,[1] 1997				Real estate and rental and leasing, 1997			
	New construction ($1,000)	Number of housing units	Number of establishments	Number of employees	Sales (mil dol)	Annual payroll (mil dol)	Number of establishments	Number of employees	Sales (mil dol)	Annual payroll (mil dol)	Number of establishments	Number of employees	Receipts (mil dol)	Annual payroll (mil dol)
	133	134	135	136	137	138	139	140	141	142	143	144	145	146
UNITED STATES............	249 693 105	1 889 214	453 471	5 794 312	4 058 480.1	214 915.5	1 118 446	13 991 004	2 460 963.0	237 201.0	288 274	1 702 540	241 268.5	41 597.5
ALABAMA	2 463 568	22 256	6 315	79 229	40 986.3	2 394.7	20 163	231 665	36 623.3	3 381.7	3 664	20 629	2 130.3	396.7
Autauga........................	14 820	283	29	81	39.7	2.1	161	2 200	367.3	32.1	21	D	D	D
Baldwin........................	437 355	3 918	151	1 248	493.5	42.9	801	7 850	1 215.3	114.8	195	1 139	81.8	19.6
Barbour........................	1 648	15	32	228	79.6	4.2	129	1 076	163.2	15.0	14	29	2.1	0.4
Bibb.............................	140	2	15	82	53.2	1.9	60	527	77.2	6.7	9	31	2.5	0.2
Blount..........................	7 036	63	51	D	D	D	143	1 328	202.0	17.8	14	42	2.4	0.4
Bullock.........................	463	11	10	D	D	D	38	289	40.3	3.8	3	13	0.7	0.3
Butler..........................	2 672	17	23	148	58.1	3.6	122	1 023	144.2	13.9	16	35	2.0	0.4
Calhoun........................	19 804	163	130	1 688	890.9	47.0	578	6 747	982.0	92.5	73	298	24.5	4.4
Chambers......................	1 183	11	23	158	89.3	3.9	131	1 502	216.0	19.7	20	58	4.0	0.7
Cherokee......................	1 900	24	22	161	65.2	4.0	88	678	123.1	9.0	10	31	2.8	0.3
Chilton.........................	4 268	29	29	193	64.2	3.8	180	1 510	246.6	21.8	21	37	3.1	0.4
Choctaw.......................	330	2	19	191	108.0	5.7	76	386	69.1	6.1	9	34	1.0	0.2
Clarke..........................	5 939	55	23	125	34.3	2.4	188	1 669	233.2	21.4	30	83	5.0	1.1
Clay.............................	568	8	4	D	D	D	49	376	45.7	4.6	6	22	1.1	0.1
Cleburne.......................	531	5	13	D	D	D	47	262	54.0	3.6	1	D	D	D
Coffee..........................	23 028	204	47	259	141.0	5.8	223	2 405	411.0	34.6	23	111	7.0	1.4
Colbert.........................	10 903	159	109	1 173	404.3	30.4	273	2 915	527.5	45.0	42	140	14.5	1.8
Conecuh........................	565	4	14	102	57.4	2.3	49	275	39.1	3.8	6	10	1.1	0.1
Coosa...........................	0	0	6	D	D	D	28	130	15.3	1.8	5	8	0.7	0.1
Covington......................	2 115	16	49	585	223.1	12.2	239	1 974	287.9	27.8	23	70	4.8	0.7
Crenshaw......................	1 967	13	15	D	D	D	54	444	56.6	5.3	5	24	1.1	0.2
Cullman........................	5 882	46	95	637	256.1	16.2	360	3 334	650.9	52.1	51	205	20.1	3.6
Dale.............................	6 354	74	37	537	118.6	8.1	182	1 402	201.8	18.1	33	152	9.0	2.4
Dallas...........................	3 297	61	52	517	213.2	12.0	232	2 430	339.0	31.9	41	110	10.0	1.6
De Kalb........................	7 124	64	62	602	309.6	12.4	269	2 576	343.0	31.3	42	144	10.2	2.1
Elmore.........................	56 118	366	47	309	116.6	7.1	199	1 780	296.8	23.7	35	D	D	D
Escambia	2 171	22	53	532	117.8	11.6	210	2 097	295.1	28.0	15	85	5.2	1.4
Etowah.........................	29 584	335	135	D	D	D	452	4 935	737.8	65.9	68	273	23.9	4.4
Fayette.........................	840	7	11	D	D	D	82	709	111.1	9.4	6	34	0.7	0.2
Franklin........................	1 468	16	27	287	99.8	6.0	144	1 167	184.5	15.5	17	35	1.8	0.4
Geneva.........................	1 326	21	28	D	D	D	124	813	108.5	10.5	15	29	2.5	0.3
Greene.........................	57	1	10	D	D	D	34	232	31.3	2.7	4	6	0.6	0.1
Hale.............................	5 583	43	5	D	D	D	45	322	52.8	4.1	7	23	3.1	0.4
Henry...........................	4 779	39	15	323	68.0	6.4	81	524	84.6	7.9	8	D	D	D
Houston........................	40 054	395	206	2 149	705.0	54.8	656	7 801	1 288.2	124.6	94	344	34.4	6.2
Jackson........................	6 916	61	47	630	203.2	12.8	218	1 849	299.8	25.7	31	94	5.6	1.2
Jefferson.......................	591 772	3 949	1 480	23 438	14 471.2	824.1	3 020	44 165	7 636.8	705.6	650	5 558	811.3	132.8
Lamar...........................	303	3	10	D	D	D	69	445	65.0	5.4	8	15	0.7	0.1
Lauderdale.....................	20 071	283	100	1 959	368.9	45.4	462	5 546	780.8	74.9	79	294	27.4	5.7
Lawrence.......................	1 083	9	19	D	D	D	100	721	116.6	9.6	4	11	1.0	0.1
Lee..............................	117 597	1 167	86	727	308.0	18.6	425	5 437	774.4	73.7	84	464	35.0	6.9
Limestone.....................	18 733	184	49	D	D	D	255	2 539	404.6	37.8	34	112	10.5	1.6
Lowndes........................	460	4	8	82	26.6	1.7	29	215	34.7	3.7	5	10	0.6	0.1
Macon..........................	1 197	17	8	D	D	D	66	437	64.1	6.0	9	D	D	D
Madison........................	116 744	2 213	471	D	D	D	1 224	17 275	2 610.7	253.6	332	1 623	167.7	30.1
Marengo........................	2 293	17	25	229	91.8	5.0	140	1 060	143.5	13.6	15	42	4.9	0.7
Marion..........................	1 571	15	44	387	243.7	10.8	138	1 063	167.6	14.2	15	48	2.5	0.4
Marshall........................	22 007	193	115	1 424	858.8	39.0	560	5 254	1 008.2	73.6	72	390	32.5	6.4
Mobile..........................	162 509	1 684	699	8 647	3 332.9	252.1	1 681	22 860	3 404.5	338.1	380	2 170	228.7	43.3
Monroe.........................	1 654	15	25	267	85.0	7.1	120	1 086	170.4	15.2	13	58	5.1	1.0
Montgomery	113 924	1 119	392	5 460	2 938.8	157.0	1 144	15 998	2 482.8	237.8	294	2 189	179.1	39.9
Morgan.........................	46 602	420	180	D	D	D	583	6 426	1 136.5	95.5	100	454	40.3	8.2
Perry............................	59	1	4	D	D	D	41	249	31.7	3.7	5	5	0.4	0.0
Pickens.........................	537	7	16	67	33.8	1.5	96	654	130.6	9.0	10	21	1.1	0.2
Pike.............................	10 124	129	44	472	177.5	9.6	145	1 559	223.2	19.9	22	87	8.8	1.0
Randolph.......................	150	1	14	74	30.6	0.9	89	722	89.4	9.3	10	33	2.9	0.4
Russell.........................	27 417	331	23	D	D	D	168	1 797	229.6	23.1	38	120	13.2	1.5
St. Clair........................	39 604	351	68	D	D	D	205	1 724	270.6	21.5	37	125	8.7	1.4
Shelby..........................	307 300	2 228	372	5 413	3 529.0	186.1	476	5 173	891.3	85.2	114	1 194	122.9	34.2
Sumter..........................	1 122	16	15	162	47.0	2.9	66	511	69.3	6.0	8	16	1.1	0.2
Talladega.......................	9 679	105	57	618	183.0	17.0	348	3 236	474.7	43.5	51	183	10.5	2.1
Tallapoosa.....................	4 482	36	37	D	D	D	196	1 800	239.0	24.1	32	127	9.1	2.4
Tuscaloosa.....................	129 426	1 150	185	1 981	858.1	61.1	790	10 852	1 543.2	151.0	161	1 079	82.6	13.7
Walker..........................	5 893	51	69	677	210.8	12.4	359	3 923	679.0	54.7	44	150	11.3	2.2

1. Establishments with payroll.

STATE County	Professional, scientific, and technical services,[1] 1997				Manufacturing, 1997				Accommodation and foodservices, 1997			
	Number of establishments	Number of employees	Receipts (mil dol)	Annual payroll (mil dol)	Number of establishments	Number of employees	Receipts (mil dol)	Annual payroll (mil dol)	Number of establishments	Number of employees	Sales (mil dol)	Annual payroll (mil dol)
	147	148	149	150	151	152	153	154	155	156	157	158
UNITED STATES............	615 305	5 212 745	579 542.1	225 376.0	363 753	16 888 016	3 842 061.4	572 101.1	545 060	9 451 056	350 389.1	97 003.9
ALABAMA	7 076	54 413	5 295.6	2 051.4	5 444	352 618	67 970.1	10 187.8	6 955	134 719	3 881.8	1 059.6
Autauga..........................	38	140	13.2	3.2	38	2 130	366.4	69.2	50	1 036	28.0	8.7
Baldwin...........................	225	981	69.6	29.2	138	5 150	809.5	127.1	303	6 337	224.3	61.0
Barbour..........................	40	110	9.8	2.5	41	3 680	689.7	93.0	42	600	17.3	4.3
Bibb...............................	8	32	2.1	0.8	27	1 218	244.3	23.9	12	D	D	D
Blount............................	34	137	8.3	3.6	60	2 742	403.5	49.5	42	461	13.7	3.3
Bullock...........................	3	D	D	D	6	D	D	D	12	D	D	D
Butler.............................	21	53	2.7	0.7	27	2 044	305.5	41.9	31	595	17.2	4.8
Calhoun..........................	149	702	45.2	13.2	149	10 841	1 504.5	257.8	185	4 262	114.4	31.3
Chambers........................	23	80	6.5	1.6	40	5 612	765.8	147.2	44	671	18.3	4.6
Cherokee.........................	15	34	2.3	0.6	21	1 194	121.2	25.4	26	251	6.9	1.8
Chilton...........................	25	58	3.2	0.8	54	1 488	162.1	30.3	50	744	18.4	5.0
Choctaw..........................	21	68	4.6	0.8	12	D	D	D	15	233	5.6	1.5
Clarke............................	29	96	7.4	1.4	32	2 888	540.1	82.7	41	665	17.2	4.2
Clay..............................	9	26	0.8	0.2	15	2 789	212.4	49.6	11	171	3.2	0.8
Cleburne.........................	9	41	1.3	0.3	10	1 108	175.1	19.9	11	D	D	D
Coffee............................	49	286	17.4	5.3	39	4 725	679.8	89.8	63	1 092	26.9	7.2
Colbert...........................	77	223	17.4	5.3	118	5 581	1 491.6	205.8	103	1 766	46.3	12.3
Conecuh..........................	7	13	1.6	0.3	21	821	98.8	17.0	17	279	6.1	1.4
Coosa............................	4	D	D	D	11	978	123.1	22.3	3	D	D	D
Covington........................	56	250	13.9	5.0	30	3 872	388.0	83.5	58	830	20.1	5.0
Crenshaw........................	8	31	1.8	0.9	15	830	26.1	9.6	11	138	3.8	0.6
Cullman..........................	82	286	17.4	5.0	123	5 994	964.1	147.4	94	1 980	52.8	14.4
Dale..............................	55	209	12.7	4.2	26	1 254	70.0	23.0	82	1 204	26.9	7.0
Dallas............................	50	355	15.9	7.2	53	5 336	1 064.8	137.6	63	887	26.0	6.3
De Kalb..........................	65	338	25.4	11.6	216	11 774	1 286.0	237.3	100	1 419	40.8	10.7
Elmore............................	55	193	14.4	4.8	51	2 340	280.3	57.1	62	1 117	33.1	9.1
Escambia........................	41	122	9.6	2.6	53	3 145	689.5	79.5	56	905	24.0	6.0
Etowah...........................	122	621	36.6	13.7	136	8 775	1 577.0	277.0	169	3 223	85.0	23.6
Fayette...........................	9	20	4.1	0.3	33	2 617	372.0	55.9	18	D	D	D
Franklin..........................	22	66	3.8	0.9	64	5 348	645.8	97.0	44	529	12.7	3.3
Geneva...........................	20	41	3.3	0.9	26	2 123	171.1	34.1	31	343	6.1	1.7
Greene............................	6	17	0.7	0.2	NA	NA	NA	NA	5	105	1.3	0.5
Hale..............................	10	24	1.1	0.2	16	1 443	210.0	28.4	12	D	D	D
Henry.............................	15	52	3.6	0.9	18	1 410	382.5	33.9	12	D	D	D
Houston..........................	169	1 171	71.3	26.7	125	9 233	1 457.7	231.9	198	3 945	121.6	31.4
Jackson..........................	49	213	17.5	5.8	83	6 557	1 253.5	182.4	70	848	25.9	6.9
Jefferson.........................	1 631	14 700	1 504.0	603.6	817	35 972	7 475.6	1 168.7	1 197	25 250	796.1	225.2
Lamar............................	12	40	1.7	0.6	22	2 589	313.4	61.3	17	106	3.5	0.9
Lauderdale.......................	148	740	50.3	17.2	115	7 545	885.1	169.9	146	2 558	67.2	19.5
Lawrence.........................	24	35	3.0	0.6	29	D	D	D	33	524	13.5	3.6
Lee...............................	129	589	50.6	16.3	88	7 016	1 232.9	194.9	199	4 165	110.3	29.6
Limestone........................	62	444	38.7	21.5	69	6 780	1 321.0	309.0	71	1 759	45.9	12.8
Lowndes..........................	7	38	3.9	1.2	10	D	D	D	4	D	D	D
Macon............................	19	65	5.8	2.7	NA	NA	NA	NA	21	393	9.9	2.3
Madison..........................	773	13 046	1 591.0	598.1	335	28 280	6 991.7	1 079.1	513	11 052	345.9	94.6
Marengo..........................	21	57	4.1	0.8	18	1 701	404.8	54.1	34	465	12.6	3.2
Marion............................	27	79	7.2	2.2	53	6 423	964.2	154.8	41	D	D	D
Marshall..........................	98	371	25.0	7.7	152	15 773	2 616.7	338.5	157	2 732	70.7	17.9
Mobile............................	769	5 949	518.6	205.9	445	22 130	5 494.8	835.3	649	12 767	370.1	102.2
Monroe...........................	17	42	3.3	0.7	28	4 748	1 094.0	165.0	34	591	15.2	3.5
Montgomery......................	553	4 447	418.0	193.5	214	11 343	2 024.6	299.4	422	10 064	279.5	77.1
Morgan...........................	169	949	71.4	28.3	214	D	D	D	185	3 752	101.1	29.0
Perry.............................	7	17	1.2	0.2	8	926	96.9	21.7	11	178	3.0	0.8
Pickens..........................	12	44	2.9	0.6	21	1 051	113.7	18.3	14	D	D	D
Pike..............................	27	105	5.8	2.1	32	2 302	356.1	47.1	58	1 135	25.8	7.2
Randolph.........................	16	36	2.2	0.9	28	2 322	218.5	39.0	27	335	8.0	2.2
Russell...........................	41	126	10.2	2.7	49	3 295	1 000.4	107.8	71	938	32.2	8.3
St. Clair..........................	68	181	11.5	4.0	85	3 180	480.2	85.1	78	1 170	31.3	8.4
Shelby............................	340	2 445	289.2	105.0	158	6 076	876.6	174.8	188	3 762	120.1	32.5
Sumter...........................	5	15	1.0	0.5	15	832	89.4	17.4	21	327	7.0	2.0
Talladega.........................	69	283	20.3	5.5	100	7 160	1 420.6	201.1	94	1 504	37.9	10.0
Tallapoosa.......................	35	129	14.8	3.8	53	5 868	1 074.8	112.8	51	788	21.4	5.7
Tuscaloosa.......................	257	1 733	134.0	51.6	160	10 738	2 557.9	378.9	317	7 396	202.5	55.6
Walker............................	76	472	26.2	9.1	72	1 709	381.3	32.8	93	1 650	43.5	10.8

1. Firms subject to federal tax.

Table B. States and Counties — Health Care and Social Assistance, Other Services, and Federal Funds

STATE County	Health care and social assistance,[1] 1997				Other services,[1] 1997				Federal funds and grants, 2002–2003 — Expenditures (mil dol)	Direct payments for individuals[2]		
	Number of establishments	Number of employees	Receipts (mil dol)	Annual payroll (mil dol)	Number of establishments	Number of employees	Receipts (mil dol)	Annual payroll (mil dol)	Total	Social Security and government retirement	Medicare	Food stamps and Supplemental Security Income
	159	160	161	162	163	164	165	166	167	168	169	170
UNITED STATES............	531 069	6 231 768	418 602.2	182 256.3	420 950	2 493 574	163 033.3	48 452.6	2 043 952.1	597 852.8	272 465.9	53 827.8
ALABAMA	7 121	104 492	7 116.7	3 104.8	6 329	37 061	2 241.7	659.3	36 870.9	11 475.6	4 832.9	1 222.5
Autauga....................	43	572	32.7	12.7	43	233	12.2	3.7	202.1	117.9	31.1	9.8
Baldwin....................	222	1 901	105.5	51.8	190	809	49.4	14.7	725.5	448.9	134.9	18.3
Barbour...................	42	446	19.7	7.7	26	93	6.1	1.3	180.6	60.3	37.1	11.1
Bibb.......................	16	140	7.0	2.7	20	194	13.5	3.6	104.4	48.1	24.9	6.5
Blount....................	30	603	23.3	12.5	62	271	18.0	4.6	192.5	93.8	44.0	8.2
Bullock...................	12	280	12.0	5.3	5	12	0.7	0.1	76.5	23.6	14.7	5.8
Butler....................	37	669	39.9	14.0	30	144	6.9	1.7	136.2	52.8	32.2	9.0
Calhoun...................	212	2 824	185.1	81.1	206	855	45.3	15.1	1 071.0	400.7	134.3	33.7
Chambers..................	53	511	29.3	12.0	39	208	9.2	2.3	202.1	94.6	48.1	9.4
Cherokee..................	16	110	9.3	4.3	23	61	5.3	1.0	127.2	55.5	24.9	4.6
Chilton...................	32	524	29.8	9.9	44	130	9.6	2.2	225.2	84.7	45.9	8.8
Choctaw...................	17	234	9.8	3.6	20	60	2.9	0.8	145.7	38.5	20.4	6.2
Clarke....................	42	557	31.5	11.2	47	169	13.5	3.1	192.0	68.1	33.2	12.4
Clay......................	17	204	8.6	3.7	14	49	2.2	0.6	80.9	39.2	18.3	2.9
Cleburne..................	7	45	2.5	1.0	9	49	3.1	1.0	70.1	34.9	12.9	3.3
Coffee....................	67	415	26.5	10.2	70	324	14.7	3.9	728.0	158.1	48.1	9.7
Colbert...................	101	1 401	99.5	44.4	103	587	33.5	9.3	471.5	183.8	66.9	10.2
Conecuh...................	14	320	14.7	6.1	21	65	6.0	1.1	102.0	35.6	22.1	6.9
Coosa.....................	7	96	4.0	1.8	4	8	1.3	0.2	58.0	30.1	11.4	3.2
Covington.................	57	1 086	64.5	24.8	56	271	12.7	3.4	253.5	109.2	56.4	10.5
Crenshaw..................	12	191	8.9	3.5	13	34	2.3	0.5	100.5	36.8	19.3	5.8
Cullman...................	120	1 694	110.0	44.5	109	462	27.6	7.0	395.8	192.0	90.5	12.3
Dale......................	60	649	28.4	12.7	63	226	8.9	2.4	524.0	139.5	54.0	14.7
Dallas....................	80	1 394	90.6	35.1	62	281	17.2	4.4	429.3	113.7	64.6	35.9
De Kalb...................	72	986	42.2	19.9	62	213	11.8	2.9	305.1	143.5	63.1	12.2
Elmore....................	74	829	37.2	15.2	70	235	12.7	3.3	315.0	185.8	53.0	12.6
Escambia	41	537	24.0	10.2	50	171	10.5	2.2	226.2	93.3	45.2	12.1
Etowah....................	199	4 291	312.8	127.9	132	570	34.8	9.5	627.0	297.7	145.6	30.8
Fayette...................	21	81	6.0	2.8	22	58	3.3	0.9	100.9	43.3	20.8	5.4
Franklin..................	63	929	50.4	20.0	47	152	8.9	2.6	194.5	78.7	43.2	7.1
Geneva....................	25	194	9.0	3.3	27	59	4.1	0.8	209.5	77.7	35.0	6.9
Greene....................	4	34	2.3	0.9	9	43	2.7	0.7	87.4	20.9	12.6	6.8
Hale......................	10	256	8.6	4.0	11	30	2.9	0.5	116.2	43.1	22.5	8.9
Henry.....................	11	101	3.9	1.7	18	56	4.3	1.4	148.3	45.8	20.2	4.7
Houston...................	223	4 564	374.4	171.6	183	1 047	56.9	17.2	521.5	235.2	78.7	24.7
Jackson...................	75	743	36.1	15.2	49	157	10.8	2.6	535.6	141.8	57.4	11.6
Jefferson	1 364	24 333	1 989.4	863.5	1 185	9 418	641.5	191.2	4 742.0	1 707.8	912.0	187.6
Lamar.....................	13	282	11.1	5.4	13	43	3.5	0.6	98.4	42.2	20.1	3.9
Lauderdale................	194	2 206	156.7	66.0	131	780	38.0	11.8	469.0	247.0	90.5	17.6
Lawrence..................	19	308	13.3	6.4	25	107	5.1	1.1	152.5	62.9	29.1	7.0
Lee.......................	133	1 478	104.9	51.3	125	661	35.6	10.2	461.3	189.2	62.1	21.8
Limestone.................	76	797	43.0	15.9	84	347	16.2	5.0	281.5	144.1	48.7	11.8
Lowndes...................	3	D	D	D	6	10	1.1	0.1	79.0	24.2	12.3	7.4
Macon.....................	18	299	12.9	5.1	21	80	4.3	1.3	250.3	61.6	24.4	13.1
Madison...................	582	6 750	496.1	209.8	446	2 526	136.6	45.8	6 842.3	812.9	177.6	48.6
Marengo...................	31	264	15.0	5.3	33	111	5.6	1.6	144.4	50.1	28.9	10.9
Marion....................	59	498	27.8	12.7	36	106	7.6	1.7	194.5	75.5	39.0	6.2
Marshall..................	143	1 600	74.9	31.4	107	519	24.9	6.4	493.8	230.1	95.9	17.8
Mobile....................	561	10 565	742.2	347.1	648	4 775	305.4	91.0	2 320.3	939.0	453.7	137.3
Monroe....................	26	257	12.0	5.6	24	85	4.6	1.3	143.3	52.4	28.3	8.0
Montgomery................	537	8 911	638.5	262.8	386	2 760	143.3	44.8	3 145.7	748.4	211.0	78.1
Morgan....................	243	2 955	184.3	85.7	172	1 310	69.3	22.4	590.1	275.5	105.3	22.2
Perry.....................	8	125	4.0	2.0	8	37	2.7	0.4	90.2	25.7	17.6	10.5
Pickens...................	20	219	9.5	4.3	15	44	3.1	0.8	145.6	54.7	30.9	8.8
Pike......................	38	702	42.2	16.8	43	136	6.9	2.1	253.3	66.2	37.8	12.5
Randolph..................	34	353	14.1	6.4	23	66	3.6	0.8	137.6	56.4	26.2	5.7
Russell...................	40	740	35.7	11.7	75	357	20.0	5.9	295.2	149.5	49.8	16.6
St. Clair.................	59	722	27.4	13.6	64	409	36.7	9.0	263.8	136.3	56.7	11.2
Shelby....................	191	1 886	113.7	50.7	177	1 096	71.3	22.2	389.4	204.5	80.8	10.9
Sumter....................	7	49	2.7	1.2	10	62	2.2	0.6	110.0	31.2	16.5	10.0
Talladega.................	90	1 150	68.2	29.3	90	454	31.6	9.0	503.9	207.6	100.9	29.7
Tallapoosa................	66	869	43.7	22.0	42	170	12.1	2.9	244.5	109.0	50.0	12.2
Tuscaloosa................	274	3 580	223.9	116.2	248	1 481	79.3	25.1	985.6	344.8	156.7	46.0
Walker....................	118	1 521	81.2	36.1	84	598	36.9	10.0	523.2	222.8	109.3	19.5

1. Firms subject to federal tax. 2. State totals may include programs not allocated by county.

STATE County	Salaries and wages	Defense	Other	Medicaid and other health-related	Nutrition and family welfare	Education	Other	Total (mil dol)	Intergovernmental (mil dol)	Total (mil dol)	Total	Property
	Procurement contract awards			Grants[1]				General revenue		Taxes	Per capita[2] (dollars)	
	171	172	173	174	175	176	177	178	179	180	181	182
UNITED STATES	209 326.6	200 182.8	125 964.9	208 825.0	61 370.6	36 926.8	127 972.9	X	X	X	X	X
ALABAMA	3 223.9	5 510.4	1 557.0	3 251.9	769.6	596.5	2 031.1	X	X	X	X	X
Autauga	7.1	0.2	1.2	23.2	3.2	2.7	2.7	87.7	49.0	18.8	411	109
Baldwin	20.8	3.1	6.0	35.3	9.1	5.6	25.8	396.4	113.7	114.0	770	319
Barbour	5.3	1.9	0.8	31.1	3.9	3.4	9.0	65.3	40.9	13.7	475	165
Bibb	3.8	0.0	1.5	13.8	2.0	2.0	1.3	44.8	22.7	4.0	183	71
Blount	5.3	0.0	1.3	23.2	2.4	2.6	10.5	73.8	45.9	15.9	301	177
Bullock	2.5	0.0	0.4	22.3	2.7	1.1	1.7	23.0	17.4	3.6	319	153
Butler	3.1	0.2	0.7	25.4	3.6	2.1	3.3	47.4	31.0	10.2	487	190
Calhoun	119.2	203.6	42.4	66.2	10.2	9.3	31.4	361.9	121.2	73.9	662	219
Chambers	6.6	1.3	3.5	26.1	4.2	2.3	3.1	55.6	29.4	16.4	452	167
Cherokee	3.2	15.2	0.7	12.6	1.6	1.8	2.8	38.9	23.1	9.4	387	198
Chilton	4.6	6.0	1.8	23.1	2.6	2.6	42.7	63.9	38.0	14.7	364	177
Choctaw	2.4	36.6	10.1	21.7	2.8	1.3	3.9	27.9	16.6	5.7	370	250
Clarke	5.8	26.6	0.9	29.4	4.5	2.6	7.7	59.5	31.0	16.2	588	198
Clay	3.8	0.0	0.6	11.9	1.1	0.8	0.7	37.0	13.9	4.4	309	158
Cleburne	3.2	0.0	0.5	10.2	1.0	0.8	3.0	26.3	15.8	4.3	297	182
Coffee	16.4	415.7	4.5	27.6	3.4	4.0	7.5	79.1	46.4	23.3	530	160
Colbert	97.1	1.7	25.9	32.9	4.2	6.7	29.9	173.9	64.1	27.8	507	185
Conecuh	2.3	0.0	0.6	22.2	2.2	1.2	4.4	26.4	18.0	4.8	351	190
Coosa	1.9	0.6	0.4	7.8	1.2	0.8	0.2	16.3	11.8	3.2	267	129
Covington	8.7	0.2	1.5	33.8	3.0	4.1	7.8	72.1	42.5	15.8	428	173
Crenshaw	3.4	0.0	0.6	21.4	1.6	1.1	3.2	24.7	16.6	3.5	258	173
Cullman	16.3	0.1	2.7	46.8	4.6	4.5	16.0	182.6	73.6	35.6	457	163
Dale	233.3	16.8	1.5	26.8	3.9	4.0	11.4	99.4	43.7	17.1	347	170
Dallas	9.3	65.0	11.7	70.5	15.3	9.8	21.5	102.6	61.6	29.7	649	304
De Kalb	9.5	0.3	1.8	49.5	7.3	4.4	7.3	112.9	63.0	27.3	416	156
Elmore	9.3	4.2	1.8	27.1	7.8	4.0	6.0	114.4	66.5	19.1	278	92
Escambia	4.8	3.0	1.1	26.0	4.2	4.0	18.3	117.3	39.8	16.6	432	135
Etowah	19.4	0.5	10.4	76.4	9.9	9.8	15.8	201.2	98.2	69.5	674	200
Fayette	3.1	6.6	0.6	15.5	1.4	1.2	1.6	28.9	18.3	3.9	215	85
Franklin	5.0	0.6	1.0	31.0	2.4	2.5	20.8	57.5	34.9	10.7	346	176
Geneva	5.8	18.6	1.0	24.7	2.4	1.6	5.1	70.4	27.7	6.8	267	132
Greene	2.2	0.0	0.5	22.5	3.2	1.4	15.1	20.2	14.2	4.0	395	235
Hale	4.5	0.4	0.7	23.7	3.8	2.5	4.9	33.4	24.3	3.5	203	100
Henry	3.1	4.9	8.2	16.7	2.1	1.2	6.5	35.1	18.7	4.9	303	137
Houston	18.9	19.7	6.0	55.9	11.5	8.6	15.1	385.9	118.2	66.4	738	241
Jackson	40.9	2.9	211.6	45.3	4.0	3.2	11.1	96.6	57.0	20.3	375	119
Jefferson	545.0	27.1	203.8	659.3	79.7	51.3	287.8	2 126.7	710.4	906.5	1 371	556
Lamar	3.7	0.0	1.0	16.2	1.1	1.3	7.4	31.6	21.9	4.9	315	85
Lauderdale	18.7	0.2	3.9	47.2	6.6	4.9	19.6	371.0	104.6	78.3	899	593
Lawrence	4.9	0.6	0.8	28.6	2.8	3.1	4.5	65.8	36.7	7.8	226	138
Lee	33.4	10.3	5.7	42.7	11.8	9.6	59.5	395.9	103.2	80.1	678	297
Limestone	8.7	0.7	2.2	33.1	3.0	3.7	7.4	133.1	58.8	20.2	297	109
Lowndes	2.8	0.5	0.3	19.1	6.0	1.9	2.1	29.2	23.4	4.0	297	142
Macon	47.9	1.8	4.0	56.4	7.6	7.7	16.0	37.0	25.3	7.5	317	166
Madison	780.0	4 039.9	671.3	95.5	16.0	21.4	140.0	1 785.1	278.3	223.7	782	312
Marengo	4.7	0.1	0.7	31.5	4.5	1.9	8.6	76.0	37.5	12.6	560	286
Marion	5.4	0.0	2.1	23.9	1.9	1.7	35.8	55.3	32.7	12.5	413	144
Marshall	18.6	1.2	44.9	56.4	4.9	4.7	13.9	261.2	91.7	48.1	575	217
Mobile	178.9	77.2	48.8	227.9	57.0	37.3	108.4	984.6	434.0	373.3	933	316
Monroe	3.9	0.0	0.8	27.3	3.3	3.5	5.2	65.7	33.3	7.0	291	153
Montgomery	555.7	319.8	113.2	233.8	184.6	197.6	455.9	460.4	207.9	178.0	797	198
Morgan	101.5	-10.3	5.7	53.8	13.2	7.5	11.1	360.6	114.5	74.7	669	378
Perry	2.4	0.0	0.3	21.0	5.0	1.8	2.2	31.0	21.4	4.3	366	152
Pickens	3.7	0.8	0.7	30.8	5.3	1.7	5.6	40.7	25.2	6.5	313	134
Pike	6.8	43.7	0.9	35.1	9.1	3.8	8.5	51.4	30.8	12.0	404	149
Randolph	3.0	3.9	9.4	20.7	2.0	1.3	2.6	39.7	24.2	10.2	452	317
Russell	5.7	2.3	1.2	40.1	7.2	3.9	10.3	95.4	53.6	28.7	582	246
St. Clair	7.8	0.0	2.1	21.0	5.2	3.6	19.0	106.2	58.3	30.4	453	186
Shelby	25.7	1.0	3.9	21.8	4.8	5.3	25.3	269.6	104.6	108.3	704	379
Sumter	3.0	0.0	0.6	24.8	6.5	2.4	10.2	31.0	20.9	7.4	517	177
Talladega	31.9	18.0	4.6	62.6	16.0	7.6	17.9	145.3	85.6	36.4	451	179
Tallapoosa	6.7	0.0	2.1	28.2	6.4	4.0	19.9	91.0	51.1	18.2	445	193
Tuscaloosa	71.8	43.3	50.1	95.7	19.5	17.8	106.8	649.0	217.0	121.4	729	260
Walker	13.7	0.4	2.5	48.8	7.0	6.0	84.0	103.4	62.9	25.4	359	111

1. State totals may include programs not allocated by county.   2. Based on the resident population estimated as of July 1 of the year shown.

Table B. States and Counties — Local Government Finances, Government Employment, and Elections

STATE County	Direct general expenditure — Total (mil dol)	Per capita[1] (dollars)	Percent of total for — Education	Health and hospitals	Police protection	Public welfare	Highways	Debt outstanding — Total (mil dol)	Per capita[1] (dollars)	Government employment, 2002 — Federal civilian	Federal military	State and local	Presidential election, 2004 Percent of vote cast — Democratic	Republican	All other
	183	184	185	186	187	188	189	190	191	192	193	194	195	196	197
UNITED STATES............	X	X	X	X	X	X	X	X	X	2 730 000	1 954 000	18 662 000	48.1	51.0	0.9
ALABAMA	X	X	X	X	X	X	X	X	X	49 517	32 104	299 867	36.8	62.5	0.7
Autauga.......................	87.4	1 916	57.5	0.1	6.0	0.4	5.4	105.0	2 303	85	201	1 845	23.7	75.7	0.6
Baldwin.......................	426.9	2 886	35.6	27.8	4.5	0.1	6.3	342.3	2 314	302	651	7 847	22.5	76.5	1.0
Barbour.......................	61.8	2 145	46.9	15.2	5.8	0.3	5.6	35.4	1 228	64	136	1 966	44.9	54.8	0.4
Bibb............................	41.2	1 888	53.7	24.2	6.4	0.0	4.0	15.1	692	71	96	1 240	27.5	72.0	0.4
Blount.........................	78.3	1 478	71.8	0.8	4.2	0.6	5.5	52.2	986	98	232	1 736	18.3	80.9	0.8
Bullock.......................	22.5	1 981	56.2	18.2	2.2	0.3	3.8	19.5	1 716	40	50	738	68.1	31.7	0.3
Butler.........................	48.6	2 323	49.2	10.7	4.2	0.0	10.5	30.8	1 471	44	92	1 032	40.5	59.2	0.3
Calhoun......................	379.7	3 402	34.7	38.7	3.7	0.0	5.3	165.2	1 480	3 928	530	7 700	33.3	65.9	0.7
Chambers....................	63.2	1 743	54.6	0.9	7.6	0.2	8.9	61.9	1 708	55	159	1 425	41.0	58.5	0.5
Cherokee.....................	37.3	1 535	67.6	0.5	4.1	0.2	11.8	12.2	503	48	107	1 118	33.6	65.5	0.9
Chilton........................	67.2	1 658	60.0	5.3	5.6	0.1	7.4	25.8	637	67	178	1 602	22.6	76.9	0.5
Choctaw......................	27.4	1 780	57.6	0.1	4.1	0.0	11.4	25.9	1 683	30	68	569	45.7	54.0	0.3
Clarke.........................	59.3	2 152	56.4	10.1	6.8	0.1	3.9	77.9	2 828	93	121	1 894	40.6	59.1	0.3
Clay............................	34.1	2 409	40.9	41.1	3.0	0.1	3.9	11.3	796	52	62	1 038	28.8	70.3	0.9
Cleburne.....................	26.9	1 845	55.5	17.5	2.5	0.1	7.6	8.3	571	76	64	728	24.0	75.4	0.6
Coffee........................	77.0	1 756	68.3	0.7	5.7	0.5	5.9	14.0	319	178	192	2 287	25.4	73.9	0.6
Colbert.......................	180.1	3 283	33.0	39.4	3.7	0.2	4.1	114.6	2 089	1 384	241	4 285	44.3	55.1	0.6
Conecuh......................	26.4	1 927	66.9	0.2	4.9	0.0	9.6	20.3	1 483	44	60	831	45.2	54.3	0.5
Coosa.........................	16.9	1 423	70.9	0.0	3.1	0.9	8.6	3.4	289	25	52	409	41.1	58.1	0.7
Covington....................	78.0	2 112	55.1	0.3	7.7	0.2	9.4	89.3	2 416	148	162	2 033	23.4	76.0	0.6
Crenshaw....................	25.9	1 898	58.5	0.6	4.9	0.3	13.1	10.7	782	47	60	612	30.9	68.7	0.5
Cullman......................	179.5	2 302	45.1	24.8	3.9	0.0	8.9	134.5	1 724	250	342	3 554	22.9	76.3	0.8
Dale...........................	99.5	2 022	43.8	27.9	5.0	0.5	4.3	55.7	1 131	2 609	4 818	2 493	24.6	74.8	0.7
Dallas.........................	92.5	2 025	62.3	0.1	4.9	0.5	3.9	52.9	1 159	164	200	2 956	60.2	39.5	0.3
De Kalb.......................	115.9	1 766	62.3	1.6	5.4	0.5	6.4	96.8	1 476	168	288	2 737	29.4	70.0	0.7
Elmore........................	116.1	1 689	57.3	15.2	4.9	0.0	7.2	57.7	839	134	302	3 410	22.6	76.9	0.5
Escambia.....................	88.5	2 309	48.3	23.0	5.4	0.5	7.1	35.5	926	70	168	3 047	30.8	68.7	0.5
Etowah........................	202.9	1 968	50.0	2.3	9.0	0.1	5.3	105.9	1 027	329	455	4 987	35.9	63.3	0.8
Fayette........................	30.4	1 664	58.9	5.4	3.8	0.6	5.1	24.6	1 346	49	80	1 286	30.1	69.2	0.7
Franklin.......................	57.3	1 858	63.7	0.1	4.7	0.7	8.8	47.0	1 523	92	135	1 999	36.8	62.7	0.5
Geneva........................	71.7	2 830	36.1	41.1	3.2	0.3	9.1	24.9	983	71	111	1 422	20.1	79.4	0.6
Greene........................	19.8	1 972	69.0	5.4	2.4	0.5	5.7	9.1	909	37	44	650	79.3	20.2	0.5
Hale............................	35.3	2 066	62.1	13.2	4.0	0.1	7.2	10.0	585	55	75	944	58.3	41.3	0.4
Henry..........................	34.1	2 092	51.4	0.9	6.5	13.5	10.7	12.6	776	68	71	749	33.2	66.4	0.4
Houston.......................	427.6	4 753	25.4	42.9	3.4	0.1	3.2	380.0	4 224	334	397	7 329	25.3	74.3	0.5
Jackson.......................	96.8	1 792	63.2	0.6	5.5	0.6	6.7	77.8	1 440	613	237	3 223	42.5	56.8	0.7
Jefferson.....................	2 646.1	4 002	30.9	6.0	5.7	0.9	3.0	4 395.8	6 649	7 983	3 313	50 644	45.2	54.2	0.6
Lamar..........................	35.7	2 304	59.7	2.5	3.6	0.1	9.1	20.0	1 291	42	68	624	28.4	71.1	0.5
Lauderdale...................	357.2	4 101	24.4	49.4	2.6	0.0	3.4	296.4	3 403	312	387	6 223	39.5	59.7	0.8
Lawrence.....................	70.6	2 036	60.2	0.4	4.1	0.7	4.7	201.2	5 805	87	152	1 506	44.0	55.2	0.8
Lee.............................	378.4	3 204	35.8	36.5	3.6	0.0	4.0	428.7	3 630	336	584	12 797	36.4	62.7	0.9
Limestone....................	143.8	2 120	52.1	25.4	3.4	0.4	5.1	125.2	1 846	1 137	298	4 362	31.6	67.7	0.8
Lowndes......................	28.6	2 119	74.6	0.2	5.4	0.0	9.9	5.2	385	20	59	652	70.3	29.7	0.0
Macon.........................	37.4	1 573	62.8	0.9	7.2	0.4	7.3	33.2	1 395	1 006	118	1 191	82.6	17.0	0.4
Madison.......................	1 067.4	3 733	30.0	34.9	3.6	0.1	2.6	1 446.3	5 059	13 800	2 763	21 017	40.2	58.9	0.9
Marengo......................	78.4	3 490	40.2	29.4	2.8	0.3	5.2	36.0	1 602	77	115	1 710	48.8	50.9	0.3
Marion.........................	59.4	1 957	60.0	2.3	2.8	0.1	3.7	37.9	1 248	96	133	1 453	29.6	69.8	0.6
Marshall.......................	257.6	3 084	39.3	35.8	3.9	0.2	3.2	196.6	2 353	282	367	5 103	26.9	72.4	0.8
Mobile.........................	1 041.5	2 603	42.1	4.4	6.2	0.8	6.3	1 005.3	2 512	2 420	2 597	25 724	40.6	58.7	0.7
Monroe........................	63.2	2 628	43.9	35.0	3.0	0.3	5.6	15.0	623	57	105	1 517	38.5	61.2	0.4
Montgomery..................	479.5	2 147	46.7	1.7	7.7	0.1	5.5	264.7	1 185	6 516	5 830	25 441	50.4	49.2	0.4
Morgan........................	371.3	3 323	37.8	27.7	3.7	0.3	3.9	380.7	3 407	296	491	7 103	30.1	69.1	0.8
Perry...........................	28.7	2 464	53.2	23.1	3.5	0.1	8.6	11.5	989	31	63	643	68.2	31.5	0.3
Pickens.......................	39.6	1 900	61.0	1.9	5.0	0.3	8.6	64.9	3 115	56	91	922	42.9	56.6	0.5
Pike............................	57.2	1 933	52.4	0.3	6.3	0.4	4.7	44.0	1 489	66	137	2 507	36.5	63.0	0.5
Randolph.....................	36.5	1 621	63.3	2.1	5.9	0.4	8.9	17.1	760	53	99	1 286	31.3	68.1	0.6
Russell........................	103.5	2 094	60.5	0.2	5.6	0.1	4.6	122.8	2 484	89	217	2 480	49.9	49.6	0.5
St. Clair.......................	130.2	1 937	63.0	0.4	5.6	0.0	8.9	78.6	1 169	112	295	2 407	18.7	80.6	0.7
Shelby.........................	278.6	1 811	58.2	2.0	5.6	0.3	4.8	253.4	1 647	274	675	5 690	18.8	80.4	0.7
Sumter........................	33.3	2 314	57.2	1.1	6.4	0.5	12.9	17.2	1 194	44	63	1 325	70.4	29.2	0.4
Talladega.....................	144.0	1 785	59.7	3.9	4.6	0.1	5.7	113.9	1 412	494	354	4 641	38.1	61.3	0.6
Tallapoosa...................	99.5	2 429	52.3	14.1	4.6	0.2	4.2	62.1	1 516	102	180	2 021	30.4	69.0	0.6
Tuscaloosa...................	703.7	4 226	31.0	42.5	3.4	0.1	5.2	426.0	2 559	1 365	755	19 202	37.9	61.4	0.7
Walker.........................	111.4	1 576	67.3	0.1	5.9	0.0	7.0	66.9	946	201	311	3 050	31.8	67.6	0.6

1. Based on the resident population estimated as of July 1 of the year shown.

Table B. States and Counties — Land Area and Population

STATE/County code	CBSA code[1]	County Type[2]	STATE County	Land area,[3] (sq km) 2000	Total persons	Rank	Per square kilometer	White	Black	Am. Indian, Alaska Native	Asian and Pacific Islander	Percent Hispanic or Latino[4]	Under 5 years	5 to 17 years	18 to 24 years	25 to 34 years	35 to 44 years	45 to 54 years
								Race alone or in combination, not Hispanic or Latino (percent)					Age (percent)					
				1	2	3	4	5	6	7	8	9	10	11	12	13	14	15
			ALABAMA—Cont'd															
01 129	...	8	Washington	2 799	17 880	1 921	6.4	65.3	26.8	7.7	0.1	0.9	6.8	20.3	9.9	11.6	14.2	13.9
01 131	...	8	Wilcox	2 302	13 024	2 237	5.7	27.0	72.0	0.1	0.1	0.8	8.0	21.5	11.2	10.6	12.7	12.8
01 133	...	6	Winston	1 591	24 620	1 594	15.5	97.1	0.6	1.0	0.2	1.7	5.9	16.9	8.6	12.6	15.2	13.8
02 000	...	X	**ALASKA**	1 481 347	648 818	X	0.4	71.1	4.4	18.5	6.0	4.6	7.5	21.7	10.7	12.7	16.1	16.3
02 013	...	9	Aleutians East Borough	18 099	2 656	3 010	0.1	19.9	1.7	32.5	32.1	14.6	3.9	10.2	11.3	17.4	24.7	20.6
02 016	...	7	Aleutians West Census Area	11 388	5 241	2 824	0.5	39.8	4.1	20.4	25.0	11.5	3.2	11.5	9.7	20.2	24.5	19.6
02 020	11260	2	Anchorage	4 396	270 951	215	61.6	72.5	7.1	10.5	8.7	6.4	7.7	20.9	10.4	14.1	16.9	15.5
02 050	...	7	Bethel	105 240	16 873	1 969	0.2	15.4	0.8	84.8	1.2	1.0	11.4	28.1	11.4	12.2	14.8	11.2
02 060	...	9	Bristol Bay	1 308	1 099	3 105	0.8	54.0	0.5	43.2	1.6	1.3	5.6	21.9	8.4	8.7	23.4	21.1
02 068	...	8	Denali Borough	33 021	1 872	3 068	0.1	89.2	1.7	6.5	1.6	3.2	4.8	16.5	8.4	13.1	19.2	23.5
02 070	...	9	Dillingham	48 367	4 933	2 849	0.1	25.6	0.4	75.5	1.0	2.1	8.0	28.3	10.0	10.4	16.2	14.6
02 090	21820	3	Fairbanks North Star	19 078	85 978	619	4.5	78.9	7.6	10.1	3.7	4.7	8.4	21.0	12.2	15.5	15.6	14.3
02 100	...	9	Haines	6 070	2 296	3 033	0.4	87.4	0.4	12.5	0.9	1.4	4.1	18.1	8.8	8.3	15.9	23.2
02 110	27940	5	Juneau	7 036	31 187	1 377	4.4	77.7	1.4	16.3	7.4	3.7	6.5	19.8	9.8	12.2	16.9	18.5
02 122	...	7	Kenai Peninsula	41 474	51 146	921	1.2	88.5	0.7	9.8	1.9	2.4	5.9	21.3	10.3	10.4	16.0	18.3
02 130	28540	7	Ketchikan Gateway	3 194	13 320	2 214	4.2	76.6	0.7	18.3	5.7	2.8	6.6	20.3	9.2	11.1	17.4	17.8
02 150	28980	7	Kodiak Island	16 990	13 419	2 203	0.8	60.6	1.1	17.4	19.1	5.7	8.1	22.8	9.5	12.9	18.5	16.1
02 164	...	9	Lake and Peninsula Borough	61 595	1 551	3 084	0.0	26.9	0.1	76.7	0.4	1.2	6.6	28.2	12.8	7.4	19.0	15.2
02 170	11260	2	Matanuska-Susitna	63 925	68 337	734	1.1	90.1	1.2	8.1	1.7	2.9	6.4	22.8	11.3	10.4	16.4	16.3
02 180	...	7	Nome	59 572	9 162	2 513	0.2	22.3	0.5	78.4	1.0	1.0	9.6	26.4	11.4	12.1	15.0	13.1
02 185	...	7	North Slope	230 035	7 218	2 663	0.0	19.5	1.2	73.4	8.1	2.8	10.7	26.8	11.7	10.8	15.7	13.4
02 188	...	7	Northwest Arctic Borough	92 976	7 373	2 650	0.1	14.9	0.2	85.2	1.2	1.2	10.8	28.8	12.5	12.5	14.0	11.1
02 201	...	9	Prince of Wales-Outer Ketchikan	19 193	5 809	2 788	0.3	57.2	0.3	45.6	0.7	1.9	7.0	21.0	10.4	9.5	16.0	18.5
02 220	...	7	Sitka	7 444	8 876	2 536	1.2	72.3	0.6	23.0	6.1	3.9	7.3	19.2	10.4	12.1	16.0	16.6
02 232	...	9	Skagway-Hoonah-Angoon	20 452	3 121	2 975	0.2	61.8	0.2	37.8	0.5	3.2	3.7	19.7	9.5	10.5	17.7	21.6
02 240	...	8	Southeast Fairbanks	64 270	5 835	2 786	0.1	83.4	1.3	15.5	1.1	2.2	7.5	23.8	10.5	8.1	13.7	17.2
02 261	...	9	Valdez-Cordova	88 886	9 933	2 449	0.1	78.4	0.6	19.0	4.1	2.3	6.2	21.8	9.7	10.0	17.4	19.7
02 270	...	9	Wade Hampton	44 531	7 314	2 657	0.2	7.0	0.1	94.4	0.2	0.5	12.1	32.8	12.4	11.6	12.1	8.7
02 280	...	7	Wrangell-Petersburg	15 112	6 296	2 746	0.4	78.7	0.2	22.2	3.5	2.1	5.7	22.0	8.5	9.3	16.2	19.0
02 282	...	9	Yakutat Borough	19 815	710	3 128	0.0	54.5	0.1	44.5	1.3	0.6	3.5	20.1	7.6	9.9	21.3	23.2
02 290	...	8	Yukon-Koyukuk	377 878	6 314	2 744	0.0	29.0	0.2	72.2	0.5	1.2	7.3	25.5	11.2	9.2	15.3	15.9
04 000	...	X	**ARIZONA**	294 312	5 580 811	X	19.0	62.4	3.3	5.1	2.6	27.8	7.8	19.4	9.9	14.4	14.1	12.4
04 001	...	6	Apache	29 021	68 129	737	2.3	17.8	0.3	78.1	0.2	4.2	8.9	28.0	11.4	10.1	12.8	11.5
04 003	43420	4	Cochise	15 979	122 161	466	7.6	61.0	3.4	1.6	2.8	32.9	7.1	19.5	10.1	10.5	13.0	13.3
04 005	22380	3	Coconino	48 219	121 301	467	2.5	56.2	1.2	31.6	1.3	11.1	7.8	20.6	13.3	14.3	13.8	13.7
04 007	37740	4	Gila	12 348	51 448	914	4.2	68.9	0.4	14.5	0.6	16.3	6.4	18.5	8.0	8.4	12.0	13.6
04 009	40940	6	Graham	11 990	33 051	1 330	2.8	54.0	1.9	16.2	0.6	27.8	7.1	21.7	13.4	13.1	13.2	11.3
04 011	40940	7	Greenlee	4 784	7 517	2 635	1.6	51.3	0.5	2.3	0.2	46.3	6.8	23.8	8.6	10.0	16.0	16.7
04 012	...	6	La Paz	11 655	19 517	1 836	1.7	63.4	0.9	13.0	0.5	23.2	4.9	15.5	7.6	7.7	11.0	12.1
04 013	38060	1	Maricopa	23 836	3 389 260	4	142.2	64.1	4.1	2.0	3.1	28.0	8.3	19.6	9.7	15.4	14.5	11.7
04 015	29420	4	Mohave	34 477	171 367	329	5.0	84.9	0.7	3.0	1.2	11.4	5.9	17.5	7.6	9.3	12.2	12.6
04 017	...	4	Navajo	25 779	104 280	520	4.0	41.3	0.9	50.2	0.5	8.0	8.3	25.5	11.3	10.8	12.7	11.5
04 019	46060	2	Pima	23 792	892 798	50	37.5	60.1	3.2	3.3	2.9	31.9	6.9	18.0	10.4	13.4	13.8	13.1
04 021	38060	1	Pinal	13 907	204 148	287	14.7	58.9	3.1	7.5	1.0	30.5	6.9	18.7	10.2	12.8	12.9	11.2
04 023	35700	4	Santa Cruz	3 205	40 267	1 129	12.6	17.1	0.2	0.3	0.5	81.9	9.1	23.9	9.5	10.9	13.5	12.6
04 025	39140	3	Yavapai	21 039	184 433	309	8.8	87.0	0.5	2.2	0.9	10.5	5.1	15.8	8.5	9.2	11.8	13.9
04 027	49740	3	Yuma	14 281	171 134	331	12.0	41.8	1.7	1.5	1.2	54.4	8.8	21.4	10.3	11.2	12.5	9.9
05 000	...	X	**ARKANSAS**	134 856	2 725 714	X	20.2	78.6	16.4	1.3	1.2	3.7	6.8	18.2	10.1	13.0	14.1	13.5
05 001	...	6	Arkansas	2 560	20 158	1 796	7.9	75.1	23.6	0.5	0.5	0.8	6.9	17.9	8.2	11.5	14.1	15.0
05 003	...	7	Ashley	2 386	23 583	1 634	9.9	68.4	27.9	0.4	0.3	3.5	6.5	19.3	9.1	12.6	14.0	13.8
05 005	34260	7	Baxter	1 436	39 113	1 156	27.2	98.0	0.2	1.3	0.5	0.9	4.4	14.1	7.5	8.6	11.8	13.1
05 007	22220	2	Benton	2 191	172 003	326	78.5	86.2	0.8	2.4	1.8	10.2	7.3	19.3	9.7	13.6	14.2	11.6
05 009	25460	7	Boone	1 531	34 740	1 282	22.7	97.7	0.2	1.5	0.5	1.0	6.1	17.1	9.1	11.9	13.9	13.5
05 011	...	6	Bradley	1 685	12 414	2 273	7.4	61.6	29.1	0.2	0.1	9.1	6.2	16.9	9.9	12.4	13.7	13.0
05 013	15780	9	Calhoun	1 627	5 626	2 800	3.5	75.5	22.6	0.3	0.1	1.8	5.0	17.9	8.4	11.3	15.6	14.5
05 015	...	6	Carroll	1 632	26 359	1 523	16.2	87.4	0.2	1.5	0.5	11.3	6.5	16.9	9.1	11.1	13.8	14.3
05 017	...	7	Chicot	1 668	13 485	2 199	8.1	41.0	55.2	0.2	0.7	3.3	7.5	19.1	9.8	11.9	13.3	13.1
05 019	11660	7	Clark	2 241	23 581	1 635	10.5	73.1	22.8	1.0	1.1	3.0	6.0	15.2	19.3	12.0	11.4	11.5
05 021	...	7	Clay	1 656	16 912	1 968	10.2	98.0	0.3	1.3	0.2	0.9	5.8	17.1	8.4	11.0	13.4	13.4
05 023	...	6	Cleburne	1 432	24 723	1 587	17.3	98.0	0.4	1.1	0.2	1.0	5.1	15.7	8.1	9.7	13.3	13.1
05 025	38220	3	Cleveland	1 548	8 709	2 551	5.6	84.0	13.8	0.5	0.2	1.9	6.8	18.5	9.2	11.8	14.4	13.2
05 027	31620	7	Columbia	1 984	25 034	1 572	12.6	60.7	37.5	0.5	0.5	1.3	5.9	18.0	12.9	11.5	13.5	12.6

1. CBSA = Core Based Statistical Area. See Appendix A for explanation. See Appendix B for list of metropolitan areas with component counties.
Service of USDA Rural-Urban Continuum Codes. See Appendix A for definition.   3. Dry land or land partially or temporarily covered by water.   2. County type code from the Economic Research   4. Hispanic or Latino persons may be of any race.

Table B. States and Counties — **Population and Households**

STATE County	55 to 64 years (16)	65 to 74 years (17)	75 years and over (18)	Percent female (19)	1990 (20)	2000 (21)	1990–2000 (22)	2000–2003 (23)	Births (24)	Deaths (25)	Net migration (26)	Number (27)	Percent change, 1990–2000 (28)	Persons per household (29)	Female family householder[1] (30)	One person (31)
ALABAMA—Cont'd																
Washington	10.4	7.2	5.4	51.2	16 694	18 097	8.4	-1.2	770	566	-414	6 705	17.4	2.69	12.5	22.8
Wilcox	9.3	6.9	6.8	54.3	13 568	13 183	-2.8	-1.2	724	454	-252	4 776	8.2	2.70	26.5	27.5
Winston	12.5	8.3	6.2	50.7	22 053	24 843	12.7	-0.9	914	937	-184	10 107	18.3	2.43	9.1	25.6
ALASKA	8.8	3.8	2.4	48.3	550 043	626 932	14.0	3.5	32 190	10 102	-117	221 600	17.3	2.74	10.8	23.5
Aleutians East Borough	8.2	1.5	1.4	33.8	2 464	2 697	9.5	-1.5	87	21	-121	526	-1.3	2.69	14.4	27.4
Aleutians West Census Area	7.5	2.0	0.7	36.2	9 478	5 465	-42.3	-4.1	108	30	-313	1 270	-31.2	2.52	7.6	32.0
Anchorage	8.0	3.6	2.2	49.4	226 338	260 283	15.0	4.1	13 375	3 874	1 457	94 822	14.7	2.67	11.5	23.4
Bethel	6.0	3.3	1.9	47.0	13 660	16 006	17.2	5.4	1 430	333	-259	4 226	17.2	3.73	15.2	19.9
Bristol Bay	9.3	3.5	1.2	44.8	1 410	1 258	-10.8	-12.6	43	28	-180	490	20.4	2.57	6.1	31.2
Denali Borough	10.4	2.6	1.1	42.3	1 682	1 893	12.5	-1.1	67	15	-72	785	NA	2.28	4.5	35.0
Dillingham	7.1	4.0	2.1	47.8	4 010	4 922	22.7	0.2	275	104	-162	1 529	25.8	3.20	15.0	23.3
Fairbanks North Star	7.2	3.0	1.8	47.9	77 720	82 840	6.6	3.8	4 843	1 196	-420	29 777	11.6	2.68	9.3	23.6
Haines	11.5	5.8	4.6	48.8	2 117	2 392	13.0	-4.0	55	51	-98	991	25.3	2.41	7.3	27.1
Juneau	9.1	3.7	2.8	49.6	26 752	30 711	14.8	1.5	1 341	453	-394	11 543	16.6	2.60	10.5	24.4
Kenai Peninsula	9.7	4.9	3.0	48.0	40 802	49 691	21.8	2.9	1 896	902	503	18 438	29.4	2.62	9.0	24.7
Ketchikan Gateway	10.3	5.0	3.6	49.1	13 828	14 070	1.8	-5.3	590	325	-1 032	5 399	7.3	2.56	11.3	26.1
Kodiak Island	7.9	3.4	2.0	47.2	13 309	13 913	4.5	-3.6	731	153	-1 104	4 424	8.4	3.07	8.8	19.9
Lake and Peninsula Borough	7.1	3.6	2.2	47.3	1 666	1 823	9.4	-14.9	74	84	-270	588	15.5	3.10	9.7	24.7
Matanuska-Susitna	7.7	3.9	2.1	47.9	39 683	59 322	49.5	15.2	2 809	1 038	7 064	20 556	53.5	2.84	9.1	20.3
Nome	7.0	3.4	2.5	46.6	8 288	9 196	11.0	-0.4	634	219	-446	2 693	13.6	3.33	15.3	23.2
North Slope	6.8	2.9	1.7	47.0	5 986	7 385	23.4	-2.3	557	103	-645	2 109	26.1	3.45	18.3	21.4
Northwest Arctic Borough	5.6	3.0	1.7	46.3	6 106	7 208	18.0	2.3	537	135	-236	1 780	16.6	3.87	19.7	16.6
Prince of Wales-Outer Ketchikan	10.1	4.8	2.1	45.3	6 278	6 146	-2.1	-5.5	256	85	-535	2 262	9.8	2.68	10.0	26.0
Sitka	9.6	5.4	3.6	48.8	8 588	8 835	2.9	0.5	423	156	-231	3 278	11.5	2.61	10.3	24.5
Skagway-Hoonah-Angoon	12.0	5.0	3.3	46.0	3 679	3 436	-6.6	-9.2	71	63	-328	1 369	NA	2.50	8.4	30.1
Southeast Fairbanks	10.0	5.3	2.5	48.1	5 925	6 174	4.2	-5.5	315	78	-616	2 098	9.9	2.80	8.6	23.5
Valdez-Cordova	10.0	3.9	2.4	47.0	9 920	10 195	2.8	-2.6	399	169	-489	3 884	13.4	2.58	8.5	27.0
Wade Hampton	4.8	3.3	1.9	47.8	5 789	7 028	21.4	4.1	695	133	-271	1 602	17.1	4.38	20.3	16.0
Wrangell-Petersburg	10.6	5.3	5.0	47.6	7 042	6 684	-5.1	-5.8	229	138	-488	2 587	2.9	2.56	9.2	26.3
Yakutat Borough	10.4	3.5	2.7	39.4	725	808	11.4	-12.1	26	15	-110	265	NA	2.59	12.1	32.1
Yukon-Koyukuk	8.6	4.8	2.8	46.4	6 798	6 551	-3.6	-3.6	324	201	-321	2 309	-16.0	2.81	16.9	30.5
ARIZONA	9.2	6.8	6.0	50.0	3 665 339	5 130 632	40.0	8.8	278 744	136 492	306 247	1 901 327	38.9	2.64	11.1	24.8
Apache	7.9	5.6	3.4	50.8	61 591	69 423	12.7	-1.9	3 668	1 791	-3 261	19 971	25.0	3.41	21.4	21.2
Cochise	10.8	8.8	6.3	50.0	97 624	117 755	20.6	3.7	5 487	3 581	2 610	43 893	27.1	2.55	11.1	25.3
Coconino	7.7	4.5	2.7	50.1	96 591	116 320	20.4	4.3	6 182	1 869	776	40 448	35.2	2.80	12.2	22.1
Gila	13.2	11.5	8.9	50.9	40 216	51 335	27.6	0.2	2 168	2 048	34	20 140	30.5	2.50	10.8	25.8
Graham	8.0	6.8	5.6	46.8	26 554	33 489	26.1	-1.3	1 439	829	-1 031	10 116	27.6	2.99	13.4	20.9
Greenlee	10.3	6.8	4.2	47.5	8 008	8 547	6.7	-12.1	307	169	-1 196	3 117	11.0	2.73	9.0	24.5
La Paz	14.7	16.2	11.0	48.9	13 844	19 715	42.4	-1.0	606	646	-124	8 362	56.4	2.32	8.2	26.6
Maricopa	8.0	5.7	5.3	49.8	2 122 101	3 072 149	44.8	10.3	181 122	76 297	211 127	1 132 886	40.3	2.67	10.7	24.5
Mohave	13.0	11.8	8.2	50.6	93 497	155 032	65.8	10.5	5 920	6 505	16 515	62 809	70.7	2.45	9.3	24.1
Navajo	8.6	6.3	3.9	50.6	77 674	97 470	25.5	7.0	5 242	2 381	3 952	30 043	35.4	3.17	16.3	19.9
Pima	9.1	7.2	6.7	51.1	666 957	843 746	26.5	5.8	39 894	24 828	34 396	332 350	27.0	2.47	11.8	28.5
Pinal	10.1	8.8	6.1	47.0	116 397	179 727	54.4	13.6	8 565	5 152	20 484	61 364	56.7	2.68	11.5	21.1
Santa Cruz	9.0	6.2	4.7	52.4	29 676	38 381	29.3	4.9	2 484	626	73	11 809	34.1	3.23	15.4	16.5
Yavapai	12.7	11.4	9.8	50.8	107 714	167 517	55.5	10.1	5 687	6 480	17 293	70 171	56.7	2.33	8.1	26.7
Yuma	8.5	9.5	7.0	49.8	106 895	160 026	49.7	6.9	9 973	3 290	4 599	53 848	50.5	2.86	11.2	18.5
ARKANSAS	10.4	7.3	6.6	51.1	2 350 624	2 673 400	13.7	2.0	122 012	92 026	22 760	1 042 696	17.0	2.49	12.1	25.6
Arkansas	11.0	8.1	8.1	52.5	21 653	20 749	-4.2	-2.8	931	945	-572	8 457	0.8	2.41	13.9	26.1
Ashley	11.3	7.4	6.5	51.5	24 319	24 209	-0.5	-2.6	1 019	954	-685	9 384	5.6	2.55	13.0	23.9
Baxter	13.8	13.8	12.6	52.0	31 186	38 386	23.1	1.9	1 090	2 012	1 628	17 052	26.4	2.21	7.7	27.5
Benton	8.8	7.1	6.1	50.5	97 530	153 406	57.3	12.1	7 776	4 268	14 710	58 212	55.0	2.60	8.2	21.1
Boone	11.3	8.8	7.8	51.4	28 297	33 948	20.0	2.3	1 383	1 313	731	13 851	24.4	2.41	8.8	25.6
Bradley	10.6	8.8	8.5	50.1	11 793	12 600	6.8	-1.5	526	624	-78	4 834	6.4	2.45	14.5	27.6
Calhoun	11.5	7.9	8.0	52.0	5 826	5 744	-1.4	-2.1	186	233	-65	2 317	6.0	2.43	11.3	27.3
Carroll	11.9	8.6	7.1	50.7	18 623	25 357	36.2	4.0	1 093	842	773	10 189	35.0	2.47	8.6	25.2
Chicot	10.3	8.4	7.2	51.3	15 713	14 117	-10.2	-4.5	717	617	-743	5 205	-6.3	2.58	22.0	26.9
Clark	9.1	7.1	7.1	51.6	21 437	23 546	9.8	0.1	910	826	-33	8 912	12.7	2.38	12.2	27.6
Clay	12.2	9.8	9.6	51.6	18 107	17 609	-2.8	-4.0	626	869	-436	7 417	-1.2	2.35	8.6	28.4
Cleburne	13.5	11.7	9.2	51.2	19 411	24 046	23.9	2.8	805	1 012	883	10 190	28.6	2.33	7.9	24.4
Cleveland	11.4	7.7	6.1	51.1	7 781	8 571	10.2	1.6	374	263	31	3 273	14.1	2.60	9.9	21.4
Columbia	9.9	7.9	8.1	52.3	25 691	25 603	-0.3	-2.2	1 037	937	-662	9 981	3.6	2.45	15.1	29.2

1. No spouse present.

STATE County	Births, average 1999–2001		Deaths, average 1999–2001				Physicians,[4] 2000		Hospitals,[4] 1998			Medicare enrollees, 2003	Serious crimes known to police,[6] 2002	
			Number		Rate					Beds			Total	
	Total	Rate[1]	Total	Infant[2]	Total[1]	Infant[3]	Number	Rate[5]	Number	Number	Rate[5]		Number	Rate[7]
	32	33	34	35	36	37	38	39	40	41	42	43	44	45
ALABAMA—Cont'd														
Washington	240	13.3	162	1	9.0	D	7	39	1	100	566	2 974	NA	NA
Wilcox	229	17.3	148	4	11.2	D	5	38	1	32	238	2 527	188	1 414
Winston	303	12.2	291	2	11.8	D	9	36	1	45	186	4 794	NA	NA
ALASKA	9 976	15.9	2 865	69	4.6	6.9	1 087	173	16	1 324	216	47 749	27 745	4 310
Aleutians East Borough	21	7.9	5	0	0.0	D	0	0	0	0	0	NA	NA	NA
Aleutians West Census Area	37	6.7	12	0	2.2	D	0	0	0	0	0	NA	NA	NA
Anchorage	4 193	16.0	1 080	23	4.1	5.5	620	238	2	603	236	19 363	NA	NA
Bethel	438	27.1	84	7	5.2	16.0	15	94	0	0	0	744	NA	NA
Bristol Bay	18	14.1	7	0	5.9	D	1	79	0	0	0	812	NA	NA
Denali Borough	92	18.8	24	1	5.0	D	7	142	0	0	0	NA	NA	NA
Dillingham	NA	NA	NA	NA	NA	NA	0	0	0	0	0	NA	NA	NA
Fairbanks North Star	1 482	17.8	343	10	4.1	6.7	161	194	1	224	266	5 233	NA	NA
Haines	20	8.3	16	1	6.9	D	4	167	0	0	0	312	NA	NA
Juneau	412	13.4	133	2	4.3	D	59	192	1	59	195	2 869	NA	NA
Kenai Peninsula	631	12.7	266	3	5.3	D	51	103	3	128	267	4 634	NA	NA
Ketchikan Gateway	184	13.1	100	1	7.1	D	30	213	1	71	528	1 372	NA	NA
Kodiak Island	233	16.9	47	1	3.4	D	23	165	1	49	337	416	NA	NA
Lake and Peninsula Borough	24	13.4	18	1	10.2	D	0	0	0	0	0	NA	NA	NA
Matanuska-Susitna	791	13.2	285	6	4.8	D	54	91	1	36	64	4 983	NA	NA
Nome	212	23.0	60	2	6.5	D	7	76	1	35	388	565	NA	NA
North Slope	154	20.9	34	1	4.7	D	4	54	0	0	0	360	NA	NA
Northwest Arctic Borough	165	22.9	37	2	5.2	D	3	42	0	0	0	NA	NA	NA
Prince of Wales-Outer Ketchikan	82	13.5	24	0	3.9	D	4	65	0	0	0	475	NA	NA
Sitka	121	13.8	52	2	6.0	D	21	238	1	28	336	843	NA	NA
Skagway-Hoonah-Angoon	24	7.1	17	0	5.0	D	0	0	0	0	0	NA	NA	NA
Southeast Fairbanks	92	15.3	26	1	4.4	D	4	65	0	0	0	536	NA	NA
Valdez-Cordova	132	13.0	48	1	4.8	D	13	128	2	43	418	748	NA	NA
Wade Hampton	212	29.9	39	3	5.5	D	0	0	0	0	0	428	NA	NA
Wrangell-Petersburg	78	11.7	43	0	6.5	D	6	90	2	48	704	728	NA	NA
Yakutat Borough	8	9.4	3	0	0.0	D	0	0	0	0	0	NA	NA	NA
Yukon-Koyukuk	119	14.2	59	0	7.0	D	0	0	0	0	0	564	NA	NA
ARIZONA	84 005	16.3	40 536	571	7.9	6.8	9 612	187	61	10 161	218	728 885	348 467	6 386
Apache	1 274	18.5	477	13	6.9	10.5	64	92	2	50	73	7 186	715	968
Cochise	1 688	14.3	1 062	12	9.0	6.9	124	105	5	250	222	19 894	4 466	3 566
Coconino	1 862	16.0	524	9	4.5	4.7	208	179	2	141	123	14 208	7 480	6 047
Gila	666	13.0	617	5	12.0	D	55	107	2	93	190	11 660	2 055	3 764
Graham	461	13.8	265	3	7.9	D	23	69	1	42	133	4 413	805	2 260
Greenlee	117	13.8	62	1	7.3	D	4	47	0	0	0	1 067	90	1 422
La Paz	184	9.4	185	3	9.5	D	20	101	1	39	262	3 801	821	3 916
Maricopa	53 917	17.4	22 731	366	7.3	6.8	6 038	197	27	6 245	224	390 110	223 985	6 936
Mohave	1 996	12.9	1 935	15	12.5	7.3	170	110	4	283	217	37 838	8 112	4 920
Navajo	1 681	17.2	679	12	7.0	7.3	88	90	2	83	86	12 559	2 909	2 806
Pima	12 184	14.4	7 383	77	8.7	6.3	2 266	269	9	2 078	263	134 558	67 628	7 537
Pinal	2 527	14.0	1 503	22	8.3	8.6	106	59	2	316	215	26 803	8 958	5 284
Santa Cruz	771	20.0	203	3	5.3	D	43	112	1	80	210	5 129	1 200	3 009
Yavapai	1 709	10.2	1 927	12	11.5	6.8	247	147	2	186	125	39 042	7 515	4 218
Yuma	2 969	18.5	985	20	6.2	6.6	156	97	1	275	208	20 451	5 671	3 685
ARKANSAS	37 174	13.9	27 967	306	10.5	8.2	4 267	160	80	10 107	398	452 676	112 672	4 158
Arkansas	273	13.1	280	2	13.5	D	16	77	2	187	900	3 841	803	3 818
Ashley	315	13.1	298	2	12.4	D	16	66	1	28	115	4 263	482	1 964
Baxter	332	8.7	618	2	16.1	D	68	177	1	207	569	11 549	498	1 280
Benton	2 284	14.8	1 258	12	8.2	5.3	163	106	4	316	236	25 122	3 523	2 265
Boone	404	11.9	393	2	11.6	D	47	138	1	125	392	7 557	675	1 961
Bradley	161	12.8	183	1	14.5	D	9	71	1	60	525	2 414	172	1 347
Calhoun	54	9.4	71	2	12.5	D	2	35	0	0	0	881	48	824
Carroll	352	13.8	257	2	10.1	D	23	91	2	60	266	4 593	732	2 848
Chicot	206	14.6	184	2	13.1	D	13	92	1	35	236	2 636	569	3 976
Clark	274	11.6	257	2	10.9	D	23	98	1	57	260	4 011	399	1 672
Clay	197	11.2	255	2	14.5	D	5	28	1	35	203	3 889	319	1 787
Cleburne	240	10.0	297	2	12.4	D	18	75	1	49	214	5 776	605	2 482
Cleveland	105	12.3	91	0	10.6	D	1	12	0	0	0	1 438	161	1 853
Columbia	307	12.0	315	3	12.3	D	15	59	1	71	283	4 862	1 010	3 892

1. Per 1,000 estimated resident population.   2. Deaths of infants under 1 year old.   3. Deaths of infants under 1 year old per 1,000 live births.   4. Data subject to copyright.   5. Per 100,000 resident population as of July 1 of the year shown.   6. Data for serious crimes have not been adjusted for underreporting; this may affect comparability between geographic areas and over time.   7. Per 100,000 population estimated by the FBI.

Table B. States and Counties — Crime, Education, Money Income, and Poverty

STATE County	Serious crimes known to police,[1] 2002 (cont'd) Rate[2] Violent	Property	Education — School enrollment and attainment, 2000 Enrollment[3] Total	Percent private	Attainment[4] (percent) High school graduate or less	Bachelor's degree or more	Local government expenditures,[5] 2000–2001 Total current expenditures (mil dol)	Current expenditures per student (dollars)	Money income, 1999 Per capita income[6] (dollars)	Households Median income Dollars	Percent change, 1989–1999 (constant 1999 dollars)	Percent with income of $100,000 or more	Percent below poverty level, 1999 Persons	Households	Families	Families with children
	46	47	48	49	50	51	52	53	54	55	56	57	58	59	60	61
ALABAMA—Cont'd																
Washington	NA	NA	4 562	4.7	71.3	8.6	20.9	5 822	14 081	30 815	14.2	2.8	18.5	19.9	14.8	19.3
Wilcox	241	1 173	3 626	12.0	70.7	10.1	16.7	6 600	10 903	16 646	-0.4	3.1	39.9	40.5	36.1	45.3
Winston	NA	NA	5 275	4.9	71.7	8.3	26.8	5 900	15 738	28 435	18.0	4.5	17.1	19.2	12.9	17.9
ALASKA	563	3 746	185 760	10.1	39.5	24.7	1 222.2	9 260	22 660	51 571	-7.3	16.1	9.4	8.3	6.7	9.3
Aleutians East Borough	NA	NA	409	1.2	74.2	4.9	6.0	20 080	18 421	47 875	-15.9	15.8	21.8	9.5	6.4	7.1
Aleutians West Census Area	NA	NA	925	11.6	55.9	11.0	8.8	15 709	24 037	61 406	29.9	21.0	11.9	4.8	3.5	4.5
Anchorage	NA	NA	74 625	12.6	33.9	28.9	366.5	7 399	25 287	55 546	-5.9	18.8	7.3	6.4	5.1	7.4
Bethel	NA	NA	5 584	3.3	67.6	13.1	76.5	16 723	12 603	35 701	4.6	9.7	20.6	19.8	18.7	21.1
Bristol Bay	NA	NA	385	4.4	45.1	21.1	16.5	15 770	22 210	52 167	-24.0	9.6	9.5	7.7	6.6	7.2
Denali Borough	NA	NA	456	7.7	38.7	22.7	NA	NA	26 251	53 654	NA	14.6	7.9	7.1	5.7	10.3
Dillingham	NA	NA	1 710	2.7	57.3	16.4	6.8	11 702	16 021	43 079	11.4	13.3	21.4	19.2	18.3	23.0
Fairbanks North Star	NA	NA	26 307	10.4	33.7	27.0	140.5	8 513	21 553	49 076	-2.5	14.1	7.8	7.9	5.5	7.6
Haines	NA	NA	584	20.4	42.2	23.8	4.4	10 858	22 090	40 772	-15.8	9.5	10.7	9.2	7.6	11.9
Juneau	NA	NA	8 777	9.1	28.8	36.0	44.8	8 160	26 719	62 034	-3.7	19.7	6.0	5.1	3.7	5.5
Kenai Peninsula	NA	NA	14 004	9.6	43.3	20.3	86.7	8 732	20 949	46 397	-18.6	12.9	10.0	9.5	7.6	10.8
Ketchikan Gateway	NA	NA	3 744	11.2	40.1	20.2	20.5	8 161	23 994	51 344	-15.4	14.1	6.5	5.9	4.5	6.1
Kodiak Island	NA	NA	3 975	13.6	45.9	18.7	26.1	9 522	22 195	54 636	-9.3	19.4	6.6	5.6	4.6	5.8
Lake and Peninsula Borough	NA	NA	645	7.3	67.1	12.4	10.5	19 860	15 361	36 442	7.5	10.1	18.9	20.1	14.8	18.8
Matanuska-Susitna	NA	NA	18 008	8.5	43.2	18.3	108.2	8 316	21 105	51 221	-6.4	13.8	11.0	9.7	7.8	11.3
Nome	NA	NA	3 129	2.5	63.3	14.7	38.3	15 355	15 476	41 250	1.9	11.8	17.4	16.7	16.0	17.9
North Slope	NA	NA	2 623	2.4	57.6	17.0	48.3	22 085	20 540	63 173	-6.8	22.6	9.1	9.9	8.6	10.4
Northwest Arctic Borough	NA	NA	2 505	2.0	68.4	12.7	35.2	16 073	15 286	45 976	2.7	12.4	17.4	15.9	15.0	17.7
Prince of Wales-Outer Ketchikan	NA	NA	1 694	4.4	57.0	14.2	17.8	12 369	18 395	40 636	-23.4	6.8	12.1	12.4	10.3	12.8
Sitka	NA	NA	2 617	13.9	34.7	29.5	14.0	8 540	23 622	51 901	-10.9	14.8	7.8	8.0	4.2	6.0
Skagway-Hoonah-Angoon	NA	NA	908	10.6	46.1	21.6	NA	NA	19 974	40 879	NA	9.0	12.8	12.6	10.5	14.1
Southeast Fairbanks	NA	NA	1 970	14.7	48.3	18.2	7.0	14 347	16 679	38 776	-4.5	9.0	18.9	15.1	12.4	15.8
Valdez-Cordova	NA	NA	2 929	8.1	41.4	21.2	24.2	10 911	23 046	48 734	-23.6	16.3	9.8	10.1	7.7	9.2
Wade Hampton	NA	NA	2 968	0.9	74.9	9.1	31.5	13 384	8 717	30 184	9.1	3.4	26.2	25.8	24.4	26.7
Wrangell-Petersburg	NA	NA	1 783	6.3	50.6	16.3	12.5	9 356	23 494	46 434	-17.8	13.6	7.9	8.6	6.1	8.2
Yakutat Borough	NA	NA	218	0.0	49.0	17.6	NA	NA	22 579	46 786	NA	6.4	13.5	13.9	11.8	17.3
Yukon-Koyukuk	NA	NA	2 278	2.8	65.0	14.2	58.0	8 141	13 720	28 666	-10.9	5.5	23.8	23.3	18.1	22.7
ARIZONA	553	5 833	1 401 840	10.6	43.3	23.5	4 703.4	5 350	20 275	40 558	9.6	10.8	13.9	11.8	9.9	15.2
Apache	145	823	25 885	4.6	61.2	11.3	117.0	8 001	8 986	23 344	23.2	3.0	37.8	36.7	33.5	37.8
Cochise	569	2 998	32 791	8.8	45.2	18.8	113.1	5 621	15 988	32 105	6.6	5.4	17.7	15.7	13.5	21.6
Coconino	575	5 472	42 187	6.7	37.9	29.9	125.4	6 231	17 139	38 256	9.0	8.5	18.2	16.1	13.1	18.8
Gila	511	3 253	12 718	7.2	50.5	13.9	49.6	5 778	16 315	30 917	9.8	5.3	17.4	14.8	12.6	22.0
Graham	197	2 064	10 949	6.2	54.5	11.8	30.3	5 372	12 139	29 668	19.7	3.3	23.0	19.9	17.7	24.9
Greenlee	111	1 311	2 476	5.0	52.6	12.2	10.4	5 376	15 814	39 384	6.6	2.9	9.9	10.9	8.0	9.5
La Paz	300	3 615	3 969	4.7	64.6	8.7	18.2	6 364	14 916	25 839	16.2	3.6	19.6	17.5	13.6	22.6
Maricopa	565	6 372	833 554	11.8	40.6	25.9	2 758.5	5 178	22 251	45 358	9.6	13.3	11.7	9.7	8.0	12.3
Mohave	305	4 615	32 934	8.3	57.4	9.9	120.8	4 812	16 788	31 521	-2.3	4.7	13.9	12.3	9.8	16.5
Navajo	321	2 682	32 682	4.9	56.6	12.3	156.0	6 409	11 609	28 569	9.3	4.3	29.5	25.9	23.4	30.6
Pima	631	6 906	236 404	10.8	39.9	26.7	721.5	5 491	19 785	36 758	7.7	9.0	14.7	13.3	10.5	16.4
Pinal	764	4 519	42 725	7.5	57.7	11.9	153.3	5 674	16 025	35 856	25.3	6.3	16.9	14.0	12.1	21.0
Santa Cruz	201	2 808	12 026	5.9	62.2	15.2	45.4	4 636	13 278	29 710	0.2	7.1	24.5	22.9	21.4	26.0
Yavapai	422	3 796	37 187	13.2	43.5	21.1	124.5	5 137	19 727	34 901	17.8	7.4	11.9	11.0	7.9	14.5
Yuma	632	3 053	43 353	4.7	59.9	11.8	159.5	5 226	14 802	32 182	1.3	6.0	19.2	15.8	15.5	24.4
ARKANSAS	424	3 733	675 109	10.7	58.8	16.7	2 633.4	5 855	16 904	32 182	13.3	6.0	15.8	15.8	12.0	18.1
Arkansas	746	3 071	5 072	11.1	67.4	12.2	20.2	5 480	16 401	30 316	15.6	4.6	17.8	17.4	14.1	20.1
Ashley	297	1 667	6 158	5.2	70.7	10.1	25.4	5 726	15 702	31 758	14.7	4.7	17.5	17.7	13.9	22.0
Baxter	98	1 182	7 019	7.4	60.0	12.8	27.3	5 438	16 859	29 106	15.1	4.1	11.1	12.0	7.9	13.4
Benton	134	2 132	36 954	13.4	52.4	20.3	135.7	5 404	19 377	40 281	15.2	8.9	10.1	9.3	7.3	11.2
Boone	212	1 749	7 417	8.9	58.2	12.7	37.3	6 283	16 175	29 988	8.1	4.5	14.8	15.9	10.7	15.8
Bradley	78	1 268	2 852	3.5	70.2	11.9	13.0	6 036	13 895	24 821	7.0	5.6	26.3	25.7	20.6	29.3
Calhoun	69	756	1 351	4.6	74.8	7.3	4.8	5 826	15 555	28 438	-0.1	4.8	16.5	17.8	13.2	17.8
Carroll	475	2 373	5 062	8.8	62.3	13.8	19.1	5 366	16 003	27 924	0.8	5.8	15.5	15.6	11.0	18.3
Chicot	517	3 459	3 640	9.4	71.0	11.7	16.5	6 369	12 825	22 024	29.3	3.9	28.6	27.5	23.1	33.6
Clark	29	1 642	7 933	21.3	57.1	19.8	19.6	6 108	14 533	28 845	18.8	3.9	19.1	21.2	13.5	19.0
Clay	162	1 625	3 670	4.4	77.2	7.4	14.5	5 291	14 512	25 345	16.3	2.9	17.5	20.2	13.4	18.8
Cleburne	176	2 306	4 705	8.9	61.6	13.9	19.4	5 592	17 250	31 531	20.7	4.9	13.1	14.1	9.0	14.9
Cleveland	58	1 796	2 085	4.1	70.3	10.0	8.5	5 545	15 362	32 405	22.4	3.9	15.2	15.5	11.4	16.6
Columbia	875	3 017	7 482	4.6	61.7	16.8	24.6	5 481	15 322	27 640	11.4	5.2	21.1	21.1	15.8	22.9

1. Data for serious crimes have not been adjusted for underreporting; this may affect comparability between geographic areas and over time.   2. Per 100,000 population estimated by the FBI.   3. All persons 3 years old and over enrolled in nursery school through college.   4. Persons 25 years old and over.   5. Elementary and secondary education expenditures.   6. Based on population enumerated as of April 1, 2000.

STATE County	Total (mil dol)	Percent change, 2001–2002	Per capita[1] Dollars	Per capita[1] Rank	Wages and salaries[2] (mil dol)	Proprietor's income (mil dol)	Dividends, interest, and rent (mil dol)	Transfer payments Total (mil dol)	Government payments to individuals Total (mil dol)	Social Security (mil dol)	Medical payments (mil dol)	Income mainte-nance (mil dol)	Unemploy-ment insurance (mil dol)
	62	63	64	65	66	67	68	69	70	71	72	73	74
ALABAMA—Cont'd													
Washington	335	0.4	18 705	2 797	210	20	49	90	86	34	35	11	3
Wilcox	221	3.2	16 996	2 996	143	14	38	82	78	23	31	20	2
Winston	496	1.3	20 114	2 518	266	41	82	134	128	47	60	12	3
ALASKA	21 040	4.5	32 799	X	14 911	2 155	3 319	3 364	3 231	545	1 096	324	160
Aleutians East Borough	65	-13.3	24 962	1 144	63	4	5	11	11	1	1	3	0
Aleutians West Census Area	132	9.9	25 637	969	158	15	13	17	16	1	3	1	2
Anchorage	10 043	4.5	37 442	96	7 505	1 199	1 583	1 369	1 314	220	440	129	51
Bethel	368	8.2	22 140	1 975	240	11	27	112	108	7	49	19	5
Bristol Bay	45	2.7	39 474	68	45	9	8	8	7	1	3	1	0
Denali Borough	75	1.6	40 019	60	91	1	12	17	17	1	9	3	1
Dillingham	136	3.1	27 323	643	90	17	15	27	26	4	9	4	1
Fairbanks North Star	2 561	5.6	30 081	344	2 018	161	407	415	399	64	137	35	19
Haines	81	1.9	35 064	140	32	16	18	15	15	3	5	1	1
Juneau	1 110	2.9	36 086	119	791	53	212	145	139	28	40	12	6
Kenai Peninsula	1 532	4.2	30 074	345	768	205	279	284	273	58	88	22	16
Ketchikan Gateway	502	0.2	37 012	105	297	69	93	81	78	17	26	8	5
Kodiak Island	400	2.0	29 255	415	286	55	68	58	55	9	16	5	4
Lake and Peninsula Borough	35	-3.0	21 783	2 069	20	3	5	10	9	1	4	1	1
Matanuska-Susitna	1 831	6.1	28 128	529	534	165	257	295	281	62	68	20	19
Nome	221	8.4	24 156	1 355	141	8	21	66	64	6	30	10	3
North Slope	257	1.5	35 905	123	812	5	35	35	33	6	10	3	2
Northwest Arctic Borough	183	1.8	25 208	1 075	156	3	13	54	53	4	27	8	3
Prince of Wales-Outer Ketchikan	122	2.6	21 238	2 229	65	11	22	30	29	5	9	2	3
Sitka	279	4.5	31 554	245	181	34	61	43	41	10	13	3	2
Skagway-Hoonah-Angoon	106	2.8	32 480	206	55	14	20	21	20	3	7	2	2
Southeast Fairbanks	147	5.5	26 146	862	74	10	22	38	36	6	13	4	2
Valdez-Cordova	325	4.6	32 369	211	241	38	54	47	45	9	12	4	3
Wade Hampton	114	7.7	15 900	3 054	56	3	7	58	57	4	29	9	3
Wrangell-Petersburg	198	0.9	30 704	291	100	33	38	41	39	9	14	3	2
Yakutat Borough	24	3.5	31 949	227	13	2	5	5	5	1	1	1	0
Yukon-Koyukuk	148	7.3	23 377	1 601	81	9	20	61	60	5	31	10	3
ARIZONA	143 429	3.9	26 360	X	95 448	11 949	25 578	21 728	20 471	8 244	8 276	1 861	506
Apache	1 111	7.0	16 457	3 030	677	36	107	435	420	59	250	66	9
Cochise	2 663	6.6	22 129	1 981	1 585	142	507	597	570	202	244	53	9
Coconino	2 943	5.4	24 543	1 249	1 847	210	654	450	423	115	185	53	13
Gila	1 064	4.5	20 646	2 385	463	58	235	349	337	134	152	29	7
Graham	533	5.4	16 046	3 050	232	28	74	172	165	48	83	17	3
Greenlee	161	-2.1	20 418	2 454	169	5	17	40	38	13	19	3	2
La Paz	369	8.9	18 943	2 766	159	53	71	100	96	40	41	8	1
Maricopa	95 619	2.9	29 020	446	68 664	8 662	15 832	11 690	10 928	4 558	4 297	935	301
Mohave	3 295	7.2	19 914	2 564	1 422	240	633	835	797	431	251	62	6
Navajo	1 623	7.2	15 917	3 053	951	72	230	514	490	125	223	79	14
Pima	22 213	4.6	25 278	1 056	13 654	1 233	4 963	3 946	3 744	1 470	1 597	322	61
Pinal	3 768	5.7	19 356	2 684	1 502	308	499	947	901	327	425	83	11
Santa Cruz	710	3.9	17 902	2 908	455	59	152	150	141	46	62	23	4
Yavapai	3 927	5.8	21 936	2 032	1 669	250	1 166	857	816	475	224	47	11
Yuma	3 431	15.6	20 561	2 416	2 000	591	440	644	606	202	222	81	54
ARKANSAS	63 750	2.6	23 556	X	40 881	5 229	10 731	12 817	12 093	4 751	4 861	1 237	406
Arkansas	479	0.0	23 551	1 548	332	34	83	107	101	39	42	12	4
Ashley	521	0.1	21 891	2 041	372	26	70	125	119	47	48	14	5
Baxter	929	3.0	23 975	1 416	434	73	276	249	239	128	80	11	7
Benton	4 427	6.0	26 789	738	3 445	310	791	571	527	280	168	38	11
Boone	749	3.8	21 636	2 111	463	76	143	176	167	75	61	14	5
Bradley	261	4.1	20 964	2 309	127	23	44	79	75	25	37	7	3
Calhoun	119	7.0	21 030	2 290	141	6	15	26	25	11	9	2	1
Carroll	504	-0.5	19 401	2 674	263	63	111	110	103	50	36	8	3
Chicot	239	-2.6	17 589	2 942	115	16	37	84	81	24	37	14	3
Clark	489	2.2	20 795	2 348	311	35	90	119	113	39	52	9	3
Clay	320	-0.3	18 748	2 789	152	17	54	97	92	37	38	8	4
Cleburne	566	3.6	23 171	1 671	198	63	127	132	125	61	44	8	3
Cleveland	190	-1.6	22 062	2 002	33	16	23	39	37	15	14	4	1
Columbia	598	1.7	23 642	1 516	337	72	110	136	129	52	49	16	3

1. Based on the resident population estimated as of July 1 of the year shown.   2. Includes other labor income.

Table B. States and Counties — Earnings, Social Security, and Housing

STATE County	Earnings, 2002 Total (mil dol)	Farm	Goods-related[1] Total	Manufacturing	Information and professional and technical services	Retail trade	Finance, insurance, and real estate	Health services	Government	Social Security beneficiaries, December 2003 Number	Rate[2]	Supplemental Security Income recipients, December 2003	Housing units, 2003 Total	Percent change, 2000–2003
	75	76	77	78	79	80	81	82	83	84	85	86	87	88
ALABAMA—Cont'd														
Washington	230	1.7	D	48.2	D	3.1	D	D	13.9	3 940	220	839	8 311	2.3
Wilcox	156	2.2	43.0	39.1	D	5.0	1.9	D	21.9	3 135	241	1 793	6 354	2.8
Winston	307	5.5	D	43.0	1.8	7.2	3.9	D	13.5	5 555	226	1 110	12 779	2.2
ALASKA	17 065	0.1	18.5	3.6	7.9	6.7	4.7	8.4	31.0	60 860	94	10 651	267 987	2.7
Aleutians East Borough	67	0.0	D	D	D	1.9	2.4	D	16.6	110	41	NA	724	0.0
Aleutians West Census Area	173	0.4	D	43.9	D	4.7	D	2.8	14.6	140	27	NA	2 317	3.7
Anchorage	8 703	0.0	15.3	2.1	11.7	7.0	5.9	9.0	27.4	23 360	86	4 969	105 336	4.9
Bethel	251	0.0	D	D	D	4.9	5.6	D	41.8	1 335	79	459	5 306	2.3
Bristol Bay	55	0.0	23.6	18.3	D	1.8	D	D	33.5	120	109	296	968	-1.1
Denali Borough	92	0.0	D	0.0	D	1.2	0.0	0.4	28.5	145	77	NA	1 363	0.9
Dillingham	108	0.0	D	11.9	D	4.2	D	D	31.0	520	105	NA	2 364	1.4
Fairbanks North Star	2 178	0.1	D	1.4	D	6.3	3.1	7.5	46.9	6 795	79	862	33 606	0.9
Haines	48	0.0	D	D	D	5.3	D	7.9	17.6	370	161	34	1 446	1.9
Juneau	844	0.0	D	1.2	4.3	6.9	3.5	6.9	50.5	3 030	97	569	12 509	1.8
Kenai Peninsula	973	0.0	28.6	7.0	D	8.2	3.8	6.4	23.6	6 390	125	725	24 999	0.5
Ketchikan Gateway	366	0.0	D	6.3	D	8.7	4.3	9.3	31.9	1 710	128	213	6 383	2.7
Kodiak Island	341	0.0	D	19.6	2.3	4.6	3.3	D	36.0	1 075	80	87	5 358	3.9
Lake and Peninsula Borough	23	0.0	D	12.8	D	4.2	D	0.6	37.6	155	100	NA	1 547	-0.6
Matanuska-Susitna	699	1.8	18.2	2.9	7.6	13.5	4.1	12.1	23.1	7 035	103	840	27 616	1.1
Nome	148	0.0	D	0.4	2.1	5.4	6.9	26.2	42.2	895	98	214	3 630	-0.5
North Slope	817	0.0	D	D	D	1.6	D	D	12.6	580	80	NA	2 634	3.8
Northwest Arctic Borough	159	0.0	D	D	D	D	D	D	28.3	580	79	NA	2 540	0.0
Prince of Wales-Outer Ketchikan	76	0.0	7.5	3.0	D	8.4	4.4	4.8	47.5	595	102	64	3 116	2.0
Sitka	215	0.0	D	5.3	2.9	7.0	3.4	17.4	32.8	995	112	87	3 749	2.7
Skagway-Hoonah-Angoon	69	0.0	D	D	D	10.2	D	1.9	31.8	355	114	NA	2 208	4.7
Southeast Fairbanks	84	0.0	13.9	1.6	2.4	7.3	D	4.6	41.1	760	130	163	3 261	1.1
Valdez-Cordova	279	0.0	D	6.5	D	4.8	3.7	2.4	24.9	1 030	104	NA	5 177	0.6
Wade Hampton	59	0.0	D	D	D	6.2	2.8	D	64.2	700	96	278	2 058	-0.2
Wrangell-Petersburg	134	0.0	D	14.6	2.2	6.0	3.5	2.8	34.0	935	149	54	3 335	1.6
Yakutat Borough	15	0.0	D	D	0.4	D	D	0.6	38.1	75	106	NA	502	0.6
Yukon-Koyukuk	90	0.0	D	D	D	5.2	D	0.6	62.9	690	109	141	3 935	0.5
ARIZONA	107 397	1.0	19.8	10.7	10.3	8.4	10.2	9.0	16.9	863 874	155	91 853	2 392 746	9.3
Apache	713	-0.5	D	D	2.3	4.3	D	4.5	69.2	8 940	131	4 609	31 811	0.6
Cochise	1 727	2.3	6.9	1.7	7.3	7.1	D	7.3	51.7	23 670	194	2 579	53 460	4.6
Coconino	2 057	-0.2	13.2	6.8	4.8	9.4	4.5	13.4	33.8	13 425	111	3 112	55 961	4.7
Gila	521	-0.3	D	8.5	D	9.6	4.3	10.9	34.1	13 900	270	1 150	29 124	3.3
Graham	260	2.4	8.4	2.7	D	13.3	2.2	11.0	45.0	5 370	162	932	11 707	2.4
Greenlee	175	1.3	D	D	D	2.2	D	D	9.5	1 260	168	125	3 772	0.7
La Paz	211	18.1	D	3.9	2.9	12.7	3.4	D	35.0	4 545	233	385	15 413	1.9
Maricopa	77 326	0.4	20.7	11.4	11.4	8.3	12.2	8.4	12.1	461 860	136	44 814	1 386 308	10.9
Mohave	1 662	0.1	D	7.5	7.8	14.1	5.4	13.3	17.5	46 135	269	2 957	87 795	9.7
Navajo	1 023	0.1	16.1	4.1	4.6	9.4	2.7	7.2	39.8	15 635	150	4 466	49 419	4.2
Pima	14 887	0.1	D	13.3	10.0	8.0	5.8	11.6	24.6	152 730	171	15 877	391 234	6.7
Pinal	1 810	11.4	13.8	6.0	D	7.2	4.0	7.5	34.6	36 310	178	3 671	92 507	14.0
Santa Cruz	514	0.2	10.6	7.6	4.2	11.7	5.1	2.8	33.9	5 840	145	1 250	14 370	10.2
Yavapai	1 919	0.1	20.2	6.1	6.6	10.8	6.1	11.7	21.6	49 885	270	2 912	90 529	10.8
Yuma	2 591	19.4	D	3.2	3.5	7.1	2.3	8.0	28.2	24 295	142	2 950	79 336	7.0
ARKANSAS	46 110	1.8	24.9	18.4	7.3	7.2	5.5	10.3	17.3	543 727	199	86 563	1 214 302	3.5
Arkansas	366	0.0	36.4	31.6	2.3	7.8	3.6	D	13.2	4 240	210	669	9 733	0.6
Ashley	398	-0.3	D	47.2	D	5.5	3.3	D	10.6	5 105	216	881	10 846	2.2
Baxter	508	1.4	D	22.2	D	10.6	5.7	23.2	11.6	13 535	346	868	20 498	3.1
Benton	3 755	1.6	20.8	15.7	D	4.7	4.6	5.0	7.0	30 060	175	1 810	70 359	9.5
Boone	539	3.2	D	18.2	5.0	9.0	5.9	7.1	19.3	8 775	253	1 002	15 729	2.0
Bradley	150	5.3	29.1	24.0	1.7	5.4	3.7	D	17.4	2 835	228	475	5 923	-0.1
Calhoun	146	0.2	D	68.6	D	D	D	1.6	12.0	1 300	231	168	3 071	2.0
Carroll	326	9.0	D	29.6	2.8	9.6	4.4	D	11.7	5 715	217	435	11 999	1.4
Chicot	130	5.0	D	12.7	D	8.3	5.0	D	28.7	2 980	221	1 018	6 065	1.5
Clark	347	1.3	D	27.8	4.1	7.4	3.9	7.7	21.2	4 420	187	619	10 511	3.4
Clay	169	2.9	36.7	31.8	D	7.7	4.1	6.4	18.8	4 565	270	733	8 582	1.0
Cleburne	261	4.5	D	25.6	D	9.6	4.6	D	12.9	7 100	287	590	14 071	2.5
Cleveland	49	18.2	D	5.2	D	D	D	D	25.2	1 740	200	234	3 913	2.1
Columbia	409	3.5	48.9	35.9	D	6.1	4.0	5.0	16.1	5 610	224	1 151	11 718	1.3

1. Covers mining, construction, and manufacturing.   2. Per 1,000 resident population estimated as of July 1 of the year shown.

Table B. States and Counties — Housing, Labor Force, and Employment

STATE County	Housing units, 2000 — Occupied units — Owner-occupied — Total (89)	Percent (90)	Median value[1] (91)	Median owner cost as a percent of income — With a mortgage (92)	Without a mortgage[2] (93)	Renter-occupied — Median rent[3] (94)	Median rent as a percent of income (95)	Sub-standard units[4] (percent) (96)	Civilian labor force, 2003 — Total (97)	Percent change, 2002–2003 (98)	Unemployment — Total (99)	Rate[5] (100)	Civilian employment,[6] 2000 — Total (101)	Percent — Management, professional and related occupations (102)	Production, transportation, and material moving occupations (103)
ALABAMA—Cont'd															
Washington	6 705	88.2	63 000	18.1	9.9	269	23.3	5.9	5 331	-0.1	878	16.5	6 778	19.6	28.7
Wilcox	4 776	83.3	52 200	24.6	11.9	250	25.6	10.9	3 644	2.0	550	15.1	3 441	20.6	26.0
Winston	10 107	80.0	60 800	19.9	9.9	329	21.4	3.2	10 078	1.1	1 099	10.9	10 646	19.6	33.2
ALASKA	221 600	62.5	144 200	22.3	9.9	720	24.8	13.0	331 675	2.5	26 561	8.0	281 532	34.4	10.8
Aleutians East Borough	526	58.4	99 500	15.8	11.1	710	18.6	6.5	1 659	4.3	81	4.9	1 086	16.4	42.1
Aleutians West Census Area	1 270	27.8	93 400	21.8	14.8	892	17.4	13.6	2 778	4.2	264	9.5	3 252	19.1	30.2
Anchorage	94 822	60.0	160 700	22.6	9.9	736	25.9	6.3	147 868	1.9	8 470	5.7	125 737	36.8	9.6
Bethel	4 226	60.9	74 900	22.3	15.5	814	21.8	60.6	6 469	5.7	995	15.4	5 481	37.9	10.5
Bristol Bay	490	51.0	139 000	21.8	11.7	778	17.3	4.9	507	2.2	57	11.2	581	34.1	8.4
Denali Borough	785	64.7	103 400	20.1	9.9	568	15.8	27.4	1 203	3.3	142	11.8	841	30.2	13.3
Dillingham	1 529	60.6	105 300	19.8	16.8	761	21.2	32.5	1 911	4.3	230	12.0	1 765	38.8	8.8
Fairbanks North Star	29 777	54.0	132 700	22.1	9.9	679	24.6	12.6	44 837	2.2	3 108	6.9	35 258	35.8	9.6
Haines	991	69.7	133 100	20.8	9.9	588	26.6	21.0	1 237	1.5	155	12.5	992	31.9	9.8
Juneau	11 543	63.8	195 100	23.0	9.9	863	25.9	6.0	16 984	1.8	1 053	6.2	16 537	42.3	7.0
Kenai Peninsula	18 438	73.7	118 000	21.2	9.9	609	24.1	13.4	22 249	1.1	2 692	12.1	20 364	27.4	13.2
Ketchikan Gateway	5 399	60.7	165 000	24.2	9.9	775	25.4	7.4	7 212	0.0	644	8.9	7 017	28.5	13.6
Kodiak Island	4 424	54.8	155 100	21.2	10.8	791	25.6	14.2	6 549	1.0	672	10.3	6 131	23.3	22.6
Lake and Peninsula Borough	588	67.5	87 400	20.3	15.7	591	18.6	30.4	566	4.8	91	16.1	581	35.5	12.9
Matanuska-Susitna	20 556	78.8	125 800	22.0	9.9	700	26.6	14.5	35 365	7.1	3 215	9.1	24 981	30.1	9.9
Nome	2 693	58.2	77 100	20.2	18.1	755	19.2	48.3	3 409	2.2	519	15.2	3 107	36.6	9.9
North Slope	2 109	48.8	113 300	17.8	10.6	902	18.2	45.7	3 416	2.4	473	13.8	2 990	34.1	10.4
Northwest Arctic Borough	1 780	56.3	89 200	24.9	16.5	842	21.5	48.5	2 422	1.8	488	20.1	2 427	33.9	11.9
Prince of Wales-Outer Ketchikan	2 262	70.1	121 800	21.0	12.6	580	20.4	13.2	2 693	0.5	390	14.5	2 614	24.8	16.1
Sitka	3 278	58.1	196 500	24.4	9.9	768	27.9	7.5	4 533	1.8	295	6.5	4 352	33.8	10.4
Skagway-Hoonah-Angoon	1 369	63.6	120 900	23.7	11.9	515	16.7	16.1	1 982	0.8	236	11.9	1 471	25.9	12.4
Southeast Fairbanks	2 098	69.1	86 000	18.1	9.9	516	22.5	28.0	2 573	0.9	325	12.6	1 932	32.6	11.7
Valdez-Cordova	3 884	67.8	141 300	19.6	11.8	634	22.1	17.2	4 971	0.3	562	11.3	4 463	30.0	13.8
Wade Hampton	1 602	66.4	38 700	22.6	15.9	552	15.6	72.6	2 339	4.9	565	24.2	1 825	36.6	7.8
Wrangell-Petersburg	2 587	70.4	156 100	24.2	14.1	648	23.0	9.4	3 339	2.2	378	11.3	3 031	27.2	12.9
Yakutat Borough	265	59.6	100 700	21.1	9.9	622	20.6	15.1	312	4.3	52	16.7	440	26.6	12.5
Yukon-Koyukuk	2 309	67.2	59 900	21.6	15.3	464	18.4	60.4	2 294	2.0	409	17.8	2 276	36.1	11.9
ARIZONA	1 901 327	68.0	121 300	22.1	9.9	619	26.6	9.3	2 690 294	0.9	150 935	5.6	2 233 004	32.7	10.9
Apache	19 971	74.3	41 700	19.9	9.9	342	14.3	44.2	21 873	-1.1	3 079	14.1	16 469	33.2	10.2
Cochise	43 893	67.3	88 200	21.1	9.9	470	24.4	6.3	45 966	1.1	2 408	5.2	42 626	30.2	9.4
Coconino	40 448	61.4	142 500	22.1	9.9	629	26.8	14.9	66 940	0.0	4 298	6.4	55 510	34.8	10.0
Gila	20 140	78.7	100 100	23.3	10.7	501	24.9	8.0	18 752	-1.2	1 463	7.8	18 051	24.3	10.9
Graham	10 116	73.2	80 900	20.8	10.2	449	24.6	10.3	11 009	-2.8	751	6.8	10 692	25.9	11.5
Greenlee	3 117	51.0	62 700	19.4	9.9	291	9.9	8.1	3 688	-6.6	275	7.5	3 460	23.0	18.4
La Paz	8 362	78.1	86 500	21.9	9.9	442	21.4	7.9	6 899	-0.9	442	6.4	6 567	23.8	12.6
Maricopa	1 132 886	67.5	129 200	22.0	9.9	666	26.6	8.8	1 730 141	0.9	85 250	4.9	1 427 292	33.9	11.0
Mohave	62 809	73.6	95 300	23.3	10.4	559	25.5	6.9	75 806	3.5	3 680	4.9	60 517	20.4	12.8
Navajo	30 043	75.5	77 000	20.4	9.9	396	21.9	25.3	35 938	1.7	3 883	10.8	29 575	27.2	13.7
Pima	332 350	64.3	114 600	22.3	9.9	544	27.7	7.5	426 018	-0.1	18 398	4.3	370 768	35.0	9.4
Pinal	61 364	77.4	93 900	22.2	9.9	509	24.4	9.7	76 415	1.1	4 995	6.5	61 291	22.1	14.7
Santa Cruz	11 809	68.0	94 700	26.1	10.3	475	27.6	16.1	14 702	2.2	1 823	12.4	12 875	25.1	14.8
Yavapai	70 171	73.4	138 000	24.3	9.9	600	28.9	4.7	81 771	2.7	2 689	3.3	68 098	28.3	11.6
Yuma	53 848	72.2	85 100	22.5	9.9	508	25.8	15.4	74 376	1.7	17 501	23.5	49 213	26.7	12.2
ARKANSAS	1 042 696	69.4	72 800	19.4	9.9	453	24.4	4.4	1 264 519	-1.3	78 132	6.2	1 173 399	27.7	21.0
Arkansas	8 457	67.8	56 800	18.8	10.3	392	23.3	3.3	10 687	-0.8	650	6.1	9 297	26.2	22.5
Ashley	9 384	76.2	55 700	18.1	10.4	414	24.4	4.0	10 103	-2.6	1 176	11.6	9 636	21.6	26.9
Baxter	17 052	79.7	84 500	21.2	9.9	435	26.6	2.2	14 275	-2.4	957	6.7	15 088	24.2	20.5
Benton	58 212	72.2	94 800	19.7	9.9	528	22.4	5.5	80 509	0.8	2 244	2.8	71 971	29.7	20.2
Boone	13 851	73.3	75 300	20.8	9.9	414	25.5	3.5	14 981	-1.5	911	6.1	15 167	24.4	21.5
Bradley	4 834	72.5	45 000	19.1	11.9	326	26.1	4.5	4 907	0.4	439	8.9	4 624	25.6	22.7
Calhoun	2 317	82.2	41 700	17.0	10.6	368	22.3	3.7	2 232	0.7	241	10.8	2 355	20.3	29.3
Carroll	10 189	73.0	83 900	23.1	11.8	433	24.8	7.4	11 737	-2.6	568	4.8	11 726	25.8	24.1
Chicot	5 205	69.6	47 300	23.5	14.8	336	23.9	6.3	5 813	-4.8	706	12.1	4 943	30.4	18.3
Clark	8 912	65.6	67 900	19.2	9.9	396	27.4	3.2	12 028	-2.3	686	5.7	10 696	29.4	20.8
Clay	7 417	74.9	39 600	18.8	11.5	320	21.7	2.2	7 142	-5.0	683	9.6	7 517	20.7	34.3
Cleburne	10 190	80.6	87 400	21.9	10.4	419	22.7	2.7	9 969	-1.1	543	5.4	9 739	25.5	23.2
Cleveland	3 273	82.2	48 900	17.7	9.9	370	21.1	3.9	3 568	-3.3	240	6.7	3 642	24.5	25.2
Columbia	9 981	71.3	55 700	21.0	11.5	381	25.9	4.2	10 902	-3.0	763	7.0	10 581	26.3	23.7

1. Specified owner-occupied units.   2. Median monthly owner costs is often in the minimum category—9.9 percent or less, which is indicated as 9.9 percent.   3. Specified renter-occupied units.   4. Overcrowded or lacking complete plumbing facilities.   5. Percent of civilian labor force.   6. Persons 16 years old and over.

Table B. States and Counties — Nonfarm Employment and Agriculture

	Private nonfarm establishments, employment and payroll, 2001									Agriculture, 2002			
STATE County		Employment						Annual payroll		Farms		Percent with—	
	Number of establishments	Total	Health care and social assistance	Manufacturing	Retail trade	Finance and insurance	Professional, scientific, and technical services	Total (mil dol)	Average per employee (dollars)	Number	Less than 50 acres	500 acres and over	Farm operators whose principal occupation is farming (percent)
	104	105	106	107	108	109	110	111	112	113	114	115	116
ALABAMA—Cont'd													
Washington	246	3 368	294	1 683	266	86	56	135	39 996	396	28.8	5.6	56.3
Wilcox	221	2 499	250	D	304	90	39	67	26 643	306	20.6	25.8	50.3
Winston	407	7 561	441	4 473	814	243	68	167	22 027	650	39.1	2.2	58.2
ALASKA	18 589	214 297	32 602	11 012	33 401	7 084	11 404	8 335	38 894	609	42.0	16.1	60.8
Aleutians East Borough	45	1 941	D	D	55	D	0	40	20 531	NA	NA	NA	NA
Aleutians West Census Area	110	4 472	79	2 462	254	D	0	87	19 515	NA	NA	NA	NA
Anchorage	7 979	119 466	16 359	1 858	15 855	4 964	8 358	5 165	43 232	251	48.6	10.4	61.8
Bethel	211	3 576	1 529	D	779	42	D	99	27 807	NA	NA	NA	NA
Bristol Bay	65	498	D	179	64	D	D	22	44 693	NA	NA	NA	NA
Denali Borough	65	310	D	0	24	0	1	20	63 874	NA	NA	NA	NA
Dillingham	90	1 317	D	192	180	21	D	44	33 074	NA	NA	NA	NA
Fairbanks North Star	2 230	23 024	4 657	459	4 519	667	1 035	789	34 247	187	24.1	24.1	66.3
Haines	115	471	D	4	109	D	2	13	27 881	NA	NA	NA	NA
Juneau	1 075	10 021	1 885	189	1 770	317	450	337	33 676	37	94.6	0.0	56.8
Kenai Peninsula	1 812	11 585	1 991	1 005	2 250	247	370	394	33 987	98	48.0	9.2	57.1
Ketchikan Gateway	577	5 226	764	291	1 166	191	97	179	34 287	NA	NA	NA	NA
Kodiak Island	465	4 255	469	1 475	541	D	74	126	29 597	NA	NA	NA	NA
Lake and Peninsula Borough	47	174	0	D	18	0	0	9	53 287	NA	NA	NA	NA
Matanuska-Susitna	1 461	9 553	1 582	171	2 497	273	373	286	29 937	NA	NA	NA	NA
Nome	191	1 844	551	D	416	D	30	54	29 486	NA	NA	NA	NA
North Slope	148	2 132	D	36	353	D	D	96	44 839	NA	NA	NA	NA
Northwest Arctic Borough	93	1 743	D	0	331	D	D	87	49 749	NA	NA	NA	NA
Prince of Wales-Outer Ketchikan	151	828	54	112	211	D	D	20	23 746	NA	NA	NA	NA
Sitka	395	2 877	848	209	424	72	60	92	31 827	NA	NA	NA	NA
Skagway-Hoonah-Angoon	154	544	18	D	126	D	D	24	43 329	NA	NA	NA	NA
Southeast Fairbanks	152	632	94	D	129	17	11	15	24 195	NA	NA	NA	NA
Valdez-Cordova	447	2 585	218	165	419	D	D	130	50 106	NA	NA	NA	NA
Wade Hampton	62	671	48	D	308	D	D	9	13 748	NA	NA	NA	NA
Wrangell-Petersburg	280	1 517	228	156	436	D	20	50	33 045	NA	NA	NA	NA
Yakutat Borough	28	217	0	D	27	0	0	9	39 447	NA	NA	NA	NA
Yukon-Koyukuk	121	573	18	0	140	D	D	16	27 469	NA	NA	NA	NA
ARIZONA	116 304	1 941 599	200 305	194 217	265 812	112 814	117 366	60 018	30 912	7 294	58.0	17.6	58.9
Apache	512	6 378	1 593	D	1 065	121	133	130	20 367	363	41.0	19.6	51.2
Cochise	2 219	23 722	3 940	679	5 228	587	2 581	529	22 279	950	33.8	26.8	61.5
Coconino	3 461	38 466	5 141	2 482	6 992	781	1 081	876	22 781	213	49.8	22.5	56.8
Gila	1 145	12 672	2 091	D	2 129	256	299	332	26 230	164	59.1	10.4	62.8
Graham	504	5 025	888	338	1 309	130	126	91	18 142	277	54.9	21.7	58.5
Greenlee	98	3 101	D	D	D	D	D	D	38 885	124	44.4	8.1	55.6
La Paz	347	5 013	396	D	794	D	D	72	19 389	101	24.8	39.6	67.3
Maricopa	73 102	1 377 298	123 387	141 310	170 471	96 992	92 187	45 515	33 047	2 110	76.7	7.7	56.6
Mohave	3 492	35 897	4 670	3 497	7 929	1 270	1 214	811	22 590	239	49.8	28.0	66.5
Navajo	1 740	16 624	2 099	648	4 210	475	359	387	23 261	291	49.5	22.7	57.7
Pima	18 828	293 987	41 187	32 749	43 012	8 963	15 860	8 327	28 324	517	72.1	11.6	54.7
Pinal	2 033	25 550	2 832	3 403	4 862	695	748	604	23 643	687	51.5	29.8	68.0
Santa Cruz	1 097	10 666	609	922	2 451	196	166	223	20 916	152	21.7	27.0	61.2
Yavapai	5 127	46 530	6 472	3 750	8 126	1 239	1 677	1 063	22 837	575	66.1	15.0	52.3
Yuma	2 539	32 820	4 881	2 317	7 076	970	863	715	21 785	531	56.9	18.3	63.7
ARKANSAS	62 725	995 521	133 950	228 671	136 513	34 376	31 999	25 788	25 904	47 483	27.3	14.5	57.7
Arkansas	571	8 301	916	3 448	1 179	267	87	201	24 210	502	10.0	51.8	77.9
Ashley	482	7 980	638	3 435	800	266	88	254	31 821	336	31.8	23.2	62.8
Baxter	1 025	11 349	2 525	2 907	2 029	316	354	271	23 881	572	32.0	8.0	56.8
Benton	3 753	69 656	4 815	12 975	6 876	1 452	2 125	2 405	34 522	2 376	44.7	4.3	55.0
Boone	926	13 237	1 673	2 588	2 267	434	217	311	23 483	1 305	24.1	9.5	54.5
Bradley	288	3 366	783	677	389	140	40	70	20 665	222	35.6	3.2	43.2
Calhoun	91	949	95	304	90	D	D	22	22 717	116	22.4	5.2	39.7
Carroll	762	8 466	872	3 607	1 299	242	124	168	19 889	1 089	24.2	10.8	60.0
Chicot	275	3 142	648	934	504	164	96	57	18 241	357	11.8	39.5	70.9
Clark	579	8 441	914	3 061	1 150	213	152	181	21 407	374	24.1	13.9	49.5
Clay	343	4 801	534	2 401	512	122	37	89	18 567	702	22.9	28.6	67.5
Cleburne	581	5 517	577	1 721	998	201	103	111	20 067	807	29.2	4.6	49.1
Cleveland	109	748	103	109	87	D	0	14	18 985	220	30.9	5.0	66.8
Columbia	629	8 748	1 155	3 102	1 123	257	211	214	24 477	339	28.3	6.2	51.9

Items 104—116

STATE County	Land in farms		Acres			Value of land and buildings (dollars)		Value of machinery and equipment average per farm (dollars)	Value of products sold		Percent from —		Percent of farms with sales of —		Government payments	
	Acreage (1,000)	Percent change, 1997–2002	Average size of farm	Total irrigated (1,000)	Total cropland (1,000)	Average per farm	Average per acre		Total (mil dol)	Average per farm (dollars)	Crops	Live-stock and poultry products	$10,000 or more	$100,000 or more	Total ($1,000)	Percent of farms
	117	118	119	120	121	122	123	124	125	126	127	128	129	130	131	132
ALABAMA—Cont'd																
Washington	74	-14.9	187	0	20	313 905	1 493	46 202	22	54 513	3.5	96.5	31.6	11.6	192	21.2
Wilcox	160	3.9	523	D	34	502 769	1 013	43 556	5	16 480	20.8	79.2	21.9	2.3	1 058	42.2
Winston	66	11.9	102	0	30	231 014	1 887	33 579	61	93 729	0.5	99.5	31.1	19.1	134	18.0
ALASKA	901	2.3	1 479	3	98	543 213	367	71 790	46	75 768	44.5	55.5	40.6	11.7	1 765	11.8
Aleutians East Borough	NA	NA	NA	NA	NA	NA	NA	NA	NA	NA	NA	NA	NA	NA	NA	NA
Aleutians West Census Area	NA	NA	NA	NA	NA	NA	NA	NA	NA	NA	NA	NA	NA	NA	NA	NA
Anchorage	47	NA	187	1	22	429 707	2 299	63 949	28	109 608	51.6	48.4	45.4	15.1	393	7.6
Bethel	NA	NA	NA	NA	NA	NA	NA	NA	NA	NA	NA	NA	NA	NA	NA	NA
Bristol Bay	NA	NA	NA	NA	NA	NA	NA	NA	NA	NA	NA	NA	NA	NA	NA	NA
Denali Borough	NA	NA	NA	NA	NA	NA	NA	NA	NA	NA	NA	NA	NA	NA	NA	NA
Dillingham	NA	NA	NA	NA	NA	NA	NA	NA	NA	NA	NA	NA	NA	NA	NA	NA
Fairbanks North Star	110	NA	588	1	69	385 526	655	72 156	5	28 261	82.3	17.7	37.4	8.6	1 267	24.6
Haines	NA	NA	NA	NA	NA	NA	NA	NA	NA	NA	NA	NA	NA	NA	NA	NA
Juneau	1	NA	15	0	0	649 659	44 679	210 596	11	296 270	5.4	94.6	64.9	29.7	0	0.0
Kenai Peninsula	36	-35.7	370	0	6	522 694	1 412	53 382	2	20 976	D	D	29.6	5.1	D	D
Ketchikan Gateway	NA	NA	NA	NA	NA	NA	NA	NA	NA	NA	NA	NA	NA	NA	NA	NA
Kodiak Island	NA	NA	NA	NA	NA	NA	NA	NA	NA	NA	NA	NA	NA	NA	NA	NA
Lake and Peninsula Borough	NA	NA	NA	NA	NA	NA	NA	NA	NA	NA	NA	NA	NA	NA	NA	NA
Matanuska-Susitna	NA	NA	NA	NA	NA	NA	NA	NA	NA	NA	NA	NA	NA	NA	NA	NA
Nome	NA	NA	NA	NA	NA	NA	NA	NA	NA	NA	NA	NA	NA	NA	NA	NA
North Slope	NA	NA	NA	NA	NA	NA	NA	NA	NA	NA	NA	NA	NA	NA	NA	NA
Northwest Arctic Borough	NA	NA	NA	NA	NA	NA	NA	NA	NA	NA	NA	NA	NA	NA	NA	NA
Prince of Wales-Outer Ketchikan	NA	NA	NA	NA	NA	NA	NA	NA	NA	NA	NA	NA	NA	NA	NA	NA
Sitka	NA	NA	NA	NA	NA	NA	NA	NA	NA	NA	NA	NA	NA	NA	NA	NA
Skagway-Hoonah-Angoon	NA	NA	NA	NA	NA	NA	NA	NA	NA	NA	NA	NA	NA	NA	NA	NA
Southeast Fairbanks	NA	NA	NA	NA	NA	NA	NA	NA	NA	NA	NA	NA	NA	NA	NA	NA
Valdez-Cordova	NA	NA	NA	NA	NA	NA	NA	NA	NA	NA	NA	NA	NA	NA	NA	NA
Wade Hampton	NA	NA	NA	NA	NA	NA	NA	NA	NA	NA	NA	NA	NA	NA	NA	NA
Wrangell-Petersburg	NA	NA	NA	NA	NA	NA	NA	NA	NA	NA	NA	NA	NA	NA	NA	NA
Yakutat Borough	NA	NA	NA	NA	NA	NA	NA	NA	NA	NA	NA	NA	NA	NA	NA	NA
Yukon-Koyukuk	NA	NA	NA	NA	NA	NA	NA	NA	NA	NA	NA	NA	NA	NA	NA	NA
ARIZONA	26 587	-1.0	3 645	932	1 262	1 456 759	398	88 651	2 395	328 413	66.3	33.7	35.7	16.3	31 760	11.4
Apache	D	NA	D	8	24	2 309 441	145	29 452	8	22 721	2.9	97.1	21.8	2.8	141	6.3
Cochise	969	-23.1	1 020	65	131	704 895	631	53 260	78	82 429	71.2	28.8	39.2	12.6	2 305	16.8
Coconino	D	D	D	2	D	4 708 165	161	45 145	11	52 183	7.0	93.0	29.1	9.9	198	7.5
Gila	D	NA	D	1	6	1 926 639	275	21 767	3	16 221	10.1	89.9	30.5	3.7	42	3.7
Graham	D	D	D	35	38	2 013 205	480	110 210	82	295 666	95.1	4.9	43.3	15.5	1 183	22.0
Greenlee	27	-6.9	221	4	6	326 621	1 505	35 245	4	33 175	22.0	78.0	20.2	4.8	181	13.7
La Paz	D	D	D	91	98	2 059 282	629	337 206	87	857 656	99.3	0.7	63.4	47.5	1 625	26.7
Maricopa	627	-11.6	297	238	288	898 974	3 026	90 386	740	350 797	52.8	47.2	31.7	16.9	9 721	7.8
Mohave	793	-20.5	3 318	21	35	1 523 894	435	98 694	16	68 354	65.9	34.1	33.1	7.5	730	13.4
Navajo	4 595	17.7	15 791	6	28	2 841 212	179	19 560	27	92 003	2.5	97.5	27.5	4.5	96	4.5
Pima	D	D	D	35	47	1 567 404	295	56 938	69	133 229	81.8	18.2	31.7	11.4	1 630	7.0
Pinal	1 162	-10.8	1 691	217	252	2 080 379	1 230	167 989	425	618 280	41.8	58.2	46.7	34.1	10 152	25.6
Santa Cruz	133	-49.8	874	2	D	1 245 033	1 434	26 929	6	38 356	4.5	95.5	38.2	4.6	64	8.6
Yavapai	720	-6.7	1 253	10	29	737 949	621	37 030	37	64 960	D	D	25.6	7.3	272	4.5
Yuma	231	-2.9	435	197	213	1 998 970	4 544	201 464	802	1 511 051	D	D	59.3	39.2	3 419	11.9
ARKANSAS	14 503	1.0	305	4 150	9 576	447 104	1 469	65 299	4 950	104 256	32.7	67.3	39.7	17.9	238 577	16.5
Arkansas	390	-8.5	777	278	339	1 078 801	1 400	212 908	96	190 833	99.1	0.9	69.5	47.0	14 404	68.5
Ashley	167	0.6	497	104	140	668 539	1 364	147 770	52	155 605	75.8	24.2	42.6	24.1	5 814	29.8
Baxter	103	-1.9	181	0	37	326 470	1 697	32 310	12	21 143	3.7	96.3	24.5	3.0	147	9.4
Benton	313	5.4	132	1	159	386 606	3 031	46 902	361	151 908	1.3	98.7	39.7	19.5	449	5.6
Boone	284	10.1	218	0	115	398 271	1 809	34 852	79	60 823	1.5	98.5	38.3	10.0	1 189	22.5
Bradley	29	0.0	132	1	14	284 438	1 898	45 781	21	96 753	31.6	68.4	35.1	15.3	D	D
Calhoun	19	5.6	165	D	8	214 978	1 278	31 513	2	19 275	8.2	91.8	25.9	3.4	19	6.9
Carroll	269	11.2	247	0	112	424 222	1 670	44 577	158	144 703	0.8	99.2	49.1	21.5	237	3.9
Chicot	269	-6.6	753	128	229	850 568	1 171	190 987	70	195 651	66.9	33.1	65.8	39.5	9 405	61.9
Clark	98	2.1	261	1	50	397 980	1 431	39 479	13	33 884	13.4	86.6	29.7	8.3	372	16.3
Clay	343	5.9	488	207	306	765 975	1 626	113 282	66	93 523	95.9	4.1	53.3	26.5	10 392	50.7
Cleburne	125	6.8	155	0	54	246 389	1 722	37 229	58	71 887	1.8	98.2	30.0	12.3	208	10.3
Cleveland	36	9.1	162	0	16	329 948	2 195	67 941	58	261 850	0.5	99.5	49.1	31.8	89	6.4
Columbia	55	-5.2	162	0	19	254 992	1 559	47 282	37	108 697	D	D	29.8	13.0	15	3.8

Table B. States and Counties — Residential Construction, Wholesale Trade, Retail Trade, and Real Estate

STATE County	Value of residential construction authorized by building permits, 2003		Wholesale trade, 1997				Retail trade,[1] 1997				Real estate and rental and leasing, 1997			
	New construction ($1,000)	Number of housing units	Number of establishments	Number of employees	Sales (mil dol)	Annual payroll (mil dol)	Number of establishments	Number of employees	Sales (mil dol)	Annual payroll (mil dol)	Number of establishments	Number of employees	Receipts (mil dol)	Annual payroll (mil dol)
	133	134	135	136	137	138	139	140	141	142	143	144	145	146
ALABAMA—Cont'd														—
Washington	215	3	11	D	D	D	53	319	52.1	4.2	2	D	D	D
Wilcox	0	0	8	36	18.3	0.7	62	331	53.0	5.0	7	9	0.4	0.0
Winston	255	2	37	560	127.2	11.6	108	751	103.8	10.8	16	37	2.8	0.4
ALASKA	560 200	3 531	784	6 860	2 989.8	256.8	2 866	32 502	6 251.4	670.5	716	4 014	543.2	98.3
Aleutians East Borough	1 012	10	2	D	D	D	6	56	7.2	1.0	2	D	D	D
Aleutians West Census Area	1 428	12	14	110	61.4	3.2	20	197	41.2	4.2	4	55	9.5	2.2
Anchorage	391 600	2 387	434	4 748	1 989.1	181.4	1 001	15 115	3 114.9	319.3	356	2 145	322.2	56.8
Bethel	7 900	53	3	9	1.1	0.2	59	829	77.2	8.5	7	33	5.3	0.7
Bristol Bay	0	0	2	D	D	D	13	91	12.8	2.1	3	15	1.4	0.2
Denali Borough	NA	NA	2	D	D	D	7	220	33.1	3.6	1	D	D	D
Dillingham	NA	NA	4	10	4.7	0.5	16	220	33.1	3.6	4	15	1.9	0.5
Fairbanks North Star	39 408	257	75	737	266.0	27.7	359	4 431	927.9	99.5	91	687	79.1	17.3
Haines	980	6	3	D	D	D	26	98	13.1	2.0	4	15	1.1	0.2
Juneau	18 208	117	33	196	96.3	8.2	173	1 807	312.7	37.2	49	249	38.3	4.0
Kenai Peninsula	17 383	125	70	337	242.0	12.6	292	2 219	426.5	45.1	49	219	21.9	4.0
Ketchikan Gateway	4 556	29	31	190	78.8	4.7	119	1 164	205.1	28.6	27	110	13.5	2.9
Kodiak Island	10 155	72	35	87	50.8	4.4	67	590	102.9	11.9	16	49	7.6	0.9
Lake and Peninsula Borough ..	NA	NA	NA	NA	NA	NA	10	D	D	D	3	6	0.3	0.0
Matanuska-Susitna	20 104	160	22	D	D	D	201	2 149	477.3	46.6	35	169	13.7	2.0
Nome	454	6	1	D	D	D	41	442	57.0	5.8	8	D	D	D
North Slope	1 104	7	4	26	42.5	2.0	22	293	45.0	7.4	3	D	D	D
Northwest Arctic Borough	0	0	NA	NA	NA	NA	30	286	40.8	5.4	1	D	D	D
Prince of Wales-Outer Ketchikan	0	0	6	32	21.6	1.0	40	158	26.0	2.7	4	D	D	D
Sitka	5 383	61	9	D	D	D	75	534	78.2	10.3	17	44	4.0	0.8
Skagway-Hoonah-Angoon	1 813	21	2	D	D	D	45	208	25.3	3.2	3	2	0.2	0.1
Southeast Fairbanks	NA	NA	3	D	D	D	30	193	28.4	2.9	4	10	0.4	0.1
Valdez-Cordova	4 662	25	20	D	D	D	78	417	81.7	8.2	15	23	3.8	0.7
Wade Hampton	NA	NA	1	D	D	D	29	353	27.3	3.1	NA	NA	NA	NA
Wrangell-Petersburg	1 683	13	7	D	D	D	61	406	54.1	8.2	5	10	0.6	0.1
Yakutat Borough	442	4	1	D	D	D	6	30	5.3	0.8	1	D	D	D
Yukon-Koyukuk	0	0	NA	NA	NA	NA	40	147	22.3	2.1	4	20	1.9	0.3
ARIZONA	10 518 958	74 996	6 689	80 155	45 763.9	2 748.9	16 283	232 050	43 960.9	4 223.9	5 450	32 529	4 110.1	747.4
Apache	12 373	103	9	D	D	D	126	1 242	170.0	17.0	13	56	6.5	0.8
Cochise	71 835	830	68	468	132.3	11.4	421	4 557	712.1	68.1	96	330	27.9	4.7
Coconino	147 566	1 189	112	D	D	D	653	7 217	1 081.2	112.1	175	662	75.3	13.0
Gila	36 533	290	42	220	60.7	6.4	176	2 040	329.6	32.9	50	111	16.5	2.1
Graham	8 157	66	25	193	59.1	3.9	110	1 377	205.4	19.4	18	47	4.0	0.7
Greenlee	173	2	7	D	D	D	22	146	20.8	1.8	1	D	D	D
La Paz	7 540	54	14	183	56.4	3.9	79	830	177.5	10.8	14	D	D	D
Maricopa	7 102 068	47 957	4 752	61 594	39 518.5	2 265.9	9 214	144 912	29 331.0	2 792.4	3 391	22 214	3 047.6	553.6
Mohave	317 257	3 387	106	D	D	D	578	6 944	1 236.9	111.1	148	486	50.0	7.6
Navajo	92 326	872	50	266	98.7	7.3	296	3 667	602.7	55.2	67	273	21.6	4.6
Pima	1 263 700	7 910	929	9 257	2 759.8	266.0	2 785	39 285	6 853.8	693.4	978	6 631	676.6	130.5
Pinal	769 103	6 903	88	690	206.4	18.1	404	4 355	680.8	63.9	111	337	32.3	4.6
Santa Cruz	66 827	534	205	1 859	1 124.9	49.9	207	2 169	320.3	30.7	49	113	11.6	1.9
Yavapai	406 155	2 984	150	1 134	480.6	29.1	757	7 325	1 203.1	120.8	226	737	88.2	15.6
Yuma	217 343	1 915	132	2 376	512.9	41.3	455	5 984	1 035.7	94.5	113	485	48.4	7.0
ARKANSAS	1 541 009	14 839	3 619	41 385	27 515.4	1 136.6	12 600	132 335	21 643.7	1 904.4	2 269	9 761	1 001.6	163.2
Arkansas	2 453	17	39	485	233.0	15.1	143	1 190	201.1	17.7	12	26	1.9	0.4
Ashley	1 242	17	28	D	D	D	117	961	133.8	12.3	12	43	1.8	0.5
Baxter	8 040	121	27	130	22.9	2.8	227	1 713	298.2	27.1	41	116	13.6	2.0
Benton	237 960	1 898	167	1 886	2 480.5	52.6	548	6 217	1 015.6	93.2	138	523	51.1	8.1
Boone	12 397	106	45	D	D	D	194	2 205	368.9	30.4	44	130	9.9	2.0
Bradley	386	9	11	37	25.6	1.0	62	385	65.1	4.9	5	14	0.5	0.1
Calhoun	67	1	2	D	D	D	22	91	13.3	1.1	1	D	D	D
Carroll	2 727	38	26	126	25.6	3.0	202	1 204	174.9	17.3	23	46	3.9	0.6
Chicot	957	20	23	216	87.6	5.7	80	627	87.1	7.1	10	D	D	D
Clark	2 009	25	25	128	39.1	3.4	116	1 100	171.3	14.8	26	70	3.9	0.6
Clay	1 366	15	23	350	98.8	7.4	86	632	106.2	8.1	10	19	1.6	0.2
Cleburne	5 365	60	33	255	63.9	5.3	111	982	135.7	12.4	20	44	4.1	0.8
Cleveland	0	0	6	D	D	D	19	94	9.2	0.8	2	D	D	D
Columbia	4 491	93	30	177	47.1	3.7	136	1 205	157.8	14.9	25	94	7.9	1.3

1. Establishments with payroll.

Table B. States and Counties — **Professional Services, Manufacturing, and Accommodation and Foodservices**

STATE County	Professional, scientific, and technical services,[1] 1997				Manufacturing, 1997				Accommodation and foodservices, 1997			
	Number of establishments	Number of employees	Receipts (mil dol)	Annual payroll (mil dol)	Number of establishments	Number of employees	Receipts (mil dol)	Annual payroll (mil dol)	Number of establishments	Number of employees	Sales (mil dol)	Annual payroll (mil dol)
	147	148	149	150	151	152	153	154	155	156	157	158
ALABAMA—Cont'd												
Washington	11	39	3.1	1.8	12	D	D	D	13	D	D	D
Wilcox	8	13	1.0	0.1	12	D	D	D	17	178	4.5	1.1
Winston	25	71	5.0	1.4	87	6 573	838.7	135.8	33	426	11.1	2.7
ALASKA	1 437	7 892	945.9	370.8	488	10 770	3 305.0	331.2	1 763	20 587	1 065.5	301.5
Aleutians East Borough	NA	NA	NA	NA	2	D	D	D	8	D	D	D
Aleutians West Census Area	1	D	D	D	8	D	D	D	11	165	7.6	3.4
Anchorage	907	5 939	767.2	301.3	187	2 022	322.3	62.9	640	11 364	574.0	165.8
Bethel	4	11	1.3	0.6	NA	NA	NA	NA	12	44	3.2	0.6
Bristol Bay	2	D	D	D	NA	NA	NA	NA	12	71	4.5	1.3
Denali Borough	NA	NA	NA	NA	NA	NA	NA	NA	18	80	8.7	2.6
Dillingham	NA	NA	NA	NA	NA	NA	NA	NA	18	73	8.9	2.2
Fairbanks North Star	167	784	70.5	28.1	NA	NA	NA	NA	184	2 488	112.1	29.4
Haines	4	8	0.5	0.3	NA	NA	NA	NA	19	84	5.3	1.4
Juneau	96	415	44.9	18.5	NA	NA	NA	NA	94	1 117	57.7	16.1
Kenai Peninsula	80	211	19.6	6.6	56	1 246	1 027.0	56.7	213	1 251	65.2	16.2
Ketchikan Gateway	25	84	9.8	3.4	18	762	131.3	31.1	57	476	25.2	7.1
Kodiak Island	20	48	3.4	1.5	25	1 576	204.3	35.4	41	378	18.4	5.3
Lake and Peninsula Borough	NA	NA	NA	NA	NA	NA	NA	NA	16	D	D	D
Matanuska-Susitna	78	251	17.2	7.0	NA	NA	NA	NA	126	928	43.9	10.2
Nome	2	D	D	D	NA	NA	NA	NA	20	215	6.6	2.1
North Slope	3	D	D	D	NA	NA	NA	NA	31	313	32.4	12.0
Northwest Arctic Borough	1	D	D	D	NA	NA	NA	NA	13	159	11.1	4.2
Prince of Wales-Outer Ketchikan	3	D	D	D	NA	NA	NA	NA	25	135	8.2	2.4
Sitka	13	34	2.6	0.6	NA	NA	NA	NA	32	331	15.5	4.4
Skagway-Hoonah-Angoon	1	D	D	D	NA	NA	NA	NA	39	120	9.4	2.7
Southeast Fairbanks	4	D	D	D	NA	NA	NA	NA	28	140	6.6	1.8
Valdez-Cordova	15	39	3.2	0.9	NA	NA	NA	NA	58	315	19.8	4.9
Wade Hampton	NA	NA	NA	NA	NA	NA	NA	NA	2	D	D	D
Wrangell-Petersburg	9	19	0.9	0.2	NA	NA	NA	NA	23	120	6.3	1.7
Yakutat Borough	NA	NA	NA	NA	NA	NA	NA	NA	6	75	2.8	0.9
Yukon-Koyukuk	2	D	D	D	NA	NA	NA	NA	17	38	4.4	0.7
ARIZONA	10 163	75 789	6 669.4	2 724.7	4 917	193 616	43 030.3	6 753.6	9 089	184 323	6 633.0	1 823.2
Apache	26	99	5.6	1.5	NA	NA	NA	NA	65	1 310	37.7	10.0
Cochise	127	1 731	148.2	61.9	53	921	153.8	20.9	270	3 310	94.2	23.9
Coconino	181	777	58.8	21.6	95	D	D	D	477	9 409	407.7	105.8
Gila	63	191	12.8	4.4	34	D	D	D	147	1 660	55.9	14.5
Graham	21	71	3.0	1.2	NA	NA	NA	NA	59	734	19.0	4.8
Greenlee	3	13	0.4	0.1	NA	NA	NA	NA	15	180	3.9	1.1
La Paz	12	39	2.3	0.7	NA	NA	NA	NA	76	795	23.2	6.5
Maricopa	7 158	57 583	5 115.0	2 134.1	3 364	143 683	32 782.1	5 045.0	4 901	112 073	4 196.1	1 170.4
Mohave	138	517	33.0	10.0	156	3 807	760.4	85.2	324	4 516	144.6	39.3
Navajo	59	234	16.2	4.4	45	1 346	275.9	44.2	222	2 890	118.5	26.2
Pima	1 811	12 214	1 124.2	430.9	764	26 746	4 455.2	1 064.7	1 524	32 305	1 041.9	292.2
Pinal	70	468	21.8	7.4	74	4 594	2 530.6	154.8	233	3 995	139.6	36.8
Santa Cruz	42	143	8.9	3.8	35	D	D	D	87	1 374	40.3	11.7
Yavapai	304	1 043	71.1	25.4	189	3 511	445.8	91.3	444	5 614	180.4	48.6
Yuma	148	666	48.1	17.3	66	3 041	389.5	54.6	245	4 158	130.0	31.3
ARKANSAS	4 125	23 094	1 825.8	719.6	3 316	230 153	45 186.0	5 778.4	4 663	73 397	2 179.7	589.9
Arkansas	25	63	3.2	0.9	28	2 768	916.2	66.4	43	340	10.5	2.8
Ashley	25	83	4.5	1.3	24	3 792	921.4	141.7	24	280	9.9	2.3
Baxter	65	312	17.1	6.4	56	3 185	350.8	74.1	106	1 060	32.3	9.1
Benton	250	1 239	155.5	46.2	194	14 220	2 491.8	346.5	230	3 585	98.9	26.9
Boone	54	137	6.8	2.2	67	2 808	495.0	70.4	65	1 015	26.7	7.0
Bradley	16	62	2.6	0.9	9	594	90.0	12.5	16	193	5.0	1.3
Calhoun	2	D	D	D	NA	NA	NA	NA	4	13	0.4	0.1
Carroll	27	76	3.4	1.3	41	3 408	426.5	62.8	157	1 117	41.3	10.9
Chicot	15	49	2.5	1.0	11	1 019	67.1	12.8	23	124	4.0	1.0
Clark	28	140	6.9	2.8	31	2 960	401.1	64.2	45	862	23.3	6.6
Clay	17	27	1.1	0.5	23	2 475	188.6	42.0	17	D	D	D
Cleburne	25	64	4.4	1.5	34	1 687	367.0	39.1	49	735	21.0	6.2
Cleveland	4	D	D	D	NA	NA	NA	NA	2	D	D	D
Columbia	40	153	7.5	3.1	39	2 957	602.3	96.6	50	755	19.5	4.8

1. Firms subject to federal tax.

Table B. States and Counties — Health Care and Social Assistance, Other Services, and Federal Funds

STATE County	Health care and social assistance,[1] 1997				Other services,[1] 1997				Federal funds and grants, 2002–2003 Expenditures (mil dol)	Direct payments for individuals[2]		
	Number of establish-ments	Number of employees	Receipts (mil dol)	Annual payroll (mil dol)	Number of establish-ments	Number of employees	Receipts (mil dol)	Annual payroll (mil dol)	Total	Social Security and government retirement	Medicare	Food stamps and Supplemental Security Income
	159	160	161	162	163	164	165	166	167	168	169	170
ALABAMA—Cont'd												
Washington	7	D	D	D	7	12	0.6	0.1	96.8	42.4	18.8	7.1
Wilcox	8	144	5.3	2.2	9	25	1.6	0.4	108.1	30.2	16.0	12.9
Winston	25	452	20.6	7.7	33	90	4.5	1.3	214.1	63.1	38.3	6.8
ALASKA	1 143	8 156	758.1	309.4	852	4 364	331.0	93.4	7 943.9	996.4	212.1	109.9
Aleutians East Borough	8	D	D	D	NA	NA	NA	NA	20.4	4.9	0.2	0.3
Aleutians West Census Area	5	22	1.6	0.5	5	42	7.8	2.2	61.5	1.8	0.6	0.1
Anchorage	599	5 053	508.6	203.9	393	2 576	185.8	54.8	3 093.7	441.1	82.9	43.0
Bethel	5	47	2.1	0.6	7	23	2.5	0.4	280.8	10.4	4.1	8.6
Bristol Bay	1	D	D	D	NA	NA	NA	NA	38.0	4.6	1.0	0.1
Denali Borough	1	D	D	D	NA	NA	NA	NA	16.5	1.3	1.3	0.0
Dillingham	1	D	D	D	4	8	0.9	0.1	74.2	9.2	0.0	1.8
Fairbanks North Star	146	1 007	96.4	45.9	129	658	52.2	14.6	1 142.2	126.7	27.4	9.7
Haines	3	D	D	D	4	5	0.7	0.2	15.1	4.9	1.6	0.4
Juneau	81	437	40.1	16.6	56	240	15.8	4.5	800.1	59.5	13.2	3.9
Kenai Peninsula	97	543	37.3	12.8	80	266	20.1	5.3	251.4	88.0	24.6	6.3
Ketchikan Gateway	24	130	9.9	3.6	21	76	6.6	1.7	117.8	22.7	8.3	2.1
Kodiak Island	14	78	6.7	3.1	20	79	6.7	1.8	145.1	9.8	2.1	2.0
Lake and Peninsula Borough..	NA	NA	NA	NA	NA	NA	NA	NA	16.9	2.7	1.5	0.7
Matanuska-Susitna	95	484	33.5	13.6	78	270	20.6	5.5	285.3	104.4	19.3	8.3
Nome	5	27	1.3	0.7	5	14	2.1	0.3	112.8	8.6	2.2	3.8
North Slope	3	11	0.4	0.1	1	D	D	D	68.5	7.2	1.4	0.5
Northwest Arctic Borough	NA	NA	NA	NA	NA	NA	NA	NA	84.0	6.1	1.5	3.1
Prince of Wales-Outer Ket-chikan	4	18	1.3	0.3	5	16	1.2	0.3	67.5	7.2	0.9	1.0
Sitka	14	76	5.2	2.3	15	41	2.5	0.6	118.4	15.5	4.8	0.9
Skagway-Hoonah-Angoon	NA	NA	NA	NA	4	3	0.2	0.0	29.1	6.3	1.6	0.5
Southeast Fairbanks	8	46	2.9	1.6	3	D	D	D	160.9	11.9	2.1	1.1
Valdez-Cordova	18	85	4.0	1.5	15	35	3.4	0.7	125.4	13.7	3.1	1.3
Wade Hampton	1	D	D	D	NA	NA	NA	NA	65.7	4.8	1.7	6.4
Wrangell-Petersburg	8	19	1.7	0.3	7	9	1.1	0.2	53.3	11.7	4.2	0.6
Yakutat Borough	NA	NA	NA	NA	NA	NA	NA	NA	3.4	0.2	0.0	0.0
Yukon-Koyukuk	2	D	D	D	NA	NA	NA	NA	175.1	11.0	0.7	3.6
ARIZONA	9 155	97 091	6 687.9	2 893.3	6 494	43 669	2 794.0	829.6	37 801.3	11 557.1	4 177.7	962.3
Apache	24	180	8.1	3.7	18	67	3.6	0.9	847.1	106.2	29.9	44.3
Cochise	145	1 432	79.1	30.7	122	514	25.0	6.7	1 514.2	425.9	91.8	27.7
Coconino	240	1 627	107.5	45.8	183	899	54.7	14.2	799.3	225.7	62.6	29.0
Gila	76	666	37.1	14.8	54	184	10.7	2.6	475.9	172.4	67.9	13.7
Graham	53	501	26.7	10.1	32	210	12.2	3.6	193.9	66.5	22.6	9.4
Greenlee	6	20	1.0	0.3	5	8	0.5	0.2	59.6	15.6	6.0	1.4
La Paz	20	100	7.9	3.8	19	80	5.0	0.8	166.3	53.7	0.0	4.9
Maricopa	5 848	63 697	4 532.2	1 979.0	4 060	30 024	2 012.8	597.3	19 061.2	6 129.8	2 430.4	480.0
Mohave	258	1 950	134.6	55.3	194	1 039	67.4	18.7	962.9	558.2	177.5	35.5
Navajo	108	675	43.0	16.3	91	424	24.5	6.3	734.5	197.3	52.5	43.9
Pima	1 614	19 280	1 283.3	563.9	1 171	7 575	437.9	138.1	8 108.7	2 213.3	782.8	163.2
Pinal	132	1 395	86.4	37.1	108	656	27.7	9.0	1 028.4	399.1	158.7	39.6
Santa Cruz	30	126	19.5	5.7	48	130	6.4	1.6	227.6	62.7	21.6	10.8
Yavapai	377	3 014	167.5	66.8	231	1 004	59.1	16.1	980.9	608.0	146.6	22.6
Yuma	224	2 428	154.1	60.1	158	855	46.5	13.6	1 021.7	321.5	126.7	36.2
ARKANSAS	4 571	59 960	3 655.1	1 609.7	3 553	18 809	1 113.9	310.5	18 340.4	6 662.4	2 636.5	680.3
Arkansas	31	362	13.8	6.2	38	138	7.5	1.5	157.1	52.1	27.5	6.3
Ashley	23	325	13.8	6.2	25	103	6.5	1.9	157.6	58.9	30.2	8.5
Baxter	99	796	62.0	28.1	83	466	25.3	8.1	267.1	166.4	56.0	6.2
Benton	207	2 285	121.6	60.2	193	1 162	72.4	22.3	588.0	364.3	102.4	13.6
Boone	64	535	32.5	12.8	54	226	12.6	3.5	195.7	105.0	33.6	6.4
Bradley	19	265	11.1	4.4	23	58	5.0	1.1	108.8	33.1	18.5	4.1
Calhoun	3	D	D	D	3	D	D	D	59.6	12.3	5.0	1.4
Carroll	35	256	12.3	4.8	34	88	5.0	1.2	114.2	65.5	22.3	3.5
Chicot	16	167	7.4	3.2	17	61	2.7	0.8	129.9	31.8	19.5	8.4
Clark	40	380	15.3	6.4	29	115	5.6	1.5	138.2	53.9	26.3	4.5
Clay	18	265	10.1	4.5	20	55	3.3	0.8	133.0	48.3	25.9	4.8
Cleburne	28	304	12.1	5.2	28	138	7.0	2.0	148.3	87.4	28.0	4.6
Cleveland	3	D	D	D	5	10	0.9	0.3	43.1	21.6	8.1	2.1
Columbia	45	375	15.7	7.0	40	165	9.1	2.8	178.2	64.5	30.0	10.9

1. Firms subject to federal tax.   2. State totals may include programs not allocated by county.

Table B. States and Counties — Federal Funds and Local Government Finances

	Federal funds and grants, 2002–2003 (cont'd)							Local government finances, 2002				
	Expenditures (mil dol) (cont'd)							General revenue				
	Procurement contract awards			Grants[1]						Taxes		
											Per capita[2] (dollars)	
STATE County	Salaries and wages	Defense	Other	Medicaid and other health-related	Nutrition and family welfare	Education	Other	Total (mil dol)	Intergovernmental (mil dol)	Total (mil dol)	Total	Property
	171	172	173	174	175	176	177	178	179	180	181	182
ALABAMA—Cont'd												
Washington	2.6	0.0	0.6	18.6	2.4	1.3	1.6	42.1	23.1	9.2	511	428
Wilcox	4.1	0.1	0.7	32.6	4.3	1.7	4.0	32.5	18.9	3.4	262	125
Winston	9.3	70.9	1.9	17.6	1.6	1.5	2.6	57.8	38.6	9.3	375	142
ALASKA	1 616.6	1 236.7	443.4	1 103.1	241.7	307.4	1 370.1	X	X	X	X	X
Aleutians East Borough	1.4	1.8	0.9	4.9	0.8	1.7	2.3	20.5	9.3	4.9	1 949	384
Aleutians West Census Area	2.7	37.0	7.3	1.9	0.7	1.6	7.9	45.2	19.5	13.0	2 271	695
Anchorage	904.9	643.2	209.1	359.0	83.8	40.8	260.5	894.6	427.7	321.8	1 196	1 070
Bethel	9.3	1.3	9.3	171.9	14.7	23.9	23.7	35.7	19.6	5.4	319	2
Bristol Bay	3.4	4.8	1.9	0.0	0.1	0.2	0.6	9.8	3.9	4.2	3 622	2 410
Denali Borough	12.7	0.1	0.2	0.0	0.1	0.2	0.6	6.0	3.6	1.8	974	105
Dillingham	3.2	0.4	1.3	31.5	3.8	6.9	14.9	23.2	15.5	3.8	749	236
Fairbanks North Star	402.7	283.0	34.3	104.7	23.9	25.0	94.3	241.4	135.7	81.5	959	865
Haines	0.6	3.5	0.1	2.8	0.2	0.3	0.7	10.5	3.3	4.4	1 014	
Juneau	65.5	1.4	11.0	61.8	45.4	98.9	435.1	179.6	44.1	64.1	2 086	869
Kenai Peninsula	28.4	4.0	9.1	34.5	5.5	5.1	41.9	179.8	72.7	74.4	1 463	856
Ketchikan Gateway	25.8	3.7	13.4	24.4	3.1	1.5	11.7	80.0	24.4	24.4	1 787	856
Kodiak Island	56.8	7.6	38.5	15.9	3.3	2.7	5.7	66.5	34.5	16.3	1 180	583
Lake and Peninsula Borough	1.5	0.3	7.6	0.0	0.4	0.2	1.5	17.4	10.8	2.1	1 281	650
Matanuska-Susitna	10.9	1.8	27.8	13.4	8.4	5.6	82.9	191.3	105.6	64.1	984	779
Nome	6.9	4.1	1.7	36.7	7.4	19.6	17.7	29.1	13.6	5.4	584	251
North Slope	1.5	21.0	2.4	12.3	1.3	11.2	8.6	323.3	42.6	226.0	31 114	30 999
Northwest Arctic Borough	4.0	0.3	2.4	43.9	2.8	10.8	8.0	67.0	43.7	6.5	883	528
Prince of Wales-Outer Ketchikan	4.9	2.5	31.5	8.0	1.0	7.5	1.6	19.8	13.0	2.3	399	70
Sitka	19.7	0.0	4.5	57.8	1.9	1.5	9.4	40.7	12.7	11.4	1 292	458
Skagway-Hoonah-Angoon	7.1	0.0	1.5	4.8	0.3	2.3	4.6	15.0	6.8	5.4	1 633	459
Southeast Fairbanks	8.1	110.8	4.2	13.9	1.2	1.8	5.5	0.6	0.5	0.0	2	0
Valdez-Cordova	14.1	33.1	4.6	8.3	1.7	2.1	41.8	89.8	10.5	25.1	2 476	2 191
Wade Hampton	2.0	0.1	0.7	29.8	2.0	15.3	2.1	8.8	3.4	0.9	121	29
Wrangell-Petersburg	9.9	0.4	12.4	4.7	1.3	1.6	5.9	41.2	14.2	9.2	1 417	754
Yakutat Borough	0.9	1.0	0.3	0.4	0.1	0.2	0.2	5.5	3.3	1.4	1 920	1 005
Yukon-Koyukuk	7.6	66.7	5.2	33.1	5.1	8.2	33.0	35.7	30.4	0.6	97	30
ARIZONA	3 334.6	7 564.1	992.9	3 688.3	1 041.7	776.7	1 728.4	X	X	X	X	X
Apache	94.6	0.4	18.3	262.5	83.1	61.1	105.2	232.8	154.8	26.8	394	345
Cochise	360.6	357.1	61.0	108.1	19.2	18.7	28.0	319.3	161.4	88.6	735	563
Coconino	141.2	4.7	33.3	140.1	26.7	46.4	64.7	381.0	180.2	132.6	1 102	703
Gila	23.1	1.2	44.6	54.5	11.2	12.5	72.9	147.8	77.6	45.0	872	546
Graham	18.8	0.1	4.5	39.6	7.1	6.4	11.3	96.4	64.5	16.5	499	302
Greenlee	2.0	0.3	0.4	6.3	1.5	0.7	25.3	29.3	12.5	9.9	1 266	1 043
La Paz	7.0	69.9	5.2	0.6	3.7	7.4	9.0	54.6	34.9	13.3	682	485
Maricopa	1 455.6	4 276.6	551.1	1 679.0	486.2	403.8	803.4	10 405.7	4 233.7	3 912.9	1 184	756
Mohave	28.6	0.9	11.5	35.3	11.3	11.1	87.2	396.5	168.1	149.8	905	656
Navajo	70.7	0.1	27.7	182.5	31.8	51.9	45.0	315.2	201.5	71.2	696	478
Pima	731.5	2 781.6	136.8	753.1	116.6	92.0	250.8	2 528.7	1 190.0	942.2	1 069	786
Pinal	40.1	1.2	53.9	183.5	39.4	25.9	54.0	503.4	257.1	169.3	863	617
Santa Cruz	37.7	0.3	3.1	56.4	7.0	6.6	20.4	114.9	68.8	32.9	822	590
Yavapai	64.5	3.2	25.4	62.4	10.8	12.2	18.8	488.0	202.0	207.2	1 157	744
Yuma	258.5	66.6	16.1	86.7	30.5	19.9	41.7	441.6	243.5	124.8	746	407
ARKANSAS	1 339.1	577.7	286.4	2 171.5	507.2	373.7	1 488.6	X	X	X	X	X
Arkansas	10.0	1.3	7.8	23.8	3.1	1.4	4.8	54.2	29.2	11.8	578	207
Ashley	4.7	1.6	1.0	31.3	3.5	2.0	6.7	57.7	28.8	10.7	449	212
Baxter	8.7	2.3	2.5	14.1	1.7	1.6	7.2	62.2	31.0	14.6	377	170
Benton	24.3	1.9	10.9	30.0	7.4	5.5	20.5	311.7	152.9	75.1	454	184
Boone	10.6	2.1	2.4	19.4	4.5	3.0	4.3	59.2	40.3	10.9	314	125
Bradley	2.6	0.0	0.4	14.2	3.2	0.7	30.3	23.8	16.3	4.0	317	157
Calhoun	0.7	29.4	0.2	9.3	0.7	0.3	0.2	16.1	6.0	2.1	362	207
Carroll	7.2	1.0	1.1	9.6	1.0	1.2	1.1	44.0	22.9	11.1	424	186
Chicot	2.5	0.0	0.4	40.5	5.2	1.9	4.7	42.9	19.4	5.5	406	240
Clark	7.6	0.5	5.5	19.5	2.3	4.7	3.2	48.4	25.2	8.9	377	150
Clay	4.8	0.3	0.9	28.4	1.9	1.2	4.1	33.2	17.8	5.2	305	149
Cleburne	5.3	0.9	1.1	14.2	1.4	1.7	2.9	33.3	21.2	7.5	307	160
Cleveland	1.1	0.0	0.3	7.6	1.3	0.7	0.1	14.9	10.1	3.6	419	358
Columbia	3.8	16.1	7.8	31.1	3.9	2.8	2.2	78.8	47.0	9.3	367	112

1. State totals may include programs not allocated by county. 2. Based on the resident population estimated as of July 1 of the year shown.

STATE County	Direct general expenditure Total (mil dol)	Per capita[1] (dollars)	Educa-tion	Health and hospitals	Police protec-tion	Public welfare	High-ways	Debt outstanding Total (mil dol)	Per capita[1] (dollars)	Federal civilian	Federal military	State and local	Demo-cratic	Republi-can	All other
	183	184	185	186	187	188	189	190	191	192	193	194	195	196	197
ALABAMA—Cont'd															
Washington	40.8	2 278	52.7	17.7	2.6	0.1	12.5	19.4	1 083	38	79	963	38.1	61.4	0.5
Wilcox	34.1	2 596	53.0	9.8	3.2	0.0	7.1	74.2	5 652	111	58	869	64.0	35.2	0.8
Winston	58.8	2 374	53.7	22.3	2.8	0.6	4.9	25.2	1 018	92	110	1 073	21.6	77.9	0.5
ALASKA	X	X	X	X	X	X	X	X	X	16 257	23 209	61 023	35.0	62.0	3.0
Aleutians East Borough	25.2	9 998	27.0	3.4	2.5	0.0	0.8	9.1	3 610	22	17	263	NA	NA	NA
Aleutians West Census Area	35.6	6 229	16.0	0.4	8.1	0.2	11.3	11.5	2 010	27	58	429	NA	NA	NA
Anchorage	1 064.2	3 957	44.2	3.0	12.9	0.0	18.4	1 371.2	5 098	9 302	11 071	19 408	NA	NA	NA
Bethel	40.0	2 364	0.0	0.5	5.9	0.0	2.6	76.3	4 512	118	112	3 002	NA	NA	NA
Bristol Bay	8.2	7 061	47.2	7.2	6.4	0.0	2.0	0.0	0	78	0	321	NA	NA	NA
Denali Borough	5.8	3 081	83.2	0.6	0.0	0.0	1.2	0.0	0	219	128	146	NA	NA	NA
Dillingham	23.8	4 711	32.0	0.5	4.3	0.0	2.5	0.2	33	46	33	852	NA	NA	NA
Fairbanks North Star	238.9	2 809	56.9	0.4	5.5	0.0	2.8	143.4	1 686	3 198	8 270	7 567	NA	NA	NA
Haines	10.3	4 425	43.5	2.6	12.0	0.1	3.8	3.8	1 625	13	15	184	NA	NA	NA
Juneau	164.4	5 345	32.0	24.6	4.8	0.0	5.1	60.7	1 973	864	417	6 480	NA	NA	NA
Kenai Peninsula	179.0	3 520	51.2	1.5	2.8	0.0	3.3	50.4	991	415	435	4 067	NA	NA	NA
Ketchikan Gateway	81.8	5 985	26.9	5.3	3.9	0.5	1.3	76.3	5 581	255	330	1 627	NA	NA	NA
Kodiak Island	63.4	4 589	46.3	0.6	2.8	0.9	2.5	19.0	1 374	210	980	1 039	NA	NA	NA
Lake and Peninsula Borough	19.9	12 297	63.0	0.1	0.1	0.0	0.0	9.8	6 067	28	11	275	NA	NA	NA
Matanuska-Susitna	206.9	3 176	68.4	1.1	1.8	0.0	4.6	137.3	2 108	166	432	3 210	NA	NA	NA
Nome	28.7	3 112	30.5	1.0	5.6	0.0	4.6	6.2	674	73	83	1 639	NA	NA	NA
North Slope	263.9	36 330	23.9	4.9	2.9	1.8	2.9	821.9	113 165	22	48	1 875	NA	NA	NA
Northwest Arctic Borough	81.7	11 153	74.4	0.1	1.2	0.0	0.3	26.3	3 587	55	49	1 194	NA	NA	NA
Prince of Wales-Outer Ket-chikan	19.2	3 335	60.3	1.6	3.7	0.0	0.8	19.9	3 455	113	38	815	NA	NA	NA
Sitka	45.8	5 185	35.6	15.7	6.3	0.6	2.2	61.3	6 939	184	238	995	NA	NA	NA
Skagway-Hoonah-Angoon	14.3	4 344	51.1	1.6	7.1	0.1	2.6	2.5	756	154	22	374	NA	NA	NA
Southeast Fairbanks	0.6	100	0.0	5.5	0.0	0.0	6.4	0.0	0	174	59	437	NA	NA	NA
Valdez-Cordova	81.1	8 009	18.9	5.5	2.3	0.2	0.5	414.1	40 895	169	190	1 171	NA	NA	NA
Wade Hampton	9.4	1 291	28.6	2.3	13.5	0.0	1.9	0.1	18	28	190	1 448	NA	NA	NA
Wrangell-Petersburg	39.8	6 130	35.9	22.8	3.4	0.1	3.2	10.1	1 557	190	48	712	NA	NA	NA
Yakutat Borough	5.0	6 570	55.1	3.0	6.1	0.0	9.1	1.3	1 741	29	0	107	NA	NA	NA
Yukon-Koyukuk	39.8	6 238	81.8	3.9	1.5	0.0	0.7	4.9	770	105	42	1 386	NA	NA	NA
ARIZONA	X	X	X	X	X	X	X	X	X	47 364	31 888	328 062	44.5	54.9	0.6
Apache	232.2	3 415	67.5	0.8	2.8	0.5	4.8	454.0	6 676	2 771	120	10 344	44.5	54.9	0.6
Cochise	319.6	2 654	46.4	3.3	6.6	8.4	6.2	160.8	1 336	4 311	5 470	6 924	64.8	34.6	0.6
Coconino	376.9	3 133	42.4	2.9	6.5	2.0	7.5	428.8	3 564	3 322	226	12 620	39.2	60.0	0.7
Gila	139.7	2 709	44.1	3.0	7.7	3.4	5.5	102.9	1 996	558	91	4 350	55.8	43.4	0.7
Graham	107.8	3 251	65.9	2.1	3.9	1.4	4.2	29.8	899	331	58	2 656	40.1	59.2	0.7
Greenlee	28.6	3 654	39.6	2.9	7.5	1.5	4.0	68.6	8 769	39	14	484	29.9	69.5	0.6
La Paz	51.6	2 646	41.1	3.8	9.4	0.0	9.3	24.2	1 238	144	34	2 081	37.4	62.0	0.6
Maricopa	10 310.7	3 121	38.5	3.2	6.8	5.5	3.8	16 575.2	5 017	19 106	12 363	170 192	36.6	62.5	0.9
Mohave	374.6	2 262	41.5	3.5	7.0	0.0	5.7	329.8	1 992	494	294	7 078	35.2	64.1	0.7
Navajo	313.5	3 067	66.5	0.4	3.4	1.2	4.7	205.1	2 006	1 607	180	9 495	46.0	53.3	0.7
Pima	2 435.1	2 763	38.6	6.8	8.1	3.0	6.7	2 753.4	3 124	8 861	7 989	65 221	52.4	47.0	0.6
Pinal	493.6	2 515	46.8	7.1	7.0	2.4	6.1	399.4	2 035	913	346	15 715	42.2	57.3	0.5
Santa Cruz	118.4	2 958	51.9	5.1	7.5	0.0	4.2	34.4	860	1 083	71	2 234	59.3	40.0	0.7
Yavapai	474.3	2 649	36.4	1.5	6.2	8.2	12.9	376.6	2 103	1 181	327	9 236	37.7	61.6	0.7
Yuma	439.5	2 625	50.0	2.0	5.4	0.6	5.7	315.9	1 887	2 643	4 305	9 432	40.6	58.9	0.6
ARKANSAS	X	X	X	X	X	X	X	X	X	20 268	17 216	171 689	44.5	54.3	1.1
Arkansas	51.4	2 526	42.4	9.0	4.4	0.0	6.5	23.9	1 175	216	91	1 137	44.8	54.5	0.7
Ashley	62.1	2 603	43.4	0.0	3.5	0.0	4.5	180.0	7 539	85	106	1 174	45.6	53.7	0.8
Baxter	59.6	1 542	47.9	0.1	5.5	2.9	10.8	118.5	3 063	165	173	1 444	38.5	60.1	1.5
Benton	296.2	1 790	56.0	6.5	8.0	0.0	5.3	234.8	1 418	394	737	6 249	30.5	68.3	1.2
Boone	59.6	1 716	61.1	0.3	4.4	0.0	6.2	23.1	667	201	154	2 628	31.4	66.3	2.3
Bradley	23.4	1 870	62.3	0.2	4.4	0.0	8.1	10.4	833	41	59	737	47.4	51.8	0.8
Calhoun	15.4	2 708	30.8	0.1	4.0	1.0	9.3	89.3	15 725	14	25	606	40.8	58.3	0.9
Carroll	42.1	1 610	50.6	0.1	6.6	0.0	9.2	32.3	1 233	111	116	953	39.7	59.0	1.3
Chicot	42.7	3 138	42.6	33.3	4.1	0.0	6.2	13.6	995	50	61	1 114	61.5	37.6	0.9
Clark	50.4	2 142	49.9	0.1	5.4	0.1	13.1	118.8	5 050	110	105	2 195	54.3	44.9	0.8
Clay	31.9	1 865	49.0	21.0	4.4	0.1	8.9	13.6	794	65	76	923	53.7	45.1	1.2
Cleburne	31.9	1 297	66.0	0.2	5.7	0.0	9.5	10.4	423	104	109	827	38.5	60.4	1.2
Cleveland	13.1	1 536	79.3	0.1	3.0	0.0	7.0	5.6	657	16	38	381	41.5	57.5	1.1
Columbia	77.2	3 046	39.3	18.7	2.4	0.0	24.4	59.6	2 350	52	113	1 879	41.5	57.8	0.7

1. Based on the resident population estimated as of July 1 of the year shown.

STATE/ County code	CBSA code[1]	County Type[2]	STATE County	Land area,[3] (sq km) 2000	Total persons	Rank	Per square kilometer	White	Black	Am. Indian, Alaska Native	Asian and Pacific Islander	Percent Hispanic or Latino[4]	Under 5 years	5 to 17 years	18 to 24 years	25 to 34 years	35 to 44 years	45 to 54 years
									Race alone or in combination, not Hispanic or Latino (percent)					Age (percent)				
				1	2	3	4	5	6	7	8	9	10	11	12	13	14	15
			ARKANSAS—Cont'd															
05 029	...	6	Conway	1 440	20 485	1 777	14.2	84.6	13.2	0.9	0.4	1.8	6.1	18.3	9.4	11.1	14.4	13.5
05 031	27860	3	Craighead	1 841	84 626	630	46.0	87.5	9.5	0.8	0.8	2.3	7.0	17.3	12.4	14.7	13.7	12.8
05 033	22900	2	Crawford	1 542	55 647	867	36.1	92.2	1.1	3.2	1.6	3.7	7.1	20.1	9.4	12.4	15.4	13.4
05 035	32820	1	Crittenden	1 580	51 155	919	32.4	47.6	50.4	0.5	0.6	1.4	8.6	22.2	10.0	13.3	14.7	13.0
05 037	...	6	Cross	1 595	19 203	1 852	12.0	74.8	23.8	0.4	0.3	1.0	6.6	20.1	9.6	12.0	14.8	13.4
05 039	...	6	Dallas	1 729	8 708	2 552	5.0	55.0	42.5	0.3	0.3	2.1	6.0	19.3	9.2	10.4	12.9	15.2
05 041	...	6	Desha	1 981	14 623	2 123	7.4	48.2	48.4	0.4	0.4	2.9	7.6	20.0	10.4	10.5	13.1	14.3
05 043	...	7	Drew	2 145	18 468	1 882	8.6	69.8	27.8	0.5	0.5	1.9	6.6	18.4	11.8	12.9	13.9	13.2
05 045	30780	2	Faulkner	1 677	92 060	585	54.9	87.5	9.5	1.0	1.0	2.1	6.7	18.1	14.6	14.7	14.5	12.0
05 047	22900	2	Franklin	1 579	18 003	1 917	11.4	95.9	0.8	1.8	0.6	1.9	6.3	18.2	9.9	11.7	13.5	13.4
05 049	...	9	Fulton	1 601	11 632	2 320	7.3	98.2	0.3	1.7	0.3	0.6	4.6	16.1	8.2	9.4	12.9	14.0
05 051	26300	3	Garland	1 754	91 188	592	52.0	88.0	8.5	1.3	0.8	2.7	5.8	15.7	8.2	10.9	13.2	13.4
05 053	30780	2	Grant	1 636	16 933	1 965	10.4	95.5	2.8	0.6	0.2	1.3	6.0	18.6	9.2	12.6	15.7	14.0
05 055	37500	6	Greene	1 496	38 353	1 175	25.6	98.2	0.3	1.4	0.2	1.1	6.8	18.3	9.3	13.2	14.4	13.2
05 057	26260	6	Hempstead	1 888	23 429	1 643	12.4	59.5	30.8	0.9	0.2	9.5	7.3	19.2	10.2	12.4	13.9	13.2
05 059	...	6	Hot Spring	1 593	30 674	1 393	19.3	87.5	10.5	1.2	0.4	1.4	6.1	18.4	8.8	11.5	14.0	14.2
05 061	...	7	Howard	1 521	14 461	2 129	9.5	70.1	22.2	0.8	0.6	6.6	7.1	19.0	9.3	12.2	14.7	12.5
05 063	12900	7	Independence	1 978	34 426	1 293	17.4	94.9	2.2	1.1	1.0	1.8	6.0	17.4	10.3	11.8	14.6	14.3
05 065	...	9	Izard	1 504	13 202	2 221	8.8	96.7	1.5	1.6	0.2	0.9	4.6	15.7	8.2	10.8	14.2	13.0
05 067	...	6	Jackson	1 641	17 443	1 939	10.6	80.1	18.0	0.7	0.3	1.4	5.7	16.2	12.2	11.3	14.2	14.1
05 069	38220	3	Jefferson	2 292	82 889	641	36.2	46.0	52.2	0.6	0.9	1.0	7.1	18.5	11.4	12.4	14.4	13.9
05 071	...	6	Johnson	1 715	23 592	1 630	13.8	90.7	1.7	1.4	0.4	6.8	7.0	17.8	10.1	12.5	13.9	12.7
05 073	...	8	Lafayette	1 364	8 310	2 575	6.1	60.3	37.7	0.5	0.3	1.3	6.1	18.2	9.0	10.3	13.7	13.3
05 075	...	6	Lawrence	1 519	17 553	1 934	11.6	98.1	0.7	1.2	0.2	0.8	6.3	17.0	10.4	11.4	13.6	12.9
05 077	...	6	Lee	1 558	11 857	2 301	7.6	39.5	57.8	0.2	0.5	2.3	6.5	18.3	11.5	14.6	14.4	13.1
05 079	38220	3	Lincoln	1 454	14 403	2 133	9.9	64.7	33.4	0.6	0.1	1.6	5.3	15.1	13.3	15.6	17.4	13.2
05 081	...	6	Little River	1 377	13 358	2 210	9.7	74.7	21.7	2.8	0.2	2.0	5.9	18.5	8.9	11.9	13.2	14.2
05 083	...	6	Logan	1 839	22 808	1 674	12.4	96.2	1.4	1.6	0.9	1.3	6.7	18.4	9.0	11.2	14.3	13.0
05 085	30780	2	Lonoke	1 984	56 718	859	28.6	90.8	6.6	0.9	0.8	1.8	6.7	20.4	9.8	12.8	16.3	13.0
05 087	22220	2	Madison	2 167	14 354	2 141	6.6	95.5	0.1	2.3	0.2	2.9	6.7	19.1	8.9	11.1	14.7	14.8
05 089	...	9	Marion	1 548	16 283	2 015	10.5	98.1	0.2	1.8	0.4	0.7	4.3	16.2	7.9	8.7	13.2	14.9
05 091	45500	3	Miller	1 616	41 892	1 083	25.9	72.6	25.4	1.3	0.6	1.1	7.1	19.0	10.1	13.4	14.0	12.8
05 093	14180	4	Mississippi	2 326	49 041	954	21.1	62.8	35.0	0.8	0.6	2.0	8.6	21.1	10.0	12.5	14.3	13.2
05 095	...	7	Monroe	1 571	9 633	2 476	6.1	58.7	40.0	0.4	0.2	1.4	6.7	20.0	9.4	9.2	12.9	13.7
05 097	...	8	Montgomery	2 023	9 120	2 516	4.5	95.1	0.3	2.0	0.5	3.1	5.1	17.3	7.8	10.0	14.2	13.7
05 099	26260	7	Nevada	1 606	9 640	2 475	6.0	65.7	32.3	0.5	0.2	1.6	6.6	17.7	9.4	11.4	14.1	13.9
05 101	25460	9	Newton	2 131	8 542	2 561	4.0	97.9	0.2	1.3	0.4	1.1	5.2	18.5	9.1	10.2	14.0	14.8
05 103	15780	7	Ouachita	1 897	27 697	1 475	14.6	58.5	40.4	0.6	0.4	1.2	6.4	18.3	8.4	11.9	14.7	13.7
05 105	30780	2	Perry	1 427	10 461	2 404	7.3	95.9	2.0	1.4	0.1	1.2	6.4	18.3	8.4	11.9	14.7	13.7
05 107	48340	7	Phillips	1 794	24 621	1 593	13.7	35.5	62.7	0.5	0.4	1.4	8.9	22.8	10.6	11.6	13.8	13.5
05 109	...	9	Pike	1 562	11 123	2 362	7.1	91.1	3.9	1.1	0.2	4.4	5.7	18.3	8.3	11.2	13.7	13.5
05 111	27860	3	Poinsett	1 963	25 415	1 554	12.9	90.8	7.4	0.5	0.2	1.6	7.0	18.8	9.2	12.2	13.7	13.5
05 113	...	7	Polk	2 226	20 224	1 789	9.1	94.2	0.3	2.9	0.4	3.6	6.6	18.3	9.0	11.1	13.1	13.1
05 115	40780	5	Pope	2 103	55 185	874	26.2	93.6	2.9	1.3	0.9	2.3	6.6	18.1	12.2	12.7	14.6	13.1
05 117	...	8	Prairie	1 673	9 344	2 498	5.6	84.0	14.7	0.4	0.2	0.8	6.2	17.0	8.3	11.1	14.1	14.0
05 119	30780	2	Pulaski	1 996	364 567	169	182.6	61.3	34.9	0.9	1.9	2.4	7.5	17.9	8.9	14.9	15.1	14.6
05 121	...	7	Randolph	1 688	18 171	1 903	10.8	97.1	1.2	1.2	0.3	1.2	5.9	17.9	9.2	11.0	13.9	13.9
05 123	22620	6	St. Francis	1 642	28 517	1 441	17.4	43.6	51.0	0.4	0.6	4.8	8.2	19.7	10.2	13.5	14.8	13.2
05 125	30780	2	Saline	1 874	87 554	612	46.7	95.1	2.4	1.0	1.0	1.5	5.9	18.4	8.8	12.8	15.6	13.8
05 127	...	6	Scott	2 315	10 963	2 370	4.7	91.7	0.5	2.5	1.5	4.9	6.6	18.8	8.9	11.4	14.4	12.8
05 129	...	9	Searcy	1 728	7 973	2 596	4.6	97.7	0.4	1.8	0.3	1.1	5.5	15.9	8.1	9.9	13.5	14.9
05 131	22900	2	Sebastian	1 389	117 252	481	84.4	80.0	7.2	3.0	4.4	7.9	7.6	18.6	9.3	13.5	14.7	13.7
05 133	...	7	Sevier	1 461	15 858	2 040	10.9	70.7	4.8	2.1	0.2	23.0	8.2	20.0	9.9	13.3	13.4	12.1
05 135	...	7	Sharp	1 565	17 461	1 936	11.2	97.7	0.6	1.7	0.2	1.0	5.2	16.0	8.0	9.9	12.4	12.8
05 137	...	9	Stone	1 571	11 632	2 320	7.4	98.0	0.3	2.1	0.1	1.0	5.3	16.1	8.1	9.3	13.0	14.4
05 139	20980	5	Union	2 691	44 829	1 028	16.7	64.5	34.0	0.6	0.8	1.0	6.5	18.6	9.5	11.5	14.4	14.2
05 141	...	8	Van Buren	1 843	16 348	2 008	8.9	97.0	0.5	1.9	0.4	1.4	5.2	15.8	8.1	9.6	12.5	12.8
05 143	22220	2	Washington	2 460	169 684	333	69.0	84.0	2.9	2.1	3.0	9.9	7.5	17.7	13.2	16.0	13.9	12.0
05 145	42620	4	White	2 678	69 981	723	26.1	93.3	4.2	1.1	0.5	2.0	6.5	17.5	13.0	12.5	13.9	12.5
05 147	...	9	Woodruff	1 519	8 244	2 581	5.4	68.7	30.3	0.3	0.2	0.8	6.6	18.9	9.4	11.1	13.4	14.6
05 149	40780	6	Yell	2 403	21 459	1 728	8.9	82.4	1.4	1.3	1.1	14.6	7.3	18.3	9.5	12.9	14.2	12.7
06 000	...	X	CALIFORNIA	403 933	35 484 453	X	87.8	46.8	6.9	1.1	13.0	34.3	7.2	19.4	10.1	14.9	15.7	13.5
06 001	41860	1	Alameda	1 910	1 461 030	24	764.9	41.6	14.8	1.1	25.7	20.2	7.0	17.5	8.8	16.0	17.0	14.6
06 003	...	8	Alpine	1 913	1 209	3 102	0.6	77.9	0.7	14.1	0.1	7.4	4.2	13.8	10.8	10.8	16.1	21.3
06 005	...	6	Amador	1 536	37 273	1 199	24.3	84.3	4.0	2.4	1.4	9.4	3.7	14.6	9.1	10.8	15.3	15.3

1. CBSA = Core Based Statistical Area. See Appendix A for explanation. See Appendix B for list of metropolitan areas with component counties. 2. County type code from the Economic Research Service of USDA Rural-Urban Continuum Codes. See Appendix A for definition. 3. Dry land or land partially or temporarily covered by water. 4. Hispanic or Latino persons may be of any race.

Table B. States and Counties — **Population and Households**

STATE County	55 to 64 years	65 to 74 years	75 years and over	Percent female	1990	2000	1990–2000	2000–2003	Births	Deaths	Net migration	Number	Percent change, 1990–2000	Persons per house-hold	Female family house-holder[1]	One person
	16	17	18	19	20	21	22	23	24	25	26	27	28	29	30	31
ARKANSAS—Cont'd																
Conway	11.1	8.1	7.7	51.2	19 151	20 336	6.2	0.7	766	713	123	7 967	11.0	2.51	11.5	25.4
Craighead	9.2	6.1	5.5	51.5	68 956	82 148	19.1	3.0	3 811	2 616	1 373	32 301	22.9	2.46	11.4	25.2
Crawford	9.9	6.4	4.9	50.3	42 493	53 247	25.3	4.5	2 501	1 559	1 478	19 702	29.2	2.68	10.9	20.0
Crittenden	8.5	5.2	4.6	52.4	49 939	50 866	1.9	0.6	3 029	1 734	-968	18 471	7.9	2.72	21.3	23.7
Cross	10.6	6.7	6.7	51.6	19 225	19 526	1.6	-1.7	860	734	-437	7 391	9.4	2.60	14.1	23.5
Dallas	10.7	8.4	8.6	51.8	9 614	9 210	-4.2	-5.5	344	444	-409	3 519	-2.3	2.48	13.8	28.3
Desha	10.9	6.9	7.2	53.3	16 798	15 341	-8.7	-4.7	765	614	-889	5 922	-0.6	2.57	19.9	26.9
Drew	9.5	6.8	6.0	51.3	17 369	18 723	7.8	-1.4	789	618	-416	7 337	15.7	2.46	14.2	26.0
Faulkner	7.8	5.0	4.3	51.1	60 006	86 014	43.3	7.0	3 950	2 036	4 105	31 882	49.5	2.57	10.2	22.5
Franklin	10.7	8.0	7.8	50.5	14 897	17 771	19.3	1.3	741	581	86	6 882	23.4	2.51	8.8	24.6
Fulton	13.1	11.5	9.7	51.3	10 037	11 642	16.0	-0.1	307	496	190	4 810	20.0	2.39	7.8	24.4
Garland	11.5	10.7	10.0	51.4	73 397	88 068	20.0	3.5	3 350	4 240	3 939	37 813	22.6	2.28	10.1	28.8
Grant	11.1	6.6	5.5	50.5	13 948	16 464	18.0	2.8	609	526	389	6 241	21.9	2.61	8.5	20.4
Greene	10.4	7.3	6.4	51.2	31 804	37 331	17.4	2.7	1 741	1 294	595	14 750	19.7	2.49	9.7	24.0
Hempstead	9.7	7.1	6.7	51.4	21 621	23 587	9.1	-0.7	1 119	887	-389	8 959	9.1	2.60	15.3	25.5
Hot Spring	11.2	8.2	7.3	51.2	26 115	30 353	16.2	1.1	1 221	1 164	290	12 004	18.7	2.50	10.6	23.5
Howard	9.9	7.0	7.7	51.0	13 569	14 300	5.4	1.1	685	529	13	5 471	10.0	2.55	12.7	25.7
Independence	10.8	7.7	6.8	50.9	31 192	34 233	9.7	0.6	1 319	1 217	130	13 467	13.7	2.47	9.2	25.5
Izard	13.0	10.9	8.8	48.6	11 364	13 249	16.6	-0.4	364	609	210	5 440	16.1	2.30	7.5	27.8
Jackson	11.7	8.1	7.8	52.1	18 944	18 418	-2.8	-5.3	691	889	-763	6 971	-5.3	2.40	13.1	27.9
Jefferson	9.5	6.4	6.5	50.9	85 487	84 278	-1.4	-1.6	4 026	2 894	-2 508	30 555	1.8	2.59	18.8	26.2
Johnson	10.4	7.5	7.0	50.2	18 221	22 781	25.0	3.6	1 115	759	477	8 738	23.8	2.54	9.5	24.6
Lafayette	12.2	8.4	9.0	51.5	9 643	8 559	-11.2	-2.9	360	334	-265	3 434	-4.2	2.46	14.4	28.4
Lawrence	11.2	8.8	8.7	51.2	17 455	17 774	1.8	-1.2	715	750	-176	7 108	3.7	2.42	9.6	26.7
Lee	9.5	7.1	6.9	47.0	13 053	12 580	-3.6	-5.7	535	451	-803	4 182	-8.7	2.59	23.1	27.2
Lincoln	8.3	6.1	5.9	40.0	13 690	14 492	5.9	-0.6	497	391	-177	4 265	12.4	2.63	14.8	23.5
Little River	12.2	8.2	7.1	51.3	13 966	13 628	-2.4	-2.0	501	576	-193	5 465	6.1	2.46	12.3	26.3
Logan	11.1	8.0	7.7	50.4	20 557	22 486	9.4	1.4	964	840	207	8 693	14.0	2.53	10.1	24.4
Lonoke	9.2	5.7	4.5	50.4	39 268	52 828	34.5	7.4	2 339	1 469	2 969	19 262	38.9	2.71	10.6	19.0
Madison	11.0	7.3	6.7	50.0	11 618	14 243	22.6	0.8	603	506	33	5 463	24.4	2.59	7.9	22.4
Marion	14.3	11.5	9.0	50.6	12 001	16 140	34.5	0.9	419	562	299	6 776	36.3	2.36	7.4	24.9
Miller	9.3	6.6	6.4	51.3	38 467	40 443	5.1	3.6	1 880	1 161	754	15 637	9.6	2.52	16.0	25.6
Mississippi	9.1	6.8	5.8	52.2	57 525	51 979	-9.6	-5.7	2 924	1 904	-4 040	19 349	-5.2	2.64	17.4	24.7
Monroe	11.0	9.1	8.7	53.3	11 333	10 254	-9.5	-6.1	411	472	-566	4 105	-5.9	2.47	16.7	30.1
Montgomery	13.0	10.7	8.5	51.1	7 841	9 245	17.9	-1.4	268	377	-2	3 785	23.6	2.41	7.0	24.5
Nevada	11.1	8.3	7.9	51.2	10 101	9 955	-1.4	-3.2	431	465	-283	3 893	2.5	2.48	14.0	27.8
Newton	13.5	7.9	7.4	49.3	7 666	8 608	12.3	-0.8	271	279	-56	3 500	24.2	2.44	7.7	26.0
Ouachita	10.4	8.4	8.6	52.7	30 574	28 790	-5.8	-3.8	1 182	1 246	-1 046	11 613	-0.8	2.45	15.6	28.0
Perry	11.3	8.2	6.8	50.1	7 969	10 209	28.1	2.5	449	359	167	3 989	30.6	2.52	8.7	23.2
Phillips	9.8	7.6	6.7	54.2	28 830	26 445	-8.3	-6.9	1 524	1 103	-2 277	9 711	-4.6	2.69	25.1	27.6
Pike	12.0	8.3	9.0	51.1	10 086	11 303	12.1	-1.6	415	440	-145	4 504	16.8	2.47	8.3	25.2
Poinsett	11.2	7.6	6.8	51.2	24 664	25 614	3.9	-0.8	1 187	978	-386	10 026	7.0	2.52	13.2	24.8
Polk	12.0	8.9	8.2	50.8	17 347	20 229	16.6	0.0	904	763	-126	8 047	17.9	2.49	8.4	25.0
Pope	9.5	6.8	6.1	50.9	45 883	54 469	18.7	1.3	2 385	1 664	54	20 701	23.0	2.55	10.2	23.0
Prairie	12.6	8.8	8.6	51.0	9 518	9 539	0.2	-2.0	392	423	-157	3 894	6.4	2.41	11.1	25.6
Pulaski	9.2	5.9	5.6	52.1	349 569	361 474	3.4	0.9	18 700	11 034	-4 379	147 942	7.8	2.39	15.1	30.0
Randolph	11.3	8.8	8.1	50.7	16 558	18 195	9.9	-0.1	671	743	68	7 265	12.7	2.46	9.9	24.7
St. Francis	9.3	6.0	5.4	48.4	28 497	29 329	2.9	-2.8	1 670	1 140	-1 356	10 043	0.9	2.65	20.8	25.1
Saline	10.7	7.6	5.3	50.3	64 183	83 529	30.1	4.8	3 141	2 351	3 254	31 778	37.9	2.57	9.7	19.6
Scott	12.3	8.2	6.6	49.9	10 205	10 996	7.8	-0.3	443	382	-82	4 323	9.2	2.52	8.5	24.8
Searcy	13.1	10.8	9.3	50.2	7 841	8 261	5.4	-3.5	288	314	-251	3 523	13.0	2.33	7.7	28.0
Sebastian	9.6	6.5	6.3	51.0	99 590	115 071	15.5	1.9	5 949	3 751	75	45 300	15.3	2.49	11.3	27.5
Sevier	9.7	6.7	6.0	50.1	13 637	15 757	15.5	0.6	879	506	-271	5 708	11.5	2.73	10.0	22.8
Sharp	12.8	12.3	10.4	51.6	14 109	17 119	21.3	2.0	557	852	632	7 211	23.9	2.34	8.1	25.6
Stone	14.0	11.3	8.1	50.7	9 775	11 499	17.6	1.2	384	457	206	4 768	23.3	2.38	7.1	24.8
Union	10.0	7.5	8.3	51.9	46 719	45 629	-2.3	-1.8	1 972	1 932	-812	17 989	1.0	2.48	15.2	26.9
Van Buren	12.7	12.0	11.2	50.8	14 008	16 192	15.6	1.0	550	733	348	6 825	19.8	2.33	7.7	26.4
Washington	7.9	5.0	4.5	49.7	113 409	157 715	39.1	7.6	8 231	3 879	7 650	60 151	38.7	2.52	9.4	25.8
White	9.7	7.1	6.4	51.1	54 676	67 165	22.8	4.2	3 007	2 266	2 095	25 148	26.9	2.53	9.5	23.4
Woodruff	11.6	7.9	8.6	52.6	9 520	8 741	-8.2	-5.7	348	440	-402	3 531	-2.7	2.44	16.7	28.2
Yell	10.3	7.5	7.0	49.8	17 759	21 139	19.0	1.5	1 090	865	99	7 922	14.7	2.61	10.1	23.2
CALIFORNIA	8.7	5.4	5.2	50.1	29 811 427	33 871 648	13.6	4.8	1 701 252	756 758	660 643	11 502 870	10.8	2.87	12.6	23.5
Alameda	8.8	5.1	5.1	50.8	1 304 347	1 443 741	10.7	1.2	70 810	31 719	-22 227	523 366	9.1	2.71	13.0	26.0
Alpine	11.1	7.2	4.2	47.6	1 113	1 208	8.5	0.1	38	18	-18	483	7.3	2.50	11.0	27.7
Amador	12.5	9.1	8.5	45.3	30 039	35 100	16.8	6.2	820	1 280	2 559	12 759	21.3	2.39	8.7	23.9

1. No spouse present.

Items 16–31

Table B. States and Counties — Vital Statistics, Health Resources, and Crime

STATE County	Births, average 1999–2001 Total	Rate[1]	Deaths, average 1999–2001 Number Total	Number Infant[2]	Rate Total[1]	Rate Infant[3]	Physicians,[4] 2000 Number	Rate[5]	Hospitals,[4] 1998 Number	Beds Number	Beds Rate[5]	Medicare enrollees, 2003	Serious crimes known to police,[6] 2002 Total Number	Rate[7]
	32	33	34	35	36	37	38	39	40	41	42	43	44	45
ARKANSAS—Cont'd														
Conway	249	12.2	222	2	10.9	D	9	44	1	60	301	4 782	442	2 144
Craighead	1 171	14.3	746	11	9.1	9.1	217	264	2	425	548	12 005	3 837	4 608
Crawford	776	14.5	479	7	9.0	9.4	34	64	1	66	131	8 672	1 104	2 045
Crittenden	894	17.6	519	11	10.2	12.3	44	87	1	122	244	6 176	2 677	5 192
Cross	262	13.4	221	4	11.3	D	9	46	1	54	596	1 724	340	3 642
Dallas	109	11.9	139	1	15.2	D	8	87	1	59	302	3 021	454	2 294
Desha	237	15.6	183	4	12.0	D	13	85	2	79	523	2 519	718	4 617
Drew	252	13.5	190	2	10.2	D	11	59	1	50	284	2 654	565	2 977
Faulkner	1 222	14.1	584	8	6.8	6.5	87	101	1	116	148	10 637	3 435	3 939
Franklin	215	12.1	199	1	11.2	D	10	56	1	39	230	3 281	190	1 055
Fulton	112	9.7	156	0	13.4	D	7	60	1	39	358	2 972	169	1 432
Garland	1 034	11.7	1 245	8	14.1	7.7	205	233	2	441	525	23 127	3 995	4 475
Grant	194	11.8	163	1	9.9	D	6	36	0	0	0	2 391	102	611
Greene	522	14.0	410	7	11.0	13.4	39	104	1	129	356	6 498	568	1 501
Hempstead	344	14.6	262	2	11.1	D	22	93	1	75	339	3 515	NA	NA
Hot Spring	375	12.4	335	2	11.0	D	13	43	1	77	265	5 383	696	2 262
Howard	212	14.8	179	1	12.5	D	11	77	1	50	364	2 669	295	2 035
Independence	418	12.2	376	3	11.0	D	46	134	1	146	442	6 317	1 462	4 213
Izard	121	9.2	200	1	15.2	D	6	45	1	27	206	3 368	170	1 266
Jackson	214	11.7	256	0	14.0	D	26	141	2	174	978	4 451	416	2 228
Jefferson	1 258	15.0	888	11	10.6	8.5	142	168	1	484	593	12 814	5 919	6 928
Johnson	327	14.4	240	3	10.5	D	19	83	1	68	318	4 000	366	1 585
Lafayette	105	12.3	111	1	13.0	D	5	58	0	0	0	1 587	27	311
Lawrence	225	12.6	247	2	13.8	D	7	39	1	202	1 167	4 103	362	2 009
Lee	157	12.5	154	3	12.3	D	8	64	0	0	0	1 897	380	2 980
Lincoln	153	10.5	126	2	8.7	D	3	21	0	0	0	1 821	123	837
Little River	156	11.5	170	2	12.6	D	6	44	1	42	318	2 411	268	1 940
Logan	294	13.2	276	1	12.3	D	13	58	2	42	198	4 575	293	1 285
Lonoke	708	13.4	452	6	8.6	D	14	27	0	0	0	7 164	1 800	3 361
Madison	180	12.7	158	3	11.1	D	3	21	0	0	0	2 494	276	1 912
Marion	137	8.5	177	0	11.0	D	10	62	0	0	0	3 488	136	831
Miller	591	14.6	376	5	9.3	D	17	42	0	0	0	6 322	2 297	5 603
Mississippi	910	17.6	587	8	11.3	8.4	41	79	2	270	533	7 635	2 703	5 130
Monroe	127	12.5	148	1	14.5	D	10	98	0	0	0	1 962	35	337
Montgomery	88	9.6	113	1	12.3	D	4	43	0	0	0	1 850	175	1 867
Nevada	136	13.6	130	1	13.0	D	2	20	1	49	488	1 891	112	1 110
Newton	88	10.3	88	0	10.3	D	2	23	0	0	0	1 668	49	561
Ouachita	360	12.6	389	3	13.6	D	20	69	1	118	423	5 797	578	1 980
Perry	133	13.0	112	1	11.0	D	2	20	0	0	0	1 993	118	1 140
Phillips	488	18.5	350	6	13.3	D	25	95	1	125	457	4 488	NA	NA
Pike	136	12.1	140	2	12.5	D	7	62	1	41	387	2 072	63	550
Poinsett	366	14.3	308	4	12.0	D	11	43	0	0	0	4 748	1 314	5 061
Polk	280	13.9	245	3	12.2	D	27	133	1	38	193	4 115	282	1 375
Pope	739	13.5	493	4	9.0	D	74	136	1	157	302	8 394	1 775	3 215
Prairie	113	11.8	120	1	12.5	D	2	21	0	0	0	1 704	126	1 303
Pulaski	5 645	15.6	3 280	57	9.1	10.1	1 582	438	8	2 569	733	53 013	31 503	8 597
Randolph	199	10.9	219	1	12.1	D	11	60	1	50	281	3 560	372	2 017
St. Francis	468	16.0	347	4	11.9	D	23	78	1	90	320	4 405	1 501	5 048
Saline	946	11.3	714	7	8.5	7.4	64	77	1	120	155	9 022	2 924	3 453
Scott	151	13.7	126	0	11.4	D	3	27	1	24	225	2 287	246	2 207
Searcy	87	10.6	110	1	13.4	D	3	36	0	0	0	2 088	39	466
Sebastian	1 805	15.7	1 145	13	10.0	7.4	323	281	2	722	680	17 834	7 832	6 714
Sevier	267	16.9	162	3	10.3	D	19	121	1	77	527	2 390	NA	NA
Sharp	166	9.7	270	1	15.8	D	13	76	1	34	200	4 820	225	1 297
Stone	127	11.1	139	1	12.1	D	11	96	1	48	430	2 699	92	789
Union	588	12.9	590	6	13.0	D	87	191	2	378	834	8 609	1 828	3 952
Van Buren	162	10.0	226	2	13.9	D	9	56	1	144	926	4 056	278	1 694
Washington	2 550	16.1	1 145	13	7.2	5.1	312	198	2	419	303	20 144	6 119	3 827
White	901	13.4	687	9	10.2	10.4	72	107	2	253	392	11 802	2 014	2 958
Woodruff	99	11.3	133	0	15.2	D	6	69	0	0	0	1 705	65	734
Yell	321	15.2	252	2	11.9	D	13	61	2	85	445	4 062	352	1 643
CALIFORNIA	526 075	15.5	230 992	2 841	6.8	5.4	75 739	224	444	90 767	278	4 078 426	1 384 872	3 944
Alameda	21 589	14.9	9 858	116	6.8	5.4	3 488	242	17	3 748	268	158 703	78 048	5 214
Alpine	11	9.4	8	0	6.6	D	0	0	0	0	0	148	131	10 463
Amador	243	6.9	378	1	10.7	D	59	168	1	89	267	7 268	1 087	2 987

1. Per 1,000 estimated resident population. 2. Deaths of infants under 1 year old. 3. Deaths of infants under 1 year old per 1,000 live births. 4. Data subject to copyright. 5. Per 100,000 resident population as of July 1 of the year shown. 6. Data for serious crimes have not been adjusted for underreporting; this may affect comparability between geographic areas and over time. 7. Per 100,000 population estimated by the FBI.

Table B. States and Counties — Crime, Education, Money Income, and Poverty

STATE County	Serious crimes known to police,[1] 2002 (cont'd) Rate[2] Violent	Property	School enrollment and attainment, 2000 Enrollment[3] Total	Percent private	Attainment[4] (percent) High school graduate or less	Bachelor's degree or more	Local government expenditures,[5] 2000-2001 Total current expenditures (mil dol)	Current expenditures per student (dollars)	Money income, 1999 Per capita income[6] (dollars)	Households Median income Dollars	Percent change, 1989-1999 (constant 1999 dollars)	Percent with income of $100,000 or more	Percent below poverty level, 1999 Persons	Households	Families	Families with children
	46	47	48	49	50	51	52	53	54	55	56	57	58	59	60	61
ARKANSAS—Cont'd																
Conway	165	1 979	4 962	8.8	68.2	11.5	23.6	7 008	16 056	31 209	13.1	5.0	16.1	15.6	12.2	19.3
Craighead	341	4 267	22 728	8.4	55.5	20.9	72.9	5 364	17 091	32 425	9.0	6.2	15.4	16.0	11.6	16.9
Crawford	161	1 884	13 483	7.1	64.5	9.7	56.3	5 450	15 015	32 871	13.4	4.4	14.2	14.1	10.9	15.8
Crittenden	780	4 412	14 577	7.9	64.0	12.8	59.4	5 540	14 424	30 109	7.0	5.1	25.3	23.1	21.0	29.0
Cross	131	2 162	5 275	5.1	69.8	9.9	21.9	5 441	15 726	29 362	14.7	4.8	19.9	19.0	16.4	23.9
Dallas	546	3 096	2 357	2.6	74.3	9.6	10.3	6 152	14 610	26 608	12.2	3.6	18.9	19.5	13.3	19.6
Desha	624	3 993	4 212	3.9	71.0	11.1	21.0	6 146	13 446	24 121	14.2	4.4	28.9	28.1	23.6	33.8
Drew	369	2 608	5 425	3.1	61.3	17.3	22.8	7 070	16 264	28 627	12.7	5.7	18.2	19.4	13.1	18.9
Faulkner	232	3 708	26 908	15.2	47.9	25.2	76.6	5 335	17 988	38 204	20.2	7.7	12.5	13.3	7.9	11.4
Franklin	28	1 027	4 051	5.4	64.3	11.0	21.0	5 819	14 616	30 848	24.7	3.6	15.2	16.0	10.6	13.6
Fulton	127	1 305	2 435	5.5	66.9	10.5	9.1	5 518	15 712	25 529	27.1	3.3	16.3	16.9	12.7	19.6
Garland	488	3 986	18 185	10.1	54.5	18.0	75.0	5 864	18 631	31 724	16.5	6.1	14.6	14.0	10.5	19.6
Grant	36	575	3 925	5.0	65.1	11.0	23.3	4 973	17 547	37 182	14.0	5.4	10.2	11.0	7.8	9.5
Greene	66	1 435	8 654	8.8	68.5	10.9	34.9	5 334	16 403	30 828	15.1	3.9	13.3	14.7	9.9	14.5
Hempstead	NA	NA	5 894	5.9	69.2	11.0	25.5	6 366	14 103	28 622	25.4	3.6	20.3	19.6	16.0	24.1
Hot Spring	442	1 820	7 183	6.8	66.4	11.2	30.3	5 476	15 216	31 543	21.3	2.9	14.0	15.1	10.3	16.4
Howard	55	1 980	3 353	7.0	67.1	11.6	16.8	5 477	15 586	28 699	0.4	5.1	15.5	16.0	11.9	17.5
Independence	107	4 106	8 165	12.1	64.2	13.7	33.5	6 016	16 163	31 920	17.6	4.1	13.0	14.3	9.9	14.3
Izard	149	1 117	2 658	6.9	63.2	11.7	13.3	6 771	14 397	25 670	13.0	2.8	17.2	18.7	13.6	20.7
Jackson	289	1 939	4 023	5.2	72.3	10.3	15.6	5 885	14 564	25 081	12.2	4.7	17.4	18.2	13.2	19.2
Jefferson	938	5 991	22 966	7.1	60.0	15.7	84.1	5 634	15 417	31 327	9.4	5.6	20.5	19.5	16.0	24.1
Johnson	26	1 559	5 363	6.1	69.0	13.1	21.6	5 392	15 097	27 910	14.0	3.6	16.4	16.9	12.9	16.9
Lafayette	92	219	2 064	2.9	70.7	9.5	9.7	6 248	14 128	24 831	33.5	3.6	23.2	23.2	18.7	29.5
Lawrence	67	1 943	4 345	10.7	73.5	8.5	20.2	6 241	13 785	27 139	31.7	2.9	18.4	19.2	13.9	20.1
Lee	455	2 525	3 184	10.6	73.4	7.3	12.0	6 387	10 983	20 510	27.8	3.1	29.9	30.7	24.7	34.3
Lincoln	88	749	2 933	6.2	72.8	7.6	11.4	5 464	12 479	29 607	19.4	3.7	19.5	19.1	15.5	24.3
Little River	188	1 752	3 128	7.1	64.7	9.9	11.7	5 595	15 899	29 417	0.5	5.2	15.4	17.3	11.9	17.3
Logan	26	1 259	5 033	7.1	68.6	9.4	19.4	5 468	14 527	28 344	11.1	3.6	15.4	16.9	11.4	16.1
Lonoke	164	3 197	14 008	7.0	58.0	14.6	56.5	5 279	17 397	40 314	25.9	6.4	10.5	11.4	8.1	11.9
Madison	485	1 427	3 198	4.6	71.0	10.1	13.2	4 938	14 736	27 895	12.9	3.5	18.6	19.6	14.7	21.1
Marion	31	801	3 301	7.8	62.3	10.4	12.3	5 328	14 588	26 737	15.6	3.0	15.2	16.0	11.5	20.6
Miller	595	5 008	9 869	10.6	61.5	12.5	38.9	5 896	16 444	30 951	13.9	5.5	19.3	18.0	15.4	22.8
Mississippi	784	4 346	13 939	7.3	67.4	11.3	55.9	5 672	13 978	27 479	10.4	4.4	23.0	22.5	19.0	26.7
Monroe	58	279	2 564	12.1	74.4	8.4	12.0	6 212	13 096	22 632	23.6	3.1	27.5	27.9	21.0	32.1
Montgomery	512	1 355	1 860	5.3	69.4	8.8	7.6	5 429	14 668	28 421	28.2	3.6	17.0	17.0	13.0	18.7
Nevada	10	1 100	2 425	3.1	70.2	10.7	10.5	5 433	14 184	26 962	6.1	3.4	22.8	23.7	18.3	25.1
Newton	11	550	1 944	5.2	67.6	11.8	9.5	7 054	13 788	24 756	21.7	3.0	20.4	21.5	15.7	22.6
Ouachita	206	1 775	7 398	6.6	61.4	12.7	33.0	6 141	15 118	29 341	3.7	3.9	19.5	19.4	14.8	23.2
Perry	77	1 063	2 325	8.1	67.6	11.1	9.7	5 251	16 216	31 083	31.3	5.2	14.0	14.8	10.5	14.1
Phillips	NA	NA	8 079	10.0	64.3	12.4	38.5	6 660	12 288	22 231	26.6	3.9	32.7	30.7	28.7	40.8
Pike	35	515	2 606	6.5	70.3	10.1	13.7	5 943	15 385	27 695	7.1	3.8	16.8	18.0	12.8	18.3
Poinsett	366	4 695	5 948	3.1	77.5	6.3	29.2	6 097	13 087	26 558	17.3	2.8	21.2	22.1	17.6	24.1
Polk	146	1 229	4 834	6.6	63.6	10.9	20.1	5 562	14 063	25 180	5.4	3.4	18.2	17.9	14.0	19.5
Pope	353	2 861	15 194	6.2	56.1	19.0	56.1	5 587	15 918	32 069	6.9	5.6	15.2	15.5	11.6	16.9
Prairie	134	1 169	2 040	6.4	70.6	9.0	8.4	5 382	15 907	29 990	31.0	4.1	15.5	17.1	12.2	17.3
Pulaski	901	7 696	94 618	20.0	42.7	28.1	374.4	7 052	21 466	38 120	5.5	10.0	13.3	12.4	10.4	16.3
Randolph	390	1 626	4 304	7.2	69.1	10.6	16.2	5 588	14 502	27 583	22.8	3.2	15.3	17.2	11.9	18.8
St. Francis	925	4 124	8 028	5.7	67.6	9.6	34.5	6 876	12 483	26 146	29.5	4.0	27.5	26.8	23.1	32.9
Saline	293	3 160	20 335	12.0	55.4	16.4	64.1	5 253	19 214	42 569	12.1	6.8	7.2	7.4	5.0	7.8
Scott	99	2 108	2 425	3.6	71.8	8.4	8.0	4 825	13 609	26 412	19.4	2.6	18.2	17.8	15.3	20.1
Searcy	191	275	1 770	3.2	72.6	8.4	8.3	6 269	12 536	21 397	20.5	1.7	23.8	25.3	17.8	26.4
Sebastian	634	6 080	27 690	11.6	54.6	16.6	109.1	5 892	18 424	33 889	4.9	7.2	13.6	13.3	10.6	16.5
Sevier	NA	NA	3 907	3.5	69.2	9.2	17.9	5 892	14 122	30 144	16.8	3.8	19.2	18.0	14.4	21.5
Sharp	75	1 222	3 404	7.4	65.4	10.3	16.3	5 304	14 143	25 152	7.8	3.7	18.2	17.5	13.2	20.8
Stone	26	763	2 284	6.0	70.4	9.8	9.6	5 575	14 134	22 209	5.6	4.0	18.9	18.3	14.1	22.1
Union	491	3 461	11 194	9.0	61.0	14.9	47.5	5 658	16 063	29 809	5.4	5.4	18.7	18.5	14.7	21.4
Van Buren	177	1 517	3 205	6.1	65.2	11.5	13.8	5 621	16 603	27 004	17.5	4.7	15.4	15.6	11.6	18.8
Washington	368	3 459	46 255	8.7	51.0	24.5	154.1	5 797	17 347	34 691	11.7	6.7	14.6	14.8	9.4	14.2
White	98	2 860	18 439	24.5	62.8	15.5	64.4	5 576	15 890	32 203	21.5	5.0	14.0	14.6	10.4	15.1
Woodruff	0	734	2 089	3.4	76.1	8.0	9.5	6 181	13 269	22 099	17.3	2.5	27.0	27.0	21.7	30.9
Yell	79	1 563	4 761	5.3	71.6	10.9	21.8	5 431	15 383	28 916	9.5	3.9	15.4	15.7	11.7	16.2
CALIFORNIA	593	3 350	10 129 990	14.1	43.3	26.6	42 176.4	6 959	22 711	47 493	-1.3	17.3	14.2	11.8	10.6	15.3
Alameda	646	4 569	417 264	16.9	36.7	34.9	1 562.3	7 152	26 680	55 946	10.9	22.2	11.0	9.8	7.7	10.9
Alpine	719	9 744	296	8.8	37.6	28.2	3.0	20 060	24 431	41 875	25.0	9.8	19.5	15.4	12.0	21.5
Amador	401	2 586	8 110	12.2	46.3	16.6	30.6	6 332	22 412	42 280	4.0	10.7	9.2	8.7	6.1	12.0

1. Data for serious crimes have not been adjusted for underreporting; this may affect comparability between geographic areas and over time. 2. Per 100,000 population estimated by the FBI. 3. All persons 3 years old and over enrolled in nursery school through college. 4. Persons 25 years old and over. 5. Elementary and secondary education expenditures. 6. Based on population enumerated as of April 1, 2000.

STATE County	Personal income, 2002 Total (mil dol)	Percent change, 2001–2002	Per capita[1] Dollars	Rank	Wages and salaries[2] (mil dol)	Proprietor's income (mil dol)	Dividends, interest, and rent (mil dol)	Transfer payments Total (mil dol)	Government payments to individuals Total (mil dol)	Social Security (mil dol)	Medical payments (mil dol)	Income maintenance (mil dol)	Unemployment insurance (mil dol)
	62	63	64	65	66	67	68	69	70	71	72	73	74
ARKANSAS—Cont'd													
Conway	466	0.5	22 762	1 798	226	56	64	114	108	42	45	10	4
Craighead	1 927	3.7	23 002	1 721	1 354	150	316	364	342	127	142	33	11
Crawford	1 088	2.6	19 798	2 589	573	79	140	239	224	90	89	23	8
Crittenden	1 087	2.2	21 278	2 218	529	79	112	228	214	67	90	43	6
Cross	352	-2.5	18 210	2 869	174	12	59	90	85	31	35	12	3
Dallas	191	1.5	21 662	2 100	99	21	25	58	56	18	29	5	2
Desha	278	-1.0	18 804	2 781	192	7	44	81	77	23	34	12	3
Drew	389	0.8	21 108	2 265	205	29	67	91	86	29	35	10	5
Faulkner	2 121	2.5	23 578	1 540	1 222	109	288	366	342	115	157	25	14
Franklin	372	0.5	20 790	2 349	145	38	59	88	83	34	33	7	2
Fulton	208	3.0	17 965	2 901	46	27	34	67	64	28	25	6	1
Garland	2 292	3.5	25 482	1 003	1 128	139	646	546	522	232	211	35	12
Grant	405	2.4	24 167	1 351	115	23	58	66	62	27	22	4	3
Greene	758	1.5	19 956	2 553	442	50	134	177	167	67	67	16	7
Hempstead	475	-0.4	20 264	2 486	283	45	77	114	108	39	47	13	3
Hot Spring	603	3.3	19 776	2 594	250	32	91	152	144	60	58	12	6
Howard	309	-4.1	21 671	2 098	236	57	43	72	68	25	32	7	2
Independence	757	2.0	22 080	1 995	519	57	128	176	166	64	69	15	7
Izard	245	3.5	18 609	2 809	85	26	43	82	78	34	28	5	3
Jackson	362	-0.5	20 435	2 449	183	26	58	115	110	35	54	10	5
Jefferson	1 771	2.9	21 277	2 220	1 332	59	265	416	394	125	145	60	15
Johnson	440	2.0	18 914	2 771	242	41	68	105	99	42	36	11	3
Lafayette	161	-1.6	19 396	2 676	62	19	24	48	46	17	20	6	1
Lawrence	322	1.4	18 228	2 867	143	28	52	102	97	36	43	9	3
Lee	201	-4.5	16 434	3 032	80	28	30	63	60	17	27	12	2
Lincoln	219	-2.0	15 128	3 073	105	11	22	57	53	19	22	7	2
Little River	287	1.9	21 414	2 177	212	26	36	68	64	26	24	6	1
Logan	438	0.4	19 412	2 670	176	45	70	127	121	44	57	10	3
Lonoke	1 288	2.6	23 296	1 632	342	58	161	221	207	75	89	16	6
Madison	288	1.7	20 112	2 519	94	44	45	57	54	25	18	5	2
Marion	301	3.6	18 529	2 825	105	26	65	87	82	39	28	7	2
Miller	960	3.1	23 275	1 635	471	120	148	190	179	64	82	25	18
Mississippi	1 011	0.4	20 137	2 512	746	62	133	263	250	78	97	42	18
Monroe	180	-2.8	18 510	2 827	75	8	33	59	56	18	25	9	2
Montgomery	179	-1.0	19 588	2 640	47	30	36	49	47	20	19	3	2
Nevada	203	2.1	20 888	2 325	79	20	32	59	57	18	30	6	1
Newton	145	3.7	17 023	2 994	29	15	24	43	40	17	15	5	1
Ouachita	585	3.4	21 067	2 278	235	32	90	157	150	60	59	18	5
Perry	230	2.5	22 060	2 003	37	22	27	49	46	19	18	4	2
Phillips	450	-2.9	17 970	2 900	227	10	56	165	158	43	70	33	5
Pike	232	-2.1	20 696	2 372	84	34	38	54	51	22	21	4	2
Poinsett	472	-1.1	18 563	2 822	197	20	71	133	126	47	52	17	6
Polk	378	-2.7	18 657	2 805	169	63	66	107	102	41	38	9	5
Pope	1 207	1.7	21 836	2 056	853	74	194	249	234	94	92	21	8
Prairie	177	-1.7	18 718	2 794	60	0	32	51	49	19	21	4	1
Pulaski	11 661	3.3	32 072	224	10 637	1 113	2 078	1 675	1 579	565	635	169	55
Randolph	328	2.6	18 031	2 894	146	22	51	100	95	38	37	9	4
St. Francis	505	4.1	17 645	2 937	306	29	59	153	145	41	62	29	6
Saline	2 126	3.3	24 674	1 220	636	83	243	366	343	153	146	18	11
Scott	209	-4.3	18 961	2 760	83	39	31	55	52	22	20	5	1
Searcy	135	3.6	16 633	3 014	41	18	21	47	45	18	19	4	1
Sebastian	3 219	2.0	27 543	609	2 618	486	536	514	482	196	191	45	18
Sevier	302	-2.4	19 223	2 709	165	34	38	69	64	24	26	7	2
Sharp	297	2.5	17 117	2 981	101	19	55	113	109	49	42	8	3
Stone	211	1.1	18 254	2 866	73	34	39	66	63	27	24	5	2
Union	1 308	7.3	28 974	453	891	119	292	247	235	96	94	27	8
Van Buren	314	3.4	19 336	2 689	104	19	63	98	94	42	36	7	2
Washington	3 946	5.1	23 810	1 468	3 104	277	643	533	488	214	179	43	15
White	1 400	3.0	20 210	2 501	768	115	213	309	290	117	114	25	10
Woodruff	154	-4.0	18 353	2 850	82	0	23	54	52	15	26	7	2
Yell	433	-0.9	20 263	2 487	197	35	72	101	96	39	40	9	2
CALIFORNIA	1 154 685	1.7	32 989	X	770 643	129 711	204 536	146 952	138 609	42 350	59 417	20 106	7 224
Alameda	55 624	-1.3	37 945	88	40 998	4 372	9 110	6 176	5 824	1 630	2 644	774	363
Alpine	34	4.8	27 538	611	27	3	6	7	7	1	4	1	0
Amador	961	7.1	26 162	858	450	89	229	178	169	83	60	10	5

1. Based on the resident population estimated as of July 1 of the year shown.   2. Includes other labor income.

Table B. States and Counties — Earnings, Social Security, and Housing

STATE County	Earnings, 2002									Social Security beneficiaries, December 2003		Supplemental Security Income recipients, December 2003	Housing units, 2003	
	Total (mil dol)	Farm	Goods-related[1]		Service-related and health				Govern-ment	Number	Rate[2]		Total	Percent change, 2000–2003
			Total	Manu-facturing	Information and professional and technical services	Retail trade	Finance, insurance, and real estate	Health services						
	75	76	77	78	79	80	81	82	83	84	85	86	87	88
ARKANSAS—Cont'd														
Conway	282	7.4	D	19.6	5.4	8.9	2.7	D	14.5	4 955	242	824	9 160	1.5
Craighead	1 504	-0.2	D	19.2	5.8	9.1	6.5	18.5	16.3	14 610	173	2 806	36 513	3.9
Crawford	652	2.8	31.3	18.9	D	6.5	3.4	6.1	12.4	11 030	198	1 682	22 014	3.3
Crittenden	608	2.2	D	12.5	3.2	9.2	4.3	9.4	17.3	8 130	159	2 836	21 369	4.2
Cross	186	-2.7	27.8	23.0	2.7	9.5	8.0	D	20.6	3 665	191	835	8 253	2.8
Dallas	120	1.2	30.2	26.7	1.5	8.4	2.6	11.3	14.1	2 025	233	426	4 440	0.9
Desha	199	1.0	33.9	22.0	2.9	8.3	3.7	5.5	19.1	2 920	200	750	6 768	1.6
Drew	235	1.2	18.6	15.4	D	10.6	4.3	D	28.3	3 460	187	592	8 606	3.8
Faulkner	1 331	0.3	D	19.4	17.1	7.7	4.2	9.9	16.7	13 120	143	1 600	37 230	7.8
Franklin	184	10.8	25.5	17.6	D	7.4	3.2	D	27.1	4 100	228	520	7 781	1.4
Fulton	73	10.0	D	4.9	D	7.0	7.8	D	25.2	3 380	291	470	6 088	1.9
Garland	1 267	0.8	19.4	11.3	5.1	10.7	5.7	21.0	15.0	24 615	270	2 631	45 670	1.6
Grant	138	1.2	D	23.8	5.4	7.6	3.8	D	21.6	3 110	184	271	7 184	3.2
Greene	492	1.0	D	39.9	D	9.0	3.7	9.7	12.8	8 140	212	1 269	16 852	4.3
Hempstead	328	8.1	38.0	35.9	1.3	6.4	3.1	D	18.1	4 440	190	816	10 307	1.4
Hot Spring	282	1.2	37.8	28.9	D	7.7	4.0	D	17.8	6 720	219	779	13 669	2.1
Howard	292	11.5	48.3	46.0	1.4	5.3	2.4	D	9.9	2 920	202	447	6 410	1.8
Independence	576	1.5	38.2	34.1	D	7.7	3.0	13.5	12.1	7 775	226	1 244	15 172	2.2
Izard	111	5.9	D	21.6	D	7.3	5.8	8.0	27.7	3 995	303	440	6 716	1.9
Jackson	209	3.9	D	18.8	3.4	7.8	4.0	D	20.0	4 165	239	861	8 054	1.2
Jefferson	1 390	0.0	25.8	22.4	D	7.0	3.9	12.1	26.7	14 660	177	3 600	34 907	1.6
Johnson	283	5.9	38.8	34.5	1.9	8.4	2.8	D	14.2	5 060	214	836	10 157	2.3
Lafayette	80	15.1	30.9	22.5	D	5.1	3.5	5.9	18.2	2 020	243	517	4 654	2.1
Lawrence	170	3.7	28.4	20.3	1.9	9.8	3.5	D	23.7	4 475	255	843	8 173	1.1
Lee	108	14.0	D	D	D	5.7	3.1	D	30.1	2 400	202	905	4 912	3.0
Lincoln	115	10.5	D	14.4	D	4.7	2.3	5.2	40.5	2 320	161	501	5 079	2.5
Little River	238	5.5	D	46.5	D	4.3	2.0	1.8	11.8	2 965	222	441	6 518	1.3
Logan	221	11.5	35.3	31.3	2.5	7.8	4.5	6.9	20.6	5 465	240	769	10 048	1.1
Lonoke	400	2.0	26.5	14.7	4.8	9.8	8.0	9.1	19.7	8 785	155	1 105	22 436	8.1
Madison	137	18.0	D	26.7	D	6.5	3.0	D	15.9	3 240	226	388	6 669	2.0
Marion	132	4.6	D	38.6	D	7.6	5.8	D	15.6	4 610	283	489	8 562	4.0
Miller	592	1.5	35.7	27.0	D	8.2	4.0	5.0	12.7	7 425	177	1 524	18 373	3.6
Mississippi	808	0.5	48.4	39.1	D	5.9	3.1	6.3	13.4	9 570	195	3 056	22 527	1.0
Monroe	83	3.0	9.5	6.4	2.8	12.4	5.7	8.7	24.4	2 315	240	644	5 157	1.8
Montgomery	77	17.1	16.7	7.5	D	7.5	5.2	D	23.0	2 380	261	260	5 163	2.3
Nevada	99	11.7	D	28.7	D	6.1	D	7.6	18.3	2 230	231	490	5 042	6.1
Newton	44	6.6	D	8.9	D	6.2	D	D	38.9	2 225	260	426	4 374	1.3
Ouachita	267	0.9	17.1	12.4	D	11.7	5.5	12.1	22.1	6 590	238	1 415	13 538	0.7
Perry	58	16.0	D	3.3	D	6.4	D	6.0	25.1	2 265	217	364	4 796	2.0
Phillips	236	-0.4	14.0	10.9	3.8	9.6	4.9	D	27.4	5 505	224	2 245	10 936	0.7
Pike	118	17.2	17.2	10.3	1.8	7.9	5.5	3.4	20.1	2 600	234	274	5 648	2.0
Poinsett	217	0.9	D	23.7	3.2	6.1	5.8	6.6	20.9	5 760	227	1 351	11 257	1.9
Polk	232	13.2	D	20.2	3.6	10.0	3.9	9.4	16.4	5 025	248	590	9 410	1.9
Pope	926	2.9	D	17.1	3.3	7.8	3.7	8.5	15.2	10 985	199	1 859	23 637	3.4
Prairie	60	-3.9	D	D	4.0	10.5	4.0	6.7	25.5	2 190	234	302	4 842	1.1
Pulaski	11 750	0.0	12.3	6.8	13.0	6.1	9.0	11.3	23.0	60 585	166	10 429	165 671	2.8
Randolph	168	3.9	D	27.5	D	8.5	3.5	D	19.8	4 560	251	667	8 477	2.5
St. Francis	336	2.7	23.2	18.3	3.2	7.5	3.9	D	27.0	5 075	178	2 088	11 488	2.2
Saline	718	0.3	D	12.9	4.3	17.8	3.8	10.0	20.7	16 090	184	1 073	36 647	8.3
Scott	122	22.6	31.6	29.2	D	5.1	1.9	D	13.7	2 835	259	397	5 026	2.1
Searcy	59	4.2	22.0	13.7	3.3	9.1	3.0	9.8	29.8	2 390	300	464	4 349	1.3
Sebastian	3 104	0.3	34.3	27.2	12.6	6.4	4.3	14.3	9.0	21 830	186	3 256	50 756	2.9
Sevier	199	11.9	D	29.9	2.3	5.5	2.8	6.7	16.4	2 795	176	331	6 524	1.4
Sharp	120	8.4	D	6.2	6.6	10.2	6.4	D	21.8	5 865	336	722	9 454	1.2
Stone	107	11.3	19.2	14.4	D	13.8	3.5	D	19.6	3 490	300	552	5 857	2.5
Union	1 010	0.7	48.9	26.7	2.6	6.2	3.3	7.7	9.5	10 280	229	1 915	20 866	0.9
Van Buren	123	2.1	20.2	13.6	3.5	12.2	4.4	D	19.0	4 960	303	498	9 322	1.7
Washington	3 381	1.6	23.6	17.6	6.0	7.5	4.9	10.9	17.3	24 080	142	2 905	69 748	8.4
White	883	0.5	28.1	21.0	3.7	8.3	3.8	D	12.7	13 680	195	2 006	28 503	3.2
Woodruff	82	1.7	22.0	19.3	D	5.4	3.8	7.7	22.0	1 985	241	511	4 139	1.2
Yell	233	7.5	D	36.0	1.9	5.2	2.8	D	21.1	4 840	226	742	9 386	2.5
CALIFORNIA	900 353	0.9	18.6	12.1	16.7	6.9	10.0	7.8	15.8	4 363 657	123	1 161 467	12 656 882	3.6
Alameda	45 369	0.0	20.9	14.1	15.8	6.8	5.6	9.3	16.5	163 830	112	48 900	549 102	1.7
Alpine	31	0.0	6.7	0.0	2.4	3.7	D	D	23.1	155	128	29	1 622	7.1
Amador	539	1.5	13.9	6.4	6.3	10.1	4.7	D	35.6	8 415	226	489	15 740	4.7

1. Covers mining, construction, and manufacturing.   2. Per 1,000 resident population estimated as of July 1 of the year shown.

STATE County	Housing units, 2000								Civilian labor force, 2003				Civilian employment,[6] 2000		
	Occupied units										Unemployment			Percent	
		Owner-occupied				Renter-occupied									
				Median owner cost as a percent of income											
	Total	Percent	Median value[1]	With a mortgage	Without a mortgage[2]	Median rent[3]	Median rent as a percent of income	Sub-standard units[4] (percent)	Total	Percent change, 2002–2003	Total	Rate[5]	Total	Management, professional and related occupations	Production, transportation, and material moving occupations
	89	90	91	92	93	94	95	96	97	98	99	100	101	102	103
ARKANSAS—Cont'd															
Conway	7 967	78.0	59 400	18.8	12.2	414	24.4	4.2	9 699	-0.3	659	6.8	8 554	23.9	23.1
Craighead	32 301	63.9	79 200	19.4	9.9	454	26.7	2.9	44 402	-0.9	2 338	5.3	40 069	28.5	20.5
Crawford	19 702	75.9	71 600	19.7	9.9	405	22.7	6.3	24 584	-1.6	1 395	5.7	23 223	21.3	26.5
Crittenden	18 471	60.3	70 500	20.8	9.9	486	27.1	6.3	22 880	0.7	1 818	7.9	20 561	25.3	19.6
Cross	7 391	70.7	61 500	20.6	11.8	420	23.2	5.7	7 911	-0.1	777	9.8	8 025	26.2	24.8
Dallas	3 519	73.9	38 700	18.3	10.2	380	23.4	4.7	3 456	-3.0	340	9.8	3 578	21.2	31.3
Desha	5 922	63.5	46 700	18.7	10.4	354	26.7	5.4	6 568	-4.2	705	10.7	5 477	24.6	23.6
Drew	7 337	68.9	60 100	18.0	11.1	374	24.1	3.3	9 447	-1.0	801	8.5	8 022	26.8	21.9
Faulkner	31 882	68.6	92 900	19.1	9.9	499	26.5	3.5	46 119	-1.2	2 648	5.7	42 479	31.3	16.7
Franklin	6 882	78.0	58 500	20.3	9.9	376	23.3	3.5	7 954	-1.4	347	4.4	7 619	25.5	27.2
Fulton	4 810	81.1	54 500	22.3	11.7	337	26.0	3.6	4 368	4.9	284	6.5	4 582	24.6	25.0
Garland	37 813	71.2	85 900	20.5	9.9	478	26.4	2.8	37 697	-0.1	2 432	6.5	36 530	27.7	14.8
Grant	6 241	80.2	70 700	17.6	9.9	435	19.5	3.0	6 824	-1.5	460	6.7	7 550	21.9	24.4
Greene	14 750	71.3	66 800	19.2	9.9	431	23.5	2.6	18 056	-1.1	1 222	6.8	16 995	22.4	31.3
Hempstead	8 959	69.3	51 400	18.7	10.4	397	22.6	6.3	11 443	-2.5	604	5.3	10 292	23.0	33.6
Hot Spring	12 004	78.0	63 100	18.7	9.9	409	22.3	4.2	12 677	-0.8	956	7.5	13 481	23.1	23.0
Howard	5 471	72.0	55 600	19.5	10.6	369	22.1	5.2	6 622	-1.4	428	6.5	6 355	22.5	32.9
Independence	13 467	74.4	64 300	19.1	10.2	423	23.3	2.6	17 053	-0.5	1 218	7.1	15 366	24.5	29.2
Izard	5 440	80.1	57 800	21.5	10.8	336	24.4	3.7	4 489	1.2	418	9.3	4 912	26.9	21.4
Jackson	6 971	69.6	45 300	18.5	12.2	339	22.8	2.9	7 754	-0.2	821	10.6	6 941	24.8	21.7
Jefferson	30 555	66.1	57 600	18.1	11.1	463	25.9	5.4	36 168	-1.4	3 429	9.5	33 198	27.2	21.8
Johnson	8 738	73.0	59 300	19.7	9.9	411	22.9	5.4	11 041	-0.4	536	4.9	9 633	21.0	30.5
Lafayette	3 434	78.4	33 600	19.7	12.0	319	26.3	5.4	3 238	-3.7	187	5.8	3 170	21.3	28.4
Lawrence	7 108	71.2	45 300	19.5	10.8	367	24.5	2.4	7 174	-1.8	762	10.6	7 255	21.8	28.8
Lee	4 182	63.6	42 800	21.5	12.1	314	28.0	5.6	4 292	-3.4	533	12.4	3 585	23.8	22.3
Lincoln	4 265	76.2	52 200	19.2	11.7	385	24.3	5.5	5 436	1.5	369	6.8	4 638	24.4	23.4
Little River	5 465	76.5	55 300	18.1	9.9	372	23.6	4.6	5 520	-3.6	280	5.1	5 928	20.8	26.4
Logan	8 693	77.2	54 000	19.1	9.9	380	21.8	4.0	9 471	0.3	559	5.9	9 205	22.9	28.3
Lonoke	19 262	75.9	85 500	18.6	9.9	490	23.9	3.1	26 884	-1.1	1 242	4.6	24 727	28.3	17.9
Madison	5 463	79.0	62 300	19.8	9.9	358	20.7	8.2	8 121	4.3	248	3.1	6 496	25.0	26.7
Marion	6 776	80.0	73 200	21.4	11.5	388	23.5	5.0	6 377	-2.1	400	6.3	6 137	21.1	29.9
Miller	15 637	67.9	63 700	17.8	10.0	439	24.5	3.6	16 806	-2.5	771	4.6	16 858	26.4	19.6
Mississippi	19 349	58.9	56 200	19.0	11.1	422	24.4	5.9	23 104	-8.0	3 397	14.7	20 462	21.1	30.5
Monroe	4 105	64.9	42 300	21.8	11.5	280	22.4	6.4	3 768	-2.8	349	9.3	3 790	22.4	25.2
Montgomery	3 785	82.8	54 000	19.5	10.1	321	22.3	4.1	4 168	0.0	215	5.2	3 749	23.3	21.7
Nevada	3 893	74.8	41 200	17.9	11.2	339	22.5	5.2	4 500	-3.6	224	5.0	4 285	21.9	27.6
Newton	3 500	81.5	50 100	21.8	9.9	335	25.2	10.5	2 855	-1.5	189	6.6	3 504	23.1	26.5
Ouachita	11 613	71.4	50 200	18.5	10.9	355	22.5	4.3	11 280	-0.3	1 158	10.3	11 384	24.3	26.7
Perry	3 989	82.1	58 700	19.9	10.1	408	20.2	4.2	3 955	4.3	366	9.3	4 435	22.0	19.2
Phillips	9 711	56.3	46 900	19.9	12.8	357	29.2	7.7	4 812	-2.6	285	5.9	4 922	21.4	27.1
Pike	4 504	78.6	49 600	20.7	10.9	366	21.2	4.8	10 004	-2.6	978	9.8	10 675	18.7	31.4
Poinsett	10 026	66.8	49 500	19.8	10.8	346	23.3	3.1	8 834	-4.6	730	8.3	8 380	25.3	24.2
Polk	8 047	78.4	57 100	21.5	10.7	361	23.5	5.1	26 646	-1.1	1 556	5.8	24 613	27.7	22.2
Pope	20 701	71.2	71 100	18.5	9.9	427	23.2	3.6							
Prairie	3 894	72.8	55 600	20.7	10.5	336	21.2	2.6	3 892	-4.4	232	6.0	4 069	26.0	25.9
Pulaski	147 942	60.9	85 300	19.4	9.9	539	24.9	3.8	191 688	-1.3	9 911	5.2	172 712	36.4	11.5
Randolph	7 265	74.5	50 600	19.0	9.9	362	24.5	3.5	7 759	-5.7	916	11.8	7 594	24.7	31.9
St. Francis	10 043	63.2	56 000	20.4	11.7	403	28.8	5.8	12 126	-0.6	1 313	10.8	9 880	23.8	23.5
Saline	31 778	80.7	93 700	18.9	9.9	525	22.8	3.2	44 092	-1.0	2 018	4.6	40 045	27.8	15.0
Scott	4 323	74.2	48 000	18.3	10.7	343	21.7	5.3	4 408	-5.8	192	4.4	4 674	25.0	32.1
Searcy	3 523	77.7	45 600	21.7	11.3	293	25.4	5.6	2 806	-0.4	176	6.3	3 120	22.4	24.6
Sebastian	45 300	63.5	73 300	18.4	9.9	428	22.6	4.8	56 760	-1.8	2 863	5.0	53 010	27.5	25.8
Sevier	5 708	74.2	51 700	18.1	9.9	398	20.5	10.0	6 982	-1.7	314	4.5	6 774	20.9	31.0
Sharp	7 211	80.1	51 900	22.0	11.7	379	24.2	3.7	6 131	-1.0	543	8.9	6 012	25.2	22.7
Stone	4 768	77.9	64 200	23.7	11.8	349	23.4	4.9	4 896	-2.2	331	6.8	4 372	24.3	22.1
Union	17 989	72.9	55 400	19.2	11.5	408	24.3	4.4	20 958	-7.8	1 909	9.1	18 655	25.6	24.5
Van Buren	6 825	81.1	63 700	22.6	9.9	372	24.6	4.4	6 428	-1.5	491	7.6	6 080	22.7	21.9
Washington	60 151	59.4	90 100	19.4	9.9	490	25.7	5.9	87 584	1.0	2 807	3.2	77 114	31.8	17.0
White	25 148	73.0	72 100	19.4	10.5	416	23.4	3.8	32 266	-0.3	1 902	5.9	29 128	24.6	22.9
Woodruff	3 531	65.6	35 500	17.8	13.0	291	23.6	4.2	3 754	-7.9	475	12.7	3 474	22.1	25.6
Yell	7 922	72.9	60 600	19.9	11.6	372	20.9	5.9	9 846	-0.9	495	5.0	9 135	22.1	29.3
CALIFORNIA	11 502 870	56.9	211 500	25.3	9.9	747	27.7	15.6	17 460 005	0.5	1 177 322	6.7	14 718 928	36.0	12.7
Alameda	523 366	54.7	303 100	25.0	9.9	852	26.8	12.7	750 278	-0.8	50 968	6.8	692 833	42.3	11.8
Alpine	483	67.9	184 200	24.2	9.9	659	21.9	11.0	481	-3.2	47	9.8	628	26.6	9.1
Amador	12 759	75.4	153 600	24.8	10.9	685	26.0	3.9	15 173	-1.3	750	4.9	13 610	30.0	11.1

1. Specified owner-occupied units.　2. Median monthly owner costs is often in the minimum category—9.9 percent or less, which is indicated as 9.9 percent.　3. Specified renter-occupied units.　4. Overcrowded or lacking complete plumbing facilities.　5. Percent of civilian labor force.　6. Persons 16 years old and over.

Table B. States and Counties — Nonfarm Employment and Agriculture

STATE County	Number of establishments	Total	Health care and social assistance	Manufacturing	Retail trade	Finance and insurance	Professional, scientific, and technical services	Total (mil dol)	Average per employee (dollars)	Number	Less than 50 acres	500 acres and over	Farm operators whose principal occupation is farming (percent)
	104	105	106	107	108	109	110	111	112	113	114	115	116
ARKANSAS—Cont'd													
Conway	398	5 505	906	972	968	121	153	134	24 384	779	22.0	8.2	60.5
Craighead	2 257	34 201	5 706	8 020	5 617	876	772	825	24 115	730	29.3	29.7	67.7
Crawford	922	16 098	1 108	4 071	1 828	325	2 303	378	23 492	916	38.0	6.7	51.4
Crittenden	943	15 402	2 016	1 894	2 595	201	299	347	22 518	238	14.3	52.9	74.4
Cross	389	4 508	640	1 255	738	216	69	91	20 172	346	19.4	49.4	74.3
Dallas	263	2 855	631	852	462	75	22	63	21 929	125	24.0	13.6	52.8
Desha	401	3 886	622	1 128	804	156	67	95	24 353	264	14.0	55.3	74.6
Drew	454	7 447	865	2 249	1 043	191	225	134	18 011	296	19.9	19.9	51.0
Faulkner	1 827	30 852	3 425	6 720	4 247	688	523	831	26 932	1 317	35.7	7.1	50.8
Franklin	280	3 260	439	1 048	504	138	45	68	20 849	832	25.8	9.4	57.3
Fulton	164	1 306	261	313	166	66	D	22	16 469	820	14.5	16.3	53.4
Garland	2 616	30 794	6 349	3 908	5 970	846	827	685	22 232	386	42.0	3.6	51.3
Grant	278	3 005	200	1 348	434	74	46	68	22 791	251	39.8	4.8	45.8
Greene	793	12 884	1 300	5 875	1 810	339	478	277	21 488	827	27.2	17.8	56.0
Hempstead	433	8 311	944	4 321	959	169	70	179	21 563	783	25.3	14.0	59.0
Hot Spring	547	5 890	878	1 832	856	214	63	134	22 807	486	28.4	4.1	60.1
Howard	322	7 283	692	4 886	664	133	62	141	19 379	642	30.5	5.8	65.9
Independence	863	14 976	2 651	5 317	1 904	313	163	345	23 057	1 117	24.1	12.8	53.8
Izard	217	1 794	282	383	436	110	9	36	20 294	741	15.7	15.4	50.5
Jackson	437	4 932	1 105	905	779	204	114	106	21 591	398	19.1	35.9	62.6
Jefferson	1 606	26 526	4 506	7 402	4 437	840	651	677	25 535	378	28.0	30.4	69.3
Johnson	384	7 287	618	3 289	898	158	84	143	19 689	694	23.5	6.3	55.5
Lafayette	126	1 367	223	403	180	70	36	30	22 080	284	22.9	15.8	64.1
Lawrence	372	4 254	469	1 458	696	111	57	79	18 670	614	18.4	27.2	63.2
Lee	152	1 035	315	31	243	57	28	23	22 107	257	9.7	45.9	77.4
Lincoln	156	1 709	308	598	241	55	22	33	19 363	315	19.4	27.3	68.9
Little River	217	3 558	303	D	370	102	43	137	38 520	424	27.8	13.2	57.3
Logan	379	4 680	545	2 096	717	197	54	91	19 426	962	22.9	7.1	55.8
Lonoke	952	9 116	1 077	1 610	1 955	367	337	181	19 872	777	26.4	23.4	61.9
Madison	199	2 026	155	904	348	92	35	46	22 575	1 270	19.8	10.6	55.9
Marion	236	3 340	304	2 003	393	112	D	63	18 777	526	20.9	14.6	52.7
Miller	733	11 158	890	2 483	1 521	348	207	269	24 065	516	29.8	14.5	58.1
Mississippi	945	15 591	1 630	5 350	2 157	496	173	426	27 310	388	13.9	54.9	86.3
Monroe	232	1 986	261	208	390	181	D	32	16 168	250	14.0	53.2	79.6
Montgomery	166	1 106	43	260	178	77	16	19	17 387	413	24.9	9.0	63.4
Nevada	153	1 892	388	D	219	D	22	45	23 529	393	21.1	9.9	56.2
Newton	105	696	128	109	143	D	11	10	13 875	613	18.8	9.3	50.2
Ouachita	613	7 508	1 253	1 841	1 248	266	512	191	25 424	195	39.0	7.7	40.0
Perry	126	633	125	27	146	53	22	11	17 646	380	28.4	8.9	55.0
Phillips	523	5 478	1 456	692	1 079	191	109	110	20 170	301	15.9	49.5	80.4
Pike	264	2 347	229	591	414	141	63	43	18 396	393	28.0	8.4	56.2
Poinsett	419	4 776	463	1 908	771	246	60	93	19 571	448	12.9	57.1	75.2
Polk	495	5 795	569	1 420	812	158	113	118	20 398	845	31.5	7.1	59.4
Pope	1 456	22 266	2 382	4 410	3 811	523	637	558	25 050	1 044	30.2	6.0	55.3
Prairie	179	1 241	192	230	294	D	D	23	18 557	431	15.8	41.5	71.9
Pulaski	11 671	225 717	36 810	18 415	26 433	13 220	12 145	6 780	30 036	575	49.0	10.3	50.3
Randolph	338	4 680	588	1 790	740	121	64	89	19 006	710	14.1	19.4	52.5
St. Francis	562	10 714	851	5 912	1 378	230	134	210	19 599	347	16.7	35.2	65.1
Saline	1 375	16 782	2 521	2 349	3 856	425	368	379	22 569	432	50.2	5.1	51.9
Scott	173	2 715	272	1 433	353	51	24	49	18 058	697	24.4	6.5	62.4
Searcy	128	1 082	200	166	209	D	24	16	14 430	615	15.9	13.5	51.9
Sebastian	3 282	72 110	10 484	23 158	8 260	1 910	1 824	1 927	26 723	812	37.4	5.3	48.8
Sevier	303	5 111	703	2 399	630	128	42	102	19 942	590	29.3	7.8	60.3
Sharp	373	3 091	606	389	680	170	55	48	15 497	680	19.6	14.0	52.9
Stone	231	2 061	68	769	484	77	32	35	16 816	681	19.5	11.9	57.3
Union	1 252	18 898	2 224	6 007	2 347	561	345	520	27 520	342	44.4	3.8	51.8
Van Buren	305	3 001	450	713	673	97	44	54	17 981	603	16.1	8.6	54.2
Washington	4 329	71 828	8 218	16 538	10 698	2 039	2 581	1 850	25 761	2 800	41.0	4.6	54.5
White	1 436	21 674	3 049	5 226	3 187	536	312	507	23 376	1 823	31.4	10.2	50.5
Woodruff	144	1 589	151	390	235	D	11	37	23 040	225	9.3	59.6	82.2
Yell	362	5 846	655	3 000	602	199	41	115	19 615	829	28.6	9.2	61.6
CALIFORNIA	806 733	13 239 616	1 374 627	1 740 754	1 531 595	649 558	1 177 669	521 765	39 409	79 631	61.7	10.5	61.7
Alameda	36 468	670 375	73 668	95 807	67 787	23 332	50 426	29 760	44 392	424	52.4	15.1	48.3
Alpine	55	1 282	D	0	D	0	D	15	11 499	14	21.4	28.6	71.4
Amador	852	7 861	1 170	850	1 710	246	216	198	25 210	451	43.2	10.9	59.9

Items 104—116

Table B. States and Counties — **Agriculture**

STATE County	Land in farms — Acreage (1,000)	Percent change, 1997–2002	Average size of farm	Total irrigated (1,000)	Total cropland (1,000)	Value of land and buildings (dollars) Average per farm	Average per acre	Value of machinery and equipment average per farm (dollars)	Value of products sold Total (mil dol)	Average per farm (dollars)	Percent from — Crops	Livestock and poultry products	Percent of farms with sales of — $10,000 or more	$100,000 or more	Government payments Total ($1,000)	Percent of farms
	117	118	119	120	121	122	123	124	125	126	127	128	129	130	131	132
ARKANSAS—Cont'd																
Conway	173	6.1	223	11	102	358 184	1 672	46 283	101	129 030	6.5	93.5	46.1	25.4	644	7.6
Craighead	350	-3.6	480	240	322	750 815	1 720	124 645	89	121 361	96.3	3.7	52.7	28.5	11 349	38.9
Crawford	151	8.6	165	4	82	268 233	1 757	41 816	57	62 225	27.6	72.4	27.7	8.6	217	4.7
Crittenden	306	-4.4	1 284	137	294	1 659 153	1 290	228 221	64	268 974	99.4	0.6	71.4	50.0	10 014	59.2
Cross	326	-5.2	942	219	294	1 298 432	1 385	220 218	67	193 397	99.0	1.0	64.5	39.9	12 432	52.3
Dallas	26	13.0	207	0	8	293 213	1 304	18 526	2	14 235	D	D	12.8	1.6	19	5.6
Desha	285	3.3	1 078	188	250	1 192 420	1 103	238 790	72	271 326	92.9	7.1	74.6	47.7	6 568	53.4
Drew	116	-5.7	393	51	81	505 386	1 255	99 965	27	91 604	71.9	28.1	45.3	18.2	2 054	26.4
Faulkner	225	6.6	171	6	120	352 252	1 823	41 772	20	15 226	28.6	71.4	21.4	3.1	951	9.0
Franklin	176	2.9	211	1	85	319 515	1 589	51 756	96	115 163	2.3	97.7	40.0	14.7	167	4.7
Fulton	250	9.6	304	0	92	328 349	1 019	26 324	16	19 115	4.2	95.8	35.1	3.2	418	14.4
Garland	46	7.0	120	0	18	258 863	2 260	23 075	10	24 939	22.9	77.1	15.0	3.4	D	D
Grant	37	12.1	147	D	17	224 379	1 716	28 799	6	24 180	18.0	82.0	22.3	2.8	13	3.2
Greene	262	-0.4	317	129	215	502 313	1 556	79 408	50	60 696	84.2	15.8	38.6	15.4	8 032	41.5
Hempstead	204	7.9	260	1	85	362 266	1 396	60 112	144	183 434	1.6	98.4	47.4	25.0	371	8.6
Hot Spring	74	-1.3	153	D	33	219 637	1 553	31 484	11	22 637	10.4	89.6	28.0	3.9	71	3.1
Howard	110	1.9	171	1	53	292 525	1 647	55 732	135	209 858	0.6	99.4	62.5	41.1	43	5.0
Independence	288	1.8	258	19	141	308 953	1 243	39 562	90	80 259	12.7	87.3	32.2	9.5	2 053	10.3
Izard	215	14.4	290	0	75	346 278	1 153	45 571	26	34 427	2.4	97.6	30.2	4.2	349	20.2
Jackson	332	-0.9	835	184	287	980 328	1 184	150 869	60	151 888	95.3	4.7	58.8	32.9	11 239	47.7
Jefferson	276	-4.5	729	176	248	902 375	1 216	153 672	69	181 648	90.0	10.0	52.4	27.2	10 475	38.6
Johnson	118	2.6	170	1	62	303 383	2 234	56 816	98	141 866	2.3	97.7	35.4	19.2	105	2.6
Lafayette	104	6.1	366	11	69	393 845	1 067	69 901	78	273 271	8.6	91.4	59.2	40.5	1 102	14.1
Lawrence	296	0.7	482	129	230	673 568	1 275	101 364	60	98 316	69.9	30.1	49.5	24.8	10 025	31.3
Lee	278	-0.7	1 082	142	259	1 140 869	1 033	201 944	68	263 419	97.5	2.5	69.6	38.9	6 341	57.6
Lincoln	199	8.2	632	113	161	743 613	1 146	131 563	97	306 477	40.4	59.6	55.9	37.5	5 560	35.6
Little River	147	0.7	347	3	77	344 992	1 121	40 283	40	94 075	14.2	85.8	38.0	17.2	737	10.6
Logan	200	0.5	208	1	100	299 801	1 522	45 503	114	118 568	2.6	97.4	40.2	16.8	282	4.4
Lonoke	361	-7.7	465	200	290	638 992	1 389	101 317	98	126 070	71.0	29.0	43.6	22.4	9 944	34.5
Madison	295	4.6	232	1	117	365 784	1 371	49 096	108	85 291	1.5	98.5	40.0	17.0	194	4.4
Marion	143	2.1	272	0	49	386 985	1 312	41 161	21	39 645	1.2	98.8	32.3	4.8	254	14.6
Miller	158	2.6	307	9	96	297 641	1 045	43 483	38	72 756	22.4	77.6	36.0	13.4	1 402	11.8
Mississippi	469	-4.1	1 207	230	458	1 644 076	1 351	294 445	136	349 301	99.8	0.2	80.4	51.8	10 365	55.4
Monroe	232	-1.7	928	156	209	1 096 647	1 169	194 713	50	200 884	91.3	8.7	74.4	44.4	6 828	54.8
Montgomery	78	5.4	189	1	39	268 784	1 499	45 939	43	103 024	1.5	98.5	46.5	24.2	9	2.4
Nevada	82	12.3	208	D	37	202 113	1 075	49 534	31	79 113	1.2	98.8	41.5	14.8	93	8.4
Newton	131	20.2	214	0	45	294 638	1 495	25 464	7	10 848	4.6	95.4	21.9	1.6	388	21.9
Ouachita	33	13.8	169	D	12	254 227	1 428	29 125	6	29 562	4.3	95.7	16.9	4.6	53	8.2
Perry	68	-6.8	178	6	41	236 689	1 772	37 158	32	85 297	13.8	86.2	36.3	16.1	196	7.9
Phillips	329	-8.9	1 093	157	315	1 141 630	1 045	191 649	83	276 948	99.2	0.8	72.1	45.8	10 381	56.1
Pike	68	-6.8	173	0	30	288 132	1 787	34 329	46	117 689	1.1	98.9	47.1	23.7	35	6.9
Poinsett	382	-4.7	852	290	353	1 314 421	1 590	205 662	92	205 600	98.3	1.7	78.8	52.0	18 235	63.8
Polk	146	9.8	173	0	61	260 900	1 713	40 108	82	96 569	0.5	99.5	39.8	22.1	23	2.1
Pope	169	11.2	161	2	83	286 656	1 946	47 120	106	101 357	2.6	97.4	35.7	18.1	257	4.4
Prairie	308	2.0	714	177	252	944 440	1 245	137 264	64	148 419	87.3	12.7	55.5	35.3	7 917	57.5
Pulaski	118	6.3	206	22	77	370 457	1 767	46 144	20	35 530	77.8	22.2	21.0	6.8	1 456	12.5
Randolph	246	-7.5	347	51	142	479 792	1 291	52 276	36	50 958	49.3	50.7	39.0	11.0	4 521	20.3
St. Francis	279	-3.8	805	148	244	985 224	1 217	161 753	54	155 342	96.2	3.8	53.0	32.9	7 655	47.6
Saline	56	12.0	130	0	25	329 640	2 393	32 799	4	8 891	34.4	65.6	16.0	1.6	20	2.3
Scott	124	6.9	177	0	59	241 397	1 584	37 216	93	132 850	0.4	99.6	43.3	24.8	32	3.9
Searcy	183	-2.7	298	0	60	347 382	994	27 937	9	15 144	4.1	95.9	30.6	3.3	285	15.8
Sebastian	122	6.1	150	1	54	316 312	2 146	29 136	50	61 598	6.0	94.0	28.4	8.6	39	2.2
Sevier	124	-6.8	210	1	54	293 648	1 698	43 397	114	193 617	0.6	99.4	46.9	32.4	182	5.4
Sharp	178	2.3	262	0	63	267 510	1 022	37 014	40	58 454	1.4	98.6	31.5	11.0	111	6.5
Stone	164	15.5	241	0	57	264 908	1 013	39 338	39	57 051	2.4	97.6	35.5	12.5	192	11.7
Union	40	17.6	118	D	15	205 137	2 138	41 024	59	173 015	0.5	99.5	30.4	20.5	24	1.5
Van Buren	132	0.0	218	0	55	296 408	1 425	43 679	15	24 816	7.4	92.6	27.9	6.1	248	7.8
Washington	368	9.9	131	1	171	363 663	2 779	36 773	314	112 012	1.4	98.6	33.9	14.6	389	2.5
White	394	0.0	216	41	224	313 848	1 586	36 140	50	27 446	42.8	57.2	25.2	4.6	4 062	19.5
Woodruff	275	-3.5	1 221	157	244	1 406 694	1 135	194 535	53	233 967	D	D	70.2	47.6	8 029	68.4
Yell	181	-3.7	219	5	90	310 329	1 277	55 224	113	136 516	3.5	96.5	41.9	23.6	381	6.4
CALIFORNIA	27 589	-0.4	346	8 709	10 994	1 206 822	3 526	81 933	25 737	323 205	74.4	25.6	54.0	24.6	168 698	9.1
Alameda	218	-15.5	514	6	32	1 373 149	2 787	41 975	43	101 962	83.8	16.2	38.2	9.9	178	4.7
Alpine	D	D	D	7	D	1 864 526	2 500	71 000	1	43 926	D	D	50.0	14.3	0	0.0
Amador	194	-4.9	430	12	22	1 038 777	1 941	22 537	21	47 079	57.8	42.2	37.3	10.2	38	1.6

STATE County	Value of residential construction authorized by building permits, 2003		Wholesale trade, 1997				Retail trade,[1] 1997				Real estate and rental and leasing, 1997			
	New construction ($1,000)	Number of housing units	Number of establishments	Number of employees	Sales (mil dol)	Annual payroll (mil dol)	Number of establishments	Number of employees	Sales (mil dol)	Annual payroll (mil dol)	Number of establishments	Number of employees	Receipts (mil dol)	Annual payroll (mil dol)
	133	134	135	136	137	138	139	140	141	142	143	144	145	146
ARKANSAS—Cont'd														
Conway	1 252	13	23	D	D	D	91	948	157.1	12.3	8	28	1.6	0.3
Craighead	57 290	646	140	1 548	509.7	35.6	480	5 589	854.3	80.8	86	349	41.5	5.9
Crawford	30 137	303	58	373	170.1	9.3	171	1 599	268.5	22.8	38	114	9.9	1.6
Crittenden	28 098	327	64	D	D	D	206	2 722	496.9	33.1	38	137	15.1	2.4
Cross	5 848	40	22	344	102.7	7.1	80	720	129.8	10.5	10	27	2.4	0.2
Dallas	392	5	13	D	D	D	63	480	63.3	6.1	5	D	D	D
Desha	2 272	33	23	D	D	D	99	859	159.4	12.2	15	48	2.3	0.6
Drew	1 218	26	21	170	78.4	4.8	102	952	153.7	12.3	17	87	6.6	1.2
Faulkner	110 728	888	76	826	242.0	17.0	309	3 423	571.2	51.5	66	145	18.6	2.3
Franklin	853	13	8	D	D	D	63	461	71.2	5.9	6	21	0.6	0.2
Fulton	0	0	8	D	D	D	40	184	21.8	1.9	6	6	1.5	0.2
Garland	14 102	129	110	898	966.5	25.5	498	5 023	875.8	74.8	106	285	33.9	5.7
Grant	2 428	28	14	113	28.7	2.2	54	450	58.5	6.0	6	8	0.9	0.2
Greene	15 007	195	55	571	115.5	9.9	183	1 649	263.2	22.0	22	43	7.2	0.8
Hempstead	1 603	19	17	D	D	D	111	925	134.4	12.0	19	69	4.7	1.0
Hot Spring	436	7	28	170	54.0	4.1	99	787	144.6	11.1	10	36	2.0	0.6
Howard	1 364	14	14	44	12.7	0.7	73	634	88.2	8.0	7	26	0.8	0.1
Independence	2 656	21	50	624	172.5	12.6	195	1 741	284.2	23.2	26	66	5.5	0.9
Izard	1 127	12	9	D	D	D	57	374	71.0	4.8	12	49	2.8	0.4
Jackson	622	7	29	D	D	D	108	862	152.4	12.0	15	51	4.7	1.0
Jefferson	11 020	212	77	780	309.8	18.9	393	4 785	726.6	71.8	58	368	23.8	5.8
Johnson	2 594	32	9	D	D	D	104	988	155.5	13.4	16	41	4.0	0.9
Lafayette	0	0	2	D	D	D	40	216	22.1	2.1	8	15	1.5	0.2
Lawrence	1 627	14	21	173	85.2	3.7	88	710	122.0	9.5	8	20	0.6	0.1
Lee	1 182	33	10	95	63.7	2.3	39	273	40.8	3.6	5	11	0.4	0.1
Lincoln	83	2	7	D	D	D	28	228	30.6	2.9	4	11	0.7	0.1
Little River	1 192	13	16	76	22.5	2.2	57	396	77.4	5.2	10	26	1.3	0.2
Logan	618	17	17	D	D	D	94	707	119.5	9.5	10	14	1.4	0.1
Lonoke	53 190	596	37	321	144.4	7.3	178	1 622	269.1	23.3	27	75	3.8	0.8
Madison	2 289	36	2	D	D	D	41	282	47.7	4.0	3	10	0.2	0.1
Marion	1 721	24	8	D	D	D	39	360	46.2	4.5	10	D	D	D
Miller	16 111	297	49	D	D	D	167	1 512	254.1	21.0	24	75	4.9	0.8
Mississippi	1 450	23	60	457	237.9	13.1	261	2 117	361.8	29.1	33	138	9.7	1.7
Monroe	1 513	31	13	65	33.6	1.7	72	488	89.8	7.2	3	D	D	D
Montgomery	NA	NA	12	34	16.6	0.6	36	174	20.9	2.4	9	10	0.9	0.2
Nevada	37 713	243	5	21	18.2	0.9	40	261	37.0	3.1	NA	NA	NA	NA
Newton	85	1	7	D	D	D	16	121	15.1	1.5	3	10	0.5	0.1
Ouachita	482	5	31	264	121.0	6.8	148	1 380	198.2	19.3	22	156	16.0	3.5
Perry	150	3	3	D	D	D	27	154	19.0	1.7	2	D	D	D
Phillips	205	2	30	D	D	D	151	1 310	187.6	16.9	18	127	9.1	2.2
Pike	NA	NA	13	107	45.5	1.6	60	441	72.7	5.2	5	36	1.0	0.4
Poinsett	3 821	44	24	267	179.0	7.7	111	760	118.1	10.0	14	52	4.3	0.8
Polk	1 528	21	18	65	10.1	0.8	99	828	121.3	10.2	19	50	2.5	0.5
Pope	10 525	109	81	543	193.9	16.6	302	3 168	502.4	45.4	52	177	10.9	2.3
Prairie	1 382	19	8	53	18.5	1.3	54	246	36.6	3.1	4	8	0.4	0.0
Pulaski	323 058	1 902	882	14 654	9 759.8	455.7	1 847	26 898	4 584.4	415.1	472	3 405	394.4	64.1
Randolph	1 331	43	16	95	28.5	2.2	73	705	96.1	9.1	8	16	0.8	0.1
St. Francis	1 532	14	36	392	303.7	9.1	144	1 485	259.3	21.3	14	29	2.3	0.3
Saline	91 904	681	78	514	204.2	14.1	250	2 860	793.4	51.9	53	125	13.7	1.7
Scott	370	5	8	84	39.4	1.2	40	343	42.2	4.1	4	7	0.6	0.1
Searcy	0	0	7	D	D	D	40	253	31.4	2.6	2	D	D	D
Sebastian	44 722	416	245	2 101	708.5	56.8	659	8 721	1 360.6	128.1	135	670	81.6	12.4
Sevier	600	8	12	88	39.7	3.1	70	710	86.4	8.1	8	18	2.4	0.4
Sharp	0	0	11	D	D	D	91	778	112.6	8.6	17	D	D	D
Stone	914	9	11	D	D	D	63	470	66.3	6.4	3	4	0.2	0.0
Union	3 234	31	78	511	119.7	12.3	263	2 603	408.6	36.5	38	234	20.3	3.8
Van Buren	210	2	9	17	4.2	0.2	78	536	71.7	6.5	5	53	5.0	1.8
Washington	335 196	4 342	278	3 203	6 815.1	101.4	762	9 555	1 444.9	141.6	184	687	90.7	11.5
White	29 057	433	85	624	243.0	14.2	312	2 997	509.0	42.5	53	162	15.1	2.1
Woodruff	165	3	17	163	112.0	5.3	48	268	34.1	3.2	4	9	0.6	0.1
Yell	1 341	27	19	68	17.0	1.3	70	638	93.2	7.3	15	46	3.0	0.5
CALIFORNIA	31 778 214	191 948	57 842	755 513	551 230.6	29 900.2	106 357	1 354 797	263 118.3	26 362.7	37 244	243 288	38 288.4	6 570.5
Alameda	942 388	4 469	3 232	51 312	47 790.8	2 155.3	4 363	59 289	12 404.9	1 227.8	1 665	10 321	1 645.6	266.1
Alpine	12 117	28	NA	NA	NA	NA	7	28	2.3	0.2	5	18	1.6	0.2
Amador	47 404	402	28	D	D	D	158	1 570	475.0	25.7	36	155	16.8	2.2

1. Establishments with payroll.

Table B. States and Counties — **Professional Services, Manufacturing, and Accommodation and Foodservices**

STATE County	Professional, scientific, and technical services,[1] 1997				Manufacturing, 1997				Accommodation and foodservices, 1997			
	Number of establishments	Number of employees	Receipts (mil dol)	Annual payroll (mil dol)	Number of establishments	Number of employees	Receipts (mil dol)	Annual payroll (mil dol)	Number of establishments	Number of employees	Sales (mil dol)	Annual payroll (mil dol)
	147	148	149	150	151	152	153	154	155	156	157	158
ARKANSAS—Cont'd												
Conway	26	60	3.3	1.0	23	2 108	334.8	49.4	29	342	10.4	2.6
Craighead	148	675	53.4	19.3	122	6 886	1 257.6	184.9	133	2 720	80.2	21.6
Crawford	51	827	26.2	17.3	62	D	D	D	65	961	32.5	7.9
Crittenden	50	300	14.1	4.8	45	2 323	620.6	56.2	84	1 561	51.1	13.3
Cross	19	55	2.3	0.6	17	1 698	286.0	37.8	21	412	8.3	2.3
Dallas	9	31	1.3	0.4	15	786	131.3	21.9	10	D	D	D
Desha	24	57	3.2	0.9	16	1 611	319.2	45.1	35	263	8.0	1.7
Drew	21	72	4.3	1.4	33	2 429	222.0	51.2	31	507	15.3	3.7
Faulkner	81	520	42.6	12.3	93	7 556	1 230.5	189.0	112	2 389	69.3	19.0
Franklin	11	30	1.7	0.5	16	1 284	216.0	24.2	27	211	5.9	1.5
Fulton	10	23	0.7	0.3	NA	NA	NA	NA	17	106	3.4	1.0
Garland	167	673	46.3	17.4	108	3 827	795.5	100.0	222	4 005	120.2	36.8
Grant	14	49	3.5	1.4	25	1 481	314.6	42.0	11	D	D	D
Greene	45	269	12.1	6.8	47	5 223	961.3	126.6	54	768	20.8	5.9
Hempstead	22	66	2.8	0.8	32	3 565	558.9	75.9	34	519	14.9	3.8
Hot Spring	29	82	3.5	1.0	47	1 764	315.2	45.3	33	454	13.5	3.6
Howard	14	34	1.8	0.6	26	5 067	1 120.2	94.5	18	224	6.7	1.8
Independence	50	157	11.6	3.3	54	5 168	1 013.3	123.3	48	812	22.6	5.8
Izard	7	7	0.4	0.1	NA	NA	NA	NA	20	88	2.1	0.6
Jackson	30	82	5.2	1.6	23	1 129	199.9	31.5	28	284	8.6	2.3
Jefferson	85	619	38.1	14.5	84	7 774	1 741.5	218.8	131	2 049	57.9	15.0
Johnson	22	58	3.2	0.9	39	3 318	409.4	65.1	36	456	13.7	3.4
Lafayette	7	27	0.7	0.2	NA	NA	NA	NA	9	61	1.6	0.4
Lawrence	18	42	1.9	0.5	37	1 615	215.5	31.2	28	284	7.7	2.1
Lee	9	70	2.6	0.7	NA	NA	NA	NA	8	D	D	D
Lincoln	4	6	0.6	0.1	8	D	D	D	7	63	1.9	0.4
Little River	11	41	2.3	0.8	16	D	D	D	23	D	D	D
Logan	19	36	2.2	0.5	36	2 569	393.0	44.8	33	335	8.7	2.2
Lonoke	57	204	10.7	3.7	39	1 739	269.8	45.4	53	728	21.3	5.3
Madison	12	32	1.8	0.5	19	738	170.7	12.8	9	79	2.1	0.6
Marion	10	22	1.4	0.5	23	1 847	133.7	29.5	30	191	6.1	1.6
Miller	38	167	12.7	4.2	25	2 274	495.6	99.7	79	1 363	45.8	11.6
Mississippi	45	125	8.0	2.7	62	7 644	2 801.7	252.7	74	1 254	36.2	8.6
Monroe	13	55	3.1	1.0	NA	NA	NA	NA	24	430	12.0	2.9
Montgomery	9	18	0.9	0.3	NA	NA	NA	NA	14	148	9.4	2.0
Nevada	8	26	1.4	0.4	8	D	D	D	9	113	3.8	1.2
Newton	3	D	D	D	NA	NA	NA	NA	10	69	1.9	0.5
Ouachita	18	99	6.5	2.6	33	2 961	854.3	96.0	40	626	18.0	4.4
Perry	6	11	0.8	0.2	NA	NA	NA	NA	8	31	1.0	0.2
Phillips	33	94	6.6	1.4	19	983	411.8	24.1	39	369	9.4	2.5
Pike	6	16	0.5	0.2	13	596	121.5	12.0	26	205	4.8	1.3
Poinsett	19	40	2.1	0.5	27	1 895	367.1	42.5	34	249	9.5	2.0
Polk	27	131	14.5	6.0	29	1 933	322.2	38.2	34	435	14.5	3.6
Pope	82	355	19.5	7.4	82	4 940	1 222.1	118.4	106	2 025	50.5	13.8
Prairie	8	20	1.1	0.3	NA	NA	NA	NA	17	132	3.5	0.8
Pulaski	1 217	9 974	918.2	406.5	431	20 557	4 342.4	572.8	801	16 728	508.0	144.7
Randolph	18	59	2.9	0.8	32	1 688	190.5	37.6	27	D	D	D
St. Francis	30	119	7.9	2.4	27	1 606	628.2	41.1	54	822	24.2	6.4
Saline	78	224	19.6	6.3	72	1 827	352.7	56.8	83	1 368	46.3	12.2
Scott	8	14	0.6	0.2	19	1 367	220.7	27.1	17	D	D	D
Searcy	4	13	0.5	0.2	NA	NA	NA	NA	10	88	2.1	0.7
Sebastian	227	1 262	101.0	29.4	233	22 891	4 319.3	582.0	257	4 669	138.9	38.1
Sevier	20	35	1.9	0.7	15	1 985	402.0	37.3	22	D	D	D
Sharp	17	35	1.9	0.7	NA	NA	NA	NA	41	379	10.1	2.6
Stone	12	37	1.5	0.5	26	602	39.8	10.4	21	278	7.6	1.9
Union	67	371	22.8	8.1	63	5 443	2 082.2	158.1	68	1 007	28.1	6.6
Van Buren	15	38	2.0	0.7	15	638	111.5	12.5	27	336	8.9	2.4
Washington	336	1 629	121.3	44.1	193	14 795	2 388.9	357.1	372	6 181	183.4	50.9
White	65	263	16.0	5.5	75	4 149	646.5	103.3	95	1 323	48.1	11.0
Woodruff	6	13	0.5	0.2	9	796	78.4	14.0	6	34	0.9	0.2
Yell	15	185	4.1	2.7	22	2 880	337.7	52.4	18	D	D	D
CALIFORNIA	78 635	805 856	89 555.7	35 258.6	49 418	1 809 667	379 612.4	65 762.8	62 532	1 052 715	42 261.1	11 437.2
Alameda	3 667	30 441	3 875.3	1 498.3	2 507	93 809	22 337.8	3 803.0	2 773	38 360	1 573.2	417.8
Alpine	1	D	D	D	NA	NA	NA	NA	16	148	6.0	1.4
Amador	50	119	9.3	2.7	51	732	136.8	19.5	105	910	29.5	8.1

1. Firms subject to federal tax.

Table B. States and Counties — Health Care and Social Assistance, Other Services, and Federal Funds

STATE County	Health care and social assistance,[1] 1997				Other services,[1] 1997				Federal funds and grants, 2002–2003 Expenditures (mil dol)			
										Direct payments for individuals[2]		
	Number of establishments	Number of employees	Receipts (mil dol)	Annual payroll (mil dol)	Number of establishments	Number of employees	Receipts (mil dol)	Annual payroll (mil dol)	Total	Social Security and government retirement	Medicare	Food stamps and Supplemental Security Income
	159	160	161	162	163	164	165	166	167	168	169	170
ARKANSAS—Cont'd												
Conway	28	745	21.8	9.7	15	75	4.2	1.3	133.1	62.0	23.9	6.0
Craighead	214	3 357	245.4	115.8	118	623	39.5	10.0	412.6	165.1	62.1	20.0
Crawford	51	957	52.0	21.2	64	364	30.8	6.5	255.0	125.4	43.1	10.8
Crittenden	66	768	42.0	16.7	64	439	25.7	7.3	337.7	84.6	47.4	23.7
Cross	26	299	12.3	5.8	21	74	4.3	1.0	129.0	39.5	19.3	7.5
Dallas	14	707	23.6	11.6	13	56	2.9	0.8	58.2	22.8	14.8	3.4
Desha	21	499	22.0	11.1	17	59	2.6	0.7	151.3	32.8	20.6	7.1
Drew	29	281	14.4	5.2	27	114	7.7	1.4	123.6	35.9	18.1	5.0
Faulkner	137	1 330	74.4	34.5	82	520	27.4	8.1	404.0	173.7	50.6	10.4
Franklin	18	243	9.6	4.8	14	100	3.3	1.2	120.4	48.3	18.3	4.0
Fulton	8	153	5.3	1.7	12	26	1.4	0.3	78.4	38.8	13.3	3.0
Garland	202	3 342	226.8	93.7	133	670	31.1	10.0	628.3	341.4	139.7	20.4
Grant	14	154	6.7	2.6	15	35	2.3	0.5	67.9	38.5	12.4	2.2
Greene	65	421	28.4	10.9	46	202	10.7	2.8	217.7	85.9	33.4	9.0
Hempstead	49	848	38.5	16.9	32	178	12.0	3.2	123.8	47.6	28.7	6.1
Hot Spring	32	331	14.0	5.8	26	78	5.1	1.3	155.0	75.6	35.3	6.1
Howard	31	404	11.8	4.8	17	74	3.9	0.9	77.9	33.8	19.3	3.4
Independence	71	792	41.5	19.2	45	182	12.5	3.3	197.2	85.2	35.7	8.1
Izard	9	336	6.8	2.6	15	25	2.5	0.5	87.8	46.5	17.3	3.2
Jackson	45	922	62.3	18.6	29	97	5.8	1.5	160.9	42.5	42.2	6.5
Jefferson	191	1 709	110.3	48.3	110	750	40.7	12.6	771.3	201.2	81.6	36.5
Johnson	24	278	12.2	5.3	28	99	6.5	1.3	111.5	55.1	20.6	5.6
Lafayette	6	109	4.4	1.8	7	32	1.7	0.5	67.0	20.4	13.6	4.0
Lawrence	16	122	6.4	2.5	26	88	5.7	1.1	130.9	49.3	24.7	5.5
Lee	11	135	4.3	1.5	11	18	1.2	0.2	112.9	20.7	13.5	8.3
Lincoln	9	206	5.2	2.4	11	54	6.3	2.0	137.1	22.7	11.5	4.0
Little River	14	155	4.5	2.0	11	34	2.6	0.7	82.3	40.5	14.6	2.9
Logan	22	238	10.5	4.5	24	100	5.8	1.3	125.8	63.6	22.4	5.3
Lonoke	51	800	29.5	13.9	50	152	8.8	2.2	265.4	137.7	41.1	7.5
Madison	10	47	2.4	1.0	8	30	4.1	1.3	63.2	33.5	10.2	2.6
Marion	8	102	4.0	1.2	12	23	2.4	0.4	91.4	52.1	15.3	4.0
Miller	34	573	23.9	8.9	41	298	14.2	4.5	251.5	89.1	51.9	14.9
Mississippi	72	731	31.3	14.0	51	341	28.0	7.8	325.4	105.6	50.7	24.1
Monroe	11	174	5.4	2.1	15	47	3.7	0.7	112.1	23.7	14.5	5.8
Montgomery	7	19	1.0	0.2	6	13	0.6	0.2	53.8	26.5	10.9	2.3
Nevada	7	193	6.6	3.2	9	33	2.2	0.6	60.4	23.9	15.5	3.3
Newton	1	D	D	D	3	3	0.2	0.0	50.4	21.4	6.6	3.2
Ouachita	40	632	28.3	10.6	37	181	10.2	2.9	194.7	78.5	38.0	11.7
Perry	9	102	3.2	1.4	2	D	D	D	54.7	29.0	10.4	2.1
Phillips	45	449	19.0	7.8	24	86	5.7	1.2	245.0	53.3	33.8	21.3
Pike	11	156	4.5	2.0	5	34	1.8	0.5	58.1	27.7	12.9	1.6
Poinsett	20	315	9.1	4.1	25	49	3.7	0.8	210.5	58.8	30.5	10.4
Polk	36	341	14.4	4.9	33	92	5.6	1.1	115.5	60.0	24.1	5.1
Pope	107	1 999	139.8	54.3	93	458	23.2	6.6	258.5	120.7	39.1	12.7
Prairie	12	207	6.6	3.0	15	48	3.6	0.5	62.3	22.2	12.8	1.9
Pulaski	1 002	12 393	955.6	448.5	698	4 422	273.2	78.7	3 664.4	1 022.1	344.9	89.5
Randolph	21	293	16.0	6.1	20	47	3.3	0.8	104.3	47.0	18.3	4.9
St. Francis	35	412	19.6	7.5	29	148	7.4	2.1	236.8	54.1	29.1	18.2
Saline	87	1 069	55.0	24.5	83	403	24.3	7.2	237.6	140.0	47.2	8.6
Scott	5	24	1.3	0.7	5	17	1.4	0.3	62.0	30.1	10.7	2.8
Searcy	6	145	3.0	1.2	1	D	D	D	60.7	25.2	9.7	2.7
Sebastian	288	4 698	337.1	152.7	192	1 278	74.3	20.6	570.6	267.1	104.5	24.5
Sevier	27	442	24.3	9.0	22	89	5.3	1.3	72.0	34.2	16.1	2.8
Sharp	21	172	6.6	2.8	15	39	1.8	0.4	132.9	65.7	25.6	4.8
Stone	13	286	19.3	4.9	7	19	1.3	0.3	76.0	37.5	13.8	3.3
Union	95	1 607	100.9	37.0	74	391	25.2	6.1	279.7	118.6	56.4	14.5
Van Buren	11	49	2.7	0.9	15	38	2.5	0.4	104.4	57.3	20.6	4.1
Washington	290	2 938	192.9	92.0	232	1 421	71.8	22.1	644.5	293.2	91.3	20.1
White	97	1 798	122.5	47.4	85	549	28.4	7.8	355.2	166.8	61.2	12.9
Woodruff	10	94	4.6	2.3	5	16	0.9	0.2	108.8	20.2	16.2	4.2
Yell	28	406	16.2	7.4	16	62	3.5	0.7	114.5	54.9	21.7	4.3
CALIFORNIA	69 857	664 539	51 968.0	20 619.3	44 642	282 762	20 521.5	5 852.2	219 705.7	56 328.7	31 692.5	6 715.7
Alameda	3 124	32 552	2 698.7	1 066.4	2 164	14 520	1 186.7	346.2	9 967.5	2 201.0	1 364.9	291.8
Alpine	2	D	D	D	1	D	D	D	7.6	4.8	0.9	0.1
Amador	70	631	26.6	8.9	32	98	8.1	1.6	190.4	105.8	46.2	2.9

1. Firms subject to federal tax.   2. State totals may include programs not allocated by county.

	Federal funds and grants, 2002–2003 (cont'd)							Local government finances, 2002				
	Expenditures (mil dol) (cont'd)							General revenue				
	Procurement contract awards			Grants[1]							Taxes	
											Per capita[2] (dollars)	
STATE County	Salaries and wages	Defense	Other	Medicaid and other health-related	Nutrition and family welfare	Education	Other	Total (mil dol)	Intergovern-mental (mil dol)	Total (mil dol)	Total	Property
	171	172	173	174	175	176	177	178	179	180	181	182
ARKANSAS—Cont'd												
Conway	4.1	0.1	1.1	22.4	2.4	1.4	4.7	34.7	22.4	6.5	318	122
Craighead	26.7	0.1	5.8	47.3	13.3	7.2	22.3	195.4	97.5	46.0	547	255
Crawford	6.6	7.8	1.7	23.6	5.4	4.2	24.8	98.7	66.0	18.4	335	148
Crittenden	7.1	1.5	1.7	79.2	9.7	5.8	61.0	121.6	70.3	28.3	552	166
Cross	4.3	9.2	0.7	21.7	3.5	1.5	1.3	38.3	27.2	6.5	336	178
Dallas	1.9	0.6	0.4	11.4	1.6	0.8	0.3	16.7	11.5	3.2	368	177
Desha	6.2	21.1	0.5	27.0	4.2	1.7	13.9	45.7	25.3	8.5	577	402
Drew	4.6	11.3	1.2	17.2	2.2	3.8	16.0	48.0	22.6	8.8	472	157
Faulkner	13.5	1.1	2.7	25.4	9.1	4.0	99.6	166.0	92.7	35.9	401	180
Franklin	13.7	2.3	1.2	10.0	1.1	1.7	19.0	31.6	22.5	5.2	292	150
Fulton	1.8	0.0	0.4	10.0	0.9	0.5	9.3	17.7	11.2	2.2	190	88
Garland	34.3	5.7	9.2	44.8	7.1	8.6	11.3	181.6	98.0	46.0	511	168
Grant	2.8	0.0	0.6	6.9	0.9	1.2	2.3	35.2	26.0	4.5	268	174
Greene	5.6	3.0	1.2	29.3	2.8	1.8	32.6	72.0	41.9	12.3	324	102
Hempstead	5.2	0.0	0.9	20.1	3.0	2.9	6.5	46.8	28.9	9.0	383	98
Hot Spring	6.6	3.2	1.0	16.9	2.8	2.4	3.2	52.3	33.8	9.0	294	158
Howard	3.8	0.0	0.6	11.5	1.4	1.0	2.6	32.6	21.1	5.6	391	163
Independence	12.1	0.0	7.8	31.4	4.2	3.4	3.0	77.1	45.6	12.6	367	192
Izard	2.2	0.0	0.5	11.9	1.0	1.5	0.8	20.1	13.6	4.1	308	141
Jackson	4.3	1.3	0.7	32.5	2.8	2.8	6.0	31.4	18.9	6.3	357	159
Jefferson	72.8	133.7	11.0	99.6	17.2	11.0	78.4	165.8	100.0	36.9	443	186
Johnson	6.4	0.1	1.2	16.3	1.7	1.6	1.1	37.2	25.5	6.5	279	138
Lafayette	1.7	5.2	0.4	15.8	1.8	0.9	0.7	16.2	10.5	3.2	382	250
Lawrence	6.1	0.0	1.0	24.3	2.0	1.5	2.1	42.3	21.5	5.7	321	143
Lee	3.0	1.4	0.6	36.1	4.9	2.2	9.1	22.0	16.5	2.7	222	87
Lincoln	1.7	1.1	0.4	20.3	2.0	0.7	64.4	19.6	14.4	2.6	180	102
Little River	2.4	0.6	0.5	11.5	1.4	0.7	4.6	39.1	16.1	6.7	494	202
Logan	7.9	0.1	1.3	19.1	2.0	1.2	1.7	33.6	23.7	5.1	230	120
Lonoke	7.3	16.1	1.6	22.2	3.2	6.7	6.2	97.4	67.2	18.3	330	119
Madison	3.0	0.0	0.5	10.5	0.9	0.8	0.8	22.5	15.8	3.1	217	130
Marion	2.0	0.2	0.4	8.4	1.1	0.8	6.9	23.0	15.6	4.1	254	135
Miller	3.9	1.7	0.3	33.9	7.4	2.7	41.4	88.4	52.6	18.0	436	188
Mississippi	7.6	0.7	2.0	72.0	15.4	5.5	7.3	159.2	66.1	20.1	400	130
Monroe	3.3	0.0	1.2	26.9	3.0	1.5	20.3	21.8	15.2	3.5	359	190
Montgomery	2.9	0.0	1.6	6.8	0.5	0.4	1.8	13.7	9.6	2.2	242	123
Nevada	2.3	0.0	0.7	11.0	1.4	0.7	1.0	22.0	12.6	2.2	226	136
Newton	3.3	0.0	0.4	12.8	1.8	0.6	0.3	13.9	11.4	1.1	132	85
Ouachita	8.3	7.3	1.6	36.8	4.3	3.4	1.9	55.5	39.4	9.5	340	155
Perry	2.3	0.1	0.9	8.2	0.7	0.5	0.2	15.5	12.3	1.7	167	103
Phillips	5.6	2.3	1.8	75.7	14.4	4.5	6.3	56.0	39.7	9.5	378	148
Pike	3.6	1.0	1.1	7.6	0.8	0.9	0.8	24.8	17.3	3.1	281	142
Poinsett	4.3	0.9	1.4	41.0	4.0	3.2	26.7	48.0	34.1	7.7	305	130
Polk	5.4	0.0	1.4	11.4	1.8	2.8	1.5	36.3	26.5	5.3	262	95
Pope	18.3	2.5	3.0	31.8	11.7	4.7	4.9	105.2	61.0	23.0	417	180
Prairie	2.0	0.0	0.5	10.1	1.1	0.7	-0.8	15.9	10.4	2.8	296	194
Pulaski	651.0	241.7	123.0	303.7	148.0	153.3	539.4	1 029.6	461.8	275.4	756	352
Randolph	2.1	0.0	0.6	17.1	3.9	1.0	0.9	26.7	18.3	4.5	251	97
St. Francis	24.1	0.6	3.6	63.3	8.8	4.0	12.6	61.6	42.9	12.0	416	119
Saline	7.5	0.2	1.6	16.3	5.9	2.8	6.7	117.7	76.4	23.6	273	151
Scott	4.0	0.0	2.3	8.2	0.9	0.7	1.4	19.9	15.5	2.1	190	94
Searcy	2.8	0.1	0.4	17.0	0.8	0.7	0.7	13.7	10.0	1.4	179	104
Sebastian	78.2	10.0	7.1	41.8	5.8	6.1	16.1	263.9	130.8	84.4	720	260
Sevier	4.4	0.1	0.5	7.3	1.2	2.1	1.3	25.7	19.3	3.8	243	116
Sharp	3.2	0.0	0.8	14.2	1.8	1.0	14.8	28.0	19.3	3.9	227	102
Stone	2.6	0.0	0.7	15.3	1.1	0.6	0.7	16.8	11.9	3.0	260	103
Union	9.8	0.0	3.2	48.5	10.4	3.6	12.1	92.3	53.7	21.2	468	170
Van Buren	2.9	2.1	1.4	13.0	1.2	0.7	0.1	22.3	16.1	3.8	235	126
Washington	70.9	20.3	17.6	41.2	9.5	12.0	51.3	359.5	185.5	106.3	638	171
White	17.4	0.1	2.5	44.4	4.5	4.8	25.8	114.5	73.8	18.3	264	97
Woodruff	2.0	0.6	0.4	26.1	2.0	0.9	20.7	20.7	15.7	2.4	289	142
Yell	7.5	0.8	1.4	17.8	1.5	1.2	2.3	38.6	28.6	4.7	220	161
CALIFORNIA	20 611.0	26 078.5	10 971.0	23 533.6	10 635.1	4 555.6	12 604.5	X	X	X	X	X
Alameda	838.9	270.7	2 307.4	1 432.7	305.1	132.0	705.3	8 019.4	3 162.1	2 436.5	1 655	1 004
Alpine	0.4	0.0	0.3	0.7	0.3	0.5	-0.7	16.9	8.3	5.4	4 526	3 569
Amador	5.1	0.3	1.5	9.5	5.5	0.7	10.6	98.2	45.9	33.3	910	744

1. State totals may include programs not allocated by county.   2. Based on the resident population estimated as of July 1 of the year shown.

Table B. States and Counties — Local Government Finances, Government Employment, and Elections

STATE County	Total (mil dol)	Per capita[1] (dollars)	Education	Health and hospitals	Police protection	Public welfare	Highways	Total (mil dol)	Per capita[1] (dollars)	Federal civilian	Federal military	State and local	Demo-cratic	Republi-can	All other
	183	184	185	186	187	188	189	190	191	192	193	194	195	196	197
ARKANSAS—Cont'd															
Conway	32.9	1 611	59.7	0.2	6.3	0.0	6.6	29.2	1 432	73	91	1 219	49.3	49.6	1.1
Craighead	184.2	2 191	47.4	0.3	4.3	0.2	9.7	412.5	4 906	427	377	6 086	45.8	53.1	1.1
Crawford	97.4	1 772	68.7	0.0	5.4	0.0	5.9	77.6	1 411	103	245	1 973	33.2	65.6	1.2
Crittenden	110.8	2 160	58.4	0.3	8.4	0.1	3.8	91.0	1 774	112	229	2 721	54.1	45.3	0.6
Cross	35.8	1 850	70.6	0.1	4.7	0.1	5.2	12.4	644	66	86	1 020	44.3	54.6	1.0
Dallas	18.8	2 143	61.5	0.1	5.6	0.4	7.8	10.7	1 220	27	39	496	49.5	50.4	0.1
Desha	42.0	2 838	53.0	14.7	6.5	0.0	4.7	24.6	1 664	123	66	1 041	60.3	38.2	1.5
Drew	45.8	2 455	45.0	24.6	3.3	0.3	7.5	17.1	918	75	83	1 824	47.2	52.2	0.6
Faulkner	150.7	1 682	57.1	0.0	5.4	0.2	5.9	182.5	2 037	203	407	5 558	39.6	58.6	1.7
Franklin	32.3	1 810	70.2	1.7	3.1	0.1	6.3	24.9	1 391	162	227	877	41.3	57.4	1.4
Fulton	16.4	1 422	61.1	13.3	3.9	0.2	8.1	5.1	444	37	51	554	48.1	50.5	1.4
Garland	178.6	1 983	51.6	0.3	7.3	0.0	5.7	145.8	1 619	593	406	3 914	44.9	54.1	0.9
Grant	32.9	1 955	75.8	0.1	3.6	0.1	6.1	17.9	1 063	33	75	848	37.3	62.1	0.6
Greene	74.3	1 953	54.2	0.1	3.8	0.0	6.0	89.2	2 346	90	169	1 615	47.0	51.9	1.1
Hempstead	43.4	1 846	59.7	0.0	4.8	0.0	7.6	23.6	1 003	103	105	1 554	51.2	48.0	0.7
Hot Spring	52.1	1 704	62.1	0.1	4.1	0.0	6.4	74.9	2 453	73	136	1 384	48.9	49.4	1.7
Howard	31.4	2 205	64.1	0.1	3.4	0.0	6.0	19.9	1 399	70	63	742	43.9	55.3	0.8
Independence	76.3	2 216	50.1	0.1	4.0	0.9	5.4	106.8	3 103	177	154	1 823	41.8	57.1	1.1
Izard	17.8	1 349	67.0	0.4	4.6	0.2	7.8	13.9	1 056	42	59	923	47.1	51.6	1.3
Jackson	30.7	1 726	55.9	0.8	6.2	0.1	6.7	11.2	629	54	79	1 344	56.4	42.0	1.6
Jefferson	162.7	1 951	52.5	0.2	8.4	0.0	5.6	107.4	1 288	1 616	420	6 684	64.5	33.5	2.0
Johnson	35.7	1 544	68.9	0.1	3.2	0.0	8.1	33.6	1 451	119	103	968	45.4	53.9	0.8
Lafayette	16.0	1 905	62.4	0.2	5.0	0.0	10.1	5.5	652	34	37	428	49.2	50.2	0.6
Lawrence	41.7	2 373	49.0	22.5	3.9	5.7	5.1	22.0	1 249	76	78	1 191	53.6	44.6	1.8
Lee	21.7	1 780	61.0	0.5	5.4	0.0	5.2	2.3	188	56	56	906	62.4	36.6	1.0
Lincoln	18.6	1 303	66.9	0.1	6.2	0.2	9.6	6.2	433	35	63	1 323	52.1	46.9	1.0
Little River	40.7	3 019	35.9	13.1	3.5	4.4	10.8	95.6	7 096	52	60	802	50.6	48.6	0.8
Logan	32.7	1 462	65.1	2.3	4.5	0.1	5.8	17.1	762	143	100	1 215	39.4	59.3	1.3
Lonoke	91.5	1 654	70.7	0.3	4.1	0.0	5.4	48.9	884	111	246	2 195	34.0	65.2	0.8
Madison	20.3	1 412	75.1	0.0	6.6	0.0	7.6	15.0	1 046	57	64	550	37.9	60.7	1.4
Marion	21.2	1 306	65.2	0.1	6.5	0.1	13.2	12.4	765	39	72	578	37.9	60.1	2.0
Miller	93.8	2 280	44.8	0.2	7.3	0.2	9.1	111.3	2 707	58	184	1 966	41.8	57.5	0.6
Mississippi	149.8	2 974	39.1	0.1	5.3	0.6	3.9	764.2	15 169	130	226	3 259	53.6	43.3	3.1
Monroe	22.1	2 282	65.2	0.5	4.9	1.2	8.1	3.5	359	46	43	566	55.8	43.4	0.8
Montgomery	12.3	1 335	68.6	0.0	3.4	2.4	8.3	9.2	999	74	41	488	38.5	59.8	1.7
Nevada	22.5	2 309	53.6	17.0	3.8	0.0	5.8	20.3	2 084	33	43	554	48.7	50.4	1.0
Newton	13.4	1 577	74.5	0.0	3.1	0.1	11.3	5.2	615	69	38	484	34.4	63.5	2.1
Ouachita	57.8	2 074	63.6	0.1	4.1	0.1	8.0	29.4	1 057	130	124	1 492	48.7	50.2	1.1
Perry	15.3	1 466	72.0	0.1	2.5	0.1	9.8	6.0	577	41	46	416	43.1	54.7	2.1
Phillips	57.4	2 297	66.6	2.3	6.2	0.1	5.6	25.4	1 015	80	112	1 942	63.5	35.8	0.7
Pike	23.8	2 135	61.6	10.3	1.9	0.0	14.7	11.9	1 068	93	50	619	39.0	59.7	1.3
Poinsett	43.2	1 699	65.3	0.3	6.6	0.2	5.1	15.9	627	77	113	1 288	52.7	46.0	1.3
Polk	34.4	1 704	68.3	0.1	5.6	0.1	9.1	18.2	900	101	90	1 107	31.7	66.6	1.7
Pope	101.0	1 828	60.0	1.0	8.4	0.1	5.7	145.7	2 639	332	251	3 248	34.0	65.1	0.9
Prairie	13.9	1 476	62.1	2.1	6.8	0.0	11.1	6.3	663	49	46	400	43.0	56.1	0.9
Pulaski	1 007.0	2 764	42.3	8.2	7.4	0.4	4.0	981.0	2 692	8 677	6 523	40 965	55.1	44.1	0.8
Randolph	26.1	1 441	64.8	0.1	6.5	0.2	8.5	7.6	419	42	81	1 000	51.2	47.4	1.5
St. Francis	59.8	2 077	62.1	0.8	6.1	0.6	5.2	19.4	674	411	128	1 823	59.9	39.4	0.7
Saline	114.1	1 322	61.5	0.3	7.9	0.0	7.9	59.1	685	97	384	3 777	36.0	63.1	0.9
Scott	17.4	1 582	53.0	0.1	4.9	0.1	29.8	5.8	526	77	49	389	36.5	62.3	1.3
Searcy	13.3	1 659	77.5	0.1	2.1	0.0	7.2	5.1	634	53	36	482	34.0	64.5	1.4
Sebastian	259.0	2 210	49.8	0.0	5.9	0.1	8.4	257.3	2 195	906	524	5 544	37.3	61.8	1.0
Sevier	25.6	1 617	74.3	0.1	5.3	0.0	6.8	5.8	368	83	70	935	44.3	54.7	1.1
Sharp	27.3	1 580	66.7	0.1	4.9	0.0	8.2	5.8	338	56	77	809	43.7	54.8	1.4
Stone	14.8	1 281	68.0	0.1	6.5	0.3	11.8	3.0	259	71	51	601	40.6	57.5	1.9
Union	86.1	1 901	60.4	0.1	6.6	0.0	6.9	82.1	1 812	196	203	2 497	39.7	58.9	1.5
Van Buren	22.5	1 381	68.9	0.5	5.0	0.4	7.4	24.1	1 475	51	73	684	46.5	52.3	1.2
Washington	336.7	2 022	53.9	0.4	6.2	0.0	5.8	277.1	1 664	1 243	755	12 908	43.0	55.7	1.2
White	114.3	1 648	67.7	0.1	5.1	0.1	5.9	126.0	1 817	181	313	3 083	34.5	64.3	1.1
Woodruff	19.9	2 345	51.4	0.3	4.8	17.9	8.7	9.5	1 123	44	38	554	65.2	33.7	1.1
Yell	37.1	1 732	69.1	0.0	6.1	0.1	9.1	19.7	918	162	95	1 206	43.8	55.2	1.0
CALIFORNIA	X	X	X	X	X	X	X	X	X	245 300	222 533	2 203 074	54.6	44.3	1.1
Alameda	7 741.5	5 258	28.3	13.0	5.4	7.5	3.5	10 734.9	7 291	10 532	3 219	108 212	74.3	24.4	1.2
Alpine	15.0	12 483	22.8	6.1	9.7	8.0	9.7	0.6	481	14	0	173	53.4	44.5	2.1
Amador	92.2	2 516	34.8	5.1	8.8	6.3	5.5	17.1	466	94	50	4 413	36.8	62.1	1.1

1. Based on the resident population estimated as of July 1 of the year shown.

STATE/ County code	CBSA code[1]	County Type[2]	STATE County	Land area[3] (sq km) 2000	Total persons	Rank	Per square kilometer	White	Black	Am. Indian, Alaska Native	Asian and Pacific Islander	Percent Hispanic or Latino[4]	Under 5 years	5 to 17 years	18 to 24 years	25 to 34 years	35 to 44 years	45 to 54 years
								Race alone or in combination, not Hispanic or Latino (percent)					Age (percent)					
				1	2	3	4	5	6	7	8	9	10	11	12	13	14	15
			CALIFORNIA—Cont'd															
06 007	17020	3	Butte	4 246	211 010	276	49.7	81.8	1.9	3.1	4.8	11.3	5.4	17.1	13.2	12.7	12.4	13.5
06 009	...	6	Calaveras	2 642	44 533	1 034	16.9	89.0	1.0	3.1	1.4	7.8	3.9	16.6	8.6	8.7	13.0	16.3
06 011	...	6	Colusa	2 980	19 678	1 824	6.6	46.4	0.7	1.9	1.8	49.7	8.3	21.8	11.9	12.3	13.3	12.5
06 013	41860	1	Contra Costa	1 865	1 001 136	36	536.8	57.8	9.9	1.2	14.2	20.1	6.6	19.1	8.7	12.6	16.2	15.0
06 015	18860	7	Del Norte	2 610	27 913	1 469	10.7	73.2	4.4	7.5	3.0	14.9	5.2	17.4	10.4	13.8	16.3	14.1
06 017	40900	1	El Dorado	4 431	168 822	335	38.1	85.9	0.9	1.8	3.2	10.4	5.1	18.6	9.2	10.3	15.8	17.2
06 019	23420	2	Fresno	15 443	850 325	54	55.1	39.5	5.5	1.3	9.2	46.0	8.1	22.3	11.8	13.8	13.8	11.7
06 021	...	6	Glenn	3 405	27 256	1 494	8.0	63.0	0.8	2.4	3.0	32.0	7.2	21.6	10.8	11.9	13.7	12.5
06 023	21700	5	Humboldt	9 253	127 915	444	13.8	85.2	1.4	7.3	2.6	7.4	5.6	16.2	11.9	13.7	13.5	15.9
06 025	20940	3	Imperial	10 813	149 232	380	13.8	19.1	3.5	1.2	1.8	74.7	8.1	22.0	11.7	13.6	14.9	11.7
06 027	13860	7	Inyo	26 426	18 326	1 886	0.7	75.3	0.2	10.2	1.2	15.1	4.9	17.2	8.6	8.6	13.9	16.7
06 029	12540	2	Kern	21 085	713 087	72	33.8	48.4	6.1	1.5	4.1	41.5	8.1	22.3	11.5	13.7	14.7	11.8
06 031	25260	3	Kings	3 603	138 564	409	38.5	42.3	8.4	1.3	3.9	45.4	7.7	20.1	12.5	17.1	16.5	10.9
06 033	17340	4	Lake	3 258	63 369	783	19.5	81.1	2.7	3.7	1.4	13.3	5.0	17.8	8.7	9.9	13.4	15.3
06 035	...	6	Lassen	11 803	33 926	1 306	2.9	72.9	9.3	3.5	1.3	14.6	3.9	15.6	12.8	17.4	18.1	14.4
06 037	31100	1	Los Angeles	10 518	9 871 506	1	938.5	31.3	9.7	0.6	13.5	46.3	7.5	19.8	10.0	16.0	15.7	12.6
06 039	31460	3	Madera	5 532	133 463	422	24.1	46.4	3.7	1.9	1.9	47.2	7.6	20.6	11.4	13.5	13.9	12.2
06 041	41860	1	Marin	1 346	246 073	242	182.8	79.9	3.2	0.8	6.2	12.0	5.5	14.6	6.3	11.5	17.2	18.5
06 043	...	8	Mariposa	3 758	17 803	1 925	4.7	87.6	0.8	4.7	1.2	8.2	4.1	15.4	10.1	8.8	14.1	16.2
06 045	46380	4	Mendocino	9 088	88 358	607	9.7	76.0	0.9	5.2	1.7	18.5	5.8	18.0	10.0	11.0	13.2	16.5
06 047	32900	3	Merced	4 995	231 574	254	46.4	39.8	4.0	1.1	7.3	49.5	8.4	24.1	12.0	13.5	13.6	10.9
06 049	...	6	Modoc	10 215	9 417	2 496	0.9	84.0	0.6	4.9	0.7	11.6	4.2	17.8	8.6	9.0	13.3	15.8
06 051	...	7	Mono	7 885	12 988	2 243	1.6	74.7	0.8	2.5	1.3	21.6	6.0	16.7	9.6	15.4	17.1	17.2
06 053	41500	2	Monterey	8 604	414 449	147	48.2	40.3	3.8	0.9	7.5	49.7	8.0	20.0	11.3	15.3	14.9	12.4
06 055	34900	3	Napa	1 952	131 607	433	67.4	66.8	1.8	1.2	5.4	26.6	5.9	17.3	9.7	12.6	14.5	14.6
06 057	46020	4	Nevada	2 480	96 099	560	38.7	91.7	0.4	1.9	1.4	6.4	4.3	16.4	8.6	9.0	13.9	17.8
06 059	31100	1	Orange	2 045	2 957 766	5	1 446.3	50.9	1.8	0.7	16.3	32.1	7.4	19.1	9.3	15.3	16.4	13.1
06 061	40900	1	Placer	3 637	292 235	199	80.4	84.0	1.4	1.6	5.2	10.4	5.5	18.2	9.3	12.0	15.3	14.4
06 063	...	7	Plumas	6 614	21 148	1 746	3.2	91.0	0.7	3.5	0.8	6.0	3.7	16.1	8.6	8.2	13.0	17.5
06 065	40140	1	Riverside	18 667	1 782 650	13	95.5	49.9	6.6	1.2	5.1	39.1	7.2	21.3	10.8	13.1	14.4	11.2
06 067	40900	1	Sacramento	2 501	1 330 711	28	532.1	58.5	11.2	1.9	14.8	17.7	7.1	19.8	9.9	14.6	15.3	13.1
06 069	41940	1	San Benito	3 598	56 300	864	15.6	46.0	0.9	0.9	3.2	50.2	8.3	22.6	10.1	13.5	16.5	12.9
06 071	40140	1	San Bernardino	51 936	1 859 678	12	35.8	42.5	9.7	1.2	6.0	42.6	7.8	23.0	11.2	13.9	15.0	12.1
06 073	41740	1	San Diego	10 878	2 930 886	6	269.4	55.5	6.1	1.1	11.2	28.7	7.2	18.4	10.8	15.4	15.7	13.0
06 075	41860	1	San Francisco	121	751 682	68	6 212.2	45.5	7.8	0.8	34.1	14.0	4.8	9.8	6.0	22.8	18.4	15.0
06 077	44700	2	San Joaquin	3 624	632 760	90	174.6	45.7	7.8	1.4	14.6	33.4	7.7	21.8	11.3	13.5	14.4	12.0
06 079	42020	3	San Luis Obispo	8 558	253 118	233	29.6	77.3	2.2	1.5	3.6	17.3	4.7	15.5	13.1	12.2	14.4	15.2
06 081	41860	1	San Mateo	1 163	697 456	75	599.7	50.7	3.5	0.6	25.4	22.3	6.8	16.1	7.4	14.5	17.3	15.3
06 083	42060	2	Santa Barbara	7 089	403 134	150	56.9	57.1	2.3	1.1	5.1	36.1	6.6	17.8	12.8	13.7	14.4	12.8
06 085	41940	1	Santa Clara	3 343	1 678 421	16	502.1	43.8	2.9	0.7	30.4	24.5	7.4	17.3	8.3	16.5	17.7	13.9
06 087	42100	2	Santa Cruz	1 153	251 584	235	218.2	67.2	1.2	1.3	4.7	27.7	6.3	16.6	11.7	13.9	15.7	16.7
06 089	39820	3	Shasta	9 804	175 650	323	17.9	88.3	1.3	4.2	2.7	6.6	5.4	18.3	10.2	10.6	13.7	14.6
06 091	...	8	Sierra	2 469	3 502	2 946	1.4	90.4	0.3	2.0	0.3	8.0	2.5	17.4	8.2	8.1	14.8	17.7
06 093	...	7	Siskiyou	16 283	44 626	1 031	2.7	85.9	1.5	5.1	1.4	8.6	4.7	16.8	9.6	8.0	12.8	16.9
06 095	46700	2	Solano	2 148	412 336	149	192.0	50.3	16.3	1.5	16.6	19.9	7.0	20.4	10.1	13.5	16.1	14.3
06 097	42220	2	Sonoma	4 082	466 725	131	114.3	74.3	1.9	1.7	4.8	19.8	5.9	17.6	9.8	12.3	15.4	16.4
06 099	33700	2	Stanislaus	3 869	492 233	120	127.2	55.7	3.1	1.5	5.9	36.0	7.6	22.0	11.1	13.8	14.5	12.1
06 101	49700	3	Sutter	1 561	84 703	629	54.3	60.5	2.2	2.3	13.2	24.1	7.0	20.1	10.6	12.8	14.1	12.5
06 103	39780	4	Tehama	7 643	58 582	837	7.7	78.8	0.7	3.2	1.2	18.1	5.8	19.5	10.2	10.7	13.9	13.2
06 105	...	8	Trinity	8 233	13 476	2 200	1.6	90.8	0.5	7.5	0.8	4.1	3.9	16.0	8.3	8.1	13.3	18.2
06 107	47300	2	Tulare	12 494	390 791	157	31.3	40.6	1.7	1.3	3.6	53.8	8.9	23.5	11.9	13.1	13.3	11.3
06 109	38020	4	Tuolumne	5 790	56 755	856	9.8	86.7	2.3	3.0	1.3	8.9	4.4	14.6	9.9	10.7	13.7	16.2
06 111	37100	2	Ventura	4 779	791 130	62	165.5	56.5	2.1	0.9	6.9	35.3	7.0	20.2	9.8	13.1	16.0	14.0
06 113	40900	1	Yolo	2 624	183 042	312	69.8	59.1	2.6	1.4	12.5	27.1	6.2	17.8	16.6	14.9	13.6	12.1
06 115	49700	3	Yuba	1 633	63 432	781	38.8	67.9	3.7	4.3	8.1	20.0	8.0	22.0	11.4	12.8	14.3	12.0
08 000	...	X	COLORADO	268 627	4 550 688	X	16.9	74.2	4.3	1.2	3.2	18.6	7.2	18.1	10.0	15.7	15.8	14.6
08 001	19740	1	Adams	3 056	380 273	162	124.4	61.3	3.3	1.2	3.9	31.7	8.0	19.4	11.0	17.8	15.4	11.9
08 003	...	7	Alamosa	1 872	15 126	2 092	8.1	53.3	0.9	1.7	1.2	43.7	7.4	19.6	15.3	12.7	13.5	13.6
08 005	19740	1	Arapahoe	2 080	516 060	111	248.1	71.3	9.8	1.1	5.7	14.5	7.1	19.3	8.9	15.1	16.3	15.4
08 007	...	7	Archuleta	3 497	11 313	2 346	3.2	82.2	0.6	1.8	0.6	15.7	5.1	17.7	8.9	10.2	14.8	17.3
08 009	...	9	Baca	6 619	4 223	2 894	0.6	90.9	0.1	2.3	0.3	7.6	5.2	17.5	7.8	8.1	13.8	14.4
08 011	...	7	Bent	3 921	5 613	2 803	1.4	64.8	3.8	1.5	0.6	29.5	6.0	16.6	11.3	13.6	15.6	14.2
08 013	14500	2	Boulder	1 898	278 231	211	146.6	83.2	1.1	0.8	4.4	11.8	6.2	16.1	12.0	17.2	16.4	15.3
08 014	19740	1	Broomfield	70	42 169	1 077	602.4	83.6	1.1	1.0	5.1	10.5	7.3	20.7	9.2	14.6	18.7	14.4
08 015	...	7	Chaffee	2 625	16 841	1 971	6.4	88.6	1.6	1.4	0.5	8.6	4.7	14.1	9.8	12.0	14.7	16.2

1. CBSA = Core Based Statistical Area. See Appendix A for explanation. See Appendix B for list of metropolitan areas with component counties. Service of USDA Rural-Urban Continuum Codes. See Appendix A for definition. 3. Dry land or land partially or temporarily covered by water. 2. County type code from the Economic Research 4. Hispanic or Latino persons may be of any race.

Table B. States and Counties — **Population and Households**

STATE County	Age (percent) (cont'd) 55 to 64 years	65 to 74 years	75 years and over	Percent female	1990	2000	1990–2000	2000–2003	Births	Deaths	Net migration	Number	Percent change, 1990–2000	Persons per household	Female family householder[1]	One person
	16	17	18	19	20	21	22	23	24	25	26	27	28	29	30	31
CALIFORNIA—Cont'd																
Butte	9.1	6.9	8.2	50.9	182 120	203 171	11.6	3.9	7 357	7 260	7 722	79 566	11.0	2.48	11.2	27.2
Calaveras	13.9	9.7	7.3	50.3	31 998	40 554	26.7	9.8	1 043	1 236	4 054	16 469	30.2	2.44	8.6	23.3
Colusa	8.1	5.5	5.4	49.2	16 275	18 804	15.5	4.6	1 128	455	212	6 097	8.6	3.01	9.6	21.5
Contra Costa	9.7	5.6	5.5	51.0	803 731	948 816	18.1	5.5	42 574	22 408	32 557	344 129	14.6	2.72	11.5	22.9
Del Norte	9.2	6.6	6.0	44.9	23 460	27 507	17.3	1.5	943	868	352	9 170	14.8	2.58	13.6	25.3
El Dorado	10.6	6.4	5.4	50.1	125 995	156 299	24.1	8.0	5 399	3 765	10 644	58 939	25.8	2.63	8.9	20.1
Fresno	7.2	4.9	4.7	49.8	667 479	799 407	19.8	6.4	46 000	17 895	23 410	252 940	14.5	3.09	15.2	20.6
Glenn	8.9	6.3	6.2	49.6	24 798	26 453	6.7	3.0	1 287	749	279	9 172	4.0	2.84	10.9	22.0
Humboldt	9.9	6.2	6.2	50.6	119 118	126 518	6.2	1.1	4 771	4 215	1 006	51 238	10.4	2.39	11.8	28.9
Imperial	6.9	5.6	4.5	48.0	109 303	142 361	30.2	4.8	8 443	2 613	1 072	39 384	19.9	3.33	17.1	17.1
Inyo	11.5	9.2	9.3	51.1	18 281	17 945	-1.8	2.1	574	685	497	7 703	1.8	2.31	9.9	31.4
Kern	7.3	4.8	4.2	48.5	544 981	661 645	21.4	7.8	38 024	15 725	29 311	208 652	15.0	3.03	14.5	20.3
Kings	6.3	3.9	3.3	42.7	101 469	129 461	27.6	7.0	7 008	2 301	4 472	34 418	18.3	3.18	14.3	17.0
Lake	11.6	8.9	8.5	50.5	50 631	58 309	15.2	8.7	1 973	2 718	5 621	23 974	15.2	2.39	11.3	29.0
Lassen	8.0	4.7	4.2	37.3	27 598	33 828	22.6	0.3	796	667	12	9 625	12.7	2.59	10.3	24.5
Los Angeles	7.8	5.1	4.7	50.5	8 863 052	9 519 338	7.4	3.7	498 085	193 782	48 018	3 133 774	4.8	2.98	14.7	24.6
Madera	7.9	5.8	4.9	51.5	88 090	123 109	39.8	8.4	6 987	3 030	6 439	36 155	27.4	3.18	12.2	16.5
Marin	13.1	6.9	7.0	50.4	230 096	247 289	7.5	-0.5	9 173	6 145	-4 264	100 650	5.9	2.34	8.5	29.8
Mariposa	12.9	9.0	7.9	48.8	14 302	17 130	19.8	3.9	471	516	723	6 613	18.0	2.37	8.0	26.5
Mendocino	11.4	6.7	6.8	50.1	80 345	86 265	7.4	2.4	3 405	2 766	1 545	33 266	9.4	2.53	11.7	27.0
Merced	6.9	4.8	4.0	49.7	178 403	210 554	18.0	10.0	12 731	4 513	12 722	63 815	15.3	3.25	14.1	17.7
Modoc	12.7	9.5	8.5	49.5	9 678	9 449	-2.4	-0.3	212	350	112	3 784	2.0	2.39	8.8	28.1
Mono	10.5	5.1	2.5	45.4	9 956	12 853	29.1	1.1	537	157	-219	5 137	29.7	2.43	6.5	26.6.
Monterey	7.7	5.1	4.7	48.2	355 660	401 762	13.0	3.2	22 995	7 909	-2 469	121 236	7.3	3.14	11.6	21.2
Napa	10.1	6.6	7.9	49.9	110 765	124 279	12.2	5.9	5 008	4 185	6 492	45 402	9.9	2.62	9.9	25.8
Nevada	12.5	8.3	8.5	50.4	78 510	92 033	17.2	4.4	2 602	3 031	4 399	36 894	19.9	2.47	8.8	22.8
Orange	8.5	5.2	4.8	50.2	2 410 668	2 846 289	18.1	3.9	146 001	54 467	20 459	935 287	13.1	3.00	10.7	21.1
Placer	9.2	6.6	6.2	50.7	172 796	248 399	43.8	17.6	9 949	6 478	39 667	93 382	45.7	2.63	9.2	21.3
Plumas	14.2	9.9	8.1	49.9	19 739	20 824	5.5	1.6	467	691	550	9 000	10.8	2.29	8.0	27.5
Riverside	7.2	5.8	5.8	50.0	1 170 413	1 545 387	32.0	15.4	81 888	41 356	192 605	506 218	25.9	2.98	12.0	20.7
Sacramento	8.0	5.5	5.2	50.9	1 066 789	1 223 499	14.7	8.8	60 820	30 600	76 268	453 602	15.0	2.64	14.1	26.7
San Benito	7.6	4.2	3.6	49.2	36 697	53 234	45.1	5.8	3 059	901	924	15 885	39.1	3.32	10.5	14.1
San Bernardino	7.0	4.4	3.7	50.0	1 418 380	1 709 434	20.5	8.8	94 524	36 956	91 989	528 594	13.7	3.15	14.8	18.4
San Diego	7.9	5.4	5.5	49.6	2 498 016	2 813 833	12.6	4.2	141 510	64 583	43 141	994 677	12.1	2.73	11.6	24.2
San Francisco	9.5	7.0	7.2	49.3	723 959	776 733	7.3	-3.2	26 466	21 387	-31 380	329 700	7.9	2.30	8.9	38.6
San Joaquin	7.5	4.9	4.9	49.9	480 628	563 598	17.3	12.3	31 670	14 415	50 843	181 629	14.8	3.00	14.0	20.7
San Luis Obispo	9.3	6.9	7.3	48.6	217 162	246 681	13.6	2.6	7 879	6 571	5 240	92 739	15.5	2.49	9.1	26.0
San Mateo	10.2	6.3	6.4	50.5	649 623	707 161	8.9	-1.4	32 709	15 542	-27 819	254 103	5.0	2.74	10.1	24.6
Santa Barbara	8.4	6.2	6.6	49.9	369 608	399 347	8.0	0.9	18 192	9 494	-5 003	136 622	5.3	2.80	10.0	24.3
Santa Clara	9.0	5.3	4.6	49.2	1 497 577	1 682 585	12.4	-0.2	85 728	28 600	-64 627	565 863	8.8	2.92	10.0	21.4
Santa Cruz	9.2	4.8	5.2	50.0	229 734	255 602	11.3	-1.6	11 161	5 501	-9 866	91 139	9.1	2.71	10.2	25.1
Shasta	10.7	7.4	7.3	51.2	147 036	163 256	11.0	7.6	6 179	5 720	11 773	63 426	13.3	2.52	11.9	24.7
Sierra	14.5	9.1	8.0	49.3	3 318	3 555	7.1	-1.5	44	119	25	1 520	13.8	2.32	7.9	29.0
Siskiyou	12.5	9.3	8.9	51.0	43 531	44 301	1.8	0.7	1 346	1 681	677	18 556	7.2	2.35	10.1	28.6
Solano	8.3	5.2	4.5	49.7	339 469	394 542	16.2	4.5	18 983	8 290	7 447	130 403	15.0	2.90	13.8	19.6
Sonoma	10.0	5.8	6.7	50.6	388 222	458 614	18.1	1.8	18 313	12 653	2 748	172 403	15.7	2.60	10.4	25.7
Stanislaus	7.5	5.1	4.8	50.5	370 522	446 997	20.6	10.1	24 333	11 511	31 924	145 146	15.8	3.03	13.7	19.4
Sutter	9.0	6.5	5.5	50.3	64 409	78 930	22.5	7.3	3 874	2 246	4 180	27 033	17.0	2.87	11.7	21.2
Tehama	10.2	7.9	7.4	50.5	49 625	56 039	12.9	4.5	2 114	2 088	2 490	21 013	12.3	2.62	11.6	24.0
Trinity	14.3	9.8	7.2	49.1	13 063	13 022	-0.3	3.5	342	463	572	5 587	8.4	2.29	10.1	29.5
Tulare	7.2	4.9	4.5	49.8	311 932	368 021	18.0	6.2	23 563	8 695	8 130	110 385	12.8	3.28	14.5	17.1
Tuolumne	11.9	9.5	8.5	47.3	48 456	54 501	12.5	4.1	1 383	1 962	2 766	21 004	17.0	2.36	9.6	26.0
Ventura	8.8	5.3	5.0	50.0	669 016	753 197	12.6	5.0	36 775	15 319	17 453	243 234	11.9	3.04	10.9	18.9
Yolo	7.3	4.6	4.5	51.1	141 212	168 660	19.4	8.5	7 444	3 783	10 791	59 375	16.5	2.71	11.1	23.3
Yuba	8.1	5.5	4.6	49.6	58 234	60 219	3.4	5.3	3 342	1 725	1 643	20 535	3.8	2.87	13.3	21.7
COLORADO	8.9	5.2	4.5	49.6	3 294 473	4 301 261	30.6	5.8	217 234	93 256	122 281	1 658 238	29.3	2.53	9.6	26.3
Adams	7.2	4.5	3.2	49.1	NA	348 618	NA	9.1	19 639	6 756	19 394	123 156	NA	2.80	11.6	21.6
Alamosa	7.9	5.2	4.4	50.3	13 617	14 966	9.9	1.1	785	368	-249	5 467	15.8	2.56	11.7	27.3
Arapahoe	8.5	4.7	4.1	50.6	391 572	487 967	24.6	5.8	23 903	9 413	13 066	190 909	23.4	2.53	10.6	27.0
Archuleta	12.5	7.5	4.1	49.2	5 345	9 898	85.2	14.3	353	177	1 202	3 980	98.0	2.47	8.2	22.1
Baca	12.1	10.8	13.2	51.0	4 556	4 517	-0.9	-6.5	146	224	-217	1 905	1.8	2.33	7.5	30.4
Bent	9.5	7.6	6.7	44.4	5 048	5 998	18.8	-6.4	214	251	-339	2 003	7.4	2.53	11.4	27.2
Boulder	8.1	4.1	3.7	49.2	NA	269 814	NA	3.1	11 731	4 394	1 102	106 658	NA	2.45	7.6	26.5
Broomfield	6.8	3.9	2.5	49.7	24 638	38 272	55.3	10.2	1 906	696	1 759	13 842	58.8	2.76	8.2	19.3
Chaffee	11.8	9.6	7.4	47.0	12 684	16 242	28.1	3.7	504	481	570	6 584	35.8	2.26	6.8	28.4

1. No spouse present.

Table B. States and Counties — Vital Statistics, Health Resources, and Crime

STATE County	Births, average 1999–2001 Total	Rate[1]	Deaths, average 1999–2001 Number Total	Infant[2]	Rate Total[1]	Infant[3]	Physicians,[4] 2000 Number	Rate[5]	Hospitals,[4] 1998 Number	Beds Number	Beds Rate[5]	Medicare enrollees, 2003	Serious crimes known to police,[6] 2002 Total Number	Rate[7]
	32	33	34	35	36	37	38	39	40	41	42	43	44	45
CALIFORNIA—Cont'd														
Butte	2 256	11.1	2 175	10	10.7	4.6	383	189	5	661	340	37 160	7 041	3 343
Calaveras	314	7.7	391	1	9.6	D	39	96	1	49	123	8 554	1 243	2 956
Colusa	341	18.1	146	2	7.7	D	11	58	1	56	302	2 705	604	3 098
Contra Costa	12 973	13.6	6 721	61	7.0	4.7	2 248	237	10	2 081	227	122 174	43 414	4 413
Del Norte	296	10.8	258	2	9.4	D	39	142	1	47	174	4 500	1 086	3 808
El Dorado	1 659	10.5	1 150	7	7.3	4.2	190	122	2	188	119	26 190	3 742	2 309
Fresno	14 193	17.7	5 492	87	6.8	6.2	1 341	168	14	2 118	280	94 572	49 847	6 015
Glenn	392	14.9	243	1	9.2	D	19	72	1	28	107	4 111	857	3 125
Humboldt	1 441	11.4	1 222	7	9.6	5.1	262	207	5	332	272	20 081	5 367	4 092
Imperial	2 599	18.2	875	13	6.1	5.1	111	78	3	221	153	18 825	5 243	3 552
Inyo	182	10.1	210	1	11.7	D	39	217	2	69	381	3 780	424	2 279
Kern	11 601	17.4	4 740	82	7.1	7.0	869	131	11	1 649	261	78 689	29 148	4 249
Kings	2 155	16.7	706	13	5.5	5.9	119	92	3	175	147	11 430	3 900	2 906
Lake	590	10.1	754	3	12.9	D	71	122	2	115	209	12 838	2 267	3 750
Lassen	304	9.0	208	3	6.2	D	27	80	1	59	177	3 972	597	1 702
Los Angeles	155 765	16.7	59 775	817	6.3	5.2	22 877	240	114	30 364	330	1 029 780	394 591	3 998
Madera	2 085	16.8	898	12	7.2	5.6	107	87	2	124	108	19 091	5 037	3 947
Marin	2 782	11.2	1 848	8	7.5	3.0	937	379	3	417	176	35 952	6 214	2 424
Mariposa	135	7.9	164	2	9.6	D	13	76	1	34	214	3 269	463	2 607
Mendocino	1 052	12.2	818	8	9.5	7.3	191	221	4	209	250	14 461	2 893	3 235
Merced	3 827	18.0	1 371	21	6.5	5.6	215	102	4	402	203	21 018	11 141	5 104
Modoc	79	8.4	101	1	10.7	D	8	85	2	113	1 202	1 826	233	2 379
Mono	147	11.5	47	1	3.7	D	20	156	1	15	146	903	636	4 773
Monterey	6 732	16.7	2 412	37	6.0	5.4	673	168	4	675	185	43 750	14 426	3 463
Napa	1 518	12.1	1 267	4	10.1	D	376	303	3	1 429	1 198	22 036	3 574	2 774
Nevada	793	8.6	895	3	9.7	D	187	203	2	193	211	16 991	2 426	2 543
Orange	46 357	16.2	16 729	215	5.9	4.6	6 371	224	37	6 889	253	309 081	82 277	2 788
Placer	3 070	12.2	1 906	18	7.6	5.9	461	186	2	310	135	39 944	8 311	3 227
Plumas	168	8.1	218	1	10.4	D	36	173	4	108	530	4 138	611	2 830
Riverside	24 604	15.8	12 360	147	7.9	6.0	1 990	129	16	3 009	203	219 960	70 046	4 372
Sacramento	18 293	14.8	9 161	111	7.4	6.1	2 913	238	11	3 174	277	160 696	69 474	5 477
San Benito	942	17.7	276	3	5.2	D	28	53	1	101	207	4 844	1 534	2 793
San Bernardino	28 799	16.7	11 230	215	6.5	7.5	2 793	163	19	3 704	227	179 248	72 908	4 114
San Diego	43 809	15.5	19 685	246	7.0	5.6	7 062	251	25	6 828	246	350 167	105 363	3 612
San Francisco	8 342	10.7	6 565	32	8.5	3.9	4 539	584	11	4 155	557	117 837	43 776	5 436
San Joaquin	9 425	16.5	4 359	59	7.6	6.3	762	135	8	1 140	207	71 307	37 878	6 483
San Luis Obispo	2 411	9.8	2 013	11	8.1	4.6	581	236	6	636	271	40 110	7 603	2 973
San Mateo	10 257	14.5	4 820	44	6.8	4.3	1 853	262	8	2 036	291	92 191	19 049	2 598
Santa Barbara	5 599	14.0	2 938	28	7.4	5.1	998	250	8	1 314	337	56 246	10 041	2 425
Santa Clara	27 041	16.0	8 907	120	5.3	4.5	4 577	272	15	4 488	273	173 115	46 147	2 645
Santa Cruz	3 658	14.3	1 682	15	6.6	4.2	531	208	2	395	163	28 062	10 136	3 825
Shasta	1 875	11.4	1 712	11	10.4	6.0	379	232	5	656	399	33 800	5 669	3 349
Sierra	22	6.3	37	0	10.6	D	3	84	1	40	1 183	677	69	1 872
Siskiyou	431	9.7	498	2	11.3	D	62	140	2	137	311	9 796	998	2 173
Solano	5 739	14.5	2 489	28	6.3	4.9	703	178	4	522	138	42 954	17 953	4 389
Sonoma	5 594	12.2	3 827	27	8.3	4.8	1 066	232	8	889	205	64 105	16 031	3 372
Stanislaus	7 322	16.2	3 453	52	7.7	7.1	648	145	7	1 478	347	58 154	27 932	6 027
Sutter	1 169	14.7	679	4	8.6	D	133	169	1	132	171	11 678	3 329	4 003
Tehama	652	11.6	625	4	11.1	D	65	116	1	76	141	9 729	1 898	3 267
Trinity	96	7.4	140	1	10.7	D	7	54	1	65	496	2 739	253	1 874
Tulare	7 116	19.3	2 634	44	7.1	6.1	431	117	7	854	240	42 622	18 592	4 873
Tuolumne	436	8.0	574	4	10.5	D	109	200	3	223	419	11 336	1 713	3 032
Ventura	11 515	15.2	4 712	55	6.2	4.8	1 299	172	8	1 451	198	91 182	17 694	2 266
Yolo	2 236	13.2	1 098	12	6.5	5.2	327	194	2	169	110	18 839	6 853	3 919
Yuba	1 040	17.2	536	8	8.9	7.7	93	154	1	128	213	8 360	3 028	4 850
COLORADO	64 871	15.0	27 565	403	6.4	6.2	9 342	217	68	9 438	238	493 454	195 936	4 348
Adams	6 085	16.7	2 070	45	5.7	7.5	308	85	4	539	166	38 254	NA	NA
Alamosa	230	15.4	110	2	7.4	D	41	274	1	70	484	1 773	438	2 793
Arapahoe	7 094	14.4	2 723	44	5.5	6.2	1 177	241	3	605	128	47 245	25 097	4 909
Archuleta	110	11.0	56	1	5.6	D	5	51	0	0	0	1 568	367	3 539
Baca	48	10.5	68	0	15.0	D	4	89	1	65	1 489	1 042	NA	NA
Bent	71	12.0	68	1	11.5	D	8	133	0	0	0	893	59	939
Boulder	3 813	13.0	1 415	20	4.8	5.2	625	215	3	360	135	30 658	7 432	2 643
Broomfield	NA	NA	NA	NA	NA	NA	NA	NA	NA	NA	NA	NA	1 750	4 364
Chaffee	148	9.1	142	0	8.7	D	18	111	1	38	252	3 234	423	2 486

1. Per 1,000 estimated resident population. 2. Deaths of infants under 1 year old. 3. Deaths of infants under 1 year old per 1,000 live births. 4. Data subject to copyright. 5. Per 100,000 resident population as of July 1 of the year shown. 6. Data for serious crimes have not been adjusted for underreporting; this may affect comparability between geographic areas and over time. 7. Per 100,000 population estimated by the FBI.

STATE County	Serious crimes known to police,[1] 2002 (cont'd) Rate[2] Violent	Property	Education — Enrollment[3] Total	Percent private	Attainment[4] (percent) High school graduate or less	Bachelor's degree or more	Local government expenditures,[5] 2000–2001 Total current expenditures (mil dol)	Current expenditures per student (dollars)	Money income, 1999 Per capita income[6] (dollars)	Households Median income Dollars	Percent change, 1989–1999 (constant 1999 dollars)	Percent with income of $100,000 or more	Percent below poverty level, 1999 Persons	Households	Families	Families with children
	46	47	48	49	50	51	52	53	54	55	56	57	58	59	60	61
CALIFORNIA—Cont'd																
Butte	257	3 086	66 431	6.9	42.1	21.8	260.5	7 564	17 517	31 924	4.3	6.7	19.8	17.6	12.2	19.8
Calaveras	478	2 478	9 406	6.7	42.9	17.1	48.0	6 887	21 420	41 022	10.4	10.1	11.8	11.3	8.7	13.2
Colusa	267	2 831	5 596	5.6	60.1	10.6	33.4	7 824	14 730	35 062	4.8	6.3	16.1	14.8	13.0	18.1
Contra Costa	433	3 980	270 131	16.7	32.9	35.0	1 058.2	6 625	30 615	63 675	5.1	26.7	7.6	6.6	5.4	7.9
Del Norte	393	3 415	7 135	12.1	55.8	11.0	36.4	7 524	14 573	29 642	-3.7	5.8	20.2	18.2	16.4	24.0
El Dorado	323	1 986	44 193	10.4	33.1	26.5	199.0	6 912	25 560	51 484	9.3	17.2	7.1	7.0	5.0	7.1
Fresno	616	5 398	263 942	7.0	53.6	17.5	1 300.6	7 181	15 495	34 725	-2.0	8.6	22.9	18.2	17.6	24.8
Glenn	270	2 855	7 721	4.9	58.3	10.7	49.9	8 089	14 069	32 107	4.7	4.8	18.1	15.4	12.5	19.4
Humboldt	384	3 708	38 481	6.8	40.8	23.0	160.6	7 578	17 203	31 226	-1.5	5.8	19.5	18.7	12.9	20.8
Imperial	461	3 092	47 441	5.4	62.9	10.3	248.7	7 487	13 239	31 870	5.7	7.2	22.6	20.1	19.4	24.6
Inyo	435	1 844	4 326	7.9	49.0	17.1	31.4	9 239	19 639	35 006	6.8	8.4	12.6	12.5	9.3	14.4
Kern	491	3 758	205 960	8.2	56.9	13.5	1 037.7	7 012	15 760	35 446	-7.9	8.3	20.8	17.7	16.8	22.9
Kings	304	2 602	37 449	9.6	60.1	10.4	177.5	7 000	15 848	35 749	4.3	7.5	19.5	15.8	15.8	22.2
Lake	447	3 303	14 144	6.4	52.5	12.1	73.7	7 255	16 825	29 627	1.2	5.5	17.6	15.8	12.9	21.6
Lassen	228	1 474	8 900	8.1	51.2	10.7	41.6	7 796	14 749	36 310	1.0	6.6	14.0	13.6	11.1	15.5
Los Angeles	902	3 096	2 931 076	15.7	48.9	24.9	11 870.8	7 063	20 683	42 189	-10.2	15.1	17.9	15.1	14.4	19.9
Madera	586	3 360	35 998	7.3	59.9	12.0	171.1	6 907	14 682	36 286	-1.3	8.2	21.4	16.5	15.9	23.1
Marin	188	2 236	57 014	25.7	21.2	51.3	242.2	8 439	44 962	71 306	9.3	35.1	6.6	5.5	3.7	6.1
Mariposa	450	2 157	4 096	11.4	41.2	20.2	20.1	7 807	18 190	34 626	2.0	7.1	14.8	12.1	10.5	16.4
Mendocino	584	2 651	22 795	7.5	45.2	20.2	135.3	8 810	19 443	35 996	1.3	8.5	15.9	13.7	10.9	17.6
Merced	645	4 458	70 396	6.8	60.1	11.0	359.3	6 963	14 257	35 532	3.5	6.9	21.7	17.8	16.9	22.8
Modoc	327	2 052	2 336	2.6	52.3	12.4	24.3	10 761	17 285	27 522	-7.0	5.1	21.5	18.1	16.4	25.7
Mono	233	4 540	2 917	10.4	32.7	28.9	21.1	9 863	23 422	44 992	4.9	11.6	11.5	9.8	6.3	10.9
Monterey	469	2 995	117 126	10.7	50.1	22.5	506.6	6 985	20 165	48 305	7.3	15.2	13.5	10.3	9.7	14.0
Napa	268	2 506	33 203	18.3	40.1	26.4	138.4	7 154	26 395	51 738	4.7	18.6	8.3	6.9	5.6	8.8
Nevada	210	2 333	23 203	9.1	33.5	26.1	99.2	6 949	24 007	45 864	6.0	13.5	8.1	7.9	5.5	8.7
Orange	278	2 510	847 671	14.8	38.0	30.8	3 173.1	6 421	25 826	58 820	-4.7	23.5	10.3	7.7	7.0	10.1
Placer	197	3 030	69 856	12.9	30.8	30.3	363.8	6 551	27 963	57 535	13.9	20.5	5.8	5.8	3.9	6.0
Plumas	296	2 534	5 030	6.8	39.7	17.5	30.0	8 844	19 391	36 351	11.3	7.4	13.1	13.3	9.0	15.9
Riverside	594	3 778	465 645	11.0	49.7	16.6	2 100.7	6 575	18 689	42 887	-3.5	12.2	14.2	12.0	10.7	15.1
Sacramento	640	4 838	366 459	12.2	39.8	24.8	1 620.8	7 302	21 142	43 816	1.0	12.3	14.1	11.5	10.3	15.4
San Benito	317	2 462	16 010	10.9	48.3	17.1	78.3	6 806	20 932	57 469	17.3	19.8	10.0	7.7	6.7	8.6
San Bernardino	563	3 551	555 363	11.0	50.8	15.9	2 481.4	6 523	16 856	42 066	-6.4	11.0	15.8	13.5	12.6	16.8
San Diego	481	3 131	827 975	13.4	37.3	29.5	3 487.5	7 141	22 926	47 067	0.0	15.7	12.4	10.3	8.9	13.3
San Francisco	758	4 679	182 963	26.4	32.7	45.0	496.3	8 035	34 556	55 221	23.0	24.7	11.3	10.2	7.8	11.8
San Joaquin	937	5 546	176 188	12.5	54.0	14.5	809.3	6 687	17 365	41 282	0.3	10.6	17.7	14.5	13.5	19.0
San Luis Obispo	273	2 700	77 496	8.9	36.2	26.7	248.6	6 727	21 864	42 428	1.3	12.0	12.8	11.8	6.8	9.9
San Mateo	284	2 314	184 928	22.9	32.2	39.0	704.9	7 728	36 045	70 819	13.5	32.3	5.8	4.9	3.5	4.9
Santa Barbara	322	2 104	127 198	13.4	39.8	29.4	454.4	6 883	23 059	46 677	-2.6	16.0	14.3	11.6	8.5	13.0
Santa Clara	357	2 288	476 333	19.9	32.5	40.5	1 837.0	7 232	32 795	74 335	15.0	34.6	7.5	6.1	4.9	6.8
Santa Cruz	415	3 410	76 840	13.1	33.3	34.2	302.9	7 493	26 396	53 998	8.3	21.9	11.9	9.5	6.7	9.8
Shasta	487	2 862	45 010	11.8	44.4	16.6	222.7	7 316	17 738	34 335	-0.1	7.2	15.4	13.9	11.3	18.1
Sierra	271	1 601	875	4.6	43.5	17.2	9.8	6 023	18 815	35 827	12.7	5.7	11.3	13.7	9.0	17.5
Siskiyou	205	1 968	11 200	7.1	44.4	17.7	63.2	8 510	17 570	29 530	0.3	5.7	18.6	16.9	14.0	23.8
Solano	545	3 844	116 471	12.9	40.7	21.4	480.2	6 572	21 731	54 099	2.9	16.5	8.3	7.4	6.1	8.5
Sonoma	309	3 063	125 553	13.6	35.5	28.5	538.1	7 302	25 724	53 076	8.8	18.1	8.1	7.0	4.7	6.9
Stanislaus	538	5 489	136 838	9.2	54.5	14.1	658.4	6 767	16 913	40 101	0.2	9.1	16.0	13.6	12.3	17.3
Sutter	385	3 683	22 869	7.8	50.6	15.3	113.3	7 042	17 428	38 375	5.4	9.1	15.5	13.3	12.1	17.9
Tehama	444	2 823	15 427	5.8	51.5	11.3	87.3	8 132	15 793	31 206	3.5	5.1	17.3	15.3	13.0	20.5
Trinity	215	1 659	3 112	5.2	48.6	15.5	24.5	11 345	16 868	27 711	0.6	5.5	18.7	17.8	14.1	26.1
Tulare	658	4 214	118 065	6.6	61.3	11.5	612.1	7 146	14 006	33 983	3.4	7.6	23.9	19.0	18.8	26.6
Tuolumne	242	2 789	13 347	10.5	45.4	16.1	60.7	7 632	21 015	38 725	6.6	8.6	11.4	10.5	8.1	15.3
Ventura	259	2 007	224 449	14.5	39.6	26.9	886.4	6 340	24 600	59 666	-2.6	22.8	9.2	7.2	6.4	9.1
Yolo	479	3 440	64 875	8.0	40.0	34.1	191.6	6 689	19 365	40 769	5.1	13.0	18.4	16.8	9.5	13.3
Yuba	594	4 256	18 858	6.4	55.4	10.3	98.1	7 241	14 124	30 460	5.3	4.6	20.8	18.7	16.3	23.1
COLORADO	352	3 995	1 166 004	13.9	36.3	32.7	4 719.9	6 521	24 049	47 203	16.6	14.2	9.3	8.8	6.2	9.2
Adams	NA	NA	90 893	10.7	51.9	16.8	359.3	5 923	19 742	NA	NA	9.7	9.1	7.9	6.6	9.5
Alamosa	421	2 372	5 251	8.2	44.5	27.0	19.8	7 164	15 037	29 447	8.2	6.5	21.3	20.6	15.6	23.5
Arapahoe	430	4 479	134 175	15.5	29.9	37.0	626.5	6 494	28 147	53 570	7.1	17.9	5.8	5.6	4.2	6.2
Archuleta	405	3 134	2 222	12.2	39.5	29.0	9.0	5 766	21 683	37 901	23.2	8.3	11.7	12.6	9.0	14.9
Baca	NA	NA	1 117	4.4	55.8	14.0	7.6	8 326	15 068	28 099	12.4	2.8	16.9	18.2	12.9	20.1
Bent	95	843	1 547	5.6	57.9	11.5	6.9	7 116	13 567	28 125	10.3	3.8	19.5	18.1	16.6	24.5
Boulder	217	2 426	83 834	14.2	22.3	53.2	301.2	6 391	29 049	NA	NA	21.5	9.9	9.5	4.8	6.9
Broomfield	95	4 270	11 520	15.3	27.9	37.9	NA	NA	26 505	63 903	NA	20.7	4.2	4.5	2.1	3.0
Chaffee	106	2 380	3 408	16.7	41.4	24.3	13.9	6 130	19 430	34 368	20.8	7.1	11.7	12.0	7.4	14.7

1. Data for serious crimes have not been adjusted for underreporting; this may affect comparability between geographic areas and over time. 2. Per 100,000 population estimated by the FBI. 3. All persons 3 years old and over enrolled in nursery school through college. 4. Persons 25 years old and over. 5. Elementary and secondary education expenditures. 6. Based on population enumerated as of April 1, 2000.

STATE County	Total (mil dol)	Percent change, 2001–2002	Per capita[1] Dollars	Rank	Wages and salaries[2] (mil dol)	Proprietor's income (mil dol)	Dividends, interest, and rent (mil dol)	Transfer payments Total (mil dol)	Government payments to individuals Total (mil dol)	Social Security (mil dol)	Medical payments (mil dol)	Income maintenance (mil dol)	Unemployment insurance (mil dol)
	62	63	64	65	66	67	68	69	70	71	72	73	74
CALIFORNIA—Cont'd													
Butte	4 999	4.5	23 944	1 422	2 555	480	1 022	1 150	1 100	396	422	153	41
Calaveras	1 128	4.9	26 165	856	297	122	265	228	218	99	81	18	7
Colusa	464	2.4	23 972	1 419	257	77	85	88	83	27	32	10	10
Contra Costa	43 854	0.2	44 326	36	20 053	4 194	7 773	3 960	3 723	1 387	1 522	355	203
Del Norte	513	2.4	18 677	2 802	251	48	93	159	152	46	65	27	6
El Dorado	6 051	4.2	36 561	111	1 914	724	1 018	669	629	271	237	48	30
Fresno	19 544	6.2	23 492	1 573	12 315	2 151	2 777	4 074	3 875	937	1 578	745	360
Glenn	552	3.3	20 605	2 402	253	77	109	131	124	43	50	17	7
Humboldt	3 189	3.9	25 039	1 117	1 713	367	661	692	661	216	267	92	27
Imperial	2 973	8.7	20 382	2 465	1 810	379	318	692	658	168	252	139	60
Inyo	480	3.7	26 246	843	266	31	125	98	94	39	39	8	3
Kern	15 674	6.4	22 635	1 839	10 220	1 685	2 129	3 018	2 853	829	1 061	541	226
Kings	2 505	7.1	18 581	2 816	1 685	182	317	492	461	118	189	80	44
Lake	1 574	6.3	25 288	1 052	523	117	289	404	389	140	160	54	14
Lassen	644	5.7	19 174	2 720	390	60	106	134	126	37	55	18	5
Los Angeles	300 898	2.6	30 804	286	215 001	39 950	50 124	43 511	41 170	10 091	19 907	7 325	1 554
Madera	2 527	6.2	19 617	2 625	1 292	281	404	571	540	171	203	90	45
Marin	16 945	-1.6	68 650	4	6 429	1 926	4 644	954	895	431	300	55	40
Mariposa	427	6.6	24 631	1 229	196	29	97	94	90	38	35	7	4
Mendocino	2 358	4.2	26 947	709	1 143	277	579	496	475	154	202	64	25
Merced	4 640	4.8	20 623	2 394	2 278	592	634	1 067	1 013	238	449	187	83
Modoc	224	9.3	24 053	1 386	96	30	46	59	57	20	24	7	2
Mono	375	6.5	28 713	477	229	51	79	31	28	11	8	3	3
Monterey	13 091	3.1	31 842	230	7 363	1 993	2 878	1 556	1 458	464	547	181	141
Napa	4 983	2.8	38 361	81	2 894	556	1 130	579	548	216	233	34	26
Nevada	3 123	4.2	32 841	194	1 129	455	851	446	423	208	146	28	16
Orange	112 267	2.8	38 367	80	73 863	14 448	18 687	9 825	9 124	3 426	3 561	1 033	410
Placer	10 328	4.7	37 083	104	5 478	950	1 901	1 101	1 034	459	353	73	45
Plumas	585	3.7	27 869	570	271	68	150	125	120	48	45	10	6
Riverside	42 068	5.7	24 814	1 172	20 480	3 536	7 591	6 957	6 551	2 461	2 518	818	314
Sacramento	38 569	4.0	29 631	377	30 293	3 037	5 765	6 129	5 818	1 578	2 664	884	259
San Benito	1 598	-0.6	28 660	478	621	178	259	168	154	54	54	19	17
San Bernardino	42 232	4.8	23 379	1 600	23 945	3 758	4 983	7 078	6 648	1 891	2 783	1 152	324
San Diego	101 293	4.3	34 872	145	68 484	10 924	18 898	11 439	10 772	3 620	4 549	1 257	398
San Francisco	41 634	-3.6	54 639	13	40 480	7 179	8 227	3 861	3 679	1 019	1 629	557	235
San Joaquin	14 788	3.6	24 119	1 365	8 507	1 152	2 195	2 960	2 813	743	1 306	435	166
San Luis Obispo	7 599	4.1	30 145	338	3 838	927	2 051	1 010	949	441	313	88	32
San Mateo	37 339	-5.8	53 315	14	25 104	4 109	9 148	2 457	2 289	1 027	769	173	140
Santa Barbara	13 701	3.2	34 103	160	7 981	1 530	3 973	1 546	1 451	611	499	164	56
Santa Clara	77 998	-7.1	46 499	28	71 870	7 290	14 764	5 990	5 588	1 829	2 184	617	523
Santa Cruz	9 707	-1.4	38 323	82	4 519	1 033	2 030	943	883	303	329	98	79
Shasta	4 558	5.7	26 532	782	2 441	529	817	1 053	1 012	355	417	124	42
Sierra	82	1.2	23 541	1 551	31	3	21	17	16	7	5	1	1
Siskiyou	1 056	3.6	23 874	1 450	474	123	238	289	278	99	112	36	11
Solano	11 912	2.7	29 089	435	5 890	539	1 605	1 475	1 379	448	519	166	96
Sonoma	17 391	1.1	37 331	98	9 003	1 770	3 922	1 863	1 751	720	667	141	95
Stanislaus	11 372	4.3	23 642	1 516	6 508	1 045	1 627	2 140	2 025	609	829	303	160
Sutter	2 114	4.9	25 698	955	905	257	342	410	390	118	148	53	32
Tehama	1 180	5.5	20 536	2 421	604	98	214	308	294	112	111	41	13
Trinity	293	5.7	22 141	1 973	106	20	66	87	84	30	36	9	4
Tulare	8 076	4.3	21 193	2 239	4 513	979	1 099	1 881	1 790	429	741	345	186
Tuolumne	1 403	5.4	25 044	1 115	621	116	346	300	286	132	102	24	9
Ventura	27 006	3.2	34 572	150	14 924	2 291	4 623	2 774	2 589	996	975	266	169
Yolo	4 881	3.4	27 114	675	3 949	456	945	667	623	195	252	87	31
Yuba	1 302	5.3	20 873	2 329	914	73	155	389	375	83	176	63	18
COLORADO	151 790	0.8	33 723	X	104 621	17 220	27 004	14 698	13 675	5 284	5 509	1 236	701
Adams	10 205	-0.9	27 389	633	6 403	779	1 068	1 164	1 079	369	476	109	60
Alamosa	351	8.4	23 183	1 669	242	39	54	71	68	16	31	12	2
Arapahoe	21 993	-0.2	43 109	43	15 850	3 850	3 874	1 325	1 209	557	377	102	90
Archuleta	219	5.2	19 869	2 571	95	24	69	36	33	18	8	3	3
Baca	101	-9.8	23 035	1 713	33	22	27	22	21	10	8	2	0
Bent	103	-3.3	18 168	2 872	43	9	21	29	27	7	13	4	1
Boulder	11 281	-6.6	40 474	58	8 697	902	2 489	662	598	257	207	46	52
Broomfield	1 321	D	32 366	212	1 542	108	239	106	97	39	39	7	4
Chaffee	389	4.0	23 113	1 691	189	32	115	75	71	33	28	5	2

1. Based on the resident population estimated as of July 1 of the year shown.   2. Includes other labor income.

STATE County	Earnings, 2002								Social Security beneficiaries, December 2003		Supplemental Security Income recipients, December 2003	Housing units, 2003	
	Total (mil dol)	Percent by selected industries											
		Farm	Goods-related[1]		Service-related and health				Govern-ment	Number	Rate[2]		Total	Percent change, 2000–2003
			Total	Manu-facturing	Infor-mation and profes-sional and technical services	Retail trade	Finance, insur-ance, and real estate	Health services						
	75	76	77	78	79	80	81	82	83	84	85	86	87	88
CALIFORNIA—Cont'd														
Butte	3 036	1.7	12.0	5.1	7.9	11.0	8.0	15.6	21.9	42 415	201	9 985	88 961	4.0
Calaveras	419	-1.4	D	4.0	7.6	9.7	8.5	D	25.1	10 085	226	1 006	24 270	5.8
Colusa	334	18.2	D	21.2	1.7	5.5	2.7	3.9	22.1	2 975	151	563	6 824	0.7
Contra Costa	24 246	0.3	20.1	9.1	17.5	7.5	13.4	9.6	11.2	132 305	132	21 990	371 177	4.7
Del Norte	299	4.2	D	3.0	3.7	8.8	2.9	12.1	46.1	5 330	191	1 953	10 604	1.6
El Dorado	2 638	0.2	19.0	3.9	16.6	9.2	10.8	9.7	16.2	27 870	165	2 754	76 405	7.2
Fresno	14 466	3.4	15.6	8.6	6.8	7.9	6.4	11.9	21.8	105 300	124	38 896	281 327	3.9
Glenn	326	13.5	D	9.0	D	6.7	3.2	D	28.9	4 885	179	968	10 130	1.5
Humboldt	2 080	2.1	D	8.6	6.2	10.8	6.7	12.0	26.2	23 295	182	6 612	57 317	2.5
Imperial	2 189	13.4	8.5	4.4	3.0	8.4	3.4	4.0	35.7	21 950	147	9 342	46 775	6.6
Inyo	297	-1.5	11.9	4.1	4.0	10.9	3.0	D	43.3	4 080	223	432	9 068	0.3
Kern	11 905	5.0	17.7	4.4	6.2	7.3	4.2	8.0	27.1	94 080	132	29 320	242 622	4.8
Kings	1 867	5.8	D	9.0	2.4	6.0	2.8	7.3	47.1	13 965	101	4 264	38 340	4.9
Lake	640	2.8	D	3.1	6.1	9.7	4.8	13.1	25.7	14 860	234	3 669	32 981	1.4
Lassen	450	0.9	D	D	2.8	7.0	3.9	8.2	54.5	4 430	131	1 069	12 279	2.3
Los Angeles	254 950	0.1	16.1	11.8	20.1	6.3	9.9	8.0	13.4	1 030 955	104	388 335	3 311 721	1.2
Madera	1 573	7.4	D	9.2	D	8.2	3.6	14.1	22.0	19 155	144	4 441	42 779	5.9
Marin	8 355	0.1	D	2.8	22.9	8.7	17.8	10.0	9.1	38 515	157	3 542	106 216	1.2
Mariposa	225	-2.6	D	1.9	D	5.9	2.8	D	35.1	4 140	233	358	9 164	3.8
Mendocino	1 420	1.7	D	12.1	6.1	11.3	5.2	10.3	22.0	16 560	187	3 900	37 775	2.3
Merced	2 870	11.5	19.2	13.6	3.2	8.6	3.3	8.8	20.8	28 230	122	10 061	72 669	6.3
Modoc	126	13.6	D	D	2.8	6.9	3.1	D	42.1	2 325	247	341	4 792	-0.3
Mono	280	-0.9	D	1.1	6.4	9.0	11.1	D	28.5	1 095	84	106	12 218	3.9
Monterey	9 356	11.1	10.8	5.1	7.0	7.5	6.3	6.6	21.8	49 470	119	8 957	135 569	2.9
Napa	3 450	4.4	D	19.1	7.7	6.8	7.7	9.8	13.6	22 055	168	2 068	50 889	4.8
Nevada	1 584	0.0	22.3	6.2	10.3	11.0	10.9	11.4	14.9	20 910	218	1 646	46 606	5.2
Orange	88 311	0.3	20.9	13.5	14.5	7.2	14.4	6.8	9.4	325 445	110	61 912	1 004 282	3.6
Placer	6 428	0.1	27.9	12.6	9.0	11.2	11.2	8.9	11.2	47 945	164	4 523	127 362	18.7
Plumas	339	3.7	D	9.3	4.4	7.9	6.0	D	30.4	5 060	239	698	13 887	3.7
Riverside	24 015	1.0	23.4	10.1	6.3	9.9	6.7	9.0	20.6	255 450	143	45 584	641 986	9.8
Sacramento	33 330	0.2	13.6	6.2	12.4	6.8	9.1	8.2	32.7	170 940	128	54 037	503 328	6.0
San Benito	799	11.7	D	14.8	3.9	9.7	5.6	3.6	18.4	5 845	104	835	17 533	6.3
San Bernardino	27 704	0.5	18.9	11.1	5.7	9.0	6.1	10.0	22.4	208 075	112	60 845	625 880	4.1
San Diego	79 407	0.5	16.7	9.9	17.3	6.7	9.8	7.0	22.8	375 965	128	79 578	1 085 515	4.4
San Francisco	47 658	0.0	5.5	2.0	26.3	4.8	22.5	4.8	14.0	104 000	138	45 681	353 506	2.0
San Joaquin	9 659	2.6	19.7	10.0	5.8	9.4	6.3	9.8	19.9	81 180	128	26 331	205 364	8.6
San Luis Obispo	4 765	2.8	17.1	6.6	9.2	9.9	7.2	10.0	21.1	44 985	178	5 345	107 819	5.4
San Mateo	29 213	0.3	16.0	9.8	28.2	7.1	11.9	5.7	6.7	93 690	134	12 577	265 362	1.8
Santa Barbara	9 511	4.1	16.3	9.4	13.1	8.0	8.2	8.7	19.8	61 505	153	9 640	146 867	2.8
Santa Clara	79 160	0.2	34.0	29.4	23.6	4.8	5.9	5.3	7.5	174 410	104	42 500	596 526	3.0
Santa Cruz	5 552	3.7	D	9.6	13.5	9.7	8.0	9.5	16.1	31 135	124	5 475	100 173	1.3
Shasta	2 970	0.4	D	5.1	7.5	10.8	5.5	16.1	20.2	38 770	221	8 991	72 193	4.9
Sierra	33	-6.4	D	6.3	D	4.2	D	4.1	58.6	760	217	82	2 213	0.5
Siskiyou	596	2.4	D	5.5	5.7	10.1	4.4	11.0	28.7	10 920	245	2 436	22 361	1.9
Solano	6 429	0.5	20.0	9.3	4.7	9.6	4.7	11.4	29.2	49 420	120	10 204	141 837	5.4
Sonoma	10 773	1.7	26.2	15.8	11.1	8.5	8.9	10.3	13.5	71 245	153	9 315	189 818	3.6
Stanislaus	7 553	3.4	21.8	13.4	5.6	10.5	5.1	11.6	17.1	66 870	136	19 593	160 358	6.3
Sutter	1 162	5.0	17.0	7.9	4.8	12.5	6.2	13.1	15.4	13 315	157	3 347	29 629	4.6
Tehama	702	4.1	D	15.2	4.2	9.7	4.3	9.1	21.9	12 315	210	2 629	24 236	2.9
Trinity	127	0.2	D	7.3	D	9.0	3.2	D	48.4	3 320	246	558	8 063	1.0
Tulare	5 492	10.6	15.4	8.9	3.8	8.1	5.0	7.0	22.9	51 120	131	17 079	124 970	4.5
Tuolumne	738	0.0	D	6.2	7.8	10.0	4.7	12.3	29.6	13 385	236	1 673	28 995	2.3
Ventura	17 215	3.3	22.7	16.6	11.1	7.4	10.9	7.2	16.5	101 275	128	14 939	262 015	4.1
Yolo	4 405	2.3	16.1	8.3	7.1	6.8	4.7	5.4	31.6	20 605	113	4 816	65 561	6.5
Yuba	988	2.2	10.5	4.6	4.6	4.9	1.9	9.2	53.4	9 585	151	3 696	23 301	2.9
COLORADO	121 841	0.5	18.7	8.6	18.3	6.6	10.5	7.3	15.5	557 253	122	54 054	1 973 622	9.2
Adams	7 182	0.1	28.4	11.5	5.7	8.5	6.0	5.7	12.6	40 225	106	4 342	147 448	11.2
Alamosa	281	8.5	9.1	1.0	7.5	11.6	5.2	15.6	26.7	2 090	138	562	6 339	4.1
Arapahoe	19 700	0.0	12.9	3.4	30.2	6.1	15.4	7.0	7.6	54 675	106	3 494	216 609	10.0
Archuleta	119	-2.9	21.1	1.2	7.3	12.8	14.7	4.4	18.1	1 995	176	112	7 291	17.4
Baca	55	28.2	D	D	D	8.0	D	1.4	33.4	1 150	272	99	2 417	2.2
Bent	52	11.8	1.7	0.6	D	4.8	D	2.1	44.5	925	165	197	2 403	1.6
Boulder	9 598	0.1	23.2	17.9	28.1	5.6	6.9	6.7	14.1	27 590	99	2 429	118 413	-1.2
Broomfield	1 650	0.1	D	15.1	44.2	7.6	5.9	1.9	2.4	3 970	NA	12	17 122	19.6
Chaffee	221	-1.0	D	3.0	5.2	12.7	12.5	D	29.0	3 640	216	207	9 151	9.0

1. Covers mining, construction, and manufacturing.   2. Per 1,000 resident population estimated as of July 1 of the year shown.

STATE County	Housing units, 2000									Civilian labor force, 2003				Civilian employment,[6] 2000		
	Occupied units											Unemployment			Percent	
			Owner-occupied			Renter-occupied										
				Median owner cost as a percent of income												
	Total	Percent	Median value[1]	With a mort-gage	Without a mort-gage[2]	Median rent[3]	Median rent as a per-cent of income	Sub-stand-ard units[4] (percent)	Total	Percent change, 2002–2003	Total	Rate[5]	Total	Management, professional and related occupations	Production, transpor-tation, and material moving occupations
	89	90	91	92	93	94	95	96	97	98	99	100	101	102	103
CALIFORNIA—Cont'd															
Butte	79 566	60.7	129 800	24.1	10.3	563	31.9	6.5	91 782	1.9	7 173	7.8	82 403	31.7	11.6
Calaveras	16 469	78.7	156 900	26.1	12.3	599	25.8	4.9	16 781	3.0	1 353	8.1	16 202	31.1	11.5
Colusa	6 097	63.3	107 500	24.5	11.3	494	23.9	18.6	8 690	-1.1	1 646	18.9	7 237	22.9	14.0
Contra Costa	344 129	69.3	267 800	24.7	9.9	898	26.8	7.7	517 730	-0.4	28 695	5.5	451 357	41.0	8.5
Del Norte	9 170	63.8	121 100	22.3	10.9	519	30.3	6.5	9 787	1.6	833	8.5	8 959	24.3	9.4
El Dorado	58 939	74.7	194 400	25.5	11.3	702	27.4	5.5	82 626	2.3	4 423	5.4	73 821	37.3	7.6
Fresno	252 940	56.5	104 900	24.2	10.8	534	28.9	17.6	399 098	1.2	56 815	14.2	301 306	29.5	13.3
Glenn	9 172	64.0	94 900	22.7	9.9	458	24.4	13.0	9 840	-1.4	1 250	12.7	10 527	24.4	15.6
Humboldt	51 238	57.6	133 500	23.8	9.9	537	32.2	5.9	59 729	-0.1	3 878	6.5	55 426	31.5	12.6
Imperial	39 384	58.3	100 000	24.5	10.9	504	28.7	23.0	57 322	3.5	11 146	19.4	44 092	24.7	11.7
Inyo	7 703	65.9	161 300	22.1	10.2	516	23.2	5.1	7 318	-1.2	465	6.4	8 007	27.6	10.8
Kern	208 652	62.1	93 300	23.5	10.5	518	28.0	15.5	302 324	2.0	37 147	12.3	232 461	27.0	13.5
Kings	34 418	55.9	97 600	23.2	9.9	533	26.9	16.0	49 138	3.7	7 162	14.6	39 511	25.9	13.7
Lake	23 974	70.5	122 600	26.7	13.8	567	28.9	6.8	25 210	1.2	2 352	9.3	20 503	27.2	11.3
Lassen	9 625	68.1	106 700	22.9	10.8	561	27.3	5.6	11 630	0.8	738	6.3	10 161	30.0	9.0
Los Angeles	3 133 774	47.9	209 300	26.6	9.9	704	28.3	23.5	4 788 827	0.0	337 116	7.0	3 953 415	34.3	15.5
Madera	36 155	66.2	118 800	25.0	10.9	562	27.7	15.8	57 114	1.3	7 213	12.6	42 166	24.7	15.2
Marin	100 650	63.6	514 600	25.2	9.9	1 162	28.3	5.0	129 749	-2.7	5 027	3.9	128 855	52.5	4.5
Mariposa	6 613	69.9	141 900	24.1	9.9	502	24.4	4.0	6 915	-4.9	512	7.4	6 833	28.7	12.0
Mendocino	33 266	61.3	170 200	24.3	11.0	600	27.1	10.1	43 954	-0.1	3 115	7.1	38 575	29.6	12.9
Merced	63 815	58.7	111 100	24.7	10.8	518	26.8	20.5	89 745	2.5	13 281	14.8	75 321	25.6	17.4
Modoc	3 784	70.7	69 100	20.0	10.3	429	26.5	6.6	4 376	3.3	367	8.4	3 635	29.9	10.7
Mono	5 137	60.1	236 300	28.1	9.9	682	25.7	8.6	7 191	5.0	404	5.6	7 153	35.4	6.7
Monterey	121 236	54.7	265 800	26.4	9.9	776	26.7	20.8	198 582	0.6	20 701	10.4	163 987	29.2	11.1
Napa	45 402	65.1	251 300	25.4	9.9	818	26.1	9.3	70 642	1.7	3 234	4.6	58 501	34.6	11.4
Nevada	36 894	75.8	205 700	26.6	11.4	746	29.0	4.5	47 870	-0.4	2 258	4.7	41 553	34.3	9.5
Orange	935 287	61.4	270 000	25.1	9.9	923	27.5	16.0	1 575 610	1.9	59 715	3.8	1 338 838	38.1	12.5
Placer	93 382	73.2	213 900	24.6	9.9	780	26.5	4.1	141 606	2.2	6 698	4.7	118 647	39.7	8.7
Plumas	9 000	70.1	137 900	23.8	10.7	525	25.8	4.3	10 519	4.8	1 111	10.6	8 520	30.0	13.5
Riverside	506 218	68.8	146 500	25.4	10.5	660	28.6	13.0	817 605	2.9	49 469	6.1	602 856	27.8	14.3
Sacramento	453 602	58.2	144 200	23.7	9.9	659	26.9	8.4	649 984	2.1	36 273	5.6	545 925	36.3	10.2
San Benito	15 885	68.1	284 000	27.0	9.9	765	25.3	15.3	28 980	3.0	2 781	9.6	23 663	30.2	13.3
San Bernardino	528 594	64.5	131 500	24.8	10.3	648	28.5	15.1	870 706	3.0	50 152	5.8	661 272	28.1	17.0
San Diego	994 677	55.4	227 200	25.6	9.9	761	28.1	12.2	1 482 241	1.7	63 137	4.3	1 241 258	37.7	9.9
San Francisco	329 700	35.0	396 400	25.2	9.9	928	24.6	14.0	403 095	-3.2	27 476	6.8	427 823	48.3	7.5
San Joaquin	181 629	60.4	142 400	24.5	9.9	617	28.2	14.4	278 922	2.4	28 154	10.1	219 000	27.1	16.8
San Luis Obispo	92 739	61.5	230 000	26.5	9.9	719	30.8	5.9	121 184	0.4	4 112	3.4	109 669	34.3	9.8
San Mateo	254 103	61.5	469 200	25.7	9.9	1 144	26.3	12.6	370 563	-2.6	18 755	5.1	361 640	42.7	8.6
Santa Barbara	136 622	56.1	293 000	26.5	9.9	830	30.6	13.2	209 136	2.4	8 433	4.0	180 716	35.4	9.6
Santa Clara	565 863	59.8	446 400	24.2	9.9	1 185	25.7	14.6	895 086	-5.1	73 474	8.2	843 912	48.5	11.2
Santa Cruz	91 139	60.0	377 500	26.7	9.9	924	29.2	11.6	139 017	-1.5	11 718	8.4	129 380	40.3	8.9
Shasta	63 426	66.1	120 800	25.2	11.6	563	29.2	5.3	81 927	2.4	6 389	7.8	65 828	30.4	12.3
Sierra	1 520	70.9	128 600	22.8	11.0	513	26.0	5.9	1 383	-0.4	164	11.9	1 515	34.7	12.1
Siskiyou	18 556	67.2	100 300	22.7	11.2	471	28.4	5.4	17 629	1.8	1 865	10.6	17 269	30.8	11.7
Solano	130 403	65.2	178 300	24.8	9.9	797	26.6	9.1	212 559	1.8	12 654	6.0	172 355	30.9	13.0
Sonoma	172 403	64.1	273 200	26.0	9.9	864	27.5	7.2	257 544	-1.9	12 578	4.9	229 227	35.0	11.4
Stanislaus	145 146	61.9	125 300	24.3	9.9	611	27.9	14.2	216 655	1.3	24 952	11.5	174 328	26.5	17.5
Sutter	27 033	61.5	120 700	23.4	9.9	506	25.8	11.7	37 611	0.7	5 112	13.6	30 980	28.5	15.5
Tehama	21 013	67.7	103 000	23.5	10.7	486	26.8	8.5	27 390	1.4	1 966	7.2	21 018	25.3	19.7
Trinity	5 587	71.3	112 000	26.4	9.9	487	28.5	7.4	5 064	0.2	566	11.2	4 529	28.3	13.9
Tulare	110 385	61.5	97 800	24.4	9.9	516	27.3	19.8	174 584	0.6	27 107	15.5	134 094	25.3	14.2
Tuolumne	21 004	71.2	149 800	25.1	10.1	611	28.9	6.2	22 723	3.0	1 508	6.6	20 419	29.7	11.3
Ventura	243 234	67.6	248 700	25.2	9.9	892	27.2	12.7	430 313	1.4	22 655	5.3	348 338	36.5	11.5
Yolo	59 375	53.1	169 800	23.9	9.9	687	32.2	11.8	98 473	3.3	5 155	5.2	76 648	41.4	10.9
Yuba	20 535	54.0	89 700	24.6	10.2	488	27.3	11.8	22 001	1.9	3 129	14.2	20 223	23.0	16.6
COLORADO	1 658 238	67.3	166 600	22.6	9.9	671	26.4	4.9	2 477 874	1.7	149 692	6.0	2 205 194	37.4	10.5
Adams	122 995	69.8	NA	NA	NA	NA	NA	7.7	201 891	6.7	14 407	7.1	173 459	26.0	16.7
Alamosa	5 467	64.0	87 900	20.7	10.1	408	27.6	6.9	9 089	5.0	609	6.7	6 849	34.6	8.5
Arapahoe	190 909	68.0	171 700	21.8	9.9	735	25.9	5.1	293 075	3.2	17 765	6.1	262 629	39.6	8.6
Archuleta	3 980	76.8	167 400	24.5	9.9	627	26.3	5.5	5 329	0.5	306	5.7	4 652	26.6	8.8
Baca	1 905	76.5	47 300	20.4	11.3	295	18.9	3.5	2 350	4.0	59	2.5	2 023	39.1	10.9
Bent	2 003	67.7	57 200	21.4	10.4	415	24.8	5.3	2 055	6.4	169	8.2	2 182	33.5	8.0
Boulder	106 534	64.4	NA	NA	NA	NA	NA	3.8	175 460	-4.4	10 147	5.8	150 999	50.5	7.5
Broomfield	13 842	76.8	182 200	22.1	9.9	856	24.9	3.6	23 683	16.7	1 451	6.1	20 612	44.2	10.9
Chaffee	6 584	73.3	152 800	24.7	9.9	517	26.9	3.3	8 484	3.9	329	3.9	6 805	30.1	8.9

1. Specified owner-occupied units.   2. Median monthly owner costs is often in the minimum category—9.9 percent or less, which is indicated as 9.9 percent.   3. Specified renter-occupied units.   4. Overcrowded or lacking complete plumbing facilities.   5. Percent of civilian labor force.   6. Persons 16 years old and over.

STATE County	Number of establishments	Total	Health care and social assistance	Manufacturing	Retail trade	Finance and insurance	Professional, scientific, and technical services	Total (mil dol)	Average per employee (dollars)	Number	Less than 50 acres	500 acres and over	Farm operators whose principal occupation is farming (percent)
	104	105	106	107	108	109	110	111	112	113	114	115	116
CALIFORNIA—Cont'd													
Butte	4 652	55 931	11 186	4 763	9 478	2 360	2 693	1 308	23 390	2 128	58.9	7.4	62.8
Calaveras	970	6 241	911	501	1 048	211	246	142	22 742	576	50.2	16.5	54.3
Colusa	362	3 400	227	636	486	111	D	91	26 791	821	23.5	26.7	71.7
Contra Costa	22 285	329 686	37 562	19 240	42 933	28 033	27 226	14 402	43 685	592	67.9	9.3	57.1
Del Norte	502	4 142	951	223	857	99	114	81	19 653	89	67.4	5.6	60.7
El Dorado	4 044	38 594	4 480	2 191	5 710	916	2 684	1 081	28 006	1 116	78.0	2.7	57.2
Fresno	15 337	218 995	33 357	25 833	32 648	10 618	9 190	6 206	28 340	6 281	58.1	11.5	69.5
Glenn	514	4 347	347	811	741	151	138	125	28 791	1 283	44.9	14.5	70.1
Humboldt	3 532	37 634	7 039	4 971	7 220	1 202	1 667	890	23 642	993	49.7	15.1	59.5
Imperial	2 270	25 103	3 401	1 588	6 484	921	662	593	23 633	537	22.0	43.9	81.2
Inyo	599	5 567	1 009	233	1 138	94	130	122	21 963	85	47.1	31.8	61.2
Kern	11 063	153 457	21 188	12 760	24 264	6 278	8 503	4 529	29 513	2 147	36.4	26.8	70.1
Kings	1 550	19 929	2 832	3 283	3 644	651	358	485	24 345	1 154	48.7	18.7	67.2
Lake	1 142	10 140	1 899	371	2 079	409	D	262	25 858	880	62.5	6.3	58.0
Lassen	501	3 906	707	336	1 036	117	81	89	22 837	419	42.5	28.6	62.1
Los Angeles	227 941	3 889 686	389 885	590 921	376 071	182 983	432 820	143 585	36 914	1 543	86.8	3.5	54.4
Madera	1 871	24 012	2 807	5 091	3 178	409	600	520	21 659	1 780	45.2	13.3	72.8
Marin	10 256	109 012	12 704	3 750	16 385	8 473	9 966	4 541	41 652	254	39.4	33.9	53.5
Mariposa	373	3 503	341	109	377	75	54	74	21 173	284	38.0	20.8	56.7
Mendocino	2 829	25 443	3 947	4 087	4 790	589	754	610	23 991	1 184	48.9	17.2	59.7
Merced	2 997	39 990	5 679	8 497	6 945	1 025	806	974	24 344	2 964	50.0	11.9	71.1
Modoc	202	1 654	509	D	D	D	D	35	20 993	428	18.0	37.9	69.2
Mono	560	6 517	269	D	828	92	173	135	20 679	63	30.2	39.7	69.8
Monterey	8 719	106 740	12 690	6 863	17 717	3 618	5 638	3 393	31 785	1 216	42.5	21.8	69.0
Napa	3 848	52 052	9 319	10 622	6 427	1 526	1 850	1 771	34 023	1 456	70.5	7.2	54.9
Nevada	3 032	28 109	3 942	2 907	4 445	880	1 179	742	26 384	599	78.1	4.2	50.8
Orange	79 937	1 409 151	111 153	216 725	144 996	90 032	107 636	54 681	38 804	348	79.3	2.3	48.0
Placer	7 685	107 395	9 954	8 772	17 125	4 666	4 690	3 676	34 225	1 438	78.2	3.3	54.4
Plumas	743	4 626	818	669	707	186	162	125	26 994	142	40.8	20.4	47.9
Riverside	27 233	410 073	45 135	54 148	65 367	10 262	11 987	11 122	27 123	3 186	81.1	4.5	52.3
Sacramento	25 909	439 198	56 604	27 419	59 000	37 493	28 746	15 146	34 485	1 513	70.0	8.9	58.4
San Benito	1 025	11 263	1 031	2 636	1 834	271	257	306	27 171	677	52.7	21.3	56.6
San Bernardino	27 352	467 422	59 300	69 851	66 128	15 327	13 069	13 305	28 464	1 386	77.9	3.7	55.4
San Diego	69 059	1 081 762	114 863	119 555	144 791	47 431	100 820	39 694	36 693	5 255	89.1	1.9	50.4
San Francisco	30 643	557 049	54 412	18 778	44 156	65 148	80 688	31 409	56 385	8	100.0	0.0	37.5
San Joaquin	10 350	163 533	21 693	24 237	23 203	6 901	4 277	4 742	28 996	4 026	62.6	8.2	67.4
San Luis Obispo	7 136	79 094	13 042	6 972	13 213	2 678	3 949	2 163	27 352	2 322	54.2	16.0	60.2
San Mateo	20 378	382 377	25 630	30 340	41 663	18 159	43 039	22 405	58 594	306	61.1	6.2	63.4
Santa Barbara	11 005	140 797	16 352	16 416	20 911	5 514	9 035	4 606	32 711	1 444	60.9	14.2	61.6
Santa Clara	45 265	1 042 998	71 678	201 577	88 367	22 019	147 352	68 288	65 473	1 026	75.6	7.7	56.6
Santa Cruz	7 001	81 466	10 424	8 247	13 207	2 065	5 641	2 605	31 976	754	74.1	2.1	64.9
Shasta	4 510	47 871	9 847	3 576	8 341	1 313	2 220	1 274	26 610	1 126	64.1	10.6	52.4
Sierra	98	589	98	D	D	D	D	15	25 336	52	13.5	28.8	69.2
Siskiyou	1 275	9 891	1 690	976	1 978	344	245	217	21 899	796	36.1	23.1	67.3
Solano	6 584	100 819	15 835	10 116	17 904	3 734	3 760	3 109	30 839	915	60.3	12.3	61.0
Sonoma	13 526	172 665	23 284	29 381	25 972	8 941	8 327	6 005	34 777	3 447	70.7	5.9	55.6
Stanislaus	8 298	125 928	18 205	22 640	20 488	3 670	3 896	3 515	27 915	4 267	66.4	6.1	64.9
Sutter	1 693	17 690	3 085	1 784	3 878	549	526	480	27 151	1 391	44.9	12.4	67.8
Tehama	1 000	11 832	1 797	2 166	1 930	507	332	310	26 207	1 573	57.0	11.0	58.1
Trinity	315	1 600	338	212	340	D	83	35	21 662	135	37.0	11.9	40.0
Tulare	5 937	79 078	11 634	12 291	13 174	3 282	2 114	2 000	25 286	5 738	61.2	8.4	66.5
Tuolumne	1 521	13 039	2 341	1 200	2 473	427	370	317	24 315	358	57.5	15.1	55.3
Ventura	17 510	249 865	23 633	35 728	34 892	17 372	15 873	8 550	34 218	2 318	73.6	4.4	57.3
Yolo	3 467	59 829	5 010	5 653	6 596	4 913	2 938	1 874	31 315	1 060	47.1	18.9	65.0
Yuba	826	8 858	1 665	1 276	1 360	336	212	233	26 360	863	50.5	10.3	55.6
COLORADO	139 225	1 986 570	196 461	162 364	260 536	105 924	149 387	71 509	35 996	31 369	32.8	29.0	58.4
Adams	7 245	127 921	8 360	13 108	15 992	2 597	3 316	4 311	33 702	728	40.2	28.2	59.1
Alamosa	520	5 279	1 119	82	1 262	265	172	114	21 651	318	14.2	34.0	67.6
Arapahoe	16 645	308 146	21 361	17 477	37 273	32 192	28 246	13 578	44 065	448	46.9	20.3	50.0
Archuleta	484	2 726	162	D	541	109	81	56	20 446	258	28.3	18.2	53.9
Baca	102	599	D	27	136	48	5	10	17 225	608	5.3	65.5	64.8
Bent	73	1 099	D	D	99	D	22	22	32 146	265	14.7	48.3	68.3
Boulder	11 361	172 266	13 152	25 438	22 524	4 549	23 845	7 626	44 267	736	63.6	6.8	48.9
Broomfield	NA	NA	NA	NA	NA	NA	NA	NA	NA	NA	NA	NA	NA
Chaffee	771	4 911	584	175	868	295	242	99	20 203	212	35.8	13.7	61.3

Table B. States and Counties — Agriculture

STATE County	Land in farms					Value of land and buildings (dollars)		Value of machinery and equipment average per farm (dollars)	Value of products sold				Percent of farms with sales of —		Government payments	
	Acreage (1,000)	Percent change, 1997–2002	Acres			Average per farm	Average per acre		Total (mil dol)	Average per farm (dollars)	Percent from —		$10,000 or more	$100,000 or more	Total ($1,000)	Percent of farms
			Average size of farm	Total irrigated (1,000)	Total cropland (1,000)						Crops	Live-stock and poultry products				
	117	118	119	120	121	122	123	124	125	126	127	128	129	130	131	132
CALIFORNIA—Cont'd																
Butte	382	-5.4	179	223	257	760 934	4 401	62 857	252	118 407	96.0	4.0	53.1	22.4	9 411	12.5
Calaveras	261	6.5	453	7	21	521 444	1 791	24 551	13	22 308	32.4	67.6	25.7	5.2	90	5.9
Colusa	485	12.5	591	291	332	1 885 392	2 636	175 235	241	293 966	97.6	2.4	80.5	45.2	12 678	44.1
Contra Costa	126	-14.9	213	33	37	1 089 622	8 044	47 274	21	239 850	50.5	49.5	28.1	18.0	118	9.0
Del Norte	13	0.0	150	7	8	650 712	4 291	67 418	16	14 071	85.7	14.3	23.3	3.1	64	1.3
El Dorado	117	13.6	105	6	16	458 380	2 846	19 399	16	14 071	77.9	22.1	71.9	32.7	18 898	8.5
Fresno	1 929	2.6	307	1 099	1 230	1 101 948	3 612	99 231	2 759	439 328	77.9	22.1	71.9	32.7	18 898	8.5
Glenn	506	4.8	395	233	271	846 235	2 396	98 679	230	179 392	74.7	25.3	70.8	34.5	8 666	25.7
Humboldt	634	8.4	638	18	54	684 583	1 187	35 922	97	97 604	45.6	54.4	42.4	14.7	1 605	11.8
Imperial	514	4.9	957	477	488	2 931 721	2 976	270 910	1 043	1 942 791	62.2	37.8	82.9	69.1	3 301	32.4
Inyo	227	14.1	2 668	23	12	2 540 925	971	48 276	14	163 167	59.9	40.1	48.2	22.4	0	0.0
Kern	2 731	-4.2	1 272	812	998	2 213 516	1 816	195 721	2 059	958 875	86.6	13.4	60.9	43.2	13 248	16.9
Kings	646	-1.7	559	407	500	2 012 543	3 643	167 431	793	687 228	49.8	50.2	65.8	42.5	10 038	25.1
Lake	144	4.3	164	23	38	637 379	4 981	35 594	65	74 143	94.9	5.1	40.6	11.1	134	2.3
Lassen	482	6.2	1 150	62	125	792 905	694	50 295	28	66 888	56.9	43.1	37.7	12.9	586	19.3
Los Angeles	111	-15.3	72	26	51	432 687	15 544	46 652	281	182 309	96.9	3.1	31.7	13.8	78	2.0
Madera	682	6.2	383	317	362	1 209 723	3 120	92 867	710	399 120	71.1	28.9	66.8	36.5	3 160	7.1
Marin	151	0.7	593	2	32	2 012 487	3 657	52 525	43	169 396	15.6	84.4	57.9	22.8	425	10.6
Mariposa	219	10.6	772	2	13	1 058 436	1 005	34 442	6	22 130	7.5	92.5	26.1	4.9	66	3.2
Mendocino	707	10.6	598	28	77	1 602 599	2 346	39 165	95	80 276	90.5	9.5	44.0	14.3	498	6.3
Merced	1 006	14.1	339	519	593	1 363 034	3 826	114 594	1 409	475 457	42.4	57.6	70.2	36.0	11 479	15.3
Modoc	609	-8.1	1 423	129	182	956 616	692	101 726	53	122 746	62.7	37.3	62.4	24.8	1 219	34.6
Mono	54	-21.7	863	26	17	1 204 840	1 561	130 519	9	141 802	64.8	35.2	61.9	27.0	8	6.3
Monterey	1 261	-18.3	1 037	253	368	3 222 212	3 248	260 030	2 190	1 801 086	98.7	1.3	61.6	43.2	1 131	7.8
Napa	238	12.3	163	53	76	2 734 325	19 350	72 725	429	294 651	99.1	0.9	67.6	30.1	225	2.1
Nevada	82	30.2	137	7	17	477 898	3 418	104 634	7	11 902	75.1	24.9	15.2	1.5	9	1.7
Orange	68	17.2	195	10	15	2 011 911	10 661	95 053	279	800 592	99.6	0.4	46.6	26.4	30	3.2
Placer	131	-6.4	91	36	50	587 380	4 849	25 720	37	25 847	76.2	23.8	18.2	4.3	1 379	3.3
Plumas	171	56.9	1 201	17	88	1 222 213	1 022	40 586	7	51 668	17.6	82.4	34.5	10.6	206	8.5
Riverside	572	12.4	180	198	282	1 089 879	4 830	63 339	1 008	316 470	66.2	33.8	45.3	17.7	1 832	3.3
Sacramento	314	1.9	208	125	161	995 091	4 485	73 699	239	158 140	68.1	31.9	35.6	18.3	3 334	10.2
San Benito	578	12.9	854	33	77	1 479 433	1 878	63 852	198	292 311	80.6	19.4	41.8	19.6	304	8.1
San Bernardino	514	-44.4	371	41	48	708 212	2 144	72 654	618	445 776	19.5	80.5	44.7	21.9	1 676	5.6
San Diego	408	-14.1	78	68	108	740 112	7 635	32 597	951	180 925	92.8	7.2	44.9	13.7	324	0.8
San Francisco	D	NA	D	0	D	32 239	32 239	1 933	1	126 530	D	D	62.5	25.0	0	0.0
San Joaquin	813	0.5	202	520	575	1 203 010	6 673	91 721	1 222	303 640	74.3	25.7	63.0	30.6	7 118	8.3
San Luis Obispo	1 318	1.2	568	74	266	1 523 567	2 676	64 723	396	170 712	92.4	7.6	46.5	16.7	2 951	11.5
San Mateo	42	-6.7	136	5	16	1 581 050	5 979	84 156	173	566 515	99.3	0.7	47.4	26.1	D	D
Santa Barbara	757	-7.3	524	108	155	1 893 146	3 684	118 593	717	496 715	95.9	4.1	54.4	29.2	538	3.3
Santa Clara	321	0.6	313	25	31	1 185 166	2 887	44 545	208	203 214	90.2	9.8	38.5	14.6	101	2.7
Santa Cruz	67	-5.6	89	24	28	1 179 533	9 335	81 260	362	479 975	97.5	2.5	59.5	31.6	233	3.6
Shasta	334	5.4	296	46	71	519 775	1 733	22 962	22	19 496	38.0	62.0	27.0	4.4	268	7.3
Sierra	59	28.3	1 128	12	17	1 295 884	1 512	70 680	2	43 635	D	D	53.8	9.6	39	17.3
Siskiyou	610	-3.0	767	160	195	854 505	1 435	89 909	109	137 390	78.0	22.0	46.1	18.7	1 944	24.4
Solano	351	-3.0	384	125	195	1 564 886	3 834	81 554	191	208 567	83.1	16.9	47.2	19.6	2 457	15.2
Sonoma	627	9.8	182	76	163	1 710 715	11 058	60 466	572	165 857	75.6	24.4	49.9	19.1	1 897	4.8
Stanislaus	790	7.8	185	401	408	1 062 751	6 068	77 381	1 229	287 932	46.2	53.8	59.2	24.6	8 589	7.8
Sutter	372	6.9	267	249	298	1 032 558	4 064	118 498	251	180 173	97.7	2.3	72.0	36.3	9 982	19.0
Tehama	862	-2.6	548	99	141	843 119	1 658	42 217	110	70 018	66.5	33.5	44.6	12.7	1 391	10.4
Trinity	105	-11.0	781	2	4	486 989	639	26 660	2	13 107	37.2	62.8	20.7	3.0	D	D
Tulare	1 393	6.3	243	652	770	948 550	3 949	90 642	2 339	407 560	51.1	48.9	68.9	33.7	12 816	9.2
Tuolumne	150	-1.3	418	4	13	809 165	1 664	23 656	24	65 836	4.8	95.2	19.8	3.9	41	3.1
Ventura	332	-4.0	143	102	124	1 441 670	8 839	66 436	1 019	439 544	98.7	1.3	61.0	31.4	1 217	4.5
Yolo	550	2.4	519	299	371	1 531 470	3 645	135 930	315	297 605	96.0	4.0	57.0	27.4	7 117	24.8
Yuba	234	12.5	271	93	97	745 087	3 444	66 261	115	133 422	78.1	21.9	45.9	20.5	3 374	15.1
COLORADO	31 093	-4.7	991	2 591	11 531	757 613	756	87 871	4 525	144 257	26.9	73.1	39.6	12.5	125 774	32.4
Adams	701	4.0	964	29	578	914 014	901	97 399	99	135 536	87.7	12.3	36.1	14.1	3 823	35.4
Alamosa	205	7.9	644	94	111	719 503	1 206	155 519	94	297 017	93.7	6.3	62.6	28.0	535	27.7
Arapahoe	333	0.0	742	3	173	600 360	853	74 232	20	44 588	76.2	23.8	26.8	6.0	1 556	33.0
Archuleta	103	-8.8	400	8	27	674 094	1 277	39 866	5	17 979	7.1	92.9	25.2	4.7	116	11.6
Baca	1 080	-5.4	1 777	48	603	593 077	292	94 358	61	100 495	28.5	71.5	46.9	14.1	7 949	75.8
Bent	736	-6.1	2 777	30	167	900 039	320	104 159	82	310 007	5.8	94.2	60.8	18.9	1 656	46.4
Boulder	108	-15.6	146	31	54	1 159 421	7 639	49 483	33	44 616	66.4	33.6	25.4	5.7	262	10.5
Broomfield	NA	NA	NA	NA	NA	NA	NA	NA	NA	NA	NA	NA	NA	NA	NA	NA
Chaffee	71	-17.4	336	9	26	777 083	2 093	122 687	9	40 266	25.7	74.3	31.6	8.5	64	7.5

Table B. States and Counties — Residential Construction, Wholesale Trade, Retail Trade, and Real Estate

STATE County	Value of residential construction authorized by building permits, 2003		Wholesale trade, 1997				Retail trade,[1] 1997				Real estate and rental and leasing, 1997			
	New construction ($1,000)	Number of housing units	Number of establish-ments	Number of employees	Sales (mil dol)	Annual payroll (mil dol)	Number of establish-ments	Number of employees	Sales (mil dol)	Annual payroll (mil dol)	Number of establish-ments	Number of employees	Receipts (mil dol)	Annual payroll (mil dol)
	133	134	135	136	137	138	139	140	141	142	143	144	145	146
CALIFORNIA—Cont'd														
Butte	208 372	1 769	179	1 792	637.9	56.9	777	9 004	1 502.6	154.0	212	1 012	80.5	13.4
Calaveras	162 653	691	27	D	D	D	136	862	135.5	14.0	36	100	10.4	1.6
Colusa	8 103	46	25	318	152.3	8.3	67	545	121.7	10.8	19	49	4.8	0.7
Contra Costa	1 451 454	6 883	1 159	11 092	14 968.0	518.5	2 705	37 550	7 376.8	752.8	1 056	6 172	972.6	172.2
Del Norte	19 503	127	15	D	D	D	88	982	123.1	12.5	20	58	4.9	0.8
El Dorado	503 913	1 850	108	684	249.7	19.3	546	4 894	926.8	91.1	180	781	68.6	9.9
Fresno	834 578	5 753	971	13 004	5 845.2	415.5	2 492	30 231	5 574.6	548.9	593	3 496	376.5	67.3
Glenn	15 034	141	36	298	125.8	8.6	79	720	98.9	10.5	18	149	7.1	1.4
Humboldt	42 697	425	128	1 306	493.6	37.1	668	6 816	1 024.0	108.7	141	494	47.1	7.9
Imperial	138 271	1 201	189	1 951	673.7	41.0	521	5 991	989.4	98.8	86	408	33.2	6.5
Inyo	4 037	19	24	D	D	D	145	1 092	171.1	17.8	18	59	4.3	1.1
Kern	798 346	5 813	612	7 930	4 313.9	256.4	1 918	22 792	4 224.4	412.1	419	2 479	220.5	43.8
Kings	102 676	1 017	60	623	411.6	15.8	316	3 690	629.3	60.0	66	235	20.8	3.3
Lake	81 360	528	39	D	D	D	197	1 954	309.3	30.7	41	89	7.0	1.0
Lassen	22 008	140	11	D	D	D	106	1 032	159.2	15.5	16	56	3.9	0.6
Los Angeles	3 049 103	20 903	21 474	259 217	177 244.9	9 450.4	27 577	343 656	69 534.2	6 769.0	10 932	76 904	13 608.6	2 256.3
Madera	164 821	1 227	87	623	265.8	18.8	313	3 173	527.3	53.0	60	217	22.3	3.8
Marin	180 017	701	570	4 167	2 414.8	170.4	1 291	14 793	2 775.7	322.0	537	2 978	556.7	91.0
Mariposa	26 072	151	7	D	D	D	78	397	57.4	6.3	14	68	4.3	1.0
Mendocino	34 238	399	108	1 095	308.7	27.0	490	4 572	711.4	76.8	109	445	35.7	5.8
Merced	369 472	2 742	117	1 333	699.9	36.4	551	6 122	1 102.1	108.0	121	461	46.0	5.7
Modoc	1 709	17	11	D	D	D	46	256	34.3	3.5	6	D	D	D
Mono	61 161	307	2	D	D	D	79	683	84.0	10.2	37	269	13.8	3.4
Monterey	351 583	1 355	473	7 530	4 747.4	267.9	1 558	16 413	3 035.9	327.9	386	1 837	236.4	38.9
Napa	183 470	607	153	1 296	533.0	46.4	525	5 292	952.6	102.8	153	1 068	84.2	15.7
Nevada	137 575	912	90	453	118.7	13.1	430	3 914	654.8	73.7	115	449	57.7	8.2
Orange	1 596 176	9 248	7 029	103 113	94 403.4	3 999.6	9 084	126 575	26 172.8	2 572.0	3 537	29 156	4 714.8	939.1
Placer	1 090 235	5 272	283	3 888	1 792.6	147.7	875	11 769	2 666.6	254.7	302	2 158	204.0	40.7
Plumas	34 711	229	12	D	D	D	119	829	127.5	16.1	26	60	4.8	0.9
Riverside	4 886 166	30 353	1 200	12 649	6 715.6	416.6	4 030	54 433	10 609.0	1 028.9	1 190	6 164	698.6	126.9
Sacramento	2 236 931	13 960	1 287	18 090	8 555.8	626.7	3 587	51 962	9 502.3	990.0	1 180	8 334	909.1	185.4
San Benito	14 687	97	43	752	211.1	21.6	117	1 731	276.8	30.9	34	95	14.5	1.4
San Bernardino	1 956 855	11 899	1 747	24 756	14 254.1	805.8	4 372	60 940	11 342.8	1 100.5	1 134	6 103	753.5	126.0
San Diego	2 999 360	18 031	4 159	53 589	26 543.9	2 273.7	9 109	119 022	22 215.3	2 241.1	3 742	23 069	3 250.0	573.9
San Francisco	118 445	1 430	1 900	17 677	12 219.1	779.8	3 841	39 693	6 795.0	830.6	1 627	14 492	2 721.2	472.9
San Joaquin	1 273 912	7 041	560	9 751	7 651.7	319.3	1 594	19 957	3 679.6	364.7	436	2 602	257.7	52.3
San Luis Obispo	414 092	2 260	244	1 904	561.5	46.8	1 132	10 917	1 780.7	182.4	319	1 243	149.7	20.9
San Mateo	376 666	1 345	1 687	21 640	14 662.6	1 088.3	2 285	33 757	7 335.4	735.4	1 003	8 940	1 496.0	270.8
Santa Barbara	292 550	1 461	469	4 282	1 636.0	137.5	1 653	19 187	3 183.5	354.0	558	2 733	708.8	71.0
Santa Clara	1 055 261	7 006	3 468	66 542	68 095.4	3 891.8	5 278	79 921	16 673.6	1 696.7	1 968	12 585	2 456.4	372.8
Santa Cruz	188 571	1 066	342	4 472	1 541.8	140.3	986	11 794	1 970.2	215.5	314	1 649	166.5	27.1
Shasta	187 920	1 358	217	1 786	566.6	51.9	713	8 113	1 354.5	140.3	199	878	80.3	14.6
Sierra	3 341	22	NA	NA	NA	NA	13	64	8.8	0.9	1	D	D	D
Siskiyou	35 335	210	35	D	D	D	233	1 770	256.1	25.4	42	89	6.6	1.0
Solano	447 292	2 642	262	3 909	2 170.1	145.7	1 116	15 046	2 789.4	281.0	321	1 344	164.9	24.5
Sonoma	394 616	2 252	619	7 430	3 069.7	259.4	1 808	22 190	4 146.2	443.7	576	2 394	329.3	48.5
Stanislaus	604 567	4 119	417	5 118	2 264.4	159.1	1 368	17 706	3 282.2	319.2	340	2 033	244.5	42.4
Sutter	155 509	989	90	D	D	D	291	3 604	606.7	61.1	85	488	40.7	6.1
Tehama	56 498	424	40	D	D	D	176	1 953	360.6	33.0	42	149	9.6	1.5
Trinity	5 920	58	6	D	D	D	54	334	38.9	4.6	7	18	0.6	0.2
Tulare	297 258	2 270	343	5 120	2 527.7	135.1	1 107	12 742	2 135.7	211.8	206	809	97.7	12.6
Tuolumne	46 543	358	37	280	96.2	8.8	228	2 343	341.4	38.0	64	198	18.0	2.6
Ventura	729 831	3 567	1 088	13 811	10 402.7	522.6	2 348	30 831	6 476.6	608.7	672	3 254	409.0	73.4
Yolo	245 296	1 750	282	7 829	5 000.2	257.8	458	5 776	1 026.7	110.6	189	1 305	177.9	30.0
Yuba	79 536	608	40	D	D	D	155	1 525	244.6	25.6	33	104	11.2	1.3
COLORADO	6 258 256	39 569	7 383	88 364	60 310.4	3 282.0	18 299	225 647	40 536.0	4 163.3	6 663	38 224	4 853.5	883.8
Adams	726 043	4 678	732	12 884	7 044.5	443.5	952	14 489	2 859.1	308.8	323	2 677	289.6	69.1
Alamosa	2 837	36	30	225	68.8	5.3	97	1 090	167.2	17.2	18	48	4.6	0.8
Arapahoe	533 981	3 311	1 156	15 912	22 395.3	813.5	2 003	30 860	6 353.6	603.5	859	5 109	766.1	157.8
Archuleta	35 366	219	9	13	10.2	0.6	67	370	54.6	5.9	25	109	19.0	4.1
Baca	450	10	11	51	24.1	1.0	27	127	18.6	1.7	2	D	D	D
Bent	0	0	2	D	D	D	16	94	11.6	1.1	3	6	0.3	0.1
Boulder	224 973	1 428	539	5 558	3 906.0	234.9	1 275	17 269	2 915.0	309.9	486	2 189	287.9	49.2
Broomfield	103 841	637	NA	NA	NA	NA	NA	NA	NA	NA	NA	NA	NA	NA
Chaffee	27 544	201	25	130	37.4	2.1	112	928	124.4	14.0	31	124	10.0	1.7

1. Establishments with payroll.

STATE County	Professional, scientific, and technical services,[1] 1997				Manufacturing, 1997				Accommodation and foodservices, 1997			
	Number of establishments	Number of employees	Receipts (mil dol)	Annual payroll (mil dol)	Number of establishments	Number of employees	Receipts (mil dol)	Annual payroll (mil dol)	Number of establishments	Number of employees	Sales (mil dol)	Annual payroll (mil dol)
	147	148	149	150	151	152	153	154	155	156	157	158
CALIFORNIA—Cont'd												
Butte	308	1 513	130.7	45.0	232	4 944	771.6	128.4	380	5 920	156.2	43.3
Calaveras	55	177	13.1	4.5	NA	NA	NA	NA	95	753	21.4	5.7
Colusa	19	37	2.6	0.6	20	651	265.8	20.8	43	508	17.1	4.9
Contra Costa	2 678	19 116	2 487.5	1 020.1	723	19 366	11 644.8	889.0	1 515	23 374	902.1	238.4
Del Norte	33	88	6.0	1.8	NA	NA	NA	NA	82	710	24.1	5.8
El Dorado	262	1 478	165.9	74.4	144	1 775	287.9	56.4	410	5 539	209.0	55.3
Fresno	1 184	11 156	584.1	234.3	696	27 552	5 667.6	704.3	1 256	19 886	631.9	169.6
Glenn	32	108	6.2	1.6	29	946	290.6	29.2	50	549	17.8	4.3
Humboldt	205	981	65.9	23.5	178	5 540	1 041.9	161.4	371	4 312	134.2	36.4
Imperial	113	519	46.2	15.8	61	1 481	241.6	40.6	238	2 723	89.3	23.0
Inyo	32	101	5.8	2.0	NA	NA	NA	NA	100	1 248	54.4	13.5
Kern	753	6 296	525.7	224.6	390	14 306	2 824.6	379.2	1 013	14 724	493.2	129.1
Kings	74	358	26.8	8.6	65	2 796	748.7	90.6	156	2 037	65.1	16.2
Lake	58	159	10.6	3.4	NA	NA	NA	NA	132	978	29.1	6.9
Lassen	22	89	4.9	1.5	NA	NA	NA	NA	68	733	25.8	7.0
Los Angeles	22 194	346 290	31 678.8	12 767.4	17 915	622 302	106 706.4	20 311.3	15 718	267 157	11 074.3	2 991.3
Madera	81	364	42.3	10.7	94	3 913	952.3	120.8	162	2 136	73.0	18.7
Marin	1 495	7 487	881.8	344.4	341	4 605	656.2	160.0	680	10 183	414.7	119.8
Mariposa	19	32	2.9	0.9	NA	NA	NA	NA	56	1 112	80.9	14.8
Mendocino	169	477	33.7	11.6	160	4 287	769.3	124.1	321	3 626	124.6	33.4
Merced	138	668	41.0	15.8	123	8 381	2 431.5	198.2	269	3 265	108.4	27.2
Modoc	6	23	0.9	0.3	NA	NA	NA	NA	27	178	4.9	1.1
Mono	26	115	10.0	3.7	NA	NA	NA	NA	133	3 192	113.3	35.1
Monterey	694	2 998	293.1	109.2	302	7 070	1 329.4	223.7	905	16 869	835.3	226.0
Napa	268	1 752	301.7	132.2	277	8 466	2 139.7	320.7	347	6 250	287.1	80.3
Nevada	220	724	60.3	21.4	174	2 311	372.9	74.1	229	3 968	117.5	33.3
Orange	8 838	75 635	9 728.8	3 540.6	5 767	215 936	39 134.1	7 643.6	5 397	105 298	4 241.7	1 133.2
Placer	526	2 488	260.0	95.9	260	9 244	3 808.4	403.4	546	10 083	334.1	94.0
Plumas	44	102	7.3	1.9	23	643	176.7	21.9	116	512	23.5	5.6
Riverside	1 642	8 798	904.9	277.4	1 420	46 134	7 736.0	1 329.1	2 159	41 940	1 619.4	447.9
Sacramento	2 731	21 959	2 343.5	892.2	910	30 493	8 939.6	1 017.0	2 185	36 413	1 195.3	320.1
San Benito	51	151	13.8	5.2	75	2 160	365.3	64.2	80	962	30.0	7.9
San Bernardino	1 482	8 262	743.8	259.7	1 992	63 448	11 618.7	1 830.4	2 323	37 291	1 279.7	335.0
San Diego	7 144	59 761	7 072.3	2 725.7	3 407	118 868	22 233.6	4 223.5	5 426	105 069	4 237.9	1 157.4
San Francisco	4 984	58 942	9 016.6	3 517.4	1 247	25 037	3 978.9	642.4	3 258	60 113	3 281.1	955.7
San Joaquin	575	3 531	277.7	111.2	553	24 646	5 879.1	749.6	826	11 413	376.9	96.5
San Luis Obispo	529	2 292	212.2	76.7	323	6 322	1 156.3	182.3	674	10 534	382.5	101.7
San Mateo	2 370	21 418	3 235.2	1 313.0	1 019	34 438	6 690.1	1 649.6	1 495	27 990	1 379.0	385.8
Santa Barbara	981	6 344	711.2	270.6	502	14 985	2 770.4	584.2	952	17 195	633.1	177.1
Santa Clara	6 338	71 612	10 440.6	4 424.1	3 464	249 947	72 528.3	13 094.0	3 495	60 330	2 590.7	677.7
Santa Cruz	678	3 073	384.1	132.1	387	10 011	2 135.0	315.2	591	8 223	305.5	80.8
Shasta	304	1 636	127.0	51.6	177	3 526	635.0	118.7	402	5 070	161.7	41.7
Sierra	4	D	D	D	NA	NA	NA	NA	22	86	5.4	1.2
Siskiyou	65	168	12.0	3.0	41	1 016	207.3	30.1	160	1 396	46.9	12.4
Solano	391	2 149	179.3	66.2	277	9 175	3 496.4	331.0	568	8 747	291.1	73.8
Sonoma	1 171	5 682	565.8	239.1	793	24 209	5 119.8	968.8	1 005	13 993	490.2	132.2
Stanislaus	478	2 974	232.5	81.3	435	25 056	6 886.6	823.1	676	9 877	312.7	80.4
Sutter	102	436	26.6	10.4	70	1 589	354.0	49.3	102	1 443	44.9	12.8
Tehama	52	194	17.7	3.8	48	2 228	455.2	62.9	102	1 128	36.7	9.2
Trinity	17	38	1.9	0.6	NA	NA	NA	NA	57	296	11.1	2.5
Tulare	335	1 788	265.6	45.0	282	11 439	3 167.3	314.5	510	7 020	232.3	56.8
Tuolumne	78	240	17.3	5.2	65	880	155.2	22.5	168	1 747	58.4	15.2
Ventura	1 597	10 829	1 229.3	464.9	1 008	33 562	6 163.4	1 136.3	1 200	21 879	775.3	209.4
Yolo	231	1 541	204.1	59.4	175	6 178	1 514.9	212.0	302	4 379	140.1	36.2
Yuba	41	136	10.7	3.9	44	1 203	248.2	26.8	85	940	31.0	9.1
COLORADO	14 315	103 008	12 887.7	4 625.1	5 480	173 069	40 012.8	6 176.8	10 064	195 126	6 705.5	1 937.4
Adams	386	2 568	205.6	86.4	436	13 151	3 045.1	428.4	512	8 990	288.8	79.3
Alamosa	43	157	8.5	3.5	NA	NA	NA	NA	49	938	20.7	5.8
Arapahoe	2 105	19 081	2 225.0	905.6	549	18 852	5 017.3	798.0	914	19 366	683.7	188.7
Archuleta	27	57	5.2	1.4	NA	NA	NA	NA	56	530	15.1	4.4
Baca	3	6	0.3	0.1	NA	NA	NA	NA	7	41	1.3	0.3
Bent	2	D	D	D	NA	NA	NA	NA	8	83	2.2	0.6
Boulder	1 612	15 458	3 081.9	760.2	686	26 225	5 196.3	1 052.1	708	13 824	453.1	131.0
Broomfield	NA	NA	NA	NA	NA	NA	NA	NA	NA	NA	NA	NA
Chaffee	42	178	7.7	2.7	NA	NA	NA	NA	100	969	30.9	8.6

1. Firms subject to federal tax.

Table B. States and Counties — Health Care and Social Assistance, Other Services, and Federal Funds

STATE County	Health care and social assistance,[1] 1997				Other services,[1] 1997				Federal funds and grants, 2002–2003 Expenditures (mil dol)			
										Direct payments for individuals[2]		
	Number of establishments	Number of employees	Receipts (mil dol)	Annual payroll (mil dol)	Number of establishments	Number of employees	Receipts (mil dol)	Annual payroll (mil dol)	Total	Social Security and government retirement	Medicare	Food stamps and Supplemental Security Income
	159	160	161	162	163	164	165	166	167	168	169	170
CALIFORNIA—Cont'd												
Butte	553	5 261	299.4	114.3	261	1 454	147.1	25.3	1 190.7	502.8	256.5	55.0
Calaveras	57	435	22.4	9.5	41	112	22.6	3.2	230.1	126.1	52.1	5.5
Colusa	23	132	7.5	2.6	24	109	6.5	1.8	131.2	35.3	20.9	2.4
Contra Costa	2 034	18 842	1 446.1	631.4	1 201	7 107	526.0	157.5	4 322.3	1 720.2	892.2	125.5
Del Norte	43	369	23.3	7.8	20	56	6.0	1.3	153.2	63.1	28.2	10.8
El Dorado	314	1 781	127.5	47.2	174	692	53.4	13.1	661.9	341.4	157.4	17.5
Fresno	1 614	15 504	1 103.7	463.9	947	6 026	458.9	120.0	4 074.2	1 210.2	529.5	237.6
Glenn	28	236	11.4	4.3	22	68	6.1	1.2	162.7	52.4	29.5	5.8
Humboldt	325	3 003	174.8	68.8	187	828	57.9	14.7	805.1	279.0	129.8	34.8
Imperial	172	1 665	103.7	40.8	107	506	34.5	9.4	765.9	210.3	123.2	41.9
Inyo	46	333	18.5	8.1	33	116	9.9	2.3	278.1	51.1	25.6	2.6
Kern	938	9 631	755.0	278.5	694	4 192	348.6	92.2	3 856.0	1 135.0	601.2	163.6
Kings	142	1 544	99.7	40.9	88	331	25.4	5.8	776.8	182.7	76.3	25.0
Lake	98	759	54.0	18.8	52	150	11.0	2.6	413.6	179.6	115.0	17.8
Lassen	43	348	19.3	5.8	28	78	5.7	1.1	197.2	65.3	23.7	5.3
Los Angeles	20 278	196 543	15 709.6	6 162.8	13 134	86 614	6 086.4	1 734.3	56 540.1	11 907.8	9 921.3	2 356.7
Madera	155	1 238	69.8	26.0	95	386	27.8	7.0	522.3	218.2	103.8	21.9
Marin	841	7 043	494.2	219.1	496	2 608	208.2	62.8	1 293.4	537.1	251.0	17.9
Mariposa	17	148	7.2	2.6	7	57	6.0	1.6	134.6	49.1	20.4	1.9
Mendocino	202	1 310	78.1	30.2	113	429	32.6	7.3	551.5	198.6	98.9	20.2
Merced	323	2 668	167.8	64.2	171	813	49.2	14.3	964.5	343.3	147.7	65.2
Modoc	7	59	2.5	1.2	8	D	D	D	90.4	26.8	10.6	1.3
Mono	15	46	5.7	2.4	10	50	3.3	0.8	46.2	14.1	4.4	0.5
Monterey	708	5 613	430.5	177.7	445	2 416	172.1	48.0	2 106.6	730.1	316.2	46.3
Napa	357	3 272	229.2	90.5	165	916	60.2	17.1	702.1	310.5	182.2	9.8
Nevada	252	1 691	100.9	37.5	107	409	33.0	8.8	534.6	250.5	100.5	7.3
Orange	6 986	66 269	5 571.4	2 170.8	4 249	28 174	2 101.9	600.0	12 437.5	4 130.4	2 435.9	351.0
Placer	585	4 845	380.4	142.6	305	3 164	239.5	83.7	1 145.9	702.2	178.3	20.8
Plumas	44	269	12.6	5.1	26	99	7.9	1.9	157.2	62.9	27.9	3.3
Riverside	2 307	24 783	1 905.2	707.4	1 499	9 119	620.7	173.1	7 028.4	3 138.7	1 595.9	221.9
Sacramento	2 383	24 874	2 014.7	870.2	1 549	10 484	731.1	214.1	14 837.0	3 361.7	1 048.4	343.3
San Benito	64	389	20.1	7.7	46	189	17.8	3.1	168.2	65.1	29.1	4.2
San Bernardino	2 314	26 710	2 051.5	798.4	1 720	12 182	804.8	232.9	7 634.8	2 571.7	1 352.6	384.7
San Diego	5 508	53 541	4 232.7	1 656.5	3 811	24 273	1 648.1	466.0	24 045.1	5 770.4	2 670.5	438.6
San Francisco	2 260	14 360	1 209.7	478.5	1 477	8 794	634.9	179.0	7 176.2	1 252.4	998.4	245.1
San Joaquin	949	9 252	664.0	273.5	690	3 838	265.3	74.2	2 675.1	986.9	462.6	158.2
San Luis Obispo	599	5 083	375.3	161.3	294	1 446	96.2	25.9	1 113.7	544.3	240.3	24.9
San Mateo	1 597	14 194	1 166.2	495.9	1 178	7 290	582.9	172.6	3 239.4	1 276.8	633.1	57.4
Santa Barbara	934	6 609	516.9	199.8	536	3 054	192.1	57.4	2 724.0	799.8	355.2	49.1
Santa Clara	3 742	38 283	3 032.2	1 240.9	2 471	16 850	1 352.9	400.5	11 239.9	2 227.7	1 164.2	261.7
Santa Cruz	631	4 739	309.8	121.7	330	1 614	112.1	31.3	992.7	370.0	219.6	29.6
Shasta	487	5 441	387.9	156.8	241	1 289	86.4	22.8	1 061.2	483.3	201.7	48.3
Sierra	2	D	D	D	NA	NA	NA	NA	27.2	9.2	5.3	0.4
Siskiyou	86	668	32.0	13.0	57	146	11.7	2.7	349.9	138.2	57.1	12.6
Solano	628	6 046	480.3	199.2	446	3 104	210.4	70.1	2 442.4	907.0	228.3	59.2
Sonoma	1 241	11 357	766.6	319.5	676	3 604	252.0	74.0	2 039.1	916.1	460.5	48.1
Stanislaus	805	9 346	656.1	253.2	538	3 154	210.7	58.7	2 046.9	764.8	389.7	105.8
Sutter	199	1 999	209.0	61.5	105	589	36.9	10.3	408.6	182.5	72.5	17.2
Tehama	89	705	37.3	14.5	62	315	21.3	5.5	321.7	134.6	60.7	14.1
Trinity	18	93	4.5	1.7	18	60	4.0	0.8	99.9	42.3	17.1	1.9
Tulare	588	5 102	334.0	127.8	308	1 544	115.2	28.7	1 634.1	521.9	277.6	91.9
Tuolumne	119	648	47.4	19.8	56	257	16.8	4.4	332.0	163.8	65.2	8.1
Ventura	1 591	13 110	1 086.6	413.1	875	5 577	442.5	126.7	4 065.6	1 343.8	636.3	72.3
Yolo	267	2 432	136.7	58.6	209	1 141	92.3	25.4	1 061.2	253.1	116.4	25.0
Yuba	53	703	39.1	17.5	43	232	17.0	4.0	557.6	134.3	62.0	22.1
COLORADO	8 611	85 370	5 790.8	2 538.1	6 793	39 363	2 571.1	770.0	28 874.2	8 115.4	2 767.7	462.6
Adams	377	4 049	262.0	117.3	505	3 508	240.0	72.5	1 474.3	489.7	238.4	37.1
Alamosa	27	213	15.8	6.3	34	168	7.6	2.2	94.1	23.0	8.8	4.4
Arapahoe	1 244	15 685	1 250.8	511.9	851	5 400	354.3	110.7	2 233.2	954.2	237.4	38.8
Archuleta	13	34	2.3	0.7	8	36	1.4	0.4	54.6	26.1	3.3	0.8
Baca	4	17	0.6	0.1	13	30	2.2	0.5	54.1	12.8	5.7	0.5
Bent	6	22	0.8	0.2	1	D	D	D	44.3	19.5	4.8	1.1
Boulder	715	6 087	405.5	170.7	482	2 945	192.2	60.9	1 864.1	443.4	154.0	18.7
Broomfield	NA	NA	NA	NA	NA	NA	NA	NA	26.3	0.0	0.0	0.0
Chaffee	28	290	11.4	5.2	28	90	6.4	1.3	88.5	46.7	12.6	1.5

1. Firms subject to federal tax.   2. State totals may include programs not allocated by county.

	Federal funds and grants, 2002–2003 (cont'd)							Local government finances, 2002				
	Expenditures (mil dol) (cont'd)							General revenue				
	Procurement contract awards			Grants[1]						Taxes		
											Per capita[2] (dollars)	
STATE County	Salaries and wages	Defense	Other	Medicaid and other health-related	Nutrition and family welfare	Education	Other	Total (mil dol)	Intergovern-mental (mil dol)	Total (mil dol)	Total	Property
	171	172	173	174	175	176	177	178	179	180	181	182
CALIFORNIA—Cont'd												
Butte	31.2	0.4	27.2	151.0	44.5	18.8	47.1	787.5	493.5	150.3	718	521
Calaveras	6.8	0.3	1.9	15.2	8.3	7.0	4.9	129.6	58.1	42.9	998	855
Colusa	3.2	1.1	2.4	10.8	5.8	1.7	4.2	102.5	54.2	19.8	1 026	849
Contra Costa	357.2	257.4	145.0	437.9	138.6	53.8	170.5	4 170.4	1 716.2	1 240.3	1 250	946
Del Norte	7.5	0.0	1.5	16.6	7.8	3.1	12.6	100.9	72.4	15.7	571	430
El Dorado	40.9	9.9	17.2	36.6	18.8	8.8	11.2	659.7	267.6	189.6	1 144	912
Fresno	539.5	119.8	131.9	579.8	256.4	97.4	205.7	3 668.6	2 338.5	634.8	761	549
Glenn	13.9	0.2	3.9	15.3	8.1	2.8	8.7	142.7	87.6	20.5	770	600
Humboldt	57.6	45.0	21.3	97.2	38.7	17.6	52.2	518.7	317.5	100.7	792	592
Imperial	82.3	19.3	21.4	115.0	40.9	28.0	64.1	844.1	474.3	103.9	710	521
Inyo	16.9	133.6	7.3	11.9	5.6	4.8	17.9	129.9	47.9	39.9	2 190	1 531
Kern	700.7	262.7	138.4	406.8	165.1	66.6	130.1	3 749.3	2 032.9	579.6	835	659
Kings	284.3	1.9	25.0	73.8	34.3	19.1	17.5	443.4	293.6	67.5	500	366
Lake	9.3	0.7	2.9	51.7	14.9	5.3	13.7	208.1	125.8	46.1	743	601
Lassen	29.0	19.2	11.1	19.4	6.3	4.1	9.5	124.8	89.0	20.4	601	487
Los Angeles	3 404.4	10 431.2	3 695.6	7 884.8	2 746.4	796.6	2 730.4	47 021.0	25 648.4	11 982.8	1 222	713
Madera	15.5	0.4	6.3	85.4	26.9	10.3	15.9	406.6	257.5	81.0	622	473
Marin	69.3	8.1	36.2	93.8	17.0	11.1	242.7	946.6	290.4	435.2	1 758	1 368
Mariposa	26.4	1.2	18.4	6.1	3.7	1.1	4.4	71.3	33.4	21.2	1 233	701
Mendocino	18.0	0.9	7.7	73.4	36.9	15.5	74.5	514.0	221.3	93.6	1 073	826
Merced	46.3	5.5	17.2	147.8	70.0	28.1	44.4	990.7	632.7	139.5	619	477
Modoc	14.7	13.2	5.0	6.6	4.0	1.9	3.5	74.9	48.0	8.6	923	819
Mono	13.9	4.2	3.8	1.8	1.5	1.3	0.1	102.8	27.1	40.5	3 091	2 132
Monterey	489.3	102.0	46.4	168.0	74.3	38.6	74.6	2 112.1	858.5	478.1	1 156	795
Napa	17.2	10.6	4.2	58.7	19.0	8.9	72.9	548.9	230.7	208.3	1 599	1 198
Nevada	20.2	72.8	13.9	31.1	9.4	4.4	21.7	354.3	128.5	101.6	1 069	862
Orange	779.9	2 137.1	634.8	935.5	313.1	162.9	411.2	10 600.7	4 526.5	3 738.3	1 272	863
Placer	54.9	11.4	19.8	80.9	26.5	10.7	28.3	1 271.4	462.2	444.2	1 595	1 079
Plumas	17.4	0.1	7.9	11.4	5.4	2.8	15.7	142.1	65.7	25.3	1 317	1 103
Riverside	386.6	251.6	86.7	551.3	261.8	122.1	322.9	6 923.3	3 844.7	1 600.7	942	695
Sacramento	621.9	737.7	262.8	1 297.6	2 715.2	1 649.3	2 605.7	6 143.7	3 344.4	1 230.6	943	595
San Benito	8.7	17.0	2.0	15.3	7.7	3.5	13.6	241.3	104.0	57.6	1 030	859
San Bernardino	1 061.0	431.8	174.8	717.3	344.3	144.8	347.4	7 937.3	4 575.4	1 360.7	749	510
San Diego	5 842.9	4 697.8	637.6	2 043.2	564.0	246.0	937.9	11 595.6	5 406.4	3 296.2	1 134	822
San Francisco	1 098.3	331.9	676.1	1 745.3	138.2	60.2	477.9	5 979.9	2 330.6	2 012.5	2 634	1 331
San Joaquin	177.1	44.9	49.9	429.5	161.4	48.4	91.3	2 641.7	1 495.5	511.3	832	572
San Luis Obispo	45.3	14.6	15.0	100.6	41.0	12.8	49.6	966.5	379.7	369.1	1 457	1 134
San Mateo	306.6	144.8	173.7	402.3	53.0	30.3	142.9	2 968.0	928.6	1 260.9	1 793	1 377
Santa Barbara	314.6	615.9	82.2	187.6	55.4	35.7	191.6	1 883.2	763.0	507.8	1 260	934
Santa Clara	723.1	3 785.9	935.1	1 037.1	216.9	110.5	705.7	8 708.9	3 107.1	3 499.0	2 078	1 468
Santa Cruz	35.4	14.0	14.3	148.3	34.6	19.4	88.5	1 096.8	493.0	328.5	1 294	927
Shasta	73.4	1.4	25.9	114.9	49.6	17.9	34.1	741.2	438.1	144.5	841	639
Sierra	2.8	0.0	1.8	3.3	0.6	0.3	3.4	29.7	17.3	5.5	1 560	1 393
Siskiyou	34.3	1.2	11.6	34.1	12.5	6.3	33.6	221.8	146.6	36.3	824	645
Solano	500.1	371.7	35.2	150.8	52.8	28.5	96.3	1 734.9	876.8	409.0	995	644
Sonoma	140.5	22.3	43.0	208.6	58.4	26.7	90.7	1 933.3	822.8	574.3	1 226	933
Stanislaus	75.9	15.0	94.6	307.5	125.7	36.8	79.6	2 047.7	1 179.3	405.9	841	554
Sutter	11.5	0.0	12.6	43.9	16.5	7.0	13.6	329.5	190.8	65.8	796	588
Tehama	14.1	0.4	7.6	35.5	14.5	14.5	21.1	211.7	142.9	37.3	650	498
Trinity	10.9	0.0	5.4	7.1	3.8	1.8	8.3	83.8	55.2	8.4	640	549
Tulare	69.4	12.0	31.8	326.2	124.7	44.4	62.1	2 104.0	1 228.0	222.4	583	408
Tuolumne	22.2	1.2	10.2	21.3	8.9	2.0	25.9	206.6	102.8	46.6	834	678
Ventura	687.9	608.4	110.8	255.1	95.7	48.1	182.2	3 092.5	1 427.8	905.2	1 155	875
Yolo	150.3	15.3	75.9	210.6	29.5	16.1	119.7	654.2	334.7	192.7	1 066	691
Yuba	184.0	0.7	9.6	71.4	25.0	13.0	14.1	270.4	194.0	31.8	510	407
COLORADO	4 329.1	2 471.0	2 670.7	2 033.6	707.9	450.0	2 823.0	X	X	X	X	X
Adams	192.2	206.2	45.8	114.8	38.9	21.7	65.9	1 210.6	392.2	501.1	1 339	730
Alamosa	8.7	0.0	5.3	25.9	5.0	3.2	3.6	48.0	24.3	17.1	1 128	658
Arapahoe	243.7	337.1	211.9	52.5	22.4	26.2	92.3	1 766.5	484.4	856.5	1 679	1 135
Archuleta	2.7	0.0	1.1	2.9	0.8	0.4	15.8	46.2	14.7	25.1	2 277	1 770
Baca	1.9	0.0	0.5	4.0	0.8	0.5	5.6	25.9	7.3	7.5	1 707	1 129
Bent	2.0	0.6	0.8	6.0	1.5	0.5	3.1	32.4	8.9	4.7	818	782
Boulder	224.5	168.1	331.8	108.8	15.6	16.8	363.0	915.5	210.7	519.9	1 862	1 118
Broomfield	0.1	18.9	5.7	0.7	0.0	0.0	1.0	104.3	3.1	81.1	1 985	251
Chaffee	5.5	0.0	3.6	8.2	2.0	0.6	7.5	56.2	13.9	17.2	1 022	660

1. State totals may include programs not allocated by county.   2. Based on the resident population estimated as of July 1 of the year shown.

STATE County	Total (mil dol)	Per capita[1] (dollars)	Education	Health and hospitals	Police protection	Public welfare	Highways	Total (mil dol)	Per capita[1] (dollars)	Federal civilian	Federal military	State and local	Democratic	Republican	All other
	183	184	185	186	187	188	189	190	191	192	193	194	195	196	197
CALIFORNIA—Cont'd															
Butte	797.8	3 814	46.6	6.2	3.7	13.6	2.9	229.5	1 097	534	298	15 051	44.4	54.0	1.6
Calaveras	126.6	2 946	47.3	5.0	5.2	9.0	6.0	79.8	1 858	128	59	2 329	37.6	60.5	1.9
Colusa	98.1	5 079	44.6	4.8	5.0	5.4	5.8	18.5	956	82	26	1 939	31.6	67.1	1.3
Contra Costa	4 285.7	4 319	39.0	12.2	5.1	7.5	4.6	3 335.0	3 361	5 733	1 401	42 329	62.3	36.7	1.0
Del Norte	99.5	3 621	42.8	6.9	4.2	13.6	4.1	15.8	573	145	48	3 192	41.4	56.8	1.9
El Dorado	635.4	3 834	41.8	3.9	4.4	5.6	5.6	359.7	2 170	828	227	8 293	37.9	60.9	1.3
Fresno	3 604.4	4 319	48.6	6.1	5.2	10.6	3.0	2 388.8	2 862	9 631	1 205	55 815	41.3	57.9	0.8
Glenn	136.9	5 142	40.2	6.2	4.5	14.7	5.0	27.5	1 033	279	36	1 914	31.7	66.9	1.4
Humboldt	521.4	4 100	44.3	9.3	4.1	10.8	4.0	133.1	1 047	854	341	12 398	58.2	39.1	2.6
Imperial	859.0	5 874	42.7	17.1	3.3	8.0	3.2	508.6	3 478	1 845	479	13 906	53.9	44.9	1.2
Inyo	129.0	7 083	31.9	31.4	4.1	4.2	4.6	17.9	981	372	25	2 580	39.1	59.1	1.8
Kern	3 450.7	4 972	42.8	8.8	3.4	9.4	1.7	1 562.6	2 251	10 102	5 185	44 510	32.2	66.9	0.9
Kings	449.9	3 332	49.2	6.1	4.1	9.2	2.8	173.7	1 286	952	6 469	10 644	34.0	65.2	0.8
Lake	204.5	3 300	43.1	7.3	5.2	14.1	4.3	50.7	818	151	90	4 212	53.3	45.1	1.7
Lassen	121.5	3 573	56.4	5.5	3.3	8.6	6.9	60.8	1 788	797	48	4 767	27.6	71.1	1.3
Los Angeles	43 227.9	4 408	37.5	9.1	6.7	10.6	3.5	42 997.4	4 385	52 776	16 711	560 846	62.9	35.9	1.2
Madera	419.7	3 222	50.5	6.2	3.9	9.8	4.8	100.3	770	340	179	7 791	34.7	64.2	1.1
Marin	1 018.7	4 115	36.1	7.2	5.8	4.5	4.6	568.0	2 294	949	538	13 363	73.1	25.8	1.1
Mariposa	68.6	3 988	33.5	17.5	5.9	8.7	6.7	13.0	759	674	24	1 082	37.7	60.4	1.9
Mendocino	518.9	5 947	32.3	9.7	2.9	9.3	2.7	182.6	2 093	296	149	7 569	63.6	34.2	2.2
Merced	967.1	4 290	51.3	4.4	3.3	11.9	2.4	342.2	1 518	788	311	13 124	42.3	56.6	1.1
Modoc	75.4	8 119	39.7	20.1	3.3	7.4	13.8	1.0	112	286	13	1 001	25.6	72.9	1.5
Mono	96.4	7 351	30.6	24.2	5.4	2.2	6.6	55.0	4 196	202	264	1 132	49.3	49.3	1.5
Monterey	2 022.0	4 891	36.9	22.1	4.3	5.7	3.6	704.5	1 704	4 724	5 785	25 661	60.0	38.9	1.1
Napa	547.2	4 201	42.0	5.2	5.9	5.6	4.7	163.3	1 254	429	179	9 198	59.7	39.0	1.3
Nevada	353.8	3 722	32.2	18.0	4.2	6.1	5.5	185.9	1 956	420	130	4 925	44.7	54.1	1.3
Orange	10 026.3	3 412	45.3	3.7	7.4	6.8	4.3	12 043.2	4 098	11 551	5 060	146 607	39.3	59.6	1.1
Placer	1 134.3	4 073	39.8	3.6	5.9	5.5	7.1	1 135.6	4 077	670	398	14 809	36.6	62.5	0.9
Plumas	136.2	6 521	31.3	31.1	3.8	4.7	7.6	19.8	948	395	29	2 182	36.5	62.2	1.3
Riverside	6 665.9	3 923	44.6	7.6	5.8	8.5	3.2	5 645.1	3 322	6 138	2 479	98 497	41.2	57.8	1.0
Sacramento	5 796.1	4 441	39.3	4.4	6.3	13.1	4.7	8 848.8	6 780	8 579	2 654	174 017	50.1	48.9	1.0
San Benito	225.3	4 028	40.6	19.5	3.3	6.3	5.2	143.8	2 570	151	77	2 744	53.6	45.5	1.0
San Bernardino	7 686.3	4 232	43.0	11.5	7.7	9.8	2.9	6 021.4	3 316	10 248	18 301	97 381	43.2	55.7	1.1
San Diego	11 583.5	3 985	43.1	8.0	5.5	6.3	2.6	8 707.3	2 996	39 014	116 506	185 393	46.9	52.2	1.0
San Francisco	5 776.2	7 560	13.9	17.3	6.5	9.1	3.5	8 638.4	11 306	17 345	1 321	77 183	83.2	15.4	1.3
San Joaquin	2 467.8	4 017	44.7	9.5	5.3	10.2	4.3	1 511.0	2 460	4 017	871	34 430	45.8	53.4	0.8
San Luis Obispo	937.7	3 700	41.2	7.9	5.0	8.4	5.6	295.7	1 167	634	379	20 722	46.1	52.5	1.4
San Mateo	2 953.7	4 200	36.6	9.7	6.5	6.0	5.6	1 988.9	2 828	3 829	1 292	27 880	69.6	29.4	1.0
Santa Barbara	1 833.5	4 549	38.8	15.6	4.6	5.5	4.2	833.6	2 068	3 760	3 872	30 539	54.9	43.9	1.3
Santa Clara	8 659.4	5 144	36.5	8.2	4.5	6.6	5.7	7 589.7	4 508	10 431	2 822	86 216	64.1	34.7	1.2
Santa Cruz	1 118.5	4 407	39.5	7.0	4.8	7.8	3.4	558.9	2 202	562	349	18 439	73.2	24.9	1.8
Shasta	693.0	4 034	41.3	8.2	4.5	11.0	3.8	441.3	2 569	1 244	238	12 962	31.2	67.5	1.2
Sierra	30.7	8 635	39.3	17.1	7.8	6.9	10.8	4.2	1 191	88	0	434	30.4	67.2	2.4
Siskiyou	201.2	4 563	44.3	6.8	6.1	9.0	9.7	11.4	258	753	60	3 686	38.1	60.5	1.4
Solano	1 732.4	4 214	35.5	4.9	6.7	7.4	4.5	1 450.9	3 530	4 257	8 157	23 296	57.8	41.2	0.9
Sonoma	1 961.9	4 189	38.0	7.8	5.4	5.7	4.3	1 544.1	3 297	1 773	1 275	27 362	67.3	31.2	1.6
Stanislaus	1 932.9	4 007	48.7	9.8	4.8	9.9	3.1	2 408.4	4 992	1 175	665	25 595	40.8	58.3	0.9
Sutter	305.4	3 699	43.5	8.8	3.7	7.4	4.5	62.6	758	173	115	4 036	32.0	67.1	0.9
Tehama	207.7	3 614	48.9	8.1	4.7	12.4	6.3	8.6	150	282	80	3 608	32.3	66.4	1.4
Trinity	81.9	6 217	32.5	20.4	3.3	7.3	9.7	20.9	1 589	280	18	1 219	43.1	54.7	2.2
Tulare	2 052.3	5 376	41.3	20.9	2.8	9.0	2.2	638.3	1 672	1 356	525	28 444	32.8	66.3	0.8
Tuolumne	190.7	3 414	35.9	18.9	5.1	7.4	3.3	74.3	1 331	365	77	4 762	38.6	60.2	1.2
Ventura	2 995.6	3 821	43.8	7.7	5.8	5.1	3.7	1 705.7	2 176	7 613	7 659	36 272	48.1	50.7	1.1
Yolo	694.7	3 841	38.8	3.8	5.3	8.9	7.7	568.8	3 145	2 381	257	26 455	59.9	38.6	1.5
Yuba	262.8	4 216	53.1	2.6	3.5	16.4	2.7	88.4	1 418	1 279	3 501	5 535	31.5	67.1	1.4
COLORADO	X	X	X	X	X	X	X	X	X	51 542	38 424	307 860	46.6	52.2	1.2
Adams	1 254.1	3 352	39.9	0.0	11.1	6.7	4.1	1 336.9	3 574	2 683	1 072	16 951	50.4	48.4	1.2
Alamosa	47.8	3 160	40.4	7.2	4.6	14.4	8.5	17.5	1 154	161	23	1 945	48.1	50.7	1.2
Arapahoe	1 922.6	3 769	41.4	1.6	6.3	2.0	13.9	2 760.0	5 410	2 567	2 024	28 914	47.3	51.7	1.0
Archuleta	30.0	2 727	34.8	2.9	1.6	5.2	8.1	22.1	2 010	63	17	558	44.3	53.7	2.0
Baca	23.7	5 403	36.9	29.3	3.1	6.8	3.8	11.1	2 517	44	0	690	22.1	76.8	1.1
Bent	31.9	5 572	24.2	1.1	2.1	11.7	4.8	16.9	2 957	47	0	635	36.1	62.4	1.5
Boulder	1 016.2	3 640	36.9	1.1	5.2	1.9	7.2	1 045.3	3 744	2 575	516	24 994	67.7	31.1	1.2
Broomfield	650.8	15 942	0.0	0.0	2.6	0.4	91.3	701.3	17 179	0	61	848	47.0	51.8	1.2
Chaffee	54.7	3 250	29.9	35.1	3.8	2.9	6.3	25.1	1 492	105	25	1 515	43.1	55.5	1.4

1. Based on the resident population estimated as of July 1 of the year shown.

Table B. States and Counties — **Land Area and Population**

STATE/County code	CBSA code[1]	County Type[2]	STATE County	Land area,[3] (sq km) 2000	Total persons	Rank	Per square kilometer	White	Black	Am. Indian, Alaska Native	Asian and Pacific Islander	Percent Hispanic or Latino[4]	Under 5 years	5 to 17 years	18 to 24 years	25 to 34 years	35 to 44 years	45 to 54 years
				1	2	3	4	5	6	7	8	9	10	11	12	13	14	15
			COLORADO—Cont'd															
08 017	...	9	Cheyenne	4 614	2 052	3 056	0.4	91.9	0.4	0.6	0.1	7.0	5.3	20.6	9.0	8.8	16.5	15.8
08 019	19740	1	Clear Creek	1 024	9 538	2 482	9.3	94.1	0.6	0.9	1.0	4.0	5.7	15.3	7.4	12.1	18.1	22.5
08 021	...	9	Conejos	3 334	8 403	2 570	2.5	40.4	0.1	0.8	0.1	58.6	7.3	22.8	11.1	9.5	12.9	12.9
08 023	...	9	Costilla	3 178	3 563	2 939	1.1	31.4	0.6	1.2	0.9	65.9	5.7	17.9	8.2	9.0	13.1	16.6
08 025	...	8	Crowley	2 043	5 449	2 814	2.7	67.0	7.1	2.6	1.0	22.9	3.8	13.4	11.5	17.3	21.8	14.2
08 027	...	8	Custer	1 914	3 784	2 927	2.0	95.9	0.6	1.4	0.4	2.4	4.6	15.8	7.3	7.6	13.5	19.2
08 029	...	6	Delta	2 958	29 409	1 418	9.9	86.5	0.5	1.1	0.6	12.1	5.6	17.3	8.6	10.1	12.8	14.3
08 031	19740	1	Denver	397	557 478	102	1 404.2	50.4	11.3	1.2	3.7	34.8	8.8	14.9	8.3	20.6	15.6	13.1
08 033	...	9	Dolores	2 763	1 825	3 072	0.7	93.0	0.2	2.2	0.6	4.2	5.9	15.7	7.9	11.4	14.2	17.5
08 035	19740	1	Douglas	2 176	223 471	260	102.7	89.1	1.6	0.7	4.3	6.0	8.6	21.6	7.8	14.9	19.2	14.0
08 037	20780	5	Eagle	4 372	46 020	1 005	10.5	72.2	0.3	0.6	1.2	26.2	8.1	15.6	8.6	23.0	18.2	14.4
08 039	19740	1	Elbert	4 794	22 254	1 694	4.6	93.5	1.1	1.2	0.8	4.7	5.7	21.7	9.3	10.2	19.9	18.0
08 041	17820	2	El Paso	5 507	550 478	105	100.0	77.6	7.7	1.6	4.2	11.9	7.8	19.8	10.5	14.3	16.4	13.9
08 043	15860	4	Fremont	3 970	47 556	970	12.0	82.3	5.4	2.3	0.7	10.4	4.5	15.2	9.2	14.8	17.5	14.5
08 045	...	5	Garfield	7 633	47 611	968	6.2	77.3	0.5	0.8	0.8	21.4	8.0	19.1	9.7	15.1	16.4	14.9
08 047	19740	1	Gilpin	388	4 845	2 851	12.5	94.0	0.6	1.5	0.9	3.8	5.5	14.3	6.4	15.3	19.9	21.3
08 049	...	8	Grand	4 783	13 173	2 224	2.8	93.2	0.7	0.6	0.9	5.0	6.3	14.9	8.8	15.8	17.0	18.5
08 051	...	7	Gunnison	8 388	14 046	2 164	1.7	93.2	0.7	1.2	0.9	5.1	5.5	12.2	16.7	20.6	13.7	14.8
08 053	...	9	Hinsdale	2 895	759	3 122	0.3	96.3	0.1	1.2	0.9	1.6	6.2	14.2	4.3	8.7	16.7	21.6
08 055	...	6	Huerfano	4 120	7 827	2 611	1.9	59.6	2.8	2.2	0.5	35.7	4.8	15.2	9.4	11.9	14.7	15.8
08 057	...	9	Jackson	4 178	1 507	3 088	0.4	92.0	0.0	0.7	0.1	7.3	6.4	18.0	7.8	8.8	15.7	17.1
08 059	19740	1	Jefferson	1 991	528 563	110	265.5	84.8	1.2	1.1	3.2	11.1	6.2	18.2	8.9	13.6	17.1	16.4
08 061	...	9	Kiowa	4 587	1 444	3 093	0.3	95.2	0.6	1.4	0.3	2.6	4.6	17.7	8.6	10.7	14.3	16.1
08 063	...	7	Kit Carson	5 597	7 911	2 600	1.4	81.4	1.7	0.7	0.4	16.0	6.2	19.2	9.7	11.6	16.3	13.1
08 065	20780	7	Lake	976	7 731	2 619	7.9	58.4	0.2	1.0	0.5	40.1	8.4	18.9	11.1	18.3	14.4	14.7
08 067	20420	6	La Plata	4 383	46 229	998	10.5	84.2	0.6	5.4	0.8	10.3	5.0	15.9	13.2	13.7	14.7	16.7
08 069	22660	2	Larimer	6 737	266 610	220	39.6	88.0	1.1	1.1	2.4	8.9	6.1	16.9	12.7	15.4	14.9	14.6
08 071	...	7	Las Animas	12 361	15 499	2 064	1.3	55.9	0.5	1.6	0.8	41.8	5.3	17.8	9.9	10.4	13.1	14.8
08 073	...	8	Lincoln	6 698	5 881	2 783	0.9	84.2	5.1	1.2	0.7	9.1	4.5	17.7	9.5	13.4	18.3	13.9
08 075	44540	7	Logan	4 762	20 928	1 754	4.4	84.7	2.3	0.8	0.6	12.3	6.1	17.7	12.2	12.7	15.0	13.8
08 077	24300	3	Mesa	8 619	124 676	454	14.5	88.0	0.6	1.3	0.9	10.3	6.1	17.7	10.6	11.8	13.7	14.5
08 079	...	9	Mineral	2 268	881	3 114	0.4	97.6	0.3	1.0	0.2	2.0	3.9	15.8	5.3	8.4	16.0	16.2
08 081	...	9	Moffat	12 282	13 527	2 196	1.1	87.7	0.2	1.7	0.6	10.9	7.5	20.0	10.1	12.0	15.6	16.2
08 083	...	6	Montezuma	5 275	24 335	1 605	4.6	80.8	0.5	10.3	0.4	9.4	6.7	19.4	8.9	10.4	14.1	15.2
08 085	33940	7	Montrose	5 803	35 984	1 239	6.2	82.2	0.3	1.6	0.7	16.1	6.9	18.7	9.3	10.9	13.6	14.3
08 087	22820	6	Morgan	3 329	27 922	1 468	8.4	67.4	0.4	0.8	0.4	31.4	8.5	21.2	10.0	12.2	14.4	12.5
08 089	...	6	Otero	3 271	19 754	1 817	6.0	57.9	0.7	1.3	0.9	38.1	7.3	19.1	10.3	9.7	13.0	14.1
08 091	...	9	Ouray	1 400	4 021	2 908	2.9	94.8	0.1	1.3	0.5	4.1	4.8	16.7	6.5	8.7	15.3	20.1
08 093	19740	1	Park	5 700	16 465	1 999	2.9	93.5	0.5	1.7	0.7	4.7	5.5	16.9	7.7	11.2	19.4	20.0
08 095	...	9	Phillips	1 781	4 511	2 872	2.5	84.7	0.4	0.4	0.4	14.4	6.7	19.4	7.6	10.0	14.6	13.8
08 097	...	7	Pitkin	2 513	15 002	2 100	6.0	91.0	0.5	0.5	1.7	6.8	4.9	11.6	6.3	19.0	18.3	19.5
08 099	...	7	Prowers	4 249	14 164	2 155	3.3	61.8	0.3	0.8	0.5	36.8	8.8	21.3	11.7	12.0	13.1	13.0
08 101	39380	3	Pueblo	6 187	148 751	382	24.0	57.5	2.0	1.1	0.9	39.3	6.7	18.5	10.4	13.0	13.9	13.4
08 103	...	9	Rio Blanco	8 342	5 938	2 776	0.7	93.0	0.4	1.2	0.4	5.7	5.6	19.1	12.3	10.1	15.0	16.7
08 105	...	7	Rio Grande	2 361	12 346	2 274	5.2	59.7	0.3	0.9	0.3	39.1	7.2	19.3	9.5	9.2	13.5	15.2
08 107	...	7	Routt	6 116	20 788	1 760	3.4	95.3	0.3	0.9	0.7	3.5	5.5	15.7	9.1	18.3	17.1	19.2
08 109	...	9	Saguache	8 206	6 708	2 712	0.8	52.0	0.1	1.7	0.5	46.2	7.1	20.0	10.9	10.5	14.4	15.8
08 111	...	9	San Juan	1 003	572	3 133	0.6	90.4	0.0	0.7	0.5	8.4	5.1	11.9	7.7	9.8	14.9	26.0
08 113	...	9	San Miguel	3 332	7 154	2 670	2.1	90.2	0.2	0.8	1.1	8.1	5.2	11.9	7.1	25.3	18.7	18.2
08 115	...	9	Sedgwick	1 420	2 683	3 005	1.9	86.6	0.4	0.1	0.9	12.1	5.8	16.5	7.8	10.1	12.6	14.3
08 117	43540	7	Summit	1 575	25 143	1 562	16.0	85.1	1.0	0.7	1.2	12.7	6.4	11.5	10.0	28.2	17.7	14.0
08 119	17820	2	Teller	1 443	21 786	1 715	15.1	93.7	0.9	1.5	1.0	4.3	5.4	18.8	8.4	9.0	18.5	20.5
08 121	...	9	Washington	6 529	4 813	2 853	0.7	92.8	0.1	0.3	0.2	6.6	5.4	18.9	8.6	9.7	14.4	15.0
08 123	24540	3	Weld	10 335	211 272	275	20.4	68.3	0.7	0.9	1.4	29.7	7.8	19.9	13.2	14.7	14.1	12.3
08 125	...	7	Yuma	6 127	9 799	2 459	1.6	83.5	0.2	0.4	0.1	16.1	6.2	20.5	9.8	10.6	13.9	13.6
09 000	...	X	CONNECTICUT	12 548	3 483 372	X	277.6	77.5	9.7	0.6	3.3	10.1	6.1	17.9	8.7	12.0	16.5	15.0
09 001	14860	2	Fairfield	1 621	899 152	48	554.7	73.0	10.5	0.3	4.2	12.9	6.7	18.6	7.5	11.9	17.2	14.6
09 003	25540	1	Hartford	1 905	871 457	51	457.5	72.7	12.4	0.5	3.3	12.2	6.0	17.9	8.4	12.2	16.2	14.6
09 005	45860	4	Litchfield	2 383	187 801	305	78.8	95.0	1.2	0.5	1.6	2.5	5.2	17.9	7.3	10.5	17.3	16.4
09 007	25540	1	Middlesex	956	161 439	345	168.9	90.3	4.8	0.6	2.1	3.3	5.6	16.8	8.2	11.9	17.3	15.5
09 009	35300	2	New Haven	1 569	841 873	55	536.6	74.2	12.1	0.6	3.2	11.1	6.0	17.8	9.2	12.8	16.0	14.2
09 011	35980	2	New London	1 725	263 992	223	153.0	85.4	6.4	1.7	3.2	5.5	5.8	17.6	9.4	12.4	17.1	14.5
09 013	25540	1	Tolland	1 062	145 039	395	136.6	91.5	3.0	0.5	2.9	3.0	5.1	16.3	14.4	11.8	16.6	14.7
09 015	48740	4	Windham	1 328	112 622	492	84.8	89.7	2.1	1.0	1.1	7.2	5.7	17.9	10.6	12.3	16.6	14.6

1. CBSA = Core Based Statistical Area. See Appendix A for explanation. See Appendix B for list of metropolitan areas with component counties. 2. County type code from the Economic Research Service of USDA Rural-Urban Continuum Codes. See Appendix A for definition. 3. Dry land or land partially or temporarily covered by water. 4. Hispanic or Latino persons may be of any race.

Table B. States and Counties — **Population and Households**

STATE County	55 to 64 years	65 to 74 years	75 years and over	Percent female	1990	2000	1990–2000	2000–2003	Births	Deaths	Net migration	Number	Percent change, 1990–2000	Persons per house-hold	Female family house-holder[1]	One person
	16	17	18	19	20	21	22	23	24	25	26	27	28	29	30	31
COLORADO—Cont'd																
Cheyenne	8.7	7.1	10.6	50.3	2 397	2 231	-6.9	-8.0	73	50	-205	880	-2.7	2.50	5.7	29.0
Clear Creek	11.6	4.6	2.6	48.3	7 619	9 322	22.4	2.3	323	129	34	4 019	27.5	2.31	6.9	27.2
Conejos	8.7	8.0	7.2	50.8	7 453	8 400	12.7	0.0	389	240	-143	2 980	19.6	2.80	12.7	23.7
Costilla	12.8	10.4	8.0	51.1	3 190	3 663	14.8	-2.7	132	112	-116	1 503	26.1	2.44	11.3	28.1
Crowley	7.6	5.5	5.3	32.7	3 946	5 518	39.8	-1.3	119	149	-33	1 358	16.6	2.59	11.0	25.7
Custer	14.5	10.3	5.3	49.2	1 926	3 503	81.9	8.0	93	77	262	1 480	92.2	2.36	5.4	23.8
Delta	11.6	9.8	9.5	50.1	20 980	27 834	32.7	5.7	1 053	1 106	1 618	11 058	32.1	2.43	7.9	24.8
Denver	7.9	5.2	5.8	49.3	467 549	554 636	18.6	0.5	37 116	14 984	-19 136	239 235	13.4	2.27	10.8	39.3
Dolores	12.0	8.7	7.9	49.3	1 504	1 844	22.6	-1.0	68	74	-11	785	35.1	2.35	8.5	26.2
Douglas	7.0	2.5	1.5	50.0	60 391	175 766	191.0	27.1	11 824	1 609	36 097	60 924	192.3	2.88	5.7	13.3
Eagle	6.8	2.2	1.0	45.2	21 928	41 659	90.0	10.5	2 547	272	2 129	15 148	81.3	2.73	5.6	20.9
Elbert	8.8	3.8	2.3	49.9	9 646	19 872	106.0	12.0	777	265	1 814	6 770	100.5	2.93	5.7	12.2
El Paso	7.9	4.8	3.8	49.8	397 014	516 929	30.2	6.5	27 822	10 115	15 864	192 409	30.9	2.61	10.2	23.9
Fremont	9.6	7.7	7.0	43.2	32 273	46 145	43.0	3.1	1 353	1 576	1 644	15 232	30.0	2.43	9.2	26.9
Garfield	7.8	4.6	3.7	48.5	29 974	43 791	46.1	8.7	2 571	882	2 125	16 229	44.1	2.65	7.8	22.8
Gilpin	11.1	3.9	2.1	47.2	3 070	4 757	55.0	1.8	155	66	4	2 043	56.2	2.32	5.7	26.8
Grand	10.1	5.3	2.4	46.8	7 966	12 442	56.2	5.9	518	221	438	5 075	60.2	2.37	5.2	24.8
Gunnison	7.7	4.4	2.7	45.5	10 273	13 956	35.9	0.6	585	204	-279	5 649	46.5	2.30	5.4	27.2
Hinsdale	17.3	8.4	4.6	50.1	467	790	69.2	-3.9	26	16	-42	359	67.8	2.20	4.7	24.8
Huerfano	12.3	8.0	9.0	46.0	6 009	7 862	30.8	-0.4	264	328	31	3 082	26.0	2.25	10.4	32.8
Jackson	14.3	8.0	6.0	50.5	1 605	1 577	-1.7	-4.4	67	41	-98	661	4.6	2.37	7.9	28.4
Jefferson	9.7	5.6	4.5	50.2	NA	525 507	NA	0.6	21 496	10 821	-7 214	205 692	NA	2.52	8.7	24.5
Kiowa	10.6	7.8	11.5	51.3	1 688	1 622	-3.9	-11.0	33	66	-151	665	1.2	2.40	6.6	29.8
Kit Carson	9.9	7.3	7.7	47.0	7 140	8 011	12.2	-1.2	306	249	-159	2 990	7.4	2.50	6.3	27.2
Lake	7.4	4.5	2.8	46.2	6 007	7 812	30.0	-1.0	448	141	-403	2 977	25.0	2.59	8.4	26.3
La Plata	9.6	5.4	4.3	49.0	32 284	43 941	36.1	5.2	1 507	777	1 552	17 342	44.8	2.43	8.7	24.8
Larimer	8.2	5.0	4.5	49.9	186 136	251 494	35.1	6.0	10 620	5 053	9 569	97 164	37.9	2.52	7.9	23.4
Las Animas	11.3	8.2	9.2	50.9	13 765	15 207	10.5	1.9	510	613	402	6 173	13.9	2.40	11.6	29.7
Lincoln	9.2	7.0	7.6	43.1	4 529	6 087	34.4	-3.4	176	214	-169	2 058	13.3	2.44	8.4	29.0
Logan	8.7	6.8	7.2	46.9	17 567	20 504	16.7	2.1	832	646	175	7 551	8.2	2.45	8.6	28.5
Mesa	9.2	7.5	7.4	51.1	93 145	116 255	24.8	7.2	4 846	3 829	6 749	45 823	26.4	2.47	9.8	25.1
Mineral	16.0	10.1	7.2	48.2	558	831	48.9	6.0	19	22	49	377	52.6	2.20	5.8	28.1
Moffat	9.3	5.0	4.1	48.0	11 357	13 184	16.1	2.6	674	326	7	4 983	19.3	2.58	8.2	23.6
Montezuma	10.9	7.6	6.4	50.6	18 672	23 830	27.6	2.1	1 017	883	385	9 201	36.1	2.54	10.6	24.6
Montrose	10.5	7.6	7.4	50.7	24 423	33 432	36.9	7.6	1 648	1 049	1 939	13 043	38.7	2.52	8.7	24.3
Morgan	8.0	6.4	6.6	49.7	21 939	27 171	23.8	2.8	1 571	860	48	9 539	17.2	2.80	9.0	23.0
Otero	10.3	8.6	8.3	51.5	20 185	20 311	0.6	-2.7	1 008	748	-833	7 920	4.3	2.49	12.0	27.8
Ouray	14.9	7.9	4.8	49.9	2 295	3 742	63.1	7.5	115	51	213	1 576	66.4	2.36	6.5	23.5
Park	10.7	5.2	2.2	48.5	7 174	14 523	102.4	13.4	548	222	1 566	5 894	112.4	2.45	4.4	21.1
Phillips	9.2	9.1	10.4	51.7	4 189	4 480	6.9	0.7	188	169	17	1 781	4.0	2.47	5.6	27.5
Pitkin	12.9	4.9	2.5	46.3	12 661	14 872	17.5	0.9	535	151	-241	6 807	15.8	2.14	5.3	25.4
Prowers	8.3	6.1	6.4	49.2	13 347	14 483	8.5	-2.2	857	460	-736	5 307	6.5	2.67	10.9	25.4
Pueblo	8.9	7.4	7.3	51.0	123 051	141 472	15.0	5.1	6 434	4 651	5 434	54 579	16.0	2.52	13.3	26.6
Rio Blanco	11.3	6.2	4.7	49.5	6 051	5 986	-1.1	-0.8	212	167	-96	2 306	5.7	2.50	7.8	24.8
Rio Grande	10.2	7.8	7.3	51.2	10 770	12 413	15.3	-0.5	566	427	-206	4 701	19.6	2.59	11.2	24.1
Routt	8.4	3.2	1.9	45.8	14 088	19 690	39.8	5.6	722	247	627	7 953	45.0	2.44	5.8	24.4
Saguache	10.2	5.6	4.4	49.6	4 619	5 917	28.1	13.4	302	167	643	2 300	40.0	2.56	11.0	26.9
San Juan	16.4	4.0	3.3	47.7	745	558	-25.1	2.5	14	7	10	269	-6.3	2.06	8.9	36.8
San Miguel	9.7	2.3	1.0	45.5	3 653	6 594	80.5	8.5	253	37	335	3 015	102.5	2.18	5.4	32.7
Sedgwick	11.4	11.6	11.1	49.6	2 690	2 747	2.1	-2.3	101	108	-61	1 165	2.1	2.31	5.4	29.4
Summit	6.8	2.8	0.8	41.8	12 881	23 548	82.8	6.8	1 084	143	658	9 120	72.2	2.48	6.6	21.6
Teller	11.2	5.5	2.4	49.3	12 468	20 555	64.9	6.0	753	282	749	7 993	69.3	2.56	4.4	19.6
Washington	10.7	9.1	9.5	49.0	4 812	4 926	2.4	-2.3	142	166	-91	1 989	3.9	2.46	6.4	26.2
Weld	7.4	4.3	3.7	49.7	NA	180 926	NA	16.8	10 243	3 831	23 269	63 197	NA	2.78	8.7	21.0
Yuma	9.7	7.9	8.2	50.6	8 954	9 841	9.9	-0.4	398	397	-40	3 800	9.4	2.55	6.8	27.4
CONNECTICUT	10.4	6.3	7.2	51.4	3 287 116	3 405 565	3.6	2.3	137 197	97 971	41 354	1 301 670	5.8	2.53	12.1	26.4
Fairfield	10.1	6.4	6.6	51.5	827 645	882 567	6.6	1.9	39 207	23 029	910	324 232	6.3	2.67	11.5	24.0
Hartford	9.9	6.7	7.6	51.8	851 783	857 183	0.6	1.7	34 241	26 197	7 154	335 098	3.2	2.48	13.5	27.9
Litchfield	10.9	6.7	7.4	51.1	174 092	182 193	4.7	3.1	6 323	5 500	4 837	71 551	7.8	2.51	8.6	25.3
Middlesex	10.4	6.5	6.9	51.2	143 196	155 071	8.3	4.1	5 665	4 360	5 142	61 341	12.2	2.43	8.8	27.2
New Haven	9.5	6.3	7.7	51.8	804 219	824 008	2.5	2.2	33 007	25 383	11 168	319 040	4.7	2.50	13.6	28.2
New London	9.7	6.4	6.5	50.5	254 957	259 088	1.6	1.9	9 822	7 209	2 585	99 835	7.1	2.48	11.0	26.4
Tolland	9.4	5.3	4.9	49.9	128 699	136 364	6.0	6.4	4 748	2 814	6 685	49 431	11.6	2.54	8.0	23.5
Windham	9.3	5.7	6.2	50.7	102 525	109 091	6.4	3.2	4 184	3 479	2 873	41 142	9.8	2.56	11.9	24.3

1. No spouse present.

Table B. States and Counties — **Vital Statistics, Health Resources, and Crime**

STATE County	Births, average 1999–2001 Total	Rate[1]	Deaths Number Total	Deaths Number Infant[2]	Deaths Rate Total[1]	Deaths Rate Infant[3]	Physicians,[4] 2000 Number	Rate[5]	Hospitals,[4] 1998 Number	Beds Number	Beds Rate[5]	Medicare enrollees, 2003	Serious crimes known to police,[6] 2002 Total Number	Rate[7]
	32	33	34	35	36	37	38	39	40	41	42	43	44	45
COLORADO—Cont'd														
Cheyenne	24	10.6	17	0	7.6	D	1	45	1	32	1 364	347	17	727
Clear Creek	97	10.4	37	0	3.9	D	3	32	0	0	0	605	344	3 987
Conejos	132	15.8	77	1	9.2	D	4	48	1	49	615	1 474	15	215
Costilla	43	11.8	37	1	10.2	D	0	0	0	0	0	865	NA	NA
Crowley	43	7.9	40	0	7.4	D	2	36	0	0	0	646	18	311
Custer	30	8.4	20	0	5.8	D	2	57	0	0	0	710	107	2 915
Delta	312	11.2	328	2	11.8	D	35	126	1	44	165	6 227	321	1 303
Denver	10 850	19.5	4 576	63	8.2	5.8	3 087	557	8	2 845	570	69 439	32 488	5 591
Dolores	21	11.2	21	0	11.6	D	0	0	0	0	0	370	31	1 605
Douglas	3 425	19.1	450	9	2.5	2.6	119	68	0	0	0	6 774	4 095	2 224
Eagle	761	18.1	70	3	1.7	D	77	185	1	49	146	1 620	1 766	4 364
Elbert	225	11.2	84	1	4.2	D	8	40	0	0	0	1 432	NA	NA
El Paso	8 339	16.0	2 963	67	5.7	8.0	963	186	4	1 008	206	55 449	23 983	4 442
Fremont	440	9.5	477	5	10.3	D	40	87	1	277	631	7 901	1 121	2 319
Garfield	758	17.2	257	4	5.8	D	67	153	2	140	356	4 505	NA	NA
Gilpin	54	11.3	19	0	3.9	D	4	84	0	0	0	202	86	1 770
Grand	154	12.4	62	1	5.0	D	13	104	1	21	209	1 133	394	3 462
Gunnison	161	11.5	59	2	4.2	D	15	107	1	24	193	1 070	420	2 872
Hinsdale	8	10.5	4	0	0.0	D	0	0	0	0	0	98	17	2 053
Huerfano	75	9.6	94	1	12.0	D	10	127	1	38	558	1 537	146	2 009
Jackson	16	10.4	13	0	8.1	D	0	0	0	0	0	237	7	423
Jefferson	6 647	12.6	3 180	41	6.0	6.1	809	153	1	322	64	58 553	19 561	3 874
Kiowa	13	8.1	18	0	11.1	D	2	123	1	42	2 572	332	0	0
Kit Carson	100	12.5	74	1	9.3	D	3	37	1	24	328	1 246	166	2 158
Lake	139	17.8	43	2	5.5	D	6	77	1	22	344	628	187	2 285
La Plata	439	10.0	239	2	5.4	D	141	321	1	96	238	5 049	1 661	3 608
Larimer	3 222	12.7	1 485	16	5.9	4.9	433	172	3	375	162	28 548	9 906	3 759
Las Animas	170	11.2	184	1	12.2	D	18	118	1	32	220	3 099	343	2 153
Lincoln	54	8.9	59	0	9.7	D	4	66	1	56	977	858	29	532
Logan	260	12.7	196	3	9.5	D	26	127	1	50	279	3 412	720	3 352
Mesa	1 464	12.6	1 135	11	9.7	7.7	286	246	3	422	374	21 588	3 955	3 451
Mineral	6	6.9	7	0	8.2	D	0	0	0	0	0	130	5	574
Moffat	187	14.2	95	1	7.2	D	13	99	1	27	215	1 499	376	2 790
Montezuma	313	13.2	247	2	10.4	D	34	143	1	137	610	3 959	614	2 459
Montrose	461	13.7	305	2	9.1	D	54	162	1	75	244	6 131	900	2 569
Morgan	488	18.0	250	3	9.2	D	31	114	2	69	275	3 885	NA	NA
Otero	300	14.8	220	2	10.8	D	35	172	1	206	997	4 085	NA	NA
Ouray	34	9.0	20	0	5.3	D	10	267	0	0	0	507		
Park	165	11.3	61	2	4.2	D	5	34	0	0	0	1 269	124	862
Phillips	58	12.9	52	0	11.5	D	5	112	2	66	1 526	968	35	746
Pitkin	163	10.9	37	1	2.5	D	72	484	1	49	365	981	632	4 056
Prowers	247	17.1	136	1	9.4	D	13	90	1	40	291	2 056	378	2 606
Pueblo	1 962	13.8	1 399	12	9.9	5.9	325	230	2	563	417	25 964	7 410	4 999
Rio Blanco	67	11.2	51	1	8.5	D	9	150	2	67	1 069	800	146	2 328
Rio Grande	179	14.6	122	1	9.9	D	10	81	0	0	0	2 068	265	2 362
Routt	215	10.9	68	1	3.5	D	36	183	1	71	405	1 284	522	2 895
Saguache	85	14.3	49	1	8.2	D	2	34	0	0	0	800	98	1 581
San Juan	4	7.8	3	0	0.0	D	0	0	0	0	0	66	27	4 615
San Miguel	70	10.5	13	0	2.0	D	7	106	0	0	0	307	307	4 443
Sedgwick	32	11.8	37	0	13.8	D	0	0	1	58	2 277	674	56	1 946
Summit	306	12.9	43	2	1.8	D	30	127	0	0	0	1 145	1 138	5 310
Teller	214	10.3	85	2	4.1	D	13	63	0	0	0	2 260	426	1 983
Washington	50	10.3	53	1	10.9	D	1	20	0	0	0	879	NA	NA
Weld	3 065	16.7	1 136	20	6.2	6.4	260	144	1	326	204	19 380	8 193	4 716
Yuma	124	12.6	105	1	10.7	D	13	132	2	39	415	1 640	136	1 319
CONNECTICUT	42 995	12.6	29 801	269	8.7	6.3	10 162	298	35	7 782	238	522 403	103 719	2 997
Fairfield	12 387	14.0	7 024	61	8.0	4.9	2 512	285	8	1 965	234	124 839	22 943	2 611
Hartford	11 037	12.9	8 155	83	9.5	7.5	2 837	331	9	2 395	289	140 430	31 368	3 690
Litchfield	2 014	11.0	1 642	10	9.0	5.0	313	172	3	279	154	29 494	NA	NA
Middlesex	1 818	11.7	1 336	9	8.6	5.1	372	240	1	158	105	23 938	NA	NA
New Haven	10 262	12.4	7 760	68	9.4	6.6	3 280	398	8	2 268	286	131 800	31 184	3 952
New London	2 671	10.3	1 998	20	7.7	7.5	539	208	2	428	174	39 390	NA	NA
Tolland	1 496	10.9	873	9	6.4	6.0	151	111	2	137	104	16 275	NA	NA
Windham	1 310	12.0	1 012	9	9.3	6.9	158	145	2	152	145	16 177	NA	NA

1. Per 1,000 estimated resident population.   2. Deaths of infants under 1 year old.   3. Deaths of infants under 1 year old per 1,000 live births.   4. Data subject to copyright.   5. Per 100,000 resident population as of July 1 of the year shown.   6. Data for serious crimes have not been adjusted for underreporting; this may affect comparability between geographic areas and over time.   7. Per 100,000 population estimated by the FBI.

Table B. States and Counties — Crime, Education, Money Income, and Poverty

STATE County	Serious crimes known to police,[1] 2002 (cont'd) Rate[2] Violent	Property	Education School enrollment and attainment, 2000 Enrollment[3] Total	Percent private	Attainment[4] (percent) High school graduate or less	Bachelor's degree or more	Local government expenditures,[5] 2000–2001 Total current expenditures (mil dol)	Current expenditures per student (dollars)	Money income, 1999 Per capita income[6] (dollars)	Households Median income Dollars	Percent change, 1989–1999 (constant 1999 dollars)	Percent with income of $100,000 or more	Percent below poverty level, 1999 Persons	House-holds	Families	Families with children
	46	47	48	49	50	51	52	53	54	55	56	57	58	59	60	61
COLORADO—Cont'd																
Cheyenne	128	599	606	3.1	50.7	14.2	4.1	8 693	17 850	37 054	13.3	7.1	11.1	12.0	8.7	11.8
Clear Creek	695	3 292	2 042	13.5	28.1	38.8	8.9	6 723	28 160	50 997	14.5	17.7	5.4	6.2	3.0	5.8
Conejos	29	187	2 611	2.0	61.8	14.4	12.2	6 227	12 050	24 744	29.8	3.7	23.0	25.0	18.6	26.7
Costilla	NA	NA	908	5.8	59.2	12.8	5.3	8 365	10 748	19 531	11.3	1.9	26.8	29.7	21.3	29.1
Crowley	225	86	1 362	10.7	57.0	11.9	3.7	6 144	12 836	26 803	24.0	3.1	18.5	18.5	15.2	22.2
Custer	817	2 098	687	12.7	37.8	26.7	3.0	6 299	19 817	34 731	29.3	8.1	13.3	14.5	9.8	15.9
Delta	93	1 210	5 975	12.3	53.9	17.6	30.6	6 387	17 152	32 785	31.7	5.0	12.1	11.5	8.5	13.5
Denver	537	5 054	130 485	19.4	41.1	34.5	506.8	7 154	24 101	39 500	17.1	11.5	14.3	12.1	10.6	16.6
Dolores	52	1 553	365	6.8	57.2	13.5	2.4	7 244	17 106	32 196	20.1	3.8	13.1	15.7	10.2	9.0
Douglas	96	2 128	51 934	19.6	16.2	51.9	225.7	6 464	34 848	82 929	19.3	36.7	2.1	2.2	1.6	1.9
Eagle	183	4 181	9 194	14.3	29.9	42.6	32.6	7 015	32 011	62 682	26.3	23.7	7.8	5.6	3.9	5.5
Elbert	NA	NA	5 926	12.1	34.9	26.6	26.3	6 528	24 960	62 480	28.2	21.0	4.0	3.8	2.5	3.7
El Paso	423	4 019	146 429	16.2	31.6	31.8	576.0	6 127	22 005	46 844	17.8	12.2	8.0	7.9	5.7	8.6
Fremont	230	2 089	10 309	12.6	56.2	13.5	37.7	5 824	17 420	34 150	27.2	4.4	11.7	12.0	8.3	14.7
Garfield	NA	NA	10 894	10.8	41.5	23.8	53.1	5 608	21 341	47 016	19.9	10.8	7.5	6.7	4.6	7.5
Gilpin	165	1 605	1 027	16.8	31.5	31.2	3.2	7 248	26 148	51 942	21.2	12.5	4.0	4.1	1.0	1.0
Grand	9	3 453	2 475	9.7	31.7	34.5	14.0	7 411	25 198	47 759	18.5	12.5	7.3	7.2	5.4	8.2
Gunnison	226	2 647	4 697	8.0	23.7	43.6	10.2	6 066	21 407	36 916	19.4	8.9	15.0	14.8	6.0	8.7
Hinsdale	483	1 570	138	21.7	27.7	34.9	0.7	11 889	22 360	37 229	5.7	10.1	7.2	9.0	4.5	0.0
Huerfano	303	1 706	1 747	16.7	54.5	16.1	7.5	6 700	15 242	25 775	30.2	4.3	18.0	18.8	14.1	23.6
Jackson	0	423	367	5.7	49.8	19.9	2.5	8 293	17 826	31 821	13.1	4.5	14.0	12.1	10.3	15.9
Jefferson	212	3 661	141 368	16.0	30.8	36.5	643.7	7 340	28 077	NA	NA	19.1	5.2	5.0	3.4	5.1
Kiowa	0	0	425	1.2	49.2	16.1	3.1	8 483	16 382	30 494	6.0	7.2	12.2	13.1	9.6	11.3
Kit Carson	156	2 002	2 120	6.2	54.6	15.4	11.7	6 959	16 964	33 152	6.7	6.1	12.1	12.0	9.4	14.7
Lake	342	1 943	2 047	4.3	47.8	19.5	12.0	9 419	18 524	37 691	13.5	6.7	12.9	11.3	9.5	12.4
La Plata	204	3 404	13 191	13.0	31.7	36.4	46.2	6 508	21 534	40 159	16.0	10.9	11.7	12.4	6.7	9.1
Larimer	272	3 488	80 102	10.7	29.0	39.5	252.8	6 292	23 689	48 655	22.0	13.9	9.2	9.1	4.3	6.1
Las Animas	207	1 946	3 954	9.0	50.3	16.2	16.5	6 929	16 829	28 273	29.2	4.4	17.3	19.3	14.0	20.4
Lincoln	92	440	1 595	11.3	53.2	13.2	11.3	11 271	15 510	31 914	15.3	5.8	11.7	11.4	8.1	11.5
Logan	223	3 128	5 725	9.2	49.7	14.6	22.2	6 356	16 721	32 724	10.4	5.2	12.2	13.1	9.0	13.5
Mesa	199	3 252	29 470	10.7	45.3	22.0	116.3	5 698	18 715	35 864	12.6	7.1	10.2	10.2	7.0	11.0
Mineral	0	574	178	3.4	36.8	31.2	1.5	8 963	24 475	34 844	30.8	5.2	10.2	10.2	9.3	12.6
Moffat	185	2 604	3 639	7.0	53.8	12.5	17.8	6 923	18 540	41 528	-2.2	2.8	8.3	8.7	6.9	9.1
Montezuma	152	2 307	5 872	5.7	51.9	21.0	28.5	6 161	17 003	32 083	6.2	5.8	16.4	15.7	13.1	20.0
Montrose	163	2 407	7 732	8.1	52.7	18.7	36.5	6 238	17 158	35 234	16.0	5.2	12.6	11.8	8.9	13.4
Morgan	NA	NA	7 075	5.9	59.6	13.5	35.2	6 395	15 492	34 568	12.6	5.1	12.4	11.5	8.5	11.9
Otero	NA	NA	5 382	5.3	55.0	15.4	28.3	7 116	15 113	29 738	21.8	4.5	18.8	17.4	14.2	22.4
Ouray	NA	NA	779	5.6	28.2	36.8	4.3	7 483	24 335	42 019	13.7	12.1	7.2	7.8	6.0	9.5
Park	63	799	3 289	13.0	33.4	30.3	13.6	6 121	25 019	51 899	20.3	12.7	5.6	5.6	3.4	4.6
Phillips	170	575	1 133	5.6	50.6	19.9	8.3	8 612	16 394	32 177	11.5	5.3	11.6	11.1	8.8	12.4
Pitkin	141	3 915	2 799	18.4	14.6	57.1	11.4	9 199	40 811	59 375	10.5	23.1	6.2	5.2	3.0	4.2
Prowers	117	2 489	4 102	2.7	56.9	11.9	19.8	6 742	14 150	29 935	8.0	4.0	19.5	17.8	14.5	22.0
Pueblo	515	4 484	37 564	8.4	49.7	18.3	144.1	5 797	17 163	32 775	13.2	5.8	14.9	14.5	11.2	17.5
Rio Blanco	446	1 881	1 726	2.7	43.6	19.5	10.9	8 208	17 344	37 711	-4.0	4.2	9.6	8.8	6.7	10.2
Rio Grande	178	2 184	3 385	6.3	51.9	18.8	15.7	6 202	15 650	31 836	23.5	4.7	14.5	14.5	11.3	16.6
Routt	244	2 651	4 656	12.0	22.4	42.5	24.0	8 312	28 792	53 612	27.0	15.9	6.1	5.6	2.8	4.3
Saguache	387	1 194	1 558	7.4	54.8	19.6	8.8	8 093	13 121	25 495	19.7	3.2	22.6	21.8	18.7	26.2
San Juan	513	4 103	111	6.3	22.4	43.7	1.0	12 190	17 584	30 764	-12.5	4.5	20.9	20.1	13.5	24.3
San Miguel	174	4 270	1 155	18.4	21.4	48.5	7.3	8 803	35 329	48 514	18.1	17.8	10.4	9.7	6.6	9.2
Sedgwick	174	1 772	601	4.0	56.2	13.4	4.2	8 667	16 125	28 278	8.9	4.0	10.0	10.2	7.8	14.7
Summit	219	5 091	4 229	11.8	24.4	48.3	20.0	7 285	28 676	56 587	19.6	19.9	9.0	6.3	3.1	4.6
Teller	233	1 750	5 228	12.5	29.5	31.7	20.7	5 126	23 412	50 165	15.9	12.9	5.4	5.4	3.4	4.7
Washington	NA	NA	1 252	3.0	51.9	14.3	8.3	8 328	17 788	32 431	17.0	6.1	11.4	9.9	8.6	13.5
Weld	336	4 380	55 843	8.6	47.2	21.6	190.5	6 264	18 958	42 321	22.8	9.5	12.5	11.7	8.0	11.9
Yuma	68	1 251	2 574	6.8	54.3	15.5	12.4	6 367	16 005	33 169	11.0	4.7	12.9	13.1	8.8	12.7
CONNECTICUT	311	2 686	910 869	19.7	44.5	31.4	5 326.0	9 872	28 766	53 935	-3.8	20.2	7.9	8.0	5.6	8.6
Fairfield	312	2 299	233 796	24.1	39.2	39.9	1 435.8	10 318	38 350	65 249	-2.7	31.0	6.9	6.9	5.0	7.2
Hartford	359	3 332	226 420	15.4	46.3	29.6	1 390.2	9 883	26 047	50 756	-7.0	17.1	9.3	9.1	7.1	10.9
Litchfield	NA	NA	45 238	16.3	45.5	27.5	265.5	9 295	28 408	56 273	-1.6	18.7	4.5	5.0	2.7	3.7
Middlesex	NA	NA	39 840	23.0	39.8	33.8	222.2	9 679	28 251	59 175	1.9	20.6	4.6	4.8	2.3	3.6
New Haven	383	3 568	225 396	23.5	47.8	27.6	1 252.1	9 757	24 439	48 834	-5.5	15.8	9.5	9.7	7.0	11.0
New London	NA	NA	67 054	16.9	46.0	26.2	392.1	9 785	24 678	50 646	0.6	14.5	6.4	6.7	4.5	7.3
Tolland	NA	NA	43 189	9.5	39.8	32.8	206.5	9 114	25 474	59 044	-2.4	19.4	5.6	5.7	2.9	3.9
Windham	NA	NA	29 936	11.1	56.1	19.0	161.6	9 456	20 443	45 115	-0.8	9.5	8.5	8.6	5.7	9.1

1. Data for serious crimes have not been adjusted for underreporting; this may affect comparability between geographic areas and over time.   2. Per 100,000 population estimated by the FBI.   3. All persons 3 years old and over enrolled in nursery school through college.   4. Persons 25 years old and over.   5. Elementary and secondary education expenditures.   6. Based on population enumerated as of April 1, 2000.

Table B. States and Counties — **Personal Income**

STATE County	Total (mil dol) [62]	Percent change, 2001–2002 [63]	Per capita Dollars [64]	Rank [65]	Wages and salaries [66]	Proprietor's income [67]	Dividends, interest, and rent [68]	Transfer payments Total [69]	Government payments to individuals Total [70]	Social Security [71]	Medical payments [72]	Income maintenance [73]	Unemployment insurance [74]
COLORADO—Cont'd													
Cheyenne	50	-14.7	23 094	1 697	28	1	16	10	9	3	5	1	0
Clear Creek	356	1.5	37 276	101	115	35	52	24	22	10	7	2	2
Conejos	140	0.6	16 634	3 013	46	7	18	48	46	12	23	8	1
Costilla	71	4.5	19 552	2 648	22	5	12	23	23	8	10	4	0
Crowley	90	-1.0	16 477	3 027	41	20	14	22	21	6	10	3	0
Custer	88	3.8	24 042	1 392	27	10	26	15	14	8	4	1	0
Delta	632	5.6	21 770	2 074	247	45	147	150	143	62	59	12	4
Denver	22 585	-0.3	40 448	59	24 855	4 508	4 197	2 612	2 485	718	1 236	265	116
Dolores	40	-2.7	21 813	2 061	13	4	9	9	9	4	3	1	1
Douglas	8 289	-1.9	39 176	71	2 831	289	1 230	268	220	136	40	8	21
Eagle	1 705	1.1	37 923	89	1 126	256	382	54	43	21	9	4	7
Elbert	673	0.7	30 543	300	135	26	92	47	42	19	13	2	5
El Paso	16 256	2.2	29 903	359	11 931	1 145	2 815	1 739	1 621	586	615	147	82
Fremont	912	2.0	19 229	2 707	499	59	178	197	186	78	72	16	5
Garfield	1 273	3.0	27 121	673	788	141	220	117	106	49	34	10	8
Gilpin	175	0.7	36 124	118	243	4	40	9	8	4	2	1	1
Grand	385	4.3	29 560	384	207	53	86	30	27	14	9	2	2
Gunnison	352	2.1	25 033	1 118	238	41	104	29	26	11	7	2	1
Hinsdale	19	1.1	24 758	1 194	7	2	8	2	2	1	0	0	0
Huerfano	146	5.7	18 486	2 833	60	10	35	48	46	15	22	5	1
Jackson	30	2.7	19 252	2 705	16	-3	12	6	6	3	2	1	0
Jefferson	20 477	-1.6	38 600	74	9 950	1 589	3 281	1 453	1 332	668	420	91	81
Kiowa	40	-21.8	27 013	699	21	6	9	7	7	3	3	0	0
Kit Carson	187	-7.5	23 495	1 570	86	28	54	30	28	14	10	2	1
Lake	162	1.5	20 718	2 365	59	11	28	23	21	8	9	2	1
La Plata	1 334	4.7	29 127	427	765	166	356	138	127	54	48	11	4
Larimer	8 296	2.4	31 420	253	5 317	742	1 569	750	690	313	249	47	36
Las Animas	340	7.7	22 025	2 010	183	10	63	102	99	28	46	10	1
Lincoln	103	-2.8	17 377	2 961	74	-3	25	21	19	8	8	2	0
Logan	534	1.0	25 436	1 015	285	94	107	83	78	35	29	8	2
Mesa	3 167	5.2	25 940	900	1 891	239	662	550	523	223	200	44	15
Mineral	21	4.5	24 188	1 346	12	3	6	3	3	2	1	0	0
Moffat	324	5.1	24 136	1 361	190	21	48	43	40	17	17	4	2
Montezuma	567	3.3	23 572	1 542	281	35	122	102	97	42	36	11	3
Montrose	843	3.7	23 849	1 456	443	117	200	144	136	64	47	13	7
Morgan	645	1.0	23 327	1 619	375	92	108	107	100	39	44	10	3
Otero	459	1.1	23 153	1 677	218	36	72	147	143	34	76	14	3
Ouray	119	5.8	30 010	351	44	15	38	12	12	7	3	1	1
Park	453	-0.2	28 140	526	73	26	64	34	30	17	7	2	2
Phillips	111	-4.9	24 548	1 248	50	19	26	21	20	10	9	1	1
Pitkin	1 041	1.8	69 681	3	697	198	399	28	25	15	6	1	2
Prowers	349	-0.1	24 499	1 262	183	64	59	70	66	20	33	8	1
Pueblo	3 489	3.5	23 689	1 503	1 928	218	551	941	907	246	499	85	18
Rio Blanco	164	8.2	27 439	625	109	32	26	22	20	9	8	1	0
Rio Grande	318	9.0	26 048	879	147	66	63	62	59	22	24	9	2
Routt	753	6.9	36 976	106	530	101	187	37	32	16	10	2	2
Saguache	113	10.9	17 467	2 954	48	14	18	23	22	6	10	4	1
San Juan	16	7.4	27 582	604	8	2	3	2	2	1	1	0	0
San Miguel	247	3.0	34 460	153	171	35	73	11	10	4	3	1	1
Sedgwick	69	4.0	25 491	1 002	26	10	15	16	15	7	6	1	0
Summit	830	0.7	33 443	173	629	74	219	34	28	15	6	2	3
Teller	639	2.4	29 604	381	215	42	107	58	53	27	14	4	3
Washington	107	-9.1	21 969	2 023	40	9	26	21	20	9	8	1	1
Weld	5 000	2.3	24 495	1 265	2 897	637	709	616	569	212	240	56	29
Yuma	244	-7.3	24 965	1 142	113	49	63	36	34	17	13	3	1
CONNECTICUT	146 881	0.6	42 468	X	96 155	14 724	26 033	17 102	16 279	6 251	7 479	1 159	851
Fairfield	53 433	-1.8	59 727	6	32 177	7 355	11 146	4 256	4 042	1 557	1 883	274	213
Hartford	33 422	1.7	38 579	77	28 715	3 206	5 277	4 671	4 464	1 643	2 106	356	227
Litchfield	7 140	0.8	38 309	84	2 845	618	1 390	782	738	360	277	31	49
Middlesex	6 198	2.0	38 854	73	3 572	432	1 026	642	604	294	224	28	35
New Haven	29 532	2.0	35 339	132	18 761	2 168	4 501	4 527	4 328	1 545	2 084	333	210
New London	9 203	3.7	35 106	139	6 759	535	1 570	1 201	1 140	454	502	76	58
Tolland	4 782	1.7	33 496	171	1 724	272	688	483	450	208	171	21	26
Windham	3 170	2.5	28 526	488	1 602	137	435	540	513	189	231	40	32

1. Based on the resident population estimated as of July 1 of the year shown.   2. Includes other labor income.

Table B. States and Counties — Earnings, Social Security, and Housing

STATE County	Earnings, 2002									Social Security beneficiaries, December 2003			Housing units, 2003	
	Total (mil dol)	Farm	Percent by selected industries							Number	Rate[2]	Supplemental Security Income recipients, December 2003	Total	Percent change, 2000–2003
			Goods-related[1]		Service-related and health				Government					
			Total	Manufacturing	Information and professional and technical services	Retail trade	Finance, insurance, and real estate	Health services						
	75	76	77	78	79	80	81	82	83	84	85	86	87	88
COLORADO—Cont'd														
Cheyenne	29	-10.4	D	D	6.8	5.5	8.9	D	32.9	380	185	14	1 132	2.4
Clear Creek	150	0.0	D	D	7.1	5.0	10.6	D	17.5	970	102	51	5 277	2.9
Conejos	53	0.8	16.7	1.9	D	8.6	D	12.1	35.3	1 660	198	434	4 149	6.8
Costilla	26	21.1	D	D	D	3.3	D	4.7	37.4	1 050	295	288	2 244	1.9
Crowley	61	32.9	D	D	D	4.3	D	D	36.9	725	133	124	1 588	3.0
Custer	37	-7.7	D	D	D	11.8	12.5	D	18.8	840	222	27	3 391	13.4
Delta	292	2.2	D	6.3	D	9.9	5.9	7.7	26.4	7 010	238	458	12 790	3.4
Denver	29 363	0.0	D	4.7	20.7	3.7	14.6	7.3	14.5	72 250	130	13 208	262 243	4.3
Dolores	17	-5.6	D	3.8	D	8.2	D	0.7	29.7	440	241	32	1 246	4.4
Douglas	3 120	-0.1	18.4	3.7	21.4	11.7	11.5	3.8	11.3	13 670	61	173	81 502	28.7
Eagle	1 381	-0.2	D	3.1	8.2	7.7	15.2	6.1	8.0	2 145	47	55	24 015	8.6
Elbert	161	-5.3	33.5	2.5	D	6.6	8.2	D	20.7	2 030	91	39	7 965	12.0
El Paso	13 076	0.0	18.1	10.8	16.5	7.1	7.2	7.1	27.8	64 350	117	5 667	222 564	9.9
Fremont	557	0.0	14.9	6.2	D	7.6	4.9	10.1	47.5	9 055	190	886	18 346	7.0
Garfield	928	-0.3	27.3	2.2	8.3	10.4	8.3	8.0	16.6	5 080	107	324	19 351	11.6
Gilpin	247	0.0	D	D	D	0.3	0.5	D	6.6	425	88	5	3 104	6.0
Grand	260	-1.5	21.6	1.3	4.4	8.1	13.8	D	17.2	1 380	105	47	12 226	12.2
Gunnison	279	-1.8	32.1	1.4	5.0	9.0	9.2	3.7	21.6	1 320	94	59	9 832	7.6
Hinsdale	9	-5.3	D	D	D	D	D	D	27.3	135	178	4	1 319	1.2
Huerfano	70	-5.1	D	7.1	D	11.9	5.9	17.0	21.7	1 785	228	272	4 825	4.9
Jackson	13	-45.4	D	D	D	16.1	D	2.9	48.8	280	186	12	1 188	3.8
Jefferson	11 538	0.0	21.3	12.9	15.3	7.8	7.1	7.9	15.8	65 735	124	3 943	220 780	3.9
Kiowa	26	44.0	D	1.2	D	2.5	D	D	27.0	335	232	17	824	0.9
Kit Carson	114	13.5	8.9	4.1	3.6	10.2	6.0	3.0	21.0	1 475	186	75	3 530	2.9
Lake	70	0.0	D	D	4.0	6.5	6.3	D	35.6	715	92	53	4 112	5.1
La Plata	931	-0.6	16.0	2.3	10.9	10.4	9.3	11.6	20.8	5 920	128	405	22 412	7.9
Larimer	6 059	0.4	31.8	20.2	9.7	7.6	6.6	8.6	19.2	32 770	123	1 851	116 467	10.5
Las Animas	194	-5.2	16.1	1.9	D	9.4	5.4	8.7	32.5	3 280	212	596	7 859	3.0
Lincoln	72	-10.3	D	D	D	11.9	7.0	5.8	51.6	960	163	47	2 443	1.5
Logan	379	12.7	11.6	3.5	4.2	9.1	5.0	D	25.2	3 755	179	310	8 641	2.6
Mesa	2 130	0.3	19.8	6.7	7.0	10.5	7.6	14.9	17.6	24 020	193	2 088	53 167	9.8
Mineral	14	-0.5	D	D	D	7.4	D	D	21.1	205	233	5	1 137	1.6
Moffat	211	-2.1	26.5	1.1	D	9.3	3.9	D	23.2	1 735	128	120	5 861	4.0
Montezuma	316	-0.1	19.1	5.0	4.9	11.9	4.9	9.8	30.5	4 705	193	450	10 977	4.6
Montrose	560	2.2	27.9	7.5	5.9	10.6	5.6	8.8	20.2	7 095	197	568	15 462	8.9
Morgan	467	11.6	30.0	21.1	2.9	6.3	5.5	D	16.4	4 370	157	320	10 840	4.1
Otero	254	5.8	D	7.4	4.9	9.6	6.2	D	24.4	4 145	210	836	8 864	0.6
Ouray	59	-2.6	D	3.4	5.9	6.7	11.9	2.9	16.3	665	165	13	2 381	11.0
Park	99	-2.0	24.9	3.1	12.2	5.6	9.1	D	28.0	1 690	103	47	11 784	10.2
Phillips	69	26.4	6.0	1.2	D	6.0	D	D	25.4	975	216	56	2 040	1.3
Pitkin	894	-0.2	15.0	0.9	D	7.6	17.5	2.6	9.6	1 390	93	20	10 626	5.2
Prowers	247	17.2	17.7	13.2	3.3	8.4	6.4	D	21.9	2 220	157	342	6 095	2.0
Pueblo	2 145	-0.5	D	10.6	4.4	9.7	6.2	17.3	22.7	28 160	189	4 876	62 798	6.6
Rio Blanco	141	-1.0	41.1	3.2	3.3	6.7	3.9	D	26.1	1 015	171	46	2 929	2.6
Rio Grande	213	18.7	D	3.3	2.8	5.7	5.0	5.3	17.4	2 655	215	352	6 326	5.4
Routt	630	-1.2	29.6	0.9	7.1	9.9	10.3	7.5	10.3	1 620	78	70	12 460	11.1
Saguache	62	24.9	D	1.9	D	5.2	D	D	30.6	685	102	132	3 456	12.0
San Juan	9	0.0	D	0.0	D	D	D	D	25.0	85	149	4	641	1.4
San Miguel	206	-0.9	D	2.2	D	6.7	14.6	2.0	14.3	385	54	21	5 507	6.0
Sedgwick	36	32.8	D	D	D	8.6	D	D	26.4	720	268	31	1 382	-0.4
Summit	703	-0.1	D	0.7	D	11.0	13.3	2.8	11.5	1 490	59	25	26 753	10.5
Teller	257	-0.4	D	D	8.2	7.0	8.0	3.0	16.5	2 880	132	89	11 202	8.1
Washington	49	8.9	D	D	D	9.9	3.6	D	29.6	990	206	45	2 352	2.0
Weld	3 534	7.4	29.4	15.5	4.9	7.4	8.2	8.2	13.4	23 325	110	2 402	79 672	20.4
Yuma	161	33.5	D	1.4	2.8	6.4	D	D	17.6	1 835	187	113	4 352	1.3
CONNECTICUT	110 879	0.1	19.7	14.5	13.0	6.5	17.6	9.9	12.5	582 877	167	51 170	1 410 459	1.8
Fairfield	39 533	0.0	D	12.0	16.1	5.8	25.4	7.4	6.7	137 055	152	10 451	344 906	1.6
Hartford	31 921	0.1	D	14.7	11.5	5.9	21.1	10.4	12.9	155 470	178	17 262	358 089	1.4
Litchfield	3 463	0.5	32.1	20.7	8.9	10.1	6.5	10.9	12.0	33 860	180	1 294	81 272	2.5
Middlesex	4 004	0.4	27.0	20.7	7.6	6.9	15.1	11.8	13.9	27 245	169	1 212	69 652	3.5
New Haven	20 929	0.1	21.0	14.9	13.5	7.6	7.3	13.4	13.2	146 070	174	15 256	344 790	1.2
New London	7 295	0.6	D	18.6	9.7	6.5	3.1	9.2	31.9	44 330	168	3 162	112 883	2.0
Tolland	1 996	0.7	D	9.3	7.7	8.1	4.2	10.6	36.1	19 730	136	599	53 680	4.1
Windham	1 740	0.6	31.1	25.1	5.6	8.7	2.8	13.4	18.7	19 110	170	1 912	45 187	2.8

1. Covers mining, construction, and manufacturing.   2. Per 1,000 resident population estimated as of July 1 of the year shown.

STATE County	Housing units, 2000								Civilian labor force, 2003				Civilian employment,[6] 2000		
	Occupied units										Unemployment			Percent	
	Owner-occupied					Renter-occupied									
				Median owner cost as a percent of income											
	Total	Percent	Median value[1]	With a mortgage	Without a mortgage[2]	Median rent[3]	Median rent as a percent of income	Substandard units[4] (percent)	Total	Percent change, 2002–2003	Total	Rate[5]	Total	Management, professional and related occupations	Production, transportation, and material moving occupations
	89	90	91	92	93	94	95	96	97	98	99	100	101	102	103
COLORADO—Cont'd															
Cheyenne	880	75.0	62 400	18.4	9.9	362	19.8	2.3	1 300	1.3	43	3.3	1 054	35.3	10.4
Clear Creek	4 019	75.9	200 400	23.4	9.9	648	25.7	3.8	5 708	5.2	313	5.5	5 661	39.6	8.5
Conejos	2 980	78.6	57 000	20.8	12.6	332	23.9	8.2	4 098	3.7	315	7.7	3 125	27.5	15.7
Costilla	1 503	78.5	61 200	28.3	14.3	316	29.1	12.9	1 672	2.0	97	5.6	1 385	31.0	13.3
Crowley	1 358	72.9	57 200	21.6	11.8	367	23.4	4.2	1 731	2.0	82	3.6	1 518	32.3	9.7
Custer	1 480	78.9	134 100	23.1	9.9	476	23.6	9.5	2 294	1.7	680	5.4	11 411	28.0	14.4
Delta	11 058	77.5	115 500	24.4	9.9	504	26.4	4.5	12 683	2.8	680	5.4	11 411	37.9	10.4
Denver	239 235	52.5	165 800	23.2	9.9	631	26.2	8.1	302 697	3.2	22 261	7.4	284 340	37.9	10.4
Dolores	785	76.1	76 800	20.1	9.9	510	23.9	5.0	789	4.6	81	10.3	818	27.8	10.1
Douglas	60 924	87.9	236 000	22.5	9.9	1 053	24.8	1.5	120 872	2.6	5 529	4.6	96 929	51.8	4.7
Eagle	15 148	63.7	369 100	25.8	9.9	1 007	24.7	7.8	21 917	-0.2	1 023	4.7	25 729	33.3	7.3
Elbert	6 770	89.4	221 600	24.9	9.9	655	23.8	2.2	16 509	4.2	674	4.1	10 777	36.2	10.3
El Paso	192 409	64.7	147 100	22.5	9.9	657	26.2	3.9	282 702	1.4	18 053	6.4	244 913	37.2	10.7
Fremont	15 232	76.0	104 900	22.8	9.9	496	27.0	3.3	18 344	1.4	1 069	5.8	16 325	28.1	12.3
Garfield	16 229	65.1	200 700	23.9	9.9	657	25.8	6.5	26 849	4.0	1 133	4.2	22 899	26.9	9.1
Gilpin	2 043	78.5	180 600	25.9	9.9	842	29.9	6.1	3 147	-3.3	173	5.5	3 077	30.0	8.2
Grand	5 075	68.3	205 500	22.6	9.9	655	22.3	4.4	6 899	6.2	287	4.2	7 520	30.0	9.1
Gunnison	5 649	58.4	189 400	25.2	9.9	593	29.0	3.5	7 912	-0.2	509	6.4	8 175	32.6	5.4
Hinsdale	359	64.9	213 300	24.0	9.9	510	26.5	4.7	684	3.8	20	2.9	449	31.2	7.1
Huerfano	3 082	70.6	75 200	24.5	12.7	419	26.1	6.4	3 832	-1.6	267	7.0	2 878	32.2	10.5
Jackson	661	67.9	86 000	21.7	9.9	388	19.0	3.9	1 097	8.3	59	5.4	793	33.7	10.0
Jefferson	205 516	72.5	NA	NA	NA	NA	NA	2.7	310 080	-3.8	17 314	5.6	290 041	41.3	8.7
Kiowa	665	71.3	46 100	18.8	11.3	366	21.8	1.5	800	-2.1	44	5.5	753	35.7	9.8
Kit Carson	2 990	72.1	80 400	19.4	9.9	420	21.1	5.2	3 893	1.2	148	3.8	3 665	33.7	10.3
Lake	2 977	68.1	115 400	22.9	9.9	558	24.3	9.2	3 157	-0.9	236	7.5	4 047	23.7	9.0
La Plata	17 342	68.4	183 900	23.3	9.9	655	29.0	3.6	26 799	3.8	1 263	4.7	22 990	36.0	7.7
Larimer	97 164	67.7	172 000	22.5	9.9	678	27.6	2.6	155 314	1.2	8 840	5.7	136 903	39.6	11.5
Las Animas	6 173	70.4	84 500	23.2	10.9	397	24.9	5.2	7 731	3.8	402	5.2	6 184	30.8	11.1
Lincoln	2 058	68.9	77 800	21.5	11.4	447	20.5	2.8	2 936	3.1	81	2.8	2 476	32.2	10.0
Logan	7 551	69.8	87 700	20.6	11.6	451	24.3	4.1	11 035	1.0	425	3.9	9 393	28.4	14.5
Mesa	45 823	72.7	118 900	23.0	9.9	527	27.8	3.3	66 793	3.8	3 806	5.7	55 046	29.3	12.9
Mineral	377	73.2	127 400	18.9	9.9	500	21.5	3.4	479	5.3	13	2.7	416	27.9	7.5
Moffat	4 983	72.0	104 600	19.2	9.9	453	20.5	4.4	6 601	3.0	462	7.0	6 499	20.9	14.4
Montezuma	9 201	74.8	109 100	21.8	9.9	459	26.5	5.1	12 031	1.1	675	5.6	10 645	32.1	10.8
Montrose	13 043	74.9	121 200	23.7	9.9	521	25.2	4.3	18 043	6.5	983	5.4	15 170	25.9	13.4
Morgan	9 539	68.5	95 900	21.9	10.3	482	23.2	9.3	14 627	6.5	575	3.9	11 888	24.4	21.9
Otero	7 920	69.2	66 300	20.1	9.9	372	25.7	5.4	8 895	1.0	566	6.4	8 345	32.1	12.4
Ouray	1 576	73.0	244 700	29.1	9.9	696	30.1	3.0	2 131	6.3	83	3.9	1 818	37.2	6.9
Park	5 894	87.8	172 100	24.5	9.9	806	25.4	4.4	9 064	0.4	431	4.8	7 902	33.2	9.9
Phillips	1 781	76.3	79 800	21.1	9.9	388	23.2	5.2	2 489	4.0	63	2.5	1 981	35.3	7.7
Pitkin	6 807	59.1	750 000	26.5	9.9	947	25.5	4.7	9 554	2.9	451	4.7	9 832	42.1	4.1
Prowers	5 307	66.2	67 900	21.0	9.9	400	23.3	7.6	7 226	1.2	325	4.5	6 681	26.3	16.5
Pueblo	54 579	70.4	95 200	22.3	9.9	489	28.4	4.5	63 232	2.2	4 599	7.3	59 715	28.2	13.3
Rio Blanco	2 306	70.4	94 700	17.7	9.9	399	19.9	2.6	3 420	1.4	118	3.5	2 948	29.8	10.1
Rio Grande	4 701	70.8	82 400	23.5	9.9	382	23.1	6.2	6 673	9.6	362	5.4	5 383	30.2	12.4
Routt	7 953	69.3	268 500	24.0	9.9	740	25.7	2.3	12 538	1.2	479	3.8	12 298	34.5	7.6
Saguache	2 300	69.4	73 900	21.8	9.9	404	26.7	10.3	3 570	9.1	201	5.6	2 504	27.9	11.7
San Juan	269	67.3	131 500	25.3	11.7	561	50.1	4.5	355	12.0	51	14.4	319	37.6	10.0
San Miguel	3 015	51.6	358 200	21.9	9.9	811	27.1	6.9	4 816	0.6	260	5.4	4 542	35.8	6.5
Sedgwick	1 165	73.4	57 100	21.1	9.9	301	18.2	2.0	1 306	0.9	44	3.4	1 321	31.7	13.1
Summit	9 120	59.0	317 500	23.3	9.9	874	24.5	5.2	13 339	0.1	665	5.0	16 596	30.8	6.8
Teller	7 993	80.9	162 000	23.7	9.9	767	23.5	3.0	13 986	1.0	667	4.8	10 980	36.6	9.0
Washington	1 989	73.7	70 800	19.6	9.9	341	18.3	2.6	2 293	-1.2	66	2.9	2 361	37.9	14.3
Weld	63 247	68.7	140 400	24.0	10.0	564	27.0	7.1	101 880	3.3	6 830	6.7	87 626	29.5	15.9
Yuma	3 800	71.1	77 100	20.2	9.9	375	21.0	4.2	5 642	5.7	126	2.2	4 803	34.0	10.6
CONNECTICUT	1 301 670	66.8	166 900	22.4	13.1	681	25.4	3.2	1 803 108	0.6	99 147	5.5	1 664 440	39.1	12.0
Fairfield	324 232	69.2	288 900	23.1	13.8	838	26.1	4.2	461 385	0.7	22 320	4.8	426 638	43.7	9.3
Hartford	335 098	64.2	147 300	21.9	12.9	645	25.1	3.5	435 935	0.3	27 094	6.2	410 771	38.8	12.5
Litchfield	71 551	75.2	156 600	22.7	13.2	660	24.4	1.5	101 761	0.9	5 150	5.1	95 626	35.8	14.5
Middlesex	61 341	72.1	166 000	22.1	12.5	701	23.2	1.4	87 136	0.5	4 191	4.8	82 040	42.1	11.0
New Haven	319 040	63.1	151 900	22.9	13.8	666	26.4	3.2	436 099	0.4	26 351	6.0	396 326	37.0	13.6
New London	99 835	66.7	142 200	21.8	11.8	646	24.1	2.2	146 905	2.2	7 069	4.8	125 194	35.6	10.8
Tolland	49 431	73.5	151 600	21.1	11.5	662	24.2	1.4	73 534	-0.1	3 209	4.4	72 743	41.3	10.6
Windham	41 142	67.4	117 200	21.6	11.4	548	23.7	2.7	60 348	0.9	3 762	6.2	55 102	28.8	18.5

1. Specified owner-occupied units.   2. Median monthly owner costs is often in the minimum category—9.9 percent or less, which is indicated as 9.9 percent.   3. Specified renter-occupied units.   4. Overcrowded or lacking complete plumbing facilities.   5. Percent of civilian labor force.   6. Persons 16 years old and over.

STATE County	Number of establishments	Total	Health care and social assistance	Manufacturing	Retail trade	Finance and insurance	Professional, scientific, and technical services	Total (mil dol)	Average per employee (dollars)	Number	Less than 50 acres	500 acres and over	Farm operators whose principal occupation is farming (percent)
	104	105	106	107	108	109	110	111	112	113	114	115	116
COLORADO—Cont'd													
Cheyenne	58	442	100	D	72	D	D	9	21 430	283	2.5	71.0	74.9
Clear Creek	341	2 635	53	71	277	60	54	62	23 625	9	0.0	55.6	77.8
Conejos	119	826	228	61	180	D	4	16	19 694	494	18.4	29.4	63.8
Costilla	60	261	59	D	D	D	D	3	13 046	205	26.3	24.4	62.4
Crowley	51	301	D	D	99	D	D	5	17 312	217	12.0	44.7	56.2
Custer	148	546	D	11	137	30	27	12	22 520	158	18.4	26.6	57.0
Delta	767	5 497	937	437	1 260	231	185	123	22 461	1 063	54.1	7.8	58.7
Denver	22 175	421 426	50 217	23 320	34 346	28 730	36 255	17 590	41 739	10	100.0	0.0	40.0
Dolores	47	179	D	14	50	D	D	3	19 039	216	17.6	37.5	63.4
Douglas	4 233	43 096	2 312	1 886	10 833	1 143	2 368	1 363	31 631	903	50.8	9.5	52.2
Eagle	2 901	29 653	1 082	398	3 951	648	1 476	824	27 790	114	30.7	23.7	57.9
Elbert	458	2 340	157	73	321	84	148	61	25 870	1 153	30.1	24.0	54.1
El Paso	13 862	216 106	23 865	22 484	29 384	11 074	17 005	7 037	32 561	1 175	35.7	23.1	54.3
Fremont	872	7 693	1 356	761	1 599	296	169	167	21 686	700	61.9	14.7	48.0
Garfield	2 113	16 390	1 724	412	3 271	645	840	487	29 717	499	46.9	19.6	51.7
Gilpin	81	3 655	D	D	D	0	16	114	31 284	26	23.1	3.8	61.5
Grand	778	6 637	187	51	824	127	155	120	18 132	173	27.7	35.8	55.5
Gunnison	885	7 077	366	103	1 051	185	220	141	19 872	186	24.2	31.7	62.9
Hinsdale	71	179	D	D	D	D	D	4	20 173	19	0.0	21.1	73.7
Huerfano	191	1 398	415	D	250	44	47	27	19 088	292	13.4	45.5	61.3
Jackson	60	231	14	D	54	D	12	5	22 974	89	10.1	74.2	77.5
Jefferson	16 202	179 920	19 853	15 963	30 686	7 898	16 909	6 248	34 726	457	65.9	8.3	46.2
Kiowa	47	238	D	9	55	D	3	5	21 391	357	1.1	67.8	64.4
Kit Carson	283	1 920	307	93	429	109	36	40	21 066	678	8.0	61.5	70.2
Lake	192	1 382	200	D	194	65	26	25	18 223	34	17.6	44.1	41.2
La Plata	2 049	17 645	2 266	1 211	3 213	572	887	433	24 557	923	38.7	14.1	51.0
Larimer	8 160	96 202	10 443	12 980	15 956	3 070	6 329	2 878	29 920	1 564	61.5	9.8	48.3
Las Animas	380	3 435	470	100	732	150	92	63	18 306	567	7.9	60.5	65.3
Lincoln	135	1 273	214	D	344	51	22	29	23 124	455	7.0	69.9	67.3
Logan	629	5 654	1 060	429	1 093	232	409	131	23 180	930	13.1	47.8	65.1
Mesa	4 073	44 063	7 127	3 790	7 602	1 437	2 019	1 164	26 406	1 599	66.4	7.6	51.2
Mineral	53	166	D	D	D	D	D	4	23 181	14	14.3	7.1	21.4
Moffat	398	3 428	493	81	814	77	93	96	27 999	443	20.5	37.0	53.5
Montezuma	760	6 740	949	366	1 609	223	276	155	22 946	829	39.2	12.6	48.3
Montrose	1 135	10 355	1 412	1 441	2 030	334	509	246	23 756	915	46.8	12.6	58.1
Morgan	640	8 290	1 126	2 979	1 068	247	110	208	25 058	761	15.2	37.8	67.8
Otero	509	4 812	1 236	303	993	230	116	98	20 454	488	31.8	24.8	58.6
Ouray	239	857	D	30	117	47	31	20	23 624	96	39.6	30.2	54.2
Park	412	1 260	45	58	185	30	85	29	23 245	217	20.7	28.1	63.1
Phillips	143	1 028	288	34	162	59	17	21	20 293	334	9.6	60.2	81.7
Pitkin	1 562	16 280	707	237	2 069	300	832	454	27 889	84	45.2	8.3	46.4
Prowers	422	4 026	529	767	959	223	106	88	21 740	531	13.4	50.8	63.5
Pueblo	3 194	44 636	9 894	4 026	7 048	1 738	1 604	1 120	25 099	801	38.2	27.3	56.7
Rio Blanco	212	1 611	264	57	192	D	37	52	32 118	245	27.3	33.9	69.0
Rio Grande	398	2 748	317	156	530	158	61	58	21 144	344	17.4	29.9	69.2
Routt	1 371	17 592	938	299	1 778	220	450	520	29 567	593	31.5	25.3	50.3
Saguache	119	676	463	47	130	20	D	12	18 263	252	9.1	54.8	77.0
San Juan	49	74	D	D	D	0	D	2	28 595	1	0.0	100.0	100.0
San Miguel	542	4 834	83	120	503	88	160	108	22 306	112	28.6	37.5	58.9
Sedgwick	89	483	131	D	106	D	7	9	18 155	188	5.9	60.6	76.6
Summit	1 888	19 991	562	136	3 339	283	625	421	21 071	36	22.2	25.0	47.2
Teller	631	5 451	247	83	663	270	362	133	24 408	118	44.1	17.8	54.2
Washington	107	732	82	D	154	30	16	15	20 400	861	5.9	58.0	69.7
Weld	4 281	58 214	5 899	9 809	8 227	3 939	2 010	1 784	30 638	3 121	31.5	21.3	57.8
Yuma	333	2 251	463	15	506	108	64	49	21 563	864	9.4	59.7	71.5
CONNECTICUT	92 105	1 555 214	220 685	233 167	187 474	136 062	95 724	68 920	44 316	4 191	62.3	2.8	49.6
Fairfield	28 673	457 272	52 229	57 990	53 304	42 016	37 964	26 468	57 882	287	76.0	0.3	51.6
Hartford	23 001	477 530	64 806	66 064	51 420	67 962	29 380	20 449	42 823	724	68.5	1.9	52.2
Litchfield	5 152	59 042	9 101	15 429	8 857	1 579	1 820	1 937	32 799	789	55.8	5.2	46.5
Middlesex	4 222	61 465	10 856	12 333	7 805	5 834	2 419	2 240	36 446	326	71.8	0.9	54.9
New Haven	20 549	335 101	58 639	51 556	42 975	15 051	16 547	12 445	37 138	486	71.4	1.2	51.9
New London	5 739	105 598	14 293	18 266	13 418	2 113	5 861	3 681	34 855	677	56.0	2.4	50.7
Tolland	2 558	28 926	5 209	4 215	4 810	882	1 214	820	28 337	398	59.0	3.3	42.2
Windham	2 211	30 280	5 552	7 314	4 885	625	519	881	29 092	504	51.6	4.8	48.0

Table B. States and Counties — **Agriculture**

	Agriculture, 2002 (cont'd)															
	Land in farms					Value of land and buildings (dollars)		Value of machinery and equipment average per farm (dollars)	Value of products sold				Percent of farms with sales of —		Government payments	
			Acres								Percent from —					
STATE County	Acreage (1,000)	Percent change, 1997–2002	Average size of farm	Total irrigated (1,000)	Total cropland (1,000)	Average per farm	Average per acre	Value of machinery and equipment average per farm (dollars)	Total (mil dol)	Average per farm (dollars)	Crops	Live-stock and poultry products	$10,000 or more	$100,000 or more	Total ($1,000)	Percent of farms
	117	118	119	120	121	122	123	124	125	126	127	128	129	130	131	132
COLORADO—Cont'd																
Cheyenne	740	-7.0	2 617	29	422	952 432	324	146 154	23	81 930	50.5	49.5	49.5	15.2	4 353	77.7
Clear Creek	D	D	D	D	D	998 450	1 665	22 541	0	882	D	D	0.0	0.0	0	0.0
Conejos	268	-6.0	542	59	138	398 956	838	91 533	23	46 259	52.5	47.5	50.4	11.5	731	29.4
Costilla	354	-2.5	1 727	35	70	846 998	501	85 908	26	128 025	86.1	13.9	44.4	9.8	214	31.2
Crowley	375	-3.8	1 730	6	55	459 908	282	87 030	53	246 008	3.0	97.0	46.5	13.4	1 188	49.8
Custer	122	-15.3	771	3	31	1 184 505	1 552	46 193	3	17 347	10.0	90.0	32.3	3.8	68	13.3
Delta	262	-7.1	247	54	79	540 121	2 093	63 553	39	36 761	36.9	63.1	36.1	6.2	847	13.7
Denver	0	-100.0	4	0	0	D	D	31 632	1	128 880	D	D	60.0	30.0	0	0.0
Dolores	159	1.9	734	10	83	650 534	946	62 668	4	17 467	47.8	52.2	21.8	4.6	1 113	59.3
Douglas	199	-2.5	221	4	51	535 049	3 065	22 423	12	12 829	56.7	43.3	13.8	1.1	84	6.5
Eagle	116	-37.3	1 018	9	17	1 500 095	1 509	105 462	4	32 887	8.1	91.9	39.5	8.8	146	18.4
Elbert	1 068	-2.5	927	6	216	577 153	694	58 353	28	24 174	18.3	81.7	29.7	4.9	2 062	21.9
El Paso	812	-6.3	691	10	109	575 409	880	57 564	32	27 204	43.7	56.3	27.5	4.6	711	18.1
Fremont	265	-6.4	378	12	33	400 072	1 044	24 646	15	20 911	31.8	68.2	16.7	2.4	167	9.4
Garfield	404	-5.4	810	34	76	1 078 254	1 293	50 972	23	45 634	31.1	68.9	30.3	8.6	559	15.4
Gilpin	6	-33.3	233	0	0	934 244	2 787	24 773	0	8 202	D	D	15.4	0.0	D	D
Grand	220	-12.4	1 269	35	50	1 521 147	1 206	99 549	7	42 155	14.7	85.3	35.8	9.2	155	8.7
Gunnison	165	-15.4	890	41	59	1 467 593	1 853	116 663	9	49 133	10.7	89.3	37.6	13.4	295	13.4
Hinsdale	9	0.0	457	2	4	1 167 571	2 926	150 161	0	16 595	D	D	31.6	0.0	13	15.8
Huerfano	608	-5.1	2 082	6	60	875 538	429	51 796	8	26 068	3.7	96.3	31.5	4.5	168	13.4
Jackson	438	-8.2	4 917	55	108	2 513 501	520	166 908	16	178 466	5.5	94.5	68.5	37.1	479	29.2
Jefferson	90	-8.2	198	2	19	752 195	4 896	35 952	20	44 854	90.3	9.7	17.7	4.6	70	3.9
Kiowa	897	-1.9	2 512	4	498	724 365	307	120 007	19	53 178	D	D	39.2	11.5	5 397	75.1
Kit Carson	1 247	-7.4	1 840	137	850	815 335	464	162 267	206	303 177	19.6	80.4	59.6	29.9	11 056	75.2
Lake	17	0.0	507	1	4	668 095	1 381	31 892	0	10 738	D	D	11.8	2.9	0	0.0
La Plata	563	-2.9	610	67	112	646 727	1 020	53 361	16	17 294	24.4	75.6	26.1	3.1	827	20.2
Larimer	522	-3.7	334	59	140	778 424	2 311	62 865	101	64 640	32.6	67.4	24.6	5.9	766	12.1
Las Animas	2 305	4.1	4 065	5	203	988 107	243	52 833	21	36 838	3.6	96.4	46.7	10.8	1 458	31.2
Lincoln	1 428	-13.3	3 139	13	488	807 513	251	164 889	36	78 262	33.7	66.3	53.8	22.0	5 960	62.6
Logan	1 111	-1.6	1 195	111	570	643 347	560	132 355	350	376 402	10.8	89.2	60.1	20.3	6 336	64.8
Mesa	385	-7.7	241	66	120	553 679	1 426	48 755	59	37 038	49.9	50.1	30.1	6.7	879	11.1
Mineral	4	NA	317	D	0	606 000	1 562	20 263	0	11 856	D	D	21.4	7.1	D	D
Moffat	1 018	-1.3	2 297	23	162	898 335	416	59 074	20	45 551	5.5	94.5	31.8	9.7	1 748	34.5
Montezuma	819	-12.4	988	49	119	536 563	516	62 927	15	17 516	44.5	55.5	27.5	3.0	598	23.3
Montrose	335	-9.9	366	75	107	497 854	1 180	45 081	58	63 378	36.3	63.7	41.4	10.6	986	18.0
Morgan	758	2.3	996	134	384	810 693	801	133 974	448	588 650	14.0	86.0	61.1	27.5	5 781	53.6
Otero	546	-5.9	1 120	39	95	427 706	382	94 102	106	217 194	11.0	89.0	55.7	15.6	1 771	44.7
Ouray	108	-7.7	1 126	11	15	1 702 053	1 505	73 127	3	33 691	12.2	87.8	40.6	10.4	108	14.6
Park	298	-4.2	1 375	11	46	1 043 968	784	40 171	4	19 346	5.5	94.5	22.1	4.1	30	6.5
Phillips	471	1.7	1 410	84	388	967 807	718	194 227	89	267 312	48.4	51.6	67.4	37.4	5 157	79.3
Pitkin	24	-4.0	284	6	5	1 656 060	5 926	70 356	1	8 975	28.9	71.1	23.8	0.0	32	11.9
Prowers	862	-0.1	1 623	94	533	690 699	417	106 521	183	343 832	15.1	84.9	55.0	20.7	6 228	59.7
Pueblo	774	-6.0	967	25	118	626 878	491	64 567	42	52 000	26.6	73.4	37.5	8.4	1 610	23.6
Rio Blanco	377	-19.1	1 537	23	73	1 207 896	669	77 784	13	52 740	8.6	91.4	49.8	18.0	634	31.4
Rio Grande	171	-26.3	497	89	111	899 346	1 827	139 541	74	216 521	92.4	7.6	60.2	29.9	626	32.0
Routt	450	-13.6	759	36	136	1 527 915	1 890	76 607	25	42 431	8.5	91.5	25.0	6.1	1 039	21.4
Saguache	477	-1.0	1 893	91	173	1 319 486	709	231 809	82	324 810	86.8	13.2	66.7	40.9	877	32.5
San Juan	D	NA	D	D	D	D	D	0	0	0	0.0	0.0	0.0	0.0	0	0.0
San Miguel	151	-6.8	1 349	5	22	1 287 758	962	68 407	4	32 247	9.1	90.8	33.0	0.8	241	25.9
Sedgwick	274	-6.8	1 459	41	185	994 695	735	184 763	58	306 920	30.6	69.4	72.9	35.6	1 933	67.0
Summit	28	-20.0	773	4	6	1 610 619	1 766	78 468	0	12 924	8.2	91.8	19.4	5.6	D	D
Teller	74	-10.8	624	1	11	815 756	1 284	32 652	2	13 196	26.1	73.9	20.3	3.4	28	10.2
Washington	1 409	1.1	1 636	43	858	676 616	417	134 302	72	83 870	46.4	53.6	54.9	18.1	10 255	74.9
Weld	1 812	-5.3	581	326	878	759 282	1 379	112 747	1 128	361 376	18.2	81.8	47.6	17.3	13 111	37.6
Yuma	1 354	-0.8	1 567	253	704	852 401	573	164 743	543	628 108	19.9	80.1	65.5	36.0	10 904	67.7
CONNECTICUT	357	-0.6	85	10	171	840 302	9 491	51 214	471	112 297	69.6	30.4	32.7	10.5	3 681	6.1
Fairfield	13	8.3	45	0	5	1 153 047	26 164	36 613	30	105 478	72.1	27.9	38.0	11.8	D	D
Hartford	50	-5.7	69	5	31	912 959	13 193	55 745	127	175 119	78.7	21.3	41.7	15.6	393	3.9
Litchfield	94	3.3	119	0	42	1 101 123	8 611	52 327	30	38 141	52.3	47.7	32.7	7.0	748	7.7
Middlesex	18	-5.3	55	1	9	543 847	12 457	36 932	44	135 588	95.9	4.1	24.8	5.5	D	D
New Haven	26	4.0	53	1	14	929 815	13 630	69 982	57	117 651	91.9	8.1	34.4	12.8	292	4.9
New London	59	-13.2	87	1	27	558 698	6 889	44 033	123	181 516	58.9	41.1	25.7	9.2	647	7.1
Tolland	37	2.8	92	1	17	567 636	5 665	67 206	28	70 747	53.2	46.8	29.6	9.3	571	5.8
Windham	61	7.0	121	0	26	850 870	6 577	38 960	31	61 632	25.5	74.5	31.9	11.5	852	11.3

Table B. States and Counties — Residential Construction, Wholesale Trade, Retail Trade, and Real Estate

STATE County	Value of residential construction authorized by building permits, 2003		Wholesale trade, 1997				Retail trade,[1] 1997				Real estate and rental and leasing, 1997			
	New construction ($1,000)	Number of housing units	Number of establish-ments	Number of employees	Sales (mil dol)	Annual payroll (mil dol)	Number of establish-ments	Number of employees	Sales (mil dol)	Annual payroll (mil dol)	Number of establish-ments	Number of employees	Receipts (mil dol)	Annual payroll (mil dol)
	133	134	135	136	137	138	139	140	141	142	143	144	145	146
COLORADO—Cont'd														
Cheyenne	49	1	5	43	39.7	1.1	13	68	11.4	0.9	2	D	D	D
Clear Creek	9 920	57	17	97	30.7	2.7	50	299	39.3	3.9	16	107	3.8	0.7
Conejos	4 733	30	6	57	11.4	0.9	22	139	22.5	2.0	3	9	0.3	0.1
Costilla	NA	NA	NA	NA	NA	NA	11	24	3.6	0.3	2	D	D	D
Crowley	85	1	NA	NA	NA	NA	10	87	12.6	1.3	3	6	0.2	0.1
Custer	19 017	129	4	8	1.6	0.1	21	100	13.9	1.4	12	29	1.6	0.4
Delta	7 004	64	26	272	40.8	4.9	129	957	156.8	15.0	24	54	5.5	1.0
Denver	339 366	3 036	1 681	26 604	16 177.1	972.8	2 410	30 080	5 600.9	628.0	1 201	11 339	1 771.9	287.0
Dolores	1 104	7	6	45	23.7	0.9	6	34	4.5	0.4	5	3	0.4	0.0
Douglas	725 454	3 693	198	967	943.9	34.5	500	8 052	1 212.0	123.5	157	397	69.9	9.6
Eagle	170 520	516	62	242	189.0	8.5	367	3 313	497.2	67.3	175	989	84.8	19.3
Elbert	22 398	166	18	60	39.3	2.8	40	188	34.9	2.8	7	8	0.9	0.2
El Paso	663 982	5 238	498	6 513	1 417.9	213.3	1 901	27 806	5 015.1	503.6	735	3 064	362.3	62.8
Fremont	36 970	304	28	120	42.8	3.0	143	1 311	203.8	21.6	30	101	10.7	1.4
Garfield	64 494	365	52	379	112.8	8.7	277	2 635	552.5	55.7	87	387	30.4	5.9
Gilpin	6 911	55	1	D	D	D	7	27	2.8	0.4	4	30	2.0	0.6
Grand	98 210	443	10	52	12.9	1.0	116	706	95.6	10.5	56	607	34.8	7.5
Gunnison	33 575	196	9	40	9.1	0.7	139	969	135.6	13.6	46	359	15.8	4.1
Hinsdale	1 966	8	1	D	D	D	14	15	5.1	0.5	6	11	1.9	0.2
Huerfano	5 352	51	7	26	2.9	0.6	39	211	33.0	3.3	10	14	1.6	0.1
Jackson	2 524	14	3	25	3.6	0.6	6	50	6.2	0.6	NA	NA	NA	NA
Jefferson	297 350	1 426	771	4 994	2 805.6	178.2	1 986	28 098	5 114.8	509.2	726	3 214	359.1	66.4
Kiowa	0	0	6	16	8.0	0.3	8	52	4.4	0.5	NA	NA	NA	NA
Kit Carson	628	5	28	241	122.5	4.8	64	462	100.1	7.6	4	11	1.6	0.2
Lake	6 248	62	4	D	D	D	33	202	25.9	2.7	12	56	4.4	0.7
La Plata	95 635	756	71	511	119.4	15.4	317	2 848	440.6	49.5	108	325	33.0	6.4
Larimer	431 406	3 003	311	2 630	805.6	75.9	1 201	13 810	2 440.5	234.2	360	1 497	190.0	27.8
Las Animas	9 418	74	17	117	33.8	3.3	54	576	84.8	8.0	8	28	4.8	0.5
Lincoln	384	5	9	61	20.6	0.9	36	320	58.3	5.1	4	D	D	D
Logan	5 345	54	32	338	97.4	6.4	115	1 149	199.5	16.5	22	61	3.2	0.8
Mesa	195 007	1 589	198	1 461	531.1	42.8	600	6 409	1 152.7	115.0	133	658	62.6	11.6
Mineral	221	17	NA	NA	NA	NA	10	34	3.7	0.5	4	D	D	D
Moffat	6 754	62	28	123	35.6	3.3	77	706	117.4	12.1	11	23	1.9	0.3
Montezuma	2 585	27	23	112	18.4	2.0	136	1 302	228.6	22.4	27	94	6.1	1.4
Montrose	44 804	368	44	377	88.7	6.7	171	1 710	304.1	31.3	44	176	11.4	2.5
Morgan	16 206	125	41	403	416.9	9.0	119	996	157.6	15.0	23	78	4.3	0.8
Otero	3 548	45	34	286	118.9	6.1	101	932	141.2	13.6	17	61	4.1	0.8
Ouray	22 277	110	2	D	D	D	41	99	11.9	1.4	12	25	2.7	0.3
Park	36 545	300	15	D	D	D	35	175	28.2	3.1	13	18	1.9	0.6
Phillips	1 268	9	15	170	142.3	4.7	23	165	28.4	2.4	3	D	D	D
Pitkin	109 767	102	26	204	79.0	9.3	265	2 264	288.9	41.0	144	644	82.0	18.2
Prowers	791	8	25	403	82.0	7.4	93	826	112.9	11.4	17	42	2.0	0.3
Pueblo	123 160	1 282	113	1 101	390.3	27.5	600	7 040	1 180.7	121.7	131	486	58.8	8.2
Rio Blanco	3 257	23	6	23	6.6	0.5	36	201	21.5	2.2	7	10	0.8	0.1
Rio Grande	15 282	101	31	564	98.1	9.1	77	476	96.8	8.6	14	29	3.0	0.5
Routt	98 751	321	31	185	51.4	5.3	184	1 484	190.3	22.5	86	633	33.9	9.1
Saguache	7 679	83	8	92	8.7	1.1	24	118	30.1	2.4	4	D	D	D
San Juan	2 673	20	NA	NA	NA	NA	18	39	5.1	0.8	1	D	D	D
San Miguel	77 473	96	5	28	2.2	0.6	76	524	44.6	6.5	44	159	17.4	3.4
Sedgwick	270	1	10	71	36.9	1.7	24	129	25.6	2.0	2	D	D	D
Summit	129 385	407	41	191	58.5	4.5	339	2 801	387.9	45.8	156	1 295	100.3	26.4
Teller	40 317	211	15	57	19.5	2.3	72	516	77.6	8.6	42	182	18.3	2.5
Washington	1 796	11	10	147	53.1	3.4	21	162	23.0	2.8	1	D	D	D
Weld	602 260	3 963	247	2 829	1 334.6	84.9	505	6 195	1 155.5	109.2	154	576	65.4	9.5
Yuma	1 092	9	30	239	112.4	4.8	68	529	89.4	8.6	1	D	D	D
CONNECTICUT	1 664 859	10 435	5 283	77 716	75 821.6	3 595.3	14 574	186 935	34 938.9	3 634.3	3 372	20 635	3 522.8	609.3
Fairfield	545 214	1 964	1 768	28 573	48 325.4	1 559.1	4 008	54 012	11 563.9	1 218.0	1 098	7 639	1 748.1	288.2
Hartford	304 212	2 585	1 369	25 741	16 831.0	1 108.2	3 683	51 121	8 829.0	943.6	874	6 243	996.4	181.9
Litchfield	122 825	732	240	2 203	779.0	90.7	816	8 193	1 611.0	158.0	141	409	48.2	9.1
Middlesex	110 388	821	218	2 045	823.0	74.2	742	8 050	1 345.0	143.1	142	765	96.3	14.8
New Haven	244 015	1 826	1 316	15 458	8 028.3	633.3	3 335	41 942	7 725.2	775.9	761	4 030	477.5	89.0
New London	173 106	1 222	201	2 279	801.6	81.9	1 182	13 923	2 405.0	240.3	188	723	82.4	13.8
Tolland	101 202	731	89	602	246.5	23.2	428	5 028	763.9	81.8	86	484	49.8	8.7
Windham	63 898	554	82	815	333.1	24.7	380	4 666	695.8	73.6	82	342	24.1	3.8

1. Establishments with payroll.

STATE County	Professional, scientific, and technical services,[1] 1997				Manufacturing, 1997				Accommodation and foodservices, 1997			
	Number of establishments	Number of employees	Receipts (mil dol)	Annual payroll (mil dol)	Number of establishments	Number of employees	Receipts (mil dol)	Annual payroll (mil dol)	Number of establishments	Number of employees	Sales (mil dol)	Annual payroll (mil dol)
	147	148	149	150	151	152	153	154	155	156	157	158
COLORADO—Cont'd												
Cheyenne	1	D	D	D	NA	NA	NA	NA	4	D	D	D
Clear Creek	31	47	5.1	1.9	NA	NA	NA	NA	48	539	18.8	5.2
Conejos	3	8	0.2	0.1	NA	NA	NA	NA	14	44	1.9	0.5
Costilla	3	4	0.3	0.1	NA	NA	NA	NA	7	D	D	D
Crowley	NA	NA	NA	NA	NA	NA	NA	NA	5	D	D	D
Custer	9	59	2.8	0.7	NA	NA	NA	NA	14	103	4.2	1.0
Delta	43	126	5.6	2.1	NA	NA	NA	NA	68	559	15.2	4.2
Denver	3 147	29 056	3 640.3	1 455.0	976	26 320	4 867.8	816.2	1 564	33 749	1 335.2	386.0
Dolores	2	D	D	D	NA	NA	NA	NA	7	D	D	D
Douglas	459	1 143	166.7	43.0	119	1 941	289.7	58.8	178	3 593	109.1	32.1
Eagle	191	755	87.3	34.2	43	502	85.3	14.9	223	7 181	288.1	100.3
Elbert	36	46	4.1	1.7	NA	NA	NA	NA	11	73	2.4	0.7
El Paso	1 384	10 515	1 199.2	467.1	499	21 593	5 698.9	700.6	998	21 480	771.9	216.9
Fremont	37	118	6.6	2.3	47	950	146.9	26.8	82	1 008	29.8	7.6
Garfield	144	508	45.5	17.1	NA	NA	NA	NA	155	1 906	72.6	21.3
Gilpin	8	111	2.5	1.0	NA	NA	NA	NA	9	647	61.1	11.4
Grand	42	99	6.9	2.4	NA	NA	NA	NA	127	1 531	51.9	15.5
Gunnison	45	144	10.4	3.6	NA	NA	NA	NA	114	2 765	84.3	22.6
Hinsdale	4	4	0.6	0.1	NA	NA	NA	NA	18	71	3.7	0.8
Huerfano	13	23	1.3	0.4	NA	NA	NA	NA	28	201	5.9	1.7
Jackson	1	D	D	D	NA	NA	NA	NA	7	48	0.9	0.3
Jefferson	1 979	11 633	1 284.3	490.7	559	17 871	3 711.2	803.0	967	18 968	585.7	172.5
Kiowa	3	4	0.3	0.1	NA	NA	NA	NA	5	D	D	D
Kit Carson	15	42	2.3	0.9	NA	NA	NA	NA	20	360	9.8	2.6
Lake	13	22	1.8	0.9	NA	NA	NA	NA	44	342	8.4	2.1
La Plata	171	639	57.9	22.1	66	752	51.8	19.3	169	4 281	143.2	44.1
Larimer	711	3 815	336.3	134.2	384	15 840	3 890.7	645.0	647	10 779	343.6	95.0
Las Animas	19	83	3.4	1.6	NA	NA	NA	NA	42	462	13.6	3.4
Lincoln	5	16	0.5	0.2	NA	NA	NA	NA	25	238	8.0	2.2
Logan	33	376	17.1	6.8	19	736	163.2	15.2	51	769	20.4	5.8
Mesa	275	1 283	91.3	39.2	167	3 605	484.2	99.2	247	4 555	124.7	36.3
Mineral	NA	NA	NA	NA	NA	NA	NA	NA	11	19	2.0	0.6
Moffat	28	55	3.3	0.9	NA	NA	NA	NA	27	372	12.0	3.4
Montezuma	50	158	11.0	3.3	NA	NA	NA	NA	82	987	27.8	7.8
Montrose	80	259	18.8	7.4	64	1 540	156.0	31.5	76	825	29.3	7.3
Morgan	33	90	5.9	1.6	25	D	D	D	63	789	19.6	5.4
Otero	24	73	4.1	1.1	17	534	36.2	10.7	63	618	15.9	3.8
Ouray	12	30	2.0	0.9	NA	NA	NA	NA	45	223	10.9	2.8
Park	21	49	3.6	1.3	NA	NA	NA	NA	38	270	9.9	2.8
Phillips	8	15	1.2	0.2	NA	NA	NA	NA	10	D	D	D
Pitkin	184	661	81.0	27.3	20	D	D	D	189	5 720	228.3	81.8
Prowers	28	111	6.5	2.5	107	4 688	1 021.3	147.0	40	470	12.3	3.5
Pueblo	192	981	49.7	19.3	NA	NA	NA	NA	321	4 969	142.4	38.1
Rio Blanco	14	37	2.4	0.9	NA	NA	NA	NA	25	182	7.5	2.3
Rio Grande	18	62	3.7	1.7	NA	NA	NA	NA	41	353	10.9	3.0
Routt	102	394	30.8	10.5	NA	NA	NA	NA	108	3 225	98.1	28.1
Saguache	6	11	0.7	0.2	NA	NA	NA	NA	10	D	D	D
San Juan	1	D	D	D	NA	NA	NA	NA	15	6	2.0	0.5
San Miguel	44	110	9.8	3.7	NA	NA	NA	NA	59	848	25.1	8.8
Sedgwick	3	D	D	D	NA	NA	NA	NA	11	D	D	D
Summit	129	531	45.2	18.3	NA	NA	NA	NA	204	7 781	226.6	67.6
Teller	50	155	16.4	5.1	NA	NA	NA	NA	68	1 848	94.8	26.0
Washington	5	16	0.8	0.2	NA	NA	NA	NA	11	D	D	D
Weld	221	964	72.2	27.9	208	10 773	4 338.5	345.4	271	4 047	106.8	29.4
Yuma	15	46	3.1	1.0	NA	NA	NA	NA	24	211	4.6	1.3
CONNECTICUT	9 393	71 058	9 115.8	3 700.1	5 844	252 330	46 938.2	10 452.1	6 903	96 556	3 746.6	1 062.8
Fairfield	3 834	31 051	4 658.6	1 932.2	1 316	57 560	12 115.5	2 495.9	1 772	24 643	1 113.3	311.3
Hartford	2 188	20 638	2 471.2	978.9	1 592	71 982	11 319.8	3 113.1	1 778	28 579	995.4	289.1
Litchfield	381	1 150	133.8	42.5	448	17 288	3 246.8	589.8	369	3 709	150.6	43.2
Middlesex	332	1 747	211.6	76.0	309	13 132	2 999.3	513.5	355	4 231	172.0	49.3
New Haven	1 885	11 285	1 191.0	466.6	1 592	59 380	12 073.9	2 285.0	1 644	21 581	804.7	221.4
New London	463	3 944	338.9	162.2	237	19 888	2 962.8	1 035.1	590	8 652	333.0	95.7
Tolland	200	883	78.1	31.5	152	4 487	739.2	145.8	208	3 148	101.4	32.6
Windham	110	360	32.6	10.2	198	8 613	1 480.9	273.8	187	2 013	76.2	20.2

1. Firms subject to federal tax.

Table B. States and Counties — Health Care and Social Assistance, Other Services, and Federal Funds

STATE County	Health care and social assistance,[1] 1997				Other services,[1] 1997				Federal funds and grants, 2002–2003 Expenditures (mil dol)			
										Direct payments for individuals[2]		
	Number of establishments	Number of employees	Receipts (mil dol)	Annual payroll (mil dol)	Number of establishments	Number of employees	Receipts (mil dol)	Annual payroll (mil dol)	Total	Social Security and government retirement	Medicare	Food stamps and Supplemental Security Income
	159	160	161	162	163	164	165	166	167	168	169	170
COLORADO—Cont'd												
Cheyenne	1	D	D	D	3	13	0.8	0.2	68.9	4.7	3.8	0.1
Clear Creek	7	24	1.5	0.6	9	25	1.8	0.5	28.5	12.8	3.9	0.5
Conejos	4	27	0.9	0.4	5	26	1.0	0.4	57.5	16.6	7.0	2.9
Costilla	NA	NA	NA	NA	1	D	D	D	33.3	11.4	3.6	1.6
Crowley	2	D	D	D	4	7	0.2	0.0	25.3	9.9	3.7	0.8
Custer	2	D	D	D	3	10	0.5	0.1	21.8	13.3	1.9	0.3
Delta	50	551	19.0	8.8	28	91	6.2	1.5	169.7	91.3	31.0	2.9
Denver	1 478	15 938	1 197.2	562.3	1 101	8 212	604.5	172.8	5 590.7	1 148.0	600.3	120.9
Dolores	1	D	D	D	NA	NA	NA	NA	14.1	5.2	1.4	0.2
Douglas	168	1 175	75.0	38.1	169	854	56.7	17.3	237.8	152.8	18.7	0.9
Eagle	79	471	41.5	18.8	78	431	25.0	8.6	72.3	26.6	5.3	0.4
Elbert	11	65	2.9	1.1	20	44	3.5	0.9	47.6	30.0	6.4	0.5
El Paso	1 134	10 522	710.1	311.1	754	4 558	264.9	89.7	5 221.7	1 377.3	278.9	55.4
Fremont	71	771	29.7	13.5	39	158	8.3	2.4	269.3	117.9	36.6	6.6
Garfield	83	686	49.7	21.2	84	479	26.8	8.6	128.7	66.2	21.5	2.7
Gilpin	2	D	D	D	5	D	D	D	10.8	4.7	1.0	0.1
Grand	11	54	3.5	1.2	15	46	3.7	1.4	47.0	19.2	6.7	0.2
Gunnison	29	102	7.0	2.4	25	94	6.3	1.7	101.5	16.0	4.0	0.5
Hinsdale	2	D	D	D	1	D	D	D	2.9	1.8	0.4	0.0
Huerfano	13	117	4.3	1.7	9	18	0.9	0.3	55.7	22.5	13.1	2.2
Jackson	1	D	D	D	2	D	D	D	7.4	3.4	0.9	0.1
Jefferson	1 065	10 148	623.1	271.6	876	4 665	284.7	88.1	3 024.2	801.2	286.0	25.6
Kiowa	1	D	D	D	2	D	D	D	36.5	4.3	2.6	0.1
Kit Carson	11	97	4.5	1.5	15	32	2.5	0.5	91.2	16.9	8.2	0.3
Lake	5	34	2.0	0.6	6	21	1.0	0.2	29.3	9.4	4.2	0.4
La Plata	109	604	46.5	19.9	74	324	19.9	5.1	177.2	74.5	26.7	3.2
Larimer	530	4 957	296.2	133.5	384	2 151	127.6	39.0	1 088.2	417.0	141.8	15.8
Las Animas	25	137	6.7	2.4	27	80	5.2	1.2	122.2	48.3	17.4	3.7
Lincoln	8	112	4.3	1.7	5	19	1.4	0.5	44.0	12.0	6.6	0.4
Logan	40	416	20.5	9.2	47	200	15.9	3.8	109.5	42.9	19.6	2.5
Mesa	264	2 504	150.7	69.9	188	1 018	73.9	19.1	641.2	309.6	97.3	17.3
Mineral	NA	NA	NA	NA	1	D	D	D	12.0	2.0	0.3	0.1
Moffat	23	263	10.9	4.1	26	67	5.5	1.1	58.8	22.1	9.3	1.1
Montezuma	44	373	19.1	7.6	43	196	12.2	2.7	156.9	55.5	18.5	3.7
Montrose	79	517	30.4	11.3	45	141	10.1	2.6	183.8	87.3	28.4	3.5
Morgan	41	728	44.0	16.0	40	120	7.6	1.8	121.0	47.5	23.6	3.0
Otero	45	239	11.8	5.2	31	126	7.2	1.7	157.6	57.4	25.6	6.2
Ouray	4	3	0.4	0.1	2	D	D	D	13.0	7.4	1.9	0.1
Park	6	16	1.0	0.7	15	31	3.2	0.6	40.5	25.8	3.3	0.5
Phillips	7	79	2.2	1.0	9	19	1.5	0.3	40.3	11.9	7.2	0.4
Pitkin	48	235	20.4	8.1	43	116	9.6	2.6	34.3	14.7	3.5	0.2
Prowers	22	198	9.3	3.7	30	75	6.9	1.5	91.5	25.6	12.1	2.8
Pueblo	299	3 459	203.9	98.4	194	912	47.5	13.9	930.9	400.6	149.8	41.0
Rio Blanco	4	12	1.0	0.2	13	34	2.4	0.6	26.3	11.8	5.2	0.3
Rio Grande	19	198	6.8	2.7	20	62	3.3	0.6	70.1	26.5	8.4	3.6
Routt	44	199	15.2	6.9	43	125	9.0	2.6	55.8	21.6	6.5	0.6
Saguache	NA	NA	NA	NA	2	D	D	D	43.0	10.6	3.6	1.8
San Juan	NA	NA	NA	NA	NA	NA	NA	NA	3.1	1.0	0.2	0.0
San Miguel	11	39	2.3	0.6	8	57	1.9	0.7	22.2	5.2	1.1	0.2
Sedgwick	4	22	0.5	0.2	7	14	1.1	0.2	24.6	8.9	5.1	0.2
Summit	36	168	9.9	4.1	49	200	12.8	3.5	56.0	23.0	2.4	0.2
Teller	26	125	5.8	2.2	28	70	5.5	1.1	72.6	48.9	6.3	1.2
Washington	3	13	0.5	0.2	3	9	0.5	0.1	51.5	12.4	5.5	0.3
Weld	209	2 279	138.2	56.5	215	1 130	67.8	17.9	651.9	262.5	105.0	18.6
Yuma	16	220	8.7	3.4	25	66	4.5	1.0	64.0	21.4	9.2	0.8
CONNECTICUT	7 515	100 363	6 849.7	3 199.3	6 121	34 089	2 370.2	727.8	28 595.2	7 287.6	3 946.2	426.6
Fairfield	2 124	25 229	1 915.4	900.3	1 497	8 289	596.6	192.2	5 777.6	1 708.5	990.7	85.7
Hartford	1 970	28 270	1 925.8	936.4	1 656	10 183	698.7	220.5	9 192.4	1 955.0	1 050.5	145.5
Litchfield	388	4 258	226.1	97.0	319	1 347	97.5	26.1	814.4	406.2	204.4	8.7
Middlesex	332	4 839	298.1	139.8	297	1 339	111.8	30.9	1 062.8	334.7	145.1	9.9
New Haven	1 855	26 597	1 750.3	800.2	1 634	9 237	633.4	191.6	5 199.6	1 786.8	1 076.5	131.0
New London	490	7 493	521.3	227.8	391	2 113	137.6	37.8	3 993.7	637.7	263.7	25.1
Tolland	188	1 657	100.0	41.5	183	1 030	61.4	18.4	495.8	233.0	97.8	4.5
Windham	168	2 020	112.6	56.3	144	551	33.3	10.4	536.3	225.2	117.4	16.2

1. Firms subject to federal tax. 2. State totals may include programs not allocated by county.

Table B. States and Counties — Federal Funds and Local Government Finances

	Federal funds and grants, 2002–2003 (cont'd)							Local government finances, 2002				
	Expenditures (mil dol) (cont'd)							General revenue				
	Procurement contract awards			Grants[1]						Taxes		
STATE County	Salaries and wages	Defense	Other	Medicaid and other health-related	Nutrition and family welfare	Education	Other	Total (mil dol)	Intergovern-mental (mil dol)	Total (mil dol)	Per capita[2] (dollars) Total	Property
	171	172	173	174	175	176	177	178	179	180	181	182
COLORADO—Cont'd												
Cheyenne	24.4	1.4	0.6	1.4	0.3	0.1	9.3	17.7	4.9	6.0	2 790	2 600
Clear Creek	2.1	0.0	0.6	1.2	0.4	0.6	6.4	33.3	7.5	19.0	2 008	1 624
Conejos	2.2	0.0	0.5	20.1	2.3	0.8	4.0	28.2	21.5	4.3	516	446
Costilla	0.9	0.0	0.2	12.1	1.3	0.4	0.9	9.0	4.9	3.3	926	853
Crowley	0.8	0.0	0.5	4.0	1.0	0.2	2.7	8.5	5.3	2.4	444	329
Custer	0.9	0.2	1.0	1.4	0.3	0.2	2.3	9.6	2.3	4.9	1 346	1 050
Delta	11.6	0.9	1.8	18.4	4.0	1.9	3.7	90.0	32.5	21.8	754	499
Denver	1 006.8	120.1	489.5	823.6	298.9	192.3	652.6	3 479.5	666.3	1 327.9	2 370	877
Dolores	0.8	0.0	0.5	1.4	0.3	0.2	2.5	7.5	4.1	2.7	1 431	1 328
Douglas	15.6	10.5	6.9	2.9	1.2	2.5	24.4	674.2	144.9	343.0	1 625	1 204
Eagle	8.7	0.4	2.5	2.0	1.3	0.9	23.9	224.3	14.1	142.2	3 154	2 056
Elbert	2.4	0.2	0.5	2.0	0.5	0.7	1.1	48.4	22.4	20.6	936	832
El Paso	1 419.6	1 517.5	213.0	128.7	49.9	44.2	98.9	1 648.8	525.2	547.9	1 007	603
Fremont	64.7	0.5	3.9	24.7	6.6	2.1	4.9	83.0	41.8	29.7	626	355
Garfield	16.5	0.2	3.5	7.0	2.2	2.0	4.5	157.3	45.0	77.7	1 645	1 087
Gilpin	0.3	0.0	3.4	0.3	0.2	0.2	0.6	48.4	13.7	26.4	5 398	1 373
Grand	5.6	0.1	1.3	0.9	0.5	0.7	11.7	77.0	10.9	38.5	2 967	2 032
Gunnison	7.5	0.2	51.5	1.7	0.6	0.7	16.6	58.6	10.8	27.5	1 941	1 231
Hinsdale	0.2	0.0	0.1	0.3	0.0	0.1	0.0	3.1	0.8	1.9	2 492	1 726
Huerfano	1.1	0.0	0.3	12.5	1.9	0.6	1.1	24.0	10.3	8.9	1 142	942
Jackson	1.5	0.0	0.5	0.3	0.1	0.2	0.2	6.9	3.4	2.2	1 426	1 118
Jefferson	600.2	19.4	1 079.2	71.1	24.1	20.7	86.9	1 392.7	416.9	683.1	1 285	952
Kiowa	0.9	0.0	0.5	0.9	0.2	0.2	1.8	14.6	5.9	4.6	3 083	2 849
Kit Carson	2.2	0.0	0.5	4.2	0.9	0.6	10.1	34.7	12.7	10.1	1 270	1 141
Lake	2.9	2.1	4.4	1.4	1.6	0.7	2.2	84.5	23.3	35.6	4 572	4 217
La Plata	22.8	0.1	8.2	16.1	5.7	5.7	8.6	130.8	35.7	71.8	1 572	1 011
Larimer	141.5	27.6	91.6	103.7	18.1	12.2	99.5	838.3	220.7	397.0	1 500	953
Las Animas	4.1	0.3	1.1	26.8	4.5	3.0	7.0	46.0	23.5	15.7	1 017	639
Lincoln	1.7	0.2	0.4	3.5	1.2	0.6	3.9	26.0	11.2	6.9	1 162	793
Logan	4.8	0.0	1.1	10.5	2.8	1.5	7.8	72.9	32.7	20.9	989	650
Mesa	66.9	17.1	21.3	54.0	11.7	6.8	29.4	324.0	129.3	132.4	1 091	610
Mineral	0.3	0.0	0.0	0.0	0.1	0.1	9.1	4.5	2.0	1.8	2 076	1 502
Moffat	8.1	0.0	4.7	2.9	1.4	0.8	6.2	84.4	15.1	28.6	2 138	1 751
Montezuma	17.0	0.0	6.9	13.6	4.1	3.9	14.2	70.9	34.3	24.2	1 003	686
Montrose	17.2	0.5	6.8	15.9	3.4	2.6	16.1	137.5	43.8	35.9	1 016	593
Morgan	7.3	0.0	2.0	13.5	4.4	1.9	4.5	81.9	32.0	33.9	1 225	1 019
Otero	7.3	0.0	1.8	29.2	12.3	2.9	8.8	64.9	39.8	15.4	777	430
Ouray	0.5	0.0	0.2	0.3	0.2	0.1	2.3	13.1	4.2	6.7	1 705	1 265
Park	2.8	0.0	1.5	0.6	0.6	0.8	4.6	40.6	15.3	18.7	1 167	1 057
Phillips	1.4	0.0	1.5	2.6	0.5	0.3	3.7	23.3	6.0	6.2	1 366	1 155
Pitkin	5.7	0.0	1.3	0.6	0.1	0.2	8.0	183.0	8.9	78.2	5 217	2 786
Prowers	2.4	0.0	0.9	12.1	3.2	1.5	14.0	63.0	23.0	14.1	991	585
Pueblo	60.8	15.4	10.3	141.0	41.8	15.0	33.6	379.0	170.7	150.6	1 026	624
Rio Blanco	3.5	0.0	0.8	1.5	0.5	0.6	0.9	48.4	18.9	12.4	2 053	1 835
Rio Grande	6.2	0.0	1.1	12.9	3.7	1.2	3.8	39.3	19.7	11.6	949	700
Routt	6.4	0.1	9.1	2.3	0.6	0.9	6.7	90.2	15.8	57.1	2 799	1 590
Saguache	2.3	0.0	0.6	6.6	2.5	1.2	11.6	18.5	10.6	6.4	1 000	932
San Juan	0.1	0.0	0.2	0.0	0.1	0.1	1.3	3.7	0.9	2.3	4 199	2 178
San Miguel	2.2	0.0	0.8	1.2	0.3	0.3	10.7	54.0	9.3	31.7	4 421	2 793
Sedgwick	0.9	0.0	0.4	2.5	0.4	0.2	0.4	14.7	4.3	3.8	1 421	1 193
Summit	3.2	0.5	1.3	1.0	0.6	0.5	23.1	139.8	7.4	90.8	3 651	2 476
Teller	2.6	0.3	4.6	1.2	1.3	0.7	5.0	71.0	24.2	31.5	1 458	848
Washington	2.6	0.5	0.7	2.8	1.0	0.4	4.4	18.8	9.5	6.7	1 367	1 288
Weld	42.1	3.9	15.1	82.0	23.2	15.0	41.0	551.1	195.4	226.8	1 106	840
Yuma	2.7	0.0	0.7	4.5	1.6	0.8	2.6	51.0	15.2	14.2	1 456	1 271
CONNECTICUT	1 516.3	7 894.8	589.5	2 623.0	695.9	388.7	1 668.5	X	X	X	X	X
Fairfield	253.1	1 574.4	172.9	486.4	110.5	52.4	292.1	3 022.0	713.7	1 983.6	2 213	2 174
Hartford	403.6	3 444.9	189.1	805.1	280.8	186.0	666.1	2 529.7	810.3	1 486.7	1 714	1 692
Litchfield	31.1	36.1	14.2	63.3	10.9	7.9	27.4	515.3	143.3	323.3	1 733	1 712
Middlesex	26.0	354.9	7.1	80.7	10.3	7.8	77.2	429.3	115.3	279.8	1 752	1 724
New Haven	351.7	113.4	148.5	924.8	135.0	71.3	388.7	2 724.1	1 145.3	1 326.0	1 587	1 559
New London	411.3	2 349.7	43.9	129.5	27.0	24.5	67.1	796.9	295.1	396.9	1 511	1 488
Tolland	21.7	6.7	5.3	39.3	6.7	12.6	55.2	364.4	145.0	182.6	1 294	1 270
Windham	17.8	14.5	8.5	76.6	18.8	8.3	22.5	297.4	157.9	113.4	1 019	1 004

1. State totals may include programs not allocated by county.   2. Based on the resident population estimated as of July 1 of the year shown.

Table B. States and Counties — Local Government Finances, Government Employment, and Elections

STATE County	Local government finances, 2002 (cont'd) Direct general expenditure — Total (mil dol)	Per capita[1] (dollars)	Percent of total for — Education	Health and hospitals	Police protection	Public welfare	High-ways	Debt outstanding — Total (mil dol)	Per capita[1] (dollars)	Government employment, 2002 — Federal civilian	Federal military	State and local	Presidential election, 2004 Percent of vote cast — Democratic	Republican	All other
	183	184	185	186	187	188	189	190	191	192	193	194	195	196	197
COLORADO—Cont'd															
Cheyenne	18.5	8 556	41.2	17.9	2.3	8.8	13.0	16.2	7 481	19	0	300	17.4	81.4	1.2
Clear Creek	44.4	4 698	51.4	2.7	6.3	5.3	9.2	46.8	4 956	47	14	625	53.0	45.1	1.9
Conejos	25.9	3 075	52.9	6.1	2.6	17.8	6.3	8.8	1 047	51	13	557	49.9	49.0	1.1
Costilla	9.4	2 605	60.4	0.3	3.2	5.1	2.8	6.6	1 839	18	0	350	66.8	31.8	1.3
Crowley	8.2	1 496	52.4	0.2	2.5	12.8	13.0	2.8	509	15	0	523	32.2	67.1	0.6
Custer	12.4	3 390	53.1	8.5	6.0	2.3	10.4	5.2	1 433	15	0	221	30.4	68.2	1.3
Delta	92.5	3 200	38.0	24.4	3.3	3.3	4.8	24.1	833	212	43	1 923	29.9	68.6	1.5
Denver	3 185.7	5 685	20.6	14.5	4.7	3.9	2.6	6 570.3	11 724	14 843	2 132	57 663	69.5	29.4	1.1
Dolores	9.8	5 244	71.3	0.6	2.6	2.9	10.4	4.9	2 613	18	0	178	29.0	68.4	2.5
Douglas	691.5	3 276	45.2	0.2	4.7	0.6	8.9	1 096.1	5 193	193	316	7 976	32.8	66.5	0.7
Eagle	215.6	4 782	22.3	1.7	5.9	1.2	6.4	289.6	6 422	151	68	2 454	52.5	46.2	1.3
Elbert	43.8	1 993	67.8	0.4	2.7	1.1	5.5	27.0	1 229	38	33	973	26.9	71.9	1.2
El Paso	1 713.9	3 152	40.4	18.1	5.9	2.0	6.5	1 981.6	3 644	9 977	29 281	30 210	32.0	66.8	1.1
Fremont	86.0	1 813	48.9	1.0	8.6	6.7	9.9	29.1	613	1 095	71	4 031	32.0	66.5	1.5
Garfield	185.3	3 922	40.5	3.1	7.7	4.4	6.0	170.3	3 604	316	71	3 575	44.7	53.9	1.4
Gilpin	30.6	6 259	13.2	1.2	12.1	3.5	15.8	65.1	13 314	0	0	362	56.5	41.6	1.9
Grand	70.9	5 462	22.6	10.1	5.3	1.2	11.4	70.5	5 433	137	19	1 034	42.5	56.1	1.4
Gunnison	58.5	4 138	18.8	16.1	5.1	3.0	14.5	38.9	2 752	160	21	1 416	56.7	41.4	1.9
Hinsdale	2.9	3 763	46.0	7.7	9.4	0.0	5.2	1.5	1 896	0	0	84	39.1	59.3	1.7
Huerfano	24.3	3 104	33.8	13.2	5.2	6.8	10.3	6.7	860	19	12	474	48.9	49.9	1.1
Jackson	6.9	4 529	43.3	5.4	3.4	1.9	17.7	4.3	2 840	36	0	162	22.4	76.1	1.5
Jefferson	1 508.8	2 838	50.9	0.8	6.8	2.4	5.6	1 279.3	2 406	8 353	803	25 976	46.6	51.9	1.5
Kiowa	13.2	8 828	23.5	2.8	1.6	28.2	10.4	3.1	2 071	20	0	242	19.4	79.7	0.9
Kit Carson	33.2	4 174	41.2	22.6	3.3	2.1	9.5	11.4	1 439	50	12	786	21.0	77.5	1.5
Lake	75.8	9 719	71.5	13.7	1.3	1.3	2.4	8.0	1 027	63	12	716	54.9	43.0	2.1
La Plata	129.2	2 830	38.3	0.0	5.8	3.4	8.5	74.3	1 628	409	68	4 559	52.6	46.0	1.5
Larimer	757.5	2 863	41.7	1.4	5.8	4.4	5.6	1 077.2	4 071	2 365	425	23 082	46.6	51.9	1.6
Las Animas	54.3	3 514	46.6	1.6	4.2	4.3	7.5	27.3	1 765	74	23	1 923	50.0	48.6	1.4
Lincoln	24.2	4 099	37.7	22.3	2.3	7.3	11.4	8.8	1 485	32	0	912	21.4	77.9	0.7
Logan	66.7	3 161	60.0	0.2	4.0	4.0	8.5	37.7	1 788	78	32	2 716	28.3	70.5	1.2
Mesa	326.3	2 688	40.5	1.7	7.5	6.2	10.2	240.1	1 977	1 149	183	7 115	31.6	67.1	1.3
Mineral	4.0	4 601	39.4	2.3	4.8	0.0	29.2	0.1	126	0	0	85	36.8	61.8	1.5
Moffat	76.8	5 744	23.0	18.5	4.1	1.6	9.6	243.4	18 204	171	21	1 085	23.7	74.2	2.1
Montezuma	66.8	2 766	44.6	3.0	7.2	4.7	6.5	35.7	1 480	383	36	2 418	35.1	63.5	1.5
Montrose	133.7	3 787	30.1	31.2	3.1	2.6	5.7	56.3	1 595	305	53	2 444	29.5	69.1	1.4
Morgan	76.1	2 745	51.9	0.8	5.9	5.4	8.6	85.8	3 095	137	42	2 169	30.6	68.3	1.1
Otero	63.6	3 213	47.9	2.1	3.9	15.1	6.7	18.5	934	123	30	1 922	38.7	60.5	0.8
Ouray	12.7	3 248	40.4	1.6	6.9	3.8	12.2	13.4	3 423	0	0	273	46.8	51.8	1.4
Park	38.4	2 402	43.0	0.8	7.7	2.4	15.1	27.4	1 710	63	24	742	41.2	57.3	1.5
Phillips	21.7	4 790	31.7	41.8	2.3	2.3	6.4	7.1	1 565	31	0	573	25.1	73.8	1.1
Pitkin	173.2	11 554	22.8	24.4	4.2	1.9	9.6	195.7	13 051	84	22	1 663	68.5	30.0	1.5
Prowers	57.3	4 035	33.9	30.9	3.5	5.3	4.4	14.3	1 003	50	21	1 562	27.6	71.5	1.0
Pueblo	360.7	2 456	44.9	1.7	5.5	6.3	5.6	425.3	2 896	676	223	10 946	52.5	46.5	1.0
Rio Blanco	47.2	7 805	46.2	20.8	4.3	3.5	8.2	10.2	1 693	83	0	1 117	18.9	80.0	1.1
Rio Grande	39.0	3 175	45.3	2.2	5.2	6.7	10.3	13.2	1 079	123	18	872	36.1	62.6	1.2
Routt	95.5	4 680	34.8	0.5	5.1	2.7	9.0	67.3	3 300	131	31	1 583	54.3	44.3	1.4
Saguache	17.2	2 667	58.0	2.2	4.6	0.0	17.4	5.7	887	80	10	533	56.9	41.4	1.6
San Juan	3.7	6 652	31.2	1.2	12.4	2.3	9.5	0.0	0	0	0	63	52.0	44.4	3.7
San Miguel	54.9	7 658	15.3	2.0	6.6	1.0	18.6	87.9	12 265	40	11	691	71.6	26.8	1.6
Sedgwick	15.4	5 757	31.6	32.5	1.9	3.5	9.8	1.7	642	23	0	317	27.7	71.3	1.0
Summit	127.2	5 113	20.1	2.9	6.0	3.3	10.7	154.3	6 206	63	37	2 002	59.2	39.2	1.6
Teller	65.0	3 013	35.9	2.5	8.9	3.2	11.6	42.9	1 990	61	32	1 092	30.0	68.4	1.6
Washington	19.0	3 884	50.3	1.4	3.3	4.0	17.8	1.7	349	56	0	456	18.0	80.9	1.0
Weld	563.2	2 747	49.2	2.2	5.1	1.3	7.8	612.1	2 986	578	312	12 235	35.9	62.7	1.3
Yuma	45.2	4 632	32.2	29.5	3.1	2.8	8.8	9.2	943	53	15	849	23.2	76.0	0.8
CONNECTICUT	X	X	X	X	X	X	X	X	X	20 649	15 474	227 547	54.3	44.0	1.7
Fairfield	3 018.2	3 368	53.0	2.4	6.2	0.5	3.6	2 549.4	2 845	3 944	1 687	42 825	51.3	47.3	1.4
Hartford	2 440.2	2 813	51.2	0.9	7.1	1.6	4.2	1 046.3	1 206	6 476	1 663	65 031	58.8	39.4	1.8
Litchfield	488.5	2 619	62.0	0.8	3.9	0.4	6.2	249.2	1 336	356	348	8 208	47.4	50.8	1.9
Middlesex	416.2	2 606	59.0	1.0	6.0	0.5	4.7	210.2	1 316	295	297	9 649	56.3	42.4	1.3
New Haven	2 648.9	3 170	52.5	1.6	5.7	1.7	3.2	2 085.5	2 496	6 464	1 729	43 378	54.2	43.9	1.9
New London	765.8	2 915	58.0	0.8	6.1	0.8	4.2	573.3	2 183	2 694	9 268	37 176	55.8	42.2	2.0
Tolland	347.6	2 463	65.8	0.5	2.6	0.5	4.9	168.5	1 194	208	275	14 422	54.7	43.3	2.0
Windham	273.1	2 453	63.7	1.0	2.0	0.4	5.3	101.1	908	212	207	6 858	52.1	45.7	2.2

1. Based on the resident population estimated as of July 1 of the year shown.

Table B. States and Counties — Land Area and Population

STATE/ County code	CBSA code[1]	County Type[2]	STATE County	Land area,[3] (sq km) 2000	Total persons	Rank	Per square kilometer	White	Black	Am. Indian, Alaska Native	Asian and Pacific Islander	Percent Hispanic or Latino[4]	Under 5 years	5 to 17 years	18 to 24 years	25 to 34 years	35 to 44 years	45 to 54 years
								Race alone or in combination, not Hispanic or Latino (percent)					Age (percent)					
				1	2	3	4	5	6	7	8	9	10	11	12	13	14	15
10 000	...	X	DELAWARE	5 060	817 491	X	161.6	72.8	19.7	0.6	2.9	5.3	6.6	17.7	10.0	13.1	15.5	13.9
10 001	20100	3	Kent	1 527	134 390	419	88.0	73.6	21.2	1.2	2.4	3.5	7.2	19.4	10.7	12.7	15.4	12.7
10 003	37980	1	New Castle	1 104	515 074	112	466.6	70.2	21.0	0.5	3.6	5.9	6.6	17.9	10.4	13.9	16.3	13.9
10 005	42580	4	Sussex	2 428	168 027	337	69.2	79.8	14.3	0.7	1.0	5.0	6.0	15.9	8.2	10.9	14.0	13.5
11 000	...	X	DISTRICT OF COLUMBIA.	159	563 384	X	3 543.3	29.2	58.6	0.7	3.6	9.4	6.0	13.3	11.4	19.4	15.0	13.2
11 001	47900	1	District of Columbia	159	563 384	101	3 543.3	29.2	58.6	0.7	3.6	9.4	6.0	13.3	11.4	19.4	15.0	13.2
12 000	...	X	FLORIDA	139 670	17 019 068	X	121.9	63.9	15.6	0.6	2.4	18.6	6.2	16.9	8.8	12.4	14.8	13.5
12 001	23540	3	Alachua	2 264	223 578	259	98.8	69.4	21.1	0.7	4.4	5.9	5.5	14.3	19.4	16.3	12.3	12.4
12 003	27260	1	Baker	1 516	23 424	1 644	15.5	83.4	14.0	0.8	0.5	1.9	7.4	19.1	11.0	13.5	15.6	13.8
12 005	37460	3	Bay	1 978	155 193	356	78.5	84.2	11.4	1.4	2.5	2.1	6.4	17.6	9.0	12.3	15.7	14.0
12 007	...	6	Bradford	759	26 928	1 506	35.5	75.0	21.6	0.8	0.7	2.5	5.5	15.7	10.6	14.2	15.3	13.6
12 009	37340	2	Brevard	2 637	505 711	118	191.8	83.9	9.1	0.8	2.3	5.2	5.1	16.5	8.2	9.7	15.2	13.6
12 011	33100	1	Broward	3 122	1 731 347	15	554.6	53.1	24.1	0.4	3.4	20.2	6.6	17.7	7.8	13.1	16.6	13.6
12 013	...	6	Calhoun	1 469	12 921	2 246	8.8	74.8	15.7	1.8	0.7	4.1	5.7	16.6	10.1	14.9	14.7	12.7
12 015	39460	3	Charlotte	1 796	153 392	366	85.4	90.3	4.8	0.4	1.2	3.8	3.8	12.2	6.0	7.4	10.6	11.5
12 017	26140	4	Citrus	1 512	126 458	449	83.6	93.2	2.6	0.9	1.1	3.0	3.7	13.5	6.5	7.6	10.8	11.8
12 019	27260	1	Clay	1 557	157 502	351	101.2	85.1	7.6	1.0	3.1	4.8	6.4	20.3	9.7	11.6	16.1	14.4
12 021	34940	2	Collier	5 246	286 634	205	54.6	70.2	5.8	0.3	0.9	23.3	6.1	14.7	7.7	10.7	12.6	11.2
12 023	29380	6	Columbia	2 064	60 244	818	29.2	78.4	17.8	1.0	0.8	2.8	6.5	18.1	10.4	11.5	13.8	13.4
12 027	11580	6	De Soto	1 651	33 879	1 308	20.5	57.5	12.3	0.4	0.5	29.4	6.7	16.1	12.9	14.1	11.7	10.2
12 029	...	6	Dixie	1 823	13 982	2 169	7.7	89.0	8.5	0.8	0.3	1.9	6.0	15.6	9.4	11.1	13.9	13.3
12 031	27260	1	Duval	2 004	817 480	59	407.9	62.4	30.0	0.7	3.9	4.5	7.7	19.1	9.6	14.5	16.0	13.6
12 033	37860	2	Escambia	1 715	295 886	197	172.5	70.9	24.0	1.8	3.5	2.0	6.7	17.3	12.4	12.9	14.4	13.3
12 035	37380	4	Flagler	1 256	62 206	797	49.5	84.1	9.1	0.6	1.5	5.5	4.0	13.8	7.5	8.5	11.1	11.7
12 037	...	6	Franklin	1 410	10 003	2 441	7.1	87.1	10.9	1.0	0.3	1.4	5.3	14.7	7.8	10.9	14.3	14.4
12 039	45220	2	Gadsden	1 337	45 134	1 021	33.8	34.8	58.0	0.4	0.3	6.7	7.4	18.6	10.1	13.2	14.9	14.5
12 041	23540	3	Gilchrist	904	15 633	2 056	17.3	89.8	6.7	1.0	0.2	3.1	5.5	17.7	15.0	10.1	13.0	12.1
12 043	...	6	Glades	2 004	11 165	2 358	5.6	68.1	10.1	5.0	0.4	16.8	5.0	15.6	9.0	12.5	13.4	11.3
12 045	...	6	Gulf	1 436	15 247	2 083	10.6	74.7	21.0	1.2	0.5	3.3	4.1	14.0	8.7	14.2	17.4	14.1
12 047	...	6	Hamilton	1 333	13 917	2 170	10.4	54.6	37.8	0.5	0.3	7.1	6.2	16.2	11.8	15.1	15.6	13.9
12 049	48100	6	Hardee	1 651	27 659	1 476	16.8	52.7	8.6	0.5	0.4	37.9	8.2	19.5	11.6	14.5	13.4	10.8
12 051	17500	4	Hendry	2 985	37 064	1 208	12.4	42.3	13.7	0.5	0.4	43.4	8.7	22.0	12.8	14.1	13.0	10.4
12 053	45300	1	Hernando	1 239	143 449	397	115.8	88.5	4.4	0.6	0.9	6.3	4.7	14.6	7.4	8.3	11.2	11.5
12 055	42700	4	Highlands	2 663	91 051	593	34.2	75.0	9.6	0.6	1.1	14.1	5.0	14.3	7.8	8.6	10.3	10.3
12 057	45300	1	Hillsborough	2 722	1 073 407	34	394.3	61.3	16.0	0.7	3.1	20.2	7.1	18.6	9.4	14.2	15.7	13.4
12 059	...	6	Holmes	1 250	18 986	1 862	15.2	89.7	6.5	2.0	0.5	2.5	5.7	16.9	10.0	13.5	14.4	12.6
12 061	46940	3	Indian River	1 303	120 463	468	92.5	82.9	8.6	0.4	1.0	7.6	4.9	14.4	7.5	9.0	12.1	12.2
12 063	...	6	Jackson	2 372	46 508	987	19.6	68.5	27.4	1.4	0.5	3.3	5.9	16.0	10.5	13.2	14.7	13.8
12 065	45220	2	Jefferson	1 548	14 037	2 165	9.1	58.3	37.8	0.6	0.3	3.4	5.4	15.3	9.2	12.8	15.8	15.4
12 067	...	8	Lafayette	1 406	7 333	2 654	5.2	73.5	14.3	0.6	0.2	11.5	6.1	15.3	11.7	17.5	15.6	11.4
12 069	36740	1	Lake	2 469	245 877	243	99.6	82.5	8.7	0.7	1.3	7.6	5.4	15.2	7.3	10.1	12.4	11.1
12 071	15980	2	Lee	2 081	492 210	121	236.5	82.3	7.5	0.5	1.2	12.2	5.7	14.9	7.3	10.3	12.6	12.0
12 073	45220	2	Leon	1 727	242 577	245	140.5	64.1	30.4	0.6	2.5	3.6	6.1	15.1	17.4	16.1	13.3	13.4
12 075	...	8	Levy	2 897	36 270	1 230	12.5	83.8	10.9	1.0	0.5	4.7	5.6	17.3	8.8	10.4	13.2	13.5
12 077	...	8	Liberty	2 165	7 315	2 656	3.4	74.4	18.1	1.7	0.2	5.7	5.8	15.5	10.3	18.3	17.8	12.4
12 079	...	6	Madison	1 792	18 766	1 872	10.5	55.4	40.4	0.7	0.4	3.6	6.1	18.3	10.4	13.3	13.5	13.4
12 081	42260	2	Manatee	1 919	286 804	204	149.5	79.1	9.0	0.5	1.4	10.8	6.0	15.6	7.5	10.6	12.9	12.3
12 083	36100	2	Marion	4 089	280 288	209	68.5	80.1	11.9	0.8	1.0	7.0	5.4	16.0	8.0	9.7	12.7	11.8
12 085	38940	2	Martin	1 439	135 122	418	93.9	85.2	5.4	0.6	0.9	8.5	4.6	14.3	6.9	8.3	12.9	12.9
12 086	33100	1	Miami-Dade	5 040	2 341 167	8	464.5	18.8	19.5	0.2	1.7	60.5	6.8	17.8	9.0	13.8	15.9	12.9
12 087	28580	4	Monroe	2 582	78 940	663	30.6	75.8	4.7	0.8	1.1	18.3	4.6	12.2	5.7	11.7	17.4	19.5
12 089	27260	1	Nassau	1 688	61 625	806	36.5	90.2	7.3	0.9	0.7	1.7	6.0	18.1	8.4	11.4	15.1	14.8
12 091	23020	3	Okaloosa	2 423	178 104	320	73.5	82.9	9.9	1.3	4.3	4.3	7.0	18.3	9.6	13.0	16.2	13.5
12 093	36380	4	Okeechobee	2 005	37 481	1 193	18.7	70.5	8.0	0.8	0.7	20.7	7.1	18.3	10.3	12.5	13.3	11.4
12 095	36740	1	Orange	2 350	964 865	38	410.6	54.6	20.3	0.6	4.7	21.2	7.5	18.5	10.1	15.9	16.3	12.8
12 097	36740	1	Osceola	3 424	205 870	284	60.1	55.4	8.0	0.6	2.9	34.3	7.0	19.6	10.0	13.6	14.9	12.2
12 099	33100	1	Palm Beach	5 113	1 216 282	30	237.9	67.6	15.7	0.4	2.3	14.9	5.8	15.9	7.5	10.9	14.4	12.6
12 101	45300	1	Pasco	1 929	388 906	158	201.6	88.8	2.8	0.8	1.5	7.0	5.4	15.6	7.5	10.0	13.1	11.7
12 103	45300	1	Pinellas	725	926 146	42	1 277.4	81.9	10.1	0.7	2.9	5.6	5.2	14.7	6.8	11.0	15.0	14.7
12 105	29460	2	Polk	4 855	510 458	115	105.1	72.9	14.6	0.7	1.4	11.4	6.8	18.0	9.1	11.6	13.3	12.2
12 107	37260	4	Putnam	1 870	71 841	707	38.4	75.1	17.4	0.8	0.5	6.8	6.4	18.2	9.0	9.9	12.7	13.4
12 109	27260	1	St. Johns	1 577	142 869	399	90.6	89.7	6.3	0.6	1.4	2.8	5.0	17.2	8.7	10.2	15.0	15.2
12 111	38940	2	St. Lucie	1 483	213 447	273	143.9	72.4	16.5	0.6	1.4	10.0	5.6	17.0	8.3	10.0	13.3	12.1
12 113	37860	2	Santa Rosa	2 634	133 092	427	50.5	91.0	4.4	1.6	2.2	2.5	6.3	19.2	9.1	11.7	16.4	14.0

1. CBSA = Core Based Statistical Area. See Appendix A for explanation. See Appendix B for list of metropolitan areas with component counties. 2. County type code from the Economic Research Service of USDA Rural-Urban Continuum Codes. See Appendix A for definition. 3. Dry land or land partially or temporarily covered by water. 4. Hispanic or Latino persons may be of any race.

STATE County	Population, 2003 (cont'd) Age (percent) (cont'd)				Population — change and components of change, 1990–2003							Households, 2000				
					Total persons		Percent change		Components of change, 2000–2003						Percent	
	55 to 64 years	65 to 74 years	75 years and over	Percent female	1990	2000	1990–2000	2000–2003	Births	Deaths	Net migration	Number	Percent change, 1990–2000	Persons per house-hold	Female family house-holder[1]	One person
	16	17	18	19	20	21	22	23	24	25	26	27	28	29	30	31
DELAWARE	10.1	7.0	6.1	51.3	666 168	783 600	17.6	4.3	35 263	23 141	22 308	298 736	20.7	2.54	13.1	25.0
Kent	9.0	6.6	5.1	51.7	110 993	126 697	14.1	6.1	6 196	3 576	5 134	47 224	19.1	2.61	13.8	23.0
New Castle	9.1	5.9	5.5	51.3	441 946	500 265	13.2	3.0	22 455	13 745	6 686	188 935	15.1	2.56	13.4	25.7
Sussex	11.8	10.4	7.9	51.1	113 229	156 638	38.3	7.3	6 612	5 820	10 488	62 577	43.3	2.45	11.3	24.3
DISTRICT OF COLUMBIA	9.8	6.1	6.0	52.8	606 900	572 059	-5.7	-1.5	25 698	19 520	-14 898	248 338	-0.5	2.16	18.9	43.8
District of Columbia	9.8	6.1	6.0	52.8	606 900	572 059	-5.7	-1.5	25 698	19 520	-14 898	248 338	-0.5	2.16	18.9	43.8
FLORIDA	10.5	8.6	8.5	51.0	12 938 071	15 982 378	23.5	6.5	675 642	543 406	889 862	6 337 929	23.4	2.46	12.0	26.6
Alachua	7.5	5.0	4.6	51.1	181 596	217 955	20.0	2.6	8 189	5 214	2 951	87 509	22.8	2.34	12.3	29.1
Baker	9.5	5.9	3.4	47.3	18 486	22 259	20.4	5.2	1 112	626	690	7 043	26.8	2.86	13.1	17.1
Bay	10.1	8.0	5.6	50.5	126 994	148 217	16.7	4.7	6 223	4 695	5 498	59 597	21.8	2.43	12.0	26.0
Bradford	10.1	7.0	5.7	43.6	22 515	26 088	15.9	3.2	970	856	717	8 497	18.1	2.58	13.3	26.0
Brevard	11.0	10.5	9.1	50.9	398 978	476 230	19.4	6.2	15 668	17 425	30 726	198 195	22.8	2.35	10.2	22.9
Broward	9.0	6.5	8.2	51.5	1 255 531	1 623 018	29.3	6.7	74 147	52 831	87 403	654 445	23.8	2.45	12.5	26.9
Calhoun	10.1	7.8	6.6	46.1	11 011	13 017	18.2	-0.7	478	461	-120	4 468	17.8	2.53	13.5	29.6
Charlotte	13.7	17.0	16.5	52.3	110 975	141 627	27.6	8.3	3 345	6 933	14 885	63 864	31.9	2.18	7.2	26.5
Citrus	14.0	16.0	14.9	52.0	93 513	118 085	26.3	7.1	2 776	6 596	11 786	52 634	29.7	2.20	7.6	26.1
Clay	9.7	5.7	3.9	50.7	105 986	140 814	32.9	11.9	6 237	3 858	14 051	50 243	37.0	2.77	10.7	16.9
Collier	11.8	12.6	10.5	49.5	152 099	251 377	65.3	14.0	11 086	7 839	31 384	102 973	66.9	2.39	7.2	24.5
Columbia	10.5	8.0	6.0	49.3	42 613	56 513	32.6	6.6	2 511	2 055	3 274	20 925	34.0	2.56	12.9	23.8
De Soto	9.6	9.5	8.0	42.2	23 865	32 209	35.0	5.2	1 447	936	1 234	10 746	30.7	2.70	10.3	21.0
Dixie	12.9	10.9	7.0	47.5	10 585	13 827	30.6	1.1	543	513	145	5 205	32.9	2.44	10.6	23.9
Duval	8.4	5.4	4.7	51.4	672 971	778 879	15.7	5.0	40 105	22 428	21 213	303 747	18.1	2.51	15.6	26.5
Escambia	9.4	7.5	6.2	50.4	262 445	294 410	12.2	0.5	12 775	9 359	-1 668	111 049	12.6	2.45	15.1	26.9
Flagler	12.9	14.3	11.2	51.8	28 701	49 832	73.6	24.8	1 370	2 142	12 800	21 294	79.2	2.32	8.1	21.6
Franklin	15.7	9.7	7.3	48.9	8 967	11 057	23.3	-9.5	305	441	316	4 096	12.9	2.28	9.8	28.7
Gadsden	9.8	6.8	5.3	52.3	41 116	45 087	9.7	0.1	2 377	1 481	-810	15 867	18.4	2.69	22.5	23.9
Gilchrist	10.3	8.2	5.7	47.4	9 667	14 437	49.3	8.3	551	493	1 139	5 021	52.9	2.61	11.2	21.1
Glades	12.1	12.0	7.4	44.7	7 591	10 576	39.3	5.6	296	315	604	3 852	33.5	2.51	8.6	22.7
Gulf	11.1	8.5	6.3	41.0	11 504	13 332	15.9	14.4	371	474	773	4 931	14.0	2.42	11.9	25.5
Hamilton	9.4	6.4	4.5	40.9	10 930	13 327	21.9	4.4	540	428	473	4 161	19.3	2.60	16.8	24.1
Hardee	8.6	7.0	6.3	44.4	19 499	26 938	38.2	2.7	1 495	705	-70	8 166	27.8	3.06	11.1	18.0
Hendry	8.1	6.0	4.2	44.2	25 773	36 210	40.5	2.4	2 169	905	-459	10 850	29.1	3.09	12.5	19.6
Hernando	11.9	14.1	14.1	52.4	101 115	130 802	29.4	9.7	3 990	6 994	15 133	55 425	31.0	2.32	8.7	23.3
Highlands	11.3	15.4	16.5	50.9	68 432	87 366	27.7	4.2	2 846	4 022	4 781	37 471	26.8	2.30	8.5	26.3
Hillsborough	8.8	6.1	5.4	50.9	834 054	998 948	19.8	7.5	48 357	28 683	54 343	391 357	20.5	2.51	13.2	26.9
Holmes	11.0	8.4	6.7	46.4	15 778	18 564	17.7	2.3	708	706	434	6 921	19.3	2.43	10.8	26.1
Indian River	11.1	13.0	14.7	51.4	90 208	112 947	25.2	6.7	3 692	5 216	8 821	49 137	29.1	2.25	8.9	28.2
Jackson	10.7	8.0	6.9	47.6	41 375	46 755	13.0	-0.5	1 782	1 746	-269	16 620	14.9	2.44	14.4	27.0
Jefferson	10.7	7.3	6.2	47.0	11 296	12 902	14.2	8.8	506	519	1 126	4 695	17.9	2.53	15.1	25.2
Lafayette	9.7	7.1	5.1	40.1	5 578	7 022	25.9	4.4	312	223	229	2 142	24.5	2.66	9.2	22.0
Lake	10.7	13.0	11.9	51.5	152 104	210 528	38.4	16.8	8 017	9 788	36 522	88 413	39.0	2.34	8.5	24.6
Lee	11.8	12.1	11.3	50.9	335 113	440 888	31.6	11.6	17 295	17 306	49 740	188 599	34.6	2.31	8.7	25.8
Leon	7.9	4.5	3.9	52.1	192 493	239 452	24.4	1.3	9 681	4 960	-1 449	96 521	29.0	2.34	13.0	29.7
Levy	12.9	9.9	7.6	51.5	25 912	34 450	32.9	5.3	1 265	1 528	2 036	13 867	37.6	2.44	11.8	24.9
Liberty	8.6	6.0	4.0	40.7	5 569	7 021	26.1	4.2	274	178	199	2 222	30.2	2.51	13.2	25.9
Madison	10.0	7.9	7.1	47.8	16 569	18 733	13.1	0.2	756	660	-41	6 629	20.0	2.57	17.5	25.4
Manatee	10.8	11.0	12.0	51.3	211 707	264 002	24.7	8.6	10 365	10 766	22 528	112 460	23.5	2.29	9.4	28.4
Marion	11.2	12.5	11.1	51.7	194 835	258 916	32.9	8.3	9 627	11 591	22 792	106 755	36.6	2.36	10.7	25.0
Martin	11.8	12.8	14.1	50.6	100 900	126 731	25.6	6.6	3 977	5 217	9 382	55 288	28.5	2.23	7.4	29.0
Miami-Dade	9.7	7.2	6.2	51.6	1 937 194	2 253 362	16.3	3.9	108 905	59 296	36 807	776 774	12.2	2.84	17.2	23.3
Monroe	14.2	8.5	6.1	46.3	78 024	79 589	2.0	-0.8	2 370	2 308	-527	35 086	4.5	2.23	7.3	28.8
Nassau	11.8	8.3	4.8	50.6	43 941	57 663	31.2	6.9	2 327	1 765	3 374	21 980	35.7	2.59	9.9	20.1
Okaloosa	9.1	7.8	4.6	49.5	143 777	170 498	18.6	4.5	7 754	4 518	4 432	66 269	24.3	2.49	10.2	23.5
Okeechobee	10.3	8.8	7.1	46.0	29 627	35 910	21.2	4.4	1 775	1 133	955	12 593	23.3	2.69	10.7	21.5
Orange	7.8	5.3	4.3	50.4	677 491	896 344	32.3	7.6	46 643	21 025	42 985	336 286	32.0	2.61	13.7	24.2
Osceola	8.4	6.0	4.6	50.4	107 728	172 493	60.1	19.3	8 743	4 403	25 734	60 977	55.8	2.79	12.8	19.1
Palm Beach	9.6	9.7	12.2	51.4	863 503	1 131 184	31.0	7.5	45 637	43 479	82 519	474 175	29.7	2.34	9.7	29.2
Pasco	10.6	11.0	12.8	51.8	281 131	344 765	22.6	12.8	12 464	17 450	47 593	147 566	21.3	2.30	8.9	27.3
Pinellas	11.3	9.8	11.7	52.2	851 659	921 482	8.2	0.5	30 583	42 180	17 212	414 968	9.0	2.17	10.5	34.1
Polk	10.2	9.3	8.4	50.8	405 382	483 924	19.4	5.5	22 432	17 252	21 204	187 233	20.0	2.52	12.0	24.1
Putnam	11.9	10.3	7.9	50.5	65 070	70 423	8.2	2.0	3 003	2 987	1 442	27 839	11.0	2.48	12.9	25.1
St. Johns	11.0	7.9	6.7	51.3	83 829	123 135	46.9	16.0	4 161	3 855	18 874	49 614	48.4	2.44	8.9	24.3
St. Lucie	10.2	11.0	10.3	51.0	150 171	192 695	28.3	10.8	7 352	7 714	20 644	76 933	32.2	2.47	11.1	23.5
Santa Rosa	9.7	6.9	4.1	49.9	81 961	117 743	43.7	13.0	4 911	3 037	13 195	43 793	46.5	2.63	10.2	19.3

1. No spouse present.

STATE County	Births, average 1999–2001 Total	Rate[1]	Deaths, average 1999–2001 Number Total	Number Infant[2]	Rate Total[1]	Rate Infant[3]	Physicians,[4] 2000 Number	Rate[5]	Hospitals,[4] 1998 Number	Beds Number	Beds Rate[5]	Medicare enrollees, 2003	Serious crimes known to police,[6] 2002 Total Number	Rate[7]
	32	33	34	35	36	37	38	39	40	41	42	43	44	45
DELAWARE	10 825	13.8	6 884	99	8.8	9.1	1 677	214	9	1 990	268	119 302	31 803	3 939
Kent	1 910	15.0	1 076	17	8.5	8.7	184	145	1	190	153	18 154	5 133	3 932
New Castle	6 947	13.9	4 084	66	8.1	9.5	1 234	247	5	1 423	295	66 500	21 855	4 240
Sussex	1 968	12.5	1 725	16	11.0	8.1	259	165	3	377	276	34 565	5 435	3 368
DISTRICT OF COLUMBIA	7 604	13.3	6 009	95	10.5	12.5	4 093	715	10	4 322	826	73 794	45 799	8 022
District of Columbia	7 604	13.3	6 009	95	10.5	12.5	4 093	715	10	4 322	826	73 794	45 799	8 022
FLORIDA	202 314	12.6	164 963	1 457	10.3	7.2	33 929	212	214	51 241	344	2 920 971	905 957	5 421
Alachua	2 484	11.4	1 530	23	7.0	9.1	1 202	551	3	1 057	532	26 956	12 955	5 684
Baker	362	16.3	192	2	8.7	D	21	94	1	93	441	2 837	502	2 157
Bay	1 960	13.2	1 413	17	9.5	8.5	239	161	2	478	325	25 461	9 673	6 241
Bradford	317	12.2	262	3	10.1	D	12	46	1	23	93	3 475	748	2 813
Brevard	4 847	10.1	5 189	24	10.9	5.0	819	172	5	1 190	255	103 480	23 277	4 674
Broward	21 837	13.4	16 201	141	9.9	6.5	3 487	215	20	5 538	368	244 892	73 096	4 307
Calhoun	143	11.2	140	1	10.9	D	8	61	1	36	290	2 144	203	1 552
Charlotte	1 010	7.1	2 139	5	15.0	D	292	206	3	652	483	41 473	4 839	3 267
Citrus	851	7.2	1 967	7	16.6	8.2	201	170	2	299	262	37 521	3 012	2 439
Clay	1 842	13.0	1 101	13	7.8	6.9	211	150	2	284	207	17 752	4 628	3 143
Collier	3 146	12.4	2 356	18	9.3	5.6	557	222	2	500	251	54 158	9 738	3 704
Columbia	761	13.5	622	8	11.0	10.1	99	175	2	145	274	9 881	2 938	4 971
De Soto	431	13.4	300	4	9.3	D	45	140	1	82	330	5 055	1 275	3 785
Dixie	171	12.4	160	1	11.6	D	4	29	0	0	0	2 790	654	4 523
Duval	12 158	15.6	6 743	126	8.6	10.4	1 907	245	7	2 615	355	98 297	53 448	6 576
Escambia	3 912	13.3	2 833	47	9.6	12.1	691	235	3	1 555	551	46 935	15 477	5 027
Flagler	391	7.7	629	3	12.4	D	45	90	1	81	171	16 858	1 357	2 604
Franklin	105	9.9	133	1	12.5	D	8	72	1	29	288	1 881	502	4 342
Gadsden	708	15.7	445	12	9.9	17.4	52	115	0	0	0	7 057	1 727	3 663
Gilchrist	170	11.8	150	2	10.5	D	9	62	0	0	0	2 526	405	2 683
Glades	86	8.2	100	0	9.5	D	3	28	0	0	0	996	323	2 920
Gulf	125	9.2	149	3	11.0	D	12	90	1	45	334	2 730	274	1 965
Hamilton	166	12.5	127	1	9.5	D	4	30	1	42	332	2 004	555	3 982
Hardee	458	17.1	211	3	7.9	D	15	56	1	50	238	3 455	1 066	3 784
Hendry	643	17.7	264	4	7.3	D	23	64	1	66	225	3 989	1 723	4 550
Hernando	1 160	8.8	2 063	7	15.7	6.3	165	126	3	316	248	42 628	6 203	4 535
Highlands	856	9.8	1 252	10	14.3	11.7	137	157	3	327	435	25 966	3 951	4 325
Hillsborough	14 663	14.6	8 596	121	8.6	8.3	2 411	241	10	2 943	318	141 837	76 215	7 296
Holmes	215	11.5	217	2	11.6	D	12	65	1	34	183	3 746	284	1 463
Indian River	1 091	9.6	1 514	8	13.4	7.3	249	220	2	480	484	32 651	4 732	4 006
Jackson	556	12.0	523	2	11.3	D	41	88	2	129	283	8 922	1 330	2 772
Jefferson	154	11.6	154	1	11.6	D	6	47	0	0	0	2 233	379	2 809
Lafayette	86	12.4	64	0	9.2	D	3	43	0	0	0	733	19	259
Lake	2 362	11.1	2 859	13	13.4	5.6	281	133	4	706	349	71 021	7 723	3 508
Lee	5 100	11.5	5 156	34	11.6	6.7	846	192	6	1 707	434	106 110	21 515	4 667
Leon	2 954	12.4	1 513	33	6.3	11.2	461	193	2	812	374	22 871	15 781	6 302
Levy	395	11.5	443	3	12.8	D	16	46	1	25	79	7 025	1 548	4 297
Liberty	81	11.5	60	0	8.5	D	0	0	0	0	0	954	95	1 294
Madison	219	11.7	203	2	10.9	D	10	53	1	57	323	3 327	1 148	5 860
Manatee	3 160	11.9	3 342	26	12.6	8.1	459	174	2	903	377	55 576	16 787	6 081
Marion	2 874	11.1	3 410	22	13.1	7.8	368	142	2	534	221	72 671	10 784	3 983
Martin	1 219	9.6	1 575	11	12.4	9.0	298	235	2	307	265	34 859	4 880	3 682
Miami-Dade	32 072	14.2	18 920	180	8.4	5.6	6 355	282	25	8 657	402	321 353	1 689 680	7 171
Monroe	769	9.7	707	4	8.9	D	188	236	4	342	421	11 152	5 214	6 265
Nassau	740	12.8	527	5	9.1	D	41	71	1	48	87	9 340	2 457	4 075
Okaloosa	2 343	13.7	1 325	17	7.8	7.3	298	175	3	433	256	26 727	5 449	3 056
Okeechobee	521	14.5	359	4	10.0	D	44	123	1	101	324	7 151	1 509	4 018
Orange	13 834	15.4	6 276	105	7.0	7.6	1 759	196	9	2 816	349	110 410	66 759	7 122
Osceola	2 559	14.7	1 308	12	7.5	4.6	207	120	3	365	251	25 561	9 853	5 462
Palm Beach	13 380	11.8	13 222	89	11.6	6.6	2 784	246	14	3 294	319	246 685	75 037	6 343
Pasco	3 712	10.7	5 273	22	15.2	5.8	509	148	5	941	289	87 092	14 916	4 137
Pinellas	9 428	10.2	12 830	75	13.9	8.0	2 342	254	15	3 931	448	197 782	50 476	5 238
Polk	6 783	14.0	5 275	53	10.9	7.9	714	148	5	1 430	316	93 608	25 818	5 133
Putnam	922	13.1	898	9	12.7	9.8	83	118	1	161	229	14 220	4 848	6 583
St. Johns	1 269	10.2	1 130	8	9.1	6.0	215	175	2	230	198	23 256	NA	NA
St. Lucie	2 210	11.4	2 300	12	11.9	5.3	282	146	2	485	271	44 255	9 742	4 835
Santa Rosa	1 529	12.9	901	8	7.6	5.0	93	79	3	237	202	18 021	2 758	2 240

1. Per 1,000 estimated resident population.   2. Deaths of infants under 1 year old.   3. Deaths of infants under 1 year old per 1,000 live births.   4. Data subject to copyright.   5. Per 100,000 resident population as of July 1 of the year shown.   6. Data for serious crimes have not been adjusted for underreporting; this may affect comparability between geographic areas and over time.   7. Per 100,000 population estimated by the FBI.

Table B. States and Counties — Crime, Education, Money Income, and Poverty

STATE County	Serious crimes known to police,[1] 2002 (cont'd) Rate[2] Violent	Property	Education — School enrollment and attainment, 2000 Enrollment[3] Total	Percent private	Attainment[4] (percent) High school graduate or less	Bachelor's degree or more	Local government expenditures,[5] 2000–2001 Total current expenditures (mil dol)	Current expenditures per student (dollars)	Money income, 1999 Per capita income[6] (dollars)	Households Median income Dollars	Percent change, 1989–1999 (constant 1999 dollars)	Percent with income of $100,000 or more	Percent below poverty level, 1999 Persons	Households	Families	Families with children
	46	47	48	49	50	51	52	53	54	55	56	57	58	59	60	61
DELAWARE	599	3 340	209 979	21.8	48.8	25.0	1 015.9	8 851	23 305	47 381	1.1	14.0	9.2	8.8	6.5	9.9
Kent	670	3 262	35 984	13.2	53.5	18.6	200.6	8 022	18 662	40 950	3.3	8.1	10.7	10.2	8.1	12.3
New Castle	636	3 604	139 816	26.4	44.2	29.5	627.9	9 243	25 413	52 419	1.0	17.4	8.4	8.0	5.6	8.4
Sussex	569	2 798	34 179	12.0	59.1	16.6	187.4	8 584	20 328	39 208	8.5	8.4	10.5	10.1	7.7	12.5
DISTRICT OF COLUMBIA	1 633	6 389	157 475	32.7	42.8	39.1	830.3	12 046	28 659	40 127	-2.8	16.4	20.2	17.1	16.7	24.5
District of Columbia	1 633	6 389	157 475	32.7	42.8	39.1	830.3	12 046	28 659	40 127	-2.8	16.4	20.2	17.1	16.7	24.5
FLORIDA	770	4 650	3 933 279	17.2	48.9	22.3	14 658.0	6 027	21 557	38 819	5.1	10.4	12.5	11.7	9.0	14.2
Alachua	817	4 867	90 184	8.2	32.2	38.7	179.4	6 038	18 465	31 426	5.9	8.7	22.8	23.2	12.2	16.9
Baker	425	1 731	5 495	8.6	69.5	8.2	25.3	5 543	15 164	40 035	15.4	5.3	14.7	13.9	11.4	16.2
Bay	748	5 492	36 970	10.0	49.6	17.7	154.3	5 992	18 700	36 092	8.8	6.6	13.0	12.7	9.8	15.9
Bradford	489	2 324	5 921	9.4	66.0	8.4	25.3	6 078	14 226	33 140	0.2	3.6	14.6	15.2	11.1	14.7
Brevard	821	3 853	112 005	18.0	42.5	23.6	393.2	5 570	21 484	40 099	-2.3	9.3	9.5	9.1	6.8	11.2
Broward	545	3 762	410 814	20.7	46.4	24.5	1 470.0	5 853	23 170	41 691	1.5	12.8	11.5	10.8	8.7	12.6
Calhoun	176	1 376	2 907	2.3	69.4	7.7	12.7	5 711	12 379	26 575	6.3	3.2	20.0	21.0	14.8	20.0
Charlotte	331	2 936	22 784	12.4	53.5	17.6	102.5	5 968	21 806	36 379	5.2	7.3	8.2	8.1	5.3	10.9
Citrus	313	2 126	19 963	10.8	59.7	13.2	88.0	5 791	18 585	31 001	8.4	5.4	11.7	11.3	8.5	16.4
Clay	424	2 718	40 121	13.1	45.3	20.1	153.7	5 468	20 868	48 854	4.3	11.4	6.8	6.1	5.1	7.2
Collier	538	3 166	46 873	13.8	44.5	27.9	228.8	6 690	31 195	48 289	5.7	18.1	10.3	7.8	6.6	13.1
Columbia	723	4 249	13 898	9.4	60.2	10.9	56.3	5 869	14 598	30 881	4.7	4.3	15.0	15.3	11.4	16.2
De Soto	621	3 165	6 014	6.5	71.8	8.4	29.0	6 285	14 000	30 714	9.1	4.1	23.6	16.3	14.2	26.2
Dixie	629	3 894	2 814	7.0	73.5	6.8	14.3	6 216	13 559	26 082	26.2	3.8	19.1	20.0	14.5	21.9
Duval	902	5 674	211 236	18.7	46.3	21.9	712.9	5 665	20 753	40 703	6.3	9.7	11.9	11.6	9.2	13.5
Escambia	703	4 324	78 198	18.7	46.3	21.0	259.1	5 757	18 641	35 234	4.2	7.0	15.4	14.6	12.1	19.4
Flagler	382	2 222	9 366	13.0	46.1	21.2	41.1	6 073	21 879	40 214	4.6	8.8	8.7	7.7	6.7	13.3
Franklin	554	3 788	1 962	5.6	68.1	12.4	9.9	6 702	16 140	26 756	15.5	4.8	17.7	18.1	11.8	16.8
Gadsden	749	2 914	11 903	11.3	65.2	12.9	50.7	6 689	14 499	31 248	16.4	4.0	19.9	19.1	16.4	23.3
Gilchrist	742	1 941	3 574	6.0	63.7	9.4	16.8	6 243	13 985	30 328	9.4	3.9	14.1	15.2	10.9	15.5
Glades	307	2 613	2 213	7.3	67.0	9.8	7.5	6 728	15 338	30 774	10.7	6.0	15.2	14.2	10.7	17.3
Gulf	516	1 449	3 072	5.4	64.6	10.1	15.0	6 645	14 449	30 276	3.1	3.8	16.7	17.9	13.7	19.4
Hamilton	840	3 143	2 853	8.2	72.2	7.3	15.1	6 931	10 562	25 638	2.0	2.4	26.0	25.7	21.7	33.1
Hardee	547	3 237	6 525	5.6	73.5	8.4	30.7	6 186	12 445	30 183	1.8	4.7	24.6	20.3	17.0	25.5
Hendry	782	3 769	9 811	6.6	74.9	8.2	46.4	6 135	13 663	33 592	0.4	5.0	24.1	19.3	16.9	24.3
Hernando	656	3 879	23 878	14.6	59.3	12.7	94.2	5 474	18 321	32 572	6.6	4.8	10.3	9.8	7.1	13.4
Highlands	478	3 846	15 766	11.2	60.1	13.6	67.2	6 001	17 222	30 160	6.2	4.8	15.2	13.5	10.2	21.5
Hillsborough	1 122	6 174	267 599	18.0	45.9	25.1	994.9	6 055	21 812	40 663	6.3	11.3	12.5	11.5	9.1	13.7
Holmes	304	1 159	4 161	7.4	72.6	8.8	21.6	6 030	14 135	27 923	20.5	3.5	19.1	20.7	15.4	22.6
Indian River	396	3 610	22 308	17.2	47.5	23.1	92.3	6 161	27 227	39 635	1.9	12.4	9.3	8.5	6.3	11.8
Jackson	442	2 330	11 144	9.5	63.5	12.8	45.2	6 086	13 905	29 744	13.7	4.6	17.2	17.8	12.8	18.9
Jefferson	623	2 186	3 050	21.7	59.1	16.9	13.1	7 130	17 006	32 998	12.8	7.1	17.1	18.1	13.3	18.6
Lafayette	41	218	1 406	8.0	71.9	7.2	6.4	5 944	13 087	30 651	10.0	4.1	17.5	14.9	12.9	21.5
Lake	608	2 900	40 624	14.1	54.5	16.6	158.8	5 423	20 199	36 903	17.4	7.1	9.6	9.1	6.9	13.0
Lee	646	4 021	81 283	15.7	50.2	21.1	354.5	6 070	24 542	40 319	5.5	10.6	9.7	8.6	6.7	12.3
Leon	838	5 464	93 932	10.1	29.8	41.7	202.8	6 326	21 024	37 517	2.2	10.4	18.2	18.8	9.4	13.1
Levy	675	3 622	7 753	6.9	64.3	10.6	37.7	6 103	14 746	26 959	6.7	4.0	18.6	18.0	15.0	24.9
Liberty	341	953	1 492	7.4	74.9	7.4	7.7	6 269	17 225	28 840	-3.5	5.0	19.9	19.1	16.8	21.0
Madison	536	5 324	4 656	10.5	66.7	10.2	21.4	6 147	12 511	26 533	8.8	3.8	23.1	24.9	18.9	25.2
Manatee	844	5 237	52 553	14.6	50.4	20.8	226.5	6 193	22 388	38 673	10.9	9.3	10.1	9.1	7.1	12.8
Marion	785	3 198	54 173	14.4	57.7	13.7	224.2	5 813	17 848	31 944	5.9	5.5	13.1	12.2	9.2	16.6
Martin	453	3 229	24 414	17.8	43.0	26.3	104.6	6 411	29 584	43 083	1.0	15.3	8.8	7.6	5.6	10.5
Miami-Dade	1 116	6 054	643 727	19.4	54.5	21.7	2 415.3	6 552	18 497	35 966	-0.5	10.8	18.0	18.1	14.5	19.3
Monroe	578	5 687	14 277	14.2	44.0	25.5	67.0	7 151	26 102	42 283	7.2	12.3	10.2	10.1	6.8	9.9
Nassau	1 264	2 811	14 083	11.4	53.4	18.9	55.1	5 391	22 836	46 022	13.3	11.4	9.1	9.2	6.4	9.4
Okaloosa	345	2 711	44 445	10.8	39.1	24.2	171.3	5 644	20 918	41 474	10.5	9.1	8.8	8.5	6.6	10.8
Okeechobee	655	3 363	8 521	5.8	68.8	8.9	39.8	5 801	14 553	30 456	5.8	5.3	16.0	15.1	11.8	17.2
Orange	1 039	6 084	248 040	17.4	44.0	26.1	862.1	5 721	20 916	41 311	1.6	10.7	12.1	10.9	8.8	13.0
Osceola	637	4 825	44 944	13.4	54.8	15.7	191.6	5 543	17 022	38 214	4.3	6.3	11.5	10.6	9.1	13.2
Palm Beach	747	5 597	254 671	20.4	43.3	27.7	964.2	6 266	28 801	45 062	3.1	16.2	9.9	9.0	6.9	11.5
Pasco	469	3 668	67 546	13.5	59.2	13.1	287.8	5 789	18 439	32 969	14.2	5.6	10.7	10.4	7.6	12.8
Pinellas	824	4 414	190 563	20.7	45.6	22.9	695.1	6 150	23 497	37 111	5.0	9.5	10.0	9.5	6.7	11.2
Polk	566	4 567	114 180	15.4	58.9	14.9	467.5	5 882	18 302	36 036	6.4	6.6	12.9	11.9	9.4	15.5
Putnam	1 134	5 449	16 240	8.0	67.0	9.4	74.1	5 867	15 603	28 180	4.1	4.6	20.9	19.3	15.8	26.6
St. Johns	NA	NA	30 609	22.5	37.3	33.1	123.6	6 154	28 674	50 099	24.6	18.3	8.0	8.2	5.1	8.4
St. Lucie	726	4 109	43 393	13.3	55.0	15.1	179.1	6 064	18 790	36 363	-2.3	6.8	13.4	11.5	9.6	16.4
Santa Rosa	337	1 903	31 346	11.5	43.8	22.9	130.6	5 771	20 089	41 881	13.0	9.4	9.8	10.0	7.9	11.6

1. Data for serious crimes have not been adjusted for underreporting; this may affect comparability between geographic areas and over time.   2. Per 100,000 population estimated by the FBI.   3. All persons 3 years old and over enrolled in nursery school through college.   4. Persons 25 years old and over.   5. Elementary and secondary education expenditures.   6. Based on population enumerated as of April 1, 2000.

STATE County	Personal income, 2002 Total (mil dol)	Percent change, 2001–2002	Per capita[1] Dollars	Per capita[1] Rank	Wages and salaries[2] (mil dol)	Proprietor's income (mil dol)	Dividends, interest, and rent (mil dol)	Transfer payments Total (mil dol)	Government payments to individuals Total (mil dol)	Social Security (mil dol)	Medical payments (mil dol)	Income maintenance (mil dol)	Unemployment insurance (mil dol)
	62	63	64	65	66	67	68	69	70	71	72	73	74
DELAWARE	25 862	3.2	32 090	X	20 262	1 661	4 587	3 627	3 413	1 447	1 417	257	142
Kent	3 286	6.4	24 987	1 131	2 357	172	475	562	528	211	204	46	27
New Castle	18 398	2.6	36 047	120	15 715	1 285	3 252	2 133	1 997	837	836	151	92
Sussex	4 178	3.7	25 471	1 005	2 190	204	859	931	887	399	377	59	24
DISTRICT OF COLUMBIA	26 636	2.7	46 800	X	52 375	3 276	4 169	3 330	3 217	624	1 742	496	160
District of Columbia	26 636	2.7	46 800	26	52 375	3 276	4 169	3 330	3 217	624	1 742	496	160
FLORIDA	496 706	3.8	29 758	X	296 922	31 330	123 134	80 711	76 636	32 033	32 764	6 171	1 700
Alachua	5 612	3.8	25 280	1 055	4 341	246	1 106	887	833	280	385	83	11
Baker	478	6.6	20 618	2 398	192	20	57	96	91	30	38	10	2
Bay	3 889	6.4	25 536	991	2 519	215	779	743	707	263	301	63	14
Bradford	518	4.3	19 819	2 582	231	26	64	115	109	32	55	13	1
Brevard	13 770	3.7	27 762	578	8 298	664	3 025	2 566	2 446	1 163	936	136	52
Broward	54 173	3.1	31 785	232	30 191	3 119	12 140	7 381	6 963	2 809	3 123	501	247
Calhoun	224	4.5	17 543	2 948	87	17	33	68	65	21	33	7	1
Charlotte	4 036	6.3	26 932	714	1 435	216	1 439	992	955	521	356	29	7
Citrus	2 887	4.3	23 341	1 615	985	124	944	851	820	450	304	38	11
Clay	4 065	4.8	26 739	746	1 264	141	645	491	455	208	156	29	11
Collier	11 601	4.1	42 050	48	4 687	892	5 559	1 214	1 146	662	398	49	16
Columbia	1 142	3.5	19 547	2 650	659	48	208	290	276	101	124	31	4
De Soto	580	4.3	17 613	2 940	271	63	114	142	134	55	61	13	3
Dixie	258	14.6	18 505	2 829	115	19	46	77	74	21	30	8	1
Duval	23 829	3.9	29 624	378	21 424	1 685	3 889	3 252	3 059	1 043	1 298	354	85
Escambia	7 404	2.5	25 017	1 123	5 452	334	1 418	1 398	1 329	484	544	145	15
Flagler	1 382	7.4	24 041	1 394	475	24	473	321	307	199	91	7	4
Franklin	223	4.2	22 300	1 933	92	26	63	56	54	21	25	5	1
Gadsden	935	4.0	20 563	2 415	461	56	135	218	207	68	88	39	3
Gilchrist	322	3.2	21 383	2 185	81	25	43	71	67	26	31	6	1
Glades	195	5.4	17 769	2 922	47	19	52	37	34	20	9	3	1
Gulf	272	4.9	18 285	2 864	120	14	56	81	77	30	36	6	1
Hamilton	185	0.6	13 519	3 096	128	9	28	60	57	19	25	9	0
Hardee	496	3.5	18 001	2 899	234	56	88	107	101	34	43	16	2
Hendry	757	6.5	20 604	2 403	436	75	105	145	136	44	62	21	6
Hernando	3 374	4.6	24 401	1 284	1 038	139	912	963	929	477	353	39	10
Highlands	1 980	5.8	22 004	2 014	777	112	587	591	569	280	223	33	5
Hillsborough	31 151	4.4	29 602	382	27 102	1 873	5 003	4 265	4 008	1 531	1 648	419	116
Holmes	352	2.8	18 830	2 776	95	40	55	107	102	36	47	11	1
Indian River	4 699	3.3	39 830	63	1 591	206	2 366	734	705	369	268	27	13
Jackson	929	5.2	20 065	2 535	443	68	153	274	262	83	140	22	2
Jefferson	321	3.8	23 362	1 608	87	23	61	65	62	23	27	8	1
Lafayette	110	-3.8	15 176	3 070	46	13	17	26	24	10	9	3	0
Lake	6 128	5.3	26 085	871	2 309	306	1 657	1 396	1 339	668	534	66	17
Lee	15 009	5.0	31 562	244	6 968	1 200	5 070	2 503	2 387	1 225	918	108	30
Leon	6 749	3.1	28 056	540	5 815	340	1 136	763	703	263	260	80	13
Levy	697	2.9	19 461	2 663	221	59	149	185	176	81	67	17	2
Liberty	138	6.6	19 297	2 697	69	10	16	27	25	9	11	3	0
Madison	329	1.3	17 581	2 944	148	21	54	97	92	31	42	13	1
Manatee	9 093	3.7	32 469	207	4 286	869	2 750	1 388	1 319	682	467	80	20
Marion	6 437	4.4	23 637	1 520	2 908	347	1 588	1 559	1 492	785	548	106	18
Martin	5 850	3.4	44 370	35	2 077	264	2 853	785	753	407	283	25	11
Miami-Dade	62 037	3.6	26 780	740	45 908	5 036	11 171	11 646	11 075	2 832	6 048	1 526	315
Monroe	3 076	3.3	38 905	72	1 414	201	1 287	323	304	131	130	20	5
Nassau	1 896	3.3	31 298	262	651	108	426	239	225	110	79	16	5
Okaloosa	5 254	7.9	29 938	357	3 904	270	1 184	739	700	264	279	47	9
Okeechobee	695	4.1	18 818	2 778	308	48	129	198	189	70	92	16	3
Orange	26 164	4.5	27 695	589	26 113	2 111	3 808	3 550	3 318	1 157	1 475	373	95
Osceola	3 883	6.5	19 992	2 550	1 856	162	523	699	652	272	297	55	18
Palm Beach	52 429	2.9	44 120	39	23 954	3 846	20 551	6 413	6 121	2 970	2 517	291	150
Pasco	8 774	4.9	23 529	1 553	2 623	227	1 870	2 211	2 120	1 010	871	99	29
Pinellas	30 688	1.9	33 167	182	18 523	1 416	7 756	5 184	4 957	2 165	2 161	291	99
Polk	12 891	4.7	25 777	935	7 193	906	2 498	2 389	2 267	1 045	838	221	44
Putnam	1 362	2.4	19 155	2 727	617	36	264	391	374	157	163	35	7
St. Johns	5 070	3.9	37 191	102	1 615	182	1 473	569	535	267	209	23	8
St. Lucie	4 813	6.4	23 458	1 581	2 007	193	1 250	1 205	1 155	529	465	82	27
Santa Rosa	3 140	4.5	24 576	1 244	1 000	102	588	492	461	200	179	32	7

1. Based on the resident population estimated as of July 1 of the year shown. 2. Includes other labor income.

STATE County	Earnings, 2002								Social Security beneficiaries, December 2003		Housing units, 2003		
	Total (mil dol)	Percent by selected industries									Supplemental Security Income recipients, December 2003		
			Goods-related[1]		Service-related and health									
		Farm	Total	Manu-facturing	Infor-mation and profes-sional and technical services	Retail trade	Finance, insur-ance, and real estate	Health services	Govern-ment	Number	Rate[2]		Total	Percent change, 2000–2003
	75	76	77	78	79	80	81	82	83	84	85	86	87	88
DELAWARE	21 923	0.4	16.8	10.7	14.3	6.6	13.7	9.4	14.4	141 488	173	12 968	357 480	4.2
Kent	2 528	0.9	D	D	D	7.8	4.4	9.2	39.8	22 725	169	2 789	53 968	6.9
New Castle	17 000	0.1	D	9.7	17.1	5.6	15.9	9.1	10.8	78 260	152	7 707	204 984	2.7
Sussex	2 394	2.2	D	D	D	12.1	7.7	12.0	13.2	40 435	241	2 456	98 528	5.9
DISTRICT OF COLUMBIA	55 651	0.0	D	D	26.3	1.0	5.3	5.1	41.0	0	0	20 393	272 394	-0.9
District of Columbia	55 651	0.0	D	D	26.3	1.0	5.3	5.1	41.0	72 209	128	20 393	272 394	-0.9
FLORIDA	328 253	0.6	13.4	6.5	12.1	8.5	10.0	10.5	16.2	3 330 425	196	410 027	7 788 543	6.6
Alachua	4 588	0.4	D	4.3	8.5	7.2	6.4	16.6	37.5	29 880	134	5 125	101 112	6.3
Baker	212	3.0	8.6	3.9	D	6.8	3.6	6.6	46.7	3 460	148	468	7 948	4.7
Bay	2 734	0.1	D	5.5	7.2	9.2	5.9	13.1	29.3	29 710	191	3 862	82 260	4.9
Bradford	257	0.9	D	10.3	4.3	6.8	2.3	D	39.7	4 095	152	734	9 775	1.8
Brevard	8 962	0.1	D	16.7	11.4	8.0	4.4	11.4	17.1	120 435	238	8 589	237 766	7.1
Broward	33 309	0.1	12.9	5.6	12.7	9.7	12.4	9.3	14.3	273 865	158	31 065	773 642	4.4
Calhoun	104	5.4	14.6	2.9	2.7	D	3.4	6.3	33.6	2 580	200	489	5 314	1.2
Charlotte	1 651	0.8	D	2.5	8.0	12.1	6.8	19.4	13.7	52 115	340	1 713	85 109	6.7
Citrus	1 109	0.2	13.5	3.1	D	12.2	5.7	19.0	14.4	46 280	366	1 768	65 650	5.5
Clay	1 405	0.1	14.7	4.6	8.1	12.8	5.1	13.4	17.4	23 035	146	1 379	60 042	11.7
Collier	5 579	2.1	17.6	2.3	9.6	9.9	12.6	10.8	9.6	62 080	217	2 131	167 244	15.7
Columbia	706	0.2	13.2	5.1	5.3	13.1	4.5	10.9	34.0	11 730	195	2 490	24 324	3.2
De Soto	334	17.3	7.7	3.0	2.1	7.6	3.2	6.7	26.8	6 120	181	757	13 908	2.2
Dixie	134	1.4	43.4	10.2	1.0	4.6	D	2.6	27.0	3 450	247	607	7 458	1.3
Duval	23 109	0.1	12.7	6.4	10.4	7.2	14.5	9.6	18.3	112 520	138	19 061	349 668	6.0
Escambia	5 786	0.1	12.0	5.6	9.2	7.6	5.0	13.2	33.8	55 635	188	8 866	129 165	3.6
Flagler	500	2.8	D	11.4	15.5	9.9	9.3	D	16.7	20 825	335	660	29 910	22.3
Franklin	118	0.0	14.6	6.8	4.1	12.2	11.5	D	22.1	2 290	229	360	7 543	5.1
Gadsden	517	11.0	17.6	9.7	D	5.6	2.0	3.6	38.8	8 485	188	2 584	17 921	1.2
Gilchrist	106	9.3	8.9	4.6	2.1	7.6	3.0	D	38.7	2 985	191	370	6 123	3.7
Glades	66	10.6	D	D	4.5	7.1	D	D	20.8	2 070	185	123	5 821	0.5
Gulf	135	0.0	8.2	2.1	9.8	5.6	3.7	D	37.5	3 135	206	356	8 094	6.7
Hamilton	137	1.3	D	D	D	3.7	0.7	6.6	37.2	2 370	170	545	5 029	1.3
Hardee	290	16.1	D	2.2	6.7	8.0	3.5	8.3	22.1	4 035	146	864	9 910	0.9
Hendry	511	15.7	D	12.8	D	6.9	2.4	3.8	17.5	4 935	133	887	12 450	1.3
Hernando	1 177	0.5	14.0	4.4	5.2	11.8	6.6	17.9	18.9	49 120	342	2 240	67 299	7.3
Highlands	889	6.5	D	5.7	4.8	10.7	5.4	16.1	17.2	29 620	325	2 145	50 057	2.5
Hillsborough	28 976	0.7	11.2	5.8	15.3	7.4	11.4	8.5	13.5	165 370	154	29 244	461 836	8.4
Holmes	135	8.7	9.6	3.8	2.5	8.5	D	D	36.7	4 475	236	693	8 102	1.3
Indian River	1 798	1.6	D	6.2	9.2	11.4	8.6	16.5	13.1	36 335	302	1 373	63 594	9.8
Jackson	511	5.9	D	5.1	4.3	9.8	2.9	8.7	44.6	10 240	220	1 998	20 043	2.8
Jefferson	110	9.3	10.8	2.4	5.8	6.0	6.3	D	30.9	2 615	186	646	5 417	3.2
Lafayette	60	21.5	D	2.3	D	7.0	D	D	37.3	1 115	152	137	2 710	1.9
Lake	2 615	2.5	19.8	5.5	7.6	10.6	5.1	16.8	15.5	71 200	290	4 148	116 142	12.9
Lee	8 169	0.5	17.9	4.8	10.0	12.4	11.7	9.4	15.4	121 810	247	6 878	276 129	12.5
Leon	6 155	0.1	D	1.6	15.6	6.4	5.9	10.6	40.5	27 290	113	4 261	110 880	6.6
Levy	280	9.8	12.2	2.4	4.3	12.2	4.9	6.1	25.2	9 245	255	1 044	16 989	2.5
Liberty	79	0.3	D	D	D	3.5	D	2.3	36.1	1 155	158	215	3 175	0.6
Madison	169	4.9	16.5	14.6	3.2	8.7	2.2	D	30.8	3 845	205	985	7 963	1.6
Manatee	5 155	2.2	18.8	11.7	13.5	9.0	4.3	9.1	10.4	69 435	242	3 820	150 537	9.0
Marion	3 255	1.7	20.0	11.7	6.4	12.5	6.8	12.4	18.0	84 365	301	6 637	133 766	9.1
Martin	2 340	0.9	D	6.0	11.5	11.2	11.2	14.1	10.2	40 450	299	1 315	69 273	5.8
Miami-Dade	50 944	0.3	9.7	4.9	14.9	7.3	10.6	9.3	16.1	332 530	142	123 324	891 553	4.6
Monroe	1 615	0.0	D	0.9	6.6	10.9	7.5	7.6	24.3	13 095	166	1 224	51 628	0.0
Nassau	759	1.9	D	12.6	6.2	7.9	7.5	4.4	25.6	11 505	187	766	28 146	8.6
Okaloosa	4 174	0.0	D	3.5	10.3	7.3	7.1	6.1	44.4	29 935	168	2 475	83 243	5.9
Okeechobee	357	10.7	D	5.5	D	11.2	2.8	17.6	21.1	7 720	206	888	15 828	2.1
Orange	28 224	0.3	12.4	6.7	14.0	6.5	10.1	8.8	10.7	126 435	131	24 279	396 150	9.6
Osceola	2 018	0.9	12.3	3.6	3.4	10.6	10.0	11.5	18.6	31 690	154	3 946	87 595	21.2
Palm Beach	27 800	0.9	13.3	5.4	14.1	7.7	11.9	11.1	10.4	271 985	224	15 805	587 491	5.6
Pasco	2 850	0.7	13.9	4.6	5.6	13.7	5.3	19.7	19.3	105 380	271	7 595	187 350	7.8
Pinellas	19 939	0.0	D	10.3	11.2	8.5	10.0	12.9	11.2	217 170	234	16 941	488 126	1.4
Polk	8 099	1.2	20.6	12.7	7.3	9.6	6.8	10.9	15.1	112 470	220	13 978	240 055	6.0
Putnam	653	2.7	32.5	22.2	3.3	8.8	3.0	9.4	26.7	17 650	246	2 727	34 334	1.4
St. Johns	1 796	0.8	17.8	9.5	7.2	9.9	7.1	10.2	15.3	27 320	191	1 749	65 820	13.5
St. Lucie	2 200	0.9	12.2	4.7	6.0	10.1	6.3	14.4	21.0	52 945	248	5 173	100 358	10.0
Santa Rosa	1 103	1.3	14.6	4.1	6.3	8.8	3.8	9.1	31.4	22 660	170	1 637	52 947	7.8

1. Covers mining, construction, and manufacturing.   2. Per 1,000 resident population estimated as of July 1 of the year shown.

Table B. States and Counties — Housing, Labor Force, and Employment

STATE County	Housing units, 2000 — Occupied units — Owner-occupied — Total	Percent	Median value[1]	Median owner cost as a percent of income — With a mortgage	Without a mortgage[2]	Renter-occupied — Median rent[3]	Median rent as a percent of income	Sub-standard units[4] (percent)	Civilian labor force, 2003 — Total	Percent change, 2002–2003	Unemployment — Total	Rate[5]	Civilian employment,[6] 2000 — Total	Percent — Management, professional and related occupations	Production, transportation and material moving occupations
	89	90	91	92	93	94	95	96	97	98	99	100	101	102	103
DELAWARE	298 736	72.3	130 400	20.8	9.9	639	24.3	3.1	417 256	-0.6	18 290	4.4	376 811	35.3	12.5
Kent	47 224	70.0	114 100	21.7	9.9	573	25.2	2.9	76 366	1.8	3 229	4.2	57 895	28.5	15.3
New Castle	188 935	70.1	136 000	20.4	9.9	670	24.5	3.1	263 653	-1.3	11 987	4.5	249 320	39.1	10.7
Sussex	62 577	80.7	122 400	21.7	9.9	507	22.3	3.4	77 237	-0.6	3 075	4.0	69 596	27.2	16.6
DISTRICT OF COLUMBIA	248 338	40.8	157 200	22.2	9.9	618	24.8	9.5	302 286	-0.3	21 096	7.0	263 108	51.1	5.2
District of Columbia	248 338	40.8	157 200	22.2	9.9	618	24.8	9.5	302 286	-0.3	21 096	7.0	263 108	51.1	5.2
FLORIDA	6 337 929	70.1	105 500	22.8	10.5	641	27.5	6.8	8 164 237	0.9	420 433	5.1	6 995 047	31.5	10.8
Alachua	87 509	54.9	97 300	20.9	9.9	553	33.6	3.9	113 942	0.6	2 718	2.4	105 293	44.0	6.7
Baker	7 043	81.3	80 900	18.4	9.9	399	21.6	6.9	10 284	0.2	456	4.4	9 329	23.6	16.6
Bay	59 597	68.6	93 500	21.1	9.9	536	25.7	3.6	71 864	2.4	3 887	5.4	64 883	28.5	10.8
Bradford	8 497	79.0	71 700	20.6	9.9	430	23.4	3.9	10 467	3.1	320	3.1	9 548	23.1	14.8
Brevard	198 195	74.6	94 400	21.6	9.9	604	26.2	2.8	224 783	0.6	11 069	4.9	207 366	34.9	10.8
Broward	654 445	69.5	128 600	24.5	13.1	757	28.6	7.7	877 270	0.9	48 646	5.5	758 939	33.3	9.3
Calhoun	4 468	80.2	58 500	21.8	10.6	353	24.4	5.3	4 800	-2.1	210	4.4	4 608	24.9	13.2
Charlotte	63 864	83.7	97 000	24.1	11.6	626	27.0	1.9	52 708	-3.2	2 297	4.4	50 690	27.2	9.3
Citrus	52 634	85.6	84 400	21.8	9.9	478	26.6	1.7	41 144	1.0	2 286	5.6	38 837	25.8	12.2
Clay	50 243	77.9	108 400	20.8	9.9	668	23.5	2.9	76 025	0.1	3 246	4.3	66 268	31.2	11.4
Collier	102 973	75.6	168 000	23.9	9.9	753	25.2	7.0	121 111	4.1	5 484	4.5	105 436	28.4	8.1
Columbia	20 925	77.1	73 600	20.8	10.3	448	23.8	4.3	25 426	0.0	1 112	4.4	23 006	23.1	13.9
De Soto	10 746	74.7	69 900	22.5	9.9	442	23.4	10.8	8 918	1.3	683	7.7	12 742	18.5	10.0
Dixie	5 205	86.5	61 700	23.4	10.8	322	20.7	5.0	4 430	-0.4	236	5.3	4 612	18.0	17.2
Duval	303 747	63.1	89 600	20.7	9.9	604	24.7	5.1	416 574	0.4	23 540	5.7	367 065	31.7	12.1
Escambia	111 049	67.3	85 700	21.0	9.9	533	26.9	3.8	125 538	1.5	5 267	4.2	120 374	30.0	11.7
Flagler	21 294	84.1	116 200	23.8	9.9	698	26.3	2.1	21 708	2.9	1 131	5.2	18 815	29.3	11.0
Franklin	4 096	79.2	105 300	24.1	11.1	419	26.7	2.8	5 476	3.9	177	3.2	3 936	21.2	11.9
Gadsden	15 867	78.0	70 100	21.1	10.1	386	24.3	7.8	19 138	-0.1	964	5.0	18 051	26.0	13.0
Gilchrist	5 021	86.2	78 000	21.9	11.1	420	22.8	4.2	5 300	5.9	209	3.9	5 756	24.3	15.1
Glades	3 852	81.6	72 400	19.7	10.4	474	18.2	8.9	3 846	-0.9	333	8.7	3 677	23.3	14.6
Gulf	4 931	81.0	77 200	22.3	10.4	413	25.6	2.1	5 370	3.8	243	4.5	4 667	23.7	13.7
Hamilton	4 161	77.3	54 600	17.9	10.9	352	24.5	5.1	3 160	3.2	199	6.3	4 139	20.7	15.9
Hardee	8 166	73.4	59 600	20.3	10.4	446	22.7	15.9	9 560	0.4	825	8.6	9 901	20.7	13.5
Hendry	10 850	72.4	71 500	19.8	9.9	479	25.6	16.2	15 583	-1.1	1 831	11.7	14 579	18.7	14.7
Hernando	55 425	86.5	87 300	23.4	10.5	550	27.4	2.2	52 304	0.6	2 697	5.2	44 071	25.3	13.1
Highlands	37 471	79.7	72 800	21.7	9.9	479	26.0	4.7	30 226	4.6	1 737	5.7	30 051	24.6	11.6
Hillsborough	391 357	64.1	97 700	21.7	10.7	623	26.0	6.6	623 614	0.6	25 668	4.1	476 023	33.8	11.0
Holmes	6 921	81.6	56 200	21.4	10.7	387	26.2	4.0	6 288	-1.4	271	4.3	6 938	19.1	21.2
Indian River	49 137	77.6	104 000	21.8	10.2	615	27.3	3.1	52 931	5.8	3 981	7.5	45 494	28.0	9.4
Jackson	16 620	77.9	66 700	19.0	9.9	368	22.0	3.7	18 280	-1.1	601	3.3	17 315	28.6	12.3
Jefferson	4 695	80.9	77 000	21.3	9.9	385	26.1	5.3	5 264	4.6	256	4.9	5 495	29.0	9.2
Lafayette	2 142	80.4	67 100	17.6	11.7	420	21.8	6.3	2 833	1.0	78	2.8	2 540	23.7	16.2
Lake	88 413	81.5	100 600	21.9	9.9	534	26.5	3.0	98 993	1.4	4 434	4.5	82 819	28.6	11.7
Lee	188 599	76.5	112 900	23.0	10.6	646	26.3	4.0	217 125	3.6	8 749	4.0	186 417	28.1	9.3
Leon	96 521	57.0	110 900	21.1	9.9	606	32.6	3.9	137 393	0.1	4 396	3.2	122 840	45.3	5.7
Levy	13 867	83.6	75 800	22.1	11.1	413	25.9	4.7	14 485	2.0	676	4.7	12 935	23.9	13.6
Liberty	2 222	81.7	66 300	18.9	9.9	350	21.9	4.4	3 008	6.2	69	2.3	2 375	22.1	15.2
Madison	6 629	78.4	54 800	23.5	12.6	347	23.2	5.7	6 796	-3.2	278	4.1	6 943	23.5	23.1
Manatee	112 460	73.7	119 400	22.9	10.5	637	26.7	4.2	139 151	2.3	5 167	3.7	111 793	29.1	13.2
Marion	106 755	79.8	81 300	21.6	9.9	513	25.5	3.5	105 823	2.1	4 731	4.5	98 248	26.4	14.5
Martin	55 288	79.8	152 400	22.2	9.9	633	27.0	3.0	56 271	3.2	2 921	5.2	51 054	32.8	8.7
Miami-Dade	776 774	57.8	124 000	26.6	13.5	647	30.5	20.6	1 103 718	-1.2	79 512	7.2	921 208	30.2	11.9
Monroe	35 086	62.4	241 200	28.0	13.4	820	29.0	6.3	48 379	1.0	1 085	2.2	41 181	27.3	8.6
Nassau	21 980	80.7	126 700	21.4	9.9	553	23.5	3.5	30 387	0.6	1 427	4.7	27 113	27.2	16.5
Okaloosa	66 269	66.4	101 200	21.2	9.9	601	24.3	3.2	91 434	2.6	2 477	2.7	71 992	32.0	9.2
Okeechobee	12 593	74.9	77 600	20.8	11.1	486	25.9	10.9	16 432	-0.4	1 158	7.0	14 169	21.5	12.6
Orange	336 286	60.7	107 500	22.9	10.5	699	27.3	7.4	547 148	1.3	26 884	4.9	447 861	32.4	10.6
Osceola	60 977	67.8	99 300	23.8	11.5	714	28.8	8.1	103 576	1.6	5 310	5.1	79 859	23.0	11.8
Palm Beach	474 175	74.7	135 200	23.2	11.1	739	28.0	5.8	584 597	0.5	32 550	5.6	484 760	34.4	8.4
Pasco	147 566	82.4	79 600	22.2	10.5	518	26.3	2.7	155 734	0.7	7 638	4.9	134 184	27.4	11.8
Pinellas	414 968	70.8	96 500	22.4	11.5	616	26.7	3.0	499 639	0.5	22 130	4.4	425 349	34.2	11.0
Polk	187 233	73.4	83 300	20.8	9.9	501	23.9	5.2	218 348	0.3	13 208	6.0	206 460	26.2	16.1
Putnam	27 839	80.0	68 500	18.9	9.9	384	25.2	5.2	29 550	3.9	1 614	5.5	26 326	22.2	18.2
St. Johns	49 614	76.4	158 400	21.9	9.9	724	26.5	2.0	68 998	0.4	2 529	3.7	59 394	37.0	8.4
St. Lucie	76 933	78.0	86 100	23.0	11.1	621	27.9	4.9	89 474	2.8	6 691	7.5	77 842	25.3	12.0
Santa Rosa	43 793	80.4	106 000	21.5	9.9	540	24.8	2.7	55 362	1.2	2 081	3.8	49 753	32.5	11.7

1. Specified owner-occupied units. 2. Median monthly owner costs is often in the minimum category—9.9 percent or less, which is indicated as 9.9 percent. 3. Specified renter-occupied units. 4. Overcrowded or lacking complete plumbing facilities. 5. Percent of civilian labor force. 6. Persons 16 years old and over.

STATE County	Number of establishments	Total	Health care and social assistance	Manufacturing	Retail trade	Finance and insurance	Professional, scientific, and technical services	Total (mil dol)	Average per employee (dollars)	Number	Less than 50 acres	500 acres and over	Farm operators whose principal occupation is farming (percent)
	104	105	106	107	108	109	110	111	112	113	114	115	116
DELAWARE	24 074	389 376	46 074	41 887	52 151	44 879	19 564	15 022	38 579	2 391	52.3	11.0	69.4
Kent	3 007	46 469	6 423	6 728	9 244	2 716	2 016	1 213	26 098	721	44.5	11.7	68.0
New Castle	16 386	291 416	31 285	24 824	32 725	40 354	16 228	12 474	42 804	358	59.5	10.6	55.9
Sussex	4 681	51 491	8 366	10 335	10 182	1 809	1 320	1 335	25 932	1 312	54.6	10.7	73.9
DISTRICT OF COLUMBIA	19 686	422 549	61 444	2 529	18 216	18 597	80 331	20 789	49 199	NA	NA	NA	NA
District of Columbia	19 686	422 549	61 444	2 529	18 216	18 597	80 331	20 789	49 199	NA	NA	NA	NA
FLORIDA	434 583	6 431 696	768 747	412 993	915 111	348 542	371 157	189 628	29 483	44 081	64.9	6.8	52.2
Alachua	5 186	84 779	17 235	4 466	13 868	4 380	5 541	2 107	24 856	1 493	64.8	4.9	48.8
Baker	305	4 040	1 631	334	629	91	D	91	22 574	204	62.3	3.9	52.0
Bay	4 179	52 887	7 902	3 165	9 851	2 836	2 320	1 235	23 348	116	73.3	2.6	59.5
Bradford	387	4 324	881	575	829	116	106	72	16 711	378	64.0	3.4	44.7
Brevard	11 484	164 500	23 839	18 049	26 086	4 589	14 872	5 003	30 413	555	73.5	7.6	53.3
Broward	51 036	640 214	77 111	36 497	99 787	37 780	39 520	20 140	31 459	494	90.3	2.6	51.0
Calhoun	198	1 943	400	183	394	74	50	33	17 231	151	31.1	15.9	49.7
Charlotte	3 149	29 956	7 007	611	7 214	1 166	1 424	711	23 732	284	60.9	13.4	45.1
Citrus	2 415	23 226	5 472	635	5 440	691	594	570	24 544	432	70.6	3.0	47.5
Clay	2 824	31 958	5 110	1 697	7 926	737	1 372	705	22 052	340	73.8	3.8	51.2
Collier	8 705	98 832	12 643	2 852	18 469	4 478	5 034	2 875	29 091	273	56.8	21.6	54.2
Columbia	1 178	15 363	3 316	925	3 027	376	517	366	23 816	688	56.4	4.8	47.8
De Soto	419	5 383	1 769	183	977	148	96	114	21 228	1 153	65.9	9.5	52.6
Dixie	189	1 311	D	379	243	25	24	26	19 972	215	56.3	6.0	35.8
Duval	21 341	413 792	44 377	28 495	46 858	52 053	20 062	12 811	30 961	382	69.9	2.9	46.6
Escambia	6 606	108 006	18 535	6 214	15 579	3 857	5 423	2 842	26 313	674	63.4	4.0	54.0
Flagler	1 120	10 337	912	1 683	2 009	336	444	231	22 355	100	35.0	22.0	42.0
Franklin	313	2 286	246	88	418	101	57	40	17 650	20	85.0	5.0	85.0
Gadsden	582	9 548	3 384	1 651	1 179	196	189	232	24 311	343	44.6	6.1	56.6
Gilchrist	177	1 169	263	131	272	D	29	21	18 321	408	48.8	9.3	53.4
Glades	126	1 548	D	D	335	56	D	35	22 872	231	34.6	23.4	53.7
Gulf	267	1 834	355	158	365	104	49	44	24 144	30	46.7	3.3	33.3
Hamilton	167	2 053	298	D	242	D	20	57	27 979	239	38.1	9.6	55.6
Hardee	365	3 644	961	D	726	184	111	87	23 871	1 142	50.6	11.6	52.7
Hendry	480	4 706	672	769	1 011	185	93	110	23 301	456	49.1	20.6	53.1
Hernando	2 380	23 756	4 688	1 119	5 394	886	719	550	23 153	617	70.5	4.5	54.3
Highlands	1 735	16 694	3 569	914	3 740	511	619	348	20 844	1 035	57.5	12.8	57.0
Hillsborough	27 430	520 203	49 944	31 267	62 169	42 699	47 388	17 588	33 809	2 969	79.3	3.2	54.2
Holmes	251	2 065	441	312	369	44	44	34	16 424	672	31.5	3.9	51.2
Indian River	3 437	39 804	6 790	3 036	8 163	1 712	1 721	992	24 923	480	64.4	12.3	55.0
Jackson	776	8 672	1 924	722	1 967	343	193	163	18 818	920	33.5	11.5	51.4
Jefferson	236	1 626	292	53	316	98	D	34	21 185	418	54.1	10.0	35.2
Lafayette	106	833	157	36	119	41	D	17	20 403	195	34.4	14.4	61.0
Lake	4 760	54 253	9 898	3 998	11 146	1 911	1 974	1 305	24 054	1 798	75.0	3.6	45.4
Lee	12 785	147 047	17 852	7 162	29 616	4 912	9 039	3 978	27 051	643	75.3	7.5	51.2
Leon	6 539	92 853	14 747	2 196	15 958	4 401	8 873	2 567	27 646	281	67.6	5.7	48.8
Levy	642	5 769	516	453	1 466	253	193	110	19 080	897	59.2	6.2	60.5
Liberty	84	824	116	46	73	D	D	20	24 801	67	52.2	4.5	44.8
Madison	306	3 568	696	973	516	85	70	65	18 149	529	29.7	12.1	49.5
Manatee	5 711	69 887	10 414	10 491	13 155	2 257	3 566	1 915	27 405	852	52.9	14.0	52.6
Marion	5 521	71 560	11 453	8 888	14 739	2 374	2 462	1 748	24 423	2 930	75.4	3.1	61.0
Martin	4 355	48 050	6 579	2 575	10 377	1 821	2 785	1 287	26 783	418	64.8	17.2	57.2
Miami-Dade	67 703	845 720	102 250	56 439	116 258	47 607	54 137	27 251	32 222	2 244	89.6	1.5	51.3
Monroe	3 722	32 202	2 574	582	6 862	1 171	1 097	733	22 750	18	100.0	0.0	44.4
Nassau	1 236	12 564	1 436	1 367	2 166	322	492	345	27 480	315	61.9	4.4	52.4
Okaloosa	4 771	60 333	7 770	2 896	11 891	2 351	4 613	1 421	23 547	465	49.7	3.4	46.5
Okeechobee	671	6 603	1 464	200	1 655	224	192	155	23 411	638	46.2	22.4	55.5
Orange	26 607	578 818	48 431	33 370	62 594	26 612	34 946	17 642	30 479	901	76.6	3.0	50.9
Osceola	3 429	48 904	5 396	1 659	8 540	864	1 016	1 116	22 824	519	63.0	14.6	53.0
Palm Beach	37 392	469 242	61 824	28 292	69 481	25 758	29 000	16 299	34 735	1 110	83.3	6.9	53.6
Pasco	6 289	64 087	13 480	3 575	15 631	2 509	2 711	1 464	22 846	1 222	75.1	4.3	50.7
Pinellas	25 825	434 866	56 097	42 580	54 034	26 438	24 932	13 000	29 894	111	93.7	0.0	41.4
Polk	9 606	155 412	18 491	16 461	23 562	11 712	5 822	4 269	27 466	3 114	65.1	6.0	52.1
Putnam	1 244	12 668	2 189	2 437	2 606	450	261	304	24 017	466	66.5	7.9	48.7
St. Johns	3 551	38 908	4 897	2 151	7 248	1 212	1 494	955	24 543	204	62.3	14.2	52.0
St. Lucie	3 859	41 422	7 570	2 620	7 490	1 400	1 917	1 031	24 894	477	53.7	13.6	55.6
Santa Rosa	1 976	18 921	2 432	1 250	3 849	520	811	401	21 193	505	60.2	8.7	52.5

Table B. States and Counties — **Agriculture**

STATE County	Land in farms					Value of land and buildings (dollars)		Value of machinery and equipment average per farm (dollars)	Value of products sold				Percent of farms with sales of —		Government payments	
	Acreage (1,000)	Percent change, 1997–2002	Acres			Average per farm	Average per acre		Total (mil dol)	Average per farm (dollars)	Percent from —		$10,000 or more	$100,000 or more	Total ($1,000)	Percent of farms
			Average size of farm	Total irrigated (1,000)	Total cropland (1,000)						Crops	Live-stock and poultry products				
	117	118	119	120	121	122	123	124	125	126	127	128	129	130	131	132
DELAWARE	540	-6.9	226	97	457	980 323	4 054	113 755	619	258 826	24.3	75.7	63.2	42.8	8 643	25.8
Kent	185	-5.1	257	29	160	905 260	3 498	127 089	129	178 468	42.3	57.7	53.0	28.7	2 930	32.7
New Castle	71	-7.8	199	3	60	1 331 761	5 681	91 665	27	76 384	84.5	15.5	39.9	11.2	1 322	24.9
Sussex	284	-7.8	216	65	238	926 312	3 951	112 411	463	352 769	15.7	84.3	75.1	59.2	4 391	22.3
DISTRICT OF COLUMBIA	NA	NA	NA	NA	NA	NA	NA	NA	NA	NA	NA	NA	NA	NA	NA	NA
District of Columbia	NA	NA	NA	NA	NA	NA	NA	NA	NA	NA	NA	NA	NA	NA	NA	NA
FLORIDA	10 415	-0.4	236	1 815	3 715	665 376	2 836	39 884	6 242	141 609	80.8	19.2	36.6	11.6	21 818	5.8
Alachua	223	12.6	149	13	80	486 109	3 222	23 887	59	39 293	64.1	35.9	27.3	6.0	567	6.2
Baker	18	38.5	89	1	4	309 168	3 954	27 867	25	124 634	37.4	62.6	28.4	12.7	D	D
Bay	11	57.1	94	0	3	243 482	2 626	20 307	2	18 592	87.2	12.7	15.5	3.4	D	D
Bradford	45	2.3	119	0	18	267 420	2 485	15 821	18	47 388	9.3	90.7	23.5	7.9	42	1.9
Brevard	188	-32.1	338	25	23	783 045	2 385	42 237	42	75 961	83.7	16.3	39.8	9.4	52	1.1
Broward	24	-22.6	48	5	7	450 331	20 423	30 471	50	100 455	89.9	10.1	43.9	10.3	163	1.6
Calhoun	49	11.4	325	2	24	485 551	1 596	59 619	14	95 300	91.4	8.6	35.1	8.6	1 046	29.1
Charlotte	192	-33.8	674	25	42	1 171 466	1 726	50 286	48	170 079	88.3	11.7	38.0	14.1	D	D
Citrus	47	-4.1	109	1	12	309 677	2 498	28 773	7	15 293	71.2	28.8	19.4	2.3	57	2.5
Clay	79	11.3	231	1	8	558 561	2 482	19 017	37	108 975	10.2	89.8	13.8	5.3	4	1.5
Collier	181	-34.7	662	55	91	1 652 022	2 660	123 655	268	980 353	98.6	1.4	56.4	29.3	D	D
Columbia	90	-7.2	131	2	27	285 920	1 515	15 318	47	67 976	17.0	83.0	17.6	4.8	168	8.0
De Soto	388	20.5	337	79	115	786 445	2 415	38 912	180	156 198	83.5	16.5	57.4	12.7	D	D
Dixie	31	-8.8	145	2	8	275 161	1 803	23 950	7	30 427	D	D	15.8	3.3	178	8.8
Duval	31	-13.9	82	2	11	496 454	6 061	34 711	22	58 775	31.2	68.8	14.9	5.8	74	2.4
Escambia	65	18.2	96	2	39	337 473	2 383	19 225	16	23 258	66.2	33.8	21.5	4.6	2 473	20.2
Flagler	68	-22.7	684	4	8	1 085 977	1 634	57 382	24	237 894	93.9	6.2	39.0	20.0	D	D
Franklin	D	D	D	0	D	356 396	1 165	30 118	0	19 257	0.0	100.0	65.0	0.0	D	D
Gadsden	68	17.2	199	4	15	550 780	2 421	38 211	91	266 404	98.8	1.2	24.8	5.0	148	18.4
Gilchrist	81	3.8	200	4	27	374 556	2 322	47 219	45	109 210	13.9	86.1	27.0	7.1	463	15.9
Glades	408	7.4	1 766	49	73	3 158 103	1 849	64 930	72	311 966	72.8	27.2	45.9	20.8	D	D
Gulf	5	25.0	151	0	1	301 835	1 886	14 707	0	16 308	D	D	26.7	3.3	0	0.0
Hamilton	52	-21.2	218	5	17	431 687	1 419	43 371	12	50 914	52.9	47.1	33.9	6.3	211	22.6
Hardee	346	0.0	303	57	116	718 746	2 341	40 190	166	145 537	78.0	22.0	60.2	18.1	230	2.0
Hendry	552	-8.8	1 211	206	296	4 518 569	3 846	123 636	376	824 149	95.0	5.0	50.9	28.3	85	1.3
Hernando	65	22.6	106	1	24	429 492	5 093	51 371	22	35 183	37.7	62.3	22.2	3.2	128	2.3
Highlands	577	17.8	557	99	169	1 206 393	2 256	48 988	236	228 024	86.8	13.2	53.8	18.6	135	1.2
Hillsborough	285	14.9	96	43	126	454 871	5 410	42 898	392	132 176	85.0	15.0	34.7	11.0	527	1.5
Holmes	91	3.4	135	1	37	223 042	1 610	26 081	30	44 975	9.7	90.3	27.5	10.0	908	27.2
Indian River	191	13.7	399	95	103	1 146 115	2 969	41 314	117	243 569	94.3	5.7	59.8	21.9	78	2.7
Jackson	227	-7.3	247	13	114	400 313	1 478	47 604	36	39 641	68.1	31.9	33.3	8.2	3 158	38.8
Jefferson	133	4.7	318	4	30	584 211	1 850	44 245	21	50 608	44.0	56.0	23.0	4.5	606	26.3
Lafayette	92	-1.1	472	4	17	619 141	1 343	66 413	48	246 751	7.0	93.0	42.6	28.2	382	17.4
Lake	180	-2.7	100	20	74	447 801	4 290	26 616	178	99 041	93.4	6.6	40.3	10.2	103	0.8
Lee	126	-2.3	197	24	36	726 318	3 293	62 165	113	176 370	96.2	3.8	35.3	11.4	86	2.3
Leon	74	8.8	263	3	11	530 636	2 085	26 624	7	23 699	66.6	33.5	16.4	2.8	201	11.7
Levy	180	14.6	201	20	70	367 195	1 899	31 845	83	92 782	31.2	68.8	31.4	8.9	708	6.4
Liberty	10	42.9	148	D	1	199 919	1 366	22 610	1	22 339	D	D	50.7	3.0	D	D
Madison	157	18.9	297	4	42	408 912	1 536	46 232	25	46 587	40.9	59.1	29.3	8.1	605	22.1
Manatee	301	12.3	354	55	117	1 086 878	3 142	50 879	268	315 118	92.0	8.0	46.2	15.8	112	0.8
Marion	271	1.9	92	6	87	443 694	4 992	27 589	88	29 874	20.9	79.1	19.6	4.3	362	1.1
Martin	206	12.0	493	56	98	1 179 554	2 604	52 195	128	305 395	78.0	22.0	42.6	15.8	700	2.9
Miami-Dade	90	5.9	40	44	67	545 496	9 726	42 997	578	257 576	99.2	0.8	55.5	18.0	136	1.2
Monroe	0	-100.0	6	D	0	104 627	20 695	31 217	3	140 738	26.5	73.5	72.2	27.8	0	0.0
Nassau	D	D	D	0	5	412 099	4 773	17 452	27	87 291	7.8	92.2	21.0	11.4	D	D
Okaloosa	55	7.8	119	0	20	292 073	2 539	70 199	7	14 065	54.7	45.3	16.1	2.6	418	21.9
Okeechobee	392	0.0	615	22	115	1 263 840	2 037	32 721	144	226 295	25.4	74.6	38.7	13.2	405	3.6
Orange	147	-16.0	163	15	25	634 638	3 931	49 786	243	269 354	98.7	1.3	50.7	23.4	45	1.7
Osceola	653	6.9	1 258	19	76	2 067 337	1 690	72 904	65	125 128	67.7	32.3	41.6	16.8	186	1.9
Palm Beach	536	-11.4	483	418	481	1 623 283	3 348	60 546	760	684 565	99.1	0.9	42.6	22.0	299	1.4
Pasco	169	4.3	138	12	53	570 545	3 863	22 407	84	68 904	41.1	58.9	26.8	6.1	213	1.6
Pinellas	2	0.0	14	0	D	362 615	31 732	32 118	8	71 710	95.8	4.2	38.7	7.2	18	3.6
Polk	627	1.0	201	116	190	588 641	2 899	36 440	285	91 454	87.5	12.5	55.2	16.4	200	1.0
Putnam	93	8.1	199	6	17	471 370	2 480	90 993	47	100 150	87.8	12.2	32.0	9.0	45	2.1
St. Johns	38	-24.0	185	22	25	808 080	4 315	106 149	60	292 552	95.4	4.6	39.2	23.5	16	2.0
St. Lucie	222	-2.2	464	103	119	1 564 070	3 239	58 765	128	268 149	87.8	12.2	61.0	26.8	93	1.7
Santa Rosa	84	-4.5	166	6	52	401 815	2 649	53 635	21	41 579	91.2	8.8	26.1	8.5	2 423	27.9

STATE County	Value of residential construction authorized by building permits, 2003		Wholesale trade, 1997				Retail trade,[1] 1997				Real estate and rental and leasing, 1997			
	New construction ($1,000)	Number of housing units	Number of establishments	Number of employees	Sales (mil dol)	Annual payroll (mil dol)	Number of establishments	Number of employees	Sales (mil dol)	Annual payroll (mil dol)	Number of establishments	Number of employees	Receipts (mil dol)	Annual payroll (mil dol)
	133	134	135	136	137	138	139	140	141	142	143	144	145	146
DELAWARE	790 664	7 760	906	13 509	12 585.5	619.5	3 736	47 116	8 237.0	798.7	1 101	5 243	5 006.5	118.3
Kent	230 804	2 167	110	D	D	D	594	7 864	1 325.4	128.3	128	506	49.4	8.0
New Castle	157 223	2 409	637	D	D	D	2 079	30 375	5 367.0	523.1	767	3 712	4 824.3	90.1
Sussex	402 637	3 184	159	1 435	481.2	35.9	1 063	8 877	1 544.5	147.4	206	1 025	132.7	20.1
DISTRICT OF COLUMBIA	95 696	1 427	348	5 008	3 918.6	223.0	2 075	19 608	2 788.8	351.5	934	7 725	1 354.2	275.4
District of Columbia	95 696	1 427	348	5 008	3 918.6	223.0	2 075	19 608	2 788.8	351.5	934	7 725	1 354.2	275.4
FLORIDA	28 351 596	213 567	31 214	296 139	187 079.9	9 678.2	66 643	841 814	151 191.2	14 169.5	20 388	118 086	15 360.4	2 652.2
Alachua	172 988	1 684	224	1 824	738.0	54.5	923	12 726	1 934.5	186.2	279	1 630	155.2	28.2
Baker	16 224	149	7	D	D	D	61	630	95.7	7.3	6	26	0.7	0.1
Bay	425 631	3 676	173	1 406	422.1	34.2	832	9 558	1 496.8	148.1	229	1 018	76.8	15.6
Bradford	6 933	93	20	78	31.1	1.7	94	930	151.7	12.7	13	38	3.5	0.4
Brevard	999 716	6 169	577	4 389	1 362.4	136.2	1 856	23 867	3 900.5	370.3	525	2 443	220.0	45.3
Broward	1 118 886	8 218	4 359	38 614	26 122.2	1 414.7	6 804	89 290	17 979.8	1 639.9	2 263	14 394	2 196.6	351.6
Calhoun	2 000	29	13	D	D	D	49	478	81.0	6.4	3	13	0.9	0.1
Charlotte	373 507	2 522	103	446	117.2	11.2	515	6 840	1 063.3	100.4	167	601	60.7	10.1
Citrus	314 355	1 850	88	383	90.4	7.1	429	5 049	800.6	71.8	107	343	33.6	5.7
Clay	291 609	2 553	104	503	220.6	12.7	516	6 956	1 100.5	106.0	114	561	62.3	11.5
Collier	977 445	5 820	350	2 076	813.8	63.0	1 343	15 366	2 627.1	274.1	509	2 874	305.2	66.0
Columbia	20 050	299	87	859	286.7	21.6	239	3 132	556.0	49.0	38	94	10.1	1.3
De Soto	11 134	95	19	D	D	D	81	937	197.0	14.9	20	61	5.7	0.8
Dixie	6 937	63	4	D	D	D	42	271	39.2	3.6	6	18	0.6	0.2
Duval	968 040	8 399	1 394	21 860	16 590.0	760.3	3 134	44 276	8 034.1	761.4	886	6 374	918.5	158.4
Escambia	280 686	2 942	388	4 769	1 616.0	128.3	1 301	16 602	2 874.7	261.4	292	1 292	131.8	22.7
Flagler	523 344	4 305	39	272	94.6	7.9	119	1 608	244.1	22.2	53	184	28.3	3.6
Franklin	39 886	195	26	309	64.1	4.4	69	389	57.0	5.6	14	85	6.5	1.4
Gadsden	19 855	128	21	D	D	D	157	1 228	179.8	16.2	15	59	4.0	0.8
Gilchrist	9 464	79	11	D	D	D	34	206	29.9	2.8	6	15	1.0	0.4
Glades	3 184	38	4	D	D	D	27	211	35.2	2.7	11	14	2.7	0.2
Gulf	27 683	181	8	24	28.2	0.6	60	404	48.9	4.7	8	18	1.5	0.2
Hamilton	5 753	62	5	D	D	D	55	393	53.6	4.3	3	33	0.5	0.3
Hardee	10 635	184	21	164	92.4	5.1	79	721	116.8	10.6	9	22	2.5	0.3
Hendry	12 553	96	23	D	D	D	104	1 030	202.6	16.8	22	50	6.8	0.7
Hernando	301 057	2 638	98	513	142.3	13.8	371	5 270	821.5	74.3	97	248	24.2	3.4
Highlands	87 674	731	85	618	184.1	13.1	349	4 035	618.2	57.1	75	249	25.0	3.8
Hillsborough	2 083 063	16 110	2 233	33 851	23 668.5	1 151.4	3 821	57 038	10 931.6	1 001.4	1 164	8 336	1 034.2	190.0
Holmes	5 641	69	11	D	D	D	55	327	46.3	3.9	6	13	0.9	0.2
Indian River	419 919	2 430	147	D	D	D	667	7 793	1 143.9	121.5	170	714	76.5	12.9
Jackson	12 320	121	42	301	86.0	7.1	221	2 289	376.9	31.6	27	48	4.5	0.7
Jefferson	9 304	78	10	D	D	D	55	426	51.5	4.3	5	19	1.1	0.2
Lafayette	2 522	23	9	D	D	D	17	93	10.0	1.2	2	D	D	D
Lake	621 746	5 163	229	2 137	680.2	48.2	760	9 663	1 514.3	148.2	217	930	82.0	17.3
Lee	1 994 695	15 675	586	4 593	1 450.3	135.3	1 924	25 417	4 367.0	430.5	642	3 328	461.1	72.2
Leon	301 413	2 858	260	D	D	D	1 038	15 478	2 244.4	229.7	301	1 835	202.3	33.1
Levy	20 126	156	21	141	37.7	2.2	132	1 455	234.5	19.2	24	61	4.1	0.8
Liberty	2 559	26	1	D	D	D	17	83	11.9	1.2	1	D	D	D
Madison	6 841	67	15	128	60.9	2.3	72	567	64.1	6.6	8	25	1.7	0.4
Manatee	645 115	3 576	270	2 348	1 087.6	76.5	938	12 165	2 141.0	194.4	265	1 002	158.6	19.4
Marion	779 354	6 475	309	3 219	999.6	80.0	1 014	13 159	2 221.4	202.1	244	786	88.4	13.8
Martin	377 023	2 006	174	695	423.8	23.7	712	8 425	1 454.0	147.5	211	986	118.6	27.7
Miami-Dade	1 697 336	15 533	8 935	70 050	43 604.4	2 235.9	9 814	110 292	20 720.6	1 995.8	3 378	19 793	2 853.9	465.8
Monroe	75 122	430	131	870	217.5	19.5	707	6 246	914.2	99.5	254	952	108.4	16.1
Nassau	137 938	799	40	238	158.4	8.9	215	2 172	332.2	28.6	43	130	28.0	2.7
Okaloosa	298 170	1 749	139	959	248.3	23.9	931	11 322	1 754.9	165.7	280	1 582	140.3	29.0
Okeechobee	14 513	171	31	D	D	D	149	1 657	270.1	23.6	29	70	8.2	1.5
Orange	1 631 140	13 950	1 931	25 730	24 089.1	868.5	3 911	53 854	10 450.9	913.6	1 309	14 060	1 952.2	345.5
Osceola	753 591	5 515	108	1 499	1 070.1	41.3	612	8 289	1 349.7	124.8	234	2 884	274.7	60.4
Palm Beach	2 481 609	15 844	2 187	17 864	11 544.5	707.0	4 967	61 563	11 731.2	1 126.1	1 716	9 409	1 323.8	248.3
Pasco	917 858	6 990	243	1 378	351.6	34.1	1 055	14 200	2 247.1	212.5	260	979	116.1	16.9
Pinellas	455 614	3 543	1 730	17 616	11 558.7	609.3	3 895	51 843	10 183.9	911.4	1 238	5 676	630.5	112.9
Polk	566 697	6 823	639	8 329	4 176.2	212.7	1 816	22 751	3 844.3	360.9	431	2 001	217.3	39.8
Putnam	25 399	337	56	D	D	D	250	2 395	397.7	36.1	45	151	12.4	1.9
St. Johns	863 890	3 921	179	1 050	428.0	31.1	549	5 640	862.5	81.0	153	505	83.4	9.6
St. Lucie	782 332	7 684	198	2 262	581.5	53.8	610	7 644	1 387.2	125.1	178	652	85.9	12.1
Santa Rosa	238 691	1 859	82	296	103.1	7.1	319	3 615	561.1	44.2	97	333	27.6	5.1

1. Establishments with payroll.

Table B. States and Counties — Professional Services, Manufacturing, and Accommodation and Foodservices

STATE County	Professional, scientific, and technical services,[1] 1997				Manufacturing, 1997				Accommodation and foodservices, 1997			
	Number of establishments	Number of employees	Receipts (mil dol)	Annual payroll (mil dol)	Number of establishments	Number of employees	Receipts (mil dol)	Annual payroll (mil dol)	Number of establishments	Number of employees	Sales (mil dol)	Annual payroll (mil dol)
	147	148	149	150	151	152	153	154	155	156	157	158
DELAWARE	1 717	12 382	1 430.4	553.4	675	41 084	13 397.3	1 474.3	1 605	26 969	1 009.0	280.8
Kent	155	1 091	69.4	30.3	82	7 985	1 965.5	209.8	234	3 796	118.4	31.9
New Castle	1 368	10 597	1 314.2	503.2	458	22 610	8 735.0	1 000.1	929	17 837	656.1	187.4
Sussex	194	694	46.8	20.0	135	10 489	2 696.8	264.4	442	5 336	234.5	61.5
DISTRICT OF COLUMBIA	3 760	61 123	10 365.2	3 935.5	200	2 858	320.2	101.1	1 700	42 650	2 263.5	701.4
District of Columbia	3 760	61 123	10 365.2	3 935.5	200	2 858	320.2	101.1	1 700	42 650	2 263.5	701.4
FLORIDA	42 403	276 263	27 231.1	10 803.5	15 992	433 149	77 477.5	13 185.1	28 999	608 834	24 165.3	6 239.5
Alachua	570	3 788	292.8	126.4	151	5 251	1 010.3	157.1	431	8 981	263.0	67.8
Baker	8	32	1.0	0.4	NA	NA	NA	NA	18	380	9.8	2.4
Bay	268	1 730	138.9	56.1	136	3 492	719.0	108.7	483	9 268	336.3	84.8
Bradford	22	72	4.8	1.9	15	698	44.1	10.7	28	698	17.3	4.8
Brevard	1 073	11 192	1 195.6	455.0	494	20 832	3 450.7	753.9	860	16 207	495.3	136.3
Broward	5 625	27 496	2 940.7	1 103.7	1 967	37 134	5 788.3	1 115.4	3 206	61 243	2 474.5	615.5
Calhoun	11	34	1.5	0.5	NA	NA	NA	NA	13	120	4.1	1.1
Charlotte	194	1 083	73.3	37.3	74	587	77.7	13.8	218	3 935	123.5	31.9
Citrus	136	602	38.8	16.0	58	1 025	92.4	18.2	166	2 393	66.3	19.0
Clay	188	685	51.8	19.8	74	1 579	247.2	43.7	195	3 990	114.6	32.7
Collier	743	3 074	414.1	196.5	205	2 305	259.0	62.4	518	11 599	536.7	140.9
Columbia	67	287	21.3	7.8	35	1 798	244.5	46.3	99	2 118	54.1	14.8
De Soto	21	83	4.1	2.0	NA	NA	NA	NA	33	412	12.4	3.0
Dixie	8	14	0.9	0.2	NA	NA	NA	NA	22	152	3.5	0.9
Duval	1 959	17 491	1 552.9	690.0	754	28 237	7 231.0	944.1	1 420	28 354	917.2	244.2
Escambia	547	3 956	306.0	132.3	236	7 526	2 214.1	294.6	493	11 101	350.9	92.3
Flagler	70	242	20.1	7.5	42	1 560	260.7	45.9	88	1 465	42.4	12.8
Franklin	14	48	2.4	0.8	NA	NA	NA	NA	43	393	14.9	3.4
Gadsden	39	133	8.1	2.4	32	1 399	187.8	32.3	39	321	10.7	2.6
Gilchrist	10	38	1.8	0.7	NA	NA	NA	NA	16	D	D	D
Glades	9	34	2.2	0.7	NA	NA	NA	NA	20	129	4.7	1.0
Gulf	15	147	7.5	2.8	12	D	D	D	21	155	4.6	1.2
Hamilton	7	D	D	D	4	D	D	D	13	161	3.7	0.9
Hardee	22	69	3.1	1.4	NA	NA	NA	NA	17	225	7.4	1.6
Hendry	23	71	3.9	1.8	22	724	437.7	26.8	48	644	18.4	5.0
Hernando	132	523	33.0	11.4	72	1 192	235.2	29.4	184	2 772	74.0	19.9
Highlands	106	410	23.4	9.8	54	1 199	191.6	27.0	118	1 817	52.3	13.8
Hillsborough	3 050	34 249	3 859.1	1 403.9	960	30 861	6 019.8	859.3	1 552	34 618	1 248.3	330.4
Holmes	14	53	2.6	0.9	NA	NA	NA	NA	13	160	4.5	1.2
Indian River	281	1 296	103.1	43.3	116	1 825	219.8	55.4	204	3 527	112.4	31.6
Jackson	35	177	11.6	4.6	26	1 344	182.1	27.3	58	931	26.0	7.6
Jefferson	16	36	2.7	0.6	NA	NA	NA	NA	13	121	3.4	0.9
Lafayette	6	D	D	D	NA	NA	NA	NA	13	94	3.1	0.7
Lake	313	1 397	87.7	37.2	164	3 730	578.5	90.2	291	5 161	154.6	42.4
Lee	997	6 053	458.2	197.4	357	5 363	741.8	141.1	824	17 424	699.1	175.2
Leon	838	6 865	702.3	292.9	127	2 676	557.6	68.0	456	9 884	296.8	77.1
Levy	30	104	5.9	2.1	NA	NA	NA	NA	57	809	19.5	5.1
Liberty	1	D	D	D	NA	NA	NA	NA	3	D	D	D
Madison	13	64	3.3	1.2	11	1 114	270.3	25.8	29	433	9.9	2.4
Manatee	445	1 884	147.8	56.1	284	11 156	2 115.7	348.4	390	7 480	241.5	64.5
Marion	361	1 882	132.9	52.8	215	9 620	1 287.8	238.0	363	6 558	200.9	54.1
Martin	409	1 598	141.8	55.5	172	3 274	555.2	101.7	258	4 676	167.8	46.4
Miami-Dade	7 821	42 781	4 640.0	1 856.0	3 031	66 391	8 523.9	1 663.8	3 835	75 597	3 199.5	878.5
Monroe	262	835	72.1	26.6	NA	NA	NA	NA	567	10 939	569.1	151.3
Nassau	65	256	25.9	11.7	34	1 790	630.6	77.3	100	3 102	143.3	37.4
Okaloosa	417	3 181	264.0	113.5	133	3 448	296.5	81.5	401	8 450	261.7	73.0
Okeechobee	28	142	5.9	2.2	NA	NA	NA	NA	60	988	34.8	8.9
Orange	2 878	25 810	2 679.2	1 077.7	889	32 437	5 786.6	1 213.4	1 720	73 124	4 058.7	962.7
Osceola	172	758	50.3	18.8	77	1 295	379.9	37.1	423	12 152	763.0	152.2
Palm Beach	4 211	21 787	2 352.0	985.5	1 051	26 262	6 344.5	1 138.1	2 087	41 031	1 659.8	440.9
Pasco	417	1 931	107.1	41.6	213	4 091	713.3	100.7	437	7 654	246.3	62.6
Pinellas	2 799	26 125	2 187.0	861.6	1 335	40 954	5 732.8	1 256.8	1 965	36 685	1 383.4	367.6
Polk	712	4 006	347.6	135.4	480	20 627	5 999.9	633.5	711	13 383	419.3	113.2
Putnam	67	171	10.8	3.5	48	2 556	730.2	88.9	88	1 318	37.5	9.8
St. Johns	294	961	96.9	34.7	88	2 277	299.6	53.8	332	6 999	263.6	71.1
St. Lucie	257	1 442	91.6	38.6	124	2 230	542.7	60.1	245	3 959	147.6	36.6
Santa Rosa	122	490	34.0	11.4	59	1 895	427.7	41.6	119	1 970	53.8	14.6

1. Firms subject to federal tax.

STATE County	Health care and social assistance,[1] 1997				Other services,[1] 1997				Federal funds and grants, 2002–2003 Expenditures (mil dol)			
										Direct payments for individuals[2]		
	Number of establishments	Number of employees	Receipts (mil dol)	Annual payroll (mil dol)	Number of establishments	Number of employees	Receipts (mil dol)	Annual payroll (mil dol)	Total	Social Security and government retirement	Medicare	Food stamps and Supplemental Security Income
	159	160	161	162	163	164	165	166	167	168	169	170
DELAWARE	1 465	15 980	1 131.6	526.4	1 198	7 006	420.5	140.7	5 060.9	1 881.0	698.3	111.8
Kent	192	2 157	137.6	59.6	215	1 016	56.0	16.8	1 158.7	359.0	86.2	22.0
New Castle	1 016	11 380	846.6	398.1	768	5 051	311.5	108.2	2 618.3	998.5	435.2	69.2
Sussex	257	2 443	147.4	68.6	215	939	53.0	15.7	936.2	523.5	176.9	20.6
DISTRICT OF COLUMBIA	1 464	13 692	1 054.8	476.7	978	6 218	404.8	111.1	34 749.8	1 826.3	770.7	198.1
District of Columbia	1 464	13 692	1 054.8	476.7	978	6 218	404.8	111.1	34 749.8	1 826.3	770.7	198.1
FLORIDA	35 568	447 117	32 559.1	13 610.7	26 121	146 360	9 123.6	2 665.7	113 340.8	43 198.3	22 773.6	2 981.3
Alachua	502	6 499	435.3	201.2	318	1 631	94.1	28.0	1 358.9	414.4	174.8	37.8
Baker	21	299	12.4	4.9	19	57	3.9	0.8	97.0	50.6	16.9	4.3
Bay	317	4 398	315.8	131.2	246	1 569	85.5	27.6	1 324.0	523.6	158.1	27.6
Bradford	27	609	22.2	9.6	17	116	7.4	1.8	130.8	55.8	27.3	5.4
Brevard	1 017	10 631	783.2	358.0	728	3 778	206.4	63.8	5 545.5	1 856.5	608.2	64.6
Broward	4 226	51 708	3 879.0	1 603.0	3 246	19 188	1 397.3	373.4	8 104.9	3 341.6	2 761.4	225.9
Calhoun	13	49	3.0	1.0	8	32	1.6	0.4	74.2	28.4	14.6	2.9
Charlotte	305	4 286	306.9	134.7	189	674	37.4	10.2	970.8	611.9	290.4	12.4
Citrus	228	3 228	205.1	85.0	150	525	29.0	7.5	823.5	525.0	226.8	16.0
Clay	250	3 913	260.4	97.6	193	970	47.8	14.3	664.0	478.7	89.2	11.4
Collier	492	5 124	404.9	175.0	431	2 035	109.6	34.8	1 224.6	761.3	273.8	17.1
Columbia	108	1 406	88.1	35.3	59	227	15.9	3.7	360.1	154.6	57.9	16.9
De Soto	37	253	14.8	5.2	26	100	5.1	1.2	149.1	64.3	48.2	6.0
Dixie	6	60	2.2	1.0	7	31	2.0	0.5	79.1	40.1	15.2	5.5
Duval	1 579	23 107	1 729.8	810.5	1 448	9 054	604.7	184.3	6 739.9	1 803.0	754.7	149.6
Escambia	535	9 282	658.6	301.3	437	3 132	176.5	64.3	2 700.2	1 008.7	292.6	71.5
Flagler	62	305	21.3	9.8	47	167	10.0	2.2	341.9	255.6	58.1	4.1
Franklin	15	279	8.9	4.0	8	15	1.1	0.2	65.7	28.5	17.8	1.9
Gadsden	26	156	11.5	3.8	37	149	7.3	2.3	268.1	89.5	45.7	17.2
Gilchrist	7	21	1.3	0.4	3	D	D	D	60.9	36.3	12.1	1.3
Glades	2	D	D	D	7	24	2.2	0.9	28.8	16.3	7.3	0.3
Gulf	16	370	20.3	8.3	19	46	3.0	0.5	89.8	43.4	23.3	2.8
Hamilton	14	188	9.0	4.3	12	28	1.9	0.3	68.6	28.7	12.1	2.5
Hardee	27	554	21.9	10.7	22	70	4.0	1.0	115.2	45.7	25.2	8.8
Hendry	28	311	12.7	5.5	29	179	7.4	3.0	144.2	53.7	28.1	10.4
Hernando	252	2 630	181.1	84.2	193	756	38.6	10.8	1 020.7	617.2	299.8	20.2
Highlands	184	1 759	134.0	47.2	110	431	21.1	5.4	624.1	351.7	180.2	13.5
Hillsborough	2 233	29 728	2 295.7	905.7	1 590	10 820	700.2	209.4	6 114.1	2 171.5	1 004.5	215.2
Holmes	16	367	25.3	7.2	8	38	2.7	0.8	134.7	58.7	25.4	6.5
Indian River	287	3 388	263.7	96.4	206	944	45.4	13.7	832.3	464.7	240.3	10.4
Jackson	62	701	36.8	14.0	51	218	13.1	3.4	359.8	121.4	55.0	13.1
Jefferson	12	77	3.8	1.2	11	30	1.0	0.2	89.4	30.6	12.7	4.6
Lafayette	4	D	D	D	5	31	2.3	0.4	24.2	11.3	4.8	1.4
Lake	376	3 834	244.4	107.5	300	1 353	71.9	21.3	1 589.6	1 025.7	354.7	30.9
Lee	825	12 968	954.5	408.4	695	3 599	224.9	68.5	2 615.3	1 516.2	674.0	47.8
Leon	441	6 479	459.0	210.2	390	2 563	144.2	46.7	3 668.7	638.4	130.0	38.1
Levy	33	534	23.8	7.8	32	108	5.9	1.5	198.5	101.6	39.5	8.6
Liberty	8	156	4.5	2.2	2	D	D	D	33.3	13.2	5.9	1.5
Madison	16	179	6.9	3.2	22	93	4.8	1.5	117.3	42.6	21.1	6.1
Manatee	472	9 114	634.7	243.7	316	1 565	84.9	25.8	1 434.3	808.9	378.6	30.9
Marion	466	6 512	466.6	185.9	369	1 680	93.9	29.4	1 647.3	987.0	364.1	48.0
Martin	317	3 142	231.3	101.1	244	1 045	63.9	18.9	855.5	499.1	231.3	10.8
Miami-Dade	6 157	60 718	4 782.5	1 877.5	3 901	22 435	1 391.0	385.8	14 036.7	3 253.7	3 662.8	854.9
Monroe	162	1 416	105.1	40.0	183	674	46.5	11.3	628.1	226.6	93.2	9.3
Nassau	56	683	38.0	16.4	79	321	19.9	6.2	339.9	170.3	46.3	4.9
Okaloosa	356	5 134	412.2	142.7	313	1 531	86.3	25.5	2 939.9	770.1	134.5	16.9
Okeechobee	68	1 153	75.0	27.1	46	184	13.2	3.2	205.9	97.9	65.5	7.9
Orange	1 792	22 044	1 627.8	774.0	1 494	11 286	713.7	216.5	6 183.0	1 709.6	800.3	163.4
Osceola	252	4 024	241.3	103.8	207	923	55.6	16.4	636.9	357.3	159.0	30.5
Palm Beach	3 280	39 623	2 981.7	1 257.5	2 113	11 678	726.5	209.6	6 913.2	3 385.4	2 101.1	120.4
Pasco	676	12 112	849.4	342.5	443	2 124	112.6	31.9	2 138.5	1 117.7	728.8	46.9
Pinellas	2 633	36 006	2 496.2	1 052.0	1 746	9 799	614.7	189.1	6 907.8	3 030.5	1 855.9	130.9
Polk	643	9 886	657.7	279.4	611	3 224	199.6	60.6	2 549.2	1 325.8	538.7	100.5
Putnam	93	1 961	120.3	47.7	74	342	21.5	5.8	427.2	200.7	98.6	21.9
St. Johns	249	2 057	152.3	66.9	139	658	42.5	12.3	755.9	374.6	129.5	12.6
St. Lucie	360	7 250	525.1	193.7	273	1 181	74.2	19.9	1 222.9	699.8	311.7	37.0
Santa Rosa	127	1 881	90.2	42.8	120	540	33.9	9.3	801.4	414.5	82.5	12.4

1. Firms subject to federal tax.   2. State totals may include programs not allocated by county.

STATE County	Salaries and wages	Defense	Other	Medicaid and other health-related	Nutrition and family welfare	Education	Other	Total (mil dol)	Intergovernmental (mil dol)	Total (mil dol)	Total	Property
	171	172	173	174	175	176	177	178	179	180	181	182
DELAWARE	489.1	164.3	80.5	475.5	144.8	114.6	445.8	X	X	X	X	X
Kent	250.0	125.4	8.3	83.0	13.0	66.9	124.8	313.3	209.7	51.1	390	357
New Castle	207.1	36.8	64.8	302.3	84.1	22.5	276.9	1 185.7	526.4	366.0	714	551
Sussex	32.0	2.2	7.4	90.3	11.5	17.0	33.0	389.8	223.0	96.4	588	432
DISTRICT OF COLUMBIA	14 760.0	1 753.1	9 622.8	1 415.5	291.2	316.2	2 287.4	X	X	X	X	X
District of Columbia	14 760.0	1 753.1	9 622.8	1 415.5	291.2	316.2	2 287.4	6 922.3	2 840.1	3 227.9	5 654	1 407
FLORIDA	9 745.9	7 998.7	2 900.3	8 388.3	2 576.4	1 704.1	4 794.4	X	X	X	X	X
Alachua	183.6	10.7	39.1	238.8	36.2	23.0	153.8	576.0	236.7	187.4	843	732
Baker	3.3	0.0	0.8	9.1	3.2	2.1	3.7	68.1	41.8	11.7	512	338
Bay	337.5	160.8	32.8	62.3	21.1	15.0	-26.3	581.6	172.5	145.7	959	630
Bradford	13.9	0.6	0.8	18.9	3.9	1.6	2.2	48.0	26.0	14.6	553	403
Brevard	432.8	1 315.8	1 016.1	88.6	37.1	24.3	79.0	1 320.3	486.6	408.5	824	650
Broward	495.5	233.2	154.2	352.9	114.7	79.0	241.6	6 696.1	1 713.2	2 278.7	1 333	1 060
Calhoun	1.4	0.0	0.5	16.5	2.9	1.1	1.3	27.5	19.2	5.7	454	286
Charlotte	18.1	0.1	4.9	9.4	9.2	4.5	7.0	373.9	76.3	176.8	1 189	823
Citrus	12.5	0.2	3.5	19.8	7.8	5.6	5.3	255.3	90.2	101.3	819	747
Clay	29.9	3.4	4.5	18.4	7.0	7.2	9.1	327.6	136.9	114.8	755	526
Collier	40.4	7.1	27.1	37.5	28.4	8.6	16.7	779.6	148.9	427.6	1 545	1 373
Columbia	53.2	0.7	6.8	41.3	10.8	5.4	7.9	142.5	71.5	38.4	662	422
De Soto	2.8	0.0	0.6	14.1	4.8	3.1	0.8	64.1	31.7	20.9	636	461
Dixie	1.1	4.6	0.2	7.8	2.6	1.2	0.3	30.0	18.0	7.3	521	406
Duval	1 722.4	847.0	196.4	435.2	122.8	67.7	568.8	2 272.8	774.2	878.4	1 090	793
Escambia	715.7	192.4	45.0	177.1	55.4	26.0	75.9	839.2	316.6	233.8	787	532
Flagler	7.5	0.0	5.3	4.1	2.8	1.7	1.7	120.0	34.0	59.0	1 028	849
Franklin	1.8	0.1	0.6	10.7	1.9	0.9	0.5	32.0	12.8	13.2	1 307	1 190
Gadsden	7.4	1.6	1.4	61.5	18.2	6.6	15.8	107.9	71.3	22.5	498	341
Gilchrist	1.6	0.0	0.6	5.2	1.6	0.8	0.3	29.9	18.3	7.6	517	418
Glades	0.5	0.1	0.2	1.5	0.9	0.7	0.3	21.7	8.1	10.5	975	677
Gulf	0.9	0.0	0.2	13.0	4.6	1.1	0.2	38.7	16.7	15.2	1 029	950
Hamilton	1.8	0.0	0.5	15.4	3.3	2.1	0.8	82.3	44.2	32.8	2 394	899
Hardee	3.2	0.3	0.6	16.7	5.3	2.2	2.0	63.5	34.3	20.0	730	584
Hendry	5.0	5.2	0.7	13.0	6.2	2.6	9.5	120.5	46.8	37.4	1 014	835
Hernando	20.6	2.2	4.9	21.2	16.7	5.7	9.6	426.3	135.7	203.5	1 470	1 408
Highlands	16.0	4.5	4.3	28.2	8.6	5.6	3.2	200.6	84.1	67.1	746	579
Hillsborough	913.7	590.2	153.5	540.8	135.0	88.7	210.6	3 477.9	1 285.5	1 197.9	1 137	874
Holmes	3.4	0.3	1.3	26.2	4.8	1.7	0.5	47.6	30.9	6.3	338	246
Indian River	25.6	33.5	6.1	22.4	10.2	5.2	10.5	335.0	68.4	175.5	1 487	1 204
Jackson	29.9	0.1	2.5	74.2	9.6	3.6	13.9	158.5	70.4	23.7	510	281
Jefferson	2.1	0.0	0.7	22.1	3.4	1.9	9.1	28.8	16.1	8.4	615	454
Lafayette	0.9	0.1	0.2	3.2	0.9	0.4	-0.4	12.3	7.4	3.1	446	370
Lake	31.7	12.3	27.1	48.4	18.5	14.0	19.0	523.9	170.7	198.0	847	588
Lee	126.7	10.8	29.9	86.4	35.5	20.4	46.4	2 118.3	519.6	618.3	1 300	1 123
Leon	121.9	43.7	36.3	497.0	493.0	594.6	935.5	771.2	281.7	239.7	982	678
Levy	5.4	0.1	1.2	18.2	4.8	4.6	3.4	78.8	40.4	24.7	686	502
Liberty	2.0	0.0	1.0	7.1	1.1	0.7	0.7	14.8	10.5	2.6	373	332
Madison	2.6	0.3	0.6	31.7	4.7	2.4	2.4	53.1	29.9	13.8	753	373
Manatee	66.7	6.9	16.2	57.5	23.7	15.1	12.1	806.3	251.6	281.3	1 003	859
Marion	40.9	8.3	18.8	94.1	35.3	15.2	21.6	601.0	256.6	174.7	641	543
Martin	17.8	21.3	19.1	18.2	9.5	5.3	16.6	400.3	87.5	216.9	1 640	1 553
Miami-Dade	1 205.6	174.8	281.6	3 318.4	369.9	151.2	486.9	9 594.8	3 185.1	2 965.2	1 271	950
Monroe	110.8	113.4	12.3	34.1	7.1	3.8	15.3	394.0	100.0	170.9	2 154	1 698
Nassau	81.7	4.3	1.9	19.9	5.4	2.8	1.1	143.7	45.2	68.3	1 127	910
Okaloosa	915.2	930.7	25.6	48.8	17.4	16.2	48.7	428.4	190.3	142.4	810	675
Okeechobee	4.0	0.6	1.1	16.9	5.2	3.3	1.2	84.4	42.2	28.1	762	544
Orange	478.8	2 025.9	266.5	266.6	87.2	56.2	251.2	3 873.7	1 034.8	1 322.5	1 397	1 054
Osceola	19.1	2.4	5.1	19.0	10.7	8.6	22.8	561.8	188.4	212.1	1 115	784
Palm Beach	356.3	114.4	125.7	240.5	87.1	47.9	284.7	4 338.5	1 004.3	2 096.5	1 761	1 477
Pasco	53.5	6.7	13.1	67.1	31.7	15.5	35.9	717.1	308.3	225.7	608	543
Pinellas	418.3	712.6	171.5	232.3	78.3	56.4	181.2	2 723.3	785.0	1 113.8	1 202	906
Polk	86.0	18.3	21.3	176.3	66.8	35.3	149.2	1 170.9	487.4	363.3	729	593
Putnam	7.9	0.3	1.9	52.2	16.2	7.2	12.9	324.0	156.4	120.0	1 689	1 613
St. Johns	25.8	70.7	4.5	36.3	8.9	6.7	80.6	372.2	106.2	157.4	1 157	1 040
St. Lucie	36.8	4.3	13.6	50.1	21.2	15.6	19.2	598.3	200.4	215.9	1 051	897
Santa Rosa	92.2	88.0	6.0	34.1	13.1	6.8	34.7	233.6	116.4	75.2	591	510

1. State totals may include programs not allocated by county.   2. Based on the resident population estimated as of July 1 of the year shown.

Table B. States and Counties — Local Government Finances, Government Employment, and Elections

STATE County	Local government finances, 2002 (cont'd) Direct general expenditure — Total (mil dol)	Per capita[1] (dollars)	Percent of total for — Education	Health and hospitals	Police protection	Public welfare	Highways	Debt outstanding Total (mil dol)	Per capita[1] (dollars)	Government employment, 2002 Federal civilian	Federal military	State and local	Presidential election, 2004 Percent of vote cast — Democratic	Republican	All other
	183	184	185	186	187	188	189	190	191	192	193	194	195	196	197
DELAWARE	X	X	X	X	X	X	X	X	X	5 321	8 856	52 744	53.3	45.8	0.9
Kent	315.7	2 409	75.8	0.8	4.3	0.0	1.2	160.7	1 226	1 683	4 775	14 117	42.6	56.4	0.9
New Castle	1 270.8	2 480	55.4	0.6	7.4	0.0	9.5	1 083.4	2 114	3 113	3 098	32 215	60.5	38.6	0.9
Sussex	363.2	2 216	71.5	1.6	3.9	0.0	2.3	250.2	1 526	525	983	6 412	38.7	60.5	0.8
DISTRICT OF COLUMBIA	X	X	X	X	X	X	X	X	X	190 821	22 324	39 315	89.5	9.3	1.2
District of Columbia	6 179.6	10 824	19.0	9.0	6.2	23.7	1.1	5 436.1	9 522	190 821	22 324	39 315	89.5	9.3	1.2
FLORIDA	X	X	X	X	X	X	X	X	X	118 725	101 909	900 416	47.1	52.1	0.8
Alachua	595.4	2 679	46.4	1.2	8.7	0.2	3.4	830.5	3 737	3 115	408	39 870	56.2	42.9	1.0
Baker	61.7	2 707	61.9	2.8	4.0	0.1	3.9	27.6	1 212	80	34	2 430	21.6	76.6	1.8
Bay	580.7	3 823	37.9	24.1	5.8	0.5	4.3	461.8	3 040	3 018	4 644	7 466	28.1	71.2	0.7
Bradford	45.4	1 726	59.0	2.1	6.5	0.9	9.3	19.3	735	36	121	2 381	29.9	69.6	0.5
Brevard	1 298.3	2 620	40.8	9.6	5.9	0.5	4.3	1 287.0	2 597	5 505	3 171	21 641	41.6	57.7	0.8
Broward	6 697.0	3 918	32.1	21.9	8.6	0.7	2.2	6 304.7	3 689	7 191	2 956	86 715	64.3	34.5	1.2
Calhoun	26.9	2 142	52.8	0.1	9.5	1.1	14.9	2.0	157	26	19	917	35.5	63.4	1.1
Charlotte	351.7	2 365	37.1	1.4	7.5	0.8	12.7	271.3	1 825	254	227	4 944	42.9	55.7	1.4
Citrus	231.5	1 871	45.8	2.7	7.0	6.1	6.8	391.9	3 168	202	188	3 926	42.1	56.9	1.0
Clay	340.7	2 240	54.1	0.5	8.7	0.4	4.9	354.9	2 333	340	231	5 317	23.3	76.2	0.5
Collier	808.8	2 923	45.1	1.0	10.2	0.6	8.9	757.3	2 737	657	420	11 002	34.1	65.0	0.9
Columbia	142.1	2 448	58.0	2.7	5.3	0.2	5.1	68.5	1 181	1 010	90	4 322	32.1	67.1	0.8
De Soto	63.5	1 934	55.0	0.5	8.3	0.0	6.4	15.2	463	52	50	2 261	41.2	58.0	0.8
Dixie	29.7	2 112	55.8	3.5	4.9	0.2	5.1	3.5	251	17	21	1 004	30.4	68.8	0.7
Duval	2 489.8	3 089	39.9	1.8	6.4	1.3	2.1	7 217.6	8 954	15 781	25 566	34 799	41.7	57.7	0.6
Escambia	857.0	2 883	44.9	1.9	6.5	0.5	5.3	1 623.1	5 460	5 981	15 386	16 850	33.7	65.3	1.0
Flagler	121.2	2 113	48.9	2.5	7.7	0.7	5.1	94.5	1 648	110	87	2 260	48.3	51.0	0.7
Franklin	27.3	2 716	41.5	1.5	9.3	1.0	4.9	12.6	1 247	20	25	692	40.5	58.5	1.0
Gadsden	108.8	2 404	59.3	1.9	6.3	0.7	7.4	35.2	778	129	68	5 128	69.7	29.8	0.5
Gilchrist	31.2	2 123	55.8	2.6	6.1	0.0	7.6	8.2	555	31	22	1 078	28.8	70.4	0.9
Glades	22.2	2 055	37.5	6.8	11.8	0.4	9.7	0.0	0	11	16	369	41.0	58.4	0.6
Gulf	36.8	2 489	47.5	0.3	6.8	1.3	3.6	19.5	1 319	16	22	1 325	32.6	66.5	0.8
Hamilton	77.0	5 620	21.8	0.8	3.0	0.0	2.1	13.8	1 006	35	21	1 313	44.6	55.0	0.5
Hardee	60.9	2 227	59.3	2.9	6.3	0.1	6.9	17.5	640	51	41	1 633	29.6	69.7	0.7
Hendry	121.3	3 287	43.3	13.2	7.8	0.5	4.5	57.2	1 551	107	56	2 181	40.5	58.9	0.6
Hernando	403.2	2 911	31.2	1.2	4.6	0.0	4.1	394.6	2 850	326	210	5 059	46.0	53.1	0.9
Highlands	219.6	2 441	52.4	2.5	6.1	0.5	7.8	161.8	1 798	296	137	3 674	37.0	62.4	0.7
Hillsborough	3 252.4	3 086	44.9	0.8	6.7	2.6	3.6	5 465.7	5 186	11 224	7 481	61 073	46.2	53.0	0.8
Holmes	47.8	2 568	46.2	17.0	2.5	0.1	6.5	15.4	826	52	28	1 362	21.8	77.2	0.9
Indian River	303.2	2 569	39.5	2.8	9.1	0.6	5.8	325.3	2 757	393	178	4 678	39.0	60.1	0.8
Jackson	162.1	3 492	47.0	25.6	2.9	4.4	7.9	26.9	579	487	74	5 494	38.1	61.2	0.7
Jefferson	27.0	1 974	48.8	2.7	9.7	0.0	8.6	2.0	147	39	21	888	55.3	44.1	0.6
Lafayette	13.7	1 961	52.0	4.4	3.3	0.8	4.0	5.0	708	17	11	571	25.4	74.0	0.6
Lake	519.6	2 222	44.1	9.9	6.9	0.8	3.7	349.3	1 494	532	355	9 657	38.9	60.0	1.1
Lee	1 884.6	3 962	25.3	25.8	5.0	0.6	5.1	2 732.0	5 744	1 932	783	25 049	39.1	59.8	1.1
Leon	744.0	3 049	40.7	0.3	7.0	1.2	6.0	2 142.7	8 782	1 670	525	54 093	62.0	37.3	0.6
Levy	72.3	2 011	54.4	2.6	7.9	1.6	7.4	18.6	517	78	86	1 894	36.5	62.5	1.0
Liberty	13.8	1 994	61.4	1.6	3.8	0.0	18.4	5.8	833	52	10	728	35.4	63.8	0.8
Madison	55.3	3 019	64.0	2.1	5.1	0.8	8.4	5.1	280	49	28	1 383	48.7	50.5	0.8
Manatee	898.0	3 201	45.8	1.7	6.5	1.9	4.1	613.4	2 187	1 064	461	11 164	42.7	56.6	0.7
Marion	560.3	2 056	51.6	0.8	7.5	0.4	5.4	482.0	1 769	716	415	14 678	41.0	58.2	0.8
Martin	335.4	2 537	39.3	0.9	9.6	2.4	2.1	317.2	2 399	275	207	4 936	41.6	57.2	1.2
Miami-Dade	9 325.1	3 998	33.6	12.0	7.2	1.3	1.1	11 299.6	4 844	18 422	6 180	132 095	53.6	45.9	0.5
Monroe	377.3	4 756	29.2	3.0	20.2	0.9	3.4	267.4	3 371	1 273	1 664	4 798	49.7	49.2	1.0
Nassau	153.2	2 530	45.9	3.9	6.9	0.1	5.7	129.7	2 142	584	91	2 818	26.2	72.7	1.2
Okaloosa	436.0	2 481	53.7	1.8	6.1	0.3	4.8	150.4	856	6 309	16 779	7 511	21.6	77.6	0.8
Okeechobee	84.5	2 289	53.3	1.0	8.9	0.4	6.2	63.4	1 719	69	56	1 723	42.3	57.2	0.5
Orange	3 869.0	4 088	35.9	2.8	5.7	1.0	6.1	8 920.5	9 425	7 855	2 041	57 343	49.8	49.6	0.6
Osceola	596.0	3 134	51.4	0.4	7.1	1.4	4.0	992.3	5 217	306	288	8 582	47.0	52.5	0.6
Palm Beach	4 250.2	3 570	35.4	3.5	8.6	1.8	3.0	4 696.4	3 945	4 145	1 893	55 760	60.4	39.0	0.6
Pasco	668.2	1 800	54.9	1.9	7.8	0.7	4.4	512.4	1 380	711	561	12 491	44.4	54.1	1.5
Pinellas	2 776.0	2 996	36.8	2.0	7.9	2.6	4.1	3 180.3	3 432	6 147	2 513	39 164	49.5	49.6	0.9
Polk	1 180.7	2 368	48.9	1.7	8.5	0.8	3.9	1 703.8	3 416	2 763	762	24 830	40.8	58.6	0.6
Putnam	184.7	2 600	56.2	2.3	4.9	0.5	3.7	255.5	3 598	150	107	4 233	40.1	59.1	0.8
St. Johns	362.7	2 666	44.5	2.8	5.2	0.0	5.1	477.9	3 513	446	215	6 065	30.6	68.6	0.8
St. Lucie	600.4	2 923	44.8	0.5	7.4	1.1	4.5	1 201.5	5 849	594	386	9 697	51.8	47.6	0.6
Santa Rosa	229.0	1 801	64.8	1.9	9.2	0.0	4.2	117.6	924	755	1 283	4 901	21.8	77.3	0.9

1. Based on the resident population estimated as of July 1 of the year shown.

Table B. States and Counties — **Land Area and Population**

STATE/County code	CBSA code[1]	County Type[2]	STATE County	Land area[3] (sq km) 2000	Population and population characteristics, 2003													
					Total persons	Rank	Per square kilometer	Race alone or in combination, not Hispanic or Latino (percent)				Percent Hispanic or Latino[4]	Age (percent)					
								White	Black	Am. Indian, Alaska Native	Asian and Pacific Islander		Under 5 years	5 to 17 years	18 to 24 years	25 to 34 years	35 to 44 years	45 to 54 years
				1	2	3	4	5	6	7	8	9	10	11	12	13	14	15
			FLORIDA—Cont'd															
12 115	42260	2	Sarasota	1 480	346 793	174	234.3	89.0	4.5	0.5	1.1	5.5	4.2	12.6	6.1	8.6	12.1	12.8
12 117	36740	1	Seminole	798	386 374	160	484.2	74.1	10.4	0.6	3.5	12.6	6.1	18.8	8.9	13.2	16.8	15.2
12 119	45540	4	Sumter	1 413	58 875	831	41.7	77.0	14.2	1.0	0.7	7.9	4.0	12.0	7.8	11.9	13.0	11.1
12 121	...	6	Suwannee	1 781	36 695	1 223	20.6	81.2	12.0	1.0	0.6	6.0	6.4	16.8	9.8	10.8	13.0	13.3
12 123	...	6	Taylor	2 699	19 415	1 840	7.2	77.8	19.3	1.7	0.5	1.6	6.5	17.3	9.6	12.3	14.7	14.4
12 125	...	6	Union	622	14 002	2 168	22.5	73.2	22.0	1.2	0.4	4.0	5.6	15.5	9.9	17.5	21.4	14.7
12 127	19660	2	Volusia	2 857	468 663	130	164.0	81.0	9.9	0.7	1.4	7.9	5.1	15.3	9.0	10.5	13.5	13.3
12 129	45220	2	Wakulla	1 571	26 131	1 534	16.6	84.3	12.6	1.1	0.4	2.4	5.8	17.6	9.7	12.8	16.8	14.4
12 131	...	6	Walton	2 739	46 373	993	16.9	89.1	6.8	2.5	0.7	2.5	5.5	16.0	8.4	11.7	14.9	13.9
12 133	...	6	Washington	1 502	21 604	1 724	14.4	81.7	14.0	2.6	0.6	2.5	5.3	17.2	9.0	12.5	15.1	13.4
13 000	...	X	**GEORGIA**	149 976	8 684 715	X	57.9	62.6	28.8	0.6	2.8	6.2	7.6	18.9	10.2	15.5	16.0	13.4
13 001	...	7	Appling	1 317	17 797	1 926	13.5	75.5	18.8	0.3	0.3	5.4	7.2	19.3	10.2	13.0	14.2	13.7
13 003	20060	9	Atkinson	876	7 891	2 605	9.0	61.7	18.5	0.4	0.3	19.1	8.5	21.7	11.1	14.0	14.0	11.5
13 005	...	7	Bacon	738	10 135	2 432	13.7	80.3	16.0	0.3	0.6	3.4	7.4	18.7	10.3	13.3	14.0	13.1
13 007	10500	3	Baker	889	4 307	2 886	4.8	45.2	51.7	0.2	0.0	2.9	6.1	20.0	11.1	11.4	13.4	12.0
13 009	33300	4	Baldwin	669	44 953	1 026	67.2	53.7	43.9	0.4	1.0	1.5	5.5	15.4	14.8	14.9	15.8	13.5
13 011	...	8	Banks	605	15 483	2 065	25.6	92.2	3.0	0.7	0.7	3.8	7.3	18.3	9.3	14.5	15.4	13.6
13 013	12060	1	Barrow	420	53 479	896	127.3	82.8	10.1	0.7	2.9	4.4	8.0	20.0	9.4	17.1	16.1	11.3
13 015	12060	1	Bartow	1 190	84 730	628	71.2	86.3	8.6	0.7	0.7	4.6	8.0	19.7	9.2	15.6	16.0	12.5
13 017	22340	7	Ben Hill	652	17 235	1 945	26.4	61.0	33.1	0.4	0.3	5.6	8.7	19.3	10.4	12.4	13.3	13.8
13 019	...	6	Berrien	1 172	16 484	1 997	14.1	86.4	10.8	0.6	0.4	2.4	7.0	19.4	9.6	13.3	14.5	12.4
13 021	31420	3	Bibb	647	154 287	363	238.5	48.0	49.5	0.5	1.4	1.4	7.8	19.2	10.0	13.5	14.5	13.6
13 023	...	6	Bleckley	563	11 842	2 303	21.0	73.4	24.3	0.2	1.0	1.4	6.6	19.4	12.3	11.4	14.3	12.3
13 025	15260	3	Brantley	1 151	15 279	2 077	13.3	94.0	4.8	0.9	0.1	1.1	5.8	20.3	10.1	14.0	15.5	13.7
13 027	46660	3	Brooks	1 278	16 242	2 017	12.7	57.9	38.6	0.6	0.5	3.5	6.6	19.4	10.1	12.2	14.0	13.1
13 029	42340	3	Bryan	1 144	26 340	1 524	23.0	83.0	13.9	0.7	1.2	2.2	7.3	21.7	10.5	12.6	16.7	14.0
13 031	44340	4	Bulloch	1 767	58 360	842	33.0	68.9	28.4	0.3	1.2	1.8	6.0	15.4	23.0	13.8	11.9	10.3
13 033	12260	2	Burke	2 151	22 949	1 668	10.7	48.1	50.3	0.5	0.5	1.3	9.1	21.9	10.6	11.8	14.2	13.2
13 035	12060	1	Butts	483	22 099	1 700	45.8	70.7	27.0	0.6	0.4	1.7	6.6	17.4	10.6	15.5	16.7	13.0
13 037	...	8	Calhoun	726	6 122	2 764	8.4	35.1	61.3	0.2	0.1	3.4	7.1	15.4	11.3	15.9	17.5	14.5
13 039	41220	4	Camden	1 631	45 470	1 010	27.9	77.2	19.3	0.9	1.7	2.5	8.5	22.8	12.2	16.0	16.4	10.9
13 043	...	7	Candler	639	10 023	2 439	15.7	64.5	24.9	0.2	0.3	10.3	8.0	18.9	9.8	12.7	12.4	12.7
13 045	12060	1	Carroll	1 292	98 525	550	76.3	79.7	16.4	0.6	0.8	3.4	7.2	18.4	12.8	15.2	14.3	11.7
13 047	16860	2	Catoosa	420	58 085	844	138.3	96.4	1.4	0.8	1.1	1.2	6.6	18.7	8.8	14.2	15.3	13.3
13 049	...	6	Charlton	2 022	10 707	2 385	5.3	70.4	28.1	0.8	0.5	0.8	6.1	19.9	12.3	13.6	17.0	11.9
13 051	42340	2	Chatham	1 135	235 270	250	207.3	55.3	40.8	0.6	2.5	2.0	7.4	17.9	10.9	14.5	14.3	13.1
13 053	17980	2	Chattahoochee	644	19 333	1 847	30.0	57.8	29.1	1.2	3.4	11.0	6.2	17.1	35.8	22.6	12.0	3.2
13 055	44900	6	Chattooga	812	26 422	1 521	32.5	86.6	10.6	0.4	0.2	2.9	6.6	16.4	10.7	14.7	14.7	12.6
13 057	12060	1	Cherokee	1 097	166 639	339	151.9	88.2	3.6	0.7	1.6	6.9	7.9	20.0	9.1	14.9	18.1	13.3
13 059	12020	3	Clarke	313	103 691	523	331.3	62.7	26.9	0.5	3.5	7.5	5.9	11.8	24.2	19.7	10.6	9.3
13 061	...	9	Clay	506	3 358	2 957	6.6	39.3	59.4	0.3	0.3	1.0	6.7	18.1	10.3	8.1	11.5	15.0
13 063	12060	1	Clayton	369	259 750	229	703.9	26.7	58.9	0.7	5.7	9.5	8.8	21.5	10.0	17.2	16.3	12.0
13 065	...	9	Clinch	2 096	6 967	2 688	3.3	68.6	30.1	0.5	0.3	0.9	9.0	19.7	9.7	12.7	14.6	13.8
13 067	12060	1	Cobb	881	651 027	86	739.0	67.1	20.2	0.6	4.1	7.6	9.3	18.4	8.5	17.1	17.6	14.3
13 069	20060	7	Coffee	1 551	38 994	1 161	25.1	65.1	26.6	0.3	0.7	7.6	8.2	19.7	11.3	14.9	14.9	12.2
13 071	34220	6	Colquitt	1 430	43 203	1 059	30.2	64.1	22.9	0.4	0.3	12.7	8.0	19.2	11.1	14.0	13.7	12.2
13 073	12260	2	Columbia	751	97 505	553	129.8	82.5	11.7	0.6	4.0	2.5	6.6	21.2	9.6	11.4	16.9	15.7
13 075	...	6	Cook	593	15 951	2 034	26.9	68.0	27.5	0.2	0.6	4.0	7.1	20.7	9.8	13.5	14.0	12.4
13 077	12060	1	Coweta	1 146	101 395	538	88.5	78.0	17.0	0.6	1.1	4.1	7.7	20.4	8.8	15.3	16.4	12.8
13 079	31420	3	Crawford	842	12 553	2 266	14.9	75.1	22.2	0.6	0.3	2.4	6.1	20.1	9.5	13.4	17.6	14.5
13 081	18380	6	Crisp	709	21 994	1 704	31.0	53.1	44.0	0.2	0.9	2.1	7.9	20.7	10.0	12.5	14.3	13.6
13 083	16860	2	Dade	451	15 910	2 036	35.3	97.1	1.1	1.0	0.4	1.0	5.8	17.1	13.1	12.7	14.3	14.3
13 085	12060	1	Dawson	547	18 575	1 879	34.0	96.4	0.6	1.1	0.4	2.3	7.0	17.9	8.7	14.5	16.1	13.1
13 087	12460	6	Decatur	1 546	28 212	1 452	18.2	56.4	39.7	0.5	0.3	3.4	7.6	20.4	10.2	12.7	14.5	13.0
13 089	12060	1	De Kalb	695	674 334	81	970.3	32.0	55.5	0.5	4.3	8.8	7.9	17.0	9.2	18.6	17.4	13.6
13 091	...	7	Dodge	1 296	19 374	1 844	14.9	68.3	29.7	0.3	0.3	1.5	6.0	19.4	9.8	13.7	15.5	12.9
13 093	...	6	Dooly	1 018	11 552	2 330	11.3	44.6	50.6	0.3	0.6	4.1	7.3	17.8	11.0	13.9	15.6	13.9
13 095	10500	3	Dougherty	854	95 684	563	112.0	35.6	62.4	0.5	0.9	1.2	8.0	19.7	11.9	13.5	13.1	13.2
13 097	12060	1	Douglas	516	102 015	534	197.7	69.9	25.6	0.8	1.5	3.6	7.5	20.1	9.8	14.6	16.7	13.6
13 099	...	6	Early	1 324	12 224	2 283	9.2	50.0	48.4	0.4	0.4	1.3	7.3	21.0	9.2	10.8	13.1	12.9
13 101	46660	3	Echols	1 047	3 999	2 910	3.8	67.6	7.8	1.2	0.1	24.0	7.0	19.6	13.2	17.0	14.2	11.1
13 103	42340	2	Effingham	1 242	42 715	1 066	34.4	84.9	12.9	0.7	0.8	1.7	7.3	20.8	10.3	13.7	16.7	13.0
13 105	...	6	Elbert	955	20 636	1 767	21.6	66.4	30.2	0.4	0.3	3.0	6.5	18.4	9.8	12.6	14.0	13.1
13 107	...	7	Emanuel	1 776	21 885	1 706	12.3	62.0	32.7	0.3	0.3	5.0	7.3	19.8	11.9	11.9	13.4	12.8
13 109	...	6	Evans	479	11 365	2 343	23.7	60.1	32.1	0.1	0.3	7.3	8.0	19.2	11.1	13.8	14.7	11.7

1. CBSA = Core Based Statistical Area. See Appendix A for explanation. See Appendix B for list of metropolitan areas with component counties. 2. County type code from the Economic Research Service of USDA Rural-Urban Continuum Codes. See Appendix A for definition. 3. Dry land or land partially or temporarily covered by water. 4. Hispanic or Latino persons may be of any race.

Table B. States and Counties — **Population and Households**

STATE County	55 to 64 years	65 to 74 years	75 years and over	Percent female	1990	2000	1990–2000	2000–2003	Births	Deaths	Net migration	Number	Percent change, 1990–2000	Persons per house-hold	Female family house-holder[1]	One person
	16	17	18	19	20	21	22	23	24	25	26	27	28	29	30	31
FLORIDA—Cont'd																
Sarasota	12.7	13.8	16.0	52.4	277 776	325 957	17.3	6.4	8 960	15 582	26 649	149 937	19.5	2.13	7.7	30.4
Seminole	9.6	5.9	4.6	50.9	287 521	365 196	27.0	5.8	14 664	8 604	15 135	139 572	29.6	2.59	11.5	22.9
Sumter	14.2	15.6	9.3	45.5	31 577	53 345	68.9	10.4	1 421	2 287	6 263	20 779	71.5	2.27	8.4	23.5
Suwannee	12.0	9.4	7.6	50.9	26 780	34 844	30.1	5.3	1 518	1 507	1 831	13 460	34.1	2.54	11.2	23.3
Taylor	11.2	8.3	5.7	48.3	17 111	19 256	12.5	0.8	828	727	84	7 176	12.1	2.51	14.4	24.2
Union	7.8	4.8	3.0	36.3	10 252	13 442	31.1	4.2	482	463	534	3 367	26.7	2.76	15.0	19.5
Volusia	11.0	10.5	10.7	51.2	370 737	443 343	19.6	5.7	15 038	18 977	28 639	184 723	20.4	2.32	10.9	27.9
Wakulla	9.9	6.4	4.0	47.6	14 202	22 863	61.0	14.3	948	567	2 846	8 450	62.2	2.57	12.4	22.0
Walton	12.0	8.9	5.9	48.8	27 759	40 601	46.3	14.2	1 471	1 414	5 511	16 548	46.5	2.35	10.1	27.1
Washington	11.8	8.1	6.9	47.8	16 919	20 973	24.0	3.0	716	764	685	7 931	23.1	2.46	11.4	25.1
GEORGIA	8.9	5.2	4.3	50.6	6 478 149	8 186 453	26.4	6.1	438 289	212 673	267 059	3 006 369	27.0	2.65	14.5	23.6
Appling	10.0	6.4	5.3	50.4	15 744	17 419	10.6	2.2	883	607	125	6 606	13.2	2.60	12.5	23.2
Atkinson	8.3	5.2	4.0	50.4	6 213	7 609	22.5	3.7	457	234	60	2 717	22.9	2.78	12.8	23.3
Bacon	9.8	7.0	5.6	51.0	9 566	10 103	5.6	0.3	490	412	-40	3 833	11.4	2.60	14.1	23.6
Baker	9.4	6.7	5.8	53.5	3 615	4 074	12.7	5.7	146	125	202	1 514	16.5	2.68	19.5	25.1
Baldwin	9.0	6.1	4.7	46.4	39 530	44 700	13.1	0.6	1 797	1 377	-116	14 758	21.3	2.50	18.2	25.6
Banks	9.8	6.2	4.2	49.7	10 308	14 422	39.9	7.4	694	462	825	5 364	42.1	2.69	7.9	19.2
Barrow	7.3	4.5	3.7	50.2	29 721	46 144	55.3	15.9	2 628	1 226	5 769	16 354	53.2	2.79	11.6	18.6
Bartow	8.3	5.2	3.9	50.4	55 915	76 019	36.0	11.5	4 420	2 021	6 185	27 176	35.3	2.76	11.1	18.7
Ben Hill	9.9	6.5	6.5	52.1	16 245	17 484	7.6	-1.4	1 057	707	-606	6 673	11.7	2.57	17.4	26.7
Berrien	10.4	7.2	5.7	50.8	14 153	16 235	14.7	1.5	751	554	55	6 261	21.6	2.57	11.7	23.6
Bibb	8.8	6.4	6.3	54.3	150 137	153 887	2.5	0.3	8 234	5 447	-2 321	59 667	6.0	2.49	20.6	28.2
Bleckley	9.8	7.3	6.5	51.8	10 430	11 666	11.9	1.5	512	363	38	4 372	14.6	2.52	15.5	25.5
Brantley	9.7	6.5	3.9	50.2	11 077	14 629	32.1	4.4	435	437	647	5 436	42.6	2.68	10.6	20.4
Brooks	10.2	7.3	7.3	52.0	15 398	16 450	6.8	-1.3	727	680	-237	6 155	14.2	2.61	18.1	25.2
Bryan	7.7	3.9	2.9	50.4	15 438	23 417	51.7	12.5	1 146	540	2 246	8 089	59.5	2.88	11.9	16.4
Bulloch	7.0	5.0	4.1	51.3	43 125	55 983	29.8	4.2	2 366	1 347	1 414	20 743	38.4	2.53	11.8	24.6
Burke	8.6	5.6	4.7	52.4	20 579	22 243	8.1	3.2	1 467	778	43	7 934	12.7	2.77	22.8	23.6
Butts	8.9	5.5	4.1	47.0	15 326	19 522	27.4	13.2	982	659	2 164	6 455	37.5	2.73	13.9	20.9
Calhoun	8.2	6.0	6.4	43.1	5 013	6 320	26.1	-3.1	325	216	-305	1 962	9.4	2.55	23.2	28.7
Camden	6.5	3.5	2.3	47.9	30 167	43 664	44.7	4.1	2 478	606	-10	14 705	55.5	2.84	11.7	17.7
Candler	9.7	6.8	7.9	50.3	7 744	9 577	23.7	4.7	556	475	358	3 375	19.3	2.72	14.3	23.9
Carroll	8.3	5.2	4.2	51.0	71 422	87 268	22.2	12.9	4 665	2 611	8 972	31 568	24.4	2.66	12.3	21.2
Catoosa	9.6	6.8	4.9	51.5	42 464	53 282	25.5	9.0	2 345	1 492	3 903	20 425	29.7	2.59	11.0	21.3
Charlton	8.9	5.6	4.2	46.7	8 496	10 282	21.0	4.1	416	300	310	3 342	14.8	2.74	15.0	21.8
Chatham	9.1	6.5	6.1	51.9	216 774	232 048	7.0	1.4	11 915	7 539	-941	89 865	10.8	2.49	17.0	27.1
Chattahoochee	1.5	1.0	0.4	31.2	16 934	14 882	-12.1	29.9	786	133	3 635	2 932	1.7	3.41	10.1	8.9
Chattooga	10.0	7.3	6.5	48.3	22 236	25 470	14.5	3.7	1 100	919	779	9 577	13.1	2.49	12.6	25.2
Cherokee	7.7	3.8	2.6	49.7	90 204	141 903	57.3	17.4	8 381	2 590	18 482	49 495	58.1	2.85	8.3	16.0
Clarke	6.3	4.0	4.1	51.0	87 594	101 489	15.9	2.2	4 331	2 049	-48	39 706	19.7	2.35	13.3	29.7
Clay	11.9	9.3	9.7	54.7	3 364	3 357	-0.2	0.0	152	140	-7	1 347	11.3	2.45	23.4	27.8
Clayton	6.6	3.8	2.4	51.2	181 436	236 517	30.4	9.8	15 081	4 463	12 736	82 243	25.5	2.84	20.3	21.8
Clinch	9.5	6.2	5.0	50.3	6 160	6 878	11.7	1.3	441	269	-80	2 512	15.6	2.60	16.9	24.6
Cobb	8.1	4.1	3.0	50.2	447 745	607 751	35.7	7.1	33 865	11 064	21 091	227 487	32.8	2.64	10.7	23.2
Coffee	8.2	5.3	4.5	49.8	29 592	37 413	26.4	4.2	2 107	1 057	553	13 354	26.7	2.69	15.2	22.6
Colquitt	9.1	6.4	6.1	50.0	36 645	42 053	14.8	2.7	2 353	1 390	238	15 495	19.4	2.63	15.5	24.9
Columbia	8.8	5.0	3.4	51.1	66 031	89 288	35.2	9.2	4 034	1 867	6 014	31 120	42.5	2.85	10.6	15.4
Cook	9.4	7.2	5.8	52.0	13 456	15 771	17.2	1.1	737	661	122	5 882	21.9	2.64	15.3	24.0
Coweta	8.4	4.6	3.4	50.3	53 853	89 215	65.7	13.7	4 977	2 118	9 144	31 442	66.1	2.81	12.2	17.6
Crawford	10.0	5.3	3.6	50.0	8 991	12 495	39.0	0.5	420	369	27	4 461	45.4	2.78	12.6	18.8
Crisp	9.0	6.7	6.3	53.1	20 011	21 996	9.9	0.0	1 167	863	-292	8 337	14.4	2.58	21.6	26.1
Dade	10.3	7.0	4.9	50.8	13 183	15 154	15.0	5.0	623	448	578	5 633	20.9	2.62	9.5	21.7
Dawson	10.2	6.2	3.1	49.8	9 429	15 999	69.7	16.1	844	376	2 053	6 069	80.6	2.62	8.2	18.6
Decatur	8.8	6.8	5.6	51.9	25 517	28 240	10.7	-0.1	1 404	991	-390	10 380	15.8	2.65	19.5	24.3
De Kalb	7.7	4.3	3.7	51.4	546 174	665 865	21.9	1.3	37 616	13 612	-16 326	249 339	19.5	2.62	17.6	26.9
Dodge	9.4	7.2	6.0	48.4	17 607	19 171	8.9	1.1	798	744	172	7 062	10.6	2.48	15.2	27.8
Dooly	9.2	5.6	5.7	48.1	9 901	11 525	16.4	0.2	575	359	-189	3 909	9.9	2.62	20.5	25.9
Dougherty	8.7	6.2	5.5	53.2	96 321	96 065	-0.3	-0.4	5 187	2 798	-2 767	35 552	4.1	2.58	23.2	26.8
Douglas	8.4	4.3	3.0	50.8	71 120	92 174	29.6	10.7	4 786	2 070	6 919	32 822	35.2	2.78	12.7	18.4
Early	9.9	7.8	8.0	53.4	11 854	12 354	4.2	-1.1	611	456	-285	4 695	10.1	2.58	20.8	26.9
Echols	6.6	5.0	2.7	45.1	2 334	3 754	60.8	6.5	181	86	158	1 264	54.9	2.97	10.8	18.7
Effingham	8.1	4.4	3.2	50.5	25 687	37 535	46.1	13.8	1 887	864	4 047	13 151	50.1	2.84	11.1	16.9
Elbert	10.1	7.9	7.0	51.9	18 949	20 511	8.2	0.6	883	778	40	8 004	12.5	2.53	15.7	25.0
Emanuel	9.8	6.6	6.4	51.5	20 546	21 837	6.3	0.2	1 151	881	-210	8 045	8.4	2.61	17.1	25.0
Evans	8.2	6.3	5.7	51.4	8 724	10 495	20.3	8.3	651	352	575	3 778	20.2	2.62	16.4	25.0

1. No spouse present.

Table B. States and Counties — Vital Statistics, Health Resources, and Crime

STATE County	Births, average 1999–2001		Deaths, average 1999–2001				Physicians,[4] 2000		Hospitals,[4] 1998			Medicare enrollees, 2003	Serious crimes known to police,[6] 2002	
			Number		Rate					Beds			Total	
	Total	Rate[1]	Total	Infant[2]	Total[1]	Infant[3]	Number	Rate[5]	Number	Number	Rate[5]		Number	Rate[7]
	32	33	34	35	36	37	38	39	40	41	42	43	44	45
FLORIDA—Cont'd														
Sarasota	2 714	8.3	4 811	14	14.7	5.3	952	292	4	1 272	419	106 049	14 609	4 286
Seminole	4 514	12.3	2 591	24	7.1	5.2	523	143	3	706	201	41 444	13 861	3 630
Sumter	443	8.3	622	4	11.7	D	21	39	0	0	0	8 630	1 478	2 682
Suwannee	465	13.3	439	6	12.6	D	16	46	1	16	49	7 665	1 437	3 944
Taylor	249	12.8	225	2	11.6	D	18	93	1	48	255	3 227	932	4 629
Union	148	10.9	148	1	10.9	D	14	104	0	0	0	1 335	148	1 053
Volusia	4 524	10.2	5 744	30	12.9	6.7	703	159	8	1 493	353	104 449	22 177	4 830
Wakulla	284	12.3	183	2	7.9	D	8	35	0	0	0	3 311	856	3 580
Walton	447	10.9	424	1	10.3	D	21	52	1	50	134	6 057	1 532	3 608
Washington	224	10.6	226	3	10.7	D	10	48	1	45	222	3 865	296	1 350
GEORGIA	130 962	15.9	63 461	1 104	7.7	8.4	17 317	212	157	24 637	322	973 794	385 830	4 507
Appling	258	14.8	186	3	10.7	D	11	63	1	43	261	2 530	NA	NA
Atkinson	169	22.2	65	3	8.5	D	1	13	0	0	0	1 076	NA	NA
Bacon	146	14.5	121	1	12.0	D	13	129	1	38	366	1 534	143	1 354
Baker	45	11.0	37	0	9.1	D	0	0	0	0	0	439	10	235
Baldwin	524	11.7	386	8	8.6	15.9	117	262	1	145	346	6 218	1 650	3 530
Banks	183	12.7	102	1	7.1	D	4	28	0	0	0	1 615	598	3 966
Barrow	821	17.7	352	3	7.6	D	26	56	1	60	149	5 535	2 013	4 172
Bartow	1 393	18.2	609	9	7.9	6.2	58	76	1	81	113	9 779	3 812	4 840
Ben Hill	316	18.1	216	3	12.3	D	14	80	1	60	343	2 970	785	4 294
Berrien	257	15.9	175	1	10.8	D	9	55	1	167	1 021	2 680	379	2 232
Bibb	2 539	16.5	1 685	34	10.9	13.5	499	324	4	964	618	26 514	13 563	8 429
Bleckley	162	13.9	122	2	10.4	D	13	111	1	45	402	2 067	NA	NA
Brantley	118	8.1	122	1	8.4	D	2	14	0	0	0	2 285	435	2 844
Brooks	188	11.5	204	1	12.4	D	7	43	0	25	156	2 776	547	3 307
Bryan	386	16.3	146	2	6.2	14.3	21	90	0	0	0	5 778	553	2 514
Bulloch	674	12.0	397	10	7.1	D	64	114	1	130	257	2 991	2 149	3 787
Burke	397	17.7	218	3	9.8	D	10	45	1	40	175	—	1 201	5 164
Butts	300	15.2	189	3	9.6	D	14	72	1	28	157	3 112	785	3 845
Calhoun	92	14.7	67	1	10.6	D	2	32	1	24	475	1 101	159	2 406
Camden	732	16.7	181	6	4.1	D	42	96	1	30	63	3 449	1 479	3 239
Candler	161	16.9	136	3	14.3	D	7	73	1	49	540	1 554	298	2 976
Carroll	1 407	16.0	757	11	8.6	7.6	94	108	3	260	313	12 671	3 469	3 802
Catoosa	697	13.0	428	4	8.0	D	50	94	1	272	538	5 633	2 072	3 719
Charlton	132	12.8	91	2	8.9	D	10	97	1	50	530	1 449	194	1 804
Chatham	3 605	15.5	2 258	31	9.7	8.6	613	264	3	1 159	514	33 598	16 662	6 937
Chattahoochee	243	16.2	34	1	2.3	D	28	188	0	0	0	387	54	347
Chattooga	338	13.2	278	3	10.9	D	10	39	1	166	728	4 560	208	796
Cherokee	2 449	17.0	775	13	5.4	5.2	87	61	1	84	62	11 767	2 703	1 822
Clarke	1 318	13.0	646	13	6.4	10.1	253	249	2	486	536	10 721	7 229	6 812
Clay	68	20.1	54	1	15.9	D	4	119	0	0	0	608	12	342
Clayton	4 267	17.9	1 295	36	5.4	8.4	324	137	1	317	152	23 241	13 774	5 569
Clinch	120	17.4	80	1	11.6	D	8	116	1	48	721	1 037	288	4 004
Cobb	10 119	16.6	3 225	68	5.3	6.7	885	146	4	1 016	179	57 101	20 905	3 290
Coffee	651	17.4	315	8	8.4	12.8	42	112	1	114	332	4 964	2 254	5 761
Colquitt	690	16.4	453	9	10.8	12.6	44	105	1	155	386	6 274	2 679	6 092
Columbia	1 212	13.5	518	8	5.8	6.9	178	199	0	0	0	10 026	2 431	2 604
Cook	235	14.9	184	3	11.7	D	9	57	1	155	1 033	2 448	369	2 688
Coweta	1 461	16.2	635	10	7.0	6.6	87	98	2	253	298	10 196	2 283	2 447
Crawford	135	10.9	105	1	8.5	D	3	24	0	0	0	897	341	2 610
Crisp	344	15.6	253	6	11.5	D	29	132	1	65	314	3 401	1 593	6 926
Dade	192	12.6	134	1	8.8	D	9	59	1	13	86	2 482	205	1 294
Dawson	268	16.7	106	2	6.6	D	6	38	0	0	0	2 187	491	2 935
Decatur	437	15.5	310	6	11.0	D	30	106	1	187	692	4 262	1 314	4 497
De Kalb	10 839	16.3	3 929	92	5.9	8.5	2 312	347	5	1 398	235	60 877	31 768	4 585
Dodge	241	12.6	224	3	11.7	D	22	115	1	95	525	2 924	575	2 915
Dooly	182	15.8	111	2	9.6	D	10	87	2	93	895	1 687	209	1 734
Dougherty	1 611	16.8	868	18	9.0	11.0	214	223	2	601	631	14 126	5 828	4 222
Douglas	1 420	15.3	603	8	6.5	5.9	92	100	2	315	351	9 386	4 070	4 223
Early	178	14.4	143	2	11.6	D	9	73	1	176	1 443	2 029	221	1 750
Echols	15	4.2	24	0	6.5	D	0	0	0	0	0	149	12	306
Effingham	527	13.9	246	4	6.5	D	13	35	1	97	266	3 746	884	2 252
Elbert	267	13.0	244	0	11.9	D	11	54	1	52	269	4 020	897	4 182
Emanuel	315	14.4	250	6	11.4	D	17	78	1	119	566	3 834	786	3 442
Evans	185	17.6	109	2	10.4	D	8	76	1	36	362	1 644	NA	NA

1. Per 1,000 estimated resident population. 2. Deaths of infants under 1 year old. 3. Deaths of infants under 1 year old per 1,000 live births. 4. Data subject to copyright. 5. Per 100,000 resident population as of July 1 of the year shown. 6. Data for serious crimes have not been adjusted for underreporting; this may affect comparability between geographic areas and over time. 7. Per 100,000 population estimated by the FBI.

Table B. States and Counties — Crime, Education, Money Income, and Poverty

STATE County	Serious crimes known to police,[1] 2002 (cont'd) Rate[2] Violent	Property	School enrollment and attainment, 2000 Enrollment[3] Total	Percent private	Attainment[4] (percent) High school grad-uate or less	Bach-elor's degree or more	Local government expenditures,[5] 2000–2001 Total current expendi-tures (mil dol)	Current expendi-tures per student (dollars)	Money income, 1999 Per capita income[6] (dollars)	Households Median income Dollars	Percent change, 1989–1999 (constant 1999 dollars)	Percent with income of $100,000 or more	Percent below poverty level, 1999 Persons	House-holds	Families	Families with children
	46	47	48	49	50	51	52	53	54	55	56	57	58	59	60	61
FLORIDA—Cont'd																
Sarasota	447	3 839	55 269	18.4	43.0	27.4	234.7	6 606	28 326	41 957	4.4	12.7	7.8	7.1	5.1	10.3
Seminole	477	3 152	99 337	18.6	35.7	31.0	335.5	5 511	24 591	49 326	3.0	15.9	7.4	7.1	5.1	7.4
Sumter	468	2 214	8 862	11.2	61.6	12.2	38.1	6 221	16 830	32 073	21.9	4.2	13.7	12.5	9.6	21.3
Suwannee	656	3 288	7 960	13.3	65.6	10.5	34.1	5 865	14 678	29 963	12.8	3.9	18.5	18.6	14.8	20.4
Taylor	829	3 799	4 676	7.6	70.9	8.9	22.3	6 012	15 281	30 032	4.5	5.0	18.0	19.1	14.5	18.5
Union	420	633	2 866	6.8	66.4	7.5	11.9	5 348	12 333	34 563	12.7	3.6	14.0	15.2	10.5	13.0
Volusia	660	4 170	101 190	21.6	50.2	17.6	357.4	5 810	19 664	35 219	5.6	7.1	11.6	11.0	7.9	14.0
Wakulla	661	2 920	5 852	5.3	56.6	15.7	27.0	5 777	17 678	37 149	10.5	6.6	11.3	12.0	9.3	13.8
Walton	610	2 998	8 374	8.1	56.4	16.2	35.9	6 108	18 198	32 407	13.3	6.4	14.4	14.1	11.6	18.9
Washington	91	1 258	4 640	5.4	67.6	9.2	25.7	7 570	14 980	27 922	13.8	5.0	19.2	19.6	15.4	22.5
GEORGIA	459	4 048	2 211 688	14.4	50.1	24.3	9 914.8	6 861	21 154	42 433	8.8	12.3	13.0	12.6	9.9	13.9
Appling	NA	NA	4 329	7.0	69.9	8.4	25.0	7 612	15 044	30 266	1.1	5.4	18.6	19.6	14.9	21.1
Atkinson	NA	NA	1 770	4.0	79.6	6.9	10.1	6 545	12 178	26 470	11.4	3.4	23.0	23.7	18.1	21.7
Bacon	57	1 297	2 262	4.1	76.3	6.6	12.1	6 305	14 289	26 910	4.8	4.7	23.7	23.6	20.2	25.5
Baker	70	164	1 114	9.7	74.4	10.7	4.7	11 214	16 969	30 338	22.1	5.2	23.4	22.1	19.9	28.2
Baldwin	246	3 284	13 169	20.0	62.8	16.2	43.8	6 911	16 271	35 159	2.6	7.5	16.8	16.8	11.8	16.9
Banks	252	3 714	3 185	8.2	72.9	8.6	13.8	5 924	17 424	38 523	18.4	6.5	12.5	13.2	9.8	12.7
Barrow	257	3 915	11 251	11.6	62.7	10.9	62.5	7 214	18 350	45 019	21.7	7.5	8.3	8.9	6.2	8.0
Bartow	221	4 619	18 576	9.5	62.4	14.1	104.6	6 539	18 989	43 660	17.9	8.1	8.6	9.0	6.6	8.3
Ben Hill	635	3 659	4 520	8.1	71.4	9.5	23.1	6 644	14 093	27 100	5.6	5.0	22.3	20.3	18.7	28.6
Berrien	389	1 844	4 085	5.1	68.6	9.4	19.1	6 097	16 375	30 044	6.6	4.0	17.7	17.0	14.6	21.0
Bibb	480	7 949	42 862	21.1	54.5	21.3	159.3	6 441	19 058	34 532	-0.4	8.8	19.1	18.5	15.5	23.4
Bleckley	NA	NA	3 502	6.5	64.0	12.5	15.0	6 275	15 934	33 448	9.7	5.9	15.9	15.4	11.7	19.1
Brantley	144	2 700	3 729	5.2	74.9	6.2	19.0	6 058	13 713	30 361	2.3	2.4	15.6	15.8	12.1	17.1
Brooks	659	2 648	4 275	6.9	69.6	11.3	17.8	6 594	13 977	26 911	2.9	3.7	23.4	22.9	19.1	27.6
Bryan	118	2 396	6 744	9.0	53.8	19.3	30.4	5 731	19 794	48 345	25.7	12.6	11.7	12.4	10.7	13.9
Bulloch	231	3 556	23 132	6.1	51.7	25.4	60.2	7 227	16 080	29 499	6.4	6.9	24.5	25.2	11.9	16.9
Burke	1 122	4 041	6 592	9.1	72.1	9.5	31.8	6 510	13 136	27 877	17.4	4.4	28.7	27.8	23.8	29.8
Butts	343	3 502	4 354	7.1	70.1	8.6	20.8	6 431	17 016	39 879	21.5	7.2	11.5	12.5	8.6	10.5
Calhoun	454	1 952	1 498	19.5	68.2	11.7	6.3	8 307	11 839	24 588	17.0	2.9	26.5	27.5	23.2	33.7
Camden	416	2 823	13 254	7.1	49.9	16.0	54.7	5 629	16 445	41 056	8.3	5.5	10.1	10.9	8.4	10.8
Candler	459	2 516	2 343	7.1	72.3	10.2	11.8	6 233	12 958	25 022	-3.9	3.6	26.1	24.0	21.4	31.7
Carroll	461	3 340	24 665	7.1	63.2	16.5	104.5	6 556	17 656	38 799	12.8	7.4	13.7	14.6	10.0	13.5
Catoosa	135	3 584	13 012	9.9	58.8	13.8	57.2	5 962	18 009	39 998	16.4	6.1	9.4	10.3	6.4	9.9
Charlton	270	1 535	2 586	6.4	77.0	6.4	12.5	6 185	12 920	27 869	-7.1	4.2	20.9	21.5	17.8	24.9
Chatham	739	6 198	64 990	22.6	46.7	25.0	233.8	6 452	21 152	37 752	5.2	10.4	15.6	15.1	11.8	18.5
Chattahoochee	45	302	4 158	9.1	34.3	25.0	4.3	8 692	14 049	37 106	9.1	3.6	10.6	11.0	8.9	9.7
Chattooga	50	746	5 264	8.5	74.2	7.7	27.6	6 691	14 508	30 664	12.2	3.5	14.3	14.6	11.3	15.4
Cherokee	126	1 696	36 937	15.9	42.9	27.0	168.0	6 452	24 871	60 896	16.1	19.9	5.3	5.4	3.5	4.2
Clarke	419	6 393	44 372	8.2	40.6	39.8	90.2	7 894	17 123	28 403	1.6	8.2	28.3	27.5	14.8	21.8
Clay	171	171	867	7.8	71.2	10.1	3.0	7 437	16 819	21 448	16.4	4.2	31.3	32.8	28.1	42.5
Clayton	476	5 093	68 358	11.2	51.8	16.6	296.3	6 314	18 079	42 697	-5.1	7.3	10.1	8.9	8.2	10.9
Clinch	1 529	2 475	1 784	2.5	73.6	10.4	10.8	7 385	13 023	26 755	10.0	4.1	23.4	26.1	22.2	23.7
Cobb	266	3 024	165 032	17.7	32.0	39.8	691.9	6 707	27 863	58 289	5.1	21.3	6.5	5.9	4.4	6.1
Coffee	435	5 327	9 786	7.3	68.1	10.0	49.3	6 401	15 530	30 710	10.7	5.5	19.1	19.6	15.3	20.6
Colquitt	1 026	5 067	10 489	5.5	70.9	11.4	54.2	6 472	14 457	28 539	4.5	4.5	19.8	20.1	16.1	21.8
Columbia	102	2 502	26 407	13.1	37.9	32.0	107.6	5 737	23 496	55 682	3.3	16.1	5.1	5.4	4.2	5.2
Cook	321	2 368	4 164	4.6	71.4	8.1	20.3	6 223	13 465	27 582	3.4	3.5	20.7	21.1	16.5	23.1
Coweta	168	2 279	23 339	14.8	51.2	20.6	106.9	6 374	21 949	52 706	22.9	14.1	7.8	8.2	6.1	8.1
Crawford	153	2 457	3 288	9.5	72.4	6.8	13.4	6 257	15 768	37 848	9.2	5.6	15.4	16.7	12.7	13.6
Crisp	600	6 326	5 839	7.8	68.6	12.8	31.3	6 896	14 695	26 547	11.0	5.5	29.3	28.3	24.6	35.4
Dade	95	1 199	3 991	22.2	63.3	10.9	17.4	6 504	16 127	35 259	30.1	4.1	9.7	11.6	7.5	8.4
Dawson	90	2 845	3 395	7.8	53.7	18.1	18.2	6 571	22 520	47 486	24.5	11.6	7.6	7.8	5.8	8.1
Decatur	394	4 104	7 686	7.1	63.9	12.1	36.8	6 303	15 063	28 820	2.9	5.3	22.7	21.0	19.2	28.4
De Kalb	460	4 125	182 326	22.4	35.3	36.3	736.8	7 471	23 968	49 117	2.3	15.5	10.8	9.1	7.8	11.1
Dodge	836	2 078	4 906	3.9	70.3	11.6	23.3	6 542	14 468	27 607	12.6	4.4	17.4	19.1	13.8	17.9
Dooly	431	1 303	3 117	13.6	69.4	9.6	13.6	7 879	13 628	27 980	27.6	4.5	22.1	22.3	18.0	23.4
Dougherty	525	5 277	28 401	11.3	54.6	17.8	121.6	7 237	16 645	30 934	-2.4	7.4	24.8	22.2	19.6	28.5
Douglas	310	3 913	25 409	15.2	53.5	19.2	114.1	6 525	21 172	50 108	0.4	11.7	7.8	7.4	5.7	8.0
Early	293	1 457	3 276	6.3	65.0	12.6	17.6	6 266	14 936	25 629	16.2	5.9	25.7	26.1	22.2	32.0
Echols	127	178	999	1.4	75.2	8.4	4.9	6 633	15 727	25 851	-10.8	5.3	28.7	23.7	22.3	29.7
Effingham	168	2 084	10 636	7.0	61.6	13.6	49.3	5 823	18 873	46 505	17.6	8.8	9.3	9.3	7.1	8.6
Elbert	947	3 236	4 834	5.5	72.0	9.8	25.6	6 759	14 535	28 724	4.3	3.8	17.3	18.2	14.6	20.3
Emanuel	1 034	2 409	5 720	5.9	73.7	10.1	30.6	6 444	13 627	24 383	1.4	4.4	27.4	25.7	21.8	31.2
Evans	NA	NA	2 588	8.3	73.5	9.0	12.5	6 152	12 758	25 447	-5.2	2.9	27.0	27.0	23.1	33.9

1. Data for serious crimes have not been adjusted for underreporting; this may affect comparability between geographic areas and over time.   2. Per 100,000 population estimated by the FBI.   3. All persons 3 years old and over enrolled in nursery school through college.   4. Persons 25 years old and over.   5. Elementary and secondary education expenditures.   6. Based on population enumerated as of April 1, 2000.

Table B. States and Counties — **Personal Income**

STATE County	Total (mil dol)	Percent change, 2001-2002	Per capita[1] Dollars	Per capita[1] Rank	Wages and salaries[2] (mil dol)	Proprietor's income (mil dol)	Dividends, interest, and rent (mil dol)	Transfer payments Total (mil dol)	Government payments to individuals Total (mil dol)	Social Security (mil dol)	Medical payments (mil dol)	Income maintenance (mil dol)	Unemployment insurance (mil dol)
	62	63	64	65	66	67	68	69	70	71	72	73	74
FLORIDA—Cont'd													
Sarasota	14 171	4.4	41 658	49	5 952	825	5 692	2 182	2 098	1 117	821	60	22
Seminole	12 256	3.5	32 110	221	6 181	823	1 912	1 287	1 193	529	398	80	43
Sumter	996	7.3	17 249	2 971	375	42	226	377	362	210	101	20	2
Suwannee	740	3.2	20 453	2 443	279	89	133	210	201	78	89	21	2
Taylor	392	4.8	20 231	2 495	241	21	62	104	99	37	43	13	2
Union	193	2.5	13 845	3 093	141	9	28	40	37	13	16	6	0
Volusia	11 380	4.7	24 747	1 197	5 112	527	3 048	2 476	2 363	1 147	946	127	42
Wakulla	542	1.8	21 514	2 145	147	27	78	87	81	31	35	9	1
Walton	889	6.8	20 018	2 546	414	79	178	192	181	80	68	15	2
Washington	394	4.6	18 419	2 838	186	18	65	122	116	41	53	11	2
GEORGIA	246 247	2.7	28 821	X	174 431	20 756	39 692	32 754	30 327	10 804	13 455	3 282	1 044
Appling	346	0.8	19 603	2 631	232	24	56	87	82	26	41	9	2
Atkinson	144	0.1	18 710	2 796	55	24	20	37	35	9	18	6	1
Bacon	201	-0.8	20 068	2 533	97	20	31	58	56	16	30	6	1
Baker	86	7.3	21 273	2 222	22	11	15	18	17	5	7	3	1
Baldwin	1 063	6.0	23 596	1 536	640	58	195	280	267	66	161	21	4
Banks	353	0.1	23 314	1 625	89	48	53	52	48	23	18	4	2
Barrow	1 204	2.2	23 501	1 568	411	76	158	177	163	61	75	17	6
Bartow	2 133	4.0	25 860	918	1 191	180	276	298	274	116	114	21	11
Ben Hill	398	5.1	22 991	1 726	274	42	65	105	100	27	50	13	3
Berrien	362	3.8	22 175	1 965	150	23	58	88	83	25	42	9	1
Bibb	4 568	4.6	29 587	383	3 491	387	849	868	824	252	398	105	20
Bleckley	283	6.3	23 969	1 420	137	12	53	61	58	18	27	6	1
Brantley	290	5.3	19 114	2 737	66	19	41	72	68	23	31	7	2
Brooks	348	3.6	21 308	2 205	97	25	67	84	79	25	36	11	3
Bryan	637	3.9	25 235	1 065	137	44	85	87	80	29	36	8	2
Bulloch	1 151	4.2	20 158	2 509	675	65	208	216	200	65	87	24	3
Burke	417	3.1	18 300	2 861	267	20	62	119	112	32	52	19	4
Butts	477	3.8	22 270	1 940	182	20	63	94	88	30	43	9	2
Calhoun	124	11.3	19 595	2 637	52	18	26	33	31	8	17	5	1
Camden	1 017	5.5	22 516	1 873	846	32	123	127	116	43	47	12	4
Candler	195	2.8	19 846	2 577	77	22	33	58	55	16	31	6	1
Carroll	2 120	3.8	22 339	1 924	1 162	155	339	396	369	137	169	34	9
Catoosa	1 303	3.4	23 086	1 700	484	101	143	201	185	90	67	13	5
Charlton	177	6.8	16 684	3 011	74	8	27	49	46	14	22	5	1
Chatham	6 877	4.0	29 274	411	5 176	338	1 463	1 136	1 070	378	474	111	24
Chattahoochee	261	4.5	13 525	3 095	810	2	32	19	16	4	5	4	1
Chattooga	491	4.3	18 783	2 785	240	28	68	125	118	47	54	10	3
Cherokee	4 855	1.9	30 450	309	1 358	303	672	388	343	159	133	18	14
Clarke	2 353	4.9	22 860	1 760	2 487	133	560	353	323	114	142	39	5
Clay	84	14.9	24 999	1 128	27	9	15	22	21	6	10	4	0
Clayton	5 471	2.7	21 585	2 124	5 568	212	523	805	733	213	348	84	37
Clinch	124	5.2	18 004	2 898	73	8	17	41	39	10	22	5	1
Cobb	23 332	0.8	36 357	115	15 537	1 992	3 219	1 699	1 514	639	620	106	77
Coffee	829	4.1	21 435	2 170	585	64	117	182	172	50	86	23	5
Colquitt	863	2.3	20 107	2 520	421	72	144	214	201	65	94	28	5
Columbia	2 881	4.0	30 345	315	749	123	494	292	265	112	100	18	6
Cook	308	5.7	19 331	2 690	151	16	50	83	78	24	39	10	2
Coweta	2 633	2.6	26 932	714	1 024	95	373	320	292	122	124	25	9
Crawford	272	4.0	21 658	2 103	44	16	38	42	39	12	17	5	2
Crisp	465	4.2	21 036	2 289	258	35	85	123	116	34	58	17	4
Dade	338	3.6	21 463	2 159	101	20	50	65	61	25	27	5	2
Dawson	478	2.5	27 106	677	152	35	78	57	52	22	22	4	2
Decatur	594	3.0	21 162	2 249	335	59	100	147	139	44	63	21	4
De Kalb	22 983	2.1	34 118	158	15 558	2 999	3 545	2 275	2 081	710	883	235	115
Dodge	380	6.9	19 687	2 613	181	19	71	97	92	28	47	11	2
Dooly	229	1.1	19 831	2 581	113	24	40	62	59	19	27	9	2
Dougherty	2 251	4.0	23 500	1 569	2 073	188	399	509	482	141	207	82	14
Douglas	2 570	2.3	26 085	871	1 123	105	288	320	292	113	130	24	11
Early	299	4.5	24 605	1 236	196	37	53	73	69	21	33	13	2
Echols	64	7.2	16 661	3 012	18	5	9	11	10	3	4	1	0
Effingham	936	3.8	22 802	1 782	285	34	104	131	119	48	49	11	3
Elbert	466	4.3	22 567	1 860	236	39	92	114	108	41	49	12	3
Emanuel	442	4.6	20 313	2 476	217	25	73	136	130	38	64	18	3
Evans	227	4.5	20 397	2 459	141	13	41	56	53	16	25	8	1

1. Based on the resident population estimated as of July 1 of the year shown. 2. Includes other labor income.

STATE County	Earnings, 2002 Total (mil dol)	Farm	Goods-related[1] Total	Manu-facturing	Information and professional and technical services	Retail trade	Finance, insurance, and real estate	Health services	Govern-ment	Social Security beneficiaries, December 2003 Number	Rate[2]	Supplemental Security Income recipients, December 2003	Housing units, 2003 Total	Percent change, 2000–2003
	75	76	77	78	79	80	81	82	83	84	85	86	87	88
FLORIDA—Cont'd														
Sarasota	6 778	0.2	D	5.9	10.7	10.1	11.0	16.1	9.0	106 145	306	3 544	195 373	7.1
Seminole	7 004	0.2	17.1	6.6	16.9	11.5	10.5	8.2	10.1	54 920	142	5 029	158 829	8.0
Sumter	417	2.5	15.4	7.7	2.2	9.1	1.8	D	41.5	21 300	362	1 223	29 306	16.3
Suwannee	368	8.9	D	D	D	10.5	4.5	D	19.2	9 130	249	1 140	16 005	2.1
Taylor	261	0.4	37.8	28.1	2.4	6.7	2.3	D	21.0	4 100	211	655	9 756	1.1
Union	150	0.8	D	3.6	D	D	D	8.3	62.4	1 595	114	312	3 814	2.1
Volusia	5 639	1.3	D	7.4	8.2	10.9	7.5	15.3	16.5	119 140	254	9 411	224 192	5.8
Wakulla	174	1.1	24.4	14.7	7.1	5.8	4.9	D	30.6	3 620	139	512	11 009	12.1
Walton	493	1.2	D	5.7	D	13.4	6.2	5.6	19.2	9 140	197	847	32 826	12.9
Washington	205	1.6	19.2	11.3	3.4	7.3	1.9	D	44.0	5 020	232	860	9 711	2.2
GEORGIA	195 187	0.8	17.8	11.7	14.6	6.9	8.5	7.7	16.5	1 168 095	135	199 991	3 576 427	9.0
Appling	257	3.9	17.9	12.8	2.3	5.5	2.5	D	16.4	3 230	181	737	8 020	2.1
Atkinson	79	26.9	32.5	30.7	D	4.2	D	2.6	17.5	1 240	157	403	3 254	2.6
Bacon	117	5.9	25.7	23.9	D	8.2	D	D	16.0	1 985	196	453	4 559	2.1
Baker	33	36.6	D	D	D	2.6	D	D	20.8	705	164	199	1 790	2.9
Baldwin	697	0.2	D	19.5	2.5	8.3	3.3	12.1	39.9	7 165	159	1 345	17 847	3.9
Banks	137	18.1	D	21.6	3.0	3.1	D	D	14.6	2 665	172	286	6 227	7.2
Barrow	487	2.6	18.6	18.6	4.4	12.3	5.4	5.3	18.9	6 915	129	1 271	20 422	18.0
Bartow	1 371	0.8	39.4	27.9	4.5	8.4	4.3	5.7	13.8	12 515	148	1 452	32 800	14.1
Ben Hill	315	5.6	45.0	42.2	D	5.4	4.9	D	16.7	3 210	186	777	7 737	1.5
Berrien	173	4.7	D	33.9	5.8	7.5	4.7	D	15.8	3 180	193	660	7 286	2.6
Bibb	3 878	0.0	D	17.2	9.7	7.5	10.4	16.9	12.7	27 890	181	6 903	68 805	2.4
Bleckley	149	0.7	D	D	D	6.4	3.4	D	23.0	2 365	200	428	4 999	2.7
Brantley	85	5.4	D	7.1	D	5.9	D	D	29.3	2 820	185	467	6 713	3.4
Brooks	122	17.5	20.8	13.5	1.9	6.8	3.6	D	20.1	3 150	194	678	7 231	1.6
Bryan	181	-0.2	21.8	5.5	6.0	9.1	13.1	D	23.7	3 190	121	471	9 831	13.3
Bulloch	740	2.3	D	9.9	D	9.7	4.4	11.0	30.2	7 400	127	1 564	24 672	8.5
Burke	287	-0.2	19.4	17.3	D	5.4	2.0	D	16.6	4 065	177	1 098	9 052	2.4
Butts	202	0.9	23.1	16.7	2.9	7.1	5.6	D	24.8	3 485	158	504	8 249	11.8
Calhoun	70	23.0	D	D	0.6	4.8	3.0	2.1	33.7	1 070	175	371	2 336	1.3
Camden	878	0.1	12.8	9.8	D	5.1	2.2	3.4	61.8	4 750	104	626	18 682	10.2
Candler	98	4.4	12.8	8.2	7.8	11.3	7.1	D	24.5	1 950	195	522	3 970	2.0
Carroll	1 317	1.7	D	27.6	5.0	9.1	4.2	11.6	17.3	14 945	152	2 456	39 805	16.8
Catoosa	586	1.4	D	15.8	3.4	11.6	5.8	16.6	12.9	9 400	162	757	23 475	7.7
Charlton	82	1.4	18.8	16.4	D	8.0	3.2	6.9	27.3	1 745	163	365	3 968	2.8
Chatham	5 515	0.0	D	13.8	7.6	7.7	5.3	13.1	19.4	38 315	163	6 436	104 609	4.9
Chattahoochee	812	0.0	D	D	D	0.6	D	D	94.9	530	27	120	3 320	0.1
Chattooga	269	0.4	53.0	47.8	D	7.8	3.0	D	20.8	5 160	195	827	10 840	1.5
Cherokee	1 660	0.7	D	8.3	7.2	11.0	7.7	7.6	15.3	16 335	98	904	63 608	22.5
Clarke	2 620	0.1	D	15.0	5.2	7.6	4.3	14.2	34.9	11 890	115	2 567	45 687	8.5
Clay	36	21.1	19.1	0.0	D	5.9	D	5.0	36.3	785	234	212	1 951	1.4
Clayton	5 779	0.0	D	5.7	5.7	6.9	2.5	7.0	11.2	23 390	90	5 465	96 865	12.0
Clinch	81	2.7	35.3	34.0	D	3.8	1.8	3.1	23.7	1 300	187	429	2 882	1.6
Cobb	17 529	0.0	13.9	4.9	19.0	7.5	9.8	7.0	8.3	60 880	94	6 213	256 274	7.9
Coffee	649	5.1	30.2	25.0	3.3	11.7	3.2	D	13.3	6 100	156	1 494	16 267	4.2
Colquitt	494	8.1	21.0	16.6	4.0	10.3	4.1	D	24.7	7 410	172	1 880	17 822	1.5
Columbia	872	0.4	D	16.1	D	10.9	6.9	7.9	15.5	11 900	122	856	36 990	11.0
Cook	167	8.3	28.2	23.2	D	7.0	5.6	8.8	17.2	2 930	184	621	6 751	2.9
Coweta	1 119	0.2	D	19.2	6.0	11.4	4.7	9.8	16.4	12 815	126	1 434	38 238	15.2
Crawford	60	8.1	D	3.7	D	7.0	D	6.5	26.0	1 845	147	270	5 330	9.4
Crisp	292	5.4	23.6	15.4	3.1	11.0	5.9	D	19.2	3 985	181	1 177	9 774	2.2
Dade	121	1.7	D	26.5	D	11.3	4.6	2.0	17.8	2 855	179	370	6 370	2.3
Dawson	188	3.5	20.9	10.7	D	16.0	6.8	2.9	16.7	2 360	127	260	8 249	15.2
Decatur	394	9.5	29.7	20.5	2.2	7.9	4.3	D	22.9	5 190	184	1 316	12 336	3.1
De Kalb	18 558	0.0	11.8	6.9	15.6	6.3	8.5	9.5	13.8	70 820	105	12 601	283 656	8.6
Dodge	199	2.9	13.6	9.4	3.4	8.3	4.2	D	37.4	3 325	172	880	8 339	1.9
Dooly	137	12.0	27.0	25.5	D	5.4	D	D	22.4	2 370	205	571	4 559	1.3
Dougherty	2 261	0.5	D	19.0	7.4	7.5	4.1	13.7	22.4	15 825	165	4 920	40 583	2.3
Douglas	1 229	-0.1	D	10.5	6.4	15.0	4.9	8.7	15.5	11 760	115	1 187	40 656	16.7
Early	233	12.7	37.3	34.8	2.1	3.6	D	D	13.0	2 420	198	730	5 433	1.8
Echols	23	15.4	D	D	D	1.2	D	1.4	22.9	420	105	47	1 534	3.5
Effingham	319	0.5	44.8	35.9	4.0	7.4	2.6	D	23.0	5 270	123	568	15 739	11.1
Elbert	276	1.2	41.9	34.2	3.4	6.6	3.4	4.7	21.5	4 630	224	933	9 321	2.0
Emanuel	242	0.9	D	24.7	4.9	8.7	3.2	D	30.6	4 535	207	1 459	9 565	1.6
Evans	154	2.7	42.1	33.6	D	7.8	2.7	D	17.0	1 960	172	530	4 493	2.6

1. Covers mining, construction, and manufacturing.   2. Per 1,000 resident population estimated as of July 1 of the year shown.

Table B. States and Counties — Housing, Labor Force, and Employment

STATE County	Housing units, 2000								Civilian labor force, 2003				Civilian employment,[6] 2000		
	Occupied units							Substandard units[4] (percent)	Total	Percent change, 2002–2003	Unemployment		Total	Percent	
	Total	Percent	Owner-occupied			Renter-occupied					Total	Rate[5]		Management, professional and related occupations	Production, transportation, and material moving occupations
			Median value[1]	Median owner cost as a percent of income		Median rent[3]	Median rent as a percent of income								
				With a mortgage	Without a mortgage[2]										
	89	90	91	92	93	94	95	96	97	98	99	100	101	102	103
FLORIDA—Cont'd															
Sarasota	149 937	79.1	122 000	23.5	10.7	711	27.6	2.3	166 718	2.4	5 482	3.3	135 419	31.7	8.9
Seminole	139 572	69.5	119 900	21.4	9.9	731	25.8	3.8	224 401	1.4	11 164	5.0	190 973	38.7	8.1
Sumter	20 779	86.4	100 400	22.1	9.9	410	25.0	3.2	18 220	6.4	641	3.5	15 109	21.2	14.9
Suwannee	13 460	81.0	68 500	20.0	10.6	394	24.2	6.5	13 742	-1.4	544	4.0	13 902	24.3	16.0
Taylor	7 176	79.8	66 000	20.7	10.0	389	22.6	4.7	7 660	-0.1	627	8.2	7 413	20.0	21.0
Union	3 367	74.5	71 700	20.3	9.9	345	19.4	6.7	3 989	0.2	133	3.3	4 018	19.4	13.2
Volusia	184 723	75.3	87 300	22.9	10.6	597	28.1	3.3	198 240	2.5	10 061	5.1	189 035	28.8	11.8
Wakulla	8 450	84.2	96 200	22.4	9.9	506	30.6	3.4	13 377	3.3	468	3.5	10 602	28.6	11.2
Walton	16 548	79.0	96 400	22.4	9.9	486	24.2	3.9	20 762	6.5	568	2.7	17 188	24.7	11.2
Washington	7 931	81.9	70 000	21.2	9.9	383	26.1	4.2	9 152	-4.0	376	4.1	8 069	25.6	14.5
GEORGIA	3 006 369	67.5	111 200	20.8	9.9	613	24.9	5.3	4 414 014	3.1	207 191	4.7	3 839 756	32.7	15.7
Appling	6 606	79.0	63 700	19.1	10.5	351	23.7	5.1	7 642	-0.6	582	7.6	7 732	21.1	24.7
Atkinson	2 717	74.2	46 700	20.5	11.1	288	19.5	8.2	3 242	11.9	242	7.5	3 193	18.6	34.0
Bacon	3 833	74.9	56 500	20.6	11.1	316	26.4	4.3	3 943	4.4	215	5.5	4 291	20.6	24.7
Baker	1 514	77.6	62 700	22.4	9.9	311	17.4	8.1	1 707	5.5	78	4.6	1 592	26.5	25.1
Baldwin	14 758	66.4	79 800	19.9	9.9	478	22.9	4.4	18 535	3.6	663	3.6	17 478	28.1	17.1
Banks	5 364	81.0	92 400	20.2	9.9	424	21.2	4.7	6 969	0.3	268	3.8	7 099	21.1	25.5
Barrow	16 354	75.5	103 400	22.5	10.7	583	23.3	4.1	25 035	2.7	1 281	5.1	22 874	22.5	21.4
Bartow	27 176	75.2	99 600	20.2	9.9	575	23.4	4.4	42 687	2.4	2 346	5.5	36 637	24.8	21.3
Ben Hill	6 673	66.7	60 700	20.5	11.8	371	27.0	4.4	8 311	-2.8	589	7.1	7 387	23.0	32.0
Berrien	6 261	75.6	70 700	19.3	9.9	369	25.0	3.3	6 826	8.5	232	3.4	7 335	22.2	25.6
Bibb	59 667	58.8	84 400	20.1	9.9	474	25.7	4.3	74 848	4.6	3 292	4.4	64 422	32.3	14.0
Bleckley	4 372	76.1	66 500	18.3	9.9	373	22.7	4.2	6 068	4.3	216	3.6	4 763	23.5	26.5
Brantley	5 436	86.9	60 900	18.2	9.9	382	21.3	5.8	7 167	1.4	421	5.9	6 154	19.9	17.8
Brooks	6 155	76.9	67 900	22.1	11.4	353	25.9	5.4	7 800	4.0	224	2.9	6 815	24.1	21.3
Bryan	8 089	78.0	115 600	20.0	11.5	541	24.2	3.8	12 207	4.5	382	3.1	10 633	30.2	15.7
Bulloch	20 743	58.1	94 300	19.1	9.9	436	32.3	4.0	29 314	5.9	869	3.0	24 775	31.5	15.4
Burke	7 934	76.0	59 800	20.8	9.9	315	25.2	6.6	9 463	3.5	979	10.3	8 220	21.4	29.5
Butts	6 455	76.6	86 700	20.9	11.0	480	24.5	4.0	9 800	6.1	452	4.6	8 114	17.7	27.1
Calhoun	1 962	71.6	48 200	20.0	11.0	291	23.2	7.0	2 431	4.4	155	6.4	2 109	22.6	26.6
Camden	14 705	63.2	85 300	21.0	10.4	551	21.5	4.1	17 285	2.1	1 034	6.0	16 495	27.9	14.1
Candler	3 375	73.2	62 700	19.1	12.2	353	26.7	9.1	3 983	2.9	146	3.7	3 630	21.5	23.2
Carroll	31 568	70.5	93 300	21.0	9.9	488	24.7	3.7	47 846	2.6	2 533	5.3	40 527	26.6	19.8
Catoosa	20 425	77.0	90 800	19.1	9.9	482	23.7	2.0	30 250	3.9	787	2.6	27 154	25.0	21.4
Charlton	3 342	80.7	67 300	21.5	14.1	394	25.8	6.3	4 532	2.0	259	5.7	3 548	14.5	28.2
Chatham	89 865	60.4	95 000	21.6	11.1	589	27.4	4.8	115 990	4.4	4 738	4.1	102 196	32.3	13.0
Chattahoochee	2 932	27.9	63 800	19.4	12.6	581	20.6	5.5	2 307	3.1	175	7.6	2 280	26.6	16.5
Chattooga	9 577	75.4	59 900	19.6	9.9	380	20.0	3.8	11 136	1.6	383	3.4	10 722	17.9	38.8
Cherokee	49 495	83.9	139 900	21.1	9.9	740	23.9	2.9	88 446	2.9	3 483	3.9	75 316	36.4	10.1
Clarke	39 706	42.1	111 300	20.2	9.9	540	32.3	5.4	51 327	4.3	1 569	3.1	49 159	36.9	14.5
Clay	1 347	74.2	53 600	22.7	11.1	265	28.3	10.4	1 843	8.5	60	3.3	1 216	23.8	18.8
Clayton	82 243	60.6	92 700	21.2	9.9	699	24.9	8.1	142 733	2.7	8 551	6.0	114 468	24.1	18.0
Clinch	2 512	72.4	54 600	17.8	9.9	256	19.8	4.9	2 887	3.9	125	4.3	2 604	20.7	30.8
Cobb	227 487	68.2	147 600	20.1	9.9	806	24.5	4.5	383 262	2.4	15 956	4.2	329 136	42.4	8.1
Coffee	13 354	74.4	68 800	20.1	9.9	380	21.2	6.2	21 283	4.2	1 354	6.4	15 660	20.2	29.1
Colquitt	15 495	66.7	65 400	19.3	11.1	370	25.4	6.2	18 109	1.0	922	5.1	17 694	23.9	23.1
Columbia	31 120	82.1	118 000	20.1	9.9	620	24.4	2.2	46 609	4.2	1 333	2.9	43 090	41.5	11.3
Cook	5 882	74.9	60 900	22.2	12.1	404	24.4	6.1	7 642	1.7	367	4.8	6 727	23.0	26.5
Coweta	31 442	78.0	121 700	20.4	9.9	628	25.6	3.9	48 663	3.0	2 249	4.6	44 098	29.6	16.6
Crawford	4 461	84.8	77 800	20.4	9.9	420	23.1	3.4	6 378	5.6	262	4.1	5 409	21.1	21.8
Crisp	8 337	60.5	74 400	19.4	11.1	368	27.8	5.7	9 220	2.3	555	6.0	8 869	25.2	19.9
Dade	5 633	80.2	79 200	20.0	9.9	406	22.1	3.6	7 940	3.3	280	3.5	7 059	22.1	24.3
Dawson	6 069	81.4	142 500	22.2	10.2	685	22.8	2.7	11 476	9.7	343	3.0	8 168	30.0	18.4
Decatur	10 380	72.5	80 200	20.7	11.1	384	22.4	6.6	11 491	3.9	697	6.1	11 346	26.3	22.0
De Kalb	249 339	58.5	135 100	21.5	9.9	767	25.7	7.6	392 478	2.2	21 769	5.5	347 410	39.6	10.9
Dodge	7 062	73.8	54 200	20.1	9.9	321	23.2	4.7	10 288	2.7	411	4.0	7 644	24.4	24.3
Dooly	3 909	71.4	62 300	18.9	11.7	313	25.9	8.3	4 528	3.7	316	7.0	4 261	23.8	22.9
Dougherty	35 552	53.5	73 900	20.5	10.9	469	25.6	7.6	43 724	4.0	2 462	5.6	37 392	29.7	17.1
Douglas	32 822	74.8	102 700	20.4	9.9	731	24.3	3.9	54 380	2.9	2 595	4.8	46 944	29.5	14.7
Early	4 695	72.4	58 600	17.8	11.5	292	27.7	7.6	5 144	7.4	366	7.1	4 845	23.2	27.6
Echols	1 264	75.7	76 000	21.4	18.5	390	25.7	7.4	1 905	5.7	47	2.5	1 683	14.7	16.8
Effingham	13 151	82.7	106 600	20.0	9.9	500	23.0	4.3	20 825	4.7	759	3.6	17 380	25.5	18.3
Elbert	8 004	75.9	66 600	21.1	9.9	327	22.0	3.9	9 709	3.1	637	6.6	8 733	20.4	32.3
Emanuel	8 045	71.2	50 800	20.1	11.6	296	25.7	6.5	8 840	7.0	532	6.0	8 897	20.6	24.7
Evans	3 778	71.4	69 000	22.5	9.9	371	26.2	4.9	5 252	1.2	167	3.2	4 240	19.6	25.1

1. Specified owner-occupied units.   2. Median monthly owner costs is often in the minimum category—9.9 percent or less, which is indicated as 9.9 percent.   3. Specified renter-occupied units.   4. Overcrowded or lacking complete plumbing facilities.   5. Percent of civilian labor force.   6. Persons 16 years old and over.

	Private nonfarm establishments, employment and payroll, 2001								Agriculture, 2002			
STATE County		Employment					Annual payroll		Farms			
											Percent with—	Farm operators whose principal occupation is farming (percent)
	Number of establishments	Total	Health care and social assistance	Manufacturing	Retail trade	Finance and insurance	Professional, scientific, and technical services	Total (mil dol)	Average per employee (dollars)	Number	Less than 50 acres	500 acres and over	
	104	105	106	107	108	109	110	111	112	113	114	115	116
FLORIDA—Cont'd													
Sarasota	11 493	156 453	21 478	7 463	22 605	5 906	8 858	4 251	27 174	371	68.7	10.2	52.3
Seminole	10 725	136 151	12 246	8 019	23 913	8 728	9 146	4 218	30 983	376	85.4	1.1	44.1
Sumter	518	5 127	278	941	1 172	125	96	114	22 147	902	61.3	4.9	53.0
Suwannee	624	7 501	1 038	D	1 481	250	170	148	19 690	1 054	45.2	5.7	58.3
Taylor	389	4 456	649	1 601	767	127	75	123	27 533	101	37.6	16.8	41.6
Union	124	1 492	464	168	155	D	D	41	27 312	275	54.2	5.8	44.0
Volusia	10 827	132 851	19 539	10 311	25 040	4 662	5 371	3 051	22 967	1 114	80.8	3.2	48.6
Wakulla	354	2 698	319	387	439	138	130	55	20 246	126	66.7	3.2	48.4
Walton	915	8 431	731	629	1 864	155	163	176	20 852	540	41.3	5.2	48.1
Washington	339	4 002	839	D	763	60	134	79	19 629	391	37.9	4.9	47.8
GEORGIA	202 505	3 498 583	361 620	491 688	464 576	174 964	205 699	115 913	33 131	49 311	39.2	9.9	50.9
Appling	373	4 653	585	984	614	138	D	149	32 123	557	37.0	10.8	56.7
Atkinson	97	1 383	D	1 033	126	45	2	32	23 267	194	21.6	22.2	67.5
Bacon	216	2 855	350	1 060	276	152	46	60	20 854	331	34.4	11.8	51.4
Baker	25	267	D	0	D	D	D	7	24 356	147	27.9	33.3	66.0
Baldwin	847	14 566	5 099	2 644	2 341	319	209	346	23 727	194	32.5	7.2	41.8
Banks	205	2 955	D	1 009	451	D	28	56	18 975	614	47.2	2.3	61.1
Barrow	850	10 276	717	2 920	1 983	300	276	263	25 622	452	56.9	1.3	54.0
Bartow	1 619	26 317	1 915	8 739	3 644	493	623	722	27 451	586	50.3	5.1	50.9
Ben Hill	380	6 604	588	3 516	959	219	106	168	25 387	174	30.5	14.4	57.5
Berrien	280	3 935	444	1 745	497	234	28	91	23 064	481	29.1	15.6	55.5
Bibb	4 575	79 713	13 569	9 358	12 241	6 527	2 985	2 280	28 588	168	41.1	8.9	39.3
Bleckley	192	3 256	368	D	456	185	D	67	20 579	265	25.3	10.6	55.1
Brantley	181	1 510	100	205	285	D	D	31	20 446	270	43.0	5.2	47.8
Brooks	200	2 190	542	638	362	106	D	45	20 550	446	24.9	20.0	50.7
Bryan	403	3 264	355	D	732	140	101	68	20 697	65	58.5	10.8	46.2
Bulloch	1 244	16 382	1 952	2 724	3 447	553	395	338	20 636	641	33.4	17.6	51.8
Burke	332	5 478	365	1 459	776	127	D	158	28 811	494	24.5	23.9	48.8
Butts	345	4 255	573	997	597	148	86	96	22 604	173	36.4	9.2	47.4
Calhoun	105	790	192	D	163	43	7	15	18 978	119	20.2	44.5	56.3
Camden	698	8 294	812	1 394	2 161	268	191	164	19 800	47	36.2	17.0	38.3
Candler	206	2 434	378	367	389	57	87	47	19 199	272	26.1	12.9	46.0
Carroll	1 868	27 174	3 275	7 962	3 951	919	574	770	28 353	975	45.4	1.9	56.7
Catoosa	768	10 345	1 940	2 207	2 381	344	195	251	24 225	296	50.3	2.4	51.4
Charlton	175	1 655	214	334	192	71	D	35	21 021	101	41.6	6.9	34.7
Chatham	6 636	110 482	15 807	13 038	16 525	3 938	3 853	3 148	28 491	58	46.6	10.3	51.7
Chattahoochee	55	1 304	D	D	D	D	71	57	29 151	16	37.5	12.5	43.8
Chattooga	334	6 409	271	4 077	855	190	54	141	22 074	329	28.9	5.8	44.1
Cherokee	3 413	31 227	2 586	4 111	6 943	1 038	1 498	790	25 301	606	71.1	1.8	55.8
Clarke	2 649	43 027	7 395	8 412	7 888	1 337	1 411	1 079	25 087	104	42.3	5.8	35.6
Clay	47	277	92	0	91	D	0	4	15 339	49	10.2	36.7	49.0
Clayton	4 340	90 040	7 283	5 753	14 396	3 969	1 735	2 536	28 161	62	71.0	0.0	33.9
Clinch	129	2 548	204	890	145	11	66	46	17 960	118	46.6	19.5	45.8
Cobb	18 024	316 010	21 593	22 505	41 830	14 241	27 179	12 150	38 449	191	74.9	2.1	52.9
Coffee	830	14 951	1 373	4 937	2 145	329	232	341	22 782	692	28.8	13.2	54.3
Colquitt	885	11 278	1 534	2 698	2 580	346	213	228	20 214	588	31.3	20.4	59.5
Columbia	1 784	26 835	6 497	4 432	3 798	734	976	770	28 685	196	54.6	4.1	38.3
Cook	335	3 931	467	1 328	631	143	67	80	20 368	254	37.0	13.4	58.3
Coweta	1 679	24 353	2 260	5 682	4 171	1 046	480	623	25 569	480	51.0	5.2	42.7
Crawford	81	692	244	162	110	41	5	12	16 723	179	31.8	6.7	43.6
Crisp	538	7 321	952	1 770	1 612	251	107	148	20 263	223	32.3	25.1	55.6
Dade	221	2 599	123	956	505	88	39	50	19 415	253	49.0	3.2	41.1
Dawson	498	4 382	159	563	1 749	87	165	93	21 326	222	56.8	6.3	51.4
Decatur	588	8 788	1 011	3 011	1 638	447	98	189	21 511	396	25.0	18.4	50.3
De Kalb	16 941	323 875	35 347	21 929	34 924	14 145	20 737	11 285	34 843	37	81.1	0.0	45.9
Dodge	369	3 667	1 007	424	754	144	110	72	19 683	491	24.6	12.8	49.1
Dooly	175	2 754	346	1 615	230	92	D	54	19 467	326	22.4	25.8	60.7
Dougherty	2 533	44 123	7 012	7 763	7 344	1 360	1 547	1 224	27 745	162	46.3	20.4	54.3
Douglas	2 168	29 650	2 666	2 784	7 989	753	915	709	23 922	153	64.1	0.7	43.1
Early	237	3 024	287	1 121	428	153	84	108	35 746	347	25.6	23.3	53.9
Echols	10	33	D	0	12	0	0	1	17 364	78	23.1	17.9	37.2
Effingham	520	5 735	509	2 017	1 086	89	219	166	28 903	206	35.0	13.1	51.0
Elbert	542	6 127	599	3 094	714	197	109	141	23 012	438	29.9	4.6	48.2
Emanuel	408	5 044	733	1 964	809	165	135	101	20 037	554	20.6	14.6	37.5
Evans	239	3 995	397	1 877	433	92	51	78	19 606	242	30.2	11.6	40.5

Table B. States and Counties — **Agriculture**

Agriculture, 2002 (cont'd)

STATE County	Land in farms — Acreage (1,000)	Percent change, 1997–2002	Average size of farm	Total irrigated (1,000)	Total cropland (1,000)	Value of land and buildings — Average per farm	Average per acre	Value of machinery and equipment average per farm (dollars)	Value of products sold — Total (mil dol)	Average per farm (dollars)	Percent from — Crops	Livestock and poultry products	Percent of farms with sales of — $10,000 or more	$100,000 or more	Government payments — Total ($1,000)	Percent of farms
	117	118	119	120	121	122	123	124	125	126	127	128	129	130	131	132
FLORIDA—Cont'd																
Sarasota	121	-6.2	327	5	33	841 623	2 995	22 024	18	47 982	75.0	25.0	31.8	8.6	D	D
Seminole	28	-24.3	74	2	4	424 814	6 137	14 884	19	51 094	93.4	6.6	31.6	8.0	0	0.8
Sumter	187	2.2	208	4	45	502 601	2 405	23 327	31	33 974	45.8	54.2	23.4	6.1	326	4.3
Suwannee	170	7.6	161	18	69	363 639	2 503	46 675	136	128 995	23.9	76.1	30.9	14.1	1 163	10.2
Taylor	54	-5.3	532	0	3	732 184	1 292	31 207	13	132 221	5.4	94.6	30.7	9.9	6	4.0
Union	60	-4.8	217	1	19	329 264	1 318	24 016	11	38 948	39.9	60.1	25.8	8.4	31	8.4
Volusia	94	-16.1	84	9	19	329 264	4 357	20 565	106	95 419	92.6	7.4	33.9	11.2	23	1.0
Wakulla	11	0.0	87	0	3	210 229	2 891	26 466	2	12 571	40.5	59.5	27.8	2.4	34	4.8
Walton	80	1.3	148	2	32	325 288	1 889	35 615	20	37 139	22.6	77.4	22.2	6.3	346	22.4
Washington	53	-3.6	136	1	18	329 229	2 288	50 772	6	14 081	41.6	58.4	16.9	3.6	411	33.5
GEORGIA	10 744	0.7	218	871	4 677	457 427	2 112	51 847	4 912	99 608	32.2	67.8	30.7	12.7	118 535	31.5
Appling	119	10.2	213	8	62	315 103	1 566	65 450	56	100 046	36.3	63.7	35.5	14.9	2 013	37.5
Atkinson	71	12.7	365	4	26	504 760	1 419	96 179	42	214 587	22.2	77.8	52.1	22.7	780	51.5
Bacon	67	-4.3	202	4	29	432 046	2 180	65 014	40	119 462	32.5	67.5	41.1	13.9	671	36.6
Baker	126	5.9	860	20	54	1 496 598	1 751	123 071	28	189 760	61.4	38.6	57.1	32.0	1 884	61.9
Baldwin	36	20.0	184	0	10	343 441	2 344	35 140	7	35 949	5.0	95.0	17.0	4.6	121	14.9
Banks	58	23.4	94	1	20	448 211	5 033	65 010	103	168 526	0.8	99.2	41.0	27.9	278	18.2
Barrow	36	-12.2	80	0	14	365 373	5 785	33 557	52	114 091	1.2	98.8	32.3	17.9	143	17.9
Bartow	82	-2.4	139	2	34	393 509	2 914	38 580	49	83 635	15.1	84.9	28.2	13.3	330	18.6
Ben Hill	57	7.5	330	8	31	501 707	1 432	67 861	14	77 811	65.4	34.6	40.2	16.7	949	41.4
Berrien	126	-3.8	262	11	58	419 823	1 680	47 846	27	55 518	76.6	23.4	39.3	11.6	1 722	43.5
Bibb	30	36.4	181	0	9	385 532	2 354	23 487	6	35 076	20.7	79.3	27.4	6.5	93	14.9
Bleckley	55	-22.5	209	7	30	327 183	1 647	46 185	6	22 053	83.7	16.3	22.6	5.7	1 229	54.3
Brantley	32	14.3	120	0	10	189 808	1 602	26 761	12	46 096	21.1	78.9	24.8	5.2	47	15.9
Brooks	203	7.4	455	17	90	672 946	1 602	83 898	55	124 011	73.3	26.7	43.3	16.4	2 813	52.2
Bryan	17	-32.0	264	D	6	442 835	1 687	21 241	1	18 978	80.2	19.7	16.9	4.6	64	21.5
Bulloch	206	3.0	322	11	114	481 079	1 629	71 515	43	66 629	77.9	22.1	36.3	11.2	3 362	47.9
Burke	219	4.3	443	16	105	626 372	1 344	92 931	26	53 131	59.1	40.9	34.6	11.9	2 232	48.0
Butts	37	37.0	212	0	9	465 477	2 036	30 068	2	14 311	32.4	67.5	24.9	2.3	124	32.9
Calhoun	118	-8.5	992	22	65	1 265 558	1 298	228 408	26	217 192	75.7	24.3	52.1	35.3	1 571	74.8
Camden	12	-36.8	264	0	1	463 421	1 615	16 788	1	21 161	83.2	16.8	12.8	2.1	27	8.5
Candler	63	-19.2	231	4	26	310 984	1 354	52 952	12	43 424	65.4	34.6	32.4	8.8	840	50.7
Carroll	94	20.5	97	1	35	381 616	3 897	35 935	106	109 085	4.6	95.4	27.2	12.6	335	17.3
Catoosa	27	22.7	92	0	13	377 949	3 877	40 839	24	81 807	3.0	97.0	23.0	8.8	90	10.8
Charlton	15	-25.0	147	0	4	280 622	1 933	25 025	4	41 240	14.5	85.5	22.8	4.0	30	9.9
Chatham	9	0.0	157	0	2	306 111	2 062	72 210	2	36 137	90.5	9.5	41.4	5.2	32	17.2
Chattahoochee	4	0.0	272	0	0	401 791	1 476	18 654	D	D	D	D	6.3	6.3	50	25.0
Chattooga	55	0.0	167	0	20	294 205	1 699	28 556	6	17 074	13.7	86.3	20.1	2.7	155	22.8
Cherokee	36	12.5	60	0	11	419 719	8 357	21 227	51	84 134	10.7	89.3	24.1	15.0	104	20.8
Clarke	14	7.7	136	0	6	546 050	4 092	30 757	35	338 101	13.9	86.1	33.7	12.5	74	23.1
Clay	42	-4.5	866	8	22	908 452	1 027	127 536	7	135 105	91.5	8.5	40.8	18.4	431	73.5
Clayton	3	-40.0	52	0	2	287 292	5 439	18 326	0	7 718	68.1	31.9	14.5	1.6	10	9.7
Clinch	31	93.8	260	0	3	446 447	1 693	30 696	6	49 507	61.8	38.2	40.7	11.0	5	5.1
Cobb	11	10.0	57	0	3	353 420	9 113	21 451	5	28 150	94.3	5.6	8.4	1.6	31	15.7
Coffee	189	-7.4	273	16	87	440 006	1 584	84 014	124	179 170	31.5	68.5	42.2	18.8	2 589	49.3
Colquitt	228	-0.4	388	34	134	592 036	1 583	94 805	129	220 179	80.5	19.5	45.7	21.8	4 638	46.3
Columbia	23	-20.7	119	0	5	390 151	4 048	26 749	5	24 808	27.5	72.6	14.3	4.6	188	21.9
Cook	68	-19.0	266	9	40	471 291	1 864	71 372	39	152 970	96.6	3.4	43.3	15.4	1 092	33.9
Coweta	61	41.9	127	1	20	698 424	5 540	27 055	7	14 789	57.5	42.5	17.7	1.3	250	13.5
Crawford	38	2.7	213	4	15	409 059	1 992	53 335	19	107 864	63.4	36.6	27.9	10.6	88	21.2
Crisp	104	-9.6	466	14	71	765 368	1 745	123 988	28	127 114	89.7	10.3	47.1	23.3	1 952	52.9
Dade	28	7.7	110	0	11	240 749	2 061	21 285	11	42 872	3.1	96.9	22.1	7.1	60	10.7
Dawson	20	5.3	91	0	6	394 667	4 574	34 532	40	177 969	2.5	97.5	35.1	23.0	83	11.7
Decatur	160	-2.4	405	49	92	678 992	1 653	104 955	101	253 809	86.3	13.7	35.6	18.9	3 160	48.5
De Kalb	1	-83.3	29	0	1	191 989	6 478	13 631	1	23 158	99.4	0.6	16.2	5.4	2	10.8
Dodge	139	-10.9	282	10	45	371 079	1 026	55 372	13	25 998	83.1	16.9	24.8	6.3	1 458	52.5
Dooly	171	3.6	524	30	117	701 021	1 304	146 590	55	167 456	62.5	37.5	56.7	29.8	4 730	65.0
Dougherty	98	18.1	603	16	32	804 439	1 329	90 539	22	138 780	94.2	5.8	25.3	14.2	738	24.1
Douglas	8	-20.0	52	0	3	304 102	5 803	22 902	2	12 906	41.6	58.4	17.6	2.6	17	13.7
Early	160	-7.5	462	25	89	566 192	1 319	91 210	26	75 647	90.8	9.2	40.9	17.9	2 874	61.1
Echols	29	61.1	376	4	11	601 249	1 602	72 948	24	305 392	98.2	1.8	37.2	10.3	55	46.2
Effingham	53	1.9	258	0	18	493 738	1 740	33 430	4	18 131	72.1	27.9	23.3	3.4	190	30.6
Elbert	63	10.5	145	0	26	290 239	2 142	20 707	23	52 821	12.9	87.1	19.2	7.1	397	39.0
Emanuel	160	4.6	288	5	56	411 634	1 225	71 058	12	21 440	67.5	32.5	22.2	4.2	1 478	50.0
Evans	48	11.6	199	3	19	315 045	1 655	48 031	23	92 983	40.0	60.0	29.3	13.2	381	43.8

STATE County	Value of residential construction authorized by building permits, 2003		Wholesale trade, 1997				Retail trade,[1] 1997				Real estate and rental and leasing, 1997			
	New construction ($1,000)	Number of housing units	Number of establish-ments	Number of employees	Sales (mil dol)	Annual payroll (mil dol)	Number of establish-ments	Number of employees	Sales (mil dol)	Annual payroll (mil dol)	Number of establish-ments	Number of employees	Receipts (mil dol)	Annual payroll (mil dol)
	133	134	135	136	137	138	139	140	141	142	143	144	145	146
FLORIDA—Cont'd														
Sarasota	931 177	5 449	527	3 122	1 035.9	86.2	1 669	20 311	3 606.6	343.8	571	2 320	290.4	48.9
Seminole	640 784	3 605	881	7 301	3 669.7	242.9	1 512	21 219	3 550.1	352.1	440	2 090	338.2	50.4
Sumter	203 919	2 280	18	236	84.4	4.5	111	1 192	185.3	14.8	22	51	6.4	0.8
Suwannee	16 309	143	35	D	D	D	137	1 333	205.0	19.2	20	64	5.3	0.7
Taylor	5 350	56	16	D	D	D	97	945	144.2	12.6	12	40	2.4	0.5
Union	3 324	39	3	D	D	D	28	180	27.2	2.8	2	D	D	D
Volusia	915 622	6 416	488	4 314	1 629.7	105.4	1 865	23 251	3 887.6	360.5	546	2 856	277.6	49.8
Wakulla	28 823	462	15	D	D	D	53	418	57.6	5.0	10	14	2.0	0.3
Walton	348 175	1 824	29	283	98.2	6.6	215	1 959	262.6	27.0	55	588	52.2	10.9
Washington	9 344	114	5	D	D	D	70	742	104.4	9.1	8	34	3.3	0.3
GEORGIA	10 837 216	96 704	13 978	191 078	163 647.5	7 519.7	33 073	420 676	72 212.5	6 943.6	7 794	47 669	6 912.9	1 308.8
Appling	850	6	14	92	41.0	2.8	88	616	116.9	9.7	7	11	1.2	0.2
Atkinson	NA	NA	9	67	11.9	0.9	30	154	20.9	1.9	3	D	D	D
Bacon	700	2	10	141	40.4	2.4	37	291	47.1	4.1	4	D	D	D
Baker	NA	NA	1	D	D	D	5	45	4.4	0.4	NA	NA	NA	NA
Baldwin	16 469	170	23	169	57.6	3.8	218	2 407	372.0	34.3	20	65	6.0	1.0
Banks	11 317	109	12	331	44.6	8.5	69	560	75.7	7.1	2	D	D	D
Barrow	100 261	1 348	30	223	73.8	5.6	145	1 798	344.8	30.8	23	65	7.7	1.0
Bartow	134 719	1 186	92	814	258.2	23.1	246	3 219	580.0	53.3	56	265	22.4	3.5
Ben Hill	3 374	70	20	D	D	D	93	884	144.0	12.3	13	44	2.5	0.6
Berrien	1 535	25	24	110	40.5	2.4	62	471	79.3	8.1	9	15	1.0	0.2
Bibb	102 180	1 198	272	3 545	1 511.7	110.7	912	12 885	1 977.3	194.2	185	1 062	148.8	26.2
Bleckley	6 307	52	4	D	D	D	53	392	59.0	4.8	3	6	0.6	0.1
Brantley	627	9	7	44	6.5	1.2	32	180	26.4	2.1	5	16	0.8	0.1
Brooks	5 361	44	9	36	5.8	0.5	57	349	63.5	5.3	2	D	D	D
Bryan	66 927	442	14	D	D	D	61	537	85.3	7.4	11	D	D	D
Bulloch	48 755	456	54	582	333.4	13.9	259	3 386	471.9	44.0	45	208	15.4	2.4
Burke	6 777	58	19	208	128.0	6.1	81	700	118.6	10.6	8	D	D	D
Butts	24 987	286	12	169	143.4	6.7	71	613	111.9	8.3	15	24	2.5	0.2
Calhoun	176	2	6	44	18.8	1.1	25	212	29.0	2.6	2	D	D	D
Camden	65 054	440	9	63	12.5	1.0	143	1 687	275.7	21.7	28	143	14.0	2.7
Candler	522	6	16	146	54.3	3.2	50	388	74.6	5.5	4	8	0.8	0.1
Carroll	179 083	1 750	84	1 232	1 286.3	48.2	348	3 505	574.5	53.2	62	232	24.1	3.7
Catoosa	66 255	644	39	638	747.7	15.7	172	2 524	406.2	35.4	30	91	8.2	1.6
Charlton	1 375	16	8	37	85.0	0.9	49	201	31.8	3.1	4	12	0.6	0.1
Chatham	203 504	1 500	348	4 347	2 445.1	142.9	1 261	15 625	2 466.9	244.0	280	1 470	195.9	36.0
Chattahoochee	475	4	1	D	D	D	6	26	4.2	0.4	1	D	D	D
Chattooga	458	7	12	54	12.4	1.0	82	922	122.5	11.9	9	13	1.0	0.2
Cherokee	479 581	3 804	201	1 103	490.8	34.7	351	5 202	968.9	86.7	93	276	33.6	5.4
Clarke	117 641	1 348	81	D	D	D	540	7 760	1 118.8	110.3	131	524	55.8	9.5
Clay	1 560	11	5	16	3.8	0.3	17	123	10.5	1.2	NA	NA	NA	NA
Clayton	299 840	2 579	316	6 142	3 345.2	217.5	832	16 204	2 731.7	285.3	197	1 326	185.6	30.9
Clinch	672	11	8	60	11.7	1.2	32	220	25.1	2.5	3	4	0.3	0.0
Cobb	783 175	5 963	1 632	24 859	23 231.5	1 270.8	2 234	37 323	6 971.6	663.6	785	5 612	989.9	183.8
Coffee	14 773	155	55	469	183.3	11.2	210	2 120	389.9	33.0	23	112	7.3	1.4
Colquitt	3 798	51	53	436	156.4	9.8	214	2 026	326.0	29.4	29	102	9.0	1.3
Columbia	194 661	1 431	91	D	D	D	247	3 731	613.0	60.0	68	285	33.0	6.3
Cook	935	49	20	231	86.0	3.9	89	824	121.1	10.7	7	12	0.9	0.1
Coweta	225 252	1 994	79	735	513.5	16.8	259	3 728	550.0	52.7	53	155	21.4	3.2
Crawford	18 957	146	2	D	D	D	14	84	11.2	1.2	NA	NA	NA	NA
Crisp	11 139	132	29	483	266.8	12.5	158	1 859	234.5	23.7	22	96	8.3	1.2
Dade	1 640	21	8	D	D	D	54	476	92.3	5.9	7	44	3.1	0.6
Dawson	66 357	378	19	56	71.0	2.1	106	704	119.4	12.2	7	10	1.0	0.2
Decatur	11 324	101	35	452	341.1	11.0	172	1 656	243.6	21.7	22	90	4.9	1.0
De Kalb	860 420	5 106	1 518	23 560	19 215.9	964.4	2 407	34 901	6 229.3	635.7	867	7 216	906.7	188.1
Dodge	3 238	48	20	D	D	D	84	799	102.4	9.0	8	161	9.3	1.6
Dooly	0	0	15	120	56.7	3.2	51	336	65.7	4.8	3	D	D	D
Dougherty	41 974	499	184	D	D	D	574	7 707	1 154.7	113.9	128	629	82.5	12.4
Douglas	131 768	2 145	105	1 492	1 100.1	43.7	312	4 781	974.7	82.6	61	263	37.5	5.6
Early	104	2	19	277	133.3	5.7	68	519	69.9	6.4	5	27	1.2	0.4
Echols	NA	NA	1	D	D	D	3	D	D	D	1	D	D	D
Effingham	82 766	584	12	D	D	D	91	1 193	165.8	15.7	21	D	D	D
Elbert	300	2	50	294	68.2	6.6	85	726	130.7	10.5	12	28	1.5	0.4
Emanuel	790	4	25	239	126.3	4.0	102	902	139.6	12.0	9	42	1.7	0.5
Evans	3 421	35	10	74	35.0	1.3	60	444	85.8	7.1	5	15	0.9	0.2

1. Establishments with payroll.

Table B. States and Counties — Professional Services, Manufacturing, and Accommodation and Foodservices

STATE County	Professional, scientific, and technical services,[1] 1997				Manufacturing, 1997				Accommodation and foodservices, 1997			
	Number of establishments	Number of employees	Receipts (mil dol)	Annual payroll (mil dol)	Number of establishments	Number of employees	Receipts (mil dol)	Annual payroll (mil dol)	Number of establishments	Number of employees	Sales (mil dol)	Annual payroll (mil dol)
	147	148	149	150	151	152	153	154	155	156	157	158
FLORIDA—Cont'd												
Sarasota	1 070	5 780	515.2	207.0	379	7 809	872.6	222.9	687	13 051	481.8	132.1
Seminole	1 102	6 182	561.6	210.7	434	9 624	1 582.2	287.1	579	12 966	423.1	117.3
Sumter	21	60	3.1	1.1	30	907	200.9	19.6	48	661	23.6	5.7
Suwannee	35	94	5.4	1.7	19	D	D	D	32	512	15.5	3.7
Taylor	18	61	3.2	1.4	20	1 594	496.1	58.0	36	364	11.9	3.0
Union	3	12	0.5	0.2	NA	NA	NA	NA	5	D	D	D
Volusia	844	4 048	346.4	120.7	392	10 216	1 212.6	263.2	1 051	19 758	635.6	167.0
Wakulla	19	72	3.7	1.4	NA	NA	NA	NA	28	293	9.8	2.3
Walton	54	162	16.4	4.6	35	937	108.7	12.5	87	2 446	107.2	29.4
Washington	19	80	3.5	1.2	14	754	85.8	15.7	22	317	8.8	2.6
GEORGIA	17 810	138 198	15 266.4	5 908.8	9 083	533 830	124 526.8	15 534.1	13 829	274 322	9 689.9	2 695.1
Appling	12	44	2.5	0.8	25	1 160	432.9	28.7	29	350	10.5	2.9
Atkinson	3	3	0.3	0.0	13	1 081	123.8	24.1	7	69	1.7	0.5
Bacon	12	39	2.1	0.7	14	1 373	210.9	27.8	17	D	D	D
Baker	1	D	D	D	NA	NA	NA	NA	3	7	0.2	0.0
Baldwin	52	172	8.1	2.4	20	3 454	624.9	91.2	66	1 507	37.8	9.8
Banks	7	15	1.0	0.2	14	D	D	D	22	372	16.7	4.6
Barrow	39	142	9.7	3.7	64	2 217	509.9	64.0	47	642	24.1	5.7
Bartow	81	315	19.5	8.2	126	10 115	2 918.4	303.1	123	1 827	65.3	17.7
Ben Hill	15	70	4.3	1.4	34	3 621	641.5	93.6	26	D	D	D
Berrien	13	30	1.6	0.5	17	1 987	231.6	45.0	15	169	5.5	1.3
Bibb	358	2 139	190.7	63.0	179	D	D	D	340	7 265	229.8	62.1
Bleckley	14	42	2.3	0.9	6	D	D	D	15	176	5.4	1.5
Brantley	2	D	D	D	NA	NA	NA	NA	10	59	2.1	0.5
Brooks	12	28	1.5	0.6	12	1 077	106.3	17.4	13	D	D	D
Bryan	23	52	4.2	1.2	NA	NA	NA	NA	29	D	D	D
Bulloch	76	353	22.7	7.9	41	3 210	493.4	84.3	99	1 894	52.5	13.5
Burke	11	36	1.2	0.5	16	1 035	84.4	21.3	21	283	7.4	1.9
Butts	13	22	1.4	0.5	18	1 127	181.4	22.3	28	272	10.5	2.8
Calhoun	1	D	D	D	3	D	D	D	8	D	D	D
Camden	41	163	10.6	3.7	21	1 364	528.8	52.7	68	1 220	35.3	9.9
Candler	15	73	3.9	1.4	NA	NA	NA	NA	17	262	7.7	2.0
Carroll	88	429	27.6	11.0	121	9 590	2 156.7	229.6	124	2 196	63.1	16.8
Catoosa	36	130	7.4	2.4	64	2 291	458.5	56.2	57	920	34.3	8.3
Charlton	4	7	0.6	0.1	NA	NA	NA	NA	11	104	3.8	1.1
Chatham	479	2 779	216.1	86.0	207	D	D	D	581	12 599	427.6	116.4
Chattahoochee	4	26	3.0	1.4	NA	NA	NA	NA	2	D	D	D
Chattooga	13	40	4.0	0.8	23	3 996	873.6	91.0	31	378	10.1	2.6
Cherokee	257	893	75.7	32.5	152	3 886	656.7	100.5	139	2 314	75.2	21.0
Clarke	156	943	54.9	22.8	90	9 388	1 368.5	234.9	240	4 371	125.5	33.8
Clay	NA	NA	NA	NA	NA	NA	NA	NA	2	D	D	D
Clayton	227	1 521	118.1	45.0	167	5 901	1 641.6	184.1	376	10 412	422.9	123.2
Clinch	8	35	3.1	1.1	11	918	148.9	18.8	8	D	D	D
Cobb	2 217	17 016	1 854.5	739.9	604	24 499	4 134.7	980.2	1 098	23 334	847.3	236.3
Coffee	52	214	12.1	3.9	45	5 377	773.8	116.1	47	810	26.1	6.5
Colquitt	44	128	9.8	3.5	55	3 503	452.2	67.1	52	754	23.3	6.4
Columbia	147	723	52.1	18.6	77	5 323	1 356.1	154.3	100	1 813	63.3	16.2
Cook	12	49	2.1	0.9	35	1 582	227.4	34.1	30	278	9.7	2.7
Coweta	85	286	22.5	8.7	76	5 589	1 093.2	147.8	103	1 880	58.5	15.2
Crawford	1	D	D	D	NA	NA	NA	NA	2	D	D	D
Crisp	25	76	4.9	1.7	27	2 067	340.5	53.1	51	913	26.2	8.0
Dade	8	30	0.7	0.2	22	907	98.5	19.9	22	319	10.5	2.5
Dawson	15	54	4.5	1.8	NA	NA	NA	NA	30	455	14.0	3.2
Decatur	21	64	5.2	1.4	35	3 538	632.8	84.2				
De Kalb	2 188	19 674	1 972.8	856.4	697	24 358	8 018.5	942.8	1 232	21 365	809.7	215.4
Dodge	21	79	4.5	1.8	16	867	155.0	17.5	22	324	8.4	2.3
Dooly	5	11	1.6	0.2	12	1 521	186.8	30.4	16	89	3.2	0.8
Dougherty	172	1 327	98.1	37.8	90	8 627	4 275.5	312.0	192	3 736	118.1	31.6
Douglas	127	438	37.7	14.7	95	2 211	371.2	54.5	127	3 049	96.8	25.5
Early	11	31	2.9	1.0	12	1 071	475.2	45.0	17	D	D	D
Echols	1	D	D	D	NA	NA	NA	NA	31	D	D	D
Effingham	26	77	4.3	1.1	112	2 954	441.7	64.6	34	396	11.6	2.7
Elbert	29	103	5.7	1.6	36	2 191	253.5	38.4	26	310	9.5	2.5
Emanuel	22	93	5.9	2.2	14	1 677	184.9	34.2	19	174	6.4	1.8
Evans	13	39	2.6	1.0								

1. Firms subject to federal tax.

Table B. States and Counties — **Health Care and Social Assistance, Other Services, and Federal Funds**

STATE County	Health care and social assistance,[1] 1997				Other services,[1] 1997				Federal funds and grants, 2002–2003			
									Expenditures (mil dol)			
										Direct payments for individuals[2]		
	Number of establish- ments	Number of employees	Receipts (mil dol)	Annual payroll (mil dol)	Number of establish- ments	Number of employees	Receipts (mil dol)	Annual payroll (mil dol)	Total	Social Security and government retirement	Medicare	Food stamps and Supplemental Security Income
	159	160	161	162	163	164	165	166	167	168	169	170
FLORIDA—Cont'd												
Sarasota	1 032	12 069	878.3	369.5	623	3 136	174.8	56.1	2 564.9	1 491.5	735.5	24.8
Seminole	716	8 306	632.6	254.9	625	3 331	198.9	60.5	1 382.5	767.0	271.2	43.3
Sumter	23	332	14.4	6.5	32	116	7.7	1.7	330.5	154.0	60.0	10.3
Suwannee	27	382	21.2	7.4	37	142	13.3	2.5	214.0	111.9	45.1	8.1
Taylor	24	325	16.1	7.8	32	222	12.5	3.2	148.4	47.3	25.4	5.1
Union	6	46	2.8	0.9	6	28	1.4	0.3	41.7	19.7	8.4	2.4
Volusia	906	10 079	596.8	253.3	707	3 094	163.6	47.8	2 878.2	1 465.3	679.7	69.4
Wakulla	8	171	5.8	2.9	14	56	4.6	0.9	85.2	42.7	14.7	3.7
Walton	31	505	27.7	11.1	35	177	9.8	3.4	230.6	113.5	32.8	6.5
Washington	27	289	12.1	5.1	18	77	4.5	1.1	144.1	59.0	30.6	5.5
GEORGIA	13 960	173 768	12 065.1	5 158.0	11 482	69 422	4 580.7	1 407.5	51 910.2	15 756.4	6 215.3	1 691.8
Appling	16	75	3.6	1.4	23	97	6.0	1.5	100.0	32.7	19.7	5.0
Atkinson	6	31	1.1	0.4	2	D	D	D	46.4	12.8	9.9	2.8
Bacon	11	71	3.3	1.1	14	53	3.1	0.7	58.1	20.2	13.7	3.3
Baker	NA	NA	NA	NA	NA	NA	NA	NA	39.7	5.6	3.5	1.2
Baldwin	101	1 868	86.1	35.0	51	329	19.6	5.6	204.5	87.6	39.6	10.4
Banks	7	32	1.3	0.6	5	22	1.8	0.4	46.1	22.8	8.7	1.8
Barrow	43	771	39.7	16.7	47	157	10.0	2.8	172.4	79.9	35.3	8.8
Bartow	98	1 471	105.2	36.6	82	514	36.9	10.0	284.2	147.0	46.4	10.6
Ben Hill	27	227	12.5	5.4	30	85	6.0	1.3	113.1	39.9	21.6	5.7
Berrien	23	505	21.0	10.2	13	40	2.3	0.6	104.9	40.6	20.0	4.8
Bibb	471	8 277	650.9	257.8	305	1 738	105.8	33.4	1 155.1	417.8	208.8	60.9
Bleckley	19	193	7.2	2.9	11	45	2.7	0.6	83.1	36.7	15.0	4.2
Brantley	8	108	5.2	1.8	9	20	1.0	0.2	66.5	32.5	13.1	4.0
Brooks	10	102	5.0	1.9	17	77	3.2	1.1	102.2	31.5	17.7	5.5
Bryan	19	238	11.8	4.7	19	54	3.2	0.9	907.1	54.9	15.5	4.0
Bulloch	97	1 668	110.2	40.7	68	289	14.6	3.7	268.4	108.7	34.3	11.3
Burke	25	364	16.4	7.3	18	53	2.6	0.6	148.3	43.8	21.1	9.0
Butts	24	419	18.7	7.9	19	112	4.3	1.3	149.2	52.3	18.5	3.7
Calhoun	5	69	2.9	1.2	5	16	0.5	0.2	71.6	13.0	8.9	2.7
Camden	63	425	25.0	9.7	37	199	9.1	2.5	534.7	83.2	17.5	6.9
Candler	10	223	6.5	2.9	8	35	2.1	0.6	60.3	19.0	12.3	4.0
Carroll	137	1 800	106.7	47.8	121	484	30.1	7.6	396.0	179.6	80.6	19.3
Catoosa	55	709	43.6	21.7	49	228	14.6	4.5	168.1	85.9	31.6	7.8
Charlton	10	39	1.8	0.6	6	10	0.9	0.1	52.1	21.5	11.1	2.9
Chatham	452	6 348	466.1	235.6	395	2 731	168.6	57.6	1 816.4	555.9	257.5	64.7
Chattahoochee	1	D	D	D	6	100	3.7	1.6	219.7	9.3	1.9	0.9
Chattooga	20	226	12.0	5.2	9	39	2.8	0.6	127.1	58.7	28.5	5.4
Cherokee	152	1 980	126.4	48.4	166	631	47.9	12.2	332.5	200.8	57.2	6.5
Clarke	260	2 017	184.6	91.6	140	817	37.2	12.0	631.4	156.7	62.6	18.9
Clay	4	D	D	D	1	D	D	D	65.3	8.9	3.2	1.9
Clayton	369	4 290	294.0	134.7	312	1 842	131.7	39.4	776.4	368.0	129.7	45.7
Clinch	11	128	5.6	1.9	3	11	0.4	0.2	46.2	13.0	10.7	3.1
Cobb	1 082	12 012	893.9	380.1	1 061	6 802	446.1	154.3	2 881.3	917.0	295.2	50.9
Coffee	61	481	29.4	11.7	52	238	12.9	3.2	192.5	65.3	35.0	11.5
Colquitt	73	616	34.5	15.0	54	321	17.3	5.4	258.1	86.6	43.5	15.5
Columbia	129	1 206	66.0	29.5	142	799	47.1	15.6	750.9	169.8	34.4	6.3
Cook	24	545	19.5	8.5	18	61	3.3	1.0	100.3	33.1	16.2	4.0
Coweta	100	1 638	119.6	53.0	72	284	19.4	5.2	322.9	169.9	62.4	12.0
Crawford	6	127	5.7	1.7	6	33	2.5	0.6	39.3	17.5	7.5	2.5
Crisp	34	293	14.1	5.8	35	118	7.3	1.9	151.3	43.9	27.1	9.7
Dade	12	243	12.2	5.0	10	25	3.0	0.5	68.1	33.9	14.3	2.7
Dawson	18	121	4.6	2.1	13	59	6.7	1.4	55.1	30.4	10.4	1.0
Decatur	44	304	17.7	7.0	41	162	7.5	1.9	181.3	53.9	24.3	11.2
De Kalb	1 360	16 256	1 184.2	486.4	1 101	7 551	535.5	175.6	2 742.2	785.2	450.1	99.9
Dodge	44	484	20.6	8.9	23	65	4.5	0.9	124.8	43.4	23.8	6.3
Dooly	13	170	7.1	2.9	8	42	1.8	0.7	101.3	23.2	13.6	4.2
Dougherty	250	3 277	239.3	110.3	169	1 163	71.1	22.5	776.3	230.3	93.7	45.3
Douglas	139	2 277	125.8	52.9	150	965	63.7	20.4	284.1	159.5	59.1	12.8
Early	10	47	1.8	0.8	10	35	1.2	0.4	113.8	25.1	13.2	5.7
Echols	NA	NA	NA	NA	NA	NA	NA	NA	11.3	2.9	1.6	0.5
Effingham	22	147	9.3	2.9	25	136	12.3	2.6	137.5	66.6	18.9	4.7
Elbert	31	375	19.0	7.7	25	64	4.8	1.0	129.5	51.2	25.8	6.2
Emanuel	40	357	16.2	6.1	24	86	4.8	1.1	155.4	47.6	26.2	8.9
Evans	15	343	17.4	6.4	8	82	5.0	1.8	58.2	23.1	10.9	3.4

1. Firms subject to federal tax.   2. State totals may include programs not allocated by county.

Table B. States and Counties — Federal Funds and Local Government Finances

STATE County	Federal funds and grants, 2002–2003 (cont'd)							Local government finances, 2002				
	Expenditures (mil dol) (cont'd)							General revenue				
	Procurement contract awards			Grants[1]						Taxes		
											Per capita[2] (dollars)	
	Salaries and wages	Defense	Other	Medicaid and other health-related	Nutrition and family welfare	Education	Other	Total (mil dol)	Intergovern-mental (mil dol)	Total (mil dol)	Total	Property
	171	172	173	174	175	176	177	178	179	180	181	182
FLORIDA—Cont'd												
Sarasota	58.9	23.0	16.1	49.6	17.0	12.6	126.5	1 369.8	175.8	461.3	1 358	1 034
Seminole	87.6	37.9	24.0	72.4	20.1	17.9	20.3	973.1	336.9	382.4	1 002	739
Sumter	65.3	0.5	5.6	20.8	5.9	2.8	1.8	87.1	37.4	34.9	607	433
Suwannee	7.1	0.1	1.3	26.2	5.0	3.4	1.5	69.7	44.0	14.2	393	311
Taylor	2.3	38.9	0.9	19.1	5.0	2.1	0.7	58.0	26.8	19.1	987	761
Union	1.3	0.0	0.3	8.4	1.9	0.7	-1.7	24.5	16.8	4.0	286	210
Volusia	93.8	111.5	30.4	133.1	32.6	28.7	195.3	1 475.6	402.7	469.9	1 023	830
Wakulla	4.2	0.1	0.9	8.5	2.8	1.5	4.5	66.6	44.9	13.3	533	405
Walton	8.8	0.4	0.9	25.5	5.0	2.5	30.7	119.8	26.6	76.7	1 748	1 386
Washington	3.1	0.4	0.9	30.9	3.3	5.6	1.0	79.4	46.9	10.4	488	358
GEORGIA	8 014.5	3 323.8	1 918.7	5 050.9	1 594.2	1 031.2	2 885.0	X	X	X	X	X
Appling	2.9	4.0	0.5	22.8	3.1	1.4	1.2	92.3	27.8	23.3	1 322	846
Atkinson	1.1	0.0	0.4	12.5	1.7	0.6	1.0	19.8	13.3	5.5	709	435
Bacon	1.2	0.0	0.3	11.0	2.6	1.0	0.7	46.6	14.7	8.4	838	466
Baker	0.5	0.0	0.1	6.3	0.7	0.5	1.2	8.9	4.0	3.6	895	730
Baldwin	5.4	0.5	1.0	31.2	7.8	4.2	6.5	160.4	57.3	32.3	721	390
Banks	1.0	0.0	0.3	8.1	0.8	0.7	1.8	30.2	11.0	16.3	1 077	531
Barrow	10.2	0.0	1.4	22.2	2.8	2.2	8.7	111.2	47.8	48.6	954	553
Bartow	11.2	4.2	9.6	24.9	8.2	4.3	15.5	233.8	84.6	99.9	1 210	661
Ben Hill	2.1	0.0	0.5	22.8	3.3	1.4	3.0	65.5	21.2	15.7	900	537
Berrien	2.0	0.6	0.5	14.7	2.2	0.9	5.1	33.6	18.4	12.0	740	405
Bibb	98.7	15.4	56.5	154.4	33.1	21.6	57.8	860.5	184.5	201.6	1 302	793
Bleckley	1.3	0.0	0.3	11.8	1.8	0.8	1.9	32.4	14.9	8.1	684	406
Brantley	1.6	-0.1	0.5	8.8	1.5	1.6	2.8	28.2	18.3	8.0	532	375
Brooks	1.7	0.0	0.4	20.1	4.0	1.8	4.6	33.1	19.8	9.2	558	399
Bryan	638.7	156.6	3.6	10.2	2.6	1.5	18.2	55.7	26.6	23.6	933	595
Bulloch	8.7	1.4	1.8	33.6	6.9	5.1	10.5	131.5	64.5	44.5	777	419
Burke	3.8	0.2	1.4	33.5	6.5	2.8	8.1	132.9	22.2	40.8	1 790	1 541
Butts	3.5	0.0	0.7	13.7	6.3	1.1	48.9	45.1	17.3	22.2	1 038	642
Calhoun	1.0	0.0	0.3	12.7	1.2	0.6	8.2	20.5	7.6	4.9	772	542
Camden	294.0	105.5	2.3	10.3	4.3	7.5	1.6	122.1	57.0	49.3	1 102	611
Candler	1.5	0.0	0.3	12.2	1.7	0.9	1.8	37.8	12.6	9.1	936	540
Carroll	14.9	16.8	3.4	46.3	7.2	6.5	12.1	201.3	90.6	81.6	859	420
Catoosa	4.8	0.2	1.5	15.1	3.8	3.3	13.0	203.3	50.1	41.7	741	349
Charlton	2.4	0.0	1.5	8.0	2.0	1.4	0.6	33.7	12.4	9.1	862	613
Chatham	318.8	234.4	20.9	170.6	50.8	22.3	74.0	784.9	244.0	361.7	1 548	984
Chattahoochee	0.4	194.9	7.6	3.0	0.5	0.8	0.0	7.5	4.3	2.1	134	57
Chattooga	2.6	0.0	1.1	21.5	3.5	2.1	3.0	54.1	28.7	16.9	645	347
Cherokee	18.3	1.0	5.5	22.3	4.1	4.2	10.0	341.5	125.8	167.8	1 053	718
Clarke	104.4	7.7	30.0	94.9	21.9	14.1	102.8	467.0	95.5	101.7	979	650
Clay	2.0	29.5	0.3	7.3	1.4	0.3	0.5	8.3	4.2	3.0	877	581
Clayton	69.7	20.2	11.6	41.7	15.3	17.9	46.0	653.1	265.5	273.9	1 084	599
Clinch	1.2	2.2	0.3	9.0	1.8	0.7	3.5	25.9	10.6	6.2	900	669
Cobb	232.5	1 132.8	58.8	68.5	19.1	22.9	62.6	1 521.0	495.3	751.4	1 153	855
Coffee	6.9	0.0	1.1	32.8	6.1	5.5	9.9	84.8	46.4	27.3	712	427
Colquitt	6.0	0.5	1.3	44.3	18.9	3.7	10.1	149.8	56.2	31.8	742	400
Columbia	377.0	113.7	4.6	17.3	4.3	2.7	18.8	205.5	85.6	90.2	949	566
Cook	1.7	0.0	0.4	15.2	2.5	2.2	14.5	41.8	23.8	12.8	797	415
Coweta	13.2	0.1	3.7	32.3	6.7	4.0	15.7	224.9	91.5	107.8	1 102	630
Crawford	0.7	0.0	0.2	6.1	1.2	0.8	1.4	24.4	14.3	7.6	605	482
Crisp	3.3	0.0	0.6	31.0	5.8	3.9	5.0	67.7	31.4	24.6	1 116	590
Dade	1.5	0.0	0.4	10.1	1.5	0.9	2.9	29.7	15.1	12.1	777	357
Dawson	2.3	0.0	0.7	6.9	0.9	0.4	1.9	45.0	13.6	26.6	1 519	844
Decatur	4.1	0.1	5.0	30.8	6.2	3.6	4.4	106.8	36.1	28.2	1 000	499
De Kalb	866.9	36.9	48.8	185.5	55.7	41.5	129.4	2 045.3	703.4	772.5	1 141	793
Dodge	2.3	1.2	0.5	27.4	4.1	1.4	3.2	84.1	23.4	11.1	582	323
Dooly	2.5	0.0	0.4	18.8	3.5	1.1	1.3	29.3	12.9	11.7	1 015	693
Dougherty	131.3	49.9	37.0	98.9	33.8	14.3	14.4	368.2	184.7	129.1	1 347	754
Douglas	11.7	0.4	3.3	20.0	4.6	4.1	7.6	252.4	94.3	115.7	1 173	702
Early	2.3	0.1	1.0	21.7	3.8	1.3	4.6	33.1	18.8	11.0	904	513
Echols	0.1	0.0	0.0	2.5	0.4	0.4	2.7	7.6	4.4	2.6	664	573
Effingham	4.3	0.2	0.9	12.2	2.7	1.5	23.3	105.8	49.6	32.8	803	492
Elbert	8.5	1.7	1.4	25.0	3.7	1.6	3.5	66.5	25.7	18.7	906	546
Emanuel	6.4	0.1	1.2	39.7	7.3	2.0	4.6	61.8	33.4	18.5	839	480
Evans	2.3	0.0	0.3	12.2	2.0	1.0	0.4	30.0	19.1	7.8	706	307

1. State totals may include programs not allocated by county.   2. Based on the resident population estimated as of July 1 of the year shown.

Table B. States and Counties — **Local Government Finances, Government Employment, and Elections**

STATE County	\[Direct general expenditure\] Total (mil dol)	Per capita[1] (dollars)	Education	Health and hospitals	Police protection	Public welfare	Highways	\[Debt outstanding\] Total (mil dol)	Per capita[1] (dollars)	Federal civilian	Federal military	State and local	Democratic	Republican	All other
	183	184	185	186	187	188	189	190	191	192	193	194	195	196	197
FLORIDA—Cont'd															
Sarasota	1 217.6	3 585	24.8	29.5	6.3	0.4	4.2	1 135.5	3 343	910	514	11 829	45.2	53.5	1.3
Seminole	897.3	2 351	50.8	0.6	9.9	0.2	8.0	508.4	1 332	1 393	578	14 698	41.3	58.1	0.6
Sumter	86.9	1 510	50.7	0.1	10.3	0.5	6.9	36.5	634	1 117	87	2 190	36.4	62.2	1.4
Suwannee	72.1	1 997	57.4	0.7	4.9	1.0	10.6	29.5	818	119	55	1 640	28.6	70.6	0.8
Taylor	63.8	3 299	62.1	1.7	8.6	0.5	4.3	34.2	1 767	36	29	1 534	35.5	63.7	0.8
Union	20.5	1 480	63.9	3.8	0.9	0.0	7.2	4.3	309	18	21	2 274	26.8	72.6	0.6
Volusia	1 512.4	3 292	34.9	21.8	6.5	0.7	4.5	1 254.8	2 731	1 321	722	20 183	50.5	48.9	0.7
Wakulla	61.4	2 465	62.5	3.0	8.2	0.3	8.7	17.4	698	88	38	1 369	41.6	57.6	0.8
Walton	115.2	2 628	42.0	4.4	7.3	2.1	11.5	45.3	1 032	163	114	2 332	25.9	73.2	0.9
Washington	78.0	3 640	47.3	16.7	2.8	0.6	5.5	18.1	845	54	32	2 151	28.1	71.1	0.8
GEORGIA	X	X	X	X	X	X	X	X	X	93 027	91 233	533 000	41.4	58.1	0.6
Appling	72.4	4 104	36.3	28.3	3.1	0.1	4.8	37.7	2 134	52	42	1 207	29.0	70.6	0.4
Atkinson	18.4	2 380	74.1	0.8	4.2	0.5	6.1	4.2	539	25	20	413	32.3	67.4	0.2
Bacon	45.1	4 488	34.5	46.5	2.6	0.2	1.8	7.8	771	25	24	561	24.5	75.3	0.2
Baker	9.5	2 353	68.6	2.0	4.1	1.2	4.6	0.0	11	13	10	221	53.1	46.5	0.4
Baldwin	167.4	3 737	37.1	41.3	2.8	0.1	2.1	86.6	1 933	68	118	7 731	46.6	53.0	0.4
Banks	24.8	1 638	60.8	1.0	4.3	0.7	6.4	29.5	1 950	16	36	611	20.6	78.9	0.6
Barrow	109.2	2 141	63.1	2.0	5.3	0.6	4.7	58.4	1 146	103	121	2 357	23.1	76.3	0.6
Bartow	223.3	2 703	57.4	1.3	6.3	0.3	4.9	226.3	2 740	179	197	4 784	25.6	73.8	0.6
Ben Hill	61.7	3 538	40.6	25.7	4.1	1.0	4.2	13.0	743	38	42	1 587	39.4	60.2	0.5
Berrien	32.0	1 966	61.4	2.4	4.6	0.2	7.9	14.9	912	40	39	790	29.3	70.0	0.7
Bibb	858.9	5 548	24.8	48.3	3.0	0.2	2.4	486.9	3 145	1 575	515	9 811	50.8	48.7	0.4
Bleckley	30.6	2 577	51.8	19.8	6.2	0.8	5.6	4.7	399	36	28	967	28.7	70.9	0.4
Brantley	28.2	1 870	77.9	0.8	2.9	0.6	3.0	6.1	402	25	64	741	22.4	77.1	0.5
Brooks	34.4	2 097	60.7	1.5	5.3	0.3	5.3	7.4	453	36	39	748	42.9	56.9	0.2
Bryan	55.0	2 177	62.1	0.7	6.2	0.7	5.3	10.0	397	40	59	1 200	26.0	73.7	0.3
Bulloch	130.4	2 276	50.4	14.1	5.1	1.6	4.9	34.1	595	142	144	5 805	35.7	63.9	0.4
Burke	130.3	5 716	30.5	0.4	2.4	0.5	3.1	902.9	39 612	58	54	1 428	49.7	49.9	0.4
Butts	46.3	2 169	61.5	1.2	5.7	0.2	4.0	26.4	1 237	38	51	1 322	33.2	66.2	0.6
Calhoun	18.7	2 917	38.1	35.0	4.2	0.9	3.3	2.9	446	29	15	746	55.4	44.1	0.5
Camden	112.5	2 516	53.5	0.8	6.3	0.2	4.6	44.9	1 004	2 255	5 601	2 323	32.7	66.9	0.4
Candler	36.2	3 709	39.3	34.3	2.8	0.3	4.3	20.0	2 045	25	23	730	34.8	65.0	0.2
Carroll	205.4	2 165	60.7	0.9	6.9	0.1	3.5	202.9	2 138	225	227	5 704	29.0	70.4	0.6
Catoosa	187.6	3 329	39.0	44.0	2.3	0.4	1.7	56.8	1 007	65	134	2 115	26.0	73.6	0.4
Charlton	29.5	2 799	47.4	23.3	4.5	0.2	4.9	13.2	1 249	46	25	618	31.4	68.2	0.4
Chatham	789.3	3 378	35.9	7.4	6.5	0.4	4.1	829.7	3 550	2 510	5 205	14 772	50.7	48.9	0.4
Chattahoochee	7.9	513	57.9	1.3	6.4	0.7	5.8	1.8	114	65	15 404	223	45.9	53.5	0.6
Chattooga	56.1	2 146	55.4	0.9	5.0	0.2	5.0	21.7	830	37	62	1 614	35.8	63.6	0.6
Cherokee	341.7	2 145	65.9	0.4	5.0	0.3	5.6	291.8	1 832	261	379	5 959	20.1	79.2	0.7
Clarke	461.5	4 443	22.0	47.4	3.6	0.1	2.5	254.6	2 451	1 544	661	16 912	58.3	40.4	1.2
Clay	7.1	2 082	51.1	2.3	6.2	0.1	5.0	1.5	455	80	0	257	61.0	38.9	0.2
Clayton	640.8	2 536	60.8	4.6	7.7	0.3	3.0	399.9	1 582	1 739	637	13 718	71.5	28.1	0.4
Clinch	24.0	3 477	49.2	25.3	3.4	0.3	3.1	2.2	320	17	16	594	33.1	66.3	0.6
Cobb	1 605.2	2 464	56.1	2.0	6.8	0.8	5.8	1 488.5	2 285	2 612	2 754	28 225	37.2	62.1	0.7
Coffee	87.8	2 294	62.8	1.2	5.4	0.1	5.0	13.1	343	123	91	2 353	32.3	67.4	0.3
Colquitt	156.9	3 665	40.7	29.9	2.7	0.1	3.3	51.1	1 195	106	102	3 406	28.8	70.7	0.5
Columbia	196.7	2 071	65.4	0.9	5.1	0.3	4.7	158.6	1 670	118	224	3 329	24.3	75.4	0.3
Cook	45.8	2 843	47.1	0.8	4.1	0.3	5.2	20.4	1 265	35	38	937	36.0	63.6	0.4
Coweta	224.4	2 295	63.1	0.7	4.9	0.3	3.5	199.1	2 037	214	233	4 251	25.0	74.5	0.5
Crawford	25.3	2 024	73.1	1.1	3.4	0.3	1.8	1.3	105	11	30	482	35.3	64.3	0.5
Crisp	66.4	3 015	52.0	1.0	6.3	0.1	6.1	54.5	2 474	60	52	1 510	37.7	61.8	0.4
Dade	30.2	1 933	61.9	1.0	4.5	0.9	5.8	1.9	120	19	37	634	29.3	70.1	0.6
Dawson	51.5	2 935	50.2	1.4	4.3	0.9	7.4	37.5	2 141	33	42	919	17.3	82.0	0.7
Decatur	102.3	3 620	41.2	32.7	5.1	1.1	3.0	21.0	743	66	67	2 690	72.7	26.6	0.6
De Kalb	2 353.5	3 476	38.6	28.9	4.1	0.3	1.8	1 213.6	1 793	11 869	2 275	32 562	39.9	59.8	0.3
Dodge	85.5	4 490	28.8	56.0	1.8	0.2	1.8	7.4	391	45	45	2 190	34.1	65.5	0.4
Dooly	28.9	2 514	56.1	0.8	5.4	0.1	8.2	12.6	1 095	52	27	886	51.3	48.2	0.5
Dougherty	383.5	4 000	36.5	15.0	4.4	0.9	3.8	226.8	2 365	2 336	970	7 800	58.9	40.8	0.4
Douglas	258.5	2 620	61.1	2.3	6.0	0.2	2.6	153.9	1 561	162	236	4 370	38.0	61.4	0.5
Early	33.4	2 747	61.1	2.6	3.7	0.1	6.1	6.8	557	51	29	853	40.3	59.3	0.4
Echols	7.2	1 881	76.0	1.5	4.2	0.7	4.0	0.4	111	0	0	183	23.3	76.4	0.3
Effingham	105.9	2 594	61.0	12.8	3.5	0.5	5.6	47.8	1 170	63	97	2 060	22.3	77.3	0.3
Elbert	71.9	3 478	45.9	19.4	3.0	0.0	2.0	38.1	1 845	157	49	1 598	39.0	60.4	0.6
Emanuel	59.6	2 696	54.2	13.6	3.6	1.0	4.1	18.9	854	102	53	2 038	37.2	62.5	0.4
Evans	24.7	2 225	61.6	1.2	4.6	0.0	6.0	1.5	138	54	26	725	34.5	65.2	0.3

1. Based on the resident population estimated as of July 1 of the year shown.

Table B. States and Counties — Land Area and Population

STATE/ County code	CBSA code[1]	County Type[2]	STATE County	Land area[3] (sq km) 2000	Population and population characteristics, 2003 — Total persons	Rank	Per square kilometer	Race alone or in combination, not Hispanic or Latino (percent) — White	Black	Am. Indian, Alaska Native	Asian and Pacific Islander	Percent Hispanic or Latino[4]	Age (percent) — Under 5 years	5 to 17 years	18 to 24 years	25 to 34 years	35 to 44 years	45 to 54 years
				1	2	3	4	5	6	7	8	9	10	11	12	13	14	15
			GEORGIA—Cont'd															
13 111	...	8	Fannin	999	21 234	1 741	21.3	97.9	0.3	1.4	0.3	1.1	5.6	15.1	8.3	11.8	13.0	14.3
13 113	12060	1	Fayette	510	98 914	547	193.9	80.8	13.9	0.7	3.2	2.6	4.9	21.3	9.6	8.9	16.2	17.8
13 115	40660	3	Floyd	1 329	93 368	577	70.3	79.1	13.4	0.5	1.2	6.5	7.1	17.7	11.2	13.5	14.2	12.8
13 117	12060	1	Forsyth	585	123 811	457	211.6	90.3	1.1	0.5	2.4	6.5	8.8	19.2	8.1	15.4	18.6	12.2
13 119	...	8	Franklin	682	21 164	1 744	31.0	89.8	8.6	0.5	0.5	1.2	6.3	17.4	10.2	12.8	14.1	12.6
13 121	12060	1	Fulton	1 369	818 322	58	597.8	46.7	43.2	0.5	4.0	6.7	7.7	17.4	9.3	18.3	16.9	14.1
13 123	...	6	Gilmer	1 105	25 973	1 538	23.5	90.6	0.3	0.9	0.3	8.5	7.1	16.9	9.4	13.6	14.3	12.8
13 125	...	9	Glascock	373	2 636	3 011	7.1	90.9	8.0	0.6	0.4	0.5	7.1	15.9	8.6	12.1	14.4	12.7
13 127	15260	3	Glynn	1 094	70 131	722	64.1	70.1	26.0	0.6	0.9	3.3	6.7	18.2	9.3	11.8	14.5	14.0
13 129	15660	6	Gordon	921	47 777	966	51.9	85.8	3.4	0.6	0.9	10.1	7.9	18.3	9.8	15.6	14.9	12.6
13 131	...	6	Grady	1 187	24 185	1 612	20.4	63.2	28.9	1.0	0.3	7.1	7.6	19.1	10.5	12.3	14.2	13.1
13 133	...	6	Greene	1 006	15 263	2 081	15.2	54.3	42.0	0.2	0.3	3.3	6.7	17.5	9.8	11.6	12.9	13.0
13 135	12060	1	Gwinnett	1 121	673 345	82	600.7	62.0	15.7	0.5	9.2	13.8	8.2	19.8	9.1	16.6	18.3	13.5
13 137	18460	6	Habersham	720	38 446	1 173	53.4	84.7	4.3	0.7	2.0	8.9	6.8	16.8	11.8	13.4	14.2	12.7
13 139	23580	3	Hall	1 020	156 101	355	153.0	69.1	6.8	0.5	1.6	22.6	8.7	18.9	10.7	16.4	14.8	11.7
13 141	33300	7	Hancock	1 226	9 977	2 444	8.1	21.7	77.4	0.2	0.1	0.5	6.2	17.3	10.7	14.7	15.7	14.2
13 143	12060	1	Haralson	731	27 460	1 487	37.6	93.5	5.6	0.6	0.3	0.7	7.1	18.7	9.3	13.8	14.6	12.4
13 145	17980	2	Harris	1 201	25 891	1 542	21.6	79.6	18.3	0.6	0.6	1.3	5.6	18.5	9.1	11.5	16.3	15.4
13 147	...	6	Hart	601	23 432	1 642	39.0	79.3	19.2	0.4	0.6	1.0	6.1	17.3	8.4	12.2	14.3	13.5
13 149	12060	1	Heard	767	11 152	2 360	14.5	88.3	10.5	0.4	0.1	1.0	7.4	21.2	8.8	14.3	16.0	12.8
13 151	12060	1	Henry	836	150 003	377	179.4	73.4	21.2	0.6	2.7	3.2	7.5	20.6	9.6	15.5	16.7	12.0
13 153	47580	3	Houston	976	120 434	469	123.4	70.0	25.3	0.8	2.5	2.9	7.1	20.3	10.5	13.1	16.5	13.2
13 155	22340	7	Irwin	924	10 060	2 436	10.9	72.4	24.5	0.1	0.4	2.6	6.7	20.9	10.2	12.4	13.3	12.2
13 157	...	6	Jackson	887	46 998	980	53.0	88.3	7.4	0.6	1.4	3.1	7.3	18.9	9.7	15.3	15.6	12.3
13 159	12060	1	Jasper	959	12 547	2 267	13.1	72.5	24.7	0.4	0.2	2.7	6.6	19.6	9.6	13.5	14.6	13.8
13 161	...	7	Jeff Davis	863	12 888	2 249	14.9	77.9	14.5	0.2	0.7	6.8	8.7	18.6	9.6	13.3	14.1	13.6
13 163	...	6	Jefferson	1 367	17 001	1 955	12.4	42.4	55.8	0.2	0.2	1.6	7.9	20.2	10.2	11.8	14.0	13.6
13 165	...	6	Jenkins	906	8 765	2 547	9.7	55.7	39.8	0.2	0.3	4.1	7.8	19.9	10.7	11.5	13.9	13.6
13 167	20140	9	Johnson	788	9 421	2 495	12.0	60.3	38.3	0.2	0.2	1.1	6.2	21.0	10.6	13.3	14.3	11.7
13 169	31420	3	Jones	1 020	25 472	1 552	25.0	76.1	22.6	0.4	0.8	0.5	6.4	19.0	10.1	12.5	15.9	14.4
13 171	12060	1	Lamar	479	16 234	2 020	33.9	69.4	28.9	0.5	0.4	1.3	6.4	18.4	10.8	13.6	14.6	14.1
13 173	46660	3	Lanier	484	7 361	2 652	15.2	71.1	26.1	0.7	0.6	2.0	6.4	19.0	11.7	13.7	15.7	12.3
13 175	20140	6	Laurens	2 104	46 108	1 003	21.9	63.5	34.3	0.4	0.9	1.3	7.2	19.1	10.2	12.7	14.3	13.6
13 177	10500	3	Lee	921	28 410	1 445	30.8	82.4	15.2	0.5	1.2	1.1	6.5	21.3	11.2	13.6	17.3	14.8
13 179	25980	3	Liberty	1 344	58 925	829	43.8	50.7	41.6	1.2	3.7	6.0	12.9	23.2	13.5	18.3	15.5	9.3
13 181	...	8	Lincoln	547	8 536	2 562	15.6	65.6	33.0	0.5	0.2	0.9	5.4	17.7	9.1	12.0	15.3	14.8
13 183	25980	3	Long	1 038	10 780	2 381	10.4	67.8	22.7	0.7	1.4	8.6	9.5	22.5	12.7	17.8	14.4	9.9
13 185	46660	3	Lowndes	1 306	94 579	568	72.4	63.2	33.3	0.8	1.6	2.2	7.4	18.5	15.4	13.8	14.5	11.8
13 187	...	6	Lumpkin	737	23 185	1 657	31.5	93.6	1.4	2.0	0.5	3.9	6.3	17.4	15.4	13.8	14.5	11.8
13 189	12260	2	McDuffie	673	21 445	1 730	31.9	60.1	38.0	0.3	0.5	1.5	7.6	19.8	9.9	12.5	14.7	13.7
13 191	15260	3	McIntosh	1 123	10 885	2 374	9.7	64.4	34.3	0.6	0.4	0.8	7.1	19.7	8.3	12.0	14.5	14.8
13 193	...	6	Macon	1 045	14 025	2 166	13.4	36.6	59.3	0.3	0.7	3.4	7.9	19.1	10.7	12.7	14.6	13.7
13 195	12020	3	Madison	735	27 075	1 504	36.8	89.0	8.4	0.7	0.6	2.1	6.6	19.1	9.3	13.7	15.6	13.9
13 197	17980	2	Marion	951	7 170	2 667	7.5	59.5	33.1	0.8	0.4	6.9	7.3	20.5	9.4	13.0	15.5	14.5
13 199	12060	1	Meriwether	1 303	22 786	1 676	17.5	57.4	40.8	0.6	0.2	1.4	7.0	19.2	10.0	12.0	14.4	13.7
13 201	...	8	Miller	733	6 328	2 742	8.6	70.9	28.1	0.3	0.1	0.7	6.7	18.8	8.6	11.5	13.8	13.1
13 205	...	6	Mitchell	1 326	23 832	1 622	18.0	49.9	47.4	0.3	0.4	2.3	7.3	19.6	10.7	13.9	14.8	13.4
13 207	31420	3	Monroe	1 025	23 244	1 653	22.7	71.9	26.1	0.6	0.5	1.4	6.3	18.7	10.3	12.5	15.7	15.1
13 209	...	9	Montgomery	635	8 691	2 555	13.7	71.7	23.9	0.2	0.4	4.0	6.4	17.9	14.6	13.5	14.9	12.4
13 211	...	6	Morgan	906	16 775	1 979	18.5	72.0	26.1	0.4	0.6	1.5	6.5	19.2	9.3	12.9	14.9	13.9
13 213	19140	6	Murray	892	39 446	1 143	44.2	89.2	0.9	0.6	0.3	9.7	7.7	19.9	10.1	16.1	15.9	12.2
13 215	17980	2	Muscogee	560	185 702	308	331.6	50.8	44.2	0.8	2.5	3.3	8.0	19.2	11.5	13.4	14.5	13.4
13 217	12060	1	Newton	716	76 144	676	106.3	69.0	27.5	0.5	1.1	2.7	7.9	19.7	10.2	16.2	14.8	11.2
13 219	12020	3	Oconee	481	28 087	1 459	58.4	88.8	6.4	0.4	1.9	3.1	6.0	22.1	9.2	11.5	16.3	15.6
13 221	12020	3	Oglethorpe	1 142	13 379	2 206	11.7	78.3	19.1	0.3	0.3	2.5	6.5	18.9	8.8	13.8	15.7	13.4
13 223	12060	1	Paulding	812	100 071	541	123.2	86.3	10.7	0.8	0.8	2.6	8.7	21.6	8.9	18.0	17.6	10.5
13 225	22980	6	Peach	391	24 320	1 606	62.2	51.7	43.5	0.4	0.3	4.4	7.1	18.4	14.5	13.2	13.9	12.9
13 227	12060	1	Pickens	601	26 905	1 507	44.8	95.6	1.3	0.9	0.4	2.5	6.4	16.8	8.9	14.3	14.7	12.5
13 229	48180	6	Pierce	889	16 327	2 012	18.4	87.1	9.8	0.4	0.3	2.8	7.2	18.8	9.8	12.5	14.1	13.9
13 231	12060	1	Pike	566	14 979	2 101	26.5	85.5	12.4	0.3	0.4	1.6	6.4	19.9	9.8	13.3	16.3	13.0
13 233	16340	6	Polk	806	39 800	1 136	49.4	77.5	13.1	0.3	0.4	9.1	8.0	18.4	10.2	14.2	14.0	12.3
13 235	...	6	Pulaski	641	9 724	2 467	15.2	63.6	32.7	0.4	0.5	3.1	6.8	16.2	10.1	14.7	15.5	13.7
13 237	...	6	Putnam	892	19 575	1 831	21.9	67.4	28.9	0.5	0.7	2.9	6.6	16.2	9.0	12.3	13.9	14.1
13 239	...	9	Quitman	392	2 480	3 022	6.3	54.8	44.2	0.3	0.0	0.8	5.5	17.1	7.5	9.3	13.1	15.7
13 241	...	6	Rabun	961	15 757	2 051	16.4	92.3	1.0	0.8	0.4	6.1	5.6	16.2	7.9	12.1	13.0	13.5
13 243	...	6	Randolph	1 112	7 465	2 640	6.7	37.3	60.5	0.3	0.4	1.6	7.4	19.5	13.7	9.7	13.5	13.3

1. CBSA = Core Based Statistical Area. See Appendix A for explanation. See Appendix B for list of metropolitan areas with component counties.
2. County type code from the Economic Research Service of USDA Rural-Urban Continuum Codes. See Appendix A for definition.
3. Dry land or land partially or temporarily covered by water.
4. Hispanic or Latino persons may be of any race.

Table B. States and Counties — **Population and Households**

STATE County	55 to 64 years (16)	65 to 74 years (17)	75 years and over (18)	Percent female (19)	1990 (20)	2000 (21)	1990–2000 (22)	2000–2003 (23)	Births (24)	Deaths (25)	Net migration (26)	Number (27)	Percent change, 1990–2000 (28)	Persons per household (29)	Female family householder[1] (30)	One person (31)
GEORGIA—Cont'd																
Fannin	12.2	10.6	8.2	51.8	15 992	19 798	23.8	7.3	779	835	1 464	8 369	32.1	2.35	8.9	25.6
Fayette	10.7	5.0	4.1	51.0	62 415	91 263	46.2	8.4	2 905	1 773	6 455	31 524	49.7	2.88	8.3	15.0
Floyd	9.4	7.1	6.5	51.5	81 251	90 565	11.5	3.1	4 401	3 160	1 631	34 028	11.5	2.55	13.0	24.5
Forsyth	8.0	3.9	2.5	49.2	44 083	98 407	123.2	25.8	6 825	1 964	19 882	34 565	116.9	2.83	6.6	14.8
Franklin	10.4	8.2	7.0	51.4	16 650	20 285	21.8	4.3	854	775	787	7 888	23.9	2.50	10.5	24.6
Fulton	8.3	4.1	3.9	50.6	648 776	816 006	25.8	0.3	44 230	19 974	-21 400	321 242	24.9	2.44	16.5	32.2
Gilmer	11.1	8.0	5.0	49.3	13 368	23 456	75.5	10.7	1 164	738	2 056	9 071	78.8	2.57	8.4	22.2
Glascock	10.5	8.2	9.4	51.6	2 357	2 556	8.4	3.1	119	99	65	1 004	15.8	2.44	9.6	26.3
Glynn	10.6	7.4	7.0	51.9	62 496	67 568	8.1	3.8	3 151	2 267	1 717	27 208	13.6	2.44	14.6	27.2
Gordon	9.1	6.0	4.4	50.2	35 067	44 104	25.8	8.3	2 572	1 359	2 448	16 173	26.6	2.70	11.1	20.3
Grady	9.7	7.0	6.2	52.2	20 279	23 659	16.7	2.2	1 287	871	128	8 797	19.6	2.66	16.2	22.4
Greene	12.7	8.8	6.0	52.1	11 793	14 406	22.2	5.9	675	535	710	5 477	34.1	2.59	18.3	23.0
Gwinnett	6.9	3.2	2.1	49.3	352 910	588 448	66.7	14.4	36 026	8 397	56 655	202 317	59.3	2.88	10.0	18.4
Habersham	9.7	7.6	6.0	48.8	27 622	35 902	30.0	7.1	1 754	1 135	1 912	13 259	33.0	2.57	9.3	22.4
Hall	8.1	5.1	3.9	49.0	95 434	139 277	45.9	12.1	9 323	3 358	10 806	47 381	36.5	2.89	10.8	19.2
Hancock	9.4	6.9	5.2	46.6	8 908	10 076	13.1	-1.0	439	356	-166	3 237	9.0	2.66	28.2	26.1
Haralson	10.1	7.1	5.7	51.2	21 966	25 690	17.0	6.9	1 283	892	1 352	9 826	19.1	2.58	11.3	23.0
Harris	10.6	6.3	5.0	50.5	17 788	23 695	33.2	9.3	915	691	1 927	8 822	36.7	2.66	10.7	17.9
Hart	11.2	9.4	7.1	50.8	19 712	22 997	16.7	1.9	887	893	451	9 106	22.1	2.47	12.0	24.4
Heard	9.5	6.0	4.8	51.0	8 628	11 012	27.6	1.3	508	348	-10	4 043	30.7	2.70	12.1	21.3
Henry	7.1	4.1	2.8	50.5	58 741	119 341	103.2	25.7	6 732	2 423	25 499	41 373	106.7	2.87	10.3	15.4
Houston	8.3	5.6	3.7	50.8	89 208	110 765	24.2	8.7	5 540	2 788	6 834	40 911	26.1	2.65	14.0	22.1
Irwin	10.1	7.5	6.6	50.8	8 649	9 931	14.8	1.3	436	401	106	3 644	16.0	2.62	14.4	23.1
Jackson	9.1	5.3	4.4	50.1	30 005	41 589	38.6	13.0	2 205	1 268	4 351	15 057	40.4	2.71	10.8	19.7
Jasper	9.8	6.2	4.6	51.2	8 453	11 426	35.2	9.8	500	376	970	4 175	37.5	2.72	13.3	21.4
Jeff Davis	10.1	6.8	5.3	50.5	12 032	12 684	5.4	1.6	736	557	42	4 828	10.8	2.61	13.6	22.3
Jefferson	9.2	6.6	6.9	53.2	17 408	17 266	-0.8	-1.5	947	706	-496	6 339	4.0	2.65	23.1	25.7
Jenkins	9.2	6.6	6.4	52.0	8 247	8 575	4.0	2.2	456	299	46	3 214	8.9	2.63	19.7	25.6
Johnson	8.9	6.9	7.2	47.2	8 329	8 560	2.8	10.1	408	319	745	3 130	4.0	2.53	18.2	26.6
Jones	9.5	6.0	4.4	51.0	20 739	23 639	14.0	7.8	990	660	1 477	8 659	18.6	2.69	13.3	20.2
Lamar	9.9	6.8	5.5	51.7	13 038	15 912	22.0	2.0	683	559	190	5 712	22.3	2.64	16.3	21.6
Lanier	8.7	6.2	4.5	49.1	5 531	7 241	30.9	1.7	270	201	49	2 593	32.0	2.69	13.7	21.8
Laurens	9.3	6.7	6.0	51.8	39 988	44 874	12.2	2.7	2 262	1 491	523	17 083	17.7	2.55	17.1	25.7
Lee	7.2	4.0	2.9	49.6	16 250	24 757	52.4	14.8	1 040	439	1 359	8 229	58.3	2.91	13.0	14.3
Liberty	5.0	2.7	1.8	47.0	52 745	61 610	16.8	-4.4	4 889	840	-6 954	19 383	28.1	2.93	14.8	16.6
Lincoln	11.2	8.6	5.8	51.7	7 442	8 348	12.2	2.3	311	334	213	3 251	20.3	2.55	15.5	23.7
Long	6.1	3.7	2.5	50.0	6 202	10 304	66.1	4.6	564	195	118	3 574	62.8	2.88	14.5	19.6
Lowndes	7.4	5.0	4.1	50.3	75 981	92 115	21.2	2.7	4 612	2 257	153	32 654	24.1	2.61	15.9	24.2
Lumpkin	8.9	5.6	3.9	50.8	14 573	21 016	44.2	10.3	958	514	1 713	7 537	51.5	2.61	9.4	22.0
McDuffie	9.7	6.4	5.4	52.8	20 119	21 231	5.5	1.0	1 094	769	-89	7 970	9.6	2.62	19.2	23.2
McIntosh	11.7	7.4	5.1	51.4	8 634	10 847	25.6	0.4	512	356	-119	4 202	31.9	2.54	14.7	24.2
Macon	8.9	6.6	6.0	50.6	13 114	14 074	7.3	-0.3	747	497	-290	4 834	10.2	2.71	24.4	25.2
Madison	10.0	6.3	4.6	50.8	21 050	25 730	22.2	5.2	1 146	772	965	9 800	26.6	2.61	10.6	21.5
Marion	9.7	5.9	4.6	50.2	5 590	7 144	27.8	0.4	362	248	-80	2 668	36.0	2.65	15.1	24.3
Meriwether	10.3	7.1	6.6	52.2	22 411	22 534	0.5	1.1	1 090	802	-24	8 248	8.0	2.68	18.4	23.8
Miller	11.0	8.4	8.9	52.7	6 280	6 383	1.6	-0.9	326	248	-132	2 487	6.5	2.51	15.5	26.7
Mitchell	9.3	6.2	5.5	48.9	20 275	23 932	18.0	-0.4	1 146	843	-385	8 063	18.6	2.72	22.5	23.3
Monroe	9.8	5.8	4.3	50.1	17 113	21 757	27.1	6.8	938	668	1 197	7 719	32.2	2.74	13.8	18.9
Montgomery	8.8	5.9	4.5	49.3	7 379	8 270	12.1	5.1	355	250	311	2 919	17.1	2.57	13.5	25.6
Morgan	9.9	6.6	5.6	51.4	12 883	15 457	20.0	8.5	734	458	1 017	5 558	26.3	2.75	14.6	19.4
Murray	8.6	5.1	3.1	49.8	26 147	36 506	39.6	8.1	1 927	831	1 822	13 286	41.9	2.73	11.1	18.8
Muscogee	8.3	6.2	5.4	51.4	179 280	186 291	3.9	-0.3	10 045	5 768	-4 841	69 819	6.0	2.54	19.6	26.7
Newton	7.9	5.0	3.8	51.1	41 808	62 001	48.3	22.8	3 846	1 824	11 722	21 997	52.7	2.77	14.1	18.3
Oconee	8.8	4.7	3.9	50.8	17 618	26 225	48.9	7.1	1 023	480	1 324	9 051	47.0	2.87	9.4	15.5
Oglethorpe	10.1	6.6	5.1	50.9	9 763	12 635	29.4	5.9	544	405	596	4 849	35.4	2.58	11.5	23.0
Paulding	6.0	3.3	2.1	49.9	41 611	81 678	96.3	22.5	5 341	1 530	14 168	28 089	96.1	2.89	9.0	14.6
Peach	8.9	5.9	4.2	51.7	21 189	23 668	11.7	2.8	1 225	698	156	8 436	18.1	2.68	19.6	22.6
Pickens	10.5	7.7	5.0	50.6	14 432	22 983	59.3	17.1	1 090	743	3 467	8 960	66.4	2.54	8.8	20.5
Pierce	10.6	6.9	5.1	50.7	13 328	15 636	17.3	4.4	775	559	506	5 958	23.9	2.61	11.6	23.1
Pike	9.4	6.0	4.5	50.0	10 224	13 688	33.9	9.4	567	381	1 079	4 755	34.9	2.81	10.5	17.5
Polk	9.6	7.0	5.9	49.8	33 815	38 127	12.8	4.4	2 228	1 336	805	14 012	11.9	2.66	13.1	22.7
Pulaski	9.9	7.1	6.2	57.1	8 108	9 588	18.3	1.4	422	298	21	3 407	10.0	2.49	15.7	27.9
Putnam	12.8	9.3	5.3	50.5	14 137	18 812	33.1	4.1	860	664	577	7 402	41.6	2.50	12.8	22.0
Quitman	13.1	11.2	9.4	53.3	2 210	2 598	17.6	-4.5	97	99	-112	1 047	22.2	2.48	18.7	24.9
Rabun	12.8	10.2	7.8	50.5	11 648	15 050	29.2	4.7	551	597	747	6 279	35.6	2.35	8.1	26.8
Randolph	9.6	7.5	7.7	54.0	8 023	7 791	-2.9	-4.2	383	388	-323	2 909	3.3	2.57	22.6	30.0

1. No spouse present.

Items 16—31

Table B. States and Counties — Vital Statistics, Health Resources, and Crime

STATE County	Births, average 1999–2001		Deaths, average 1999–2001				Physicians[4] 2000		Hospitals[4] 1998			Medicare enrollees, 2003	Serious crimes known to police[6] 2002	
			Number		Rate					Beds			Total	
	Total	Rate[1]	Total	Infant[2]	Total[1]	Infant[3]	Number	Rate[5]	Number	Number	Rate[5]		Number	Rate[7]
	32	33	34	35	36	37	38	39	40	41	42	43	44	45

GEORGIA—Cont'd														
Fannin	245	12.3	241	3	12.1	D	15	76	1	51	274	4 645	151	729
Fayette	911	9.9	520	4	5.7	D	123	135	0	0	0	9 817	1 486	1 557
Floyd	1 303	14.4	973	9	10.7	7.2	239	264	2	505	593	15 212	3 756	3 966
Forsyth	1 923	19.2	533	10	5.3	5.0	50	51	1	28	33	7 568	2 501	2 430
Franklin	257	12.6	222	1	10.9	D	16	79	1	333	1 745	4 326	612	2 885
Fulton	13 769	16.8	6 263	111	7.7	8.1	2 808	344	13	4 287	580	72 466	70 048	8 209
Gilmer	357	15.2	217	2	9.2	D	14	60	1	50	268	4 346	256	1 044
Glascock	34	13.1	35	0	13.5	D	0	0	0	0	0	569	4	150
Glynn	953	14.1	689	10	10.2	10.1	159	235	1	337	501	11 410	6 021	8 522
Gordon	784	17.6	395	7	8.9	8.5	44	100	1	50	122	6 490	1 306	2 832
Grady	357	15.1	262	5	11.0	D	17	72	1	49	228	3 520	834	3 371
Greene	190	13.2	163	2	11.3	D	12	83	1	58	425	2 758	368	2 443
Gwinnett	10 289	17.3	2 390	64	4.0	6.2	552	94	3	428	82	37 759	19 765	3 278
Habersham	549	15.2	331	5	9.1	D	29	81	1	137	430	6 091	691	1 841
Hall	2 744	19.5	1 007	20	7.2	7.4	213	153	2	447	375	17 273	5 230	3 594
Hancock	132	13.1	105	2	10.5	D	5	50	1	52	569	1 527	109	1 035
Haralson	379	14.7	274	3	10.6	D	14	54	1	59	239	4 421	854	3 179
Harris	293	12.3	193	3	8.1	D	13	55	0	0	0	2 971	365	1 473
Hart	265	11.6	276	2	12.0	D	20	87	1	41	188	3 527	509	2 117
Heard	144	13.2	101	2	9.2	D	2	18	0	0	0	1 258	193	1 826
Henry	2 069	17.1	724	15	6.0	7.2	70	59	1	119	114	12 901	3 601	2 886
Houston	1 562	14.1	775	15	7.0	9.8	127	115	2	236	223	13 146	5 250	4 533
Irwin	114	11.5	109	2	11.0	D	4	40	1	34	379	1 324	312	3 004
Jackson	703	16.7	387	5	9.2	D	17	41	1	233	619	6 237	1 392	3 201
Jasper	126	11.0	109	2	9.5	D	9	79	1	68	670	1 473	NA	NA
Jeff Davis	240	18.9	136	3	10.7	D	9	71	1	50	392	2 071	690	5 202
Jefferson	279	16.2	206	4	12.0	D	14	81	1	37	208	3 085	328	1 817
Jenkins	134	15.7	89	1	10.4	D	5	58	1	38	450	1 395	169	1 885
Johnson	128	14.9	100	1	11.7	D	3	35	0	0	0	1 483	NA	NA
Jones	268	11.3	188	2	8.0	D	7	30	0	0	0	2 064	676	2 735
Lamar	202	12.7	161	2	10.1	D	6	38	0	0	0	2 468	397	2 386
Lanier	79	11.0	61	1	8.5	D	3	41	1	40	573	877	121	1 598
Laurens	663	14.8	449	6	10.0	D	90	201	1	190	434	7 467	1 857	3 957
Lee	317	12.6	120	1	4.7	D	3	12	0	0	0	1 815	793	3 063
Liberty	1 482	24.1	259	16	4.2	11.0	54	88	1	49	83	3 448	2 524	3 989
Lincoln	90	10.8	97	1	11.6	D	1	12	0	0	0	1 433	155	1 775
Long	170	16.7	60	1	5.9	D	0	0	0	0	0	673	224	2 079
Lowndes	1 489	16.2	702	19	7.6	12.5	160	174	2	359	421	11 312	4 577	4 752
Lumpkin	265	12.5	158	1	7.5	D	16	76	1	52	274	2 475	511	2 325
McDuffie	344	16.2	234	5	11.0	D	16	75	1	47	216	3 106	756	3 405
McIntosh	157	14.5	103	2	9.5	D	4	37	0	0	0	1 773	344	3 033
Macon	226	16.1	155	2	11.0	D	9	64	0	0	0	1 854	330	2 242
Madison	362	14.1	232	3	9.0	D	2	8	0	0	0	3 971	685	2 595
Marion	108	15.2	68	1	9.6	D	4	56	0	0	0	744	117	1 566
Meriwether	302	13.4	248	3	11.0	D	9	40	1	96	415	3 415	857	3 637
Miller	87	13.5	76	0	11.9	D	3	47	1	135	2 106	1 130	82	1 228
Mitchell	346	14.5	247	4	10.3	D	14	58	1	26	123	3 281	NA	NA
Monroe	263	12.1	200	4	9.2	D	7	32	1	40	204	2 660	388	1 705
Montgomery	115	13.8	73	1	8.8	D	1	12	0	0	0	1 282	NA	NA
Morgan	220	14.1	149	2	9.5	D	10	65	1	26	172	2 436	NA	NA
Murray	521	14.3	247	3	6.8	D	9	25	1	42	129	4 237	1 109	2 905
Muscogee	3 091	16.6	1 760	52	9.5	16.7	393	211	3	871	477	25 883	12 473	6 421
Newton	1 129	17.9	500	6	7.9	D	40	65	1	90	156	8 809	2 192	3 381
Oconee	299	11.4	153	3	5.9	D	21	80	0	0	0	2 809	559	2 039
Oglethorpe	145	11.5	115	1	9.1	D	3	24	0	0	0	1 196	NA	NA
Paulding	1 473	17.8	413	5	5.0	D	24	29	1	175	238	5 281	2 149	2 516
Peach	403	17.0	225	4	9.5	D	13	55	1	36	147	3 951	935	3 778
Pickens	323	13.9	209	3	9.0	D	16	70	1	91	462	3 614	228	949
Pierce	238	15.2	173	2	11.1	D	7	45	0	0	0	2 803	NA	NA
Pike	188	13.7	119	1	8.7	D	2	15	0	0	0	2 056	240	1 719
Polk	669	17.4	422	5	11.0	D	24	63	1	35	96	6 853	1 419	3 559
Pulaski	134	14.0	104	0	10.8	D	14	146	1	55	655	1 612	248	2 474
Putnam	251	13.3	172	4	9.1	D	9	48	1	50	285	3 010	497	2 527
Quitman	36	13.7	31	1	11.8	D	0	0	0	0	0	590	49	1 803
Rabun	178	11.8	174	2	11.5	D	25	166	2	66	492	3 059	281	1 786
Randolph	112	14.4	115	2	14.9	D	7	90	1	120	1 523	1 317	158	2 281

1. Per 1,000 estimated resident population.   2. Deaths of infants under 1 year old.   3. Deaths of infants under 1 year old per 1,000 live births.   4. Data subject to copyright.   5. Per 100,000 resident population as of July 1 of the year shown.   6. Data for serious crimes have not been adjusted for underreporting; this may affect comparability between geographic areas and over time.   7. Per 100,000 population estimated by the FBI.

Table B. States and Counties — Crime, Education, Money Income, and Poverty

STATE County	Serious crimes known to police,[1] 2002 (cont'd) — Rate[2] Violent (46)	Property (47)	Education — School enrollment and attainment, 2000 — Enrollment[3] Total (48)	Percent private (49)	Attainment[4] (percent) High school graduate or less (50)	Bachelor's degree or more (51)	Local government expenditures,[5] 2000–2001 Total current expenditures (mil dol) (52)	Current expenditures per student (dollars) (53)	Money income, 1999 — Per capita income[6] (dollars) (54)	Households — Median income Dollars (55)	Percent change, 1989–1999 (constant 1999 dollars) (56)	Percent with income of $100,000 or more (57)	Percent below poverty level, 1999 — Persons (58)	House-holds (59)	Families (60)	Families with children (61)
GEORGIA—Cont'd																
Fannin	10	720	3 861	6.4	68.0	10.4	21.6	6 948	16 269	30 612	19.8	4.1	12.4	13.9	10.2	14.0
Fayette	46	1 511	27 262	14.8	31.6	36.2	129.9	6 631	29 464	71 227	5.7	28.8	2.6	2.8	2.0	2.7
Floyd	338	3 628	23 133	18.5	61.8	15.8	103.2	6 603	17 808	35 615	3.8	7.3	14.4	14.3	10.8	16.1
Forsyth	223	2 208	23 873	17.9	37.8	34.6	115.8	6 759	29 114	68 890	39.9	27.2	5.5	5.6	3.9	4.6
Franklin	335	2 551	5 002	15.4	70.4	10.3	23.5	6 545	15 767	32 134	10.4	4.2	13.9	15.7	11.0	13.8
Fulton	1 356	6 853	219 663	23.4	35.4	41.4	1 179.8	9 303	30 003	47 321	17.5	21.5	15.7	13.9	12.4	18.2
Gilmer	29	1 015	4 750	10.2	67.3	12.9	23.3	6 270	17 147	35 140	22.2	5.7	12.5	13.4	9.3	12.1
Glascock	37	112	564	8.7	74.2	6.5	4.0	7 197	14 185	29 743	1.5	3.8	17.2	17.0	9.4	11.6
Glynn	773	7 749	16 443	11.2	47.0	23.8	83.4	6 921	21 707	38 765	3.5	11.1	15.1	13.9	11.6	18.6
Gordon	134	2 697	10 354	7.7	68.2	10.6	56.0	6 522	17 586	38 831	7.1	6.3	9.9	10.6	7.5	11.2
Grady	437	2 935	6 185	7.5	70.3	10.6	29.5	6 471	14 278	28 656	9.3	4.3	21.3	21.0	16.7	23.3
Greene	199	2 244	3 385	14.4	63.2	17.6	18.9	7 944	23 389	33 479	23.0	13.3	22.3	19.3	16.0	27.1
Gwinnett	255	3 023	161 510	14.2	34.7	34.1	752.0	6 701	25 006	60 537	3.5	19.8	5.7	4.8	3.8	5.0
Habersham	160	1 681	8 166	14.3	62.9	15.8	37.5	6 630	17 706	36 321	10.9	6.5	12.2	12.9	8.8	12.6
Hall	320	3 274	33 309	10.4	59.1	18.7	156.2	6 427	19 690	44 908	12.3	11.0	12.4	11.0	8.5	11.9
Hancock	228	807	2 704	8.5	72.2	9.8	12.0	6 879	10 916	22 003	-8.1	2.6	29.4	28.7	26.1	36.8
Haralson	194	2 986	5 956	6.7	73.1	9.0	32.6	6 252	15 823	31 656	3.5	4.8	15.5	16.2	11.4	16.1
Harris	109	1 364	6 252	13.2	50.5	21.1	27.3	6 395	21 680	47 763	28.7	14.1	8.2	9.2	6.5	8.8
Hart	295	1 821	4 886	7.2	65.8	13.5	24.5	7 136	16 714	32 833	0.4	4.9	14.8	15.1	12.2	18.6
Heard	208	1 617	2 767	6.1	75.7	7.3	12.6	5 971	15 132	33 038	14.3	4.0	13.6	14.4	10.5	13.8
Henry	209	2 676	32 860	15.3	50.1	19.5	138.3	5 861	22 945	57 309	13.6	14.4	4.9	4.9	3.7	4.8
Houston	265	4 268	32 495	10.5	48.1	19.8	141.5	6 571	19 515	43 638	4.0	8.5	10.2	9.8	8.4	12.3
Irwin	645	2 359	2 682	4.1	70.8	9.9	14.5	7 654	14 867	30 257	11.7	4.9	17.8	18.7	13.5	18.1
Jackson	212	2 989	9 885	8.8	67.5	11.7	53.3	6 716	17 808	40 349	18.2	7.9	12.0	13.2	9.9	13.1
Jasper	NA	NA	2 876	13.1	67.4	11.5	13.2	6 317	19 249	39 890	15.4	6.3	14.2	13.7	10.9	15.3
Jeff Davis	422	4 780	2 880	7.4	72.1	9.4	18.0	6 808	13 780	27 310	-5.3	4.9	19.4	20.6	16.8	19.2
Jefferson	199	1 617	4 628	11.4	75.4	9.1	23.0	6 258	13 491	26 120	13.9	3.9	23.0	24.0	19.3	25.5
Jenkins	256	1 628	2 381	5.7	70.8	10.8	11.1	6 174	13 400	24 025	5.4	4.9	28.4	26.4	22.3	31.9
Johnson	NA	NA	2 318	5.6	77.0	7.8	9.9	7 036	12 384	23 848	-1.7	4.9	22.6	25.1	20.9	27.5
Jones	105	2 630	6 342	11.0	63.2	15.0	26.5	5 526	19 126	43 301	0.9	8.7	10.2	10.6	7.7	10.3
Lamar	427	1 959	4 354	9.3	65.7	11.3	16.1	6 093	16 666	37 087	18.3	6.1	11.2	13.1	8.1	13.6
Lanier	515	1 083	1 834	6.5	67.2	8.8	9.8	7 310	13 690	29 171	23.2	2.8	18.5	19.7	15.3	18.4
Laurens	356	3 602	11 544	6.6	66.8	14.4	60.7	6 681	16 763	32 010	9.3	6.2	18.4	18.3	14.7	21.0
Lee	116	2 947	7 626	9.2	54.6	17.0	30.5	5 655	19 897	48 600	16.8	12.4	8.2	8.5	6.5	8.8
Liberty	335	3 654	17 177	8.3	47.5	14.5	67.9	5 922	13 855	33 477	15.4	4.3	15.0	14.9	13.5	17.4
Lincoln	367	1 409	1 953	3.5	65.3	10.1	9.9	6 784	15 351	31 952	10.8	5.1	15.3	17.5	12.4	16.7
Long	130	1 949	2 788	6.8	67.3	5.8	10.7	5 417	12 586	30 640	21.3	2.3	19.5	18.4	17.6	22.0
Lowndes	399	4 353	30 067	9.0	52.9	19.7	105.2	6 494	16 683	32 132	2.7	6.6	18.3	18.5	13.9	19.4
Lumpkin	114	2 212	6 383	7.9	58.4	17.6	21.3	6 527	18 062	39 167	11.6	7.8	13.2	13.8	9.0	11.8
McDuffie	225	3 180	5 669	9.3	68.5	11.7	28.0	6 308	18 005	31 920	11.6	6.6	18.4	18.5	14.1	19.1
McIntosh	150	2 883	2 737	11.8	66.7	11.1	12.2	6 205	14 253	30 102	16.8	3.5	18.7	18.9	15.7	21.9
Macon	299	1 943	3 765	12.2	72.0	10.0	17.4	7 607	11 820	24 224	2.9	2.9	25.8	25.8	22.1	33.4
Madison	193	2 402	5 893	10.5	70.0	10.9	28.9	6 334	16 998	36 347	7.8	4.4	11.6	12.6	9.2	12.5
Marion	107	1 459	1 824	6.6	70.7	8.9	11.5	6 575	14 044	29 145	18.3	3.9	22.4	22.4	17.8	23.4
Meriwether	301	3 336	5 667	11.7	69.9	10.8	30.9	7 589	15 708	31 870	17.4	5.0	17.8	17.6	13.6	19.4
Miller	195	1 034	1 707	11.7	66.9	11.3	8.8	7 115	15 445	27 335	-0.7	5.4	21.2	20.4	16.9	25.4
Mitchell	NA	NA	6 545	11.8	70.1	9.1	29.5	6 548	13 042	26 581	4.5	4.7	26.4	25.4	22.3	32.1
Monroe	26	1 679	5 835	15.8	61.0	17.1	24.7	6 577	19 580	44 195	18.5	10.4	9.8	11.3	7.3	10.9
Montgomery	NA	NA	2 506	23.1	68.0	13.5	8.5	6 419	14 182	30 240	12.2	5.8	19.9	20.8	15.8	18.6
Morgan	NA	NA	3 886	13.3	63.1	18.7	20.3	6 768	18 823	40 249	15.1	9.8	10.9	11.1	8.9	12.9
Murray	291	2 614	8 373	5.1	74.3	7.2	40.0	5 790	16 230	36 996	3.8	4.5	12.7	13.1	9.2	12.8
Muscogee	428	5 992	50 950	10.9	49.3	20.3	224.7	6 826	18 262	34 798	7.7	8.0	15.7	15.1	12.8	18.6
Newton	211	3 170	16 015	15.8	60.0	14.5	73.9	6 298	19 317	44 875	19.3	9.2	10.0	9.3	7.2	10.4
Oconee	73	1 966	7 782	16.7	36.7	39.8	33.1	6 093	24 153	55 211	18.9	18.8	6.5	6.2	4.9	6.5
Oglethorpe	NA	NA	3 078	12.6	65.4	15.6	14.1	6 552	17 089	35 578	7.4	5.9	13.2	14.2	10.0	13.3
Paulding	269	2 247	21 260	11.2	58.3	15.2	97.7	5 889	19 974	52 161	17.3	8.8	5.5	5.8	4.0	5.0
Peach	517	3 261	7 642	15.4	59.8	16.8	26.3	6 278	16 031	34 453	0.2	6.8	20.2	19.8	15.2	21.9
Pickens	42	907	4 808	7.6	62.9	15.6	26.4	7 008	19 774	41 387	22.0	8.4	9.2	9.2	6.2	10.3
Pierce	NA	NA	3 931	3.8	71.4	10.1	19.9	6 170	14 230	29 895	8.5	3.7	18.4	19.7	14.4	21.9
Pike	186	1 533	3 534	14.3	64.8	14.0	14.0	5 250	17 661	44 370	19.1	8.8	9.6	10.1	6.9	9.3
Polk	261	3 298	9 338	7.5	71.8	8.0	43.3	5 617	15 617	32 328	7.8	4.7	15.5	15.4	11.2	16.6
Pulaski	658	1 815	2 205	10.5	62.8	12.9	11.6	7 146	16 435	31 895	11.1	6.1	16.4	17.8	12.3	17.4
Putnam	361	2 166	4 207	18.9	65.1	14.4	17.2	6 806	20 161	36 956	13.1	9.5	14.6	13.8	10.5	18.8
Quitman	184	1 619	609	7.7	76.3	6.1	2.6	9 584	14 301	25 875	20.6	3.7	21.9	21.6	16.1	24.2
Rabun	127	1 659	2 961	14.4	59.6	17.6	14.8	6 916	20 608	33 899	19.1	7.0	11.1	11.7	8.1	10.3
Randolph	303	1 977	2 230	20.4	70.1	9.5	13.9	8 512	11 809	22 004	17.2	3.1	27.7	28.3	22.0	30.7

1. Data for serious crimes have not been adjusted for underreporting; this may affect comparability between geographic areas and over time. 2. Per 100,000 population estimated by the FBI. 3. All persons 3 years old and over enrolled in nursery school through college. 4. Persons 25 years old and over. 5. Elementary and secondary education expenditures. 6. Based on population enumerated as of April 1, 2000.

Table B. States and Counties — **Personal Income**

STATE County	Personal income, 2002 Total (mil dol) 62	Percent change, 2001-2002 63	Per capita[1] Dollars 64	Rank 65	Wages and salaries[2] (mil dol) 66	Proprietor's income (mil dol) 67	Dividends, interest, and rent (mil dol) 68	Transfer payments Total (mil dol) 69	Government payments to individuals Total (mil dol) 70	Social Security (mil dol) 71	Medical payments (mil dol) 72	Income maintenance (mil dol) 73	Unemployment insurance (mil dol) 74
GEORGIA—Cont'd													
Fannin	466	6.5	22 300	1 933	153	49	87	122	116	51	49	8	3
Fayette	3 626	2.5	37 553	94	1 421	205	632	278	251	129	84	14	5
Floyd	2 346	4.5	25 337	1 034	1 570	129	405	476	449	177	206	40	10
Forsyth	3 861	0.9	33 108	183	1 710	68	651	241	207	106	81	6	10
Franklin	468	-1.4	22 451	1 890	236	62	85	111	105	42	49	8	2
Fulton	38 921	1.6	47 478	21	46 426	6 266	7 525	3 099	2 864	889	1 260	400	133
Gilmer	535	5.0	21 166	2 246	226	62	91	120	113	44	55	8	2
Glascock	55	2.6	21 005	2 301	19	2	8	17	16	5	10	1	0
Glynn	2 111	4.6	30 459	306	1 289	112	594	355	335	136	148	29	7
Gordon	1 064	4.1	22 806	1 778	699	98	147	193	179	71	79	17	6
Grady	501	2.7	20 900	2 324	184	49	90	107	100	37	42	15	2
Greene	367	3.3	24 302	1 309	157	31	74	87	82	32	34	9	5
Gwinnett	19 553	0.9	30 138	339	14 681	1 146	2 335	1 347	1 161	495	483	70	69
Habersham	868	2.4	22 981	1 731	470	81	184	158	147	64	62	10	3
Hall	3 795	3.4	25 040	1 116	2 540	323	704	524	481	201	210	41	10
Hancock	154	6.1	15 310	3 067	46	6	25	60	58	15	31	8	2
Haralson	600	4.5	22 320	1 927	218	35	92	131	123	48	56	11	3
Harris	792	3.4	31 554	245	136	51	133	89	82	37	28	7	2
Hart	501	1.2	21 535	2 139	250	30	105	114	107	46	45	9	2
Heard	215	2.1	19 117	2 735	118	13	23	46	43	16	20	4	1
Henry	3 732	3.3	26 658	756	1 377	145	472	384	344	155	136	23	11
Houston	3 027	7.0	25 876	916	2 510	128	476	399	367	118	170	41	12
Irwin	211	6.5	21 087	2 272	75	23	37	53	50	16	25	5	1
Jackson	1 094	1.8	24 074	1 378	506	102	134	183	170	64	79	16	5
Jasper	283	3.5	23 226	1 651	90	15	56	49	46	19	19	5	1
Jeff Davis	270	1.7	20 983	2 302	155	23	44	68	65	23	31	7	2
Jefferson	334	3.0	19 503	2 660	186	16	56	105	100	30	47	16	4
Jenkins	162	2.1	18 598	2 814	76	10	25	49	46	13	23	7	1
Johnson	164	2.0	17 368	2 963	60	8	24	51	49	14	25	7	1
Jones	595	4.1	23 998	1 408	105	21	77	87	80	35	30	7	2
Lamar	379	3.7	23 347	1 612	115	21	55	76	71	27	29	7	1
Lanier	148	8.4	20 693	2 374	37	6	21	38	36	10	19	4	1
Laurens	1 057	5.3	23 238	1 647	701	54	172	232	219	74	100	28	5
Lee	614	3.5	22 158	1 967	127	35	65	69	61	23	26	7	2
Liberty	1 115	4.7	18 210	2 869	1 359	31	149	165	151	36	67	23	5
Lincoln	178	2.9	21 088	2 271	41	13	31	41	38	15	16	4	1
Long	175	6.3	16 265	3 039	24	5	23	36	33	8	16	5	1
Lowndes	2 230	8.1	23 808	1 469	1 682	133	384	409	383	115	180	45	10
Lumpkin	505	3.6	22 356	1 920	218	38	91	81	74	30	33	6	1
McDuffie	523	3.2	24 529	1 255	253	30	94	112	106	32	51	15	3
McIntosh	215	6.0	19 599	2 635	64	14	38	56	53	19	25	6	1
Macon	266	0.1	18 953	2 763	143	30	43	73	69	15	40	11	2
Madison	634	1.5	23 762	1 480	117	55	85	113	106	41	48	10	2
Marion	156	1.2	21 678	2 097	60	16	20	29	27	7	13	5	1
Meriwether	474	3.9	20 764	2 350	191	33	75	117	111	37	48	15	3
Miller	150	8.9	23 485	1 574	47	22	28	36	34	11	17	4	1
Mitchell	448	4.3	18 809	2 780	238	38	74	117	110	33	52	20	3
Monroe	572	3.4	25 275	1 057	178	23	76	89	83	34	36	8	2
Montgomery	159	2.0	18 767	2 788	53	9	27	40	38	12	17	5	1
Morgan	454	2.7	27 708	588	205	35	94	71	66	28	28	7	2
Murray	788	4.2	20 400	2 458	408	32	82	132	121	46	53	13	4
Muscogee	5 168	3.9	27 892	566	3 945	307	996	895	844	271	342	108	27
Newton	1 632	3.7	22 749	1 802	710	45	218	266	245	97	114	23	7
Oconee	825	3.3	30 263	326	227	38	115	74	66	31	26	5	1
Oglethorpe	297	0.7	22 624	1 841	53	21	42	47	44	19	17	4	1
Paulding	2 189	2.7	23 207	1 658	486	112	182	217	191	84	75	16	8
Peach	563	4.8	23 370	1 604	301	25	99	117	110	35	45	16	3
Pickens	712	3.4	27 743	583	209	55	138	114	106	47	45	6	3
Pierce	337	3.5	21 071	2 277	119	23	52	86	81	27	35	9	1
Pike	345	3.3	23 615	1 530	69	21	47	54	50	21	21	4	1
Polk	793	5.4	20 107	2 520	372	37	115	207	196	71	85	17	4
Pulaski	241	3.8	24 779	1 185	103	13	41	48	45	15	22	6	2
Putnam	483	5.0	24 939	1 151	212	29	108	92	86	36	35	8	3
Quitman	55	4.5	21 568	2 132	10	2	9	16	15	5	6	2	1
Rabun	369	1.6	23 720	1 493	175	22	106	74	69	27	34	5	1
Randolph	155	9.3	20 424	2 453	76	16	29	43	41	12	18	7	1

1. Based on the resident population estimated as of July 1 of the year shown.   2. Includes other labor income.

STATE County	Earnings, 2002 — Total (mil dol)	Farm	Goods-related[1] Total	Manufacturing	Information and professional and technical services	Retail trade	Finance, insurance, and real estate	Health services	Government	Social Security beneficiaries, Dec. 2003 — Number	Rate[2]	Supplemental Security Income recipients, December 2003	Housing units, 2003 — Total	Percent change, 2000–2003
	75	76	77	78	79	80	81	82	83	84	85	86	87	88
GEORGIA—Cont'd														
Fannin	202	1.4	D	9.6	5.1	13.1	8.5	13.6	16.1	5 535	261	645	13 683	22.9
Fayette	1 626	0.2	D	13.7	7.3	9.5	7.2	9.1	12.9	12 345	125	421	35 694	9.1
Floyd	1 699	0.3	D	26.7	5.9	7.1	4.6	16.5	14.2	18 285	196	2 918	38 009	3.8
Forsyth	1 778	1.0	34.1	17.7	12.9	6.8	4.5	4.3	10.0	10 960	89	531	45 243	23.9
Franklin	298	10.7	D	20.8	D	9.8	3.4	D	12.2	4 755	225	722	9 507	2.2
Fulton	52 692	0.0	9.3	5.9	26.8	4.0	13.8	5.8	11.3	89 725	110	19 822	377 765	2.2
Gilmer	287	6.6	D	33.1	6.4	9.1	4.4	5.3	14.9	4 980	192	554	13 667	14.6
Glascock	21	-1.8	D	0.0	D	D	D	D	26.1	575	218	103	1 212	1.7
Glynn	1 401	0.0	D	12.4	5.8	8.6	5.4	8.9	25.8	13 710	195	1 696	34 727	6.4
Gordon	797	2.2	D	45.0	5.8	6.9	2.8	D	11.7	7 855	164	990	18 920	10.4
Grady	233	9.9	18.5	12.7	D	9.8	4.3	D	19.2	4 560	189	1 018	10 242	2.5
Greene	187	4.1	D	12.0	D	7.4	7.2	D	17.7	3 500	229	550	7 132	7.2
Gwinnett	15 827	0.0	D	11.0	15.4	9.6	9.7	4.6	8.1	49 545	74	4 378	246 000	17.3
Habersham	551	4.9	D	27.8	5.4	8.3	4.6	D	19.1	7 080	184	763	15 868	8.4
Hall	2 863	0.9	34.4	27.0	5.4	7.3	4.6	12.3	9.1	21 105	135	2 276	57 011	11.7
Hancock	52	3.7	D	D	D	6.6	D	D	58.9	1 885	189	476	4 453	3.9
Haralson	254	1.3	D	31.0	D	8.2	2.3	5.8	21.2	5 275	192	804	11 325	5.7
Harris	187	0.7	26.2	16.2	D	5.4	6.0	D	20.1	4 000	154	422	11 236	9.2
Hart	280	3.6	D	37.6	D	5.7	3.5	D	14.5	5 165	220	620	11 326	1.9
Heard	131	4.6	D	D	0.7	1.4	D	D	14.3	1 840	165	276	4 725	4.7
Henry	1 522	0.1	D	10.5	6.9	11.2	6.3	8.3	22.4	16 585	111	1 295	56 353	30.5
Houston	2 638	0.1	9.1	6.6	6.7	5.8	2.5	4.8	61.1	15 195	126	2 426	49 774	11.8
Irwin	97	16.5	17.6	12.0	D	3.9	D	D	25.2	1 865	185	369	4 218	1.7
Jackson	608	11.6	D	25.8	D	10.5	2.7	2.5	15.4	7 170	153	1 168	18 865	16.3
Jasper	105	4.7	D	35.9	4.0	3.6	2.5	D	19.2	2 180	174	225	5 355	11.4
Jeff Davis	179	2.5	32.0	30.2	D	10.2	2.1	3.0	16.3	2 580	200	470	5 709	2.3
Jefferson	201	2.2	D	31.4	D	7.6	4.1	D	19.5	3 565	210	1 178	7 309	1.2
Jenkins	86	5.1	40.4	38.7	1.1	4.8	D	4.8	22.7	1 670	191	479	3 935	0.7
Johnson	68	6.5	18.2	13.9	D	4.3	D	6.5	30.5	1 765	187	483	3 683	1.3
Jones	126	1.7	D	1.7	D	6.9	3.8	7.4	27.3	4 045	159	353	10 101	8.9
Lamar	136	3.6	31.1	24.6	2.3	7.5	5.1	D	25.5	3 045	188	368	6 542	6.5
Lanier	43	2.9	D	D	D	8.5	D	D	31.1	1 260	171	255	3 116	3.5
Laurens	755	1.2	D	23.2	5.3	9.0	3.4	D	24.2	8 780	190	1 943	20 093	2.1
Lee	163	10.6	D	1.5	D	6.1	2.1	7.1	26.6	2 630	93	352	10 122	14.9
Liberty	1 390	0.0	4.6	3.4	D	2.8	1.6	1.4	80.4	4 570	78	989	23 029	4.8
Lincoln	54	3.0	14.2	3.7	D	8.4	3.5	2.5	27.5	1 755	206	249	4 626	2.5
Long	30	4.2	D	D	D	D	D	D	47.4	1 035	96	153	4 375	3.4
Lowndes	1 815	0.5	D	11.3	4.6	10.1	4.8	9.4	35.5	13 085	138	2 877	38 821	6.2
Lumpkin	256	3.5	25.3	17.6	D	9.7	4.3	10.6	29.5	3 390	146	408	9 316	12.7
McDuffie	283	2.8	31.7	21.1	4.1	10.0	6.0	D	21.0	3 740	174	848	9 136	2.5
McIntosh	79	0.0	5.4	1.6	D	12.0	3.3	4.3	29.0	2 320	213	397	6 076	5.9
Macon	173	15.0	33.3	28.9	2.4	4.6	1.6	6.6	20.4	1 920	137	755	5 582	1.6
Madison	172	13.9	27.2	10.4	4.6	6.0	2.9	D	21.6	4 770	176	773	11 068	5.2
Marion	76	7.2	41.2	37.0	D	5.1	D	4.8	19.7	1 055	147	243	3 225	3.0
Meriwether	224	1.6	29.9	22.3	2.7	10.0	4.9	D	28.6	4 225	185	942	9 791	6.3
Miller	69	28.6	D	D	D	8.6	4.0	D	30.6	1 290	204	294	2 815	1.6
Mitchell	275	11.8	29.1	26.3	D	7.7	3.3	D	22.5	4 110	172	1 120	9 166	3.2
Monroe	201	2.0	D	3.9	3.4	4.8	2.2	D	31.5	3 860	166	428	8 777	4.2
Montgomery	61	4.4	14.6	8.1	D	7.5	D	1.4	26.3	1 495	172	380	3 622	3.7
Morgan	240	5.0	30.8	24.1	4.6	7.9	5.0	D	15.1	3 060	182	381	6 601	7.7
Murray	440	1.4	D	48.9	D	5.4	2.7	3.3	12.8	5 495	139	864	15 159	5.9
Muscogee	4 252	0.0	D	12.3	14.3	6.9	11.7	10.1	23.1	29 730	160	6 012	78 815	3.5
Newton	755	0.0	D	30.1	D	7.4	3.2	10.2	17.3	10 550	139	2 009	29 222	26.9
Oconee	265	3.8	20.8	9.7	9.2	8.2	10.2	6.4	16.4	3 375	120	293	10 530	10.5
Oglethorpe	74	23.5	17.1	4.9	D	6.1	D	D	23.8	2 270	170	305	5 537	3.1
Paulding	598	-0.2	D	7.5	8.2	13.1	5.6	5.2	23.1	9 260	93	623	38 000	29.8
Peach	327	3.2	17.9	12.1	D	10.1	3.2	3.4	26.9	3 920	161	866	9 555	5.1
Pickens	264	4.6	D	12.6	5.9	9.1	8.9	D	16.9	4 960	184	408	11 989	12.2
Pierce	142	5.4	19.1	8.2	2.3	8.9	6.3	D	19.1	3 195	196	720	6 965	3.7
Pike	90	6.6	D	16.1	D	3.0	8.1	D	24.6	2 460	164	291	5 725	13.0
Polk	409	1.1	D	27.4	7.3	8.7	3.2	4.8	20.4	7 935	199	1 271	15 892	5.5
Pulaski	116	5.8	10.9	4.4	8.5	8.5	4.7	20.2	24.5	2 055	211	385	4 110	4.2
Putnam	241	2.2	29.4	19.9	3.1	6.5	4.8	D	17.9	3 820	195	383	11 055	7.1
Quitman	12	6.3	D	D	0.8	7.4	D	D	37.1	610	246	160	1 818	2.5
Rabun	197	1.4	D	26.6	3.8	11.3	6.4	D	15.9	3 575	227	423	11 016	7.9
Randolph	92	14.5	15.4	12.9	D	4.5	2.7	D	29.4	1 555	208	466	3 416	0.4

1. Covers mining, construction, and manufacturing.   2. Per 1,000 resident population estimated as of July 1 of the year shown.

Table B. States and Counties — Housing, Labor Force, and Employment

STATE County	Total	Percent	Median value[1]	With a mortgage	Without a mortgage[2]	Median rent[3]	Median rent as a percent of income	Sub-standard units[4] (percent)	Total	Percent change, 2002–2003	Total	Rate[5]	Total	Management, professional and related occupations	Production, transportation, and material moving occupations
	89	90	91	92	93	94	95	96	97	98	99	100	101	102	103
GEORGIA—Cont'd															
Fannin	8 369	82.6	86 200	23.0	9.9	391	22.3	2.1	9 611	0.0	581	6.0	8 331	22.4	25.3
Fayette	31 524	86.6	171 500	21.4	9.9	890	25.4	1.4	50 721	3.0	1 558	3.1	45 423	40.9	11.8
Floyd	34 028	66.8	83 500	20.2	9.9	476	23.1	4.6	48 176	4.3	2 090	4.3	40 403	27.1	22.7
Forsyth	34 565	88.1	184 600	20.7	9.9	683	23.5	2.8	63 722	2.5	2 173	3.4	51 779	41.1	9.1
Franklin	7 888	79.3	84 600	21.8	9.9	377	23.2	2.5	11 360	5.7	508	4.5	9 007	24.0	25.1
Fulton	321 242	52.0	180 700	21.8	10.7	709	26.0	6.4	431 182	2.3	24 922	5.8	392 627	43.6	9.1
Gilmer	9 071	78.1	95 700	23.0	9.9	482	22.0	5.2	9 672	5.7	441	4.6	10 447	22.9	29.5
Glascock	1 004	80.2	48 600	17.1	11.9	313	18.3	2.0	1 042	2.7	51	4.9	1 080	18.6	26.0
Glynn	27 208	65.5	114 500	21.5	10.7	533	25.1	4.0	36 657	2.2	1 299	3.5	31 858	31.3	13.3
Gordon	16 173	71.7	83 600	19.2	9.9	486	22.0	5.3	22 580	2.9	1 138	5.0	22 451	20.9	31.6
Grady	8 797	73.3	74 900	22.2	13.1	368	25.3	6.1	9 348	1.8	460	4.9	10 068	24.1	21.9
Greene	5 477	76.2	87 100	21.1	10.6	386	24.9	5.0	5 821	2.3	424	7.3	5 709	25.9	23.6
Gwinnett	202 317	72.4	142 100	20.7	9.9	824	24.8	6.0	389 991	2.5	15 919	4.1	314 471	39.7	9.6
Habersham	13 259	76.2	99 700	22.3	9.9	467	22.9	4.8	16 999	5.8	585	3.4	16 777	25.0	23.6
Hall	47 381	71.1	120 200	21.3	9.9	619	24.0	8.8	80 368	3.9	2 832	3.5	66 587	26.3	24.0
Hancock	3 237	76.5	53 000	26.7	13.7	277	26.9	8.9	3 713	1.6	284	7.6	2 931	18.4	31.5
Haralson	9 826	75.2	76 500	20.6	10.2	395	23.6	3.8	10 775	5.2	565	5.2	11 258	20.3	24.4
Harris	8 822	86.1	122 700	20.9	9.9	411	21.5	3.5	13 742	4.1	438	3.2	11 821	33.6	15.6
Hart	9 106	80.8	89 900	21.4	9.9	381	23.5	2.6	9 496	2.0	497	5.2	10 409	24.6	23.9
Heard	4 043	77.3	72 900	22.1	9.9	428	23.8	5.9	5 242	0.7	293	5.6	4 619	18.3	26.5
Henry	41 373	85.3	122 400	21.5	9.9	740	22.8	2.8	74 722	3.2	3 151	4.2	60 999	30.3	14.6
Houston	40 911	68.5	88 900	19.2	9.9	558	23.5	3.7	58 123	4.9	1 783	3.1	48 653	31.7	12.6
Irwin	3 644	76.8	58 100	21.2	12.3	343	22.8	4.9	4 755	-3.6	280	5.9	4 107	23.6	24.6
Jackson	15 057	74.9	102 900	21.7	10.2	501	22.1	4.3	25 176	6.5	960	3.8	19 542	22.5	22.6
Jasper	4 175	79.1	81 000	21.6	9.9	442	19.4	5.7	5 390	6.0	296	5.5	5 258	19.4	25.7
Jeff Davis	4 828	77.4	61 000	21.2	10.8	368	19.8	6.2	5 024	-2.7	479	9.5	5 266	20.5	29.2
Jefferson	6 339	72.2	56 900	22.0	10.7	300	23.5	7.4	7 328	4.1	667	9.1	5 952	22.8	30.4
Jenkins	3 214	73.4	49 400	24.1	10.2	327	24.0	8.2	4 034	2.0	213	5.3	3 328	23.5	28.4
Johnson	3 130	79.8	48 000	21.0	10.8	259	30.1	5.8	3 380	9.3	278	8.2	3 017	20.2	26.9
Jones	8 659	85.8	91 200	20.0	9.9	447	20.2	2.4	13 069	4.7	433	3.3	10 819	30.5	14.4
Lamar	5 712	72.4	79 900	20.9	9.9	441	22.6	4.1	6 612	3.7	419	6.3	7 243	21.3	25.5
Lanier	2 593	76.3	62 200	22.5	12.9	394	24.2	5.2	3 690	5.0	102	2.8	2 990	22.1	23.6
Laurens	17 083	71.3	73 900	19.2	9.9	392	24.3	4.8	23 286	2.7	1 364	5.9	19 250	26.5	23.4
Lee	8 229	78.3	102 900	19.4	9.9	587	23.0	5.3	13 786	4.7	413	3.0	11 989	29.5	13.8
Liberty	19 383	50.7	79 800	22.6	11.0	529	23.5	6.2	19 529	2.5	1 049	5.4	17 344	24.4	15.8
Lincoln	3 251	81.8	82 000	21.8	13.1	377	18.6	5.1	2 589	0.2	255	9.8	3 377	23.8	24.3
Long	3 574	66.2	71 100	26.7	11.3	456	22.8	8.1	5 023	3.0	153	3.0	3 854	18.8	17.3
Lowndes	32 654	60.8	87 600	20.5	9.9	495	26.4	5.0	47 300	5.6	1 447	3.1	39 305	26.9	16.0
Lumpkin	7 537	72.3	111 800	22.1	9.9	534	25.6	4.4	12 158	6.6	377	3.1	10 130	25.3	19.0
McDuffie	7 970	71.4	74 600	20.7	9.9	389	25.1	5.0	9 779	2.8	660	6.7	8 931	24.7	22.4
McIntosh	4 202	83.5	81 700	24.2	11.6	369	19.3	5.7	5 079	3.5	223	4.4	4 424	21.5	17.0
Macon	4 834	73.2	54 200	20.2	12.2	331	24.6	7.7	5 344	2.9	439	8.2	4 802	21.9	26.7
Madison	9 800	80.2	87 300	20.0	9.9	452	21.9	3.2	14 045	3.9	510	3.6	12 498	21.9	22.7
Marion	2 668	78.1	70 400	20.9	13.4	317	31.2	5.1	2 859	-0.3	180	6.3	3 015	20.7	30.8
Meriwether	8 248	74.1	66 300	19.4	10.4	427	25.3	5.6	9 360	4.4	638	6.8	9 157	20.3	28.3
Miller	2 487	76.9	57 600	22.4	11.6	317	22.9	4.3	3 406	3.8	180	5.3	2 863	26.3	24.0
Mitchell	8 063	72.0	64 500	20.0	12.2	337	24.6	7.7	12 103	4.1	555	4.6	8 883	24.2	23.2
Monroe	7 719	79.4	103 600	19.5	9.9	461	21.9	3.5	7 997	7.6	430	5.4	10 410	28.3	19.5
Montgomery	2 919	78.2	68 300	21.0	9.9	323	22.3	4.6	3 784	4.9	248	6.6	3 554	26.7	18.1
Morgan	5 558	77.6	99 700	22.4	9.9	470	23.2	4.6	8 117	3.1	338	4.2	7 414	26.4	19.5
Murray	13 286	73.7	85 700	19.8	9.9	446	20.8	5.1	19 028	-1.6	806	4.2	17 802	16.6	38.8
Muscogee	69 819	56.4	84 000	21.1	9.9	500	24.5	4.9	89 672	3.7	4 424	4.9	75 677	30.7	16.5
Newton	21 997	77.7	101 300	21.7	10.1	597	25.1	4.3	34 720	3.3	1 984	5.7	29 136	26.2	19.1
Oconee	9 051	80.2	151 600	20.5	9.9	589	21.3	3.6	14 554	4.4	279	1.9	13 054	44.2	10.7
Oglethorpe	4 849	82.5	87 500	22.5	11.0	457	23.6	4.5	6 915	6.4	269	3.9	6 003	26.8	22.8
Paulding	28 089	86.8	106 100	21.1	9.9	628	23.4	2.6	48 795	3.1	1 991	4.1	41 472	28.2	14.6
Peach	8 436	68.4	78 300	20.6	10.7	412	25.6	6.5	11 415	6.2	714	6.3	9 766	26.1	17.1
Pickens	8 960	82.1	113 100	21.3	9.9	470	23.5	3.2	12 942	3.3	543	4.2	11 275	24.1	19.9
Pierce	5 958	80.7	64 300	22.0	10.9	328	25.7	4.3	8 493	7.4	283	3.3	6 962	22.2	19.7
Pike	4 755	81.5	103 000	20.8	9.9	470	21.2	4.8	8 195	7.9	383	4.7	6 312	24.5	20.0
Polk	14 012	71.3	73 900	20.4	9.9	425	24.0	6.0	19 568	6.7	876	4.5	15 904	19.5	28.7
Pulaski	3 407	73.7	75 400	21.3	12.1	369	24.4	4.3	4 278	4.2	149	3.5	3 972	25.4	21.4
Putnam	7 402	79.5	102 300	20.0	9.9	355	23.1	5.0	10 021	0.6	358	3.6	8 264	21.4	25.3
Quitman	1 047	80.4	51 300	16.8	11.3	323	18.4	5.4	1 486	8.6	46	3.1	924	13.7	33.9
Rabun	6 279	79.4	112 400	23.4	9.9	439	22.4	4.7	7 651	3.5	180	2.4	6 582	22.2	22.8
Randolph	2 909	68.8	48 600	23.5	12.6	251	24.0	8.5	3 120	2.1	230	7.4	2 691	26.2	25.3

1. Specified owner-occupied units. 2. Median monthly owner costs is often in the minimum category—9.9 percent or less, which is indicated as 9.9 percent. 3. Specified renter-occupied units. 4. Overcrowded or lacking complete plumbing facilities. 5. Percent of civilian labor force. 6. Persons 16 years old and over.

STATE County	Number of establishments	Total	Health care and social assistance	Manufacturing	Retail trade	Finance and insurance	Professional, scientific, and technical services	Total (mil dol)	Average per employee (dollars)	Number	Less than 50 acres	500 acres and over	Farm operators whose principal occupation is farming (percent)
	104	105	106	107	108	109	110	111	112	113	114	115	116
GEORGIA—Cont'd													
Fannin	450	4 231	658	883	939	188	137	89	20 985	208	54.8	1.0	49.0
Fayette	2 493	32 773	2 900	4 878	6 164	1 168	1 189	943	28 761	235	55.3	0.9	43.8
Floyd	2 026	36 749	6 806	7 953	4 842	1 105	961	925	25 158	663	41.2	4.7	45.6
Forsyth	2 463	30 225	1 422	5 122	4 641	635	1 186	911	30 134	528	65.5	1.5	51.5
Franklin	489	6 579	678	2 126	1 068	180	67	166	25 185	825	41.1	2.1	62.2
Fulton	31 327	759 306	63 966	31 810	60 455	60 990	87 323	34 646	45 629	328	69.5	4.9	54.0
Gilmer	445	6 391	456	3 062	831	225	162	135	21 128	303	50.5	1.3	57.4
Glascock	22	175	D	0	D	D	0	2	13 651	100	13.0	11.0	47.0
Glynn	2 378	30 479	3 895	3 592	4 689	864	854	731	23 987	59	45.8	5.1	44.1
Gordon	986	17 038	1 145	7 791	2 378	293	294	427	25 038	804	51.6	2.2	50.9
Grady	384	3 809	433	657	827	164	80	80	20 971	501	35.9	11.2	52.3
Greene	342	4 623	369	1 400	468	566	64	100	21 559	255	29.0	11.8	52.9
Gwinnett	18 360	301 501	16 242	28 392	45 024	20 740	19 973	11 309	37 510	312	75.0	1.3	42.9
Habersham	825	11 465	919	3 790	1 833	461	249	266	23 171	517	60.3	1.2	58.0
Hall	3 403	56 748	5 893	19 007	7 021	2 303	1 288	1 617	28 501	834	61.0	1.4	54.9
Hancock	79	683	332	D	97	D	13	10	14 751	144	12.5	16.0	49.3
Haralson	445	5 567	516	1 887	1 036	129	92	134	24 119	332	36.7	3.0	45.8
Harris	403	4 525	185	1 624	338	106	95	88	19 432	298	33.6	10.4	39.3
Hart	372	5 803	633	2 685	719	140	99	142	24 397	567	40.7	3.4	55.9
Heard	122	1 452	126	327	172	25	28	28	19 063	209	34.9	8.1	44.0
Henry	2 406	31 645	2 900	3 386	5 834	1 282	964	799	25 247	439	63.8	4.1	41.0
Houston	1 996	27 694	3 789	2 595	5 746	929	3 462	640	23 098	360	48.6	10.3	44.7
Irwin	131	2 020	519	738	143	46	D	38	18 847	349	21.5	20.9	53.3
Jackson	1 050	14 420	890	4 628	2 488	361	218	356	24 689	915	50.8	3.8	59.3
Jasper	159	1 913	164	861	134	67	36	47	24 652	210	27.1	9.0	52.9
Jeff Davis	300	4 548	291	1 831	697	90	61	95	20 803	254	34.3	11.4	48.0
Jefferson	345	4 455	400	1 538	740	180	46	113	25 270	388	15.5	18.3	53.6
Jenkins	145	2 057	245	1 133	220	50	17	42	20 198	240	20.4	24.6	42.1
Johnson	141	1 406	159	443	143	30	34	29	20 349	286	21.7	12.2	47.9
Jones	229	1 717	247	90	265	84	40	41	23 775	194	31.4	8.8	53.1
Lamar	228	2 882	269	1 024	390	114	44	57	19 738	243	37.0	7.0	47.3
Lanier	123	951	253	126	145	90	22	17	17 497	134	35.1	14.9	44.0
Laurens	1 051	17 239	2 949	4 880	2 850	459	251	420	24 389	709	30.3	9.7	45.8
Lee	221	1 992	269	232	326	70	D	44	21 971	171	30.4	35.7	47.4
Liberty	704	9 619	1 655	1 009	2 128	510	285	204	21 233	68	33.8	13.2	29.4
Lincoln	160	1 147	55	181	158	39	34	20	17 051	207	36.2	5.3	44.9
Long	49	337	D	0	68	D	0	3	9 721	76	21.1	21.1	48.7
Lowndes	2 417	36 361	5 651	5 028	6 636	910	1 419	834	22 924	462	48.1	7.1	43.9
Lumpkin	388	4 099	646	885	689	115	95	100	24 457	250	59.2	1.6	56.8
McDuffie	473	7 033	746	2 003	1 507	298	153	159	22 543	296	48.3	9.5	47.0
McIntosh	217	1 718	164	D	708	96	12	31	17 990	39	25.6	12.8	38.5
Macon	210	2 457	417	872	370	64	24	67	27 452	360	28.6	15.3	54.2
Madison	493	4 846	368	1 295	609	272	205	124	25 669	763	48.6	1.4	56.9
Marion	81	2 495	141	D	221	15	3	37	14 854	181	24.3	14.4	53.0
Meriwether	342	4 400	1 046	1 358	687	128	D	107	24 300	339	27.4	10.0	51.6
Miller	138	891	224	D	259	41	27	15	16 942	207	16.9	29.0	63.8
Mitchell	401	6 452	461	3 279	946	172	120	118	18 365	496	31.5	21.0	52.2
Monroe	374	3 535	502	421	516	89	86	89	25 190	236	31.4	14.0	56.4
Montgomery	105	1 148	D	197	110	97	10	26	23 048	252	23.4	15.1	42.1
Morgan	412	5 524	272	1 626	848	127	182	125	22 698	525	36.8	7.2	52.0
Murray	459	10 183	296	6 583	772	156	97	250	24 594	306	44.8	4.6	49.3
Muscogee	4 240	84 793	10 317	14 320	11 375	7 143	3 380	2 350	27 713	96	47.9	9.4	41.7
Newton	1 201	15 561	1 356	4 826	2 410	443	306	443	28 483	355	54.4	5.4	43.7
Oconee	600	6 079	564	825	1 119	234	487	142	23 229	411	45.3	5.6	51.1
Oglethorpe	146	902	128	97	131	41	83	18	20 104	362	36.2	5.0	63.3
Paulding	1 030	9 574	739	1 166	2 498	237	336	228	23 819	265	58.1	0.0	52.8
Peach	456	6 686	419	3 077	920	255	88	159	23 841	217	41.9	6.9	49.8
Pickens	495	4 838	629	1 201	778	212	117	125	25 859	243	57.6	0.8	49.4
Pierce	301	2 576	144	352	388	168	64	54	21 148	434	40.6	11.8	49.1
Pike	215	1 324	233	176	133	146	41	30	22 992	327	38.8	4.6	54.4
Polk	632	8 551	843	2 864	1 267	242	148	200	23 501	428	48.6	3.5	49.1
Pulaski	200	2 370	617	446	259	106	97	48	20 286	187	33.7	19.8	50.8
Putnam	375	5 333	324	1 983	994	118	95	130	24 421	225	35.1	9.8	55.1
Quitman	35	224	D	D	82	D	0	4	17 388	23	13.0	34.8	47.8
Rabun	492	5 484	462	1 752	939	199	107	116	21 075	146	63.7	2.1	43.8
Randolph	154	1 454	167	377	245	58	D	32	22 080	136	12.5	30.9	55.1

Table B. States and Counties — Agriculture

	Agriculture, 2002 (cont'd)															
	Land in farms					Value of land and buildings (dollars)			Value of products sold				Percent of farms with sales of —		Government payments	
			Acres								Percent from —					
STATE County	Acreage (1,000)	Percent change, 1997–2002	Average size of farm	Total irrigated (1,000)	Total cropland (1,000)	Average per farm	Average per acre	Value of machinery and equipment average per farm (dollars)	Total (mil dol)	Average per farm (dollars)	Crops	Live-stock and poultry products	$10,000 or more	$100,000 or more	Total ($1,000)	Percent of farms
	117	118	119	120	121	122	123	124	125	126	127	128	129	130	131	132

GEORGIA—Cont'd

STATE County	117	118	119	120	121	122	123	124	125	126	127	128	129	130	131	132
Fannin	15	0.0	74	0	6	324 480	3 549	30 350	11	51 117	9.1	90.9	21.6	7.7	23	14.4
Fayette	18	0.0	77	0	9	376 992	5 006	21 168	4	17 857	78.5	21.5	23.4	2.1	97	13.6
Floyd	91	9.6	138	1	31	358 778	2 650	28 802	29	43 163	7.9	92.1	17.5	4.2	317	14.2
Forsyth	34	9.7	64	0	14	430 810	7 482	31 118	56	105 773	10.2	89.8	25.8	13.8	156	15.5
Franklin	86	11.7	104	0	37	429 163	4 557	36 194	181	219 071	0.8	99.2	40.5	27.0	568	27.3
Fulton	28	3.7	85	0	9	547 490	5 806	20 496	6	18 220	61.7	38.3	18.3	3.4	77	11.0
Gilmer	25	8.7	82	0	8	327 573	4 590	42 794	99	326 263	1.4	98.6	57.4	43.2	149	21.8
Glascock	21	5.0	210	D	6	315 238	1 563	24 763	2	18 706	16.4	83.6	24.0	4.0	128	40.0
Glynn	8	0.0	129	0	1	244 820	1 804	18 281	0	3 068	43.1	56.9	3.4	0.0	3	6.8
Gordon	76	10.1	95	2	38	327 582	3 896	46 501	100	124 724	3.5	96.5	31.0	17.7	286	15.9
Grady	127	0.0	254	7	59	460 479	1 824	69 044	74	146 795	78.3	21.7	38.9	12.0	1 739	39.1
Greene	52	0.0	205	0	20	477 497	2 908	42 139	25	97 881	D	D	31.4	15.7	321	23.9
Gwinnett	18	-41.9	56	0	6	425 587	6 474	21 593	21	68 909	87.4	12.6	15.7	5.4	45	12.2
Habersham	39	25.8	75	0	13	417 455	5 286	33 783	120	231 333	0.8	99.2	46.8	36.4	147	15.1
Hall	62	21.6	74	0	21	336 075	5 384	37 639	170	204 137	0.8	99.2	34.5	21.6	491	20.9
Hancock	42	23.5	293	0	8	360 507	1 178	26 301	2	10 762	16.6	83.4	20.1	1.4	126	24.3
Haralson	40	29.0	120	0	11	280 381	2 827	27 451	19	57 110	3.4	96.6	16.0	4.8	101	16.6
Harris	67	42.6	225	0	14	507 227	1 887	25 392	3	8 995	53.5	46.5	16.1	2.0	74	9.1
Hart	65	12.1	115	1	33	451 033	3 394	48 283	82	145 452	2.4	97.6	32.1	19.8	701	36.9
Heard	42	50.0	201	D	9	411 044	2 175	42 048	22	105 344	1.3	98.7	26.3	7.7	35	14.8
Henry	58	28.9	132	0	17	495 460	4 226	21 588	6	13 431	58.2	41.8	21.4	2.5	211	19.4
Houston	75	-13.8	210	5	39	469 980	2 197	73 606	24	65 567	34.0	66.0	27.2	9.7	930	23.1
Irwin	138	4.5	396	22	81	585 917	1 417	84 821	29	84 158	80.8	19.2	53.3	18.9	2 401	60.7
Jackson	100	29.9	109	1	43	464 331	5 565	36 741	154	168 690	1.7	98.3	36.5	21.2	332	18.3
Jasper	51	-1.9	243	D	14	536 577	2 249	48 782	26	122 545	8.4	91.6	29.0	9.0	214	30.0
Jeff Davis	56	-21.1	221	4	27	308 298	1 509	49 436	11	41 564	61.6	38.4	29.5	7.5	654	31.5
Jefferson	137	-3.5	354	19	73	429 035	1 323	58 431	38	98 779	76.4	23.6	34.0	14.2	1 735	54.9
Jenkins	95	2.2	394	7	39	573 924	1 337	53 678	14	58 566	52.5	47.5	28.8	11.3	1 372	57.9
Johnson	76	-20.8	266	1	29	433 677	1 587	51 313	4	15 524	57.7	42.3	19.6	2.8	410	39.5
Jones	35	12.9	181	0	9	335 153	2 110	34 960	8	41 392	6.5	93.5	27.8	5.7	203	19.1
Lamar	42	10.5	172	2	17	483 271	2 450	61 191	23	94 728	17.4	82.6	26.3	9.5	411	24.7
Lanier	52	20.9	386	8	20	432 171	1 181	77 544	10	75 025	94.9	5.2	23.1	9.0	827	27.6
Laurens	194	-2.0	273	6	68	364 175	1 359	36 340	13	18 215	71.0	29.0	19.3	5.2	1 848	46.3
Lee	147	6.5	858	22	53	1 364 904	1 544	130 785	24	137 550	68.3	31.7	47.4	21.1	1 512	48.5
Liberty	16	-23.8	234	0	4	474 243	2 325	26 287	0	4 598	63.6	36.4	8.8	0.0	10	14.7
Lincoln	31	0.0	149	0	9	362 394	2 657	40 701	3	12 137	8.6	91.4	23.2	2.4	227	33.8
Long	24	26.3	311	1	6	455 515	1 454	34 897	8	104 605	19.2	80.8	38.2	15.8	67	23.7
Lowndes	74	2.8	160	7	31	350 002	2 046	37 541	24	51 794	93.5	6.5	30.5	7.1	831	31.2
Lumpkin	21	-16.0	85	0	6	556 950	6 096	50 763	44	176 494	7.6	92.4	35.2	23.6	130	16.8
McDuffie	47	14.6	158	1	16	360 513	1 991	37 225	30	102 961	D	D	16.9	3.4	134	20.3
McIntosh	11	175.0	290	0	1	469 457	1 618	31 998	D	D	D	D	20.5	2.6	D	D
Macon	114	-4.2	318	17	62	549 163	1 687	95 334	123	342 699	15.5	84.5	48.3	26.7	1 837	48.6
Madison	76	8.6	100	0	30	478 648	4 630	29 512	123	161 275	1.2	98.8	34.3	20.1	487	31.6
Marion	52	0.0	286	1	18	425 177	1 539	53 113	13	71 120	20.8	79.2	29.3	9.4	251	32.6
Meriwether	84	21.7	248	1	20	549 210	1 998	41 982	7	20 646	46.0	54.0	21.8	4.1	213	22.1
Miller	95	-18.1	460	37	70	732 392	1 638	151 731	29	138 426	81.1	18.9	52.7	27.5	2 245	51.7
Mitchell	185	-16.3	373	45	109	607 203	1 448	113 036	128	257 485	37.9	62.1	47.2	23.6	4 152	42.5
Monroe	62	8.8	261	0	13	550 307	2 169	61 270	45	190 695	3.3	96.7	32.2	14.0	264	23.7
Montgomery	74	-1.3	294	3	22	341 105	1 400	45 146	9	35 586	61.5	38.5	21.0	3.2	570	45.2
Morgan	89	1.1	170	1	40	551 072	3 517	38 288	48	91 179	7.2	92.8	27.8	15.2	960	31.8
Murray	42	20.0	137	1	15	435 878	3 028	56 852	27	88 517	5.8	94.2	29.7	16.0	364	17.0
Muscogee	15	87.5	161	0	7	355 133	3 225	31 922	1	11 819	83.8	16.1	13.5	3.1	25	19.8
Newton	45	-2.2	126	0	15	489 659	4 116	21 238	8	22 110	6.9	93.1	20.6	3.7	242	19.2
Oconee	54	5.9	132	1	21	577 961	4 845	33 200	51	123 611	15.7	84.3	33.6	14.6	403	31.4
Oglethorpe	56	-11.1	155	1	18	593 945	3 328	34 154	80	219 714	2.1	97.9	34.8	20.2	298	24.3
Paulding	17	-5.6	63	0	6	374 667	6 524	22 207	14	53 664	20.5	79.5	14.7	5.3	61	14.0
Peach	39	-23.5	179	6	23	433 544	2 375	45 717	20	90 285	81.9	18.1	28.6	7.4	288	24.4
Pickens	17	6.3	71	0	7	441 193	5 781	29 825	48	196 685	1.2	98.8	30.0	19.3	73	14.8
Pierce	99	-1.0	227	7	40	378 644	1 537	48 512	29	67 165	65.1	34.9	33.6	10.8	967	39.2
Pike	44	-8.3	134	1	17	506 590	3 751	25 675	10	30 617	28.8	71.2	21.4	3.7	235	25.4
Polk	52	4.0	122	0	21	262 418	2 398	26 235	19	45 145	5.6	94.4	18.0	6.1	303	19.2
Pulaski	67	-27.2	360	8	46	511 770	1 401	92 631	13	70 129	75.9	24.1	35.3	15.5	1 580	56.1
Putnam	41	32.3	181	1	14	489 866	2 723	46 315	27	118 216	2.7	97.3	25.8	15.1	458	22.2
Quitman	14	27.3	623	D	5	814 011	1 362	91 246	D	D	D	D	30.4	8.7	D	D
Rabun	10	-9.1	68	0	4	427 587	6 087	32 784	11	72 163	22.2	77.8	24.0	8.2	14	10.3
Randolph	79	-16.0	583	15	48	700 471	1 204	131 128	13	98 258	86.7	13.3	40.4	22.1	1 220	66.9

STATE County	Value of residential construction authorized by building permits, 2003		Wholesale trade, 1997				Retail trade,[1] 1997				Real estate and rental and leasing, 1997			
	New construction ($1,000)	Number of housing units	Number of establishments	Number of employees	Sales (mil dol)	Annual payroll (mil dol)	Number of establishments	Number of employees	Sales (mil dol)	Annual payroll (mil dol)	Number of establishments	Number of employees	Receipts (mil dol)	Annual payroll (mil dol)
	133	134	135	136	137	138	139	140	141	142	143	144	145	146
GEORGIA—Cont'd														
Fannin	110 038	1 011	16	56	21.1	1.4	103	779	126.7	10.7	12	15	2.0	0.2
Fayette	182 240	907	135	1 236	545.5	42.3	298	4 697	677.6	69.9	91	287	42.0	6.2
Floyd	61 712	502	112	1 163	523.3	35.8	442	4 991	808.1	75.0	56	313	26.8	5.2
Forsyth	361 652	3 147	228	3 138	1 140.8	110.0	255	3 503	653.9	63.5	88	208	44.8	6.5
Franklin	1 947	24	32	208	56.5	3.9	92	937	202.3	15.2	16	43	3.6	0.8
Fulton	1 085 142	12 296	2 462	40 435	55 915.1	1 823.9	3 569	51 556	9 248.2	990.1	1 496	14 372	2 523.5	516.3
Gilmer	62 383	670	17	170	44.4	2.9	89	778	136.1	11.9	18	69	4.4	0.6
Glascock	0	0	NA	NA	NA	NA	7	30	2.9	0.3	NA	NA	NA	NA
Glynn	104 834	722	118	903	461.5	30.7	504	4 847	716.1	69.6	122	622	51.4	9.9
Gordon	51 821	504	57	675	150.6	16.5	241	2 260	360.1	33.9	24	84	8.1	2.0
Grady	7 952	66	24	272	125.3	5.7	111	824	130.1	12.2	16	33	3.2	0.5
Greene	51 636	187	16	90	102.0	2.2	56	465	66.8	6.2	14	37	5.6	0.7
Gwinnett	992 694	9 617	1 959	31 305	29 114.6	1 365.0	2 013	33 639	6 829.0	632.5	580	3 193	492.4	89.2
Habersham	53 365	505	34	203	35.1	4.8	153	1 677	256.3	24.1	21	71	9.7	1.6
Hall	221 199	1 830	238	3 407	1 777.8	100.6	548	6 357	1 240.8	114.6	105	398	44.3	9.0
Hancock	7 396	63	3	D	D	D	24	149	17.0	2.0	1	D	D	D
Haralson	14 894	124	16	121	50.8	4.3	98	845	145.7	11.3	5	21	1.1	0.1
Harris	88 895	430	9	D	D	D	59	259	31.3	3.2	8	D	D	D
Hart	1 561	13	25	113	35.6	2.6	78	778	96.9	9.6	7	24	1.1	0.2
Heard	7 626	60	2	D	D	D	21	117	17.2	1.7	2	D	D	D
Henry	426 004	4 466	84	1 136	377.1	29.1	300	3 580	660.7	58.9	77	313	33.3	4.7
Houston	149 639	1 648	54	454	236.5	14.7	403	5 818	941.2	86.6	88	347	43.4	5.1
Irwin	0	0	10	54	13.3	1.1	31	226	28.3	3.1	2	D	D	D
Jackson	128 469	841	48	867	502.2	25.4	218	1 673	288.4	25.5	24	49	5.4	0.9
Jasper	13 902	141	3	D	D	D	21	148	19.9	2.0	3	12	0.3	0.1
Jeff Davis	47	2	23	228	177.9	6.1	79	660	127.9	9.2	4	19	1.7	0.3
Jefferson	2 705	27	19	188	59.8	3.1	83	681	94.3	10.2	6	33	0.9	0.4
Jenkins	700	7	8	44	10.9	0.7	34	235	38.0	3.2	2	D	D	D
Johnson	0	0	13	56	25.4	0.9	29	250	27.3	2.9	1	D	D	D
Jones	40 563	265	15	D	D	D	36	249	37.7	3.6	8	D	D	D
Lamar	11 348	191	6	63	10.0	1.2	51	440	74.1	6.8	5	6	0.3	0.1
Lanier	1 830	21	3	D	D	D	29	167	24.0	2.3	3	10	0.9	0.1
Laurens	3 279	40	64	390	125.3	9.5	265	2 872	417.5	38.4	35	149	14.8	2.3
Lee	39 886	349	7	D	D	D	39	362	54.0	4.4	5	7	0.9	0.1
Liberty	40 194	336	14	D	D	D	165	1 762	255.0	22.2	39	261	24.7	4.4
Lincoln	7 372	51	6	33	4.1	0.6	21	118	15.9	1.4	1	D	D	D
Long	NA	NA	1	D	D	D	9	37	7.1	0.4	1	D	D	D
Lowndes	94 828	985	135	1 155	452.9	31.5	533	6 187	1 008.5	91.3	88	517	52.4	8.2
Lumpkin	54 015	375	10	42	8.1	0.7	64	740	120.1	11.8	14	34	4.3	0.4
McDuffie	8 830	74	12	D	D	D	112	1 382	312.3	25.0	12	42	2.5	0.5
McIntosh	11 058	107	7	D	D	D	106	732	104.9	9.1	5	D	D	D
Macon	2 742	25	15	129	63.6	2.6	52	409	57.7	5.5	6	39	1.3	0.2
Madison	17 301	138	47	1 146	514.3	39.3	74	453	76.4	5.9	19	51	4.6	0.8
Marion	NA	NA	4	11	1.2	0.1	23	181	30.1	2.7	3	2	0.2	0.1
Meriwether	19 201	178	8	21	3.1	0.3	85	556	99.4	9.4	8	27	1.9	0.2
Miller	262	2	7	D	D	D	43	286	39.2	3.4	1	D	D	D
Mitchell	6 460	84	39	408	148.5	8.2	107	897	122.3	12.1	12	51	2.8	1.0
Monroe	39 510	226	13	59	26.4	1.0	75	503	70.3	6.7	7	13	1.4	0.2
Montgomery	5 700	60	5	106	36.5	2.7	29	138	20.2	1.9	1	D	D	D
Morgan	28 841	232	17	186	66.7	4.2	71	886	166.3	15.6	6	18	3.2	0.7
Murray	26 815	232	33	320	537.2	10.5	108	743	166.9	13.6	15	45	2.7	0.4
Muscogee	109 656	1 226	208	2 884	1 316.5	91.3	845	11 718	1 950.9	186.6	224	1 197	142.7	27.3
Newton	291 864	2 263	52	D	D	D	173	2 023	319.8	32.4	33	114	16.1	2.8
Oconee	96 170	470	22	D	D	D	55	799	166.6	14.7	18	86	10.8	1.2
Oglethorpe	NA	NA	10	84	6.3	1.2	25	140	27.9	1.9	2	D	D	D
Paulding	237 646	2 763	45	260	98.6	7.4	124	2 137	390.8	31.4	18	48	3.2	0.7
Peach	19 466	174	18	D	D	D	110	862	146.7	11.5	15	45	7.4	0.9
Pickens	70 360	595	23	D	D	D	74	694	238.5	12.9	22	33	4.8	0.7
Pierce	13 725	127	15	D	D	D	69	417	68.6	6.5	7	15	2.1	0.1
Pike	23 746	221	13	44	14.4	1.4	23	109	15.9	1.4	2	D	D	D
Polk	30 027	446	20	318	121.5	9.5	146	1 377	183.9	18.3	26	90	6.8	1.4
Pulaski	4 217	49	16	215	162.7	5.5	53	319	48.8	4.6	3	6	0.3	0.0
Putnam	34 062	230	8	88	63.7	2.6	56	490	83.7	8.3	8	21	0.9	0.3
Quitman	100	1	2	D	D	D	6	30	4.1	0.4	1	D	D	D
Rabun	24 873	365	8	D	D	D	91	561	97.6	8.7	22	63	7.7	1.2
Randolph	142	1	10	54	33.5	1.2	40	261	27.5	3.3	5	4	0.6	0.2

1. Establishments with payroll.

STATE County	Professional, scientific, and technical services,[1] 1997				Manufacturing, 1997				Accommodation and foodservices, 1997			
	Number of establishments	Number of employees	Receipts (mil dol)	Annual payroll (mil dol)	Number of establishments	Number of employees	Receipts (mil dol)	Annual payroll (mil dol)	Number of establishments	Number of employees	Sales (mil dol)	Annual payroll (mil dol)
	147	148	149	150	151	152	153	154	155	156	157	158
GEORGIA—Cont'd												
Fannin	26	76	3.0	1.2	28	922	146.6	15.7	35	431	11.3	3.3
Fayette	212	719	69.7	27.1	85	5 595	1 345.1	170.2	118	2 750	102.3	27.6
Floyd	131	650	61.6	19.7	120	9 583	1 892.4	280.0	151	2 572	87.8	22.9
Forsyth	206	824	83.2	30.1	129	4 337	701.3	127.7	89	1 523	54.5	15.0
Franklin	18	53	3.3	0.9	46	1 852	281.1	43.2	35	621	16.8	4.3
Fulton	4 614	56 202	7 607.2	2 846.1	897	37 948	14 240.9	1 283.6	2 292	57 973	2 364.4	682.1
Gilmer	28	90	4.4	1.7	34	3 404	303.0	52.3	30	428	11.1	2.9
Glascock	1	D	D	D	NA	NA	NA	NA	2	D	D	D
Glynn	179	579	43.4	16.6	71	3 784	993.6	124.9	214	7 051	251.5	84.3
Gordon	34	235	10.8	4.6	102	10 527	2 419.0	255.4	76	1 201	40.8	11.3
Grady	13	45	2.9	0.8	19	1 402	153.7	29.6	26	300	8.2	2.0
Greene	25	51	3.1	1.3	19	1 533	448.4	33.1	19	208	6.3	1.6
Gwinnett	1 939	12 871	1 326.6	534.3	737	29 121	6 241.7	1 071.3	896	19 623	720.4	199.8
Habersham	37	112	9.8	2.5	69	4 354	681.2	111.8	64	879	26.0	7.3
Hall	217	972	91.6	32.0	226	16 519	4 293.7	443.1	202	4 192	148.5	41.6
Hancock	5	13	2.2	0.3	NA	NA	NA	NA	5	46	1.2	0.3
Haralson	19	75	4.7	1.3	35	2 552	340.0	59.4	31	D	D	D
Harris	16	82	3.9	1.7	19	D	D	D	35	D	D	D
Hart	22	55	4.0	1.5	36	2 540	465.6	61.1	22	268	9.0	2.4
Heard	4	22	0.6	0.2	9	550	77.6	12.8	5	D	D	D
Henry	122	499	48.5	15.4	68	3 392	854.8	106.1	139	2 485	74.5	20.0
Houston	135	1 504	111.5	44.5	66	D	D	D	183	3 753	102.5	28.4
Irwin	5	25	2.0	0.9	7	746	38.5	13.7	9	70	2.0	0.5
Jackson	33	95	8.5	2.0	65	5 896	1 204.5	135.8	53	1 318	65.3	16.7
Jasper	6	19	1.4	0.4	19	737	176.7	21.4	7	78	2.2	0.6
Jeff Davis	15	49	2.4	0.8	23	2 493	304.4	49.0	20	D	D	D
Jefferson	11	36	2.0	1.1	28	1 999	294.2	51.9	17	207	6.4	1.5
Jenkins	7	15	0.7	0.1	4	1 294	154.3	25.0	12	D	D	D
Johnson	4	16	0.8	0.3	8	762	34.9	8.8	7	D	D	D
Jones	12	24	1.4	0.5	NA	NA	NA	NA	8	D	D	D
Lamar	16	27	1.7	0.5	13	1 605	190.9	35.1	18	217	6.6	1.6
Lanier	6	13	0.8	0.1	NA	NA	NA	NA	5	D	D	D
Laurens	44	197	12.4	5.1	43	5 703	888.6	134.2	76	1 448	40.9	10.0
Lee	7	7	0.7	0.1	NA	NA	NA	NA	9	94	2.4	0.8
Liberty	30	182	18.3	3.0	14	1 020	319.0	33.9	65	1 209	35.8	9.0
Lincoln	4	10	0.4	0.2	7	688	55.8	10.9	12	D	D	D
Long	2	D	D	D	NA	NA	NA	NA	6	39	1.1	0.3
Lowndes	132	738	46.2	18.5	98	5 492	1 468.9	146.7	194	3 700	109.3	30.8
Lumpkin	16	34	3.4	1.1	17	879	85.9	21.0	34	465	16.5	4.0
McDuffie	24	105	10.4	4.0	26	1 677	297.8	41.7	34	572	17.8	4.8
McIntosh	6	16	0.7	0.1	NA	NA	NA	NA	23	332	9.0	2.7
Macon	5	17	1.8	0.6	14	1 624	369.0	46.7	15	D	D	D
Madison	58	332	45.7	31.2	31	826	69.0	18.9	50	1 032	33.4	9.8
Marion	2	D	D	D	5	D	D	D	5	D	D	D
Meriwether	15	47	3.4	0.8	22	2 105	273.7	46.1	29	269	9.0	2.5
Miller	7	25	1.2	0.4	NA	NA	NA	NA	7	121	2.7	0.7
Mitchell	21	103	5.1	1.9	17	1 016	72.2	15.4	30	292	11.6	4.0
Monroe	23	63	3.8	1.1	21	515	57.1	10.7	33	616	21.6	4.7
Montgomery	5	13	0.4	0.2	NA	NA	NA	NA	7	90	2.0	0.5
Morgan	21	58	6.3	2.3	20	1 512	262.1	39.8	37	574	16.8	4.4
Murray	19	140	3.9	1.8	100	5 321	1 201.9	121.8	39	493	20.0	5.1
Muscogee	264	1 607	146.2	43.6	158	D	D	D	365	D	D	D
Newton	62	169	13.9	4.0	62	3 976	1 348.8	146.4	58	1 074	30.9	8.2
Oconee	44	158	15.7	5.3	30	746	208.8	20.8	13	134	3.5	0.8
Oglethorpe	10	20	1.4	0.8	NA	NA	NA	NA	8	59	1.4	0.4
Paulding	45	176	10.6	3.8	38	1 161	137.3	26.0	51	D	D	D
Peach	21	63	3.6	1.2	32	D	D	D	44	D	D	D
Pickens	30	69	5.2	2.0	35	1 155	135.8	26.7	25	331	11.3	3.0
Pierce	12	32	2.3	0.8	17	521	77.2	9.1	21	229	5.6	1.8
Pike	13	23	3.2	0.6	NA	NA	NA	NA	10	77	2.1	0.7
Polk	25	110	7.6	2.9	35	2 273	423.1	62.1	43	D	D	D
Pulaski	13	31	2.5	1.1	11	D	D	D	16	326	5.6	1.9
Putnam	21	48	3.4	0.7	24	2 030	424.8	56.8	22	191	6.1	1.3
Quitman	1	D	D	D	NA	NA	NA	NA	1	D	D	D
Rabun	25	72	4.2	1.5	27	1 870	316.0	44.1	47	573	19.0	5.3
Randolph	10	35	3.1	0.9	NA	NA	NA	NA	14	88	2.6	0.6

1. Firms subject to federal tax.

STATE County	Health care and social assistance,[1] 1997				Other services,[1] 1997				Federal funds and grants, 2002–2003 Expenditures (mil dol)			
										Direct payments for individuals[2]		
	Number of establishments	Number of employees	Receipts (mil dol)	Annual payroll (mil dol)	Number of establishments	Number of employees	Receipts (mil dol)	Annual payroll (mil dol)	Total	Social Security and government retirement	Medicare	Food stamps and Supplemental Security Income
	159	160	161	162	163	164	165	166	167	168	169	170
GEORGIA—Cont'd												
Fannin	32	418	29.7	9.2	12	39	2.5	0.6	131.5	66.5	27.7	4.0
Fayette	150	1 197	86.9	37.1	129	777	41.6	13.2	332.0	213.3	40.4	2.9
Floyd	165	4 018	345.6	131.4	95	721	41.6	14.1	440.4	205.1	92.4	22.0
Forsyth	90	1 115	50.4	22.3	105	607	34.8	10.9	215.4	120.1	33.8	4.6
Franklin	20	177	10.4	4.5	33	222	18.2	4.6	125.7	55.0	25.0	4.0
Fulton	2 252	26 639	2 258.3	1 009.7	1 543	12 781	928.9	270.3	9 110.5	1 706.1	688.7	255.3
Gilmer	22	437	23.5	8.8	18	87	6.2	1.7	109.0	60.6	23.2	3.7
Glascock	2	D	D	D	1	D	D	D	17.9	7.2	4.1	0.3
Glynn	205	2 257	149.3	60.7	123	557	36.0	10.5	556.2	192.8	85.8	15.3
Gordon	42	373	26.1	9.9	37	174	12.3	3.1	164.1	88.2	34.9	5.6
Grady	24	263	11.0	4.0	17	84	6.2	1.3	119.0	46.3	18.9	8.1
Greene	13	139	7.3	3.2	15	70	4.1	1.0	88.8	40.8	15.3	4.4
Gwinnett	927	9 585	656.4	265.8	1 032	7 165	510.3	173.4	1 233.4	587.1	162.0	30.1
Habersham	60	488	26.5	10.7	42	149	10.8	2.8	159.1	81.8	32.9	4.7
Hall	245	2 626	230.0	95.8	184	860	56.2	15.3	565.8	247.7	93.8	17.6
Hancock	12	267	8.2	3.3	9	11	1.1	0.2	75.1	27.8	14.4	4.0
Haralson	28	319	12.8	5.3	25	100	8.0	1.7	122.5	59.0	26.4	5.2
Harris	9	D	D	D	13	27	1.9	0.4	100.0	57.0	12.8	2.7
Hart	27	509	24.8	9.2	22	110	8.9	1.8	116.2	49.0	21.8	3.5
Heard	8	111	3.1	1.6	6	12	0.8	0.2	40.5	16.9	8.5	3.1
Henry	127	1 299	66.8	31.8	120	586	34.0	10.3	471.4	238.8	58.4	9.2
Houston	181	1 927	125.5	52.7	162	744	38.3	11.3	1 769.9	376.4	69.1	20.4
Irwin	8	146	4.2	2.1	11	29	1.7	0.3	75.4	16.9	9.3	2.3
Jackson	39	317	19.5	11.1	43	185	10.8	2.8	179.0	87.4	33.7	7.6
Jasper	7	37	1.5	0.5	11	21	1.7	0.3	46.5	22.5	8.3	2.2
Jeff Davis	11	61	2.9	0.8	20	67	4.5	0.9	75.5	28.1	13.6	3.6
Jefferson	22	248	9.7	3.5	19	61	2.8	0.8	128.6	39.7	23.6	6.8
Jenkins	8	60	3.4	1.2	8	20	1.0	0.2	67.8	17.2	11.5	3.2
Johnson	5	136	6.9	3.0	9	21	1.4	0.3	57.5	19.1	12.2	2.3
Jones	16	335	14.8	6.7	15	48	2.3	0.5	84.1	36.8	14.2	2.6
Lamar	16	186	6.8	2.4	14	84	8.1	1.9	75.3	35.5	14.6	2.9
Lanier	8	128	2.7	1.3	5	13	1.1	0.2	37.3	13.7	8.4	2.3
Laurens	96	1 855	135.5	48.9	54	212	11.1	2.9	322.5	113.3	44.4	12.9
Lee	7	142	3.9	1.6	16	51	3.5	1.1	82.6	34.1	8.6	3.0
Liberty	45	586	25.5	9.2	60	379	16.7	5.2	311.0	112.4	19.6	11.0
Lincoln	10	44	3.0	1.3	14	31	2.4	0.4	47.4	21.6	10.9	1.7
Long	3	16	0.2	0.1	2	D	D	D	28.7	15.2	3.9	2.1
Lowndes	185	2 740	162.4	76.4	142	695	37.7	10.6	687.7	193.5	72.6	25.9
Lumpkin	28	456	30.7	9.5	15	69	4.0	0.8	90.8	44.4	11.8	3.0
McDuffie	41	873	29.9	17.2	38	110	7.4	1.6	115.3	48.1	23.3	7.0
McIntosh	5	40	2.3	0.9	13	26	1.4	0.4	59.0	27.9	12.5	3.2
Macon	20	417	22.7	9.0	10	53	4.9	1.5	94.3	25.1	18.4	4.4
Madison	33	311	16.5	7.3	31	256	22.7	4.7	113.6	55.3	21.1	6.4
Marion	5	38	1.8	0.6	2	D	D	D	37.5	11.9	4.7	2.5
Meriwether	24	203	7.4	3.7	15	56	3.7	0.8	117.2	48.4	21.5	7.3
Miller	9	46	1.8	0.7	12	24	1.8	0.5	66.9	13.5	7.3	2.4
Mitchell	14	160	8.6	3.0	26	118	6.1	1.7	160.2	42.0	21.7	9.5
Monroe	20	256	9.8	4.0	20	74	6.8	1.4	89.0	39.8	15.2	3.6
Montgomery	4	12	0.5	0.1	2	D	D	D	50.7	16.4	8.7	2.8
Morgan	16	169	7.9	2.5	12	52	2.5	0.7	73.8	34.4	14.9	3.0
Murray	17	248	17.3	5.8	14	59	4.1	1.4	104.9	54.4	21.3	3.2
Muscogee	343	5 225	439.9	171.5	305	2 004	104.6	35.8	1 910.0	551.2	157.4	60.8
Newton	80	747	40.7	17.9	61	248	19.3	5.8	262.4	125.9	50.6	16.1
Oconee	34	202	11.4	4.9	32	260	12.3	4.9	77.4	45.0	13.7	2.8
Oglethorpe	9	97	4.6	1.8	6	9	0.7	0.1	48.1	17.3	8.1	3.3
Paulding	39	339	13.2	5.5	58	226	14.5	4.7	156.6	89.1	26.8	6.2
Peach	22	196	9.9	3.9	27	122	8.3	1.7	180.9	69.3	21.8	7.4
Pickens	22	476	24.6	9.5	12	30	1.9	0.4	98.8	57.8	18.0	2.3
Pierce	13	106	4.3	2.3	20	61	2.8	0.6	89.3	43.4	15.1	4.6
Pike	5	102	3.3	1.6	4	7	0.6	0.1	70.7	29.3	10.5	1.8
Polk	42	505	24.8	8.8	42	312	24.4	5.3	247.0	102.9	45.0	7.9
Pulaski	18	333	12.5	5.4	10	35	1.6	0.4	75.3	26.3	11.8	2.4
Putnam	14	243	10.8	4.2	14	43	2.6	0.7	94.9	48.2	17.0	3.3
Quitman	1	D	D	D	1	D	D	D	22.5	7.7	3.6	1.3
Rabun	27	276	14.7	5.9	18	41	3.5	0.8	85.6	42.0	20.2	2.1
Randolph	3	27	0.7	0.5	13	34	1.9	0.4	77.4	16.6	9.3	4.0

1. Firms subject to federal tax.   2. State totals may include programs not allocated by county.

STATE County	Salaries and wages	Defense	Other	Medicaid and other health-related	Nutrition and family welfare	Education	Other	Total (mil dol)	Intergovern-mental (mil dol)	Total (mil dol)	Per capita[2] (dollars) Total	Property
	171	172	173	174	175	176	177	178	179	180	181	182
GEORGIA—Cont'd												
Fannin	4.5	0.0	0.8	19.7	2.1	1.2	4.3	42.9	18.7	19.2	916	500
Fayette	54.6	2.7	4.9	5.9	2.5	2.2	0.8	260.5	92.8	134.2	1 389	1 111
Floyd	16.6	1.5	3.1	56.0	11.9	6.4	14.8	423.0	134.3	90.6	978	581
Forsyth	11.3	0.3	3.4	15.8	2.1	2.4	21.4	265.7	79.8	154.1	1 318	718
Franklin	3.3	0.1	0.9	20.5	1.7	1.4	12.1	52.3	24.1	21.4	1 031	521
Fulton	1 511.4	558.1	1 172.1	986.8	446.8	440.1	1 178.5	4 499.7	1 204.7	1 923.6	2 330	1 575
Gilmer	4.0	0.0	0.8	13.2	1.7	1.1	0.1	49.8	20.8	22.6	898	513
Glascock	0.5	0.0	0.1	4.4	0.3	0.2	0.4	6.8	3.9	2.4	917	693
Glynn	103.1	15.3	64.2	32.8	14.8	5.0	21.8	335.4	67.0	112.3	1 626	1 029
Gordon	6.6	0.1	3.3	16.1	3.3	2.5	2.6	112.1	48.3	43.0	923	374
Grady	2.2	1.0	0.6	21.5	3.4	2.5	1.6	50.0	26.3	17.6	737	461
Greene	3.9	0.2	0.8	16.3	2.6	1.4	1.9	49.6	14.2	22.5	1 487	967
Gwinnett	194.5	58.1	92.0	40.2	12.2	14.5	33.6	1 831.9	573.2	951.9	1 463	990
Habersham	6.7	0.0	2.3	19.6	2.0	0.9	4.8	111.9	35.1	34.3	904	524
Hall	28.7	27.7	28.8	49.0	27.9	6.8	31.3	652.1	168.3	182.4	1 198	673
Hancock	1.0	0.0	0.3	19.3	4.6	1.0	1.2	32.2	13.3	10.2	1 018	868
Haralson	3.3	0.4	1.0	16.6	2.8	1.8	5.3	63.2	32.6	23.4	874	519
Harris	3.3	0.0	0.6	14.5	2.1	1.1	4.9	50.5	21.7	23.0	915	631
Hart	4.6	9.3	0.6	21.5	2.2	1.6	1.2	53.5	22.7	22.7	974	615
Heard	1.0	0.0	0.3	7.3	1.5	0.7	0.6	32.9	14.3	14.5	1 280	609
Henry	116.3	0.1	5.9	19.5	4.2	3.7	13.4	370.5	123.4	176.9	1 266	871
Houston	884.5	277.8	53.4	36.5	16.8	7.2	16.3	385.5	129.5	108.3	927	511
Irwin	2.1	0.2	0.3	12.4	1.8	0.8	2.9	22.7	13.5	7.2	728	524
Jackson	8.0	0.4	3.1	27.1	2.9	2.4	5.7	123.9	45.1	44.8	987	541
Jasper	1.5	0.0	0.4	8.3	2.2	0.7	0.0	30.3	12.5	12.2	991	719
Jeff Davis	1.6	0.0	0.4	13.2	2.0	0.8	7.6	39.1	17.5	10.3	795	419
Jefferson	2.4	0.1	0.5	37.2	5.4	2.9	4.1	52.0	23.6	14.8	864	563
Jenkins	1.1	0.0	0.4	16.6	2.4	1.5	5.1	22.6	11.8	5.9	681	391
Johnson	1.0	0.1	0.3	15.5	1.8	0.9	2.1	16.0	10.8	3.8	437	268
Jones	1.9	2.6	0.3	10.3	2.2	1.3	11.2	45.8	25.4	16.6	677	402
Lamar	2.3	0.0	0.5	10.8	2.0	0.9	1.1	33.3	13.9	11.8	716	485
Lanier	0.7	0.0	0.2	8.5	1.4	0.6	-0.1	14.4	9.1	4.1	570	345
Laurens	44.4	1.6	8.0	50.9	8.0	3.9	23.2	134.8	79.9	34.1	743	365
Lee	1.9	0.0	0.5	7.8	1.8	1.1	1.7	59.3	29.7	23.5	860	552
Liberty	65.1	53.5	1.7	17.4	8.3	11.0	7.0	155.4	79.1	44.3	717	395
Lincoln	1.0	0.0	0.2	8.1	1.3	0.8	1.6	20.4	9.5	7.6	898	685
Long	0.6	0.3	0.2	4.9	1.0	0.7	-0.5	17.7	11.2	5.4	504	376
Lowndes	180.5	93.0	4.1	57.6	18.8	8.2	17.4	412.5	117.6	99.7	1 064	504
Lumpkin	14.1	0.6	0.7	11.7	1.3	0.6	0.4	51.8	17.7	25.8	1 138	666
McDuffie	4.5	0.0	0.6	23.2	3.9	1.8	1.6	76.2	27.9	21.1	986	510
McIntosh	1.4	0.4	0.3	9.8	2.1	0.9	-0.1	24.4	11.2	10.8	970	529
Macon	1.9	0.8	0.4	23.2	4.9	1.6	2.7	34.8	18.8	10.8	771	526
Madison	3.2	0.0	0.9	19.5	2.2	1.6	2.8	50.1	26.5	19.4	724	494
Marion	1.5	0.0	0.1	10.7	1.3	0.8	1.0	18.2	12.0	4.7	651	437
Meriwether	2.8	0.0	0.6	27.6	4.6	2.2	0.9	54.5	30.9	17.5	776	548
Miller	1.1	0.0	0.2	8.3	1.3	0.6	2.4	15.3	8.7	5.2	810	588
Mitchell	3.4	0.0	0.6	34.0	6.5	2.6	4.9	61.6	30.9	19.5	815	505
Monroe	3.4	0.0	0.6	10.5	1.3	1.1	13.0	75.6	16.0	29.1	1 285	831
Montgomery	1.2	0.0	0.3	12.7	1.3	0.7	3.0	13.8	8.6	4.0	477	292
Morgan	2.3	0.0	0.6	12.2	2.1	0.9	1.2	47.4	16.8	21.1	1 297	910
Murray	4.9	1.5	2.3	10.7	2.3	2.1	1.2	68.6	36.8	23.1	599	381
Muscogee	891.9	7.1	8.5	123.6	38.2	18.9	26.4	520.5	256.8	177.0	952	652
Newton	10.4	2.3	2.2	26.2	6.5	3.8	17.7	219.6	64.1	74.4	1 040	652
Oconee	5.6	0.1	1.0	6.1	1.0	1.0	0.4	66.9	28.1	32.7	1 198	779
Oglethorpe	1.0	0.0	0.3	10.2	1.7	0.9	4.9	22.9	12.6	7.5	570	392
Paulding	7.8	1.8	1.7	15.4	3.2	2.1	1.5	191.0	87.1	84.0	892	522
Peach	5.5	22.6	0.8	19.3	7.6	6.0	13.1	76.6	27.7	25.8	1 063	496
Pickens	3.5	0.2	0.9	10.5	2.0	1.0	1.3	54.7	22.8	26.3	1 028	733
Pierce	2.5	0.0	1.7	12.9	2.0	1.1	1.3	33.2	18.3	11.6	725	407
Pike	17.2	0.0	1.3	8.3	1.0	0.7	0.3	24.7	13.6	9.2	628	405
Polk	5.5	20.3	2.0	32.5	5.3	2.4	20.2	83.4	42.9	31.3	794	476
Pulaski	1.2	0.0	0.3	13.5	2.0	0.6	1.6	20.7	10.6	7.1	728	442
Putnam	3.2	0.0	0.6	10.2	3.8	0.9	5.7	57.5	15.0	25.2	1 301	739
Quitman	0.5	0.0	0.1	5.2	0.7	0.3	1.0	5.9	3.2	1.9	739	565
Rabun	3.1	0.4	0.6	15.2	1.0	0.3	0.1	51.7	9.4	23.7	1 526	983
Randolph	1.2	0.1	0.5	16.6	3.5	2.6	0.9	32.5	14.3	6.1	814	542

1. State totals may include programs not allocated by county.   2. Based on the resident population estimated as of July 1 of the year shown.

Table B. States and Counties — Local Government Finances, Government Employment, and Elections

STATE County	Local government finances, 2002 (cont'd)									Government employment, 2002			Presidential election, 2004		
	Direct general expenditure							Debt outstanding					Percent of vote cast —		
	Total (mil dol)	Per capita[1] (dollars)	Percent of total for —					Total (mil dol)	Per capita[1] (dollars)	Federal civilian	Federal military	State and local	Demo-cratic	Republi-can	All other
			Educa-tion	Health and hospitals	Police protec-tion	Public welfare	High-ways								
	183	184	185	186	187	188	189	190	191	192	193	194	195	196	197
GEORGIA—Cont'd															
Fannin	40.0	1 904	59.3	4.3	3.7	0.3	13.3	6.9	327	71	50	865	28.3	71.1	0.6
Fayette	285.4	2 954	58.3	0.9	6.7	0.2	4.0	270.2	2 797	319	230	4 487	28.3	71.1	0.6
Floyd	388.5	4 195	34.5	40.8	2.7	0.1	2.0	198.0	2 139	160	246	6 115	31.7	67.7	0.6
Forsyth	344.1	2 943	58.1	0.3	3.3	0.3	8.5	336.2	2 875	162	278	4 188	16.2	83.2	0.6
Franklin	45.3	2 181	56.1	2.3	7.5	1.4	4.9	27.2	1 310	51	49	1 061	29.9	69.5	0.5
Fulton	3 736.5	4 527	38.8	1.2	6.3	2.1	2.4	10 755.5	13 030	22 909	3 981	79 744	60.2	39.2	0.7
Gilmer	49.5	1 962	67.3	2.5	4.0	0.0	5.7	16.4	650	74	60	1 090	25.1	74.2	0.7
Glascock	6.9	2 650	69.2	1.5	2.2	0.8	5.4	0.9	359	14	0	192	19.7	80.1	0.2
Glynn	303.7	4 399	28.8	39.7	8.7	0.1	1.5	112.4	1 629	1 341	167	5 803	32.4	67.2	0.4
Gordon	114.0	2 450	55.9	1.3	4.4	0.1	5.4	43.7	940	97	111	2 372	25.5	74.0	0.5
Grady	52.1	2 186	64.9	1.0	4.6	0.1	4.3	14.2	598	44	57	1 252	37.8	61.9	0.4
Greene	47.9	3 170	43.8	17.9	5.8	0.7	9.0	15.1	998	45	36	896	40.4	59.2	0.4
Gwinnett	1 731.4	2 660	59.9	2.7	4.1	0.2	3.9	1 349.0	2 073	3 537	1 555	22 793	33.5	65.8	0.7
Habersham	103.1	2 713	41.2	34.6	3.1	0.0	2.4	47.8	1 260	133	90	2 695	20.8	78.8	0.5
Hall	668.4	4 391	31.7	37.6	2.7	0.5	2.5	434.4	2 854	485	364	8 263	21.2	78.2	0.6
Hancock	33.7	3 358	43.4	20.3	3.6	1.4	4.7	15.6	1 561	15	24	1 023	76.5	23.2	0.4
Haralson	60.0	2 242	63.3	1.0	4.9	0.1	3.8	28.9	1 081	51	64	1 498	23.9	75.6	0.5
Harris	48.5	1 933	62.9	0.8	4.2	0.7	4.5	22.1	881	59	60	1 108	27.6	72.0	0.4
Hart	56.7	2 439	67.0	2.1	3.6	0.1	4.1	17.8	766	101	55	1 065	38.5	61.0	0.5
Heard	32.7	2 886	65.9	0.4	3.3	1.1	8.4	26.0	2 297	15	27	573	29.0	70.5	0.5
Henry	372.3	2 665	56.5	0.2	4.4	0.8	4.5	647.1	4 632	926	333	5 422	32.9	66.7	0.5
Houston	393.5	3 370	40.8	29.0	3.9	0.0	2.2	133.7	1 145	12 657	5 716	7 277	33.3	66.1	0.5
Irwin	23.5	2 365	67.4	1.4	4.1	0.2	5.6	2.5	247	29	24	767	30.8	68.7	0.5
Jackson	138.3	3 048	51.6	15.3	4.0	0.3	4.7	105.1	2 316	116	108	2 592	21.4	78.0	0.5
Jasper	30.2	2 460	48.1	14.3	5.5	0.1	5.5	17.5	1 429	23	29	595	32.9	66.6	0.5
Jeff Davis	37.3	2 890	49.2	20.6	4.7	0.2	3.6	16.7	1 294	35	31	799	26.4	73.3	0.4
Jefferson	49.0	2 857	50.2	18.0	3.9	1.2	3.7	21.2	1 236	44	41	1 188	52.7	46.9	0.3
Jenkins	22.7	2 631	57.3	18.9	3.0	0.6	3.6	4.9	569	27	21	624	43.9	55.8	0.3
Johnson	16.5	1 903	66.1	1.2	4.4	0.4	6.6	1.8	203	17	21	628	35.5	64.1	0.3
Jones	43.9	1 794	68.3	0.4	5.6	0.5	4.9	20.0	818	34	58	973	35.5	64.0	0.5
Lamar	33.8	2 057	50.8	1.4	5.3	0.1	8.7	22.4	1 364	41	39	896	37.4	62.0	0.5
Lanier	14.7	2 037	71.5	1.4	5.3	0.5	6.4	2.2	306	14	17	390	36.0	63.5	0.5
Laurens	136.5	2 975	50.6	16.2	4.4	0.9	4.9	34.4	750	868	109	3 286	36.4	63.1	0.4
Lee	62.1	2 267	62.7	0.7	3.4	0.1	3.9	43.1	1 573	34	65	1 232	21.0	78.8	0.3
Liberty	150.0	2 430	57.8	11.4	4.6	1.4	3.8	43.8	710	2 814	15 610	3 360	51.7	47.9	0.4
Lincoln	20.3	2 396	56.3	3.2	2.2	0.5	3.8	7.1	841	17	20	468	36.6	63.1	0.3
Long	17.5	1 623	70.3	0.5	6.2	2.6	3.7	9.1	847	11	25	482	34.0	65.7	0.3
Lowndes	414.1	4 422	31.2	44.0	4.0	0.4	4.2	60.5	646	934	4 203	8 972	39.6	60.0	0.4
Lumpkin	66.9	2 950	56.1	2.1	3.1	0.8	2.3	66.8	2 947	67	275	1 479	23.6	75.6	0.8
McDuffie	66.0	3 077	48.5	28.8	3.5	0.9	2.4	8.7	407	48	111	1 576	37.3	62.1	0.6
McIntosh	27.0	2 420	53.4	2.9	6.2	0.5	5.2	2.9	256	23	27	703	46.9	52.8	0.3
Macon	36.5	2 598	52.8	0.9	5.2	1.2	5.8	25.5	1 817	34	33	1 061	60.8	38.7	0.4
Madison	48.1	1 799	64.2	2.7	3.7	0.4	6.0	7.8	291	51	64	1 117	25.7	73.8	0.5
Marion	18.8	2 592	77.3	1.9	2.2	0.2	3.5	7.2	992	41	17	438	43.2	56.6	0.2
Meriwether	59.2	2 616	69.0	2.3	4.3	0.3	3.0	34.6	1 527	49	54	1 839	45.5	54.0	0.4
Miller	15.8	2 465	61.6	3.7	8.3	0.3	4.7	2.5	383	31	15	583	30.2	69.3	0.5
Mitchell	63.6	2 651	52.5	2.6	6.5	0.1	4.9	34.8	1 450	78	57	1 772	46.2	53.5	0.3
Monroe	78.3	3 453	37.4	12.8	5.0	0.1	3.7	228.6	10 080	44	54	1 644	32.9	66.7	0.5
Montgomery	14.3	1 702	65.9	3.1	3.5	1.6	6.6	1.8	220	26	20	478	31.8	67.9	0.3
Morgan	46.2	2 835	47.8	10.6	4.4	0.8	10.7	6.3	386	46	39	1 017	31.8	67.7	0.5
Murray	64.7	1 678	70.2	0.8	3.0	0.6	4.5	35.6	924	104	92	1 503	27.1	72.5	0.4
Muscogee	545.2	2 932	49.9	7.2	6.9	0.1	2.7	350.0	1 882	5 076	5 153	12 397	51.5	48.1	0.4
Newton	239.5	3 346	38.0	27.5	4.1	0.2	3.6	138.9	1 941	129	173	3 324	37.5	62.0	0.5
Oconee	60.5	2 218	67.4	1.2	3.1	0.7	5.3	32.3	1 184	97	65	1 196	26.7	72.5	0.7
Oglethorpe	21.3	1 620	75.1	2.3	2.8	0.9	3.3	4.8	366	16	31	518	33.8	65.5	0.7
Paulding	187.3	1 989	67.3	0.7	4.5	1.9	4.5	109.6	1 164	108	224	3 469	23.3	76.2	0.5
Peach	70.2	2 897	41.1	22.1	5.3	0.2	1.9	24.8	1 022	108	63	2 041	46.3	53.3	0.4
Pickens	53.4	2 086	67.3	2.3	3.0	0.3	7.0	18.5	720	52	61	1 228	22.8	76.5	0.7
Pierce	31.1	1 943	71.5	3.1	3.3	0.2	3.0	5.1	321	49	38	803	20.8	79.0	0.2
Pike	24.2	1 658	66.3	1.5	4.2	0.3	7.3	12.9	883	32	35	648	22.3	77.0	0.6
Polk	88.5	2 244	61.9	2.2	5.9	0.2	4.0	40.8	1 036	71	94	2 159	31.2	68.3	0.5
Pulaski	22.4	2 302	56.5	1.3	6.1	0.3	4.8	4.0	409	17	23	837	36.9	62.7	0.4
Putnam	58.2	3 004	42.5	22.3	4.9	2.0	5.2	37.2	1 917	81	46	1 140	35.5	64.0	0.5
Quitman	5.5	2 113	50.9	1.9	5.5	0.3	5.7	4.7	1 791	0	0	131	56.3	42.4	1.3
Rabun	43.2	2 783	38.3	28.5	5.5	1.0	3.7	14.0	900	67	37	884	29.0	70.2	0.9
Randolph	31.2	4 184	50.0	27.5	2.3	0.4	3.2	1.9	251	26	18	880	52.9	46.5	0.6

1. Based on the resident population estimated as of July 1 of the year shown.

Table B. States and Counties — **Land Area and Population**

STATE/ County code	CBSA code[1]	County Type[2]	STATE County	Land area,[3] (sq km) 2000	Total persons	Rank	Per square kilometer	White	Black	Am. Indian, Alaska Native	Asian and Pacific Islander	Percent Hispanic or Latino[4]	Under 5 years	5 to 17 years	18 to 24 years	25 to 34 years	35 to 44 years	45 to 54 years
					1	2	3	4	5	6	7	8	9	10	11	12	13	14	15
			GEORGIA—Cont'd															
13 245	12260	2	Richmond	839	198 149	291	236.2	45.3	51.3	0.8	2.2	2.2	8.1	19.2	11.5	14.4	14.2	13.3
13 247	12060	1	Rockdale	338	74 941	685	221.7	63.2	27.6	0.6	2.2	7.3	6.8	20.4	10.3	12.0	16.3	14.8
13 249	11140	8	Schley	434	3 935	2 912	9.1	70.1	27.3	0.3	0.1	2.6	6.4	21.1	9.7	13.3	14.9	12.2
13 251	...	6	Screven	1 679	15 407	2 068	9.2	53.8	44.7	0.1	0.3	1.1	6.5	21.2	10.0	11.0	14.1	14.2
13 253	...	6	Seminole	617	9 270	2 503	15.0	62.4	34.0	0.2	0.2	3.3	7.2	18.5	9.5	11.5	13.9	12.5
13 255	12060	1	Spalding	513	60 483	815	117.9	65.1	32.3	0.5	0.9	1.9	7.7	19.8	9.7	13.6	14.8	12.9
13 257	45740	7	Stephens	464	25 264	1 558	54.4	86.4	12.0	0.6	0.7	1.1	6.4	17.4	10.4	12.8	13.6	13.5
13 259	...	8	Stewart	1 188	5 001	2 845	4.2	37.5	60.7	0.3	0.4	1.5	5.8	18.4	8.8	10.9	13.8	14.4
13 261	11140	6	Sumter	1 257	33 217	1 324	26.4	46.5	50.0	0.3	0.6	2.9	8.0	20.2	11.7	13.4	13.3	12.3
13 263	...	8	Talbot	1 018	6 562	2 729	6.4	39.4	58.2	0.3	0.3	1.9	6.8	17.7	8.6	12.1	14.6	15.6
13 265	...	8	Taliaferro	506	1 957	3 063	3.9	40.2	58.8	0.1	0.3	0.9	4.7	16.8	8.7	10.1	13.7	13.5
13 267	...	6	Tattnall	1 253	22 385	1 687	17.9	59.6	29.8	0.2	0.3	10.3	6.7	16.3	12.1	17.2	16.3	11.8
13 269	...	8	Taylor	978	8 901	2 534	9.1	56.3	41.6	0.1	0.2	2.0	6.7	19.7	10.1	13.2	14.7	12.6
13 271	...	7	Telfair	1 142	11 523	2 332	10.1	59.5	37.5	0.0	0.2	3.0	6.6	15.7	11.3	13.7	15.2	14.0
13 273	10500	6	Terrell	869	10 854	2 378	12.5	37.3	60.8	0.3	0.5	1.3	8.1	20.4	10.3	11.0	14.0	13.2
13 275	45620	4	Thomas	1 420	43 667	1 052	30.8	59.1	38.4	0.7	0.5	1.8	7.1	19.3	9.6	11.8	14.8	13.6
13 277	45700	4	Tift	686	39 523	1 142	57.6	62.7	27.3	0.3	1.1	9.0	7.6	19.6	11.9	13.6	13.5	12.6
13 279	...	7	Toombs	950	26 469	1 519	27.9	65.5	24.1	0.2	0.5	9.8	8.0	20.3	10.1	12.7	14.1	12.5
13 281	...	9	Towns	432	9 901	2 452	22.9	97.8	0.7	0.3	0.4	1.0	4.5	12.5	10.0	10.1	10.8	11.8
13 283	...	7	Treutlen	520	6 952	2 691	13.4	64.5	33.7	0.1	0.4	1.4	6.5	18.3	14.1	13.4	13.0	12.2
13 285	29300	4	Troup	1 072	60 218	820	56.2	65.4	32.2	0.4	0.7	1.9	7.4	20.2	10.1	13.0	14.5	13.7
13 287	...	6	Turner	741	9 570	2 481	12.9	55.1	41.0	0.2	0.3	3.4	8.0	21.0	11.3	12.5	13.4	12.5
13 289	31420	3	Twiggs	933	10 466	2 402	11.2	56.5	42.0	0.4	0.2	1.2	6.5	19.3	10.8	13.1	15.2	13.7
13 291	...	9	Union	835	19 119	1 855	22.9	97.6	0.9	0.7	0.3	1.0	4.7	14.9	8.3	10.5	12.3	12.7
13 293	45580	6	Upson	843	27 978	1 466	33.2	69.7	28.3	0.5	0.5	1.5	6.9	18.5	9.2	12.2	14.9	13.3
13 295	16860	2	Walker	1 157	62 584	790	54.1	95.0	3.7	0.6	0.5	0.9	6.3	17.9	9.4	13.3	14.7	14.0
13 297	12060	1	Walton	853	69 381	728	81.3	82.9	14.2	0.7	0.9	2.1	7.6	19.9	9.4	14.6	16.0	12.3
13 299	48180	4	Ware	2 337	35 503	1 258	15.2	69.5	27.8	0.3	0.5	2.3	6.9	17.9	9.9	13.3	14.1	13.4
13 301	...	8	Warren	739	6 129	2 763	8.3	40.4	58.4	0.2	0.1	1.0	7.2	18.9	9.6	11.5	13.5	14.3
13 303	...	7	Washington	1 762	20 780	1 762	11.8	45.2	53.7	0.2	0.4	0.7	6.0	19.6	10.6	12.2	16.7	13.7
13 305	27700	8	Wayne	1 670	27 509	1 484	16.5	76.1	19.6	0.4	0.5	3.9	6.8	18.5	9.7	14.3	15.4	13.7
13 307	...	8	Webster	543	2 295	3 034	4.2	48.8	47.5	0.3	0.0	3.7	5.8	18.8	9.3	12.0	14.1	14.5
13 309	...	9	Wheeler	771	6 593	2 722	8.6	61.3	34.5	0.1	0.2	4.0	5.2	15.0	12.2	16.6	16.9	14.8
13 311	...	8	White	626	22 815	1 672	36.4	95.1	2.4	1.1	0.6	1.7	6.0	16.8	10.3	13.3	14.2	12.4
13 313	19140	3	Whitfield	751	87 833	609	117.0	70.6	3.6	0.5	1.3	24.7	9.3	19.5	9.7	14.6	14.7	12.5
13 315	...	9	Wilcox	985	8 764	2 548	8.9	62.6	35.8	0.1	0.2	1.3	6.5	16.0	10.3	14.4	15.8	14.3
13 317	...	6	Wilkes	1 221	10 653	2 388	8.7	55.1	42.3	0.3	0.3	2.2	6.0	17.1	9.8	11.5	14.2	13.5
13 319	...	8	Wilkinson	1 157	10 267	2 420	8.9	58.1	40.1	0.2	0.2	1.5	7.8	18.4	10.0	12.2	15.1	14.3
13 321	10500	3	Worth	1 476	21 849	1 710	14.8	68.8	29.5	0.5	0.3	1.2	6.7	20.4	9.9	11.4	14.6	14.3
15 000	...	X	HAWAII	16 635	1 257 608	X	75.6	35.3	3.1	1.5	74.8	7.6	6.8	16.9	10.0	13.1	14.7	14.7
15 001	25900	5	Hawaii	10 433	158 423	350	15.2	47.1	1.1	2.3	67.5	10.9	6.5	19.2	10.5	10.1	13.1	15.9
15 003	26180	2	Honolulu	1 553	902 709	47	581.3	31.2	3.9	1.3	77.7	6.8	6.8	16.2	10.0	14.0	15.0	13.8
15 005	...	9	Kalawao	34	129	3 140	3.8	34.1	0.0	0.0	61.2	4.7	0.0	2.3	0.8	2.3	14.0	24.8
15 007	28180	5	Kauai	1 612	60 747	812	37.7	42.8	0.7	1.5	69.7	8.6	6.5	18.5	9.1	10.3	14.1	16.6
15 009	27980	5	Maui	3 002	135 605	416	45.2	45.5	1.0	1.5	66.4	8.1	6.6	17.7	9.2	12.5	15.7	16.1
16 000	...	X	IDAHO	214 314	1 366 332	X	6.4	88.4	0.7	1.9	1.6	8.7	7.4	19.8	11.2	13.1	13.9	13.8
16 001	14260	2	Ada	2 732	325 151	183	119.0	91.4	1.1	1.2	3.0	5.1	7.4	19.0	9.8	15.4	15.8	13.9
16 003	...	8	Adams	3 534	3 515	2 943	1.0	96.7	0.1	1.7	0.2	1.5	3.7	17.4	7.9	6.3	13.6	18.2
16 005	38540	3	Bannock	2 883	75 630	678	26.2	90.1	0.9	3.5	1.9	5.1	8.6	19.0	12.8	14.3	12.8	13.4
16 007	...	7	Bear Lake	2 516	6 306	2 745	2.5	96.8	0.2	0.6	0.1	2.3	6.3	22.5	11.4	7.7	13.0	13.4
16 009	...	6	Benewah	2 010	9 029	2 519	4.5	90.2	0.3	9.2	0.2	1.6	6.4	18.7	8.7	9.0	13.7	15.9
16 011	13940	6	Bingham	5 425	42 926	1 062	7.9	79.3	0.3	6.5	1.0	13.8	8.6	24.0	11.9	10.7	13.1	12.4
16 013	...	7	Blaine	6 850	20 791	1 759	3.0	85.2	0.1	0.6	1.2	13.6	6.1	16.9	8.2	13.9	16.4	17.9
16 015	14260	2	Boise	4 927	7 236	2 662	1.5	95.3	0.1	1.9	0.6	3.4	5.5	18.9	8.5	8.6	15.6	17.9
16 017	...	6	Bonner	4 501	39 162	1 150	8.7	96.9	0.2	2.1	0.6	1.7	5.2	18.1	9.1	9.1	13.7	18.0
16 019	26820	3	Bonneville	4 839	87 007	617	18.0	89.8	0.7	1.0	1.3	8.2	8.2	22.2	10.9	11.7	13.8	13.3
16 021	...	7	Boundary	3 286	10 173	2 429	3.1	93.7	0.1	2.5	0.8	3.5	6.5	20.2	9.4	9.3	13.4	16.3
16 023	...	8	Butte	5 783	2 873	2 993	0.5	93.2	0.7	1.3	0.2	5.2	6.9	20.4	8.5	8.4	13.9	15.5
16 025	...	9	Camas	2 784	1 049	3 107	0.4	93.5	0.3	0.7	0.4	6.1	5.0	17.3	8.6	10.2	17.2	14.2
16 027	14260	2	Canyon	1 527	151 508	372	99.2	78.1	0.5	1.3	1.5	19.9	8.9	21.4	11.3	14.4	12.9	11.1
16 029	...	6	Caribou	4 574	7 152	2 671	1.6	95.5	0.1	0.3	0.3	4.2	7.0	21.9	10.4	9.5	13.9	14.3
16 031	15420	7	Cassia	6 647	21 610	1 723	3.3	78.0	0.2	1.1	0.8	20.7	8.6	23.6	10.8	10.5	12.8	12.2
16 033	...	8	Clark	4 570	904	3 112	0.2	57.5	0.6	1.1	0.3	40.9	10.0	22.3	11.6	11.2	15.2	11.9
16 035	...	6	Clearwater	6 375	8 401	2 571	1.3	94.9	0.2	4.0	0.6	1.9	4.4	15.7	7.9	9.0	15.7	16.9

1. CBSA = Core Based Statistical Area. See Appendix A for explanation. See Appendix B for list of metropolitan areas with component counties. 2. County type code from the Economic Research Service of USDA Rural-Urban Continuum Codes. See Appendix A for definition. 3. Dry land or land partially or temporarily covered by water. 4. Hispanic or Latino persons may be of any race.

Table B. States and Counties — Population and Households

STATE County	Population, 2003 (cont'd) Age (percent) (cont'd) 55 to 64 years	65 to 74 years	75 years and over	Percent female	Population — change and components of change, 1990–2003 Total persons 1990	2000	Percent change 1990–2000	2000–2003	Components of change, 2000–2003 Births	Deaths	Net migration	Households, 2000 Number	Percent change, 1990–2000	Persons per house-hold	Female family house-holder[1]	One person
	16	17	18	19	20	21	22	23	24	25	26	27	28	29	30	31
GEORGIA—Cont'd																
Richmond	8.5	5.9	5.0	51.8	189 719	199 775	5.3	-0.8	11 010	6 334	-6 301	73 920	7.6	2.55	20.8	27.7
Rockdale	9.2	5.2	3.8	50.1	54 091	70 111	29.6	6.9	3 338	1 648	3 162	24 052	31.2	2.87	12.4	16.9
Schley	11.4	5.7	4.9	52.1	3 590	3 766	4.9	4.5	138	149	179	1 435	9.1	2.62	15.7	24.8
Screven	9.2	7.2	6.8	51.8	13 842	15 374	11.1	0.2	657	553	-73	5 797	14.8	2.60	18.3	26.5
Seminole	11.2	9.2	7.1	52.8	9 010	9 369	4.0	-1.1	426	398	-119	3 573	13.9	2.54	17.9	24.3
Spalding	9.4	6.2	5.3	51.5	54 457	58 417	7.3	3.5	3 063	2 023	-239	21 519	10.8	2.67	18.2	22.3
Stephens	10.6	7.9	8.0	52.1	23 436	25 435	8.5	-0.7	1 119	1 029	-239	9 951	11.2	2.46	11.1	25.5
Stewart	10.3	8.6	10.3	51.8	5 654	5 252	-7.1	-4.8	177	230	-198	2 007	1.3	2.48	23.1	29.5
Sumter	8.8	5.7	6.3	52.6	30 232	33 200	9.8	0.1	1 771	1 102	-636	12 025	14.7	2.64	22.0	25.0
Talbot	11.3	8.3	5.6	52.8	6 524	6 498	-0.4	1.0	310	268	28	2 538	8.2	2.55	20.2	25.4
Taliaferro	12.7	10.2	10.6	52.3	1 915	2 077	8.5	-5.8	62	77	-103	870	19.7	2.36	20.0	33.3
Tattnall	8.4	5.8	5.3	42.4	17 722	22 305	25.9	0.4	1 017	692	-240	7 057	20.7	2.60	13.4	26.7
Taylor	10.2	6.6	6.5	51.0	7 642	8 815	15.3	1.0	389	343	43	3 281	17.0	2.56	20.1	27.6
Telfair	9.0	7.5	7.4	47.7	11 000	11 794	7.2	-2.3	486	542	-207	4 140	3.1	2.48	16.7	28.4
Terrell	10.5	6.6	6.2	52.9	10 653	10 970	3.0	-1.1	617	403	-323	4 002	7.1	2.69	24.0	24.3
Thomas	9.7	6.9	6.6	52.9	38 943	42 737	9.7	2.2	2 090	1 718	602	16 309	13.9	2.55	18.4	25.8
Tift	8.9	6.0	5.5	51.3	34 998	38 407	9.7	2.9	2 002	1 136	289	13 919	14.2	2.65	16.9	23.3
Toombs	9.8	6.4	5.8	52.2	24 072	26 067	8.3	1.5	1 414	936	-63	9 877	12.2	2.59	15.6	27.0
Towns	13.8	14.3	11.0	51.9	6 754	9 319	38.0	6.2	281	415	697	3 998	42.2	2.20	6.3	26.0
Treutlen	9.3	6.5	6.5	49.4	5 994	6 854	14.3	1.4	291	249	59	2 531	17.3	2.55	17.3	25.3
Troup	8.6	6.2	5.9	52.1	55 532	58 779	5.8	2.4	3 018	2 206	673	21 920	7.6	2.61	17.9	24.9
Turner	9.0	6.6	6.0	52.1	8 703	9 504	9.2	0.7	517	356	-85	3 435	12.9	2.72	18.6	23.2
Twiggs	10.2	6.4	4.9	51.9	9 806	10 590	8.0	-1.2	419	365	-156	3 832	16.3	2.73	17.5	22.3
Union	12.6	12.3	9.2	51.0	11 993	17 289	44.2	10.6	548	631	1 872	7 159	52.0	2.35	7.1	24.2
Upson	10.1	7.6	7.0	52.3	26 300	27 597	4.9	1.4	1 259	1 212	365	10 722	8.2	2.53	16.9	25.2
Walker	10.3	7.5	6.1	51.3	58 310	61 053	4.7	2.5	2 471	2 204	1 284	23 605	8.8	2.54	12.0	22.9
Walton	8.5	5.3	4.2	51.1	38 586	60 687	57.3	14.3	3 274	1 660	6 972	21 307	58.6	2.82	12.8	16.6
Ware	9.5	7.5	7.6	50.4	35 471	35 483	0.0	0.1	1 625	1 450	-137	13 475	3.3	2.47	14.8	27.9
Warren	10.3	7.7	8.2	53.8	6 078	6 336	4.2	-3.3	293	266	-221	2 435	14.3	2.55	22.1	27.4
Washington	8.8	6.6	6.0	54.9	19 112	21 176	10.8	-1.9	822	800	-405	7 435	10.3	2.65	21.5	24.8
Wayne	9.6	6.6	4.7	48.1	22 356	26 565	18.8	3.6	1 207	833	581	9 324	17.7	2.62	14.0	22.6
Webster	10.7	7.5	7.0	49.5	2 263	2 390	5.6	-4.0	83	82	-93	911	14.2	2.62	16.8	23.5
Wheeler	8.6	5.2	5.6	40.2	4 903	6 179	26.0	6.7	202	202	396	2 011	12.6	2.54	13.0	27.8
White	10.6	7.9	6.1	50.7	13 006	19 944	53.3	14.4	868	631	2 570	7 731	57.6	2.51	8.7	21.7
Whitfield	9.1	5.8	4.5	50.0	72 462	83 525	15.3	5.2	5 649	2 216	859	29 385	9.4	2.82	10.8	20.6
Wilcox	8.6	6.8	6.7	43.9	7 008	8 577	22.4	2.2	391	279	70	2 785	10.9	2.55	15.0	26.7
Wilkes	11.3	8.3	8.8	52.4	10 597	10 687	0.8	-0.3	446	501	34	4 314	7.3	2.45	17.3	28.1
Wilkinson	10.1	7.2	5.9	52.6	10 228	10 220	-0.1	0.5	539	374	-110	3 827	5.7	2.65	18.4	24.1
Worth	10.2	6.8	5.6	52.1	19 744	21 967	11.3	-0.5	969	619	-444	8 106	17.6	2.68	15.7	21.5
HAWAII	10.5	6.6	6.8	49.9	1 108 229	1 211 537	9.3	3.8	59 044	29 180	16 797	403 240	13.2	2.92	12.4	21.9
Hawaii	9.9	6.9	6.3	49.7	120 317	148 677	23.6	6.6	7 046	4 030	6 695	52 985	27.8	2.75	13.2	23.1
Honolulu	9.7	6.7	6.8	49.9	836 231	876 156	4.8	3.0	43 246	20 749	4 569	286 450	8.0	2.95	12.3	21.6
Kalawao	26.4	23.3	10.1	49.6	130	147	13.1	-12.2	0	6	-10	115	85.5	1.28	2.6	79.1
Kauai	10.4	6.7	7.0	50.0	51 177	58 463	14.2	3.9	2 690	1 514	1 160	20 183	23.9	2.87	12.8	21.4
Maui	9.8	5.8	5.5	49.5	100 374	128 094	27.6	5.9	6 062	2 881	4 383	43 507	31.3	2.91	12.0	21.9
IDAHO	9.3	5.9	5.5	49.9	1 006 734	1 293 953	28.5	5.6	66 337	32 085	36 648	469 645	30.2	2.69	8.7	22.4
Ada	7.9	4.5	4.5	49.8	205 775	300 904	46.2	8.1	15 516	6 054	14 779	113 408	46.4	2.59	9.4	23.8
Adams	14.8	11.0	6.7	49.0	3 254	3 476	6.8	1.1	77	106	94	1 421	13.6	2.42	5.7	23.2
Bannock	8.0	5.3	5.1	50.6	66 026	75 565	14.4	0.1	4 417	1 877	-2 494	27 192	16.1	2.69	10.0	22.8
Bear Lake	9.7	8.3	7.9	50.2	6 084	6 411	5.4	-1.6	258	203	-156	2 259	12.7	2.81	6.4	22.2
Benewah	12.6	8.5	6.6	49.1	7 937	9 171	15.5	-1.5	378	300	-218	3 580	19.7	2.52	7.7	24.0
Bingham	8.2	5.8	4.6	50.2	37 583	41 735	11.0	2.9	2 459	966	-272	13 317	15.7	3.10	9.8	17.1
Blaine	11.0	4.8	2.9	48.2	13 552	18 991	40.1	9.5	848	240	1 182	7 780	41.3	2.40	7.2	27.3
Boise	13.0	6.7	3.8	48.5	3 509	6 670	90.1	8.5	237	115	437	2 616	92.8	2.52	5.8	21.8
Bonner	12.1	7.6	5.5	50.2	26 622	36 835	38.4	6.3	1 253	1 052	2 099	14 693	43.1	2.49	7.5	24.0
Bonneville	8.5	5.3	4.8	50.1	72 207	82 522	14.3	5.4	4 706	2 036	1 921	28 753	18.4	2.83	9.3	21.4
Boundary	11.0	7.3	5.6	49.7	8 332	9 871	18.5	3.1	417	288	170	3 707	29.8	2.61	7.5	23.1
Butte	12.1	8.5	7.1	49.3	2 918	2 899	-0.7	-0.9	138	75	-93	1 089	9.2	2.64	7.4	23.6
Camas	13.0	7.8	6.2	49.7	727	991	36.3	5.9	39	20	38	396	44.0	2.49	4.5	22.2
Canyon	7.5	4.9	5.1	50.2	90 076	131 441	45.9	15.3	8 674	3 191	14 251	45 018	43.9	2.85	10.1	19.8
Caribou	9.9	7.2	6.4	50.0	6 963	7 304	4.9	-2.1	325	198	-271	2 560	13.2	2.83	5.2	20.4
Cassia	8.5	6.3	6.5	50.0	19 532	21 416	9.6	0.9	1 257	582	-476	7 060	10.8	2.99	8.8	19.5
Clark	11.2	6.5	4.3	46.2	762	1 022	34.1	-11.5	61	37	-148	340	22.7	3.01	7.1	20.0
Clearwater	14.1	9.9	7.5	46.2	8 505	8 930	5.0	-5.9	244	328	-452	3 456	7.6	2.41	6.9	24.0

1. No spouse present.

STATE County	Births, average 1999-2001 Total	Rate[1]	Deaths, average 1999-2001 Number Total	Infant[2]	Rate Total[1]	Infant[3]	Physicians,[4] 2000 Number	Rate[5]	Hospitals,[4] 1998 Number	Beds Number	Rate[5]	Medicare enrollees, 2003	Serious crimes known to police,[6] 2002 Total Number	Rate[7]
	32	33	34	35	36	37	38	39	40	41	42	43	44	45
GEORGIA—Cont'd														
Richmond	3 276	16.4	1 916	34	9.6	10.5	1 047	524	4	1 571	821	26 368	12 569	6 017
Rockdale	987	14.0	495	4	7.0	D	96	137	1	107	157	7 802	3 752	5 118
Schley	48	12.8	40	0	10.7	D	1	27	0	0	0	503	52	1 320
Screven	199	13.1	168	3	11.0	D	11	72	1	40	277	2 466	347	2 158
Seminole	137	14.7	111	2	11.9	D	11	117	1	62	633	1 805	157	1 603
Spalding	895	15.3	622	10	10.6	10.8	79	135	1	160	278	8 936	3 296	5 396
Stephens	368	14.4	314	2	12.3	D	44	173	1	96	378	5 545	NA	NA
Stewart	59	11.3	69	0	13.3	D	4	76	1	32	585	957	171	3 114
Sumter	545	16.5	337	4	10.2	D	44	133	1	152	485	4 550	1 648	4 840
Talbot	86	13.2	85	1	13.0	D	1	15	0	0	0	1 094	91	1 339
Taliaferro	22	10.9	28	1	13.7	D	0	0	0	0	0	414	32	1 473
Tattnall	307	13.8	215	2	9.6	D	14	63	1	40	211	3 230	335	1 767
Taylor	123	14.0	105	1	11.9	D	2	23	0	0	0	1 603	122	1 323
Telfair	165	14.0	152	1	12.9	D	6	51	1	52	450	2 286	200	1 622
Terrell	183	16.7	130	2	11.9	D	5	46	0	0	0	1 709	343	2 990
Thomas	651	15.2	502	7	11.8	10.8	125	292	1	264	615	8 047	1 927	4 374
Tift	624	16.2	348	7	9.0	10.7	78	203	1	168	458	5 671	2 448	6 096
Toombs	446	17.1	287	4	11.0	D	33	127	1	122	472	4 393	850	3 118
Towns	96	10.3	127	1	13.6	D	9	97	1	101	1 184	2 730	131	1 344
Treutlen	94	13.8	76	1	11.3	D	3	44	0	0	0	1 054	NA	NA
Troup	939	15.9	667	9	11.3	9.6	87	148	1	364	619	9 429	3 931	6 396
Turner	159	16.7	109	2	11.4	D	3	32	0	0	0	1 581	175	1 761
Twiggs	133	12.6	113	2	10.7	D	4	38	0	0	0	1 471	79	713
Union	174	10.1	205	2	11.8	D	11	64	1	145	878	4 524	NA	NA
Upson	365	13.2	355	2	12.8	D	38	138	1	119	440	4 848	845	2 928
Walker	808	13.2	703	6	11.5	D	15	25	0	0	0	11 591	2 085	3 266
Walton	1 027	16.8	467	6	7.6	D	35	58	1	135	248	8 690	1 782	3 014
Ware	493	13.9	427	4	12.0	D	66	186	1	125	353	7 136	1 717	4 628
Warren	85	13.4	89	2	14.1	D	5	79	0	0	0	1 060	93	1 404
Washington	261	12.4	231	2	11.0	D	15	71	1	114	569	3 165	733	3 392
Wayne	356	13.4	246	4	9.2	D	36	136	1	123	484	4 045	NA	NA
Webster	26	10.9	30	0	12.7	D	0	0	0	0	0	298	NA	NA
Wheeler	68	11.0	63	0	10.2	D	3	49	0	40	821	877	NA	NA
White	262	13.1	195	3	9.7	D	8	40	0	0	0	3 781	604	2 896
Whitfield	1 783	21.2	696	12	8.3	6.5	137	164	1	282	344	11 618	4 795	5 590
Wilcox	118	13.7	91	2	10.5	D	4	47	0	0	0	1 411	NA	NA
Wilkes	133	12.4	145	2	13.5	D	12	112	1	44	416	2 246	239	2 139
Wilkinson	174	16.9	108	2	10.6	D	3	29	0	0	0	1 853	269	2 680
Worth	276	12.5	200	2	9.1	D	10	46	1	50	222	2 646	425	1 850
HAWAII	17 220	14.2	8 318	123	6.8	7.1	3 138	259	19	3 166	265	174 633	75 238	6 044
Hawaii	2 309	15.4	1 191	14	8.0	6.2	272	183	5	435	304	22 986	6 936	4 540
Honolulu	12 421	14.1	5 896	92	6.7	7.4	2 518	287	10	2 316	265	126 752	57 271	6 360
Kalawao	13	78.8	4	0	0.0	D	0	0	NA	NA	NA	54	NA	NA
Kauai	743	12.7	444	3	7.6	D	101	173	2	240	424	8 799	3 045	5 069
Maui	1 734	13.5	783	13	6.1	7.3	247	193	2	175	145	15 966	7 986	6 067
IDAHO	20 309	15.7	9 632	139	7.4	6.8	1 831	142	43	3 271	266	177 700	42 547	3 173
Ada	4 805	15.9	1 800	26	5.9	5.5	606	201	3	596	216	34 011	12 647	4 055
Adams	24	6.9	36	0	10.4	D	3	86	1	26	683	800	81	2 248
Bannock	1 378	18.2	575	9	7.6	6.5	132	175	2	248	331	9 441	2 391	3 053
Bear Lake	83	12.9	64	0	10.0	D	4	62	1	58	887	1 139	21	316
Benewah	119	13.1	95	1	10.5	D	9	98	1	33	362	1 663	111	1 168
Bingham	754	18.0	286	4	6.8	D	25	60	1	120	287	5 273	769	1 778
Blaine	245	12.8	76	2	4.0	D	61	321	2	88	512	1 726	433	2 441
Boise	79	11.8	31	0	4.7	D	0	0	0	0	0	758	111	1 606
Bonner	376	10.2	317	3	8.6	D	42	114	1	62	176	6 054	939	2 460
Bonneville	1 425	17.2	578	9	7.0	6.3	150	182	1	270	335	10 532	3 007	3 516
Boundary	129	13.1	82	0	8.3	D	5	51	1	62	633	1 665	149	1 456
Butte	36	12.6	25	0	8.7	D	1	34	1	43	1 418	550	29	965
Camas	11	10.6	5	0	0.0	D	0	0	0	0	0	146	1	97
Canyon	2 538	19.2	995	16	7.5	6.4	144	110	2	274	228	18 009	6 120	4 492
Caribou	110	15.1	57	1	7.8	D	5	68	1	65	875	1 110	93	1 229
Cassia	394	18.4	180	4	8.4	D	32	149	1	70	328	2 999	637	2 870
Clark	19	19.0	9	0	8.7	D	0	0	0	0	0	106	18	1 700
Clearwater	74	8.4	95	1	10.8	D	13	146	1	22	236	1 749	150	1 621

1. Per 1,000 estimated resident population.   2. Deaths of infants under 1 year old.   3. Deaths of infants under 1 year old per 1,000 live births.   4. Data subject to copyright.   5. Per 100,000 resident population as of July 1 of the year shown.   6. Data for serious crimes have not been adjusted for underreporting; this may affect comparability between geographic areas and over time.   7. Per 100,000 population estimated by the FBI.

STATE County	Serious crimes known to police,[1] 2002 (cont'd) Rate[2]		Education						Money income, 1999				Percent below poverty level, 1999			
			School enrollment and attainment, 2000				Local government expenditures,[5] 2000–2001			Households						
			Enrollment[3]		Attainment[4] (percent)					Median income						
	Violent	Property	Total	Percent private	High school graduate or less	Bachelor's degree or more	Total current expenditures (mil dol)	Current expenditures per student (dollars)	Per capita income[6] (dollars)	Dollars	Percent change, 1989–1999 (constant 1999 dollars)	Percent with income of $100,000 or more	Persons	Households	Families	Families with children
	46	47	48	49	50	51	52	53	54	55	56	57	58	59	60	61
GEORGIA—Cont'd																
Richmond	387	5 630	56 607	11.6	51.7	18.7	228.4	6 447	17 088	33 086	-2.5	6.4	19.6	17.9	16.2	23.1
Rockdale	445	4 673	19 019	11.4	47.0	23.4	91.1	6 740	22 300	53 599	1.3	16.7	8.2	7.0	5.7	8.0
Schley	76	1 244	1 062	11.6	70.1	13.7	5.4	5 580	14 981	32 035	11.3	3.7	19.9	19.5	15.8	21.3
Screven	149	2 009	4 374	5.7	71.7	10.2	20.2	6 396	13 894	29 312	6.3	2.9	20.1	21.7	15.5	20.6
Seminole	459	1 143	2 359	9.4	68.9	8.6	12.4	6 565	14 635	27 094	9.4	4.9	23.2	20.1	15.8	25.6
Spalding	488	4 908	14 632	12.1	67.0	12.5	72.8	7 045	16 791	36 221	5.2	6.8	15.5	15.5	12.4	18.7
Stephens	NA	NA	6 355	23.4	64.7	14.1	29.8	6 833	15 529	29 466	-1.2	4.9	15.1	16.3	11.3	15.0
Stewart	1 056	2 058	1 265	12.8	73.9	9.3	6.9	8 574	16 071	24 789	18.2	4.1	22.2	22.2	17.2	26.9
Sumter	455	4 385	9 860	13.0	60.3	19.3	37.1	6 501	15 083	30 904	9.8	5.7	21.4	21.2	17.6	25.5
Talbot	74	1 266	1 505	15.0	75.5	7.9	6.6	7 759	14 539	26 611	-3.3	4.4	24.2	24.8	19.9	31.2
Taliaferro	230	1 243	463	13.4	76.4	8.4	2.3	12 177	15 498	23 750	20.3	6.2	23.4	25.2	22.3	30.8
Tattnall	195	1 571	4 802	15.9	72.9	7.9	21.0	6 301	13 439	28 664	5.1	4.4	23.9	22.5	18.6	26.3
Taylor	163	1 161	2 199	4.5	75.4	8.5	11.2	6 287	13 432	25 148	15.5	4.0	26.0	27.1	20.2	29.0
Telfair	519	1 103	2 480	5.0	76.5	8.3	12.8	6 922	14 197	26 097	17.2	4.7	21.2	23.4	17.3	22.2
Terrell	523	2 467	2 960	13.0	68.3	10.7	13.0	7 077	13 894	26 969	11.3	5.0	28.6	27.2	22.7	32.6
Thomas	372	4 002	11 646	13.0	60.0	16.8	58.9	6 755	16 211	31 115	10.8	6.0	17.4	18.6	13.6	19.3
Tift	732	5 364	10 744	9.5	62.4	15.6	46.7	6 273	16 833	32 616	8.3	7.4	19.9	18.7	15.5	22.9
Toombs	462	2 656	6 704	7.0	67.6	12.7	31.1	5 997	14 252	26 811	2.5	5.3	23.9	22.4	17.8	26.9
Towns	92	1 252	1 865	26.0	58.3	17.4	7.1	6 680	18 221	31 950	22.9	7.1	11.8	13.4	8.8	13.0
Treutlen	NA	NA	1 671	7.9	77.8	8.5	8.4	6 902	13 122	24 644	5.5	3.4	26.3	27.8	20.8	27.8
Troup	384	6 012	15 898	13.8	60.7	18.0	78.6	6 764	17 626	35 469	6.5	8.0	14.8	15.2	12.2	17.3
Turner	453	1 308	2 621	3.5	71.0	10.5	13.9	6 958	13 454	25 676	7.6	4.7	26.7	23.0	20.5	28.1
Twiggs	135	578	2 644	18.3	77.6	5.4	12.8	7 437	14 259	31 608	22.4	5.4	19.7	20.3	15.5	20.8
Union	NA	NA	3 414	9.8	60.9	12.5	18.4	6 821	18 845	31 893	17.1	5.2	12.5	14.1	9.3	9.9
Upson	308	2 620	6 844	9.4	70.5	11.5	31.1	6 243	17 053	31 201	2.1	4.7	14.7	14.7	11.2	17.2
Walker	111	3 155	13 598	10.3	68.2	10.2	64.4	6 338	15 867	32 406	0.2	3.9	12.5	13.5	10.0	15.7
Walton	242	2 772	15 459	13.9	62.1	13.0	71.0	6 369	19 470	46 479	22.7	10.7	9.7	9.9	8.0	10.9
Ware	334	4 293	8 641	5.6	68.4	11.4	45.5	7 078	14 384	28 360	3.3	3.8	20.5	20.1	15.9	24.8
Warren	257	1 147	1 645	8.4	77.6	8.0	6.8	7 070	14 022	27 366	17.8	3.7	27.0	26.4	24.1	32.9
Washington	435	2 957	5 802	10.5	70.5	10.5	25.9	6 598	15 565	29 910	3.7	6.1	22.9	22.1	18.7	25.3
Wayne	NA	NA	6 292	6.6	66.9	11.6	33.3	6 418	15 628	32 766	4.6	6.4	16.7	17.3	13.4	19.1
Webster	NA	NA	549	14.2	72.7	9.1	3.2	8 517	14 772	27 992	9.5	3.7	19.3	17.3	13.4	22.9
Wheeler	NA	NA	1 358	5.4	74.0	7.1	7.8	6 968	13 005	24 053	7.9	4.3	25.3	28.1	21.6	29.1
White	326	2 570	4 506	16.1	59.2	15.4	22.2	6 357	17 193	36 084	10.8	4.8	10.5	11.9	8.4	10.4
Whitfield	407	5 183	19 439	7.5	66.0	12.8	121.2	7 125	18 515	39 377	5.4	8.9	11.5	11.4	8.6	11.6
Wilcox	NA	NA	1 855	8.2	75.5	7.0	9.5	6 840	14 014	27 483	25.2	5.1	21.0	21.7	16.8	24.5
Wilkes	385	1 754	2 461	6.7	70.9	12.0	13.6	7 088	15 020	27 644	10.4	4.1	17.5	18.8	13.0	17.9
Wilkinson	428	2 252	2 710	15.5	71.0	9.6	13.8	7 966	14 658	32 723	-3.2	3.2	17.9	18.3	14.6	21.8
Worth	109	1 741	6 158	8.4	69.8	8.6	28.6	6 481	15 856	32 384	13.1	5.4	18.5	17.9	14.7	20.6
HAWAII	262	5 782	320 842	20.5	43.9	26.2	1 216.6	6 558	21 525	49 820	-4.5	16.6	10.7	10.5	7.6	11.3
Hawaii	145	4 395	40 194	12.3	46.8	22.1	[7]0.0	[7]NA	18 791	39 805	-0.3	10.5	15.7	14.8	11.0	17.1
Honolulu	289	6 072	234 038	23.3	43.0	27.9	[7]1 216.6	[7]6 558	21 998	51 914	-4.8	18.2	9.9	9.7	7.0	10.3
Kalawao	NA	NA	0	0.0	80.3	10.2	[7]0.0	[7]NA	13 756	9 333	-30.5	0.0	40.1	44.7	0.0	0.0
Kauai	298	4 771	14 881	10.2	46.4	19.4	[7]0.0	[7]NA	20 301	45 020	-10.5	12.2	10.5	10.6	8.4	12.3
Maui	198	5 869	31 729	15.0	46.1	22.4	[7]0.0	[7]NA	22 033	49 489	-5.0	15.5	10.5	10.1	7.7	10.6
IDAHO	255	2 918	368 579	12.2	43.8	21.7	1 382.4	5 642	17 841	37 572	10.7	7.3	11.8	11.2	8.3	12.2
Ada	300	3 755	81 730	12.3	32.3	31.2	307.4	5 755	22 519	46 140	13.5	12.0	7.7	7.4	5.4	7.9
Adams	139	2 109	774	9.4	56.6	14.9	4.0	7 584	14 908	28 423	-5.8	3.6	15.1	14.5	11.7	16.0
Bannock	318	2 735	25 491	7.5	38.4	24.9	76.3	5 479	17 148	36 683	3.9	7.2	13.9	14.1	9.8	14.5
Bear Lake	30	286	1 933	2.9	56.7	11.7	8.4	5 345	13 592	32 162	10.6	2.0	9.6	10.3	7.1	10.4
Benewah	231	936	2 139	10.6	61.3	11.4	11.7	6 953	15 285	31 517	9.1	3.9	14.1	13.3	10.5	16.4
Bingham	132	1 646	13 297	4.5	50.5	14.4	56.2	5 429	14 365	36 423	7.8	5.3	12.4	11.5	9.9	14.2
Blaine	288	2 153	4 341	17.2	25.7	43.1	24.2	8 033	31 346	50 496	20.5	18.3	7.8	7.3	4.9	8.6
Boise	203	1 403	1 611	10.7	46.2	19.9	7.2	6 793	18 787	38 651	10.4	8.2	12.9	12.5	9.0	14.5
Bonner	173	2 287	8 413	18.5	47.9	16.9	32.2	5 786	17 263	32 803	13.7	4.9	15.5	14.6	11.9	17.7
Bonneville	229	3 287	24 784	7.2	38.7	26.1	96.9	5 228	18 326	41 805	2.1	8.9	10.1	10.0	7.4	11.2
Boundary	342	1 114	2 237	18.3	55.9	14.7	9.8	6 122	14 636	31 250	7.4	3.3	15.7	15.1	11.5	17.5
Butte	100	865	758	4.1	50.4	13.0	3.8	6 533	14 948	30 473	-13.7	4.4	18.2	15.9	14.7	26.0
Camas	0	97	250	5.2	43.0	22.2	1.4	7 899	19 550	34 167	4.1	6.0	8.3	9.0	7.2	8.0
Canyon	382	4 110	35 560	14.6	54.3	14.9	130.1	5 104	15 155	35 884	16.2	5.0	12.0	11.3	8.7	12.9
Caribou	106	1 123	2 190	3.5	47.6	15.9	11.8	6 360	15 179	37 609	-6.6	5.6	9.6	10.7	7.0	10.1
Cassia	257	2 613	6 560	6.5	52.9	13.9	27.0	5 268	14 087	33 322	6.1	4.3	13.6	13.0	11.1	16.6
Clark	0	1 700	289	3.1	60.5	12.6	1.8	7 456	11 141	31 576	-4.4	0.9	19.9	18.9	18.7	25.3
Clearwater	205	1 415	2 056	11.0	57.2	13.4	10.2	7 037	15 463	32 071	-0.2	3.0	13.5	12.1	9.7	16.4

1. Data for serious crimes have not been adjusted for underreporting; this may affect comparability between geographic areas and over time.   2. Per 100,000 population estimated by the FBI.   3. All persons 3 years old and over enrolled in nursery school through college.   4. Persons 25 years old and over.   5. Elementary and secondary education expenditures.   6. Based on population enumerated as of April 1, 2000.   7. Hawaii, Kalawao, Kaui, and Maui Counties included with Honolulu County.

STATE County	Personal income, 2002 Total (mil dol)	Percent change, 2001–2002	Per capita¹ Dollars	Per capita¹ Rank	Wages and salaries² (mil dol)	Proprietor's income (mil dol)	Dividends, interest, and rent (mil dol)	Transfer payments Total (mil dol)	Government payments to individuals Total (mil dol)	Social Security (mil dol)	Medical payments (mil dol)	Income maintenance (mil dol)	Unemployment insurance (mil dol)
	62	63	64	65	66	67	68	69	70	71	72	73	74
GEORGIA—Cont'd													
Richmond	4 755	5.0	23 994	1 410	4 691	164	826	1 071	1 017	288	473	133	33
Rockdale	2 114	3.5	28 903	459	1 379	85	298	240	219	96	91	18	7
Schley	76	1.3	19 262	2 702	37	6	10	16	15	5	7	2	0
Screven	289	4.0	18 719	2 793	119	12	53	79	75	25	35	11	2
Seminole	223	2.9	23 881	1 446	80	22	38	59	56	19	27	8	1
Spalding	1 439	4.2	24 126	1 362	802	90	224	287	270	99	121	32	8
Stephens	612	3.5	23 935	1 427	351	46	101	144	136	54	61	12	4
Stewart	110	4.5	21 608	2 120	32	7	15	32	30	8	16	5	1
Sumter	752	4.9	22 647	1 837	452	65	144	176	167	47	79	26	5
Talbot	130	4.8	19 801	2 586	33	5	23	34	32	12	12	5	1
Taliaferro	37	0.7	18 549	2 823	6	2	7	12	11	3	5	2	1
Tattnall	428	0.7	19 276	2 701	174	65	62	99	92	29	44	13	2
Taylor	171	2.0	19 189	2 717	72	14	28	50	47	14	21	8	1
Telfair	218	4.7	18 818	2 778	97	12	41	79	76	21	40	9	2
Terrell	227	5.1	20 973	2 305	76	22	44	60	57	17	25	11	2
Thomas	1 115	3.0	25 896	913	750	66	222	251	239	76	117	29	8
Tift	911	4.7	23 342	1 614	677	71	161	185	174	56	82	24	3
Toombs	569	5.2	21 647	2 108	299	44	92	154	147	44	72	21	4
Towns	247	9.7	25 588	979	79	17	72	69	66	35	25	2	0
Treutlen	115	4.6	16 482	3 024	31	6	20	35	33	10	16	5	1
Troup	1 503	2.7	25 121	1 097	1 226	65	257	280	263	99	110	32	8
Turner	194	7.3	20 124	2 516	72	23	30	53	50	13	25	7	2
Twiggs	207	4.9	19 742	2 606	76	7	22	48	45	17	20	5	1
Union	428	7.1	23 270	1 637	161	37	107	109	104	48	44	5	2
Upson	565	2.4	20 339	2 469	254	36	92	149	142	55	59	14	7
Walker	1 378	4.1	22 201	1 957	496	56	188	323	305	116	141	24	8
Walton	1 643	3.4	24 502	1 261	551	67	198	237	218	85	103	16	6
Ware	745	4.9	21 019	2 295	531	45	121	235	225	61	103	25	5
Warren	122	0.6	19 625	2 624	50	4	17	39	38	11	19	5	2
Washington	482	2.3	23 137	1 682	323	21	108	108	102	33	47	14	3
Wayne	569	5.6	21 037	2 288	324	32	80	137	129	44	63	14	2
Webster	52	1.6	22 536	1 868	11	7	10	10	9	3	4	1	0
Wheeler	98	6.3	14 928	3 079	33	7	13	31	29	8	15	4	1
White	503	3.6	22 816	1 774	187	46	117	99	93	42	38	6	2
Whitfield	2 295	3.6	26 485	791	2 343	161	409	353	328	131	148	29	10
Wilcox	174	2.9	20 088	2 526	43	23	27	48	45	11	26	6	1
Wilkes	227	2.2	21 293	2 210	112	16	48	65	62	22	28	7	3
Wilkinson	215	3.9	20 958	2 310	134	9	29	54	51	19	21	7	1
Worth	484	4.5	22 186	1 962	106	41	63	100	94	31	42	15	3
HAWAII	37 064	5.5	29 875	X	26 011	2 777	6 521	4 723	4 478	1 856	1 599	584	204
Hawaii	3 646	7.1	23 547	1 549	2 135	373	684	688	656	258	221	108	37
Honolulu	28 301	5.1	31 707	236	20 522	1 893	4 924	3 277	3 104	1 317	1 067	401	139
Kalawao	[3]	[3]	[3]	[3]	[3]	[3]	[3]	[3]	[3]	[3]	[3]	[3]	[3]
Kauai	1 507	6.4	25 132	1 095	959	118	284	253	241	97	94	28	15
Maui	[3]3 611	[3]5.9	[3]27 087	[3]686	[3]2 395	[3]393	[3]628	[3]505	[3]477	[3]183	[3]217	[3]46	[3]14
IDAHO	34 217	3.8	25 476	X	21 052	4 173	6 302	4 974	4 676	1 952	1 711	345	250
Ada	10 892	3.1	34 072	163	7 808	1 560	2 029	1 007	935	386	330	61	58
Adams	81	3.9	23 189	1 666	30	7	27	18	17	8	5	1	2
Bannock	1 726	2.5	22 754	1 801	1 073	121	256	303	286	96	94	24	14
Bear Lake	121	1.4	19 320	2 692	41	13	23	26	25	11	9	1	1
Benewah	201	2.2	22 271	1 939	121	20	36	47	45	18	17	3	4
Bingham	883	7.2	20 839	2 338	448	121	124	152	143	60	55	13	7
Blaine	909	4.2	44 641	34	498	129	323	49	45	22	13	2	5
Boise	157	5.0	22 309	1 932	45	7	25	22	20	10	6	1	1
Bonner	836	5.3	21 865	2 047	392	97	205	159	150	69	50	10	10
Bonneville	2 198	3.7	25 815	931	1 480	222	372	314	295	123	120	22	12
Boundary	183	6.6	18 316	2 859	107	18	35	44	41	18	14	3	3
Butte	66	1.7	22 436	1 897	369	7	11	14	14	6	6	1	0
Camas	24	8.3	23 267	1 639	8	3	5	3	3	2	1	0	0
Canyon	2 824	2.8	19 432	2 667	1 568	246	410	538	506	183	209	48	33
Caribou	158	1.1	21 749	2 077	141	15	32	24	23	13	6	1	4
Cassia	525	4.3	24 324	1 300	268	111	96	82	77	33	30	7	4
Clark	25	-7.2	25 950	896	18	4	3	3	2	1	1	0	0
Clearwater	193	4.4	22 805	1 780	101	19	41	48	46	21	15	3	4

1. Based on the resident population estimated as of July 1 of the year shown.   2. Includes other labor income.   3. Kalawao County included with Maui County.

Table B. States and Counties — Earnings, Social Security, and Housing

STATE County	Earnings, 2002									Social Security beneficiaries, December 2003		Supplemental Security Income recipients, December 2003	Housing units, 2003	
	Total (mil dol)	Farm	Goods-related[1]		Service-related and health				Government	Number	Rate[2]		Total	Percent change, 2000-2003
			Total	Manufacturing	Information and professional and technical services	Retail trade	Finance, insurance, and real estate	Health services						
	75	76	77	78	79	80	81	82	83	84	85	86	87	88
GEORGIA—Cont'd														
Richmond	4 855	0.0	16.8	12.6	6.1	6.8	3.8	12.7	38.4	31 910	161	7 040	84 204	2.3
Rockdale	1 464	0.0	D	20.7	13.4	9.1	3.5	8.8	10.4	9 605	128	933	27 772	10.7
Schley	43	8.6	49.6	44.4	0.3	3.4	D	1.1	18.4	635	161	147	1 657	2.8
Screven	130	3.4	30.5	26.5	D	7.4	3.6	D	27.1	2 960	192	763	7 013	2.3
Seminole	102	15.1	D	12.9	D	8.3	3.8	14.3	17.4	2 150	232	480	4 837	2.0
Spalding	892	0.0	D	24.9	D	9.5	4.4	10.3	18.6	10 825	179	2 070	24 423	6.2
Stephens	397	2.4	D	30.8	3.5	9.1	4.1	D	16.7	5 880	233	1 065	12 057	3.5
Stewart	38	9.3	D	D	D	9.9	D	16.2	27.3	1 055	211	325	2 357	0.1
Sumter	518	8.1	D	21.3	4.3	6.6	3.2	11.4	21.8	5 395	162	1 411	13 975	2.0
Talbot	38	0.9	D	0.0	D	4.0	D	1.4	27.8	1 335	203	323	3 004	4.6
Taliaferro	8	14.5	D	D	0.0	D	D	D	54.0	450	230	117	1 106	1.9
Tattnall	239	22.7	4.5	0.9	2.6	6.3	3.1	D	34.4	3 660	164	956	8 673	1.1
Taylor	85	11.6	D	5.1	D	9.2	3.5	D	22.2	1 765	198	561	4 072	2.4
Telfair	109	4.5	D	D	2.2	7.9	3.4	D	30.6	2 635	229	635	5 145	1.2
Terrell	98	18.0	15.8	14.0	4.1	7.2	4.3	D	25.9	2 090	193	609	4 575	2.6
Thomas	816	1.2	D	17.8	D	7.9	4.9	D	17.3	8 830	202	2 264	18 836	3.0
Tift	749	4.2	21.5	15.2	5.4	8.3	3.4	9.9	23.1	6 540	165	1 594	15 881	3.0
Toombs	342	4.6	19.1	11.2	4.4	11.8	3.9	15.2	15.0	5 190	196	1 500	11 587	1.9
Towns	95	-0.1	D	2.3	6.5	9.4	8.0	D	16.1	3 105	314	225	6 956	10.7
Treutlen	37	3.7	D	D	D	9.4	4.4	D	37.9	1 350	194	373	2 916	1.8
Troup	1 291	0.0	D	34.0	5.2	11.7	4.0	D	16.0	10 865	180	2 219	25 201	5.8
Turner	95	20.4	10.7	7.9	D	8.8	5.5	3.8	22.3	1 810	189	471	3 982	1.7
Twiggs	83	5.2	D	D	D	2.5	D	2.5	18.2	2 115	202	390	4 390	2.3
Union	198	3.6	D	5.2	4.4	11.6	5.2	D	22.8	5 410	283	471	11 251	12.5
Upson	290	0.6	30.1	25.8	3.6	9.2	4.4	D	21.2	6 000	214	879	11 948	2.9
Walker	552	0.9	D	37.9	3.3	8.2	3.9	D	20.3	12 380	198	1 637	26 768	4.7
Walton	618	1.4	D	17.1	4.1	11.2	3.4	D	19.6	9 320	134	1 336	26 348	17.1
Ware	576	1.0	15.0	8.1	D	11.0	3.6	15.6	23.0	7 240	204	2 024	16 156	2.1
Warren	54	5.0	D	32.4	D	5.1	D	D	19.4	1 285	210	301	2 807	1.4
Washington	344	0.6	32.3	4.5	3.2	5.6	2.2	D	22.7	3 915	188	913	8 476	1.8
Wayne	356	0.9	34.7	27.6	2.3	9.9	1.8	D	31.6	4 975	181	949	11 084	2.4
Webster	18	38.0	D	D	D	3.7	D	0.3	25.3	440	192	88	1 138	2.1
Wheeler	40	12.4	D	D	D	3.8	D	D	28.4	1 055	160	282	2 487	1.6
White	232	6.8	27.6	15.1	3.0	13.3	5.8	2.5	19.2	4 600	202	424	10 507	11.1
Whitfield	2 504	0.3	43.3	40.8	13.1	6.5	3.1	7.7	8.8	13 640	155	1 777	32 986	7.4
Wilcox	66	30.8	5.4	2.4	D	4.8	D	6.6	32.4	1 535	175	418	3 373	1.6
Wilkes	128	4.8	27.8	24.1	D	8.1	4.0	5.5	23.1	2 525	237	536	5 098	1.5
Wilkinson	143	0.9	58.6	4.4	2.0	2.3	D	2.0	12.0	2 135	208	340	4 543	2.1
Worth	147	22.1	9.3	5.2	D	10.4	4.0	8.9	24.1	3 670	168	802	9 317	2.5
HAWAII	28 788	0.7	9.3	2.6	8.9	7.4	6.3	8.9	30.8	194 019	154	21 757	475 972	3.4
Hawaii	2 508	2.4	D	3.3	D	9.0	D	10.1	21.8	27 690	175	3 544	66 896	6.7
Honolulu	22 415	0.3	7.9	2.1	9.9	6.7	6.4	9.0	34.2	136 730	151	15 918	322 845	2.2
Kalawao	(4)	(4)	(4)	(4)	(4)	(4)	(4)	(4)	(4)	0	NA	1	170	-1.2
Kauai	1 077	1.5	D	1.4	D	10.4	D	D	20.3	10 445	172	862	26 514	4.7
Maui	(4)2 788	(4)2.1	(4)D	(4)6.9	(4)5.6	(4)10.0	(4)5.2	(4)D	(4)15.0	19 145	141	1 418	59 547	5.6
IDAHO	25 224	4.5	21.9	13.5	9.7	8.3	5.9	8.9	18.5	211 528	155	20 279	564 474	6.9
Ada	9 368	0.4	26.2	17.9	9.8	7.3	8.4	9.9	14.0	40 330	124	3 824	131 303	10.8
Adams	37	1.2	D	D	D	7.8	D	0.7	39.2	975	277	50	2 140	8.0
Bannock	1 193	0.7	D	10.5	6.9	9.1	5.8	10.5	28.3	10 125	134	1 462	29 903	2.8
Bear Lake	54	12.7	8.4	3.9	D	12.2	4.2	3.9	36.4	1 240	197	83	3 419	4.6
Benewah	141	2.2	D	16.9	4.2	6.7	1.3	D	29.3	2 010	223	199	4 290	1.2
Bingham	569	15.1	D	16.2	2.5	6.0	2.5	4.0	26.6	6 480	151	641	14 704	2.8
Blaine	627	0.7	23.9	2.9	13.6	8.5	10.8	5.3	8.0	2 135	103	41	13 129	7.7
Boise	52	0.7	D	4.3	D	4.6	D	D	41.2	1 120	155	48	4 551	4.6
Bonner	488	0.7	24.1	13.5	7.3	15.7	6.2	6.3	17.6	7 685	196	587	19 619	-0.1
Bonneville	1 702	1.7	12.6	4.5	23.5	9.6	4.3	12.7	13.9	12 845	148	1 450	32 539	6.7
Boundary	125	6.7	19.5	13.9	6.2	7.2	1.5	11.9	29.0	2 080	204	214	4 214	2.9
Butte	375	1.3	D	D	D	0.5	D	1.1	2.1	640	223	54	1 287	-0.2
Camas	11	25.2	D	D	D	D	D	D	33.0	170	162	8	649	8.0
Canyon	1 814	5.4	30.6	20.6	4.9	9.3	4.2	10.4	14.2	20 865	138	2 817	55 332	15.4
Caribou	156	6.8	D	D	2.2	5.0	1.4	1.7	14.5	1 275	178	56	3 234	1.4
Cassia	380	25.4	17.6	10.1	3.5	10.6	2.9	D	15.4	3 625	168	349	7 980	1.5
Clark	22	25.5	D	D	D	D	2.8	D	27.5	120	133	8	527	1.2
Clearwater	120	0.5	13.3	6.5	3.4	7.3	3.2	9.8	38.5	2 235	266	196	4 252	2.6

1. Covers mining, construction, and manufacturing.　　2. Per 1,000 resident population estimated as of July 1 of the year shown.　　4. Kalawao County included with Maui County.

STATE County	Housing units, 2000								Civilian labor force, 2003		Unemployment		Civilian employment,[6] 2000		
	Occupied units													Percent	
		Owner-occupied				Renter-occupied									
				Median owner cost as a percent of income											
	Total	Percent	Median value[1]	With a mortgage	Without a mortgage[2]	Median rent[3]	Median rent as a percent of income	Substandard units[4] (percent)	Total	Percent change, 2002–2003	Total	Rate[5]	Total	Management, professional and related occupations	Production, transportation, and material moving occupations
	89	90	91	92	93	94	95	96	97	98	99	100	101	102	103
GEORGIA—Cont'd															
Richmond	73 920	57.9	76 800	21.5	9.9	505	25.8	5.7	84 447	3.9	4 570	5.4	78 906	30.5	16.0
Rockdale	24 052	74.5	118 000	19.9	9.9	757	24.3	4.3	40 423	2.9	1 850	4.6	33 611	33.6	14.6
Schley	1 435	76.3	57 400	21.8	12.0	358	22.8	4.3	1 835	6.3	88	4.8	1 582	26.0	28.1
Screven	5 797	77.7	64 600	21.3	11.8	341	26.4	5.8	5 646	5.7	365	6.5	5 941	21.7	28.8
Seminole	3 573	80.8	58 600	19.7	11.4	362	26.5	5.8	4 685	3.0	193	4.1	3 609	22.0	24.2
Spalding	21 519	62.8	86 600	21.1	10.1	537	25.6	5.2	29 172	2.7	1 953	6.7	25 438	22.5	24.6
Stephens	9 951	72.7	80 900	21.6	11.5	422	24.1	2.8	12 008	-0.7	804	6.7	12 018	23.2	27.2
Stewart	2 007	72.5	44 000	18.0	10.3	245	21.8	9.3	2 456	14.4	153	6.2	1 904	24.8	25.8
Sumter	12 025	63.9	66 900	19.9	9.9	399	23.5	8.0	14 579	2.1	858	5.9	14 174	29.9	20.0
Talbot	2 538	82.7	57 700	18.9	11.4	307	26.1	5.6	2 890	-0.9	165	5.7	2 533	21.2	34.2
Taliaferro	870	77.1	40 300	18.6	9.9	285	31.5	7.8	822	5.1	64	7.8	757	17.6	36.1
Tattnall	7 057	70.5	67 300	19.7	12.0	338	23.1	7.5	6 942	3.6	312	4.5	7 996	23.3	16.7
Taylor	3 281	76.8	56 300	19.3	11.9	302	26.7	5.5	3 627	0.9	179	4.9	3 051	22.5	24.3
Telfair	4 140	78.3	47 600	19.5	11.6	311	23.7	4.3	4 139	8.8	349	8.4	4 148	22.2	31.5
Terrell	4 002	66.3	59 300	22.1	11.7	314	24.6	9.3	4 093	3.4	284	6.9	4 183	23.6	28.4
Thomas	16 309	70.0	76 900	20.7	11.2	446	23.3	5.0	22 816	1.6	878	3.8	17 983	32.0	17.7
Tift	13 919	67.2	82 600	19.1	9.9	431	23.0	5.9	21 028	3.3	779	3.7	17 008	26.5	19.8
Toombs	9 877	65.5	66 400	20.5	9.9	393	24.7	6.2	11 835	4.4	805	6.8	10 987	27.0	17.6
Towns	3 998	85.2	127 500	22.8	9.9	435	26.0	2.2	5 033	10.2	126	2.5	3 703	27.7	11.0
Treutlen	2 531	74.9	56 600	22.8	9.9	309	24.3	4.9	2 999	4.8	188	6.3	2 307	25.5	16.7
Troup	21 920	64.5	83 700	19.5	11.1	482	24.0	4.4	31 075	2.5	1 763	5.7	26 669	27.6	23.4
Turner	3 435	71.4	57 600	19.9	13.6	347	24.3	5.5	4 537	1.1	372	8.2	3 930	23.7	25.8
Twiggs	3 832	82.7	61 800	18.0	12.0	390	19.4	6.7	4 508	3.2	233	5.2	4 203	15.4	23.7
Union	7 159	82.3	111 100	22.8	9.9	389	24.5	2.1	9 453	6.8	319	3.4	7 198	22.4	18.6
Upson	10 722	69.9	66 100	20.3	10.7	414	23.9	3.5	10 475	-2.3	697	6.7	11 529	23.0	29.5
Walker	23 605	77.0	71 200	21.0	9.9	441	24.0	3.1	32 209	3.7	1 110	3.4	27 753	20.9	27.1
Walton	21 307	76.5	113 300	21.2	9.9	558	25.0	4.3	32 744	2.8	1 372	4.2	29 353	25.2	16.6
Ware	13 475	70.3	56 700	19.5	10.9	401	24.7	4.4	15 863	6.0	707	4.5	13 798	24.5	18.9
Warren	2 435	76.8	48 700	19.2	13.7	317	26.3	6.0	2 349	-5.1	292	12.4	2 339	20.4	36.0
Washington	7 435	74.1	66 900	21.2	10.8	342	25.3	7.4	9 270	1.5	510	5.5	7 804	22.8	22.8
Wayne	9 324	76.5	71 200	18.0	9.9	371	22.1	5.6	11 614	3.2	554	4.8	10 188	24.3	20.2
Webster	911	81.4	49 300	17.2	9.9	282	19.4	6.0	1 191	10.2	55	4.6	985	23.2	30.5
Wheeler	2 011	77.4	49 800	18.4	12.6	249	25.4	5.8	2 093	11.3	144	6.9	2 081	23.4	26.8
White	7 731	79.3	114 000	24.0	9.9	525	27.0	3.4	10 025	4.0	317	3.2	9 668	25.4	16.2
Whitfield	29 385	67.6	91 800	18.7	9.9	484	20.7	9.9	51 044	4.6	1 653	3.2	39 593	21.9	34.1
Wilcox	2 785	79.9	51 400	19.5	10.4	298	25.5	5.2	3 443	3.1	202	5.9	2 964	24.9	22.5
Wilkes	4 314	75.5	65 100	22.5	12.7	359	25.8	4.1	4 967	-2.2	398	8.0	4 547	20.9	28.2
Wilkinson	3 827	82.3	61 500	21.3	9.9	366	19.6	5.3	4 346	1.5	243	5.6	4 123	22.0	20.3
Worth	8 106	76.2	68 000	21.0	9.9	367	23.5	5.9	9 722	9.5	491	5.1	9 343	22.8	22.9
HAWAII	403 240	56.5	272 700	26.3	9.9	779	27.2	16.1	618 310	1.9	26 512	4.3	537 909	32.2	8.9
Hawaii	52 985	64.5	153 700	24.7	9.9	645	26.7	14.9	75 369	3.1	4 718	6.3	64 979	30.2	8.9
Honolulu	286 450	54.5	309 000	26.4	9.9	802	27.5	16.4	436 442	1.7	16 901	3.9	383 148	33.8	8.8
Kalawao	115	0.0	0	0.0	0.0	525	17.5	0.0	NA	NA	NA	NA	58	0.0	25.9
Kauai	20 183	61.3	216 100	26.0	9.9	739	25.8	13.0	30 761	3.7	1 534	5.0	26 789	29.0	9.1
Maui	43 507	57.5	249 900	27.9	9.9	788	25.5	17.1	75 738	1.8	3 359	4.4	62 935	26.3	9.4
IDAHO	469 645	72.4	106 300	21.5	9.9	515	25.3	5.4	692 543	1.0	37 440	5.4	599 453	31.4	14.2
Ada	113 408	70.7	124 700	21.1	9.9	617	26.3	3.8	177 174	-0.7	8 272	4.7	156 634	38.2	10.2
Adams	1 421	79.0	88 800	23.9	9.9	395	26.6	3.2	1 830	14.8	259	14.2	1 403	27.7	12.9
Bannock	27 192	70.6	90 000	20.0	9.9	443	26.4	4.3	40 604	-0.7	2 107	5.2	35 641	32.3	13.1
Bear Lake	2 259	83.2	72 600	20.3	10.0	345	23.0	5.0	4 237	7.6	160	5.2	2 482	25.9	17.8
Benewah	3 580	78.4	89 000	21.5	9.9	380	22.1	6.6	4 237	-0.6	429	10.1	3 472	21.4	22.8
Bingham	13 317	79.4	84 400	19.5	9.9	411	24.7	6.7	22 636	3.0	977	4.3	17 841	28.7	18.2
Blaine	7 780	68.7	288 800	25.5	9.9	740	25.4	5.2	12 497	3.3	502	4.0	10 846	35.6	5.9
Boise	2 616	83.3	126 000	23.9	9.9	495	22.3	6.8	2 679	-1.3	176	6.6	3 088	33.1	12.2
Bonner	14 693	77.8	124 500	24.2	11.2	518	27.6	6.8	17 906	0.0	1 355	7.6	15 890	26.8	17.0
Bonneville	28 753	74.7	93 500	19.5	9.9	485	25.2	5.0	49 932	3.0	1 669	3.3	38 309	36.0	11.1
Boundary	3 707	78.4	96 900	23.7	9.9	452	22.8	6.7	4 456	1.4	386	8.7	3 875	25.1	20.8
Butte	1 089	77.1	68 700	18.2	10.1	335	27.9	6.1	1 593	3.7	76	4.8	1 226	36.7	12.0
Camas	396	77.8	86 400	24.5	10.6	477	21.3	4.0	482	14.8	32	6.6	499	29.5	13.8
Canyon	45 018	73.3	96 300	22.3	9.9	509	24.1	7.7	70 399	-0.5	4 741	6.7	59 634	26.1	19.1
Caribou	2 560	79.5	80 400	18.5	9.9	398	18.8	3.9	3 293	0.7	235	7.1	2 981	27.9	17.6
Cassia	7 060	72.6	83 100	20.5	9.9	403	23.1	8.4	9 938	1.5	662	6.7	8 942	26.2	19.4
Clark	340	68.2	64 600	18.9	10.1	347	18.2	15.0	615	11.4	29	4.7	448	21.7	19.0
Clearwater	3 456	77.9	80 500	20.4	9.9	396	22.6	3.2	3 753	0.6	373	9.9	3 270	25.0	17.8

1. Specified owner-occupied units.   2. Median monthly owner costs is often in the minimum category—9.9 percent or less, which is indicated as 9.9 percent.   3. Specified renter-occupied units.   4. Overcrowded or lacking complete plumbing facilities.   5. Percent of civilian labor force.   6. Persons 16 years old and over.

Table B. States and Counties — Nonfarm Employment and Agriculture

	Private nonfarm establishments, employment and payroll, 2001									Agriculture, 2002			
	Employment						Annual payroll		Farms			
											Percent with—		
STATE County	Number of establish-ments	Total	Health care and social assistance	Manufac-turing	Retail trade	Finance and insurance	Professional, scientific, and technical services	Total (mil dol)	Average per employee (dollars)	Number	Less than 50 acres	500 acres and over	Farm operators whose principal occupation is farming (percent)
	104	105	106	107	108	109	110	111	112	113	114	115	116
GEORGIA—Cont'd													
Richmond	4 465	85 931	18 784	11 293	12 687	2 742	2 744	2 343	27 261	140	58.6	1.4	49.3
Rockdale	2 034	33 748	3 292	6 718	5 184	648	1 208	1 003	29 735	140	70.7	1.4	38.6
Schley	61	1 021	D	638	89	D	D	23	22 384	115	13.0	20.9	34.8
Screven	240	2 716	284	1 018	511	94	35	55	20 135	347	15.6	23.9	42.9
Seminole	189	1 518	418	56	416	77	24	31	20 107	206	22.8	21.8	63.1
Spalding	1 189	18 822	3 031	5 290	3 354	605	354	447	23 768	249	47.0	3.2	40.6
Stephens	607	9 494	1 094	3 613	1 249	242	141	232	24 399	238	52.1	1.3	60.9
Stewart	89	804	199	182	165	38	D	15	18 774	85	12.9	31.8	50.6
Sumter	699	12 047	2 765	2 687	1 902	427	143	279	23 130	381	27.0	21.3	56.7
Talbot	62	521	D	D	56	D	9	12	22 104	160	23.1	16.9	49.4
Taliaferro	20	60	D	D	10	0	D	1	15 367	73	11.0	19.2	43.8
Tattnall	296	2 809	491	62	584	180	62	52	18 540	644	35.2	7.5	50.9
Taylor	136	1 308	291	130	241	13	15	29	22 092	227	13.2	18.1	45.8
Telfair	242	3 639	416	1 916	386	96	41	53	14 474	304	18.1	12.5	46.1
Terrell	190	2 199	222	973	365	79	37	43	19 436	239	18.4	29.7	53.6
Thomas	1 064	18 142	2 860	3 945	2 296	466	295	455	25 088	510	33.7	16.7	48.8
Tift	1 158	17 308	2 383	3 713	2 417	475	411	417	24 102	398	41.7	11.3	48.7
Toombs	706	9 720	1 372	2 022	1 733	311	197	197	20 255	382	20.4	12.3	51.0
Towns	290	1 874	93	89	379	127	46	40	21 471	148	56.1	0.7	46.6
Treutlen	90	786	197	134	161	35	D	11	13 588	182	31.9	12.6	40.7
Troup	1 421	31 760	3 277	10 020	3 650	620	438	918	28 919	294	29.9	10.5	49.0
Turner	170	1 760	131	219	226	95	22	31	17 867	282	22.3	18.1	54.3
Twiggs	90	1 346	122	D	147	D	17	17	33 410	119	40.3	16.8	52.9
Union	487	3 915	662	354	737	155	144	82	20 940	330	57.3	1.5	48.2
Upson	494	7 766	1 320	3 350	962	265	101	175	22 528	291	40.2	7.2	45.7
Walker	904	16 130	1 258	6 741	2 028	392	1 157	374	23 185	642	38.6	4.2	48.4
Walton	1 270	12 273	1 182	2 119	1 686	549	377	313	25 465	679	51.3	2.2	46.7
Ware	981	12 328	2 981	1 502	2 705	413	212	259	21 049	323	42.4	10.8	55.4
Warren	76	1 365	179	779	132	32	7	30	22 018	165	26.1	16.4	53.3
Washington	390	6 636	823	635	895	198	150	186	27 961	411	29.4	16.5	41.1
Wayne	526	7 403	1 649	1 639	1 568	158	107	173	23 346	341	39.3	7.0	47.2
Webster	23	295	D	D	39	0	0	6	20 959	98	4.1	30.6	67.3
Wheeler	75	1 013	228	D	94	D	D	20	19 546	156	12.8	26.9	55.1
White	602	4 428	291	627	1 012	168	130	104	23 581	376	58.0	2.1	57.7
Whitfield	2 546	54 520	3 536	23 328	7 384	890	868	1 539	28 228	418	45.2	2.4	47.1
Wilcox	105	640	123	137	172	50	0	11	17 861	311	28.9	16.1	60.8
Wilkes	266	3 200	364	1 327	397	87	54	74	23 060	349	22.1	12.9	53.6
Wilkinson	163	2 911	109	1 449	143	63	32	97	33 271	127	32.3	10.2	37.0
Worth	295	2 382	473	219	518	108	D	48	20 275	487	35.1	20.5	49.7
HAWAII	30 175	441 856	51 024	15 221	64 822	18 104	19 500	12 684	28 707	5 398	88.0	3.1	57.9
Hawaii	3 688	46 711	5 591	1 662	8 104	954	1 338	1 168	24 995	3 216	87.9	2.9	56.9
Honolulu	20 801	320 461	38 942	11 549	43 687	15 971	16 596	9 624	30 033	794	91.4	2.4	69.9
Kalawao	NA	NA	NA	NA	NA	NA	NA	NA	NA	NA	NA	NA	NA
Kauai	1 731	20 529	2 255	276	3 827	392	553	486	23 650	565	84.8	4.8	54.2
Maui	3 955	54 155	4 236	1 734	9 204	787	1 013	1 407	25 975	823	87.1	3.6	52.7
IDAHO	37 622	467 316	56 537	66 507	71 669	17 676	29 655	12 358	26 444	25 017	49.2	18.0	55.4
Ada	10 275	161 511	18 547	20 512	20 041	8 239	7 885	4 946	30 621	1 420	76.4	4.9	45.3
Adams	104	580	D	D	117	25	D	16	26 919	316	42.4	25.0	55.4
Bannock	1 868	25 310	3 654	3 331	4 625	1 488	1 577	608	24 037	1 030	58.9	15.3	43.3
Bear Lake	131	906	217	71	280	57	D	16	17 285	424	30.7	22.9	55.7
Benewah	276	2 470	487	D	269	47	D	65	26 508	241	32.4	24.5	55.2
Bingham	774	9 757	1 228	2 322	1 558	227	222	212	21 721	1 273	56.2	19.6	55.4
Blaine	1 309	10 743	495	356	1 437	267	741	296	27 577	224	48.2	24.6	62.9
Boise	121	507	D	D	93	0	D	9	17 963	89	47.2	15.7	49.4
Bonner	1 266	10 517	1 026	1 709	2 202	256	363	267	25 367	743	59.6	3.6	52.5
Bonneville	2 661	37 947	5 004	2 469	6 081	1 110	9 204	1 170	30 826	963	55.9	17.7	50.6
Boundary	336	2 273	216	396	342	62	D	52	22 934	432	54.9	9.0	52.8
Butte	69	331	D	D	89	27	D	6	18 039	197	28.4	29.4	65.5
Camas	20	89	D	D	D	D	0	1	13 989	106	17.0	41.5	67.0
Canyon	3 063	42 147	4 821	11 508	5 923	898	923	1 061	25 169	2 233	70.1	6.2	51.8
Caribou	188	2 062	179	D	428	43	D	72	35 115	490	23.9	36.7	60.4
Cassia	595	6 318	890	1 137	1 195	221	166	135	21 289	692	37.6	34.2	64.5
Clark	14	101	D	0	D	D	0	2	16 970	85	21.2	54.1	69.4
Clearwater	253	1 644	333	186	270	49	D	41	24 765	193	32.6	21.2	50.8

Table B. States and Counties — **Agriculture**

Agriculture, 2002 (cont'd)

STATE County	Land in farms — Acreage (1,000)	Percent change, 1997-2002	Acres — Average size of farm	Total irrigated (1,000)	Total cropland (1,000)	Value of land and buildings (dollars) — Average per farm	Average per acre	Value of machinery and equipment average per farm (dollars)	Value of products sold — Total (mil dol)	Average per farm (dollars)	Percent from — Crops	Live-stock and poultry products	Percent of farms with sales of — $10,000 or more	$100,000 or more	Government payments — Total ($1,000)	Percent of farms
	117	118	119	120	121	122	123	124	125	126	127	128	129	130	131	132
GEORGIA—Cont'd																
Richmond	12	-20.0	89	0	5	255 709	2 917	26 417	3	22 312	54.0	46.0	28.6	4.3	15	9.3
Rockdale	9	-25.0	63	0	3	387 949	5 718	28 266	1	6 083	45.2	54.8	12.1	0.7	67	10.7
Schley	35	-14.6	308	0	13	484 589	1 586	64 822	10	83 984	15.3	84.7	27.0	8.7	304	48.7
Screven	184	11.5	531	12	87	653 203	1 355	82 840	19	54 162	85.7	14.3	32.3	10.1	2 245	55.9
Seminole	93	-13.1	451	21	56	688 023	1 547	103 321	24	116 683	82.0	18.0	55.8	17.5	1 461	49.0
Spalding	26	-3.7	103	0	9	458 587	4 594	25 558	4	17 781	15.0	85.0	14.5	1.6	108	14.5
Stephens	20	0.0	82	0	8	365 486	4 447	45 813	44	186 646	0.5	99.5	26.9	14.7	72	17.6
Stewart	34	-39.3	398	0	13	540 468	1 406	70 915	4	47 291	51.5	48.5	32.9	9.4	205	45.9
Sumter	167	-10.2	437	28	84	615 227	1 421	80 546	49	128 331	64.8	35.2	36.7	15.7	3 119	47.2
Talbot	45	25.0	283	D	8	507 676	1 705	26 395	2	10 149	20.0	80.0	21.9	1.3	130	27.5
Taliaferro	19	18.8	254	D	6	374 849	1 666	35 060	3	42 007	2.7	97.3	28.8	8.2	122	24.7
Tattnall	143	4.4	223	12	58	423 199	1 987	51 861	139	216 203	29.9	70.1	41.9	22.7	936	31.7
Taylor	75	7.1	328	5	30	458 157	1 611	49 987	24	107 681	42.2	57.8	30.0	9.7	660	48.0
Telfair	73	-15.1	240	6	27	333 103	1 561	47 890	8	24 889	83.9	16.1	29.6	6.6	683	59.5
Terrell	123	-11.5	516	22	69	693 983	1 356	73 879	19	81 010	97.0	3.0	35.1	14.2	2 434	72.8
Thomas	198	10.0	389	7	63	557 480	1 548	70 316	26	51 734	71.4	28.6	37.8	10.8	2 299	37.5
Tift	98	-7.5	246	22	55	474 179	2 035	74 966	45	113 404	94.4	5.6	42.2	13.8	2 298	42.7
Toombs	93	-7.0	243	10	37	423 022	1 528	74 210	33	86 752	82.3	17.7	31.2	9.7	783	40.8
Towns	11	22.2	74	0	4	321 082	3 878	25 765	2	13 529	33.4	66.7	14.9	3.4	21	14.9
Treutlen	35	-16.7	191	1	11	322 408	1 371	31 228	4	19 803	84.8	15.2	14.8	3.8	249	48.9
Troup	61	41.9	208	D	14	386 340	1 625	23 180	3	10 381	22.8	77.2	18.0	1.4	168	18.0
Turner	98	0.0	348	20	64	592 259	1 619	104 510	35	124 830	68.5	31.5	54.6	15.6	1 764	60.6
Twiggs	40	53.8	338	3	12	512 579	1 451	50 006	2	19 323	76.9	23.1	20.2	3.4	458	29.4
Union	25	13.6	75	0	10	391 506	5 435	26 168	16	48 194	26.4	73.6	27.0	3.0	168	17.6
Upson	47	23.7	160	1	13	374 209	2 235	38 773	14	46 448	10.3	89.7	17.5	4.5	196	26.8
Walker	82	-4.7	127	0	34	341 389	2 554	24 448	34	53 652	3.4	96.6	21.3	6.5	379	19.0
Walton	66	10.0	97	1	27	515 694	6 507	30 760	32	47 330	24.5	75.5	20.5	7.8	304	25.3
Ware	65	1.6	202	4	19	320 369	1 523	36 226	23	69 819	41.2	58.8	30.3	7.4	274	24.5
Warren	48	9.1	291	D	14	438 688	1 352	31 541	4	27 263	8.3	91.7	23.0	5.5	269	38.8
Washington	124	11.7	302	8	47	403 789	1 537	51 517	16	37 870	76.7	23.3	19.5	5.6	742	42.3
Wayne	64	-1.5	189	3	26	404 749	1 794	52 026	16	47 975	55.2	44.8	29.6	8.2	424	30.8
Webster	66	13.8	676	3	33	1 017 604	1 430	118 547	9	89 272	79.8	20.2	49.0	27.6	775	60.2
Wheeler	60	-15.5	383	4	17	419 757	1 214	58 778	10	63 829	95.2	4.8	25.6	8.3	338	54.5
White	30	15.4	81	0	13	459 943	6 020	35 159	73	195 320	1.6	98.4	42.3	25.8	206	15.7
Whitfield	43	10.3	104	0	20	401 085	2 460	46 700	74	177 383	1.3	98.7	25.4	12.0	88	11.2
Wilcox	102	-17.1	329	15	53	424 592	1 313	102 277	48	154 308	41.9	58.1	37.3	14.5	2 140	56.6
Wilkes	99	4.2	284	0	30	495 592	1 743	40 014	21	60 717	8.2	91.8	28.9	8.0	410	36.1
Wilkinson	31	10.7	241	0	8	299 680	1 382	25 889	1	9 115	68.1	31.9	15.0	0.8	208	18.1
Worth	179	-6.3	368	23	110	563 924	1 558	109 602	38	79 035	80.8	19.2	37.0	17.0	4 353	51.7
HAWAII	1 300	-9.7	241	69	211	842 875	3 507	35 568	533	98 819	83.5	16.5	43.7	9.0	886	2.1
Hawaii	821	-5.6	255	9	91	724 308	2 822	23 981	188	58 375	76.7	23.3	41.8	7.4	397	1.3
Honolulu	71	-11.3	89	14	29	738 577	8 358	37 543	179	225 845	83.1	16.9	58.2	17.1	60	1.8
Kalawao	NA	NA	NA	NA	NA	NA	NA	NA	NA	NA	NA	NA	NA	NA	NA	NA
Kauai	152	-22.8	269	20	31	1 068 439	3 989	66 074	42	74 080	85.4	14.6	35.0	6.0	165	5.0
Maui	257	-12.0	312	27	61	1 251 598	4 112	58 849	125	151 289	93.7	6.3	43.3	9.5	264	3.4
IDAHO	11 767	-0.5	470	3 289	6 153	613 303	1 270	91 746	3 908	156 224	45.7	54.3	37.2	15.6	93 934	28.4
Ada	223	-3.5	157	71	75	496 948	3 471	44 795	127	89 246	33.9	66.1	21.6	7.1	1 201	9.2
Adams	196	-2.0	622	25	36	335 413	568	42 670	8	25 191	10.1	89.9	24.4	4.7	224	12.7
Bannock	357	15.5	347	55	237	273 174	731	46 676	32	31 259	74.5	25.5	19.1	5.0	3 986	26.9
Bear Lake	212	-4.5	499	43	113	409 502	790	69 509	13	30 544	25.4	74.6	37.3	9.9	1 585	44.6
Benewah	138	9.5	572	0	92	617 245	1 212	73 249	14	59 804	95.6	4.4	24.9	12.4	860	35.7
Bingham	821	3.1	645	323	390	832 438	1 151	144 797	269	211 224	73.6	26.4	40.7	19.4	5 838	26.9
Blaine	226	5.1	1 009	40	53	1 271 837	1 304	72 071	19	85 818	43.6	56.4	40.6	16.5	709	25.4
Boise	50	11.1	563	2	6	545 144	1 010	25 083	3	28 710	72.7	27.3	20.2	4.5	D	D
Bonner	91	-8.1	122	2	33	399 591	2 909	22 952	7	9 623	61.7	38.3	13.7	1.6	117	3.0
Bonneville	478	6.5	496	142	333	559 753	1 303	86 224	119	123 717	75.1	24.9	30.3	12.4	6 010	32.2
Boundary	77	5.5	177	3	48	485 079	2 391	69 156	23	52 829	87.5	12.5	27.8	8.8	312	10.2
Butte	121	-6.9	616	58	65	593 220	879	80 485	49	246 582	21.7	78.3	56.3	20.8	545	48.7
Camas	134	4.7	1 266	17	84	882 029	697	140 652	6	60 037	84.8	15.2	45.3	16.0	567	43.4
Canyon	272	-23.4	122	206	203	464 797	4 219	78 116	269	120 443	49.7	50.3	33.0	12.7	2 359	14.0
Caribou	427	-9.0	871	67	225	619 359	676	99 535	42	85 191	D	D	41.6	21.8	4 310	51.8
Cassia	744	13.2	1 076	262	422	1 087 864	986	207 676	383	552 789	37.5	62.5	61.0	31.9	8 285	39.7
Clark	178	-17.2	2 092	31	42	1 337 246	647	147 264	28	330 124	88.2	11.8	50.6	23.5	747	38.8
Clearwater	71	-2.7	366	0	38	442 562	1 285	36 663	6	29 250	67.5	32.5	29.0	6.7	586	29.5

Table B. States and Counties — Residential Construction, Wholesale Trade, Retail Trade, and Real Estate

STATE County	Value of residential construction authorized by building permits, 2003		Wholesale trade, 1997				Retail trade,[1] 1997				Real estate and rental and leasing, 1997			
	New construction ($1,000)	Number of housing units	Number of establishments	Number of employees	Sales (mil dol)	Annual payroll (mil dol)	Number of establishments	Number of employees	Sales (mil dol)	Annual payroll (mil dol)	Number of establishments	Number of employees	Receipts (mil dol)	Annual payroll (mil dol)
	133	134	135	136	137	138	139	140	141	142	143	144	145	146
GEORGIA—Cont'd														
Richmond	90 758	888	245	2 262	756.9	68.8	912	12 332	1 909.9	189.3	223	1 064	114.0	20.4
Rockdale	122 567	903	124	1 267	1 230.4	47.3	281	4 411	766.0	71.4	58	250	36.6	4.9
Schley	380	2	9	57	21.5	1.5	14	96	9.9	1.1	1	D	D	D
Screven	140	1	8	41	9.8	0.7	56	483	82.1	7.0	7	7	0.6	0.1
Seminole	999	12	14	182	83.0	2.0	61	413	71.5	5.4	5	13	1.0	0.1
Spalding	53 127	506	49	611	338.5	18.4	248	3 119	521.5	52.1	47	170	13.9	2.5
Stephens	9 398	77	28	222	50.8	5.1	121	1 247	203.9	17.8	14	31	4.7	0.5
Stewart	463	8	5	39	9.7	1.2	26	133	14.5	1.3	2	D	D	D
Sumter	8 920	77	42	430	168.9	11.0	162	1 984	283.9	28.1	23	62	6.3	1.0
Talbot	0	0	2	D	D	D	13	68	7.1	0.7	NA	NA	NA	NA
Taliaferro	NA	NA	2	D	D	D	4	D	D	D	1	D	D	D
Tattnall	4 455	52	19	389	58.4	7.3	78	581	76.2	6.7	6	10	1.0	0.1
Taylor	3 853	33	7	D	D	D	36	227	36.5	2.8	4	3	0.4	0.0
Telfair	65	2	14	237	53.6	4.5	60	407	49.5	4.9	3	7	0.8	0.1
Terrell	1 917	28	17	198	125.8	4.3	57	321	55.3	4.2	2	D	D	D
Thomas	34 691	306	64	701	293.0	21.0	256	2 661	395.8	39.0	32	135	15.9	2.6
Tift	13 120	129	88	1 117	459.4	26.6	260	2 500	440.4	36.1	37	127	11.4	1.7
Toombs	8 802	126	39	333	203.6	8.4	152	1 706	253.7	23.1	17	67	5.7	0.9
Towns	30 383	239	7	D	D	D	52	289	42.4	3.9	13	22	2.6	0.3
Treutlen	0	0	2	D	D	D	23	111	14.2	1.3	3	5	0.2	0.0
Troup	43 969	459	69	681	270.8	22.6	293	3 500	526.0	52.7	45	175	18.9	3.4
Turner	1 149	9	16	230	203.8	5.8	54	316	58.3	4.4	6	40	4.4	0.6
Twiggs	4 693	36	3	D	D	D	14	116	17.2	1.6	2	D	D	D
Union	66 244	517	15	92	37.3	2.1	75	592	101.8	8.2	16	22	3.7	0.3
Upson	10 931	113	17	112	17.0	1.4	121	1 119	174.5	14.5	12	39	3.3	0.5
Walker	43 016	439	58	D	D	D	180	1 515	240.1	22.4	22	67	4.5	0.9
Walton	152 792	1 460	45	322	239.9	10.4	162	1 567	247.6	25.0	35	108	12.7	1.4
Ware	10 444	93	62	493	169.4	10.4	226	2 628	390.1	35.8	26	131	14.9	2.1
Warren	170	1	3	6	0.8	0.1	22	128	12.5	1.9	1	D	D	D
Washington	518	7	24	157	37.8	4.0	108	925	139.3	13.2	12	26	3.4	0.4
Wayne	1 352	17	17	159	50.7	3.9	125	1 145	172.5	16.6	9	57	2.6	0.5
Webster	NA	NA	2	D	D	D	8	80	7.6	0.8	NA	NA	NA	NA
Wheeler	30	1	3	D	D	D	13	64	11.1	0.7	1	D	D	D
White	42 493	339	12	110	23.6	1.8	139	1 028	230.4	18.3	20	36	4.4	0.5
Whitfield	58 416	627	340	4 254	3 475.7	122.9	508	5 908	1 068.1	103.7	87	365	61.3	8.2
Wilcox	0	0	5	D	D	D	30	138	20.1	1.8	2	D	D	D
Wilkes	2 735	25	18	138	61.5	3.1	65	414	56.3	5.2	3	6	0.5	0.1
Wilkinson	NA	NA	7	125	24.8	3.3	29	190	29.5	2.3	NA	NA	NA	NA
Worth	3 550	31	32	308	118.7	7.9	62	461	101.5	8.1	10	24	2.2	0.3
HAWAII	1 316 090	7 284	1 872	18 532	7 147.5	576.0	5 088	64 218	11 317.8	1 161.8	1 753	12 446	1 824.1	311.9
Hawaii	411 542	2 180	179	1 362	457.3	35.9	688	7 587	1 183.1	128.5	211	1 838	196.9	39.0
Honolulu	589 007	3 473	1 463	15 423	6 079.9	487.0	3 269	44 960	8 264.7	823.6	1 221	7 746	1 219.9	208.4
Kalawao	NA	NA	NA	NA	NA	NA	NA	NA	NA	NA	NA	NA	NA	NA
Kauai	149 644	543	64	423	176.7	11.9	326	3 427	510.7	59.0	108	1 166	131.7	24.8
Maui	165 896	1 088	166	1 324	433.6	41.2	805	8 244	1 359.3	150.7	213	1 696	275.6	39.7
IDAHO	1 942 662	15 091	1 980	22 828	10 127.8	628.0	5 848	63 732	11 649.6	1 079.7	1 236	4 870	450.3	73.9
Ada	706 833	4 679	578	7 610	5 362.7	273.5	1 264	16 663	3 163.2	300.9	379	1 860	197.1	33.5
Adams	9 400	56	1	D	D	D	16	81	13.4	0.9	1	D	D	D
Bannock	41 576	401	104	935	282.6	25.2	343	4 177	705.7	65.1	64	255	23.5	3.5
Bear Lake	7 587	68	3	88	20.2	1.5	34	271	40.2	3.3	7	60	1.2	0.4
Benewah	2 361	21	8	52	17.6	1.2	41	313	50.2	4.9	4	17	0.9	0.3
Bingham	19 524	184	54	974	189.4	18.0	125	1 363	243.8	22.0	14	44	1.8	0.4
Blaine	117 592	285	41	301	172.3	12.3	189	1 372	226.9	26.3	73	292	31.0	4.9
Boise	9 986	113	NA	NA	NA	NA	18	65	6.6	0.5	NA	NA	NA	NA
Bonner	5 661	81	37	256	69.8	6.2	200	2 325	573.8	41.5	46	170	14.4	2.9
Bonneville	81 613	948	181	2 484	808.0	63.2	480	5 615	933.4	90.1	69	368	19.2	3.6
Boundary	7 949	53	12	89	16.7	2.9	54	373	61.6	6.1	8	22	1.8	0.3
Butte	283	5	3	D	D	D	15	81	10.6	0.9	NA	NA	NA	NA
Camas	2 056	23	1	D	D	D	4	11	3.0	0.1	NA	NA	NA	NA
Canyon	315 142	2 766	157	1 512	555.2	38.4	429	4 724	1 014.1	88.9	88	268	22.9	3.6
Caribou	1 357	12	15	64	25.3	1.6	42	301	57.8	4.5	3	7	0.3	0.1
Cassia	8 707	62	40	271	218.6	6.3	116	1 144	193.0	19.2	17	39	3.0	0.6
Clark	349	7	1	D	D	D	4	40	4.5	0.3	NA	NA	NA	NA
Clearwater	2 400	17	5	D	D	D	45	331	56.8	5.0	6	D	D	D

1. Establishments with payroll.

Table B. States and Counties — Professional Services, Manufacturing, and Accommodation and Foodservices

STATE County	Professional, scientific, and technical services,[1] 1997				Manufacturing, 1997				Accommodation and foodservices, 1997			
	Number of establishments	Number of employees	Receipts (mil dol)	Annual payroll (mil dol)	Number of establishments	Number of employees	Receipts (mil dol)	Annual payroll (mil dol)	Number of establishments	Number of employees	Sales (mil dol)	Annual payroll (mil dol)
	147	148	149	150	151	152	153	154	155	156	157	158
GEORGIA—Cont'd												
Richmond	324	1 931	147.2	58.3	134	12 084	4 092.6	423.4	400	8 301	255.6	70.4
Rockdale	141	777	55.7	22.2	116	6 730	1 625.1	200.0	122	2 657	86.6	23.5
Schley	2	D	D	D	9	589	115.4	14.6	4	6	0.3	0.1
Screven	12	28	1.2	0.4	13	1 289	127.8	33.9	18	89	4.0	0.9
Seminole	8	30	1.5	0.5	NA	NA	NA	NA	10	82	2.9	0.6
Spalding	65	302	23.2	8.0	70	6 328	1 118.8	150.7	92	1 524	46.7	12.6
Stephens	33	111	7.9	2.4	64	3 970	634.8	88.4	44	844	21.3	5.7
Stewart	1	D	D	D	NA	NA	NA	NA	6	30	1.7	0.4
Sumter	31	136	9.5	3.3	38	3 163	475.4	71.3	51	770	23.5	6.2
Talbot	3	7	0.3	0.1	NA	NA	NA	NA	6	D	D	D
Taliaferro	NA	NA	NA	NA	NA	NA	NA	NA	1	D	D	D
Tattnall	12	51	2.4	0.8	12	762	62.9	8.4	19	241	6.6	1.6
Taylor	8	21	1.0	0.4	14	1 946	566.3	37.0	6	48	1.3	0.3
Telfair	12	19	1.0	0.3	13	786	141.6	15.1	19	175	4.9	1.1
Terrell	5	41	2.1	0.8	72	4 926	933.7	108.6	9	D	D	D
Thomas	45	221	18.1	6.6	72	4 926	933.7	108.6	64	1 100	36.9	9.6
Tift	55	297	25.1	8.6	51	4 449	613.3	103.7	80	1 434	44.3	12.8
Toombs	39	174	13.5	4.5	38	2 516	169.3	41.6	60	814	22.8	5.7
Towns	9	34	1.5	0.7	NA	NA	NA	NA	24	381	14.8	4.8
Treutlen	4	12	0.5	0.2	NA	NA	NA	NA	8	131	2.3	0.7
Troup	71	301	21.0	8.6	101	9 369	1 807.7	284.2	111	1 757	50.6	12.8
Turner	7	16	0.7	0.2	10	686	66.1	11.8	16	194	6.0	0.9
Twiggs	4	7	0.4	0.2	NA	NA	NA	NA	4	D	D	D
Union	25	69	3.9	1.8	NA	NA	NA	NA	27	272	8.4	2.3
Upson	24	57	4.0	0.9	26	4 241	555.1	82.9	46	502	14.6	3.8
Walker	46	197	12.7	4.6	77	6 555	1 207.7	159.9	51	658	20.0	5.1
Walton	62	160	10.9	3.7	55	2 611	441.5	70.4	45	D	D	D
Ware	55	161	10.2	3.5	42	2 121	287.4	55.8	63	1 180	34.4	9.9
Warren	2	D	D	D	6	798	131.0	20.0	1	D	D	D
Washington	18	132	6.0	2.9	18	917	131.7	22.3	20	D	D	D
Wayne	25	74	4.1	1.4	23	1 816	460.6	56.0	34	555	15.7	4.1
Webster	NA	NA	NA	NA	NA	NA	NA	NA	NA	NA	NA	NA
Wheeler	2	D	D	D	NA	NA	NA	NA	3	8	0.4	0.0
White	20	49	2.7	0.7	28	952	172.8	27.0	73	666	25.3	6.6
Whitfield	144	856	64.4	29.3	379	27 373	6 166.5	687.5	143	2 565	92.0	25.4
Wilcox	NA	NA	NA	NA	NA	NA	NA	NA	1	D	D	D
Wilkes	10	35	1.6	0.3	23	1 584	315.4	36.8	13	D	D	D
Wilkinson	6	15	1.0	0.3	14	1 307	391.2	49.7	8	D	D	D
Worth	10	26	1.4	0.5	NA	NA	NA	NA	18	D	D	D
HAWAII	2 480	15 743	1 574.0	606.5	921	15 109	3 192.5	405.0	3 081	88 083	5 007.9	1 507.5
Hawaii	246	933	73.3	24.9	106	1 588	192.5	37.5	326	10 441	546.6	188.1
Honolulu	1 917	13 729	1 400.6	546.8	685	11 161	2 692.2	300.9	2 125	53 916	3 036.8	852.8
Kalawao	NA	NA	NA	NA	NA	NA	NA	NA	210	5 775	293.8	102.3
Kauai	90	327	25.0	9.0	100	1 919	259.6	51.3	420	17 951	1 130.7	364.4
Maui	227	754	75.2	25.7								
IDAHO	2 364	19 669	2 046.1	756.2	1 647	66 184	16 952.9	2 099.8	2 978	42 067	1 232.5	345.7
Ada	805	6 419	903.2	264.2	395	20 850	6 318.4	862.6	648	12 105	370.1	103.9
Adams	2	D	D	D	NA	NA	NA	NA	14	134	3.4	1.7
Bannock	108	934	47.4	22.5	62	3 482	775.1	119.2	188	2 792	75.3	20.5
Bear Lake	2	D	D	D	NA	NA	NA	NA	13	90	2.8	0.7
Benewah	13	44	1.6	0.7	8	586	141.8	20.2	26	181	4.2	1.3
Bingham	26	110	6.4	2.6	44	2 413	366.1	64.2	51	583	12.6	3.7
Blaine	102	524	55.0	19.2	NA	NA	NA	NA	131	3 365	115.3	34.3
Boise	5	13	1.5	0.4	NA	NA	NA	NA	23	110	3.1	0.7
Bonner	86	214	13.6	5.5	86	1 898	382.1	56.8	115	1 385	33.6	11.1
Bonneville	210	7 327	748.5	338.6	115	2 550	267.9	55.8	180	3 381	90.3	25.9
Boundary	11	31	1.3	0.5	NA	NA	NA	NA	24	276	13.3	2.5
Butte	1	D	D	D	NA	NA	NA	NA	9	50	1.5	0.3
Camas	NA	NA	NA	NA	NA	NA	NA	NA	5	D	D	D
Canyon	128	553	35.4	12.7	176	9 817	3 581.7	268.2	188	2 619	71.4	19.1
Caribou	14	26	1.2	0.3	7	D	D	D	16	129	2.7	0.7
Cassia	30	D	D	D	24	D	D	D	48	653	17.9	4.8
Clark	NA	NA	NA	NA	NA	NA	NA	NA	3	D	D	D
Clearwater	9	40	1.7	0.6	NA	NA	NA	NA	31	186	4.7	1.3

1. Firms subject to federal tax.

STATE County	Health care and social assistance,[1] 1997				Other services,[1] 1997				Federal funds and grants, 2002–2003 Expenditures (mil dol)			
										Direct payments for individuals[2]		
	Number of establishments	Number of employees	Receipts (mil dol)	Annual payroll (mil dol)	Number of establishments	Number of employees	Receipts (mil dol)	Annual payroll (mil dol)	Total	Social Security and government retirement	Medicare	Food stamps and Supplemental Security Income
	159	160	161	162	163	164	165	166	167	168	169	170
GEORGIA—Cont'd												
Richmond	500	5 944	498.0	212.2	282	1 997	102.3	33.3	1 395.8	523.6	176.6	71.9
Rockdale	127	1 615	94.8	43.0	109	518	35.0	9.4	211.0	123.5	40.9	5.6
Schley	2	D	D	D	2	D	D	D	22.3	7.0	3.8	1.2
Screven	13	173	6.4	2.9	13	36	2.9	0.7	97.7	31.0	18.0	5.3
Seminole	15	95	5.8	2.8	17	60	3.6	1.0	79.5	24.4	11.2	4.1
Spalding	103	1 979	107.0	45.3	71	438	28.3	8.5	292.5	124.6	58.1	16.2
Stephens	36	531	32.4	10.2	38	116	8.7	1.8	151.0	71.0	32.5	6.9
Stewart	3	140	6.9	2.2	4	9	0.8	0.1	47.1	12.3	8.6	2.6
Sumter	64	787	38.5	17.5	39	195	10.8	3.0	213.8	60.2	30.9	12.0
Talbot	3	19	1.7	0.6	5	12	0.4	0.1	43.2	20.2	5.8	2.6
Taliaferro	2	D	D	D	2	D	D	D	15.4	5.0	3.7	0.8
Tattnall	19	518	17.2	7.5	18	52	3.7	0.8	121.4	48.6	21.5	6.6
Taylor	1	D	D	D	10	22	1.7	0.3	60.5	22.9	10.0	4.0
Telfair	16	464	19.3	8.3	14	62	4.4	1.1	95.3	29.8	19.6	4.4
Terrell	13	127	4.7	1.7	15	52	2.8	0.6	97.0	21.4	12.9	5.2
Thomas	86	960	70.2	33.6	74	282	17.6	4.6	270.2	105.1	47.2	15.1
Tift	83	1 157	69.5	37.1	57	584	43.3	12.3	210.5	76.3	34.5	11.8
Toombs	67	804	35.1	15.7	37	263	10.6	4.1	147.6	56.1	27.9	9.0
Towns	14	284	14.6	6.3	8	18	0.9	0.2	64.3	38.0	11.6	1.0
Treutlen	9	79	2.8	1.2	4	D	D	D	50.5	12.6	6.5	2.6
Troup	91	1 173	73.7	36.9	94	410	26.5	8.1	311.9	126.7	58.5	15.8
Turner	6	104	3.7	1.5	13	34	2.8	0.5	86.4	19.2	12.4	3.7
Twiggs	5	143	5.2	2.1	7	8	0.9	0.1	52.8	21.0	9.3	2.5
Union	30	171	9.4	4.5	19	59	6.3	1.0	107.7	62.7	19.9	2.3
Upson	48	515	26.9	11.9	39	140	9.6	2.5	148.2	68.0	29.3	7.9
Walker	52	507	25.5	11.2	64	377	22.6	6.3	315.3	156.5	77.6	11.9
Walton	59	639	28.4	12.2	49	152	12.0	3.2	242.8	124.0	46.9	10.0
Ware	90	1 100	62.7	29.8	60	292	16.6	4.4	277.9	105.7	50.1	14.6
Warren	7	234	6.0	3.5	6	19	0.9	0.1	47.2	13.8	9.8	2.5
Washington	41	508	20.6	9.3	30	95	5.9	1.4	123.7	42.2	26.1	8.4
Wayne	46	530	30.1	11.9	26	118	8.3	2.4	164.6	59.6	30.6	7.8
Webster	NA	NA	NA	NA	1	D	D	D	21.3	4.1	2.4	0.6
Wheeler	6	164	9.7	3.3	2	D	D	D	37.0	10.9	7.2	1.5
White	24	269	14.5	4.6	20	69	4.8	1.0	93.5	55.0	15.3	2.1
Whitfield	129	1 442	114.0	52.5	123	672	47.2	14.6	331.0	153.8	67.4	14.6
Wilcox	5	208	6.4	3.0	8	18	0.7	0.2	71.1	20.6	11.0	2.9
Wilkes	22	159	8.6	3.4	21	64	5.4	1.6	73.6	29.2	17.0	3.5
Wilkinson	6	108	4.6	1.6	8	30	1.9	0.5	65.2	27.7	12.4	3.0
Worth	21	316	15.4	5.8	16	51	3.1	0.9	146.3	37.5	16.7	6.9
HAWAII	2 360	18 221	1 646.3	730.8	1 476	10 375	683.2	206.4	11 269.3	2 905.2	874.1	265.1
Hawaii	321	2 441	224.8	76.2	157	808	50.3	14.5	803.6	340.9	104.7	53.4
Honolulu	1 730	13 474	1 231.7	563.1	1 097	8 402	560.8	170.7	9 056.3	2 219.8	645.0	179.5
Kalawao	NA	NA	NA	NA	NA	NA	NA	NA	0.8	0.0	0.8	0.0
Kauai	79	745	51.4	27.6	59	281	17.9	5.1	339.3	122.1	45.6	13.2
Maui	230	1 561	138.4	63.9	163	884	54.2	16.2	537.7	222.3	78.1	18.9
IDAHO	2 551	26 365	1 548.3	680.1	1 858	9 461	550.6	151.7	8 654.5	2 769.0	789.0	172.1
Ada	711	6 993	484.7	228.8	462	3 185	171.1	51.3	1 711.1	609.8	144.6	28.9
Adams	2	D	D	D	1	D	D	D	29.2	12.3	2.6	0.5
Bannock	157	1 421	79.8	39.1	108	564	33.5	9.5	365.8	154.1	42.7	14.0
Bear Lake	7	33	1.6	0.6	6	10	1.3	0.2	44.9	16.5	4.7	0.7
Benewah	9	9	1.4	0.4	15	136	7.2	2.0	73.1	26.0	9.3	1.9
Bingham	51	391	17.2	7.9	39	215	15.7	4.2	190.0	74.1	21.1	6.4
Blaine	52	239	21.1	10.0	44	188	11.8	3.3	54.2	26.6	6.8	0.5
Boise	NA	NA	NA	NA	3	D	D	D	84.2	14.0	2.9	0.4
Bonner	70	535	26.3	10.0	54	166	11.4	3.0	184.1	96.5	24.6	5.5
Bonneville	241	3 151	229.1	91.6	140	709	49.5	13.0	1 357.1	161.0	50.1	13.0
Boundary	16	48	2.2	0.6	17	43	4.1	0.9	64.5	25.6	5.4	2.0
Butte	3	27	1.0	0.3	3	17	1.3	0.2	36.0	7.7	2.9	0.5
Camas	1	D	D	D	NA	NA	NA	NA	7.2	2.3	0.4	0.1
Canyon	182	2 692	161.3	74.9	158	697	39.0	10.9	631.3	250.2	78.4	23.1
Caribou	14	76	3.5	1.2	13	37	1.9	0.4	37.5	15.8	4.1	0.5
Cassia	56	421	20.6	6.4	44	176	10.7	2.7	95.5	40.6	15.0	3.0
Clark	2	D	D	D	NA	NA	NA	NA	14.8	1.8	0.6	0.1
Clearwater	9	94	3.9	1.3	13	39	2.6	0.8	68.7	26.1	8.2	1.5

1. Firms subject to federal tax.   2. State totals may include programs not allocated by county.

STATE County	Salaries and wages	Defense	Other	Medicaid and other health-related	Nutrition and family welfare	Education	Other	Total (mil dol)	Intergovernmental (mil dol)	Total (mil dol)	Total	Property
	171	172	173	174	175	176	177	178	179	180	181	182
GEORGIA—Cont'd												
Richmond	230.6	10.2	41.4	194.9	47.8	20.3	50.3	524.2	243.1	170.0	859	528
Rockdale	8.6	0.8	2.1	14.6	3.4	3.1	6.7	192.6	62.9	100.3	1 363	867
Schley	0.5	0.1	1.2	4.7	0.7	0.4	0.1	9.8	5.8	2.7	685	500
Screven	2.3	0.0	0.6	22.5	3.5	1.3	1.2	42.5	22.7	10.5	693	437
Seminole	1.1	0.0	0.3	12.7	2.0	1.0	1.1	21.9	11.0	8.8	947	583
Spalding	9.3	3.1	2.3	46.5	8.6	5.3	16.0	172.3	75.0	25.6	1 104	655
Stephens	4.5	0.2	1.1	22.0	2.6	2.3	4.9	91.2	41.7	25.1	975	575
Stewart	0.7	0.0	0.2	13.0	2.1	0.6	1.2	12.4	7.4	3.9	772	541
Sumter	7.3	0.0	1.1	36.5	8.4	3.2	25.9	149.9	54.5	28.5	857	560
Talbot	1.2	0.0	0.3	8.6	1.6	0.6	1.9	13.2	6.1	5.5	826	575
Taliaferro	0.3	0.0	0.1	5.1	0.6	0.2	-0.8	6.7	4.3	1.6	821	632
Tattnall	2.4	0.2	0.5	26.6	4.2	1.3	1.3	41.3	23.8	13.2	584	375
Taylor	1.2	0.0	0.3	14.0	2.1	0.9	2.2	18.9	10.6	6.0	677	385
Telfair	2.1	0.2	1.3	21.0	3.1	1.2	7.1	24.7	13.1	8.6	732	384
Terrell	4.1	0.0	2.5	20.5	3.2	1.2	1.7	24.7	14.0	8.1	741	421
Thomas	9.8	0.1	1.7	50.6	7.9	5.6	12.4	124.9	68.0	26.4	615	358
Tift	12.2	0.1	1.2	33.7	6.1	3.4	4.6	187.8	44.2	39.4	1 001	511
Toombs	4.2	0.0	1.0	31.4	5.3	2.4	3.2	61.7	33.4	17.7	670	262
Towns	1.7	0.0	1.3	7.4	0.6	0.3	2.0	18.6	7.4	8.4	864	409
Treutlen	0.8	0.6	0.2	12.2	1.5	0.5	12.2	13.9	8.8	3.0	435	291
Troup	8.3	6.1	2.0	51.8	15.4	4.7	17.8	190.3	85.2	68.1	1 139	669
Turner	1.7	0.0	0.3	12.2	2.8	1.6	7.7	26.0	13.7	8.7	893	532
Twiggs	0.6	1.8	0.2	10.8	2.5	1.0	0.1	20.3	10.5	8.2	781	614
Union	4.0	0.0	0.8	13.4	1.2	0.5	2.7	63.7	19.8	15.4	844	450
Upson	3.4	0.4	0.9	24.5	4.9	1.9	5.1	58.0	28.0	22.3	803	513
Walker	7.0	0.9	2.0	33.8	13.2	4.5	1.6	117.7	62.4	34.3	554	321
Walton	17.8	0.3	6.9	25.5	4.3	3.3	2.2	205.0	63.6	83.1	1 239	726
Ware	9.2	0.0	2.1	47.1	14.8	4.3	25.1	116.8	59.8	38.8	1 090	566
Warren	1.2	0.0	0.4	14.0	1.8	0.9	1.9	14.5	6.8	5.2	833	560
Washington	2.6	0.0	0.6	29.8	7.0	1.8	2.3	71.0	21.2	21.8	1 048	686
Wayne	24.0	0.0	1.5	25.9	4.3	2.1	4.2	86.8	33.2	22.5	830	560
Webster	0.6	0.0	0.1	3.2	0.5	0.1	0.8	7.0	4.3	2.0	851	672
Wheeler	0.7	0.0	0.2	10.7	1.6	0.5	1.5	12.5	8.2	3.2	514	351
White	2.8	0.0	0.8	9.1	0.9	4.3	2.1	47.4	18.2	23.9	1 091	629
Whitfield	11.5	2.7	7.2	38.7	6.5	7.0	17.6	337.2	126.2	113.7	1 306	742
Wilcox	1.2	0.0	0.3	13.5	1.6	0.7	1.6	16.9	10.3	5.3	624	433
Wilkes	2.1	0.0	0.4	15.7	2.5	0.9	1.4	35.9	18.4	9.8	914	643
Wilkinson	1.5	0.0	0.4	10.5	2.2	1.0	5.6	25.7	10.0	13.8	1 331	759
Worth	2.2	0.1	0.5	18.9	4.7	2.5	12.2	47.4	27.3	15.5	710	455
HAWAII	2 863.7	1 750.2	228.2	657.0	278.7	236.3	738.9	X	X	X	X	X
Hawaii	56.7	23.9	17.0	61.2	27.9	12.0	94.1	214.7	74.5	118.0	762	638
Honolulu	2 737.5	1 624.6	179.2	520.9	176.9	179.9	537.8	1 021.2	176.7	534.4	596	427
Kalawao	0.0	0.0	0.0	0.0	0.0	0.0	0.0	101.5	37.2	48.5	810	635
Kauai	29.2	57.4	3.1	29.3	5.8	1.6	30.6	205.2	48.2	117.9	880	713
Maui	40.4	44.2	28.8	38.3	13.2	2.7	43.8	X	X	X	X	X
IDAHO	834.2	207.2	1 324.2	743.3	215.2	175.6	724.2	X	X	X	X	X
Ada	287.5	30.0	98.1	137.3	57.5	71.3	217.1	779.2	290.9	301.3	942	876
Adams	4.0	0.0	1.9	1.5	2.2	0.1	3.4	12.8	5.8	2.9	844	744
Bannock	31.0	1.5	11.5	50.3	6.3	3.5	25.6	242.5	83.4	51.0	673	646
Bear Lake	3.5	0.0	0.5	4.1	5.2	0.1	7.6	24.0	9.9	3.8	600	573
Benewah	3.7	0.7	0.6	11.5	4.4	1.8	10.9	29.5	11.2	5.9	658	632
Bingham	13.2	0.3	12.5	29.3	5.4	3.4	8.6	106.7	61.3	19.6	461	448
Blaine	5.4	0.6	2.7	2.1	1.0	0.3	6.2	70.9	16.9	43.0	2 109	1 858
Boise	5.2	4.7	3.7	1.5	0.9	0.2	50.5	14.6	8.2	4.5	634	606
Bonner	9.7	2.1	2.3	19.4	2.0	1.0	19.9	72.1	30.4	29.4	770	749
Bonneville	50.3	14.9	982.2	36.8	8.3	1.5	26.0	199.4	106.3	54.1	635	614
Boundary	6.0	0.0	3.8	6.7	0.9	0.4	12.3	28.3	12.7	6.7	662	639
Butte	8.0	0.0	0.2	5.1	6.7	0.1	3.1	13.1	4.1	2.3	802	771
Camas	0.9	0.0	0.3	0.5	1.1	0.0	1.0	3.6	2.4	0.9	861	834
Canyon	22.7	52.5	59.9	102.2	13.2	4.5	13.2	311.9	151.5	93.6	646	601
Caribou	2.1	0.0	1.2	1.6	2.0	0.2	4.9	30.8	13.7	7.9	1 077	1 066
Cassia	8.5	0.0	1.5	10.7	2.4	0.8	2.7	56.0	32.0	13.7	633	569
Clark	1.8	0.0	0.3	0.0	9.4	0.1	0.1	4.5	2.8	1.1	1 093	1 046
Clearwater	11.5	2.0	3.2	11.2	0.9	0.2	3.2	25.3	13.5	7.0	830	799

1. State totals may include programs not allocated by county.   2. Based on the resident population estimated as of July 1 of the year shown.

Table B. States and Counties — Local Government Finances, Government Employment, and Elections

STATE County	Direct general expenditure — Total (mil dol)	Per capita[1] (dollars)	Percent of total for — Education	Health and hospitals	Police protection	Public welfare	Highways	Debt outstanding — Total (mil dol)	Per capita[1] (dollars)	Federal civilian	Federal military	State and local	Presidential election, 2004 — Democratic	Republican	All other
	183	184	185	186	187	188	189	190	191	192	193	194	195	196	197
GEORGIA—Cont'd															
Richmond	532.3	2 690	47.8	7.2	5.5	0.2	3.0	524.4	2 651	5 575	10 632	21 716	56.7	43.0	0.4
Rockdale	175.8	2 391	61.0	0.4	6.5	0.4	1.4	216.4	2 942	123	175	3 976	38.9	60.5	0.5
Schley	9.5	2 382	69.2	2.0	4.6	0.2	4.8	7.9	1 996	0	0	232	30.3	69.5	0.2
Screven	39.4	2 594	60.5	14.3	3.4	0.3	3.8	5.0	332	45	36	1 002	42.8	56.7	0.5
Seminole	21.4	2 297	64.6	2.8	4.1	0.1	3.4	0.7	77	17	22	518	39.1	60.4	0.6
Spalding	186.5	3 140	44.0	9.3	5.2	0.1	5.4	106.0	1 783	129	141	4 328	35.5	64.1	0.4
Stephens	89.5	3 480	38.5	35.5	2.7	0.3	1.8	69.8	2 715	67	61	1 790	28.1	71.5	0.4
Stewart	14.1	2 791	55.1	0.9	4.9	0.1	3.7	1.2	232	11	12	344	60.1	39.2	0.7
Sumter	147.3	4 429	26.9	46.8	3.1	0.2	1.7	48.5	1 459	139	79	2 925	49.3	50.4	0.3
Talbot	13.2	1 962	56.4	1.5	4.7	1.1	7.3	3.7	550	15	16	320	62.2	37.5	0.3
Taliaferro	8.1	4 102	73.4	1.6	5.5	1.3	5.6	0.3	149	0	0	138	64.4	35.2	0.4
Tattnall	38.4	1 703	58.8	2.4	4.9	0.1	5.0	17.9	795	34	54	2 424	27.6	72.1	0.3
Taylor	18.1	2 033	66.1	2.7	7.5	0.4	7.4	8.2	921	25	21	549	43.1	56.6	0.3
Telfair	23.8	2 018	60.2	3.3	6.8	0.5	4.6	5.3	448	37	28	992	42.1	57.5	0.4
Terrell	25.9	2 383	56.3	2.8	5.5	0.2	4.1	2.5	232	81	26	634	51.0	48.6	0.4
Thomas	129.8	3 020	48.6	13.4	4.3	0.1	4.0	30.5	710	199	103	3 694	38.2	61.5	0.3
Tift	204.0	5 187	26.7	49.2	2.7	0.1	2.3	69.3	1 762	194	95	4 470	30.9	68.8	0.3
Toombs	56.9	2 155	63.3	1.3	3.8	0.1	4.6	12.5	474	70	63	1 471	29.1	70.3	0.6
Towns	17.6	1 807	55.5	6.0	4.8	2.5	3.9	12.7	1 296	26	23	476	27.1	72.4	0.5
Treutlen	14.2	2 075	61.7	3.0	4.8	1.5	3.7	1.4	206	13	16	418	38.2	61.3	0.5
Troup	193.7	3 241	50.5	11.9	5.3	0.1	3.1	113.9	1 906	141	142	5 398	34.8	64.7	0.5
Turner	27.4	2 829	57.2	2.8	5.7	0.7	10.4	7.3	750	32	23	526	38.3	61.3	0.3
Twiggs	20.3	1 925	69.2	1.1	4.3	1.3	4.7	0.3	31	12	25	484	50.9	48.4	0.8
Union	63.6	3 482	39.9	33.4	2.0	0.2	9.9	16.8	922	85	44	1 280	25.2	74.2	0.6
Upson	55.7	2 004	57.1	1.9	5.7	0.7	3.6	30.5	1 097	50	66	1 780	34.0	65.8	0.3
Walker	122.4	1 976	58.0	11.7	5.1	0.5	3.9	28.5	460	136	147	3 116	27.9	71.5	0.6
Walton	193.4	2 884	54.1	15.6	4.4	0.2	3.7	104.1	1 551	137	160	2 948	21.3	78.2	0.5
Ware	112.9	3 175	46.9	24.3	4.3	0.3	3.7	56.0	1 576	152	86	3 495	29.3	70.3	0.4
Warren	19.9	3 199	68.0	2.0	3.4	0.5	3.9	5.2	837	20	15	329	54.6	45.1	0.3
Washington	73.9	3 551	40.9	31.0	3.9	0.1	5.4	21.7	1 043	52	50	2 274	47.6	52.0	0.4
Wayne	90.8	3 357	43.4	31.0	3.4	0.3	4.8	16.7	615	395	64	2 470	28.1	71.5	0.4
Webster	7.0	3 031	68.8	3.6	4.6	0.4	7.5	6.6	2 872	14	0	145	51.3	48.3	0.4
Wheeler	12.5	2 017	72.7	1.6	4.0	0.4	3.2	0.9	147	12	15	348	41.3	58.2	0.5
White	45.7	2 084	59.1	1.6	5.0	0.9	8.2	24.2	1 107	47	52	1 178	21.3	78.1	0.7
Whitfield	339.4	3 899	45.4	16.6	3.1	0.2	4.9	394.1	4 527	188	207	5 228	26.3	73.2	0.5
Wilcox	16.4	1 920	65.1	3.3	5.6	1.0	7.7	1.1	131	31	20	634	34.5	65.3	0.2
Wilkes	35.6	3 312	40.2	30.5	4.5	0.6	3.8	7.6	708	43	26	879	44.7	54.8	0.6
Wilkinson	24.6	2 378	62.9	2.2	6.7	1.3	9.2	4.8	459	22	25	527	49.5	50.1	0.4
Worth	48.4	2 224	65.0	1.5	4.3	0.1	7.2	3.6	166	45	52	1 075	30.2	69.5	0.3
HAWAII	X	X	X	X	X	X	X	X	X	29 734	54 135	87 156	54.0	45.3	0.7
Hawaii	216.0	1 396	0.0	5.5	15.4	0.0	15.1	155.9	1 007	1 038	1 220	10 317	60.9	38.2	1.0
Honolulu	1 197.5	1 336	0.0	1.6	14.0	0.0	9.1	2 297.0	2 564	27 715	51 297	64 964	51.1	48.3	0.6
Kalawao	NA	NA	NA	NA	NA	NA	NA	NA	NA	(3)	(3)	(3)	NA	NA	NA
Kauai	110.7	1 847	0.0	0.0	20.3	4.4	15.2	83.1	1 386	396	567	3 879	60.0	39.2	0.9
Maui	212.1	1 582	0.0	0.4	11.7	11.6	11.5	255.9	1 910	(3)585	(3)1 051	(3)7 996	60.7	38.3	0.9
IDAHO	X	X	X	X	X	X	X	X	X	13 174	9 352	97 689	30.4	68.5	1.2
Ada	805.3	2 519	46.7	2.1	7.1	0.7	7.4	453.9	1 420	4 779	1 207	23 994	37.9	61.1	1.0
Adams	12.0	3 473	39.4	20.6	6.7	0.8	7.2	4.8	1 398	125	12	220	26.9	71.2	1.8
Bannock	233.7	3 083	35.1	29.5	5.5	0.6	3.7	76.3	1 007	509	277	8 305	37.1	61.8	1.1
Bear Lake	22.8	3 581	44.1	31.0	3.6	0.5	6.5	2.8	440	60	23	538	16.3	82.6	1.1
Benewah	29.9	3 320	42.8	32.8	2.5	0.3	6.1	6.4	706	80	32	1 064	28.4	69.9	1.7
Bingham	106.4	2 506	56.6	17.1	5.5	0.3	6.2	29.1	686	338	152	3 604	21.8	76.9	1.3
Blaine	65.1	3 194	56.4	1.2	5.5	0.4	5.9	29.0	1 423	106	73	1 058	59.2	39.8	1.0
Boise	15.0	2 119	52.8	1.8	7.7	0.9	13.2	5.0	714	183	25	354	27.6	71.1	1.3
Bonner	71.5	1 872	48.8	0.8	8.5	0.5	10.7	13.2	345	254	137	2 066	37.7	60.7	1.6
Bonneville	197.0	2 313	52.4	4.5	6.3	0.7	4.2	78.8	925	779	306	4 510	21.5	77.4	1.1
Boundary	27.3	2 705	41.1	26.3	4.1	0.8	9.7	5.9	589	139	36	901	29.1	69.1	1.9
Butte	11.4	3 955	33.7	46.7	3.1	0.4	1.2	5.7	1 969	44	13	185	22.8	76.6	0.6
Camas	3.3	3 179	46.1	0.0	8.2	0.3	29.8	0.8	807	21	0	94	23.4	75.8	0.8
Canyon	322.7	2 226	54.0	2.6	6.6	0.6	4.8	190.2	1 312	382	527	6 413	24.1	74.8	1.1
Caribou	28.4	3 875	45.9	20.5	4.3	0.3	9.5	9.1	1 244	56	26	623	15.0	84.1	0.9
Cassia	54.5	2 508	54.9	0.2	7.4	0.7	9.3	23.9	1 101	186	78	1 433	14.7	83.9	1.3
Clark	6.6	6 605	71.9	0.6	4.0	0.5	11.5	3.9	3 958	43	0	133	13.0	85.6	1.4
Clearwater	21.5	2 541	48.6	1.2	5.4	0.7	18.4	0.8	91	278	30	878	27.7	70.4	1.9

1. Based on the resident population estimated as of July 1 of the year shown. 3. Kalawao County included with Maui County.

Table B. States and Counties — Land Area and Population

STATE/ County code	CBSA code[1]	County Type[2]	STATE County	Land area,[3] (sq km) 2000	Population and population characteristics, 2003												
								Race alone or in combination, not Hispanic or Latino (percent)					Age (percent)					
					Total persons	Rank	Per square kilometer	White	Black	Am. Indian, Alaska Native	Asian and Pacific Islander	Percent Hispanic or Latino[4]	Under 5 years	5 to 17 years	18 to 24 years	25 to 34 years	35 to 44 years	45 to 54 years
					1	2	3	4	5	6	7	8	9	10	11	12	13	14	15

(Header columns 1–15 correspond to: Total persons, Rank, Per square kilometer, White, Black, Am. Indian Alaska Native, Asian and Pacific Islander, Percent Hispanic or Latino, Under 5 years, 5 to 17 years, 18 to 24 years, 25 to 34 years, 35 to 44 years, 45 to 54 years.)

IDAHO—Cont'd

STATE/ County code	CBSA code	County Type	County	Land area	Total persons	Rank	Per sq km	White	Black	Am. Ind.	Asian/PI	Hispanic	Under 5	5-17	18-24	25-34	35-44	45-54
16 037	...	9	Custer	12 757	4 090	2 905	0.3	94.1	0.0	1.1	0.0	5.3	4.6	18.1	7.0	8.4	15.8	18.6
16 039	34300	4	Elmore	7 971	28 872	1 434	3.6	80.1	4.1	1.4	3.5	13.1	8.7	19.5	12.2	18.6	18.1	9.9
16 041	30860	3	Franklin	1 723	11 874	2 299	6.9	93.4	0.1	0.5	0.2	5.9	9.2	25.8	11.3	11.9	11.8	10.8
16 043	39940	6	Fremont	4 835	12 107	2 287	2.5	87.0	0.2	0.9	0.6	12.0	8.6	22.4	11.7	10.3	13.1	12.0
16 045	14260	2	Gem	1 457	15 795	2 049	10.8	91.3	0.2	1.4	0.8	7.5	6.6	19.7	9.8	10.4	13.4	13.4
16 047	...	7	Gooding	1 893	14 329	2 143	7.6	79.3	0.2	0.9	0.4	19.7	7.4	20.6	9.9	11.2	13.0	12.1
16 049	...	6	Idaho	21 976	15 413	2 067	0.7	94.9	0.1	4.0	0.5	1.7	4.9	17.2	9.8	7.7	13.5	16.7
16 051	26820	3	Jefferson	2 836	20 194	1 792	7.1	89.4	0.2	0.7	0.6	9.6	8.6	25.1	12.1	10.3	13.3	12.2
16 053	46300	7	Jerome	1 554	18 913	1 865	12.2	77.4	0.2	0.9	0.5	21.5	8.4	21.8	10.6	11.4	14.0	12.9
16 055	17660	3	Kootenai	3 225	117 481	479	36.4	95.3	0.4	2.0	1.1	2.6	6.5	19.1	9.8	11.7	14.2	14.5
16 057	34140	4	Latah	2 789	35 087	1 272	12.6	93.6	1.0	1.7	3.1	2.1	5.6	13.6	19.9	16.7	11.8	12.5
16 059	...	7	Lemhi	11 821	7 731	2 619	0.7	96.7	0.1	1.4	0.2	2.5	4.5	18.6	8.6	7.1	13.5	17.0
16 061	...	8	Lewis	1 241	3 748	2 930	3.0	92.7	0.4	4.7	0.6	2.0	5.1	18.5	8.0	7.7	13.1	14.2
16 063	...	9	Lincoln	3 122	4 321	2 883	1.4	83.8	0.2	1.1	0.5	14.7	8.3	21.8	10.4	11.0	13.0	13.4
16 065	39940	6	Madison	1 221	29 878	1 408	24.5	94.6	0.4	0.5	1.3	3.8	8.0	17.2	35.1	9.2	7.2	7.3
16 067	15420	7	Minidoka	1 967	19 349	1 845	9.8	72.2	0.2	1.0	0.5	26.5	8.2	21.6	10.7	10.0	13.4	12.9
16 069	30300	3	Nez Perce	2 199	37 699	1 189	17.1	91.8	0.4	6.1	1.1	1.8	5.9	16.5	10.1	11.6	13.7	14.2
16 071	...	8	Oneida	3 109	4 132	2 902	1.3	97.0	0.1	0.4	0.2	2.3	7.5	21.4	11.4	8.8	12.7	13.4
16 073	14260	2	Owyhee	19 886	11 186	2 356	0.6	73.0	0.2	3.7	0.6	23.5	7.9	22.2	10.1	11.2	13.7	12.1
16 075	36620	6	Payette	1 055	21 466	1 727	20.3	85.4	0.2	1.3	1.4	13.0	7.5	21.8	9.7	11.5	13.5	12.4
16 077	38540	3	Power	3 640	7 373	2 650	2.0	72.7	0.1	3.3	0.5	23.6	7.2	23.9	10.0	10.7	13.5	14.3
16 079	...	6	Shoshone	6 822	12 993	2 241	1.9	96.0	0.2	2.6	0.3	2.2	5.0	16.5	7.5	8.9	14.5	16.6
16 081	27220	9	Teton	1 166	7 058	2 682	6.1	85.2	0.1	0.5	0.5	13.9	9.0	22.0	9.6	14.6	16.8	13.4
16 083	46300	7	Twin Falls	4 986	67 082	751	13.5	87.4	0.4	1.2	1.2	10.7	7.3	19.4	11.4	11.4	13.1	12.9
16 085	...	8	Valley	9 526	7 743	2 618	0.8	96.4	0.2	1.1	0.6	2.4	4.3	16.4	8.2	6.9	14.3	19.9
16 087	...	6	Washington	3 772	9 995	2 443	2.6	82.2	0.2	1.2	1.3	15.9	6.5	19.6	8.8	9.5	12.5	13.9
17 000	...	X	**ILLINOIS**	143 961	12 653 544	X	87.9	67.3	15.3	0.4	4.3	13.6	7.0	18.5	9.9	14.3	15.2	13.9
17 001	39500	5	Adams	2 219	67 582	744	30.5	95.1	3.7	0.4	0.6	1.0	6.2	17.6	10.0	11.2	14.2	13.6
17 003	16020	7	Alexander	612	9 327	2 499	15.2	62.5	35.7	0.5	0.4	1.5	6.9	18.1	9.4	12.2	14.2	14.1
17 005	41180	1	Bond	985	17 941	1 919	18.2	90.4	6.9	0.8	0.3	2.0	5.4	15.2	12.9	13.9	15.2	13.7
17 007	40420	2	Boone	728	46 477	989	63.8	82.4	1.5	0.6	1.1	15.4	6.8	20.9	10.0	13.0	15.4	12.6
17 009	...	7	Brown	792	6 879	2 700	8.7	77.2	18.3	0.1	0.2	4.3	3.9	12.3	13.6	19.0	18.1	12.2
17 011	36860	6	Bureau	2 250	35 221	1 264	15.7	93.1	0.7	0.4	0.6	5.7	5.8	17.5	9.2	10.7	14.5	14.4
17 013	41180	1	Calhoun	657	5 069	2 837	7.7	98.9	0.0	0.5	0.2	0.7	4.9	16.1	9.0	10.4	14.8	13.3
17 015	...	7	Carroll	1 151	16 242	2 017	14.1	96.4	1.2	0.6	0.7	2.0	5.0	17.2	8.6	10.1	14.4	14.4
17 017	...	6	Cass	974	13 841	2 177	14.2	84.5	0.6	0.3	0.4	14.6	7.3	17.6	9.3	12.1	14.3	13.4
17 019	16580	3	Champaign	2 582	186 800	306	72.3	72.5	11.9	0.6	8.2	3.5	6.0	14.6	20.3	15.7	12.5	11.6
17 021	45380	6	Christian	1 836	35 127	1 270	19.1	95.9	2.4	0.2	0.5	1.2	5.6	17.4	8.8	12.1	15.4	13.9
17 023	...	6	Clark	1 299	16 998	1 956	13.1	98.8	0.5	0.3	0.2	0.5	5.7	17.7	9.0	11.1	14.7	13.7
17 025	...	7	Clay	1 215	14 316	2 144	11.8	98.3	0.3	0.3	0.7	0.7	6.5	16.8	8.9	10.8	14.1	13.7
17 027	41180	1	Clinton	1 228	36 135	1 234	29.4	93.7	4.0	0.3	0.5	1.9	5.5	17.5	10.4	12.8	16.3	13.4
17 029	16660	5	Coles	1 316	51 880	908	39.4	94.8	2.6	0.4	1.1	1.9	5.6	13.6	19.9	12.6	12.0	12.5
17 031	16980	1	Cook	2 449	5 351 552	2	2 185.2	47.0	26.3	0.4	5.8	21.5	7.4	18.5	9.2	15.9	15.4	13.2
17 033	...	6	Crawford	1 149	19 899	1 811	17.3	93.3	4.3	0.4	0.5	1.8	4.9	16.3	10.3	12.4	15.4	14.0
17 035	16660	9	Cumberland	896	11 063	2 366	12.3	98.9	0.3	0.4	0.2	0.5	5.7	18.7	9.6	11.5	14.9	13.8
17 037	16980	1	De Kalb	1 642	94 041	571	57.3	85.1	5.1	0.5	2.8	7.4	6.2	16.0	19.8	14.5	13.2	11.2
17 039	...	6	De Witt	1 030	16 679	1 983	16.2	97.6	0.7	0.3	0.5	1.4	6.2	17.4	8.8	11.9	14.9	14.5
17 041	...	6	Douglas	1 080	19 923	1 809	18.4	94.9	0.5	0.3	0.4	4.3	7.4	18.6	9.3	11.3	14.6	13.7
17 043	16980	1	Du Page	864	925 188	43	1 070.8	76.1	3.8	0.4	10.1	10.7	7.0	18.9	8.7	13.9	17.0	15.1
17 045	...	6	Edgar	1 615	19 396	1 842	12.0	96.4	2.0	0.3	0.3	1.2	5.4	16.8	9.4	11.3	14.5	14.2
17 047	...	9	Edwards	576	6 850	2 702	11.9	98.8	0.1	0.1	0.4	0.6	5.8	16.2	8.7	11.1	13.8	14.3
17 049	20820	7	Effingham	1 240	34 529	1 291	27.8	98.2	0.3	0.3	0.5	1.0	6.6	20.0	9.5	12.0	15.2	13.4
17 051	...	6	Fayette	1 856	21 539	1 725	11.6	93.8	5.0	0.3	0.3	0.9	5.7	16.8	10.2	13.1	15.4	13.5
17 053	16580	3	Ford	1 258	14 094	2 159	11.2	97.4	0.5	0.3	0.5	1.6	6.3	18.2	8.5	10.6	14.9	13.5
17 055	16660	5	Franklin	1 067	39 117	1 155	36.7	98.7	0.2	0.7	0.3	0.7	5.8	16.4	8.9	11.8	13.8	14.0
17 057	15900	6	Fulton	2 242	37 658	1 190	16.8	94.4	3.8	0.4	0.3	1.4	5.2	15.9	9.4	12.7	14.4	14.0
17 059	...	8	Gallatin	838	6 220	2 753	7.4	98.5	0.3	0.4	0.1	0.8	5.5	15.8	9.3	10.8	13.7	13.9
17 061	...	6	Greene	1 407	14 708	2 119	10.4	98.1	1.0	0.6	0.1	0.6	5.7	18.1	10.1	11.2	14.0	13.3
17 063	16980	1	Grundy	1 088	39 528	1 141	36.3	94.1	0.5	0.5	0.5	5.0	6.1	18.5	9.9	12.9	15.8	14.4
17 065	34500	7	Hamilton	1 127	8 334	2 574	7.4	98.3	0.7	0.2	0.2	0.7	5.4	16.8	9.1	10.5	13.6	14.6
17 067	...	7	Hancock	2 058	19 393	1 843	9.4	98.7	0.3	0.4	0.3	0.7	5.3	17.4	8.9	10.4	14.4	15.3
17 069	...	9	Hardin	462	4 711	2 858	10.2	96.1	2.3	0.4	0.6	1.0	5.0	13.9	9.3	11.3	14.6	15.4
17 071	15460	9	Henderson	981	8 073	2 591	8.2	98.3	0.5	0.2	0.3	1.3	4.8	16.3	9.4	10.2	14.8	15.3
17 073	19340	2	Henry	2 132	50 644	927	23.8	95.2	1.5	0.4	0.4	3.2	5.5	17.9	9.5	10.5	14.4	15.0
17 075	...	6	Iroquois	2 892	30 684	1 392	10.6	94.0	1.0	0.4	0.4	4.5	5.7	18.2	8.8	10.0	14.5	14.1

1. CBSA = Core Based Statistical Area. See Appendix A for explanation. See Appendix B for list of metropolitan areas with component counties.
2. County type code from the Economic Research Service of USDA Rural-Urban Continuum Codes. See Appendix A for definition.
3. Dry land or land partially or temporarily covered by water.
4. Hispanic or Latino persons may be of any race.

Table B. States and Counties — Population and Households

STATE County	55 to 64 years	65 to 74 years	75 years and over	Percent female	1990	2000	1990–2000	2000–2003	Births	Deaths	Net migration	Number	Percent change, 1990–2000	Persons per household	Female family householder[1]	One person
	Age (percent) (cont'd)				**Total persons**		**Percent change**		**Components of change, 2000–2003**			**Households, 2000**			**Percent**	
	16	17	18	19	20	21	22	23	24	25	26	27	28	29	30	31
IDAHO—Cont'd																
Custer	14.0	7.8	7.1	49.4	4 133	4 342	5.1	-5.8	118	109	-262	1 770	13.4	2.41	4.4	27.7
Elmore	6.2	4.5	3.0	44.9	21 205	29 130	37.4	-0.9	1 674	507	-1 448	9 092	27.4	2.76	7.5	20.7
Franklin	7.3	5.4	6.1	49.6	9 232	11 329	22.7	4.8	686	306	178	3 476	23.1	3.24	5.8	16.0
Fremont	8.7	7.1	5.1	48.5	10 937	11 819	8.1	2.4	681	331	-51	3 885	12.5	2.96	6.9	19.5
Gem	10.4	7.4	8.0	50.4	11 844	15 181	28.2	4.0	654	544	513	5 539	25.2	2.70	8.4	20.8
Gooding	9.8	7.6	7.6	48.8	11 633	14 155	21.7	1.2	670	476	-15	5 046	16.8	2.76	7.6	22.0
Idaho	13.2	9.3	8.1	48.7	13 768	15 511	12.7	-0.6	488	471	-99	6 084	17.3	2.46	6.3	25.3
Jefferson	7.9	4.9	4.3	49.5	16 543	19 155	15.8	5.4	1 171	456	331	5 901	21.1	3.23	6.8	15.2
Jerome	8.2	6.2	5.7	48.9	15 138	18 342	21.2	3.1	1 038	453	-5	6 298	18.3	2.89	7.6	19.5
Kootenai	9.7	6.5	5.9	50.5	69 795	108 685	55.7	8.1	4 866	2 929	6 871	41 308	53.3	2.60	9.2	21.9
Latah	7.8	4.5	5.1	48.1	30 617	34 935	14.1	0.4	1 325	659	-499	13 059	16.3	2.38	6.1	26.3
Lemhi	13.8	8.8	8.3	50.5	6 899	7 806	13.1	-1.0	219	286	-11	3 275	18.3	2.38	6.9	27.7
Lewis	13.4	9.8	9.7	49.4	3 516	3 747	6.6	0.0	132	112	-23	1 554	11.6	2.39	6.4	28.1
Lincoln	8.7	6.2	6.3	49.0	3 308	4 044	22.2	6.8	233	109	158	1 447	21.5	2.77	5.5	22.0
Madison	4.8	3.1	2.9	52.8	23 674	27 467	16.0	8.8	1 585	370	-113	7 129	22.9	3.66	5.7	12.7
Minidoka	9.5	6.8	7.1	50.3	19 361	20 174	4.2	-4.1	1 112	612	-1 376	6 973	7.7	2.87	8.2	20.0
Nez Perce	10.1	7.9	8.8	50.9	33 754	37 410	10.8	0.8	1 450	1 287	153	15 286	12.2	2.40	9.3	26.7
Oneida	8.7	7.1	8.8	49.3	3 492	4 125	18.1	0.2	195	153	-34	1 430	23.4	2.85	4.5	22.5
Owyhee	9.2	6.5	5.7	47.6	8 392	10 644	26.8	5.1	611	285	221	3 710	31.6	2.85	8.7	21.8
Payette	9.9	6.5	6.4	50.3	16 434	20 578	25.2	4.3	1 025	614	492	7 371	22.0	2.78	9.3	20.6
Power	9.4	5.9	5.2	50.3	7 086	7 538	6.4	-2.2	333	128	-381	2 560	8.0	2.92	8.8	20.3
Shoshone	13.0	9.5	8.8	50.1	13 931	13 771	-1.1	-5.6	444	579	-655	5 906	3.8	2.87	5.8	29.4
Teton	6.1	3.7	2.8	46.8	3 439	5 999	74.4	17.7	437	92	697	2 078	85.0	2.87	5.8	21.3
Twin Falls	9.1	6.6	7.3	51.0	53 580	64 284	20.0	4.4	3 218	2 044	1 674	23 853	20.9	2.64	9.2	23.6
Valley	13.7	9.4	6.1	48.5	6 109	7 651	25.2	1.2	231	170	41	3 208	33.4	2.36	5.4	24.8
Washington	10.9	9.0	8.9	50.9	8 550	9 977	16.7	0.2	437	335	-74	3 762	15.5	2.61	8.2	23.5
ILLINOIS	9.3	5.9	6.0	50.9	11 430 602	12 419 293	8.6	1.9	598 234	347 071	-20 773	4 591 779	9.3	2.63	12.3	26.8
Adams	9.7	8.0	9.7	52.1	66 090	68 277	3.3	-1.0	2 792	2 676	-770	26 860	5.3	2.44	9.8	28.5
Alexander	9.8	8.2	8.5	50.7	10 626	9 590	-9.7	-2.7	459	367	-348	3 808	-10.1	2.36	17.5	32.3
Bond	9.0	7.0	7.3	46.3	14 991	17 633	17.6	1.7	632	563	258	6 155	8.9	2.47	8.1	25.6
Boone	8.9	5.4	4.8	49.8	30 806	41 786	35.6	11.2	1 988	992	3 624	14 597	33.3	2.84	8.7	19.0
Brown	7.8	6.1	6.6	35.9	5 836	6 950	19.1	-1.0	192	160	-98	2 108	5.9	2.36	6.8	30.8
Bureau	10.6	7.8	9.7	51.4	35 688	35 503	-0.5	-0.8	1 358	1 292	-311	14 182	2.8	2.47	8.0	27.0
Calhoun	12.0	9.5	9.3	49.4	5 322	5 084	-4.5	-0.3	157	234	69	2 046	-0.1	2.46	5.7	26.5
Carroll	11.3	9.8	9.9	50.5	16 805	16 674	-0.8	-2.6	479	652	-254	6 794	2.4	2.42	7.4	27.3
Cass	9.8	7.5	8.2	49.8	13 437	13 695	1.9	1.1	673	508	-25	5 347	2.9	2.52	9.2	26.1
Champaign	7.0	4.9	4.7	49.6	173 025	179 669	3.8	4.0	7 482	3 960	3 793	70 597	10.5	2.33	9.2	31.4
Christian	10.2	8.0	9.8	49.8	34 418	35 372	2.8	-0.7	1 276	1 395	-89	13 921	2.4	2.41	9.1	28.4
Clark	10.4	8.2	9.4	51.2	15 921	17 008	6.8	-0.1	637	716	92	6 971	9.0	2.41	8.7	28.1
Clay	10.1	8.5	10.7	52.1	14 460	14 560	0.7	-1.7	623	572	-290	5 839	2.3	2.40	8.6	27.9
Clinton	8.8	7.3	7.1	48.6	33 944	35 535	4.7	1.7	1 267	1 012	381	12 754	10.1	2.60	8.4	24.2
Coles	8.2	6.5	7.1	52.1	51 644	53 196	3.0	-2.5	1 938	1 672	-1 607	21 043	11.0	2.31	8.3	31.2
Cook	8.7	5.9	5.7	51.4	5 105 044	5 376 741	5.3	-0.5	276 520	149 864	-155 349	1 974 181	5.0	2.68	15.6	29.4
Crawford	10.2	8.4	8.5	48.4	19 464	20 452	5.1	-2.7	635	729	-451	7 842	0.6	2.41	8.6	26.8
Cumberland	10.0	7.5	8.4	51.3	10 670	11 253	5.5	-1.7	400	433	-151	4 368	8.4	2.55	7.6	25.5
De Kalb	6.9	4.6	4.8	50.3	77 932	88 969	14.2	5.7	3 828	1 895	3 185	31 674	19.9	2.56	8.5	25.5
De Witt	10.5	7.6	8.4	51.1	16 516	16 798	1.7	-0.7	701	625	-178	6 770	4.3	2.44	8.5	26.8
Douglas	9.5	8.0	8.0	51.2	19 464	19 922	2.4	0.0	1 033	676	-334	7 574	5.1	2.59	7.9	24.7
Du Page	9.2	5.0	4.9	50.5	781 689	904 161	15.7	2.3	42 789	18 563	-2 920	325 601	16.6	2.73	7.9	22.9
Edgar	10.4	8.3	9.7	50.9	19 595	19 704	0.6	-1.6	692	733	-260	7 874	0.2	2.40	7.9	22.9
Edwards	11.2	8.6	10.0	51.6	7 440	6 971	-6.3	-1.7	272	255	-133	2 905	-3.7	2.37	9.6	28.5
Effingham	9.0	6.8	7.2	50.5	31 704	34 264	8.1	0.8	1 493	1 121	-66	13 001	13.4	2.60	8.2	26.1
Fayette	9.8	7.8	8.0	47.9	20 893	21 802	4.4	-1.2	782	823	-204	8 146	5.5	2.46	9.1	27.2
Ford	9.7	8.4	10.2	51.7	14 275	14 241	-0.2	-1.0	569	693	-3	5 639	0.7	2.45	8.0	28.0
Franklin	11.1	8.3	9.8	52.0	40 319	39 018	-3.2	0.3	1 550	1 930	490	16 408	-0.9	2.34	10.1	29.8
Fulton	10.2	8.3	9.4	48.6	38 080	38 250	0.4	-1.5	1 300	1 512	-363	14 877	-0.1	2.40	8.8	27.5
Gallatin	12.8	9.4	9.4	51.7	6 909	6 445	-6.7	-3.5	241	295	-169	2 726	-2.1	2.34	9.8	29.4
Greene	10.0	8.3	9.2	50.9	15 317	14 761	-3.6	-0.4	560	513	-88	5 757	-2.6	2.51	9.2	25.7
Grundy	9.1	5.8	6.0	50.2	32 337	37 535	16.1	5.3	1 561	1 020	1 444	14 293	19.3	2.60	8.6	23.5
Hamilton	11.0	9.1	10.4	51.7	8 499	8 621	1.4	-3.3	288	334	-232	3 462	-0.4	2.43	7.9	27.3
Hancock	10.9	8.7	9.7	51.4	21 373	20 121	-5.9	-3.6	684	734	-660	8 069	-4.0	2.45	7.6	26.9
Hardin	12.5	9.3	8.8	49.8	5 189	4 800	-7.5	-1.9	129	238	24	1 987	-3.0	2.30	8.8	28.6
Henderson	12.7	9.4	7.7	50.7	8 096	8 213	1.4	-1.7	243	292	-81	3 365	4.0	2.42	7.1	25.3
Henry	10.7	7.8	8.5	51.0	51 159	51 020	-0.3	-0.7	1 772	1 803	-317	20 056	2.8	2.51	8.0	25.1
Iroquois	10.9	8.4	9.7	50.9	30 787	31 334	1.8	-2.1	1 153	1 260	-531	12 220	3.7	2.51	8.5	25.2

1. No spouse present.

Table B. States and Counties — Vital Statistics, Health Resources, and Crime

STATE County	Births, average 1999–2001 Total	Rate[1]	Deaths, average 1999–2001 Number Total	Infant[2]	Rate Total[1]	Infant[3]	Physicians,[4] 2000 Number	Rate[5]	Hospitals,[4] 1998 Number	Beds Number	Rate[5]	Medicare enrollees, 2003	Serious crimes known to police,[6] 2002 Total Number	Rate[7]
	32	33	34	35	36	37	38	39	40	41	42	43	44	45
IDAHO—Cont'd														
Custer	36	8.4	35	0	8.2	D	1	23	0	0	0	709	74	1 644
Elmore	520	17.9	151	4	5.2	D	26	89	1	78	310	2 480	691	2 289
Franklin	226	19.9	86	2	7.5	D	3	26	1	65	585	1 536	98	835
Fremont	204	17.3	100	1	8.5	D	5	42	0	0	0	1 746	137	1 118
Gem	197	12.9	171	0	11.2	D	4	26	1	24	162	2 692	198	1 258
Gooding	219	15.5	129	1	9.2	D	6	42	1	27	198	2 329	288	1 963
Idaho	156	10.1	150	1	9.7	D	12	77	2	41	272	2 817	211	1 313
Jefferson	352	18.4	124	3	6.5	D	2	10	0	0	0	2 298	224	1 128
Jerome	328	17.9	138	2	7.6	D	13	71	1	73	406	2 487	625	3 288
Kootenai	1 502	13.8	845	11	7.8	7.5	156	144	1	187	184	17 754	4 366	3 876
Latah	414	11.8	203	3	5.8	D	30	86	1	40	125	3 876	792	2 187
Lemhi	67	8.6	93	1	11.9	D	6	77	1	28	349	1 595	NA	NA
Lewis	40	10.9	36	0	9.7	D	1	27	0	0	0	1 330	68	1 751
Lincoln	71	17.4	32	0	7.8	D	0	0	0	0	0	554	NA	NA
Madison	476	17.4	100	3	3.7	D	30	109	1	52	221	1 971	376	1 321
Minidoka	346	17.3	179	7	8.9	19.2	11	55	1	103	510	3 115	333	1 593
Nez Perce	445	11.9	401	4	10.8	D	92	246	1	120	326	7 211	1 375	3 657
Oneida	64	15.5	41	0	9.8	D	2	48	1	52	1 284	694	55	1 286
Owyhee	180	16.9	84	2	7.8	D	0	0	0	0	0	1 330	321	2 910
Payette	302	14.7	186	3	9.0	D	10	49	0	0	0	3 182	643	3 015
Power	110	14.5	48	0	6.4	D	7	93	1	41	493	865	164	2 099
Shoshone	148	10.8	189	3	13.8	D	20	145	1	69	497	2 928	330	2 312
Teton	123	20.3	31	1	5.1	D	6	100	1	13	237	586	94	1 512
Twin Falls	967	15.0	604	7	9.4	7.6	134	208	2	171	275	10 317	2 846	4 271
Valley	69	9.0	54	1	7.0	D	17	222	2	23	287	1 511	354	4 465
Washington	144	14.4	116	2	11.6	D	5	50	1	27	265	2 003	228	2 205
ILLINOIS	183 723	14.8	106 833	1 510	8.6	8.2	25 778	208	206	40 475	336	1 661 454	506 086	4 016
Adams	845	12.4	820	5	12.0	D	126	185	2	500	745	12 669	NA	NA
Alexander	129	13.5	118	1	12.3	D	4	42	1	50	315	1 912	NA	NA
Bond	189	10.7	176	2	10.0	D	7	40	1	50	315	2 849	NA	NA
Boone	606	14.4	307	3	7.3	D	33	79	2	129	333	5 170	NA	NA
Brown	57	8.2	56	0	8.0	D	0	0	0	0	0	959	NA	NA
Bureau	417	11.8	409	2	11.5	D	41	115	2	214	602	6 613	NA	NA
Calhoun	49	9.7	69	0	13.6	D	2	39	0	0	0	1 058	NA	NA
Carroll	168	10.1	200	2	12.0	D	9	54	0	0	0	3 607	NA	NA
Cass	196	14.3	158	2	11.5	D	5	37	0	0	0	2 480	NA	NA
Champaign	2 302	12.8	1 136	21	6.3	9.0	393	219	2	555	331	19 780	NA	NA
Christian	399	11.3	435	4	12.3	D	31	88	2	165	478	6 606	NA	NA
Clark	190	11.2	222	1	13.0	D	7	41	0	0	0	3 223	NA	NA
Clay	184	12.7	181	0	12.5	D	22	62	1	40	276	2 929	NA	NA
Clinton	404	11.4	324	2	9.1	D	86	162	1	54	152	5 022	NA	NA
Coles	602	11.3	528	6	9.9	D	86	162	1	176	344	7 831	NA	NA
Cook	84 728	15.8	46 453	825	8.6	9.7	15 095	281	63	19 465	375	666 722	NA	NA
Crawford	214	10.4	235	1	11.5	D	21	103	1	102	487	3 886	NA	NA
Cumberland	128	11.4	121	1	10.8	D	2	18	0	0	0	1 820	NA	NA
De Kalb	1 141	12.8	605	8	6.8	7.3	102	115	3	221	263	10 513	NA	NA
De Witt	209	12.4	192	3	11.5	D	11	65	1	36	214	3 003	NA	NA
Douglas	304	15.3	201	2	10.1	D	11	55	0	0	0	2 883	NA	NA
Du Page	13 470	14.9	5 643	87	6.2	6.4	2 064	228	8	1 880	214	98 797	NA	NA
Edgar	216	11.0	240	3	12.2	D	10	51	1	49	249	3 719	NA	NA
Edwards	78	11.3	88	1	12.7	D	2	29	0	0	0	1 307	NA	NA
Effingham	466	13.6	336	5	9.8	D	72	210	1	143	427	5 669	NA	NA
Fayette	252	11.6	248	2	11.4	D	10	46	1	170	774	3 708	NA	NA
Ford	181	12.7	212	1	14.9	D	12	84	1	56	398	2 647	NA	NA
Franklin	479	12.3	578	5	14.8	D	28	72	2	150	371	8 574	NA	NA
Fulton	408	10.7	485	2	12.7	D	36	94	1	124	320	7 505	NA	NA
Gallatin	72	11.2	82	0	12.7	D	1	16	0	0	0	1 379	NA	NA
Greene	172	11.7	180	1	12.2	D	8	54	1	73	469	3 032	NA	NA
Grundy	493	13.1	322	3	8.6	D	50	133	1	82	224	5 405	NA	NA
Hamilton	94	10.9	107	1	12.4	D	7	81	1	91	1 057	1 770	NA	NA
Hancock	224	11.2	233	0	11.6	D	13	65	1	67	318	4 112	NA	NA
Hardin	43	8.9	73	0	15.3	D	3	63	1	48	979	942	NA	NA
Henderson	77	9.4	83	0	10.2	D	6	73	0	0	0	1 370	NA	NA
Henry	579	11.4	541	5	10.6	D	39	76	2	168	326	8 828	NA	NA
Iroquois	362	11.6	384	2	12.3	D	23	73	2	99	317	6 204	NA	NA

1. Per 1,000 estimated resident population.　2. Deaths of infants under 1 year old.　3. Deaths of infants under 1 year old per 1,000 live births.　4. Data subject to copyright.　5. Per 100,000 resident population as of July 1 of the year shown.　6. Data for serious crimes have not been adjusted for underreporting; this may affect comparability between geographic areas and over time.　7. Per 100,000 population estimated by the FBI.

Table B. States and Counties — Crime, Education, Money Income, and Poverty

STATE County	Serious crimes known to police,[1] 2002 (cont'd) Rate[2] Violent	Property	Education — School enrollment and attainment, 2000 Enrollment[3] Total	Percent private	Attainment[4] (percent) High school graduate or less	Bachelor's degree or more	Local government expenditures,[5] 2000–2001 Total current expenditures (mil dol)	Current expenditures per student (dollars)	Money income, 1999 Per capita income[6] (dollars)	Households Median income Dollars	Percent change, 1989–1999 (constant 1999 dollars)	Percent with income of $100,000 or more	Percent below poverty level, 1999 Persons	House-holds	Families	Families with children
	46	47	48	49	50	51	52	53	54	55	56	57	58	59	60	61
IDAHO—Cont'd																
Custer	244	1 400	1 018	2.8	53.0	17.4	6.1	6 992	15 783	32 174	-1.8	3.6	14.3	14.3	10.7	14.0
Elmore	222	2 067	7 773	8.7	37.8	17.3	27.3	5 303	16 773	35 256	10.5	4.0	11.2	10.0	8.8	13.2
Franklin	17	818	3 506	4.1	51.8	13.6	14.2	4 800	13 702	36 061	5.5	4.8	7.4	6.8	5.4	7.1
Fremont	98	1 020	3 534	7.0	54.2	12.0	13.9	5 940	13 965	33 424	5.9	3.8	14.2	12.9	10.3	14.4
Gem	140	1 119	3 788	8.9	55.6	11.4	14.8	4 948	15 340	34 460	19.3	5.0	13.1	13.7	11.6	15.4
Gooding	150	1 813	3 470	6.3	62.1	12.0	17.5	6 067	14 612	31 888	19.7	4.0	13.8	14.0	11.2	16.7
Idaho	149	1 163	3 608	13.2	55.4	14.4	14.2	6 590	14 411	29 515	-0.6	2.6	16.3	15.7	12.5	18.5
Jefferson	156	972	6 224	6.6	45.0	15.2	28.0	5 225	13 838	37 737	15.0	5.4	10.4	9.7	8.0	11.4
Jerome	268	3 019	5 187	10.1	51.7	14.0	19.1	5 059	15 530	34 696	21.8	4.8	13.9	11.3	10.7	16.4
Kootenai	287	3 589	28 610	13.1	43.0	19.1	94.0	5 145	18 430	37 754	9.8	6.6	10.5	10.2	7.7	11.7
Latah	94	2 093	14 797	8.5	31.6	41.0	33.6	7 502	16 690	32 524	6.6	5.9	16.7	18.4	7.9	9.8
Lemhi	NA	NA	1 763	10.4	48.8	17.9	7.8	5 896	16 037	30 185	14.1	4.7	15.3	15.0	10.6	17.2
Lewis	232	1 519	885	7.2	50.5	14.8	8.0	7 503	15 942	31 413	11.7	3.4	12.0	12.1	8.7	14.0
Lincoln	NA	NA	1 127	2.4	55.5	13.0	6.1	6 956	14 257	32 484	11.7	3.7	13.1	11.8	9.3	13.1
Madison	116	1 205	15 041	58.0	33.8	24.4	27.8	5 232	10 956	32 607	5.5	4.5	30.5	24.8	10.1	11.2
Minidoka	100	1 492	5 884	7.1	59.1	10.1	24.1	5 375	13 813	32 021	2.2	3.6	14.8	13.8	11.9	18.0
Nez Perce	146	3 511	9 620	9.5	46.3	18.9	41.0	6 996	18 544	36 282	7.1	5.6	12.2	12.5	8.6	14.3
Oneida	140	1 146	1 245	3.0	45.3	15.0	5.2	5 432	13 829	34 309	13.1	3.1	10.8	10.9	6.7	11.7
Owyhee	263	2 647	2 883	7.7	67.0	10.2	16.0	6 272	13 405	28 339	13.4	4.7	16.9	16.0	14.2	19.3
Payette	211	2 804	5 547	6.0	57.5	10.6	22.3	5 120	14 924	33 046	20.8	5.0	13.2	12.7	9.7	13.6
Power	179	1 920	2 319	4.8	58.1	14.3	12.4	6 653	14 007	32 226	-3.2	5.4	16.1	14.9	10.8	15.7
Shoshone	378	1 934	2 907	4.3	62.4	10.2	17.4	7 493	15 934	28 535	1.2	3.2	16.4	15.9	12.4	20.4
Teton	113	1 399	1 655	14.8	35.3	28.1	6.6	5 004	17 778	41 968	37.0	5.7	12.9	9.6	9.7	10.5
Twin Falls	360	3 911	17 741	9.5	49.1	16.0	62.8	5 278	16 678	34 506	9.2	5.7	12.7	11.9	9.7	14.8
Valley	492	3 973	1 634	5.4	40.2	26.3	10.0	7 071	19 246	36 927	13.4	6.0	9.3	11.9	9.1	13.9
Washington	193	2 012	2 400	5.6	58.9	12.7	11.7	5 889	15 464	30 625	27.2	4.6	13.3	12.6	9.4	15.7
ILLINOIS	621	3 396	3 450 604	19.2	46.3	26.1	15 475.9	7 641	23 104	46 590	7.5	14.4	10.7	10.1	7.8	11.6
Adams	NA	NA	17 661	23.8	53.8	17.6	68.0	6 522	17 894	34 784	11.0	5.7	10.0	10.8	7.4	11.6
Alexander	NA	NA	2 413	6.0	67.7	6.9	13.7	8 221	16 084	26 042	31.1	3.8	26.1	24.8	21.2	32.7
Bond	NA	NA	4 596	25.6	61.4	15.0	13.9	5 662	17 947	37 680	18.1	5.3	9.3	10.3	6.7	9.4
Boone	NA	NA	11 539	17.3	57.5	14.5	43.7	5 514	21 590	52 397	11.1	13.0	7.0	6.8	5.1	7.2
Brown	NA	NA	1 306	9.3	65.6	9.2	5.1	6 169	14 629	35 445	29.0	3.4	8.5	10.7	4.8	7.2
Bureau	NA	NA	8 576	10.6	54.9	15.7	42.9	7 072	19 542	40 233	14.1	6.1	7.3	7.1	5.4	8.2
Calhoun	NA	NA	1 192	17.2	64.7	9.4	5.0	7 224	16 785	34 375	20.9	2.9	9.0	10.7	7.3	9.7
Carroll	NA	NA	4 020	4.7	60.7	13.1	20.4	6 529	18 688	37 148	7.3	5.3	9.6	8.7	7.4	12.0
Cass	NA	NA	3 273	10.8	64.3	12.6	15.0	6 615	16 532	35 243	11.0	3.8	12.0	10.9	9.2	14.6
Champaign	NA	NA	73 433	7.3	33.3	38.0	171.3	7 250	19 708	37 780	5.9	9.0	16.1	16.9	6.9	10.3
Christian	NA	NA	8 254	11.8	62.6	10.5	33.8	6 160	17 937	36 561	11.0	5.5	9.5	9.9	6.5	10.2
Clark	NA	NA	4 100	3.7	59.3	13.6	17.3	5 592	17 655	35 967	15.0	4.9	9.2	10.3	6.4	10.6
Clay	NA	NA	3 331	1.1	62.3	9.7	16.6	6 139	15 771	30 599	13.8	3.7	11.8	12.2	9.0	12.3
Clinton	NA	NA	9 052	16.0	57.6	13.0	33.7	5 998	19 109	44 618	11.1	7.2	6.4	6.8	4.6	6.6
Coles	NA	NA	19 136	5.0	49.7	20.8	57.5	8 265	17 370	32 286	-0.5	6.2	17.5	18.4	7.5	10.2
Cook	NA	NA	1 491 276	23.8	46.5	28.0	6 635.2	8 226	23 227	45 922	4.6	15.1	13.5	12.2	10.6	15.4
Crawford	NA	NA	5 498	5.1	57.6	10.3	26.6	7 514	16 869	32 531	1.3	5.0	11.2	11.3	8.5	13.0
Cumberland	NA	NA	2 845	7.5	62.8	10.1	11.0	5 390	16 953	36 149	13.9	3.2	9.5	9.9	7.8	11.6
De Kalb	NA	NA	35 173	6.6	42.4	26.8	114.6	7 431	19 462	45 828	10.5	10.1	11.4	12.5	5.1	7.3
De Witt	NA	NA	4 046	7.2	60.1	13.4	24.4	7 490	20 488	41 256	12.9	9.6	8.2	8.3	5.8	9.5
Douglas	NA	NA	4 859	12.7	60.3	13.8	18.8	6 091	18 474	39 439	9.7	5.8	6.4	7.0	4.2	6.6
Du Page	NA	NA	254 238	22.6	30.6	41.7	1 273.7	8 163	31 315	67 887	3.4	27.5	3.6	3.5	2.4	3.5
Edgar	NA	NA	4 346	7.2	60.5	13.3	25.4	6 965	17 857	35 203	21.0	4.3	10.5	11.3	7.6	11.7
Edwards	NA	NA	1 626	5.3	56.6	9.8	6.0	5 785	16 187	31 816	11.5	3.6	9.8	10.3	6.3	10.6
Effingham	NA	NA	9 514	15.3	54.7	15.1	35.5	5 520	18 301	39 379	7.6	6.2	8.1	8.7	6.0	8.9
Fayette	NA	NA	4 939	7.2	68.7	9.0	18.6	5 664	15 357	31 873	7.7	3.5	12.2	13.0	8.4	12.8
Ford	NA	NA	3 420	7.5	56.0	13.9	15.0	6 047	18 860	38 073	9.8	5.3	7.0	7.2	5.7	8.6
Franklin	NA	NA	9 032	5.2	57.7	11.3	44.4	6 924	15 407	28 411	13.1	3.4	16.2	16.0	12.6	19.9
Fulton	NA	NA	8 460	5.2	59.7	11.4	41.0	7 031	17 373	33 952	16.4	4.7	9.9	9.8	7.3	11.4
Gallatin	NA	NA	1 474	3.7	63.3	7.7	7.2	7 047	15 575	26 118	1.8	3.4	20.7	20.8	15.3	24.7
Greene	NA	NA	3 569	9.8	64.9	10.1	16.3	6 556	15 246	31 754	13.9	3.2	12.4	13.2	10.1	13.5
Grundy	NA	NA	10 016	10.2	52.0	15.2	60.3	7 193	22 591	51 719	7.7	12.5	4.8	5.8	3.2	4.4
Hamilton	NA	NA	1 983	7.6	57.6	10.5	9.8	7 056	16 262	30 496	24.2	4.4	12.9	13.3	8.5	14.5
Hancock	NA	NA	4 985	6.7	55.8	15.6	29.5	7 484	17 478	36 654	13.5	4.3	8.3	8.3	5.4	8.4
Hardin	NA	NA	953	4.1	60.9	9.6	5.1	7 627	15 984	27 693	33.0	3.4	18.6	17.6	14.7	24.1
Henderson	NA	NA	1 882	7.7	63.9	10.0	8.4	7 071	17 456	36 405	22.2	4.3	9.5	8.6	6.1	9.6
Henry	NA	NA	12 859	8.8	52.7	15.7	61.9	6 555	18 716	39 854	13.2	6.6	8.0	8.2	5.6	8.8
Iroquois	NA	NA	7 606	9.0	60.3	11.8	41.5	7 700	18 435	38 071	11.4	5.7	8.7	8.5	6.8	10.9

1. Data for serious crimes have not been adjusted for underreporting; this may affect comparability between geographic areas and over time.   2. Per 100,000 population estimated by the FBI.   3. All persons 3 years old and over enrolled in nursery school through college.   4. Persons 25 years old and over.   5. Elementary and secondary education expenditures.   6. Based on population enumerated as of April 1, 2000.

Table B. States and Counties — **Personal Income**

STATE County	Total (mil dol) 62	Percent change, 2001–2002 63	Per capita[1] Dollars 64	Per capita[1] Rank 65	Wages and salaries[2] (mil dol) 66	Proprietor's income (mil dol) 67	Dividends, interest, and rent (mil dol) 68	Transfer payments Total (mil dol) 69	Gov't payments to individuals Total (mil dol) 70	Social Security (mil dol) 71	Medical payments (mil dol) 72	Income maintenance (mil dol) 73	Unemployment insurance (mil dol) 74
IDAHO—Cont'd													
Custer	100	-2.3	24 023	1 399	49	13	28	17	16	7	6	1	1
Elmore	652	7.1	22 138	1 978	470	42	89	79	73	25	24	6	5
Franklin	231	1.4	19 610	2 628	77	31	35	34	32	17	11	2	1
Fremont	241	10.1	20 322	2 473	98	25	49	43	40	18	15	3	2
Gem	308	0.0	19 753	2 600	85	19	55	67	64	30	21	4	4
Gooding	393	0.4	27 589	603	157	117	60	57	54	24	22	4	2
Idaho	322	4.0	20 764	2 350	143	32	84	74	71	33	25	4	4
Jefferson	407	8.9	20 619	2 396	150	59	57	63	59	26	22	4	3
Jerome	463	2.3	24 787	1 181	217	127	59	68	64	27	26	6	3
Kootenai	2 761	4.6	24 164	1 353	1 472	264	521	476	450	200	158	29	26
Latah	846	5.0	24 141	1 360	463	77	177	110	103	43	34	6	3
Lemhi	168	3.2	21 645	2 109	73	20	44	40	38	16	15	2	2
Lewis	94	3.7	25 154	1 090	34	9	26	25	24	10	10	2	1
Lincoln	90	4.9	21 184	2 242	41	14	16	15	14	7	4	1	1
Madison	434	8.6	15 000	3 077	313	57	63	68	62	22	21	4	1
Minidoka	382	5.7	19 664	2 616	234	48	51	77	73	29	28	7	5
Nez Perce	988	3.0	26 578	770	762	81	183	193	185	80	72	12	5
Oneida	73	0.3	17 620	2 939	24	5	14	16	15	7	6	1	0
Owyhee	217	2.6	19 799	2 588	64	38	31	36	33	15	12	4	1
Payette	424	3.2	20 016	2 547	179	43	75	79	74	35	25	7	2
Power	160	9.1	21 512	2 147	123	31	25	27	25	11	9	2	2
Shoshone	271	1.9	20 714	2 368	126	18	49	83	80	35	31	7	5
Teton	137	4.9	20 072	2 531	52	9	29	16	15	7	6	1	1
Twin Falls	1 624	5.5	24 814	1 172	942	229	321	272	257	110	99	20	8
Valley	231	4.5	30 551	314	104	27	66	39	37	17	11	2	3
Washington	202	4.0	20 281	2 484	86	16	40	45	43	20	15	4	1
ILLINOIS	416 018	1.4	33 053	X	288 565	34 240	76 685	52 527	49 265	19 196	20 018	4 944	3 051
Adams	1 797	3.7	26 515	785	1 142	112	433	310	292	138	103	24	10
Alexander	167	2.2	17 607	2 941	76	8	26	61	59	19	23	12	1
Bond	438	2.6	24 541	1 250	162	24	74	74	70	31	26	5	3
Boone	1 225	2.0	27 357	637	647	64	215	146	135	67	42	8	15
Brown	121	1.1	17 707	2 931	99	10	24	23	22	10	8	2	1
Bureau	930	0.3	26 358	817	458	50	201	156	147	73	51	8	10
Calhoun	119	2.3	23 718	1 495	24	12	23	24	23	11	9	1	1
Carroll	420	-0.5	25 720	947	148	49	100	82	78	35	27	5	5
Cass	331	-0.2	24 270	1 320	190	24	69	63	60	26	24	4	3
Champaign	4 967	3.7	26 947	709	3 898	244	1 093	536	489	199	166	53	25
Christian	876	1.0	24 902	1 159	378	52	184	186	177	82	68	11	9
Clark	394	1.2	23 166	1 675	155	27	84	81	76	35	28	5	4
Clay	332	2.2	23 222	1 654	201	30	61	82	78	30	36	5	4
Clinton	1 008	1.9	28 131	528	370	72	184	150	141	61	60	7	7
Coles	1 247	0.2	24 046	1 390	888	68	251	218	204	81	77	16	12
Cook	189 054	1.0	35 224	136	147 639	21 242	34 115	24 879	23 484	7 656	10 691	2 954	1 403
Crawford	473	0.4	23 620	1 527	304	32	106	94	89	43	30	6	5
Cumberland	270	-2.0	24 331	1 298	70	32	48	47	44	20	15	4	3
De Kalb	2 419	1.5	26 208	854	1 293	149	475	288	264	115	91	16	18
De Witt	442	-1.1	26 482	794	229	27	85	82	78	34	27	5	5
Douglas	512	1.4	25 626	971	328	40	101	82	76	39	25	5	4
Du Page	41 663	0.5	45 214	32	31 923	3 238	7 699	2 891	2 651	1 314	916	108	221
Edgar	398	-10.9	20 508	2 430	202	7	87	95	90	40	34	7	4
Edwards	161	2.3	23 554	1 546	115	11	38	30	28	15	9	2	1
Effingham	911	2.1	26 477	798	683	63	220	138	129	59	48	9	8
Fayette	427	1.3	19 807	2 585	194	33	90	103	97	41	39	8	6
Ford	403	1.1	28 485	490	150	29	85	65	61	30	23	3	2
Franklin	843	2.4	21 622	2 119	312	54	158	232	222	93	84	21	10
Fulton	896	2.3	23 833	1 462	266	43	171	202	192	84	78	13	10
Gallatin	133	-0.5	21 377	2 187	47	6	35	37	35	15	14	4	1
Greene	299	0.5	20 329	2 472	83	26	59	71	68	30	25	5	3
Grundy	1 191	4.7	30 767	288	812	50	225	146	136	67	47	6	13
Hamilton	182	1.6	21 690	2 093	52	13	36	47	44	18	19	4	2
Hancock	486	1.3	24 686	1 214	180	51	104	89	84	42	29	6	3
Hardin	94	3.0	19 905	2 567	31	8	19	30	28	11	12	2	1
Henderson	190	-2.0	23 263	1 640	38	12	34	34	32	16	10	2	1
Henry	1 357	1.3	26 912	718	460	77	289	213	200	102	66	13	12
Iroquois	746	-0.7	24 224	1 335	258	45	181	152	144	70	53	9	7

1. Based on the resident population estimated as of July 1 of the year shown.   2. Includes other labor income.

Table B. States and Counties — Earnings, Social Security, and Housing

STATE County	Earnings, 2002									Social Security beneficiaries, December 2003		Supplemental Security Income recipients, December 2003	Housing units, 2003	
	Total (mil dol)	Farm	Goods-related[1]		Service-related and health									
			Total	Manu-facturing	Information and professional and technical services	Retail trade	Finance, insurance, and real estate	Health services	Govern-ment	Number	Rate[2]		Total	Percent change, 2000–2003
	75	76	77	78	79	80	81	82	83	84	85	86	87	88
IDAHO—Cont'd														
Custer	62	8.3	D	0.3	D	7.2	2.5	D	32.1	875	214	57	3 016	1.1
Elmore	512	7.3	D	1.2	D	4.8	2.1	2.4	70.6	2 955	102	234	11 044	4.9
Franklin	108	24.6	D	9.8	4.4	8.2	2.7	3.3	22.5	1 820	153	105	4 065	5.0
Fremont	123	17.6	D	1.3	D	6.0	3.3	D	31.8	2 065	171	127	7 108	3.2
Gem	104	6.6	D	3.0	D	8.4	4.6	D	27.8	3 370	213	219	6 212	5.5
Gooding	273	48.2	12.9	8.8	D	3.2	D	D	12.3	2 730	191	210	5 712	3.8
Idaho	175	1.9	20.6	11.4	3.8	7.8	D	D	31.8	3 820	248	351	7 646	1.4
Jefferson	208	19.5	22.7	12.4	D	6.0	2.1	D	18.5	2 915	144	199	6 641	5.6
Jerome	344	34.7	14.3	9.6	3.7	8.9	1.7	3.5	9.6	2 925	155	280	6 896	2.7
Kootenai	1 736	0.1	20.2	8.9	8.7	11.4	6.3	10.4	19.4	21 605	184	1 815	50 643	8.7
Latah	539	1.9	D	2.9	7.0	9.1	2.6	7.9	47.2	4 385	125	267	14 306	3.4
Lemhi	93	4.3	D	4.3	4.1	10.4	3.9	D	40.4	1 960	254	136	4 267	2.7
Lewis	43	11.4	D	6.9	D	8.9	D	4.4	28.7	1 225	327	156	1 800	0.3
Lincoln	55	29.0	D	D	D	1.7	1.1	8.2	34.1	885	205	45	1 703	3.1
Madison	370	5.5	D	8.2	D	8.9	3.0	D	14.6	2 410	81	160	9 038	18.5
Minidoka	282	17.3	29.9	25.9	3.7	4.4	1.5	D	16.1	3 290	170	328	7 558	0.8
Nez Perce	843	1.0	D	16.8	5.1	9.3	6.7	15.0	18.1	8 270	219	905	16 490	1.8
Oneida	29	10.7	D	D	D	7.3	D	4.7	40.6	810	196	48	1 801	2.6
Owyhee	101	39.8	D	4.7	2.0	4.1	D	3.2	20.5	1 755	157	124	4 591	3.1
Payette	223	12.0	D	24.4	D	6.7	3.5	6.2	15.9	3 985	186	352	8 324	4.7
Power	154	25.1	36.8	31.5	D	2.8	1.6	D	14.9	1 120	152	83	2 921	2.7
Shoshone	144	-0.1	22.8	4.8	6.1	18.5	D	D	26.3	3 565	274	390	7 032	-0.4
Teton	61	8.9	D	4.2	10.6	9.2	5.1	D	23.7	765	108	30	3 284	24.8
Twin Falls	1 172	8.4	16.8	10.5	8.9	11.1	5.2	9.1	17.9	11 920	178	1 278	26 688	4.3
Valley	131	1.5	D	5.2	D	10.2	7.4	D	34.0	1 770	229	61	8 444	4.5
Washington	102	12.0	20.3	15.0	7.2	6.6	2.3	6.5	23.8	2 360	236	218	4 172	0.8
ILLINOIS	322 805	0.2	20.7	13.9	14.5	5.9	11.6	8.5	13.5	1 867 671	148	255 262	5 030 728	3.0
Adams	1 253	1.3	27.5	20.9	5.5	9.2	6.5	14.9	13.9	14 260	211	1 211	29 753	1.2
Alexander	84	2.4	D	8.2	D	4.0	2.2	D	33.6	2 160	232	634	4 622	0.7
Bond	186	4.1	D	15.4	D	6.0	4.1	D	26.0	3 260	182	233	6 905	3.2
Boone	711	1.9	D	44.3	D	6.5	3.6	D	9.2	6 680	144	261	16 612	7.8
Brown	109	6.1	D	D	D	2.2	2.2	D	23.6	1 070	156	104	2 496	1.6
Bureau	508	3.5	28.4	19.2	D	15.8	4.7	D	16.6	7 410	210	289	15 338	0.0
Calhoun	36	18.5	D	D	D	12.1	8.6	D	24.6	1 235	244	86	2 721	1.5
Carroll	197	10.9	D	24.4	2.8	5.7	5.7	5.3	15.6	3 810	235	189	8 042	1.2
Cass	214	4.6	38.8	35.7	D	5.2	4.4	D	14.0	2 640	191	183	5 774	-0.2
Champaign	4 142	0.1	16.1	10.4	8.4	6.2	5.5	11.6	35.5	21 870	117	2 466	78 575	4.4
Christian	430	1.5	D	15.9	3.6	9.6	4.7	11.5	17.8	7 760	221	558	15 152	1.1
Clark	182	2.2	41.9	32.5	2.9	6.9	4.3	D	15.2	3 700	218	247	7 961	1.9
Clay	231	2.5	49.8	42.7	4.6	5.2	3.2	D	14.5	3 315	232	298	6 516	1.9
Clinton	442	6.1	D	9.5	4.7	11.0	5.4	10.3	21.6	6 500	180	245	14 235	3.1
Coles	956	0.1	19.7	13.1	12.4	7.0	3.8	14.4	24.7	8 515	164	989	23 014	1.1
Cook	168 881	0.0	16.5	10.7	18.7	4.6	15.1	7.9	11.7	730 380	136	155 278	2 117 761	1.0
Crawford	335	0.1	48.7	39.3	3.3	6.0	3.2	4.5	20.7	4 340	218	285	8 889	1.2
Cumberland	103	11.7	D	10.4	D	13.6	D	9.5	16.3	2 115	191	158	4 992	2.4
De Kalb	1 442	1.1	25.3	17.0	3.9	8.7	5.6	10.3	29.8	11 410	121	420	34 735	5.3
De Witt	256	1.3	17.4	12.4	D	6.9	4.0	2.5	16.8	3 290	197	233	7 381	1.4
Douglas	368	0.2	D	46.8	2.3	9.7	3.2	D	8.4	3 850	193	176	8 144	1.7
Du Page	35 160	0.0	19.1	11.6	17.1	6.7	9.9	6.4	7.1	114 610	124	6 098	348 260	3.8
Edgar	209	-6.2	D	28.0	5.6	9.2	6.6	D	23.3	4 280	221	383	8 718	1.2
Edwards	127	0.5	D	D	D	4.8	D	2.0	7.8	1 575	230	79	3 279	2.5
Effingham	746	1.3	D	21.0	D	8.8	3.5	14.3	10.8	6 265	181	420	14 252	2.1
Fayette	228	2.1	24.7	17.2	3.8	9.3	3.8	D	25.1	4 540	211	482	9 227	1.9
Ford	179	2.0	24.0	17.6	4.2	7.3	4.4	11.8	15.7	3 000	213	129	6 115	0.9
Franklin	366	1.0	27.2	20.9	5.9	11.9	3.5	8.6	24.4	9 820	251	1 345	18 255	0.8
Fulton	309	3.7	D	2.5	D	11.4	4.8	D	31.1	8 510	226	577	16 256	0.1
Gallatin	53	4.8	D	3.6	D	7.3	D	D	19.4	1 565	252	229	3 158	2.8
Greene	109	11.6	D	8.4	D	9.9	D	D	23.7	3 315	225	325	6 415	1.3
Grundy	862	-0.4	22.4	12.1	3.4	5.8	2.9	6.8	9.6	6 260	158	151	15 872	5.5
Hamilton	65	4.3	11.3	2.8	D	8.1	D	5.1	31.2	2 030	244	210	4 061	2.0
Hancock	231	10.5	D	29.7	4.1	5.5	3.9	D	16.7	4 385	226	252	9 062	1.7
Hardin	39	4.0	D	D	D	D	D	15.8	22.7	1 215	258	177	2 525	1.2
Henderson	50	6.0	D	D	D	5.6	D	6.4	28.6	1 685	209	92	4 171	1.1
Henry	537	2.0	D	10.7	8.1	10.0	6.3	9.1	21.4	10 220	202	408	21 406	0.6
Iroquois	303	4.6	D	9.9	D	8.6	7.5	D	16.8	7 040	229	369	13 422	0.4

1. Covers mining, construction, and manufacturing.   2. Per 1,000 resident population estimated as of July 1 of the year shown.

Table B. States and Counties — Housing, Labor Force, and Employment

STATE County	Total	Percent	Median value[1]	With a mortgage	Without a mortgage[2]	Median rent[3]	Median rent as a percent of income	Substandard units[4] (percent)	Total	Percent change, 2002–2003	Total	Rate[5]	Total	Management, professional and related occupations	Production, transportation, and material moving occupations
	Housing units, 2000									Civilian labor force, 2003		Unemployment		Civilian employment,[6] 2000		
	Occupied units													Percent		
			Owner-occupied			Renter-occupied									
				Median owner cost as a percent of income											
	89	90	91	92	93	94	95	96	97	98	99	100	101	102	103
IDAHO—Cont'd															
Custer	1 770	74.7	90 400	19.6	9.9	378	18.9	3.6	2 254	11.4	151	6.7	1 941	35.1	9.1
Elmore	9 092	57.4	93 200	21.8	9.9	473	22.4	5.8	9 655	-0.6	677	7.0	9 492	27.1	14.2
Franklin	3 476	80.8	94 300	21.5	9.9	481	21.5	7.1	5 416	6.4	182	3.4	4 911	25.1	22.1
Fremont	3 885	84.3	82 200	22.2	9.9	420	20.2	7.6	4 803	-5.5	293	6.1	5 101	22.7	20.7
Gem	5 539	79.9	97 600	22.8	10.0	502	28.5	6.0	5 877	-3.4	452	7.7	6 376	21.9	21.0
Gooding	5 046	72.4	82 500	21.4	9.9	480	20.8	9.4	7 579	7.4	280	3.7	6 259	24.1	15.1
Idaho	6 084	77.0	88 600	21.6	9.9	410	22.2	5.7	6 659	3.4	584	8.8	5 925	28.9	16.0
Jefferson	5 901	84.7	91 900	21.9	9.9	433	22.3	6.6	10 453	2.8	385	3.7	8 289	30.4	16.6
Jerome	6 298	70.0	89 800	22.0	10.5	480	24.2	8.2	10 116	7.3	414	4.1	8 084	27.6	16.1
Kootenai	41 308	74.5	120 100	23.8	9.9	571	27.9	3.7	59 593	0.3	4 260	7.1	50 162	27.8	13.5
Latah	13 059	58.7	126 400	21.4	9.9	469	32.1	3.7	15 832	1.5	520	3.3	17 223	39.5	9.1
Lemhi	3 275	76.1	91 500	23.8	9.9	390	23.1	2.6	4 008	8.2	263	6.6	3 196	33.6	11.5
Lewis	1 554	74.5	78 900	19.6	10.7	342	20.0	1.4	1 502	1.0	59	3.9	1 514	28.9	18.8
Lincoln	1 447	74.4	75 700	20.5	9.9	464	24.1	7.3	2 195	10.2	116	5.3	1 799	27.7	14.9
Madison	7 129	59.2	106 800	21.6	9.9	298	19.4	18.1	11 477	-2.0	211	1.8	11 659	31.6	12.4
Minidoka	6 973	76.9	74 600	21.5	9.9	394	21.1	9.8	9 714	1.8	807	8.3	8 788	24.8	23.0
Nez Perce	15 286	68.7	105 800	19.9	9.9	462	25.6	2.4	24 128	-1.5	847	3.5	17 856	27.3	17.6
Oneida	1 430	82.3	88 400	23.1	9.9	484	26.7	4.2	1 811	7.2	69	3.8	1 751	28.6	26.1
Owyhee	3 710	69.7	82 500	23.1	9.9	383	22.1	9.0	4 266	-2.7	98	2.3	4 389	24.8	20.0
Payette	7 371	74.2	87 900	23.3	9.9	460	23.8	6.6	9 697	1.5	900	9.3	8 765	23.8	19.9
Power	2 560	74.5	89 000	22.1	14.1	388	19.5	6.8	3 207	1.4	299	9.3	3 325	27.8	21.0
Shoshone	5 906	72.6	70 200	20.6	10.8	389	23.2	3.4	6 226	0.9	718	11.5	5 377	24.7	14.2
Teton	2 078	73.7	133 000	23.9	9.9	603	21.9	9.1	4 043	10.4	154	3.8	3 030	29.3	9.1
Twin Falls	23 853	68.3	93 800	21.0	9.9	489	24.6	4.9	36 572	7.1	1 475	4.0	29 916	27.4	16.4
Valley	3 208	79.1	141 200	24.9	9.9	505	25.8	2.9	4 158	2.4	345	8.3	3 599	29.7	9.9
Washington	3 762	73.8	90 200	22.6	11.8	457	22.3	6.1	4 231	1.9	446	10.5	4 245	26.5	21.8
ILLINOIS	4 591 779	67.3	130 800	21.7	11.1	605	24.4	5.3	6 330 059	-0.6	422 263	6.7	5 833 185	34.2	15.7
Adams	26 860	73.8	75 600	18.6	10.2	402	23.1	1.5	37 478	0.5	1 757	4.7	33 344	27.7	18.8
Alexander	3 808	72.0	33 400	19.7	11.6	265	26.7	4.0	3 800	-3.2	409	10.8	3 256	24.6	21.6
Bond	6 155	79.6	68 900	18.3	9.9	385	23.8	2.8	9 381	2.5	463	4.9	7 718	26.8	20.7
Boone	14 597	78.6	123 600	22.2	10.5	531	20.8	4.4	23 004	-1.3	1 913	8.3	20 149	25.3	26.3
Brown	2 108	74.1	47 400	15.3	9.9	316	23.1	2.5	3 067	0.7	127	4.1	2 528	24.7	21.7
Bureau	14 182	76.0	77 800	19.1	10.8	432	19.6	1.6	18 657	0.2	1 442	7.7	17 395	26.2	24.0
Calhoun	2 046	80.8	61 600	19.2	11.7	350	17.0	2.9	3 036	-0.6	170	5.6	2 332	26.1	15.7
Carroll	6 794	76.7	68 700	19.3	9.9	385	19.7	0.7	8 150	1.9	752	9.2	7 724	25.8	27.9
Cass	5 347	75.2	54 900	17.7	10.3	419	20.0	3.6	7 645	0.4	414	5.4	6 476	25.3	26.4
Champaign	70 597	55.7	94 700	19.2	9.9	540	29.6	3.0	100 196	0.1	3 292	3.3	93 236	42.2	11.1
Christian	13 921	76.2	61 000	18.5	11.3	407	21.9	1.8	19 059	0.5	1 131	5.9	15 941	25.0	19.5
Clark	6 971	77.5	63 300	18.2	10.4	422	20.3	2.0	10 016	-1.9	620	6.2	7 890	26.1	24.3
Clay	5 839	79.8	51 500	19.0	9.9	348	20.9	1.8	7 241	1.9	484	6.7	6 531	23.4	27.6
Clinton	12 754	80.3	83 700	19.9	10.3	430	20.0	1.6	17 136	0.9	1 039	6.1	17 153	28.7	21.0
Coles	21 043	61.9	71 500	19.4	9.9	438	28.9	2.3	27 764	0.6	1 516	5.5	26 381	27.2	19.8
Cook	1 974 181	57.9	157 700	23.1	11.9	648	25.0	8.3	2 620 397	-0.9	191 032	7.3	2 421 287	35.2	15.1
Crawford	7 842	80.2	54 200	18.6	10.4	372	22.4	1.6	9 503	-1.9	682	7.2	8 594	24.3	28.0
Cumberland	4 368	82.0	68 700	20.4	9.9	372	20.3	3.2	5 595	1.2	396	7.1	5 411	21.2	29.4
De Kalb	31 674	59.6	135 900	22.7	11.7	577	26.8	3.2	47 832	-0.3	2 817	5.9	45 909	32.7	15.5
De Witt	6 770	74.9	74 300	17.8	9.9	409	21.7	1.8	6 784	-1.7	541	8.0	8 380	26.1	19.9
Douglas	7 574	76.9	70 500	18.6	9.9	431	19.8	3.4	13 431	-0.2	554	4.1	9 571	25.3	24.1
Du Page	325 601	76.4	195 000	22.3	11.4	837	23.6	3.7	515 705	-0.8	26 904	5.2	476 172	43.7	10.1
Edgar	7 874	74.6	54 300	18.1	10.7	391	22.1	2.2	11 262	3.7	554	4.9	8 934	25.7	27.7
Edwards	2 905	81.2	46 700	18.8	10.9	319	22.8	1.7	3 670	2.4	151	4.1	3 314	23.6	29.7
Effingham	13 001	76.0	85 400	19.2	10.8	436	20.6	2.7	18 432	1.0	1 070	5.8	17 234	25.1	23.1
Fayette	8 146	79.7	59 500	19.2	10.2	384	21.5	2.2	10 595	1.8	798	7.5	9 356	19.9	27.0
Ford	5 639	76.0	70 600	18.7	9.9	412	21.1	0.9	6 794	0.9	322	4.7	6 883	26.9	22.3
Franklin	16 408	77.7	45 100	19.9	12.6	380	24.2	2.4	17 380	1.4	1 428	8.2	16 017	24.6	20.0
Fulton	14 877	76.3	58 100	18.6	11.0	390	22.8	2.1	13 898	0.5	1 372	9.9	16 137	27.6	19.6
Gallatin	2 726	81.1	46 300	19.7	11.5	272	24.0	2.2	2 705	3.0	229	8.5	2 600	27.1	21.3
Greene	5 757	76.4	47 900	19.3	10.2	369	19.4	1.6	6 755	0.4	372	5.5	6 301	27.5	22.5
Grundy	14 293	72.3	128 600	20.8	10.3	602	21.6	2.3	19 113	0.4	1 764	9.2	18 567	25.2	19.4
Hamilton	3 462	81.5	47 800	18.2	10.1	308	24.4	2.7	3 709	0.8	266	7.2	3 698	26.7	20.0
Hancock	8 069	80.3	58 200	17.5	9.9	363	19.7	1.2	12 162	-0.4	759	6.2	10 016	26.0	25.6
Hardin	1 987	80.5	40 800	16.9	10.0	246	23.8	2.7	1 849	2.3	155	8.4	1 788	27.8	19.1
Henderson	3 365	78.9	57 300	17.3	9.9	374	18.9	1.7	5 368	-5.1	309	5.8	4 005	22.7	27.0
Henry	20 056	78.8	77 700	18.9	10.7	419	20.9	1.6	25 948	-0.2	1 650	6.4	24 999	28.4	19.0
Iroquois	12 220	76.4	77 900	18.9	11.5	446	19.8	1.6	15 518	2.3	917	5.9	14 980	26.4	22.5

1. Specified owner-occupied units.   2. Median monthly owner costs is often in the minimum category—9.9 percent or less, which is indicated as 9.9 percent.   3. Specified renter-occupied units.   4. Overcrowded or lacking complete plumbing facilities.   5. Percent of civilian labor force.   6. Persons 16 years old and over.

	Private nonfarm establishments, employment and payroll, 2001									Agriculture, 2002			
	Employment							Annual payroll		Farms			
											Percent with—		
STATE County	Number of establishments	Total	Health care and social assistance	Manufacturing	Retail trade	Finance and insurance	Professional, scientific, and technical services	Total (mil dol)	Average per employee (dollars)	Number	Less than 50 acres	500 acres and over	Farm operators whose principal occupation is farming (percent)
	104	105	106	107	108	109	110	111	112	113	114	115	116
IDAHO—Cont'd													
Custer	142	814	76	D	112	24	D	19	23 248	285	38.6	20.4	59.6
Elmore	396	4 014	831	365	1 118	158	54	79	19 730	364	49.7	23.6	55.5
Franklin	231	1 764	261	325	443	61	D	32	17 919	792	43.2	17.6	46.2
Fremont	258	1 447	177	D	311	53	D	29	19 945	518	36.3	24.1	57.1
Gem	308	2 093	362	407	326	57	D	41	19 627	802	66.1	8.5	56.9
Gooding	315	2 293	356	282	440	65	70	47	20 422	663	50.8	12.8	59.0
Idaho	436	2 618	363	338	570	103	58	57	21 811	663	19.6	35.7	62.4
Jefferson	363	3 394	163	690	608	74	55	64	18 954	784	51.0	16.7	53.7
Jerome	431	4 437	335	827	1 084	74	108	93	20 983	635	52.1	15.4	62.8
Kootenai	3 642	36 660	5 295	4 399	6 266	997	1 938	874	23 845	828	58.0	7.7	48.4
Latah	853	8 037	1 172	361	1 990	243	293	151	18 767	890	32.2	19.7	47.3
Lemhi	308	1 634	295	143	426	38	D	31	19 069	303	45.9	28.1	63.0
Lewis	122	689	20	210	141	32	D	15	21 611	177	12.4	50.3	65.5
Lincoln	78	594	66	D	83	D	D	13	21 170	280	28.6	24.6	70.7
Madison	531	12 035	998	1 384	1 539	294	518	182	15 082	479	48.4	19.4	52.6
Minidoka	375	5 417	431	1 995	905	58	102	121	22 281	694	51.2	14.1	58.6
Nez Perce	1 164	15 971	2 743	2 963	2 727	1 089	429	441	27 620	441	41.0	32.9	59.0
Oneida	71	546	171	D	109	36	D	10	18 266	428	23.1	34.6	58.6
Owyhee	151	1 523	113	528	157	D	D	41	27 126	571	34.9	23.6	68.1
Payette	404	3 863	370	1 295	579	108	111	86	22 211	639	61.2	5.8	52.0
Power	149	1 940	159	719	290	D	D	40	20 564	334	18.6	49.4	64.4
Shoshone	369	3 206	430	178	705	64	200	73	22 865	46	58.7	0.0	80.4
Teton	244	1 164	156	D	252	D	D	25	21 660	302	36.4	22.5	61.6
Twin Falls	2 234	23 789	3 390	3 254	4 669	817	992	526	22 130	1 297	47.3	14.7	63.2
Valley	475	2 445	256	105	476	50	78	43	17 769	156	56.4	19.2	55.1
Washington	223	2 153	272	319	328	56	58	38	17 472	495	36.4	26.5	60.0
ILLINOIS	307 356	5 447 349	643 977	820 179	608 957	343 237	353 262	204 268	37 499	73 027	26.9	24.0	64.1
Adams	1 890	29 775	4 751	5 739	4 658	1 382	694	771	25 896	1 347	23.8	21.8	62.0
Alexander	154	1 697	334	293	214	D	D	37	22 027	149	14.1	24.2	62.4
Bond	349	4 068	549	718	542	154	68	91	22 338	668	33.8	19.8	60.6
Boone	722	11 596	711	5 363	1 155	307	99	400	34 467	476	40.8	17.0	65.1
Brown	127	1 918	171	D	135	69	D	53	27 385	417	23.3	19.4	48.0
Bureau	847	11 040	1 935	2 429	1 404	432	266	294	26 658	1 091	18.2	31.8	74.9
Calhoun	105	760	107	D	145	83	D	13	17 253	480	24.2	7.3	45.4
Carroll	437	3 912	473	1 058	521	207	64	86	21 905	656	25.3	22.1	65.9
Cass	313	4 617	456	2 222	454	197	63	105	22 702	427	24.4	28.6	67.7
Champaign	4 097	71 162	10 225	9 875	10 650	2 903	3 508	1 903	26 735	1 285	21.4	32.1	72.5
Christian	816	10 498	1 705	1 838	1 723	338	170	235	22 424	796	25.8	34.4	65.5
Clark	391	4 591	357	2 002	535	162	70	100	21 825	581	28.6	28.1	60.9
Clay	381	5 242	627	2 131	490	157	94	124	23 730	703	31.3	23.5	56.2
Clinton	819	8 095	1 588	1 131	1 295	298	268	180	22 250	915	29.2	16.4	65.4
Coles	1 299	20 735	3 033	5 614	3 198	718	546	537	25 881	684	29.5	26.6	65.9
Cook	127 162	2 515 882	301 331	323 894	233 438	189 328	214 653	106 288	42 247	211	60.7	4.7	52.6
Crawford	474	6 828	658	2 390	820	258	120	218	31 976	567	33.9	23.3	55.7
Cumberland	183	1 619	402	354	241	74	D	28	17 219	583	30.4	18.5	61.2
De Kalb	1 937	26 061	3 842	6 297	4 322	1 123	712	686	26 333	816	23.8	32.6	77.1
De Witt	406	5 179	452	786	726	D	72	232	44 834	459	27.7	32.0	68.6
Douglas	630	7 443	354	2 935	1 635	206	95	188	25 238	576	28.0	28.3	72.0
Du Page	32 543	622 033	46 264	69 364	66 183	33 654	50 197	25 777	41 440	79	64.6	5.1	48.1
Edgar	412	5 363	786	1 826	838	259	114	115	21 456	667	20.5	37.0	70.5
Edwards	172	2 892	101	D	199	69	D	75	25 915	379	32.5	23.5	53.6
Effingham	1 122	19 142	2 869	5 006	2 956	486	434	480	25 089	1 134	29.4	13.5	57.6
Fayette	486	4 965	774	1 208	893	192	114	104	20 995	1 248	32.1	18.2	60.5
Ford	422	4 025	667	850	711	159	80	93	22 984	530	16.2	40.0	74.3
Franklin	837	8 584	1 404	1 708	1 676	260	177	180	20 925	727	40.0	12.7	45.0
Fulton	715	7 094	1 792	249	1 630	318	170	138	19 445	1 055	21.4	24.0	64.2
Gallatin	132	1 022	D	D	131	D	D	30	29 426	187	23.0	35.3	63.6
Greene	277	1 925	319	251	484	127	98	35	18 050	678	22.1	27.7	72.7
Grundy	916	10 904	1 284	1 537	1 893	465	319	401	36 756	407	19.2	34.6	72.7
Hamilton	184	1 105	402	50	202	D	D	18	16 426	694	31.4	15.4	47.3
Hancock	484	5 097	573	2 299	607	209	103	104	20 413	1 095	18.4	25.6	68.9
Hardin	70	812	375	D	66	D	D	17	20 825	179	12.8	9.5	50.8
Henderson	119	648	123	D	125	D	D	11	17 701	392	17.1	36.2	74.2
Henry	1 147	14 103	1 365	4 280	2 381	557	297	317	22 476	1 284	22.7	26.7	74.8
Iroquois	731	7 076	1 649	1 187	1 100	366	101	148	20 921	1 386	18.8	34.3	75.7

STATE County	Land in farms Acreage (1,000) [117]	Percent change, 1997-2002 [118]	Acres Average size of farm [119]	Total irrigated (1,000) [120]	Total cropland (1,000) [121]	Value of land and buildings (dollars) Average per farm [122]	Average per acre [123]	Value of machinery and equipment average per farm (dollars) [124]	Value of products sold Total (mil dol) [125]	Average per farm (dollars) [126]	Percent from — Crops [127]	Live-stock and poultry products [128]	Percent of farms with sales of — $10,000 or more [129]	$100,000 or more [130]	Government payments Total ($1,000) [131]	Percent of farms [132]
IDAHO—Cont'd																
Custer	132	-10.8	462	55	55	739 598	1 836	52 701	13	44 668	23.6	76.4	38.2	13.3	292	17.5
Elmore	346	-2.8	951	91	124	676 926	719	124 954	293	804 545	D	D	33.5	18.1	1 157	19.8
Franklin	244	-0.8	308	46	132	318 843	1 078	61 999	49	62 385	15.5	84.5	37.0	13.0	2 733	36.1
Fremont	287	-14.1	555	103	168	599 950	1 148	113 951	72	139 054	88.8	11.2	38.8	18.7	2 701	41.7
Gem	221	20.8	276	33	42	449 989	1 234	36 071	27	34 248	32.2	67.8	26.9	6.1	615	15.5
Gooding	195	-11.4	294	118	120	795 709	2 535	137 759	353	531 928	-9.9	90.1	54.0	25.5	2 569	23.8
Idaho	639	-1.7	963	1	217	777 859	745	81 943	35	53 163	66.6	33.4	43.4	14.6	2 588	38.6
Jefferson	305	-8.4	389	203	221	643 066	1 758	98 575	159	202 423	62.7	37.3	43.6	20.4	2 982	29.7
Jerome	186	-4.1	293	140	145	652 684	1 887	153 933	289	454 752	26.1	73.9	51.5	29.0	2 091	26.5
Kootenai	154	17.6	186	13	68	487 329	2 265	30 418	14	17 078	85.2	14.8	15.2	3.3	685	12.4
Latah	340	4.6	382	0	252	579 759	1 400	61 583	40	44 789	93.2	6.8	27.1	12.5	4 496	59.9
Lemhi	174	-11.7	573	75	70	652 328	1 228	59 888	17	55 914	7.6	92.4	47.2	17.2	446	23.1
Lewis	217	11.9	1 224	1	157	976 948	830	163 864	28	156 792	94.1	5.9	58.2	35.6	1 755	57.6
Lincoln	128	-2.3	457	66	70	605 784	943	148 280	54	192 513	28.4	71.6	52.9	20.7	1 061	38.2
Madison	190	-14.8	397	116	152	914 039	2 283	179 093	93	193 470	93.6	6.4	48.6	22.3	3 128	37.0
Minidoka	228	10.1	329	197	204	670 789	2 000	154 999	191	274 994	76.1	23.9	52.3	28.1	3 314	30.0
Nez Perce	343	1.2	779	1	196	773 951	853	168 315	40	91 614	87.4	12.6	37.4	19.7	2 837	32.7
Oneida	363	33.9	848	32	238	521 988	667	66 516	16	38 165	56.3	43.7	40.9	13.1	3 552	58.6
Owyhee	571	-16.4	1 000	123	153	779 529	689	127 029	127	222 019	29.3	70.7	56.0	28.0	1 613	31.5
Payette	155	4.7	242	55	58	402 068	1 735	79 528	107	167 003	23.7	76.3	36.6	12.8	736	18.0
Power	425	0.2	1 273	114	331	1 135 300	986	210 893	112	333 969	71.3	28.7	47.3	25.7	8 402	67.7
Shoshone	4	0.0	94	0	2	331 599	3 442	34 571	0	1 929	14.6	85.4	4.3	0.0	D	D
Teton	125	-6.0	413	56	92	1 205 545	2 462	74 977	24	79 886	82.9	17.1	41.4	13.9	829	28.8
Twin Falls	441	-3.3	340	238	268	614 239	1 946	120 236	292	225 021	36.8	63.2	54.7	25.4	3 548	35.9
Valley	66	3.1	420	20	17	662 593	1 524	36 737	3	22 397	27.6	72.4	23.1	5.1	91	11.5
Washington	472	6.5	954	43	104	709 632	736	65 891	45	91 000	44.1	55.9	42.4	13.3	1 452	34.3
ILLINOIS	27 311	0.4	374	391	24 171	913 251	2 425	102 242	7 676	105 115	76.5	23.5	58.6	26.7	412 636	65.5
Adams	444	0.5	330	2	354	684 179	2 030	90 740	124	92 258	60.8	39.2	59.5	23.5	5 924	60.4
Alexander	78	9.9	526	D	63	658 128	1 305	119 919	10	68 678	96.3	3.7	51.7	18.8	887	59.7
Bond	193	7.2	288	0	169	528 189	2 103	88 173	41	61 848	71.2	28.8	42.4	19.2	3 236	71.0
Boone	147	4.3	309	2	135	1 000 594	3 424	78 974	48	100 505	78.5	21.5	59.5	24.6	2 176	51.9
Brown	144	-5.3	346	D	91	550 809	1 662	57 675	24	57 356	74.5	25.5	41.5	14.6	1 871	71.5
Bureau	491	1.4	450	6	450	1 241 444	2 655	128 112	204	186 914	84.9	15.1	78.6	41.2	9 463	72.9
Calhoun	90	-9.1	188	0	56	288 086	1 558	49 647	13	26 397	78.8	21.2	39.2	6.5	1 200	63.1
Carroll	248	2.1	377	12	215	956 194	2 377	140 480	111	169 162	56.2	43.8	61.6	36.1	5 282	68.9
Cass	199	3.6	465	12	166	1 032 531	2 102	111 119	64	149 717	66.8	33.2	56.2	30.7	3 199	76.1
Champaign	577	1.6	449	5	559	1 284 092	2 890	132 373	168	130 928	95.0	5.0	79.1	38.0	8 982	74.9
Christian	411	5.4	516	0	389	1 339 210	2 530	129 646	111	138 962	93.3	6.7	66.5	37.4	5 752	72.4
Clark	275	2.2	474	5	239	783 541	1 950	105 225	60	102 620	84.8	15.2	53.2	25.1	3 286	65.1
Clay	243	1.7	346	0	210	701 724	1 585	72 938	37	53 059	74.8	25.2	46.1	14.1	3 041	70.7
Clinton	255	9.0	278	0	228	694 495	2 466	96 461	141	153 809	29.8	70.2	64.9	26.7	4 825	70.3
Coles	261	1.6	382	0	239	977 295	2 716	96 799	61	89 166	92.4	7.6	60.1	26.2	3 280	67.0
Cook	24	-38.5	113	0	19	816 215	6 286	63 348	21	100 867	98.6	1.4	40.3	13.7	263	28.4
Crawford	214	2.4	377	7	184	711 835	1 713	101 073	46	80 489	82.3	17.7	43.7	21.5	3 737	70.5
Cumberland	173	1.8	297	D	154	604 166	2 123	89 019	51	87 097	61.8	38.2	56.8	22.6	2 367	67.4
De Kalb	359	-2.4	440	1	346	1 694 178	3 759	146 357	175	213 897	53.3	46.7	76.8	42.6	6 619	66.7
De Witt	203	-1.0	442	D	193	1 403 056	3 012	139 139	56	122 581	88.9	11.1	69.3	37.5	3 049	66.9
Douglas	233	-6.8	404	0	223	1 105 880	2 970	94 937	63	108 701	90.7	9.3	69.3	33.3	3 896	62.3
Du Page	8	-52.9	97	0	6	462 187	5 056	52 451	9	115 466	98.1	1.9	48.1	19.0	138	24.1
Edgar	355	0.9	532	D	330	1 284 359	2 341	120 223	140	209 367	D	D	68.4	37.8	5 048	63.9
Edwards	123	8.8	325	D	105	526 568	1 591	67 208	22	58 064	68.6	31.4	46.4	19.3	1 725	76.8
Effingham	278	8.2	245	0	238	487 464	2 170	68 262	72	63 752	52.6	47.4	54.5	18.0	3 821	63.0
Fayette	366	9.9	293	0	313	515 871	1 714	59 276	66	53 278	84.2	15.8	43.5	15.9	4 899	65.6
Ford	286	-9.2	540	1	277	1 437 155	2 608	137 998	82	155 426	87.7	12.3	79.4	44.9	3 886	76.4
Franklin	180	0.0	247	0	155	468 860	1 573	75 087	27	36 993	61.1	38.9	27.2	8.8	2 641	69.2
Fulton	413	-2.8	392	1	309	746 430	1 886	79 302	90	85 393	74.8	25.2	59.0	21.8	4 330	59.6
Gallatin	154	-19.4	826	18	131	1 218 072	1 497	206 004	29	155 641	61.9	38.1	60.3	27.3	3 578	67.6
Greene	315	-4.0	464	8	252	864 713	1 855	116 361	88	129 162	61.9	38.1	75.7	38.1	2 996	71.5
Grundy	213	6.0	524	0	200	1 528 380	3 096	141 653	53	129 643	94.1	5.9	32.7	9.8	3 843	77.2
Hamilton	234	8.8	338	D	206	521 984	1 622	64 950	30	42 538	89.1	10.9	66.4	27.0	7 126	66.9
Hancock	432	-1.4	394	1	360	1 023 254	2 544	121 448	117	106 723	69.6	30.4	34.1	2.2	317	39.7
Hardin	40	2.6	222	0	22	389 986	1 736	35 978	3	16 248	D	D	79.1	40.3	2 852	62.8
Henderson	201	-0.5	513	10	164	1 056 522	2 253	109 419	59	151 048	72.6	27.4	70.2	36.6	9 455	70.1
Henry	481	5.3	375	5	439	942 531	2 458	113 472	180	140 566	63.6	36.4	77.3	41.0	12 473	79.4
Iroquois	679	1.8	490	3	648	1 140 149	2 402	147 839	229	164 907	81.4	18.6				

Table B. States and Counties — Residential Construction, Wholesale Trade, Retail Trade, and Real Estate

STATE County	Value of residential construction authorized by building permits, 2003		Wholesale trade, 1997				Retail trade,[1] 1997				Real estate and rental and leasing, 1997			
	New construction ($1,000)	Number of housing units	Number of establish-ments	Number of employees	Sales (mil dol)	Annual payroll (mil dol)	Number of establish-ments	Number of employees	Sales (mil dol)	Annual payroll (mil dol)	Number of establish-ments	Number of employees	Receipts (mil dol)	Annual payroll (mil dol)
	133	134	135	136	137	138	139	140	141	142	143	144	145	146
IDAHO—Cont'd														
Custer	843	6	3	D	D	D	25	106	14.7	1.2	4	D	D	D
Elmore	12 675	131	11	64	20.1	1.6	84	894	231.0	17.3	10	43	3.7	0.5
Franklin	7 929	62	19	122	30.1	2.9	45	383	55.1	4.8	5	13	0.6	0.1
Fremont	21 949	144	17	235	83.0	4.2	50	285	53.0	4.2	4	D	D	D
Gem	13 786	107	18	155	35.7	3.0	42	326	49.5	5.4	9	22	1.2	0.2
Gooding	7 742	74	13	197	58.5	3.3	54	480	66.8	6.5	10	31	0.9	0.3
Idaho	552	4	15	168	38.6	2.8	81	540	75.2	8.0	7	16	0.6	0.2
Jefferson	27 397	235	30	511	101.2	8.0	48	438	59.9	5.7	7	8	0.7	0.1
Jerome	8 243	77	37	312	251.9	6.1	57	624	107.6	10.3	4	4	0.6	0.1
Kootenai	247 100	1 837	121	1 171	402.9	35.7	545	5 590	1 022.7	100.5	143	379	47.7	6.1
Latah	15 094	123	44	255	111.6	6.0	176	1 982	253.8	26.7	39	185	12.8	2.4
Lemhi	5 736	46	10	28	8.0	0.6	54	384	54.5	5.1	8	12	1.7	0.2
Lewis	500	6	8	87	27.2	1.8	27	137	21.0	2.5	3	16	0.9	0.2
Lincoln	2 144	22	1	D	D	D	12	57	11.2	0.7	1	D	D	D
Madison	57 550	900	40	605	94.3	8.4	93	1 286	211.9	18.9	19	80	5.6	0.6
Minidoka	3 343	22	42	776	158.4	16.8	76	775	130.4	12.1	6	22	1.3	0.3
Nez Perce	17 400	109	66	725	214.1	16.9	231	2 832	464.3	48.7	39	178	11.5	2.5
Oneida	3 030	19	1	D	D	D	11	78	10.3	0.9	3	11	0.4	0.1
Owyhee	4 860	59	13	161	40.6	4.0	33	202	31.6	2.9	4	D	D	D
Payette	12 638	139	25	308	58.0	5.0	66	490	89.5	8.8	10	18	2.0	0.3
Power	1 641	11	11	143	72.9	3.2	23	191	35.9	3.1	1	D	D	D
Shoshone	70	1	13	95	33.1	2.6	76	687	243.5	12.8	16	58	3.3	0.5
Teton	23 134	155	4	6	0.5	0.1	37	217	34.7	3.0	8	16	2.1	0.1
Twin Falls	72 026	778	159	1 600	450.7	37.9	378	4 721	837.9	76.8	65	241	25.9	4.0
Valley	31 184	212	9	21	3.8	0.9	65	436	66.2	6.7	25	49	5.5	0.6
Washington	3 721	31	9	322	46.7	4.2	40	341	58.7	5.5	7	22	1.1	0.2
ILLINOIS	9 105 577	62 211	21 956	325 847	275 978.4	13 325.5	44 568	610 790	108 002.2	10 596.0	11 411	73 819	12 830.0	2 101.4
Adams	18 109	138	127	1 650	686.7	45.7	341	4 752	669.5	68.2	60	256	25.3	3.7
Alexander	0	0	10	D	D	D	35	237	29.1	2.9	5	14	1.0	0.3
Bond	10 800	80	19	264	143.4	6.5	60	496	97.7	7.1	12	20	1.8	0.2
Boone	83 606	596	43	D	D	D	91	1 156	198.7	19.4	34	86	10.9	1.5
Brown	95	1	11	D	D	D	21	138	16.5	1.5	5	14	0.4	0.2
Bureau	8 988	66	58	D	D	D	145	1 379	229.5	20.7	16	41	3.3	0.5
Calhoun	3 986	35	4	D	D	D	24	134	26.8	2.0	4	D	D	D
Carroll	10 228	64	26	190	111.6	5.0	72	560	81.4	7.1	9	24	1.4	0.2
Cass	2 151	24	20	193	240.0	5.4	59	520	68.3	6.3	5	18	1.7	0.4
Champaign	160 307	1 266	199	3 737	2 419.0	111.5	675	10 645	1 556.7	151.9	203	1 356	179.7	27.3
Christian	11 075	118	51	482	363.6	15.0	156	1 644	283.1	24.7	20	67	5.9	0.9
Clark	594	6	22	199	104.8	4.6	77	627	106.7	8.5	6	14	0.5	0.1
Clay	777	11	31	316	84.2	6.1	66	662	92.1	7.4	9	38	1.7	0.5
Clinton	17 922	142	54	D	D	D	136	1 373	243.8	30.9	18	136	9.7	3.2
Coles	5 891	80	67	663	327.2	15.4	233	3 210	526.5	46.2	49	195	14.3	2.6
Cook	2 014 963	15 085	9 574	149 994	120 551.8	6 467.2	17 318	240 539	42 547.2	4 369.9	5 614	42 649	8 711.0	1 393.7
Crawford	630	12	24	151	246.8	3.4	93	907	136.4	12.5	16	30	2.5	0.3
Cumberland	836	12	16	87	48.7	1.9	42	253	37.2	3.3	4	9	0.5	0.0
De Kalb	117 514	902	75	835	871.8	32.2	309	4 008	642.3	63.1	63	275	34.4	3.9
De Witt	5 364	53	22	127	138.0	5.5	70	756	142.0	12.4	9	16	1.0	0.1
Douglas	6 390	83	33	370	203.4	8.6	165	1 299	185.8	16.7	10	46	4.1	0.6
Du Page	733 681	2 909	3 351	64 415	74 318.8	2 918.5	3 625	64 962	12 825.3	1 231.1	1 134	9 484	1 480.5	293.4
Edgar	2 287	21	31	260	163.8	5.4	68	721	108.3	9.8	12	33	1.4	0.2
Edwards	NA	NA	15	188	105.7	6.1	34	235	28.4	2.4	2	D	D	D
Effingham	9 474	63	58	879	265.9	29.6	236	3 205	561.3	50.2	27	119	8.6	1.3
Fayette	1 164	10	27	372	186.3	8.8	103	933	153.3	12.7	12	24	1.7	0.3
Ford	3 437	27	33	335	298.9	11.4	93	716	120.2	9.6	12	13	1.2	0.1
Franklin	2 022	49	47	258	72.6	6.1	192	1 707	276.9	27.1	22	62	9.1	0.8
Fulton	6 715	65	36	235	95.4	5.0	156	1 718	248.4	24.8	21	52	3.3	0.5
Gallatin	0	0	8	D	D	D	29	144	23.4	2.0	NA	NA	NA	NA
Greene	744	5	22	108	70.1	2.4	70	480	71.1	6.6	5	D	D	D
Grundy	133 520	883	40	347	387.3	12.3	137	1 604	288.0	27.2	39	199	16.7	4.2
Hamilton	NA	NA	13	68	54.3	1.4	37	207	37.7	2.7	2	D	D	D
Hancock	3 977	18	32	220	211.9	5.1	101	601	101.5	8.8	7	33	4.0	1.1
Hardin	10	1	NA	NA	NA	NA	15	60	8.6	0.8	1	D	D	D
Henderson	2 015	32	10	40	21.6	0.7	23	125	21.0	1.7	2	D	D	D
Henry	11 488	87	81	775	521.6	19.9	217	2 583	371.9	37.1	28	83	4.9	1.3
Iroquois	8 658	71	65	524	405.3	12.8	118	1 139	176.1	17.2	11	25	2.5	0.3

1. Establishments with payroll.

Table B. States and Counties — Professional Services, Manufacturing, and Accommodation and Foodservices

STATE County	Professional, scientific, and technical services,[1] 1997				Manufacturing, 1997				Accommodation and foodservices, 1997			
	Number of establishments	Number of employees	Receipts (mil dol)	Annual payroll (mil dol)	Number of establishments	Number of employees	Receipts (mil dol)	Annual payroll (mil dol)	Number of establishments	Number of employees	Sales (mil dol)	Annual payroll (mil dol)
	147	148	149	150	151	152	153	154	155	156	157	158
IDAHO—Cont'd												
Custer	8	18	0.9	0.2	NA	NA	NA	NA	26	131	5.8	1.7
Elmore	11	40	1.8	0.7	NA	NA	NA	NA	53	479	13.5	3.9
Franklin	9	16	0.7	0.1	NA	NA	NA	NA	14	171	3.3	0.9
Fremont	5	10	0.4	0.0	NA	NA	NA	NA	32	172	8.6	2.0
Gem	16	50	1.8	0.5	NA	NA	NA	NA	22	189	5.4	1.2
Gooding	13	45	2.6	1.0	NA	NA	NA	NA	28	254	5.0	1.5
Idaho	21	70	3.1	1.0	NA	NA	NA	NA	56	323	9.7	2.5
Jefferson	16	39	2.0	0.6	17	664	94.4	11.9	18	D	D	D
Jerome	17	54	3.9	1.4	19	803	176.3	15.9	30	210	6.9	1.7
Kootenai	245	1 121	81.8	32.8	195	4 472	592.1	116.9	298	4 086	137.7	37.9
Latah	69	230	13.3	5.2	NA	NA	NA	NA	91	1 348	33.5	8.6
Lemhi	21	45	2.6	0.7	NA	NA	NA	NA	36	209	6.5	2.0
Lewis	5	13	0.6	0.2	NA	NA	NA	NA	18	109	4.2	1.2
Lincoln	1	D	D	D	NA	NA	NA	NA	7	63	1.5	0.4
Madison	23	158	10.7	5.2	21	1 326	141.4	25.5	40	D	D	D
Minidoka	16	69	3.5	1.1	18	1 638	425.7	44.3	25	274	5.7	1.9
Nez Perce	69	349	24.0	9.4	55	3 263	769.1	128.0	103	1 439	43.0	12.5
Oneida	1	D	D	D	NA	NA	NA	NA	7	D	D	D
Owyhee	4	15	0.7	0.2	5	613	225.2	12.2	18	107	2.4	0.7
Payette	27	90	5.8	1.9	24	D	D	D	25	208	4.7	1.1
Power	6	17	0.6	0.2	8	889	155.3	21.3	16	76	2.3	0.6
Shoshone	24	132	9.2	4.2	NA	NA	NA	NA	49	326	8.1	2.3
Teton	11	33	4.1	0.8	NA	NA	NA	NA	19	104	4.1	1.1
Twin Falls	140	574	41.2	16.7	95	3 588	723.3	82.9	148	2 303	62.7	18.1
Valley	22	61	3.7	1.4	NA	NA	NA	NA	65	484	13.9	3.9
Washington	12	39	2.0	0.6	NA	NA	NA	NA	21	D	D	D
ILLINOIS	30 378	274 714	33 855.1	13 105.4	17 953	887 350	200 020.0	31 837.9	23 984	397 300	14 826.8	4 018.7
Adams	112	504	42.2	13.9	85	5 707	1 868.3	190.4	139	2 204	65.9	18.2
Alexander	11	35	1.6	0.7	NA	NA	NA	NA	23	130	4.3	1.0
Bond	14	51	2.3	0.8	16	695	166.0	19.2	36	407	11.0	3.1
Boone	34	D	D	D	63	5 846	2 300.0	283.9	53	556	18.6	4.7
Brown	7	15	0.6	0.1	NA	NA	NA	NA	12	77	1.8	0.5
Bureau	39	198	9.8	3.9	41	2 499	413.7	72.0	86	766	20.7	5.4
Calhoun	6	9	0.4	0.1	NA	NA	NA	NA	18	96	3.6	0.8
Carroll	18	42	2.2	0.6	33	1 015	235.2	27.0	55	317	9.0	2.1
Cass	16	44	2.4	0.5	13	D	D	D	36	237	7.7	1.8
Champaign	336	2 660	263.2	91.6	152	10 857	2 689.5	292.4	449	8 944	248.6	70.6
Christian	35	140	6.9	2.3	30	1 388	479.3	53.2	76	763	21.6	5.4
Clark	20	61	3.6	1.4	24	1 682	435.5	44.6	40	530	12.4	3.2
Clay	18	60	5.2	1.6	23	2 453	480.1	62.8	30	216	5.8	1.6
Clinton	34	197	8.6	3.7	39	963	175.9	22.4	92	D	D	D
Coles	77	387	37.5	12.2	57	5 754	1 455.6	182.9	136	2 058	59.8	15.4
Cook	15 689	178 223	23 915.1	9 267.6	7 966	362 364	74 563.3	13 032.0	9 912	177 351	7 770.0	2 092.4
Crawford	27	108	8.4	2.5	20	2 547	2 175.4	90.4	34	D	D	D
Cumberland	6	11	0.9	0.2	NA	NA	NA	NA	14	D	D	D
De Kalb	106	321	28.2	7.8	137	6 957	1 511.7	207.7	190	2 664	73.2	17.8
De Witt	21	63	4.5	1.5	15	1 300	267.1	39.6	42	384	11.1	2.9
Douglas	23	58	3.3	1.1	65	2 711	481.7	79.2	47	692	17.3	4.8
Du Page	4 099	32 018	4 200.8	1 475.6	2 033	71 351	11 938.5	2 503.0	1 698	37 452	1 495.4	405.7
Edgar	29	127	7.4	2.2	27	1 539	248.7	36.9	31	264	6.1	1.6
Edwards	8	15	0.7	0.1	8	D	D	D	7	D	D	D
Effingham	47	560	72.5	15.4	59	5 660	978.7	148.7	90	2 061	59.2	15.8
Fayette	18	93	4.0	1.8	22	1 529	277.9	37.8	39	477	12.5	3.5
Ford	21	52	3.1	1.0	22	951	322.4	23.7	32	290	7.5	2.0
Franklin	40	133	8.9	2.3	43	1 632	233.7	36.6	82	983	26.7	7.5
Fulton	25	90	5.2	1.8	NA	NA	NA	NA	81	837	20.4	5.8
Gallatin	7	14	0.7	0.3	NA	NA	NA	NA	8	45	1.3	0.3
Greene	14	56	2.0	0.8	NA	NA	NA	NA	31	D	D	D
Grundy	53	194	17.3	6.6	33	2 015	875.4	87.8	72	999	32.8	8.4
Hamilton	10	23	1.3	0.3	NA	NA	NA	NA	7	88	2.1	0.5
Hancock	14	43	2.9	0.7	28	1 862	193.2	42.5	44	321	7.8	2.0
Hardin	5	9	0.3	0.1	NA	NA	NA	NA	6	D	D	D
Henderson	5	15	0.7	0.1	NA	NA	NA	NA	12	83	2.0	0.3
Henry	52	185	11.0	4.0	53	4 019	1 288.0	124.3	113	1 309	32.9	9.1
Iroquois	27	68	5.1	1.4	30	1 723	296.9	43.0	67	435	14.5	3.3

1. Firms subject to federal tax.

STATE County	Health care and social assistance,[1] 1997				Other services,[1] 1997				Federal funds and grants, 2002–2003 Expenditures (mil dol)			
										Direct payments for individuals[2]		
	Number of establishments	Number of employees	Receipts (mil dol)	Annual payroll (mil dol)	Number of establishments	Number of employees	Receipts (mil dol)	Annual payroll (mil dol)	Total	Social Security and government retirement	Medicare	Food stamps and Supplemental Security Income
	159	160	161	162	163	164	165	166	167	168	169	170
IDAHO—Cont'd												
Custer	8	62	1.2	0.6	3	5	0.3	0.1	32.0	10.8	3.7	0.4
Elmore	27	195	8.7	3.0	35	152	7.9	1.9	360.1	66.3	10.4	2.6
Franklin	11	86	3.1	1.1	10	33	2.1	0.3	44.0	21.9	6.4	1.0
Fremont	16	78	4.0	1.8	9	20	1.5	0.3	52.3	24.0	7.0	1.1
Gem	19	293	9.0	4.1	22	76	3.6	1.0	73.9	40.4	11.6	1.7
Gooding	19	207	6.9	3.1	17	69	4.0	0.9	89.5	30.6	11.2	2.2
Idaho	26	147	6.7	1.9	21	62	4.4	0.8	106.1	40.5	13.3	3.1
Jefferson	19	127	4.7	1.8	12	26	2.2	0.4	63.9	34.0	10.2	1.4
Jerome	15	102	5.4	2.8	23	83	4.8	1.3	79.1	32.7	12.4	2.6
Kootenai	267	2 561	137.1	55.6	176	836	47.5	12.9	607.8	283.4	71.2	14.1
Latah	57	389	22.8	10.9	38	201	13.6	3.8	221.6	59.4	16.4	2.8
Lemhi	20	162	6.3	2.7	14	39	2.8	0.6	65.0	25.4	9.5	1.0
Lewis	6	8	0.7	0.1	2	D	D	D	44.8	18.0	4.6	0.9
Lincoln	5	63	3.4	1.3	2	D	D	D	25.8	8.0	2.5	0.3
Madison	49	463	21.9	7.3	27	109	5.2	1.2	74.4	27.2	8.3	1.4
Minidoka	26	185	7.8	3.2	23	117	11.5	2.2	87.1	39.4	16.1	3.0
Nez Perce	111	1 454	82.2	34.0	87	534	28.4	8.1	252.1	103.5	38.5	6.6
Oneida	5	35	1.3	0.5	5	7	0.9	0.1	27.2	10.0	3.4	0.5
Owyhee	5	180	4.2	2.4	6	6	0.6	0.1	42.0	19.6	5.0	1.4
Payette	33	466	12.4	4.5	18	67	3.1	0.7	95.2	44.3	13.8	3.9
Power	7	29	1.7	0.7	15	64	3.3	1.0	37.4	12.0	3.6	1.2
Shoshone	25	308	11.1	4.8	26	56	3.7	1.0	102.0	45.0	18.1	4.6
Teton	7	15	1.4	0.4	4	7	0.8	0.1	23.2	8.1	3.5	0.2
Twin Falls	154	2 301	116.0	52.5	114	630	31.9	9.3	308.9	143.3	48.0	9.2
Valley	19	130	6.3	2.5	20	41	2.8	0.7	60.1	31.8	7.0	0.9
Washington	12	178	7.7	3.1	9	32	2.4	0.6	65.1	28.0	8.6	1.8
ILLINOIS	21 122	248 667	16 870.2	7 441.8	18 806	118 317	8 296.8	2 503.0	73 019.6	23 396.6	11 991.7	2 442.2
Adams	122	1 605	96.3	50.9	146	749	43.3	13.2	362.5	162.5	69.4	11.5
Alexander	2	D	D	D	5	16	0.9	0.2	87.6	24.3	14.6	6.0
Bond	20	217	7.2	3.7	32	79	5.9	1.4	106.8	37.8	17.0	2.2
Boone	34	535	21.9	10.1	53	248	17.6	6.1	123.2	73.8	23.6	3.0
Brown	4	109	3.0	1.7	10	23	1.2	0.3	31.7	11.8	5.1	0.6
Bureau	54	629	30.7	15.4	57	197	10.4	2.5	172.7	89.8	40.6	2.8
Calhoun	5	72	3.8	1.1	5	38	1.8	1.0	75.3	13.7	6.7	0.7
Carroll	20	159	5.2	2.6	30	101	6.2	1.4	98.5	51.9	19.4	2.8
Cass	20	283	7.7	4.0	20	87	4.5	1.2	72.8	33.3	15.8	1.6
Champaign	204	4 973	367.9	182.4	244	1 241	65.0	21.0	923.8	273.6	92.7	22.5
Christian	45	798	30.5	11.8	63	195	12.4	2.7	181.4	90.2	47.4	5.0
Clark	17	102	5.3	1.8	27	74	4.2	0.8	83.9	42.3	20.2	2.1
Clay	23	249	12.6	3.9	24	67	5.8	1.3	89.7	35.9	19.6	2.0
Clinton	51	699	27.3	11.1	47	147	10.9	2.6	149.1	81.3	33.9	2.4
Coles	90	1 224	61.2	27.9	85	428	25.7	6.9	221.7	96.9	48.5	7.7
Cook	9 558	108 873	7 974.7	3 416.1	7 707	55 223	4 042.9	1 211.5	31 374.9	8 853.6	6 063.5	1 541.9
Crawford	37	354	14.6	5.5	33	117	6.6	2.0	101.7	51.7	22.0	2.6
Cumberland	5	84	2.5	1.5	13	35	2.4	0.4	52.9	23.3	10.6	1.7
De Kalb	104	1 453	87.5	40.2	131	495	31.6	8.4	298.4	139.7	57.7	4.3
De Witt	23	218	9.9	4.9	22	65	5.8	1.3	81.9	42.5	18.3	2.3
Douglas	30	399	12.7	5.2	26	117	11.4	2.7	81.3	39.9	16.1	1.6
Du Page	2 117	23 540	1 852.3	807.3	1 706	12 714	931.0	310.5	3 024.3	1 465.9	607.2	39.6
Edgar	24	270	11.5	4.6	22	64	4.5	0.9	102.1	49.8	23.0	3.3
Edwards	10	88	2.5	1.2	16	27	1.6	0.3	34.4	16.4	7.6	0.9
Effingham	90	895	63.5	25.7	70	426	26.4	6.1	160.8	73.7	31.2	3.5
Fayette	33	321	11.7	5.1	31	129	17.7	2.6	108.3	46.9	22.7	3.6
Ford	20	271	12.5	5.0	20	64	4.3	1.0	75.6	38.4	15.3	1.1
Franklin	63	474	19.2	7.1	55	168	11.2	2.8	261.7	122.6	55.2	13.2
Fulton	44	1 104	43.1	21.8	38	154	9.7	2.2	205.4	97.2	54.8	6.0
Gallatin	3	148	2.7	1.4	3	D	D	D	63.6	18.5	9.4	2.0
Greene	21	172	5.1	2.3	18	35	2.4	0.4	99.3	39.2	19.1	2.7
Grundy	62	670	34.5	15.0	58	300	21.1	5.2	164.9	79.0	35.0	1.9
Hamilton	8	70	3.2	1.5	11	28	2.5	0.3	58.4	21.4	11.0	1.8
Hancock	30	238	10.8	4.4	25	52	4.0	0.8	108.4	53.6	21.5	2.4
Hardin	8	76	2.2	0.8	2	D	D	D	32.4	13.1	7.6	1.3
Henderson	7	29	1.5	0.8	7	20	0.6	0.3	41.1	19.4	7.3	0.7
Henry	50	399	16.7	6.2	84	273	19.3	4.2	218.1	124.8	50.0	4.8
Iroquois	35	208	13.3	6.2	45	129	10.7	2.4	165.9	81.9	34.7	3.6

1. Firms subject to federal tax.   2. State totals may include programs not allocated by county.

Table B. States and Counties — Federal Funds and Local Government Finances

	Federal funds and grants, 2002–2003 (cont'd)							Local government finances, 2002				
	Expenditures (mil dol) (cont'd)							General revenue				
	Procurement contract awards			Grants[1]						Taxes		
											Per capita[2] (dollars)	
STATE County	Salaries and wages	Defense	Other	Medicaid and other health-related	Nutrition and family welfare	Education	Other	Total (mil dol)	Intergovern-mental (mil dol)	Total (mil dol)	Total	Property
	171	172	173	174	175	176	177	178	179	180	181	182
IDAHO—Cont'd												
Custer	6.2	0.0	2.9	1.5	1.0	0.2	5.2	14.8	7.3	5.7	1 370	1 346
Elmore	179.2	70.0	2.6	6.7	2.0	4.4	11.5	55.5	33.7	12.7	429	408
Franklin	2.0	0.1	0.4	3.6	0.8	0.3	2.5	30.0	16.4	5.1	439	395
Fremont	4.9	0.0	1.5	5.6	1.0	0.6	1.4	31.5	15.9	11.4	959	895
Gem	5.2	0.0	0.9	9.7	1.7	0.4	1.1	32.1	16.7	6.9	443	417
Gooding	3.4	0.0	1.0	11.7	1.2	0.5	22.0	38.8	19.8	7.7	538	533
Idaho	16.1	0.1	10.5	12.7	1.6	1.4	3.1	38.2	21.3	6.3	409	396
Jefferson	3.1	0.0	1.0	6.2	2.0	0.5	0.6	43.2	31.2	8.3	421	403
Jerome	3.3	0.7	1.0	12.1	1.4	1.0	6.2	39.8	22.3	10.1	541	523
Kootenai	36.2	17.4	50.6	50.5	7.3	2.6	66.9	479.5	116.1	89.3	784	737
Latah	13.7	1.4	29.8	19.6	5.4	7.4	47.9	78.1	34.5	25.8	732	685
Lemhi	12.5	1.4	4.8	5.2	0.8	0.3	4.2	22.8	11.5	4.0	521	500
Lewis	1.9	0.0	1.0	9.6	2.5	0.3	3.0	12.0	8.0	2.8	670	625
Lincoln	4.7	0.0	2.9	1.0	0.5	0.2	1.6	19.5	12.5	4.7	1 267	1 247
Madison	3.5	0.0	0.8	4.2	2.0	1.0	3.8	71.9	29.6	10.9	393	360
Minidoka	4.1	0.1	1.8	9.7	1.9	0.7	0.8	57.8	27.6	9.1	468	441
Nez Perce	11.8	0.1	7.6	42.8	7.9	4.4	20.4	99.1	38.7	37.5	1 011	967
Oneida	1.0	0.0	0.4	1.5	2.1	0.1	3.6	13.6	6.8	2.7	657	572
Owyhee	1.5	0.0	1.3	7.1	1.1	0.6	1.3	28.8	18.2	6.9	634	611
Payette	2.7	0.0	1.5	16.9	6.0	0.7	1.4	43.0	23.4	11.9	566	487
Power	1.4	0.0	0.4	2.6	0.6	0.4	2.0	31.0	12.7	11.5	1 555	1 544
Shoshone	3.7	5.4	1.8	12.2	0.9	0.5	9.6	49.9	22.9	10.8	824	803
Teton	2.0	0.0	0.6	5.1	0.6	0.5	1.0	17.3	6.6	3.7	540	508
Twin Falls	21.0	1.3	7.6	42.0	9.0	2.0	9.1	248.4	101.3	42.5	649	615
Valley	11.6	0.1	2.3	2.6	0.7	0.2	2.4	43.0	12.3	14.0	1 856	1 761
Washington	2.4	0.0	1.1	8.6	1.0	0.3	11.9	33.7	14.4	9.0	911	881
ILLINOIS	6 552.6	2 513.7	3 215.1	7 013.3	2 603.5	1 461.9	4 641.3	X	X	X	X	X
Adams	19.3	17.0	4.9	42.9	7.6	3.8	9.3	150.2	75.5	47.5	703	635
Alexander	2.1	0.2	0.5	24.9	3.1	1.0	5.9	25.8	16.8	3.7	390	338
Bond	19.6	1.6	1.3	7.8	1.3	0.5	9.0	32.4	17.5	8.7	486	472
Boone	4.7	0.0	1.4	5.2	1.6	0.7	4.1	115.8	37.4	58.0	1 300	1 215
Brown	1.9	1.3	0.3	1.9	3.2	0.1	1.8	13.8	7.6	3.7	542	521
Bureau	9.2	0.1	1.9	6.5	2.0	1.0	6.6	106.3	34.4	33.3	944	910
Calhoun	1.7	45.1	0.4	3.5	0.4	0.2	0.5	10.8	5.9	2.8	564	560
Carroll	4.5	3.0	2.3	4.7	1.2	0.8	2.7	37.7	15.0	17.8	1 087	1 025
Cass	4.5	3.2	0.8	5.5	1.1	0.5	2.8	34.1	18.2	9.9	723	661
Champaign	80.0	15.6	15.7	107.8	15.9	18.4	240.3	494.2	195.7	200.2	1 093	919
Christian	5.5	0.0	1.4	13.8	2.5	1.0	2.7	72.0	34.7	26.1	740	719
Clark	3.4	0.1	0.8	6.3	1.0	0.5	0.6	35.7	18.4	10.1	598	577
Clay	3.1	0.0	0.7	11.3	1.3	0.5	4.3	46.6	20.5	7.6	537	518
Clinton	5.5	2.0	2.7	6.6	2.0	0.9	1.5	65.7	31.0	22.1	617	607
Coles	11.0	0.0	3.3	20.3	3.2	2.0	10.1	156.9	71.3	52.4	998	921
Cook	2 878.3	1 068.1	1 992.9	4 507.9	964.6	299.8	2 236.6	21 454.9	7 357.8	10 019.9	1 863	1 399
Crawford	3.6	0.1	1.1	7.7	1.3	0.6	2.2	58.3	21.7	14.6	725	697
Cumberland	1.8	0.0	0.5	4.0	3.7	0.3	2.3	23.5	13.9	6.5	586	577
De Kalb	13.1	0.1	3.2	15.2	3.1	8.6	26.1	242.9	82.7	119.1	1 300	1 186
De Witt	3.4	0.0	0.8	4.8	1.1	0.5	2.6	58.4	12.2	24.7	1 490	1 468
Douglas	3.7	0.8	1.0	4.0	1.0	0.5	6.4	43.3	19.4	17.4	870	847
Du Page	355.1	121.5	116.1	88.2	16.8	11.7	173.6	3 062.1	665.4	1 773.0	1 918	1 712
Edgar	4.4	0.5	1.4	8.3	1.7	0.7	1.6	45.1	21.9	16.0	832	771
Edwards	1.4	0.0	0.4	2.1	0.6	0.2	1.1	11.9	6.5	3.5	518	516
Effingham	12.9	0.7	2.5	10.0	4.8	1.2	10.4	78.9	40.4	26.0	758	714
Fayette	3.8	0.1	0.9	10.3	1.8	0.8	7.4	45.4	26.8	11.0	510	494
Ford	3.1	0.0	0.8	2.8	0.9	0.3	5.2	42.1	15.5	18.4	1 297	1 276
Franklin	11.1	1.6	7.2	29.3	5.0	2.8	4.3	87.5	54.3	17.6	450	420
Fulton	11.6	0.6	1.9	11.7	3.8	1.8	6.6	104.9	51.3	33.5	887	861
Gallatin	1.7	0.0	9.6	7.3	0.9	0.3	5.0	14.1	7.6	5.0	804	532
Greene	3.4	0.4	0.9	10.8	1.7	0.6	13.9	30.2	16.5	8.6	593	569
Grundy	6.7	0.2	1.9	3.1	1.2	0.7	29.9	123.5	26.9	74.2	1 909	1 863
Hamilton	2.0	0.0	0.5	6.8	0.8	0.3	2.5	25.0	10.2	4.2	498	497
Hancock	5.2	0.2	1.3	7.1	1.5	1.0	4.9	50.2	27.8	15.5	787	769
Hardin	1.0	0.0	0.3	6.1	0.8	0.2	1.1	11.2	9.0	0.8	177	175
Henderson	1.9	0.1	0.4	3.5	0.7	0.3	3.0	17.1	8.4	5.7	703	693
Henry	10.6	0.1	2.1	8.0	3.2	1.5	1.3	139.1	56.1	42.2	833	801
Iroquois	7.0	0.0	2.4	5.2	1.9	1.2	12.0	71.5	33.7	28.2	912	879

1. State totals may include programs not allocated by county. 2. Based on the resident population estimated as of July 1 of the year shown.

STATE County	Total (mil dol)	Per capita[1] (dollars)	Education	Health and hospitals	Police protection	Public welfare	Highways	Total (mil dol)	Per capita[1] (dollars)	Federal civilian	Federal military	State and local	Democratic	Republican	All other
	183	184	185	186	187	188	189	190	191	192	193	194	195	196	197
IDAHO—Cont'd															
Custer	11.9	2 849	57.4	6.3	3.7	3.0	9.0	0.6	136	183	15	313	23.8	75.0	1.2
Elmore	51.5	1 747	62.7	3.7	5.9	1.1	7.4	13.1	443	1 146	4 515	1 312	24.3	74.8	0.9
Franklin	27.6	2 357	56.1	21.8	2.7	2.0	4.8	2.1	176	32	42	791	9.0	89.6	1.4
Fremont	30.3	2 557	50.1	1.3	4.4	1.3	9.2	12.1	1 020	109	42	903	13.0	86.0	1.0
Gem	31.4	2 029	52.4	17.9	6.3	0.1	5.4	15.0	967	89	55	711	22.9	76.1	1.0
Gooding	34.9	2 441	56.6	15.3	2.2	0.8	7.1	24.5	1 710	68	51	1 026	24.1	74.8	1.1
Idaho	38.5	2 515	47.1	13.1	3.2	3.8	12.8	8.7	571	446	55	915	21.2	75.7	3.1
Jefferson	49.2	2 488	79.7	0.4	2.2	0.8	4.2	17.8	897	48	71	1 174	12.2	86.6	1.3
Jerome	39.5	2 113	60.0	0.5	4.4	0.8	9.2	8.0	427	53	67	889	20.5	78.8	0.7
Kootenai	399.0	3 501	37.8	32.2	3.5	0.5	4.6	105.2	924	660	410	7 815	32.3	66.4	1.3
Latah	77.3	2 196	47.1	0.3	7.0	7.0	9.0	25.9	736	218	175	6 726	48.2	49.7	2.1
Lemhi	20.5	2 686	41.5	27.8	2.8	1.2	6.7	3.6	471	299	27	581	22.6	76.1	1.3
Lewis	20.0	5 369	46.2	1.5	6.5	0.6	23.0	3.2	872	30	13	365	24.2	74.8	0.9
Lincoln	10.9	2 580	63.2	0.2	4.2	0.8	12.3	5.5	1 302	127	15	390	24.9	74.1	1.0
Madison	68.5	2 473	43.5	31.2	4.3	0.3	6.1	23.4	844	54	99	1 633	7.1	92.0	0.9
Minidoka	60.7	3 116	53.2	15.3	3.9	6.0	5.5	19.7	1 011	71	70	1 364	18.5	80.6	0.9
Nez Perce	99.0	2 667	45.1	3.9	7.2	0.6	8.8	37.1	998	176	137	3 860	36.6	62.3	1.1
Oneida	13.5	3 265	41.0	23.8	4.6	0.2	10.5	4.4	1 055	33	15	385	14.3	83.9	1.8
Owyhee	26.4	2 433	67.4	0.3	3.4	0.0	7.9	10.6	973	34	39	622	19.1	79.7	1.2
Payette	40.4	1 922	62.5	0.3	5.8	0.6	5.1	12.8	611	48	75	994	22.6	76.5	0.9
Power	33.7	4 566	60.4	11.7	4.2	0.2	8.7	21.7	2 945	27	32	672	28.0	71.2	0.8
Shoshone	42.7	3 266	44.4	22.4	5.5	1.4	8.4	14.0	1 068	115	47	964	43.8	54.8	1.4
Teton	16.3	2 379	45.5	30.0	2.4	0.1	4.1	9.2	1 341	39	25	390	41.7	57.7	0.7
Twin Falls	237.7	3 630	48.7	30.2	3.3	0.9	4.5	68.3	1 043	350	235	5 066	24.4	74.6	1.0
Valley	42.8	5 681	25.4	25.7	4.7	0.4	10.9	26.3	3 495	301	27	772	38.8	60.2	1.0
Washington	31.1	3 134	41.7	19.3	3.9	0.3	8.2	8.2	830	56	36	683	23.7	75.1	1.1
ILLINOIS	X	X	X	X	X	X	X	X	X	89 765	51 640	759 199	54.7	44.7	0.6
Adams	163.7	2 420	56.6	2.1	5.3	0.3	6.7	75.4	1 115	320	126	4 433	33.4	66.2	0.4
Alexander	26.6	2 813	47.3	0.0	5.6	4.4	7.0	4.0	427	41	17	665	51.7	47.6	0.7
Bond	37.7	2 101	57.9	4.7	4.2	0.1	11.8	17.3	964	339	33	670	43.8	55.2	0.9
Boone	103.5	2 320	52.2	0.9	3.6	3.3	9.2	81.4	1 825	82	82	1 560	42.4	57.0	0.5
Brown	14.7	2 134	49.3	3.1	4.4	0.1	13.5	5.3	775	64	13	476	34.5	65.1	0.4
Bureau	110.6	3 137	40.8	21.4	4.1	3.2	8.3	29.0	824	151	65	2 379	44.5	54.9	0.5
Calhoun	12.3	2 429	53.9	0.0	2.8	0.0	17.2	3.5	700	30	0	246	50.5	48.7	0.8
Carroll	39.5	2 413	56.2	0.6	5.4	0.2	9.9	25.0	1 532	86	31	869	43.5	55.8	0.7
Cass	35.5	2 594	44.6	6.8	3.4	0.1	8.3	10.1	741	76	25	850	43.7	55.5	0.8
Champaign	525.2	2 867	54.6	1.7	4.5	2.0	5.6	216.6	1 182	1 329	386	31 470	50.5	48.5	1.0
Christian	73.4	2 083	55.3	1.1	5.7	0.2	8.5	23.3	661	95	65	2 031	40.1	59.3	0.7
Clark	43.4	2 562	43.2	2.0	4.3	0.1	9.1	10.1	599	59	31	833	36.0	63.5	0.5
Clay	46.7	3 294	44.3	26.6	2.9	0.1	4.5	19.9	1 407	57	26	879	32.1	67.4	0.5
Clinton	70.6	1 970	52.7	1.2	5.4	0.0	12.1	37.8	1 054	114	65	2 346	39.7	59.7	0.6
Coles	188.5	3 588	65.3	1.8	4.1	0.0	4.6	63.3	1 204	141	101	5 918	42.1	57.2	0.7
Cook	22 384.0	4 163	37.3	5.3	7.7	0.8	5.2	30 870.8	5 741	45 137	10 303	304 493	70.0	29.4	0.6
Crawford	58.0	2 878	42.9	29.9	3.0	0.1	6.3	18.0	894	64	37	1 894	34.2	65.2	0.5
Cumberland	25.1	2 268	58.5	1.9	4.6	0.2	8.7	14.4	1 299	36	20	481	34.4	64.6	0.9
De Kalb	239.5	2 616	46.8	2.1	5.5	3.6	10.0	166.6	1 820	208	174	11 292	47.4	51.9	0.8
De Witt	62.3	3 767	42.6	17.8	3.5	3.7	9.6	17.1	1 033	57	30	1 154	36.4	63.1	0.5
Douglas	46.2	2 311	54.5	1.0	5.2	0.3	9.5	27.5	1 377	64	37	861	32.4	66.8	0.8
Du Page	3 096.4	3 349	52.1	1.0	5.8	1.4	7.1	2 661.5	2 879	4 778	1 703	44 220	45.0	54.3	0.7
Edgar	45.7	2 373	58.7	3.1	4.5	0.1	9.3	12.4	646	71	35	1 202	36.7	62.4	0.9
Edwards	11.5	1 694	53.5	0.9	4.1	0.1	11.8	5.3	781	24	12	269	27.7	71.7	0.6
Effingham	78.1	2 277	52.5	2.5	5.7	0.0	10.6	37.0	1 079	181	64	1 861	26.9	72.4	0.7
Fayette	47.5	2 194	58.8	4.4	4.5	0.0	7.5	15.2	702	73	40	1 383	37.4	61.6	1.0
Ford	37.3	2 628	45.3	0.7	6.2	4.8	13.5	15.9	1 122	56	26	744	29.5	69.7	0.8
Franklin	81.3	2 077	57.0	0.9	7.3	0.9	6.5	37.7	963	247	72	2 110	45.6	53.7	0.7
Fulton	102.4	2 710	61.4	3.9	4.3	1.9	5.5	41.5	1 098	117	69	2 562	53.3	45.9	0.7
Gallatin	11.9	1 928	58.2	0.2	4.1	0.3	11.0	3.9	622	31	11	298	48.9	50.2	1.0
Greene	33.4	2 301	56.9	4.8	4.1	0.3	11.9	6.5	448	60	27	745	40.5	58.7	0.9
Grundy	130.2	3 351	62.2	0.7	5.2	4.0	6.2	88.9	2 288	117	71	2 179	42.7	56.5	0.7
Hamilton	28.8	3 424	50.0	29.3	1.1	0.0	4.7	8.7	1 030	42	15	590	40.2	58.8	1.0
Hancock	48.9	2 481	53.2	2.6	3.1	0.2	13.5	10.4	527	92	36	1 239	40.2	59.0	0.9
Hardin	9.2	1 934	56.6	1.4	3.6	2.2	8.2	0.6	119	27	0	261	37.9	61.6	0.5
Henderson	17.6	2 165	48.0	6.5	3.4	0.0	13.8	4.7	572	47	15	427	54.7	44.8	0.6
Henry	147.0	2 904	42.4	15.0	4.8	3.7	5.8	49.9	985	166	93	3 334	47.1	52.4	0.5
Iroquois	78.3	2 530	55.4	2.4	3.4	0.5	12.3	20.8	671	126	57	1 429	27.7	71.7	0.6

1. Based on the resident population estimated as of July 1 of the year shown.

Table B. States and Counties — Land Area and Population

STATE/ County code	CBSA code[1]	County Type[2]	STATE County	Land area,[3] (sq km) 2000	Population and population characteristics, 2003			Race alone or in combination, not Hispanic or Latino (percent)					Age (percent)					
					Total persons	Rank	Per square kilometer	White	Black	Am. Indian, Alaska Native	Asian and Pacific Islander	Percent Hispanic or Latino[4]	Under 5 years	5 to 17 years	18 to 24 years	25 to 34 years	35 to 44 years	45 to 54 years
				1	2	3	4	5	6	7	8	9	10	11	12	13	14	15
			ILLINOIS—Cont'd															
17 077	16060	5	Jackson	1 523	58 976	828	38.7	80.0	13.4	0.9	4.3	3.0	5.4	13.7	20.0	17.1	11.3	11.3
17 079	...	7	Jasper	1 280	9 955	2 446	7.8	99.1	0.2	0.1	0.2	0.5	5.3	18.3	10.3	10.8	15.2	14.6
17 081	34500	7	Jefferson	1 479	40 334	1 128	27.3	89.9	8.3	0.6	0.9	1.3	5.7	17.4	9.7	12.9	14.8	14.3
17 083	41180	1	Jersey	956	22 188	1 697	23.2	98.2	0.8	0.4	0.3	0.7	5.3	17.7	11.9	10.9	15.5	13.8
17 085	...	6	Jo Daviess	1 557	22 526	1 682	14.5	97.0	0.4	0.4	0.4	2.3	5.2	16.3	8.4	10.8	13.9	14.9
17 087	...	7	Johnson	893	12 951	2 244	14.5	84.0	12.4	0.6	0.2	3.2	4.7	13.2	12.2	16.9	16.0	12.6
17 089	16980	1	Kane	1 348	457 122	137	339.1	65.8	5.7	0.4	2.9	26.2	8.5	20.9	10.1	14.8	15.7	12.8
17 091	28100	3	Kankakee	1 753	105 625	518	60.3	77.7	15.9	0.5	1.0	5.9	7.1	19.2	10.7	12.6	14.3	13.6
17 093	16980	1	Kendall	830	66 565	755	80.2	86.3	2.6	0.4	1.6	9.9	7.2	19.8	10.1	13.7	16.0	12.5
17 095	23660	4	Knox	1 855	54 491	882	29.4	88.7	7.2	0.4	0.9	3.8	5.6	15.9	10.3	12.1	13.9	14.6
17 097	16980	1	Lake	1 159	685 019	77	591.0	71.3	7.3	0.5	5.6	16.6	7.6	20.7	10.2	12.9	16.8	14.1
17 099	36860	4	La Salle	2 939	112 037	494	38.1	91.8	1.7	0.4	0.8	6.0	6.2	17.8	9.4	11.5	15.3	13.9
17 101	...	7	Lawrence	963	15 287	2 075	15.9	97.6	1.1	0.4	0.2	1.2	5.4	16.2	9.0	11.2	14.2	14.0
17 103	19940	4	Lee	1 879	35 537	1 256	18.9	91.3	4.7	0.4	0.9	3.4	5.0	17.8	9.4	11.9	16.7	14.8
17 105	38700	4	Livingston	2 703	39 208	1 147	14.5	91.9	5.2	0.4	0.6	2.5	6.4	17.7	9.7	12.4	15.4	14.3
17 107	30660	6	Logan	1 601	30 716	1 391	19.2	90.6	6.9	0.3	0.8	1.8	5.0	15.5	12.9	13.4	15.3	13.8
17 109	31380	5	McDonough	1 526	32 852	1 338	21.5	92.0	4.1	0.4	2.8	1.6	4.4	12.3	25.4	12.1	10.5	11.5
17 111	16980	1	McHenry	1 563	286 091	206	183.0	87.9	1.0	0.4	2.5	9.2	7.2	21.0	9.0	13.0	18.0	13.9
17 113	14060	3	McLean	3 065	156 879	353	51.2	87.4	7.2	0.4	3.1	3.2	6.3	16.5	16.8	14.8	14.2	12.5
17 115	19500	3	Macon	1 504	111 175	499	73.9	83.6	15.3	0.5	1.0	1.1	6.4	17.6	10.1	11.2	13.9	15.3
17 117	41180	1	Macoupin	2 237	49 055	953	21.9	97.9	1.1	0.5	0.3	0.7	5.8	17.3	10.2	10.9	14.6	14.3
17 119	41180	1	Madison	1 878	261 689	226	139.3	89.7	7.9	0.6	0.9	1.8	6.2	17.7	10.0	12.9	15.2	14.1
17 121	16460	4	Marion	1 482	40 751	1 117	27.5	94.2	4.4	0.7	0.7	1.0	6.3	18.2	9.1	11.2	14.4	13.9
17 123	37900	2	Marshall	1 000	13 039	2 235	13.0	97.6	0.6	0.5	0.3	1.5	4.9	17.1	8.6	10.4	13.9	15.1
17 125	...	6	Mason	1 396	15 884	2 038	11.4	98.7	0.3	0.4	0.3	0.6	5.8	17.4	8.7	11.0	14.9	14.2
17 127	37140	7	Massac	619	15 138	2 091	24.5	92.4	6.5	0.7	0.3	1.1	6.0	16.4	8.9	12.4	14.4	13.6
17 129	44100	3	Menard	814	12 593	2 264	15.5	98.2	0.5	0.2	0.2	0.9	5.1	19.1	9.2	10.3	16.9	15.5
17 131	19340	2	Mercer	1 453	17 003	1 954	11.7	98.0	0.5	0.3	0.3	1.3	6.0	17.4	9.1	10.4	15.0	15.0
17 133	41180	1	Monroe	1 006	29 723	1 411	29.5	98.4	0.1	0.3	0.4	1.2	5.8	18.4	9.3	11.9	16.9	14.3
17 135	...	6	Montgomery	1 823	30 352	1 398	16.6	94.5	4.0	0.3	0.3	1.2	5.4	16.9	9.8	12.9	15.5	14.0
17 137	27300	4	Morgan	1 473	35 990	1 238	24.4	92.5	5.7	0.5	0.7	1.5	5.6	16.2	11.9	11.7	14.6	14.3
17 139	...	6	Moultrie	869	14 469	2 128	16.7	98.9	0.4	0.4	0.1	0.6	6.5	18.0	9.1	10.8	14.1	13.9
17 141	40300	4	Ogle	1 965	52 858	899	26.9	91.4	0.9	0.4	0.6	7.3	5.8	19.5	9.3	11.4	15.8	14.2
17 143	37900	2	Peoria	1 605	182 335	313	113.6	78.5	17.8	0.6	2.4	2.5	7.1	17.9	10.4	13.1	13.6	14.1
17 145	...	7	Perry	1 142	22 684	1 678	19.9	89.2	8.5	0.6	0.4	1.9	5.1	15.7	11.0	13.6	15.0	14.0
17 147	16580	3	Piatt	1 140	16 426	2 002	14.4	98.5	0.6	0.3	0.4	0.8	5.2	17.8	8.9	10.0	15.5	15.4
17 149	...	7	Pike	2 150	16 927	1 967	7.9	97.3	1.5	0.3	0.3	0.8	5.4	17.1	9.2	11.5	13.6	14.2
17 151	...	9	Pope	961	4 261	2 891	4.4	93.5	4.6	1.2	0.3	1.0	3.8	15.6	11.9	9.7	14.0	14.9
17 153	...	9	Pulaski	520	7 077	2 680	13.6	65.9	32.1	0.2	1.0	1.4	6.7	19.7	9.8	10.3	14.1	13.9
17 155	36860	8	Putnam	414	6 119	2 766	14.8	95.1	0.9	0.2	0.4	3.7	5.0	17.9	8.9	10.1	15.5	14.8
17 157	...	6	Randolph	1 498	33 244	1 321	22.2	89.3	9.0	0.5	0.3	1.5	5.4	15.8	10.6	13.4	15.7	14.1
17 159	...	7	Richland	933	15 997	2 031	17.1	98.1	0.6	0.2	0.7	0.9	5.8	17.0	9.7	11.3	14.6	13.4
17 161	19340	2	Rock Island	1 105	147 912	384	133.9	81.0	8.6	0.6	1.4	9.8	6.5	16.9	10.3	12.3	14.1	14.6
17 163	41180	1	St. Clair	1 719	258 606	230	150.4	66.7	29.6	0.6	1.6	2.8	6.9	19.7	9.9	12.7	15.4	13.8
17 165	25380	7	Saline	993	26 158	1 533	26.3	94.1	4.6	0.6	0.3	1.1	5.7	17.5	9.3	10.7	13.6	13.8
17 167	44100	3	Sangamon	2 249	191 875	300	85.3	86.9	10.9	0.6	1.6	1.3	6.5	17.7	8.7	12.9	15.6	15.3
17 169	...	7	Schuyler	1 133	7 021	2 684	6.2	98.7	0.3	0.2	0.1	0.9	5.4	16.4	8.5	10.8	14.0	14.8
17 171	27300	9	Scott	650	5 505	2 809	8.5	99.5	0.0	0.2	0.1	0.2	5.5	17.6	9.6	11.0	15.3	14.2
17 173	...	6	Shelby	1 965	22 407	1 684	11.4	98.9	0.2	0.2	0.3	0.6	5.1	18.0	9.0	10.7	14.8	14.1
17 175	37900	2	Stark	746	6 198	2 755	8.3	98.8	0.1	0.3	0.2	0.9	6.1	17.7	8.4	10.6	13.9	14.1
17 177	23300	4	Stephenson	1 461	48 151	961	33.0	89.5	8.5	0.4	1.1	1.9	6.0	18.2	8.8	11.0	14.9	14.2
17 179	37900	2	Tazewell	1 681	128 056	443	76.2	97.2	1.0	0.5	0.7	1.2	6.0	17.2	9.0	12.5	15.1	15.0
17 181	...	7	Union	1 078	18 170	1 904	16.9	95.0	1.0	0.7	0.4	3.5	5.5	16.9	8.9	11.3	14.7	14.4
17 183	19180	3	Vermilion	2 329	82 804	643	35.6	85.0	11.3	0.5	0.7	3.3	6.6	17.7	9.2	12.2	14.1	14.0
17 185	...	6	Wabash	579	12 680	2 262	21.9	97.9	0.8	0.3	0.6	1.0	5.9	16.9	10.6	10.7	14.7	14.9
17 187	23660	7	Warren	1 405	18 246	1 893	13.0	93.4	2.2	0.3	0.6	4.1	5.4	16.4	13.8	10.1	13.4	14.3
17 189	...	6	Washington	1 457	15 179	2 089	10.4	98.2	0.6	0.5	0.3	0.8	5.7	18.4	9.2	10.8	15.6	14.3
17 191	...	7	Wayne	1 849	16 944	1 961	9.2	98.4	0.4	0.4	0.4	0.7	5.8	16.7	8.9	11.0	14.1	13.7
17 193	...	6	White	1 282	15 106	2 096	11.8	98.5	0.4	0.7	0.3	0.7	5.3	15.3	8.6	10.7	14.4	14.2
17 195	44580	4	Whiteside	1 774	59 886	823	33.8	88.8	1.4	0.4	0.6	9.5	6.1	17.8	9.2	11.4	14.4	14.7
17 197	16980	1	Will	2 168	586 706	97	270.6	76.0	10.6	0.5	3.3	10.7	7.6	20.9	9.9	13.9	16.6	12.8
17 199	32060	5	Williamson	1 097	62 448	794	56.9	95.0	3.0	0.6	0.7	1.5	5.8	16.2	9.1	13.1	14.4	13.8
17 201	40420	2	Winnebago	1 331	284 313	207	213.6	78.4	11.5	0.6	2.3	8.5	6.9	18.9	9.1	13.3	15.2	14.1
17 203	37900	2	Woodford	1 367	36 367	1 229	26.6	98.2	0.7	0.4	0.5	0.8	6.1	18.9	10.5	10.3	15.3	15.3

1. CBSA = Core Based Statistical Area. See Appendix A for explanation. See Appendix B for list of metropolitan areas with component counties. 2. County type code from the Economic Research Service of USDA Rural-Urban Continuum Codes. See Appendix A for definition. 3. Dry land or land partially or temporarily covered by water. 4. Hispanic or Latino persons may be of any race.

Table B. States and Counties — Population and Households

STATE County	55 to 64 years (16)	65 to 74 years (17)	75 years and over (18)	Percent female (19)	1990 (20)	2000 (21)	1990–2000 (22)	2000–2003 (23)	Births (24)	Deaths (25)	Net migration (26)	Number (27)	Percent change, 1990–2000 (28)	Persons per household (29)	Female family householder[1] (30)	One person (31)
ILLINOIS—Cont'd																
Jackson	7.5	5.4	5.6	48.9	61 067	59 612	-2.4	-1.1	2 205	1 574	-1 317	24 215	3.2	2.21	9.7	34.9
Jasper	9.7	7.5	8.8	51.1	10 609	10 117	-4.6	-1.6	348	345	-154	3 930	-0.8	2.55	7.0	24.7
Jefferson	9.8	7.0	8.2	48.9	37 020	40 045	8.2	0.7	1 559	1 340	124	15 374	5.3	2.44	9.9	27.6
Jersey	9.8	7.4	7.0	51.0	20 539	21 668	5.5	2.4	759	725	503	8 096	10.2	2.57	9.1	23.9
Jo Daviess	12.2	9.4	8.8	49.8	21 821	22 289	2.1	1.1	768	722	209	9 218	10.1	2.40	6.5	27.5
Johnson	10.2	7.3	6.3	41.4	11 347	12 878	13.5	0.6	379	397	80	4 183	12.3	2.43	7.1	24.2
Kane	7.5	4.1	3.7	49.5	317 471	404 119	27.3	13.1	25 751	8 204	34 765	133 901	24.9	2.97	10.0	19.6
Kankakee	9.1	6.6	6.3	51.3	96 255	103 833	7.9	1.7	5 078	3 809	660	38 182	10.3	2.61	13.1	24.9
Kendall	8.1	4.2	3.8	50.1	39 413	54 544	38.4	22.0	3 013	1 001	9 731	18 798	41.3	2.89	7.5	16.4
Knox	10.5	8.6	9.1	50.1	56 393	55 836	-1.0	-2.4	2 030	2 229	-1 133	22 056	0.7	2.33	10.6	29.6
Lake	8.3	4.6	3.9	49.6	516 418	644 356	24.8	6.3	34 413	12 388	19 046	216 297	24.3	2.88	9.2	19.7
La Salle	9.5	7.5	8.7	50.7	106 913	111 509	4.3	0.5	4 600	3 962	-43	43 417	5.2	2.49	9.2	27.4
Lawrence	10.2	9.0	10.9	52.1	15 972	15 452	-3.3	-1.1	520	687	14	6 309	-0.2	2.36	9.0	29.2
Lee	9.6	7.4	7.4	49.2	34 392	36 062	4.9	-1.5	1 152	1 295	-353	13 253	6.2	2.49	9.3	26.5
Livingston	9.2	7.1	8.1	50.7	39 301	39 678	1.0	-1.2	1 789	1 226	-1 010	14 374	4.6	2.51	8.8	26.3
Logan	9.3	6.9	8.0	49.8	30 798	31 183	1.3	-1.5	997	1 153	-286	11 113	0.7	2.42	9.3	27.8
McDonough	8.2	6.5	7.3	51.1	35 244	32 913	-6.6	-0.2	944	1 044	69	12 360	0.9	2.28	7.5	31.8
McHenry	8.0	4.3	3.7	49.8	183 241	260 077	41.9	10.0	13 189	4 951	17 679	89 403	42.0	2.89	7.6	18.0
McLean	7.3	4.8	4.7	51.6	129 180	150 433	16.5	4.3	6 527	3 319	3 356	56 746	21.3	2.45	8.8	27.6
Macon	10.4	7.8	7.9	52.3	117 206	114 706	-2.1	-3.1	4 692	3 726	-4 550	46 561	1.2	2.39	12.2	28.8
Macoupin	9.8	8.1	9.1	51.3	47 679	49 019	2.8	0.1	1 871	1 929	143	19 253	5.9	2.48	8.9	25.6
Madison	9.6	7.0	7.0	51.7	249 238	258 941	3.9	1.1	10 664	8 816	1 168	101 953	7.5	2.48	11.8	26.3
Marion	10.6	7.9	8.9	51.8	41 561	41 691	0.3	-2.3	1 693	1 743	-883	16 619	2.1	2.45	11.6	27.2
Marshall	11.2	8.9	9.8	50.5	12 846	13 180	2.6	-1.1	425	567	34	5 225	6.6	2.47	6.7	25.0
Mason	11.1	8.4	8.8	50.8	16 269	16 038	-1.4	-1.0	609	660	-89	6 389	0.7	2.48	9.0	24.9
Massac	10.7	8.2	9.3	52.2	14 752	15 161	2.8	-0.2	582	686	105	6 261	6.0	2.37	10.0	28.0
Menard	10.4	6.9	6.6	50.7	11 164	12 486	11.8	0.9	450	431	104	4 873	16.1	2.52	9.1	23.8
Mercer	11.4	7.8	8.1	50.6	17 290	16 957	-1.9	0.3	682	598	-20	6 624	0.8	2.53	7.2	22.8
Monroe	8.7	6.7	6.2	50.6	22 422	27 619	23.2	7.6	1 125	759	1 721	10 275	25.5	2.65	7.3	21.3
Montgomery	9.2	7.6	9.2	48.3	30 728	30 652	-0.2	-1.0	1 092	1 151	-207	11 507	0.2	2.44	8.9	27.8
Morgan	10.2	7.3	8.3	50.2	36 397	36 616	0.6	-1.7	1 369	1 325	-648	14 039	2.6	2.37	10.0	29.3
Moultrie	9.9	8.1	9.4	51.4	13 930	14 287	2.6	1.3	638	622	190	5 405	5.5	2.56	7.1	23.6
Ogle	9.8	6.7	6.6	50.4	45 957	51 032	11.0	3.6	1 895	1 484	1 465	19 278	12.5	2.62	8.3	22.5
Peoria	9.7	6.8	7.3	51.9	182 827	183 433	0.3	-0.6	8 548	5 726	-3 879	72 733	2.7	2.43	12.9	29.7
Perry	9.8	7.5	8.4	46.5	21 412	23 094	7.9	-1.8	766	885	-277	8 504	2.4	2.43	9.7	27.9
Piatt	10.8	7.9	7.9	51.1	15 548	16 365	5.3	0.4	544	485	17	6 475	9.1	2.50	6.8	23.7
Pike	10.4	8.2	11.0	50.1	17 577	17 384	-1.1	-2.6	593	728	-313	6 876	-2.0	2.42	7.8	27.8
Pope	12.9	9.5	8.8	48.7	4 373	4 413	0.9	-3.4	97	146	-97	1 769	9.8	2.33	7.6	27.9
Pulaski	9.4	8.3	8.9	52.4	7 523	7 348	-2.3	-3.7	342	337	-275	2 893	-2.2	2.44	15.8	30.0
Putnam	11.6	7.9	8.2	50.5	5 730	6 086	6.2	0.5	192	171	20	2 415	9.6	2.52	7.0	24.6
Randolph	9.4	7.2	8.4	46.6	34 583	33 893	-2.0	-1.9	1 202	1 327	-511	12 084	1.1	2.46	9.2	26.9
Richland	10.4	9.0	9.2	51.4	16 545	16 149	-2.4	-0.9	606	562	-190	6 660	2.4	2.40	8.8	27.7
Rock Island	10.3	7.4	7.8	51.3	148 723	149 374	0.4	-1.0	6 334	4 762	-3 019	60 712	2.4	2.38	11.6	30.2
St. Clair	8.4	6.5	6.3	52.2	262 852	256 082	-2.6	1.0	12 404	8 422	-1 189	96 810	1.5	2.59	17.1	25.9
Saline	10.7	9.1	9.9	51.5	26 551	26 733	0.7	-2.2	976	1 346	-183	10 992	1.4	2.32	10.2	31.3
Sangamon	9.6	6.5	6.8	52.2	178 386	188 951	5.9	1.5	8 318	5 969	-264	78 722	9.1	2.36	11.7	31.0
Schuyler	10.9	8.9	10.3	50.4	7 498	7 189	-4.1	-2.3	264	325	-105	2 975	-0.9	2.38	7.1	27.3
Scott	10.2	8.7	8.2	51.4	5 644	5 537	-1.9	-0.6	203	218	-11	2 222	1.5	2.47	8.3	26.1
Shelby	10.6	8.8	9.3	50.6	22 261	22 893	2.8	-2.1	710	866	-308	9 056	5.8	2.50	7.1	25.4
Stark	10.9	8.7	10.4	51.5	6 534	6 332	-3.1	-2.1	235	327	-34	2 525	0.5	2.46	7.0	27.1
Stephenson	10.2	8.1	8.8	51.8	48 052	48 979	1.9	-1.7	1 869	1 739	-958	19 785	4.6	2.43	9.5	27.6
Tazewell	10.2	7.8	7.3	50.8	123 692	128 485	3.9	-0.3	5 011	3 991	-1 343	50 327	6.7	2.49	8.7	24.8
Union	11.5	8.2	8.8	51.3	17 619	18 293	3.8	-0.7	678	906	122	7 290	6.6	2.38	9.5	28.4
Vermilion	10.3	8.0	8.1	50.8	88 257	83 919	-4.9	-1.3	3 688	3 070	-1 711	33 406	-2.0	2.42	12.2	28.9
Wabash	9.9	7.9	8.9	51.0	13 111	12 937	-1.3	-2.0	474	420	-292	5 192	3.2	2.46	8.7	27.0
Warren	10.5	8.0	8.6	51.5	19 181	18 735	-2.3	-2.6	622	648	-462	7 166	-3.1	2.44	8.8	26.7
Washington	10.0	7.7	8.6	50.6	14 965	15 148	1.2	0.2	610	562	2	5 848	3.4	2.55	7.1	24.3
Wayne	11.0	9.0	10.0	51.4	17 241	17 151	-0.5	-1.2	647	610	-225	7 143	3.0	2.37	8.3	27.6
White	11.5	9.3	11.5	52.3	16 522	15 371	-7.0	-1.7	552	735	-67	6 534	-4.5	2.29	7.6	29.8
Whiteside	10.3	8.0	8.5	51.1	60 186	60 653	0.8	-1.3	2 367	1 935	-1 177	23 684	4.2	2.51	9.5	25.1
Will	7.5	4.2	3.6	50.1	357 313	502 266	40.6	16.8	27 780	10 161	65 092	167 542	43.3	2.94	9.6	17.8
Williamson	10.7	8.0	8.4	51.3	57 733	61 296	6.2	1.9	2 324	2 448	1 306	25 358	9.7	2.35	10.2	28.9
Winnebago	9.4	6.3	6.3	51.0	252 913	278 418	10.1	2.1	12 862	8 139	1 416	107 980	11.6	2.53	11.8	26.3
Woodford	9.7	6.5	7.8	51.0	32 653	35 469	8.6	2.5	1 460	1 125	591	12 797	12.3	2.69	6.6	20.5

1. No spouse present.

Table B. States and Counties — Vital Statistics, Health Resources, and Crime

STATE County	Births, average 1999-2001 Total	Rate[1]	Deaths, average 1999-2001 Number Total	Infant[2]	Rate Total[1]	Infant[3]	Physicians, 2000 Number	Rate[5]	Hospitals, 1998 Number	Beds Number	Rate[5]	Medicare enrollees, 2003	Serious crimes known to police, 2002 Total Number	Rate[7]
	32	33	34	35	36	37	38	39	40	41	42	43	44	45
ILLINOIS—Cont'd														
Jackson	683	11.4	492	6	8.2	D	121	203	2	192	318	7 694	NA	NA
Jasper	109	10.7	110	2	10.8	D	1	10	0	0	0	1 730	NA	NA
Jefferson	470	11.7	417	3	10.4	D	54	135	2	207	554	6 688	NA	NA
Jersey	234	10.8	229	1	10.6	D	16	74	1	67	313	3 076	NA	NA
Jo Daviess	241	10.8	224	1	10.0	D	10	45	1	85	396	4 535	NA	NA
Johnson	125	9.7	117	1	9.1	D	2	16	0	0	0	2 293	NA	NA
Kane	7 751	18.9	2 456	52	6.0	6.8	561	139	4	850	217	43 169	NA	NA
Kankakee	1 536	14.8	1 109	14	10.7	9.3	172	166	2	482	472	16 616	NA	NA
Kendall	876	15.9	310	7	5.6	7.6	16	29	0	0	0	4 864	NA	NA
Knox	636	11.4	695	5	12.5	D	80	143	2	330	594	10 688	NA	NA
Lake	10 634	16.4	3 760	54	5.8	5.1	1 157	180	7	1 473	243	64 930	NA	NA
La Salle	1 425	12.8	1 209	8	10.8	5.4	117	105	4	466	423	20 135	NA	NA
Lawrence	162	10.5	232	0	15.1	D	7	45	1	59	385	3 239	NA	NA
Lee	370	10.3	401	3	11.1	D	52	144	1	101	280	6 214	NA	NA
Livingston	512	12.9	398	3	10.0	D	28	71	1	84	212	6 216	NA	NA
Logan	327	10.5	351	2	11.3	D	20	64	1	66	211	5 039	NA	NA
McDonough	307	9.3	301	1	9.1	D	55	167	1	144	425	4 924	NA	NA
McHenry	4 074	15.6	1 525	20	5.8	5.0	238	92	3	378	157	28 118	NA	NA
McLean	1 997	13.3	1 003	12	6.7	6.2	242	161	2	322	226	17 106	NA	NA
Macon	1 474	12.9	1 169	14	10.2	9.7	198	173	2	581	511	20 177	NA	NA
Macoupin	564	11.5	611	3	12.5	D	16	33	2	90	184	9 628	NA	NA
Madison	3 299	12.7	2 689	24	10.4	7.2	325	126	6	961	371	42 767	NA	NA
Marion	533	12.8	523	4	12.6	D	56	134	2	324	774	8 944	NA	NA
Marshall	132	10.1	167	1	12.7	D	8	61	0	0	0	2 374	NA	NA
Mason	181	11.3	196	1	12.2	D	11	69	1	36	214	3 343	NA	NA
Massac	198	13.0	230	0	15.2	D	8	53	1	53	340	3 006	NA	NA
Menard	138	11.1	126	1	10.1	D	2	16	0	0	0	1 902	NA	NA
Mercer	197	11.6	185	0	10.9	D	4	24	1	45	255	2 784	NA	NA
Monroe	344	12.4	234	1	8.4	D	14	51	0	0	0	4 178	NA	NA
Montgomery	346	11.3	381	1	12.4	D	17	55	2	189	602	5 860	NA	NA
Morgan	415	11.4	407	2	11.1	D	57	156	1	159	450	6 516	NA	NA
Moultrie	203	14.2	202	2	14.1	D	8	56	0	0	0	3 049	NA	NA
Ogle	604	11.8	454	5	8.9	D	25	49	1	42	83	7 620	NA	NA
Peoria	2 618	14.3	1 775	23	9.7	8.9	612	334	3	1 074	591	29 343	NA	NA
Perry	235	10.2	253	2	10.9	D	14	61	2	125	594	4 099	NA	NA
Piatt	176	10.8	153	2	9.3	D	12	73	1	18	110	3 039	NA	NA
Pike	185	10.7	228	0	13.2	D	10	58	1	59	340	3 553	NA	NA
Pope	35	8.0	48	0	11.0	D	0	0	0	0	0	1 410	NA	NA
Pulaski	102	13.9	107	1	14.7	D	0	0	0	0	0	1 098	NA	NA
Putnam	65	10.7	56	0	9.2	D	0	0	0	0	0	5 875	NA	NA
Randolph	373	11.0	389	5	11.5	D	41	121	3	199	594	3 335	NA	NA
Richland	198	12.3	186	2	11.5	D	34	211	1	134	799	25 333	NA	NA
Rock Island	1 961	13.1	1 514	15	10.1	7.5	255	171	3	648	439	38 124	NA	NA
St. Clair	3 724	14.5	2 579	37	10.1	10.0	400	156	4	965	368	38 124	NA	NA
Saline	294	11.0	420	4	15.8	D	37	138	2	130	497	5 612	NA	NA
Sangamon	2 547	13.5	1 803	18	9.5	7.1	643	340	3	1 336	698	29 398	NA	NA
Schuyler	77	10.8	95	1	13.2	D	4	56	1	53	694	1 343	NA	NA
Scott	65	11.8	65	0	11.8	D	1	18	0	0	0	946	NA	NA
Shelby	243	10.6	247	2	10.8	D	8	35	1	53	233	4 285	NA	NA
Stark	76	12.1	92	1	14.5	D	1	16	0	0	0	1 254	NA	NA
Stephenson	590	12.1	528	4	10.8	D	66	135	1	166	339	9 395	NA	NA
Tazewell	1 571	12.2	1 223	12	9.5	7.6	94	73	1	154	120	21 899	NA	NA
Union	206	11.3	265	0	14.5	D	25	137	1	94	522	3 577	NA	NA
Vermilion	1 167	13.9	956	15	11.4	12.6	141	168	2	233	277	15 773	NA	NA
Wabash	136	10.6	139	1	10.8	D	9	70	1	56	443	2 303	NA	NA
Warren	205	11.0	214	0	11.5	D	14	75	1	77	409	2 598	NA	NA
Washington	174	11.4	178	2	11.7	D	5	33	1	61	397	3 427	NA	NA
Wayne	198	11.6	205	2	11.9	D	10	58	1	81	477	3 716	NA	NA
White	163	10.6	244	0	15.9	D	11	72	1	126	805	11 444	NA	NA
Whiteside	749	12.4	608	5	10.0	D	56	92	2	182	305	50 517	NA	NA
Will	8 240	16.2	2 998	55	5.9	6.7	432	86	2	646	141	11 226	NA	NA
Williamson	709	11.5	742	4	12.1	D	104	170	2	181	298		NA	NA
Winnebago	3 971	14.3	2 490	33	8.9	8.3	619	222	3	897	335	41 594	NA	NA
Woodford	442	12.4	340	3	9.6	D	21	59	1	34	97	4 939	NA	NA

1. Per 1,000 estimated resident population.   2. Deaths of infants under 1 year old.   3. Deaths of infants under 1 year old per 1,000 live births.   4. Data subject to copyright.   5. Per 100,000 resident population as of July 1 of the year shown.   6. Data for serious crimes have not been adjusted for underreporting; this may affect comparability between geographic areas and over time.   7. Per 100,000 population estimated by the FBI.

Table B. States and Counties — Crime, Education, Money Income, and Poverty

STATE County	Serious crimes known to police,[1] 2002 (cont'd) Rate[2] Violent	Property	Education School enrollment and attainment, 2000 Enrollment[3] Total	Percent private	Attainment[4] (percent) High school graduate or less	Bachelor's degree or more	Local government expenditures,[5] 2000–2001 Total current expenditures (mil dol)	Current expenditures per student (dollars)	Money income, 1999 Per capita income[6] (dollars)	Households Median income Dollars	Percent change, 1989–1999 (constant 1999 dollars)	Percent with income of $100,000 or more	Percent below poverty level, 1999 Persons	Households	Families	Families with children
	46	47	48	49	50	51	52	53	54	55	56	57	58	59	60	61
ILLINOIS—Cont'd																
Jackson	NA	NA	26 116	4.8	39.7	32.0	62.4	7 951	15 755	24 946	5.7	5.4	25.2	27.3	14.7	20.7
Jasper	NA	NA	2 708	8.3	58.0	11.2	12.7	7 498	16 649	34 721	13.6	4.0	9.9	10.0	8.5	13.2
Jefferson	NA	NA	9 817	6.9	56.0	13.7	47.9	7 147	16 644	33 555	11.5	5.2	12.3	13.7	9.1	12.6
Jersey	NA	NA	5 988	20.4	56.8	12.6	20.1	6 431	19 581	42 065	15.4	7.8	7.1	7.6	5.3	8.0
Jo Daviess	NA	NA	5 104	14.0	58.0	15.2	24.7	7 003	21 497	40 411	11.9	7.3	6.7	7.4	4.0	6.2
Johnson	NA	NA	2 829	4.7	60.7	11.7	12.0	6 792	17 990	33 326	13.0	5.1	11.3	13.0	8.1	11.3
Kane	NA	NA	114 833	17.9	44.8	27.7	709.3	6 993	24 315	59 351	10.2	20.4	6.7	5.8	4.9	7.1
Kankakee	NA	NA	28 166	18.3	56.0	15.0	132.9	7 117	19 055	41 532	9.3	7.9	11.4	10.5	8.7	13.3
Kendall	NA	NA	15 369	16.3	40.2	25.3	72.7	6 586	25 188	64 625	12.3	18.5	3.0	3.2	2.0	2.6
Knox	NA	NA	13 125	18.0	54.9	14.6	57.0	7 016	17 985	35 407	7.5	5.3	11.1	10.2	7.7	14.0
Lake	NA	NA	185 035	19.0	34.8	38.6	1 082.8	8 578	32 102	66 973	8.3	29.1	5.7	5.3	4.0	5.7
La Salle	NA	NA	27 018	13.7	57.2	13.3	131.0	7 595	19 185	40 308	10.7	6.7	9.1	8.9	6.9	11.3
Lawrence	NA	NA	3 396	5.0	60.6	9.7	15.7	6 501	17 070	30 361	14.8	4.1	13.7	13.7	10.7	18.8
Lee	NA	NA	9 047	14.3	56.5	13.2	39.6	7 323	18 650	40 967	7.8	6.8	7.7	7.3	4.9	7.0
Livingston	NA	NA	9 388	9.7	63.2	12.6	53.7	7 047	18 347	41 342	3.1	6.8	8.8	8.4	5.8	8.5
Logan	NA	NA	7 826	25.3	60.0	14.2	28.7	7 480	17 953	39 389	6.5	6.2	8.1	8.1	6.2	9.4
McDonough	NA	NA	13 645	4.1	46.5	26.9	29.0	7 295	15 890	32 141	9.9	5.0	19.8	19.9	9.6	16.8
McHenry	NA	NA	76 811	14.2	39.1	27.7	293.1	6 596	26 476	64 826	11.0	21.8	3.7	3.5	2.5	3.7
McLean	NA	NA	52 781	12.9	37.5	36.2	164.6	7 125	22 227	47 021	11.6	13.5	9.7	10.1	4.1	6.3
Macon	NA	NA	29 235	19.9	54.9	16.9	125.4	6 925	20 067	37 859	-1.5	7.8	12.9	12.1	9.3	15.9
Macoupin	NA	NA	12 504	10.3	59.5	11.8	56.7	5 837	17 298	36 190	12.6	5.1	9.4	9.9	7.1	11.5
Madison	NA	NA	70 430	15.4	49.7	19.2	292.9	6 847	20 509	41 541	3.5	8.9	9.8	9.9	7.2	11.1
Marion	NA	NA	10 286	9.0	56.8	12.1	55.5	7 053	17 235	35 227	14.9	5.1	11.3	11.4	8.6	15.0
Marshall	NA	NA	3 090	6.9	55.2	14.5	12.6	7 819	19 065	41 576	17.0	5.4	5.6	5.7	3.8	7.0
Mason	NA	NA	3 734	4.4	62.2	11.2	24.4	6 917	17 357	35 985	19.4	4.4	9.7	10.0	7.8	13.3
Massac	NA	NA	3 373	2.6	58.3	10.7	15.5	5 985	16 334	31 498	19.4	3.6	13.5	15.1	10.4	16.0
Menard	NA	NA	3 307	8.3	50.0	20.5	15.4	5 490	21 584	46 596	18.3	8.7	8.2	7.8	6.1	10.4
Mercer	NA	NA	4 186	6.3	58.7	12.6	21.7	6 217	18 645	40 893	14.4	5.6	7.8	7.7	5.8	8.5
Monroe	NA	NA	7 520	20.5	45.4	20.4	28.0	6 250	22 954	55 320	17.4	12.1	3.4	4.0	2.3	2.8
Montgomery	NA	NA	7 203	7.0	63.9	11.2	31.2	5 801	16 272	33 123	3.2	4.5	13.4	13.7	10.6	16.0
Morgan	NA	NA	9 652	24.4	57.2	19.9	41.1	7 591	18 205	36 933	4.1	5.7	9.7	10.2	6.0	9.2
Moultrie	NA	NA	3 304	11.7	59.1	14.7	11.2	5 859	18 562	40 084	11.1	5.9	7.8	8.1	5.3	8.5
Ogle	NA	NA	13 620	6.7	53.3	17.0	75.8	7 234	20 515	45 448	9.3	10.0	7.1	7.4	5.3	8.0
Peoria	NA	NA	49 942	25.6	45.6	23.3	217.5	7 460	21 219	39 978	5.5	9.8	13.7	12.2	10.0	16.7
Perry	NA	NA	5 382	9.6	61.9	10.1	19.5	6 424	15 935	33 281	7.8	3.5	13.2	13.9	10.1	14.5
Piatt	NA	NA	4 303	6.4	48.5	21.0	20.7	6 087	21 075	45 752	8.6	7.7	5.0	5.7	3.6	5.3
Pike	NA	NA	4 152	7.6	64.2	9.9	20.1	6 381	15 946	31 127	12.9	2.6	12.4	13.4	9.8	13.3
Pope	NA	NA	959	5.6	57.3	10.5	4.3	6 729	16 440	30 048	17.5	3.3	18.2	14.9	9.8	16.8
Pulaski	NA	NA	2 064	3.1	60.9	7.1	13.5	9 609	13 325	25 361	20.8	2.2	24.7	24.4	20.5	29.0
Putnam	NA	NA	1 497	10.0	54.2	12.1	6.3	6 207	19 792	45 492	12.4	7.0	5.5	5.0	4.2	7.7
Randolph	NA	NA	7 438	16.4	65.9	8.6	33.5	7 157	17 696	37 013	6.5	5.2	10.0	10.0	7.1	11.4
Richland	NA	NA	4 095	8.7	49.4	15.2	17.0	6 288	16 847	31 185	0.9	4.6	12.9	13.1	9.8	15.0
Rock Island	NA	NA	37 839	17.5	51.5	17.1	163.3	7 128	20 164	38 608	7.2	7.6	10.7	10.4	8.1	13.8
St. Clair	NA	NA	73 803	15.1	48.2	19.3	328.8	7 144	18 932	39 148	8.7	8.5	14.5	13.4	11.8	17.5
Saline	NA	NA	6 262	2.6	54.1	12.1	28.6	6 523	15 590	28 768	16.7	3.8	14.2	15.2	10.4	16.2
Sangamon	NA	NA	48 266	17.9	43.0	28.6	194.1	6 725	23 173	42 957	5.3	10.5	9.3	8.5	6.5	10.4
Schuyler	NA	NA	1 580	5.4	62.6	11.7	7.7	6 673	17 158	35 233	24.4	4.4	10.1	11.2	6.8	9.6
Scott	NA	NA	1 315	11.7	63.5	12.1	6.5	6 416	16 998	36 566	15.1	4.1	9.7	10.7	6.5	9.6
Shelby	NA	NA	5 454	7.4	61.0	11.5	26.7	6 297	17 313	37 313	6.7	4.4	9.1	9.9	6.5	9.6
Stark	NA	NA	1 457	10.8	55.7	13.4	8.6	7 063	16 767	35 826	6.1	4.1	8.6	9.5	6.3	9.0
Stephenson	NA	NA	12 693	14.1	54.2	15.6	52.7	6 653	19 794	40 366	6.0	6.5	9.0	9.1	6.5	10.3
Tazewell	NA	NA	31 754	12.4	49.4	18.1	133.3	6 713	21 511	45 250	8.9	9.2	6.3	6.6	4.4	6.6
Union	NA	NA	4 290	5.2	56.2	15.8	23.2	6 814	16 450	30 994	14.4	4.2	16.5	15.0	10.8	18.1
Vermilion	NA	NA	19 917	9.2	59.6	12.5	104.9	7 356	16 787	34 071	6.4	4.3	13.3	12.9	9.7	15.2
Wabash	NA	NA	3 334	8.4	48.7	12.5	12.9	6 007	16 747	34 473	-1.4	5.3	14.1	14.8	9.5	16.8
Warren	NA	NA	5 142	22.9	57.3	15.8	19.5	6 565	16 946	36 224	21.1	4.7	9.2	9.1	6.8	10.5
Washington	NA	NA	3 895	13.4	55.8	13.4	15.3	6 771	19 108	40 932	20.0	6.4	6.0	6.6	3.7	5.2
Wayne	NA	NA	3 981	3.1	59.5	10.0	18.7	6 497	15 793	30 481	9.8	3.1	12.4	13.4	9.4	14.4
White	NA	NA	3 321	4.0	61.0	10.4	25.0	9 173	16 412	29 601	6.6	3.6	12.5	12.7	8.7	13.6
Whiteside	NA	NA	14 998	11.3	58.0	11.3	75.2	7 230	19 296	40 354	10.9	6.1	8.5	7.9	6.2	9.9
Will	NA	NA	147 354	17.9	42.2	25.5	535.7	6 557	24 613	62 238	12.4	21.0	4.9	4.7	3.4	4.6
Williamson	NA	NA	14 961	9.2	52.6	17.2	62.1	6 557	17 779	31 991	8.0	5.8	14.6	15.2	11.4	18.1
Winnebago	NA	NA	72 350	21.4	51.4	19.4	344.0	7 747	21 194	43 886	4.2	10.0	9.6	9.3	6.9	10.7
Woodford	NA	NA	9 879	14.2	47.5	21.1	51.4	6 780	21 956	51 394	11.3	12.1	4.3	4.4	2.9	4.7

1. Data for serious crimes have not been adjusted for underreporting; this may affect comparability between geographic areas and over time.   2. Per 100,000 population estimated by the FBI.   3. All persons 3 years old and over enrolled in nursery school through college.   4. Persons 25 years old and over.   5. Elementary and secondary education expenditures.   6. Based on population enumerated as of April 1, 2000.

Table B. States and Counties — Personal Income

STATE County	Total (mil dol)	Percent change, 2001–2002	Per capita Dollars	Per capita Rank	Wages and salaries[2] (mil dol)	Proprietor's income (mil dol)	Dividends, interest, and rent (mil dol)	Transfer payments Total (mil dol)	Govt payments Total (mil dol)	Social Security (mil dol)	Medical payments (mil dol)	Income maintenance (mil dol)	Unemployment insurance (mil dol)
	62	63	64	65	66	67	68	69	70	71	72	73	74
ILLINOIS—Cont'd													
Jackson	1 387	3.7	23 628	1 525	1 017	98	252	236	221	71	77	28	9
Jasper	239	-2.4	23 728	1 488	91	27	59	43	40	20	14	3	2
Jefferson	939	4.0	23 319	1 623	721	68	170	198	188	72	78	18	8
Jersey	582	1.9	26 449	807	148	22	106	94	88	43	33	6	4
Jo Daviess	673	2.0	29 956	355	265	52	195	94	88	51	26	4	4
Johnson	235	4.5	18 394	2 845	77	17	49	53	50	23	17	4	2
Kane	13 434	1.7	30 394	312	8 605	642	2 116	1 247	1 132	449	431	92	120
Kankakee	2 716	2.5	25 901	912	1 598	119	456	513	486	187	200	47	28
Kendall	1 884	1.9	30 530	302	717	55	269	156	140	77	34	6	14
Knox	1 329	1.1	24 189	1 345	847	74	245	312	298	113	121	21	16
Lake	31 253	2.0	46 343	30	19 844	2 218	6 912	1 956	1 786	825	637	112	149
La Salle	2 903	1.3	25 980	891	1 631	144	588	514	485	243	157	28	38
Lawrence	374	1.5	24 506	1 260	147	33	92	91	87	36	41	6	3
Lee	857	1.3	24 084	1 376	472	46	183	158	149	71	56	8	8
Livingston	1 071	0.6	27 230	664	616	53	205	167	156	77	57	9	8
Logan	709	-0.1	22 984	1 729	351	42	146	132	124	56	47	8	6
McDonough	710	0.4	21 516	2 144	452	35	156	131	123	55	40	10	4
McHenry	9 299	2.2	33 507	170	3 902	257	1 393	755	683	343	214	28	74
McLean	4 798	3.9	30 892	276	4 138	245	778	450	410	196	127	33	20
Macon	3 157	-0.4	28 094	532	2 275	191	615	574	545	231	185	55	37
Macoupin	1 209	1.8	24 671	1 221	400	52	233	237	224	102	87	15	10
Madison	7 290	3.2	27 947	558	3 850	316	1 246	1 212	1 145	491	443	100	43
Marion	966	0.8	23 515	1 563	528	34	187	262	251	80	114	21	13
Marshall	355	0.7	27 206	667	119	19	82	62	59	30	20	3	3
Mason	402	0.1	25 143	1 092	134	24	85	87	83	39	31	6	4
Massac	347	2.8	22 920	1 746	189	19	64	85	81	33	35	8	2
Menard	355	0.5	28 223	518	65	23	68	50	46	22	17	3	2
Mercer	436	1.3	25 613	977	96	28	85	74	69	35	22	5	5
Monroe	915	1.4	31 488	249	248	38	180	102	94	49	33	3	3
Montgomery	679	0.9	22 215	1 955	345	36	153	152	144	64	56	11	7
Morgan	869	1.2	24 079	1 377	528	41	210	171	161	72	61	13	7
Moultrie	342	-0.2	23 755	1 482	130	21	66	67	64	30	25	3	3
Ogle	1 353	0.6	25 916	906	662	80	257	192	178	92	56	10	13
Peoria	5 389	1.9	29 496	391	4 393	302	1 100	829	782	345	271	89	42
Perry	438	-0.1	19 242	2 706	206	20	86	109	103	45	36	8	7
Piatt	492	-0.6	30 192	333	121	27	84	67	63	31	23	3	4
Pike	372	-1.6	21 830	2 058	127	25	91	84	80	36	32	6	3
Pope	85	3.5	19 568	2 643	22	7	15	23	21	10	8	2	1
Pulaski	134	3.0	18 639	2 806	61	7	19	44	42	14	17	6	1
Putnam	152	-4.1	24 902	1 159	59	8	35	26	25	13	7	1	3
Randolph	714	2.2	21 479	2 154	456	30	159	153	144	66	54	11	6
Richland	369	0.7	22 937	1 740	209	30	87	85	81	36	30	7	3
Rock Island	4 079	2.1	27 469	621	3 623	179	856	661	623	289	213	64	27
St. Clair	6 928	4.2	26 909	719	4 098	266	1 182	1 252	1 187	413	483	163	39
Saline	588	2.0	22 451	1 890	321	42	111	162	156	59	65	15	6
Sangamon	6 061	2.5	31 640	240	4 740	420	1 161	805	756	334	275	78	33
Schuyler	178	5.5	25 424	1 020	74	17	34	30	29	15	9	2	2
Scott	113	-0.5	20 509	2 429	51	3	22	24	23	11	8	2	2
Shelby	494	-2.9	21 905	2 036	176	31	99	101	95	42	37	6	6
Stark	159	-4.7	25 439	1 014	40	9	38	32	30	14	12	2	2
Stephenson	1 323	0.3	27 480	620	814	61	300	220	208	103	67	17	12
Tazewell	3 772	2.1	29 403	403	2 530	167	741	554	520	257	185	33	29
Union	396	4.5	21 807	2 066	170	23	69	102	98	35	45	9	4
Vermilion	1 870	1.5	22 484	1 883	1 168	75	350	423	401	173	136	45	21
Wabash	299	1.2	23 528	1 554	140	20	68	58	55	26	20	4	2
Warren	391	-0.3	21 288	2 214	177	20	72	78	73	31	27	6	4
Washington	406	-0.4	26 811	733	218	27	86	67	63	29	25	3	3
Wayne	390	1.0	22 925	1 744	142	37	83	87	83	37	34	6	3
White	376	0.5	24 691	1 213	153	28	93	88	84	38	34	6	2
Whiteside	1 475	-0.6	24 473	1 270	743	74	326	297	281	132	108	16	16
Will	16 445	1.7	29 461	395	6 852	520	2 142	1 584	1 439	638	500	93	144
Williamson	1 497	4.8	24 101	1 371	847	84	282	310	294	126	106	26	13
Winnebago	7 636	2.3	27 103	679	5 784	332	1 312	1 181	1 107	507	382	103	85
Woodford	1 010	1.5	28 039	544	339	41	198	126	117	63	39	5	5

1. Based on the resident population estimated as of July 1 of the year shown. 2. Includes other labor income.

Table B. States and Counties — Earnings, Social Security, and Housing

STATE County	Earnings, 2002 Total (mil dol)	Farm	Goods-related[1] Total	Manufacturing	Information and professional and technical services	Retail trade	Finance, insurance, and real estate	Health services	Government	Social Security beneficiaries, December 2003 Number	Rate[2]	Supplemental Security Income recipients, December 2003	Housing units, 2003 Total	Percent change, 2000–2003
	75	76	77	78	79	80	81	82	83	84	85	86	87	88
ILLINOIS—Cont'd														
Jackson	1 115	0.7	10.5	3.9	D	7.4	3.9	13.8	45.2	8 125	138	1 362	27 522	2.5
Jasper	118	11.2	13.2	7.8	3.0	9.7	3.4	D	21.3	2 175	218	138	4 399	2.4
Jefferson	788	0.6	D	19.6	6.7	7.2	5.3	D	14.0	7 605	189	960	17 390	2.4
Jersey	169	-1.0	D	2.7	6.3	13.7	4.7	D	26.7	4 360	197	255	9 205	3.2
Jo Daviess	317	3.0	D	24.2	D	8.2	6.5	D	14.5	5 255	233	154	12 352	2.9
Johnson	95	3.5	D	D	D	7.1	4.0	D	42.1	2 520	195	254	5 198	3.0
Kane	9 246	0.2	31.7	21.3	8.4	7.1	7.0	8.6	14.3	42 405	93	4 158	154 252	11.0
Kankakee	1 717	1.5	27.8	21.2	D	9.2	5.3	15.6	15.7	18 995	180	2 573	41 752	2.8
Kendall	772	0.4	D	32.1	D	7.9	5.2	2.6	13.9	7 425	112	117	24 284	24.4
Knox	921	1.9	D	20.3	4.1	8.0	3.7	16.0	15.6	11 330	208	1 224	23 858	0.6
Lake	22 062	0.0	D	20.4	10.7	8.2	10.2	6.2	14.0	74 900	109	5 096	238 605	5.6
La Salle	1 775	0.1	25.3	17.1	5.8	10.6	5.5	9.8	15.2	23 275	208	1 162	47 447	2.2
Lawrence	180	4.4	D	14.0	2.9	6.3	10.6	D	17.2	3 775	247	320	7 115	1.4
Lee	518	1.3	D	24.2	3.1	5.8	3.5	14.4	21.5	7 075	199	525	14 486	1.2
Livingston	669	1.7	D	29.4	D	6.7	3.4	7.9	20.4	7 640	195	413	15 410	0.7
Logan	392	0.2	D	18.1	2.6	9.8	D	11.8	25.9	5 570	181	284	11 873	0.0
McDonough	487	1.4	D	12.2	4.0	6.9	4.5	6.3	47.1	5 895	179	504	13 719	3.2
McHenry	4 159	0.2	38.2	24.1	7.2	8.4	4.4	8.5	12.2	32 350	113	1 110	103 182	11.1
McLean	4 384	0.0	16.3	10.8	17.4	5.8	21.3	8.8	12.7	19 295	123	1 392	63 841	6.5
Macon	2 466	0.0	36.6	29.2	4.7	7.5	4.3	10.8	10.1	22 655	204	3 125	50 908	1.3
Macoupin	452	1.0	D	9.8	4.6	8.0	5.4	D	20.4	10 470	213	809	21 511	2.0
Madison	4 166	0.0	33.6	24.8	5.9	8.7	5.0	10.8	15.9	48 580	186	4 701	112 401	3.2
Marion	562	0.7	33.5	25.8	D	6.2	3.1	15.4	17.0	8 700	213	1 138	18 296	1.5
Marshall	138	3.0	D	36.3	1.9	5.6	4.8	D	13.6	2 885	221	98	6 038	2.1
Mason	158	7.0	D	12.3	D	8.0	4.8	D	27.7	3 865	243	252	7 039	0.1
Massac	208	1.3	22.5	20.2	2.0	5.7	4.3	5.0	15.5	3 540	234	427	7 052	1.5
Menard	87	7.6	D	0.7	5.4	7.9	8.1	D	26.5	2 235	177	120	5 470	3.5
Mercer	124	10.3	17.1	10.6	4.2	7.6	D	D	32.0	3 555	209	140	7 133	0.3
Monroe	286	2.6	19.6	4.3	D	12.7	D	7.5	15.8	4 900	165	155	11 567	7.6
Montgomery	381	1.3	22.6	14.4	4.4	9.0	5.4	D	20.3	6 695	221	610	12 627	0.8
Morgan	569	0.0	31.1	26.4	D	7.1	6.1	12.4	17.7	7 410	206	756	15 538	1.6
Moultrie	151	2.4	37.4	27.7	4.8	8.0	4.5	D	14.4	3 010	208	130	5 850	1.9
Ogle	741	0.8	35.1	29.3	D	5.5	4.6	4.9	14.5	9 185	174	323	20 959	2.6
Peoria	4 695	0.2	21.6	15.8	14.4	5.7	6.2	19.7	12.0	33 260	182	4 788	79 880	2.1
Perry	227	0.4	D	29.8	3.7	9.0	4.3	8.0	24.8	4 510	199	404	9 682	2.4
Piatt	148	-1.6	D	14.3	D	6.9	5.8	D	20.5	3 085	188	111	6 959	2.4
Pike	153	8.8	D	3.9	4.2	10.6	7.3	D	23.9	3 960	234	334	8 070	0.7
Pope	29	2.4	D	D	D	2.8	6.9	D	41.2	1 090	256	118	2 392	1.7
Pulaski	68	0.8	D	7.6	D	4.9	D	D	43.5	1 580	223	335	3 416	1.9
Putnam	67	8.2	D	32.5	D	4.6	D	2.5	12.9	1 305	213	45	2 985	3.4
Randolph	487	2.2	D	24.5	3.7	6.9	2.9	7.0	27.7	6 495	195	428	13 464	1.0
Richland	239	2.8	20.8	13.6	3.1	8.2	6.7	D	15.5	3 895	243	358	7 668	2.7
Rock Island	3 802	0.1	21.6	15.6	D	5.7	6.2	8.3	21.6	28 605	193	2 915	64 662	0.3
St. Clair	4 363	0.3	D	7.6	9.0	7.2	4.0	12.2	32.2	42 870	166	8 606	108 193	3.6
Saline	363	-0.3	D	3.5	3.7	6.8	4.7	D	22.0	6 295	241	1 167	12 646	2.3
Sangamon	5 160	0.1	D	3.4	9.3	6.0	10.0	15.8	32.9	34 440	179	4 726	87 668	2.6
Schuyler	92	9.7	D	3.6	5.9	5.4	2.7	4.2	18.6	1 590	226	90	3 373	2.1
Scott	55	3.2	D	D	D	D	D	D	20.9	1 095	199	61	2 510	1.9
Shelby	207	3.3	D	21.3	4.7	6.6	4.4	9.7	19.5	4 790	214	286	10 172	1.1
Stark	49	11.7	16.3	10.3	D	12.5	D	6.6	22.4	1 360	219	48	2 767	1.5
Stephenson	875	1.4	44.0	34.1	3.2	5.4	9.7	D	12.4	10 355	215	819	21 869	0.7
Tazewell	2 698	0.5	48.6	40.6	3.4	6.2	4.5	5.1	9.7	24 690	193	1 684	54 134	2.2
Union	194	4.1	D	11.8	3.2	8.7	4.1	D	35.4	4 050	223	699	8 044	1.9
Vermilion	1 243	0.1	D	21.9	5.1	6.9	5.7	10.0	23.4	17 745	214	2 538	36 512	0.4
Wabash	160	-0.4	47.2	19.0	3.8	6.4	3.8	D	20.0	2 605	205	175	5 824	1.1
Warren	197	2.5	D	30.1	3.9	8.1	4.6	D	15.0	3 125	171	271	7 767	-0.3
Washington	245	3.5	D	35.2	3.1	8.2	3.5	4.6	12.8	3 055	201	120	6 536	2.4
Wayne	180	5.1	35.3	24.0	2.8	8.1	D	9.2	17.6	4 030	238	276	8 175	2.8
White	181	1.8	27.8	5.5	3.3	14.2	4.6	D	17.1	4 060	269	380	7 557	2.2
Whiteside	817	1.8	35.7	28.1	4.1	9.2	4.6	8.9	19.0	13 070	218	950	25 231	0.8
Will	7 372	0.2	30.1	14.5	6.1	8.2	4.9	8.3	15.7	64 780	110	4 176	199 661	13.8
Williamson	931	0.1	D	13.5	D	9.4	7.3	10.4	27.6	13 295	213	1 366	28 389	2.5
Winnebago	6 116	0.1	35.6	29.2	5.4	6.8	6.9	13.8	10.8	48 920	172	5 611	118 146	3.3
Woodford	380	1.0	D	26.0	4.2	8.4	3.7	7.1	16.5	6 040	166	154	14 025	4.0

1. Covers mining, construction, and manufacturing. 2. Per 1,000 resident population estimated as of July 1 of the year shown.

STATE County	Housing units, 2000								Civilian labor force, 2003				Civilian employment,[6] 2000		
	Occupied units										Unemployment			Percent	
			Owner-occupied			Renter-occupied									
				Median owner cost as a percent of income											
	Total	Percent	Median value[1]	With a mortgage	Without a mortgage[2]	Median rent[3]	Median rent as a percent of income	Substandard units[4] (percent)	Total	Percent change, 2002–2003	Total	Rate[5]	Total	Management, professional and related occupations	Production, transportation, and material moving occupations
	89	90	91	92	93	94	95	96	97	98	99	100	101	102	103
ILLINOIS—Cont'd															
Jackson	24 215	53.3	68 200	19.0	10.1	409	33.4	3.1	31 542	1.8	1 413	4.5	28 213	35.8	10.5
Jasper	3 930	83.2	65 000	17.6	9.9	363	23.8	1.9	3 713	1.5	367	9.9	4 935	24.2	23.6
Jefferson	15 374	74.4	63 800	19.8	11.7	392	22.9	2.8	19 614	0.1	1 191	6.1	17 592	26.2	20.0
Jersey	8 096	77.7	82 800	18.6	11.0	424	21.7	2.3	10 470	-0.2	605	5.8	11 528	26.8	18.0
Jo Daviess	9 218	77.3	89 100	20.7	9.9	393	22.9	1.4	13 024	-0.5	690	5.3	11 528	27.8	19.5
Johnson	4 183	84.9	64 700	19.2	9.9	351	24.2	2.4	5 179	2.3	341	6.6	4 398	29.7	13.9
Kane	133 901	76.0	160 400	23.1	11.9	686	24.2	7.3	230 734	-0.3	16 239	7.0	196 184	32.4	18.3
Kankakee	38 182	69.4	99 200	21.6	11.3	539	24.6	3.7	52 354	-0.3	4 027	7.7	48 227	26.1	20.7
Kendall	18 798	84.1	154 900	23.8	12.3	720	23.0	2.3	32 763	-0.2	1 981	6.0	28 842	34.0	15.4
Knox	22 056	71.6	63 500	18.2	10.4	411	22.5	1.4	28 517	-1.3	2 132	7.5	25 485	26.7	23.2
Lake	216 297	77.8	198 200	23.1	12.2	742	24.8	4.9	342 646	-0.5	20 664	6.0	310 396	41.1	11.6
La Salle	43 417	75.1	87 000	19.9	11.4	474	21.7	2.2	56 310	-1.0	4 567	8.1	51 042	25.0	21.7
Lawrence	6 309	77.0	45 800	18.8	11.2	360	19.6	1.6	7 488	0.1	479	6.4	7 042	25.6	21.2
Lee	13 253	73.9	83 400	19.9	9.9	468	21.0	1.8	17 927	-0.8	1 082	6.0	16 325	26.1	23.7
Livingston	14 374	74.2	79 700	19.7	10.1	464	21.7	2.4	20 057	-0.9	1 050	5.2	17 952	25.1	23.9
Logan	11 113	71.3	75 700	19.2	11.0	455	21.1	1.5	12 517	-4.8	899	7.2	13 932	27.5	17.7
McDonough	12 360	63.1	61 200	17.7	9.9	393	28.8	1.3	16 537	-0.8	730	4.4	15 934	33.3	13.0
McHenry	89 403	83.1	168 100	23.4	12.1	761	25.1	2.8	147 893	-0.2	9 331	6.3	135 269	34.6	15.2
McLean	56 746	66.4	114 800	19.5	9.9	533	23.9	1.7	93 019	-1.0	2 634	2.8	80 759	37.3	10.8
Macon	46 561	71.7	69 800	18.1	10.0	448	24.1	1.8	55 790	-2.1	4 134	7.4	52 584	28.4	19.6
Macoupin	19 253	79.0	66 700	19.2	11.0	422	22.5	1.7	24 054	1.8	1 486	6.2	22 672	25.9	19.3
Madison	101 953	73.8	77 200	19.0	10.6	490	23.8	2.1	128 321	0.4	8 027	6.3	123 468	30.9	16.6
Marion	16 619	76.6	53 700	18.5	9.9	371	23.4	2.4	18 473	-1.5	1 913	10.4	18 873	24.8	28.1
Marshall	5 225	80.2	75 900	19.0	9.9	410	19.5	1.3	7 029	1.5	345	4.9	6 568	25.5	22.5
Mason	6 389	76.7	61 200	18.9	10.4	390	21.1	2.1	8 504	-1.4	663	7.8	7 087	24.9	21.0
Massac	6 261	78.6	63 300	19.2	11.1	373	26.0	1.7	7 845	-1.2	378	4.8	6 730	24.6	18.1
Menard	4 873	78.9	93 600	19.5	9.9	455	23.1	1.7	6 053	-3.1	279	4.6	6 486	34.9	10.3
Mercer	6 624	79.7	68 500	19.1	9.9	392	18.0	0.9	9 146	2.0	612	6.7	8 031	26.9	21.8
Monroe	10 275	80.2	125 500	19.8	9.9	562	21.1	1.5	14 958	0.4	674	4.5	14 526	33.4	13.3
Montgomery	11 507	78.4	54 800	19.3	10.7	388	22.5	1.8	14 905	1.1	1 269	8.5	12 951	26.0	18.1
Morgan	14 039	70.3	75 800	19.1	9.9	420	22.0	1.9	19 129	1.7	1 000	5.2	17 425	30.8	18.0
Moultrie	5 405	78.4	72 800	18.6	10.5	436	19.7	2.8	8 371	-2.1	391	4.7	6 927	26.2	27.2
Ogle	19 278	74.5	102 700	20.7	10.0	489	21.6	3.2	26 339	-0.8	1 907	7.2	24 812	28.3	23.1
Peoria	72 733	67.8	85 800	19.2	9.9	490	24.0	2.3	93 141	-0.9	5 604	6.0	85 258	35.2	14.1
Perry	8 504	78.6	55 000	17.9	10.6	370	24.0	2.0	9 130	0.6	846	9.3	9 197	23.6	23.9
Piatt	6 475	80.3	82 600	19.0	10.1	460	20.3	0.9	8 242	-0.2	436	5.3	8 502	32.3	18.0
Pike	6 876	77.2	54 000	18.6	10.2	341	20.8	2.1	9 032	-0.2	497	5.5	7 718	25.8	21.0
Pope	1 769	82.1	50 600	19.5	11.1	257	24.4	1.5	1 631	1.7	156	9.6	1 885	26.4	18.4
Pulaski	2 893	75.7	33 300	17.6	10.3	305	24.6	4.0	2 901	-3.1	323	11.1	2 848	23.1	21.6
Putnam	2 415	82.3	89 100	19.3	9.9	445	22.0	0.9	3 285	-3.0	238	7.2	2 855	23.4	23.9
Randolph	12 084	79.4	65 700	18.7	9.9	393	19.8	2.1	14 505	-1.7	854	5.9	13 993	24.1	23.4
Richland	6 660	76.4	62 500	20.0	10.1	385	24.6	1.6	7 904	-2.4	513	6.5	7 270	30.1	18.7
Rock Island	60 712	69.7	78 900	18.9	10.6	450	22.9	2.7	74 261	-0.3	4 532	6.1	71 446	27.2	19.1
St. Clair	96 810	67.0	77 700	20.0	11.2	503	24.5	3.3	113 479	0.3	8 447	7.4	110 505	30.1	14.7
Saline	10 992	76.5	48 300	19.1	11.9	347	25.0	2.1	10 632	2.6	854	8.0	10 650	27.5	14.0
Sangamon	78 722	70.0	91 200	19.9	9.9	503	22.6	1.8	98 826	-2.5	5 227	5.3	97 526	39.3	8.2
Schuyler	2 975	79.0	54 000	18.3	11.1	341	17.7	1.6	4 592	1.7	223	4.9	3 621	27.9	20.8
Scott	2 222	77.6	57 800	17.7	11.0	326	16.6	0.8	2 809	1.4	185	6.6	2 736	26.1	18.0
Shelby	9 056	81.0	66 600	18.7	9.9	418	20.4	1.7	11 285	0.6	718	6.4	10 698	24.4	26.1
Stark	2 525	77.4	61 800	18.4	11.1	397	20.5	1.5	2 852	-0.9	239	8.4	2 658	28.1	20.0
Stephenson	19 785	74.8	81 400	19.7	10.7	433	22.7	1.6	24 185	-1.1	1 889	7.8	23 536	28.5	22.5
Tazewell	50 327	76.1	89 200	18.7	9.9	471	21.7	1.4	67 991	-0.9	3 621	5.3	62 984	29.3	17.7
Union	7 290	75.4	59 900	18.6	11.5	341	25.6	2.6	8 945	1.7	584	6.5	7 581	31.2	13.5
Vermilion	33 406	71.8	56 000	17.6	10.6	420	23.4	2.5	37 418	0.0	3 130	8.4	35 735	24.3	23.1
Wabash	5 192	75.2	56 200	19.4	9.9	337	22.5	2.1	4 579	-2.1	380	8.3	6 265	22.9	23.1
Warren	7 166	74.4	57 600	17.8	9.9	376	21.1	1.2	9 407	-1.3	583	6.2	9 205	27.5	23.2
Washington	5 848	81.0	74 300	19.7	10.8	424	18.7	1.8	8 833	0.9	435	4.9	7 669	28.2	21.1
Wayne	7 143	79.6	48 600	17.9	9.9	308	19.5	1.9	7 607	-0.6	491	6.5	7 649	24.2	28.9
White	6 534	78.0	43 100	18.2	10.6	313	20.8	1.5	7 634	0.9	402	5.3	6 772	24.2	22.8
Whiteside	23 684	74.5	75 700	18.8	9.9	463	22.8	2.3	29 847	-1.9	2 163	7.2	28 343	24.7	27.0
Will	167 542	83.2	154 300	22.7	11.3	630	23.4	2.8	278 231	-0.2	19 273	6.9	246 431	33.9	14.4
Williamson	25 358	73.6	63 300	19.5	11.0	400	24.3	2.0	30 543	2.7	1 945	6.4	27 266	28.4	16.0
Winnebago	107 980	70.1	91 900	20.6	11.7	514	23.3	3.2	146 159	-0.7	12 666	8.7	134 952	29.7	22.0
Woodford	12 797	82.7	102 900	19.2	9.9	484	19.0	1.3	18 927	-0.8	742	3.9	17 681	33.6	16.7

1. Specified owner-occupied units. 2. Median monthly owner costs is often in the minimum category—9.9 percent or less, which is indicated as 9.9 percent. 3. Specified renter-occupied units. 4. Overcrowded or lacking complete plumbing facilities. 5. Percent of civilian labor force. 6. Persons 16 years old and over.

Table B. States and Counties — Nonfarm Employment and Agriculture

	Private nonfarm establishments, employment and payroll, 2001									Agriculture, 2002			
		Employment						Annual payroll		Farms			
												Percent with—	
STATE County	Number of establishments	Total	Health care and social assistance	Manufacturing	Retail trade	Finance and insurance	Professional, scientific, and technical services	Total (mil dol)	Average per employee (dollars)	Number	Less than 50 acres	500 acres and over	Farm operators whose principal occupation is farming (percent)
	104	105	106	107	108	109	110	111	112	113	114	115	116
ILLINOIS—Cont'd													
Jackson	1 373	18 609	3 784	982	3 754	649	884	391	20 986	740	28.9	13.2	52.4
Jasper	242	2 394	112	378	340	D	D	69	28 904	791	26.2	25.2	67.9
Jefferson	1 075	15 695	3 050	2 695	2 692	379	495	404	25 767	1 168	33.4	11.9	46.8
Jersey	412	4 569	858	105	974	200	140	90	19 627	520	26.7	21.0	56.2
Jo Daviess	757	7 577	545	1 742	868	227	163	157	20 701	989	24.4	13.7	61.4
Johnson	196	1 167	127	D	263	D	139	20	17 386	636	26.6	7.4	54.4
Kane	10 499	179 345	18 580	39 743	20 271	9 487	9 516	6 043	33 693	619	42.6	20.5	44.8
Kankakee	2 275	37 535	5 922	6 877	5 669	1 816	682	1 066	28 401	722	22.6	32.3	68.2
													72.2
Kendall	1 201	13 572	643	2 871	2 131	454	429	378	27 885	412	24.5	29.6	71.8
Knox	1 272	20 629	4 765	4 528	3 266	481	344	496	24 027	921	23.9	26.0	65.7
Lake	18 388	312 014	27 787	53 177	40 880	19 105	22 115	14 122	45 262	337	69.7	6.2	46.3
La Salle	2 942	38 888	5 154	6 632	7 087	1 441	1 053	1 050	27 006	1 478	19.1	27.8	73.3
Lawrence	350	4 230	1 070	706	458	D	D	88	20 848	355	25.6	32.1	63.4
Lee	811	10 660	1 868	3 358	1 269	252	239	290	27 214	842	21.4	30.8	74.2
Livingston	930	11 749	1 518	4 075	1 816	525	231	361	30 761	1 330	17.1	35.3	74.5
Logan	695	8 633	1 286	1 468	1 176	347	160	195	22 616	692	21.5	37.7	73.3
McDonough	771	9 359	1 253	1 690	1 568	427	191	204	21 834	752	19.8	28.9	63.0
McHenry	7 022	89 910	7 376	27 763	11 219	2 470	3 192	3 014	33 524	870	49.0	14.5	59.1
McLean	3 506	79 778	7 046	7 046	9 252	22 295	2 169	2 855	35 787	1 442	21.3	35.0	68.7
Macon	2 685	53 746	6 856	9 487	6 821	1 619	1 028	1 702	31 661	646	28.3	36.1	73.4
Macoupin	1 068	10 396	1 552	952	1 625	523	411	242	23 270	1 214	26.6	21.7	69.4
Madison	5 770	83 264	12 534	16 791	11 937	2 878	2 738	2 321	27 876	1 152	37.2	14.6	57.1
Marion	1 156	15 103	2 844	5 599	1 938	415	313	361	23 903	1 095	34.6	14.0	49.4
Marshall	293	3 036	333	1 074	381	123	51	69	22 778	454	17.4	27.5	72.9
Mason	335	2 796	422	439	520	209	D	63	22 631	443	19.2	42.9	69.5
Massac	270	4 464	641	638	353	138	52	129	28 814	434	29.3	14.5	55.5
Menard	248	1 422	151	D	337	100	52	31	21 700	329	25.2	31.3	58.7
Mercer	331	2 307	408	367	571	D	D	47	20 247	746	26.3	25.6	66.8
Monroe	668	6 448	697	285	1 142	337	439	164	25 386	531	32.8	20.7	60.5
Montgomery	777	8 502	1 419	1 348	1 560	418	230	207	24 331	1 001	26.7	24.0	61.3
Morgan	921	14 728	2 591	3 801	2 016	857	284	340	23 088	682	22.6	30.1	67.6
Moultrie	308	3 519	779	897	390	146	109	84	23 729	441	29.9	30.2	70.3
Ogle	1 014	15 064	1 111	5 550	1 589	527	206	443	29 409	1 129	30.9	21.1	64.8
Peoria	4 763	104 939	17 914	12 748	10 963	4 554	5 092	3 685	35 117	892	29.1	18.0	63.5
Perry	451	5 700	838	2 106	762	160	67	127	22 330	549	25.7	20.8	64.7
Piatt	368	2 918	461	378	583	192	120	65	22 187	442	20.1	42.1	77.8
Pike	397	3 195	669	155	713	215	68	59	18 495	1 041	21.0	23.8	62.6
Pope	70	328	128	D	D	D	D	5	16 637	341	21.1	10.9	45.7
Pulaski	120	912	242	D	119	D	D	19	21 309	253	26.5	19.4	56.9
Putnam	122	1 554	19	900	123	D	D	55	35 518	175	20.0	25.1	64.6
Randolph	724	10 333	2 236	2 364	1 505	324	129	256	24 762	823	24.5	17.9	58.8
Richland	506	6 243	982	460	949	243	72	143	22 925	506	29.6	26.1	63.8
Rock Island	3 613	67 466	8 467	9 255	8 321	3 825	2 182	2 211	32 769	659	34.1	16.8	64.8
St. Clair	5 420	75 592	12 709	6 724	12 872	3 204	4 685	1 958	25 908	811	28.9	21.5	65.2
Saline	665	7 811	2 233	402	1 279	308	158	172	21 968	446	38.3	17.3	49.6
Sangamon	5 275	83 346	17 999	4 058	12 061	5 752	3 917	2 357	28 279	970	33.5	27.8	62.9
Schuyler	165	1 323	298	110	252	D	D	32	24 037	538	20.8	21.0	58.6
Scott	99	686	11	D	115	D	9	25	35 914	291	26.5	26.1	69.1
Shelby	471	4 528	708	1 256	528	213	136	106	23 362	1 228	27.0	22.9	65.6
Stark	129	909	174	181	143	D	66	18	19 435	335	21.2	37.0	73.1
Stephenson	1 126	18 650	2 640	5 717	2 396	1 660	355	559	29 974	1 075	29.0	16.7	70.2
Tazewell	2 850	41 918	4 512	6 658	7 086	1 767	953	1 226	29 244	918	28.8	24.9	63.4
Union	363	4 494	1 964	550	685	D	80	102	22 653	666	28.5	11.6	51.8
Vermilion	1 700	28 457	4 539	6 537	3 989	1 368	492	759	26 677	909	26.7	35.4	69.6
Wabash	301	3 777	851	584	493	105	110	90	23 905	199	24.6	36.2	71.4
Warren	384	5 292	816	1 520	650	238	85	108	20 387	633	14.1	38.1	76.6
Washington	418	5 367	645	1 798	713	185	107	130	24 268	756	18.8	28.7	69.2
Wayne	354	3 630	608	983	641	198	76	81	22 418	1 092	29.4	17.1	53.6
White	410	3 517	729	382	614	160	95	79	22 428	482	26.8	27.0	62.0
Whiteside	1 442	20 963	3 449	6 363	3 268	747	449	499	23 792	1 001	24.5	23.7	71.1
Will	10 373	145 697	13 641	25 517	18 645	4 455	5 846	5 122	35 153	830	38.2	20.8	64.7
Williamson	1 575	20 358	3 977	2 689	3 769	1 174	475	476	23 390	631	35.8	7.3	42.5
Winnebago	7 033	133 124	17 648	35 283	17 026	5 682	4 947	4 135	31 059	695	39.9	16.5	63.6
Woodford	724	8 187	1 141	2 252	1 142	245	197	206	25 204	919	25.0	22.4	66.3

Items 104—116

IL(Jackson)—IL(Woodford) 219

STATE County	Acreage (1,000)	Percent change, 1997–2002	Average size of farm	Total irrigated (1,000)	Total cropland (1,000)	Average per farm	Average per acre	Value of machinery and equipment average per farm (dollars)	Total (mil dol)	Average per farm (dollars)	Crops	Live-stock and poultry products	$10,000 or more	$100,000 or more	Total ($1,000)	Percent of farms
	117	118	119	120	121	122	123	124	125	126	127	128	129	130	131	132
ILLINOIS—Cont'd																
Jackson	200	-1.5	270	0	159	504 574	1 672	68 200	29	38 972	73.6	26.4	35.5	11.4	2 461	50.9
Jasper	271	7.5	343	0	243	692 078	2 008	86 322	69	87 102	63.9	36.1	60.3	27.1	3 525	75.1
Jefferson	259	12.6	222	1	215	319 517	1 333	53 455	32	27 451	73.9	26.1	31.8	7.5	3 709	63.2
Jersey	173	5.5	333	0	138	781 684	2 152	75 242	41	78 964	79.5	20.5	52.1	21.5	1 852	60.4
Jo Daviess	264	-4.3	267	D	183	566 478	2 190	68 868	70	70 943	42.5	57.5	47.8	19.1	5 437	70.8
Johnson	121	16.3	190	0	74	228 368	1 363	33 026	11	17 045	52.3	47.7	20.6	4.6	1 813	55.7
Kane	198	-5.7	320	2	185	1 247 695	3 857	124 787	116	187 487	87.2	12.8	61.9	29.7	3 193	42.5
Kankakee	347	-1.4	481	14	334	1 342 239	2 812	137 679	120	166 150	92.0	8.0	74.4	37.5	4 886	66.1
Kendall	168	0.6	408	D	161	1 811 831	4 206	126 318	58	141 094	89.0	11.0	75.0	31.3	2 572	62.4
Knox	394	1.0	428	0	329	983 435	2 380	119 161	130	140 777	67.1	33.0	58.8	30.0	6 713	66.4
Lake	39	-23.5	115	1	33	631 641	4 655	83 011	28	83 855	86.2	13.8	42.4	15.1	446	16.0
La Salle	579	-1.5	392	2	546	1 302 657	3 106	118 395	162	109 407	90.5	9.5	76.0	33.4	9 450	70.6
Lawrence	192	4.9	541	8	176	1 042 745	1 766	136 198	56	158 992	59.7	40.3	57.5	33.0	2 962	72.4
Lee	389	-1.0	462	19	370	1 506 408	2 998	136 565	129	153 754	83.5	16.5	77.2	41.4	6 471	69.2
Livingston	636	3.6	479	D	612	1 262 005	2 658	126 245	183	137 794	82.4	17.6	80.8	40.8	7 890	74.1
Logan	359	-5.8	518	2	343	1 395 884	2 808	126 370	110	159 285	85.6	14.4	74.0	44.4	4 900	75.0
McDonough	325	-4.4	432	0	281	936 447	2 247	96 630	82	109 676	86.8	13.2	62.8	30.7	4 276	63.0
McHenry	233	-3.7	268	7	212	1 153 206	4 262	94 750	92	105 306	75.3	24.7	55.1	23.1	3 912	37.9
McLean	688	-1.3	477	1	659	1 281 279	2 912	117 586	207	143 669	86.8	13.2	76.0	41.7	10 513	71.4
Macon	321	-0.6	496	0	303	1 504 821	3 057	131 746	91	140 646	93.5	6.5	69.0	39.8	4 688	62.1
Macoupin	427	7.8	352	0	370	868 096	2 363	97 813	129	106 409	71.8	28.2	57.4	25.2	5 167	64.7
Madison	296	4.2	257	1	262	710 104	2 477	86 597	78	67 878	83.4	16.6	53.1	17.1	3 592	50.9
Marion	262	5.2	239	0	215	333 367	1 608	52 156	39	35 526	73.5	26.5	31.1	10.3	3 938	76.3
Marshall	191	-16.2	421	3	171	1 195 983	2 704	158 258	53	115 642	88.8	11.2	74.0	34.4	2 601	61.9
Mason	285	-2.4	644	92	260	1 390 934	2 183	179 762	72	163 594	93.2	6.8	67.7	43.1	3 394	74.3
Massac	125	20.2	287	8	100	380 524	1 251	62 050	17	38 946	67.8	32.2	38.9	10.6	1 945	63.4
Menard	155	-8.8	471	2	140	1 141 510	2 421	113 686	42	126 986	82.7	17.3	62.3	33.7	2 209	74.2
Mercer	293	-5.5	392	6	252	885 546	2 216	111 197	90	120 823	75.5	24.5	61.4	29.9	5 514	68.1
Monroe	177	-5.3	334	1	148	892 111	2 542	89 100	39	72 589	66.3	33.7	49.0	19.4	1 948	58.0
Montgomery	362	0.3	362	D	327	784 478	2 033	108 531	93	92 756	82.3	17.7	57.2	26.4	5 281	67.1
Morgan	293	-4.2	429	2	254	950 646	2 400	128 533	84	123 178	79.9	20.1	65.1	33.6	3 780	67.9
Moultrie	186	7.5	423	0	177	1 129 060	2 952	138 390	49	110 789	89.0	11.0	68.0	34.0	3 045	56.2
Ogle	372	-1.8	330	1	331	1 054 831	3 131	120 204	131	116 434	65.0	35.0	63.1	24.8	8 289	65.4
Peoria	266	-0.4	299	4	228	863 792	2 754	80 623	78	87 015	81.2	18.8	56.7	21.2	3 666	52.4
Perry	194	12.8	353	1	165	517 946	1 423	102 177	24	43 843	79.4	20.6	46.6	12.9	2 208	68.5
Piatt	258	2.0	583	0	251	1 827 180	2 981	171 835	72	162 002	96.1	3.9	76.2	47.5	3 836	75.8
Pike	426	-7.6	409	2	324	772 242	1 840	84 037	100	95 924	68.8	31.2	51.9	20.4	6 613	68.6
Pope	77	6.9	226	0	49	233 006	1 155	27 515	4	12 630	67.5	32.5	21.7	2.3	1 054	71.0
Pulaski	86	3.6	341	2	73	494 380	1 418	76 003	15	58 040	86.9	13.1	43.5	15.0	1 235	68.4
Putnam	71	-7.8	407	D	63	1 159 919	2 888	101 943	43	242 876	93.7	6.3	70.9	32.0	1 260	63.4
Randolph	254	-3.1	308	D	206	565 052	1 939	85 492	39	47 644	71.3	28.7	49.9	13.7	3 776	61.4
Richland	209	6.1	414	0	191	782 155	1 794	120 792	53	104 782	56.7	43.3	54.5	23.9	3 288	73.7
Rock Island	170	0.0	257	3	140	584 878	2 642	59 900	46	69 178	76.7	23.3	51.6	19.3	3 162	59.9
St. Clair	270	1.9	333	1	250	920 870	2 759	104 587	70	86 773	86.1	13.9	63.3	22.8	3 485	51.4
Saline	130	-0.8	291	1	113	449 805	1 538	65 573	20	45 471	65.6	34.4	35.4	12.8	1 648	57.4
Sangamon	468	0.2	483	1	436	1 318 704	2 829	132 730	146	150 422	90.0	10.0	55.2	32.7	6 386	60.9
Schuyler	207	-1.0	386	0	143	686 664	1 599	70 725	42	77 795	68.0	32.0	49.1	18.6	2 941	75.5
Scott	116	-20.5	398	5	94	785 502	2 053	100 019	27	93 668	81.3	18.7	56.0	25.1	1 432	64.3
Shelby	420	0.2	342	0	375	788 230	2 341	91 751	95	77 328	77.1	22.9	59.0	24.0	5 805	69.0
Stark	174	-3.3	520	D	163	1 430 555	2 631	146 311	57	169 328	85.1	14.9	77.3	46.3	2 584	72.8
Stephenson	324	4.9	302	D	293	734 711	2 388	95 882	125	116 224	47.8	52.2	64.0	31.1	6 579	60.3
Tazewell	327	-0.3	356	31	302	994 355	2 862	100 956	107	116 227	83.8	16.2	65.4	31.3	4 783	68.6
Union	152	11.8	229	1	103	431 271	1 944	43 321	23	33 788	80.5	19.5	27.5	6.0	2 142	59.0
Vermilion	450	-7.2	495	D	429	1 268 611	2 467	135 076	125	137 202	93.6	6.4	68.2	38.6	7 525	64.0
Wabash	111	-9.0	556	D	102	938 325	1 722	135 456	23	113 189	87.7	12.3	63.3	32.2	1 466	71.4
Warren	327	3.8	516	D	287	1 223 078	2 518	175 466	106	167 773	77.9	22.1	79.9	46.6	5 264	67.0
Washington	332	7.4	440	2	302	793 128	1 900	124 344	80	105 380	58.5	41.5	67.9	28.4	4 701	73.5
Wayne	356	10.9	326	D	308	480 360	1 239	76 951	57	51 885	69.3	30.7	34.8	13.3	5 566	78.8
White	281	9.8	583	11	246	860 245	1 609	116 234	44	91 052	88.3	11.7	46.9	21.4	4 211	75.7
Whiteside	379	-1.6	379	42	348	955 300	2 540	106 898	144	143 962	66.7	33.3	67.6	33.8	7 440	69.2
Will	265	-9.9	320	2	253	1 417 074	4 652	101 114	82	99 062	93.0	7.0	60.4	23.3	3 993	45.9
Williamson	105	14.1	167	0	76	408 688	2 011	34 809	10	15 491	59.9	40.1	19.8	4.0	1 440	44.4
Winnebago	191	-2.6	275	1	175	859 303	2 956	94 293	62	89 467	73.0	27.0	51.8	23.2	3 613	56.7
Woodford	310	3.3	337	1	283	1 025 183	2 993	102 711	104	112 976	75.2	24.8	68.7	30.3	4 011	64.6

STATE County	Value of residential construction authorized by building permits, 2003		Wholesale trade, 1997				Retail trade,[1] 1997				Real estate and rental and leasing, 1997			
	New construction ($1,000)	Number of housing units	Number of establishments	Number of employees	Sales (mil dol)	Annual payroll (mil dol)	Number of establishments	Number of employees	Sales (mil dol)	Annual payroll (mil dol)	Number of establishments	Number of employees	Receipts (mil dol)	Annual payroll (mil dol)
	133	134	135	136	137	138	139	140	141	142	143	144	145	146
ILLINOIS—Cont'd														
Jackson	6 766	161	45	289	78.4	7.6	287	3 992	551.9	60.7	81	414	29.2	5.3
Jasper	150	1	22	206	120.1	5.1	45	366	78.5	5.9	6	D	D	D
Jefferson	2 716	20	64	667	362.9	18.5	216	2 678	385.2	36.8	31	98	6.4	1.1
Jersey	14 202	125	28	D	D	D	82	1 031	171.0	14.2	3	4	0.3	0.0
Jo Daviess	32 070	185	31	176	130.4	5.5	144	897	150.2	12.4	24	64	8.9	1.2
Johnson	NA	NA	12	90	38.5	1.7	34	235	42.8	4.1	2	D	D	D
Kane	1 003 163	5 632	787	9 948	8 557.1	392.4	1 353	19 688	3 116.6	331.1	318	1 620	212.1	35.8
Kankakee	97 360	671	126	1 628	809.3	47.2	388	5 594	907.0	88.5	85	348	34.9	5.9
Kendall	207 421	1 297	61	585	348.0	18.6	118	1 755	371.0	36.6	34	127	15.1	2.0
Knox	6 972	55	75	933	381.7	25.2	252	3 785	489.9	52.5	40	164	12.6	2.0
Lake	757 388	4 406	1 411	20 149	19 079.1	932.4	2 391	38 002	8 562.3	785.9	626	3 563	725.4	95.7
La Salle	38 562	292	168	1 729	1 292.6	55.8	502	6 352	1 047.7	96.8	72	296	23.3	4.0
Lawrence	225	2	16	248	64.0	6.7	63	535	71.8	6.9	4	D	D	D
Lee	16 994	102	55	525	248.5	14.7	138	1 379	234.8	23.6	28	133	7.1	1.5
Livingston	10 499	87	48	431	255.6	11.1	186	1 909	336.3	28.7	20	72	3.1	0.6
Logan	11 768	106	45	433	252.3	12.2	140	1 283	238.0	20.3	33	87	8.6	0.9
McDonough	7 484	238	37	233	164.8	5.6	167	1 870	246.6	24.8	29	205	9.5	2.6
McHenry	632 170	3 917	497	5 381	2 874.1	210.7	813	10 457	2 034.6	188.3	184	807	106.8	15.2
McLean	150 034	1 643	212	2 268	1 348.4	87.1	632	9 242	1 474.6	142.3	134	704	99.8	14.6
Macon	63 005	526	158	1 815	3 249.3	57.4	506	6 967	1 129.6	110.4	98	515	39.9	8.5
Macoupin	5 651	48	76	749	238.9	19.6	188	1 695	309.4	26.0	27	68	5.7	0.9
Madison	243 370	1 709	259	2 860	2 264.4	91.6	969	11 722	2 057.0	181.4	190	885	106.9	14.0
Marion	5 974	66	53	474	166.7	11.8	226	2 119	309.4	30.2	28	153	8.1	1.4
Marshall	1 809	18	16	127	232.5	3.9	49	395	68.7	6.4	10	16	0.9	0.1
Mason	2 501	35	32	225	305.2	5.6	59	601	98.4	9.5	4	D	D	D
Massac	483	5	6	D	D	D	55	414	79.7	6.4	7	19	1.1	0.2
Menard	11 001	84	15	104	74.7	2.7	41	320	58.3	4.6	11	48	2.2	0.4
Mercer	4 571	41	21	103	102.2	3.1	57	586	88.5	8.6	7	12	0.3	0.2
Monroe	52 567	346	29	D	D	D	85	858	175.2	15.4	22	56	5.1	0.8
Montgomery	206	2	46	351	215.1	9.0	142	1 344	236.6	19.3	17	37	2.3	0.3
Morgan	2 731	20	45	D	D	D	192	2 207	344.7	31.9	20	65	6.0	1.0
Moultrie	5 503	54	28	211	103.2	5.1	46	303	42.5	3.9	6	16	0.8	0.1
Ogle	37 667	330	54	D	D	D	150	1 491	268.3	24.0	35	80	8.3	0.9
Peoria	84 712	725	299	4 755	5 876.5	171.6	801	11 817	1 847.4	182.6	192	1 163	115.3	20.6
Perry	NA	NA	14	D	D	D	98	789	113.8	14.3	9	22	1.1	0.2
Piatt	12 174	80	29	335	332.4	7.6	55	432	99.4	7.8	8	37	2.0	0.4
Pike	4 691	64	37	319	175.1	8.0	85	725	119.9	10.6	6	17	1.1	0.2
Pope	0	0	2	D	D	D	12	36	7.5	0.5	3	5	0.2	0.0
Pulaski	0	0	9	D	D	D	27	127	15.5	1.4	3	4	0.4	0.0
Putnam	5 182	38	7	D	D	D	22	126	23.4	1.9	2	D	D	D
Randolph	11 117	89	32	D	D	D	140	1 601	261.7	27.3	17	45	2.4	0.3
Richland	1 771	15	38	641	266.2	14.0	94	940	149.0	13.8	10	45	1.1	0.3
Rock Island	42 179	274	239	4 530	2 042.8	148.4	623	8 593	1 427.4	142.2	136	650	81.8	13.6
St. Clair	236 089	1 719	214	2 169	1 615.1	64.2	965	12 887	2 048.5	197.7	207	961	90.5	18.9
Saline	0	0	26	D	D	D	154	1 404	232.5	32.3	14	56	2.7	0.5
Sangamon	115 807	991	259	3 517	1 513.4	119.7	836	12 054	1 991.9	187.0	204	837	85.3	14.3
Schuyler	NA	NA	8	93	62.5	2.3	37	303	45.5	4.3	6	22	0.5	0.1
Scott	0	0	13	123	152.5	3.4	13	113	20.5	1.5	2	D	D	D
Shelby	5 739	51	37	237	153.1	5.6	86	554	123.9	7.7	9	22	0.8	0.2
Stark	300	3	12	73	52.0	1.6	23	124	27.4	2.4	1	D	D	D
Stephenson	16 566	112	54	429	129.6	10.0	191	2 522	414.6	40.3	30	111	9.7	1.7
Tazewell	110 585	771	140	D	D	D	473	6 813	1 275.2	112.1	82	419	45.2	9.6
Union	4 731	49	14	93	25.0	2.6	66	641	96.8	9.4	12	30	1.9	0.5
Vermilion	7 032	70	102	2 221	1 257.5	68.5	351	4 505	639.2	64.4	63	265	17.6	4.2
Wabash	1 130	8	21	116	52.3	2.8	49	508	75.6	6.7	6	16	1.0	0.2
Warren	5 802	73	23	274	164.4	7.3	67	632	97.7	9.1	7	31	1.7	0.4
Washington	8 850	72	27	245	128.9	6.9	83	662	157.1	13.0	5	16	1.0	0.1
Wayne	538	4	32	176	113.3	4.2	80	703	103.6	9.9	10	17	1.1	0.1
White	0	0	33	152	104.7	3.7	84	644	109.7	9.3	10	22	1.2	0.2
Whiteside	12 689	109	75	522	481.9	15.3	241	3 303	515.4	54.1	55	181	13.3	2.4
Will	1 386 309	9 070	577	6 563	3 946.2	230.2	1 157	17 267	3 286.2	301.3	287	1 191	129.0	23.0
Williamson	24 742	316	80	629	189.3	15.0	306	3 405	576.2	51.1	39	185	16.3	2.4
Winnebago	141 625	2 029	510	6 308	2 530.0	216.5	1 090	17 044	2 754.5	270.3	217	1 169	160.4	24.2
Woodford	32 818	240	55	D	D	D	101	1 009	229.4	16.8	15	66	3.5	1.1

1. Establishments with payroll.

Table B. States and Counties — Professional Services, Manufacturing, and Accommodation and Foodservices

STATE County	Professional, scientific, and technical services,[1] 1997				Manufacturing, 1997				Accommodation and foodservices, 1997			
	Number of establishments	Number of employees	Receipts (mil dol)	Annual payroll (mil dol)	Number of establishments	Number of employees	Receipts (mil dol)	Annual payroll (mil dol)	Number of establishments	Number of employees	Sales (mil dol)	Annual payroll (mil dol)
	147	148	149	150	151	152	153	154	155	156	157	158
ILLINOIS—Cont'd												
Jackson	96	664	37.2	14.6	35	1 062	151.8	29.0	156	2 379	65.4	17.8
Jasper	9	72	2.7	1.7	15	874	66.4	15.2	18	87	2.3	0.5
Jefferson	61	386	29.1	12.2	44	2 922	743.1	104.5	72	1 270	41.9	11.3
Jersey	20	85	6.3	3.1	NA	NA	NA	NA	50	612	16.0	4.6
Jo Daviess	46	116	14.0	4.0	33	1 590	312.6	46.2	101	1 755	61.8	16.0
Johnson	12	55	3.1	0.9	NA	NA	NA	NA	15	111	3.6	1.1
Kane	955	6 298	541.4	225.7	877	40 200	8 226.1	1 443.8	633	11 078	367.0	106.3
Kankakee	132	507	32.7	12.7	116	6 937	2 253.2	263.8	229	3 563	100.4	27.4
Kendall	48	135	7.6	2.8	66	2 303	369.6	69.5	76	869	28.2	6.6
Knox	52	263	19.6	7.1	56	5 528	1 058.8	165.0	132	1 863	54.5	14.8
Lake	2 204	14 385	1 676.3	697.1	969	62 535	13 686.2	2 660.2	1 245	20 090	775.8	210.3
La Salle	154	877	56.0	24.0	152	6 752	1 732.6	232.1	332	3 830	109.7	30.8
Lawrence	20	75	4.8	1.9	NA	NA	NA	NA	24	199	5.6	1.5
Lee	35	186	14.5	6.2	35	3 798	739.4	115.3	68	638	20.1	5.0
Livingston	49	154	10.5	4.0	51	4 573	1 055.8	170.5	86	1 001	26.5	7.2
Logan	32	101	7.6	2.0	24	1 401	318.2	44.9	77	864	24.0	6.4
McDonough	39	169	10.1	2.6	30	1 956	255.9	61.2	78	1 303	29.8	8.1
McHenry	594	2 115	176.6	65.5	583	22 949	3 930.4	760.4	409	5 347	175.8	46.4
McLean	234	1 382	111.6	57.9	112	8 388	3 870.3	357.7	336	7 104	200.5	58.3
Macon	156	1 101	90.0	36.1	134	11 616	6 114.2	479.4	233	4 105	123.6	35.7
Macoupin	46	254	23.3	7.0	35	697	156.5	18.9	90	783	24.7	5.7
Madison	392	2 162	167.1	73.2	224	19 074	7 676.5	743.8	537	8 326	253.8	68.1
Marion	56	238	18.4	5.3	65	5 220	768.3	152.6	95	1 056	31.4	8.5
Marshall	16	56	3.9	1.4	18	921	179.6	28.2	31	422	7.7	2.1
Mason	13	33	2.1	0.6	NA	NA	NA	NA	48	294	8.3	2.1
Massac	13	57	2.1	0.9	12	732	191.5	31.2	38	343	10.3	2.6
Menard	18	40	3.2	1.2	NA	NA	NA	NA	24	D	D	D
Mercer	14	29	1.7	0.4	NA	NA	NA	NA	34	215	5.6	1.5
Monroe	42	245	18.1	9.1	NA	NA	NA	NA	51	D	D	D
Montgomery	41	203	12.1	5.1	37	1 752	300.7	48.3	77	924	25.7	6.5
Morgan	42	223	15.4	7.4	36	3 566	1 213.4	110.6	78	1 165	34.0	9.5
Moultrie	20	57	4.1	0.9	20	796	210.8	19.8	27	283	6.2	1.9
Ogle	52	D	D	D	70	5 859	1 020.5	166.2	93	999	27.6	7.2
Peoria	361	4 635	378.4	167.7	177	14 351	4 392.7	610.6	494	8 204	246.3	70.7
Perry	24	77	3.7	1.2	22	1 481	262.3	35.3	34	428	10.4	2.9
Piatt	25	90	4.6	2.2	NA	NA	NA	NA	28	D	D	D
Pike	16	52	2.0	0.8	NA	NA	NA	NA	39	389	9.3	2.4
Pope	3	D	D	D	NA	NA	NA	NA	8	36	1.8	0.4
Pulaski	4	D	D	D	NA	NA	NA	NA	10	64	1.6	0.4
Putnam	5	22	1.0	0.3	9	D	D	D	11	D	D	D
Randolph	33	99	6.0	2.2	32	2 353	398.6	51.8	75	749	20.4	5.3
Richland	24	67	3.9	1.4	34	1 814	218.3	37.0	34	439	12.9	3.4
Rock Island	238	2 124	164.9	72.3	197	10 675	3 508.8	493.8	373	5 780	161.4	43.9
St. Clair	395	3 109	284.7	119.2	198	7 123	1 763.5	249.3	477	8 481	245.0	66.7
Saline	39	134	11.2	2.9	NA	NA	NA	NA	58	709	19.7	5.1
Sangamon	471	3 283	277.1	117.6	134	D	D	D	497	D	D	D
Schuyler	9	56	3.6	1.8	NA	NA	NA	NA	15	D	D	D
Scott	6	15	0.6	0.1	NA	NA	NA	NA	9	90	1.2	0.3
Shelby	24	97	5.7	2.0	14	1 191	205.7	32.4	40	473	15.4	4.2
Stark	7	64	1.8	0.7	NA	NA	NA	NA	6	D	D	D
Stephenson	62	243	17.5	6.8	62	8 386	1 239.2	300.3	103	1 259	37.1	8.7
Tazewell	153	731	53.9	26.7	118	7 015	2 512.9	311.1	265	4 329	115.8	33.7
Union	17	65	3.8	1.5	11	616	132.2	17.0	26	D	D	D
Vermilion	94	331	27.9	8.6	104	7 055	1 696.1	228.9	185	2 570	68.5	20.0
Wabash	22	93	7.3	2.4	15	611	55.8	20.5	24	367	7.9	2.4
Warren	17	42	2.7	0.6	19	D	D	D	37	334	9.8	2.7
Washington	14	63	3.7	1.7	16	1 397	222.4	44.5	43	380	10.9	2.6
Wayne	23	77	4.6	1.4	20	D	D	D	20	D	D	D
White	20	80	3.4	1.1	NA	NA	NA	NA	28	404	10.7	3.3
Whiteside	56	236	19.2	7.6	102	7 374	1 381.8	245.0	112	1 567	42.9	10.9
Will	689	2 966	285.4	113.7	527	24 090	7 594.7	988.2	646	9 054	291.6	75.2
Williamson	89	381	29.5	8.6	51	2 551	425.1	69.2	135	2 155	68.1	18.1
Winnebago	567	5 447	327.5	128.6	779	39 740	6 608.4	1 483.6	556	9 693	306.3	84.1
Woodford	35	144	14.6	6.1	55	2 272	644.9	74.7	63	789	18.8	4.7

1. Firms subject to federal tax.

Table B. States and Counties — Health Care and Social Assistance, Other Services, and Federal Funds

STATE County	Health care and social assistance,[1] 1997				Other services,[1] 1997				Federal funds and grants, 2002–2003 Expenditures (mil dol)			
										Direct payments for individuals[2]		
	Number of establishments	Number of employees	Receipts (mil dol)	Annual payroll (mil dol)	Number of establishments	Number of employees	Receipts (mil dol)	Annual payroll (mil dol)	Total	Social Security and government retirement	Medicare	Food stamps and Supplemental Security Income
	159	160	161	162	163	164	165	166	167	168	169	170
ILLINOIS—Cont'd												
Jackson	118	1 698	96.9	46.9	85	338	20.3	4.7	291.4	99.2	44.4	13.7
Jasper	8	109	3.6	1.7	21	62	4.7	0.8	51.5	21.1	9.9	1.1
Jefferson	92	1 088	69.7	23.8	64	384	24.9	7.7	213.6	89.4	49.5	9.1
Jersey	28	387	15.4	6.1	28	63	4.4	0.9	89.4	46.7	19.6	2.5
Jo Daviess	26	224	9.6	4.6	41	130	11.6	1.9	109.1	62.0	21.5	1.2
Johnson	12	112	3.7	1.5	8	21	2.2	0.4	62.8	31.7	11.8	1.8
Kane	620	6 731	522.4	241.2	604	3 897	259.3	84.5	1 696.9	621.4	257.9	39.5
Kankakee	168	1 730	107.6	53.0	162	954	59.8	18.3	522.8	224.7	122.7	23.2
Kendall	43	464	20.9	8.9	69	391	26.3	7.1	145.6	75.0	20.7	1.4
Knox	72	1 213	71.7	27.1	86	390	24.4	6.4	293.9	148.8	68.5	10.1
Lake	1 210	12 163	896.3	414.7	975	5 862	468.9	140.9	3 275.3	1 041.1	374.5	42.5
La Salle	199	1 663	93.8	38.9	208	933	65.7	16.9	524.0	273.6	115.2	11.6
Lawrence	31	533	18.9	7.4	20	58	4.4	1.0	94.9	42.3	22.3	3.1
Lee	47	537	39.8	16.5	56	245	15.0	3.9	167.5	84.2	33.7	4.1
Livingston	41	265	15.3	7.0	59	206	14.1	3.7	183.3	82.5	39.9	3.8
Logan	31	366	17.4	5.8	37	133	7.7	1.9	140.3	66.4	32.6	3.2
McDonough	58	480	25.5	12.4	64	230	12.6	3.2	205.7	58.2	28.0	4.5
McHenry	410	4 539	226.2	108.2	401	2 001	126.7	38.8	679.3	411.8	141.3	8.6
McLean	228	2 901	190.8	91.6	226	1 433	85.6	26.8	529.3	233.8	85.2	12.0
Macon	204	2 546	155.6	70.3	189	1 456	86.0	28.7	599.4	278.9	114.2	28.0
Macoupin	65	943	29.1	12.4	65	208	13.4	3.1	257.4	133.6	64.0	7.3
Madison	501	5 457	307.2	141.5	438	2 526	158.9	45.8	1 381.6	653.3	289.2	49.3
Marion	96	1 070	62.4	23.6	71	242	13.3	3.5	274.3	124.8	69.5	10.0
Marshall	19	255	9.8	4.7	14	33	1.7	0.3	62.2	32.8	13.6	1.2
Mason	20	157	6.7	2.2	21	54	3.9	0.9	96.8	44.6	23.7	2.8
Massac	23	320	11.7	5.6	18	61	3.9	1.0	93.7	40.4	22.0	3.4
Menard	14	146	4.3	2.1	15	67	3.9	1.0	54.8	27.5	11.0	1.1
Mercer	15	132	5.5	2.6	21	66	3.8	0.8	77.5	39.9	15.9	1.7
Monroe	34	366	14.5	6.7	48	297	13.7	4.8	108.3	63.5	20.7	0.9
Montgomery	47	634	27.8	10.9	48	188	14.8	2.9	162.5	77.3	36.1	6.0
Morgan	75	792	33.0	14.7	58	246	15.6	4.5	179.3	83.9	38.0	6.4
Moultrie	16	195	8.2	2.8	15	49	3.5	0.7	71.5	40.1	16.7	0.8
Ogle	58	564	22.9	9.2	75	264	16.6	4.3	194.5	102.0	36.7	3.0
Peoria	365	4 477	369.3	193.7	291	2 391	172.4	56.2	1 165.3	411.6	184.6	47.0
Perry	35	368	13.4	5.1	31	106	7.0	1.7	113.0	58.0	25.7	4.1
Piatt	14	159	6.5	2.8	20	66	4.5	1.3	81.6	41.5	16.3	1.0
Pike	20	348	11.8	5.2	28	67	4.8	1.1	111.8	43.8	21.9	2.4
Pope	2	D	D	D	2	D	D	D	29.9	11.6	5.4	1.1
Pulaski	2	D	D	D	9	19	1.5	0.3	104.6	18.2	10.3	2.8
Putnam	4	13	0.5	0.1	6	8	0.7	0.1	29.2	16.8	5.8	0.4
Randolph	53	608	22.8	9.8	57	170	10.3	2.7	164.5	81.2	38.4	4.4
Richland	24	403	19.8	9.9	37	124	8.3	1.7	93.9	41.6	17.3	3.0
Rock Island	290	3 073	192.2	87.6	255	1 782	114.3	31.9	1 042.0	387.5	149.5	28.1
St. Clair	469	6 013	346.2	156.5	423	2 147	124.4	40.7	2 649.5	685.9	285.3	90.2
Saline	55	1 048	42.5	19.7	42	100	7.2	1.7	206.3	76.8	34.1	10.3
Sangamon	356	7 594	478.1	204.4	347	2 285	142.3	46.4	3 161.6	721.1	190.6	36.1
Schuyler	9	129	4.2	1.8	9	11	1.6	0.1	40.5	17.1	7.2	0.9
Scott	3	6	0.2	0.1	6	12	2.1	0.1	28.3	12.6	5.7	0.6
Shelby	26	337	14.9	5.8	33	123	9.5	2.1	126.6	55.9	27.7	2.2
Stark	5	25	0.6	0.2	4	14	1.3	0.2	35.8	16.0	9.3	0.5
Stephenson	67	713	37.8	19.4	86	395	21.8	6.4	237.0	119.8	45.0	7.3
Tazewell	152	1 931	88.1	40.6	221	1 122	72.3	22.3	534.5	286.4	120.5	12.4
Union	35	930	22.9	9.6	16	66	4.7	1.0	104.1	44.8	20.7	5.0
Vermilion	103	1 343	83.4	38.6	133	627	33.3	9.9	529.3	230.6	91.1	22.6
Wabash	22	499	9.3	3.9	19	91	6.0	1.5	59.4	30.9	13.5	1.3
Warren	17	331	10.0	3.9	23	83	4.1	0.9	94.3	42.4	19.5	2.4
Washington	17	295	10.9	4.6	29	94	5.4	1.3	82.2	37.1	21.1	1.1
Wayne	20	129	5.5	2.1	22	72	4.9	1.1	104.2	42.5	22.0	2.4
White	24	265	8.2	3.7	19	59	5.2	0.8	123.5	48.0	23.0	3.2
Whiteside	71	1 087	66.0	27.2	135	691	37.5	10.1	308.9	180.5	63.6	8.2
Will	558	5 682	377.4	173.6	617	3 523	251.6	76.8	1 376.1	755.9	269.6	38.8
Williamson	122	2 043	123.4	38.9	59	430	25.3	6.4	461.9	165.4	65.0	12.8
Winnebago	433	5 688	458.3	222.2	479	3 651	225.9	72.3	1 232.4	561.7	209.2	49.0
Woodford	27	265	10.3	4.8	47	159	10.5	2.8	119.0	64.8	27.3	1.7

1. Firms subject to federal tax.   2. State totals may include programs not allocated by county.

Items 159—170

STATE County	Federal funds and grants, 2002–2003 (cont'd)							Local government finances, 2002				
	Expenditures (mil dol) (cont'd)							General revenue				
	Procurement contract awards			Grants[1]						Taxes		
											Per capita[2] (dollars)	
	Salaries and wages	Defense	Other	Medicaid and other health-related	Nutrition and family welfare	Education	Other	Total (mil dol)	Intergovern-mental (mil dol)	Total (mil dol)	Total	Property
	171	172	173	174	175	176	177	178	179	180	181	182
ILLINOIS—Cont'd												
Jackson	19.0	6.4	5.7	38.8	8.9	5.6	19.2	143.8	73.9	42.0	705	534
Jasper	2.4	0.0	0.6	4.0	0.7	0.4	2.6	24.1	11.0	9.6	954	943
Jefferson	10.5	0.8	1.7	25.3	5.3	2.5	8.7	108.5	64.9	25.6	637	539
Jersey	3.0	0.1	0.8	8.5	1.2	0.5	2.0	55.5	19.5	9.9	452	431
Jo Daviess	4.8	0.0	1.2	4.5	1.0	0.5	3.7	69.4	19.8	33.4	1 490	1 397
Johnson	3.8	0.0	0.9	7.5	1.0	0.5	1.0	19.3	12.4	4.4	336	328
Kane	186.5	40.5	336.8	83.6	25.2	12.1	75.3	1 607.0	501.9	808.8	1 826	1 659
Kankakee	30.5	2.1	4.3	55.7	16.2	6.1	23.9	284.4	141.0	98.1	937	882
Kendall	21.0	0.1	2.0	2.1	0.9	0.6	16.1	160.2	53.7	83.2	1 360	1 292
Knox	12.1	0.2	2.7	21.3	5.0	2.7	9.2	156.0	68.2	49.1	893	814
Lake	1 028.5	278.2	91.4	109.6	29.5	21.0	102.0	2 414.5	638.2	1 344.7	1 993	1 860
La Salle	22.5	0.1	4.9	30.3	6.4	4.1	35.0	307.4	118.8	132.2	1 180	1 076
Lawrence	3.4	0.0	1.4	9.2	1.4	0.6	4.4	30.2	19.5	6.5	424	419
Lee	5.6	0.2	1.4	9.3	1.8	1.0	13.8	94.8	33.6	37.9	1 051	970
Livingston	6.9	0.1	1.7	6.9	2.2	1.0	22.5	113.7	40.4	46.7	1 179	1 159
Logan	6.9	0.0	1.4	8.5	3.8	2.2	2.4	56.5	23.8	24.5	799	790
McDonough	5.7	65.6	1.4	8.9	2.3	4.6	9.2	110.0	31.1	25.1	767	751
McHenry	38.8	7.3	10.1	18.9	6.0	3.0	21.0	738.5	212.7	391.8	1 411	1 326
McLean	53.8	1.0	13.0	31.1	9.1	6.4	47.9	410.4	126.2	208.4	1 349	1 140
Macon	26.3	0.3	21.5	62.5	14.2	5.1	27.4	327.5	134.9	106.3	949	833
Macoupin	8.5	2.9	2.2	15.7	5.6	1.5	3.9	106.6	63.7	29.1	598	579
Madison	41.6	48.7	23.7	125.8	38.5	11.6	71.3	667.1	321.0	213.1	815	747
Marion	11.6	0.6	3.3	25.6	6.6	2.1	6.7	146.6	69.2	29.3	714	662
Marshall	2.7	0.0	0.6	2.1	0.7	0.3	3.9	28.6	11.4	13.4	1 028	986
Mason	3.6	2.5	1.0	6.3	1.8	0.6	4.3	51.3	19.4	16.9	1 060	1 030
Massac	2.5	0.8	2.2	13.0	1.7	0.6	3.7	58.1	33.9	9.5	630	599
Menard	2.1	0.0	0.5	5.4	0.8	0.4	1.3	33.7	15.5	12.1	960	952
Mercer	3.5	2.6	0.9	3.3	1.3	0.5	0.8	49.1	20.7	13.4	793	786
Monroe	4.4	2.2	1.1	7.4	0.7	0.3	2.3	60.8	20.7	23.7	816	758
Montgomery	8.4	4.1	1.6	12.6	2.4	1.4	3.2	67.1	35.8	21.2	693	672
Morgan	6.1	0.1	1.6	25.7	2.7	2.7	4.9	69.3	30.5	27.4	757	710
Moultrie	2.7	0.0	0.5	3.3	0.6	0.4	1.4	33.1	11.9	14.5	1 015	1 007
Ogle	8.6	1.8	6.0	7.5	2.2	1.0	13.8	170.0	52.5	83.4	1 600	1 537
Peoria	137.8	114.4	31.7	77.9	27.0	9.3	100.7	502.2	228.8	164.8	904	738
Perry	3.1	0.0	0.8	9.2	1.8	0.8	3.7	54.1	23.4	9.8	427	385
Piatt	3.3	0.1	0.8	2.9	0.8	0.3	7.1	52.2	24.3	18.7	1 147	1 119
Pike	4.1	0.0	1.0	9.7	1.6	0.7	16.6	37.4	19.6	10.9	640	634
Pope	3.6	1.5	0.8	3.1	0.6	0.2	0.3	9.9	7.0	2.0	460	433
Pulaski	3.1	20.5	0.4	15.5	6.0	1.9	20.1	19.1	13.8	2.3	323	263
Putnam	1.7	0.0	0.4	0.5	0.4	0.1	0.9	11.5	5.2	4.5	736	727
Randolph	6.5	0.3	5.3	11.1	4.1	1.0	2.5	96.7	34.5	18.1	538	511
Richland	3.5	0.0	0.8	9.2	1.4	1.7	3.2	65.1	36.8	12.5	786	744
Rock Island	234.3	82.3	12.9	49.7	18.9	6.0	54.0	448.0	197.3	152.2	1 027	921
St. Clair	544.5	320.3	299.3	255.3	48.8	25.1	63.0	789.3	461.5	194.4	754	681
Saline	6.9	8.6	17.5	28.6	2.8	1.8	9.8	77.6	49.8	15.7	603	588
Sangamon	132.1	5.4	22.4	302.4	778.9	414.5	527.7	523.0	202.6	212.5	1 115	1 009
Schuyler	1.6	0.0	0.4	3.8	0.6	0.2	3.1	28.2	9.3	4.9	700	698
Scott	1.2	0.3	0.3	3.8	0.5	0.2	0.2	13.2	6.4	3.4	621	578
Shelby	5.3	7.5	1.1	8.9	1.4	0.7	3.1	40.8	19.4	15.0	667	655
Stark	1.8	0.0	0.5	1.9	0.5	0.2	1.1	16.9	5.5	9.1	1 463	1 456
Stephenson	9.1	1.1	2.0	17.2	4.2	1.9	5.7	133.5	54.2	52.5	1 092	1 016
Tazewell	31.2	3.2	7.5	31.5	7.7	3.5	21.0	360.1	149.3	132.7	1 036	915
Union	3.3	0.0	0.8	21.4	1.7	0.8	1.2	63.5	32.4	10.7	591	584
Vermilion	64.3	1.8	8.2	45.1	13.9	4.0	32.5	228.2	119.0	64.3	774	681
Wabash	1.7	0.0	0.5	5.2	1.0	0.5	1.1	37.3	14.4	6.6	525	498
Warren	4.2	0.0	0.9	8.5	3.6	0.6	4.0	39.3	17.5	14.3	784	740
Washington	3.5	0.0	0.8	5.0	1.1	0.4	0.6	39.6	13.7	10.3	681	674
Wayne	3.6	0.1	0.9	9.4	1.4	0.7	5.1	33.9	20.1	8.5	502	474
White	3.6	0.2	11.5	12.6	5.7	0.7	3.0	33.0	18.8	8.5	560	505
Whiteside	10.9	0.3	2.3	15.0	8.2	1.5	7.8	211.9	58.6	50.3	833	807
Will	62.8	11.8	17.2	66.1	25.8	9.5	94.1	1 453.9	476.7	680.6	1 216	1 096
Williamson	67.1	78.4	6.5	39.2	4.6	2.6	9.5	154.9	83.5	43.8	709	638
Winnebago	67.5	101.8	19.7	105.8	23.9	14.7	52.4	815.2	333.3	337.6	1 195	1 140
Woodford	4.5	0.0	1.3	4.5	1.6	0.7	5.5	81.6	32.7	38.7	1 072	1 010

1. State totals may include programs not allocated by county.   2. Based on the resident population estimated as of July 1 of the year shown.

	Local government finances, 2002 (cont'd)									Government employment, 2002			Presidential election, 2004		
	Direct general expenditure							Debt outstanding					Percent of vote cast —		
			Percent of total for —												
STATE County	Total (mil dol)	Per capita[1] (dollars)	Education	Health and hospitals	Police protection	Public welfare	Highways	Total (mil dol)	Per capita[1] (dollars)	Federal civilian	Federal military	State and local	Democratic	Republican	All other
	183	184	185	186	187	188	189	190	191	192	193	194	195	196	197
ILLINOIS—Cont'd															
Jackson	161.9	2 716	54.1	3.2	5.3	4.4	8.0	95.7	1 606	316	126	12 641	55.4	43.4	1.2
Jasper	23.7	2 369	50.8	6.2	4.3	0.1	14.8	3.3	328	48	18	703	33.4	66.1	0.5
Jefferson	115.7	2 872	66.3	0.9	4.6	0.2	4.8	20.2	501	164	75	2 702	39.6	60.0	0.4
Jersey	57.1	2 612	35.2	36.3	3.3	0.1	4.8	5.6	254	53	40	1 166	45.3	53.6	1.0
Jo Daviess	75.8	3 384	42.9	9.1	3.5	0.0	6.1	24.2	1 081	87	41	1 259	45.9	53.3	0.8
Johnson	21.3	1 625	62.5	1.1	5.0	0.3	11.2	13.5	1 025	89	24	815	31.0	68.2	0.8
Kane	1 829.5	4 129	54.4	0.4	5.5	0.2	5.1	2 021.2	4 562	1 823	816	25 007	44.2	55.0	0.8
Kankakee	301.3	2 878	54.3	1.0	5.9	0.2	7.0	143.9	1 375	329	193	6 097	44.4	54.9	0.7
Kendall	162.2	2 649	58.8	0.0	4.1	1.9	5.0	144.6	2 362	95	112	2 565	38.1	61.1	0.8
Knox	144.8	2 631	46.1	0.9	5.9	4.8	5.9	66.6	1 210	200	101	3 571	54.3	45.0	0.7
Lake	2 444.4	3 622	55.5	1.7	5.1	0.9	4.0	2 240.2	3 320	5 633	22 866	32 710	47.8	51.5	0.7
La Salle	317.7	2 837	57.6	1.2	5.2	1.3	8.7	178.3	1 592	346	206	6 268	48.9	50.6	0.6
Lawrence	36.0	2 366	63.6	0.7	4.6	0.1	7.7	9.2	602	53	28	998	37.5	61.9	0.7
Lee	94.5	2 624	62.5	1.5	4.5	3.6	7.1	21.4	593	98	66	2 412	40.4	58.6	0.9
Livingston	106.0	2 676	49.4	3.6	4.1	4.0	6.8	31.9	806	118	73	3 055	35.1	64.4	0.5
Logan	56.9	1 853	51.0	4.0	7.7	0.1	11.7	9.6	313	120	56	2 235	31.8	67.7	0.5
McDonough	105.8	3 239	27.7	39.2	2.9	3.5	5.6	22.4	685	103	66	6 044	47.8	51.4	0.7
McHenry	820.7	2 955	53.7	1.7	5.0	0.9	5.4	686.9	2 474	551	510	11 881	39.4	59.8	0.8
McLean	476.9	3 087	46.0	1.2	4.6	1.3	5.4	298.1	1 930	956	291	13 222	41.8	57.7	0.5
Macon	302.2	2 698	44.9	2.6	6.0	1.0	6.3	175.3	1 565	356	215	6 298	45.1	54.4	0.5
Macoupin	112.5	2 312	61.9	1.8	4.6	0.1	7.5	39.8	818	149	89	2 694	49.2	50.1	0.7
Madison	654.5	2 504	50.7	2.5	6.9	1.5	6.7	438.1	1 676	647	505	15 610	51.3	48.1	0.6
Marion	149.2	3 635	50.7	17.5	3.4	0.2	4.9	36.1	879	196	75	2 430	44.7	54.7	0.6
Marshall	29.1	2 232	40.3	1.4	4.1	0.0	9.9	10.9	837	50	24	529	42.7	56.8	0.6
Mason	52.9	3 325	46.9	22.7	2.9	0.1	3.7	11.7	735	67	29	1 196	44.8	54.4	0.8
Massac	54.7	3 642	42.0	20.2	4.2	0.0	5.9	12.8	854	50	28	885	37.8	61.7	0.4
Menard	31.2	2 480	50.6	2.3	3.3	12.1	6.7	18.6	1 483	41	23	713	32.5	67.1	0.4
Mercer	52.7	3 119	53.1	17.5	2.6	0.2	9.1	16.9	997	69	31	1 141	50.3	49.1	0.6
Monroe	62.7	2 156	45.9	1.6	4.7	9.4	7.8	51.7	1 779	71	53	1 201	41.5	57.9	0.7
Montgomery	73.4	2 404	50.2	2.7	5.8	0.3	10.7	31.4	1 028	117	56	1 935	46.3	53.0	0.7
Morgan	66.8	1 848	55.6	2.1	6.7	3.3	6.3	14.9	411	108	66	2 454	37.2	61.9	0.9
Moultrie	34.6	2 421	42.7	1.6	3.1	0.0	11.1	15.5	1 082	40	26	607	37.0	62.4	0.7
Ogle	193.1	3 705	60.4	1.1	2.9	0.4	8.5	127.5	2 445	145	96	2 729	37.5	62.0	0.5
Peoria	504.8	2 768	43.1	1.8	4.7	2.4	6.1	293.8	1 611	2 147	393	9 937	49.8	49.7	0.5
Perry	52.2	2 283	37.6	27.3	2.9	1.7	7.1	24.1	1 056	58	42	1 386	45.8	53.6	0.6
Piatt	56.1	3 440	52.9	2.9	3.0	8.0	10.3	26.2	1 609	57	30	906	36.4	62.8	0.8
Pike	40.7	2 384	55.6	5.2	2.7	0.2	8.2	16.1	943	74	31	983	35.7	63.1	1.2
Pope	10.4	2 436	41.5	0.6	2.9	0.4	12.2	1.2	286	89	0	235	37.7	61.6	0.7
Pulaski	19.0	2 654	53.9	3.6	5.4	3.0	9.4	4.2	581	69	13	876	44.1	55.3	0.5
Putnam	11.5	1 870	53.8	2.3	5.0	0.0	13.7	0.5	85	25	11	286	50.8	48.4	0.7
Randolph	96.0	2 854	37.1	30.2	3.8	2.9	7.6	37.7	1 122	104	62	3 014	45.3	54.0	0.7
Richland	72.9	4 577	79.3	0.3	1.8	0.1	4.8	21.7	1 359	66	29	983	32.7	66.6	0.8
Rock Island	441.2	2 978	51.4	1.3	6.4	2.3	3.9	245.3	1 655	5 535	414	8 898	57.0	42.4	0.5
St. Clair	803.0	3 114	56.1	2.0	4.8	0.2	6.3	480.0	1 861	5 054	6 543	12 683	55.2	44.4	0.4
Saline	81.1	3 110	71.4	0.0	5.4	0.6	4.3	38.4	1 470	130	48	2 004	39.8	59.8	0.4
Sangamon	558.3	2 929	45.8	1.2	7.0	0.1	7.7	587.2	3 080	2 086	370	28 551	40.5	58.7	0.8
Schuyler	29.5	4 199	26.5	40.8	1.1	0.2	10.3	9.0	1 274	33	13	542	39.6	59.7	0.8
Scott	14.1	2 570	47.0	0.0	4.4	13.4	5.3	0.6	114	23	10	355	35.2	64.4	0.5
Shelby	38.4	1 704	48.1	2.4	4.4	0.3	11.0	8.9	393	115	41	1 116	35.5	63.9	0.6
Stark	17.2	2 762	55.4	0.9	2.9	0.0	7.4	3.3	530	33	11	322	38.8	60.1	1.0
Stephenson	137.4	2 857	51.5	1.6	4.7	4.6	8.4	67.3	1 398	147	89	2 945	41.9	57.3	0.8
Tazewell	355.1	2 772	56.8	1.1	4.8	0.3	6.6	122.5	956	505	235	6 429	41.4	57.9	0.7
Union	70.4	3 878	60.0	16.8	2.6	0.2	5.0	13.1	720	66	33	1 746	41.0	58.5	0.5
Vermilion	237.7	2 859	57.8	1.5	5.5	2.7	5.8	72.5	872	1 485	153	4 785	43.7	55.6	0.7
Wabash	41.1	3 260	39.9	31.2	4.8	0.2	6.6	16.9	1 344	38	23	925	29.2	70.2	0.7
Warren	38.2	2 096	49.1	0.7	5.3	1.4	7.3	18.8	1 028	79	33	838	46.6	52.9	0.5
Washington	37.4	2 470	40.9	29.6	2.1	0.0	7.9	13.9	918	66	28	903	36.9	62.6	0.5
Wayne	35.7	2 103	58.3	1.7	3.9	0.0	11.9	3.3	192	70	31	936	25.8	73.6	0.5
White	34.6	2 295	53.9	1.2	4.8	0.3	10.0	7.0	461	64	28	877	37.0	62.5	0.5
Whiteside	215.0	3 563	36.1	33.3	2.9	0.8	4.5	51.2	848	185	112	3 891	51.1	48.2	0.7
Will	1 552.7	2 773	50.0	1.1	5.8	0.8	8.2	1 463.3	2 614	880	1 048	25 488	47.0	52.4	0.6
Williamson	150.3	2 436	61.8	0.8	4.4	0.5	7.8	79.7	1 292	1 232	114	4 397	39.0	60.4	0.6
Winnebago	879.8	3 113	51.9	1.4	5.9	2.5	5.2	609.9	2 158	1 079	523	13 821	49.3	50.0	0.6
Woodford	91.0	2 522	64.8	0.6	3.3	0.4	8.2	43.1	1 195	78	66	1 715	31.9	67.6	0.5

1. Based on the resident population estimated as of July 1 of the year shown.

STATE/ County code	CBSA code[1]	County Type[2]	STATE County	Land area,[3] (sq km) 2000	Total persons	Rank	Per square kilometer	White	Black	Am. Indian, Alaska Native	Asian and Pacific Islander	Percent Hispanic or Latino[4]	Under 5 years	5 to 17 years	18 to 24 years	25 to 34 years	35 to 44 years	45 to 54 years
				1	2	3	4	5	6	7	8	9	10	11	12	13	14	15
18 000	...	X	INDIANA	92 895	6 195 643	X	66.7	86.2	8.9	0.6	1.5	3.9	6.9	18.9	10.2	13.2	14.8	14.1
18 001	19540	6	Adams	879	33 592	1 312	38.2	96.3	0.3	0.4	0.2	3.1	8.2	22.8	9.9	11.5	13.2	12.5
18 003	23060	2	Allen	1 702	340 153	177	199.9	81.9	12.2	0.7	2.1	4.7	7.8	20.3	9.4	13.5	14.8	14.0
18 005	18020	3	Bartholomew	1 054	72 341	701	68.6	93.2	2.0	0.4	2.4	2.7	7.1	19.5	7.7	12.9	15.1	14.4
18 007	29140	3	Benton	1 052	9 189	2 509	8.7	97.0	0.4	0.7	0.2	2.6	5.8	21.1	8.4	11.4	14.4	13.4
18 009	...	6	Blackford	428	13 876	2 175	32.4	98.7	0.3	0.8	0.2	0.7	6.4	18.4	8.1	11.8	14.4	14.4
18 011	26900	1	Boone	1 095	49 370	944	45.1	97.2	0.6	0.5	1.0	1.2	6.6	20.8	8.6	11.7	16.4	14.7
18 013	26900	1	Brown	809	15 313	2 073	18.9	98.3	0.5	0.5	0.5	0.9	5.2	17.2	8.5	10.6	15.7	17.0
18 015	29140	3	Carroll	964	20 499	1 775	21.3	96.2	0.3	0.3	0.0	3.4	5.8	19.5	8.6	12.0	15.1	14.5
18 017	30900	4	Cass	1 069	40 415	1 125	37.8	89.9	1.5	0.5	0.6	8.1	7.1	19.0	9.0	12.4	14.9	13.9
18 019	31140	1	Clark	971	99 482	544	102.5	90.5	7.2	0.6	0.8	2.1	6.7	17.7	9.0	13.8	15.2	14.6
18 021	45460	3	Clay	926	26 772	1 514	28.9	98.5	0.6	0.5	0.3	0.7	6.3	19.2	9.7	11.5	14.6	14.0
18 023	23140	6	Clinton	1 049	33 947	1 305	32.4	89.9	0.2	0.4	0.2	9.5	7.3	20.0	9.3	12.2	14.9	13.3
18 025	...	8	Crawford	792	11 146	2 361	14.1	98.0	0.2	0.5	0.2	1.2	6.3	19.1	9.1	12.2	15.2	14.6
18 027	47780	7	Daviess	1 115	30 047	1 403	26.9	96.3	0.7	0.4	0.3	2.7	7.6	21.3	9.6	11.2	13.8	12.9
18 029	17140	1	Dearborn	790	47 849	965	60.6	98.3	0.7	0.5	0.5	0.6	6.2	20.0	9.4	11.8	16.4	14.8
18 031	24700	6	Decatur	965	24 747	1 586	25.6	98.2	0.2	0.3	1.1	0.6	7.6	19.0	8.6	12.9	15.0	13.5
18 033	12140	4	De Kalb	940	41 129	1 107	43.8	97.3	0.5	0.5	0.5	1.8	7.2	20.6	9.0	12.8	15.5	13.9
18 035	34620	3	Delaware	1 019	117 488	478	115.3	91.2	7.1	0.6	1.1	1.1	5.9	16.2	15.5	12.8	12.8	12.7
18 037	27540	7	Dubois	1 114	40 200	1 131	36.1	96.2	0.2	0.2	0.3	3.4	6.6	20.0	8.9	11.8	16.3	14.1
18 039	21140	3	Elkhart	1 201	188 779	303	157.2	82.9	5.7	0.7	1.3	10.7	8.3	21.0	9.5	13.6	14.5	13.0
18 041	18220	7	Fayette	557	24 999	1 574	44.9	97.5	1.8	0.3	0.4	0.6	6.2	17.9	8.8	12.3	13.8	15.2
18 043	31140	1	Floyd	383	71 148	713	185.8	93.6	4.9	0.5	0.9	1.2	6.2	19.2	8.9	12.3	16.2	15.2
18 045	...	6	Fountain	1 025	17 750	1 927	17.3	98.1	0.2	0.3	0.3	1.3	6.5	19.4	8.1	11.5	15.0	13.2
18 047	17140	1	Franklin	1 000	22 773	1 677	22.8	99.0	0.1	0.4	0.4	0.5	5.9	20.5	9.4	11.9	15.5	14.1
18 049	...	7	Fulton	954	20 508	1 774	21.5	96.0	0.8	0.8	0.4	2.6	6.4	19.0	8.8	11.6	14.9	13.8
18 051	21780	2	Gibson	1 266	32 991	1 335	26.1	96.5	2.4	0.3	0.6	0.7	6.3	18.1	9.6	11.5	15.1	14.0
18 053	31980	4	Grant	1 072	71 572	710	66.8	89.5	7.6	0.8	0.8	2.5	6.0	17.8	11.9	10.8	13.5	14.0
18 055	14020	3	Greene	1 403	33 244	1 321	23.7	98.4	0.4	0.7	0.3	0.8	6.0	18.5	8.7	11.8	15.2	14.2
18 057	26900	1	Hamilton	1 031	216 826	269	210.3	91.9	2.7	0.4	4.1	2.0	7.9	21.8	8.5	13.8	17.6	13.3
18 059	26900	1	Hancock	793	59 446	826	75.0	97.4	1.2	0.5	0.8	1.1	6.2	19.3	9.1	11.7	16.1	14.7
18 061	31140	1	Harrison	1 257	35 706	1 254	28.4	98.0	0.5	0.5	0.3	1.1	6.4	18.6	9.9	11.8	16.4	14.8
18 063	26900	1	Hendricks	1 058	118 850	473	112.3	94.6	2.5	0.6	1.6	1.6	6.6	20.3	9.5	13.2	16.6	13.6
18 065	35220	4	Henry	1 018	47 699	967	46.9	98.0	1.0	0.3	0.3	0.8	6.0	18.1	8.0	11.7	15.1	14.5
18 067	29020	3	Howard	759	84 880	626	111.8	89.9	7.6	0.8	1.3	1.8	7.2	19.0	8.4	12.4	14.4	14.3
18 069	26540	6	Huntington	991	38 143	1 181	38.5	98.1	0.4	0.7	0.4	1.0	6.1	19.2	10.5	11.8	15.0	13.9
18 071	42980	4	Jackson	1 319	41 639	1 093	31.6	95.0	0.8	0.5	0.9	3.4	7.2	18.6	8.8	13.6	15.4	13.4
18 073	16980	1	Jasper	1 450	31 078	1 382	21.4	96.1	0.4	0.4	0.4	3.1	6.3	19.9	11.4	12.1	14.3	13.3
18 075	...	6	Jay	994	21 732	1 718	21.9	97.1	0.3	0.3	0.5	2.1	7.1	20.1	8.2	11.8	14.1	13.3
18 077	31500	6	Jefferson	936	32 250	1 355	34.5	96.7	1.7	0.7	0.8	0.9	5.8	18.0	11.4	12.1	15.1	13.8
18 079	35860	6	Jennings	977	28 111	1 458	28.8	98.0	0.9	0.6	0.5	0.8	7.2	20.6	8.9	13.8	15.6	13.6
18 081	26900	1	Johnson	829	123 256	459	148.7	96.4	1.0	0.3	1.2	1.6	6.9	19.8	9.6	13.6	15.9	13.6
18 083	47180	4	Knox	1 336	38 745	1 169	29.0	96.3	2.1	0.5	0.8	0.9	5.7	16.6	14.8	10.5	13.6	13.5
18 085	47700	4	Kosciusko	1 392	75 301	682	54.1	93.1	0.8	0.5	0.7	5.4	7.4	20.1	9.2	12.7	14.7	13.8
18 087	...	6	Lagrange	983	36 026	1 236	36.6	95.9	0.3	0.4	0.4	3.1	9.7	23.8	10.9	12.3	12.7	11.3
18 089	16980	1	Lake	1 287	487 476	123	378.8	61.2	25.4	0.6	1.2	12.6	7.0	19.5	9.4	12.2	14.7	14.5
18 091	33140	3	La Porte	1 549	109 878	503	70.9	85.8	10.6	0.8	0.6	3.5	6.4	18.1	8.3	12.3	14.5	14.6
18 093	13260	4	Lawrence	1 162	46 201	999	39.8	98.2	0.4	0.8	0.5	0.8	6.4	17.7	9.1	12.7	14.6	14.2
18 095	11300	3	Madison	1 171	131 121	435	112.0	89.7	8.4	0.7	0.5	1.7	6.4	18.8	8.7	15.8	16.0	13.4
18 097	26900	1	Marion	1 026	863 251	52	841.4	68.2	25.9	0.6	2.0	4.8	8.1	20.2	9.7	11.9	14.6	13.6
18 099	38500	6	Marshall	1 151	46 352	994	40.3	92.3	0.5	0.5	0.6	6.8	7.4	20.2	9.7	11.9	14.6	13.6
18 101	...	6	Martin	871	10 347	2 412	11.9	99.1	0.4	0.2	0.2	0.4	6.1	18.5	8.5	11.6	14.6	15.4
18 103	37940	6	Miami	973	36 177	1 233	37.2	94.5	2.9	1.9	0.5	1.4	6.4	19.2	8.9	12.8	15.8	14.6
18 105	14020	3	Monroe	1 021	122 903	461	120.4	91.0	3.3	0.7	4.7	1.8	5.0	12.7	23.6	16.0	11.9	11.2
18 107	18820	6	Montgomery	1 307	37 911	1 185	29.0	96.3	1.0	0.5	0.7	2.1	6.6	19.3	9.7	12.0	15.5	13.2
18 109	26900	1	Morgan	1 053	68 656	732	65.2	98.6	0.3	0.7	0.4	0.8	6.7	19.8	9.1	11.3	15.7	14.7
18 111	16980	1	Newton	1 041	14 403	2 133	13.8	90.8	0.5	0.5	0.3	3.4	6.1	19.1	9.7	13.5	15.2	13.4
18 113	28340	6	Noble	1 065	47 039	978	44.2	90.8	0.5	0.5	0.5	8.2	7.6	21.1	9.5	11.6	16.0	14.7
18 115	17140	1	Ohio	225	5 732	2 794	25.5	98.9	0.5	0.0	0.2	0.4	5.9	18.0	9.2	11.6	16.0	14.7
18 117	...	6	Orange	998	19 616	1 829	19.0	98.1	0.8	0.6	0.3	0.7	6.8	19.1	8.6	11.6	15.1	13.6
18 119	14020	3	Owen	1 035	22 827	1 670	22.9	98.5	0.4	0.7	0.2	0.7	6.0	19.6	9.3	11.2	14.6	14.5
18 121	...	6	Parke	1 152	17 329	1 941	15.0	96.8	2.1	0.5	0.3	0.6	5.1	17.7	8.9	11.9	16.2	14.1
18 123	...	6	Perry	988	18 717	1 874	18.9	97.3	1.6	0.3	0.2	0.8	5.8	16.4	10.9	12.1	15.9	15.1
18 125	27540	6	Pike	871	12 931	2 245	14.8	99.0	0.2	0.2	0.2	0.6	6.1	17.6	8.6	11.7	15.5	14.3
18 127	16980	1	Porter	1 083	152 533	368	140.8	92.3	1.6	0.6	1.4	5.1	6.1	18.7	10.8	12.0	15.0	15.7
18 129	21780	2	Posey	1 058	26 876	1 509	25.4	98.2	1.1	0.4	0.3	0.4	5.6	20.4	8.9	10.6	16.7	15.5
18 131	...	6	Pulaski	1 123	13 835	2 179	12.3	97.1	0.9	0.4	0.4	1.6	5.8	19.4	9.1	10.9	15.0	13.6

1. CBSA = Core Based Statistical Area. See Appendix A for explanation. See Appendix B for list of metropolitan areas with component counties.   2. County type code from the Economic Research Service of USDA Rural-Urban Continuum Codes. See Appendix A for definition.   3. Dry land or land partially or temporarily covered by water.   4. Hispanic or Latino persons may be of any race.

Table B. States and Counties — **Population and Households**

STATE County	55 to 64 years	65 to 74 years	75 years and over	Percent female	1990	2000	1990–2000	2000–2003	Births	Deaths	Net migration	Number	Percent change, 1990–2000	Persons per house-hold	Female family house-holder[1]	One person
	16	**17**	**18**	**19**	**20**	**21**	**22**	**23**	**24**	**25**	**26**	**27**	**28**	**29**	**30**	**31**
INDIANA	9.5	6.2	6.1	50.8	5 544 156	6 080 485	9.7	1.9	277 808	181 651	21 305	2 336 306	13.1	2.53	11.1	25.9
Adams	8.5	5.9	7.4	50.4	31 095	33 625	8.1	-0.1	1 853	1 011	-869	11 818	12.9	2.81	8.3	24.0
Allen	8.5	5.6	5.6	50.9	300 836	331 849	10.3	2.5	17 246	8 521	-131	128 745	13.6	2.53	11.7	27.4
Bartholomew	10.4	6.8	5.6	50.8	63 657	71 435	12.2	1.3	3 270	2 095	-234	27 936	15.5	2.52	9.7	24.0
Benton	9.9	6.8	8.6	50.3	9 441	9 421	-0.2	-2.5	329	301	-249	3 558	1.0	2.59	8.5	24.5
Blackford	11.3	7.9	7.6	50.6	14 067	14 048	-0.1	-1.2	548	490	-218	5 690	4.7	2.44	10.0	25.9
Boone	9.2	5.5	5.6	50.8	38 147	46 107	20.9	7.1	1 998	1 431	2 654	17 081	22.7	2.65	7.8	21.1
Brown	12.8	7.8	5.3	49.4	14 080	14 957	6.2	2.4	491	460	330	5 897	9.8	2.51	6.5	20.6
Carroll	10.1	6.8	7.0	50.0	18 809	20 165	7.2	1.7	672	535	225	7 718	9.2	2.59	6.5	22.8
Cass	9.8	7.0	7.3	49.6	38 413	40 930	6.6	-1.3	1 850	1 452	-887	15 715	7.2	2.53	9.4	25.9
Clark	9.8	6.6	5.7	51.1	87 774	96 472	9.9	3.1	4 230	3 190	2 080	38 751	16.4	2.45	12.5	26.3
Clay	9.3	7.4	7.5	51.5	24 705	26 556	7.5	0.8	1 073	992	160	10 216	8.9	2.57	9.4	23.8
Clinton	8.9	6.8	7.4	50.7	30 974	33 866	9.3	0.2	1 669	1 164	-424	12 545	9.6	2.63	9.0	23.6
Crawford	10.7	7.2	5.3	49.9	9 914	10 743	8.4	3.8	451	366	319	4 181	14.2	2.55	9.5	22.5
Daviess	9.2	6.9	7.4	50.5	27 533	29 820	8.3	0.8	1 494	987	-261	10 894	8.8	2.69	8.7	25.0
Dearborn	9.4	6.0	5.1	50.3	38 835	46 109	18.7	3.8	1 793	1 099	1 049	16 832	23.4	2.71	9.6	20.1
Decatur	9.4	7.2	6.5	50.3	23 645	24 555	3.8	0.8	1 189	730	-257	9 389	11.4	2.58	9.2	22.8
De Kalb	8.8	5.8	5.6	50.0	35 324	40 285	14.0	2.1	1 925	1 116	77	15 134	18.9	2.63	8.8	23.4
Delaware	9.8	7.0	6.6	52.0	119 659	118 769	-0.7	-1.1	4 429	3 793	-1 849	47 131	4.3	2.37	10.9	28.2
Dubois	9.0	6.7	6.3	50.7	36 616	39 674	8.4	1.3	1 667	1 119	23	14 813	13.7	2.63	7.4	23.5
Elkhart	8.5	5.5	5.3	50.1	156 198	182 791	17.0	3.3	10 127	4 675	620	66 154	16.6	2.72	10.5	22.6
Fayette	10.4	7.9	7.9	51.6	26 015	25 588	-1.6	-2.3	992	1 020	-558	10 199	2.6	2.46	10.2	25.8
Floyd	9.8	6.3	5.9	51.6	64 404	70 823	10.0	0.5	2 757	2 254	-118	27 511	14.2	2.54	12.4	23.5
Fountain	10.5	8.3	7.7	50.3	17 808	17 954	0.8	-1.1	751	655	-292	7 041	2.7	2.52	8.0	24.8
Franklin	9.2	6.7	6.0	50.0	19 580	22 151	13.1	2.8	786	468	322	7 868	18.6	2.77	8.0	19.0
Fulton	10.6	7.7	7.7	50.5	18 840	20 511	8.9	0.0	813	741	-53	8 082	10.0	2.52	7.5	24.9
Gibson	9.8	7.7	7.6	50.9	31 913	32 500	1.8	1.5	1 268	1 151	403	12 847	4.5	2.48	9.2	25.7
Grant	10.7	8.1	7.5	52.0	74 169	73 403	-1.0	-2.5	2 762	2 555	-2 030	28 319	2.2	2.43	11.5	26.7
Greene	10.5	7.5	7.6	50.8	30 410	33 157	9.0	0.3	1 288	1 259	104	13 372	12.3	2.44	8.4	26.5
Hamilton	7.4	3.9	3.1	50.5	108 936	182 740	67.7	18.7	10 334	3 267	26 286	65 933	69.8	2.75	7.0	18.6
Hancock	10.5	6.2	4.9	50.6	45 527	55 391	21.7	7.3	2 285	1 400	3 128	20 718	29.8	2.65	7.4	18.8
Harrison	9.8	6.2	5.0	50.2	29 890	34 325	14.8	4.0	1 446	997	952	12 917	24.1	2.63	8.8	20.7
Hendricks	8.7	5.2	4.3	49.8	75 717	104 093	37.5	14.2	4 852	2 322	11 942	37 275	42.8	2.71	7.7	18.3
Henry	11.2	8.1	7.8	51.6	48 139	48 508	0.8	-1.7	1 819	1 903	-688	19 486	4.5	2.45	9.9	24.8
Howard	10.9	7.3	6.2	51.5	80 827	84 964	5.1	-0.1	3 893	2 986	-933	34 800	10.4	2.41	11.5	28.2
Huntington	9.0	6.6	7.6	51.4	35 427	38 075	7.5	0.2	1 442	1 340	12	14 242	11.0	2.57	9.1	23.6
Jackson	9.7	6.9	6.4	50.7	37 730	41 335	9.6	0.7	2 011	1 389	-291	16 052	14.4	2.54	9.9	23.5
Jasper	9.4	6.7	5.8	50.3	24 823	30 043	21.0	3.4	1 153	836	740	10 686	25.3	2.72	7.7	19.9
Jay	10.7	7.2	7.6	51.1	21 512	21 806	1.4	-0.3	975	745	-286	8 405	3.0	2.57	9.1	24.8
Jefferson	10.4	6.9	6.3	50.4	29 797	31 705	6.4	1.7	1 189	934	307	12 148	11.5	2.46	10.6	25.7
Jennings	10.1	5.8	4.8	50.5	23 661	27 554	16.5	2.0	1 278	815	110	10 134	21.4	2.67	9.5	20.6
Johnson	8.9	5.6	5.2	50.9	88 109	115 209	30.8	7.0	5 303	3 144	5 876	42 434	35.3	2.63	9.0	21.2
Knox	9.8	7.5	8.0	50.2	39 884	39 256	-1.6	-1.3	1 442	1 521	-414	15 552	2.7	2.36	10.2	29.7
Kosciusko	9.6	6.3	5.8	49.9	65 294	74 057	13.4	1.7	3 669	1 923	-436	27 283	16.4	2.66	8.3	21.9
Lagrange	8.4	5.7	4.5	49.2	29 477	34 909	18.4	3.2	2 240	680	-410	11 225	21.9	3.09	6.5	18.0
Lake	9.4	6.7	6.3	51.9	475 594	484 564	1.9	0.6	22 724	15 811	-3 574	181 633	6.4	2.64	16.6	25.8
La Porte	9.7	6.8	6.7	48.6	107 066	110 106	2.8	-0.2	4 533	3 446	-1 229	41 050	6.7	2.52	11.7	25.2
Lawrence	10.9	7.9	7.1	51.1	42 836	45 922	7.2	0.6	1 823	1 674	187	18 535	14.2	2.44	9.0	25.5
Madison	10.6	7.6	7.4	50.7	130 669	133 358	2.1	-1.7	5 418	4 817	-2 789	53 052	6.5	2.41	11.8	27.2
Marion	8.0	5.6	5.4	51.5	797 159	860 454	7.9	0.3	47 089	25 260	-18 989	352 164	10.2	2.39	14.9	31.8
Marshall	8.9	6.6	6.4	50.1	42 182	45 128	7.0	2.7	2 259	1 277	283	16 519	9.1	2.69	8.3	22.3
Martin	11.0	7.8	6.6	49.4	10 369	10 369	0.0	-0.2	421	376	-54	4 183	9.0	2.45	8.2	27.6
Miami	9.7	6.8	6.1	49.2	36 897	36 082	-2.2	0.3	1 536	1 112	-293	13 716	1.7	2.52	9.8	24.6
Monroe	7.1	4.9	4.5	50.9	108 978	120 563	10.6	1.9	3 996	2 455	859	46 898	19.2	2.27	8.1	32.4
Montgomery	10.2	7.2	6.7	49.8	34 436	37 629	9.3	0.7	1 615	1 221	-79	14 595	10.3	2.50	8.6	25.3
Morgan	10.0	6.1	4.6	50.3	55 920	66 689	19.3	2.9	2 744	1 765	1 037	24 437	24.7	2.70	8.6	18.4
Newton	10.6	6.8	6.1	50.2	13 551	14 566	7.5	-1.1	521	472	-201	5 340	10.4	2.69	7.8	20.9
Noble	8.5	5.6	5.3	49.5	37 877	46 275	22.2	1.7	2 292	1 179	-334	16 696	24.4	2.73	9.0	21.9
Ohio	11.1	7.6	6.3	50.7	5 315	5 623	5.8	1.9	227	160	44	2 201	11.2	2.53	8.5	23.2
Orange	10.3	7.6	6.9	50.9	18 409	19 306	4.9	1.6	872	742	198	7 621	9.7	2.49	8.6	26.2
Owen	10.3	7.2	5.3	50.4	17 281	21 786	26.1	4.8	835	603	808	8 282	29.5	2.60	8.5	21.3
Parke	11.3	7.7	6.9	52.5	15 410	17 241	11.9	0.5	545	557	118	6 415	9.8	2.51	8.3	24.1
Perry	9.5	7.4	7.4	48.1	19 107	18 899	-1.1	-1.0	717	643	-228	7 270	6.2	2.45	9.0	26.7
Pike	11.0	8.0	7.3	50.1	12 509	12 837	2.6	0.7	486	484	104	5 119	3.9	2.47	8.4	24.9
Porter	9.8	5.7	5.1	50.7	128 932	146 798	13.9	3.9	5 871	3 674	3 612	54 649	21.0	2.62	9.2	22.2
Posey	10.0	6.8	5.7	50.1	25 968	27 061	4.2	-0.7	871	801	-225	10 205	7.3	2.63	7.8	22.1
Pulaski	10.0	7.5	7.9	49.9	12 780	13 755	7.6	0.6	479	417	29	5 170	9.5	2.59	7.3	23.5

1. No spouse present.

Table B. States and Counties — Vital Statistics, Health Resources, and Crime

STATE County	Births, average 1999–2001 Total	Rate[1]	Deaths, average 1999–2001 Number Total	Infant[2]	Rate Total[1]	Infant[3]	Physicians,[4] 2000 Number	Rate[5]	Hospitals,[4] 1998 Number	Beds Number	Rate[5]	Medicare enrollees, 2003	Serious crimes known to police,[6] 2002 Total Number	Rate[7]
	32	33	34	35	36	37	38	39	40	41	42	43	44	45
INDIANA	86 730	14.3	55 323	674	9.1	7.8	10 572	174	117	19 596	332	877 954	230 966	3 750
Adams	596	17.7	294	5	8.7	D	17	51	1	87	263	4 637	NA	NA
Allen	5 228	15.7	2 626	34	7.9	6.6	681	205	3	1 042	332	43 686	14 351	4 269
Bartholomew	1 069	15.0	634	9	8.9	8.4	157	220	1	237	341	10 575	2 482	3 444
Benton	153	16.2	100	1	10.6	D	2	21	0	0	0	1 673	NA	NA
Blackford	175	12.5	149	2	10.6	D	7	50	1	28	201	2 495	275	1 953
Boone	627	13.6	423	4	9.2	D	78	169	1	49	112	5 772	NA	NA
Brown	147	9.8	128	0	8.6	D	7	47	0	0	0	1 370	145	957
Carroll	236	11.7	176	1	8.7	D	10	50	0	0	0	2 665	NA	NA
Cass	592	14.5	433	4	10.6	D	65	159	1	112	290	6 605	1 081	2 607
Clark	1 335	13.8	952	10	9.9	7.5	147	152	2	376	401	15 482	4 955	5 071
Clay	346	13.0	306	4	11.5	D	20	75	1	55	206	5 001	486	1 807
Clinton	551	16.3	378	5	11.1	D	20	59	1	53	160	5 213	1 189	3 466
Crawford	131	12.2	107	0	10.0	D	2	19	0	0	0	1 951	NA	NA
Daviess	472	15.8	312	4	10.5	D	22	74	1	85	293	4 476	NA	NA
Dearborn	657	14.2	377	7	8.1	11.2	44	95	1	76	161	6 563	494	1 177
Decatur	386	15.7	229	3	9.3	D	20	81	1	73	286	4 070	NA	NA
De Kalb	576	14.3	344	4	8.5	D	31	77	1	45	114	5 506	NA	NA
Delaware	1 411	11.9	1 153	15	9.7	10.4	267	225	1	428	366	18 631	4 320	3 591
Dubois	539	13.6	366	3	9.2	D	52	131	2	191	481	5 818	NA	NA
Elkhart	3 187	17.4	1 425	24	7.8	7.5	228	125	2	476	276	23 188	7 821	4 224
Fayette	344	13.5	305	3	11.9	D	19	74	1	140	539	4 760	NA	NA
Floyd	882	12.4	691	4	9.7	D	114	161	1	174	242	10 368	3 760	5 241
Fountain	237	13.2	215	3	12.0	D	5	28	0	0	0	3 663	254	1 630
Franklin	286	12.9	164	1	7.4	D	12	54	0	0	0	2 934	319	1 615
Fulton	267	13.0	208	3	10.1	D	21	102	1	49	238	3 496	NA	NA
Gibson	390	12.0	355	3	10.9	D	23	71	2	135	420	5 689	NA	NA
Grant	882	12.0	788	8	10.8	8.7	126	172	1	212	292	13 095	2 800	3 766
Greene	358	10.8	351	5	10.6	D	18	54	1	76	227	5 689	NA	NA
Hamilton	3 098	16.8	935	19	5.1	6.2	312	171	2	199	122	16 110	3 234	1 747
Hancock	738	13.3	426	2	7.6	D	67	121	1	70	128	7 514	665	1 185
Harrison	450	13.1	295	2	8.6	D	29	84	1	45	130	5 159	1 227	3 529
Hendricks	1 380	13.2	687	6	6.6	D	107	103	1	127	133	11 998	NA	NA
Henry	584	12.1	544	5	11.2	D	47	97	1	107	219	8 952	2 720	5 536
Howard	1 212	14.3	870	8	10.2	6.3	143	168	2	300	359	13 825	3 789	4 403
Huntington	492	12.9	392	2	10.3	D	22	58	1	75	201	6 411	731	1 895
Jackson	594	14.4	410	4	9.9	D	37	90	1	107	261	6 755	NA	NA
Jasper	388	12.9	255	1	8.5	D	17	57	1	69	236	4 654	NA	NA
Jay	316	14.5	235	2	10.8	D	12	55	1	71	327	3 896	NA	NA
Jefferson	371	11.7	312	2	9.8	D	43	136	1	119	378	5 072	371	1 329
Jennings	407	14.7	236	4	8.6	D	10	36	1	34	122	3 866	NA	NA
Johnson	1 624	14.0	945	11	8.2	6.6	107	93	2	180	165	15 570	1 566	4 309
Knox	452	11.5	479	4	12.2	D	77	196	1	301	764	7 105	1 306	1 840
Kosciusko	1 156	15.6	607	8	8.2	7.2	56	76	1	113	159	10 317	234	662
Lagrange	712	20.4	216	4	6.2	D	12	34	1	62	185	3 730	NA	NA
Lake	7 031	14.5	4 788	65	9.9	9.3	912	188	8	2 289	479	72 840	21 628	4 608
La Porte	1 404	12.7	1 051	11	9.5	7.6	160	145	3	468	428	16 605	5 027	4 568
Lawrence	585	12.7	491	5	10.7	D	45	98	2	245	537	7 927	839	2 003
Madison	1 709	12.8	1 443	15	10.8	9.0	171	128	3	659	502	22 828	NA	NA
Marion	14 472	16.8	7 748	138	9.0	9.5	3 152	366	11	4 037	496	112 896	51 494	5 908
Marshall	697	15.4	408	2	9.0	D	44	98	2	63	139	6 734	NA	NA
Martin	141	13.6	108	1	10.4	D	3	29	0	0	0	1 910	111	1 057
Miami	464	12.9	324	3	9.0	D	28	78	1	135	402	5 426	NA	NA
Monroe	1 262	10.5	739	10	6.1	7.9	235	195	1	265	230	13 324	4 225	3 460
Montgomery	506	13.4	383	5	10.2	D	54	144	1	120	330	6 012	NA	NA
Morgan	933	14.0	526	4	7.9	D	53	79	2	191	292	8 567	216	1 464
Newton	183	12.6	138	1	9.5	D	7	48	0	0	0	1 894	216	1 464
Noble	715	15.4	380	4	8.2	D	27	58	1	51	120	5 873	610	1 369
Ohio	64	11.4	46	0	8.2	D	1	18	0	0	0	844	NA	NA
Orange	264	13.7	218	1	11.3	D	14	73	1	37	189	3 342	57	291
Owen	256	11.8	178	2	8.2	D	3	14	0	0	0	2 992	NA	NA
Parke	178	10.3	165	2	9.6	D	11	64	0	0	0	2 836	NA	NA
Perry	221	11.7	195	4	10.3	D	11	58	1	44	227	3 179	NA	NA
Pike	158	12.3	139	3	10.8	D	5	39	0	0	0	2 274	NA	NA
Porter	1 833	12.5	1 125	12	7.6	6.5	176	120	1	367	252	18 387	4 193	2 820
Posey	271	10.0	238	3	8.8	D	10	37	0	0	0	3 666	NA	NA
Pulaski	173	12.6	129	1	9.3	D	8	58	1	47	355	2 400	90	646

1. Per 1,000 estimated resident population.   2. Deaths of infants under 1 year old.   3. Deaths of infants under 1 year old per 1,000 live births.   4. Data subject to copyright.   5. Per 100,000 resident population as of July 1 of the year shown.   6. Data for serious crimes have not been adjusted for underreporting; this may affect comparability between geographic areas and over time.   7. Per 100,000 population estimated by the FBI.

Table B. States and Counties — Crime, Education, Money Income, and Poverty

STATE County	Serious crimes known to police,[1] 2002 (cont'd) Rate[2] Violent	Property	Education Enrollment[3] Total	Percent private	Attainment[4] (percent) High school graduate or less	Bachelor's degree or more	Local government expenditures,[5] 2000–2001 Total current expenditures (mil dol)	Current expenditures per student (dollars)	Money income, 1999 Per capita income[6] (dollars)	Households Median income Dollars	Percent change, 1989–1999 (constant 1999 dollars)	Percent with income of $100,000 or more	Percent below poverty level, 1999 Persons	Households	Families	Families with children
	46	47	48	49	50	51	52	53	54	55	56	57	58	59	60	61
INDIANA	357	3 393	1 603 554	16.6	55.1	19.4	7 208.3	7 296	20 397	41 567	7.4	9.2	9.5	9.5	6.7	10.2
Adams	NA	NA	9 020	19.5	65.1	10.7	35.7	7 012	16 704	40 625	5.0	5.9	9.1	7.7	6.1	9.0
Allen	294	3 975	91 489	24.7	46.3	22.7	391.8	7 570	21 544	42 671	-0.2	10.2	9.1	8.6	6.7	10.3
Bartholomew	137	3 307	17 865	15.6	52.4	22.0	86.2	7 423	21 536	44 184	6.2	9.9	7.3	7.9	5.9	8.7
Benton	NA	NA	2 424	14.4	61.9	13.0	16.1	7 585	17 220	39 813	10.3	4.3	5.5	5.6	3.5	5.2
Blackford	64	1 889	3 178	9.8	68.2	10.3	17.7	7 646	16 543	34 760	1.4	2.8	8.7	9.2	6.0	9.6
Boone	NA	NA	11 649	12.2	49.6	27.6	55.0	6 373	24 182	49 632	6.6	16.3	5.2	5.6	3.8	4.3
Brown	40	917	3 303	9.1	55.2	18.5	16.9	7 017	20 548	43 708	10.6	9.1	8.9	9.3	7.7	8.1
Carroll	NA	NA	4 612	10.6	64.5	12.9	19.6	6 723	19 436	42 677	11.4	7.3	6.8	5.8	4.3	6.6
Cass	130	2 477	9 488	9.7	63.7	12.0	45.5	6 554	18 892	39 193	12.4	6.7	7.6	7.2	4.7	7.6
Clark	334	4 737	21 962	14.5	56.6	14.3	105.3	7 376	19 936	40 111	9.0	7.2	8.1	8.7	6.0	8.9
Clay	164	1 643	6 549	9.5	63.3	12.8	31.4	6 713	16 364	36 865	16.9	4.6	8.7	8.8	6.4	9.8
Clinton	283	3 183	7 947	8.2	70.2	10.1	41.6	6 570	17 862	40 759	16.0	6.3	8.6	8.7	6.3	9.1
Crawford	NA	NA	2 346	9.2	74.5	8.4	13.6	7 359	15 926	32 646	19.3	3.4	16.8	16.6	11.1	18.5
Daviess	NA	NA	7 094	18.5	68.1	9.7	28.8	6 427	16 015	34 064	11.2	5.0	13.8	12.6	9.6	13.9
Dearborn	86	1 092	11 922	16.8	59.2	15.4	59.2	6 725	20 431	48 899	15.9	10.0	6.6	6.7	4.8	6.8
Decatur	NA	NA	5 684	11.7	68.4	11.5	27.7	6 544	18 582	40 401	8.6	5.7	9.3	8.8	6.6	10.2
De Kalb	NA	NA	10 316	10.4	61.2	12.4	52.1	7 425	19 448	44 909	7.9	7.4	5.9	6.2	3.7	5.3
Delaware	293	3 297	37 225	5.9	55.6	20.4	133.1	7 891	19 233	34 659	5.6	7.3	15.1	15.4	9.0	13.7
Dubois	NA	NA	10 124	11.2	64.3	14.5	53.0	7 163	20 225	44 169	5.3	7.6	5.3	6.1	2.9	4.9
Elkhart	275	3 949	44 933	14.6	61.3	15.5	225.3	6 878	20 250	44 478	6.9	9.0	7.8	7.3	5.8	8.8
Fayette	NA	NA	5 544	10.2	72.8	7.8	30.2	7 134	18 624	38 840	13.1	7.0	7.9	8.9	6.0	9.3
Floyd	408	4 833	18 474	17.2	50.7	20.4	85.7	7 710	21 852	44 022	15.1	10.8	8.7	9.1	6.9	11.4
Fountain	269	1 360	4 260	7.9	66.8	10.1	21.5	6 553	17 779	38 119	14.5	4.1	8.5	8.7	6.2	8.6
Franklin	116	1 499	5 644	21.8	68.1	12.5	19.0	6 315	18 624	43 530	16.8	8.1	7.1	6.9	4.7	7.2
Fulton	NA	NA	4 904	8.2	69.0	10.3	17.8	6 291	17 950	38 290	9.0	4.7	7.6	7.5	5.0	7.9
Gibson	NA	NA	7 933	18.5	60.1	12.4	36.0	7 116	18 169	37 515	7.5	5.5	8.2	9.5	6.6	10.5
Grant	387	3 379	19 117	26.6	62.7	14.1	88.0	7 746	18 003	36 162	2.5	6.0	11.8	11.4	8.4	13.8
Greene	NA	NA	7 678	7.7	64.3	10.5	41.7	7 155	16 834	33 998	9.4	4.2	11.0	11.1	8.4	13.4
Hamilton	106	1 641	51 209	20.8	25.6	48.9	232.8	6 750	33 109	71 026	15.6	28.8	2.9	3.1	2.0	2.6
Hancock	71	1 114	14 151	14.8	49.7	22.2	64.0	6 257	24 966	56 416	12.5	16.8	3.0	3.3	1.9	2.8
Harrison	124	3 405	8 341	14.7	60.8	13.1	41.8	6 922	19 643	43 423	18.7	7.6	6.4	6.8	4.9	6.2
Hendricks	NA	NA	27 181	13.8	48.7	23.1	123.8	6 448	23 129	55 208	3.0	14.8	3.6	4.5	2.8	3.1
Henry	83	5 452	10 911	8.4	64.8	11.7	58.1	6 871	19 355	38 150	10.6	7.8	7.8	8.0	6.0	9.3
Howard	401	4 002	20 385	12.7	54.7	18.1	111.9	7 928	22 049	43 487	2.7	10.3	9.5	9.1	6.6	11.1
Huntington	70	1 825	9 918	18.5	61.7	14.2	42.2	6 476	19 480	41 620	4.4	6.7	5.5	5.6	3.7	5.5
Jackson	NA	NA	9 233	15.3	66.9	11.5	42.6	6 685	18 400	39 401	13.8	5.8	8.5	8.9	6.5	9.2
Jasper	NA	NA	8 012	21.2	64.0	13.0	31.6	6 386	19 012	43 369	13.1	7.6	6.7	7.7	4.6	6.9
Jay	NA	NA	5 006	7.3	71.0	9.9	30.4	7 729	16 686	35 700	12.1	3.3	9.1	9.4	5.8	10.3
Jefferson	NA	NA	8 115	23.4	59.1	16.4	42.9	8 619	17 412	38 189	14.5	5.1	9.6	9.5	7.6	11.0
Jennings	82	1 247	6 562	13.8	70.8	8.4	32.5	6 341	17 059	39 402	19.1	5.7	9.2	9.0	6.0	9.2
Johnson	NA	NA	29 119	18.1	50.5	23.1	136.5	6 552	22 976	52 693	11.9	14.2	5.6	5.3	3.3	4.7
Knox	206	4 103	11 067	7.0	55.6	14.4	42.8	7 189	16 085	31 362	8.3	5.3	16.0	17.0	11.6	18.7
Kosciusko	56	1 784	18 081	14.8	60.5	14.9	99.5	7 073	19 806	43 939	3.3	8.4	6.4	6.3	4.4	6.2
Lagrange	42	619	7 998	22.1	73.7	8.9	44.3	6 940	16 481	42 848	16.8	6.2	7.7	7.6	5.4	7.0
Lake	537	4 070	130 977	15.3	56.6	16.2	656.6	7 979	19 639	41 829	2.3	9.4	12.2	11.9	9.7	15.1
La Porte	245	4 322	27 395	14.3	60.4	14.0	126.6	7 089	18 913	41 430	8.3	7.1	8.7	8.7	6.3	9.7
Lawrence	69	1 934	9 850	8.5	69.0	10.7	50.2	6 795	17 653	36 280	4.8	4.9	9.8	10.7	7.3	11.5
Madison	NA	NA	31 151	16.5	59.9	14.4	154.0	7 660	20 090	38 925	5.6	7.6	9.3	9.3	7.0	11.3
Marion	894	5 014	218 164	22.1	48.0	25.4	1 035.0	8 113	21 789	40 421	3.2	9.9	11.4	10.6	8.7	13.1
Marshall	NA	NA	11 369	14.5	61.3	14.9	58.9	7 488	18 427	42 581	11.9	6.8	6.8	6.2	4.8	6.7
Martin	105	952	2 269	10.5	68.1	8.8	12.3	6 646	17 054	36 411	16.1	4.3	11.2	11.4	8.1	11.0
Miami	NA	NA	8 768	9.7	64.3	10.4	51.1	6 749	17 726	39 184	19.3	5.5	8.0	8.0	6.0	9.8
Monroe	211	3 248	52 065	7.0	37.7	39.6	96.1	7 241	18 534	33 311	0.0	8.6	18.9	18.9	7.1	10.0
Montgomery	NA	NA	9 352	14.8	61.2	14.7	46.1	6 889	18 938	41 297	9.7	6.2	8.3	8.3	6.1	9.9
Morgan	NA	NA	15 760	10.7	64.3	12.6	73.9	6 545	20 657	47 739	8.5	9.4	6.6	7.1	5.3	6.9
Newton	75	1 389	3 438	8.1	71.1	9.6	19.6	6 936	17 755	40 944	6.5	5.0	6.9	8.5	4.8	5.3
Noble	85	1 284	11 357	12.7	66.3	11.1	53.5	6 725	17 896	42 700	6.5	6.4	7.9	7.3	5.6	7.9
Ohio	NA	NA	1 310	7.5	66.3	11.6	6.4	6 264	19 627	41 348	17.3	4.6	7.1	8.5	5.8	6.1
Orange	87	205	4 377	8.1	71.4	10.2	22.7	6 567	16 717	31 564	11.8	4.4	12.4	13.1	9.0	11.9
Owen	NA	NA	5 037	9.0	68.6	9.2	22.8	7 191	16 884	36 529	16.2	5.0	9.4	9.0	6.1	10.3
Parke	NA	NA	4 019	9.8	65.1	11.6	17.4	6 514	16 986	35 724	8.5	5.5	11.5	10.5	9.3	15.9
Perry	NA	NA	4 257	7.0	70.7	9.6	21.0	6 707	16 673	36 246	11.7	4.4	9.4	10.1	7.1	11.4
Pike	NA	NA	2 792	5.9	69.9	8.4	14.5	6 563	16 217	34 759	12.0	2.9	8.0	8.9	5.1	7.7
Porter	146	2 674	39 988	19.0	49.8	22.6	183.8	7 184	23 957	53 100	6.4	12.9	5.9	6.2	3.9	6.2
Posey	NA	NA	7 225	17.6	57.4	14.8	37.2	7 909	19 516	44 209	4.4	7.9	7.4	9.0	6.0	9.3
Pulaski	122	524	3 478	7.2	65.3	10.3	17.6	6 925	16 835	35 422	3.7	5.8	8.3	8.5	6.3	8.9

1. Data for serious crimes have not been adjusted for underreporting; this may affect comparability between geographic areas and over time.   2. Per 100,000 population estimated by the FBI.   3. All persons 3 years old and over enrolled in nursery school through college.   4. Persons 25 years old and over.   5. Elementary and secondary education expenditures.   6. Based on population enumerated as of April 1, 2000.

Items 46—61

Table B. States and Counties — **Personal Income**

STATE County	Personal income, 2002 Total (mil dol) [62]	Percent change, 2001–2002 [63]	Per capita[1] Dollars [64]	Per capita[1] Rank [65]	Wages and salaries[2] (mil dol) [66]	Proprietor's income (mil dol) [67]	Dividends, interest, and rent (mil dol) [68]	Transfer payments Total (mil dol) [69]	Government payments to individuals Total (mil dol) [70]	Social Security (mil dol) [71]	Medical payments (mil dol) [72]	Income maintenance (mil dol) [73]	Unemployment insurance (mil dol) [74]
INDIANA	172 592	2.0	28 032	X	117 565	11 809	29 127	25 298	23 762	10 386	9 450	1 980	876
Adams	787	1.4	23 512	1 565	490	60	145	116	107	55	41	6	3
Allen	9 948	2.0	29 493	392	7 896	721	1 833	1 295	1 211	532	481	108	41
Bartholomew	2 172	2.2	30 261	327	1 818	155	424	283	266	130	105	19	5
Benton	230	-0.1	24 731	1 204	82	14	48	36	34	18	12	2	1
Blackford	318	1.8	22 894	1 753	143	21	59	65	62	30	23	5	2
Boone	1 868	2.2	38 585	76	564	182	412	159	147	75	56	7	4
Brown	450	3.1	29 476	394	81	44	102	57	53	30	16	3	3
Carroll	552	-0.7	27 146	672	177	48	107	73	68	38	21	3	3
Cass	1 014	1.4	25 000	1 127	590	41	162	191	181	73	80	12	4
Clark	2 699	1.7	27 541	610	1 667	179	393	438	413	172	175	31	17
Clay	593	2.3	22 359	1 919	217	50	99	124	117	51	48	10	4
Clinton	775	1.1	22 803	1 781	404	45	131	137	128	57	51	9	4
Crawford	235	3.0	21 172	2 243	67	20	31	54	51	19	22	5	3
Daviess	687	0.8	23 029	1 714	310	44	137	131	124	45	57	10	5
Dearborn	1 343	2.9	28 438	497	550	86	205	177	165	79	65	10	6
Decatur	648	2.8	26 295	833	484	21	130	101	95	45	38	6	2
De Kalb	1 080	3.5	26 551	775	920	73	169	146	135	65	51	8	4
Delaware	2 992	1.6	25 313	1 041	1 987	152	541	549	520	225	207	46	19
Dubois	1 258	1.8	31 466	251	1 034	75	329	152	142	68	58	6	5
Elkhart	5 145	4.6	27 665	592	4 843	372	847	661	614	278	227	58	31
Fayette	653	0.9	26 004	887	434	25	107	143	136	56	62	10	5
Floyd	2 202	1.8	30 865	279	993	124	347	315	297	120	122	26	12
Fountain	419	-0.6	23 565	1 544	180	32	75	82	77	38	29	5	3
Franklin	617	3.0	27 418	628	122	16	143	87	81	44	26	5	3
Fulton	493	1.0	23 891	1 442	242	38	96	89	84	42	31	5	3
Gibson	835	4.3	25 555	988	645	29	151	145	137	63	53	8	3
Grant	1 764	2.7	24 474	1 269	1 176	86	298	384	366	155	153	30	10
Greene	752	3.0	22 714	1 816	243	31	124	151	142	59	59	10	7
Hamilton	8 847	1.7	42 891	44	4 073	762	1 620	457	406	220	140	16	14
Hancock	1 965	1.8	33 741	166	708	162	320	202	188	95	71	8	4
Harrison	901	1.4	25 564	986	428	24	141	135	126	57	50	9	4
Hendricks	3 441	2.6	29 999	353	1 267	221	495	325	297	152	107	11	12
Henry	1 236	2.4	25 704	952	598	48	207	239	227	106	93	16	5
Howard	2 408	2.5	28 402	504	2 484	98	366	395	374	174	150	31	8
Huntington	982	1.2	25 715	949	529	36	164	150	141	69	50	8	6
Jackson	1 007	1.1	24 227	1 334	770	68	143	167	157	74	62	11	5
Jasper	777	0.6	25 331	1 036	370	60	129	117	109	55	38	6	6
Jay	451	-1.4	20 816	2 342	246	17	67	95	89	44	34	6	3
Jefferson	727	2.1	22 546	1 865	467	34	140	154	146	58	67	11	5
Jennings	617	0.6	21 876	2 045	279	19	73	136	129	45	68	9	3
Johnson	3 635	2.4	29 936	358	1 421	223	566	403	373	184	141	20	13
Knox	966	1.8	24 936	1 152	562	71	177	221	212	77	101	17	3
Kosciusko	2 045	3.9	27 287	656	1 432	93	379	265	247	127	84	13	16
Lagrange	699	4.1	19 615	2 626	466	37	116	97	88	45	30	5	6
Lake	12 987	0.7	26 730	747	8 088	684	1 924	2 340	2 219	898	893	259	86
La Porte	2 729	1.2	24 773	1 189	1 728	125	495	477	450	203	173	36	21
Lawrence	1 131	3.3	24 540	1 252	582	56	168	217	206	85	90	13	10
Madison	3 430	1.9	26 005	886	1 835	202	483	650	617	278	253	50	19
Marion	27 711	2.2	32 129	218	29 056	2 744	4 536	3 741	3 526	1 301	1 440	394	150
Marshall	1 114	1.4	24 319	1 304	627	72	199	167	155	79	55	10	6
Martin	236	2.4	22 847	1 764	431	6	45	45	42	17	18	3	2
Miami	795	1.0	21 881	2 042	386	27	122	150	141	55	54	11	6
Monroe	2 939	3.4	24 212	1 340	2 239	168	632	395	364	158	144	25	14
Montgomery	938	2.0	24 725	1 206	673	40	155	158	149	70	60	10	5
Morgan	1 853	2.1	27 294	651	505	55	212	242	225	105	86	17	9
Newton	326	1.6	22 701	1 822	126	19	45	56	53	25	19	4	3
Noble	1 115	2.3	23 728	1 488	747	69	150	158	146	71	55	10	6
Ohio	142	2.3	24 661	1 222	67	6	20	21	20	10	8	1	0
Orange	416	1.3	21 393	2 183	198	21	70	96	91	36	40	8	5
Owen	491	3.1	21 862	2 049	148	23	62	91	85	37	33	7	5
Parke	364	1.1	21 127	2 259	101	17	65	79	74	33	31	6	2
Perry	441	2.9	23 396	1 595	219	21	83	80	76	35	31	6	3
Pike	279	0.9	21 571	2 130	137	6	45	64	61	26	25	4	2
Porter	4 650	0.5	30 892	276	2 217	197	701	546	509	249	189	26	25
Posey	767	0.7	28 401	505	467	29	155	104	97	46	37	7	3
Pulaski	330	0.3	24 065	1 381	162	37	67	59	55	27	21	4	2

1. Based on the resident population estimated as of July 1 of the year shown.   2. Includes other labor income.

Table B. States and Counties — Earnings, Social Security, and Housing

STATE County	Total (mil dol)	Farm	Goods-related[1] Total	Manu-facturing	Information and professional and technical services	Retail trade	Finance, insurance, and real estate	Health services	Govern-ment	Social Security beneficiaries, December 2003 Number	Rate[2]	Supplemental Security Income recipients, December 2003	Housing units, 2003 Total	Percent change, 2000–2003
	75	76	77	78	79	80	81	82	83	84	85	86	87	88
INDIANA	129 374	0.1	33.3	26.4	6.5	6.9	7.0	9.7	13.5	1 032 417	167	94 027	2 651 165	4.7
Adams	550	-0.6	D	48.8	3.8	7.2	3.6	D	12.4	5 360	160	213	12 701	2.4
Allen	8 617	0.0	28.4	21.7	7.8	6.3	9.5	14.2	9.4	51 440	151	4 973	145 300	4.6
Bartholomew	1 973	-0.1	D	43.1	4.9	5.2	7.1	7.2	11.3	12 875	178	1 185	30 523	2.2
Benton	96	3.9	22.1	17.3	1.9	7.3	D	4.9	23.8	1 860	202	97	3 844	0.7
Blackford	165	-0.6	D	44.7	1.8	9.3	3.9	6.4	15.4	3 110	224	188	6 302	2.4
Boone	746	1.0	D	12.1	6.3	7.4	6.1	6.9	13.6	7 155	145	248	19 548	9.0
Brown	125	0.0	D	6.5	10.3	10.3	5.4	5.3	21.0	2 905	190	78	7 582	5.8
Carroll	225	2.8	D	36.3	3.5	7.1	5.9	D	13.1	3 770	184	95	8 934	3.0
Cass	631	0.8	D	35.6	2.2	7.6	3.6	6.3	22.2	7 430	184	588	16 972	2.1
Clark	1 846	-0.1	D	19.2	2.9	9.5	4.6	7.4	16.8	17 915	180	1 760	44 342	7.7
Clay	266	1.3	35.1	29.8	3.3	12.0	4.8	6.5	16.1	5 390	201	505	11 453	3.2
Clinton	449	1.3	48.7	44.5	2.5	6.2	3.0	D	13.8	5 800	171	369	13 450	1.4
Crawford	86	0.5	D	D	0.8	6.8	7.4	4.3	21.2	2 275	204	286	5 341	4.0
Daviess	354	-1.2	37.1	19.4	2.6	8.0	4.0	D	18.5	5 240	174	481	12 141	2.0
Dearborn	636	-0.4	D	18.1	3.3	9.1	4.7	6.5	15.8	7 880	165	417	18 861	6.0
Decatur	504	-0.8	D	50.2	D	7.4	3.2	3.5	10.3	4 670	189	298	10 407	4.2
De Kalb	993	0.5	63.0	56.0	2.1	4.5	2.2	D	7.6	6 570	160	431	16 675	3.3
Delaware	2 139	0.3	D	22.1	5.2	7.7	5.6	17.9	19.4	22 030	188	2 653	51 938	1.8
Dubois	1 109	-0.2	50.1	43.0	2.5	8.6	2.3	D	7.3	6 970	173	302	16 133	4.0
Elkhart	5 215	0.1	D	53.7	3.3	4.9	3.4	6.6	6.3	27 005	143	2 265	73 973	6.0
Fayette	458	-1.1	D	54.1	2.3	6.6	2.6	10.3	12.1	5 675	227	539	11 206	2.0
Floyd	1 117	0.0	D	26.0	6.3	7.4	6.6	10.2	18.7	12 145	171	1 489	30 164	3.7
Fountain	212	1.2	46.7	42.6	2.7	7.8	5.7	D	15.1	3 835	216	284	7 825	1.7
Franklin	138	-5.0	D	11.3	D	8.7	D	D	23.6	4 425	194	238	8 960	4.2
Fulton	279	2.0	D	37.1	D	8.4	5.2	D	14.7	4 280	209	209	9 340	2.4
Gibson	674	-0.3	59.2	50.9	3.0	5.1	1.7	4.8	7.1	6 410	194	375	14 726	4.3
Grant	1 262	0.2	D	38.4	3.0	7.3	3.8	10.7	15.8	15 375	215	1 616	31 323	2.5
Greene	274	0.2	D	5.9	8.1	9.9	4.4	D	26.9	6 665	200	605	15 614	3.7
Hamilton	4 835	0.2	D	6.8	11.9	8.1	22.7	6.3	8.2	21 030	97	661	83 003	19.5
Hancock	870	-0.1	D	18.0	14.0	7.5	6.5	5.6	15.6	9 470	159	331	24 444	12.4
Harrison	451	-1.1	32.2	26.9	D	8.4	3.6	D	15.6	6 275	176	480	14 409	5.2
Hendricks	1 487	-0.1	D	6.5	5.1	12.6	5.6	6.2	18.6	14 685	124	378	46 702	19.0
Henry	646	-0.2	D	40.1	3.0	8.2	3.6	D	19.6	10 660	223	742	21 178	2.8
Howard	2 581	0.3	D	61.1	3.5	5.3	2.9	5.5	9.4	16 600	196	1 671	38 700	2.9
Huntington	565	0.4	41.7	36.6	D	8.2	5.2	D	11.5	6 945	182	340	15 641	2.4
Jackson	838	0.8	D	40.1	3.1	7.0	3.7	D	12.2	7 780	187	636	17 832	4.1
Jasper	431	3.2	27.8	15.1	10.3	9.8	4.3	D	15.0	5 450	175	246	12 067	7.4
Jay	263	-1.1	D	48.9	D	5.7	3.5	9.1	16.2	4 540	209	308	9 266	2.1
Jefferson	500	-0.7	D	32.8	D	7.7	2.9	D	16.9	6 250	194	711	13 871	3.6
Jennings	297	-0.1	D	25.8	D	6.0	2.5	5.5	24.6	4 945	176	467	12 309	7.3
Johnson	1 644	-0.1	28.2	18.6	7.3	11.8	8.5	8.2	14.7	17 885	145	730	49 525	9.8
Knox	633	0.4	18.9	9.5	4.6	8.2	4.6	11.6	30.1	8 250	213	1 058	17 392	0.5
Kosciusko	1 525	0.5	D	55.9	3.2	6.1	2.8	6.2	7.5	12 335	164	544	33 839	5.1
Lagrange	503	2.2	D	56.0	1.6	6.0	2.4	D	11.2	4 675	130	199	13 546	4.7
Lake	8 772	0.0	29.6	21.0	4.8	7.9	4.9	13.1	13.4	85 305	175	10 982	200 407	2.8
La Porte	1 853	0.2	32.3	24.6	4.1	7.5	3.8	12.5	16.4	19 650	179	1 673	46 699	2.4
Lawrence	638	-0.3	46.0	40.2	4.0	8.6	3.7	9.3	15.5	9 165	198	798	21 043	2.3
Madison	2 037	0.2	D	36.4	3.8	7.3	4.2	11.4	14.6	26 740	204	2 671	57 881	1.7
Marion	31 801	0.0	24.9	18.3	10.2	5.8	10.4	10.0	12.2	128 355	149	17 487	403 480	4.2
Marshall	698	0.6	D	39.8	3.7	6.8	5.6	6.9	12.4	7 845	169	366	18 752	3.6
Martin	437	-0.2	D	5.4	2.8	1.4	1.2	0.7	75.9	2 110	204	215	4 905	3.7
Miami	413	-0.4	34.8	28.1	1.9	7.4	4.0	3.6	32.6	5 800	160	530	15 646	2.3
Monroe	2 408	0.0	21.6	15.5	7.0	7.3	4.7	12.1	30.4	15 545	126	1 437	53 492	5.2
Montgomery	713	0.8	50.9	47.0	D	5.8	2.8	D	10.2	7 140	188	498	16 107	2.7
Morgan	561	-0.6	31.1	18.3	D	12.2	5.1	8.7	19.5	10 460	152	636	27 622	6.6
Newton	146	3.3	D	31.6	D	4.3	4.0	2.2	20.0	2 535	176	117	5 916	3.3
Noble	816	0.1	D	59.4	3.1	4.6	2.3	4.3	9.2	7 270	155	395	18 906	3.7
Ohio	73	-2.1	D	D	D	3.0	D	3.6	15.0	995	174	36	2 528	4.3
Orange	219	-1.0	44.6	26.0	D	7.2	2.8	8.8	15.5	4 140	211	433	8 651	3.6
Owen	171	-1.2	43.5	36.0	4.3	7.1	5.1	5.4	18.0	4 020	176	229	10 221	3.7
Parke	118	-1.8	D	16.8	2.7	8.5	4.8	D	35.0	3 445	199	318	7 707	2.2
Perry	240	-0.5	D	36.4	D	6.7	4.4	4.8	23.9	3 670	196	279	8 404	2.2
Pike	143	0.2	33.3	4.4	D	4.2	D	D	14.9	2 750	213	214	5 899	5.1
Porter	2 414	0.0	D	29.1	5.7	7.2	4.3	8.0	14.2	23 210	152	1 340	61 242	6.3
Posey	496	-0.2	57.9	48.6	5.1	4.3	2.4	D	10.1	4 610	172	303	11 398	2.9
Pulaski	199	5.2	D	37.5	2.0	7.1	3.8	D	18.6	2 790	202	192	6 139	3.7

1. Covers mining, construction, and manufacturing. 2. Per 1,000 resident population estimated as of July 1 of the year shown.

Table B. States and Counties — Housing, Labor Force, and Employment

STATE County	Housing units, 2000 Total	Occupied units Percent	Owner-occupied Median value[1]	Median owner cost as a percent of income With a mortgage	Without a mortgage[2]	Renter-occupied Median rent[3]	Median rent as a percent of income	Substandard units[4] (percent)	Civilian labor force, 2003 Total	Percent change, 2002-2003	Unemployment Total	Rate[5]	Civilian employment,[6] 2000 Total	Percent Management, professional and related occupations	Production, transportation, and material moving occupations
	89	90	91	92	93	94	95	96	97	98	99	100	101	102	103
INDIANA	2 336 306	71.4	94 300	19.3	9.9	521	23.9	2.7	3 187 734	0.6	163 367	5.1	2 965 174	28.7	21.4
Adams	11 818	77.0	85 400	18.1	9.9	393	18.8	7.2	15 857	-1.2	674	4.3	15 962	22.6	27.5
Allen	128 745	71.0	88 700	18.4	9.9	506	22.9	2.6	180 377	-0.6	9 846	5.5	167 203	31.9	19.4
Bartholomew	27 936	74.2	105 300	19.8	9.9	570	23.5	2.0	37 961	-0.4	1 558	4.1	35 744	31.6	24.8
Benton	3 558	75.8	75 000	19.7	11.7	488	19.9	2.4	4 940	1.3	266	5.4	4 655	25.0	24.2
Blackford	5 690	78.6	58 900	18.4	9.9	396	21.2	1.4	6 212	0.0	553	8.9	6 746	19.8	36.5
Boone	17 081	78.7	131 100	20.3	10.4	545	22.8	1.3	26 596	1.2	939	3.5	23 059	34.5	15.3
Brown	5 897	85.0	114 500	22.2	9.9	569	23.7	2.6	7 895	-0.4	372	4.7	7 445	28.4	18.2
Carroll	7 718	79.7	87 200	18.4	9.9	453	19.5	2.4	11 964	-0.1	628	5.2	10 087	23.3	29.7
Cass	15 715	73.6	71 500	17.1	9.9	440	20.0	2.9	19 674	-0.7	1 265	6.4	19 502	22.6	30.9
Clark	38 751	70.0	89 900	19.4	9.9	511	23.3	2.0	53 699	-0.8	2 212	4.1	49 327	26.0	21.0
Clay	10 216	79.1	72 600	19.0	10.6	419	22.3	1.6	12 764	1.8	709	5.6	12 112	22.9	27.6
Clinton	12 545	72.9	85 000	18.5	11.5	495	21.6	3.3	15 959	-1.4	816	5.1	15 359	18.6	33.6
Crawford	4 181	82.9	64 600	20.0	10.7	390	23.0	3.9	5 859	0.0	375	6.4	4 664	18.2	28.7
Daviess	10 894	78.6	70 800	18.1	9.9	363	22.3	4.1	13 842	-0.2	516	3.7	13 305	25.4	24.1
Dearborn	16 832	78.6	120 600	19.9	9.9	504	23.6	1.6	23 813	0.8	1 149	4.8	23 083	26.2	20.6
Decatur	9 389	73.2	86 400	19.3	9.9	490	19.9	2.7	15 470	-7.7	539	3.5	12 592	21.7	33.4
De Kalb	15 134	81.5	88 000	19.2	9.9	480	22.3	2.1	21 690	-0.3	1 371	6.3	20 628	21.5	35.9
Delaware	47 131	67.2	75 400	18.5	9.9	465	27.2	1.5	60 050	-0.5	3 470	5.8	55 773	30.1	17.6
Dubois	14 813	78.0	92 700	18.3	9.9	440	19.8	2.0	22 797	-0.2	726	3.2	20 885	24.3	29.8
Elkhart	66 154	72.2	98 100	18.7	9.9	541	22.0	4.1	98 759	2.4	4 612	4.7	93 074	23.8	32.7
Fayette	10 199	71.6	78 500	17.9	9.9	442	20.9	2.3	37 950	-0.6	1 404	3.7	35 899	29.8	19.1
Floyd	27 511	72.5	104 300	19.7	9.9	517	24.3	1.6	8 283	-0.9	465	5.6	8 197	20.7	34.2
Fountain	7 041	77.9	69 200	18.2	9.9	439	20.7	2.3	12 605	7.2	645	5.1	10 672	23.9	27.9
Franklin	7 868	81.4	100 100	20.0	9.9	407	19.2	3.1	9 355	0.0	665	7.1	10 066	20.8	34.0
Fulton	8 082	78.3	77 000	18.3	10.0	456	21.7	2.6	21 841	13.2	716	3.3	15 826	21.4	26.9
Gibson	12 847	77.9	74 700	18.6	10.0	427	22.0	2.2	32 172	-6.6	2 627	8.2	33 119	24.9	26.7
Grant	28 319	73.2	68 500	18.2	9.9	428	22.5	2.0	13 525	-2.5	1 121	8.3	15 219	25.0	21.5
Greene	13 372	80.0	66 800	18.2	10.1	375	25.1	2.6	116 591	1.0	3 101	2.7	95 694	49.1	7.4
Hamilton	65 933	80.9	166 300	19.8	9.9	709	22.7	1.3	31 957	1.1	1 244	3.9	28 881	32.4	15.1
Hancock	20 718	81.4	129 700	19.7	9.9	571	22.4	0.7	18 594	0.0	780	4.2	17 600	25.3	24.4
Harrison	12 917	84.1	95 700	19.2	9.9	475	20.7	2.5	63 034	1.5	2 450	3.9	54 349	32.8	14.7
Hendricks	37 275	82.9	133 300	19.7	9.9	644	22.0	1.2	23 732	1.1	1 308	5.5	22 135	23.5	25.3
Henry	19 486	77.1	84 100	18.0	9.9	464	23.9	1.5	42 183	0.8	2 846	6.7	39 421	26.6	27.2
Howard	34 800	71.7	89 000	17.5	9.9	509	23.9	1.8	20 124	-1.1	1 140	5.7	19 688	22.9	30.0
Huntington	14 242	77.0	81 600	18.5	9.9	488	21.7	1.4	22 579	0.7	988	4.4	20 385	22.1	32.7
Jackson	16 052	74.2	87 500	18.6	9.9	495	22.2	2.6	14 834	2.7	854	5.8	13 901	25.5	23.5
Jasper	10 686	77.5	105 700	19.1	9.9	486	20.4	2.4	10 421	0.2	870	8.3	10 419	18.2	36.7
Jay	8 405	77.8	62 500	18.1	10.1	387	20.0	3.4	14 289	3.2	699	4.9	15 327	25.8	25.1
Jefferson	12 148	74.6	85 800	19.0	9.9	419	21.0	2.5	14 044	-0.6	858	6.1	13 244	21.0	31.9
Jennings	10 134	79.1	81 900	19.4	9.9	490	20.7	3.5	67 706	1.1	2 486	3.7	60 047	33.9	16.4
Johnson	42 434	76.5	122 500	19.9	9.9	599	23.5	1.5	19 441	3.0	686	3.5	18 256	27.2	16.7
Knox	15 552	68.9	63 600	18.2	9.9	403	25.8	1.9	39 420	0.0	1 727	4.4	37 387	23.1	33.1
Kosciusko	27 283	78.9	95 500	18.9	9.9	502	21.0	3.2	16 614	-0.3	773	4.7	15 966	18.5	38.5
Lagrange	11 225	81.4	99 800	20.1	9.9	477	20.4	5.8	228 057	0.5	13 716	6.0	213 404	26.1	19.1
Lake	181 633	69.0	97 500	19.9	10.9	544	24.8	4.6	54 146	-1.6	3 725	6.9	51 097	24.5	23.4
La Porte	41 050	75.2	93 500	19.8	9.9	495	23.6	2.6	22 011	-1.5	1 664	7.6	21 666	21.9	29.9
Lawrence	18 535	78.9	75 400	18.8	9.9	447	22.6	2.2	65 856	1.0	3 971	6.0	60 207	25.2	22.3
Madison	53 052	74.2	81 600	18.9	9.9	490	24.5	1.8	476 091	1.0	25 555	5.4	432 302	32.9	15.1
Marion	352 164	59.3	99 000	20.2	9.9	567	24.5	3.5	23 031	-0.2	1 246	5.4	22 087	22.5	31.4
Marshall	16 519	76.8	88 100	19.1	9.9	500	21.5	3.6	5 050	-0.3	261	5.2	4 793	26.2	28.0
Martin	4 183	81.3	64 200	18.9	9.9	356	20.5	3.0	16 093	-2.0	1 421	8.8	16 617	21.2	29.4
Miami	13 716	76.0	71 100	17.3	9.9	452	20.1	2.2	66 289	4.6	2 013	3.0	61 988	39.4	10.7
Monroe	46 898	53.9	113 100	19.5	9.9	560	33.6	2.3	17 868	2.5	712	4.0	18 490	23.7	30.0
Montgomery	14 595	73.3	88 800	18.9	9.9	477	22.0	2.2	36 208	1.0	1 751	4.8	33 764	23.4	21.5
Morgan	24 437	79.7	116 200	19.7	10.2	531	22.8	2.5	6 256	-0.6	388	6.2	6 936	19.2	28.5
Newton	5 340	80.0	87 500	20.7	11.9	472	23.4	2.7	24 240	0.5	1 638	6.8	23 021	19.7	39.9
Noble	16 696	78.0	88 600	19.0	9.9	470	20.6	3.7	2 870	1.7	126	4.4	2 817	23.9	22.8
Ohio	2 201	77.6	97 100	19.4	10.1	463	24.1	1.0	8 142	-1.2	777	9.5	8 764	20.6	31.7
Orange	7 621	79.2	63 500	19.8	9.9	385	22.5	3.3	11 512	-0.4	669	5.8	10 354	19.7	28.4
Owen	8 282	81.6	84 600	20.7	9.9	455	20.6	4.0	7 457	0.7	427	5.7	7 432	24.4	25.5
Parke	6 415	80.3	64 900	17.5	9.9	381	21.2	3.1	9 303	1.3	486	5.2	8 741	18.4	33.7
Perry	7 270	79.2	71 200	17.6	9.9	370	22.8	2.0	6 264	0.3	343	5.5	5 918	19.9	29.9
Pike	5 119	82.7	59 300	18.1	9.9	339	19.1	2.1	77 821	1.2	3 812	4.9	73 823	30.5	17.3
Porter	54 649	76.6	127 000	19.6	9.9	625	23.2	2.1	14 699	0.1	536	3.6	13 149	29.9	21.2
Posey	10 205	81.9	89 800	18.3	9.9	419	23.8	2.1	5 791	-0.8	394	6.8	6 249	23.3	29.1
Pulaski	5 170	80.7	72 500	19.0	9.9	397	19.1	3.1							

1. Specified owner-occupied units.   2. Median monthly owner costs is often in the minimum category—9.9 percent or less, which is indicated as 9.9 percent.   3. Specified renter-occupied units.   4. Overcrowded or lacking complete plumbing facilities.   5. Percent of civilian labor force.   6. Persons 16 years old and over.

Table B. States and Counties — Nonfarm Employment and Agriculture

STATE County	Number of establishments	Total	Health care and social assistance	Manufacturing	Retail trade	Finance and insurance	Professional, scientific, and technical services	Total (mil dol)	Average per employee (dollars)	Number	Less than 50 acres	500 acres and over	Farm operators whose principal occupation is farming (percent)
	104	105	106	107	108	109	110	111	112	113	114	115	116
INDIANA	145 580	2 601 738	327 896	604 255	351 024	106 107	91 045	79 317	30 486	60 296	39.9	13.8	55.7
Adams	784	13 017	1 377	5 703	1 900	326	136	327	25 128	1 296	48.4	9.4	54.8
Allen	8 984	172 197	22 089	33 058	21 906	10 125	7 239	5 363	31 144	1 550	46.5	9.1	55.8
Bartholomew	1 914	37 892	3 964	13 199	4 373	1 157	877	1 300	34 300	608	42.3	15.1	56.7
Benton	250	2 027	227	587	454	114	D	42	20 778	394	16.8	42.9	71.1
Blackford	287	3 666	382	1 782	459	135	36	89	24 393	279	34.8	21.1	57.0
Boone	1 294	12 809	1 843	2 191	1 788	238	514	323	25 234	672	48.7	20.2	58.2
Brown	363	2 155	181	230	390	30	110	40	18 445	222	53.2	2.3	53.2
Carroll	413	4 580	240	2 181	662	141	97	105	22 940	529	31.0	23.6	65.2
Cass	842	16 074	2 755	6 840	2 098	320	228	391	24 345	717	36.8	18.7	58.0
Clark	2 483	42 154	4 444	7 182	7 471	772	917	1 117	26 502	638	41.2	7.8	54.4
Clay	527	5 637	638	1 608	1 180	183	163	120	21 212	555	40.5	16.2	51.9
Clinton	656	9 584	1 345	4 053	1 127	262	136	235	24 506	604	36.9	27.8	63.6
Crawford	149	1 150	141	D	312	63	13	20	17 747	427	26.7	2.8	50.8
Daviess	737	8 613	1 281	1 956	1 472	236	114	177	20 532	1 138	45.8	7.7	57.1
Dearborn	963	13 561	1 682	2 284	2 159	420	243	355	26 170	676	32.4	2.7	46.4
Decatur	616	12 562	1 055	5 759	1 661	193	1 210	328	26 135	676	29.3	18.3	64.9
De Kalb	1 005	21 009	1 404	12 294	1 677	317	454	657	31 272	1 000	41.0	8.8	49.3
Delaware	2 649	48 787	7 993	8 718	6 956	1 615	2 012	1 324	27 143	687	48.5	13.5	60.0
Dubois	1 259	28 913	2 685	13 042	3 457	584	432	794	27 455	758	24.9	12.9	57.7
Elkhart	5 031	109 759	8 461	55 051	10 745	1 747	1 780	3 219	29 330	1 516	52.8	5.9	55.5
Fayette	533	9 534	1 442	4 484	1 153	213	152	298	31 265	424	36.1	14.9	53.5
Floyd	1 723	26 827	3 862	7 176	3 173	749	1 358	723	26 937	299	56.5	2.7	53.8
Fountain	396	4 967	468	2 440	701	184	90	122	24 476	487	27.7	24.4	66.3
Franklin	343	4 077	506	865	473	173	64	92	22 563	817	31.6	7.1	50.8
Fulton	480	6 202	615	2 613	914	183	102	154	24 900	616	36.0	18.7	59.9
Gibson	736	12 060	1 101	4 462	1 603	189	224	393	32 620	557	32.1	22.6	64.5
Grant	1 507	29 987	4 832	8 192	3 671	686	460	789	26 308	598	36.3	22.6	59.0
Greene	623	5 798	1 234	558	1 374	245	402	106	18 245	822	34.5	8.4	48.9
Hamilton	5 503	80 950	7 878	5 816	11 105	11 742	5 261	2 936	36 263	726	57.4	10.2	56.2
Hancock	1 281	14 432	1 971	2 832	1 943	329	407	498	34 477	616	51.4	14.6	57.0
Harrison	660	9 236	1 182	3 235	1 521	289	204	209	22 659	1 176	37.8	4.6	51.3
Hendricks	2 192	28 315	3 499	2 057	6 160	597	967	771	27 238	703	54.9	12.9	48.5
Henry	936	12 186	2 182	3 278	2 259	413	256	362	29 699	745	46.6	13.7	60.1
Howard	1 966	41 872	4 994	16 021	6 180	1 059	555	1 699	40 587	536	39.2	18.7	66.2
Huntington	863	15 332	1 639	5 884	1 874	259	358	375	24 469	675	38.8	19.0	54.1
Jackson	1 072	19 108	2 189	6 980	2 510	493	309	508	26 597	806	36.7	16.6	61.4
Jasper	780	10 689	1 004	1 519	1 492	235	264	275	25 710	641	35.4	30.9	64.6
Jay	436	6 860	1 042	3 055	629	168	142	163	23 784	857	39.8	11.8	53.0
Jefferson	733	11 834	2 073	3 587	1 941	283	173	307	25 924	778	42.4	5.0	47.3
Jennings	440	6 984	582	2 578	870	149	65	159	22 748	669	45.3	10.0	52.2
Johnson	2 630	39 781	4 989	7 503	8 852	1 112	1 011	1 000	25 150	598	53.3	14.0	53.7
Knox	1 023	13 842	3 309	1 374	2 413	445	256	323	23 351	508	26.1	31.3	69.1
Kosciusko	1 870	31 885	2 565	15 709	3 458	757	488	998	31 291	1 203	42.3	11.6	51.1
Lagrange	702	10 577	715	5 464	1 232	244	151	288	27 193	1 551	41.6	4.4	62.0
Lake	9 952	177 320	26 715	33 669	25 708	5 361	6 112	5 428	30 609	482	51.7	15.8	54.6
La Porte	2 625	39 545	4 989	9 587	6 450	773	1 030	1 086	27 467	817	41.2	17.6	57.0
Lawrence	948	13 490	1 970	4 426	2 246	374	295	380	28 145	825	35.2	7.4	45.9
Madison	2 719	42 861	5 985	9 741	6 965	1 443	892	1 192	27 811	807	45.2	19.1	59.0
Marion	24 021	564 810	73 208	65 610	62 325	34 147	30 779	20 992	37 166	303	74.6	3.3	44.2
Marshall	1 117	17 313	1 746	7 138	2 180	343	274	438	25 273	842	35.7	13.4	55.5
Martin	248	2 211	D	591	383	99	189	55	24 692	350	32.0	6.6	50.0
Miami	684	7 974	1 029	2 739	1 161	279	119	185	23 187	685	36.4	16.9	59.4
Monroe	2 928	46 678	7 338	7 959	7 281	1 179	1 942	1 160	24 849	547	41.7	3.5	47.9
Montgomery	915	14 893	1 557	6 183	1 837	360	410	437	29 361	644	37.6	24.8	63.0
Morgan	1 302	13 972	2 042	2 667	2 704	471	249	331	23 661	690	57.1	7.5	45.9
Newton	292	3 052	147	1 355	424	103	46	72	23 608	344	28.2	36.3	66.0
Noble	921	18 647	1 227	11 358	1 704	272	212	515	27 626	1 029	39.7	8.6	49.6
Ohio	75	1 586	70	D	129	D	D	39	24 393	213	41.8	2.3	46.0
Orange	389	6 467	1 047	1 803	829	146	82	149	22 969	535	26.4	7.9	50.5
Owen	314	3 654	389	1 407	498	139	73	83	22 587	588	34.0	6.1	41.3
Parke	308	2 560	562	620	438	94	47	51	20 057	470	33.2	17.7	50.4
Perry	389	4 710	721	1 580	864	168	74	115	24 492	470	24.3	6.0	53.0
Pike	195	2 144	297	184	254	102	30	77	36 070	288	30.2	14.2	54.9
Porter	3 293	48 330	5 423	10 737	6 726	1 030	1 513	1 503	31 092	606	49.5	16.0	53.8
Posey	524	7 181	544	2 576	896	109	270	281	39 196	396	29.3	29.3	64.6
Pulaski	350	3 507	563	1 096	547	140	65	91	25 981	524	33.4	24.2	64.3

STATE County	Acreage (1,000) [117]	Percent change, 1997-2002 [118]	Average size of farm [119]	Total irrigated (1,000) [120]	Total cropland (1,000) [121]	Average per farm [122]	Average per acre [123]	Value of machinery and equipment average per farm (dollars) [124]	Total (mil dol) [125]	Average per farm (dollars) [126]	Crops [127]	Live-stock and poultry products [128]	$10,000 or more [129]	$100,000 or more [130]	Total ($1,000) [131]	Percent of farms [132]
INDIANA	15 059	-0.3	250	313	12 909	637 645	2 567	80 240	4 783	79 328	62.6	37.4	46.0	17.2	224 701	44.5
Adams	229	9.6	177	0	209	533 632	2 880	77 073	99	76 090	39.3	60.7	55.5	17.0	3 498	39.3
Allen	284	2.9	183	1	257	578 090	3 349	69 002	75	48 167	75.0	25.0	46.6	12.5	4 128	45.4
Bartholomew	161	-3.6	264	9	143	765 489	2 958	86 508	42	69 689	83.0	17.0	50.2	17.1	2 365	49.5
Benton	248	-3.5	629	D	237	1 536 791	2 494	155 254	70	176 604	96.5	3.5	80.5	51.3	3 236	75.6
Blackford	97	12.8	348	D	88	748 414	2 200	110 396	26	92 839	78.1	21.9	52.0	21.5	1 508	62.4
Boone	226	-0.9	336	0	213	1 038 939	3 194	107 950	75	111 260	85.6	14.4	50.7	25.1	3 819	40.2
Brown	20	-9.1	92	0	10	232 521	2 766	21 071	2	8 775	65.2	34.8	14.0	0.9	89	19.8
Carroll	202	-7.3	381	D	185	1 012 034	2 733	130 376	95	179 992	54.0	46.0	66.5	35.3	3 355	52.4
Cass	208	1.5	291	2	187	680 158	2 389	120 044	72	100 875	68.5	31.5	54.5	22.2	3 439	55.5
Clark	101	-7.3	158	0	72	407 383	3 276	61 790	22	34 481	73.8	26.2	32.1	8.8	896	32.9
Clay	152	-4.4	273	0	126	511 180	2 026	66 464	32	58 422	82.3	17.7	45.2	17.5	2 266	50.6
Clinton	245	3.8	405	0	231	1 091 042	2 728	143 909	105	174 402	64.6	35.4	63.6	36.6	3 971	56.3
Crawford	55	-9.8	129	0	26	235 106	1 825	25 972	4	8 421	36.8	63.2	16.4	1.6	276	31.1
Daviess	207	-4.6	182	2	179	386 494	2 025	60 812	104	91 186	31.2	68.8	48.2	19.2	2 878	24.3
Dearborn	74	-8.6	110	0	41	349 286	3 242	26 496	7	10 193	64.0	36.0	19.1	2.4	268	24.3
Decatur	207	4.0	306	0	181	845 999	2 641	112 891	87	128 631	54.7	45.3	62.6	25.6	4 026	58.3
De Kalb	179	9.8	179	1	153	428 844	2 203	61 446	42	42 338	58.2	41.8	32.9	9.4	3 597	67.3
Delaware	190	9.8	276	D	177	684 845	2 540	101 639	50	73 048	86.9	13.1	47.6	15.7	2 239	45.6
Dubois	189	-1.0	249	0	141	551 884	2 316	79 787	105	138 863	19.2	80.8	54.4	24.1	2 621	51.2
Elkhart	201	9.8	133	23	176	493 262	3 803	63 874	136	89 718	30.6	69.4	58.0	24.7	3 441	23.7
Fayette	107	0.0	252	D	85	541 283	2 292	65 032	20	46 572	76.1	23.9	46.2	13.9	1 524	52.6
Floyd	24	-17.2	80	0	16	472 906	3 666	61 692	4	11 717	69.2	30.8	20.4	3.3	145	24.7
Fountain	205	0.0	422	0	182	899 507	2 217	101 065	52	107 464	89.8	10.2	54.6	26.3	2 957	52.0
Franklin	139	0.0	171	0	93	434 649	2 491	51 222	25	30 464	56.9	43.1	37.2	8.9	1 807	42.6
Fulton	193	12.9	313	16	174	700 249	2 045	73 411	53	85 395	73.6	26.4	57.0	22.9	3 392	52.9
Gibson	211	-9.4	379	1	191	856 391	2 280	123 734	54	97 826	81.3	18.7	56.4	26.9	2 837	54.4
Grant	198	3.1	332	0	185	837 813	2 532	116 411	54	90 006	81.5	18.5	57.0	25.4	3 595	50.5
Greene	171	-17.0	207	2	118	376 084	2 000	44 008	41	50 027	41.6	58.4	30.4	7.5	1 334	30.5
Hamilton	140	-0.7	193	1	128	725 243	4 062	55 946	56	76 616	91.8	8.2	44.1	13.4	1 871	32.4
Hancock	162	-1.2	262	0	152	874 580	3 220	88 199	44	71 689	82.1	17.9	48.2	17.2	2 584	36.9
Harrison	160	-0.6	136	0	108	389 487	2 568	47 425	42	36 080	31.1	68.9	25.7	4.2	1 397	31.3
Hendricks	182	9.0	259	D	166	883 031	3 403	83 090	52	74 329	86.4	13.6	41.7	15.9	3 027	28.7
Henry	173	-2.8	232	0	157	648 457	2 738	84 478	47	63 601	74.1	25.9	47.0	15.8	2 550	45.0
Howard	156	5.4	291	0	147	771 459	3 064	99 463	57	105 958	68.7	31.3	61.6	25.6	2 829	50.7
Huntington	200	8.7	296	0	183	669 968	2 492	96 831	63	93 605	66.7	33.3	52.0	20.6	3 173	59.3
Jackson	207	3.0	257	2	162	670 131	2 443	104 564	80	99 783	39.4	60.6	47.1	16.6	2 932	50.7
Jasper	280	-1.1	437	21	260	1 127 911	2 436	125 049	133	207 341	54.2	45.9	65.7	37.4	4 757	55.2
Jay	195	8.3	228	0	173	611 526	2 552	104 828	94	109 740	29.1	70.9	46.0	17.9	2 937	52.5
Jefferson	109	-13.5	140	D	70	301 335	2 397	29 935	16	20 226	75.8	24.2	27.5	4.9	932	30.7
Jennings	143	10.0	213	D	109	482 737	2 179	90 554	41	61 019	50.3	49.7	31.1	9.9	1 561	39.5
Johnson	135	-0.7	226	1	121	883 541	3 776	71 110	49	82 672	69.3	30.7	40.5	15.9	1 863	31.8
Knox	300	6.8	591	25	273	1 211 208	2 156	160 277	86	169 764	84.1	15.9	73.2	36.6	3 530	55.9
Kosciusko	262	6.1	218	19	225	584 537	2 720	68 504	122	101 634	39.8	60.2	46.1	18.0	4 372	47.1
Lagrange	189	-0.5	122	22	153	460 784	3 544	46 138	107	69 090	38.3	61.7	62.3	13.1	1 987	15.0
Lake	128	-14.1	265	7	117	839 628	3 392	111 948	39	80 796	92.6	7.4	44.8	18.0	1 800	41.1
La Porte	243	-2.0	298	32	222	787 647	2 653	100 522	79	97 139	70.2	29.8	48.3	21.1	4 367	48.7
Lawrence	147	-14.0	179	D	87	273 654	1 575	32 396	15	17 613	43.3	56.7	27.8	3.4	1 557	37.9
Madison	244	8.9	302	1	229	834 889	2 816	95 767	75	93 311	90.1	9.9	49.4	20.4	3 535	45.2
Marion	24	-17.2	78	1	20	485 528	4 413	66 003	33	110 348	D	D	30.4	11.9	277	16.2
Marshall	204	1.0	243	9	179	514 579	2 357	68 526	63	74 790	63.3	36.7	54.2	19.6	3 093	46.2
Martin	64	-8.6	181	D	42	404 330	1 938	59 970	28	79 016	16.5	83.5	40.6	15.1	883	32.6
Miami	191	-3.0	279	1	172	698 287	2 406	90 346	59	85 699	60.9	39.1	51.4	21.2	3 409	53.3
Monroe	61	-1.6	111	0	34	268 058	2 444	37 452	7	12 591	49.9	50.1	21.9	2.7	233	24.1
Montgomery	273	0.0	425	1	246	1 024 846	2 424	146 320	94	146 592	74.0	26.0	56.7	28.4	5 146	51.6
Morgan	112	-16.4	162	D	89	588 920	3 161	55 085	25	36 679	77.9	22.1	25.9	7.8	1 506	26.8
Newton	182	-12.1	528	4	169	1 275 863	2 392	131 928	119	346 619	39.9	60.1	68.3	40.7	2 941	67.2
Noble	173	-4.9	168	6	146	536 478	2 742	60 168	51	49 214	48.6	51.4	41.6	11.6	3 075	52.3
Ohio	24	-20.0	112	1	14	274 165	3 262	27 369	2	11 044	82.2	17.8	26.7	1.9	89	23.5
Orange	106	-13.8	198	D	66	374 551	1 901	46 280	18	34 401	44.2	55.8	26.7	4.9	1 361	50.7
Owen	99	-7.5	168	0	62	350 320	2 031	42 408	13	22 132	72.7	27.3	26.7	4.4	1 166	34.9
Parke	165	-12.7	351	1	123	734 636	2 051	77 449	33	70 468	80.3	19.7	48.7	18.1	2 171	43.4
Perry	76	-9.5	162	D	39	265 093	1 809	43 476	9	18 580	30.4	69.6	24.5	4.3	499	35.3
Pike	76	-9.5	263	0	63	500 431	2 051	74 204	15	53 301	70.5	29.5	41.0	14.9	1 041	50.3
Porter	146	8.1	241	8	133	764 999	3 150	79 740	37	61 579	83.7	16.3	45.7	18.5	2 064	42.2
Posey	192	-1.5	485	7	174	1 136 934	2 237	144 743	50	127 373	84.5	15.5	63.6	32.3	2 773	53.0
Pulaski	223	-5.5	425	19	206	980 877	2 321	145 202	81	155 352	61.9	38.1	58.0	27.9	3 826	66.8

Table B. States and Counties — Residential Construction, Wholesale Trade, Retail Trade, and Real Estate

STATE County	Value of residential construction authorized by building permits, 2003 New construction ($1,000)	Number of housing units	Wholesale trade, 1997 Number of establishments	Number of employees	Sales (mil dol)	Annual payroll (mil dol)	Retail trade,[1] 1997 Number of establishments	Number of employees	Sales (mil dol)	Annual payroll (mil dol)	Real estate and rental and leasing, 1997 Number of establishments	Number of employees	Receipts (mil dol)	Annual payroll (mil dol)
	133	134	135	136	137	138	139	140	141	142	143	144	145	146
INDIANA	5 392 722	39 421	8 896	112 705	66 350.1	3 737.8	24 954	337 867	57 241.6	5 273.8	5 427	28 948	3 269.1	572.6
Adams	9 216	98	43	314	151.3	7.5	172	1 824	344.6	27.9	14	54	5.3	0.9
Allen	357 800	2 312	686	10 861	6 586.2	357.8	1 320	21 917	3 534.6	351.1	336	1 988	254.8	43.2
Bartholomew	43 725	283	114	910	714.3	29.8	397	4 658	680.6	66.1	68	268	37.2	5.8
Benton	1 775	15	27	181	109.0	4.3	59	413	70.0	7.0	6	D	D	D
Blackford	4 015	47	15	110	20.8	2.9	56	515	82.9	6.8	14	29	2.5	0.4
Boone	94 997	490	94	629	500.9	18.8	173	1 632	261.0	25.3	33	135	11.2	2.0
Brown	8 519	144	9	D	D	D	102	432	42.1	5.3	9	34	2.8	0.6
Carroll	10 398	128	33	224	145.8	6.4	61	574	90.9	8.8	17	47	2.7	0.5
Cass	6 857	53	49	453	220.0	13.7	169	2 046	339.1	31.5	22	76	4.4	0.9
Clark	99 729	909	128	1 486	686.5	37.8	471	7 887	1 261.0	114.9	98	477	59.4	8.2
Clay	2 138	19	18	D	D	D	105	1 076	190.1	16.1	16	42	4.5	0.5
Clinton	10 216	72	47	D	D	D	126	1 200	193.5	18.8	23	70	5.8	1.1
Crawford	167	2	4	D	D	D	36	322	36.3	4.0	6	8	1.1	0.3
Daviess	2 809	17	22	233	76.6	6.0	145	1 490	260.5	21.4	15	60	4.3	0.7
Dearborn	55 281	374	37	D	D	D	158	1 896	344.3	29.0	37	D	D	D
Decatur	13 897	127	36	423	231.2	10.4	128	1 414	230.9	20.2	19	46	4.6	0.8
De Kalb	34 007	252	49	413	254.5	15.6	152	1 667	291.8	25.1	27	112	10.4	2.3
Delaware	130 660	563	119	1 501	653.4	45.8	548	7 340	1 118.7	105.4	119	433	46.9	8.4
Dubois	33 593	225	72	1 417	781.8	52.1	231	2 951	551.7	50.7	36	184	9.8	2.2
Elkhart	145 593	1 175	382	5 031	2 246.1	160.0	751	10 866	1 973.6	179.6	171	884	78.1	13.9
Fayette	4 223	59	19	227	69.5	6.2	94	1 202	193.4	16.8	24	83	4.9	1.0
Floyd	84 902	476	97	1 076	298.0	30.1	231	2 366	331.0	36.8	54	233	20.7	3.7
Fountain	694	10	22	D	D	D	75	675	120.4	8.9	9	30	1.0	0.2
Franklin	15 530	102	14	81	28.1	2.1	63	443	66.5	6.5	7	23	1.5	0.4
Fulton	2 760	24	35	175	70.0	4.0	91	936	143.8	11.6	15	39	2.5	0.9
Gibson	5 564	46	38	D	D	D	148	1 694	252.0	21.9	12	33	3.3	0.4
Grant	22 457	186	72	770	200.2	20.4	318	3 864	629.5	54.8	56	284	24.9	4.9
Greene	0	0	30	145	89.2	3.1	135	1 252	178.5	16.7	19	66	2.4	0.4
Hamilton	770 080	4 588	508	5 552	5 171.0	223.2	574	9 896	1 786.5	176.8	168	1 267	172.7	29.9
Hancock	134 545	997	62	665	258.7	17.9	149	1 639	341.4	25.4	39	121	12.5	2.1
Harrison	27 221	186	27	264	70.9	6.0	133	1 540	234.9	20.6	24	54	5.8	0.8
Hendricks	345 720	2 692	100	725	263.9	23.2	289	4 363	756.5	65.5	72	348	27.7	4.6
Henry	13 449	94	46	498	197.3	13.8	189	2 107	426.6	33.4	24	63	6.9	0.9
Howard	53 594	353	110	D	D	D	409	6 078	959.6	89.1	84	306	38.5	5.4
Huntington	23 519	166	54	485	265.1	12.9	169	1 943	312.8	28.1	28	86	7.2	1.3
Jackson	20 026	182	46	553	206.0	14.7	242	2 444	389.5	36.6	41	115	9.9	1.8
Jasper	27 180	258	43	299	283.7	8.6	149	1 718	278.5	24.7	20	113	29.2	2.6
Jay	4 336	44	21	231	122.7	5.2	82	707	115.0	17.0	20	99	3.4	0.6
Jefferson	12 708	125	27	226	40.3	4.8	167	1 766	281.2	24.5	24	76	7.8	1.1
Jennings	11 544	139	16	115	39.9	2.7	72	764	136.0	12.1	18	37	3.4	0.4
Johnson	186 067	1 335	113	788	659.9	26.6	490	7 338	1 171.2	109.2	99	362	42.1	6.1
Knox	4 715	39	68	842	373.7	19.3	234	2 668	399.9	36.7	28	120	10.9	1.7
Kosciusko	72 283	586	105	737	372.3	22.4	333	3 460	551.9	55.3	64	169	18.0	2.7
Lagrange	14 460	177	31	479	132.4	9.6	145	1 184	203.9	17.6	16	44	3.0	0.6
Lake	411 021	3 008	547	7 094	3 876.3	249.7	1 736	25 503	4 380.6	398.6	403	2 001	240.6	44.1
La Porte	50 610	417	135	1 525	658.5	44.6	552	6 312	1 041.7	95.7	95	313	31.0	4.9
Lawrence	3 260	43	26	228	54.7	5.3	207	2 108	372.1	31.6	24	179	22.3	4.2
Madison	71 940	581	105	1 157	428.6	31.3	521	6 790	1 123.4	101.3	112	439	35.0	7.0
Marion	652 943	4 978	1 953	32 619	21 284.8	1 245.4	3 654	59 830	10 757.4	1 038.3	1 106	9 086	1 137.7	212.1
Marshall	23 049	179	71	696	265.5	18.4	202	2 103	367.9	31.2	38	149	15.8	3.4
Martin	340	3	6	D	D	D	52	385	58.6	4.7	7	D	D	D
Miami	12 800	161	41	564	270.9	16.4	121	1 068	205.0	17.9	24	52	3.6	0.5
Monroe	130 921	1 173	102	D	D	D	514	6 846	1 073.7	97.5	162	869	83.1	15.3
Montgomery	21 744	177	56	271	176.4	8.9	167	1 947	293.8	27.2	30	97	8.8	1.2
Morgan	51 833	346	56	303	150.5	8.8	207	2 372	432.9	35.7	52	185	16.9	2.8
Newton	4 978	51	24	131	82.4	4.1	53	418	70.6	5.7	6	12	2.3	0.3
Noble	28 051	248	39	392	208.3	13.0	157	1 642	258.3	23.5	23	73	4.0	0.7
Ohio	6 000	63	NA	NA	NA	NA	12	108	13.7	1.4	2	D	D	D
Orange	131	1	19	109	33.4	2.0	89	574	103.2	9.0	6	47	2.9	0.5
Owen	220	3	15	60	13.0	1.4	59	510	71.3	6.1	8	D	D	D
Parke	3 514	39	12	67	21.0	1.1	50	367	48.8	4.8	8	33	3.2	0.6
Perry	5 094	40	15	178	77.3	5.8	85	974	131.2	11.7	16	35	4.3	0.5
Pike	2 988	30	12	113	37.1	3.2	38	266	41.1	3.1	1	D	D	D
Porter	174 363	1 090	174	1 823	941.7	56.1	436	6 231	1 040.3	98.6	133	593	74.4	10.2
Posey	14 457	94	30	D	D	D	95	906	151.5	13.9	8	27	1.5	0.2
Pulaski	8 227	62	36	356	167.3	9.7	58	419	73.9	6.9	15	36	1.5	0.3

1. Establishments with payroll.

STATE County	Professional, scientific, and technical services,¹ 1997				Manufacturing, 1997				Accommodation and foodservices, 1997			
	Number of establish-ments	Number of employees	Receipts (mil dol)	Annual payroll (mil dol)	Number of establish-ments	Number of employees	Receipts (mil dol)	Annual payroll (mil dol)	Number of establish-ments	Number of employees	Sales (mil dol)	Annual payroll (mil dol)
	147	148	149	150	151	152	153	154	155	156	157	158
INDIANA	9 795	69 393	5 974.2	2 207.5	9 303	625 692	142 270.7	22 121.4	11 705	215 710	6 646.3	1 865.3
Adams	39	115	6.7	2.1	67	6 536	1 428.9	189.6	61	1 103	27.4	7.9
Allen	658	5 508	463.9	162.4	576	36 585	9 182.2	1 362.0	626	13 472	414.0	122.2
Bartholomew	152	777	58.5	24.7	145	13 311	3 096.7	412.1	135	3 114	102.4	28.4
Benton	14	37	1.6	0.6	16	562	58.8	12.6	19	D	D	D
Blackford	14	32	2.0	0.5	28	2 081	299.2	58.6	21	D	D	D
Boone	76	245	26.4	7.7	73	1 769	190.9	48.5	85	1 303	37.5	11.0
Brown	36	107	5.8	2.5	NA	NA	NA	NA	46	623	18.4	6.1
Carroll	21	73	3.9	1.1	33	2 191	500.8	50.3	26	339	9.8	3.0
Cass	35	141	10.8	3.2	60	6 129	994.3	157.9	88	1 125	30.7	9.0
Clark	138	563	43.5	12.8	163	D	D	D	192	3 876	121.7	34.8
Clay	24	105	4.0	1.7	34	D	D	D	50	516	13.7	3.8
Clinton	35	104	6.0	1.6	49	4 959	1 565.1	148.1	63	753	19.4	5.2
Crawford	8	13	0.7	0.2	NA	NA	NA	NA	18	D	D	D
Daviess	30	127	6.1	1.8	51	1 947	350.0	37.4	59	899	20.4	5.6
Dearborn	46	149	8.8	2.9	39	D	D	D	79	1 068	31.7	8.6
Decatur	26	486	11.8	7.9	52	4 926	847.9	155.6	47	765	19.6	5.7
De Kalb	52	255	12.2	4.0	119	11 000	2 040.2	364.3	78	1 008	34.0	8.8
Delaware	153	1 691	87.8	37.3	176	9 972	1 764.5	402.6	228	4 981	126.7	35.6
Dubois	61	236	16.1	6.1	114	12 450	1 637.0	327.9	91	1 480	39.4	11.5
Elkhart	246	1 465	111.6	36.0	894	56 087	8 999.9	1 610.8	354	6 202	189.4	51.7
Fayette	32	132	6.7	2.8	36	4 809	1 254.3	217.0	49	759	22.0	5.9
Floyd	146	975	77.7	28.3	135	7 499	1 243.2	204.0	107	1 830	54.9	15.8
Fountain	12	47	2.6	0.7	22	2 616	282.8	67.8	48	546	16.4	5.1
Franklin	18	45	3.8	0.9	19	812	134.5	23.3	38	554	12.6	3.5
Fulton	23	56	4.6	1.0	52	3 004	424.4	79.1	46	551	14.2	3.9
Gibson	37	193	11.6	5.2	42	2 142	336.1	54.3	62	894	21.0	6.3
Grant	66	360	16.0	5.6	80	9 375	1 784.4	395.2	140	2 579	74.3	20.2
Greene	31	343	21.1	9.0	26	1 136	171.7	18.5	49	D	D	D
Hamilton	515	4 169	435.2	168.7	191	5 687	836.3	185.8	252	5 154	165.6	49.2
Hancock	81	247	21.9	6.9	66	2 564	712.9	88.4	79	1 470	41.5	11.0
Harrison	24	92	4.2	1.7	38	D	D	D	44	690	21.4	5.5
Hendricks	148	507	33.2	12.1	80	1 537	248.4	48.5	127	2 581	72.2	20.9
Henry	46	205	15.1	4.3	57	3 516	688.7	164.8	68	1 082	30.4	8.3
Howard	98	410	30.8	10.3	80	20 018	4 732.2	1 077.9	182	3 913	115.1	31.7
Huntington	33	239	14.3	6.7	78	7 451	1 245.5	207.8	85	1 260	32.3	9.0
Jackson	43	284	15.8	6.1	90	5 848	1 182.7	179.4	72	1 042	35.3	10.1
Jasper	28	107	5.8	1.6	33	1 479	279.4	35.2	57	810	24.1	6.6
Jay	19	99	3.7	1.2	39	3 751	539.1	86.6	41	528	14.4	3.8
Jefferson	29	124	7.9	2.4	51	3 655	548.9	97.3	77	1 068	29.6	8.7
Jennings	12	54	2.2	0.7	42	2 410	263.2	55.7	31	392	10.0	2.7
Johnson	187	890	54.9	22.1	126	6 486	1 305.5	204.6	214	4 190	121.6	34.9
Knox	47	189	12.1	3.6	44	1 715	289.1	46.2	80	1 375	36.1	10.3
Kosciusko	96	395	27.1	8.3	186	14 949	2 969.2	514.1	152	2 116	58.7	16.6
Lagrange	38	97	5.1	1.6	77	4 765	887.4	154.3	60	702	24.0	6.9
Lake	728	5 402	455.5	154.3	423	37 109	14 297.9	1 748.3	931	15 407	463.1	126.0
La Porte	145	707	40.1	13.9	189	10 835	2 007.9	351.2	234	3 394	106.1	29.0
Lawrence	37	175	9.6	3.6	75	5 322	1 063.0	195.0	74	1 321	38.0	10.5
Madison	187	1 152	62.2	31.9	133	12 144	2 256.8	534.3	244	4 794	139.8	38.4
Marion	2 264	23 108	2 423.6	899.9	1 194	66 571	19 561.3	2 898.6	1 893	43 946	1 523.7	432.4
Marshall	51	250	13.2	4.6	143	8 588	1 516.0	230.2	97	1 418	37.1	10.0
Martin	13	87	5.5	2.7	9	575	133.4	17.7	21	D	D	D
Miami	27	94	5.0	1.4	50	2 491	385.9	64.0	58	706	18.2	5.1
Monroe	196	1 360	97.0	34.0	122	8 817	2 444.2	302.6	302	6 312	176.6	48.8
Montgomery	44	137	9.5	3.5	67	7 634	1 878.7	264.1	88	1 054	33.7	8.6
Morgan	61	193	12.5	4.7	65	2 869	472.3	78.7	80	1 411	45.1	13.3
Newton	11	33	1.4	0.4	29	1 474	176.5	34.4	28	D	D	D
Noble	45	243	19.9	4.5	143	10 818	1 821.7	309.2	69	961	29.8	7.7
Ohio	3	8	0.3	0.2	NA	NA	NA	NA	9	D	D	D
Orange	22	39	2.3	0.7	34	2 478	296.4	55.3	35	610	10.0	3.1
Owen	15	55	2.2	0.7	24	1 242	109.2	31.5	20	D	D	D
Parke	16	48	2.5	0.9	17	641	92.1	13.7	34	D	D	D
Perry	19	55	2.8	0.7	27	1 211	141.1	33.6	44	465	14.1	3.6
Pike	9	30	1.2	0.4	NA	NA	NA	NA	12	D	D	D
Porter	237	1 217	109.8	42.1	146	12 353	4 353.6	624.5	259	4 385	126.5	35.9
Posey	35	247	18.0	9.3	31	D	D	D	35	D	D	D
Pulaski	25	82	3.3	0.8	20	1 353	218.1	41.1	22	D	D	D

1. Firms subject to federal tax.

Table B. States and Counties — Health Care and Social Assistance, Other Services, and Federal Funds

STATE County	Health care and social assistance,[1] 1997				Other services,[1] 1997				Federal funds and grants, 2002–2003 Expenditures (mil dol)			
									Total	Direct payments for individuals[2]		
	Number of establishments	Number of employees	Receipts (mil dol)	Annual payroll (mil dol)	Number of establishments	Number of employees	Receipts (mil dol)	Annual payroll (mil dol)		Social Security and government retirement	Medicare	Food stamps and Supplemental Security Income
	159	160	161	162	163	164	165	166	167	168	169	170
INDIANA	10 236	132 416	8 132.3	3 675.3	9 243	60 711	3 701.4	1 127.8	35 524.7	12 920.1	5 374.0	957.4
Adams	35	238	14.6	6.5	58	223	12.9	3.2	131.0	61.0	27.2	2.7
Allen	580	9 292	618.5	281.0	584	4 490	272.7	86.3	1 741.6	621.5	235.6	51.9
Bartholomew	142	1 633	106.6	57.3	101	703	39.4	13.8	369.7	151.1	58.1	8.7
Benton	11	191	5.5	2.8	10	43	2.4	0.7	47.7	22.7	9.7	0.9
Blackford	18	209	10.7	3.5	18	54	3.0	1.0	65.8	35.1	13.7	2.3
Boone	71	686	40.3	19.1	67	303	26.2	6.2	152.5	84.5	35.2	2.4
Brown	12	177	6.4	3.2	8	18	1.1	0.2	40.1	23.2	6.4	1.2
Carroll	23	194	8.1	3.0	20	50	3.8	1.1	74.1	37.5	14.3	1.0
Cass	56	777	36.0	18.5	58	226	11.3	3.3	216.8	94.0	40.8	6.1
Clark	155	2 188	119.7	52.0	157	1 165	63.3	21.3	572.3	234.9	100.8	16.7
Clay	34	257	10.7	3.8	40	132	6.6	1.9	143.7	71.2	30.8	4.1
Clinton	31	237	12.8	4.7	46	176	11.4	3.0	133.1	72.1	31.5	3.8
Crawford	5	90	3.4	1.4	5	18	1.3	0.4	60.6	27.1	11.4	2.1
Daviess	59	700	31.5	12.9	52	257	42.4	6.9	150.0	71.7	29.8	4.1
Dearborn	66	759	38.1	17.2	62	182	13.5	3.1	171.9	94.7	35.6	4.4
Decatur	29	406	14.3	6.5	39	153	8.7	2.6	109.1	54.0	21.2	2.9
De Kalb	55	695	37.3	15.6	51	208	12.0	3.7	142.0	77.3	27.0	3.3
Delaware	223	3 304	200.9	94.2	186	1 530	98.7	24.4	596.1	259.5	108.0	26.7
Dubois	86	798	49.6	18.1	69	341	27.5	6.4	172.1	80.8	32.4	2.0
Elkhart	233	3 281	187.7	78.0	345	2 427	164.1	47.3	594.4	318.4	109.1	21.1
Fayette	55	667	27.4	12.4	42	214	11.5	3.4	139.6	65.5	29.5	5.5
Floyd	154	1 835	109.0	45.7	108	628	35.9	11.6	331.8	157.0	68.7	12.2
Fountain	19	298	9.5	4.1	24	81	7.4	1.2	96.8	51.5	19.5	2.5
Franklin	22	230	8.7	3.7	16	70	3.1	1.4	80.7	38.5	14.1	2.6
Fulton	22	133	9.7	3.4	34	104	6.5	2.2	85.4	47.5	19.4	2.1
Gibson	54	556	23.7	9.0	40	153	8.2	2.5	154.6	78.8	35.3	3.6
Grant	124	1 834	80.6	37.2	106	573	32.6	9.2	452.4	195.9	76.0	17.3
Greene	52	739	19.0	7.6	41	101	6.9	1.5	190.5	92.4	31.8	5.0
Hamilton	341	3 816	244.6	108.6	245	1 499	100.2	30.5	417.9	266.0	68.4	5.3
Hancock	78	849	43.8	20.0	80	398	21.4	6.2	196.8	124.1	37.2	3.0
Harrison	40	341	16.0	6.7	24	93	5.9	1.6	141.7	77.2	26.7	4.1
Hendricks	149	1 959	101.8	48.7	131	610	36.0	11.3	334.1	189.0	57.0	3.4
Henry	70	986	43.0	23.3	61	264	13.8	3.9	246.5	122.4	52.2	7.8
Howard	162	1 947	115.9	53.3	131	961	44.4	14.1	415.1	206.6	86.8	15.8
Huntington	46	604	25.0	10.8	58	247	12.2	3.5	152.4	87.6	28.7	3.3
Jackson	59	598	34.0	15.7	64	304	19.0	5.0	184.3	90.2	33.7	5.6
Jasper	33	161	10.9	4.2	40	205	10.9	3.1	147.4	67.1	25.3	2.7
Jay	24	397	18.1	7.0	28	79	4.8	1.4	118.2	51.5	23.2	3.1
Jefferson	51	671	38.8	16.7	36	183	8.5	2.5	173.5	74.4	32.5	5.6
Jennings	23	255	10.8	5.1	21	67	6.8	1.1	109.1	54.8	19.2	4.5
Johnson	158	2 065	123.1	53.3	174	1 031	62.3	20.2	409.6	235.3	75.4	8.2
Knox	81	1 315	65.7	31.0	63	404	24.0	7.2	264.2	99.0	51.3	8.9
Kosciusko	79	851	48.9	22.4	138	708	44.6	13.5	243.9	141.9	47.0	5.1
Lagrange	26	468	24.9	9.2	41	151	14.3	2.7	89.1	51.0	17.2	1.5
Lake	1 013	10 528	697.3	317.5	740	6 006	373.9	123.8	2 710.2	1 107.3	577.5	137.7
La Porte	181	1 995	137.2	64.5	189	929	49.9	17.3	494.0	237.9	110.2	18.1
Lawrence	73	627	28.5	12.6	58	252	14.2	4.5	233.2	119.5	46.2	6.1
Madison	206	2 232	119.4	53.5	199	1 133	60.5	19.2	710.0	351.6	153.8	27.8
Marion	1 847	27 477	1 891.6	876.8	1 442	12 491	742.6	236.4	7 391.5	1 871.6	851.5	193.0
Marshall	53	775	37.0	14.3	65	301	19.5	5.7	175.1	90.6	31.5	2.6
Martin	19	145	5.0	2.0	14	29	1.8	0.3	312.1	32.3	10.5	1.6
Miami	39	352	16.1	6.5	40	162	6.8	1.8	239.5	88.5	32.2	5.8
Monroe	243	2 384	162.1	76.2	160	1 124	64.3	20.0	603.9	194.3	66.3	13.6
Montgomery	61	1 161	70.6	26.5	67	540	37.3	10.8	164.6	81.8	34.4	4.0
Morgan	86	877	48.2	23.3	94	472	26.7	7.8	243.3	127.0	48.7	6.5
Newton	6	44	1.7	0.7	11	26	1.9	0.3	59.6	26.7	12.5	1.4
Noble	50	392	21.4	8.9	71	258	16.9	4.8	146.8	81.1	31.7	3.3
Ohio	3	60	3.0	1.0	6	20	0.7	0.2	22.3	11.9	4.7	0.3
Orange	28	431	15.5	6.5	17	54	3.7	0.8	100.9	46.1	19.3	3.4
Owen	14	212	9.1	4.4	24	92	6.0	1.3	77.1	42.7	13.4	2.8
Parke	20	323	12.2	5.7	18	50	8.5	0.9	81.3	39.3	15.0	2.5
Perry	21	216	10.2	4.3	24	72	4.9	1.1	97.9	41.5	18.8	2.5
Pike	14	188	6.7	3.1	14	44	3.6	0.6	72.3	32.5	14.9	2.2
Porter	263	2 434	158.6	74.5	239	1 330	77.3	24.2	531.0	288.2	110.5	11.7
Posey	25	317	13.4	4.6	31	90	4.9	1.2	119.7	51.6	23.7	3.1
Pulaski	18	137	5.3	2.6	24	76	9.1	1.4	64.7	33.0	12.7	1.3

1. Firms subject to federal tax.   2. State totals may include programs not allocated by county.

	Federal funds and grants, 2002–2003 (cont'd)							Local government finances, 2002				
	Expenditures (mil dol) (cont'd)							General revenue				
		Procurement contract awards		Grants[1]						Taxes		
											Per capita[2] (dollars)	
STATE County	Salaries and wages	Defense	Other	Medicaid and other health-related	Nutrition and family welfare	Education	Other	Total (mil dol)	Intergovern-mental (mil dol)	Total (mil dol)	Total	Property
	171	172	173	174	175	176	177	178	179	180	181	182
INDIANA	2 338.4	2 566.7	734.8	3 628.8	941.8	627.4	2 115.1	X	X	X	X	X
Adams	3.9	0.0	1.2	20.8	1.5	0.9	4.2	99.1	28.8	29.2	871	807
Allen	146.8	363.4	72.3	142.4	32.3	7.9	40.7	815.4	285.2	371.9	1 102	982
Bartholomew	21.5	32.0	4.0	39.0	9.0	1.1	37.9	298.9	67.7	75.7	1 057	877
Benton	2.2	0.0	0.5	3.5	0.3	0.2	2.3	28.8	11.6	12.4	1 344	1 222
Blackford	2.1	0.0	0.5	6.9	1.2	0.2	1.1	42.3	14.4	12.9	813	813
Boone	6.3	0.2	1.6	7.8	1.4	0.6	7.0	174.8	43.4	59.6	1 234	997
Brown	1.0	0.0	0.2	3.5	0.9	0.2	3.2	39.2	16.4	14.0	924	735
Carroll	4.3	0.0	0.7	5.6	1.1	0.3	4.6	44.9	16.2	19.5	965	828
Cass	7.1	29.0	2.5	19.9	5.9	0.8	5.9	136.2	41.7	39.6	973	864
Clark	73.8	6.7	8.1	54.6	11.1	2.2	58.5	311.7	89.3	85.8	874	851
Clay	5.4	0.0	1.2	21.6	1.7	0.5	2.9	67.8	26.3	18.4	697	594
Clinton	4.2	0.0	1.0	14.3	2.6	0.5	-2.2	86.3	37.4	31.6	929	806
Crawford	2.2	0.1	0.8	13.0	1.0	0.4	1.9	24.7	12.7	6.7	605	545
Daviess	4.9	0.0	0.9	16.9	2.2	1.0	7.3	90.2	25.4	23.4	784	672
Dearborn	5.9	0.0	1.5	19.0	5.1	0.8	3.4	211.3	78.8	51.4	1 086	985
Decatur	3.6	0.1	0.8	13.4	1.7	0.4	3.8	85.2	20.1	24.0	978	831
De Kalb	5.0	0.2	1.2	10.4	2.2	0.5	9.5	134.2	39.5	41.6	1 025	857
Delaware	23.5	1.8	7.5	91.0	15.5	6.7	35.7	283.9	129.8	110.7	937	845
Dubois	7.2	13.0	15.3	7.4	0.3	5.1	5.1	105.4	37.4	42.8	1 070	940
Elkhart	18.3	11.7	7.0	59.7	9.7	3.9	26.7	466.6	185.0	204.3	1 095	928
Fayette	3.4	0.0	2.1	20.8	4.3	0.5	4.2	65.2	31.2	25.7	1 019	855
Floyd	16.1	0.9	3.7	52.5	8.0	1.2	3.8	288.0	70.1	67.5	942	914
Fountain	3.4	0.0	0.8	8.7	3.4	0.3	1.4	39.3	18.1	14.8	838	648
Franklin	2.5	0.0	1.6	13.0	0.9	0.3	2.7	36.8	18.0	13.8	612	501
Fulton	2.6	0.0	0.7	5.6	1.1	0.3	1.6	64.0	16.7	18.6	899	786
Gibson	4.3	0.0	1.1	15.1	2.3	1.4	2.7	81.2	24.4	33.4	1 025	996
Grant	45.8	0.0	16.1	53.3	10.4	2.4	20.4	160.6	72.6	65.9	913	763
Greene	5.8	18.4	1.3	19.5	1.9	0.9	7.9	106.3	40.0	28.4	858	734
Hamilton	26.5	1.1	6.3	22.9	3.2	1.0	11.6	604.8	141.2	284.5	1 384	1 113
Hancock	7.9	0.3	1.7	9.5	1.9	0.5	6.0	254.3	52.5	59.3	1 016	816
Harrison	6.7	0.0	1.5	16.4	2.3	0.5	1.4	116.5	52.2	27.7	786	690
Hendricks	12.8	1.1	4.8	13.0	2.3	0.8	45.8	335.0	87.9	129.2	1 130	946
Henry	6.9	0.6	1.5	34.6	6.1	1.0	7.2	172.4	54.1	43.7	910	736
Howard	19.1	0.2	4.6	47.2	10.4	1.8	14.5	293.5	83.5	115.0	1 356	1 209
Huntington	5.3	0.4	1.2	9.1	2.0	0.4	5.6	91.3	39.2	36.3	950	817
Jackson	6.4	0.1	2.2	23.4	3.3	0.7	11.6	142.8	38.2	30.1	725	595
Jasper	5.2	23.7	2.1	8.2	1.5	0.4	4.0	97.8	24.1	31.3	1 015	895
Jay	3.0	2.4	0.7	13.4	4.0	0.4	3.9	72.6	22.7	18.5	856	800
Jefferson	6.5	10.3	1.4	26.4	4.2	0.8	7.7	79.6	29.5	32.7	1 019	996
Jennings	3.8	0.5	0.7	18.2	1.4	0.5	1.1	58.4	27.6	20.8	738	522
Johnson	19.0	1.1	19.2	30.8	4.0	1.3	10.0	362.1	99.8	118.9	978	815
Knox	10.8	9.0	7.6	34.6	7.2	3.2	14.0	194.5	41.0	30.0	778	745
Kosciusko	12.0	1.5	4.1	13.0	5.5	0.8	6.4	178.1	64.7	78.1	1 044	935
Lagrange	3.9	0.3	1.0	5.6	0.6	0.8	1.3	74.9	31.1	31.7	896	741
Lake	104.9	20.2	27.9	414.2	101.9	18.2	167.2	1 815.2	664.5	671.8	1 379	1 309
La Porte	15.2	4.7	4.3	50.2	12.1	2.8	26.5	338.0	125.1	134.8	1 221	1 132
Lawrence	9.7	3.5	2.2	31.4	5.0	0.9	4.7	126.4	46.9	36.7	796	708
Madison	19.5	0.6	8.5	93.2	15.4	3.5	26.9	320.4	143.3	113.0	856	759
Marion	877.8	999.2	244.0	731.0	339.7	234.8	748.7	3 122.7	1 222.9	1 243.4	1 440	1 268
Marshall	6.4	2.4	10.7	11.3	3.5	0.7	9.0	100.5	41.7	41.7	911	855
Martin	177.1	74.6	0.5	10.0	1.1	0.3	1.4	22.7	10.7	9.1	873	569
Miami	67.1	17.1	1.4	15.1	2.9	0.8	2.3	131.4	51.2	25.2	697	617
Monroe	26.9	7.4	10.4	188.9	8.1	8.4	59.3	299.2	72.1	105.7	872	703
Montgomery	6.7	0.4	1.4	16.0	1.8	2.7	7.9	106.1	40.2	44.5	1 173	1 032
Morgan	8.1	7.5	2.0	26.8	3.4	0.9	8.4	159.7	67.7	53.0	781	624
Newton	2.4	0.0	0.6	3.5	0.9	0.3	6.6	41.9	15.9	16.4	1 139	1 021
Noble	5.4	0.6	1.3	11.7	1.5	0.6	3.8	103.1	44.2	40.2	851	738
Ohio	0.9	0.0	0.2	3.5	0.3	0.1	0.0	28.5	10.4	15.0	2 581	526
Orange	2.9	0.4	1.3	18.2	1.8	0.6	3.6	52.5	20.5	13.5	693	578
Owen	2.8	0.2	0.7	10.0	1.2	0.6	1.1	42.8	21.3	13.6	605	498
Parke	3.6	0.0	0.8	10.4	1.5	0.5	2.4	34.1	16.7	12.1	703	591
Perry	6.9	2.2	1.3	13.8	3.2	0.4	5.6	61.7	18.7	19.0	1 007	687
Pike	2.1	2.5	0.5	9.5	0.9	0.3	2.7	33.1	12.7	12.7	987	873
Porter	26.6	4.4	8.4	31.6	7.0	2.1	33.6	469.9	120.3	132.7	882	825
Posey	3.8	1.2	0.9	10.8	1.8	0.4	16.0	65.9	21.9	36.2	1 342	1 334
Pulaski	2.7	0.9	0.6	5.6	0.8	0.3	1.6	54.4	16.4	14.4	1 046	904

1. State totals may include programs not allocated by county.　　2. Based on the resident population estimated as of July 1 of the year shown.

STATE County	Total (mil dol)	Per capita[1] (dollars)	Education	Health and hospitals	Police protection	Public welfare	Highways	Total (mil dol)	Per capita[1] (dollars)	Federal civilian	Federal military	State and local	Democratic	Republican	All other
	183	184	185	186	187	188	189	190	191	192	193	194	195	196	197
INDIANA	X	X	X	X	X	X	X	X	X	36 078	17 619	375 677	39.2	60.1	0.8
Adams	95.9	2 862	38.1	28.4	2.3	1.0	4.2	37.2	1 112	75	89	2 015	26.3	73.0	0.7
Allen	837.6	2 482	52.6	0.7	4.2	4.1	4.5	554.8	1 644	2 187	904	16 263	36.0	63.4	0.6
Bartholomew	303.3	4 234	32.8	39.5	2.1	2.0	2.6	152.4	2 128	247	191	5 162	32.3	67.0	0.7
Benton	29.9	3 247	57.5	0.3	1.4	2.7	10.0	11.9	1 296	35	25	646	28.5	70.2	1.4
Blackford	42.9	3 109	41.1	23.5	3.0	2.7	3.6	31.8	2 305	31	37	679	35.4	64.1	0.6
Boone	172.0	3 562	36.7	24.5	2.5	0.9	6.3	230.7	4 779	99	129	2 398	24.6	74.5	0.8
Brown	29.9	1 965	62.4	1.4	2.3	1.9	7.0	8.8	580	17	41	739	37.3	61.6	1.1
Carroll	45.2	2 234	41.8	1.7	2.9	3.1	9.2	28.6	1 416	71	54	779	31.2	67.9	0.9
Cass	153.1	3 757	41.6	26.7	2.6	2.5	2.4	48.8	1 197	119	109	3 644	31.0	68.1	0.9
Clark	312.6	3 183	37.1	29.2	3.3	2.5	3.0	128.2	1 305	1 683	264	5 569	41.7	57.9	0.5
Clay	68.3	2 592	53.2	14.3	1.9	1.9	3.2	37.0	1 405	87	70	1 157	30.9	68.3	0.7
Clinton	79.3	2 336	54.0	1.2	3.0	4.9	4.9	30.6	901	72	91	1 517	28.1	71.3	0.6
Crawford	22.8	2 062	60.0	2.1	1.5	7.9	2.3	17.9	1 615	31	30	613	42.2	57.0	0.7
Daviess	88.3	2 956	33.6	38.9	2.0	1.6	4.2	66.8	2 238	84	80	1 620	24.3	74.9	0.8
Dearborn	200.2	4 230	31.4	23.4	2.3	0.4	2.0	87.1	1 839	93	127	2 316	31.4	67.9	0.7
Decatur	99.2	4 045	31.6	23.0	1.5	1.2	14.0	49.2	2 006	73	65	1 275	31.5	67.9	0.6
De Kalb	140.0	3 455	42.3	20.1	2.8	1.9	5.6	79.5	1 962	89	108	1 849	25.7	73.5	0.8
Delaware	276.4	2 339	51.4	0.9	5.4	4.7	3.6	98.3	832	392	321	10 375	42.7	56.5	0.8
Dubois	105.2	2 630	60.3	0.7	2.6	1.2	7.0	85.7	2 141	114	107	1 858	30.6	68.8	0.7
Elkhart	481.9	2 584	53.9	0.9	5.2	4.1	3.5	396.6	2 127	295	499	7 485	29.3	70.1	0.6
Fayette	70.8	2 804	56.6	0.7	4.6	4.2	5.4	20.8	823	61	67	1 306	38.3	60.8	0.9
Floyd	275.7	3 848	43.4	26.3	3.0	1.9	3.4	97.2	1 357	177	191	5 159	40.9	58.7	0.5
Fountain	43.6	2 461	51.6	1.7	2.1	3.2	6.1	23.8	1 345	63	47	845	31.8	67.5	0.8
Franklin	39.7	1 756	58.6	0.5	1.3	2.4	11.3	12.2	538	50	60	824	23.0	69.9	7.1
Fulton	61.3	2 957	31.5	29.9	2.5	2.1	5.9	39.5	1 905	52	55	1 048	30.0	69.3	0.7
Gibson	80.4	2 468	43.4	0.6	4.7	2.2	6.1	209.6	6 433	87	87	1 109	36.8	62.5	0.7
Grant	165.4	2 291	54.3	0.6	5.7	4.4	5.2	60.1	832	1 006	194	3 351	31.0	68.4	0.6
Greene	90.0	2 715	48.1	20.5	1.6	3.8	4.8	28.4	856	87	88	1 940	34.3	64.8	0.9
Hamilton	619.3	3 012	42.9	12.1	3.7	0.5	5.3	593.5	2 887	370	553	8 663	25.2	74.3	0.6
Hancock	270.0	4 628	30.6	21.9	1.6	0.9	15.5	192.5	3 299	112	156	3 326	24.8	74.6	0.6
Harrison	110.0	3 120	40.7	22.0	0.8	1.7	3.4	51.1	1 451	118	94	1 741	35.7	63.7	0.6
Hendricks	337.5	2 953	41.6	21.2	2.1	0.7	2.2	423.4	3 704	182	305	6 456	25.9	73.5	0.6
Henry	188.2	3 923	36.2	28.7	1.4	2.9	3.2	67.6	1 409	104	128	3 385	35.0	64.1	0.9
Howard	296.4	3 494	38.6	18.0	5.2	1.7	3.2	172.8	2 037	302	227	5 938	35.1	64.1	0.7
Huntington	99.8	2 610	47.7	1.9	2.7	2.1	6.6	50.8	1 329	93	102	1 572	24.8	74.4	0.8
Jackson	132.4	3 186	35.0	34.1	3.1	2.4	3.2	72.5	1 744	112	111	2 417	31.3	68.0	0.7
Jasper	92.4	3 000	35.9	23.8	2.9	1.1	5.0	180.2	5 846	83	82	1 755	31.1	68.1	0.9
Jay	72.4	3 345	44.2	25.2	2.4	1.9	6.1	17.7	817	50	58	1 158	33.3	66.0	0.7
Jefferson	82.4	2 565	47.3	1.1	2.9	3.3	13.3	44.6	1 388	98	86	2 385	39.4	59.8	0.7
Jennings	57.1	2 026	61.8	0.8	2.7	2.1	4.1	48.9	1 733	66	75	1 840	33.6	65.3	1.1
Johnson	344.8	2 835	43.8	17.0	2.5	0.7	3.6	274.3	2 255	348	324	5 553	25.6	73.8	0.6
Knox	200.0	5 191	22.5	58.1	2.2	1.0	1.9	93.2	2 418	176	104	5 128	35.9	63.5	0.7
Kosciusko	169.6	2 268	57.2	0.9	3.4	1.8	6.0	85.9	1 149	189	201	2 764	21.1	78.1	0.9
Lagrange	80.4	2 270	63.4	0.5	1.4	2.0	4.9	66.2	1 869	69	94	1 385	28.0	71.4	0.6
Lake	1 776.3	3 647	39.4	0.9	5.1	7.1	2.8	1 033.2	2 121	1 627	1 301	26 881	49.6	49.1	1.3
La Porte	303.9	2 753	45.7	1.3	4.3	4.5	4.2	168.5	1 526	225	313	7 606	60.8	38.5	0.7
Lawrence	123.8	2 685	43.8	25.5	1.6	1.6	5.2	66.9	1 451	171	123	2 365	30.2	69.0	0.8
Madison	318.6	2 412	50.0	0.7	4.7	2.4	3.5	148.2	1 122	305	353	6 616	39.9	59.3	0.8
Marion	3 290.3	3 811	36.5	12.2	4.7	2.2	3.1	4 369.7	5 061	12 480	3 175	63 341	50.6	48.7	0.7
Marshall	109.7	2 399	57.6	1.2	3.9	2.7	5.3	72.2	1 580	104	122	2 214	31.4	67.8	0.7
Martin	21.2	2 043	59.2	1.1	4.4	3.6	7.4	10.1	969	3 602	89	461	30.5	68.4	1.2
Miami	128.4	3 548	41.2	21.4	2.5	2.1	4.4	33.8	935	556	122	2 518	28.6	70.6	0.9
Monroe	316.6	2 612	33.0	1.4	3.3	3.3	4.3	219.3	1 809	405	346	18 738	53.7	45.4	0.9
Montgomery	105.6	2 781	54.9	0.4	3.2	2.1	4.5	90.1	2 373	103	101	1 886	24.3	75.0	0.7
Morgan	152.6	2 251	51.1	18.8	2.8	0.9	4.2	52.1	769	121	181	2 732	25.5	73.8	0.7
Newton	40.7	2 836	50.7	3.1	1.9	1.6	5.7	22.7	1 580	43	38	802	34.8	64.3	0.9
Noble	103.6	2 195	52.9	0.3	4.2	1.5	5.7	75.5	1 599	97	126	1 880	30.0	69.3	0.7
Ohio	29.5	5 091	22.2	0.5	1.8	1.0	3.2	4.6	795	15	15	300	38.5	60.7	0.8
Orange	51.2	2 634	45.9	23.4	1.8	0.9	5.4	40.5	2 083	50	52	868	33.4	65.7	0.9
Owen	38.8	1 721	62.4	2.0	1.6	2.3	8.4	31.2	1 386	41	60	852	33.4	65.8	0.9
Parke	32.8	1 903	56.9	2.1	4.6	1.9	9.5	14.1	820	59	46	1 197	33.9	65.3	0.8
Perry	62.2	3 306	35.7	24.5	2.1	0.8	4.5	70.0	3 720	83	50	1 450	50.2	49.3	0.5
Pike	47.8	3 699	69.2	0.2	0.4	4.3	7.0	25.3	1 962	39	34	603	38.9	60.3	0.8
Porter	504.0	3 351	45.6	26.3	2.3	0.7	3.1	378.7	2 518	437	403	8 206	45.3	53.6	1.0
Posey	64.0	2 372	56.2	1.9	2.2	2.9	10.0	50.1	1 855	81	72	1 188	34.1	65.3	0.6
Pulaski	49.0	3 572	36.5	27.4	2.5	2.3	6.3	33.3	2 428	48	37	962	31.2	67.8	1.0

1. Based on the resident population estimated as of July 1 of the year shown.

Table B. States and Counties — Land Area and Population

STATE/ County code	CBSA code[1]	County Type[2]	STATE County	Land area,[3] (sq km) 2000	Population and population characteristics, 2003												
					Total persons	Rank	Per square kilometer	White	Black	Am. Indian, Alaska Native	Asian and Pacific Islander	Percent Hispanic or Latino[4]	Under 5 years	5 to 17 years	18 to 24 years	25 to 34 years	35 to 44 years	45 to 54 years
				1	2	3	4	5	6	7	8	9	10	11	12	13	14	15
			INDIANA—Cont'd															
18 133	26900	1	Putnam	1 244	36 692	1 224	29.5	95.1	3.0	0.6	0.8	1.2	5.7	17.4	14.1	12.3	15.7	12.5
18 135	...	6	Randolph	1 173	26 833	1 512	22.9	97.8	0.5	0.5	0.4	1.5	6.5	18.6	8.4	11.8	14.7	14.1
18 137	...	6	Ripley	1 156	27 316	1 491	23.6	98.2	0.2	0.4	0.5	1.0	7.0	20.7	8.7	12.3	15.4	13.1
18 139	...	6	Rush	1 057	18 016	1 916	17.0	98.1	0.9	0.5	0.6	0.6	6.9	20.3	8.1	11.5	15.5	13.8
18 141	43780	2	St. Joseph	1 185	266 348	221	224.8	81.5	12.2	0.8	2.1	5.1	7.2	18.9	11.6	12.6	14.1	13.7
18 143	42500	6	Scott	493	23 556	1 637	47.8	98.6	0.2	0.3	0.2	1.0	6.9	19.2	9.4	13.7	15.7	13.6
18 145	26900	1	Shelby	1 069	43 717	1 051	40.9	96.3	1.0	0.5	0.9	1.9	6.7	19.6	8.7	12.2	16.8	14.3
18 147	...	8	Spencer	1 033	20 343	1 782	19.7	97.5	0.6	0.4	0.3	1.5	6.1	19.5	8.7	11.3	15.9	14.9
18 149	...	6	Starke	801	23 139	1 659	28.9	97.4	0.2	0.6	0.4	2.0	6.7	19.9	8.5	10.1	14.6	14.5
18 151	11420	7	Steuben	800	33 706	1 311	42.1	97.0	0.5	0.6	0.4	2.1	6.4	18.7	11.0	12.2	14.9	14.0
18 153	45460	3	Sullivan	1 158	21 861	1 708	18.9	94.4	4.4	0.6	0.2	0.9	5.7	16.5	10.5	14.1	15.4	14.5
18 155	...	8	Switzerland	573	9 435	2 494	16.5	98.6	0.2	0.2	0.1	1.0	5.9	19.2	9.5	12.5	15.4	13.7
18 157	29140	3	Tippecanoe	1 294	154 848	359	119.7	86.3	2.8	0.6	5.8	5.6	6.0	14.8	22.1	15.5	11.8	10.9
18 159	29020	3	Tipton	674	16 422	2 003	24.4	97.9	0.3	0.2	0.4	1.3	5.8	18.7	8.5	11.9	14.9	15.2
18 161	...	8	Union	418	7 238	2 661	17.3	98.9	0.3	0.3	0.3	0.3	5.7	19.9	9.3	11.8	15.7	14.4
18 163	21780	2	Vanderburgh	608	171 889	327	282.7	89.7	8.8	0.5	1.3	1.0	6.6	17.0	11.3	12.4	14.4	13.9
18 165	45460	3	Vermillion	665	16 572	1 992	24.9	98.6	0.4	0.6	0.2	0.7	6.0	17.6	8.6	11.8	14.2	15.0
18 167	45460	3	Vigo	1 045	104 540	519	100.0	91.3	6.4	0.8	1.8	1.0	6.2	16.8	13.7	12.9	13.6	13.5
18 169	47340	6	Wabash	1 070	34 339	1 294	32.1	97.2	0.6	1.0	0.6	1.2	5.7	18.1	10.8	11.0	13.9	14.1
18 171	...	8	Warren	945	8 703	2 554	9.2	99.2	0.1	0.2	0.2	0.4	5.6	19.5	8.0	11.8	15.6	14.5
18 173	21780	2	Warrick	995	54 744	878	55.0	97.0	1.3	0.3	1.0	0.9	6.2	19.6	8.9	11.2	16.2	15.5
18 175	31140	1	Washington	1 332	27 618	1 478	20.7	98.8	0.3	0.6	0.3	0.7	6.6	19.6	9.4	13.2	15.6	14.2
18 177	39980	3	Wayne	1 045	70 235	719	67.2	92.7	5.8	0.6	0.7	1.5	6.5	18.0	9.7	11.9	14.3	13.9
18 179	23060	5	Wells	958	27 912	1 470	29.1	97.8	0.4	0.4	0.3	1.6	6.0	20.1	9.6	10.8	15.4	14.2
18 181	...	6	White	1 309	24 852	1 580	19.0	93.1	0.2	0.5	0.3	6.2	6.9	18.7	8.5	12.0	14.5	14.5
18 183	23060	2	Whitley	869	31 651	1 367	36.4	98.2	0.3	0.6	0.5	0.9	6.6	19.7	9.3	11.9	15.2	14.8
19 000	...	X	IOWA	144 701	2 944 062	X	20.3	92.7	2.6	0.6	1.9	3.1	6.2	17.4	10.8	12.3	14.3	14.5
19 001	...	8	Adair	1 474	7 922	2 599	5.4	98.9	0.1	0.2	0.3	0.7	4.4	16.8	8.8	9.0	14.3	14.9
19 003	...	9	Adams	1 097	4 371	2 881	4.0	98.4	0.0	0.5	0.6	0.5	4.9	16.9	8.2	9.0	14.3	13.8
19 005	...	6	Allamakee	1 656	14 551	2 124	8.8	94.0	0.2	0.2	0.7	5.3	5.7	17.9	8.7	10.1	14.7	14.1
19 007	...	7	Appanoose	1 285	13 590	2 192	10.6	98.0	0.5	0.6	0.4	1.0	5.2	16.7	9.2	10.0	13.5	13.9
19 009	...	8	Audubon	1 148	6 479	2 734	5.6	99.0	0.3	0.2	0.2	0.5	4.9	19.2	9.4	11.2	16.9	13.3
19 011	16300	3	Benton	1 855	26 243	1 529	14.1	98.6	0.4	0.4	0.3	0.7	5.8	19.2	9.4	11.2	16.9	13.3
19 013	47940	3	Black Hawk	1 469	126 418	450	86.1	88.3	8.8	0.5	1.6	2.0	6.0	16.0	14.0	12.5	12.7	14.4
19 015	14340	6	Boone	1 480	26 247	1 528	17.7	98.3	0.5	0.4	0.4	0.8	5.4	17.5	9.5	11.3	15.0	15.1
19 017	47940	3	Bremer	1 134	23 368	1 647	20.6	98.2	0.6	0.1	0.9	0.6	4.9	16.9	13.7	9.3	13.4	14.3
19 019	...	6	Buchanan	1 480	20 903	1 756	14.1	98.4	0.3	0.5	0.5	0.7	7.0	19.7	9.5	10.5	14.7	14.0
19 021	44740	7	Buena Vista	1 489	20 205	1 791	13.6	78.8	0.5	0.1	5.1	15.9	5.4	18.3	13.0	10.4	14.3	14.1
19 023	...	8	Butler	1 503	14 968	2 102	10.0	99.1	0.2	0.3	0.3	0.6	4.9	17.1	8.3	9.5	14.5	15.5
19 025	...	9	Calhoun	1 477	10 653	2 388	7.2	97.6	0.9	0.4	0.3	1.1	4.4	15.9	8.5	9.8	14.5	15.5
19 027	...	7	Carroll	1 475	21 086	1 750	14.3	98.6	0.3	0.1	0.4	0.8	5.5	18.6	8.9	9.8	14.8	14.2
19 029	...	6	Cass	1 462	14 314	2 145	9.8	98.7	0.3	0.3	0.2	0.7	5.2	16.6	8.6	9.1	14.4	14.7
19 031	...	6	Cedar	1 501	18 264	1 891	12.2	98.3	0.3	0.3	0.5	1.0	5.3	17.4	9.2	10.5	15.9	15.2
19 033	32380	5	Cerro Gordo	1 472	45 118	1 023	30.7	95.4	1.3	0.4	1.1	2.7	5.4	16.6	9.9	10.6	14.7	15.2
19 035	...	6	Cherokee	1 495	12 541	2 268	8.4	97.6	0.4	0.2	0.7	1.3	4.8	17.3	8.4	8.7	14.1	15.7
19 037	...	6	Chickasaw	1 307	12 702	2 261	9.7	98.8	0.3	0.3	0.5	0.8	5.5	18.5	8.5	9.1	15.3	14.7
19 039	...	6	Clarke	1 117	9 242	2 505	8.3	93.9	0.4	0.4	0.7	4.9	6.3	18.2	9.0	10.8	15.1	13.9
19 041	43980	7	Clay	1 473	17 073	1 952	11.6	97.3	0.4	0.2	1.0	1.5	5.6	17.0	8.7	10.5	14.6	15.4
19 043	...	8	Clayton	2 017	18 454	1 884	9.1	98.7	0.2	0.2	0.2	0.9	5.6	17.7	8.4	9.9	14.7	14.9
19 045	17540	4	Clinton	1 800	49 804	935	27.7	95.7	2.5	0.7	0.8	1.3	6.0	17.8	9.4	10.9	15.0	14.3
19 047	...	6	Crawford	1 850	16 930	1 966	9.2	85.9	0.9	0.3	0.6	12.5	6.3	18.5	9.0	10.6	14.3	13.8
19 049	19780	2	Dallas	1 519	46 148	1 001	30.4	92.0	1.0	0.4	1.8	5.5	6.3	18.9	10.5	14.1	16.4	13.2
19 051	...	9	Davis	1 303	8 557	2 560	6.6	98.6	0.3	0.7	0.3	0.8	6.4	19.2	8.9	10.5	14.1	14.0
19 053	...	9	Decatur	1 377	8 706	2 553	6.3	96.0	1.1	0.6	1.6	1.9	5.1	15.5	17.2	9.8	11.9	12.5
19 055	...	6	Delaware	1 497	18 140	1 906	12.1	98.9	0.1	0.2	0.2	0.8	5.6	20.0	9.4	9.9	16.3	14.2
19 057	15460	5	Des Moines	1 078	41 247	1 101	38.3	93.6	4.2	0.5	0.9	1.9	5.9	17.1	9.3	11.0	14.1	15.3
19 059	44020	7	Dickinson	987	16 399	2 004	16.6	98.7	0.4	0.3	0.2	0.7	4.9	15.1	8.1	10.0	13.2	16.0
19 061	20220	3	Dubuque	1 575	90 049	597	57.2	96.7	1.4	0.4	1.1	1.2	6.2	17.7	11.1	11.3	14.6	14.3
19 063	...	7	Emmet	1 025	10 805	2 380	10.5	94.7	0.4	0.3	0.4	4.4	5.5	16.7	11.4	9.7	13.3	14.3
19 065	...	6	Fayette	1 893	21 408	1 733	11.3	97.1	1.0	0.3	0.5	1.5	5.1	17.5	9.9	9.8	14.3	14.1
19 067	...	7	Floyd	1 296	16 608	1 988	12.8	97.6	0.3	0.2	0.8	1.5	5.7	17.6	8.4	10.2	13.8	14.2
19 069	...	7	Franklin	1 508	10 693	2 386	7.1	91.6	0.3	0.0	0.3	8.0	5.4	16.7	9.1	9.8	13.4	14.8
19 071	...	8	Fremont	1 324	7 862	2 609	5.9	97.1	0.1	0.3	0.3	2.4	5.3	17.5	8.1	9.6	13.8	15.0
19 073	...	6	Greene	1 472	10 047	2 437	6.8	97.8	0.3	0.2	0.4	1.5	5.2	18.1	8.3	8.9	14.4	14.5
19 075	47940	3	Grundy	1 302	12 341	2 275	9.5	98.9	0.2	0.2	0.5	0.6	4.9	17.9	8.7	9.5	14.5	14.8

1. CBSA = Core Based Statistical Area. See Appendix A for explanation. See Appendix B for list of metropolitan areas with component counties. 2. County type code from the Economic Research Service of USDA Rural-Urban Continuum Codes. See Appendix A for definition. 3. Dry land or land partially or temporarily covered by water. 4. Hispanic or Latino persons may be of any race.

Table B. States and Counties — **Population and Households**

STATE County	55 to 64 years	65 to 74 years	75 years and over	Percent female	1990	2000	1990–2000	2000–2003	Births	Deaths	Net migration	Number	Percent change, 1990–2000	Persons per house-hold	Female family house-holder[1]	One person
	16	17	18	19	20	21	22	23	24	25	26	27	28	29	30	31
INDIANA—Cont'd																
Putnam	9.5	6.9	5.6	47.9	30 315	36 019	18.8	1.9	1 292	957	376	12 374	23.8	2.56	7.7	22.4
Randolph	10.7	8.1	7.8	50.9	27 148	27 401	0.9	-2.1	1 085	1 009	-620	10 937	4.7	2.48	8.7	25.0
Ripley	9.5	6.8	6.5	50.6	24 616	26 523	7.7	3.0	1 264	670	226	9 842	12.1	2.66	8.7	22.7
Rush	9.6	7.4	7.4	50.7	18 129	18 261	0.7	-1.3	829	617	-455	6 923	6.4	2.60	8.4	23.3
St. Joseph	8.3	6.2	7.1	51.6	247 052	265 559	7.5	0.3	12 500	8 051	-3 558	100 743	9.1	2.50	12.4	27.9
Scott	10.0	6.3	4.8	50.3	20 991	22 960	9.4	2.6	998	761	380	8 832	16.3	2.58	11.3	22.5
Shelby	9.6	6.4	5.9	50.4	40 307	43 445	7.8	0.6	1 948	1 284	-362	16 561	12.2	2.58	9.3	22.7
Spencer	10.5	7.3	5.9	49.9	19 490	20 391	4.6	-0.2	830	603	-261	7 569	8.7	2.65	7.2	20.8
Starke	11.0	8.0	6.6	50.6	22 747	23 556	3.6	-1.8	1 024	867	-579	8 740	7.4	2.66	9.9	22.4
Steuben	10.3	6.6	5.4	49.7	27 446	33 214	21.0	1.5	1 441	879	-43	12 738	25.0	2.53	8.5	24.3
Sullivan	9.8	6.9	6.8	46.4	18 993	21 751	14.5	0.5	839	883	175	7 819	6.2	2.49	9.3	25.3
Switzerland	11.1	7.1	5.4	49.7	7 738	9 065	17.1	4.1	338	283	313	3 435	21.0	2.61	10.2	21.7
Tippecanoe	6.8	4.4	4.5	48.4	130 598	148 955	14.1	4.0	6 107	3 308	3 227	55 226	21.1	2.42	8.3	28.0
Tipton	11.2	6.9	7.5	51.0	16 119	16 577	2.8	-0.9	598	525	-202	6 469	7.4	2.53	7.7	23.1
Union	10.7	6.9	6.2	50.2	6 976	7 349	5.3	-1.5	246	180	-170	2 793	8.4	2.60	8.2	22.4
Vanderburgh	9.1	7.1	7.9	52.4	165 058	171 922	4.2	0.0	7 373	6 192	-1 045	70 623	5.8	2.33	11.9	31.0
Vermillion	11.1	7.6	8.2	50.9	16 773	16 788	0.1	-1.3	611	738	-75	6 762	1.9	2.44	9.0	26.6
Vigo	9.0	6.4	7.5	50.5	106 107	105 848	-0.2	-1.2	4 185	3 910	-1 539	40 998	3.0	2.38	11.7	30.0
Wabash	10.3	7.8	8.4	51.5	35 069	34 960	-0.3	-1.8	1 266	1 274	-594	13 215	4.6	2.50	8.5	24.9
Warren	11.5	7.3	6.2	49.3	8 176	8 419	3.0	3.4	295	305	292	3 219	6.8	2.58	6.8	21.2
Warrick	10.4	5.9	5.0	50.7	44 920	52 383	16.6	4.5	2 168	1 432	1 671	19 438	22.9	2.66	8.2	18.6
Washington	9.8	6.4	5.5	50.0	23 717	27 223	14.8	1.5	1 166	874	127	10 264	18.5	2.62	9.2	22.2
Wayne	10.3	7.8	7.9	51.8	71 951	71 097	-1.2	-1.2	2 877	2 647	-1 038	28 469	3.2	2.42	11.4	27.4
Wells	9.3	6.8	7.4	50.6	25 948	27 600	6.4	1.1	1 043	805	117	10 402	10.2	2.61	8.3	23.3
White	10.4	8.0	7.4	50.7	23 265	25 267	8.6	-1.6	1 207	861	-744	9 727	9.0	2.57	8.4	22.6
Whitley	9.3	6.4	6.4	50.2	27 651	30 707	11.1	3.1	1 352	958	571	11 711	17.0	2.58	8.3	22.4
IOWA	9.8	6.9	7.8	50.8	2 776 831	2 926 324	5.4	0.6	121 048	91 168	-10 393	1 149 276	8.0	2.46	8.6	27.2
Adair	10.3	9.5	12.8	51.0	8 409	8 243	-2.0	-3.9	210	373	-150	3 398	-0.6	2.37	5.7	28.1
Adams	11.9	9.6	12.1	50.4	4 866	4 482	-7.9	-2.5	125	170	-60	1 867	-6.9	2.34	5.5	30.0
Allamakee	10.8	8.5	9.4	49.7	13 855	14 675	5.9	-0.8	544	548	-114	5 722	8.6	2.49	6.6	27.5
Appanoose	11.0	8.9	11.1	52.1	13 743	13 721	-0.2	-1.0	451	543	-33	5 779	3.0	2.34	8.8	29.9
Audubon	11.4	10.3	13.2	52.0	7 334	6 830	-6.9	-5.1	195	332	-208	2 773	-4.5	2.40	5.6	28.2
Benton	8.9	6.9	7.8	50.3	22 429	25 308	12.8	3.7	983	753	702	9 746	14.4	2.56	6.5	23.4
Black Hawk	9.2	6.6	7.5	52.0	123 798	128 012	3.4	-1.2	5 149	3 775	-3 004	49 683	5.9	2.45	10.8	27.1
Boone	9.8	7.5	8.4	51.1	25 186	26 224	4.1	0.1	942	954	61	10 374	5.6	2.44	7.8	26.7
Bremer	10.8	7.4	8.6	51.6	22 813	23 325	2.2	0.2	759	783	84	8 860	5.6	2.47	6.2	24.7
Buchanan	9.9	7.1	7.7	50.3	20 844	21 093	1.2	-0.9	968	600	-551	7 933	5.7	2.61	7.4	24.7
Buena Vista	8.1	7.1	9.2	49.6	19 965	20 411	2.2	-1.0	751	675	-281	7 499	-0.2	2.54	7.2	27.0
Butler	11.0	8.9	11.0	50.4	15 731	15 305	-2.7	-2.2	458	674	-111	6 175	2.3	2.43	6.3	25.0
Calhoun	10.3	9.7	12.6	49.8	11 508	11 115	-3.4	-4.2	315	515	-250	4 513	-3.7	2.31	6.6	30.5
Carroll	9.2	8.2	10.8	51.1	21 423	21 421	0.0	-1.6	766	639	-458	8 486	6.6	2.46	6.8	29.6
Cass	10.9	9.1	11.7	51.3	15 128	14 684	-2.9	-2.5	492	655	-203	6 120	-0.9	2.32	7.2	29.8
Cedar	10.0	7.2	8.8	50.8	17 444	18 187	4.3	0.4	628	601	67	7 147	6.9	2.51	6.7	23.7
Cerro Gordo	9.9	8.5	9.3	51.9	46 733	46 447	-0.6	-2.9	1 533	1 723	-1 129	19 374	1.6	2.32	9.1	30.9
Cherokee	10.6	10.1	10.8	50.9	14 098	13 035	-7.5	-3.8	392	513	-361	5 378	-2.5	2.35	6.5	29.5
Chickasaw	10.8	8.6	9.6	49.9	13 295	13 095	-1.5	-3.0	476	456	-412	5 192	3.0	2.48	6.3	26.1
Clarke	9.6	7.7	9.0	50.1	8 287	9 133	10.2	1.2	393	314	35	3 584	7.2	2.50	8.3	25.9
Clay	9.4	8.2	10.1	51.6	17 585	17 372	-1.2	-1.7	654	543	-408	7 259	2.6	2.35	6.8	29.8
Clayton	10.4	9.0	9.6	50.4	19 054	18 678	-2.0	-1.2	687	723	-178	7 375	2.2	2.47	6.1	26.3
Clinton	10.4	7.5	8.5	51.4	51 040	50 149	-1.7	-0.7	1 940	1 729	-526	20 155	1.8	2.44	9.8	27.4
Crawford	10.2	7.8	9.1	49.5	16 775	16 942	1.0	-0.1	699	551	-148	6 441	0.7	2.53	7.0	26.2
Dallas	8.0	4.8	5.0	50.5	29 755	40 750	37.0	13.2	1 696	992	4 558	15 584	39.1	2.59	8.0	23.6
Davis	9.9	8.2	8.9	50.2	8 312	8 541	2.8	0.2	405	287	-92	3 207	3.7	2.61	5.2	25.0
Decatur	9.5	8.0	9.4	51.0	8 338	8 689	4.2	0.2	264	299	58	3 337	4.1	2.37	7.2	30.3
Delaware	9.4	7.5	8.0	50.5	18 035	18 404	2.0	-1.4	648	555	-342	6 834	7.0	2.66	6.2	23.0
Des Moines	10.8	7.6	9.0	51.7	42 614	42 351	-0.6	-2.6	1 629	1 399	-1 332	17 270	2.3	2.40	10.5	28.6
Dickinson	11.7	10.3	10.4	51.1	14 909	16 424	10.2	-0.2	492	618	116	7 103	15.3	2.27	6.7	28.6
Dubuque	9.3	7.2	7.5	51.2	86 403	89 143	3.2	1.0	3 783	2 831	29	33 690	9.4	2.51	8.7	26.7
Emmet	9.8	8.3	11.2	50.9	11 569	11 027	-4.7	-2.0	404	447	-175	4 450	-0.2	2.36	7.8	30.3
Fayette	10.3	8.9	10.4	50.6	21 843	22 008	0.8	-2.7	676	897	-373	8 778	3.4	2.41	7.4	28.2
Floyd	10.9	8.6	10.8	51.7	17 058	16 900	-0.9	-1.7	618	681	-220	6 828	1.6	2.40	7.7	28.0
Franklin	10.8	9.1	10.8	50.1	11 364	10 704	-5.8	-0.1	388	407	17	4 356	-4.9	2.41	6.4	27.6
Fremont	10.8	9.1	10.9	50.7	8 226	8 010	-2.6	-1.8	283	325	-99	3 199	-0.6	2.45	8.2	26.3
Greene	9.8	9.2	12.5	51.2	10 045	10 366	3.2	-3.1	350	491	-179	4 205	0.2	2.41	7.2	29.1
Grundy	10.9	8.4	10.5	51.2	12 029	12 369	2.8	-0.2	407	426	7	4 984	4.4	2.45	5.5	25.5

1. No spouse present.

STATE County	Births, average 1999–2001 Total	Rate[1]	Deaths, average 1999–2001 Number Total	Infant[2]	Rate Total[1]	Infant[3]	Physicians,[4] 2000 Number	Rate[5]	Hospitals,[4] 1998 Number	Beds Number	Rate[5]	Medicare enrollees, 2003	Serious crimes known to police,[6] 2002 Total Number	Rate[7]
	32	33	34	35	36	37	38	39	40	41	42	43	44	45
INDIANA—Cont'd														
Putnam	414	11.5	295	2	8.2	D	16	44	1	85	247	4 967	NA	NA
Randolph	352	12.9	299	4	10.9	D	18	66	1	27	98	4 948	369	1 329
Ripley	398	14.9	234	1	8.8	D	27	102	1	73	268	4 685	426	1 586
Rush	247	13.5	199	0	10.9	D	14	77	1	44	240	2 907	NA	NA
St. Joseph	3 901	14.7	2 461	33	9.3	8.4	542	204	4	836	324	40 501	15 025	5 586
Scott	298	13.0	241	2	10.5	D	12	52	1	46	201	3 870	NA	NA
Shelby	609	14.0	374	6	8.6	D	29	67	1	59	136	5 842	NA	NA
Spencer	284	13.9	177	1	8.7	D	5	25	0	0	0	3 141	NA	NA
Starke	307	13.2	261	2	11.2	D	10	42	1	35	146	3 883	676	2 833
Steuben	431	13.0	276	4	8.3	D	18	54	1	57	181	5 081	1 185	3 522
Sullivan	259	11.9	260	3	11.9	D	12	55	1	53	275	3 622	NA	NA
Switzerland	108	11.9	88	1	9.7	D	2	22	0	0	0	1 304	NA	NA
Tippecanoe	1 896	12.7	1 035	17	6.9	9.0	288	193	2	477	343	15 691	5 421	3 609
Tipton	186	11.2	164	1	9.9	D	19	115	1	116	694	2 490	NA	NA
Union	95	12.9	63	1	8.5	D	0	0	0	0	0	1 135	90	1 209
Vanderburgh	2 308	13.4	1 902	17	11.1	7.4	540	314	3	1 127	670	30 238	7 560	4 341
Vermillion	210	12.5	215	1	12.9	D	6	36	1	56	331	2 857	NA	NA
Vigo	1 319	12.5	1 220	11	11.5	8.3	220	208	2	550	523	16 943	NA	NA
Wabash	421	12.1	384	3	11.0	D	43	123	1	69	200	6 334	NA	NA
Warren	95	11.2	92	1	10.8	D	3	36	1	35	424	1 014	7	82
Warrick	654	12.5	429	2	8.2	D	53	101	1	34	66	6 827	885	1 668
Washington	350	12.8	254	1	9.3	D	12	44	1	68	244	3 936	NA	NA
Wayne	914	12.9	821	9	11.6	10.2	138	194	1	250	351	13 249	2 598	3 718
Wells	337	12.2	256	2	9.3	D	60	217	2	144	536	3 929	380	1 359
White	363	14.4	259	2	10.2	D	17	67	1	59	233	4 884	NA	NA
Whitley	420	13.6	274	3	8.9	D	25	81	1	100	328	4 830	NA	NA
IOWA	37 814	12.9	28 087	225	9.6	5.9	5 236	179	120	13 473	471	482 340	101 265	3 448
Adair	68	8.3	119	0	14.5	D	5	61	1	34	422	1 562	34	411
Adams	40	9.0	57	0	12.7	D	4	89	1	22	506	972	49	1 089
Allamakee	171	11.7	167	1	11.4	D	6	41	0	0	0	2 819	NA	NA
Appanoose	147	10.7	172	0	12.6	D	11	80	1	60	441	3 085	494	3 588
Audubon	58	8.5	98	1	14.5	D	2	29	1	29	427	1 547	63	919
Benton	298	11.7	226	1	8.9	D	7	28	1	116	456	4 026	241	949
Black Hawk	1 582	12.4	1 153	9	9.0	5.7	283	221	3	609	503	20 139	5 978	4 653
Boone	309	11.8	305	3	11.6	D	27	103	1	65	248	4 393	294	1 117
Bremer	242	10.3	228	1	9.7	D	13	56	2	74	316	4 239	246	1 051
Buchanan	300	14.2	192	1	9.1	D	19	90	1	109	514	3 506	519	2 452
Buena Vista	243	11.9	216	0	10.6	D	17	83	1	41	211	3 569	558	2 724
Butler	155	10.1	196	1	12.9	D	1	7	0	0	0	3 324	44	286
Calhoun	102	9.2	161	0	14.5	D	7	63	1	49	431	2 538	121	1 085
Carroll	247	11.6	232	1	10.8	D	28	131	2	181	834	4 354	403	1 875
Cass	157	10.7	205	1	14.0	D	16	109	2	71	487	3 365	269	1 825
Cedar	192	10.5	173	1	9.5	D	10	55	0	0	0	2 914	226	1 238
Cerro Gordo	519	11.2	522	3	11.3	D	135	291	1	285	617	9 204	2 154	4 621
Cherokee	132	10.2	165	1	12.7	D	17	130	1	67	508	2 825	191	1 460
Chickasaw	149	11.4	140	1	10.6	D	3	23	1	55	409	2 548	118	898
Clarke	113	12.5	101	0	11.2	D	5	55	1	48	574	1 557	278	3 033
Clay	201	11.6	175	1	10.1	D	30	173	1	86	491	3 293	438	2 512
Clayton	201	10.7	229	1	12.3	D	9	48	2	54	288	3 748	0	0
Clinton	612	12.2	538	3	10.7	D	69	138	2	250	501	9 066	NA	NA
Crawford	205	12.1	178	2	10.5	D	9	53	1	72	438	3 147	119	700
Dallas	532	13.0	314	4	7.7	D	39	96	1	53	144	5 262	809	1 978
Davis	119	13.8	87	1	10.2	D	8	94	1	80	952	1 532	20	233
Decatur	91	10.5	101	1	11.7	D	8	92	1	50	608	1 729	0	0
Delaware	209	11.4	160	1	8.7	D	12	65	1	49	264	2 833	120	650
Des Moines	526	12.4	436	3	10.3	D	75	177	1	388	925	7 725	1 759	4 139
Dickinson	162	9.9	185	1	11.2	D	17	104	1	49	302	3 787	79	479
Dubuque	1 184	13.3	873	7	9.8	5.6	179	201	3	670	763	15 114	2 420	2 705
Emmet	126	11.5	134	1	12.2	D	9	82	1	58	533	2 256	268	2 422
Fayette	223	10.2	265	0	12.1	D	21	95	3	119	547	4 308	315	1 426
Floyd	193	11.5	212	0	12.6	D	13	77	1	20	122	3 579	242	1 427
Franklin	120	11.2	134	0	12.5	D	6	56	1	92	847	2 046	150	1 396
Fremont	90	11.3	103	1	12.9	D	5	62	1	36	465	1 634	111	1 381
Greene	110	10.7	142	1	13.8	D	8	77	1	115	1 143	2 311	NA	NA
Grundy	121	9.8	130	2	10.5	D	8	65	1	88	722	2 339	110	886

1. Per 1,000 estimated resident population. 2. Deaths of infants under 1 year old. 3. Deaths of infants under 1 year old per 1,000 live births. 4. Data subject to copyright. 5. Per 100,000 resident population as of July 1 of the year shown. 6. Data for serious crimes have not been adjusted for underreporting; this may affect comparability between geographic areas and over time. 7. Per 100,000 population estimated by the FBI.

Table B. States and Counties — Crime, Education, Money Income, and Poverty

STATE County	Serious crimes known to police,[1] 2002 (cont'd) Rate[2]		Education School enrollment and attainment, 2000 Enrollment[3]		Attainment[4] (percent)		Local government expenditures,[5] 2000–2001		Money income, 1999	Households Median income			Percent below poverty level, 1999			
	Violent	Property	Total	Percent private	High school graduate or less	Bachelor's degree or more	Total current expenditures (mil dol)	Current expenditures per student (dollars)	Per capita income[6] (dollars)	Dollars	Percent change, 1989–1999 (constant 1999 dollars)	Percent with income of $100,000 or more	Persons	Households	Families	Families with children
	46	47	48	49	50	51	52	53	54	55	56	57	58	59	60	61
INDIANA—Cont'd																
Putnam	NA	NA	9 600	26.2	67.0	13.1	44.7	6 550	17 163	38 882	4.4	6.7	8.0	8.7	6.4	8.5
Randolph	83	1 247	6 095	5.1	67.9	9.9	34.6	7 213	16 954	34 544	3.8	3.6	11.1	11.1	8.3	13.0
Ripley	506	1 079	6 526	14.9	67.9	11.5	39.7	7 338	17 559	41 426	15.9	5.7	7.5	8.3	6.3	8.3
Rush	NA	NA	4 229	13.6	71.3	10.3	17.7	6 627	17 997	38 152	13.1	6.0	7.3	9.0	5.5	7.8
St. Joseph	404	5 181	76 955	32.8	50.1	23.6	323.6	8 161	19 756	40 420	6.6	8.9	10.4	9.7	7.6	12.3
Scott	NA	NA	5 152	8.7	71.1	8.8	26.9	6 569	16 065	34 656	18.7	5.1	13.1	12.7	10.5	16.5
Shelby	NA	NA	10 554	9.7	64.9	12.7	51.9	6 606	20 324	43 649	7.0	9.1	7.6	7.1	4.8	7.4
Spencer	NA	NA	5 109	10.0	61.6	13.0	25.6	6 641	18 000	42 451	9.8	6.5	6.9	6.9	4.8	6.6
Starke	126	2 707	5 722	9.8	71.5	8.4	30.0	6 801	16 466	37 243	21.7	5.2	11.1	10.9	8.8	13.4
Steuben	155	3 368	8 611	17.7	58.7	15.5	33.9	6 774	20 647	44 089	12.4	7.4	6.7	7.3	4.9	6.0
Sullivan	NA	NA	5 101	7.1	63.6	9.4	26.3	7 395	16 234	32 976	7.0	5.0	10.9	11.3	8.5	13.3
Switzerland	NA	NA	2 017	6.0	73.1	7.6	10.5	6 381	17 466	37 092	15.7	4.3	13.9	12.2	10.6	15.3
Tippecanoe	211	3 398	60 819	7.8	42.7	33.2	129.5	6 819	19 375	38 652	4.1	9.5	15.4	15.5	7.3	10.7
Tipton	NA	NA	3 883	11.3	64.7	12.4	19.0	6 542	21 926	48 546	15.8	10.2	5.1	6.2	2.9	4.1
Union	309	900	1 818	6.2	65.7	11.1	10.1	6 279	19 549	36 672	10.8	5.7	9.7	8.2	7.9	12.1
Vanderburgh	478	3 863	44 775	22.5	52.6	19.3	176.2	7 704	20 655	36 823	6.2	7.7	11.2	11.0	7.8	12.9
Vermillion	NA	NA	3 892	6.7	64.0	11.2	20.2	7 240	18 579	34 837	16.1	5.7	9.5	10.7	6.3	8.2
Vigo	NA	NA	31 055	12.8	53.8	21.4	113.3	6 848	17 620	33 184	5.1	6.3	14.1	14.6	10.3	15.8
Wabash	NA	NA	8 948	18.7	64.3	13.7	41.5	6 910	18 192	40 413	12.6	5.1	6.9	7.0	5.1	7.6
Warren	12	70	2 032	7.8	61.7	14.0	9.1	6 638	18 070	41 825	21.2	7.0	6.5	6.1	4.0	6.3
Warrick	241	1 427	13 756	15.5	47.3	21.8	55.0	6 119	21 893	48 814	6.6	11.7	5.3	5.1	3.5	5.5
Washington	NA	NA	6 407	9.0	68.9	10.2	34.5	7 234	16 748	36 630	19.1	4.7	10.6	11.0	7.3	10.7
Wayne	318	3 401	17 570	12.6	61.4	13.7	83.0	7 206	17 727	34 885	10.6	5.4	11.4	11.5	8.5	14.1
Wells	43	1 316	7 028	11.4	59.2	14.3	34.3	6 632	19 158	43 934	4.6	6.9	5.9	6.1	4.2	6.8
White	NA	NA	5 855	5.2	65.6	10.5	32.4	5 798	18 323	40 707	13.9	5.4	7.0	6.1	4.3	5.5
Whitley	NA	NA	7 674	10.9	59.2	13.3	34.1	6 746	20 519	45 503	8.8	8.2	4.9	5.8	3.3	4.9
IOWA	286	3 163	792 057	15.4	50.0	21.2	3 421.9	6 911	19 674	39 469	12.0	7.3	9.1	9.3	6.0	9.3
Adair	24	387	1 856	5.6	60.6	11.2	7.9	6 582	17 262	35 179	22.2	3.6	7.6	8.8	4.9	8.6
Adams	111	978	1 039	3.4	56.9	12.0	4.6	6 418	15 550	30 453	10.2	3.1	9.3	9.5	6.4	8.2
Allamakee	NA	NA	3 436	12.3	62.8	14.4	16.2	6 226	16 599	33 967	19.8	3.9	9.6	9.5	6.4	10.7
Appanoose	291	3 297	3 296	7.7	59.7	12.2	15.7	6 654	14 644	28 612	19.4	2.5	14.5	16.5	10.1	13.7
Audubon	15	905	1 616	3.0	62.2	12.3	7.1	6 200	17 489	32 215	11.5	5.0	7.7	9.3	6.7	9.0
Benton	35	913	6 744	9.0	55.5	13.9	26.6	6 194	18 891	42 427	21.6	4.8	6.1	7.0	4.6	6.6
Black Hawk	357	4 296	40 461	13.0	48.7	23.0	130.3	7 386	18 885	37 266	8.0	7.1	13.1	12.8	7.9	12.7
Boone	34	1 083	6 393	8.6	49.2	18.8	27.3	6 477	19 943	40 763	16.2	6.0	7.6	7.7	4.5	6.5
Bremer	64	987	6 970	24.7	50.0	21.5	29.0	5 728	19 199	40 826	11.2	6.8	5.1	5.6	2.9	4.6
Buchanan	61	2 390	5 468	12.0	59.0	12.7	19.8	6 294	18 405	38 036	21.1	5.5	9.4	9.2	6.8	10.3
Buena Vista	190	2 534	5 960	27.9	54.8	18.7	26.1	6 780	16 042	35 300	3.8	5.0	10.5	10.9	7.6	12.0
Butler	13	273	3 667	5.0	59.3	12.4	12.9	6 041	17 036	35 883	14.7	4.0	8.0	8.7	6.5	9.4
Calhoun	36	1 049	2 485	4.8	52.7	15.4	15.9	6 522	17 498	33 286	10.1	4.9	10.1	10.5	7.1	10.7
Carroll	33	1 842	5 715	30.1	56.1	16.0	21.4	6 339	18 595	37 275	13.7	5.8	6.5	8.6	4.5	6.4
Cass	34	1 792	3 431	6.9	54.5	16.6	18.6	6 348	17 067	32 922	12.4	4.5	11.1	10.8	7.2	10.8
Cedar	77	1 162	4 574	5.9	54.2	16.3	22.0	5 962	19 200	42 198	13.3	5.1	5.5	6.4	4.0	5.0
Cerro Gordo	163	4 458	11 271	13.2	46.0	20.3	54.1	7 756	19 184	35 867	6.3	5.9	8.5	9.5	5.9	9.7
Cherokee	54	1 407	2 998	5.1	55.2	15.2	14.7	6 787	17 934	35 142	13.9	4.0	7.3	7.3	5.5	8.8
Chickasaw	91	807	3 365	13.6	61.8	12.2	15.4	6 023	18 237	37 649	13.7	3.9	8.3	8.0	5.9	7.9
Clarke	55	2 978	2 192	5.8	58.6	12.1	11.4	6 042	16 409	34 474	18.1	4.4	8.5	8.1	6.2	10.4
Clay	23	2 490	4 161	8.5	48.8	16.3	17.8	6 246	19 451	35 799	6.5	5.7	8.2	9.1	6.3	10.7
Clayton	0	0	4 406	9.1	63.0	12.8	38.2	11 189	16 930	34 068	18.5	3.9	8.6	9.1	5.7	8.3
Clinton	NA	NA	12 977	13.1	55.9	14.4	57.0	6 589	17 724	37 423	9.6	4.1	10.2	10.1	7.7	12.4
Crawford	59	641	4 224	12.0	64.3	12.4	17.6	6 530	15 851	33 922	13.7	3.1	11.1	9.6	6.9	10.0
Dallas	125	1 853	10 346	13.3	43.2	26.8	54.7	6 279	22 970	48 528	25.1	13.1	5.6	5.8	4.0	5.6
Davis	35	198	2 038	16.2	62.5	11.4	7.7	5 880	15 127	32 864	22.0	3.3	11.9	11.8	9.0	12.5
Decatur	0	0	2 733	35.3	59.8	15.1	10.0	6 719	14 209	27 343	12.4	3.5	15.5	18.6	10.9	15.2
Delaware	76	574	5 181	16.4	62.1	13.0	21.5	6 035	17 327	37 168	7.4	5.5	7.9	9.2	6.3	8.1
Des Moines	409	3 729	10 167	14.5	53.5	16.0	53.1	7 611	19 701	36 790	3.2	5.4	10.7	9.8	8.2	14.6
Dickinson	18	461	3 611	5.8	46.1	21.3	18.0	6 388	21 929	39 020	15.2	7.6	6.0	7.2	4.2	6.1
Dubuque	224	2 482	24 497	39.1	55.0	21.3	80.7	6 386	19 600	39 582	4.2	7.2	7.8	7.9	4.9	7.4
Emmet	289	2 133	2 916	6.2	53.8	13.0	19.1	9 806	16 619	33 305	8.8	4.5	8.2	9.1	5.2	8.7
Fayette	72	1 354	5 850	13.9	59.0	13.8	28.0	6 540	17 271	32 453	14.4	3.8	10.8	11.5	8.2	10.7
Floyd	47	1 380	4 072	12.3	55.0	13.8	19.4	6 623	17 091	35 237	12.3	3.7	9.3	8.9	6.5	10.3
Franklin	56	1 340	2 506	5.3	54.6	14.5	12.6	6 739	18 767	36 042	13.0	5.1	8.0	7.8	5.7	8.2
Fremont	162	1 219	1 936	3.8	57.4	14.0	10.4	6 449	18 081	38 345	24.4	4.7	9.5	10.6	6.5	9.9
Greene	NA	NA	2 518	7.4	56.7	14.6	13.5	6 396	16 866	33 883	13.0	3.3	8.1	9.3	4.8	8.6
Grundy	24	862	3 156	6.1	51.7	17.2	15.6	6 192	19 142	39 396	11.4	5.4	4.6	5.5	3.3	4.1

1. Data for serious crimes have not been adjusted for underreporting; this may affect comparability between geographic areas and over time.   2. Per 100,000 population estimated by the FBI.   3. All persons 3 years old and over enrolled in nursery school through college.   4. Persons 25 years old and over.   5. Elementary and secondary education expenditures.   6. Based on population enumerated as of April 1, 2000.

Table B. States and Counties — **Personal Income**

STATE County	Personal income, 2002 Total (mil dol)	Percent change, 2001–2002	Per capita[1] Dollars	Per capita[1] Rank	Wages and salaries[2] (mil dol)	Proprietor's income (mil dol)	Dividends, interest, and rent (mil dol)	Transfer payments Total (mil dol)	Government payments to individuals Total (mil dol)	Social Security (mil dol)	Medical payments (mil dol)	Income maintenance (mil dol)	Unemployment insurance (mil dol)
	62	63	64	65	66	67	68	69	70	71	72	73	74
INDIANA—Cont'd													
Putnam	883	2.1	24 250	1 328	426	72	131	128	119	61	44	7	2
Randolph	626	-0.8	23 084	1 702	288	33	101	124	117	56	46	9	3
Ripley	661	4.0	24 217	1 338	616	16	107	107	100	43	43	6	4
Rush	457	-1.6	25 456	1 010	199	21	64	78	73	34	31	4	3
St. Joseph	7 656	2.9	28 742	475	5 083	896	1 375	1 108	1 041	467	411	99	32
Scott	507	1.5	21 682	2 096	237	13	60	108	102	40	44	12	2
Shelby	1 187	1.4	27 093	684	669	47	153	173	162	72	69	10	7
Spencer	504	0.7	24 795	1 177	279	25	77	79	74	36	29	4	3
Starke	446	1.3	19 382	2 681	135	13	65	112	106	48	40	10	4
Steuben	834	2.5	24 913	1 157	541	44	152	123	115	58	40	7	5
Sullivan	434	-0.1	19 849	2 575	187	17	75	103	98	40	43	7	3
Switzerland	193	-3.2	20 435	2 449	86	4	21	37	35	14	15	3	2
Tippecanoe	3 767	1.7	24 737	1 201	3 200	251	714	446	409	189	141	33	13
Tipton	484	2.0	29 269	412	166	24	64	69	65	33	24	3	3
Union	167	-1.8	22 773	1 791	47	10	22	28	26	11	11	2	2
Vanderburgh	5 298	3.6	30 842	282	4 427	477	1 042	850	807	343	332	70	23
Vermillion	403	1.4	24 308	1 307	207	23	63	77	73	34	28	5	2
Vigo	2 505	3.2	23 930	1 428	1 908	118	505	518	491	192	211	46	16
Wabash	872	0.9	25 282	1 054	484	57	157	164	155	75	64	9	2
Warren	195	-2.1	22 450	1 892	58	12	30	33	31	16	10	2	1
Warrick	1 623	3.6	30 240	330	590	64	260	192	178	86	70	10	5
Washington	619	-0.8	22 382	1 913	213	30	83	115	108	46	43	9	6
Wayne	1 742	1.7	24 696	1 212	1 237	78	287	360	343	151	140	29	9
Wells	704	0.4	25 300	1 047	400	37	118	100	93	49	34	5	2
White	571	-1.3	22 718	1 814	289	18	101	114	108	51	42	6	3
Whitley	833	1.5	26 539	780	401	27	125	118	110	55	39	5	6
IOWA	82 465	2.8	28 089	X	53 326	7 001	15 396	12 962	12 180	5 351	5 024	781	442
Adair	213	1.2	26 554	774	89	26	51	37	35	17	14	2	1
Adams	104	1.3	23 732	1 486	40	14	23	24	23	10	10	1	1
Allamakee	357	3.9	24 681	1 217	164	62	75	63	74	30	31	7	2
Appanoose	298	5.7	22 199	1 959	148	29	58	78	74	30	31	1	1
Audubon	173	0.4	26 279	836	53	36	47	30	28	16	9	1	1
Benton	692	1.4	26 509	786	182	70	137	102	95	47	36	5	5
Black Hawk	3 349	4.0	26 470	800	2 638	216	574	610	576	235	242	49	20
Boone	762	5.3	29 162	426	335	38	158	164	157	52	89	5	3
Bremer	653	2.6	28 022	548	314	58	129	105	99	47	41	4	3
Buchanan	521	1.6	25 017	1 123	197	52	114	91	86	38	36	5	4
Buena Vista	499	0.4	24 627	1 230	307	50	108	89	84	38	34	5	2
Butler	372	1.4	24 796	1 176	97	46	76	71	67	33	27	3	3
Calhoun	273	3.8	25 218	1 072	85	42	65	60	57	28	24	2	2
Carroll	583	1.2	27 597	601	344	67	138	105	99	44	46	5	2
Cass	368	2.9	25 675	962	182	37	78	80	77	34	34	4	3
Cedar	518	1.5	28 531	486	156	52	114	72	67	35	25	3	2
Cerro Gordo	1 289	3.9	28 460	496	868	96	257	234	222	102	89	13	7
Cherokee	347	2.3	27 337	641	178	42	82	68	64	31	26	3	2
Chickasaw	328	2.7	25 461	1 009	138	47	74	59	56	28	22	3	3
Clarke	220	4.4	23 940	1 424	138	30	34	40	38	16	15	3	3
Clay	463	1.9	27 061	688	301	51	102	79	74	37	29	4	3
Clayton	461	1.4	25 028	1 120	209	52	113	86	81	38	32	4	4
Clinton	1 275	3.3	25 586	981	745	106	223	264	251	102	109	18	10
Crawford	397	2.2	23 365	1 606	230	46	76	77	73	32	32	4	2
Dallas	1 413	4.0	31 912	228	482	81	226	138	126	61	49	6	5
Davis	180	1.8	20 845	2 333	64	25	31	38	36	15	16	2	1
Decatur	165	3.2	19 043	2 748	64	16	28	43	41	16	18	3	1
Delaware	457	-0.8	24 945	1 150	185	74	91	70	66	30	25	4	4
Des Moines	1 137	1.0	27 442	624	843	95	216	222	211	89	81	17	10
Dickinson	515	4.4	31 359	257	265	56	138	81	76	42	26	3	3
Dubuque	2 442	3.4	27 294	651	1 809	178	535	393	369	168	151	23	13
Emmet	274	2.2	25 362	1 028	141	38	49	59	56	24	23	3	2
Fayette	499	2.1	23 167	1 674	222	61	102	111	105	45	42	7	4
Floyd	411	4.3	24 766	1 190	184	41	93	91	87	39	37	5	3
Franklin	283	0.1	26 462	802	118	41	69	53	50	25	20	2	2
Fremont	206	1.6	26 310	828	124	11	48	40	38	18	16	2	0
Greene	244	3.3	23 895	1 440	100	21	64	52	49	25	18	3	1
Grundy	352	1.2	28 488	489	123	41	79	53	50	29	17	2	1

1. Based on the resident population estimated as of July 1 of the year shown. 2. Includes other labor income.

STATE County	Earnings, 2002									Social Security beneficiaries, December 2003			Housing units, 2003	
			Percent by selected industries											
			Goods-related[1]		Service-related and health									
	Total (mil dol)	Farm	Total	Manu-facturing	Infor-mation and profes-sional and technical services	Retail trade	Finance, insur-ance, and real estate	Health services	Govern-ment	Number	Rate[2]	Supple-mental Security Income recipients, December 2003	Total	Percent change, 2000–2003
	75	76	77	78	79	80	81	82	83	84	85	86	87	88
INDIANA—Cont'd														
Putnam	498	0.6	36.8	32.7	D	6.5	2.8	D	20.5	6 120	167	344	13 851	2.6
Randolph	321	-0.8	D	42.0	D	5.4	2.8	D	15.0	5 730	214	339	11 886	0.9
Ripley	632	-0.9	D	35.8	D	4.5	3.7	D	8.5	4 785	175	344	11 125	6.1
Rush	220	-1.2	D	32.5	3.3	6.5	4.4	6.7	20.1	3 510	195	218	7 480	1.9
St. Joseph	5 979	0.1	29.4	23.0	8.4	7.2	5.9	12.7	9.9	44 690	168	4 163	110 359	3.1
Scott	249	-0.7	D	40.7	D	10.2	3.2	D	19.2	4 580	194	736	10 453	7.4
Shelby	716	0.3	50.0	42.3	2.8	5.7	2.9	D	14.2	7 230	165	494	18 017	2.2
Spencer	304	-1.6	36.4	30.5	D	4.9	4.0	D	12.0	3 705	182	230	8 777	5.3
Starke	148	0.2	31.0	26.1	2.7	10.3	2.6	D	24.2	5 190	224	438	10 506	3.0
Steuben	584	0.2	D	46.3	D	8.6	4.0	D	10.0	5 780	171	300	18 163	4.8
Sullivan	204	-0.3	D	8.6	3.8	7.7	4.7	D	38.2	4 220	193	359	9 036	2.6
Switzerland	90	-4.8	D	5.8	D	3.7	2.6	4.3	17.4	1 595	169	168	4 663	10.3
Tippecanoe	3 451	0.3	D	26.7	4.3	6.7	5.6	11.6	25.3	18 370	119	1 498	62 942	7.9
Tipton	189	3.1	34.9	28.9	3.7	12.8	2.8	D	23.2	3 160	192	132	6 973	1.8
Union	57	-6.0	28.4	22.0	D	11.4	D	D	25.5	1 315	182	113	3 249	5.6
Vanderburgh	4 904	0.0	D	18.7	8.2	7.4	6.7	13.9	8.7	34 115	198	3 989	78 560	3.0
Vermillion	230	-1.1	D	32.8	D	9.4	2.5	D	13.4	3 430	207	238	7 490	1.1
Vigo	2 026	0.1	27.1	20.7	4.8	11.5	4.5	13.3	18.6	19 630	188	2 648	45 906	1.6
Wabash	542	0.3	D	40.5	3.3	6.8	3.9	7.4	14.1	7 435	217	458	14 272	1.7
Warren	69	7.1	D	18.8	D	5.4	D	12.0	22.5	1 610	185	76	3 678	5.8
Warrick	654	-0.3	46.0	37.0	3.8	4.7	6.7	10.3	11.5	8 600	157	472	21 973	6.9
Washington	243	-1.1	D	33.9	3.8	8.2	3.5	4.9	21.6	5 045	183	529	11 720	4.7
Wayne	1 315	-0.4	33.7	29.1	D	8.5	4.6	D	13.8	15 315	218	1 673	30 684	0.7
Wells	437	1.3	D	35.2	2.5	6.0	3.3	D	12.1	4 840	173	164	11 345	3.4
White	307	2.4	D	28.1	D	12.2	3.3	D	18.7	5 230	210	233	12 542	3.8
Whitley	428	0.7	D	41.7	D	7.6	2.9	6.0	13.2	5 395	170	170	13 168	5.0
IOWA	60 327	2.6	25.0	18.7	7.1	7.9	9.1	10.0	16.5	546 065	185	41 890	1 269 685	3.0
Adair	115	11.8	D	23.5	3.6	6.1	D	D	15.4	1 870	236	78	3 748	1.6
Adams	54	9.0	D	14.7	D	9.2	D	17.6	17.1	1 150	263	111	2 098	-0.5
Allamakee	226	9.8	D	26.9	3.0	9.2	3.6	D	14.7	3 165	218	171	7 299	2.2
Appanoose	177	3.2	D	25.8	3.2	8.6	3.2	11.4	17.6	3 420	252	453	6 700	0.0
Audubon	89	12.3	16.8	9.7	D	8.1	4.8	6.2	16.3	1 810	279	72	3 005	0.3
Benton	252	6.7	D	15.0	D	10.8	5.9	D	21.7	4 805	183	223	10 704	3.2
Black Hawk	2 854	0.6	D	28.3	6.0	7.7	5.8	12.4	16.0	23 055	182	2 866	52 961	2.3
Boone	373	2.4	D	9.1	5.6	13.1	3.9	7.4	24.2	5 315	202	273	11 247	2.5
Bremer	372	6.9	D	19.1	3.5	6.8	16.3	D	13.6	4 770	204	184	9 602	2.8
Buchanan	249	7.5	D	22.6	2.9	9.0	4.6	D	24.3	3 860	185	275	8 873	2.0
Buena Vista	357	6.3	30.9	28.0	D	7.9	5.7	D	15.2	3 815	189	235	8 113	-0.4
Butler	143	15.9	D	13.0	3.7	7.0	4.5	7.0	18.2	3 585	240	152	6 591	0.2
Calhoun	127	20.8	9.2	4.9	3.4	6.4	5.4	D	22.1	2 890	271	137	5 177	-0.8
Carroll	411	6.3	D	10.4	D	10.8	9.1	D	11.1	4 705	223	267	9 094	0.8
Cass	219	3.3	D	13.9	D	9.4	5.4	D	24.1	3 640	254	308	6 574	-0.2
Cedar	208	8.3	23.6	16.5	D	10.6	3.9	D	17.7	3 495	191	117	7 707	1.8
Cerro Gordo	964	2.2	D	17.8	6.3	10.1	6.1	21.0	12.4	10 175	226	768	21 560	0.3
Cherokee	220	8.2	D	19.2	4.0	8.5	D	D	17.9	3 125	249	133	5 851	0.0
Chickasaw	185	13.5	D	21.8	2.4	8.4	4.6	D	12.9	2 915	229	125	5 637	0.8
Clarke	167	6.0	D	29.2	2.1	7.2	3.4	D	16.0	1 910	207	138	4 021	2.2
Clay	352	2.5	D	17.5	5.9	14.3	4.5	11.0	17.0	3 815	223	228	7 942	1.5
Clayton	262	10.0	D	13.0	2.6	7.6	4.5	D	18.2	4 390	238	258	8 873	2.9
Clinton	851	2.9	D	29.8	3.6	8.3	3.9	D	11.5	10 305	207	932	21 830	1.1
Crawford	276	5.6	35.2	30.6	3.5	8.0	4.0	7.5	16.5	3 540	209	204	6 985	0.4
Dallas	563	3.6	D	13.5	7.2	6.4	5.7	10.1	14.8	6 005	130	314	18 390	11.3
Davis	89	6.3	D	21.1	5.1	10.2	3.5	8.4	23.0	1 715	200	134	3 599	2.0
Decatur	81	7.9	D	6.5	D	6.6	D	D	28.6	1 845	212	189	3 852	0.5
Delaware	259	12.0	D	22.9	D	9.1	5.0	D	15.9	3 380	186	206	7 769	1.1
Des Moines	938	0.6	D	33.0	4.2	8.2	3.5	12.3	10.8	8 720	211	891	18 768	0.7
Dickinson	322	1.7	D	28.1	4.1	11.0	6.8	7.6	12.4	4 275	261	165	11 799	3.7
Dubuque	1 987	1.2	D	23.7	8.7	9.0	5.6	14.5	8.1	17 160	191	1 357	36 884	3.9
Emmet	179	8.9	D	20.2	D	9.1	3.6	11.3	17.2	2 385	221	121	4 920	0.6
Fayette	283	11.7	D	13.4	D	8.1	3.9	D	16.2	4 950	231	371	9 575	0.7
Floyd	225	6.6	35.5	28.3	D	7.8	4.6	D	17.0	4 085	246	315	7 296	-0.3
Franklin	159	10.7	D	18.9	3.8	8.1	3.8	D	16.7	2 530	237	109	4 731	-0.7
Fremont	135	5.0	D	49.9	2.1	7.1	D	6.9	12.3	1 860	237	117	3 538	0.7
Greene	122	6.7	D	16.6	5.8	8.3	5.5	D	25.3	2 545	253	157	4 628	0.1
Grundy	164	16.2	26.3	14.1	3.1	7.9	7.4	D	13.5	2 845	231	60	5 462	3.0

1. Covers mining, construction, and manufacturing.　　2. Per 1,000 resident population estimated as of July 1 of the year shown.

Table B. States and Counties — Housing, Labor Force, and Employment

STATE County	Housing units, 2000 Occupied units Total	Percent	Owner-occupied Median value[1]	Median owner cost as a percent of income With a mortgage	Without a mortgage[2]	Renter-occupied Median rent[3]	Median rent as a percent of income	Substandard units[4] (percent)	Civilian labor force, 2003 Total	Percent change, 2002–2003	Unemployment Total	Rate[5]	Civilian employment,[6] 2000 Total	Percent Management, professional and related occupations	Production, transportation, and material moving occupations
	89	90	91	92	93	94	95	96	97	98	99	100	101	102	103
INDIANA—Cont'd															
Putnam	12 374	78.6	94 300	20.8	10.1	462	21.7	2.5	19 147	12.0	805	4.2	16 183	24.2	24.5
Randolph	10 937	75.9	64 600	17.9	10.4	392	22.6	2.4	11 348	-1.6	952	8.4	12 624	22.4	30.4
Ripley	9 842	76.9	94 900	19.2	9.9	478	21.4	2.3	15 142	8.0	690	4.6	12 837	23.2	31.5
Rush	6 923	74.1	82 300	18.3	10.8	446	20.6	1.7	8 963	-3.2	430	4.8	8 790	22.2	31.6
St. Joseph	100 743	71.7	85 700	19.2	9.9	535	24.3	3.0	137 041	0.1	6 472	4.7	127 563	32.1	18.2
Scott	8 832	75.8	76 900	19.3	9.9	463	23.7	2.6	11 091	0.1	668	6.0	10 590	20.1	34.3
Shelby	16 561	73.4	98 600	18.5	9.9	528	20.7	1.7	23 418	0.8	1 143	4.9	22 307	25.6	25.6
Spencer	7 569	83.4	85 100	18.6	9.9	423	20.4	2.3	11 840	7.8	560	4.7	10 073	23.1	28.2
Starke	8 740	80.8	80 000	20.5	9.9	431	23.2	3.8	9 869	-1.0	817	8.3	10 012	20.9	32.6
Steuben	12 738	78.3	106 200	19.1	9.9	520	21.3	2.0	15 962	-0.4	1 151	7.2	17 437	24.1	30.3
Sullivan	7 819	79.8	58 900	18.6	11.1	375	22.2	1.9	9 209	0.4	587	6.4	8 594	23.6	22.1
Switzerland	3 435	77.8	78 400	20.8	11.4	444	21.2	4.4	3 804	0.4	246	6.5	4 135	20.5	29.1
Tippecanoe	55 226	55.9	112 200	19.7	9.9	565	28.7	3.8	77 108	-1.8	3 111	4.0	74 947	36.7	16.6
Tipton	6 469	79.9	88 300	16.6	9.9	489	18.9	0.9	8 515	-0.2	441	5.2	8 296	23.0	25.1
Union	2 793	75.0	82 600	19.8	10.8	450	21.6	2.4	3 840	0.1	196	5.1	3 492	24.7	24.6
Vanderburgh	70 623	66.8	82 400	18.8	9.9	458	24.3	2.0	96 298	0.5	4 000	4.2	85 080	27.9	18.1
Vermillion	6 762	79.2	59 500	18.1	9.9	378	23.2	2.1	7 875	2.4	513	6.5	7 630	22.6	24.3
Vigo	40 998	67.4	72 500	18.5	9.9	445	26.0	2.2	52 114	2.3	2 857	5.5	47 977	29.4	15.7
Wabash	13 215	75.9	78 400	17.3	9.9	425	20.8	1.3	17 099	0.8	969	5.7	17 127	23.3	31.2
Warren	3 219	80.9	74 100	20.2	9.9	419	18.5	2.0	4 101	-0.7	198	4.8	4 220	26.0	28.3
Warrick	19 438	83.3	104 400	19.4	9.9	478	20.5	1.1	30 810	0.7	1 134	3.7	26 815	31.1	16.5
Washington	10 264	81.1	77 500	19.5	9.9	418	22.3	3.4	11 333	-0.5	786	6.9	13 181	20.8	34.0
Wayne	28 469	68.7	80 300	19.1	9.9	446	24.5	1.6	36 456	0.4	2 260	6.2	33 829	24.8	25.2
Wells	10 402	80.8	87 900	18.6	9.9	458	20.0	1.6	14 547	-0.3	712	4.9	14 219	24.2	26.0
White	9 727	76.6	86 200	19.5	10.8	526	21.4	3.5	11 610	-4.0	985	8.5	12 656	22.8	29.9
Whitley	11 711	83.3	96 000	19.0	9.9	453	19.4	1.6	16 556	-0.2	1 051	6.3	16 302	24.6	28.1
IOWA	1 149 276	72.3	82 500	19.1	9.9	470	23.2	2.3	1 612 328	-3.0	72 223	4.5	1 489 816	31.3	18.1
Adair	3 398	75.3	59 300	17.6	9.9	373	18.9	0.7	4 480	-5.0	159	3.5	4 165	27.9	20.4
Adams	1 867	74.8	46 500	17.1	11.1	333	21.1	1.0	1 984	-5.9	103	5.2	2 230	32.6	19.5
Allamakee	5 722	76.5	68 100	19.0	10.2	348	19.0	2.7	7 849	-5.5	493	6.3	7 260	28.6	22.9
Appanoose	5 779	74.1	45 400	17.9	10.4	346	24.7	2.3	6 899	-0.9	347	5.0	5 897	25.2	25.6
Audubon	2 773	79.0	48 700	17.1	9.9	351	16.6	1.3	3 299	-6.2	126	3.8	3 214	34.6	17.4
Benton	9 746	79.4	82 700	19.6	9.9	385	20.0	2.1	12 075	-5.3	718	5.9	12 798	27.7	20.8
Black Hawk	49 683	68.9	77 000	18.4	11.0	472	26.3	2.8	70 821	-1.7	3 400	4.8	64 135	30.3	17.8
Boone	10 374	75.6	74 900	18.8	11.0	443	21.6	0.9	14 051	-2.5	499	3.6	13 619	27.3	16.2
Bremer	8 860	78.1	88 000	18.6	9.9	400	19.5	1.2	12 223	-6.1	430	3.5	12 016	32.4	17.6
Buchanan	7 933	78.1	73 900	19.0	10.3	376	19.6	3.1	11 386	-0.6	525	4.6	9 939	28.1	22.3
Buena Vista	7 499	70.5	64 900	18.3	10.2	417	20.3	6.1	11 144	-4.5	312	2.8	9 828	27.8	23.7
Butler	6 175	80.4	62 200	18.0	10.8	351	20.1	1.1	7 562	-4.7	427	5.6	7 377	27.8	20.6
Calhoun	4 513	77.4	54 700	18.9	9.9	315	20.7	1.4	4 526	-6.7	188	4.2	4 993	32.8	14.6
Carroll	8 486	74.3	75 900	18.6	9.9	403	19.8	1.5	12 848	-2.7	332	2.6	10 982	28.3	16.4
Cass	6 120	74.6	59 500	17.6	9.9	357	19.9	1.0	7 097	-4.7	394	5.6	7 338	28.6	21.1
Cedar	7 147	76.9	84 600	19.4	10.6	441	19.0	2.0	9 371	-4.7	363	3.9	9 753	28.3	20.0
Cerro Gordo	19 374	71.5	75 400	19.1	10.7	404	23.3	1.0	26 496	-1.4	1 011	3.8	23 581	28.3	19.3
Cherokee	5 378	73.5	57 300	18.2	10.6	353	18.2	1.8	6 686	-6.5	264	3.9	6 536	29.2	21.2
Chickasaw	5 192	80.4	71 200	18.5	9.9	325	17.9	1.3	6 540	-4.7	417	6.4	6 197	28.4	25.6
Clarke	3 584	72.3	64 700	19.1	12.1	449	21.7	4.1	5 279	-4.1	474	9.0	4 534	26.7	24.1
Clay	7 259	69.2	74 400	18.5	9.9	379	19.4	2.1	10 362	-0.8	411	4.0	9 142	26.0	23.6
Clayton	7 375	76.6	66 400	18.7	9.9	353	18.3	1.6	9 631	-6.9	664	6.9	9 427	28.1	24.0
Clinton	20 105	72.9	70 900	18.5	9.9	399	22.4	1.9	26 867	-4.3	1 510	5.6	24 226	25.1	24.6
Crawford	6 441	73.1	58 200	18.6	9.9	362	19.4	3.0	8 797	-4.4	297	3.4	8 260	24.5	28.6
Dallas	15 584	76.4	108 000	20.7	9.9	529	24.1	2.3	23 816	-1.4	730	3.1	21 978	35.9	12.6
Davis	3 207	79.8	55 000	17.9	12.6	352	21.0	5.1	4 566	-0.8	198	4.3	3 931	28.2	25.3
Decatur	3 337	71.1	45 400	19.2	11.9	340	25.3	2.3	3 680	-3.7	274	7.4	4 092	29.3	16.7
Delaware	6 834	78.0	79 700	19.5	10.8	370	21.7	1.6	9 532	-7.2	584	6.1	9 298	29.2	24.7
Des Moines	17 270	74.2	70 100	18.4	9.9	439	23.1	1.8	22 735	-2.7	1 527	6.7	20 927	24.9	24.3
Dickinson	7 103	78.0	96 800	20.3	9.9	416	21.0	1.4	10 840	2.3	437	4.0	8 468	29.9	19.2
Dubuque	33 690	73.5	93 300	19.4	9.9	434	22.4	1.8	50 076	-0.9	1 996	4.0	45 728	29.7	19.7
Emmet	4 450	75.2	53 000	17.2	10.0	322	18.3	1.5	5 550	-3.6	323	5.8	5 524	24.3	26.5
Fayette	8 778	75.6	58 300	18.1	9.9	360	21.3	1.3	10 901	-4.9	574	5.3	10 424	29.3	22.4
Floyd	6 828	74.1	64 700	18.6	10.0	357	20.6	1.3	7 979	-3.8	439	5.5	7 849	32.0	17.8
Franklin	4 356	74.8	55 200	16.8	9.9	374	20.8	2.2	5 543	-8.0	241	4.3	5 324	31.4	21.3
Fremont	3 199	74.5	64 400	17.7	9.9	391	20.9	2.5	4 442	-3.5	119	2.7	3 887	29.6	22.0
Greene	4 205	75.6	51 800	18.0	10.7	342	20.4	1.1	4 934	-2.7	171	3.5	4 632	31.7	20.7
Grundy	4 984	79.7	72 500	18.4	9.9	376	18.6	1.2	6 446	-2.4	223	3.5	6 121	30.8	20.1

1. Specified owner-occupied units.   2. Median monthly owner costs is often in the minimum category—9.9 percent or less, which is indicated as 9.9 percent.   3. Specified renter-occupied units.   4. Overcrowded or lacking complete plumbing facilities.   5. Percent of civilian labor force.   6. Persons 16 years old and over.

Table B. States and Counties — Nonfarm Employment and Agriculture

STATE County	Number of establishments	Total	Health care and social assistance	Manufacturing	Retail trade	Finance and insurance	Professional, scientific, and technical services	Total (mil dol)	Average per employee (dollars)	Number	Less than 50 acres	500 acres and over	Farm operators whose principal occupation is farming (percent)
	104	105	106	107	108	109	110	111	112	113	114	115	116
INDIANA—Cont'd													
Putnam	662	11 135	1 080	2 780	1 283	277	160	256	23 020	853	44.3	10.8	48.2
Randolph	565	6 694	569	3 150	932	204	106	178	26 624	786	34.9	21.2	61.7
Ripley	715	11 718	1 415	3 650	1 265	567	136	394	33 591	904	36.4	9.2	57.7
Rush	421	4 822	741	1 398	801	122	105	109	22 564	606	26.7	25.9	71.3
St. Joseph	6 456	121 271	15 164	19 965	17 726	4 901	4 984	3 588	29 585	855	52.2	9.8	56.6
Scott	441	6 511	626	2 772	1 052	135	84	147	22 540	387	44.2	7.5	48.3
Shelby	952	15 535	1 645	6 666	1 604	252	260	453	29 136	651	41.3	20.1	60.2
Spencer	408	5 796	329	1 930	838	128	95	170	29 284	593	30.7	14.5	52.4
Starke	347	3 672	693	1 181	760	D	38	74	20 212	518	47.7	13.7	48.8
Steuben	1 007	16 154	974	7 106	2 657	252	502	395	24 461	674	38.1	6.5	46.9
Sullivan	377	3 548	499	486	642	152	99	86	24 348	437	29.1	21.5	62.0
Switzerland	119	2 289	155	162	137	44	12	55	24 232	464	35.8	2.6	45.7
Tippecanoe	3 167	62 470	8 026	17 178	9 912	3 367	2 239	1 884	30 159	705	49.6	17.2	52.9
Tipton	327	3 770	600	1 043	514	102	95	104	27 587	360	28.3	26.9	64.4
Union	141	986	67	71	244	106	19	20	19 872	262	22.1	25.2	66.4
Vanderburgh	5 166	106 306	16 074	16 270	14 565	3 851	3 894	3 025	28 454	306	44.4	16.7	61.1
Vermillion	299	4 896	611	1 277	688	113	17	162	33 091	221	29.4	26.2	65.2
Vigo	2 633	47 506	8 224	7 699	9 658	1 386	1 112	1 202	25 307	476	46.8	16.6	47.7
Wabash	845	13 792	1 774	5 551	1 717	327	190	339	24 568	799	35.2	14.8	54.3
Warren	109	1 065	241	363	D	D	D	26	24 346	346	33.5	26.0	52.9
Warrick	1 041	11 092	1 840	2 662	1 418	401	303	314	28 296	401	45.9	13.7	48.6
Washington	485	6 049	665	2 949	703	158	122	133	21 920	977	34.8	7.1	55.5
Wayne	1 677	31 424	4 915	8 183	5 091	972	762	784	24 947	850	38.5	11.8	52.0
Wells	624	10 760	1 559	3 193	1 201	216	148	271	25 190	631	29.5	24.7	67.0
White	691	8 633	665	3 381	1 499	224	137	203	23 521	589	33.6	29.5	68.6
Whitley	699	11 258	1 054	4 663	1 727	276	204	298	26 492	840	41.0	10.5	54.0
IOWA	80 392	1 255 162	181 023	237 779	181 794	81 243	38 349	34 451	27 448	90 655	23.3	22.7	68.3
Adair	219	2 165	441	571	329	82	37	48	22 258	843	16.7	27.2	69.4
Adams	120	853	321	D	D	48	D	17	19 651	567	16.4	28.4	69.8
Allamakee	406	4 968	798	1 670	661	143	183	106	21 305	1 083	19.5	17.4	64.9
Appanoose	314	3 760	641	1 241	699	117	59	78	20 731	816	20.0	17.3	56.3
Audubon	205	1 302	288	238	224	60	56	26	19 629	638	22.4	26.2	69.9
Benton	628	4 612	664	693	827	261	94	106	23 013	1 186	24.1	23.1	68.0
Black Hawk	3 152	60 268	9 401	13 056	9 102	2 630	1 775	1 619	26 865	939	30.6	18.8	61.9
Boone	573	6 915	1 789	842	1 080	217	121	171	24 773	827	29.9	25.8	67.8
Bremer	615	7 730	1 183	1 817	1 019	1 106	146	198	25 566	956	27.5	15.3	66.9
Buchanan	520	5 397	1 025	1 433	915	228	87	127	23 494	1 067	24.7	20.5	71.7
Buena Vista	585	8 207	1 068	2 959	1 275	308	165	182	22 190	825	20.8	32.2	77.8
Butler	366	2 135	365	409	391	118	71	45	21 073	1 076	30.4	19.6	68.8
Calhoun	295	2 325	932	148	498	130	53	45	19 182	762	24.5	33.3	74.8
Carroll	853	10 082	1 723	1 285	1 827	889	176	222	21 990	1 045	22.3	22.4	77.1
Cass	491	5 288	1 169	1 072	947	203	120	115	21 670	764	19.8	30.6	72.1
Cedar	494	4 114	502	925	692	143	294	83	20 139	971	24.5	23.3	66.9
Cerro Gordo	1 466	22 434	5 070	4 021	3 798	1 241	511	567	25 287	795	31.2	28.4	76.4
Cherokee	390	4 522	957	934	823	175	80	110	24 410	837	19.6	27.7	76.3
Chickasaw	401	3 550	500	1 007	476	146	54	77	21 796	951	26.5	18.1	70.9
Clarke	221	3 848	419	1 338	506	106	D	85	22 038	726	16.9	15.8	59.6
Clay	641	8 237	1 334	1 433	1 867	266	197	188	22 814	691	20.4	33.1	80.6
Clayton	555	5 283	884	1 236	707	212	104	125	23 617	1 601	17.3	15.2	69.4
Clinton	1 282	19 459	3 037	4 942	2 906	761	271	479	24 601	1 219	25.5	20.9	67.1
Crawford	464	5 930	881	2 080	925	197	123	133	22 487	927	24.2	29.4	73.8
Dallas	856	10 047	1 521	2 457	1 431	353	257	276	27 450	938	37.4	20.9	54.2
Davis	185	1 537	408	308	284	D	60	31	20 332	1 007	17.5	14.4	58.4
Decatur	170	2 346	381	191	235	64	34	35	15 046	788	17.8	18.3	54.2
Delaware	494	4 822	642	1 469	735	214	114	110	22 770	1 253	18.8	14.9	75.7
Des Moines	1 215	20 787	2 909	6 914	3 286	521	269	528	25 392	674	28.8	16.5	56.5
Dickinson	694	7 377	722	2 412	1 158	263	165	185	25 070	492	21.5	30.9	72.8
Dubuque	2 645	48 677	6 525	10 458	6 749	2 289	1 018	1 247	25 621	1 481	19.9	8.5	71.2
Emmet	320	3 618	783	964	540	116	71	81	22 469	510	20.0	36.9	72.2
Fayette	645	6 980	1 220	1 196	1 169	270	157	136	19 516	1 344	26.4	19.6	68.2
Floyd	460	4 510	986	965	765	182	83	102	22 565	895	26.6	22.2	69.1
Franklin	329	3 016	532	810	440	107	80	74	24 503	825	22.9	29.5	75.5
Fremont	185	1 471	324	229	319	78	88	29	19 861	547	15.2	36.0	78.6
Greene	295	2 588	759	480	349	138	59	54	20 793	727	22.4	34.1	72.1
Grundy	317	2 816	349	564	426	170	D	77	27 433	724	25.8	28.9	74.4

Table B. States and Counties — Agriculture

STATE County	Land in farms					Value of land and buildings (dollars)		Value of machinery and equipment average per farm (dollars)	Value of products sold				Percent of farms with sales of —		Government payments	
	Acreage (1,000)	Percent change, 1997–2002	Acres Average size of farm	Total irrigated (1,000)	Total cropland (1,000)	Average per farm	Average per acre		Total (mil dol)	Average per farm (dollars)	Percent from — Crops	Live-stock and poultry products	$10,000 or more	$100,000 or more	Total ($1,000)	Percent of farms
	117	118	119	120	121	122	123	124	125	126	127	128	129	130	131	132
INDIANA—Cont'd																
Putnam	181	-7.2	212	D	144	512 108	2 426	70 059	45	52 183	74.9	25.1	34.9	12.3	2 667	39.6
Randolph	258	15.2	328	0	237	715 791	2 122	114 016	70	89 451	68.3	31.7	55.9	21.9	3 375	53.2
Ripley	173	8.8	191	0	133	420 969	2 517	56 253	44	48 770	71.0	29.0	40.2	10.0	2 265	47.7
Rush	224	-1.8	369	0	205	906 396	2 624	123 169	67	111 101	66.5	33.5	72.4	34.0	3 485	57.9
St. Joseph	165	7.1	193	20	149	457 761	2 914	61 082	50	58 936	74.7	25.3	42.2	14.2	2 546	43.6
Scott	69	21.1	179	0	53	363 821	2 223	53 650	13	32 343	83.4	16.6	26.1	7.5	874	42.1
Shelby	200	-0.5	307	3	185	842 101	2 801	105 369	59	90 702	86.1	13.9	58.2	24.0	3 647	47.3
Spencer	155	-10.4	261	0	125	454 472	1 941	79 602	35	58 611	59.6	40.4	46.7	14.3	1 925	47.9
Starke	134	-1.5	259	11	116	512 305	2 045	71 616	28	54 792	93.2	6.8	33.4	14.5	2 292	64.9
Steuben	113	-8.9	167	1	90	419 697	2 292	44 482	21	30 533	61.1	38.9	28.2	5.9	2 281	65.6
Sullivan	179	1.1	409	7	153	783 206	1 975	103 243	38	87 916	87.7	12.3	50.6	21.5	2 372	52.4
Switzerland	60	-11.8	130	0	32	273 230	2 439	30 576	6	13 939	72.8	27.2	25.4	2.2	302	24.1
Tippecanoe	221	-8.7	313	4	200	894 728	2 864	111 868	78	110 791	78.2	21.8	48.5	20.4	3 546	41.4
Tipton	152	-3.8	421	D	143	1 325 147	3 265	122 497	56	154 769	78.6	21.4	72.2	30.3	2 231	61.4
Union	85	3.7	325	D	72	815 644	2 475	109 936	22	82 604	68.1	31.9	64.9	25.6	1 338	59.5
Vanderburgh	82	13.9	268	0	76	672 256	2 562	105 404	20	66 551	90.3	9.7	51.3	21.2	1 134	53.9
Vermillion	110	-6.8	497	D	96	1 096 408	2 291	98 419	28	128 413	78.5	21.5	53.8	25.8	2 036	52.9
Vigo	123	7.0	258	1	105	529 783	2 165	77 770	28	59 657	91.2	8.8	41.0	13.4	1 551	37.2
Wabash	215	14.4	269	1	190	665 476	2 540	91 492	103	129 191	37.0	63.0	50.8	21.8	4 583	59.6
Warren	167	-9.7	482	1	152	1 180 732	2 445	161 534	52	151 592	D	D	48.6	25.1	2 931	57.8
Warrick	94	-5.1	236	0	75	536 405	2 399	69 464	17	42 499	83.7	16.4	37.2	15.0	1 556	46.4
Washington	181	0.0	185	0	123	450 571	2 238	53 748	40	41 121	36.6	63.4	33.5	8.6	2 393	38.6
Wayne	171	-1.2	201	0	142	507 014	2 224	54 757	45	52 660	72.8	27.2	41.3	13.3	3 368	51.3
Wells	226	15.3	359	D	211	835 578	2 356	107 265	62	98 961	71.4	28.6	65.9	25.8	3 818	56.1
White	284	4.4	482	3	260	1 216 336	2 535	113 448	116	197 775	60.8	39.2	65.5	37.2	4 716	60.4
Whitley	172	4.2	205	D	150	537 258	2 515	74 213	46	54 907	59.6	40.4	41.0	13.1	2 846	55.1
IOWA	31 729	1.8	350	142	27 153	707 730	2 005	100 422	12 274	135 388	49.5	50.5	64.6	30.2	538 896	69.6
Adair	373	11.0	443	D	307	620 870	1 464	108 285	93	110 654	57.6	42.4	64.9	27.5	4 872	68.1
Adams	238	1.3	419	D	182	538 843	1 421	51 903	51	69 833	55.6	44.4	56.3	21.7	4 150	75.0
Allamakee	326	10.1	301	0	192	471 249	1 524	106 884	91	84 049	31.3	68.7	52.5	21.5	7 183	73.8
Appanoose	236	-2.1	289	0	160	287 881	926	39 327	25	30 984	51.3	48.7	47.2	7.0	3 629	65.4
Audubon	261	-4.0	409	0	234	740 445	1 840	109 315	113	176 658	41.5	58.5	65.4	34.2	4 678	75.2
Benton	401	-4.1	338	0	358	789 874	2 374	102 187	148	124 750	64.4	35.6	70.0	33.9	7 104	69.5
Black Hawk	275	-3.8	293	0	253	838 929	2 786	106 687	114	121 814	60.9	39.1	67.9	27.4	4 967	67.6
Boone	313	-4.9	378	0	281	936 262	2 151	128 757	106	128 093	71.4	28.6	65.3	30.5	4 303	62.9
Bremer	255	6.7	267	D	231	674 166	2 588	121 400	108	113 041	58.0	42.0	67.5	29.0	4 239	70.0
Buchanan	340	0.9	319	D	311	718 027	2 449	105 191	142	132 719	59.3	40.7	74.8	34.3	5 799	62.3
Buena Vista	342	-4.2	414	D	315	1 082 507	2 465	124 771	213	257 862	37.3	62.7	78.7	47.9	4 814	77.8
Butler	328	1.2	305	D	296	664 074	2 233	82 455	135	125 040	55.4	44.6	64.8	28.0	6 543	75.1
Calhoun	341	1.2	447	D	320	1 071 168	2 460	148 418	141	184 459	58.7	41.3	75.6	44.1	4 808	73.5
Carroll	364	3.1	348	0	331	798 845	2 210	128 632	264	252 648	28.6	71.4	78.7	43.1	4 879	68.2
Cass	337	1.8	441	D	296	695 234	1 639	118 000	117	153 289	44.7	55.3	64.8	31.2	4 879	71.7
Cedar	338	3.7	349	0	298	763 552	2 081	104 630	123	126 674	66.9	33.1	66.5	33.5	7 124	74.0
Cerro Gordo	323	7.3	407	0	303	824 072	2 114	131 548	112	141 204	74.6	25.4	67.2	35.3	5 483	72.6
Cherokee	335	1.5	401	D	290	871 557	2 274	99 972	155	184 780	42.9	57.1	81.4	42.3	3 888	64.4
Chickasaw	271	-0.4	285	0	242	608 608	2 169	113 298	120	126 073	46.9	53.1	65.9	30.6	4 694	72.2
Clarke	216	-2.7	298	D	143	356 121	995	51 455	44	60 132	26.3	73.7	48.6	9.0	2 941	65.8
Clay	312	9.1	451	0	285	1 010 030	2 252	120 950	157	227 306	40.6	59.4	73.4	38.4	4 485	72.8
Clayton	433	-4.2	270	0	315	528 238	1 903	91 835	160	99 905	33.6	66.4	57.2	28.6	10 384	72.5
Clinton	388	5.4	318	0	345	708 713	2 309	97 349	138	113 456	63.9	36.1	65.2	31.3	8 617	69.2
Crawford	446	3.2	481	D	395	890 588	1 903	120 858	157	169 540	57.2	42.8	72.1	37.2	5 943	66.1
Dallas	309	-4.6	330	1	270	874 630	2 537	83 227	92	98 610	69.9	30.1	53.9	22.4	4 613	61.6
Davis	291	9.0	289	0	204	321 559	1 136	44 614	50	49 293	41.4	58.6	48.8	11.2	4 952	62.6
Decatur	278	6.1	353	D	172	357 162	945	83 147	42	53 275	34.3	65.7	44.7	11.0	4 078	68.8
Delaware	345	5.8	276	D	300	676 998	2 375	115 184	190	151 863	33.1	66.9	75.9	42.3	8 283	73.3
Des Moines	181	-5.7	269	4	152	581 231	2 216	88 925	47	70 473	78.4	21.6	60.5	20.3	3 043	70.9
Dickinson	203	1.0	413	0	188	787 747	1 936	114 663	76	155 302	56.2	43.8	71.5	39.0	2 824	73.4
Dubuque	316	-6.0	213	0	242	478 042	2 134	88 728	152	102 612	22.7	77.3	67.5	30.2	7 915	65.7
Emmet	235	6.8	462	D	219	872 403	1 906	117 558	107	209 445	49.4	50.6	73.9	41.8	3 671	71.6
Fayette	415	2.7	309	D	358	626 654	2 160	116 543	181	134 548	44.2	55.8	66.4	33.6	8 969	74.9
Floyd	291	-3.0	325	1	268	769 694	2 278	112 522	116	129 964	61.1	38.9	64.0	32.8	5 133	76.2
Franklin	337	-2.0	409	0	313	910 618	2 154	115 608	160	193 896	51.7	48.3	75.3	41.8	5 171	72.6
Fremont	318	0.0	582	1	280	920 640	1 610	112 553	62	114 207	79.6	20.4	67.6	32.9	4 287	73.5
Greene	347	1.2	477	D	317	1 053 534	2 093	132 408	120	165 154	65.4	34.6	73.9	42.8	5 343	66.9
Grundy	324	0.9	448	0	306	1 161 631	2 576	151 066	140	193 844	65.9	34.1	74.6	43.5	5 451	69.2

Table B. States and Counties — Residential Construction, Wholesale Trade, Retail Trade, and Real Estate

STATE County	Value of residential construction authorized by building permits, 2003		Wholesale trade, 1997				Retail trade,[1] 1997				Real estate and rental and leasing, 1997			
	New construction ($1,000)	Number of housing units	Number of establishments	Number of employees	Sales (mil dol)	Annual payroll (mil dol)	Number of establishments	Number of employees	Sales (mil dol)	Annual payroll (mil dol)	Number of establishments	Number of employees	Receipts (mil dol)	Annual payroll (mil dol)
	133	134	135	136	137	138	139	140	141	142	143	144	145	146
INDIANA—Cont'd														
Putnam	5 706	52	24	110	39.2	2.7	126	1 278	186.0	18.4	30	65	4.6	0.9
Randolph	5 706	58	21	120	76.5	3.1	111	978	152.2	13.7	8	19	1.0	0.1
Ripley	16 756	208	34	532	108.0	25.5	130	1 124	197.4	18.4	23	104	4.3	1.3
Rush	7 676	58	30	189	119.0	3.9	75	678	114.8	10.3	12	30	4.6	0.4
St. Joseph	166 052	1 062	472	7 080	3 389.0	230.7	1 069	16 822	2 782.9	249.0	215	1 274	127.8	25.5
Scott	8 619	89	15	83	13.9	1.8	105	1 134	168.2	15.9	11	52	5.9	1.0
Shelby	25 781	162	49	530	215.6	18.4	146	1 577	310.8	26.3	34	89	11.8	1.2
Spencer	13 457	108	24	308	217.5	8.4	80	661	94.6	9.7	13	49	2.1	0.6
Starke	14 550	118	20	127	75.8	3.2	95	812	110.3	11.2	13	54	3.7	1.0
Steuben	48 748	321	39	252	98.7	5.9	238	2 280	397.5	35.5	31	87	14.7	1.5
Sullivan	447	4	23	155	113.6	3.7	68	648	95.3	8.6	10	D	D	D
Switzerland	7 633	131	3	D	D	D	20	125	17.1	1.4	1	D	D	D
Tippecanoe	156 064	1 376	117	D	D	D	564	9 688	1 479.8	137.8	148	748	81.0	12.0
Tipton	7 875	50	20	D	D	D	52	478	118.1	7.3	11	23	1.2	0.2
Union	2 948	29	10	94	44.9	1.7	31	221	28.9	3.5	3	D	D	D
Vanderburgh	96 827	1 055	352	D	D	D	932	14 807	2 282.8	229.6	222	1 495	170.5	27.2
Vermillion	4 511	38	15	D	D	D	61	726	123.8	9.4	3	23	1.0	0.2
Vigo	34 395	298	143	1 646	682.4	43.0	509	9 685	2 321.3	158.4	87	480	39.5	8.6
Wabash	9 152	86	38	233	86.4	6.0	169	1 853	289.8	27.5	43	136	13.0	1.8
Warren	3 920	56	12	129	74.8	3.5	16	101	19.8	1.4	4	6	0.7	0.0
Warrick	77 484	532	48	D	D	D	170	1 438	219.1	20.2	33	139	14.7	2.0
Washington	2 439	22	16	D	D	D	88	731	176.1	11.8	15	47	5.2	0.6
Wayne	18 528	138	96	1 657	1 256.3	53.8	338	4 233	690.6	64.3	61	226	23.1	4.1
Wells	16 482	109	38	1 735	455.3	37.9	116	1 113	164.0	16.1	29	97	15.9	1.5
White	11 343	95	46	358	196.7	8.5	131	1 173	209.7	19.6	16	64	4.0	0.8
Whitley	28 172	210	29	240	168.0	6.1	108	1 657	221.0	22.8	21	66	9.1	1.3
IOWA	2 062 916	16 082	5 399	63 596	35 453.7	1 820.1	14 695	175 694	26 723.8	2 633.4	2 518	12 619	1 457.5	249.0
Adair	1 494	14	16	142	83.1	3.7	49	320	46.2	3.7	1	D	D	D
Adams	675	7	9	52	18.5	0.9	22	131	16.0	1.5	1	D	D	D
Allamakee	5 820	73	34	512	158.2	9.8	95	652	101.2	8.1	9	24	1.5	0.1
Appanoose	617	10	12	65	25.7	1.0	73	702	92.4	9.4	7	57	1.3	0.6
Audubon	741	7	24	169	76.2	3.5	34	254	51.9	4.0	3	11	0.7	0.1
Benton	12 297	79	40	506	186.3	12.5	101	789	144.1	12.2	11	39	1.3	0.4
Black Hawk	71 362	511	169	2 690	952.7	77.0	598	9 386	1 344.8	139.3	126	549	60.9	10.3
Boone	8 794	85	25	216	155.2	5.2	98	1 134	173.2	15.5	11	23	2.6	0.3
Bremer	20 640	120	42	293	151.8	6.0	115	1 037	144.7	13.7	14	26	2.9	0.5
Buchanan	5 096	50	38	311	222.7	8.4	106	911	154.9	13.8	16	32	1.3	0.2
Buena Vista	5 350	51	42	392	287.3	11.3	122	1 450	192.1	20.1	18	45	2.5	0.6
Butler	5 936	45	42	257	158.5	6.1	86	428	67.6	5.5	2	D	D	D
Calhoun	1 448	12	15	222	184.9	6.3	71	484	81.3	6.1	8	32	1.3	0.4
Carroll	12 067	80	53	868	354.5	21.4	176	1 706	226.0	22.9	23	122	10.9	1.9
Cass	4 187	33	41	D	D	D	99	927	122.3	11.9	11	21	2.8	0.4
Cedar	13 194	100	39	370	137.8	8.3	85	689	100.8	8.6	11	24	1.0	0.2
Cerro Gordo	19 339	134	85	875	489.6	24.5	292	3 995	609.9	54.9	52	164	16.2	2.3
Cherokee	4 651	24	22	184	59.1	3.9	83	787	107.7	10.3	5	7	0.9	0.1
Chickasaw	1 352	11	32	362	179.2	9.6	62	480	73.4	6.4	6	D	D	D
Clarke	3 391	50	8	D	D	D	39	402	51.3	5.3	7	9	2.2	0.2
Clay	4 942	36	58	612	246.8	14.8	141	1 529	215.0	25.7	19	69	4.8	0.8
Clayton	9 022	105	52	335	269.9	7.1	120	670	133.4	10.4	11	20	1.1	0.3
Clinton	19 572	148	68	492	217.7	12.1	227	2 523	418.3	43.3	50	177	12.2	1.9
Crawford	3 698	31	27	309	191.4	6.0	97	919	111.7	9.9	9	14	0.9	0.1
Dallas	79 919	510	53	D	D	D	134	1 371	220.7	21.1	10	20	1.8	0.3
Davis	894	10	15	136	62.6	2.4	42	294	43.4	4.2	5	12	0.7	0.1
Decatur	1 330	8	11	129	68.3	2.0	35	205	24.8	2.4	1	D	D	D
Delaware	2 194	20	39	444	250.5	10.0	80	726	110.8	10.7	2	D	D	D
Des Moines	5 384	75	67	618	375.8	14.5	238	3 724	499.9	51.7	43	422	48.5	10.2
Dickinson	31 764	215	26	738	176.1	17.6	143	1 087	172.2	17.0	38	236	21.5	4.7
Dubuque	75 481	541	157	1 845	926.5	50.8	525	6 583	935.5	100.2	89	341	32.8	4.9
Emmet	3 315	24	14	260	56.8	4.5	61	550	79.2	7.7	1	D	D	D
Fayette	1 819	21	41	D	D	D	133	1 089	174.3	16.6	10	39	1.3	0.3
Floyd	7 492	93	31	258	112.2	5.3	95	839	119.3	10.5	12	33	3.9	0.3
Franklin	1 252	9	24	241	144.8	5.2	65	459	61.1	5.8	15	27	2.1	0.2
Fremont	2 247	14	15	108	97.4	3.6	32	212	26.8	2.5	2	D	D	D
Greene	2 083	17	19	207	116.8	4.7	47	381	53.1	4.8	5	17	2.7	0.3
Grundy	8 507	59	20	231	171.9	8.2	49	377	61.4	5.3	7	37	9.3	2.2

1. Establishments with payroll.

Table B. States and Counties — Professional Services, Manufacturing, and Accommodation and Foodservices

STATE County	Professional, scientific, and technical services,[1] 1997				Manufacturing, 1997				Accommodation and foodservices, 1997			
	Number of establishments	Number of employees	Receipts (mil dol)	Annual payroll (mil dol)	Number of establishments	Number of employees	Receipts (mil dol)	Annual payroll (mil dol)	Number of establishments	Number of employees	Sales (mil dol)	Annual payroll (mil dol)
	147	148	149	150	151	152	153	154	155	156	157	158
INDIANA—Cont'd												
Putnam	34	123	7.3	2.8	25	2 482	421.7	64.8	75	1 022	27.8	7.5
Randolph	25	79	3.6	1.1	54	3 080	361.0	86.5	44	438	11.9	3.1
Ripley	27	117	7.5	2.6	35	3 168	755.2	109.9	58	787	19.8	5.2
Rush	22	81	3.8	1.2	32	1 081	289.1	32.4	30	D	D	D
St. Joseph	520	4 003	369.9	154.8	457	20 435	4 149.7	698.9	537	10 620	305.2	86.9
Scott	20	51	2.7	0.9	34	D	D	D	38	716	19.6	5.9
Shelby	63	228	15.3	5.3	86	6 656	1 188.8	218.5	57	1 059	31.2	9.3
Spencer	15	54	3.0	0.9	19	1 369	134.0	36.3	28	D	D	D
Starke	13	40	1.8	0.5	19	1 357	143.3	29.7	37	D	D	D
Steuben	47	172	10.0	2.8	110	6 774	1 056.5	189.0	88	1 300	41.6	11.8
Sullivan	24	88	4.4	1.4	18	579	73.0	14.3	28	D	D	D
Switzerland	4	11	0.6	0.1	6	619	58.7	10.7	9	D	D	D
Tippecanoe	207	1 232	104.4	36.5	113	16 695	7 519.0	692.2	312	6 722	194.3	56.0
Tipton	24	93	4.6	1.4	22	954	199.3	30.5	25	319	9.2	2.5
Union	4	6	0.3	0.1	NA	NA	NA	NA	10	D	D	D
Vanderburgh	404	3 594	258.6	99.3	271	17 536	3 824.6	607.7	426	8 841	267.3	78.5
Vermillion	9	12	1.0	0.2	10	D	D	D	35	463	13.7	3.4
Vigo	160	955	70.4	21.3	137	7 464	1 891.8	255.2	268	5 027	148.9	42.7
Wabash	39	130	10.0	3.2	77	5 300	812.8	156.3	71	D	D	D
Warren	6	14	0.7	0.2	NA	NA	NA	NA	68	D	D	D
Warrick	67	254	12.3	4.3	53	D	D	D	68	D	D	D
Washington	26	81	4.3	1.4	40	2 824	298.7	66.9	31	D	D	D
Wayne	76	420	26.5	11.8	132	8 940	1 598.7	270.0	145	2 808	83.7	24.2
Wells	24	127	8.8	2.8	49	3 615	490.2	106.2	36	597	15.3	4.4
White	40	126	16.8	4.8	56	3 402	638.0	90.6	66	459	17.2	4.6
Whitley	32	92	6.1	2.1	66	4 327	908.8	117.3	61	871	23.3	6.6
IOWA	4 670	31 115	2 435.6	887.9	3 749	235 880	62 413.7	7 573.3	6 830	99 148	2 762.8	769.5
Adair	13	39	1.9	0.7	8	527	101.9	15.1	19	246	5.4	1.4
Adams	5	19	0.7	0.2	NA	NA	NA	NA	9	55	1.2	0.3
Allamakee	20	62	2.3	0.9	26	1 505	209.7	27.4	42	293	6.1	1.5
Appanoose	16	43	1.9	0.6	15	1 070	156.5	30.1	35	284	7.4	1.8
Audubon	10	23	1.4	0.4	NA	NA	NA	NA	16	D	D	D
Benton	24	64	3.0	1.1	NA	NA	NA	NA	43	249	6.1	1.6
Black Hawk	193	1 530	100.9	44.9	165	13 542	5 133.1	555.7	293	5 544	135.8	39.2
Boone	27	92	8.1	2.4	26	914	131.9	22.5	48	574	15.1	4.4
Bremer	35	82	6.3	1.7	39	1 993	446.3	58.6	47	578	13.6	4.0
Buchanan	22	66	4.1	1.4	35	1 230	277.7	31.7	38	D	D	D
Buena Vista	34	147	9.3	3.7	28	2 546	688.6	55.2	47	604	15.0	4.0
Butler	19	51	2.6	0.6	23	601	70.7	16.3	29	D	D	D
Calhoun	10	20	1.1	0.2	NA	NA	NA	NA	17	D	D	D
Carroll	37	124	7.6	2.3	39	1 588	423.8	41.7	64	785	19.3	4.9
Cass	20	86	5.6	2.3	25	1 112	150.7	29.8	43	443	10.2	2.8
Cedar	21	211	7.2	3.3	25	810	122.3	19.4	37	375	8.1	1.9
Cerro Gordo	78	376	27.5	10.5	61	3 703	719.8	98.9	139	2 286	61.0	16.7
Cherokee	15	58	2.9	1.1	15	904	188.5	24.6	35	350	8.3	2.2
Chickasaw	16	43	3.0	0.7	25	1 674	414.4	42.2	33	D	D	D
Clarke	12	30	1.4	0.4	19	1 152	209.4	21.4	26	399	12.2	2.8
Clay	28	145	11.1	3.1	28	1 180	202.3	34.9	53	682	17.2	4.8
Clayton	22	66	3.9	1.4	31	1 538	184.6	28.6	51	266	7.2	1.5
Clinton	57	183	12.3	3.8	59	5 148	2 106.9	175.6	132	1 516	39.3	10.9
Crawford	19	120	6.7	2.8	22	1 879	908.9	49.5	49	477	11.4	2.9
Dallas	38	135	8.5	2.8	41	2 489	451.2	59.7	55	596	13.1	3.9
Davis	8	62	2.2	1.0	NA	NA	NA	NA	13	126	2.6	0.7
Decatur	8	22	0.7	0.2	NA	NA	NA	NA	16	110	2.2	0.6
Delaware	19	68	3.8	1.7	34	1 144	327.5	33.7	34	269	5.6	1.3
Des Moines	61	240	16.7	5.2	66	6 772	1 320.8	228.8	109	1 841	47.8	13.4
Dickinson	33	145	10.1	3.0	31	2 386	353.4	60.3	98	857	29.1	8.3
Dubuque	117	802	56.4	23.5	133	10 687	3 074.9	386.9	233	3 838	94.7	27.4
Emmet	18	76	4.9	1.7	15	752	115.8	18.2	25	218	5.5	1.4
Fayette	34	120	6.1	2.1	24	1 539	262.4	38.9	50	504	10.8	3.0
Floyd	24	75	3.9	1.1	17	591	94.5	16.6	37	368	8.9	2.0
Franklin	14	63	2.7	1.2	22	790	83.9	21.6	19	164	3.1	0.9
Fremont	9	58	2.0	0.7	NA	NA	NA	NA	18	83	2.6	0.6
Greene	12	67	3.2	1.4	17	525	83.4	14.4	22	D	D	D
Grundy	15	50	3.2	1.2	NA	NA	NA	NA	23	D	D	D

1. Firms subject to federal tax.

Table B. States and Counties — Health Care and Social Assistance, Other Services, and Federal Funds

STATE County	Health care and social assistance,[1] 1997				Other services,[1] 1997				Federal funds and grants, 2002–2003			
										Expenditures (mil dol)		
											Direct payments for individuals[2]	
	Number of establishments	Number of employees	Receipts (mil dol)	Annual payroll (mil dol)	Number of establishments	Number of employees	Receipts (mil dol)	Annual payroll (mil dol)	Total	Social Security and government retirement	Medicare	Food stamps and Supplemental Security Income
	159	160	161	162	163	164	165	166	167	168	169	170
INDIANA—Cont'd												
Putnam	40	436	17.7	7.6	37	149	10.4	2.4	140.3	69.5	26.1	2.8
Randolph	23	241	9.2	4.1	34	124	8.4	1.8	141.6	69.0	27.4	4.3
Ripley	56	501	21.8	10.7	53	177	11.0	2.8	136.8	62.6	26.4	3.2
Rush	26	442	15.2	6.4	20	75	5.8	1.4	87.2	38.7	19.3	1.6
St. Joseph	496	5 999	458.0	212.7	452	3 851	256.3	81.0	1 964.1	548.1	243.5	45.3
Scott	28	224	11.7	4.6	25	76	5.4	1.3	121.5	53.3	25.0	6.6
Shelby	61	830	39.5	18.4	57	387	18.6	5.5	173.9	85.1	38.0	4.5
Spencer	14	245	9.8	4.2	21	54	3.7	1.0	104.7	43.5	17.3	2.4
Starke	16	176	6.8	2.9	18	41	2.9	0.8	103.7	54.3	18.2	4.5
Steuben	57	454	25.4	9.7	50	381	15.7	5.6	128.9	69.4	27.0	3.3
Sullivan	25	369	15.4	6.3	27	66	4.1	0.9	120.7	51.5	27.6	3.2
Switzerland	6	D	D	D	4	D	D	D	44.3	18.7	8.1	1.4
Tippecanoe	181	2 830	217.1	103.0	227	1 619	102.3	30.6	621.3	228.5	79.4	14.3
Tipton	27	216	11.6	4.2	21	129	6.8	2.3	70.0	36.2	17.3	1.3
Union	8	100	3.0	1.4	9	23	1.4	0.3	32.8	15.9	5.8	0.8
Vanderburgh	396	7 805	496.6	237.0	338	2 995	179.7	56.2	1 127.5	415.4	192.8	37.8
Vermillion	19	304	10.5	4.7	12	33	1.4	0.4	111.5	42.6	17.3	2.3
Vigo	249	3 340	243.7	76.8	170	1 395	66.2	20.2	676.3	239.2	127.4	22.7
Wabash	44	712	28.5	11.8	53	170	10.6	3.4	163.9	85.3	28.1	3.7
Warren	4	D	D	D	4	D	D	D	39.1	15.0	7.0	0.6
Warrick	73	931	44.7	18.5	57	275	16.6	5.2	181.7	102.9	34.2	4.4
Washington	31	335	12.9	4.8	33	98	4.5	1.1	124.8	55.2	21.3	6.5
Wayne	134	1 754	95.8	47.4	118	564	29.2	9.3	393.0	176.8	73.3	16.6
Wells	28	484	33.4	17.5	53	237	17.2	4.9	101.5	53.1	20.9	1.5
White	35	285	9.4	3.6	35	89	6.6	1.3	124.9	66.7	26.4	2.2
Whitley	30	314	16.1	7.1	46	302	16.4	6.0	135.7	68.2	23.9	1.5
IOWA	4 876	56 374	3 183.2	1 540.6	5 234	24 383	1 486.5	411.3	17 549.7	6 590.0	2 559.2	339.2
Adair	14	208	5.6	2.9	16	31	1.8	0.4	47.8	18.6	8.3	0.6
Adams	7	92	1.9	1.0	8	16	1.3	0.2	29.0	12.0	5.5	0.5
Allamakee	22	159	6.7	2.8	34	82	6.8	1.1	74.2	34.0	10.9	1.3
Appanoose	18	155	8.3	3.0	26	80	4.7	1.0	97.1	39.4	15.5	3.5
Audubon	8	117	3.5	1.7	20	50	2.9	0.6	42.6	18.2	8.6	0.8
Benton	23	150	5.5	2.3	43	99	6.3	1.3	103.1	53.5	20.8	1.8
Black Hawk	228	2 173	167.9	83.0	213	1 513	80.2	25.9	633.9	274.1	119.7	24.2
Boone	32	287	13.9	6.9	38	122	6.8	1.9	124.2	62.0	22.7	2.4
Bremer	41	333	16.1	7.0	59	153	10.1	2.3	107.6	55.5	22.4	1.1
Buchanan	20	235	8.9	3.5	40	115	7.8	1.7	94.9	46.1	19.4	2.1
Buena Vista	28	397	16.5	8.0	45	145	8.3	1.8	101.7	43.9	20.7	1.5
Butler	19	317	9.1	4.5	25	61	4.5	0.9	86.1	40.2	18.6	1.2
Calhoun	16	272	8.6	4.2	19	58	2.5	0.5	66.1	31.8	14.1	0.9
Carroll	44	305	20.6	8.4	47	174	11.1	2.3	114.1	52.2	21.0	1.5
Cass	27	294	13.5	5.5	43	102	7.3	1.4	89.9	40.9	19.0	1.9
Cedar	31	114	5.1	2.0	29	70	6.7	1.5	79.0	38.4	15.1	1.0
Cerro Gordo	80	1 328	81.5	50.1	97	437	20.3	6.6	247.3	118.6	46.5	5.6
Cherokee	25	250	8.8	4.6	28	53	4.4	1.0	76.3	35.6	14.4	0.7
Chickasaw	17	349	11.6	4.5	38	79	6.9	1.2	77.7	30.5	12.9	0.8
Clarke	12	46	3.9	1.5	18	36	2.4	0.5	44.1	19.3	8.4	1.1
Clay	31	315	24.1	11.4	37	224	11.6	3.4	110.3	42.3	15.4	1.6
Clayton	25	195	9.1	4.3	39	78	4.8	1.0	104.5	45.8	18.7	1.6
Clinton	95	922	46.4	18.0	97	374	21.8	6.1	246.8	123.8	54.1	8.6
Crawford	25	362	14.8	6.7	34	79	5.7	1.1	103.0	37.4	17.5	1.7
Dallas	61	693	39.5	21.5	50	130	10.2	1.7	141.1	72.8	27.6	2.4
Davis	18	210	8.4	3.3	7	20	1.2	0.3	46.7	19.2	7.8	1.0
Decatur	10	136	4.9	2.0	5	11	1.5	0.5	55.8	20.0	7.5	1.7
Delaware	20	127	7.0	2.7	39	96	5.4	1.2	85.4	35.3	12.8	1.4
Des Moines	100	910	54.1	24.0	62	345	16.6	4.5	276.7	107.6	44.2	7.1
Dickinson	37	373	17.5	8.6	37	116	6.5	1.6	87.6	48.6	16.0	1.1
Dubuque	124	2 376	185.8	89.3	172	889	51.2	14.9	438.3	199.4	82.4	8.9
Emmet	27	360	13.3	6.4	20	63	3.3	0.9	71.8	29.0	13.0	1.1
Fayette	44	534	17.8	8.2	50	180	12.7	3.4	118.8	53.6	22.5	2.6
Floyd	30	394	16.5	8.1	34	137	9.0	2.0	101.3	46.4	19.8	2.4
Franklin	16	166	6.0	2.9	23	67	7.4	1.7	63.2	25.7	10.4	0.8
Fremont	13	267	9.5	5.2	12	27	2.3	0.4	60.7	21.7	10.9	1.0
Greene	15	137	7.6	3.1	26	68	4.5	0.8	64.7	28.5	10.8	1.1
Grundy	15	181	6.3	2.6	26	55	4.8	0.8	63.6	30.8	12.2	0.5

1. Firms subject to federal tax.   2. State totals may include programs not allocated by county.

STATE County	Salaries and wages	Defense	Other	Medicaid and other health-related	Nutrition and family welfare	Education	Other	Total (mil dol)	Intergovern-mental (mil dol)	Total (mil dol)	Per capita (dollars) Total	Property
	171	172	173	174	175	176	177	178	179	180	181	182
INDIANA—Cont'd												
Putnam	4.9	0.0	1.0	12.6	4.8	0.6	11.8	111.0	36.3	35.6	976	859
Randolph	5.0	0.0	3.7	15.6	2.6	0.7	5.2	76.7	29.9	23.2	852	721
Ripley	5.3	1.7	9.5	16.9	1.9	0.8	1.4	63.4	28.6	24.7	896	754
Rush	3.4	0.0	0.8	10.0	1.1	0.3	5.0	53.3	16.0	16.4	916	818
St. Joseph	75.5	619.6	117.2	155.2	26.0	7.7	97.3	795.2	272.3	312.6	1 170	1 094
Scott	3.7	0.5	0.7	24.2	3.3	0.8	1.8	74.7	23.9	17.3	743	619
Shelby	11.7	3.8	1.2	18.6	2.3	0.7	2.2	148.4	41.9	40.5	926	788
Spencer	4.6	0.3	1.0	10.8	0.9	0.3	17.3	51.1	16.9	25.8	1 268	1 161
Starke	3.5	0.0	0.8	13.4	2.4	0.7	2.0	69.4	25.1	18.4	806	759
Steuben	5.0	1.2	1.1	8.7	2.3	0.5	3.7	76.0	26.3	33.6	1 005	860
Sullivan	3.8	5.7	1.2	14.7	1.3	0.5	3.5	74.7	21.9	20.0	914	900
Switzerland	1.5	0.0	0.4	9.1	0.4	0.3	3.1	35.0	22.0	6.8	728	624
Tippecanoe	34.4	23.2	10.2	74.0	8.9	6.6	117.3	346.0	115.3	156.4	1 029	880
Tipton	2.5	0.0	1.4	6.1	0.7	0.2	0.5	61.8	15.6	18.3	1 108	889
Union	0.9	0.0	0.2	3.5	1.2	0.1	1.5	20.2	9.6	7.7	1 033	908
Vanderburgh	58.7	167.3	0.2	137.8	24.4	4.5	74.2	443.6	160.0	190.9	1 111	888
Vermillion	4.0	27.2	1.0	10.0	1.5	0.3	3.4	36.3	14.5	17.7	1 070	1 050
Vigo	97.7	8.9	25.7	94.1	13.6	5.7	22.9	216.1	94.7	95.6	910	894
Wabash	4.9	0.0	1.2	19.5	2.3	0.6	8.3	105.6	33.7	31.5	910	795
Warren	1.5	0.0	0.3	3.0	0.6	0.1	6.2	20.3	8.6	7.2	824	704
Warrick	7.4	1.4	1.7	17.3	2.8	0.6	3.1	120.7	40.1	56.7	1 057	957
Washington	6.4	0.0	0.9	19.9	2.4	0.7	4.5	78.7	31.4	20.0	722	636
Wayne	10.1	1.7	3.4	67.5	12.1	1.9	14.9	181.7	79.7	73.7	1 044	853
Wells	5.3	0.0	1.1	7.4	1.6	0.4	2.4	61.0	26.1	22.9	825	698
White	4.6	0.0	1.0	8.2	2.6	0.4	6.6	85.1	28.4	32.7	1 307	1 167
Whitley	4.3	23.8	1.1	6.5	1.0	0.3	0.6	84.8	29.1	44.0	1 402	1 084
IOWA	1 129.3	658.2	451.0	1 838.7	520.4	338.6	1 179.5	X	X	X	X	X
Adair	1.8	0.0	0.4	8.3	0.8	0.3	2.1	18.7	9.1	7.3	908	869
Adams	1.6	0.0	0.3	2.5	0.5	0.2	0.6	11.0	5.0	4.1	928	910
Allamakee	3.7	0.1	1.3	8.4	1.5	0.9	1.6	42.2	17.1	13.9	954	900
Appanoose	4.2	0.4	0.8	18.8	2.5	1.3	5.4	33.8	19.8	10.4	776	743
Audubon	1.9	0.0	0.8	2.6	0.5	0.2	2.0	16.9	8.3	6.6	999	964
Benton	3.9	0.0	1.0	7.7	2.0	0.5	1.4	56.6	28.1	20.1	772	749
Black Hawk	35.1	0.9	7.2	87.9	23.4	12.0	27.1	379.4	147.1	141.2	1 108	862
Boone	12.1	0.3	1.1	10.9	2.4	0.7	3.1	76.2	27.8	24.8	946	821
Bremer	3.5	0.5	0.8	7.3	1.8	0.5	6.3	74.6	27.5	22.6	973	901
Buchanan	3.8	0.0	0.9	8.7	2.1	1.9	2.9	54.5	21.8	16.6	797	723
Buena Vista	7.2	0.0	1.0	8.7	1.7	1.4	3.7	67.8	24.6	19.2	943	851
Butler	3.1	0.0	0.7	9.4	1.3	0.8	3.0	33.4	15.1	13.2	877	828
Calhoun	2.5	0.0	0.7	5.8	1.0	0.4	1.3	33.5	15.6	13.9	1 281	1 257
Carroll	6.1	0.0	2.5	12.4	3.0	0.5	3.8	57.8	22.1	22.2	1 053	1 030
Cass	4.5	0.0	0.8	8.0	1.7	0.5	4.7	56.2	17.0	15.4	1 081	1 002
Cedar	5.3	0.0	1.5	5.8	1.3	0.3	1.8	45.9	18.9	19.3	1 053	967
Cerro Gordo	10.6	0.2	2.3	29.8	6.6	1.8	10.6	139.5	56.6	52.7	1 162	983
Cherokee	2.9	0.2	0.7	6.9	1.2	0.7	4.2	30.9	13.9	12.2	955	886
Chickasaw	3.1	0.0	0.6	5.8	1.1	0.4	15.6	32.8	14.6	13.7	1 060	972
Clarke	1.7	0.1	0.5	5.4	1.2	0.3	1.6	33.5	12.2	10.6	1 166	1 048
Clay	4.9	0.4	0.9	10.2	1.8	0.4	5.5	84.1	21.3	17.2	1 006	859
Clayton	5.3	0.3	1.0	14.2	1.9	0.5	1.1	49.9	22.5	20.2	1 102	932
Clinton	7.9	0.2	1.8	21.1	6.0	3.5	8.3	132.1	59.4	54.1	1 089	882
Crawford	5.8	0.7	15.0	10.5	1.9	0.8	3.0	52.9	20.3	15.8	933	824
Dallas	6.8	0.0	1.6	9.1	2.7	0.7	10.7	115.8	45.1	48.2	1 089	1 026
Davis	2.0	0.0	0.4	6.5	0.8	0.4	1.5	32.1	10.0	10.4	1 207	1 189
Decatur	2.4	0.0	0.6	8.8	3.1	1.9	2.6	28.9	13.4	7.2	838	764
Delaware	3.4	0.0	0.7	8.4	1.7	0.4	8.9	57.8	20.8	17.9	976	886
Des Moines	10.4	51.0	2.2	23.3	8.4	2.1	9.5	136.1	57.9	49.8	1 202	899
Dickinson	2.6	0.0	0.7	6.6	1.2	0.4	3.8	64.5	13.3	29.3	1 771	1 414
Dubuque	18.9	4.1	3.8	48.4	10.0	2.0	39.8	234.8	96.8	85.9	961	793
Emmet	3.1	0.0	5.1	6.2	1.4	2.0	3.1	56.2	23.5	14.6	1 357	1 202
Fayette	5.3	-0.1	1.7	12.4	2.5	0.9	1.8	54.9	26.9	19.6	904	796
Floyd	3.3	0.0	0.7	15.9	1.9	0.5	2.9	56.4	20.0	17.6	1 059	939
Franklin	2.5	0.3	0.6	6.2	0.9	0.4	7.9	37.3	12.5	12.5	1 164	1 023
Fremont	2.1	0.0	0.5	6.2	0.9	0.3	3.3	23.0	10.8	9.6	1 237	1 087
Greene	2.8	0.0	0.6	7.3	1.0	0.3	5.4	42.1	14.6	12.6	1 242	1 198
Grundy	2.2	0.0	0.6	3.3	0.7	0.2	6.5	36.3	13.7	13.1	1 056	967

1. State totals may include programs not allocated by county. 2. Based on the resident population estimated as of July 1 of the year shown.

Table B. States and Counties — Local Government Finances, Government Employment, and Elections

STATE County	Total (mil dol)	Per capita[1] (dollars)	Educa-tion	Health and hospitals	Police protec-tion	Public welfare	High-ways	Total (mil dol)	Per capita[1] (dollars)	Federal civilian	Federal military	State and local	Demo-cratic	Republi-can	All other
	183	184	185	186	187	188	189	190	191	192	193	194	195	196	197
INDIANA—Cont'd															
Putnam	116.8	3 206	45.4	12.8	0.7	1.5	5.4	109.4	3 002	82	97	2 670	31.2	67.9	0.9
Randolph	78.4	2 885	45.8	19.4	2.2	2.8	5.3	13.6	501	83	73	1 275	34.4	64.7	1.0
Ripley	60.8	2 208	66.8	0.4	2.0	2.1	4.9	24.0	871	89	73	1 292	29.7	69.6	0.8
Rush	50.6	2 822	38.3	22.9	2.9	1.8	6.4	18.4	1 028	58	48	1 136	26.9	72.3	0.8
St. Joseph	839.8	3 144	44.8	0.4	4.1	4.0	2.7	712.6	2 668	1 152	779	12 848	48.5	50.9	0.6
Scott	66.8	2 861	43.6	25.1	2.8	1.1	3.4	55.2	2 366	60	62	1 215	44.1	55.3	0.6
Shelby	146.1	3 346	34.8	27.7	3.5	1.8	3.5	155.4	3 558	159	117	2 394	28.2	71.1	0.7
Spencer	48.5	2 381	56.1	0.4	0.8	2.1	7.1	41.2	2 025	83	54	908	39.6	59.8	0.6
Starke	68.8	3 015	49.2	24.0	1.8	2.1	4.4	73.4	3 215	58	61	965	44.6	54.2	1.1
Steuben	77.1	2 307	48.2	0.4	3.4	2.7	5.7	64.1	1 918	78	89	1 523	33.7	65.5	0.8
Sullivan	74.6	3 419	36.4	17.9	1.0	1.5	4.7	218.4	10 007	69	58	2 156	39.8	59.6	0.6
Switzerland	30.0	3 189	43.3	7.4	0.5	1.6	4.5	7.5	793	31	25	400	40.3	58.9	0.8
Tippecanoe	326.5	2 148	47.4	0.5	5.6	2.6	4.3	183.9	1 210	549	451	20 362	39.8	59.2	1.0
Tipton	65.7	3 971	30.6	36.1	1.7	3.5	2.6	34.0	2 059	40	44	1 241	28.2	71.0	0.8
Union	18.8	2 531	57.3	1.0	2.6	2.3	8.4	18.1	2 439	14	20	430	31.3	67.8	1.0
Vanderburgh	460.3	2 680	40.2	1.4	7.0	3.4	2.6	194.0	1 130	907	473	9 225	40.7	58.7	0.6
Vermillion	37.2	2 254	61.9	0.6	1.3	1.5	5.0	34.2	2 072	74	50	725	48.6	50.7	0.8
Vigo	225.2	2 143	52.3	0.2	3.4	1.9	4.3	92.9	884	1 164	304	7 724	46.4	52.8	0.8
Wabash	104.6	3 017	43.4	24.2	2.2	3.3	3.9	51.9	1 497	86	92	1 979	28.7	70.8	0.5
Warren	20.6	2 354	56.9	1.5	2.4	3.5	12.3	5.8	663	27	29	389	34.2	64.8	1.0
Warrick	116.9	2 179	50.2	0.4	3.2	1.8	5.0	112.4	2 097	130	143	1 713	34.5	65.0	0.5
Washington	75.2	2 724	48.0	19.7	1.6	1.7	5.2	26.0	942	63	74	1 337	35.7	63.6	0.7
Wayne	193.9	2 749	49.1	1.4	4.6	1.8	5.9	57.5	815	164	189	4 824	39.0	60.0	1.1
Wells	66.3	2 384	53.1	0.7	3.9	2.7	6.2	64.7	2 326	64	74	1 340	25.2	74.2	0.6
White	86.7	3 468	52.2	16.4	1.2	0.2	4.6	83.8	3 354	75	67	1 555	31.7	67.4	0.9
Whitley	94.3	3 010	37.0	0.1	1.8	3.4	4.8	43.9	1 400	78	84	1 378	28.8	70.6	0.6
IOWA	X	X	X	X	X	X	X	X	X	18 744	12 188	222 835	49.2	50.1	0.8
Adair	18.6	2 332	44.6	4.7	4.4	0.4	20.2	12.0	1 496	39	32	501	43.1	56.3	0.6
Adams	12.5	2 854	40.0	5.8	5.2	0.5	14.4	7.5	1 710	29	17	251	42.1	56.8	1.1
Allamakee	40.7	2 788	43.2	20.6	3.9	1.0	11.8	11.5	786	79	58	1 000	49.4	50.6	0.0
Appanoose	33.3	2 482	51.2	6.4	5.9	0.4	14.1	10.5	784	75	53	757	47.5	51.8	0.7
Audubon	16.7	2 518	46.2	7.2	3.0	0.3	15.5	3.1	459	42	26	410	44.7	54.6	0.7
Benton	52.5	2 011	57.2	3.1	4.0	1.2	13.6	42.9	1 643	73	104	1 461	49.9	49.5	0.6
Black Hawk	364.2	2 859	47.5	2.4	4.3	5.8	7.9	239.2	1 877	542	527	11 072	55.1	44.3	0.7
Boone	72.9	2 786	41.4	24.8	3.3	0.7	9.7	86.9	3 323	111	104	2 261	50.2	49.1	0.7
Bremer	74.9	3 216	40.5	21.9	3.8	0.5	12.8	41.3	1 772	73	93	1 415	47.2	52.2	0.6
Buchanan	50.6	2 420	41.0	20.3	4.4	0.9	10.1	16.6	795	137	83	1 529	53.4	46.0	0.6
Buena Vista	64.3	3 158	42.3	27.3	4.0	0.8	8.0	25.5	1 252	64	81	1 552	41.5	57.6	0.9
Butler	32.8	2 180	42.1	6.4	4.1	0.8	21.2	14.5	964	61	60	760	40.2	59.1	0.7
Calhoun	32.9	3 045	52.8	11.6	4.3	4.6	10.6	6.2	568	50	43	772	40.7	59.1	0.2
Carroll	55.2	2 614	45.5	4.2	3.5	4.5	13.2	34.3	1 624	105	84	1 214	44.6	54.8	0.7
Cass	57.3	4 027	35.3	37.8	3.2	0.6	9.4	27.1	1 900	87	57	1 348	35.5	63.7	0.8
Cedar	46.4	2 526	52.9	5.3	3.2	1.5	12.7	19.4	1 055	110	73	952	48.9	50.3	0.8
Cerro Gordo	131.9	2 910	55.8	5.9	5.0	1.0	8.9	44.8	988	167	181	2 841	54.5	44.9	0.7
Cherokee	32.6	2 551	49.4	3.2	3.7	0.2	18.9	21.1	1 653	54	51	1 022	44.0	55.4	0.7
Chickasaw	32.3	2 508	51.4	4.7	3.3	1.4	14.1	9.9	768	63	51	635	54.5	44.7	0.8
Clarke	32.6	3 600	38.1	24.4	3.7	0.9	11.6	24.4	2 689	37	36	703	50.8	48.3	0.8
Clay	80.2	4 701	23.9	41.2	2.9	0.3	6.6	45.5	2 664	86	69	1 423	41.1	57.4	1.5
Clayton	46.1	2 507	49.3	3.5	3.7	3.1	14.0	10.2	557	115	73	1 152	51.6	47.1	1.2
Clinton	132.4	2 666	48.3	5.5	5.5	0.7	12.5	90.5	1 822	140	197	2 634	55.6	43.5	0.9
Crawford	54.1	3 189	36.3	29.0	3.1	1.4	12.4	7.5	442	104	67	1 116	44.5	54.6	0.9
Dallas	128.7	2 910	61.1	10.5	4.3	0.6	6.0	112.0	2 532	109	176	2 162	41.7	57.6	0.7
Davis	26.4	3 067	31.7	38.4	3.1	0.4	12.5	11.1	1 295	44	34	561	44.2	54.9	0.9
Decatur	28.8	3 339	46.2	23.8	2.2	1.1	10.6	8.1	934	51	34	706	46.4	52.1	1.6
Delaware	55.5	3 031	41.9	28.0	2.9	0.5	11.9	16.2	884	66	73	1 109	45.9	53.5	0.6
Des Moines	136.6	3 294	57.6	3.1	4.7	1.4	9.1	71.2	1 719	181	167	2 425	59.6	39.6	0.8
Dickinson	67.8	4 102	37.0	23.4	3.1	0.3	12.1	49.2	2 978	53	66	1 073	43.3	56.0	0.7
Dubuque	235.6	2 636	39.3	5.5	5.5	4.0	9.4	66.9	749	276	382	3 684	56.4	42.8	0.7
Emmet	57.5	5 361	74.3	3.1	2.6	0.3	6.3	10.2	951	49	43	801	46.7	52.3	1.0
Fayette	58.2	2 684	59.4	4.3	3.3	0.3	10.1	15.6	720	98	86	1 237	49.9	49.4	0.7
Floyd	55.3	3 337	38.5	25.7	3.0	0.9	12.1	18.0	1 086	63	66	1 029	53.3	45.9	0.8
Franklin	37.7	3 516	38.0	29.1	4.5	3.1	10.1	9.4	877	51	43	742	42.4	56.8	0.7
Fremont	21.3	2 754	54.6	5.4	2.1	1.0	16.7	7.9	1 014	44	31	483	38.6	60.5	0.9
Greene	34.1	3 363	42.1	34.8	3.1	0.0	4.6	9.1	895	48	40	900	48.3	51.4	0.3
Grundy	35.9	2 887	42.3	16.3	3.7	0.2	15.6	15.8	1 276	45	49	635	34.9	64.8	0.4

1. Based on the resident population estimated as of July 1 of the year shown.

Table B. States and Counties — Land Area and Population

STATE/ County code	CBSA code[1]	County Type[2]	STATE County	Land area,[3] (sq km) 2000	Population and population characteristics, 2003			Race alone or in combination, not Hispanic or Latino (percent)					Age (percent)					
					Total persons	Rank	Per square kilometer	White	Black	Am. Indian, Alaska Native	Asian and Pacific Islander	Percent Hispanic or Latino[4]	Under 5 years	5 to 17 years	18 to 24 years	25 to 34 years	35 to 44 years	45 to 54 years
				1	2	3	4	5	6	7	8	9	10	11	12	13	14	15
			IOWA—Cont'd															
19 077	19780	2	Guthrie	1 530	11 500	2 334	7.5	98.3	0.2	0.3	0.3	1.4	5.6	16.2	8.3	9.3	14.4	14.4
19 079	...	6	Hamilton	1 494	16 316	2 014	10.9	96.0	0.5	0.2	1.9	1.7	5.8	17.6	8.5	11.1	15.0	14.0
19 081	...	7	Hancock	1 479	11 945	2 295	8.1	96.3	0.1	0.1	0.9	2.9	5.4	18.4	8.9	8.7	14.8	15.3
19 083	...	6	Hardin	1 474	18 297	1 889	12.4	96.0	0.7	0.2	0.6	2.7	5.7	17.2	10.0	8.8	13.8	14.2
19 085	36540	2	Harrison	1 805	15 667	2 054	8.7	98.7	0.2	0.6	0.2	0.8	5.3	18.6	8.7	10.5	15.3	14.0
19 087	...	7	Henry	1 125	20 023	1 803	17.8	94.5	1.8	0.5	2.8	1.3	5.7	17.3	10.2	12.6	15.8	14.4
19 089	...	7	Howard	1 226	9 784	2 461	8.0	98.9	0.3	0.2	0.3	0.6	5.6	18.5	8.4	10.0	14.7	13.4
19 091	...	7	Humboldt	1 125	10 090	2 434	9.0	97.9	0.1	0.1	0.5	1.5	5.3	17.1	9.3	8.5	14.4	14.9
19 093	...	8	Ida	1 118	7 512	2 636	6.7	98.9	0.2	0.1	0.4	0.6	5.0	17.9	8.1	8.9	14.0	15.2
19 095	...	8	Iowa	1 519	15 920	2 035	10.5	98.3	0.3	0.1	0.4	1.1	5.4	18.9	8.3	10.1	16.2	14.3
19 097	...	6	Jackson	1 647	20 221	1 790	12.3	98.8	0.3	0.2	0.4	0.6	5.5	18.3	8.7	9.8	15.4	14.3
19 099	35500	6	Jasper	1 891	37 708	1 188	19.9	97.1	1.0	0.5	0.9	1.1	5.9	17.2	8.6	11.8	15.6	14.5
19 101	...	7	Jefferson	1 128	16 022	2 029	14.2	95.0	1.0	0.4	2.3	1.9	4.8	16.7	9.6	9.7	13.0	21.8
19 103	26980	3	Johnson	1 591	115 548	408	72.6	88.4	3.7	0.5	6.1	2.6	5.6	13.6	18.7	18.4	13.6	12.6
19 105	16300	3	Jones	1 490	20 299	1 785	13.6	96.3	2.1	0.6	0.4	1.1	5.0	17.0	9.4	12.0	16.1	14.6
19 107	...	8	Keokuk	1 500	11 352	2 344	7.6	98.8	0.1	0.2	0.4	0.7	5.9	17.8	9.0	9.7	14.6	14.1
19 109	...	7	Kossuth	2 520	16 443	2 000	6.5	98.5	0.2	0.2	0.6	0.7	4.8	17.7	8.6	8.0	14.6	15.3
19 111	28460	5	Lee	1 340	36 714	1 221	27.4	94.1	3.2	0.7	0.8	2.3	5.6	17.1	8.7	10.5	15.0	15.7
19 113	16300	3	Linn	1 858	196 202	293	105.6	93.8	3.6	0.6	2.0	1.5	6.9	17.6	10.2	13.7	15.4	14.1
19 115	34700	8	Louisa	1 041	12 201	2 286	11.7	85.6	0.4	0.3	0.3	13.6	6.3	19.6	8.6	12.2	15.8	13.5
19 117	...	6	Lucas	1 115	9 501	2 485	8.5	98.6	0.2	0.2	0.3	0.9	5.7	18.4	9.0	10.0	14.0	13.2
19 119	...	8	Lyon	1 522	11 746	2 309	7.7	98.8	0.2	0.3	0.4	0.5	6.2	19.1	9.3	10.6	13.7	13.7
19 121	19780	2	Madison	1 453	14 510	2 126	10.0	98.6	0.1	0.5	0.3	0.8	6.4	18.7	9.4	11.3	15.1	14.9
19 123	36820	7	Mahaska	1 479	22 303	1 691	15.1	96.7	1.1	0.5	1.4	1.1	6.4	17.5	11.0	11.4	14.5	14.1
19 125	...	6	Marion	1 435	32 425	1 350	22.6	97.2	0.7	0.5	1.3	0.9	5.9	17.6	11.8	11.1	14.5	13.8
19 127	32260	4	Marshall	1 482	39 103	1 157	26.4	87.0	1.3	0.7	1.2	10.7	6.7	17.5	9.1	11.3	14.1	15.0
19 129	36540	2	Mills	1 131	14 909	2 107	13.2	97.7	0.3	0.7	0.4	1.4	5.7	18.8	9.4	11.1	15.7	16.1
19 131	...	7	Mitchell	1 215	10 946	2 371	9.0	98.9	0.2	0.1	0.2	0.6	6.1	18.8	8.2	8.5	13.9	13.3
19 133	...	6	Monona	1 795	9 746	2 464	5.4	98.1	0.3	1.0	0.2	0.7	5.2	16.5	8.2	9.1	13.6	13.7
19 135	...	7	Monroe	1 123	7 796	2 613	6.9	98.4	0.4	0.4	0.5	0.6	5.5	18.1	8.8	9.8	14.2	13.5
19 137	...	6	Montgomery	1 098	11 289	2 347	10.3	97.3	0.2	0.5	0.3	1.9	5.8	17.6	7.6	10.4	13.7	15.3
19 139	34700	4	Muscatine	1 136	42 093	1 078	37.1	85.6	0.9	0.6	1.1	12.5	7.1	18.4	9.3	12.3	15.4	14.8
19 141	...	7	O'Brien	1 484	14 627	2 122	9.9	96.8	0.3	0.2	0.7	2.1	5.1	17.0	9.6	9.6	13.5	14.7
19 143	...	7	Osceola	1 033	6 819	2 704	6.6	97.0	0.4	0.4	0.3	2.2	5.3	18.4	9.2	9.3	14.9	14.3
19 145	...	7	Page	1 385	16 346	2 009	11.8	95.3	2.0	0.7	0.8	1.6	5.0	16.6	8.8	11.5	14.2	14.6
19 147	...	7	Palo Alto	1 460	9 705	2 470	6.6	98.6	0.1	0.4	0.4	0.8	5.2	16.4	11.4	9.1	13.4	14.0
19 149	...	6	Plymouth	2 237	24 719	1 589	11.1	97.3	0.5	0.4	0.6	1.7	5.9	19.6	9.6	10.1	14.9	15.1
19 151	...	9	Pocahontas	1 496	8 251	2 579	5.5	98.3	0.3	0.2	0.3	1.1	4.1	18.3	7.2	7.0	14.4	15.6
19 153	19780	2	Polk	1 475	388 606	159	263.5	86.6	5.5	0.6	3.7	5.0	7.5	17.7	9.3	15.2	15.8	14.0
19 155	36540	2	Pottawattamie	2 472	88 477	606	35.8	94.6	1.1	0.7	1.0	3.5	6.5	17.8	10.1	12.4	15.2	14.3
19 157	...	7	Poweshiek	1 515	19 033	1 860	12.6	96.4	0.8	0.3	1.7	1.4	5.1	15.9	14.0	9.6	13.7	13.5
19 159	...	9	Ringgold	1 393	5 421	2 815	3.9	99.1	0.1	0.3	0.2	0.4	5.9	16.2	9.0	7.7	12.7	13.2
19 161	...	9	Sac	1 491	10 872	2 376	7.3	98.3	0.6	0.2	0.4	1.0	4.9	17.3	8.0	8.7	13.8	15.0
19 163	19340	2	Scott	1 186	159 414	348	134.4	87.5	7.0	0.8	2.3	4.1	6.8	18.2	9.6	13.6	15.0	14.9
19 165	...	6	Shelby	1 530	12 717	2 260	8.3	98.5	0.2	0.4	0.4	0.7	4.9	18.6	8.3	8.9	15.1	14.5
19 167	...	6	Sioux	1 989	32 104	1 356	16.1	95.6	0.4	0.3	0.8	3.3	6.7	18.3	17.0	9.7	12.6	12.6
19 169	11180	3	Story	1 484	83 021	640	55.9	90.1	2.1	0.4	6.7	1.6	5.2	12.4	24.2	15.6	11.3	11.3
19 171	...	6	Tama	1 868	17 876	1 923	9.6	89.3	0.5	7.0	0.4	3.9	6.5	18.7	8.4	10.0	14.0	13.8
19 173	...	9	Taylor	1 383	6 793	2 706	4.9	95.5	0.0	0.2	0.4	4.0	5.6	16.7	9.2	9.2	13.3	13.9
19 175	...	6	Union	1 099	11 932	2 297	10.9	98.2	0.3	0.4	0.4	1.1	5.1	16.2	9.8	10.5	14.6	14.4
19 177	...	9	Van Buren	1 256	7 777	2 614	6.2	98.7	0.2	0.4	0.3	0.9	5.6	17.5	8.9	9.7	13.4	15.0
19 179	36900	5	Wapello	1 118	35 885	1 243	32.1	93.2	1.2	0.5	1.0	4.6	5.9	16.6	10.1	11.5	13.8	14.7
19 181	19780	2	Warren	1 481	41 997	1 080	28.4	98.0	0.5	0.5	0.6	1.1	6.0	18.7	11.5	10.8	15.8	14.6
19 183	26980	3	Washington	1 473	21 314	1 736	14.5	96.1	0.5	0.4	0.4	3.0	6.8	18.1	8.5	10.6	15.0	14.1
19 185	...	9	Wayne	1 361	6 669	2 716	4.9	98.8	0.2	0.2	0.3	0.9	5.4	16.8	8.5	7.8	13.8	13.3
19 187	22700	5	Webster	1 852	39 590	1 139	21.4	92.9	3.8	0.6	1.0	2.5	6.1	17.1	12.3	10.7	13.7	14.1
19 189	...	7	Winnebago	1 037	11 445	2 337	11.0	96.5	0.3	0.2	1.0	2.3	5.4	17.1	10.9	9.3	13.2	16.0
19 191	...	7	Winneshiek	1 786	21 307	1 738	11.9	97.4	0.7	0.2	1.1	0.9	4.6	15.8	18.5	9.2	13.9	13.4
19 193	43580	3	Woodbury	2 260	103 220	526	45.7	83.8	2.7	2.3	3.1	9.6	7.5	19.0	10.5	13.1	14.4	13.8
19 195	32380	9	Worth	1 036	7 773	2 616	7.5	97.6	0.4	0.5	0.2	1.8	5.4	16.8	8.1	9.9	15.0	15.4
19 197	...	7	Wright	1 504	13 765	2 184	9.2	93.2	0.4	0.2	0.2	6.3	5.5	17.5	7.7	9.4	14.1	15.3
20 000	...	X	KANSAS	211 900	2 723 507	X	12.9	83.4	6.4	1.5	2.5	7.8	6.9	18.6	10.9	12.9	14.4	14.1
20 001	...	7	Allen	1 303	13 907	2 172	10.7	95.0	2.0	1.7	0.4	2.1	6.0	17.7	11.8	9.8	13.5	14.3
20 003	...	6	Anderson	1 510	8 208	2 582	5.4	97.5	0.5	1.1	0.3	1.2	6.4	18.3	9.2	9.9	13.8	12.2
20 005	11860	6	Atchison	1 120	16 741	1 980	14.9	91.7	6.1	1.2	0.5	1.9	6.2	19.0	12.7	10.4	13.0	13.0

1. CBSA = Core Based Statistical Area. See Appendix A for explanation. See Appendix B for list of metropolitan areas with component counties. 2. County type code from the Economic Research Service of USDA Rural-Urban Continuum Codes. See Appendix A for definition. 3. Dry land or land partially or temporarily covered by water. 4. Hispanic or Latino persons may be of any race.

STATE County	55 to 64 years	65 to 74 years	75 years and over	Percent female	Total persons 1990	Total persons 2000	Percent change 1990–2000	Percent change 2000–2003	Births	Deaths	Net migration	Number	Percent change, 1990–2000	Persons per household	Female family householder[1]	One person
	16	17	18	19	20	21	22	23	24	25	26	27	28	29	30	31
IOWA—Cont'd																
Guthrie	11.2	9.6	10.3	50.5	10 935	11 353	3.8	1.3	424	481	215	4 641	5.3	2.39	6.6	26.1
Hamilton	9.6	8.5	9.6	50.5	16 071	16 438	2.3	-0.7	574	613	-76	6 692	5.3	2.43	7.6	27.5
Hancock	10.3	8.1	10.0	51.2	12 638	12 100	-4.3	-1.3	422	440	-136	4 795	-1.5	2.48	6.0	26.5
Hardin	10.1	8.8	12.0	51.0	19 094	18 812	-1.5	-2.7	731	799	-444	7 628	0.2	2.35	6.5	29.4
Harrison	10.0	8.1	9.2	50.9	14 730	15 666	6.4	0.0	530	633	113	6 115	8.1	2.51	7.6	26.1
Henry	9.7	6.5	8.0	49.2	19 226	20 336	5.8	-1.5	729	710	-315	7 626	7.6	2.46	8.2	26.8
Howard	9.7	8.6	11.2	50.2	9 809	9 932	1.3	-1.5	365	397	-108	3 974	3.1	2.43	6.6	29.5
Humboldt	10.1	9.4	11.5	51.3	10 756	10 381	-3.5	-2.8	371	401	-251	4 295	-1.0	2.38	6.4	29.8
Ida	9.9	9.8	12.3	51.3	8 365	7 837	-6.3	-4.1	254	303	-267	3 213	-0.3	2.39	5.9	29.3
Iowa	9.4	7.8	9.3	51.1	14 630	15 671	7.1	1.6	579	572	253	6 163	7.9	2.50	6.6	25.9
Jackson	10.6	8.8	8.6	50.8	19 950	20 296	1.7	-0.4	763	654	-162	8 078	7.3	2.47	7.7	27.0
Jasper	10.1	7.8	8.0	49.3	34 795	37 213	6.9	1.3	1 478	1 156	217	14 689	7.8	2.42	7.4	26.1
Jefferson	10.5	6.1	7.7	51.0	16 310	16 181	-0.8	-1.0	486	465	-175	6 649	5.4	2.34	8.0	30.4
Johnson	6.7	3.9	3.6	50.3	96 119	111 006	15.5	4.1	4 390	1 660	1 971	44 080	22.2	2.34	6.8	30.2
Jones	9.9	7.5	8.2	47.3	19 444	20 221	4.0	0.4	645	602	61	7 560	9.3	2.47	7.9	25.3
Keokuk	9.7	8.6	11.0	51.3	11 624	11 400	-1.9	-0.4	433	414	-55	4 586	0.3	2.45	6.5	27.8
Kossuth	10.7	9.6	11.1	51.0	18 591	17 163	-7.7	-4.2	504	615	-599	6 974	-3.1	2.42	5.8	28.7
Lee	11.0	7.9	9.0	50.5	38 687	38 052	-1.6	-3.5	1 325	1 423	-1 253	15 161	1.5	2.41	10.3	28.3
Linn	9.1	6.1	6.2	50.9	168 767	191 701	13.6	2.3	9 021	4 684	357	76 753	17.2	2.43	9.0	27.5
Louisa	9.6	7.1	7.0	50.3	11 592	12 183	5.1	0.1	503	357	-120	4 519	5.2	2.66	8.2	22.5
Lucas	11.0	8.5	10.2	51.6	9 070	9 422	3.9	0.8	359	371	98	3 811	1.2	2.42	7.0	28.7
Lyon	8.8	8.3	10.0	50.2	11 952	11 763	-1.6	-0.1	466	382	-89	4 428	3.2	2.61	4.4	24.3
Madison	9.7	6.5	7.4	50.6	12 483	14 019	12.3	3.5	580	499	415	5 326	13.0	2.58	5.9	22.7
Mahaska	9.1	7.3	8.7	50.0	21 532	22 335	3.7	-0.1	938	706	-248	8 880	6.9	2.45	7.0	26.6
Marion	9.5	7.1	8.7	50.6	30 001	32 052	6.8	1.2	1 231	1 089	247	12 017	11.1	2.50	6.9	25.6
Marshall	10.5	7.7	8.3	50.5	38 276	39 311	2.7	-0.5	1 750	1 712	-224	15 338	3.0	2.48	9.3	26.9
Mills	10.3	6.3	6.0	49.7	13 202	14 547	10.2	2.5	563	426	240	5 324	14.1	2.60	8.9	22.3
Mitchell	9.9	9.1	12.3	51.0	10 928	10 874	-0.5	0.7	467	426	51	4 294	1.0	2.47	5.7	27.6
Monona	10.8	10.0	13.4	51.3	10 034	10 020	-0.1	-2.7	339	579	-23	4 211	2.8	2.31	7.1	31.0
Monroe	11.1	8.6	10.5	51.1	8 114	8 016	-1.2	-2.7	271	358	-130	3 228	1.0	2.43	8.6	28.0
Montgomery	10.3	8.8	11.2	52.4	12 076	11 771	-2.5	-4.1	440	538	-391	4 886	-1.4	2.36	8.7	29.5
Muscatine	9.8	6.3	6.5	50.3	39 907	41 722	4.5	0.9	2 062	1 233	-427	15 847	7.0	2.59	9.3	24.1
O'Brien	9.4	9.7	11.8	50.9	15 444	15 102	-2.2	-3.1	507	613	-374	6 001	0.4	2.42	5.4	28.0
Osceola	10.1	9.1	9.9	51.2	7 267	7 003	-3.6	-2.6	242	310	-108	2 778	-1.4	2.48	4.9	28.0
Page	9.8	9.2	10.7	48.9	16 870	16 976	0.6	-3.7	512	777	-354	6 708	0.3	2.32	8.1	29.9
Palo Alto	9.5	10.2	11.8	50.8	10 669	10 147	-4.9	-4.4	330	468	-303	4 119	-1.5	2.37	5.9	30.4
Plymouth	8.9	7.5	8.2	50.2	23 388	24 849	6.2	-0.5	937	793	-256	9 372	11.3	2.61	6.2	24.0
Pocahontas	11.2	9.7	13.1	50.8	9 525	8 662	-9.1	-4.7	211	362	-261	3 617	-5.3	2.35	5.9	30.2
Polk	8.7	5.5	5.4	51.2	327 140	374 601	14.5	3.7	19 714	9 144	3 868	149 112	15.4	2.45	10.3	28.1
Pottawattamie	9.5	7.1	6.5	51.0	82 628	87 704	6.1	0.9	3 895	2 811	-329	33 844	8.3	2.54	11.8	24.9
Poweshiek	10.1	7.9	9.6	51.8	19 033	18 815	-1.1	1.2	648	712	302	7 398	3.4	2.35	7.4	29.2
Ringgold	11.4	10.8	12.4	51.2	5 420	5 469	0.9	-0.9	216	293	34	2 245	1.2	2.37	5.5	28.6
Sac	10.1	10.1	13.1	51.1	12 324	11 529	-6.5	-5.7	346	487	-509	4 746	-3.4	2.37	6.2	29.4
Scott	9.5	6.0	5.9	50.9	150 973	158 668	5.1	0.5	7 277	4 219	-2 260	62 334	8.5	2.49	11.4	26.9
Shelby	9.8	9.3	11.1	51.0	13 230	13 173	-0.4	-3.5	393	520	-209	5 173	3.0	2.49	6.8	25.2
Sioux	7.9	6.7	8.2	50.8	29 903	31 589	5.6	1.6	1 495	764	-186	10 693	7.7	2.71	4.2	22.2
Story	6.6	4.7	5.1	48.6	74 252	79 981	7.7	3.8	2 957	1 443	1 548	29 383	13.3	2.39	5.9	26.7
Tama	10.4	8.4	9.9	50.8	17 419	18 103	3.9	-1.3	766	720	-254	7 018	3.7	2.51	8.0	25.3
Taylor	10.6	9.3	12.6	51.4	7 114	6 958	-2.2	-2.4	266	311	-119	2 824	-1.2	2.40	5.9	27.8
Union	10.8	8.5	10.5	52.0	12 750	12 309	-3.5	-3.1	423	480	-316	5 242	1.3	2.29	8.0	31.3
Van Buren	10.7	8.8	10.4	50.5	7 676	7 809	1.7	-0.4	297	346	22	3 181	4.1	2.41	6.0	28.0
Wapello	10.0	8.1	9.2	51.0	35 696	36 051	1.0	-0.5	1 417	1 337	-200	14 784	1.6	2.37	9.9	28.2
Warren	9.8	6.1	5.8	51.2	36 033	40 671	12.9	3.3	1 600	1 100	854	14 708	16.2	2.65	8.8	19.9
Washington	9.3	7.5	9.8	51.7	19 612	20 670	5.4	3.1	1 015	758	403	8 056	8.1	2.50	6.7	26.4
Wayne	11.3	10.0	13.3	52.4	7 067	6 730	-4.8	-0.9	270	314	-12	2 821	-4.5	2.34	6.4	29.8
Webster	9.2	7.9	9.1	49.6	40 342	40 235	-0.3	-1.6	1 620	1 531	-715	15 878	-0.5	2.38	9.5	30.3
Winnebago	9.6	8.4	10.4	51.3	12 122	11 723	-3.3	-2.4	424	469	-239	4 749	1.0	2.36	7.2	29.4
Winneshiek	8.9	7.0	8.5	50.8	20 847	21 310	2.2	0.0	654	636	0	7 734	6.6	2.46	5.5	27.6
Woodbury	8.4	6.2	6.9	50.9	98 276	103 877	5.7	-0.6	5 293	2 964	-3 016	39 151	6.1	2.58	11.3	26.6
Worth	10.3	8.3	11.0	50.2	7 991	7 909	-1.0	-1.7	268	319	-80	3 278	1.2	2.38	7.3	27.6
Wright	10.3	8.9	12.1	50.6	14 269	14 334	0.5	-4.0	509	672	-406	5 940	0.7	2.36	6.2	30.2
KANSAS	9.2	6.2	6.7	50.4	2 477 588	2 688 418	8.5	1.3	125 734	80 523	-10 108	1 037 891	9.9	2.51	9.3	27.0
Allen	10.2	8.2	9.8	51.0	14 638	14 385	-1.7	-3.3	568	610	-429	5 775	1.2	2.43	8.9	28.5
Anderson	10.1	8.8	11.1	50.7	7 803	8 110	3.9	1.2	346	324	80	3 221	5.0	2.48	6.9	26.8
Atchison	9.8	7.3	8.6	51.8	16 932	16 774	-0.9	-0.2	663	574	-106	6 275	2.4	2.51	10.0	27.6

1. No spouse present.

Table B. States and Counties — Vital Statistics, Health Resources, and Crime

STATE County	Births, average 1999–2001 Total	Rate[1]	Deaths, average 1999–2001 Number Total	Number Infant[2]	Rate Total[1]	Rate Infant[3]	Physicians,[4] 2000 Number	Rate[5]	Hospitals,[4] 1998 Number	Beds Number	Beds Rate[5]	Medicare enrollees, 2003	Serious crimes known to police,[6] 2002 Total Number	Rate[7]
	32	33	34	35	36	37	38	39	40	41	42	43	44	45
IOWA—Cont'd														
Guthrie	136	12.0	144	0	12.6	D	9	79	1	26	225	2 520	72	632
Hamilton	193	11.8	180	2	11.0	D	19	116	1	42	262	3 127	449	2 722
Hancock	130	10.8	140	0	11.6	D	5	41	1	26	216	2 246	98	807
Hardin	225	12.0	254	1	13.6	D	12	64	2	76	412	4 227	484	2 564
Harrison	177	11.3	200	0	12.8	D	8	51	1	37	241	2 974	199	1 266
Henry	242	11.9	212	2	10.4	D	21	103	1	61	305	3 342	152	745
Howard	113	11.4	131	0	13.2	D	6	60	1	32	330	1 966	233	2 338
Humboldt	112	10.8	121	1	11.7	D	9	87	1	49	475	2 188	80	768
Ida	76	9.8	103	1	13.2	D	4	51	1	36	455	1 660	51	648
Iowa	181	11.5	175	1	11.1	D	10	64	1	44	283	2 848	108	687
Jackson	238	11.8	216	1	10.7	D	14	69	1	67	334	3 838	262	1 286
Jasper	458	12.3	361	2	9.7	D	23	89	1	61	170	6 294	967	2 589
Jefferson	152	9.4	139	0	8.6	D	23	142	1	83	485	2 355	454	2 796
Johnson	1 362	12.2	504	7	4.5	4.9	1 045	941	2	1 002	975	9 946	3 885	3 487
Jones	206	10.2	182	1	9.0	D	14	69	1	38	187	3 422	298	1 468
Keokuk	135	11.9	132	0	11.6	D	1	9	1	33	287	2 566	31	271
Kossuth	163	9.5	200	1	11.7	D	8	47	1	24	135	3 591	195	1 132
Lee	429	11.3	444	4	11.7	D	53	139	2	155	403	6 728	1 239	3 245
Linn	2 769	14.4	1 448	15	7.5	5.4	353	184	2	877	480	27 690	8 345	4 489
Louisa	162	13.3	107	0	8.8	D	2	16	0	0	0	1 885	125	1 022
Lucas	108	11.4	115	1	12.2	D	6	64	1	83	907	1 991	327	3 458
Lyon	152	12.9	126	2	10.7	D	3	26	1	30	250	2 195	112	949
Madison	185	13.2	152	2	10.8	D	5	36	1	23	166	2 207	72	512
Mahaska	294	13.2	218	4	9.7	D	18	81	1	53	242	3 858	553	2 467
Marion	399	12.4	319	2	9.9	D	48	150	2	215	686	5 596	629	1 955
Marshall	557	14.1	512	3	13.0	D	74	188	1	158	408	7 116	1 687	4 276
Mills	165	11.3	140	0	9.6	D	10	69	0	0	0	2 404	456	3 124
Mitchell	138	12.8	135	1	12.4	D	5	46	1	30	272	2 525	98	898
Monona	108	10.8	169	0	16.9	D	10	100	1	48	475	2 311	201	1 999
Monroe	95	11.9	104	0	13.0	D	5	62	1	46	572	1 605	124	1 542
Montgomery	140	12.0	163	2	13.9	D	10	85	1	40	336	2 509	222	1 879
Muscatine	636	15.2	375	1	9.0	D	24	58	1	80	195	6 419	1 317	3 145
O'Brien	172	11.4	185	2	12.3	D	7	46	2	121	812	3 465	196	1 293
Osceola	74	10.6	86	0	12.2	D	4	57	1	32	458	1 378	66	939
Page	175	10.3	240	2	14.1	D	17	100	2	137	793	3 626	454	2 665
Palo Alto	106	10.5	139	0	13.7	D	6	59	1	54	539	2 323	NA	NA
Plymouth	293	11.8	254	3	10.2	D	15	60	1	44	177	4 198	353	1 416
Pocahontas	73	8.5	108	0	12.5	D	3	35	1	20	228	2 065	35	403
Polk	6 096	16.2	2 770	41	7.4	6.7	1 049	280	6	1 879	522	48 540	20 032	5 454
Pottawattamie	1 208	13.8	849	8	9.7	6.3	115	131	2	545	632	14 266	7 561	8 921
Poweshiek	196	10.4	219	1	11.6	D	31	165	1	46	244	3 594	450	2 383
Ringgold	67	12.3	89	0	16.4	D	8	146	1	36	672	1 211	0	0
Sac	121	10.5	163	1	14.1	D	6	52	1	54	453	2 654	83	717
Scott	2 276	14.3	1 306	18	8.2	7.9	314	198	3	660	416	22 069	11 162	7 010
Shelby	135	10.3	158	1	12.0	D	5	38	1	52	401	2 722	9	68
Sioux	444	14.0	234	1	7.4	D	28	89	4	295	943	5 076	NA	NA
Story	916	11.5	456	5	5.7	D	144	180	2	338	449	9 020	2 853	3 554
Tama	242	13.4	218	2	12.1	D	10	55	0	0	0	3 539	239	1 549
Taylor	79	11.3	94	0	13.5	D	3	43	1	0	0	1 595	53	759
Union	134	10.9	153	2	12.5	D	6	49	1	53	422	2 648	241	1 951
Van Buren	92	11.8	105	0	13.5	D	7	90	1	40	507	1 802	41	523
Wapello	424	11.8	431	2	12.0	D	71	197	1	137	387	7 296	1 485	4 104
Warren	502	12.3	324	4	8.0	D	23	57	0	0	0	5 180	879	2 154
Washington	309	14.9	226	1	10.9	D	17	82	1	83	396	4 086	301	1 451
Wayne	80	11.9	102	1	15.1	D	3	45	1	28	420	1 683	86	1 273
Webster	497	12.4	479	2	11.9	D	73	181	1	182	470	7 692	2 202	5 453
Winnebago	129	11.1	149	0	12.8	D	5	43	0	0	0	2 467	23	239
Winneshiek	194	9.1	190	0	8.9	D	22	103	1	83	396	3 460	190	888
Woodbury	1 647	15.9	917	11	8.8	6.9	227	219	2	681	670	15 679	6 097	5 849
Worth	83	10.5	101	1	12.9	D	2	25	0	0	0	1 472	0	0
Wright	163	11.4	201	1	14.0	D	7	49	2	54	386	3 150	124	862
KANSAS	39 106	14.5	24 612	279	9.1	7.1	0	0	132	11 383	433	394 206	110 997	4 087
Allen	185	12.9	185	1	12.9	D	15	104	1	40	275	2 774	501	3 448
Anderson	106	13.0	98	1	12.1	D	5	62	1	60	744	1 785	243	3 337
Atchison	205	12.2	183	3	10.9	D	17	101	1	160	946	2 938	509	3 004

1. Per 1,000 estimated resident population.   2. Deaths of infants under 1 year old.   3. Deaths of infants under 1 year old per 1,000 live births.   4. Data subject to copyright.   5. Per 100,000 resident population as of July 1 of the year shown.   6. Data for serious crimes have not been adjusted for underreporting; this may affect comparability between geographic areas and over time.   7. Per 100,000 population estimated by the FBI.

Table B. States and Counties — Crime, Education, Money Income, and Poverty

STATE County	Serious crimes known to police,[1] 2002 (cont'd) Rate[2] Violent	Property	Enrollment[3] Total	Percent private	High school graduate or less	Bachelor's degree or more	Local govt expenditures,[5] 2000–2001 Total current expenditures (mil dol)	Current expenditures per student (dollars)	Per capita income[6] (dollars)	Median income Dollars	Percent change, 1989–1999 (constant 1999 dollars)	Percent with income of $100,000 or more	Persons	House-holds	Families	Families with children
	46	47	48	49	50	51	52	53	54	55	56	57	58	59	60	61
IOWA—Cont'd																
Guthrie	0	632	2 510	5.4	59.5	14.9	14.7	6 206	19 726	36 495	16.3	6.6	8.0	8.7	5.8	7.3
Hamilton	121	2 600	4 022	9.7	53.1	17.5	19.3	6 598	18 801	38 658	11.3	4.9	6.3	6.4	4.3	7.2
Hancock	66	741	3 128	9.1	52.8	15.4	13.6	6 641	17 957	37 703	10.3	4.5	6.0	6.9	5.2	7.3
Hardin	101	2 463	4 772	5.0	51.3	17.1	23.1	7 043	17 537	35 429	12.4	4.2	8.0	7.9	5.5	8.5
Harrison	38	1 228	3 914	7.9	59.1	12.7	21.0	6 289	17 662	38 141	27.5	4.6	7.1	7.5	5.0	8.0
Henry	98	647	5 245	16.9	53.5	16.2	23.5	6 130	18 192	39 087	16.6	5.7	8.8	10.1	6.7	10.2
Howard	110	2 227	2 395	15.9	63.7	12.6	12.9	6 381	17 842	34 641	17.7	4.7	9.3	9.1	5.6	6.3
Humboldt	38	730	2 621	12.0	52.0	15.4	12.5	6 568	18 300	38 201	15.8	5.7	8.3	8.2	5.3	9.9
Ida	64	585	1 914	4.0	58.3	13.6	8.8	6 278	18 675	34 805	13.3	4.6	8.8	9.4	5.7	8.6
Iowa	51	636	3 952	10.9	55.1	15.8	18.4	6 282	18 884	41 222	15.4	4.1	5.0	6.9	3.4	4.9
Jackson	59	1 227	5 091	15.0	63.2	12.1	24.4	6 909	17 329	34 529	14.3	3.7	10.3	9.9	7.7	12.0
Jasper	64	2 525	8 568	9.8	58.0	15.9	40.2	6 236	19 622	41 683	8.1	6.3	6.5	7.2	4.8	6.5
Jefferson	135	2 660	4 260	29.0	43.3	31.2	13.3	6 492	19 579	33 851	11.3	8.2	10.9	12.0	7.4	12.3
Johnson	440	3 048	45 029	8.4	26.1	47.6	84.3	6 369	22 220	40 060	7.0	11.9	15.0	15.5	5.2	7.7
Jones	69	1 399	4 977	11.1	57.0	12.7	22.1	6 373	17 816	37 449	13.9	4.6	8.6	8.7	6.2	9.5
Keokuk	0	271	2 751	2.7	62.3	11.6	15.8	6 702	17 329	34 025	13.9	4.1	10.1	10.3	7.5	11.0
Kossuth	75	1 057	4 259	20.0	53.4	13.6	18.6	7 651	16 598	34 562	10.3	4.7	10.2	10.1	7.5	10.3
Lee	466	2 778	8 838	15.4	59.1	12.5	38.6	6 443	18 430	36 193	9.2	5.4	9.7	10.4	7.1	12.2
Linn	259	4 230	51 126	19.5	39.8	27.7	288.5	8 725	22 977	46 206	7.0	10.2	6.5	6.7	4.3	6.9
Louisa	8	1 014	3 131	4.0	61.3	12.7	19.4	6 541	17 644	39 086	13.7	4.7	9.3	8.9	7.0	10.7
Lucas	74	3 384	2 236	9.3	65.4	11.1	9.4	5 978	15 341	30 876	7.8	2.8	13.7	13.6	8.4	13.9
Lyon	93	856	3 024	14.3	59.6	14.2	13.0	6 581	16 081	36 878	21.0	4.4	7.0	8.4	4.9	6.7
Madison	43	469	3 444	7.7	53.4	14.4	18.6	6 265	19 357	41 845	16.9	7.7	6.7	8.1	4.6	5.3
Mahaska	156	2 311	5 587	18.0	58.6	16.5	20.8	6 153	18 232	37 314	20.2	4.7	9.8	10.3	7.5	10.7
Marion	152	1 803	8 619	25.3	56.6	18.9	35.4	5 910	18 717	42 401	12.7	6.4	7.6	7.9	5.2	8.5
Marshall	578	3 698	9 625	9.2	54.9	17.0	50.7	7 590	19 176	38 268	0.5	5.5	10.2	9.7	7.1	11.7
Mills	349	2 774	3 900	9.5	53.5	16.3	18.0	6 455	18 736	42 428	15.2	8.0	8.3	7.8	5.8	9.6
Mitchell	64	834	2 586	11.3	60.0	12.8	11.8	6 302	16 809	34 843	5.8	3.5	10.7	9.9	7.0	10.8
Monona	179	1 820	2 215	5.6	61.2	13.4	11.1	6 895	17 477	33 235	19.4	4.0	9.4	10.9	6.6	8.4
Monroe	286	1 256	1 956	6.1	62.1	12.6	8.3	6 509	17 155	34 877	25.1	4.3	9.0	8.6	5.6	9.6
Montgomery	119	1 761	2 706	6.8	58.8	12.9	13.2	6 321	16 373	33 214	6.0	4.0	9.1	10.4	6.5	11.3
Muscatine	447	2 699	10 777	7.8	54.2	17.2	48.2	6 339	19 625	41 803	4.5	7.3	8.9	8.4	6.3	9.1
O'Brien	73	1 221	3 545	16.9	58.3	14.7	23.1	8 333	17 281	35 758	15.1	3.7	7.3	8.4	4.6	6.4
Osceola	14	925	1 719	11.3	56.5	13.4	5.9	6 076	16 463	34 274	10.7	4.8	7.0	7.8	6.0	6.4
Page	170	2 495	3 956	8.3	53.8	16.6	19.3	6 549	16 670	35 466	19.7	4.5	12.5	12.2	8.1	14.9
Palo Alto	NA	NA	2 695	12.4	51.3	13.9	13.1	7 066	17 733	32 409	13.7	4.8	10.6	10.8	6.6	10.7
Plymouth	80	1 335	6 856	19.9	51.7	19.3	26.9	6 004	19 442	41 638	15.7	7.7	6.0	6.3	4.4	6.5
Pocahontas	58	345	2 189	10.4	53.2	15.0	9.0	6 749	17 006	33 362	5.6	4.7	9.1	9.8	6.6	12.3
Polk	319	5 135	96 530	19.8	41.1	29.7	423.4	6 786	23 654	46 116	9.9	11.7	7.9	7.6	5.3	8.3
Pottawattamie	650	8 271	21 969	10.5	55.3	15.0	120.7	6 852	19 275	40 089	12.0	6.8	8.4	8.5	6.4	10.3
Poweshiek	138	2 246	5 335	26.5	55.8	18.5	20.1	6 550	18 629	37 836	8.1	6.3	9.8	9.9	6.2	10.5
Ringgold	0	0	1 271	9.6	61.6	13.4	7.3	7 716	15 023	29 110	4.4	3.3	14.3	14.8	9.4	14.8
Sac	61	657	2 717	5.4	58.8	13.6	13.2	6 010	16 902	32 874	12.1	3.7	9.9	10.2	6.8	12.1
Scott	1 077	5 933	44 556	19.9	44.4	24.9	208.4	7 585	21 310	42 701	6.0	9.5	10.5	10.0	7.7	12.1
Shelby	0	68	3 210	11.4	59.3	15.3	15.9	6 420	16 969	37 442	22.8	4.7	6.0	7.7	4.3	6.1
Sioux	NA	NA	10 299	48.6	53.3	19.8	26.1	6 129	16 532	40 536	17.4	5.4	6.4	6.8	4.6	6.8
Story	221	3 334	35 450	4.7	27.8	44.5	73.2	6 703	19 949	40 442	12.9	9.5	14.1	14.5	5.5	7.2
Tama	344	1 206	4 440	6.4	56.6	12.9	21.4	6 070	17 097	37 419	14.6	4.3	10.5	9.8	7.6	11.9
Taylor	0	759	1 605	3.1	63.3	12.0	8.8	7 222	15 082	31 297	25.0	2.4	12.1	12.6	8.5	11.5
Union	105	1 846	3 013	8.5	55.9	14.7	18.7	8 780	16 690	31 905	10.2	3.7	11.4	12.0	7.4	12.1
Van Buren	64	459	1 753	12.7	63.5	11.8	9.4	6 830	15 748	31 094	20.3	2.9	12.7	13.3	8.7	11.1
Wapello	522	3 582	8 657	7.9	58.4	14.6	50.5	7 653	16 500	32 188	13.8	3.8	13.2	13.7	9.4	16.6
Warren	145	2 009	11 429	16.9	47.8	21.2	48.0	6 183	20 558	50 349	15.5	9.3	5.1	5.3	3.7	6.0
Washington	342	1 109	4 958	11.9	56.6	16.4	22.7	6 416	18 221	39 103	12.7	4.5	7.6	7.7	5.1	8.0
Wayne	104	1 170	1 566	5.9	62.0	12.1	8.2	6 780	15 613	29 380	24.3	4.1	14.0	15.1	10.8	14.9
Webster	520	4 933	10 158	14.0	52.6	16.9	50.1	8 863	17 857	35 334	11.0	4.7	10.0	10.2	6.7	10.7
Winnebago	62	177	3 008	13.9	50.8	16.5	17.7	6 300	18 494	38 381	21.7	4.3	8.4	8.2	5.0	8.7
Winneshiek	103	786	7 105	43.8	53.2	20.5	18.1	6 456	17 047	38 908	18.8	5.6	10.3	10.3	5.1	6.6
Woodbury	565	5 284	27 592	18.7	53.6	18.9	133.3	7 190	18 771	38 509	13.8	5.6	10.3	9.7	7.2	11.0
Worth	0	0	1 848	3.6	53.6	12.7	7.1	6 255	16 952	36 444	18.4	2.9	8.3	9.0	6.3	9.2
Wright	70	792	3 218	3.9	54.7	13.5	19.1	6 522	18 247	36 197	9.6	4.4	7.0	7.6	4.2	6.8
KANSAS	377	3 710	756 960	13.5	43.8	25.8	3 068.7	6 552	20 506	40 624	10.8	9.3	9.9	10.1	6.7	10.0
Allen	275	3 172	3 682	4.1	52.7	15.2	15.7	5 964	15 640	31 481	12.8	3.3	14.9	13.8	11.3	17.1
Anderson	398	2 939	1 952	10.0	60.4	11.7	9.0	6 189	16 458	33 244	12.7	3.3	12.8	12.4	10.6	14.9
Atchison	260	2 744	4 863	33.9	56.9	18.0	18.0	7 171	15 207	34 355	14.5	3.9	13.3	13.5	7.9	10.9

1. Data for serious crimes have not been adjusted for underreporting; this may affect comparability between geographic areas and over time.   2. Per 100,000 population estimated by the FBI.   3. All persons 3 years old and over enrolled in nursery school through college.   4. Persons 25 years old and over.   5. Elementary and secondary education expenditures.   6. Based on population enumerated as of April 1, 2000.

Table B. States and Counties — **Personal Income**

STATE County	Total (mil dol) [62]	Percent change, 2001–2002 [63]	Per capita[1] Dollars [64]	Rank [65]	Wages and salaries[2] (mil dol) [66]	Proprietor's income (mil dol) [67]	Dividends, interest, and rent (mil dol) [68]	Transfer payments Total (mil dol) [69]	Gov't payments to individuals Total (mil dol) [70]	Social Security (mil dol) [71]	Medical payments (mil dol) [72]	Income maintenance (mil dol) [73]	Unemployment insurance (mil dol) [74]
IOWA—Cont'd													
Guthrie	298	3.6	26 380	814	86	29	61	56	53	27	21	2	1
Hamilton	431	2.7	26 433	808	263	49	89	71	67	34	26	4	2
Hancock	332	5.9	28 019	551	283	43	65	50	47	25	18	2	1
Hardin	467	0.0	25 316	1 040	256	44	99	98	93	44	39	4	3
Harrison	400	2.7	25 650	966	118	27	63	79	75	30	35	4	1
Henry	498	2.4	24 766	1 190	376	33	99	84	78	36	29	5	4
Howard	255	5.6	25 943	899	135	39	62	44	41	20	16	2	1
Humboldt	278	3.6	27 525	613	126	39	62	51	48	25	19	2	1
Ida	192	-0.2	25 179	1 083	120	19	46	34	32	17	11	1	1
Iowa	488	4.1	30 884	278	367	57	101	65	61	32	23	2	2
Jackson	488	3.7	24 106	1 370	180	42	102	101	95	40	42	6	4
Jasper	1 026	1.7	27 300	649	598	61	184	164	154	75	62	8	6
Jefferson	427	-0.2	26 772	741	265	46	102	67	63	26	27	5	4
Johnson	3 503	3.6	30 636	296	2 890	277	631	303	273	122	103	18	10
Jones	455	0.7	22 415	1 904	184	36	95	57	54	24	23	3	2
Keokuk	283	2.4	24 800	1 175	86	26	63	57	54	24	23	4	2
Kossuth	462	5.2	27 845	574	191	91	105	82	78	41	29	4	2
Lee	905	1.3	24 455	1 277	610	53	185	202	193	76	80	14	11
Linn	6 183	1.0	31 677	238	5 068	390	1 062	787	735	331	278	46	42
Louisa	301	1.5	24 682	1 216	117	23	60	49	45	21	18	3	2
Lucas	206	2.7	21 808	2 063	108	18	45	45	43	19	16	3	1
Lyon	270	-2.3	23 168	1 672	94	36	66	44	41	22	14	2	1
Madison	395	4.4	27 437	627	110	43	63	59	55	25	23	3	3
Mahaska	562	0.4	25 121	1 097	245	46	120	101	95	42	36	7	6
Marion	851	1.5	26 143	864	645	52	162	140	132	60	50	6	6
Marshall	1 079	2.1	27 486	617	676	83	205	202	191	81	77	12	6
Mills	465	7.5	31 575	243	128	25	57	132	128	25	95	4	1
Mitchell	272	2.2	24 959	1 147	115	36	66	51	48	24	20	2	1
Monona	239	1.1	24 516	1 258	95	23	51	60	57	24	27	3	1
Monroe	206	0.8	26 381	813	107	19	37	43	41	17	18	2	2
Montgomery	287	1.2	25 233	1 067	147	24	70	67	64	27	29	4	3
Muscatine	1 177	3.4	27 953	557	904	61	262	177	165	74	66	14	6
O'Brien	393	0.8	26 632	759	168	50	89	79	75	35	32	3	1
Osceola	158	-1.6	23 057	1 706	67	25	32	27	26	15	9	1	0
Page	399	0.5	24 200	1 343	191	43	86	90	86	38	39	6	2
Palo Alto	224	-2.2	22 659	1 833	102	24	50	50	47	23	19	2	1
Plymouth	689	2.0	27 979	553	358	73	135	98	92	46	37	4	3
Pocahontas	209	3.3	24 929	1 153	78	35	45	46	44	21	18	2	1
Polk	13 188	4.1	34 287	155	11 831	1 075	2 077	1 493	1 390	572	586	107	61
Pottawattamie	2 402	3.5	27 256	661	1 242	135	334	410	387	149	159	32	7
Poweshiek	539	2.2	28 417	502	354	53	103	85	80	39	31	4	3
Ringgold	117	1.1	21 863	2 048	41	21	26	27	26	12	11	2	1
Sac	289	-0.2	26 148	861	97	42	71	58	55	27	22	2	1
Scott	4 772	2.7	30 000	352	3 202	329	850	661	619	256	249	61	22
Shelby	336	0.1	26 236	846	142	33	83	66	63	29	28	3	1
Sioux	824	1.7	25 690	958	504	127	185	116	107	53	43	4	3
Story	2 173	3.3	26 479	797	1 639	144	396	250	229	105	86	11	6
Tama	432	1.6	24 112	1 367	166	46	81	79	75	38	28	4	3
Taylor	154	1.9	22 427	1 901	49	22	31	36	34	15	15	2	1
Union	287	3.8	23 645	1 514	183	27	52	65	62	25	24	4	2
Van Buren	159	2.0	20 472	2 439	62	9	34	40	38	17	16	2	2
Wapello	853	4.5	23 769	1 477	544	48	144	212	202	77	85	17	8
Warren	1 140	4.4	27 507	615	285	48	149	144	133	63	52	6	5
Washington	584	2.6	27 607	600	216	40	117	96	90	44	38	4	3
Wayne	142	6.5	21 338	2 199	51	17	28	38	36	16	16	3	1
Webster	1 026	3.4	25 748	941	697	75	196	213	202	86	87	14	5
Winnebago	288	5.9	25 167	1 086	148	33	55	52	49	24	19	2	1
Winneshiek	571	4.0	26 708	750	339	84	115	82	76	36	27	3	3
Woodbury	2 778	2.0	26 877	721	1 781	253	482	457	429	170	188	35	14
Worth	172	0.9	22 103	1 989	49	17	38	33	31	16	11	2	1
Wright	395	-0.4	28 378	506	186	38	100	79	75	33	34	3	2
KANSAS	78 382	1.9	28 905	X	52 384	6 345	14 163	11 261	10 521	4 442	4 289	710	414
Allen	311	-1.0	22 065	2 001	176	23	63	75	71	30	30	5	2
Anderson	176	-1.2	21 575	2 129	59	10	39	41	38	18	16	2	2
Atchison	362	0.5	21 596	2 122	218	23	71	77	72	30	31	5	2

1. Based on the resident population estimated as of July 1 of the year shown.　2. Includes other labor income.

Table B. States and Counties — **Earnings, Social Security, and Housing**

STATE County	Total (mil dol)	Farm	Goods-related[1] Total	Manu-facturing	Information and professional and technical services	Retail trade	Finance, insurance, and real estate	Health services	Govern-ment	Social Security beneficiaries December 2003 Number	Rate[2]	Supplemental Security Income recipients, December 2003	Housing units, 2003 Total	Percent change, 2000–2003
	75	76	77	78	79	80	81	82	83	84	85	86	87	88
IOWA—Cont'd														
Guthrie	114	12.3	15.9	6.5	4.7	5.3	10.0	D	23.4	2 815	245	130	5 570	1.9
Hamilton	313	9.1	D	37.5	D	4.5	4.4	D	13.9	3 515	215	190	7 158	1.1
Hancock	326	6.1	D	61.3	1.9	3.4	2.4	D	7.5	2 545	213	105	5 228	1.2
Hardin	299	9.2	20.5	12.9	3.5	7.0	3.9	D	20.2	4 365	239	178	8 346	0.3
Harrison	146	6.8	D	6.5	D	11.0	4.1	D	21.7	3 265	208	230	6 770	2.5
Henry	410	1.6	34.0	29.0	6.0	5.5	2.5	D	17.5	3 725	186	213	8 325	1.0
Howard	174	11.2	41.6	37.4	2.6	6.7	3.9	D	14.8	2 305	236	117	4 372	1.0
Humboldt	165	10.8	D	22.7	3.2	8.3	3.8	D	15.3	2 480	246	125	4 734	1.9
Ida	139	5.8	43.6	35.3	1.8	6.2	4.8	D	10.8	1 845	246	66	3 486	-0.6
Iowa	424	4.6	53.2	48.9	2.8	8.5	1.9	D	8.0	3 265	205	118	6 659	1.7
Jackson	222	5.6	24.0	17.4	4.5	9.6	4.8	D	20.4	4 410	218	305	9 136	2.1
Jasper	659	3.8	D	40.4	6.0	9.0	3.3	5.9	14.9	7 425	197	364	15 894	1.5
Jefferson	311	2.2	D	18.5	14.8	14.6	6.7	D	13.7	2 775	173	265	7 397	2.2
Johnson	3 167	0.4	D	8.0	8.8	6.5	4.6	7.2	43.7	11 795	102	1 032	49 760	8.6
Jones	221	6.8	D	17.6	4.6	10.8	3.7	D	23.5	4 090	201	181	8 201	0.9
Keokuk	112	8.2	D	17.1	2.9	12.1	4.7	7.0	18.2	2 595	229	186	4 998	-0.3
Kossuth	282	11.3	D	20.0	4.9	8.0	8.0	D	14.0	4 305	262	191	7 588	-0.2
Lee	662	0.8	D	34.4	D	7.1	3.1	D	15.0	7 670	209	723	16 721	0.7
Linn	5 457	0.3	D	22.0	10.8	7.2	9.2	9.4	10.0	31 875	162	2 344	85 531	6.2
Louisa	140	7.1	D	38.1	2.4	4.5	3.0	4.3	19.5	2 135	175	116	5 172	0.8
Lucas	126	2.2	D	7.6	2.9	8.3	6.3	6.4	19.9	2 145	226	220	4 255	0.4
Lyon	130	12.8	D	17.1	7.7	6.2	4.9	6.5	16.0	2 425	206	76	4 831	1.5
Madison	153	4.9	D	23.9	D	7.3	5.4	D	21.1	2 640	182	117	5 921	4.6
Mahaska	291	4.7	D	21.1	D	9.0	5.3	6.1	15.8	4 530	203	422	9 728	1.9
Marion	697	1.0	D	47.4	D	5.5	2.7	8.1	14.2	6 330	195	353	13 376	4.9
Marshall	758	2.1	D	36.9	3.2	7.1	3.5	9.6	16.6	8 105	207	573	16 577	1.5
Mills	153	1.4	D	4.9	4.7	8.8	7.2	D	41.7	2 655	178	261	5 780	1.9
Mitchell	151	15.9	D	24.3	2.9	6.0	4.5	D	15.7	2 550	233	97	4 626	0.7
Monona	118	8.5	9.9	3.6	D	8.0	5.0	D	25.2	2 605	267	166	4 691	0.7
Monroe	125	4.3	D	39.0	D	6.3	2.7	D	14.6	1 810	232	141	3 570	-0.5
Montgomery	170	6.6	D	18.9	9.3	7.3	4.6	D	20.3	2 815	249	215	5 355	-0.8
Muscatine	964	0.9	D	43.5	D	5.7	3.2	5.4	11.5	7 240	172	570	17 167	2.3
O'Brien	218	8.8	D	11.9	5.2	8.0	D	15.1	16.0	3 715	254	198	6 562	0.8
Osceola	93	19.1	D	22.7	D	5.5	D	D	12.7	1 545	227	65	2 985	-0.9
Page	234	2.3	D	20.3	D	11.9	3.7	D	23.6	4 005	245	311	7 269	-0.5
Palo Alto	127	12.2	D	10.6	D	8.5	4.7	D	26.8	2 405	248	147	4 679	1.0
Plymouth	431	6.8	D	29.0	3.4	6.4	4.9	5.8	11.7	4 845	196	179	10 135	2.6
Pocahontas	114	20.5	D	18.5	D	5.5	4.4	D	18.5	2 210	268	105	3 918	-1.8
Polk	12 905	0.1	13.5	6.8	10.4	7.6	22.5	9.7	12.8	55 360	142	5 687	166 010	6.1
Pottawattamie	1 376	0.6	D	15.0	4.4	11.2	5.8	12.6	15.9	15 655	177	1 606	37 192	4.0
Poweshiek	407	5.5	D	18.1	7.1	5.4	9.5	D	8.7	3 965	208	163	8 707	1.8
Ringgold	63	16.8	D	5.7	D	7.9	D	10.4	27.4	1 395	257	106	2 811	0.8
Sac	139	16.2	D	7.2	D	9.1	5.1	D	16.7	2 850	262	120	5 609	2.7
Scott	3 531	0.3	25.5	18.9	7.6	9.3	6.3	12.7	10.1	25 635	161	2 885	67 687	3.1
Shelby	175	7.7	14.2	7.3	9.2	9.0	6.7	D	18.8	3 075	242	149	5 416	-0.8
Sioux	631	13.8	D	28.5	4.3	5.4	3.9	6.5	10.7	5 535	172	211	11 527	2.4
Story	1 783	0.7	D	12.3	5.9	6.2	3.6	6.8	44.2	9 865	119	542	32 176	5.0
Tama	212	12.2	14.6	9.8	2.8	5.7	3.5	D	38.9	3 965	222	160	7 611	0.4
Taylor	71	19.3	D	19.9	2.7	5.3	D	5.1	21.5	1 750	258	126	3 212	0.4
Union	209	3.5	D	22.1	D	9.3	3.8	8.0	22.5	2 805	235	335	5 739	1.4
Van Buren	71	4.1	D	31.4	D	5.9	3.5	D	28.9	1 930	248	144	3 609	0.8
Wapello	592	0.6	D	26.7	3.9	8.9	3.1	16.0	17.0	8 125	226	1 132	15 944	0.4
Warren	334	2.0	D	7.3	5.1	12.9	4.8	9.8	22.0	6 390	152	202	16 122	5.4
Washington	256	5.3	29.6	18.2	4.9	8.4	4.9	D	18.2	4 465	209	235	8 718	2.0
Wayne	68	11.7	D	20.3	3.7	7.6	3.5	6.8	29.4	1 870	280	169	3 378	0.6
Webster	772	1.8	D	19.2	6.2	8.4	4.0	15.5	16.7	8 670	219	753	17 145	1.0
Winnebago	181	6.1	D	27.9	3.6	8.0	4.3	D	15.1	2 565	224	124	5 126	1.2
Winneshiek	423	6.3	34.8	24.2	D	6.9	3.4	D	15.1	3 950	185	189	8 347	1.7
Woodbury	2 033	0.6	20.5	14.3	5.8	8.7	7.8	16.2	14.7	17 370	172	1 938	41 674	0.7
Worth	66	13.4	D	16.7	D	6.7	4.6	6.8	20.4	1 645	212	87	3 516	-0.5
Wright	224	11.4	D	23.7	8.3	5.9	3.8	5.9	17.3	3 370	245	179	6 535	-0.4
KANSAS	58 729	0.8	23.8	16.9	11.5	7.0	7.4	9.4	18.1	443 706	163	37 813	1 170 718	3.5
Allen	199	-2.5	40.7	33.2	4.2	7.6	3.7	D	23.0	3 170	228	390	6 456	0.1
Anderson	69	-2.2	23.1	11.4	D	11.5	6.8	D	24.8	1 890	230	87	3 630	0.9
Atchison	241	-0.9	35.8	30.0	4.2	6.7	3.7	D	15.3	3 195	191	293	6 855	0.5

1. Covers mining, construction, and manufacturing.   2. Per 1,000 resident population estimated as of July 1 of the year shown.

STATE County	Housing units, 2000 — Occupied units — Total [89]	Owner-occupied Percent [90]	Median value[1] [91]	Median owner cost as a percent of income — With a mortgage [92]	Without a mortgage[2] [93]	Renter-occupied Median rent[3] [94]	Median rent as a percent of income [95]	Substandard units[4] (percent) [96]	Civilian labor force, 2003 Total [97]	Percent change, 2002–2003 [98]	Unemployment Total [99]	Rate[5] [100]	Civilian employment,[6] 2000 Total [101]	Percent Management, professional and related occupations [102]	Production, transportation, and material moving occupations [103]
IOWA—Cont'd															
Guthrie	4 641	79.6	61 800	19.5	11.7	389	20.0	1.8	5 754	-5.1	226	3.9	5 655	31.5	16.8
Hamilton	6 692	72.8	70 500	18.5	10.8	422	18.9	1.8	8 463	-3.9	356	4.2	8 485	30.2	23.2
Hancock	4 795	78.2	59 600	18.2	9.9	353	17.3	1.8	7 175	-3.9	220	3.1	6 036	28.3	28.4
Hardin	7 628	74.6	57 200	18.1	10.2	403	21.0	1.4	8 949	-6.5	443	5.0	8 934	29.8	21.0
Harrison	6 115	76.6	74 900	19.6	10.5	418	23.2	2.6	7 682	-3.2	384	5.0	7 489	29.2	17.7
Henry	7 626	73.1	76 700	17.7	9.9	428	21.6	1.5	10 702	-3.4	740	6.9	9 876	25.6	27.3
Howard	3 974	79.2	59 500	19.8	10.3	333	19.7	2.7	5 567	-5.0	221	4.0	4 764	27.0	26.1
Humboldt	4 295	75.9	71 700	17.9	9.9	362	21.6	1.2	5 453	-4.1	199	3.6	4 913	29.5	20.9
Ida	3 213	73.2	55 500	17.1	9.9	338	17.7	1.1	3 871	-7.3	146	3.8	3 739	29.7	21.6
Iowa	6 163	77.9	85 600	19.0	9.9	412	19.9	1.1	9 047	-6.3	297	3.3	8 292	28.0	24.7
Jackson	8 078	75.8	76 500	19.4	10.9	386	20.1	2.3	10 769	-5.2	794	7.4	10 299	25.3	25.0
Jasper	14 689	75.7	82 500	19.3	10.4	448	20.5	1.4	19 534	-5.7	986	5.0	18 606	28.8	23.7
Jefferson	6 649	67.4	72 500	19.3	10.5	426	22.9	2.0	8 778	-5.6	469	5.3	8 412	35.0	16.8
Johnson	44 080	56.7	131 500	20.3	9.9	564	30.5	2.5	72 752	-3.9	2 386	3.3	64 255	43.3	8.9
Jones	7 560	75.8	80 400	20.0	9.9	416	20.2	1.4	9 812	-4.7	549	5.6	9 721	29.0	20.9
Keokuk	4 586	78.8	51 900	17.7	10.4	372	22.3	1.6	5 338	-5.5	285	5.3	5 335	27.5	22.4
Kossuth	6 974	77.6	54 300	17.6	9.9	347	18.0	1.1	8 561	-5.8	408	4.8	8 240	32.2	19.5
Lee	15 161	75.5	60 300	18.2	10.5	398	23.8	1.7	17 879	-4.2	1 476	8.3	17 345	23.2	27.9
Linn	76 753	72.7	99 400	19.3	9.9	510	22.4	2.1	116 620	-2.8	5 489	4.7	103 761	34.8	14.7
Louisa	4 519	77.3	66 600	17.6	9.9	419	20.4	4.8	5 864	-4.1	288	4.9	5 828	22.5	31.6
Lucas	3 811	78.4	50 900	18.8	12.0	326	22.7	2.5	4 270	-1.6	258	6.0	4 384	22.2	23.0
Lyon	4 428	81.7	64 000	18.0	9.9	350	18.8	1.6	5 453	-7.5	211	3.9	5 931	29.9	19.6
Madison	5 326	78.0	87 700	21.2	11.8	445	22.3	1.6	7 348	-4.3	345	4.7	7 054	32.4	14.3
Mahaska	8 880	71.1	68 100	16.6	9.9	420	22.4	1.9	11 277	-4.2	556	4.9	10 762	27.7	25.7
Marion	12 017	75.5	88 300	18.8	9.9	472	24.5	1.9	18 645	-3.2	756	4.1	16 251	30.5	22.6
Marshall	15 338	73.8	71 200	19.0	10.8	458	24.0	4.3	20 760	-1.4	1 125	5.4	19 142	27.6	23.1
Mills	5 324	79.5	92 900	20.5	11.5	465	24.8	1.5	6 376	-2.0	239	3.7	7 373	30.1	13.7
Mitchell	4 294	81.5	66 500	18.2	9.9	334	22.4	1.7	5 352	-5.3	168	3.1	5 104	31.9	20.7
Monona	4 211	76.2	54 400	19.5	9.9	384	18.8	1.9	4 876	-5.5	246	5.0	4 658	28.6	15.2
Monroe	3 228	78.5	52 400	17.3	11.7	399	26.3	1.6	3 875	-4.5	196	5.1	3 618	27.1	28.2
Montgomery	4 886	73.2	55 900	19.5	10.1	361	22.7	1.4	5 538	-5.7	281	5.1	5 484	24.4	21.6
Muscatine	15 847	75.4	84 700	19.1	9.9	460	22.7	3.5	22 125	-1.1	923	4.2	20 765	26.1	27.2
O'Brien	6 001	76.8	58 300	17.4	9.9	373	20.1	1.6	7 549	-6.7	256	3.4	7 379	28.3	23.9
Osceola	2 778	77.8	53 400	17.7	9.9	374	19.8	0.7	3 593	-5.4	117	3.3	3 373	28.9	23.8
Page	6 708	71.7	60 000	17.4	9.9	407	23.4	1.2	7 729	-6.0	308	4.0	7 679	28.0	25.3
Palo Alto	4 119	74.0	53 500	17.7	10.7	337	20.2	0.9	5 072	-5.4	171	3.4	4 912	31.6	19.0
Plymouth	9 372	77.4	88 200	19.2	10.7	416	21.1	1.2	14 001	-1.9	522	3.7	12 583	31.2	18.5
Pocahontas	3 617	79.2	40 400	17.0	9.9	315	17.9	0.7	3 522	-11.3	233	6.6	3 920	35.5	17.8
Polk	149 112	68.8	103 100	20.2	10.8	574	23.9	3.6	224 977	-1.4	8 982	4.0	200 662	36.1	11.4
Pottawattamie	33 844	71.1	84 900	19.6	10.8	537	24.1	2.9	51 049	-0.8	2 678	5.2	44 658	26.5	17.3
Poweshiek	7 398	71.9	81 600	18.9	9.9	432	20.8	1.2	10 184	-9.1	483	4.7	9 773	29.7	22.1
Ringgold	2 245	75.5	45 000	18.2	10.7	368	24.9	2.6	2 591	-6.1	106	4.1	2 388	33.3	16.2
Sac	4 746	76.8	50 000	17.9	9.9	329	20.2	1.2	5 648	-7.2	225	4.0	5 560	28.2	19.0
Scott	62 334	70.5	92 400	19.2	9.9	496	24.5	2.0	86 767	-1.8	3 798	4.4	79 475	31.7	16.9
Shelby	5 173	77.1	73 800	19.0	9.9	399	21.2	1.1	6 865	-3.7	234	3.4	6 594	29.0	16.7
Sioux	10 693	80.4	84 700	19.1	9.9	385	21.2	2.0	18 508	-1.9	511	2.8	16 827	31.0	18.4
Story	29 383	58.3	115 800	19.6	9.9	575	28.3	2.1	48 532	-2.7	1 304	2.7	44 535	43.0	9.1
Tama	7 018	77.6	64 200	18.3	11.1	418	19.8	2.3	8 505	-5.5	866	10.2	8 500	26.0	20.5
Taylor	2 824	76.6	37 900	17.2	10.4	352	19.0	2.8	3 287	-5.8	128	3.9	3 257	25.3	27.4
Union	5 242	72.0	55 600	17.0	11.1	344	19.9	2.1	6 321	-3.6	359	5.7	6 176	26.3	24.0
Van Buren	3 181	79.3	43 100	18.2	11.5	334	20.0	3.4	3 933	-4.9	233	5.9	3 760	27.2	28.5
Wapello	14 784	75.6	50 100	18.4	10.5	419	24.5	2.3	19 205	-0.5	1 109	5.8	16 493	24.5	24.7
Warren	14 708	79.9	102 000	19.7	9.9	494	22.3	1.6	23 602	-1.4	825	3.5	22 009	31.3	13.3
Washington	8 056	75.3	83 600	19.4	9.9	424	20.5	1.9	11 918	-3.0	450	3.8	10 766	31.5	18.1
Wayne	2 821	79.5	35 600	18.3	11.6	303	19.6	1.8	2 876	-8.4	131	4.6	3 061	30.2	21.0
Webster	15 878	71.2	66 000	17.3	10.4	408	22.1	1.7	20 213	-2.3	887	4.4	18 705	28.0	19.8
Winnebago	4 749	76.1	61 200	16.4	9.9	341	18.4	0.9	6 141	-6.0	200	3.3	6 045	27.3	28.6
Winneshiek	7 734	73.6	86 000	19.1	9.9	389	21.5	1.6	12 292	-7.1	586	4.8	11 764	33.4	17.4
Woodbury	39 151	68.6	76 400	19.3	10.6	494	23.5	4.6	53 020	-4.3	2 709	5.1	51 827	27.9	19.3
Worth	3 278	79.0	55 900	17.6	9.9	357	20.3	0.6	4 211	-1.7	164	3.9	4 065	22.7	27.0
Wright	5 940	74.1	52 500	17.3	9.9	350	20.0	2.0	6 455	-6.2	291	4.5	6 929	28.2	25.6
KANSAS	1 037 891	69.3	83 500	19.3	9.9	498	23.4	3.4	1 434 070	1.7	77 299	5.4	1 316 283	33.9	15.0
Allen	5 775	74.9	40 900	17.4	9.9	365	22.2	2.9	6 921	2.9	307	4.4	6 840	24.9	26.1
Anderson	3 221	80.0	49 300	19.6	9.9	365	19.8	3.4	4 024	-0.2	212	5.3	3 767	28.0	20.1
Atchison	6 275	73.5	56 500	18.6	10.8	378	20.8	1.7	8 491	1.9	409	4.8	7 788	30.7	19.1

1. Specified owner-occupied units. 2. Median monthly owner costs is often in the minimum category—9.9 percent or less, which is indicated as 9.9 percent. 3. Specified renter-occupied units. 4. Overcrowded or lacking complete plumbing facilities. 5. Percent of civilian labor force. 6. Persons 16 years old and over.

STATE County	Number of establishments	Total	Health care and social assistance	Manufacturing	Retail trade	Finance and insurance	Professional, scientific, and technical services	Total (mil dol)	Average per employee (dollars)	Number	Less than 50 acres	500 acres and over	Farm operators whose principal occupation is farming (percent)
	104	105	106	107	108	109	110	111	112	113	114	115	116
IOWA—Cont'd													
Guthrie	296	1 850	381	184	342	135	53	34	18 647	885	22.5	21.0	65.3
Hamilton	437	6 173	549	2 758	702	167	100	163	26 465	797	28.1	30.4	75.5
Hancock	329	3 148	462	1 190	475	126	89	71	22 533	827	23.9	27.8	79.1
Hardin	624	7 045	1 170	1 516	922	244	129	158	22 483	829	27.3	28.7	69.5
Harrison	349	3 199	678	283	688	140	64	61	18 947	828	20.7	32.0	68.7
Henry	562	11 989	1 109	2 757	898	177	118	286	23 882	857	27.0	16.6	58.7
Howard	258	3 445	516	1 568	355	120	59	77	22 438	891	25.5	17.7	68.2
Humboldt	320	3 369	447	1 156	489	102	52	85	25 189	606	19.3	30.2	77.4
Ida	263	3 298	425	1 224	376	130	41	82	24 751	618	26.5	27.3	73.9
Iowa	493	9 459	598	5 421	1 249	116	96	274	28 927	1 024	21.3	18.0	66.1
Jackson	585	5 202	856	1 330	907	234	132	94	18 042	1 336	20.6	14.4	62.1
Jasper	831	13 854	1 255	4 495	1 840	311	644	469	33 868	1 212	27.7	24.1	68.7
Jefferson	670	7 393	699	1 648	1 392	295	705	200	27 078	808	20.8	18.1	61.0
Johnson	2 638	52 276	12 619	4 843	8 239	1 451	1 835	1 402	26 819	1 261	27.0	13.3	66.1
Jones	494	4 457	714	870	909	178	155	91	20 485	1 024	21.3	20.1	69.5
Keokuk	269	1 753	342	246	411	113	43	38	21 918	1 093	23.0	21.0	69.2
Kossuth	542	5 451	706	1 263	991	436	156	124	22 659	1 340	18.8	32.8	75.8
Lee	1 009	15 285	2 079	5 130	2 057	472	244	409	26 785	945	24.1	18.1	60.3
Linn	5 283	111 650	11 623	20 403	13 896	7 070	4 276	3 687	33 025	1 445	32.5	13.3	61.6
Louisa	224	2 816	282	1 392	224	88	40	64	22 689	601	21.5	21.8	64.9
Lucas	210	2 767	420	D	422	129	D	70	25 214	747	19.3	16.1	54.4
Lyon	368	2 611	567	411	455	112	102	50	19 016	1 045	20.8	21.9	76.6
Madison	342	2 824	575	530	542	141	107	60	21 376	990	23.3	17.5	57.6
Mahaska	601	6 411	800	927	1 258	244	119	135	21 044	1 043	19.8	20.5	69.1
Marion	807	18 204	2 534	8 512	1 768	265	182	489	26 835	1 051	27.8	15.4	59.8
Marshall	918	15 553	1 953	5 433	2 407	391	304	412	26 472	848	30.0	27.1	67.9
Mills	254	2 848	1 527	53	342	87	D	71	24 822	462	19.3	39.2	67.7
Mitchell	338	2 995	549	990	437	123	58	68	22 674	828	22.8	25.6	71.1
Monona	277	2 576	768	124	510	111	60	50	19 406	625	13.1	39.2	80.0
Monroe	203	2 472	439	903	389	64	33	62	25 277	714	16.2	20.3	61.2
Montgomery	331	4 067	832	601	583	177	82	85	20 901	583	19.9	29.3	65.5
Muscatine	990	19 974	1 765	7 817	2 220	417	901	650	32 554	816	27.9	19.0	64.5
O'Brien	549	5 207	1 199	744	971	227	115	102	19 618	993	18.6	26.4	77.5
Osceola	202	1 860	317	535	175	90	35	40	21 694	636	20.3	30.7	80.5
Page	492	6 213	1 129	2 224	949	147	157	152	24 421	873	17.6	29.0	63.1
Palo Alto	330	2 522	545	421	470	138	53	50	19 811	783	23.9	30.5	80.1
Plymouth	663	9 023	949	1 725	1 160	319	125	243	26 913	1 339	17.2	27.4	76.8
Pocahontas	264	2 079	343	592	292	103	62	42	20 416	730	17.7	37.9	81.1
Polk	11 577	246 513	29 455	17 843	31 006	40 738	11 121	8 159	33 099	764	41.4	17.8	55.9
Pottawattamie	1 901	30 412	4 075	4 425	6 150	1 399	740	753	24 747	1 255	25.7	31.4	74.1
Poweshiek	579	9 039	1 135	1 769	1 028	802	260	236	26 146	925	21.6	26.2	69.3
Ringgold	130	1 033	314	155	199	D	19	23	22 028	758	14.5	22.2	61.1
Sac	376	2 640	652	221	483	140	71	49	18 418	791	21.4	31.4	75.5
Scott	4 452	82 860	9 701	13 174	11 732	2 596	2 302	2 468	29 786	750	27.5	19.5	68.9
Shelby	418	4 601	930	243	683	215	294	93	20 145	868	15.9	30.3	77.0
Sioux	1 109	14 118	1 494	3 965	1 645	527	300	324	22 947	1 673	25.5	18.5	77.4
Story	1 927	27 973	4 414	3 727	4 971	858	1 128	669	23 900	977	30.9	24.5	64.2
Tama	394	4 273	518	459	596	137	63	93	21 710	1 159	19.4	23.3	68.1
Taylor	161	1 329	D	D	210	36	D	28	21 224	794	14.9	22.5	61.7
Union	366	5 012	957	915	872	152	80	99	19 846	698	20.3	19.9	62.9
Van Buren	165	1 637	349	703	170	67	31	37	22 505	870	18.0	16.0	56.9
Wapello	848	13 584	2 449	3 361	2 419	376	305	339	24 953	845	25.9	14.1	58.2
Warren	763	7 510	959	279	1 735	218	205	139	18 480	1 338	34.6	11.7	53.7
Washington	683	5 783	1 086	1 286	1 146	243	126	127	21 951	1 200	26.4	18.4	69.1
Wayne	177	1 394	366	437	231	D	45	25	18 053	788	12.6	23.0	59.6
Webster	1 151	16 183	2 924	2 127	3 046	509	356	434	26 837	932	22.4	30.3	75.3
Winnebago	370	7 700	571	4 377	622	175	76	197	25 554	631	30.3	25.4	60.4
Winneshiek	618	10 155	1 480	2 014	1 247	234	210	218	21 513	1 501	23.3	15.9	66.2
Woodbury	2 906	47 646	7 918	6 907	7 507	1 538	1 324	1 178	24 723	1 148	24.0	24.2	63.3
Worth	182	1 313	202	330	204	70	20	27	20 220	588	28.2	30.3	75.7
Wright	429	4 812	690	1 354	650	147	280	107	22 223	752	24.9	33.5	72.9
KANSAS	74 565	1 118 898	157 316	191 013	152 328	52 857	52 362	33 304	29 765	64 414	17.4	34.6	63.1
Allen	414	5 270	606	2 081	608	134	99	111	21 035	619	17.1	27.5	66.1
Anderson	239	1 604	374	208	280	118	43	27	17 144	654	16.8	30.6	68.7
Atchison	404	5 938	1 046	1 773	842	141	70	144	24 237	619	19.1	20.7	61.2

Table B. States and Counties — **Agriculture**

Agriculture, 2002 (cont'd)

STATE County	Land in farms — Acreage (1,000)	Percent change, 1997–2002	Average size of farm (Acres)	Total irrigated (1,000)	Total cropland (1,000)	Value of land and buildings — Average per farm (dollars)	Average per acre (dollars)	Value of machinery and equipment average per farm (dollars)	Value of products sold — Total (mil dol)	Average per farm (dollars)	Percent from — Crops	Percent from — Livestock and poultry products	Percent of farms with sales of — $10,000 or more	$100,000 or more	Government payments Total ($1,000)	Percent of farms
	117	118	119	120	121	122	123	124	125	126	127	128	129	130	131	132
IOWA—Cont'd																
Guthrie	324	6.6	366	D	261	627 640	1 813	87 331	111	125 631	46.6	53.4	56.6	21.6	5 501	72.1
Hamilton	348	-0.3	437	0	327	1 013 638	2 324	163 962	235	294 730	37.3	62.7	72.6	40.9	4 837	76.0
Hancock	322	-3.6	390	1	309	756 135	2 095	111 500	142	171 209	56.6	43.4	76.4	42.0	5 067	73.8
Hardin	328	-3.5	395	0	298	1 033 567	2 463	129 699	252	303 944	32.2	67.8	70.6	38.4	5 438	71.8
Harrison	428	8.9	517	26	368	881 870	1 692	104 822	111	134 289	76.3	23.7	65.7	32.0	6 244	69.2
Henry	251	2.4	293	0	198	575 938	2 019	82 950	79	91 717	50.5	49.5	52.0	21.5	5 365	70.7
Howard	269	-0.4	302	D	237	589 597	1 992	99 933	105	118 110	52.0	48.0	63.0	26.6	5 613	79.2
Humboldt	271	5.4	447	0	253	1 041 524	2 487	118 522	97	159 466	68.1	31.9	80.7	40.9	3 758	74.4
Ida	266	5.1	430	D	240	915 772	2 059	102 219	111	180 229	52.9	47.1	73.1	40.0	4 238	67.8
Iowa	340	2.4	332	D	277	548 590	1 706	99 784	133	129 877	67.0	33.0	56.1	25.4	7 172	72.6
Jackson	349	4.2	261	0	238	425 523	1 849	66 794	107	80 011	31.1	68.9	58.5	20.7	7 546	67.1
Jasper	410	-2.6	339	1	355	693 496	2 040	97 775	149	122 889	59.5	40.5	65.2	31.0	6 418	66.2
Jefferson	233	2.2	289	0	177	425 473	1 492	70 786	49	60 096	54.6	45.4	47.6	15.7	5 093	74.9
Johnson	301	4.5	239	0	258	546 917	2 377	72 228	105	82 971	54.2	45.8	60.7	21.8	6 135	61.3
Jones	312	-3.1	304	D	259	668 794	2 202	96 787	119	116 670	48.3	51.7	65.8	32.3	6 650	69.9
Keokuk	344	6.5	315	0	280	541 271	1 519	105 400	99	90 431	51.1	48.9	53.4	24.7	8 559	76.8
Kossuth	592	1.9	442	0	560	1 026 962	2 338	129 429	261	194 789	55.7	44.3	82.0	44.9	10 247	77.5
Lee	270	5.1	286	1	202	478 396	1 778	72 127	66	69 398	58.1	41.9	47.6	17.5	4 961	66.0
Linn	349	2.9	241	0	292	641 286	2 577	80 812	105	72 910	69.6	30.4	56.9	18.9	6 016	60.3
Louisa	201	0.0	334	6	169	688 491	2 150	97 746	70	117 008	60.9	39.1	59.2	29.1	4 547	75.9
Lucas	222	-2.2	298	D	134	331 099	1 093	40 668	27	35 930	41.4	58.6	41.9	6.8	3 644	66.3
Lyon	342	-1.7	327	0	305	742 370	2 356	91 649	248	237 221	27.1	72.9	86.0	48.3	4 860	66.1
Madison	304	-4.1	307	0	210	520 520	1 757	63 505	71	71 215	47.3	52.7	50.8	13.5	6 330	75.1
Mahaska	329	0.0	315	D	278	675 409	1 852	92 229	133	127 275	42.0	58.0	60.0	28.4	4 733	66.5
Marion	277	-3.1	263	0	214	399 258	1 491	50 739	68	65 140	67.4	32.6	46.1	16.2	5 757	69.8
Marshall	335	5.0	395	D	302	870 878	2 009	137 296	132	155 772	64.8	35.2	63.9	34.4		
Mills	247	6.5	535	2	220	965 971	1 803	100 195	48	104 151	88.6	11.4	71.4	34.0	3 585	69.9
Mitchell	289	9.1	349	D	263	767 313	2 222	120 240	155	186 700	40.4	59.6	73.1	43.5	4 379	70.4
Monona	392	6.5	628	54	335	1 106 554	1 792	115 976	105	168 136	67.4	32.6	76.0	39.0	4 401	72.6
Monroe	253	16.6	354	0	165	345 299	1 008	71 219	41	57 329	36.7	63.3	50.3	11.9	3 413	64.4
Montgomery	243	0.0	416	0	205	565 380	1 420	84 549	83	141 559	59.7	40.3	63.3	29.5	4 252	75.8
Muscatine	230	5.0	282	5	197	633 878	2 283	87 967	72	88 416	70.8	29.2	57.0	24.3	5 376	69.6
O'Brien	362	1.1	365	0	332	949 993	2 545	117 677	204	205 752	40.4	59.6	85.6	45.7	5 705	70.6
Osceola	257	6.6	404	1	243	975 939	2 475	99 245	163	255 830	35.1	64.9	80.0	45.7	4 611	75.8
Page	339	9.7	388	0	278	509 083	1 256	73 068	69	79 211	61.8	38.2	64.5	23.3	4 664	73.9
Palo Alto	327	-0.3	417	3	308	844 947	2 356	114 313	191	244 070	39.3	60.7	73.9	40.9	5 135	76.5
Plymouth	531	3.7	397	2	472	904 120	2 267	100 211	278	207 911	38.2	61.8	79.1	43.6	6 441	63.9
Pocahontas	354	-0.8	485	D	333	1 199 126	2 377	135 369	142	194 684	61.2	38.8	82.5	49.0	4 661	78.8
Polk	227	0.4	297	D	204	747 561	2 156	124 636	69	89 682	86.3	13.7	52.5	20.5	3 259	53.4
Pottawattamie	540	0.6	431	3	488	928 528	2 028	113 421	163	130 093	65.5	34.5	65.2	33.9	8 636	64.1
Poweshiek	345	3.0	373	0	294	633 723	1 832	92 144	111	120 066	60.1	39.9	59.2	28.6	6 234	77.9
Ringgold	299	13.3	395	0	216	458 545	1 015	54 702	52	67 967	35.2	64.8	51.5	13.6	4 874	74.5
Sac	339	-1.7	429	1	313	1 180 995	2 438	137 699	183	231 793	44.3	55.7	82.0	44.8	4 644	71.3
Scott	229	1.8	305	1	210	942 443	3 003	131 268	96	127 620	66.5	33.5	72.4	31.6	4 675	62.4
Shelby	348	1.8	401	0	323	761 140	2 044	157 948	124	142 761	59.9	40.1	81.2	41.4	5 470	71.8
Sioux	505	2.2	302	8	463	776 515	2 655	109 603	617	368 711	17.6	82.4	86.6	52.2	8 198	59.5
Story	360	5.6	368	0	330	950 209	2 342	121 033	119	121 525	77.9	22.1	68.0	29.7	5 577	64.6
Tama	418	5.6	361	0	371	826 772	2 253	112 228	128	110 464	75.5	24.5	68.1	31.7	7 708	70.4
Taylor	308	5.8	388	0	239	495 960	1 226	56 804	60	75 831	51.2	48.8	52.8	16.9	6 650	77.8
Union	238	5.8	341	D	176	450 018	1 309	85 551	63	90 100	36.8	63.2	54.4	18.6	3 563	70.3
Van Buren	253	-1.6	291	0	175	349 272	1 220	72 611	48	55 026	42.5	57.5	44.6	10.9	3 646	64.9
Wapello	206	-1.0	244	0	156	390 388	1 540	44 919	38	44 765	66.3	33.8	39.8	12.5	3 909	60.9
Warren	299	-0.3	224	0	217	351 293	1 468	50 364	53	39 941	65.1	34.9	39.2	10.2	4 503	59.3
Washington	335	5.3	279	0	284	618 883	2 271	113 339	175	145 682	34.7	65.3	61.3	31.7	8 663	73.2
Wayne	305	6.6	387	D	235	408 974	1 001	56 127	41	52 348	58.5	41.5	50.6	13.5	5 133	71.8
Webster	417	1.0	447	0	387	942 349	2 206	129 882	154	165 206	69.4	30.6	74.4	39.5	6 320	73.8
Winnebago	240	-0.8	381	D	225	901 384	2 101	112 511	98	155 036	56.1	43.9	63.7	33.1	4 546	76.9
Winneshiek	380	5.3	253	0	303	496 455	1 808	99 197	148	98 886	33.2	66.8	60.4	27.4	8 014	67.4
Woodbury	442	-11.1	385	8	384	698 733	1 794	103 817	142	123 994	57.8	42.2	59.1	27.0	7 205	60.4
Worth	224	-1.8	381	1	209	826 029	2 153	114 695	68	115 372	78.0	22.0	65.6	35.7	3 723	77.2
Wright	345	-1.4	459	0	327	1 111 023	2 479	135 317	226	300 196	38.9	61.1	72.9	40.6	5 048	77.3
KANSAS	47 228	2.5	733	2 678	29 542	505 999	687	95 124	8 746	135 782	27.7	72.3	51.7	17.1	328 244	60.8
Allen	280	3.3	453	D	170	419 305	821	78 680	25	40 068	49.6	50.4	50.7	11.6	1 785	58.2
Anderson	379	3.3	579	3	228	505 793	899	81 370	44	67 844	46.7	53.3	56.1	14.5	1 924	54.7
Atchison	227	-6.2	366	1	156	402 638	1 057	61 163	32	51 928	49.4	50.6	52.0	12.8	1 869	53.3

Table B. States and Counties — Residential Construction, Wholesale Trade, Retail Trade, and Real Estate

STATE County	Value of residential construction authorized by building permits, 2003		Wholesale trade, 1997				Retail trade,[1] 1997				Real estate and rental and leasing, 1997			
	New construction ($1,000)	Number of housing units	Number of establishments	Number of employees	Sales (mil dol)	Annual payroll (mil dol)	Number of establishments	Number of employees	Sales (mil dol)	Annual payroll (mil dol)	Number of establishments	Number of employees	Receipts (mil dol)	Annual payroll (mil dol)
	133	134	135	136	137	138	139	140	141	142	143	144	145	146
IOWA—Cont'd														
Guthrie	6 988	46	14	121	70.6	2.1	53	359	57.9	5.0	11	31	2.1	0.4
Hamilton	3 066	24	36	D	D	D	82	747	90.8	9.0	11	28	1.3	0.2
Hancock	3 465	27	30	285	179.8	6.7	55	425	55.4	4.4	9	30	1.5	0.2
Hardin	3 750	32	63	1 095	554.5	31.5	114	1 097	151.0	13.6	14	46	2.3	0.5
Harrison	7 063	58	26	228	106.5	5.1	78	647	166.9	11.5	14	42	2.3	0.3
Henry	5 973	71	34	246	93.6	5.4	88	970	161.8	13.5	18	82	5.8	1.3
Howard	651	8	22	159	102.6	3.9	54	361	54.4	4.0	8	D	D	D
Humboldt	2 770	23	37	285	199.0	7.7	56	496	71.3	7.3	8	19	1.7	0.4
Ida	1 013	8	23	166	211.1	5.0	44	389	52.8	4.6	9	20	1.5	0.3
Iowa	3 073	25	28	217	112.4	4.8	164	1 250	153.6	14.7	4	3	0.8	0.1
Jackson	10 132	82	35	197	73.7	4.3	110	889	165.5	12.0	13	32	1.8	0.2
Jasper	17 501	121	47	465	465.2	11.3	175	1 703	232.3	25.2	21	73	4.5	0.6
Jefferson	1 626	15	50	275	78.3	6.6	107	1 165	279.2	38.5	14	29	1.9	0.4
Johnson	218 230	1 517	89	D	D	D	467	6 924	990.9	104.7	120	566	66.7	10.2
Jones	2 516	27	34	236	101.6	5.6	90	771	124.4	11.4	10	12	1.1	0.1
Keokuk	600	6	21	178	90.8	3.9	55	449	94.3	6.6	5	D	D	D
Kossuth	2 366	15	32	279	176.3	6.7	118	1 091	152.2	13.6	15	28	2.2	0.3
Lee	2 903	17	50	486	178.8	11.9	194	2 166	344.2	34.0	37	101	5.5	1.1
Linn	146 378	1 709	375	5 653	2 324.1	166.0	874	13 337	2 040.9	213.9	199	1 135	128.8	25.6
Louisa	1 889	16	14	185	70.9	5.1	39	256	45.7	3.6	6	D	D	D
Lucas	166	2	14	134	35.0	2.8	45	399	50.2	4.8	3	4	0.4	0.0
Lyon	3 336	24	24	243	133.7	5.7	62	476	63.8	5.5	3	D	D	D
Madison	18 736	118	15	89	62.8	2.3	61	522	82.8	7.1	11	26	1.7	0.2
Mahaska	4 014	47	43	374	192.8	10.3	114	1 246	190.8	17.1	21	57	3.8	0.5
Marion	19 951	165	42	510	98.6	7.2	156	1 519	243.1	22.4	23	78	5.4	0.9
Marshall	19 690	137	58	488	227.6	16.6	182	2 457	319.9	33.9	32	247	20.6	6.1
Mills	2 750	36	15	110	51.1	2.8	41	322	52.8	4.4	5	19	4.1	0.2
Mitchell	3 084	28	24	D	D	D	91	541	71.0	6.0	3	7	0.2	0.0
Monona	2 327	25	22	159	88.1	4.3	61	576	95.4	8.4	6	15	0.8	0.1
Monroe	1 656	17	11	73	20.9	1.4	43	363	51.7	4.7	1	D	D	D
Montgomery	1 257	12	30	214	151.3	5.1	68	581	82.8	7.4	6	14	0.7	0.2
Muscatine	24 097	269	63	381	264.1	10.1	177	2 390	337.6	34.5	36	140	11.4	2.4
O'Brien	3 232	19	41	367	201.1	8.9	111	976	169.5	14.0	7	28	3.1	0.6
Osceola	900	6	13	128	65.8	4.8	36	211	32.0	2.6	4	7	0.3	0.0
Page	1 805	18	26	223	87.4	5.0	108	1 185	148.5	14.3	11	42	6.8	1.0
Palo Alto	805	8	22	172	164.6	4.2	60	479	75.4	6.5	7	8	0.9	0.2
Plymouth	15 642	123	39	938	401.8	27.2	118	1 052	194.9	16.2	17	63	6.3	0.7
Pocahontas	1 615	13	18	277	197.4	6.8	46	301	43.4	3.4	5	9	0.5	0.1
Polk	632 461	4 565	901	D	D	D	1 680	28 123	4 454.0	461.4	456	3 433	584.7	84.4
Pottawattamie	59 530	539	101	D	D	D	382	5 742	978.5	87.1	63	D	D	D
Poweshiek	9 025	66	36	298	124.9	8.0	103	1 122	190.6	15.4	20	38	2.7	0.4
Ringgold	360	3	8	35	19.6	0.9	28	214	38.2	2.7	2	D	D	D
Sac	460	7	37	230	144.5	6.6	76	491	83.7	6.2	6	12	0.8	0.1
Scott	105 496	877	389	4 535	3 366.3	151.6	747	11 397	1 831.5	187.3	165	1 424	144.1	33.3
Shelby	2 093	13	27	D	D	D	80	645	117.4	9.6	5	18	0.9	0.1
Sioux	19 471	116	92	1 144	470.8	27.7	182	1 557	285.2	21.4	19	49	4.2	0.8
Story	102 460	744	95	772	321.2	21.7	359	4 729	631.3	65.8	68	366	24.4	5.6
Tama	6 146	46	31	221	215.9	4.9	90	646	90.8	8.1	8	22	1.3	0.2
Taylor	140	3	15	72	26.2	1.4	34	193	24.8	2.3	2	D	D	D
Union	1 649	14	24	318	108.9	5.6	72	800	114.6	11.5	22	63	5.3	1.1
Van Buren	336	5	8	69	35.2	0.5	34	154	19.8	1.9	3	5	0.4	0.1
Wapello	7 845	93	38	321	140.6	9.1	185	2 538	330.9	32.7	31	79	11.8	0.9
Warren	41 357	263	54	D	D	D	113	1 314	244.8	20.8	22	47	5.0	0.7
Washington	4 820	38	40	298	134.2	6.5	128	1 036	155.6	16.2	16	28	1.3	0.2
Wayne	145	1	17	130	53.5	2.2	38	252	31.6	3.5	1	D	D	D
Webster	8 890	70	71	885	710.2	31.4	252	3 142	438.7	44.9	47	168	13.3	2.4
Winnebago	2 267	16	17	D	D	D	74	573	81.6	6.2	7	15	1.0	0.1
Winneshiek	3 996	24	39	449	131.4	10.5	124	1 113	180.1	15.0	10	16	3.0	0.4
Woodbury	24 929	210	209	2 476	1 222.1	70.5	523	7 771	1 143.5	116.0	111	D	D	D
Worth	949	8	17	97	85.6	2.6	41	213	28.8	2.3	3	9	0.1	0.0
Wright	1 713	15	28	D	D	D	83	639	73.9	7.8	13	49	2.0	0.4
KANSAS	1 895 406	15 049	5 085	59 954	42 209.9	1 946.8	12 271	140 412	22 571.9	2 191.1	2 602	13 005	1 525.8	259.6
Allen	1 772	15	18	186	35.5	3.2	83	590	85.3	8.1	7	20	1.3	0.2
Anderson	475	3	12	77	48.4	1.4	38	207	43.0	2.9	3	9	0.3	0.0
Atchison	2 530	35	17	449	270.8	9.9	68	659	86.1	7.9	14	45	3.5	0.6

1. Establishments with payroll.

Table B. States and Counties — **Professional Services, Manufacturing, and Accommodation and Foodservices**

STATE County	Professional, scientific, and technical services,[1] 1997				Manufacturing, 1997				Accommodation and foodservices, 1997			
	Number of establishments	Number of employees	Receipts (mil dol)	Annual payroll (mil dol)	Number of establishments	Number of employees	Receipts (mil dol)	Annual payroll (mil dol)	Number of establishments	Number of employees	Sales (mil dol)	Annual payroll (mil dol)
	147	148	149	150	151	152	153	154	155	156	157	158
IOWA—Cont'd												
Guthrie	11	58	1.7	0.5	NA	NA	NA	NA	30	158	5.8	1.4
Hamilton	24	103	4.8	1.7	30	2 861	472.0	75.8	35	311	8.4	2.2
Hancock	12	33	1.5	0.4	27	1 126	221.2	29.7	22	199	3.9	0.9
Hardin	27	111	5.5	2.0	39	1 580	375.8	34.8	43	371	9.4	2.4
Harrison	12	36	1.5	0.6	NA	NA	NA	NA	30	318	8.6	2.5
Henry	24	94	4.5	2.0	34	2 839	717.4	85.2	44	612	16.7	4.5
Howard	15	45	2.5	0.9	20	1 405	177.7	29.2	29	D	D	D
Humboldt	13	40	2.5	0.7	28	1 257	159.7	31.8	21	210	4.5	1.3
Ida	12	28	1.8	0.5	9	1 112	165.0	32.5	22	D	D	D
Iowa	18	40	4.9	0.9	31	4 698	678.8	144.7	54	999	30.4	8.5
Jackson	26	74	3.6	0.9	34	1 208	194.5	25.7	58	515	11.4	2.6
Jasper	41	586	124.4	13.1	46	3 702	740.0	132.4	74	961	25.9	7.3
Jefferson	122	538	51.0	20.9	37	1 751	256.6	56.4	41	365	10.7	2.7
Johnson	164	1 085	81.9	29.3	89	3 639	2 510.4	121.1	271	5 496	144.3	40.8
Jones	21	78	4.5	1.5	23	889	170.1	23.5	37	366	7.7	1.9
Keokuk	7	25	0.8	0.3	NA	NA	NA	NA	20	86	1.7	0.5
Kossuth	23	89	5.6	1.3	30	1 126	207.3	33.7	42	417	9.2	2.2
Lee	50	182	11.7	3.4	70	6 397	1 671.5	209.0	108	1 257	33.0	8.8
Linn	369	2 936	268.6	106.7	239	22 877	6 376.1	935.0	439	7 853	240.1	68.2
Louisa	10	40	1.5	0.5	11	D	D	D	27	191	4.0	1.0
Lucas	9	23	1.0	0.3	NA	NA	NA	NA	18	148	3.5	0.8
Lyon	15	80	5.8	2.6	NA	NA	NA	NA	26	D	D	1.3
Madison	19	65	3.8	1.5	26	1 020	230.6	26.3	43	656	15.6	4.3
Mahaska	24	98	6.5	2.9	44	6 687	1 388.5	229.8	59	900	20.5	5.4
Marion	35	144	7.9	3.1	44	5 363	1 413.2	174.0	86	1 070	29.7	8.4
Marshall	50	201	13.4	4.9								
Mills	9	43	2.1	0.8	NA	NA	NA	NA	23	221	5.7	1.6
Mitchell	7	37	1.7	0.6	16	1 021	186.3	27.4	21	D	D	D
Monona	15	53	3.5	1.1	NA	NA	NA	NA	36	267	6.4	1.6
Monroe	11	26	1.5	0.3	18	863	593.2	32.8	18	D	D	D
Montgomery	19	48	2.7	1.1	11	1 365	185.0	32.4	32	291	7.0	1.8
Muscatine	53	1 020	75.8	22.7	70	6 523	2 631.1	252.7	85	1 057	29.3	8.0
O'Brien	25	76	5.1	1.4	NA	NA	NA	NA	44	392	8.1	1.9
Osceola	7	35	1.7	0.3	NA	NA	NA	NA	14	117	2.3	0.5
Page	19	143	3.7	1.5	27	2 271	477.3	78.0	41	466	10.1	3.1
Palo Alto	12	31	2.1	0.5	NA	NA	NA	NA	30	D	D	D
Plymouth	29	108	5.6	2.0	26	D	D	D	57	D	D	D
Pocahontas	19	46	2.4	0.7	19	821	91.8	20.3	25	179	3.0	0.8
Polk	954	10 594	845.8	346.1	410	19 790	5 054.9	688.6	897	17 068	534.4	156.1
Pottawattamie	99	656	47.0	16.4	59	4 109	888.7	113.2	197	3 782	186.1	48.4
Poweshiek	33	115	7.2	2.0	32	1 533	226.6	42.7	43	677	13.2	4.1
Ringgold	3	10	0.3	0.1	NA	NA	NA	NA	9	64	1.3	0.3
Sac	20	65	3.3	1.0	NA	NA	NA	NA	25	207	3.9	1.1
Scott	315	1 999	177.4	58.0	210	11 845	4 614.8	478.3	378	8 050	234.2	70.0
Shelby	19	80	3.8	1.5	NA	NA	NA	NA	34	343	7.4	2.1
Sioux	43	192	12.7	4.2	67	4 610	822.0	104.6	71	1 098	19.8	5.0
Story	148	970	97.9	34.7	75	3 577	988.6	108.4	202	3 598	89.1	24.5
Tama	15	48	2.4	0.5	14	911	236.1	22.5	33	311	7.8	1.8
Taylor	10	26	1.1	0.4	NA	NA	NA	NA	11	77	1.4	0.3
Union	18	64	3.2	1.6	19	1 031	113.2	24.6	28	379	10.0	2.7
Van Buren	11	31	1.4	0.7	14	653	54.4	14.8	10	83	2.0	0.3
Wapello	45	206	12.9	4.2	22	2 701	741.8	92.5	85	1 076	29.8	7.8
Warren	35	108	6.2	2.0	NA	NA	NA	NA	58	809	18.3	5.1
Washington	33	133	5.8	1.7	32	1 441	196.2	41.2	42	506	10.8	3.1
Wayne	8	28	2.2	0.3	13	D	D	D	17	99	1.7	0.4
Webster	69	319	22.8	8.5	60	2 554	1 110.9	81.7	93	1 322	37.1	10.5
Winnebago	19	83	4.8	1.4	13	4 006	640.5	105.5	28	259	6.2	1.4
Winneshiek	21	90	5.6	2.6	29	1 453	215.0	38.0	51	573	14.5	4.0
Woodbury	178	946	73.6	23.9	113	D	D	D	246	3 812	109.2	29.9
Worth	6	18	0.8	0.1	12	596	49.2	12.5	9	D	D	D
Wright	27	173	8.8	2.5	25	1 318	546.5	39.2	40	292	7.3	1.8
KANSAS	5 345	39 534	3 559.3	1 396.0	3 309	193 742	46 296.4	6 532.5	5 677	91 173	2 685.7	757.1
Allen	25	94	4.5	1.8	28	1 722	277.3	45.7	38	534	13.7	4.1
Anderson	12	28	1.9	0.4	NA	NA	NA	NA	22	206	4.9	1.1
Atchison	16	48	2.7	1.0	24	1 753	360.1	53.7	32	340	8.2	2.2

1. Firms subject to federal tax.

Table B. States and Counties — **Health Care and Social Assistance, Other Services, and Federal Funds**

STATE County	Health care and social assistance,[1] 1997				Other services,[1] 1997				Federal funds and grants, 2002–2003 Expenditures (mil dol)			
									Total	Direct payments for individuals[2]		
	Number of establishments	Number of employees	Receipts (mil dol)	Annual payroll (mil dol)	Number of establishments	Number of employees	Receipts (mil dol)	Annual payroll (mil dol)		Social Security and government retirement	Medicare	Food stamps and Supplemental Security Income
	159	160	161	162	163	164	165	166	167	168	169	170
IOWA—Cont'd												
Guthrie	17	36	2.6	0.6	13	36	2.2	0.5	74.3	31.0	12.3	1.1
Hamilton	30	292	14.8	7.3	23	86	5.9	1.2	85.0	38.6	19.1	1.4
Hancock	11	244	7.8	3.7	29	71	4.2	1.1	56.9	28.0	11.3	0.8
Hardin	24	257	8.9	4.0	41	103	7.0	1.5	148.1	53.0	22.0	1.8
Harrison	14	289	10.0	5.4	23	49	4.2	0.8	93.6	40.6	17.7	1.8
Henry	38	487	18.0	8.1	31	93	6.8	1.1	100.6	44.4	15.9	2.0
Howard	13	182	5.0	2.9	16	32	3.6	0.5	55.2	22.7	10.1	0.8
Humboldt	14	199	6.9	2.9	21	52	4.9	1.0	58.3	28.3	12.1	1.0
Ida	15	192	7.0	3.0	18	50	2.4	0.6	46.5	19.5	8.4	0.4
Iowa	22	244	8.4	4.1	22	73	4.2	1.2	72.1	36.5	13.6	1.0
Jackson	34	424	14.4	6.7	43	114	9.4	1.6	112.1	49.8	21.3	2.4
Jasper	42	664	22.5	12.4	58	198	11.9	3.1	163.3	82.8	33.4	2.8
Jefferson	37	466	17.7	8.4	30	78	5.5	1.2	75.2	30.1	13.2	2.0
Johnson	181	1 907	97.5	41.4	152	767	43.3	12.5	645.8	148.5	44.4	7.4
Jones	22	299	12.1	5.0	34	91	5.7	1.2	95.1	43.3	15.8	1.6
Keokuk	12	201	5.5	2.7	15	29	2.4	0.4	73.5	30.9	14.1	1.6
Kossuth	24	321	7.9	2.7	43	106	6.6	1.4	103.9	44.6	16.9	1.3
Lee	87	1 008	40.8	18.4	68	308	18.4	4.6	199.7	93.6	43.0	6.2
Linn	340	3 925	267.5	138.3	350	2 296	143.5	43.3	1 259.7	389.9	126.2	19.8
Louisa	10	193	5.6	2.7	11	31	1.7	0.3	56.5	25.4	8.5	1.3
Lucas	15	78	4.0	1.8	5	15	1.3	0.3	61.1	25.8	10.2	1.7
Lyon	16	113	4.6	1.8	26	59	4.6	1.0	57.5	26.7	10.2	0.6
Madison	17	305	8.4	4.4	24	53	3.0	0.7	61.9	30.3	13.5	1.1
Mahaska	28	249	11.2	5.5	46	143	10.3	2.0	112.3	48.6	19.6	3.2
Marion	41	479	16.6	7.6	56	208	10.5	2.9	195.1	86.8	26.5	2.6
Marshall	60	612	35.9	17.4	57	250	15.0	3.9	216.3	100.7	33.3	5.0
Mills	14	452	8.5	5.6	29	163	9.4	2.8	76.8	35.1	14.1	1.5
Mitchell	15	97	6.0	2.6	26	95	5.1	1.2	59.2	29.8	12.6	0.5
Monona	17	448	13.9	7.4	21	51	3.9	0.8	78.2	29.3	16.3	1.1
Monroe	12	144	4.2	2.0	10	29	1.6	0.4	57.6	22.3	11.2	1.1
Montgomery	18	231	12.9	4.5	31	76	6.0	1.2	71.0	31.9	16.7	1.6
Muscatine	60	606	28.7	14.8	61	296	17.6	5.5	190.8	87.9	29.1	5.7
O'Brien	33	275	11.2	4.8	45	146	8.5	1.9	88.3	41.3	16.9	1.2
Osceola	11	150	4.4	1.9	14	41	2.6	0.5	38.1	16.8	7.2	0.3
Page	33	569	26.0	10.3	41	105	7.7	1.7	101.9	44.8	19.4	2.1
Palo Alto	24	304	10.3	4.7	16	31	1.8	0.5	71.2	28.3	12.2	1.0
Plymouth	35	436	15.6	7.5	48	176	12.5	2.5	104.5	50.8	20.4	1.3
Pocahontas	17	190	6.1	2.9	17	26	1.8	0.4	59.0	26.1	12.0	0.7
Polk	766	9 160	632.7	311.0	674	4 664	294.6	90.9	2 569.8	797.8	275.9	51.1
Pottawattamie	103	1 322	74.8	41.9	142	684	43.8	12.5	441.4	210.6	79.1	13.1
Poweshiek	39	328	18.8	8.1	30	91	6.1	1.6	90.8	45.6	18.5	1.2
Ringgold	7	149	4.4	1.8	9	23	1.9	0.4	38.6	14.3	6.3	0.7
Sac	14	178	6.6	3.0	27	75	4.2	1.1	64.7	31.9	13.5	0.9
Scott	324	3 126	236.5	111.7	296	2 042	115.7	37.8	777.6	366.4	109.9	29.9
Shelby	19	218	6.7	3.1	29	79	5.4	0.9	82.6	33.7	18.0	1.2
Sioux	50	356	16.7	7.4	75	233	18.9	3.9	147.6	60.9	23.3	1.5
Story	91	1 545	88.0	47.2	107	617	33.9	9.3	488.6	128.4	46.8	4.7
Tama	18	247	7.9	3.8	27	93	6.1	0.9	92.7	43.6	17.9	1.3
Taylor	7	107	2.6	1.2	10	26	1.4	0.3	48.2	18.4	8.1	0.9
Union	17	283	11.1	5.7	20	86	8.3	1.8	82.4	34.4	13.4	2.1
Van Buren	5	9	0.5	0.1	10	13	1.8	0.2	49.4	22.1	9.1	0.9
Wapello	66	723	45.9	22.9	62	284	15.7	4.0	228.3	97.0	42.7	8.4
Warren	49	532	22.3	8.9	48	140	9.1	2.0	139.1	75.0	24.8	2.3
Washington	39	486	16.6	7.8	36	120	11.3	2.0	100.4	50.3	19.7	1.8
Wayne	7	82	2.9	1.3	14	38	2.2	0.6	56.8	20.3	10.1	1.4
Webster	85	809	53.3	25.5	80	448	24.0	7.2	252.5	101.0	46.4	6.4
Winnebago	22	236	8.6	3.8	18	37	3.2	0.6	65.7	29.6	12.0	0.6
Winneshiek	28	219	13.0	5.2	40	102	6.5	1.5	103.6	41.3	15.4	1.1
Woodbury	223	2 111	186.1	89.6	181	1 319	66.4	21.2	567.7	210.8	94.0	14.3
Worth	6	31	1.4	0.9	7	17	1.7	0.3	41.0	18.3	8.1	0.5
Wright	20	310	10.2	4.5	22	91	3.5	0.8	85.7	40.4	17.7	1.2
KANSAS	4 793	66 613	4 116.1	1 771.8	4 604	24 081	1 548.4	452.9	18 208.1	6 015.1	2 476.0	321.2
Allen	28	312	9.1	4.4	24	94	6.3	1.6	84.6	36.9	16.1	2.6
Anderson	14	152	4.7	2.2	14	31	2.4	0.4	46.7	22.8	10.2	0.8
Atchison	35	230	12.8	5.9	23	82	4.7	1.5	100.0	39.7	19.0	2.5

1. Firms subject to federal tax.   2. State totals may include programs not allocated by county.

STATE County	Salaries and wages	Defense	Other	Medicaid and other health-related	Nutrition and family welfare	Education	Other	Total (mil dol)	Intergovern-mental (mil dol)	Total (mil dol)	Total	Property
	171	172	173	174	175	176	177	178	179	180	181	182
IOWA—Cont'd												
Guthrie	3.2	0.0	0.7	6.9	1.1	0.4	1.2	39.4	18.4	12.3	1 090	1 044
Hamilton	3.1	0.0	0.8	7.8	1.4	0.3	4.6	60.4	19.7	20.2	1 247	1 199
Hancock	3.0	0.0	0.6	3.3	0.9	0.3	1.1	35.5	13.9	13.1	1 105	1 026
Hardin	5.0	0.0	34.6	9.8	1.8	0.7	10.4	64.8	21.9	22.3	1 210	1 069
Harrison	5.0	0.0	1.5	9.9	1.8	0.5	5.4	41.1	20.4	16.8	1 079	1 003
Henry	4.2	0.0	0.9	8.7	1.5	1.3	13.5	67.2	21.2	20.4	1 013	910
Howard	1.8	0.0	0.7	7.6	1.1	0.5	2.3	33.5	12.4	11.1	1 130	1 001
Humboldt	3.3	0.0	0.7	5.1	0.9	0.4	1.0	32.2	10.4	11.4	1 124	1 093
Ida	2.0	0.0	0.4	3.6	0.7	0.2	1.4	18.7	8.4	7.7	1 001	966
Iowa	4.0	0.0	0.9	4.8	0.8	0.3	1.0	45.7	17.4	17.8	1 125	915
Jackson	4.8	1.3	1.0	14.2	2.4	0.7	4.1	57.2	23.4	16.3	806	693
Jasper	6.6	0.4	1.7	15.3	3.2	0.7	6.6	131.0	41.8	41.5	1 110	1 024
Jefferson	4.9	0.0	0.7	8.8	1.2	0.3	4.7	43.6	13.3	14.1	883	784
Johnson	79.2	3.0	76.0	215.9	5.0	6.2	39.9	259.4	93.7	111.7	978	891
Jones	3.3	0.0	0.9	8.0	1.8	0.5	11.8	47.6	21.8	18.0	880	804
Keokuk	3.3	0.0	0.8	8.0	1.1	0.5	2.5	33.5	14.8	12.6	1 102	1 044
Kossuth	5.0	0.0	1.0	10.2	1.1	0.5	2.7	55.4	18.2	21.4	1 286	1 147
Lee	8.0	0.2	1.6	20.4	4.8	2.5	12.8	95.2	41.7	40.0	1 085	827
Linn	65.7	439.4	46.5	82.2	22.0	5.1	29.3	624.6	239.9	230.7	1 183	1 091
Louisa	3.0	0.0	1.6	6.5	1.4	0.4	0.8	44.3	18.9	14.0	1 144	1 098
Lucas	2.5	2.0	0.5	9.4	1.4	0.4	2.5	33.3	12.3	8.6	914	820
Lyon	2.3	0.0	0.6	4.7	0.8	0.3	4.2	29.5	13.0	12.3	1 048	932
Madison	2.9	0.0	0.6	7.3	1.2	0.3	0.5	59.3	21.2	14.3	985	953
Mahaska	4.7	0.0	1.0	14.9	2.3	1.4	6.2	65.2	20.9	22.8	1 026	882
Marion	34.4	0.7	4.4	15.6	2.6	2.6	9.6	77.9	36.2	29.7	910	829
Marshall	8.2	0.1	1.7	22.5	7.3	2.5	26.4	118.9	54.0	41.3	1 045	894
Mills	2.8	0.0	0.6	10.9	1.3	0.4	2.4	35.6	17.7	14.0	954	918
Mitchell	2.4	0.1	0.6	4.7	0.7	0.4	0.6	33.6	11.5	10.6	995	910
Monona	2.7	0.7	0.7	10.5	1.4	0.5	5.2	27.9	11.9	12.5	1 274	1 106
Monroe	2.1	0.9	0.3	8.3	1.2	0.4	4.1	25.4	9.3	7.7	983	958
Montgomery	3.6	0.1	0.7	7.3	1.3	0.4	1.8	50.4	13.2	14.5	1 264	1 043
Muscatine	7.3	14.4	6.6	16.0	5.4	1.2	5.6	120.7	48.5	47.3	1 125	907
O'Brien	4.0	0.0	0.9	11.6	1.0	0.9	1.5	47.8	19.0	17.7	1 193	1 102
Osceola	1.6	0.1	0.4	3.0	0.5	0.1	1.1	14.4	6.3	6.0	880	845
Page	4.2	0.0	1.0	13.4	1.9	1.0	3.8	49.9	18.9	16.0	969	818
Palo Alto	2.6	0.0	0.6	10.2	4.0	0.3	1.7	38.6	11.7	11.9	1 203	1 095
Plymouth	6.1	0.0	1.1	8.4	3.4	0.6	2.7	71.7	25.1	23.4	951	864
Pocahontas	4.2	0.0	0.5	4.7	0.9	0.3	0.7	23.8	8.2	8.5	1 015	954
Polk	345.9	54.7	71.0	265.3	151.1	115.8	391.3	1 353.6	450.3	556.1	1 442	1 235
Pottawattamie	14.3	0.0	3.1	62.7	11.3	4.0	26.6	273.2	109.4	110.2	1 251	972
Poweshiek	3.1	0.1	0.8	6.8	1.3	1.1	4.3	45.5	19.9	18.7	992	895
Ringgold	2.1	0.0	0.5	4.7	0.9	0.9	1.4	21.3	7.3	5.6	1 055	1 039
Sac	2.9	0.0	0.7	4.8	1.1	0.5	1.6	27.9	12.9	11.4	1 025	1 005
Scott	35.1	46.1	19.6	80.3	25.6	11.5	26.2	502.1	192.4	213.1	1 337	1 044
Shelby	3.2	0.0	0.7	9.4	4.3	0.4	3.7	54.7	16.3	17.0	1 308	1 187
Sioux	5.6	0.1	2.6	20.1	1.5	0.8	11.9	90.8	27.0	27.4	861	758
Story	57.7	6.3	70.6	35.9	4.0	4.1	105.6	289.1	71.3	82.8	1 026	910
Tama	3.8	0.0	0.9	8.3	1.7	1.1	3.3	49.9	24.0	19.1	1 067	971
Taylor	2.2	0.0	0.5	6.2	1.2	0.4	0.8	19.5	10.6	5.7	832	764
Union	4.5	0.0	0.9	12.0	2.8	1.2	5.1	62.7	23.9	12.4	1 025	1 013
Van Buren	2.4	0.0	0.6	4.4	0.8	0.4	3.0	27.1	11.2	6.1	787	743
Wapello	7.9	0.1	1.7	39.8	7.6	3.3	9.7	129.7	57.0	39.2	1 095	870
Warren	6.1	0.0	1.7	12.1	2.8	1.0	5.0	94.0	45.7	35.1	845	813
Washington	4.0	0.0	0.8	8.7	1.4	2.1	0.8	61.7	21.8	19.8	940	886
Wayne	2.3	0.0	0.6	9.8	1.2	0.5	1.9	22.8	8.8	6.1	910	880
Webster	21.2	11.1	3.1	27.6	6.6	2.0	13.5	126.2	49.2	42.9	1 076	927
Winnebago	2.9	0.0	0.7	7.6	0.8	0.3	1.9	36.5	16.2	14.5	1 248	1 132
Winneshiek	4.9	0.2	0.9	7.3	3.6	2.2	5.4	84.4	29.8	23.4	1 093	904
Woodbury	62.8	16.4	6.6	67.2	17.5	8.6	40.0	334.3	147.7	124.0	1 200	936
Worth	1.9	0.0	0.5	3.6	0.6	0.3	1.7	18.8	8.2	7.7	992	917
Wright	4.6	0.0	0.9	7.6	1.4	0.7	2.7	47.4	17.2	17.9	1 280	1 145
KANSAS	2 108.4	1 219.2	800.9	1 422.1	483.1	394.5	1 115.3	X	X	X	X	X
Allen	3.9	0.0	0.6	15.4	1.7	1.0	0.8	43.8	23.0	12.2	855	635
Anderson	2.3	0.1	0.5	2.9	0.6	0.3	2.1	20.0	9.6	7.6	938	820
Atchison	3.2	1.6	0.8	9.9	2.4	0.9	11.0	41.5	20.0	14.9	894	669

1. State totals may include programs not allocated by county. 2. Based on the resident population estimated as of July 1 of the year shown.

STATE County	Total (mil dol)	Per capita[1] (dollars)	Educa- tion	Health and hospitals	Police protec- tion	Public welfare	High- ways	Total (mil dol)	Per capita[1] (dollars)	Federal civilian	Federal military	State and local	Demo- cratic	Republi- can	All other
	183	184	185	186	187	188	189	190	191	192	193	194	195	196	197
IOWA—Cont'd															
Guthrie	37.5	3 313	49.6	14.6	3.0	1.6	16.2	15.3	1 354	64	45	787	43.5	55.7	0.8
Hamilton	59.6	3 669	34.8	26.6	3.6	0.6	12.7	36.5	2 247	62	65	1 170	46.7	52.5	0.8
Hancock	32.1	2 714	46.7	20.2	4.8	2.7	13.0	10.9	921	56	47	709	42.1	57.1	0.9
Hardin	61.3	3 335	42.8	21.7	4.1	0.3	10.5	24.7	1 344	87	73	1 679	44.8	54.5	0.7
Harrison	40.1	2 572	57.4	1.6	5.7	0.1	13.8	22.7	1 456	84	62	798	37.9	61.0	1.1
Henry	63.9	3 178	39.9	31.0	3.1	1.0	8.0	51.8	2 574	72	80	1 767	43.6	55.3	1.1
Howard	35.4	3 615	47.5	21.2	2.3	0.9	9.2	9.5	968	40	39	822	55.8	43.1	1.1
Humboldt	32.4	3 189	42.4	24.6	3.3	0.4	10.0	11.6	1 141	62	40	655	40.1	59.2	0.7
Ida	18.1	2 366	51.9	2.9	3.9	0.9	19.3	7.2	934	42	30	420	37.5	62.1	0.4
Iowa	44.8	2 832	55.5	11.2	4.1	1.8	12.6	15.0	948	72	63	939	45.4	53.8	0.8
Jackson	56.7	2 806	47.6	22.3	3.0	0.5	9.4	10.9	541	92	80	1 235	56.3	42.5	1.1
Jasper	131.3	3 514	34.7	34.0	3.3	2.1	7.2	49.1	1 313	117	149	2 357	52.0	47.2	0.7
Jefferson	42.5	2 665	33.9	36.2	4.4	0.7	8.6	10.1	635	84	63	1 060	54.1	44.4	1.5
Johnson	272.6	2 385	37.3	5.1	4.7	0.6	11.0	386.8	3 384	1 504	476	27 375	63.7	35.1	1.1
Jones	46.5	2 279	52.3	6.0	3.0	0.9	15.7	28.3	1 387	62	81	1 320	50.6	48.6	0.8
Keokuk	32.2	2 818	54.1	11.1	2.6	0.2	14.0	15.2	1 333	66	45	546	41.9	57.0	1.1
Kossuth	53.1	3 188	37.0	22.9	2.5	1.8	15.7	11.5	691	85	66	1 088	44.6	54.5	0.9
Lee	97.2	2 635	54.1	6.7	5.4	1.3	8.7	55.5	1 504	109	188	2 262	56.3	42.4	1.2
Linn	667.3	3 423	53.4	4.3	4.4	1.1	7.4	476.9	2 446	1 147	786	11 206	54.5	44.8	0.7
Louisa	44.9	3 665	51.2	3.2	3.3	0.7	8.9	113.8	9 293	63	49	687	46.5	52.6	0.9
Lucas	30.0	3 173	35.6	33.7	2.6	0.3	10.6	10.5	1 115	42	38	711	43.9	56.1	0.0
Lyon	32.0	2 734	43.9	4.7	4.3	0.3	12.0	11.3	964	49	47	588	21.3	77.9	0.7
Madison	59.9	4 134	39.4	34.4	2.7	0.6	7.8	100.0	6 897	56	58	825	42.1	56.8	1.1
Mahaska	65.5	2 945	35.4	35.5	3.8	0.2	8.7	34.3	1 543	74	88	1 183	35.3	64.0	0.7
Marion	74.5	2 280	53.0	6.1	4.2	0.7	11.5	67.2	2 056	744	130	1 547	39.4	59.9	0.7
Marshall	117.1	2 965	63.8	3.0	4.9	0.3	7.7	48.2	1 222	137	157	3 267	49.2	50.1	0.8
Mills	34.8	2 366	57.9	6.7	6.2	2.2	10.7	10.7	726	50	58	1 632	33.2	65.7	1.0
Mitchell	32.1	3 006	39.1	26.9	3.7	1.2	11.8	12.1	1 128	50	42	640	50.8	48.4	0.8
Monona	28.1	2 861	44.7	6.3	4.8	0.5	20.2	4.3	434	50	39	926	47.6	51.1	1.3
Monroe	24.2	3 090	35.3	33.9	4.4	0.9	13.1	6.3	801	44	31	465	46.9	52.2	0.9
Montgomery	52.3	4 573	38.5	34.4	2.1	0.3	7.1	23.7	2 077	61	45	888	34.0	65.0	1.0
Muscatine	109.6	2 608	50.1	5.5	5.2	0.6	8.4	162.3	3 862	122	167	2 607	50.9	48.4	0.8
O'Brien	49.3	3 324	66.2	1.0	3.4	0.1	9.1	21.2	1 426	63	59	1 011	30.1	69.0	0.9
Osceola	13.6	1 999	47.5	3.7	6.5	1.0	15.8	7.7	1 123	36	27	314	28.7	70.3	1.1
Page	56.6	3 423	47.7	18.6	3.8	0.1	12.6	26.8	1 618	77	66	1 433	29.4	69.8	0.7
Palo Alto	40.1	4 059	35.4	29.3	3.1	0.8	13.6	10.6	1 068	52	39	984	47.9	51.5	0.6
Plymouth	69.8	2 835	48.0	18.8	3.5	2.5	9.4	27.9	1 134	79	98	1 310	35.0	64.0	1.1
Pocahontas	23.0	2 757	40.5	19.1	3.4	1.2	13.6	8.1	975	52	33	564	42.3	56.6	1.1
Polk	1 400.6	3 631	40.7	8.3	4.4	1.3	4.9	1 193.1	3 093	5 144	1 878	27 360	51.8	47.5	0.7
Pottawattamie	287.9	3 266	53.2	3.3	5.0	0.6	10.0	151.4	1 717	233	352	4 929	40.8	58.4	0.8
Poweshiek	45.5	2 410	52.9	2.1	4.9	2.8	10.1	23.8	1 261	67	75	989	49.9	49.3	0.8
Ringgold	21.1	3 992	41.1	35.1	1.3	0.0	10.2	1.9	352	40	21	522	46.3	52.8	0.8
Sac	27.3	2 461	54.8	7.0	4.8	0.3	14.2	6.2	554	50	44	663	41.2	58.2	0.6
Scott	527.1	3 306	54.1	3.4	3.3	0.4	8.5	409.1	2 566	545	639	7 744	50.9	48.4	0.7
Shelby	48.7	3 751	36.6	27.4	3.1	0.2	9.9	28.8	2 221	60	52	903	35.2	64.0	0.8
Sioux	90.8	2 853	32.5	28.0	3.3	0.6	12.2	69.9	2 196	106	127	1 846	13.6	85.9	0.5
Story	275.8	3 420	29.1	35.7	3.2	0.7	9.4	131.1	1 625	1 062	348	17 856	52.1	46.8	1.1
Tama	47.1	2 627	61.0	4.3	3.5	0.3	13.2	9.9	554	74	71	2 365	49.9	49.5	0.6
Taylor	19.2	2 778	51.5	4.1	4.0	1.6	17.4	9.1	1 325	50	27	454	39.3	59.9	0.8
Union	58.6	4 834	43.3	26.2	2.1	0.2	9.1	21.7	1 788	86	48	1 213	46.1	52.9	1.1
Van Buren	28.4	3 640	43.8	29.2	2.6	1.9	9.9	11.4	1 461	46	31	615	40.9	57.9	1.3
Wapello	124.7	3 486	62.5	4.5	2.7	0.6	6.3	50.6	1 415	144	143	2 662	54.9	44.2	0.9
Warren	96.8	2 332	60.0	5.9	5.0	0.7	5.7	68.5	1 649	112	165	1 893	46.6	52.8	0.7
Washington	57.8	2 737	44.2	25.2	3.3	0.4	8.2	43.2	2 049	76	84	1 275	42.8	56.2	1.0
Wayne	23.0	3 462	38.3	30.3	3.2	0.4	11.5	4.7	701	48	26	597	44.0	55.3	0.6
Webster	130.2	3 271	61.1	4.4	3.2	0.3	7.1	54.7	1 375	281	161	2 920	51.2	48.2	0.6
Winnebago	39.2	3 388	55.4	5.0	4.4	0.3	9.7	14.6	1 260	54	46	746	45.4	53.5	1.0
Winneshiek	70.1	3 271	50.6	24.5	3.1	0.6	10.2	20.0	934	87	85	1 818	49.7	49.4	0.9
Woodbury	339.4	3 285	51.4	3.1	5.4	0.7	6.9	203.3	1 967	829	419	5 977	48.5	51.0	0.6
Worth	15.9	2 049	48.6	4.8	4.0	2.2	15.9	10.4	1 335	39	31	347	55.4	43.6	1.0
Wright	43.6	3 116	51.5	17.6	4.1	0.5	10.5	15.0	1 074	82	56	1 036	44.4	55.0	0.6
KANSAS	X	X	X	X	X	X	X	X	X	25 457	24 089	231 564	36.5	62.2	1.4
Allen	43.6	3 060	61.3	1.6	3.2	0.0	5.5	17.7	1 242	59	40	1 593	32.6	65.9	1.5
Anderson	19.7	2 422	51.1	1.8	3.9	0.0	12.3	28.3	3 474	43	23	561	33.6	64.7	1.7
Atchison	42.9	2 570	47.1	0.7	4.9	4.5	6.1	36.3	2 177	54	47	1 154	43.8	54.5	1.6

1. Based on the resident population estimated as of July 1 of the year shown.

Table B. States and Counties — Land Area and Population

STATE/ County code	CBSA code[1]	County Type[2]	STATE County	Land area,[3] (sq km) 2000	Total persons	Rank	Per square kilometer	White	Black	Am. Indian, Alaska Native	Asian and Pacific Islander	Percent Hispanic or Latino[4]	Under 5 years	5 to 17 years	18 to 24 years	25 to 34 years	35 to 44 years	45 to 54 years
				1	2	3	4	5	6	7	8	9	10	11	12	13	14	15
			KANSAS—Cont'd															
20 007	...	9	Barber	2 937	5 034	2 840	1.7	96.9	0.5	0.9	0.2	1.9	4.0	18.2	8.2	7.6	13.8	15.4
20 009	24460	7	Barton	2 315	27 467	1 486	11.9	87.9	1.7	1.0	0.3	9.9	6.1	18.5	10.6	9.5	14.0	14.5
20 011	...	6	Bourbon	1 650	15 086	2 098	9.1	94.3	3.5	1.4	0.4	1.4	6.2	18.1	11.3	10.6	13.1	13.3
20 013	...	6	Brown	1 478	10 442	2 407	7.1	88.0	2.3	8.9	0.5	2.0	6.3	18.2	9.4	9.1	13.1	14.8
20 015	48620	2	Butler	3 698	61 127	809	16.5	94.6	1.8	1.9	0.7	2.5	6.3	20.1	10.7	11.0	15.8	14.7
20 017	21380	8	Chase	2 010	3 107	2 976	1.5	94.7	1.8	0.8	0.5	2.8	13.0	15.3	7.9	9.5	14.0	13.8
20 019	...	9	Chautauqua	1 662	4 185	2 897	2.5	94.3	0.5	4.6	0.2	1.9	4.4	17.5	9.2	7.3	12.8	12.6
20 021	...	6	Cherokee	1 521	21 815	1 712	14.3	94.8	0.8	5.5	0.4	1.2	6.2	18.6	9.6	11.6	14.4	13.8
20 023	...	9	Cheyenne	2 641	2 955	2 987	1.1	95.3	0.0	0.1	0.7	4.0	4.7	17.1	7.2	8.3	13.2	15.3
20 025	...	9	Clark	2 524	2 333	3 030	0.9	93.4	0.3	0.9	0.2	5.4	5.9	18.1	8.7	8.2	13.2	14.4
20 027	...	7	Clay	1 668	8 573	2 559	5.1	98.0	0.6	0.9	0.3	0.8	5.3	17.8	8.5	9.6	13.6	15.1
20 029	...	7	Cloud	1 853	9 859	2 458	5.3	98.3	0.4	0.7	0.4	0.8	5.0	15.5	12.8	8.5	12.7	13.3
20 031	...	6	Coffey	1 631	8 815	2 540	5.4	97.1	0.3	1.4	0.6	1.7	5.6	18.7	9.8	9.9	15.3	15.4
20 033	...	9	Comanche	2 042	1 915	3 066	0.9	97.3	0.3	0.3	0.7	2.0	5.5	16.4	6.5	8.6	12.2	14.0
20 035	49060	4	Cowley	2 917	35 860	1 246	12.3	88.5	3.6	2.9	1.6	5.1	6.6	18.3	11.9	11.2	14.2	13.3
20 037	38260	4	Crawford	1 536	38 398	1 174	25.0	92.7	2.3	1.8	1.9	2.8	6.7	15.6	15.3	13.0	12.2	12.2
20 039	...	9	Decatur	2 314	3 295	2 963	1.4	97.9	0.5	0.3	0.3	1.5	4.5	16.9	7.2	7.7	14.0	15.2
20 041	...	7	Dickinson	2 196	19 255	1 849	8.8	95.9	0.4	1.3	0.7	2.6	5.7	18.2	8.9	9.9	14.8	14.0
20 043	41140	3	Doniphan	1 016	8 149	2 585	8.0	94.5	2.8	1.6	0.3	1.6	5.5	17.9	13.6	10.5	13.5	14.2
20 045	29940	3	Douglas	1 183	102 983	529	87.1	86.3	4.9	3.3	4.3	3.5	5.7	14.1	21.5	17.2	12.3	11.6
20 047	...	9	Edwards	1 611	3 275	2 964	2.0	87.1	0.3	0.4	0.4	11.9	6.2	17.4	8.3	8.9	14.9	14.3
20 049	...	8	Elk	1 676	3 167	2 969	1.9	96.3	0.2	2.8	0.3	2.3	4.6	16.2	8.4	8.0	11.5	14.5
20 051	25700	5	Ellis	2 331	27 212	1 496	11.7	95.6	1.0	0.4	1.0	2.8	6.0	15.0	17.0	12.8	12.5	13.4
20 053	...	7	Ellsworth	1 854	6 347	2 740	3.4	91.8	3.8	0.6	0.4	3.7	4.4	15.0	10.1	10.3	15.6	15.7
20 055	23780	3	Finney	3 372	39 176	1 148	11.6	52.9	1.1	0.7	2.8	43.0	10.2	24.0	10.6	14.2	15.3	12.1
20 057	19980	5	Ford	2 845	33 012	1 334	11.6	53.3	1.6	0.8	1.9	43.0	9.3	21.7	11.3	14.7	13.6	11.3
20 059	28140	1	Franklin	1 486	25 540	1 550	17.2	94.8	1.6	1.8	0.4	2.8	6.9	19.3	10.5	11.7	15.2	13.1
20 061	31740	5	Geary	996	26 313	1 525	26.4	67.4	22.2	1.7	5.2	7.8	10.0	19.9	11.2	15.3	14.1	11.5
20 063	...	9	Gove	2 775	2 910	2 990	1.0	98.4	0.2	0.3	0.3	1.3	5.8	18.3	7.2	6.4	13.9	15.3
20 065	...	9	Graham	2 327	2 808	2 998	1.2	95.4	3.2	0.4	0.4	0.8	3.3	15.3	8.3	6.7	16.0	14.3
20 067	...	7	Grant	1 489	7 745	2 617	5.2	63.4	0.2	0.8	0.3	35.5	8.9	22.2	9.9	12.4	15.3	14.4
20 069	...	9	Gray	2 250	6 063	2 769	2.7	87.4	0.3	0.4	0.2	12.1	7.9	22.2	9.9	12.4	14.1	13.0
20 071	...	9	Greeley	2 015	1 420	3 094	0.7	89.2	0.4	0.2	0.3	10.1	6.2	20.0	7.7	7.0	17.5	15.6
20 073	...	6	Greenwood	2 952	7 485	2 639	2.5	96.8	0.4	1.8	0.3	2.0	4.9	17.2	8.7	9.7	13.5	13.9
20 075	...	9	Hamilton	2 581	2 666	3 007	1.0	77.1	0.5	0.5	0.6	21.4	7.3	19.2	9.5	10.9	14.0	12.4
20 077	...	8	Harper	2 076	6 206	2 754	3.0	97.5	0.5	1.4	0.4	1.1	5.3	17.7	8.9	8.4	12.3	14.7
20 079	48620	2	Harvey	1 397	33 502	1 316	24.0	89.0	2.0	1.2	0.8	8.3	6.4	18.2	10.7	11.2	14.1	13.6
20 081	...	9	Haskell	1 495	4 246	2 892	2.8	72.9	0.2	1.3	0.7	25.6	8.0	23.1	10.4	12.8	13.6	13.9
20 083	...	9	Hodgeman	2 227	2 151	3 046	1.0	95.8	1.2	0.2	0.0	3.2	4.4	20.2	9.5	8.6	15.8	14.0
20 085	45820	3	Jackson	1 698	13 017	2 239	7.7	91.2	0.7	7.5	0.3	2.0	6.4	19.8	9.7	10.6	14.6	14.3
20 087	45820	3	Jefferson	1 389	18 798	1 871	13.5	97.1	0.6	1.7	0.4	1.5	5.7	19.0	9.9	9.9	16.3	15.2
20 089	...	9	Jewell	2 355	3 433	2 953	1.5	98.9	0.1	0.6	0.1	0.7	3.2	15.7	7.3	5.8	13.2	17.5
20 091	28140	1	Johnson	1 235	486 515	124	393.9	87.9	3.8	0.7	4.3	4.6	7.1	18.9	8.8	14.5	16.5	14.8
20 093	...	9	Kearny	2 256	4 591	2 864	2.0	71.8	0.9	1.0	0.4	26.4	9.1	24.1	9.9	10.7	15.3	12.9
20 095	...	6	Kingman	2 236	8 382	2 572	3.7	96.7	0.2	1.6	0.4	2.1	5.2	19.9	8.3	8.0	14.9	13.8
20 097	...	9	Kiowa	1 871	3 152	2 973	1.7	96.5	0.3	0.9	0.5	2.4	6.1	16.8	9.5	7.4	12.2	15.2
20 099	37660	7	Labette	1 680	22 259	1 693	13.2	89.7	5.8	3.3	0.5	3.0	6.2	18.5	10.4	10.4	14.1	13.6
20 101	...	9	Lane	1 858	1 946	3 064	1.0	98.0	0.5	0.3	0.2	1.8	4.4	18.0	8.0	7.5	15.1	15.9
20 103	28140	1	Leavenworth	1 200	71 546	711	59.6	83.6	11.0	1.4	2.0	3.9	6.4	18.7	10.4	13.4	18.3	14.3
20 105	...	9	Lincoln	1 862	3 498	2 947	1.9	98.1	0.1	0.6	0.1	1.1	5.2	16.9	7.8	8.6	13.7	16.3
20 107	28140	1	Linn	1 551	9 722	2 468	6.3	97.9	0.9	0.9	0.2	1.0	6.3	17.4	8.9	9.9	13.8	14.7
20 109	...	9	Logan	2 779	2 855	2 994	1.0	97.3	1.0	0.2	0.5	1.9	5.5	17.9	8.4	9.3	14.1	15.1
20 111	21380	5	Lyon	2 204	35 805	1 248	16.2	76.7	2.3	0.8	2.0	19.1	7.2	17.6	15.2	13.2	13.5	13.0
20 113	32700	6	McPherson	2 330	29 346	1 421	12.6	96.3	1.2	0.9	0.6	2.1	5.9	17.7	12.0	9.9	14.1	14.2
20 115	...	6	Marion	2 443	13 299	2 215	5.4	96.7	0.7	0.9	0.3	2.1	5.2	17.8	10.3	8.5	14.0	13.1
20 117	...	7	Marshall	2 338	10 589	2 393	4.5	98.3	0.3	0.7	0.6	0.8	5.5	17.1	8.9	7.6	14.7	14.6
20 119	...	9	Meade	2 534	4 662	2 861	1.8	86.6	0.4	0.7	0.3	12.5	7.8	20.8	8.5	11.6	13.9	12.3
20 121	28140	1	Miami	1 494	29 187	1 429	19.5	96.0	2.0	1.4	0.3	1.6	6.7	19.6	9.7	10.8	16.8	14.6
20 123	...	7	Mitchell	1 813	6 707	2 713	3.7	97.6	0.7	0.8	0.4	1.0	4.6	18.0	10.6	7.6	13.3	14.6
20 125	17700	5	Montgomery	1 671	34 934	1 275	20.9	87.0	6.8	5.5	0.8	3.0	6.3	17.7	10.4	10.1	13.5	13.9
20 127	...	9	Morris	1 806	5 995	2 773	3.3	96.6	0.3	0.7	0.3	2.6	5.1	18.1	8.1	8.3	14.3	15.5
20 129	...	9	Morton	1 890	3 317	2 959	1.8	82.3	0.3	1.1	1.2	15.3	8.8	20.3	9.2	10.5	14.5	13.9
20 131	...	8	Nemaha	1 860	10 500	2 397	5.6	98.2	0.8	0.4	0.2	0.8	6.9	20.1	8.6	8.5	13.9	12.5
20 133	...	7	Neosho	1 481	16 580	1 991	11.2	94.8	1.0	2.1	0.5	3.0	5.8	18.0	10.6	10.1	14.1	14.0
20 135	...	9	Ness	2 784	3 158	2 970	1.1	97.5	0.0	0.3	0.3	2.3	4.7	15.4	7.2	6.7	16.0	16.0
20 137	...	7	Norton	2 274	5 796	2 790	2.5	92.2	4.2	0.5	0.7	2.5	4.4	15.8	10.0	11.8	15.5	14.3

1. CBSA = Core Based Statistical Area. See Appendix A for explanation. See Appendix B for list of metropolitan areas with component counties.   2. County type code from the Economic Research Service of USDA Rural-Urban Continuum Codes. See Appendix A for definition.   3. Dry land or land partially or temporarily covered by water.   4. Hispanic or Latino persons may be of any race.

Table B. States and Counties — **Population and Households**

STATE County	Population, 2003 (cont'd) — Age (percent) (cont'd) 55 to 64 years (16)	65 to 74 years (17)	75 years and over (18)	Percent female (19)	Population — change and components of change, 1990–2003 — Total persons 1990 (20)	2000 (21)	Percent change 1990–2000 (22)	2000–2003 (23)	Components of change, 2000–2003 Births (24)	Deaths (25)	Net migration (26)	Households, 2000 Number (27)	Percent change, 1990–2000 (28)	Persons per household (29)	Percent Female family householder[1] (30)	One person (31)
KANSAS—Cont'd																
Barber	11.7	10.1	11.7	52.0	5 874	5 307	-9.7	-5.1	127	220	-177	2 235	-5.2	2.35	6.5	29.9
Barton	9.4	8.4	9.4	51.2	29 382	28 205	-4.0	-2.6	1 085	1 065	-769	11 393	-1.5	2.41	7.8	30.2
Bourbon	10.0	7.9	9.9	51.6	14 966	15 379	2.8	-1.9	618	633	-263	6 161	4.5	2.44	9.2	29.0
Brown	10.1	8.2	11.1	51.2	11 128	10 724	-3.6	-2.6	448	427	-307	4 318	-0.7	2.44	9.2	28.8
Butler	8.3	6.2	6.3	49.6	50 580	59 482	17.6	2.8	2 436	1 673	925	21 527	16.4	2.67	8.3	21.9
Chase	9.9	8.5	9.6	49.3	3 021	3 030	0.3	2.5	320	125	-118	1 246	2.6	2.34	7.6	31.1
Chautauqua	13.5	10.1	13.5	51.7	4 407	4 359	-1.1	-4.0	102	242	-33	1 796	-2.1	2.34	7.9	29.4
Cherokee	10.8	7.3	8.0	51.2	21 374	22 605	5.8	-3.5	875	843	-820	8 875	5.7	2.51	9.7	26.3
Cheyenne	9.7	11.4	15.4	50.8	3 243	3 165	-2.4	-6.6	94	138	-164	1 360	-2.1	2.29	5.1	30.8
Clark	11.0	8.8	12.9	51.1	2 418	2 390	-1.2	-2.4	78	71	-61	979	-2.7	2.39	6.2	29.6
Clay	10.6	8.6	12.0	49.9	9 158	8 822	-3.7	-2.8	282	334	-191	3 617	-0.7	2.39	6.1	27.7
Cloud	10.2	9.1	13.9	52.4	11 023	10 268	-6.8	-4.0	328	506	-230	4 163	-7.1	2.31	6.6	30.8
Coffey	10.0	7.0	8.7	50.6	8 404	8 865	5.5	-0.6	344	389	7	3 489	5.4	2.49	6.9	26.0
Comanche	14.3	9.6	15.2	51.9	2 313	1 967	-15.0	-2.6	74	82	-44	872	-8.2	2.18	6.2	35.9
Cowley	9.7	7.4	8.3	50.8	36 915	36 291	-1.7	-1.2	1 604	1 436	-608	14 039	-0.1	2.46	9.6	27.9
Crawford	8.9	6.2	8.6	51.2	35 582	38 242	7.5	0.4	1 641	1 469	7	15 504	6.1	2.35	9.3	30.6
Decatur	10.0	12.1	14.3	51.0	4 021	3 472	-13.7	-5.1	100	186	-91	1 494	-9.5	2.24	5.6	32.8
Dickinson	10.2	8.8	9.5	50.8	18 958	19 344	2.0	-0.5	718	729	-72	7 903	4.8	2.40	7.7	28.1
Doniphan	9.3	7.2	8.5	50.5	8 134	8 249	1.4	-1.2	272	317	-49	3 173	3.2	2.48	8.7	27.6
Douglas	6.4	4.0	4.0	50.2	81 798	99 962	22.2	3.0	3 856	1 805	1 092	38 486	27.7	2.37	8.5	28.5
Edwards	10.5	9.3	11.8	50.9	3 787	3 449	-8.9	-5.0	134	136	-173	1 455	-8.2	2.33	6.0	32.0
Elk	12.5	12.2	12.5	52.2	3 327	3 261	-2.0	-2.9	100	194	5	1 412	-1.7	2.25	6.1	32.9
Ellis	7.7	6.8	7.5	50.9	26 004	27 507	5.8	-1.1	1 115	805	-600	11 193	10.9	2.35	7.8	30.1
Ellsworth	10.8	8.4	10.7	46.7	6 586	6 525	-0.9	-2.7	156	313	-11	2 481	-1.6	2.30	6.2	31.4
Finney	6.9	3.9	3.4	49.2	33 070	40 523	22.5	-3.3	2 723	684	-3 546	12 948	19.5	3.09	10.5	19.6
Ford	6.9	4.9	5.5	48.1	27 463	32 458	18.2	1.7	2 074	949	-629	10 852	9.9	2.92	9.2	22.7
Franklin	9.1	6.7	7.0	50.1	21 994	24 784	12.7	3.1	1 205	789	364	9 452	13.8	2.56	8.9	24.8
Geary	7.2	5.4	4.8	51.0	30 453	27 947	-8.2	-5.8	1 913	656	-3 000	10 458	-2.0	2.61	12.3	22.5
Gove	10.5	11.3	12.6	51.6	3 231	3 068	-5.0	-5.1	116	130	-144	1 245	-3.0	2.42	3.5	29.7
Graham	12.5	12.7	12.1	51.1	3 543	2 946	-16.9	-4.7	56	121	-70	1 263	-12.0	2.28	5.9	30.1
Grant	8.1	5.7	4.1	49.7	7 159	7 909	10.5	-2.1	490	176	-489	2 742	14.6	2.86	7.1	21.0
Gray	8.3	5.4	6.9	50.0	5 396	5 904	9.4	2.7	305	168	23	2 045	6.9	2.82	5.6	21.2
Greeley	9.2	9.6	9.8	51.1	1 774	1 534	-13.5	-7.4	62	50	-130	602	-8.2	2.50	4.5	28.6
Greenwood	11.2	10.3	12.1	50.7	7 847	7 673	-2.2	-2.5	255	417	-20	3 234	-1.6	2.31	6.6	30.3
Hamilton	9.4	7.8	10.2	50.5	2 388	2 670	11.8	-0.1	143	105	-43	1 054	6.9	2.49	7.6	29.4
Harper	10.9	9.5	13.7	51.3	7 124	6 536	-8.3	-5.0	194	332	-184	2 773	-7.8	2.30	6.9	32.1
Harvey	9.0	7.4	9.1	51.3	31 028	32 869	5.9	1.9	1 373	1 099	391	12 581	8.6	2.50	7.7	25.8
Haskell	7.3	5.9	4.9	49.1	3 886	4 307	10.8	-1.4	219	131	-151	1 481	7.9	2.88	5.9	20.1
Hodgeman	9.4	8.6	9.5	50.4	2 177	2 085	-4.2	3.2	56	70	82	796	-3.6	2.58	4.4	24.7
Jackson	9.9	7.0	7.5	50.7	11 525	12 657	9.8	2.8	519	462	313	4 727	10.5	2.63	8.2	22.7
Jefferson	10.7	6.7	6.2	49.7	15 905	18 426	15.9	2.0	685	496	200	6 830	18.2	2.66	7.0	20.1
Jewell	12.9	12.8	13.6	50.3	4 251	3 791	-10.8	-9.4	58	194	-227	1 695	-6.1	2.21	4.8	32.4
Johnson	8.4	4.9	4.8	50.8	355 021	451 086	27.1	7.9	22 454	9 195	21 763	174 570	28.0	2.56	7.8	24.5
Kearny	7.8	5.6	5.1	48.7	4 027	4 531	12.5	1.3	273	106	-112	1 542	11.8	2.91	8.3	20.2
Kingman	10.9	9.0	10.8	50.6	8 292	8 673	4.6	-3.4	271	357	-204	3 371	6.2	2.51	7.1	26.0
Kiowa	10.6	10.9	10.7	51.4	3 660	3 278	-10.4	-3.8	123	155	-98	1 365	-6.9	2.32	5.3	30.5
Labette	10.2	7.5	9.5	51.0	23 693	22 835	-3.6	-2.5	889	1 009	-451	9 194	-2.0	2.39	10.2	29.8
Lane	11.3	9.6	11.9	50.2	2 375	2 155	-9.3	-9.7	48	55	-199	910	-5.8	2.34	5.1	30.3
Leavenworth	8.4	5.2	4.3	46.9	64 371	68 691	6.7	4.2	3 002	1 735	1 618	23 071	17.0	2.69	9.5	21.7
Lincoln	10.2	9.9	12.4	50.4	3 653	3 578	-2.1	-2.2	118	231	34	1 529	-0.1	2.29	6.4	29.6
Linn	11.6	9.1	8.7	50.0	8 254	9 570	15.9	1.6	391	409	173	3 807	18.4	2.48	6.2	24.0
Logan	10.2	9.6	11.6	51.2	3 081	3 046	-1.1	-6.3	94	142	-136	1 243	1.8	2.40	6.3	28.6
Lyon	7.9	5.3	6.1	50.6	34 732	35 935	3.5	-0.4	1 729	952	-927	13 691	4.8	2.51	8.4	28.5
McPherson	9.2	7.3	9.7	50.7	27 268	29 554	8.4	-0.7	1 135	1 124	-193	11 205	9.5	2.49	6.0	25.5
Marion	10.5	8.8	12.1	51.0	12 888	13 361	3.7	-0.5	443	487	5	5 114	2.8	2.46	5.5	25.2
Marshall	10.2	9.9	12.3	50.5	11 705	10 965	-6.3	-3.4	395	466	-303	4 458	-4.9	2.40	5.4	29.5
Meade	8.0	8.5	9.3	50.2	4 247	4 631	9.0	0.7	239	141	-63	1 728	-4.9	2.61	4.9	25.6
Miami	9.6	6.2	5.5	50.3	23 466	28 351	20.8	2.9	1 240	837	448	10 365	23.4	2.66	8.0	21.0
Mitchell	10.2	9.5	11.8	50.4	7 203	6 932	-3.8	-3.2	209	279	-154	2 850	0.1	2.31	5.3	31.2
Montgomery	10.9	8.1	10.2	51.8	38 816	36 252	-6.6	-3.6	1 536	1 578	-1 279	14 903	-4.9	2.37	10.1	29.7
Morris	10.3	9.4	11.2	50.5	6 198	6 104	-1.5	-1.8	203	251	-53	2 539	0.4	2.37	6.6	28.0
Morton	9.7	7.8	6.8	52.1	3 480	3 496	0.5	-5.1	210	86	-309	1 306	1.2	2.63	6.8	24.3
Nemaha	8.5	8.7	12.7	50.5	10 446	10 717	2.6	-2.0	436	530	-119	3 959	-0.9	2.58	5.1	28.0
Neosho	10.2	8.3	9.4	51.8	17 035	16 997	-0.2	-2.5	662	648	-420	6 739	-0.1	2.45	8.5	27.1
Ness	11.2	11.1	14.6	50.3	4 033	3 454	-14.4	-8.6	101	146	-252	1 516	-9.2	2.23	4.7	33.5
Norton	10.1	7.9	11.1	44.2	5 947	5 953	0.1	-2.6	167	232	-86	2 266	-2.7	2.28	7.0	32.3

1. No spouse present.

Table B. States and Counties — Vital Statistics, Health Resources, and Crime

STATE County	Births, average 1999–2001 Total	Births Rate[1]	Deaths, avg 1999–2001 Number Total	Number Infant[2]	Deaths Rate Total[1]	Rate Infant[3]	Physicians 2000 Number	Physicians Rate[5]	Hospitals 1998 Number	Beds Number	Beds Rate[5]	Medicare enrollees, 2003	Serious crimes 2002 Total Number	Rate[7]
	32	33	34	35	36	37	38	39	40	41	42	43	44	45
KANSAS—Cont'd														
Barber	45	8.5	71	0	13.4	D	5	94	2	66	1 235	1 236	23	429
Barton	351	12.4	339	1	12.0	D	39	138	3	238	861	5 314	815	2 897
Bourbon	195	12.7	202	1	13.2	D	23	150	1	114	747	3 023	697	4 486
Brown	135	12.6	133	1	12.4	D	11	103	2	70	632	2 190	226	2 086
Butler	762	12.8	529	3	8.9	D	38	64	2	234	378	8 102	1 760	2 961
Chase	79	26.0	43	0	14.2	D	0	0	0	0	0	546	1	33
Chautauqua	33	7.7	66	0	15.3	D	4	92	2	73	1 674	995	101	2 294
Cherokee	282	12.5	265	2	11.8	D	7	31	1	39	173	3 850	603	2 641
Cheyenne	28	8.8	39	0	12.4	D	2	63	1	23	725	800	6	188
Clark	28	11.8	29	0	12.3	D	3	126	2	63	2 668	538	44	1 823
Clay	92	10.4	108	0	12.2	D	8	91	1	32	350	1 873	150	1 683
Cloud	103	10.1	160	1	15.6	D	18	175	1	39	389	2 436	165	1 591
Coffey	104	11.7	103	0	11.7	D	3	34	1	26	299	1 523	177	2 117
Comanche	22	10.9	32	0	16.1	D	1	51	1	14	696	492	NA	NA
Cowley	493	13.6	451	5	12.4	D	38	105	2	178	490	6 313	2 686	7 104
Crawford	536	14.0	464	3	12.1	D	61	160	2	175	481	6 491		
Decatur	29	8.3	52	0	14.9	D	6	173	1	74	2 141	904	29	827
Dickinson	228	11.8	243	2	12.6	D	9	47	2	102	517	3 907	585	3 193
Doniphan	90	11.0	93	0	11.3	D	4	48	0	0	0	1 375	135	1 620
Douglas	1 195	11.9	529	5	5.3	D	135	135	1	167	179	9 567	4 651	4 606
Edwards	43	12.5	47	1	13.6	D	4	116	1	49	1 479	732	19	545
Elk	28	8.7	64	1	19.7	D	0	0	0	0	0	781	101	3 065
Ellis	351	12.7	240	2	8.7	D	73	265	1	104	395	4 206	815	3 068
Ellsworth	54	8.3	89	1	13.7	D	6	92	1	22	350	1 241	118	2 117
Finney	877	21.8	209	6	5.2	D	45	111	1	93	255	3 607	2 550	6 229
Ford	657	20.3	279	8	8.6	12.7	40	123	1	105	357	3 599	1 678	5 235
Franklin	367	14.8	238	2	9.6	D	16	65	1	45	182	4 065	773	3 087
Geary	584	21.0	210	10	7.6	17.1	43	154	1	49	193	2 948	1 602	5 674
Gove	34	11.1	40	0	13.2	D	5	163	1	123	4 028	753	NA	NA
Graham	22	7.4	40	0	13.5	D	2	68	1	42	1 311	710	31	1 042
Grant	152	19.2	53	1	6.7	D	7	89	1	45	562	848	162	2 028
Gray	92	15.6	46	1	7.8	D	2	34	0	0	0	836	31	520
Greeley	19	12.2	16	0	10.2	D	1	65	1	50	2 934	283	5	323
Greenwood	82	10.6	129	1	16.7	D	6	78	1	46	565	1 925	109	1 406
Hamilton	46	17.0	32	0	11.9	D	2	75	1	77	3 286	489	46	1 705
Harper	66	10.1	104	0	16.0	D	12	184	2	50	778	1 465	89	1 493
Harvey	441	13.4	349	1	10.6	D	91	277	2	221	643	6 170	772	2 497
Haskell	76	17.8	35	1	8.2	D	3	70	1	42	1 056	479	76	1 747
Hodgeman	20	9.5	22	0	10.4	D	1	48	1	54	2 445	384	64	3 037
Jackson	156	12.4	138	3	10.9	D	3	24	1	17	140	2 055	277	2 263
Jefferson	212	11.5	159	1	8.6	D	10	54	1	118	647	2 849	471	2 530
Jewell	24	6.3	63	0	16.9	D	0	0	1	57	1 474	935	8	209
Johnson	6 878	15.2	2 736	39	6.0	5.7	1 116	247	4	849	198	51 292	12 657	3 050
Kearny	83	18.2	38	0	8.3	D	2	44	1	20	479	512	129	2 818
Kingman	93	10.8	112	1	13.0	D	6	69	1	49	574	1 679	147	1 678
Kiowa	38	11.5	45	0	13.8	D	2	61	1	24	692	755	56	1 691
Labette	276	12.1	304	2	13.3	D	32	140	2	91	395	4 334	611	2 698
Lane	18	8.3	24	0	11.4	D	2	93	1	31	1 369	472	30	1 378
Leavenworth	899	13.0	510	7	7.4	7.4	87	127	1	136	191	7 335	2 170	3 127
Lincoln	40	11.1	58	1	16.2	D	2	56	1	34	1 019	777	91	2 518
Linn	120	12.5	125	1	13.1	D	2	21	0	0	0	1 943	235	2 504
Logan	36	12.0	44	0	14.4	D	1	33	1	51	1 707	680	76	2 469
Lyon	536	14.9	296	1	8.2	D	43	120	1	152	448	4 646	1 871	5 292
McPherson	346	11.7	339	2	11.5	D	27	91	3	83	290	5 385	432	1 618
Marion	142	10.6	178	1	13.3	D	11	82	2	152	1 118	2 836	167	1 380
Marshall	113	10.3	148	0	13.5	D	9	82	1	55	500	2 464	88	794
Meade	72	15.6	48	0	10.4	D	2	43	1	26	588	865	NA	NA
Miami	383	13.5	250	3	8.8	D	26	92	1	22	83	3 594	797	2 783
Mitchell	63	9.1	98	0	14.2	D	7	101	1	89	1 283	1 532	142	2 193
Montgomery	472	13.0	479	4	13.2	D	44	121	2	182	491	7 471	1 847	5 043
Morris	63	10.3	78	0	12.8	D	6	98	1	22	357	1 278	129	2 092
Morton	62	17.9	28	0	8.1	D	8	229	1	100	2 907	542	69	1 954
Nemaha	141	13.3	155	0	14.6	D	8	75	2	51	503	2 212	172	1 589
Neosho	196	11.5	203	2	11.9	D	16	94	1	60	325	3 325	588	3 424
Ness	30	8.7	47	0	13.8	D	3	87	2	104	2 883	892	NA	NA
Norton	54	9.1	77	0	13.0	D	6	101	1	43	748	1 215	90	1 497

1. Per 1,000 estimated resident population. 2. Deaths of infants under 1 year old. 3. Deaths of infants under 1 year old per 1,000 live births. 4. Data subject to copyright. 5. Per 100,000 resident population as of July 1 of the year shown. 6. Data for serious crimes have not been adjusted for underreporting; this may affect comparability between geographic areas and over time. 7. Per 100,000 population estimated by the FBI.

STATE County	Serious crimes known to police,[1] 2002 (cont'd) Rate[2]		Education						Money income, 1999				Percent below poverty level, 1999			
			School enrollment and attainment, 2000				Local government expenditures,[5] 2000–2001			Households						
			Enrollment[3]		Attainment[4] (percent)					Median income						
	Violent	Property	Total	Percent private	High school graduate or less	Bachelor's degree or more	Total current expenditures (mil dol)	Current expenditures per student (dollars)	Per capita income[6] (dollars)	Dollars	Percent change, 1989–1999 (constant 1999 dollars)	Percent with income of $100,000 or more	Persons	Households	Families	Families with children
	46	47	48	49	50	51	52	53	54	55	56	57	58	59	60	61
KANSAS—Cont'd																
Barber	56	373	1 355	7.6	47.0	21.0	6.6	6 301	16 627	33 407	15.8	4.7	10.1	10.2	7.5	10.5
Barton	437	2 460	7 446	11.3	49.1	16.6	31.6	6 411	16 695	32 176	2.2	4.7	12.9	12.4	7.9	15.0
Bourbon	367	4 119	4 181	12.9	47.5	17.8	14.5	5 459	16 393	31 199	14.0	3.7	13.5	13.8	9.9	15.1
Brown	148	1 938	2 732	6.0	54.5	19.0	11.1	6 068	15 163	31 971	16.7	2.5	12.9	14.1	9.5	15.6
Butler	172	2 789	16 975	12.0	45.0	20.4	83.2	6 211	20 150	45 474	9.1	9.6	7.3	7.5	10.6	8.1
Chase	0	33	709	5.9	52.6	19.6	3.5	7 187	17 422	32 656	20.8	4.2	8.6	10.0	5.4	7.0
Chautauqua	318	1 976	1 055	6.8	59.7	12.3	4.8	6 678	16 280	28 717	25.2	3.9	12.2	13.1	4.1	13.7
Cherokee	267	2 373	5 494	5.8	58.5	11.3	24.2	6 143	14 710	30 505	19.5	3.0	14.3	14.3	9.0	16.2
Cheyenne	0	188	734	3.0	50.2	16.0	4.5	7 395	17 862	30 599	4.7	4.4	9.4	10.1	11.4	11.1
Clark	207	1 616	582	2.2	40.1	22.1	4.4	8 296	17 795	33 857	5.0	6.3	12.7	10.8	7.4	15.8
Clay	168	1 515	2 148	2.3	52.5	16.5	11.1	7 072	17 939	33 965	15.5	4.4	10.1	10.5	11.3	12.2
Cloud	116	1 475	2 741	5.1	52.6	18.0	12.4	8 164	17 536	31 758	13.7	4.6	10.8	10.7	6.8	11.3
Coffey	156	1 962	2 325	5.2	53.7	20.1	14.6	7 631	18 337	37 839	15.3	5.4	6.6	8.7	6.4	4.9
Comanche	NA	NA	393	2.3	45.8	15.1	2.7	8 433	17 037	29 415	12.7	3.3	10.2	10.7	5.0	12.9
Cowley	NA	NA	10 397	16.2	45.6	18.3	42.4	6 457	17 509	34 406	2.2	4.8	12.9	11.9	8.5	14.4
Crawford	481	6 623	11 944	7.7	46.2	23.9	43.2	7 241	16 245	29 409	11.6	4.6	16.0	17.3	9.2	14.8
Decatur	29	798	833	2.3	53.6	15.4	5.0	8 267	16 348	30 257	11.9	2.7	11.6	10.3	9.4	14.6
Dickinson	175	3 018	4 917	6.9	52.9	15.2	25.3	6 079	17 780	35 975	16.7	3.9	7.5	8.7	8.0	7.7
Doniphan	192	1 428	2 377	4.0	56.5	14.8	11.4	6 749	14 849	32 537	9.6	2.8	11.9	13.7	5.3	12.9
Douglas	361	4 244	42 645	9.3	29.9	42.7	85.5	6 563	19 952	37 547	10.7	9.0	15.9	17.1	9.0	8.9
Edwards	29	516	836	10.3	51.1	16.3	3.8	7 587	17 586	30 530	3.7	4.2	10.4	11.1	6.2	11.8
Elk	182	2 883	730	3.4	61.6	10.6	6.7	8 879	16 066	27 267	14.5	3.2	13.8	15.4	7.0	17.0
Ellis	162	2 906	9 329	9.4	42.7	29.2	29.0	7 060	18 259	32 339	7.1	6.4	12.9	15.3	9.2	9.2
Ellsworth	90	2 027	1 343	4.3	50.7	16.4	8.8	6 981	16 569	35 772	32.7	4.2	7.2	8.5	6.5	6.2
Finney	608	5 621	12 187	6.4	57.5	14.3	53.0	6 032	15 377	38 474	3.6	5.9	14.2	11.8	4.0	14.0
Ford	446	4 788	8 955	7.2	53.2	16.4	32.8	5 276	15 721	37 860	12.5	6.1	12.4	11.1	10.0	14.2
Franklin	272	2 816	6 652	13.9	54.2	16.5	28.9	5 888	17 311	39 052	16.4	4.3	7.7	8.6	9.9	7.5
Geary	921	4 753	8 115	9.0	44.0	17.1	39.6	6 127	16 199	31 917	8.4	5.1	12.1	11.7	5.6	14.3
Gove	NA	NA	753	4.5	50.7	18.4	6.1	8 575	17 852	33 510	6.7	4.5	10.3	10.0	9.7	11.9
Graham	101	941	685	4.1	50.4	17.4	3.9	8 207	18 050	31 286	5.6	5.1	11.5	11.6	8.0	12.1
Grant	238	1 790	2 281	6.8	56.5	15.2	9.8	5 487	17 072	39 854	-1.7	7.3	10.1	8.7	8.6	10.6
Gray	84	436	1 565	17.5	52.1	16.3	8.9	6 830	18 632	40 000	15.1	7.7	9.1	7.4	6.5	10.1
Greeley	0	323	395	4.8	45.6	17.4	2.3	7 119	19 974	34 605	0.2	9.3	11.6	10.8	6.5	13.9
Greenwood	206	1 200	1 640	2.4	57.7	14.5	8.8	7 601	15 976	30 169	15.3	4.9	12.5	14.1	8.2	13.1
Hamilton	334	1 371	711	9.4	53.7	17.4	3.6	6 517	16 484	32 033	6.0	5.4	15.7	13.4	10.9	19.5
Harper	151	1 342	1 554	5.3	55.3	14.0	8.2	6 765	16 368	29 776	4.4	3.4	11.6	12.3	8.5	13.3
Harvey	188	2 309	8 739	20.1	44.9	23.0	38.5	6 549	18 715	40 907	10.6	6.0	6.4	7.6	4.2	6.3
Haskell	276	1 471	1 258	9.6	50.6	17.5	6.9	7 122	17 349	38 634	7.5	7.3	11.6	9.5	8.0	10.8
Hodgeman	47	2 990	615	4.6	43.8	19.7	3.4	6 889	15 599	35 994	12.6	5.1	11.5	12.5	10.7	16.1
Jackson	229	2 035	3 284	8.8	58.2	15.4	18.5	7 421	18 606	40 451	18.5	6.1	8.8	8.9	6.4	9.7
Jefferson	301	2 230	4 722	7.2	53.7	17.9	26.7	6 228	19 373	45 535	16.7	4.9	6.7	7.8	6.4	6.4
Jewell	26	183	773	4.1	51.9	13.8	5.1	8 129	16 644	30 538	20.7	3.9	11.6	13.0	5.3	11.9
Johnson	232	2 817	124 515	21.2	22.6	47.7	513.8	6 744	30 919	61 455	7.0	22.7	3.4	3.6	8.4	3.0
Kearny	459	2 360	1 379	7.2	51.9	15.0	8.3	7 224	15 708	40 149	2.0	7.1	11.7	10.3	2.1	12.1
Kingman	114	1 564	2 284	9.2	49.0	17.8	9.4	5 902	18 533	37 790	23.6	6.0	10.6	9.7	8.4	13.2
Kiowa	211	1 479	826	16.1	44.8	18.9	5.0	8 507	17 207	31 576	3.9	4.1	10.8	11.2	7.4	11.2
Labette	314	2 385	5 956	4.1	48.9	15.9	24.2	5 587	15 525	30 875	5.1	2.8	12.7	12.5	8.9	13.3
Lane	0	1 378	514	3.5	45.6	18.5	3.6	8 532	18 606	36 047	14.0	6.0	8.2	8.6	5.4	9.0
Leavenworth	434	2 693	18 935	15.9	47.4	23.1	74.6	6 018	20 292	48 114	10.2	9.0	6.7	6.8	4.8	7.2
Lincoln	387	2 131	803	5.2	50.6	17.4	4.4	7 394	15 788	30 893	23.3	3.4	9.7	10.3	7.3	10.1
Linn	245	2 259	2 094	10.9	58.6	12.7	15.0	7 306	17 009	35 906	25.5	3.9	11.0	11.3	7.8	12.9
Logan	65	2 404	723	10.5	52.0	17.5	5.0	8 732	17 294	32 131	8.1	5.9	7.3	9.0	4.7	6.7
Lyon	362	4 930	11 701	4.2	50.0	23.0	44.4	6 994	15 724	32 819	1.6	4.3	14.5	15.4	9.6	14.4
McPherson	172	1 446	8 098	14.4	46.2	22.2	34.4	6 678	18 921	41 138	13.4	6.1	6.6	8.1	4.2	5.4
Marion	141	1 240	3 472	19.0	54.2	17.2	17.2	6 674	16 100	34 500	18.2	3.5	8.3	8.0	4.8	7.8
Marshall	63	731	2 606	13.0	60.6	13.2	17.7	7 357	17 090	32 089	16.0	4.9	9.2	10.5	6.4	9.1
Meade	NA	NA	1 272	9.4	48.2	19.6	5.1	7 436	16 824	36 761	16.9	6.3	9.3	8.9	6.7	9.9
Miami	279	2 503	7 575	12.0	49.2	19.4	32.8	6 866	21 408	46 665	18.7	10.8	5.5	6.9	3.6	5.2
Mitchell	77	2 116	1 866	14.4	48.1	16.9	12.3	9 321	17 653	33 385	12.1	5.1	9.5	9.8	6.5	12.1
Montgomery	535	4 508	9 206	9.9	49.0	16.0	32.9	5 370	16 421	30 997	10.6	4.2	12.6	13.0	9.2	14.2
Morris	162	1 930	1 419	3.7	56.1	16.0	6.1	5 840	18 491	32 163	7.8	5.0	9.0	10.0	6.7	8.2
Morton	340	1 614	1 005	4.3	52.7	17.6	6.2	8 168	17 076	37 232	8.0	5.1	10.5	9.7	8.5	12.4
Nemaha	129	1 459	2 698	8.1	62.5	14.6	13.2	7 088	17 121	34 296	15.3	4.1	9.1	10.0	6.5	8.2
Neosho	314	3 110	4 518	8.6	51.7	15.0	17.3	5 509	16 539	32 167	7.4	4.8	13.0	13.3	10.0	16.7
Ness	NA	NA	769	8.8	52.1	17.9	5.0	8 101	17 787	32 340	2.0	4.7	8.7	9.7	6.5	8.0
Norton	33	1 463	1 349	9.7	52.8	15.4	7.4	7 312	16 835	31 050	8.7	4.0	10.5	10.0	6.1	10.3

1. Data for serious crimes have not been adjusted for underreporting; this may affect comparability between geographic areas and over time. 2. Per 100,000 population estimated by the FBI. 3. All persons 3 years old and over enrolled in nursery school through college. 4. Persons 25 years old and over. 5. Elementary and secondary education expenditures. 6. Based on population enumerated as of April 1, 2000.

STATE County	Personal income, 2002							Transfer payments					
			Per capita[1]						Government payments to individuals				
	Total (mil dol)	Percent change, 2001–2002	Dollars	Rank	Wages and salaries[2] (mil dol)	Proprietor's income (mil dol)	Dividends, interest, and rent (mil dol)	Total (mil dol)	Total (mil dol)	Social Security (mil dol)	Medical payments (mil dol)	Income maintenance (mil dol)	Unemployment insurance (mil dol)
	62	63	64	65	66	67	68	69	70	71	72	73	74
KANSAS—Cont'd													
Barber	118	2.9	23 117	1 690	54	9	32	29	28	13	11	1	1
Barton	731	1.6	26 465	801	413	73	165	139	131	60	54	7	4
Bourbon	343	2.4	22 585	1 854	194	23	74	83	79	31	35	6	2
Brown	255	-0.5	24 299	1 310	141	17	57	55	52	22	22	4	2
Butler	1 674	2.2	27 710	587	530	140	239	237	220	101	82	13	11
Chase	91	7.7	29 813	364	21	25	15	14	14	6	5	1	0
Chautauqua	101	4.8	24 013	1 400	25	13	26	28	27	11	13	2	1
Cherokee	481	1.0	21 879	2 044	197	56	73	117	111	42	49	11	4
Cheyenne	66	-6.7	21 650	2 107	26	5	21	17	16	8	6	1	0
Clark	59	6.0	24 801	1 174	27	3	16	12	12	6	5	0	0
Clay	218	-1.3	25 072	1 111	81	24	54	43	41	20	15	2	1
Cloud	213	-2.1	21 392	2 184	94	8	58	58	55	25	24	2	1
Coffey	242	2.0	27 450	623	169	20	50	44	41	17	18	2	2
Comanche	39	-1.0	19 929	2 559	17	-1	13	11	11	5	5	0	0
Cowley	881	1.8	24 239	1 330	517	54	141	191	181	71	78	12	7
Crawford	857	2.2	22 482	1 886	564	13	170	199	188	68	85	15	4
Decatur	83	-4.5	24 638	1 226	28	7	31	19	18	9	7	1	0
Dickinson	448	0.5	23 423	1 589	205	14	100	88	83	38	30	4	3
Doniphan	173	2.5	21 186	2 240	78	17	28	38	36	15	14	2	3
Douglas	2 658	2.8	26 010	885	1 674	139	461	294	266	113	104	18	11
Edwards	90	-4.3	26 954	707	32	19	20	19	18	8	8	1	0
Elk	66	1.0	20 624	2 393	19	6	13	20	19	9	8	1	0
Ellis	733	2.8	26 851	727	457	92	133	115	107	45	47	5	2
Ellsworth	145	0.3	22 746	1 803	71	12	39	32	30	14	13	1	1
Finney	829	0.8	21 025	2 291	580	117	115	115	104	37	46	14	4
Ford	743	2.9	22 905	1 751	534	70	119	109	100	41	41	9	2
Franklin	620	2.7	24 499	1 262	311	26	90	114	107	44	46	8	4
Geary	715	3.8	27 077	687	954	28	107	91	86	30	30	9	3
Gove	74	-10.2	24 971	1 136	32	7	21	16	15	7	7	0	0
Graham	76	-9.9	26 400	811	30	12	17	19	18	8	9	1	0
Grant	179	-3.7	22 658	1 834	126	21	32	24	22	10	9	2	1
Gray	154	-1.3	25 441	1 012	76	34	25	20	18	9	7	1	1
Greeley	35	-8.8	23 817	1 466	19	3	9	7	6	3	2	0	0
Greenwood	168	0.9	21 991	2 018	52	18	35	46	44	20	19	2	1
Hamilton	70	-4.5	26 140	865	29	18	15	12	11	6	5	1	0
Harper	155	6.0	24 634	1 228	64	14	37	35	34	16	14	2	1
Harvey	904	2.6	27 106	677	468	114	153	163	154	65	64	7	5
Haskell	123	-2.3	28 974	453	49	39	21	13	12	6	5	1	0
Hodgeman	50	1.5	23 143	1 681	15	9	14	10	9	5	3	0	0
Jackson	333	2.3	25 947	897	132	26	54	52	49	23	17	3	2
Jefferson	449	2.6	24 009	1 401	114	9	68	72	67	32	24	3	3
Jewell	80	-8.3	22 827	1 771	26	7	24	19	18	10	6	1	0
Johnson	20 581	2.3	43 237	42	14 078	1 876	3 980	1 430	1 300	637	484	41	64
Kearny	97	-0.7	21 022	2 293	36	18	21	15	14	6	6	1	0
Kingman	195	2.9	23 235	1 648	74	11	42	42	39	19	16	2	1
Kiowa	73	1.6	23 321	1 621	32	0	21	20	19	8	9	1	0
Labette	532	4.1	23 833	1 462	301	40	80	151	145	44	79	10	3
Lane	61	-1.8	30 285	321	23	14	16	11	11	5	4	0	0
Leavenworth	1 831	3.6	25 806	932	1 156	99	292	234	216	84	85	15	10
Lincoln	73	-2.9	20 972	2 306	24	5	22	17	16	8	6	1	0
Linn	219	-0.3	22 550	1 864	73	8	40	49	46	21	18	3	2
Logan	62	-4.5	21 106	2 266	32	0	19	15	14	7	5	1	0
Lyon	780	1.9	21 808	2 063	569	32	137	141	131	48	53	10	5
McPherson	806	4.3	27 438	626	490	97	150	134	126	61	53	5	2
Marion	281	0.7	21 075	2 275	106	16	59	65	62	30	26	2	1
Marshall	276	-6.3	25 917	904	162	19	72	55	52	24	19	2	2
Meade	108	-0.9	23 098	1 695	46	11	26	20	19	10	8	1	0
Miami	807	3.1	27 884	568	270	21	103	119	111	43	52	6	5
Mitchell	162	-2.0	24 176	1 349	101	10	40	35	33	16	14	1	0
Montgomery	795	2.6	22 562	1 862	493	46	137	206	196	81	83	17	6
Morris	139	-0.1	23 059	1 705	51	6	32	29	27	13	10	1	1
Morton	67	-0.5	19 917	2 562	43	-5	19	15	14	6	6	1	0
Nemaha	244	-4.5	23 345	1 613	127	8	77	47	44	22	18	2	1
Neosho	374	1.8	22 378	1 916	226	28	67	91	86	34	38	6	2
Ness	93	1.3	28 361	507	37	12	25	19	18	9	8	0	0
Norton	129	-1.6	22 145	1 970	73	7	35	27	25	13	10	1	0

1. Based on the resident population estimated as of July 1 of the year shown.   2. Includes other labor income.

STATE County	Earnings, 2002									Social Security beneficiaries, December 2003		Supple-mental Security Income recipients, December 2003	Housing units, 2003	
	Total (mil dol)	Farm	Goods-related[1]		Service-related and health									
			Total	Manu-facturing	Infor-mation and profes-sional and technical services	Retail trade	Finance, insur-ance, and real estate	Health services	Govern-ment	Number	Rate[2]		Total	Percent change, 2000–2003
	75	76	77	78	79	80	81	82	83	84	85	86	87	88
KANSAS—Cont'd														
Barber	63	-8.0	27.2	11.9	D	7.4	7.3	4.6	30.1	1 340	266	74	2 738	-0.1
Barton	486	1.9	27.0	9.5	5.0	D	7.4	D	15.3	5 850	213	361	12 937	0.4
Bourbon	217	0.5	D	22.1	4.1	8.7	3.7	14.7	16.7	3 475	230	313	7 252	1.6
Brown	159	1.5	D	16.2	3.7	5.8	4.6	D	36.3	2 390	229	218	4 859	0.9
Butler	670	1.0	26.6	15.0	D	8.3	6.3	11.1	23.9	9 750	160	401	24 495	5.7
Chase	46	31.1	D	D	D	2.7	D	D	17.3	625	201	36	1 532	0.2
Chautauqua	38	10.2	D	4.0	D	7.5	D	18.8	21.6	1 195	286	113	2 206	1.7
Cherokee	252	2.6	D	30.3	4.2	4.9	4.7	8.5	15.6	4 670	214	597	10 218	1.9
Cheyenne	30	4.9	D	D	D	9.7	D	13.1	25.0	880	298	20	1 629	-0.4
Clark	30	13.4	D	D	D	6.3	D	D	41.5	575	246	23	1 123	1.1
Clay	104	-1.7	20.8	12.1	6.1	10.9	6.0	9.4	23.9	2 090	244	101	4 094	0.2
Cloud	102	-3.0	10.0	6.4	5.5	13.6	5.1	D	24.9	2 625	266	164	4 817	-0.4
Coffey	189	0.2	10.0	5.1	1.5	4.7	3.0	D	18.7	1 900	216	148	3 982	2.7
Comanche	15	-31.7	20.1	13.7	D	7.0	13.1	D	46.1	520	272	23	1 076	-1.1
Cowley	571	0.9	34.1	29.5	D	7.4	7.5	D	20.9	7 085	198	755	15 969	1.9
Crawford	577	0.2	28.3	25.0	4.5	7.4	2.7	11.2	26.0	7 115	185	939	17 637	2.4
Decatur	35	9.9	D	D	D	8.8	D	18.5	25.2	985	299	29	1 818	-0.2
Dickinson	219	-0.6	22.4	17.7	3.1	8.7	5.1	5.2	21.0	4 150	216	247	8 762	0.9
Doniphan	95	10.5	24.4	20.2	D	3.8	4.0	D	23.9	1 555	191	116	3 520	0.9
Douglas	1 812	0.0	D	9.0	15.0	6.8	5.0	7.4	30.7	10 925	106	922	43 026	6.9
Edwards	51	29.4	D	14.5	D	5.5	2.5	5.0	14.8	790	241	38	1 753	-0.1
Elk	25	5.4	D	0.4	D	5.9	3.7	0.8	40.0	990	313	64	1 891	1.7
Ellis	549	0.5	16.3	5.0	9.1	12.1	4.6	20.3	20.7	4 660	171	354	12 247	1.4
Ellsworth	82	1.5	D	15.9	8.5	5.5	4.2	8.7	32.9	1 470	232	61	3 264	1.1
Finney	697	6.9	28.8	18.0	4.2	9.9	4.4	D	16.2	3 760	96	463	14 017	1.8
Ford	603	4.2	D	32.8	4.3	8.2	4.2	D	15.4	4 105	124	376	11 900	2.1
Franklin	338	-1.3	19.6	12.0	2.9	8.5	3.2	D	18.2	4 600	180	466	10 645	4.1
Geary	982	-0.3	D	2.4	D	3.6	1.6	2.3	77.2	3 525	134	408	12 104	1.2
Gove	40	10.5	D	6.3	D	10.0	D	4.4	31.9	755	259	16	1 440	1.2
Graham	41	0.6	19.3	2.8	D	7.4	D	9.5	27.1	910	324	46	1 557	0.3
Grant	148	9.0	28.5	4.9	D	5.5	4.1	D	15.9	980	127	69	3 098	2.3
Gray	110	26.0	13.8	2.6	4.1	4.3	D	2.9	21.9	880	145	22	2 252	3.3
Greeley	23	24.8	D	0.0	D	6.7	3.3	D	20.9	320	225	8	718	0.8
Greenwood	70	13.2	D	7.8	D	6.2	D	11.1	22.3	2 025	271	172	4 299	0.6
Hamilton	46	41.3	6.1	0.2	D	3.8	5.3	D	22.8	520	195	33	1 225	1.2
Harper	78	1.9	22.8	12.4	3.2	8.8	D	D	31.7	1 605	259	90	3 256	-0.4
Harvey	582	1.5	35.3	26.0	D	7.4	4.7	16.0	10.8	6 470	193	279	13 788	3.1
Haskell	89	46.4	D	D	1.6	2.5	D	0.4	18.9	580	137	33	1 681	2.6
Hodgeman	24	32.9	D	D	D	4.8	D	0.3	36.3	450	209	4	960	1.6
Jackson	158	-3.5	D	7.4	5.2	10.3	5.6	D	25.7	2 580	198	105	5 242	2.9
Jefferson	124	-0.9	D	6.7	3.4	5.5	4.4	D	29.6	3 340	178	128	7 810	4.3
Jewell	33	5.0	D	D	2.3	7.6	9.7	1.5	37.3	1 095	319	50	2 102	0.0
Johnson	15 954	0.1	13.5	7.1	25.4	7.6	12.9	7.8	8.0	57 380	118	2 424	198 710	9.4
Kearny	54	38.0	D	D	D	1.7	3.2	2.1	34.2	615	134	46	1 718	3.7
Kingman	85	-4.8	31.5	15.8	7.5	6.5	8.9	13.0	20.3	1 945	232	79	3 879	0.7
Kiowa	32	-8.9	D	D	4.9	7.2	4.7	D	34.1	800	254	70	1 647	0.2
Labette	341	0.7	D	25.5	D	6.5	4.2	D	26.6	4 850	218	607	10 351	0.4
Lane	37	39.5	D	D	D	3.1	4.6	0.4	20.4	505	260	18	1 059	-0.6
Leavenworth	1 255	0.2	D	2.7	11.0	4.2	4.8	D	56.1	9 210	129	536	25 896	6.1
Lincoln	29	-2.1	D	2.1	D	10.5	8.5	5.5	42.4	885	253	32	1 846	-0.4
Linn	81	-1.9	18.0	3.7	2.4	6.8	D	3.0	28.0	2 240	230	133	4 839	2.5
Logan	33	-12.1	D	D	D	10.2	8.7	D	37.8	705	247	31	1 424	0.1
Lyon	601	0.7	33.8	29.6	5.6	7.1	2.5	6.3	25.5	5 005	140	553	14 818	0.4
McPherson	588	2.0	35.7	28.1	3.0	5.6	5.9	D	10.5	5 920	202	201	12 151	2.7
Marion	122	3.0	16.8	9.9	5.6	8.8	4.8	D	24.6	3 060	230	135	5 992	1.9
Marshall	181	-1.7	D	20.0	D	8.9	12.8	8.6	13.0	2 635	249	141	5 003	0.1
Meade	57	26.1	D	1.2	D	4.7	3.7	4.1	26.4	960	206	31	1 977	0.5
Miami	291	-1.1	26.5	8.6	4.7	12.6	6.1	D	24.1	4 415	151	375	11 509	4.8
Mitchell	111	2.2	19.2	15.2	3.7	13.1	4.5	14.0	22.7	1 605	239	60	3 320	-0.6
Montgomery	539	0.6	33.7	30.0	3.1	7.8	3.6	14.7	15.7	8 485	243	994	17 208	0.0
Morris	58	-0.3	25.4	14.0	6.5	7.9	D	4.9	25.6	1 460	244	68	3 192	1.0
Morton	39	-12.4	D	D	D	8.6	D	2.7	48.9	635	191	35	1 560	2.7
Nemaha	135	-0.5	D	22.3	5.7	6.9	D	D	17.3	2 395	228	99	4 385	1.0
Neosho	254	-1.3	34.1	25.5	3.7	9.2	D	9.1	22.3	3 625	219	322	7 494	0.4
Ness	49	-4.2	D	1.7	D	6.2	5.4	D	28.2	940	298	17	1 837	0.1
Norton	81	1.4	D	6.4	4.5	5.6	D	11.6	35.9	1 320	228	80	2 666	-0.3

1. Covers mining, construction, and manufacturing.   2. Per 1,000 resident population estimated as of July 1 of the year shown.

	Housing units, 2000								Civilian labor force, 2003				Civilian employment,[6] 2000		
	Occupied units										Unemployment			Percent	
		Owner-occupied				Renter-occupied									
				Median owner cost as a percent of income											
STATE County	Total	Percent	Median value[1]	With a mortgage	Without a mortgage[2]	Median rent[3]	Median rent as a percent of income	Sub-standard units[4] (percent)	Total	Percent change, 2002–2003	Total	Rate[5]	Total	Management, professional and related occupations	Production, transportation, and material moving occupations
	89	90	91	92	93	94	95	96	97	98	99	100	101	102	103
KANSAS—Cont'd															
Barber	2 235	75.3	33 000	17.1	9.9	354	17.1	2.7	2 387	5.7	70	2.9	2 554	34.3	16.9
Barton	11 393	72.0	55 500	19.0	11.0	390	22.5	3.2	14 086	-1.4	545	3.9	13 563	27.6	16.3
Bourbon	6 161	74.1	46 200	19.0	11.4	356	24.1	2.4	7 105	1.1	371	5.2	7 377	26.5	22.5
Brown	4 318	71.3	50 800	18.3	10.9	342	21.2	2.1	5 432	1.5	234	4.3	4 947	31.5	13.0
Butler	21 527	77.7	83 900	19.2	10.8	485	23.3	2.1	30 163	-0.1	1 952	6.5	28 121	31.7	16.5
Chase	1 246	73.5	39 800	18.5	9.9	349	18.8	2.6	1 460	2.9	70	4.8	1 533	32.4	18.6
Chautauqua	1 796	81.8	26 200	16.2	12.1	365	23.2	2.1	1 707	1.5	80	4.7	1 737	33.0	16.5
Cherokee	8 875	76.2	46 900	18.1	10.5	381	23.4	3.3	10 025	5.4	749	7.5	10 253	24.5	26.6
Cheyenne	1 360	77.4	48 500	17.4	11.0	314	17.3	2.1	1 501	5.9	25	1.7	1 509	33.8	10.2
Clark	979	76.5	42 600	18.7	9.9	386	21.3	1.8	1 333	2.1	28	2.1	1 134	37.3	11.4
Clay	3 617	77.0	52 900	18.5	9.9	333	20.9	0.6	4 644	1.5	167	3.6	4 266	31.4	16.0
Cloud	4 163	74.4	42 400	17.3	9.9	312	19.3	1.5	4 764	3.3	143	3.0	4 933	27.3	19.8
Coffey	3 489	78.3	60 700	15.7	9.9	394	19.1	2.5	4 073	0.2	301	7.4	4 431	31.4	15.9
Comanche	872	73.5	29 700	18.0	9.9	294	18.1	0.5	960	-1.3	16	1.7	970	40.2	13.7
Cowley	14 039	70.9	54 100	18.8	11.6	417	22.3	3.0	19 389	2.3	1 216	6.3	16 413	28.7	21.4
Crawford	15 504	64.3	54 000	19.2	11.3	451	26.9	2.4	18 890	1.5	917	4.9	18 321	30.9	19.1
Decatur	1 494	76.0	43 600	19.4	12.0	354	16.2	0.5	1 657	0.9	40	2.4	1 597	34.4	11.7
Dickinson	7 903	74.8	62 800	19.1	9.9	377	20.3	2.1	10 104	2.6	408	4.0	9 626	25.9	18.9
Doniphan	3 173	74.6	54 700	16.7	10.9	379	24.1	2.2	3 543	-4.0	360	10.2	3 871	29.0	20.6
Douglas	38 486	51.9	117 800	20.5	9.9	560	29.3	2.7	58 116	0.9	2 705	4.7	55 212	40.4	10.1
Edwards	1 455	77.5	36 300	18.2	11.0	350	18.4	2.6	1 531	-0.5	42	2.7	1 593	34.3	15.5
Elk	1 412	80.8	24 700	19.4	11.3	301	20.4	1.9	1 321	0.0	72	5.5	1 307	33.4	18.8
Ellis	11 193	63.3	85 500	20.6	10.2	431	25.3	1.6	17 873	3.1	464	2.6	14 882	33.2	10.7
Ellsworth	2 481	79.6	43 400	16.9	11.2	336	19.8	1.1	2 783	1.2	80	2.9	2 975	32.9	14.9
Finney	12 948	64.8	83 800	20.6	9.9	491	23.9	13.5	17 610	0.2	585	3.3	18 595	24.5	25.9
Ford	10 852	64.8	69 200	19.3	10.9	451	21.1	11.7	16 025	3.8	444	2.8	15 266	24.5	26.0
Franklin	9 452	73.5	73 800	19.1	11.7	465	22.7	3.3	14 714	3.0	733	5.0	12 346	25.2	20.4
Geary	10 458	50.4	69 400	20.9	12.1	461	22.5	5.3	11 168	2.9	719	6.4	10 947	25.4	16.7
Gove	1 245	79.7	48 100	18.4	9.9	330	19.2	0.7	1 529	1.9	27	1.8	1 484	37.5	12.7
Graham	1 263	79.3	41 300	20.1	10.6	320	18.4	2.5	1 496	2.8	25	1.7	1 422	35.0	11.1
Grant	2 742	74.7	78 600	19.4	9.9	436	18.6	8.6	3 675	0.4	114	3.1	3 500	25.8	15.3
Gray	2 045	72.7	76 000	18.3	9.9	418	17.7	4.8	3 498	3.3	74	2.1	2 828	33.9	13.0
Greeley	602	75.1	57 700	20.1	10.3	383	19.1	5.3	821	0.4	28	3.4	702	35.2	13.5
Greenwood	3 234	75.3	35 300	19.3	11.1	322	22.8	3.1	3 153	0.4	190	6.0	3 440	29.7	17.3
Hamilton	1 054	69.7	59 400	18.6	11.0	373	19.8	5.5	1 320	4.1	20	1.5	1 197	32.0	10.2
Harper	2 773	74.6	44 100	17.6	12.1	356	22.5	1.8	3 005	2.7	119	4.0	2 992	30.0	18.1
Harvey	12 581	71.9	76 400	18.4	9.9	448	21.3	2.3	16 720	0.6	909	5.4	16 285	31.6	17.9
Haskell	1 481	72.2	76 100	18.6	9.9	446	22.0	9.0	2 170	3.1	39	1.8	1 944	32.8	15.5
Hodgeman	796	78.4	45 000	17.7	9.9	360	17.3	2.9	1 008	4.3	27	2.7	994	38.5	10.8
Jackson	4 727	80.6	70 200	19.1	10.4	453	21.0	2.7	9 318	3.5	486	5.2	6 140	28.3	16.4
Jefferson	6 830	85.1	83 100	19.9	9.9	447	20.7	2.5	10 685	3.1	489	4.6	9 036	28.5	15.6
Jewell	1 695	79.9	24 000	17.2	9.9	266	17.0	1.3	2 098	3.3	35	1.7	1 809	35.0	12.3
Johnson	174 570	72.3	150 100	19.7	9.9	702	23.0	2.0	280 910	2.0	12 529	4.5	247 166	47.5	7.1
Kearny	1 542	73.5	77 500	19.3	9.9	465	21.7	7.3	1 932	0.9	68	3.5	1 956	31.0	16.7
Kingman	3 371	78.1	56 800	18.2	9.9	397	17.6	3.3	4 157	2.9	213	5.1	4 015	31.6	17.6
Kiowa	1 365	71.8	44 200	16.7	10.0	336	19.3	2.1	1 573	6.2	30	1.9	1 581	35.3	11.7
Labette	9 194	73.3	39 600	18.5	11.3	375	20.0	2.3	10 938	0.8	641	5.9	10 820	30.8	22.8
Lane	910	77.0	48 500	17.3	11.1	365	19.5	1.6	1 136	5.0	42	3.7	1 071	33.1	13.4
Leavenworth	23 071	67.0	96 900	19.7	9.9	551	22.0	2.6	28 005	2.1	1 933	6.9	29 178	31.0	13.3
Lincoln	1 529	76.2	33 900	19.7	9.9	296	18.2	0.6	1 732	6.3	79	4.6	1 830	36.7	16.7
Linn	3 807	82.5	56 100	18.9	10.9	412	24.8	3.3	3 259	2.5	294	9.0	4 382	25.3	20.2
Logan	1 243	76.3	55 000	18.9	9.9	360	20.6	2.7	1 574	2.4	34	2.2	1 511	30.8	12.8
Lyon	13 691	60.9	67 900	19.1	10.6	420	24.6	5.5	20 367	3.2	928	4.6	18 095	25.7	23.3
McPherson	11 205	73.9	82 700	18.6	9.9	416	20.9	1.4	16 568	2.6	463	2.8	15 038	29.7	22.1
Marion	5 114	79.9	52 300	18.8	10.4	374	21.5	1.8	6 836	2.4	241	3.5	6 324	32.1	19.3
Marshall	4 458	79.7	46 200	17.1	9.9	324	18.5	2.2	6 215	1.7	167	2.7	5 254	30.3	21.3
Meade	1 728	73.9	52 900	18.3	9.9	395	18.1	3.4	2 202	5.7	45	2.0	2 035	35.2	12.5
Miami	10 365	78.5	106 300	20.6	12.1	499	21.4	2.6	14 805	2.2	871	5.9	14 403	29.6	15.6
Mitchell	2 850	74.7	55 600	19.3	11.0	346	18.9	1.1	3 664	5.7	87	2.4	3 383	33.4	14.2
Montgomery	14 903	71.7	44 400	18.6	11.3	401	23.8	2.0	17 361	0.4	1 094	6.3	16 444	26.9	22.6
Morris	2 539	78.2	48 400	17.7	9.9	368	18.7	2.2	3 263	4.9	102	3.1	2 975	29.2	18.2
Morton	1 306	71.6	67 700	16.6	9.9	413	19.6	5.8	1 597	4.9	33	2.1	1 635	33.4	13.0
Nemaha	3 959	80.5	58 200	18.8	9.9	321	21.2	1.9	5 530	5.4	132	2.4	4 951	31.3	17.3
Neosho	6 739	74.5	44 900	17.9	10.4	375	20.8	2.7	8 890	4.7	381	4.3	7 961	27.0	24.7
Ness	1 516	76.1	40 600	18.4	9.9	340	18.6	0.7	1 827	2.7	31	1.7	1 687	39.3	12.4
Norton	2 266	77.9	46 800	19.8	10.9	329	22.1	0.7	3 071	3.8	57	1.9	2 519	33.4	8.6

1. Specified owner-occupied units.   2. Median monthly owner costs is often in the minimum category—9.9 percent or less, which is indicated as 9.9 percent.   3. Specified renter-occupied units.   4. Overcrowded or lacking complete plumbing facilities.   5. Percent of civilian labor force.   6. Persons 16 years old and over.

Table B. States and Counties — **Nonfarm Employment and Agriculture**

STATE County	Private nonfarm establishments, employment and payroll, 2001									Agriculture, 2002			
	Number of establishments	Employment						Annual payroll		Farms			Farm operators whose principal occupation is farming (percent)
		Total	Health care and social assistance	Manufacturing	Retail trade	Finance and insurance	Professional, scientific, and technical services	Total (mil dol)	Average per employee (dollars)	Number	Percent with—		
											Less than 50 acres	500 acres and over	
	104	105	106	107	108	109	110	111	112	113	114	115	116
KANSAS—Cont'd													
Barber	209	1 333	248	D	278	66	43	30	22 263	471	8.3	52.7	62.6
Barton	1 016	10 412	1 923	1 643	1 698	401	369	247	23 758	772	13.3	41.8	69.0
Bourbon	416	6 635	1 046	1 356	739	785	132	150	22 613	838	14.7	22.6	56.9
Brown	265	3 290	646	299	406	140	89	71	21 617	591	16.4	31.0	71.4
Butler	1 264	11 880	2 010	1 548	2 169	531	330	280	23 578	1 309	27.7	21.5	51.0
Chase	71	454	D	64	72	26	D	7	15 700	260	14.2	45.0	70.4
Chautauqua	90	589	233	D	91	D	7	9	16 008	371	7.0	39.4	63.1
Cherokee	398	5 193	552	2 060	593	118	93	129	24 783	746	26.9	20.5	60.5
Cheyenne	113	546	136	D	105	33	18	11	19 590	441	7.7	54.0	73.2
Clark	80	479	181	D	46	51	19	10	21 292	302	7.0	46.7	63.9
Clay	289	2 548	499	369	542	108	53	51	19 925	571	14.4	42.6	68.3
Cloud	340	3 147	684	335	567	177	66	64	20 294	520	10.2	47.7	69.0
Coffey	252	2 817	416	142	386	90	D	101	35 701	607	15.2	29.7	60.6
Comanche	78	443	136	73	65	35	5	7	15 542	274	7.7	57.3	71.9
Cowley	825	11 235	2 036	3 433	1 573	388	191	283	25 228	1 004	18.3	28.6	59.2
Crawford	994	13 804	2 161	3 341	1 921	340	319	327	23 708	825	22.1	21.6	61.1
Decatur	123	798	241	13	133	28	40	13	16 090	350	14.3	55.7	75.7
Dickinson	564	5 760	879	1 303	780	212	137	120	20 759	976	17.3	34.4	64.8
Doniphan	167	1 742	178	728	216	66	27	44	25 001	469	18.1	26.0	62.9
Douglas	2 599	36 544	4 767	4 024	6 266	837	1 568	828	22 668	874	35.8	11.3	51.5
Edwards	97	675	140	208	53	33	14	15	22 599	353	4.8	47.3	70.5
Elk	60	310	21	D	37	34	6	4	13 458	407	11.1	38.1	66.1
Ellis	1 032	12 221	3 008	1 094	2 268	349	986	268	21 904	758	12.5	39.4	61.5
Ellsworth	195	1 665	433	339	205	72	76	39	23 149	478	17.2	40.2	62.8
Finney	1 007	14 568	2 065	3 753	2 544	409	380	345	23 679	485	8.5	59.2	73.0
Ford	851	13 099	1 283	5 008	1 946	293	461	336	25 639	701	14.4	46.6	68.0
Franklin	573	7 522	906	1 179	1 247	211	170	184	24 502	977	26.0	17.6	56.6
Geary	577	8 510	1 201	783	1 247	238	212	172	20 182	245	18.8	40.8	65.7
Gove	133	867	257	113	181	29	7	16	18 106	395	10.4	58.7	81.5
Graham	105	695	256	D	108	47	25	11	16 494	431	10.0	42.5	63.1
Grant	243	1 969	173	169	341	95	32	59	29 726	304	10.2	48.0	69.4
Gray	217	1 324	168	116	169	59	88	31	23 474	470	8.1	51.9	67.4
Greeley	57	340	D	0	82	18	D	7	19 626	303	5.0	51.8	65.3
Greenwood	231	1 232	314	71	212	85	30	24	19 302	575	11.5	38.6	63.0
Hamilton	81	606	D	0	101	36	21	12	20 373	393	7.4	51.4	55.7
Harper	239	1 476	292	218	211	112	35	29	19 693	523	9.9	45.1	68.3
Harvey	814	11 890	2 605	3 199	1 683	278	176	296	24 908	832	26.0	26.7	62.7
Haskell	118	792	D	D	92	67	19	19	23 977	227	5.3	70.0	82.8
Hodgeman	49	297	D	D	52	D	13	5	18 455	381	5.5	59.3	75.6
Jackson	279	3 264	351	D	554	105	68	67	20 666	1 099	22.7	17.1	53.7
Jefferson	362	2 374	385	165	332	106	82	61	25 885	1 041	23.4	11.8	54.8
Jewell	100	536	D	D	107	58	11	8	14 375	572	11.0	45.8	78.0
Johnson	15 938	285 510	23 723	19 592	37 694	19 934	24 444	10 518	36 840	659	45.5	11.1	48.7
Kearny	91	580	D	0	59	44	12	14	23 634	347	9.5	45.2	66.3
Kingman	213	2 036	426	381	307	120	48	44	21 393	837	14.6	36.0	62.0
Kiowa	114	856	234	D	126	24	16	18	20 855	379	8.4	47.2	60.4
Labette	516	7 844	2 197	2 317	970	246	147	178	22 711	889	18.9	22.8	58.0
Lane	85	376	D	D	D	36	12	8	20 372	312	6.1	59.9	70.8
Leavenworth	1 113	14 438	2 991	753	2 356	789	801	375	25 939	1 094	34.8	7.0	51.1
Lincoln	106	608	179	D	96	45	17	10	15 775	458	10.9	48.9	68.3
Linn	174	1 271	121	125	214	72	17	38	29 833	903	16.9	17.9	56.6
Logan	150	757	117	D	140	50	28	15	19 439	318	7.5	62.6	70.8
Lyon	910	15 212	2 169	5 341	2 408	337	356	335	22 022	898	19.3	29.4	61.5
McPherson	958	12 716	1 941	3 858	1 284	702	200	330	25 979	1 161	17.5	31.0	64.6
Marion	338	3 221	746	317	530	126	108	57	17 660	996	19.4	34.6	64.8
Marshall	375	3 564	616	909	440	184	206	72	20 268	954	12.5	42.6	69.0
Meade	146	865	180	11	190	60	15	19	21 992	454	6.4	52.6	74.2
Miami	619	6 742	1 688	473	1 494	300	253	154	22 875	1 424	37.6	10.1	49.5
Mitchell	265	2 530	511	402	436	118	85	55	21 710	473	11.6	49.7	71.9
Montgomery	998	14 377	2 312	4 943	2 568	378	234	335	23 272	983	23.3	16.5	51.7
Morris	150	1 167	217	220	219	59	47	23	19 837	466	16.5	41.0	67.4
Morton	116	789	D	D	86	36	13	20	25 909	309	7.1	46.0	56.6
Nemaha	384	3 809	750	1 054	542	160	106	89	23 421	1 020	12.0	27.5	68.1
Neosho	531	6 751	1 085	1 893	1 205	295	118	147	21 709	769	18.1	25.1	59.0
Ness	156	1 060	255	34	112	52	41	21	19 942	547	9.7	55.8	63.6
Norton	212	1 767	402	176	204	101	56	40	22 397	482	16.6	43.6	68.5

STATE County	Acreage (1,000) 117	Percent change, 1997–2002 118	Average size of farm 119	Total irrigated (1,000) 120	Total cropland (1,000) 121	Average per farm 122	Average per acre 123	Value of machinery and equipment average per farm (dollars) 124	Total (mil dol) 125	Average per farm (dollars) 126	Crops 127	Livestock and poultry products 128	$10,000 or more 129	$100,000 or more 130	Total ($1,000) 131	Percent of farms 132
KANSAS—Cont'd																
Barber	697	17.1	1 480	6	224	624 528	441	88 065	50	105 816	29.6	70.4	61.6	25.7	2 471	63.1
Barton	650	6.0	842	43	487	531 316	591	103 913	171	221 708	26.3	73.7	60.1	24.0	4 230	68.8
Bourbon	339	3.0	405	D	169	258 047	720	49 148	29	35 045	23.9	76.1	47.5	7.6	1 836	48.9
Brown	324	-2.7	548	1	253	650 612	1 164	103 259	53	89 091	59.3	40.7	61.1	21.5	3 804	68.2
Butler	701	-7.6	536	5	308	526 418	1 002	73 989	116	88 939	20.9	79.1	41.6	13.1	2 332	34.9
Chase	362	-11.5	1 391	0	82	821 715	618	72 201	44	167 593	11.2	88.8	61.9	23.1	759	52.7
Chautauqua	390	-0.3	1 052	D	66	490 627	535	55 255	30	81 950	23.8	76.2	50.4	13.7	630	42.9
Cherokee	291	8.2	389	0	219	415 511	968	71 877	50	66 470	58.1	41.9	45.8	14.9	1 683	39.8
Cheyenne	576	2.5	1 307	41	367	627 176	480	143 923	54	123 402	36.3	63.7	54.0	22.7	4 123	79.1
Clark	492	-9.9	1 628	6	193	649 369	395	95 289	98	324 080	5.1	94.9	45.7	17.2	2 856	80.1
Clay	393	6.5	689	19	262	639 101	907	84 906	49	85 279	53.9	46.1	62.9	24.7	3 155	72.9
Cloud	431	9.7	829	19	266	553 649	604	113 230	38	72 722	64.1	35.9	64.0	23.1	2 997	71.2
Coffey	336	9.4	553	1	193	439 172	755	83 264	38	63 194	44.3	55.7	48.4	14.5	2 303	66.4
Comanche	447	-11.3	1 631	3	171	656 317	408	109 371	26	93 998	D	D	57.7	24.1	2 660	78.1
Cowley	690	7.3	687	4	287	536 050	775	71 227	62	62 157	36.6	63.4	49.2	13.1	2 669	48.0
Crawford	341	17.2	413	3	205	365 040	875	63 091	42	50 889	51.7	48.3	49.1	10.9	2 071	45.0
Decatur	469	-8.9	1 340	10	282	614 513	485	118 607	108	308 264	14.2	85.8	68.6	23.7	2 238	73.1
Dickinson	551	7.2	564	7	376	381 611	666	78 435	97	98 950	30.9	69.1	53.6	20.6	4 975	70.8
Doniphan	206	-7.2	439	D	155	643 024	1 281	137 681	32	68 446	78.2	21.8	53.5	20.7	2 933	65.9
Douglas	201	-8.2	230	2	129	411 999	2 010	49 084	24	27 446	53.3	46.7	29.9	6.4	1 360	39.7
Edwards	420	17.6	1 190	88	311	717 601	579	159 896	131	372 249	28.6	71.4	55.8	29.7	3 449	79.6
Elk	370	11.8	910	2	74	464 132	496	50 517	26	63 307	15.6	84.4	53.3	10.3	688	45.7
Ellis	578	14.0	762	2	316	415 437	528	93 580	52	68 961	26.9	73.1	58.2	10.0	2 928	65.3
Ellsworth	413	9.8	864	1	219	414 310	518	116 925	25	51 659	54.2	45.8	53.1	17.2	2 289	78.0
Finney	802	5.4	1 653	199	601	946 701	616	234 835	488	1 005 611	16.0	84.0	65.2	40.2	6 855	73.6
Ford	649	-3.0	926	79	508	538 092	578	116 112	215	306 217	17.4	82.6	50.4	19.0	5 892	72.9
Franklin	339	11.9	347	1	197	457 603	1 240	62 037	41	41 512	37.1	62.9	37.3	7.5	2 168	42.0
Geary	180	16.9	733	3	76	610 494	859	83 213	17	68 187	38.1	61.9	54.3	13.9	796	61.6
Gove	592	-8.8	1 498	17	385	673 018	449	170 722	110	278 339	17.5	82.5	71.9	28.9	3 492	71.6
Graham	517	6.4	1 200	7	304	535 676	453	80 766	32	75 299	40.3	59.6	45.9	17.9	3 784	81.9
Grant	302	-9.3	993	85	250	666 523	664	179 616	317	1 041 153	9.8	90.2	55.9	35.9	3 200	76.6
Gray	501	-9.9	1 066	131	422	827 769	791	167 151	354	752 205	16.1	83.9	59.4	36.6	5 518	76.4
Greeley	456	3.2	1 506	14	419	767 447	504	179 206	52	171 705	17.6	82.4	33.7	12.9	4 225	79.9
Greenwood	594	-6.3	1 034	1	143	565 136	552	64 312	51	88 670	12.5	87.5	56.5	16.9	1 032	38.8
Hamilton	536	1.5	1 363	24	405	641 765	465	132 708	176	447 653	7.2	92.8	37.4	14.8	6 419	86.8
Harper	470	2.0	898	1	347	569 541	623	134 653	63	120 437	44.3	55.7	63.7	25.4	3 691	75.5
Harvey	352	9.7	423	27	274	409 353	928	84 481	60	72 475	57.6	42.4	54.9	20.0	2 858	51.8
Haskell	406	10.0	1 788	162	339	1 316 845	744	333 943	482	2 124 121	12.5	87.5	73.6	58.6	3 751	72.7
Hodgeman	471	-2.9	1 235	22	308	641 663	512	131 500	98	257 620	13.7	86.3	59.6	25.7	3 968	82.7
Jackson	337	5.0	307	1	179	261 013	832	45 923	28	25 280	35.6	64.4	40.8	6.0	2 263	47.5
Jefferson	280	4.1	269	2	169	302 175	1 067	51 091	35	33 463	37.3	62.7	37.8	6.6	1 984	41.4
Jewell	496	8.1	867	11	318	601 228	656	133 537	50	87 448	53.1	46.9	61.9	24.3	4 168	75.2
Johnson	149	9.6	226	2	88	555 417	1 978	47 466	27	40 616	65.1	34.9	26.3	6.5	987	25.5
Kearny	558	6.1	1 607	86	398	752 565	479	150 695	181	520 733	20.6	79.4	50.1	28.5	4 662	75.8
Kingman	556	6.7	664	18	362	431 030	683	88 272	52	61 879	52.8	47.2	52.7	15.4	3 626	72.6
Kiowa	435	-1.6	1 147	44	228	491 857	441	115 282	36	96 282	56.1	43.9	50.1	19.8	4 248	83.6
Labette	361	9.1	406	1	205	316 819	746	66 312	62	70 229	27.9	72.1	48.7	11.6	2 035	44.3
Lane	460	5.7	1 476	15	343	733 084	468	178 101	124	397 628	11.7	88.3	59.6	25.0	3 716	75.0
Leavenworth	197	-2.5	180	1	120	301 996	1 589	36 367	22	20 181	48.0	52.0	28.2	3.2	1 431	31.4
Lincoln	446	4.2	974	1	239	444 923	439	76 087	35	76 833	49.0	51.0	64.0	20.5	2 967	78.4
Linn	311	11.9	344	1	169	328 727	1 003	62 263	23	25 540	45.0	55.0	33.6	5.6	1 955	48.5
Logan	610	-2.9	1 918	19	377	749 243	417	173 127	40	126 410	32.3	67.7	63.5	23.9	2 881	78.3
Lyon	494	-0.4	550	1	262	416 459	778	63 078	76	84 523	24.3	75.7	48.0	11.8	2 474	56.3
McPherson	575	9.9	495	32	420	574 947	1 151	94 736	99	85 640	49.7	50.3	63.9	19.2	4 356	62.9
Marion	588	4.4	591	3	359	401 821	731	79 129	81	81 618	38.8	61.2	60.1	20.0	3 603	69.4
Marshall	581	13.0	609	2	383	645 660	917	119 799	64	67 452	49.3	50.7	64.4	18.1	4 929	69.0
Meade	611	10.1	1 345	104	340	784 736	584	158 677	106	233 673	40.4	59.6	56.6	31.5	4 281	75.1
Miami	320	14.3	225	2	188	429 055	1 755	49 158	44	30 964	36.2	63.8	29.6	4.4	1 484	30.0
Mitchell	449	-1.3	949	7	322	672 573	724	123 117	74	156 219	37.0	63.0	66.0	29.4	3 271	74.8
Montgomery	346	5.5	352	2	186	323 688	884	59 763	40	40 192	41.8	58.2	38.9	6.9	1 427	38.9
Morris	386	-2.5	828	2	157	529 910	632	97 963	54	114 818	20.8	79.2	63.7	15.5	1 514	63.3
Morton	353	-16.4	1 141	38	283	562 862	466	117 263	41	133 732	31.3	68.7	37.5	16.8	4 133	86.1
Nemaha	417	-0.2	408	1	275	405 610	998	70 609	79	77 841	23.3	76.7	63.9	18.0	4 729	64.0
Neosho	341	-1.2	444	0	188	345 121	763	96 767	39	50 552	42.8	57.2	46.2	10.9	1 699	50.3
Ness	655	5.1	1 198	3	404	504 882	413	93 327	31	57 025	50.3	49.7	64.0	18.6	3 622	79.2
Norton	517	7.9	1 074	11	289	470 057	447	85 309	54	112 323	27.5	72.5	53.7	17.8	3 452	72.6

Table B. States and Counties — Residential Construction, Wholesale Trade, Retail Trade, and Real Estate

STATE County	Value of residential construction authorized by building permits, 2003		Wholesale trade, 1997				Retail trade,[1] 1997				Real estate and rental and leasing, 1997			
	New construction ($1,000)	Number of housing units	Number of establishments	Number of employees	Sales (mil dol)	Annual payroll (mil dol)	Number of establishments	Number of employees	Sales (mil dol)	Annual payroll (mil dol)	Number of establishments	Number of employees	Receipts (mil dol)	Annual payroll (mil dol)
	133	134	135	136	137	138	139	140	141	142	143	144	145	146
KANSAS—Cont'd														
Barber	560	5	12	97	35.7	2.0	39	271	35.1	3.9	2	D	D	D
Barton	5 093	50	92	737	206.2	18.2	185	1 803	282.8	28.7	17	48	3.4	1.0
Bourbon	467	9	24	475	233.2	9.8	69	606	95.2	8.8	11	38	2.4	0.6
Brown	614	7	27	152	73.6	3.7	51	407	67.1	5.4	5	12	1.0	0.2
Butler	52 863	409	67	368	136.2	8.8	194	1 875	350.3	29.3	38	96	7.0	1.4
Chase	0	0	2	D	D	D	14	103	8.3	0.8	NA	NA	NA	NA
Chautauqua	NA	NA	7	39	9.3	0.8	19	98	10.9	0.9	NA	NA	NA	NA
Cherokee	969	21	18	134	210.5	3.4	91	621	93.2	7.8	9	26	0.8	0.2
Cheyenne	200	4	11	118	57.8	2.7	30	125	17.7	1.4	3	4	0.3	0.1
Clark	250	1	5	D	D	D	19	62	7.6	0.8	NA	NA	NA	NA
Clay	3 232	33	18	140	55.4	3.2	61	487	63.4	6.3	5	12	1.1	0.1
Cloud	971	5	22	238	110.5	5.5	71	608	83.2	7.7	8	D	D	D
Coffey	2 743	29	9	76	38.5	2.1	50	418	58.8	5.2	6	11	0.4	0.1
Comanche	0	0	4	D	D	D	14	71	8.4	0.8	NA	NA	NA	NA
Cowley	5 842	41	38	343	118.9	8.9	173	1 682	255.5	24.2	22	67	4.7	1.5
Crawford	17 164	204	53	624	173.3	17.0	180	2 132	296.5	27.7	29	112	9.2	1.5
Decatur	344	3	15	144	74.3	2.9	23	108	10.2	1.1	5	3	1.4	0.2
Dickinson	4 873	47	25	365	220.6	8.8	110	900	125.0	11.4	10	D	D	D
Doniphan	1 490	16	11	D	D	D	27	322	43.2	4.0	4	7	0.6	0.0
Douglas	115 372	1 060	88	777	248.8	21.0	453	5 664	758.5	80.3	122	434	46.4	6.6
Edwards	383	2	8	87	57.6	2.6	15	64	7.6	0.7	NA	NA	NA	NA
Elk	NA	NA	6	18	10.9	0.4	8	30	3.7	0.2	2	D	D	D
Ellis	10 674	127	46	411	93.1	8.3	216	2 207	326.7	32.3	36	122	10.3	1.8
Ellsworth	306	4	12	D	D	D	41	242	30.3	2.5	3	3	0.1	0.0
Finney	3 785	32	84	791	495.5	26.2	186	2 502	405.0	38.3	45	147	16.2	3.1
Ford	8 533	98	55	607	347.8	17.3	169	2 016	367.4	31.9	37	114	11.0	1.7
Franklin	20 266	201	29	487	298.4	11.4	89	1 114	167.2	15.3	16	47	2.5	0.5
Geary	6 111	51	18	153	60.1	2.7	99	1 174	181.1	17.9	33	121	10.7	1.6
Gove	0	0	11	74	31.8	1.7	22	122	19.3	1.4	1	D	D	D
Graham	0	0	9	39	16.9	1.0	21	133	25.3	2.1	NA	NA	NA	NA
Grant	1 084	6	20	165	97.8	4.9	39	371	60.1	6.1	5	26	1.8	0.3
Gray	2 557	23	23	189	126.5	6.0	28	163	33.2	2.7	2	D	D	D
Greeley	150	1	3	D	D	D	11	59	9.2	0.9	2	D	D	D
Greenwood	485	4	14	70	6.2	D	41	215	36.6	2.9	5	10	0.3	0.0
Hamilton	90	1	11	136	53.8	3.0	16	81	14.3	1.0	2	D	D	D
Harper	244	3	18	168	76.8	3.8	39	266	38.7	2.9	3	8	0.2	0.1
Harvey	14 463	130	35	280	181.2	7.7	156	1 608	185.8	19.1	27	56	4.7	0.7
Haskell	125	1	13	146	92.3	4.7	15	84	10.6	0.9	NA	NA	NA	NA
Hodgeman	NA	NA	4	D	D	D	9	55	11.3	0.6	NA	NA	NA	NA
Jackson	4 708	60	12	45	25.0	0.8	50	489	73.9	6.4	6	D	D	D
Jefferson	12 655	114	10	30	9.6	0.5	60	353	51.4	4.2	8	D	D	D
Jewell	150	1	8	76	50.2	1.2	27	89	9.3	0.9	1	D	D	D
Johnson	818 018	5 353	1 502	19 597	21 107.6	789.6	1 903	30 545	5 418.8	543.2	646	4 947	681.3	119.5
Kearny	246	2	7	35	24.1	1.0	14	69	5.8	0.6	1	D	D	D
Kingman	988	8	15	129	51.6	3.7	41	290	36.2	3.6	4	12	0.4	0.1
Kiowa	0	0	7	50	30.2	1.4	21	176	20.2	1.9	NA	NA	NA	NA
Labette	1 870	26	29	214	81.7	4.6	120	1 021	147.5	14.1	10	37	3.4	0.6
Lane	90	1	9	69	36.0	1.6	17	62	8.9	0.8	NA	NA	NA	NA
Leavenworth	64 251	567	24	D	D	D	178	2 081	359.2	31.6	39	152	16.0	2.2
Lincoln	48	1	15	93	37.5	1.4	22	104	14.6	1.2	1	D	D	D
Linn	6 445	55	6	24	8.6	0.4	34	241	30.1	2.7	2	D	D	D
Logan	246	2	8	72	30.6	1.5	28	249	43.9	3.1	NA	NA	NA	NA
Lyon	5 714	91	41	571	197.3	14.0	172	1 982	285.5	29.3	32	118	7.7	1.6
McPherson	14 180	107	52	337	165.6	9.4	155	1 378	213.7	19.4	20	50	3.8	0.7
Marion	3 425	35	17	215	79.0	4.6	80	482	97.3	7.8	5	12	0.8	0.1
Marshall	1 146	8	24	206	115.2	5.6	74	490	76.5	6.0	5	5	0.2	0.0
Meade	200	2	10	87	66.8	2.4	32	171	21.3	2.0	3	D	D	D
Miami	31 411	203	21	D	D	D	91	1 163	170.6	16.3	17	65	6.2	0.9
Mitchell	921	6	25	247	133.5	6.1	61	448	79.7	6.7	3	11	0.3	0.0
Montgomery	1 266	16	52	472	124.4	10.9	223	2 013	264.2	25.4	36	130	7.0	1.7
Morris	439	3	6	24	8.0	0.5	39	239	40.1	2.9	3	9	0.5	0.1
Morton	335	2	13	146	78.8	3.7	19	84	10.8	1.2	NA	NA	NA	NA
Nemaha	2 599	17	21	135	58.5	3.0	82	490	88.1	6.5	5	D	D	D
Neosho	1 249	12	37	297	125.2	8.2	107	925	149.1	12.7	8	18	1.2	0.2
Ness	195	3	18	118	39.4	2.9	25	103	13.3	1.2	1	D	D	D
Norton	426	6	15	92	66.1	1.5	37	263	32.7	2.8	2	D	D	D

1. Establishments with payroll.

Table B. States and Counties — Professional Services, Manufacturing, and Accommodation and Foodservices

STATE County	Professional, scientific, and technical services,[1] 1997				Manufacturing, 1997				Accommodation and foodservices, 1997			
	Number of establishments	Number of employees	Receipts (mil dol)	Annual payroll (mil dol)	Number of establishments	Number of employees	Receipts (mil dol)	Annual payroll (mil dol)	Number of establishments	Number of employees	Sales (mil dol)	Annual payroll (mil dol)
	147	148	149	150	151	152	153	154	155	156	157	158
KANSAS—Cont'd												
Barber	7	27	1.7	0.4	NA	NA	NA	NA	16	121	2.4	0.7
Barton	65	699	26.0	13.5	45	1 608	308.1	34.0	71	959	26.8	7.2
Bourbon	23	111	7.0	3.4	29	1 295	149.0	29.4	60	D	D	D
Brown	12	70	4.3	1.8	18	820	75.8	18.0	20	248	5.4	1.4
Butler	63	198	11.2	3.9	52	1 704	1 132.7	58.8	96	1 400	37.6	10.6
Chase	4	9	0.4	0.1	NA	NA	NA	NA	8	D	D	D
Chautauqua	5	6	0.3	0.1	NA	NA	NA	NA	10	58	1.0	0.2
Cherokee	21	86	8.2	1.8	44	2 291	343.5	59.6	29	285	7.3	2.0
Cheyenne	4	11	0.7	0.2	NA	NA	NA	NA	9	51	1.2	0.3
Clark	5	12	0.4	0.2	NA	NA	NA	NA	6	D	D	D
Clay	10	41	1.6	0.7	NA	NA	NA	NA	21	256	4.6	1.3
Cloud	9	55	2.3	1.2	NA	NA	NA	NA	28	314	7.9	2.0
Coffey	11	20	0.8	0.3	NA	NA	NA	NA	21	172	4.6	1.2
Comanche	3	4	0.1	0.0	NA	NA	NA	NA	10	32	1.0	0.2
Cowley	36	148	8.2	3.2	47	3 793	1 176.7	107.3	74	1 002	25.6	6.5
Crawford	53	354	18.1	7.2	74	3 206	519.3	77.2	96	1 623	50.7	14.0
Decatur	7	43	1.9	0.7	NA	NA	NA	NA	7	D	D	D
Dickinson	24	95	7.9	1.7	25	1 161	160.9	24.6	49	494	12.6	3.6
Doniphan	7	24	0.7	0.2	8	D	D	D	10	51	1.3	0.4
Douglas	192	1 280	84.5	33.1	76	4 240	728.8	120.0	240	4 627	120.7	34.2
Edwards	5	14	0.4	0.1	NA	NA	NA	NA	11	D	D	D
Elk	4	4	0.2	0.1	NA	NA	NA	NA	8	D	D	D
Ellis	58	262	17.7	6.3	28	1 061	95.1	20.6	89	1 717	43.6	11.8
Ellsworth	8	77	4.7	2.1	NA	NA	NA	NA	16	122	3.5	0.9
Finney	59	450	22.3	9.2	38	5 416	2 420.2	123.4	68	1 310	40.2	11.1
Ford	49	439	27.6	12.5	29	D	D	D	69	1 102	35.4	9.6
Franklin	31	123	7.1	2.4	25	806	151.0	22.0	43	603	17.1	4.7
Geary	23	136	7.6	2.8	NA	NA	NA	NA	77	1 128	28.7	9.5
Gove	4	4	0.2	0.0	NA	NA	NA	NA	7	D	D	D
Graham	4	13	0.4	0.2	NA	NA	NA	NA	10	108	1.4	0.3
Grant	10	26	1.9	0.4	NA	NA	NA	NA	23	243	7.0	1.6
Gray	12	41	1.7	0.6	NA	NA	NA	NA	9	44	1.0	0.3
Greeley	2	D	D	D	NA	NA	NA	NA	5	30	0.5	0.1
Greenwood	13	29	1.0	0.3	NA	NA	NA	NA	27	D	D	D
Hamilton	7	18	0.9	0.2	NA	NA	NA	NA	7	59	1.2	0.3
Harper	12	33	1.3	0.4	NA	NA	NA	NA	22	172	4.4	1.1
Harvey	40	140	9.4	3.8	55	2 855	446.6	87.9	65	942	25.5	7.5
Haskell	3	11	0.7	0.3	NA	NA	NA	NA	8	51	1.2	0.3
Hodgeman	3	5	0.1	0.0	NA	NA	NA	NA	4	D	D	D
Jackson	11	39	1.4	0.4	NA	NA	NA	NA	20	271	5.8	1.6
Jefferson	16	35	1.5	0.5	NA	NA	NA	NA	33	148	4.2	0.7
Jewell	4	11	0.6	0.2	NA	NA	NA	NA	11	75	1.2	0.4
Johnson	1 780	18 416	2 032.6	810.1	551	20 590	3 659.3	662.8	827	19 029	636.3	188.5
Kearny	2	D	D	D	NA	NA	NA	NA	6	47	1.1	0.2
Kingman	12	44	1.9	0.8	NA	NA	NA	NA	18	197	4.4	1.2
Kiowa	5	9	0.3	0.1	NA	NA	NA	NA	11	89	1.8	0.6
Labette	23	103	5.6	2.6	40	2 298	254.5	64.4	45	548	13.3	3.7
Lane	4	9	0.4	0.1	NA	NA	NA	NA	4	D	D	D
Leavenworth	71	680	75.5	20.2	36	645	62.3	16.2	85	1 409	37.4	10.8
Lincoln	7	18	0.6	0.2	NA	NA	NA	NA	7	62	1.0	0.2
Linn	12	21	1.0	0.4	NA	NA	NA	NA	12	54	1.8	0.4
Logan	5	8	0.3	0.1	NA	NA	NA	NA	11	77	2.1	0.5
Lyon	38	200	9.6	4.3	40	6 478	2 054.1	167.1	104	1 633	37.3	10.0
McPherson	47	154	9.3	2.6	68	3 845	1 633.5	131.2	64	992	22.9	6.3
Marion	17	81	19.7	1.8	NA	NA	NA	NA	34	264	5.4	1.5
Marshall	10	37	1.7	0.6	21	880	106.8	23.0	36	257	6.1	1.5
Meade	6	20	0.8	0.2	NA	NA	NA	NA	8	62	1.4	0.3
Miami	32	95	6.9	2.0	31	682	58.2	19.1	36	456	11.2	3.3
Mitchell	12	35	2.3	0.6	NA	NA	NA	NA	24	274	5.1	1.5
Montgomery	59	209	12.7	4.4	61	4 590	1 482.9	121.6	87	1 164	30.3	8.5
Morris	8	51	2.4	0.6	NA	NA	NA	NA	10	D	D	D
Morton	6	19	1.0	0.3	NA	NA	NA	NA	10	90	2.4	0.6
Nemaha	20	62	3.9	1.7	19	1 047	209.5	30.3	31	256	5.0	1.4
Neosho	30	119	5.8	2.2	40	2 281	289.0	53.7	41	497	11.1	3.0
Ness	7	24	1.1	0.3	NA	NA	NA	NA	14	D	D	D
Norton	11	41	2.3	0.6	NA	NA	NA	NA	14	157	4.0	0.9

1. Firms subject to federal tax.

Table B. States and Counties — Health Care and Social Assistance, Other Services, and Federal Funds

STATE County	Health care and social assistance,[1] 1997				Other services,[1] 1997				Federal funds and grants, 2002–2003 Expenditures (mil dol)	Direct payments for individuals[2]		
	Number of establishments	Number of employees	Receipts (mil dol)	Annual payroll (mil dol)	Number of establishments	Number of employees	Receipts (mil dol)	Annual payroll (mil dol)	Total	Social Security and government retirement	Medicare	Food stamps and Supplemental Security Income
	159	160	161	162	163	164	165	166	167	168	169	170
KANSAS—Cont'd												
Barber	8	87	2.5	1.2	13	28	2.3	0.4	36.2	16.7	8.8	0.5
Barton	72	723	38.8	18.6	66	275	19.3	5.2	141.5	70.4	34.0	3.8
Bourbon	32	509	20.9	11.7	19	52	3.8	0.7	107.9	40.3	21.9	3.0
Brown	18	226	9.0	4.4	20	41	3.7	0.7	83.4	28.5	13.5	1.7
Butler	82	966	45.9	19.3	81	263	17.3	3.9	224.1	125.4	41.9	5.0
Chase	2	D	D	D	5	8	0.7	0.1	18.9	8.2	4.0	0.3
Chautauqua	8	165	3.9	2.2	2	D	D	D	28.7	13.5	7.0	0.7
Cherokee	21	290	9.2	4.1	14	37	2.4	0.6	127.2	52.9	27.3	5.0
Cheyenne	7	27	1.2	0.5	3	3	0.4	0.0	31.6	10.0	5.5	0.1
Clark	4	D	D	D	6	18	0.8	0.2	20.1	7.6	4.2	0.1
Clay	14	191	6.4	3.4	22	65	3.9	0.7	61.0	27.6	11.7	0.9
Cloud	23	149	7.5	3.6	19	93	6.6	2.0	86.3	31.1	17.2	1.1
Coffey	13	125	3.6	1.5	15	25	2.3	0.4	44.6	21.0	12.0	0.9
Comanche	5	D	D	D	5	31	1.1	0.3	17.5	7.0	3.2	0.1
Cowley	57	801	34.7	14.6	52	197	11.2	2.5	280.3	90.5	37.3	6.0
Crawford	82	1 022	38.8	17.0	59	519	48.0	12.7	236.9	90.2	46.2	6.9
Decatur	6	37	2.1	1.0	4	5	0.8	0.2	38.6	11.6	5.5	0.2
Dickinson	35	237	8.5	3.8	37	115	10.9	1.5	121.5	60.7	21.2	1.7
Doniphan	8	129	2.6	1.6	10	26	2.3	0.5	48.5	17.9	8.9	1.1
Douglas	175	1 648	88.7	41.8	132	782	42.5	13.5	398.2	143.7	45.8	7.4
Edwards	7	72	3.6	1.3	9	20	1.2	0.3	29.4	9.5	6.5	0.3
Elk	NA	NA	NA	NA	5	13	0.8	0.2	27.9	10.7	5.5	0.6
Ellis	70	623	42.9	19.4	71	302	23.1	5.2	134.1	54.5	28.1	2.5
Ellsworth	10	145	6.7	3.0	11	27	1.9	0.3	39.7	16.7	10.8	0.4
Finney	48	576	40.4	19.0	75	399	23.1	6.8	124.1	50.4	19.5	3.9
Ford	60	774	65.7	24.5	51	227	13.6	3.6	134.4	51.0	22.7	3.4
Franklin	41	417	17.7	8.4	33	126	8.8	2.1	126.1	55.6	26.8	3.8
Geary	39	283	13.0	5.4	54	529	20.8	10.3	651.3	84.0	11.2	4.9
Gove	2	D	D	D	13	30	2.6	0.4	37.1	9.6	5.0	0.1
Graham	7	25	2.1	0.5	6	15	1.2	0.2	32.0	9.6	5.1	0.3
Grant	9	35	3.3	1.1	15	59	5.3	1.1	34.6	11.6	5.0	0.7
Gray	5	D	D	D	11	22	2.9	0.4	35.4	11.3	4.2	0.2
Greeley	2	D	D	D	6	19	1.7	0.3	31.3	4.1	1.4	0.0
Greenwood	8	186	6.7	3.2	16	32	2.4	0.4	60.7	25.7	13.0	1.3
Hamilton	2	D	D	D	9	23	1.4	0.2	30.2	6.4	4.0	0.1
Harper	11	66	2.6	1.0	17	35	2.0	0.5	46.5	19.9	10.8	0.8
Harvey	51	1 052	66.3	33.2	45	205	12.4	3.7	166.5	86.1	35.2	2.7
Haskell	6	9	0.6	0.0	8	26	3.2	0.4	25.3	6.9	2.8	0.4
Hodgeman	1	D	D	D	3	6	0.2	0.1	20.4	5.8	3.2	0.0
Jackson	16	148	4.0	2.0	23	92	6.5	1.2	63.5	31.1	9.9	1.3
Jefferson	18	231	6.8	3.0	22	63	4.6	1.2	79.1	45.3	13.3	1.4
Jewell	2	D	D	D	10	27	1.7	0.3	37.3	12.2	5.0	0.4
Johnson	1 050	14 539	1 046.2	449.9	765	5 116	347.7	107.9	1 785.2	812.0	296.6	17.3
Kearny	5	17	1.2	0.4	8	16	1.2	0.2	38.9	7.6	3.6	0.4
Kingman	10	189	4.6	2.2	11	24	1.5	0.2	51.4	22.8	11.8	0.7
Kiowa	3	60	1.6	0.7	7	17	1.0	0.2	25.6	9.6	5.9	0.3
Labette	37	430	20.8	8.8	31	262	15.9	4.8	153.2	58.5	30.5	4.8
Lane	3	D	D	D	5	7	0.5	0.1	26.0	6.3	3.4	0.1
Leavenworth	87	906	44.8	20.7	82	545	22.7	7.4	1 065.0	195.5	47.8	6.4
Lincoln	7	71	1.6	0.8	5	12	0.6	0.1	27.9	10.4	4.6	0.2
Linn	14	127	2.8	1.1	9	18	1.9	0.3	58.7	26.6	13.4	1.2
Logan	5	55	2.6	1.1	9	50	2.4	0.6	32.8	9.0	4.4	0.2
Lyon	67	754	33.8	17.2	64	289	14.5	4.2	174.7	65.8	26.5	4.8
McPherson	47	489	19.7	8.2	70	297	21.6	5.7	129.3	70.4	28.6	1.6
Marion	20	193	7.4	3.3	19	47	2.9	0.5	76.9	36.3	16.4	0.8
Marshall	28	190	8.6	4.1	33	74	5.0	0.9	91.2	33.6	14.4	1.1
Meade	3	18	1.1	0.3	9	14	1.2	0.2	28.3	11.4	6.3	0.2
Miami	39	623	22.0	9.7	41	112	7.7	1.8	111.6	52.9	26.1	2.2
Mitchell	12	235	6.6	3.5	19	81	3.6	1.1	49.9	19.5	9.8	0.4
Montgomery	80	1 233	49.5	22.8	58	211	11.6	3.3	225.1	101.8	48.2	7.7
Morris	9	109	4.4	1.5	15	23	1.9	0.3	42.2	20.3	7.6	0.6
Morton	6	17	1.1	0.5	8	13	1.2	0.2	29.4	7.6	4.2	0.3
Nemaha	25	367	8.3	3.2	24	75	5.4	1.1	73.6	27.0	12.4	0.4
Neosho	32	513	21.5	8.7	33	132	9.5	2.3	99.9	44.6	20.4	2.8
Ness	6	18	0.9	0.4	10	28	2.1	0.4	32.1	11.2	7.4	0.1
Norton	14	76	4.1	1.4	14	32	3.5	0.6	51.2	15.8	7.6	0.7

1. Firms subject to federal tax. 2. State totals may include programs not allocated by county.

Items 159—170

	Federal funds and grants, 2002–2003 (cont'd)							Local government finances, 2002				
	Expenditures (mil dol) (cont'd)							General revenue				
	Procurement contract awards			Grants[1]						Taxes		
											Per capita[2] (dollars)	
STATE County	Salaries and wages	Defense	Other	Medicaid and other health-related	Nutrition and family welfare	Education	Other	Total (mil dol)	Intergovernmental (mil dol)	Total (mil dol)	Total	Property
	171	172	173	174	175	176	177	178	179	180	181	182
KANSAS—Cont'd												
Barber	1.5	0.0	0.8	2.2	0.4	0.2	1.3	25.5	6.0	8.3	1 633	1 373
Barton	5.5	0.0	1.2	8.3	3.1	1.8	3.9	93.2	39.7	31.4	1 130	916
Bourbon	5.6	0.2	3.6	12.4	1.9	1.2	12.0	41.3	20.5	12.7	838	660
Brown	3.9	0.0	1.2	6.8	5.3	0.8	5.9	25.1	12.5	8.9	845	700
Butler	8.8	1.3	2.0	15.7	5.9	1.4	7.0	194.6	97.8	56.3	930	818
Chase	1.5	0.0	0.4	1.5	0.3	0.5	0.9	9.5	4.0	3.8	1 312	1 275
Chautauqua	1.0	0.0	0.3	4.0	0.5	0.2	0.8	10.2	5.9	2.9	697	604
Cherokee	3.2	1.6	0.9	26.0	3.8	1.3	1.5	45.0	25.8	12.7	576	454
Cheyenne	0.8	0.0	0.2	1.8	0.2	0.1	1.8	9.0	4.2	3.8	1 209	997
Clark	0.5	0.0	0.1	0.7	0.1	0.1	2.8	18.9	3.9	5.1	2 158	2 128
Clay	2.3	0.4	0.8	3.7	2.4	0.3	2.2	31.7	10.6	8.2	945	827
Cloud	2.8	1.8	0.7	9.9	0.9	0.2	9.2	36.4	17.1	11.3	1 141	946
Coffey	2.4	0.4	0.5	2.9	0.6	0.5	-0.1	51.5	8.7	28.7	3 224	3 201
Comanche	0.5	0.0	0.1	1.1	0.1	0.1	2.4	9.6	2.0	4.1	2 087	1 973
Cowley	6.5	86.1	6.4	21.4	4.7	3.2	9.5	130.6	56.8	30.3	832	713
Crawford	8.1	0.1	3.1	38.7	9.0	2.5	23.0	92.6	40.6	31.2	820	528
Decatur	1.2	0.0	0.3	1.5	0.3	0.2	3.4	10.4	4.4	4.0	1 168	1 079
Dickinson	6.0	0.1	1.8	10.2	2.0	0.5	6.1	55.7	25.2	15.8	828	700
Doniphan	1.9	0.0	1.2	7.0	1.0	1.0	1.4	31.9	17.9	6.1	737	618
Douglas	31.1	10.9	4.0	56.3	7.1	35.3	38.8	308.3	70.1	106.8	1 044	743
Edwards	1.3	0.0	0.3	3.3	0.3	0.1	1.0	10.0	3.8	5.2	1 568	1 471
Elk	1.2	0.0	0.3	3.3	0.4	0.2	4.9	13.3	6.9	2.8	894	819
Ellis	10.5	0.2	1.4	11.7	2.7	0.9	10.5	63.5	27.4	26.0	955	780
Ellsworth	1.4	0.4	0.3	1.8	0.4	0.2	3.1	19.7	8.0	9.4	1 457	1 302
Finney	7.5	0.0	1.1	13.8	3.7	3.0	4.5	142.6	57.2	52.9	1 331	1 086
Ford	13.1	0.0	1.4	9.1	5.0	3.3	7.1	106.8	50.1	39.4	1 206	921
Franklin	5.3	0.3	1.0	13.5	4.6	0.7	6.2	87.9	32.1	25.1	990	714
Geary	460.1	49.3	0.9	15.6	6.6	11.5	3.6	112.4	45.7	22.7	858	556
Gove	1.0	0.0	0.3	0.7	0.1	0.2	5.3	17.9	6.6	3.9	1 289	1 142
Graham	1.2	0.0	0.3	2.2	0.3	0.1	2.1	13.9	3.6	4.0	1 411	1 323
Grant	1.0	0.0	1.9	1.1	0.8	0.5	1.7	29.2	5.1	20.9	2 648	2 545
Gray	1.2	0.0	0.2	2.2	0.4	0.2	1.6	18.4	8.7	7.9	1 306	1 190
Greeley	0.4	0.0	0.1	1.7	0.1	0.1	3.7	6.6	2.0	4.0	2 727	2 607
Greenwood	2.6	0.0	0.6	6.6	0.9	0.3	8.6	18.6	9.0	7.7	1 002	915
Hamilton	0.4	0.0	0.1	0.7	0.2	0.1	3.9	11.4	3.2	6.9	2 604	2 459
Harper	2.0	0.3	0.5	2.9	0.6	0.2	2.6	30.4	8.5	8.7	1 380	1 238
Harvey	4.7	0.2	1.2	7.7	2.8	0.8	18.8	84.5	36.3	29.8	894	673
Haskell	0.9	0.0	0.1	1.1	0.3	0.7	0.9	20.8	3.5	11.6	2 713	2 609
Hodgeman	0.8	0.0	0.2	0.7	0.1	0.1	1.6	11.9	3.5	3.6	1 666	1 529
Jackson	3.7	0.0	0.9	5.9	1.8	1.7	1.8	31.4	18.4	8.6	675	556
Jefferson	4.0	1.0	0.9	4.1	1.3	0.5	2.5	49.1	28.2	15.6	833	759
Jewell	1.9	0.0	0.4	3.7	0.3	0.1	3.0	15.4	5.6	4.9	1 407	1 234
Johnson	278.1	46.9	190.5	53.7	13.9	5.9	51.9	1 544.1	410.6	782.7	1 643	1 194
Kearny	0.5	0.0	0.1	1.8	0.5	0.2	14.3	26.2	4.5	14.6	3 219	3 142
Kingman	2.1	0.0	0.5	2.6	0.6	0.3	4.4	22.7	11.5	8.2	976	959
Kiowa	1.3	0.0	0.3	1.5	0.3	0.2	1.0	11.2	4.2	5.4	1 748	1 642
Labette	4.9	17.1	1.1	24.2	3.2	2.5	1.3	89.5	30.6	18.5	830	626
Lane	0.5	0.0	0.1	2.6	0.1	0.1	3.3	10.3	3.0	3.7	1 871	1 791
Leavenworth	258.0	123.9	375.1	21.6	5.3	10.8	15.5	161.5	81.0	56.6	799	635
Lincoln	1.5	0.1	0.3	1.5	0.3	0.1	3.5	14.5	4.5	4.5	1 256	1 166
Linn	2.5	0.0	1.1	7.7	0.9	0.4	0.8	32.6	12.6	14.6	1 509	1 471
Logan	0.7	0.0	0.1	0.7	1.6	0.1	4.0	13.5	4.3	4.4	1 462	1 333
Lyon	8.8	0.6	1.3	10.5	2.8	5.1	39.3	144.2	45.9	28.2	785	625
McPherson	4.9	2.3	1.2	7.0	2.6	0.4	1.3	79.6	31.6	32.1	1 092	924
Marion	3.6	0.2	0.9	5.1	0.8	0.3	4.2	35.7	17.7	12.5	946	825
Marshall	3.6	2.2	0.8	7.8	0.9	0.3	7.1	32.1	16.3	11.2	1 059	954
Meade	0.7	0.0	0.1	1.8	0.2	0.2	0.6	22.6	4.2	8.2	1 782	1 633
Miami	4.2	0.1	2.3	11.0	1.8	0.5	7.3	66.6	28.5	29.0	1 005	834
Mitchell	2.0	0.0	0.5	3.7	0.6	0.2	2.8	23.4	10.1	8.8	1 321	1 062
Montgomery	9.0	0.4	1.9	37.0	5.6	2.6	4.9	143.3	40.6	34.0	964	668
Morris	2.0	1.3	0.4	2.9	0.5	0.6	2.2	11.9	6.7	3.7	612	499
Morton	0.9	0.0	0.1	0.7	0.3	0.5	2.8	29.8	4.6	10.8	3 225	3 106
Nemaha	3.5	0.0	1.1	5.1	0.7	0.3	4.2	26.7	13.5	8.9	848	737
Neosho	3.7	0.9	0.8	10.6	1.9	1.3	8.6	65.0	22.9	13.0	784	509
Ness	1.7	0.0	0.4	1.1	0.2	0.1	2.2	16.1	4.4	5.2	1 554	1 505
Norton	1.6	0.0	0.9	2.2	0.4	0.2	9.9	23.5	7.4	7.6	1 299	1 234

1. State totals may include programs not allocated by county.   2. Based on the resident population estimated as of July 1 of the year shown.

Table B. States and Counties — Local Government Finances, Government Employment, and Elections

STATE County	Total (mil dol)	Per capita[1] (dollars)	Educa-tion	Health and hospitals	Police protec-tion	Public welfare	High-ways	Total (mil dol)	Per capita[1] (dollars)	Federal civilian	Federal military	State and local	Demo-cratic	Republi-can	All other
	183	184	185	186	187	188	189	190	191	192	193	194	195	196	197
KANSAS—Cont'd															
Barber	26.0	5 116	29.4	39.8	2.5	0.0	9.9	6.0	1 190	32	14	662	24.7	73.9	1.4
Barton	99.5	3 585	60.6	2.1	3.3	0.0	5.7	74.8	2 697	91	78	2 495	24.6	74.0	1.4
Bourbon	41.1	2 712	65.4	0.5	3.5	0.1	6.4	29.2	1 922	94	42	1 172	33.2	65.4	1.5
Brown	25.1	2 392	52.7	1.4	4.5	0.0	14.4	20.8	1 979	65	29	1 935	28.5	70.2	1.3
Butler	198.8	3 285	63.4	1.2	2.9	0.0	6.0	259.8	4 292	134	169	4 965	28.4	70.3	1.3
Chase	11.0	3 751	38.3	2.0	2.8	0.0	8.8	4.0	1 356	36	0	271	27.8	70.3	1.9
Chautauqua	10.7	2 538	52.4	6.4	3.4	0.0	9.1	3.3	786	19	12	275	20.8	77.8	1.4
Cherokee	44.2	2 013	63.7	2.1	5.3	0.0	7.7	10.4	474	58	61	1 294	37.5	61.4	1.1
Cheyenne	8.5	2 731	60.6	0.2	2.9	0.0	13.1	0.1	27	22	0	250	18.8	80.0	1.1
Clark	19.6	8 223	24.2	54.4	2.3	0.0	5.6	1.7	711	15	0	446	20.0	78.5	1.6
Clay	30.5	3 506	35.2	29.5	3.1	0.0	9.0	15.1	1 736	41	24	849	19.7	79.2	1.1
Cloud	37.0	3 723	67.4	2.1	2.7	0.0	6.3	13.3	1 340	47	28	917	26.9	71.5	1.6
Coffey	50.0	5 620	34.1	27.1	3.0	0.0	9.5	15.6	1 750	45	25	1 132	24.8	73.9	1.2
Comanche	9.5	4 782	32.2	28.5	2.9	0.0	9.7	1.5	766	14	0	298	20.3	78.5	1.1
Cowley	131.1	3 599	49.5	21.8	2.5	0.0	4.2	68.1	1 868	117	102	3 752	33.4	65.1	1.5
Crawford	88.5	2 326	49.2	13.3	5.8	0.0	5.2	57.8	1 519	128	110	4 867	46.2	52.1	1.7
Decatur	10.3	3 026	54.1	2.3	3.0	0.0	12.8	1.8	533	27	10	358	20.4	77.9	1.7
Dickinson	54.8	2 861	50.7	16.9	3.8	0.0	8.3	24.4	1 277	112	54	1 528	26.8	71.7	1.5
Doniphan	30.9	3 758	68.0	2.7	1.4	0.0	7.6	9.1	1 111	39	23	838	29.5	69.2	1.2
Douglas	294.3	2 876	32.9	29.8	4.6	0.1	4.0	258.6	2 528	554	332	15 516	56.7	41.4	1.8
Edwards	9.8	2 930	45.7	8.8	1.8	0.0	13.7	1.4	423	28	0	246	25.9	72.4	1.7
Elk	12.9	4 103	55.7	1.7	0.5	18.1	6.3	2.7	850	22	0	388	24.3	73.9	1.8
Ellis	66.3	2 430	49.2	2.7	4.6	0.0	7.6	30.6	1 122	167	76	3 511	33.2	64.7	2.1
Ellsworth	19.9	3 103	52.5	4.3	3.8	0.0	10.8	21.9	3 417	27	18	868	25.8	72.9	1.3
Finney	134.7	3 390	62.4	1.0	5.5	0.0	5.0	110.6	2 783	136	112	3 210	23.6	75.4	1.0
Ford	107.3	3 286	54.2	2.5	3.7	0.0	4.5	89.9	2 753	237	92	2 459	25.2	73.7	1.1
Franklin	84.2	3 326	39.0	21.1	3.4	1.7	5.3	45.8	1 808	88	71	1 749	34.2	64.3	1.4
Geary	106.2	4 022	45.2	25.6	5.2	0.0	3.1	48.9	1 853	2 097	10 316	2 391	34.4	64.3	1.3
Gove	17.5	5 855	38.1	35.1	1.6	0.0	5.8	3.6	1 215	24	0	479	16.9	81.5	1.7
Graham	12.8	4 512	28.7	37.2	1.3	0.0	10.2	1.9	657	31	0	381	23.2	75.1	1.7
Grant	27.4	3 464	41.5	8.8	4.4	0.0	12.3	16.8	2 134	23	22	788	20.7	78.4	0.9
Gray	18.2	3 004	58.1	2.4	3.8	0.0	12.2	10.9	1 803	25	17	951	18.1	80.9	1.0
Greeley	5.9	4 001	45.2	4.9	4.0	0.0	14.1	5.0	3 404	14	0	183	18.8	79.4	1.8
Greenwood	18.6	2 431	51.8	2.1	5.0	0.0	12.8	14.1	1 844	51	21	508	28.1	70.3	1.6
Hamilton	10.3	3 889	45.6	2.4	6.9	0.0	9.5	8.8	3 321	15	0	395	20.0	78.9	1.1
Harper	30.4	4 842	29.2	41.4	2.5	0.0	8.4	12.0	1 910	43	18	913	24.8	73.5	1.6
Harvey	80.3	2 407	51.3	2.0	4.9	0.1	6.8	114.0	3 414	82	93	1 921	35.3	63.1	1.6
Haskell	21.5	5 014	35.1	27.7	3.4	0.0	15.9	11.2	2 603	22	12	535	14.3	84.7	1.0
Hodgeman	12.0	5 596	32.4	38.1	2.3	0.0	9.1	0.0	0	18	0	332	18.9	80.6	0.5
Jackson	31.6	2 484	61.1	0.6	7.8	0.0	7.8	19.6	1 538	59	36	1 178	34.9	63.5	1.6
Jefferson	45.9	2 462	66.8	3.4	4.5	0.0	7.5	24.9	1 333	72	52	1 171	37.1	61.4	1.5
Jewell	13.1	3 742	43.0	12.8	2.1	0.0	12.9	1.3	380	35	10	470	20.1	78.1	1.8
Johnson	1 450.6	3 044	46.2	2.9	7.6	1.3	6.5	2 327.5	4 884	4 009	1 337	24 828	37.8	61.2	1.0
Kearny	23.4	5 147	39.5	25.6	4.4	0.0	7.9	13.5	2 978	18	13	645	18.9	80.7	0.4
Kingman	24.4	2 899	43.6	2.7	3.5	0.0	12.7	22.8	2 708	43	24	595	24.0	74.4	1.6
Kiowa	11.2	3 604	57.8	2.4	2.0	0.0	11.5	3.2	1 038	24	0	388	16.5	81.4	2.2
Labette	92.6	4 155	42.9	34.1	2.6	0.0	4.3	29.1	1 306	87	62	2 840	39.6	59.1	1.4
Lane	10.9	5 432	35.1	35.3	3.1	0.0	5.8	2.9	1 471	15	0	311	17.8	81.2	1.0
Leavenworth	153.1	2 163	56.5	1.4	5.1	1.5	5.7	123.9	1 751	3 075	3 206	3 960	40.4	58.4	1.2
Lincoln	14.3	4 038	34.0	32.6	2.8	0.0	9.4	3.3	936	38	10	426	21.9	75.8	2.3
Linn	31.4	3 242	53.4	1.7	3.7	0.0	7.2	31.0	3 207	44	27	748	34.6	64.1	1.3
Logan	13.9	4 632	38.3	30.7	3.4	0.0	8.0	1.3	443	22	0	454	16.3	82.4	1.3
Lyon	137.6	3 834	36.6	29.9	3.5	0.0	4.7	121.8	3 393	152	101	4 678	38.9	59.2	1.9
McPherson	81.5	2 771	46.6	2.8	3.5	0.0	12.6	112.8	3 835	97	82	1 850	27.0	71.7	1.3
Marion	34.9	2 637	55.5	2.7	3.3	0.0	11.5	28.4	2 141	70	37	1 113	25.0	73.3	1.7
Marshall	32.1	3 036	59.5	1.3	3.0	0.0	10.6	15.1	1 429	65	30	887	34.9	64.0	1.1
Meade	21.8	4 727	26.8	23.5	2.6	15.6	10.2	9.8	2 128	16	13	534	16.7	82.5	0.8
Miami	64.3	2 225	52.9	1.2	6.3	0.0	10.5	90.1	3 117	70	81	2 080	34.7	64.1	1.1
Mitchell	23.2	3 466	52.6	4.1	4.8	0.0	9.8	3.3	488	41	19	810	20.8	77.9	1.4
Montgomery	134.5	3 808	47.0	23.3	2.7	0.0	3.6	93.2	2 640	150	99	2 819	30.7	68.1	1.3
Morris	10.8	1 768	63.8	1.6	3.9	0.0	2.7	4.7	771	38	17	518	31.7	66.9	1.5
Morton	25.1	7 461	32.0	44.4	1.1	0.0	5.6	6.7	1 994	22	0	604	17.8	81.4	0.8
Nemaha	26.1	2 498	53.2	1.7	1.8	0.2	14.4	14.7	1 406	67	29	735	24.8	73.7	1.5
Neosho	68.3	4 102	42.9	26.6	2.5	0.0	5.0	83.2	5 003	66	47	1 655	33.4	65.2	1.4
Ness	17.0	5 112	31.1	41.1	2.6	0.2	8.5	2.4	732	33	0	514	21.1	77.4	1.5
Norton	21.8	3 709	36.0	31.5	1.4	0.0	7.8	2.5	422	36	16	875	18.3	80.3	1.3

1. Based on the resident population estimated as of July 1 of the year shown.

STATE/ County code	CBSA code[1]	County Type[2]	STATE County	Land area,[3] (sq km) 2000	Population and population characteristics, 2003												
								Race alone or in combination, not Hispanic or Latino (percent)					Age (percent)					
					Total persons	Rank	Per square kilometer	White	Black	Am. Indian, Alaska Native	Asian and Pacific Islander	Percent Hispanic or Latino[4]	Under 5 years	5 to 17 years	18 to 24 years	25 to 34 years	35 to 44 years	45 to 54 years
				1	2	3	4	5	6	7	8	9	10	11	12	13	14	15
			KANSAS—Cont'd															
20 139	45820	3	Osage	1 822	16 784	1 977	9.2	97.2	0.6	1.2	0.4	1.7	5.1	19.5	9.1	10.0	15.5	14.5
20 141	...	9	Osborne	2 311	4 179	2 899	1.8	99.1	0.1	0.2	0.3	0.4	4.3	17.3	7.1	7.0	14.0	15.3
20 143	41460	9	Ottawa	1 868	6 177	2 757	3.3	97.2	0.6	0.7	0.3	1.7	6.1	17.5	9.2	9.8	15.4	15.0
20 145	...	7	Pawnee	1 953	6 796	2 705	3.5	88.9	5.4	0.9	0.6	4.5	5.1	17.6	9.0	9.8	14.2	16.1
20 147	...	7	Phillips	2 295	5 657	2 797	2.5	97.9	0.3	0.5	0.5	1.1	4.9	17.3	7.5	8.7	13.8	15.7
20 149	31740	6	Pottawatomie	2 187	18 714	1 875	8.6	95.7	1.1	1.4	0.7	2.5	6.9	20.6	9.8	11.3	15.0	13.9
20 151	...	7	Pratt	1 904	9 437	2 493	5.0	94.8	1.2	0.5	0.5	3.4	5.7	16.7	12.0	9.3	13.9	15.1
20 153	...	9	Rawlins	2 770	2 843	2 996	1.0	98.5	0.5	0.3	0.1	0.9	4.2	16.5	7.7	6.3	13.9	15.3
20 155	26740	4	Reno	3 249	63 832	776	19.6	90.2	3.1	1.2	0.8	6.0	6.5	17.0	10.4	11.2	14.3	14.5
20 157	...	9	Republic	1 855	5 307	2 820	2.9	98.0	0.4	0.4	0.2	1.2	4.3	15.5	6.8	6.7	13.6	16.0
20 159	...	7	Rice	1 882	10 412	2 409	5.5	91.0	1.3	1.1	0.6	6.8	6.3	17.0	15.0	8.6	13.0	13.2
20 161	31740	5	Riley	1 579	62 291	796	39.4	84.1	7.6	1.2	4.6	4.6	6.6	12.7	27.2	17.7	10.0	8.9
20 163	...	9	Rooks	2 301	5 417	2 816	2.4	96.9	1.3	0.5	0.2	1.2	5.7	18.1	7.9	9.5	15.0	13.6
20 165	...	9	Rush	1 860	3 418	2 865	1.8	98.0	0.3	0.4	0.3	1.1	4.8	16.1	7.1	8.6	13.5	15.9
20 167	...	7	Russell	2 291	6 907	2 697	3.0	97.0	1.0	0.7	0.4	1.2	4.9	15.5	8.1	7.7	14.1	14.8
20 169	41460	5	Saline	1 864	53 737	893	28.8	87.7	3.8	1.0	2.3	6.9	6.9	18.5	10.0	12.5	14.8	14.2
20 171	...	7	Scott	1 858	4 806	2 855	2.6	91.9	0.3	0.3	0.1	7.6	6.1	19.1	9.0	9.4	14.6	16.8
20 173	48620	2	Sedgwick	2 588	462 896	132	178.9	76.7	10.1	1.9	4.4	9.1	7.8	19.8	9.8	13.9	15.1	13.8
20 175	30580	7	Seward	1 656	23 091	1 661	13.9	44.4	3.5	0.9	3.0	48.7	10.0	22.0	12.0	15.3	14.0	11.2
20 177	45820	3	Shawnee	1 424	170 902	332	120.0	80.7	10.0	1.9	1.5	8.0	7.0	17.9	9.5	12.5	14.6	15.1
20 179	...	7	Sheridan	2 322	2 662	3 009	1.1	98.2	0.3	0.0	0.2	1.5	5.1	19.0	8.2	6.6	14.5	15.7
20 181	...	7	Sherman	2 735	6 277	2 749	2.3	90.7	0.6	0.5	0.4	8.1	5.8	16.9	12.6	9.5	13.1	14.4
20 183	...	9	Smith	2 319	4 181	2 898	1.8	98.5	0.3	0.3	0.2	1.0	3.4	16.1	7.0	7.0	13.9	14.5
20 185	...	7	Stafford	2 051	4 589	2 865	2.2	92.6	0.3	0.5	0.3	6.9	5.6	18.7	7.9	7.7	15.5	14.5
20 187	...	9	Stanton	1 761	2 404	3 027	1.4	70.3	0.2	1.2	0.3	28.2	8.2	20.7	9.4	11.9	15.0	12.9
20 189	...	7	Stevens	1 884	5 389	2 817	2.9	75.0	0.8	1.0	0.3	22.9	8.2	21.5	10.2	10.9	14.8	12.4
20 191	48620	2	Sumner	3 061	25 256	1 559	8.3	94.2	1.2	2.1	0.4	3.6	6.4	20.1	9.5	9.5	14.9	15.2
20 193	...	7	Thomas	2 784	7 933	2 598	2.8	96.8	0.6	0.7	0.4	2.1	5.9	18.3	14.6	10.0	13.6	14.2
20 195	...	9	Trego	2 301	3 103	2 977	1.3	98.0	0.4	0.8	0.5	0.8	4.6	15.9	8.8	7.0	14.0	15.4
20 197	45820	3	Wabaunsee	2 065	6 767	2 708	3.3	96.8	0.5	1.1	0.1	2.0	6.0	18.2	9.2	9.2	15.9	15.7
20 199	...	9	Wallace	2 367	1 621	3 081	0.7	92.2	0.7	0.9	0.3	5.9	5.7	20.0	10.2	6.9	14.3	16.0
20 201	...	9	Washington	2 327	6 131	2 762	2.6	98.6	0.4	0.3	0.1	1.0	5.4	17.0	7.7	8.2	13.7	13.8
20 203	...	9	Wichita	1 861	2 447	3 026	1.3	78.1	0.2	0.9	0.1	21.0	6.0	20.2	8.2	11.9	14.4	14.6
20 205	...	7	Wilson	1 486	10 080	2 435	6.8	96.6	0.5	1.6	0.3	1.8	5.3	18.3	9.1	9.7	13.6	14.2
20 207	...	9	Woodson	1 297	3 631	2 936	2.8	96.9	0.8	0.9	0.1	1.4	4.6	15.0	9.7	7.8	13.3	15.1
20 209	28140	1	Wyandotte	392	157 092	352	400.7	50.2	28.8	1.3	2.2	19.2	8.4	19.9	10.3	14.4	14.7	12.9
21 000	...	X	KENTUCKY	102 896	4 117 827	X	40.0	89.6	7.9	0.6	1.2	1.7	6.6	17.6	10.0	13.7	15.1	14.4
21 001	...	7	Adair	1 054	17 458	1 937	16.6	95.7	3.2	0.6	0.4	0.8	5.9	16.8	11.6	12.1	14.4	13.5
21 003	...	6	Allen	896	18 262	1 892	20.4	97.7	1.2	0.4	0.2	1.0	6.4	18.3	9.8	13.4	14.8	13.0
21 005	23180	6	Anderson	525	19 812	1 814	37.7	96.5	2.6	0.3	0.2	0.9	6.5	19.4	7.9	13.9	16.8	14.4
21 007	37140	9	Ballard	651	8 193	2 584	12.6	95.8	3.4	0.9	0.3	0.8	5.4	16.9	8.3	11.7	14.5	14.8
21 009	23980	6	Barren	1 272	39 133	1 153	30.8	94.3	4.3	0.4	0.6	1.1	6.3	17.4	8.9	12.7	14.8	14.0
21 011	34660	8	Bath	724	11 413	2 341	15.8	97.2	1.9	0.5	0.1	0.9	6.8	17.2	9.1	13.3	14.6	14.4
21 013	33180	7	Bell	934	29 953	1 405	32.1	96.1	2.7	0.8	0.4	0.7	5.9	17.5	9.6	13.1	14.9	14.2
21 015	17140	1	Boone	638	97 139	555	152.3	93.9	2.3	0.6	2.0	2.2	7.7	20.1	9.7	14.5	16.6	13.5
21 017	30460	2	Bourbon	755	19 598	1 830	26.0	89.7	7.3	0.3	0.1	3.3	6.3	18.4	8.7	11.9	15.5	14.8
21 019	26580	2	Boyd	415	49 554	939	119.4	95.6	2.9	0.7	0.3	1.3	5.3	15.8	9.0	12.7	15.1	15.3
21 021	19220	7	Boyle	471	27 837	1 472	59.1	88.1	9.7	0.5	1.0	1.6	5.4	16.7	11.8	12.5	14.7	14.4
21 023	17140	1	Bracken	526	8 487	2 564	16.1	98.4	0.7	0.4	0.1	0.6	6.4	18.4	9.4	13.2	15.2	13.8
21 025	...	7	Breathitt	1 283	15 850	2 041	12.4	98.4	0.4	0.3	0.4	0.7	5.1	18.8	10.6	12.5	15.6	15.3
21 027	...	8	Breckinridge	1 483	19 011	1 861	12.8	96.4	2.7	0.6	0.1	0.9	5.7	18.0	9.5	11.5	14.6	14.7
21 029	31140	1	Bullitt	775	64 909	763	83.8	98.2	0.7	0.7	0.5	0.7	6.2	19.3	9.8	14.2	16.7	14.5
21 031	...	6	Butler	1 109	13 199	2 222	11.9	97.4	0.5	0.6	0.3	1.5	6.2	17.8	9.8	13.2	15.1	13.8
21 033	...	6	Caldwell	899	12 824	2 253	14.3	94.1	5.0	0.3	0.4	0.6	5.3	16.1	8.3	11.5	13.5	15.0
21 035	34660	7	Calloway	1 000	34 671	1 284	34.7	92.8	3.9	0.4	1.9	1.6	4.9	13.3	17.5	13.3	12.1	12.0
21 037	17140	1	Campbell	393	87 970	608	223.8	96.3	2.2	0.5	0.8	1.0	6.9	18.3	9.8	13.5	16.0	14.0
21 039	...	9	Carlisle	499	5 384	2 818	10.8	97.5	1.3	0.5	0.1	1.0	6.5	16.2	9.1	11.1	14.4	14.5
21 041	...	6	Carroll	337	10 230	2 424	30.4	93.9	2.3	0.4	0.3	3.7	6.9	17.8	9.6	13.6	15.7	14.0
21 043	...	6	Carter	1 063	27 144	1 500	25.5	98.9	0.2	0.5	0.2	0.6	6.3	17.6	10.8	13.5	14.5	13.7
21 045	...	9	Casey	1 154	15 977	2 032	13.8	97.5	0.4	0.4	0.1	1.8	6.3	17.5	9.3	12.4	13.9	13.7
21 047	17300	3	Christian	1 868	69 912	724	37.4	67.8	26.8	1.2	2.3	4.5	10.5	19.3	13.4	18.1	12.8	9.7
21 049	30460	2	Clark	659	33 958	1 304	51.5	93.3	5.0	0.4	0.4	1.4	6.3	17.7	8.7	13.3	15.8	14.6
21 051	...	7	Clay	1 220	24 346	1 604	20.0	93.5	4.8	0.5	0.2	1.4	5.9	18.5	9.6	15.4	16.6	13.8
21 053	...	9	Clinton	511	9 605	2 479	18.8	97.6	0.1	0.3	0.0	2.0	6.4	15.7	8.8	12.5	14.7	13.9
21 055	...	6	Crittenden	938	9 092	2 517	9.7	98.3	0.8	0.4	0.3	0.7	4.7	17.0	9.0	10.7	14.4	14.6

1. CBSA = Core Based Statistical Area. See Appendix A for explanation. See Appendix B for list of metropolitan areas with component counties.
Service of USDA Rural-Urban Continuum Codes. See Appendix A for definition. 3. Dry land or land partially or temporarily covered by water.   2. County type code from the Economic Research   4. Hispanic or Latino persons may be of any race.

Table B. States and Counties — Population and Households

	Population, 2003 (cont'd)				Population — change and components of change, 1990–2003							Households, 2000				
	Age (percent) (cont'd)				Total persons		Percent change		Components of change, 2000–2003						Percent	
STATE County	55 to 64 years	65 to 74 years	75 years and over	Percent female	1990	2000	1990–2000	2000–2003	Births	Deaths	Net migration	Number	Percent change, 1990–2000	Persons per household	Female family householder[1]	One person
	16	17	18	19	20	21	22	23	24	25	26	27	28	29	30	31
KANSAS—Cont'd																
Osage	10.6	8.0	7.7	50.9	15 248	16 712	9.6	0.4	524	604	165	6 490	11.8	2.54	8.1	23.5
Osborne	10.0	10.7	15.8	49.6	4 867	4 452	-8.5	-6.1	107	230	-154	1 940	-5.7	2.23	5.2	35.2
Ottawa	10.3	8.3	8.8	49.6	5 634	6 163	9.4	0.2	254	267	33	2 430	7.2	2.46	6.3	25.7
Pawnee	10.8	8.3	10.6	46.8	7 555	7 233	-4.3	-6.0	201	309	-330	2 739	-6.3	2.31	7.3	32.2
Phillips	11.0	9.7	12.8	51.5	6 590	6 001	-8.9	-5.7	196	286	-260	2 496	-7.4	2.35	5.5	28.6
Pottawatomie	8.8	6.4	6.6	50.2	16 128	18 209	12.9	2.8	846	544	218	6 771	14.0	2.65	7.2	23.2
Pratt	9.5	8.4	10.6	51.3	9 702	9 647	-0.6	-2.2	346	412	-139	3 963	0.7	2.35	7.5	30.4
Rawlins	11.7	11.7	14.2	50.1	3 404	2 966	-12.9	-4.1	76	142	-56	1 269	-6.8	2.29	4.9	31.4
Reno	9.8	7.7	8.9	49.8	62 389	64 790	3.8	-1.5	2 742	2 280	-1 415	25 498	5.2	2.41	8.7	27.9
Republic	11.9	12.3	14.9	51.8	6 482	5 835	-10.0	-9.0	149	352	-328	2 557	-7.7	2.23	4.8	31.8
Rice	9.6	8.7	9.4	51.7	10 610	10 761	1.4	-3.2	445	444	-345	4 050	-2.8	2.44	7.2	27.8
Riley	5.2	3.6	4.0	46.5	67 139	62 843	-6.4	-0.9	2 961	1 079	-2 524	22 137	4.0	2.42	6.8	27.5
Rooks	9.9	10.1	11.5	50.3	6 039	5 685	-5.9	-4.7	205	250	-218	2 362	-3.4	2.32	7.2	31.8
Rush	11.0	10.5	14.2	51.2	3 842	3 551	-7.6	-3.7	102	186	-47	1 548	-5.7	2.24	5.8	31.7
Russell	11.5	10.9	13.9	51.7	7 835	7 370	-5.9	-6.3	208	338	-332	3 207	-4.9	2.23	7.1	32.8
Saline	9.2	6.9	7.1	50.5	49 301	53 597	8.7	0.3	2 447	1 683	-596	21 436	8.1	2.43	9.7	28.3
Scott	10.6	7.4	9.0	50.6	5 289	5 120	-3.2	-6.1	189	152	-342	2 045	1.1	2.46	6.7	27.3
Sedgwick	8.1	5.7	5.5	50.4	403 662	452 869	12.2	2.2	24 194	12 007	-1 900	176 444	12.7	2.53	10.9	28.2
Seward	6.6	4.5	4.2	48.4	18 743	22 510	20.1	2.6	1 636	520	-576	7 419	12.2	2.98	10.0	20.6
Shawnee	9.7	6.9	6.8	51.3	160 976	169 871	5.5	0.6	7 906	5 805	-940	68 920	8.1	2.39	11.6	29.8
Sheridan	10.6	10.9	9.9	49.7	3 043	2 813	-7.6	-5.4	97	130	-118	1 124	-4.0	2.46	4.5	27.6
Sherman	10.9	8.8	9.3	48.9	6 926	6 760	-2.4	-7.1	242	224	-512	2 758	0.9	2.40	6.0	29.2
Smith	11.4	12.1	16.2	51.8	5 078	4 536	-10.7	-7.8	98	255	-193	1 953	-9.8	2.27	4.7	30.2
Stafford	10.1	9.7	11.4	51.2	5 365	4 789	-10.7	-4.2	158	227	-130	2 010	-8.8	2.34	5.9	33.0
Stanton	8.1	7.6	6.2	48.8	2 333	2 406	3.1	-0.1	140	61	-87	858	3.2	2.74	6.8	22.6
Stevens	8.7	6.3	7.0	51.1	5 048	5 463	8.2	-1.4	288	196	-170	1 988	5.5	2.72	7.1	24.3
Sumner	9.4	7.5	8.5	50.9	25 841	25 946	0.4	-2.7	1 060	833	-924	9 888	2.1	2.58	8.0	25.6
Thomas	8.7	7.2	8.1	51.5	8 258	8 180	-0.9	-3.0	318	252	-314	3 226	3.3	2.45	6.9	28.4
Trego	10.3	11.8	13.8	51.9	3 694	3 319	-10.2	-6.5	102	154	-167	1 412	-3.6	2.27	6.3	31.4
Wabaunsee	10.4	8.4	7.3	49.2	6 603	6 885	4.3	-1.7	247	246	-111	2 633	6.1	2.57	6.3	23.0
Wallace	9.9	9.3	9.9	51.2	1 821	1 749	-4.0	-7.3	72	68	-135	674	-0.4	2.56	4.0	27.6
Washington	11.2	10.7	14.1	49.3	7 073	6 483	-8.3	-5.4	204	355	-195	2 673	-6.6	2.35	4.2	31.2
Wichita	9.7	7.7	8.6	48.0	2 758	2 531	-8.2	-3.3	84	79	-85	967	-2.9	2.59	5.8	23.7
Wilson	10.7	8.9	10.7	51.2	10 289	10 332	0.4	-2.4	321	469	-94	4 203	0.2	2.40	7.8	29.1
Woodson	11.0	10.5	13.8	50.9	4 116	3 788	-8.0	-4.1	98	196	-61	1 642	-3.4	2.24	7.4	33.3
Wyandotte	8.3	5.8	5.6	51.1	162 026	157 882	-2.6	-0.5	9 173	5 062	-4 949	59 700	-2.9	2.62	17.8	28.9
KENTUCKY	10.2	6.6	5.8	51.0	3 686 892	4 041 769	9.6	1.9	177 581	130 520	30 493	1 590 647	15.3	2.47	11.8	26.0
Adair	10.7	7.8	6.9	51.3	15 360	17 244	12.3	1.2	695	539	81	6 747	16.3	2.44	10.2	26.2
Allen	10.4	7.3	6.1	51.0	14 628	17 800	21.7	2.6	721	599	353	6 910	23.5	2.55	9.8	23.1
Anderson	9.3	5.9	5.0	51.0	14 571	19 111	31.2	3.7	771	522	452	7 320	34.6	2.59	9.2	20.5
Ballard	12.2	8.2	7.8	50.0	7 902	8 286	4.9	-1.1	278	349	-22	3 395	6.4	2.39	8.0	25.8
Barren	10.7	7.6	7.0	51.7	34 001	38 033	11.9	2.9	1 587	1 412	937	15 346	16.8	2.44	9.8	25.6
Bath	10.0	7.9	6.4	50.7	9 692	11 085	14.4	3.0	505	429	254	4 445	21.5	2.47	10.3	25.3
Bell	11.0	7.2	6.4	51.9	31 506	30 060	-4.6	-0.4	1 173	1 167	-105	12 004	4.3	2.44	15.7	26.8
Boone	8.0	4.6	3.2	50.4	57 589	85 991	49.3	13.0	4 733	1 763	8 022	31 258	55.3	2.73	9.8	20.2
Bourbon	10.6	7.1	6.4	51.5	19 236	19 360	0.6	1.2	796	664	128	7 681	5.9	2.49	12.3	24.8
Boyd	11.4	8.4	7.1	50.8	51 096	49 752	-2.6	-0.4	1 719	2 004	146	20 010	0.7	2.38	11.6	26.5
Boyle	10.3	7.2	6.6	50.4	25 590	27 697	8.2	0.5	1 010	1 073	229	10 574	11.5	2.38	12.5	27.1
Bracken	9.8	7.4	5.9	50.6	7 766	8 279	6.6	2.5	340	299	171	3 228	12.4	2.55	10.7	23.9
Breathitt	10.4	6.9	4.9	50.8	15 703	16 100	2.5	-1.6	526	584	-176	6 170	11.1	2.54	14.2	23.8
Breckinridge	11.4	8.0	6.0	50.3	16 312	18 648	14.3	1.9	655	620	346	7 324	18.9	2.52	8.9	24.6
Bullitt	10.1	5.0	2.9	50.4	47 567	61 236	28.7	6.0	2 338	1 198	2 509	22 171	38.9	2.75	10.4	16.4
Butler	10.8	6.9	5.9	50.3	11 245	13 010	15.7	1.5	502	401	105	5 059	21.0	2.52	9.3	23.7
Caldwell	12.5	9.2	8.6	52.0	13 232	13 060	-1.3	-1.8	406	587	-42	5 431	3.0	2.36	9.8	27.5
Calloway	10.1	7.1	7.5	51.5	30 735	34 177	11.2	1.4	1 071	1 206	651	13 862	19.4	2.25	8.1	29.7
Campbell	9.0	6.6	6.1	51.7	83 866	88 616	5.7	-0.7	3 959	2 799	-1 784	34 742	11.5	2.49	12.3	28.6
Carlisle	10.4	9.6	8.2	51.3	5 238	5 351	2.2	0.6	211	238	72	2 208	4.8	2.40	9.3	26.3
Carroll	10.5	6.4	5.6	49.7	9 292	10 155	9.3	0.7	460	405	31	3 940	12.4	2.51	11.7	25.3
Carter	10.6	7.4	5.4	51.0	24 340	26 889	10.5	0.9	1 128	986	139	10 342	19.2	2.54	10.7	22.3
Casey	11.4	7.6	7.2	51.1	14 211	15 447	8.7	3.4	611	585	507	6 260	15.2	2.44	10.8	26.8
Christian	6.9	5.4	4.7	48.5	68 941	72 265	4.8	-3.3	5 143	1 901	-5 742	24 857	14.9	2.66	13.6	22.5
Clark	10.7	6.7	5.6	51.5	29 496	33 144	12.4	2.5	1 368	987	461	13 015	18.6	2.51	12.1	22.8
Clay	9.8	6.0	4.5	47.0	21 746	24 556	12.9	-0.9	1 017	743	-467	8 556	16.1	2.62	12.4	22.5
Clinton	12.5	8.5	7.0	51.8	9 135	9 634	5.5	-0.3	402	368	-46	4 086	13.8	2.34	9.7	28.4
Crittenden	13.3	8.7	8.0	51.7	9 196	9 384	2.0	-3.1	281	480	-86	3 829	5.0	2.42	8.9	27.0

1. No spouse present.

Items 16—31

Table B. States and Counties — Vital Statistics, Health Resources, and Crime

STATE County	Births, average 1999–2001 Total	Rate¹	Deaths, average 1999–2001 Number Total	Infant²	Deaths Rate Total¹	Infant³	Physicians,⁴ 2000 Number	Rate⁵	Hospitals,⁴ 1998 Number	Beds Number	Rate⁵	Medicare enrollees, 2003	Serious crimes known to police,⁶ 2002 Total Number	Rate⁷
	32	33	34	35	36	37	38	39	40	41	42	43	44	45
KANSAS—Cont'd														
Osage	179	10.7	183	1	11.0	D	6	36	0	0	0	2 955	418	2 802
Osborne	37	8.4	74	0	16.8	D	3	67	1	29	615	1 132	NA	NA
Ottawa	76	12.4	84	1	13.6	D	3	49	1	53	898	1 088	78	1 253
Pawnee	72	10.1	92	1	12.9	D	29	401	1	79	1 062	1 325	271	3 709
Phillips	66	11.0	84	1	14.1	D	7	117	1	62	1 020	1 363	22	363
Pottawatomie	260	14.3	173	2	9.5	D	11	60	3	109	583	2 586	317	1 723
Pratt	110	11.4	125	0	13.0	D	17	176	1	99	1 021	1 838	330	3 386
Rawlins	22	7.5	44	0	14.9	D	3	101	1	28	896	746	34	1 135
Reno	856	13.2	700	6	10.8	D	112	173	1	160	253	11 580	1 136	1 736
Republic	45	7.8	109	0	18.8	D	5	86	1	86	1 409	1 466	112	1 900
Rice	128	11.9	133	0	12.4	D	6	56	1	44	425	2 139	155	1 584
Riley	932	14.9	318	3	5.1	D	99	158	2	155	244	5 333	1 900	2 993
Rooks	61	10.8	78	0	13.8	D	5	88	1	27	477	1 272	31	540
Rush	37	10.3	58	0	16.4	D	2	56	1	76	2 227	950	NA	NA
Russell	68	9.2	106	0	14.5	D	4	54	1	60	794	1 884	196	2 632
Saline	738	13.8	495	5	9.2	D	111	207	1	187	362	8 497	3 177	5 916
Scott	66	12.9	54	0	10.6	D	4	78	1	27	538	442	128	2 475
Sedgwick	7 599	16.7	3 603	64	7.9	8.5	1 007	222	5	1 770	395	59 041	25 988	5 759
Seward	524	23.3	146	5	6.5	D	28	124	1	77	385	2 068	1 390	6 113
Shawnee	2 416	14.2	1 758	25	10.3	10.3	479	282	2	642	388	27 949	12 581	7 390
Sheridan	27	9.8	38	0	13.6	D	6	0	1	69	2 517	540	NA	NA
Sherman	85	12.7	72	1	10.8	D	6	89	1	49	753	1 245	259	3 793
Smith	28	6.2	79	0	17.4	D	4	88	1	54	1 177	1 209	NA	NA
Stafford	53	11.0	71	0	14.9	D	1	21	1	25	500	1 021	81	1 674
Stanton	43	17.7	20	0	8.3	D	1	42	1	46	2 031	371	13	535
Stevens	92	17.0	51	1	9.4	D	5	92	1	17	317	795	176	3 189
Sumner	327	12.6	282	1	10.9	D	16	62	2	118	436	4 727	657	2 887
Thomas	98	12.0	79	1	9.6	D	8	98	1	40	498	1 284	313	3 788
Trego	32	9.7	51	0	15.5	D	7	211	1	73	2 224	779	42	1 253
Wabaunsee	81	11.9	78	0	11.4	D	3	44	0	0	0	1 166	131	2 021
Wallace	22	12.4	20	0	11.4	D	1	57	0	0	0	345	7	396
Washington	67	10.4	103	0	15.9	D	2	31	2	75	1 156	1 663	36	550
Wichita	33	12.9	24	0	9.4	D	2	79	1	43	1 627	415	47	1 838
Wilson	116	11.2	153	0	14.8	D	9	87	2	80	783	2 063	143	1 370
Woodson	33	8.6	59	0	15.5	D	4	106	0	0	0	958	67	1 751
Wyandotte	2 797	17.7	1 573	25	9.9	8.8	499	316	3	1 102	723	21 531	NA	NA
KENTUCKY	55 030	13.6	39 562	379	9.8	6.9	7 010	173	105	16 966	431	648 400	118 799	2 903
Adair	209	12.1	175	4	10.2	D	18	104	1	85	517	3 133	NA	NA
Allen	240	13.5	186	1	10.5	D	6	34	1	62	375	2 949	NA	NA
Anderson	251	13.1	161	1	8.4	D	11	58	0	0	0	2 545	NA	NA
Ballard	95	11.5	112	0	13.6	D	2	24	0	0	0	1 931	NA	NA
Barren	487	12.8	410	2	10.8	D	43	113	1	194	525	6 763	NA	NA
Bath	160	14.4	128	1	11.5	D	7	63	0	0	0	2 098	NA	NA
Bell	366	12.2	352	2	11.8	D	44	146	2	247	848	6 241	NA	NA
Boone	1 419	16.4	522	11	6.0	8.0	85	99	1	155	195	9 911	2 775	3 187
Bourbon	241	12.4	208	1	10.7	D	24	124	1	68	351	3 093	NA	NA
Boyd	536	10.8	610	4	12.3	D	115	231	2	539	1 088	10 403	NA	NA
Boyle	315	11.4	317	2	11.4	D	61	220	1	168	618	4 887	NA	NA
Bracken	108	13.0	95	1	11.4	D	2	24	0	0	0	1 463	NA	NA
Breathitt	166	10.3	175	2	10.9	D	20	124	1	59	376	2 834	NA	NA
Breckinridge	221	11.8	201	1	10.8	D	12	64	1	45	258	3 310	NA	NA
Bullitt	726	11.9	368	4	6.0	D	13	21	0	0	0	5 900	NA	NA
Butler	161	12.3	135	2	10.3	D	5	38	0	0	0	1 987	NA	NA
Caldwell	130	10.0	172	0	13.2	D	12	92	1	50	376	2 712	NA	NA
Calloway	336	9.8	354	1	10.3	D	39	114	1	360	1 075	5 751	NA	NA
Campbell	1 262	14.2	860	9	9.7	6.9	107	121	1	267	306	12 727	NA	NA
Carlisle	69	12.8	77	0	14.3	D	1	19	0	0	0	1 148	NA	NA
Carroll	143	14.1	117	2	11.5	D	10	98	1	53	552	1 655	NA	NA
Carter	361	13.4	300	2	11.2	D	9	33	0	0	0	4 781	NA	NA
Casey	197	12.8	182	1	11.8	D	8	52	0	0	0	2 650	NA	NA
Christian	1 582	21.9	602	10	8.3	6.1	92	127	1	226	312	8 355	NA	NA
Clark	428	12.9	307	3	9.2	D	29	87	1	109	341	5 195	NA	NA
Clay	301	12.3	225	3	9.2	D	17	69	1	62	272	3 805	NA	NA
Clinton	127	13.2	108	1	11.2	D	4	42	1	36	385	2 125	NA	NA
Crittenden	101	10.8	140	0	15.0	D	8	85	1	46	480	1 771	NA	NA

1. Per 1,000 estimated resident population. 2. Deaths of infants under 1 year old. 3. Deaths of infants under 1 year old per 1,000 live births. 4. Data subject to copyright. 5. Per 100,000 resident population as of July 1 of the year shown. 6. Data for serious crimes have not been adjusted for underreporting; this may affect comparability between geographic areas and over time. 7. Per 100,000 population estimated by the FBI.

Table B. States and Counties — Crime, Education, Money Income, and Poverty

STATE County	Serious crimes known to police,[1] 2002 (cont'd) Rate[2] Violent	Property	Education — Enrollment[3] Total	Percent private	Attainment[4] (percent) High school graduate or less	Bachelor's degree or more	Local government expenditures,[5] 2000–2001 Total current expenditures (mil dol)	Current expenditures per student (dollars)	Money income, 1999 Per capita income[6] (dollars)	Households Median income Dollars	Percent change, 1989–1999 (constant 1999 dollars)	Percent with income of $100,000 or more	Percent below poverty level, 1999 Persons	Households	Families	Families with children
	46	47	48	49	50	51	52	53	54	55	56	57	58	59	60	61
KANSAS—Cont'd																
Osage	402	2 400	4 279	5.1	56.8	14.3	20.2	6 137	17 691	37 928	13.5	4.0	8.4	9.6	6.4	8.8
Osborne	NA	NA	1 033	4.8	55.5	15.5	3.1	6 692	16 236	29 145	18.1	3.7	10.4	11.7	7.2	11.8
Ottawa	64	1 189	1 514	9.2	51.7	16.3	9.0	6 739	17 663	38 009	29.5	4.5	8.6	9.2	5.1	8.7
Pawnee	452	3 257	1 676	8.1	45.0	21.8	11.6	9 557	17 584	35 175	9.6	6.2	11.8	7.7	5.4	6.6
Phillips	0	363	1 384	2.0	52.5	16.1	12.0	11 163	17 121	35 013	24.6	4.0	10.0	10.5	7.2	11.3
Pottawatomie	190	1 533	5 159	12.7	48.2	22.7	27.1	7 193	17 785	40 176	18.2	6.1	9.7	9.5	6.4	10.1
Pratt	277	3 109	2 533	9.5	41.4	21.0	10.3	6 015	17 906	35 529	10.8	4.6	9.4	10.3	6.7	11.8
Rawlins	33	1 101	666	4.7	49.9	15.9	4.1	8 424	17 161	32 105	12.0	4.4	12.5	12.9	7.9	14.4
Reno	93	1 642	15 601	11.6	47.8	17.3	65.1	6 246	18 520	35 510	7.2	5.8	10.9	11.3	8.1	12.4
Republic	17	1 883	1 306	4.0	52.7	14.9	8.2	8 029	17 433	30 494	12.2	4.8	9.1	9.7	6.0	11.2
Rice	245	1 339	3 243	11.7	50.2	17.5	15.4	7 980	16 064	35 671	25.9	4.6	10.7	10.7	8.5	13.5
Riley	310	2 683	28 110	5.1	28.6	40.5	46.4	7 040	16 349	32 042	9.9	7.2	20.6	20.8	8.5	10.9
Rooks	104	435	1 330	8.3	54.3	15.4	7.7	7 522	15 588	30 457	12.7	2.3	9.8	11.0	7.3	10.3
Rush	NA	NA	790	4.9	49.6	16.4	4.7	7 139	18 033	31 268	20.2	4.0	9.7	10.2	6.7	10.4
Russell	175	2 458	1 627	6.5	52.7	16.7	9.2	7 348	17 073	29 284	4.6	5.8	12.0	13.3	9.1	15.3
Saline	304	5 612	14 039	15.6	47.5	20.4	63.8	7 208	19 073	37 308	7.9	5.9	8.8	9.0	6.0	9.0
Scott	193	2 282	1 229	6.9	44.3	23.0	6.2	5 828	20 443	40 534	18.4	8.7	5.1	5.5	2.1	4.2
Sedgwick	557	5 202	129 180	17.6	44.2	25.4	474.2	6 154	20 907	42 485	4.7	9.1	9.5	9.4	7.0	10.5
Seward	374	5 739	6 348	4.7	63.1	13.6	29.6	5 908	15 059	36 752	5.0	6.6	16.9	14.6	13.9	19.3
Shawnee	651	6 740	43 314	16.9	45.5	26.0	171.7	6 445	20 904	40 988	2.1	8.4	9.6	9.6	6.3	10.2
Sheridan	NA	NA	757	0.8	48.8	15.9	3.7	8 584	16 299	33 547	15.9	5.1	15.7	12.4	12.0	21.2
Sherman	483	3 309	1 793	4.7	49.3	15.0	7.4	6 343	16 761	32 684	15.1	3.7	12.9	11.9	9.7	15.2
Smith	NA	NA	979	3.7	53.4	16.7	5.5	7 050	14 983	28 486	12.6	2.6	10.7	12.1	8.8	11.0
Stafford	83	1 592	1 201	3.2	46.2	18.4	8.0	7 430	16 409	31 107	17.1	3.1	11.8	11.7	8.7	11.7
Stanton	82	453	644	7.8	53.0	16.9	4.2	7 377	18 043	40 172	21.8	7.7	14.9	13.0	10.7	15.4
Stevens	199	2 990	1 570	3.5	51.5	17.5	8.4	6 451	17 814	41 830	13.0	5.9	10.3	8.0	8.3	13.2
Sumner	185	2 702	7 299	8.3	51.4	15.7	29.6	6 367	18 305	39 415	9.1	5.6	9.5	10.2	7.2	11.3
Thomas	266	3 521	2 545	8.5	37.5	25.0	10.7	7 433	19 028	37 034	23.9	7.6	9.7	12.9	6.6	9.5
Trego	30	1 223	807	5.9	53.3	14.0	4.0	7 755	16 239	29 677	10.9	3.4	12.3	13.1	11.2	14.2
Wabaunsee	309	1 712	1 699	5.6	55.6	17.3	8.4	7 406	17 704	41 710	12.0	4.1	7.3	7.5	5.8	8.4
Wallace	113	283	470	9.1	52.7	17.2	3.2	7 702	17 016	33 000	20.3	7.9	16.1	13.2	10.7	15.8
Washington	61	489	1 403	12.0	56.9	15.2	10.2	7 409	15 515	29 363	12.5	3.3	10.1	10.9	7.3	9.8
Wichita	0	1 838	617	8.8	55.1	15.5	3.3	6 730	16 720	33 462	6.5	6.3	14.8	11.4	11.2	18.2
Wilson	115	1 255	2 434	3.1	56.1	10.9	13.3	6 386	14 910	29 747	17.9	2.8	11.3	12.8	7.5	12.1
Woodson	366	1 385	862	3.8	56.8	11.4	3.9	6 683	14 283	25 335	-4.0	2.6	13.2	17.0	10.2	18.4
Wyandotte	NA	NA	42 334	13.1	60.3	12.0	192.3	6 756	16 005	33 784	5.7	4.7	16.5	15.7	12.5	18.5
KENTUCKY	279	2 624	1 007 452	14.7	59.4	17.1	4 046.2	6 285	18 093	33 672	11.2	7.2	15.8	16.2	12.7	18.1
Adair	NA	NA	4 198	22.8	71.1	10.9	16.2	6 184	14 931	24 055	13.3	4.7	24.0	24.8	18.2	22.8
Allen	NA	NA	3 983	8.9	74.7	9.1	16.1	5 394	14 506	31 238	29.8	3.2	17.3	18.0	13.2	17.8
Anderson	NA	NA	4 641	6.8	62.6	12.0	18.4	4 925	18 621	45 433	21.9	5.4	7.5	9.1	4.8	7.3
Ballard	NA	NA	1 785	4.0	64.1	10.6	8.9	5 917	19 035	32 130	23.5	4.7	13.6	14.0	10.7	15.6
Barren	NA	NA	8 256	9.5	70.9	11.1	42.1	6 168	16 816	31 240	19.0	4.3	15.6	16.6	11.4	16.4
Bath	NA	NA	2 341	5.1	75.5	10.1	12.0	6 336	15 326	26 018	21.5	3.9	21.9	23.6	16.4	24.8
Bell	NA	NA	6 872	8.3	76.5	9.0	35.4	6 263	11 526	19 057	8.5	2.4	31.1	32.1	26.7	38.6
Boone	220	2 966	23 160	22.5	47.7	22.8	83.2	5 757	23 535	53 593	15.7	14.9	5.6	6.2	4.4	6.4
Bourbon	NA	NA	4 539	8.1	63.3	13.5	22.3	6 368	18 335	35 038	16.2	7.2	14.0	15.2	12.3	19.6
Boyd	NA	NA	11 748	10.3	57.3	14.1	50.0	6 681	18 212	32 749	2.3	6.4	15.5	15.6	11.5	18.8
Boyle	NA	NA	7 043	20.6	57.7	19.3	29.7	6 332	18 288	35 241	13.4	7.2	11.9	13.4	9.1	14.6
Bracken	NA	NA	1 978	6.9	71.0	9.5	8.1	5 246	16 478	34 823	31.7	3.9	10.8	13.2	7.6	10.2
Breathitt	NA	NA	4 131	9.7	73.6	10.0	20.4	7 018	11 044	19 155	15.1	2.1	33.2	34.2	28.1	37.9
Breckinridge	NA	NA	4 228	11.4	75.3	7.4	19.8	6 522	15 402	30 554	28.6	3.5	15.8	17.1	11.8	16.0
Bullitt	NA	NA	14 974	14.3	65.1	9.2	59.7	5 505	18 339	45 106	14.0	7.6	7.9	8.0	6.2	9.5
Butler	NA	NA	2 925	3.7	79.7	6.4	14.2	6 171	14 617	29 405	25.0	2.6	16.0	18.5	13.1	18.5
Caldwell	NA	NA	2 797	6.8	68.1	10.0	12.2	5 888	16 264	28 686	18.6	4.2	15.9	16.7	12.2	17.7
Calloway	NA	NA	11 875	4.9	52.4	24.0	27.9	5 881	16 566	30 134	15.6	5.4	16.6	17.5	9.8	14.8
Campbell	NA	NA	23 663	24.0	53.9	20.5	77.6	6 233	20 637	41 903	6.7	9.0	9.3	9.7	7.3	11.5
Carlisle	NA	NA	1 185	10.2	66.1	10.6	5.4	6 046	16 276	30 087	15.4	5.0	13.1	14.0	10.5	17.5
Carroll	NA	NA	2 243	9.4	69.4	8.3	13.3	7 508	17 057	35 925	32.5	3.4	14.9	15.5	10.4	17.4
Carter	NA	NA	6 517	12.5	72.9	8.9	29.5	6 198	13 442	26 427	15.1	2.6	22.3	22.2	19.2	25.4
Casey	NA	NA	3 103	9.3	79.3	7.4	14.7	6 175	12 867	21 580	7.1	3.0	25.5	26.5	20.7	27.4
Christian	NA	NA	18 278	11.7	56.1	12.5	59.4	6 407	14 611	31 177	10.3	4.2	15.0	14.8	12.1	16.0
Clark	NA	NA	7 482	13.8	61.2	15.6	30.6	5 824	19 170	39 946	17.4	7.2	10.6	11.0	8.3	13.0
Clay	NA	NA	5 678	10.1	79.5	8.0	29.4	6 991	9 716	16 271	-4.9	1.5	39.7	39.5	35.4	43.3
Clinton	NA	NA	2 011	4.7	78.1	8.0	12.0	7 709	13 286	19 563	28.3	2.4	25.8	29.3	20.2	28.2
Crittenden	NA	NA	2 030	10.5	73.2	7.3	9.1	6 365	15 262	29 060	16.5	3.3	19.1	17.8	14.7	23.2

1. Data for serious crimes have not been adjusted for underreporting; this may affect comparability between geographic areas and over time.   2. Per 100,000 population estimated by the FBI.   3. All persons 3 years old and over enrolled in nursery school through college.   4. Persons 25 years old and over.   5. Elementary and secondary education expenditures.   6. Based on population enumerated as of April 1, 2000.

STATE County	Total (mil dol)	Percent change, 2001–2002	Per capita[1] Dollars	Rank	Wages and salaries[2] (mil dol)	Proprietor's income (mil dol)	Dividends, interest, and rent (mil dol)	Transfer payments Total (mil dol)	Government payments to individuals Total (mil dol)	Social Security (mil dol)	Medical payments (mil dol)	Income mainte- nance (mil dol)	Unemploy- ment insurance (mil dol)
	62	63	64	65	66	67	68	69	70	71	72	73	74
KANSAS—Cont'd													
Osage	382	0.7	22 760	1 800	83	4	71	76	71	31	27	4	3
Osborne	93	-2.0	21 780	2 070	36	10	27	25	24	12	10	1	0
Ottawa	142	0.1	22 863	1 759	37	6	37	26	24	12	9	1	0
Pawnee	156	-6.3	22 628	1 840	94	9	33	33	31	15	13	1	0
Phillips	149	-2.0	25 828	926	76	12	43	31	30	14	12	1	0
Pottawatomie	485	1.6	26 330	825	252	39	100	66	61	29	24	3	2
Pratt	230	2.8	24 031	1 396	132	13	55	50	47	21	20	2	1
Rawlins	70	-7.8	24 107	1 369	26	8	21	17	16	8	7	1	0
Reno	1 586	1.5	24 789	1 180	971	89	324	305	288	132	117	20	8
Republic	120	-1.8	22 034	2 008	58	7	32	29	28	14	11	1	1
Rice	212	1.5	20 131	2 513	96	11	49	50	47	23	18	3	1
Riley	1 500	3.2	24 377	1 287	899	43	238	162	147	56	49	9	6
Rooks	128	-2.2	23 402	1 594	59	14	30	30	28	14	12	1	1
Rush	79	0.9	22 773	1 791	36	2	22	22	21	10	9	1	1
Russell	164	0.7	23 327	1 619	67	13	48	46	44	20	21	2	1
Saline	1 495	2.3	27 726	584	1 085	151	285	230	215	95	86	15	7
Scott	142	-1.5	28 806	467	63	26	36	19	17	10	6	1	0
Sedgwick	13 959	1.9	30 302	319	10 824	1 404	2 311	1 888	1 762	716	714	159	91
Seward	511	-0.7	22 222	1 954	403	64	65	73	67	24	30	7	2
Shawnee	5 068	3.0	29 757	368	4 097	317	875	828	782	299	313	56	23
Sheridan	70	-12.1	26 237	845	26	12	21	13	12	6	5	0	0
Sherman	156	-4.2	24 222	1 337	91	8	31	36	35	14	16	2	1
Smith	99	-6.5	22 977	1 732	40	4	32	24	23	13	9	1	1
Stafford	112	0.8	24 069	1 379	41	15	27	27	26	12	12	1	1
Stanton	55	-0.3	22 606	1 849	28	5	16	9	8	4	3	0	0
Stevens	123	-4.0	22 953	1 737	68	7	34	21	19	10	8	1	1
Sumner	621	1.9	24 358	1 290	197	31	95	122	115	48	45	6	6
Thomas	202	-4.3	25 139	1 093	116	26	41	35	33	15	14	2	1
Trego	65	2.1	20 668	2 380	28	1	18	18	17	8	8	1	0
Wabaunsee	169	-0.3	24 960	1 146	37	12	27	28	26	12	9	1	1
Wallace	36	-2.1	21 355	2 194	16	1	11	9	8	4	4	0	1
Washington	130	-2.3	20 924	2 319	52	3	34	34	32	16	13	1	1
Wichita	73	-3.9	29 185	424	28	25	14	10	9	5	3	1	0
Wilson	214	3.4	21 116	2 263	125	8	41	57	54	23	23	4	2
Woodson	69	-2.2	18 933	2 769	20	8	15	22	21	9	9	1	1
Wyandotte	3 364	2.9	21 332	2 202	3 753	139	330	771	728	230	321	81	47
KENTUCKY	104 264	2.7	25 494	X	69 823	7 352	17 458	19 517	18 474	6 934	7 626	2 053	648
Adair	334	3.0	19 192	2 716	131	20	54	101	96	30	48	10	3
Allen	389	2.7	21 498	2 149	172	33	65	80	76	30	33	8	3
Anderson	484	2.3	24 766	1 190	149	14	82	68	63	30	22	5	4
Ballard	215	-2.8	26 426	809	133	22	30	46	44	17	20	3	2
Barren	872	3.5	22 491	1 880	588	67	145	183	173	69	73	19	6
Bath	218	4.1	19 131	2 733	65	4	32	56	53	18	22	9	2
Bell	525	2.2	17 521	2 950	299	23	73	207	199	61	90	32	4
Boone	2 781	3.3	29 703	372	3 217	173	364	280	256	117	91	17	11
Bourbon	547	1.7	28 045	543	250	63	111	84	79	34	32	7	2
Boyd	1 281	4.3	25 795	933	1 160	54	234	298	285	112	116	30	7
Boyle	701	3.7	25 327	1 037	626	38	149	128	121	51	46	12	5
Bracken	176	1.2	20 887	2 326	44	1	26	37	35	14	14	4	1
Breathitt	280	4.0	17 559	2 946	105	15	38	109	105	28	49	22	4
Breckinridge	384	1.9	20 317	2 475	88	23	80	89	84	33	35	9	4
Bullitt	1 524	1.5	23 927	1 429	382	79	180	213	197	89	69	16	9
Butler	246	0.2	18 737	2 792	117	11	34	64	61	21	27	7	3
Caldwell	289	2.2	22 578	1 856	126	25	53	71	67	28	27	6	2
Calloway	823	0.6	23 927	1 429	482	102	155	156	148	64	55	10	7
Campbell	2 479	2.6	28 049	542	966	131	396	369	347	148	132	27	13
Carlisle	117	-6.0	21 733	2 081	24	12	23	27	26	11	11	2	1
Carroll	237	2.2	23 036	1 711	260	9	36	50	47	18	20	5	4
Carter	482	5.0	17 798	2 918	167	21	59	144	137	45	57	20	6
Casey	289	3.3	18 276	2 865	98	25	40	85	81	25	37	11	5
Christian	1 666	5.3	23 444	1 586	2 494	81	272	266	252	87	108	32	5
Clark	906	3.5	26 944	712	524	64	157	145	136	56	53	15	5
Clay	361	2.7	14 798	3 081	150	11	43	150	144	34	66	34	3
Clinton	183	3.6	19 031	2 750	94	13	23	72	70	17	38	9	4
Crittenden	184	0.8	20 040	2 541	59	13	28	51	49	21	21	4	1

1. Based on the resident population estimated as of July 1 of the year shown.   2. Includes other labor income.

Table B. States and Counties — Earnings, Social Security, and Housing

STATE County	Earnings, 2002									Social Security beneficiaries, December 2003		Supplemental Security Income recipients, December 2003	Housing units, 2003	
		Percent by selected industries												
		Goods-related[1]			Service-related and health									
	Total (mil dol)	Farm	Total	Manu-facturing	Information and professional and technical services	Retail trade	Finance, insurance, and real estate	Health services	Govern-ment	Number	Rate[2]	Total	Total	Percent change, 2000–2003
	75	76	77	78	79	80	81	82	83	84	85	86	87	88
KANSAS—Cont'd														
Osage	87	-4.4	D	9.4	D	11.6	6.0	D	42.1	3 285	196	202	7 239	3.1
Osborne	46	-1.4	D	11.1	6.8	10.6	D	D	22.7	1 215	291	45	2 409	-0.4
Ottawa	43	1.9	D	9.8	D	4.8	D	16.0	30.9	1 245	202	53	2 771	0.6
Pawnee	104	4.5	D	1.9	D	5.3	5.0	7.5	54.0	1 450	213	73	3 121	0.2
Phillips	87	0.6	D	19.7	4.1	6.9	D	9.1	24.7	1 530	270	57	3 093	0.2
Pottawatomie	291	0.1	25.2	15.1	D	10.9	D	D	13.6	3 120	167	162	7 644	4.6
Pratt	145	0.1	13.7	3.2	5.6	9.7	6.5	D	23.7	2 080	220	102	4 708	1.6
Rawlins	34	-0.7	10.5	3.9	D	4.7	D	8.1	31.1	830	292	36	1 563	-0.1
Reno	1 060	0.5	26.4	16.8	5.4	8.6	4.5	15.3	16.8	12 980	203	1 105	27 832	0.7
Republic	66	1.2	D	12.5	4.5	8.4	8.1	9.8	26.6	1 545	291	74	3 113	0.0
Rice	106	3.5	23.4	14.4	D	5.3	5.2	D	26.2	2 365	227	121	4 595	-0.3
Riley	942	-0.4	D	1.8	5.6	7.4	6.6	10.5	48.1	5 740	92	512	23 973	2.5
Rooks	73	-0.6	26.0	17.1	D	8.2	7.3	2.8	26.3	1 415	261	63	2 748	-0.4
Rush	38	-4.3	D	27.3	D	3.6	D	7.0	26.7	990	290	65	1 933	0.3
Russell	80	1.2	23.4	11.4	4.6	6.9	5.5	13.5	23.3	2 020	292	122	3 837	-0.9
Saline	1 236	-0.1	D	22.9	8.3	8.3	5.0	13.9	12.2	9 615	179	866	23 140	2.0
Scott	89	30.1	D	0.6	D	5.6	D	D	18.9	965	201	32	2 317	1.1
Sedgwick	12 228	0.0	40.5	34.1	6.5	6.2	5.1	10.7	11.9	68 545	148	7 853	197 816	3.5
Seward	467	3.2	D	D	3.7	7.2	3.7	D	16.7	2 410	104	282	8 122	1.2
Shawnee	4 415	0.0	15.1	9.4	10.0	8.0	9.9	12.9	22.7	30 360	178	3 738	75 908	2.9
Sheridan	38	12.2	5.8	0.8	D	8.2	7.6	3.5	22.4	640	240	17	1 289	2.1
Sherman	99	0.5	D	2.6	4.0	10.4	7.0	21.8	24.6	1 410	225	102	3 239	1.7
Smith	44	2.8	D	16.3	2.2	9.5	D	13.4	24.6	1 325	317	49	2 333	0.3
Stafford	57	20.8	D	D	D	3.9	D	4.4	30.9	1 155	252	51	2 451	-0.3
Stanton	32	22.6	D	D	D	3.1	5.5	1.9	26.3	395	164	8	1 029	-0.2
Stevens	75	4.8	17.2	1.6	D	4.5	4.5	D	29.9	920	171	37	2 303	1.7
Sumner	228	1.6	23.7	18.3	D	8.4	5.4	8.2	27.5	4 795	190	285	11 028	1.4
Thomas	142	10.4	D	1.7	5.6	8.1	7.2	10.7	22.7	1 455	183	66	3 581	0.5
Trego	30	-10.1	D	1.5	10.7	9.1	D	3.0	36.8	905	292	42	1 705	-1.0
Wabaunsee	49	1.5	D	18.3	D	5.8	5.0	4.7	26.4	1 345	199	59	3 098	2.1
Wallace	17	2.5	5.0	0.5	D	8.3	D	D	28.1	350	216	10	798	0.9
Washington	55	4.4	D	6.3	D	6.7	D	6.9	36.7	1 790	292	70	3 154	0.4
Wichita	53	53.0	D	D	D	2.4	D	D	14.5	470	192	14	1 132	1.2
Wilson	133	-1.5	D	39.5	4.8	3.5	3.7	3.7	21.5	2 430	241	201	4 976	0.8
Woodson	28	12.5	D	7.7	D	7.6	D	5.1	25.7	995	274	73	2 078	0.1
Wyandotte	3 893	0.0	D	21.7	3.2	D	2.5	7.2	22.8	23 650	151	4 386	66 281	0.6
KENTUCKY	77 175	0.8	26.5	18.9	7.3	7.4	6.0	10.6	18.4	768 861	187	178 852	1 814 575	3.6
Adair	151	3.1	18.7	9.7	3.1	8.3	4.8	D	22.4	3 860	221	1 189	7 820	0.4
Allen	205	0.5	D	35.7	D	12.9	3.7	D	12.3	3 665	201	833	8 234	2.2
Anderson	163	-2.6	D	39.8	3.6	8.6	4.1	D	18.6	3 260	165	329	8 217	6.0
Ballard	155	7.2	D	35.8	D	3.8	1.7	D	9.5	1 860	227	258	3 912	2.0
Barren	654	2.0	42.5	37.0	D	8.5	3.2	12.6	11.9	8 400	215	1 706	17 321	1.3
Bath	69	-4.8	36.5	22.0	2.7	8.7	4.5	6.0	28.8	2 425	212	952	5 134	2.8
Bell	322	0.0	22.3	8.2	4.2	12.3	4.4	D	22.1	7 260	242	3 473	13 622	2.1
Boone	3 390	0.0	D	16.2	5.0	7.5	8.3	3.4	7.0	12 095	125	1 308	38 506	15.5
Bourbon	312	14.5	D	25.6	D	6.3	3.4	D	11.6	3 850	196	651	8 632	3.4
Boyd	1 214	0.0	D	18.4	9.2	8.8	3.9	16.7	12.1	11 350	229	2 669	22 098	0.6
Boyle	664	-0.5	D	32.0	D	7.6	3.8	15.8	10.9	5 655	203	1 232	11 786	3.2
Bracken	46	-7.1	D	D	D	7.9	4.1	5.4	28.1	1 730	204	330	3 762	1.3
Breathitt	120	-0.7	D	2.1	3.1	13.1	4.8	17.5	35.8	3 640	230	2 364	7 030	3.2
Breckinridge	111	-1.6	16.5	6.1	3.1	12.8	6.1	10.6	27.5	3 990	210	884	10 092	2.0
Bullitt	461	-0.7	D	24.7	D	8.9	4.7	3.4	17.6	9 565	147	927	25 488	9.8
Butler	127	0.5	D	39.0	1.4	5.8	2.5	D	18.6	2 750	208	583	5 945	2.2
Caldwell	151	2.8	30.7	24.0	3.6	13.7	4.8	D	19.9	3 185	248	511	6 228	1.7
Calloway	584	5.8	D	17.4	3.4	12.0	3.5	6.9	28.3	6 830	197	719	16 481	2.6
Campbell	1 097	-0.2	D	14.2	6.7	8.5	7.1	11.8	19.9	14 610	166	1 813	37 298	1.1
Carlisle	36	14.0	15.8	5.1	D	10.8	D	6.2	22.5	1 315	244	170	2 537	1.9
Carroll	269	-0.4	D	52.2	D	7.1	D	D	9.1	1 995	195	486	4 491	1.2
Carter	188	-1.2	D	12.9	4.2	13.8	4.1	D	24.6	5 540	204	1 850	11 940	3.5
Casey	123	1.8	D	22.9	D	10.2	D	10.7	18.0	3 430	215	1 279	7 413	2.4
Christian	2 575	0.3	D	12.1	2.4	3.2	1.4	4.0	68.1	9 960	142	2 334	28 039	3.2
Clark	588	0.3	D	30.0	8.4	8.4	3.6	8.6	10.4	6 380	188	1 191	14 686	6.8
Clay	161	-1.2	7.7	2.9	5.3	10.1	2.9	D	48.1	4 630	190	3 687	9 710	2.9
Clinton	107	6.5	44.5	39.4	D	6.1	D	D	18.6	2 475	258	1 014	4 954	1.4
Crittenden	72	4.8	D	18.4	D	9.1	4.4	18.0	19.2	2 245	247	317	4 507	2.2

1. Covers mining, construction, and manufacturing.   2. Per 1,000 resident population estimated as of July 1 of the year shown.

Table B. States and Counties — Housing, Labor Force, and Employment

	Housing units, 2000								Civilian labor force, 2003				Civilian employment,[6] 2000		
	Occupied units										Unemployment			Percent	
			Owner-occupied			Renter-occupied									
				Median owner cost as a percent of income											Production, transportation, and material moving occupations
STATE County	Total	Percent	Median value[1]	With a mortgage	Without a mortgage[2]	Median rent[3]	Median rent as a percent of income	Substandard units[4] (percent)	Total	Percent change, 2002–2003	Total	Rate[5]	Total	Management, professional and related occupations	
	89	90	91	92	93	94	95	96	97	98	99	100	101	102	103
KANSAS—Cont'd															
Osage	6 490	79.8	67 600	19.3	9.9	398	21.2	2.7	8 145	9.6	506	6.2	8 120	27.4	17.0
Osborne	1 940	78.6	32 000	17.5	9.9	314	20.2	1.3	2 322	4.7	79	3.4	2 112	35.1	18.6
Ottawa	2 430	82.2	58 900	19.0	9.9	372	21.9	2.3	3 235	1.1	124	3.8	3 103	28.4	16.9
Pawnee	2 739	74.4	48 800	18.4	9.9	332	19.6	1.4	3 552	2.7	84	2.4	3 275	34.6	8.5
Phillips	2 496	77.9	48 200	17.4	9.9	296	18.9	1.5	3 229	1.4	75	2.3	2 868	33.1	14.6
Pottawatomie	6 771	78.5	81 100	19.2	9.9	464	19.3	3.5	11 352	2.9	360	3.2	9 070	32.8	14.0
Pratt	3 963	73.4	56 600	18.9	9.9	389	23.2	2.1	5 161	2.7	121	2.3	4 788	32.3	12.5
Rawlins	1 269	76.8	41 300	20.8	11.2	328	21.2	1.8	1 447	2.3	33	2.3	1 364	40.8	7.9
Reno	25 498	70.7	66 600	19.0	9.9	442	23.3	2.7	31 986	-0.1	1 461	4.6	30 395	27.9	18.5
Republic	2 557	78.9	35 300	19.0	10.2	288	21.9	1.4	3 068	4.6	115	3.7	2 803	35.1	17.1
Rice	4 050	76.6	42 900	18.5	9.9	340	19.6	2.7	4 642	-2.3	176	3.8	4 991	28.2	18.8
Riley	22 137	47.3	93 700	18.7	9.9	475	28.4	2.8	31 035	3.0	1 078	3.5	30 067	38.4	7.4
Rooks	2 362	77.1	38 300	18.9	11.6	325	18.2	1.9	3 134	7.5	138	4.4	2 613	32.3	14.5
Rush	1 548	82.4	32 200	17.9	11.4	328	18.4	1.8	1 796	5.4	52	2.9	1 652	33.0	17.4
Russell	3 207	75.2	41 100	19.6	10.3	325	26.1	2.2	3 168	3.4	95	3.0	3 383	30.6	13.9
Saline	21 436	69.0	85 300	19.6	9.9	457	23.1	3.0	30 804	1.1	1 247	4.0	27 665	28.0	18.6
Scott	2 045	74.4	72 100	17.9	10.9	402	21.5	1.7	2 628	0.2	57	2.2	2 748	34.7	9.0
Sedgwick	176 444	66.2	83 600	19.3	9.9	511	23.2	4.3	239 790	0.4	17 597	7.3	219 098	32.1	16.0
Seward	7 419	64.1	72 400	19.4	9.9	467	22.6	13.7	10 831	1.1	314	2.9	9 724	21.0	26.2
Shawnee	68 920	67.5	81 600	19.0	9.9	494	24.3	2.8	89 865	0.1	4 448	4.9	84 676	34.2	12.4
Sheridan	1 124	82.3	56 000	20.2	10.9	286	18.3	3.6	1 427	1.8	25	1.8	1 388	39.0	10.2
Sherman	2 758	68.9	63 900	19.9	12.9	414	21.8	3.2	4 631	3.2	89	1.9	3 393	25.9	11.6
Smith	1 953	79.7	37 400	17.6	10.9	283	17.9	2.3	2 404	2.3	46	1.9	2 071	35.5	14.0
Stafford	2 010	77.7	34 400	18.6	10.8	353	18.6	1.9	2 308	1.7	64	2.8	2 182	37.6	15.7
Stanton	858	67.8	73 400	18.2	9.9	406	18.9	7.2	1 032	0.7	22	2.1	1 161	28.7	12.0
Stevens	1 988	75.4	79 000	18.8	9.9	450	23.1	8.7	2 637	5.2	52	2.0	2 430	31.4	13.1
Sumner	9 888	76.7	62 100	18.5	11.1	416	23.0	2.7	14 339	2.0	1 111	7.7	11 767	31.9	20.6
Thomas	3 226	69.0	75 500	18.0	9.9	373	21.3	2.4	4 751	4.0	85	1.8	4 021	35.6	10.2
Trego	1 412	81.4	47 400	18.5	11.6	326	15.0	1.3	1 781	2.7	39	2.2	1 556	33.0	10.3
Wabaunsee	2 633	82.9	62 600	18.1	9.9	378	19.2	2.7	3 783	3.8	135	3.6	3 492	33.3	15.9
Wallace	674	76.6	45 700	19.5	10.3	361	19.7	2.4	852	2.1	18	2.1	872	33.4	10.8
Washington	2 673	79.5	32 200	17.2	9.9	286	18.9	2.5	3 290	1.8	89	2.7	3 197	33.0	16.5
Wichita	967	74.3	55 300	17.9	10.6	451	20.7	5.6	1 244	2.7	38	3.1	1 152	31.5	13.7
Wilson	4 203	78.1	37 700	18.5	11.6	382	24.2	3.6	5 539	5.6	239	4.3	4 725	25.1	25.7
Woodson	1 642	81.4	34 300	20.9	12.2	321	20.1	1.0	1 617	3.7	109	6.7	1 616	26.4	24.3
Wyandotte	59 700	62.9	54 300	19.5	11.1	492	24.2	6.8	79 542	3.2	9 443	11.9	68 084	22.0	21.2
KENTUCKY	1 590 647	70.7	86 700	19.6	9.9	445	24.0	2.9	1 956 384	1.2	120 475	6.2	1 798 264	28.7	19.7
Adair	6 747	80.1	60 800	20.6	9.9	315	25.6	4.2	7 745	-0.9	483	6.2	7 331	26.3	22.8
Allen	6 910	79.0	69 300	20.0	9.9	357	21.7	4.2	8 196	-4.7	642	7.8	7 768	22.1	33.5
Anderson	7 320	79.8	89 500	18.9	9.9	523	19.8	2.0	9 992	0.0	397	4.0	9 486	25.9	26.6
Ballard	3 395	81.9	58 800	17.6	9.9	349	21.7	2.0	3 967	1.2	374	9.4	3 848	21.7	20.2
Barren	15 346	72.3	77 900	19.1	9.9	383	21.3	2.6	17 641	-0.1	873	4.9	17 552	23.9	25.5
Bath	4 445	79.8	65 000	20.0	9.9	317	23.0	4.0	6 025	2.6	427	7.1	4 384	25.7	26.1
Bell	12 004	67.5	52 500	21.8	9.9	309	25.3	3.2	9 686	-0.8	756	7.8	8 939	24.2	20.0
Boone	31 258	74.2	131 800	19.9	9.9	596	23.0	1.9	50 539	2.4	2 469	4.9	45 323	32.0	16.9
Bourbon	7 681	65.5	84 500	19.8	9.9	416	22.7	1.8	9 321	1.4	528	5.7	9 273	25.2	22.7
Boyd	20 010	72.9	68 800	18.7	9.9	407	24.7	1.4	22 403	3.6	1 573	7.0	19 515	28.3	14.8
Boyle	10 574	69.3	86 400	18.7	9.9	419	23.2	2.0	14 603	1.5	1 302	8.9	12 476	29.6	21.6
Bracken	3 228	76.9	69 000	18.5	9.9	337	20.5	3.3	3 770	3.7	243	6.4	3 885	23.1	27.8
Breathitt	6 170	76.5	46 500	21.5	9.9	297	27.3	6.0	4 251	3.2	449	10.6	4 868	27.8	17.2
Breckinridge	7 324	81.9	64 600	20.5	9.9	360	26.2	3.6	8 074	1.4	673	8.3	7 900	21.9	29.3
Bullitt	22 171	83.9	105 100	19.8	9.9	499	21.9	2.3	34 098	0.6	1 938	5.7	30 901	21.7	24.4
Butler	5 059	79.5	59 900	19.3	9.9	338	21.7	3.4	6 322	-0.6	552	8.7	5 926	16.5	32.2
Caldwell	5 431	77.4	53 600	19.9	9.9	348	22.9	1.8	6 523	2.1	358	5.5	5 708	23.9	23.9
Calloway	13 862	68.3	83 100	20.8	9.9	427	27.1	1.8	17 749	-0.7	1 193	6.7	16 007	31.4	19.3
Campbell	34 742	69.0	101 000	19.8	9.9	512	23.9	1.8	45 098	2.0	2 174	4.8	43 371	31.4	14.4
Carlisle	2 208	84.0	49 400	21.0	9.9	273	21.4	0.8	2 674	3.6	248	9.3	2 221	20.2	26.0
Carroll	3 940	66.8	79 900	18.6	9.9	389	21.3	3.1	5 626	2.1	417	7.4	4 577	19.0	27.2
Carter	10 342	81.0	57 100	18.6	10.9	365	25.3	3.7	11 609	2.5	1 321	11.4	10 456	22.7	20.6
Casey	6 260	81.1	49 500	22.1	11.1	295	24.4	5.6	6 891	-0.6	501	7.3	6 259	19.5	33.0
Christian	24 857	55.3	72 500	20.0	9.9	458	23.4	4.0	28 250	4.2	1 968	7.0	24 162	25.2	22.8
Clark	13 015	68.6	93 700	19.3	9.9	476	22.2	2.3	15 736	1.0	864	5.5	15 695	26.8	20.8
Clay	8 556	74.8	43 800	21.0	12.1	292	28.8	6.5	7 811	-1.6	646	8.3	6 439	23.1	24.9
Clinton	4 086	77.2	50 200	19.3	13.4	294	27.7	2.9	6 397	1.5	532	8.3	4 002	21.6	28.4
Crittenden	3 829	80.3	48 300	19.0	9.9	331	23.8	2.8	3 844	3.4	301	7.8	3 890	21.9	24.6

1. Specified owner-occupied units.   2. Median monthly owner costs is often in the minimum category—9.9 percent or less, which is indicated as 9.9 percent.   3. Specified renter-occupied units.   4. Overcrowded or lacking complete plumbing facilities.   5. Percent of civilian labor force.   6. Persons 16 years old and over.

STATE County	Number of establishments	Employment — Total	Health care and social assistance	Manufacturing	Retail trade	Finance and insurance	Professional, scientific, and technical services	Annual payroll — Total (mil dol)	Average per employee (dollars)	Farms — Number	Percent with — Less than 50 acres	Percent with — 500 acres and over	Farm operators whose principal occupation is farming (percent)
	104	105	106	107	108	109	110	111	112	113	114	115	116
KANSAS—Cont'd													
Osage	332	3 213	1 359	D	502	201	47	54	16 920	925	20.5	21.4	56.2
Osborne	164	1 303	260	239	241	74	44	22	16 826	449	8.7	52.1	74.8
Ottawa	131	775	208	59	96	110	27	17	21 293	512	11.1	41.4	65.2
Pawnee	187	1 984	877	86	273	103	46	43	21 898	430	13.5	45.1	66.7
Phillips	229	1 651	286	D	262	121	68	36	22 002	531	16.2	47.8	67.0
Pottawatomie	482	5 840	1 221	699	1 129	203	133	133	22 842	842	18.8	29.3	59.0
Pratt	390	3 142	630	124	609	147	94	72	22 932	591	10.3	39.6	63.3
Rawlins	100	569	154	29	105	72	18	12	20 467	405	8.6	65.4	73.3
Reno	1 758	25 311	3 917	4 993	3 793	847	560	674	26 626	1 570	21.7	26.4	61.4
Republic	216	1 878	320	531	277	100	30	35	18 638	642	9.7	42.8	74.6
Rice	310	2 652	340	376	316	150	D	57	21 373	500	18.4	41.2	67.8
Riley	1 416	19 867	3 105	679	3 570	1 191	1 301	392	19 745	493	23.5	29.0	58.6
Rooks	214	1 330	102	324	227	82	54	30	22 280	485	12.8	46.2	63.1
Rush	106	912	171	196	124	47	38	21	22 886	504	11.1	41.5	70.4
Russell	275	1 916	218	180	319	77	58	37	19 143	617	13.6	37.1	60.8
Saline	1 687	26 606	3 762	5 793	4 433	758	1 207	682	25 627	758	19.7	29.8	57.5
Scott	203	1 410	281	33	276	93	68	29	20 661	327	14.1	56.0	71.6
Sedgwick	11 911	234 158	29 788	64 008	26 773	8 485	7 505	7 788	33 260	1 355	32.3	21.1	56.3
Seward	667	10 177	1 182		1 586	216	217	240	23 607	350	10.0	39.4	64.0
Shawnee	4 587	79 338	16 628	7 277	10 905	5 518	4 023	2 274	28 658	903	35.8	13.1	50.5
Sheridan	110	628	147	15	117	47	17	13	20 826	404	5.9	63.1	75.5
Sherman	283	2 098	376	D	523	154	71	42	20 072	443	5.6	57.6	69.3
Smith	162	1 046	203	193	159	71	24	19	17 968	546	11.9	53.7	77.7
Stafford	147	748	156	58	112	70	11	16	21 664	534	9.9	44.2	65.9
Stanton	77	418	D	D	59	28	15	9	21 983	313	4.5	52.7	73.5
Stevens	163	1 224	234	10	190	79	37	29	23 996	401	9.7	46.4	69.1
Sumner	538	4 731	960	1 122	773	301	69	105	22 091	1 072	15.8	39.1	68.5
Thomas	351	2 581	342	24	540	133	50	50	19 230	476	7.8	59.7	67.0
Trego	122	707	D	19	120	35	16	13	17 859	423	11.6	54.4	71.4
Wabaunsee	120	924	131	75	168	44	7	15	16 713	631	16.0	30.7	54.8
Wallace	67	369	38	D	56	29	D	6	16 412	290	7.6	61.0	54.8
Washington	235	1 542	384	46	230	83	39	24	15 586	796	16.5	35.9	68.6
Wichita	91	406	D	37	103	11	D	8	20 906	326	9.2	58.9	66.1
Wilson	262	3 728	545	1 460	313	85	44	93	24 956	556	13.1	35.3	75.5
Woodson	109	597	146	D	90	35	16	10	16 144	308	13.0	41.9	71.1
Wyandotte	2 991	60 983	9 654	13 495	5 090	1 168	2 128	2 110	34 605	161	68.3	3.1	39.8
KENTUCKY	89 501	1 497 466	212 423	279 836	221 103	65 166	56 400	42 597	28 446	86 541	34.8	5.6	54.2
Adair	301	3 706	1 189	331	534	110	34	71	19 052	1 395	31.5	2.9	58.4
Allen	208	4 099	433	1 724	445	137	56	96	23 441	1 191	30.4	2.9	54.3
Anderson	268	3 384	256	1 395	572	93	81	91	27 000	748	37.3	1.7	45.7
Ballard	160	1 944	163	730	248	61	63	65	33 684	486	33.7	11.3	47.7
Barren	835	14 649	2 029	4 805	2 264	356	385	353	24 116	2 021	37.4	3.8	59.7
Bath	165	1 444	202	470	206	89	29	30	20 538	692	28.3	6.1	57.9
Bell	617	7 774	1 515	917	1 862	256	193	167	21 418	63	33.3	3.2	36.5
Boone	2 409	55 444	2 670	9 746	8 975	2 652	1 163	1 774	31 992	743	50.1	2.4	48.9
Bourbon	379	5 211	567	1 337	660	178	59	142	27 332	913	38.2	11.0	61.2
Boyd	1 484	27 015	5 276	3 984	4 639	1 461	645	830	30 739	274	36.5	2.6	40.5
Boyle	787	15 016	2 409	4 761	1 981	362	347	379	25 260	715	41.1	5.0	51.7
Bracken	114	1 051	85	D	151	46	D	21	19 932	639	27.4	3.8	55.7
Breathitt	209	2 397	807	28	525	133	62	42	17 511	209	29.7	13.9	44.5
Breckinridge	317	2 317	431	236	548	132	50	42	18 094	1 443	25.6	7.6	54.3
Bullitt	938	11 062	518	3 321	1 830	261	205	258	23 293	616	50.3	2.9	52.3
Butler	213	3 381	292	1 545	334	83	D	62	18 395	729	19.1	9.2	47.3
Caldwell	267	3 098	524	768	709	122	47	68	21 791	673	25.0	9.2	49.6
Calloway	770	11 831	1 643	2 939	2 103	287	601	276	23 337	819	42.5	9.8	52.6
Campbell	1 590	23 312	2 884	3 112	4 574	518	800	625	26 793	581	43.4	0.9	49.1
Carlisle	75	579	72	130	136	59	D	10	18 029	380	33.4	10.3	54.2
Carroll	240	5 259	349	2 595	753	51	48	188	35 751	339	27.4	5.6	49.0
Carter	429	4 434	599	403	1 063	197	167	73	16 459	925	28.6	3.0	49.3
Casey	191	2 640	442	568	386	84	D	45	16 906	1 353	29.7	3.9	57.9
Christian	1 301	23 036	5 275	5 473	3 041	671	519	555	24 100	1 267	27.8	12.0	61.0
Clark	735	12 585	1 160	4 450	1 870	229	331	316	25 119	861	41.0	7.4	57.1
Clay	302	2 974	805	428	613	103	81	57	19 146	386	28.2	4.1	53.9
Clinton	194	3 781	402	2 415	370	78	28	63	16 576	629	39.1	3.2	53.7
Crittenden	173	1 730	443	220	279	77	57	29	16 962	698	20.1	8.5	51.1

Table B. States and Counties — Agriculture

STATE County	Agriculture, 2002 (cont'd)														
	Land in farms					Value of land and buildings (dollars)		Value of machinery and equipment average per farm (dollars)	Value of products sold				Percent of farms with sales of —		Government payments	
			Acres								Percent from —					
	Acreage (1,000)	Percent change, 1997–2002	Average size of farm	Total irrigated (1,000)	Total cropland (1,000)	Average per farm	Average per acre		Total (mil dol)	Average per farm (dollars)	Crops	Live-stock and poultry products	$10,000 or more	$100,000 or more	Total ($1,000)	Percent of farms
	117	118	119	120	121	122	123	124	125	126	127	128	129	130	131	132
KANSAS—Cont'd																
Osage	367	1.9	397	0	216	368 808	899	56 333	33	35 489	47.6	52.4	42.9	9.2	2 001	56.0
Osborne	499	-1.2	1 111	10	308	526 109	497	95 489	34	76 799	51.8	48.2	68.6	26.9	2 656	79.3
Ottawa	416	4.0	812	4	229	481 577	577	91 061	49	95 961	41.5	58.5	59.2	21.9	2 801	67.2
Pawnee	520	8.3	1 210	61	362	724 996	563	141 633	139	324 383	22.4	77.6	56.7	25.6	3 548	77.9
Phillips	587	5.8	1 106	10	298	521 061	461	102 422	48	90 349	27.9	72.1	57.1	19.2	3 177	74.2
Pottawatomie	465	5.0	553	16	192	460 953	722	57 020	54	63 899	24.0	76.0	48.1	12.0	2 168	56.3
Pratt	501	14.6	848	80	350	498 067	633	157 866	131	221 095	30.0	70.0	46.9	22.8	4 849	80.0
Rawlins	651	0.6	1 607	11	403	638 956	416	127 350	35	85 247	51.4	48.6	72.6	25.7	3 295	75.1
Reno	735	11.0	468	42	532	410 721	875	70 644	112	71 127	49.5	50.5	43.2	14.3	7 818	64.6
Republic	424	-0.9	660	41	298	507 215	819	109 427	83	129 276	46.7	53.3	67.0	26.5	3 924	69.6
Rice	416	-9.2	832	16	312	571 122	667	130 241	106	211 575	31.7	68.3	61.2	28.4	3 315	68.4
Riley	222	-6.7	451	3	107	444 559	1 035	100 574	24	47 992	39.0	61.0	48.7	11.4	1 084	53.8
Rooks	560	-1.8	1 155	3	299	537 662	448	97 617	40	82 790	34.3	65.7	56.3	17.3	3 234	76.9
Rush	418	1.5	829	9	315	379 214	472	82 930	29	57 724	58.5	41.5	56.7	17.9	2 861	79.2
Russell	484	12.8	784	2	269	333 830	430	71 840	28	45 628	47.4	52.6	48.1	12.8	2 963	78.4
Saline	437	5.6	576	3	281	440 491	748	114 024	41	54 428	53.7	46.3	52.0	13.9	2 918	64.6
Scott	495	4.0	1 515	47	392	836 477	555	172 008	335	1 025 687	8.0	92.0	65.7	34.9	3 225	70.3
Sedgwick	534	-1.1	394	39	410	471 676	1 197	74 462	75	55 664	63.8	36.2	47.6	12.6	3 904	44.9
Seward	363	10.7	1 036	76	243	667 877	647	199 005	276	788 894	11.2	88.8	44.6	23.7	3 384	68.0
Shawnee	217	-3.1	240	14	136	300 264	1 265	61 030	22	24 336	69.7	30.3	31.7	6.3	1 459	38.2
Sheridan	511	0.8	1 266	66	360	828 512	596	150 355	142	352 633	22.3	77.7	72.8	34.4	3 400	67.8
Sherman	607	-7.0	1 369	96	504	790 826	622	179 056	68	153 736	52.3	47.7	63.0	27.3	5 290	79.7
Smith	518	5.3	949	7	338	645 966	663	110 501	46	83 651	48.8	51.2	64.5	20.9	3 583	72.0
Stafford	473	8.7	885	77	348	639 087	764	125 507	111	207 401	37.7	62.3	56.9	27.7	4 654	73.6
Stanton	438	9.5	1 399	107	381	796 279	573	193 517	105	337 020	34.4	65.6	46.0	28.4	5 388	86.3
Stevens	491	-4.1	1 223	160	404	830 287	677	203 129	152	378 732	37.6	62.4	43.9	27.9	4 895	82.0
Sumner	732	9.7	683	8	620	486 920	682	102 270	78	72 634	74.3	25.7	59.0	22.7	5 092	61.5
Thomas	690	1.6	1 450	87	566	848 225	607	179 986	93	195 253	48.0	52.0	71.6	31.7	6 035	76.7
Trego	455	-1.5	1 075	6	268	462 411	462	93 808	40	93 563	29.5	70.5	59.8	17.7	2 412	84.2
Wabaunsee	464	-2.9	736	7	140	578 922	726	72 464	35	55 189	21.0	79.0	51.3	12.8	1 564	56.4
Wallace	415	-13.5	1 431	45	262	589 102	444	141 773	24	82 409	52.2	47.8	51.0	18.6	3 741	83.8
Washington	497	-7.3	624	12	310	549 198	804	113 013	82	102 698	30.9	69.1	60.8	18.7	4 545	67.7
Wichita	471	4.7	1 444	60	366	673 525	503	179 406	314	964 600	D	D	57.4	27.9	4 154	77.3
Wilson	337	12.0	607	2	202	456 804	770	86 021	32	57 001	64.8	35.2	54.7	16.0	1 589	50.9
Woodson	255	0.4	828	D	111	488 351	589	65 020	28	91 103	30.5	69.5	58.8	19.8	702	50.3
Wyandotte	14	-36.4	86	0	10	281 088	3 915	29 959	3	18 062	79.2	20.8	23.0	4.3	52	9.3
KENTUCKY	13 844	3.8	160	37	8 412	294 056	1 824	41 458	3 080	35 591	36.0	64.0	32.7	5.9	94 053	26.4
Adair	170	6.3	122	0	96	191 623	1 784	32 367	31	22 429	19.3	80.7	33.4	4.8	972	25.4
Allen	168	5.7	141	0	95	255 011	1 789	33 201	41	34 665	15.1	84.9	35.0	3.3	656	28.6
Anderson	84	0.0	112	0	47	326 883	2 407	29 810	9	11 964	31.6	68.4	22.9	1.2	169	12.0
Ballard	113	-5.0	233	0	90	412 092	1 695	50 268	34	70 647	44.7	55.3	38.5	12.1	1 382	44.2
Barren	240	-4.0	119	0	166	191 457	1 609	38 742	63	31 071	25.5	74.5	38.2	6.9	1 959	24.6
Bath	108	-16.3	155	0	67	211 617	1 373	33 591	13	18 427	48.4	51.6	39.2	3.0	362	21.4
Bell	7	75.0	110	D	3	140 614	1 326	20 593	0	3 424	27.8	71.8	11.1	0.0	3	12.7
Boone	75	-6.3	101	1	44	340 579	3 633	37 573	18	24 426	62.3	37.7	26.6	4.6	284	15.7
Bourbon	185	-6.1	202	0	127	622 296	2 664	69 697	98	107 129	18.0	82.0	51.0	14.9	1 052	25.6
Boyd	34	30.8	122	0	13	186 965	1 446	22 110	1	4 591	35.0	65.0	9.9	0.0	51	19.0
Boyle	99	4.2	138	0	65	292 492	2 136	32 433	22	31 465	19.7	80.3	36.2	7.0	378	15.1
Bracken	94	2.2	148	1	50	183 729	1 534	25 652	10	16 208	58.0	42.0	33.2	2.3	266	19.6
Breathitt	51	8.5	245	0	8	203 300	923	20 994	1	6 425	72.0	28.0	16.7	0.5	21	19.6
Breckinridge	276	3.0	192	0	150	326 835	1 507	45 520	29	19 899	44.0	56.0	33.9	3.8	2 183	42.8
Bullitt	61	7.0	100	0	31	300 167	2 742	43 507	7	11 735	48.4	51.6	19.2	2.6	226	12.8
Butler	162	7.3	222	0	80	324 269	1 537	37 124	19	26 197	37.0	63.0	22.9	4.8	1 011	40.5
Caldwell	147	-0.7	219	2	98	236 258	1 156	50 206	18	26 665	68.1	31.9	27.2	6.2	1 799	56.5
Calloway	169	15.8	207	1	131	384 589	1 862	49 703	54	65 903	51.7	48.3	37.9	12.1	2 512	50.4
Campbell	50	11.1	87	0	29	306 013	3 836	22 472	6	10 074	51.2	48.8	16.0	1.5	57	7.7
Carlisle	107	18.9	283	0	84	412 259	1 410	60 444	31	82 823	49.1	50.9	33.4	14.7	2 172	63.4
Carroll	61	1.7	180	0	29	354 772	2 071	36 354	8	23 620	76.8	23.2	37.2	3.8	79	22.7
Carter	120	10.1	130	0	46	154 748	1 496	31 133	7	7 603	50.5	49.5	18.2	0.8	62	11.9
Casey	191	0.0	141	0	88	163 067	1 168	30 545	22	16 052	38.0	62.0	31.4	3.2	735	20.2
Christian	342	10.3	270	2	238	429 627	1 696	57 395	77	60 798	69.7	30.3	43.7	13.4	5 106	47.2
Clark	143	-2.7	166	0	90	387 108	2 182	43 229	25	29 367	28.3	71.7	39.8	7.4	473	20.0
Clay	55	-3.5	143	0	16	136 386	959	16 147	4	9 619	80.8	19.2	17.6	1.8	51	13.5
Clinton	72	-7.7	114	0	39	152 870	1 529	31 887	21	32 769	14.0	86.0	31.0	3.8	195	23.2
Crittenden	157	10.6	224	0	89	228 868	1 043	23 525	12	17 576	36.8	63.2	26.5	2.3	1 820	49.0

Table B. States and Counties — Residential Construction, Wholesale Trade, Retail Trade, and Real Estate

STATE County	Value of residential construction authorized by building permits, 2003		Wholesale trade, 1997				Retail trade,[1] 1997				Real estate and rental and leasing, 1997			
	New construction ($1,000)	Number of housing units	Number of establishments	Number of employees	Sales (mil dol)	Annual payroll (mil dol)	Number of establishments	Number of employees	Sales (mil dol)	Annual payroll (mil dol)	Number of establishments	Number of employees	Receipts (mil dol)	Annual payroll (mil dol)
	133	134	135	136	137	138	139	140	141	142	143	144	145	146
KANSAS—Cont'd														
Osage	12 509	76	9	90	45.7	1.6	65	444	67.7	5.7	8	13	1.0	0.2
Osborne	17	1	13	156	65.9	2.8	45	244	34.2	2.8	1	D	D	D
Ottawa	979	8	12	92	72.1	2.6	24	132	16.8	1.7	NA	NA	NA	NA
Pawnee	249	3	11	92	43.1	2.3	42	298	40.8	4.2	3	7	0.2	0.0
Phillips	939	12	16	138	58.8	2.9	39	281	34.7	3.0	1	D	D	D
Pottawatomie	17 713	122	22	266	113.9	5.0	94	854	119.6	12.1	18	35	2.5	0.5
Pratt	2 076	31	30	357	258.0	8.7	62	632	88.0	9.5	10	D	D	D
Rawlins	0	0	12	77	47.0	2.0	23	114	13.8	1.2	1	D	D	D
Reno	16 352	120	94	1 239	474.6	36.3	327	3 961	667.0	65.7	55	185	54.9	2.4
Republic	0	0	24	153	85.8	2.3	51	255	34.5	3.6	3	4	0.3	0.0
Rice	414	4	19	116	47.7	3.1	50	337	40.1	4.1	5	D	D	D
Riley	52 451	590	42	493	140.7	12.1	305	3 331	442.9	43.6	73	245	18.4	2.8
Rooks	40	1	17	114	53.8	2.6	43	258	37.3	3.0	2	D	D	D
Rush	13	1	16	160	58.8	4.2	18	93	13.5	1.2	NA	NA	NA	NA
Russell	194	2	17	138	108.7	3.2	53	310	42.0	4.2	2	D	D	D
Saline	18 752	141	103	1 261	841.2	36.0	313	4 340	679.3	63.8	70	279	34.4	4.3
Scott	1 080	4	22	149	67.4	3.7	40	297	48.9	3.9	5	D	D	D
Sedgwick	308 544	3 072	798	9 903	5 875.1	336.3	1 804	25 223	4 265.4	423.1	541	2 663	340.6	54.2
Seward	1 554	17	48	299	133.3	9.2	135	1 394	249.1	21.5	31	112	12.1	2.3
Shawnee	158 942	1 092	204	2 298	947.1	65.9	768	10 625	1 619.6	166.7	199	1 216	88.8	22.4
Sheridan	NA	NA	9	109	56.6	3.1	22	110	15.9	1.4	NA	NA	NA	NA
Sherman	158	2	21	203	126.6	5.7	62	453	88.7	7.4	6	10	1.0	0.1
Smith	0	0	15	133	61.4	2.4	39	230	25.7	2.5	2	D	D	D
Stafford	0	0	15	157	57.1	3.4	21	108	12.0	1.1	1	D	D	D
Stanton	525	2	16	132	65.5	3.7	12	61	13.1	1.2	NA	NA	NA	NA
Stevens	575	4	19	181	113.9	4.9	23	138	26.4	2.1	2	D	D	D
Sumner	3 606	37	33	212	143.2	6.1	93	733	114.5	9.4	16	42	2.2	0.4
Thomas	356	3	28	255	207.8	6.5	70	606	81.5	8.0	9	35	2.3	0.4
Trego	117	1	11	52	38.6	1.1	29	177	21.4	2.0	2	D	D	D
Wabaunsee	3 116	36	5	21	6.7	0.2	30	139	18.4	1.9	2	D	D	D
Wallace	0	0	6	D	D	D	12	68	7.7	0.7	NA	NA	NA	NA
Washington	100	1	21	226	83.8	4.7	42	211	19.6	1.8	NA	NA	NA	NA
Wichita	80	1	8	43	31.7	1.2	22	104	19.1	1.7	2	D	D	D
Wilson	190	2	11	D	D	D	38	253	26.8	2.6	6	13	0.3	0.1
Woodson	108	1	9	D	D	D	25	101	11.7	1.2	3	6	0.1	0.0
Wyandotte	33 357	280	311	6 891	4 013.4	224.7	436	5 172	932.9	91.8	126	758	84.9	15.9
KENTUCKY	2 346 693	20 404	5 051	69 309	37 242.9	2 071.2	17 369	212 189	33 332.7	3 128.1	3 227	16 284	1 961.6	314.3
Adair	0	0	16	131	29.4	3.6	65	525	83.0	6.3	10	31	1.5	0.2
Allen	NA	NA	11	102	15.3	1.8	70	469	78.6	5.9	5	20	1.3	0.2
Anderson	17 703	212	10	D	D	D	54	528	92.7	8.0	7	D	D	D
Ballard	NA	NA	5	50	28.7	1.1	37	264	49.0	3.6	3	12	0.5	0.0
Barren	9 349	72	35	328	97.6	8.1	208	2 171	355.5	31.2	26	55	6.6	0.7
Bath	566	9	1	D	D	D	42	238	38.5	2.9	6	11	0.3	0.1
Bell	3 436	63	26	328	88.9	7.6	163	1 955	299.2	36.2	12	34	2.8	0.8
Boone	158 774	1 650	122	1 683	1 005.0	59.6	435	8 561	1 666.2	132.5	92	676	101.9	13.5
Bourbon	9 530	72	18	D	D	D	75	781	127.9	10.1	10	54	2.8	0.7
Boyd	2 248	19	94	1 435	515.3	38.7	345	4 313	641.6	60.8	63	215	25.8	4.4
Boyle	18 901	167	33	285	197.0	4.8	149	2 152	301.8	29.0	20	74	7.8	1.3
Bracken	NA	NA	4	47	18.2	1.0	27	127	19.7	1.5	3	14	0.5	0.1
Breathitt	0	0	5	75	40.1	1.7	52	715	102.8	8.7	5	15	1.6	0.3
Breckinridge	927	20	10	D	D	D	69	525	95.1	7.4	5	36	1.9	0.5
Bullitt	126 669	903	31	288	92.8	7.1	151	1 547	243.3	22.5	33	89	10.7	1.3
Butler	0	0	8	31	13.9	0.5	41	270	35.7	3.1	8	21	1.0	0.2
Caldwell	731	6	11	61	27.2	1.3	64	752	126.3	11.8	3	D	D	D
Calloway	4 067	85	53	D	D	D	192	2 020	336.5	28.4	25	94	7.6	1.1
Campbell	46 838	433	78	649	230.1	26.0	266	3 874	644.1	57.6	68	507	58.9	15.8
Carlisle	NA	NA	8	28	22.0	0.6	19	134	20.3	3.0	4	D	D	D
Carroll	294	4	13	234	63.4	3.6	59	549	121.8	8.7	3	D	D	D
Carter	798	7	12	D	D	D	130	1 071	179.2	14.8	14	D	D	D
Casey	219	2	17	87	18.2	1.4	53	310	44.2	4.2	3	11	0.4	0.1
Christian	18 901	121	79	1 281	682.5	39.9	301	2 836	464.9	43.7	74	266	26.6	4.0
Clark	33 926	356	34	D	D	D	147	1 922	348.2	30.3	24	60	6.0	0.5
Clay	0	0	14	70	13.4	1.1	78	812	110.2	9.4	11	35	1.2	0.2
Clinton	515	21	8	55	12.8	1.0	55	374	47.2	4.5	4	18	1.8	0.4
Crittenden	NA	NA	7	D	D	D	29	261	28.9	3.2	4	D	D	D

1. Establishments with payroll.

Table B. States and Counties — Professional Services, Manufacturing, and Accommodation and Foodservices

STATE County	Professional, scientific, and technical services,[1] 1997				Manufacturing, 1997				Accommodation and foodservices, 1997			
	Number of establishments	Number of employees	Receipts (mil dol)	Annual payroll (mil dol)	Number of establishments	Number of employees	Receipts (mil dol)	Annual payroll (mil dol)	Number of establishments	Number of employees	Sales (mil dol)	Annual payroll (mil dol)
	147	148	149	150	151	152	153	154	155	156	157	158
KANSAS—Cont'd												
Osage	13	52	2.4	0.9	NA	NA	NA	NA	32	189	5.2	1.1
Osborne	5	22	1.7	0.5	NA	NA	NA	NA	11	83	1.4	0.5
Ottawa	4	D	D	D	NA	NA	NA	NA	14	50	1.4	0.3
Pawnee	11	30	2.1	0.8	NA	NA	NA	NA	18	195	8.6	1.3
Phillips	14	51	3.4	1.5	NA	NA	NA	NA	18	150	3.1	0.8
Pottawatomie	27	83	4.9	1.4	22	720	134.2	25.8	32	320	7.3	1.9
Pratt	25	91	5.1	1.9	NA	NA	NA	NA	34	478	10.3	3.0
Rawlins	5	15	0.7	0.2	NA	NA	NA	NA	7	D	D	D
Reno	89	453	26.9	11.5	97	5 141	849.7	161.3	141	2 382	67.5	17.6
Republic	8	29	1.5	0.5	8	D	D	D	12	172	3.1	0.8
Rice	15	33	1.6	0.4	NA	NA	NA	NA	28	317	6.2	1.7
Riley	91	660	54.8	21.0	28	533	75.8	14.4	156	2 998	74.6	21.0
Rooks	7	18	1.3	0.5	NA	NA	NA	NA	19	79	1.6	0.4
Rush	7	15	0.9	0.4	NA	NA	NA	NA	8	D	D	D
Russell	14	57	2.5	0.8	NA	NA	NA	NA	21	288	6.2	1.6
Saline	84	702	52.1	20.4	87	6 434	1 212.2	193.2	136	2 464	68.9	21.0
Scott	14	36	1.8	0.5	NA	NA	NA	NA	12	148	3.3	0.8
Sedgwick	957	6 367	537.9	217.7	595	61 675	10 638.7	2 569.7	969	17 828	585.6	166.7
Seward	31	209	12.3	4.7	10	D	D	D	56	820	24.2	6.2
Shawnee	405	3 227	233.6	94.7	140	7 722	1 805.6	265.4	374	D	D	D
Sheridan	5	15	0.8	0.2	NA	NA	NA	NA	4	D	D	D
Sherman	18	57	2.6	0.7	NA	NA	NA	NA	20	246	6.6	1.7
Smith	9	22	0.7	0.2	NA	NA	NA	NA	14	81	2.3	0.6
Stafford	8	18	0.9	0.2	NA	NA	NA	NA	14	D	D	D
Stanton	5	13	0.6	0.2	NA	NA	NA	NA	6	D	D	D
Stevens	14	41	2.3	0.8	NA	NA	NA	NA	13	94	3.0	0.6
Sumner	27	70	3.4	1.1	44	1 262	194.6	45.1	36	444	10.7	3.2
Thomas	20	55	3.6	0.8	NA	NA	NA	NA	34	487	13.5	3.9
Trego	6	12	0.6	0.2	NA	NA	NA	NA	13	D	D	D
Wabaunsee	4	8	0.3	0.1	NA	NA	NA	NA	8	21	1.4	0.2
Wallace	1	D	D	D	NA	NA	NA	NA	2	D	D	D
Washington	10	28	1.4	0.3	NA	NA	NA	NA	17	159	2.8	0.7
Wichita	3	9	0.3	0.1	NA	NA	NA	NA	1	D	D	D
Wilson	12	29	1.8	0.3	29	1 256	261.5	35.0	13	D	D	D
Woodson	4	11	0.3	0.1	NA	NA	NA	NA	10	55	1.3	0.4
Wyandotte	157	1 127	88.8	33.4	262	15 083	7 678.2	638.9	230	3 191	109.3	30.3
KENTUCKY	6 189	41 991	3 820.3	1 260.1	4 218	288 405	86 636.1	9 198.1	6 546	129 442	4 056.1	1 140.6
Adair	16	28	1.9	0.6	20	533	30.8	8.3	19	221	7.3	2.0
Allen	8	38	1.5	0.5	12	1 858	285.1	41.6	20	232	6.3	1.7
Anderson	16	44	3.0	1.1	20	D	D	D	19	283	6.5	2.2
Ballard	7	54	2.0	1.1	12	D	D	D	6	D	D	D
Barren	44	204	13.5	4.5	55	5 672	796.0	154.5	85	1 338	44.6	11.9
Bath	12	25	1.1	0.3	NA	NA	NA	NA	11	105	2.7	0.7
Bell	36	157	9.4	4.1	22	858	125.8	18.6	50	766	26.0	6.5
Boone	125	857	117.1	35.9	134	9 050	1 857.4	305.7	171	4 381	156.0	43.2
Bourbon	23	58	2.6	0.8	19	D	D	D	27	308	9.9	2.6
Boyd	97	624	53.0	26.6	42	4 395	2 930.8	203.4	109	2 172	68.7	18.1
Boyle	46	208	16.9	5.9	33	4 604	778.3	130.5	54	1 088	32.5	8.8
Bracken	7	9	0.6	0.2	NA	NA	NA	NA	11	329	10.0	2.7
Breathitt	13	34	3.9	0.8	NA	NA	NA	NA	19	188	4.7	1.5
Breckinridge	11	41	1.4	0.4	49	2 959	344.8	85.6	56	1 169	36.0	10.4
Bullitt	45	143	8.5	2.6	15	1 886	355.1	37.6	12	134	3.0	0.9
Butler	6	21	0.7	0.2	19	659	121.6	18.7	24	283	7.2	2.0
Caldwell	16	38	2.0	0.5	NA	NA	NA	NA	NA	NA	NA	NA
Calloway	37	169	10.9	3.0	28	2 983	817.4	69.1	63	995	26.5	7.2
Campbell	101	387	30.0	9.8	83	3 043	726.1	105.0	169	D	D	D
Carlisle	4	12	0.4	0.1	NA	NA	NA	NA	7	D	D	D
Carroll	8	37	1.8	1.2	18	2 378	1 408.7	94.8	27	430	12.7	3.3
Carter	24	82	3.7	1.1	18	612	40.0	8.9	33	445	14.2	4.0
Casey	11	331	8.1	6.3	27	946	80.3	16.0	16	D	D	D
Christian	79	320	25.3	7.6	56	4 469	780.8	115.4	101	2 208	55.5	18.2
Clark	46	271	16.8	8.5	46	3 635	661.1	87.0	58	1 105	31.1	8.5
Clay	21	64	3.4	0.9	NA	NA	NA	NA	20	281	9.6	2.4
Clinton	12	21	1.3	0.2	15	671	45.7	9.9	16	155	6.5	1.8
Crittenden	9	29	1.3	0.5	NA	NA	NA	NA	12	D	D	D

1. Firms subject to federal tax.

STATE County	Health care and social assistance,[1] 1997				Other services,[1] 1997				Federal funds and grants, 2002–2003			
									Expenditures (mil dol)			
										Direct payments for individuals[2]		
	Number of establish-ments	Number of employees	Receipts (mil dol)	Annual payroll (mil dol)	Number of establish-ments	Number of employees	Receipts (mil dol)	Annual payroll (mil dol)	Total	Social Security and government retirement	Medicare	Food stamps and Supplemental Security Income
	159	160	161	162	163	164	165	166	167	168	169	170
KANSAS—Cont'd												
Osage	22	317	9.0	4.2	21	38	3.6	0.6	86.2	46.4	15.4	1.6
Osborne	11	169	4.9	2.5	9	22	1.0	0.2	37.5	14.2	8.1	0.3
Ottawa	8	112	3.1	1.7	9	34	4.6	0.8	34.7	15.4	6.4	0.4
Pawnee	16	142	8.2	3.0	12	39	2.8	1.2	43.8	18.5	8.9	0.6
Phillips	15	50	2.6	0.7	15	42	2.5	0.6	46.5	18.0	9.6	0.4
Pottawatomie	27	322	10.2	5.2	27	73	4.9	1.1	79.9	39.9	17.2	1.4
Pratt	29	244	11.7	4.7	32	83	5.9	1.0	60.3	26.4	15.2	0.7
Rawlins	3	9	0.4	0.1	6	9	0.5	0.1	36.0	9.6	4.4	0.2
Reno	86	1 387	98.3	48.0	118	586	32.0	9.7	326.5	155.8	72.2	9.6
Republic	10	55	3.6	1.2	18	37	2.7	0.4	60.2	18.1	8.1	0.4
Rice	13	89	5.6	2.3	15	57	3.4	0.9	59.9	28.5	11.9	1.2
Riley	100	949	55.4	22.0	94	463	20.0	6.4	394.7	100.4	24.7	4.4
Rooks	7	41	1.4	0.6	12	33	2.0	0.6	42.0	16.8	10.6	0.5
Rush	4	15	1.1	0.7	5	11	0.6	0.2	30.8	11.8	7.2	0.5
Russell	14	170	6.8	2.7	18	46	4.5	0.7	62.6	24.1	13.3	0.7
Saline	125	1 149	91.8	36.6	110	697	49.0	15.8	274.1	123.8	49.9	6.6
Scott	7	44	3.4	1.6	19	37	3.0	0.5	35.7	6.9	4.7	0.3
Sedgwick	776	15 442	1 149.0	469.4	787	5 172	322.6	100.3	2 958.7	909.4	385.9	72.8
Seward	46	314	22.2	8.9	53	167	15.3	3.4	78.2	28.5	12.3	3.2
Shawnee	322	5 720	309.5	159.9	296	1 914	127.2	41.7	1 680.9	527.5	145.7	29.1
Sheridan	4	10	0.6	0.3	5	9	1.0	0.1	38.3	7.3	3.4	0.1
Sherman	12	144	5.9	2.3	23	151	5.8	1.7	65.2	17.2	9.4	0.8
Smith	11	160	4.2	2.0	11	29	1.6	0.3	41.0	15.0	7.0	0.3
Stafford	7	150	4.0	2.5	10	18	2.1	0.3	35.0	13.8	7.3	0.5
Stanton	4	31	0.5	0.2	3	D	D	D	29.1	4.9	1.8	0.1
Stevens	9	25	1.3	0.5	15	29	2.7	0.4	37.6	10.8	5.4	0.4
Sumner	44	444	15.2	6.6	33	101	7.0	1.6	139.0	72.1	28.8	2.3
Thomas	14	141	8.3	3.3	23	72	5.9	1.1	76.0	17.9	9.1	0.6
Trego	6	55	1.2	0.4	10	22	1.8	0.3	25.6	9.7	6.1	0.2
Wabaunsee	4	110	3.1	1.6	7	11	0.8	0.2	64.7	50.5	6.2	0.3
Wallace	1	D	D	D	4	7	0.6	0.1	26.3	4.7	2.9	0.1
Washington	14	116	3.3	1.3	16	29	1.8	0.4	56.5	20.4	9.3	0.4
Wichita	2	D	D	D	7	7	1.2	0.2	49.4	5.8	2.2	0.2
Wilson	19	229	8.3	3.7	17	37	2.8	0.6	61.1	27.3	13.0	1.9
Woodson	5	93	2.7	0.9	6	33	3.6	0.8	26.5	12.4	5.7	0.4
Wyandotte	223	4 049	301.9	108.6	231	1 379	78.5	25.1	1 115.7	315.7	197.4	40.0
KENTUCKY	6 805	94 720	5 936.2	2 620.3	5 383	31 164	1 870.3	551.4	31 153.1	9 305.1	3 788.0	1 349.7
Adair	23	353	14.7	7.6	13	31	2.3	0.6	110.8	36.0	21.8	7.0
Allen	13	55	2.7	1.1	9	27	2.0	0.3	93.9	36.1	17.3	5.6
Anderson	19	192	9.2	3.7	20	91	4.2	1.1	66.5	38.7	11.4	2.3
Ballard	5	154	3.7	1.7	9	43	2.4	0.7	57.6	26.1	14.0	1.5
Barren	75	1 002	53.7	26.1	40	198	12.3	3.0	190.0	83.1	32.9	10.3
Bath	10	102	2.6	1.2	13	20	1.3	0.2	68.5	24.5	7.7	4.5
Bell	61	557	28.5	11.7	39	184	9.3	2.9	74.3	81.2	40.4	26.3
Boone	142	1 452	94.8	38.1	132	1 244	68.7	19.5	396.5	158.7	44.2	8.8
Bourbon	32	274	21.4	6.9	23	94	4.0	1.1	135.4	44.6	18.6	5.2
Boyd	164	1 480	124.4	69.4	97	644	32.7	10.2	367.6	154.4	71.7	20.3
Boyle	76	724	49.1	24.4	41	195	7.9	2.4	133.8	65.0	25.8	8.5
Bracken	7	36	1.3	0.5	4	10	0.6	0.1	44.1	19.0	8.5	2.1
Breathitt	19	290	26.0	8.5	18	54	5.0	1.3	131.9	36.9	15.5	18.3
Breckinridge	18	144	6.7	2.0	20	80	4.5	1.1	101.8	46.6	17.8	5.9
Bullitt	47	537	21.8	10.3	69	285	18.2	4.6	349.0	97.0	29.9	8.4
Butler	10	78	2.9	1.4	12	62	7.6	0.9	64.6	25.5	13.5	3.1
Caldwell	18	93	8.1	1.9	17	55	3.7	0.7	77.1	36.3	15.2	3.8
Calloway	81	936	50.4	26.5	56	235	12.3	3.2	164.6	79.1	35.8	4.2
Campbell	117	1 487	84.5	41.8	116	640	41.1	12.2	391.9	186.8	85.2	16.4
Carlisle	4	70	2.6	1.0	5	11	0.6	0.1	32.9	14.5	7.7	1.2
Carroll	12	140	5.1	2.4	10	39	2.4	0.6	62.0	22.1	10.0	3.3
Carter	23	231	8.2	3.3	28	85	5.3	1.2	222.4	61.9	25.5	13.9
Casey	12	109	6.3	2.4	9	21	1.4	0.4	83.1	31.0	14.5	7.4
Christian	96	1 231	64.9	29.6	84	320	18.6	5.0	1 617.2	133.5	49.2	18.2
Clark	58	470	25.2	9.8	49	212	11.1	3.1	165.9	80.4	24.5	9.6
Clay	19	209	8.4	3.2	14	49	3.2	1.0	190.5	45.7	21.4	28.6
Clinton	13	200	9.0	4.2	4	9	0.7	0.1	88.8	21.3	17.9	5.9
Crittenden	9	153	5.2	3.0	13	30	2.2	0.4	56.5	24.7	13.1	2.4

1. Firms subject to federal tax.   2. State totals may include programs not allocated by county.

STATE County	Salaries and wages	Defense	Other	Medicaid and other health-related	Nutrition and family welfare	Education	Other	Total (mil dol)	Intergovern-mental (mil dol)	Total (mil dol)	Total	Property
	171	172	173	174	175	176	177	178	179	180	181	182
KANSAS—Cont'd												
Osage	4.1	1.4	0.8	5.9	1.3	0.9	3.5	37.8	20.9	10.7	634	567
Osborne	1.7	0.0	0.4	4.0	0.4	0.2	1.2	9.7	3.7	4.4	1 044	954
Ottawa	1.3	0.1	0.4	3.3	0.5	0.2	1.1	18.9	9.3	6.5	1 027	903
Pawnee	2.2	0.0	0.3	2.6	1.3	0.2	1.7	23.9	10.9	8.6	1 236	1 095
Phillips	2.3	0.0	0.6	4.8	0.4	0.2	2.3	23.9	10.5	9.1	1 555	1 484
Pottawatomie	3.2	0.2	0.8	5.9	1.3	0.6	4.5	66.1	24.2	25.4	1 375	1 321
Pratt	2.0	0.0	0.4	2.2	0.6	0.3	4.1	32.6	12.3	12.8	1 339	1 186
Rawlins	1.0	0.0	0.2	2.6	0.2	0.1	3.7	8.9	3.9	4.1	1 415	1 303
Reno	16.1	0.2	2.8	30.7	9.9	4.1	10.7	181.3	72.6	71.6	1 122	854
Republic	2.1	0.0	0.5	2.6	0.4	0.2	17.1	18.1	7.5	7.9	1 451	1 347
Rice	2.5	0.1	3.1	3.3	1.2	0.4	0.5	33.4	14.6	12.1	1 156	1 028
Riley	23.6	134.6	9.8	20.4	5.5	8.4	42.2	104.9	43.5	45.5	740	537
Rooks	1.6	0.0	0.4	2.6	0.5	0.2	2.4	23.3	7.5	7.0	1 270	1 188
Rush	1.4	0.0	0.3	1.8	0.3	0.1	1.7	14.5	4.8	5.5	1 576	1 529
Russell	2.3	0.1	0.5	3.3	0.6	0.2	5.0	31.0	8.9	9.6	1 366	1 187
Saline	20.2	2.0	4.9	22.8	8.6	2.3	22.0	153.0	59.6	63.6	1 180	783
Scott	1.1	0.0	0.3	1.8	0.3	0.1	3.9	16.1	5.8	7.3	1 476	1 346
Sedgwick	413.1	685.8	58.9	231.0	66.1	20.4	77.1	1 218.2	527.5	426.5	923	676
Seward	5.6	0.1	2.1	8.1	2.6	1.9	2.9	113.3	33.0	30.6	1 328	931
Shawnee	188.6	26.2	29.1	160.5	125.3	120.1	310.9	562.4	190.4	222.6	1 304	999
Sheridan	0.7	0.0	0.1	1.5	0.2	0.2	6.5	12.3	3.4	4.2	1 573	1 465
Sherman	3.3	0.0	0.3	2.9	0.7	0.2	5.9	28.0	8.2	8.8	1 382	1 059
Smith	2.3	0.0	0.4	2.2	0.3	0.2	3.7	12.9	5.7	5.0	1 156	1 113
Stafford	2.0	0.0	0.7	1.5	0.4	0.2	1.2	20.4	7.4	8.1	1 740	1 603
Stanton	0.4	0.0	0.1	0.4	0.2	0.1	3.5	14.2	2.8	8.6	3 583	3 490
Stevens	1.2	0.0	0.2	1.8	0.4	0.2	0.9	28.6	2.5	17.6	3 302	3 202
Sumner	5.4	1.1	1.3	10.6	2.8	1.3	3.2	77.1	31.4	20.6	805	725
Thomas	2.7	0.0	0.5	2.9	0.6	0.4	12.9	31.7	13.3	10.0	1 238	1 047
Trego	0.8	0.0	0.2	2.2	0.2	0.1	1.1	14.7	3.7	4.3	1 368	1 325
Wabaunsee	1.6	0.1	0.4	1.5	0.5	0.2	0.5	16.5	8.0	6.2	929	825
Wallace	0.6	0.0	1.1	0.7	0.2	0.1	3.7	6.4	3.1	2.6	1 532	1 507
Washington	3.2	0.0	0.7	4.4	0.5	0.3	2.6	27.2	11.1	7.5	1 195	1 102
Wichita	0.6	11.4	5.9	1.1	0.3	0.1	7.5	11.7	3.2	4.5	1 797	1 597
Wilson	2.4	0.1	0.6	10.6	1.4	0.4	1.0	29.3	14.5	8.2	807	694
Woodson	1.3	0.0	1.3	3.3	0.3	0.1	0.2	8.4	3.8	3.5	943	915
Wyandotte	153.4	3.5	42.4	244.0	49.1	8.6	47.4	540.0	204.9	180.0	1 137	897
KENTUCKY	3 112.4	3 223.4	1 895.7	3 246.3	848.1	567.1	1 972.6	X	X	X	X	X
Adair	2.5	0.0	0.5	25.4	2.0	1.7	8.1	22.7	15.1	4.8	277	174
Allen	2.1	0.0	0.6	21.2	1.4	1.1	7.6	28.5	16.5	7.7	421	254
Anderson	2.4	0.0	0.5	6.8	1.1	1.0	1.8	31.8	16.3	10.2	523	390
Ballard	2.0	2.6	0.5	5.1	0.9	1.6	1.2	25.0	9.4	4.4	538	338
Barren	7.5	0.8	8.8	33.8	3.2	1.8	4.0	82.0	38.9	23.4	603	359
Bath	1.6	0.0	0.7	15.0	1.7	1.0	10.8	16.3	11.8	3.0	263	195
Bell	12.2	0.8	-159.5	52.0	10.0	3.2	6.1	54.6	36.9	11.4	379	190
Boone	78.6	57.7	6.2	10.9	3.6	2.6	23.1	205.1	49.5	105.2	1 127	668
Bourbon	2.2	21.8	15.8	12.6	3.0	1.8	6.2	39.0	19.5	12.8	653	349
Boyd	34.1	3.9	10.6	37.7	8.4	5.9	19.1	104.7	45.8	31.8	641	429
Boyle	5.0	0.8	1.0	21.7	2.4	2.0	0.3	58.9	26.5	21.0	754	428
Bracken	1.6	0.0	0.4	8.2	0.8	0.7	2.0	13.9	9.1	3.3	389	295
Breathitt	3.8	1.7	0.4	43.3	7.1	1.7	2.7	30.6	20.4	5.1	323	159
Breckinridge	3.8	0.7	0.7	17.2	3.3	1.4	2.3	30.5	19.9	6.2	325	248
Bullitt	4.0	171.4	14.7	13.6	4.3	3.1	1.9	87.3	50.7	29.4	461	349
Butler	2.0	0.0	0.5	14.3	1.3	0.9	1.9	29.5	19.5	6.2	469	176
Caldwell	2.7	0.0	1.0	10.7	1.3	1.0	2.3	20.6	10.5	5.9	453	212
Calloway	5.9	0.0	2.4	12.7	6.7	3.1	3.9	120.3	25.7	15.9	462	327
Campbell	18.3	8.3	3.2	32.8	8.9	4.5	17.3	143.8	56.1	69.5	784	472
Carlisle	1.1	0.1	0.2	3.4	0.6	0.5	1.7	7.5	5.3	1.4	260	188
Carroll	2.0	3.2	0.4	8.8	2.1	0.8	8.8	115.7	9.9	8.6	844	480
Carter	4.9	20.9	1.1	34.2	6.9	2.8	46.9	40.9	29.0	6.7	249	155
Casey	1.8	0.0	0.6	23.1	2.1	1.4	0.5	21.8	14.2	4.4	276	198
Christian	1 012.4	297.3	3.4	41.6	10.4	4.4	35.3	110.1	60.6	30.5	428	208
Clark	7.9	0.5	1.4	19.9	3.1	2.2	14.9	67.7	26.4	22.6	671	370
Clay	22.3	0.4	1.1	57.1	6.4	3.4	3.4	36.5	27.8	4.9	204	113
Clinton	2.3	0.3	1.5	22.8	1.7	1.5	13.0	17.1	12.5	3.1	317	162
Crittenden	3.2	0.0	0.4	7.1	0.9	0.8	1.8	12.3	7.9	2.7	289	195

1. State totals may include programs not allocated by county.　2. Based on the resident population estimated as of July 1 of the year shown.

STATE County	Total (mil dol)	Per capita[1] (dollars)	Education	Health and hospitals	Police protection	Public welfare	Highways	Total (mil dol)	Per capita[1] (dollars)	Federal civilian	Federal military	State and local	Democratic	Republican	All other
	Direct general expenditure — Percent of total for —							Debt outstanding		Government employment, 2002			Presidential election, 2004 Percent of vote cast —		
	183	184	185	186	187	188	189	190	191	192	193	194	195	196	197
KANSAS—Cont'd															
Osage	38.9	2 297	60.4	1.5	4.8	0.0	9.4	29.3	1 733	94	47	1 242	34.0	64.4	1.6
Osborne	8.6	2 027	41.0	5.4	2.3	0.0	13.7	3.6	856	34	12	392	21.9	76.5	1.7
Ottawa	18.6	2 957	52.8	3.3	3.3	0.0	14.7	6.7	1 063	27	18	463	20.1	78.6	1.4
Pawnee	23.2	3 342	50.5	2.6	4.7	0.0	10.0	5.8	835	50	19	1 721	25.8	72.8	1.5
Phillips	22.8	3 886	40.4	4.8	1.1	1.4	9.2	9.0	1 538	47	16	828	19.7	79.1	1.2
Pottawatomie	59.4	3 211	48.0	14.5	3.0	0.0	10.3	54.7	2 960	61	51	1 326	24.7	71.6	3.7
Pratt	33.6	3 522	59.2	5.1	2.2	0.0	8.6	27.0	2 829	42	27	1 195	27.4	71.2	1.4
Rawlins	8.4	2 892	53.1	3.5	4.3	0.0	15.4	1.1	369	21	0	358	16.8	82.3	0.9
Reno	174.7	2 739	58.6	2.0	4.2	0.0	5.8	118.7	1 862	245	178	5 197	33.2	65.1	1.7
Republic	17.7	3 243	48.3	1.9	2.7	0.0	13.4	10.1	1 854	39	15	687	21.1	77.4	1.5
Rice	32.8	3 125	50.5	11.2	4.6	0.0	11.3	15.8	1 503	51	29	1 036	25.9	72.6	1.4
Riley	99.0	1 610	53.0	0.3	2.5	0.0	6.0	113.3	1 843	514	169	11 655	37.9	60.5	1.6
Rooks	22.8	4 158	36.1	16.5	4.4	6.7	8.3	6.7	1 213	30	15	715	19.6	78.4	2.0
Rush	13.3	3 797	39.8	22.0	3.3	0.0	10.1	2.7	783	31	10	357	28.9	68.5	2.6
Russell	32.1	4 552	30.7	29.2	5.3	0.0	9.4	12.2	1 726	42	20	657	22.9	75.8	1.2
Saline	147.3	2 733	47.9	1.0	4.8	0.0	6.0	181.1	3 360	307	152	4 087	32.7	65.5	1.8
Scott	14.3	2 903	52.5	3.8	4.5	0.0	7.8	21.2	4 313	25	14	518	15.0	83.8	1.2
Sedgwick	1 189.3	2 575	45.7	2.0	5.7	0.3	9.7	1 891.8	4 095	4 733	4 264	25 081	36.3	62.3	1.4
Seward	118.4	5 130	43.2	30.0	2.9	0.0	2.9	74.3	3 221	104	64	2 301	20.6	78.6	0.8
Shawnee	531.1	3 110	51.8	2.5	5.8	0.6	2.9	972.5	5 696	2 682	693	20 110	44.3	54.3	1.4
Sheridan	9.5	3 600	39.6	19.3	2.9	0.2	9.2	1.0	365	18	0	307	16.7	81.6	1.7
Sherman	30.0	4 683	28.3	32.1	3.1	0.2	10.5	5.3	826	58	18	717	23.0	75.5	1.5
Smith	13.2	3 014	45.8	5.3	3.1	0.0	11.6	2.1	484	40	12	376	22.8	75.6	1.6
Stafford	20.2	4 329	46.8	14.0	1.3	0.0	12.8	4.3	916	44	13	682	23.3	75.3	1.4
Stanton	12.8	5 312	36.6	24.8	4.7	0.0	10.0	2.1	888	12	0	293	16.9	82.5	0.5
Stevens	28.1	5 266	38.2	23.9	3.5	0.0	10.1	6.7	1 250	23	15	729	13.6	85.4	0.8
Sumner	77.8	3 047	42.4	20.1	2.6	0.1	7.5	86.3	3 379	96	71	1 910	30.6	67.7	1.7
Thomas	32.3	3 993	68.0	1.6	3.5	0.0	5.8	9.1	1 121	51	23	1 130	21.1	77.7	1.2
Trego	15.9	5 054	29.6	34.7	1.6	0.0	6.1	7.9	2 513	18	0	423	25.8	72.6	1.6
Wabaunsee	16.0	2 384	56.6	2.4	3.7	0.0	10.6	15.3	2 280	33	19	448	27.9	70.1	2.0
Wallace	6.2	3 657	55.9	1.6	2.2	0.0	11.3	2.7	1 608	16	0	176	12.8	84.8	2.4
Washington	25.5	4 059	43.1	20.5	1.3	0.0	10.7	6.1	967	55	18	803	20.3	78.2	1.5
Wichita	11.1	4 428	37.6	29.4	4.6	0.0	9.6	1.4	549	16	0	291	17.4	81.7	0.9
Wilson	31.0	3 051	51.8	19.1	3.7	0.0	6.8	12.3	1 214	45	28	941	24.0	74.3	1.7
Woodson	11.7	3 189	36.7	1.5	3.9	0.0	12.8	1.1	287	25	10	256	30.0	68.4	1.7
Wyandotte	543.5	3 433	45.0	0.7	7.0	0.0	4.0	1 602.1	10 118	2 268	445	15 134	64.7	34.2	1.1
KENTUCKY	X	X	X	X	X	X	X	X	X	36 729	39 402	265 614	39.7	59.5	0.8
Adair	22.9	1 319	69.5	4.0	2.6	0.0	6.7	28.2	1 626	52	16	879	23.7	75.6	0.7
Allen	26.4	1 454	57.8	5.8	5.4	0.1	6.6	37.7	2 073	48	17	699	26.8	72.6	0.5
Anderson	28.1	1 439	62.9	6.0	4.1	0.0	4.6	33.6	1 716	39	18	883	32.7	57.2	0.9
Ballard	23.1	2 827	38.4	3.4	1.5	0.0	6.5	134.2	16 441	39	0	423	42.1	57.2	0.7
Barren	82.9	2 138	49.7	1.4	4.0	0.1	5.1	130.5	3 367	126	37	2 085	32.3	67.1	0.6
Bath	15.9	1 390	75.2	3.8	1.5	0.1	5.5	9.5	836	36	11	567	53.0	46.1	0.9
Bell	54.9	1 824	62.8	2.0	3.1	0.0	3.3	25.9	859	156	28	1 784	38.3	61.1	0.6
Boone	193.5	2 074	41.3	1.2	5.6	0.6	4.3	562.4	6 029	1 126	90	3 978	27.5	71.7	0.8
Bourbon	37.8	1 931	56.7	4.7	3.8	0.4	3.3	36.0	1 840	50	19	978	38.9	60.3	0.8
Boyd	106.5	2 148	44.9	4.5	3.9	0.7	3.1	262.1	5 283	540	48	3 131	46.5	52.8	0.7
Boyle	55.6	1 994	52.0	4.3	4.2	3.0	5.1	71.7	2 573	81	26	1 867	37.2	62.2	0.6
Bracken	12.7	1 496	60.8	5.9	1.8	0.0	7.6	8.9	1 044	34	0	384	33.6	65.5	0.9
Breathitt	29.2	1 838	64.8	10.1	2.1	0.0	5.8	23.8	1 501	68	15	1 137	56.0	42.8	1.3
Breckinridge	28.5	1 502	67.1	3.4	2.0	0.0	6.8	33.2	1 752	74	18	843	33.8	65.5	0.7
Bullitt	81.6	1 278	65.0	3.8	3.4	0.0	4.1	45.2	709	71	60	2 057	31.6	67.9	0.5
Butler	24.7	1 877	55.1	2.5	1.7	0.0	5.9	43.0	3 267	38	12	697	25.7	73.7	0.6
Caldwell	19.9	1 541	57.9	0.6	4.6	0.0	6.9	46.1	3 571	53	12	829	35.4	64.0	0.6
Calloway	113.7	3 307	24.0	59.7	2.0	0.0	2.1	46.1	1 342	85	33	5 076	37.8	61.4	0.8
Campbell	156.5	1 767	47.6	0.5	8.6	0.1	5.7	327.6	3 698	299	84	5 374	35.5	63.6	1.0
Carlisle	7.3	1 367	68.8	5.1	2.1	0.0	7.2	6.6	1 238	23	0	223	38.7	60.9	0.3
Carroll	106.5	10 422	11.6	8.6	0.6	0.0	1.3	1 600.5	156 555	38	10	715	43.3	55.8	0.9
Carter	43.6	1 613	64.1	6.7	2.4	0.0	2.9	35.2	1 302	83	26	1 281	50.2	48.8	1.1
Casey	20.1	1 277	70.9	4.8	1.4	0.0	6.5	9.2	584	37	15	652	18.6	80.8	0.6
Christian	104.8	1 471	52.8	2.6	5.3	0.2	4.5	155.4	2 181	3 865	25 360	3 643	33.2	66.3	0.5
Clark	67.9	2 014	42.7	6.5	4.1	0.1	3.4	126.1	3 740	134	32	1 452	37.0	62.3	0.8
Clay	37.1	1 528	76.9	3.2	1.7	0.0	5.3	23.4	966	385	23	1 381	24.7	74.5	0.8
Clinton	16.2	1 675	69.1	4.5	3.8	0.0	8.4	9.8	1 013	53	0	570	21.9	77.4	0.7
Crittenden	12.6	1 362	62.7	0.9	3.4	0.0	7.7	16.8	1 820	37	0	375	34.3	65.1	0.6

1. Based on the resident population estimated as of July 1 of the year shown.

Table B. States and Counties — Land Area and Population

Population and population characteristics, 2003

STATE/County code	CBSA code[1]	County Type[2]	STATE County	Land area[3] (sq km) 2000	Total persons (1)	Rank (2)	Per square kilometer (3)	White (4)	Black (5)	Am. Indian, Alaska Native (6)	Asian and Pacific Islander (7)	Percent Hispanic or Latino[4] (8)	Under 5 years (9)	5 to 17 years (10)	18 to 24 years (11)	25 to 34 years (12)	35 to 44 years (13)	45 to 54 years (14)
			KENTUCKY—Cont'd															
21 057	...	9	Cumberland	792	7 159	2 669	9.0	95.5	4.1	0.2	0.0	0.7	5.3	17.2	8.6	11.1	14.7	13.5
21 059	36980	3	Daviess	1 198	92 540	584	77.2	93.9	5.1	0.4	0.6	1.0	7.2	18.2	9.8	11.9	14.8	14.2
21 061	14540	3	Edmonson	784	11 869	2 300	15.1	98.4	0.6	0.5	0.1	0.6	5.7	16.9	9.7	13.1	14.2	13.8
21 063	...	9	Elliott	606	6 935	2 695	11.4	99.4	0.1	0.5	0.1	0.6	6.4	18.2	10.4	12.0	13.5	14.3
21 065	...	6	Estill	658	15 192	2 086	23.1	98.8	0.3	0.5	0.1	0.7	6.1	17.4	9.4	13.4	15.7	13.7
21 067	30460	2	Fayette	737	266 798	218	362.0	78.6	14.6	0.6	3.4	4.2	6.5	18.2	9.4	13.3	14.4	14.1
21 069	...	7	Fleming	909	14 379	2 139	15.8	97.6	1.6	0.4	0.2	0.7	6.0	16.6	9.9	13.7	15.6	15.5
21 071	...	7	Floyd	1 021	42 272	1 075	41.4	97.6	1.4	0.4	0.3	0.7	6.0	16.6	9.9	13.7	15.6	15.5
21 073	23180	4	Franklin	545	48 051	962	88.2	87.9	10.0	0.6	1.2	1.6	6.3	16.1	9.5	13.9	15.7	15.5
21 075	46460	7	Fulton	541	7 419	2 647	13.7	74.4	24.7	0.2	0.4	0.8	6.6	17.2	10.2	11.5	13.8	14.1
21 077	17140	1	Gallatin	256	7 995	2 594	31.2	96.5	2.0	0.4	0.6	1.4	6.7	21.0	8.4	12.7	16.4	13.5
21 079	...	6	Garrard	599	15 850	2 041	26.5	95.3	3.2	0.2	0.1	1.6	5.5	17.8	9.5	13.4	16.2	13.9
21 081	17140	1	Grant	673	23 983	1 615	35.6	97.9	0.3	0.6	0.5	1.1	7.7	20.4	10.0	14.8	15.6	12.2
21 083	32460	7	Graves	1 439	37 252	1 201	25.9	91.4	5.0	0.7	0.4	3.5	6.4	17.8	9.0	11.9	14.4	13.8
21 085	...	6	Grayson	1 305	24 600	1 596	18.9	98.3	0.7	0.5	0.2	0.8	6.3	17.7	9.5	12.5	14.4	14.1
21 087	...	8	Green	748	11 787	2 306	15.8	95.9	2.9	0.4	0.2	1.2	5.5	16.6	9.0	11.2	14.6	14.4
21 089	26580	2	Greenup	896	36 952	1 212	41.2	98.2	0.7	0.6	0.5	0.6	5.4	17.0	8.8	11.7	14.6	15.2
21 091	36980	3	Hancock	489	8 433	2 568	17.2	97.6	1.0	0.3	0.3	1.0	6.7	19.6	8.7	12.7	15.3	14.6
21 093	21060	3	Hardin	1 626	96 052	561	59.1	81.5	13.4	1.0	3.3	3.2	7.1	19.5	11.2	13.3	16.5	13.6
21 095	...	7	Harlan	1 210	32 095	1 357	26.5	96.0	2.7	1.0	0.4	0.7	6.0	18.1	9.5	11.8	14.8	16.0
21 097	...	6	Harrison	802	18 227	1 895	22.7	95.6	2.7	0.5	0.2	1.5	6.4	17.7	9.0	12.7	15.6	14.5
21 099	...	8	Hart	1 077	17 879	1 922	16.6	93.1	5.7	0.7	0.2	1.0	6.2	18.4	9.7	11.9	15.4	13.3
21 101	21780	2	Henderson	1 140	45 129	1 022	39.6	90.9	7.6	0.5	0.5	1.3	6.4	17.4	9.2	12.7	15.8	15.0
21 103	31140	1	Henry	749	15 543	2 060	20.8	93.4	3.8	0.4	0.4	2.6	7.0	18.4	8.7	12.3	15.7	14.4
21 105	...	8	Hickman	633	5 165	2 831	8.2	88.9	10.1	0.5	0.1	1.2	5.4	15.8	8.1	11.2	14.9	14.1
21 107	31580	4	Hopkins	1 426	46 839	983	32.8	92.0	6.7	0.6	0.6	1.0	6.4	17.4	8.8	12.1	14.5	15.0
21 109	...	9	Jackson	897	13 595	2 190	15.2	99.0	0.2	0.4	0.1	0.7	6.5	18.7	10.2	13.7	15.3	14.0
21 111	31140	1	Jefferson	997	699 017	74	701.1	76.1	20.3	0.6	2.1	2.1	6.9	17.4	8.6	13.7	15.6	14.8
21 113	30460	2	Jessamine	448	41 508	1 097	92.7	94.6	3.5	0.6	1.0	1.4	6.8	18.8	11.6	14.7	15.1	13.8
21 115	...	7	Johnson	677	23 647	1 627	34.9	98.5	0.3	0.4	0.5	0.8	6.5	16.6	9.6	12.8	14.9	15.3
21 117	17140	1	Kenton	419	152 287	369	363.5	93.5	4.9	0.5	1.0	1.3	7.5	18.9	8.9	14.4	16.1	14.2
21 119	...	9	Knott	912	17 614	1 932	19.3	98.3	0.9	0.4	0.2	0.6	6.9	18.9	10.0	13.1	14.3	13.5
21 121	...	6	Knox	1 004	31 708	1 364	31.6	98.0	1.1	0.8	0.3	0.6	6.2	17.5	9.3	11.5	15.4	14.3
21 123	21060	3	Larue	682	13 437	2 202	19.7	95.5	3.4	0.7	0.2	1.1	6.2	17.5	9.3	11.5	15.4	14.3
21 125	30940	7	Laurel	1 128	55 488	869	49.2	97.9	0.8	1.0	0.5	0.8	6.3	18.0	9.6	13.9	15.3	14.0
21 127	...	6	Lawrence	1 085	15 895	2 037	14.6	99.0	0.2	0.6	0.1	0.5	6.0	18.0	9.7	13.3	14.9	14.7
21 129	...	9	Lee	544	7 900	2 601	14.5	95.3	3.8	0.7	0.2	0.4	4.9	16.5	10.3	13.7	16.4	13.7
21 131	...	9	Leslie	1 046	12 203	2 285	11.7	99.1	0.1	0.3	0.2	0.6	5.9	17.3	9.3	13.1	16.6	15.6
21 133	...	9	Letcher	878	24 843	1 581	28.3	98.5	0.6	0.3	0.3	0.5	5.6	16.7	9.8	12.4	15.7	16.1
21 135	32500	8	Lewis	1 255	13 796	2 182	11.0	99.0	0.4	0.4	0.1	0.5	6.0	18.1	9.5	13.4	15.2	14.7
21 137	19220	7	Lincoln	871	24 535	1 600	28.2	96.3	2.6	0.4	0.1	1.1	6.9	18.4	9.0	13.4	15.2	13.0
21 139	37140	9	Livingston	819	9 726	2 466	11.9	98.5	0.2	0.8	0.1	0.8	4.9	16.3	8.1	12.2	15.5	15.0
21 141	...	6	Logan	1 439	26 841	1 511	18.7	90.5	8.0	0.6	0.4	1.5	6.8	18.1	9.5	12.2	15.0	13.6
21 143	...	8	Lyon	559	8 078	2 590	14.5	91.9	6.8	0.4	0.3	0.8	3.1	11.9	8.4	14.6	17.6	15.1
21 145	37140	5	McCracken	650	64 768	766	99.6	86.9	11.8	0.7	0.8	1.2	6.3	16.8	8.3	11.8	14.7	15.4
21 147	...	9	McCreary	1 108	17 190	1 947	15.5	98.0	0.8	1.1	0.1	0.7	6.7	20.1	10.4	12.9	14.7	13.5
21 149	36980	3	McLean	659	9 872	2 456	15.0	98.3	0.4	0.4	0.1	1.1	6.6	17.0	8.9	12.7	14.6	14.4
21 151	40020	4	Madison	1 141	74 814	686	65.6	93.4	4.9	0.7	1.2	1.0	6.6	15.6	15.8	15.9	13.8	12.1
21 153	...	9	Magoffin	801	13 334	2 213	16.6	99.0	0.2	0.2	0.1	0.5	7.1	18.5	10.4	13.5	15.8	14.2
21 155	...	6	Marion	897	18 533	1 880	20.7	89.3	9.4	0.3	0.7	1.0	6.6	17.9	10.4	13.5	16.0	13.7
21 157	...	6	Marshall	790	30 559	1 396	38.7	98.7	0.2	0.8	0.2	0.8	5.0	15.8	8.7	11.0	14.7	14.5
21 159	...	8	Martin	598	12 521	2 269	20.9	99.1	0.2	0.4	0.2	0.6	7.1	19.4	10.5	12.8	15.6	15.1
21 161	32500	6	Mason	624	16 815	1 973	26.9	91.1	7.7	0.4	0.6	1.0	6.1	17.4	8.6	12.4	15.0	15.4
21 163	31140	1	Meade	799	27 619	1 477	34.6	92.6	4.3	1.0	1.2	2.2	7.0	21.1	9.5	15.1	16.7	12.9
21 165	34460	9	Menifee	528	6 618	2 721	12.5	97.7	1.1	0.4	0.1	1.1	5.3	17.7	11.0	12.8	14.7	14.6
21 167	...	6	Mercer	650	21 410	1 732	32.9	93.8	4.3	0.5	0.8	1.4	6.5	17.8	8.1	12.0	15.3	14.1
21 169	23980	9	Metcalfe	753	10 042	2 438	13.3	97.4	1.8	0.5	0.1	0.6	6.5	17.7	8.5	12.1	15.1	13.6
21 171	...	9	Monroe	857	11 740	2 311	13.7	95.3	3.1	0.3	0.1	1.8	6.0	17.0	9.5	12.1	14.5	14.1
21 173	34460	6	Montgomery	514	23 535	1 638	45.8	95.2	3.6	0.5	0.2	1.2	6.9	17.7	8.7	14.3	14.9	14.2
21 175	...	9	Morgan	987	14 278	2 148	14.5	94.8	4.4	0.4	0.1	0.6	5.4	15.8	11.4	15.5	16.5	14.2
21 177	16420	6	Muhlenberg	1 230	31 691	1 365	25.8	94.4	4.7	0.5	0.2	0.8	6.0	16.2	9.5	12.3	14.6	14.5
21 179	31140	1	Nelson	1 095	39 635	1 138	36.2	92.8	5.5	0.4	0.8	1.1	6.8	19.6	9.7	13.0	16.2	14.1
21 181	...	8	Nicholas	509	6 937	2 694	13.6	98.2	0.8	0.3	0.2	0.6	6.5	16.4	8.7	12.4	14.8	14.2
21 183	...	6	Ohio	1 538	23 165	1 658	15.1	97.5	0.9	0.5	0.3	1.2	6.2	17.5	9.6	12.7	14.5	14.2
21 185	31140	1	Oldham	490	50 517	930	103.1	93.2	4.5	0.6	0.9	1.7	5.6	19.9	9.5	11.4	18.7	16.7
21 187	...	8	Owen	912	11 092	2 363	12.2	97.2	1.2	0.6	0.4	1.2	6.1	18.2	9.4	12.2	15.0	14.4

1. CBSA = Core Based Statistical Area. See Appendix A for explanation. See Appendix B for list of metropolitan areas with component counties.
2. County type code from the Economic Research Service of USDA Rural-Urban Continuum Codes. See Appendix A for definition.
3. Dry land or land partially or temporarily covered by water.
4. Hispanic or Latino persons may be of any race.

Table B. States and Counties — Population and Households

STATE County	Age (percent) (cont'd) 55 to 64 years	65 to 74 years	75 years and over	Percent female	Total persons 1990	2000	Percent change 1990–2000	2000–2003	Components of change, 2000–2003 Births	Deaths	Net migration	Households, 2000 Number	Percent change, 1990–2000	Persons per house-hold	Female family house-holder[1]	One person
	16	17	18	19	20	21	22	23	24	25	26	27	28	29	30	31
KENTUCKY—Cont'd																
Cumberland	11.7	9.6	8.1	51.0	6 784	7 147	5.4	0.2	256	361	123	2 976	9.7	2.37	11.2	28.9
Daviess	9.8	7.1	6.7	51.7	87 189	91 545	5.0	1.1	4 393	2 995	-327	36 033	9.1	2.47	11.8	27.1
Edmonson	12.2	7.9	6.2	50.7	10 357	11 644	12.4	1.9	444	359	150	4 648	20.9	2.47	8.9	22.4
Elliott	11.0	7.0	6.2	51.2	6 455	6 748	4.5	2.8	287	234	141	2 638	13.5	2.54	9.7	24.7
Estill	11.3	7.5	5.9	51.3	14 614	15 307	4.7	-0.8	623	612	-103	6 108	14.0	2.48	12.9	24.6
Fayette	8.3	5.2	4.8	50.6	225 366	260 512	15.6	2.4	12 032	6 619	1 011	108 288	21.0	2.29	11.5	31.7
Fleming	10.1	7.1	6.0	50.9	12 292	13 792	12.2	4.3	612	507	482	5 367	16.0	2.55	9.6	23.3
Floyd	10.4	6.6	5.7	50.9	43 586	42 441	-2.6	-0.4	1 726	1 508	-351	16 881	7.8	2.45	12.3	25.2
Franklin	10.5	6.5	5.7	51.5	44 143	47 687	8.0	0.8	1 995	1 489	-101	19 907	14.5	2.30	12.2	30.4
Fulton	10.6	7.9	9.5	53.6	8 271	7 752	-6.3	-4.3	327	356	-304	3 237	-4.2	2.32	18.0	32.3
Gallatin	9.7	5.4	4.9	50.3	5 393	7 870	45.9	1.6	338	263	45	2 902	49.5	2.68	10.7	22.0
Garrard	10.1	6.8	5.6	50.7	11 579	14 792	27.7	7.2	521	437	955	5 741	29.4	2.56	9.4	21.1
Grant	9.0	4.8	4.2	50.4	15 737	22 384	42.2	7.1	1 238	701	1 042	8 175	46.4	2.72	11.1	19.8
Graves	10.8	7.4	8.2	51.1	33 550	37 028	10.4	0.6	1 554	1 540	250	14 841	10.9	2.44	10.0	26.2
Grayson	11.0	7.9	5.8	50.5	21 050	24 053	14.3	2.3	1 012	992	542	9 596	20.1	2.47	10.0	24.1
Green	11.3	8.6	8.1	50.6	10 371	11 518	11.1	2.3	439	439	272	4 706	15.1	2.41	8.5	25.4
Greenup	11.9	8.7	6.4	51.8	36 796	36 891	0.3	0.2	1 323	1 313	97	14 536	8.4	2.51	10.4	21.7
Hancock	11.3	6.1	4.9	50.3	7 864	8 392	6.7	0.5	383	237	-96	3 215	15.0	2.59	8.3	21.2
Hardin	8.3	5.8	4.2	49.7	89 240	94 174	5.5	2.0	4 543	2 241	-321	34 497	17.5	2.62	11.9	22.8
Harlan	10.9	7.3	6.6	52.0	36 574	33 202	-9.2	-3.3	1 252	1 444	-899	13 291	0.2	2.47	13.2	27.0
Harrison	10.5	6.6	6.5	51.1	16 248	17 983	10.7	1.4	754	625	136	7 012	15.2	2.53	10.3	24.0
Hart	10.7	7.6	6.1	50.7	14 890	17 445	17.2	2.5	711	585	299	6 769	17.9	2.54	10.4	25.3
Henderson	10.1	6.9	6.1	51.6	43 044	44 829	4.1	0.7	1 843	1 458	-27	18 095	9.3	2.43	11.6	26.4
Henry	10.7	6.5	5.5	50.3	12 823	15 060	17.4	3.2	713	515	297	5 844	19.4	2.57	10.4	22.0
Hickman	12.9	9.2	9.6	51.6	5 566	5 262	-5.5	-1.8	163	226	-32	2 188	0.0	2.34	10.8	27.6
Hopkins	10.7	7.4	7.2	52.0	46 126	46 519	0.9	0.7	1 970	1 717	83	18 820	6.0	2.43	11.9	25.8
Jackson	10.0	6.5	5.1	50.4	11 955	13 495	12.9	0.7	573	497	41	5 307	21.1	2.52	10.3	23.0
Jefferson	9.4	6.9	6.5	52.0	665 123	693 604	4.3	0.8	32 261	23 179	-3 143	287 012	8.7	2.37	14.7	30.5
Jessamine	8.4	5.2	4.3	51.0	30 508	39 041	28.0	6.3	1 717	1 020	1 782	13 867	30.8	2.69	11.1	18.5
Johnson	11.2	7.1	5.5	51.5	23 248	23 445	0.8	0.9	1 005	858	83	9 103	7.5	2.52	11.3	22.3
Kenton	8.8	5.7	5.2	50.8	142 005	151 464	6.7	0.5	7 499	4 372	-2 188	59 444	12.8	2.52	12.1	27.8
Knott	10.4	6.3	5.3	50.9	17 906	17 649	-1.4	-0.2	525	563	15	6 717	10.4	2.54	12.6	23.6
Knox	10.7	6.6	6.0	51.9	29 676	31 795	7.1	-0.3	1 421	1 090	-377	12 416	15.8	2.51	13.6	25.7
Larue	11.0	7.8	7.4	51.4	11 679	13 373	14.5	0.5	521	439	-4	5 275	17.1	2.49	10.5	23.7
Laurel	9.8	6.6	4.6	51.1	43 438	52 715	21.4	5.3	2 663	1 685	1 790	20 353	30.6	2.56	11.4	21.7
Lawrence	10.4	7.1	5.4	50.5	13 998	15 569	11.2	2.1	638	581	277	5 954	18.9	2.59	10.5	22.4
Lee	10.3	7.9	6.3	47.7	7 422	7 916	6.7	-0.2	260	327	58	2 985	8.2	2.41	12.8	26.6
Leslie	10.3	7.1	4.9	51.4	13 642	12 401	-9.1	-1.6	494	443	-245	4 885	3.7	2.52	12.9	22.4
Letcher	11.0	7.2	5.6	50.9	27 000	25 277	-6.4	-1.7	942	1 007	-346	10 085	3.6	2.48	11.5	24.1
Lewis	10.6	7.0	5.8	50.2	13 029	14 092	8.2	-2.1	555	454	-383	5 422	15.0	2.56	9.7	22.5
Lincoln	10.4	7.0	5.8	50.9	20 096	23 361	16.2	5.0	1 117	767	816	9 206	23.9	2.51	10.3	23.6
Livingston	13.2	8.4	6.9	50.3	9 062	9 804	8.2	-0.8	300	359	-7	3 996	11.2	2.42	7.9	24.4
Logan	10.6	7.2	6.6	51.7	24 416	26 573	8.8	1.0	1 196	952	51	10 506	12.9	2.50	11.2	25.0
Lyon	12.6	10.1	7.1	42.5	6 624	8 080	22.0	0.0	160	349	194	2 898	23.1	2.26	8.1	26.8
McCracken	10.9	7.8	8.2	52.5	62 879	65 514	4.2	-1.1	2 728	2 494	-950	27 736	8.2	2.31	12.2	29.7
McCreary	11.0	6.3	4.5	50.7	15 603	17 080	9.5	0.6	782	560	-95	6 520	19.0	2.55	13.8	24.7
McLean	12.1	7.6	6.7	50.5	9 628	9 938	3.2	-0.7	435	388	-111	3 984	8.5	2.47	8.7	24.7
Madison	8.3	5.4	4.3	51.6	57 508	70 872	23.2	5.6	3 180	1 742	2 494	27 152	35.7	2.42	10.7	25.2
Magoffin	9.3	6.0	4.7	50.7	13 077	13 332	1.9	0.0	625	454	-164	5 024	13.2	2.62	11.2	21.4
Marion	9.1	6.5	6.0	49.4	16 499	18 212	10.4	1.8	768	646	223	6 613	16.3	2.58	13.7	24.4
Marshall	12.1	9.5	8.2	50.9	27 205	30 125	10.7	1.4	985	1 175	635	12 412	15.0	2.38	7.9	25.0
Martin	9.3	6.0	4.0	50.4	12 526	12 578	0.4	-0.5	570	419	-193	4 776	11.1	2.62	12.5	21.8
Mason	9.9	7.6	7.6	51.5	16 666	16 800	0.8	0.1	667	642	9	6 847	4.7	2.41	11.1	27.6
Meade	8.5	5.1	3.2	49.8	24 170	26 349	9.0	4.8	993	557	829	9 470	17.2	2.77	9.7	18.4
Menifee	11.7	7.6	4.9	50.0	5 092	6 556	28.8	0.9	227	215	56	2 537	37.7	2.49	8.8	22.1
Mercer	10.9	7.5	6.9	51.2	19 148	20 817	8.7	2.8	884	741	483	8 423	13.6	2.45	10.4	25.1
Metcalfe	10.9	8.6	6.7	50.8	8 963	10 037	12.0	0.0	419	447	37	4 016	17.0	2.47	10.0	25.2
Monroe	11.5	8.3	7.0	51.4	11 401	11 756	3.1	-0.1	453	432	-26	4 741	5.2	2.45	10.4	26.3
Montgomery	9.9	6.6	5.9	51.3	19 561	22 554	15.3	4.3	1 042	738	682	8 900	21.7	2.49	11.2	23.9
Morgan	9.2	6.7	5.1	44.9	11 648	13 948	19.7	2.4	505	366	207	4 752	16.2	2.55	9.2	22.6
Muhlenberg	11.4	8.1	7.3	50.7	31 318	31 839	1.7	-0.5	1 240	1 264	-93	12 357	5.8	2.45	10.4	24.3
Nelson	9.0	5.8	4.7	50.9	29 710	37 477	26.1	5.8	1 638	1 025	1 548	13 953	33.9	2.64	12.1	22.3
Nicholas	11.1	7.8	7.4	51.2	6 725	6 813	1.3	1.8	292	264	99	2 710	3.4	2.48	10.0	24.6
Ohio	11.2	7.3	6.8	50.5	21 105	22 916	8.6	1.1	913	868	226	8 899	13.9	2.54	9.2	23.2
Oldham	9.7	4.1	2.8	47.0	33 263	46 178	38.8	9.4	1 727	844	2 955	14 856	39.2	2.85	7.8	14.9
Owen	10.6	6.9	6.3	49.9	9 035	10 547	16.7	5.2	428	354	462	4 086	19.8	2.55	8.0	23.1

1. No spouse present.

STATE County	Births, average 1999–2001 Total	Rate[1]	Deaths, average 1999–2001 Number Total	Infant[2]	Rate Total[1]	Infant[3]	Physicians,[4] 2000 Number	Rate[5]	Hospitals,[4] 1998 Number	Beds Number	Rate[5]	Medicare enrollees, 2003	Serious crimes known to police,[6] 2002 Total Number	Rate[7]
	32	33	34	35	36	37	38	39	40	41	42	43	44	45
KENTUCKY—Cont'd														
Cumberland	79	11.1	110	1	15.4	D	3	42	1	31	454	1 525	NA	NA
Daviess	1 328	14.5	910	9	9.9	7.0	145	158	2	526	577	15 692	3 184	3 435
Edmonson	136	11.6	104	1	8.9	D	3	26	0	0	0	1 695	NA	NA
Elliott	80	11.9	72	1	10.8	D	3	44	0	0	0	860	NA	NA
Estill	194	12.7	173	2	11.3	D	12	78	1	26	167	3 247	NA	NA
Fayette	3 594	13.8	1 969	29	7.6	8.2	1 297	498	5	1 906	788	31 266	13 306	5 044
Fleming	180	13.0	146	0	10.5	D	7	51	1	45	335	2 469	NA	NA
Floyd	537	12.7	464	3	10.9	D	56	132	3	295	681	8 497	NA	NA
Franklin	613	12.8	447	5	9.4	D	87	182	1	154	332	8 956	NA	NA
Fulton	101	12.9	114	0	14.6	D	20	258	1	65	862	1 808	NA	NA
Gallatin	110	13.9	77	1	9.7	D	3	38	0	0	0	982	NA	NA
Garrard	173	11.6	136	1	9.1	D	9	61	1	131	941	2 426	NA	NA
Grant	392	17.4	190	2	8.5	D	14	63	1	30	147	3 201	NA	NA
Graves	486	13.1	462	2	12.5	D	38	103	1	101	282	7 294	NA	NA
Grayson	318	13.2	281	2	11.7	D	23	96	1	71	299	4 515	NA	NA
Green	122	10.6	127	1	11.0	D	9	78	1	58	545	2 138	NA	NA
Greenup	408	11.1	403	4	10.9	D	44	119	0	0	0	6 848	NA	NA
Hancock	124	14.7	66	0	7.8	D	2	24	0	0	0	1 181	NA	NA
Hardin	1 458	15.5	677	16	7.2	10.7	174	185	1	296	324	12 341	NA	NA
Harlan	408	12.3	428	4	12.9	D	48	145	1	132	378	7 065	NA	NA
Harrison	235	13.1	198	2	11.0	D	14	78	1	81	461	2 991	NA	NA
Hart	227	13.1	194	2	11.2	D	14	80	1	36	215	2 935	NA	NA
Henderson	595	13.3	460	5	10.2	D	67	149	1	233	524	7 240	NA	NA
Henry	216	14.3	160	1	10.6	D	14	93	0	0	0	2 562	NA	NA
Hickman	51	9.8	67	0	12.8	D	3	57	0	0	0	852	NA	NA
Hopkins	603	13.0	528	2	11.4	D	103	221	1	429	925	8 701	NA	NA
Jackson	183	13.5	143	1	10.6	D	3	22	0	0	0	2 273	NA	NA
Jefferson	9 897	14.3	7 104	68	10.2	6.9	2 154	311	10	3 761	560	111 466	28 721	4 596
Jessamine	551	14.1	296	2	7.6	D	26	67	0	0	0	4 755	NA	NA
Johnson	315	13.4	252	2	10.7	D	30	128	1	78	325	4 560	NA	NA
Kenton	2 351	15.5	1 284	18	8.5	7.7	296	195	2	521	355	19 532	NA	NA
Knott	183	10.4	170	1	9.7	D	6	34	0	0	0	2 704	NA	NA
Knox	456	14.4	341	4	10.7	D	19	60	1	62	194	4 563	NA	NA
Larue	168	12.6	134	2	10.0	D	8	60	0	0	0	2 299	NA	NA
Laurel	787	14.9	496	4	9.4	D	47	89	1	80	158	7 930	NA	NA
Lawrence	199	12.8	174	0	11.2	D	17	109	1	106	677	2 837	NA	NA
Lee	85	10.7	88	1	11.2	D	4	51	0	0	0	1 510	NA	NA
Leslie	156	12.6	130	2	10.5	D	9	73	1	36	265	2 476	NA	NA
Letcher	298	11.8	291	2	11.5	D	35	138	2	149	569	5 083	NA	NA
Lewis	179	12.8	152	1	10.9	D	5	35	0	0	0	2 396	NA	NA
Lincoln	329	14.1	235	2	10.0	D	11	47	1	73	326	4 374	NA	NA
Livingston	97	9.9	109	0	11.1	D	8	82	1	26	276	1 996	NA	NA
Logan	378	14.2	290	2	10.9	D	19	72	1	106	405	4 639	NA	NA
Lyon	57	7.1	104	0	12.9	D	3	37	0	0	0	1 648	NA	NA
McCracken	840	12.9	775	6	11.9	D	178	272	2	769	1 193	11 983	NA	NA
McCreary	231	13.6	169	2	9.9	D	8	47	0	0	0	2 927	NA	NA
McLean	137	13.9	119	0	12.1	D	4	40	1	26	264	1 852	NA	NA
Madison	980	13.8	528	7	7.4	6.8	83	117	2	227	341	9 487	NA	NA
Magoffin	199	14.9	136	1	10.2	D	5	38	0	0	0	2 207	NA	NA
Marion	249	13.7	185	2	10.2	D	14	77	1	82	482	3 120	NA	NA
Marshall	309	10.2	357	1	11.8	D	18	60	1	41	135	6 288	603	1 977
Martin	184	14.7	122	3	9.7	D	7	56	0	0	0	2 193	NA	NA
Mason	229	13.6	205	2	12.2	D	27	161	1	117	687	2 937	NA	NA
Meade	307	11.7	173	3	6.6	D	13	49	0	0	0	2 572	NA	NA
Menifee	79	12.1	62	1	9.6	D	2	31	0	0	0	1 153	NA	NA
Mercer	274	13.1	234	1	11.2	D	14	67	1	59	285	3 769	NA	NA
Metcalfe	133	13.2	120	1	11.9	D	2	20	0	0	0	2 064	NA	NA
Monroe	147	12.5	136	1	11.6	D	7	60	1	49	437	2 580	NA	NA
Montgomery	344	15.2	229	4	10.1	D	20	89	1	97	463	3 681	NA	NA
Morgan	154	11.0	117	2	8.4	D	8	57	1	24	177	2 237	NA	NA
Muhlenberg	406	12.7	381	2	12.0	D	24	75	1	112	348	6 111	NA	NA
Nelson	535	14.2	312	2	8.3	D	28	75	1	47	131	5 772	NA	NA
Nicholas	97	14.1	82	0	11.9	D	8	117	1	73	1 043	1 349	NA	NA
Ohio	294	12.8	257	2	11.2	D	26	113	1	52	236	3 929	NA	NA
Oldham	537	11.6	249	3	5.4	D	42	91	1	123	277	3 936	NA	NA
Owen	127	12.0	108	2	10.2	D	8	76	1	50	487	1 293	NA	NA

1. Per 1,000 estimated resident population. 2. Deaths of infants under 1 year old. 3. Deaths of infants under 1 year old per 1,000 live births. 4. Data subject to copyright. 5. Per 100,000 resident population as of July 1 of the year shown. 6. Data for serious crimes have not been adjusted for underreporting; this may affect comparability between geographic areas and over time. 7. Per 100,000 population estimated by the FBI.

Table B. States and Counties — Crime, Education, Money Income, and Poverty

STATE County	Serious crimes known to police,[1] 2002 (cont'd) Rate[2] Violent	Property	Education School enrollment and attainment, 2000 Enrollment[3] Total	Percent private	Attainment[4] (percent) High school graduate or less	Bachelor's degree or more	Local government expenditures,[5] 2000–2001 Total current expenditures (mil dol)	Current expenditures per student (dollars)	Money income, 1999 Per capita income[6] (dollars)	Households Median income Dollars	Percent change, 1989–1999 (constant 1999 dollars)	Percent with income of $100,000 or more	Percent below poverty level, 1999 Persons	House-holds	Families	Families with children
	46	47	48	49	50	51	52	53	54	55	56	57	58	59	60	61
KENTUCKY—Cont'd																
Cumberland	NA	NA	1 566	4.2	80.4	7.1	7.9	6 757	12 643	21 572	23.6	2.3	23.8	26.8	16.4	24.8
Daviess	231	3 204	23 030	21.1	56.9	17.0	93.0	6 414	18 739	36 813	12.3	6.2	12.3	12.7	9.4	14.6
Edmonson	NA	NA	2 541	1.6	78.4	4.9	11.8	5 993	14 480	25 413	25.0	2.8	18.4	20.1	14.2	22.8
Elliott	NA	NA	1 524	2.2	78.5	7.8	8.1	6 700	12 067	21 014	12.6	3.7	25.9	26.0	20.8	27.1
Estill	NA	NA	3 394	4.1	78.8	6.9	15.8	5 911	12 285	23 318	8.1	2.4	26.4	27.4	22.5	31.7
Fayette	547	4 496	76 330	15.4	36.6	35.6	228.0	6 883	23 109	39 813	5.6	11.5	12.9	12.9	8.2	12.6
Fleming	NA	NA	3 295	8.2	71.5	8.8	15.6	6 430	14 214	27 990	15.6	3.5	18.6	19.8	14.8	18.2
Floyd	NA	NA	9 447	8.3	68.6	9.7	45.7	6 309	12 442	21 168	0.6	3.2	30.3	30.7	26.9	35.2
Franklin	NA	NA	11 593	16.0	52.6	23.8	40.5	5 871	21 229	40 011	8.4	8.9	10.7	11.6	6.9	11.6
Fulton	NA	NA	1 835	6.0	69.4	11.5	9.6	7 303	14 309	24 382	12.8	3.1	23.1	24.6	20.1	30.7
Gallatin	NA	NA	1 911	8.0	76.4	6.9	8.2	5 466	16 416	36 422	26.4	6.0	13.4	15.0	11.6	16.1
Garrard	NA	NA	3 317	7.4	66.3	10.5	14.0	5 678	16 915	34 284	21.2	4.1	14.7	15.0	11.6	17.3
Grant	NA	NA	5 436	8.3	71.8	9.4	23.9	5 441	16 776	38 438	16.8	5.6	11.1	11.3	9.0	13.0
Graves	NA	NA	8 421	11.1	65.5	12.6	33.2	5 644	16 834	30 874	11.3	5.8	16.4	17.6	13.1	20.5
Grayson	NA	NA	5 375	6.0	74.3	7.7	22.7	5 491	14 759	27 639	18.9	3.5	18.1	19.4	13.9	21.4
Green	NA	NA	2 523	8.2	74.8	9.1	10.1	5 994	16 107	25 463	2.8	4.5	18.4	19.5	15.2	19.9
Greenup	NA	NA	8 244	8.2	62.6	11.5	36.2	5 804	17 137	32 142	-2.5	5.8	14.1	15.0	11.6	17.8
Hancock	NA	NA	1 977	9.0	68.5	8.1	9.9	6 361	16 623	36 914	5.3	5.1	13.6	14.0	11.4	15.0
Hardin	NA	NA	25 768	10.4	52.0	15.4	89.9	5 794	17 487	37 744	15.0	5.7	10.0	9.9	8.2	11.5
Harlan	NA	NA	7 775	6.0	75.6	8.9	38.3	6 206	11 585	18 665	-6.0	2.3	32.5	31.9	29.1	36.0
Harrison	NA	NA	4 119	7.1	68.5	10.6	18.9	5 929	17 478	36 210	23.7	6.4	12.0	12.8	9.4	13.4
Hart	NA	NA	3 765	8.2	76.9	7.0	15.1	6 334	13 495	25 378	20.5	3.1	22.4	23.1	18.6	24.2
Henderson	NA	NA	10 565	11.8	59.5	13.8	42.3	5 942	18 470	35 892	4.5	6.3	12.3	12.9	9.7	15.8
Henry	NA	NA	3 368	11.1	71.1	9.8	16.4	6 459	17 846	37 263	23.1	7.6	13.7	14.9	10.4	14.3
Hickman	NA	NA	1 077	2.8	74.7	8.8	5.5	6 522	17 279	31 615	15.6	4.7	17.4	16.3	14.2	24.1
Hopkins	NA	NA	10 750	9.1	67.0	10.6	46.6	5 948	17 382	30 868	3.7	5.1	16.5	16.2	13.6	21.1
Jackson	NA	NA	2 999	6.2	80.5	6.8	16.6	6 986	10 711	20 177	26.4	1.1	30.2	30.5	25.8	33.1
Jefferson	595	4 001	175 028	24.7	47.2	24.8	688.8	7 079	22 352	39 457	8.4	10.7	12.4	12.2	9.5	15.3
Jessamine	NA	NA	11 132	28.3	53.3	21.5	38.5	5 759	18 842	40 096	10.3	10.1	10.5	11.2	8.4	11.9
Johnson	NA	NA	5 335	4.1	71.4	9.3	28.3	6 324	14 051	24 911	17.5	3.9	26.6	26.1	21.7	30.5
Kenton	NA	NA	38 232	28.3	50.4	22.9	134.1	6 248	22 085	43 906	7.1	11.1	9.0	9.0	7.1	10.8
Knott	NA	NA	4 684	11.1	72.1	10.2	20.1	6 522	11 297	20 373	13.8	2.6	31.1	31.0	26.2	35.6
Knox	NA	NA	7 599	10.0	78.5	8.8	34.0	6 032	10 660	18 294	7.2	2.2	34.8	35.1	29.6	36.9
Larue	NA	NA	3 123	8.7	69.2	10.9	14.3	6 142	15 865	32 056	6.5	4.8	15.4	16.6	12.6	17.5
Laurel	NA	NA	11 653	8.9	71.0	10.6	52.4	5 841	14 165	27 015	8.2	4.1	21.3	21.3	17.8	24.7
Lawrence	NA	NA	3 631	3.3	74.8	6.6	17.1	6 067	12 008	21 610	5.3	3.1	30.7	29.6	25.3	34.1
Lee	NA	NA	1 738	14.0	79.9	6.3	8.9	6 585	13 325	18 544	10.8	3.6	30.4	30.8	25.2	34.6
Leslie	NA	NA	2 862	6.5	77.6	6.3	15.6	6 569	10 429	18 546	0.8	1.3	32.7	33.8	30.2	36.5
Letcher	NA	NA	5 801	5.2	74.4	7.7	29.9	6 966	11 984	21 110	4.0	2.1	27.1	27.9	23.7	32.0
Lewis	NA	NA	3 393	5.0	77.3	6.4	15.4	6 172	12 031	22 208	4.8	2.1	28.5	27.8	23.5	33.0
Lincoln	NA	NA	5 338	5.6	76.1	8.4	26.4	6 301	13 602	26 542	15.1	3.3	21.1	21.4	16.4	22.0
Livingston	NA	NA	2 160	5.6	66.4	8.4	8.8	6 038	17 072	31 776	13.2	4.4	10.3	11.8	7.6	9.5
Logan	NA	NA	5 915	7.8	71.0	9.6	27.3	5 830	15 962	32 474	13.6	4.1	15.5	15.7	10.8	16.3
Lyon	NA	NA	1 466	16.0	68.5	10.1	5.9	5 507	16 016	31 694	16.6	5.7	12.7	14.0	10.2	16.4
McCracken	NA	NA	15 279	13.8	53.1	18.1	68.0	6 859	19 533	33 865	11.5	7.3	15.1	15.5	11.4	18.9
McCreary	NA	NA	4 288	6.1	78.4	6.7	21.8	6 246	9 896	19 348	35.9	1.1	32.2	32.6	26.1	36.7
McLean	NA	NA	2 167	7.8	67.8	8.7	9.8	5 995	16 046	29 675	7.9	3.3	16.0	16.7	13.7	20.4
Madison	NA	NA	22 171	12.2	54.5	21.8	58.9	5 692	16 790	32 861	14.4	5.7	16.8	18.3	12.0	17.6
Magoffin	NA	NA	3 284	3.2	78.1	6.3	16.8	6 704	10 685	19 421	18.9	2.4	36.6	35.7	31.2	37.1
Marion	NA	NA	4 229	13.7	73.4	9.1	18.7	6 137	14 472	30 387	24.4	3.9	18.6	19.2	15.8	20.8
Marshall	144	1 832	6 568	9.5	61.1	13.7	26.4	5 455	18 069	35 573	18.1	5.7	9.5	10.7	6.6	9.8
Martin	NA	NA	3 166	2.2	75.6	9.0	17.9	8 064	10 650	18 279	-10.2	1.8	37.0	36.3	33.3	40.6
Mason	NA	NA	3 816	10.0	62.5	14.4	16.7	6 105	16 589	30 195	9.2	5.8	16.8	16.5	12.9	19.3
Meade	NA	NA	6 800	7.4	62.0	11.3	24.5	5 281	16 000	36 966	16.2	5.0	11.3	11.4	9.3	11.0
Menifee	NA	NA	1 478	3.5	81.7	8.4	7.6	6 669	11 399	22 064	12.1	1.7	29.6	28.5	23.4	35.3
Mercer	NA	NA	4 555	8.5	65.8	13.5	20.4	5 645	17 972	35 555	16.2	4.8	12.9	12.7	10.0	14.7
Metcalfe	NA	NA	2 146	8.4	79.6	6.6	10.9	6 877	13 236	23 540	18.3	2.9	23.6	25.9	18.8	25.9
Monroe	NA	NA	2 660	4.1	76.8	8.4	12.4	6 075	14 365	22 356	9.4	2.9	23.4	25.6	20.0	24.4
Montgomery	NA	NA	4 925	7.6	68.8	13.4	24.1	5 860	16 701	31 746	18.0	5.1	15.2	17.4	12.5	17.1
Morgan	NA	NA	3 092	9.4	76.4	7.7	14.9	6 652	12 657	21 869	23.0	3.1	27.2	28.4	23.5	31.8
Muhlenberg	NA	NA	6 747	7.1	74.9	8.1	33.6	6 497	14 798	28 566	13.8	3.8	19.7	19.8	15.5	22.4
Nelson	NA	NA	9 404	18.3	64.1	13.4	38.0	6 155	18 120	39 010	19.9	6.9	12.2	12.8	10.0	14.5
Nicholas	NA	NA	1 392	0.6	74.7	7.5	7.1	5 997	15 880	29 886	23.1	4.1	13.2	15.7	9.7	12.8
Ohio	NA	NA	5 308	4.9	74.5	7.4	23.5	5 757	15 317	29 557	20.9	3.5	17.3	17.9	13.9	18.5
Oldham	NA	NA	13 104	20.8	40.0	30.6	49.2	5 606	25 374	63 229	22.5	23.5	4.1	4.7	2.9	4.1
Owen	NA	NA	2 396	6.1	73.3	9.1	10.7	5 505	15 521	33 310	17.7	4.5	15.5	17.6	12.1	14.7

1. Data for serious crimes have not been adjusted for underreporting; this may affect comparability between geographic areas and over time.　2. Per 100,000 population estimated by the FBI.　3. All persons 3 years old and over enrolled in nursery school through college.　4. Persons 25 years old and over.　5. Elementary and secondary education expenditures.　6. Based on population enumerated as of April 1, 2000.

Table B. States and Counties — **Personal Income**

STATE County	Personal income, 2002 Total (mil dol)	Percent change, 2001-2002	Per capita[1] Dollars	Per capita[1] Rank	Wages and salaries[2] (mil dol)	Proprietor's income (mil dol)	Dividends, interest, and rent (mil dol)	Transfer payments Total (mil dol)	Government payments to individuals Total (mil dol)	Social Security (mil dol)	Medical payments (mil dol)	Income maintenance (mil dol)	Unemployment insurance (mil dol)
	62	63	64	65	66	67	68	69	70	71	72	73	74
KENTUCKY—Cont'd													
Cumberland	131	2.7	18 328	2 856	48	10	19	50	48	13	26	6	1
Daviess	2 326	2.3	25 310	1 043	1 501	124	422	448	424	177	174	38	18
Edmonson	198	3.5	16 728	3 009	48	4	34	54	51	20	21	6	2
Elliott	99	6.3	14 601	3 084	20	3	12	36	34	11	14	7	1
Estill	272	3.5	17 747	2 925	76	9	35	87	83	24	38	13	2
Fayette	8 681	3.3	32 932	187	7 117	854	1 640	999	931	354	334	83	27
Fleming	263	1.4	18 606	2 811	108	11	47	64	60	23	25	8	3
Floyd	828	4.0	19 568	2 643	415	54	105	290	280	90	121	43	5
Franklin	1 371	3.4	28 481	492	1 354	65	244	230	217	96	83	18	8
Fulton	169	0.7	22 398	1 909	105	20	31	48	46	16	19	7	2
Gallatin	163	2.1	20 828	2 339	81	5	15	31	29	9	14	3	2
Garrard	321	2.2	20 513	2 426	72	19	59	64	60	25	23	7	3
Grant	498	3.7	21 195	2 238	175	19	60	94	88	34	35	10	5
Graves	818	-0.3	22 070	1 998	412	69	147	198	188	77	82	16	6
Grayson	462	3.1	19 038	2 749	243	27	61	125	119	43	52	14	6
Green	211	3.1	18 091	2 884	59	11	40	64	61	21	30	6	2
Greenup	839	3.9	22 795	1 784	368	31	99	208	198	65	71	18	7
Hancock	171	-0.4	20 219	2 498	250	5	22	33	30	14	11	3	2
Hardin	2 439	2.3	25 468	1 007	2 042	118	368	389	367	117	155	35	15
Harlan	564	2.9	17 354	2 964	295	17	71	228	219	77	88	34	3
Harrison	405	2.7	22 423	1 902	185	15	62	75	70	31	27	7	3
Hart	302	3.4	17 110	2 983	122	21	45	83	79	27	35	11	3
Henderson	1 141	3.1	25 356	1 029	823	47	178	213	201	84	86	15	8
Henry	356	0.7	23 222	1 654	96	16	56	66	62	25	26	6	2
Hickman	169	-3.3	32 359	213	35	67	18	29	27	11	12	2	1
Hopkins	1 070	3.5	23 039	1 710	616	63	191	243	231	98	88	24	5
Jackson	199	3.1	14 588	3 085	80	8	24	72	68	20	30	13	2
Jefferson	23 300	2.3	33 466	172	19 365	2 180	4 638	3 362	3 183	1 256	1 321	297	131
Jessamine	1 036	2.8	25 429	1 019	477	114	149	136	126	54	45	14	3
Johnson	473	3.2	20 159	2 508	208	29	62	146	140	47	59	21	3
Kenton	4 600	3.1	30 332	316	2 523	217	733	588	549	224	212	50	21
Knott	302	4.0	17 047	2 988	143	9	39	109	104	31	46	19	1
Knox	575	4.5	18 139	2 875	251	64	76	192	183	53	79	38	3
Larue	327	2.5	24 295	1 312	78	19	48	65	61	23	27	6	2
Laurel	1 115	2.5	20 468	2 442	745	70	158	265	251	89	103	35	8
Lawrence	268	4.7	16 853	3 005	108	10	31	94	90	29	39	15	2
Lee	130	4.6	16 433	3 033	54	8	17	52	50	14	24	9	1
Leslie	215	1.7	17 513	2 951	101	7	18	90	87	27	40	14	1
Letcher	481	2.2	19 337	2 688	231	18	50	172	166	55	72	25	3
Lewis	208	4.3	15 057	3 074	54	11	28	73	69	21	30	12	3
Lincoln	446	2.9	18 458	2 834	124	23	60	114	108	38	45	14	6
Livingston	222	2.3	22 623	1 842	82	13	36	53	51	22	21	3	2
Logan	574	0.7	21 476	2 156	330	43	90	134	127	47	56	12	7
Lyon	164	2.9	20 095	2 524	59	10	33	42	40	20	15	2	1
McCracken	1 898	2.8	29 313	407	1 442	134	394	347	330	135	132	31	11
McCreary	255	3.1	14 912	3 080	93	15	29	117	112	28	54	22	3
McLean	262	-9.8	26 351	820	50	71	31	49	46	20	19	4	2
Madison	1 527	3.8	20 808	2 345	949	56	227	288	269	96	106	30	8
Magoffin	231	1.5	17 389	2 959	78	11	26	87	83	21	40	17	3
Marion	390	4.4	21 105	2 267	208	20	71	86	81	28	36	11	4
Marshall	749	2.1	24 792	1 178	441	54	135	158	150	73	55	9	6
Martin	215	2.7	17 152	2 978	143	7	30	84	81	28	33	16	1
Mason	390	2.6	23 126	1 686	317	16	81	78	74	30	30	9	3
Meade	595	-0.1	21 687	2 095	124	28	89	90	83	33	30	7	3
Menifee	103	4.8	15 356	3 065	28	6	12	36	34	11	15	6	1
Mercer	483	2.4	22 911	1 749	282	22	86	90	84	40	30	8	3
Metcalfe	178	2.8	17 761	2 924	70	14	24	53	50	17	23	7	2
Monroe	224	3.4	19 098	2 742	95	22	32	73	70	21	35	9	3
Montgomery	497	4.3	21 398	2 180	319	27	78	103	97	37	39	13	4
Morgan	216	3.7	15 153	3 072	100	8	26	69	65	19	28	11	3
Muhlenberg	654	2.6	20 632	2 391	351	48	122	172	163	68	64	16	5
Nelson	1 001	3.4	25 732	946	485	54	161	159	149	60	57	15	12
Nicholas	145	2.3	21 052	2 280	34	-1	15	38	36	13	17	4	1
Ohio	450	2.0	19 435	2 665	182	20	72	119	113	44	46	12	6
Oldham	1 580	1.5	32 120	220	437	71	263	127	115	53	44	6	4
Owen	199	3.5	18 053	2 888	58	0	31	43	40	16	16	5	1

1. Based on the resident population estimated as of July 1 of the year shown.   2. Includes other labor income.

STATE County	Earnings, 2002									Social Security beneficiaries, December 2003		Supplemental Security Income recipients, December 2003	Housing units, 2003	
			Percent by selected industries											
			Goods-related[1]		Service-related and health									
	Total (mil dol)	Farm	Total	Manu-facturing	Information and professional and technical services	Retail trade	Finance, insurance, and real estate	Health services	Govern-ment	Number	Rate[2]		Total	Percent change, 2000–2003
	75	76	77	78	79	80	81	82	83	84	85	86	87	88
KENTUCKY—Cont'd														
Cumberland	57	8.7	D	15.4	D	8.6	8.4	18.3	24.4	1 780	249	642	3 572	0.1
Daviess	1 624	0.0	26.9	17.8	D	8.7	5.9	10.9	18.7	18 660	202	3 078	41 081	6.9
Edmonson	52	-2.9	D	D	D	6.8	4.7	D	51.2	2 595	219	520	6 273	2.8
Elliott	23	-3.5	D	0.0	D	8.7	D	12.0	44.7	1 480	213	539	3 195	2.8
Estill	85	-2.2	D	12.1	3.0	14.0	4.3	12.1	28.2	3 110	205	1 244	6 948	1.8
Fayette	7 971	1.2	18.5	11.8	14.1	7.5	6.5	11.1	19.8	35 890	135	6 020	122 513	5.5
Fleming	119	-3.5	D	20.8	3.4	12.3	3.9	D	29.1	2 950	205	770	6 210	1.5
Floyd	469	0.0	D	2.2	9.5	8.6	3.0	16.2	19.7	10 735	254	4 240	19 048	2.7
Franklin	1 419	-0.2	D	10.7	5.1	6.1	3.4	5.7	56.0	10 425	217	1 864	22 039	2.9
Fulton	125	9.4	30.9	28.9	D	11.9	3.5	10.1	17.7	1 860	251	549	3 686	-0.3
Gallatin	85	-0.9	D	41.2	D	5.2	2.1	D	15.7	1 050	131	230	3 430	2.0
Garrard	91	-5.6	D	D	3.3	8.3	5.3	12.2	25.6	3 080	194	580	6 525	1.7
Grant	194	-2.6	29.8	21.9	3.8	16.8	4.6	8.7	20.1	3 915	163	676	9 880	6.2
Graves	481	3.5	37.9	32.0	D	8.9	3.8	D	15.1	8 450	227	1 474	16 585	1.5
Grayson	270	1.0	D	32.8	D	8.1	3.1	D	18.9	5 290	215	1 331	12 825	0.2
Green	69	-0.2	D	15.6	D	9.7	6.2	D	33.0	2 765	235	708	5 407	-0.2
Greenup	399	0.3	D	10.3	D	7.1	7.8	D	13.4	7 190	195	1 488	16 214	1.5
Hancock	255	-0.2	D	79.6	D	2.1	1.0	1.4	5.9	1 530	181	233	3 652	1.4
Hardin	2 160	-0.1	D	16.5	4.8	6.9	3.5	6.7	46.7	14 170	148	2 808	39 625	5.2
Harlan	312	0.0	31.7	1.7	D	7.5	3.2	D	22.9	8 575	267	3 060	15 265	1.7
Harrison	200	-3.2	45.0	35.3	3.0	7.8	4.0	12.5	16.3	3 635	199	688	7 817	2.0
Hart	143	2.0	47.8	36.9	D	8.9	3.8	D	19.8	3 670	205	1 103	8 155	1.4
Henderson	870	0.2	D	36.3	3.1	5.8	3.1	10.5	10.9	8 710	193	1 488	19 875	2.1
Henry	113	-1.6	D	28.8	D	10.7	6.0	5.5	22.9	2 860	184	532	6 659	4.4
Hickman	102	57.2	D	D	D	4.0	2.5	3.5	9.0	1 235	239	173	2 485	2.0
Hopkins	679	2.2	29.0	18.6	4.6	9.2	4.1	18.8	16.9	10 215	218	1 949	21 044	1.8
Jackson	89	-2.4	D	27.6	D	7.9	D	8.5	27.3	2 760	203	1 471	6 208	2.4
Jefferson	21 545	0.0	22.9	16.9	10.1	6.2	9.7	12.1	10.7	123 870	177	19 487	314 607	2.9
Jessamine	591	7.4	D	19.7	D	12.2	3.2	D	13.4	6 015	145	990	16 225	10.8
Johnson	236	-0.3	D	5.8	7.3	13.7	3.5	11.2	23.3	5 440	230	1 916	10 346	1.1
Kenton	2 739	-0.1	D	9.4	9.3	5.4	7.1	14.2	19.0	22 385	147	3 348	65 405	2.9
Knott	153	-0.1	D	D	5.6	4.7	D	D	20.5	3 735	212	1 812	7 820	3.2
Knox	316	-0.1	D	12.4	D	13.1	4.5	D	22.0	6 880	217	3 767	14 386	2.8
Larue	97	-0.6	33.5	22.0	D	9.8	6.2	D	22.8	2 815	209	478	6 179	5.4
Laurel	815	-0.3	27.3	17.5	D	10.0	3.7	10.3	14.0	10 685	193	3 269	23 020	3.2
Lawrence	118	-1.0	D	D	2.9	9.2	2.2	17.4	20.9	3 425	215	1 444	7 217	2.5
Lee	62	-0.2	D	D	D	9.9	D	7.6	27.5	1 760	223	913	3 416	2.9
Leslie	108	0.0	D	D	4.2	5.6	D	D	21.2	3 210	263	1 351	5 700	3.6
Letcher	248	0.0	34.3	3.7	4.1	6.9	1.9	D	18.1	6 325	255	2 403	11 676	2.4
Lewis	65	-0.1	18.3	9.3	D	8.3	5.3	D	32.6	2 715	197	986	6 330	2.5
Lincoln	146	1.2	D	24.7	D	10.4	3.8	8.2	26.0	5 020	205	1 501	10 772	6.4
Livingston	96	3.4	D	D	D	8.9	2.4	10.6	20.7	2 410	248	307	4 898	2.6
Logan	373	1.4	D	46.5	D	6.4	2.8	7.7	11.6	5 490	205	1 064	11 990	1.0
Lyon	69	0.2	D	D	D	7.2	2.3	8.4	40.5	2 075	257	187	4 297	2.6
McCracken	1 576	0.6	18.9	13.0	8.8	10.4	3.8	19.2	12.6	13 880	214	2 242	30 859	1.6
McCreary	108	-0.7	D	19.0	D	11.5	4.1	D	31.7	3 670	213	2 134	7 472	0.9
McLean	121	51.3	D	5.2	D	7.1	2.6	D	13.9	2 135	216	307	4 500	2.5
Madison	1 005	-0.7	D	26.2	4.7	8.4	3.0	9.8	27.0	11 255	212	2 709	30 956	4.6
Magoffin	88	-1.3	D	D	6.2	6.9	D	10.8	26.3	2 780	150	1 618	5 645	3.6
Marion	228	2.7	49.5	44.2	2.8	6.3	2.7	11.6	13.3	3 550	208	1 158	7 354	1.1
Marshall	495	1.5	50.0	40.5	4.0	8.7	3.3	D	12.0	7 465	244	667	15 208	3.2
Martin	150	0.0	D	D	D	5.5	D	3.2	16.4	2 940	235	1 398	5 758	3.7
Mason	332	-1.6	D	33.6	D	10.2	3.1	D	11.8	3 500	208	756	7 781	0.3
Meade	152	5.2	25.9	14.7	D	12.4	4.9	D	22.7	3 815	138	488	10 607	3.1
Menifee	34	-1.1	D	12.8	D	6.9	D	12.1	40.2	1 460	221	578	3 785	2.0
Mercer	304	-1.0	D	49.6	3.0	5.9	2.9	D	11.0	4 530	212	703	9 584	3.2
Metcalfe	84	9.3	D	38.4	1.7	6.2	D	3.5	21.2	2 355	235	686	4 698	2.3
Monroe	116	9.1	D	26.2	1.2	10.6	3.0	5.9	24.8	2 905	247	1 047	5 403	2.2
Montgomery	346	-0.9	D	38.0	D	11.1	4.0	9.3	12.7	4 475	190	1 153	10 199	5.3
Morgan	109	-2.6	D	7.5	D	11.1	D	D	35.9	2 615	183	1 102	5 670	3.3
Muhlenberg	400	5.9	27.5	8.7	D	7.8	3.0	D	27.5	7 460	235	1 437	13 927	1.8
Nelson	539	-0.3	D	33.3	5.0	7.7	3.0	9.5	11.5	6 890	174	1 094	16 355	9.5
Nicholas	33	-11.1	D	D	D	8.3	D	19.5	32.8	1 590	229	405	3 085	1.1
Ohio	201	1.7	33.0	28.8	D	10.6	3.1	8.1	23.2	4 990	215	1 057	10 163	2.6
Oldham	508	0.8	D	9.1	D	7.8	6.5	9.0	24.6	5 360	106	315	17 744	14.2
Owen	58	-7.9	D	D	D	6.2	5.4	12.3	31.0	1 875	169	387	5 438	1.7

1. Covers mining, construction, and manufacturing.   2. Per 1,000 resident population estimated as of July 1 of the year shown.

Table B. States and Counties — Housing, Labor Force, and Employment

STATE County	Housing units, 2000 Occupied units Owner-occupied Total	Percent	Median value[1]	Median owner cost as a percent of income With a mortgage	Without a mortgage[2]	Renter-occupied Median rent[3]	Median rent as a percent of income	Sub-standard units[4] (percent)	Civilian labor force, 2003 Total	Percent change, 2002–2003	Unemployment Total	Rate[5]	Civilian employment,[6] 2000 Total	Percent Management, professional and related occupations	Production, transportation, and material moving occupations
	89	90	91	92	93	94	95	96	97	98	99	100	101	102	103
KENTUCKY—Cont'd															
Cumberland	2 976	77.6	50 300	20.9	10.8	242	21.2	4.4	2 892	1.5	256	8.9	2 849	25.0	30.9
Daviess	36 033	70.3	81 800	18.4	9.9	415	22.8	2.5	48 349	1.0	3 004	6.2	43 000	28.1	20.3
Edmonson	4 648	85.6	63 700	21.9	12.2	310	25.3	2.1	4 965	1.5	364	7.3	4 633	17.9	27.1
Elliott	2 638	82.3	54 800	22.0	10.8	232	31.5	5.1	2 758	1.1	247	9.0	2 155	19.7	22.5
Estill	6 108	73.9	50 200	21.4	9.9	332	25.7	6.0	5 576	-1.7	430	7.7	5 491	19.3	30.4
Fayette	108 288	55.3	110 800	19.2	9.9	528	25.4	2.5	141 070	1.4	5 394	3.8	139 174	40.4	11.2
Fleming	5 367	78.8	63 600	18.9	9.9	318	21.2	5.0	6 311	-1.6	386	6.1	5 960	25.8	24.5
Floyd	16 881	76.2	53 100	21.0	9.9	332	27.0	2.8	14 020	4.2	1 124	8.0	12 558	29.2	14.3
Franklin	19 907	64.8	91 600	18.5	9.9	482	23.2	2.2	24 709	0.9	918	3.7	23 721	35.1	14.2
Fulton	3 237	64.2	40 500	18.4	10.1	343	26.7	3.4	3 505	0.2	432	12.3	2 844	22.5	32.4
Gallatin	2 902	77.0	87 100	20.3	10.2	422	21.9	4.0	3 845	1.1	220	5.7	3 625	17.4	28.3
Garrard	5 741	76.4	81 300	20.1	9.9	390	23.6	3.4	7 865	-0.4	456	5.8	6 933	27.0	22.1
Grant	8 175	74.1	93 100	20.6	9.9	505	22.4	4.0	11 392	2.0	744	6.5	10 634	19.9	28.1
Graves	14 841	77.9	63 600	19.9	9.9	354	26.0	3.0	17 332	0.6	1 322	7.6	15 911	24.9	23.7
Grayson	9 596	77.3	65 600	21.3	9.9	353	22.8	3.0	12 951	1.0	1 329	10.3	10 130	18.5	32.1
Green	4 706	78.4	52 500	19.4	10.6	326	26.9	2.4	4 656	0.9	341	7.3	4 803	23.5	28.7
Greenup	14 536	81.8	67 500	18.8	9.9	412	23.8	2.5	16 333	3.8	1 135	6.9	14 370	26.1	18.1
Hancock	3 215	82.5	71 800	18.2	9.9	438	19.2	2.8	3 840	-0.9	325	8.5	3 801	19.0	31.6
Hardin	34 497	66.9	88 300	19.6	9.9	443	21.5	3.2	40 923	4.9	2 608	6.4	39 858	26.2	21.0
Harlan	13 291	73.5	43 000	22.7	11.3	306	25.1	3.9	9 444	4.7	1 073	11.4	8 946	27.8	12.0
Harrison	7 012	70.5	83 100	18.0	9.9	403	21.6	2.8	7 262	0.2	524	7.2	8 442	22.3	28.8
Hart	6 769	77.3	60 100	20.3	10.3	312	21.7	5.0	7 635	0.6	459	6.0	7 022	24.1	28.5
Henderson	18 095	67.3	76 600	18.2	9.9	408	23.4	1.9	24 221	0.6	1 393	5.8	21 199	25.4	25.2
Henry	5 844	77.4	82 100	19.9	9.9	444	22.0	4.0	7 559	10.2	354	4.7	7 208	22.5	25.9
Hickman	2 188	81.4	49 200	18.2	9.9	282	19.9	1.7	2 473	4.0	242	9.8	2 195	21.5	31.2
Hopkins	18 820	74.7	57 200	18.3	9.9	363	21.5	2.0	19 329	2.9	1 481	7.7	19 524	23.8	22.0
Jackson	5 307	80.2	48 300	25.9	11.3	301	28.6	6.4	6 897	1.1	363	5.3	4 598	19.5	31.9
Jefferson	287 012	64.9	103 000	19.7	9.9	494	23.9	2.6	372 219	0.5	22 425	6.0	334 938	33.0	15.7
Jessamine	13 867	67.1	102 100	20.4	9.9	535	24.4	3.2	20 833	1.5	751	3.6	19 193	31.0	16.5
Johnson	9 103	76.4	64 700	19.7	11.0	338	23.7	2.7	9 588	2.7	598	6.2	8 211	25.2	15.1
Kenton	59 444	66.4	105 600	19.6	9.9	517	23.6	2.0	80 254	1.8	3 834	4.8	77 247	31.9	14.8
Knott	6 717	79.6	46 500	21.6	9.9	293	26.0	4.5	5 868	0.9	287	4.9	5 144	29.3	15.8
Knox	12 416	71.4	59 400	23.6	10.9	327	28.4	4.2	11 283	1.5	880	7.8	10 076	22.8	21.0
Larue	5 275	80.3	72 100	20.6	9.9	342	25.5	3.2	6 744	4.8	318	4.7	5 937	24.2	25.0
Laurel	20 353	77.0	77 300	21.8	9.9	377	24.2	2.9	24 629	2.3	1 858	7.5	21 652	22.9	22.6
Lawrence	5 954	78.0	56 300	20.4	9.9	362	27.9	4.6	5 531	1.5	515	9.3	5 005	20.3	20.1
Lee	2 985	76.8	52 300	23.4	12.1	268	26.6	5.2	2 709	1.9	250	9.2	2 267	24.3	24.9
Leslie	4 885	82.1	36 900	22.1	10.7	278	25.1	5.9	4 326	2.6	362	8.4	3 478	24.1	18.3
Letcher	10 085	80.8	39 500	20.9	9.9	309	23.5	3.7	8 109	2.7	1 001	12.3	7 758	23.9	15.1
Lewis	5 422	81.2	44 700	21.9	10.2	269	25.7	6.0	4 300	2.8	446	10.4	4 920	19.7	31.2
Lincoln	9 206	78.9	65 100	20.2	11.0	378	23.0	4.7	11 438	-0.6	918	8.0	9 929	22.0	29.3
Livingston	3 996	85.2	58 200	19.1	9.9	362	18.8	2.9	4 776	0.1	345	7.0	4 514	23.2	18.6
Logan	10 506	75.2	67 100	19.6	10.6	415	23.9	3.2	11 691	-3.9	809	6.9	12 386	21.6	33.1
Lyon	2 898	82.2	80 700	17.7	9.9	398	22.7	1.8	3 320	1.6	279	8.4	2 840	26.3	19.2
McCracken	27 736	68.7	84 300	18.9	9.9	419	24.0	1.9	32 496	0.2	1 950	6.0	29 359	29.0	15.3
McCreary	6 520	75.6	46 300	23.0	9.9	320	26.7	6.2	5 921	-6.2	630	10.6	5 464	20.5	33.3
McLean	3 984	80.3	58 200	18.1	10.7	318	23.4	2.4	4 229	0.6	369	8.7	4 320	23.7	23.9
Madison	27 152	59.7	93 500	19.1	9.9	428	24.1	1.8	36 033	1.4	1 859	5.2	34 948	29.0	17.1
Magoffin	5 024	81.9	55 600	22.0	14.3	294	30.1	3.7	5 031	1.1	666	13.2	3 870	23.2	21.9
Marion	6 613	78.2	70 300	19.9	9.9	353	25.5	3.6	11 815	4.1	531	4.5	7 750	24.3	30.1
Marshall	12 412	82.6	82 800	19.2	9.9	407	22.7	1.5	14 198	-0.6	1 136	8.0	13 374	25.2	21.2
Martin	4 776	79.3	62 100	23.5	12.0	286	28.1	3.7	3 699	6.5	311	8.4	3 105	27.1	16.3
Mason	6 847	67.4	71 900	20.5	9.9	369	23.6	2.7	8 267	3.8	520	6.3	7 690	25.8	25.0
Meade	9 470	73.9	85 500	19.5	9.9	431	20.2	4.0	11 071	5.7	740	6.7	10 713	20.9	23.5
Menifee	2 537	81.2	54 500	26.4	10.1	233	27.7	4.3	3 254	3.4	261	8.0	2 296	23.3	30.1
Mercer	8 423	74.5	83 800	19.2	9.9	411	21.2	2.3	10 527	-2.4	639	6.1	9 821	24.7	24.4
Metcalfe	4 016	79.3	52 600	19.9	11.8	310	23.9	4.7	4 594	-0.6	201	4.4	4 198	20.3	34.1
Monroe	4 741	75.1	57 600	22.5	11.3	304	26.5	5.0	4 531	0.2	385	8.5	4 815	24.8	31.2
Montgomery	8 902	71.5	82 100	20.2	9.9	420	22.8	2.8	13 305	1.9	785	5.9	10 123	24.7	25.4
Morgan	4 752	79.9	55 400	23.2	10.0	310	24.7	4.9	5 041	-0.9	531	10.5	4 364	23.0	18.2
Muhlenberg	12 357	82.9	58 200	18.9	9.9	330	24.7	2.6	12 503	-0.9	1 089	8.7	11 989	20.4	27.3
Nelson	13 953	78.0	87 100	19.1	9.9	426	23.4	3.2	19 866	1.9	1 248	6.3	17 961	22.6	28.7
Nicholas	2 710	74.8	62 000	18.4	9.9	296	21.7	2.7	2 332	-3.6	209	9.0	2 983	23.1	28.7
Ohio	8 899	80.2	56 600	18.2	10.2	350	24.1	3.7	10 188	2.4	978	9.6	9 558	19.6	26.3
Oldham	14 856	86.8	158 600	19.6	9.9	499	23.2	1.1	25 546	0.4	814	3.2	22 003	40.1	13.0
Owen	4 086	78.2	72 800	21.5	9.9	357	22.7	5.4	4 173	-2.2	197	4.7	4 622	25.4	22.5

1. Specified owner-occupied units.　2. Median monthly owner costs is often in the minimum category—9.9 percent or less, which is indicated as 9.9 percent.　3. Specified renter-occupied units.　4. Overcrowded or lacking complete plumbing facilities.　5. Percent of civilian labor force.　6. Persons 16 years old and over.

Table B. States and Counties — Nonfarm Employment and Agriculture

STATE County	Private nonfarm establishments, employment and payroll, 2001									Agriculture, 2002			
	Number of establish-ments	Employment						Annual payroll		Farms			Farm operators whose principal occu-pation is farming (percent)
		Total	Health care and social assistance	Manufac-turing	Retail trade	Finance and insurance	Professional, scientific, and technical services	Total (mil dol)	Average per employee (dollars)	Number	Percent with—		
											Less than 50 acres	500 acres and over	
	104	105	106	107	108	109	110	111	112	113	114	115	116

KENTUCKY—Cont'd

Cumberland	122	1 259	445	204	248	63	11	23	17 973	473	24.9	6.8	57.9
Daviess	2 374	39 424	6 507	6 891	6 148	1 539	1 311	1 041	26 406	1 062	43.6	11.1	56.8
Edmonson	107	782	235	16	129	60	14	14	18 193	670	30.3	3.9	58.5
Elliott	57	394	104	D	64	D	D	6	16 350	427	26.5	3.5	47.1
Estill	227	1 946	313	288	409	96	32	34	17 383	457	25.6	3.7	53.4
Fayette	7 869	147 715	25 126	16 402	21 522	6 374	11 112	4 520	30 600	738	47.0	8.0	60.6
Fleming	290	2 744	650	608	621	118	47	57	20 921	1 071	24.7	6.8	61.7
Floyd	826	9 200	1 930	249	1 440	250	299	247	26 808	68	45.6	1.5	38.2
Franklin	1 173	16 302	2 044	3 155	3 131	854	1 039	414	25 405	689	35.8	2.9	46.4
Fulton	203	2 707	323	1 114	488	105	D	60	22 015	193	31.1	28.5	63.7
Gallatin	102	1 269	176	D	172	34	15	26	20 378	247	28.7	5.3	51.4
Garrard	224	1 967	357	317	219	58	45	39	19 679	873	31.0	3.9	59.6
Grant	451	4 662	457	968	1 198	199	81	96	20 682	1 020	32.4	1.7	51.2
Graves	669	9 625	1 574	3 021	1 525	326	177	221	22 990	1 712	39.7	7.0	53.0
Grayson	457	7 513	882	2 922	912	179	97	143	18 978	1 650	30.1	4.3	54.0
Green	175	1 549	520	333	273	78	20	27	17 275	1 134	35.3	3.2	61.6
Greenup	487	4 950	649	572	759	253	165	108	21 793	728	29.4	3.6	52.7
Hancock	128	3 408	129	2 335	179	57	29	123	36 051	418	25.8	5.3	53.1
Hardin	1 977	33 130	7 076	6 882	5 887	886	1 264	801	24 174	1 732	44.5	5.7	53.4
Harlan	517	5 281	1 217	262	1 148	176	208	120	22 718	23	47.8	0.0	13.0
Harrison	306	4 208	678	1 575	631	119	50	111	26 371	1 085	30.7	5.2	57.4
Hart	255	2 667	472	796	476	103	69	46	17 309	1 392	27.1	3.4	57.0
Henderson	1 077	19 980	2 326	8 040	2 243	789	341	538	26 917	525	44.0	18.9	51.8
Henry	242	2 561	202	761	503	151	45	56	21 913	883	27.5	4.8	59.2
Hickman	91	1 256	149	469	120	53	D	25	19 579	347	32.6	14.1	58.8
Hopkins	1 064	14 656	3 211	2 569	2 576	419	357	374	25 504	678	29.9	9.7	47.6
Jackson	139	2 177	248	966	202	17	5	41	19 037	727	35.2	1.8	49.1
Jefferson	19 774	410 939	53 884	52 959	48 315	27 986	18 851	13 705	33 350	526	63.9	2.5	50.0
Jessamine	879	12 832	429	2 484	2 235	192	249	302	23 537	770	50.5	3.8	56.0
Johnson	479	4 758	655	382	1 410	217	192	100	21 063	195	35.4	2.6	52.3
Kenton	3 156	63 699	8 139	7 190	6 196	1 523	2 661	2 066	32 441	495	38.4	1.8	47.5
Knott	218	2 488	306	17	347	47	63	77	30 879	22	22.7	9.1	36.4
Knox	417	5 525	1 334	727	1 288	157	134	107	19 426	347	37.8	4.3	47.3
Larue	211	1 869	270	671	233	124	42	35	18 699	888	36.1	4.3	53.8
Laurel	1 053	18 469	1 553	3 351	2 793	948	441	475	25 731	1 137	48.7	1.7	53.4
Lawrence	205	2 172	513	D	515	65	37	53	24 584	318	20.8	6.3	50.3
Lee	110	1 684	751	167	211	D	12	25	14 807	173	32.9	4.0	48.6
Leslie	130	1 268	409	0	207	D	D	27	21 439	20	50.0	5.0	25.0
Letcher	424	5 174	853	108	770	161	178	137	26 410	46	54.3	0.0	60.9
Lewis	146	1 043	198	242	230	93	35	18	17 210	733	22.5	7.9	54.0
Lincoln	299	2 901	524	738	529	262	76	60	20 590	1 275	38.5	4.9	58.2
Livingston	159	1 808	279	81	192	31	23	53	29 278	518	18.7	13.3	51.0
Logan	503	7 619	696	3 802	905	194	117	192	25 216	1 212	29.8	9.2	55.8
Lyon	165	1 345	245	D	355	32	D	23	16 934	304	23.4	6.3	45.4
McCracken	2 058	35 276	6 018	3 841	6 526	827	1 238	951	26 953	531	50.3	6.0	46.1
McCreary	174	1 743	302	452	390	93	47	28	16 186	154	42.9	0.6	36.4
McLean	178	1 427	137	193	254	141	22	33	22 884	413	33.2	17.2	64.2
Madison	1 438	22 493	3 314	6 128	3 904	531	382	538	23 931	1 396	38.8	6.2	54.2
Magoffin	190	1 681	342	D	260	61	93	37	21 757	345	38.3	3.8	44.1
Marion	331	5 725	926	2 224	627	141	107	129	22 584	1 054	33.2	5.6	52.6
Marshall	625	8 491	871	2 535	1 224	342	170	286	33 707	902	40.7	4.4	43.2
Martin	178	1 973	186	D	385	146	31	65	32 779	13	0.0	23.1	38.5
Mason	451	8 283	1 089	2 621	1 389	206	100	200	24 152	726	31.3	8.0	61.0
Meade	292	2 950	218	D	696	216	56	69	23 541	955	43.1	4.5	54.1
Menifee	68	577	166	234	94	16	14	11	18 744	334	33.2	2.1	48.2
Mercer	413	5 799	497	2 532	693	123	77	184	31 751	1 086	41.0	3.0	54.2
Metcalfe	131	2 468	D	1 687	251	67	13	56	22 767	950	33.2	3.9	62.5
Monroe	214	2 834	453	1 064	596	85	D	54	18 907	980	31.5	7.0	56.7
Montgomery	531	8 116	919	2 790	1 550	229	178	176	21 709	676	37.9	4.7	50.1
Morgan	191	2 078	368	367	387	237	38	55	26 469	804	25.5	4.4	50.5
Muhlenberg	605	6 751	1 206	1 280	1 335	214	156	152	22 485	667	28.3	8.1	54.1
Nelson	890	12 386	1 155	3 330	1 781	323	208	305	24 643	1 407	39.2	4.1	56.7
Nicholas	95	800	293	D	123	D	8	14	17 354	582	27.8	6.5	59.3
Ohio	364	4 864	820	1 583	800	163	82	97	19 958	1 006	29.7	5.1	49.8
Oldham	1 008	9 297	1 194	1 128	1 370	304	466	221	23 729	481	53.2	5.4	51.4
Owen	111	1 093	261	120	196	71	D	27	24 376	788	18.5	7.7	51.5

Items 104—116

Table B. States and Counties — **Agriculture**

STATE County	\[117\] Land in farms Acreage (1,000)	\[118\] Percent change, 1997–2002	\[119\] Acres Average size of farm	\[120\] Total irrigated (1,000)	\[121\] Total cropland (1,000)	\[122\] Value of land and buildings (dollars) Average per farm	\[123\] Average per acre	\[124\] Value of machinery and equipment average per farm (dollars)	\[125\] Value of products sold Total (mil dol)	\[126\] Average per farm (dollars)	\[127\] Percent from — Crops	\[128\] Live-stock and poultry products	\[129\] Percent of farms with sales of — $10,000 or more	\[130\] $100,000 or more	\[131\] Government payments Total ($1,000)	\[132\] Percent of farms

KENTUCKY—Cont'd

County	117	118	119	120	121	122	123	124	125	126	127	128	129	130	131	132
Cumberland	89	-17.6	189	0	34	261 254	1 038	28 927	7	15 697	33.0	67.0	29.2	1.5	117	27.1
Daviess	254	1.2	239	2	215	487 146	2 041	66 904	63	59 070	73.4	26.6	39.4	12.1	2 964	33.7
Edmonson	94	4.4	140	0	48	181 216	1 176	53 704	10	14 859	33.5	66.5	23.9	2.7	354	32.7
Elliott	56	-3.4	131	0	21	129 817	906	39 943	3	6 601	64.6	35.3	18.5	0.5	45	12.6
Estill	64	3.2	140	0	28	161 611	1 112	46 673	4	8 444	41.8	58.2	21.0	0.4	105	20.8
Fayette	119	-12.5	161	1	67	714 656	4 589	61 677	179	242 401	8.1	91.9	54.2	20.7	314	12.2
Fleming	184	-2.6	171	0	111	218 114	1 273	46 176	34	31 698	26.2	73.8	43.1	7.7	926	27.6
Floyd	7	0.0	99	D	2	168 092	1 536	15 433	1	7 497	87.1	12.9	10.3	1.5	D	D
Franklin	82	-1.2	119	1	48	283 032	2 350	42 105	12	17 625	60.6	39.4	30.8	2.9	121	13.4
Fulton	112	19.1	581	1	101	832 372	1 450	119 738	30	156 341	65.7	34.3	53.9	33.2	1 392	68.9
Gallatin	38	5.6	152	0	16	383 650	2 155	31 305	4	15 349	64.6	35.4	25.9	2.4	77	15.4
Garrard	120	-4.0	137	0	73	237 159	1 852	47 562	21	24 281	29.4	70.6	39.7	5.4	205	14.5
Grant	116	0.9	114	0	62	271 952	2 545	38 221	13	12 940	41.8	58.2	23.9	1.0	146	12.3
Graves	300	26.6	175	2	225	313 934	1 659	54 815	150	87 741	26.9	73.1	30.8	12.7	5 934	60.2
Grayson	233	11.5	141	0	129	167 516	1 378	28 726	32	19 177	23.9	76.1	25.6	4.3	1 818	33.1
Green	135	4.7	119	0	81	203 011	1 522	33 692	21	18 635	35.6	64.4	35.8	3.9	488	25.1
Greenup	103	5.1	142	0	37	150 779	1 204	25 916	5	7 471	56.5	43.5	17.3	0.5	69	16.3
Hancock	69	6.2	165	0	39	236 566	1 333	39 138	9	22 681	54.3	45.7	27.0	4.5	538	30.9
Hardin	240	7.6	138	0	151	264 759	1 895	36 225	36	20 726	51.2	48.8	27.1	4.3	1 515	23.8
Harlan	2	0.0	81	0	1	179 532	2 249	20 224	0	5 394	75.0	25.0	13.0	0.0	0	0.0
Harrison	159	-5.9	147	1	103	243 897	1 867	33 605	21	19 393	51.1	48.9	37.4	3.6	374	20.7
Hart	195	4.8	140	0	106	206 017	1 387	39 033	30	21 392	35.3	64.7	38.6	4.5	884	27.4
Henderson	192	-2.0	366	2	166	710 507	1 933	117 150	52	98 849	55.8	44.2	41.0	17.9	2 855	41.0
Henry	142	-4.7	160	1	85	358 936	2 398	41 720	26	29 034	56.8	43.2	44.5	5.9	444	21.6
Hickman	125	8.7	361	2	102	538 663	1 498	84 640	66	189 060	31.2	68.8	38.9	25.1	1 942	68.0
Hopkins	164	16.3	242	0	108	331 154	1 301	51 452	38	56 618	34.9	65.1	27.9	6.6	1 906	46.5
Jackson	82	10.8	113	0	38	159 067	1 194	36 767	8	10 866	56.1	43.9	23.2	1.4	166	14.3
Jefferson	41	20.6	78	1	25	408 793	4 917	32 210	13	25 338	74.6	25.4	25.7	5.9	83	6.5
Jessamine	82	-7.9	107	1	52	371 815	3 699	41 636	50	64 594	15.9	84.1	35.8	5.7	183	13.0
Johnson	24	20.0	122	0	5	175 194	1 522	47 216	1	6 311	81.2	18.8	17.4	0.0	5	6.7
Kenton	46	21.1	94	0	27	310 436	3 775	32 786	5	10 730	53.2	46.8	23.2	2.4	106	12.7
Knott	4	0.0	204	0	2	313 246	1 599	29 780	0	2 857	6.3	93.7	4.5	0.0	D	D
Knox	41	-10.9	119	0	18	194 823	1 545	30 579	2	7 198	65.9	34.1	17.3	1.2	87	8.9
Larue	134	14.5	151	0	92	334 103	1 936	48 615	21	23 712	50.5	49.5	34.6	5.0	1 175	27.9
Laurel	108	12.5	95	0	63	239 290	2 305	27 052	16	13 822	43.7	56.3	25.5	2.6	216	10.5
Lawrence	57	16.3	179	0	16	150 039	910	25 733	2	5 636	58.0	42.0	13.5	0.0	31	11.3
Lee	23	-4.2	136	0	9	164 062	1 139	20 503	1	6 650	54.1	45.9	13.3	1.7	24	20.8
Leslie	3	0.0	174	0	0	123 193	786	19 558	0	1 687	82.4	17.6	0.0	0.0	0	0.0
Letcher	3	0.0	62	D	1	66 640	1 038	23 673	0	3 931	66.9	33.1	8.7	0.0	1	6.5
Lewis	144	0.7	196	0	49	215 066	894	28 438	9	12 951	59.4	40.6	30.7	1.5	290	20.9
Lincoln	171	0.6	134	0	104	216 160	1 745	35 523	35	27 512	32.7	67.3	36.5	7.5	857	20.9
Livingston	146	24.8	282	0	87	265 821	1 024	32 733	11	21 834	33.7	66.3	25.9	4.4	1 473	55.8
Logan	276	1.1	228	0	199	394 621	1 593	50 209	56	45 901	68.9	31.1	39.5	9.7	4 091	44.0
Lyon	56	16.7	186	0	36	227 808	1 187	34 368	5	15 475	63.1	36.9	17.8	3.9	723	50.7
McCracken	85	26.9	161	0	68	254 329	1 753	34 300	16	29 777	73.7	26.3	27.5	7.3	920	38.0
McCreary	15	36.4	97	D	7	220 560	2 246	37 232	1	3 678	22.3	77.7	7.8	0.0	10	16.2
McLean	129	-3.7	312	0	104	595 108	1 696	79 901	65	156 815	32.0	68.0	56.2	28.1	1 302	51.6
Madison	218	-1.8	156	0	131	344 029	2 266	29 911	36	25 530	34.1	65.9	40.9	5.7	510	19.9
Magoffin	46	12.2	132	D	14	145 848	1 120	15 202	2	4 805	71.2	28.8	14.8	0.0	28	10.7
Marion	171	3.0	162	0	98	297 048	1 771	37 049	29	27 281	30.1	69.9	40.9	5.9	1 456	35.4
Marshall	121	36.0	134	0	82	238 467	1 757	31 198	27	29 946	32.3	67.7	21.8	4.5	1 455	46.1
Martin	5	150.0	365	0	1	237 979	610	32 825	0	9 118	7.6	92.4	15.4	0.0	D	D
Mason	128	-2.3	176	0	87	369 664	1 889	58 431	22	30 791	42.7	57.3	45.0	6.9	735	28.4
Meade	135	11.6	141	0	82	300 598	2 068	46 825	16	16 933	42.5	57.5	28.5	2.9	869	33.1
Menifee	37	-2.6	111	0	14	218 226	1 942	16 653	3	7 759	66.6	33.4	21.0	0.3	33	9.3
Mercer	134	6.3	123	0	86	329 046	2 852	47 025	29	26 611	31.0	69.0	35.9	5.2	493	20.4
Metcalfe	132	-1.5	139	0	73	216 482	1 594	35 184	30	31 349	19.8	80.2	39.1	7.2	520	19.8
Monroe	162	-3.0	166	0	87	215 598	1 312	31 956	33	33 616	15.4	84.6	36.7	6.3	848	29.1
Montgomery	91	-18.8	135	0	56	260 834	1 912	43 841	16	23 146	32.8	67.2	38.3	4.6	259	21.2
Morgan	116	4.5	144	0	38	137 528	969	25 039	8	9 505	54.9	45.1	20.6	0.7	118	12.2
Muhlenberg	138	20.0	207	0	85	262 870	1 261	43 041	42	62 678	22.0	78.0	32.1	7.0	1 444	31.6
Nelson	189	7.4	134	0	120	305 588	2 154	40 304	33	23 626	33.2	66.8	34.0	5.6	1 214	26.4
Nicholas	106	0.0	181	0	68	246 861	1 260	59 123	12	20 404	51.4	48.6	35.1	2.9	216	16.8
Ohio	167	3.1	166	0	95	259 750	1 716	47 515	61	61 087	18.5	81.5	30.9	9.3	916	29.3
Oldham	63	-11.3	130	0	35	654 268	4 562	43 565	21	44 214	42.1	57.9	31.6	7.9	357	12.9
Owen	155	3.3	196	1	85	338 898	1 664	56 937	17	21 380	47.4	52.6	41.1	4.6	309	20.4

STATE County	Value of residential construction authorized by building permits, 2003		Wholesale trade, 1997				Retail trade,¹ 1997				Real estate and rental and leasing, 1997			
	New construction ($1,000)	Number of housing units	Number of establish-ments	Number of employees	Sales (mil dol)	Annual payroll (mil dol)	Number of establish-ments	Number of employees	Sales (mil dol)	Annual payroll (mil dol)	Number of establish-ments	Number of employees	Receipts (mil dol)	Annual payroll (mil dol)
	133	134	135	136	137	138	139	140	141	142	143	144	145	146
KENTUCKY—Cont'd														
Cumberland	141	3	2	D	D	D	34	231	35.1	3.1	6	17	2.2	0.7
Daviess	45 173	582	141	1 678	872.9	43.7	470	6 011	853.8	84.5	75	476	33.9	7.7
Edmonson	NA	NA	2	D	D	D	22	140	18.9	1.5	2	D	D	D
Elliott	NA	NA	NA	NA	NA	NA	20	87	11.5	0.9	1	D	D	D
Estill	70	1	11	D	D	D	61	375	58.9	4.5	7	31	1.8	0.4
Fayette	285 972	2 309	492	6 529	4 181.5	203.8	1 251	20 363	3 133.1	308.7	368	2 018	289.5	40.7
Fleming	0	0	20	126	58.2	2.1	68	526	108.2	9.5	4	8	1.0	0.1
Floyd	1 872	28	55	771	312.6	19.7	185	1 568	259.4	22.9	30	156	17.1	2.7
Franklin	33 496	277	33	D	D	D	202	3 096	443.4	39.2	34	130	12.5	1.9
Fulton	600	10	12	D	D	D	61	498	70.5	7.0	5	9	0.8	0.1
Gallatin	0	0	6	D	D	D	19	179	21.6	2.0	5	D	D	D
Garrard	1 336	19	5	D	D	D	44	238	33.8	3.0	6	D	D	D
Grant	15 665	137	18	D	D	D	100	1 098	181.3	16.5	11	D	D	D
Graves	934	17	37	571	201.8	14.3	141	1 580	286.2	24.4	24	93	7.2	1.5
Grayson	200	4	17	D	D	D	103	942	131.4	12.0	13	70	3.2	1.0
Green	0	0	7	31	6.7	0.3	41	230	33.4	3.1	5	11	1.0	0.1
Greenup	5 850	47	18	D	D	D	111	788	119.7	11.2	15	33	3.2	0.4
Hancock	2 023	18	1	D	D	D	22	168	29.3	2.3	5	D	D	D
Hardin	97 523	895	68	596	134.7	13.1	422	5 431	897.0	82.9	83	241	23.6	3.6
Harlan	0	0	31	242	108.9	6.3	132	1 261	168.8	17.1	24	D	D	D
Harrison	5 065	63	11	D	D	D	64	695	106.6	9.0	9	46	2.8	0.5
Hart	2 306	35	10	D	D	D	90	589	76.7	7.3	7	D	D	D
Henderson	19 793	173	71	798	728.4	23.9	208	2 252	422.2	36.8	43	181	16.0	3.4
Henry	9 184	82	18	247	114.4	5.7	53	470	90.5	7.0	10	14	1.2	0.2
Hickman	NA	NA	6	97	40.4	2.3	19	93	13.5	1.4	5	31	0.5	0.2
Hopkins	17 120	149	57	435	190.0	10.5	246	2 805	409.0	39.9	37	114	8.6	1.3
Jackson	0	0	2	D	D	D	30	179	31.2	2.3	2	D	D	D
Jefferson	457 019	3 995	1 509	24 651	15 932.9	852.5	2 950	47 517	7 200.8	761.6	811	5 810	766.7	126.8
Jessamine	58 166	461	46	1 010	513.7	27.9	132	2 078	394.0	32.7	27	81	6.0	1.0
Johnson	633	4	24	187	60.1	5.4	127	1 606	229.2	20.7	10	32	1.6	0.3
Kenton	129 508	1 222	198	3 123	1 370.3	109.3	452	5 904	829.4	86.6	131	823	90.0	16.8
Knott	NA	NA	6	59	3.6	0.7	48	242	35.4	3.4	6	14	1.5	0.2
Knox	290	6	14	140	52.4	3.4	123	1 556	254.4	20.6	13	48	3.4	0.6
Larue	5 941	62	7	19	3.4	0.2	41	294	42.5	4.3	6	10	0.4	0.1
Laurel	1 534	13	67	1 239	520.2	28.3	230	2 827	499.8	40.6	31	108	10.2	2.2
Lawrence	0	0	9	D	D	D	51	440	63.7	5.5	4	16	0.7	0.2
Lee	NA	NA	6	50	16.3	2.0	27	179	25.8	2.8	5	D	D	D
Leslie	NA	NA	2	D	D	D	42	215	30.2	2.8	4	35	1.9	0.6
Letcher	0	0	14	374	111.3	5.1	92	837	110.2	10.8	3	16	1.0	0.2
Lewis	0	0	5	13	5.6	0.2	34	241	22.6	2.0	3	8	0.2	0.0
Lincoln	21 164	163	13	68	12.1	0.8	64	471	70.9	6.6	6	15	1.2	0.1
Livingston	NA	NA	4	39	4.4	0.4	33	188	22.7	2.7	3	13	1.1	0.2
Logan	1 820	31	27	203	79.8	3.5	106	975	147.8	13.8	13	34	6.1	0.3
Lyon	1 481	11	4	27	42.7	0.7	68	461	52.4	5.2	8	39	4.0	0.8
McCracken	30 379	215	136	2 700	1 557.0	72.3	515	6 266	1 012.0	91.1	79	418	62.7	11.3
McCreary	NA	NA	4	18	1.0	0.2	50	318	52.4	4.2	7	51	6.6	1.2
McLean	280	3	11	134	52.5	2.4	30	209	40.8	3.4	5	8	0.3	0.1
Madison	33 968	452	49	720	285.7	24.8	288	3 824	565.0	51.4	55	184	17.1	2.0
Magoffin	NA	NA	6	36	45.2	0.9	47	314	46.9	3.5	4	D	D	D
Marion	850	8	14	143	40.3	1.9	79	642	84.8	7.1	6	12	1.7	0.3
Marshall	10 725	93	38	292	124.2	7.6	128	1 054	179.2	16.4	16	110	11.7	2.3
Martin	NA	NA	8	48	73.9	2.1	51	344	58.0	5.3	4	D	D	D
Mason	4 445	35	31	394	93.7	7.4	109	1 467	246.3	20.2	12	28	3.7	0.6
Meade	390	6	12	51	59.0	1.5	85	570	122.8	9.4	14	35	2.6	0.3
Menifee	NA	NA	NA	NA	NA	NA	16	81	11.8	0.8	2	D	D	D
Mercer	13 574	162	18	67	23.7	1.2	84	637	125.6	10.1	11	100	2.6	0.5
Metcalfe	NA	NA	3	44	11.8	1.2	40	272	39.8	3.5	3	6	0.6	0.1
Monroe	NA	NA	12	D	D	D	64	405	63.7	5.3	6	7	1.2	0.1
Montgomery	14 833	184	31	243	126.7	5.2	117	1 479	225.2	18.1	25	75	6.0	1.0
Morgan	NA	NA	4	D	D	D	52	388	65.7	5.6	3	D	D	D
Muhlenberg	2 327	23	16	D	D	D	130	1 405	198.7	20.0	17	89	4.5	0.8
Nelson	46 959	482	41	448	133.3	12.8	178	1 445	218.8	19.5	27	80	7.9	1.1
Nicholas	519	4	1	D	D	D	14	114	18.5	1.6	5	11	0.5	0.0
Ohio	876	11	8	198	45.4	3.0	75	614	89.8	8.2	5	9	1.3	0.2
Oldham	161 985	831	58	451	272.6	15.0	113	1 209	192.1	19.1	23	108	12.2	1.5
Owen	105	2	6	17	3.0	0.2	23	220	50.4	2.9	4	14	0.5	0.1

1. Establishments with payroll.

Table B. States and Counties — **Professional Services, Manufacturing, and Accommodation and Foodservices**

STATE County	Professional, scientific, and technical services,[1] 1997				Manufacturing, 1997				Accommodation and foodservices, 1997			
	Number of establishments	Number of employees	Receipts (mil dol)	Annual payroll (mil dol)	Number of establishments	Number of employees	Receipts (mil dol)	Annual payroll (mil dol)	Number of establishments	Number of employees	Sales (mil dol)	Annual payroll (mil dol)
	147	148	149	150	151	152	153	154	155	156	157	158
KENTUCKY—Cont'd												
Cumberland	5	8	0.8	0.1	NA	NA	NA	NA	12	123	4.3	1.2
Daviess	145	857	56.4	23.3	114	8 011	2 938.2	276.8	150	3 331	100.6	26.6
Edmonson	4	D	D	D	NA	NA	NA	NA	11	179	6.1	1.9
Elliott	1	D	D	D	NA	NA	NA	NA	4	D	D	D
Estill	5	11	0.3	0.1	NA	NA	NA	NA	17	D	D	D
Fayette	765	8 482	1 043.1	292.0	283	17 403	4 313.9	654.0	610	15 216	508.1	146.9
Fleming	7	71	1.7	0.5	19	650	54.8	14.6	9	143	3.6	1.0
Floyd	56	300	21.7	8.5	NA	NA	NA	NA	43	608	19.3	5.4
Franklin	104	669	61.1	25.0	40	3 435	592.4	97.8	89	1 518	47.2	13.2
Fulton	9	15	0.9	0.2	14	1 087	194.1	23.4	15	D	D	D
Gallatin	3	6	0.4	0.1	NA	NA	NA	NA	9	103	4.7	0.7
Garrard	8	21	1.3	0.3	16	D	D	NA	13	112	2.7	0.7
Grant	18	51	2.5	1.0	16	D	D	D	37	D	D	D
Graves	38	142	7.9	2.9	50	3 053	537.6	101.4	49	592	15.7	4.2
Grayson	19	57	2.7	0.9	31	2 462	382.5	47.8	36	370	12.9	3.0
Green	5	19	0.9	0.3	NA	NA	NA	NA	11	115	3.2	0.8
Greenup	29	130	6.5	2.0	13	600	108.6	23.4	33	789	20.3	5.6
Hancock	8	17	0.8	0.1	13	1 862	1 049.0	80.9	8	D	D	D
Hardin	109	509	34.2	13.0	68	7 162	1 633.9	216.8	141	2 975	85.7	24.3
Harlan	34	184	11.2	4.8	NA	NA	NA	NA	32	457	15.0	3.9
Harrison	13	36	1.7	0.6	19	1 730	353.3	54.9	18	D	D	D
Hart	13	38	2.4	0.6	10	D	D	D	17	189	5.5	1.5
Henderson	73	284	18.8	5.7	78	6 862	1 722.9	208.0	81	1 403	41.3	11.8
Henry	12	31	1.3	0.6	8	555	213.9	17.1	7	99	3.1	0.8
Hickman	4	14	0.9	0.4	NA	NA	NA	NA	3	D	D	D
Hopkins	69	334	23.3	7.7	55	2 606	572.8	89.7	74	982	30.4	8.3
Jackson	4	7	0.3	0.1	13	1 940	173.3	28.4	8	D	D	D
Jefferson	1 811	15 317	1 479.9	503.7	873	56 948	30 261.6	2 201.4	1 394	34 303	1 081.9	314.8
Jessamine	48	173	10.6	3.3	67	2 379	675.4	67.9	44	799	23.6	6.2
Johnson	34	189	14.2	3.6	NA	NA	NA	NA	28	470	15.3	4.3
Kenton	263	2 441	162.3	71.1	161	6 810	1 482.8	233.4	294	6 542	236.9	65.5
Knott	14	47	2.8	1.2	NA	NA	NA	NA	10	D	D	D
Knox	28	196	14.9	6.1	17	877	160.6	20.6	33	561	15.9	4.3
Larue	16	30	2.1	0.8	12	641	25.3	10.1	10	D	D	D
Laurel	60	246	18.6	4.7	44	2 595	319.1	57.4	64	1 698	50.9	14.4
Lawrence	10	34	2.5	0.8	NA	NA	NA	NA	18	280	8.3	2.2
Lee	5	8	0.3	0.1	NA	NA	NA	NA	8	D	D	D
Leslie	10	47	4.4	0.7	NA	NA	NA	NA	6	D	D	D
Letcher	27	169	9.5	3.2	NA	NA	NA	NA	19	314	9.5	2.7
Lewis	6	27	0.9	0.3	15	804	89.9	15.7	14	D	D	D
Lincoln	19	65	4.8	1.7	18	737	54.7	18.9	15	176	4.7	1.3
Livingston	9	31	1.3	0.4	NA	NA	NA	NA	11	249	8.7	3.1
Logan	23	83	5.1	1.8	41	4 650	781.7	126.0	29	479	11.6	2.6
Lyon	10	24	0.9	0.3	NA	NA	NA	NA	21	216	7.2	1.8
McCracken	133	947	67.3	21.8	58	4 081	978.9	155.2	184	4 116	125.1	35.3
McCreary	7	23	0.7	0.2	16	D	D	D	10	117	3.0	0.9
McLean	8	18	0.9	0.2	NA	NA	NA	NA	10	58	1.6	0.4
Madison	77	273	14.7	4.6	68	5 460	1 576.1	160.3	126	2 664	75.5	21.2
Magoffin	12	72	5.6	1.8	NA	NA	NA	NA	11	161	4.8	1.4
Marion	19	78	5.1	1.7	22	1 554	175.1	34.4	28	296	8.3	2.5
Marshall	37	224	12.8	6.4	35	2 881	1 715.5	141.0	72	774	24.0	6.3
Martin	13	31	2.5	0.6	NA	NA	NA	NA	15	235	7.6	2.1
Mason	20	72	4.2	1.4	19	3 167	545.5	85.6	42	526	20.2	4.9
Meade	10	36	1.6	0.5	NA	NA	NA	NA	24	284	9.4	2.7
Menifee	2	D	D	D	NA	NA	NA	NA	4	D	D	D
Mercer	24	52	3.7	1.0	16	3 053	888.7	94.9	36	403	14.0	3.7
Metcalfe	6	9	0.4	0.1	13	1 829	231.4	37.0	9	83	2.0	0.4
Monroe	7	14	0.8	0.1	32	1 966	160.9	35.8	21	D	D	D
Montgomery	23	101	5.9	1.6	32	2 124	281.4	45.4	38	785	20.5	5.5
Morgan	9	23	0.9	0.2	NA	NA	NA	NA	9	D	D	D
Muhlenberg	38	148	6.0	2.1	36	1 399	130.1	26.8	41	502	13.2	3.8
Nelson	46	181	11.5	3.2	56	3 616	960.2	99.0	55	863	27.2	7.5
Nicholas	4	6	0.3	0.1	5	D	D	D	4	59	0.8	0.2
Ohio	23	75	4.5	1.4	27	2 010	177.1	37.4	24	363	10.3	2.4
Oldham	78	261	23.2	9.3	41	1 004	252.5	37.5	51	957	29.2	8.4
Owen	5	25	2.4	1.4	NA	NA	NA	NA	6	75	1.8	0.5

1. Firms subject to federal tax.

STATE County	Health care and social assistance,[1] 1997				Other services,[1] 1997				Federal funds and grants, 2002–2003 Expenditures (mil dol)			
										Direct payments for individuals[2]		
	Number of establishments	Number of employees	Receipts (mil dol)	Annual payroll (mil dol)	Number of establishments	Number of employees	Receipts (mil dol)	Annual payroll (mil dol)	Total	Social Security and government retirement	Medicare	Food stamps and Supplemental Security Income
	159	160	161	162	163	164	165	166	167	168	169	170
KENTUCKY—Cont'd												
Cumberland	10	165	8.3	3.7	4	7	0.8	0.1	51.7	16.4	11.6	4.2
Daviess	202	2 568	184.0	76.4	144	829	50.4	14.5	467.1	210.8	89.3	24.1
Edmonson	8	137	5.3	2.2	3	13	1.3	0.2	60.5	22.6	9.6	3.5
Elliott	5	76	2.5	0.8	4	18	0.6	0.1	32.9	11.1	3.6	3.7
Estill	11	126	6.5	2.2	13	26	3.0	0.8	106.9	42.5	20.3	9.8
Fayette	612	10 905	793.3	352.1	456	3 266	177.5	56.7	1 624.7	468.5	168.4	46.8
Fleming	14	195	8.4	3.9	26	43	2.8	0.5	76.0	29.1	11.7	5.3
Floyd	85	702	40.1	16.3	43	155	12.0	3.2	310.4	122.7	53.7	36.4
Franklin	88	1 258	87.8	36.3	69	408	22.4	9.1	1 364.7	255.5	53.7	11.6
Fulton	19	322	18.7	7.7	9	32	2.2	0.5	65.7	23.4	12.7	3.7
Gallatin	4	D	D	D	4	6	0.5	0.1	31.6	13.2	5.7	1.9
Garrard	10	61	2.6	1.2	7	22	1.4	0.4	66.6	33.0	10.9	4.0
Grant	22	316	12.5	6.7	19	65	2.6	0.7	101.3	44.8	16.0	4.5
Graves	50	898	53.3	21.8	33	293	10.3	3.5	210.0	94.8	48.0	11.3
Grayson	23	204	10.6	5.2	27	93	4.5	1.3	142.8	58.1	26.1	9.9
Green	16	267	11.0	4.9	9	17	1.3	0.2	61.0	24.8	14.5	4.3
Greenup	48	444	21.5	8.3	32	104	6.6	1.6	196.3	108.0	40.3	10.9
Hancock	6	74	2.8	0.9	9	13	0.8	0.2	34.1	17.1	5.7	1.7
Hardin	189	2 319	154.9	71.4	136	825	43.5	14.2	932.1	300.3	60.2	19.7
Harlan	26	429	22.7	13.7	32	132	8.3	1.9	393.2	104.9	37.5	124.0
Harrison	31	295	13.2	6.0	22	69	4.4	1.0	81.7	39.5	14.5	3.1
Hart	17	266	10.4	4.7	16	38	2.9	0.5	103.3	35.2	15.8	8.3
Henderson	92	687	48.5	19.4	68	503	32.0	10.4	224.5	100.3	49.4	11.5
Henry	14	150	6.2	3.3	16	44	3.5	0.8	67.7	28.7	15.4	3.1
Hickman	6	120	3.7	1.5	4	14	1.1	0.3	29.5	10.3	6.5	1.3
Hopkins	55	1 047	38.3	18.6	71	449	28.0	8.6	342.8	128.2	45.9	15.9
Jackson	5	160	6.5	2.9	7	22	1.4	0.3	109.2	27.0	13.0	9.6
Jefferson	1 622	27 669	1 872.1	835.3	1 317	9 422	586.0	187.4	6 107.4	1 634.4	765.1	72.4
Jessamine	37	286	10.8	3.8	51	227	13.6	4.1	158.2	71.3	19.1	8.1
Johnson	52	525	47.1	13.8	32	116	5.5	1.5	159.7	64.1	25.9	13.4
Kenton	219	2 729	173.5	89.7	221	1 586	103.2	31.0	840.8	291.1	128.7	30.5
Knott	8	142	7.5	3.1	9	30	2.3	0.5	117.9	36.6	15.3	14.9
Knox	33	269	14.1	6.1	20	86	5.7	1.3	197.4	56.9	26.8	22.8
Larue	11	86	3.4	1.5	11	34	2.4	0.6	81.3	32.3	14.8	3.4
Laurel	46	292	22.1	8.5	53	273	19.1	4.3	267.1	108.3	34.9	27.9
Lawrence	24	441	27.4	9.7	19	76	4.4	1.1	99.2	38.6	14.9	12.0
Lee	4	26	1.4	0.9	5	16	0.8	0.2	58.3	18.5	8.7	7.6
Leslie	9	154	6.6	2.8	5	15	1.5	0.5	98.7	34.1	15.3	11.7
Letcher	21	329	17.2	6.3	23	79	5.5	1.1	177.9	73.2	29.3	21.0
Lewis	7	161	7.0	3.4	4	7	0.6	0.1	77.1	28.7	12.6	7.8
Lincoln	13	217	9.3	4.1	16	31	3.0	0.7	134.1	51.5	21.2	9.5
Livingston	8	62	3.8	1.5	6	14	0.9	0.1	93.4	28.2	13.2	2.2
Logan	40	479	28.4	10.3	33	127	9.9	2.3	145.6	59.5	33.4	7.2
Lyon	9	207	7.3	3.3	6	14	1.0	0.2	42.9	24.1	8.6	1.3
McCracken	191	2 250	186.3	91.5	117	737	49.6	12.3	1 577.6	173.2	79.6	17.7
McCreary	12	271	11.3	5.2	6	14	1.1	0.3	143.5	38.7	18.7	16.5
McLean	13	143	5.4	2.3	12	38	3.7	0.8	53.9	24.9	11.9	2.2
Madison	116	1 034	52.1	23.6	63	316	13.3	3.9	378.1	134.3	46.8	18.3
Magoffin	11	237	9.2	3.4	6	24	3.7	0.4	98.7	26.4	13.2	13.4
Marion	27	519	31.3	12.0	14	56	3.9	0.9	93.8	35.7	16.3	7.7
Marshall	36	428	21.6	9.1	31	175	15.2	4.3	154.3	87.2	34.5	4.7
Martin	12	140	5.1	2.0	11	101	5.2	2.8	95.0	33.7	10.4	10.2
Mason	39	770	53.8	18.1	30	167	6.5	2.0	90.8	35.2	17.4	4.7
Meade	22	135	5.5	2.0	12	47	2.8	0.6	92.6	57.6	13.5	4.0
Menifee	3	D	D	D	3	D	D	D	45.3	14.4	4.7	3.6
Mercer	21	231	9.8	4.2	20	57	3.0	0.8	92.7	49.4	15.8	4.2
Metcalfe	6	59	3.0	1.1	6	9	0.6	0.1	57.1	21.9	10.5	4.2
Monroe	16	189	8.8	2.8	15	56	3.0	0.6	87.4	27.6	18.8	5.9
Montgomery	47	446	21.0	9.1	33	174	9.4	3.0	116.3	47.9	18.9	10.9
Morgan	11	122	5.6	2.0	15	38	2.3	0.4	79.7	25.8	10.9	9.5
Muhlenberg	37	532	25.4	11.7	35	136	9.3	2.1	305.7	90.4	36.7	9.9
Nelson	43	521	22.4	9.2	39	166	6.5	1.8	157.4	70.2	28.3	8.1
Nicholas	6	27	1.4	0.8	7	15	0.5	0.2	40.5	16.3	7.4	2.3
Ohio	31	619	28.7	11.5	22	107	15.2	2.3	115.0	54.7	23.1	8.4
Oldham	57	256	14.6	5.8	52	248	14.4	4.9	88.4	49.6	18.5	2.3
Owen	11	285	11.4	5.0	11	34	1.5	0.5	40.9	17.1	8.3	3.1

1. Firms subject to federal tax.   2. State totals may include programs not allocated by county.

	Federal funds and grants, 2002–2003 (cont'd)							Local government finances, 2002				
	Expenditures (mil dol) (cont'd)							General revenue				
	Procurement contract awards			Grants[1]							Taxes	
											Per capita[2] (dollars)	
STATE County	Salaries and wages	Defense	Other	Medicaid and other health-related	Nutrition and family welfare	Education	Other	Total (mil dol)	Intergovern-mental (mil dol)	Total (mil dol)	Total	Property
	171	172	173	174	175	176	177	178	179	180	181	182
KENTUCKY—Cont'd												
Cumberland	0.9	0.4	0.2	14.8	1.3	0.7	0.4	12.6	7.7	2.4	330	153
Daviess	18.9	3.0	4.5	39.7	20.2	5.2	43.1	230.3	81.0	60.4	658	405
Edmonson	8.6	0.1	2.2	10.4	1.3	1.1	0.4	17.6	12.7	3.1	264	202
Elliott	0.4	0.0	0.1	10.4	1.5	0.7	1.0	11.5	9.9	1.1	164	130
Estill	2.4	0.2	0.7	24.1	2.9	1.5	2.0	23.4	16.8	4.1	268	174
Fayette	207.7	202.6	57.1	181.6	30.6	26.6	133.5	545.2	126.5	326.2	1 237	491
Fleming	2.6	0.1	0.6	15.8	4.3	1.2	2.2	35.7	14.5	4.6	324	234
Floyd	11.2	1.0	7.0	55.0	7.2	3.8	5.9	80.9	51.5	17.5	414	320
Franklin	31.7	0.2	2.7	154.7	181.8	184.1	456.9	103.9	31.2	47.0	974	451
Fulton	2.8	1.2	0.7	12.1	1.7	1.8	2.1	21.2	12.4	4.0	528	303
Gallatin	1.4	0.6	0.2	4.1	0.7	0.5	3.1	24.9	7.4	4.0	515	369
Garrard	1.9	0.0	0.5	9.3	1.3	0.9	4.2	29.0	12.9	7.0	449	328
Grant	3.2	1.0	0.7	9.9	2.8	1.4	16.3	38.2	22.3	9.7	411	302
Graves	10.3	0.8	2.2	25.3	3.5	1.9	3.9	57.2	29.6	15.6	419	227
Grayson	3.9	0.0	1.1	26.0	4.5	1.6	9.8	43.1	26.1	9.7	398	204
Green	1.4	0.0	0.3	9.9	1.1	0.8	3.0	25.6	9.4	3.1	267	169
Greenup	3.9	0.9	1.1	21.9	3.7	2.0	2.7	59.6	33.0	15.6	424	363
Hancock	1.3	0.0	0.3	5.4	0.7	0.5	0.8	68.3	7.4	6.9	809	333
Hardin	476.6	7.0	7.3	33.3	8.6	5.1	6.9	254.3	80.1	45.7	478	279
Harlan	10.5	0.6	51.5	46.7	7.9	5.2	3.5	65.2	40.9	9.8	301	223
Harrison	3.9	0.1	0.8	13.1	1.8	1.2	2.5	30.0	16.7	9.1	501	233
Hart	2.2	0.0	0.6	18.9	2.1	1.5	17.4	23.4	15.1	5.5	309	187
Henderson	6.7	13.3	1.5	19.8	4.1	2.6	11.7	113.0	40.3	24.6	548	320
Henry	3.0	0.0	1.3	11.6	1.8	0.9	0.9	24.1	13.2	6.3	408	307
Hickman	1.1	0.0	0.2	4.6	0.7	0.5	1.4	7.9	5.6	1.7	319	234
Hopkins	9.9	1.4	89.4	29.4	4.8	3.2	10.1	85.9	46.7	26.2	562	313
Jackson	2.1	20.6	0.5	27.5	3.0	2.0	3.5	19.4	15.9	2.6	189	137
Jefferson	411.2	2 199.4	98.9	409.1	94.0	65.6	287.5	1 802.2	523.0	767.6	1 100	563
Jessamine	5.1	0.5	19.5	12.4	2.4	1.8	15.5	66.9	30.1	25.9	636	400
Johnson	3.4	1.2	1.3	33.0	11.2	2.2	3.4	49.5	29.8	12.2	523	276
Kenton	196.2	12.3	17.3	54.6	16.5	7.0	72.2	425.3	101.4	148.3	974	549
Knott	2.8	0.2	0.9	31.4	8.2	1.9	3.4	34.2	24.5	4.8	273	209
Knox	13.3	0.0	0.8	57.2	14.5	3.4	0.0	63.1	36.9	9.9	311	186
Larue	2.5	0.1	0.8	9.9	1.4	0.9	13.7	21.4	14.9	4.0	300	226
Laurel	19.4	0.2	5.3	43.0	7.0	3.7	16.5	92.5	47.5	22.5	415	221
Lawrence	2.4	0.2	0.5	23.6	2.8	2.2	1.6	42.8	21.7	3.9	247	176
Lee	1.1	0.0	0.4	15.8	1.8	1.1	3.3	15.3	9.4	2.3	285	194
Leslie	1.9	0.0	1.0	26.2	3.3	1.7	3.3	24.2	19.9	3.4	273	215
Letcher	4.5	0.0	1.5	38.2	5.1	2.3	2.4	41.3	29.6	7.8	313	221
Lewis	1.2	0.0	0.3	21.8	2.3	1.0	0.6	22.3	17.3	3.6	255	179
Lincoln	8.4	0.0	0.8	30.2	4.6	3.0	2.7	37.7	27.4	7.0	293	175
Livingston	4.6	17.2	15.4	6.3	0.9	0.6	2.6	13.5	7.8	3.9	400	261
Logan	3.8	0.0	1.0	27.5	2.6	1.9	2.3	42.4	25.8	11.9	445	252
Lyon	1.7	0.0	0.0	3.7	0.4	0.4	1.3	15.6	8.2	4.1	499	366
McCracken	47.3	0.3	1 188.4	36.9	9.0	3.8	17.3	145.0	59.9	54.3	841	428
McCreary	5.4	28.2	1.1	25.3	4.6	2.4	2.3	29.1	24.0	3.3	196	160
McLean	1.9	0.0	0.4	5.4	0.9	0.7	1.9	21.1	8.8	4.1	404	256
Madison	31.6	25.6	2.7	44.8	10.2	6.4	34.2	124.5	55.4	44.4	606	298
Magoffin	1.2	0.5	0.3	30.6	3.8	1.8	6.4	24.2	18.0	3.5	260	178
Marion	3.1	0.0	0.8	19.0	6.0	1.4	1.6	33.3	17.3	9.5	518	269
Marshall	6.2	0.9	2.0	10.9	2.2	1.4	1.9	90.2	22.8	22.7	749	426
Martin	6.6	1.0	2.1	18.7	3.0	1.3	7.6	24.9	19.9	3.5	283	219
Mason	3.9	0.0	0.7	16.1	1.9	1.2	7.7	57.0	16.8	13.7	808	402
Meade	2.3	0.0	0.6	6.8	1.9	1.3	2.7	36.9	22.9	8.6	313	247
Menifee	9.0	2.1	1.2	8.5	0.9	0.4	0.4	9.2	6.9	1.7	252	185
Mercer	3.1	0.0	0.8	12.2	1.6	1.0	3.5	34.8	18.2	12.2	578	322
Metcalfe	1.8	0.0	0.5	13.9	1.3	0.9	0.6	14.8	10.4	3.7	367	180
Monroe	3.0	0.0	0.5	25.1	1.7	0.9	2.7	20.5	14.6	4.4	372	233
Montgomery	4.2	0.0	1.4	17.7	2.6	2.2	9.3	56.6	24.9	14.2	612	334
Morgan	1.9	0.0	0.4	22.3	5.0	1.5	2.3	26.7	20.9	3.8	269	177
Muhlenberg	39.9	0.2	97.7	21.7	3.6	1.7	1.9	47.2	29.7	9.5	299	253
Nelson	16.2	3.1	1.3	18.0	3.4	2.3	3.9	71.3	30.8	18.3	472	373
Nicholas	1.5	0.0	0.2	8.0	0.9	0.5	1.6	11.4	7.7	2.6	377	240
Ohio	4.9	0.0	1.0	15.0	2.9	1.8	1.2	50.1	27.3	8.4	362	218
Oldham	4.9	0.1	1.2	5.8	2.2	1.7	1.2	73.8	33.6	33.4	678	552
Owen	1.3	0.0	0.3	7.3	1.1	0.9	1.2	16.5	9.9	3.8	351	251

1. State totals may include programs not allocated by county.   2. Based on the resident population estimated as of July 1 of the year shown.

STATE County	Total (mil dol)	Per capita[1] (dollars)	Education	Health and hospitals	Police protection	Public welfare	Highways	Total (mil dol)	Per capita[1] (dollars)	Federal civilian	Federal military	State and local	Democratic	Republican	All other
	183	184	185	186	187	188	189	190	191	192	193	194	195	196	197
KENTUCKY—Cont'd															
Cumberland	11.5	1 603	66.2	0.7	3.5	0.0	13.9	4.1	567	20	0	403	26.2	72.7	1.1
Daviess	225.4	2 458	40.4	6.4	3.9	0.7	2.8	1 014.9	11 069	292	105	7 909	38.1	61.2	0.8
Edmonson	16.7	1 412	72.2	4.0	1.8	0.0	5.0	21.5	1 819	210	11	537	33.9	65.6	0.5
Elliott	10.9	1 615	75.5	0.8	0.7	0.0	5.6	7.8	1 162	0	0	306	69.8	29.5	0.7
Estill	23.0	1 497	68.2	6.3	1.8	0.1	3.6	18.9	1 234	27	15	649	34.2	65.2	0.6
Fayette	574.0	2 177	37.6	2.2	7.4	2.6	4.3	695.2	2 637	4 038	310	30 204	46.2	52.9	0.9
Fleming	34.0	2 413	41.7	40.0	1.2	0.0	3.5	21.9	1 554	50	13	896	38.8	60.4	0.8
Floyd	76.8	1 818	58.0	1.2	1.6	0.0	7.8	71.1	1 684	148	40	2 604	62.2	37.0	0.8
Franklin	101.3	2 101	37.8	6.4	4.3	1.9	2.9	115.0	2 386	500	63	16 392	48.1	50.9	1.0
Fulton	21.6	2 859	42.8	1.3	4.1	0.0	5.6	30.5	4 038	39	25	603	46.4	52.8	0.8
Gallatin	26.8	3 424	31.9	2.0	1.5	0.0	2.5	208.9	26 655	33	0	366	38.7	60.8	0.5
Garrard	26.4	1 691	51.8	25.6	1.4	0.0	3.6	12.1	774	35	15	662	27.7	71.9	0.5
Grant	37.6	1 594	61.1	0.3	4.9	0.1	4.8	31.9	1 351	59	22	1 056	31.9	67.4	0.6
Graves	63.7	1 710	51.0	0.2	1.8	0.0	5.7	198.2	5 325	183	35	1 783	38.2	61.0	0.7
Grayson	42.4	1 738	51.9	0.7	3.0	0.9	5.4	77.7	3 183	63	23	1 533	28.6	70.7	0.7
Green	22.9	1 948	41.0	44.1	1.8	0.0	4.3	13.7	1 167	34	11	694	25.2	74.3	0.5
Greenup	60.4	1 642	56.7	3.4	3.7	0.1	3.9	32.7	889	80	35	1 456	46.4	52.9	0.7
Hancock	67.4	7 860	14.0	0.3	0.5	0.1	1.9	679.6	79 272	27	0	452	42.4	56.7	0.8
Hardin	259.0	2 706	33.6	43.7	2.5	0.2	2.3	206.7	2 159	4 396	9 954	6 231	31.6	67.6	0.8
Harlan	64.6	1 982	54.3	23.7	2.6	0.1	4.7	24.5	752	107	31	2 036	39.5	59.8	0.7
Harrison	29.6	1 637	61.4	1.1	4.9	0.3	9.0	37.8	2 091	57	17	893	36.3	62.8	0.9
Hart	23.6	1 335	60.7	3.8	3.1	0.2	4.7	26.3	1 490	43	17	783	36.4	62.9	0.7
Henderson	108.1	2 403	36.4	0.3	4.5	0.2	1.6	489.5	10 879	131	43	2 419	43.3	56.0	0.7
Henry	24.1	1 567	67.5	8.6	3.3	0.0	4.4	21.6	1 402	59	15	665	36.4	63.0	0.6
Hickman	7.7	1 487	67.1	0.0	2.6	0.0	7.9	6.8	1 310	28	0	247	39.5	59.6	0.9
Hopkins	86.4	1 854	52.6	2.5	4.9	0.0	5.4	85.7	1 840	163	44	3 138	34.1	65.4	0.6
Jackson	19.0	1 382	84.0	0.7	0.6	0.0	3.3	9.1	664	42	13	685	14.9	84.4	0.8
Jefferson	1 907.7	2 733	35.2	3.0	6.4	1.2	2.3	4 774.5	6 840	6 566	877	41 368	50.4	48.8	0.8
Jessamine	67.6	1 659	57.2	1.8	5.5	0.1	2.6	71.6	1 758	77	39	2 124	29.5	69.8	0.7
Johnson	45.1	1 929	60.9	7.0	2.2	0.2	4.5	37.4	1 599	64	22	1 481	35.3	63.8	0.8
Kenton	466.7	3 067	27.3	2.7	5.4	0.2	4.3	1 381.4	9 078	4 786	143	6 519	34.0	65.1	0.9
Knott	30.2	1 701	62.9	11.8	0.9	0.0	9.6	13.3	749	53	17	822	63.4	35.8	0.8
Knox	62.0	1 946	53.1	23.6	1.8	0.0	5.7	30.8	966	168	31	1 814	31.8	67.4	0.8
Larue	20.3	1 519	69.2	1.8	1.2	0.1	5.9	22.0	1 644	52	13	594	30.5	68.9	0.6
Laurel	73.2	1 347	67.0	2.7	3.0	0.1	5.2	79.2	1 459	335	51	2 677	23.8	75.5	0.7
Lawrence	40.2	2 549	41.6	0.2	0.7	0.0	3.5	374.4	23 723	46	15	695	41.5	57.7	0.8
Lee	15.0	1 889	60.7	9.7	2.7	0.1	4.9	15.2	1 913	27	0	533	30.1	69.1	0.8
Leslie	20.6	1 675	72.7	0.1	0.4	0.0	7.1	7.7	628	32	12	641	25.5	73.8	0.7
Letcher	41.4	1 661	69.4	0.2	1.7	0.0	4.0	18.7	750	76	24	1 248	46.2	53.0	0.8
Lewis	27.0	1 938	56.8	1.5	1.7	0.0	5.1	105.5	7 568	22	13	677	30.4	68.9	0.7
Lincoln	38.3	1 592	69.9	2.2	1.7	0.1	5.4	33.7	1 399	59	23	1 173	31.5	67.7	0.8
Livingston	13.7	1 393	60.0	8.3	1.7	0.1	12.2	6.3	641	101	0	465	42.6	56.8	0.5
Logan	40.9	1 526	64.2	0.1	5.8	0.0	4.4	38.1	1 421	72	25	1 258	35.4	64.0	0.6
Lyon	15.0	1 842	36.5	4.1	3.4	0.2	4.3	17.2	2 101	34	0	775	45.1	54.3	0.6
McCracken	142.5	2 208	42.8	7.2	5.3	0.2	4.3	124.7	1 932	700	79	4 031	38.1	61.1	0.7
McCreary	29.7	1 747	75.2	2.0	0.2	0.0	3.1	16.2	956	119	16	856	26.9	72.4	0.7
McLean	19.5	1 941	46.9	18.8	1.9	0.0	4.4	34.4	3 419	42	0	508	41.1	58.3	0.6
Madison	127.7	1 742	45.8	9.8	2.9	0.0	3.0	212.2	2 894	637	78	6 177	37.5	61.6	0.8
Magoffin	25.3	1 892	69.3	3.8	0.9	0.3	7.3	18.0	1 348	22	13	744	49.7	49.6	0.7
Marion	32.5	1 764	55.2	4.1	3.7	0.0	4.8	57.9	3 143	59	17	851	46.2	53.1	0.7
Marshall	79.6	2 630	31.6	2.7	4.3	0.4	5.0	441.0	14 575	84	29	1 778	41.1	58.3	0.6
Martin	26.4	2 104	64.5	3.6	1.0	3.6	4.0	13.4	1 073	34	12	707	33.1	66.0	0.9
Mason	54.9	3 245	29.7	2.6	2.8	0.0	5.2	339.3	20 060	65	16	1 074	37.3	61.9	0.8
Meade	33.9	1 237	70.5	2.7	1.1	0.0	3.9	34.5	1 257	39	26	950	34.0	65.3	0.7
Menifee	9.0	1 346	78.0	0.6	0.2	0.0	1.3	10.3	1 532	57	0	322	50.8	48.1	1.1
Mercer	32.5	1 543	59.8	5.1	3.3	0.0	4.6	49.2	2 340	52	20	905	32.1	67.3	0.6
Metcalfe	17.3	1 726	59.0	1.1	2.9	0.0	5.0	12.5	1 245	28	0	569	35.4	63.6	1.0
Monroe	19.2	1 630	62.9	3.5	2.6	0.0	9.6	10.5	890	41	11	891	19.8	79.7	0.5
Montgomery	55.5	2 386	42.4	12.4	3.0	0.0	3.5	139.3	5 989	79	22	1 065	44.0	55.2	0.8
Morgan	21.4	1 505	68.4	4.0	2.7	0.0	3.6	7.2	508	36	13	1 132	47.9	50.8	1.3
Muhlenberg	53.3	1 681	58.5	2.3	2.8	0.0	3.9	72.7	2 292	626	30	1 698	49.2	50.1	0.7
Nelson	69.1	1 780	54.8	2.3	2.9	0.5	4.3	180.6	4 653	95	37	1 632	38.7	60.3	0.9
Nicholas	10.8	1 563	60.1	0.5	3.4	0.7	7.2	9.5	1 374	16	0	307	43.5	55.6	0.9
Ohio	45.6	1 961	51.5	2.0	2.7	0.3	2.4	246.6	10 598	95	22	1 302	36.2	62.9	0.9
Oldham	71.4	1 447	67.3	4.0	4.5	0.0	3.1	232.0	4 705	74	48	3 159	29.8	69.3	0.9
Owen	15.3	1 395	68.3	7.9	1.3	0.0	6.4	11.9	1 088	30	10	471	34.1	65.0	0.9

1. Based on the resident population estimated as of July 1 of the year shown.

Table B. States and Counties — **Land Area and Population**

STATE/ County code	CBSA code[1]	County Type[2]	STATE County	Land area,[3] (sq km) 2000	Population and population characteristics, 2003			Race alone or in combination, not Hispanic or Latino (percent)				Percent Hispanic or Latino[4]	Age (percent)					
					Total persons	Rank	Per square kilometer	White	Black	Am. Indian, Alaska Native	Asian and Pacific Islander		Under 5 years	5 to 17 years	18 to 24 years	25 to 34 years	35 to 44 years	45 to 54 years
				1	2	3	4	5	6	7	8	9	10	11	12	13	14	15
			KENTUCKY—Cont'd															
21 189	...	9	Owsley	513	4 755	2 857	9.3	99.1	0.2	0.2	0.1	0.7	5.9	17.4	9.9	11.4	14.4	15.0
21 191	17140	1	Pendleton	727	15 090	2 097	20.8	98.4	0.6	0.4	0.2	0.7	7.0	20.3	9.6	13.0	16.4	13.1
21 193	...	7	Perry	886	29 492	1 417	33.3	97.1	1.9	0.2	0.6	0.6	6.4	17.3	9.6	13.7	15.8	15.6
21 195	...	7	Pike	2 040	67 495	746	33.1	98.4	0.5	0.4	0.5	0.6	5.5	17.1	9.2	13.6	15.6	15.8
21 197	...	6	Powell	467	13 347	2 211	28.6	98.6	0.6	0.4	0.1	0.7	6.6	18.2	9.7	13.3	15.5	13.8
21 199	43700	5	Pulaski	1 714	58 013	845	33.8	97.3	1.2	0.6	0.5	0.9	6.3	16.7	8.7	12.4	14.8	14.2
21 201	...	8	Robertson	259	2 320	3 032	9.0	98.2	0.3	0.4	0.0	1.6	5.1	18.4	8.4	11.3	15.0	12.9
21 203	40020	7	Rockcastle	822	16 644	1 987	20.2	98.8	0.2	0.6	0.2	0.6	6.0	17.6	9.1	14.0	15.5	13.9
21 205	...	7	Rowan	727	22 397	1 685	30.8	96.0	1.6	0.7	1.4	1.2	5.6	14.4	21.4	13.4	12.6	11.7
21 207	...	9	Russell	657	16 586	1 990	25.2	98.2	0.7	0.4	0.2	1.0	5.6	16.5	8.6	12.3	14.5	14.3
21 209	30460	2	Scott	737	36 726	1 220	49.8	91.8	5.6	0.5	1.3	1.8	7.3	18.7	12.0	15.0	15.7	13.1
21 211	31140	1	Shelby	995	35 900	1 242	36.1	83.9	9.1	0.6	0.7	6.7	7.1	17.9	9.8	13.5	16.1	14.1
21 213	...	6	Simpson	612	16 664	1 985	27.2	88.1	10.2	0.3	0.9	1.1	7.0	18.9	8.7	13.0	15.5	13.5
21 215	31140	1	Spencer	481	14 301	2 146	29.7	97.0	1.7	0.5	0.4	1.1	6.7	19.1	10.0	14.1	17.0	13.4
21 217	15820	7	Taylor	699	23 347	1 650	33.4	93.6	5.3	0.3	0.3	0.9	6.0	16.6	11.1	11.1	14.6	13.8
21 219	...	8	Todd	975	12 019	2 291	12.3	89.2	8.6	0.3	0.2	1.9	7.4	18.8	9.0	12.9	14.8	13.0
21 221	17300	3	Trigg	1 148	12 877	2 250	11.2	89.0	9.8	0.7	0.4	0.9	5.4	17.0	7.4	11.9	14.4	14.1
21 223	31140	1	Trimble	386	8 759	2 549	22.7	97.8	0.3	0.7	0.2	1.3	5.8	19.3	9.0	14.3	15.9	14.0
21 225	...	6	Union	894	15 751	2 052	17.6	84.9	13.4	0.6	0.3	1.6	6.3	18.4	14.7	11.0	13.2	14.0
21 227	14540	3	Warren	1 412	95 778	562	67.8	86.1	9.3	0.6	1.9	3.2	6.4	16.3	14.5	14.5	14.2	13.1
21 229	...	8	Washington	779	11 260	2 348	14.5	90.3	7.7	0.3	0.6	1.8	5.9	18.5	10.1	11.3	15.5	13.7
21 231	...	7	Wayne	1 190	20 277	1 787	17.0	96.0	1.5	0.6	0.1	2.4	6.0	18.2	9.7	13.0	14.2	13.7
21 233	21780	2	Webster	867	14 051	2 162	16.2	91.9	4.4	0.3	0.1	3.6	6.4	17.0	9.6	12.7	14.4	13.9
21 235	18340	7	Whitley	1 140	37 261	1 200	32.7	98.2	0.5	0.8	0.4	0.8	6.6	18.4	11.4	12.4	13.8	13.3
21 237	...	9	Wolfe	577	6 939	2 693	12.0	99.0	0.4	0.1	0.1	0.7	7.1	18.4	9.7	12.1	15.1	13.9
21 239	30460	2	Woodford	494	23 659	1 626	47.9	90.4	5.7	0.4	0.4	3.7	6.4	18.3	8.8	12.1	16.9	16.3
22 000	...	X	**LOUISIANA**	112 825	4 496 334	X	39.9	62.6	33.0	0.9	1.7	2.6	7.2	19.0	11.1	13.2	14.5	13.9
22 001	18940	4	Acadia	1 697	59 246	827	34.9	80.3	18.5	0.4	0.3	0.9	7.8	20.7	10.9	11.7	14.6	13.1
22 003	...	6	Allen	1 980	25 268	1 557	12.8	72.1	24.6	2.3	0.7	4.5	6.6	17.5	10.5	15.6	16.5	12.4
22 005	12940	2	Ascension	755	84 424	632	111.8	76.7	19.5	0.4	0.8	3.0	8.0	20.5	10.9	14.2	16.3	12.9
22 007	38200	6	Assumption	877	23 269	1 652	26.5	66.8	31.4	0.4	0.3	1.4	6.9	19.8	10.9	12.0	15.3	13.8
22 009	...	6	Avoyelles	2 156	41 791	1 089	19.4	67.4	30.5	1.2	0.2	1.0	7.2	18.6	10.8	12.9	14.8	12.8
22 011	19760	6	Beauregard	3 005	33 514	1 315	11.2	83.5	13.6	1.2	0.7	1.8	6.5	19.4	10.2	12.7	14.9	13.7
22 013	...	6	Bienville	2 100	15 320	2 072	7.3	56.2	42.4	0.3	0.2	1.1	6.2	18.8	10.5	10.2	13.5	12.7
22 015	43340	2	Bossier	2 174	101 999	535	46.9	73.4	21.5	1.0	2.0	3.4	7.4	19.5	10.4	13.8	15.5	13.2
22 017	43340	2	Caddo	2 284	250 342	237	109.6	51.4	46.0	0.7	1.2	1.6	7.2	18.7	10.5	12.9	13.7	13.9
22 019	29340	3	Calcasieu	2 774	183 889	311	66.3	72.9	25.0	0.7	0.9	1.5	7.3	18.8	11.1	12.6	14.7	13.8
22 021	...	8	Caldwell	1 371	10 599	2 392	7.7	80.0	17.7	0.7	0.2	1.6	5.9	17.6	10.8	13.2	14.7	13.7
22 023	...	9	Cameron	3 401	9 708	2 469	2.9	92.5	4.3	0.4	0.5	2.4	6.2	19.7	10.9	11.4	17.3	13.3
22 025	...	9	Catahoula	1 822	10 615	2 391	5.8	71.4	27.4	0.4	0.3	1.0	6.3	17.8	11.7	11.1	14.5	14.7
22 027	...	7	Claiborne	1 955	16 534	1 994	8.5	51.7	47.8	0.2	0.1	0.8	5.4	18.2	10.0	12.1	14.3	14.3
22 029	35020	7	Concordia	1 802	19 730	1 819	10.9	60.2	37.9	0.3	0.3	1.6	7.1	19.2	10.2	10.4	14.2	14.3
22 031	43340	2	De Soto	2 272	25 990	1 537	11.4	57.5	40.3	0.7	0.2	1.7	7.1	19.6	10.2	11.3	14.1	13.7
22 033	12940	2	East Baton Rouge	1 180	412 447	148	349.5	53.6	42.1	0.5	2.7	2.0	7.2	18.2	13.5	14.1	14.0	13.7
22 035	...	7	East Carroll	1 092	8 997	2 523	8.2	30.5	67.7	0.2	0.4	1.3	8.0	21.2	12.7	13.2	13.4	11.8
22 037	12940	2	East Feliciana	1 174	21 095	1 749	18.0	53.0	45.8	0.3	0.3	0.8	6.9	17.5	10.5	13.2	15.9	15.2
22 039	...	6	Evangeline	1 720	35 149	1 269	20.4	69.7	28.8	0.3	0.3	1.2	7.5	20.6	11.1	12.1	14.6	12.5
22 041	...	7	Franklin	1 615	20 860	1 757	12.9	66.6	32.2	0.5	0.2	0.8	7.5	19.5	10.0	11.3	13.5	13.1
22 043	10780	3	Grant	1 671	18 887	1 866	11.3	86.2	11.6	1.7	0.3	1.4	7.1	20.0	9.5	11.9	14.5	13.7
22 045	35340	4	Iberia	1 490	74 146	690	49.8	64.6	31.6	0.8	2.5	1.5	8.0	20.8	10.5	12.1	15.0	13.0
22 047	12940	2	Iberville	1 602	32 811	1 340	20.5	48.5	49.9	0.3	0.3	1.1	7.3	18.0	11.5	13.5	16.3	14.0
22 049	40820	6	Jackson	1 476	15 259	2 082	10.3	71.8	27.1	0.3	0.2	0.6	6.9	17.5	10.5	11.6	13.7	13.3
22 051	35380	1	Jefferson	794	452 459	139	569.8	63.2	25.5	0.8	4.0	7.6	6.9	17.7	9.4	13.5	15.4	14.8
22 053	27660	6	Jefferson Davis	1 689	31 113	1 381	18.4	80.8	17.8	0.5	0.4	1.0	7.5	20.5	10.4	11.6	14.2	12.8
22 055	29180	3	Lafayette	699	194 239	297	277.9	72.1	24.7	0.6	1.5	1.9	7.3	18.9	11.7	14.4	15.5	13.9
22 057	26380	3	Lafourche	2 809	91 281	591	32.5	82.3	13.2	2.9	0.9	1.5	6.4	19.1	11.5	12.7	15.7	13.1
22 059	...	6	La Salle	1 616	14 179	2 154	8.8	86.4	12.1	0.8	0.2	0.8	6.5	18.4	10.5	12.1	14.2	13.5
22 061	40820	4	Lincoln	1 221	42 413	1 074	34.7	57.5	39.6	0.4	1.4	1.5	6.3	15.2	22.5	13.3	11.1	10.9
22 063	12940	2	Livingston	1 678	102 046	533	60.8	94.1	4.0	0.7	0.4	1.3	7.2	20.1	11.1	14.2	15.6	12.9
22 065	45260	7	Madison	1 616	13 079	2 233	8.1	35.6	61.1	0.2	0.2	3.0	8.3	22.7	12.0	13.0	12.4	12.6
22 067	12820	6	Morehouse	2 057	30 671	1 394	14.9	54.9	44.0	0.2	0.2	0.8	7.5	18.9	10.7	11.8	13.2	13.8
22 069	35060	6	Natchitoches	3 252	39 002	1 160	12.0	57.7	39.5	1.4	0.6	1.4	7.4	17.5	18.0	11.8	12.1	11.9
22 071	35380	1	Orleans	468	469 032	129	1 002.2	27.2	67.3	0.5	2.6	3.1	7.5	18.6	10.9	14.3	14.4	14.1
22 073	33740	3	Ouachita	1 581	147 898	385	93.5	63.5	34.3	0.5	0.9	1.3	7.4	19.7	11.6	13.7	13.6	12.9
22 075	35380	1	Plaquemines	2 187	28 025	1 464	12.8	69.7	22.6	2.6	3.8	2.2	7.1	20.2	10.8	12.8	16.0	13.2

1. CBSA = Core Based Statistical Area. See Appendix A for explanation. See Appendix B for list of metropolitan areas with component counties.   2. County type code from the Economic Research Service of USDA Rural-Urban Continuum Codes. See Appendix A for definition.   3. Dry land or land partially or temporarily covered by water.   4. Hispanic or Latino persons may be of any race.

Table B. States and Counties — **Population and Households**

STATE County	55 to 64 years	65 to 74 years	75 years and over	Percent female	1990	2000	1990–2000	2000–2003	Births	Deaths	Net migration	Number	Percent change, 1990–2000	Persons per house-hold	Female family house-holder[1]	One person
	16	17	18	19	20	21	22	23	24	25	26	27	28	29	30	31
KENTUCKY—Cont'd																
Owsley	10.8	8.6	6.8	49.8	5 036	4 858	-3.5	-2.1	201	262	-34	1 894	2.5	2.51	12.7	24.5
Pendleton	9.5	5.5	4.7	50.0	12 062	14 390	19.3	4.9	706	406	406	5 170	19.3	2.75	9.6	20.1
Perry	10.3	6.3	5.0	51.3	30 283	29 390	-2.9	0.3	1 321	1 098	-95	11 460	8.1	2.53	13.2	23.3
Pike	10.9	7.0	5.5	51.1	72 584	68 736	-5.3	-1.8	2 458	2 509	-1 173	27 612	5.6	2.46	11.4	24.1
Powell	10.3	7.1	4.6	50.4	11 686	13 237	13.3	0.8	594	458	-8	5 044	24.3	2.60	12.4	21.8
Pulaski	11.0	8.4	6.9	51.3	49 489	56 217	13.6	3.2	2 463	2 038	1 396	22 719	20.4	2.42	10.1	24.9
Robertson	12.3	8.8	7.5	50.8	2 124	2 266	6.7	2.4	85	130	103	866	5.6	2.54	9.1	24.7
Rockcastle	10.7	7.5	5.9	50.4	14 803	16 582	12.0	0.4	672	574	-15	6 544	19.8	2.49	11.4	24.4
Rowan	8.8	6.3	4.7	51.4	20 353	22 094	8.6	1.4	833	528	20	7 927	17.4	2.39	10.2	27.0
Russell	12.0	8.9	7.2	51.6	14 716	16 315	10.9	1.7	642	639	280	6 941	17.7	2.33	10.2	28.0
Scott	7.5	4.6	3.7	51.0	23 867	33 061	38.5	11.1	1 712	746	2 638	12 110	42.5	2.61	11.5	21.0
Shelby	10.0	5.5	4.6	50.9	24 824	33 337	34.3	7.7	1 689	897	1 757	12 104	33.8	2.63	10.6	20.2
Simpson	10.2	6.4	6.4	51.0	15 145	16 405	8.3	1.6	728	562	108	6 415	11.2	2.52	11.5	24.2
Spencer	8.4	4.6	3.4	49.5	6 801	11 766	73.0	21.5	566	314	2 196	4 251	73.4	2.74	7.6	17.1
Taylor	10.9	8.6	6.7	52.1	21 146	22 927	8.4	1.8	919	897	426	9 233	12.4	2.41	11.5	26.0
Todd	10.2	7.3	6.6	51.1	10 940	11 971	9.4	0.4	611	394	-160	4 569	11.3	2.59	11.6	23.0
Trigg	12.6	9.5	7.2	51.0	10 361	12 597	21.6	2.2	420	523	380	5 215	27.1	2.39	8.4	25.0
Trimble	9.8	5.8	5.0	50.9	6 090	8 125	33.4	7.8	306	255	566	3 137	39.7	2.57	8.5	22.0
Union	9.3	6.8	5.9	49.4	16 557	15 637	-5.6	0.7	662	570	41	5 710	2.3	2.50	11.4	26.1
Warren	8.8	5.6	4.8	50.8	77 720	92 522	19.0	3.5	3 944	2 552	1 958	35 365	22.7	2.46	11.2	26.1
Washington	9.8	7.3	7.1	50.5	10 441	10 916	4.5	3.2	436	392	305	4 121	11.1	2.57	10.0	24.0
Wayne	10.9	7.7	5.9	50.5	17 468	19 923	14.1	1.8	750	699	315	7 913	21.4	2.49	10.6	23.9
Webster	10.5	7.6	7.4	51.1	13 955	14 120	1.2	-0.5	608	534	-130	5 560	3.5	2.49	10.3	24.3
Whitley	10.4	7.0	5.9	51.6	33 326	35 865	7.6	3.9	1 654	1 387	1 153	13 780	13.4	2.52	13.0	25.2
Wolfe	10.8	7.2	6.0	50.5	6 503	7 065	8.6	-1.8	361	277	-215	2 816	14.9	2.45	12.5	27.0
Woodford	10.5	5.9	4.7	51.6	19 955	23 208	16.3	1.9	1 034	621	60	8 893	23.1	2.57	9.7	21.0
LOUISIANA	9.4	6.2	5.5	51.5	4 221 826	4 468 976	5.9	0.6	219 361	135 991	-55 144	1 656 053	10.5	2.62	16.6	25.3
Acadia	9.0	6.6	5.6	51.6	55 882	58 861	5.3	0.7	3 022	2 092	-499	21 142	9.6	2.74	14.9	22.6
Allen	8.8	6.6	5.3	44.2	21 226	25 440	19.9	-0.7	1 108	745	-518	8 102	14.4	2.62	15.2	24.3
Ascension	7.8	4.2	3.2	50.6	58 214	76 627	31.6	10.2	4 473	1 624	4 858	26 691	38.0	2.85	13.3	18.3
Assumption	9.9	6.0	5.0	51.4	22 753	23 388	2.8	-0.5	1 062	639	-535	8 239	11.4	2.81	14.9	20.3
Avoyelles	9.4	6.8	6.5	50.7	39 159	41 481	5.9	0.7	2 008	1 517	-147	14 736	9.3	2.60	15.7	25.0
Beauregard	10.0	6.8	5.0	49.5	30 083	32 986	9.6	1.6	1 358	1 060	261	12 104	16.8	2.63	10.9	22.2
Bienville	10.7	8.9	8.8	52.1	16 232	15 752	-3.0	-2.7	632	759	-295	6 108	4.4	2.52	17.7	28.8
Bossier	8.6	6.3	4.4	50.8	86 088	98 310	14.2	3.8	4 957	2 488	1 238	36 628	19.2	2.63	14.1	22.9
Caddo	9.2	6.9	6.8	52.6	248 253	252 161	1.6	-0.7	12 607	8 808	-5 466	97 974	5.1	2.51	18.9	28.9
Calcasieu	9.0	6.7	5.4	51.2	168 134	183 577	9.2	0.2	8 930	5 626	-2 917	68 613	13.7	2.61	14.7	24.0
Caldwell	10.2	7.4	6.4	49.2	9 806	10 560	7.7	0.4	433	395	11	3 941	10.2	2.50	12.6	25.4
Cameron	10.1	6.7	4.6	49.7	9 260	9 991	7.9	-2.8	359	264	-379	3 592	13.9	2.76	9.0	20.9
Catahoula	10.1	8.1	6.4	50.0	11 065	10 920	-1.3	-2.8	433	433	-296	4 082	3.9	2.55	14.5	24.3
Claiborne	9.9	8.1	6.9	51.0	17 405	16 851	-3.2	-1.9	550	723	-121	6 270	3.4	2.50	17.6	28.5
Concordia	9.8	6.6	5.6	52.1	20 828	20 247	-2.8	-2.6	912	703	-718	7 521	2.5	2.60	19.0	25.3
De Soto	10.1	6.9	6.7	52.2	25 668	25 494	-0.7	1.9	1 223	895	190	9 691	6.2	2.60	18.6	25.4
East Baton Rouge	8.5	5.3	4.8	52.0	380 105	412 852	8.6	-0.1	20 271	10 758	-9 997	156 365	12.8	2.55	16.8	26.9
East Carroll	7.8	6.6	5.9	48.9	9 709	9 421	-3.0	-4.5	517	311	-636	2 969	-5.1	2.82	27.7	25.6
East Feliciana	9.7	6.3	4.7	46.7	19 211	21 360	11.2	-1.2	964	726	-498	6 699	19.9	2.76	18.0	22.5
Evangeline	9.0	6.7	6.0	49.8	33 274	35 434	6.5	-0.8	1 693	1 303	-655	12 736	8.0	2.64	15.5	25.8
Franklin	9.7	8.1	7.4	52.3	22 387	21 263	-5.0	-1.9	1 098	980	-520	7 754	-0.3	2.64	16.5	23.9
Grant	10.5	6.7	5.8	50.8	17 526	18 698	6.7	1.0	874	610	-53	7 073	13.0	2.61	12.9	22.6
Iberia	8.7	6.1	5.3	51.8	68 297	73 266	7.3	1.2	3 969	2 158	-878	25 381	11.1	2.82	17.2	21.1
Iberville	9.0	5.9	5.1	50.1	31 049	33 320	7.3	-1.5	1 678	1 020	-1 163	10 674	8.1	2.81	20.4	21.9
Jackson	10.8	8.0	7.8	52.0	15 859	15 397	-2.9	-0.9	725	708	-140	6 086	4.6	2.48	14.4	27.0
Jefferson	10.0	6.4	5.7	51.9	448 306	455 466	1.6	-0.7	20 969	13 485	-10 541	176 234	5.9	2.56	15.4	26.7
Jefferson Davis	9.5	7.1	6.4	51.8	30 722	31 435	2.3	-1.0	1 549	1 048	-825	11 480	7.6	2.70	13.7	22.6
Lafayette	7.8	5.4	4.2	51.3	164 762	190 503	15.6	2.0	9 492	4 523	-1 094	72 372	19.8	2.57	14.0	25.4
Lafourche	9.3	6.3	5.0	51.2	85 860	89 974	4.8	1.5	3 790	2 384	-19	32 057	11.2	2.75	12.4	19.6
La Salle	10.0	7.9	7.0	49.8	13 662	14 282	4.5	-0.7	631	557	-166	5 291	4.0	2.52	9.8	25.7
Lincoln	7.5	5.6	5.8	51.4	41 745	42 509	1.8	-0.2	1 819	1 040	-859	15 235	11.5	2.44	15.3	27.0
Livingston	8.5	4.9	3.4	50.4	70 523	91 814	30.2	11.1	4 783	2 289	7 546	32 630	37.0	2.80	10.7	18.2
Madison	8.0	5.9	5.7	49.5	12 463	13 728	10.2	-4.7	744	555	-857	4 469	5.1	2.74	24.2	26.6
Morehouse	8.9	7.8	7.3	52.1	31 938	31 021	-2.9	-1.1	1 569	1 188	-733	11 382	3.8	2.64	19.8	24.4
Natchitoches	8.6	6.2	5.7	52.4	37 254	39 080	4.9	-0.2	2 032	1 133	-966	14 263	12.8	2.56	17.7	27.1
Orleans	8.6	5.8	5.9	53.0	496 938	484 674	-2.5	-3.2	25 062	16 476	-24 463	188 251	0.0	2.48	24.5	33.2
Ouachita	8.5	6.4	5.5	52.6	142 191	147 250	3.6	0.4	7 535	4 582	-2 232	55 216	9.3	2.58	17.9	25.8
Plaquemines	8.7	5.9	3.8	50.1	25 575	26 757	4.6	4.7	1 299	734	716	9 021	9.8	2.89	14.6	18.6

1. No spouse present.

Table B. States and Counties — Vital Statistics, Health Resources, and Crime

STATE County	Births, average 1999–2001		Deaths, average 1999–2001				Physicians,[4] 2000		Hospitals,[4] 1998			Medicare enrollees, 2003	Serious crimes known to police,[6] 2002	
			Number		Rate					Beds			Total	
	Total	Rate[1]	Total	Infant[2]	Total[1]	Infant[3]	Number	Rate[5]	Number	Number	Rate[5]		Number	Rate[7]
	32	33	34	35	36	37	38	39	40	41	42	43	44	45

KENTUCKY—Cont'd

STATE County	Total	Rate	Total	Infant	Total	Infant	Number	Rate	Number	Number	Rate	Medicare	Number	Rate
Owsley	58	11.9	75	0	15.4	D	2	41	0	0	0	1 131	NA	NA
Pendleton	199	13.9	124	2	8.6	D	2	14	0	0	0	1 896	NA	NA
Perry	407	13.8	324	2	11.0	D	75	255	1	295	950	6 065	NA	NA
Pike	779	11.3	773	8	11.2	9.8	113	164	2	354	491	13 933	NA	NA
Powell	185	14.0	132	1	10.0	D	4	30	0	0	0	1 624	NA	NA
Pulaski	744	13.2	616	3	10.9	D	82	146	1	248	441	12 373	NA	NA
Robertson	25	10.8	32	0	13.9	D	0	0	0	0	0	391	NA	NA
Rockcastle	202	12.2	176	1	10.6	D	10	60	1	28	176	2 605	NA	NA
Rowan	259	11.7	167	0	7.5	D	44	199	1	169	761	3 168	NA	NA
Russell	193	11.8	196	2	12.0	D	12	74	1	47	290	3 510	NA	NA
Scott	521	15.7	243	3	7.3	D	27	82	1	79	257	3 839	NA	NA
Shelby	481	14.4	288	3	8.6	D	32	96	1	78	264	4 074	NA	NA
Simpson	236	14.3	170	2	10.3	D	11	67	1	58	354	2 523	NA	NA
Spencer	167	14.1	92	0	7.8	D	2	17	0	0	0	1 423	NA	NA
Taylor	285	12.4	266	2	11.6	D	29	126	1	98	427	4 935	NA	NA
Todd	184	15.3	130	3	10.9	D	4	33	0	0	0	1 853	NA	NA
Trigg	135	10.7	149	1	11.9	D	5	40	1	42	339	2 684	NA	NA
Trimble	99	12.1	81	0	9.9	D	3	37	0	0	0	1 195	NA	NA
Union	197	12.6	176	2	11.2	D	8	51	1	42	253	2 561	NA	NA
Warren	1 227	13.2	759	9	8.2	7.6	176	190	2	623	713	13 174	NA	NA
Washington	134	12.3	122	0	11.1	D	7	64	0	0	0	1 954	NA	NA
Wayne	242	12.2	211	2	10.6	D	16	80	1	30	157	3 577	NA	NA
Webster	184	13.0	156	3	11.1	D	4	28	0	0	0	2 640	NA	NA
Whitley	509	14.1	411	2	11.4	D	57	159	1	286	796	8 817	NA	NA
Wolfe	109	15.5	90	1	12.9	D	2	28	0	0	0	1 439	NA	NA
Woodford	303	13.0	192	2	8.3	D	21	90	1	66	289	3 000	381	1 621
LOUISIANA	66 795	14.9	41 378	624	9.3	9.3	9 061	203	133	18 314	419	620 196	228 528	5 098
Acadia	931	15.8	603	7	10.3	7.9	45	76	2	217	376	8 793	2 033	3 543
Allen	342	13.5	229	2	9.0	D	17	67	2	87	364	3 436	NA	NA
Ascension	1 337	17.4	494	11	6.4	8.2	47	61	3	189	264	7 703	3 427	4 531
Assumption	315	13.5	201	3	8.6	D	11	47	1	38	165	3 106	462	1 969
Avoyelles	618	14.9	487	5	11.7	D	22	53	2	103	252	6 939	434	1 067
Beauregard	433	13.1	314	4	9.5	D	24	73	2	193	604	4 879	681	2 058
Bienville	193	12.3	224	1	14.3	D	5	32	0	0	0	3 019	134	848
Bossier	1 509	15.3	780	12	7.9	8.0	110	112	2	214	229	12 167	5 243	5 317
Caddo	3 739	14.8	2 636	52	10.5	14.0	888	352	7	1 611	664	38 925	18 085	7 150
Calcasieu	2 798	15.3	1 713	28	9.3	10.0	304	166	6	862	478	26 680	10 808	5 980
Caldwell	131	12.4	115	1	10.9	D	14	133	2	89	859	1 855	136	1 284
Cameron	116	11.7	77	1	7.8	D	3	30	1	27	298	900	232	2 315
Catahoula	137	12.6	122	1	11.1	D	6	55	0	0	0	2 014	218	1 990
Claiborne	176	10.5	217	2	12.9	D	13	77	1	40	236	2 817	310	1 834
Concordia	299	14.8	213	3	10.5	D	10	49	1	46	222	3 534	533	2 624
De Soto	388	15.2	294	5	11.5	D	9	35	1	35	140	4 275	1 029	4 024
East Baton Rouge	6 134	14.9	3 244	60	7.9	9.7	1 033	250	5	1 557	394	47 196	32 682	7 892
East Carroll	155	16.6	105	2	11.2	D	9	96	1	29	326	1 400	NA	NA
East Feliciana	304	14.3	219	2	10.3	D	9	42	0	0	0	2 850	NA	NA
Evangeline	528	14.9	395	6	11.2	D	42	119	2	311	912	5 953	455	1 662
Franklin	331	15.6	292	6	13.8	D	8	38	1	46	208	3 684	389	1 824
Grant	270	14.4	200	3	10.7	D	5	27	0	0	0	2 897	372	1 983
Iberia	1 212	16.5	651	11	8.9	9.1	78	106	2	156	213	10 414	NA	NA
Iberville	494	14.8	309	5	9.3	D	32	96	1	151	484	4 467	1 555	5 049
Jackson	206	13.3	206	0	13.4	D	11	71	1	66	424	2 892	128	829
Jefferson	6 355	14.0	4 086	47	9.0	7.4	1 456	320	7	1 772	393	64 634	24 250	5 308
Jefferson Davis	505	16.1	341	3	10.9	D	24	76	2	70	221	4 996	1 669	5 293
Lafayette	2 867	15.0	1 394	26	7.3	9.1	455	239	5	1 024	549	22 430	10 549	5 803
Lafourche	1 203	13.3	713	16	7.9	13.0	106	118	3	251	281	12 006	2 587	2 953
La Salle	187	13.1	170	1	11.9	D	14	98	2	114	834	2 503	148	1 305
Lincoln	543	12.8	337	4	8.0	D	55	129	1	107	257	5 445	1 839	4 953
Livingston	1 474	15.9	669	9	7.2	6.1	14	15	0	0	0	10 265	2 925	3 176
Madison	247	18.1	165	3	12.1	D	6	44	1	50	390	1 759	NA	NA
Morehouse	471	15.2	371	5	12.0	D	32	103	1	119	378	5 602	NA	NA
Natchitoches	597	15.4	381	6	9.8	D	35	90	1	196	529	5 496	2 006	5 117
Orleans	7 500	15.5	5 059	68	10.5	9.1	2 192	452	14	3 229	694	65 485	31 922	6 566
Ouachita	2 249	15.3	1 383	27	9.4	12.0	317	215	5	1 012	689	20 118	NA	NA
Plaquemines	399	14.9	217	2	8.1	D	15	56	0	0	0	3 365	535	1 993

1. Per 1,000 estimated resident population.   2. Deaths of infants under 1 year old.   3. Deaths of infants under 1 year old per 1,000 live births.   4. Data subject to copyright.   5. Per 100,000 resident population as of July 1 of the year shown.   6. Data for serious crimes have not been adjusted for underreporting; this may affect comparability between geographic areas and over time.   7. Per 100,000 population estimated by the FBI.

Table B. States and Counties — Crime, Education, Money Income, and Poverty

STATE County	Serious crimes known to police,[1] 2002 (cont'd) Rate[2] Violent	Property	Education — School enrollment and attainment, 2000 Enrollment[3] Total	Percent private	Attainment[4] (percent) High school graduate or less	Bachelor's degree or more	Local government expenditures,[5] 2000–2001 Total current expenditures (mil dol)	Current expenditures per student (dollars)	Money income, 1999 Per capita income[6] (dollars)	Households Median income Dollars	Percent change, 1989–1999 (constant 1999 dollars)	Percent with income of $100,000 or more	Percent below poverty level, 1999 Persons	Households	Families	Families with children
	46	47	48	49	50	51	52	53	54	55	56	57	58	59	60	61
KENTUCKY—Cont'd																
Owsley	NA	NA	1 167	7.6	78.7	7.7	7.1	7 763	10 742	15 805	36.9	1.9	45.4	43.9	41.7	53.0
Pendleton	NA	NA	3 590	6.2	74.1	9.7	16.4	5 415	16 551	38 125	26.1	3.9	11.4	11.6	9.8	13.3
Perry	NA	NA	6 979	4.4	73.0	8.9	39.0	6 452	12 224	22 089	1.5	3.0	29.1	29.3	26.1	33.0
Pike	NA	NA	15 519	7.7	72.6	9.9	76.4	6 551	14 005	23 930	2.0	3.7	23.4	24.4	20.6	27.8
Powell	NA	NA	3 021	4.2	80.4	6.5	16.3	6 268	13 060	25 515	12.9	3.1	23.5	24.2	18.9	27.0
Pulaski	NA	NA	12 531	7.3	69.2	10.5	57.6	5 897	15 352	27 370	11.9	4.2	19.1	20.2	16.2	21.6
Robertson	NA	NA	519	5.2	75.5	8.7	2.4	6 342	13 404	30 581	15.2	2.3	22.2	20.2	14.8	23.0
Rockcastle	NA	NA	3 509	2.7	79.3	8.3	18.3	6 209	12 337	23 475	16.7	2.4	23.1	25.3	19.1	25.6
Rowan	NA	NA	8 071	6.2	58.1	21.9	19.7	6 412	13 888	28 055	31.1	4.8	21.3	22.7	15.9	20.1
Russell	NA	NA	3 471	5.4	72.6	9.6	16.8	6 085	13 183	22 042	-2.3	3.4	24.3	26.3	20.4	27.3
Scott	NA	NA	9 002	23.3	52.8	20.3	35.7	6 020	21 490	47 081	27.1	12.6	8.8	9.3	7.3	10.0
Shelby	NA	NA	7 538	16.2	55.4	18.7	28.8	5 600	20 195	45 534	18.9	10.3	9.9	9.6	6.5	10.1
Simpson	NA	NA	3 705	8.8	67.4	11.9	16.8	5 560	17 150	36 432	24.4	4.2	11.6	12.9	8.5	11.2
Spencer	NA	NA	2 845	13.6	65.0	11.1	12.8	5 923	19 848	47 042	54.4	8.5	8.8	10.8	7.7	10.9
Taylor	NA	NA	5 780	22.5	68.1	12.2	24.1	6 257	15 162	28 089	-0.8	4.1	17.5	19.1	14.2	20.6
Todd	NA	NA	2 687	10.0	73.2	9.2	12.4	5 880	15 462	29 718	8.9	3.4	17.2	18.6	14.7	20.1
Trigg	NA	NA	2 654	3.8	64.6	12.0	11.9	5 749	17 184	33 002	23.7	4.4	12.3	14.7	8.8	12.1
Trimble	NA	NA	2 007	7.5	70.2	7.6	8.4	5 577	16 354	36 192	20.4	5.2	13.6	14.9	10.0	13.1
Union	NA	NA	3 952	12.7	66.0	10.9	17.2	6 830	17 465	35 018	9.5	5.8	17.7	12.7	9.3	14.4
Warren	NA	NA	28 046	7.3	51.0	24.7	82.6	5 694	18 847	36 151	11.3	8.0	15.4	16.0	10.8	15.9
Washington	NA	NA	2 699	19.5	69.7	13.3	10.7	5 740	15 722	33 136	19.7	5.0	13.5	14.8	10.3	13.8
Wayne	NA	NA	4 496	2.3	78.0	7.2	23.1	6 523	12 601	20 863	23.6	3.0	29.4	30.0	24.6	30.6
Webster	NA	NA	3 296	7.9	72.6	7.1	14.6	5 972	15 657	31 529	10.8	3.4	15.4	15.7	12.4	16.3
Whitley	NA	NA	9 292	15.0	70.1	13.4	47.0	6 233	12 777	22 075	9.7	3.5	26.4	27.7	21.6	30.7
Wolfe	NA	NA	1 649	6.2	77.1	10.6	10.3	7 716	10 321	19 310	30.7	1.4	35.9	34.3	29.9	45.0
Woodford	230	1 391	5 753	23.7	46.9	25.9	20.9	5 476	22 839	49 491	12.1	12.2	7.3	8.1	5.2	7.5
LOUISIANA	662	4 436	1 271 299	18.9	57.6	18.7	4 409.7	5 981	16 912	32 566	10.4	7.4	19.6	19.1	15.8	22.1
Acadia	281	3 263	16 063	20.9	73.4	9.4	52.9	5 302	13 424	26 684	24.0	4.6	24.5	25.6	21.0	27.0
Allen	NA	NA	6 125	10.8	74.8	9.3	26.4	5 996	13 101	27 777	30.5	4.5	19.9	21.3	17.9	21.9
Ascension	551	3 980	21 867	17.1	62.1	14.5	91.6	6 088	17 858	44 288	20.2	8.3	12.9	12.6	10.7	13.7
Assumption	332	1 637	6 255	11.2	77.5	7.4	29.5	6 408	14 008	31 168	15.9	4.8	21.8	21.2	19.5	24.7
Avoyelles	224	843	10 352	12.1	77.3	8.3	37.7	5 330	12 146	23 851	32.0	3.6	25.9	26.8	21.7	27.7
Beauregard	178	1 880	8 255	10.7	64.5	13.8	34.2	5 664	15 514	32 582	8.1	5.6	15.6	15.8	13.0	17.6
Bienville	82	766	4 152	10.6	69.4	11.5	18.4	7 103	12 471	23 663	9.8	2.6	26.1	25.8	21.8	29.1
Bossier	631	4 686	27 569	9.4	49.5	18.1	102.2	5 439	18 119	39 203	12.0	7.3	13.7	13.6	10.6	15.8
Caddo	880	6 270	68 792	11.2	53.5	20.6	291.8	6 467	17 839	31 467	4.6	7.8	21.1	19.5	17.1	25.5
Calcasieu	662	5 318	50 285	13.8	57.5	16.9	181.9	5 637	17 710	35 372	8.0	7.6	15.4	15.8	12.8	17.7
Caldwell	245	1 039	2 531	3.9	73.2	8.8	11.2	5 943	13 884	26 972	24.9	3.8	21.2	21.1	17.7	23.5
Cameron	349	1 966	2 578	7.2	74.7	7.9	13.8	7 043	15 348	34 232	1.3	4.4	12.3	13.4	9.1	9.3
Catahoula	146	1 844	2 633	6.6	75.3	9.4	12.1	6 316	12 608	22 528	12.1	3.8	28.1	26.7	22.6	35.3
Claiborne	337	1 497	4 244	13.5	69.5	12.4	17.3	6 077	13 825	25 344	17.4	4.2	26.5	26.1	21.4	28.8
Concordia	483	2 142	5 092	10.2	69.9	9.6	22.8	5 811	11 966	22 742	-2.0	3.0	29.1	27.2	24.3	33.2
De Soto	735	3 289	6 702	7.5	70.3	10.2	32.7	6 464	13 606	28 252	28.9	3.4	25.1	24.9	21.0	29.1
East Baton Rouge	817	7 075	134 817	21.7	42.5	30.8	372.2	6 861	19 790	37 224	1.8	10.9	17.9	17.3	13.2	19.0
East Carroll	NA	NA	2 997	12.2	73.3	12.3	11.6	6 295	9 629	20 723	57.5	2.7	40.5	36.0	32.6	47.0
East Feliciana	NA	NA	5 150	24.7	68.8	11.3	16.0	6 069	15 428	31 631	16.9	6.0	23.0	20.8	18.3	26.5
Evangeline	183	1 480	9 554	10.1	75.2	9.5	33.8	5 276	11 432	20 532	10.8	3.0	32.2	33.9	27.2	35.1
Franklin	375	1 449	5 329	13.8	75.1	9.8	22.0	5 606	12 675	22 964	12.8	3.1	28.4	27.8	23.1	35.0
Grant	299	1 685	4 695	7.0	68.5	9.8	19.7	5 471	14 410	29 622	24.5	4.4	21.5	20.8	16.9	24.1
Iberia	NA	NA	20 021	12.6	71.6	11.2	90.3	6 209	14 145	31 204	11.5	5.6	23.6	22.7	20.2	27.1
Iberville	1 224	3 825	8 553	20.8	73.2	9.6	33.8	6 819	13 272	29 039	6.1	5.8	23.1	23.1	19.5	25.7
Jackson	168	660	3 746	8.0	66.1	12.9	17.4	6 769	15 354	28 352	12.2	4.6	19.8	21.1	16.0	23.9
Jefferson	624	4 684	121 830	37.3	50.7	21.5	315.3	6 195	19 953	38 435	2.5	9.2	13.7	12.6	10.8	16.6
Jefferson Davis	1 189	4 104	8 365	13.1	71.8	9.9	34.8	5 924	13 398	27 736	11.8	3.9	20.9	21.9	18.1	22.3
Lafayette	709	5 094	56 319	20.0	49.2	25.5	160.9	5 560	19 371	36 518	11.7	9.5	15.7	15.9	11.8	15.8
Lafourche	293	2 659	24 776	15.7	71.7	12.4	90.5	5 968	15 809	34 910	21.3	5.6	16.5	16.8	13.2	18.3
La Salle	185	1 119	3 312	4.7	70.0	11.2	15.5	5 825	14 033	28 189	12.8	4.2	18.7	20.9	14.9	21.4
Lincoln	461	4 492	17 955	9.1	44.3	31.8	38.3	5 713	14 313	26 977	4.3	5.1	26.5	27.9	18.2	26.9
Livingston	471	2 705	25 283	8.9	66.0	11.4	97.6	4 949	16 282	38 887	13.6	5.8	11.4	12.5	9.1	11.1
Madison	NA	NA	4 076	12.1	70.3	11.0	14.3	5 516	10 114	20 509	19.3	2.1	36.7	32.0	29.7	41.0
Morehouse	NA	NA	7 885	13.5	72.2	9.7	30.0	5 585	13 197	25 124	8.0	4.0	26.8	26.1	21.3	31.5
Natchitoches	735	4 383	13 663	8.8	59.4	18.4	40.5	5 771	13 743	25 722	21.3	4.9	26.5	27.0	20.9	28.9
Orleans	941	5 625	150 096	27.0	48.8	25.8	449.3	5 789	17 258	27 133	9.3	7.8	27.9	25.6	23.7	33.5
Ouachita	NA	NA	44 054	11.0	51.4	22.7	155.4	5 552	17 084	32 047	12.9	7.6	20.7	19.5	15.8	23.2
Plaquemines	209	1 785	7 807	18.5	65.5	10.8	29.5	5 927	15 937	38 173	18.0	7.7	18.0	17.0	15.4	18.3

1. Data for serious crimes have not been adjusted for underreporting; this may affect comparability between geographic areas and over time.   2. Per 100,000 population estimated by the FBI.   3. All persons 3 years old and over enrolled in nursery school through college.   4. Persons 25 years old and over.   5. Elementary and secondary education expenditures.   6. Based on population enumerated as of April 1, 2000.

Table B. States and Counties — **Personal Income**

STATE County	Total (mil dol)	Percent change, 2001–2002	Per capita[1] Dollars	Per capita[1] Rank	Wages and salaries[2] (mil dol)	Proprietor's income (mil dol)	Dividends, interest, and rent (mil dol)	Transfer payments Total (mil dol)	Government payments to individuals Total (mil dol)	Social Security (mil dol)	Medical payments (mil dol)	Income maintenance (mil dol)	Unemployment insurance (mil dol)
	62	63	64	65	66	67	68	69	70	71	72	73	74
KENTUCKY—Cont'd													
Owsley	84	1.0	17 644	2 938	19	4	8	41	40	8	21	9	0
Pendleton	303	2.6	20 445	2 445	96	5	46	53	49	20	19	6	1
Perry	615	4.3	20 926	2 317	462	36	78	217	209	61	93	35	4
Pike	1 435	1.8	21 172	2 243	902	116	204	439	422	158	162	57	7
Powell	244	4.4	18 341	2 851	84	22	24	66	62	22	24	11	2
Pulaski	1 259	3.9	21 986	2 019	760	73	191	372	357	119	173	36	12
Robertson	40	-0.8	17 227	2 973	9	-1	5	11	11	3	5	1	0
Rockcastle	277	3.9	16 615	3 016	97	9	33	86	82	25	39	11	2
Rowan	431	6.8	19 309	2 695	312	23	57	106	101	32	40	12	2
Russell	315	3.5	19 139	2 730	153	30	43	105	100	33	44	12	7
Scott	993	2.8	28 022	548	1 289	76	115	108	99	41	39	10	3
Shelby	982	2.8	28 034	546	558	40	162	116	107	49	40	9	5
Simpson	384	2.2	23 107	1 693	284	34	64	70	66	27	27	6	3
Spencer	287	0.6	21 150	2 252	46	3	33	44	41	17	17	3	2
Taylor	473	5.0	20 391	2 462	277	23	73	133	127	48	55	13	5
Todd	242	-0.8	20 121	2 517	93	25	39	53	50	18	22	5	2
Trigg	324	4.5	25 419	1 021	118	15	54	66	62	29	22	4	3
Trimble	148	2.8	17 109	2 984	33	2	21	36	34	13	15	3	1
Union	359	0.0	22 934	1 741	208	24	64	77	73	31	32	6	1
Warren	2 377	4.6	25 183	1 081	1 827	147	375	409	384	137	168	40	10
Washington	231	3.3	20 732	2 360	105	11	42	54	51	20	22	4	3
Wayne	346	3.8	17 231	2 972	172	21	48	111	106	33	49	17	3
Webster	358	-2.0	25 417	1 022	152	62	55	68	65	29	24	6	2
Whitley	714	3.6	19 388	2 678	396	25	96	252	242	63	114	35	5
Wolfe	114	2.9	16 407	3 035	33	6	10	52	50	13	24	11	1
Woodford	804	2.2	34 135	157	409	115	130	76	70	37	22	5	2
LOUISIANA	113 231	3.4	25 296	X	72 279	9 728	17 722	21 690	20 537	6 586	9 891	2 661	398
Acadia	1 225	2.1	20 750	2 356	443	71	192	288	272	88	134	37	5
Allen	451	3.8	17 948	2 903	270	45	54	113	107	36	50	14	2
Ascension	2 078	3.9	25 432	1 017	1 296	232	221	276	255	93	113	31	10
Assumption	572	6.5	24 657	1 223	244	33	80	100	94	35	39	15	3
Avoyelles	761	2.2	18 331	2 855	297	59	110	216	205	61	99	34	3
Beauregard	666	2.9	20 089	2 525	305	38	96	137	129	47	57	14	3
Bienville	308	4.1	19 969	2 552	127	24	53	87	83	28	38	11	2
Bossier	2 399	4.1	23 811	1 467	1 548	109	346	416	391	131	177	40	10
Caddo	6 856	2.8	27 397	632	4 643	642	1 279	1 339	1 275	408	610	165	26
Calcasieu	4 526	2.8	24 708	1 208	3 214	284	728	868	821	301	378	83	18
Caldwell	203	4.4	19 162	2 725	72	11	29	66	64	16	37	6	1
Cameron	176	-2.0	18 031	2 894	131	15	31	29	26	13	9	2	1
Catahoula	194	1.7	18 059	2 886	62	24	28	57	54	18	25	8	1
Claiborne	342	3.5	20 580	2 407	144	28	73	83	79	29	34	12	1
Concordia	356	3.3	17 869	2 913	147	15	66	107	101	36	42	18	2
De Soto	535	3.2	20 757	2 354	224	69	80	117	111	43	40	20	3
East Baton Rouge	11 704	3.4	28 474	493	9 595	625	2 004	1 716	1 609	524	767	194	32
East Carroll	142	-0.4	15 630	3 061	65	7	19	53	51	11	24	13	1
East Feliciana	455	5.4	21 571	2 130	172	28	63	111	105	26	59	15	2
Evangeline	636	1.5	18 015	2 896	237	39	97	215	206	55	113	30	2
Franklin	365	0.4	17 489	2 952	148	18	54	127	121	32	63	19	3
Grant	366	4.4	19 538	2 652	113	22	49	83	78	28	32	11	2
Iberia	1 629	3.1	22 107	1 986	1 101	118	292	322	302	111	128	48	7
Iberville	689	4.7	20 796	2 347	724	65	95	164	156	47	79	23	3
Jackson	363	3.2	23 794	1 473	141	29	70	89	85	31	41	9	1
Jefferson	13 678	3.2	30 280	323	8 128	1 418	2 230	2 123	2 006	740	938	208	37
Jefferson Davis	574	0.9	18 449	2 835	216	23	99	143	135	51	60	16	3
Lafayette	5 717	2.7	29 646	374	4 846	511	980	811	761	240	382	82	14
Lafourche	2 344	4.2	25 835	923	1 229	253	377	395	371	143	166	43	6
La Salle	270	4.1	19 002	2 754	116	26	39	76	72	26	35	6	2
Lincoln	926	4.2	21 965	2 025	617	82	155	202	191	49	92	21	2
Livingston	2 110	4.4	21 336	2 200	507	118	219	338	313	122	133	35	12
Madison	217	2.0	16 461	3 029	117	10	28	71	67	16	33	14	1
Morehouse	597	2.7	19 560	2 645	286	29	84	188	180	54	86	30	4
Natchitoches	798	2.8	20 497	2 432	416	110	118	180	170	49	69	29	3
Orleans	13 767	3.7	29 100	433	11 500	2 267	2 160	2 832	2 711	667	1 376	476	37
Ouachita	3 730	5.0	25 354	1 030	2 524	364	589	729	691	212	337	89	12
Plaquemines	631	2.6	23 091	1 698	794	68	85	141	134	37	78	13	2

1. Based on the resident population estimated as of July 1 of the year shown.   2. Includes other labor income.

STATE County	Earnings, 2002									Social Security beneficiaries, December 2003			Housing units, 2003	
				Percent by selected industries								Supple-mental Security Income recipients, December 2003		
			Goods-related[1]		Service-related and health									
	Total (mil dol)	Farm	Total	Manu-facturing	Infor-mation and profes-sional and technical services	Retail trade	Finance, insur-ance, and real estate	Health services	Govern-ment	Number	Rate[2]		Total	Percent change, 2000–2003
	75	76	77	78	79	80	81	82	83	84	85	86	87	88
KENTUCKY—Cont'd														
Owsley	23	-1.5	D	D	D	D	2.2	17.7	46.6	1 225	258	1 005	2 302	2.4
Pendleton	101	-3.5	D	17.7	2.6	5.3	5.1	6.2	23.9	2 400	159	433	5 832	1.3
Perry	497	0.0	24.0	3.2	D	9.3	3.3	D	18.8	7 250	246	3 279	13 087	2.7
Pike	1 018	0.0	34.8	2.3	5.9	10.0	3.7	D	14.0	17 345	257	5 397	31 968	3.4
Powell	106	0.6	D	23.1	2.1	9.8	3.3	D	25.0	2 815	211	999	5 702	3.2
Pulaski	833	0.3	D	16.0	D	11.3	4.2	D	17.8	14 520	250	4 106	27 350	0.6
Robertson	8	-21.1	D	0.0	D	D	D	18.0	61.3	450	194	110	1 043	0.9
Rockcastle	106	-2.1	D	15.4	D	7.5	3.6	19.8	26.1	3 365	202	1 207	7 553	2.7
Rowan	335	0.2	D	15.4	3.3	8.0	2.9	19.5	32.0	3 870	173	1 174	9 232	2.7
Russell	183	-0.2	D	27.9	4.6	10.5	4.4	D	19.4	4 290	259	1 397	9 147	0.9
Scott	1 365	3.1	D	65.8	1.5	2.6	1.5	D	5.0	4 595	125	797	13 815	6.5
Shelby	598	0.2	48.0	44.4	D	7.0	4.8	7.9	10.2	5 270	147	633	14 021	9.1
Simpson	318	1.0	D	53.3	D	10.1	2.6	3.6	9.4	3 090	185	477	7 402	5.5
Spencer	49	-8.7	D	D	4.1	10.0	6.9	D	35.3	1 910	134	264	5 446	19.6
Taylor	301	-0.6	D	19.7	D	12.9	4.1	D	19.6	5 700	244	1 466	10 205	0.2
Todd	118	11.9	D	35.3	2.4	5.4	2.4	D	15.8	2 255	188	432	5 190	1.3
Trigg	133	0.5	D	37.2	D	8.3	3.5	D	20.6	3 250	252	394	6 837	2.1
Trimble	34	-6.9	D	D	D	4.5	D	7.5	33.8	1 565	179	228	3 516	2.3
Union	232	-1.0	47.9	16.8	D	7.6	2.7	D	11.7	3 070	195	344	6 300	1.1
Warren	1 974	0.0	29.9	22.1	5.2	8.6	5.1	12.4	16.0	15 000	157	3 363	40 553	5.7
Washington	116	2.1	D	34.3	2.8	7.8	4.6	D	15.2	2 470	219	477	4 587	1.0
Wayne	193	5.0	D	32.7	7.6	10.3	3.1	8.5	18.3	4 485	221	1 929	9 821	0.3
Webster	214	23.6	41.1	11.1	0.9	4.3	2.4	D	10.6	3 065	218	496	6 327	1.2
Whitley	421	-0.4	D	11.6	D	10.9	3.2	D	18.0	7 755	208	3 561	15 674	2.5
Wolfe	39	-0.7	D	8.5	1.7	14.0	D	D	40.6	1 825	263	1 288	3 372	3.3
Woodford	524	17.7	D	29.7	5.7	4.1	3.2	D	7.4	3 720	157	337	9 769	4.2
LOUISIANA	82 007	0.4	23.4	11.2	8.7	7.1	6.2	10.0	19.2	731 511	163	167 800	1 896 748	2.7
Acadia	515	-0.1	28.3	10.6	4.7	9.5	6.1	10.4	19.1	10 645	180	2 820	23 730	2.2
Allen	315	0.0	9.1	6.2	D	6.6	3.0	D	54.5	4 320	171	912	9 297	1.5
Ascension	1 528	0.3	D	29.0	6.0	6.3	7.1	6.6	9.0	10 000	118	1 659	32 237	10.5
Assumption	277	3.0	59.1	51.9	1.7	4.5	2.1	3.5	13.8	4 085	176	1 046	9 984	3.6
Avoyelles	356	2.6	D	5.8	3.9	9.9	4.8	12.2	36.6	8 065	193	2 762	17 181	3.6
Beauregard	343	0.4	32.8	23.2	D	9.4	8.2	D	16.3	5 480	164	987	14 744	1.7
Bienville	151	2.4	30.5	23.3	D	6.2	5.1	8.7	17.1	3 325	217	796	7 968	1.8
Bossier	1 657	-0.1	13.3	5.8	D	7.6	3.9	7.3	40.3	14 695	144	2 059	42 592	5.7
Caddo	5 286	0.1	21.2	11.8	7.9	7.1	5.4	15.7	19.0	43 605	174	10 094	109 738	1.3
Calcasieu	3 498	-0.1	34.9	21.1	8.6	6.9	3.8	10.0	14.0	31 385	171	5 036	79 341	4.4
Caldwell	83	-2.1	D	2.0	D	12.2	D	D	24.9	1 960	185	453	5 089	1.1
Cameron	146	-0.7	29.9	10.1	D	D	D	D	19.8	1 420	146	122	5 455	2.2
Catahoula	86	14.4	D	3.4	D	10.4	4.3	D	25.7	2 230	210	619	5 445	1.8
Claiborne	172	6.7	21.3	10.5	3.2	6.0	2.2	D	34.5	3 360	203	841	7 919	1.3
Concordia	162	2.6	D	D	D	10.4	3.0	D	31.0	4 135	210	1 122	9 363	2.4
De Soto	293	1.9	51.4	21.2	2.1	5.4	3.1	D	16.9	4 985	192	1 240	11 452	2.2
East Baton Rouge	10 220	0.0	21.5	8.7	11.2	6.9	6.8	9.8	20.7	55 255	134	11 210	173 866	2.8
East Carroll	71	11.7	6.9	4.3	D	6.1	5.0	D	35.3	1 535	171	723	3 247	-1.7
East Feliciana	200	1.4	11.4	7.5	D	4.7	5.2	D	54.7	3 085	146	872	8 070	2.0
Evangeline	276	3.0	18.8	14.7	6.8	9.1	4.5	22.9	21.1	6 990	199	2 673	14 616	2.5
Franklin	166	3.8	11.8	6.0	D	13.7	5.0	D	29.4	4 240	203	1 301	8 759	1.6
Grant	135	0.1	D	13.8	D	4.2	D	3.4	46.7	3 460	183	703	8 720	2.2
Iberia	1 219	1.2	39.4	15.4	4.2	7.5	7.0	6.8	11.9	12 545	169	2 952	28 376	1.9
Iberville	789	1.1	55.3	47.1	2.4	3.5	1.4	D	15.0	5 295	161	1 474	12 189	2.0
Jackson	170	4.8	41.7	34.9	D	7.7	3.5	5.3	18.3	3 260	214	559	7 437	1.3
Jefferson	9 546	0.0	18.5	8.1	11.8	9.2	8.4	11.0	10.7	75 320	166	13 486	190 578	1.4
Jefferson Davis	238	-0.9	16.0	7.7	3.7	12.4	8.3	D	22.4	5 915	190	1 073	13 041	1.7
Lafayette	5 357	0.1	30.8	5.9	9.9	7.9	8.0	11.6	10.0	26 545	137	5 007	81 960	4.9
Lafourche	1 482	0.6	20.7	10.1	4.4	6.3	7.4	5.7	17.5	15 555	170	2 739	35 995	2.7
La Salle	141	0.0	23.7	7.4	D	9.9	D	6.6	26.7	2 900	205	456	6 379	1.7
Lincoln	700	1.3	26.3	16.1	3.6	7.6	5.8	D	26.4	5 850	138	1 244	17 401	2.4
Livingston	625	0.2	24.8	10.7	D	11.3	4.6	6.1	22.8	13 435	132	1 812	39 259	8.4
Madison	127	8.5	10.7	8.9	1.8	9.4	2.3	D	40.3	2 120	162	832	5 019	0.8
Morehouse	315	3.1	D	23.3	3.3	9.5	3.5	12.3	15.8	6 030	197	1 845	12 956	1.9
Natchitoches	527	2.0	D	23.6	6.9	6.5	3.1	4.4	27.6	6 200	159	1 961	17 415	3.1
Orleans	13 766	0.0	14.0	3.7	13.2	4.2	7.1	8.9	21.5	75 185	160	26 714	212 394	-1.3
Ouachita	2 888	0.1	19.8	14.1	12.9	8.5	7.8	13.8	16.2	23 330	158	5 151	61 597	2.4
Plaquemines	862	0.2	40.9	18.2	D	D	4.8	D	18.0	4 110	147	843	10 911	4.1

1. Covers mining, construction, and manufacturing.   2. Per 1,000 resident population estimated as of July 1 of the year shown.

Table B. States and Counties — **Housing, Labor Force, and Employment**

	Housing units, 2000								Civilian labor force, 2003				Civilian employment,[6] 2000		
	Occupied units										Unemployment			Percent	
		Owner-occupied				Renter-occupied									
				Median owner cost as a percent of income											
STATE County	Total	Percent	Median value[1]	With a mortgage	Without a mortgage[2]	Median rent[3]	Median rent as a percent of income	Substandard units[4] (percent)	Total	Percent change, 2002–2003	Total	Rate[5]	Total	Management, professional and related occupations	Production, transportation, and material moving occupations
	89	90	91	92	93	94	95	96	97	98	99	100	101	102	103
KENTUCKY—Cont'd															
Owsley	1 894	78.4	40 800	26.4	18.3	276	32.1	5.9	1 788	-1.0	135	7.6	1 373	29.4	21.0
Pendleton	5 170	77.9	77 700	20.5	9.9	428	24.1	4.5	7 009	3.1	470	6.7	6 606	20.5	25.1
Perry	11 460	77.4	52 500	21.0	9.9	302	26.8	4.6	11 746	2.8	985	8.4	8 966	24.1	15.8
Pike	27 612	78.7	65 900	21.6	9.9	352	28.2	2.8	25 717	-2.6	1 706	6.6	22 230	25.0	15.1
Powell	5 044	74.0	63 000	22.0	10.3	406	26.2	6.1	6 198	0.8	633	10.2	5 275	15.8	33.7
Pulaski	22 719	76.0	74 100	19.1	9.9	360	25.3	3.1	26 999	0.0	1 785	6.6	23 328	24.3	23.7
Robertson	866	77.9	58 500	16.9	9.9	250	24.2	4.8	1 038	4.3	68	6.6	933	27.0	24.7
Rockcastle	6 544	79.6	57 000	21.6	10.1	282	26.3	4.9	6 152	0.9	338	5.5	6 616	19.6	28.4
Rowan	7 927	69.7	80 000	19.2	9.9	421	26.8	2.8	11 275	9.3	557	4.9	9 715	29.1	15.5
Russell	6 941	79.4	62 000	23.3	10.5	313	24.2	4.4	5 817	-0.1	609	10.5	6 572	23.6	24.9
Scott	12 110	69.8	107 900	17.9	9.9	513	22.5	2.0	18 255	2.0	959	5.3	16 879	26.9	24.2
Shelby	12 104	72.7	114 600	19.8	9.9	495	21.9	3.1	18 803	0.8	878	4.7	16 953	30.4	22.8
Simpson	6 415	71.8	81 400	20.7	9.9	469	20.5	2.4	8 418	0.7	497	5.9	7 861	21.2	33.5
Spencer	4 251	82.6	122 400	20.1	9.9	426	22.6	2.2	5 850	2.1	281	4.8	5 952	22.2	23.3
Taylor	9 233	72.3	70 700	20.5	9.9	349	25.7	3.3	9 474	0.0	690	7.3	9 953	25.5	24.8
Todd	4 569	76.5	58 300	20.5	10.8	388	23.1	4.4	4 960	-0.3	219	4.4	5 438	21.4	34.6
Trigg	5 215	81.3	74 300	19.6	9.9	399	20.0	2.7	6 014	-1.2	336	5.6	5 434	24.0	25.5
Trimble	3 137	80.6	82 500	20.2	9.9	392	22.8	4.0	3 538	5.0	212	6.0	3 752	19.8	26.8
Union	5 710	77.9	59 400	18.7	9.9	337	21.9	2.3	5 845	-1.5	421	7.2	6 869	24.9	23.2
Warren	35 365	64.0	100 400	19.4	9.9	490	24.4	3.1	51 777	2.1	2 720	5.3	46 803	30.0	18.0
Washington	4 121	79.9	72 000	20.1	9.9	352	23.4	3.5	6 093	2.9	308	5.1	4 833	26.5	28.5
Wayne	7 913	76.4	55 400	20.2	10.5	313	26.0	5.6	8 841	1.5	587	6.6	7 363	19.9	29.0
Webster	5 560	78.0	45 800	17.5	9.9	331	22.5	3.0	5 574	3.3	465	8.3	6 212	18.9	29.9
Whitley	13 780	72.7	62 100	20.5	10.4	352	27.8	4.4	14 490	-0.3	945	6.5	13 020	26.3	22.5
Wolfe	2 816	73.8	45 300	25.2	9.9	250	26.6	7.1	2 911	-3.0	254	8.7	2 265	24.3	31.6
Woodford	8 893	72.4	117 100	19.0	9.9	488	23.6	2.4	12 495	0.8	374	3.0	12 496	36.0	15.6
LOUISIANA	1 656 053	67.9	85 000	19.6	9.9	466	25.8	5.8	2 037 050	1.9	133 531	6.6	1 851 777	29.9	14.1
Acadia	21 142	72.2	61 700	18.3	10.4	332	24.1	6.2	23 990	2.5	1 675	7.0	21 517	24.0	19.7
Allen	8 102	76.0	58 100	20.8	9.9	350	22.4	6.0	9 648	4.1	795	8.2	7 991	23.3	15.6
Ascension	26 691	82.2	103 800	18.5	9.9	450	21.9	6.2	38 695	3.2	3 027	7.8	35 151	26.3	16.8
Assumption	8 239	84.1	78 800	17.7	9.9	368	23.8	6.7	9 719	2.3	811	8.3	8 856	22.5	22.1
Avoyelles	14 736	74.4	54 800	20.8	9.9	320	27.0	5.5	16 258	3.0	1 506	9.3	14 134	23.6	17.1
Beauregard	12 104	79.8	64 800	18.1	9.9	383	19.5	4.5	12 079	3.0	1 064	8.8	12 743	25.5	17.1
Bienville	6 108	77.8	46 700	19.7	11.4	335	27.5	5.2	5 394	2.4	583	10.8	5 348	22.6	26.5
Bossier	36 628	69.5	87 600	19.1	9.9	488	23.2	4.0	47 823	1.7	3 117	6.5	42 873	29.1	13.1
Caddo	97 974	63.8	75 100	19.1	9.9	463	25.9	6.0	117 699	1.6	8 761	7.4	104 650	29.3	14.9
Calcasieu	68 613	71.5	80 500	17.8	9.9	465	24.5	5.1	88 299	1.0	5 823	6.6	79 408	27.2	14.8
Caldwell	3 941	79.2	53 800	19.3	11.0	334	27.4	3.8	4 159	2.2	518	12.5	3 897	23.8	19.3
Cameron	3 592	85.2	59 600	17.7	9.9	412	23.2	7.5	3 118	-2.3	199	6.4	4 184	18.5	22.6
Catahoula	4 082	83.0	48 800	19.2	11.2	267	24.3	5.6	4 498	0.2	484	10.8	3 667	24.2	18.4
Claiborne	6 270	75.8	55 400	21.1	11.2	318	24.7	6.5	5 843	2.8	482	8.2	5 702	23.2	21.3
Concordia	7 521	76.1	55 600	21.5	11.7	305	31.4	4.9	7 577	-0.1	1 042	13.8	6 859	23.9	15.7
De Soto	9 691	76.6	58 100	18.9	11.2	313	23.0	6.1	10 683	1.7	1 121	10.5	9 707	21.1	22.5
East Baton Rouge	156 365	61.6	98 800	19.2	9.9	510	26.6	5.2	213 788	3.2	12 035	5.6	192 715	36.7	10.9
East Carroll	2 969	62.1	35 900	25.8	13.3	277	24.2	8.1	3 007	-0.8	579	19.3	2 673	30.0	17.6
East Feliciana	6 699	82.4	76 600	20.2	9.9	344	22.7	8.4	7 987	2.1	593	7.4	7 601	24.7	16.1
Evangeline	12 736	69.4	53 000	20.4	10.2	289	30.5	8.0	11 614	-0.7	939	8.1	11 149	25.9	16.0
Franklin	7 754	76.2	48 700	20.9	12.0	313	26.3	6.1	9 275	-2.2	970	10.5	7 273	27.3	16.3
Grant	7 073	81.7	58 500	19.8	10.0	374	23.8	4.3	6 790	4.4	687	10.1	7 112	25.2	18.1
Iberia	25 381	73.4	75 500	18.6	9.9	388	26.1	7.9	32 424	-0.4	2 038	6.3	27 472	23.6	18.2
Iberville	10 674	77.3	76 700	18.4	9.9	341	23.0	7.4	12 718	2.2	1 319	10.4	11 443	23.5	18.9
Jackson	6 086	77.3	53 100	18.5	10.1	325	23.5	4.9	5 854	4.9	631	10.8	6 150	23.8	23.7
Jefferson	176 234	63.9	105 300	20.5	9.9	544	24.7	5.7	225 953	1.9	11 398	5.0	212 477	32.4	11.3
Jefferson Davis	11 480	74.9	60 500	19.5	10.6	353	24.3	5.1	11 937	3.6	722	6.0	11 606	24.9	15.5
Lafayette	72 372	66.1	100 500	18.6	9.9	475	23.8	5.0	100 469	2.1	4 441	4.4	88 603	34.7	11.2
Lafourche	32 057	77.9	78 900	18.4	9.9	402	23.5	6.1	46 726	3.2	1 806	3.9	37 207	25.4	20.2
La Salle	5 291	83.5	53 200	19.1	12.7	329	24.9	2.6	5 096	0.4	561	11.0	5 360	23.8	20.7
Lincoln	15 235	59.9	79 800	19.7	9.9	436	34.0	3.9	19 009	-1.6	899	4.7	17 550	33.3	13.1
Livingston	32 630	83.8	96 100	19.4	9.9	481	22.1	4.7	47 058	3.5	3 490	7.4	40 890	24.8	14.2
Madison	4 469	61.9	46 900	21.7	11.7	334	26.3	8.8	5 723	0.2	735	12.8	4 273	23.6	17.0
Morehouse	11 382	71.6	50 400	19.7	10.4	362	26.7	5.9	11 832	2.9	1 613	13.6	11 016	21.9	21.3
Natchitoches	14 263	64.5	70 400	20.2	9.9	370	29.7	5.4	17 938	1.7	1 313	7.3	14 909	27.3	16.6
Orleans	188 251	46.5	87 300	22.9	11.4	488	28.6	8.3	194 424	1.9	12 863	6.6	191 739	34.7	10.4
Ouachita	55 216	64.1	80 000	18.9	9.9	444	26.8	5.4	73 699	1.4	4 395	6.0	64 071	30.8	12.6
Plaquemines	9 021	78.9	110 100	19.8	9.9	521	18.7	7.3	10 698	1.5	611	5.7	9 960	24.7	18.9

1. Specified owner-occupied units.   2. Median monthly owner costs is often in the minimum category—9.9 percent or less, which is indicated as 9.9 percent.   3. Specified renter-occupied units.   4. Overcrowded or lacking complete plumbing facilities.   5. Percent of civilian labor force.   6. Persons 16 years old and over.

Table B. States and Counties — Nonfarm Employment and Agriculture

STATE County	Private nonfarm establishments, employment and payroll, 2001									Agriculture, 2002			
		Employment						Annual payroll		Farms			
											Percent with—		Farm operators whose principal occupation is farming (percent)
	Number of establishments	Total	Health care and social assistance	Manufacturing	Retail trade	Finance and insurance	Professional, scientific, and technical services	Total (mil dol)	Average per employee (dollars)	Number	Less than 50 acres	500 acres and over	
	104	105	106	107	108	109	110	111	112	113	114	115	116
KENTUCKY—Cont'd													
Owsley	42	295	161	0	78	D	D	5	17 061	227	24.7	4.4	51.1
Pendleton	194	1 687	203	556	240	88	38	37	22 009	964	25.1	2.5	47.2
Perry	713	9 226	2 215	821	1 731	282	592	255	27 663	44	38.6	15.9	40.9
Pike	1 504	20 014	3 252	627	4 272	780	1 361	539	26 918	45	35.6	4.4	55.6
Powell	172	2 384	346	1 017	316	58	19	44	18 643	239	28.9	4.6	52.3
Pulaski	1 452	20 680	3 606	3 997	3 867	729	817	440	21 286	1 977	36.3	2.5	57.9
Robertson	22	137	D	D	D	D	D	2	12 540	247	20.2	5.7	55.1
Rockcastle	213	2 917	652	647	476	98	37	53	18 217	803	36.5	2.9	57.4
Rowan	455	7 087	1 653	1 311	1 272	173	72	148	20 901	436	40.1	4.1	50.9
Russell	361	4 227	330	1 307	780	121	86	84	19 916	930	44.3	2.7	58.8
Scott	682	19 866	1 221	9 864	1 578	234	259	808	40 650	848	37.6	6.5	58.7
Shelby	740	11 777	1 023	4 847	1 722	314	209	336	28 499	1 557	44.4	4.1	51.7
Simpson	359	7 424	399	3 471	998	135	74	199	26 853	550	38.4	10.4	57.5
Spencer	176	1 030	230	D	185	45	33	19	18 238	623	41.3	2.4	48.8
Taylor	677	8 822	1 097	2 010	2 914	229	102	204	23 177	957	39.1	3.7	52.8
Todd	191	2 347	163	1 329	231	86	75	49	20 918	676	25.0	12.9	62.0
Trigg	241	2 929	281	1 350	336	71	61	59	20 211	425	28.0	11.5	50.8
Trimble	75	487	126	D	115	44	7	14	29 372	562	40.0	3.0	48.8
Union	290	6 816	1 047	928	1 289	94	537	182	26 684	328	30.2	25.0	60.4
Warren	2 527	42 788	6 693	8 030	7 330	1 383	1 176	1 126	26 318	1 881	44.3	4.1	53.4
Washington	221	2 670	238	944	338	71	38	61	22 733	1 119	27.8	2.7	56.6
Wayne	307	4 203	489	1 803	720	153	43	81	19 198	860	35.3	7.0	57.6
Webster	255	2 855	268	647	413	214	42	82	28 561	595	26.4	10.9	50.4
Whitley	840	13 808	2 634	1 882	2 427	440	234	294	21 327	530	34.5	2.8	51.5
Wolfe	77	671	197	169	145	D	D	11	15 855	371	26.7	6.5	46.1
Woodford	515	7 522	548	3 061	854	202	245	226	30 039	708	43.1	9.7	60.5
LOUISIANA	100 780	1 599 482	234 842	159 039	228 767	66 937	79 445	45 161	28 235	27 413	41.2	13.9	54.0
Acadia	1 018	12 059	1 636	2 239	2 415	439	241	269	22 287	751	42.9	20.0	62.5
Allen	364	3 536	567	465	672	220	57	71	20 208	360	40.3	15.6	55.3
Ascension	1 523	25 488	1 586	5 809	4 380	1 201	621	813	31 898	329	61.4	6.7	40.1
Assumption	247	2 507	407	317	643	116	43	55	21 775	105	38.1	43.8	61.0
Avoyelles	694	8 386	1 801	682	1 381	407	139	151	17 959	890	39.3	16.2	61.1
Beauregard	605	6 789	965	1 026	1 229	882	131	178	26 191	793	36.7	7.3	44.9
Bienville	264	3 322	388	1 281	377	148	57	69	20 636	222	37.8	5.4	62.2
Bossier	2 012	31 062	3 405	3 027	5 228	888	806	692	22 281	456	46.7	12.1	47.8
Caddo	6 230	110 420	20 878	11 531	14 025	3 479	3 981	3 007	27 231	555	39.1	16.6	58.0
Calcasieu	4 187	69 244	9 740	10 205	10 246	1 821	3 104	1 959	28 290	870	49.3	11.5	46.6
Caldwell	203	2 040	531	59	375	118	50	38	18 431	285	38.6	11.6	60.7
Cameron	176	2 211	183	219	238	D	145	66	29 785	409	30.3	27.1	46.5
Catahoula	194	1 745	248	253	419	83	55	30	17 430	435	21.4	26.9	58.2
Claiborne	273	2 829	458	402	440	94	47	72	25 321	275	26.2	10.2	55.6
Concordia	323	3 038	336	D	719	171	102	63	20 730	336	19.0	34.5	60.1
De Soto	357	4 248	392	1 076	616	168	71	116	27 223	628	35.7	9.7	44.3
East Baton Rouge	11 415	211 070	27 212	11 444	27 432	10 654	15 197	6 158	29 175	489	56.9	5.1	35.0
East Carroll	138	1 128	214	D	204	66	19	23	20 342	234	11.5	41.0	80.3
East Feliciana	255	3 554	1 830	227	373	123	69	82	23 143	460	41.3	13.5	44.6
Evangeline	552	5 717	1 991	665	1 073	319	147	123	21 538	648	38.9	15.3	54.2
Franklin	417	4 188	969	300	1 003	229	525	73	17 415	856	28.6	16.7	60.9
Grant	200	1 335	105	453	174	49	18	30	22 178	196	41.8	9.7	53.1
Iberia	1 588	26 689	2 996	3 619	3 813	969	806	807	30 246	340	60.9	17.6	65.9
Iberville	546	10 793	937	3 669	1 087	260	156	438	40 623	183	36.1	28.4	60.7
Jackson	278	3 292	529	D	576	142	57	82	24 937	235	47.7	1.7	43.8
Jefferson	12 694	212 766	29 491	16 386	32 443	9 288	10 871	6 124	28 784	52	40.4	7.7	48.1
Jefferson Davis	590	5 345	981	135	1 332	309	178	102	19 073	641	37.4	30.9	63.0
Lafayette	6 730	105 419	15 572	6 624	14 318	2 970	7 327	3 104	29 441	715	71.2	5.0	52.2
Lafourche	1 857	26 189	3 327	3 084	4 332	738	1 280	746	28 486	405	38.5	11.9	55.3
La Salle	310	2 911	663	419	518	164	78	65	22 496	161	41.0	1.9	40.4
Lincoln	908	13 379	2 391	1 777	2 369	775	335	307	22 933	392	35.7	6.4	53.1
Livingston	1 257	11 762	1 060	1 311	2 829	349	425	254	21 593	451	65.6	2.4	44.1
Madison	203	2 124	688	90	478	D	64	33	15 437	274	18.2	43.8	67.2
Morehouse	521	6 706	1 373	1 114	1 050	195	113	166	24 718	412	21.6	34.2	63.6
Natchitoches	781	10 858	1 255	2 697	1 895	282	246	219	20 210	565	28.7	14.7	52.0
Orleans	10 628	214 914	31 885	9 371	19 985	11 138	14 399	6 557	30 510	8	100.0	0.0	75.0
Ouachita	4 033	62 292	10 030	8 103	8 974	6 252	3 830	1 633	26 215	493	44.0	10.3	40.8
Plaquemines	744	11 368	238	1 963	716	129	790	450	39 581	192	75.0	6.3	47.4

Table B. States and Counties — **Agriculture**

STATE County	Land in farms — Acreage (1,000)	Percent change, 1997–2002	Average size of farm	Total irrigated (1,000)	Total cropland (1,000)	Value of land and buildings (dollars) Average per farm	Average per acre	Value of machinery and equipment average per farm (dollars)	Value of products sold Total (mil dol)	Average per farm (dollars)	Percent from — Crops	Livestock and poultry products	Percent of farms with sales of — $10,000 or more	$100,000 or more	Government payments Total ($1,000)	Percent of farms
	117	118	119	120	121	122	123	124	125	126	127	128	129	130	131	132
KENTUCKY—Cont'd																
Owsley	33	3.1	145	0	9	182 344	1 319	23 314	2	7 531	83.0	16.9	20.7	0.0	33	9.7
Pendleton	132	12.8	137	1	69	227 985	1 479	27 585	9	9 130	61.8	38.2	20.9	1.3	219	12.0
Perry	7	0.0	161	0	3	174 718	1 137	30 350	1	13 037	40.8	59.1	22.7	0.0	3	15.9
Pike	7	16.7	160	D	2	179 043	1 114	25 220	0	3 312	53.0	47.0	11.1	0.0	D	D
Powell	38	35.7	157	0	16	228 819	1 813	25 442	2	10 394	59.2	40.8	21.8	1.7	76	20.9
Pulaski	232	7.9	117	0	136	217 177	1 871	41 252	35	17 712	35.4	64.6	32.4	3.6	1 028	20.3
Robertson	43	-10.4	174	0	20	192 519	1 073	27 348	2	10 065	63.3	36.7	26.3	0.4	74	18.2
Rockcastle	94	0.0	117	0	42	171 516	1 737	39 207	9	11 480	41.2	58.8	28.5	2.1	155	18.1
Rowan	51	21.4	117	0	25	140 876	1 330	20 252	6	12 933	43.4	56.6	18.6	2.1	50	12.8
Russell	97	2.1	105	0	61	206 616	1 953	47 778	23	24 263	21.2	78.8	33.2	6.1	500	20.6
Scott	137	-6.2	162	2	84	449 122	3 146	54 599	49	57 236	27.1	72.9	41.9	8.7	340	16.9
Shelby	202	1.5	130	2	141	441 808	3 221	41 231	46	29 311	57.3	42.7	38.3	6.6	1 328	17.9
Simpson	128	11.3	233	0	102	489 210	2 021	69 899	42	75 688	51.3	48.7	41.5	12.5	1 282	39.5
Spencer	78	-3.7	124	1	47	326 013	2 540	37 571	11	18 268	61.2	38.8	36.0	2.9	312	20.9
Taylor	112	0.0	117	0	65	201 124	1 689	42 722	20	20 972	39.9	60.1	38.7	5.4	667	32.0
Todd	184	-3.2	272	0	135	491 077	1 734	69 954	62	92 414	51.7	48.3	47.9	18.8	2 384	53.4
Trigg	123	5.1	289	0	75	386 859	1 476	58 456	20	47 048	71.6	28.4	37.4	7.8	1 146	42.6
Trimble	65	1.6	115	0	28	191 238	1 510	28 439	6	11 512	70.2	29.8	27.8	1.1	122	18.7
Union	209	-1.4	637	1	177	1 083 325	1 730	124 634	43	132 156	87.7	12.3	56.1	26.2	3 091	50.9
Warren	255	0.0	136	0	172	287 956	2 054	38 939	61	32 684	38.7	61.3	29.6	5.6	2 005	22.4
Washington	150	-4.5	134	0	98	215 431	1 776	45 184	27	24 182	44.9	55.1	37.7	3.8	547	23.4
Wayne	139	6.1	162	0	59	321 665	2 216	30 161	44	50 917	13.0	87.0	32.0	5.1	252	19.1
Webster	159	16.9	268	D	124	370 747	1 410	59 153	77	129 994	22.1	77.9	36.3	15.6	2 894	59.8
Whitley	64	45.5	121	0	31	201 704	1 530	27 852	5	9 138	24.8	75.2	14.3	1.9	123	20.0
Wolfe	60	5.3	161	0	18	197 425	1 111	25 593	3	6 749	78.6	21.4	18.9	0.0	58	11.9
Woodford	123	0.0	174	1	67	772 037	3 755	58 833	172	242 821	5.6	94.4	51.3	16.8	267	15.7
LOUISIANA	7 831	-0.6	286	939	5 072	444 007	1 534	64 379	1 816	66 239	58.7	41.3	33.5	12.5	123 599	27.6
Acadia	257	-5.9	342	87	221	593 093	1 773	93 611	33	44 150	89.8	10.2	34.9	12.5	9 094	37.4
Allen	103	-11.2	286	22	63	398 810	1 229	60 523	8	23 457	61.0	39.0	28.9	6.7	1 773	25.3
Ascension	50	-9.1	151	0	31	445 676	2 779	59 744	19	57 325	88.1	11.9	21.9	5.8	146	16.1
Assumption	66	3.1	628	0	53	1 014 530	1 597	289 306	36	343 231	93.9	6.1	64.8	49.5	50	20.0
Avoyelles	272	5.0	305	15	211	386 187	1 300	75 538	52	58 941	90.9	9.1	35.6	11.6	4 725	43.0
Beauregard	143	-13.3	180	3	59	265 863	1 339	33 281	11	14 351	21.5	78.5	22.8	4.3	815	20.6
Bienville	44	-6.4	198	D	14	333 415	1 529	45 077	24	108 227	1.5	98.5	31.1	11.3	57	17.1
Bossier	107	-3.6	235	1	51	357 307	1 668	50 510	9	19 938	35.6	64.4	23.7	5.3	1 007	20.4
Caddo	172	-0.6	309	6	95	419 483	1 428	48 538	24	44 036	64.2	35.8	28.8	10.1	2 987	21.4
Calcasieu	303	-2.9	349	18	128	592 337	1 425	37 110	16	18 120	50.5	49.5	24.6	4.3	2 033	13.6
Caldwell	61	-12.9	213	3	30	284 785	1 350	36 400	5	17 416	79.1	20.9	24.6	6.0	1 184	37.5
Cameron	249	1.6	608	12	75	825 369	1 438	40 752	6	15 352	D	D	24.0	3.4	1 797	11.0
Catahoula	232	1.3	534	18	178	577 352	1 164	79 463	29	65 706	83.7	16.3	42.1	18.2	5 969	50.8
Claiborne	56	-3.4	202	0	17	320 106	1 586	48 265	52	189 051	1.5	98.5	36.4	21.5	301	23.3
Concordia	212	-16.2	630	20	175	690 699	1 127	100 943	29	87 143	89.8	10.2	47.9	25.6	4 666	58.9
De Soto	137	-12.7	218	0	45	304 576	1 278	31 286	18	28 318	8.0	92.0	22.5	5.6	398	15.9
East Baton Rouge	61	-7.6	126	0	30	436 718	3 074	31 778	11	23 101	51.1	48.9	22.9	5.7	151	11.7
East Carroll	217	3.3	925	60	191	1 101 056	1 194	221 301	45	192 137	97.1	2.9	69.2	38.5	5 809	65.0
East Feliciana	123	7.0	268	0	42	553 455	1 927	38 751	7	16 219	16.0	84.0	25.7	3.0	340	23.0
Evangeline	184	1.7	284	58	141	367 702	1 261	65 466	22	34 573	81.6	18.4	33.0	11.3	6 371	39.7
Franklin	258	-4.1	302	71	197	334 280	1 191	70 069	60	69 565	74.4	25.6	43.7	15.0	4 842	46.0
Grant	36	-26.5	182	0	20	206 414	1 332	35 775	3	16 965	56.1	43.9	25.5	5.1	372	25.5
Iberia	111	7.8	327	1	89	617 930	1 883	176 638	53	155 064	98.0	2.0	40.0	23.2	252	11.8
Iberville	97	1.0	528	1	76	995 497	1 852	223 483	44	243 151	95.6	4.4	49.2	25.7	389	25.1
Jackson	21	31.3	89	0	6	226 895	2 627	28 236	32	136 464	2.7	97.3	29.8	21.3	30	14.9
Jefferson	8	60.0	147	0	3	318 941	2 204	20 742	2	32 345	90.3	9.7	36.5	5.8	D	D
Jefferson Davis	323	6.3	504	94	271	586 401	1 089	69 656	32	50 416	86.6	13.4	43.8	16.7	11 752	47.7
Lafayette	75	-14.8	105	6	58	324 440	3 161	48 211	20	28 354	88.3	11.7	15.8	3.2	817	6.9
Lafourche	151	11.9	373	0	58	512 552	1 470	89 611	27	66 067	83.5	16.5	35.6	11.9	65	12.3
La Salle	17	-37.0	105	D	6	176 363	1 688	22 420	1	6 345	18.3	81.7	19.9	0.0	37	11.2
Lincoln	66	61.0	168	0	18	312 943	1 953	43 110	70	179 239	3.3	96.7	38.3	21.2	186	19.1
Livingston	34	-15.0	76	0	13	301 191	2 916	19 124	7	15 684	18.3	81.7	20.6	3.5	42	8.2
Madison	237	-10.9	865	25	211	928 926	1 105	115 313	45	164 826	98.7	1.3	55.1	37.6	4 208	66.8
Morehouse	245	-5.0	595	120	211	680 428	1 172	117 543	51	123 911	97.3	2.7	54.6	29.4	7 657	45.6
Natchitoches	193	2.1	341	7	103	475 721	1 363	45 316	57	101 314	16.2	83.8	33.8	11.3	2 011	32.0
Orleans	D	NA	D	0	0	106 952	43 753	15 540	0	5 063	D	D	25.0	0.0	0	0.0
Ouachita	95	6.7	192	9	57	370 669	1 743	58 248	20	40 164	50.3	49.7	26.2	7.3	1 674	22.5
Plaquemines	35	-5.4	181	0	7	486 671	2 889	33 301	7	34 391	67.9	32.1	39.6	7.8	6	4.2

Table B. States and Counties — Residential Construction, Wholesale Trade, Retail Trade, and Real Estate

STATE County	Value of residential construction authorized by building permits, 2003		Wholesale trade, 1997				Retail trade,[1] 1997				Real estate and rental and leasing, 1997			
	New construction ($1,000)	Number of housing units	Number of establishments	Number of employees	Sales (mil dol)	Annual payroll (mil dol)	Number of establishments	Number of employees	Sales (mil dol)	Annual payroll (mil dol)	Number of establishments	Number of employees	Receipts (mil dol)	Annual payroll (mil dol)
	133	134	135	136	137	138	139	140	141	142	143	144	145	146
KENTUCKY—Cont'd														
Owsley	NA	NA	NA	NA	NA	NA	16	99	25.9	1.0	2	D	D	D
Pendleton	100	2	10	D	D	D	40	287	35.5	2.9	6	D	D	D
Perry	994	13	50	467	233.7	14.4	183	1 917	294.6	25.7	17	78	17.7	1.5
Pike	3 041	43	78	711	318.4	21.3	347	4 618	664.7	61.2	42	140	21.7	3.3
Powell	NA	NA	8	115	23.2	2.2	39	297	38.1	3.0	6	20	0.8	0.2
Pulaski	3 774	29	76	1 068	318.4	21.1	336	3 508	543.3	48.7	57	203	16.3	3.3
Robertson	NA	NA	NA	NA	NA	NA	7	25	2.4	0.2	1	D	D	D
Rockcastle	NA	NA	9	62	11.4	0.9	54	365	44.3	4.3	4	33	1.5	0.2
Rowan	754	21	28	230	61.2	4.2	131	1 319	180.7	15.6	18	52	3.3	0.7
Russell	300	4	10	356	83.2	7.2	88	797	104.9	14.0	9	36	7.4	0.3
Scott	79 989	618	25	816	319.5	26.3	115	1 396	230.7	17.5	17	76	8.2	1.1
Shelby	66 902	496	46	375	140.4	11.2	111	1 338	253.0	19.6	32	108	10.7	1.5
Simpson	8 079	85	18	411	130.6	4.6	77	914	205.7	13.9	12	28	2.2	0.4
Spencer	32 696	244	7	D	D	D	23	147	16.9	2.5	2	D	D	D
Taylor	916	12	33	175	37.1	3.1	152	1 555	252.8	22.5	19	55	4.8	0.9
Todd	90	2	16	227	54.1	2.8	48	274	45.7	3.3	5	D	D	D
Trigg	1 302	17	10	66	18.3	1.8	52	324	51.8	4.1	8	36	3.4	0.5
Trimble	NA	NA	1	D	D	D	14	96	11.1	1.1	3	6	0.3	0.0
Union	1 244	12	21	226	66.8	4.4	77	623	91.4	7.7	5	16	0.6	0.1
Warren	117 378	1 046	155	2 029	1 367.4	57.4	525	7 144	1 108.8	102.5	100	407	38.9	6.0
Washington	645	4	10	D	D	D	41	301	44.6	3.9	5	11	0.9	0.1
Wayne	0	0	10	113	15.2	1.3	65	663	99.0	13.0	4	16	1.9	0.3
Webster	470	4	3	D	D	D	59	431	73.3	6.5	6	D	D	D
Whitley	2 740	43	28	D	D	D	164	1 609	275.6	23.5	29	99	8.1	1.4
Wolfe	NA	NA	3	15	3.9	0.1	27	161	25.7	1.7	1	D	D	D
Woodford	26 792	159	20	D	D	D	75	724	124.9	9.7	16	47	29.2	0.9
LOUISIANA	2 595 720	22 220	6 390	76 350	46 972.3	2 375.2	17 863	224 412	35 807.9	3 307.9	4 151	28 571	3 342.1	642.2
Acadia	20 375	208	61	598	280.7	12.9	199	2 093	278.0	27.9	34	96	8.1	1.6
Allen	1 402	24	16	113	37.7	2.0	93	672	99.1	7.8	13	37	1.9	0.4
Ascension	111 519	1 182	94	950	314.1	26.8	304	3 777	578.0	48.9	54	288	52.4	7.4
Assumption	8 879	69	15	114	32.5	2.7	59	599	75.1	7.5	8	D	D	D
Avoyelles	13 600	134	26	236	83.3	3.3	169	1 606	212.0	18.2	22	67	3.4	0.5
Beauregard	879	11	21	130	43.4	2.2	115	1 293	222.4	18.9	22	69	4.1	0.7
Bienville	0	0	10	76	188.8	2.2	65	414	57.3	5.0	10	51	5.6	1.3
Bossier	134 148	1 353	121	D	D	D	363	4 838	834.1	72.9	73	327	28.5	5.3
Caddo	129 948	889	451	5 864	2 586.1	176.2	1 053	13 945	2 338.2	221.5	247	1 185	120.6	22.9
Calcasieu	113 403	1 398	244	3 136	1 732.7	90.8	775	10 400	1 606.2	147.1	210	1 164	106.0	20.6
Caldwell	890	9	12	D	D	D	34	274	48.4	3.7	5	6	0.6	0.1
Cameron	5 391	60	19	115	416.8	4.7	34	240	29.1	2.4	4	11	1.5	0.2
Catahoula	3 104	42	15	193	111.8	3.0	52	407	62.2	4.9	3	D	D	D
Claiborne	0	0	20	173	121.7	4.2	63	486	63.7	6.3	7	17	1.0	0.2
Concordia	419	24	17	224	113.6	4.7	94	853	126.0	10.8	3	25	2.0	0.5
De Soto	248	1	17	D	D	D	83	748	116.3	9.6	48	129	9.6	1.7
East Baton Rouge	226 255	2 763	764	9 966	4 006.6	345.9	1 822	27 428	4 468.8	423.7	502	3 760	330.1	73.5
East Carroll	45	2	9	147	97.5	4.4	36	245	41.3	3.5	5	13	1.3	0.2
East Feliciana	0	3	11	D	D	D	45	373	45.0	4.3	13	38	2.2	0.7
Evangeline	8 474	133	17	122	30.4	2.3	129	1 012	144.5	13.4	21	73	4.0	0.7
Franklin	5 363	52	29	D	D	D	90	1 119	168.1	13.7	11	30	3.3	0.4
Grant	58	1	4	D	D	D	31	168	49.3	3.3	4	D	D	D
Iberia	28 768	241	118	1 447	359.2	44.4	282	3 354	613.9	54.1	82	1 274	218.2	47.5
Iberville	12 263	102	27	251	89.7	5.7	100	1 036	159.1	14.3	21	128	13.0	2.3
Jackson	125	1	8	36	28.0	1.1	53	521	59.8	5.6	10	28	2.1	0.4
Jefferson	165 023	1 195	1 168	15 313	10 041.1	500.0	2 038	32 403	5 787.0	535.8	533	5 485	627.9	121.6
Jefferson Davis	10 356	83	36	359	270.7	9.7	131	1 406	232.9	18.7	23	181	9.8	4.2
Lafayette	168 546	1 379	484	6 260	2 620.5	223.5	990	14 462	2 465.4	231.6	347	2 953	394.1	85.7
Lafourche	42 908	340	88	722	328.5	18.8	323	3 869	570.0	50.4	81	426	56.1	9.4
La Salle	0	0	8	43	8.8	0.8	64	515	68.4	6.0	4	12	0.4	0.1
Lincoln	12 849	145	34	376	105.8	9.1	163	2 233	328.0	28.8	41	150	10.0	1.4
Livingston	119 939	1 025	55	502	140.1	12.8	213	2 403	368.9	32.4	39	214	14.2	2.2
Madison	1 164	8	14	D	D	D	53	512	83.8	6.5	14	50	1.9	0.8
Morehouse	511	20	15	143	45.8	4.0	126	1 263	216.2	16.3	14	27	4.3	0.4
Natchitoches	15 770	217	33	247	91.0	4.6	141	1 612	230.4	19.7	34	82	6.5	0.7
Orleans	281 293	917	484	6 086	2 450.5	210.2	1 871	20 405	2 771.3	315.6	481	3 538	407.4	72.3
Ouachita	64 378	536	248	2 912	1 257.2	82.4	753	9 649	1 483.5	134.0	176	805	79.7	12.7
Plaquemines	19 450	202	87	1 168	837.8	36.4	76	674	85.8	8.4	44	286	45.0	8.4

1. Establishments with payroll.

Table B. States and Counties — Professional Services, Manufacturing, and Accommodation and Foodservices

STATE County	Professional, scientific, and technical services,[1] 1997				Manufacturing, 1997				Accommodation and foodservices, 1997			
	Number of establishments	Number of employees	Receipts (mil dol)	Annual payroll (mil dol)	Number of establishments	Number of employees	Receipts (mil dol)	Annual payroll (mil dol)	Number of establishments	Number of employees	Sales (mil dol)	Annual payroll (mil dol)
	147	148	149	150	151	152	153	154	155	156	157	158
KENTUCKY—Cont'd												
Owsley	3	D	D	D	NA	NA	NA	NA	2	D	D	D
Pendleton	8	12	0.7	0.2	12	D	D	D	12	D	D	D
Perry	54	211	14.1	5.9	9	614	91.4	16.5	51	1 008	34.6	8.7
Pike	102	627	49.3	19.6	26	587	74.3	10.7	84	1 425	44.9	10.9
Powell	6	10	0.5	0.1	16	1 185	175.3	19.2	15	D	D	D
Pulaski	79	686	29.2	11.1	84	4 564	672.1	107.1	82	1 548	45.4	13.2
Robertson	1	D	D	D	NA	NA	NA	NA	3	12	0.1	0.0
Rockcastle	11	36	1.7	0.4	11	D	D	D	17	270	8.6	2.3
Rowan	18	70	2.9	1.1	13	647	111.6	10.5	43	899	24.0	6.8
Russell	16	40	2.7	0.6	24	2 098	348.9	40.5	29	324	9.8	2.7
Scott	44	182	52.5	4.7	45	D	D	D	51	1 209	43.2	12.2
Shelby	49	129	9.3	3.3	42	4 095	942.2	126.2	43	685	21.4	5.8
Simpson	16	63	3.5	1.0	34	3 390	549.4	107.2	37	697	23.7	6.3
Spencer	7	21	1.2	0.3	NA	NA	NA	NA	7	D	D	D
Taylor	40	62	5.7	1.7	38	4 088	599.8	96.6	45	685	18.8	5.0
Todd	10	34	1.3	0.5	19	1 299	147.3	25.7	10	75	2.0	0.5
Trigg	8	37	2.4	0.9	19	1 083	158.0	26.5	18	224	6.1	1.8
Trimble	3	5	0.6	0.1	NA	NA	NA	NA	7	30	0.6	0.2
Union	13	41	2.1	0.6	18	1 214	167.0	29.3	23	D	D	D
Warren	146	946	58.1	20.2	104	D	D	D	192	4 375	136.0	40.0
Washington	11	25	2.0	0.4	13	1 049	179.6	25.1	13	131	4.1	1.0
Wayne	20	44	2.9	0.7	33	1 877	190.0	33.4	20	D	D	D
Webster	10	28	1.3	0.3	19	798	82.5	16.4	15	138	3.1	0.9
Whitley	39	130	9.2	2.9	33	1 927	201.1	43.5	68	1 128	35.1	9.4
Wolfe	4	7	0.6	0.1	NA	NA	NA	NA	6	D	D	D
Woodford	37	124	9.9	2.9	22	D	D	D	41	529	14.9	4.3
LOUISIANA	9 077	63 642	5 754.6	2 159.0	3 545	165 777	80 424.0	6 054.5	7 151	147 016	5 259.9	1 408.9
Acadia	54	233	18.1	5.7	47	2 247	283.9	38.5	58	D	D	D
Allen	17	35	2.2	0.6	11	658	97.5	16.7	26	288	10.9	2.3
Ascension	80	820	34.7	15.5	86	5 577	7 012.9	300.0	103	1 729	58.8	15.9
Assumption	15	45	2.2	0.7	NA	NA	NA	NA	13	116	3.3	0.9
Avoyelles	46	132	9.6	2.5	20	622	92.8	11.4	37	1 931	131.2	34.6
Beauregard	28	68	4.0	1.1	26	1 413	627.1	63.0	32	449	15.7	3.2
Bienville	11	15	1.5	0.4	14	1 052	226.3	33.0	16	D	D	D
Bossier	95	440	29.0	10.4	76	2 578	376.5	65.4	173	5 610	300.8	69.8
Caddo	557	3 317	277.3	102.7	216	11 997	4 515.6	445.7	408	7 743	236.9	66.0
Calcasieu	348	2 432	183.4	69.2	134	11 274	10 153.5	542.4	294	8 019	306.4	75.4
Caldwell	12	38	3.3	0.6	NA	NA	NA	NA	8	D	D	D
Cameron	11	118	6.7	3.0	NA	NA	NA	NA	11	54	2.0	0.4
Catahoula	11	24	1.3	0.4	10	507	109.5	11.5	11	100	2.7	0.7
Claiborne	16	36	2.6	0.5	16	1 166	493.3	43.9	18	D	D	D
Concordia	21	59	3.7	0.9	NA	NA	NA	NA	27	D	D	D
De Soto	20	75	3.4	0.9	16	1 166	493.3	43.9	15	D	D	D
East Baton Rouge	1 376	12 183	1 200.8	452.8	354	12 159	9 831.6	570.1	754	16 452	504.7	138.3
East Carroll	11	20	1.9	0.9	NA	NA	NA	NA	6	D	D	D
East Feliciana	15	29	1.9	0.9	NA	NA	NA	NA	17	150	3.4	0.9
Evangeline	34	100	5.4	1.8	18	944	191.0	36.0	34	D	D	D
Franklin	24	494	7.5	4.8	13	506	36.1	6.9	18	D	D	D
Grant	5	D	D	D	NA	NA	NA	NA	3	D	D	D
Iberia	113	562	34.6	13.4	100	4 962	911.0	141.8	83	1 302	33.9	9.0
Iberville	36	158	11.7	4.4	39	4 360	4 176.1	270.0	31	478	13.0	3.5
Jackson	14	45	2.4	0.6	5	D	D	D	18	D	D	D
Jefferson	1 359	9 307	861.4	333.4	444	16 356	2 893.2	508.6	948	18 676	681.2	185.7
Jefferson Davis	35	119	10.4	2.6	21	598	110.2	13.9	44	684	20.4	5.4
Lafayette	786	5 714	535.5	207.1	215	5 419	868.5	150.1	382	9 058	270.1	78.8
Lafourche	139	1 486	123.5	41.5	66	2 464	424.2	72.9	129	1 554	48.6	10.9
La Salle	20	56	2.7	0.9	8	D	D	D	13	150	4.6	1.2
Lincoln	55	222	16.6	4.9	35	1 788	346.0	53.0	66	1 206	34.5	8.4
Livingston	76	255	17.1	5.1	54	1 342	227.4	39.6	84	1 282	37.1	9.5
Madison	15	65	2.2	0.7	NA	NA	NA	NA	15	D	D	D
Morehouse	18	65	4.5	1.9	14	D	D	D	28	D	D	D
Natchitoches	47	280	21.6	6.1	18	1 664	537.9	42.5	65	1 370	40.9	11.2
Orleans	1 420	12 469	1 401.8	551.5	261	10 453	2 305.0	362.2	1 105	32 081	1 371.8	377.5
Ouachita	358	2 042	145.3	50.7	152	8 235	1 983.4	287.6	265	5 360	170.1	42.6
Plaquemines	38	489	28.1	13.1	44	2 231	2 779.2	102.1	51	1 600	55.5	20.4

1. Firms subject to federal tax.

Table B. States and Counties — Health Care and Social Assistance, Other Services, and Federal Funds

STATE County	Health care and social assistance,[1] 1997				Other services,[1] 1997				Federal funds and grants, 2002–2003 Expenditures (mil dol)			
										Direct payments for individuals[2]		
	Number of establishments	Number of employees	Receipts (mil dol)	Annual payroll (mil dol)	Number of establishments	Number of employees	Receipts (mil dol)	Annual payroll (mil dol)	Total	Social Security and government retirement	Medicare	Food stamps and Supplemental Security Income
	159	160	161	162	163	164	165	166	167	168	169	170
KENTUCKY—Cont'd												
Owsley	4	31	1.3	0.6	2	D	D	D	46.8	11.8	6.9	5.4
Pendleton	14	D	D	D	18	39	5.0	0.6	58.5	26.0	10.3	3.8
Perry	55	636	43.9	21.3	41	166	9.5	2.2	232.5	90.5	32.6	25.5
Pike	131	1 233	70.2	28.3	83	408	24.0	6.5	499.8	215.5	72.2	40.8
Powell	14	169	5.9	2.4	10	34	1.3	0.4	57.6	23.5	6.3	6.7
Pulaski	129	2 367	158.7	61.0	67	316	17.8	5.1	412.6	158.5	48.7	25.4
Robertson	4	D	D	D	1	D	D	D	12.3	4.7	2.5	0.8
Rockcastle	12	141	6.4	3.2	11	42	2.4	0.5	109.4	32.3	14.2	10.4
Rowan	29	540	28.3	15.3	19	91	4.6	1.0	120.9	39.7	14.6	8.6
Russell	18	233	9.9	3.9	15	56	3.0	0.9	119.6	41.1	18.0	9.0
Scott	42	634	34.9	14.3	45	276	12.2	4.5	109.0	53.8	19.7	6.0
Shelby	39	500	20.8	9.6	46	316	33.4	7.2	120.0	56.1	20.8	4.3
Simpson	27	232	11.2	4.3	28	180	11.5	3.1	74.3	32.0	17.7	3.3
Spencer	10	116	5.8	2.4	8	37	2.1	0.4	37.8	20.2	6.9	1.6
Taylor	59	421	22.6	10.3	41	134	7.7	1.6	136.7	59.4	26.8	8.7
Todd	11	147	5.3	2.1	12	41	2.2	0.7	61.9	23.3	13.3	2.8
Trigg	18	146	5.6	2.3	12	33	3.0	0.6	84.0	41.7	14.5	2.4
Trimble	4	86	2.9	1.3	6	17	0.7	0.3	32.1	16.6	7.0	1.8
Union	19	796	35.6	17.3	13	52	4.3	1.0	280.1	37.4	17.0	3.1
Warren	232	3 877	262.9	105.0	133	1 020	43.6	14.1	478.7	176.5	80.4	23.9
Washington	17	137	6.1	2.1	7	51	2.5	0.9	57.0	22.1	11.2	2.9
Wayne	27	310	13.0	6.6	21	50	3.8	0.8	125.7	38.9	21.3	13.5
Webster	11	191	6.2	2.9	18	71	5.4	1.3	80.1	36.8	14.6	3.2
Whitley	65	770	44.2	20.3	51	225	12.8	3.4	346.8	119.3	50.3	31.6
Wolfe	4	194	6.3	2.7	3	14	1.1	0.2	61.0	16.1	6.1	8.4
Woodford	28	124	9.0	3.0	34	142	7.5	2.0	77.8	45.8	11.4	2.8
LOUISIANA	8 580	129 773	7 967.6	3 341.5	5 998	39 764	2 595.2	767.2	31 646.3	8 759.3	5 253.1	1 485.4
Acadia	74	930	39.7	16.2	65	296	20.8	5.4	372.5	106.0	63.7	21.7
Allen	30	435	29.0	9.1	14	46	3.7	0.6	197.6	46.3	29.5	8.4
Ascension	92	1 542	68.9	30.3	92	571	37.7	12.0	269.7	113.3	65.7	15.7
Assumption	13	307	8.8	4.1	17	117	6.0	1.3	118.5	40.0	30.4	7.8
Avoyelles	55	954	39.7	16.3	44	121	7.7	1.9	275.0	80.0	54.6	19.7
Beauregard	42	349	21.5	9.1	39	117	7.0	1.6	166.4	80.7	32.6	7.6
Bienville	10	191	7.1	2.7	16	197	10.3	3.3	107.6	38.3	27.1	6.6
Bossier	112	1 773	93.6	37.7	154	830	48.5	13.8	862.5	251.9	71.4	57.0
Caddo	549	8 870	622.6	278.6	379	2 579	169.1	49.7	1 494.6	545.8	300.3	53.4
Calcasieu	405	4 756	319.7	131.7	262	1 914	122.2	35.7	1 033.6	373.6	200.8	42.8
Caldwell	22	532	25.4	10.0	9	26	2.3	0.5	70.1	23.4	20.1	3.5
Cameron	4	23	1.5	0.8	8	30	2.7	0.6	42.1	12.5	7.8	1.3
Catahoula	10	92	4.3	2.3	9	30	1.2	0.2	103.1	23.1	15.8	5.0
Claiborne	13	112	5.9	2.2	10	28	2.2	0.4	99.2	33.5	21.7	6.5
Concordia	32	372	20.2	8.4	20	74	4.0	1.3	153.2	43.6	25.9	8.8
De Soto	15	199	8.6	3.8	22	80	5.1	1.3	148.9	53.5	31.1	10.9
East Baton Rouge	983	14 707	973.8	426.5	724	5 646	355.3	111.1	3 174.1	850.8	401.7	111.1
East Carroll	8	138	2.3	1.3	11	28	1.3	0.4	85.5	13.6	16.3	7.2
East Feliciana	14	300	9.9	4.8	15	136	8.9	3.3	122.4	34.3	28.2	7.7
Evangeline	81	1 528	71.9	27.1	17	48	2.8	0.5	262.1	67.5	47.2	21.4
Franklin	40	767	26.9	11.7	28	114	5.6	1.3	163.0	39.3	36.1	7.7
Grant	13	111	4.4	1.6	7	30	2.2	0.6	244.1	43.3	23.7	6.0
Iberia	149	1 810	115.1	42.6	129	827	65.4	18.9	362.0	133.6	69.0	25.4
Iberville	50	989	54.2	21.8	25	194	11.2	4.5	194.6	57.9	50.0	11.7
Jackson	14	396	11.4	5.7	14	70	3.3	0.8	104.6	39.1	29.2	4.7
Jefferson	1 170	17 797	1 165.4	469.1	865	6 614	431.3	135.6	2 141.9	854.7	557.5	113.7
Jefferson Davis	51	471	20.9	6.9	35	118	5.6	1.6	226.9	63.0	34.2	9.0
Lafayette	616	7 560	589.9	228.8	359	2 443	160.6	49.2	814.2	301.2	151.2	40.0
Lafourche	144	1 330	85.6	41.3	95	1 011	79.9	23.4	475.1	160.2	94.0	24.5
La Salle	19	136	6.2	2.9	13	34	2.3	0.6	78.7	32.5	22.1	3.0
Lincoln	61	1 299	85.0	25.4	41	223	15.6	3.7	204.6	66.0	40.0	10.7
Livingston	71	1 458	41.3	18.7	62	346	19.9	6.0	310.0	149.3	77.7	15.9
Madison	26	458	17.1	8.3	12	30	1.8	0.4	115.3	20.2	20.8	7.3
Morehouse	66	688	33.6	15.2	35	105	6.5	1.5	243.0	66.3	51.7	15.1
Natchitoches	51	516	24.7	10.0	45	180	10.0	2.3	258.9	68.3	39.8	16.6
Orleans	1 022	19 447	1 245.4	530.6	605	4 684	257.7	77.8	5 930.9	971.4	765.3	293.3
Ouachita	355	5 465	339.6	153.9	224	1 332	74.1	22.2	765.0	265.5	172.1	49.4
Plaquemines	23	258	13.7	6.3	46	400	41.8	15.4	241.2	48.1	27.3	7.9

1. Firms subject to federal tax.　　2. State totals may include programs not allocated by county.

STATE County	Salaries and wages	Defense	Other	Medicaid and other health-related	Nutrition and family welfare	Education	Other	Total (mil dol)	Intergovern-mental (mil dol)	Total (mil dol)	Per capita (dollars) Total	Property
	171	172	173	174	175	176	177	178	179	180	181	182
KENTUCKY—Cont'd												
Owsley	0.9	0.0	0.2	16.8	2.2	1.0	1.6	9.7	8.2	1.0	202	134
Pendleton	1.7	0.2	0.5	7.3	1.4	0.8	5.5	28.8	20.2	5.3	357	267
Perry	9.7	0.4	11.4	43.3	6.0	3.8	7.8	82.0	51.7	14.0	477	319
Pike	16.7	2.5	8.5	59.3	8.9	5.1	66.8	119.0	76.8	30.4	448	314
Powell	1.9	0.0	0.4	14.1	2.4	1.2	0.9	21.8	15.3	3.7	284	146
Pulaski	14.2	1.0	2.2	61.0	6.4	4.9	88.4	100.7	55.2	31.2	545	320
Robertson	0.3	0.0	0.1	2.2	0.3	0.3	0.2	3.5	2.7	0.6	259	186
Rockcastle	1.7	0.4	0.5	24.1	2.6	1.3	21.0	45.6	25.4	4.9	292	207
Rowan	5.7	0.1	1.1	21.2	2.2	5.8	8.6	35.4	17.5	12.0	538	210
Russell	2.9	1.2	0.5	24.2	7.1	1.2	13.3	27.6	17.4	6.1	369	224
Scott	3.7	0.0	1.0	13.1	1.9	1.6	5.9	123.4	24.1	40.4	1 143	328
Shelby	5.7	0.0	1.8	14.4	6.2	2.3	6.1	60.2	22.7	26.5	755	511
Simpson	2.1	0.1	0.6	10.9	1.5	1.0	2.6	36.9	14.5	9.8	586	345
Spencer	1.6	0.0	0.4	4.2	0.9	0.5	0.7	21.6	11.6	8.1	602	526
Taylor	5.4	6.8	0.9	17.7	2.3	1.7	3.1	76.5	38.9	11.7	503	259
Todd	2.1	0.0	0.4	13.3	1.4	0.8	0.6	19.7	12.4	3.6	303	175
Trigg	4.8	0.0	6.6	8.5	1.1	1.1	1.6	18.3	11.1	5.4	424	291
Trimble	1.2	0.0	0.3	3.4	1.3	0.6	-0.3	38.7	7.6	4.0	457	278
Union	3.1	0.1	203.1	7.1	1.5	1.3	2.6	25.2	15.8	6.4	409	303
Warren	41.3	3.9	10.1	45.8	12.9	11.9	49.9	186.4	79.2	69.5	733	374
Washington	2.1	0.0	0.4	9.7	1.4	0.8	3.9	18.9	11.9	5.2	472	226
Wayne	2.5	1.5	0.4	38.9	3.5	1.9	2.6	28.9	16.4	5.6	395	296
Webster	2.5	0.0	6.0	8.7	1.6	1.1	2.3	67.8	45.8	12.2	332	175
Whitley	7.8	63.1	10.7	46.6	6.6	2.8	4.6	11.9	9.9	1.5	223	118
Wolfe	2.0	0.0	0.5	20.2	2.0	1.0	4.1	39.1	15.2	19.7	840	433
Woodford	3.0	0.0	0.9	7.3	1.4	1.2	0.5	X	X	X	X	X
LOUISIANA	2 647.8	1 951.3	1 243.4	4 071.3	1 008.4	693.7	2 046.9	X	X	X	X	X
Acadia	7.1	1.5	11.6	81.8	9.7	4.4	33.6	116.6	58.4	41.3	701	198
Allen	38.6	0.4	4.3	27.3	4.4	1.6	30.0	55.2	27.7	17.5	690	284
Ascension	10.7	0.2	2.2	31.6	8.0	4.2	16.1	215.7	66.6	116.3	1 422	483
Assumption	3.5	3.0	0.7	24.3	3.9	2.0	2.2	49.2	28.8	16.1	692	264
Avoyelles	6.7	0.4	4.8	76.7	8.2	3.5	6.5	83.6	52.7	17.4	420	100
Beauregard	7.8	0.2	1.2	24.0	2.6	2.4	4.4	87.7	35.0	28.3	848	377
Bienville	3.3	0.0	0.7	25.1	2.2	1.3	2.4	39.7	21.8	15.6	1 007	560
Bossier	333.8	64.6	2.7	39.4	9.8	6.3	16.6	241.6	89.5	114.6	1 138	375
Caddo	134.0	5.4	47.3	226.9	38.5	23.3	96.7	716.1	275.4	343.8	1 369	680
Calcasieu	39.3	120.7	49.7	97.3	18.1	13.2	56.4	587.9	166.1	270.2	1 474	527
Caldwell	1.7	0.8	0.3	13.8	1.5	1.1	1.7	24.9	17.3	5.6	528	238
Cameron	2.0	1.9	5.9	2.8	1.1	0.7	2.2	46.7	12.1	18.6	1 926	1 870
Catahoula	3.0	0.0	0.5	21.2	4.1	1.1	5.7	22.5	14.1	6.0	555	245
Claiborne	2.7	0.0	1.6	27.4	2.3	1.4	1.4	48.2	22.5	10.9	662	347
Concordia	4.9	4.7	0.6	33.6	4.2	1.8	10.5	70.8	33.2	15.4	770	418
De Soto	3.8	-0.3	0.9	36.0	4.0	2.2	4.2	77.2	36.0	27.0	1 038	607
East Baton Rouge	155.4	16.4	28.0	272.8	244.3	277.1	753.3	1 074.0	291.7	549.2	1 333	460
East Carroll	1.4	1.4	0.4	24.7	3.9	1.4	3.8	30.6	19.7	4.6	505	240
East Feliciana	4.6	0.0	0.7	25.3	3.0	1.9	15.1	27.7	16.9	8.8	417	175
Evangeline	3.9	0.3	1.0	87.4	8.4	3.2	3.5	63.0	38.3	18.3	516	207
Franklin	4.3	0.0	0.7	45.1	4.9	2.2	7.5	59.6	30.8	12.8	613	176
Grant	27.0	0.5	98.4	20.6	3.2	1.6	18.6	30.0	23.4	4.6	248	128
Iberia	8.5	6.3	3.0	65.4	8.1	8.7	31.1	200.3	90.5	60.6	821	271
Iberville	5.2	5.9	4.1	43.5	8.2	3.7	3.2	84.8	31.9	43.5	1 315	522
Jackson	4.5	0.0	0.6	17.4	4.0	1.2	2.4	33.9	16.5	12.5	810	250
Jefferson	138.8	37.1	101.7	164.6	38.3	28.2	76.0	1 442.6	369.9	524.5	1 158	410
Jefferson Davis	5.5	0.0	3.5	29.1	5.4	2.8	53.8	66.1	33.6	24.1	774	339
Lafayette	63.3	14.6	38.4	96.2	20.5	18.4	43.0	400.6	128.9	191.5	993	317
Lafourche	9.9	77.3	16.3	45.6	11.9	8.4	14.9	325.9	119.5	83.5	915	402
La Salle	2.4	-0.2	0.4	14.4	1.1	1.0	0.9	51.5	21.1	10.0	701	433
Lincoln	7.0	0.1	1.4	33.7	5.9	7.1	10.7	82.7	34.2	36.6	864	366
Livingston	9.3	0.0	3.8	31.3	6.0	4.4	9.2	165.0	95.0	54.3	548	151
Madison	2.3	0.9	0.3	29.2	5.5	2.1	10.0	30.1	19.8	7.6	573	268
Morehouse	4.2	0.0	0.9	58.1	7.8	3.6	7.6	106.5	41.1	22.2	730	302
Natchitoches	11.1	2.3	2.0	66.7	7.8	4.7	18.6	139.1	59.1	28.6	739	297
Orleans	792.3	1 047.0	625.6	787.2	118.1	70.7	309.6	1 536.7	582.5	641.6	1 355	540
Ouachita	33.6	5.3	7.5	121.5	18.1	12.5	55.5	424.0	181.0	196.2	1 332	466
Plaquemines	30.6	77.9	19.6	14.9	3.0	1.9	8.2	112.7	38.1	46.2	1 690	1 068

1. State totals may include programs not allocated by county.   2. Based on the resident population estimated as of July 1 of the year shown.

STATE County	Local government finances, 2002 (cont'd)									Government employment, 2002			Presidential election, 2004		
	Direct general expenditure							Debt outstanding					Percent of vote cast —		
			Percent of total for —												
	Total (mil dol)	Per capita[1] (dollars)	Educa-tion	Health and hospitals	Police protec-tion	Public welfare	High-ways	Total (mil dol)	Per capita[1] (dollars)	Federal civilian	Federal military	State and local	Demo-cratic	Republi-can	All other
	183	184	185	186	187	188	189	190	191	192	193	194	195	196	197
KENTUCKY—Cont'd															
Owsley	9.5	1 988	81.4	0.3	1.3	0.0	5.8	5.5	1 151	15	0	352	21.5	77.9	0.6
Pendleton	26.5	1 792	60.3	14.4	1.7	1.0	4.3	12.9	873	33	14	705	32.2	67.1	0.7
Perry	88.3	3 007	41.2	17.6	1.2	0.0	3.2	226.0	7 695	166	28	2 755	46.3	53.1	0.6
Pike	118.2	1 744	61.9	2.5	1.2	0.3	5.0	64.3	948	299	66	3 403	52.3	47.1	0.6
Powell	21.6	1 633	71.1	5.1	3.0	0.0	2.8	14.4	1 088	45	12	773	45.3	54.2	0.5
Pulaski	100.3	1 755	55.2	12.0	2.8	0.1	4.2	99.3	1 738	204	55	4 333	22.8	76.6	0.6
Robertson	3.6	1 522	64.2	0.4	1.9	0.0	15.8	1.3	549	0	0	176	37.9	61.5	0.6
Rockcastle	44.2	2 633	40.5	41.3	1.0	0.0	3.2	23.0	1 368	35	16	786	21.4	77.9	0.7
Rowan	37.1	1 666	49.6	1.4	3.1	0.1	8.1	26.2	1 177	94	26	2 995	52.3	46.7	1.0
Russell	25.0	1 501	68.0	3.3	3.5	0.0	3.9	22.7	1 362	68	16	1 002	22.7	76.8	0.5
Scott	133.8	3 788	25.6	0.5	3.5	0.1	3.4	690.9	19 561	66	33	1 852	37.1	62.2	0.7
Shelby	52.3	1 488	53.4	9.7	3.1	0.1	3.4	65.4	1 861	92	33	1 601	32.3	66.9	0.8
Simpson	36.6	2 196	44.7	21.3	3.8	0.0	4.8	36.9	2 215	42	16	869	38.8	60.7	0.6
Spencer	20.3	1 504	62.1	1.5	2.2	0.0	4.8	13.8	1 020	29	13	477	28.9	70.6	0.5
Taylor	71.3	3 071	32.2	51.9	2.4	0.6	2.3	28.8	1 241	95	22	1 576	28.9	70.4	0.7
Todd	18.6	1 553	65.1	3.6	3.7	0.0	4.4	93.1	7 766	44	11	560	31.4	68.2	0.4
Trigg	17.6	1 389	65.7	2.0	3.1	0.0	6.6	11.6	917	99	12	673	33.5	65.8	0.7
Trimble	38.3	4 417	22.2	0.5	0.1	0.0	2.1	405.9	46 807	18	0	317	37.7	61.5	0.8
Union	28.1	1 809	55.9	0.8	4.8	0.1	7.7	17.2	1 107	54	15	777	40.1	59.1	0.8
Warren	175.6	1 853	46.7	5.5	4.5	0.6	4.2	567.9	5 995	765	94	8 104	36.1	63.2	0.7
Washington	18.4	1 660	55.7	2.6	3.1	1.3	9.7	39.4	3 545	43	10	468	32.9	66.4	0.6
Wayne	30.7	1 527	72.5	0.4	3.3	0.0	4.9	21.2	1 056	40	19	1 013	34.0	65.4	0.5
Webster	25.1	1 784	53.8	2.4	3.4	0.4	4.6	31.4	2 228	48	13	685	41.6	57.8	0.6
Whitley	69.8	1 905	66.5	7.5	4.0	0.2	4.3	42.0	1 146	103	35	2 278	29.2	70.1	0.6
Wolfe	11.4	1 644	83.3	0.0	0.7	0.0	6.1	3.9	557	35	0	440	55.3	43.9	0.8
Woodford	41.5	1 772	47.1	5.3	9.3	0.7	5.6	36.6	1 566	51	22	1 086	38.9	60.3	0.7
LOUISIANA	X	X	X	X	X	X	X	X	X	34 149	38 867	336 269	42.2	56.8	1.1
Acadia	111.3	1 889	52.6	6.6	6.3	0.0	5.9	51.2	869	109	251	3 122	35.4	63.7	0.8
Allen	51.3	2 028	56.7	6.9	6.6	0.1	7.6	17.9	706	671	108	4 465	41.5	56.3	2.1
Ascension	230.8	2 822	58.8	8.4	4.7	0.0	4.0	163.2	1 995	132	348	3 713	35.7	63.1	1.2
Assumption	45.2	1 946	72.8	0.2	4.2	0.8	3.3	9.9	425	32	99	1 230	52.0	46.3	1.7
Avoyelles	85.1	2 052	48.8	9.0	11.7	0.0	3.6	16.7	403	94	177	4 559	44.9	53.5	1.6
Beauregard	87.1	2 614	44.4	29.1	5.1	0.2	5.4	36.7	1 101	113	140	1 597	27.6	71.3	1.1
Bienville	35.6	2 305	55.2	0.8	5.8	0.2	2.1	15.8	1 020	59	66	713	47.2	50.9	1.9
Bossier	216.8	2 152	52.9	1.2	7.0	0.0	5.9	124.2	1 233	1 781	6 502	5 601	28.6	70.6	0.8
Caddo	709.9	2 827	48.5	1.3	6.1	0.0	3.3	757.1	3 015	2 598	1 065	19 241	48.5	51.0	0.5
Calcasieu	571.0	3 114	41.9	7.1	6.1	0.3	5.9	774.1	4 222	602	810	12 827	41.2	57.8	1.0
Caldwell	23.8	2 232	51.8	0.5	4.6	0.1	6.4	4.3	403	37	45	736	29.1	69.6	1.3
Cameron	46.6	4 832	41.4	28.8	3.7	0.2	7.2	13.8	1 428	37	41	818	29.5	68.8	1.8
Catahoula	25.5	2 345	51.6	0.7	4.6	0.0	7.7	8.0	738	60	46	704	33.8	64.9	1.3
Claiborne	49.2	2 989	41.6	28.4	5.5	0.7	4.7	23.8	1 445	48	70	1 760	43.0	55.9	1.1
Concordia	56.4	2 818	51.7	22.0	6.2	0.0	4.0	20.6	1 030	79	85	1 498	38.4	60.4	1.2
De Soto	76.8	2 952	51.1	0.0	3.5	0.6	5.0	170.5	6 556	56	111	1 403	44.3	54.8	0.9
East Baton Rouge	1 019.4	2 474	41.2	4.4	5.5	0.2	4.8	1 073.2	2 605	2 131	1 876	50 166	44.8	54.4	0.8
East Carroll	31.0	3 402	43.6	15.6	4.2	0.9	3.6	2.6	290	27	39	877	58.3	40.0	1.7
East Feliciana	26.0	1 230	71.5	0.1	7.0	0.0	2.7	13.3	628	44	91	3 181	44.5	54.6	1.0
Evangeline	63.5	1 793	63.9	0.1	6.0	0.5	5.9	20.8	586	67	151	1 973	41.2	56.9	2.0
Franklin	55.9	2 683	42.2	24.7	5.3	0.0	6.2	7.8	372	67	89	1 437	31.1	67.5	1.5
Grant	28.0	1 494	81.5	0.3	1.8	0.0	2.0	6.9	368	467	89	1 066	24.7	74.0	1.3
Iberia	192.2	2 603	50.4	18.0	4.1	0.2	2.2	86.9	1 177	128	316	4 413	38.5	60.2	1.3
Iberville	86.1	2 602	47.5	1.5	9.1	1.5	6.8	70.9	2 143	100	145	3 261	54.3	44.2	1.5
Jackson	28.5	1 853	67.9	0.9	3.3	0.0	8.4	114.6	7 452	34	65	929	33.0	65.9	1.1
Jefferson	1 411.5	3 117	25.2	31.6	5.9	1.5	7.0	1 356.4	2 996	1 626	2 063	22 216	37.6	61.5	0.9
Jefferson Davis	67.1	2 153	63.9	1.3	6.4	0.2	4.0	36.9	1 182	76	133	1 595	36.5	61.9	1.6
Lafayette	427.3	2 215	44.7	1.1	6.7	0.1	7.1	713.6	3 699	996	847	10 991	18.5	80.4	1.1
Lafourche	292.4	3 205	39.0	31.4	4.1	0.3	5.3	147.5	1 617	160	401	7 195	34.7	64.2	1.1
La Salle	49.4	3 477	36.7	38.3	3.3	0.1	3.5	6.5	459	34	61	1 231	38.1	60.0	1.9
Lincoln	79.2	1 870	54.6	1.0	5.8	0.6	5.4	28.4	671	114	195	5 287	39.8	59.2	1.0
Livingston	162.8	1 644	72.2	0.3	4.3	0.0	7.9	43.1	436	138	422	4 350	22.4	76.8	0.9
Madison	28.4	2 134	55.8	0.1	4.8	0.4	5.4	18.2	1 366	49	57	1 492	49.9	49.0	1.0
Morehouse	103.1	3 387	35.0	31.3	4.7	0.0	1.5	163.2	5 360	70	130	1 454	41.1	57.6	1.3
Natchitoches	131.9	3 411	36.7	28.3	3.6	0.8	1.9	66.5	1 719	203	171	4 217	43.6	54.6	1.8
Orleans	1 386.4	2 927	37.2	1.5	7.6	0.3	3.5	2 046.4	4 320	12 409	5 665	44 337	77.4	21.8	0.8
Ouachita	456.0	3 095	47.7	3.1	4.5	0.2	5.6	343.4	2 331	499	636	12 605	34.2	64.8	1.1
Plaquemines	102.8	3 762	37.1	5.1	6.5	0.7	6.5	81.3	2 973	530	798	2 409	34.4	64.7	0.9

1. Based on the resident population estimated as of July 1 of the year shown.

Table B. States and Counties — Land Area and Population

STATE/ County code	CBSA code[1]	County Type[2]	STATE County	Land area,[3] (sq km) 2000	Total persons	Rank	Per square kilometer	White	Black	Am. Indian, Alaska Native	Asian and Pacific Islander	Percent Hispanic or Latino[4]	Under 5 years	5 to 17 years	18 to 24 years	25 to 34 years	35 to 44 years	45 to 54 years
				1	2	3	4	5	6	7	8	9	10	11	12	13	14	15
			LOUISIANA—Cont'd															
22 077	12940	2	Pointe Coupee	1 444	22 564	1 681	15.6	61.2	37.3	0.2	0.3	1.1	7.1	18.3	10.3	10.6	14.7	14.3
22 079	10780	3	Rapides	3 425	127 394	445	37.2	65.8	31.2	1.2	1.1	1.6	7.3	18.8	10.7	12.1	14.6	13.5
22 081	...	6	Red River	1 008	9 524	2 484	9.4	56.1	42.6	0.3	0.1	1.1	7.4	21.2	11.3	10.9	13.7	12.3
22 083	...	6	Richland	1 446	20 623	1 769	14.3	60.4	38.1	0.2	0.3	1.2	7.5	18.9	10.6	11.7	14.4	13.2
22 085	...	6	Sabine	2 241	23 406	1 645	10.4	73.2	16.6	8.7	0.3	3.0	6.7	18.5	9.9	10.7	13.2	12.3
22 087	35380	1	St. Bernard	1 204	66 113	758	54.9	83.9	9.1	0.8	2.0	5.2	6.3	17.9	9.9	12.3	15.6	14.7
22 089	35380	1	St. Charles	735	49 353	946	67.1	69.9	25.8	0.5	0.9	3.5	7.0	21.1	10.4	11.6	17.5	14.8
22 091	12940	2	St. Helena	1 058	10 307	2 415	9.7	45.0	53.6	0.2	0.3	1.3	6.9	20.8	10.4	11.8	13.9	14.7
22 093	...	6	St. James	637	21 118	1 747	33.2	49.1	50.1	0.2	0.1	0.7	7.2	20.6	11.2	10.9	15.6	13.8
22 095	35380	1	St. John the Baptist	567	44 816	1 029	79.0	49.0	46.9	0.4	0.8	3.3	7.6	21.7	11.5	12.5	15.6	14.0
22 097	36660	4	St. Landry	2 405	89 041	604	37.0	56.4	42.5	0.4	0.4	1.0	7.9	20.1	10.9	11.3	13.9	12.8
22 099	29180	3	St. Martin	1 916	49 911	934	26.0	65.8	32.2	0.4	1.1	0.9	7.6	20.4	11.0	12.5	15.5	13.4
22 101	34020	4	St. Mary	1 587	52 357	903	33.0	62.4	32.4	1.8	1.7	2.4	7.4	20.6	10.2	11.5	15.4	13.5
22 103	35380	1	St. Tammany	2 212	207 743	282	93.9	84.9	11.2	0.9	1.4	2.8	6.6	19.8	9.9	11.5	15.9	15.2
22 105	25220	4	Tangipahoa	2 047	103 591	524	50.6	68.8	28.9	0.5	0.6	1.9	7.4	19.2	12.9	13.2	13.7	13.3
22 107	...	9	Tensas	1 560	6 247	2 750	4.0	42.3	55.9	0.1	0.2	1.7	7.0	18.1	12.1	10.7	14.0	15.0
22 109	26380	3	Terrebonne	3 250	106 107	516	32.6	73.9	18.3	6.1	1.1	1.8	7.6	20.0	11.3	12.7	15.6	13.2
22 111	33740	3	Union	2 273	22 966	1 665	10.1	69.3	27.7	0.3	0.3	2.6	7.3	17.7	9.9	12.1	13.5	13.8
22 113	10020	4	Vermilion	3 040	54 222	886	17.8	82.0	14.2	0.4	2.3	1.6	7.5	19.3	10.7	11.7	15.2	13.1
22 115	22860	4	Vernon	3 441	50 669	925	14.7	72.5	19.1	2.3	3.6	5.8	9.5	20.2	12.9	17.6	14.0	10.1
22 117	14220	6	Washington	1 734	43 947	1 046	25.3	66.8	31.8	0.5	0.2	1.0	7.4	18.5	10.7	12.1	13.8	13.5
22 119	33380	6	Webster	1 542	41 404	1 098	26.9	65.4	33.0	0.7	0.5	1.1	6.6	18.0	9.8	11.4	13.8	13.5
22 121	12940	2	West Baton Rouge	495	21 717	1 719	43.9	63.0	34.6	0.4	0.3	2.0	6.7	19.4	11.3	12.8	16.4	14.2
22 123	...	9	West Carroll	931	12 236	2 282	13.1	79.8	18.3	0.4	0.2	1.4	6.6	17.4	11.5	11.3	13.9	13.0
22 125	12940	2	West Feliciana	1 052	15 235	2 084	14.5	49.0	49.6	0.2	0.2	1.1	4.3	14.0	10.6	17.0	21.4	17.0
22 127	...	6	Winn	2 462	16 397	2 005	6.7	66.1	32.4	0.7	0.3	0.9	6.2	17.3	10.8	13.5	15.0	13.6
23 000	...	X	MAINE	79 931	1 305 728	X	16.3	97.2	0.8	1.0	1.1	0.8	5.1	16.8	9.3	11.2	15.9	16.1
23 001	30340	3	Androscoggin	1 218	106 115	515	87.1	97.0	1.3	0.8	1.0	1.1	5.7	17.0	9.9	12.0	16.3	14.4
23 003	...	7	Aroostook	17 279	73 428	694	4.2	96.9	0.5	1.8	0.7	0.7	4.7	16.1	9.3	9.8	14.8	15.9
23 005	38860	2	Cumberland	2 164	270 923	216	125.2	95.7	1.6	0.7	2.2	1.1	5.4	16.8	8.9	12.6	17.0	15.7
23 007	...	6	Franklin	4 397	29 763	1 410	6.8	98.3	0.3	0.8	0.6	0.6	4.6	16.4	12.1	10.2	15.0	15.3
23 009	...	6	Hancock	4 112	52 792	900	12.8	98.1	0.5	1.0	0.8	0.6	4.6	15.8	9.1	10.2	15.3	16.7
23 011	12300	4	Kennebec	2 247	119 683	471	53.3	97.8	0.6	0.9	0.8	0.8	5.2	16.9	9.8	10.8	15.9	15.9
23 013	40500	7	Knox	947	40 406	1 126	42.7	98.5	0.3	0.6	0.5	0.6	4.7	16.0	7.7	11.2	14.9	16.1
23 015	...	8	Lincoln	1 181	34 729	1 283	29.4	98.7	0.2	0.6	0.4	0.5	4.2	16.3	7.6	9.4	14.8	16.1
23 017	...	6	Oxford	5 382	56 151	865	10.4	98.6	0.2	0.7	0.5	0.6	4.6	17.1	8.4	10.1	16.1	16.2
23 019	12620	3	Penobscot	8 795	146 982	388	16.7	97.1	0.7	1.3	1.1	0.6	5.1	16.1	11.6	11.9	15.8	15.4
23 021	...	8	Piscataquis	10 272	17 394	1 940	1.7	98.4	0.3	1.0	0.3	0.5	4.2	16.5	8.3	9.0	14.9	16.7
23 023	38860	2	Sagadahoc	658	36 455	1 227	55.4	96.9	1.3	0.6	1.0	1.1	5.4	18.3	8.2	11.4	16.8	16.0
23 025	...	6	Somerset	10 170	51 154	920	5.0	98.4	0.3	0.9	0.6	0.5	5.2	17.6	8.5	11.1	16.0	15.9
23 027	...	6	Waldo	1 890	38 248	1 179	20.2	98.6	0.2	1.1	0.4	0.7	5.3	17.0	8.8	11.5	15.0	16.9
23 029	...	7	Washington	6 652	33 479	1 317	5.0	94.0	0.3	5.1	0.4	0.9	5.0	16.3	9.1	10.3	14.5	15.6
23 031	38860	2	York	2 566	198 030	292	77.2	97.7	0.6	0.6	1.1	0.8	5.3	17.7	8.4	11.3	16.7	15.9
24 000	...	X	MARYLAND	25 314	5 508 909	X	217.6	62.6	28.4	0.6	5.0	4.8	6.6	18.4	9.2	13.1	16.5	14.8
24 001	19060	3	Allegany	1 102	73 668	692	66.8	93.4	5.5	0.3	0.6	0.8	4.8	14.9	11.9	12.3	14.0	13.5
24 003	12580	1	Anne Arundel	1 077	506 620	116	470.4	81.2	13.8	0.7	3.1	2.7	6.7	18.1	9.0	13.5	17.5	14.8
24 005	12580	1	Baltimore	1 550	777 184	64	501.4	72.2	22.4	0.4	4.0	2.0	5.9	17.1	9.2	12.9	15.7	14.7
24 009	47900	1	Calvert	557	84 110	635	151.0	85.1	12.4	0.7	1.3	1.7	6.0	20.9	9.3	11.3	18.0	14.5
24 011	...	6	Caroline	829	30 861	1 387	37.2	82.7	13.7	0.6	0.6	3.1	6.0	19.4	9.4	11.7	15.9	13.9
24 013	12580	1	Carroll	1 163	163 207	341	140.3	95.2	2.5	0.4	1.3	1.1	5.9	19.8	9.5	11.0	17.6	14.8
24 015	37980	1	Cecil	902	92 746	582	102.8	93.9	3.9	0.6	0.9	1.5	6.4	19.7	9.0	13.0	16.4	14.1
24 017	47900	1	Charles	1 194	133 049	428	111.4	65.2	30.8	1.3	2.6	2.2	6.8	20.6	9.6	12.9	17.8	13.9
24 019	15700	6	Dorchester	1 444	30 612	1 395	21.2	70.6	27.1	0.4	0.8	1.4	5.3	17.0	8.1	10.7	15.0	14.8
24 021	47900	1	Frederick	1 717	213 662	270	124.4	88.5	6.9	0.5	2.6	2.9	6.8	19.6	9.1	12.9	17.8	14.5
24 023	...	6	Garrett	1 678	30 049	1 402	17.9	98.8	0.5	0.2	0.2	0.4	5.4	17.9	9.5	11.9	14.9	14.0
24 025	12580	1	Harford	1 140	232 175	253	203.7	86.8	10.1	0.6	2.1	1.8	6.5	20.0	8.6	11.8	17.4	14.7
24 027	12580	1	Howard	653	264 265	222	404.7	72.5	15.1	0.6	10.5	3.3	6.9	20.3	7.5	13.3	18.7	15.5
24 029	...	6	Kent	724	19 680	1 823	27.2	81.2	15.5	0.2	0.8	2.6	4.3	15.1	12.7	9.4	13.3	13.6
24 031	47900	1	Montgomery	1 283	918 881	45	716.2	60.1	15.0	0.6	13.8	12.3	7.0	18.1	7.3	13.3	17.1	15.5
24 033	47900	1	Prince George's	1 257	838 716	56	667.2	22.9	64.9	0.9	4.4	8.5	7.3	19.2	10.2	14.5	16.8	14.2
24 035	12580	1	Queen Anne's	964	44 108	1 043	45.8	90.3	7.9	0.5	1.0	1.0	5.8	18.3	8.1	10.9	17.0	14.7
24 037	30500	4	St. Mary's	936	92 754	581	99.1	83.0	13.5	0.8	2.4	1.9	6.9	19.8	10.5	12.8	17.3	13.4
24 039	41540	3	Somerset	847	25 447	1 553	30.0	57.1	40.6	0.7	0.8	1.5	4.8	13.1	17.1	13.7	15.4	12.9
24 041	20660	6	Talbot	697	34 670	1 285	49.7	82.8	14.6	0.3	0.7	2.1	5.0	15.8	7.4	9.8	14.1	14.4

1. CBSA = Core Based Statistical Area. See Appendix A for explanation. See Appendix B for list of metropolitan areas with component counties. 2. County type code from the Economic Research Service of USDA Rural-Urban Continuum Codes. See Appendix A for definition. 3. Dry land or land partially or temporarily covered by water. 4. Hispanic or Latino persons may be of any race.

Table B. States and Counties — **Population and Households**

STATE County	55 to 64 years	65 to 74 years	75 years and over	Percent female	1990	2000	1990– 2000	2000– 2003	Births	Deaths	Net migration	Number	Percent change, 1990– 2000	Persons per house-hold	Female family house-holder[1]	One person
	16	17	18	19	20	21	22	23	24	25	26	27	28	29	30	31
LOUISIANA—Cont'd																
Pointe Coupee	10.2	7.6	6.5	51.5	22 540	22 763	1.0	-0.9	1 103	773	-512	8 397	8.5	2.67	15.3	23.4
Rapides	9.6	7.0	6.0	52.0	131 556	126 337	-4.0	0.8	6 370	4 414	-800	47 120	2.6	2.56	16.8	26.0
Red River	9.9	7.0	7.1	52.8	9 526	9 622	1.0	-1.0	443	425	-109	3 414	2.8	2.74	18.6	23.1
Richland	8.9	7.5	7.2	53.0	20 629	20 981	1.7	-1.7	1 052	838	-570	7 490	5.8	2.65	18.8	24.0
Sabine	12.1	8.8	7.4	51.0	22 646	23 459	3.6	-0.2	1 017	878	-152	9 221	10.3	2.50	12.0	26.0
St. Bernard	9.6	7.4	6.4	51.5	66 631	67 229	0.9	-1.7	2 727	2 353	-1 462	25 123	8.5	2.64	14.6	22.9
St. Charles	8.1	5.1	3.9	51.1	42 437	48 072	13.3	2.7	2 306	1 053	82	16 422	14.6	2.90	14.7	19.7
St. Helena	10.0	6.8	5.3	51.8	9 874	10 525	6.6	-2.1	439	318	-312	3 873	16.4	2.70	18.4	25.4
St. James	9.1	6.5	4.9	51.7	20 879	21 216	1.6	-0.5	1 087	641	-517	6 992	8.7	3.00	19.3	18.4
St. John the Baptist	8.4	4.4	3.3	51.3	39 996	43 044	7.6	4.1	2 275	979	512	14 283	12.4	2.98	18.1	17.5
St. Landry	9.5	7.1	6.1	51.9	80 312	87 700	9.2	1.5	4 639	2 968	-227	32 328	17.7	2.67	17.9	25.4
St. Martin	8.9	5.5	4.5	50.8	44 097	48 583	10.2	2.7	2 478	1 272	190	17 164	17.3	2.78	15.9	20.7
St. Mary	9.6	6.7	5.0	51.2	58 086	53 500	-7.9	-2.1	2 603	1 527	-2 249	19 317	-0.7	2.74	16.5	23.2
St. Tammany	9.2	5.7	4.4	50.9	144 500	191 268	32.4	8.6	8 796	4 840	12 410	69 253	37.6	2.73	11.0	19.7
Tangipahoa	8.7	5.7	4.6	51.6	85 709	100 588	17.4	3.0	5 311	3 210	995	36 558	23.2	2.66	16.2	24.0
Tensas	9.8	7.5	7.7	49.7	7 103	6 618	-6.8	-5.6	313	251	-429	2 416	-3.9	2.54	20.2	29.3
Terrebonne	9.0	5.7	4.3	50.8	96 982	104 503	7.8	1.5	5 608	2 742	-1 195	35 997	13.1	2.86	14.1	19.3
Union	10.4	8.1	6.7	51.3	20 796	22 803	9.7	0.7	1 119	836	-96	8 857	17.7	2.52	13.7	24.9
Vermilion	8.9	7.0	6.5	51.5	50 055	53 807	7.5	0.8	2 663	1 706	-490	19 832	11.7	2.67	13.0	23.1
Vernon	7.1	5.1	3.5	47.6	61 961	52 531	-15.2	-3.5	3 256	1 132	-4 090	18 260	-4.5	2.69	10.7	22.0
Washington	10.0	7.2	6.9	51.1	43 185	43 926	1.7	0.0	2 183	1 740	-382	16 467	6.4	2.56	17.1	26.6
Webster	10.8	8.6	7.7	52.0	41 989	41 831	-0.4	-1.0	1 862	1 769	-491	16 501	4.1	2.48	16.3	27.0
West Baton Rouge	8.9	5.6	4.4	51.0	19 419	21 601	11.2	0.5	956	546	-272	7 663	16.0	2.74	18.2	21.5
West Carroll	10.4	8.0	7.7	49.2	12 093	12 314	1.8	-0.6	534	473	-131	4 458	1.5	2.59	12.3	24.8
West Feliciana	8.0	4.1	3.2	34.7	12 915	15 111	17.0	0.8	406	288	26	3 645	33.0	2.73	15.6	23.1
Winn	10.0	7.4	6.7	47.0	16 498	16 894	2.4	-2.9	685	680	-507	5 930	2.5	2.55	15.3	26.2
MAINE	11.2	7.3	7.1	51.2	1 227 928	1 274 923	3.8	2.4	43 434	40 920	28 848	518 200	11.4	2.39	9.5	27.0
Androscoggin	9.7	6.9	7.2	51.3	105 259	103 793	-1.4	2.2	3 914	3 427	1 886	42 028	5.0	2.38	10.8	28.3
Aroostook	11.9	9.2	8.1	51.2	86 936	73 938	-15.0	-0.7	2 276	2 692	-56	30 356	-3.2	2.36	8.1	27.6
Cumberland	9.7	6.4	6.8	51.5	243 135	265 612	9.2	2.0	9 500	7 878	4 008	107 989	14.3	2.38	9.5	28.4
Franklin	11.1	7.6	6.7	51.7	29 008	29 467	1.6	1.0	850	921	402	11 806	9.5	2.40	9.2	28.4
Hancock	11.7	8.2	7.6	50.9	46 948	51 791	10.3	1.9	1 554	1 924	1 398	21 864	19.2	2.31	8.1	27.9
Kennebec	10.5	7.2	6.9	51.3	115 904	117 114	1.0	2.2	4 060	3 737	2 300	47 683	8.6	2.38	10.0	27.6
Knox	11.4	8.1	9.0	51.2	36 310	39 618	9.1	2.4	1 209	1 512	1 096	16 608	15.8	2.31	9.0	29.0
Lincoln	13.0	9.3	8.7	51.4	30 357	33 616	10.7	3.3	929	1 311	1 491	14 158	18.3	2.35	7.7	26.7
Oxford	10.9	8.3	7.7	51.1	52 602	54 755	4.1	2.5	1 644	1 974	1 721	22 314	11.2	2.42	9.5	25.6
Penobscot	10.0	7.1	6.0	51.2	146 601	144 919	-1.1	1.4	4 897	4 400	1 686	58 096	7.5	2.38	9.9	26.7
Piscataquis	12.6	8.5	8.8	51.0	18 653	17 235	-7.6	0.9	481	673	354	7 278	1.2	2.34	8.4	27.8
Sagadahoc	10.4	6.5	6.0	50.8	33 535	35 214	5.0	3.5	1 221	922	967	14 117	12.2	2.47	9.6	25.2
Somerset	11.2	7.6	6.7	51.0	49 767	50 888	2.3	0.5	1 746	1 734	312	20 496	10.7	2.44	10.1	24.6
Waldo	10.9	7.5	6.0	50.8	33 018	36 280	9.9	5.4	1 311	1 136	1 755	14 726	18.6	2.43	9.0	24.9
Washington	11.5	9.1	8.3	51.2	35 308	33 941	-3.9	-1.4	1 138	1 412	-174	14 118	5.2	2.34	9.0	24.9
York	10.2	7.0	6.4	51.2	164 587	186 742	13.5	6.0	6 704	5 267	9 702	74 563	20.6	2.47	9.5	24.9
MARYLAND	10.0	5.9	5.5	51.6	4 780 753	5 296 486	10.8	4.0	241 352	144 272	111 121	1 980 859	13.3	2.61	14.1	25.0
Allegany	10.7	8.6	9.4	50.2	74 946	74 930	0.0	-1.7	2 328	2 892	-627	29 322	-1.1	2.35	10.3	30.1
Anne Arundel	10.2	5.6	4.4	50.1	427 239	489 656	14.6	3.5	22 256	11 708	6 791	178 670	19.8	2.65	11.1	21.3
Baltimore	9.5	6.9	7.5	52.5	692 134	754 292	9.0	3.0	29 984	25 269	18 864	299 877	11.8	2.46	12.8	27.3
Calvert	9.0	4.7	3.9	50.7	51 372	74 563	45.1	12.8	3 171	1 660	7 856	25 447	49.8	2.91	9.9	16.3
Caroline	9.7	6.6	6.5	50.9	27 035	29 772	10.1	3.7	1 283	1 046	861	11 097	11.2	2.64	13.6	21.5
Carroll	9.4	5.5	5.1	50.7	123 372	150 897	22.3	8.2	6 052	3 941	10 117	52 503	24.3	2.81	8.3	17.5
Cecil	9.5	5.7	4.6	50.5	71 347	85 951	20.5	7.9	3 757	2 408	5 365	31 223	26.3	2.71	11.1	19.9
Charles	9.0	4.4	3.2	51.0	101 154	120 546	19.2	10.4	5 698	2 656	9 242	41 668	26.5	2.86	14.5	17.2
Dorchester	11.7	8.9	8.5	52.8	30 236	30 674	1.4	-0.2	1 078	1 337	226	12 706	4.9	2.36	15.5	28.2
Frederick	8.7	4.9	4.5	50.7	150 208	195 277	30.0	9.4	9 368	4 386	13 215	70 060	33.3	2.72	9.4	20.1
Garrett	11.0	8.0	7.2	50.6	28 138	29 846	6.1	0.7	1 043	1 025	211	11 476	13.5	2.55	8.4	23.5
Harford	9.6	5.8	4.5	51.0	182 132	218 590	20.0	6.2	9 382	5 076	9 289	79 667	26.1	2.72	10.2	19.7
Howard	9.4	4.4	3.3	50.8	187 328	247 842	32.3	6.6	11 564	4 234	9 239	90 043	31.8	2.71	9.5	20.8
Kent	12.0	9.4	9.8	52.0	17 842	19 197	7.6	2.5	537	760	712	7 666	14.4	2.33	11.1	27.8
Montgomery	9.9	5.6	5.6	51.9	762 875	873 341	14.5	5.2	42 796	18 138	21 555	324 565	15.0	2.66	10.5	24.4
Prince George's	9.0	4.7	3.2	52.0	722 705	801 515	10.9	4.6	41 654	16 874	13 324	286 610	11.1	2.74	19.6	24.1
Queen Anne's	11.2	6.9	5.5	50.4	33 953	40 563	19.5	8.7	1 529	1 181	3 141	15 315	22.6	2.62	9.5	19.6
St. Mary's	8.7	4.8	4.1	49.8	75 974	86 211	13.5	7.6	4 143	1 857	4 224	30 642	20.2	2.72	10.6	21.3
Somerset	9.2	7.1	6.5	46.8	23 440	24 747	5.6	2.8	831	837	709	8 361	4.8	2.37	15.1	29.4
Talbot	12.4	10.2	10.7	52.2	30 549	33 812	10.7	2.5	1 186	1 372	1 086	14 307	12.9	2.32	9.8	27.8

1. No spouse present.

Table B. States and Counties — **Vital Statistics, Health Resources, and Crime**

STATE County	Births, average 1999–2001 Total	Births Rate[1]	Deaths avg 1999–2001 Number Total	Deaths Number Infant[2]	Deaths Rate Total[1]	Deaths Rate Infant[3]	Physicians[4] 2000 Number	Physicians Rate[5]	Hospitals[4] 1998 Number	Beds Number	Beds Rate[5]	Medicare enrollees, 2003	Serious crimes known to police[6] 2002 Total Number	Total Rate[7]
	32	33	34	35	36	37	38	39	40	41	42	43	44	45
LOUISIANA—Cont'd														
Pointe Coupee	349	15.4	237	3	10.4	D	20	88	1	32	136	3 425	374	2 095
Rapides	1 957	15.5	1 338	22	10.6	11.1	285	226	3	746	588	20 718	8 242	6 681
Red River	138	14.3	115	2	12.0	D	7	73	1	74	771	1 539	182	1 886
Richland	335	16.0	266	5	12.7	D	18	86	2	101	480	3 611	209	1 244
Sabine	321	13.7	274	3	11.7	D	12	51	2	104	437	4 197	506	2 150
St. Bernard	824	12.3	730	8	10.9	9.3	61	91	2	226	342	10 649	1 505	2 232
St. Charles	699	14.5	329	3	6.8	D	16	33	1	104	215	5 269	1 821	3 777
St. Helena	130	12.4	101	1	9.7	D	6	57	1	25	261	978	243	2 302
St. James	338	15.9	184	4	8.6	D	13	61	1	41	194	3 028	1 275	5 991
St. John the Baptist	699	16.2	305	5	7.1	D	46	107	1	102	241	4 560	1 243	2 879
St. Landry	1 385	15.8	897	16	10.2	11.3	109	124	3	274	327	14 517	3 803	4 639
St. Martin	764	15.7	386	8	7.9	10.9	16	33	1	12	25	6 009	505	1 049
St. Mary	831	15.5	479	9	9.0	10.8	62	116	2	147	257	8 039	2 753	5 381
St. Tammany	2 708	14.1	1 436	16	7.5	6.0	368	192	4	610	323	25 120	6 848	5 321
Tangipahoa	1 617	16.0	959	13	9.5	7.8	116	115	4	385	397	14 331	NA	NA
Tensas	107	16.2	77	2	11.7	D	3	45	0	0	0	1 088		
Terrebonne	1 697	16.2	807	20	7.7	12.0	194	186	2	396	379	14 486	6 118	5 837
Union	334	14.6	266	2	11.7	D	8	35	2	60	273	3 847	571	2 496
Vermilion	821	15.3	510	7	9.5	8.9	41	76	2	150	288	8 316	635	1 510
Vernon	1 015	19.4	344	5	6.6	D	48	91	1	66	128	5 017	643	1 279
Washington	663	15.1	541	6	12.3	D	51	116	3	235	546	7 962	1 868	4 240
Webster	561	13.4	550	6	13.1	D	33	79	3	266	623	7 986	740	1 764
West Baton Rouge	302	14.0	168	3	7.8	D	7	32	0	0	0	2 642	219	1 773
West Carroll	160	13.0	153	0	12.5	D	7	57	1	50	409	2 294	1 178	5 998
West Feliciana	136	9.0	87	0	5.8	D	27	179	1	24	178	1 117	230	1 517
Winn	211	12.5	208	2	12.4	D	11	65	1	73	412	2 422	170	1 003
MAINE	13 659	10.7	12 345	72	9.7	5.3	2 816	221	40	4 371	351	226 696	34 381	2 656
Androscoggin	1 213	11.7	1 047	7	10.1	5.8	247	238	2	440	434	18 740	3 547	3 366
Aroostook	715	9.7	821	3	11.1	D	130	176	5	459	603	16 002	1 490	1 985
Cumberland	2 991	11.3	2 355	17	8.9	5.6	960	361	6	1 049	414	42 336	8 489	3 148
Franklin	283	9.6	278	1	9.4	D	44	149	1	70	242	5 062	908	3 035
Hancock	494	9.5	544	2	10.5	D	101	195	3	139	278	9 562	1 141	2 170
Kennebec	1 232	10.5	1 125	6	9.6	D	288	246	3	451	391	21 523	3 165	2 662
Knox	503	12.6	452	2	11.4	D	95	240	1	157	415	7 794	1 037	2 578
Lincoln	290	8.6	383	2	11.4	D	66	196	2	82	258	7 043	569	1 667
Oxford	514	9.4	590	3	10.8	D	65	119	2	99	184	10 479	1 328	2 389
Penobscot	1 543	10.6	1 356	11	9.3	6.9	353	244	4	633	445	25 114	4 112	2 805
Piscataquis	153	8.9	203	1	11.8	D	20	116	2	96	525	3 974	520	2 972
Sagadahoc	401	11.3	280	0	7.9	D	53	151	1	53	148	5 274	849	2 375
Somerset	552	10.8	522	2	10.3	D	47	130	2	100	191	9 307	1 355	2 623
Waldo	412	11.3	338	2	9.3	D	63	124	1	49	134	6 342	694	1 884
Washington	357	10.5	425	1	12.6	D	46	136	2	95	268	7 325	685	2 161
York	2 008	10.7	1 626	11	8.7	5.5	238	127	3	399	228	30 718	4 392	2 316
MARYLAND	73 167	13.8	43 560	586	8.2	8.0	16 561	313	48	13 611	265	674 448	259 120	4 747
Allegany	766	10.2	921	7	12.3	8.7	172	230	2	462	648	15 389	2 368	3 067
Anne Arundel	6 535	13.3	3 515	49	7.2	7.4	813	166	3	996	209	58 064	21 884	4 337
Baltimore	8 766	11.6	7 560	70	10.0	8.0	2 713	360	4	1 514	210	119 838	36 969	4 756
Calvert	994	13.2	478	5	6.4	D	98	131	1	157	218	4 695		
Caroline	391	13.1	324	7	10.8	17.1	13	44	0	0	0		985	3 210
Carroll	2 014	13.3	1 153	9	7.6	4.3	192	127	1	166	201	21 594	3 001	1 930
Cecil	1 171	13.6	714	11	8.3	9.4	93	108	1	131	111	11 198	3 052	3 446
Charles	1 672	13.8	744	12	6.1	7.4	153	127	1	131	111	11 245	4 943	3 979
Dorchester	327	10.7	402	3	13.1	D	51	166	1	114	386	5 762	1 321	4 179
Frederick	2 688	13.7	1 293	13	6.6	4.8	277	142	1	248	133	21 686	5 303	2 635
Garrett	325	10.9	300	3	10.1	D	28	94	2	76	260	4 819	537	1 746
Harford	2 887	13.2	1 489	14	6.8	4.7	313	143	1	494	230	26 526	7 855	3 075
Howard	3 525	14.2	1 194	18	4.8	5.2	690	278	1	223	94			
Kent	207	10.7	239	2	12.4	D	38	198	1	64	338	4 724	508	2 568
Montgomery	13 028	14.8	5 216	65	5.9		4 803	550	5	1 493	178	102 284	29 791	3 310
Prince George's	12 118	15.0	5 190	135	6.4	11.1	1 291	161	5	1 281	165	74 589	62 117	7 520
Queen Anne's	465	11.4	341	2	8.4	D	20	49	0	0	0	5 172	1 025	2 452
St. Mary's	1 294	15.0	566	8	6.5	6.4	71	82	1	107	122	9 046	2 142	2 411
Somerset	248	9.9	255	2	10.2	D	26	105	1	39	161	4 008	767	3 007
Talbot	357	10.5	411	1	12.2	D	138	408	1	191	578	7 699	899	2 580

1. Per 1,000 estimated resident population. 2. Deaths of infants under 1 year old. 3. Deaths of infants under 1 year old per 1,000 live births. 4. Data subject to copyright. 5. Per 100,000 resident population as of July 1 of the year shown. 6. Data for serious crimes have not been adjusted for underreporting; this may affect comparability between geographic areas and over time. 7. Per 100,000 population estimated by the FBI.

Table B. States and Counties — Crime, Education, Money Income, and Poverty

STATE County	Serious crimes known to police,[1] 2002 (cont'd) Rate[2] Violent	Property	Education — School enrollment and attainment, 2000 — Enrollment[3] Total	Percent private	Attainment[4] (percent) High school graduate or less	Bachelor's degree or more	Local government expenditures,[5] 2000–2001 Total current expenditures (mil dol)	Current expenditures per student (dollars)	Money income, 1999 Per capita income[6] (dollars)	Households — Median income Dollars	Percent change, 1989–1999 (constant 1999 dollars)	Percent with income of $100,000 or more	Percent below poverty level, 1999 Persons	House-holds	Families	Families with children
	46	47	48	49	50	51	52	53	54	55	56	57	58	59	60	61
LOUISIANA—Cont'd																
Pointe Coupee	387	1 709	5 974	27.2	70.0	12.8	20.1	5 972	15 387	30 618	21.4	5.8	23.1	22.5	18.7	24.8
Rapides	1 027	5 654	33 345	13.6	59.1	16.5	140.1	5 971	16 088	29 856	6.8	6.5	20.5	19.5	16.4	22.5
Red River	363	1 523	2 747	10.3	74.4	8.7	12.4	6 448	12 119	23 153	16.2	2.9	29.9	27.3	26.0	35.1
Richland	48	1 196	5 489	13.6	70.3	12.8	22.0	5 849	12 479	23 668	15.2	4.2	27.9	26.4	23.1	32.9
Sabine	548	1 602	5 663	5.3	70.1	11.1	24.7	5 653	15 199	26 655	18.2	4.6	21.5	21.7	16.3	25.9
St. Bernard	305	1 926	17 654	29.9	64.8	8.9	51.8	6 067	16 718	35 939	5.0	5.3	13.1	13.7	10.5	14.7
St. Charles	624	3 152	14 720	17.5	56.1	17.5	74.2	7 502	19 054	45 139	5.7	11.1	11.4	11.7	9.3	12.1
St. Helena	493	1 809	2 993	18.4	72.0	11.2	8.9	6 109	12 318	24 970	20.1	4.0	26.8	26.4	22.8	29.8
St. James	2 472	3 520	6 103	19.0	71.2	10.1	28.3	6 767	14 381	35 277	13.6	6.5	20.7	20.5	18.0	25.0
St. John the Baptist	294	2 585	13 204	32.7	62.1	12.9	42.7	6 634	15 445	39 456	1.1	6.8	16.7	15.8	13.9	17.7
St. Landry	707	3 931	24 609	13.3	71.2	10.7	90.9	5 879	12 042	22 855	16.0	3.5	29.3	29.5	24.7	32.7
St. Martin	214	835	13 235	15.8	74.9	8.5	48.7	5 640	13 619	30 701	19.5	3.8	21.5	21.8	18.4	24.2
St. Mary	839	4 543	14 750	13.2	72.3	9.4	64.0	5 966	13 399	28 072	-0.4	3.9	23.6	23.2	20.6	27.5
St. Tammany	335	3 271	54 129	23.5	48.2	28.3	207.6	6 408	22 514	47 883	16.3	15.6	9.7	10.2	7.6	10.6
Tangipahoa	886	4 435	30 230	13.5	62.8	16.3	96.6	5 311	14 461	29 412	29.9	5.2	22.7	23.2	18.0	24.0
Tensas	NA	NA	1 750	17.7	68.3	14.8	8.1	7 352	12 622	19 799	23.5	5.9	36.3	33.7	30.0	41.8
Terrebonne	695	5 141	28 789	16.3	68.7	12.3	113.3	5 730	16 051	35 235	20.5	6.5	19.1	17.6	15.8	20.9
Union	359	2 138	5 345	8.8	68.4	11.8	18.2	5 059	14 819	29 061	19.6	4.0	18.6	18.7	14.3	19.9
Vermilion	233	1 277	14 156	12.2	72.4	10.7	48.9	5 491	14 201	29 500	20.6	4.7	22.1	21.8	17.4	24.5
Vernon	167	1 112	14 157	6.2	56.3	13.5	60.3	5 908	14 036	31 216	21.3	3.3	15.3	15.1	12.2	15.9
Washington	540	3 699	10 968	9.4	71.9	10.9	47.9	6 120	12 915	24 264	11.2	3.4	24.7	24.8	19.4	26.6
Webster	214	1 549	10 694	7.1	65.1	12.6	42.5	5 501	15 203	28 408	13.0	4.6	20.2	19.4	15.3	24.2
West Baton Rouge	621	5 377	5 967	17.8	67.2	11.1	23.3	6 166	15 773	37 117	11.2	7.4	17.0	16.1	13.2	18.2
West Carroll	154	1 619	2 913	3.3	75.3	9.5	12.7	5 152	12 302	24 637	22.9	3.2	23.4	22.5	18.2	25.2
West Feliciana	277	1 240	3 830	19.4	70.8	10.6	18.4	7 727	16 201	39 667	52.2	10.0	19.9	19.0	15.0	19.3
Winn	195	808	4 107	4.3	74.6	9.4	18.1	6 166	11 794	25 462	11.7	3.6	21.5	23.3	17.0	22.6
MAINE	108	2 548	321 041	14.3	50.8	22.9	1 684.2	8 146	19 533	37 240	-0.5	7.1	10.9	11.5	7.8	11.9
Androscoggin	130	3 236	25 970	19.7	60.3	14.4	130.8	7 890	18 734	35 793	-1.3	5.4	11.1	12.1	7.5	12.3
Aroostook	81	1 904	17 892	4.5	61.6	14.6	97.7	8 031	15 033	28 837	-3.4	3.1	14.3	16.1	9.8	14.9
Cumberland	138	3 009	68 515	17.6	38.1	34.2	334.1	8 431	23 949	44 048	1.5	11.7	7.9	8.0	5.2	8.4
Franklin	70	2 965	8 413	7.6	55.8	20.9	41.5	8 136	15 796	31 459	-4.2	3.8	14.6	15.1	10.7	17.2
Hancock	82	2 088	12 336	14.0	46.7	27.1	69.7	8 878	19 809	35 811	5.6	7.0	10.2	10.8	7.0	10.7
Kennebec	117	2 545	30 287	16.3	52.4	20.7	144.7	7 989	18 520	36 498	-5.1	5.8	11.1	12.0	8.5	12.5
Knox	45	2 533	8 546	14.3	48.9	26.2	58.3	8 335	19 981	36 774	7.7	7.4	10.1	10.2	6.4	10.1
Lincoln	53	1 614	7 510	17.6	47.2	26.6	38.2	10 279	20 760	38 686	1.5	7.8	10.1	10.0	6.6	10.9
Oxford	117	2 272	12 792	12.1	60.7	15.7	85.0	8 059	16 945	33 435	1.4	4.2	11.8	12.0	8.3	13.2
Penobscot	73	2 732	40 435	12.0	52.7	20.3	191.4	7 780	17 801	34 274	-4.2	5.8	13.7	14.4	9.7	14.6
Piscataquis	211	2 760	3 892	10.2	63.4	13.3	24.3	8 247	14 374	28 250	-5.0	2.4	14.8	15.7	11.2	16.8
Sagadahoc	92	2 282	8 939	12.0	47.8	25.0	56.1	8 195	20 378	41 908	-2.4	7.5	8.6	8.2	6.9	11.6
Somerset	105	2 518	11 942	9.8	64.5	11.8	75.2	8 372	15 474	30 731	0.2	3.7	14.9	14.9	11.1	16.8
Waldo	106	1 778	8 692	11.5	54.2	12.3	44.0	8 514	17 438	33 986	9.3	5.1	13.9	14.2	10.9	16.1
Washington	129	2 032	8 044	7.8	62.0	14.7	46.2	9 364	14 119	25 869	-3.7	3.1	19.0	20.9	14.2	20.3
York	109	2 208	46 836	15.9	48.5	22.9	246.9	7 581	21 225	43 630	0.1	8.8	8.2	8.7	5.9	8.9
MARYLAND	770	3 978	1 475 484	20.4	42.9	31.4	6 888.6	8 076	25 614	52 868	-0.1	18.1	8.5	8.3	6.1	8.7
Allegany	304	2 762	18 070	8.1	62.5	14.1	81.9	7 863	16 780	30 821	6.5	4.3	14.8	15.3	9.7	16.2
Anne Arundel	734	3 602	131 201	20.6	41.5	30.6	580.5	7 793	27 578	61 768	1.8	21.8	5.1	4.9	3.6	5.1
Baltimore	844	3 912	201 904	23.4	43.2	30.6	860.6	8 051	26 167	50 667	-2.9	15.3	6.5	6.4	4.5	6.5
Calvert	483	1 597	21 773	12.4	47.5	22.5	116.0	7 171	25 410	65 945	3.1	22.0	4.4	4.1	3.1	4.4
Caroline	619	2 591	7 456	9.6	67.0	12.1	38.7	6 973	17 275	38 832	4.1	5.9	11.7	11.9	9.0	12.6
Carroll	251	1 678	41 776	18.4	48.0	24.8	195.8	7 112	23 829	60 021	5.4	18.0	3.8	3.9	2.7	3.7
Cecil	470	2 976	22 438	14.5	56.7	16.4	114.1	7 175	21 384	50 510	4.4	11.8	7.2	6.9	5.4	7.9
Charles	704	3 275	35 134	17.5	47.5	20.0	169.6	7 225	24 285	62 199	-0.3	20.2	5.5	5.2	3.7	5.3
Dorchester	671	3 508	7 043	11.4	67.8	12.0	40.2	8 261	18 929	34 077	1.8	5.9	13.8	13.7	10.1	15.9
Frederick	444	2 191	54 005	16.0	43.0	30.0	258.4	7 004	25 404	60 276	8.4	19.0	4.5	4.6	2.9	4.1
Garrett	143	1 603	6 978	8.4	64.4	13.8	39.6	8 005	16 219	32 238	5.5	5.5	13.3	14.5	9.8	14.2
Harford	373	2 692	61 532	17.7	41.5	27.3	275.0	6 958	24 232	57 234	2.2	16.3	4.9	5.2	3.6	5.1
Howard	185	2 890	73 343	19.8	23.1	52.9	381.6	8 490	32 402	74 167	1.6	31.9	3.9	3.6	2.5	3.5
Kent	455	2 113	4 940	31.5	57.1	21.7	24.5	8 760	21 573	39 869	-1.4	9.2	13.0	11.6	9.3	14.5
Montgomery	234	3 076	240 098	25.1	24.2	54.6	1 280.5	9 543	35 684	71 551	-1.5	32.4	5.4	4.9	3.7	5.0
Prince George's	1 026	6 494	249 844	19.7	42.4	27.2	1 019.6	7 625	23 360	55 256	-4.6	17.0	7.7	7.0	5.3	7.2
Queen Anne's	433	2 019	9 899	13.0	46.0	25.4	53.0	7 343	26 364	57 037	8.3	17.4	6.3	6.5	4.4	6.6
St. Mary's	423	1 988	25 031	18.0	49.6	22.6	111.9	7 385	22 662	54 706	9.6	14.5	7.2	6.7	5.2	7.3
Somerset	463	2 545	7 036	10.9	67.2	11.6	26.2	8 569	15 965	29 903	-4.8	5.7	20.1	20.6	15.0	22.8
Talbot	253	2 328	7 292	23.1	46.3	27.8	34.3	7 582	28 164	43 532	1.6	14.8	8.3	8.4	5.3	9.2

1. Data for serious crimes have not been adjusted for underreporting; this may affect comparability between geographic areas and over time.   2. Per 100,000 population estimated by the FBI.   3. All persons 3 years old and over enrolled in nursery school through college.   4. Persons 25 years old and over.   5. Elementary and secondary education expenditures.   6. Based on population enumerated as of April 1, 2000.

Table B. States and Counties — **Personal Income**

STATE County	Personal income, 2002 Total (mil dol)	Percent change, 2001–2002	Per capita[1] Dollars	Per capita[1] Rank	Wages and salaries[2] (mil dol)	Proprietor's income (mil dol)	Dividends, interest, and rent (mil dol)	Transfer payments Total (mil dol)	Government payments to individuals Total (mil dol)	Social Security (mil dol)	Medical payments (mil dol)	Income maintenance (mil dol)	Unemployment insurance (mil dol)
	62	63	64	65	66	67	68	69	70	71	72	73	74
LOUISIANA—Cont'd													
Pointe Coupee	489	3.0	21 701	2 088	185	24	88	97	91	33	37	15	2
Rapides	3 395	4.1	26 827	730	1 947	312	555	915	882	194	549	86	10
Red River	170	2.2	17 817	2 915	77	17	22	51	49	14	24	8	1
Richland	393	0.8	18 985	2 756	163	10	56	136	131	32	75	17	3
Sabine	452	2.0	19 324	2 691	163	52	78	121	115	44	48	13	3
St. Bernard	1 589	3.7	23 944	1 422	580	76	213	346	329	121	158	29	7
St. Charles	1 237	4.2	25 202	1 078	1 107	51	153	165	152	64	59	19	4
St. Helena	188	2.3	18 034	2 892	46	19	23	47	45	19	16	8	1
St. James	422	5.2	19 848	2 576	335	11	67	94	89	34	36	14	4
St. John the Baptist	948	5.0	21 477	2 155	533	57	101	165	154	56	62	25	5
St. Landry	1 693	3.7	19 171	2 721	704	70	247	483	460	133	224	74	9
St. Martin	919	1.0	18 572	2 820	276	36	118	193	180	66	72	30	5
St. Mary	1 262	3.1	24 059	1 383	1 102	68	220	257	244	94	99	40	6
St. Tammany	6 235	3.9	30 899	275	2 036	476	993	800	748	297	347	59	13
Tangipahoa	2 158	4.4	21 067	2 278	1 037	129	265	594	567	129	316	79	11
Tensas	109	-1.1	16 939	2 999	50	0	24	33	31	9	13	7	0
Terrebonne	2 429	3.5	23 036	1 711	1 882	81	332	472	445	166	209	53	7
Union	494	3.7	21 655	2 104	168	48	63	111	105	39	48	12	2
Vermilion	1 073	1.0	19 842	2 578	491	41	192	235	221	85	98	25	6
Vernon	1 187	4.7	23 168	1 672	941	29	128	173	162	48	77	18	4
Washington	845	2.8	19 297	2 697	356	50	120	274	262	82	128	38	3
Webster	907	2.9	21 856	2 051	393	58	131	237	226	82	104	24	5
West Baton Rouge	517	4.2	23 859	1 454	422	46	60	88	82	29	33	14	2
West Carroll	215	0.3	17 699	2 932	83	10	34	70	67	21	34	8	2
West Feliciana	264	4.1	17 377	2 961	293	11	36	39	35	12	16	5	1
Winn	283	2.6	17 114	2 982	150	19	35	84	79	25	39	10	1
MAINE	36 307	4.1	28 038	X	22 801	2 733	6 369	6 565	6 268	2 321	2 779	614	157
Androscoggin	2 809	5.5	26 721	749	1 779	154	348	580	556	190	265	59	14
Aroostook	1 690	5.2	23 125	1 687	1 003	120	226	466	449	149	209	48	11
Cumberland	9 278	3.7	34 498	151	7 462	675	1 855	1 229	1 168	451	527	102	18
Franklin	688	4.5	23 180	1 670	425	59	117	160	153	56	66	15	6
Hancock	1 527	3.6	29 243	417	806	165	404	254	242	101	101	20	7
Kennebec	3 239	4.5	27 324	642	2 274	195	488	631	604	216	256	64	14
Knox	1 186	5.2	29 390	405	629	160	310	198	189	80	80	17	3
Lincoln	1 013	4.5	29 420	399	362	87	310	170	162	76	63	13	3
Oxford	1 283	4.0	22 999	1 723	600	85	208	316	303	112	135	31	10
Penobscot	3 817	4.1	26 123	866	2 643	358	509	761	728	253	321	78	17
Piscataquis	391	3.5	22 699	1 823	180	41	65	105	101	36	42	10	3
Sagadahoc	1 005	3.5	27 955	556	681	50	176	149	141	58	57	12	3
Somerset	1 170	3.5	22 933	1 742	669	111	136	290	278	88	128	34	12
Waldo	896	3.5	23 775	1 476	369	79	158	185	176	63	76	20	7
Washington	750	3.6	22 469	1 888	372	65	111	236	229	69	112	24	8
York	5 566	3.5	28 482	491	2 547	328	950	835	790	324	340	66	20
MARYLAND	197 869	4.0	36 303	X	124 381	12 391	33 655	21 587	20 212	7 430	9 180	1 707	724
Allegany	1 681	4.8	22 703	1 820	1 077	79	281	499	481	156	234	28	18
Anne Arundel	19 756	4.5	39 273	70	12 544	1 269	3 140	1 742	1 617	667	669	97	77
Baltimore	29 376	3.2	38 159	87	17 447	1 590	5 949	3 533	3 337	1 449	1 450	187	139
Calvert	2 650	4.9	32 732	197	813	84	398	241	221	91	96	15	7
Caroline	682	2.3	22 502	1 877	288	37	109	138	130	53	61	11	1
Carroll	5 434	4.6	34 117	159	1 885	273	865	580	539	232	221	23	39
Cecil	2 626	3.7	29 078	438	1 057	122	356	339	316	127	141	23	8
Charles	4 156	5.1	32 254	215	1 575	145	546	384	351	120	160	31	11
Dorchester	756	1.3	24 725	1 206	399	42	160	175	168	62	76	16	9
Frederick	7 215	3.9	34 478	152	3 713	404	1 073	622	569	254	219	34	22
Garrett	709	4.3	23 686	1 505	320	105	125	154	147	53	67	12	6
Harford	7 558	4.1	33 249	179	3 264	295	1 063	786	729	307	298	46	28
Howard	11 830	4.2	45 464	31	7 204	814	1 781	622	557	251	211	33	21
Kent	641	2.7	32 730	198	267	53	234	116	111	52	46	5	3
Montgomery	47 032	3.8	51 750	17	28 205	4 000	9 884	2 745	2 516	1 066	1 075	165	54
Prince George's	25 287	4.8	30 489	305	16 501	998	3 029	2 566	2 357	715	1 112	235	81
Queen Anne's	1 506	3.7	35 172	137	410	88	277	146	135	65	53	8	3
St. Mary's	2 764	6.4	30 658	295	2 155	112	427	287	265	91	126	23	7
Somerset	499	1.1	19 594	2 638	258	19	83	123	116	40	51	11	4
Talbot	1 459	3.6	42 497	45	696	109	541	189	181	89	72	9	4

1. Based on the resident population estimated as of July 1 of the year shown.   2. Includes other labor income.

Table B. States and Counties — Earnings, Social Security, and Housing

STATE County	Earnings, 2002									Social Security beneficiaries, December 2003		Supplemental Security Income recipients, December 2003	Housing units, 2003	
			Percent by selected industries											
			Goods-related[1]		Service-related and health									
	Total (mil dol)	Farm	Total	Manu-facturing	Information and professional and technical services	Retail trade	Finance, insurance, and real estate	Health services	Govern-ment	Number	Rate[2]		Total	Percent change, 2000–2003
	75	76	77	78	79	80	81	82	83	84	85	86	87	88
LOUISIANA—Cont'd														
Pointe Coupee	208	1.1	22.0	8.6	3.9	9.8	4.2	D	20.6	3 925	174	1 104	10 605	3.0
Rapides	2 258	0.5	18.5	10.6	6.8	8.2	4.4	17.7	25.5	23 170	182	6 215	53 380	2.6
Red River	94	1.6	31.0	16.1	D	5.2	4.5	D	19.7	1 760	185	482	4 075	2.2
Richland	172	-1.4	D	10.1	4.5	9.3	4.7	D	22.5	3 900	189	1 171	8 469	1.6
Sabine	215	9.1	24.5	19.5	D	10.1	4.6	D	17.9	5 050	216	991	13 960	2.1
St. Bernard	656	0.1	D	17.9	4.1	8.6	4.1	D	15.8	12 575	190	1 805	27 167	1.4
St. Charles	1 157	0.1	47.5	40.3	3.0	4.0	2.9	2.0	11.5	6 660	135	969	18 035	3.5
St. Helena	65	12.2	D	9.6	D	4.0	D	D	29.7	2 530	245	458	5 118	1.7
St. James	347	2.2	D	49.9	D	4.2	3.5	D	15.0	3 640	172	597	7 759	2.0
St. John the Baptist	590	0.3	44.8	28.1	3.4	6.3	3.5	7.1	12.8	6 145	137	1 363	16 351	5.3
St. Landry	774	0.4	22.0	11.3	5.4	11.4	4.2	12.9	24.1	16 930	190	5 980	37 024	2.2
St. Martin	312	3.3	24.7	9.3	3.4	12.2	4.5	D	24.8	8 140	163	1 773	20 865	3.1
St. Mary	1 170	0.8	35.9	14.5	D	5.4	5.7	D	15.1	10 250	196	2 399	22 015	1.7
St. Tammany	2 511	0.1	15.6	3.5	9.3	11.0	7.3	15.1	19.7	30 870	149	3 730	81 942	8.7
Tangipahoa	1 166	1.7	13.6	7.6	5.0	13.4	3.5	8.2	31.2	15 650	151	5 582	42 801	4.9
Tensas	50	4.8	D	D	6.6	5.4	4.3	D	30.9	1 150	184	434	3 367	0.2
Terrebonne	1 963	0.2	37.8	12.0	4.7	7.7	7.2	9.6	10.4	18 220	172	4 090	41 559	4.1
Union	216	10.6	D	D	3.2	6.5	2.3	D	16.9	4 365	190	786	11 181	2.8
Vermilion	531	0.3	33.9	7.9	4.2	8.7	6.2	D	19.1	10 070	186	1 652	22 998	2.4
Vernon	970	0.1	4.5	1.8	2.0	3.3	1.2	3.6	76.9	6 035	119	1 153	21 373	1.6
Washington	406	2.0	24.4	17.4	6.5	8.8	3.7	D	30.2	9 570	218	2 930	19 477	1.9
Webster	451	0.2	34.8	23.5	3.7	10.7	5.0	D	16.0	8 890	215	1 752	19 496	2.7
West Baton Rouge	468	1.7	D	28.2	2.6	4.4	1.3	D	11.0	3 205	148	616	8 639	3.2
West Carroll	94	6.5	15.1	8.0	D	7.2	3.8	D	29.2	2 585	211	542	5 090	2.2
West Feliciana	304	0.2	D	19.6	D	1.8	1.2	2.3	35.3	1 385	91	318	4 670	4.1
Winn	169	0.0	D	23.6	D	7.3	3.0	12.5	17.8	2 980	182	609	7 612	1.5
MAINE	25 533	0.4	20.2	13.6	8.3	9.2	7.6	13.9	18.8	262 533	201	31 438	671 089	2.9
Androscoggin	1 933	0.7	21.7	15.1	9.8	10.4	D	16.2	12.1	21 455	202	3 436	46 971	2.2
Aroostook	1 124	2.5	D	16.0	5.4	8.7	4.5	15.9	22.4	18 395	251	2 986	39 097	1.0
Cumberland	8 137	0.1	13.8	8.0	12.2	8.4	13.1	14.2	14.3	47 405	175	4 952	127 437	3.9
Franklin	484	0.1	D	26.8	D	8.7	5.4	D	16.2	6 375	214	701	19 455	1.5
Hancock	971	0.6	24.9	15.3	11.5	10.8	4.7	11.7	13.9	11 155	211	790	35 144	3.5
Kennebec	2 469	0.2	11.8	6.5	6.8	9.7	3.5	14.5	33.4	26 005	217	3 810	57 838	2.6
Knox	789	0.1	D	10.2	7.6	10.2	11.3	12.1	15.2	8 840	219	812	22 357	3.4
Lincoln	449	0.4	18.6	8.1	D	11.4	5.4	12.6	14.5	8 190	236	500	21 450	2.9
Oxford	685	0.6	D	D	3.9	9.2	3.9	11.8	16.9	12 790	228	1 349	33 106	2.5
Penobscot	3 001	0.2	D	13.6	7.2	9.8	4.2	17.2	20.1	29 005	197	4 503	68 504	2.5
Piscataquis	221	0.7	D	26.3	D	9.0	2.5	D	19.9	4 250	244	465	13 865	0.6
Sagadahoc	730	0.1	D	D	4.4	5.1	2.2	4.9	16.4	6 290	173	411	16 997	3.1
Somerset	780	0.6	42.8	28.4	3.4	8.0	2.3	12.1	14.5	10 355	202	1 783	28 527	1.1
Waldo	448	0.5	D	12.8	D	9.1	2.2	13.9	14.4	7 565	198	985	19 683	4.1
Washington	437	3.2	D	16.1	2.3	8.8	3.6	14.9	25.3	8 490	254	1 166	22 231	1.4
York	2 875	0.2	23.5	16.0	5.4	9.9	4.4	11.9	25.9	35 950	182	2 742	98 427	4.4
MARYLAND	136 772	0.2	14.6	7.2	15.5	6.8	8.9	9.6	23.2	751 358	136	90 983	2 219 423	3.5
Allegany	1 156	0.0	19.9	14.0	3.8	8.6	4.0	18.6	25.0	16 160	219	1 885	32 534	-1.4
Anne Arundel	13 813	0.0	D	9.6	12.4	6.6	5.7	5.9	33.6	65 990	130	5 097	194 405	4.0
Baltimore	19 036	0.2	D	10.4	12.1	8.8	11.1	11.9	17.9	134 850	174	12 425	320 902	2.3
Calvert	897	-0.5	17.2	4.9	9.4	8.0	4.3	12.6	19.4	9 720	116	635	30 258	9.7
Caroline	325	0.4	D	17.2	2.6	14.1	4.3	D	19.7	5 690	184	676	12 376	2.9
Carroll	2 158	0.6	D	11.7	6.9	9.2	6.0	10.8	14.9	22 775	140	1 149	58 258	7.4
Cecil	1 179	1.9	28.0	19.8	D	9.1	3.6	8.6	21.4	13 565	146	1 269	36 892	7.1
Charles	1 721	-0.2	D	3.6	6.9	13.0	6.3	8.5	29.0	13 565	102	1 276	47 982	9.3
Dorchester	440	1.5	31.2	25.3	2.8	6.3	4.0	11.6	22.7	6 660	218	896	14 824	1.0
Frederick	4 117	0.6	20.6	8.9	14.8	8.0	10.5	9.0	19.3	26 360	123	1 385	79 222	8.5
Garrett	424	2.1	23.4	7.1	6.2	9.5	7.2	D	15.6	5 940	198	663	17 334	3.4
Harford	3 559	0.6	D	6.2	9.7	10.0	6.1	8.0	34.0	31 740	137	2 061	88 370	6.3
Howard	8 019	0.2	D	5.6	21.9	8.0	10.4	6.3	9.8	24 300	92	1 670	98 071	5.7
Kent	320	6.2	15.4	9.1	7.7	7.0	5.3	14.0	15.7	5 190	264	330	10 330	9.8
Montgomery	32 205	0.1	11.0	4.9	24.5	5.5	10.1	7.8	21.2	101 635	111	10 823	349 678	4.5
Prince George's	17 498	0.1	14.8	4.1	13.3	7.7	4.7	7.4	32.0	81 200	97	10 995	311 132	2.9
Queen Anne's	498	0.0	22.1	11.0	8.0	12.3	6.7	4.1	19.2	6 555	149	280	18 011	8.0
St. Mary's	2 267	-0.4	5.2	1.2	20.7	4.4	2.8	6.1	47.3	10 150	109	1 061	36 629	7.5
Somerset	277	-2.6	7.8	2.1	D	5.8	2.8	D	46.5	4 530	178	632	10 069	-0.2
Talbot	805	0.0	D	11.6	D	10.7	8.7	16.0	10.5	8 615	248	530	17 364	5.2

1. Covers mining, construction, and manufacturing.   2. Per 1,000 resident population estimated as of July 1 of the year shown.

Table B. States and Counties — Housing, Labor Force, and Employment

STATE County	Housing units, 2000								Civilian labor force, 2003				Civilian employment,[6] 2000		
	Occupied units		Owner-occupied			Renter-occupied		Sub-standard units[4] (percent)			Unemployment			Percent	
				Median owner cost as a percent of income										Management, professional and related occupations	Production, transportation, and material moving occupations
	Total	Percent	Median value[1]	With a mortgage	Without a mortgage[2]	Median rent[3]	Median rent as a percent of income		Total	Percent change, 2002–2003	Total	Rate[5]	Total		
	89	90	91	92	93	94	95	96	97	98	99	100	101	102	103
LOUISIANA—Cont'd															
Pointe Coupee	8 397	77.7	80 100	21.2	9.9	343	21.2	6.3	9 160	-1.2	816	8.9	8 911	25.2	19.5
Rapides	47 120	68.0	74 000	19.9	9.9	434	26.4	4.2	60 265	1.9	3 630	6.0	50 576	31.4	11.3
Red River	3 414	76.2	48 500	23.9	10.7	325	23.4	6.8	3 526	1.3	441	12.5	3 139	22.2	21.8
Richland	7 490	72.3	55 400	20.7	10.3	329	28.1	6.8	7 950	1.5	964	12.1	7 682	26.8	17.2
Sabine	9 221	81.0	61 400	19.7	10.2	309	25.3	4.5	7 922	-0.4	662	8.4	8 466	24.2	21.6
St. Bernard	25 123	74.7	85 200	19.4	9.9	489	23.9	4.5	30 377	2.0	2 029	6.7	29 303	24.4	14.8
St. Charles	16 422	81.4	104 200	19.5	9.9	507	23.0	4.5	22 473	1.9	1 320	5.9	21 610	30.0	15.9
St. Helena	3 873	85.0	71 400	20.6	12.1	326	21.3	8.9	4 319	2.6	270	6.3	3 735	23.7	20.9
St. James	6 992	85.6	81 500	17.9	9.9	317	19.7	7.3	9 034	2.8	1 080	12.0	7 679	23.7	24.6
St. John the Baptist	14 283	81.0	83 500	19.7	9.9	489	23.5	5.9	19 746	1.9	1 593	8.1	17 864	24.1	17.2
St. Landry	32 328	70.7	59 600	19.6	11.3	320	28.0	7.2	33 805	2.2	2 633	7.8	29 334	26.2	16.7
St. Martin	17 164	81.7	71 800	19.5	9.9	353	23.1	7.3	22 257	0.2	1 315	5.9	19 111	20.2	22.8
St. Mary	19 317	73.9	74 200	18.5	11.1	397	21.9	6.3	22 804	1.2	1 892	8.3	20 176	22.1	20.9
St. Tammany	69 253	80.5	123 900	19.9	9.9	593	25.2	2.9	92 277	1.7	4 152	4.5	88 044	37.0	8.9
Tangipahoa	36 558	73.3	85 400	21.0	9.9	427	27.8	5.4	47 034	2.6	3 741	8.0	40 689	27.5	15.5
Tensas	2 416	69.4	45 300	24.8	13.0	265	24.4	4.8	2 808	-1.9	274	9.8	2 165	28.3	14.7
Terrebonne	35 997	75.5	80 500	18.9	9.9	460	23.0	7.0	52 662	3.1	2 045	3.9	41 406	25.0	17.8
Union	8 857	81.2	63 900	19.6	10.8	351	22.4	5.6	12 496	2.8	855	6.8	9 262	24.7	22.5
Vermilion	19 832	77.0	68 000	19.0	9.9	342	22.3	6.9	20 755	-0.1	1 560	7.5	21 103	23.5	19.8
Vernon	18 260	56.7	66 900	19.2	9.9	411	20.4	4.5	17 146	1.2	1 107	6.5	16 520	26.1	13.4
Washington	16 467	76.5	54 200	22.5	11.3	330	27.1	5.1	15 666	-0.4	1 282	8.2	15 014	23.5	19.5
Webster	16 501	74.5	57 200	19.0	9.9	360	26.7	4.4	18 035	1.8	1 802	10.0	16 648	22.9	21.2
West Baton Rouge	7 663	78.8	87 400	18.7	9.9	439	24.1	5.2	10 428	4.4	781	7.5	9 408	22.5	17.5
West Carroll	4 458	79.0	48 200	18.0	12.6	326	22.7	5.1	5 279	-2.2	901	17.1	4 139	25.9	20.5
West Feliciana	3 645	74.5	107 500	21.5	9.9	411	19.4	8.5	3 554	-2.2	233	6.6	4 369	31.7	16.0
Winn	5 930	74.7	43 000	20.2	11.6	341	25.9	3.8	5 771	1.4	508	8.8	5 488	21.1	22.1
MAINE	518 200	71.6	98 700	21.4	12.1	497	25.3	2.1	693 083	1.9	35 015	5.1	624 011	31.5	15.3
Androscoggin	42 028	63.4	89 900	21.4	12.5	433	24.1	2.0	61 734	1.7	2 994	4.8	51 522	26.0	19.0
Aroostook	30 356	73.1	60 200	19.2	12.1	364	25.2	2.2	37 640	2.7	2 218	5.9	32 461	27.4	18.1
Cumberland	107 989	66.7	131 200	21.9	12.6	615	25.5	1.5	148 402	2.0	4 484	3.0	138 612	38.8	11.1
Franklin	11 806	76.0	78 300	21.3	11.6	432	26.7	2.9	14 363	1.7	907	6.3	13 737	27.6	18.0
Hancock	21 864	75.6	108 600	22.4	11.6	514	26.6	2.6	29 736	3.4	1 503	5.1	25 034	30.7	11.9
Kennebec	47 683	71.2	87 200	20.8	12.0	439	25.1	2.0	60 208	0.9	3 177	5.3	57 050	33.2	13.7
Knox	16 608	74.0	112 200	22.7	12.0	517	25.1	2.7	21 647	2.7	856	4.0	19 263	29.7	13.4
Lincoln	14 158	83.1	119 900	22.7	11.8	541	26.5	2.5	18 361	3.3	668	3.6	16 197	31.7	13.2
Oxford	22 314	77.0	82 800	21.3	11.7	418	23.7	2.7	26 728	2.3	1 829	6.8	25 686	26.6	20.1
Penobscot	58 096	69.8	82 400	20.5	12.1	468	26.3	2.1	81 205	1.9	4 958	6.1	69 846	30.3	15.1
Piscataquis	7 278	79.4	62 300	20.2	12.8	373	25.4	2.8	8 145	1.0	672	8.3	7 280	25.1	23.5
Sagadahoc	14 117	72.0	110 200	21.9	11.1	551	25.3	2.2	15 577	1.4	604	3.9	17 745	33.1	14.0
Somerset	20 496	77.9	70 100	20.2	11.6	421	25.3	3.2	25 414	1.6	2 264	8.9	23 205	23.9	24.1
Waldo	14 726	79.8	90 100	21.7	11.8	494	24.8	3.5	23 736	3.0	1 170	4.9	17 315	30.3	16.5
Washington	14 118	77.6	68 700	20.7	13.2	408	25.9	3.5	16 196	2.4	1 572	9.7	14 042	25.4	17.1
York	74 563	72.6	122 600	22.0	12.2	568	25.3	1.5	103 994	1.0	5 139	4.9	95 016	31.0	16.7
MARYLAND	1 980 859	67.7	146 000	22.2	9.9	689	24.7	4.0	2 904 139	0.3	130 827	4.5	2 608 457	41.3	9.5
Allegany	29 322	70.1	71 100	19.8	10.9	381	25.5	1.3	32 082	-0.3	2 047	6.4	30 031	27.1	17.5
Anne Arundel	178 670	75.5	159 300	22.4	9.9	798	23.9	2.3	264 939	-0.4	9 667	3.6	250 254	40.5	9.1
Baltimore	299 877	67.6	127 300	21.3	9.9	670	24.3	2.3	414 099	0.0	20 493	4.9	379 705	39.5	10.2
Calvert	25 447	85.2	169 200	22.4	9.9	837	25.5	2.0	41 289	0.9	1 227	3.0	37 604	36.8	8.8
Caroline	11 097	74.0	101 700	23.4	10.5	482	23.1	3.3	16 697	0.6	888	5.3	14 297	24.8	18.3
Carroll	52 503	82.0	162 500	22.8	9.9	638	24.8	1.3	84 878	-0.2	2 828	3.3	78 444	37.1	10.4
Cecil	31 223	74.9	132 300	22.2	9.9	617	23.4	2.3	43 128	0.9	3 120	7.2	42 953	28.1	17.2
Charles	41 668	78.2	153 000	22.6	9.9	858	25.9	3.0	65 669	0.8	2 022	3.1	60 836	35.7	9.2
Dorchester	12 706	70.1	92 300	22.5	11.3	456	24.0	3.1	14 916	-1.0	1 396	9.4	14 225	23.3	21.5
Frederick	70 060	75.8	160 200	22.4	9.9	719	24.0	1.7	110 154	0.9	3 416	3.1	102 856	40.5	9.3
Garrett	11 476	77.9	86 400	21.6	9.9	382	24.0	1.7	13 863	0.6	909	6.6	13 069	25.7	17.6
Harford	79 667	78.0	149 800	21.8	9.9	648	23.2	1.9	118 426	0.0	5 551	4.7	111 792	38.0	11.2
Howard	90 043	73.8	206 300	21.9	9.9	879	23.7	2.5	151 685	-0.4	4 326	2.9	135 504	57.0	4.9
Kent	7 666	70.3	115 500	22.2	11.3	526	23.4	2.4	10 691	0.2	484	4.5	9 294	31.6	12.7
Montgomery	324 565	68.7	221 800	21.5	9.9	914	24.6	5.7	505 536	0.5	13 317	2.6	458 824	56.6	4.6
Prince George's	286 610	61.8	145 600	23.9	9.9	737	24.6	7.8	469 785	0.6	22 268	4.7	399 355	38.9	9.0
Queen Anne's	15 315	83.2	160 000	23.2	11.0	622	24.3	2.4	22 169	0.2	843	3.8	21 186	36.3	10.6
St. Mary's	30 642	71.8	150 000	22.0	9.9	719	23.5	3.6	58 013	2.6	1 651	2.8	41 453	39.1	9.3
Somerset	8 361	69.7	81 100	21.5	11.7	429	28.1	3.1	11 123	-2.4	751	6.8	9 368	24.8	15.1
Talbot	14 307	71.6	149 200	22.5	9.9	552	25.4	1.6	19 709	0.7	832	4.2	16 208	34.9	11.5

1. Specified owner-occupied units.   2. Median monthly owner costs is often in the minimum category—9.9 percent or less, which is indicated as 9.9 percent.   3. Specified renter-occupied units.   4. Overcrowded or lacking complete plumbing facilities.   5. Percent of civilian labor force.   6. Persons 16 years old and over.

STATE County	Private nonfarm establishments, employment and payroll, 2001									Agriculture, 2002			
	Number of establishments	Employment						Annual payroll		Farms			Farm operators whose principal occupation is farming (percent)
		Total	Health care and social assistance	Manufacturing	Retail trade	Finance and insurance	Professional, scientific, and technical services	Total (mil dol)	Average per employee (dollars)	Number	Percent with—		
											Less than 50 acres	500 acres and over	
	104	105	106	107	108	109	110	111	112	113	114	115	116

STATE County	104	105	106	107	108	109	110	111	112	113	114	115	116
LOUISIANA—Cont'd													
Pointe Coupee	351	3 830	603	535	900	135	96	82	21 395	465	35.3	21.7	46.7
Rapides	3 093	47 228	11 696	3 299	7 248	1 749	2 113	1 191	25 220	996	47.3	9.7	57.2
Red River	149	1 813	399	440	291	96	31	42	22 892	236	30.5	20.8	63.1
Richland	399	4 894	1 504	524	740	165	82	100	20 515	536	22.8	24.1	61.2
Sabine	457	4 390	575	865	758	363	47	92	20 896	403	34.7	6.5	52.6
St. Bernard	1 191	14 150	2 695	1 681	2 881	366	386	347	24 547	24	58.3	8.3	58.3
St. Charles	885	18 945	1 096	5 148	1 749	274	588	793	41 871	62	38.7	4.8	62.9
St. Helena	89	745	89	164	98	83	34	16	21 012	326	31.3	6.1	54.0
St. James	301	5 560	364	2 265	734	206	54	217	39 002	69	26.1	42.0	72.5
St. John the Baptist	657	11 336	952	2 321	1 415	235	269	335	29 543	34	29.4	32.4	61.8
St. Landry	1 531	17 319	3 956	1 761	3 432	866	603	397	22 899	1 228	52.4	12.0	54.0
St. Martin	668	7 717	922	1 834	1 421	305	128	163	21 175	328	52.7	16.2	59.1
St. Mary	1 414	22 322	1 353	4 412	2 482	504	1 659	724	32 452	99	23.2	47.5	68.7
St. Tammany	4 744	52 273	10 214	2 434	11 025	1 928	2 992	1 260	24 096	603	71.5	3.2	48.4
Tangipahoa	1 989	25 918	5 041	2 627	5 882	866	720	534	20 616	1 065	49.8	3.3	53.3
Tensas	103	708	114	D	105	73	18	14	19 730	228	11.4	45.2	71.5
Terrebonne	2 713	40 848	5 026	3 899	6 927	1 030	1 176	1 205	29 489	156	45.5	19.2	42.3
Union	332	4 636	682	D	662	168	39	90	19 421	504	38.7	4.4	60.9
Vermilion	965	9 917	1 450	1 020	2 209	430	286	236	23 795	1 116	43.0	16.9	63.5
Vernon	593	7 397	1 742	129	1 626	250	891	142	19 253	460	45.4	3.0	47.4
Washington	701	7 841	1 435	1 652	1 648	292	188	173	22 042	836	42.0	2.2	50.7
Webster	821	10 404	1 950	2 294	1 861	364	184	244	23 445	426	39.2	4.7	49.5
West Baton Rouge	436	8 610	365	2 473	1 036	228	49	259	30 107	108	57.4	10.2	41.7
West Carroll	184	1 924	530	182	390	74	32	39	20 436	709	24.1	15.1	51.6
West Feliciana	176	2 715	229	D	244	D	90	129	47 562	165	30.3	23.0	46.7
Winn	327	3 792	602	942	626	101	23	90	23 684	130	26.9	4.6	56.9
MAINE	39 650	500 030	88 153	77 091	79 629	24 473	22 612	14 205	28 408	7 196	38.6	8.0	47.4
Androscoggin	2 799	45 920	7 581	7 675	6 492	2 763	2 337	1 203	26 198	334	40.7	7.5	55.4
Aroostook	2 286	25 517	6 016	4 218	4 338	791	372	573	22 467	1 084	15.9	17.8	44.4
Cumberland	10 410	151 555	24 547	13 709	21 950	13 362	10 027	4 978	32 848	596	60.7	3.2	43.5
Franklin	852	10 229	1 778	2 279	1 604	292	112	259	25 363	317	32.2	5.3	45.4
Hancock	2 108	17 417	2 677	2 266	3 154	675	1 504	498	28 615	317	46.1	6.3	36.9
Kennebec	3 225	45 804	10 078	4 554	8 249	1 183	1 630	1 191	26 010	575	36.5	7.6	51.8
Knox	1 549	14 676	2 648	1 509	2 567	563	458	399	27 187	275	50.9	6.6	53.5
Lincoln	1 374	8 525	1 637	D	1 739	254	282	207	24 321	292	45.9	2.2	50.7
Oxford	1 410	15 945	2 488	4 007	2 224	359	255	391	24 548	469	48.0	2.7	55.4
Penobscot	4 156	59 142	12 560	7 793	10 329	1 828	2 600	1 624	27 452	575	35.8	6.8	47.0
Piscataquis	487	4 538	1 050	1 292	825	80	129	105	23 045	201	32.3	9.4	26.4
Sagadahoc	785	14 335	994	D	1 250	228	865	441	30 773	158	37.3	10.0	46.2
Somerset	1 203	16 667	2 648	4 152	2 398	333	275	480	28 818	504	25.6	4.4	55.2
Waldo	905	9 897	1 626	1 424	1 376	106	180	247	24 982	415	35.7	10.9	55.2
Washington	892	7 646	1 827	1 230	1 795	278	70	183	23 956	399	40.9	6.7	47.7
York	5 209	52 217	7 998	12 433	9 339	1 378	1 516	1 423	27 255	685	55.8	2.3	43.9
MARYLAND	129 301	2 091 198	270 239	157 084	284 759	115 169	207 526	74 187	35 476	12 198	47.8	7.8	57.2
Allegany	1 821	25 376	5 453	4 263	4 359	864	696	628	24 734	278	30.2	5.8	45.3
Anne Arundel	12 281	191 828	18 700	13 650	30 001	6 979	16 023	6 641	34 620	432	65.0	3.0	53.2
Baltimore	18 877	313 427	45 831	28 918	49 877	21 952	22 382	10 577	33 746	784	62.6	3.1	56.4
Calvert	1 538	15 495	2 683	626	2 681	338	721	456	29 430	321	51.7	1.9	54.2
Caroline	618	6 587	D	1 814	898	196	D	155	23 581	506	39.9	14.2	63.4
Carroll	4 119	44 518	6 657	3 896	7 177	1 166	1 963	1 161	26 090	1 058	52.6	5.0	56.0
Cecil	1 656	21 380	3 422	4 002	3 731	504	616	688	32 231	468	51.5	7.9	54.5
Charles	2 462	30 316	3 489	969	8 650	934	1 430	776	25 594	418	49.5	4.1	56.2
Dorchester	713	10 099	1 851	3 362	1 137	273	190	253	25 035	351	38.5	22.5	55.0
Frederick	5 075	74 219	7 732	8 722	11 658	8 433	4 913	2 353	31 701	1 273	44.1	5.8	56.1
Garrett	892	9 413	1 282	1 052	1 718	312	171	191	20 291	634	24.6	4.9	54.3
Harford	4 838	58 859	6 503	6 322	10 768	2 031	4 016	1 601	27 204	683	58.9	4.8	53.4
Howard	7 373	139 779	11 450	9 535	14 587	6 135	24 839	5 681	40 645	346	64.2	5.5	49.4
Kent	676	7 149	1 267	1 018	1 072	254	273	166	23 234	318	25.8	19.5	66.4
Montgomery	25 967	408 770	43 897	12 660	49 678	21 976	67 690	17 824	43 604	577	60.3	5.7	50.4
Prince George's	13 960	252 837	24 073	10 612	37 941	9 634	25 907	8 714	34 467	452	58.8	3.8	55.3
Queen Anne's	1 212	9 879	682	1 048	1 935	238	468	239	24 169	443	35.9	21.7	58.0
St. Mary's	1 684	23 124	2 909	579	4 288	459	6 336	733	31 714	577	46.3	3.6	64.1
Somerset	403	3 062	768	383	D	D	61	64	20 746	301	43.9	10.0	65.1
Talbot	1 485	17 476	2 940	2 843	2 733	674	921	473	27 075	288	36.1	20.5	56.9

Table B. States and Counties — **Agriculture**

STATE County	Land in farms Acreage (1,000)	Percent change, 1997–2002	Acres Average size of farm	Total irrigated (1,000)	Total cropland (1,000)	Value of land and buildings (dollars) Average per farm	Average per acre	Value of machinery and equipment average per farm (dollars)	Value of products sold Total (mil dol)	Average per farm (dollars)	Percent from Crops	Livestock and poultry products	Percent of farms with sales of $10,000 or more	$100,000 or more	Government payments Total ($1,000)	Percent of farms
	117	118	119	120	121	122	123	124	125	126	127	128	129	130	131	132
LOUISIANA—Cont'd																
Pointe Coupee	199	-1.0	429	6	155	687 881	1 423	107 689	52	111 133	89.9	10.1	46.2	18.3	2 795	33.1
Rapides	201	3.6	202	8	121	305 555	1 704	61 939	67	66 976	82.4	17.6	41.5	15.3	2 261	18.0
Red River	138	22.1	587	2	60	527 769	895	66 131	11	44 820	53.6	46.4	36.0	8.5	1 484	41.9
Richland	216	-8.9	403	56	164	494 785	1 045	81 372	28	51 396	86.9	13.1	40.5	14.6	5 601	60.1
Sabine	63	10.5	155	0	21	293 989	1 894	42 848	67	165 502	0.7	99.3	46.2	23.1	421	20.8
St. Bernard	D	D	D	0	1	388 986	4 246	34 742	0	15 654	67.8	32.2	25.0	4.2	D	D
St. Charles	9	-57.1	141	0	5	586 307	4 152	36 201	5	85 544	D	D	38.7	3.2	0	0.0
St. Helena	51	-22.7	156	0	22	335 249	1 982	30 029	20	62 822	2.7	97.3	32.8	10.7	610	33.1
St. James	53	17.8	765	D	45	1 017 420	1 300	255 859	27	386 211	99.5	0.5	65.2	49.3	48	39.1
St. John the Baptist	22	120.0	647	0	15	2 205 253	3 410	160 358	6	170 345	99.5	0.5	35.3	23.5	16	14.7
St. Landry	290	9.4	236	29	223	325 464	1 384	60 581	52	42 331	83.8	16.2	28.5	8.6	4 802	26.2
St. Martin	81	3.8	246	7	68	358 114	1 666	105 985	28	86 330	92.5	7.5	36.3	15.2	334	12.5
St. Mary	73	-12.0	742	0	63	1 161 115	1 477	321 234	36	358 871	98.2	1.8	69.7	51.5	17	9.1
St. Tammany	51	21.4	85	0	16	402 072	3 907	23 483	13	20 748	52.5	47.5	20.2	3.6	153	6.6
Tangipahoa	118	-1.7	111	2	67	292 021	2 780	36 632	57	53 275	15.1	84.9	35.4	15.8	2 148	22.9
Tensas	226	-6.2	992	21	176	1 047 322	1 055	188 555	49	213 975	99.7	0.3	60.5	37.3	4 865	66.7
Terrebonne	53	0.0	340	D	32	636 927	1 823	102 217	15	98 230	62.1	37.9	41.0	12.8	92	15.4
Union	73	15.9	144	0	27	341 892	1 974	45 042	121	239 568	0.7	99.3	51.4	35.1	164	14.1
Vermilion	359	9.1	322	101	272	568 012	1 632	87 877	53	47 046	86.4	13.6	37.1	10.2	8 098	32.3
Vernon	50	13.6	108	0	18	187 596	1 813	28 112	9	18 810	4.7	95.3	18.0	2.6	89	12.4
Washington	102	2.0	122	1	52	255 422	2 201	37 856	35	42 197	21.2	78.8	26.7	12.6	1 287	24.2
Webster	57	14.0	133	0	22	331 635	2 887	36 061	8	17 687	7.9	92.1	19.7	3.1	123	14.8
West Baton Rouge	22	-24.1	199	0	18	399 728	1 965	81 364	29	265 358	D	D	29.6	13.0	86	14.8
West Carroll	184	10.2	259	41	129	384 114	1 781	57 634	31	44 016	91.7	8.3	30.9	11.0	2 876	65.6
West Feliciana	68	-10.5	413	0	18	704 347	1 817	49 227	5	30 947	64.5	35.5	29.7	1.2	1 047	29.7
Winn	21	16.7	159	D	9	233 381	1 584	20 601	5	38 626	10.4	89.6	20.0	3.8	149	19.2
MAINE	1 370	13.0	190	20	537	322 690	1 637	54 316	464	64 425	48.0	52.0	29.2	9.4	8 664	17.3
Androscoggin	56	0.0	167	1	22	443 764	2 421	72 201	97	289 367	7.4	92.6	38.9	15.0	606	13.8
Aroostook	392	20.6	361	6	198	322 820	897	86 980	121	111 770	96.8	3.2	33.1	20.0	2 333	49.9
Cumberland	54	8.0	91	1	22	422 906	4 043	45 387	18	29 519	66.9	33.1	26.8	7.7	294	8.9
Franklin	50	25.0	157	0	15	235 156	1 459	38 147	6	18 874	24.2	75.8	26.5	5.0	287	16.7
Hancock	50	16.3	156	0	12	338 912	1 960	43 565	29	90 467	D	D	27.8	4.7	51	12.3
Kennebec	86	-2.3	150	0	40	331 957	1 924	60 051	30	52 571	22.8	77.2	27.7	10.3	971	13.0
Knox	29	16.0	104	0	12	278 992	2 833	34 933	5	18 348	69.7	30.3	28.7	4.4	76	5.1
Lincoln	31	19.2	105	0	11	297 470	2 744	43 287	8	25 829	47.0	53.0	30.5	6.2	66	7.2
Oxford	67	4.7	144	1	21	320 518	2 397	28 625	15	31 238	76.6	23.4	22.4	5.1	241	11.1
Penobscot	107	-8.5	186	2	48	245 401	1 266	54 487	29	50 357	34.9	65.1	30.6	9.4	1 417	16.9
Piscataquis	39	14.7	196	0	10	170 812	1 015	32 078	4	19 075	D	D	19.4	5.5	127	12.4
Sagadahoc	20	11.1	128	0	6	427 082	2 873	42 837	4	27 034	D	D	22.8	7.6	81	5.7
Somerset	110	8.9	219	0	35	259 206	1 305	66 063	24	48 200	26.3	73.7	34.1	10.7	1 107	18.7
Waldo	69	0.0	167	0	23	287 272	1 668	37 945	15	35 318	20.0	80.0	27.7	7.5	680	10.4
Washington	152	55.1	382	7	41	363 334	856	57 667	41	103 544	43.8	56.2	34.3	4.3	58	8.3
York	57	-1.7	84	1	22	361 456	3 761	45 720	19	27 372	76.8	23.2	25.5	6.3	270	7.2
MARYLAND	2 078	-3.6	170	81	1 487	694 061	4 084	74 528	1 293	106 026	34.8	65.2	39.5	17.2	33 131	27.6
Allegany	39	-7.1	142	0	19	315 842	2 447	24 657	2	7 679	45.2	54.8	19.4	0.7	76	19.1
Anne Arundel	35	0.0	82	1	24	566 783	7 475	53 737	11	25 413	90.3	9.7	28.5	5.3	220	9.5
Baltimore	71	-6.6	91	1	49	614 858	6 824	58 984	62	79 286	74.3	25.7	33.4	11.2	823	13.3
Calvert	30	-9.1	94	0	17	410 285	3 980	30 516	3	10 105	87.5	12.5	23.1	0.6	178	17.4
Caroline	115	3.6	227	19	94	623 769	2 951	104 701	104	206 242	27.6	72.4	56.9	35.4	1 870	39.3
Carroll	147	-8.1	139	1	115	751 710	5 629	67 770	69	65 175	45.2	54.8	37.1	11.1	2 715	27.0
Cecil	77	-10.5	165	1	57	976 857	5 799	94 059	69	146 606	44.1	55.9	35.7	13.0	1 297	28.6
Charles	52	-7.1	125	1	30	504 614	3 342	39 723	6	15 272	74.3	25.6	22.7	4.1	401	16.0
Dorchester	125	1.6	357	16	91	1 008 456	2 704	109 155	84	238 934	30.6	69.4	53.8	36.5	1 752	61.0
Frederick	196	-9.3	154	1	148	754 746	5 325	76 343	97	76 004	21.4	78.6	37.0	9.5	4 175	28.0
Garrett	101	-6.5	160	0	51	306 298	2 179	54 229	21	32 897	18.0	82.0	36.9	9.5	390	12.3
Harford	81	-13.8	119	0	55	610 832	4 903	64 258	26	38 205	49.6	50.4	30.2	9.1	1 417	23.3
Howard	38	-5.0	109	0	26	717 316	6 071	62 954	22	62 603	75.8	24.2	27.5	8.4	569	19.1
Kent	117	-0.8	369	8	95	1 235 084	3 380	163 848	67	210 175	56.8	43.2	56.9	23.9	3 000	67.0
Montgomery	75	-2.6	130	1	53	793 623	5 979	64 128	42	72 156	87.0	13.0	31.0	9.5	1 071	15.4
Prince George's	45	-6.3	101	0	24	694 515	6 531	50 922	12	27 009	86.2	13.8	23.7	4.0	191	10.2
Queen Anne's	156	-7.1	351	12	132	1 144 839	3 144	149 908	66	149 038	68.8	31.1	52.1	26.9	4 031	61.8
St. Mary's	68	-5.6	118	1	42	409 009	2 831	56 964	12	21 137	73.7	26.3	36.0	4.9	655	17.5
Somerset	57	3.6	188	1	39	473 486	2 516	60 546	127	422 848	7.0	93.0	64.5	51.5	1 027	45.8
Talbot	106	-3.6	367	3	86	1 583 295	4 203	126 207	33	116 149	42.8	57.2	43.1	24.3	2 035	64.6

Table B. States and Counties — Residential Construction, Wholesale Trade, Retail Trade, and Real Estate

STATE County	Value of residential construction authorized by building permits, 2003		Wholesale trade, 1997				Retail trade,[1] 1997				Real estate and rental and leasing, 1997			
	New construction ($1,000)	Number of housing units	Number of establishments	Number of employees	Sales (mil dol)	Annual payroll (mil dol)	Number of establishments	Number of employees	Sales (mil dol)	Annual payroll (mil dol)	Number of establishments	Number of employees	Receipts (mil dol)	Annual payroll (mil dol)
	133	134	135	136	137	138	139	140	141	142	143	144	145	146
LOUISIANA—Cont'd														
Pointe Coupee	9 983	76	13	D	D	D	84	807	159.0	11.6	8	17	0.6	0.2
Rapides	64 208	579	173	1 789	581.1	45.6	586	7 397	1 188.3	108.5	92	660	57.8	12.4
Red River	100	1	6	53	13.8	0.9	39	265	53.6	3.7	4	13	0.7	0.2
Richland	8 180	68	28	259	160.4	5.6	85	844	188.0	12.8	14	40	2.9	0.7
Sabine	253	2	13	D	D	D	93	840	120.2	11.2	8	19	1.5	0.2
St. Bernard	8 480	108	62	D	D	D	214	2 887	362.7	33.6	37	148	13.2	3.0
St. Charles	47 234	319	84	1 485	2 627.1	50.7	119	1 316	210.8	17.5	29	109	14.5	2.1
St. Helena	961	16	1	D	D	D	17	101	11.1	1.1	1	D	D	D
St. James	3 666	29	15	282	277.7	10.5	55	609	72.4	7.4	10	20	2.2	0.3
St. John the Baptist	30 064	265	30	D	D	D	119	1 643	231.5	19.9	30	365	45.0	9.8
St. Landry	34 901	331	85	948	415.1	21.5	327	3 522	515.8	43.9	48	146	12.7	1.9
St. Martin	22 022	195	36	332	116.5	8.2	121	1 260	192.4	17.2	27	224	24.1	4.7
St. Mary	11 732	106	124	1 384	705.3	46.9	256	2 829	396.1	38.3	80	522	178.5	16.7
St. Tammany	419 240	3 123	252	2 070	6 604.0	75.3	749	9 479	1 511.5	135.3	156	739	86.4	14.5
Tangipahoa	83 319	848	106	1 482	725.4	38.0	415	5 442	894.8	74.6	72	309	29.5	5.4
Tensas	2 813	27	8	103	50.5	3.3	22	114	27.5	1.5	3	11	0.7	0.2
Terrebonne	55 212	713	212	2 467	790.5	69.5	482	6 237	1 064.1	93.3	137	1 651	247.6	54.0
Union	735	7	11	75	9.0	1.3	73	578	92.3	7.8	9	22	1.8	0.3
Vermilion	25 646	268	66	738	361.9	19.6	198	1 836	277.5	23.7	27	129	10.9	1.4
Vernon	603	25	30	221	53.6	4.8	143	1 392	216.1	19.3	29	78	6.4	0.8
Washington	12 634	137	28	178	57.0	3.7	184	1 627	241.2	20.0	13	44	2.4	0.5
Webster	3 384	23	36	D	D	D	197	1 844	293.5	24.5	25	116	9.2	1.4
West Baton Rouge	15 639	133	38	575	444.2	19.1	63	843	124.3	11.9	11	68	7.4	1.1
West Carroll	250	1	9	19	8.9	0.4	37	426	54.0	4.6	8	20	1.0	0.2
West Feliciana	6 721	51	7	30	11.7	0.8	35	275	40.7	3.5	2	D	D	D
Winn	0	0	17	159	56.7	4.9	65	692	81.1	7.9	8	20	1.4	0.3
MAINE	1 066 671	7 933	1 726	19 932	7 305.6	616.2	7 074	72 897	12 737.1	1 164.2	1 343	5 929	601.7	114.2
Androscoggin	66 287	508	126	1 244	277.8	35.7	533	6 362	1 247.1	96.4	109	418	46.9	7.2
Aroostook	12 636	136	101	766	211.1	19.8	471	4 285	591.9	57.9	71	197	13.1	2.2
Cumberland	261 001	1 698	574	8 884	3 673.3	296.8	1 570	20 735	3 825.9	346.5	407	2 731	293.4	63.5
Franklin	30 348	219	16	91	26.8	2.7	179	1 537	245.5	22.4	37	130	6.8	1.4
Hancock	70 318	478	73	354	138.6	8.4	388	2 895	490.0	49.3	63	127	13.9	2.2
Kennebec	59 882	596	133	2 135	821.9	67.6	589	7 166	1 289.7	120.5	109	439	37.7	7.6
Knox	51 707	371	79	550	171.7	13.8	278	2 309	394.0	35.8	42	92	11.1	1.3
Lincoln	41 540	272	52	259	66.5	5.5	236	1 545	299.7	25.2	28	58	11.6	1.2
Oxford	37 724	352	36	366	122.2	9.8	280	2 104	320.4	30.6	48	127	16.0	2.4
Penobscot	70 909	638	196	2 786	938.0	85.6	796	9 433	1 654.6	148.0	146	620	66.9	9.5
Piscataquis	7 306	88	11	D	D	D	100	871	120.6	12.3	17	37	2.6	0.5
Sagadahoc	33 651	208	21	111	78.7	1.9	124	1 044	183.5	17.1	27	93	8.1	1.6
Somerset	8 288	114	30	473	120.9	18.9	260	2 234	356.5	35.1	32	124	5.8	1.8
Waldo	23 942	200	29	165	149.2	4.2	165	1 226	192.5	18.2	15	41	3.0	0.4
Washington	18 798	203	50	D	D	D	204	1 712	260.2	23.5	13	38	2.5	0.4
York	238 737	1 599	199	1 479	438.6	41.1	901	7 439	1 265.1	125.1	179	657	62.1	11.1
MARYLAND	3 723 627	29 914	6 283	92 458	54 906.6	3 656.3	19 798	274 260	46 428.2	4 914.0	5 065	39 502	4 764.7	971.3
Allegany	12 840	107	71	D	D	D	385	4 719	663.5	63.5	56	198	23.7	3.4
Anne Arundel	293 569	3 001	653	9 148	8 829.7	366.4	1 863	27 922	4 757.6	487.0	415	3 531	407.1	82.4
Baltimore	333 392	2 599	1 003	12 047	6 707.2	491.6	3 138	49 690	8 243.4	902.7	743	7 047	947.9	182.5
Calvert	120 475	791	29	202	61.7	4.8	190	2 566	404.0	42.7	60	151	19.3	2.7
Caroline	32 859	260	26	325	163.2	9.1	104	901	191.3	13.7	17	36	2.1	0.4
Carroll	142 714	1 065	146	966	292.9	27.8	604	7 366	1 160.6	116.5	121	395	56.1	6.8
Cecil	157 001	1 089	53	D	D	D	284	3 526	613.4	58.2	60	177	20.3	3.0
Charles	187 566	1 244	75	1 088	234.9	27.6	490	7 750	1 243.6	128.0	84	290	31.2	5.7
Dorchester	37 220	287	51	402	121.6	10.7	132	1 476	285.9	27.7	30	97	5.8	1.3
Frederick	225 534	1 837	212	2 783	847.7	94.0	741	10 644	1 839.3	186.8	185	862	88.0	18.2
Garrett	66 622	334	40	303	121.7	5.7	157	1 367	222.9	20.6	20	113	8.5	1.5
Harford	296 516	1 976	198	1 502	1 024.7	47.1	741	10 518	1 755.4	174.6	170	780	74.1	13.8
Howard	210 731	1 479	631	13 185	9 392.3	528.3	766	11 823	2 010.8	216.2	254	1 899	335.2	64.7
Kent	48 418	429	25	162	49.8	3.5	125	908	132.3	13.9	31	65	9.3	0.8
Montgomery	440 212	4 428	971	14 752	8 795.9	778.9	3 000	46 311	8 914.4	957.8	1 123	11 375	1 321.4	305.1
Prince George's	414 651	2 938	759	13 904	9 053.7	542.9	2 425	38 214	6 390.5	675.8	599	5 013	638.5	110.7
Queen Anne's	54 434	318	71	526	209.0	14.3	217	1 833	321.5	28.7	31	62	8.4	1.0
St. Mary's	118 113	1 094	27	D	D	D	278	3 615	553.2	55.4	55	241	27.0	3.6
Somerset	19 726	230	19	D	D	D	73	485	68.0	6.1	10	30	1.6	0.3
Talbot	86 129	522	69	527	243.4	15.5	262	2 621	457.5	47.0	71	179	20.8	3.4

1. Establishments with payroll.

STATE County	Professional, scientific, and technical services,[1] 1997				Manufacturing, 1997				Accommodation and foodservices, 1997			
	Number of establishments	Number of employees	Receipts (mil dol)	Annual payroll (mil dol)	Number of establishments	Number of employees	Receipts (mil dol)	Annual payroll (mil dol)	Number of establishments	Number of employees	Sales (mil dol)	Annual payroll (mil dol)
	147	148	149	150	151	152	153	154	155	156	157	158
LOUISIANA—Cont'd												
Pointe Coupee	23	79	5.4	1.7	11	539	146.1	12.9	26	D	D	D
Rapides	247	1 956	124.2	42.2	73	3 179	1 165.9	103.0	224	3 985	119.8	31.7
Red River	6	17	1.0	0.2	NA	NA	NA	NA	6	D	D	D
Richland	24	85	5.9	1.9	14	600	132.1	16.6	27	296	8.7	2.1
Sabine	24	74	3.6	1.3	19	1 121	253.1	28.8	24	217	7.6	2.2
St. Bernard	69	224	17.9	4.9	54	1 769	2 603.6	83.1	107	1 431	43.0	11.6
St. Charles	63	430	30.1	15.1	37	5 068	8 501.5	302.2	47	701	19.0	5.2
St. Helena	7	D	D	D	NA	NA	NA	NA	5	D	D	D
St. James	14	39	2.7	1.0	26	2 858	3 842.3	149.5	14	203	6.6	1.8
St. John the Baptist	42	194	11.6	3.4	29	2 304	3 057.5	104.2	36	783	21.8	5.7
St. Landry	113	490	35.1	12.3	57	1 919	904.7	50.8	76	1 034	32.2	8.6
St. Martin	42	170	12.3	4.4	44	3 501	1 259.8	69.7	52	D	D	D
St. Mary	94	1 044	139.2	32.8	67	5 098	944.4	163.6	91	1 385	41.3	10.3
St. Tammany	401	1 789	125.4	45.5	127	2 699	373.7	61.3	345	5 415	170.7	44.8
Tangipahoa	133	530	36.2	12.0	74	2 933	420.4	59.5	159	2 898	79.7	21.9
Tensas	9	15	1.6	0.3	NA	NA	NA	NA	8	25	1.6	0.2
Terrebonne	190	1 111	93.2	36.8	119	3 990	539.5	129.3	173	3 133	105.9	31.1
Union	12	29	1.7	0.4	NA	NA	NA	NA	19	D	D	D
Vermilion	64	225	12.1	5.1	27	1 348	203.9	28.6	64	775	22.6	5.5
Vernon	31	599	21.0	12.9	NA	NA	NA	NA	58	782	23.0	5.9
Washington	43	148	11.7	2.8	28	1 536	466.3	54.7	49	626	18.3	4.4
Webster	43	151	8.7	3.3	45	2 336	504.6	67.2	56	637	18.1	4.2
West Baton Rouge	16	79	10.7	2.4	39	2 452	1 376.7	84.0	31	591	18.1	4.5
West Carroll	6	D	D	D	NA	NA	NA	NA	7	D	D	D
West Feliciana	12	25	1.5	0.4	6	D	D	D	18	176	7.1	1.8
Winn	13	22	1.2	0.3	24	1 252	300.0	37.8	20	209	6.2	1.5
MAINE	2 552	13 747	1 215.6	474.8	1 812	82 288	14 097.6	2 591.1	3 714	39 624	1 509.3	428.8
Androscoggin	151	1 672	191.6	54.3	183	8 233	1 218.6	226.6	180	2 438	77.4	23.3
Aroostook	89	342	18.1	7.2	89	3 906	895.0	125.4	162	1 807	50.0	14.8
Cumberland	973	6 408	614.6	253.8	382	14 304	2 232.7	477.2	792	11 749	429.9	121.3
Franklin	36	95	5.0	2.0	53	3 457	867.8	110.3	94	1 328	33.6	11.0
Hancock	111	309	24.2	8.7	94	2 397	551.0	103.8	315	1 741	105.0	28.4
Kennebec	230	926	71.1	26.3	129	5 488	753.4	165.8	257	3 282	109.1	32.0
Knox	74	275	15.0	6.2	92	1 602	267.7	44.3	131	1 306	58.0	17.5
Lincoln	74	D	D	D	68	D	D	D	158	870	49.1	14.4
Oxford	56	149	8.9	3.6	84	4 038	758.5	118.7	140	1 203	44.2	12.2
Penobscot	271	1 388	102.7	45.9	155	8 897	1 658.6	285.9	344	4 778	151.3	45.8
Piscataquis	13	D	D	D	26	1 905	114.7	36.1	50	351	10.8	2.8
Sagadahoc	62	535	42.7	19.4	29	D	D	D	64	743	25.6	7.7
Somerset	58	221	16.6	6.1	76	4 441	1 239.9	143.7	105	778	26.0	6.8
Waldo	40	100	7.4	2.8	53	1 180	117.8	24.8	86	546	23.2	6.2
Washington	34	82	3.7	1.1	41	1 676	364.8	52.6	113	707	22.0	6.3
York	280	973	77.7	30.7	258	11 649	2 093.5	360.2	723	5 997	294.1	78.1
MARYLAND	14 115	146 814	15 940.2	6 483.8	3 996	163 992	36 505.9	5 840.5	9 049	161 273	5 972.5	1 644.7
Allegany	94	515	25.5	13.9	67	4 169	785.9	139.2	165	2 434	75.5	19.8
Anne Arundel	1 321	9 033	1 025.4	366.7	339	14 878	2 703.8	618.4	852	17 645	637.3	175.6
Baltimore	2 132	17 132	1 708.2	682.1	575	31 065	6 883.3	1 235.1	1 359	24 414	842.4	233.5
Calvert	105	516	38.9	17.2	NA	NA	NA	NA	94	1 859	56.9	15.5
Caroline	21	70	2.7	1.0	31	1 533	167.6	36.6	27	255	7.9	1.9
Carroll	289	1 073	67.4	27.5	144	4 330	716.9	131.1	214	3 906	110.3	31.4
Cecil	109	363	27.3	9.7	55	2 766	678.3	100.9	131	2 011	75.2	20.1
Charles	145	993	91.9	33.0	58	1 100	170.3	38.5	186	3 895	125.3	33.5
Dorchester	42	126	7.3	3.1	48	3 580	867.2	86.9	60	765	21.3	6.0
Frederick	449	3 821	296.2	130.2	162	7 795	1 509.1	268.5	304	6 028	193.2	54.5
Garrett	36	151	7.6	3.2	49	1 135	103.5	22.8	73	961	26.7	8.0
Harford	408	2 608	237.5	90.5	152	5 301	1 274.6	178.8	293	5 777	185.9	51.6
Howard	1 050	15 883	1 950.3	772.1	245	6 927	1 177.3	257.2	366	7 078	242.5	68.5
Kent	39	284	13.1	4.3	27	1 031	189.4	25.4	66	585	20.1	5.7
Montgomery	4 314	49 186	5 997.5	2 419.3	527	15 190	3 111.9	680.5	1 407	25 248	1 062.1	298.0
Prince George's	1 364	23 023	2 186.8	967.6	372	11 179	2 008.1	408.5	1 027	20 122	718.4	193.8
Queen Anne's	71	291	20.7	8.5	34	877	106.7	21.8	80	1 482	54.9	15.7
St. Mary's	166	4 226	364.8	177.5	NA	NA	NA	NA	111	2 017	62.6	17.5
Somerset	18	81	4.0	1.8	NA	NA	NA	NA	28	335	10.5	3.0
Talbot	112	604	58.9	27.6	54	3 035	836.1	69.1	96	1 639	69.8	20.0

1. Firms subject to federal tax.

Table B. States and Counties — Health Care and Social Assistance, Other Services, and Federal Funds

STATE County	Health care and social assistance,[1] 1997				Other services,[1] 1997				Federal funds and grants, 2002–2003 Expenditures (mil dol)			
										Direct payments for individuals[2]		
	Number of establishments	Number of employees	Receipts (mil dol)	Annual payroll (mil dol)	Number of establishments	Number of employees	Receipts (mil dol)	Annual payroll (mil dol)	Total	Social Security and government retirement	Medicare	Food stamps and Supplemental Security Income
	159	160	161	162	163	164	165	166	167	168	169	170
LOUISIANA—Cont'd												
Pointe Coupee	20	235	9.0	4.0	20	66	4.9	1.1	133.3	41.0	22.6	9.2
Rapides	335	5 666	306.0	129.1	170	984	55.3	16.7	847.5	304.7	163.1	44.8
Red River	13	294	17.3	6.4	7	32	2.5	0.9	74.6	18.5	13.6	3.3
Richland	52	908	32.1	13.7	20	103	5.4	1.7	158.9	39.3	33.6	9.3
Sabine	21	393	22.5	8.6	25	89	6.8	1.6	151.5	60.4	29.6	7.2
St. Bernard	111	2 263	135.1	53.5	93	459	31.3	9.6	338.0	153.0	108.7	13.8
St. Charles	58	771	39.0	14.3	32	314	40.7	7.6	231.6	77.3	42.1	8.9
St. Helena	7	39	2.4	0.7	2	D	D	D	50.7	11.7	11.6	3.6
St. James	23	289	14.6	6.5	8	91	3.6	1.2	111.5	41.2	28.5	6.8
St. John the Baptist	59	990	57.4	26.7	42	211	9.9	3.0	190.4	69.5	38.5	13.8
St. Landry	163	2 333	130.3	51.2	98	441	26.6	8.0	580.5	164.9	112.4	43.2
St. Martin	34	584	19.4	10.2	30	91	7.0	1.8	216.0	74.9	42.4	13.9
St. Mary	73	809	41.9	19.2	96	479	46.4	10.3	298.9	106.7	60.3	23.1
St. Tammany	444	5 248	345.0	141.4	239	1 263	81.4	21.6	854.6	407.0	167.3	30.3
Tangipahoa	158	1 778	95.5	42.6	121	704	49.7	12.3	583.7	179.5	135.0	45.4
Tensas	8	149	4.8	2.6	3	D	D	D	72.1	11.7	11.5	4.0
Terrebonne	175	2 234	145.0	69.3	172	1 457	132.1	35.6	503.6	199.0	105.5	35.0
Union	20	352	12.6	5.1	14	54	3.1	0.7	132.6	49.2	32.8	5.5
Vermilion	73	805	36.6	12.5	61	384	24.5	9.2	275.7	101.0	59.9	14.1
Vernon	34	531	51.6	14.3	48	196	12.0	3.1	895.2	115.1	40.6	9.1
Washington	72	1 369	62.2	29.3	33	201	9.0	2.5	321.1	104.9	96.6	22.9
Webster	59	1 449	82.0	34.8	41	183	8.8	2.6	265.4	109.3	64.3	14.0
West Baton Rouge	20	439	11.9	6.1	21	151	11.2	3.2	156.9	36.2	24.6	6.5
West Carroll	7	254	7.7	3.7	17	54	2.8	0.7	92.9	25.5	20.6	4.1
West Feliciana	12	137	4.6	2.1	4	24	2.4	0.7	48.1	13.8	8.9	2.0
Winn	24	388	26.3	10.0	14	47	3.2	0.8	96.8	31.8	24.9	5.7
MAINE	2 727	28 944	1 608.4	766.3	1 923	8 820	612.3	169.6	9 965.7	3 259.8	1 114.3	267.0
Androscoggin	221	2 542	149.6	68.4	191	714	46.2	12.9	597.3	248.1	104.0	29.1
Aroostook	140	1 681	78.7	34.0	108	448	32.3	5.6	604.2	215.6	78.9	23.5
Cumberland	764	9 092	602.3	303.5	503	3 458	226.7	71.3	1 713.6	604.7	220.3	41.5
Franklin	51	709	28.8	12.0	37	120	9.8	2.0	155.8	68.1	26.3	6.6
Hancock	79	888	42.5	20.5	75	256	22.8	8.4	371.2	136.8	46.6	6.7
Kennebec	316	2 870	143.3	68.7	170	655	43.2	10.7	1 225.1	338.0	93.4	29.3
Knox	95	747	41.2	18.0	78	324	22.4	6.5	248.0	106.6	39.0	7.4
Lincoln	49	361	20.5	10.2	50	160	11.7	2.9	189.6	100.3	32.3	4.7
Oxford	84	834	38.1	18.2	71	220	15.6	4.0	322.3	142.9	56.5	12.5
Penobscot	310	3 432	209.8	98.2	208	980	82.3	20.4	963.2	356.9	125.6	36.8
Piscataquis	36	310	12.7	5.7	13	47	2.9	0.7	116.2	56.2	18.2	4.2
Sagadahoc	68	589	25.4	11.7	48	176	11.1	2.6	932.6	93.9	20.2	3.7
Somerset	75	1 024	35.6	15.8	68	200	13.2	3.2	307.5	125.8	43.8	15.6
Waldo	49	448	21.3	7.9	43	115	10.1	2.0	299.8	87.0	25.9	9.3
Washington	53	721	23.9	10.4	41	132	10.1	1.9	282.2	99.8	37.5	10.6
York	337	2 696	134.8	63.0	219	815	51.8	14.4	1 172.7	478.9	145.6	25.5
MARYLAND	10 841	116 241	8 060.7	3 538.0	7 871	55 241	3 561.3	1 129.2	57 646.3	12 831.4	5 056.5	732.0
Allegany	170	1 348	98.4	47.9	135	790	39.2	11.7	549.0	217.0	135.7	14.9
Anne Arundel	864	8 875	598.3	264.2	771	5 428	360.2	103.3	4 676.1	1 427.1	397.0	31.9
Baltimore	2 003	25 262	1 700.4	764.7	1 244	8 780	510.4	177.5	4 850.1	1 852.6	902.0	75.5
Calvert	108	971	59.8	29.7	69	397	20.7	6.5	309.8	196.6	45.9	6.0
Caroline	22	154	6.5	2.4	31	143	11.6	3.4	162.8	68.5	31.7	5.2
Carroll	265	2 346	130.7	56.9	271	1 596	86.9	26.7	656.6	354.6	131.5	6.6
Cecil	97	1 047	59.1	27.8	107	495	31.4	9.3	416.1	193.7	70.9	9.2
Charles	209	1 836	101.8	46.6	174	1 111	77.1	22.3	715.4	335.7	72.4	11.2
Dorchester	57	715	35.9	14.7	48	176	9.0	2.4	236.2	78.5	45.0	5.8
Frederick	315	3 258	203.2	96.0	280	1 384	102.0	28.8	1 874.0	421.2	109.4	10.3
Garrett	42	436	21.6	9.7	45	313	17.2	5.1	169.4	68.9	30.7	5.0
Harford	354	3 253	197.9	84.0	322	1 824	96.7	31.8	1 736.0	507.9	156.8	15.4
Howard	486	7 205	525.2	216.7	328	2 830	228.5	66.1	1 080.9	414.0	94.1	11.9
Kent	37	319	17.0	6.4	35	128	7.7	2.1	142.5	68.8	29.0	1.8
Montgomery	2 438	19 961	1 704.3	701.7	1 398	9 308	650.5	221.9	13 341.4	2 098.3	646.0	67.7
Prince George's	1 396	13 111	939.8	408.1	1 025	9 635	647.1	207.1	9 127.7	1 993.9	531.5	89.9
Queen Anne's	42	430	16.7	7.3	58	221	15.2	4.3	192.1	93.0	28.4	1.9
St. Mary's	108	1 289	66.1	30.8	97	526	28.6	8.7	2 181.7	239.3	60.2	9.4
Somerset	19	251	13.0	5.9	16	67	6.8	0.8	148.2	52.3	25.3	4.5
Talbot	97	1 195	76.2	37.2	88	482	26.6	8.5	228.8	117.5	44.0	3.3

1. Firms subject to federal tax.   2. State totals may include programs not allocated by county.

Table B. States and Counties — Federal Funds and Local Government Finances

	Federal funds and grants, 2002–2003 (cont'd)							Local government finances, 2002				
	Expenditures (mil dol) (cont'd)							General revenue				
STATE County	Procurement contract awards			Grants[1]							Taxes	
											Per capita[2] (dollars)	
	Salaries and wages	Defense	Other	Medicaid and other health-related	Nutrition and family welfare	Education	Other	Total (mil dol)	Intergovernmental (mil dol)	Total (mil dol)	Total	Property
	171	172	173	174	175	176	177	178	179	180	181	182
LOUISIANA—Cont'd												
Pointe Coupee	3.4	1.7	0.7	37.4	4.8	1.9	3.1	68.4	29.4	21.3	943	425
Rapides	114.6	10.3	18.2	119.7	20.7	12.9	19.2	309.1	148.8	117.8	928	411
Red River	1.6	8.5	0.3	18.3	1.9	0.9	5.3	24.2	14.9	6.7	700	365
Richland	5.8	0.0	0.9	41.2	4.1	1.9	8.2	72.6	35.0	13.5	653	206
Sabine	3.1	3.1	0.8	35.4	3.7	2.1	5.3	47.8	28.9	14.9	633	272
St. Bernard	7.5	4.5	2.7	23.7	5.4	4.3	6.3	131.6	51.6	60.5	914	300
St. Charles	8.7	11.6	49.8	19.1	5.3	2.8	3.2	222.4	44.0	115.6	2 347	1 439
St. Helena	0.9	0.0	0.3	16.2	2.1	1.0	2.2	20.9	11.2	4.1	398	185
St. James	4.0	0.0	5.4	16.7	4.6	1.8	1.3	87.6	22.7	44.9	2 103	1 306
St. John the Baptist	5.2	0.3	30.7	16.1	6.2	2.5	5.4	110.8	40.5	45.3	1 017	444
St. Landry	11.7	0.5	9.5	177.5	20.6	10.9	8.6	231.5	111.7	50.1	568	185
St. Martin	5.5	3.0	1.8	55.3	5.3	4.6	6.7	91.8	52.2	26.2	527	303
St. Mary	10.6	22.4	2.0	44.8	12.4	6.1	4.9	209.1	84.5	54.8	1 045	488
St. Tammany	47.7	38.8	9.7	46.1	19.5	9.1	28.6	626.8	199.8	226.1	1 122	448
Tangipahoa	19.6	0.4	3.4	126.1	15.8	12.0	16.6	342.1	115.4	72.3	705	191
Tensas	1.0	3.8	0.3	17.7	2.6	1.1	3.0	19.8	13.5	4.7	728	425
Terrebonne	17.4	9.9	3.9	58.9	10.2	9.3	22.9	402.5	136.5	100.8	954	270
Union	5.3	0.0	1.7	27.3	2.4	1.6	5.6	43.4	21.8	11.1	486	144
Vermilion	9.0	2.6	1.7	42.2	5.4	4.0	10.8	130.0	54.5	38.6	713	316
Vernon	412.1	262.2	1.8	30.3	5.9	9.4	5.4	100.7	66.0	25.8	505	169
Washington	7.6	3.4	1.4	65.9	6.5	3.7	3.4	103.4	55.8	29.4	669	250
Webster	6.7	1.7	1.5	49.3	7.2	3.3	6.2	88.4	48.4	30.3	729	258
West Baton Rouge	3.2	57.6	0.6	15.9	2.3	1.4	6.6	65.2	23.1	26.1	1 205	557
West Carroll	2.6	0.0	0.4	24.0	2.0	1.0	3.1	21.6	13.6	6.0	499	177
West Feliciana	1.1	8.3	0.3	9.1	1.8	0.8	1.3	75.0	12.7	22.7	1 497	1 078
Winn	3.9	-0.1	0.7	20.6	2.5	1.6	4.4	30.3	18.6	9.2	560	249
MAINE	888.5	1 175.6	136.1	1 428.7	292.0	181.3	707.8	X	X	X	X	X
Androscoggin	22.7	1.6	4.4	117.2	17.3	6.3	38.2	276.0	110.3	134.3	1 282	1 255
Aroostook	40.9	9.4	11.3	146.7	18.2	5.1	34.9	250.3	92.8	103.6	1 417	1 377
Cumberland	285.9	132.5	34.8	217.8	29.0	12.8	95.4	807.3	189.2	468.7	1 742	1 704
Franklin	5.1	1.8	1.3	25.5	5.1	1.8	10.0	96.6	26.1	53.9	1 816	1 772
Hancock	22.9	3.3	15.6	104.3	7.3	2.7	20.4	133.0	30.4	87.3	1 668	1 623
Kennebec	92.2	10.8	11.3	201.0	95.4	72.9	259.0	292.6	122.1	141.6	1 197	1 168
Knox	11.3	0.0	3.1	53.2	5.3	2.0	17.7	95.9	17.8	69.8	1 725	1 702
Lincoln	7.1	2.5	1.9	27.9	4.1	1.2	6.7	105.5	27.7	70.3	2 043	1 998
Oxford	10.1	9.9	2.7	55.8	11.0	2.1	14.3	147.0	55.9	82.4	1 483	1 457
Penobscot	97.1	20.2	24.3	164.7	24.3	13.1	75.0	376.2	131.2	174.7	1 197	1 136
Piscataquis	3.4	0.0	0.8	22.4	2.9	0.8	4.8	63.8	19.8	20.2	1 174	1 117
Sagadahoc	25.2	752.1	1.5	17.3	4.8	1.2	10.7	100.4	33.7	57.4	1 595	1 570
Somerset	9.3	0.1	10.7	69.1	8.7	2.4	18.6	141.5	59.7	72.2	1 416	1 396
Waldo	7.4	107.8	1.8	41.7	5.8	3.6	5.6	87.4	29.5	51.4	1 367	1 313
Washington	16.6	9.9	2.6	69.0	9.4	3.5	14.8	82.9	35.6	41.7	1 248	1 203
York	231.1	113.9	8.0	95.2	17.8	6.8	43.4	474.9	143.4	284.7	1 457	1 414
MARYLAND	10 331.3	7 171.2	9 044.7	4 437.8	963.9	583.2	2 647.3	X	X	X	X	X
Allegany	39.2	3.9	13.5	69.9	12.5	5.3	26.8	215.5	107.5	64.7	872	555
Anne Arundel	939.1	1 159.6	307.2	174.7	39.9	19.7	161.7	1 444.3	336.7	854.5	1 697	906
Baltimore	1 009.3	304.8	240.2	214.3	35.8	18.6	184.3	2 130.6	586.1	1 216.1	1 579	862
Calvert	14.1	4.0	5.4	21.8	3.7	1.8	9.1	238.0	76.2	120.5	1 490	917
Caroline	5.1	0.6	3.8	29.2	3.1	1.2	6.7	78.0	45.9	23.5	775	438
Carroll	25.7	60.5	7.7	36.4	4.5	2.2	17.3	415.1	136.6	217.2	1 366	815
Cecil	76.7	4.7	15.5	24.3	6.4	2.1	5.8	231.0	92.5	109.5	1 212	744
Charles	160.1	45.3	15.1	38.7	12.2	3.6	15.4	388.8	129.7	185.6	1 438	882
Dorchester	8.8	14.4	16.5	31.8	5.4	1.6	22.5	90.1	44.9	31.8	1 046	675
Frederick	222.1	290.0	515.0	243.2	9.7	3.6	32.5	699.3	212.3	378.5	1 810	1 119
Garrett	4.9	2.5	10.6	22.1	6.5	1.5	11.6	84.9	39.7	32.3	1 083	629
Harford	418.9	507.7	24.2	48.9	11.1	6.0	32.1	600.8	191.0	319.6	1 403	806
Howard	66.4	248.9	114.8	27.6	6.8	6.8	82.9	891.5	190.0	544.6	2 094	1 224
Kent	5.1	5.5	1.7	12.1	1.8	2.6	4.0	51.1	20.2	26.0	1 326	803
Montgomery	3 586.9	1 263.3	4 410.7	667.2	37.3	32.7	499.1	3 785.6	686.7	2 429.2	2 669	1 481
Prince George's	2 229.9	1 033.9	2 299.9	295.4	70.0	46.4	483.5	2 454.0	922.9	1 053.5	1 265	670
Queen Anne's	6.5	13.6	10.3	11.8	2.5	1.1	15.8	142.0	45.0	75.3	1 757	1 023
St. Mary's	561.9	1 239.2	-1.7	38.6	5.9	5.3	18.2	248.0	86.6	125.3	1 392	785
Somerset	5.7	0.4	6.2	28.7	3.1	5.8	8.1	59.6	32.1	15.7	614	389
Talbot	18.1	3.0	7.6	18.1	2.3	1.2	6.0	104.6	19.9	62.3	1 819	1 085

1. State totals may include programs not allocated by county.   2. Based on the resident population estimated as of July 1 of the year shown.

Table B. States and Counties — Local Government Finances, Government Employment, and Elections

STATE County	Local government finances, 2002 (cont'd) Direct general expenditure Total (mil dol)	Per capita¹ (dollars)	Percent of total for — Educa-tion	Health and hospitals	Police protec-tion	Public welfare	High-ways	Debt outstanding Total (mil dol)	Per capita¹ (dollars)	Government employment, 2002 Federal civilian	Federal military	State and local	Presidential election, 2004 Percent of vote cast — Demo-cratic	Republi-can	All other
	183	184	185	186	187	188	189	190	191	192	193	194	195	196	197
LOUISIANA—Cont'd															
Pointe Coupee	65.5	2 901	37.0	15.6	6.4	4.4	2.7	63.3	2 804	68	96	1 241	50.7	48.2	1.2
Rapides	329.5	2 597	53.5	0.3	7.8	0.0	3.7	249.8	1 969	2 078	548	11 691	35.0	63.8	1.2
Red River	27.6	2 882	66.6	0.2	4.6	0.0	1.8	10.8	1 130	32	41	608	45.2	52.9	1.9
Richland	73.3	3 540	38.8	33.3	2.8	0.0	3.8	16.9	818	113	88	1 173	35.6	63.1	1.3
Sabine	49.8	2 112	68.8	0.2	3.4	0.1	6.9	31.7	1 341	49	100	1 214	28.7	70.1	1.3
St. Bernard	122.3	1 847	48.3	0.3	6.0	0.4	4.5	131.7	1 988	118	283	2 977	33.4	65.7	1.0
St. Charles	207.5	4 214	43.6	10.6	5.1	0.4	3.0	517.3	10 504	162	210	3 209	37.3	61.8	0.9
St. Helena	21.7	2 087	43.5	30.7	3.6	0.0	7.5	5.1	492	12	48	719	57.6	40.6	1.8
St. James	78.9	3 697	43.9	8.8	4.7	2.4	2.8	138.9	6 507	69	91	1 449	57.7	40.9	1.4
St. John the Baptist	118.4	2 658	44.2	0.7	5.1	1.3	3.4	186.7	4 193	92	190	1 812	52.8	45.8	1.4
St. Landry	217.9	2 470	45.1	25.1	4.1	0.0	3.0	53.7	608	202	376	5 339	49.4	49.8	0.8
St. Martin	97.2	1 957	60.2	7.7	8.7	0.4	3.6	41.8	842	67	211	2 308	45.2	53.0	1.8
St. Mary	182.9	3 488	38.6	22.8	5.3	0.2	4.2	79.3	1 513	145	318	4 832	42.1	56.7	1.2
St. Tammany	691.5	3 432	36.6	34.3	3.8	0.2	4.6	510.2	2 532	604	860	11 377	24.5	74.7	0.8
Tangipahoa	322.8	3 147	34.7	40.1	4.3	0.1	4.3	139.9	1 364	276	439	10 246	36.4	62.1	1.4
Tensas	24.0	3 692	39.3	2.7	12.2	0.0	2.0	18.6	2 857	20	28	573	49.6	49.1	1.4
Terrebonne	394.8	3 738	32.3	39.2	3.5	0.7	1.8	165.6	1 568	271	478	6 462	33.7	65.0	1.3
Union	43.5	1 912	48.0	18.1	3.7	0.0	6.0	7.6	334	93	97	1 062	28.8	69.6	1.6
Vermilion	132.3	2 444	43.3	22.9	4.9	0.2	5.0	30.0	554	155	244	2 853	37.0	61.4	1.6
Vernon	98.8	1 937	66.7	0.4	4.6	0.2	6.0	23.9	468	2 632	9 075	3 030	26.4	72.1	1.6
Washington	101.6	2 316	52.2	14.2	5.5	0.2	2.2	20.7	471	102	187	3 561	36.7	61.7	1.6
Webster	90.1	2 169	55.9	0.1	6.3	1.3	5.1	47.2	1 136	116	177	1 975	37.0	60.0	3.0
West Baton Rouge	66.1	3 058	38.8	0.5	9.0	0.2	4.6	112.1	5 183	68	92	1 428	45.5	53.7	0.7
West Carroll	20.8	1 721	64.6	4.9	3.5	0.1	6.6	3.8	316	43	52	853	24.5	74.3	1.2
West Feliciana	64.8	4 283	31.0	9.2	2.5	0.1	2.8	475.4	31 401	15	64	2 721	43.3	55.3	1.4
Winn	31.7	1 923	67.3	0.4	5.4	0.3	4.2	15.1	917	70	70	887	31.6	67.1	1.3
MAINE	X	X	X	X	X	X	X	X	X	13 515	9 186	87 447	53.1	45.0	1.9
Androscoggin	249.1	2 377	50.8	0.1	3.9	0.3	6.4	178.3	1 701	342	415	5 326	54.3	43.8	1.9
Aroostook	223.8	3 061	45.5	15.4	1.9	0.3	6.9	69.6	951	732	334	5 375	51.6	46.9	1.5
Cumberland	767.5	2 852	44.2	0.4	3.8	2.5	5.2	629.3	2 339	2 958	4 029	18 305	56.8	41.5	1.7
Franklin	79.3	2 673	52.7	1.1	4.5	0.3	7.3	87.8	2 956	95	116	1 969	55.0	42.6	2.4
Hancock	122.6	2 341	60.0	0.3	2.6	0.2	5.2	63.1	1 204	391	359	3 058	54.4	43.5	2.0
Kennebec	283.2	2 395	62.2	0.7	3.3	0.3	5.1	194.5	1 645	1 651	470	14 825	52.8	45.1	2.1
Knox	89.0	2 198	54.4	0.4	3.2	0.2	7.1	51.8	1 279	121	250	2 700	53.0	42.6	4.4
Lincoln	86.2	2 505	62.7	0.8	3.1	0.2	6.3	25.8	750	101	157	1 603	50.3	47.9	1.8
Oxford	132.1	2 376	69.0	0.3	2.7	0.3	7.9	62.3	1 120	167	218	3 124	52.7	45.1	2.2
Penobscot	374.1	2 562	47.3	5.5	3.7	0.1	3.9	206.3	1 413	1 360	587	12 988	49.4	48.9	1.7
Piscataquis	57.7	3 354	41.4	35.0	2.2	0.1	5.1	18.6	1 084	61	67	1 129	44.3	53.3	2.4
Sagadahoc	93.5	2 599	69.5	0.3	3.9	0.1	4.0	57.0	1 585	346	483	1 697	52.5	45.2	2.2
Somerset	148.4	2 913	75.9	0.5	2.8	0.3	4.2	56.2	1 104	163	199	2 827	49.9	47.9	2.3
Waldo	71.8	1 908	66.3	1.1	3.8	0.3	7.1	36.9	980	114	147	1 666	52.0	46.1	2.0
Washington	70.8	2 120	66.9	0.2	4.0	0.1	6.6	24.5	734	300	177	2 593	48.2	49.9	1.8
York	439.0	2 245	60.5	0.4	5.7	1.4	4.9	262.9	1 345	4 613	1 178	8 262	53.3	45.1	1.7
MARYLAND	X	X	X	X	X	X	X	X	X	154 514	46 257	324 826	55.7	43.3	1.0
Allegany	210.8	2 841	52.0	0.7	3.2	4.5	6.6	131.4	1 771	586	180	5 720	35.1	64.0	1.0
Anne Arundel	1 402.1	2 785	53.5	1.8	5.6	0.6	5.3	1 532.4	3 044	35 716	15 964	27 640	42.9	55.9	1.2
Baltimore	2 026.4	2 631	58.2	1.8	6.6	0.6	2.9	1 244.5	1 616	15 128	1 873	42 062	51.6	47.1	1.3
Calvert	229.3	2 834	56.4	1.2	3.3	2.9	4.2	136.5	1 687	112	241	3 352	40.3	58.8	0.8
Caroline	83.3	2 750	56.2	2.1	3.8	0.1	4.5	40.1	1 323	78	73	1 450	33.3	65.4	1.2
Carroll	375.0	2 358	60.8	1.1	3.1	0.8	4.8	310.1	1 950	311	389	6 809	28.6	70.1	1.3
Cecil	213.3	2 361	66.6	1.6	4.1	0.5	5.1	99.7	1 104	1 399	217	3 456	38.7	60.2	1.1
Charles	366.5	2 840	61.0	1.9	7.5	0.3	3.3	172.6	1 337	2 204	844	5 658	50.7	48.6	0.7
Dorchester	85.8	2 817	50.6	1.2	5.0	2.4	3.8	35.8	1 174	127	82	2 144	40.3	58.8	0.9
Frederick	667.7	3 193	56.2	3.0	5.1	1.9	4.8	485.6	2 322	3 064	1 940	9 792	38.9	60.1	1.0
Garrett	84.2	2 819	60.3	0.8	1.9	0.0	15.1	27.7	927	79	72	1 647	25.7	73.5	0.8
Harford	577.1	2 534	59.3	0.7	5.3	2.3	5.7	315.1	1 384	7 004	3 399	8 953	34.9	63.9	1.2
Howard	890.3	3 423	58.1	0.9	4.8	1.0	3.5	701.7	2 698	682	627	15 303	53.9	44.9	1.2
Kent	49.6	2 529	54.5	1.4	4.5	3.1	7.1	14.0	711	78	48	1 089	46.2	52.8	1.0
Montgomery	3 226.1	3 545	51.6	2.2	5.4	3.3	3.2	3 341.8	3 672	42 815	6 128	42 122	65.7	33.2	1.0
Prince George's	2 376.8	2 853	52.1	2.4	6.5	0.1	2.8	1 915.3	2 299	25 493	8 190	51 783	81.8	17.5	0.7
Queen Anne's	141.9	3 312	61.7	2.0	3.4	1.0	3.8	71.2	1 662	91	103	2 139	32.5	66.5	1.0
St. Mary's	242.3	2 691	63.4	0.9	4.4	0.6	3.5	221.6	2 461	6 696	3 196	4 073	36.1	62.9	1.0
Somerset	56.2	2 198	48.3	1.9	3.6	0.1	3.7	17.4	679	71	93	2 910	44.4	54.8	0.8
Talbot	98.6	2 876	50.2	1.6	5.2	2.0	5.5	66.1	1 930	266	87	1 612	38.5	60.4	1.0

1. Based on the resident population estimated as of July 1 of the year shown.

STATE/ County code	CBSA code[1]	County Type[2]	STATE County	Land area,[3] (sq km) 2000	Population and population characteristics, 2003												
								Race alone or in combination, not Hispanic or Latino (percent)					Age (percent)					
					Total persons	Rank	Per square kilometer	White	Black	Am. Indian, Alaska Native	Asian and Pacific Islander	Percent Hispanic or Latino[4]	Under 5 years	5 to 17 years	18 to 24 years	25 to 34 years	35 to 44 years	45 to 54 years
					1	2	3	4	5	6	7	8	9	10	11	12	13	14	15

STATE/ County code	CBSA code[1]	County Type[2]	STATE County	Land area	Total persons	Rank	Per sq km	White	Black	Am.Ind.	Asian/PI	Hisp	Under 5	5-17	18-24	25-34	35-44	45-54
			MARYLAND—Cont'd															
24 043	25180	3	Washington	1 187	136 796	413	115.2	89.8	8.3	0.4	1.0	1.3	5.9	16.8	9.2	13.6	16.3	13.8
24 045	41540	3	Wicomico	977	87 375	613	89.4	73.2	23.2	0.4	2.0	2.2	6.3	17.5	12.3	14.8	14.8	14.0
24 047	36180	4	Worcester	1 226	49 604	938	40.5	83.4	14.7	0.4	0.7	1.4	5.1	14.8	7.4	10.9	14.6	13.7
24 510	12580	1	Baltimore city	209	628 670	92	3 008.0	31.4	65.2	0.7	2.0	1.8	7.0	17.8	10.7	14.1	15.4	13.8
25 000	...	X	MASSACHUSETTS	20 306	6 433 422	X	316.8	82.1	6.2	0.5	4.9	7.4	6.2	16.9	9.3	13.8	16.3	14.4
25 001	12700	3	Barnstable	1 024	229 545	255	224.2	95.1	2.4	0.9	1.0	1.5	4.4	14.7	7.0	9.9	14.6	14.7
25 003	38340	3	Berkshire	2 412	133 310	424	55.3	94.5	2.6	0.5	1.4	2.0	4.7	16.2	9.8	10.4	14.8	15.4
25 005	39300	1	Bristol	1 440	547 008	106	379.9	90.9	3.4	0.6	2.0	4.3	6.0	17.6	9.3	13.4	16.3	13.9
25 007	...	7	Dukes	269	15 601	2 058	58.0	93.9	3.1	2.2	0.7	1.1	4.8	15.7	7.3	11.5	16.6	18.4
25 009	14460	1	Essex	1 297	737 848	70	568.9	81.6	2.8	0.4	3.1	13.2	6.8	18.1	8.3	12.3	16.8	14.8
25 011	44140	2	Franklin	1 818	72 204	703	39.7	95.6	1.3	0.8	1.3	2.1	4.9	16.7	9.1	11.7	15.6	17.6
25 013	44140	2	Hampden	1 602	461 190	133	287.9	73.8	8.4	0.5	1.7	16.6	6.2	18.7	10.1	12.1	15.2	13.9
25 015	44140	2	Hampshire	1 370	155 101	357	113.2	90.5	2.5	0.6	4.1	3.6	4.2	13.9	19.1	11.7	14.2	14.9
25 017	14460	1	Middlesex	2 133	1 471 724	21	690.0	83.7	4.0	0.4	8.2	4.8	6.2	16.2	8.6	15.2	17.3	14.5
25 019	...	7	Nantucket	124	10 724	2 383	86.5	86.9	8.9	0.1	0.9	3.5	6.3	13.4	7.2	18.5	19.6	15.0
25 021	14460	1	Norfolk	1 035	654 331	85	632.2	87.0	4.2	0.4	7.2	2.1	6.2	16.9	7.3	13.2	17.2	15.1
25 023	14460	1	Plymouth	1 712	487 521	122	284.8	88.9	7.4	0.6	1.4	2.7	6.6	19.0	8.5	12.0	17.0	15.1
25 025	14460	1	Suffolk	152	680 705	78	4 478.3	53.1	22.9	0.6	8.2	16.5	6.5	14.2	12.3	21.1	15.6	11.6
25 027	49340	2	Worcester	3 919	776 610	65	198.2	86.1	3.3	0.5	3.7	7.3	6.4	18.3	9.2	13.0	16.9	14.3
26 000	...	X	MICHIGAN	147 121	10 079 985	X	68.5	79.5	14.8	1.1	2.5	3.5	6.4	18.8	9.8	13.0	15.3	14.7
26 001	...	9	Alcona	1 747	11 572	2 329	6.6	98.0	0.4	1.0	0.2	0.8	3.3	13.9	7.2	7.4	12.6	14.1
26 003	...	9	Alger	2 377	9 767	2 463	4.1	89.4	6.2	4.4	0.4	1.2	3.9	14.8	9.5	12.0	15.4	16.1
26 005	10880	4	Allegan	2 143	110 331	501	51.5	91.6	1.5	0.9	0.8	5.9	6.5	20.3	9.8	12.2	16.2	14.4
26 007	10980	7	Alpena	1 487	30 781	1 389	20.7	98.2	0.5	0.7	0.5	0.6	5.3	16.8	9.6	9.6	15.3	15.2
26 009	...	9	Antrim	1 235	24 094	1 614	19.5	97.1	0.6	1.5	0.3	1.4	4.7	17.5	8.8	10.6	14.2	13.9
26 011	...	8	Arenac	950	17 309	1 943	18.2	95.5	1.9	1.5	0.3	1.5	4.8	16.5	9.7	10.7	15.2	14.1
26 013	...	9	Baraga	2 341	8 782	2 543	3.8	81.4	5.9	14.2	0.4	0.9	5.4	16.1	8.8	12.7	14.9	15.0
26 015	24340	2	Barry	1 440	58 774	836	40.8	97.2	0.5	1.1	0.5	1.7	6.0	19.3	9.4	11.5	15.8	15.0
26 017	13020	3	Bay	1 151	109 452	504	95.1	93.7	1.8	1.0	0.6	4.0	5.9	17.6	9.1	11.4	15.3	15.4
26 019	45900	9	Benzie	832	17 078	1 951	20.5	96.5	0.6	2.2	0.2	1.4	5.3	16.7	8.4	11.0	14.8	14.2
26 021	35660	3	Berrien	1 479	162 766	342	110.1	79.0	16.4	0.9	1.7	3.4	6.4	18.6	9.5	11.4	14.7	14.6
26 023	17740	3	Branch	1 314	46 414	990	35.3	92.8	1.1	0.9	0.7	3.4	6.0	17.8	9.7	13.1	16.2	14.1
26 025	12980	3	Calhoun	1 836	138 854	406	75.6	83.9	11.8	1.4	1.5	3.3	6.5	18.7	9.9	12.3	14.7	14.5
26 027	43780	2	Cass	1 275	51 385	916	40.3	90.3	6.8	1.8	0.6	2.4	5.4	18.4	9.2	10.9	15.2	15.6
26 029	...	7	Charlevoix	1 080	26 712	1 516	24.7	96.5	0.6	2.4	0.4	1.2	5.7	18.5	8.3	10.6	14.9	14.8
26 031	...	7	Cheboygan	1 853	27 405	1 488	14.8	96.2	0.6	3.7	0.3	0.9	5.2	16.8	8.5	11.1	13.8	14.1
26 033	42300	5	Chippewa	4 043	38 822	1 166	9.6	79.3	5.9	16.1	0.7	1.7	4.8	14.9	12.7	14.5	16.5	14.0
26 035	...	7	Clare	1 468	31 589	1 369	21.5	97.6	0.5	1.3	0.2	1.1	5.4	17.6	8.9	10.9	13.7	13.7
26 037	29620	7	Clinton	1 480	67 609	743	45.7	95.4	1.4	0.8	0.8	2.6	5.7	19.9	9.6	11.2	16.1	15.4
26 039	...	7	Crawford	1 446	14 808	2 115	10.2	96.0	1.8	1.1	0.5	1.1	4.6	17.5	9.2	10.7	14.9	14.2
26 041	21540	5	Delta	3 030	38 317	1 176	12.6	96.8	0.3	3.2	0.4	0.5	5.4	16.7	9.7	9.9	14.5	16.0
26 043	27020	2	Dickinson	1 985	27 186	1 498	13.7	98.2	0.2	0.8	0.7	0.7	4.9	18.2	8.6	9.8	15.6	15.6
26 045	29620	2	Eaton	1 493	106 197	513	71.1	88.8	6.4	1.0	1.6	3.5	5.9	18.5	10.2	12.4	15.1	15.7
26 047	...	7	Emmet	1 212	32 741	1 342	27.0	95.2	0.4	3.8	0.7	0.9	5.6	17.8	8.9	11.6	15.0	16.1
26 049	22420	2	Genesee	1 657	442 250	142	266.9	75.9	21.1	1.4	1.2	2.4	6.9	19.8	9.4	13.0	15.2	14.3
26 051	...	6	Gladwin	1 313	26 939	1 505	20.5	97.9	0.4	1.1	0.3	1.1	5.3	16.7	8.7	10.2	13.2	13.6
26 053	...	7	Gogebic	2 854	17 329	1 941	6.1	92.4	4.1	2.8	0.4	1.2	3.6	14.2	11.3	11.1	13.8	13.9
26 055	45900	5	Grand Traverse	1 205	82 011	645	68.1	96.2	0.9	1.4	0.7	1.7	5.6	17.6	9.7	12.3	15.9	15.6
26 057	10940	6	Gratiot	1 477	42 501	1 069	28.8	90.7	4.2	1.0	0.6	4.3	5.6	16.9	12.3	13.2	15.4	13.4
26 059	...	6	Hillsdale	1 551	47 230	976	30.5	97.5	0.6	0.9	0.5	1.3	6.3	18.5	11.3	11.1	14.4	14.2
26 061	26340	5	Houghton	2 620	36 249	1 231	13.8	96.1	1.1	0.9	1.8	0.7	5.3	15.3	18.3	11.0	11.8	12.6
26 063	...	7	Huron	2 167	35 216	1 265	16.3	97.5	0.4	0.6	0.5	1.6	4.9	17.3	8.5	9.6	14.3	14.7
26 065	29620	2	Ingham	1 448	282 030	208	194.8	78.1	12.3	1.2	4.9	6.0	6.4	16.7	16.0	14.8	13.6	13.4
26 067	24340	2	Ionia	1 485	63 573	778	42.8	91.4	5.3	1.2	0.6	2.7	6.2	18.9	13.1	14.1	15.7	13.5
26 069	...	7	Iosco	1 422	26 888	1 508	18.9	97.6	0.7	1.3	0.5	0.9	4.6	16.0	7.7	8.4	13.7	13.8
26 071	...	7	Iron	3 021	12 787	2 256	4.2	97.2	1.2	1.4	0.3	0.7	3.7	14.7	8.6	8.0	13.4	15.3
26 073	34380	5	Isabella	1 487	64 663	769	43.5	91.4	2.3	3.2	2.0	2.3	5.3	14.1	24.6	13.7	11.7	11.2
26 075	27100	3	Jackson	1 830	162 321	343	88.8	88.8	8.6	1.0	0.8	2.4	6.1	18.6	9.3	12.9	16.0	14.6
26 077	28020	2	Kalamazoo	1 455	242 110	246	166.4	84.7	10.9	1.1	2.6	2.8	6.4	17.3	13.6	14.0	13.8	13.8
26 079	45900	7	Kalkaska	1 453	17 177	1 948	11.8	97.7	0.5	1.4	0.3	1.0	6.2	18.3	8.9	11.5	15.9	14.1
26 081	24340	2	Kent	2 217	590 417	96	266.3	80.2	9.9	0.9	2.5	8.1	7.7	19.9	10.4	14.4	15.6	13.5
26 083	26340	9	Keweenaw	1 401	2 227	3 039	1.6	97.3	2.0	0.2	0.1	0.6	4.5	15.1	7.4	7.5	13.5	17.4
26 085	...	8	Lake	1 470	11 795	2 305	8.0	85.6	12.1	1.6	0.2	1.8	4.5	16.1	10.6	9.4	12.9	13.1
26 087	19820	1	Lapeer	1 694	91 314	590	53.9	94.9	1.0	0.8	0.6	3.4	5.7	19.9	9.7	11.7	17.3	15.6

1. CBSA = Core Based Statistical Area. See Appendix A for explanation. See Appendix B for list of metropolitan areas with component counties. Service of USDA Rural-Urban Continuum Codes. See Appendix A for definition. 3. Dry land or land partially or temporarily covered by water. 2. County type code from the Economic Research 4. Hispanic or Latino persons may be of any race.

Table B. States and Counties — **Population and Households**

STATE County	55 to 64 years	65 to 74 years	75 years and over	Percent female	1990	2000	1990–2000	2000–2003	Births	Deaths	Net migration	Number	Percent change, 1990–2000	Persons per house-hold	Female family house-holder[1]	One person
	16	17	18	19	20	21	22	23	24	25	26	27	28	29	30	31
MARYLAND—Cont'd																
Washington	9.5	7.0	6.9	48.9	121 393	131 923	8.7	3.7	5 149	4 220	3 986	49 726	11.1	2.46	10.7	26.0
Wicomico	9.4	6.6	6.0	52.3	74 339	84 644	13.9	3.2	3 741	2 641	1 721	32 218	16.0	2.53	14.1	24.8
Worcester	12.3	11.5	8.6	51.4	35 028	46 543	32.9	6.6	1 669	1 918	3 263	19 694	39.3	2.33	10.8	26.3
Baltimore city	8.9	6.5	6.5	53.4	736 014	651 154	-11.5	-3.5	31 153	26 836	-33 249	257 996	-6.7	2.42	25.0	34.9
MASSACHUSETTS	9.8	6.3	7.0	51.7	6 016 425	6 349 097	5.5	1.3	265 871	185 556	5 832	2 443 580	8.7	2.51	11.9	28.0
Barnstable	11.6	11.0	11.7	52.6	186 605	222 230	19.1	3.3	6 517	9 116	9 808	94 822	22.2	2.28	9.4	29.5
Berkshire	10.9	8.3	9.5	52.0	139 352	134 953	-3.2	-1.2	3 956	5 157	-329	56 006	3.1	2.30	11.0	31.6
Bristol	9.4	6.4	7.3	51.8	506 325	534 678	5.6	2.3	21 482	16 987	8 217	205 411	9.5	2.54	13.0	26.5
Dukes	10.7	7.0	7.2	50.8	11 639	14 987	28.8	4.1	434	397	582	6 421	28.3	2.30	9.8	32.0
Essex	9.5	6.5	7.1	51.9	670 080	723 419	8.0	2.0	33 668	21 370	2 712	275 419	9.6	2.57	12.4	27.1
Franklin	10.1	6.3	7.7	51.4	70 086	71 535	2.1	0.9	2 241	2 093	600	29 466	6.6	2.38	10.6	29.0
Hampden	9.2	6.5	7.7	51.9	456 310	456 228	0.0	1.1	18 641	14 897	1 619	175 288	3.2	2.52	15.9	28.4
Hampshire	8.7	5.4	6.4	53.3	146 568	152 251	3.9	1.9	4 093	3 814	2 658	55 991	11.9	2.39	9.8	28.6
Middlesex	9.5	6.3	6.4	51.3	1 398 468	1 465 396	4.8	0.4	60 821	38 426	-17 147	561 220	8.0	2.52	9.9	27.1
Nantucket	8.8	5.1	4.6	48.7	6 012	9 520	58.3	12.6	443	202	945	3 699	42.4	2.37	8.0	29.8
Norfolk	10.0	6.9	7.3	52.1	616 087	650 308	5.6	0.6	26 543	18 935	-3 211	248 827	9.2	2.54	9.5	26.8
Plymouth	10.0	5.9	5.7	51.2	435 276	472 822	8.6	3.1	20 839	13 424	7 747	168 361	12.6	2.74	11.9	22.2
Suffolk	7.8	5.4	5.6	51.7	663 906	689 807	3.9	-1.3	33 243	18 385	-25 019	278 722	5.6	2.34	16.3	36.3
Worcester	8.8	5.8	6.7	51.1	709 711	750 963	5.8	3.4	32 950	22 353	16 650	283 927	9.1	2.56	11.4	26.2
MICHIGAN	9.8	6.2	6.1	50.9	9 295 287	9 938 444	6.9	1.4	428 261	285 979	3 918	3 785 661	10.7	2.56	12.5	26.2
Alcona	16.5	14.1	11.3	49.5	10 145	11 719	15.5	-1.3	206	527	186	5 132	20.4	2.24	5.8	26.6
Alger	11.2	8.8	8.9	46.1	8 972	9 862	9.9	-1.0	259	411	73	3 785	13.4	2.35	7.6	26.8
Allegan	8.8	5.6	5.3	50.1	90 509	105 665	16.7	4.4	4 575	2 828	2 964	38 165	20.4	2.72	9.1	20.7
Alpena	11.2	8.9	8.5	51.5	30 605	31 314	2.3	-1.7	1 077	1 119	-449	12 818	8.3	2.40	9.0	27.8
Antrim	12.0	9.7	7.7	50.2	18 185	23 110	27.1	4.3	685	807	1 087	9 222	32.1	2.47	7.9	23.4
Arenac	12.0	9.8	7.2	48.7	14 906	17 269	15.9	0.2	521	645	180	6 710	18.9	2.45	9.0	25.5
Baraga	10.9	7.3	8.9	46.7	7 954	8 746	10.0	0.4	321	353	76	3 353	9.4	2.37	10.1	29.5
Barry	10.4	6.5	5.3	50.1	50 057	56 755	13.4	3.6	2 243	1 523	1 317	21 035	18.4	2.68	7.7	19.5
Bay	10.5	7.1	7.7	51.3	111 723	110 157	-1.4	-0.6	4 222	3 584	-1 261	43 930	4.1	2.47	10.9	27.2
Benzie	11.1	9.5	7.9	50.3	12 200	15 998	31.1	6.8	585	552	1 025	6 500	36.2	2.42	7.7	24.1
Berrien	10.2	7.2	7.2	51.4	161 378	162 453	0.7	0.2	7 022	5 285	-1 342	63 569	4.2	2.49	13.2	27.1
Branch	9.9	6.9	6.3	49.3	41 502	45 787	10.3	1.4	1 839	1 323	141	16 349	9.6	2.61	9.9	24.2
Calhoun	9.7	7.0	6.7	51.3	135 982	137 985	1.5	0.6	6 028	4 914	-107	54 100	4.4	2.47	13.0	27.8
Cass	11.5	7.5	6.3	50.1	49 477	51 104	3.3	0.5	1 687	1 520	176	19 676	7.9	2.56	9.9	22.6
Charlevoix	11.3	8.1	7.1	50.6	21 468	26 090	21.5	2.4	986	782	436	10 400	26.2	2.48	8.1	25.2
Cheboygan	12.3	9.6	8.2	50.3	21 398	26 448	23.6	3.6	910	940	970	10 835	32.1	2.41	8.6	25.8
Chippewa	9.2	6.9	5.9	44.4	34 604	38 543	11.4	0.7	1 280	1 044	81	13 474	16.7	2.42	10.7	27.5
Clare	12.5	10.3	7.4	50.7	24 952	31 252	25.2	1.1	1 109	1 153	403	12 686	30.8	2.42	9.4	26.2
Clinton	10.1	5.9	5.0	50.2	57 893	64 753	11.8	4.4	2 400	1 452	1 903	23 653	17.0	2.70	8.4	19.8
Crawford	11.6	9.5	7.1	49.1	12 260	14 273	16.4	3.7	425	503	602	5 625	26.7	2.45	9.7	24.0
Delta	10.7	8.6	8.6	50.8	37 780	38 520	2.0	-0.5	1 393	1 388	-171	15 836	9.0	2.40	8.3	28.0
Dickinson	9.8	7.7	10.1	51.0	26 831	27 472	2.4	-1.0	875	1 045	-95	11 386	7.1	2.37	8.4	29.4
Eaton	10.1	6.0	5.5	51.2	92 879	103 655	11.6	2.5	4 079	2 599	1 175	40 167	18.0	2.54	10.3	24.5
Emmet	9.9	7.4	7.0	51.1	25 040	31 437	25.5	4.1	1 143	940	1 114	12 557	32.2	2.44	8.5	26.9
Genesee	9.3	6.5	5.3	51.9	430 459	436 141	1.3	1.4	20 460	12 979	-836	169 825	5.3	2.54	16.3	26.6
Gladwin	13.5	10.9	7.6	50.3	21 896	26 023	18.8	3.5	926	1 021	997	10 561	26.4	2.43	8.0	24.0
Gogebic	10.6	9.5	12.7	47.9	18 052	17 370	-3.8	-0.2	409	799	338	7 425	-0.3	2.20	9.3	34.2
Grand Traverse	9.3	6.5	6.6	50.7	64 273	77 654	20.8	5.6	3 004	2 058	3 389	30 396	26.8	2.49	9.2	25.0
Gratiot	9.3	6.4	7.1	47.8	38 982	42 285	8.5	0.5	1 545	1 342	54	14 501	6.2	2.57	10.2	23.7
Hillsdale	10.4	7.2	6.2	50.3	43 431	46 527	7.1	1.5	1 953	1 527	322	17 335	10.9	2.60	8.4	22.9
Houghton	9.3	6.6	8.3	46.7	35 446	36 016	1.6	0.6	1 264	1 283	274	13 793	4.7	2.39	8.0	32.6
Huron	11.3	9.7	10.1	50.6	34 951	36 079	3.2	-2.4	1 125	1 486	-475	14 597	10.0	2.42	7.4	27.3
Ingham	7.9	4.8	4.7	51.6	281 912	279 320	-0.9	1.0	11 835	6 049	-3 152	108 593	5.8	2.42	12.1	30.2
Ionia	8.3	5.2	4.6	46.1	57 024	61 518	7.9	3.3	2 594	1 534	1 028	20 606	11.7	2.70	10.1	21.9
Iosco	13.7	12.6	10.0	51.0	30 209	27 339	-9.5	-1.6	817	1 190	-50	11 727	1.2	2.30	8.4	28.6
Iron	11.4	10.7	14.4	50.7	13 175	13 138	-0.3	-2.7	285	615	-12	5 748	1.6	2.19	8.4	33.7
Isabella	7.0	4.7	4.4	52.2	54 624	63 351	16.0	2.1	2 270	1 364	486	22 425	27.5	2.55	8.9	23.8
Jackson	9.4	6.3	6.3	48.9	149 756	158 422	5.8	2.5	6 524	4 684	2 170	58 168	8.4	2.55	12.0	24.6
Kalamazoo	8.5	5.6	5.7	51.5	223 411	238 603	6.8	1.5	10 141	6 363	-75	93 479	11.7	2.43	11.0	28.0
Kalkaska	10.9	7.9	5.8	49.6	13 497	16 571	22.8	3.7	711	508	409	6 428	30.3	2.55	9.0	22.3
Kent	7.7	5.0	5.2	50.6	500 631	574 335	14.7	2.8	30 000	13 277	-271	212 890	17.1	2.64	11.6	25.6
Keweenaw	13.9	11.5	9.6	48.0	1 701	2 301	35.3	-3.2	70	84	-56	998	28.4	2.13	5.7	35.8
Lake	13.1	11.4	8.0	47.6	8 583	11 333	32.0	4.1	312	516	650	4 704	33.0	2.28	8.7	29.6
Lapeer	9.8	5.5	4.3	49.3	74 768	87 904	17.6	3.9	3 404	1 886	1 931	30 729	24.6	2.80	8.1	18.5

1. No spouse present.

STATE County	Births, average 1999–2001 Total	Rate[1]	Deaths, average 1999–2001 Number Total	Infant[2]	Rate Total[1]	Infant[3]	Physicians,[4] 2000 Number	Rate[5]	Hospitals,[4] 1998 Number	Beds Number	Rate[5]	Medicare enrollees, 2003	Serious crimes known to police,[6] 2002 Total Number	Rate[7]
	32	33	34	35	36	37	38	39	40	41	42	43	44	45
MARYLAND—Cont'd														
Washington	1 615	12.2	1 278	8	9.7	4.7	254	193	1	320	251	21 145	3 600	2 648
Wicomico	1 151	13.6	802	13	9.5	11.3	218	258	1	400	504	12 492	4 396	5 040
Worcester	518	11.1	550	4	11.8	D	52	112	1	32	75	10 812	2 699	5 627
Baltimore city	10 108	15.5	8 626	125	13.2	12.4	4 044	621	12	4 945	766	95 297	57 270	8 535
MASSACHUSETTS	81 210	12.8	56 425	399	8.9	4.9	20 757	327	90	20 369	331	965 943	198 890	3 094
Barnstable	2 019	9.1	2 738	11	12.3	5.4	453	204	2	385	185	57 608	6 117	2 761
Berkshire	1 237	9.2	1 592	3	11.8	D	327	242	4	595	447	26 737	2 845	2 156
Bristol	6 644	12.4	5 094	41	9.5	6.1	704	132	5	1 232	238	88 786	17 159	3 204
Dukes	151	10.1	125	0	8.3	D	33	220	1	80	576	2 557	380	2 563
Essex	9 668	13.3	6 509	47	9.0	4.9	1 314	182	9	2 044	292	111 346	19 966	2 805
Franklin	711	9.9	671	2	9.4	D	106	148	1	128	181	11 634	1 553	2 477
Hampden	5 824	12.8	4 684	31	10.3	5.3	1 120	245	7	1 746	397	76 370	26 313	5 758
Hampshire	1 282	8.4	1 208	5	7.9	D	333	219	2	227	152	20 873	3 756	2 480
Middlesex	19 075	13.0	11 691	80	8.0	4.2	4 526	309	21	4 066	286	205 867	29 820	2 095
Nantucket	133	13.9	66	3	6.9	D	12	126	1	39	497	1 165	612	6 350
Norfolk	8 391	12.9	5 784	24	8.9	2.9	2 413	371	6	1 317	205	97 928	11 495	1 783
Plymouth	6 465	13.6	3 961	34	8.4	5.3	645	136	4	741	158	66 366	10 791	2 526
Suffolk	9 605	13.9	5 536	63	8.0	6.6	6 743	978	15	5 521	860	86 349	42 410	6 073
Worcester	10 006	13.3	6 766	55	9.0	5.5	2 028	270	12	2 248	307	112 188	19 590	2 688
MICHIGAN	134 402	13.5	86 870	1 088	8.7	8.1	21 114	212	167	31 719	323	1 444 987	389 366	3 874
Alcona	76	6.5	168	0	14.4	D	6	51	0	0	0	3 240	205	1 730
Alger	86	8.7	116	0	11.7	D	8	81	1	40	405	2 052	170	1 705
Allegan	1 470	13.9	842	10	7.9	7.0	121	115	2	106	104	12 422	2 077	1 955
Alpena	339	10.8	353	3	11.3	D	59	188	1	169	556	6 803	844	2 665
Antrim	240	10.4	239	2	10.4	D	16	69	0	0	0	4 573	462	1 977
Arenac	172	10.0	189	1	11.0	D	16	93	1	81	494	3 891	327	1 872
Baraga	97	11.1	112	0	12.8	D	8	91	1	61	725	1 692	NA	NA
Barry	728	12.8	467	5	8.2	D	41	72	1	91	167	7 011	1 133	2 103
Bay	1 308	11.9	1 086	7	9.9	5.4	143	130	1	341	310	18 613	3 487	3 130
Benzie	185	11.6	164	1	10.2	D	16	100	1	48	327	3 347	533	3 295
Berrien	2 182	13.4	1 639	22	10.1	10.1	268	165	4	733	457	29 034	6 883	4 190
Branch	580	12.7	395	5	8.6	D	42	92	1	130	298	6 892	1 302	2 812
Calhoun	1 873	13.6	1 461	19	10.6	10.1	211	153	4	527	374	22 972	8 601	6 164
Cass	560	11.0	474	3	9.3	D	14	27	1	57	115	7 217	1 589	3 601
Charlevoix	314	12.0	233	2	8.9	D	38	146	1	40	164	4 732	334	1 266
Cheboygan	277	10.5	285	2	10.8	D	38	144	1	129	543	5 001	574	2 146
Chippewa	398	10.3	315	2	8.2	D	37	96	1	137	361	6 052	678	1 739
Clare	348	11.2	372	3	12.0	D	30	96	1	64	216	7 258	1 285	4 066
Clinton	767	11.8	457	4	7.1	D	31	48	1	48	76	6 660	881	1 345
Crawford	144	10.0	153	2	10.7	D	26	182	1	130	919	2 493	377	2 612
Delta	433	11.2	413	4	10.7	D	56	145	1	66	169	7 946	NA	NA
Dickinson	277	10.1	314	1	11.4	D	66	240	2	126	465	5 483	638	2 297
Eaton	1 248	12.0	788	3	7.6	D	72	69	2	81	80	10 895	2 937	2 889
Emmet	377	12.0	292	3	9.3	D	131	417	1	249	868	5 530	818	2 573
Genesee	6 409	14.7	3 910	73	9.0	11.4	853	196	5	1 779	408	65 570	21 597	4 901
Gladwin	302	11.6	302	3	11.6	D	13	50	1	42	166	6 073	500	1 900
Gogebic	139	7.9	255	1	14.6	D	25	144	1	53	310	4 496	266	1 612
Grand Traverse	954	12.2	613	7	7.8	7.0	279	359	1	328	442	14 003	2 309	2 940
Gratiot	508	12.2	419	3	10.1	D	57	135	1	100	249	6 641	898	2 100
Hillsdale	627	13.5	442	5	9.5	D	47	101	1	68	146	7 271	1 170	2 487
Houghton	400	11.1	418	2	11.6	D	43	119	2	122	342	6 126	636	1 746
Huron	370	10.3	457	3	12.7	D	50	139	3	207	586	7 888	738	2 222
Ingham	3 720	13.3	1 879	25	6.7	6.8	900	322	4	1 503	527	37 833	12 406	4 392
Ionia	825	13.4	457	6	7.4	D	38	62	1	77	125	7 379	1 631	2 622
Iosco	260	9.5	350	2	12.8	D	25	91	1	69	275	7 211	812	2 937
Iron	93	7.1	210	1	16.1	D	13	99	2	71	551	3 577	306	2 303
Isabella	704	11.1	387	7	6.1	9.5	67	106	1	118	203	6 595	2 199	3 432
Jackson	2 048	12.9	1 428	21	9.0	10.4	220	139	2	507	325	24 460	5 750	3 754
Kalamazoo	3 163	13.3	1 915	26	8.0	8.2	758	318	2	817	356	31 996	12 683	5 349
Kalkaska	226	13.6	153	1	9.2	D	6	36	1	81	520	2 390	517	3 085
Kent	9 433	16.4	4 067	76	7.1	8.0	1 318	229	4	1 405	258	71 228	23 805	4 099
Keweenaw	22	9.5	25	0	11.0	D	4	174	0	0	0	504	52	2 235
Lake	114	10.1	151	1	13.4	D	3	26	0	0	0	2 650	459	4 005
Lapeer	1 088	12.3	598	6	6.8	D	81	92	1	182	206	9 920	1 875	2 109

1. Per 1,000 estimated resident population.   2. Deaths of infants under 1 year old.   3. Deaths of infants under 1 year old per 1,000 live births.   4. Data subject to copyright.   5. Per 100,000 resident population as of July 1 of the year shown.   6. Data for serious crimes have not been adjusted for underreporting; this may affect comparability between geographic areas and over time.   7. Per 100,000 population estimated by the FBI.

Table B. States and Counties — Crime, Education, Money Income, and Poverty

STATE County	Violent	Property	Total	Percent private	High school graduate or less	Bachelor's degree or more	Total current expenditures (mil dol)	Current expenditures per student (dollars)	Per capita income[6] (dollars)	Dollars	Percent change, 1989–1999 (constant 1999 dollars)	Percent with income of $100,000 or more	Persons	Households	Families	Families with children
	46	47	48	49	50	51	52	53	54	55	56	57	58	59	60	61
MARYLAND—Cont'd																
Washington	348	2 300	29 792	13.6	61.1	14.6	139.8	7 068	20 062	40 617	2.0	7.5	9.5	9.7	7.0	10.5
Wicomico	903	4 136	24 554	11.7	53.7	21.9	108.7	7 692	19 171	39 035	1.9	8.4	12.8	12.0	8.7	13.3
Worcester	995	4 633	9 832	10.5	52.5	21.6	58.4	8 477	22 505	40 650	9.7	8.8	9.6	9.1	7.2	13.6
Baltimore city	2 072	6 463	184 513	23.1	59.8	19.1	879.8	8 810	16 978	30 078	-6.9	6.3	22.9	21.8	18.8	26.2
MASSACHUSETTS	484	2 610	1 726 111	26.0	42.5	33.2	9 125.0	9 346	25 952	50 502	1.7	17.7	9.3	9.8	6.7	10.1
Barnstable	418	2 344	47 762	14.8	35.4	33.6	286.9	9 102	25 318	45 933	7.6	12.4	6.9	7.0	4.6	8.1
Berkshire	359	1 797	34 081	18.8	49.1	26.0	205.6	9 940	21 807	39 047	-4.6	9.7	9.5	10.2	6.5	11.6
Bristol	521	2 683	137 870	17.8	56.4	19.9	786.8	8 485	20 978	43 496	2.7	11.0	10.0	11.3	7.8	11.5
Dukes	378	2 185	3 307	10.6	32.8	38.4	32.9	13 465	26 472	45 559	6.0	13.0	7.3	7.2	5.0	8.5
Essex	398	2 407	194 443	21.4	43.5	31.3	1 046.1	8 941	26 358	51 576	1.3	19.0	8.9	9.5	6.6	10.1
Franklin	640	1 838	18 575	12.1	43.3	29.1	115.3	10 243	20 672	40 768	0.0	8.0	9.4	10.4	6.5	10.5
Hampden	1 022	4 736	127 601	18.1	53.4	20.5	736.6	9 596	19 541	39 718	-4.9	8.8	14.7	14.1	11.4	18.7
Hampshire	374	2 107	55 111	22.4	36.4	37.9	190.6	9 230	21 685	46 098	0.5	12.4	9.4	9.7	5.1	7.7
Middlesex	221	1 873	391 638	32.1	34.9	43.6	2 107.8	10 131	31 199	60 821	3.2	24.9	6.5	7.0	4.3	6.3
Nantucket	643	5 707	1 800	23.7	36.1	38.4	17.4	14 448	31 314	55 522	2.5	22.6	7.5	5.3	3.0	2.0
Norfolk	203	1 580	169 601	30.4	33.0	42.9	880.3	9 079	32 484	63 432	2.2	26.3	4.6	5.3	3.0	4.1
Plymouth	449	2 077	128 952	16.8	43.1	27.8	670.9	8 432	24 789	55 615	1.2	18.8	6.6	5.5	2.9	4.1
Suffolk	1 251	4 822	209 914	42.3	47.6	32.5	926.5	12 057	22 766	39 355	-0.4	12.4	19.0	18.4	14.9	21.6
Worcester	453	2 235	205 456	21.3	46.7	26.9	1 121.4	8 610	22 983	47 874	-0.4	14.8	9.2	9.6	6.8	9.9
MICHIGAN	540	3 334	2 780 378	13.8	47.9	21.8	13 995.5	8 208	22 168	44 667	7.2	12.7	10.5	10.1	7.4	11.3
Alcona	93	1 637	2 113	5.4	62.1	10.9	7.8	7 459	17 653	31 362	29.6	4.1	12.6	12.5	9.1	15.2
Alger	130	1 574	2 015	5.5	60.8	14.7	10.8	6 945	18 210	35 892	23.9	4.5	10.3	10.7	7.2	11.3
Allegan	286	1 669	28 058	14.7	56.8	15.8	135.4	7 388	19 918	45 813	11.4	8.6	7.3	7.5	5.0	7.0
Alpena	202	2 463	7 992	10.6	52.6	13.2	43.0	7 978	17 566	34 177	12.6	4.1	10.5	11.3	7.7	11.8
Antrim	98	1 878	5 301	5.0	52.5	19.4	30.7	7 329	19 485	38 107	25.3	6.8	9.0	8.6	6.2	10.3
Arenac	281	1 592	4 010	5.2	65.4	9.1	18.7	6 336	16 300	32 805	25.3	4.9	13.9	13.3	11.3	19.1
Baraga	NA	NA	2 051	6.6	58.4	10.9	10.1	7 159	15 860	33 673	29.0	3.8	11.1	9.8	7.2	12.2
Barry	230	1 873	14 796	10.7	52.5	14.7	56.8	6 893	20 636	46 820	14.2	9.9	5.5	5.3	3.9	6.1
Bay	259	2 871	27 880	16.3	54.5	14.2	142.8	8 216	19 698	38 646	2.9	8.7	9.7	10.1	6.7	10.9
Benzie	223	3 072	3 445	10.0	51.0	20.0	17.5	6 878	18 524	37 350	28.8	5.6	7.0	7.4	4.7	7.7
Berrien	541	3 649	42 978	20.4	49.9	19.6	229.5	8 196	19 952	38 567	5.4	8.7	12.7	11.6	9.3	14.4
Branch	281	2 531	11 468	9.9	60.8	10.6	53.5	8 704	17 552	38 760	13.9	5.7	9.3	8.0	6.0	9.3
Calhoun	985	5 178	36 415	13.9	52.4	16.0	199.4	8 201	19 230	38 918	5.4	7.7	11.3	10.9	8.1	12.5
Cass	276	3 325	12 592	8.8	57.2	12.1	52.5	7 012	19 474	41 264	9.7	7.7	9.9	9.6	6.8	11.1
Charlevoix	91	1 175	6 278	8.9	49.1	19.8	45.0	10 092	20 130	39 788	19.7	7.9	8.0	8.2	5.4	8.7
Cheboygan	183	1 963	5 790	10.8	58.7	13.9	33.5	8 480	18 088	33 417	18.4	5.7	12.2	12.1	8.7	15.1
Chippewa	159	1 580	10 308	6.4	53.6	15.0	55.3	7 762	15 858	34 464	19.6	3.9	12.8	13.6	8.9	14.7
Clare	361	3 705	7 307	6.4	64.3	8.8	44.5	7 992	15 922	28 845	25.1	4.5	16.0	15.5	12.1	18.0
Clinton	92	1 254	18 094	12.5	43.7	21.2	71.7	7 192	22 913	52 806	8.6	13.0	4.6	5.1	3.3	5.0
Crawford	263	2 349	3 404	5.4	56.8	12.9	14.9	6 871	16 903	33 364	15.5	5.2	12.7	11.5	10.0	16.0
Delta	NA	NA	9 845	8.2	49.7	17.1	56.9	8 139	18 667	35 511	16.0	5.9	9.5	10.8	7.0	9.9
Dickinson	137	2 160	6 743	6.1	55.6	16.7	40.5	7 894	18 516	34 825	4.5	5.7	9.1	9.6	7.1	10.5
Eaton	246	2 643	28 631	13.0	40.8	21.7	124.5	7 444	22 411	49 588	3.3	11.1	5.8	6.2	4.1	6.6
Emmet	170	2 403	7 935	9.8	42.4	26.2	37.3	6 941	21 070	40 222	15.1	9.5	7.4	8.2	4.5	6.5
Genesee	627	4 273	120 255	11.2	50.2	16.2	633.0	7 905	20 883	41 951	0.6	10.7	13.1	12.2	10.2	16.2
Gladwin	232	1 668	5 597	9.6	63.3	9.2	25.8	6 660	16 614	32 019	28.2	5.3	13.8	12.9	10.4	17.9
Gogebic	170	1 442	3 902	11.1	53.0	15.8	22.6	9 313	16 169	27 405	17.6	3.9	14.4	14.3	10.6	17.6
Grand Traverse	225	2 715	19 918	15.7	38.6	25.4	111.9	8 833	22 111	43 169	10.7	10.4	5.9	6.2	3.8	5.5
Gratiot	215	1 885	11 080	17.7	58.6	12.9	65.0	8 307	17 118	37 262	13.1	5.8	10.3	9.8	7.3	10.1
Hillsdale	295	2 191	12 176	15.8	59.8	12.0	57.6	7 520	18 255	40 396	15.6	6.8	8.2	8.2	5.2	7.3
Houghton	85	1 661	12 652	5.7	51.4	23.0	45.2	7 769	15 078	28 817	21.5	4.4	16.8	18.2	9.9	14.9
Huron	151	2 071	8 425	12.1	64.7	10.9	56.7	7 644	17 851	35 315	20.3	5.0	10.2	10.4	7.3	10.6
Ingham	623	3 769	102 939	8.8	35.3	33.0	426.8	9 083	21 079	40 774	0.6	10.8	14.6	14.2	8.3	12.8
Ionia	254	2 368	15 973	11.9	57.0	10.8	88.8	7 257	17 451	43 074	8.9	6.8	8.7	8.7	6.8	9.9
Iosco	286	2 651	5 740	7.0	62.3	11.3	46.6	7 563	17 115	31 321	16.0	4.2	12.7	12.4	9.5	15.3
Iron	203	2 100	2 727	2.6	60.8	13.7	81.1	6 231	16 506	28 560	30.4	2.8	11.3	11.8	7.1	14.7
Isabella	237	3 195	28 337	6.3	47.8	23.9	93.8	6 774	16 242	34 262	12.5	6.8	20.4	19.8	7.4	10.4
Jackson	505	3 249	41 089	15.4	48.6	16.3	213.1	8 263	20 171	43 171	10.2	8.9	9.0	8.7	6.5	10.5
Kalamazoo	535	4 814	78 268	12.9	37.2	31.2	277.9	8 239	21 739	42 022	0.7	11.4	12.0	11.6	6.5	10.7
Kalkaska	239	2 846	3 785	6.0	64.7	9.7	19.2	6 856	16 309	36 072	21.6	4.3	10.5	10.7	8.2	13.5
Kent	541	3 558	165 304	21.2	43.6	25.8	800.1	8 221	21 629	45 980	5.8	11.4	8.9	8.4	6.3	9.2
Keweenaw	172	2 063	501	13.2	53.5	19.1	0.1	12 714	16 769	28 140	51.5	4.7	12.7	13.8	7.4	14.9
Lake	497	3 508	2 313	7.9	67.5	7.8	7.2	9 331	14 457	26 622	36.1	3.6	19.4	18.6	14.7	25.5
Lapeer	178	1 931	24 153	11.8	54.0	12.7	104.7	6 978	21 462	51 717	7.3	13.8	5.4	5.5	3.8	5.0

1. Data for serious crimes have not been adjusted for underreporting; this may affect comparability between geographic areas and over time. 2. Per 100,000 population estimated by the FBI. 3. All persons 3 years old and over enrolled in nursery school through college. 4. Persons 25 years old and over. 5. Elementary and secondary education expenditures. 6. Based on population enumerated as of April 1, 2000.

Table B. States and Counties — **Personal Income**

STATE County	Personal income, 2002 Total (mil dol)	Percent change, 2001–2002	Per capita[1] Dollars	Rank	Wages and salaries[2] (mil dol)	Proprietor's income (mil dol)	Dividends, interest, and rent (mil dol)	Transfer payments Total (mil dol)	Government payments to individuals Total (mil dol)	Social Security (mil dol)	Medical payments (mil dol)	Income maintenance (mil dol)	Unemployment insurance (mil dol)
	62	63	64	65	66	67	68	69	70	71	72	73	74
MARYLAND—Cont'd													
Washington	3 643	4.1	27 052	691	2 435	136	594	595	561	234	233	34	25
Wicomico	2 213	3.1	25 708	951	1 558	110	389	401	379	141	174	33	11
Worcester	1 445	3.4	29 637	376	727	97	408	269	256	124	94	14	16
Baltimore city	16 949	3.3	26 629	761	19 585	1 411	1 939	4 334	4 172	990	2 238	612	132
MASSACHUSETTS	250 994	0.7	39 085	X	178 663	20 634	43 996	33 635	32 105	10 542	15 492	2 396	2 536
Barnstable	9 021	3.5	39 589	67	3 699	914	2 436	1 423	1 369	649	532	56	81
Berkshire	4 437	4.2	33 263	178	2 561	377	978	848	816	300	394	55	44
Bristol	16 678	3.0	30 674	294	9 167	808	2 092	3 065	2 936	922	1 439	249	234
Dukes	641	5.8	41 508	50	297	86	227	69	66	30	24	3	7
Essex	28 204	0.2	38 309	84	14 886	1 631	4 904	3 855	3 679	1 231	1 702	295	337
Franklin	2 183	3.9	30 291	320	1 021	138	353	433	416	123	218	27	27
Hampden	13 422	3.1	29 239	418	8 748	686	1 892	3 171	3 062	807	1 680	311	171
Hampshire	4 461	3.7	29 026	445	2 311	271	833	555	518	221	185	30	39
Middlesex	68 485	-1.0	46 499	28	52 501	5 674	13 394	6 498	6 147	2 336	2 663	349	577
Nantucket	493	4.5	47 104	25	267	80	164	33	31	15	12	1	2
Norfolk	31 469	-0.1	48 081	20	18 096	2 518	6 012	2 880	2 723	1 122	1 140	121	224
Plymouth	17 548	2.1	36 214	117	7 763	1 190	2 519	2 296	2 181	749	1 021	146	173
Suffolk	28 374	0.8	41 227	52	42 360	4 663	4 766	4 702	4 538	793	2 823	481	291
Worcester	25 580	0.8	33 229	180	14 986	1 600	3 427	3 807	3 624	1 243	1 658	272	328
MICHIGAN	299 449	1.5	29 816	X	211 788	20 565	47 374	45 387	43 001	17 645	17 271	4 279	2 364
Alcona	242	3.0	20 956	2 311	55	17	68	79	76	40	25	5	3
Alger	191	2.7	19 495	2 661	114	11	34	51	49	23	18	3	2
Allegan	2 925	0.7	26 769	742	1 428	251	461	385	359	166	129	28	28
Alpena	748	1.4	24 151	1 356	457	39	144	195	188	76	80	14	10
Antrim	620	2.6	26 059	876	196	53	192	126	121	59	47	7	5
Arenac	373	2.7	21 545	2 138	150	34	67	99	95	40	38	8	5
Baraga	169	0.8	19 280	2 699	110	10	32	45	43	19	16	3	3
Barry	1 658	1.9	28 530	487	455	108	320	210	196	100	63	16	12
Bay	2 861	1.1	26 067	874	1 634	92	497	566	540	229	213	47	27
Benzie	418	3.9	24 949	1 148	141	27	110	83	79	38	27	5	4
Berrien	4 305	1.9	26 482	794	2 753	269	729	830	791	325	317	93	32
Branch	996	2.0	21 419	2 174	582	56	171	202	191	84	76	15	11
Calhoun	3 621	4.2	26 097	868	2 893	141	532	701	668	268	261	70	31
Cass	1 290	2.3	25 100	1 105	377	54	197	225	213	100	76	20	7
Charlevoix	746	3.6	28 169	524	423	93	160	116	110	54	39	7	7
Cheboygan	622	2.5	22 807	1 776	254	37	158	147	140	65	47	11	13
Chippewa	748	2.0	19 298	2 696	499	25	120	175	166	64	68	14	9
Clare	638	2.5	20 147	2 510	239	53	115	187	180	81	66	18	6
Clinton	1 999	3.0	29 978	354	584	117	339	203	188	104	58	12	8
Crawford	302	3.9	20 634	2 389	155	24	60	73	69	32	25	6	3
Delta	924	1.8	24 050	1 387	570	50	159	211	202	86	72	15	12
Dickinson	744	3.6	27 298	650	563	28	142	148	141	61	57	8	7
Eaton	2 927	2.9	27 748	582	1 363	82	450	363	338	179	105	24	14
Emmet	965	4.2	29 722	371	639	108	222	155	147	60	64	9	10
Genesee	11 446	1.6	25 977	892	7 611	509	1 632	2 337	2 233	822	883	297	150
Gladwin	547	2.0	20 482	2 437	161	20	90	158	151	73	56	11	6
Gogebic	365	2.1	20 905	2 323	190	18	63	115	111	45	48	8	4
Grand Traverse	2 370	3.6	29 250	416	1 782	270	498	348	329	150	127	20	19
Gratiot	917	1.7	21 661	2 101	498	62	158	194	184	74	82	15	8
Hillsdale	1 106	2.6	23 564	1 545	643	62	167	201	189	87	71	16	10
Houghton	733	0.5	20 319	2 474	444	31	135	187	178	69	80	13	7
Huron	915	2.9	25 875	917	471	71	222	199	191	89	75	12	11
Ingham	7 689	2.8	27 313	644	8 104	427	1 082	1 151	1 084	395	463	124	50
Ionia	1 347	1.8	21 329	2 203	645	52	162	213	198	87	75	19	10
Iosco	559	1.8	20 724	2 363	258	29	120	189	182	83	72	12	8
Iron	288	2.5	22 525	1 871	124	14	53	92	89	38	39	5	3
Isabella	1 397	2.1	21 771	2 074	960	71	218	288	272	84	141	21	8
Jackson	4 030	2.6	25 011	1 125	2 539	167	650	731	693	295	264	68	38
Kalamazoo	6 918	2.8	28 742	475	5 285	378	1 192	980	923	398	354	96	36
Kalkaska	312	1.5	18 340	2 853	156	14	42	78	74	34	26	6	5
Kent	17 638	2.1	30 068	346	15 219	1 782	2 614	2 188	2 049	839	728	230	163
Keweenaw	50	0.7	22 288	1 936	14	2	10	13	13	6	5	1	1
Lake	233	3.3	20 129	2 514	62	14	48	75	72	31	27	8	3
Lapeer	2 496	1.4	27 547	606	818	114	336	317	296	135	108	19	26

1. Based on the resident population estimated as of July 1 of the year shown.　2. Includes other labor income.

Table B. States and Counties — Earnings, Social Security, and Housing

STATE County	Earnings, 2002 Total (mil dol)	Farm	Goods-related[1] Total	Manu-facturing	Information and professional and technical services	Retail trade	Finance, insurance, and real estate	Health services	Govern-ment	Social Security beneficiaries, December 2003 Number	Rate[2]	Supplemental Security Income recipients, December 2003	Housing units, 2003 Total	Percent change, 2000–2003
	75	76	77	78	79	80	81	82	83	84	85	86	87	88
MARYLAND—Cont'd														
Washington	2 570	0.2	24.2	17.3	5.8	10.2	11.6	13.4	14.5	24 030	176	2 137	55 211	4.2
Wicomico	1 668	1.2	D	12.2	D	8.7	5.3	17.1	17.0	14 695	168	1 729	36 318	5.6
Worcester	824	1.2	D	7.5	4.8	13.8	7.8	6.0	17.9	12 640	255	681	48 786	3.0
Baltimore city	20 996	0.0	D	6.7	13.5	3.1	12.9	14.6	21.2	104 800	167	30 529	294 467	-2.0
MASSACHUSETTS	199 297	0.1	18.5	12.3	17.1	5.8	13.4	10.6	11.4	1 061 851	165	167 883	2 660 847	1.5
Barnstable	4 614	0.1	12.9	3.2	11.4	11.2	13.0	13.2	15.8	63 295	276	3 463	151 161	2.8
Berkshire	2 938	0.1	23.7	16.8	8.0	8.8	6.9	16.7	11.4	30 225	227	3 770	66 915	0.9
Bristol	9 975	0.2	D	21.2	7.5	10.1	4.8	12.8	13.9	101 625	186	18 830	220 737	1.8
Dukes	383	0.2	D	D	D	13.0	9.1	9.4	14.5	2 850	183	151	15 345	3.4
Essex	16 517	0.1	28.7	22.1	13.3	7.6	5.9	11.8	12.0	122 570	166	20 322	291 037	1.4
Franklin	1 159	0.7	D	22.8	7.7	7.4	4.4	10.9	16.0	13 295	184	1 950	32 406	1.5
Hampden	9 434	0.1	20.6	14.9	7.4	7.7	9.9	15.5	17.6	86 010	186	22 178	187 451	0.8
Hampshire	2 581	0.4	13.7	8.2	7.3	7.8	3.7	10.8	28.7	23 220	150	2 261	59 669	1.7
Middlesex	58 175	0.0	21.6	15.5	26.1	4.9	6.6	7.1	8.4	221 055	150	24 511	582 755	1.1
Nantucket	347	0.0	D	D	D	13.4	8.5	4.1	11.6	1 345	125	46	9 769	6.1
Norfolk	20 614	0.0	18.7	10.3	13.9	7.7	17.2	9.0	8.1	105 255	161	8 331	258 873	1.5
Plymouth	8 953	0.1	16.8	7.8	10.1	9.1	7.3	12.7	17.1	76 635	157	8 560	186 338	2.7
Suffolk	47 023	0.0	D	3.2	18.3	2.1	29.6	12.0	11.0	87 985	129	34 573	292 496	0.0
Worcester	16 585	0.1	23.8	17.5	10.8	7.2	7.8	12.6	14.4	126 480	163	18 745	305 895	2.6
MICHIGAN	232 353	0.2	29.3	23.1	12.0	6.6	6.7	9.2	13.7	1 699 384	169	216 629	4 383 456	3.5
Alcona	72	-0.6	D	13.1	D	D	5.4	11.6	19.4	4 125	356	245	10 870	2.7
Alger	125	0.1	34.9	30.7	D	4.8	6.3	5.1	32.6	2 355	241	175	6 122	2.6
Allegan	1 679	2.4	50.7	41.4	3.4	7.0	6.3	4.9	10.9	16 885	153	1 276	45 598	5.3
Alpena	497	-0.5	26.0	19.0	D	10.0	4.5	10.9	27.0	7 765	252	920	15 430	0.9
Antrim	248	1.4	31.8	21.1	6.7	7.4	6.1	D	19.8	5 945	247	343	15 949	5.7
Arenac	184	3.6	18.5	12.3	D	8.9	5.8	D	21.8	4 235	245	464	9 794	2.4
Baraga	119	-0.1	20.5	17.4	2.9	5.0	D	D	53.0	1 930	220	186	4 714	1.8
Barry	563	-0.2	D	25.7	D	7.8	8.6	10.6	16.7	9 725	165	512	24 837	4.0
Bay	1 726	0.4	25.5	20.5	12.2	10.9	4.0	12.3	16.9	22 420	205	2 374	47 217	1.7
Benzie	168	0.4	D	9.4	6.0	9.5	6.9	D	18.2	3 950	231	227	10 957	6.3
Berrien	3 021	0.3	37.9	33.2	5.0	7.0	4.2	9.2	11.8	32 180	198	4 957	74 788	1.8
Branch	638	1.0	D	23.9	D	9.9	6.0	D	23.6	8 615	186	654	20 300	2.4
Calhoun	3 035	0.2	D	31.8	6.3	6.6	3.2	9.9	19.2	27 245	196	4 103	59 818	1.9
Cass	430	0.7	D	30.0	3.3	7.6	5.8	D	21.3	10 100	197	819	24 693	3.4
Charlevoix	515	-0.1	D	29.8	8.9	7.2	5.6	6.8	15.2	5 380	201	321	16 335	6.3
Cheboygan	291	0.1	22.4	8.2	3.6	14.8	5.7	D	18.9	6 775	247	438	17 153	3.4
Chippewa	524	-0.2	D	4.9	2.4	8.6	3.1	D	55.6	7 155	184	770	19 919	2.5
Clare	292	0.3	22.9	12.6	4.4	14.6	5.5	D	22.0	8 410	266	1 064	22 622	1.8
Clinton	701	1.8	32.9	21.5	D	8.3	4.9	7.0	19.8	10 125	150	410	27 428	11.4
Crawford	180	0.0	D	19.3	4.9	8.9	4.0	18.7	23.6	3 410	230	269	10 295	2.5
Delta	620	0.2	33.7	27.4	D	8.7	4.1	9.9	16.8	9 025	236	871	19 630	2.1
Dickinson	590	0.0	D	23.6	D	8.7	3.7	D	22.7	6 425	236	457	13 818	0.8
Eaton	1 444	-0.1	20.2	9.5	9.3	9.5	14.9	5.4	20.2	17 235	162	810	43 930	4.3
Emmet	748	-0.1	22.9	10.3	D	11.9	7.9	18.3	14.2	6 095	186	578	19 665	6.0
Genesee	8 120	0.0	33.8	28.2	9.3	7.3	4.8	11.6	14.6	77 725	176	13 190	192 176	4.7
Gladwin	181	0.1	D	24.1	2.6	10.3	3.5	8.1	22.6	7 370	274	583	17 623	4.7
Gogebic	209	-0.1	15.3	11.0	4.4	7.5	5.0	D	37.1	4 655	269	426	10 833	-0.1
Grand Traverse	2 052	0.0	23.8	12.5	9.4	11.4	7.9	17.9	12.7	14 850	181	1 185	37 235	6.9
Gratiot	560	2.3	23.2	19.7	2.8	7.5	4.8	D	20.5	7 645	180	892	15 760	1.6
Hillsdale	705	0.5	46.4	41.8	D	6.5	4.2	D	14.6	8 765	186	795	21 011	4.1
Houghton	475	0.0	14.3	6.5	4.4	8.5	4.5	D	41.8	7 155	197	739	17 873	0.7
Huron	542	5.2	35.3	29.0	5.4	7.1	4.9	D	15.2	9 120	259	697	20 806	1.8
Ingham	8 531	0.1	21.6	17.0	8.8	6.2	8.2	9.8	29.5	37 950	135	6 672	118 162	2.7
Ionia	697	1.2	D	27.0	4.7	8.1	4.3	6.2	27.5	9 115	143	843	23 054	4.8
Iosco	286	0.6	22.1	13.0	3.8	11.4	6.0	D	24.5	8 480	315	583	20 747	1.5
Iron	138	-0.2	D	5.4	4.8	9.3	4.3	D	31.9	3 950	309	280	8 809	0.4
Isabella	1 030	0.5	21.5	9.6	3.9	7.3	5.6	7.3	36.7	8 490	131	1 247	26 995	10.1
Jackson	2 705	0.0	27.4	21.4	4.0	9.4	5.1	11.6	17.8	28 775	177	3 587	65 532	4.2
Kalamazoo	5 663	0.5	34.8	28.0	6.2	7.6	7.2	11.6	14.2	38 155	158	4 810	103 135	3.9
Kalkaska	170	0.4	34.1	10.2	2.3	8.1	3.6	D	19.5	3 530	206	298	11 234	3.8
Kent	17 001	0.2	32.9	26.5	9.4	7.0	7.6	10.0	8.2	81 995	139	11 651	233 478	4.2
Keweenaw	15	0.0	D	3.3	D	5.7	D	D	27.1	590	265	40	2 336	0.4
Lake	75	-0.1	13.6	4.0	D	D	D	D	27.9	3 355	284	540	13 847	2.6
Lapeer	932	0.2	34.4	24.5	4.6	9.9	6.2	4.4	21.2	13 180	144	579	34 296	4.8

1. Covers mining, construction, and manufacturing.   2. Per 1,000 resident population estimated as of July 1 of the year shown.

Table B. States and Counties — Housing, Labor Force, and Employment

	Housing units, 2000								Civilian labor force, 2003				Civilian employment,[6] 2000		
	Occupied units										Unemployment			Percent	
			Owner-occupied			Renter-occupied									
				Median owner cost as a percent of income											
STATE County	Total	Percent	Median value[1]	With a mortgage	Without a mortgage[2]	Median rent[3]	Median rent as a percent of income	Sub-standard units[4] (percent)	Total	Percent change, 2002–2003	Total	Rate[5]	Total	Management, professional and related occupations	Production, transportation, and material moving occupations
	89	90	91	92	93	94	95	96	97	98	99	100	101	102	103
MARYLAND—Cont'd															
Washington	49 726	65.6	115 000	21.4	10.4	482	22.2	1.5	71 065	-0.3	3 264	4.6	61 442	26.6	17.7
Wicomico	32 218	66.5	94 500	20.5	10.6	567	26.8	2.6	48 340	-2.2	2 448	5.1	42 211	30.8	14.3
Worcester	19 694	75.0	121 500	22.6	9.9	574	24.8	2.2	27 435	3.3	2 271	8.3	21 510	29.3	9.2
Baltimore city	257 996	50.3	69 100	22.5	12.5	498	26.9	5.3	288 454	0.3	24 810	8.6	256 036	32.4	13.4
MASSACHUSETTS	2 443 580	61.7	185 700	21.9	12.4	684	25.5	3.4	3 415 518	-1.5	198 311	5.8	3 161 087	41.1	11.3
Barnstable	94 822	77.8	178 800	23.1	12.4	723	27.7	1.4	120 232	2.5	6 206	5.2	100 780	35.1	7.5
Berkshire	56 006	66.9	116 800	21.2	11.7	499	25.3	1.2	68 651	-0.2	3 493	5.1	65 253	35.1	11.9
Bristol	205 411	61.6	151 500	21.6	11.9	499	23.8	2.3	279 230	-0.1	19 451	7.0	258 909	30.7	17.8
Dukes	6 421	71.3	304 000	25.9	13.9	741	24.8	1.7	10 535	3.9	488	4.6	7 929	31.8	7.5
Essex	275 419	63.5	220 000	22.3	12.6	665	25.7	3.8	380 796	-2.0	25 886	6.8	349 835	39.4	12.4
Franklin	29 466	67.0	119 000	21.7	12.2	541	26.1	1.5	40 055	-0.2	1 805	4.5	37 577	35.3	15.6
Hampden	175 288	61.9	117 400	21.6	12.7	535	26.3	4.2	222 415	-0.8	14 945	6.7	206 062	31.0	17.3
Hampshire	55 991	65.0	142 400	21.4	11.5	631	26.3	2.0	82 999	-1.1	3 314	4.0	82 826	42.9	10.9
Middlesex	561 220	61.8	247 900	21.7	12.1	835	24.8	3.0	839 603	-2.7	42 732	5.1	776 273	49.7	8.4
Nantucket	3 699	63.1	577 500	26.3	11.8	1 016	29.5	1.6	7 195	4.0	173	2.4	5 451	30.0	6.3
Norfolk	248 827	69.7	230 400	21.7	12.4	853	25.1	2.0	360 461	-2.2	17 299	4.8	337 538	48.1	6.9
Plymouth	168 361	75.6	179 200	22.5	12.7	679	25.8	2.3	255 213	-0.9	14 344	5.6	235 921	35.8	11.7
Suffolk	278 722	33.9	187 300	22.9	13.0	791	27.3	8.3	359 571	-2.2	22 267	6.2	329 791	41.0	9.2
Worcester	283 927	64.1	146 000	21.2	12.3	580	24.0	2.7	388 557	-0.7	25 906	6.7	366 942	37.6	14.7
MICHIGAN	3 785 661	73.8	115 600	19.6	9.9	546	24.4	3.4	5 042 094	0.8	368 121	7.3	4 637 461	31.5	18.5
Alcona	5 132	89.5	83 700	21.0	9.9	411	25.7	2.5	4 480	0.7	514	11.5	3 898	23.8	19.2
Alger	3 785	82.4	75 900	19.9	9.9	376	20.2	3.0	4 421	0.2	314	7.1	3 776	26.0	17.0
Allegan	38 165	82.9	115 500	20.2	9.9	515	22.4	2.9	56 635	0.0	3 888	6.9	52 100	24.0	27.7
Alpena	12 818	79.3	78 100	18.7	9.9	370	24.9	1.9	15 645	0.4	1 458	9.3	13 782	27.2	18.4
Antrim	9 222	85.0	110 000	21.8	10.7	460	23.6	3.2	10 954	0.8	1 039	9.5	10 018	24.9	21.6
Arenac	6 710	84.3	77 700	19.8	10.8	399	27.1	3.0	7 086	1.0	777	11.0	6 593	22.3	21.1
Baraga	3 353	77.7	67 100	18.3	9.9	339	22.3	2.8	4 115	2.1	404	9.8	3 504	21.4	19.7
Barry	21 035	85.9	107 100	20.4	9.9	493	22.7	1.9	31 882	0.1	1 671	5.2	27 538	27.4	25.6
Bay	43 930	79.3	84 900	18.8	10.8	440	25.3	1.8	53 797	0.2	4 334	8.1	50 804	26.9	18.0
Benzie	6 500	85.8	107 400	22.2	9.9	486	24.0	2.9	8 402	4.7	736	8.8	7 257	24.2	17.6
Berrien	63 569	72.2	94 700	19.4	9.9	476	24.7	3.4	80 294	1.6	5 873	7.3	76 557	29.3	21.3
Branch	16 349	78.9	85 000	19.3	9.9	477	22.6	3.5	23 628	2.2	1 634	6.9	21 133	22.7	31.3
Calhoun	54 100	73.0	81 000	19.0	10.1	484	23.6	2.8	65 876	1.3	4 850	7.4	62 956	26.9	23.8
Cass	19 676	81.9	91 800	19.5	9.9	471	19.8	2.7	25 942	1.1	1 334	5.1	24 788	22.6	28.5
Charlevoix	10 400	81.2	112 700	20.4	9.9	470	23.5	3.0	13 811	0.2	1 213	8.8	12 001	27.2	18.3
Cheboygan	10 835	82.8	94 500	21.5	9.9	440	26.7	2.6	12 329	2.3	1 353	11.0	10 263	23.4	16.9
Chippewa	13 474	74.0	77 300	18.9	9.9	426	24.7	2.3	17 643	2.3	1 480	8.4	15 002	26.2	10.8
Clare	12 686	82.2	70 500	20.8	9.9	397	26.1	4.1	11 135	4.2	1 210	10.9	11 675	22.6	21.6
Clinton	23 653	85.2	120 500	19.2	9.9	511	20.8	1.7	36 344	0.9	1 501	4.1	32 920	31.0	16.9
Crawford	5 625	82.8	79 500	19.8	9.9	453	26.2	3.4	5 580	1.3	498	8.9	5 869	24.3	17.6
Delta	15 836	79.6	80 000	18.6	9.9	383	24.7	1.5	19 532	1.6	1 747	8.9	17 453	25.3	21.0
Dickinson	11 386	80.1	64 600	18.4	11.0	417	23.9	1.8	14 595	0.9	994	6.8	12 362	28.0	17.5
Eaton	40 167	74.1	113 700	19.2	9.9	569	23.0	1.8	59 139	0.8	2 514	4.3	53 442	30.5	18.3
Emmet	12 577	75.5	131 500	22.2	9.9	513	24.2	2.5	19 334	3.1	1 604	8.3	15 204	30.7	11.7
Genesee	169 825	73.2	95 000	18.8	9.9	507	25.6	3.3	186 236	-0.5	18 113	9.7	192 969	27.0	21.4
Gladwin	10 561	85.6	86 800	22.0	10.0	395	23.0	3.6	9 463	4.4	1 073	11.3	9 738	24.1	21.2
Gogebic	7 425	78.7	39 700	18.7	11.5	340	22.5	1.8	8 248	1.0	661	8.0	6 713	26.1	17.8
Grand Traverse	30 396	77.3	130 400	21.0	9.9	614	24.4	2.2	47 099	3.8	3 040	6.5	39 964	31.4	12.8
Gratiot	14 501	77.5	75 300	18.1	9.9	424	22.7	2.2	20 178	2.8	1 365	6.8	17 806	25.1	22.7
Hillsdale	17 335	79.9	85 800	19.5	9.9	434	20.0	2.9	23 670	1.8	1 843	7.8	22 023	23.2	32.5
Houghton	13 793	71.5	54 800	18.5	10.4	368	26.8	3.5	17 133	1.2	1 104	6.4	15 219	34.4	10.0
Huron	14 597	83.5	78 000	18.6	9.9	383	23.0	2.0	17 687	2.3	1 766	10.0	15 579	26.2	26.3
Ingham	108 593	60.7	98 400	19.5	9.9	542	27.2	3.3	154 290	1.1	8 285	5.4	142 675	36.9	12.2
Ionia	20 606	80.1	94 400	18.8	9.9	468	23.0	3.0	27 821	1.6	2 094	7.5	27 065	22.4	25.9
Iosco	11 727	82.0	77 100	21.0	10.1	416	26.2	2.6	10 488	-1.0	1 115	10.6	10 155	22.3	21.7
Iron	5 748	82.5	47 500	18.7	11.1	346	23.9	2.6	5 493	2.4	386	7.0	4 994	24.8	14.5
Isabella	22 425	63.3	91 800	18.6	9.9	462	28.7	3.5	33 371	-0.2	1 495	4.5	31 677	28.4	11.8
Jackson	58 168	76.5	96 900	19.0	9.9	505	24.3	2.4	79 492	1.5	6 331	8.0	71 695	27.5	21.7
Kalamazoo	93 479	65.8	108 000	19.1	9.9	529	25.8	2.6	129 631	1.4	6 926	5.3	120 740	34.7	15.4
Kalkaska	6 428	85.4	85 100	21.4	10.3	468	24.1	4.0	8 047	3.8	767	9.5	7 410	19.7	23.4
Kent	212 890	70.3	115 100	19.4	9.9	554	23.3	3.7	329 193	0.5	25 874	7.9	289 158	31.1	20.7
Keweenaw	998	89.3	44 100	18.9	9.9	263	25.9	3.3	898	3.5	109	12.1	916	32.6	14.5
Lake	4 704	82.9	61 300	22.5	11.2	387	28.8	4.1	3 798	4.2	433	11.4	3 918	19.8	25.7
Lapeer	30 729	85.0	134 600	20.3	9.9	541	22.9	2.7	44 920	0.2	3 857	8.6	41 012	26.9	24.2

1. Specified owner-occupied units.   2. Median monthly owner costs is often in the minimum category—9.9 percent or less, which is indicated as 9.9 percent.   3. Specified renter-occupied units.   4. Overcrowded or lacking complete plumbing facilities.   5. Percent of civilian labor force.   6. Persons 16 years old and over.

Table B. States and Counties — **Nonfarm Employment and Agriculture**

STATE County	Private nonfarm establishments, employment and payroll, 2001									Agriculture, 2002			
	Number of establishments	Employment						Annual payroll		Farms			Farm operators whose principal occupation is farming (percent)
		Total	Health care and social assistance	Manufacturing	Retail trade	Finance and insurance	Professional, scientific, and technical services	Total (mil dol)	Average per employee (dollars)	Number	Percent with—		
											Less than 50 acres	500 acres and over	
	104	105	106	107	108	109	110	111	112	113	114	115	116
MARYLAND—Cont'd													
Washington	3 362	58 243	9 005	9 665	9 556	6 694	1 233	1 640	28 155	775	40.1	5.4	61.8
Wicomico	2 507	37 542	6 717	5 306	6 672	1 215	1 164	972	25 887	512	54.9	9.8	66.2
Worcester	2 155	18 462	1 261	1 654	3 310	445	430	469	25 407	403	43.7	16.1	64.0
Baltimore city	13 583	305 394	60 872	24 185	19 872	23 073	23 035	11 479	37 587	NA	NA	NA	NA
MASSACHUSETTS	177 434	3 129 980	454 041	390 351	352 124	215 087	257 577	134 667	43 025	6 075	60.0	2.7	54.0
Barnstable	8 442	73 481	13 312	3 287	14 586	3 004	4 026	2 243	30 527	285	89.1	0.0	51.2
Berkshire	4 414	57 538	10 120	7 781	8 787	2 514	2 027	1 717	29 838	401	43.9	10.2	58.1
Bristol	13 364	199 307	30 815	44 066	34 421	5 926	5 642	5 858	29 390	624	66.8	1.1	51.6
Dukes	994	5 027	672	92	1 062	260	D	181	36 002	83	86.7	2.4	67.5
Essex	18 634	284 473	43 563	56 055	38 534	10 977	14 962	10 542	37 057	400	71.5	3.0	52.3
Franklin	1 786	24 338	3 189	7 712	3 051	682	383	643	26 436	586	36.5	4.3	53.2
Hampden	11 992	181 495	34 302	31 772	24 811	11 309	7 288	5 679	31 291	458	54.4	1.7	50.4
Hampshire	3 671	46 790	7 223	5 028	7 505	1 144	1 263	1 255	26 827	542	50.6	2.4	50.9
Middlesex	43 079	871 013	88 550	118 115	84 016	27 402	110 239	43 567	50 018	579	68.0	0.9	55.6
Nantucket	772	3 837	D	43	D	D	D	159	41 442	13	84.6	0.0	46.2
Norfolk	19 738	344 196	44 975	31 437	40 622	32 369	28 209	14 879	43 229	208	81.3	2.4	46.6
Plymouth	11 977	150 808	24 884	14 917	26 268	6 554	8 192	4 949	32 818	794	70.7	2.3	62.6
Suffolk	20 395	579 254	99 369	17 729	30 322	95 794	61 863	32 042	55 316	8	87.5	0.0	25.0
Worcester	18 129	299 548	52 786	52 317	36 430	16 991	12 813	10 392	34 693	1 094	51.4	2.4	52.5
MICHIGAN	236 711	4 008 572	506 185	755 635	543 649	162 700	212 598	142 939	35 658	53 315	41.1	9.0	54.5
Alcona	241	1 406	291	255	305	D	62	29	20 728	244	27.9	9.4	56.1
Alger	340	2 958	290	801	416	111	D	62	20 907	67	23.9	11.9	53.7
Allegan	2 237	35 695	2 517	15 849	4 157	551	398	1 080	30 249	1 489	49.4	7.0	53.9
Alpena	906	10 878	2 499	2 118	1 801	370	201	293	26 932	460	28.7	6.3	55.0
Antrim	659	5 403	607	1 478	696	134	663	126	23 305	382	33.8	6.0	51.0
Arenac	475	5 836	1 343	760	885	134	109	124	21 216	381	32.5	12.1	51.7
Baraga	234	2 153	449	602	318	66	14	47	21 745	63	27.0	12.7	41.3
Barry	994	11 242	1 175	3 330	1 866	729	309	300	26 675	1 063	40.9	7.4	49.6
Bay	2 563	34 861	5 988	5 030	7 013	1 040	1 044	1 052	30 172	787	38.8	13.6	61.8
Benzie	478	3 226	415	378	584	134	85	71	21 982	181	35.4	3.3	50.8
Berrien	3 956	59 622	7 936	15 058	7 663	1 360	1 554	1 813	30 415	1 093	53.4	7.6	62.4
Branch	911	13 110	1 751	3 565	2 571	431	320	341	26 024	1 123	36.7	11.1	52.8
Calhoun	3 029	58 793	8 539	14 325	8 011	3 263	1 140	1 859	31 622	1 147	32.8	10.1	53.1
Cass	809	8 802	951	3 423	1 041	225	196	224	25 495	808	41.6	11.9	52.7
Charlevoix	1 074	10 613	1 096	3 329	1 347	230	278	312	29 415	299	42.1	4.3	46.2
Cheboygan	905	6 168	1 018	667	1 422	197	146	158	25 544	268	35.1	7.5	47.8
Chippewa	878	9 362	1 486	702	1 584	250	169	212	22 649	372	16.7	12.4	50.5
Clare	627	6 273	1 025	980	1 564	194	114	139	22 208	414	30.9	6.0	53.4
Clinton	1 195	13 358	1 240	2 850	2 274	261	531	391	29 266	1 179	39.5	10.1	54.7
Crawford	308	3 263	779	479	603	99	85	76	23 338	47	46.8	10.6	59.6
Delta	1 188	13 633	1 654	2 840	2 466	479	837	368	26 980	273	19.0	15.4	52.4
Dickinson	957	14 933	2 246	2 418	2 250	338	290	407	27 283	146	32.2	7.5	49.3
Eaton	1 977	29 158	2 573	5 465	6 760	1 360	819	827	28 369	1 221	41.0	9.0	52.2
Emmet	1 399	14 445	2 433	1 548	2 511	348	926	394	27 289	274	33.9	6.2	54.7
Genesee	9 087	145 300	22 241	24 689	25 376	5 543	5 585	4 789	32 956	1 051	59.1	6.6	56.8
Gladwin	459	4 488	476	1 280	890	133	76	110	24 472	534	29.4	4.9	48.1
Gogebic	483	4 986	730	636	915	120	111	87	17 508	49	32.7	0.0	38.8
Grand Traverse	3 568	43 070	7 028	5 426	7 797	1 813	2 110	1 252	29 071	489	49.9	5.1	53.0
Gratiot	874	12 751	3 073	2 824	1 741	333	100	311	24 396	1 018	35.6	15.3	60.9
Hillsdale	913	14 714	1 341	6 834	1 688	378	189	377	25 625	1 509	40.1	8.1	48.8
Houghton	919	9 953	2 519	815	2 128	490	384	195	19 611	158	29.1	5.1	45.6
Huron	1 007	10 655	1 477	3 859	1 606	386	203	264	24 814	1 189	29.4	21.6	67.1
Ingham	7 098	125 445	17 827	14 469	18 381	9 234	7 026	4 030	32 122	1 018	54.9	8.4	48.8
Ionia	1 057	11 696	1 206	3 452	2 202	631	278	313	26 786	1 146	41.4	10.6	57.5
Iosco	675	5 908	698	1 429	1 269	327	111	127	21 464	285	37.2	7.4	57.2
Iron	411	3 173	651	376	597	150	107	65	20 556	106	25.5	10.4	56.6
Isabella	1 340	19 541	2 958	1 581	3 572	510	1 026	429	21 930	953	31.1	9.0	53.7
Jackson	3 398	53 738	7 815	11 774	8 516	1 506	1 294	1 608	29 930	1 265	46.2	6.0	48.4
Kalamazoo	5 884	112 186	15 865	18 782	15 249	4 514	5 056	3 839	34 218	808	53.7	9.5	56.8
Kalkaska	401	3 895	388	1 176	563	76	53	116	29 820	175	38.3	4.0	48.6
Kent	15 428	333 135	36 165	75 888	41 048	15 503	15 704	11 383	34 169	1 212	51.5	5.5	50.9
Keweenaw	71	439	D	D	16	D	D	7	15 303	11	54.5	0.0	45.5
Lake	179	1 217	244	100	256	70	12	22	17 913	173	31.2	5.2	45.1
Lapeer	1 799	20 545	2 086	6 002	3 980	525	622	532	25 918	1 187	47.7	8.6	57.2

STATE County	Acreage (1,000)	Percent change, 1997–2002	Average size of farm	Total irrigated (1,000)	Total cropland (1,000)	Average per farm	Average per acre	Value of machinery and equipment average per farm (dollars)	Total (mil dol)	Average per farm (dollars)	Crops	Live-stock and poultry products	$10,000 or more	$100,000 or more	Total ($1,000)	Percent of farms
	117	118	119	120	121	122	123	124	125	126	127	128	129	130	131	132
MARYLAND—Cont'd																
Washington	125	-0.8	161	1	89	600 354	3 804	69 730	60	76 874	18.6	81.4	47.9	24.0	1 809	23.9
Wicomico	88	-3.3	173	8	63	573 235	3 413	88 748	175	341 003	15.0	85.0	61.5	45.3	1 492	33.2
Worcester	131	17.0	326	4	91	760 657	2 394	85 958	123	306 328	13.1	86.9	63.3	48.6	1 939	39.0
Baltimore city	NA	NA	NA	NA	NA	NA	NA	NA	NA	NA	NA	NA	NA	NA	NA	NA
MASSACHUSETTS	519	0.2	85	24	208	755 254	9 234	50 243	384	63 262	72.1	27.9	36.4	11.4	4 268	6.8
Barnstable	6	20.0	21	2	3	447 947	21 421	32 869	14	48 517	62.2	37.8	42.1	12.3	D	D
Berkshire	69	9.5	171	0	26	783 518	5 639	58 867	22	54 178	44.7	55.3	36.9	11.7	330	6.2
Bristol	36	-2.7	58	2	15	780 190	12 750	36 804	29	47 053	76.0	24.0	35.3	10.3	256	6.6
Dukes	8	60.0	94	0	1	1 081 431	11 343	30 726	1	17 524	61.6	38.4	36.1	4.8	D	D
Essex	28	7.7	70	1	13	1 167 953	14 560	51 248	24	61 173	82.0	18.0	35.5	13.3	166	4.3
Franklin	74	-1.3	127	2	26	550 794	3 989	61 289	43	73 200	63.4	36.6	36.2	14.8	765	10.2
Hampden	38	2.7	82	1	16	460 886	6 404	35 433	24	51 717	85.3	14.7	29.9	10.0	180	7.2
Hampshire	51	-1.9	94	1	24	591 829	6 601	56 507	35	64 722	68.7	31.3	37.5	13.5	542	10.5
Middlesex	33	6.5	57	1	16	1 031 520	20 975	43 038	66	113 844	83.7	16.3	33.2	11.1	267	4.1
Nantucket	D	D	D	D	1	2 494 308	50 824	D	3	205 939	100.0	0.0	46.2	15.4	0	0.0
Norfolk	13	30.0	61	0	4	974 228	15 960	44 484	11	54 357	93.1	6.9	28.8	10.6	D	D
Plymouth	59	-19.2	75	12	22	869 228	12 635	71 318	43	54 142	94.1	5.9	48.0	10.2	515	5.9
Suffolk	D	NA	D	D	0	784 292	56 021	D	0	44 250	80.2	19.8	75.0	25.0	0	0.0
Worcester	104	1.0	95	1	42	661 544	7 378	46 309	69	62 682	50.8	49.2	32.5	10.1	1 098	8.4
MICHIGAN	10 143	2.7	190	456	7 984	509 299	2 667	73 910	3 772	70 757	62.6	37.4	37.8	12.2	144 771	34.0
Alcona	41	-4.7	168	D	27	353 515	2 157	56 682	6	22 818	49.6	50.4	29.1	7.8	154	21.3
Alger	15	-6.3	223	0	10	294 462	1 556	43 071	2	22 547	33.2	66.8	34.3	7.5	168	17.9
Allegan	243	2.5	163	15	198	514 851	3 159	82 427	230	154 646	48.9	51.1	40.8	16.0	3 884	23.2
Alpena	74	-5.1	160	0	50	277 594	1 939	46 865	13	27 290	33.4	66.6	28.9	7.8	538	26.5
Antrim	63	14.5	166	2	36	452 419	2 589	51 547	16	41 501	69.8	30.2	29.6	7.3	365	24.6
Arenac	84	-2.3	220	0	67	464 953	2 033	61 832	23	59 137	72.6	27.4	32.0	14.4	1 240	58.0
Baraga	15	0.0	241	D	8	275 665	1 241	45 908	1	17 786	57.8	42.2	31.7	7.9	2	14.3
Barry	182	10.3	171	3	130	501 497	2 557	54 139	48	45 007	39.9	60.1	23.5	7.5	2 656	37.3
Bay	186	5.7	236	4	167	543 065	2 573	102 824	59	75 442	91.9	8.1	51.5	19.8	2 073	47.8
Benzie	23	0.0	127	0	12	360 074	3 075	73 625	4	23 324	79.2	20.8	34.3	7.7	146	11.6
Berrien	174	0.0	159	19	143	604 737	3 898	89 999	97	88 487	87.4	12.6	48.9	15.6	3 016	30.2
Branch	254	8.5	226	39	199	556 637	2 452	75 769	65	57 796	60.5	39.5	36.3	11.5	4 575	51.5
Calhoun	240	-1.2	209	10	190	505 642	2 314	61 196	64	56 184	56.1	43.9	41.6	10.7	3 437	39.9
Cass	189	6.8	234	25	148	521 896	2 280	100 279	64	79 545	59.4	40.6	38.2	13.7	3 025	41.0
Charlevoix	39	25.8	130	0	22	414 924	3 178	40 980	4	13 349	46.1	53.9	18.7	3.3	139	17.7
Cheboygan	50	-2.0	187	0	25	412 509	2 079	46 550	7	24 612	43.2	56.8	29.1	6.7	323	14.2
Chippewa	94	-5.1	252	0	62	337 749	1 304	39 122	6	15 566	45.1	54.9	32.8	2.4	147	17.7
Clare	64	1.6	155	1	41	385 382	2 051	41 307	12	27 922	18.0	82.0	30.7	7.2	475	24.2
Clinton	256	4.9	217	3	219	522 632	2 371	80 149	99	83 681	42.0	58.0	43.1	13.4	4 602	46.6
Crawford	6	100.0	134	0	1	353 662	2 537	37 682	0	3 161	D	D	8.5	0.0	0	0.0
Delta	74	5.7	272	0	42	385 550	1 445	48 265	10	37 433	47.2	52.8	34.4	9.2	405	20.1
Dickinson	29	3.6	196	0	14	286 007	1 407	42 338	4	25 798	43.7	56.2	26.7	7.5	194	21.2
Eaton	238	2.6	195	2	194	521 167	2 838	64 233	53	43 435	76.2	23.8	36.9	10.2	3 058	36.6
Emmet	44	10.0	159	0	25	460 595	2 983	41 337	6	21 412	48.6	51.4	28.8	5.5	147	12.0
Genesee	143	21.2	136	1	116	512 373	3 853	55 786	29	28 004	73.6	26.4	25.5	7.3	1 601	20.7
Gladwin	72	5.9	135	0	52	261 086	2 177	31 849	8	15 572	58.6	41.4	28.8	3.0	657	33.3
Gogebic	4	0.0	82	D	2	153 151	1 821	20 498	0	4 093	78.1	21.4	14.3	0.0	0	6.1
Grand Traverse	62	0.0	127	2	43	557 942	4 139	52 300	11	23 243	66.5	33.5	32.5	4.9	639	18.4
Gratiot	289	4.3	284	5	254	596 630	2 020	97 459	115	112 697	56.2	43.8	47.5	19.5	5 139	56.4
Hillsdale	275	7.0	182	4	217	458 441	2 400	52 741	79	52 296	51.8	48.2	29.3	8.2	5 403	55.4
Houghton	26	13.0	164	0	13	198 904	1 326	41 237	3	17 853	48.4	51.5	27.2	3.8	70	16.5
Huron	432	1.9	363	2	394	704 043	1 998	149 928	211	177 056	51.6	48.4	57.9	31.1	7 598	65.2
Ingham	185	-2.6	182	2	155	548 872	2 879	73 993	51	50 438	67.3	32.7	34.3	11.5	2 880	23.3
Ionia	230	-3.0	201	3	190	576 416	2 786	93 986	113	98 668	32.0	68.0	40.1	14.7	4 277	44.4
Iosco	45	4.7	156	D	32	368 737	2 280	46 359	13	45 570	20.2	79.8	28.4	8.1	616	29.5
Iron	31	29.2	296	1	15	409 911	1 494	52 001	3	30 318	84.6	15.4	31.1	6.6	15	18.9
Isabella	195	-10.1	205	4	156	404 161	2 004	56 505	50	52 598	48.4	51.6	43.7	11.4	2 188	47.2
Jackson	193	6.6	153	5	145	453 511	2 902	48 062	43	34 068	49.2	50.8	31.1	6.5	2 994	28.4
Kalamazoo	148	0.7	183	30	119	724 272	3 535	83 756	155	191 310	70.5	29.5	40.3	19.3	2 015	26.7
Kalkaska	24	14.3	138	2	13	284 699	2 175	35 095	6	32 203	87.2	12.8	21.1	5.1	55	12.6
Kent	173	-7.0	143	9	133	612 465	4 023	71 537	150	123 490	75.5	24.5	36.5	13.7	3 967	25.2
Keweenaw	1	NA	65	0	1	151 254	2 218	19 123	D	D	D	D	9.1	0.0	0	0.0
Lake	23	0.0	135	0	14	307 384	2 213	23 567	2	12 235	46.6	53.3	15.6	2.3	96	18.5
Lapeer	189	6.2	159	2	153	650 013	3 867	73 619	51	42 641	65.8	34.2	35.2	9.6	2 610	24.5

STATE County	Value of residential construction authorized by building permits, 2003		Wholesale trade, 1997				Retail trade,[1] 1997				Real estate and rental and leasing, 1997			
	New construction ($1,000)	Number of housing units	Number of establishments	Number of employees	Sales (mil dol)	Annual payroll (mil dol)	Number of establishments	Number of employees	Sales (mil dol)	Annual payroll (mil dol)	Number of establishments	Number of employees	Receipts (mil dol)	Annual payroll (mil dol)
	133	134	135	136	137	138	139	140	141	142	143	144	145	146
MARYLAND—Cont'd														
Washington	142 761	1 105	156	2 184	922.7	62.9	598	7 450	1 220.5	117.3	105	479	43.4	7.3
Wicomico	102 459	1 068	130	1 410	502.1	41.7	464	6 111	994.1	100.0	91	580	52.9	11.1
Worcester	128 263	1 018	76	1 181	476.0	39.1	505	3 285	546.0	59.1	137	1 095	53.9	16.5
Baltimore city	51 421	695	792	14 152	6 171.2	499.2	2 256	23 159	3 438.4	414.7	597	4 807	568.2	124.9
MASSACHUSETTS	3 141 366	20 257	9 993	146 827	112 792.4	6 484.8	26 209	335 736	58 578.0	5 894.8	5 834	41 233	5 925.4	1 214.1
Barnstable	284 753	1 228	259	1 361	462.8	45.5	1 592	13 675	2 518.8	256.5	286	917	138.1	21.4
Berkshire	79 197	417	136	D	D	D	832	8 513	1 280.7	137.7	122	410	43.9	7.5
Bristol	231 456	1 749	709	12 089	11 586.3	471.3	2 365	32 400	5 158.7	511.1	375	1 564	193.6	31.8
Dukes	49 021	239	22	D	D	D	222	931	207.6	24.3	45	112	19.3	2.9
Essex	301 808	2 058	1 071	14 836	9 270.7	671.4	2 703	34 590	6 156.2	585.5	563	2 555	319.4	58.2
Franklin	33 636	244	87	782	349.0	29.3	295	2 880	410.8	46.2	45	101	13.6	1.6
Hampden	140 425	867	573	7 696	4 481.2	285.4	1 862	24 675	3 919.9	384.7	373	1 852	238.0	40.2
Hampshire	80 011	552	109	D	D	D	604	6 976	964.6	107.5	128	500	61.1	8.7
Middlesex	531 944	3 388	2 914	49 166	33 893.5	2 386.3	5 701	78 812	14 462.1	1 491.7	1 412	9 998	1 669.0	305.0
Nantucket	82 960	212	13	D	D	D	178	799	195.7	23.0	37	124	27.3	6.5
Norfolk	333 625	1 908	1 451	23 872	21 949.4	1 128.8	2 599	38 832	7 332.9	715.5	687	5 682	981.6	196.0
Plymouth	327 114	2 000	700	9 214	5 772.6	361.1	1 917	27 147	4 895.9	472.3	337	1 399	243.6	31.3
Suffolk	137 082	1 766	923	11 910	10 935.6	523.8	2 543	30 091	4 842.5	532.2	887	13 000	1 585.4	432.5
Worcester	528 334	3 629	1 026	12 865	12 038.3	493.9	2 796	35 415	6 231.7	606.7	537	3 019	391.6	70.5
MICHIGAN	7 052 549	53 913	13 936	189 057	158 757.3	7 629.6	39 564	529 441	93 706.1	8 922.3	8 302	50 941	6 492.7	1 126.2
Alcona	7 455	79	1	D	D	D	40	290	49.7	3.9	2	D	D	D
Alger	6 346	85	7	D	D	D	55	294	37.1	3.3	9	24	11.0	0.8
Allegan	112 577	826	100	1 003	369.4	29.9	365	3 757	642.0	59.5	64	258	23.5	3.7
Alpena	5 254	38	45	396	143.3	10.3	162	1 719	288.5	25.0	23	127	9.1	2.0
Antrim	43 860	324	24	96	32.5	3.0	96	628	106.5	11.6	24	74	6.6	1.1
Arenac	7 618	86	27	227	74.6	5.3	79	758	127.8	10.6	13	31	4.1	0.4
Baraga	4 421	42	6	67	27.0	1.8	43	337	48.8	4.2	3	D	D	D
Barry	50 037	381	50	317	87.0	8.4	180	1 697	262.3	24.0	28	80	6.2	1.1
Bay	63 809	438	123	1 393	600.0	41.7	541	6 661	1 101.7	104.8	89	364	35.4	6.8
Benzie	46 081	298	9	48	4.6	0.7	78	532	104.8	10.0	16	27	3.3	0.8
Berrien	114 986	608	193	1 887	938.3	60.0	674	8 078	1 302.5	125.6	164	627	186.3	10.5
Branch	21 526	203	49	639	411.8	19.0	174	2 002	321.3	30.4	28	84	14.4	1.6
Calhoun	50 283	394	145	1 646	1 392.4	60.8	567	7 779	1 239.0	114.7	88	425	44.2	6.7
Cass	44 905	304	54	351	252.5	11.1	143	985	159.0	14.6	28	67	7.1	0.8
Charlevoix	35 150	274	14	113	33.9	3.4	172	1 288	202.8	19.3	29	96	9.1	1.3
Cheboygan	23 644	187	21	85	48.9	3.0	195	1 475	254.0	24.0	24	49	6.5	1.1
Chippewa	15 532	189	21	140	24.9	3.2	187	1 839	289.6	25.5	26	107	8.4	1.6
Clare	10 145	137	15	90	47.2	2.8	140	1 319	217.8	21.4	16	32	3.6	0.4
Clinton	125 959	909	56	685	522.2	23.2	207	2 378	426.2	40.1	38	152	17.8	3.3
Crawford	8 142	108	11	D	D	D	65	629	116.0	9.3	11	33	2.6	0.4
Delta	18 611	164	59	452	95.5	10.9	232	2 552	380.0	35.7	24	77	7.5	1.0
Dickinson	9 518	103	54	505	119.1	14.1	177	2 222	316.6	31.4	23	71	4.8	0.7
Eaton	109 113	810	86	774	673.9	25.1	342	5 587	898.7	82.4	77	342	40.7	6.4
Emmet	41 692	280	32	228	75.4	6.7	298	2 509	404.7	41.9	41	120	12.0	2.0
Genesee	310 073	2 240	422	5 884	1 899.4	217.2	1 809	25 369	4 521.3	409.3	350	1 613	193.6	28.7
Gladwin	30 826	256	15	40	11.2	1.1	90	895	152.8	14.2	22	36	4.2	0.6
Gogebic	5 913	53	16	115	35.4	2.6	102	920	135.0	11.4	17	160	3.1	0.9
Grand Traverse	90 139	776	167	1 580	729.9	51.9	634	7 300	1 232.7	117.5	113	441	52.7	9.7
Gratiot	7 762	60	37	493	196.0	14.1	200	1 891	295.8	26.9	20	55	5.5	0.7
Hillsdale	29 113	280	48	416	215.6	12.7	163	1 556	255.8	23.2	29	81	5.8	0.9
Houghton	13 477	124	27	179	33.7	5.3	181	2 052	262.3	25.4	24	80	5.9	0.7
Huron	21 029	173	51	536	194.5	14.0	211	1 800	262.6	23.3	22	41	3.6	0.7
Ingham	141 386	1 437	365	5 830	3 313.4	213.5	1 207	18 762	2 992.6	301.9	295	2 999	223.2	54.1
Ionia	39 257	344	42	325	143.5	11.1	184	2 189	331.2	32.1	17	109	6.2	1.9
Iosco	14 543	145	11	79	7.9	1.4	160	1 475	224.3	21.7	25	60	5.0	0.6
Iron	7 757	61	17	86	18.4	2.1	77	632	92.9	9.2	15	70	1.6	0.3
Isabella	41 854	592	69	817	327.9	23.7	220	3 187	458.6	44.0	46	581	21.3	7.0
Jackson	99 930	831	196	2 339	1 047.2	83.7	564	8 108	1 289.4	126.9	96	465	41.9	7.3
Kalamazoo	262 045	1 996	337	6 278	1 870.1	233.2	978	15 421	2 388.2	230.2	237	2 032	180.7	40.8
Kalkaska	13 131	155	27	225	76.2	8.2	70	660	144.3	11.6	15	56	5.3	1.1
Kent	488 166	3 279	1 314	28 386	15 882.2	1 043.6	2 194	38 200	6 491.8	658.0	567	4 030	493.9	88.5
Keweenaw	2 813	26	3	7	0.7	0.2	10	19	2.7	0.3	3	2	0.2	0.0
Lake	3 554	121	7	27	4.0	0.5	36	244	36.8	3.7	6	11	1.6	0.2
Lapeer	64 815	500	68	373	136.0	13.2	278	3 706	705.7	58.2	52	170	14.9	2.6

1. Establishments with payroll.

Table B. States and Counties — **Professional Services, Manufacturing, and Accommodation and Foodservices**

STATE County	Professional, scientific, and technical services,[1] 1997				Manufacturing, 1997				Accommodation and foodservices, 1997			
	Number of establishments	Number of employees	Receipts (mil dol)	Annual payroll (mil dol)	Number of establishments	Number of employees	Receipts (mil dol)	Annual payroll (mil dol)	Number of establishments	Number of employees	Sales (mil dol)	Annual payroll (mil dol)
	147	148	149	150	151	152	153	154	155	156	157	158
MARYLAND—Cont'd												
Washington	163	854	63.5	22.7	147	9 173	1 924.5	294.2	230	4 135	127.6	36.4
Wicomico	169	967	76.5	29.2	95	5 690	1 041.6	158.1	159	2 964	86.8	25.0
Worcester	103	319	23.1	8.7	38	1 754	275.4	30.9	393	5 697	309.7	77.8
Baltimore city	1 395	14 695	1 645.0	666.3	688	30 216	9 822.2	1 006.2	1 328	20 021	849.9	232.0
MASSACHUSETTS	18 086	177 345	22 744.1	9 261.4	9 554	417 135	77 876.6	16 379.0	14 800	227 476	9 269.9	2 575.6
Barnstable	571	1 919	173.7	63.9	226	2 561	349.4	82.4	1 144	11 852	624.3	177.3
Berkshire	247	1 420	129.3	50.6	207	9 176	1 423.0	344.7	485	7 060	247.3	75.6
Bristol	793	4 101	324.7	112.5	915	49 363	7 651.4	1 654.2	1 112	16 980	557.3	152.7
Dukes	44	109	10.3	4.3	NA	NA	NA	NA	139	888	87.9	25.3
Essex	1 735	9 589	1 058.1	377.4	1 200	57 660	13 728.1	2 362.4	1 573	22 544	872.0	238.5
Franklin	110	359	28.8	9.0	119	5 700	756.0	182.2	150	1 715	49.8	14.3
Hampden	738	5 108	398.3	173.7	802	33 350	5 953.5	1 204.0	931	13 492	430.3	119.7
Hampshire	265	1 411	93.8	34.2	180	5 760	1 048.3	192.3	332	4 816	147.8	42.8
Middlesex	5 744	73 319	9 250.9	4 134.1	2 437	118 002	22 587.1	5 216.5	3 045	48 816	2 055.4	558.2
Nantucket	44	133	14.3	6.0	NA	NA	NA	NA	106	899	69.1	20.1
Norfolk	2 286	16 489	1 983.8	768.5	863	36 648	6 528.4	1 515.2	1 299	21 115	802.5	222.0
Plymouth	937	5 219	530.4	228.1	613	16 063	2 210.8	534.4	887	14 410	482.0	135.0
Suffolk	3 140	50 260	7 923.2	2 969.3	624	21 366	4 317.9	745.4	2 075	41 647	2 129.0	598.5
Worcester	1 432	7 909	824.4	329.8	1 336	61 344	11 303.4	2 340.9	1 522	21 242	715.1	195.6
MICHIGAN	18 614	162 971	16 231.7	6 882.9	16 045	833 429	214 900.7	34 418.9	18 958	320 014	10 158.7	2 835.8
Alcona	10	94	3.4	1.7	NA	NA	NA	NA	38	194	5.5	1.3
Alger	8	13	1.1	0.3	13	873	195.8	29.7	57	392	12.6	3.1
Allegan	82	330	17.3	7.1	203	15 984	3 108.9	585.9	174	2 136	65.6	18.1
Alpena	33	127	8.6	3.5	58	2 445	480.1	90.8	74	1 130	27.2	7.4
Antrim	31	589	11.2	5.9	56	1 323	164.9	38.7	71	930	49.3	15.6
Arenac	20	54	4.4	1.5	37	732	91.8	18.9	51	499	14.7	3.8
Baraga	3	5	0.1	0.0	26	715	115.2	21.6	21	211	4.6	1.3
Barry	45	170	12.9	4.8	71	3 145	525.2	102.1	84	1 095	28.0	7.9
Bay	138	834	62.8	28.6	152	7 459	1 928.6	347.0	241	3 922	106.5	29.6
Benzie	19	49	2.6	0.9	23	657	70.1	12.3	60	819	28.7	8.0
Berrien	255	1 338	124.6	48.9	397	16 996	2 394.2	539.1	383	5 328	163.5	44.0
Branch	35	212	15.3	6.2	90	3 572	516.5	102.4	78	1 026	30.0	7.4
Calhoun	168	836	68.8	29.1	222	16 973	4 514.8	613.8	307	5 010	147.5	42.5
Cass	52	193	11.8	4.3	87	3 384	570.8	95.9	76	708	20.0	5.2
Charlevoix	57	191	14.1	5.4	69	3 624	724.1	116.9	84	1 384	45.0	16.4
Cheboygan	40	145	10.3	3.4	37	711	76.6	17.9	128	715	33.6	8.6
Chippewa	44	198	10.2	4.5	31	818	63.2	15.0	147	1 475	49.0	12.3
Clare	31	109	7.4	3.2	28	924	120.9	23.9	80	895	25.2	6.7
Clinton	84	410	39.2	13.6	62	2 586	450.3	100.3	83	1 213	32.4	9.2
Crawford	16	52	2.9	1.1	17	503	104.3	15.8	47	409	14.7	3.9
Delta	47	730	23.3	12.8	59	2 834	702.4	124.3	132	1 529	40.0	10.5
Dickinson	51	224	19.4	6.4	50	2 478	655.3	100.6	92	1 124	26.7	7.7
Eaton	133	580	38.1	17.3	94	D	D	D	156	3 008	88.4	25.4
Emmet	86	312	24.7	9.7	57	1 377	168.2	39.1	143	1 970	88.5	24.7
Genesee	660	4 149	274.3	125.2	355	34 414	11 240.3	1 744.6	794	13 618	403.9	111.2
Gladwin	22	64	5.3	1.2	46	1 406	206.8	42.1	42	475	11.7	3.4
Gogebic	25	103	4.9	2.2	27	709	62.5	14.8	70	1 175	40.0	10.5
Grand Traverse	284	1 990	133.7	58.1	190	5 867	875.9	177.1	233	3 895	134.2	37.3
Gratiot	38	94	5.7	1.9	51	2 282	265.7	77.0	67	1 009	29.8	7.6
Hillsdale	38	123	6.5	2.8	104	6 510	1 134.5	176.1	75	815	23.6	6.3
Houghton	48	266	15.4	7.1	43	698	72.1	16.3	118	1 272	30.3	8.3
Huron	38	150	7.1	3.2	67	4 216	612.8	126.9	103	719	23.2	6.1
Ingham	680	5 171	520.7	222.7	272	D	D	D	597	13 137	368.9	104.8
Ionia	56	205	12.3	4.5	80	4 308	852.8	138.0	85	893	26.0	6.5
Iosco	33	101	5.3	2.3	34	1 299	164.7	31.5	88	795	25.8	6.6
Iron	30	105	6.6	2.7	NA	NA	NA	NA	49	577	11.5	3.9
Isabella	86	457	39.4	16.2	58	2 221	402.5	61.2	103	2 498	68.5	19.5
Jackson	200	1 354	90.8	45.5	351	12 248	2 271.8	422.0	267	4 467	137.0	37.7
Kalamazoo	481	3 366	306.0	134.4	399	22 007	4 108.6	820.9	452	9 317	260.6	78.2
Kalkaska	13	42	3.5	1.3	19	1 187	178.2	34.5	29	296	9.0	2.4
Kent	1 303	11 722	1 113.1	457.4	1 205	80 020	14 765.5	3 189.9	954	20 741	617.5	181.6
Keweenaw	NA	NA	NA	NA	NA	NA	NA	NA	21	D	D	D
Lake	6	15	0.7	0.2	NA	NA	NA	NA	36	201	7.9	1.9
Lapeer	98	430	28.6	10.1	139	6 118	837.2	155.6	119	2 045	52.1	14.1

1. Firms subject to federal tax.

Table B. States and Counties — **Health Care and Social Assistance, Other Services, and Federal Funds**

STATE County	Health care and social assistance,[1] 1997				Other services,[1] 1997				Federal funds and grants, 2002–2003 Expenditures (mil dol)			
										Direct payments for individuals[2]		
	Number of establishments	Number of employees	Receipts (mil dol)	Annual payroll (mil dol)	Number of establishments	Number of employees	Receipts (mil dol)	Annual payroll (mil dol)	Total	Social Security and government retirement	Medicare	Food stamps and Supplemental Security Income
	159	160	161	162	163	164	165	166	167	168	169	170
MARYLAND—Cont'd												
Washington	225	3 006	208.0	95.5	207	1 524	81.7	25.4	690.8	315.5	124.8	15.3
Wicomico	200	2 520	159.9	86.6	146	986	60.1	18.1	422.0	179.6	73.9	12.7
Worcester	67	597	27.2	11.1	85	364	19.7	6.0	510.0	171.7	52.4	5.1
Baltimore city	1 220	16 856	1 093.8	486.1	891	6 733	426.4	131.5	9 446.9	1 363.1	1 217.8	311.7
MASSACHUSETTS	11 887	182 902	11 361.4	5 310.5	10 806	61 557	4 359.8	1 338.6	51 264.8	13 033.5	8 141.4	1 014.1
Barnstable	482	5 989	336.5	163.8	439	1 819	124.6	36.0	1 767.5	809.4	390.2	20.2
Berkshire	268	4 334	254.6	113.7	231	1 074	62.7	18.7	1 087.9	342.7	213.0	21.7
Bristol	844	12 815	711.6	350.6	878	4 340	295.9	79.6	3 276.2	1 101.4	678.5	100.9
Dukes	33	D	D	D	36	D	D	D	68.4	34.3	17.8	0.4
Essex	1 317	19 159	1 104.7	558.8	1 181	6 614	441.3	149.5	5 356.7	1 474.6	904.4	126.9
Franklin	107	1 502	72.7	35.1	116	471	29.1	7.9	374.9	151.9	79.9	10.0
Hampden	806	13 261	794.1	367.4	742	4 092	278.1	85.2	2 916.3	982.6	556.8	147.0
Hampshire	225	2 407	143.5	65.9	195	818	56.7	16.1	785.2	279.7	129.6	10.8
Middlesex	2 991	42 136	2 707.8	1 227.3	2 661	16 875	1 307.7	428.7	12 515.4	2 764.7	1 802.9	129.9
Nantucket	20	D	D	D	20	D	D	D	36.7	17.1	8.7	0.1
Norfolk	1 672	25 589	1 542.9	714.3	1 266	7 302	501.0	159.0	3 551.9	1 116.3	881.2	34.1
Plymouth	811	13 663	737.4	372.8	702	3 550	243.6	70.3	2 214.4	950.3	509.8	48.6
Suffolk	1 067	20 943	1 517.1	737.0	1 157	8 142	558.9	160.9	9 797.1	1 540.3	1 036.7	245.9
Worcester	1 244	20 902	1 425.3	599.7	1 182	6 312	444.3	122.9	3 926.5	1 467.5	931.8	117.7
MICHIGAN	18 943	186 954	11 811.5	5 696.8	14 705	93 792	6 159.1	1 893.8	57 870.1	20 916.6	10 192.5	1 908.8
Alcona	7	153	5.4	2.6	8	19	1.7	0.2	89.9	48.2	17.4	1.6
Alger	12	147	4.8	1.9	13	31	1.9	0.4	64.1	29.1	12.5	1.1
Allegan	98	1 251	64.8	32.7	125	560	33.5	9.6	377.0	169.4	66.6	10.5
Alpena	72	661	33.8	15.2	61	393	18.3	6.8	207.3	92.8	40.4	7.8
Antrim	31	277	10.2	5.2	32	94	6.4	1.7	119.8	62.9	23.3	2.8
Arenac	39	938	21.1	9.2	28	107	6.8	1.7	118.0	52.8	22.8	3.2
Baraga	16	104	3.9	2.0	7	20	1.4	0.2	58.8	23.8	9.5	1.5
Barry	61	498	26.9	11.5	86	415	26.0	7.9	182.8	103.6	34.4	5.3
Bay	210	2 225	132.9	65.2	198	1 004	55.9	16.2	582.9	258.2	121.5	20.5
Benzie	22	146	7.0	3.2	19	48	2.7	0.7	85.8	46.8	13.8	1.8
Berrien	281	2 395	154.1	71.3	262	1 452	77.6	25.1	876.4	389.3	172.5	41.6
Branch	72	570	34.3	13.7	59	199	13.9	3.3	183.0	93.6	40.2	4.2
Calhoun	300	3 100	176.3	79.3	207	1 433	91.5	26.9	971.2	352.9	149.8	33.3
Cass	46	233	11.0	4.7	60	216	11.8	3.3	199.7	99.6	37.4	7.7
Charlevoix	48	216	12.2	4.5	59	208	15.3	4.0	123.5	64.2	21.5	2.1
Cheboygan	53	295	15.9	6.9	53	237	10.2	3.1	132.2	69.4	27.2	3.8
Chippewa	40	366	19.1	9.7	56	193	10.8	2.8	249.2	92.1	31.0	5.3
Clare	40	456	19.3	7.3	35	77	5.1	1.1	193.0	98.4	41.3	9.1
Clinton	65	666	30.8	13.3	71	268	17.6	5.2	207.0	99.3	34.7	3.9
Crawford	21	141	10.0	4.3	13	59	3.5	1.2	76.6	37.4	13.7	2.1
Delta	61	443	20.4	9.1	79	450	27.9	6.8	237.8	113.8	43.7	6.2
Dickinson	85	755	37.3	16.9	69	301	20.2	5.0	204.5	80.2	26.1	3.3
Eaton	158	1 269	59.5	26.2	103	592	32.4	9.3	382.9	158.0	60.3	6.4
Emmet	85	1 233	114.2	52.0	52	193	10.2	3.3	139.9	74.9	25.7	3.0
Genesee	1 037	9 466	610.5	310.7	627	4 165	255.2	74.4	2 292.2	940.7	510.5	128.4
Gladwin	22	191	7.3	3.3	23	81	5.0	1.3	150.3	82.8	34.2	5.0
Gogebic	26	364	14.3	9.2	31	113	6.8	1.7	133.4	59.7	27.2	3.4
Grand Traverse	272	2 175	157.5	72.2	187	1 045	70.5	22.1	399.3	196.5	64.4	7.4
Gratiot	76	885	44.7	21.8	63	234	17.2	4.4	206.6	88.0	41.7	7.1
Hillsdale	66	411	22.7	10.6	57	219	12.8	3.4	196.5	98.9	36.6	5.9
Houghton	60	650	26.5	12.7	54	175	12.9	3.1	211.4	82.5	37.8	5.2
Huron	88	566	27.3	12.9	53	190	12.1	2.8	218.1	100.2	44.8	5.1
Ingham	659	5 597	407.3	198.4	438	3 073	162.9	53.7	3 641.0	958.5	248.4	59.0
Ionia	78	747	34.4	14.9	75	354	21.5	6.2	209.1	101.3	42.9	7.0
Iosco	35	226	11.1	5.5	45	159	7.8	2.2	192.0	107.4	39.7	4.3
Iron	21	295	15.3	7.6	17	57	3.0	0.7	93.6	46.6	20.5	1.9
Isabella	101	1 005	50.8	23.8	80	414	22.7	5.6	213.0	90.5	33.8	8.1
Jackson	299	2 649	180.0	85.7	238	1 294	77.2	22.2	722.6	342.1	148.3	29.2
Kalamazoo	467	5 746	407.2	205.0	412	2 814	176.6	55.9	1 064.8	448.6	177.9	38.7
Kalkaska	14	73	4.3	2.1	26	174	10.8	3.6	66.2	32.8	13.4	1.9
Kent	1 075	12 469	832.0	420.3	975	7 146	503.4	149.3	2 354.9	981.5	378.9	90.0
Keweenaw	2	D	D	D	2	D	D	D	14.0	7.2	3.3	0.2
Lake	11	182	7.4	4.1	6	D	D	D	76.6	35.5	14.9	4.0
Lapeer	116	915	51.3	26.9	95	454	30.0	7.9	274.5	146.4	56.1	5.9

1. Firms subject to federal tax.   2. State totals may include programs not allocated by county.

Table B. States and Counties — **Federal Funds and Local Government Finances**

STATE County	Federal funds and grants, 2002–2003 (cont'd)							Local government finances, 2002				
	Expenditures (mil dol) (cont'd)							General revenue				
	Procurement contract awards		Grants[1]							Taxes		
											Per capita[2] (dollars)	
	Salaries and wages	Defense	Other	Medicaid and other health-related	Nutrition and family welfare	Education	Other	Total (mil dol)	Intergovern-mental (mil dol)	Total (mil dol)	Total	Property
	171	172	173	174	175	176	177	178	179	180	181	182
MARYLAND—Cont'd												
Washington	34.2	48.8	17.7	64.9	13.7	3.6	39.8	331.3	116.3	147.3	1 097	663
Wicomico	25.5	18.2	4.0	50.8	15.2	4.2	27.1	221.3	86.3	94.4	1 094	662
Worcester	13.6	201.6	3.4	25.2	3.9	2.6	24.4	184.9	33.1	115.7	2 379	1 560
Baltimore city	853.5	696.3	995.5	2 242.0	553.1	250.1	792.7	2 566.1	1 483.1	809.8	1 268	781
MASSACHUSETTS	3 446.4	6 364.8	1 992.7	7 346.5	1 275.8	816.7	3 889.4	X	X	X	X	X
Barnstable	140.3	107.1	33.9	101.7	18.6	13.7	124.2	725.6	178.1	427.6	1 871	1 751
Berkshire	66.8	103.1	141.4	107.8	22.6	13.0	48.5	377.7	177.4	160.5	1 203	1 160
Bristol	100.5	368.4	37.5	561.1	91.5	48.0	152.4	1 438.8	750.5	521.4	960	923
Dukes	3.8	0.0	1.2	5.6	1.0	0.7	2.9	94.2	22.6	54.5	3 533	3 367
Essex	240.2	1 581.2	164.6	490.1	102.7	66.6	176.1	2 119.9	875.0	952.9	1 295	1 261
Franklin	14.5	12.5	3.8	44.9	15.6	5.6	29.5	218.1	107.9	90.0	1 255	1 225
Hampden	305.9	40.0	77.1	407.2	121.4	48.7	183.4	1 445.6	814.5	468.4	1 020	999
Hampshire	80.0	40.1	17.4	74.1	11.1	15.0	101.4	343.4	145.0	152.2	992	968
Middlesex	935.4	3 180.5	1 060.8	1 424.6	125.1	314.5	692.8	4 607.7	1 470.2	2 391.0	1 622	1 575
Nantucket	4.8	0.0	1.0	2.4	0.2	0.2	1.6	56.3	3.5	39.8	3 818	3 538
Norfolk	138.2	658.5	81.8	274.0	39.5	37.1	110.6	1 782.2	469.4	1 061.4	1 617	1 571
Plymouth	164.5	30.5	46.5	261.7	52.4	34.0	97.6	1 354.8	576.2	648.1	1 334	1 277
Suffolk	1 032.2	136.0	302.7	2 930.1	456.4	108.6	1 845.5	3 923.3	2 355.9	1 137.8	1 649	1 540
Worcester	219.1	106.7	22.9	626.8	101.6	67.0	225.1	2 425.0	1 185.9	967.1	1 255	1 188
MICHIGAN	3 417.9	2 494.2	1 389.6	6 173.8	2 317.3	1 193.3	3 285.5	X	X	X	X	X
Alcona	2.5	0.1	0.6	16.9	1.5	0.9	-0.2	28.2	9.9	9.1	798	774
Alger	3.9	0.1	1.1	9.2	1.3	1.6	3.8	27.2	16.5	6.4	648	634
Allegan	10.8	1.1	2.9	36.0	10.1	48.7	10.7	261.2	151.1	66.7	610	596
Alpena	11.1	2.4	1.5	18.6	20.7	2.5	5.4	211.4	79.0	22.0	710	698
Antrim	3.9	4.0	2.9	11.8	2.1	1.3	3.8	79.1	35.0	28.1	1 180	1 156
Arenac	3.8	4.8	1.0	14.0	3.1	2.7	6.6	41.7	25.6	10.6	617	610
Baraga	2.4	0.0	0.7	9.7	1.6	1.4	7.7	40.1	14.8	6.1	697	693
Barry	6.1	2.2	1.6	16.5	4.7	1.9	1.6	121.8	74.9	25.9	448	441
Bay	17.4	3.9	5.0	57.2	17.9	8.6	48.7	427.7	207.7	91.4	833	816
Benzie	2.9	0.0	2.6	10.4	1.3	0.9	5.0	54.8	21.3	16.4	974	960
Berrien	25.5	2.1	13.7	137.2	29.5	14.1	36.4	472.4	270.6	114.2	704	684
Branch	5.4	0.0	1.5	20.0	6.8	3.4	2.4	178.1	74.2	23.1	499	479
Calhoun	172.0	25.9	34.3	107.1	31.3	15.1	37.4	455.1	257.8	100.2	724	603
Cass	5.6	0.1	1.3	25.7	5.9	4.5	5.1	125.7	75.3	24.8	484	470
Charlevoix	6.4	7.5	3.0	9.9	2.5	1.6	3.9	100.8	40.5	32.8	1 244	1 238
Cheboygan	8.0	0.0	0.9	15.5	3.2	1.5	2.0	62.8	32.8	20.2	747	734
Chippewa	21.2	8.0	3.4	43.3	13.4	6.7	17.6	111.7	62.8	21.6	555	552
Clare	3.5	0.1	1.0	19.6	7.7	2.3	5.6	97.0	60.0	18.7	589	577
Clinton	33.5	0.0	5.8	10.0	4.4	2.6	4.7	142.9	85.3	30.7	460	444
Crawford	10.3	2.8	0.5	4.7	2.2	1.0	0.9	37.3	19.9	11.8	798	751
Delta	13.2	5.2	2.3	24.9	8.5	4.8	10.4	117.3	64.4	26.1	680	679
Dickinson	33.2	19.0	13.9	10.6	4.2	1.4	11.4	119.7	40.5	23.2	849	842
Eaton	29.4	0.8	2.3	23.1	6.4	4.5	84.4	239.7	141.3	59.1	560	534
Emmet	6.5	0.0	1.5	15.3	3.1	2.0	5.4	151.3	45.1	50.8	1 570	1 539
Genesee	92.6	0.4	27.2	283.2	106.8	41.4	96.3	1 332.5	824.1	232.4	526	510
Gladwin	3.5	0.0	0.9	13.9	4.4	2.0	2.4	54.0	32.6	14.7	550	539
Gogebic	11.0	2.6	4.5	16.7	3.5	2.0	1.2	73.3	38.2	11.3	650	646
Grand Traverse	35.8	0.4	16.9	39.2	12.5	3.5	17.4	313.9	156.0	74.4	915	886
Gratiot	8.1	0.6	2.6	28.6	5.6	3.6	10.6	102.1	70.6	16.6	391	384
Hillsdale	6.4	0.6	1.6	24.3	6.2	2.6	5.1	121.3	76.7	20.1	428	423
Houghton	13.2	6.0	3.3	27.6	7.9	2.9	18.8	132.8	80.1	15.7	439	433
Huron	6.6	0.0	1.7	24.9	4.5	2.5	14.8	113.0	56.4	29.8	842	825
Ingham	123.3	115.5	32.1	375.1	501.6	349.6	800.4	1 129.9	585.6	285.9	1 016	873
Ionia	6.9	0.1	1.8	24.7	6.6	3.4	6.8	158.5	107.0	25.7	408	404
Iosco	6.6	2.6	1.6	10.8	4.3	2.3	9.4	97.8	56.6	22.7	840	824
Iron	3.5	0.1	1.2	11.4	1.7	0.9	5.3	46.6	24.9	10.3	812	805
Isabella	8.5	0.0	1.9	30.3	6.0	4.9	8.4	203.6	121.9	26.0	402	378
Jackson	28.2	14.6	10.5	77.6	27.2	10.4	21.7	465.9	306.5	75.2	467	411
Kalamazoo	76.3	39.7	22.6	129.0	32.6	24.2	49.3	664.6	329.5	187.5	777	758
Kalkaska	1.8	2.7	0.6	8.4	2.1	1.2	0.8	48.6	17.7	12.3	723	705
Kent	193.2	124.8	69.1	237.8	55.8	34.9	145.3	1 965.6	1 023.4	483.1	822	714
Keweenaw	0.9	0.1	0.1	1.0	0.3	0.3	0.4	6.4	2.7	1.4	635	615
Lake	3.2	0.0	0.5	12.2	2.7	1.3	1.7	28.8	15.8	8.9	767	765
Lapeer	10.5	0.9	2.8	32.1	7.4	4.1	4.5	217.2	133.6	41.9	462	425

1. State totals may include programs not allocated by county.   2. Based on the resident population estimated as of July 1 of the year shown.

Local Government Finances, Government Employment, and Elections

STATE County	Local government finances, 2002 (cont'd)									Government employment, 2002			Presidential election, 2004		
	Direct general expenditure							Debt outstanding					Percent of vote cast —		
			Percent of total for —												
	Total (mil dol)	Per capita[1] (dollars)	Education	Health and hospitals	Police protection	Public welfare	Highways	Total (mil dol)	Per capita[1] (dollars)	Federal civilian	Federal military	State and local	Democratic	Republican	All other
	183	184	185	186	187	188	189	190	191	192	193	194	195	196	197
MARYLAND—Cont'd															
Washington	305.7	2 277	59.8	1.1	4.7	0.9	4.3	201.6	1 502	615	345	7 582	34.9	64.2	1.0
Wicomico	230.2	2 667	56.2	1.1	5.0	3.6	5.4	142.2	1 647	331	212	6 078	40.3	58.8	0.9
Worcester	198.6	4 085	35.4	1.2	7.3	0.5	4.4	170.2	3 499	236	154	3 109	38.0	61.2	0.9
Baltimore city	2 375.4	3 720	40.5	2.7	10.8	0.3	4.9	1 959.9	3 069	11 332	1 800	68 343	82.2	16.8	1.0
MASSACHUSETTS	X	X	X	X	X	X	X	X	X	51 524	19 064	381 624	62.1	37.0	0.9
Barnstable	714.2	3 124	42.5	1.2	5.8	0.6	3.8	635.1	2 779	1 490	1 142	12 327	54.2	43.9	1.9
Berkshire	399.3	2 992	58.5	0.4	3.4	0.1	5.9	295.9	2 217	429	309	7 695	73.3	25.8	0.8
Bristol	1 545.3	2 844	54.0	0.7	5.4	0.6	3.0	1 045.8	1 924	1 148	1 460	26 314	63.7	35.6	0.7
Dukes	103.5	6 710	39.8	1.4	4.6	0.0	4.0	93.8	6 078	44	35	1 277	72.9	26.2	0.9
Essex	2 162.0	2 939	54.2	2.5	5.1	0.5	2.8	1 967.1	2 674	4 120	1 767	36 504	58.5	40.7	0.8
Franklin	207.8	2 898	58.8	0.5	3.2	0.2	6.8	164.0	2 287	179	163	5 301	68.6	29.7	1.6
Hampden	1 447.6	3 153	54.3	0.5	5.7	0.9	2.8	1 915.8	4 173	4 805	1 241	31 000	61.1	38.1	0.8
Hampshire	359.0	2 340	57.4	0.7	4.4	0.1	4.3	278.7	1 817	1 224	368	14 944	69.8	28.8	1.3
Middlesex	4 760.9	3 230	50.3	9.2	5.1	0.3	3.0	2 965.5	2 012	13 692	5 210	71 159	64.2	34.7	1.0
Nantucket	57.0	5 473	34.7	0.3	4.8	5.3	0.6	49.1	4 714	48	55	633	63.3	35.9	0.8
Norfolk	1 852.4	2 822	53.6	2.1	5.9	0.1	3.8	1 165.4	1 775	2 249	1 513	29 899	60.4	38.8	0.8
Plymouth	1 507.5	3 104	58.4	0.4	4.7	0.2	2.8	930.7	1 916	4 259	1 175	25 052	53.8	45.4	0.7
Suffolk	2 923.7	4 238	32.9	6.4	9.3	4.1	2.1	5 909.6	8 566	14 904	2 689	72 832	76.1	23.0	0.9
Worcester	2 314.6	3 005	56.5	0.7	4.3	0.1	3.5	2 689.5	3 491	2 933	1 937	46 687	56.5	42.6	0.9
MICHIGAN	X	X	X	X	X	X	X	X	X	54 068	19 652	624 588	51.2	47.8	1.0
Alcona	30.5	2 664	38.6	17.6	2.9	7.6	6.5	22.3	1 949	46	20	353	44.0	55.0	1.0
Alger	29.5	3 008	42.2	1.5	2.5	2.0	20.2	18.2	1 863	92	17	887	50.2	48.6	1.2
Allegan	265.3	2 427	58.0	7.7	3.8	5.1	5.0	245.0	2 241	192	187	4 467	36.5	62.5	1.0
Alpena	207.4	6 684	27.6	53.8	1.1	0.4	4.6	49.5	1 596	106	55	3 146	48.7	50.4	0.9
Antrim	76.4	3 207	43.4	8.8	3.8	12.3	9.4	38.4	1 614	60	41	1 376	37.2	61.5	1.2
Arenac	48.7	2 832	64.7	1.2	2.9	0.5	10.6	36.9	2 145	52	29	921	49.6	49.5	0.8
Baraga	37.1	4 265	31.1	41.9	2.0	0.0	9.3	21.4	2 456	41	38	1 735	45.1	53.7	1.3
Barry	111.8	1 929	55.2	5.5	3.4	7.9	7.0	80.2	1 384	104	99	2 164	37.4	61.6	1.1
Bay	406.3	3 705	49.6	17.0	3.7	3.4	5.6	135.6	1 236	289	215	6 437	54.4	44.6	1.0
Benzie	52.1	3 100	38.8	2.0	2.2	0.4	9.6	26.2	1 556	39	38	755	44.8	54.0	1.1
Berrien	478.0	2 946	53.4	6.6	4.0	1.1	6.7	224.8	1 385	419	305	8 228	44.0	55.0	1.0
Branch	176.0	3 811	34.9	38.3	1.9	3.2	4.5	83.1	1 800	103	79	3 395	39.0	60.0	1.0
Calhoun	466.0	3 368	55.5	5.1	4.6	3.0	5.3	311.7	2 252	3 351	299	7 897	47.7	51.2	1.1
Cass	120.6	2 352	64.3	6.1	3.1	1.1	4.5	88.3	1 722	98	88	2 362	42.1	57.1	0.9
Charlevoix	116.0	4 395	47.1	11.2	2.0	5.3	10.6	73.8	2 797	59	113	1 825	40.5	58.1	1.4
Cheboygan	62.9	2 325	49.9	2.5	3.9	1.6	13.0	38.6	1 425	68	127	1 126	42.8	56.1	1.1
Chippewa	118.9	3 057	47.0	11.3	2.7	1.0	10.9	113.5	2 919	320	203	6 888	43.7	55.3	1.0
Clare	92.6	2 923	60.0	0.6	3.1	0.6	9.1	41.5	1 309	60	54	1 583	49.1	49.8	1.1
Clinton	134.3	2 015	55.0	0.6	4.1	0.8	8.6	183.4	2 751	315	409	2 138	41.0	58.2	0.9
Crawford	36.2	2 455	47.5	0.2	5.3	2.1	12.6	26.3	1 783	168	25	710	43.2	55.5	1.3
Delta	118.8	3 100	61.8	8.8	1.8	0.0	2.9	86.7	2 262	224	66	2 177	48.8	50.3	0.9
Dickinson	117.9	4 313	30.7	39.2	2.5	0.5	6.5	67.5	2 470	596	48	2 331	41.7	57.0	1.2
Eaton	253.2	2 398	59.2	2.8	4.1	2.4	7.1	275.4	2 608	264	186	5 986	45.6	53.4	1.0
Emmet	151.7	4 691	43.5	21.5	1.8	4.1	4.8	183.3	5 670	105	56	2 606	39.4	59.5	1.1
Genesee	1 364.2	3 090	58.8	8.6	2.8	1.0	3.5	603.3	1 367	1 454	761	24 332	60.0	39.2	0.7
Gladwin	51.6	1 930	56.2	2.1	3.2	1.0	13.0	21.6	807	61	46	1 099	48.0	51.2	0.9
Gogebic	70.7	4 062	41.6	14.3	3.3	9.2	10.1	30.3	1 741	182	30	1 947	52.3	46.6	1.1
Grand Traverse	312.9	3 850	45.0	12.8	2.4	5.9	5.3	441.3	5 431	453	272	5 511	39.5	59.4	1.1
Gratiot	103.7	2 449	58.8	5.7	3.5	1.3	7.7	61.3	1 446	116	73	2 574	42.5	56.6	1.0
Hillsdale	128.7	2 739	53.3	0.6	2.6	17.5	8.5	153.6	3 269	123	81	2 440	35.2	63.3	1.4
Houghton	127.9	3 564	33.5	26.7	1.7	9.2	8.4	94.1	2 622	210	96	4 398	42.5	56.1	1.5
Huron	122.0	3 445	44.3	6.9	2.7	6.2	13.3	88.5	2 498	116	66	2 082	43.7	55.4	1.0
Ingham	1 194.3	4 245	48.0	7.8	3.8	6.2	3.1	1 325.5	4 711	2 166	613	48 763	57.8	41.1	1.1
Ionia	159.7	2 537	58.4	5.7	2.8	0.8	6.1	207.3	3 294	121	108	3 978	38.6	60.1	1.3
Iosco	90.7	3 361	49.6	14.9	1.5	4.4	4.3	80.7	2 990	122	68	1 728	46.8	52.1	1.1
Iron	44.1	3 459	34.8	8.1	2.1	14.8	13.4	20.6	1 617	58	22	1 175	48.8	50.1	1.1
Isabella	212.0	3 286	26.9	33.2	2.7	10.3	5.3	118.8	1 841	149	118	10 133	50.6	48.2	1.2
Jackson	500.8	3 111	50.0	14.1	2.7	2.1	4.6	312.3	1 940	434	278	10 032	43.4	55.6	1.0
Kalamazoo	658.2	2 726	52.5	6.5	7.6	1.3	5.5	883.8	3 660	1 165	423	16 387	51.3	47.7	1.0
Kalkaska	46.3	2 716	31.8	29.1	5.6	3.8	11.0	19.0	1 118	38	29	879	38.0	60.7	1.3
Kent	2 157.0	3 669	46.3	6.2	5.0	1.0	4.1	2 642.2	4 494	2 980	1 054	25 230	40.2	58.9	1.0
Keweenaw	6.3	2 836	1.6	0.5	3.5	2.2	35.2	0.6	294	31	0	123	43.8	54.3	1.9
Lake	24.1	2 070	33.8	2.7	5.1	2.8	16.3	12.1	1 041	59	20	474	51.0	47.7	1.3
Lapeer	203.3	2 240	50.9	16.0	5.1	0.1	8.5	118.2	1 302	165	157	4 676	41.0	57.9	1.1

1. Based on the resident population estimated as of July 1 of the year shown.

Table B. States and Counties — **Land Area and Population**

| STATE/ County code | CBSA code[1] | County Type[2] | STATE County | Land area,[3] (sq km) 2000 | Population and population characteristics, 2003 | | | Race alone or in combination, not Hispanic or Latino (percent) | | | | | Age (percent) | | | | | |
| | | | | | Total persons | Rank | Per square kilometer | White | Black | Am. Indian, Alaska Native | Asian and Pacific Islander | Percent Hispanic or Latino[4] | Under 5 years | 5 to 17 years | 18 to 24 years | 25 to 34 years | 35 to 44 years | 45 to 54 years |
				1	2	3	4	5	6	7	8	9	10	11	12	13	14	15
			MICHIGAN—Cont'd															
26 089	45900	9	Leelanau	903	21 860	1 709	24.2	92.7	0.5	3.9	0.3	3.2	4.2	17.8	8.4	8.4	13.7	17.6
26 091	10300	4	Lenawee	1 944	100 786	539	51.8	90.0	2.3	0.7	0.7	7.2	5.9	18.5	10.4	12.2	15.1	15.0
26 093	19820	1	Livingston	1 472	172 881	325	117.4	96.9	0.7	0.9	1.0	1.4	6.0	20.2	9.2	11.6	17.7	15.8
26 095	...	7	Luce	2 339	6 919	2 696	3.0	85.0	7.7	6.6	0.6	1.8	4.0	15.1	10.3	14.9	15.7	14.8
26 097	...	7	Mackinac	2 646	11 470	2 336	4.3	85.4	0.4	17.3	0.3	0.9	4.1	16.1	7.6	10.0	14.1	15.8
26 099	19820	1	Macomb	1 244	813 948	60	654.3	91.0	4.5	0.8	3.2	1.8	6.1	17.5	8.3	13.9	16.4	14.3
26 101	...	7	Manistee	1 408	25 317	1 556	18.0	94.0	1.9	2.2	0.5	2.4	4.9	16.1	8.9	11.0	14.3	15.2
26 103	32100	5	Marquette	4 717	64 616	771	13.7	95.7	1.6	2.3	0.7	0.8	4.5	14.9	13.7	12.0	14.3	16.2
26 105	...	7	Mason	1 282	28 685	1 437	22.4	94.9	1.0	1.4	0.3	3.4	5.2	17.3	9.2	10.5	14.5	15.2
26 107	13660	6	Mecosta	1 439	41 728	1 091	29.0	93.6	4.3	1.3	1.1	1.2	5.7	15.9	18.1	12.2	11.8	11.7
26 109	31940	7	Menominee	2 703	25 084	1 566	9.3	96.7	0.4	2.5	0.3	0.7	5.4	16.8	9.4	9.7	15.2	15.9
26 111	33220	4	Midland	1 350	84 492	631	62.6	95.2	1.4	0.7	1.9	1.6	5.9	19.3	10.0	11.4	16.2	15.0
26 113	15620	9	Missaukee	1 468	15 189	2 088	10.3	97.5	0.5	1.2	0.4	1.2	5.8	19.1	9.8	10.9	15.0	13.4
26 115	33780	3	Monroe	1 427	150 673	375	105.6	95.0	2.3	0.8	0.8	2.2	5.8	19.5	9.8	12.0	16.1	15.2
26 117	...	6	Montcalm	1 834	62 926	785	34.3	94.2	2.3	1.2	0.6	2.8	6.4	19.2	9.9	12.9	15.8	13.6
26 119	...	9	Montmorency	1 418	10 492	2 400	7.4	98.3	0.4	0.8	0.1	0.8	3.9	14.5	8.5	8.2	12.4	14.6
26 121	34740	3	Muskegon	1 319	173 090	324	131.2	80.9	14.8	1.5	0.7	3.8	6.7	19.7	9.8	12.4	15.2	14.2
26 123	24340	2	Newaygo	2 182	49 271	948	22.6	93.5	1.4	1.3	0.4	4.4	6.2	21.1	9.5	10.8	15.3	13.8
26 125	19820	1	Oakland	2 260	1 207 869	31	534.5	81.0	11.5	0.7	5.6	2.6	6.4	18.1	7.7	13.6	17.0	15.7
26 127	...	8	Oceana	1 400	28 074	1 461	20.1	85.0	0.6	1.5	0.3	13.3	6.5	19.5	10.3	10.9	14.6	13.6
26 129	...	9	Ogemaw	1 462	21 792	1 714	14.9	97.4	0.4	1.4	0.5	1.2	5.0	16.8	8.7	9.3	13.9	14.0
26 131	...	9	Ontonagon	3 397	7 571	2 629	2.2	97.7	0.5	1.7	0.2	0.7	3.5	14.4	7.0	8.7	13.9	16.4
26 133	...	7	Osceola	1 466	23 509	1 640	16.0	97.8	0.6	1.3	0.3	1.1	5.9	19.4	9.9	10.9	14.8	13.9
26 135	...	9	Oscoda	1 463	9 461	2 490	6.5	97.9	0.3	1.2	0.1	1.1	4.4	16.8	8.7	8.3	13.2	14.2
26 137	...	7	Otsego	1 333	24 268	1 610	18.2	97.9	0.4	1.3	0.5	0.8	5.7	18.9	9.0	11.3	16.1	14.1
26 139	26100	3	Ottawa	1 465	249 391	238	170.2	88.8	1.4	0.6	2.7	7.4	7.1	20.0	12.5	12.7	15.2	13.1
26 141	...	7	Presque Isle	1 710	14 286	2 147	8.4	98.1	0.6	0.9	0.2	0.6	4.5	14.8	8.6	8.6	13.1	15.5
26 143	...	7	Roscommon	1 350	26 230	1 531	19.4	97.8	0.5	1.0	0.3	0.9	4.1	14.9	8.0	8.1	12.1	13.9
26 145	40980	3	Saginaw	2 095	209 327	281	99.9	72.8	19.7	0.8	1.1	6.9	6.5	19.2	9.8	12.0	14.4	14.7
26 147	19820	1	St. Clair	1 876	169 063	334	90.1	94.7	2.5	1.0	0.6	2.3	6.0	19.2	9.4	12.0	16.3	14.6
26 149	44780	4	St. Joseph	1 305	62 864	786	48.2	91.5	3.1	0.9	0.7	4.9	7.1	19.3	10.0	12.1	14.5	13.7
26 151	...	6	Sanilac	2 496	44 583	1 033	17.9	96.3	0.5	0.9	0.3	2.7	5.9	19.2	9.1	10.9	15.2	13.8
26 153	...	7	Schoolcraft	3 051	8 772	2 546	2.9	91.0	1.9	8.0	0.5	1.0	4.8	16.2	8.9	10.3	14.3	15.2
26 155	37020	4	Shiawassee	1 395	72 543	699	52.0	97.0	0.4	1.1	0.4	2.0	6.2	19.2	9.6	11.7	15.9	14.9
26 157	...	6	Tuscola	2 104	58 382	841	27.7	95.7	1.2	1.1	0.4	2.3	5.7	19.2	9.9	11.2	15.4	14.8
26 159	28020	2	Van Buren	1 582	78 210	668	49.4	85.6	5.5	1.7	0.6	8.2	6.7	19.9	9.9	10.9	15.3	14.9
26 161	11460	2	Washtenaw	1 839	338 562	178	184.1	76.9	13.2	0.9	8.4	2.8	6.0	15.6	14.8	16.8	15.0	13.6
26 163	19820	1	Wayne	1 591	2 028 778	11	1 275.2	51.0	42.8	0.9	2.6	4.2	7.2	20.6	8.6	14.0	15.4	14.0
26 165	15620	7	Wexford	1 465	31 251	1 374	21.3	97.4	0.7	1.1	0.6	1.1	6.0	18.7	9.9	11.0	15.4	14.1
27 000	...	X	MINNESOTA	206 189	5 059 375	X	24.5	88.4	4.4	1.5	3.8	3.3	6.4	18.2	10.3	13.3	15.9	14.6
27 001	...	8	Aitkin	4 712	15 782	2 050	3.3	96.6	0.3	2.5	0.2	0.8	4.3	14.8	8.5	8.2	12.9	13.9
27 003	33460	1	Anoka	1 097	314 074	188	286.3	92.3	2.9	1.2	3.3	2.0	6.9	20.4	9.5	13.9	18.3	14.1
27 005	...	6	Becker	3 394	31 174	1 380	9.2	91.0	0.4	9.2	0.5	0.8	5.7	18.3	10.0	10.2	13.9	14.5
27 007	13420	7	Beltrami	6 489	41 797	1 087	6.4	77.9	0.6	21.3	1.0	0.9	6.7	19.5	14.9	11.7	13.0	12.8
27 009	41060	3	Benton	1 057	36 925	1 214	34.9	94.1	1.7	0.6	1.4	1.0	6.9	18.2	12.0	16.3	15.1	12.2
27 011	...	9	Big Stone	1 287	5 653	2 799	4.4	98.5	0.2	0.6	0.4	0.3	4.4	17.6	8.5	7.0	14.0	14.3
27 013	31860	5	Blue Earth	1 949	57 306	850	29.4	94.4	1.9	0.4	2.2	1.8	5.6	14.2	19.8	13.9	12.4	12.3
27 015	35580	7	Brown	1 582	26 505	1 518	16.8	97.5	0.3	0.2	0.5	1.9	4.9	17.6	11.7	9.7	14.9	14.3
27 017	20260	2	Carlton	2 228	33 044	1 331	14.8	92.3	1.1	6.2	0.6	0.9	5.5	17.3	10.4	11.4	15.5	14.9
27 019	33460	1	Carver	925	78 960	662	85.4	94.1	1.0	0.4	2.3	2.8	7.5	21.5	9.5	12.5	19.4	13.6
27 021	14660	9	Cass	5 226	28 205	1 453	5.4	88.4	0.3	11.5	0.3	0.8	5.2	17.1	9.4	9.5	13.3	13.9
27 023	...	7	Chippewa	1 509	12 808	2 255	8.5	95.5	0.3	1.1	0.4	3.0	4.8	17.9	9.1	9.6	13.9	15.4
27 025	33460	1	Chisago	1 082	46 165	1 000	42.7	96.3	0.9	0.9	1.2	1.5	6.7	20.4	10.3	13.6	17.4	12.8
27 027	22020	3	Clay	2 707	51 983	907	19.2	94.1	0.8	1.9	1.4	2.9	6.0	17.6	17.5	10.8	14.0	13.1
27 029	...	8	Clearwater	2 576	8 424	2 569	3.3	90.2	0.3	9.5	0.4	0.8	6.2	18.0	9.8	10.1	13.8	14.2
27 031	...	9	Cook	3 757	5 282	2 822	1.4	90.7	0.3	9.0	0.4	1.2	3.9	14.6	7.5	9.2	15.4	18.3
27 033	...	7	Cottonwood	1 658	12 019	2 291	7.2	93.7	0.5	0.3	2.3	3.4	5.8	18.0	8.3	8.7	13.1	14.1
27 035	14660	5	Crow Wing	2 581	58 430	839	22.6	97.6	0.6	1.3	0.5	0.7	6.0	17.0	10.1	10.7	14.0	13.7
27 037	33460	1	Dakota	1 475	373 311	166	253.1	89.6	3.7	0.8	4.2	3.4	7.0	20.6	8.8	14.2	18.3	14.5
27 039	40340	3	Dodge	1 138	18 931	1 864	16.6	96.1	0.3	0.3	0.7	3.0	6.8	20.5	10.3	12.1	16.6	13.9
27 041	10820	7	Douglas	1 643	34 117	1 301	20.8	98.3	0.4	0.5	0.5	0.7	5.2	16.3	11.4	10.7	13.5	13.8
27 043	...	7	Faribault	1 848	15 737	2 053	8.5	95.2	0.4	0.2	0.5	4.0	4.7	17.5	8.8	8.2	13.9	14.7
27 045	...	8	Fillmore	2 231	21 314	1 736	9.6	98.9	0.4	0.2	0.3	0.5	5.5	18.2	9.3	10.0	14.2	14.0
27 047	10660	7	Freeborn	1 833	31 961	1 358	17.4	92.8	0.5	0.4	0.6	6.1	5.2	16.7	9.1	9.9	14.7	14.4
27 049	39860	4	Goodhue	1 964	45 167	1 019	23.0	96.2	0.9	1.3	0.7	1.4	5.6	18.3	9.9	10.9	15.9	14.9

1. CBSA = Core Based Statistical Area. See Appendix A for explanation. See Appendix B for list of metropolitan areas with component counties. 2. County type code from the Economic Research Service of USDA Rural-Urban Continuum Codes. See Appendix A for definition. 3. Dry land or land partially or temporarily covered by water. 4. Hispanic or Latino persons may be of any race.

Table B. States and Counties — **Population and Households**

STATE County	Age (percent) 55 to 64 years	65 to 74 years	75 years and over	Percent female	Total persons 1990	2000	Percent change 1990–2000	2000–2003	Components of change, 2000–2003 Births	Deaths	Net migration	Households, 2000 Number	Percent change, 1990–2000	Persons per house-hold	Female family house-holder[1]	One person
	16	17	18	19	20	21	22	23	24	25	26	27	28	29	30	31
MICHIGAN—Cont'd																
Leelanau	11.7	9.6	8.1	50.0	16 527	21 119	27.8	3.5	579	563	728	8 436	34.5	2.48	7.1	22.3
Lenawee	9.8	6.4	6.2	50.0	91 476	98 890	8.1	1.9	3 867	2 917	979	35 930	13.6	2.61	10.0	22.9
Livingston	9.5	4.6	3.8	49.6	115 645	156 951	35.7	10.1	6 470	3 098	12 359	55 384	42.4	2.80	6.8	17.1
Luce	10.1	8.8	7.1	44.4	5 763	7 024	21.9	-1.5	196	274	-23	2 481	15.2	2.40	8.5	26.3
Mackinac	13.1	10.8	8.6	50.1	10 674	11 943	11.9	-4.0	311	477	-300	5 067	19.5	2.32	8.1	28.0
Macomb	9.6	6.7	6.7	50.9	717 400	788 149	9.9	3.3	32 188	23 753	17 833	309 203	16.7	2.52	10.1	26.9
Manistee	11.3	9.4	8.6	49.0	21 265	24 527	15.3	3.2	825	944	903	9 860	14.9	2.37	9.1	27.3
Marquette	9.8	6.9	6.8	49.8	70 887	64 634	-8.8	0.0	1 929	2 092	234	25 767	1.3	2.35	8.9	28.9
Mason	11.5	8.2	8.5	50.8	25 537	28 274	10.7	1.5	1 009	1 163	593	11 406	14.2	2.43	9.2	26.5
Mecosta	9.7	7.4	5.8	49.2	37 308	40 553	8.7	2.9	1 529	1 176	838	14 915	21.7	2.49	9.3	24.5
Menominee	10.6	8.4	8.8	50.4	24 920	25 326	1.6	-1.0	870	997	-92	10 529	7.8	2.36	8.8	29.2
Midland	9.5	6.4	5.9	50.9	75 651	82 874	9.5	2.0	3 279	2 011	428	31 769	14.3	2.56	8.1	23.5
Missaukee	10.6	7.7	6.9	50.2	12 147	14 478	19.2	4.9	567	427	567	5 450	24.2	2.62	7.4	21.5
Monroe	9.6	6.0	5.2	50.4	133 600	145 945	9.2	3.2	5 460	4 025	3 397	53 772	15.6	2.69	10.1	21.7
Montcalm	9.5	6.6	5.7	48.9	53 059	61 266	15.5	2.7	2 723	1 803	783	22 079	18.9	2.65	9.7	21.9
Montmorency	14.0	13.3	10.6	51.3	8 936	10 315	15.4	1.7	270	565	477	4 455	23.8	2.29	7.1	27.5
Muskegon	8.9	6.3	6.4	50.3	158 983	170 200	7.1	1.7	7 737	5 286	643	63 330	9.6	2.59	13.9	25.2
Newaygo	10.1	7.0	5.8	50.2	38 206	47 874	25.3	2.9	1 957	1 409	870	17 599	27.8	2.68	9.0	22.2
Oakland	9.9	5.7	5.6	50.9	1 083 592	1 194 156	10.2	1.1	50 593	29 410	-7 081	471 115	14.8	2.51	9.5	27.3
Oceana	10.1	7.6	6.3	49.6	22 455	26 873	19.7	4.5	1 197	728	746	9 778	21.1	2.67	9.2	21.6
Ogemaw	13.0	11.1	8.2	50.3	18 681	21 645	15.9	0.7	738	978	399	8 842	23.0	2.41	8.8	25.7
Ontonagon	14.2	11.6	11.1	49.3	8 854	7 818	-11.7	-3.2	145	344	-37	3 456	-5.1	2.21	6.3	31.5
Osceola	10.9	8.1	6.3	50.7	20 146	23 197	15.1	1.3	905	796	224	8 861	20.6	2.58	9.7	22.6
Oscoda	14.0	11.5	9.2	51.1	7 842	9 418	20.1	0.5	271	382	158	3 921	24.1	2.39	7.5	26.0
Otsego	10.3	7.9	6.1	50.3	17 957	23 301	29.8	4.2	906	668	721	8 995	37.9	2.56	8.3	22.5
Ottawa	8.0	5.0	5.1	50.8	187 768	238 314	26.9	4.6	11 508	4 731	4 522	81 662	30.3	2.81	7.5	19.6
Presque Isle	12.7	11.8	10.8	50.3	13 743	14 411	4.9	-0.9	422	619	89	6 155	14.5	2.31	6.3	28.4
Roscommon	14.7	13.3	10.4	50.7	19 776	25 469	28.8	3.0	668	1 247	1 311	11 250	32.1	2.23	7.7	28.1
Saginaw	9.9	6.8	6.8	51.8	211 946	210 039	-0.9	-0.3	9 008	6 848	-2 753	80 430	2.8	2.54	15.4	26.0
St. Clair	9.6	6.1	5.9	50.7	145 607	164 235	12.8	2.9	6 464	4 789	3 257	62 072	17.4	2.62	10.4	23.4
St. Joseph	9.7	6.8	6.3	50.5	58 913	62 422	6.0	0.7	3 012	1 875	-658	23 381	8.4	2.63	10.4	23.6
Sanilac	10.2	8.0	7.7	50.6	39 928	44 547	11.6	0.1	1 714	1 493	-129	16 871	15.1	2.64	8.6	24.3
Schoolcraft	11.9	9.4	9.4	49.8	8 302	8 903	7.2	-1.5	275	341	-54	3 606	9.5	2.36	8.1	27.4
Shiawassee	10.0	6.4	5.7	50.9	69 770	71 687	2.7	1.2	2 899	2 091	109	26 896	8.2	2.64	10.3	21.7
Tuscola	10.7	6.7	6.4	50.0	55 498	58 266	5.0	0.2	2 207	1 820	-219	21 454	10.2	2.65	9.2	21.9
Van Buren	9.7	6.5	5.8	50.4	70 060	76 263	8.9	2.6	3 387	2 187	823	27 982	10.2	2.66	11.2	22.5
Washtenaw	8.0	4.3	3.9	50.2	282 937	322 895	14.1	4.9	13 323	6 034	8 923	125 327	19.9	2.41	9.3	29.5
Wayne	8.6	5.9	6.0	52.0	2 111 687	2 061 162	-2.4	-1.6	100 123	66 808	-65 834	768 440	-1.5	2.64	20.6	28.3
Wexford	9.7	7.5	6.7	50.4	26 360	30 484	15.6	2.5	1 211	1 008	579	11 824	19.2	2.55	10.3	24.2
MINNESOTA	9.2	5.8	6.2	50.4	4 375 665	4 919 479	12.4	2.8	216 100	122 759	46 271	1 895 127	15.0	2.52	8.9	26.9
Aitkin	14.1	12.8	10.3	49.8	12 425	15 301	23.1	3.1	453	608	627	6 644	29.6	2.28	6.3	28.7
Anoka	8.5	4.4	3.0	49.7	243 641	298 084	22.3	5.4	13 977	4 720	6 920	106 428	29.1	2.77	9.8	19.3
Becker	10.7	8.3	7.7	50.2	27 881	30 000	7.6	3.9	1 162	1 044	1 047	11 844	13.0	2.49	7.9	26.9
Beltrami	8.1	5.8	5.7	50.7	34 384	39 650	15.3	5.4	1 871	1 168	1 460	14 337	20.8	2.63	13.6	24.8
Benton	6.9	4.9	5.4	50.1	30 185	34 226	13.4	7.9	1 748	999	1 950	13 065	19.5	2.56	8.8	25.8
Big Stone	11.3	10.6	13.2	51.1	6 285	5 820	-7.4	-2.9	166	264	-65	2 377	-3.5	2.38	5.3	30.2
Blue Earth	7.4	5.2	6.6	50.1	54 044	55 941	3.5	2.4	2 125	1 339	635	21 062	9.3	2.46	7.8	27.1
Brown	9.6	7.9	9.7	50.4	26 984	26 911	-0.3	-1.5	848	831	-407	10 598	2.7	2.43	6.9	29.0
Carlton	9.3	7.2	7.5	49.3	29 259	31 671	8.2	4.3	1 180	1 067	1 262	12 064	11.3	2.50	9.0	26.1
Carver	6.8	3.7	3.4	50.0	47 915	70 205	46.5	12.5	3 781	914	5 775	24 356	46.7	2.84	7.3	18.1
Cass	13.0	10.4	7.6	49.8	21 791	27 150	24.6	3.9	1 021	1 087	1 110	10 893	31.2	2.45	8.0	25.0
Chippewa	9.8	8.1	12.1	51.3	13 228	13 088	-1.1	-2.1	386	494	-165	5 361	2.2	2.39	6.6	29.5
Chisago	7.8	4.7	4.5	49.0	30 521	41 101	34.7	12.3	2 099	970	3 835	14 454	37.0	2.79	8.0	18.4
Clay	7.9	5.9	6.7	51.7	50 422	51 229	1.6	1.5	1 445	1 192	558	18 670	6.7	2.53	8.8	26.1
Clearwater	11.0	8.1	9.1	49.8	8 309	8 423	1.4	0.0	365	345	-14	3 330	8.7	2.48	7.5	27.9
Cook	13.6	9.1	7.8	50.2	3 868	5 168	33.6	2.2	132	152	140	2 350	44.0	2.17	6.1	32.5
Cottonwood	10.6	8.8	13.3	51.2	12 694	12 167	-4.2	-1.2	483	461	-161	4 917	-2.8	2.39	6.9	28.9
Crow Wing	10.4	8.7	8.1	50.9	44 249	55 099	24.5	6.0	2 279	1 690	2 699	22 250	29.3	2.43	8.0	26.4
Dakota	8.2	4.2	3.3	50.5	275 210	355 904	29.3	4.9	16 707	5 384	6 435	131 151	33.4	2.70	9.1	21.7
Dodge	8.1	5.3	6.1	50.5	15 731	17 731	12.7	6.8	841	429	781	6 420	15.9	2.73	7.2	20.2
Douglas	10.3	8.3	9.4	50.0	28 674	32 821	14.5	3.9	1 150	1 045	1 192	13 276	20.8	2.42	6.4	26.5
Faribault	10.8	9.7	12.5	50.3	16 937	16 181	-4.5	-2.7	495	692	-237	6 652	-1.8	2.36	6.1	29.7
Fillmore	9.8	8.3	10.6	50.4	20 777	21 122	1.7	0.9	796	794	210	8 228	5.2	2.50	6.1	26.6
Freeborn	11.2	8.7	10.3	50.6	33 060	32 584	-1.4	-1.9	1 104	1 183	-534	13 356	2.5	2.40	7.5	28.2
Goodhue	9.5	6.9	7.9	50.2	40 690	44 127	8.4	2.4	1 661	1 470	885	16 983	11.7	2.53	7.2	25.2

1. No spouse present.

STATE County	Births, average 1999-2001 Total	Rate[1]	Deaths, average 1999-2001 Number Total	Infant[2]	Rate Total[1]	Infant[3]	Physicians,[4] 2000 Number	Rate[5]	Hospitals,[4] 1998 Number	Beds Number	Beds Rate[5]	Medicare enrollees, 2003	Serious crimes known to police,[6] 2002 Total Number	Rate[7]
	32	33	34	35	36	37	38	39	40	41	42	43	44	45
MICHIGAN—Cont'd														
Leelanau	193	9.2	169	0	8.0	D	23	109	1	90	470	3 426	251	1 175
Lenawee	1 234	12.5	882	8	8.9	6.2	118	119	4	317	322	15 758	2 346	2 346
Livingston	2 014	12.8	921	10	5.8	5.1	135	86	1	93	64	14 500	2 362	1 488
Luce	64	9.2	76	1	10.9	D	11	157	1	69	1 039	1 344	NA	NA
Mackinac	109	9.2	148	1	12.5	D	11	92	1	75	676	2 379	549	4 545
Macomb	10 118	12.8	7 227	68	9.1	6.7	1 225	155	7	1 466	186	122 065	23 268	2 936
Manistee	252	10.3	278	1	11.3	D	30	122	1	173	742	5 315	630	2 540
Marquette	597	9.3	629	3	9.7	D	166	257	2	376	611	10 465	1 387	2 244
Mason	315	11.1	333	3	11.8	D	49	173	1	85	304	5 566	1 029	3 599
Mecosta	488	12.0	341	3	8.4	D	38	94	1	74	185	6 464	1 521	3 709
Menominee	273	10.8	304	2	12.0	D	8	32	1	78	319	4 718	649	2 534
Midland	1 040	12.5	609	9	7.3	8.3	181	218	1	307	375	11 819	1 646	1 964
Missaukee	180	12.4	132	1	9.1	D	3	21	0	0	0	2 400	379	2 589
Monroe	1 824	12.5	1 165	10	8.0	5.3	114	78	1	173	121	19 848	4 409	2 987
Montcalm	846	13.8	546	5	8.9	D	83	135	4	300	495	10 169	1 799	3 157
Montmorency	87	8.4	154	0	14.9	D	5	48	0	0	0	3 327	148	1 419
Muskegon	2 386	14.0	1 608	25	9.4	10.6	296	174	3	618	371	27 920	10 117	5 878
Newaygo	629	13.1	413	4	8.6	D	31	65	1	73	159	7 029	1 334	2 755
Oakland	16 050	13.4	9 018	97	7.5	6.0	4 194	351	12	3 458	294	154 708	33 310	2 758
Oceana	366	13.6	242	1	9.0	D	16	60	1	35	141	4 965	560	2 097
Ogemaw	222	10.3	285	1	13.2	D	31	143	1	92	434	4 758	601	2 746
Ontonagon	57	7.3	110	0	14.1	D	7	90	1	87	1 104	1 999	129	1 632
Osceola	290	12.5	240	3	10.3	D	12	52	1	110	498	4 698	485	2 068
Oscoda	91	9.6	106	1	11.2	D	6	64	0	0	0	1 838	332	3 486
Otsego	281	12.0	197	0	8.4	D	38	163	1	111	502	4 217	686	2 911
Ottawa	3 652	15.3	1 444	25	6.0	6.9	205	86	3	336	150	29 533	5 435	2 255
Presque Isle	134	9.3	190	3	13.2	D	7	49	0	0	0	3 880	164	1 125
Roscommon	216	8.5	367	1	14.4	D	15	59	0	0	0	7 726	805	3 125
Saginaw	2 835	13.5	2 001	26	9.5	9.1	442	210	3	848	404	34 090	10 242	4 822
St. Clair	2 090	12.7	1 477	16	9.0	7.5	226	138	4	473	296	24 189	4 516	2 719
St. Joseph	926	14.8	600	7	9.6	7.9	56	90	2	117	191	9 631	2 324	3 682
Sanilac	551	12.4	472	5	10.6	D	31	70	3	144	335	8 013	856	1 900
Schoolcraft	92	10.3	111	1	12.5	D	9	101	1	47	534	2 020	NA	NA
Shiawassee	922	12.8	619	5	8.6	D	82	114	1	155	214	11 061	1 697	2 410
Tuscola	688	11.8	526	5	9.0	D	35	60	2	109	187	9 644	799	1 602
Van Buren	1 042	13.6	660	7	8.6	6.7	45	59	2	224	296	11 822	2 772	3 594
Washtenaw	4 085	12.6	1 844	33	5.7	8.0	2 127	659	5	1 637	540	32 544	12 099	3 705
Wayne	30 886	15.0	20 360	320	9.9	10.3	4 658	226	27	8 232	389	287 693	124 239	6 022
Wexford	395	13.0	303	5	9.9	D	51	167	1	154	528	5 625	1 303	4 227
MINNESOTA	67 045	13.6	37 987	382	7.7	5.7	10 124	206	142	17 140	363	676 156	177 454	3 535
Aitkin	138	9.0	183	1	12.0	D	8	52	1	84	594	4 006	576	3 689
Anoka	4 294	14.4	1 397	21	4.7	4.9	321	108	2	470	161	25 651	12 412	4 081
Becker	373	12.4	324	5	10.8	D	36	120	1	160	545	5 496	939	3 067
Beltrami	574	14.4	333	4	8.4	D	65	164	1	98	253	5 882	1 381	3 413
Benton	533	15.5	307	3	8.9	D	6	18	0	0	0	3 341	1 035	2 964
Big Stone	52	9.0	94	0	16.2	D	8	137	2	137	2 423	1 496	85	1 431
Blue Earth	672	12.0	430	3	7.7	D	123	220	1	153	285	8 805	2 254	3 949
Brown	286	10.6	278	1	10.3	D	29	108	3	126	466	5 348	449	1 635
Carlton	358	11.3	309	2	9.7	D	29	92	2	253	821	5 778	878	2 717
Carver	1 139	16.1	301	6	4.3	D	69	98	1	106	164	6 010	1 202	1 678
Cass	303	11.2	308	2	11.3	D	16	59	0	0	0	5 592	1 361	4 913
Chippewa	133	10.2	150	1	11.5	D	8	61	1	35	268	2 501	202	1 513
Chisago	638	15.4	297	2	7.2	D	33	80	2	115	282	5 716	1 282	3 057
Clay	631	12.3	407	6	7.9	D	21	41	0	0	0	7 196	1 470	2 812
Clearwater	104	12.3	109	1	12.9	D	7	83	1	18	217	1 559	210	2 444
Cook	40	7.7	50	1	9.8	D	10	193	1	63	1 315	972	184	3 489
Cottonwood	139	11.4	155	1	12.8	D	9	74	2	43	357	2 774	437	3 520
Crow Wing	689	12.5	518	2	9.4	D	87	158	2	322	623	11 549	2 451	4 360
Dakota	5 283	14.8	1 623	23	4.5	4.4	311	87	3	304	89	26 327	10 882	3 096
Dodge	250	14.1	130	2	7.3	D	7	39	0	0	0	2 291	315	1 741
Douglas	357	10.9	323	1	9.8	D	50	152	1	110	354	6 863	716	2 138
Faribault	153	9.5	212	1	13.1	D	14	87	1	43	265	3 735	217	1 314
Fillmore	241	11.4	252	2	11.9	D	14	66	2	129	620	4 419	138	640
Freeborn	387	11.9	375	2	11.5	D	36	110	1	115	364	6 510	687	2 066
Goodhue	514	11.6	465	3	10.5	D	53	120	3	124	287	7 188	1 577	3 502

1. Per 1,000 estimated resident population.   2. Deaths of infants under 1 year old.   3. Deaths of infants under 1 year old per 1,000 live births.   4. Data subject to copyright.   5. Per 100,000 resident population as of July 1 of the year shown.   6. Data for serious crimes have not been adjusted for underreporting; this may affect comparability between geographic areas and over time.   7. Per 100,000 population estimated by the FBI.

Table B. States and Counties — Crime, Education, Money Income, and Poverty

STATE County	Serious crimes known to police,[1] 2002 (cont'd) Rate[2] Violent	Property	Education: Enrollment[3] Total	Percent private	Attainment[4] (percent) High school graduate or less	Bachelor's degree or more	Local government expenditures,[5] 2000–2001 Total current expenditures (mil dol)	Current expenditures per student (dollars)	Money income, 1999 Per capita income[6] (dollars)	Households Median income Dollars	Percent change, 1989–1999 (constant 1999 dollars)	Percent with income of $100,000 or more	Percent below poverty level, 1999 Persons	Households	Families	Families with children
	46	47	48	49	50	51	52	53	54	55	56	57	58	59	60	61
MICHIGAN—Cont'd																
Leelanau	94	1 082	5 224	15.0	35.7	31.4	20.5	7 457	24 686	47 062	22.5	11.9	5.4	5.5	3.3	5.9
Lenawee	231	2 115	26 304	15.9	55.1	16.3	146.3	7 955	20 186	45 739	9.8	9.8	6.7	6.9	4.4	6.4
Livingston	114	1 374	44 359	12.2	36.9	28.2	195.3	7 172	28 069	67 400	10.4	25.5	3.4	3.4	2.4	3.5
Luce	NA	NA	1 638	10.4	61.9	11.8	8.9	7 167	16 828	32 031	17.0	3.0	14.9	13.2	12.0	17.1
Mackinac	290	4 256	2 544	3.8	58.8	14.9	14.1	7 943	17 777	33 356	28.0	4.5	10.5	10.7	7.2	12.5
Macomb	310	2 627	200 126	13.6	49.8	17.6	1 045.7	8 231	24 446	52 102	-0.4	15.3	5.6	5.9	4.0	6.3
Manistee	218	2 322	5 638	12.2	58.0	14.2	31.5	8 676	17 204	34 208	27.5	4.6	10.3	10.7	6.9	10.9
Marquette	149	2 095	18 785	5.8	46.9	23.7	82.0	8 073	18 070	35 548	5.3	5.1	10.9	12.3	6.0	10.5
Mason	374	3 225	6 780	9.4	52.8	15.9	46.1	8 945	17 713	34 704	19.0	5.9	11.0	10.7	8.2	14.1
Mecosta	302	3 406	14 409	6.0	52.7	19.1	82.2	7 483	16 372	33 849	21.2	6.2	16.1	16.3	9.6	14.6
Menominee	164	2 370	5 896	7.4	62.9	11.0	29.0	7 555	16 909	32 888	13.4	3.3	11.5	12.0	8.0	13.1
Midland	204	1 760	23 890	15.1	41.0	29.3	119.1	8 179	23 383	45 674	0.1	15.5	8.4	8.6	5.7	8.2
Missaukee	137	2 452	3 629	13.0	64.0	10.2	14.9	6 267	16 072	35 224	25.2	4.3	10.7	10.7	8.2	11.5
Monroe	274	2 714	39 786	13.7	54.2	14.3	195.6	7 909	22 458	51 743	8.6	13.7	7.0	7.3	4.8	6.7
Montcalm	316	2 841	15 656	9.1	58.8	10.8	101.1	7 477	16 183	37 218	16.0	4.3	10.9	10.5	7.4	11.2
Montmorency	201	1 218	1 978	6.2	66.9	8.2	8.6	7 693	16 493	30 005	25.3	3.6	12.8	12.2	9.8	17.3
Muskegon	629	5 249	46 749	9.7	52.4	13.9	261.8	8 001	17 967	38 008	10.4	6.6	11.4	11.1	8.8	13.8
Newaygo	308	2 448	12 809	9.4	61.7	11.4	76.8	7 618	16 976	37 130	17.8	4.7	11.6	11.0	9.0	13.0
Oakland	316	2 443	326 864	17.5	32.8	38.2	1 771.1	9 068	32 534	61 907	6.2	25.3	5.5	5.4	3.8	5.5
Oceana	187	1 909	7 065	7.6	59.6	12.6	31.3	7 589	15 878	35 307	17.4	4.3	14.7	12.3	11.0	17.8
Ogemaw	329	2 417	5 004	8.7	64.9	9.6	18.9	7 006	15 768	30 474	28.4	3.8	14.0	13.4	11.0	16.1
Ontonagon	316	1 315	1 534	2.7	59.7	13.0	9.0	7 768	16 695	29 552	4.0	3.7	10.4	11.8	5.8	11.8
Osceola	175	1 893	5 867	9.1	63.3	11.3	37.1	6 701	15 632	34 102	21.6	3.9	12.7	12.3	9.5	13.2
Oscoda	241	3 244	2 015	10.4	66.8	8.0	9.8	7 324	15 697	28 228	18.2	3.3	14.6	13.8	10.3	16.6
Otsego	221	2 691	5 748	16.4	50.9	17.4	31.4	6 775	19 810	40 876	15.4	8.0	6.8	7.0	5.3	6.7
Ottawa	170	2 085	73 944	22.2	44.5	26.0	365.8	7 518	21 676	52 347	6.7	12.8	5.5	5.3	3.1	4.4
Presque Isle	103	1 022	3 000	12.7	61.3	11.5	13.4	6 665	17 363	31 656	12.5	3.9	10.3	10.9	6.8	11.3
Roscommon	171	2 955	5 232	9.3	59.8	10.9	36.5	8 813	17 837	30 029	31.1	4.3	12.4	11.8	8.6	17.6
Saginaw	971	3 851	58 489	11.9	54.6	15.9	292.1	7 956	19 438	38 637	2.8	9.3	13.9	13.1	11.0	17.4
St. Clair	279	2 440	42 822	10.9	54.4	12.6	208.5	7 476	21 582	46 313	12.3	11.0	7.8	8.2	5.8	8.3
St. Joseph	407	3 274	15 335	9.9	59.7	12.7	87.4	7 216	18 247	40 355	9.2	6.5	11.3	10.2	8.2	13.2
Sanilac	189	1 711	11 139	7.2	64.2	10.0	62.3	7 142	17 089	36 870	18.8	4.8	10.4	10.0	7.6	11.3
Schoolcraft	NA	NA	1 881	10.7	64.5	11.3	7.8	6 603	17 137	31 140	15.2	4.5	12.2	11.8	9.1	14.9
Shiawassee	254	2 156	19 093	10.9	54.1	13.7	106.2	7 330	19 229	42 553	4.6	7.8	7.8	8.2	5.7	8.3
Tuscola	207	1 396	15 594	12.1	60.6	10.6	96.0	7 890	17 985	40 174	9.2	6.9	8.2	7.8	5.4	8.0
Van Buren	419	3 175	20 117	8.9	57.0	14.3	139.8	8 008	17 878	39 365	14.9	6.6	11.1	10.7	7.8	11.1
Washtenaw	333	3 372	117 309	10.6	25.8	48.1	413.0	8 660	27 173	51 990	6.6	19.8	11.1	10.8	5.1	7.4
Wayne	1 176	4 846	587 853	14.3	53.7	17.2	3 024.1	8 684	20 058	40 776	8.4	11.5	16.4	14.9	12.7	18.5
Wexford	383	3 844	7 690	10.2	56.7	15.3	46.3	8 234	17 144	35 363	14.9	6.1	10.3	11.1	7.7	11.2
MINNESOTA	268	3 268	1 362 507	15.8	40.9	27.4	6 433.9	7 608	23 198	47 111	13.4	12.6	7.9	7.9	5.1	7.6
Aitkin	160	3 529	3 142	3.4	59.2	11.3	16.6	7 265	17 848	31 139	32.0	4.6	11.6	12.1	8.2	14.1
Anoka	182	3 898	83 625	12.3	41.4	21.3	431.2	6 690	23 297	57 754	7.3	13.9	4.2	4.1	2.9	4.3
Becker	95	2 973	7 526	4.9	51.7	16.7	34.4	7 082	17 085	34 797	23.8	5.3	12.2	12.9	8.5	14.0
Beltrami	148	3 265	13 148	7.1	45.2	23.5	73.3	9 070	15 497	33 392	18.8	5.5	17.6	16.8	12.9	19.1
Benton	149	2 815	9 595	11.9	49.9	17.2	32.9	6 304	19 008	41 968	17.3	5.9	7.7	7.3	5.5	6.9
Big Stone	101	1 330	1 443	4.6	61.1	11.4	9.4	7 673	15 708	30 721	17.8	3.0	7.1	8.5	4.5	5.3
Blue Earth	130	3 819	20 028	11.1	40.4	26.6	68.2	6 732	18 712	38 940	14.3	6.8	12.0	11.8	7.8	12.2
Brown	73	1 562	7 413	37.1	56.8	16.5	28.4	6 680	19 535	39 800	18.3	5.8	6.4	7.7	4.4	7.2
Carlton	161	2 556	8 607	8.6	53.1	14.9	46.3	7 223	18 073	40 021	19.6	5.5	7.9	8.9	5.4	8.1
Carver	92	1 586	21 079	25.1	35.3	34.3	91.6	7 706	28 486	65 540	24.5	24.1	3.5	3.8	2.3	3.1
Cass	260	4 653	6 556	4.7	52.5	16.6	38.0	7 807	17 189	34 332	36.4	5.4	13.6	12.9	9.5	15.8
Chippewa	127	1 385	3 082	5.3	56.0	13.7	20.9	8 149	18 039	35 582	19.2	4.0	8.6	8.8	4.8	8.0
Chisago	124	2 933	11 266	9.4	48.4	15.3	50.0	6 026	21 013	52 012	23.8	10.9	5.1	5.1	3.2	4.6
Clay	189	2 623	17 797	19.7	41.5	24.7	61.0	6 814	17 557	37 889	8.9	6.4	13.2	13.4	7.4	11.5
Clearwater	198	2 246	2 066	4.1	59.0	14.7	12.9	7 309	15 694	30 517	28.0	4.2	15.1	16.9	11.0	15.3
Cook	114	3 376	962	6.4	39.9	28.8	5.4	7 231	21 775	36 640	19.0	6.4	10.1	10.7	8.1	14.3
Cottonwood	161	3 359	2 897	9.8	56.8	14.2	14.7	7 823	16 647	31 943	9.8	4.0	11.7	10.3	7.4	12.7
Crow Wing	212	4 148	13 331	6.7	47.2	18.4	70.7	6 905	19 174	37 589	25.7	5.9	9.8	10.2	6.5	10.4
Dakota	143	2 953	101 596	15.9	30.3	34.9	489.1	6 778	27 008	61 863	9.1	20.1	3.6	3.8	2.4	3.3
Dodge	94	1 647	4 988	6.1	49.2	17.1	24.3	6 106	19 259	47 437	21.5	7.8	5.8	6.7	4.4	5.8
Douglas	87	2 051	8 170	10.0	47.5	17.3	37.6	6 863	18 850	37 703	27.2	6.3	8.5	10.2	5.6	8.7
Faribault	109	1 205	3 880	7.7	57.2	13.8	17.3	6 881	17 193	34 440	14.3	4.1	8.6	9.8	5.5	8.7
Fillmore	65	575	5 095	8.3	55.2	15.1	22.2	6 771	17 067	36 651	23.1	4.6	10.1	9.9	6.8	9.9
Freeborn	72	1 994	7 375	6.9	56.5	12.8	33.1	6 723	18 325	36 964	11.1	4.8	8.4	8.8	5.6	8.9
Goodhue	135	3 367	11 305	8.9	49.8	19.1	51.7	6 712	21 934	46 972	19.6	9.7	5.7	6.7	3.7	5.2

1. Data for serious crimes have not been adjusted for underreporting; this may affect comparability between geographic areas and over time.　2. Per 100,000 population estimated by the FBI.　3. All persons 3 years old and over enrolled in nursery school through college.　4. Persons 25 years old and over.　5. Elementary and secondary education expenditures.　6. Based on population enumerated as of April 1, 2000.

Table B. States and Counties — **Personal Income**

STATE County	Total (mil dol)	Percent change, 2001–2002	Per capita[1] Dollars	Per capita Rank	Wages and salaries[2] (mil dol)	Proprietor's income (mil dol)	Dividends, interest, and rent (mil dol)	Transfer payments Total (mil dol)	Government payments to individuals Total (mil dol)	Social Security (mil dol)	Medical payments (mil dol)	Income mainte-nance (mil dol)	Unemploy-ment insurance (mil dol)
	62	63	64	65	66	67	68	69	70	71	72	73	74
MICHIGAN—Cont'd													
Leelanau	630	2.1	29 201	422	206	35	161	93	88	52	26	4	3
Lenawee	2 638	2.6	26 276	837	1 309	83	367	434	410	186	156	30	26
Livingston	5 851	1.5	34 639	148	2 140	291	816	462	422	227	139	18	25
Luce	130	3.1	18 547	2 824	80	8	23	39	37	14	17	4	2
Mackinac	300	0.6	25 910	910	159	16	65	67	64	28	23	4	7
Macomb	26 282	1.3	32 571	201	17 681	1 264	3 889	3 485	3 293	1 541	1 312	168	208
Manistee	560	1.3	22 320	1 927	294	23	123	151	145	62	63	9	6
Marquette	1 504	1.9	23 262	1 641	1 007	61	234	331	316	118	134	20	17
Mason	685	3.1	23 865	1 452	380	43	131	164	157	63	58	12	14
Mecosta	814	3.0	19 601	2 633	406	53	151	178	168	76	53	17	7
Menominee	559	2.0	22 245	1 948	288	30	103	115	109	51	36	9	6
Midland	2 601	-0.1	30 964	270	1 832	100	553	341	321	150	121	24	15
Missaukee	294	2.0	19 638	2 623	88	21	49	67	64	29	23	6	3
Monroe	4 328	2.2	29 015	447	2 140	158	607	587	552	251	212	38	29
Montcalm	1 235	1.6	19 752	2 601	728	48	146	265	250	109	96	24	14
Montmorency	203	4.3	19 370	2 683	73	12	47	74	71	34	27	5	3
Muskegon	4 082	1.7	23 707	1 498	2 579	187	571	863	823	329	308	109	55
Newaygo	1 046	1.0	21 375	2 189	398	57	149	219	207	91	73	20	14
Oakland	57 033	1.0	47 394	24	43 930	6 210	10 188	4 642	4 357	2 030	1 712	266	249
Oceana	551	2.3	19 856	2 573	225	20	95	132	125	53	45	14	9
Ogemaw	422	2.9	19 399	2 675	198	24	70	133	128	59	48	12	6
Ontonagon	166	1.5	21 631	2 113	77	10	26	52	50	23	20	3	2
Osceola	477	4.0	20 287	2 482	315	19	69	117	111	49	41	12	5
Oscoda	156	4.5	16 580	3 021	54	14	25	56	53	26	18	4	3
Otsego	588	1.7	24 417	1 283	405	62	108	105	100	48	34	8	7
Ottawa	6 769	1.5	27 485	618	4 942	326	1 161	755	696	351	222	42	53
Presque Isle	306	1.9	21 353	2 195	119	9	62	86	82	42	28	5	5
Roscommon	544	3.5	21 075	2 275	195	27	121	189	183	89	70	14	5
Saginaw	5 306	1.0	25 297	1 048	4 257	237	798	1 105	1 055	418	401	149	56
St. Clair	4 660	2.0	27 864	572	2 034	186	695	716	677	292	255	56	46
St. Joseph	1 458	3.1	23 352	1 609	954	52	221	279	264	117	100	24	16
Sanilac	1 071	3.4	23 973	1 417	414	55	184	234	223	92	95	17	14
Schoolcraft	190	1.6	21 651	2 106	101	10	35	57	55	21	25	4	3
Shiawassee	1 659	2.0	22 999	1 723	609	44	214	322	305	129	124	25	17
Tuscola	1 240	2.9	21 299	2 207	497	33	173	275	261	112	104	21	18
Van Buren	1 755	2.4	22 673	1 829	879	40	223	358	339	137	139	39	16
Washtenaw	11 801	3.0	35 282	134	10 504	694	2 113	1 037	958	424	375	73	32
Wayne	56 477	-0.1	27 684	590	46 126	4 093	7 527	11 018	10 533	3 475	4 761	1 500	504
Wexford	689	3.5	22 362	1 918	550	29	109	158	151	62	62	14	8
MINNESOTA	167 434	2.6	33 322	X	121 766	11 185	30 809	20 721	19 405	7 417	8 403	1 478	1 043
Aitkin	364	5.8	23 241	1 645	126	30	86	96	92	37	40	6	4
Anoka	9 733	2.7	31 385	256	5 062	350	1 189	943	862	344	342	56	75
Becker	788	4.2	25 590	978	389	82	157	163	155	57	62	14	7
Beltrami	982	4.4	23 864	1 453	596	95	180	212	201	56	92	32	7
Benton	975	4.1	26 877	721	511	81	174	120	111	41	46	7	9
Big Stone	143	4.4	25 072	1 111	56	12	42	34	33	14	16	2	1
Blue Earth	1 577	3.5	27 763	577	1 224	144	346	216	202	82	80	15	8
Brown	722	0.0	27 027	696	476	54	173	128	121	54	51	5	5
Carlton	830	5.2	25 503	998	525	37	130	170	162	61	70	11	8
Carver	3 012	1.5	39 611	66	1 405	192	476	191	172	75	68	7	15
Cass	730	4.3	26 164	857	284	67	188	166	159	66	63	15	5
Chippewa	361	4.3	27 925	561	197	41	86	63	59	24	26	3	3
Chisago	1 274	4.0	28 424	499	485	64	212	165	154	62	62	8	13
Clay	1 268	4.3	24 470	1 273	581	52	225	221	207	75	90	18	4
Clearwater	180	5.1	21 306	2 206	94	19	27	49	47	14	22	5	4
Cook	155	4.7	29 550	385	79	19	45	24	23	11	9	1	1
Cottonwood	300	1.9	24 968	1 138	150	39	72	65	61	27	27	4	2
Crow Wing	1 432	5.3	24 978	1 134	962	53	288	299	284	121	110	19	11
Dakota	13 755	2.8	37 289	100	7 583	525	2 140	1 030	933	402	343	50	76
Dodge	536	4.9	28 883	460	182	51	97	67	62	25	29	3	3
Douglas	895	5.5	26 594	767	560	71	204	157	148	68	58	8	4
Faribault	417	9.3	26 234	847	207	31	106	88	84	37	38	5	3
Fillmore	548	3.6	25 713	950	214	60	116	102	96	40	46	4	5
Freeborn	823	3.2	25 659	964	432	61	166	165	157	72	64	9	5
Goodhue	1 316	2.3	29 287	409	827	77	268	185	173	77	72	8	10

1. Based on the resident population estimated as of July 1 of the year shown.   2. Includes other labor income.

Table B. States and Counties — Earnings, Social Security, and Housing

STATE County	Earnings, 2002 Total (mil dol)	Farm	Goods-related[1] Total	Manufacturing	Information and professional and technical services	Retail trade	Finance, insurance, and real estate	Health services	Government	Social Security beneficiaries, December 2003 Number	Rate[2]	Supplemental Security Income recipients, December 2003	Housing units, 2003 Total	Percent change, 2000–2003
	75	76	77	78	79	80	81	82	83	84	85	86	87	88
MICHIGAN—Cont'd														
Leelanau	242	1.5	D	2.9	6.3	7.1	8.5	6.7	33.9	5 070	232	94	13 960	5.0
Lenawee	1 392	-0.1	39.4	33.6	D	10.0	6.2	8.0	17.4	18 385	182	1 671	41 161	3.5
Livingston	2 431	0.1	37.4	24.0	7.2	8.1	10.4	5.4	11.6	21 645	125	587	66 711	13.2
Luce	88	1.2	D	15.6	1.9	7.4	3.3	2.0	45.5	1 535	222	205	4 103	2.4
Mackinac	175	-0.3	D	2.6	2.8	10.2	3.4	D	30.5	3 005	262	180	9 642	2.4
Macomb	18 945	0.1	46.0	37.6	7.4	7.0	4.4	7.2	11.5	140 145	172	9 440	337 823	5.5
Manistee	317	0.0	25.8	20.2	3.6	8.2	3.1	D	35.6	6 320	250	513	14 699	3.0
Marquette	1 068	0.0	17.6	3.1	5.8	8.0	5.0	21.3	26.1	12 055	187	979	33 298	1.3
Mason	423	0.8	32.8	26.4	4.1	10.2	4.5	11.2	18.7	6 590	230	677	16 448	2.4
Mecosta	459	1.1	19.7	14.9	D	9.8	3.5	7.0	39.5	7 910	190	931	20 429	4.3
Menominee	318	0.6	35.6	31.7	3.2	6.8	3.3	D	26.5	5 460	218	410	13 966	2.4
Midland	1 932	-0.1	D	11.6	D	5.3	3.2	10.4	8.8	14 580	173	1 095	34 835	3.1
Missaukee	110	4.8	31.3	19.5	D	9.0	4.4	D	18.1	3 180	209	206	8 902	3.3
Monroe	2 298	0.6	42.4	32.3	D	7.6	3.5	6.5	12.9	24 210	161	1 966	60 164	6.5
Montcalm	776	2.0	41.6	35.6	2.4	9.1	2.7	9.7	19.4	11 335	180	1 240	26 682	3.0
Montmorency	85	-0.1	D	15.2	5.3	8.5	4.3	D	19.3	3 520	335	273	9 443	2.2
Muskegon	2 765	0.3	D	27.2	6.2	10.9	4.4	12.8	16.0	33 510	194	5 267	71 302	4.0
Newaygo	454	1.8	D	25.0	4.9	8.7	6.2	8.9	23.0	9 610	195	874	24 060	3.7
Oakland	50 140	0.0	D	16.2	23.2	5.6	11.0	8.4	6.0	176 705	146	15 100	509 640	3.6
Oceana	245	7.1	D	16.4	6.1	7.6	3.5	4.2	24.1	5 700	203	636	15 305	2.0
Ogemaw	222	1.0	19.0	12.3	3.1	16.0	5.8	9.5	23.5	6 120	281	678	15 694	1.9
Ontonagon	87	-0.1	D	D	D	8.9	4.0	5.2	29.7	2 355	311	195	5 451	0.9
Osceola	334	0.1	D	45.2	1.8	5.7	2.2	D	14.9	5 225	222	662	13 219	2.8
Oscoda	68	0.0	D	21.4	2.0	10.6	4.4	D	23.1	2 745	290	186	9 083	4.5
Otsego	467	0.0	31.6	13.5	6.9	11.8	4.9	10.8	14.2	4 940	204	368	14 218	6.3
Ottawa	5 268	1.5	48.9	42.0	4.5	6.2	4.5	5.1	11.9	34 135	137	1 924	93 282	7.4
Presque Isle	128	1.3	D	5.7	2.7	11.1	4.8	D	20.7	4 315	302	309	10 205	3.0
Roscommon	222	0.0	D	D	2.9	17.6	5.3	9.8	31.1	8 845	337	669	24 006	3.9
Saginaw	4 494	0.2	D	31.6	5.8	7.5	5.7	13.3	12.6	40 415	193	7 107	87 439	2.3
St. Clair	2 221	0.0	27.7	20.9	5.7	8.7	5.3	13.4	15.7	28 730	170	2 651	71 890	6.2
St. Joseph	1 006	0.8	D	51.3	D	7.2	2.5	4.3	16.0	11 590	184	1 002	27 038	2.0
Sanilac	468	4.1	35.5	28.1	2.1	9.8	5.7	D	19.5	9 550	214	692	21 743	2.0
Schoolcraft	111	-0.2	27.5	12.2	2.1	9.1	7.4	4.6	34.3	2 275	259	226	5 816	2.0
Shiawassee	653	0.1	24.4	17.3	D	12.2	3.5	D	23.5	12 825	177	1 290	29 859	2.7
Tuscola	531	3.4	27.2	21.4	D	9.8	3.5	7.3	30.1	11 300	194	1 007	23 914	2.3
Van Buren	919	1.8	D	21.0	4.9	8.4	4.7	4.5	23.6	14 115	180	1 845	35 254	3.8
Washtenaw	11 198	0.0	23.4	18.7	17.0	5.5	4.0	8.5	27.0	37 955	112	3 692	139 708	6.6
Wayne	50 219	0.0	25.0	20.7	12.1	5.2	5.2	9.4	13.2	332 540	164	75 834	831 285	0.6
Wexford	579	0.2	D	28.2	D	9.6	2.7	11.7	15.3	6 575	210	880	15 556	4.6
MINNESOTA	132 951	0.5	22.1	15.5	11.1	6.6	10.0	10.1	13.7	765 228	151	69 020	2 167 054	4.9
Aitkin	156	-0.5	D	9.7	4.2	10.6	4.0	D	22.4	4 110	260	258	14 862	4.9
Anoka	5 412	0.0	D	28.5	4.7	7.9	4.4	9.3	12.1	34 205	109	1 857	115 543	6.9
Becker	471	2.4	D	15.2	4.2	9.8	4.4	D	22.9	6 715	215	519	17 216	3.6
Beltrami	691	0.0	D	11.0	4.5	10.1	3.2	14.6	30.7	6 570	157	1 077	17 622	3.7
Benton	592	1.0	41.9	29.7	9.2	7.3	3.2	D	10.0	4 730	128	290	14 863	10.4
Big Stone	69	3.9	D	2.0	D	D	6.4	11.6	31.3	1 635	289	97	3 179	0.3
Blue Earth	1 368	2.2	D	12.0	8.8	9.3	5.5	15.1	17.2	8 650	151	949	23 310	6.1
Brown	529	3.2	D	29.8	6.5	7.7	4.1	10.9	12.0	5 800	219	253	11 274	1.0
Carlton	561	-0.3	35.0	22.9	2.4	5.8	5.8	D	28.9	6 435	195	508	14 490	5.6
Carver	1 597	0.2	D	33.6	8.6	5.3	5.9	8.4	10.5	7 255	92	210	29 052	16.8
Cass	351	-0.5	12.9	4.5	D	8.4	7.7	D	40.3	7 405	263	562	22 666	6.5
Chippewa	238	6.7	D	19.7	D	7.7	4.6	D	16.0	2 780	217	151	5 909	0.9
Chisago	549	0.3	32.5	18.0	D	8.4	3.8	19.5	18.0	6 475	140	302	17 525	12.8
Clay	633	1.2	D	7.4	3.6	10.6	4.4	D	27.8	8 020	154	814	20 697	4.8
Clearwater	113	-0.4	39.4	17.3	D	7.0	2.6	5.0	26.5	1 800	214	196	4 207	2.3
Cook	97	0.0	D	D	3.1	9.1	3.3	2.6	36.3	1 135	215	35	5 000	6.2
Cottonwood	190	6.3	D	17.6	2.7	8.2	4.4	D	17.9	3 020	251	194	5 385	0.2
Crow Wing	1 015	-0.4	D	13.4	9.1	12.0	6.8	D	19.6	12 975	222	952	35 867	7.1
Dakota	8 108	0.1	23.2	13.5	14.5	8.3	8.7	6.3	11.3	39 350	105	1 875	144 184	7.8
Dodge	233	5.5	D	25.2	3.6	5.1	4.5	D	17.9	2 675	141	127	7 226	8.8
Douglas	631	0.2	D	18.8	D	10.0	4.8	8.4	18.0	7 815	229	464	18 042	8.1
Faribault	239	3.0	30.6	24.3	5.2	5.5	5.5	D	16.5	4 000	254	203	7 218	-0.4
Fillmore	274	6.9	D	22.0	3.5	8.5	5.3	D	16.8	4 580	215	218	9 251	3.9
Freeborn	494	3.1	D	23.2	4.0	10.6	5.1	D	12.8	7 580	237	422	14 091	0.7
Goodhue	904	1.7	D	23.0	D	6.3	3.8	9.1	20.4	7 980	177	344	18 790	5.1

1. Covers mining, construction, and manufacturing.   2. Per 1,000 resident population estimated as of July 1 of the year shown.

Table B. States and Counties — Housing, Labor Force, and Employment

STATE County	Total [89]	Percent [90]	Median value[1] [91]	With a mortgage [92]	Without a mortgage[2] [93]	Median rent[3] [94]	Median rent as a percent of income [95]	Substandard units[4] (percent) [96]	Total [97]	Percent change, 2002–2003 [98]	Total [99]	Rate[5] [100]	Total [101]	Management, professional and related occupations [102]	Production, transportation, and material moving occupations [103]
MICHIGAN—Cont'd															
Leelanau	8 436	84.7	165 400	22.4	9.9	565	21.0	2.4	11 875	4.1	618	5.2	9 945	35.1	11.0
Lenawee	35 930	78.2	109 500	19.5	9.9	517	23.3	2.3	46 778	1.8	3 537	7.6	46 895	25.3	24.8
Livingston	55 384	88.1	187 500	20.2	9.9	681	24.1	1.7	86 667	1.0	3 635	4.2	81 087	36.8	13.9
Luce	2 481	79.6	67 800	19.3	9.9	430	24.2	3.1	2 749	2.4	206	7.5	2 375	24.5	11.4
Mackinac	5 067	79.1	91 800	21.3	10.1	429	22.0	3.0	7 181	1.3	662	9.2	4 738	26.0	10.6
Macomb	309 203	78.9	139 200	19.6	10.2	603	23.1	2.7	440 956	0.2	29 104	6.6	390 791	30.9	17.7
Manistee	9 860	81.0	77 400	18.8	10.3	424	23.4	2.5	11 279	0.4	1 047	9.3	10 321	23.5	18.7
Marquette	25 767	69.8	77 200	18.0	9.9	398	24.6	1.7	32 887	1.5	2 219	6.7	30 639	29.3	11.3
Mason	11 406	78.3	81 500	18.9	10.3	425	23.9	2.3	15 649	1.0	1 949	12.5	12 646	28.5	20.2
Mecosta	14 915	73.6	90 100	19.6	9.9	470	30.3	2.9	18 876	5.0	1 212	6.4	17 470	27.3	20.0
Menominee	10 529	79.5	63 400	18.4	9.9	353	21.2	1.7	11 916	0.9	882	7.4	11 839	21.3	31.3
Midland	31 769	78.4	101 800	18.1	9.9	498	25.9	1.7	42 921	0.2	2 686	6.3	38 813	37.4	13.2
Missaukee	5 450	83.5	78 700	20.0	10.0	460	22.2	3.2	6 714	0.3	539	8.0	6 288	22.5	24.2
Monroe	53 772	80.9	132 000	19.2	9.9	549	24.3	2.2	75 335	1.1	5 477	7.3	70 344	24.8	24.1
Montcalm	22 079	81.6	84 900	20.3	10.3	455	23.0	3.2	26 060	0.9	2 424	9.3	26 560	22.0	28.2
Montmorency	4 455	86.1	76 900	22.7	9.9	431	23.5	2.1	3 836	3.8	514	13.4	3 372	21.5	20.6
Muskegon	63 330	77.7	85 900	19.2	9.9	453	25.2	3.0	82 442	0.3	8 745	10.6	76 788	24.3	25.8
Newaygo	17 599	84.5	88 700	20.2	10.9	447	24.4	4.3	21 928	3.5	2 231	10.2	20 569	22.7	25.9
Oakland	471 115	74.8	181 200	20.0	10.1	707	23.3	2.8	669 884	-0.2	34 536	5.2	614 377	44.6	10.9
Oceana	9 778	82.7	82 500	20.0	10.1	427	23.6	4.9	14 534	1.6	1 414	9.7	11 367	23.8	26.6
Ogemaw	8 842	85.0	72 900	22.2	9.9	432	23.0	3.3	9 504	1.0	896	9.4	8 221	24.0	18.9
Ontonagon	3 456	84.9	41 400	16.7	9.9	321	22.9	3.2	2 793	-0.2	251	9.0	3 169	23.8	18.0
Osceola	8 861	81.3	70 000	19.2	10.4	409	23.8	3.4	10 585	1.4	912	8.6	10 012	23.0	30.8
Oscoda	3 921	85.3	67 300	22.8	9.9	393	25.9	4.0	3 328	0.4	454	13.6	3 294	21.3	23.9
Otsego	8 995	81.9	102 500	20.1	9.9	540	25.4	2.2	13 693	0.4	1 121	8.2	10 887	27.5	17.4
Ottawa	81 662	80.8	133 000	19.6	9.9	579	21.9	3.0	139 957	-0.3	8 625	6.2	123 168	31.8	21.7
Presque Isle	6 155	85.5	77 800	19.9	10.0	345	23.9	2.6	6 438	2.0	795	12.3	5 400	25.7	17.1
Roscommon	11 250	85.8	78 900	20.7	9.9	420	24.9	2.5	8 657	3.5	848	9.8	8 996	27.3	13.8
Saginaw	80 430	73.8	85 200	18.3	9.9	497	26.7	3.4	100 157	1.5	9 393	9.4	91 113	27.3	18.0
St. Clair	62 072	79.6	125 200	20.5	10.5	537	24.7	1.9	83 649	0.9	7 699	9.2	77 966	24.0	24.8
St. Joseph	23 381	76.9	85 000	18.6	9.9	456	21.9	3.5	31 543	0.7	2 401	7.6	29 816	22.1	34.3
Sanilac	16 871	81.9	88 900	19.9	10.4	448	22.4	3.1	20 527	1.0	2 324	11.3	19 529	24.8	26.9
Schoolcraft	3 606	81.8	64 900	19.4	10.3	345	27.4	1.9	4 339	2.7	441	10.2	3 285	24.3	15.6
Shiawassee	26 896	80.1	95 900	19.2	9.9	482	23.5	2.1	34 030	2.8	2 752	8.1	34 205	25.2	24.5
Tuscola	21 454	84.1	87 100	18.7	9.9	445	21.8	2.8	28 597	3.3	2 834	9.9	25 823	23.1	25.7
Van Buren	27 982	79.5	94 200	19.5	9.9	451	22.7	3.8	36 730	1.8	2 885	7.9	35 625	25.4	24.6
Washtenaw	125 327	59.7	174 300	20.5	9.9	687	26.7	3.5	179 803	0.9	5 770	3.2	172 373	48.3	9.7
Wayne	768 440	66.6	99 400	19.8	11.1	530	25.0	5.6	922 787	1.2	83 066	9.0	851 110	28.1	19.6
Wexford	11 824	79.2	79 900	19.9	10.4	451	23.5	2.8	14 758	1.4	1 442	9.8	13 924	25.5	25.5
MINNESOTA	1 895 127	74.5	122 400	20.0	9.9	566	24.7	3.3	2 923 083	0.3	145 399	5.0	2 580 046	35.8	14.9
Aitkin	6 644	85.3	93 200	21.6	9.9	409	25.2	4.4	6 783	1.9	525	7.7	6 242	26.1	17.4
Anoka	106 428	83.4	131 300	20.4	9.9	649	24.8	2.6	189 407	0.3	9 442	5.0	165 101	32.2	17.1
Becker	11 844	80.4	87 400	20.5	10.2	364	24.7	3.7	16 106	1.6	1 071	6.6	13 811	29.3	17.4
Beltrami	14 337	74.5	79 800	19.2	9.9	414	26.8	5.0	22 133	-0.3	1 239	5.6	18 085	32.5	13.7
Benton	13 065	67.1	99 100	19.6	9.9	480	22.3	3.2	22 622	0.0	1 246	5.5	18 905	25.8	22.0
Big Stone	2 377	85.1	41 900	18.8	9.9	231	21.3	1.3	2 939	0.5	125	4.3	2 517	33.8	14.4
Blue Earth	21 062	66.4	98 200	19.8	9.9	487	26.0	2.1	36 992	-0.3	1 335	3.6	31 468	29.8	17.8
Brown	10 598	80.1	85 400	18.8	9.9	399	22.4	1.2	15 411	-0.5	903	5.9	13 834	28.4	23.4
Carlton	12 064	82.0	85 400	19.6	10.1	395	23.1	3.0	16 714	-1.6	1 122	6.7	14 345	27.1	18.7
Carver	24 356	83.5	170 200	21.7	9.9	637	24.2	2.1	45 678	0.2	1 902	4.2	37 796	40.7	13.0
Cass	10 893	86.0	105 900	22.3	10.6	371	23.8	4.2	13 699	2.0	1 070	7.8	11 658	27.8	14.5
Chippewa	5 361	76.5	62 200	18.8	10.1	401	24.3	1.5	7 166	-2.8	383	5.3	6 329	30.5	18.5
Chisago	14 454	87.0	132 500	22.0	9.9	506	24.1	2.4	23 338	0.8	1 583	6.8	21 084	28.9	19.0
Clay	18 670	71.6	85 400	20.0	9.9	421	28.9	2.2	31 480	1.5	969	3.1	25 843	31.9	12.7
Clearwater	3 330	81.6	51 300	17.9	9.9	340	25.0	3.6	4 179	-6.2	544	13.0	3 574	31.1	15.2
Cook	2 350	78.2	107 700	22.0	9.9	456	22.7	8.8	3 130	-0.1	146	4.7	2 668	32.7	10.0
Cottonwood	4 917	80.4	50 600	17.0	9.9	308	23.5	1.7	6 415	6.5	301	4.7	5 869	30.6	20.6
Crow Wing	22 250	79.6	107 500	20.3	9.9	458	26.1	3.0	32 012	1.2	1 918	6.0	25 712	29.4	15.5
Dakota	131 151	78.2	152 400	20.3	9.9	722	24.4	2.4	228 748	0.2	9 639	4.2	200 612	39.5	11.0
Dodge	6 420	84.4	97 100	19.7	10.4	386	20.2	1.9	10 138	-0.7	514	5.1	9 368	32.2	17.5
Douglas	13 276	77.2	102 300	20.6	9.9	411	25.5	1.5	19 470	3.2	698	3.6	16 490	29.6	19.5
Faribault	6 652	80.6	50 300	16.8	9.9	347	20.1	1.2	8 302	-2.3	444	5.3	7 735	29.7	20.6
Fillmore	8 228	80.7	74 400	19.2	9.9	350	21.0	3.3	10 470	0.4	614	5.9	10 802	32.1	17.1
Freeborn	13 356	78.7	71 400	18.3	9.9	368	22.7	2.7	16 747	-2.2	889	5.3	16 032	25.8	25.5
Goodhue	16 983	78.9	116 000	20.3	9.9	477	23.6	1.9	24 297	-1.8	1 277	5.3	23 363	29.5	19.8

1. Specified owner-occupied units.   2. Median monthly owner costs is often in the minimum category—9.9 percent or less, which is indicated as 9.9 percent.   3. Specified renter-occupied units.   4. Overcrowded or lacking complete plumbing facilities.   5. Percent of civilian labor force.   6. Persons 16 years old and over.

	Private nonfarm establishments, employment and payroll, 2001								Agriculture, 2002			
STATE County	Number of establishments	Employment						Annual payroll		Farms			Farm operators whose principal occupation is farming (percent)
		Total	Health care and social assistance	Manufacturing	Retail trade	Finance and insurance	Professional, scientific, and technical services	Total (mil dol)	Average per employee (dollars)	Number	Percent with—		
											Less than 50 acres	500 acres and over	
	104	105	106	107	108	109	110	111	112	113	114	115	116
MICHIGAN—Cont'd													
Leelanau	701	4 254	429	240	681	108	131	112	26 252	429	35.2	4.9	58.5
Lenawee	2 152	29 989	3 599	8 586	5 031	951	513	826	27 549	1 446	37.6	13.7	53.1
Livingston	3 820	44 562	3 387	10 991	8 080	929	2 273	1 406	31 547	877	60.2	4.6	45.7
Luce	193	1 782	295	D	458	93	17	39	21 750	30	33.3	23.3	60.0
Mackinac	515	2 588	265	97	489	96	56	78	29 963	76	17.1	13.2	67.1
Macomb	18 739	317 262	30 825	83 939	48 002	7 711	15 052	11 937	37 626	512	58.2	5.9	55.7
Manistee	619	5 542	1 042	1 137	964	164	87	138	24 972	315	31.4	5.1	55.7
Marquette	1 598	21 272	5 307	953	3 643	883	558	591	27 783	160	39.4	8.1	51.7
Mason	877	9 480	1 125	2 552	1 979	211	265	246	25 993	478	32.8	7.3	52.5
Mecosta	905	9 344	1 211	1 947	2 019	260	189	206	22 079	794	27.3	5.4	51.9
Menominee	527	6 783	585	2 936	737	231	116	161	23 723	372	17.2	13.7	53.9
Midland	1 944	36 792	5 618	5 268	5 159	790	1 069	1 607	43 672	510	43.5	8.2	54.6
Missaukee	322	1 965	D	385	435	54	43	43	22 041	412	23.5	12.4	57.1
Monroe	2 502	39 441	4 133	9 349	6 830	947	914	1 368	34 696	1 183	51.2	10.1	61.2
Montcalm	1 119	16 301	1 783	6 747	2 742	440	245	398	24 418	1 139	35.2	9.3	55.9
Montmorency	251	1 792	191	389	335	57	24	38	21 222	139	23.0	4.3	53.6
Muskegon	3 583	56 495	8 196	15 757	8 389	1 286	1 746	1 700	30 084	545	55.2	5.1	51.1
Newaygo	781	8 870	1 184	1 904	1 511	243	279	257	28 992	902	37.7	6.3	53.0
Oakland	42 013	779 062	87 901	78 200	86 999	45 162	79 934	33 518	43 024	643	71.4	1.9	52.8
Oceana	583	4 537	590	1 541	792	118	116	101	22 350	648	33.0	9.0	50.1
Ogemaw	616	5 344	1 084	783	1 294	157	115	115	21 536	256	23.8	14.8	49.7
Ontonagon	230	1 697	334	D	354	83	D	41	24 273	108	9.3	18.5	59.4
Osceola	417	6 795	736	3 552	715	99	89	164	24 113	591	25.7	8.3	59.3
Oscoda	263	1 825	D	401	333	156	D	46	25 065	123	33.3	3.3	55.2
Otsego	901	11 139	1 214	1 586	1 990	232	250	279	25 018	170	32.9	12.9	68.3
Ottawa	5 995	105 640	9 837	40 168	12 908	2 372	3 441	3 286	31 105	1 291	54.3	5.0	58.2
Presque Isle	440	3 322	324	185	858	122	67	74	22 352	303	19.8	9.2	56.8
Roscommon	727	5 079	543	430	1 590	231	78	109	21 520	46	39.1	8.7	53.5
Saginaw	4 905	91 399	15 479	19 306	14 202	2 859	3 172	2 982	32 625	1 359	38.8	12.1	37.0
St. Clair	3 559	46 885	7 081	11 770	8 167	1 247	1 340	1 352	28 837	1 260	48.7	5.2	58.9
St. Joseph	1 277	19 976	1 935	9 847	2 785	495	296	583	29 161	907	40.2	12.7	54.4
Sanilac	986	10 492	1 323	4 030	1 881	383	207	246	23 405	1 595	29.8	15.4	58.9
Schoolcraft	270	1 834	261	240	488	92	45	47	25 411	51	33.3	15.7	66.6
Shiawassee	1 323	15 605	2 480	3 279	2 989	429	563	375	24 050	1 037	38.2	12.2	60.8
Tuscola	1 066	11 540	2 655	2 192	2 240	428	133	271	23 495	1 292	35.9	13.5	55.0
													59.1
Van Buren	1 549	17 288	1 926	4 808	2 572	357	815	448	25 931	1 160	45.3	4.6	53.7
Washtenaw	8 270	157 248	27 705	27 425	19 877	4 185	12 105	6 588	41 892	1 325	51.4	6.5	49.4
Wayne	35 887	750 087	96 439	118 155	82 608	32 981	35 448	29 780	39 703	319	74.0	2.5	43.9
Wexford	839	13 503	1 605	4 378	2 625	265	363	324	23 996	395	40.5	3.0	44.8
MINNESOTA	140 968	2 418 159	331 939	373 586	315 883	139 830	123 646	84 861	35 093	80 839	24.9	19.0	62.9
Aitkin	426	3 247	570	597	572	89	54	71	21 821	674	16.9	11.9	49.0
Anoka	6 786	105 114	11 918	24 781	15 260	1 857	3 223	3 737	35 552	552	55.8	4.9	46.7
Becker	1 057	16 472	1 688	1 778	2 275	221	210	425	25 812	1 254	15.3	14.2	53.2
Beltrami	1 035	13 189	2 804	1 311	2 807	365	337	304	23 054	746	14.3	17.0	53.2
Benton	766	10 440	667	2 612	1 631	130	156	288	27 576	965	27.4	8.3	58.8
Big Stone	186	1 492	464	61	337	99	D	26	17 135	446	14.1	40.8	77.1
Blue Earth	1 700	28 252	5 329	4 144	5 897	910	769	691	24 460	1 125	27.3	25.0	68.9
Brown	671	12 529	1 937	3 859	1 879	370	340	300	23 945	1 047	19.0	22.4	77.3
Carlton	681	8 989	1 249	2 070	1 482	355	150	279	31 033	607	15.7	5.6	52.4
Carver	1 817	29 199	3 357	9 986	3 089	501	1 435	1 001	34 270	820	35.6	8.9	63.4
Cass	811	4 541	651	200	999	203	183	92	20 237	646	11.8	13.8	56.5
Chippewa	395	4 057	669	850	746	198	130	90	22 145	694	21.6	32.0	67.9
Chisago	1 152	11 058	2 915	2 026	1 824	319	295	286	25 859	943	46.1	3.5	48.5
Clay	1 139	14 826	2 114	961	2 794	492	356	299	20 169	877	20.2	33.1	64.5
Clearwater	178	1 822	463	461	267	74	69	40	22 001	627	10.2	17.9	54.4
Cook	263	2 125	176	D	348	D	D	43	20 375	20	25.0	5.0	45.0
Cottonwood	376	4 043	881	1 189	749	139	67	76	18 837	832	21.8	33.5	72.4
Crow Wing	1 974	22 346	3 745	2 878	4 263	607	1 576	582	26 057	755	24.2	7.4	50.1
Dakota	9 021	159 175	12 615	18 192	23 799	7 375	6 584	5 666	35 598	997	44.1	11.7	59.6
Dodge	447	4 260	222	1 237	672	153	71	121	28 288	697	34.4	20.1	63.0
Douglas	1 297	14 425	2 029	2 787	2 942	354	545	350	24 273	1 177	22.8	10.9	56.3
Faribault	443	4 747	829	1 487	691	235	107	104	21 935	909	22.9	33.3	75.1
Fillmore	635	5 574	997	1 191	966	243	87	114	20 458	1 600	25.8	16.5	64.6
Freeborn	1 041	13 123	2 310	3 016	2 138	470	257	300	22 881	1 172	31.7	23.8	64.9
Goodhue	1 285	19 561	2 885	4 903	2 434	453	463	514	26 263	1 679	35.4	12.0	60.2

STATE County	Land in farms		Acres			Value of land and buildings (dollars)		Value of machinery and equipment average per farm (dollars)	Value of products sold		Percent from —		Percent of farms with sales of —		Government payments	
	Acreage (1,000)	Percent change, 1997–2002	Average size of farm	Total irrigated (1,000)	Total cropland (1,000)	Average per farm	Average per acre		Total (mil dol)	Average per farm (dollars)	Crops	Live-stock and poultry products	$10,000 or more	$100,000 or more	Total ($1,000)	Percent of farms
	117	118	119	120	121	122	123	124	125	126	127	128	129	130	131	132
MICHIGAN—Cont'd																
Leelanau	62	0.0	145	2	38	714 551	4 684	76 938	16	37 268	78.4	21.6	41.5	8.2	968	15.2
Lenawee	353	5.1	244	4	314	585 178	2 516	73 823	103	71 478	62.2	37.8	39.7	13.6	7 897	59.1
Livingston	96	-2.0	110	1	69	520 447	4 782	57 430	25	29 032	64.6	35.4	25.8	5.7	1 130	13.6
Luce	10	NA	342	D	6	543 869	1 367	62 331	3	87 848	85.1	15.0	50.0	16.7	13	20.0
Mackinac	20	-9.1	269	D	12	410 189	1 547	48 680	3	37 062	17.4	82.6	32.9	6.6	110	13.2
Macomb	68	-1.4	133	3	59	695 732	6 107	104 880	44	85 532	91.2	8.8	42.2	17.8	939	22.3
Manistee	46	-4.2	147	2	27	337 720	2 222	48 988	8	25 494	85.9	14.1	28.3	6.3	204	14.6
Marquette	30	11.1	188	0	11	305 139	1 632	47 461	4	23 107	48.9	51.1	13.8	5.6	147	3.8
Mason	80	3.9	167	2	57	355 507	1 983	73 615	25	52 207	66.3	33.7	39.3	10.9	707	28.5
Mecosta	120	7.1	151	6	84	351 212	2 202	38 160	31	38 544	43.8	56.2	33.4	5.5	1 051	32.9
Menominee	99	-10.0	265	D	57	376 098	1 322	56 120	21	56 963	14.4	85.6	42.5	15.6	1 138	26.3
Midland	85	6.3	166	1	67	426 823	2 607	75 001	22	42 627	66.3	33.7	36.7	8.6	1 083	37.6
Missaukee	98	8.9	237	3	70	461 562	2 199	71 960	40	95 983	27.1	72.9	44.2	18.7	1 601	29.6
Monroe	217	3.3	184	6	200	578 759	3 152	79 298	92	77 973	93.4	6.6	45.4	12.5	4 129	34.1
Montcalm	255	7.1	224	47	198	507 601	2 205	98 166	106	93 338	68.3	31.7	35.6	12.6	2 934	38.5
Montmorency	21	0.0	152	0	13	293 201	1 937	51 627	3	23 987	34.6	65.4	27.3	6.5	133	16.5
Muskegon	74	1.4	136	7	49	356 820	3 008	63 674	46	84 955	63.8	36.2	33.0	12.3	1 134	18.5
Newaygo	135	10.7	150	7	93	370 501	2 689	57 251	61	67 481	34.1	65.9	30.9	11.2	2 178	27.6
Oakland	41	-8.9	64	1	25	369 447	7 428	47 468	45	70 699	91.3	8.7	22.1	5.1	177	6.4
Oceana	127	-0.8	197	4	89	532 675	2 701	93 785	58	90 096	68.1	31.9	46.0	15.0	1 234	24.4
Ogemaw	68	-6.8	265	0	47	585 978	2 159	93 600	23	88 830	18.2	81.8	44.5	17.2	1 003	37.1
Ontonagon	34	3.0	312	D	20	354 577	1 138	47 202	2	22 343	20.3	79.7	30.6	4.6	109	17.6
Osceola	116	7.4	196	2	75	417 586	2 050	46 075	19	32 461	24.0	76.0	28.4	7.8	1 247	32.7
Oscoda	17	21.4	138	0	10	294 110	2 220	39 069	3	27 973	9.8	90.2	43.9	6.5	50	7.3
Otsego	35	2.9	203	0	20	491 835	2 419	67 976	5	27 856	72.6	27.4	30.6	5.9	146	20.0
Ottawa	165	-3.5	128	14	138	574 104	4 352	85 231	278	214 952	59.4	40.6	49.6	22.3	3 435	23.3
Presque Isle	68	-17.1	225	2	42	465 527	1 997	60 488	11	37 308	65.2	34.8	34.7	7.6	388	25.7
Roscommon	7	75.0	161	0	3	337 978	3 186	23 106	D	D	0.0	0.0	26.1	2.2	6	13.0
Saginaw	325	9.1	239	3	287	469 112	2 068	82 227	91	67 131	88.2	11.8	48.9	14.6	4 927	50.3
St. Clair	182	11.7	145	1	154	565 329	3 970	63 838	40	31 909	78.0	21.9	32.0	7.2	1 612	23.3
St. Joseph	231	6.5	254	104	196	579 889	2 314	122 928	94	103 264	81.2	18.8	42.7	17.6	3 970	43.7
Sanilac	435	1.2	273	1	382	609 400	2 097	128 298	137	85 826	56.2	43.8	50.6	20.7	8 140	54.0
Schoolcraft	14	-12.5	266	0	8	483 445	1 638	39 408	2	29 809	54.9	45.1	0.0	9.8	13	17.6
Shiawassee	235	9.8	226	2	201	470 760	2 163	77 924	44	42 906	72.5	27.5	42.3	11.1	3 535	42.9
Tuscola	336	0.9	260	6	297	633 362	2 297	107 161	94	72 599	77.6	22.4	44.3	17.3	5 069	49.6
Van Buren	176	-0.6	152	24	133	399 485	2 806	73 513	97	83 382	87.7	12.3	41.9	12.0	2 092	24.1
Washtenaw	175	-2.8	132	2	140	622 942	4 739	56 441	55	41 221	68.6	31.4	35.0	9.3	2 251	22.9
Wayne	21	-46.2	67	1	18	443 608	6 829	53 727	28	86 390	97.8	2.2	36.1	11.9	134	10.3
Wexford	46	7.0	116	0	29	284 587	2 779	26 412	10	24 101	66.9	33.1	26.6	4.6	147	16.2
MINNESOTA	27 512	5.8	340	455	22 729	517 132	1 513	86 369	8 576	106 083	53.2	46.8	51.8	22.9	350 709	54.3
Aitkin	174	6.1	259	6	93	249 071	879	46 930	12	18 081	56.3	43.7	24.2	3.7	285	14.5
Anoka	60	5.3	109	3	43	571 529	6 025	35 753	50	90 113	86.5	13.5	29.5	7.8	198	17.6
Becker	417	7.2	332	5	295	307 095	951	49 512	98	78 441	47.2	52.8	35.1	12.4	4 126	50.5
Beltrami	233	3.6	312	4	125	214 777	734	41 275	17	23 209	26.5	73.5	33.8	5.0	1 024	20.4
Benton	196	11.4	203	12	144	397 407	2 024	63 700	88	91 518	21.9	78.1	46.4	16.6	2 369	41.9
Big Stone	274	7.9	614	2	248	586 661	1 041	108 512	58	129 304	77.9	22.1	69.5	37.0	3 061	70.2
Blue Earth	406	0.7	361	0	374	752 842	2 168	103 590	210	186 960	44.6	53.6	68.4	36.5	5 055	64.7
Brown	348	-0.6	333	3	317	620 629	1 967	94 331	165	157 983	44.0	56.0	76.5	36.4	4 631	64.0
Carlton	114	6.5	188	0	59	208 297	1 036	27 577	8	13 337	34.8	65.2	24.7	1.8	166	6.4
Carver	172	12.4	210	0	149	621 363	2 956	104 186	62	76 066	48.3	51.7	57.2	23.3	2 661	47.2
Cass	197	2.6	305	3	101	270 470	957	39 817	14	22 177	27.6	72.4	35.1	4.3	300	13.8
Chippewa	340	6.9	489	D	312	692 323	1 502	124 731	103	148 243	85.3	14.7	62.5	34.1	4 671	75.8
Chisago	117	-4.1	124	2	80	390 987	2 897	41 908	29	30 487	70.1	29.9	31.3	6.7	894	24.4
Clay	601	3.4	685	4	543	733 548	1 070	142 428	135	153 847	83.5	16.5	56.0	31.6	6 479	66.8
Clearwater	226	6.6	361	12	121	225 761	626	50 008	20	31 940	45.0	55.0	40.2	6.4	900	32.2
Cook	3	NA	163	D	2	288 264	1 764	28 775	0	17 398	81.0	19.0	0.0	0.0	0	0.0
Cottonwood	375	1.9	450	2	346	776 154	1 780	115 533	147	176 511	51.9	48.1	70.9	42.9	4 892	67.5
Crow Wing	145	7.4	192	2	69	220 511	1 105	29 794	14	18 181	36.5	63.5	25.0	3.8	339	15.1
Dakota	236	6.8	236	47	207	737 030	3 453	86 099	112	112 337	66.5	33.5	51.1	21.0	3 003	40.6
Dodge	233	-5.7	335	D	214	799 060	2 341	110 176	109	156 150	52.4	47.6	60.7	29.0	3 885	56.0
Douglas	273	1.9	232	2	207	304 536	1 272	48 879	53	45 200	47.2	52.8	40.2	13.0	3 679	63.9
Faribault	432	4.6	475	0	410	985 809	2 104	147 922	167	183 323	68.3	31.7	78.2	47.3	6 184	63.3
Fillmore	441	1.4	276	0	340	495 990	1 754	74 912	143	89 221	45.2	54.8	56.9	22.4	6 684	55.4
Freeborn	394	3.7	337	1	365	726 289	2 197	96 690	167	142 314	60.3	39.7	62.6	32.9	6 195	63.7
Goodhue	384	-0.3	229	2	313	526 713	2 396	87 231	157	93 515	41.1	58.9	56.9	22.6	5 869	51.2

STATE County	New construction ($1,000)	Number of housing units	Number of establishments	Number of employees	Sales (mil dol)	Annual payroll (mil dol)	Number of establishments	Number of employees	Sales (mil dol)	Annual payroll (mil dol)	Number of establishments	Number of employees	Receipts (mil dol)	Annual payroll (mil dol)
	Value of residential construction authorized by building permits, 2003		Wholesale trade, 1997				Retail trade,[1] 1997				Real estate and rental and leasing, 1997			
	133	134	135	136	137	138	139	140	141	142	143	144	145	146
MICHIGAN—Cont'd														
Leelanau	35 299	255	18	90	20.0	1.7	143	661	92.0	10.5	23	59	4.6	1.0
Lenawee	72 011	556	92	685	429.5	22.6	375	4 859	826.3	75.8	80	270	31.5	4.1
Livingston	285 795	2 000	246	1 859	1 064.1	73.2	476	6 435	1 308.4	121.7	117	439	55.5	7.7
Luce	2 257	57	10	61	10.8	1.2	36	333	64.7	4.6	5	28	4.0	0.3
Mackinac	22 217	199	12	92	29.6	1.6	133	448	83.7	8.2	16	22	2.0	0.6
Macomb	675 288	5 276	1 040	12 592	6 608.7	521.7	2 901	47 125	9 010.8	859.9	625	3 058	456.3	64.0
Manistee	6 900	70	26	D	D	D	116	947	189.8	16.3	15	44	3.9	0.7
Marquette	34 546	399	68	545	159.1	15.4	331	3 822	522.7	51.1	66	286	21.8	4.2
Mason	13 245	161	25	118	41.0	3.2	159	1 470	223.0	21.0	19	62	7.4	0.8
Mecosta	21 590	259	31	187	43.0	4.9	175	1 925	301.1	25.6	46	115	10.2	1.7
Menominee	9 640	119	24	337	192.4	10.5	85	967	162.0	12.5	9	30	3.8	0.6
Midland	29 438	255	73	758	311.0	29.0	353	4 449	722.1	72.2	60	223	27.2	3.5
Missaukee	10 984	90	11	57	17.6	1.3	57	506	103.1	7.8	9	18	1.5	0.2
Monroe	153 782	1 160	96	1 213	731.5	46.2	448	5 489	1 035.0	91.1	74	278	30.0	4.4
Montcalm	27 819	327	48	287	158.7	7.1	217	2 613	403.7	36.5	20	64	7.2	1.0
Montmorency	9 808	96	3	D	D	D	48	312	49.9	4.1	10	47	1.6	0.3
Muskegon	105 853	969	162	1 852	891.4	57.6	591	8 672	1 365.4	132.3	112	469	55.5	7.2
Newaygo	18 737	280	27	323	56.0	9.4	156	1 394	244.2	22.8	21	54	4.5	0.7
Oakland	974 791	5 573	3 526	45 311	68 519.0	2 332.1	5 530	83 826	16 585.0	1 623.9	1 772	14 568	1 987.1	390.9
Oceana	11 773	119	11	72	14.6	2.3	110	786	124.3	10.7	13	24	2.3	0.4
Ogemaw	8 042	147	18	207	69.9	6.0	148	1 351	230.8	20.1	23	58	4.1	0.7
Ontonagon	2 465	27	2	D	D	D	51	388	60.4	5.2	3	2	0.1	0.0
Osceola	9 269	95	11	129	51.2	3.0	88	694	105.5	9.8	4	19	2.4	0.3
Oscoda	4 424	56	3	D	D	D	44	318	44.7	4.2	9	16	1.3	0.3
Otsego	23 600	213	38	387	207.8	11.3	163	1 903	334.8	29.9	31	184	12.1	1.9
Ottawa	340 051	2 451	326	3 471	2 213.3	110.2	828	12 375	1 920.7	193.1	168	774	93.6	15.9
Presque Isle	13 908	145	15	181	41.7	3.6	93	768	122.5	11.0	9	21	1.6	0.3
Roscommon	28 077	344	22	72	10.5	1.3	149	1 553	267.0	25.5	26	51	3.5	0.6
Saginaw	94 363	699	269	3 643	1 614.3	120.1	1 101	14 917	2 477.0	228.2	155	820	80.1	14.0
St. Clair	113 215	913	131	1 415	596.4	50.6	629	7 801	1 315.1	124.8	102	444	53.9	7.6
St. Joseph	23 659	197	59	680	252.1	27.8	230	2 627	399.3	37.4	52	199	19.7	3.0
Sanilac	14 784	126	37	238	99.5	5.2	183	1 707	287.6	25.7	29	105	9.3	2.2
Schoolcraft	4 053	70	12	D	D	D	56	410	78.6	6.2	8	17	0.9	0.2
Shiawassee	26 825	257	67	476	182.6	11.5	234	3 080	571.4	46.6	37	148	63.8	3.8
Tuscola	14 742	131	54	408	202.4	9.8	212	2 048	412.6	33.1	22	68	6.2	0.8
Van Buren	41 093	466	61	405	160.5	11.7	267	2 694	503.8	44.2	48	169	11.8	2.1
Washtenaw	380 475	2 527	435	4 778	3 338.4	182.3	1 204	18 464	3 371.9	329.6	315	2 147	184.5	47.9
Wayne	686 927	5 638	2 357	40 193	37 963.4	1 614.4	6 690	85 476	15 852.1	1 483.7	1 256	9 014	1 478.6	225.7
Wexford	25 324	220	29	334	83.5	9.0	174	2 127	359.1	33.1	28	156	12.7	2.2
MINNESOTA	6 269 475	42 046	9 348	131 787	99 444.5	5 024.0	20 883	282 282	48 077.7	4 525.7	5 051	30 172	3 886.4	687.2
Aitkin	39 955	374	16	D	D	D	60	490	77.7	6.5	9	26	1.3	0.2
Anoka	454 519	2 930	351	4 520	1 824.1	161.2	826	13 478	2 232.6	206.0	235	1 166	117.9	18.0
Becker	33 805	324	42	263	78.6	7.4	182	1 609	258.6	22.7	29	107	7.8	1.7
Beltrami	13 922	142	44	414	101.2	10.0	200	2 453	365.8	34.5	24	89	18.4	1.1
Benton	42 089	348	45	1 083	535.4	28.4	102	1 356	186.8	20.6	15	65	6.8	1.2
Big Stone	3 033	31	15	D	D	D	42	254	26.9	2.6	4	D	D	D
Blue Earth	97 726	888	108	1 520	558.0	39.0	325	5 166	744.4	70.4	62	344	29.2	6.2
Brown	16 144	180	41	438	417.7	9.8	152	1 850	234.7	22.2	23	84	9.2	1.4
Carlton	34 076	280	25	417	193.2	11.5	129	1 364	226.6	19.5	12	62	5.7	0.7
Carver	254 871	1 463	122	2 205	570.1	59.8	177	2 389	413.8	40.0	61	320	32.3	8.1
Cass	71 609	558	18	D	D	D	163	959	164.8	15.9	17	45	4.9	0.9
Chippewa	1 991	15	27	240	191.4	6.9	75	844	125.9	10.8	13	51	1.6	0.3
Chisago	92 718	664	33	D	D	D	148	1 421	221.9	20.0	39	171	7.4	1.5
Clay	57 854	539	67	765	410.6	17.8	193	2 828	458.0	37.8	38	127	10.1	1.4
Clearwater	130	1	10	75	17.7	1.4	40	260	34.5	3.0	3	8	0.3	0.1
Cook	12 183	110	2	D	D	D	48	271	44.0	4.5	19	30	3.9	0.5
Cottonwood	2 911	21	28	206	169.6	4.5	72	665	103.2	8.7	7	21	1.1	0.4
Crow Wing	130 285	1 045	79	713	178.7	16.4	376	3 749	708.3	61.9	76	220	28.3	3.5
Dakota	657 036	4 186	686	9 650	5 578.3	359.6	1 140	22 202	4 010.9	374.2	331	1 597	237.1	34.3
Dodge	26 153	205	22	321	156.1	10.1	68	448	70.5	6.5	6	23	16.6	0.5
Douglas	77 452	599	56	488	174.6	13.1	233	2 472	368.7	33.3	48	126	13.1	1.9
Faribault	3 551	28	40	D	D	D	84	634	80.5	7.7	6	7	0.9	0.1
Fillmore	19 052	147	35	319	240.8	8.4	135	810	149.2	12.7	9	11	1.7	0.1
Freeborn	5 981	48	68	646	522.1	19.1	183	1 965	310.8	29.5	21	61	6.6	0.6
Goodhue	61 394	385	63	1 051	680.4	31.3	244	2 390	337.0	32.7	43	107	10.9	1.6

1. Establishments with payroll.

Table B. States and Counties — **Professional Services, Manufacturing, and Accommodation and Foodservices**

STATE County	Professional, scientific, and technical services,¹ 1997				Manufacturing, 1997				Accommodation and foodservices, 1997			
	Number of establishments	Number of employees	Receipts (mil dol)	Annual payroll (mil dol)	Number of establishments	Number of employees	Receipts (mil dol)	Annual payroll (mil dol)	Number of establishments	Number of employees	Sales (mil dol)	Annual payroll (mil dol)
	147	148	149	150	151	152	153	154	155	156	157	158
MICHIGAN—Cont'd												
Leelanau	36	220	11.5	4.4	NA	NA	NA	NA	78	884	32.5	10.1
Lenawee	106	371	23.5	9.4	163	8 940	1 736.1	359.3	182	2 485	73.5	19.6
Livingston	288	1 629	103.7	50.5	264	10 560	2 782.8	374.1	193	3 494	116.1	29.9
Luce	7	16	0.7	0.2	NA	NA	NA	NA	33	275	7.3	2.0
Mackinac	21	109	10.2	4.9	NA	NA	NA	NA	129	723	50.4	13.3
Macomb	1 305	11 709	1 069.4	509.2	2 116	93 551	23 988.0	4 321.9	1 342	24 413	796.5	216.4
Manistee	28	77	4.7	2.0	31	1 300	244.6	48.4	73	671	18.5	5.2
Marquette	120	590	35.2	16.7	39	730	81.0	16.0	175	2 642	64.7	20.1
Mason	53	190	12.6	4.9	40	2 682	435.8	84.2	80	1 010	29.5	8.4
Mecosta	41	141	9.6	3.8	41	1 837	363.2	50.7	87	1 587	41.2	11.4
Menominee	26	92	5.0	2.5	56	2 901	425.2	78.0	51	D	D	D
Midland	142	697	71.5	23.4	71	5 613	1 690.8	285.4	132	2 688	78.1	22.9
Missaukee	9	32	2.4	0.8	23	548	73.0	17.5	25	179	4.6	1.2
Monroe	120	501	36.3	14.1	138	9 278	2 560.1	425.6	219	3 339	98.0	26.2
Montcalm	35	134	5.7	1.4	77	5 456	923.8	172.0	89	1 027	27.7	7.5
Montmorency	12	25	1.6	0.7	NA	NA	NA	NA	38	275	7.1	1.7
Muskegon	229	1 087	91.2	40.4	335	16 398	2 903.3	562.1	321	5 256	153.8	42.2
Newaygo	37	258	11.6	4.7	46	1 727	484.7	51.7	62	686	19.9	5.4
Oakland	5 522	60 999	6 922.0	2 990.6	2 366	90 481	27 172.7	3 747.5	2 453	48 174	1 668.0	478.6
Oceana	21	96	5.6	1.7	51	1 385	214.5	31.2	66	410	16.9	5.2
Ogemaw	24	78	7.4	2.1	29	872	85.9	23.3	69	654	20.8	5.7
Ontonagon	9	15	0.8	0.4	NA	NA	NA	NA	40	303	6.5	1.8
Osceola	20	58	3.9	1.8	36	3 582	661.3	99.2	43	334	10.6	2.6
Oscoda	6	27	0.8	0.3	NA	NA	NA	NA	24	210	5.6	1.7
Otsego	51	317	19.4	8.0	39	1 870	255.5	53.8	69	1 686	56.9	18.3
Ottawa	344	2 565	192.0	91.9	591	38 244	7 688.1	1 310.8	328	6 073	173.2	50.4
Presque Isle	14	59	2.2	1.3	NA	NA	NA	NA	57	295	9.1	2.5
Roscommon	28	61	3.8	1.5	NA	NA	NA	NA	79	994	26.5	7.5
Saginaw	320	2 908	195.1	86.5	239	20 681	5 172.2	1 148.6	408	9 236	270.5	78.9
St. Clair	176	851	56.8	25.2	294	14 162	2 667.6	431.5	290	4 520	138.3	38.4
St. Joseph	49	244	12.6	6.1	163	10 651	2 402.7	371.4	128	1 436	45.5	11.4
Sanilac	42	164	9.7	2.3	88	5 244	726.3	123.6	75	736	21.3	6.1
Schoolcraft	9	24	0.9	0.4	NA	NA	NA	NA	43	221	7.5	1.9
Shiawassee	70	334	26.5	11.9	86	4 139	453.8	99.6	110	1 467	41.1	11.0
Tuscola	43	127	9.0	3.0	65	2 818	486.4	96.9	84	1 101	29.0	8.2
Van Buren	77	439	37.2	13.7	127	4 879	1 007.8	152.1	146	1 677	51.6	15.1
Washtenaw	993	7 818	954.4	380.0	412	29 254	7 350.2	1 395.5	627	13 266	430.2	119.5
Wayne	2 512	29 950	3 133.0	1 233.0	2 390	133 703	54 375.0	6 514.3	3 313	58 336	2 023.7	542.5
Wexford	42	257	18.2	8.4	57	4 331	719.1	126.7	88	1 487	39.7	11.6
MINNESOTA	12 391	96 677	10 447.9	4 091.3	8 091	382 530	76 244.9	13 126.1	9 982	179 487	5 934.2	1 688.8
Aitkin	15	87	3.1	1.6	NA	NA	NA	NA	59	469	16.5	4.4
Anoka	533	2 440	167.8	68.0	614	24 754	3 860.7	908.7	351	7 744	215.4	62.3
Becker	45	157	9.9	4.2	42	1 320	193.0	35.7	104	973	33.3	8.4
Beltrami	47	208	13.3	6.0	43	1 112	175.9	32.0	100	1 339	40.9	11.4
Benton	25	179	12.9	5.4	53	2 797	300.2	71.4	53	962	26.8	7.5
Big Stone	8	28	1.5	0.8	NA	NA	NA	NA	21	155	3.3	0.8
Blue Earth	90	596	48.6	16.6	78	4 144	1 160.8	126.7	137	2 657	72.6	19.5
Brown	44	367	23.1	9.7	41	4 292	1 580.8	113.0	62	1 044	23.5	6.5
Carlton	33	133	7.2	3.1	30	2 131	425.0	89.8	74	808	23.4	6.4
Carver	140	1 096	75.2	31.5	143	10 470	1 920.0	391.7	109	1 566	43.6	12.8
Cass	34	100	6.6	2.5	NA	NA	NA	NA	121	669	26.8	6.0
Chippewa	13	61	3.4	1.5	24	1 498	116.3	34.5	30	329	7.6	2.0
Chisago	63	297	13.0	6.3	101	2 462	282.1	70.3	67	772	18.5	5.2
Clay	56	307	24.9	9.6	38	1 225	229.4	35.7	107	1 615	40.7	11.4
Clearwater	10	D	D	D	NA	NA	NA	NA	20	D	D	D
Cook	13	D	D	D	NA	NA	NA	NA	71	748	36.1	9.8
Cottonwood	18	66	3.4	1.7	16	930	486.9	20.5	24	258	6.0	1.6
Crow Wing	94	784	67.1	25.1	95	2 957	458.3	91.2	211	2 480	121.3	33.2
Dakota	854	4 016	399.0	151.1	439	17 957	5 922.4	636.3	488	11 244	344.9	100.8
Dodge	18	50	2.7	1.0	29	1 322	398.6	37.5	24	D	D	D
Douglas	54	270	15.7	7.8	72	2 806	448.4	76.0	106	1 258	42.2	11.1
Faribault	22	85	3.3	1.3	28	1 578	260.6	36.5	31	D	D	D
Fillmore	28	87	3.5	1.2	42	1 122	224.8	27.9	60	D	D	D
Freeborn	33	202	14.6	5.9	66	3 062	564.5	86.7	79	978	26.5	7.0
Goodhue	66	286	27.2	9.5	81	5 522	972.8	166.6	104	1 623	39.4	12.0

1. Firms subject to federal tax.

STATE County	Health care and social assistance,[1] 1997				Other services,[1] 1997				Federal funds and grants, 2002–2003 Expenditures (mil dol)			
									Total	Direct payments for individuals[2]		
	Number of establishments	Number of employees	Receipts (mil dol)	Annual payroll (mil dol)	Number of establishments	Number of employees	Receipts (mil dol)	Annual payroll (mil dol)		Social Security and government retirement	Medicare	Food stamps and Supplemental Security Income
	159	160	161	162	163	164	165	166	167	168	169	170
MICHIGAN—Cont'd												
Leelanau	34	147	8.8	3.7	26	145	11.3	2.7	84.9	46.9	14.9	1.1
Lenawee	183	1 335	71.3	33.2	134	605	38.8	12.0	435.2	215.1	93.7	12.0
Livingston	246	2 017	98.3	49.0	209	1 109	82.4	25.5	392.6	221.3	77.1	5.5
Luce	11	D	D	D	7	37	2.6	0.5	42.2	17.4	9.2	1.7
Mackinac	17	76	3.5	1.5	14	57	2.9	0.8	65.9	32.3	13.3	1.1
Macomb	1 492	14 800	995.8	477.1	1 366	8 618	573.3	184.6	5 061.1	1 726.5	943.4	70.8
Manistee	59	448	18.3	8.4	32	101	6.0	1.5	143.4	71.0	29.7	4.2
Marquette	137	1 582	98.4	56.2	99	485	29.1	7.9	338.2	164.5	63.1	7.8
Mason	74	509	27.3	12.9	36	166	9.6	2.9	148.5	76.5	28.8	5.0
Mecosta	68	612	27.1	13.5	61	276	14.2	4.1	176.2	87.4	28.7	7.4
Menominee	32	351	11.6	5.6	32	106	7.7	1.8	121.9	62.5	22.3	2.8
Midland	202	1 822	112.6	56.3	124	698	46.4	12.0	299.2	164.4	58.0	9.4
Missaukee	21	154	5.6	2.5	13	27	2.7	0.4	63.3	32.2	11.8	1.7
Monroe	171	1 480	90.2	41.9	141	892	60.7	22.4	574.9	291.7	131.4	15.8
Montcalm	73	596	31.7	13.9	76	350	22.4	6.5	281.2	133.7	56.9	9.5
Montmorency	13	179	6.2	3.1	11	30	2.4	0.5	83.9	43.8	18.2	2.3
Muskegon	272	2 682	157.8	82.2	234	1 299	67.2	21.8	877.4	381.0	154.5	42.7
Newaygo	43	542	26.3	12.3	53	187	12.4	2.7	189.0	98.3	35.9	7.4
Oakland	3 713	35 580	2 427.4	1 186.9	2 108	16 274	1 133.6	363.1	4 933.9	2 346.9	1 204.0	118.7
Oceana	31	192	7.4	3.9	41	107	6.0	1.4	137.9	64.3	24.2	5.6
Ogemaw	52	499	21.9	9.8	37	169	9.2	2.6	128.3	64.0	27.1	6.4
Ontonagon	10	120	3.9	2.0	8	32	2.8	0.4	61.2	27.7	11.5	1.3
Osceola	24	178	9.9	3.9	29	80	4.5	1.1	132.0	63.0	23.1	5.5
Oscoda	11	D	D	D	11	31	2.4	0.4	46.4	24.7	10.7	1.6
Otsego	66	499	28.1	12.1	55	250	20.9	4.9	112.0	57.6	17.7	2.6
Ottawa	332	4 128	213.1	105.4	346	2 032	141.6	40.5	801.3	409.4	118.4	9.7
Presque Isle	25	247	12.7	4.2	27	74	5.8	1.1	93.5	51.0	17.8	1.8
Roscommon	40	473	21.2	9.2	48	125	7.8	2.1	175.3	102.1	45.9	5.0
Saginaw	410	3 465	248.1	121.5	336	2 127	126.7	39.1	1 153.2	484.0	217.6	63.8
St. Clair	271	2 176	148.7	72.5	242	1 229	87.2	24.0	659.2	286.0	148.7	20.0
St. Joseph	98	805	36.6	15.3	97	578	40.2	13.8	258.2	131.1	55.1	8.1
Sanilac	82	527	25.2	10.5	59	443	15.2	2.8	228.5	104.8	51.6	6.0
Schoolcraft	8	136	5.7	3.5	19	55	3.6	0.8	60.0	27.6	12.3	1.6
Shiawassee	114	972	54.2	28.1	84	443	25.8	8.1	315.4	157.3	72.0	10.4
Tuscola	81	923	32.6	15.5	72	352	19.4	5.8	298.1	131.8	55.7	7.7
Van Buren	94	688	34.6	16.0	95	330	18.4	5.4	370.4	160.0	70.5	14.5
Washtenaw	703	6 534	525.1	228.3	392	2 628	158.7	53.6	1 943.9	483.8	213.2	31.3
Wayne	3 115	35 576	2 186.2	1 040.1	2 621	20 451	1 407.6	440.8	13 268.4	4 137.1	2 913.7	767.0
Wexford	67	477	33.2	15.5	51	304	17.4	5.0	243.0	76.9	27.8	6.4
MINNESOTA	8 033	106 839	5 864.5	2 946.0	7 614	55 723	3 394.6	1 103.6	27 580.0	9 284.4	3 537.5	569.7
Aitkin	12	264	7.3	3.6	11	30	3.0	0.6	103.7	52.7	17.1	1.8
Anoka	384	5 016	282.6	143.4	399	2 502	170.0	49.4	603.8	341.4	98.9	12.6
Becker	30	424	21.0	8.4	63	668	21.5	8.5	194.4	74.5	24.3	4.6
Beltrami	65	995	47.5	25.5	62	574	23.3	6.6	250.7	81.3	29.5	10.2
Benton	29	491	18.8	9.2	38	174	13.7	2.9	136.5	81.9	14.7	4.5
Big Stone	8	48	2.7	0.8	14	34	2.4	0.4	41.1	16.5	7.3	0.5
Blue Earth	118	2 027	103.3	53.6	101	662	36.1	10.6	297.1	110.3	35.7	6.0
Brown	35	414	18.1	9.9	47	190	12.4	3.3	133.7	63.2	23.0	2.0
Carlton	39	292	16.0	7.3	43	110	8.0	2.1	185.4	83.9	27.4	4.2
Carver	79	922	51.3	29.7	76	675	46.5	18.7	176.9	83.8	27.1	1.1
Cass	20	193	7.9	3.6	21	62	4.2	1.0	206.2	78.8	27.6	4.6
Chippewa	21	171	8.6	4.0	20	86	7.6	1.6	68.4	29.7	10.0	1.0
Chisago	49	1 150	47.6	27.8	50	192	11.8	2.6	144.6	84.2	26.9	2.8
Clay	56	496	24.9	11.6	76	299	17.9	4.9	250.5	98.8	35.1	8.8
Clearwater	12	71	3.6	2.0	8	21	2.2	0.2	59.3	18.2	8.8	1.4
Cook	2	D	D	D	4	8	0.7	0.2	31.9	13.7	3.6	0.3
Cottonwood	28	310	9.6	4.6	29	76	5.9	1.2	74.8	31.5	13.0	1.2
Crow Wing	99	1 353	63.0	35.8	84	352	21.1	5.2	306.6	156.8	51.5	6.9
Dakota	501	7 009	344.1	156.2	488	4 515	279.0	101.7	967.7	465.3	110.8	14.8
Dodge	16	66	3.3	1.5	34	173	14.3	4.7	66.4	29.0	12.9	1.1
Douglas	61	573	34.2	16.9	65	241	15.1	3.6	168.3	85.0	27.2	2.9
Faribault	33	150	7.0	2.8	27	55	5.3	0.9	95.5	43.4	17.8	1.4
Fillmore	27	263	10.5	4.7	32	74	7.0	1.2	120.1	49.6	23.4	1.6
Freeborn	47	447	33.3	14.2	50	225	9.8	2.4	175.0	83.0	32.0	3.5
Goodhue	65	764	39.2	14.2	74	383	29.0	6.3	183.8	93.4	33.4	2.2

1. Firms subject to federal tax.   2. State totals may include programs not allocated by county.

STATE County	Salaries and wages	Defense	Other	Medicaid and other health-related	Nutrition and family welfare	Education	Other	Total (mil dol)	Intergovern-mental (mil dol)	Total (mil dol)	Total	Property
		Procurement contract awards			Grants[1]				General revenue		Taxes / Per capita[2] (dollars)	
	171	172	173	174	175	176	177	178	179	180	181	182
MICHIGAN—Cont'd												
Leelanau	6.3	0.2	1.0	3.8	1.8	1.6	5.5	51.1	19.8	22.2	1 022	995
Lenawee	14.0	1.8	3.6	48.0	13.3	7.2	10.3	258.6	161.6	52.5	525	506
Livingston	17.1	15.6	9.2	22.9	7.5	5.6	7.7	401.0	211.9	102.4	606	593
Luce	1.0	0.3	0.3	9.8	1.2	0.8	0.4	44.1	15.9	4.0	573	562
Mackinac	5.3	0.0	0.6	6.7	1.6	1.4	3.3	52.0	16.6	15.9	1 382	1 343
Macomb	394.4	1 531.5	44.1	180.6	48.7	40.1	67.9	2 422.3	1 199.9	696.2	861	835
Manistee	7.0	0.1	8.7	9.9	3.2	5.6	2.3	103.6	37.0	20.2	806	795
Marquette	21.0	5.2	2.8	32.1	9.3	5.3	15.5	222.7	127.8	45.2	702	685
Mason	6.0	0.1	5.6	13.1	6.5	1.6	1.7	119.1	62.4	29.0	1 003	993
Mecosta	5.8	0.0	1.6	18.0	3.8	2.6	6.0	119.5	53.5	24.1	582	531
Menominee	4.3	0.0	1.2	13.4	3.1	2.1	5.9	58.4	38.2	12.6	502	494
Midland	10.2	0.6	2.6	27.5	8.4	4.6	6.7	277.9	131.4	91.7	1 090	1 078
Missaukee	2.0	1.0	1.7	6.1	1.7	1.3	0.2	40.9	27.1	8.5	566	505
Monroe	16.0	2.2	5.5	40.7	18.0	8.1	37.5	438.2	204.5	119.6	801	773
Montcalm	9.3	0.0	2.2	34.7	12.9	4.5	8.8	175.2	116.1	35.5	568	550
Montmorency	1.3	0.0	0.3	7.5	1.5	0.9	7.6	23.3	11.4	7.4	703	683
Muskegon	28.2	60.1	20.7	109.3	36.4	15.7	21.0	619.9	331.1	112.8	656	590
Newaygo	5.4	2.3	2.1	19.0	6.7	3.0	5.1	148.0	97.7	25.4	518	505
Oakland	304.0	91.8	176.1	339.6	83.8	58.7	173.7	4 135.1	1 922.5	1 548.4	1 287	1 235
Oceana	3.9	0.0	11.6	13.1	4.5	2.0	5.3	66.1	35.6	18.2	660	604
Ogemaw	3.7	0.0	0.8	12.7	3.3	1.4	6.3	74.8	27.9	13.6	624	601
Ontonagon	3.4	3.2	1.0	8.0	1.3	0.8	2.7	23.7	14.1	5.8	755	752
Osceola	3.7	3.9	1.0	18.8	3.6	1.8	5.2	73.0	44.8	14.1	600	597
Oscoda	2.2	0.4	0.7	2.9	1.3	0.8	0.9	19.5	11.8	6.2	653	644
Otsego	13.3	0.6	2.8	11.0	2.0	1.0	2.0	70.1	30.4	27.5	1 137	1 132
Ottawa	32.6	56.8	67.8	37.7	10.4	11.3	30.9	628.1	341.6	174.1	708	690
Presque Isle	3.2	0.0	0.7	11.2	1.5	1.0	4.4	31.9	18.7	8.9	624	623
Roscommon	2.0	0.0	0.5	11.8	3.8	1.5	0.4	77.2	34.9	29.4	1 139	1 124
Saginaw	86.4	6.0	30.6	146.5	54.0	19.2	29.8	617.3	369.5	118.5	564	468
St. Clair	29.1	24.6	7.3	67.4	23.7	10.5	34.5	493.1	251.8	129.2	770	714
St. Joseph	8.0	1.0	1.9	28.8	6.9	4.7	5.7	237.6	103.1	39.9	640	632
Sanilac	7.4	7.5	1.9	24.3	5.7	3.0	3.7	128.0	73.9	27.4	616	606
Schoolcraft	3.6	0.0	1.1	10.6	1.4	1.3	0.1	32.1	16.5	6.1	698	693
Shiawassee	12.3	0.0	2.3	30.6	9.4	4.6	10.0	194.8	129.3	32.5	451	434
Tuscola	9.0	26.8	2.1	30.9	8.7	5.4	5.1	154.7	104.2	28.5	490	477
Van Buren	9.8	0.4	9.0	65.8	19.0	5.3	8.1	296.4	153.7	53.3	690	667
Washtenaw	195.0	103.0	78.3	501.1	27.0	25.6	237.0	1 017.0	452.0	370.0	1 106	1 079
Wayne	1 042.7	55.4	568.2	2 044.8	630.4	198.9	794.7	9 102.1	5 083.5	2 250.0	1 100	833
Wexford	9.5	89.7	1.4	18.6	4.0	1.9	5.8	104.7	65.3	17.8	577	575
MINNESOTA	2 119.9	1 541.9	864.0	3 363.4	1 061.8	542.5	1 945.9	X	X	X	X	X
Aitkin	3.1	0.0	0.9	20.3	2.5	0.9	3.6	52.1	29.2	15.0	970	956
Anoka	15.0	17.3	9.7	50.5	24.0	13.0	17.9	999.3	507.0	274.1	885	842
Becker	12.8	2.2	5.0	36.5	12.4	2.8	8.0	91.7	51.4	23.5	762	748
Beltrami	19.4	1.3	2.9	55.1	15.3	11.3	14.3	145.7	92.9	26.2	638	622
Benton	4.3	0.4	0.5	15.2	3.1	1.3	3.2	90.8	49.3	25.5	702	675
Big Stone	2.5	0.0	0.4	5.6	1.0	0.5	1.7	37.9	15.1	4.5	799	787
Blue Earth	21.7	0.1	5.1	33.7	8.1	4.0	52.2	195.7	98.1	54.5	961	868
Brown	5.1	0.1	6.3	11.3	2.2	1.3	6.7	85.2	43.4	19.3	724	679
Carlton	5.8	0.0	2.4	32.2	7.7	4.2	13.4	137.4	67.6	25.4	780	765
Carver	15.2	0.5	5.1	9.4	6.6	2.5	5.4	264.7	108.4	99.0	1 309	1 218
Cass	11.9	0.4	2.3	46.3	10.5	5.9	13.4	103.3	54.4	31.5	1 131	1 119
Chippewa	3.3	0.1	0.6	7.3	3.4	0.8	1.7	51.7	29.1	10.7	828	816
Chisago	7.0	0.1	1.8	11.3	3.2	1.6	3.7	133.5	71.0	34.0	763	713
Clay	8.3	0.1	1.8	27.2	8.6	3.2	32.6	177.0	104.3	29.7	572	553
Clearwater	2.0	0.0	1.0	18.0	2.6	1.1	4.1	29.6	19.1	8.3	984	982
Cook	5.1	0.0	1.2	4.3	0.6	0.4	2.7	40.2	11.1	8.2	1 581	1 305
Cottonwood	3.7	0.0	0.9	6.8	1.4	1.1	5.1	50.1	23.4	11.2	926	922
Crow Wing	11.3	2.4	3.0	44.5	8.6	3.7	12.6	191.5	85.0	54.2	953	926
Dakota	149.6	81.8	20.6	38.1	16.8	12.6	45.0	1 197.9	529.6	374.8	1 016	969
Dodge	2.4	0.0	1.4	6.8	1.7	0.9	1.4	63.5	32.9	14.3	769	755
Douglas	7.4	0.2	1.6	25.6	3.8	1.7	3.3	156.1	57.7	26.2	783	760
Faribault	3.5	0.0	1.1	10.7	1.0	1.2	2.7	63.9	29.1	12.2	767	751
Fillmore	4.5	0.0	1.3	16.9	4.0	1.4	2.6	62.6	38.4	13.1	612	603
Freeborn	6.3	0.0	2.7	19.2	4.4	2.3	9.3	92.1	51.6	23.4	730	667
Goodhue	7.4	0.1	2.1	16.7	4.5	2.3	10.3	179.5	73.2	59.0	1 317	1 291

1. State totals may include programs not allocated by county.   2. Based on the resident population estimated as of July 1 of the year shown.

	Local government finances, 2002 (cont'd)									Government employment, 2002			Presidential election, 2004		
STATE County	Direct general expenditure							Debt outstanding					Percent of vote cast —		
			Percent of total for —												
	Total (mil dol)	Per capita[1] (dollars)	Education	Health and hospitals	Police protection	Public welfare	High-ways	Total (mil dol)	Per capita[1] (dollars)	Federal civilian	Federal military	State and local	Demo-cratic	Republi-can	All other
	183	184	185	186	187	188	189	190	191	192	193	194	195	196	197
MICHIGAN—Cont'd															
Leelanau	56.0	2 580	55.4	1.0	3.1	2.5	10.4	40.5	1 865	137	37	2 123	43.5	55.6	1.0
Lenawee	257.0	2 567	60.7	4.0	4.2	2.8	4.8	155.7	1 555	222	172	5 551	44.2	54.6	1.2
Livingston	411.2	2 435	63.1	2.2	3.0	0.4	5.0	681.6	4 037	265	289	6 271	36.3	62.8	1.0
Luce	44.3	6 303	23.1	54.2	0.8	0.2	7.0	4.8	688	17	12	938	36.9	61.8	1.2
Mackinac	51.9	4 515	29.8	27.1	2.6	1.5	11.3	38.5	3 350	63	67	1 385	42.6	56.3	1.1
Macomb	2 445.2	3 024	56.1	5.9	6.2	1.9	5.3	1 970.7	2 437	6 635	1 752	32 117	48.8	50.2	1.0
Manistee	100.4	4 003	36.9	28.5	2.0	6.6	5.0	72.4	2 887	104	64	2 786	49.3	49.4	1.3
Marquette	228.1	3 545	31.9	15.8	2.9	5.7	10.7	145.8	2 266	299	133	6 319	53.6	45.2	1.2
Mason	123.5	4 278	43.7	14.9	2.0	5.1	6.2	22.6	781	109	59	2 008	43.3	55.6	1.1
Mecosta	125.4	3 025	45.8	18.9	3.0	1.1	2.2	91.4	2 204	93	72	4 316	44.0	55.2	0.8
Menominee	58.6	2 332	49.5	6.0	5.1	1.1	12.5	31.0	1 234	73	43	2 365	46.6	52.0	1.3
Midland	243.0	2 888	55.0	4.1	3.1	0.1	7.7	297.5	3 536	170	145	3 733	42.4	56.3	1.3
Missaukee	41.6	2 780	41.1	24.7	3.2	1.9	11.8	13.8	926	31	26	560	31.2	68.1	0.6
Monroe	424.3	2 843	53.7	6.5	3.4	1.0	6.5	559.2	3 747	259	258	6 305	48.7	50.5	0.8
Montcalm	181.3	2 905	68.2	3.6	1.9	0.4	8.6	163.1	2 614	142	107	3 398	42.9	56.0	1.1
Montmorency	23.6	2 237	40.9	0.2	3.1	1.7	9.6	17.2	1 629	20	18	427	39.5	59.3	1.2
Muskegon	618.9	3 603	53.7	6.7	3.4	4.0	11.4	463.2	2 696	396	310	9 238	55.2	43.9	0.9
Newaygo	154.4	3 150	56.9	11.9	2.0	4.3	6.7	97.6	1 991	89	84	2 613	39.6	59.5	0.9
Oakland	4 390.5	3 651	52.3	5.8	5.5	0.1	6.3	3 606.0	2 998	4 863	2 162	54 500	49.8	49.3	0.9
Oceana	63.6	2 301	52.0	5.2	2.9	0.8	11.0	38.1	1 379	64	47	1 567	44.2	54.3	1.5
Ogemaw	83.4	3 832	37.3	36.2	1.9	2.1	6.8	42.6	1 960	64	37	1 397	48.3	50.5	1.2
Ontonagon	21.9	2 846	42.8	1.6	2.2	0.6	25.6	16.0	2 075	52	13	626	44.5	54.1	1.4
Osceola	68.6	2 919	62.2	1.5	2.0	1.2	5.7	31.3	1 331	60	40	1 254	39.9	59.0	1.1
Oscoda	18.6	1 972	52.9	0.8	3.3	4.5	15.5	5.7	602	49	16	380	40.6	58.3	1.1
Otsego	70.1	2 900	51.2	3.0	2.4	2.5	9.7	61.4	2 543	204	42	1 230	38.0	60.7	1.3
Ottawa	642.3	2 612	53.7	7.0	2.6	0.8	8.9	849.9	3 456	470	489	13 760	27.6	71.6	0.8
Presque Isle	29.8	2 082	50.3	1.1	3.6	1.8	14.0	8.5	590	60	25	651	45.7	53.0	1.4
Roscommon	78.4	3 036	64.8	1.0	2.9	1.5	6.3	22.5	870	34	44	1 597	47.4	51.3	1.3
Saginaw	630.6	3 001	50.1	11.1	4.7	0.9	5.2	427.0	2 033	1 283	382	11 146	53.4	45.9	0.8
St. Clair	472.1	2 815	50.3	9.6	4.2	1.2	7.4	338.9	2 021	486	362	7 081	45.4	53.6	1.0
St. Joseph	234.9	3 766	47.4	29.0	2.9	0.7	3.8	150.2	2 408	134	107	4 062	38.2	60.8	1.0
Sanilac	140.9	3 163	54.5	7.6	4.0	4.6	12.9	99.0	2 223	130	76	2 180	38.0	60.8	1.2
Schoolcraft	30.9	3 519	30.8	26.2	4.5	0.7	16.1	11.3	1 288	68	15	903	48.1	51.0	0.8
Shiawassee	189.6	2 628	57.5	7.1	3.0	6.3	7.8	103.4	1 434	145	124	3 936	46.0	52.9	1.0
Tuscola	162.5	2 790	60.1	7.2	3.7	3.4	9.0	78.4	1 346	151	101	3 613	44.6	54.3	1.1
Van Buren	324.4	4 200	47.3	20.3	2.3	1.1	5.0	286.9	3 715	164	132	5 278	47.3	51.6	1.1
Washtenaw	1 073.1	3 210	53.7	5.2	4.9	1.2	2.8	1 110.5	3 321	2 620	642	65 927	63.5	35.5	1.1
Wayne	10 348.5	5 059	38.0	7.3	5.7	2.0	4.6	10 316.2	5 043	16 294	3 978	109 689	69.3	29.9	0.8
Wexford	106.3	3 454	39.5	24.6	2.6	1.6	8.2	70.5	2 291	175	54	1 904	40.0	60.0	0.0
MINNESOTA	X	X	X	X	X	X	X	X	X	32 033	18 119	358 856	51.1	47.6	1.2
Aitkin	51.7	3 336	39.8	1.1	4.0	7.8	18.2	34.7	2 241	74	53	837	48.1	50.5	1.4
Anoka	1 012.5	3 268	55.7	0.6	4.1	6.6	5.7	1 037.6	3 349	214	1 062	13 826	46.1	52.8	1.1
Becker	84.8	2 755	43.8	0.2	4.1	15.8	11.4	51.9	1 687	239	105	2 486	40.2	58.3	1.4
Beltrami	148.4	3 618	55.6	1.4	3.3	10.6	6.0	140.4	3 422	345	142	5 007	50.0	48.6	1.4
Benton	97.9	2 695	58.3	0.4	3.4	8.0	9.8	150.0	4 131	55	125	1 372	43.9	54.7	1.3
Big Stone	36.2	6 384	29.2	24.9	2.3	4.8	22.4	255.7	45 047	46	19	630	43.9	54.7	1.4
Blue Earth	202.2	3 566	43.8	0.3	4.2	7.0	14.4	187.0	3 297	373	198	4 927	50.1	48.4	1.4
Brown	85.1	3 190	36.2	6.0	3.9	8.1	12.5	108.3	4 061	87	91	1 566	37.5	61.1	1.5
Carlton	131.7	4 043	39.5	18.8	3.3	7.0	8.1	178.3	5 473	80	112	4 206	62.6	36.3	1.1
Carver	282.0	3 729	41.6	0.7	3.4	5.4	10.4	409.8	5 419	228	259	3 796	36.3	62.8	0.9
Cass	110.3	3 964	50.3	2.1	3.2	10.2	10.3	76.7	2 757	239	95	3 698	42.9	55.9	1.2
Chippewa	51.5	3 985	44.0	0.3	4.8	13.8	13.9	44.0	3 401	56	44	1 006	51.9	46.8	1.3
Chisago	129.4	2 903	45.6	4.1	3.6	7.1	13.6	157.5	3 533	116	153	2 301	43.3	55.6	1.2
Clay	203.1	3 910	36.7	1.4	4.8	9.9	12.1	274.7	5 288	132	179	4 277	46.9	51.8	1.3
Clearwater	28.8	3 433	53.2	0.0	4.2	10.2	9.2	26.4	3 145	38	29	831	42.9	56.0	1.1
Cook	37.1	7 143	15.0	39.8	3.7	3.2	10.7	29.2	5 629	145	18	769	52.6	45.2	2.3
Cottonwood	53.5	4 438	41.5	14.8	2.7	7.5	7.9	42.8	3 557	66	41	871	42.8	55.9	1.3
Crow Wing	196.1	3 446	42.7	11.9	5.7	7.0	11.4	168.0	2 952	167	197	4 337	41.8	57.0	1.2
Dakota	1 227.4	3 327	48.3	0.8	4.5	6.4	7.7	1 501.0	4 068	1 483	1 268	16 608	48.5	50.5	1.0
Dodge	65.0	3 502	42.8	0.9	4.6	15.6	13.2	58.2	3 138	49	64	1 159	41.8	56.7	1.5
Douglas	143.3	4 276	27.0	35.3	2.7	5.0	9.4	68.0	2 029	129	115	2 787	40.5	58.1	1.4
Faribault	61.2	3 845	31.1	19.7	3.7	0.0	20.1	48.2	3 029	68	55	1 130	43.4	55.2	1.3
Fillmore	62.6	2 922	39.4	3.1	2.9	5.5	21.8	41.6	1 942	86	73	1 262	49.8	48.7	1.5
Freeborn	93.0	2 896	39.6	1.3	4.5	11.0	15.8	61.6	1 920	103	110	1 485	55.1	43.5	1.4
Goodhue	170.4	3 807	42.0	6.7	4.1	4.8	8.9	270.7	6 046	124	153	4 553	47.3	51.3	1.4

1. Based on the resident population estimated as of July 1 of the year shown.

Table B. States and Counties — Land Area and Population

MINNESOTA—Cont'd

STATE/ County code	CBSA code[1]	County Type[2]	STATE County	Land area[3] (sq km) 2000 (1)	Total persons (2)	Rank (3)	Per square kilometer (4)	White (5)	Black (6)	Am. Indian, Alaska Native (7)	Asian and Pacific Islander (8)	Percent Hispanic or Latino[4] (9)	Under 5 years (10)	5 to 17 years (11)	18 to 24 years (12)	25 to 34 years (13)	35 to 44 years (14)	45 to 54 years (15)
27 051	...	9	Grant	1 415	6 243	2 751	4.4	98.7	0.3	0.4	0.2	0.7	4.5	16.9	8.9	9.0	13.6	13.7
27 053	33460	1	Hennepin	1 442	1 121 035	32	777.4	78.9	10.7	1.4	6.0	4.9	6.9	16.8	8.7	16.0	16.9	14.9
27 055	29100	3	Houston	1 446	19 980	1 807	13.8	98.3	0.7	0.2	0.6	0.6	5.1	19.4	9.0	9.9	15.5	15.3
27 057	...	7	Hubbard	2 389	18 635	1 876	7.8	97.1	0.3	2.4	0.3	0.7	5.0	17.1	8.9	9.2	14.0	14.7
27 059	33460	1	Isanti	1 137	35 372	1 261	31.1	97.3	0.6	1.2	0.8	1.1	5.9	19.3	11.4	12.4	16.4	13.5
27 061	...	6	Itasca	6 902	44 265	1 038	6.4	95.4	0.3	4.5	0.4	0.6	4.8	17.1	10.3	9.2	13.8	16.3
27 063	...	7	Jackson	1 817	11 170	2 357	6.1	96.2	0.2	0.2	1.7	1.9	4.7	17.1	9.5	10.0	14.4	14.8
27 065	...	6	Kanabec	1 360	15 867	2 039	11.7	97.3	0.4	1.4	0.6	1.2	5.7	18.9	10.3	11.2	14.7	14.2
27 067	48820	4	Kandiyohi	2 062	41 148	1 105	20.0	90.3	0.6	0.4	0.6	8.4	6.0	18.4	11.1	10.7	14.0	14.9
27 069	...	9	Kittson	2 841	4 968	2 848	1.7	97.7	0.3	0.4	0.5	1.4	5.0	18.7	6.7	8.1	13.9	15.8
27 071	...	7	Koochiching	8 035	14 018	2 167	1.7	96.6	0.3	3.2	0.2	0.7	5.0	16.7	8.5	8.8	15.0	16.1
27 073	...	9	Lac qui Parle	1 981	7 867	2 607	4.0	99.0	0.2	0.3	0.3	0.3	4.1	17.6	8.7	7.4	13.8	15.5
27 075	...	6	Lake	5 437	11 160	2 359	2.1	98.5	0.1	1.3	0.2	0.5	4.3	15.8	8.8	8.9	14.6	15.9
27 077	...	9	Lake of the Woods	3 358	4 384	2 880	1.3	97.3	0.4	1.7	0.5	0.7	4.0	18.3	7.4	7.7	15.8	17.0
27 079	...	6	Le Sueur	1 162	26 763	1 515	23.0	95.5	0.3	0.5	0.5	3.6	5.9	18.8	10.0	10.8	15.6	14.2
27 081	...	9	Lincoln	1 391	6 159	2 760	4.4	98.4	0.1	0.3	0.3	0.9	4.8	16.8	8.2	9.0	13.4	13.1
27 083	32140	7	Lyon	1 850	24 819	1 583	13.4	93.0	1.1	0.5	2.2	3.8	6.3	17.8	13.6	11.6	14.0	13.5
27 085	26780	8	McLeod	1 274	35 864	1 245	28.2	94.7	0.3	0.5	0.7	4.2	6.7	19.3	9.4	13.0	15.5	13.3
27 087	...	8	Mahnomen	1 440	5 113	2 835	3.6	70.1	0.3	35.9	0.1	1.1	7.2	20.1	9.7	9.3	13.2	13.6
27 089	...	8	Marshall	4 590	9 997	2 442	2.2	95.5	0.1	0.6	0.3	3.8	4.9	17.5	9.3	8.9	14.4	15.5
27 091	21860	7	Martin	1 837	21 221	1 742	11.6	97.1	0.4	0.1	0.5	2.0	5.5	17.3	8.7	8.8	13.9	16.2
27 093	...	6	Meeker	1 576	23 205	1 655	14.7	96.7	0.3	0.2	0.5	2.5	6.2	18.4	9.7	10.8	14.6	14.4
27 095	...	6	Mille Lacs	1 488	24 317	1 607	16.3	93.8	0.5	5.1	0.4	1.0	5.4	18.6	10.3	11.3	14.8	13.0
27 097	...	6	Morrison	2 912	32 589	1 347	11.2	98.4	0.4	0.6	0.3	0.7	6.4	19.2	10.3	11.1	14.8	13.6
27 099	12380	6	Mower	1 843	38 823	1 165	21.1	92.2	1.3	0.3	1.6	5.2	6.4	17.5	9.8	10.7	14.1	13.4
27 101	...	9	Murray	1 824	8 981	2 526	4.9	97.4	0.1	0.4	0.3	2.0	4.9	17.5	8.0	8.7	13.6	15.3
27 103	31860	5	Nicollet	1 171	30 733	1 390	26.2	95.4	1.2	0.4	1.4	2.1	6.0	16.8	16.8	11.9	14.2	14.1
27 105	49380	7	Nobles	1 853	20 621	1 770	11.1	82.8	1.1	0.3	4.0	12.2	6.9	18.1	9.5	10.8	14.3	13.7
27 107	...	6	Norman	2 270	7 191	2 665	3.2	94.2	0.1	2.8	0.4	3.4	4.7	18.4	8.4	8.9	14.8	13.9
27 109	40340	3	Olmsted	1 691	131 384	434	77.7	89.2	3.5	0.5	5.5	2.4	6.9	18.5	9.0	14.2	16.8	13.7
27 111	22260	6	Otter Tail	5 127	58 847	833	11.5	97.0	0.5	0.8	0.6	1.6	4.9	17.5	10.0	9.0	14.1	14.4
27 113	...	6	Pennington	1 597	13 636	2 188	8.5	96.5	0.5	1.4	0.8	1.5	5.9	16.4	11.7	11.8	13.9	14.3
27 115	...	6	Pine	3 655	27 746	1 473	7.6	93.8	1.6	3.3	0.5	1.7	5.3	17.7	10.3	11.6	15.6	14.0
27 117	...	6	Pipestone	1 207	9 681	2 471	8.0	96.9	0.3	1.8	0.6	0.8	5.5	18.0	9.0	9.3	14.3	13.5
27 119	24220	3	Polk	5 103	30 905	1 385	6.1	93.8	0.5	1.9	0.6	5.3	4.8	18.1	11.9	9.4	14.1	13.5
27 121	...	8	Pope	1 736	11 252	2 349	6.5	98.7	0.3	0.3	0.1	0.7	4.7	17.1	9.5	8.9	13.6	14.7
27 123	33460	1	Ramsey	403	506 355	117	1 256.5	75.3	9.5	1.3	10.4	5.7	7.0	18.1	10.3	14.8	15.4	14.1
27 125	...	8	Red Lake	1 120	4 319	2 884	3.9	97.8	0.3	1.3	0.1	0.6	5.6	16.5	10.6	9.3	14.1	14.8
27 127	...	7	Redwood	2 278	16 231	2 021	7.1	93.6	0.4	3.8	1.7	1.1	5.5	18.3	8.8	9.9	14.0	13.9
27 129	...	9	Renville	2 546	16 851	1 970	6.6	93.9	0.3	0.9	0.2	5.2	5.6	18.8	8.7	9.7	14.5	14.5
27 131	22060	4	Rice	1 289	59 667	824	46.3	90.2	1.7	0.5	2.0	6.4	5.8	17.4	17.1	11.5	14.9	12.8
27 133	...	6	Rock	1 250	9 614	2 478	7.7	97.4	0.6	0.5	0.2	0.7	5.6	18.1	9.5	10.0	13.8	14.1
27 135	...	7	Roseau	4 306	16 318	2 013	3.8	95.7	0.2	2.1	2.0	0.5	6.2	21.4	8.8	11.6	16.9	13.7
27 137	20260	2	St. Louis	16 123	198 799	290	12.3	95.5	1.3	2.8	1.0	0.8	4.9	15.6	12.8	10.8	14.1	16.0
27 139	33460	1	Scott	924	108 578	508	117.5	90.7	1.8	1.3	4.4	3.2	8.2	20.9	9.4	15.8	19.0	11.8
27 141	33460	1	Sherburne	1 130	74 667	687	66.1	96.4	1.0	1.2	0.8	1.0	7.4	20.6	11.7	15.0	17.2	12.0
27 143	...	8	Sibley	1 525	15 277	2 078	10.0	93.6	0.2	0.4	0.5	5.6	6.0	19.5	9.2	11.1	15.6	13.2
27 145	41060	3	Stearns	3 482	137 149	411	39.4	95.2	1.5	0.6	2.0	1.6	6.2	17.4	15.9	12.9	14.6	12.7
27 147	36940	5	Steele	1 113	34 753	1 281	31.2	93.3	2.2	0.3	0.8	3.9	6.6	19.4	9.8	12.1	15.7	14.2
27 149	...	7	Stevens	1 456	9 888	2 455	6.8	96.0	1.2	1.3	1.2	0.9	4.9	14.1	21.7	8.2	12.0	12.7
27 151	...	7	Swift	1 926	11 656	2 318	6.1	88.8	3.4	0.6	5.9	2.8	4.4	15.1	9.0	11.8	16.5	13.8
27 153	...	6	Todd	2 440	24 309	1 608	10.0	96.4	0.2	0.6	0.5	2.7	5.4	19.0	11.1	9.8	14.4	14.3
27 155	...	9	Traverse	1 487	3 911	2 917	2.6	95.1	0.2	3.1	0.4	1.4	4.2	17.8	8.5	7.5	12.8	13.4
27 157	40340	3	Wabasha	1 360	22 144	1 698	16.3	97.0	0.3	0.4	0.5	2.0	5.6	18.9	9.8	10.5	15.5	14.4
27 159	...	7	Wadena	1 386	13 603	2 189	9.8	97.5	0.3	0.9	0.2	0.9	5.8	18.2	9.6	9.5	13.5	13.3
27 161	...	7	Waseca	1 096	19 435	1 838	17.7	93.9	2.5	0.7	0.7	2.5	6.2	17.8	10.0	13.1	16.1	14.8
27 163	33460	1	Washington	1 015	213 564	272	210.4	91.7	2.8	0.8	3.9	2.2	6.6	20.6	9.0	12.4	18.3	15.3
27 165	...	7	Watonwan	1 125	11 621	2 323	10.3	82.3	0.4	0.2	1.0	16.2	6.9	19.2	9.0	9.9	13.1	13.9
27 167	47420	6	Wilkin	1 946	6 945	2 692	3.6	97.8	0.4	0.8	0.1	1.4	5.6	19.6	9.4	9.1	16.4	14.2
27 169	49100	4	Winona	1 622	49 482	940	30.5	95.7	0.9	0.5	2.2	1.3	5.2	15.5	18.8	11.1	13.2	13.4
27 171	33460	1	Wright	1 711	102 529	530	59.9	97.2	0.7	0.6	1.0	1.3	7.3	20.9	10.3	13.8	16.9	12.3
27 173	...	9	Yellow Medicine	1 963	10 677	2 387	5.4	95.4	0.1	2.3	0.2	2.1	5.5	17.8	9.8	8.6	14.3	14.0

Population and population characteristics, 2003. Race alone or in combination, not Hispanic or Latino (percent). Age (percent).

1. CBSA = Core Based Statistical Area. See Appendix A for explanation. See Appendix B for list of metropolitan areas with component counties. 2. County type code from the Economic Research Service of USDA Rural-Urban Continuum Codes. See Appendix A for definition. 3. Dry land or land partially or temporarily covered by water. 4. Hispanic or Latino persons may be of any race.

Table B. States and Counties — Population and Households

STATE County	Population, 2003 (cont'd) — Age (percent) (cont'd)				Population — change and components of change, 1990–2003							Households, 2000				
					Total persons		Percent change		Components of change, 2000–2003						Percent	
	55 to 64 years	65 to 74 years	75 years and over	Percent female	1990	2000	1990–2000	2000–2003	Births	Deaths	Net migration	Number	Percent change, 1990–2000	Persons per household	Female family householder[1]	One person
	16	17	18	19	20	21	22	23	24	25	26	27	28	29	30	31
MINNESOTA—Cont'd																
Grant	10.2	9.8	13.4	51.3	6 246	6 289	0.7	-0.7	186	263	39	2 534	3.3	2.40	6.5	28.0
Hennepin	8.7	5.2	5.7	50.6	1 032 431	1 116 200	8.1	0.4	53 259	26 097	-22 455	456 129	8.8	2.39	9.9	31.8
Houston	9.3	7.6	8.6	50.7	18 497	19 718	6.6	1.3	700	588	168	7 633	11.5	2.53	7.4	25.4
Hubbard	12.4	10.1	8.3	50.4	14 939	18 376	23.0	1.4	600	537	221	7 435	28.6	2.45	7.1	24.2
Isanti	8.5	5.0	5.1	49.9	25 921	31 287	20.7	13.1	1 294	715	3 414	11 236	27.5	2.74	8.4	20.1
Itasca	11.4	8.6	8.2	50.1	40 844	43 992	7.7	0.6	1 402	1 563	470	17 789	15.1	2.43	7.6	26.0
Jackson	9.8	8.5	11.5	49.7	11 677	11 268	-3.5	-0.9	344	424	-13	4 556	-0.1	2.40	5.4	28.5
Kanabec	9.9	7.4	6.4	49.7	12 802	14 996	17.1	5.8	591	432	704	5 759	21.2	2.58	8.4	23.8
Kandiyohi	9.3	7.0	8.2	50.6	38 761	41 203	6.3	-0.1	1 705	1 157	-596	15 936	11.5	2.53	7.5	25.7
Kittson	10.6	9.8	12.6	50.7	5 767	5 285	-8.4	-6.0	157	231	-247	2 167	-4.7	2.37	6.0	30.5
Koochiching	11.5	9.4	9.2	50.5	16 299	14 355	-11.9	-2.3	447	498	-283	6 040	0.2	2.33	8.5	30.4
Lac qui Parle	10.7	9.2	13.8	50.2	8 924	8 067	-9.6	-2.5	223	337	-77	3 316	-5.4	2.37	4.1	30.2
Lake	11.4	10.8	9.6	50.0	10 415	11 058	6.2	0.9	301	427	236	4 646	9.5	2.32	6.6	28.0
Lake of the Woods	11.7	8.9	9.3	49.3	4 076	4 522	10.9	-3.1	120	175	-84	1 903	20.7	2.35	5.3	29.7
Le Sueur	9.7	6.4	7.2	50.0	23 239	25 426	9.4	5.3	1 083	777	1 037	9 630	13.7	2.61	6.8	23.7
Lincoln	10.8	10.6	14.4	50.5	6 890	6 429	-6.7	-4.2	190	296	-158	2 653	-1.9	2.35	4.6	30.5
Lyon	8.3	6.1	8.4	51.0	24 789	25 425	2.6	-2.4	1 076	727	-969	9 715	7.1	2.49	7.1	27.9
McLeod	9.0	6.3	7.5	50.3	32 030	34 898	9.0	2.8	1 647	931	293	13 449	13.8	2.56	7.3	25.0
Mahnomen	10.9	7.9	9.3	50.1	5 044	5 190	2.9	-1.5	256	173	-156	1 969	9.1	2.60	11.6	27.0
Marshall	10.7	8.6	10.1	49.1	10 993	10 155	-7.6	-1.6	315	326	-137	4 101	-2.2	2.45	5.4	28.7
Martin	10.2	8.7	11.4	51.2	22 914	21 802	-4.9	-2.7	793	835	-532	9 067	-0.7	2.35	7.2	30.0
Meeker	9.4	7.6	8.5	49.2	20 846	22 644	8.6	2.5	980	735	331	8 590	12.3	2.58	6.3	24.4
Mille Lacs	9.5	7.6	7.8	50.7	18 670	22 330	19.6	8.9	825	837	1 970	8 638	25.0	2.53	9.5	25.9
Morrison	9.1	7.4	7.8	49.6	29 604	31 712	7.1	2.8	1 397	944	442	11 816	13.6	2.64	7.8	24.9
Mower	9.3	8.2	10.7	50.5	37 385	38 603	3.3	0.6	1 706	1 309	-125	15 582	3.7	2.42	8.0	29.1
Murray	11.1	10.2	11.4	50.3	9 660	9 165	-5.1	-2.0	293	335	-135	3 722	-1.0	2.42	4.6	27.1
Nicollet	8.4	5.4	5.3	50.1	28 076	29 771	6.0	3.2	1 223	576	345	10 642	12.3	2.56	7.9	24.0
Nobles	9.7	7.5	9.6	50.1	20 098	20 832	3.7	-1.0	969	570	-613	7 939	3.3	2.58	6.9	26.5
Norman	10.8	9.6	11.8	50.4	7 975	7 442	-6.7	-3.4	195	317	-125	3 010	-3.5	2.41	5.9	31.3
Olmsted	8.8	5.4	5.5	50.8	106 470	124 277	16.7	5.7	6 093	2 451	3 611	47 807	19.3	2.53	5.8	25.8
Otter Tail	10.9	9.2	9.5	50.0	50 714	57 159	12.7	3.0	1 817	2 075	1 932	22 671	16.2	2.46	8.0	25.8
Pennington	9.8	6.9	8.8	50.3	13 306	13 584	2.1	0.4	547	470	-27	5 525	6.8	2.38	6.1	26.6
Pine	10.2	8.1	6.9	48.1	21 264	26 530	24.8	4.6	958	774	1 018	9 939	31.2	2.53	9.1	29.5
Pipestone	9.5	9.1	12.4	51.4	10 491	9 895	-5.7	-2.2	384	412	-185	4 069	-0.2	2.38	8.7	25.1
Polk	9.6	7.6	9.8	50.5	32 589	31 369	-3.7	-1.5	926	1 126	-251	12 070	0.7	2.47	8.5	28.9
Pope	10.2	9.3	11.8	50.8	10 745	11 236	4.6	0.1	367	457	123	4 513	9.1	2.42	5.9	28.7
Ramsey	8.5	5.6	6.3	51.7	485 760	511 035	5.2	-0.9	24 012	13 096	-16 135	201 236	5.6	2.45	11.9	32.0
Red Lake	10.4	8.3	10.0	49.7	4 525	4 299	-5.0	0.5	164	144	3	1 727	-0.2	2.39	6.8	30.5
Redwood	10.4	8.4	11.5	49.9	17 254	16 815	-2.5	-3.5	579	672	-493	6 674	1.8	2.44	7.1	28.8
Renville	9.6	8.5	10.6	50.3	17 673	17 154	-2.9	-1.8	618	701	-208	6 779	-0.2	2.48	5.6	28.5
Rice	8.2	5.7	5.5	49.5	49 183	56 665	15.2	5.3	2 262	1 475	2 224	18 888	15.5	2.65	8.6	23.9
Rock	9.7	8.2	11.5	51.1	9 806	9 721	-0.9	-1.1	379	447	-26	3 843	2.4	2.47	5.5	27.0
Roseau	8.8	5.5	6.9	48.5	15 026	16 338	8.7	-0.1	643	429	-226	6 190	14.3	2.60	6.8	24.6
St. Louis	9.9	7.3	8.6	50.7	198 232	200 528	1.2	-0.9	6 283	7 096	-752	82 619	4.7	2.32	9.4	31.2
Scott	6.7	3.1	2.6	49.7	57 846	89 498	54.7	21.3	5 665	1 308	14 232	30 692	58.5	2.89	7.4	16.0
Sherburne	6.6	3.5	3.2	49.0	41 945	64 417	53.6	15.9	3 626	1 149	7 574	21 581	58.2	2.91	7.5	15.7
Sibley	9.3	7.9	8.4	49.5	14 366	15 356	6.9	-0.5	599	491	-172	5 772	8.4	2.60	5.8	25.4
Stearns	7.5	5.7	5.4	49.8	119 324	133 166	11.6	3.0	5 612	2 553	1 060	47 604	19.7	2.64	7.5	23.6
Steele	8.6	6.3	6.8	50.5	30 729	33 680	9.6	3.2	1 533	935	499	12 846	13.3	2.57	7.4	24.6
Stevens	7.8	7.0	9.8	51.4	10 634	10 053	-5.5	-1.6	320	288	-198	3 751	-1.9	2.43	5.1	29.1
Swift	8.9	7.7	11.0	43.8	10 724	11 956	11.5	-2.5	346	401	-261	4 353	2.0	2.39	6.1	30.9
Todd	10.6	7.9	8.1	49.5	23 363	24 426	4.5	-0.5	881	758	-197	9 342	8.8	2.58	6.1	26.3
Traverse	9.5	11.7	16.0	50.8	4 463	4 134	-7.4	-5.4	102	181	-146	1 717	-3.4	2.34	6.0	32.0
Wabasha	10.0	7.0	7.9	49.9	19 744	21 610	9.5	2.5	869	612	296	8 277	13.6	2.57	6.5	24.3
Wadena	10.2	9.5	10.9	50.3	13 154	13 713	4.2	-0.8	499	633	50	5 426	9.0	2.45	7.6	29.2
Waseca	8.4	6.2	7.8	47.6	18 079	19 526	8.0	-0.5	786	582	-283	7 059	6.2	2.56	7.8	25.1
Washington	9.1	4.5	3.3	50.3	145 860	201 130	37.9	6.2	8 996	3 283	6 752	71 462	45.1	2.77	7.3	18.7
Watonwan	9.6	8.6	10.4	50.7	11 682	11 876	1.7	-2.1	547	430	-381	4 627	2.1	2.53	8.5	28.7
Wilkin	9.4	8.0	8.4	51.0	7 516	7 138	-5.0	-2.7	230	256	-161	2 752	-1.9	2.54	7.3	28.7
Winona	8.4	6.1	7.1	51.3	47 828	49 985	4.5	-1.0	1 710	1 424	-775	18 744	10.7	2.46	7.0	25.9
Wright	7.6	4.3	4.0	49.8	68 710	89 986	31.0	13.9	4 798	1 754	9 245	31 465	36.7	2.83	7.8	28.2
Yellow Medicine	10.1	8.6	12.1	50.2	11 684	11 080	-5.2	-3.6	397	422	-374	4 439	-3.6	2.42	5.7	29.3

1. No spouse present.

Table B. States and Counties — Vital Statistics, Health Resources, and Crime

STATE County	Births, average 1999–2001		Deaths, average 1999–2001				Physicians,[4] 2000		Hospitals,[4] 1998			Medicare enrollees, 2003	Serious crimes known to police,[6] 2002	
			Number		Rate					Beds			Total	
	Total	Rate[1]	Total	Infant[2]	Total[1]	Infant[3]	Number	Rate[5]	Number	Number	Rate[5]		Number	Rate[7]
	32	33	34	35	36	37	38	39	40	41	42	43	44	45
MINNESOTA—Cont'd														
Grant	56	9.0	86	0	13.7	D	4	64	1	20	324	1 555	102	1 590
Hennepin	16 355	14.6	8 037	94	7.2	5.7	3 827	343	8	3 411	322	137 676	52 129	4 577
Houston	212	10.7	192	2	9.7	D	10	51	1	89	462	3 512	329	1 635
Hubbard	181	9.9	177	1	9.7	D	15	82	1	45	266	3 755	401	2 139
Isanti	381	12.1	218	1	6.9	D	43	137	1	86	286	3 790	678	2 124
Itasca	445	10.1	461	2	10.5	D	54	123	3	244	556	8 707	553	1 232
Jackson	112	9.9	132	1	11.7	D	9	80	1	41	356	2 077	228	1 983
Kanabec	168	11.2	136	0	9.0	D	6	40	1	49	346	2 442	380	2 483
Kandiyohi	515	12.5	366	2	8.9	D	106	257	1	122	297	6 967	1 204	2 864
Kittson	54	10.3	73	0	13.9	D	4	76	2	205	3 852	1 154	80	1 483
Koochiching	146	10.2	168	2	11.8	D	12	84	1	44	283	3 062	369	2 519
Lac qui Parle	72	8.9	119	0	14.8	D	7	87	2	106	1 321	1 786	86	1 045
Lake	101	9.1	123	2	11.1	D	13	118	1	80	757	2 374	146	1 294
Lake of the Woods	40	8.8	48	0	10.5	D	6	133	1	73	1 600	892	85	1 842
Le Sueur	313	12.3	229	1	9.0	D	8	31	2	131	517	4 574	177	682
Lincoln	64	9.9	95	0	14.8	D	8	124	3	231	3 576	1 548	76	1 159
Lyon	335	13.2	232	3	9.1	D	29	114	2	145	596	4 309	630	2 428
McLeod	487	13.9	302	4	8.6	D	34	97	2	215	632	5 464	857	2 407
Mahnomen	76	14.6	57	0	10.9	D	3	58	1	66	1 300	1 016	242	4 569
Marshall	105	10.4	101	1	10.0	D	1	10	1	18	175	2 088	123	1 187
Martin	236	10.9	247	1	11.4	D	23	105	1	108	491	4 630	646	2 904
Meeker	295	13.0	232	1	10.3	D	15	66	1	38	175	3 764	612	2 649
Mille Lacs	259	11.6	253	1	11.3	D	24	107	2	149	708	4 864	826	3 625
Morrison	411	12.9	289	3	9.1	D	24	76	1	55	180	5 528	850	2 627
Mower	513	13.3	435	3	11.3	D	71	184	1	94	254	8 093	1 540	3 910
Murray	83	9.0	110	0	12.0	D	4	44	1	32	336	1 975	106	1 133
Nicollet	370	12.4	172	1	5.8	D	36	121	1	121	409	2 837	723	2 380
Nobles	291	14.0	203	1	9.8	D	25	120	2	146	756	3 852	426	2 004
Norman	81	10.9	100	0	13.5	D	4	54	1	77	1 022	1 591	71	935
Olmsted	1 856	14.9	780	11	6.3	5.7	1 511	1 216	3	1 343	1 151	15 448	3 434	2 708
Otter Tail	578	10.1	653	3	11.4	D	67	117	2	267	486	11 522	1 241	2 128
Pennington	171	12.6	150	2	11.1	D	20	147	1	150	1 106	2 374	384	2 770
Pine	313	11.8	242	3	9.1	D	8	30	2	233	974	4 720	1 133	4 185
Pipestone	110	11.0	131	2	13.2	D	7	71	1	87	862	2 211	105	1 040
Polk	350	11.2	363	2	11.6	D	21	67	2	252	814	5 685	865	2 702
Pope	107	9.5	149	1	13.3	D	8	71	2	53	487	2 388	152	1 326
Ramsey	7 541	14.7	4 109	60	8.0	8.0	1 369	268	6	1 514	312	78 175	26 727	5 126
Red Lake	52	12.0	48	0	11.0	D	1	23	0	0	0	810	32	729
Redwood	189	11.3	211	0	12.6	D	10	59	1	35	212	3 503	375	2 186
Renville	202	11.8	221	0	12.9	D	8	47	1	30	177	3 304	326	1 862
Rice	686	12.1	422	5	7.4	D	69	122	2	114	211	7 232	1 936	3 348
Rock	116	11.9	129	1	13.2	D	6	62	1	38	390	1 966	117	1 179
Roseau	207	12.7	138	2	8.5	D	10	61	1	101	627	2 285	301	1 806
St. Louis	2 021	10.1	2 217	14	11.1	7.1	448	223	8	1 368	707	36 042	8 328	4 070
Scott	1 663	18.3	388	5	4.3	D	44	49	1	67	85	6 433	2 630	2 880
Sherburne	1 087	16.7	347	4	5.3	D	24	37	0	0	0	5 619	1 967	2 993
Sibley	196	12.7	155	1	10.1	D	3	20	1	17	117	2 559	79	504
Stearns	1 755	13.2	788	11	5.9	6.1	299	225	5	655	511	19 286	4 325	3 183
Steele	460	13.6	277	3	8.2	D	35	104	1	65	205	5 024	1 051	3 058
Stevens	111	11.0	93	0	9.2	D	9	90	1	38	375	1 780	187	1 823
Swift	118	10.0	130	1	11.0	D	7	59	2	138	1 277	2 360	185	1 516
Todd	270	11.1	224	2	9.2	D	6	25	2	262	1 091	4 181	641	2 572
Traverse	36	8.9	61	0	15.0	D	4	97	1	35	824	1 082	31	735
Wabasha	246	11.3	186	2	8.6	D	18	83	2	112	535	3 891	351	1 867
Wadena	162	11.8	198	0	14.5	D	12	88	1	48	365	3 158	378	2 702
Waseca	248	12.7	179	0	9.2	D	17	87	1	26	143	2 959	398	1 998
Washington	2 794	13.8	976	13	4.8	4.8	177	88	2	92	47	13 813	6 261	3 051
Watonwan	170	14.3	133	1	11.2	D	8	67	2	37	323	2 386	284	2 344
Wilkin	85	12.0	78	1	11.0	D	4	56	1	171	2 339	1 273	180	2 472
Winona	542	10.9	430	3	8.6	D	46	92	1	203	422	7 073	1 057	2 072
Wright	1 441	15.9	525	5	5.8	D	49	54	2	147	173	10 133	2 559	3 054
Yellow Medicine	128	11.5	134	0	12.1	D	4	36	2	193	1 691	2 517	96	849

1. Per 1,000 estimated resident population.   2. Deaths of infants under 1 year old.   3. Deaths of infants under 1 year old per 1,000 live births.   4. Data subject to copyright.   5. Per 100,000 resident population as of July 1 of the year shown.   6. Data for serious crimes have not been adjusted for underreporting; this may affect comparability between geographic areas and over time.   7. Per 100,000 population estimated by the FBI.

Table B. States and Counties — Crime, Education, Money Income, and Poverty

STATE County	Violent	Property	Total	Percent private	High school graduate or less	Bachelor's degree or more	Total current expenditures (mil dol)	Current expenditures per student (dollars)	Per capita income (dollars)	Dollars	Percent change, 1989–1999 (constant 1999 dollars)	Percent with income of $100,000 or more	Persons	Households	Families	Families with children
	46	47	48	49	50	51	52	53	54	55	56	57	58	59	60	61
MINNESOTA—Cont'd																
Grant	47	1 543	1 476	3.9	51.8	15.7	9.7	6 936	17 131	33 775	27.1	4.4	8.4	9.5	6.0	9.6
Hennepin	479	4 098	297 966	17.9	30.5	39.1	1 395.0	8 894	28 789	51 711	7.9	17.9	8.3	7.4	5.0	8.0
Houston	84	1 551	5 283	14.1	49.2	20.5	24.6	6 743	18 826	40 680	17.1	6.0	6.5	7.6	4.2	5.6
Hubbard	107	2 032	4 254	6.0	48.3	20.2	20.5	7 290	18 115	35 321	30.5	5.5	9.7	10.3	7.5	11.4
Isanti	97	2 027	8 631	8.1	51.8	14.5	39.7	7 027	20 348	50 127	19.2	9.1	5.7	6.0	4.0	5.8
Itasca	87	1 145	10 950	7.3	47.7	17.6	59.8	7 883	17 717	36 234	20.2	4.9	10.6	10.6	7.7	13.0
Jackson	43	1 939	2 795	8.3	53.9	14.2	12.3	7 196	17 499	36 746	18.1	3.8	8.6	8.6	5.2	8.9
Kanabec	137	2 346	3 844	5.4	61.6	10.5	17.1	6 218	17 741	38 520	27.5	5.1	9.5	10.0	6.4	9.8
Kandiyohi	200	2 664	10 814	8.7	47.7	18.3	46.8	7 316	19 627	39 772	16.7	7.2	9.2	9.7	5.9	9.2
Kittson	0	1 483	1 288	8.5	54.8	14.8	8.1	7 835	16 525	32 515	2.9	3.2	10.2	11.2	8.0	11.2
Koochiching	164	2 355	3 451	9.9	55.5	15.1	18.4	7 788	19 167	36 262	15.3	4.8	12.1	13.1	8.4	14.7
Lac qui Parle	24	1 020	1 860	5.3	56.9	13.0	14.2	7 402	17 399	32 626	12.2	4.4	8.5	10.2	5.6	8.3
Lake	97	1 196	2 402	7.0	51.1	19.5	14.8	7 248	19 761	40 402	28.1	5.0	7.4	7.7	5.5	9.5
Lake of the Woods	65	1 777	1 073	2.9	52.8	17.2	5.8	7 375	16 976	32 861	0.3	4.3	9.8	11.7	6.7	8.6
Le Sueur	62	621	6 677	11.3	53.7	16.9	30.1	6 200	20 151	45 933	23.4	7.8	6.9	7.5	4.8	5.8
Lincoln	137	1 021	1 465	6.0	58.7	14.1	7.3	7 969	16 009	31 607	22.5	2.6	9.7	11.5	7.0	7.8
Lyon	123	2 305	7 659	13.3	49.8	21.4	43.1	9 033	18 013	38 996	17.6	5.5	10.1	10.9	6.3	8.4
McLeod	166	2 241	9 193	15.9	52.6	15.4	37.3	6 129	20 137	45 953	15.7	6.8	4.8	5.2	2.8	4.2
Mahnomen	661	3 909	1 414	5.7	59.0	12.4	13.2	9 833	13 438	30 053	32.2	2.1	16.7	14.9	11.8	19.2
Marshall	39	1 148	2 429	4.0	57.9	12.0	14.4	8 625	16 317	34 804	19.3	3.4	9.8	11.0	6.9	8.8
Martin	157	2 747	5 316	13.1	54.2	16.1	28.9	7 870	18 529	34 810	6.1	4.3	10.5	10.8	7.1	12.3
Meeker	138	2 510	5 764	4.9	56.8	13.9	40.3	6 520	18 628	40 908	24.2	7.1	7.1	9.1	4.7	6.4
Mille Lacs	167	3 458	5 643	10.7	59.0	12.2	42.4	6 682	17 766	36 977	21.3	5.9	9.6	10.5	6.7	9.8
Morrison	93	2 534	8 143	9.5	59.0	12.6	43.2	7 219	16 566	37 047	24.8	4.9	11.1	12.2	7.5	10.3
Mower	234	3 676	9 295	11.0	53.0	14.7	41.3	6 940	19 795	36 654	14.8	6.2	9.2	8.7	6.3	10.3
Murray	53	1 080	2 144	11.7	58.7	11.9	9.9	6 829	17 936	34 966	14.8	4.1	8.3	9.4	6.3	8.4
Nicollet	105	2 275	9 887	34.7	37.6	29.3	24.4	10 179	20 517	46 170	12.7	9.2	7.5	7.6	4.3	6.5
Nobles	118	1 887	5 134	9.2	58.5	13.5	26.9	7 384	16 987	35 684	15.8	5.0	11.7	11.4	8.2	10.7
Norman	119	817	1 769	3.3	54.8	13.1	11.8	8 614	15 895	32 535	14.0	3.7	10.3	12.4	7.1	9.0
Olmsted	201	2 507	34 049	17.1	32.9	34.7	153.7	7 184	24 939	51 316	6.7	15.1	6.4	6.2	3.8	5.9
Otter Tail	158	1 970	14 133	9.1	51.7	17.2	91.5	10 265	18 014	35 395	20.2	5.5	10.1	11.0	6.7	9.7
Pennington	130	2 641	3 589	6.6	49.8	14.9	19.4	8 251	17 346	34 216	18.1	4.1	11.1	12.5	7.7	9.6
Pine	266	3 919	6 412	8.6	61.9	10.3	31.2	6 937	17 445	37 379	31.3	5.2	11.3	11.4	7.8	11.7
Pipestone	59	980	2 509	12.2	58.5	13.9	13.2	6 445	16 450	31 909	14.5	3.5	9.5	11.3	7.8	11.3
Polk	222	2 481	8 889	8.2	49.8	17.6	43.1	7 391	17 279	35 105	15.8	5.5	10.9	11.5	7.3	11.5
Pope	131	1 195	2 750	6.0	51.7	14.7	12.1	7 056	19 032	35 633	31.7	5.2	8.8	10.4	5.8	7.8
Ramsey	511	4 614	148 722	25.3	37.7	34.3	732.8	8 316	23 536	45 722	6.2	13.1	10.6	9.2	7.4	11.9
Red Lake	23	707	1 072	8.6	59.4	10.7	6.8	8 459	15 372	32 052	19.7	2.7	10.8	12.2	8.4	10.1
Redwood	245	1 941	4 054	11.6	56.8	13.4	22.9	6 608	18 903	37 352	21.8	5.0	7.7	8.5	5.5	7.6
Renville	40	1 822	4 278	10.1	57.1	12.6	18.6	7 008	17 770	37 652	20.4	4.5	8.8	8.4	6.3	9.2
Rice	164	3 184	18 631	37.8	47.8	22.4	56.3	6 900	19 695	48 651	22.4	9.8	6.9	6.8	4.0	5.3
Rock	202	978	2 525	9.7	54.2	15.4	11.9	7 139	17 411	38 102	15.8	4.4	8.0	9.5	5.5	7.2
Roseau	30	1 776	4 373	3.5	55.3	14.9	24.7	6 750	17 053	39 852	14.5	4.3	6.6	7.8	4.6	5.6
St. Louis	257	3 814	54 961	10.9	44.6	21.9	233.5	7 740	18 982	36 306	12.2	6.1	12.1	12.3	7.2	11.7
Scott	157	2 723	25 390	17.4	37.4	29.4	95.0	6 937	26 418	66 612	21.5	21.2	3.4	3.7	2.0	2.8
Sherburne	123	2 869	19 430	11.7	42.6	19.4	89.3	6 353	21 322	57 014	19.3	11.6	4.4	4.4	2.3	3.1
Sibley	0	504	3 952	13.2	60.9	11.6	18.0	7 428	18 004	41 458	23.6	5.5	8.1	7.7	5.1	7.9
Stearns	182	3 001	43 624	20.0	47.1	22.0	183.8	7 526	19 211	42 426	14.8	8.7	8.7	9.0	4.3	6.1
Steele	163	2 895	8 991	13.6	49.4	20.1	42.3	6 501	20 328	46 106	12.3	8.0	6.2	6.5	4.2	6.2
Stevens	127	1 696	3 536	4.8	49.7	20.6	11.4	7 054	17 569	37 267	26.5	5.9	13.6	15.4	5.7	7.2
Swift	90	1 426	2 722	5.3	54.8	14.0	12.5	6 761	16 360	34 820	38.3	3.8	8.4	10.4	5.3	6.5
Todd	112	2 459	6 472	11.3	62.0	10.0	59.1	13 213	15 658	32 281	27.6	4.3	12.9	13.7	9.6	13.1
Traverse	119	616	1 000	2.4	57.4	10.7	5.3	7 664	16 378	30 617	9.8	5.3	12.0	13.8	9.3	14.9
Wabasha	32	1 835	5 671	8.7	51.8	15.6	33.2	6 210	19 664	42 117	16.1	6.7	6.0	6.9	4.1	5.6
Wadena	179	2 523	3 538	6.1	57.4	13.4	21.6	6 980	15 146	30 651	31.6	3.3	14.1	15.0	9.7	14.2
Waseca	196	1 802	4 864	11.8	53.7	16.2	27.6	7 004	18 631	42 440	17.0	5.9	6.5	6.0	4.5	5.6
Washington	128	2 923	58 157	16.4	32.0	33.9	265.6	7 544	28 148	66 305	11.9	23.1	2.9	2.8	2.0	2.9
Watonwan	58	2 286	3 074	10.5	63.1	13.7	15.1	7 049	16 413	35 441	17.3	3.5	9.8	9.5	7.8	11.3
Wilkin	110	2 362	1 839	12.6	48.0	14.0	9.6	7 121	16 873	38 093	22.8	4.6	8.1	10.0	6.2	8.5
Winona	69	2 004	17 104	20.4	46.2	23.2	47.5	7 178	18 077	38 700	11.1	6.3	12.0	12.3	5.6	8.0
Wright	88	2 966	25 341	10.6	48.7	17.9	126.7	6 721	21 844	53 945	20.0	12.7	4.7	5.0	3.6	4.8
Yellow Medicine	62	787	2 864	4.6	53.4	14.4	15.8	7 562	17 120	34 393	18.9	3.8	10.4	12.1	7.1	10.1

1. Data for serious crimes have not been adjusted for underreporting; this may affect comparability between geographic areas and over time. 2. Per 100,000 population estimated by the FBI. 3. All persons 3 years old and over enrolled in nursery school through college. 4. Persons 25 years old and over. 5. Elementary and secondary education expenditures. 6. Based on population enumerated as of April 1, 2000.

STATE County	Total (mil dol)	Percent change, 2001–2002	Per capita[1] Dollars	Per capita[1] Rank	Wages and salaries[2] (mil dol)	Proprietor's income (mil dol)	Dividends, interest, and rent (mil dol)	Transfer payments Total (mil dol)	Government payments to individuals Total (mil dol)	Social Security (mil dol)	Medical payments (mil dol)	Income maintenance (mil dol)	Unemployment insurance (mil dol)
	62	63	64	65	66	67	68	69	70	71	72	73	74
MINNESOTA—Cont'd													
Grant	161	3.0	25 766	936	64	19	42	36	34	15	15	2	1
Hennepin	49 702	1.3	44 302	37	49 123	4 961	9 580	4 879	4 585	1 580	2 132	410	253
Houston	559	3.2	28 071	537	157	33	117	85	80	35	34	4	3
Hubbard	436	8.1	23 528	1 554	199	19	90	100	95	40	40	7	4
Isanti	933	5.0	27 546	607	348	83	126	126	117	48	46	8	10
Itasca	1 059	4.3	24 056	1 385	577	69	212	242	230	96	95	17	10
Jackson	280	2.8	24 897	1 161	139	29	70	49	46	21	20	2	1
Kanabec	352	4.5	22 723	1 813	132	22	63	70	66	26	25	5	5
Kandiyohi	1 188	4.1	29 095	434	743	88	281	190	179	70	74	14	6
Kittson	126	13.5	25 033	1 118	55	8	33	28	26	11	12	1	1
Koochiching	376	3.3	26 848	728	236	16	65	81	78	33	33	5	3
Lac qui Parle	197	2.7	24 782	1 183	71	31	46	43	41	18	19	2	1
Lake	317	3.9	28 465	495	152	23	69	65	62	25	25	3	2
Lake of the Woods	91	3.5	20 640	2 386	50	4	24	21	20	9	8	1	1
Le Sueur	738	3.6	28 249	517	299	55	150	108	101	41	44	6	7
Lincoln	145	-1.8	23 199	1 663	48	15	32	35	33	14	16	1	1
Lyon	706	2.1	28 259	514	535	53	147	110	103	41	45	7	4
McLeod	971	3.8	27 224	665	699	55	196	135	126	57	51	6	7
Mahnomen	106	-3.6	20 547	2 420	74	-3	22	31	29	8	15	4	1
Marshall	239	6.3	23 993	1 411	88	5	61	51	48	19	22	3	2
Martin	621	3.3	29 065	440	333	70	145	115	109	49	46	7	4
Meeker	585	4.8	25 434	1 016	237	53	120	95	89	38	36	5	6
Mille Lacs	535	3.8	22 570	1 859	311	20	93	128	122	46	55	9	7
Morrison	719	4.3	22 142	1 972	357	39	140	149	140	53	62	9	8
Mower	1 053	5.1	27 149	671	596	61	216	204	194	84	82	12	5
Murray	226	0.0	24 968	1 138	81	26	60	45	43	20	18	2	2
Nicollet	841	2.0	27 590	602	483	31	159	102	94	41	34	6	5
Nobles	520	1.3	25 241	1 061	319	61	112	93	88	38	38	6	2
Norman	170	-4.5	23 321	1 621	69	6	45	42	40	15	20	2	1
Olmsted	4 572	4.4	35 389	131	4 156	307	763	480	446	184	194	31	21
Otter Tail	1 423	4.1	24 461	1 276	695	102	346	285	269	119	109	15	11
Pennington	386	5.1	28 354	508	291	23	89	66	63	22	27	4	3
Pine	628	7.0	22 769	1 794	282	20	114	134	127	50	51	10	8
Pipestone	266	-1.2	27 260	660	141	41	56	49	46	19	21	3	1
Polk	751	2.1	24 292	1 313	397	27	141	162	154	56	72	12	6
Pope	292	2.7	26 066	875	121	28	68	58	55	23	25	3	1
Ramsey	18 033	2.6	35 304	133	17 333	863	3 534	2 502	2 368	724	1 157	253	105
Red Lake	88	-1.1	20 667	2 381	36	5	16	21	20	7	9	1	1
Redwood	409	1.7	24 967	1 140	220	25	113	80	76	34	32	4	3
Renville	433	3.9	25 515	996	211	26	112	84	80	33	35	4	4
Rice	1 468	3.6	24 981	1 133	889	58	266	204	189	81	77	12	11
Rock	242	0.0	24 974	1 135	105	19	59	45	43	20	18	2	1
Roseau	425	1.7	26 233	849	326	5	95	61	57	22	25	3	4
St. Louis	5 573	3.9	27 879	569	3 775	363	1 046	1 102	1 050	391	451	84	43
Scott	3 362	3.0	32 391	208	1 658	138	438	239	212	87	79	10	23
Sherburne	1 869	4.4	25 998	888	811	74	249	188	169	72	60	10	18
Sibley	366	4.1	23 877	1 449	121	7	77	67	63	27	28	3	3
Stearns	3 618	5.1	26 559	773	2 961	193	629	488	453	178	173	32	26
Steele	977	3.5	28 406	503	756	44	186	133	124	54	51	8	6
Stevens	259	2.9	26 152	860	172	23	65	44	41	16	19	2	1
Swift	255	4.3	22 229	1 952	132	16	61	56	53	21	25	3	2
Todd	505	3.5	20 696	2 372	216	27	88	115	109	39	49	9	4
Traverse	96	4.0	24 550	1 247	38	10	31	25	24	10	11	1	1
Wabasha	633	3.8	28 835	464	253	24	132	93	87	39	38	4	4
Wadena	293	7.0	21 335	2 201	200	10	57	82	78	28	38	6	3
Waseca	484	1.7	24 759	1 193	285	23	97	76	71	33	27	5	3
Washington	7 928	2.1	37 679	91	3 007	202	1 381	555	500	243	166	26	38
Watonwan	283	0.4	24 049	1 389	150	22	60	55	52	23	22	3	1
Wilkin	165	3.4	23 788	1 475	76	1	42	33	31	12	15	2	0
Winona	1 267	2.8	25 583	982	856	64	269	196	183	76	76	12	6
Wright	2 761	3.4	28 083	535	1 191	117	365	306	280	115	110	16	28
Yellow Medicine	256	0.0	23 686	1 505	124	19	54	61	58	23	26	3	2

1. Based on the resident population estimated as of July 1 of the year shown. 2. Includes other labor income.

Table B. States and Counties — Earnings, Social Security, and Housing

STATE County	Earnings, 2002									Social Security beneficiaries, December 2003			Housing units, 2003	
			Percent by selected industries											
			Goods-related[1]		Service-related and health							Supplemental Security Income recipients, December 2003		Percent change, 2000–2003
	Total (mil dol)	Farm	Total	Manufacturing	Information and professional and technical services	Retail trade	Finance, insurance, and real estate	Health services	Government	Number	Rate[2]	Total	Total	
	75	76	77	78	79	80	81	82	83	84	85	86	87	88
MINNESOTA—Cont'd														
Grant	83	10.8	14.6	5.4	7.6	7.9	D	11.9	17.4	1 735	278	71	3 122	0.8
Hennepin	54 084	0.0	16.1	11.7	16.1	5.3	15.3	7.8	9.6	147 790	132	19 829	482 787	3.0
Houston	190	0.2	D	13.0	10.6	8.3	D	D	19.7	3 820	191	195	8 343	2.1
Hubbard	218	1.3	D	25.1	D	8.6	3.9	D	18.1	4 575	246	307	12 573	2.8
Isanti	431	-1.3	27.3	18.0	D	9.9	5.3	D	17.9	4 920	139	251	13 704	13.6
Itasca	646	-0.2	D	14.5	D	9.6	3.8	11.0	21.4	10 260	232	774	25 491	3.9
Jackson	169	8.7	29.8	24.4	D	4.7	D	D	18.0	2 380	213	95	5 106	0.3
Kanabec	154	-2.5	32.5	14.3	3.9	10.7	5.2	6.5	26.7	2 975	187	184	7 219	5.4
Kandiyohi	831	2.1	D	14.5	5.3	9.0	4.6	D	22.8	7 795	189	582	18 992	3.1
Kittson	62	10.1	D	3.0	D	8.2	5.4	12.7	28.0	1 250	252	66	2 730	0.4
Koochiching	252	-0.3	35.9	30.2	3.0	7.2	12.4	D	18.7	3 435	245	283	7 874	2.0
Lac qui Parle	102	18.3	D	12.0	D	7.5	4.9	9.7	24.4	2 035	259	94	3 757	-0.5
Lake	175	-0.1	D	13.8	2.1	6.4	3.8	D	21.5	2 620	235	101	7 100	3.8
Lake of the Woods	54	-6.2	D	D	D	8.7	D	D	24.5	1 020	233	41	3 352	3.5
Le Sueur	354	1.7	45.7	33.1	D	5.2	4.4	5.8	13.7	4 380	164	219	11 483	5.8
Lincoln	63	9.3	9.3	1.2	D	7.2	3.5	D	20.3	1 685	274	80	3 061	0.6
Lyon	588	2.5	D	31.3	D	6.4	7.2	6.0	19.3	4 490	181	358	10 619	3.1
McLeod	753	1.5	D	43.9	3.1	6.7	3.4	7.4	13.0	6 145	171	194	14 733	4.6
Mahnomen	71	-7.5	D	D	D	4.3	2.8	D	64.5	980	192	125	2 758	2.1
Marshall	93	-2.0	23.8	13.2	2.7	8.5	D	7.2	27.9	2 330	233	118	4 880	1.9
Martin	403	8.7	23.3	17.7	4.7	6.7	4.5	D	12.9	5 300	250	334	9 898	1.0
Meeker	290	2.6	D	22.5	3.6	6.5	4.7	D	18.0	4 400	190	175	10 216	4.0
Mille Lacs	331	0.4	D	16.0	2.3	6.6	3.4	20.6	29.9	5 070	208	347	11 153	6.6
Morrison	396	0.9	D	19.8	4.9	9.2	3.6	D	22.7	6 535	201	465	14 799	6.7
Mower	657	3.2	40.2	34.8	D	6.7	4.1	D	15.2	8 740	225	647	16 627	2.3
Murray	107	9.3	D	9.1	4.4	5.6	5.4	8.8	19.1	2 305	257	82	4 424	1.5
Nicollet	514	3.3	D	31.9	4.8	3.7	3.2	D	19.9	4 275	139	236	11 896	5.8
Nobles	380	1.2	31.0	26.4	3.4	12.9	3.9	D	17.6	4 195	203	302	8 473	0.1
Norman	75	-2.9	D	D	13.4	9.7	D	12.9	28.3	1 820	253	113	3 449	-0.2
Olmsted	4 464	0.3	D	19.2	5.4	5.8	3.4	39.4	8.5	18 420	140	1 618	54 301	9.9
Otter Tail	797	2.5	24.2	16.3	5.4	9.7	4.7	12.3	18.5	13 220	225	824	34 440	1.7
Pennington	314	0.5	24.4	21.3	3.2	6.5	2.6	D	19.7	2 465	181	204	6 188	2.6
Pine	302	-0.3	D	3.5	2.3	7.9	3.1	8.8	50.1	5 710	206	414	15 832	3.1
Pipestone	181	5.7	20.2	14.6	6.1	7.4	3.4	D	16.2	2 280	236	131	4 457	0.5
Polk	425	3.2	20.7	14.7	5.2	6.6	3.6	D	25.1	6 380	206	589	14 217	1.5
Pope	149	3.7	D	19.0	2.9	7.8	4.2	8.1	19.5	2 630	234	118	6 463	10.9
Ramsey	18 196	0.0	D	13.3	10.8	5.4	8.9	9.9	16.8	70 270	139	13 278	208 970	1.2
Red Lake	41	2.5	D	D	D	D	D	D	25.4	870	201	52	1 916	1.8
Redwood	245	4.2	D	14.2	4.0	8.1	4.8	D	28.8	3 825	236	201	7 277	0.7
Renville	237	11.4	D	19.9	6.0	4.7	5.4	7.0	17.9	3 720	221	159	7 420	0.1
Rice	948	0.3	33.1	25.1	3.6	7.0	4.6	8.0	18.3	8 435	141	502	21 527	7.3
Rock	124	8.7	D	12.0	6.1	7.8	10.0	14.1	20.4	2 190	228	72	4 171	0.8
Roseau	331	-3.6	64.2	62.5	D	4.8	2.6	D	13.6	2 640	162	144	7 336	3.3
St. Louis	4 138	0.0	16.7	6.1	6.6	7.6	7.0	18.5	21.2	40 700	205	4 606	96 481	0.7
Scott	1 796	0.0	33.4	16.6	9.0	5.1	3.4	5.8	20.0	8 900	82	335	38 074	20.5
Sherburne	885	1.0	D	15.8	4.7	10.6	4.5	5.8	18.3	7 550	101	323	26 600	16.5
Sibley	128	1.6	27.6	15.0	D	5.8	D	D	24.9	3 010	197	91	6 178	2.6
Stearns	3 154	0.9	24.6	17.4	5.9	10.4	6.6	13.8	16.4	20 380	149	1 815	53 534	6.4
Steele	800	0.8	D	35.2	D	7.9	14.3	8.1	10.1	5 710	164	289	13 903	4.5
Stevens	194	8.2	D	12.3	4.5	5.9	4.2	D	27.9	1 845	187	107	4 116	1.0
Swift	148	7.0	D	18.4	D	6.1	3.7	D	24.1	2 445	210	153	4 855	0.7
Todd	243	0.8	D	31.6	2.4	7.3	4.7	8.2	21.6	4 820	198	454	12 209	2.6
Traverse	47	12.8	8.8	4.3	D	6.5	D	7.3	30.7	1 170	299	46	2 213	0.6
Wabasha	276	2.5	40.5	32.3	3.1	7.5	3.5	11.6	15.2	4 285	194	176	9 512	4.9
Wadena	211	-0.3	20.6	16.4	3.8	11.8	3.6	D	23.2	3 635	267	364	6 521	3.0
Waseca	308	2.1	D	19.4	D	5.0	3.9	D	19.4	3 550	183	176	7 609	2.5
Washington	3 209	0.6	30.8	22.5	5.8	9.4	9.6	9.0	13.7	23 880	112	757	79 808	8.4
Watonwan	172	6.5	D	31.3	D	5.1	3.3	D	16.1	2 540	219	94	5 043	0.1
Wilkin	76	2.5	D	0.7	1.7	6.9	6.6	19.9	22.8	1 415	204	66	3 142	1.2
Winona	920	1.8	D	28.9	7.0	11.8	3.3	8.7	16.0	8 220	166	589	20 109	2.9
Wright	1 308	0.0	D	17.0	D	10.5	4.7	7.6	16.1	12 210	119	520	39 655	15.4
Yellow Medicine	143	8.9	D	12.7	3.1	5.1	3.5	D	33.3	2 630	246	142	4 889	0.3

1. Covers mining, construction, and manufacturing.   2. Per 1,000 resident population estimated as of July 1 of the year shown.

STATE County	Housing units, 2000								Civilian labor force, 2003				Civilian employment,[6] 2000		
	Occupied units										Unemployment			Percent	
	Owner-occupied					Renter-occupied									
				Median owner cost as a percent of income											
	Total	Percent	Median value[1]	With a mortgage	Without a mortgage[2]	Median rent[3]	Median rent as a percent of income	Substandard units[4] (percent)	Total	Percent change, 2002–2003	Total	Rate[5]	Total	Management, professional and related occupations	Production, transportation, and material moving occupations
	89	90	91	92	93	94	95	96	97	98	99	100	101	102	103
MINNESOTA—Cont'd															
Grant	2 534	82.2	52 900	18.5	10.5	359	22.0	2.2	2 883	-0.7	218	7.6	2 998	33.3	15.7
Hennepin	456 129	66.2	143 400	20.1	9.9	654	25.2	4.5	693 591	0.1	32 383	4.7	616 729	42.5	10.8
Houston	7 633	81.1	88 600	19.2	9.9	392	20.7	1.2	11 548	0.2	577	5.0	10 105	33.6	16.7
Hubbard	7 435	83.4	97 300	20.4	9.9	382	24.0	3.8	9 708	0.3	609	6.3	8 004	30.2	14.9
Isanti	11 236	85.2	110 700	21.2	9.9	527	27.0	3.1	17 849	0.9	1 211	6.8	16 370	27.2	21.7
Itasca	17 789	82.9	81 700	19.9	9.9	406	25.5	3.7	21 660	1.2	1 810	8.4	19 222	26.2	19.3
Jackson	4 556	79.1	56 800	17.9	9.9	357	18.9	1.8	6 712	0.8	260	3.9	5 659	31.5	17.9
Kanabec	5 759	84.0	90 400	21.2	9.9	446	23.7	3.9	6 904	-1.9	733	10.6	7 180	23.5	23.0
Kandiyohi	15 936	75.5	90 400	20.3	9.9	435	24.2	3.2	23 193	1.6	1 061	4.6	21 131	30.8	18.7
Kittson	2 167	82.7	39 400	17.1	9.9	347	19.8	2.0	2 372	-1.6	223	9.4	2 295	32.5	18.8
Koochiching	6 040	80.4	65 400	17.9	9.9	348	24.4	2.6	6 392	-0.6	457	7.1	6 489	24.0	23.1
Lac qui Parle	3 316	80.7	43 100	17.5	9.9	348	22.0	1.3	3 818	0.3	162	4.2	3 839	32.9	18.0
Lake	4 646	84.0	71 300	17.5	9.9	435	23.4	3.2	5 900	-0.2	249	4.2	5 208	29.7	16.4
Lake of the Woods	1 903	85.4	74 000	21.0	9.9	338	28.1	1.9	2 562	2.7	134	5.2	2 177	27.2	22.9
Le Sueur	9 630	82.9	105 500	20.2	9.9	433	20.3	2.8	15 932	-0.4	919	5.8	13 417	27.9	24.0
Lincoln	2 653	80.4	43 700	18.8	10.5	326	20.3	1.5	3 128	0.5	114	3.6	3 105	33.3	16.5
Lyon	9 715	68.4	81 000	18.6	9.9	445	23.9	2.4	15 238	-0.1	619	4.1	13 402	31.6	18.6
McLeod	13 449	78.5	104 800	20.1	9.9	465	22.6	2.2	19 744	-0.4	987	5.0	18 449	27.7	26.4
Mahnomen	1 969	77.3	53 100	17.9	9.9	302	22.3	4.7	2 530	-0.6	147	5.8	2 221	32.1	10.2
Marshall	4 101	83.8	50 500	17.5	9.9	317	22.7	2.8	4 849	1.3	501	10.3	4 524	31.2	20.6
Martin	9 067	77.4	62 200	18.1	9.9	342	22.5	1.8	11 461	-1.2	554	4.8	10 757	30.1	20.9
Meeker	8 590	81.5	89 200	19.3	9.9	441	23.7	2.1	10 594	0.9	811	7.7	11 176	27.6	25.3
Mille Lacs	8 638	79.8	91 000	21.0	11.0	409	24.1	3.3	10 483	1.7	1 033	9.9	10 660	24.1	24.6
Morrison	11 816	82.0	82 800	19.2	10.1	404	24.8	2.9	16 739	3.9	1 270	7.6	15 077	29.2	21.8
Mower	15 582	78.3	71 400	18.5	9.9	380	22.8	3.1	20 991	0.4	863	4.1	18 620	26.9	21.7
Murray	3 722	84.5	50 900	18.6	9.9	373	20.3	2.2	4 587	1.8	250	5.5	4 560	32.0	17.9
Nicollet	10 642	75.6	113 400	19.2	9.9	488	23.3	1.8	20 006	-0.5	676	3.4	16 757	35.7	17.7
Nobles	7 939	75.1	61 400	18.1	9.9	388	21.0	5.8	10 165	1.0	387	3.8	10 185	25.6	24.4
Norman	3 010	81.1	43 600	17.2	10.7	374	22.7	2.0	3 355	-0.6	199	5.9	3 380	30.1	12.1
Olmsted	47 807	76.0	117 000	18.5	9.9	556	24.3	2.9	84 164	1.5	3 545	4.2	66 973	44.5	10.2
Otter Tail	22 671	80.0	84 000	19.1	9.9	391	25.2	2.7	28 859	1.4	1 665	5.8	26 470	31.2	17.5
Pennington	5 525	74.6	63 300	17.4	9.9	349	22.1	2.4	8 609	1.7	507	5.9	6 688	28.6	20.1
Pine	9 939	83.7	89 700	21.0	9.9	431	24.5	5.1	13 299	1.1	1 124	8.5	11 895	24.4	18.6
Pipestone	4 069	77.5	49 000	17.7	10.3	365	19.7	1.6	5 350	-0.8	207	3.9	4 948	30.1	18.7
Polk	12 070	74.0	75 000	19.0	9.9	396	26.0	2.8	18 137	1.0	843	4.6	14 301	30.3	14.8
Pope	4 513	80.8	74 100	19.4	10.1	363	23.2	2.5	6 016	4.1	246	4.1	5 341	33.8	16.6
Ramsey	201 236	63.5	126 400	19.9	9.9	606	25.5	5.4	296 651	0.3	14 400	4.9	264 914	39.9	12.8
Red Lake	1 727	79.4	43 200	17.3	9.9	282	20.4	1.7	1 902	-1.3	202	10.6	1 930	30.2	20.2
Redwood	6 674	80.0	57 900	17.6	9.9	371	21.1	1.8	9 125	-0.9	408	4.5	8 175	29.6	18.2
Renville	6 779	81.0	57 700	17.7	9.9	382	20.3	2.1	8 481	0.8	517	6.1	8 307	30.9	22.4
Rice	18 888	77.9	123 600	20.9	10.6	519	21.9	3.1	31 300	0.0	1 597	5.1	29 029	30.6	19.1
Rock	3 843	78.0	68 500	18.4	10.4	394	24.5	1.2	4 803	-0.8	159	3.3	4 904	33.2	14.4
Roseau	6 190	84.1	76 300	19.1	9.9	442	21.9	3.2	10 187	5.7	952	9.3	8 491	26.0	35.5
St. Louis	82 619	74.7	75 000	18.9	9.9	415	26.3	2.8	109 408	0.2	6 137	5.6	94 095	30.5	12.8
Scott	30 692	86.6	157 300	21.4	9.9	655	26.4	2.7	61 365	0.2	2 695	4.4	49 491	36.1	13.7
Sherburne	21 581	84.0	137 500	21.4	9.9	570	23.9	2.6	39 279	0.5	2 259	5.8	34 509	29.0	19.2
Sibley	5 772	80.9	80 700	19.4	9.9	426	20.9	2.5	7 443	2.0	474	6.4	7 966	26.7	28.2
Stearns	47 604	73.8	100 300	19.6	9.9	473	23.1	2.2	83 792	-0.1	4 044	4.8	72 511	30.2	18.6
Steele	12 846	80.2	102 300	20.2	9.9	471	21.6	2.6	20 229	-0.8	1 023	5.1	18 005	29.6	20.4
Stevens	3 751	70.2	67 100	17.8	9.9	385	23.6	1.7	5 921	0.8	179	3.0	5 266	37.3	12.6
Swift	4 353	77.1	58 200	17.9	9.9	362	21.4	1.4	5 483	-0.9	240	4.4	5 199	33.3	17.9
Todd	9 342	82.9	64 400	19.9	10.1	346	24.4	3.4	10 328	0.8	668	6.5	11 200	25.0	26.8
Traverse	1 717	80.5	34 100	19.5	10.0	374	25.6	1.5	1 768	0.5	82	4.6	1 668	35.2	14.2
Wabasha	8 277	82.5	95 000	19.9	9.9	434	22.1	2.2	12 270	-5.8	568	4.6	11 335	32.1	18.4
Wadena	5 426	77.4	56 900	17.9	11.3	337	24.5	4.1	7 617	1.0	471	6.2	5 949	29.3	21.5
Waseca	7 059	80.0	87 700	19.5	10.1	402	20.5	1.8	9 888	0.4	506	5.1	9 761	26.8	24.6
Washington	71 462	85.8	156 200	20.9	9.9	699	25.6	1.6	122 685	0.2	5 055	4.1	108 822	41.0	11.2
Watonwan	4 627	77.0	56 600	17.2	9.9	338	19.3	3.8	5 709	-1.0	305	5.3	5 606	26.3	29.8
Wilkin	2 752	80.6	64 100	18.0	9.9	339	21.9	2.7	4 012	1.1	166	4.1	3 414	32.8	17.9
Winona	18 744	71.0	95 800	19.7	9.9	425	23.6	2.7	29 301	-1.5	1 345	4.6	26 688	30.0	20.9
Wright	31 465	84.3	135 300	21.2	9.9	526	22.9	2.5	54 879	0.4	3 138	5.7	48 045	29.2	19.1
Yellow Medicine	4 439	79.3	52 400	17.8	9.9	357	23.2	1.6	5 554	2.4	349	6.3	5 208	33.4	20.9

1. Specified owner-occupied units.   2. Median monthly owner costs is often in the minimum category—9.9 percent or less, which is indicated as 9.9 percent.   3. Specified renter-occupied units.   4. Overcrowded or lacking complete plumbing facilities.   5. Percent of civilian labor force.   6. Persons 16 years old and over.

STATE County	Number of establish-ments	Total	Health care and social assistance	Manufac-turing	Retail trade	Finance and insurance	Professional, scientific, and technical services	Total (mil dol)	Average per employee (dollars)	Number	Less than 50 acres	500 acres and over	Farm operators whose principal occu-pation is farming (percent)
	104	105	106	107	108	109	110	111	112	113	114	115	116
MINNESOTA—Cont'd													
Grant	208	1 437	305	170	262	102	61	30	20 769	606	24.6	27.4	67.2
Hennepin	39 022	859 442	91 859	99 889	89 617	76 746	68 833	36 915	42 952	626	60.7	4.3	51.0
Houston	388	3 536	719	525	526	198	99	77	21 888	1 031	19.0	11.1	61.7
Hubbard	534	6 107	998	1 092	886	176	68	133	21 845	535	17.2	10.5	48.8
Isanti	769	7 727	1 681	1 358	1 519	251	262	191	24 657	952	46.7	6.5	48.8
Itasca	1 228	13 954	2 141	2 454	2 667	361	502	362	25 943	494	23.7	10.9	48.6
Jackson	346	4 275	888	948	420	269	79	111	26 049	989	21.9	28.4	74.0
Kanabec	290	3 351	710	594	700	120	128	73	21 735	796	26.4	7.9	49.9
Kandiyohi	1 344	20 585	4 549	3 179	2 926	649	471	490	23 814	1 286	28.3	17.5	58.6
Kittson	154	1 091	336	29	225	77	D	22	19 728	659	6.4	42.2	56.3
Koochiching	466	4 753	605	1 262	769	356	55	121	25 461	258	8.1	16.7	41.1
Lac qui Parle	290	2 424	504	329	411	106	29	56	23 260	910	15.9	34.8	72.9
Lake	287	3 176	561	443	422	131	136	79	24 895	46	32.6	2.2	52.2
Lake of the Woods	149	1 213	D	251	210	D	D	25	20 627	266	12.4	27.4	50.4
Le Sueur	771	9 593	814	2 790	1 022	248	850	256	26 711	974	29.8	12.6	60.0
Lincoln	179	1 310	534	20	198	48	29	24	18 134	761	22.9	23.0	66.4
Lyon	780	13 292	1 731	2 094	2 012	768	176	336	25 246	949	22.2	32.2	74.4
McLeod	881	15 642	1 965	6 926	2 299	387	207	479	30 609	987	29.7	15.4	69.9
Mahnomen	138	980	190	D	257	65	16	21	21 157	363	16.0	31.1	66.1
Marshall	359	2 338	345	261	385	134	19	53	22 562	1 409	8.3	36.1	62.9
Martin	707	9 031	1 624	2 489	1 501	326	256	228	25 212	954	22.2	31.2	77.7
Meeker	599	6 216	973	1 714	848	188	176	148	23 879	1 141	28.7	16.2	61.7
Mille Lacs	627	9 289	1 447	910	1 115	195	85	208	22 412	847	29.5	5.8	52.9
Morrison	843	8 881	1 596	1 958	1 747	296	104	194	21 808	1 924	16.6	9.5	65.7
Mower	920	13 409	2 837	3 238	1 912	473	208	376	28 038	1 088	33.6	23.2	73.2
Murray	295	2 265	434	432	349	144	100	45	19 889	911	21.1	32.6	73.0
Nicollet	712	13 596	1 753	5 144	932	203	490	340	25 024	730	21.0	22.6	73.4
Nobles	632	8 361	1 387	2 378	1 480	294	185	181	21 617	1 043	22.0	24.9	81.9
Norman	211	1 397	440	D	221	102	65	30	21 805	660	13.2	42.6	67.9
Olmsted	3 032	78 480	29 225	13 328	10 160	1 736	1 869	2 785	35 483	1 395	36.3	11.9	55.6
Otter Tail	1 600	17 673	3 270	3 848	3 057	450	340	395	22 371	3 013	16.2	15.3	57.1
Pennington	325	6 052	957	1 299	938	138	70	160	26 403	610	11.3	29.3	64.4
Pine	669	5 106	878	440	1 096	239	95	108	21 054	1 199	19.7	8.3	51.3
Pipestone	299	3 830	590	728	518	118	D	70	18 273	703	23.9	24.6	70.0
Polk	817	8 753	1 956	1 375	1 433	275	245	183	20 859	1 518	11.9	39.4	63.2
Pope	303	3 252	670	543	345	110	172	95	29 125	924	19.6	20.6	64.7
Ramsey	13 836	305 934	42 113	35 342	34 191	18 484	16 860	11 902	38 905	36	77.8	0.0	58.3
Red Lake	122	1 366	306	365	172	57	3	31	23 021	378	9.8	34.7	64.8
Redwood	648	5 615	1 007	1 060	987	218	177	120	21 314	1 198	19.2	34.4	81.1
Renville	646	6 153	869	1 149	785	213	188	143	23 309	1 164	19.5	35.8	77.4
Rice	1 475	23 754	3 267	5 163	3 082	534	457	598	25 186	1 296	37.9	9.6	52.8
Rock	243	2 994	443	362	524	421	63	62	20 708	721	26.4	25.0	75.7
Roseau	389	7 583	780	4 244	767	200	83	194	25 562	1 238	10.3	29.1	54.7
St. Louis	5 586	81 132	18 221	5 545	12 993	3 026	3 427	2 191	27 000	978	25.9	6.6	52.1
Scott	2 363	31 225	2 610	5 304	2 885	542	771	1 023	32 776	1 004	56.4	5.0	49.2
Sherburne	1 386	15 700	1 889	3 397	3 311	431	310	429	27 335	677	50.2	9.0	52.6
Sibley	347	3 138	428	932	488	170	65	65	20 582	963	22.2	18.7	74.5
Stearns	4 029	72 629	11 161	14 138	12 489	2 492	1 852	1 955	26 916	3 152	23.7	8.1	67.5
Steele	967	19 021	1 612	6 612	2 803	2 445	164	603	31 696	899	36.3	15.5	64.2
Stevens	346	3 740	920	278	588	140	210	85	22 834	556	26.4	37.2	69.6
Swift	320	3 507	736	664	511	128	31	67	19 096	807	18.8	32.6	74.2
Todd	541	4 622	367	1 657	705	201	102	106	22 949	1 825	18.1	7.8	60.8
Traverse	131	890	D	68	D	D	D	15	17 002	452	22.1	45.8	71.9
Wabasha	683	6 982	1 192	1 967	1 109	192	176	161	23 028	999	22.3	14.0	68.8
Wadena	333	4 844	1 821	923	678	99	88	97	20 044	734	17.3	8.0	51.9
Waseca	464	6 739	1 205	2 621	759	201	100	167	24 744	759	28.5	20.2	68.1
Washington	4 660	62 693	6 385	11 578	10 968	5 197	2 165	2 100	33 497	810	56.2	5.9	48.5
Watonwan	321	3 487	561	1 017	412	137	62	76	21 714	601	22.8	28.8	77.9
Wilkin	180	1 632	486	37	252	D	D	34	20 775	414	14.0	51.9	76.1
Winona	1 307	22 974	2 991	6 615	2 633	552	692	559	24 315	1 125	20.1	14.4	66.3
Wright	2 501	26 774	4 172	4 887	4 793	745	1 004	718	26 820	1 646	40.7	7.5	54.6
Yellow Medicine	349	4 120	881	560	537	123	50	93	22 452	989	23.9	32.8	67.5

Table B. States and Counties — **Agriculture**

STATE County	Acreage (1,000) [117]	Percent change, 1997–2002 [118]	Average size of farm [119]	Total irrigated (1,000) [120]	Total cropland (1,000) [121]	Average per farm [122]	Average per acre [123]	Value of machinery and equipment average per farm (dollars) [124]	Total (mil dol) [125]	Average per farm (dollars) [126]	Crops [127]	Live-stock and poultry products [128]	$10,000 or more [129]	$100,000 or more [130]	Total ($1,000) [131]	Percent of farms [132]
MINNESOTA—Cont'd																
Grant	317	14.0	524	4	289	691 969	1 285	118 010	69	114 444	89.8	10.2	46.0	26.4	4 489	82.2
Hennepin	65	-5.8	105	1	49	626 969	5 558	62 545	58	92 086	88.8	11.2	37.4	12.1	891	25.4
Houston	254	-14.8	246	0	152	343 138	1 305	64 234	67	64 558	28.8	71.2	52.4	16.9	4 651	62.3
Hubbard	140	6.9	262	23	75	254 689	868	41 819	23	42 912	75.4	24.6	24.1	4.9	429	19.1
Isanti	139	0.0	146	1	97	361 948	2 294	49 831	26	26 887	63.5	36.5	24.7	6.5	1 145	28.4
Itasca	120	15.4	243	1	57	248 176	998	35 870	6	13 037	52.7	47.3	24.1	2.4	93	7.7
Jackson	398	3.6	402	0	373	748 864	1 858	107 846	159	161 140	51.9	48.1	74.0	36.3	4 860	66.0
Kanabec	159	14.4	199	2	86	276 049	1 287	42 356	19	23 862	33.1	66.9	29.1	6.8	922	21.6
Kandiyohi	408	7.7	317	12	354	488 220	1 602	93 135	231	179 546	36.0	64.0	49.1	25.3	6 904	67.7
Kittson	556	11.0	843	D	471	487 738	563	94 289	70	106 169	86.5	13.5	44.9	23.8	7 859	84.8
Koochiching	74	-3.9	288	0	40	200 621	703	35 042	4	14 795	36.1	63.9	29.1	2.3	D	D
Lac qui Parle	435	9.3	478	5	391	582 260	1 222	97 008	113	124 343	69.1	30.9	64.9	34.2	5 747	76.8
Lake	5	25.0	105	D	2	172 827	1 733	19 499	0	7 633	80.6	19.4	0.0	0.0	D	D
Lake of the Woods	152	28.8	573	0	103	340 818	590	62 845	6	21 056	79.1	20.9	27.1	6.8	695	41.7
Le Sueur	238	10.7	244	1	204	613 276	2 245	86 009	88	90 560	51.5	48.5	49.8	19.7	3 955	64.9
Lincoln	271	0.4	357	D	239	438 086	1 164	72 624	73	96 373	50.6	49.4	56.6	24.0	4 675	73.9
Lyon	404	0.2	426	0	367	628 848	1 451	113 771	157	165 526	47.9	52.1	69.0	40.3	5 225	68.2
McLeod	263	5.2	266	D	235	562 239	2 095	93 747	81	82 160	63.8	36.2	63.4	25.4	3 781	55.3
Mahnomen	195	2.6	537	D	156	375 685	671	74 141	24	66 046	72.3	27.7	55.1	19.8	2 575	71.1
Marshall	935	20.8	664	1	811	403 826	611	105 344	107	76 267	91.4	8.6	41.0	18.9	15 538	80.9
Martin	423	0.5	443	1	398	1 021 699	2 047	196 624	249	260 786	41.3	58.7	80.4	47.5	5 663	64.9
Meeker	341	16.4	298	5	287	533 011	1 793	101 665	129	113 120	45.9	54.1	52.0	22.3	5 293	66.5
Mille Lacs	132	-2.2	156	0	81	280 556	1 731	47 324	23	26 581	36.6	63.4	33.8	5.7	826	27.3
Morrison	452	5.1	235	18	262	314 697	1 338	80 906	166	86 119	18.2	81.8	49.4	17.0	4 627	40.7
Mower	412	2.0	379	1	383	773 356	1 959	115 300	179	164 229	59.0	41.0	67.0	34.9	6 693	60.3
Murray	407	6.0	447	0	376	705 374	1 545	113 721	139	152 366	54.4	45.6	73.4	43.1	5 553	74.2
Nicollet	257	3.2	352	0	234	798 939	2 263	125 256	148	203 199	38.9	61.1	75.1	41.4	4 183	63.2
Nobles	404	3.6	388	D	374	648 161	1 679	115 994	188	179 825	40.0	60.0	77.1	37.9	5 382	67.5
Norman	527	9.1	799	D	478	684 816	835	133 832	91	137 457	82.9	17.1	57.6	29.5	6 453	77.7
Olmsted	313	3.0	224	D	255	497 719	2 214	91 973	104	74 668	55.2	44.8	46.6	18.1	5 100	55.6
Otter Tail	881	4.9	292	56	614	317 973	1 047	59 295	220	73 118	40.8	59.2	42.1	14.8	9 899	65.1
Pennington	332	6.1	544	0	274	266 566	524	72 954	24	40 048	89.2	10.8	37.7	11.5	4 793	74.4
Pine	255	3.2	213	1	131	311 142	1 269	30 648	34	28 683	36.9	63.1	31.6	6.1	1 079	20.5
Pipestone	249	2.0	355	1	214	555 293	1 407	91 903	106	150 532	35.0	65.0	66.6	32.4	3 133	61.5
Polk	1 111	5.6	732	11	986	595 853	828	158 634	197	129 900	93.0	7.0	48.6	27.6	16 559	76.7
Pope	350	7.7	379	33	290	454 080	1 233	89 703	91	98 037	57.5	42.5	49.9	23.5	5 116	69.6
Ramsey	1	NA	29	0	0	497 635	19 011	44 866	4	122 353	79.6	20.4	66.7	27.8	0	0.0
Red Lake	227	10.7	600	D	191	401 885	630	78 811	23	61 157	76.4	23.6	48.7	16.1	3 322	80.7
Redwood	545	7.3	455	0	510	755 890	1 722	108 372	220	184 048	55.3	44.7	76.7	45.5	6 971	72.4
Renville	664	10.5	570	2	628	1 053 600	1 889	156 900	317	272 348	64.3	35.7	76.1	45.5	7 214	64.9
Rice	249	-0.8	192	1	206	524 704	2 732	65 828	99	76 640	45.7	54.3	45.8	16.7	4 157	58.0
Rock	299	6.4	415	0	269	714 333	1 395	93 508	152	211 395	35.9	64.1	76.3	39.5	3 789	61.6
Roseau	703	21.8	568	1	582	303 612	527	75 572	45	35 981	59.4	40.6	34.1	9.1	8 669	67.7
St. Louis	175	12.9	179	0	89	200 393	1 377	20 990	11	11 409	52.6	47.4	19.4	2.4	223	4.4
Scott	131	11.0	130	0	109	471 348	3 496	54 322	54	53 297	52.1	47.9	35.8	12.9	1 635	30.5
Sherburne	126	20.0	186	38	97	465 532	2 816	55 429	49	71 696	77.9	22.1	31.3	10.9	1 143	27.9
Sibley	339	9.4	352	0	310	829 466	2 234	116 801	169	175 079	49.4	50.6	75.6	35.5	4 769	60.7
Stearns	681	5.4	216	40	531	358 266	1 579	78 322	344	109 029	20.2	79.8	58.9	25.9	12 085	52.5
Steele	282	24.2	314	1	258	635 872	2 126	124 419	128	142 327	62.7	37.3	53.3	27.4	4 801	65.1
Stevens	313	4.7	563	15	291	791 920	1 472	123 018	120	216 203	54.2	45.8	61.9	42.1	4 055	73.0
Swift	416	7.2	515	23	377	650 187	1 250	115 769	158	195 438	55.4	44.6	60.0	34.9	6 247	81.8
Todd	370	-4.4	203	11	233	220 720	1 164	47 337	96	52 645	26.8	73.2	41.5	11.3	3 385	44.6
Traverse	344	9.2	761	D	325	876 908	1 131	179 022	80	177 512	90.9	9.1	66.6	41.8	3 598	79.6
Wabasha	267	5.5	267	2	193	482 790	1 875	92 513	96	95 795	39.5	60.5	61.3	26.5	4 537	57.3
Wadena	166	-5.1	226	18	96	221 706	1 015	45 579	39	53 555	33.5	66.5	31.6	7.4	980	42.5
Waseca	231	-1.7	305	0	211	669 559	2 345	93 613	111	145 944	51.0	49.0	66.1	33.6	3 758	66.9
Washington	96	6.7	119	3	72	656 084	5 200	64 708	62	76 228	89.8	10.2	34.2	9.5	938	20.6
Watonwan	272	6.3	452	1	254	839 418	1 858	128 348	127	211 435	51.6	48.4	74.2	41.8	3 593	66.7
Wilkin	425	-7.2	1 025	1	404	1 113 545	1 068	187 060	106	256 605	92.3	7.7	71.0	46.9	4 546	76.3
Winona	311	7.2	276	0	210	503 713	1 989	82 532	125	111 132	25.3	74.7	60.7	26.3	4 751	50.9
Wright	266	5.6	161	3	214	443 986	2 772	61 426	94	57 214	53.0	47.0	42.2	12.8	3 185	40.0
Yellow Medicine	448	8.0	453	1	408	557 181	1 286	99 102	139	140 393	62.4	37.6	64.5	37.2	5 938	75.2

Table B. States and Counties — Residential Construction, Wholesale Trade, Retail Trade, and Real Estate

STATE County	Value of residential construction authorized by building permits, 2003		Wholesale trade, 1997				Retail trade,[1] 1997				Real estate and rental and leasing, 1997			
	New construction ($1,000)	Number of housing units	Number of establish-ments	Number of employees	Sales (mil dol)	Annual payroll (mil dol)	Number of establish-ments	Number of employees	Sales (mil dol)	Annual payroll (mil dol)	Number of establish-ments	Number of employees	Receipts (mil dol)	Annual payroll (mil dol)
	133	134	135	136	137	138	139	140	141	142	143	144	145	146
MINNESOTA—Cont'd														
Grant	583	4	18	168	209.1	3.8	44	287	53.4	4.1	7	D	D	D
Hennepin	1 018 080	5 636	3 723	61 454	59 929.0	2 700.6	4 644	78 226	14 615.8	1 409.6	1 796	14 720	2 205.9	409.7
Houston	14 862	96	31	536	70.0	10.1	70	500	76.3	6.0	5	11	1.8	0.1
Hubbard	3 387	35	22	111	29.0	2.2	107	846	125.2	11.4	9	42	3.3	0.8
Isanti	57 954	467	19	D	D	D	103	1 195	193.6	15.7	18	54	3.7	0.5
Itasca	45 808	377	43	395	467.5	9.7	256	2 376	361.0	34.0	31	83	7.1	1.1
Jackson	2 355	23	23	254	131.3	6.9	55	478	57.6	5.6	3	7	0.5	0.1
Kanabec	12 063	113	9	D	D	D	75	665	114.0	9.5	7	D	D	D
Kandiyohi	36 232	261	73	1 071	548.8	31.5	267	3 022	447.6	44.2	52	189	31.4	3.0
Kittson	695	4	20	171	89.3	3.3	36	220	38.0	2.7	6	10	0.4	0.0
Koochiching	3 790	52	10	D	D	D	104	787	124.6	11.9	12	35	3.9	0.7
Lac qui Parle	1 132	8	21	207	124.6	5.2	56	355	50.1	3.8	7	12	0.6	0.1
Lake	11 844	89	9	D	D	D	53	407	121.4	9.3	2	D	D	D
Lake of the Woods	304	3	8	43	15.8	0.8	29	202	26.2	2.5	6	14	1.3	0.2
Le Sueur	23 031	163	30	415	154.0	11.6	117	955	150.1	13.1	19	35	2.8	0.4
Lincoln	675	6	15	99	40.2	1.9	34	228	35.9	4.2	5	9	0.5	0.0
Lyon	17 328	124	54	889	915.8	31.7	155	2 013	290.5	27.6	26	87	5.4	0.8
McLeod	41 416	294	43	413	239.0	13.6	188	2 079	286.6	27.7	28	72	8.7	1.0
Mahnomen	0	0	8	48	29.7	1.2	28	147	28.8	2.7	3	7	0.3	0.1
Marshall	198	5	32	D	D	D	45	293	72.0	5.6	2	D	D	D
Martin	7 783	54	53	377	419.4	12.6	131	1 552	250.4	21.3	18	47	4.2	0.7
Meeker	26 420	188	26	203	100.8	5.3	103	787	128.2	11.9	19	36	3.9	0.3
Mille Lacs	41 647	337	27	219	87.1	5.1	118	997	133.1	12.2	12	23	1.7	0.2
Morrison	31 816	345	31	282	161.5	5.3	141	1 468	247.8	20.1	13	42	4.3	0.5
Mower	21 681	145	44	279	443.3	9.8	191	1 957	269.0	26.0	21	112	4.2	1.0
Murray	4 993	51	15	124	78.6	3.0	53	335	54.0	4.3	3	D	D	D
Nicollet	35 133	291	41	492	207.3	21.1	80	756	121.7	10.3	19	72	3.8	0.7
Nobles	5 238	36	43	D	D	D	155	1 376	206.6	19.0	12	51	2.6	0.5
Norman	1 371	13	15	141	57.6	3.3	43	357	80.5	5.7	4	D	D	D
Olmsted	256 057	1 562	125	1 176	605.4	37.5	583	9 254	1 431.6	136.5	124	654	72.9	9.7
Otter Tail	22 701	203	73	602	233.4	10.2	317	2 922	474.8	43.3	47	113	10.4	1.4
Pennington	4 193	34	19	939	302.9	21.0	85	1 000	149.5	15.3	13	37	3.2	0.6
Pine	11 452	112	14	101	25.4	2.0	116	875	153.2	12.3	26	111	5.3	1.0
Pipestone	2 457	20	31	457	256.1	9.1	67	557	94.3	6.6	6	D	D	D
Polk	18 915	162	57	415	206.2	10.0	152	1 377	211.7	19.7	15	66	3.3	0.9
Pope	9 847	89	22	290	192.2	8.0	54	379	58.7	5.1	4	11	0.6	0.1
Ramsey	234 620	1 846	927	15 680	9 328.6	633.3	1 878	32 511	5 485.7	564.7	625	4 875	560.0	111.9
Red Lake	445	6	10	70	35.0	1.8	30	150	32.5	2.6	NA	NA	NA	NA
Redwood	2 723	18	51	478	400.0	16.1	87	927	126.9	11.7	26	40	2.3	0.2
Renville	3 538	26	31	478	364.7	13.3	104	681	111.7	9.8	9	29	1.4	0.3
Rice	93 802	567	63	1 009	543.5	32.2	242	2 788	416.8	40.5	37	130	11.7	1.5
Rock	3 735	26	22	126	108.5	3.2	50	517	85.6	7.2	8	16	0.9	0.1
Roseau	4 194	43	20	145	69.7	4.0	89	769	119.7	10.3	12	40	1.9	0.3
St. Louis	102 038	817	280	D	D	D	1 087	12 385	1 892.0	186.2	175	918	85.3	14.8
Scott	441 182	2 703	153	1 613	1 917.8	64.5	229	2 318	419.3	37.0	67	204	23.2	2.8
Sherburne	232 211	1 596	51	351	78.5	7.1	154	2 120	502.9	34.4	38	133	13.5	1.5
Sibley	13 219	80	13	110	146.7	3.6	62	497	63.1	5.3	8	14	1.0	0.2
Stearns	205 211	1 667	193	3 688	1 068.9	117.1	661	9 866	1 664.3	149.4	135	668	57.4	10.3
Steele	45 179	354	55	415	225.7	13.1	174	2 042	272.4	27.5	17	125	7.3	1.4
Stevens	2 892	18	22	379	151.6	11.0	64	569	119.4	8.5	12	17	1.6	0.2
Swift	1 969	18	21	266	180.6	6.5	65	486	68.5	6.7	7	39	1.2	0.3
Todd	21 132	186	32	217	49.3	4.1	112	780	124.1	10.1	13	28	1.8	0.2
Traverse	960	8	8	72	96.4	2.9	31	213	31.6	2.7	4	D	D	D
Wabasha	34 222	249	25	199	49.0	4.3	107	882	124.7	13.1	12	28	3.3	0.6
Wadena	7 328	99	17	D	D	D	66	589	104.8	9.0	7	18	1.7	0.2
Waseca	12 126	90	26	156	62.6	3.3	70	742	106.3	10.0	6	13	0.8	0.1
Washington	439 174	2 290	205	1 471	2 029.3	69.8	601	9 304	1 674.4	142.6	160	702	84.5	12.0
Watonwan	4 312	31	24	219	211.8	6.0	59	427	55.3	5.0	3	5	1.1	0.1
Wilkin	1 543	17	20	260	149.7	6.8	36	272	38.1	3.8	3	5	0.5	0.1
Winona	42 110	374	80	682	418.3	17.8	224	2 506	384.8	36.5	41	129	19.7	1.9
Wright	308 949	1 940	85	669	221.2	18.2	283	3 870	682.9	59.7	70	248	26.1	3.3
Yellow Medicine	6 783	64	24	124	91.7	2.7	66	514	79.7	6.5	6	18	1.0	0.1

1. Establishments with payroll.

Table B. States and Counties — Professional Services, Manufacturing, and Accommodation and Foodservices

STATE County	Professional, scientific, and technical services,[1] 1997				Manufacturing, 1997				Accommodation and foodservices, 1997			
	Number of establishments	Number of employees	Receipts (mil dol)	Annual payroll (mil dol)	Number of establishments	Number of employees	Receipts (mil dol)	Annual payroll (mil dol)	Number of establishments	Number of employees	Sales (mil dol)	Annual payroll (mil dol)
	147	148	149	150	151	152	153	154	155	156	157	158
MINNESOTA—Cont'd												
Grant	9	19	1.2	0.7	NA	NA	NA	NA	11	D	D	D
Hennepin	5 655	58 051	7 181.2	2 758.4	2 404	106 772	17 291.6	4 090.1	2 196	54 567	2 078.4	616.4
Houston	20	53	4.7	0.7	NA	NA	NA	NA	33	260	6.9	1.3
Hubbard	24	73	3.4	1.0	32	940	166.1	19.6	70	429	16.9	3.8
Isanti	41	149	10.7	4.1	59	1 330	153.5	35.6	43	570	14.5	4.1
Itasca	61	472	20.9	8.8	58	2 432	534.3	92.0	116	1 365	41.9	10.9
Jackson	12	122	15.9	3.4	18	D	D	D	16	D	D	D
Kanabec	13	46	2.7	0.8	17	803	96.7	19.4	23	D	D	D
Kandiyohi	74	381	27.4	9.7	66	3 265	605.5	84.0	88	1 551	41.5	11.0
Kittson	5	23	1.6	0.9	NA	NA	NA	NA	11	D	D	D
Koochiching	18	65	3.2	1.2	11	D	D	D	52	599	18.1	5.1
Lac qui Parle	10	D	D	D	NA	NA	NA	NA	17	D	D	D
Lake	10	27	1.4	0.3	12	507	84.4	18.6	49	481	15.6	3.9
Lake of the Woods	4	D	D	D	NA	NA	NA	NA	35	304	11.3	2.6
Le Sueur	31	575	40.4	24.6	51	2 751	728.9	79.5	47	D	D	D
Lincoln	5	D	D	D	NA	NA	NA	NA	15	83	2.3	0.4
Lyon	32	134	9.2	3.6	28	1 833	456.0	40.5	52	879	22.0	6.4
McLeod	49	195	9.1	3.5	67	9 080	1 670.5	291.0	67	1 040	26.9	7.1
Mahnomen	4	D	D	D	NA	NA	NA	NA	14	D	D	D
Marshall	9	28	1.5	0.6	NA	NA	NA	NA	27	D	D	D
Martin	31	207	13.6	5.7	44	2 111	294.1	61.6	52	775	18.1	5.2
Meeker	26	99	6.2	2.2	58	1 740	356.8	41.1	36	D	D	D
Mille Lacs	26	54	2.2	0.8	38	1 029	158.0	24.4	65	D	D	D
Morrison	21	67	4.0	1.3	44	1 883	256.3	47.3	91	804	22.4	5.6
Mower	38	191	13.3	5.1	37	D	D	D	87	1 211	31.5	8.5
Murray	14	89	5.2	2.0	NA	NA	NA	NA	22	D	D	D
Nicollet	34	207	12.4	4.7	34	3 748	868.2	79.9	44	826	22.9	6.1
Nobles	25	87	4.9	1.5	24	2 690	823.8	62.9	44	737	17.6	5.5
Norman	6	55	5.0	2.4	NA	NA	NA	NA	26	D	D	D
Olmsted	206	2 145	164.4	84.1	77	10 477	3 085.4	482.1	274	5 924	204.3	58.5
Otter Tail	65	199	12.0	4.0	91	3 732	661.7	82.1	138	1 354	37.9	9.7
Pennington	20	68	4.8	1.8	16	2 047	594.7	50.9	32	839	22.0	7.0
Pine	21	56	3.3	1.1	NA	NA	NA	NA	68	911	27.7	7.9
Pipestone	13	23	1.1	0.2	15	652	96.9	16.6	28	D	D	D
Polk	29	154	9.7	4.5	40	1 350	300.3	36.3	80	1 127	25.0	6.7
Pope	14	142	7.6	4.3	29	529	84.6	13.3	36	D	D	D
Ramsey	1 569	12 225	1 240.6	530.7	765	41 550	9 294.6	1 581.6	1 011	20 952	654.9	196.6
Red Lake	3	D	D	D	NA	NA	NA	NA	9	D	D	D
Redwood	23	94	4.7	1.8	21	1 250	165.9	34.9	41	397	10.5	2.9
Renville	26	104	8.7	3.5	34	884	155.7	21.5	33	1 068	39.9	12.5
Rice	81	254	23.0	7.6	86	4 838	954.9	161.3	110	1 825	55.0	15.5
Rock	12	21	1.6	0.3	NA	NA	NA	NA	20	D	D	D
Roseau	17	54	2.6	0.9	18	D	D	D	44	718	14.6	5.2
St. Louis	318	2 186	147.8	66.6	228	5 446	879.4	155.8	591	8 610	289.8	73.3
Scott	157	395	40.2	15.5	148	5 039	989.5	180.8	122	2 049	57.0	16.1
Sherburne	59	167	11.7	5.0	96	3 278	463.2	103.2	74	1 095	33.4	9.7
Sibley	17	42	3.2	1.1	25	1 054	352.1	28.7	18	180	4.2	0.8
Stearns	224	1 325	100.8	41.9	219	12 609	2 216.6	369.1	309	5 558	150.4	40.0
Steele	55	162	10.5	3.6	67	6 292	1 006.9	191.7	65	1 004	26.4	7.0
Stevens	17	131	9.0	4.0	NA	NA	NA	NA	24	D	D	D
Swift	16	58	3.0	1.3	13	829	56.5	19.3	28	219	6.6	1.5
Todd	16	76	3.4	1.4	47	1 519	278.2	46.4	49	D	D	D
Traverse	1	D	D	D	NA	NA	NA	NA	10	D	D	D
Wabasha	29	71	5.1	1.6	39	1 934	368.5	51.3	51	D	D	D
Wadena	14	52	2.4	0.7	21	784	74.4	19.8	22	D	D	D
Waseca	29	103	4.9	1.6	29	3 298	467.1	108.6	32	D	D	D
Washington	443	1 180	135.0	44.3	210	9 456	2 795.0	436.0	296	5 543	165.2	51.0
Watonwan	12	68	3.4	1.0	21	1 102	139.3	22.7	20	D	D	D
Wilkin	9	149	3.4	2.7	NA	NA	NA	NA	19	D	D	D
Winona	71	569	33.2	10.9	116	7 115	1 071.9	196.1	115	1 725	45.7	11.9
Wright	129	693	44.3	17.5	179	4 315	583.6	127.4	130	2 159	54.3	15.1
Yellow Medicine	13	47	4.3	1.1	NA	NA	NA	NA	21	D	D	D

1. Firms subject to federal tax.

Table B. States and Counties — Health Care and Social Assistance, Other Services, and Federal Funds

STATE County	Health care and social assistance,[1] 1997				Other services,[1] 1997				Federal funds and grants, 2002–2003 Expenditures (mil dol)			
										Direct payments for individuals[2]		
	Number of establishments	Number of employees	Receipts (mil dol)	Annual payroll (mil dol)	Number of establishments	Number of employees	Receipts (mil dol)	Annual payroll (mil dol)	Total	Social Security and government retirement	Medicare	Food stamps and Supplemental Security Income
	159	160	161	162	163	164	165	166	167	168	169	170
MINNESOTA—Cont'd												
Grant	13	221	5.3	2.9	11	33	2.3	0.4	53.2	17.8	7.8	0.5
Hennepin	2 292	32 525	2 031.0	1 019.3	1 929	23 352	1 348.6	514.2	7 240.7	1 970.1	918.7	179.6
Houston	17	174	7.5	3.3	33	77	6.5	1.3	96.7	44.0	14.6	1.3
Hubbard	26	238	14.5	5.0	19	48	3.5	0.7	97.9	48.5	18.2	2.0
Isanti	43	519	28.4	13.5	45	166	10.7	2.4	105.8	52.8	18.2	2.0
Itasca	75	855	39.9	18.9	61	216	14.4	3.4	248.7	122.3	40.1	6.3
Jackson	15	462	8.9	5.2	31	87	7.3	1.3	57.9	23.6	10.1	0.8
Kanabec	13	192	8.0	4.8	15	48	2.6	0.6	65.5	32.4	9.4	1.4
Kandiyohi	77	1 519	69.9	41.4	70	266	17.5	4.4	233.3	87.5	30.1	6.8
Kittson	10	157	4.7	1.7	7	18	1.5	0.3	56.5	13.7	6.7	0.4
Koochiching	21	230	9.5	5.0	17	67	4.1	0.8	90.8	42.0	13.4	2.2
Lac qui Parle	15	98	3.5	1.5	19	67	5.5	0.8	50.0	20.0	9.1	0.5
Lake	13	87	2.0	0.6	18	93	5.7	1.5	68.4	36.5	10.6	0.9
Lake of the Woods	5	10	0.6	0.1	7	12	1.1	0.2	26.9	11.3	4.0	0.2
Le Sueur	40	344	12.4	5.4	36	107	8.0	1.6	108.5	57.0	19.4	1.2
Lincoln	8	66	2.7	1.1	9	14	1.0	0.2	44.5	16.0	8.5	0.6
Lyon	50	707	27.0	14.0	56	168	11.9	2.2	121.9	50.6	19.7	2.1
McLeod	68	586	33.4	15.0	64	278	21.8	4.9	126.6	67.2	24.6	1.7
Mahnomen	7	29	1.2	0.4	5	D	D	D	45.3	12.1	4.3	1.1
Marshall	10	81	1.9	0.9	24	74	7.3	0.9	96.5	24.2	12.1	0.8
Martin	47	448	27.8	10.2	37	113	7.8	1.7	115.6	56.0	23.2	2.3
Meeker	23	215	10.2	5.7	19	56	3.1	0.9	95.8	45.9	17.0	1.4
Mille Lacs	28	285	11.7	6.1	38	121	10.1	2.3	133.7	63.0	25.7	2.4
Morrison	40	490	24.1	12.2	48	172	14.5	2.9	185.2	71.5	26.3	3.2
Mower	71	637	26.3	11.7	75	377	19.9	4.7	214.1	100.6	43.7	4.4
Murray	12	176	5.6	3.3	13	27	2.2	0.4	53.5	22.4	9.6	0.6
Nicollet	31	225	12.2	5.7	48	202	10.5	2.8	83.0	39.2	12.9	1.8
Nobles	28	455	21.2	9.5	43	149	8.7	2.1	111.6	46.7	17.6	2.1
Norman	10	42	1.9	0.8	10	37	1.9	0.3	73.0	19.3	8.7	0.9
Olmsted	168	2 241	102.8	50.7	180	1 363	69.8	20.4	639.1	202.8	76.7	13.0
Otter Tail	73	896	41.7	22.6	81	320	18.4	4.2	318.5	144.6	53.3	5.2
Pennington	15	183	12.9	3.8	29	92	5.4	1.5	88.0	29.4	11.3	1.3
Pine	34	587	25.8	10.7	22	51	3.2	0.7	145.3	63.3	20.3	3.0
Pipestone	16	88	4.1	1.8	20	72	4.9	1.0	60.5	23.4	10.5	0.8
Polk	49	475	16.0	7.0	55	237	12.7	3.1	236.9	70.8	32.2	4.9
Pope	15	77	3.6	1.3	24	50	3.7	0.7	66.2	29.0	12.8	1.0
Ramsey	1 030	15 342	939.0	502.5	826	6 378	401.6	124.5	4 264.2	1 153.2	492.0	116.0
Red Lake	2	D	D	D	2	D	D	D	31.3	9.2	4.8	0.3
Redwood	41	587	14.3	6.9	32	64	5.2	1.1	98.1	41.4	15.1	1.3
Renville	26	518	14.4	7.6	32	65	6.5	1.1	106.4	39.0	15.7	1.5
Rice	84	1 398	64.4	35.5	81	331	23.6	6.3	203.1	96.7	31.1	3.8
Rock	10	106	3.6	1.8	22	89	7.1	1.6	52.5	24.3	9.4	0.6
Roseau	19	134	5.5	1.6	17	66	4.2	1.1	92.6	27.2	12.1	1.1
St. Louis	376	5 334	240.6	125.7	327	1 807	124.4	35.9	1 338.6	532.4	197.4	36.8
Scott	99	1 131	53.9	25.5	120	607	51.1	12.6	178.5	97.5	24.0	1.9
Sherburne	77	665	30.5	15.1	59	302	14.8	4.5	148.4	85.3	19.0	2.4
Sibley	15	57	3.2	1.0	27	62	4.4	0.8	67.7	29.0	14.3	0.6
Stearns	238	3 178	239.5	121.3	243	1 493	89.0	24.7	580.4	225.3	77.0	11.1
Steele	46	667	33.2	17.2	55	223	18.0	4.1	130.0	62.9	22.9	2.2
Stevens	15	54	3.7	1.3	25	116	6.0	1.3	63.8	20.7	10.4	0.7
Swift	14	189	6.6	3.3	21	68	6.4	1.3	70.7	26.3	12.6	1.0
Todd	24	150	10.0	4.6	30	68	6.5	1.2	131.7	50.8	19.9	3.0
Traverse	7	55	2.7	1.2	8	14	1.4	0.3	33.2	11.8	5.7	0.5
Wabasha	27	316	15.6	6.0	34	90	6.1	1.3	122.1	49.6	19.0	1.2
Wadena	17	156	9.5	4.5	18	48	3.5	0.7	86.1	36.0	15.2	2.4
Waseca	42	585	18.7	8.5	37	98	6.7	1.2	105.3	36.2	13.1	1.4
Washington	265	3 251	177.8	89.2	219	1 700	99.3	29.4	375.9	198.8	58.5	6.3
Watonwan	20	216	8.9	3.6	17	49	4.5	0.7	64.2	27.8	10.5	0.9
Wilkin	6	52	1.3	0.5	6	8	1.0	0.2	43.9	15.6	5.6	0.7
Winona	71	705	38.2	17.1	67	296	16.9	4.3	196.2	92.5	34.2	4.1
Wright	126	1 244	56.2	26.7	124	482	29.2	7.4	258.7	138.8	45.0	4.6
Yellow Medicine	22	191	6.9	3.4	31	175	10.6	3.0	72.6	28.1	12.8	0.9

1. Firms subject to federal tax.   2. State totals may include programs not allocated by county.

Items 159—170

STATE County	Salaries and wages	Defense	Other	Medicaid and other health-related	Nutrition and family welfare	Education	Other	Total (mil dol)	Intergovernmental (mil dol)	Total (mil dol)	Total	Property
	171	172	173	174	175	176	177	178	179	180	181	182
MINNESOTA—Cont'd												
Grant	1.6	0.0	0.4	6.2	3.5	0.5	6.7	25.2	13.8	6.2	994	972
Hennepin	821.8	1 035.6	402.9	1 046.0	171.1	78.9	488.5	5 060.5	2 058.1	1 614.5	1 439	1 332
Houston	3.8	0.3	0.8	11.3	1.6	1.0	11.9	57.6	36.0	12.0	607	598
Hubbard	2.6	0.0	0.7	18.0	3.4	1.4	1.5	58.2	33.7	16.5	896	878
Isanti	4.5	0.0	1.0	12.4	3.1	1.2	7.9	92.3	53.8	25.3	749	711
Itasca	10.6	0.3	8.6	39.1	11.4	4.2	3.2	183.9	77.5	45.1	1 022	1 016
Jackson	2.2	0.0	0.5	6.2	1.4	0.7	1.7	40.7	19.7	9.7	858	854
Kanabec	2.5	0.0	0.5	9.6	4.5	0.8	2.5	60.2	25.5	8.5	553	543
Kandiyohi	11.8	0.0	12.4	27.9	7.3	2.6	28.5	195.3	66.0	34.7	850	787
Kittson	2.8	0.0	0.8	6.2	0.8	0.5	9.5	23.2	12.8	6.6	1 297	1 295
Koochiching	6.4	0.0	1.8	14.1	3.5	1.2	5.1	52.4	29.1	7.9	565	553
Lac qui Parle	2.6	0.0	0.6	4.5	0.9	0.5	1.5	38.8	20.7	7.1	897	893
Lake	1.8	0.0	0.5	7.3	1.5	0.6	8.4	51.0	26.6	9.9	897	868
Lake of the Woods	1.3	0.0	0.2	5.1	0.6	0.3	1.2	19.8	11.0	3.0	689	675
Le Sueur	4.2	0.0	1.1	14.1	2.2	1.5	2.1	75.6	43.1	18.2	700	687
Lincoln	1.7	0.0	0.4	6.2	0.5	1.0	0.9	19.3	11.4	5.2	833	830
Lyon	7.8	0.0	1.9	13.5	5.4	2.3	6.0	112.5	43.4	20.8	827	799
McLeod	5.3	0.1	2.5	10.1	2.1	1.7	2.8	168.2	59.0	26.7	755	733
Mahnomen	1.2	0.2	0.4	9.0	2.0	3.1	4.7	29.4	18.6	4.0	777	773
Marshall	4.2	0.2	0.9	10.1	1.5	1.9	8.9	39.5	24.7	8.4	849	846
Martin	4.5	0.4	1.0	9.0	4.5	1.7	2.9	65.8	31.6	17.8	838	825
Meeker	4.6	0.1	0.9	10.7	2.8	1.3	2.4	97.3	52.1	17.0	744	731
Mille Lacs	4.1	0.0	2.4	20.0	4.7	2.3	4.5	84.4	53.9	19.5	827	808
Morrison	20.1	3.2	1.6	28.7	7.8	2.8	7.1	90.4	56.0	19.2	593	582
Mower	8.7	3.3	1.6	26.4	4.7	2.4	5.3	132.2	69.1	21.3	550	539
Murray	2.5	0.0	0.6	5.6	0.6	0.6	1.2	34.9	18.3	7.0	778	773
Nicollet	3.3	0.1	0.6	7.9	1.9	1.2	2.5	87.5	40.1	18.1	597	580
Nobles	5.9	0.0	1.0	15.2	3.3	1.5	5.9	87.3	40.0	14.9	728	718
Norman	2.4	0.1	0.7	6.8	1.0	0.6	9.5	38.2	19.0	8.6	1 178	1 163
Olmsted	58.4	8.1	16.8	196.4	9.9	6.8	37.5	459.9	205.9	112.1	869	750
Otter Tail	14.0	0.1	5.8	47.3	7.6	3.2	8.2	178.6	89.6	39.6	683	671
Pennington	4.6	0.0	0.7	18.6	2.5	1.2	5.1	50.6	28.7	10.9	810	795
Pine	19.9	0.2	1.8	22.5	4.2	1.9	4.6	78.5	48.8	17.4	635	620
Pipestone	3.5	0.0	0.7	9.6	1.5	0.8	2.9	47.0	20.6	9.3	957	938
Polk	7.8	18.4	6.0	31.2	11.9	2.9	13.5	159.3	96.5	25.1	805	776
Pope	2.2	0.2	0.6	7.3	1.5	0.7	1.3	46.7	19.4	9.9	881	697
Ramsey	333.0	326.1	163.2	481.3	286.2	214.1	604.5	2 884.2	1 356.4	682.5	1 337	1 230
Red Lake	1.2	0.0	0.3	3.9	2.3	0.4	2.6	16.4	10.4	3.3	763	758
Redwood	4.6	0.0	1.0	13.5	1.7	1.2	4.8	71.1	33.5	14.0	863	849
Renville	4.2	0.0	1.6	13.0	1.7	1.5	9.0	66.9	28.7	15.3	895	882
Rice	9.3	1.0	2.2	31.3	4.1	3.8	8.5	205.7	74.1	36.9	630	597
Rock	2.1	0.0	0.4	3.9	0.9	0.7	2.8	35.8	20.0	7.4	758	719
Roseau	4.0	0.0	1.0	11.8	3.2	1.0	11.1	71.2	34.1	9.6	594	586
St. Louis	149.5	15.6	29.6	198.4	48.8	17.2	88.5	862.8	416.6	173.4	867	772
Scott	16.7	0.3	6.2	9.0	6.1	3.1	5.3	264.6	113.1	89.4	862	789
Sherburne	13.7	0.2	1.9	11.3	3.5	2.3	5.8	227.1	98.2	80.8	1 130	1 095
Sibley	2.7	0.0	1.6	6.2	1.2	0.8	0.6	54.8	26.0	11.8	765	755
Stearns	80.3	1.2	23.1	61.5	14.4	10.9	29.0	467.4	238.3	117.6	866	798
Steele	4.7	3.8	7.5	10.7	2.2	1.6	3.5	101.2	55.7	24.3	707	688
Stevens	5.0	0.4	2.9	7.9	1.1	0.8	3.6	31.3	19.8	7.1	717	713
Swift	4.1	0.2	1.0	9.6	1.6	0.8	3.4	52.8	29.4	5.8	499	493
Todd	4.9	0.0	1.1	28.2	4.5	2.2	7.9	77.7	51.8	15.0	614	589
Traverse	1.1	0.0	0.4	2.8	0.7	0.5	1.6	26.0	10.6	4.3	1 088	954
Wabasha	4.1	1.0	22.6	10.7	1.8	1.3	1.9	67.6	39.0	14.6	667	649
Wadena	3.2	0.1	0.7	20.4	2.6	1.1	1.5	52.5	32.3	8.8	645	635
Waseca	16.5	8.0	8.5	7.9	1.9	1.3	3.1	67.6	37.2	16.1	830	797
Washington	18.8	1.1	4.5	24.5	9.1	6.6	45.4	610.0	254.9	214.0	1 018	964
Watonwan	3.5	0.0	10.5	2.8	0.7	0.8	0.5	40.8	25.0	9.2	786	777
Wilkin	1.8	1.3	0.5	5.1	1.0	0.7	2.5	29.3	17.4	5.8	826	818
Winona	8.2	2.3	3.4	22.9	4.4	2.7	4.1	124.8	68.0	30.6	619	583
Wright	14.0	1.0	3.6	23.2	7.3	4.2	9.5	323.9	139.2	88.9	906	862
Yellow Medicine	2.7	0.0	1.2	9.6	1.5	0.8	2.5	55.2	25.1	10.1	931	921

1. State totals may include programs not allocated by county.   2. Based on the resident population estimated as of July 1 of the year shown.

Table B. States and Counties — Local Government Finances, Government Employment, and Elections

STATE County	Direct general expenditure Total (mil dol)	Per capita¹ (dollars)	Education	Health and hospitals	Police protection	Public welfare	Highways	Debt outstanding Total (mil dol)	Per capita¹ (dollars)	Federal civilian	Federal military	State and local	Democratic	Republican	All other
	183	184	185	186	187	188	189	190	191	192	193	194	195	196	197
MINNESOTA—Cont'd															
Grant	28.3	4 517	46.8	2.3	3.1	7.7	19.6	24.0	3 835	32	21	379	48.7	49.6	1.7
Hennepin	4 872.3	4 341	35.0	13.0	5.3	7.6	5.6	6 308.9	5 622	12 489	4 481	82 868	59.4	39.5	1.1
Houston	75.6	3 811	59.3	2.0	2.6	5.0	11.9	47.9	2 415	82	68	1 052	47.4	50.6	1.9
Hubbard	71.5	3 881	59.2	0.1	3.2	7.2	12.3	75.2	4 081	43	63	1 077	41.8	56.9	1.3
Isanti	89.4	2 646	47.6	1.1	5.8	10.3	10.6	86.7	2 566	76	116	1 802	39.2	57.5	3.3
Itasca	193.9	4 392	38.1	12.5	2.9	11.1	11.5	184.9	4 188	211	151	3 248	54.6	44.0	1.5
Jackson	41.2	3 656	33.4	3.7	3.2	18.7	15.4	38.9	3 449	39	39	914	45.9	52.4	1.8
Kanabec	58.8	3 807	34.1	34.7	3.9	6.3	6.1	48.0	3 105	47	53	1 000	43.6	54.9	1.5
Kandiyohi	194.0	4 752	24.1	29.4	2.9	8.2	6.8	176.5	4 322	188	141	4 164	43.8	54.9	1.4
Kittson	23.5	4 637	45.6	0.2	2.5	3.2	22.0	8.8	1 730	65	17	355	49.8	48.8	1.4
Koochiching	54.5	3 897	36.9	2.0	4.9	14.7	15.2	49.0	3 509	151	48	956	50.5	48.1	1.3
Lac qui Parle	38.9	4 903	41.5	17.5	2.7	4.6	15.2	16.7	2 112	46	27	714	52.6	46.1	1.3
Lake	52.5	4 733	30.1	0.8	5.2	12.1	20.8	56.4	5 082	42	38	912	59.6	39.2	1.2
Lake of the Woods	19.1	4 345	32.5	0.4	4.0	4.7	19.0	332.7	75 881	29	19	273	38.5	59.6	1.9
Le Sueur	72.8	2 800	46.8	2.1	3.9	7.5	13.3	56.8	2 183	72	89	1 369	44.9	53.8	1.4
Lincoln	19.2	3 079	39.9	0.1	9.7	0.0	23.6	11.8	1 893	38	21	341	46.6	52.0	1.3
Lyon	123.7	4 924	34.4	23.2	3.5	1.4	9.7	108.4	4 316	136	86	2 711	41.8	56.9	1.3
McLeod	175.4	4 954	23.9	34.3	3.7	7.5	10.5	115.7	3 267	90	121	2 441	36.5	62.0	1.5
Mahnomen	29.8	5 787	49.8	14.5	4.5	9.7	8.1	5.1	994	27	18	1 606	53.4	45.2	1.4
Marshall	40.2	4 062	39.6	0.3	3.1	6.1	23.5	11.5	1 156	78	34	649	41.5	57.3	1.1
Martin	60.8	2 865	50.5	0.1	6.3	2.9	16.2	41.5	1 956	75	73	1 383	41.6	57.2	1.3
Meeker	101.3	4 426	47.1	13.9	3.4	8.2	7.7	88.5	3 868	82	78	1 295	42.9	55.6	1.5
Mille Lacs	79.7	3 372	59.0	0.9	3.2	8.3	9.0	77.8	3 291	65	81	2 666	43.4	55.1	1.5
Morrison	86.4	2 669	49.4	1.5	3.1	9.4	12.6	63.9	1 975	404	111	1 643	40.5	57.9	1.6
Mower	140.8	3 631	40.6	1.3	3.2	10.2	11.8	1 186.5	30 592	146	133	2 385	61.0	37.6	1.4
Murray	34.1	3 786	31.5	13.4	3.6	0.0	17.8	15.4	1 707	52	31	540	44.4	54.5	1.1
Nicollet	90.8	2 999	19.7	14.3	4.2	3.3	14.7	62.0	2 049	57	104	2 364	49.6	49.0	1.3
Nobles	89.7	4 387	34.2	22.7	3.4	6.9	10.9	61.9	3 027	112	70	1 757	42.4	56.1	1.4
Norman	37.4	5 115	32.9	21.4	2.4	5.1	14.5	18.0	2 466	49	25	574	51.4	47.2	1.4
Olmsted	474.3	3 678	39.8	1.4	3.7	9.3	7.5	1 422.0	11 026	876	446	6 977	46.6	52.3	1.2
Otter Tail	166.7	2 872	38.2	8.5	4.3	9.0	12.1	154.2	2 657	246	199	3 366	37.5	61.4	1.2
Pennington	46.4	3 436	41.3	0.1	6.0	14.1	12.0	29.8	2 203	81	46	1 543	44.4	53.7	1.8
Pine	83.3	3 048	45.9	1.6	3.5	9.4	19.8	64.4	2 355	312	94	3 782	49.5	48.9	1.6
Pipestone	53.9	5 521	46.0	21.4	2.2	4.2	8.4	36.1	3 697	61	33	815	37.8	60.9	1.3
Polk	133.5	4 289	35.5	1.7	3.9	11.3	10.5	112.8	3 627	135	106	2 651	43.0	55.8	1.2
Pope	42.2	3 769	31.6	26.5	4.1	3.2	11.8	20.3	1 818	48	38	716	49.3	49.3	1.4
Ramsey	2 928.0	5 735	30.4	1.4	3.5	6.4	3.3	4 454.9	8 725	4 648	1 881	51 294	63.3	35.4	1.2
Red Lake	16.9	3 930	41.1	0.4	5.0	6.7	22.2	10.2	2 369	27	15	282	44.3	53.5	2.2
Redwood	68.5	4 206	36.0	15.5	2.9	14.4	12.1	61.8	3 798	79	56	2 269	38.2	60.2	1.6
Renville	69.3	4 061	27.1	10.1	3.4	13.2	17.0	55.9	3 278	77	58	1 172	45.4	53.1	1.5
Rice	207.0	3 534	33.0	25.4	3.8	4.2	8.6	244.4	4 171	148	201	3 962	53.5	45.2	1.4
Rock	32.0	3 265	39.9	0.2	3.7	7.0	22.2	40.1	4 098	41	34	696	38.5	60.0	1.5
Roseau	69.0	4 249	40.0	24.7	2.7	3.7	10.8	57.0	3 514	82	56	1 141	30.9	67.7	1.4
St. Louis	826.9	4 135	30.2	6.2	4.4	11.8	9.7	608.9	3 045	1 981	808	17 283	65.2	33.6	1.2
Scott	305.8	2 950	49.7	0.4	3.7	4.7	11.0	416.4	4 016	264	355	8 462	39.5	59.5	1.0
Sherburne	273.3	3 824	63.6	0.5	3.0	3.9	4.6	438.9	6 141	190	245	3 211	38.2	60.8	1.0
Sibley	51.7	3 362	32.9	12.3	4.1	12.5	14.4	39.0	2 532	50	53	898	39.1	58.8	2.1
Stearns	465.6	3 427	43.9	3.5	4.1	6.0	11.8	715.7	5 267	1 429	472	9 599	43.7	54.8	1.5
Steele	106.9	3 107	50.3	0.9	4.5	5.5	10.7	87.4	2 540	82	118	1 855	42.8	55.6	1.6
Stevens	30.5	3 090	38.6	2.6	4.3	9.1	19.7	18.4	1 865	91	35	1 323	47.5	51.0	1.5
Swift	46.4	3 996	29.1	17.5	4.5	13.3	14.1	25.6	2 207	62	40	923	55.2	43.3	1.5
Todd	75.4	3 082	48.0	3.4	3.7	9.5	14.1	38.4	1 569	86	84	1 408	41.2	56.9	1.8
Traverse	26.1	6 606	24.7	16.8	2.8	13.5	18.6	9.1	2 305	31	14	438	47.9	50.3	1.8
Wabasha	69.9	3 190	39.9	2.1	4.0	5.0	13.5	52.2	2 383	68	75	1 063	46.9	51.7	1.4
Wadena	52.8	3 885	46.4	2.1	3.6	16.9	9.2	40.9	3 013	55	47	1 343	39.4	59.5	1.1
Waseca	66.5	3 422	47.3	0.7	4.8	13.5	12.0	50.6	2 605	274	67	1 207	42.7	55.8	1.5
Washington	661.3	3 145	51.1	1.9	5.4	4.9	9.2	750.9	3 571	245	720	9 047	47.8	51.2	0.9
Watonwan	47.7	4 088	46.7	1.1	3.6	7.9	13.7	28.4	2 436	62	40	761	45.1	53.3	1.6
Wilkin	29.0	4 155	38.0	2.3	4.7	7.4	18.0	24.2	3 475	36	24	404	33.2	65.3	1.5
Winona	121.3	2 458	40.1	2.0	5.7	8.0	11.4	108.5	2 199	148	169	3 394	52.4	46.5	1.1
Wright	352.1	3 590	51.3	8.4	3.3	4.2	7.3	548.6	5 593	198	336	4 851	38.0	60.9	1.1
Yellow Medicine	59.8	5 535	30.4	17.9	2.2	9.6	14.0	33.9	3 139	55	37	1 555	48.7	50.1	1.3

1. Based on the resident population estimated as of July 1 of the year shown.

MN(Grant)—MN(Yellow Medicine) 379

Table B. States and Counties — Land Area and Population

STATE/ County code	CBSA code[1]	County Type[2]	STATE County	Land area[3] (sq km) 2000	Total persons	Rank	Per square kilometer	White	Black	Am. Indian, Alaska Native	Asian and Pacific Islander	Percent Hispanic or Latino[4]	Under 5 years	5 to 17 years	18 to 24 years	25 to 34 years	35 to 44 years	45 to 54 years
				1	2	3	4	5	6	7	8	9	10	11	12	13	14	15
28 000	...	X	MISSISSIPPI	121 488	2 881 281	X	23.7	60.4	37.0	0.7	1.0	1.5	7.3	19.1	11.2	13.3	14.1	13.4
28 001	35020	5	Adams	1 192	33 233	1 323	27.9	44.2	54.6	0.4	0.4	0.9	6.8	18.7	9.5	10.5	13.8	15.1
28 003	18420	7	Alcorn	1 036	34 930	1 276	33.7	86.8	11.5	0.4	0.4	1.5	6.7	16.8	9.2	12.8	14.2	13.8
28 005	32620	8	Amite	1 890	13 594	2 191	7.2	56.1	42.5	0.3	0.2	1.2	6.4	18.0	9.9	10.8	13.6	14.2
28 007	...	6	Attala	1 904	19 673	1 825	10.3	57.6	40.3	0.3	0.3	1.7	6.9	18.2	9.9	11.9	12.9	13.0
28 009	...	8	Benton	1 054	7 774	2 615	7.4	63.1	35.5	0.6	0.1	0.9	7.2	18.7	10.0	12.0	13.7	12.3
28 011	17380	5	Bolivar	2 270	39 235	1 146	17.3	32.2	66.2	0.2	0.6	1.1	7.9	20.5	14.5	12.7	12.6	12.6
28 013	...	7	Calhoun	1 519	14 827	2 114	9.8	67.5	29.4	0.4	0.1	3.0	7.1	17.5	9.2	12.4	13.6	13.6
28 015	24900	9	Carroll	1 626	10 462	2 403	6.4	64.1	34.6	0.1	0.2	1.0	5.3	17.1	10.6	11.1	14.7	15.2
28 017	...	7	Chickasaw	1 299	19 204	1 850	14.8	55.3	41.8	0.3	0.4	2.5	7.9	20.3	9.5	12.3	14.5	12.9
28 019	...	9	Choctaw	1 085	9 661	2 473	8.9	67.6	30.9	0.4	0.2	0.9	5.9	19.6	10.0	10.8	14.0	14.0
28 021	...	6	Claiborne	1 261	11 502	2 333	9.1	14.5	84.5	0.1	0.3	0.9	7.3	18.6	22.4	10.5	11.9	12.1
28 023	32940	9	Clarke	1 790	17 746	1 928	9.9	64.7	34.5	0.1	0.1	0.7	6.9	18.7	9.4	11.6	14.1	13.8
28 025	...	7	Clay	1 058	21 625	1 721	20.4	41.2	57.8	0.2	0.5	1.1	7.6	20.0	11.0	11.9	13.6	14.3
28 027	17260	5	Coahoma	1 435	29 546	1 416	20.6	26.3	72.4	0.2	0.6	0.9	9.4	23.2	11.5	11.1	13.2	12.6
28 029	27140	2	Copiah	2 011	28 928	1 433	14.4	47.6	51.0	0.2	0.2	1.3	7.2	18.8	13.2	11.2	14.0	13.6
28 031	...	8	Covington	1 072	20 177	1 795	18.8	63.2	35.8	0.3	0.1	0.8	7.6	20.2	10.6	12.4	13.6	12.2
28 033	32820	1	De Soto	1 238	124 378	456	100.5	81.0	15.2	0.6	1.2	2.7	7.4	20.1	9.5	15.0	15.5	13.9
28 035	25620	3	Forrest	1 208	74 386	689	61.6	62.9	34.8	0.5	1.1	1.4	7.0	17.1	16.1	15.1	12.8	11.1
28 037	...	9	Franklin	1 462	8 340	2 573	5.7	63.3	35.9	0.4	0.1	0.6	6.9	18.2	10.6	10.4	14.3	14.2
28 039	37700	3	George	1 239	20 407	1 780	16.5	88.4	9.0	0.6	0.3	2.1	8.1	20.3	10.5	13.6	14.4	11.8
28 041	...	8	Greene	1 846	13 169	2 225	7.1	72.9	25.9	0.4	0.2	0.8	6.0	16.7	13.2	16.6	15.4	12.6
28 043	24980	7	Grenada	1 092	22 809	1 673	20.9	57.1	41.6	0.3	0.5	0.6	6.4	19.8	9.6	12.3	14.4	13.5
28 045	25060	3	Hancock	1 235	45 145	1 020	36.6	90.1	6.7	1.2	1.1	1.9	6.1	18.0	8.6	11.8	14.9	14.2
28 047	25060	3	Harrison	1 505	189 614	302	126.0	71.4	23.1	1.0	3.8	2.4	7.5	18.5	10.7	14.2	15.5	13.3
28 049	27140	2	Hinds	2 251	249 087	239	110.7	34.9	63.9	0.4	0.9	0.8	7.7	19.6	11.7	13.8	14.2	13.7
28 051	...	6	Holmes	1 958	21 347	1 735	10.9	18.6	80.4	0.2	0.3	0.8	8.7	22.2	13.8	11.4	12.9	11.3
28 053	...	7	Humphreys	1 083	10 722	2 384	9.9	25.3	72.5	0.2	0.3	1.8	9.6	22.2	11.9	11.5	13.1	12.6
28 055	...	9	Issaquena	1 070	2 016	3 059	1.9	35.1	64.4	0.1	0.0	0.5	5.1	20.1	11.8	13.6	17.5	12.0
28 057	46180	7	Itawamba	1 379	22 964	1 666	16.7	92.1	6.5	0.3	0.3	1.0	6.0	17.6	11.3	13.0	14.1	13.1
28 059	37700	3	Jackson	1 883	133 928	421	71.1	73.7	22.2	0.7	2.4	2.1	7.0	19.5	10.0	12.9	15.5	13.9
28 061	29860	9	Jasper	1 751	18 280	1 890	10.4	45.8	53.3	0.2	0.1	0.9	7.4	19.4	10.5	12.1	13.6	13.3
28 063	...	7	Jefferson	1 345	9 533	2 483	7.1	12.4	86.7	0.1	0.1	0.7	7.3	19.9	12.9	12.2	15.6	13.2
28 065	...	8	Jefferson Davis	1 058	13 399	2 204	12.7	40.6	58.2	0.2	0.3	0.9	6.8	20.0	10.4	11.8	13.1	13.6
28 067	29860	4	Jones	1 797	65 168	760	36.3	69.5	27.0	0.6	0.4	2.9	7.5	17.6	11.0	12.5	13.9	13.5
28 069	32940	9	Kemper	1 984	10 435	2 408	5.3	38.4	58.6	2.1	0.2	0.9	6.4	17.6	13.0	12.3	13.2	10.4
28 071	37060	6	Lafayette	1 635	40 188	1 132	24.6	71.5	25.4	0.4	2.1	1.2	5.5	13.5	23.0	15.5	11.9	10.4
28 073	25620	3	Lamar	1 287	41 957	1 082	32.6	84.7	13.4	0.5	0.8	1.1	7.3	19.6	11.0	14.3	15.0	13.4
28 075	32940	5	Lauderdale	1 822	77 706	669	42.6	58.4	39.9	0.4	0.9	1.1	7.5	18.6	10.3	13.2	14.0	13.3
28 077	...	8	Lawrence	1 115	13 520	2 197	12.1	67.0	31.8	0.2	0.4	0.7	7.3	18.8	10.6	11.8	14.4	13.8
28 079	...	6	Leake	1 509	21 820	1 711	14.5	54.2	38.4	4.6	0.3	2.7	7.8	20.4	10.4	12.8	12.9	12.7
28 081	46180	5	Lee	1 164	77 690	670	66.7	72.4	26.1	0.4	0.8	1.2	7.8	19.5	9.1	13.4	15.4	13.5
28 083	24900	7	Leflore	1 533	36 470	1 226	23.8	28.0	69.4	0.2	0.7	2.0	7.7	21.2	13.6	13.1	12.9	12.2
28 085	15020	6	Lincoln	1 517	33 549	1 314	22.1	68.4	30.4	0.3	0.3	0.7	7.0	18.5	10.1	12.9	14.2	13.8
28 087	18060	5	Lowndes	1 301	60 658	813	46.6	55.1	43.1	0.6	1.0	1.1	7.6	20.1	10.4	13.6	14.8	13.2
28 089	27140	2	Madison	1 857	79 758	653	42.9	59.9	37.4	0.3	1.9	1.1	7.9	20.0	9.5	14.1	16.3	13.6
28 091	...	6	Marion	1 405	25 090	1 565	17.9	66.7	32.2	0.6	0.3	0.7	6.9	19.8	10.1	12.0	13.8	13.8
28 093	32820	1	Marshall	1 829	35 442	1 259	19.4	48.2	50.4	0.5	0.2	1.3	7.3	18.7	12.3	12.7	14.7	13.3
28 095	...	7	Monroe	1 979	37 842	1 187	19.1	68.2	30.9	0.3	0.2	0.8	6.7	19.1	9.8	12.5	14.1	13.4
28 097	...	7	Montgomery	1 054	11 935	2 296	11.3	53.4	45.3	0.2	0.3	1.0	6.4	19.3	9.8	10.3	13.6	13.7
28 099	...	7	Neshoba	1 476	29 134	1 430	19.7	64.0	20.4	14.9	0.4	1.2	8.2	19.7	10.0	12.4	13.5	13.1
28 101	...	7	Newton	1 497	22 044	1 701	14.7	65.0	30.1	3.9	0.2	0.9	7.2	18.4	11.5	12.3	12.5	13.0
28 103	...	7	Noxubee	1 799	12 318	2 277	6.8	28.3	70.2	0.2	0.2	1.3	8.5	21.4	10.8	11.6	13.6	13.0
28 105	44260	5	Oktibbeha	1 185	42 573	1 067	35.9	58.3	37.9	0.3	3.0	1.0	6.2	14.1	23.5	16.2	10.9	10.1
28 107	...	6	Panola	1 772	35 243	1 263	19.9	50.3	48.4	0.3	0.2	1.1	8.4	20.3	10.9	12.5	13.9	12.7
28 109	38100	6	Pearl River	2 101	50 894	924	24.2	85.4	12.3	1.1	0.6	1.6	6.6	19.0	10.3	12.1	14.2	13.6
28 111	25620	3	Perry	1 676	12 288	2 279	7.3	76.3	22.3	0.5	0.2	1.0	7.0	19.6	10.8	12.9	14.3	13.6
28 113	32620	7	Pike	1 059	38 935	1 163	36.8	50.0	48.7	0.4	0.6	0.7	7.9	19.0	10.8	11.6	13.5	13.7
28 115	46180	7	Pontotoc	1 288	27 575	1 482	21.4	83.0	14.4	0.4	0.2	2.3	6.8	19.6	9.7	12.9	15.0	13.3
28 117	...	7	Prentiss	1 075	25 581	1 549	23.8	85.6	13.5	0.5	0.2	0.7	6.2	17.7	11.8	12.7	13.7	12.8
28 119	...	6	Quitman	1 049	9 740	2 465	9.3	29.3	69.8	0.2	0.2	0.6	8.4	22.7	10.0	12.6	13.3	12.0
28 121	27140	2	Rankin	2 006	124 695	453	62.2	79.4	18.2	0.4	1.2	1.4	6.8	18.0	10.0	14.9	15.9	14.0
28 123	...	6	Scott	1 578	28 450	1 443	18.0	54.4	39.5	0.5	0.3	5.9	7.5	20.1	10.0	12.8	14.0	13.3
28 125	...	9	Sharkey	1 108	6 224	2 752	5.6	29.2	68.9	0.2	0.4	1.4	8.7	22.7	11.3	10.9	13.1	14.3
28 127	27140	2	Simpson	1 525	27 592	1 479	18.1	63.7	34.7	0.3	0.2	1.5	7.1	19.8	9.5	12.4	14.4	13.6
28 129	...	8	Smith	1 647	15 834	2 046	9.6	76.2	22.9	0.1	0.1	0.8	6.7	19.5	9.7	12.4	14.0	13.6
28 131	25060	3	Stone	1 153	14 206	2 150	12.3	78.3	19.9	0.6	0.3	1.4	7.0	18.8	12.9	12.6	14.2	13.5

1. CBSA = Core Based Statistical Area. See Appendix A for explanation. See Appendix B for list of metropolitan areas with component counties. 2. County type code from the Economic Research Service of USDA Rural-Urban Continuum Codes. See Appendix A for definition. 3. Dry land or land partially or temporarily covered by water. 4. Hispanic or Latino persons may be of any race.

Table B. States and Counties — Population and Households

STATE County	Population, 2003 (cont'd) Age (percent) (cont'd) 55 to 64 years	65 to 74 years	75 years and over	Percent female	Population — change and components of change, 1990–2003 Total persons 1990	2000	Percent change 1990–2000	2000–2003	Components of change, 2000–2003 Births	Deaths	Net migration	Households, 2000 Number	Percent change, 1990–2000	Persons per household	Percent Female family householder[1]	One person
	16	17	18	19	20	21	22	23	24	25	26	27	28	29	30	31
MISSISSIPPI	9.5	6.5	5.7	51.5	2 575 475	2 844 658	10.5	1.3	141 826	92 710	-11 761	1 046 434	14.8	2.63	17.3	24.6
Adams	10.0	8.5	7.4	53.7	35 356	34 340	-2.9	-3.2	1 538	1 415	-1 239	13 677	3.1	2.48	21.5	28.0
Alcorn	11.2	7.9	7.0	51.5	31 722	34 558	8.9	1.1	1 573	1 398	238	14 224	14.3	2.39	11.5	27.6
Amite	11.3	8.0	7.6	51.6	13 328	13 599	2.0	0.0	587	475	-99	5 271	9.1	2.58	16.3	24.5
Attala	10.4	8.6	8.3	52.3	18 481	19 661	6.4	0.1	931	861	-37	7 567	9.0	2.55	16.7	26.4
Benton	10.6	8.5	7.3	51.3	8 046	8 026	-0.2	-3.1	383	332	-304	2 999	5.5	2.64	14.8	23.8
Bolivar	8.4	5.3	5.5	53.3	41 875	40 633	-3.0	-3.4	2 203	1 458	-2 178	13 776	3.6	2.79	27.3	25.3
Calhoun	10.6	8.1	8.5	52.1	14 908	15 069	1.1	-1.6	724	640	-318	6 019	6.3	2.46	15.4	27.1
Carroll	12.1	7.4	6.6	50.4	9 237	10 769	16.6	-2.9	365	313	-340	4 071	21.4	2.57	15.2	22.4
Chickasaw	9.5	6.9	6.6	51.9	18 085	19 440	7.5	-1.2	1 058	745	-534	7 253	11.9	2.65	18.0	24.9
Choctaw	10.3	8.0	7.5	51.9	9 071	9 758	7.6	-1.0	338	341	-86	3 686	14.6	2.56	14.6	25.0
Claiborne	7.5	5.0	5.3	53.2	11 370	11 831	4.1	-2.8	604	385	-545	3 685	10.3	2.72	26.9	28.0
Clarke	10.3	8.1	7.2	52.2	17 313	17 955	3.7	-1.2	847	648	-401	6 978	10.2	2.55	15.9	25.5
Clay	8.8	6.7	6.6	52.8	21 120	21 979	4.1	-1.6	1 112	775	-690	8 152	12.4	2.64	22.4	25.5
Coahoma	7.9	6.0	6.0	53.7	31 665	30 622	-3.3	-3.5	2 006	1 112	-1 994	10 553	0.2	2.83	28.7	26.2
Copiah	9.0	6.6	5.9	51.9	27 592	28 757	4.2	0.6	1 462	977	-292	10 142	9.0	2.71	20.1	23.6
Covington	9.5	6.8	6.0	52.4	16 527	19 407	17.4	4.0	1 040	709	449	7 126	23.2	2.68	17.2	23.6
De Soto	8.6	5.3	3.4	50.3	67 910	107 199	57.9	16.0	5 765	2 591	13 654	38 792	66.7	2.75	11.6	18.1
Forrest	7.7	5.8	5.5	52.7	68 314	72 604	6.3	2.5	3 544	2 340	678	27 183	8.1	2.47	17.2	28.5
Franklin	10.0	7.6	7.3	52.1	8 377	8 448	0.8	-1.3	385	332	-152	3 211	4.1	2.60	14.6	25.6
George	9.9	6.0	4.5	49.3	16 673	19 144	14.8	6.6	1 082	653	828	6 742	16.7	2.78	10.4	19.1
Greene	9.2	5.7	4.5	42.7	10 220	13 299	30.1	-1.0	478	388	-210	4 148	24.7	2.67	11.9	22.0
Grenada	9.8	7.4	7.0	53.1	21 555	23 263	7.9	-2.0	987	1 007	-422	8 820	14.5	2.58	18.6	25.3
Hancock	11.5	8.0	6.0	50.4	31 760	42 967	35.3	5.1	1 752	1 450	1 846	16 897	43.0	2.52	11.3	24.7
Harrison	8.9	6.6	4.9	50.3	165 365	189 601	14.7	0.0	9 457	5 726	-3 637	71 538	20.1	2.55	15.1	25.8
Hinds	8.2	5.5	5.4	52.8	254 441	250 800	-1.4	-0.7	13 173	6 784	-7 980	91 030	0.0	2.64	22.7	26.7
Holmes	7.9	6.0	6.1	52.8	21 604	21 609	0.0	-1.2	1 350	806	-795	7 314	2.5	2.86	31.2	26.3
Humphreys	8.1	5.6	6.2	53.6	12 134	11 206	-7.6	-4.3	761	375	-885	3 765	-4.1	2.95	27.7	24.9
Issaquena	11.3	6.6	5.1	47.5	1 909	2 274	19.1	-11.3	71	43	-286	726	14.7	2.77	16.0	26.2
Itawamba	11.2	7.6	6.2	51.4	20 017	22 770	13.8	0.9	865	972	313	8 773	17.0	2.51	9.9	23.4
Jackson	10.0	6.4	4.3	50.3	115 243	131 420	14.0	1.9	6 208	3 737	156	47 676	17.9	2.72	14.5	20.8
Jasper	9.7	7.1	6.5	52.0	17 114	18 149	6.0	0.7	963	613	-210	6 708	12.6	2.68	18.2	24.2
Jefferson	8.2	5.8	5.2	50.3	8 653	9 740	12.6	-2.1	469	295	-374	3 308	17.6	2.75	28.5	27.1
Jefferson Davis	10.4	7.1	6.9	52.6	14 051	13 962	-0.6	-4.0	594	480	-670	5 177	8.1	2.68	21.6	25.0
Jones	9.5	7.7	6.5	51.4	62 031	64 958	4.7	0.3	3 369	2 310	-815	24 275	7.9	2.61	15.1	24.4
Kemper	9.5	7.2	7.6	50.7	10 356	10 453	0.9	-0.2	455	369	-97	3 909	7.8	2.57	20.2	26.4
Lafayette	7.1	5.2	4.6	50.7	31 826	38 744	21.7	3.7	1 480	966	970	14 373	29.6	2.36	11.4	29.1
Lamar	8.5	5.4	4.0	51.6	30 424	39 070	28.4	7.4	2 003	934	1 799	14 396	32.3	2.68	11.5	20.4
Lauderdale	8.9	7.0	7.2	52.2	75 555	78 161	3.4	-0.6	3 987	3 099	-1 306	29 990	6.2	2.49	18.3	28.0
Lawrence	9.9	7.4	5.7	51.9	12 458	13 258	6.4	2.0	650	478	102	5 040	11.9	2.61	14.4	24.1
Leake	8.9	7.4	6.5	50.1	18 436	20 940	13.6	4.2	1 183	761	461	7 611	12.1	2.65	16.5	24.3
Lee	9.4	6.1	5.3	51.7	65 579	75 755	15.5	2.6	4 063	2 427	373	29 200	19.4	2.55	14.6	25.0
Leflore	7.9	5.6	6.2	52.1	37 341	37 947	1.6	-3.9	2 035	1 340	-2 228	12 956	1.6	2.70	27.6	28.2
Lincoln	9.6	7.3	6.3	52.0	30 278	33 166	9.5	1.2	1 489	1 353	291	12 538	13.1	2.59	14.7	24.4
Lowndes	8.6	6.1	5.5	52.6	59 308	61 586	3.8	-1.5	3 093	1 709	-2 343	22 849	6.8	2.61	18.7	24.6
Madison	7.3	5.1	4.7	52.3	53 794	74 674	38.8	6.8	4 226	2 788	3 765	27 219	41.2	2.67	15.6	25.0
Marion	9.3	7.5	6.8	51.6	25 544	25 595	0.2	-2.0	1 173	1 063	-613	9 336	2.5	2.64	15.6	24.2
Marshall	9.5	6.3	4.8	50.8	30 361	34 993	15.3	1.3	1 773	1 094	-198	12 163	20.7	2.74	20.1	22.0
Monroe	10.1	7.2	7.1	52.6	36 582	38 014	3.9	-0.5	1 692	1 284	-533	14 603	9.4	2.57	17.2	24.7
Montgomery	10.2	8.5	8.5	53.0	12 387	12 189	-1.6	-2.1	527	404	-372	4 690	3.5	2.57	18.8	26.1
Neshoba	9.1	6.9	6.5	52.0	24 800	28 684	15.7	1.6	1 594	1 153	24	10 694	20.9	2.63	15.6	24.7
Newton	9.6	7.7	7.2	51.9	20 291	21 838	7.6	0.9	1 088	783	-82	8 221	11.7	2.57	16.0	24.6
Noxubee	8.3	6.5	6.4	52.4	12 604	12 548	-0.4	-1.8	744	374	-602	4 470	8.0	2.77	24.7	25.9
Oktibbeha	6.8	4.8	4.1	49.6	38 375	42 902	11.8	-0.8	1 853	831	-1 363	15 945	23.5	2.42	14.8	27.7
Panola	8.8	6.3	5.6	52.0	29 996	34 274	14.3	2.8	2 031	1 184	160	12 232	20.8	2.75	19.9	23.2
Pearl River	10.6	7.3	5.2	51.3	38 714	48 621	25.6	4.7	2 108	1 537	1 686	18 078	31.4	2.65	12.5	21.7
Perry	9.7	6.8	4.7	51.1	10 865	12 138	11.7	1.2	535	412	45	4 420	16.3	2.72	13.2	21.9
Pike	9.3	7.3	6.9	53.0	36 882	38 940	5.6	0.0	2 109	1 408	-675	14 792	10.3	2.57	19.9	26.5
Pontotoc	9.0	6.6	6.0	51.2	22 237	26 726	20.2	3.2	1 182	795	494	10 097	21.0	2.62	11.9	22.7
Prentiss	10.6	7.2	6.9	51.6	23 278	25 556	9.8	0.1	1 006	756	-191	9 821	13.6	2.52	12.6	24.9
Quitman	8.8	6.7	6.5	53.0	10 490	10 117	-3.6	-3.7	580	380	-578	3 565	1.2	2.80	26.8	26.9
Rankin	9.1	5.8	3.8	51.0	87 161	115 327	32.3	8.1	5 491	2 669	6 456	42 089	41.0	2.62	12.2	21.9
Scott	9.4	6.6	5.9	50.9	24 137	28 423	17.8	0.1	1 447	998	-418	10 183	19.6	2.76	18.8	22.2
Sharkey	8.3	5.4	6.0	52.5	7 066	6 580	-6.9	-5.4	384	212	-539	2 163	3.8	2.99	26.8	23.5
Simpson	9.8	7.1	6.0	51.4	23 953	27 639	15.4	-0.2	1 274	1 055	-247	10 076	20.6	2.65	14.8	24.0
Smith	10.7	7.8	6.3	51.1	14 798	16 182	9.4	-2.2	675	561	-447	6 046	14.6	2.65	11.9	23.0
Stone	9.8	6.3	4.5	49.8	10 750	13 622	26.7	4.3	654	504	423	4 747	28.8	2.72	13.3	20.6

1. No spouse present.

Table B. States and Counties — Vital Statistics, Health Resources, and Crime

STATE County	Births, average 1999–2001		Deaths, average 1999–2001				Physicians,[4] 2000		Hospitals,[4] 1998			Medicare enrollees, 2003	Serious crimes known to police,[6] 2002	
			Number		Rate					Beds			Total	
	Total	Rate[1]	Total	Infant[2]	Total[1]	Infant[3]	Number	Rate[5]	Number	Number	Rate[5]		Number	Rate[7]
	32	33	34	35	36	37	38	39	40	41	42	43	44	45
MISSISSIPPI	43 014	15.1	28 366	449	10.0	10.4	4 116	145	104	12 563	456	436 677	119 442	4 159
Adams	467	13.6	431	6	12.6	D	65	189	2	238	695	6 334	1 786	5 152
Alcorn	454	13.1	442	4	12.8	D	35	101	1	150	458	6 966	NA	NA
Amite	174	12.8	144	1	10.6	D	5	37	0	0	0	2 336	NA	NA
Attala	278	14.1	257	2	13.1	D	13	66	1	72	391	3 968	366	1 844
Benton	124	15.5	98	2	12.2	D	3	37	0	0	0	1 598	NA	NA
Bolivar	658	16.2	446	7	11.0	11.1	18	44	1	119	295	5 950	NA	NA
Calhoun	207	13.8	196	1	13.0	D	5	33	2	77	519	3 013	NA	NA
Carroll	109	10.2	98	1	9.1	D	5	46	0	0	0	1 559	NA	NA
Chickasaw	324	16.6	224	4	11.5	D	10	51	2	160	888	3 788	106	540
Choctaw	111	11.5	100	1	10.3	D	6	61	1	88	938	1 447	NA	NA
Claiborne	175	14.9	115	2	9.7	D	4	34	1	27	232	1 437	179	1 499
Clarke	249	13.9	200	2	11.2	D	5	28	1	42	230	3 332	NA	NA
Clay	333	15.2	229	5	10.4	D	24	109	1	60	277	3 390	NA	NA
Coahoma	596	19.5	355	7	11.6	11.2	40	131	1	195	627	4 653	492	1 592
Copiah	433	15.0	300	8	10.4	19.3	14	49	1	49	169	5 548	NA	NA
Covington	302	15.6	199	4	10.3	D	12	62	1	82	461	3 338	213	1 087
De Soto	1 734	16.1	796	16	7.4	9.0	70	65	1	130	134	13 091	NA	NA
Forrest	1 075	14.8	737	9	10.1	8.7	151	208	2	672	904	12 041	NA	NA
Franklin	120	14.2	101	2	12.0	D	2	24	1	53	637	1 427	NA	NA
George	333	17.3	197	4	10.2	D	12	63	1	53	270	3 316	NA	NA
Greene	160	12.1	103	1	7.8	D	3	23	0	0	0	1 461	NA	NA
Grenada	298	12.8	307	3	13.2	D	33	142	1	118	526	4 113	1 025	4 364
Hancock	552	12.8	455	4	10.6	D	52	121	1	66	164	6 829	NA	NA
Harrison	2 955	15.6	1 760	30	9.3	10.2	447	236	4	722	406	27 994	12 531	6 547
Hinds	3 907	15.6	2 175	56	8.7	14.3	959	382	5	2 038	825	33 009	18 168	9 724
Holmes	406	18.7	252	5	11.6	D	13	60	2	113	525	3 665	NA	NA
Humphreys	210	18.7	128	3	11.4	D	12	107	1	28	247	1 676	NA	NA
Issaquena	23	10.1	15	0	6.7	D	0	0	0	0	0	160	0	0
Itawamba	271	11.9	275	2	12.1	D	6	26	0	0	0	3 336	NA	NA
Jackson	1 886	14.3	1 138	13	8.6	6.9	203	154	2	446	341	17 153	6 065	4 571
Jasper	278	15.2	197	3	10.8	D	5	28	1	114	645	3 204	NA	NA
Jefferson	144	14.8	90	2	9.3	D	4	41	1	30	356	1 342	NA	NA
Jefferson Davis	190	13.6	151	3	10.9	D	11	79	1	101	729	2 084	NA	NA
Jones	1 021	15.7	692	10	10.7	9.5	87	134	2	301	474	11 788	NA	NA
Kemper	136	12.9	103	2	9.8	D	5	48	1	24	227	1 699	NA	NA
Lafayette	440	11.4	282	4	7.3	D	63	163	1	150	434	4 187	NA	NA
Lamar	605	15.4	285	6	7.3	D	117	299	1	23	62	4 083	851	2 158
Lauderdale	1 188	15.2	957	15	12.3	12.9	225	288	3	619	813	13 034	2 398	3 039
Lawrence	187	14.1	144	1	10.8	D	9	68	1	53	406	3 076	NA	NA
Leake	351	16.7	234	4	11.1	D	13	62	1	76	392	3 949	NA	NA
Lee	1 245	16.4	741	10	9.8	8.0	185	244	1	607	813	12 458	2 933	4 092
Leflore	607	16.0	416	10	11.0	15.9	58	153	1	187	506	5 513	2 156	5 628
Lincoln	463	14.0	433	2	13.1	D	34	103	1	95	299	5 419	1 096	3 273
Lowndes	951	15.5	501	10	8.2	10.9	84	136	2	404	660	8 724	2 526	4 063
Madison	1 242	16.6	759	12	10.1	9.4	127	170	1	127	174	9 058	1 907	3 058
Marion	369	14.4	332	2	13.0	D	15	59	1	90	341	4 888	NA	NA
Marshall	535	15.3	349	7	10.0	12.5	14	40	1	40	124	5 183	1 182	3 346
Monroe	507	13.3	401	6	10.5	D	55	145	2	122	319	6 331	745	1 941
Montgomery	157	12.9	141	3	11.5	D	7	57	2	68	547	2 554	NA	NA
Neshoba	486	17.0	318	5	11.1	D	18	63	2	224	810	3 919	NA	NA
Newton	328	15.0	238	3	10.9	D	15	69	1	39	181	4 773	NA	NA
Noxubee	230	18.3	126	4	10.0	D	6	48	1	109	881	2 159	NA	NA
Oktibbeha	551	12.9	274	4	6.4	D	36	84	1	96	244	4 895	NA	NA
Panola	596	17.4	358	7	10.4	11.8	15	44	1	70	210	5 631	906	2 781
Pearl River	668	13.7	454	3	9.3	D	26	53	2	145	309	8 002	1 593	3 245
Perry	182	15.0	133	1	11.0	D	3	25	1	82	695	1 722	NA	NA
Pike	644	16.6	431	5	11.1	D	52	134	2	166	438	7 271	NA	NA
Pontotoc	373	14.0	248	2	9.3	D	11	41	1	61	240	4 126	195	723
Prentiss	324	12.7	236	3	9.3	D	25	98	1	78	321	5 201	591	2 474
Quitman	174	17.2	125	2	12.4	D	5	49	1	96	968	1 815	NA	NA
Rankin	1 655	14.3	799	13	6.9	7.9	185	160	3	233	213	14 634	3 134	2 749
Scott	443	15.6	291	7	10.2	15.8	12	42	2	104	416	4 694	NA	NA
Sharkey	112	17.1	63	0	9.6	D	2	30	1	29	436	983	NA	NA
Simpson	392	14.3	309	4	11.2	D	15	54	2	113	446	4 404	NA	NA
Smith	194	12.1	172	1	10.7	D	4	25	1	22	144	2 385	NA	NA
Stone	207	15.0	148	1	10.8	D	10	73	1	34	258	2 444	510	3 709

1. Per 1,000 estimated resident population.　2. Deaths of infants under 1 year old.　3. Deaths of infants under 1 year old per 1,000 live births.　4. Data subject to copyright.　5. Per 100,000 resident population as of July 1 of the year shown.　6. Data for serious crimes have not been adjusted for underreporting; this may affect comparability between geographic areas and over time.　7. Per 100,000 population estimated by the FBI.

Table B. States and Counties — Crime, Education, Money Income, and Poverty

STATE County	Serious crimes known to police,[1] 2002 (cont'd) Rate[2] — Violent	Property	Education — School enrollment and attainment, 2000 — Enrollment — Total	Percent private	Attainment (percent) — High school graduate or less	Bachelor's degree or more	Local government expenditures,[5] 2000–2001 — Total current expenditures (mil dol)	Current expenditures per student (dollars)	Money income, 1999 — Per capita income[6] (dollars)	Households — Median income — Dollars	Percent change, 1989–1999 (constant 1999 dollars)	Percent with income of $100,000 or more	Percent below poverty level, 1999 — Persons	Households	Families	Families with children
	46	47	48	49	50	51	52	53	54	55	56	57	58	59	60	61
MISSISSIPPI	343	3 816	789 903	12.8	56.5	16.9	2 578.5	5 193	15 853	31 330	15.8	6.0	19.9	19.7	16.0	22.2
Adams	257	4 895	9 809	19.6	58.3	17.5	29.6	5 848	15 778	25 234	9.1	5.0	25.9	25.6	22.9	32.9
Alcorn	NA	NA	7 421	7.8	66.8	11.7	30.5	5 609	15 418	29 041	16.6	4.1	16.6	19.6	13.1	17.2
Amite	NA	NA	3 261	23.1	68.4	9.4	9.3	5 738	14 048	26 033	23.7	3.5	22.6	23.0	19.3	27.1
Attala	343	1 501	5 044	11.6	66.4	11.6	18.5	5 265	13 782	24 794	20.0	4.4	21.8	22.1	18.3	24.9
Benton	NA	NA	2 002	9.5	73.3	7.8	6.8	5 454	12 212	24 149	13.8	3.0	23.2	24.0	19.2	24.1
Bolivar	NA	NA	14 277	7.3	59.1	18.8	48.3	5 848	12 088	23 428	24.4	4.3	33.3	31.5	27.9	37.3
Calhoun	NA	NA	3 470	11.4	70.2	10.2	13.3	5 270	15 106	27 113	11.0	3.8	18.1	20.5	14.9	21.0
Carroll	NA	NA	2 647	25.0	68.1	10.9	6.4	5 297	15 744	28 878	29.2	5.4	16.0	19.1	13.7	19.8
Chickasaw	158	382	4 950	8.7	71.0	9.5	17.3	5 046	13 279	26 364	7.5	2.7	20.0	22.2	16.8	20.1
Choctaw	NA	NA	2 513	11.8	67.6	11.2	10.1	5 252	13 474	27 020	16.2	4.4	24.7	23.2	17.7	27.6
Claiborne	243	1 256	4 792	4.9	53.7	18.9	12.1	6 025	11 244	22 615	30.7	5.1	32.4	31.9	27.9	34.8
Clarke	NA	NA	4 411	6.7	68.0	9.6	17.4	5 084	14 288	26 610	3.9	3.1	23.0	23.5	18.8	26.4
Clay	NA	NA	6 257	15.4	63.1	14.6	18.9	4 699	14 512	27 372	11.1	6.0	23.5	23.7	19.2	28.0
Coahoma	146	1 446	9 446	10.9	59.3	16.2	32.0	5 074	12 558	22 338	20.7	5.1	35.9	32.6	29.8	37.9
Copiah	NA	NA	8 378	17.2	60.9	11.6	24.7	5 068	12 408	26 358	18.3	3.6	25.1	24.7	22.0	29.6
Covington	235	852	5 285	7.2	64.7	11.4	17.4	4 893	14 506	26 669	12.9	4.6	23.5	22.7	18.7	27.2
De Soto	NA	NA	27 677	16.4	52.5	14.3	80.9	4 084	20 468	48 206	13.0	9.0	7.1	7.3	5.6	7.1
Forrest	NA	NA	24 754	11.7	48.6	22.8	65.6	5 651	15 160	27 420	13.5	5.3	22.5	22.3	17.1	24.2
Franklin	NA	NA	2 176	6.6	66.3	10.5	10.3	6 186	13 643	24 885	29.2	2.9	24.1	25.2	20.6	27.0
George	NA	NA	4 817	5.1	68.9	9.1	17.3	4 265	14 337	34 730	40.5	4.1	16.7	17.4	13.0	17.8
Greene	NA	NA	2 768	5.9	70.6	8.0	9.9	5 208	11 868	28 336	17.4	3.2	19.6	20.1	16.5	21.0
Grenada	447	3 917	6 164	11.8	63.8	13.5	21.2	4 594	13 786	27 385	7.5	4.1	20.9	22.3	17.6	24.5
Hancock	NA	NA	10 176	17.2	51.4	17.3	35.0	5 412	17 748	35 202	26.5	5.9	14.4	15.1	11.2	15.7
Harrison	387	6 160	48 256	14.6	48.1	18.4	171.6	5 592	18 024	35 624	19.7	6.5	14.6	14.0	11.6	17.0
Hinds	971	8 753	78 720	19.5	41.5	27.2	238.4	5 611	17 785	33 991	2.5	7.7	19.9	18.4	16.1	22.4
Holmes	NA	NA	7 369	9.1	67.0	11.2	21.1	4 642	10 683	17 235	30.8	3.3	41.1	40.6	35.9	45.1
Humphreys	NA	NA	3 643	13.5	67.9	11.6	10.9	4 793	10 926	20 566	20.6	2.6	38.2	35.6	32.4	42.5
Issaquena	0	0	658	9.1	72.4	7.1	NA	NA	10 581	19 936	14.1	3.1	33.2	31.9	25.9	36.4
Itawamba	NA	NA	5 744	3.5	65.6	8.8	17.9	4 726	14 956	31 156	11.6	4.1	14.0	17.0	10.1	12.7
Jackson	315	4 256	34 736	8.3	51.1	16.5	130.8	5 107	17 768	39 118	10.1	7.4	12.7	12.9	9.9	15.5
Jasper	NA	NA	4 891	9.3	67.8	9.8	16.9	5 473	12 889	24 441	12.8	3.4	22.7	24.6	19.3	25.3
Jefferson	NA	NA	2 748	6.2	68.5	10.6	9.4	5 455	9 709	18 447	33.7	1.7	36.0	35.9	32.5	39.7
Jefferson Davis	NA	NA	3 815	13.8	68.4	10.4	12.6	5 262	11 974	21 834	5.2	3.2	28.2	28.2	23.2	31.6
Jones	NA	NA	16 331	8.2	58.4	14.0	57.8	5 248	14 820	28 786	11.4	4.8	19.8	18.5	14.3	21.3
Kemper	NA	NA	2 955	13.7	67.8	10.3	8.2	5 822	11 985	23 998	24.8	3.8	26.0	27.5	21.2	30.9
Lafayette	NA	NA	16 076	6.0	44.2	31.1	29.0	5 634	16 406	28 517	16.7	6.1	21.3	23.0	10.2	13.6
Lamar	127	2 031	11 465	11.7	44.0	26.8	35.9	4 805	18 849	37 628	20.4	9.4	13.3	12.9	9.7	12.5
Lauderdale	262	2 777	20 890	9.9	53.2	16.2	74.2	5 433	16 026	30 768	12.2	5.9	20.8	21.0	17.1	24.2
Lawrence	NA	NA	3 493	7.5	61.2	12.0	12.6	5 120	14 469	28 495	21.1	3.2	19.6	20.7	16.6	21.0
Leake	NA	NA	5 007	19.7	67.7	11.6	15.4	4 767	13 365	27 055	26.1	4.1	23.3	23.4	18.1	25.1
Lee	258	3 834	19 509	8.3	53.5	18.1	78.5	5 276	18 956	36 165	9.2	7.0	13.4	14.4	10.5	15.1
Leflore	608	5 020	11 798	12.7	63.7	15.9	35.8	5 226	12 553	21 518	5.2	5.3	34.8	31.7	29.1	39.8
Lincoln	290	2 984	8 437	11.1	59.6	12.4	29.5	4 953	13 961	27 279	11.6	5.2	19.2	19.7	16.0	21.8
Lowndes	238	3 825	18 414	14.8	54.3	20.5	56.1	5 211	16 514	32 123	4.0	6.5	21.3	20.7	18.0	27.0
Madison	244	2 815	21 716	27.3	35.3	37.9	58.5	4 640	23 469	46 970	35.0	16.4	14.0	12.2	10.6	14.7
Marion	NA	NA	6 517	10.9	66.9	11.5	24.8	5 383	12 301	24 555	13.6	3.3	24.8	25.5	20.7	28.3
Marshall	481	2 865	8 919	21.7	71.5	9.0	24.1	4 636	14 028	28 756	15.7	4.7	21.9	22.3	18.0	24.4
Monroe	91	1 850	9 518	7.8	66.9	10.9	32.4	4 995	14 072	30 307	12.5	3.3	17.2	19.7	13.6	18.8
Montgomery	NA	NA	3 213	9.0	69.9	11.0	12.7	5 828	14 040	25 270	22.2	4.6	24.3	25.6	21.9	30.2
Neshoba	NA	NA	7 642	18.0	64.0	11.4	20.6	5 215	14 964	28 300	15.5	4.7	21.0	21.9	17.9	24.4
Newton	NA	NA	6 028	10.6	60.5	12.1	19.8	5 360	14 008	28 735	10.8	3.4	19.9	20.7	16.4	24.0
Noxubee	NA	NA	3 505	17.4	72.2	10.9	12.5	5 436	12 018	22 330	17.0	4.8	32.8	31.9	29.2	37.9
Oktibbeha	NA	NA	19 744	9.1	41.8	34.8	33.9	6 342	14 998	24 899	0.1	7.1	28.2	28.5	18.0	26.3
Panola	454	2 327	9 472	9.1	66.1	10.8	33.5	4 987	13 075	26 785	12.7	4.7	25.3	24.3	21.2	27.3
Pearl River	132	3 113	12 637	10.0	56.6	13.9	41.5	4 819	15 160	30 912	14.3	5.4	18.4	18.0	15.5	22.7
Perry	NA	NA	2 986	6.4	66.1	7.7	12.7	5 567	12 837	27 189	24.7	2.7	22.0	22.7	19.6	24.9
Pike	NA	NA	10 215	12.3	61.7	12.5	38.0	5 351	14 040	24 562	20.7	4.7	25.3	24.5	21.5	29.9
Pontotoc	11	712	6 412	6.4	67.1	11.4	24.9	4 764	15 658	32 055	18.0	4.3	13.8	16.4	10.2	12.9
Prentiss	54	2 420	6 548	2.9	66.4	9.9	25.8	5 408	14 131	28 446	19.4	4.1	16.5	19.3	13.1	16.7
Quitman	NA	NA	2 901	13.0	69.9	10.6	8.6	5 075	10 817	20 636	11.9	2.5	33.1	33.3	28.6	37.3
Rankin	196	2 552	28 701	14.2	45.6	23.8	87.9	4 698	20 412	44 946	5.6	10.4	9.5	9.5	7.3	10.2
Scott	NA	NA	7 148	8.8	70.0	8.6	26.3	4 678	14 013	26 686	16.6	3.8	20.7	21.4	16.5	22.1
Sharkey	NA	NA	2 026	11.5	68.2	12.6	8.6	5 533	11 396	22 285	24.7	3.4	38.3	32.7	30.5	43.2
Simpson	NA	NA	6 941	11.6	66.5	10.9	21.3	4 811	13 344	28 343	10.7	3.6	21.6	21.2	17.5	24.1
Smith	NA	NA	4 070	8.9	67.5	9.1	15.2	4 839	14 752	30 840	20.1	4.2	16.9	17.6	12.9	18.1
Stone	480	3 229	3 916	6.5	55.4	12.4	13.2	4 958	14 693	30 495	19.2	5.7	17.5	17.4	14.5	19.9

1. Data for serious crimes have not been adjusted for underreporting; this may affect comparability between geographic areas and over time.   2. Per 100,000 population estimated by the FBI.   3. All persons 3 years old and over enrolled in nursery school through college.   4. Persons 25 years old and over.   5. Elementary and secondary education expenditures.   6. Based on population enumerated as of April 1, 2000.

STATE County	Total (mil dol)	Percent change, 2001–2002	Per capita[1] Dollars	Rank	Wages and salaries[2] (mil dol)	Proprietor's income (mil dol)	Dividends, interest, and rent (mil dol)	Total (mil dol)	Total (mil dol)	Social Security (mil dol)	Medical payments (mil dol)	Income mainte-nance (mil dol)	Unemploy-ment insurance (mil dol)
	62	63	64	65	66	67	68	69	70	71	72	73	74
MISSISSIPPI	64 645	3.0	22 550	X	39 270	4 770	10 023	13 963	13 224	4 644	5 845	1 724	273
Adams	764	5.6	22 821	1 772	458	64	133	193	184	71	76	26	4
Alcorn	735	2.8	21 158	2 250	448	39	114	193	184	74	83	16	5
Amite	262	2.6	19 429	2 668	78	28	43	68	65	24	29	8	1
Attala	436	19.0	22 109	1 984	255	27	67	110	105	37	47	15	2
Benton	133	3.2	16 902	3 002	43	4	19	43	41	13	19	6	1
Bolivar	715	-0.9	18 111	2 877	398	19	112	215	204	55	88	46	7
Calhoun	319	0.9	21 454	2 164	113	38	53	87	84	31	38	10	1
Carroll	211	0.2	19 972	2 551	38	5	33	47	45	18	19	6	1
Chickasaw	375	1.9	19 392	2 677	195	36	60	105	100	36	44	13	3
Choctaw	156	1.8	16 064	3 049	66	15	22	46	44	15	20	6	1
Claiborne	192	3.7	16 478	3 026	6	6	25	64	61	15	26	11	1
Clarke	349	4.1	19 578	2 642	124	35	55	99	95	36	39	10	7
Clay	457	2.2	20 914	2 320	283	34	85	105	99	37	40	15	2
Coahoma	641	-0.8	21 404	2 179	338	29	114	190	182	46	88	37	4
Copiah	544	2.9	18 922	2 770	224	39	76	162	155	49	67	22	2
Covington	364	2.5	18 415	2 843	143	50	51	98	93	32	42	13	1
De Soto	3 231	4.2	27 261	659	1 225	297	347	357	327	159	116	25	7
Forrest	1 751	4.9	23 804	1 470	1 303	186	367	378	359	113	164	42	5
Franklin	147	3.6	17 733	2 929	56	6	21	44	42	16	18	5	1
George	388	3.5	19 385	2 679	121	20	50	98	93	34	44	9	3
Greene	201	1.8	15 174	3 071	62	20	20	51	48	13	25	6	1
Grenada	491	2.7	21 372	2 190	357	27	87	131	125	43	61	14	3
Hancock	1 043	4.6	23 370	1 604	630	74	210	208	196	80	88	15	2
Harrison	4 883	4.0	25 693	957	3 850	332	817	884	837	283	390	85	13
Hinds	6 594	3.3	26 494	789	5 891	713	1 132	1 156	1 092	374	448	169	21
Holmes	324	3.8	15 053	3 075	109	0	46	148	142	30	68	32	3
Humphreys	188	-5.5	17 442	2 956	92	2	37	69	66	16	32	15	2
Issaquena	25	-16.1	11 864	3 106	9	-1	4	7	6	2	3	2	0
Itawamba	495	4.0	21 562	2 136	168	35	75	108	102	46	39	7	2
Jackson	3 109	1.2	23 350	1 610	2 005	136	479	570	536	224	222	46	13
Jasper	339	3.2	18 571	2 821	138	31	42	94	90	30	41	14	2
Jefferson	129	2.0	13 305	3 098	37	2	13	51	49	13	22	10	1
Jefferson Davis	234	2.5	17 296	2 968	65	19	32	73	69	24	29	12	1
Jones	1 482	2.5	22 780	1 788	939	130	222	401	384	123	202	36	4
Kemper	191	1.2	18 104	2 879	55	16	31	58	55	17	21	7	2
Lafayette	915	5.1	23 147	1 678	581	82	161	156	146	46	77	10	1
Lamar	933	5.7	22 683	1 827	415	59	90	147	137	59	55	15	2
Lauderdale	1 883	4.0	24 264	1 323	1 344	101	311	408	389	133	173	50	7
Lawrence	284	0.5	21 102	2 268	119	24	33	80	77	29	35	9	1
Leake	433	0.8	19 933	2 558	191	52	56	117	112	37	54	13	2
Lee	2 095	4.8	27 206	667	1 965	141	328	343	323	133	136	35	9
Leflore	720	2.7	19 604	2 629	507	44	127	221	211	54	98	41	5
Lincoln	728	2.6	21 699	2 089	402	94	104	175	167	65	73	18	4
Lowndes	1 361	2.0	22 382	1 913	1 001	80	223	266	251	91	103	37	5
Madison	2 561	3.8	32 896	191	1 120	192	457	286	266	105	108	38	4
Marion	492	2.7	19 530	2 654	229	32	90	152	145	52	67	19	2
Marshall	669	3.7	19 019	2 751	210	31	62	161	152	53	63	24	4
Monroe	784	3.3	20 734	2 358	390	44	123	187	178	70	74	20	5
Montgomery	237	1.4	19 800	2 587	73	31	35	75	72	23	35	10	2
Neshoba	688	5.7	23 921	1 434	453	78	94	144	137	48	65	15	3
Newton	460	0.4	21 045	2 284	194	53	66	129	124	41	58	13	2
Noxubee	219	0.7	17 668	2 933	97	21	35	69	66	19	29	15	1
Oktibbeha	911	4.2	21 426	2 172	609	61	161	158	147	47	59	21	2
Panola	646	2.4	18 510	2 827	331	49	91	174	165	57	69	28	6
Pearl River	957	4.8	19 002	2 754	284	62	134	256	243	95	101	24	3
Perry	209	3.2	16 994	2 997	99	10	27	65	62	26	25	7	1
Pike	775	2.8	19 916	2 563	450	44	121	231	221	70	95	33	4
Pontotoc	549	5.1	20 245	2 488	328	42	64	112	105	43	46	10	2
Prentiss	468	5.7	18 295	2 863	273	16	64	126	119	47	52	11	3
Quitman	158	-8.2	15 854	3 055	-3	-3	21	61	58	15	29	12	1
Rankin	3 287	2.8	27 034	693	1 842	201	437	483	451	179	215	31	6
Scott	536	-2.3	18 958	2 762	305	74	69	143	136	44	65	19	2
Sharkey	101	-5.7	16 082	3 048	45	-6	18	39	37	9	18	9	1
Simpson	564	-0.1	20 425	2 452	190	62	62	162	155	45	87	15	2
Smith	336	-4.7	21 048	2 283	135	52	41	79	75	33	31	8	1
Stone	286	4.9	20 302	2 477	116	8	31	82	78	24	33	8	0

1. Based on the resident population estimated as of July 1 of the year shown. 2. Includes other labor income.

Table B. States and Counties — Earnings, Social Security, and Housing

STATE County	Earnings, 2002									Social Security beneficiaries, December 2003		Supplemental Security Income recipients, December 2003	Housing units, 2003	
	Total (mil dol)	Farm	Goods-related[1] Total	Manufacturing	Information and professional and technical services	Retail trade	Finance, insurance, and real estate	Health services	Government	Number	Rate[2]		Total	Percent change, 2000–2003
	75	76	77	78	79	80	81	82	83	84	85	86	87	88
MISSISSIPPI	44 040	1.0	23.7	16.7	6.4	8.1	5.1	9.7	22.9	533 375	185	126 282	1 206 630	3.8
Adams	522	-0.2	34.7	15.0	D	10.1	5.1	D	15.5	7 570	228	1 967	15 259	0.6
Alcorn	487	0.1	39.2	35.1	2.9	11.5	3.5	D	19.0	8 700	249	1 881	16 115	1.9
Amite	106	6.6	D	27.9	D	6.5	3.8	D	15.3	3 125	230	666	6 577	2.0
Attala	281	-0.2	48.4	12.2	D	7.7	3.3	D	14.2	4 325	220	1 113	8 850	2.4
Benton	47	-3.3	D	22.8	D	9.5	1.6	10.1	20.8	1 815	233	506	3 520	1.9
Bolivar	417	0.9	20.4	17.2	D	11.8	3.6	12.8	24.2	6 965	178	3 574	15 181	1.6
Calhoun	151	6.7	39.8	37.8	2.4	8.8	D	D	16.8	3 735	252	857	7 024	1.8
Carroll	44	-6.1	D	D	D	6.5	D	D	29.8	2 200	210	491	5 005	2.4
Chickasaw	230	2.6	52.5	49.7	2.1	7.5	2.3	6.0	12.2	4 110	214	1 065	8 148	2.1
Choctaw	81	1.3	D	14.8	D	5.4	D	D	18.8	1 995	207	493	4 321	1.7
Claiborne	214	0.8	D	7.6	D	2.9	D	2.6	27.7	1 880	163	755	4 347	2.2
Clarke	159	1.9	47.1	23.0	1.8	4.2	3.0	7.6	15.8	4 025	227	770	8 291	2.4
Clay	316	-0.6	D	45.7	3.4	6.9	2.5	D	10.8	4 195	194	1 107	8 969	1.8
Coahoma	366	-0.4	D	10.1	9.3	8.7	6.9	D	19.7	5 605	190	2 595	11 566	0.7
Copiah	263	2.7	35.1	29.5	3.5	7.5	2.2	6.3	24.0	5 900	204	1 759	11 265	1.5
Covington	193	5.8	D	20.9	D	6.6	2.6	3.1	19.9	3 940	195	1 106	8 301	2.7
De Soto	1 521	-0.4	D	17.8	4.5	10.7	6.1	8.4	9.9	16 750	135	1 541	48 039	17.8
Forrest	1 489	0.4	13.8	9.0	5.6	9.1	5.7	13.8	30.9	12 345	166	3 016	30 952	3.5
Franklin	62	-0.5	13.3	6.1	11.8	5.3	D	5.9	33.0	1 790	215	403	4 220	2.5
George	140	2.5	D	9.6	D	13.2	D	4.7	30.4	3 940	193	656	7 673	2.1
Greene	82	4.8	D	D	1.4	4.5	D	4.8	43.4	1 630	124	427	5 086	2.8
Grenada	385	-0.2	D	35.3	D	10.3	4.4	D	18.0	5 090	223	1 315	10 189	2.2
Hancock	704	-0.2	D	11.2	13.1	5.1	3.7	D	33.8	8 635	191	1 077	22 698	7.7
Harrison	4 182	0.0	D	4.9	5.4	7.0	3.6	7.6	35.7	32 655	172	6 173	84 869	6.6
Hinds	6 604	0.1	11.9	5.8	14.1	6.8	8.4	12.7	24.8	39 810	160	10 439	102 703	2.4
Holmes	109	-5.1	D	12.2	D	11.9	6.3	D	37.4	4 160	195	2 225	8 650	2.5
Humphreys	95	5.3	D	D	D	9.2	2.8	D	20.8	2 080	194	1 010	4 138	0.0
Issaquena	7	0.0	D	1.3	D	1.6	D	D	38.3	200	99	99	882	0.6
Itawamba	203	2.2	D	24.8	D	7.2	2.5	8.0	18.3	5 280	230	558	10 069	2.7
Jackson	2 141	-0.1	D	35.3	6.2	6.1	3.1	6.7	23.5	23 645	177	2 671	54 783	6.0
Jasper	169	6.3	36.1	26.9	D	6.5	3.1	D	18.1	3 810	208	1 061	7 913	3.2
Jefferson	39	0.2	D	D	D	4.3	D	9.1	49.2	1 785	187	819	3 929	2.9
Jefferson Davis	84	6.9	19.6	1.9	D	10.3	D	D	27.8	2 855	213	730	6 021	2.2
Jones	1 070	3.1	35.6	20.4	3.9	7.4	3.3	6.0	20.0	14 160	217	3 102	27 387	1.7
Kemper	71	8.0	22.6	11.1	D	7.9	3.2	D	28.8	1 710	164	585	4 634	2.2
Lafayette	662	-0.4	D	10.3	6.7	8.0	4.3	15.1	38.3	5 395	134	888	17 456	5.2
Lamar	474	1.2	15.8	8.5	D	13.5	5.2	21.8	11.3	6 625	158	865	15 775	2.2
Lauderdale	1 445	0.1	D	12.0	4.4	9.2	4.4	18.8	23.4	14 740	190	3 726	33 858	1.3
Lawrence	143	7.0	45.6	41.4	D	4.7	1.6	4.0	16.1	3 240	240	645	5 829	2.5
Leake	243	14.0	D	D	D	8.1	4.0	D	15.5	4 620	212	1 082	8 782	2.3
Lee	2 106	-0.2	35.6	32.8	4.9	7.8	5.7	17.5	9.2	14 670	189	2 838	32 302	1.3
Leflore	551	0.0	22.7	17.0	6.6	7.2	3.6	D	27.6	6 490	178	2 961	14 275	1.3
Lincoln	495	1.7	28.0	19.5	3.3	8.6	4.4	9.9	11.3	7 030	210	1 455	14 324	1.9
Lowndes	1 081	0.9	27.4	19.4	4.3	9.4	3.3	9.9	25.3	10 335	170	2 593	25 634	2.1
Madison	1 313	-0.1	19.3	9.9	12.8	9.9	15.1	7.9	10.6	11 265	141	2 148	31 323	8.8
Marion	261	3.8	31.9	12.8	3.2	9.7	4.8	D	19.4	5 925	236	1 378	10 555	1.5
Marshall	242	-1.1	27.1	17.9	2.3	11.3	5.6	D	18.8	6 360	179	2 009	13 647	3.0
Monroe	434	-0.1	49.4	41.6	2.6	6.8	2.3	D	13.5	8 180	216	1 460	16 521	1.8
Montgomery	105	-0.3	10.3	6.0	18.9	11.8	D	D	21.9	2 760	231	783	5 700	5.5
Neshoba	532	3.3	25.7	8.7	2.1	6.9	1.8	D	44.7	5 985	205	1 160	12 209	1.9
Newton	247	11.9	D	26.3	2.3	7.5	1.9	D	25.0	4 815	218	1 118	9 450	2.1
Noxubee	118	6.4	D	37.3	D	7.8	2.6	D	21.6	2 675	217	1 221	5 336	2.1
Oktibbeha	670	0.0	D	11.2	3.8	6.6	2.8	4.7	51.5	5 510	129	1 729	18 581	7.1
Panola	380	-0.5	28.7	23.2	7.2	10.2	5.5	6.8	21.1	6 880	195	2 059	14 105	2.7
Pearl River	346	-0.8	D	9.4	7.2	15.6	5.8	D	23.8	10 755	211	1 589	21 789	5.7
Perry	109	3.7	D	50.6	D	5.1	2.8	5.0	16.3	2 860	233	530	5 230	2.4
Pike	494	1.4	D	16.4	4.5	12.3	3.9	D	24.8	8 145	209	2 317	16 919	1.2
Pontotoc	370	0.0	59.2	56.8	D	5.5	2.6	D	10.1	5 545	201	803	11 188	3.4
Prentiss	289	-0.8	D	42.5	3.6	6.0	3.0	D	18.5	5 750	225	1 015	10 936	2.4
Quitman	56	-11.6	D	11.3	D	12.0	7.4	D	26.1	1 945	200	976	3 939	0.4
Rankin	2 042	0.7	19.7	10.8	5.6	8.6	8.4	9.1	15.5	18 820	151	2 245	48 636	7.9
Scott	379	14.0	D	35.8	1.7	7.5	2.5	5.7	12.4	5 455	192	1 419	11 401	2.6
Sharkey	39	-8.8	2.8	0.0	D	10.3	6.4	D	37.6	1 210	194	535	2 457	1.7
Simpson	252	13.3	D	2.9	2.4	10.8	4.7	D	22.0	5 370	195	1 184	11 463	1.4
Smith	186	22.8	41.2	35.0	2.5	3.6	1.5	D	11.6	3 640	230	635	7 175	2.4
Stone	124	-0.2	D	20.4	3.8	8.5	4.5	6.4	30.9	2 835	200	494	5 512	3.2

1. Covers mining, construction, and manufacturing.   2. Per 1,000 resident population estimated as of July 1 of the year shown.

Table B. States and Counties — Housing, Labor Force, and Employment

STATE County	Housing units, 2000 Total	Occupied units Percent	Owner-occupied Median value[1]	Median owner cost as a percent of income With a mortgage	Without a mortgage[2]	Renter-occupied Median rent[3]	Median rent as a percent of income	Sub-standard units[4] (percent)	Civilian labor force, 2003 Total	Percent change, 2002–2003	Unemployment Total	Rate[5]	Civilian employment,[6] 2000 Total	Percent Management, professional and related occupations	Production, transportation, and material moving occupations
	89	90	91	92	93	94	95	96	97	98	99	100	101	102	103
MISSISSIPPI	1 046 434	72.4	71 400	20.4	9.9	439	25.0	5.7	1 312 127	1.6	83 135	6.3	1 173 314	27.4	20.4
Adams	13 677	70.2	60 200	22.3	11.1	375	28.2	4.0	13 992	1.1	1 333	9.5	12 853	27.8	15.9
Alcorn	14 224	73.5	62 100	19.6	9.9	355	22.5	2.4	15 208	-0.7	1 197	7.9	14 861	22.4	30.5
Amite	5 271	85.9	54 100	20.8	10.7	291	27.1	6.5	5 488	3.7	499	9.1	4 985	20.9	26.3
Attala	7 567	77.7	49 900	21.2	9.9	349	24.6	5.3	8 986	-0.7	733	8.2	7 334	23.6	24.6
Benton	2 999	84.3	55 500	21.6	10.6	368	21.9	9.2	2 910	-3.9	343	11.8	2 880	17.8	34.6
Bolivar	13 776	61.1	57 200	20.3	11.1	377	27.0	10.0	16 950	-1.7	1 474	8.7	14 161	31.2	20.2
Calhoun	6 019	76.2	46 500	20.4	10.1	321	22.6	4.1	6 031	-0.5	509	8.4	6 266	20.1	39.0
Carroll	4 071	84.8	57 800	19.3	12.3	340	16.1	4.5	4 738	-0.6	321	6.8	4 416	24.4	21.6
Chickasaw	7 253	77.8	51 400	21.0	11.8	349	24.5	5.8	7 195	-0.7	802	11.1	8 022	17.6	44.1
Choctaw	3 686	81.3	55 300	21.4	11.2	332	24.4	4.8	3 414	1.5	467	13.7	3 537	24.0	29.0
Claiborne	3 685	80.3	48 200	22.0	12.5	312	29.3	9.8	3 098	-4.1	442	14.3	3 780	25.1	24.3
Clarke	6 978	84.2	53 600	18.5	9.9	355	24.7	5.0	8 521	-5.3	802	9.4	6 669	20.8	29.9
Clay	8 152	73.4	60 900	19.8	9.9	364	25.8	5.9	8 915	-1.4	1 106	12.4	8 698	22.6	33.2
Coahoma	10 553	57.3	51 200	21.3	12.7	360	26.3	8.6	11 779	-0.7	1 184	10.1	10 117	24.2	11.8
Copiah	10 142	79.8	54 800	21.7	12.5	353	24.9	8.0	11 766	1.8	788	6.7	10 808	22.3	24.8
Covington	7 126	84.9	55 000	22.0	11.1	343	23.8	6.4	8 903	3.1	421	4.7	7 454	23.8	25.5
De Soto	38 792	79.2	103 100	20.3	9.9	657	23.1	3.5	64 458	3.8	2 346	3.6	53 773	26.5	16.7
Forrest	27 183	60.4	69 100	21.1	10.9	438	28.1	4.7	34 858	3.5	1 583	4.5	31 852	30.1	14.4
Franklin	3 211	86.1	47 300	23.0	9.9	273	28.0	6.8	2 826	1.2	294	10.4	3 060	23.3	20.3
George	6 742	86.2	66 500	19.2	9.9	428	23.5	5.7	9 731	7.6	992	10.2	7 334	22.2	23.0
Greene	4 148	86.9	57 900	19.4	11.4	338	26.5	6.1	5 676	5.2	509	9.0	4 150	21.3	22.4
Grenada	8 820	69.1	68 300	21.5	9.9	371	24.2	5.3	10 208	3.9	641	6.3	9 275	23.8	27.5
Hancock	16 897	79.6	92 500	21.4	9.9	510	24.9	3.7	18 843	2.3	813	4.3	17 473	27.9	12.7
Harrison	71 538	62.7	87 200	20.4	9.9	543	25.0	5.3	87 766	2.0	3 901	4.4	81 944	27.5	11.6
Hinds	91 030	63.9	73 100	20.8	9.9	503	26.6	7.2	131 808	2.9	6 615	5.0	109 552	32.7	12.9
Holmes	7 314	73.2	44 900	26.1	14.1	265	24.5	11.6	5 984	3.8	926	15.5	6 283	23.5	28.8
Humphreys	3 765	61.4	49 600	20.5	14.1	313	23.4	12.0	5 085	-5.3	525	10.3	3 656	26.1	26.3
Issaquena	726	67.4	58 600	21.3	13.6	225	29.0	11.3	896	-4.2	111	12.4	704	26.0	18.0
Itawamba	8 773	82.5	58 600	19.0	9.9	384	21.5	2.3	11 611	0.2	625	5.4	10 003	19.6	33.9
Jackson	47 676	74.6	80 300	19.5	9.9	522	24.8	4.9	67 659	2.0	3 689	5.5	56 553	27.9	15.6
Jasper	6 708	86.8	51 200	23.7	11.4	315	23.7	5.6	7 985	-1.2	514	6.4	6 620	19.4	32.8
Jefferson	3 308	80.4	48 700	22.8	15.8	276	28.1	8.8	2 492	4.1	460	18.5	2 655	21.9	24.1
Jefferson Davis	5 177	84.5	47 700	24.8	11.7	321	26.7	9.4	4 191	4.4	424	10.1	4 702	22.9	28.6
Jones	24 275	76.8	59 000	19.8	9.9	374	23.0	4.8	30 703	-0.3	1 232	4.0	26 990	24.0	23.6
Kemper	3 909	83.9	48 400	22.2	11.2	233	20.9	6.8	4 297	1.0	448	10.4	3 860	20.6	28.8
Lafayette	14 373	60.6	101 100	20.8	10.2	507	34.8	3.4	17 853	4.0	864	4.8	17 731	36.9	12.9
Lamar	14 396	75.8	93 000	20.1	9.9	523	24.9	3.3	20 122	3.8	598	3.0	18 247	32.9	13.1
Lauderdale	29 990	67.8	67 600	19.9	9.9	404	24.5	4.7	34 636	2.4	2 385	6.9	31 126	29.6	16.9
Lawrence	5 040	84.3	56 400	20.4	10.6	351	30.2	5.8	4 786	7.6	332	6.9	5 100	22.5	24.1
Leake	7 611	82.0	53 000	20.8	9.9	345	23.0	6.9	9 877	-11.9	502	5.1	7 750	25.1	25.0
Lee	29 200	69.2	85 500	19.0	9.9	441	22.3	3.4	39 621	0.0	2 275	5.7	36 171	26.8	27.4
Leflore	12 956	53.3	56 800	22.7	10.6	325	26.4	8.1	16 046	2.2	1 964	12.2	12 430	28.1	21.3
Lincoln	12 538	78.1	64 400	20.7	10.9	366	26.7	4.3	14 173	0.2	798	5.6	13 153	24.2	21.6
Lowndes	22 849	66.6	74 700	20.5	9.9	416	25.9	5.4	25 693	-1.7	2 074	8.1	24 726	27.8	21.1
Madison	27 219	70.8	117 000	18.9	9.9	590	24.2	6.0	39 985	3.0	1 577	3.9	35 310	43.1	10.7
Marion	9 336	80.4	57 600	22.2	12.2	345	26.6	6.1	10 688	4.9	573	5.4	9 619	23.5	23.8
Marshall	12 163	80.5	67 400	23.5	11.1	375	22.0	7.1	13 825	0.2	1 581	11.4	13 815	18.9	27.7
Monroe	14 603	79.0	64 200	20.9	9.9	362	24.4	4.0	15 510	5.5	1 571	10.1	15 601	21.8	34.2
Montgomery	4 690	76.9	51 000	22.0	11.5	347	26.9	4.9	5 299	0.6	488	9.2	4 720	23.5	28.6
Neshoba	10 694	79.5	55 800	20.6	11.2	343	22.1	6.2	17 635	3.5	783	4.4	11 952	25.7	20.4
Newton	8 221	81.8	54 300	20.1	10.3	345	23.5	4.9	8 288	0.1	436	5.3	8 896	25.1	30.2
Noxubee	4 470	79.7	46 800	22.8	11.1	270	24.1	9.8	4 269	-0.4	530	12.4	4 050	20.1	34.9
Oktibbeha	15 945	55.6	89 400	19.7	9.9	473	33.6	4.4	22 598	5.4	873	3.9	18 840	39.6	12.9
Panola	12 232	77.9	57 700	21.5	10.4	387	25.9	7.7	13 215	2.3	1 605	12.1	12 891	20.8	26.0
Pearl River	18 078	79.8	76 500	21.5	10.4	421	24.6	3.9	21 371	4.3	881	4.1	19 165	27.6	16.8
Perry	4 420	84.6	56 100	20.9	11.1	310	22.1	7.9	4 085	2.5	367	9.0	4 636	23.0	26.4
Pike	14 792	74.3	59 700	22.7	12.6	380	27.5	4.9	16 270	-1.3	898	5.5	14 266	24.3	24.5
Pontotoc	10 097	78.1	66 400	19.5	9.9	391	23.1	3.9	13 595	-0.1	681	5.0	12 404	18.7	41.1
Prentiss	9 821	78.0	56 400	19.9	9.9	325	20.1	3.0	12 238	0.3	773	6.3	10 978	20.2	34.9
Quitman	3 565	68.8	37 100	22.6	12.7	303	26.5	7.0	3 545	-0.5	424	12.0	3 487	21.0	24.5
Rankin	42 089	77.2	98 600	19.0	9.9	576	21.6	4.2	67 565	3.2	2 125	3.1	57 105	34.8	12.2
Scott	10 183	78.4	48 200	22.0	10.8	370	23.0	9.9	12 250	-0.3	663	5.4	11 459	18.1	31.4
Sharkey	2 163	65.7	49 300	20.2	9.9	283	26.2	14.3	2 414	-4.5	311	12.9	2 198	27.4	19.2
Simpson	10 076	81.2	58 800	22.6	12.6	376	21.5	8.2	11 102	3.8	531	4.8	10 609	25.8	18.7
Smith	6 046	87.0	58 400	19.6	11.1	331	19.6	6.4	5 875	1.0	270	4.6	6 558	25.8	31.3
Stone	4 747	81.3	71 100	20.0	12.9	429	24.4	5.8	5 524	6.3	339	6.1	5 855	24.3	18.2

1. Specified owner-occupied units.   2. Median monthly owner costs is often in the minimum category—9.9 percent or less, which is indicated as 9.9 percent.   3. Specified renter-occupied units.   4. Overcrowded or lacking complete plumbing facilities.   5. Percent of civilian labor force.   6. Persons 16 years old and over.

Table B. States and Counties — Nonfarm Employment and Agriculture

STATE County	Private nonfarm establishments, employment and payroll, 2001									Agriculture, 2002			
	Number of establishments	Employment						Annual payroll		Farms			Farm operators whose principal occupation is farming (percent)
		Total	Health care and social assistance	Manufacturing	Retail trade	Finance and insurance	Professional, scientific, and technical services	Total (mil dol)	Average per employee (dollars)	Number	Percent with—		
											Less than 50 acres	500 acres and over	
	104	105	106	107	108	109	110	111	112	113	114	115	116
MISSISSIPPI	59 056	926 868	126 406	200 793	139 590	33 097	28 387	22 718	24 510	42 186	30.0	9.9	48.8
Adams	973	11 493	1 883	1 594	2 272	417	239	252	21 936	269	32.0	11.5	41.3
Alcorn	841	12 663	1 764	4 686	2 146	330	192	315	24 886	564	35.3	5.5	37.2
Amite	167	1 633	124	677	241	D	D	35	21 697	626	27.8	7.5	45.5
Attala	396	5 496	473	1 019	1 002	258	77	115	20 844	526	21.7	8.4	52.9
Benton	65	609	153	147	109	D	D	15	25 328	302	24.2	10.3	38.7
Bolivar	764	10 226	1 762	2 961	1 728	305	161	206	20 146	435	20.0	40.9	69.0
Calhoun	304	2 855	182	1 417	457	92	49	58	20 212	634	20.8	10.4	47.5
Carroll	106	685	D	D	129	10	3	13	19 074	556	18.3	14.7	52.7
Chickasaw	408	5 922	350	3 659	694	96	D	123	20 767	655	25.0	10.7	43.8
Choctaw	134	1 479	182	439	194	53	12	35	23 463	284	22.9	8.8	46.8
Claiborne	144	2 272	273	467	218	71	D	87	38 081	298	20.1	16.1	56.0
Clarke	305	3 610	350	1 921	248	107	28	73	20 335	362	33.1	5.8	43.9
Clay	407	8 450	617	4 157	746	145	146	204	24 107	497	23.1	10.3	44.7
Coahoma	636	8 419	1 529	1 185	1 367	294	246	206	24 455	255	20.0	43.1	67.1
Copiah	458	5 887	624	2 333	974	141	73	118	20 110	690	28.7	8.8	46.8
Covington	293	4 140	564	1 647	436	99	68	85	20 461	565	26.5	6.5	49.9
De Soto	1 860	30 336	2 405	6 162	5 743	710	515	739	24 370	639	53.2	7.7	47.9
Forrest	2 153	33 946	7 524	4 601	5 406	1 369	1 532	817	24 070	440	45.0	2.5	46.4
Franklin	135	1 309	248	192	195	D	37	29	22 505	208	23.1	9.6	49.0
George	309	2 720	532	162	722	73	114	51	18 775	537	56.1	2.8	41.9
Greene	125	1 033	152	D	220	53	D	15	14 972	393	29.5	3.8	47.8
Grenada	626	10 571	1 264	3 783	1 535	260	232	242	22 929	339	20.9	10.6	44.2
Hancock	747	9 163	807	659	1 626	198	1 354	240	26 245	298	41.6	3.0	44.0
Harrison	4 395	78 236	12 514	3 729	11 476	2 550	2 422	1 901	24 296	418	66.7	1.0	47.1
Hinds	6 670	130 056	22 755	8 599	16 850	7 541	6 287	3 780	29 067	1 247	37.3	8.4	41.8
Holmes	269	2 429	226	844	615	95	71	47	19 361	516	18.2	18.0	50.8
Humphreys	172	2 515	103	1 200	344	98	35	46	18 208	289	18.7	30.8	77.9
Issaquena	12	79	D	0	0	D	D	1	10 468	91	14.3	44.0	81.3
Itawamba	331	4 275	360	1 077	612	65	40	102	23 856	514	25.3	5.8	45.3
Jackson	2 330	40 848	4 641	13 912	5 531	922	2 362	1 228	30 053	568	63.2	1.6	49.1
Jasper	257	3 621	255	1 414	464	108	155	74	20 456	475	27.4	6.5	46.5
Jefferson	72	723	206	D	105	D	D	13	18 241	315	14.9	12.4	50.8
Jefferson Davis	178	1 392	329	D	299	D	33	29	20 676	442	26.9	4.1	51.6
Jones	1 442	21 943	2 573	7 391	3 190	553	391	547	24 929	1 080	40.7	2.3	52.9
Kemper	123	932	110	292	180	56	7	16	17 692	503	20.7	9.3	48.7
Lafayette	891	11 082	2 001	2 017	1 980	301	681	247	22 286	572	22.6	8.6	39.5
Lamar	691	7 350	737	490	2 113	364	237	157	21 325	565	40.5	4.2	44.6
Lauderdale	2 053	29 855	5 617	4 672	5 258	1 083	736	770	25 799	505	37.2	6.5	41.6
Lawrence	219	2 133	279	D	311	50	D	63	29 726	424	28.1	5.2	54.2
Leake	340	6 246	690	3 318	752	189	80	106	16 927	742	25.6	5.1	49.3
Lee	2 222	47 300	6 570	16 377	6 510	1 878	1 390	1 274	26 941	613	40.3	9.8	44.7
Leflore	824	13 053	2 508	3 318	1 802	365	406	293	22 453	287	10.8	42.9	71.4
Lincoln	768	10 821	1 473	1 413	1 632	284	247	258	23 887	643	27.8	4.4	48.5
Lowndes	1 641	24 247	2 623	5 869	4 149	621	1 242	595	24 551	492	30.5	17.1	43.9
Madison	1 980	29 326	2 431	2 478	5 655	2 009	1 332	752	25 645	719	30.2	11.4	39.1
Marion	568	6 333	777	1 123	1 079	252	148	131	20 746	581	29.1	4.6	38.6
Marshall	421	6 851	1 310	1 357	735	263	46	131	19 176	670	28.8	12.7	43.4
Monroe	694	9 204	1 402	3 484	1 446	263	119	239	25 931	713	27.3	7.9	51.2
Montgomery	255	2 960	654	776	595	135	41	51	17 336	352	16.8	11.9	46.0
Neshoba	543	8 096	931	2 187	1 346	255	95	249	30 792	692	23.6	5.3	60.5
Newton	356	4 502	596	1 944	811	117	57	95	21 159	745	34.9	4.7	54.2
Noxubee	214	2 652	228	1 022	432	102	12	50	18 970	571	22.1	18.0	52.9
Oktibbeha	794	10 406	1 335	2 000	2 491	387	315	185	17 761	502	34.9	9.6	41.4
Panola	634	8 786	666	2 336	1 456	379	211	190	21 637	725	16.3	15.4	45.2
Pearl River	754	7 339	997	849	2 069	286	209	147	20 014	881	49.0	4.4	44.9
Perry	148	1 925	240	861	229	58	D	54	27 909	331	40.8	2.1	44.7
Pike	974	13 025	1 715	4 047	2 559	385	237	268	20 595	563	33.2	3.6	48.0
Pontotoc	479	10 019	602	6 992	786	176	138	221	22 076	864	30.1	6.4	38.3
Prentiss	522	8 203	871	3 948	869	174	157	169	20 596	572	29.2	5.9	40.4
Quitman	146	1 172	242	233	269	81	17	22	18 473	243	15.6	32.1	63.0
Rankin	2 553	39 918	6 095	6 210	5 470	2 084	871	1 001	25 067	804	41.4	4.7	55.5
Scott	504	8 610	659	4 611	1 021	230	79	179	20 733	771	35.9	4.2	58.6
Sharkey	126	727	163	D	165	54	18	14	19 820	101	6.9	64.4	73.3
Simpson	422	4 963	1 399	576	1 084	220	133	83	16 646	684	26.9	4.1	59.5
Smith	195	2 848	144	1 671	250	63	54	68	23 860	727	29.0	4.3	60.8
Stone	291	2 534	196	687	414	123	75	54	21 406	330	36.7	5.8	45.2

Items 104—116

Table B. States and Counties — **Agriculture**

STATE County	Land in farms Acreage (1,000)	Percent change, 1997–2002	Average size of farm	Total irrigated (1,000)	Total cropland (1,000)	Value of land and buildings (dollars) Average per farm	Average per acre	Value of machinery and equipment average per farm (dollars)	Value of products sold Total (mil dol)	Average per farm (dollars)	Percent from — Crops	Live-stock and poultry products	Percent of farms with sales of — $10,000 or more	$100,000 or more	Government payments Total ($1,000)	Percent of farms
	117	118	119	120	121	122	123	124	125	126	127	128	129	130	131	132
MISSISSIPPI	11 098	9.6	263	1 176	5 823	370 689	1 381	51 839	3 116	73 870	32.9	67.1	25.9	10.3	145 508	29.4
Adams	91	40.0	340	0	40	336 308	1 004	38 922	6	21 672	70.0	30.0	15.2	3.0	884	23.4
Alcorn	93	14.8	166	0	52	267 804	1 355	30 745	8	14 191	80.3	19.7	17.7	2.1	511	40.8
Amite	157	33.1	250	0	41	348 222	1 572	28 821	30	48 523	2.3	97.7	19.3	5.8	530	28.6
Attala	126	-2.3	240	0	36	341 175	1 285	55 110	9	16 976	48.6	51.4	15.4	2.9	1 034	34.2
Benton	100	23.5	333	0	44	333 066	970	39 250	9	28 571	89.5	10.5	18.2	4.3	1 185	46.0
Bolivar	440	-3.3	1 011	228	394	1 103 209	1 098	230 495	107	246 125	98.3	1.7	63.7	39.8	11 654	52.9
Calhoun	170	19.7	268	1	86	238 795	953	61 352	32	50 824	79.7	20.3	22.6	7.1	1 689	55.2
Carroll	168	17.5	302	9	66	341 589	991	31 700	14	25 583	62.4	37.6	25.4	4.7	1 691	35.6
Chickasaw	172	24.6	263	1	80	221 273	923	34 638	24	35 963	28.3	71.7	25.5	7.8	1 377	44.9
Choctaw	64	10.3	225	0	21	306 936	1 174	28 127	10	36 606	8.1	91.9	14.4	3.2	428	44.4
Claiborne	101	24.7	339	D	32	380 948	1 203	25 746	6	19 972	57.4	42.6	19.8	3.7	1 053	31.9
Clarke	56	7.7	155	D	14	255 561	1 710	27 293	8	21 936	8.3	91.7	15.2	2.5	48	9.1
Clay	129	-2.3	260	1	45	384 589	1 130	39 230	12	23 304	23.5	76.5	23.5	4.4	965	37.0
Coahoma	272	-0.4	1 068	112	240	1 235 790	1 157	257 939	80	312 554	93.0	7.0	67.1	42.4	8 194	57.6
Copiah	158	30.6	228	1	45	350 023	1 646	23 963	41	58 811	6.7	93.3	22.8	6.7	502	19.0
Covington	103	19.8	183	0	37	319 800	1 572	37 349	62	110 572	3.6	96.4	30.1	13.6	246	22.7
De Soto	143	-4.0	224	12	104	469 682	1 961	37 701	21	33 483	86.5	13.5	16.4	4.4	2 417	13.0
Forrest	45	-2.2	103	1	15	271 985	2 709	33 440	14	31 019	14.4	85.6	19.1	7.5	340	13.0
Franklin	44	4.8	214	D	14	392 149	1 644	29 059	4	17 832	11.8	88.2	16.8	3.4	102	20.2
George	63	50.0	117	1	26	338 428	3 023	31 198	13	24 302	76.3	23.7	21.0	3.5	147	11.7
Greene	59	0.0	151	0	20	262 468	1 629	29 298	18	45 122	6.9	93.1	22.9	7.6	26	5.3
Grenada	91	0.0	268	5	40	309 607	1 215	39 474	6	17 105	75.5	24.5	21.5	2.9	1 004	46.3
Hancock	38	5.6	127	0	15	328 455	2 376	20 376	3	8 488	27.0	73.0	17.8	2.0	96	10.1
Harrison	25	38.9	60	0	10	239 686	3 852	17 871	3	7 982	54.6	45.4	15.6	1.4	36	3.6
Hinds	279	42.3	223	0	109	343 373	1 348	47 174	51	40 987	19.3	80.7	16.4	2.6	2 287	23.3
Holmes	219	15.3	425	31	126	489 263	1 230	84 422	32	62 647	87.3	12.7	22.9	8.5	4 613	49.6
Humphreys	182	-8.1	628	52	136	695 752	1 128	205 444	75	258 982	51.9	48.1	61.6	38.4	4 150	47.1
Issaquena	117	3.5	1 281	12	89	1 529 891	1 169	224 665	22	242 097	D	D	59.3	37.4	3 327	69.2
Itawamba	96	17.1	187	0	38	237 289	1 124	40 911	22	42 456	15.5	84.5	23.5	9.5	507	39.9
Jackson	43	30.3	76	0	16	205 525	3 846	16 418	6	11 252	48.9	51.1	16.4	1.6	262	5.1
Jasper	80	6.7	168	0	23	218 479	1 385	33 654	40	83 800	2.0	98.0	29.1	15.4	255	18.5
Jefferson	91	42.2	289	D	31	419 870	1 467	25 564	13	40 831	26.8	73.2	24.1	7.6	698	26.7
Jefferson Davis	64	-19.0	145	0	22	191 111	1 325	33 588	22	50 762	5.8	94.1	20.8	5.2	191	21.0
Jones	132	45.1	122	0	48	240 397	2 223	36 112	130	120 242	1.7	98.3	34.6	18.3	598	12.6
Kemper	123	26.8	245	0	35	246 222	1 134	31 695	10	19 512	8.1	91.9	16.9	3.4	281	22.3
Lafayette	135	32.4	236	0	42	311 817	1 394	31 132	6	9 646	58.4	41.6	13.6	1.7	675	33.6
Lamar	75	1.4	133	0	24	290 602	1 988	31 932	28	49 430	7.1	92.9	28.1	10.1	117	11.2
Lauderdale	93	24.0	183	0	23	335 887	1 392	37 219	7	14 095	33.8	66.2	14.7	2.0	142	12.3
Lawrence	66	20.0	156	D	26	229 218	1 561	42 058	33	77 484	5.4	94.6	19.8	7.8	308	17.9
Leake	110	5.8	148	D	37	189 994	1 489	55 707	121	162 481	0.8	99.2	36.8	24.8	493	19.7
Lee	144	6.7	235	D	93	326 927	1 337	42 635	18	29 353	53.8	46.2	23.2	5.5	1 192	29.7
Leflore	283	6.0	986	116	228	1 076 105	1 110	213 139	104	361 361	61.0	39.0	63.8	41.1	7 459	59.9
Lincoln	112	13.1	174	0	33	446 949	2 255	32 205	28	43 395	4.2	95.8	23.2	6.1	456	16.8
Lowndes	150	3.4	304	0	74	370 458	1 126	60 106	39	79 313	20.0	80.0	22.8	7.1	1 294	40.9
Madison	192	5.5	268	1	80	478 466	1 622	49 322	16	22 740	74.9	25.1	16.8	5.4	2 836	35.0
Marion	99	2.1	170	0	29	267 778	1 356	24 967	37	63 774	2.2	97.8	24.1	8.8	465	25.5
Marshall	193	6.6	287	0	83	403 055	1 347	39 606	14	20 647	57.6	42.4	21.9	4.2	1 229	26.9
Monroe	183	13.0	257	1	109	326 707	1 173	45 722	32	44 252	38.8	61.2	24.4	5.6	1 820	38.6
Montgomery	86	-6.5	244	D	28	201 763	909	42 076	7	18 918	45.2	54.8	20.5	4.3	610	36.6
Neshoba	146	3.5	211	0	39	185 464	2 133	35 143	125	181 312	0.6	99.4	36.8	23.4	186	13.4
Newton	119	19.0	160	0	45	408 440	3 072	38 972	95	127 273	1.1	98.9	30.2	16.4	517	16.4
Noxubee	210	8.2	368	4	98	371 300	1 064	54 119	50	87 739	29.0	71.0	24.7	17.2	1 744	45.0
Oktibbeha	94	10.6	186	1	37	300 507	1 712	35 444	10	18 941	22.5	77.5	17.3	3.0	625	23.9
Panola	272	14.3	375	28	159	454 112	1 106	60 481	30	41 557	86.3	13.7	23.2	5.9	4 176	37.7
Pearl River	120	16.5	136	1	42	386 964	2 786	22 858	12	13 304	28.4	71.6	18.6	2.7	307	9.5
Perry	35	9.4	106	0	11	241 204	2 143	30 802	12	36 586	3.3	96.7	16.6	7.9	148	18.4
Pike	80	12.7	142	0	34	235 826	1 928	26 023	50	87 944	3.2	96.8	23.8	9.8	363	17.4
Pontotoc	140	21.7	162	0	70	184 720	1 176	37 881	11	12 680	41.8	58.2	14.5	2.0	1 333	51.9
Prentiss	102	15.9	179	0	54	194 464	924	23 876	7	11 404	67.5	32.5	18.2	2.8	1 277	59.4
Quitman	182	7.1	751	42	154	759 695	984	144 954	32	133 575	97.3	2.7	50.2	24.3	5 215	60.5
Rankin	131	12.0	163	0	42	351 427	1 485	49 628	62	77 153	8.8	91.2	24.5	9.6	866	17.8
Scott	114	6.5	148	0	42	236 678	1 611	35 829	205	265 710	1.0	99.0	40.3	26.1	478	18.0
Sharkey	165	-0.6	1 632	37	148	1 727 477	1 064	332 780	48	477 017	84.2	15.8	0.0	59.4	4 778	77.2
Simpson	104	10.6	152	0	33	289 082	2 044	37 438	127	185 896	1.7	98.3	34.8	21.2	406	18.9
Smith	104	9.5	143	0	33	285 543	1 960	47 719	154	212 280	2.2	97.8	44.7	32.2	177	12.8
Stone	57	35.7	174	0	12	319 887	1 826	27 830	7	21 089	45.6	54.4	26.4	3.3	65	8.8

STATE County	Value of residential construction authorized by building permits, 2003		Wholesale trade, 1997				Retail trade,¹ 1997				Real estate and rental and leasing, 1997			
	New construction ($1,000)	Number of housing units	Number of establishments	Number of employees	Sales (mil dol)	Annual payroll (mil dol)	Number of establishments	Number of employees	Sales (mil dol)	Annual payroll (mil dol)	Number of establishments	Number of employees	Receipts (mil dol)	Annual payroll (mil dol)
	133	134	135	136	137	138	139	140	141	142	143	144	145	146
MISSISSIPPI	1 268 335	12 010	3 173	36 520	18 445.2	1 012.1	12 791	138 372	20 774.5	1 935.3	2 125	8 354	794.2	132.1
Adams	415	6	57	369	80.4	9.2	225	2 356	328.9	33.3	46	128	9.3	2.1
Alcorn	4 289	38	49	692	264.3	16.9	200	2 152	315.1	29.4	28	128	7.2	1.9
Amite	420	19	7	D	D	D	44	228	34.6	3.1	2	D	D	D
Attala	2 526	24	18	210	46.2	3.9	93	1 022	146.7	13.9	9	23	0.5	0.1
Benton	5	1	1	D	D	D	24	178	23.6	1.8	1	D	D	D
Bolivar	4 213	47	41	685	355.4	18.8	187	1 775	296.3	24.1	33	77	6.2	0.9
Calhoun	150	1	12	130	27.3	2.7	86	525	63.2	6.6	4	8	0.2	0.0
Carroll	NA	NA	9	32	17.3	0.9	24	161	15.5	1.9	NA	NA	NA	NA
Chickasaw	806	15	29	244	66.6	3.3	94	741	102.0	9.1	14	39	6.6	1.0
Choctaw	392	4	5	D	D	D	29	183	26.5	2.3	1	D	D	D
Claiborne	125	1	1	D	D	D	34	229	46.8	4.3	2	D	D	D
Clarke	431	6	14	142	33.1	2.3	63	325	38.3	3.7	7	13	0.7	0.1
Clay	130	11	18	217	561.8	14.1	94	771	109.5	9.4	12	26	2.9	0.4
Coahoma	1 837	25	37	529	203.2	14.3	160	1 613	250.4	22.2	39	100	11.1	1.4
Copiah	990	13	20	187	66.4	3.6	107	815	100.1	9.4	5	30	0.7	0.2
Covington	220	4	15	150	426.1	2.6	63	479	92.4	7.2	7	16	1.0	0.2
De Soto	265 325	2 437	78	D	D	D	278	4 248	663.2	58.5	69	205	31.8	4.1
Forrest	12 340	116	113	1 602	1 282.5	37.6	427	5 509	852.4	77.9	97	410	34.3	5.5
Franklin	235	1	5	D	D	D	37	198	25.4	2.2	4	14	1.4	0.3
George	15	1	12	D	D	D	70	706	92.4	8.0	5	10	0.5	0.1
Greene	389	14	5	92	18.6	1.9	36	203	28.2	2.1	2	D	D	D
Grenada	1 653	20	34	252	123.2	5.6	139	1 506	249.5	20.9	25	99	8.3	1.3
Hancock	16 705	165	30	251	68.8	7.6	128	1 583	214.2	19.9	34	124	9.1	1.7
Harrison	234 714	1 779	195	2 082	650.9	51.9	883	10 553	1 613.9	153.3	208	841	75.3	12.7
Hinds	81 980	1 026	454	6 671	2 600.7	206.0	1 092	17 356	2 760.8	280.3	295	1 560	152.6	24.6
Holmes	994	17	10	73	22.5	0.6	95	673	95.0	8.6	10	24	2.1	0.3
Humphreys	736	13	14	D	D	D	44	334	70.4	5.0	7	16	1.1	0.2
Issaquena	0	0	2	D	D	D	2	D	D	D	NA	NA	NA	NA
Itawamba	1 603	22	13	188	43.2	3.9	65	555	85.1	6.8	7	11	0.4	0.1
Jackson	94 545	896	70	576	272.6	16.7	512	6 119	948.6	82.3	100	367	29.4	5.6
Jasper	591	19	9	61	11.1	1.5	63	480	76.1	7.2	6	31	4.0	0.7
Jefferson	260	5	4	D	2.0	D	22	D	D	D	1	D	D	D
Jefferson Davis	0	0	4	17	2.0	0.2	51	357	45.5	4.6	4	8	0.7	0.1
Jones	3 971	48	102	764	211.8	20.8	303	3 059	467.1	43.3	49	275	19.1	6.0
Kemper	0	0	4	D	D	D	37	176	27.7	2.5	1	D	D	D
Lafayette	28 688	407	22	89	46.8	2.0	174	2 099	254.2	26.4	36	150	11.0	1.7
Lamar	810	10	29	D	D	D	170	2 250	283.4	28.0	22	67	7.2	1.3
Lauderdale	6 822	51	106	1 869	973.6	50.4	496	5 305	793.7	76.2	74	259	23.7	3.7
Lawrence	0	0	9	43	8.5	0.6	62	350	40.1	4.0	4	8	0.8	0.0
Leake	1 088	10	17	105	17.7	1.5	99	769	125.2	10.9	4	D	D	D
Lee	23 094	204	201	2 121	831.0	56.7	541	6 341	975.8	92.3	73	353	32.9	6.0
Leflore	5 959	36	56	803	905.1	23.4	222	2 033	277.8	26.4	40	95	9.7	1.3
Lincoln	1 396	17	37	762	415.6	17.9	164	1 809	315.2	24.7	20	75	7.2	1.5
Lowndes	20 679	284	93	1 098	333.5	30.0	367	3 856	601.2	54.3	58	332	27.5	5.2
Madison	179 375	1 069	118	1 565	1 180.0	45.4	377	4 987	679.8	69.6	72	235	28.6	4.5
Marion	442	5	29	D	D	D	130	1 154	167.4	15.0	14	41	4.2	0.6
Marshall	16 630	150	14	99	46.1	2.1	115	892	102.0	10.8	14	38	2.1	0.5
Monroe	696	9	33	200	104.5	5.4	169	1 525	228.1	21.3	18	50	3.1	0.5
Montgomery	4 240	86	10	57	20.7	1.0	68	507	63.1	5.5	2	D	D	D
Neshoba	1 185	16	32	297	85.3	5.9	117	1 384	226.0	18.4	9	150	17.5	3.0
Newton	425	14	8	D	D	D	91	829	116.0	10.6	9	18	1.1	0.4
Noxubee	361	4	9	57	21.2	0.9	62	378	50.9	4.3	4	4	0.3	0.1
Oktibbeha	13 733	179	11	63	25.3	1.5	172	2 029	241.4	23.5	37	109	12.7	2.0
Panola	2 197	38	37	465	248.0	14.6	186	1 525	239.7	20.8	14	32	2.3	0.4
Pearl River	36 376	388	34	276	58.0	3.8	178	2 086	336.3	30.2	26	83	9.5	1.1
Perry	462	7	3	D	D	D	36	253	29.4	2.7	4	7	0.7	0.1
Pike	1 322	22	64	527	164.0	11.9	252	2 339	343.0	33.2	34	130	9.6	1.6
Pontotoc	2 211	26	24	204	73.1	4.6	103	808	120.2	9.7	10	37	2.1	0.7
Prentiss	4 007	53	29	223	85.3	4.7	129	891	138.4	11.5	16	28	1.9	0.2
Quitman	577	11	4	D	D	D	35	249	44.4	3.9	4	4	0.8	0.1
Rankin	128 915	1 416	200	3 150	1 609.8	112.2	350	5 001	808.9	72.9	92	429	74.2	9.6
Scott	1 550	12	34	208	103.6	3.6	144	1 216	156.2	14.6	8	28	1.3	0.3
Sharkey	205	1	10	91	18.3	1.8	33	204	25.4	2.8	6	11	1.0	0.1
Simpson	4 026	45	13	76	31.3	1.6	103	1 039	147.9	13.3	13	33	1.9	0.3
Smith	438	5	7	D	D	D	49	279	35.5	3.4	5	16	2.3	0.3
Stone	1 224	18	17	76	17.0	1.3	59	425	63.6	6.7	7	26	1.8	0.3

1. Establishments with payroll.

Table B. States and Counties — Professional Services, Manufacturing, and Accommodation and Foodservices

STATE County	Professional, scientific, and technical services,[1] 1997				Manufacturing, 1997				Accommodation and foodservices, 1997			
	Number of establishments	Number of employees	Receipts (mil dol)	Annual payroll (mil dol)	Number of establishments	Number of employees	Receipts (mil dol)	Annual payroll (mil dol)	Number of establishments	Number of employees	Sales (mil dol)	Annual payroll (mil dol)
	147	148	149	150	151	152	153	154	155	156	157	158
MISSISSIPPI	3 627	21 671	1 761.6	662.1	3 008	227 800	39 658.3	5 599.4	4 050	84 834	3 064.8	814.5
Adams	66	234	14.9	3.9	38	2 299	550.0	76.0	88	1 189	37.7	10.3
Alcorn	43	191	10.7	3.6	58	4 918	955.6	150.8	66	913	26.9	6.8
Amite	11	22	4.2	0.3	10	691	97.3	17.2	4	D	D	D
Attala	17	39	8.5	2.2	22	1 267	119.9	21.8	28	373	10.8	2.3
Benton	3	D	D	D	NA	NA	NA	NA	1	D	D	D
Bolivar	42	139	10.2	3.6	22	2 724	417.8	67.0	49	626	D	4.3
Calhoun	15	47	4.0	1.1	34	1 874	296.2	35.4	16	D	D	D
Carroll	4	7	0.5	0.1	NA	NA	NA	NA	2	D	D	D
Chickasaw	16	62	2.2	0.7	80	4 896	420.8	93.4	27	D	D	D
Choctaw	3	D	D	D	10	598	105.0	13.9	5	D	D	D
Claiborne	7	15	1.1	0.2	10	629	88.6	13.9	6	46	1.5	0.4
Clarke	15	41	2.4	0.8	18	2 084	304.1	51.4	12	94	3.4	0.9
Clay	18	103	5.8	2.3	25	3 640	926.0	113.6	32	408	11.5	3.1
Coahoma	44	246	19.3	7.9	28	1 353	236.6	35.6	37	540	17.2	4.3
Copiah	15	50	3.5	0.8	32	2 735	407.7	52.6	30	425	12.6	3.0
Covington	12	37	2.5	0.7	17	1 950	194.2	32.2	15	D	D	D
De Soto	83	445	24.4	8.7	131	7 232	1 369.6	213.4	114	2 639	72.7	18.6
Forrest	166	799	61.1	19.8	84	5 170	1 037.1	116.3	163	D	D	D
Franklin	7	39	2.2	0.8	NA	NA	NA	NA	4	D	D	D
George	19	73	4.4	1.9	NA	NA	NA	NA	25	D	D	D
Greene	5	9	0.3	0.1	NA	NA	NA	NA	9	78	1.8	0.5
Grenada	29	127	8.8	4.1	24	4 194	571.8	109.5	46	806	24.4	5.9
Hancock	55	614	54.2	23.5	NA	NA	NA	NA	72	784	24.7	6.2
Harrison	335	2 049	152.0	55.6	139	4 498	1 079.7	133.6	377	9 573	323.4	87.8
Hinds	652	5 400	544.0	216.5	208	11 540	2 484.4	314.8	449	10 351	322.4	92.6
Holmes	7	27	3.2	0.5	14	1 674	214.5	31.4	18	113	3.1	0.8
Humphreys	7	21	1.4	0.4	4	D	D	D	9	D	D	D
Issaquena	NA	NA	NA	NA	NA	NA	NA	NA	NA	NA	NA	NA
Itawamba	10	31	1.3	0.5	40	1 366	371.6	30.1	29	341	6.9	1.5
Jackson	161	1 603	134.3	61.4	98	16 340	4 447.7	534.5	191	3 469	97.4	25.5
Jasper	16	150	6.8	3.3	15	1 720	151.3	30.0	12	D	D	D
Jefferson	4	12	1.3	0.1	NA	NA	NA	NA	5	131	2.3	0.5
Jefferson Davis	7	13	0.5	0.1	9	769	56.0	8.9	16	D	D	D
Jones	83	478	48.2	12.1	68	6 820	991.3	162.7	84	1 309	37.3	10.0
Kemper	2	D	D	D	NA	NA	NA	NA	4	30	0.6	0.2
Lafayette	70	422	27.6	14.1	29	2 017	304.5	43.2	109	1 665	43.2	11.5
Lamar	36	195	14.1	6.4	22	770	116.8	16.4	48	D	D	D
Lauderdale	117	483	33.9	10.6	83	6 076	916.6	164.2	147	2 855	87.4	23.9
Lawrence	4	10	0.6	0.1	9	D	D	D	15	126	2.9	0.7
Leake	16	36	1.5	0.3	18	2 481	242.0	29.8	20	D	D	D
Lee	140	865	64.0	26.6	191	17 717	2 708.4	472.9	158	3 037	84.7	23.2
Leflore	63	324	23.6	7.8	40	3 572	510.9	76.6	51	841	28.0	7.3
Lincoln	41	298	17.0	7.0	28	1 383	301.4	35.1	42	715	21.2	5.2
Lowndes	90	459	31.4	12.3	71	7 611	1 313.9	223.2	105	2 071	59.5	14.9
Madison	131	1 042	103.7	32.2	57	2 414	396.6	57.2	113	2 402	78.8	20.8
Marion	21	112	5.7	2.9	26	1 000	103.9	15.7	32	434	10.5	2.8
Marshall	20	32	4.3	0.6	29	1 777	201.3	41.2	19	322	7.7	1.9
Monroe	35	114	5.5	1.5	71	4 889	1 121.2	124.8	46	503	13.4	3.1
Montgomery	10	54	3.2	0.7	21	1 165	116.6	21.8	20	196	5.4	1.3
Neshoba	18	69	4.7	1.7	32	2 572	347.8	57.1	37	725	17.1	3.8
Newton	16	232	5.9	3.1	20	2 256	165.7	49.5	26	D	D	D
Noxubee	8	27	0.6	0.1	20	1 201	210.8	22.8	8	105	3.0	1.0
Oktibbeha	61	286	12.6	4.1	35	2 132	372.3	49.8	85	1 546	40.2	10.2
Panola	30	201	11.0	5.4	44	2 943	575.0	68.5	46	829	23.0	5.6
Pearl River	49	174	13.6	5.2	47	905	190.3	20.3	66	877	23.2	5.7
Perry	5	14	0.8	0.2	7	D	D	D	6	68	1.5	0.4
Pike	52	163	10.7	3.2	36	3 924	580.3	64.7	61	923	26.0	6.5
Pontotoc	19	75	4.3	1.1	92	5 549	720.2	116.5	25	340	8.0	1.9
Prentiss	21	87	7.5	2.0	46	4 507	702.2	86.1	34	425	10.9	2.8
Quitman	6	21	0.7	0.2	NA	NA	NA	NA	5	D	D	D
Rankin	129	740	73.8	24.4	127	5 763	1 088.2	150.3	127	2 286	78.1	20.7
Scott	19	66	2.9	1.1	28	5 487	607.4	95.8	36	448	13.0	3.4
Sharkey	7	22	1.4	0.6	NA	NA	NA	NA	3	D	D	D
Simpson	22	86	6.0	2.1	15	1 182	360.4	22.2	21	D	D	D
Smith	13	41	4.0	0.5	17	1 801	392.8	41.2	8	53	1.6	0.4
Stone	13	65	5.2	1.8	15	682	124.6	15.3	18	D	D	D

1. Firms subject to federal tax.

STATE County	Health care and social assistance,[1] 1997				Other services,[1] 1997				Federal funds and grants, 2002–2003 Expenditures (mil dol)			
										Direct payments for individuals[2]		
	Number of establishments	Number of employees	Receipts (mil dol)	Annual payroll (mil dol)	Number of establishments	Number of employees	Receipts (mil dol)	Annual payroll (mil dol)	Total	Social Security and government retirement	Medicare	Food stamps and Supplemental Security Income
	159	160	161	162	163	164	165	166	167	168	169	170
MISSISSIPPI	4 139	55 529	3 632.3	1 547.0	3 491	17 449	1 057.1	299.6	21 740.6	6 354.0	2 802.5	904.0
Adams	82	1 136	74.8	29.7	55	260	13.0	4.0	214.8	85.3	34.8	15.1
Alcorn	73	540	32.5	11.9	55	163	9.2	2.5	189.1	86.9	40.3	10.5
Amite	5	20	1.5	0.7	5	42	1.3	0.4	78.3	30.7	15.6	4.4
Attala	21	309	15.3	6.6	29	132	12.2	2.3	124.5	48.4	26.2	7.1
Benton	6	112	3.8	1.9	3	3	0.2	0.0	50.4	19.1	9.7	4.8
Bolivar	48	735	38.7	15.2	49	167	12.9	2.7	292.3	67.8	40.6	26.4
Calhoun	19	153	8.2	2.6	12	55	2.5	0.6	97.1	35.9	20.0	4.8
Carroll	6	23	0.9	0.4	8	17	1.8	0.2	52.0	19.9	9.5	3.5
Chickasaw	27	396	20.7	8.0	22	64	3.2	0.8	118.1	45.6	22.8	6.0
Choctaw	8	37	2.7	0.8	7	18	1.6	0.3	48.9	17.7	7.8	5.0
Claiborne	12	149	5.8	2.9	7	14	0.6	0.1	73.1	19.5	12.2	6.4
Clarke	17	185	7.8	3.0	16	53	2.9	0.7	97.9	43.6	19.7	5.5
Clay	34	271	12.4	4.8	29	150	10.7	3.1	115.5	45.6	18.6	8.5
Coahoma	63	1 435	96.3	31.8	45	169	7.8	2.3	240.6	54.3	40.3	19.6
Copiah	26	431	16.0	6.5	27	109	8.1	1.7	198.1	72.8	35.5	13.0
Covington	13	130	5.7	2.3	16	66	6.0	1.3	118.9	45.5	20.5	6.1
De Soto	87	859	62.2	26.0	112	533	35.9	9.8	366.0	213.5	56.0	10.3
Forrest	122	2 562	159.7	91.3	101	753	45.2	12.9	484.1	181.7	78.6	21.2
Franklin	7	92	3.6	1.8	6	27	1.3	0.4	49.7	19.1	9.4	3.1
George	12	166	8.9	3.1	27	79	4.0	0.9	97.7	49.8	22.4	5.4
Greene	6	103	3.7	1.3	8	32	1.9	0.7	58.0	19.7	11.4	3.4
Grenada	59	652	39.1	14.4	29	133	10.6	2.3	146.9	54.1	33.9	9.0
Hancock	48	322	19.4	7.8	45	187	8.8	2.9	493.4	116.9	43.2	9.6
Harrison	372	5 503	407.7	157.6	284	1 663	89.6	28.6	1 874.7	565.8	194.8	45.7
Hinds	528	7 452	562.2	250.5	391	3 003	176.0	55.8	2 496.6	594.8	232.3	94.3
Holmes	20	267	14.0	6.0	15	43	2.0	0.4	185.8	39.9	34.0	17.0
Humphreys	14	159	6.7	3.0	15	36	2.9	0.5	88.0	18.9	17.9	5.8
Issaquena	NA	NA	NA	NA	NA	NA	NA	NA	15.5	1.9	1.5	0.6
Itawamba	19	309	9.6	4.2	19	60	2.7	0.6	105.3	42.4	20.4	2.7
Jackson	237	1 763	124.0	53.4	162	744	41.0	11.7	2 048.8	323.8	109.3	25.3
Jasper	14	64	2.5	1.0	16	82	5.5	1.4	107.5	40.5	19.7	5.7
Jefferson	3	15	0.8	0.1	4	9	0.4	0.1	81.6	16.5	9.8	5.9
Jefferson Davis	12	62	3.1	1.2	7	19	1.3	0.3	86.6	27.3	15.3	6.2
Jones	76	1 147	65.7	32.0	101	543	33.3	8.9	368.7	158.5	75.0	19.8
Kemper	4	140	3.7	1.9	6	11	0.7	0.2	69.5	21.7	10.2	3.3
Lafayette	72	713	58.8	25.9	40	238	10.1	3.3	181.4	59.6	19.2	2.5
Lamar	61	745	67.0	29.7	27	107	8.4	2.0	120.8	59.8	23.4	6.5
Lauderdale	149	2 063	164.4	82.5	136	690	36.6	10.7	623.3	194.3	88.0	25.5
Lawrence	11	120	4.3	1.4	7	27	2.5	0.5	93.0	41.6	19.5	4.0
Leake	25	775	37.9	18.5	18	44	3.8	0.8	134.4	50.3	29.5	6.8
Lee	161	2 064	168.4	92.8	127	859	52.7	21.9	379.0	171.2	63.8	15.0
Leflore	67	954	61.6	26.2	57	325	17.6	5.4	275.2	65.5	48.1	21.8
Lincoln	55	739	42.8	16.4	34	191	11.7	2.7	167.2	72.7	30.7	9.6
Lowndes	132	1 159	79.5	29.4	102	540	33.1	9.5	453.5	133.8	44.3	18.8
Madison	87	758	46.4	21.7	74	482	45.1	11.4	530.5	141.3	45.7	18.7
Marion	32	419	22.4	8.8	37	142	8.8	2.1	165.8	63.5	33.5	10.7
Marshall	19	332	17.2	5.9	16	86	3.8	1.1	204.6	66.5	29.7	12.6
Monroe	46	586	27.8	12.0	60	182	13.3	2.8	206.5	85.7	41.4	9.4
Montgomery	17	210	9.1	4.1	17	59	3.6	0.6	106.1	30.7	19.5	5.0
Neshoba	22	535	31.8	15.0	38	133	9.9	2.4	160.2	53.7	30.6	8.4
Newton	27	432	21.9	8.3	22	46	3.2	0.8	150.1	61.5	34.9	6.4
Noxubee	12	53	2.5	1.2	9	22	1.6	0.3	86.5	23.2	10.9	7.9
Oktibbeha	63	625	32.7	12.6	58	252	11.4	3.4	248.6	69.6	22.0	10.7
Panola	50	646	33.1	13.2	25	84	4.4	1.0	192.9	69.8	32.4	13.7
Pearl River	59	451	23.7	9.1	43	206	10.1	2.9	259.7	124.8	53.0	11.5
Perry	6	41	2.0	0.6	10	38	2.3	0.7	58.6	25.0	10.2	5.8
Pike	72	680	40.7	18.4	48	245	12.8	3.7	248.3	96.3	49.7	17.9
Pontotoc	28	285	10.6	4.1	32	104	5.2	1.3	123.0	52.0	23.3	4.5
Prentiss	37	331	14.7	6.3	37	148	10.1	2.8	140.1	61.9	26.1	5.8
Quitman	7	219	11.3	4.1	12	36	2.1	0.3	90.6	19.4	14.1	6.9
Rankin	154	3 534	269.9	104.4	143	744	55.9	13.4	433.1	218.9	67.7	12.5
Scott	25	290	15.0	6.2	32	173	10.1	2.9	158.5	59.3	33.9	8.7
Sharkey	11	138	6.3	2.5	10	19	1.0	0.2	51.0	11.0	8.6	5.6
Simpson	35	855	31.4	12.9	23	65	4.5	0.9	133.7	59.4	29.5	7.2
Smith	8	171	4.7	2.3	8	10	1.1	0.2	76.4	32.0	14.2	4.0
Stone	18	390	31.8	9.3	12	34	2.3	0.7	94.3	39.6	16.6	3.8

1. Firms subject to federal tax.   2. State totals may include programs not allocated by county.

Table B. States and Counties — Federal Funds and Local Government Finances

	Federal funds and grants, 2002–2003 (cont'd)							Local government finances, 2002				
	Expenditures (mil dol) (cont'd)							General revenue				
	Procurement contract awards		Grants[1]							Taxes		
STATE County											Per capita[2] (dollars)	
	Salaries and wages	Defense	Other	Medicaid and other health-related	Nutrition and family welfare	Education	Other	Total (mil dol)	Intergovern-mental (mil dol)	Total (mil dol)	Total	Property
	171	172	173	174	175	176	177	178	179	180	181	182
MISSISSIPPI	1 969.9	2 126.4	499.3	2 763.2	689.0	474.2	1 392.1	X	X	X	X	X
Adams	7.4	0.5	3.0	41.9	11.5	2.6	10.8	107.1	38.5	25.4	757	646
Alcorn	5.5	0.0	1.4	32.5	2.1	1.7	2.0	145.1	46.4	17.0	489	456
Amite	3.7	0.0	0.9	17.0	1.6	0.9	2.4	16.6	9.8	4.0	300	274
Attala	3.7	0.0	1.2	29.4	2.4	1.6	2.8	51.1	19.8	10.0	508	472
Benton	1.3	0.0	0.6	13.0	2.1	0.4	-1.6	13.7	9.4	2.9	365	364
Bolivar	8.6	0.1	1.1	83.2	16.1	4.8	11.0	81.8	48.5	22.4	562	521
Calhoun	3.2	0.6	1.2	21.9	1.6	0.6	3.5	27.6	13.9	6.7	449	414
Carroll	1.4	0.1	0.3	12.2	1.1	0.5	0.5	13.2	6.8	4.5	424	420
Chickasaw	3.4	0.2	1.4	28.1	2.1	1.1	3.3	35.5	20.4	8.2	421	386
Choctaw	2.4	0.0	0.7	11.8	1.2	0.7	0.8	17.6	10.5	3.9	405	379
Claiborne	1.5	0.1	0.7	16.9	2.1	0.8	11.0	37.2	19.2	3.9	329	292
Clarke	2.2	0.0	0.5	21.6	2.0	1.0	1.1	29.8	17.5	7.9	441	394
Clay	4.4	0.0	1.2	24.1	3.3	2.7	2.6	38.4	22.1	12.4	566	536
Coahoma	5.7	0.4	1.3	63.1	11.6	5.3	12.3	83.3	45.2	23.2	768	634
Copiah	8.1	3.9	9.7	37.1	3.9	2.7	4.0	83.9	37.8	14.9	517	484
Covington	3.7	0.0	0.6	24.2	2.4	1.7	12.4	45.1	18.8	7.7	391	365
De Soto	10.3	4.3	4.2	30.5	3.9	1.8	28.5	192.7	99.9	68.6	579	544
Forrest	38.3	17.0	6.7	48.4	12.1	6.2	47.4	405.5	72.4	56.6	771	677
Franklin	3.2	0.0	1.2	9.5	1.2	0.5	1.8	17.4	10.6	3.9	468	459
George	2.9	0.0	0.8	8.4	2.8	0.8	1.8	49.8	19.1	8.5	431	399
Greene	1.0	0.0	0.7	10.6	1.2	2.3	7.5	18.6	11.6	5.1	390	374
Grenada	10.8	1.6	2.0	24.1	2.4	1.4	4.9	82.7	27.8	14.4	629	584
Hancock	113.9	26.2	134.5	9.9	3.0	1.6	24.9	122.7	38.2	34.0	760	680
Harrison	642.6	160.6	64.9	86.6	23.7	12.3	60.0	718.3	238.6	172.9	906	755
Hinds	269.9	50.7	59.8	313.3	188.7	186.2	434.4	652.1	313.3	220.0	882	820
Holmes	3.7	3.8	1.2	59.0	6.2	3.2	3.6	56.5	37.3	10.0	461	437
Humphreys	1.6	0.0	0.4	25.0	3.0	1.2	1.7	25.0	11.5	6.4	592	547
Issaquena	0.4	3.8	0.1	2.3	0.6	0.2	0.3	5.5	0.9	1.2	527	508
Itawamba	2.6	2.6	0.7	18.2	1.3	0.8	4.0	66.2	38.2	13.0	564	555
Jackson	140.0	1 359.3	5.4	28.4	13.2	7.9	31.6	429.5	126.0	117.6	883	805
Jasper	3.4	0.1	0.5	26.5	2.5	1.2	6.6	36.5	16.7	9.9	541	491
Jefferson	1.7	0.1	0.4	20.7	2.0	4.5	10.7	21.5	10.7	4.4	457	412
Jefferson Davis	1.8	0.0	0.3	21.2	8.4	1.9	3.5	28.2	20.8	4.8	355	346
Jones	18.4	0.5	10.4	55.1	6.1	4.2	8.1	206.2	83.2	36.1	556	514
Kemper	2.7	0.0	0.4	17.8	1.4	0.7	1.8	51.4	22.4	6.7	632	606
Lafayette	22.1	7.5	4.0	22.9	2.3	1.7	24.4	65.2	31.4	22.4	568	513
Lamar	3.3	0.0	0.7	14.8	2.3	1.6	5.8	64.6	34.1	22.7	552	524
Lauderdale	117.2	64.2	7.1	73.8	8.1	4.8	28.6	178.3	95.6	50.3	648	600
Lawrence	3.7	0.0	1.7	15.6	1.6	1.5	3.3	27.5	12.8	7.8	578	562
Leake	4.5	0.0	0.9	31.5	2.2	1.4	6.0	30.9	16.8	7.3	339	317
Lee	31.4	0.5	6.7	44.4	10.2	4.4	22.4	177.3	89.8	54.7	708	670
Leflore	11.5	8.0	1.0	61.0	7.5	9.0	14.7	138.2	41.5	21.3	573	545
Lincoln	6.5	0.0	1.0	26.8	3.3	1.8	13.3	58.8	32.8	16.8	502	463
Lowndes	88.7	85.6	3.2	49.4	5.9	3.8	12.7	135.8	75.1	38.2	626	576
Madison	14.5	159.7	66.3	46.6	6.6	3.5	21.1	164.9	71.4	59.6	766	710
Marion	3.8	2.9	2.0	32.5	10.8	1.6	3.0	61.8	26.7	11.5	455	425
Marshall	5.9	0.0	1.6	44.6	27.5	3.5	6.4	45.8	25.0	16.0	456	427
Monroe	6.0	0.1	10.8	35.9	3.6	2.1	6.5	61.4	34.1	17.6	467	433
Montgomery	7.1	0.0	0.5	24.9	8.6	1.0	7.7	23.6	13.7	5.5	464	418
Neshoba	5.9	0.0	1.0	27.9	5.0	4.5	10.4	41.0	25.5	10.1	349	317
Newton	6.1	0.0	0.9	26.8	2.0	1.2	2.4	50.8	31.3	9.2	418	382
Noxubee	2.3	0.0	2.5	29.6	3.0	1.1	1.8	31.3	13.0	6.3	503	466
Oktibbeha	18.6	12.1	3.9	36.1	4.1	6.3	49.7	95.7	36.0	20.0	467	459
Panola	6.2	1.0	5.4	42.6	4.8	2.1	2.1	69.6	38.2	17.1	490	435
Pearl River	10.0	5.1	9.6	22.7	4.6	2.4	6.8	109.5	60.8	26.1	518	485
Perry	1.6	0.1	0.6	10.9	1.5	0.8	0.4	69.6	14.1	6.4	523	490
Pike	11.3	0.0	4.7	43.5	5.3	6.0	6.9	157.2	50.6	20.5	525	508
Pontotoc	3.6	0.0	0.8	21.9	1.6	0.9	11.9	52.3	30.2	11.6	430	391
Prentiss	3.7	0.0	0.6	27.5	1.7	1.6	4.4	69.7	41.0	11.9	463	451
Quitman	1.6	0.0	0.3	26.6	2.5	1.6	3.4	16.2	9.7	5.0	510	463
Rankin	39.3	5.3	2.2	29.8	4.3	3.8	45.1	189.0	91.0	66.8	549	518
Scott	9.7	0.1	3.2	30.5	3.5	1.5	7.3	47.8	30.0	12.2	430	386
Sharkey	1.9	0.3	0.5	12.1	1.6	0.8	1.4	14.3	9.0	3.8	609	568
Simpson	3.3	0.1	0.8	23.4	2.5	2.7	3.5	43.5	24.1	9.5	344	315
Smith	3.4	0.0	0.4	18.9	1.4	0.9	0.1	26.2	16.8	6.5	411	374
Stone	4.9	0.0	1.2	6.1	1.2	1.1	6.7	81.0	41.6	18.4	1 290	1 248

1. State totals may include programs not allocated by county.   2. Based on the resident population estimated as of July 1 of the year shown.

Table B. States and Counties — Local Government Finances, Government Employment, and Elections

STATE County	Total (mil dol)	Per capita[1] (dollars)	Education	Health and hospitals	Police protection	Public welfare	Highways	Total (mil dol)	Per capita[1] (dollars)	Federal civilian	Federal military	State and local	Democratic	Republican	All other
	183	184	185	186	187	188	189	190	191	192	193	194	195	196	197
MISSISSIPPI	X	X	X	X	X	X	X	X	X	25 005	32 400	217 272	39.6	59.6	0.8
Adams	111.8	3 331	29.6	20.4	6.1	0.1	11.0	150.1	4 472	129	180	2 182	54.6	45.1	0.3
Alcorn	148.4	4 273	21.3	50.1	2.4	0.3	3.9	74.6	2 149	98	182	2 451	38.3	60.7	1.1
Amite	16.1	1 195	63.4	0.7	6.3	0.0	11.4	2.5	183	63	70	435	41.8	57.7	0.5
Attala	50.1	2 539	41.6	29.1	3.0	0.1	5.2	13.0	658	70	103	1 187	37.9	61.4	0.6
Benton	13.8	1 738	62.1	0.3	3.7	0.0	7.3	2.6	324	25	41	298	52.8	46.4	0.8
Bolivar	81.0	2 034	63.7	0.8	6.8	0.3	5.9	44.8	1 125	95	208	3 289	63.8	35.2	1.1
Calhoun	26.3	1 765	52.9	13.0	5.0	0.2	7.5	11.5	769	44	78	776	34.9	64.7	0.4
Carroll	15.4	1 445	46.0	0.5	5.2	0.3	10.7	11.4	1 070	26	56	402	34.0	65.5	0.5
Chickasaw	34.0	1 740	57.2	8.1	5.7	0.1	5.7	12.2	627	53	102	821	48.9	50.3	0.9
Choctaw	16.2	1 683	61.9	0.6	5.1	2.7	7.3	7.9	819	71	50	423	33.0	66.5	0.5
Claiborne	35.5	3 029	36.4	13.9	2.8	0.2	5.0	149.1	12 705	35	61	1 942	81.5	17.7	0.8
Clarke	28.1	1 561	67.3	0.4	4.0	0.2	9.3	11.0	612	39	94	791	32.0	67.6	0.5
Clay	37.9	1 732	58.9	0.2	6.1	0.6	7.1	33.5	1 532	76	114	921	51.9	47.6	0.5
Coahoma	82.3	2 729	57.0	0.5	5.3	0.2	7.2	102.4	3 394	89	159	2 088	64.1	34.6	1.3
Copiah	81.5	2 828	58.4	15.8	4.0	0.1	6.2	36.9	1 281	75	151	1 945	43.5	56.0	0.5
Covington	40.7	2 065	45.5	33.1	3.3	0.3	6.7	6.9	348	69	103	1 155	38.3	61.1	0.6
De Soto	195.4	1 650	51.8	1.1	8.1	0.0	7.4	170.7	1 441	151	619	4 213	27.0	72.3	0.6
Forrest	375.0	5 105	18.0	62.8	2.6	0.1	2.8	204.3	2 781	706	622	11 820	37.7	61.6	0.7
Franklin	15.3	1 833	71.7	1.7	4.3	0.0	4.0	1.8	210	78	44	515	35.0	64.5	0.5
George	48.7	2 459	39.4	39.0	3.9	0.0	6.4	28.2	1 423	46	103	1 240	21.6	77.8	0.7
Greene	18.5	1 415	62.7	0.4	6.0	0.0	7.9	2.5	189	17	68	1 144	26.8	72.6	0.5
Grenada	91.4	3 991	24.8	44.3	5.1	0.1	6.6	46.0	2 007	251	120	1 636	41.3	58.1	0.5
Hancock	125.8	2 816	29.9	27.4	4.5	0.1	6.3	83.8	1 876	1 535	528	2 194	28.6	70.3	1.1
Harrison	733.5	3 842	29.7	27.2	6.6	0.4	6.0	399.9	2 094	6 108	12 434	12 027	36.5	62.7	0.8
Hinds	662.9	2 656	54.6	0.5	7.1	0.9	5.2	738.3	2 958	4 452	1 513	34 463	59.5	39.7	0.7
Holmes	55.5	2 564	77.1	0.8	3.2	0.3	5.9	22.5	1 038	65	113	1 230	75.8	23.6	0.6
Humphreys	24.2	2 256	45.0	19.8	5.3	0.0	8.3	11.5	1 069	31	56	606	64.0	35.0	1.1
Issaquena	4.8	2 210	0.0	3.5	12.6	0.0	14.4	5.0	2 276	0	11	97	53.0	45.4	1.6
Itawamba	63.6	2 768	79.5	0.2	1.8	0.1	6.5	32.4	1 411	52	120	917	28.9	70.4	0.8
Jackson	421.3	3 162	34.1	27.9	4.0	0.2	4.7	515.4	3 868	786	2 878	8 822	30.4	68.9	0.7
Jasper	35.8	1 959	49.3	17.2	3.7	0.2	8.3	13.8	755	57	96	941	51.5	48.0	0.5
Jefferson	19.8	2 054	48.2	11.2	9.9	0.1	7.7	14.3	1 479	23	54	610	81.3	18.2	0.4
Jefferson Davis	25.1	1 860	56.4	0.9	3.8	0.3	7.3	8.6	637	30	71	816	51.3	46.3	2.4
Jones	216.1	3 322	43.6	28.6	3.1	0.2	4.8	180.5	2 775	252	340	6 275	27.7	71.8	0.5
Kemper	51.8	4 893	80.3	0.3	1.6	0.1	5.7	9.0	845	37	55	548	53.5	45.9	0.6
Lafayette	68.1	1 724	47.8	0.4	6.2	0.1	9.8	81.4	2 059	356	230	6 487	40.4	58.5	1.1
Lamar	64.7	1 570	62.7	0.4	3.8	0.2	12.4	53.3	1 295	52	215	1 699	19.1	80.3	0.6
Lauderdale	180.2	2 323	58.3	2.7	5.6	0.2	7.0	113.8	1 467	771	1 900	5 667	33.9	65.6	0.5
Lawrence	26.9	2 002	51.3	18.9	3.7	0.1	9.9	6.3	470	54	70	718	36.1	63.2	0.7
Leake	31.2	1 450	50.7	0.2	9.8	0.2	11.2	19.5	906	85	113	1 120	39.3	60.3	0.4
Lee	184.9	2 395	53.5	0.2	7.2	0.1	6.4	198.2	2 567	495	440	4 669	33.0	66.2	0.8
Leflore	136.6	3 682	27.7	47.8	4.7	0.2	4.9	45.3	1 222	174	200	4 258	62.0	37.9	0.1
Lincoln	60.4	1 805	57.7	0.3	5.9	0.2	9.1	48.7	1 455	107	175	1 660	30.5	69.0	0.5
Lowndes	127.3	2 088	51.1	0.3	6.7	0.1	7.5	172.5	2 828	860	1 719	3 840	42.9	56.4	0.7
Madison	192.2	2 468	50.6	8.2	5.9	1.1	5.8	218.6	2 807	210	407	3 670	34.8	64.6	0.5
Marion	58.9	2 326	45.2	24.3	7.6	0.0	4.6	36.4	1 439	60	132	1 512	32.6	66.9	0.5
Marshall	49.1	1 395	55.9	1.4	5.9	0.3	11.1	32.8	933	117	184	1 227	58.5	40.9	0.6
Monroe	65.5	1 735	55.9	0.6	6.6	0.2	8.0	29.9	793	153	197	1 518	39.8	59.7	0.6
Montgomery	23.0	1 943	59.3	0.6	5.4	0.2	10.5	5.7	478	36	62	748	44.9	54.7	0.4
Neshoba	41.7	1 436	55.6	0.6	6.8	0.2	6.8	22.9	789	96	152	7 257	24.8	74.8	0.4
Newton	52.4	2 385	76.0	0.5	3.7	0.2	6.5	12.4	566	90	115	1 819	26.8	72.7	0.5
Noxubee	37.5	3 014	51.9	20.1	3.4	0.6	9.7	14.3	1 148	52	65	723	71.3	28.2	0.5
Oktibbeha	92.7	2 169	42.7	29.9	3.9	0.0	3.6	44.1	1 031	329	233	9 089	43.1	55.7	1.2
Panola	69.6	1 994	51.6	9.9	7.2	0.2	7.7	35.7	1 023	133	182	2 255	49.1	50.5	0.4
Pearl River	100.9	2 000	72.1	0.2	4.1	0.2	5.4	24.7	490	124	263	2 571	23.0	76.4	0.6
Perry	70.5	5 780	19.3	10.3	1.9	0.1	4.0	578.3	47 399	22	64	608	25.1	74.4	0.4
Pike	153.2	3 931	36.1	44.0	2.6	1.2	2.8	33.6	861	140	205	3 288	46.7	52.7	0.6
Pontotoc	48.2	1 783	56.0	0.3	4.9	0.2	11.1	21.2	783	59	141	1 079	23.4	75.7	0.9
Prentiss	68.5	2 662	75.9	0.4	3.6	0.2	3.9	37.4	1 453	56	135	1 479	33.5	65.8	0.7
Quitman	16.3	1 662	58.5	1.0	6.9	0.4	8.7	7.5	761	32	51	442	59.5	39.8	0.7
Rankin	178.0	1 464	55.7	0.6	7.9	0.3	7.0	209.2	1 721	453	638	8 846	20.1	78.6	1.2
Scott	47.7	1 684	61.9	0.5	6.8	0.1	9.0	28.5	1 005	202	148	1 163	37.1	62.5	0.3
Sharkey	13.4	2 143	64.4	1.1	7.1	0.5	8.3	4.1	654	42	33	418	50.4	36.2	13.4
Simpson	41.9	1 514	57.0	15.9	3.0	0.0	6.5	11.0	398	49	145	1 750	32.4	67.6	0.0
Smith	23.9	1 502	66.2	0.5	7.4	0.0	9.4	4.1	256	60	83	611	21.0	78.3	0.7
Stone	80.3	5 623	84.4	0.2	4.4	0.0	4.0	15.4	1 077	91	75	1 035	26.7	72.3	1.0

1. Based on the resident population estimated as of July 1 of the year shown.

Table B. States and Counties — Land Area and Population

STATE/ County code	CBSA code[1]	County Type[2]	STATE County	Land area,[3] (sq km) 2000	Total persons	Rank	Per square kilometer	White	Black	Am. Indian, Alaska Native	Asian and Pacific Islander	Percent Hispanic or Latino[4]	Under 5 years	5 to 17 years	18 to 24 years	25 to 34 years	35 to 44 years	45 to 54 years
								(Race alone or in combination, not Hispanic or Latino, percent)					(Age, percent)					
				1	2	3	4	5	6	7	8	9	10	11	12	13	14	15
			MISSISSIPPI—Cont'd															
28 133	26940	5	Sunflower	1 797	33 374	1 318	18.6	26.4	71.5	0.1	0.5	1.5	7.4	19.0	15.0	15.3	15.2	12.6
28 135	...	7	Tallahatchie	1 668	14 394	2 135	8.6	38.8	59.7	0.2	0.4	1.0	7.1	21.7	10.6	11.5	13.6	13.0
28 137	32820	1	Tate	1 048	25 794	1 544	24.6	68.1	30.5	0.5	0.2	1.1	7.0	19.1	12.6	11.7	14.6	13.5
28 139	...	7	Tippah	1 186	20 920	1 755	17.6	79.8	17.1	0.5	0.2	3.0	7.1	17.7	10.4	12.9	14.5	12.9
28 141	...	8	Tishomingo	1 098	18 966	1 863	17.3	94.2	3.3	0.6	0.1	2.2	5.8	16.5	8.3	12.3	14.5	13.9
28 143	32820	1	Tunica	1 178	9 917	2 450	8.4	24.6	72.4	0.2	0.6	2.6	9.1	22.0	11.8	13.3	13.3	12.3
28 145	...	7	Union	1 076	26 113	1 535	24.3	82.6	14.9	0.3	0.3	2.3	7.3	18.4	9.4	13.2	14.4	13.1
28 147	...	9	Walthall	1 046	15 191	2 087	14.5	54.5	44.0	0.3	0.3	1.2	7.1	19.9	10.8	11.5	13.1	12.8
28 149	46980	4	Warren	1 519	48 993	955	32.3	52.9	45.1	0.6	0.9	1.0	7.6	20.1	9.7	12.2	14.6	14.7
28 151	24740	5	Washington	1 875	60 347	817	32.2	31.8	66.7	0.3	0.7	0.9	8.7	21.8	10.8	12.4	13.1	13.8
28 153	...	7	Wayne	2 099	21 149	1 745	10.1	61.7	37.5	0.1	0.2	0.7	7.4	20.2	10.5	12.4	14.3	13.2
28 155	...	9	Webster	1 094	10 159	2 430	9.3	77.6	20.8	0.2	0.2	1.3	7.1	17.9	9.9	11.3	14.8	13.2
28 157	...	8	Wilkinson	1 753	10 241	2 422	5.8	30.4	69.1	0.1	0.1	0.4	6.6	17.8	12.5	13.8	14.8	13.1
28 159	...	7	Winston	1 572	19 911	1 810	12.7	54.1	43.9	0.7	0.1	1.4	7.1	18.5	10.0	11.9	13.2	13.9
28 161	...	7	Yalobusha	1 210	13 347	2 211	11.0	59.9	38.8	0.3	0.2	1.0	6.5	18.1	9.7	12.0	13.4	13.8
28 163	49540	6	Yazoo	2 381	28 272	1 449	11.9	40.2	54.5	0.4	0.5	4.8	7.6	19.8	10.7	13.3	14.8	12.9
29 000	...	X	**MISSOURI**	178 414	5 704 484	X	32.0	84.4	11.9	1.0	1.7	2.3	6.5	18.1	10.1	12.9	14.9	14.1
29 001	28860	7	Adair	1 469	24 790	1 584	16.9	95.3	1.5	0.5	1.9	1.5	5.4	13.1	25.0	11.9	11.2	11.2
29 003	41140	3	Andrew	1 127	16 813	1 974	14.9	97.8	0.7	0.6	0.3	0.9	5.5	18.9	9.7	11.3	15.6	15.0
29 005	...	9	Atchison	1 411	6 286	2 747	4.5	96.6	2.4	0.2	0.2	0.7	4.8	18.0	8.4	9.9	13.3	14.0
29 007	33020	6	Audrain	1 795	25 716	1 547	14.3	90.8	8.0	0.6	0.4	0.9	6.4	17.4	8.9	12.4	15.1	13.7
29 009	...	6	Barry	2 018	34 629	1 288	17.2	92.9	0.2	1.8	0.4	5.8	6.3	18.9	9.1	10.9	14.1	13.2
29 011	...	6	Barton	1 539	12 999	2 240	8.4	97.4	0.4	1.7	0.4	1.2	6.8	19.2	10.1	11.3	14.1	13.4
29 013	28140	1	Bates	2 198	16 937	1 963	7.7	97.4	0.9	1.1	0.2	1.2	6.0	18.9	9.8	10.9	14.6	13.3
29 015	...	9	Benton	1 827	18 076	1 912	9.9	98.3	0.2	1.3	0.4	0.9	4.4	14.9	8.0	8.6	12.3	14.0
29 017	16020	9	Bollinger	1 608	12 318	2 277	7.7	98.3	0.3	1.3	0.3	0.6	6.0	18.7	9.6	11.6	14.5	14.3
29 019	17860	3	Boone	1 775	141 122	403	79.5	85.5	9.6	1.0	3.8	1.9	6.3	16.1	16.8	16.1	13.9	12.6
29 021	41140	3	Buchanan	1 061	84 909	625	80.0	92.2	5.0	0.9	0.8	2.4	6.4	17.5	11.0	12.8	15.1	13.6
29 023	38740	7	Butler	1 807	40 854	1 113	22.6	92.4	5.5	1.3	0.7	1.2	6.7	17.1	9.3	12.0	13.8	14.1
29 025	28140	1	Caldwell	1 112	9 159	2 514	8.2	98.6	0.5	0.5	0.2	0.7	6.2	19.7	9.1	10.0	14.0	13.6
29 027	27620	3	Callaway	2 173	42 225	1 076	19.4	92.5	5.7	1.1	0.8	0.9	5.9	18.3	12.5	13.7	16.5	13.9
29 029	...	7	Camden	1 697	38 302	1 177	22.6	97.6	0.4	1.2	0.7	1.0	4.8	14.6	8.0	9.5	13.1	14.8
29 031	16020	5	Cape Girardeau	1 499	69 876	725	46.6	92.1	6.1	0.8	1.1	0.9	6.2	16.6	12.8	13.1	14.1	13.6
29 033	...	6	Carroll	1 799	10 149	2 431	5.6	97.0	2.0	0.5	0.5	0.7	5.7	18.3	8.5	10.7	13.4	13.7
29 035	...	9	Carter	1 315	5 974	2 774	4.5	97.2	0.1	2.5	0.1	1.3	6.4	18.1	9.1	10.8	13.8	14.1
29 037	28140	1	Cass	1 810	88 834	605	49.1	94.2	2.3	1.1	1.0	2.6	6.6	20.3	9.3	12.4	16.0	13.4
29 039	...	6	Cedar	1 233	13 838	2 178	11.2	97.3	0.4	1.6	0.7	1.0	5.3	18.0	8.6	9.4	12.9	13.3
29 041	...	9	Chariton	1 958	8 251	2 579	4.2	95.8	3.2	0.3	0.2	0.6	4.7	16.4	9.5	9.0	13.4	14.2
29 043	44180	2	Christian	1 459	61 571	807	42.2	97.3	0.5	1.2	0.6	1.6	6.9	19.3	9.7	14.3	15.5	13.0
29 045	28460	9	Clark	1 314	7 420	2 646	5.6	98.8	0.5	0.3	0.1	0.7	5.8	18.1	9.0	10.6	14.3	14.3
29 047	28140	1	Clay	1 027	194 247	296	189.1	90.4	3.9	1.0	2.3	3.9	7.2	18.3	9.1	14.8	16.1	14.0
29 049	28140	1	Clinton	1 085	20 140	1 798	18.6	97.0	1.7	0.8	0.2	1.1	6.3	18.6	9.9	10.9	15.6	13.5
29 051	27620	3	Cole	1 014	72 454	700	71.5	86.8	10.7	0.8	1.3	1.5	6.3	17.0	10.1	14.7	16.4	14.8
29 053	...	6	Cooper	1 463	17 009	1 953	11.6	89.4	9.2	0.9	0.4	1.0	5.6	16.3	15.0	12.9	13.8	12.9
29 055	...	6	Crawford	1 923	23 513	1 639	12.2	98.2	0.2	1.1	0.2	1.0	6.2	18.6	9.7	11.0	14.7	13.1
29 057	...	8	Dade	1 270	7 845	2 610	6.2	97.8	0.3	1.5	0.3	0.9	5.5	17.0	8.8	9.4	13.8	14.2
29 059	44180	2	Dallas	1 403	16 113	2 025	11.5	97.8	0.3	1.9	0.3	1.2	6.5	19.7	9.3	10.4	14.3	13.7
29 061	...	8	Daviess	1 468	8 004	2 593	5.5	98.4	0.2	0.4	0.4	0.8	7.2	18.8	9.1	10.7	13.0	13.5
29 063	41140	3	De Kalb	1 099	13 063	2 234	11.9	86.2	11.6	1.0	0.4	1.2	4.2	12.8	9.4	16.9	21.8	13.2
29 065	...	7	Dent	1 952	14 921	2 106	7.6	97.7	0.4	2.0	0.3	0.8	5.9	17.9	9.2	10.3	14.2	13.7
29 067	...	6	Douglas	2 110	13 363	2 209	6.3	97.7	0.1	2.4	0.2	1.0	5.1	18.6	9.3	10.2	13.8	14.0
29 069	28380	7	Dunklin	1 413	32 654	1 346	23.1	87.2	9.6	0.8	0.4	2.9	7.1	18.6	8.9	11.9	13.5	13.2
29 071	41180	1	Franklin	2 390	96 905	557	40.5	97.8	1.0	0.6	0.5	0.7	6.6	19.4	9.7	12.1	16.2	13.8
29 073	...	6	Gasconade	1 349	15 542	2 061	11.5	99.1	0.2	0.5	0.2	0.5	5.7	17.6	8.8	10.0	14.8	14.1
29 075	...	8	Gentry	1 273	6 566	2 728	5.2	98.2	0.3	0.4	0.6	0.7	5.5	18.9	8.8	9.2	13.8	12.4
29 077	44180	2	Greene	1 748	245 765	244	140.6	93.9	2.8	1.4	1.6	1.8	6.1	15.6	12.7	14.1	14.0	13.4
29 079	...	7	Grundy	1 129	10 311	2 414	9.1	97.2	0.5	0.6	0.2	2.0	5.7	16.7	9.6	9.5	12.8	13.3
29 081	...	7	Harrison	1 878	8 828	2 539	4.7	98.5	0.5	0.5	0.5	1.0	6.1	16.5	8.8	9.8	13.1	12.7
29 083	...	6	Henry	1 819	22 419	1 683	12.3	96.9	1.3	1.4	0.3	1.1	6.2	17.1	9.0	11.1	13.6	13.3
29 085	...	8	Hickory	1 032	9 005	2 522	8.7	98.4	0.3	1.3	0.2	0.8	4.4	14.6	7.7	7.2	11.1	13.3
29 087	...	8	Holt	1 196	5 145	2 834	4.3	98.9	0.1	0.7	0.1	0.5	4.0	17.3	8.3	9.0	14.0	14.6
29 089	17860	3	Howard	1 206	10 007	2 440	8.3	92.2	6.8	0.7	0.2	0.7	5.6	16.6	14.5	9.9	14.1	13.8
29 091	48460	7	Howell	2 403	37 499	1 192	15.6	97.1	0.4	2.0	0.7	1.2	6.3	18.4	9.3	11.3	13.7	13.2
29 093	...	6	Iron	1 428	10 306	2 416	7.2	97.3	1.7	0.9	0.1	0.6	5.9	17.8	9.4	10.6	14.1	14.5
29 095	28140	1	Jackson	1 567	659 723	83	421.0	68.0	24.7	1.1	2.1	5.9	7.4	18.3	8.9	14.4	15.7	13.9

1. CBSA = Core Based Statistical Area. See Appendix A for explanation. See Appendix B for list of metropolitan areas with component counties. See Service of USDA Rural-Urban Continuum Codes. See Appendix A for definition. 3. Dry land or land partially or temporarily covered by water. 2. County type code from the Economic Research Service of USDA Rural-Urban Continuum Codes. See Appendix A for definition. 4. Hispanic or Latino persons may be of any race.

Table B. States and Counties — **Population and Households**

STATE County	55 to 64 years (16)	65 to 74 years (17)	75 years and over (18)	Percent female (19)	Total persons 1990 (20)	Total persons 2000 (21)	Percent change 1990–2000 (22)	Percent change 2000–2003 (23)	Births (24)	Deaths (25)	Net migration (26)	Households 2000 Number (27)	Percent change 1990–2000 (28)	Persons per household (29)	Female family householder[1] (30)	One person (31)
MISSISSIPPI—Cont'd																
Sunflower	6.9	4.9	4.7	45.5	35 129	34 369	-2.2	-2.9	1 723	1 040	-1 672	9 637	-0.1	3.01	28.4	21.2
Tallahatchie	9.4	6.7	6.7	53.3	15 210	14 903	-2.0	-3.4	713	535	-683	5 263	4.5	2.81	23.5	24.6
Tate	9.7	6.0	5.4	51.5	21 432	25 370	18.4	1.7	1 269	843	34	8 850	26.0	2.74	15.5	21.3
Tippah	10.2	7.5	6.7	51.6	19 523	20 826	6.7	0.5	1 062	881	-66	8 108	13.3	2.52	11.8	24.9
Tishomingo	12.0	9.2	7.9	51.7	17 683	19 163	8.4	-1.0	691	909	46	7 917	12.2	2.39	10.1	27.5
Tunica	7.8	4.9	4.6	52.4	8 164	9 227	13.0	7.5	634	339	396	3 258	29.0	2.80	26.9	26.9
Union	9.8	7.3	6.4	51.3	22 085	25 362	14.8	3.0	1 215	890	449	9 786	17.0	2.57	11.1	23.4
Walthall	10.2	7.3	6.7	51.9	14 352	15 156	5.6	0.2	708	538	-132	5 571	13.0	2.69	16.9	24.0
Warren	9.4	6.0	5.8	52.9	47 880	49 644	3.7	-1.3	2 543	1 751	-1 441	18 756	7.7	2.61	19.1	25.8
Washington	8.5	6.0	5.7	53.4	67 935	62 977	-7.3	-4.2	3 665	2 190	-4 201	22 158	-1.9	2.80	26.0	24.6
Wayne	9.8	6.7	5.3	52.1	19 517	21 216	8.7	-0.3	1 047	674	-417	7 857	14.6	2.67	17.2	23.1
Webster	9.9	8.7	7.9	51.9	10 222	10 294	0.7	-1.3	496	458	-162	3 905	2.1	2.59	13.1	24.0
Wilkinson	8.4	6.8	6.7	47.6	9 678	10 312	6.6	-0.7	464	443	-79	3 578	6.9	2.59	24.5	27.9
Winston	9.8	8.0	7.5	51.6	19 433	20 160	3.7	-1.2	919	696	-466	7 578	7.3	2.59	18.1	25.2
Yalobusha	10.8	7.9	7.7	52.1	12 033	13 051	8.5	2.3	600	434	139	5 260	14.0	2.46	17.6	28.7
Yazoo	8.4	6.1	5.9	48.6	25 506	28 149	10.4	0.4	1 449	922	-392	9 178	4.1	2.81	23.7	24.5
MISSOURI	10.0	6.8	6.6	51.2	5 116 901	5 595 211	9.3	2.0	245 375	180 689	45 116	2 194 594	11.9	2.48	11.6	27.3
Adair	8.1	5.6	6.3	53.0	24 577	24 977	1.6	-0.7	889	765	-295	9 669	6.7	2.29	7.2	31.5
Andrew	9.8	6.6	7.1	51.0	14 632	16 492	12.7	1.9	549	555	341	6 273	15.5	2.59	7.4	22.3
Atchison	11.5	8.7	11.7	50.0	7 457	6 430	-13.8	-2.2	218	305	-55	2 722	-8.1	2.25	6.1	31.5
Audrain	9.8	7.6	9.1	55.1	23 599	25 853	9.6	-0.5	1 153	899	-376	9 844	6.9	2.43	9.9	27.8
Barry	11.3	8.6	7.2	50.4	27 547	34 010	23.5	1.8	1 463	1 140	351	13 398	23.4	2.51	8.4	24.7
Barton	9.2	7.2	8.4	51.0	11 312	12 541	10.9	3.7	549	438	349	4 895	8.2	2.53	8.5	26.4
Bates	10.2	8.1	8.5	51.5	15 025	16 653	10.8	1.7	688	743	342	6 511	10.0	2.51	7.6	26.1
Benton	14.5	13.3	9.0	50.9	13 859	17 180	24.0	5.2	483	798	1 185	7 420	28.7	2.28	6.8	26.3
Bollinger	10.7	8.2	6.5	50.6	10 619	12 029	13.3	2.4	486	428	236	4 576	16.0	2.59	8.4	21.6
Boone	7.0	4.4	4.2	51.5	112 379	135 454	20.5	4.2	5 675	2 780	2 901	53 094	26.6	2.38	10.4	28.7
Buchanan	8.9	7.1	7.8	50.6	83 083	85 998	3.5	-1.3	3 567	3 070	-1 543	33 557	3.3	2.42	12.0	28.9
Butler	10.6	8.6	8.0	52.0	38 765	40 867	5.4	0.0	1 798	1 714	-41	16 718	9.0	2.39	11.6	28.0
Caldwell	10.7	7.7	8.7	51.0	8 380	8 969	7.0	2.1	377	363	183	3 523	9.3	2.51	8.0	25.5
Callaway	8.7	5.7	4.9	48.5	32 809	40 766	24.3	3.6	1 590	1 155	1 018	14 416	24.8	2.56	10.4	23.0
Camden	15.7	12.0	7.1	50.0	27 495	37 051	34.8	3.4	1 151	1 173	1 284	15 779	39.6	2.31	6.6	23.3
Cape Girardeau	9.1	6.6	7.1	51.8	61 633	68 693	11.5	1.7	2 916	2 260	626	26 980	15.3	2.42	9.8	27.3
Carroll	10.6	8.6	10.9	51.1	10 748	10 285	-4.3	-1.3	363	453	-29	4 169	-3.8	2.42	8.0	27.8
Carter	11.7	9.2	6.5	51.4	5 515	5 941	7.7	0.6	250	243	31	2 378	11.7	2.46	8.9	26.7
Cass	9.4	6.3	5.2	50.8	63 808	82 092	28.7	8.2	3 579	2 359	5 470	30 168	31.8	2.69	9.1	20.0
Cedar	12.3	10.8	9.8	50.9	12 093	13 733	13.6	0.8	476	644	279	5 685	13.6	2.35	7.9	28.1
Chariton	11.1	10.3	11.9	52.0	9 202	8 438	-8.3	-2.2	248	442	18	3 469	-5.2	2.38	6.5	29.8
Christian	8.5	5.6	4.6	51.1	32 644	54 285	66.3	13.4	2 664	1 321	5 821	20 425	71.1	2.63	9.3	19.1
Clark	11.7	8.0	8.4	50.8	7 547	7 416	-1.7	0.1	274	256	-12	2 966	3.7	2.46	7.0	26.4
Clay	9.1	5.6	4.9	51.2	153 411	184 006	19.9	5.6	9 043	4 647	5 890	72 558	23.2	2.50	10.2	25.2
Clinton	10.4	6.7	6.9	50.9	16 595	18 979	14.4	6.1	810	657	1 009	7 152	17.0	2.59	8.8	22.0
Cole	8.9	5.7	5.5	48.6	63 579	71 397	12.3	1.5	2 969	2 030	192	27 040	17.7	2.43	10.0	28.7
Cooper	8.8	6.7	8.1	45.9	14 835	16 670	12.4	2.0	601	553	297	5 932	10.7	2.46	9.0	26.1
Crawford	10.5	8.4	7.1	50.6	19 173	22 804	18.9	3.1	965	855	610	8 858	21.4	2.53	9.0	24.3
Dade	11.4	10.5	9.9	50.6	7 449	7 923	6.4	-1.0	254	418	92	3 202	7.6	2.44	6.5	26.5
Dallas	10.8	8.2	6.7	50.3	12 646	15 661	23.8	2.9	692	580	347	6 030	23.1	2.57	8.4	23.7
Daviess	11.0	8.9	7.8	52.1	7 865	8 016	1.9	-0.1	379	316	-61	3 178	4.5	2.50	7.5	25.7
De Kalb	8.4	6.2	6.8	35.0	9 967	11 597	16.4	12.6	348	370	32	3 528	15.5	2.50	7.4	26.9
Dent	11.4	9.0	8.5	51.4	13 702	14 927	8.9	0.0	571	724	152	5 982	12.3	2.45	9.1	25.0
Douglas	12.1	9.2	7.7	50.8	11 876	13 084	10.2	2.1	425	495	352	5 201	13.4	2.49	7.2	26.1
Dunklin	11.2	7.9	8.3	52.5	33 112	33 155	0.1	-1.5	1 527	1 508	-476	13 411	2.2	2.42	13.2	28.1
Franklin	9.6	6.6	5.5	50.4	80 603	93 807	16.4	3.3	4 166	2 917	1 930	34 945	21.1	2.66	9.0	22.1
Gasconade	10.5	9.0	7.4	51.5	14 006	15 342	9.5	1.3	548	671	339	6 171	11.3	2.44	7.6	27.0
Gentry	10.7	9.9	12.0	51.1	6 854	6 861	0.1	-4.3	228	306	-209	2 747	-0.3	2.42	7.2	29.3
Greene	9.1	6.7	6.9	51.3	207 949	240 391	15.6	2.2	9 742	7 899	3 830	97 859	20.1	2.34	9.8	29.1
Grundy	11.5	9.6	11.0	52.6	10 536	10 432	-1.0	-1.2	398	483	-35	4 382	0.8	2.30	8.0	30.8
Harrison	11.5	9.9	11.7	51.1	8 469	8 850	4.5	-0.2	322	421	77	3 658	2.4	2.36	7.7	28.8
Henry	11.5	8.8	9.3	50.8	20 044	21 997	9.7	1.9	976	947	407	9 133	11.5	2.37	9.3	27.7
Hickory	15.4	14.7	11.3	51.6	7 335	8 940	21.9	0.7	243	458	283	3 911	22.9	2.26	6.7	26.5
Holt	11.1	9.3	12.8	50.7	6 034	5 351	-11.3	-3.8	138	209	-133	2 237	-8.3	2.35	6.1	29.7
Howard	9.3	7.1	9.0	51.3	9 631	10 212	6.0	-2.0	356	308	-241	3 836	7.4	2.46	9.5	27.3
Howell	10.6	8.8	8.1	51.5	31 447	37 238	18.4	0.7	1 481	1 525	346	14 762	20.2	2.47	9.9	25.0
Iron	12.0	9.1	7.9	51.2	10 726	10 697	-0.3	-3.7	412	555	-244	4 197	5.1	2.46	9.4	25.8
Jackson	9.0	6.2	6.1	51.7	633 234	654 880	3.4	0.7	33 426	20 044	-8 112	266 294	5.4	2.42	14.7	31.2

1. No spouse present.

STATE County	Births, average 1999–2001		Deaths, average 1999–2001				Physicians,[4] 2000		Hospitals,[4] 1998			Medicare enrollees, 2003	Serious crimes known to police,[6] 2002	
			Number		Rate					Beds			Total	
	Total	Rate[1]	Total	Infant[2]	Total[1]	Infant[3]	Number	Rate[5]	Number	Number	Rate[5]		Number	Rate[7]
	32	33	34	35	36	37	38	39	40	41	42	43	44	45
MISSISSIPPI—Cont'd														
Sunflower	543	15.8	327	7	9.5	12.9	18	52	2	155	448	3 969	NA	NA
Tallahatchie	209	14.1	158	2	10.6	D	5	34	1	77	517	2 361	NA	NA
Tate	387	15.3	247	4	9.7	D	12	47	1	52	217	3 803	NA	NA
Tippah	328	15.7	261	1	12.5	D	9	43	1	106	504	4 586	255	1 213
Tishomingo	230	12.0	275	2	14.4	D	9	47	1	88	472	4 748	NA	NA
Tunica	176	19.1	100	4	10.8	D	3	33	0	0	0	1 279	610	6 549
Union	393	15.5	263	3	10.4	D	23	91	1	153	642	4 429	660	2 578
Walthall	220	14.4	172	2	11.3	D	21	139	1	49	341	2 264	NA	NA
Warren	801	16.1	525	9	10.6	11.2	81	163	2	343	694	6 973	2 819	5 625
Washington	1 104	17.5	673	13	10.7	11.8	87	138	2	287	440	9 170	4 636	9 081
Wayne	316	14.9	202	3	9.5	D	14	66	1	77	378	2 933	73	451
Webster	149	14.5	140	2	13.6	D	6	58	1	76	721	2 100	NA	NA
Wilkinson	134	13.0	130	1	12.6	D	9	87	1	66	719	1 618	NA	NA
Winston	292	14.5	232	3	11.6	D	8	40	1	185	954	3 479	NA	NA
Yalobusha	186	14.2	147	2	11.3	D	5	38	1	85	687	3 164	NA	NA
Yazoo	447	15.9	309	5	11.0	D	21	75	1	34	133	4 188	NA	NA
MISSOURI	75 786	13.5	55 259	563	9.9	7.4	11 883	212	134	21 768	400	884 449	261 077	4 602
Adair	271	10.9	231	1	9.2	D	81	324	2	194	799	3 361	832	3 286
Andrew	179	10.8	165	1	10.0	D	5	30	1	205	1 317	2 022	218	1 304
Atchison	57	8.8	94	0	14.5	D	5	78	1	44	629	1 351	65	997
Audrain	361	14.0	299	3	11.6	D	47	182	1	165	700	4 564	531	2 026
Barry	466	13.7	366	3	10.8	D	23	68	2	71	214	6 956	965	2 799
Barton	179	14.3	132	0	10.5	D	8	64	1	44	364	2 187	374	2 942
Bates	209	12.6	220	2	13.3	D	5	30	1	33	209	3 167	364	2 156
Benton	148	8.6	245	1	14.3	D	7	41	0	0	0	4 929	395	2 268
Bollinger	154	12.8	128	2	10.6	D	2	17	0	0	0	2 077	91	746
Boone	1 766	13.0	835	13	6.2	7.4	775	572	3	931	721	15 115	5 326	3 878
Buchanan	1 126	13.1	942	10	11.0	8.6	162	188	1	277	339	15 091	5 004	5 757
Butler	558	13.7	515	6	12.6	D	92	225	2	376	927	8 372	1 828	4 412
Caldwell	113	12.5	116	1	12.9	D	2	22	0	0	0	1 731	112	1 232
Callaway	490	12.0	342	2	8.4	D	36	88	1	36	96	5 577	888	2 149
Camden	372	10.1	369	4	10.0	D	37	100	1	91	268	7 026	1 043	2 797
Cape Girardeau	879	12.8	690	7	10.0	7.6	182	265	2	510	769	10 763	2 882	4 138
Carroll	115	11.2	140	1	13.6	D	10	97	1	52	509	2 154	153	1 467
Carter	77	13.0	81	0	13.7	D	1	17	0	0	0	1 355	61	1 013
Cass	1 114	13.5	697	6	8.4	D	31	38	2	89	111	11 342	2 289	2 761
Cedar	155	11.3	209	1	15.2	D	11	80	1	34	257	3 366	395	2 837
Chariton	78	9.2	132	0	15.7	D	4	47	0	0	0	1 698	274	3 203
Christian	827	15.1	402	3	7.4	D	7	13	0	0	0	7 748	1 257	2 284
Clark	89	12.0	85	1	11.4	D	2	27	0	0	0	1 294	170	2 261
Clay	2 734	14.8	1 385	16	7.5	6.0	328	178	3	608	345	24 237	11 715	6 280
Clinton	246	12.9	201	0	10.6	D	7	37	1	38	199	3 248	459	2 385
Cole	921	12.9	623	6	8.7	D	178	249	3	290	418	9 812	2 089	2 886
Cooper	181	10.9	171	0	10.3	D	12	72	1	49	306	2 829	498	2 947
Crawford	310	13.6	259	1	11.4	D	16	70	0	0	0	4 126	813	3 516
Dade	86	10.9	123	1	15.6	D	2	25	0	0	0	1 812	109	1 357
Dallas	213	13.6	176	1	11.2	D	6	38	0	0	0	2 765	296	1 864
Daviess	120	14.9	98	2	12.3	D	3	37	0	0	0	1 501	119	1 464
De Kalb	115	9.9	124	1	10.7	D	2	17	0	0	0	1 428	187	1 591
Dent	184	12.3	200	1	13.4	D	12	80	1	46	326	3 134	449	2 967
Douglas	135	10.3	151	1	11.6	D	3	23	0	0	0	2 346	78	588
Dunklin	486	14.7	475	4	14.3	D	30	90	1	116	355	6 705	840	2 499
Franklin	1 284	13.7	856	7	9.1	5.5	84	90	2	194	211	15 074	3 048	3 205
Gasconade	175	11.4	204	1	13.3	D	13	85	1	41	275	3 302	347	2 231
Gentry	81	11.8	104	0	15.2	D	4	58	1	35	504	1 769	30	431
Greene	3 093	12.9	2 354	23	9.8	7.3	663	276	5	1 657	731	38 750	14 221	5 835
Grundy	127	12.2	140	0	13.4	D	10	96	1	48	472	2 339	273	2 581
Harrison	110	12.5	129	0	14.6	D	7	79	1	23	270	2 103	198	2 306
Henry	289	13.1	295	1	13.4	D	25	114	1	108	509	5 109	862	3 955
Hickory	73	8.1	131	0	14.7	D	0	0	0	0	0	2 422	150	1 655
Holt	43	8.1	70	1	13.1	D	3	56	0	0	0	1 200	146	2 691
Howard	118	11.6	107	0	10.5	D	5	49	0	0	0	1 751	89	860
Howell	482	13.0	472	1	12.7	D	37	99	2	140	391	8 008	1 287	3 409
Iron	129	12.1	178	1	16.7	D	11	103	1	50	460	2 265	119	1 457
Jackson	10 113	15.4	6 186	75	9.4	7.4	1 890	289	14	3 347	511	95 540	49 529	7 460

1. Per 1,000 estimated resident population. 2. Deaths of infants under 1 year old. 3. Deaths of infants under 1 year old per 1,000 live births. 4. Data subject to copyright. 5. Per 100,000 resident population as of July 1 of the year shown. 6. Data for serious crimes have not been adjusted for underreporting; this may affect comparability between geographic areas and over time. 7. Per 100,000 population estimated by the FBI.

STATE County	Violent	Property	Total	Percent private	High school graduate or less	Bachelor's degree or more	Total current expenditures (mil dol)	Current expenditures per student (dollars)	Per capita income[6] (dollars)	Dollars	Percent change, 1989-1999 (constant 1999 dollars)	Percent with income of $100,000 or more	Persons	Households	Families	Families with children
	46	47	48	49	50	51	52	53	54	55	56	57	58	59	60	61
MISSISSIPPI—Cont'd																
Sunflower	NA	NA	10 048	13.2	66.3	12.0	30.3	5 086	11 365	24 970	28.8	4.2	30.0	27.6	24.6	32.7
Tallahatchie	NA	NA	4 489	8.2	69.8	10.9	16.8	5 581	10 749	22 229	21.7	2.4	32.2	30.8	26.8	36.8
Tate	NA	NA	7 177	12.3	60.8	12.3	22.8	4 909	16 154	35 836	20.1	6.0	13.5	15.5	10.6	12.5
Tippah	176	1 037	4 775	8.8	70.3	9.0	19.9	4 886	14 041	29 300	21.2	3.1	16.9	19.6	14.0	18.6
Tishomingo	NA	NA	3 842	4.2	71.3	8.7	16.3	5 128	15 395	28 315	20.4	4.3	14.1	16.2	11.0	14.2
Tunica	526	6 023	2 471	9.9	69.6	9.1	14.7	7 316	11 978	23 270	58.0	3.6	33.1	31.0	28.1	35.1
Union	94	2 484	5 916	5.0	65.3	13.2	23.6	5 078	15 700	32 682	15.1	3.4	12.6	15.5	9.6	11.4
Walthall	NA	NA	4 094	4.9	67.1	10.4	14.4	5 279	12 563	22 945	20.8	3.3	27.8	25.9	22.4	32.1
Warren	674	4 950	13 651	14.9	49.5	20.8	48.9	5 331	17 527	35 056	14.4	8.1	18.7	16.8	15.0	22.2
Washington	727	8 354	19 083	13.7	62.2	16.4	66.2	5 302	13 430	25 757	9.6	5.2	29.2	27.9	24.6	31.3
Wayne	6	445	5 535	8.3	70.1	9.5	20.1	4 982	12 757	25 918	19.9	4.5	25.4	25.6	21.4	28.2
Webster	NA	NA	2 474	10.3	66.3	13.0	9.8	4 999	14 109	28 834	25.5	3.0	18.7	20.0	14.8	22.0
Wilkinson	NA	NA	2 669	21.3	75.0	10.0	8.9	5 380	10 868	18 929	18.3	3.6	37.7	36.2	33.1	43.1
Winston	NA	NA	5 032	16.1	65.1	13.8	17.0	5 149	14 548	28 256	14.8	4.0	23.7	23.0	19.4	26.4
Yalobusha	NA	NA	3 267	9.7	68.6	9.6	11.5	5 500	14 953	26 315	23.3	3.9	21.8	22.1	19.5	28.2
Yazoo	NA	NA	7 155	19.3	66.0	11.8	25.2	5 338	12 062	24 795	29.7	3.6	31.9	29.0	25.4	35.8
MISSOURI	539	4 064	1 479 573	18.5	51.4	21.6	6 018.0	6 601	19 936	37 934	7.1	8.8	11.7	11.8	8.6	12.8
Adair	178	3 108	10 082	9.9	48.9	28.5	17.7	5 973	15 484	26 677	14.9	5.5	23.3	24.4	11.9	17.7
Andrew	54	1 250	4 144	9.7	56.8	18.8	16.8	5 787	19 375	40 688	16.0	8.2	8.2	9.0	6.4	9.2
Atchison	123	874	1 417	5.4	59.2	16.6	7.8	6 467	16 956	30 959	14.5	4.5	11.6	12.0	9.3	12.4
Audrain	160	1 866	5 632	14.0	67.8	12.7	21.5	5 828	16 441	32 057	1.9	4.6	14.8	12.9	11.1	17.0
Barry	107	2 691	7 860	5.6	65.4	10.7	37.3	5 609	14 980	28 906	12.2	3.7	16.6	15.4	11.8	17.7
Barton	582	2 360	2 959	7.1	65.7	10.6	12.5	5 756	13 987	29 275	9.2	2.7	13.0	14.6	11.0	13.3
Bates	314	1 842	3 883	9.7	68.4	10.1	17.1	5 548	15 477	30 731	13.9	4.0	14.5	14.7	11.5	15.3
Benton	327	1 941	3 197	7.6	66.8	8.8	15.0	5 419	15 457	26 646	17.2	3.1	15.7	15.7	10.2	20.2
Bollinger	156	590	2 686	9.8	75.8	6.9	11.5	5 562	13 641	30 462	16.7	2.4	13.8	15.8	10.9	14.5
Boone	355	3 523	49 784	10.7	34.1	41.7	136.8	6 522	19 844	37 485	8.8	9.2	14.5	15.2	7.6	10.9
Buchanan	245	5 512	21 945	12.5	56.5	16.9	85.0	6 095	17 882	34 704	12.2	5.4	12.2	12.7	8.5	13.3
Butler	840	3 572	9 296	8.7	63.8	11.6	36.9	5 600	15 721	27 228	24.4	4.7	18.6	18.9	14.0	21.7
Caldwell	198	1 034	2 186	5.1	64.7	11.7	12.9	6 956	15 343	31 240	19.6	4.0	11.9	12.9	9.7	13.1
Callaway	174	1 974	10 500	19.8	58.2	16.5	32.6	6 003	17 005	39 110	9.2	5.6	8.5	8.4	6.0	8.7
Camden	365	2 432	6 943	8.5	54.4	17.7	31.7	5 930	20 197	35 840	18.2	6.6	11.4	9.9	8.0	14.9
Cape Girardeau	266	3 873	19 596	14.5	52.2	24.2	51.7	5 340	18 593	36 458	10.7	7.0	11.1	12.5	6.7	9.8
Carroll	125	1 343	2 272	5.9	67.3	14.0	12.1	6 451	15 522	30 643	15.8	4.5	13.7	14.2	9.7	12.7
Carter	166	847	1 441	3.3	68.7	10.8	9.0	6 707	13 349	22 863	10.8	4.0	25.2	23.2	19.6	28.1
Cass	226	2 536	21 176	14.9	51.0	17.7	92.3	5 885	21 073	49 562	17.6	9.8	5.8	6.1	4.2	6.3
Cedar	151	2 686	3 058	11.8	69.8	10.0	13.1	5 461	14 356	26 694	17.3	2.7	17.4	18.6	11.6	20.4
Chariton	222	2 981	1 908	10.6	68.6	11.4	9.1	6 733	15 515	32 285	15.4	2.7	11.6	13.5	8.8	9.2
Christian	140	2 144	14 178	12.5	48.3	20.9	52.9	5 215	18 422	38 085	9.0	6.4	9.1	8.8	7.1	11.2
Clark	213	2 048	1 778	9.7	65.7	10.7	7.5	5 968	15 988	29 457	11.4	3.3	14.1	12.9	10.8	15.7
Clay	812	5 468	47 240	17.2	43.3	24.9	198.2	6 137	23 144	48 347	4.7	10.7	5.5	5.4	3.8	5.5
Clinton	390	1 996	4 790	7.5	56.4	14.5	22.7	6 817	19 056	41 629	17.8	8.3	9.3	9.3	7.3	9.5
Cole	497	2 389	18 439	26.9	46.7	27.4	60.5	5 743	20 739	42 924	5.2	8.1	8.7	8.7	5.8	8.7
Cooper	225	2 722	4 281	15.8	63.5	13.7	17.2	6 814	15 648	35 313	15.4	3.4	10.7	11.6	8.3	12.3
Crawford	376	3 140	5 230	9.7	69.8	8.4	18.1	5 203	14 825	30 860	16.5	3.6	16.3	15.9	12.7	19.4
Dade	187	1 170	1 758	9.7	66.9	9.9	8.6	6 640	14 254	29 097	15.7	2.4	13.4	14.2	9.3	16.4
Dallas	258	1 606	3 824	10.1	68.7	9.5	12.3	5 639	15 106	27 346	22.1	3.4	17.9	17.9	14.2	19.8
Daviess	172	1 292	1 830	9.4	63.2	12.0	10.2	7 378	15 953	30 855	25.1	4.5	15.2	15.2	11.4	18.1
De Kalb	111	1 480	2 508	10.0	64.2	10.7	8.9	6 146	12 687	31 654	3.5	3.2	10.8	13.4	7.2	9.9
Dent	383	2 584	3 282	8.4	69.5	10.1	13.6	5 280	14 463	27 193	22.0	2.8	17.2	16.4	12.7	19.4
Douglas	75	513	3 163	10.5	69.1	9.9	10.1	5 435	13 785	25 918	19.2	3.0	17.5	19.6	13.0	17.0
Dunklin	211	2 288	7 596	4.5	73.7	9.1	35.2	5 634	13 561	24 878	20.3	2.9	24.5	25.0	19.4	27.7
Franklin	499	2 705	23 737	16.4	57.9	12.8	93.8	5 499	19 705	43 474	13.1	7.4	7.0	7.4	4.5	6.3
Gasconade	463	1 768	3 449	10.0	66.2	10.4	16.9	5 414	17 319	35 047	16.8	4.4	9.5	10.6	7.0	10.2
Gentry	29	403	1 682	6.8	63.8	14.5	9.5	6 873	15 879	28 750	21.6	3.6	12.0	12.8	9.0	13.3
Greene	514	5 321	67 577	17.1	46.1	24.2	200.6	5 564	19 185	34 157	4.7	7.1	12.1	12.5	7.6	11.8
Grundy	66	2 515	2 421	5.6	60.4	12.5	10.9	5 968	15 432	27 333	12.5	4.2	15.8	16.0	12.3	20.4
Harrison	303	2 003	1 871	7.5	67.8	9.3	10.9	7 279	14 192	28 707	22.4	2.6	13.5	14.7	9.9	13.4
Henry	468	3 487	4 848	6.6	66.6	11.7	20.6	6 236	16 468	30 949	24.7	4.2	14.3	15.0	11.4	17.2
Hickory	276	1 379	1 551	4.5	68.8	7.7	11.4	6 039	13 536	25 346	17.8	2.3	19.7	18.1	13.0	25.1
Holt	221	2 470	1 239	4.0	67.6	11.7	5.9	6 475	15 876	29 461	17.1	3.3	13.0	13.7	10.5	15.2
Howard	155	705	3 018	33.3	61.7	17.9	10.0	6 301	15 198	31 614	10.1	3.0	11.6	11.6	7.5	12.3
Howell	392	3 017	9 017	7.1	65.5	10.9	42.8	5 808	13 959	25 628	15.2	3.1	18.7	17.9	14.0	22.0
Iron	369	729	2 522	3.6	69.9	8.4	14.9	6 164	14 227	26 080	12.2	2.7	18.7	18.7	13.8	22.8
Jackson	850	6 610	171 287	17.8	46.6	23.4	788.6	7 326	20 788	39 277	5.0	8.8	11.9	11.5	9.0	13.9

1. Data for serious crimes have not been adjusted for underreporting; this may affect comparability between geographic areas and over time.　　2. Per 100,000 population estimated by the FBI.　　3. All persons 3 years old and over enrolled in nursery school through college.　　4. Persons 25 years old and over.　　5. Elementary and secondary education expenditures.　　6. Based on population enumerated as of April 1, 2000.

Table B. States and Counties — **Personal Income**

STATE County	Total (mil dol)	Percent change, 2001–2002	Per capita Dollars	Per capita Rank	Wages and salaries[2] (mil dol)	Proprietor's income (mil dol)	Dividends, interest, and rent (mil dol)	Transfer payments Total (mil dol)	Government payments to individuals Total (mil dol)	Social Security (mil dol)	Medical payments (mil dol)	Income maintenance (mil dol)	Unemployment insurance (mil dol)
	62	63	64	65	66	67	68	69	70	71	72	73	74
MISSISSIPPI—Cont'd													
Sunflower	526	-2.7	15 537	3 063	329	21	71	163	154	37	67	35	5
Tallahatchie	249	-1.5	17 185	2 976	79	0	43	83	79	27	34	15	2
Tate	567	3.1	22 175	1 965	195	38	70	115	108	40	41	12	2
Tippah	421	2.3	20 077	2 529	228	18	60	119	113	41	56	11	2
Tishomingo	365	4.1	19 138	2 731	189	14	64	113	108	44	48	8	3
Tunica	172	-3.1	17 763	2 923	548	-3	31	46	44	13	20	9	1
Union	529	3.2	20 418	2 454	280	30	85	115	108	48	46	9	2
Walthall	254	0.3	16 808	3 006	81	20	32	79	75	25	34	12	1
Warren	1 336	3.4	27 189	669	940	79	226	238	225	73	105	31	6
Washington	1 192	1.3	19 504	2 659	715	76	191	334	318	96	130	74	10
Wayne	382	0.3	18 035	2 891	170	42	58	100	95	33	41	15	3
Webster	185	-2.3	18 045	2 889	61	8	34	66	64	25	28	7	2
Wilkinson	165	3.3	16 041	3 051	54	9	28	55	52	15	25	9	2
Winston	368	1.4	18 416	2 841	170	27	63	105	100	38	42	14	1
Yalobusha	269	3.2	20 235	2 491	112	7	44	82	78	28	36	10	2
Yazoo	522	1.0	18 633	2 807	240	40	97	149	141	43	65	26	2
MISSOURI	161 648	2.7	28 512	X	111 609	12 270	29 008	26 341	24 999	9 871	10 959	2 159	734
Adair	525	2.3	21 021	2 294	327	42	107	115	109	36	58	8	2
Andrew	443	1.8	26 528	783	71	33	83	60	56	25	23	3	2
Atchison	144	-9.8	22 917	1 747	52	7	36	39	37	14	19	2	0
Audrain	572	-0.9	22 158	1 967	317	52	118	129	123	53	55	8	3
Barry	730	0.9	21 282	2 217	475	68	141	172	164	65	73	15	4
Barton	270	0.0	21 011	2 300	161	23	54	61	58	24	26	5	2
Bates	389	-1.0	22 945	1 739	103	42	70	86	82	35	37	6	2
Benton	367	5.7	20 713	2 369	93	39	72	121	117	52	49	8	2
Bollinger	230	4.2	18 682	2 800	50	24	32	61	58	22	26	5	2
Boone	3 894	3.6	27 947	558	2 949	283	662	501	468	172	211	42	7
Buchanan	2 139	3.2	25 103	1 103	1 625	144	348	435	414	161	184	35	11
Butler	969	4.0	23 752	1 483	598	94	144	275	266	84	129	27	6
Caldwell	215	1.9	23 722	1 491	46	23	36	43	41	17	18	3	1
Callaway	901	2.2	21 340	2 198	497	51	137	167	157	64	71	12	4
Camden	975	3.6	25 699	953	458	95	229	203	194	96	73	11	5
Cape Girardeau	1 865	4.0	26 802	735	1 406	142	379	298	282	118	115	23	7
Carroll	223	0.4	21 777	2 071	78	14	55	54	52	21	24	4	1
Carter	116	8.2	19 601	2 633	36	15	17	41	40	13	20	5	1
Cass	2 385	2.7	27 380	634	680	133	343	334	314	134	125	16	12
Cedar	271	2.7	19 510	2 657	82	30	57	83	80	33	36	6	1
Chariton	199	2.9	24 059	1 383	61	25	47	47	45	19	20	2	2
Christian	1 389	4.5	23 449	1 585	384	120	214	209	195	86	78	15	6
Clark	150	1.8	20 067	2 534	40	9	31	37	35	14	15	2	2
Clay	5 960	3.2	31 171	267	3 897	425	770	676	631	287	256	32	21
Clinton	495	1.9	25 206	1 077	139	12	79	80	75	31	33	4	3
Cole	2 164	2.4	30 149	337	2 032	164	400	281	264	112	111	18	6
Cooper	363	4.1	21 270	2 223	172	28	70	75	70	30	32	4	1
Crawford	538	4.3	23 156	1 676	183	57	78	127	121	48	55	10	2
Dade	168	0.0	21 295	2 209	61	21	33	42	40	17	17	3	1
Dallas	338	5.0	21 244	2 228	76	43	52	79	75	31	31	7	2
Daviess	165	-0.2	20 764	2 350	49	17	38	37	35	16	14	2	1
De Kalb	185	0.2	14 218	3 089	82	10	26	44	42	19	18	2	1
Dent	307	3.2	20 667	2 381	120	31	53	91	87	32	42	8	3
Douglas	233	2.2	17 466	2 955	71	28	43	67	64	25	27	7	3
Dunklin	679	1.3	20 704	2 370	306	34	99	230	222	65	115	32	4
Franklin	2 571	2.7	26 783	739	1 213	112	418	389	366	166	148	24	13
Gasconade	359	1.6	23 230	1 649	157	19	83	77	73	34	32	4	2
Gentry	148	-3.0	22 249	1 947	56	8	33	43	41	17	20	2	1
Greene	6 842	4.0	28 122	530	5 265	950	1 268	1 085	1 027	412	419	87	21
Grundy	221	1.4	21 689	2 094	104	17	44	60	58	22	26	4	1
Harrison	177	2.6	20 142	2 511	70	11	41	52	50	19	26	3	1
Henry	516	1.9	23 187	1 668	240	29	111	132	126	53	57	10	3
Hickory	160	4.3	17 935	2 906	29	12	36	65	63	29	26	4	1
Holt	117	-2.0	22 833	1 770	39	6	27	30	29	13	12	2	1
Howard	237	2.5	23 644	1 515	65	11	47	50	48	18	23	3	1
Howell	762	4.0	20 442	2 447	423	70	137	219	210	82	91	21	4
Iron	210	4.7	20 021	2 545	101	11	30	75	72	24	36	7	2
Jackson	20 257	2.6	30 714	290	18 593	2 056	3 116	3 127	2 970	1 098	1 345	282	107

1. Based on the resident population estimated as of July 1 of the year shown.   2. Includes other labor income.

Table B. States and Counties — Earnings, Social Security, and Housing

STATE County	Earnings, 2002									Social Security beneficiaries, December 2003			Housing units, 2003	
			Percent by selected industries											
			Goods-related[1]		Service-related and health							Supplemental Security Income recipients, December 2003		
	Total (mil dol)	Farm	Total	Manu-facturing	Information and professional and technical services	Retail trade	Finance, insurance, and real estate	Health services	Govern-ment	Number	Rate[2]		Total	Percent change, 2000–2003
	75	76	77	78	79	80	81	82	83	84	85	86	87	88
MISSISSIPPI—Cont'd														
Sunflower	349	1.5	13.7	11.5	1.9	13.0	3.6	D	38.6	4 610	138	2 033	10 490	1.5
Tallahatchie	79	-8.7	D	6.8	D	10.0	5.1	D	36.4	3 425	238	1 281	5 824	2.0
Tate	233	1.8	D	13.1	D	14.4	3.5	D	23.9	4 610	179	880	9 946	6.3
Tippah	246	0.8	48.7	41.3	D	6.8	3.4	D	14.2	5 220	250	1 268	9 063	2.2
Tishomingo	203	0.0	48.5	42.2	2.3	7.5	3.4	D	13.1	5 130	270	904	9 691	1.4
Tunica	545	0.0	4.3	3.0	0.7	1.8	0.7	D	5.4	1 685	170	672	4 216	13.8
Union	310	0.2	37.4	33.4	2.9	8.0	2.6	10.2	12.3	5 645	216	816	10 907	2.0
Walthall	101	10.9	D	18.5	1.7	8.8	D	8.5	23.1	3 235	213	862	6 549	2.0
Warren	1 020	-0.2	D	18.1	D	7.3	3.1	D	27.2	8 340	170	1 866	21 015	1.1
Washington	791	1.7	D	15.0	7.0	9.7	3.4	10.0	22.8	11 175	185	4 942	24 966	2.4
Wayne	212	8.2	30.7	15.8	D	11.4	2.7	D	17.6	4 095	194	1 100	9 296	2.7
Webster	69	-1.8	22.6	18.3	D	13.6	D	D	21.2	3 005	296	579	4 418	1.7
Wilkinson	63	0.9	11.0	7.5	D	7.5	4.5	D	30.4	2 055	201	819	5 223	2.3
Winston	197	0.9	D	29.9	3.1	10.0	3.1	D	13.9	4 420	222	948	8 629	1.9
Yalobusha	119	-2.7	D	43.1	D	8.7	3.2	3.6	21.4	3 310	248	917	6 388	2.6
Yazoo	280	0.9	D	22.5	3.2	7.3	4.2	D	26.9	5 160	183	1 822	10 128	1.1
MISSOURI	123 878	0.2	21.2	14.1	11.2	7.2	7.9	9.7	15.4	1 033 886	181	115 131	2 532 960	3.7
Adair	368	0.5	18.3	13.8	3.6	10.3	5.5	D	25.7	3 990	161	569	11 107	2.6
Andrew	104	-0.2	D	2.9	5.1	14.1	6.4	7.7	22.4	2 830	168	142	6 879	3.3
Atchison	58	-15.4	5.3	0.7	D	8.9	8.7	21.1	23.4	1 525	243	96	3 117	0.5
Audrain	369	2.3	D	24.8	3.4	10.3	4.9	D	25.1	5 365	209	395	11 031	1.4
Barry	542	2.1	D	38.5	D	7.3	3.0	D	11.8	7 680	222	759	16 607	4.0
Barton	183	1.3	D	41.1	D	7.2	4.3	4.2	15.0	2 745	211	243	5 526	2.2
Bates	145	2.0	D	10.1	4.7	9.4	6.1	D	26.0	3 890	230	313	7 421	2.4
Benton	131	0.7	D	8.3	4.4	15.6	8.6	5.5	24.7	5 705	316	427	13 022	2.6
Bollinger	74	2.1	D	7.3	3.8	13.4	5.5	6.6	21.9	2 770	225	339	5 701	3.2
Boone	3 232	0.0	D	7.2	5.8	7.8	7.1	10.9	37.1	17 705	125	2 028	61 189	8.0
Buchanan	1 769	0.0	D	19.9	4.6	8.1	6.3	14.1	15.2	16 630	196	2 053	36 921	0.9
Butler	693	0.6	D	16.4	4.4	9.4	4.0	20.0	19.0	10 160	249	2 312	19 185	2.6
Caldwell	69	-2.1	21.5	1.1	5.0	9.8	9.5	D	26.5	1 870	204	145	4 550	1.3
Callaway	547	0.5	23.1	14.8	3.0	5.8	3.6	4.1	26.6	6 905	164	557	16 884	4.4
Camden	553	0.2	D	7.6	6.1	16.7	9.3	12.5	11.2	9 775	255	393	34 363	2.7
Cape Girardeau	1 548	-0.2	D	16.7	7.8	9.0	5.7	19.9	13.4	12 505	179	1 425	30 456	3.5
Carroll	92	1.5	D	14.3	4.2	9.3	6.8	9.0	21.8	2 370	234	213	4 943	0.9
Carter	51	0.4	19.3	12.4	D	9.0	5.5	D	30.7	1 630	273	331	3 135	3.5
Cass	813	0.4	24.5	5.7	5.9	13.0	6.0	6.5	21.4	13 985	157	496	34 862	10.1
Cedar	113	0.2	D	12.3	4.5	11.5	4.5	9.0	24.8	3 780	273	374	6 986	2.5
Chariton	86	4.3	19.7	13.1	2.7	12.5	7.3	D	17.5	2 075	251	151	4 326	1.8
Christian	504	0.1	D	13.4	D	12.8	7.9	5.6	14.9	9 830	160	709	24 331	11.5
Clark	49	-5.8	14.6	9.7	D	11.4	6.4	5.0	34.4	1 590	214	105	3 553	2.0
Clay	4 321	0.0	D	23.1	10.1	10.5	4.9	6.7	12.0	27 870	143	1 529	80 126	5.1
Clinton	151	-3.1	D	4.0	3.5	12.1	12.0	D	26.4	3 275	163	218	8 339	5.9
Cole	2 196	0.0	D	6.3	7.2	8.4	6.3	10.3	40.1	11 800	163	1 083	30 708	6.2
Cooper	200	1.3	D	15.2	3.1	7.4	4.8	D	21.5	3 235	190	197	6 901	3.4
Crawford	239	0.4	D	26.9	3.2	16.2	4.7	D	13.1	5 335	227	531	11 194	3.2
Dade	82	5.2	D	8.1	D	6.1	D	1.4	21.6	2 005	256	170	3 827	1.8
Dallas	118	1.6	D	8.5	D	13.6	7.7	6.3	20.7	3 685	229	426	7 181	3.9
Daviess	67	2.3	D	18.5	2.7	10.1	D	4.6	25.8	1 840	230	100	3 931	2.0
De Kalb	92	-0.1	D	D	D	8.2	4.6	D	50.0	2 110	162	85	3 973	3.5
Dent	151	0.4	D	10.9	2.3	11.1	5.4	D	20.6	3 715	249	485	7 188	2.8
Douglas	99	3.7	D	22.1	4.3	8.7	4.9	D	18.5	3 200	239	411	6 109	3.2
Dunklin	340	-0.8	22.7	17.2	3.6	12.4	4.2	14.8	17.9	8 015	245	2 435	15 071	2.6
Franklin	1 326	0.0	D	31.3	5.2	9.8	4.8	8.3	12.1	17 330	179	1 432	40 270	5.2
Gasconade	176	0.2	D	28.3	D	10.2	4.0	4.8	17.7	3 685	237	187	8 012	2.5
Gentry	65	-0.2	16.3	12.8	D	14.7	6.4	19.0	23.7	1 985	302	139	3 245	1.0
Greene	6 214	0.0	D	15.6	8.1	10.4	7.4	16.2	12.1	44 090	179	5 337	110 837	6.0
Grundy	121	1.6	23.7	19.6	4.6	13.9	3.7	12.3	24.9	2 560	248	231	5 173	1.4
Harrison	81	1.7	D	1.8	4.2	20.0	6.0	9.7	28.0	2 305	261	189	4 382	1.5
Henry	269	-0.2	D	20.8	3.3	11.2	5.1	D	20.3	5 850	261	634	10 521	2.5
Hickory	41	0.6	D	4.9	D	13.9	5.6	6.7	29.7	3 220	358	213	6 448	4.3
Holt	46	3.1	D	9.8	5.1	10.5	5.0	7.5	25.6	1 370	266	75	2 963	1.1
Howard	76	1.8	D	16.7	D	7.5	D	D	21.5	1 990	199	209	4 438	2.1
Howell	492	0.7	26.5	22.3	D	11.0	4.4	15.2	16.8	10 020	267	1 495	16 941	3.7
Iron	113	0.1	D	22.7	D	6.5	2.7	D	16.0	2 795	271	508	5 044	2.8
Jackson	20 650	0.0	14.9	7.8	19.3	5.9	11.1	9.1	15.7	109 420	166	13 311	299 311	3.8

1. Covers mining, construction, and manufacturing.   2. Per 1,000 resident population estimated as of July 1 of the year shown.

Table B. States and Counties — Housing, Labor Force, and Employment

STATE County	Housing units, 2000 Total	Percent	Median value[1]	With a mortgage	Without a mortgage[2]	Median rent[3]	Median rent as a percent of income	Substandard units[4] (percent)	Civilian labor force, 2003 Total	Percent change, 2002–2003	Unemployment Total	Rate[5]	Civilian employment,[6] 2000 Total	Percent Management, professional and related occupations	Production, transportation, and material moving occupations
	89	90	91	92	93	94	95	96	97	98	99	100	101	102	103
MISSISSIPPI—Cont'd															
Sunflower	9 637	61.9	50 000	21.5	11.3	357	24.0	12.4	10 455	-4.0	1 100	10.5	10 369	25.5	25.1
Tallahatchie	5 263	76.1	42 300	24.0	12.9	285	22.0	9.0	6 076	6.3	711	11.7	5 079	24.9	27.6
Tate	8 850	78.3	80 000	20.1	9.9	410	24.5	6.2	10 311	2.0	744	7.2	10 654	23.1	22.9
Tippah	8 108	78.1	57 200	21.5	10.2	353	21.1	2.9	9 116	-0.1	864	9.5	8 716	20.5	38.1
Tishomingo	7 917	78.7	60 200	19.1	9.9	353	22.3	2.9	8 842	-5.1	864	9.8	7 986	19.6	32.8
Tunica	3 258	51.8	56 800	19.4	12.6	459	24.9	10.0	6 895	6.4	587	8.5	3 627	18.7	13.7
Union	9 786	77.6	68 300	20.0	9.9	401	21.2	4.1	12 934	-0.6	710	5.5	11 322	21.3	37.3
Walthall	5 571	83.2	60 500	23.9	11.7	346	29.1	7.5	5 162	-5.1	401	7.8	5 663	23.1	26.6
Warren	18 756	68.3	79 100	19.9	9.9	466	25.6	5.3	25 371	-0.6	1 477	5.8	21 899	31.5	17.6
Washington	22 158	59.5	55 400	21.2	11.7	423	27.8	8.4	25 541	-2.2	2 783	10.9	22 691	27.2	21.2
Wayne	7 857	84.9	54 400	20.1	10.1	334	22.1	5.9	8 457	-1.1	802	9.5	7 781	19.9	28.6
Webster	3 905	78.4	55 600	20.5	11.0	319	21.6	4.6	2 926	-15.9	455	15.6	3 010	22.1	21.2
Wilkinson	3 578	83.1	43 800	24.7	12.8	269	22.9	6.1	3 485	23.4	403	11.6	7 803	23.7	27.3
Winston	7 578	79.6	56 700	19.7	9.9	370	26.6	5.8	6 963	-1.3	651	9.3	5 077	18.3	35.3
Yalobusha	5 260	79.0	51 600	21.0	10.7	304	23.1	4.2	5 064	7.8	517	10.2	9 325	23.9	24.1
Yazoo	9 178	68.9	54 700	21.3	9.9	346	27.3	9.3	9 608	0.9	925	9.6			
MISSOURI	2 194 594	70.3	89 900	19.5	9.9	484	24.0	2.9	3 020 592	1.3	170 126	5.6	2 657 924	31.5	16.3
Adair	9 669	60.4	73 900	18.7	9.9	418	31.0	2.3	13 619	0.2	516	3.8	12 126	35.2	14.5
Andrew	6 273	80.0	89 000	18.0	9.9	435	20.0	2.1	8 968	-0.6	458	5.1	8 153	30.0	18.0
Atchison	2 722	69.2	49 800	17.4	10.8	317	18.6	1.2	2 910	-2.4	96	3.3	3 025	32.1	18.9
Audrain	9 844	74.1	62 400	18.2	9.9	384	21.8	3.6	12 070	-5.3	716	5.9	11 463	28.3	24.3
Barry	13 398	75.7	70 600	21.3	9.9	377	23.5	5.0	15 335	-1.0	790	5.2	14 836	22.3	29.2
Barton	4 895	73.4	55 800	18.1	10.9	354	20.6	2.7	7 137	-3.4	318	4.5	5 882	24.5	27.0
Bates	6 511	75.0	58 000	19.5	11.2	413	24.2	3.2	7 227	-1.8	536	7.4	7 386	23.6	19.6
Benton	7 420	82.2	65 700	22.2	9.9	364	24.9	3.2	6 776	2.7	506	7.5	6 613	23.0	19.8
Bollinger	4 576	81.6	58 400	19.3	9.9	337	21.8	3.8	5 623	-0.9	375	6.7	5 323	18.3	30.6
Boone	53 094	57.5	107 400	19.7	9.9	523	27.4	2.2	89 183	-0.5	2 046	2.3	72 978	41.8	9.4
Buchanan	33 557	67.5	72 700	18.5	9.9	435	23.7	1.9	43 896	-0.8	2 595	5.9	39 031	27.4	18.1
Butler	16 718	68.9	59 400	18.4	9.9	354	24.3	3.0	21 416	1.6	1 138	5.3	16 803	26.8	22.7
Caldwell	3 523	77.4	53 800	19.9	10.2	336	21.6	3.1	3 309	-3.7	272	8.2	4 057	24.4	19.8
Callaway	14 416	76.8	85 800	18.9	9.9	418	21.2	2.4	24 195	2.3	920	3.8	19 719	27.8	16.0
Camden	15 779	82.3	124 300	21.9	9.9	454	21.7	2.1	18 309	0.6	1 121	6.1	16 339	27.4	12.7
Cape Girardeau	26 980	68.4	94 700	18.9	9.9	440	24.4	2.0	38 536	-0.1	1 529	4.0	34 821	30.9	16.0
Carroll	4 169	74.0	48 900	18.9	11.2	323	19.5	3.0	4 874	-2.9	269	5.5	4 647	30.0	23.6
Carter	2 378	76.7	51 900	21.4	9.9	303	22.4	4.0	2 758	1.2	188	6.8	2 214	24.6	23.3
Cass	30 168	79.6	104 200	19.6	9.9	543	22.8	2.1	48 271	2.6	2 460	5.1	40 924	30.2	14.8
Cedar	5 685	78.3	57 900	21.0	10.5	324	26.8	2.8	5 318	0.1	381	7.2	5 323	25.3	21.7
Chariton	3 469	80.5	43 800	17.2	9.9	317	18.0	2.7	4 029	-6.8	264	6.6	3 842	29.4	23.0
Christian	20 425	75.9	97 900	20.7	9.9	511	24.3	2.3	31 922	2.0	1 501	4.7	27 770	30.7	15.2
Clark	2 966	78.5	51 300	18.7	9.9	316	22.6	3.1	3 645	-3.1	287	7.9	3 462	22.3	30.7
Clay	72 558	70.7	104 900	19.7	9.9	576	22.4	2.1	114 314	2.3	5 112	4.5	98 141	32.5	13.8
Clinton	7 152	79.0	86 400	19.7	10.2	442	23.2	2.2	10 002	2.0	552	5.5	9 092	25.3	18.5
Cole	27 040	67.8	97 200	18.8	9.9	441	21.5	1.8	41 742	2.2	1 285	3.1	36 120	35.6	11.5
Cooper	5 932	74.2	74 200	19.6	9.9	426	19.5	2.4	8 777	-3.2	341	3.9	7 423	26.3	17.9
Crawford	8 858	76.7	66 100	21.5	9.9	387	23.2	3.6	10 681	-0.3	798	7.5	9 698	19.2	27.7
Dade	3 202	78.8	54 500	20.4	10.2	297	21.3	2.5	3 382	-2.8	162	4.8	3 427	24.9	26.6
Dallas	6 030	79.2	72 300	22.9	10.2	353	25.8	3.3	6 911	-0.7	462	6.7	6 461	21.3	24.6
Daviess	3 178	76.8	56 700	19.2	10.7	331	20.6	3.7	3 393	-4.5	222	6.5	3 575	25.2	19.1
De Kalb	3 528	73.4	64 800	19.0	9.9	332	23.3	2.3	4 631	2.8	245	5.3	4 023	29.3	17.5
Dent	5 982	74.1	61 000	20.5	9.9	337	23.3	3.1	5 564	-4.5	382	6.9	6 107	22.4	24.3
Douglas	5 201	73.0	54 100	22.3	11.3	305	21.3	4.2	5 011	-6.6	445	8.9	5 416	24.5	29.3
Dunklin	13 411	65.9	48 500	18.1	10.2	323	25.5	3.8	14 236	-0.6	1 185	8.3	13 179	21.9	27.1
Franklin	34 945	78.0	96 400	19.1	9.9	471	21.5	3.0	50 296	1.9	3 032	6.0	46 027	23.8	24.1
Gasconade	6 171	80.3	70 500	19.6	9.9	374	20.2	3.4	7 559	-2.1	492	6.5	7 068	21.6	32.5
Gentry	2 747	74.5	47 200	18.5	10.7	294	19.8	1.9	3 585	-3.7	134	3.7	2 969	30.2	19.6
Greene	97 859	63.6	88 200	20.2	9.9	462	25.6	2.2	130 890	1.6	5 000	3.8	121 148	29.8	15.4
Grundy	4 382	71.8	42 500	17.6	9.9	325	23.2	2.4	4 722	-3.6	287	6.1	4 726	24.5	23.1
Harrison	3 658	74.7	41 500	18.1	10.4	336	21.3	2.4	4 045	-3.7	188	4.6	4 182	26.8	16.9
Henry	9 133	73.0	64 200	19.6	10.7	394	22.3	2.3	10 462	-0.3	838	8.0	9 897	24.4	22.6
Hickory	3 911	84.5	62 600	22.2	9.9	342	27.1	3.3	2 689	0.5	266	9.9	2 907	22.1	22.3
Holt	2 237	74.4	50 100	17.7	9.9	272	19.6	2.6	2 456	-8.5	136	5.5	2 487	30.7	18.0
Howard	3 836	75.2	59 500	19.1	9.9	380	24.1	2.2	4 460	1.0	183	4.1	4 949	27.9	18.2
Howell	14 762	73.5	67 700	21.2	9.9	350	24.6	3.7	18 189	0.9	1 054	5.8	15 758	24.0	25.0
Iron	4 197	75.9	51 800	19.8	9.9	347	24.7	4.0	4 567	-2.9	396	8.7	4 165	23.7	20.8
Jackson	266 294	62.9	85 000	19.8	10.6	536	24.3	3.7	372 046	2.2	25 206	6.8	315 967	33.0	13.5

1. Specified owner-occupied units. 2. Median monthly owner costs is often in the minimum category—9.9 percent or less, which is indicated as 9.9 percent. 3. Specified renter-occupied units. 4. Overcrowded or lacking complete plumbing facilities. 5. Percent of civilian labor force. 6. Persons 16 years old and over.

	Private nonfarm establishments, employment and payroll, 2001								Agriculture, 2002			
STATE County	Number of establish-ments	Employment					Annual payroll		Farms			
		Total	Health care and social assistance	Manufac-turing	Retail trade	Finance and insurance	Professional, scientific, and technical services	Total (mil dol)	Average per employee (dollars)	Number	Percent with—		Farm operators whose principal occu-pation is farming (percent)
											Less than 50 acres	500 acres and over	
	104	105	106	107	108	109	110	111	112	113	114	115	116
MISSISSIPPI—Cont'd													
Sunflower	488	6 989	996	1 998	1 055	307	91	136	19 479	343	9.6	41.7	70.0
Tallahatchie	197	1 496	289	260	277	37	17	29	19 270	417	15.8	26.9	51.1
Tate	392	4 924	438	1 427	1 237	199	74	101	20 455	662	32.9	10.1	48.5
Tippah	380	7 322	549	3 415	858	142	83	159	21 763	733	28.2	4.1	45.4
Tishomingo	396	5 098	526	2 403	612	148	60	112	22 053	358	28.5	3.9	42.2
Tunica	192	16 826	243	614	374	39	11	372	22 138	98	5.1	62.2	80.6
Union	477	9 419	759	3 939	1 025	173	112	215	22 856	819	30.3	4.4	42.0
Walthall	225	2 374	424	651	422	62	22	43	18 243	662	24.8	4.7	49.1
Warren	1 171	20 621	2 377	5 090	2 932	374	651	511	24 762	281	33.5	20.6	43.4
Washington	1 467	19 433	3 114	3 914	3 339	407	483	440	22 630	333	19.8	39.9	67.3
Wayne	376	5 041	611	1 109	875	167	40	111	21 968	547	33.3	5.3	59.0
Webster	192	2 536	374	1 216	337	64	58	44	17 259	351	19.1	10.8	51.3
Wilkinson	170	1 649	309	212	262	67	16	31	18 976	298	21.1	18.8	39.9
Winston	388	4 613	397	1 490	806	95	93	103	22 336	530	26.2	8.1	44.9
Yalobusha	240	2 678	276	1 175	391	96	44	64	23 891	374	21.1	12.6	41.7
Yazoo	418	5 082	630	1 676	976	208	72	113	22 226	566	17.1	25.6	49.3
MISSOURI	144 071	2 404 489	331 323	335 403	317 459	134 293	121 844	74 428	30 954	106 797	23.1	14.0	57.2
Adair	625	8 496	1 760	1 249	1 636	254	118	186	21 841	915	17.9	17.0	49.4
Andrew	247	2 220	D	50	976	67	D	39	17 359	847	23.8	15.5	58.9
Atchison	204	1 435	461	34	306	82	D	28	19 507	465	12.3	43.4	70.3
Audrain	651	8 361	1 474	2 576	1 387	376	139	196	23 449	1 089	20.6	21.7	65.3
Barry	819	14 639	1 102	7 073	1 582	328	D	390	26 620	1 669	28.6	7.4	58.5
Barton	288	4 722	601	D	635	165	123	111	23 468	960	20.1	21.8	59.9
Bates	393	3 065	542	370	586	171	145	57	18 458	1 293	19.0	17.8	61.4
Benton	412	2 489	228	450	712	120	73	41	16 536	839	16.3	15.4	60.1
Bollinger	207	1 421	265	283	332	40	D	24	16 728	913	14.9	11.7	56.7
Boone	3 785	63 207	13 699	5 847	8 984	5 286	2 432	1 571	24 855	1 388	34.1	8.5	48.8
Buchanan	2 317	36 860	6 135	6 222	4 900	2 015	891	973	26 400	848	29.8	12.6	55.1
Butler	1 028	15 041	3 468	3 150	2 442	427	396	334	22 203	673	23.5	20.5	62.3
Caldwell	180	930	170	47	175	91	D	21	22 086	959	23.4	11.5	49.0
Callaway	671	10 737	2 125	1 886	1 253	252	96	285	26 570	1 494	24.6	11.6	50.8
Camden	1 624	13 328	1 755	1 287	3 186	521	382	282	21 149	623	12.4	14.8	57.1
Cape Girardeau	2 324	37 306	7 797	6 290	6 398	1 208	959	932	24 977	1 204	22.8	9.6	57.6
Carroll	245	2 047	367	453	295	119	D	37	18 081	1 081	16.3	20.0	58.4
Carter	143	692	84	158	170	37	D	12	17 169	228	18.0	16.2	40.4
Cass	1 756	16 171	2 282	1 365	3 225	503	380	356	21 989	1 635	37.7	7.7	51.7
Cedar	308	2 661	629	472	530	101	68	47	17 761	952	19.4	10.3	58.0
Chariton	205	1 275	131	239	285	111	D	24	18 874	1 095	14.0	20.6	62.5
Christian	1 238	11 014	906	2 418	2 143	397	246	225	20 406	1 294	35.3	6.1	54.0
Clark	140	900	183	79	283	68	14	15	16 299	685	13.4	23.6	60.0
Clay	4 668	82 250	9 322	13 800	12 799	2 522	5 715	2 765	33 613	683	43.3	9.4	49.0
Clinton	429	3 557	877	290	882	220	76	68	19 132	889	30.1	10.7	55.8
Cole	2 204	36 958	5 607	2 830	5 232	1 890	1 268	941	25 465	1 098	25.1	4.4	51.6
Cooper	425	3 635	648	552	768	148	69	67	18 515	923	16.7	17.9	63.9
Crawford	484	4 987	580	1 595	782	150	193	104	20 937	751	17.7	16.0	47.9
Dade	146	1 358	123	262	127	46	D	25	18 116	893	20.3	16.2	61.5
Dallas	265	2 431	949	189	433	131	D	33	13 395	1 243	26.0	7.8	56.0
Daviess	169	1 122	87	392	232	57	D	18	16 052	1 029	16.8	15.8	48.9
De Kalb	192	1 510	335	51	235	222	D	29	19 259	833	19.8	15.0	53.8
Dent	339	3 675	524	755	686	129	50	81	22 165	693	15.0	17.3	52.2
Douglas	197	2 098	260	749	347	63	D	34	16 398	1 160	17.1	12.1	57.3
Dunklin	764	8 137	2 070	1 056	1 787	418	125	151	18 584	429	18.4	42.4	72.3
Franklin	2 410	31 097	3 391	9 994	4 974	834	869	784	25 210	1 833	30.7	5.9	52.3
Gasconade	424	4 502	479	1 771	657	132	78	97	21 471	877	14.1	10.9	51.9
Gentry	212	1 752	496	317	283	59	D	34	19 359	821	18.3	19.9	57.2
Greene	7 684	136 859	22 864	17 565	19 260	6 749	6 028	3 478	25 416	2 122	44.3	4.8	50.3
Grundy	267	3 188	584	1 243	437	100	52	67	20 914	735	18.6	14.3	58.6
Harrison	232	2 178	539	D	699	102	D	37	17 090	1 101	18.6	17.6	54.3
Henry	638	7 186	1 483	1 895	1 333	243	112	160	22 257	1 010	21.7	18.1	60.7
Hickory	161	653	115	D	146	32	D	10	15 129	534	13.9	15.5	65.9
Holt	136	921	147	153	217	53	D	20	21 368	486	14.0	27.2	68.7
Howard	214	1 684	320	254	205	80	37	32	19 127	806	17.1	16.6	56.5
Howell	1 004	13 281	2 770	3 880	2 234	302	248	261	19 667	1 743	25.0	9.5	56.2
Iron	256	2 116	463	376	314	62	D	48	22 913	299	10.7	13.4	59.2
Jackson	17 659	374 329	46 380	35 091	40 008	29 092	26 237	13 198	35 258	807	53.3	6.6	52.2

STATE County	Land in farms Acreage (1,000)	Percent change, 1997–2002	Acres Average size of farm	Acres Total irrigated (1,000)	Acres Total cropland (1,000)	Value of land and buildings (dollars) Average per farm	Average per acre	Value of machinery and equipment average per farm (dollars)	Value of products sold Total (mil dol)	Average per farm (dollars)	Percent from — Crops	Percent from — Live-stock and poultry products	Percent of farms with sales of — $10,000 or more	$100,000 or more	Government payments Total ($1,000)	Percent of farms
	117	118	119	120	121	122	123	124	125	126	127	128	129	130	131	132
MISSISSIPPI—Cont'd																
Sunflower	336	-3.4	981	161	285	1 053 946	1 063	243 077	119	347 230	58.2	41.8	66.8	43.4	11 337	56.6
Tallahatchie	293	-1.3	703	72	226	686 715	905	146 267	45	108 254	95.0	5.0	36.2	20.4	7 547	58.0
Tate	155	14.8	234	2	79	321 831	1 699	36 024	24	36 919	46.2	53.8	25.1	6.0	1 801	27.5
Tippah	121	6.1	165	0	50	201 590	1 238	20 225	13	17 147	49.7	50.3	15.1	2.0	819	42.3
Tishomingo	53	17.8	147	D	19	134 581	1 311	20 214	3	9 130	32.1	67.9	11.5	1.1	260	38.8
Tunica	201	-0.5	2 053	71	186	2 088 513	1 000	503 794	53	545 342	87.3	12.7	70.4	55.1	5 058	68.4
Union	139	36.3	170	0	62	197 261	1 549	26 198	10	12 195	47.8	52.2	15.0	2.4	1 051	44.3
Walthall	107	-2.7	162	0	45	440 004	2 899	41 642	51	77 641	1.5	98.5	25.1	13.4	961	30.4
Warren	115	17.3	408	2	53	471 906	1 095	73 002	10	37 016	87.3	12.7	27.8	8.5	1 259	36.3
Washington	321	-6.4	963	137	291	1 195 760	1 260	228 547	94	283 569	86.0	14.0	60.4	38.1	10 622	51.4
Wayne	84	10.5	154	0	25	312 268	1 570	67 940	101	183 969	2.0	98.0	39.9	26.3	108	6.6
Webster	77	-2.5	220	0	32	200 328	817	44 822	14	39 382	45.3	54.7	21.4	6.3	763	55.6
Wilkinson	105	-3.7	353	0	26	498 361	1 379	44 531	3	9 628	D	D	15.8	1.7	563	24.5
Winston	101	14.8	190	0	32	293 075	1 670	38 720	13	24 930	9.3	90.7	19.1	3.6	411	26.8
Yalobusha	100	16.3	268	0	41	367 285	1 207	36 007	8	20 363	78.4	21.6	16.0	3.7	786	42.8
Yazoo	360	15.4	636	25	216	729 113	1 102	89 666	67	118 606	79.8	20.2	32.3	12.9	7 077	52.7
MISSOURI	29 946	3.9	280	1 033	18 885	424 347	1 508	49 940	4 983	46 661	40.0	60.0	41.0	8.8	264 475	40.6
Adair	269	0.4	294	0	165	341 003	1 012	39 127	20	22 150	51.7	48.3	38.8	4.9	3 010	53.6
Andrew	223	-1.8	264	D	172	512 909	1 838	66 163	31	36 407	69.9	30.1	45.6	9.8	3 003	60.2
Atchison	318	8.2	683	8	277	1 093 447	1 642	128 387	48	104 029	88.5	11.5	74.2	33.5	3 849	69.9
Audrain	415	8.6	381	18	345	607 021	1 601	74 225	90	82 299	58.4	41.6	59.1	19.7	7 485	57.7
Barry	321	12.6	193	0	160	346 202	1 678	33 665	201	120 670	1.9	98.1	42.4	15.0	1 046	22.0
Barton	337	0.6	351	13	245	370 333	1 000	67 018	66	69 142	41.0	59.0	52.2	11.9	3 192	55.7
Bates	468	5.2	362	3	317	432 249	1 199	73 236	57	44 336	46.1	53.9	46.9	9.9	3 691	48.6
Benton	259	11.6	309	D	121	359 371	1 115	43 377	31	37 196	19.0	81.0	44.1	5.8	836	30.5
Bollinger	228	9.1	250	7	115	327 779	1 292	36 801	20	21 451	D	D	34.2	3.3	886	32.5
Boone	270	8.0	194	5	170	487 493	2 544	31 838	36	25 793	55.0	45.0	33.9	4.5	1 857	32.3
Buchanan	200	9.9	236	D	153	457 309	1 790	85 723	28	32 996	76.0	24.0	44.0	7.8	2 489	52.4
Butler	248	-2.7	368	115	210	546 636	1 499	81 193	43	64 248	92.1	7.9	48.6	17.8	5 748	44.3
Caldwell	230	1.3	240	0	156	336 037	1 369	35 140	25	25 689	36.7	63.3	33.2	4.1	3 361	60.6
Callaway	358	8.5	239	5	220	495 552	1 780	45 654	51	34 159	42.7	57.3	35.1	7.0	2 634	38.9
Camden	178	3.5	287	0	70	354 482	1 254	25 578	16	26 276	5.4	94.6	28.1	4.8	236	20.2
Cape Girardeau	261	0.0	217	11	192	438 403	1 891	43 342	44	36 809	53.7	46.3	41.9	7.7	2 505	44.2
Carroll	417	5.3	386	3	325	476 784	1 295	64 659	62	57 192	76.2	23.8	49.2	13.3	5 813	73.0
Carter	93	47.6	406	0	24	393 932	1 048	30 697	3	12 113	8.3	91.7	25.0	1.8	83	16.2
Cass	314	1.3	192	6	225	381 457	1 844	56 520	48	29 612	59.7	40.3	32.4	4.7	2 059	33.5
Cedar	228	11.8	240	0	117	260 876	1 146	41 953	24	24 765	13.6	86.4	41.1	4.2	745	33.5
Chariton	379	-8.5	346	1	292	411 966	1 333	63 345	66	60 223	58.6	41.4	52.1	13.8	4 105	62.1
Christian	213	4.9	165	0	125	435 525	2 387	32 409	27	20 840	11.1	88.9	35.5	4.3	687	21.6
Clark	254	2.4	370	1	171	419 594	1 165	54 825	29	41 945	68.7	31.3	49.2	11.5	2 832	65.3
Clay	128	-4.5	188	0	79	542 603	3 392	39 225	25	35 872	36.5	63.5	31.3	6.7	888	23.4
Clinton	226	4.6	255	0	159	390 694	1 541	50 706	31	35 321	50.7	49.3	37.2	7.4	2 827	44.4
Cole	186	3.9	169	1	97	315 767	1 974	30 819	25	22 458	24.5	75.5	34.9	3.6	807	32.0
Cooper	294	-2.6	318	0	204	400 949	1 332	48 610	47	51 243	43.3	56.7	50.5	10.9	2 658	55.0
Crawford	218	19.8	290	0	85	346 279	1 247	30 118	9	12 484	20.3	79.7	31.4	0.9	301	20.8
Dade	296	18.9	332	7	171	404 349	1 277	54 308	41	46 023	32.3	67.7	50.4	9.2	1 443	36.8
Dallas	235	5.9	189	0	121	256 325	1 396	29 362	37	29 501	6.2	93.8	36.4	6.3	827	23.0
Daviess	330	9.3	321	0	222	384 819	1 176	55 141	45	43 404	40.1	59.9	38.2	7.9	4 977	67.2
De Kalb	225	4.7	271	D	156	332 420	1 139	41 800	28	33 062	39.1	60.9	42.7	7.1	3 540	64.5
Dent	210	-5.4	303	0	80	326 109	991	26 796	10	14 741	9.9	90.1	35.6	2.0	304	24.8
Douglas	312	3.3	269	D	120	241 049	1 071	21 406	26	22 719	3.9	96.1	33.6	5.3	935	23.6
Dunklin	297	-5.1	692	125	289	1 298 121	1 936	176 288	82	191 820	98.4	1.6	70.9	41.5	4 290	47.1
Franklin	300	3.4	164	1	177	407 182	2 431	42 605	40	21 588	38.8	61.2	28.8	3.7	1 593	28.4
Gasconade	222	18.1	253	0	105	422 430	1 586	55 493	19	21 232	30.5	69.5	35.2	3.8	811	35.7
Gentry	292	17.3	355	D	214	415 581	1 156	41 201	54	66 308	26.1	73.9	42.0	9.4	4 567	70.4
Greene	275	-0.7	130	0	163	372 072	3 299	36 834	39	18 434	16.5	83.5	29.3	3.7	886	17.3
Grundy	212	-4.5	288	1	157	274 567	1 024	35 109	27	37 201	58.2	41.8	37.3	9.0	3 638	66.1
Harrison	388	0.3	353	0	260	326 501	951	37 578	48	43 156	40.9	59.1	37.1	7.7	5 664	66.5
Henry	338	7.3	335	0	222	437 005	1 209	49 174	45	44 484	31.2	68.8	47.7	10.0	2 665	40.2
Hickory	156	-9.3	292	0	73	278 163	1 082	34 995	16	30 106	10.0	90.0	47.0	5.1	514	34.6
Holt	252	9.1	519	9	212	743 307	1 491	87 437	48	98 348	84.6	15.4	72.4	22.2	2 553	61.9
Howard	270	11.6	335	3	170	442 717	1 334	42 739	29	36 325	67.2	32.8	40.9	8.6	2 716	54.1
Howell	414	7.0	237	1	156	358 331	1 372	35 418	44	25 111	8.2	91.8	36.9	5.1	1 404	20.7
Iron	71	12.7	236	0	28	284 801	1 332	24 511	4	12 172	12.4	87.6	27.8	0.7	69	16.1
Jackson	145	-4.0	180	0	106	567 789	3 675	55 331	21	26 448	74.3	25.7	27.5	5.2	909	22.3

STATE County	New construction ($1,000)	Number of housing units	Number of establish-ments	Number of employees	Sales (mil dol)	Annual payroll (mil dol)	Number of establish-ments	Number of employees	Sales (mil dol)	Annual payroll (mil dol)	Number of establish-ments	Number of employees	Receipts (mil dol)	Annual payroll (mil dol)
	Value of residential construction authorized by building permits, 2003		**Wholesale trade, 1997**				**Retail trade,[1] 1997**				**Real estate and rental and leasing, 1997**			
	133	134	135	136	137	138	139	140	141	142	143	144	145	146
MISSISSIPPI—Cont'd														
Sunflower	2 954	49	31	D	D	D	144	1 250	212.3	16.8	13	49	2.8	0.6
Tallahatchie	610	12	10	59	24.2	1.5	45	276	35.3	3.3	5	16	6.3	1.5
Tate	17 886	211	15	151	34.2	2.1	93	1 182	220.4	17.0	13	31	2.1	0.3
Tippah	1 750	25	20	181	59.9	2.8	105	831	106.7	10.2	11	38	6.1	0.7
Tishomingo	220	3	31	288	82.7	6.3	98	635	91.1	8.7	9	52	1.3	0.3
Tunica	5 867	117	11	109	110.6	2.9	40	304	61.8	4.8	10	20	1.6	0.2
Union	1 613	17	21	217	334.5	9.2	107	1 084	138.3	12.8	11	34	3.3	0.4
Walthall	0	0	14	181	53.3	1.9	54	378	56.2	5.3	2	D	D	D
Warren	3 401	25	46	359	151.6	10.6	281	3 316	454.7	43.7	46	127	14.2	2.0
Washington	7 767	107	78	795	393.8	24.5	324	3 441	507.2	48.2	78	305	25.5	4.0
Wayne	777	10	25	159	174.4	7.6	99	868	124.1	12.7	8	21	1.9	0.2
Webster	860	10	6	D	D	D	45	329	42.4	3.9	3	5	0.7	0.1
Wilkinson	0	0	12	88	27.3	1.5	31	228	31.1	2.7	3	8	0.7	0.1
Winston	682	6	13	242	98.0	8.6	90	741	103.9	10.2	7	123	5.6	1.9
Yalobusha	1 678	29	11	36	48.9	1.1	50	372	41.0	4.2	6	17	0.8	0.1
Yazoo	134	2	28	224	93.5	6.1	121	1 043	196.5	16.0	17	45	3.3	0.5
MISSOURI	3 596 524	29 309	9 522	125 929	91 411.9	4 639.8	24 181	297 556	51 269.9	4 945.0	5 500	31 301	3 991.1	698.1
Adair	3 993	44	30	376	87.6	6.8	143	1 595	225.2	21.7	26	198	11.1	2.5
Andrew	2 092	14	9	D	D	D	47	513	86.8	7.1	9	21	1.5	0.2
Atchison	56	1	13	D	D	D	45	376	59.5	4.8	5	12	0.8	0.1
Audrain	3 640	45	46	356	125.1	7.4	122	1 108	166.5	16.8	16	33	2.9	0.7
Barry	6 836	77	39	252	98.1	5.3	160	1 383	255.3	19.8	26	85	4.9	0.8
Barton	3 379	45	17	D	D	D	58	546	78.4	6.7	6	18	1.8	0.4
Bates	902	8	23	183	72.0	3.7	82	636	81.4	7.8	4	12	0.8	0.1
Benton	786	8	13	131	29.6	1.9	82	587	99.3	8.2	18	40	4.9	0.9
Bollinger	60	1	16	135	56.6	3.4	41	274	40.5	3.8	3	5	0.5	0.1
Boone	229 128	2 094	138	1 651	684.7	49.9	602	8 880	1 469.7	135.3	173	642	75.2	11.0
Buchanan	32 154	268	153	D	D	D	399	4 841	797.9	73.4	86	433	32.3	5.8
Butler	2 485	41	66	523	170.0	12.2	248	2 419	425.7	35.9	25	122	8.1	1.9
Caldwell	0	0	14	57	22.9	0.9	31	175	25.4	2.2	4	D	D	D
Callaway	12 165	96	35	238	130.0	5.0	119	1 109	208.2	16.3	19	56	4.2	0.8
Camden	9 380	153	58	244	88.4	5.0	328	2 639	437.0	42.1	80	272	26.8	4.6
Cape Girardeau	25 893	230	144	1 585	647.2	42.0	473	5 997	959.5	88.0	87	273	27.7	4.9
Carroll	400	2	24	105	78.8	2.1	52	286	36.3	3.2	7	15	0.7	0.1
Carter	0	0	5	20	4.7	0.4	29	149	17.9	1.3	7	17	1.3	0.2
Cass	110 954	937	58	D	D	D	218	2 833	492.9	44.4	60	176	17.5	3.3
Cedar	1 019	17	12	40	11.4	0.6	67	416	70.0	5.5	8	D	D	D
Chariton	541	5	20	190	121.4	4.2	49	260	47.9	3.6	9	D	D	D
Christian	67 440	791	58	403	134.3	8.6	176	1 298	247.7	20.7	42	109	7.9	1.2
Clark	530	4	17	155	69.1	3.5	38	327	44.2	3.8	5	D	D	D
Clay	110 611	865	334	4 707	5 773.2	165.4	721	11 919	2 476.5	211.4	179	1 179	169.4	27.9
Clinton	28 810	239	14	D	D	D	72	787	129.3	11.5	14	29	3.5	0.4
Cole	50 544	399	100	3 286	897.5	65.9	349	4 884	764.1	72.0	74	194	23.5	3.7
Cooper	11 620	104	26	125	63.2	2.8	71	640	96.5	8.6	10	36	1.7	0.3
Crawford	1 494	33	19	117	46.3	3.8	83	1 014	224.5	14.2	23	39	4.2	0.7
Dade	0	0	8	328	104.6	8.0	27	156	20.9	1.7	3	5	0.2	0.0
Dallas	NA	NA	17	75	23.8	1.2	59	423	80.9	6.8	13	22	0.9	0.2
Daviess	168	3	13	119	41.6	2.1	45	203	24.8	2.3	2	D	D	D
De Kalb	540	6	12	77	29.6	2.2	28	232	44.9	3.1	2	D	D	D
Dent	269	5	11	D	D	D	77	675	105.5	9.1	19	34	2.9	0.7
Douglas	390	3	8	56	27.1	0.8	40	324	46.6	4.3	3	9	0.8	0.1
Dunklin	3 681	28	53	384	134.3	9.0	186	1 690	256.6	25.2	27	98	6.4	1.2
Franklin	100 820	672	104	753	185.3	19.5	398	4 495	803.1	74.5	86	254	20.8	3.8
Gasconade	623	6	26	D	D	D	84	605	91.2	9.8	13	102	6.8	2.3
Gentry	40	1	12	D	D	D	48	304	40.9	4.1	3	10	0.5	0.0
Greene	311 994	2 366	576	8 856	5 101.7	263.9	1 302	17 819	3 271.8	294.0	336	1 736	151.7	32.3
Grundy	1 671	21	13	136	59.1	2.6	54	451	65.7	6.5	11	21	1.2	0.2
Harrison	745	10	19	225	74.6	4.6	56	605	92.7	8.7	9	23	1.2	0.2
Henry	3 188	27	48	534	218.6	14.2	136	1 126	177.1	15.0	18	37	2.7	0.4
Hickory	0	0	4	3	2.0	0.2	28	141	22.5	1.7	6	D	D	D
Holt	570	7	6	34	45.7	1.2	28	191	39.4	2.9	2	D	D	D
Howard	790	7	13	129	48.4	3.1	41	199	24.8	2.1	3	9	0.3	0.1
Howell	6 567	89	55	418	273.4	10.5	213	2 123	351.7	30.1	38	155	9.4	2.2
Iron	60	1	5	D	D	D	53	317	56.1	4.3	9	20	0.9	0.3
Jackson	681 465	5 570	1 197	19 252	11 305.8	712.5	2 670	39 198	7 239.1	704.8	746	4 888	793.7	127.3

1. Establishments with payroll.

Table B. States and Counties — Professional Services, Manufacturing, and Accommodation and Foodservices

STATE County	Professional, scientific, and technical services,[1] 1997				Manufacturing, 1997				Accommodation and foodservices, 1997			
	Number of establishments	Number of employees	Receipts (mil dol)	Annual payroll (mil dol)	Number of establishments	Number of employees	Receipts (mil dol)	Annual payroll (mil dol)	Number of establishments	Number of employees	Sales (mil dol)	Annual payroll (mil dol)
	147	148	149	150	151	152	153	154	155	156	157	158
MISSISSIPPI—Cont'd												
Sunflower	27	90	6.5	1.7	22	2 654	508.3	48.3	27	299	9.8	2.5
Tallahatchie	10	19	1.6	0.5	7	500	41.2	5.6	11	56	1.1	0.3
Tate	21	54	2.8	0.8	16	2 047	199.9	45.3	25	357	10.4	2.4
Tippah	12	42	2.3	0.9	42	3 247	344.1	71.2	21	D	D	D
Tishomingo	16	43	3.1	1.5	46	3 361	321.6	70.8	21	D	D	D
Tunica	6	19	2.5	0.5	NA	NA	NA	NA	26	11 575	826.9	226.1
Union	27	75	4.8	1.4	39	4 204	445.8	97.2	38	D	D	D
Walthall	7	19	0.9	0.2	24	940	68.9	15.8	17	149	4.3	1.2
Warren	76	577	34.2	17.4	43	4 698	1 181.8	131.7	97	3 294	160.8	38.0
Washington	83	361	36.2	10.5	65	5 067	1 030.3	121.8	95	1 486	47.5	12.3
Wayne	15	37	1.7	0.4	16	1 323	294.9	28.7	20	D	D	D
Webster	11	52	3.2	1.1	17	1 567	149.8	25.2	5	D	D	D
Wilkinson	6	13	0.7	0.1	NA	NA	NA	NA	9	79	2.2	0.6
Winston	20	176	5.9	3.2	26	1 850	318.3	53.5	22	326	8.9	2.4
Yalobusha	10	54	2.4	0.9	17	1 576	224.2	33.4	10	D	D	D
Yazoo	19	67	9.4	1.3	21	1 987	236.1	52.1	24	340	9.9	2.5
MISSOURI	10 601	93 792	9 953.3	3 643.6	7 497	371 448	93 115.5	11 647.0	11 150	203 849	6 780.8	1 933.3
Adair	34	112	6.8	2.2	10	1 619	412.4	39.8	59	1 364	29.0	8.7
Andrew	10	18	0.9	0.4	NA	NA	NA	NA	14	149	3.5	1.0
Atchison	6	13	0.7	0.2	NA	NA	NA	NA	21	D	D	D
Audrain	24	137	7.7	4.2	38	2 721	531.3	79.7	46	626	17.1	4.2
Barry	39	D	D	D	61	7 537	1 096.2	154.3	66	667	17.9	4.6
Barton	19	122	6.4	2.8	19	2 080	269.6	52.0	25	324	7.2	2.0
Bates	16	56	2.4	0.8	NA	NA	NA	NA	23	282	7.1	1.8
Benton	16	49	2.0	0.6	NA	NA	NA	NA	43	427	9.6	2.5
Bollinger	10	16	0.7	0.2	NA	NA	NA	NA	10	61	1.5	0.3
Boone	272	1 588	112.4	39.1	87	5 703	1 595.0	165.3	312	5 983	180.1	48.4
Buchanan	133	779	64.4	21.7	96	7 365	2 293.8	235.1	196	3 208	96.2	26.7
Butler	44	245	14.8	5.5	53	3 010	494.5	66.7	76	1 210	36.4	9.3
Caldwell	6	13	0.4	0.1	NA	NA	NA	NA	9	58	1.0	0.4
Callaway	22	85	5.5	1.9	37	1 896	320.6	59.6	48	739	22.6	5.9
Camden	73	275	19.9	6.4	53	1 269	132.0	32.6	200	2 412	103.9	31.4
Cape Girardeau	119	731	48.4	16.3	93	5 912	1 569.7	163.3	137	3 017	89.4	24.9
Carroll	11	21	1.0	0.2	NA	NA	NA	NA	13	D	D	D
Carter	5	D	D	D	NA	NA	NA	NA	18	63	2.0	0.5
Cass	80	209	16.5	5.3	71	1 057	116.6	24.6	104	1 647	50.4	12.8
Cedar	12	40	2.5	0.4	15	505	76.5	9.9	33	291	6.4	1.7
Chariton	11	18	1.0	0.2	NA	NA	NA	NA	11	39	1.1	0.2
Christian	44	156	8.1	2.9	101	D	D	D	62	841	20.3	5.9
Clark	5	D	D	D	NA	NA	NA	NA	4	31	0.8	0.3
Clay	337	3 362	401.0	154.3	214	14 743	9 891.7	569.6	320	12 228	527.2	145.2
Clinton	17	48	2.2	0.7	NA	NA	NA	NA	22	D	D	D
Cole	173	910	75.1	29.8	53	D	D	D	134	2 751	84.5	24.6
Cooper	17	64	3.6	1.0	16	865	138.6	19.2	32	391	10.2	2.8
Crawford	23	63	3.8	0.9	52	1 639	142.9	33.8	47	447	11.6	3.1
Dade	6	17	0.6	0.2	NA	NA	NA	NA	11	D	D	D
Dallas	11	25	1.1	0.3	11	530	40.2	8.7	27	298	6.7	1.9
Daviess	7	13	0.8	0.2	NA	NA	NA	NA	10	79	2.2	0.5
De Kalb	11	28	0.9	0.3	NA	NA	NA	NA	27	415	10.3	2.9
Dent	18	51	2.0	0.7	27	951	84.3	17.3	22	300	8.3	2.2
Douglas	8	10	0.7	0.2	NA	NA	NA	NA	8	148	3.6	1.0
Dunklin	39	113	6.9	1.5	26	1 281	259.7	28.5	51	563	14.6	3.7
Franklin	125	578	39.4	15.8	210	10 641	1 836.3	284.4	160	2 514	70.9	20.2
Gasconade	26	67	5.2	1.0	38	1 643	161.8	41.9	36	357	7.4	2.0
Gentry	6	15	0.8	0.3	NA	NA	NA	NA	12	62	1.3	0.3
Greene	574	4 028	363.7	121.3	371	19 475	3 788.6	513.1	595	11 812	350.3	100.0
Grundy	10	40	2.1	0.4	11	798	242.4	20.7	17	238	5.0	1.5
Harrison	8	25	0.8	0.2	NA	NA	NA	NA	17	320	8.8	2.2
Henry	28	85	4.9	1.2	32	1 780	390.1	33.0	53	568	16.2	4.1
Hickory	6	16	0.6	0.2	NA	NA	NA	NA	20	121	3.5	0.8
Holt	3	8	0.2	0.1	NA	NA	NA	NA	12	99	2.7	0.7
Howard	8	19	1.2	0.4	NA	NA	NA	NA	12	152	2.9	0.8
Howell	41	160	9.2	4.1	70	3 690	485.6	72.5	76	1 093	29.3	8.0
Iron	8	17	0.6	0.2	NA	NA	NA	NA	18	151	3.8	1.0
Jackson	1 728	19 506	2 015.2	843.0	907	38 785	8 984.7	1 301.5	1 393	28 200	1 005.3	292.5

1. Firms subject to federal tax.

Table B. States and Counties — Health Care and Social Assistance, Other Services, and Federal Funds

STATE County	Health care and social assistance,[1] 1997				Other services,[1] 1997				Federal funds and grants, 2002–2003 Expenditures (mil dol)	Direct payments for individuals[2]		
	Number of establishments	Number of employees	Receipts (mil dol)	Annual payroll (mil dol)	Number of establishments	Number of employees	Receipts (mil dol)	Annual payroll (mil dol)	Total	Social Security and government retirement	Medicare	Food stamps and Supplemental Security Income
	159	160	161	162	163	164	165	166	167	168	169	170
MISSISSIPPI—Cont'd												
Sunflower	35	457	25.5	9.4	41	172	10.4	3.0	201.9	45.9	34.7	14.4
Tallahatchie	8	122	7.2	2.5	13	34	1.5	0.3	127.2	24.8	17.9	8.4
Tate	27	335	18.8	6.6	31	111	7.4	1.8	134.9	51.2	21.3	5.3
Tippah	20	253	9.6	4.7	12	34	1.8	0.5	128.8	52.7	28.2	7.0
Tishomingo	19	303	14.4	5.1	23	64	4.5	1.1	163.6	60.0	25.8	4.0
Tunica	7	166	5.9	2.9	12	34	1.3	0.4	68.3	15.0	9.0	2.8
Union	35	280	17.6	6.5	25	94	6.1	1.4	122.3	55.5	23.8	4.7
Walthall	18	230	11.3	4.8	11	41	2.3	0.5	83.3	28.6	17.7	5.3
Warren	66	1 867	143.5	54.9	69	278	15.5	4.5	415.9	120.0	61.8	15.6
Washington	125	1 267	84.3	32.9	111	508	27.8	7.9	424.2	118.4	64.0	44.2
Wayne	27	268	14.6	5.6	18	57	3.3	0.8	113.9	37.8	16.4	8.2
Webster	12	176	7.9	3.2	8	19	1.8	0.3	64.3	26.2	12.5	3.8
Wilkinson	13	200	9.1	4.3	10	43	5.6	0.6	60.4	19.1	11.1	5.8
Winston	21	205	9.2	4.6	20	67	3.5	0.8	109.7	45.2	20.0	5.4
Yalobusha	14	62	4.2	1.1	5	17	1.1	0.2	119.9	40.4	21.2	5.3
Yazoo	24	326	17.6	6.8	35	106	6.7	1.6	206.7	52.8	33.8	14.6
MISSOURI	10 213	131 485	7 885.4	3 596.7	9 427	52 060	3 203.3	963.1	43 873.7	12 964.1	5 852.7	1 112.1
Adair	77	2 068	114.5	51.6	45	211	9.9	2.5	124.2	42.0	27.0	4.1
Andrew	14	131	5.1	2.5	18	69	4.4	1.2	79.4	41.5	11.9	1.4
Atchison	10	412	17.1	7.5	17	25	2.3	0.3	52.4	17.6	8.4	0.9
Audrain	60	452	26.1	11.8	49	241	15.7	4.2	143.9	61.8	36.2	3.7
Barry	36	277	9.9	4.2	46	139	8.8	2.1	181.6	94.1	35.7	5.9
Barton	17	199	7.5	2.9	24	90	4.6	1.0	63.5	27.5	13.9	2.2
Bates	23	272	12.1	4.4	33	62	4.1	0.8	94.8	42.5	20.5	2.8
Benton	16	190	7.6	3.1	28	45	3.5	0.7	125.6	70.2	25.9	3.5
Bollinger	6	79	2.4	1.0	14	59	3.5	0.8	70.0	27.0	11.0	3.4
Boone	328	4 024	321.4	129.7	230	1 269	67.1	20.6	707.2	231.0	95.7	20.9
Buchanan	174	2 235	138.5	62.8	161	786	46.6	13.2	495.9	206.4	103.1	21.5
Butler	92	2 502	160.4	53.5	64	243	13.6	4.1	334.7	115.2	50.3	16.4
Caldwell	4	D	D	D	11	18	1.4	0.2	56.3	23.4	10.8	1.4
Callaway	34	395	14.9	5.9	46	267	13.6	4.1	177.5	78.5	35.8	5.1
Camden	61	569	32.8	13.3	82	293	14.3	4.0	183.3	106.9	40.3	4.5
Cape Girardeau	201	2 170	162.1	73.5	129	584	36.4	10.6	366.8	146.7	51.8	12.0
Carroll	16	136	6.4	2.3	16	45	2.8	1.0	87.1	27.0	14.7	2.0
Carter	8	98	2.9	1.4	3	15	2.1	0.3	66.4	18.9	7.1	2.8
Cass	83	713	31.4	14.9	115	487	27.9	8.2	383.6	191.6	57.3	6.1
Cedar	14	211	8.0	3.6	13	28	1.6	0.3	88.0	44.0	18.8	3.0
Chariton	8	151	4.3	1.9	14	31	1.6	0.4	57.2	21.9	12.3	1.2
Christian	49	672	22.6	8.7	67	256	18.2	3.9	196.5	117.8	30.3	5.4
Clark	5	33	2.0	0.6	10	19	1.5	0.2	40.4	16.3	8.3	1.1
Clay	382	4 689	308.2	148.7	317	1 839	115.9	35.2	575.4	261.7	150.4	10.2
Clinton	24	177	7.8	3.2	33	101	5.1	1.2	99.2	47.4	19.6	2.2
Cole	160	1 936	127.1	70.5	115	609	30.8	9.4	1 497.7	306.4	64.1	9.8
Cooper	22	199	7.9	3.2	34	151	8.3	2.5	88.1	38.1	18.2	1.7
Crawford	26	412	10.8	4.5	27	71	7.5	1.1	107.7	55.6	22.5	5.0
Dade	4	12	0.7	0.1	10	28	2.1	0.4	50.4	23.8	9.8	1.6
Dallas	18	176	4.7	1.9	17	38	2.7	0.5	81.7	37.0	14.8	3.5
Daviess	8	51	1.6	0.5	10	30	0.8	0.1	50.4	19.9	9.0	1.2
De Kalb	13	214	7.6	2.9	9	30	2.3	0.6	41.1	18.8	7.5	1.0
Dent	21	213	7.9	3.3	20	61	3.3	0.7	112.3	41.6	19.3	3.9
Douglas	11	150	6.2	2.3	10	33	1.6	0.5	74.4	29.4	12.2	3.2
Dunklin	57	1 841	75.0	29.9	45	129	8.6	1.8	280.3	81.0	46.0	19.3
Franklin	159	1 507	74.1	30.9	140	561	34.3	11.0	407.4	212.0	80.1	12.1
Gasconade	23	309	9.9	4.5	19	66	4.6	1.2	77.4	42.6	18.9	1.7
Gentry	22	216	7.1	3.2	9	32	1.8	0.4	58.2	20.8	12.8	0.8
Greene	457	7 245	532.1	253.3	514	3 519	184.4	56.9	1 246.5	552.0	203.7	44.6
Grundy	17	159	4.9	2.0	23	94	4.1	1.0	76.6	29.0	14.6	2.1
Harrison	16	133	5.0	1.9	24	63	4.3	0.8	71.0	25.2	14.6	1.7
Henry	35	581	30.9	14.1	37	156	7.7	2.0	140.2	69.3	31.4	5.2
Hickory	5	D	D	D	9	17	1.2	0.2	62.4	33.9	14.4	2.2
Holt	5	114	4.2	1.7	11	17	1.3	0.2	44.0	15.9	8.4	0.7
Howard	16	298	8.4	3.7	10	24	1.4	0.2	62.7	22.6	14.2	1.9
Howell	63	631	29.1	10.9	61	218	16.0	3.3	265.6	102.2	39.4	10.8
Iron	19	151	5.3	1.7	15	57	2.9	0.9	72.5	30.1	14.6	3.4
Jackson	1 334	18 242	1 254.8	614.8	1 265	8 921	539.1	170.9	5 697.4	1 652.6	775.5	105.2

1. Firms subject to federal tax. 2. State totals may include programs not allocated by county.

Table B. States and Counties — Federal Funds and Local Government Finances

	Federal funds and grants, 2002–2003 (cont'd) — Expenditures (mil dol) (cont'd)							Local government finances, 2002 — General revenue				
	Salaries and wages	Procurement contract awards		Grants[1]				Total (mil dol)	Intergovern- mental (mil dol)	Taxes Total (mil dol)	Taxes Per capita[2] (dollars) Total	Taxes Per capita[2] (dollars) Property
STATE County		Defense	Other	Medicaid and other health- related	Nutrition and family welfare	Education	Other					
	171	172	173	174	175	176	177	178	179	180	181	182
MISSISSIPPI—Cont'd												
Sunflower	4.0	0.3	1.1	48.4	9.8	4.8	9.5	88.3	44.9	16.4	485	453
Tallahatchie	3.1	8.2	0.5	33.5	3.6	1.5	8.5	35.2	21.3	6.6	461	433
Tate	4.4	2.3	0.8	24.1	2.8	1.2	8.1	82.1	43.1	17.7	686	655
Tippah	3.5	0.9	0.8	28.0	1.7	1.0	3.2	46.9	22.9	8.7	414	358
Tishomingo	3.8	43.2	0.8	20.7	1.4	0.6	1.2	27.4	15.7	7.3	382	345
Tunica	1.1	0.0	0.2	17.8	2.6	1.4	6.6	71.7	51.2	9.6	1 006	922
Union	3.6	0.0	0.9	21.1	1.6	0.9	8.5	43.0	24.3	12.0	460	435
Walthall	1.7	0.0	0.3	23.7	2.5	1.1	0.3	30.9	15.2	5.6	369	338
Warren	89.5	52.2	16.9	39.6	5.7	2.5	6.7	116.9	57.9	38.7	782	741
Washington	27.1	3.1	5.2	89.1	20.5	11.2	19.7	230.0	85.2	44.2	721	649
Wayne	2.2	0.0	0.7	23.0	3.1	1.1	20.1	58.3	23.9	8.8	413	378
Webster	2.2	0.0	0.4	13.5	1.2	0.5	1.6	17.1	10.4	4.6	446	416
Wilkinson	0.6	0.0	0.1	19.0	1.9	0.8	0.7	19.0	11.4	4.1	400	379
Winston	2.9	0.0	0.6	27.3	2.8	1.3	2.7	34.2	19.1	7.7	383	338
Yalobusha	4.4	22.1	1.1	19.9	1.4	0.9	0.8	33.0	15.0	5.7	429	399
Yazoo	20.7	5.1	2.1	45.3	7.5	2.2	6.9	48.7	27.1	14.8	525	498
MISSOURI	3 831.6	6 243.8	1 747.9	4 617.2	1 033.0	684.0	2 320.9	X	X	X	X	X
Adair	4.5	2.5	1.0	27.7	3.8	2.2	3.0	57.9	23.2	23.8	953	624
Andrew	4.6	0.0	0.6	6.3	1.1	0.5	6.4	25.6	14.3	7.3	434	371
Atchison	2.0	0.0	0.4	3.9	0.6	0.4	1.2	18.5	8.0	7.6	1 205	842
Audrain	4.5	0.1	1.0	14.4	2.3	1.6	7.9	49.3	19.5	19.3	752	460
Barry	7.6	0.3	1.4	27.1	2.9	2.5	1.9	78.6	33.3	26.8	776	498
Barton	2.7	0.0	0.6	6.8	0.9	1.5	1.6	31.1	9.7	8.5	660	467
Bates	3.5	0.0	0.8	13.2	1.7	1.0	3.0	32.8	13.2	11.2	661	433
Benton	4.7	0.9	0.8	11.5	1.5	1.0	4.2	28.1	12.2	9.4	536	365
Bollinger	2.0	0.0	0.5	21.0	1.2	0.8	0.8	17.0	9.9	5.3	437	335
Boone	111.4	11.7	15.0	90.2	11.2	19.4	75.4	345.4	114.1	144.7	1 037	620
Buchanan	30.3	1.9	11.3	70.2	11.6	5.7	23.6	201.9	76.0	86.8	1 017	553
Butler	25.9	0.0	8.3	80.8	6.4	4.6	9.8	80.0	38.8	27.7	681	361
Caldwell	2.3	0.0	0.6	4.9	0.7	0.6	6.5	31.4	17.1	8.6	949	774
Callaway	27.5	0.5	3.6	20.4	2.3	1.6	-4.0	65.8	27.3	26.2	621	479
Camden	4.5	0.0	1.3	14.7	1.8	1.9	6.5	77.3	22.5	38.5	1 018	607
Cape Girardeau	27.0	2.3	50.0	41.2	4.2	5.5	14.5	169.7	57.9	88.8	1 277	812
Carroll	3.5	0.0	0.7	8.2	1.2	0.9	19.9	20.7	11.0	7.5	728	568
Carter	3.7	0.0	3.4	9.5	1.4	0.6	18.6	11.0	7.8	2.5	421	345
Cass	54.7	9.3	2.8	14.4	3.4	3.6	32.3	223.3	81.1	83.3	954	722
Cedar	2.6	0.6	0.7	15.0	1.1	0.6	0.7	30.1	12.0	8.0	579	485
Chariton	2.8	0.0	0.8	9.3	0.7	0.6	0.6	15.3	7.1	5.5	667	558
Christian	7.3	0.1	1.7	17.5	2.2	3.1	8.6	95.6	46.2	37.2	630	427
Clark	2.1	0.1	0.5	3.8	0.8	0.6	1.4	17.8	7.0	4.7	637	495
Clay	52.9	0.6	23.6	32.8	5.4	7.1	26.2	695.1	130.8	223.3	1 167	798
Clinton	3.9	0.0	1.1	10.9	1.1	1.0	7.2	37.6	17.8	14.1	718	512
Cole	19.0	3.1	4.3	140.6	230.0	208.1	497.7	128.0	40.7	65.5	911	562
Cooper	3.2	0.1	1.1	13.9	1.3	1.0	4.6	43.0	15.1	11.8	695	445
Crawford	2.4	0.0	0.6	16.7	2.1	1.5	0.9	28.9	16.1	9.7	417	318
Dade	2.0	0.1	0.5	8.5	0.8	1.4	0.6	17.9	7.1	3.7	470	417
Dallas	2.1	0.3	0.5	18.6	1.2	0.8	1.7	21.2	15.2	5.2	328	216
Daviess	2.6	2.1	0.6	5.5	0.9	0.8	0.8	17.0	9.7	5.4	671	572
De Kalb	1.7	0.0	0.4	2.5	0.6	0.8	1.6	13.3	7.6	4.2	360	298
Dent	3.8	16.3	0.5	24.4	2.0	1.2	-1.1	44.9	12.3	11.2	751	607
Douglas	2.7	0.0	0.6	21.0	1.5	1.2	1.1	17.2	10.3	4.1	311	247
Dunklin	5.7	1.9	1.5	95.1	8.3	3.4	2.8	60.9	34.1	19.1	582	407
Franklin	18.4	1.1	3.4	34.3	5.3	5.7	29.6	177.5	67.9	82.4	859	592
Gasconade	2.4	0.1	0.6	8.8	0.8	0.8	0.0	37.0	13.1	13.3	863	637
Gentry	3.1	0.2	0.6	7.6	0.9	0.6	3.1	15.7	8.8	5.0	760	611
Greene	146.3	1.6	37.0	129.8	27.7	14.1	52.4	535.2	167.7	242.7	997	505
Grundy	3.2	0.0	0.6	9.7	2.6	1.2	5.8	31.1	15.9	6.9	676	473
Harrison	3.6	0.0	1.8	8.2	0.9	1.0	5.0	24.4	8.2	6.0	687	536
Henry	5.5	0.3	1.3	17.5	1.7	1.4	3.2	84.1	20.7	20.3	910	484
Hickory	2.1	0.3	0.4	6.8	1.0	0.4	0.2	15.4	9.4	4.8	536	430
Holt	2.3	0.0	1.4	4.6	0.5	0.3	4.2	13.5	6.1	5.6	1 086	797
Howard	2.2	0.9	1.0	12.8	0.8	0.9	0.9	16.5	9.2	5.2	519	409
Howell	9.8	20.0	1.4	45.5	8.3	2.6	20.6	68.9	37.4	21.8	585	379
Iron	1.6	0.0	0.8	18.6	1.7	1.3	0.1	21.7	11.5	8.2	789	659
Jackson	948.1	417.5	790.9	462.6	90.2	57.2	336.2	2 453.9	787.4	1 166.6	1 766	849

1. State totals may include programs not allocated by county.   2. Based on the resident population estimated as of July 1 of the year shown.

STATE County	Total (mil dol) 183	Per capita¹ (dollars) 184	Education 185	Health and hospitals 186	Police protection 187	Public welfare 188	Highways 189	Total (mil dol) 190	Per capita¹ (dollars) 191	Federal civilian 192	Federal military 193	State and local 194	Democratic 195	Republican 196	All other 197
MISSISSIPPI—Cont'd															
Sunflower	87.4	2 579	61.3	13.2	4.3	0.3	5.6	30.7	907	63	177	4 028	62.7	36.1	1.2
Tallahatchie	34.7	2 408	54.6	11.5	5.4	0.3	5.4	7.2	498	50	75	924	54.8	44.2	1.0
Tate	75.1	2 917	77.3	0.1	3.4	0.0	4.0	43.2	1 679	87	135	1 584	38.9	60.6	0.5
Tippah	51.4	2 444	41.2	18.3	8.9	0.2	7.3	3.5	166	62	110	1 051	32.7	66.4	0.9
Tishomingo	26.3	1 381	54.4	0.6	6.1	0.2	10.3	5.0	263	69	100	744	34.0	64.8	1.2
Tunica	74.1	7 743	37.8	0.2	5.0	0.5	11.6	32.3	3 373	21	50	789	68.7	30.0	1.3
Union	49.4	1 891	68.0	0.3	4.2	0.3	7.7	37.0	1 419	61	136	1 087	26.6	72.8	0.7
Walthall	30.2	1 992	51.4	25.2	4.8	0.0	6.8	3.1	207	26	79	773	39.5	60.0	0.6
Warren	113.2	2 289	46.4	1.6	9.6	0.3	8.1	80.8	1 634	2 123	288	2 560	41.0	58.5	0.5
Washington	220.6	3 598	33.5	31.8	6.0	0.2	5.2	95.7	1 561	556	341	4 148	59.1	39.3	1.6
Wayne	55.8	2 630	38.6	32.2	4.6	0.2	8.4	18.7	879	39	111	1 152	37.0	62.5	0.5
Webster	16.8	1 631	59.6	0.6	6.3	0.0	11.6	10.9	1 060	42	54	438	26.3	73.3	0.3
Wilkinson	17.0	1 658	57.4	0.6	6.1	0.3	13.6	5.3	520	10	53	568	63.7	35.6	0.7
Winston	31.8	1 589	57.1	0.2	5.6	0.1	9.5	17.5	873	47	105	810	42.2	57.3	0.5
Yalobusha	31.1	2 334	41.0	29.8	4.8	0.6	7.5	18.6	1 397	98	70	708	44.5	54.9	0.6
Yazoo	54.6	1 935	60.7	0.6	6.5	0.1	9.4	38.9	1 379	351	147	1 462	45.6	51.6	2.7
MISSOURI	X	X	X	X	X	X	X	X	X	57 805	33 598	375 999	46.1	53.4	0.6
Adair	53.8	2 158	62.7	2.0	6.2	0.0	4.8	20.3	814	88	77	2 751	43.3	55.8	0.9
Andrew	23.2	1 387	79.5	3.5	6.6	0.1	2.9	3.3	196	49	50	689	37.2	62.2	0.7
Atchison	19.5	3 079	46.3	4.5	5.6	0.0	21.0	1.5	235	41	19	403	31.9	67.7	0.4
Audrain	51.3	2 003	53.6	1.0	4.4	6.4	11.3	24.7	964	87	76	2 686	40.4	58.9	0.6
Barry	82.3	2 384	51.3	13.6	2.7	0.7	11.8	20.5	593	150	103	1 759	30.3	68.9	0.8
Barton	33.0	2 565	42.0	31.9	4.3	0.0	6.3	12.4	963	44	38	909	23.0	76.4	0.6
Bates	34.7	2 043	62.6	0.0	5.8	5.3	11.0	31.9	1 877	70	50	1 123	40.1	59.2	0.7
Benton	28.1	1 599	57.8	2.5	4.7	11.9	6.9	9.0	512	111	52	808	37.6	61.9	0.5
Bollinger	17.2	1 401	78.0	1.2	3.5	0.1	6.0	0.4	34	35	36	472	29.8	69.6	0.7
Boone	351.5	2 520	50.8	2.7	4.8	1.3	7.1	344.3	2 468	1 908	455	28 356	49.7	49.7	0.6
Buchanan	219.4	2 572	54.1	1.4	3.9	0.2	7.4	261.9	3 070	517	261	6 461	46.9	52.2	0.9
Butler	79.8	1 957	68.7	0.0	3.5	0.0	4.2	22.8	560	530	122	2 828	28.4	71.2	0.5
Caldwell	28.9	3 181	49.4	0.8	0.9	6.1	3.7	6.9	757	44	27	596	38.5	60.8	0.7
Callaway	67.6	1 601	55.4	2.8	5.4	0.1	8.6	52.0	1 232	199	144	4 194	36.9	62.5	0.6
Camden	79.2	2 092	48.6	2.2	4.7	9.8	10.1	79.5	2 100	60	113	1 758	32.3	67.2	0.5
Cape Girardeau	188.8	2 717	68.9	0.6	4.4	0.0	5.7	113.4	1 632	411	219	5 537	30.6	68.9	0.5
Carroll	22.3	2 168	60.7	3.5	1.5	0.1	12.2	6.0	582	56	31	607	33.1	66.5	0.4
Carter	11.2	1 908	85.9	1.2	1.2	0.0	3.0	3.6	615	83	17	386	34.7	64.7	0.6
Cass	219.1	2 510	58.6	10.5	4.7	0.0	5.8	242.0	2 772	247	716	3 804	37.8	61.7	0.6
Cedar	27.6	1 996	61.2	16.8	1.9	0.0	6.8	4.9	351	62	41	749	30.8	68.4	0.8
Chariton	17.3	2 109	67.4	2.7	2.8	0.1	10.4	3.1	381	58	24	467	43.7	55.9	0.5
Christian	101.9	1 723	64.5	0.5	2.7	0.0	6.3	82.1	1 389	120	176	1 993	28.9	70.6	0.4
Clark	17.9	2 402	52.1	2.1	2.1	21.0	12.2	6.6	888	42	22	571	48.1	50.9	1.1
Clay	794.6	4 152	33.6	41.8	2.2	0.5	2.9	391.8	2 047	309	1 004	11 877	46.3	53.1	0.5
Clinton	35.5	1 806	69.1	1.6	5.6	0.0	7.3	27.6	1 405	68	58	1 060	43.8	55.5	0.7
Cole	133.3	1 854	52.4	1.1	5.6	0.0	7.1	101.0	1 405	539	214	20 913	32.0	67.5	0.5
Cooper	46.8	2 754	43.8	18.1	3.1	4.0	7.0	24.6	1 449	55	51	1 278	32.0	67.4	0.5
Crawford	29.1	1 255	73.5	6.2	3.8	0.0	2.9	9.7	419	41	69	893	38.7	60.6	0.7
Dade	20.5	2 599	51.5	0.2	0.8	31.9	8.9	3.5	445	41	23	612	27.0	72.5	0.5
Dallas	17.9	1 129	74.4	0.0	3.1	0.0	10.8	3.6	225	42	47	677	33.2	66.0	0.8
Daviess	16.8	2 098	65.5	4.3	2.4	0.0	10.6	5.2	644	66	24	445	37.0	62.0	1.1
De Kalb	13.2	1 144	77.0	2.9	2.4	0.0	5.6	1.8	158	35	34	1 317	36.5	62.8	0.7
Dent	45.3	3 038	34.8	39.2	2.0	0.0	2.2	5.6	374	87	44	881	29.6	69.3	1.1
Douglas	14.5	1 089	81.5	0.5	2.1	0.0	6.9	1.6	123	62	40	467	27.6	71.2	1.2
Dunklin	61.6	1 877	67.4	4.5	3.6	0.0	8.0	24.0	733	107	98	1 650	42.0	57.6	0.3
Franklin	181.5	1 893	62.3	1.9	5.7	0.8	9.7	133.0	1 387	240	286	4 044	41.0	58.3	0.7
Gasconade	37.6	2 435	53.4	20.7	4.6	1.3	7.6	19.7	1 274	49	46	960	32.8	66.3	0.9
Gentry	15.6	2 356	66.8	4.3	2.2	0.0	10.3	4.5	675	44	20	445	36.3	63.0	0.7
Greene	620.2	2 549	44.9	0.9	6.3	1.2	4.9	597.1	2 454	2 164	762	15 664	37.3	62.2	0.6
Grundy	31.3	3 066	64.3	2.2	2.9	11.8	5.4	29.1	2 851	52	30	963	32.5	66.1	1.4
Harrison	25.5	2 901	49.8	30.8	0.6	0.0	8.3	5.0	572	57	26	688	31.6	67.4	0.9
Henry	83.8	3 768	30.1	40.6	4.1	0.0	6.0	30.0	1 347	92	66	1 525	41.0	58.5	0.5
Hickory	15.1	1 691	82.2	0.0	2.7	0.0	4.4	7.5	847	48	26	312	42.0	57.4	0.6
Holt	13.8	2 678	45.0	0.6	1.7	0.0	15.6	2.4	475	48	15	331	30.2	69.3	0.5
Howard	19.9	1 988	67.9	0.2	2.7	0.0	9.1	7.2	719	48	30	485	40.1	59.3	0.6
Howell	66.1	1 773	76.5	0.7	4.8	0.0	2.9	25.7	689	111	111	2 447	31.3	67.8	0.9
Iron	21.2	2 040	74.5	0.0	4.5	0.0	9.5	3.3	322	25	31	580	46.2	53.0	0.8
Jackson	2 422.5	3 666	46.3	2.2	7.1	0.5	5.4	2 077.9	3 145	16 229	2 179	46 746	57.9	41.5	0.6

1. Based on the resident population estimated as of July 1 of the year shown.

Table B. States and Counties — **Land Area and Population**

STATE/ County code	CBSA code[1]	County Type[2]	STATE County	Land area,[3] (sq km) 2000	Population and population characteristics, 2003			Race alone or in combination, not Hispanic or Latino (percent)					Age (percent)					
					Total persons	Rank	Per square kilometer	White	Black	Am. Indian, Alaska Native	Asian and Pacific Islander	Percent Hispanic or Latino[4]	Under 5 years	5 to 17 years	18 to 24 years	25 to 34 years	35 to 44 years	45 to 54 years
					1	2	3	4	5	6	7	8	9	10	11	12	13	14	15
			MISSOURI—Cont'd															
29 097	27900	3	Jasper	1 657	108 112	510	65.2	92.1	2.1	2.5	1.0	4.2	7.6	18.1	10.8	13.5	13.9	13.0
29 099	41180	1	Jefferson	1 701	206 786	283	121.6	97.4	0.9	0.7	0.8	1.1	6.6	19.7	10.0	12.9	17.1	14.3
29 101	47660	4	Johnson	2 151	50 262	931	23.4	90.8	4.9	1.3	2.4	2.4	6.9	17.2	18.3	13.9	14.1	10.9
29 103	...	9	Knox	1 310	4 311	2 885	3.3	99.3	0.4	0.3	0.1	0.6	6.9	17.6	8.1	8.5	14.2	13.4
29 105	30060	6	Laclede	1 984	33 326	1 320	16.8	97.6	0.7	1.0	0.6	1.3	6.6	18.6	9.7	11.8	14.8	13.2
29 107	28140	1	Lafayette	1 630	32 951	1 336	20.2	96.1	2.6	0.7	0.4	1.2	6.0	18.8	9.3	11.2	15.3	13.8
29 109	...	6	Lawrence	1 588	36 426	1 228	22.9	94.8	0.4	1.6	0.3	3.9	6.6	19.5	9.3	11.9	14.1	13.0
29 111	39500	9	Lewis	1 308	10 226	2 425	7.8	95.9	3.3	0.2	0.5	0.8	5.7	18.1	13.3	10.7	13.5	12.6
29 113	41180	1	Lincoln	1 633	44 207	1 039	27.1	96.4	2.1	1.0	0.4	1.2	6.6	21.2	10.6	12.2	15.9	12.6
29 115	...	7	Linn	1 607	13 460	2 201	8.4	97.8	1.0	0.5	0.2	0.9	6.3	18.0	9.1	10.1	13.4	13.2
29 117	...	6	Livingston	1 384	14 387	2 137	10.4	96.1	2.6	0.5	0.4	0.8	5.9	16.9	9.1	11.1	13.8	14.0
29 119	22220	2	McDonald	1 397	21 973	1 705	15.7	86.5	0.2	5.0	0.6	10.1	7.8	20.6	9.5	12.5	14.8	12.8
29 121	...	7	Macon	2 082	15 577	2 059	7.5	96.2	2.7	0.7	0.2	0.9	6.0	17.3	9.1	10.3	13.3	13.7
29 123	...	7	Madison	1 287	11 804	2 304	9.2	98.7	0.2	0.6	0.3	0.7	5.8	17.3	9.5	11.1	14.8	13.1
29 125	...	8	Maries	1 367	8 841	2 537	6.5	97.9	0.5	1.0	0.1	1.2	6.3	18.7	8.7	10.5	13.4	13.4
29 127	25300	5	Marion	1 135	28 289	1 447	24.9	93.5	5.7	0.7	0.5	0.8	7.1	18.3	10.4	11.3	13.8	13.8
29 129	...	9	Mercer	1 176	3 596	2 938	3.1	98.7	0.2	0.8	0.0	0.4	5.5	15.9	8.6	9.1	14.5	14.5
29 131	...	6	Miller	1 534	24 255	1 611	15.8	98.0	0.4	1.1	0.2	1.1	6.6	18.3	9.9	11.9	14.7	13.5
29 133	...	7	Mississippi	1 070	14 386	2 138	13.4	76.3	21.6	0.5	0.8	1.4	7.1	16.7	9.9	12.0	14.3	13.1
29 135	27620	3	Moniteau	1 079	14 965	2 103	13.9	94.3	3.6	1.1	0.4	2.4	6.2	18.3	9.6	14.1	16.5	13.1
29 137	...	9	Monroe	1 673	9 396	2 497	5.6	94.6	4.3	0.6	0.3	0.7	6.6	18.3	9.1	10.0	14.0	13.4
29 139	...	8	Montgomery	1 392	12 068	2 289	8.7	96.3	2.5	0.8	0.7	0.9	6.3	18.2	9.0	10.3	14.2	14.2
29 141	...	8	Morgan	1 547	20 000	1 805	12.9	97.8	0.6	1.3	0.2	0.9	5.6	17.3	8.1	9.6	12.8	13.0
29 143	27900	7	New Madrid	1 756	19 187	1 853	10.9	83.4	15.6	0.4	0.3	0.9	6.7	18.6	10.1	11.3	14.2	13.7
29 145	27900	3	Newton	1 622	54 033	890	33.3	92.8	0.9	3.5	1.1	2.6	6.7	18.6	10.1	11.3	14.2	13.7
29 147	32340	6	Nodaway	2 270	21 743	1 717	9.6	96.5	1.4	0.5	1.2	0.7	4.7	13.0	23.4	11.2	12.2	11.3
29 149	...	9	Oregon	2 050	10 301	2 417	5.0	95.8	0.1	4.9	0.1	1.1	5.5	17.4	8.6	10.0	13.4	13.8
29 151	27620	3	Osage	1 570	13 134	2 228	8.4	99.1	0.1	0.7	0.1	0.6	6.2	18.6	11.0	12.0	15.0	12.9
29 153	...	9	Ozark	1 922	9 498	2 486	4.9	98.2	0.2	1.4	0.1	1.0	5.5	15.4	8.4	8.9	13.0	14.4
29 155	...	7	Pemiscot	1 277	19 729	1 820	15.4	71.8	26.3	0.4	0.3	1.7	8.2	21.5	9.5	11.5	12.9	12.8
29 157	...	7	Perry	1 229	18 225	1 896	14.8	98.2	0.3	0.5	0.8	0.6	6.6	18.4	9.3	12.2	15.0	13.9
29 159	42740	4	Pettis	1 774	39 344	1 144	22.2	91.1	3.5	0.8	0.9	4.9	7.0	18.8	9.9	12.0	15.0	13.0
29 161	40620	5	Phelps	1 743	41 668	1 092	23.9	94.1	1.9	1.3	2.8	1.2	6.0	16.9	14.0	12.6	13.6	12.5
29 163	...	6	Pike	1 743	18 519	1 881	10.6	88.3	9.5	0.4	0.2	2.1	5.4	16.8	10.6	13.1	15.5	13.3
29 165	28140	1	Platte	1 089	79 390	656	72.9	90.1	4.4	1.0	2.6	3.2	6.5	18.2	8.9	14.0	16.8	15.5
29 167	44180	2	Polk	1 650	28 081	1 460	17.0	97.1	0.6	1.3	0.5	1.5	6.2	18.1	13.2	11.8	13.2	11.6
29 169	22780	5	Pulaski	1 417	45 254	1 015	31.9	77.4	13.1	2.0	4.5	6.0	7.1	19.0	20.3	14.9	14.5	9.9
29 171	...	9	Putnam	1 341	5 148	2 833	3.8	99.1	0.0	0.2	0.2	0.6	6.0	17.1	7.6	10.1	13.3	13.3
29 173	25300	9	Ralls	1 220	9 653	2 474	7.9	98.2	1.0	0.5	0.1	0.5	4.6	18.1	9.1	10.3	15.3	16.2
29 175	33620	6	Randolph	1 475	25 045	1 571	20.1	90.9	7.1	1.1	0.6	1.3	6.6	17.1	10.2	13.1	15.1	13.8
29 177	28140	1	Ray	1 475	23 926	1 616	16.2	96.9	1.6	1.0	0.4	1.1	6.0	19.9	9.6	11.0	15.7	14.2
29 179	...	9	Reynolds	2 101	6 581	2 726	3.1	97.1	0.6	2.9	0.3	0.9	5.6	16.9	8.3	10.5	13.6	14.2
29 181	...	9	Ripley	1 630	13 781	2 183	8.5	97.6	0.1	2.0	0.3	1.0	6.4	17.8	9.5	10.5	13.7	12.9
29 183	41180	1	St. Charles	1 451	311 531	191	214.7	93.8	3.6	0.6	1.6	1.6	6.9	20.3	9.9	13.0	17.1	13.7
29 185	...	8	St. Clair	1 753	9 679	2 472	5.5	97.7	0.5	1.6	0.2	1.0	5.1	16.7	7.6	9.0	13.1	13.3
29 186	...	6	Ste. Genevieve	1 301	18 094	1 910	13.9	98.0	0.8	0.6	0.2	0.7	5.4	19.0	9.8	10.5	16.1	14.5
29 187	22100	4	St. Francois	1 164	57 929	846	49.8	96.1	2.4	0.8	0.6	0.8	6.0	16.9	10.5	13.0	15.0	13.1
29 189	41180	1	St. Louis	1 315	1 013 123	35	770.4	74.7	21.2	0.5	3.3	1.5	6.1	18.2	8.7	12.2	15.6	15.2
29 195	32180	6	Saline	1 957	22 887	1 669	11.7	90.4	5.7	0.6	0.7	3.7	6.5	17.0	12.7	10.2	13.9	13.7
29 197	28860	9	Schuyler	797	4 209	2 896	5.3	98.8	0.3	0.7	0.2	0.7	5.4	17.6	8.5	9.7	14.1	13.1
29 199	...	9	Scotland	1 136	4 905	2 850	4.3	98.8	0.2	0.1	0.1	0.9	6.5	20.3	9.8	9.2	14.1	11.8
29 201	43460	5	Scott	1 090	40 779	1 114	37.4	86.9	11.6	0.7	0.4	1.2	7.0	19.6	9.5	12.1	14.3	13.7
29 203	...	9	Shannon	2 600	8 293	2 576	3.2	96.9	0.2	4.1	0.0	1.1	5.6	18.7	9.2	10.8	14.5	14.1
29 205	...	9	Shelby	1 297	6 702	2 714	5.2	97.7	1.3	0.3	0.1	0.6	5.9	18.4	9.2	9.2	14.0	14.0
29 207	...	7	Stoddard	2 142	29 626	1 414	13.8	97.5	1.3	1.0	0.2	0.9	5.4	17.3	9.6	11.7	14.0	13.5
29 209	14700	8	Stone	1 200	29 941	1 406	25.0	97.9	0.4	1.4	0.3	1.1	4.9	15.5	8.0	9.8	12.6	14.0
29 211	...	9	Sullivan	1 686	7 080	2 679	4.2	90.1	0.7	0.2	0.2	8.9	7.6	17.6	7.9	12.1	14.2	13.3
29 213	14700	6	Taney	1 638	41 403	1 099	25.3	95.5	0.6	1.5	0.8	2.7	6.4	15.8	10.5	12.0	13.2	13.3
29 215	...	9	Texas	3 052	24 142	1 613	7.9	95.5	2.4	2.2	0.6	1.2	5.5	17.0	9.7	10.7	14.9	14.1
29 217	...	7	Vernon	2 160	20 283	1 786	9.4	97.0	0.9	1.5	0.5	1.0	6.5	19.3	10.3	10.9	13.6	13.7
29 219	41180	1	Warren	1 117	26 862	1 510	24.0	95.5	2.5	0.9	0.3	1.6	6.3	19.1	9.8	11.2	15.8	13.4
29 221	41180	1	Washington	1 967	23 884	1 618	12.1	95.6	2.9	1.4	0.2	0.8	7.0	18.3	11.1	13.0	15.1	13.4
29 223	...	9	Wayne	1 971	13 090	2 232	6.6	98.5	0.4	1.7	0.2	0.5	5.9	16.6	9.0	9.1	13.4	13.1
29 225	44180	2	Webster	1 537	33 124	1 326	21.6	96.4	1.4	1.4	0.5	1.3	7.0	20.5	9.7	12.9	14.3	12.9
29 227	...	9	Worth	690	2 270	3 035	3.3	99.1	0.2	0.4	0.3	0.3	4.7	16.6	10.2	7.3	14.9	13.2
29 229	...	6	Wright	1 767	18 186	1 901	10.3	97.7	0.5	1.4	0.3	1.0	7.1	19.1	9.7	10.7	13.6	13.0

1. CBSA = Core Based Statistical Area. See Appendix A for explanation. See Appendix B for list of metropolitan areas with component counties. 2. County type code from the Economic Research Service of USDA Rural-Urban Continuum Codes. See Appendix A for definition. 3. Dry land or land partially or temporarily covered by water. 4. Hispanic or Latino persons may be of any race.

Table B. States and Counties — Population and Households

STATE County	55 to 64 years (16)	65 to 74 years (17)	75 years and over (18)	Percent female (19)	Total persons 1990 (20)	Total persons 2000 (21)	Percent change 1990–2000 (22)	Percent change 2000–2003 (23)	Births (24)	Deaths (25)	Net migration (26)	Households 2000 Number (27)	Percent change 1990–2000 (28)	Persons per household (29)	Female family householder[1] (30)	One person (31)
MISSOURI—Cont'd																
Jasper	8.9	6.6	6.7	51.3	90 465	104 686	15.7	3.3	5 496	3 613	1 650	41 412	14.6	2.46	11.1	27.2
Jefferson	9.3	5.4	3.9	50.2	171 380	198 099	15.6	4.4	8 493	4 975	5 227	71 499	20.8	2.74	10.4	18.9
Johnson	7.5	5.1	4.2	49.4	42 514	48 258	13.5	4.2	2 230	1 076	909	17 410	19.4	2.58	8.5	22.7
Knox	11.1	10.1	10.5	51.4	4 482	4 361	-2.7	-1.1	195	204	-34	1 791	-1.5	2.38	6.9	29.3
Laclede	10.1	7.6	6.8	50.8	27 158	32 513	19.7	2.5	1 392	1 107	553	12 760	22.5	2.52	9.4	24.0
Lafayette	10.5	7.5	7.8	50.9	31 107	32 960	6.0	0.0	1 309	1 278	-7	12 569	7.1	2.55	9.4	24.0
Lawrence	10.1	7.5	7.8	50.8	30 236	35 204	16.4	3.5	1 557	1 391	1 071	13 568	15.7	2.55	9.0	24.5
Lewis	10.3	7.9	8.6	50.8	10 233	10 494	2.6	-2.6	334	356	-236	3 956	5.6	2.46	8.3	27.4
Lincoln	8.4	5.2	4.6	50.3	28 892	38 944	34.8	13.5	1 856	1 047	4 321	13 851	34.3	2.77	10.1	19.7
Linn	10.6	9.0	11.1	52.9	13 885	13 754	-0.9	-2.1	586	668	-196	5 697	-0.1	2.37	8.9	30.3
Livingston	10.3	8.3	10.9	53.9	14 592	14 558	-0.2	-1.2	526	550	-133	5 736	1.6	2.38	8.4	30.5
McDonald	10.4	6.3	4.9	49.2	16 938	21 681	28.0	1.3	1 159	656	-188	8 113	27.0	2.65	9.6	23.3
Macon	11.3	8.4	10.4	50.7	15 345	15 762	2.7	-1.2	615	742	-56	6 501	5.5	2.38	9.4	29.0
Madison	11.0	8.7	9.1	52.2	11 127	11 800	6.0	0.0	448	472	35	4 711	8.4	2.46	10.1	25.9
Maries	11.8	8.5	6.8	49.8	7 976	8 903	11.6	-0.7	355	307	-104	3 519	16.2	2.51	7.7	25.7
Marion	9.0	7.2	9.0	52.5	27 682	28 289	2.2	0.0	1 367	1 085	-280	11 066	3.2	2.44	11.4	28.1
Mercer	11.3	10.6	11.1	50.7	3 723	3 757	0.9	-4.3	110	150	-113	1 600	1.5	2.31	6.7	29.3
Miller	10.0	7.7	7.4	50.8	20 700	23 564	13.8	2.9	1 018	897	573	9 284	16.4	2.50	9.2	26.1
Mississippi	10.7	6.9	7.5	50.1	14 442	13 427	-7.0	7.1	703	541	755	5 383	-0.5	2.44	17.3	28.5
Moniteau	8.7	6.4	7.0	46.9	12 298	14 827	20.6	0.9	593	486	49	5 259	14.8	2.56	8.6	25.6
Monroe	11.5	8.2	9.2	50.6	9 104	9 311	2.3	0.9	383	362	75	3 656	5.3	2.50	7.7	26.5
Montgomery	10.8	8.3	9.1	50.7	11 355	12 136	6.9	-0.6	528	525	-59	4 775	10.0	2.47	8.6	26.3
Morgan	13.3	11.5	8.3	51.0	15 574	19 309	24.0	3.6	736	846	791	7 850	25.2	2.42	7.1	25.1
New Madrid	11.0	7.9	7.8	52.1	20 928	19 760	-5.6	-2.9	801	845	-525	7 824	0.4	2.48	14.6	26.5
Newton	10.8	7.2	6.5	50.9	44 445	52 636	18.4	2.7	2 342	1 803	897	20 140	19.3	2.57	8.8	22.7
Nodaway	8.1	6.3	7.6	50.0	21 709	21 912	0.9	-0.8	694	634	-212	8 138	6.8	2.33	6.2	30.0
Oregon	13.1	9.5	8.3	51.2	9 470	10 344	9.2	-0.4	354	473	84	4 263	10.7	2.40	8.4	26.2
Osage	9.9	7.2	7.0	49.0	12 018	13 062	8.7	0.6	504	425	15	4 922	15.5	2.61	6.7	23.8
Ozark	14.4	11.7	8.1	50.4	8 598	9 542	11.0	-0.5	332	397	31	3 950	13.3	2.40	6.9	24.4
Pemiscot	9.5	7.1	7.5	53.3	21 921	20 047	-8.5	-1.6	1 161	757	-720	7 855	-4.3	2.52	18.5	28.8
Perry	9.3	7.4	7.9	49.9	16 648	18 132	8.9	0.5	816	635	-69	6 904	13.0	2.57	7.9	24.5
Pettis	9.1	7.6	7.7	51.2	35 437	39 403	11.2	-0.1	1 784	1 397	-407	15 568	10.8	2.49	10.5	27.0
Phelps	9.8	6.7	6.6	49.0	35 248	39 825	13.0	4.6	1 605	1 417	1 667	15 683	18.1	2.38	9.5	28.6
Pike	10.2	7.3	7.5	45.2	15 969	18 351	14.9	0.9	685	637	140	6 451	6.0	2.50	9.6	26.7
Platte	10.0	4.8	4.1	50.4	57 867	73 781	27.5	7.6	3 355	1 548	3 785	29 278	32.2	2.49	8.8	24.9
Polk	9.3	7.8	7.5	51.3	21 826	26 992	23.7	4.0	1 100	892	897	9 917	23.5	2.56	8.2	23.2
Pulaski	6.0	4.3	3.0	45.9	41 307	41 165	-0.3	9.9	1 968	944	2 984	13 433	8.4	2.68	9.7	21.6
Putnam	12.4	10.5	10.3	50.7	5 079	5 223	2.9	-1.4	186	253	-1	2 228	2.9	2.32	7.2	28.7
Ralls	11.9	7.6	7.1	49.9	8 476	9 626	13.6	0.3	261	332	105	3 736	15.8	2.55	6.5	21.2
Randolph	9.1	7.1	7.3	48.2	24 370	24 663	1.2	1.5	1 124	967	251	9 199	2.9	2.43	11.1	27.9
Ray	10.8	6.8	5.7	49.9	21 968	23 354	6.3	2.4	921	723	389	8 743	9.0	2.63	8.0	22.1
Reynolds	14.5	9.6	7.0	49.6	6 661	6 689	0.4	-1.6	239	273	-75	2 721	7.0	2.40	7.8	26.0
Ripley	11.5	9.4	7.8	51.5	12 303	13 509	9.8	2.0	602	582	256	5 416	13.1	2.46	9.6	25.9
St. Charles	8.4	5.1	3.8	50.7	212 751	283 883	33.4	9.7	13 486	5 497	19 423	101 663	36.8	2.76	9.2	19.4
St. Clair	13.9	11.3	10.1	50.3	8 457	9 652	14.1	0.3	322	436	146	4 040	15.5	2.34	7.7	27.4
Ste. Genevieve	10.0	7.8	6.6	49.9	16 037	17 842	11.3	1.4	586	651	322	6 586	15.4	2.66	7.6	21.8
St. Francois	9.6	7.5	6.9	48.7	48 904	55 641	13.8	4.1	2 354	2 379	2 313	20 793	17.7	2.48	11.3	24.9
St. Louis	10.0	7.0	7.1	52.5	993 508	1 016 315	2.3	-0.3	40 763	31 888	-11 514	404 312	6.4	2.47	12.7	28.0
Saline	10.3	7.4	8.9	50.7	23 523	23 756	1.0	-3.7	972	947	-909	9 015	1.3	2.45	10.3	28.2
Schuyler	11.9	9.3	10.4	51.8	4 236	4 170	-1.6	0.9	142	184	86	1 725	-0.2	2.39	7.2	28.2
Scotland	10.2	7.9	10.4	51.2	4 822	4 983	3.3	-1.6	206	248	-32	1 902	-2.8	2.55	7.0	28.2
Scott	10.1	6.7	6.8	52.1	39 376	40 422	2.7	0.9	1 873	1 265	-212	15 626	5.9	2.55	13.4	25.0
Shannon	12.6	8.4	6.7	51.0	7 613	8 324	9.3	-0.4	302	295	-29	3 319	13.8	2.49	8.2	25.8
Shelby	10.7	8.3	10.9	51.9	6 942	6 799	-2.1	-1.4	276	285	-79	2 745	-2.3	2.38	7.3	30.3
Stoddard	11.3	8.6	8.9	51.8	28 895	29 705	2.8	-0.3	1 016	1 255	178	12 064	6.0	2.39	9.4	26.6
Stone	14.8	11.9	7.4	51.0	19 078	28 658	50.2	4.5	911	1 062	1 416	11 822	49.9	2.40	7.2	21.4
Sullivan	11.0	8.1	9.9	49.7	6 326	7 219	14.1	-1.9	363	307	-190	2 925	11.9	2.42	9.1	29.1
Taney	11.5	9.0	7.2	51.7	25 561	39 703	55.3	4.3	1 795	1 466	1 388	16 158	56.6	2.37	8.6	25.7
Texas	11.4	9.4	7.9	50.0	21 476	23 003	7.1	5.0	882	901	1 113	9 378	11.1	2.42	8.9	26.0
Vernon	9.8	8.0	8.1	51.7	19 041	20 454	7.4	-0.8	842	750	-240	7 966	9.1	2.44	9.6	28.1
Warren	10.1	7.1	5.4	50.4	19 534	24 525	25.6	9.5	1 064	671	1 893	9 185	29.9	2.64	8.9	20.8
Washington	10.0	6.9	4.8	48.3	20 380	23 344	14.5	2.3	1 075	699	181	8 406	20.4	2.64	10.6	22.0
Wayne	13.6	11.3	9.0	50.6	11 543	13 259	14.9	-1.3	562	611	-91	5 551	20.5	2.36	9.2	27.2
Webster	9.3	6.3	5.1	49.6	23 753	31 045	30.7	6.7	1 516	871	1 430	11 073	32.0	2.72	8.3	20.4
Worth	11.0	10.5	12.2	51.3	2 440	2 382	-2.4	-4.7	60	121	-44	1 009	-2.7	2.31	7.7	30.0
Wright	10.5	8.7	7.8	51.4	16 758	17 955	7.1	1.3	829	691	108	7 081	8.8	2.50	8.8	26.3

1. No spouse present.

Table B. States and Counties — Vital Statistics, Health Resources, and Crime

STATE County	Births, average 1999–2001		Deaths, average 1999–2001				Physicians,[4] 2000		Hospitals,[4] 1998			Medicare enrollees, 2003	Serious crimes known to police,[6] 2002 Total	
			Number		Rate					Beds				
	Total	Rate[1]	Total	Infant[2]	Total[1]	Infant[3]	Number	Rate[5]	Number	Number	Rate[5]		Number	Rate[7]
	32	33	34	35	36	37	38	39	40	41	42	43	44	45

MISSOURI—Cont'd

STATE County	32	33	34	35	36	37	38	39	40	41	42	43	44	45
Jasper	1 693	16.1	1 105	12	10.5	7.1	151	144	4	705	708	19 963	4 835	4 556
Jefferson	2 727	13.7	1 510	16	7.6	5.9	96	48	1	228	117	22 288	6 818	3 395
Johnson	705	14.6	327	3	6.7	D	41	85	1	70	147	5 229	1 229	2 512
Knox	56	12.9	65	0	14.9	D	2	46	0	0	0	932	170	3 845
Laclede	441	13.6	338	3	10.4	D	23	71	1	48	155	5 893	1 182	3 586
Lafayette	400	12.1	382	3	11.6	D	25	76	1	37	113	5 807	774	2 316
Lawrence	492	14.0	402	4	11.4	D	31	88	2	174	525	6 017	696	1 950
Lewis	115	11.1	127	0	12.2	D	4	38	0	0	0	1 930	166	1 560
Lincoln	549	14.0	311	3	7.9	D	33	85	1	36	98	5 068	1 083	2 743
Linn	174	12.7	207	1	15.0	D	10	73	1	34	246	3 133	215	1 542
Livingston	161	11.1	189	2	13.0	D	9	62	1	80	565	2 942	397	2 690
McDonald	359	16.6	199	3	9.2	D	1	5	0	0	0	2 938	453	2 254
Macon	179	11.4	216	2	13.7	D	12	76	1	38	249	3 280	417	2 610
Madison	137	11.6	154	0	13.1	D	13	110	1	147	1 280	2 536	284	2 374
Maries	106	12.0	95	0	10.8	D	2	22	0	0	0	1 267	83	920
Marion	416	14.7	344	2	12.2	D	50	177	1	105	378	5 432	1 332	4 644
Mercer	37	10.0	49	0	13.2	D	1	27	0	0	0	774	57	1 496
Miller	316	13.4	269	2	11.4	D	6	25	0	0	0	4 642	777	3 252
Mississippi	213	15.9	172	2	12.9	D	5	37	0	0	0	2 728	515	3 783
Moniteau	189	12.8	159	2	10.8	D	9	61	0	0	0	2 241	231	1 537
Monroe	116	12.5	111	1	12.0	D	4	43	0	0	0	1 867	137	1 451
Montgomery	154	12.7	164	1	13.5	D	10	82	0	0	0	2 407	340	2 764
Morgan	231	12.0	252	1	13.0	D	13	67	0	0	0	4 555	635	3 296
New Madrid	244	12.3	250	3	12.6	D	10	51	0	0	0	3 442	215	1 092
Newton	706	13.4	550	7	10.5	9.9	150	285	1	54	110	6 434	2 559	4 795
Nodaway	211	9.7	198	0	9.0	D	22	100	1	55	265	3 268	374	1 684
Oregon	112	10.9	144	1	13.9	D	1	10	0	0	0	2 304	47	448
Osage	160	12.3	138	3	10.6	D	4	31	0	0	0	1 873	112	846
Ozark	100	10.5	129	1	13.6	D	2	21	0	0	0	2 261	162	1 675
Pemiscot	350	17.4	255	4	12.7	D	18	90	1	209	971	3 721	718	3 533
Perry	254	14.0	197	2	10.9	D	13	72	1	55	316	2 926	443	2 410
Pettis	577	14.7	420	5	10.7	D	40	102	1	147	397	6 927	1 943	4 864
Phelps	484	12.1	427	3	10.7	D	75	188	1	227	588	6 882	1 405	3 523
Pike	202	11.0	197	1	10.8	D	14	76	1	25	153	3 085	229	1 231
Platte	1 018	13.7	467	7	6.3	6.5	67	91	1	55	78	7 936	4 643	6 207
Polk	359	13.3	288	2	10.7	D	26	96	1	74	290	5 392	955	3 490
Pulaski	609	14.8	277	7	6.7	10.9	47	114	0	0	0	4 587	729	1 747
Putnam	62	11.9	75	0	14.5	D	4	77	1	26	529	1 136	60	1 133
Ralls	86	9.0	95	1	9.9	D	1	10	0	0	0	1 215	200	2 049
Randolph	337	13.6	311	5	12.6	D	31	126	1	101	420	4 282	967	3 867
Ray	295	12.6	228	2	9.7	D	8	34	1	50	211	3 066	522	2 277
Reynolds	74	11.1	79	0	12.0	D	4	60	1	29	438	1 350	74	1 091
Ripley	174	12.9	181	0	13.4	D	8	59	1	26	185	3 027	392	2 862
St. Charles	4 167	14.6	1 663	22	5.8	5.4	284	100	4	659	242	33 024	7 770	2 700
St. Clair	96	10.0	126	0	13.1	D	8	83	2	72	793	2 184	234	2 391
Ste. Genevieve	187	10.5	175	0	9.8	D	14	78	1	34	194	2 874	228	1 261
St. Francois	716	12.9	704	6	12.6	D	82	147	2	210	378	10 932	1 558	2 762
St. Louis	12 616	12.4	9 695	96	9.5	7.6	3 188	314	12	3 981	399	159 375	37 060	3 635
Saline	295	12.5	297	1	12.5	D	24	101	1	56	247	4 415	543	2 255
Schuyler	46	10.9	60	1	14.5	D	2	48	0	0	0	1 108	38	899
Scotland	60	12.1	82	0	16.4	D	3	60	1	32	665	944	64	1 267
Scott	566	14.0	413	5	10.2	D	51	126	1	148	368	7 431	1 106	2 699
Shannon	91	10.9	88	1	10.6	D	1	12	0	0	0	1 396	111	1 315
Shelby	85	12.5	98	0	14.4	D	4	59	0	0	0	1 506	81	1 306
Stoddard	334	11.2	381	2	12.8	D	15	50	1	50	169	6 373	572	1 899
Stone	309	10.8	294	3	10.3	D	10	35	0	0	0	5 990	1 188	4 089
Sullivan	111	15.4	102	0	14.1	D	3	42	1	47	668	1 388	69	943
Taney	546	13.8	430	3	10.9	D	38	96	1	99	287	7 987	1 721	4 276
Texas	268	11.4	278	3	11.9	D	10	43	1	53	237	4 756	340	1 458
Vernon	279	13.7	233	4	11.4	D	27	132	1	97	499	3 748	708	3 414
Warren	329	13.3	207	1	8.4	D	6	24	0	0	0	3 852	663	2 666
Washington	325	14.0	224	2	9.6	D	11	47	1	42	183	3 355	437	1 846
Wayne	161	12.2	178	3	13.4	D	6	45	0	0	0	3 701	260	1 934
Webster	485	15.6	260	3	8.3	D	8	26	0	0	0	5 565	678	2 154
Worth	24	10.2	37	0	15.7	D	0	0	0	0	0	569	46	1 905
Wright	259	14.4	218	2	12.1	D	8	45	0	0	0	4 138	241	1 324

1. Per 1,000 estimated resident population.   2. Deaths of infants under 1 year old.   3. Deaths of infants under 1 year old per 1,000 live births.   4. Data subject to copyright.   5. Per 100,000 resident population as of July 1 of the year shown.   6. Data for serious crimes have not been adjusted for underreporting; this may affect comparability between geographic areas and over time.   7. Per 100,000 population estimated by the FBI.

Table B. States and Counties — Crime, Education, Money Income, and Poverty

STATE County	Serious crimes known to police,[1] 2002 (cont'd) Rate[2]		Education — School enrollment and attainment, 2000 Enrollment[3]		Education — Attainment[4] (percent)		Local government expenditures,[5] 2000-2001		Money income, 1999	Money income, 1999 Households Median income			Percent below poverty level, 1999			
	Violent	Property	Total	Percent private	High school graduate or less	Bachelor's degree or more	Total current expenditures (mil dol)	Current expenditures per student (dollars)	Per capita income[6] (dollars)	Dollars	Percent change, 1989-1999 (constant 1999 dollars)	Percent with income of $100,000 or more	Persons	Households	Families	Families with children
	46	47	48	49	50	51	52	53	54	55	56	57	58	59	60	61
MISSOURI—Cont'd																
Jasper	279	4 277	26 027	12.0	55.9	16.5	101.9	5 478	16 227	31 323	11.4	4.5	14.5	14.1	10.4	16.1
Jefferson	375	3 020	52 378	14.7	57.0	12.1	200.5	5 664	19 435	46 338	6.8	8.1	6.8	6.7	4.9	7.1
Johnson	211	2 301	17 035	6.2	46.5	23.2	47.8	5 878	16 037	35 391	14.3	5.4	14.9	15.3	9.5	13.0
Knox	204	3 642	900	12.9	66.6	12.8	5.1	7 443	13 075	27 124	16.7	1.2	18.0	17.6	12.9	18.5
Laclede	397	3 188	7 953	8.0	68.2	11.3	31.2	5 233	15 572	29 562	9.3	4.5	14.3	15.4	11.5	16.3
Lafayette	224	2 092	8 064	11.5	62.3	13.8	37.5	6 326	18 493	38 235	15.4	6.3	8.8	10.0	6.9	10.9
Lawrence	126	1 824	8 171	10.9	64.1	12.1	33.7	5 630	15 399	31 239	12.6	3.5	14.1	14.3	11.0	16.2
Lewis	160	1 401	2 870	29.3	65.0	13.0	9.8	5 691	14 746	30 651	10.9	3.9	16.1	14.3	10.7	18.8
Lincoln	555	2 188	10 611	15.9	66.5	9.7	36.4	4 984	17 149	42 592	13.0	6.1	8.3	8.1	6.2	8.1
Linn	273	1 269	3 150	5.8	69.0	10.8	19.5	6 816	15 378	28 242	21.0	3.2	14.9	14.8	11.3	16.5
Livingston	210	2 480	3 413	8.8	65.1	13.1	17.0	7 006	16 685	32 290	11.0	5.7	12.4	13.7	8.6	13.8
McDonald	279	1 975	5 135	7.9	69.1	7.0	15.7	4 571	13 175	27 010	16.1	3.0	20.7	20.5	15.6	23.6
Macon	601	2 009	3 393	8.5	67.0	13.0	15.2	6 097	16 189	30 195	10.9	3.7	12.5	13.7	8.3	12.2
Madison	711	1 663	2 620	4.5	70.4	7.8	12.1	5 736	13 215	25 601	11.4	2.3	17.2	18.1	12.8	19.1
Maries	188	731	2 034	14.8	67.7	11.0	8.5	5 894	15 662	31 925	24.8	2.8	13.1	13.4	10.1	15.7
Marion	335	4 310	6 983	19.8	61.4	15.6	28.8	5 477	16 964	31 774	10.4	4.6	12.1	12.8	9.3	14.5
Mercer	105	1 391	809	6.1	64.0	12.2	5.4	8 090	15 140	29 640	32.7	3.4	13.3	14.3	10.2	13.8
Miller	758	2 495	5 473	8.5	66.3	11.4	30.1	5 888	15 144	30 977	21.4	3.7	14.2	14.3	10.8	15.9
Mississippi	1 175	2 608	3 143	3.9	76.6	9.6	15.2	6 011	13 038	23 012	6.0	3.6	23.7	25.0	19.0	27.7
Moniteau	246	1 291	3 474	15.9	66.3	13.0	14.1	5 812	16 609	37 168	25.1	4.3	9.9	10.2	7.3	10.2
Monroe	95	1 356	2 126	11.5	67.9	9.5	11.3	6 220	14 695	30 871	16.0	2.8	11.9	12.3	8.3	12.4
Montgomery	374	2 390	2 798	10.1	70.4	9.9	11.4	5 733	15 092	32 772	12.3	2.8	11.8	12.5	8.4	14.0
Morgan	592	2 704	3 916	13.9	66.1	10.7	12.1	5 218	15 950	30 659	19.1	5.0	16.2	14.6	12.1	20.6
New Madrid	295	797	4 677	3.4	76.0	9.6	22.3	6 295	14 204	26 826	14.2	3.2	22.1	22.2	18.6	27.6
Newton	1 049	3 746	12 541	12.3	54.6	16.1	46.9	5 620	17 502	35 041	17.1	5.8	11.6	12.0	8.1	12.0
Nodaway	167	1 517	8 420	7.5	54.1	23.6	22.5	7 356	15 384	31 781	16.3	4.4	16.5	18.7	8.3	9.8
Oregon	67	381	2 232	4.9	72.3	9.1	11.5	5 784	12 812	22 359	21.4	2.9	22.0	23.0	16.3	24.2
Osage	30	816	3 316	23.4	68.9	10.4	11.5	6 564	17 245	39 565	17.9	4.1	8.3	9.7	5.9	8.4
Ozark	651	1 023	1 902	7.3	70.0	8.3	10.8	5 964	14 133	25 861	17.2	2.9	21.6	21.1	16.1	24.7
Pemiscot	738	2 795	5 262	2.0	75.6	8.4	29.5	6 540	12 968	21 911	17.2	3.5	30.4	29.2	24.8	36.3
Perry	430	1 980	4 250	27.1	73.2	9.9	14.9	6 056	16 554	36 632	14.5	3.7	9.0	11.0	5.2	6.7
Pettis	528	4 336	9 733	13.4	55.5	15.0	33.8	5 440	16 251	31 822	7.2	4.2	12.8	12.4	10.2	14.4
Phelps	288	3 234	12 582	10.4	53.9	21.1	38.3	5 745	16 084	29 378	4.7	5.0	16.4	17.7	11.3	17.9
Pike	183	1 048	4 039	12.4	68.2	10.2	18.1	6 107	14 462	32 373	13.8	3.9	15.5	15.2	11.9	16.3
Platte	775	5 432	19 324	15.7	34.8	33.3	84.4	6 712	26 356	55 849	8.9	16.4	4.8	4.8	3.3	4.9
Polk	395	3 095	7 619	28.7	62.2	14.6	30.5	5 985	13 645	29 656	18.2	3.5	16.3	16.2	11.1	17.4
Pulaski	266	1 481	11 608	10.4	48.5	18.8	52.3	6 304	14 586	34 247	18.2	3.5	10.3	11.1	8.0	10.5
Putnam	132	1 001	1 139	5.4	64.8	11.2	5.5	6 571	14 647	26 282	25.8	2.2	16.0	16.1	13.2	21.9
Ralls	430	1 619	2 197	9.6	67.8	12.3	4.9	5 446	16 456	37 094	25.1	3.4	8.7	9.7	6.6	9.9
Randolph	464	3 403	5 935	12.6	61.2	11.7	23.8	6 254	15 010	31 464	9.3	3.7	12.5	12.4	9.2	13.9
Ray	244	2 033	5 815	8.5	66.6	10.8	22.6	5 815	18 685	41 886	14.9	6.5	6.8	8.0	5.3	7.8
Reynolds	546	546	1 519	4.5	74.5	7.5	9.0	7 143	13 065	25 867	13.2	1.8	20.1	20.3	16.1	23.6
Ripley	818	2 044	2 972	7.6	71.0	7.8	13.2	5 815	12 889	22 761	23.3	2.6	22.0	23.5	16.9	25.6
St. Charles	198	2 501	82 278	23.2	40.5	26.3	296.8	5 994	23 592	57 258	5.7	15.1	4.0	3.9	2.8	4.2
St. Clair	235	2 156	1 941	5.2	72.6	9.0	9.6	6 353	14 025	25 321	9.2	2.2	19.6	20.3	16.2	23.4
Ste. Genevieve	77	1 183	4 398	23.8	69.0	8.1	12.6	5 710	17 283	39 200	9.2	4.8	8.2	7.5	6.0	8.7
St. Francois	438	2 324	13 139	8.4	62.3	10.2	58.7	5 622	15 273	31 199	11.9	4.1	14.9	14.9	11.0	17.5
St. Louis	297	3 338	281 608	31.5	36.0	35.4	1 271.1	8 210	27 595	50 532	-1.4	17.5	6.9	6.7	5.0	7.9
Saline	183	2 072	6 338	21.3	64.2	15.8	26.0	6 586	16 132	32 743	12.4	4.9	13.2	12.9	10.5	17.1
Schuyler	24	875	919	5.0	65.2	11.6	5.1	6 575	15 850	27 385	21.8	2.6	17.0	18.8	13.2	19.0
Scotland	119	1 148	1 129	18.2	67.8	11.2	4.9	6 477	14 474	27 409	28.0	4.4	16.8	17.6	13.4	16.5
Scott	403	2 296	10 018	10.6	69.8	10.6	41.6	5 368	15 620	31 352	12.4	3.9	16.1	16.0	12.3	19.7
Shannon	427	889	2 042	4.5	75.6	7.6	5.8	6 503	11 492	20 878	4.2	1.9	26.9	26.1	21.0	31.3
Shelby	81	1 225	1 592	10.4	66.4	12.5	8.0	6 559	15 632	29 448	19.9	3.3	16.3	14.6	13.0	17.8
Stoddard	395	1 504	6 629	4.6	72.0	10.1	31.8	5 635	14 656	26 987	10.0	3.4	16.5	17.4	12.8	18.6
Stone	1 325	2 764	5 502	6.7	58.5	14.2	25.9	5 953	18 036	32 637	15.4	5.2	12.8	12.6	8.5	16.9
Sullivan	191	751	1 520	4.6	72.4	8.4	7.4	6 431	13 392	26 107	22.8	2.5	16.5	17.9	11.0	16.1
Taney	539	3 736	8 973	19.6	56.4	14.9	35.1	5 719	17 267	30 898	13.5	4.5	12.4	11.9	9.4	14.7
Texas	197	1 261	5 405	9.4	68.3	10.8	25.3	5 855	13 799	24 545	9.0	3.3	21.4	21.3	16.5	24.4
Vernon	183	3 231	5 081	14.5	63.3	14.2	21.1	6 272	15 047	30 021	13.8	3.8	14.9	15.1	10.1	15.1
Warren	261	2 405	5 978	18.8	60.8	11.1	19.2	4 923	19 690	41 016	5.5	7.7	8.6	9.6	6.4	10.0
Washington	439	1 407	5 577	7.3	72.9	7.5	22.2	5 459	12 934	27 112	17.9	2.6	20.8	20.9	17.1	23.9
Wayne	379	1 555	2 743	5.4	74.6	6.8	11.9	5 759	13 434	24 007	29.3	2.5	21.9	21.8	17.9	27.3
Webster	674	1 481	7 879	11.0	65.0	11.0	25.0	5 336	14 502	31 929	15.8	4.2	14.8	13.3	9.6	14.6
Worth	41	1 863	565	1.8	65.5	11.3	2.8	6 843	14 367	27 471	40.4	2.6	14.3	16.0	10.9	15.5
Wright	126	1 198	4 349	7.6	69.6	9.8	25.1	6 509	13 135	24 691	16.5	3.4	21.7	22.1	17.3	25.7

1. Data for serious crimes have not been adjusted for underreporting; this may affect comparability between geographic areas and over time.   2. Per 100,000 population estimated by the FBI.   3. All persons 3 years old and over enrolled in nursery school through college.   4. Persons 25 years old and over.   5. Elementary and secondary education expenditures.   6. Based on population enumerated as of April 1, 2000.

STATE County	Total (mil dol)	Percent change, 2001–2002	Per capita[1] Dollars	Per capita[1] Rank	Wages and salaries[2] (mil dol)	Proprietor's income (mil dol)	Dividends, interest, and rent (mil dol)	Transfer payments Total (mil dol)	Government payments to individuals Total (mil dol)	Social Security (mil dol)	Medical payments (mil dol)	Income mainte-nance (mil dol)	Unemploy-ment insurance (mil dol)
	62	63	64	65	66	67	68	69	70	71	72	73	74
MISSOURI—Cont'd													
Jasper	2 501	2.5	23 407	1 592	1 895	187	436	544	519	189	242	50	12
Jefferson	5 190	2.4	25 465	1 008	1 470	207	578	736	688	299	280	46	27
Johnson	1 096	6.2	22 007	2 012	725	75	183	172	161	58	66	17	3
Knox	90	-3.7	20 845	2 333	30	8	23	23	22	9	11	1	0
Laclede	689	4.2	20 932	2 315	400	61	130	157	150	58	64	16	4
Lafayette	890	1.8	26 959	704	260	76	142	177	169	65	85	9	4
Lawrence	700	1.9	19 373	2 682	243	41	107	172	163	68	70	14	4
Lewis	196	1.7	18 872	2 773	83	6	36	45	43	18	19	3	1
Lincoln	977	4.1	23 050	1 708	318	48	139	161	151	63	67	12	5
Linn	304	1.4	22 478	1 887	155	23	62	80	77	27	34	5	3
Livingston	368	2.1	25 565	985	193	37	97	76	73	30	34	5	2
McDonald	436	3.7	20 107	2 520	172	35	53	91	86	32	38	11	3
Macon	344	3.2	22 292	1 935	143	25	75	88	85	33	39	5	2
Madison	222	2.8	18 675	2 804	77	16	39	72	70	27	32	6	2
Maries	188	2.3	21 451	2 166	42	17	33	40	38	15	17	3	1
Marion	655	1.8	23 384	1 598	456	36	114	160	153	54	76	14	4
Mercer	73	-12.4	19 938	2 557	47	3	13	18	17	8	7	1	0
Miller	468	2.0	19 345	2 686	216	27	73	118	112	41	52	9	4
Mississippi	274	3.8	19 506	2 658	112	29	42	88	85	27	42	12	2
Moniteau	320	-0.7	21 428	2 171	115	24	61	58	55	24	23	4	2
Monroe	193	-1.5	20 669	2 378	79	12	47	46	44	19	19	2	1
Montgomery	277	0.3	22 968	1 733	104	18	53	65	62	24	30	4	2
Morgan	402	1.8	20 357	2 468	113	27	100	115	110	49	46	8	3
New Madrid	396	-2.2	20 559	2 418	282	25	49	124	119	35	63	15	3
Newton	1 246	2.6	23 439	1 587	650	117	167	223	211	92	83	17	7
Nodaway	431	0.4	19 717	2 608	288	21	88	78	73	32	29	4	1
Oregon	178	3.8	17 408	2 957	63	18	29	64	62	21	28	6	1
Osage	323	0.8	24 703	1 211	99	20	56	50	47	21	19	2	2
Ozark	168	3.4	17 770	2 921	40	11	33	57	55	24	22	5	1
Pemiscot	401	1.2	20 211	2 500	178	24	53	138	133	35	68	24	3
Perry	404	2.4	22 210	1 956	272	22	72	80	75	31	35	5	2
Pettis	942	1.5	23 915	1 437	617	65	170	203	194	72	86	16	6
Phelps	954	6.1	23 221	1 656	582	62	167	202	192	68	91	16	3
Pike	363	2.3	19 797	2 590	178	19	68	89	85	34	40	7	2
Platte	2 652	2.3	34 083	162	1 522	134	345	232	213	101	79	10	8
Polk	528	3.8	19 085	2 744	214	36	97	144	137	48	68	11	2
Pulaski	1 052	7.9	23 884	1 445	930	28	122	145	137	41	60	13	3
Putnam	99	3.0	19 005	2 753	27	11	23	28	27	11	12	2	1
Ralls	213	-1.4	21 955	2 030	82	5	37	45	42	17	15	2	1
Randolph	527	5.0	21 327	2 204	319	37	77	138	132	40	63	11	3
Ray	590	2.7	24 855	1 167	147	42	69	97	91	40	37	6	3
Reynolds	131	6.2	19 914	2 564	56	8	21	52	51	15	29	4	1
Ripley	252	6.4	18 522	2 826	66	24	35	98	95	30	49	10	2
St. Charles	9 151	4.0	30 181	335	4 140	314	1 161	909	837	412	315	39	30
St. Clair	184	1.7	19 104	2 741	57	12	39	58	56	24	23	4	1
Ste. Genevieve	411	1.4	22 775	1 790	189	16	79	78	73	34	30	4	2
St. Francois	1 179	4.0	20 762	2 353	589	70	171	325	312	117	140	30	8
St. Louis	41 755	2.0	41 126	53	32 117	2 854	9 818	4 364	4 123	1 937	1 653	258	132
Saline	558	0.6	24 231	1 333	273	48	98	162	156	45	92	9	3
Schuyler	82	2.0	19 433	2 666	20	8	17	23	22	8	11	1	0
Scotland	99	3.0	20 238	2 490	34	14	23	24	23	9	12	1	1
Scott	952	3.5	23 493	1 572	460	109	143	236	227	75	109	26	5
Shannon	142	4.8	17 001	2 995	49	16	19	47	45	15	21	5	1
Shelby	146	-6.5	21 711	2 086	51	15	33	35	34	14	15	2	1
Stoddard	630	1.9	21 121	2 261	300	57	100	177	170	64	81	15	4
Stone	696	5.3	23 680	1 508	189	93	138	158	151	74	54	10	6
Sullivan	150	-4.2	20 579	2 408	93	16	22	40	38	12	21	3	1
Taney	948	4.6	23 309	1 626	663	83	175	214	204	87	82	13	10
Texas	407	2.0	16 765	3 008	167	26	73	119	113	40	50	12	3
Vernon	441	-0.2	21 717	2 085	225	26	74	130	125	38	70	10	2
Warren	662	3.8	25 398	1 024	207	26	101	113	106	49	44	6	3
Washington	423	4.3	17 893	2 910	123	19	41	131	125	39	63	16	4
Wayne	240	5.3	18 297	2 862	62	14	32	99	95	34	46	9	2
Webster	608	2.9	18 606	2 811	181	38	84	133	126	51	56	11	4
Worth	44	1.5	19 312	2 694	12	6	10	12	11	5	5	1	0
Wright	312	2.2	17 206	2 974	120	16	57	105	101	38	45	11	3

1. Based on the resident population estimated as of July 1 of the year shown.   2. Includes other labor income.

Table B. States and Counties — Earnings, Social Security, and Housing

STATE County	Earnings, 2002 Total (mil dol)	Farm	Goods-related[1] Total	Manu-facturing	Information and professional and technical services	Retail trade	Finance, insurance, and real estate	Health services	Govern-ment	Social Security beneficiaries, December 2003 Number	Rate[2]	Supplemental Security Income recipients, December 2003	Housing units, 2003 Total	Percent change, 2000–2003
	75	76	77	78	79	80	81	82	83	84	85	86	87	88
MISSOURI—Cont'd														
Jasper	2 082	0.5	28.7	24.0	4.7	9.3	4.7	11.9	11.3	20 860	193	3 064	47 097	3.3
Jefferson	1 677	0.0	26.8	12.5	5.0	10.2	5.6	10.1	18.1	30 875	149	2 048	80 540	6.6
Johnson	800	0.3	D	10.6	D	5.5	4.1	3.8	57.3	6 490	129	564	19 625	3.9
Knox	39	12.9	D	6.8	D	9.5	D	3.5	28.2	1 085	252	113	2 351	1.5
Laclede	461	0.3	D	39.8	4.2	12.7	3.5	D	11.3	7 020	211	1 002	15 022	4.9
Lafayette	336	2.6	25.7	9.9	D	11.5	5.5	D	22.3	6 840	208	440	13 995	2.1
Lawrence	285	3.7	D	19.0	3.6	12.9	4.4	5.8	21.3	7 935	218	666	15 195	2.7
Lewis	89	-0.3	D	11.2	D	8.2	3.8	D	23.3	2 075	203	162	4 717	2.5
Lincoln	365	-1.0	32.9	18.0	4.5	11.0	5.7	D	19.5	6 635	150	477	16 443	6.0
Linn	179	2.8	D	22.1	D	7.2	3.6	6.9	16.4	3 180	236	308	6 604	0.8
Livingston	230	2.9	D	15.2	5.3	11.6	6.8	D	18.1	3 340	232	387	6 616	2.3
McDonald	207	5.5	45.7	38.3	2.6	7.8	2.8	3.4	14.5	3 785	172	478	9 622	3.6
Macon	168	1.1	D	11.9	D	11.2	5.1	4.6	34.0	3 775	242	268	7 621	1.6
Madison	93	0.2	19.4	13.7	4.6	15.0	4.7	D	25.3	3 075	261	387	5 791	2.4
Maries	59	0.6	D	17.6	D	7.2	10.3	7.4	16.9	1 730	196	124	4 286	3.3
Marion	492	-0.8	D	25.0	4.4	8.8	4.0	D	14.3	5 980	211	973	12 586	1.1
Mercer	50	51.0	D	D	D	4.5	D	3.0	16.7	955	266	69	2 171	2.2
Miller	243	0.3	D	13.2	D	14.1	4.5	D	16.5	4 715	194	463	11 756	4.4
Mississippi	141	10.0	7.8	5.5	3.5	10.3	4.8	D	22.4	3 175	221	696	5 947	1.8
Moniteau	139	4.6	D	23.4	2.9	8.9	4.1	D	24.1	2 670	178	150	5 885	2.5
Monroe	92	-0.1	D	33.6	D	7.3	3.0	4.3	26.4	2 090	222	132	4 703	3.0
Montgomery	121	-3.1	33.6	19.6	2.4	8.2	6.3	6.1	19.7	2 715	225	213	5 938	3.7
Morgan	140	6.8	22.9	14.1	3.6	15.4	5.1	D	20.7	5 425	271	371	14 268	2.7
New Madrid	308	5.8	44.4	43.1	D	7.9	2.5	D	11.5	4 245	221	1 066	8 848	2.9
Newton	767	1.7	D	27.7	2.4	8.5	2.3	22.6	10.1	10 405	193	682	22 716	3.7
Nodaway	309	-1.9	D	31.0	3.0	7.8	4.6	D	27.2	3 675	169	287	9 169	2.9
Oregon	81	2.0	D	11.7	3.2	13.2	6.4	8.0	20.3	2 710	263	551	5 136	2.8
Osage	120	1.8	35.8	26.9	D	10.7	4.4	4.6	19.1	2 375	181	110	6 035	2.2
Ozark	52	2.5	16.3	10.2	3.9	9.5	8.6	D	27.2	2 835	298	375	5 297	3.6
Pemiscot	202	5.0	D	16.1	D	8.5	4.0	5.5	29.6	4 500	228	1 669	8 966	2.0
Perry	294	-0.3	D	36.3	D	9.1	4.1	4.6	12.2	3 490	191	270	8 024	2.7
Pettis	682	0.6	37.0	30.6	7.5	8.3	3.8	8.2	15.7	8 075	205	944	17 161	1.2
Phelps	644	0.0	13.9	8.8	4.2	9.1	3.7	11.7	38.1	8 020	192	1 082	18 411	5.2
Pike	198	0.9	26.8	16.9	5.6	9.2	4.4	6.4	28.0	3 660	198	355	7 627	1.8
Platte	1 656	-0.1	D	9.7	6.6	5.2	8.1	4.9	8.8	9 735	123	284	33 534	8.5
Polk	250	1.0	D	7.4	6.0	10.9	6.0	D	25.7	5 710	203	675	11 682	4.5
Pulaski	959	0.0	D	0.4	D	3.8	1.8	2.1	79.4	5 225	115	705	15 956	3.6
Putnam	38	2.5	8.4	3.1	2.2	11.9	9.7	3.8	34.6	1 395	271	158	2 970	1.9
Ralls	86	1.0	D	36.9	D	6.1	3.3	3.4	15.0	1 935	200	103	4 690	2.8
Randolph	356	0.5	D	15.0	D	12.0	7.2	D	19.3	4 440	177	685	10 925	1.7
Ray	188	-0.2	D	13.3	D	9.5	7.9	5.3	24.2	4 225	177	192	9 703	3.5
Reynolds	65	0.8	D	15.6	D	5.3	D	7.0	19.2	1 840	280	290	3 879	3.2
Ripley	90	1.9	19.0	15.4	2.6	13.0	4.9	8.7	26.7	3 780	274	795	6 614	3.5
St. Charles	4 454	0.0	30.6	17.3	9.5	9.3	5.2	9.8	11.7	40 185	129	1 602	119 076	12.9
St. Clair	68	0.2	D	D	3.9	11.5	D	13.3	31.3	2 720	281	249	5 376	3.3
Ste. Genevieve	205	0.1	46.3	30.1	D	8.5	3.4	D	15.7	3 570	197	194	8 217	2.5
St. Francois	659	0.4	21.7	13.5	3.6	11.6	4.9	14.8	24.0	13 065	226	1 949	25 211	3.1
St. Louis	34 971	0.0	21.8	14.2	13.8	6.4	10.0	9.2	7.6	176 580	174	12 023	429 993	1.5
Saline	321	2.1	D	19.5	4.1	6.9	4.1	D	23.6	4 945	216	563	10 208	1.9
Schuyler	28	5.3	D	D	D	12.6	D	3.7	33.8	1 015	241	133	2 100	3.6
Scotland	48	11.9	D	9.5	D	9.5	D	1.9	37.9	1 055	215	82	2 317	1.1
Scott	569	1.1	16.4	10.9	11.7	8.9	4.7	D	16.1	8 670	213	1 726	17 447	2.9
Shannon	65	0.2	D	28.3	D	6.0	4.4	3.4	25.9	2 010	242	330	3 992	3.4
Shelby	66	9.0	D	15.7	D	6.4	4.9	3.1	25.1	1 610	240	118	3 286	1.3
Stoddard	357	4.0	D	25.3	2.4	11.1	4.2	D	14.4	7 610	257	1 110	13 602	2.9
Stone	282	0.2	D	D	D	12.9	8.6	D	12.5	7 820	261	420	16 794	3.4
Sullivan	109	15.1	D	D	4.2	5.7	5.5	4.2	15.3	1 545	218	203	3 435	2.1
Taney	747	0.0	10.9	3.0	5.2	11.8	11.9	8.4	9.0	9 560	231	564	21 239	7.9
Texas	193	1.9	19.1	15.4	2.1	10.6	5.2	D	33.3	4 990	207	835	11 124	3.3
Vernon	251	-2.5	D	22.6	3.6	8.7	5.9	D	26.3	4 505	222	699	9 045	1.9
Warren	233	-0.6	D	30.2	D	10.3	4.4	D	14.9	5 115	190	227	12 169	10.2
Washington	142	0.2	D	17.3	1.5	9.5	3.2	D	37.8	4 600	193	941	10 304	4.1
Wayne	76	1.0	D	14.5	7.3	11.2	D	5.9	28.2	4 030	308	800	7 796	4.0
Webster	219	0.4	27.6	16.7	D	13.0	6.5	D	20.8	6 110	184	679	12 639	4.9
Worth	16	9.0	D	D	D	7.9	D	4.5	36.7	615	271	40	1 251	0.5
Wright	136	3.1	D	13.5	3.4	13.4	4.4	6.9	25.4	4 840	266	821	8 114	2.0

1. Covers mining, construction, and manufacturing. 2. Per 1,000 resident population estimated as of July 1 of the year shown.

STATE County	Housing units, 2000								Civilian labor force, 2003				Civilian employment,[6] 2000		
	Occupied units										Unemployment			Percent	
	Owner-occupied					Renter-occupied									
				Median owner cost as a percent of income											Production, transportation, and material moving occupations
	Total	Percent	Median value[1]	With a mortgage	Without a mortgage[2]	Median rent[3]	Median rent as a percent of income	Substandard units[4] (percent)	Total	Percent change, 2002–2003	Total	Rate[5]	Total	Management, professional and related occupations	
	89	90	91	92	93	94	95	96	97	98	99	100	101	102	103
MISSOURI—Cont'd															
Jasper	41 412	67.0	67 700	18.5	9.9	441	23.8	2.9	56 074	0.3	2 772	4.9	49 046	25.9	22.6
Jefferson	71 499	83.4	99 200	19.1	9.9	502	22.1	2.6	109 831	2.0	6 172	5.6	99 837	23.8	18.6
Johnson	17 410	61.5	86 500	19.6	9.9	475	25.0	2.9	23 960	0.5	957	4.0	21 815	28.2	18.2
Knox	1 791	77.1	37 800	17.7	12.2	282	20.4	2.8	1 965	-3.2	80	4.1	1 907	29.1	17.0
Laclede	12 760	72.8	73 000	19.7	9.9	371	22.9	3.6	16 712	-0.5	1 636	9.8	14 885	21.6	31.3
Lafayette	12 569	75.4	74 400	18.7	9.9	426	21.5	2.0	16 785	1.9	922	5.5	15 977	23.8	19.8
Lawrence	13 568	74.3	65 500	20.6	9.9	404	24.1	3.8	16 474	-1.2	820	5.0	15 973	26.2	24.7
Lewis	3 956	76.5	52 400	16.2	9.9	273	21.5	2.6	5 981	-4.0	305	5.1	5 075	25.4	26.2
Lincoln	13 851	80.8	102 200	19.4	9.9	460	22.5	3.9	21 529	2.3	1 299	6.0	18 600	21.1	23.2
Linn	5 697	77.0	42 200	18.6	11.5	322	21.3	1.8	6 419	-1.7	611	9.5	6 269	25.9	26.1
Livingston	5 736	70.8	61 400	18.7	9.9	357	24.1	1.8	7 103	-5.5	344	4.8	6 615	27.5	18.0
McDonald	8 113	71.5	55 800	18.7	10.8	382	23.8	7.3	9 232	0.2	583	6.3	9 757	19.7	29.5
Macon	6 501	75.9	55 900	19.3	9.9	308	22.1	2.4	7 108	-1.0	410	5.8	7 465	23.8	21.9
Madison	4 711	76.0	54 800	20.4	11.4	354	23.9	3.0	5 027	-0.1	369	7.8	4 852	18.1	25.9
Maries	3 519	81.5	64 400	18.9	9.9	351	20.1	3.5	5 027	1.8	205	4.1	4 126	24.1	23.8
Marion	11 066	70.4	66 600	17.3	9.9	358	22.7	1.9	15 160	-1.7	872	5.8	12 884	24.7	23.9
Mercer	1 600	76.8	32 300	17.1	10.9	286	20.8	3.1	1 439	-5.4	91	6.3	1 757	32.8	15.9
Miller	9 284	75.0	69 900	20.8	9.9	367	22.6	2.6	11 995	0.2	791	6.6	10 926	23.2	20.0
Mississippi	5 383	63.5	47 000	19.2	11.4	327	27.6	2.4	6 215	-0.4	461	7.4	5 395	21.7	25.7
Moniteau	5 259	77.7	69 900	18.5	9.9	370	19.6	3.2	8 353	1.3	286	3.4	6 747	26.2	18.7
Monroe	3 656	78.5	55 300	18.3	9.9	337	20.0	2.6	3 855	-4.7	281	7.3	4 286	24.5	26.2
Montgomery	4 775	78.7	59 300	18.5	10.2	385	21.2	3.6	5 805	-2.0	411	7.1	5 519	21.6	27.2
Morgan	7 850	82.9	79 500	20.1	9.9	367	24.2	3.8	8 373	-2.2	572	6.8	8 202	23.0	21.0
New Madrid	7 824	66.1	48 100	17.3	10.2	330	23.6	3.5	8 539	1.0	926	10.8	8 140	22.1	27.1
Newton	20 140	76.6	74 200	19.1	9.9	421	21.3	3.9	28 392	0.4	1 678	5.9	24 915	26.1	25.9
Nodaway	8 138	63.8	71 100	17.7	9.9	392	25.8	1.4	13 424	3.9	268	2.0	11 099	32.9	18.1
Oregon	4 263	78.3	45 900	24.2	11.3	339	26.3	4.7	4 359	-0.1	197	4.5	3 856	23.3	27.4
Osage	4 922	83.0	81 400	18.8	9.9	343	19.7	2.3	7 786	1.6	364	4.7	6 620	26.1	22.0
Ozark	3 950	81.6	62 600	22.6	9.9	336	24.2	5.2	4 211	-1.0	236	5.6	3 855	25.2	23.9
Pemiscot	7 855	58.4	44 200	19.3	12.1	333	28.0	4.4	8 220	-3.7	955	11.6	7 262	21.4	26.0
Perry	6 904	79.9	80 000	18.6	9.9	422	21.7	2.2	11 076	1.1	366	3.3	9 014	21.3	27.5
Pettis	15 568	72.5	66 400	19.1	9.9	426	23.6	3.4	21 732	-1.3	1 278	5.9	18 333	26.4	25.3
Phelps	15 683	65.6	74 800	18.1	9.9	396	26.1	2.9	22 997	2.9	780	3.4	17 616	33.6	14.3
Pike	6 451	74.1	63 400	19.3	9.9	356	22.0	4.2	8 041	-3.9	430	5.3	7 650	23.5	22.6
Platte	29 278	67.4	126 700	19.4	9.9	640	20.7	2.2	48 152	1.9	1 973	4.1	41 276	38.8	10.6
Polk	9 917	73.0	77 000	21.0	9.9	391	25.2	4.0	12 846	-2.3	620	4.8	11 948	27.9	19.3
Pulaski	13 433	58.0	78 300	20.6	9.9	439	19.7	3.0	14 405	4.0	674	4.7	12 950	28.5	15.3
Putnam	2 228	77.2	44 500	20.0	12.9	278	20.7	2.2	2 032	2.8	134	6.6	2 184	31.7	22.7
Ralls	3 736	82.3	67 400	18.2	9.9	400	21.7	2.4	5 503	-1.4	345	6.3	4 888	25.7	23.2
Randolph	9 199	72.0	49 300	18.5	10.7	384	22.6	3.1	11 767	0.9	664	5.6	10 724	25.4	23.2
Ray	8 743	79.5	81 000	18.4	10.9	455	23.4	2.3	11 577	2.8	703	6.1	10 974	22.5	24.5
Reynolds	2 721	77.1	47 200	19.5	10.5	317	25.0	3.8	2 446	1.7	223	9.1	2 446	21.0	27.8
Ripley	5 416	78.0	49 100	21.0	11.5	306	24.5	5.2	5 625	1.6	403	7.2	4 948	23.0	30.2
St. Charles	101 663	82.0	126 200	19.5	9.9	624	22.4	1.7	176 493	2.1	7 197	4.1	150 836	34.6	12.5
St. Clair	4 040	79.5	48 500	20.3	10.7	290	20.5	4.1	4 211	0.7	326	7.7	3 860	26.6	19.7
Ste. Genevieve	6 586	82.3	83 700	18.5	9.9	396	23.1	2.9	8 996	0.9	493	5.5	8 507	21.8	25.8
St. Francois	20 793	73.2	68 200	19.0	9.9	402	25.2	2.5	26 471	3.5	1 877	7.1	22 256	23.6	19.8
St. Louis	404 312	74.1	116 600	19.3	9.9	601	23.8	2.0	579 331	2.3	29 327	5.1	505 250	41.6	10.0
Saline	9 015	69.1	59 700	18.0	9.9	391	22.2	3.3	11 303	-0.3	591	5.2	11 351	27.0	22.9
Schuyler	1 725	75.2	38 500	17.0	10.1	276	21.4	2.1	2 200	0.5	136	6.2	1 931	27.4	18.2
Scotland	1 902	76.7	43 300	19.0	10.2	313	20.5	4.0	2 085	-4.6	89	4.3	2 315	32.9	21.3
Scott	15 626	69.3	68 200	18.5	9.9	393	24.3	2.9	20 157	-0.1	1 197	5.9	18 220	22.7	23.4
Shannon	3 319	79.7	41 400	21.3	10.4	283	24.5	5.8	4 076	1.1	311	7.6	3 151	18.5	34.4
Shelby	2 745	75.1	44 000	17.9	9.9	294	21.4	2.7	3 010	-2.6	178	5.9	3 177	27.5	25.5
Stoddard	12 064	72.3	57 200	18.9	10.5	352	23.8	2.1	13 888	-0.6	911	6.6	13 023	21.5	27.7
Stone	11 822	81.2	102 700	22.7	9.9	468	26.4	3.1	14 570	3.4	1 450	10.0	11 816	23.5	13.8
Sullivan	2 925	71.7	37 700	18.6	12.2	328	20.7	3.9	3 468	-10.8	388	11.2	3 285	23.7	29.8
Taney	16 158	68.9	93 500	21.8	9.9	483	23.8	4.0	32 650	2.1	2 507	7.7	18 817	25.9	10.1
Texas	9 378	76.6	61 000	21.6	9.9	308	25.5	4.5	9 221	-1.5	806	8.7	9 110	26.3	23.7
Vernon	7 966	72.3	58 500	18.8	10.8	364	25.3	3.0	8 941	-1.4	447	5.0	9 225	28.2	21.3
Warren	9 185	83.1	108 600	19.4	9.9	466	21.9	3.2	13 548	2.5	836	6.2	12 170	23.5	21.3
Washington	8 406	79.9	57 600	18.8	10.3	364	24.0	4.5	10 296	3.2	936	9.1	8 721	17.9	25.6
Wayne	5 551	78.2	44 700	18.9	9.9	317	23.5	3.6	3 781	0.1	424	11.2	4 647	22.7	28.8
Webster	11 073	78.0	80 900	21.2	9.9	398	20.8	5.6	15 283	0.6	653	4.3	13 696	23.2	24.7
Worth	1 009	76.8	27 200	18.6	9.9	258	21.9	1.8	788	-3.4	35	4.4	1 078	30.0	19.1
Wright	7 081	73.1	57 000	23.4	10.5	308	23.7	3.7	6 667	-5.1	516	7.7	7 370	27.9	25.1

1. Specified owner-occupied units.　2. Median monthly owner costs is often in the minimum category—9.9 percent or less, which is indicated as 9.9 percent.　3. Specified renter-occupied units.　4. Overcrowded or lacking complete plumbing facilities.　5. Percent of civilian labor force.　6. Persons 16 years old and over.

Table B. States and Counties — Nonfarm Employment and Agriculture

STATE County	Private nonfarm establishments, employment and payroll, 2001									Agriculture, 2002			
	Number of establishments	Employment						Annual payroll		Farms			Farm operators whose principal occupation is farming (percent)
		Total	Health care and social assistance	Manufacturing	Retail trade	Finance and insurance	Professional, scientific, and technical services	Total (mil dol)	Average per employee (dollars)	Number	Percent with—		
											Less than 50 acres	500 acres and over	
	104	105	106	107	108	109	110	111	112	113	114	115	116

MISSOURI—Cont'd

STATE County	104	105	106	107	108	109	110	111	112	113	114	115	116
Jasper	3 090	54 674	7 171	11 524	8 091	1 163	1 097	1 360	24 877	1 390	32.9	9.2	53.5
Jefferson	3 494	37 310	5 122	5 498	6 692	970	2 023	891	23 874	764	33.1	5.2	48.7
Johnson	847	9 613	1 711	1 703	1 787	426	201	199	20 731	1 811	28.3	10.8	54.4
Knox	122	681	D	D	118	D	D	13	18 583	643	8.9	23.5	59.7
Laclede	832	11 606	1 080	5 072	2 018	312	137	248	21 370	1 394	22.7	11.8	53.7
Lafayette	781	6 799	841	1 058	1 631	255	134	129	18 947	1 286	27.4	14.9	64.8
Lawrence	642	6 959	1 125	1 488	1 142	165	105	155	22 247	1 852	34.5	7.3	58.5
Lewis	218	1 953	340	D	313	96	D	43	21 847	838	19.9	16.7	60.9
Lincoln	778	7 463	973	1 220	1 445	243	141	193	25 815	1 102	31.3	12.2	51.3
Linn	332	4 322	536	1 795	572	145	71	94	21 830	969	17.6	20.8	56.7
Livingston	430	5 206	923	846	1 019	249	207	110	21 162	903	19.2	15.5	57.8
McDonald	343	4 877	220	2 880	501	95	69	103	21 036	1 113	23.9	8.3	54.8
Macon	365	3 172	482	480	654	159	76	61	19 291	1 351	16.1	14.5	56.0
Madison	273	2 399	399	435	474	78	63	41	17 213	463	18.1	12.3	55.5
Maries	135	1 066	123	255	237	71	D	23	21 691	883	12.6	12.9	56.5
Marion	805	11 414	1 984	2 931	1 870	353	263	268	23 498	744	19.8	16.7	60.3
Mercer	75	434	58	D	88	41	D	9	21 062	569	12.7	20.6	59.9
Miller	574	5 645	462	1 098	1 053	163	163	129	22 895	1 111	16.7	11.2	56.8
Mississippi	283	2 871	478	352	605	114	D	52	18 099	247	15.4	56.7	81.0
Moniteau	334	2 957	342	900	515	92	D	61	20 717	1 139	19.8	10.3	56.9
Monroe	209	2 061	289	D	267	69	D	42	20 533	960	19.0	16.5	56.7
Montgomery	330	2 848	370	712	415	159	D	57	19 908	761	19.1	19.2	58.0
Morgan	475	3 323	154	720	960	108	123	57	17 048	930	18.7	9.4	66.6
New Madrid	344	6 022	666	2 485	1 143	203	50	164	27 162	364	9.1	62.4	80.5
Newton	994	16 520	4 000	4 450	1 761	445	211	386	23 371	1 752	35.1	5.1	59.6
Nodaway	513	6 899	988	1 995	1 169	226	116	150	21 674	1 396	15.1	22.3	63.3
Oregon	219	1 613	236	275	449	74	D	26	15 901	843	16.1	15.4	57.4
Osage	262	2 624	118	973	391	96	D	61	23 436	1 219	12.6	12.5	57.3
Ozark	171	1 101	D	154	362	85	25	18	16 095	820	12.1	17.1	63.7
Pemiscot	335	4 325	1 054	856	725	136	D	85	19 555	258	15.5	55.4	84.5
Perry	464	7 529	774	3 008	1 048	200	92	174	23 048	914	19.1	10.6	54.5
Pettis	1 042	17 074	2 238	5 514	2 485	442	299	377	22 091	1 278	20.3	16.2	61.2
Phelps	1 077	12 219	2 909	1 633	2 458	348	413	256	20 972	824	24.2	11.0	50.7
Pike	403	3 688	605	746	618	151	164	89	24 253	1 061	19.1	17.2	53.5
Platte	1 880	36 720	1 885	1 883	3 578	3 866	1 209	1 103	30 029	736	34.6	11.5	51.2
Polk	594	7 581	1 726	877	1 229	222	321	140	18 423	1 768	28.2	9.2	58.8
Pulaski	662	5 688	1 076	82	1 306	296	259	108	18 925	573	18.5	14.3	57.6
Putnam	96	634	123	D	124	64	D	10	16 077	723	15.9	20.9	57.7
Ralls	159	2 395	275	1 214	218	D	21	60	24 929	674	18.7	17.8	55.3
Randolph	575	7 384	1 303	1 463	1 172	610	117	168	22 718	971	23.5	11.2	56.5
Ray	393	3 913	613	636	753	153	123	81	20 668	1 231	26.3	10.6	52.8
Reynolds	148	1 512	247	375	135	36	D	34	22 572	379	15.6	14.0	56.2
Ripley	247	1 984	563	479	427	71	D	33	16 679	478	17.6	16.1	61.5
St. Charles	6 321	95 775	10 582	14 953	15 319	2 431	4 933	2 737	28 577	739	34.2	13.8	57.0
St. Clair	175	1 344	583	28	279	83	D	21	15 297	766	15.4	20.5	65.8
Ste. Genevieve	363	4 778	712	1 660	422	133	71	121	25 227	677	19.4	11.7	53.9
St. Francois	1 275	17 370	4 766	2 379	2 944	476	394	348	20 043	735	28.8	5.6	50.1
St. Louis	30 086	594 898	71 186	59 048	74 170	37 391	39 169	21 918	36 843	328	57.6	6.1	46.3
Saline	559	7 703	1 404	2 472	1 008	216	84	143	18 538	945	19.0	26.2	66.2
Schuyler	92	376	D	13	140	24	D	7	17 535	480	14.8	16.7	62.7
Scotland	141	821	175	144	169	62	17	14	16 867	654	14.4	21.4	64.5
Scott	1 110	13 407	2 655	2 459	1 853	449	285	291	21 724	514	28.8	23.0	66.9
Shannon	140	1 226	212	550	173	46	D	18	14 941	516	21.3	15.1	56.0
Shelby	184	1 390	75	378	230	69	D	29	20 976	676	13.2	27.8	62.6
Stoddard	710	8 212	1 445	2 246	1 269	239	106	156	18 985	960	29.7	20.9	62.4
Stone	611	5 254	370	198	966	165	99	114	21 769	645	25.1	6.8	56.1
Sullivan	124	2 462	208	D	169	34	D	55	22 340	850	12.8	26.5	55.6
Taney	1 715	19 257	1 689	594	3 587	389	699	447	23 221	512	18.9	12.7	57.4
Texas	484	5 077	846	1 052	855	210	76	107	21 163	1 600	18.6	13.4	61.1
Vernon	516	6 242	1 260	1 364	913	409	114	126	20 181	1 399	23.8	14.9	55.7
Warren	542	6 067	490	1 952	1 204	142	68	133	21 855	670	33.7	10.1	51.6
Washington	312	2 947	552	740	510	102	D	53	17 941	576	19.6	8.5	55.7
Wayne	245	1 867	322	562	419	87	77	33	17 419	445	13.3	11.9	58.7
Webster	644	5 409	562	1 221	1 079	264	125	104	19 241	1 962	33.6	6.4	57.3
Worth	55	227	D	D	D	16	D	3	14 216	368	12.8	22.6	57.6
Wright	387	3 847	504	851	937	181	63	77	20 072	1 348	18.9	11.9	60.9

STATE County	\multicolumn{5}{c}{Land in farms}					Value of land and buildings (dollars)			\multicolumn{5}{c}{Value of products sold}					Percent of farms with sales of —		Government payments	
	Acreage (1,000)	Percent change, 1997–2002	\multicolumn{3}{c}{Acres}			Average per farm	Average per acre	Value of machinery and equipment average per farm (dollars)	Total (mil dol)	Average per farm (dollars)	\multicolumn{2}{c}{Percent from —}		$10,000 or more	$100,000 or more	Total ($1,000)	Percent of farms
			Average size of farm	Total irrigated (1,000)	Total cropland (1,000)							Crops	Live-stock and poultry products				
	117	118	119	120	121	122	123	124	125	126	127	128	129	130	131	132
MISSOURI—Cont'd																
Jasper	289	6.6	208	6	168	278 912	1 494	35 287	66	47 716	33.5	66.5	35.3	6.5	1 747	32.7
Jefferson	125	14.7	163	1	62	449 722	2 635	28 577	11	13 857	41.6	58.4	20.0	2.4	363	13.9
Johnson	413	3.3	228	0	263	418 934	1 693	47 456	56	30 864	34.5	65.5	37.8	4.9	3 181	41.0
Knox	249	-11.4	387	D	170	701 312	1 391	55 440	27	42 012	56.8	43.2	49.3	12.0	4 115	74.5
Laclede	319	0.6	229	0	152	318 596	1 377	29 450	31	22 518	8.2	91.8	34.1	6.0	1 164	24.0
Lafayette	363	4.0	282	3	285	505 944	1 831	80 942	76	59 010	64.5	35.5	49.7	12.6	3 818	47.6
Lawrence	316	-6.5	171	2	195	288 775	1 777	45 768	110	59 338	10.5	89.5	39.9	6.8	2 260	30.0
Lewis	284	5.6	339	2	199	390 651	1 106	81 928	49	58 647	47.1	52.9	43.3	11.7	3 950	60.0
Lincoln	252	-3.8	228	2	178	553 291	2 172	70 422	49	44 582	50.7	49.3	39.4	8.6	2 758	45.7
Linn	340	-1.7	351	1	240	378 057	1 005	77 134	38	39 160	40.2	59.8	46.6	10.2	4 846	68.5
Livingston	300	9.9	332	1	220	431 680	1 285	71 830	39	43 004	68.6	31.4	41.0	8.3	4 605	64.1
McDonald	216	-6.9	194	D	85	366 746	2 029	31 522	120	107 717	1.1	98.9	35.0	12.1	564	21.8
Macon	406	6.6	301	0	246	344 776	1 072	41 879	41	30 454	46.4	53.6	38.7	7.3	4 208	59.1
Madison	123	11.8	265	0	47	225 433	973	28 490	9	19 369	7.2	92.8	30.7	2.8	231	20.1
Maries	234	2.2	265	0	106	283 706	1 032	37 234	20	22 275	11.9	88.1	44.8	3.3	580	27.9
Marion	230	4.1	309	4	161	431 602	1 226	62 400	40	53 717	57.9	42.1	47.0	12.1	2 574	59.5
Mercer	212	-7.8	373	D	134	1 980 042	5 358	54 294	83	146 538	D	D	45.2	7.9	3 028	68.5
Miller	268	5.1	241	2	114	396 158	1 479	29 583	72	64 756	3.9	96.1	39.2	8.7	416	23.7
Mississippi	272	3.0	1 100	75	265	2 051 905	1 855	312 739	66	267 244	97.3	2.7	82.6	56.7	2 878	66.0
Moniteau	258	15.7	227	0	161	338 641	1 380	37 200	84	74 010	13.4	86.6	48.8	9.0	1 584	41.1
Monroe	316	-3.7	329	1	224	413 601	1 183	57 442	49	51 415	51.0	49.0	44.6	11.7	4 308	64.0
Montgomery	259	4.4	340	4	178	513 507	1 639	69 905	36	47 466	68.8	31.2	46.9	12.4	2 713	57.6
Morgan	222	9.9	239	0	120	352 949	1 553	44 054	81	87 626	7.5	92.5	51.7	15.4	762	24.1
New Madrid	395	2.3	1 085	199	390	1 910 391	1 837	232 073	99	270 765	98.9	1.1	87.9	58.8	7 281	69.2
Newton	269	5.1	153	3	150	277 802	1 760	31 832	138	78 565	4.9	95.1	34.2	8.4	1 062	23.7
Nodaway	506	2.8	362	D	390	453 013	1 195	55 990	69	49 688	60.7	39.3	56.7	13.6	6 028	63.0
Oregon	266	7.3	316	0	92	304 609	1 004	23 030	23	27 857	8.0	92.0	40.6	5.2	681	27.4
Osage	315	3.3	258	2	133	348 967	1 400	61 465	53	43 308	9.1	90.9	44.7	8.5	1 189	34.5
Ozark	282	11.5	343	0	82	450 766	1 366	21 628	26	31 978	4.0	96.0	40.4	7.3	807	25.4
Pemiscot	296	0.0	1 149	91	288	1 963 953	1 772	226 288	70	269 816	99.6	0.4	81.4	52.3	4 907	51.9
Perry	222	10.4	243	1	137	320 095	1 487	55 067	31	33 573	47.4	52.6	43.1	8.5	1 871	49.3
Pettis	402	9.8	315	2	278	406 697	1 388	58 925	102	79 714	23.9	76.1	50.9	12.0	3 827	48.6
Phelps	201	2.6	244	0	73	364 484	1 519	22 578	10	12 535	13.3	86.7	28.3	2.1	337	22.1
Pike	344	8.5	325	2	233	542 207	1 618	54 749	55	51 759	51.2	48.8	47.0	12.1	3 392	52.4
Platte	185	2.8	251	1	139	579 673	2 306	43 141	28	37 416	77.5	22.5	37.5	8.7	1 646	38.0
Polk	369	6.0	209	0	205	287 746	1 409	30 529	60	33 917	7.4	92.6	41.1	6.8	1 277	25.0
Pulaski	142	1.4	247	0	63	288 816	1 310	43 684	11	19 275	12.3	87.7	32.1	3.1	175	21.5
Putnam	293	12.3	406	D	142	342 730	866	42 027	57	78 530	12.0	88.0	49.5	8.7	2 697	46.7
Ralls	253	9.1	376	1	184	535 869	1 437	86 052	36	52 787	65.8	34.2	41.8	12.2	3 161	66.5
Randolph	246	7.0	253	0	148	307 652	1 174	46 025	33	33 775	34.0	66.0	34.8	4.8	2 790	50.2
Ray	292	6.6	237	3	210	357 488	1 490	58 952	35	28 499	60.6	39.4	33.1	6.4	2 766	45.3
Reynolds	118	4.4	311	0	37	318 869	1 048	22 980	4	10 740	12.1	87.9	26.9	1.1	87	22.2
Ripley	140	-7.9	293	7	64	314 585	1 016	43 994	10	20 187	47.7	52.3	34.7	4.4	507	29.7
St. Charles	185	-1.1	250	2	145	977 340	3 991	66 429	34	45 518	80.0	20.0	45.2	10.8	2 171	42.1
St. Clair	268	1.9	350	0	152	310 185	1 018	39 377	23	29 790	40.5	59.5	44.6	7.2	1 301	39.4
Ste. Genevieve	184	9.5	272	0	103	367 279	1 446	37 723	18	26 312	44.5	55.5	37.2	5.5	882	39.0
St. Francois	129	14.2	175	0	64	290 069	2 033	37 471	15	20 792	46.4	53.6	26.3	1.9	259	17.8
St. Louis	39	-13.3	120	1	29	509 557	3 627	36 846	21	64 896	92.5	7.5	29.6	10.1	457	19.5
Saline	413	-4.0	437	D	326	576 841	1 368	90 369	92	97 019	63.9	36.1	61.3	22.1	4 517	61.1
Schuyler	146	-8.8	305	D	90	252 359	811	35 476	12	25 917	29.6	70.4	45.6	6.3	1 387	61.3
Scotland	234	4.0	358	D	164	467 439	1 122	64 210	32	48 222	52.4	47.6	53.4	13.9	3 731	65.1
Scott	224	-7.1	435	63	203	734 247	1 745	100 195	71	138 321	62.3	37.7	51.8	25.1	2 979	49.8
Shannon	135	1.5	262	0	57	231 033	1 052	32 885	6	11 606	7.1	92.9	33.1	1.0	176	21.9
Shelby	299	9.9	442	1	230	507 508	1 187	79 930	59	87 281	50.1	49.9	58.0	19.2	3 169	63.2
Stoddard	415	-7.6	432	188	375	864 499	2 048	99 413	127	132 758	69.6	30.4	45.0	22.5	8 822	58.9
Stone	114	-16.2	176	0	46	328 926	1 927	26 692	12	19 193	8.6	91.4	31.2	5.7	504	26.0
Sullivan	365	12.0	429	0	211	428 338	814	51 449	74	86 863	D	D	48.5	9.3	4 331	63.6
Taney	154	-2.5	301	0	46	464 433	1 728	28 257	10	19 887	6.0	94.0	29.1	2.5	239	23.2
Texas	472	9.8	295	0	178	298 447	1 027	33 511	40	24 981	10.2	89.8	37.2	6.1	1 345	23.0
Vernon	426	9.5	305	4	274	303 758	1 105	49 899	80	57 415	27.9	72.1	41.9	7.5	3 909	48.1
Warren	142	6.8	211	1	90	479 699	2 312	53 598	19	28 489	62.8	37.2	30.7	8.5	1 516	40.7
Washington	133	4.7	230	D	55	288 974	1 477	26 243	8	13 268	14.9	85.1	28.1	2.3	110	15.1
Wayne	114	16.3	256	D	37	220 960	1 034	40 866	5	10 460	20.0	80.0	24.5	1.8	349	28.3
Webster	320	7.7	163	0	168	291 800	1 722	33 015	62	31 471	5.4	94.6	37.4	6.7	1 340	18.5
Worth	140	-6.7	381	D	93	329 342	916	49 839	11	29 730	47.5	52.5	43.5	7.1	2 157	73.6
Wright	318	1.9	236	0	150	356 682	1 259	34 494	44	32 716	6.1	93.9	43.0	10.6	1 747	27.4

Table B. States and Counties — Residential Construction, Wholesale Trade, Retail Trade, and Real Estate

STATE County	Value of residential construction authorized by building permits, 2003		Wholesale trade, 1997				Retail trade,[1] 1997				Real estate and rental and leasing, 1997			
	New construction ($1,000)	Number of housing units	Number of establishments	Number of employees	Sales (mil dol)	Annual payroll (mil dol)	Number of establishments	Number of employees	Sales (mil dol)	Annual payroll (mil dol)	Number of establishments	Number of employees	Receipts (mil dol)	Annual payroll (mil dol)
	133	134	135	136	137	138	139	140	141	142	143	144	145	146
MISSOURI—Cont'd														
Jasper	49 018	533	198	2 164	897.0	54.3	597	7 658	1 153.1	108.8	115	455	39.7	7.5
Jefferson	201 215	1 774	158	1 115	352.6	35.7	549	6 265	1 110.0	99.9	134	460	42.5	8.4
Johnson	19 100	246	37	373	93.8	8.0	154	1 551	243.8	22.1	29	79	6.8	1.1
Knox	180	2	7	D	D	D	31	115	20.4	1.3	1	D	D	D
Laclede	10 655	138	44	337	126.4	7.3	191	1 964	318.9	28.1	35	89	7.0	1.3
Lafayette	18 565	138	48	362	220.3	9.1	185	1 516	201.4	19.3	16	49	7.8	0.5
Lawrence	4 179	59	26	108	205.6	2.2	120	1 202	270.8	21.4	17	36	4.6	0.3
Lewis	2 383	15	13	D	D	D	49	261	47.2	4.0	16	15	1.2	0.1
Lincoln	17 613	171	47	254	144.2	6.5	110	1 249	234.1	18.9	26	60	7.8	0.9
Linn	902	10	23	123	34.0	2.8	71	531	80.4	7.0	8	19	0.6	0.1
Livingston	4 554	42	36	591	196.3	12.6	83	987	150.4	14.8	12	32	5.2	0.6
McDonald	530	11	16	D	D	D	79	478	82.6	6.4	11	22	1.6	0.3
Macon	953	7	23	227	82.9	3.7	73	642	85.6	7.7	8	21	1.2	0.1
Madison	1 218	37	11	64	19.0	0.6	53	475	62.9	7.0	4	13	0.9	0.1
Maries	NA	NA	8	142	87.0	0.7	30	199	31.5	2.3	3	7	0.5	0.2
Marion	6 032	60	37	437	138.6	8.4	178	1 889	298.6	25.4	26	85	4.8	1.0
Mercer	0	0	4	33	11.8	0.6	16	78	17.5	1.1	NA	NA	NA	NA
Miller	5 139	89	22	182	62.8	2.9	130	1 004	208.1	17.8	33	73	8.0	1.4
Mississippi	1 013	14	22	236	313.2	6.2	67	588	94.7	7.6	6	10	0.7	0.1
Moniteau	200	1	19	D	D	D	59	447	108.9	7.2	10	19	0.8	0.1
Monroe	6 392	52	13	40	17.0	0.9	42	267	47.1	3.8	3	4	0.6	0.1
Montgomery	1 652	27	21	180	93.7	4.0	67	438	74.4	6.3	5	12	0.6	0.1
Morgan	NA	NA	23	129	31.1	2.0	112	921	146.0	12.8	20	D	D	D
New Madrid	1 026	11	31	482	310.5	11.2	95	741	145.0	10.4	11	53	1.6	0.4
Newton	5 807	66	52	411	195.1	10.0	193	1 644	291.2	24.8	36	130	10.6	1.8
Nodaway	4 616	40	29	266	240.0	5.0	100	1 029	128.1	12.5	20	51	3.3	0.4
Oregon	1 655	5	14	113	29.0	2.0	46	378	57.1	4.9	5	13	0.7	0.1
Osage	NA	NA	15	34	24.4	0.9	52	387	91.9	7.1	4	D	D	D
Ozark	252	4	8	D	D	D	37	249	39.6	3.2	4	16	0.7	0.1
Pemiscot	929	15	25	239	213.8	5.7	91	667	129.8	10.4	9	D	D	D
Perry	5 224	60	17	122	39.1	3.9	83	880	170.2	14.7	14	36	1.7	0.4
Pettis	3 413	54	67	765	211.6	18.3	204	2 230	355.7	33.5	40	142	12.0	2.4
Phelps	17 413	224	44	428	99.0	9.6	209	2 352	375.8	33.7	27	88	6.3	1.2
Pike	679	13	28	D	D	D	95	636	86.1	9.0	7	19	0.8	0.1
Platte	70 908	368	119	1 943	3 334.6	92.4	204	2 471	581.5	40.4	74	731	99.4	13.0
Polk	6 105	86	26	788	120.2	7.0	110	919	167.2	14.6	16	52	3.2	0.5
Pulaski	2 419	24	15	D	D	D	143	1 041	178.8	15.6	29	88	7.6	1.2
Putnam	145	1	10	D	D	D	18	116	17.7	1.4	5	D	D	D
Ralls	25	1	12	86	61.3	2.6	31	172	23.2	2.3	3	D	D	D
Randolph	3 139	33	26	188	76.9	4.7	110	1 384	211.7	19.1	16	98	13.9	1.4
Ray	16 085	151	19	D	D	D	72	608	109.9	8.9	13	34	1.9	0.3
Reynolds	NA	NA	7	59	8.3	0.7	27	123	19.1	1.5	2	D	D	D
Ripley	408	8	7	32	11.0	0.5	54	371	68.4	5.1	3	D	D	D
St. Charles	542 473	4 066	345	2 729	1 831.7	91.9	934	13 688	2 343.7	220.7	189	1 095	304.6	24.6
St. Clair	NA	NA	8	38	34.4	0.5	48	314	42.5	3.5	3	4	0.3	0.0
Ste. Genevieve	320	3	24	137	36.0	3.2	64	469	82.5	6.7	5	D	D	D
St. Francois	36 262	365	51	556	145.1	14.4	260	2 792	440.1	39.9	39	121	9.1	1.6
St. Louis	419 411	2 257	2 639	38 765	39 755.5	1 890.0	4 287	72 497	12 385.5	1 347.8	1 319	10 396	1 405.8	275.6
Saline	4 036	52	41	459	226.2	12.0	122	1 025	140.9	12.9	16	71	2.7	0.5
Schuyler	1 844	15	3	D	D	D	22	138	22.6	1.6	1	D	D	D
Scotland	175	2	9	56	25.3	0.7	33	170	24.2	2.1	3	D	D	D
Scott	14 442	101	80	1 142	629.5	30.8	243	2 248	355.1	34.3	33	81	5.7	1.0
Shannon	15	10	10	61	22.3	1.5	29	128	19.1	1.5	10	11	0.9	0.2
Shelby	492	4	20	98	32.3	1.9	45	233	28.0	2.8	4	D	D	D
Stoddard	4 125	58	52	355	177.2	8.1	152	1 292	245.1	18.7	24	41	3.9	0.6
Stone	2 474	20	17	51	28.0	1.2	131	828	134.0	13.1	32	61	6.4	0.9
Sullivan	100	1	2	D	D	D	31	191	34.4	2.7	4	5	0.2	0.0
Taney	58 693	554	40	302	73.0	6.9	391	2 976	442.6	47.3	78	831	66.0	18.1
Texas	1 178	16	26	184	66.7	3.0	105	916	136.7	11.9	11	50	3.5	0.9
Vernon	1 604	17	29	164	56.3	3.3	89	1 003	143.7	14.5	13	37	4.2	0.8
Warren	48 631	394	26	145	53.7	4.3	114	1 027	188.8	15.3	17	45	7.1	0.8
Washington	100	1	15	65	11.3	1.0	67	633	101.7	11.6	8	31	1.0	0.3
Wayne	NA	NA	5	18	3.6	0.2	53	457	57.5	5.2	4	7	0.4	0.1
Webster	20 075	212	23	120	25.8	2.2	114	876	146.3	11.9	19	46	2.5	0.6
Worth	0	0	7	D	D	D	14	58	6.1	0.6	3	D	D	D
Wright	1 072	13	20	147	94.8	2.4	94	795	130.4	10.7	14	39	2.3	0.4

1. Establishments with payroll.

Items 133—146

Table B. States and Counties — Professional Services, Manufacturing, and Accommodation and Foodservices

STATE County	Professional, scientific, and technical services,[1] 1997				Manufacturing, 1997				Accommodation and foodservices, 1997			
	Number of establishments	Number of employees	Receipts (mil dol)	Annual payroll (mil dol)	Number of establishments	Number of employees	Receipts (mil dol)	Annual payroll (mil dol)	Number of establishments	Number of employees	Sales (mil dol)	Annual payroll (mil dol)
	147	148	149	150	151	152	153	154	155	156	157	158
MISSOURI—Cont'd												
Jasper	145	948	53.9	23.0	198	11 904	2 154.6	289.8	222	4 100	109.5	31.7
Jefferson	152	570	40.9	16.0	182	5 304	1 199.3	168.2	214	3 981	113.8	31.8
Johnson	42	108	15.2	2.5	31	1 856	183.2	46.7	83	1 144	31.5	8.2
Knox	6	15	0.7	0.2	NA	NA	NA	NA	4	24	0.7	0.2
Laclede	31	101	6.0	2.2	57	5 177	809.7	130.4	62	827	27.9	6.9
Lafayette	36	117	11.5	2.4	42	1 166	130.4	22.9	70	D	D	D
Lawrence	26	63	3.6	1.3	54	1 614	259.0	34.8	54	690	17.6	4.8
Lewis	6	D	D	D	NA	NA	NA	NA	18	66	2.1	0.4
Lincoln	27	296	4.2	1.4	43	1 078	176.8	29.0	48	700	19.4	5.1
Linn	11	52	2.2	1.0	24	1 739	137.8	45.0	26	241	6.6	1.7
Livingston	22	123	8.2	2.6	28	903	117.1	23.6	28	405	11.7	3.1
McDonald	11	29	3.2	0.7	34	3 052	469.8	52.5	34	218	7.2	2.0
Macon	16	76	3.6	1.4	15	D	D	D	26	355	9.8	3.0
Madison	8	77	2.8	0.8	16	553	28.7	8.3	23	278	5.7	1.6
Maries	5	D	D	D	NA	NA	NA	NA	9	D	D	D
Marion	44	226	15.0	5.5	46	3 179	1 707.1	87.5	69	1 053	28.9	8.2
Mercer	2	D	D	D	NA	NA	NA	NA	8	49	0.8	0.3
Miller	36	180	16.7	3.7	29	1 500	128.5	31.8	63	1 090	40.0	12.5
Mississippi	9	21	1.3	0.2	14	571	66.4	10.7	16	D	D	D
Moniteau	14	35	1.9	0.5	22	1 095	173.8	19.5	21	210	5.5	1.4
Monroe	7	14	0.8	0.1	7	1 047	74.8	27.9	22	160	3.4	0.9
Montgomery	9	16	0.7	0.1	32	811	82.1	16.6	17	240	4.7	1.2
Morgan	20	80	3.6	1.3	29	649	115.0	12.0	51	330	11.4	3.2
New Madrid	17	39	2.5	1.3	17	2 504	529.8	83.4	26	298	7.9	2.2
Newton	37	144	6.8	2.3	63	4 315	692.9	109.8	87	1 664	50.0	14.3
Nodaway	22	92	5.6	1.6	23	1 677	647.2	48.2	41	764	18.4	4.7
Oregon	9	17	0.7	0.2	NA	NA	NA	NA	18	139	4.2	1.1
Osage	7	11	0.6	0.2	24	914	169.8	20.3	21	D	D	D
Ozark	5	17	0.6	0.2	NA	NA	NA	NA	14	63	2.3	0.5
Pemiscot	13	28	1.9	0.5	12	893	131.1	19.8	36	404	10.6	3.0
Perry	14	75	4.1	1.8	31	2 855	609.3	61.9	39	469	12.5	3.5
Pettis	50	215	13.2	4.9	69	5 324	958.9	130.2	76	1 313	36.2	10.8
Phelps	64	282	18.0	7.0	55	1 132	218.2	29.6	103	1 346	45.1	12.1
Pike	16	87	6.0	2.2	27	771	277.4	25.7	25	304	8.7	2.3
Platte	138	830	105.3	34.1	47	1 599	344.7	52.4	157	3 218	139.2	38.3
Polk	27	93	4.2	1.6	34	859	81.1	13.9	40	462	12.0	3.3
Pulaski	27	144	9.8	3.0	18	682	36.4	9.4	77	914	29.5	10.7
Putnam	3	20	0.8	0.3	NA	NA	NA	NA	5	D	D	D
Ralls	3	17	1.3	0.4	10	913	253.9	21.6	17	239	6.1	2.1
Randolph	17	83	5.9	1.3	37	1 381	182.6	30.5	45	656	16.1	4.2
Ray	31	104	14.4	2.4	21	654	63.9	16.5	26	244	7.1	1.8
Reynolds	6	D	D	D	33	634	52.7	10.9	14	70	3.0	1.0
Ripley	5	14	0.6	0.2	42	629	42.8	10.0	16	156	4.1	1.0
St. Charles	446	2 971	208.6	71.0	279	12 160	4 432.9	431.9	418	8 656	245.2	71.3
St. Clair	6	13	0.8	0.2	NA	NA	NA	NA	14	D	D	D
Ste. Genevieve	17	73	3.9	1.2	32	1 752	208.2	47.8	32	399	9.5	2.6
St. Francois	73	330	16.5	5.7	66	3 797	394.6	80.3	100	1 602	45.1	13.1
St. Louis	3 296	35 334	4 078.7	1 437.2	1 272	78 218	25 347.9	3 359.8	2 030	46 507	1 579.7	465.7
Saline	23	56	3.1	0.8	24	2 530	647.5	55.4	50	603	15.3	4.0
Schuyler	1	D	D	D	NA	NA	NA	NA	8	51	0.8	0.2
Scotland	5	D	D	D	NA	NA	NA	NA	10	66	2.3	0.5
Scott	59	209	16.2	5.6	77	3 008	532.6	66.1	78	1 102	35.1	9.8
Shannon	3	D	D	D	22	710	40.9	8.1	16	44	2.1	0.5
Shelby	10	41	3.8	1.0	5	D	D	D	11	94	1.5	0.4
Stoddard	26	103	5.5	2.1	40	2 372	264.0	42.4	47	504	14.6	4.1
Stone	23	60	3.6	0.8	NA	NA	NA	NA	86	530	19.2	5.8
Sullivan	4	13	1.1	0.8	5	D	D	D	7	D	D	D
Taney	80	295	18.9	6.5	59	798	87.8	15.8	328	4 947	245.4	68.6
Texas	16	39	2.4	0.8	53	1 399	169.6	26.2	32	212	4.7	1.3
Vernon	25	89	4.9	1.6	21	1 561	425.8	44.0	41	520	13.8	3.6
Warren	19	49	2.8	0.8	37	2 042	242.7	50.1	34	503	14.3	4.1
Washington	13	30	1.0	0.4	NA	NA	NA	NA	17	D	D	D
Wayne	9	22	1.6	0.3	28	510	44.0	8.3	20	144	3.5	0.9
Webster	24	75	3.3	1.2	44	D	D	D	38	420	11.7	3.1
Worth	2	D	D	D	NA	NA	NA	NA	6	13	0.4	0.1
Wright	13	31	1.2	0.3	18	730	102.0	14.2	40	303	8.3	2.0

1. Firms subject to federal tax.

Table B. States and Counties — Health Care and Social Assistance, Other Services, and Federal Funds

STATE County	Health care and social assistance,[1] 1997				Other services,[1] 1997				Federal funds and grants, 2002–2003 Expenditures (mil dol)			
									Total	Direct payments for individuals[2]		
	Number of establishments	Number of employees	Receipts (mil dol)	Annual payroll (mil dol)	Number of establishments	Number of employees	Receipts (mil dol)	Annual payroll (mil dol)		Social Security and government retirement	Medicare	Food stamps and Supplemental Security Income
	159	160	161	162	163	164	165	166	167	168	169	170
MISSOURI—Cont'd												
Jasper	235	2 360	144.4	65.4	227	1 189	69.2	18.9	755.8	262.8	116.0	25.9
Jefferson	216	2 633	108.7	48.1	291	1 426	83.0	24.4	672.7	355.5	133.8	24.4
Johnson	59	650	26.9	11.0	55	212	10.9	2.8	410.3	95.5	28.7	5.9
Knox	7	53	1.6	0.8	11	51	11.7	0.7	36.8	10.9	8.3	0.7
Laclede	41	492	26.2	10.3	48	133	8.4	2.0	173.1	88.0	27.6	7.4
Lafayette	45	489	18.8	8.6	48	146	7.6	2.0	167.0	81.4	40.1	4.6
Lawrence	36	211	12.7	4.3	44	106	6.4	1.6	165.2	80.3	32.2	5.6
Lewis	8	120	3.3	1.8	19	52	3.7	0.8	62.0	23.8	11.6	1.6
Lincoln	39	376	12.6	4.6	53	155	9.6	2.5	146.4	73.8	30.0	5.3
Linn	24	476	13.8	5.9	31	86	6.0	1.1	97.8	41.1	23.9	2.2
Livingston	34	537	19.3	7.4	32	97	6.5	1.6	93.9	36.6	19.4	2.8
McDonald	15	148	6.1	2.8	18	64	1.6	0.6	100.4	40.7	16.3	5.6
Macon	20	226	7.2	3.0	29	73	4.5	1.0	114.8	43.5	23.6	2.7
Madison	16	150	4.5	1.5	11	24	2.3	0.4	71.6	33.7	15.0	3.6
Maries	9	145	5.1	1.9	10	28	1.8	0.4	41.3	19.5	9.6	1.4
Marion	61	798	39.7	19.7	43	216	15.0	3.8	170.8	68.7	35.6	7.4
Mercer	6	85	2.6	1.3	5	9	0.9	0.2	26.2	9.6	5.2	0.7
Miller	26	261	9.4	5.0	43	141	8.0	2.2	138.4	64.1	29.0	3.9
Mississippi	13	255	7.5	3.1	20	56	3.2	0.8	117.3	33.1	16.2	7.2
Moniteau	19	158	7.3	2.6	18	63	2.7	0.8	64.0	30.5	15.3	1.3
Monroe	14	78	2.8	1.2	12	25	1.7	0.4	69.2	25.1	13.1	1.1
Montgomery	19	268	8.9	4.1	25	245	8.4	3.2	79.4	31.1	15.9	2.0
Morgan	13	61	2.7	1.4	33	87	4.9	0.9	114.1	64.1	24.2	4.4
New Madrid	14	479	14.5	6.5	21	86	6.0	1.0	174.2	41.5	20.6	8.9
Newton	63	1 108	60.4	21.3	72	222	10.3	2.5	195.9	93.6	37.3	6.5
Nodaway	29	391	13.5	5.6	43	136	8.3	1.9	107.5	40.3	18.4	2.1
Oregon	8	203	7.2	3.2	14	28	2.1	0.5	77.1	31.4	11.7	3.7
Osage	10	229	6.6	2.4	15	33	2.7	0.4	53.7	24.5	13.8	0.9
Ozark	4	93	3.1	1.4	11	19	1.1	0.2	67.7	30.4	10.6	2.8
Pemiscot	26	361	11.3	4.5	21	102	5.8	1.4	222.8	43.0	27.6	14.0
Perry	29	255	8.8	3.2	31	106	10.2	2.1	79.5	38.2	18.0	1.9
Pettis	89	998	43.5	19.4	77	821	36.8	13.8	216.0	98.7	42.5	8.1
Phelps	88	1 529	56.6	27.3	66	306	16.7	4.4	304.1	112.8	37.5	9.0
Pike	24	273	9.1	4.0	23	68	6.9	1.3	110.8	40.7	20.9	3.3
Platte	101	1 309	60.2	28.5	106	604	59.2	11.3	275.0	63.7	39.0	57.6
Polk	32	626	15.1	6.8	41	111	7.1	1.2	149.3	70.5	28.3	4.4
Pulaski	26	300	9.1	3.4	54	204	11.1	2.9	811.1	113.4	23.7	7.2
Putnam	9	31	1.3	0.4	8	17	1.0	0.2	39.5	14.2	8.6	1.1
Ralls	8	260	8.2	3.7	9	34	1.8	0.4	48.5	18.0	8.5	1.0
Randolph	44	864	45.9	18.2	48	189	10.3	2.6	144.5	59.2	33.7	5.8
Ray	21	164	5.7	2.9	42	113	6.3	1.7	121.3	45.6	22.5	2.5
Reynolds	10	194	5.7	2.5	3	7	0.6	0.1	47.7	18.4	8.5	2.3
Ripley	15	251	9.3	3.9	13	23	1.7	0.4	109.5	39.8	16.4	6.6
St. Charles	417	5 042	344.0	161.4	425	2 506	145.7	48.2	1 162.4	533.5	156.0	18.0
St. Clair	8	213	5.9	2.8	5	11	1.8	0.2	65.8	29.8	12.5	2.2
Ste. Genevieve	26	189	7.0	2.9	21	75	4.5	1.2	74.2	40.4	15.8	2.1
St. Francois	123	1 649	68.7	33.9	83	271	15.1	3.9	323.9	148.2	67.3	16.7
St. Louis	2 719	29 766	2 077.0	972.8	1 877	12 884	819.2	270.5	5 423.7	2 390.4	1 119.9	125.1
Saline	44	499	18.7	7.7	43	141	9.0	2.3	143.8	56.3	30.7	4.2
Schuyler	6	22	1.0	0.5	6	11	0.8	0.1	35.6	13.4	7.0	2.1
Scotland	3	21	0.5	0.2	15	32	2.4	0.4	35.7	11.0	7.6	0.8
Scott	87	1 452	56.1	23.1	57	262	19.8	5.0	243.8	99.5	41.0	13.7
Shannon	4	9	0.5	0.3	7	13	1.1	0.2	54.4	19.3	7.7	3.3
Shelby	7	44	2.4	1.6	15	52	2.4	0.7	52.5	18.9	10.5	1.5
Stoddard	47	977	33.1	15.6	40	169	10.3	3.2	220.0	80.3	35.3	8.4
Stone	19	195	10.8	3.5	37	117	7.1	2.0	140.1	87.1	26.3	4.0
Sullivan	9	177	6.1	2.7	11	24	1.9	0.5	54.0	16.7	11.4	1.3
Taney	64	537	31.1	11.8	66	267	14.0	4.4	213.8	111.6	40.6	5.2
Texas	17	295	8.3	3.7	32	77	5.9	0.9	146.2	69.6	21.7	6.7
Vernon	48	639	24.7	9.7	27	77	4.3	1.1	114.2	48.7	21.9	4.9
Warren	27	210	7.2	2.6	29	81	5.4	2.1	102.6	55.1	22.7	3.8
Washington	18	83	4.8	2.0	17	37	2.0	0.5	114.8	44.7	18.9	9.5
Wayne	10	244	7.5	2.6	9	26	2.1	0.5	109.5	48.3	19.2	5.8
Webster	22	150	4.4	2.0	36	112	6.8	1.6	148.7	73.4	25.5	5.3
Worth	6	27	1.0	0.3	4	10	0.7	0.1	18.6	6.8	2.7	0.4
Wright	23	351	13.7	6.1	29	72	5.4	1.1	129.0	51.4	22.3	6.3

1. Firms subject to federal tax.   2. State totals may include programs not allocated by county.

Table B. States and Counties — Federal Funds and Local Government Finances

	Federal funds and grants, 2002–2003 (cont'd)							Local government finances, 2002				
	Expenditures (mil dol) (cont'd)							General revenue				
		Procurement contract awards		Grants[1]						Taxes		
											Per capita[2] (dollars)	
STATE County	Salaries and wages	Defense	Other	Medicaid and other health-related	Nutrition and family welfare	Education	Other	Total (mil dol)	Intergovern-mental (mil dol)	Total (mil dol)	Total	Property
	171	172	173	174	175	176	177	178	179	180	181	182
MISSOURI—Cont'd												
Jasper	24.2	9.9	176.3	82.5	14.9	7.2	22.8	232.9	87.3	97.2	908	512
Jefferson	21.2	13.8	5.1	47.3	11.8	8.3	45.7	351.8	152.5	144.7	709	489
Johnson	169.2	62.0	2.7	13.5	3.1	8.1	7.8	115.4	41.8	31.1	625	399
Knox	2.1	0.1	0.5	4.4	0.4	0.4	1.1	10.2	3.9	3.1	713	560
Laclede	5.5	0.2	1.1	33.4	3.0	1.9	1.7	55.7	26.4	20.6	629	368
Lafayette	8.0	2.0	1.3	13.5	1.7	2.7	4.6	59.1	30.5	19.7	596	434
Lawrence	9.6	0.0	1.2	23.9	2.8	2.6	2.9	65.3	30.9	16.1	445	333
Lewis	3.1	0.0	1.3	8.5	1.0	0.8	2.1	20.4	8.6	5.8	554	393
Lincoln	6.3	0.1	1.6	17.0	1.7	0.8	5.9	86.6	31.0	27.1	642	407
Linn	3.9	0.1	1.0	13.4	1.4	1.1	3.1	29.9	17.4	8.1	597	467
Livingston	6.0	0.0	1.7	16.1	1.3	0.9	1.6	36.5	15.3	11.3	788	484
McDonald	5.5	0.0	0.7	22.3	2.0	1.5	4.9	29.1	19.3	6.6	305	245
Macon	5.4	0.1	0.9	12.7	1.2	1.1	16.9	46.6	14.0	10.0	642	420
Madison	1.3	0.3	0.5	13.7	1.6	0.8	0.6	27.2	10.1	4.9	412	342
Maries	0.9	0.0	0.2	7.4	0.6	0.6	0.7	11.9	5.7	5.0	580	405
Marion	3.8	2.2	0.6	30.7	6.7	1.8	4.8	102.6	50.3	34.5	1 230	833
Mercer	1.1	0.0	0.2	4.4	0.4	0.2	0.4	9.3	4.5	3.2	867	767
Miller	3.3	0.1	0.8	17.0	2.0	1.5	15.3	49.7	21.3	21.3	882	646
Mississippi	2.2	0.6	0.5	41.4	4.6	1.9	2.2	28.0	15.3	8.2	590	402
Moniteau	2.8	0.0	0.6	8.5	0.8	1.0	0.9	21.2	10.2	7.2	480	395
Monroe	3.4	3.5	0.6	9.8	0.7	0.8	2.7	24.3	10.3	7.1	770	563
Montgomery	2.9	0.2	8.1	11.0	1.0	1.1	1.8	18.4	9.6	6.7	553	422
Morgan	2.6	0.0	0.7	12.6	1.4	1.1	1.7	24.0	10.8	10.3	526	385
New Madrid	4.0	4.9	0.9	57.3	12.7	2.2	4.4	39.8	19.3	14.9	779	621
Newton	10.9	0.5	3.3	25.9	4.1	6.4	2.8	90.4	45.6	27.1	511	362
Nodaway	6.3	0.1	1.3	11.9	2.9	3.6	5.8	43.4	18.2	18.3	847	554
Oregon	1.9	2.1	0.5	21.9	1.7	1.0	0.5	16.8	10.8	4.5	436	292
Osage	2.2	0.0	0.5	8.5	0.3	0.6	0.2	15.9	8.6	5.6	427	335
Ozark	1.6	0.1	0.5	17.7	1.3	1.2	0.8	18.9	12.4	4.9	526	414
Pemiscot	3.5	2.9	0.8	82.4	8.2	6.0	16.8	48.6	31.1	10.7	541	414
Perry	3.4	0.3	0.7	11.9	1.4	0.7	0.6	40.7	9.8	13.7	752	445
Pettis	8.7	0.5	1.6	34.8	4.9	3.1	2.3	141.0	34.9	30.9	782	425
Phelps	38.5	26.7	4.9	33.0	3.3	3.0	30.4	172.8	39.8	36.7	895	517
Pike	3.9	13.0	1.3	15.0	1.8	1.9	3.2	38.0	14.5	9.9	536	354
Platte	50.8	27.1	3.6	8.5	2.3	3.3	3.6	161.1	49.9	82.5	1 063	767
Polk	4.9	0.1	1.2	25.5	1.9	3.6	3.6	85.3	30.1	15.9	572	357
Pulaski	447.5	152.6	1.4	24.6	7.8	26.4	3.5	84.1	58.0	18.0	415	319
Putnam	1.5	0.0	0.4	5.8	0.5	0.4	3.6	12.2	5.6	4.7	901	725
Ralls	4.1	0.1	1.0	4.1	0.5	0.4	4.2	9.7	4.3	4.1	429	321
Randolph	4.9	0.0	1.0	20.5	2.5	1.6	8.3	66.9	27.5	22.5	913	573
Ray	3.8	0.0	1.2	7.4	2.0	1.3	29.1	59.2	21.9	14.2	595	435
Reynolds	1.6	0.6	0.5	12.8	1.1	0.9	1.1	12.5	7.3	4.1	613	554
Ripley	2.7	1.6	3.9	30.8	3.0	1.1	2.6	19.2	11.9	5.1	378	284
St. Charles	52.0	258.1	21.9	40.6	11.2	8.2	50.8	708.3	215.9	370.6	1 223	860
St. Clair	1.7	0.0	0.4	9.6	5.2	0.9	1.7	30.8	12.9	4.4	457	388
Ste. Genevieve	1.7	0.0	0.6	7.4	1.1	0.8	2.8	42.4	18.5	9.5	523	436
St. Francois	9.0	0.0	1.7	49.2	10.9	5.2	10.2	119.1	63.1	35.4	624	400
St. Louis	395.5	229.8	123.1	737.5	51.7	50.3	144.2	2 667.5	733.0	1 538.2	1 511	1 044
Saline	5.2	0.0	1.2	23.2	5.5	1.8	4.9	65.3	23.5	15.9	690	450
Schuyler	2.5	0.0	0.4	4.6	0.5	0.4	2.6	10.3	4.9	2.6	613	501
Scotland	1.5	0.0	0.3	3.9	0.5	0.4	3.6	20.3	7.3	3.1	638	531
Scott	6.7	0.6	1.7	57.8	6.8	3.2	6.1	80.4	38.6	27.8	690	470
Shannon	3.0	0.1	0.3	13.1	4.5	0.6	2.2	11.9	7.2	2.8	334	213
Shelby	2.6	0.7	0.6	5.7	0.6	0.6	6.3	16.2	8.2	5.0	752	576
Stoddard	10.3	0.7	2.0	49.5	3.9	2.4	1.8	54.0	26.9	18.6	625	445
Stone	2.4	0.1	0.6	12.0	1.9	2.3	2.4	49.9	20.9	24.3	829	699
Sullivan	2.9	0.4	2.0	12.9	0.8	0.4	0.2	17.0	6.8	4.9	664	532
Taney	6.1	14.5	1.1	15.7	1.6	1.2	12.3	103.6	32.2	55.1	1 357	535
Texas	5.0	0.0	1.1	26.5	2.9	2.9	6.7	50.2	25.4	9.6	390	309
Vernon	5.8	0.1	1.0	15.9	2.1	1.4	4.2	45.1	18.1	18.7	921	402
Warren	3.9	0.3	0.8	7.5	1.2	0.9	4.3	39.7	14.4	19.7	753	463
Washington	3.8	0.0	0.9	28.2	4.0	1.8	2.8	48.2	19.9	8.7	371	279
Wayne	3.3	3.7	0.6	23.5	2.2	1.2	1.4	19.8	12.3	5.8	443	296
Webster	4.8	2.6	1.2	27.3	1.9	2.4	1.6	45.8	22.7	12.5	383	243
Worth	1.6	0.0	0.4	2.5	0.2	0.2	0.8	5.9	2.9	1.2	535	488
Wright	3.4	0.0	0.9	34.7	2.2	1.6	2.1	50.8	24.2	19.5	1 082	318

1. State totals may include programs not allocated by county.   2. Based on the resident population estimated as of July 1 of the year shown.

Table B. States and Counties — Local Government Finances, Government Employment, and Elections

STATE County	Local government finances, 2002 (cont'd)									Government employment, 2002			Presidential election, 2004		
	Direct general expenditure							Debt outstanding					Percent of vote cast —		
			Percent of total for —												
	Total (mil dol)	Per capita¹ (dollars)	Educa-tion	Health and hospitals	Police protec-tion	Public welfare	High-ways	Total (mil dol)	Per capita¹ (dollars)	Federal civilian	Federal military	State and local	Demo-cratic	Republi-can	All other
	183	184	185	186	187	188	189	190	191	192	193	194	195	196	197
MISSOURI—Cont'd															
Jasper	235.9	2 204	52.2	8.8	5.2	0.5	11.2	84.7	791	342	322	6 464	28.8	70.6	0.5
Jefferson	364.0	1 784	71.2	2.0	4.1	0.1	5.9	229.3	1 124	341	606	7 513	49.4	50.0	0.6
Johnson	124.3	2 498	44.4	32.1	4.3	0.0	4.4	57.8	1 161	813	3 849	5 502	38.6	60.6	0.8
Knox	9.8	2 287	50.5	2.4	1.6	17.1	11.9	3.6	832	48	13	371	38.6	61.1	0.3
Laclede	66.5	2 030	67.6	0.6	3.2	0.1	10.5	29.8	911	91	97	1 443	28.3	71.2	0.5
Lafayette	57.7	1 742	74.3	0.6	2.2	0.0	8.2	49.4	1 492	124	105	2 115	39.6	59.7	0.6
Lawrence	66.3	1 839	58.5	16.8	1.8	4.5	7.7	21.3	591	83	107	1 768	28.5	70.9	0.6
Lewis	20.9	2 017	59.0	2.4	2.7	16.4	4.4	4.6	439	71	31	602	37.8	61.7	0.5
Lincoln	86.8	2 053	50.3	25.6	4.8	0.0	10.0	55.9	1 323	118	126	1 766	42.2	57.1	0.7
Linn	32.4	2 399	69.3	0.0	1.6	0.0	10.8	13.8	1 017	71	40	836	41.4	58.0	0.6
Livingston	37.3	2 611	55.4	3.0	3.3	4.9	9.8	3.8	266	98	42	1 102	35.9	63.5	0.6
McDonald	23.8	1 098	72.9	0.8	2.0	3.3	5.8	1.3	60	99	64	750	28.7	70.5	0.8
Macon	48.4	3 123	37.0	26.0	1.9	16.3	7.4	10.8	697	85	46	1 670	37.7	61.7	0.5
Madison	27.6	2 336	47.0	42.6	0.9	0.0	3.5	1.7	140	27	35	778	37.2	62.0	0.8
Maries	12.9	1 477	74.0	2.9	2.3	0.0	8.6	0.3	29	15	26	329	35.3	63.9	0.8
Marion	129.4	4 610	70.8	2.1	2.8	4.2	4.5	100.4	3 576	96	83	1 927	36.7	62.8	0.5
Mercer	10.0	2 724	61.1	4.6	2.2	0.0	13.8	2.7	745	23	11	239	32.0	66.4	1.5
Miller	48.2	1 992	73.7	2.1	2.2	4.2	3.1	26.7	1 103	55	72	1 173	27.3	72.0	0.6
Mississippi	27.0	1 931	60.0	2.6	5.2	0.5	6.7	10.5	754	48	42	898	44.8	54.8	0.3
Moniteau	23.3	1 548	75.3	4.1	2.5	0.0	4.5	12.5	832	51	45	1 026	28.6	70.9	0.5
Monroe	24.3	2 623	55.3	3.4	3.9	13.0	6.8	34.0	3 666	86	28	731	38.2	61.2	0.6
Montgomery	19.7	1 630	75.4	3.3	2.9	0.0	6.4	4.5	370	59	36	694	37.3	61.9	0.7
Morgan	25.0	1 276	63.8	0.8	4.2	6.9	9.4	3.4	174	50	58	946	37.3	61.9	0.7
New Madrid	39.2	2 047	60.9	5.7	4.6	0.0	7.9	9.8	514	66	57	1 014	47.0	52.6	0.5
Newton	93.2	1 753	76.2	2.9	3.4	0.0	3.0	17.2	323	146	158	2 181	27.5	72.0	0.5
Nodaway	42.4	1 958	60.6	1.4	4.4	0.0	9.7	27.7	1 278	100	64	2 706	37.9	61.6	0.5
Oregon	17.5	1 702	82.5	0.4	0.3	0.0	6.5	2.0	193	34	31	507	39.0	59.3	1.6
Osage	16.5	1 267	79.0	1.0	2.4	0.1	7.6	7.3	558	41	39	720	25.1	74.6	0.3
Ozark	19.1	2 036	67.9	6.3	0.9	0.0	5.1	5.3	567	25	28	480	33.2	65.6	1.2
Pemiscot	48.8	2 457	73.0	0.0	4.1	0.0	4.7	8.6	434	70	59	1 794	49.7	49.9	0.4
Perry	44.1	2 412	36.3	30.2	4.2	0.0	6.6	27.5	1 506	57	54	1 022	31.8	67.7	0.5
Pettis	138.7	3 508	41.3	39.5	2.6	0.0	4.1	69.8	1 765	158	119	2 900	33.2	66.3	0.5
Phelps	167.0	4 080	32.2	45.9	1.8	0.2	4.4	64.5	1 576	530	343	5 559	35.7	63.5	0.8
Pike	38.8	2 108	52.9	26.1	4.8	0.0	5.2	7.4	403	84	55	1 684	45.7	53.7	0.6
Platte	170.2	2 192	64.0	0.8	5.2	0.5	4.8	158.5	2 041	348	234	3 056	43.9	55.6	0.5
Polk	88.9	3 209	42.1	41.2	2.4	0.0	8.1	18.5	667	83	82	1 810	30.3	69.0	0.7
Pulaski	78.1	1 805	81.4	5.3	2.1	0.2	2.5	8.4	194	2 818	10 825	1 772	29.1	70.6	0.3
Putnam	12.6	2 422	46.5	1.0	4.9	12.0	12.8	6.9	1 332	29	15	424	31.6	68.0	0.3
Ralls	9.4	983	62.1	3.3	4.2	0.2	14.7	9.5	987	44	28	370	40.4	59.4	0.2
Randolph	65.2	2 638	63.7	4.5	4.3	0.0	7.3	24.6	994	87	73	2 022	35.2	64.3	0.5
Ray	56.6	2 376	46.9	21.0	2.1	7.9	7.5	27.8	1 167	65	71	1 299	46.7	52.6	0.8
Reynolds	14.0	2 107	74.1	1.9	2.4	0.0	7.2	1.6	239	23	20	401	43.1	56.3	0.6
Ripley	18.8	1 400	77.4	5.2	1.8	0.0	8.6	1.2	91	56	40	661	33.8	65.4	0.8
St. Charles	775.4	2 559	52.8	1.3	6.2	0.5	6.6	1 019.4	3 364	627	902	11 782	40.9	58.6	0.5
St. Clair	32.0	3 315	33.6	34.7	1.6	0.0	5.1	5.5	568	37	29	650	37.1	62.5	0.4
Ste. Genevieve	46.3	2 555	30.7	27.1	2.9	4.5	4.1	14.6	806	34	54	904	52.6	46.5	0.9
St. Francois	121.1	2 132	76.2	0.8	5.0	0.0	3.8	68.2	1 202	134	169	4 488	46.9	52.7	0.4
St. Louis	2 638.4	2 592	57.9	1.8	7.0	0.6	6.7	1 793.9	1 762	5 972	3 073	50 855	54.4	45.1	0.5
Saline	45.9	1 992	63.2	3.0	4.1	0.0	6.5	18.9	821	104	68	2 286	45.1	54.3	0.7
Schuyler	9.9	2 357	55.0	5.6	1.7	18.5	10.1	5.3	1 247	38	13	305	44.0	55.3	0.6
Scotland	19.1	3 929	27.7	36.3	1.4	21.1	6.3	2.3	463	31	14	569	37.7	61.6	0.7
Scott	81.0	2 012	60.0	2.5	4.9	0.0	4.9	240.8	5 978	113	120	2 370	34.7	65.0	0.3
Shannon	12.8	1 522	60.7	0.0	2.1	0.0	21.1	3.2	383	85	25	444	35.4	63.6	1.1
Shelby	15.5	2 326	57.0	4.6	2.2	13.0	10.3	3.7	554	49	20	570	34.3	65.2	0.5
Stoddard	53.8	1 803	65.5	3.4	5.8	0.0	9.8	13.3	446	202	89	1 325	29.8	69.8	0.4
Stone	43.7	1 489	82.5	0.6	2.3	0.3	1.8	37.3	1 269	39	87	984	30.2	69.4	0.4
Sullivan	17.2	2 354	49.2	24.3	3.3	0.0	12.4	3.1	418	58	22	464	38.1	60.9	1.0
Taney	95.9	2 362	53.6	1.3	4.9	0.0	7.5	136.2	3 355	108	121	1 733	29.1	70.5	0.4
Texas	50.5	2 052	58.4	21.2	2.3	0.0	7.9	8.6	348	93	73	1 835	33.3	65.7	1.1
Vernon	59.7	2 942	40.7	1.0	0.8	0.1	7.5	38.6	1 902	97	60	1 873	35.7	63.8	0.6
Warren	35.8	1 365	64.4	4.0	5.9	0.0	6.8	26.8	1 022	60	78	992	40.7	58.7	0.6
Washington	44.7	1 900	53.9	28.2	3.7	0.0	4.4	12.7	540	80	70	1 508	48.6	50.6	0.8
Wayne	19.4	1 480	67.0	7.9	4.6	0.0	8.2	3.6	275	92	39	582	36.3	63.2	0.5
Webster	49.1	1 504	65.9	0.1	3.4	9.1	6.1	21.3	652	81	97	1 215	31.2	68.3	0.5
Worth	6.0	2 624	50.4	1.7	1.7	23.2	11.7	3.8	1 654	27	0	192	38.5	61.0	0.4
Wright	49.7	2 756	56.6	0.0	16.1	5.2	7.6	6.5	360	59	54	946	26.3	73.1	0.7

1. Based on the resident population estimated as of July 1 of the year shown.

STATE/ County code	CBSA code[1]	County Type[2]	STATE County	Land area,[3] (sq km) 2000	Population and population characteristics, 2003													
								Race alone or in combination, not Hispanic or Latino (percent)					Age (percent)					
					Total persons	Rank	Per square kilometer	White	Black	Am. Indian, Alaska Native	Asian and Pacific Islander	Percent Hispanic or Latino[4]	Under 5 years	5 to 17 years	18 to 24 years	25 to 34 years	35 to 44 years	45 to 54 years
				1	2	3	4	5	6	7	8	9	10	11	12	13	14	15
			MISSOURI—Cont'd															
29 510	41180	1	St. Louis city	160	332 223	179	2 076.4	43.5	52.6	0.8	2.6	2.1	7.4	18.4	9.5	15.7	15.3	13.3
30 000	...	X	MONTANA	376 979	917 621	X	2.4	90.5	0.6	7.4	1.0	2.1	5.8	17.7	10.5	11.3	14.1	16.1
30 001	...	7	Beaverhead	14 355	8 919	2 531	0.6	95.0	0.2	2.3	0.4	3.0	5.3	17.1	12.8	9.5	13.6	16.4
30 003	...	6	Big Horn	12 936	12 894	2 248	1.0	35.4	0.1	62.5	0.5	3.6	9.5	24.4	10.6	11.4	13.8	12.7
30 005	...	9	Blaine	10 946	6 729	2 710	0.6	51.3	0.2	48.3	0.3	1.0	7.7	22.5	10.8	9.1	14.5	14.4
30 007	...	9	Broadwater	3 086	4 430	2 878	1.4	96.5	0.3	1.9	0.2	1.5	3.8	17.6	8.0	8.3	15.8	15.9
30 009	13740	3	Carbon	5 304	9 770	2 462	1.8	96.8	0.4	0.9	0.5	1.8	4.6	16.9	8.4	9.2	14.9	18.0
30 011	...	9	Carter	8 649	1 333	3 098	0.2	98.6	0.1	0.5	0.3	0.6	3.1	18.9	9.3	8.3	15.4	16.1
30 013	24500	3	Cascade	6 988	79 561	654	11.4	90.3	1.9	5.9	1.7	2.6	6.4	18.1	10.0	11.7	13.8	14.1
30 015	...	8	Chouteau	10 291	5 576	2 805	0.5	84.1	0.0	14.8	0.3	0.7	4.4	20.4	8.8	7.8	13.8	16.7
30 017	...	7	Custer	9 798	11 369	2 342	1.2	96.5	0.3	1.8	0.4	1.7	5.9	17.3	10.0	9.3	14.1	15.6
30 019	...	9	Daniels	3 694	1 940	3 065	0.5	96.4	0.1	1.5	0.5	2.0	3.8	14.8	7.5	5.9	12.0	17.7
30 021	...	7	Dawson	6 146	8 776	2 545	1.4	97.3	0.4	1.4	0.2	1.0	5.2	15.7	10.8	8.9	13.3	17.1
30 023	...	7	Deer Lodge	1 909	8 953	2 527	4.7	95.7	0.2	3.1	0.6	1.8	4.7	16.1	9.5	8.5	13.9	17.2
30 025	...	9	Fallon	4 197	2 752	3 000	0.7	98.5	0.2	0.4	0.4	0.5	4.4	17.3	9.7	7.8	14.9	17.4
30 027	...	7	Fergus	11 238	11 695	2 314	1.0	97.6	0.1	2.1	0.5	0.6	4.9	16.6	8.8	8.1	13.5	16.1
30 029	28060	5	Flathead	13 205	79 485	655	6.0	96.4	0.4	2.0	1.0	1.6	5.9	17.8	9.6	10.3	14.7	16.8
30 031	14580	5	Gallatin	6 749	73 243	695	10.9	95.9	0.5	1.5	1.4	1.7	5.5	15.2	15.4	16.1	14.1	14.4
30 033	...	9	Garfield	12 090	1 233	3 101	0.1	98.6	0.1	0.7	0.2	0.4	5.6	16.4	8.6	8.2	13.1	17.8
30 035	...	7	Glacier	7 756	13 250	2 217	1.7	34.8	0.7	65.1	0.1	1.4	8.6	23.8	11.4	9.9	15.2	13.0
30 037	...	8	Golden Valley	3 044	1 047	3 108	0.3	97.8	0.0	0.9	0.1	1.2	7.4	18.9	9.3	9.6	12.6	15.1
30 039	...	8	Granite	4 474	2 894	2 992	0.6	97.2	0.0	2.0	0.4	1.3	3.4	17.5	8.5	8.6	14.0	17.1
30 041	25660	7	Hill	7 502	16 350	2 007	2.2	79.0	0.2	20.7	0.7	1.4	7.8	19.0	12.1	10.3	14.0	14.8
30 043	25740	3	Jefferson	4 291	10 499	2 398	2.4	96.4	0.2	2.4	0.7	1.7	4.3	20.0	9.1	8.0	16.2	19.4
30 045	...	8	Judith Basin	4 843	2 192	3 042	0.5	98.9	0.0	1.0	0.1	0.6	3.3	18.8	7.8	6.9	14.8	17.8
30 047	...	6	Lake	3 869	27 197	1 497	7.0	73.0	0.2	26.6	0.4	2.5	6.4	19.5	10.1	9.6	13.5	15.0
30 049	25740	5	Lewis and Clark	8 964	57 137	851	6.4	95.5	0.4	2.8	1.0	1.6	5.7	17.6	9.9	10.5	15.2	17.5
30 051	...	9	Liberty	3 703	2 055	3 054	0.6	99.3	0.1	0.1	0.4	0.2	4.5	16.7	9.4	6.6	14.0	15.8
30 053	...	7	Lincoln	9 357	18 835	1 867	2.0	96.7	0.3	2.6	0.6	1.4	4.8	17.7	8.5	7.7	14.0	17.5
30 055	...	9	McCone	6 844	1 818	3 073	0.3	96.8	0.4	1.9	0.6	1.0	5.0	18.1	6.9	6.2	15.1	17.4
30 057	...	9	Madison	9 289	6 967	2 688	0.8	97.1	0.1	1.4	0.3	2.0	4.5	15.3	8.0	9.2	14.3	17.7
30 059	...	9	Meagher	6 195	1 967	3 062	0.3	97.5	0.1	1.1	0.2	1.3	4.6	17.6	8.8	7.6	13.4	17.6
30 061	...	8	Mineral	3 159	3 884	2 921	1.2	95.2	0.5	3.2	0.8	2.0	4.4	16.4	9.0	8.4	14.8	16.8
30 063	33540	3	Missoula	6 729	98 616	549	14.7	94.3	0.6	3.4	1.7	1.7	5.6	15.9	13.3	14.9	14.2	15.2
30 065	...	8	Musselshell	4 836	4 464	2 876	0.9	96.6	0.2	1.8	0.2	1.6	4.7	15.4	9.0	7.9	13.8	19.7
30 067	...	7	Park	7 258	15 840	2 044	2.2	95.9	0.5	1.9	0.6	2.1	5.5	16.4	7.9	10.5	15.7	18.4
30 069	...	9	Petroleum	4 284	491	3 136	0.1	98.2	0.0	0.6	0.0	1.2	5.5	17.9	9.2	9.8	12.0	14.3
30 071	...	9	Phillips	13 311	4 271	2 889	0.3	91.0	0.1	9.0	0.3	1.2	4.5	19.5	8.6	6.3	15.7	15.6
30 073	...	7	Pondera	4 208	6 166	2 759	1.5	84.3	0.2	15.1	0.2	1.0	5.4	20.4	9.8	8.3	14.5	15.6
30 075	...	9	Powder River	8 540	1 834	3 070	0.2	97.0	0.0	2.1	0.2	0.7	4.8	18.6	7.5	7.7	14.5	17.2
30 077	...	7	Powell	6 024	7 006	2 686	1.2	93.0	0.6	5.2	0.6	2.1	4.4	15.1	9.7	11.4	18.1	16.8
30 079	...	9	Prairie	4 498	1 154	3 103	0.3	98.6	0.0	0.7	0.3	0.7	3.7	12.7	7.5	8.3	11.2	19.3
30 081	...	6	Ravalli	6 201	38 662	1 171	6.2	96.2	0.3	1.9	0.7	2.1	5.3	18.0	9.0	9.4	13.4	16.2
30 083	...	7	Richland	5 398	9 155	2 515	1.7	95.4	0.1	2.3	0.2	2.4	5.1	19.3	8.8	8.6	15.3	16.9
30 085	...	7	Roosevelt	6 101	10 451	2 406	1.7	39.7	0.1	60.3	0.6	1.4	9.0	24.3	10.2	9.2	13.9	14.5
30 087	...	9	Rosebud	12 982	9 303	2 501	0.7	61.6	0.3	36.9	0.5	2.4	7.8	22.9	9.8	8.7	14.5	16.9
30 089	...	8	Sanders	7 154	10 455	2 405	1.5	92.9	0.2	6.6	0.5	1.9	4.9	16.6	8.5	8.0	12.3	17.3
30 091	...	9	Sheridan	4 342	3 668	2 934	0.8	97.1	0.1	1.5	0.4	1.3	2.7	15.5	7.9	5.5	13.4	19.3
30 093	15580	5	Silver Bow	1 860	33 208	1 325	17.9	94.6	0.2	2.8	0.7	2.8	5.5	16.9	9.7	10.5	14.8	15.3
30 095	...	8	Stillwater	4 649	8 459	2 566	1.8	96.4	0.3	1.2	0.4	2.4	5.1	17.9	8.4	9.9	14.9	17.6
30 097	...	9	Sweet Grass	4 805	3 604	2 937	0.8	97.0	0.2	1.0	0.6	1.9	5.8	18.7	6.9	9.5	13.8	16.5
30 099	...	8	Teton	5 886	6 369	2 738	1.1	96.8	0.3	2.5	0.1	1.3	5.1	19.0	9.3	7.6	14.8	15.2
30 101	...	7	Toole	4 949	5 337	2 819	1.1	93.9	0.3	5.2	0.7	1.6	5.3	17.5	9.5	11.4	16.5	16.7
30 103	...	8	Treasure	2 535	735	3 127	0.3	95.6	0.1	1.9	0.7	1.8	3.8	20.1	8.8	6.5	15.1	18.5
30 105	...	7	Valley	12 745	7 349	2 653	0.6	89.4	0.2	10.5	0.4	0.8	5.9	17.3	8.4	7.9	14.3	16.1
30 107	...	9	Wheatland	3 686	2 106	3 048	0.6	97.2	0.5	1.8	0.4	1.1	6.5	19.2	7.3	9.2	11.3	15.4
30 109	...	9	Wibaux	2 303	977	3 110	0.4	98.8	0.5	0.5	0.4	0.4	3.7	17.5	8.4	7.1	14.6	17.9
30 111	13740	3	Yellowstone	6 825	133 191	425	19.5	91.8	0.8	4.0	1.2	3.8	6.3	17.8	9.8	12.2	15.0	15.0
31 000	...	X	NEBRASKA	199 099	1 739 291	X	8.7	87.3	4.5	1.2	1.9	6.1	6.9	18.4	10.8	13.0	14.3	14.1
31 001	25580	5	Adams	1 459	30 890	1 386	21.2	91.8	0.8	0.6	2.3	5.1	6.3	17.5	12.1	11.4	13.6	14.1
31 003	...	9	Antelope	2 220	7 211	2 664	3.2	98.5	0.1	0.3	0.1	1.1	5.2	19.1	9.1	7.6	13.9	15.0
31 005	...	9	Arthur	1 853	398	3 138	0.2	97.5	0.0	0.5	0.8	1.8	4.8	17.8	7.0	8.3	16.8	12.8
31 007	42420	9	Banner	1 933	774	3 120	0.4	93.7	0.1	0.0	0.1	6.1	2.5	22.1	7.4	5.9	15.6	18.0

1. CBSA = Core Based Statistical Area. See Appendix A for explanation. See Appendix B for list of metropolitan areas with component counties.   2. County type code from the Economic Research Service of USDA Rural-Urban Continuum Codes. See Appendix A for definition.   3. Dry land or land partially or temporarily covered by water.   4. Hispanic or Latino persons may be of any race.

STATE County	55 to 64 years	65 to 74 years	75 years and over	Percent female	Total persons 1990	Total persons 2000	Percent change 1990–2000	Percent change 2000–2003	Births	Deaths	Net migration	Number	Percent change 1990–2000	Persons per household	Female family householder[1]	One person
	16	17	18	19	20	21	22	23	24	25	26	27	28	29	30	31
MISSOURI—Cont'd																
St. Louis city	7.8	6.1	7.1	52.9	396 685	348 189	-12.2	-4.6	17 929	13 741	-20 394	147 076	-10.8	2.30	21.3	40.3
MONTANA	10.9	7.0	6.7	50.1	799 065	902 195	12.9	1.7	35 234	27 673	7 907	358 667	17.1	2.45	8.9	27.4
Beaverhead	10.8	7.7	6.7	49.0	8 424	9 202	9.2	-3.1	306	306	-285	3 684	14.7	2.36	6.2	29.7
Big Horn	8.9	4.7	4.0	50.6	11 337	12 671	11.8	1.8	873	333	-308	3 924	13.8	3.17	17.6	19.3
Blaine	9.3	6.5	6.4	50.6	6 728	7 009	4.2	-4.0	332	286	-325	2 501	5.1	2.78	14.4	26.0
Broadwater	12.0	10.0	7.9	49.2	3 318	4 385	32.2	1.0	101	161	111	1 752	36.9	2.47	6.9	24.1
Carbon	11.6	8.2	8.0	49.8	8 080	9 552	18.2	2.3	269	303	254	4 065	24.3	2.32	6.7	28.8
Carter	12.2	9.7	8.7	51.7	1 503	1 360	-9.5	-2.0	23	60	10	543	-7.8	2.47	7.0	27.1
Cascade	10.0	7.4	7.0	50.6	77 691	80 357	3.4	-1.0	3 337	2 682	-1 431	32 547	8.0	2.41	9.9	28.8
Chouteau	10.1	8.9	9.6	50.0	5 452	5 970	9.5	-6.6	126	216	-313	2 226	7.8	2.59	8.4	24.9
Custer	10.6	8.4	8.9	50.9	11 697	11 696	0.0	-2.8	436	448	-316	4 768	3.0	2.36	10.0	29.9
Daniels	14.6	10.9	13.6	50.4	2 266	2 017	-11.0	-3.8	45	85	-36	892	-2.9	2.22	5.5	33.6
Dawson	10.8	8.9	9.4	50.5	9 505	9 059	-4.7	-3.1	297	336	-250	3 625	-1.8	2.37	6.8	28.4
Deer Lodge	12.1	9.3	9.7	50.2	10 356	9 417	-9.1	-4.9	287	475	-275	3 995	-1.6	2.26	9.4	33.4
Fallon	9.6	10.0	8.7	49.6	3 103	2 837	-8.6	-3.0	75	103	-58	1 140	-2.2	2.45	6.0	26.6
Fergus	11.8	9.4	10.6	50.9	12 083	11 893	-1.6	-1.7	359	531	-15	4 860	5.6	2.33	6.7	30.5
Flathead	10.5	6.8	6.1	50.4	59 218	74 471	25.8	6.7	3 135	2 212	4 058	29 588	29.6	2.48	8.3	25.2
Gallatin	7.5	4.3	4.1	48.0	50 484	67 831	34.4	8.0	2 643	1 195	3 913	26 323	38.4	2.46	6.6	24.1
Garfield	10.6	8.5	11.3	47.7	1 589	1 279	-19.5	-3.6	49	41	-50	532	-7.8	2.38	4.5	28.2
Glacier	8.2	5.3	4.3	50.3	12 121	13 247	9.3	0.0	785	372	-414	4 304	12.8	3.03	16.2	21.6
Golden Valley	13.3	9.1	6.2	48.6	912	1 042	14.3	0.5	45	26	-15	365	10.6	2.41	3.3	24.4
Granite	14.1	8.7	7.1	49.6	2 548	2 830	11.1	2.3	64	101	101	1 200	14.2	2.33	7.4	30.1
Hill	8.7	6.6	6.4	50.1	17 654	16 673	-5.6	-1.9	866	525	-670	6 457	0.5	2.53	10.9	28.6
Jefferson	12.1	6.1	4.0	50.1	7 939	10 049	26.6	4.5	280	311	474	3 747	30.7	2.62	5.9	20.2
Judith Basin	14.1	8.4	9.3	47.6	2 282	2 329	2.1	-5.9	49	52	-132	951	4.7	2.45	4.3	27.5
Lake	10.9	7.8	6.7	51.0	21 041	26 507	26.0	2.6	1 114	923	515	10 192	30.4	2.54	11.5	24.5
Lewis and Clark	10.7	6.2	5.7	50.7	47 495	55 716	17.3	2.6	2 138	1 583	929	22 850	22.5	2.38	9.2	29.1
Liberty	11.1	9.6	11.6	50.3	2 295	2 158	-6.0	-4.8	70	70	-107	833	5.7	2.51	5.6	27.9
Lincoln	13.6	9.4	6.7	49.3	17 481	18 837	7.8	0.0	595	627	47	7 764	16.4	2.40	7.8	26.7
McCone	13.0	9.7	10.0	49.4	2 276	1 977	-13.1	-8.0	61	56	-166	810	-4.0	2.44	3.8	24.6
Madison	13.9	9.5	7.8	49.6	5 989	6 851	14.4	1.7	195	246	171	2 956	23.8	2.29	4.4	29.3
Meagher	11.9	9.9	8.3	50.6	1 819	1 932	6.2	1.8	62	49	22	803	13.3	2.37	6.1	31.0
Mineral	13.3	9.7	6.1	48.8	3 315	3 884	17.2	0.0	113	116	1	1 584	23.6	2.41	6.0	26.6
Missoula	9.0	5.0	5.0	50.0	78 687	95 802	21.8	2.9	3 614	2 186	1 476	38 439	24.9	2.40	9.2	28.0
Musselshell	12.5	7.9	9.3	51.3	4 106	4 497	9.5	-0.7	136	197	32	1 878	13.1	2.33	6.6	30.1
Park	10.9	7.2	7.6	50.4	14 515	15 694	8.1	0.9	571	528	115	6 828	21.5	2.27	7.3	32.4
Petroleum	14.9	7.9	8.1	48.3	519	493	-5.0	-0.4	13	17	4	211	1.0	2.34	5.7	31.3
Phillips	11.2	9.1	10.0	50.0	5 163	4 601	-10.9	-7.2	146	208	-273	1 848	-4.3	2.45	6.8	29.1
Pondera	10.2	8.3	8.4	50.6	6 433	6 424	-0.1	-4.0	205	251	-213	2 410	7.3	2.63	8.4	25.5
Powder River	11.2	10.2	8.2	51.4	2 090	1 858	-11.1	-1.3	49	72	0	737	-8.4	2.48	4.1	24.8
Powell	10.7	7.8	6.9	41.1	6 620	7 180	8.5	-2.4	203	233	-140	2 422	8.4	2.39	7.7	28.6
Prairie	15.3	10.2	14.1	49.4	1 383	1 199	-13.3	-3.8	28	59	-14	537	-5.5	2.19	2.4	31.3
Ravalli	12.1	8.0	7.1	50.2	25 010	36 070	44.2	7.2	1 282	1 140	2 393	14 289	47.3	2.48	7.5	24.1
Richland	10.6	7.7	8.4	50.4	10 716	9 667	-9.8	-5.3	292	342	-469	3 878	-2.0	2.46	7.4	28.8
Roosevelt	7.8	5.7	5.7	50.5	10 999	10 620	-3.4	-1.6	652	404	-421	3 581	-3.1	2.89	18.9	23.6
Rosebud	9.9	5.6	3.8	50.3	10 505	9 383	-10.7	-0.9	490	218	-357	3 307	-4.9	2.81	11.8	24.3
Sanders	14.9	10.0	7.7	49.7	8 669	10 227	18.0	2.2	347	373	255	4 273	25.8	2.35	7.1	28.0
Sheridan	12.3	12.2	13.4	50.5	4 732	4 105	-13.3	-10.6	46	215	-280	1 741	-8.3	2.29	4.8	32.3
Silver Bow	11.0	7.8	8.6	50.6	33 941	34 606	2.0	-4.0	1 188	1 406	-1 203	14 432	3.8	2.32	10.5	32.8
Stillwater	11.9	7.6	6.6	49.1	6 536	8 195	25.4	3.2	310	226	178	3 234	28.2	2.48	5.0	24.1
Sweet Grass	12.5	8.2	8.6	49.8	3 154	3 609	14.4	-0.1	147	127	-20	1 476	15.2	2.41	4.5	28.9
Teton	11.7	8.2	8.9	50.6	6 271	6 445	2.8	-1.2	204	211	-62	2 538	9.0	2.51	5.9	27.3
Toole	9.4	7.7	7.4	47.3	5 046	5 267	4.4	-1.0	199	169	-103	1 962	2.1	2.47	6.5	30.2
Treasure	13.2	9.4	9.4	48.2	874	861	-1.5	-14.6	16	23	-111	357	5.3	2.41	4.2	30.0
Valley	11.2	10.2	10.0	50.6	8 239	7 675	-6.8	-4.2	315	322	-320	3 150	-3.6	2.38	8.2	29.3
Wheatland	12.8	8.7	11.3	50.2	2 246	2 259	0.6	-6.8	75	91	-136	853	0.5	2.24	4.9	34.5
Wibaux	9.6	11.5	10.7	52.5	1 191	1 068	-10.3	-8.5	21	65	-47	421	-7.3	2.45	5.9	29.0
Yellowstone	9.6	6.7	6.7	51.1	113 419	129 352	14.0	3.0	5 555	3 760	2 183	52 084	16.5	2.43	10.1	27.9
NEBRASKA	9.2	6.5	6.9	50.6	1 578 417	1 711 263	8.4	1.6	80 474	50 477	-979	666 184	10.6	2.49	9.1	27.6
Adams	9.2	6.7	9.0	51.1	29 625	31 151	5.2	-0.8	1 297	965	-592	12 141	4.7	2.43	8.3	28.6
Antelope	10.4	8.9	11.3	50.4	7 965	7 452	-6.4	-3.2	224	281	-182	2 953	-3.0	2.49	5.5	27.8
Arthur	12.3	12.8	7.3	49.5	462	444	-3.9	-10.4	12	10	-49	185	-1.1	2.40	7.6	21.6
Banner	11.6	10.3	6.7	48.3	852	819	-3.9	-5.5	10	16	-39	311	2.0	2.63	4.2	19.9

1. No spouse present.

Table B. States and Counties — Vital Statistics, Health Resources, and Crime

STATE County	Births, average 1999–2001 Total	Rate[1]	Deaths, average 1999–2001 Number Total	Number Infant[2]	Rate Total[1]	Rate Infant[3]	Physicians,[4] 2000 Number	Rate[5]	Hospitals,[4] 1998 Number	Beds Number	Beds Rate[5]	Medicare enrollees, 2003	Serious crimes known to police,[6] 2002 Total Number	Rate[7]
	32	33	34	35	36	37	38	39	40	41	42	43	44	45
MISSOURI—Cont'd														
St. Louis city	5 418	15.6	4 320	73	12.4	13.4	2 098	603	12	3 411	1 005	51 929	50 429	14 286
MONTANA	10 904	12.1	8 163	71	9.1	6.5	1 646	182	54	4 084	464	142 457	31 948	3 513
Beaverhead	95	10.4	79	0	8.6	D	17	185	1	31	350	1 439	136	1 466
Big Horn	238	18.7	104	2	8.2	D	12	95	1	54	428	1 236	303	2 372
Blaine	103	14.8	73	1	10.0	D	5	71	0	0	0	930	141	1 995
Broadwater	37	8.4	44	1	10.0	D	6	137	1	42	1 016	887	123	2 783
Carbon	93	9.7	97	1	10.2	D	12	126	1	46	487	1 679	117	1 215
Carter	8	6.1	16	0	11.7	D	1	74	1	10	651	254	NA	NA
Cascade	1 053	13.1	764	10	9.5	9.2	198	246	2	402	509	13 233	5 043	6 226
Chouteau	39	6.7	68	0	11.6	D	1	17	2	82	1 581	1 053	117	1 944
Custer	137	11.7	144	1	12.4	D	30	256	1	141	1 172	2 279	NA	NA
Daniels	16	7.9	23	0	11.2	D	2	99	1	54	2 699	490	NA	NA
Dawson	96	10.6	99	0	11.0	D	8	88	1	104	1 175	1 696	214	2 343
Deer Lodge	83	8.8	139	0	14.8	D	16	170	2	134	1 340	2 109	187	1 970
Fallon	25	8.8	29	0	10.1	D	1	35	1	52	1 768	553	10	350
Fergus	109	9.2	164	1	13.8	D	17	143	1	132	1 076	2 510	215	1 793
Flathead	946	12.6	669	6	9.0	D	144	193	2	249	347	12 638	NA	NA
Gallatin	805	11.8	358	5	5.3	D	121	178	1	86	138	7 070	NA	NA
Garfield	16	12.2	12	0	9.6	D	0	0	0	0	0	235	NA	NA
Glacier	237	18.0	107	1	8.1	D	12	91	1	59	470	1 451	289	2 164
Golden Valley	12	11.1	8	0	7.3	D	0	0	0	0	0	206	19	1 808
Granite	20	7.2	30	0	10.7	D	2	71	1	31	1 162	458	13	456
Hill	281	16.8	153	1	9.2	D	25	150	1	140	806	2 423	772	4 593
Jefferson	92	9.1	86	0	8.5	D	11	109	0	0	0	1 389	61	672
Judith Basin	16	7.1	20	0	8.7	D	0	0	0	0	0	423	30	1 278
Lake	344	13.0	265	5	10.0	D	36	136	2	121	472	4 276	910	3 406
Lewis and Clark	663	11.9	469	4	8.4	D	125	224	1	79	147	8 182	NA	NA
Liberty	21	9.9	22	0	10.1	D	1	46	1	67	2 884	680	NA	NA
Lincoln	182	9.7	196	1	10.4	D	16	85	1	26	139	3 843	668	3 719
McCone	15	7.8	17	0	8.7	D	1	51	0	0	0	353	NA	NA
Madison	54	7.8	76	0	11.0	D	7	102	2	23	335	1 249	49	710
Meagher	20	10.3	21	0	10.7	D	4	207	1	37	2 059	385	50	2 567
Mineral	43	11.0	34	0	8.9	D	2	51	1	30	800	887	100	2 554
Missoula	1 110	11.6	654	4	6.8	D	257	268	2	336	378	11 664	NA	NA
Musselshell	47	10.5	61	1	13.6	D	2	44	1	48	1 042	899	147	3 243
Park	181	11.6	152	1	9.7	D	14	89	1	35	221	2 596	NA	NA
Petroleum	4	8.8	3	0	0.0	D	0	0	0	0	0	77	NA	NA
Phillips	41	9.0	59	0	12.9	D	5	109	1	21	436	897	64	1 380
Pondera	73	11.3	78	1	12.2	D	6	93	1	94	1 468	1 193	82	1 266
Powder River	16	8.7	23	0	12.7	D	0	0	0	0	0	293	NA	NA
Powell	61	8.6	61	1	8.5	D	6	84	1	35	500	1 132	242	3 344
Prairie	11	9.3	16	0	12.9	D	0	0	1	21	1 575	295	10	828
Ravalli	410	11.3	313	3	8.7	D	36	100	1	48	137	6 815	436	1 199
Richland	100	10.4	100	0	10.4	D	12	124	1	49	485	1 698	NA	NA
Roosevelt	206	19.3	106	2	10.0	D	11	104	3	116	1 056	1 406	NA	NA
Rosebud	163	17.4	70	2	7.4	D	5	53	1	75	746	1 122	113	1 195
Sanders	107	10.4	106	1	10.3	D	11	108	1	44	432	2 273	283	2 745
Sheridan	27	6.6	64	0	15.7	D	3	73	1	103	2 413	988	NA	NA
Silver Bow	380	11.1	431	1	12.6	D	72	208	1	115	333	6 381	1 693	4 853
Stillwater	88	10.7	75	0	9.1	D	5	61	1	23	285	1 330	58	702
Sweet Grass	37	10.3	41	0	11.5	D	2	55	0	0	0	602	46	1 264
Teton	68	10.6	65	1	10.1	D	2	31	0	0	0	1 188	108	1 662
Toole	54	10.3	52	0	9.9	D	9	171	1	83	1 756	512	NA	NA
Treasure	6	7.1	8	0	9.0	D	0	0	0	0	0	177	NA	NA
Valley	88	11.5	90	0	11.7	D	10	130	1	42	513	1 678	148	1 913
Wheatland	25	11.2	25	0	11.4	D	3	133	1	44	1 854	454	1	44
Wibaux	9	8.8	17	0	15.7	D	0	0	0	0	0	215	NA	NA
Yellowstone	1 692	13.1	1 108	11	8.6	6.3	342	264	2	520	412	20 036	6 020	4 617
NEBRASKA	24 458	14.3	15 248	170	8.9	7.0	3 091	181	89	7 870	473	257 171	73 606	4 257
Adams	405	13.0	298	4	9.6	D	62	199	1	190	645	5 194	1 544	4 905
Antelope	73	9.9	89	0	12.1	D	7	94	1	49	682	1 409	53	904
Arthur	3	7.7	2	0	0.0	D	0	0	0	0	0	113	0	0
Banner	3	3.7	4	0	0.0	D	0	0	0	0	0	91	NA	NA

1. Per 1,000 estimated resident population.   2. Deaths of infants under 1 year old.   3. Deaths of infants under 1 year old per 1,000 live births.   4. Data subject to copyright.   5. Per 100,000 resident population as of July 1 of the year shown.   6. Data for serious crimes have not been adjusted for underreporting; this may affect comparability between geographic areas and over time.   7. Per 100,000 population estimated by the FBI.

STATE County	Serious crimes known to police,[1] 2002 (cont'd) Rate[2]		Education School enrollment and attainment, 2000				Local government expenditures,[5] 2000–2001		Money income, 1999	Households Median income			Percent below poverty level, 1999			
			Enrollment[3]		Attainment[4] (percent)				Per capita income[6] (dollars)							Families with children
	Violent	Property	Total	Percent private	High school graduate or less	Bachelor's degree or more	Total current expenditures (mil dol)	Current expenditures per student (dollars)		Dollars	Percent change, 1989–1999 (constant 1999 dollars)	Percent with income of $100,000 or more	Persons	Households	Families	
	46	47	48	49	50	51	52	53	54	55	56	57	58	59	60	61
MISSOURI—Cont'd																
St. Louis city	2 124	12 161	98 331	27.4	56.2	19.1	405.3	9 127	16 108	27 156	3.9	4.6	24.6	22.1	20.8	29.8
MONTANA	352	3 161	241 754	10.2	44.1	24.4	1 033.1	6 678	17 151	33 024	6.9	5.6	14.6	14.1	10.5	16.4
Beaverhead	129	1 337	2 812	7.8	39.8	26.4	10.2	6 743	15 621	28 962	3.0	4.0	17.1	19.2	12.8	18.2
Big Horn	478	1 895	4 140	11.0	53.8	14.3	24.4	9 914	10 792	27 684	7.9	2.1	29.2	24.5	23.7	31.2
Blaine	410	1 585	2 097	7.1	49.3	17.4	13.6	9 231	12 101	25 247	1.5	3.7	28.1	24.8	23.4	32.4
Broadwater	543	2 240	1 046	9.5	54.5	15.0	4.1	5 345	16 237	32 689	20.1	4.9	10.8	11.9	7.6	13.4
Carbon	114	1 101	2 219	8.6	48.0	23.3	11.6	7 081	17 204	32 139	25.6	3.7	11.6	11.7	8.2	12.8
Carter	NA	NA	335	11.9	52.5	13.6	1.8	8 587	13 280	26 313	19.0	2.4	18.1	18.6	15.9	13.9
Cascade	389	5 837	20 212	14.0	46.2	21.5	82.1	5 982	17 566	32 971	3.5	5.4	13.5	13.4	10.4	17.1
Chouteau	199	1 745	1 675	5.3	43.3	20.5	7.7	8 463	14 851	29 150	-3.0	4.2	20.5	16.4	16.5	23.3
Custer	NA	NA	2 903	8.5	44.9	18.8	12.0	6 133	15 876	30 000	4.6	4.6	15.1	14.6	10.1	16.7
Daniels	NA	NA	405	2.7	51.0	14.1	3.7	10 665	16 055	27 306	-5.2	4.0	16.9	17.4	13.4	22.2
Dawson	230	2 113	2 206	6.4	47.8	15.1	11.1	7 433	15 368	31 393	-0.2	3.0	14.9	15.6	11.7	17.2
Deer Lodge	558	1 412	2 218	5.4	58.4	14.7	8.8	5 794	15 580	26 305	-3.5	2.4	15.8	16.7	11.6	19.7
Fallon	70	280	653	2.8	57.7	14.4	7.1	12 159	16 014	29 944	-3.8	3.1	12.5	11.5	9.5	14.7
Fergus	459	1 335	2 689	5.0	50.4	19.1	16.4	7 593	15 808	30 409	5.8	4.2	15.4	14.4	10.6	15.8
Flathead	NA	NA	17 987	11.6	43.2	22.4	76.8	5 755	18 112	34 466	6.2	6.0	13.0	12.7	9.4	14.9
Gallatin	NA	NA	22 806	9.1	27.9	41.0	55.8	5 217	19 074	38 120	21.5	8.0	12.8	12.3	6.3	9.6
Garfield	NA	NA	277	6.5	54.1	16.8	1.9	9 043	13 930	25 917	12.1	2.4	21.5	20.1	16.7	26.5
Glacier	749	1 415	4 330	4.4	48.7	16.5	26.5	8 815	11 597	27 921	11.7	3.1	27.3	24.9	23.5	29.2
Golden Valley	285	1 522	242	9.5	58.4	16.2	1.8	8 859	13 573	27 308	12.5	3.9	25.8	17.2	16.5	23.2
Granite	105	351	622	9.2	47.1	22.1	3.6	7 796	16 636	27 813	13.3	4.9	16.8	14.8	13.9	21.9
Hill	488	4 105	5 291	8.0	45.3	20.0	26.5	8 146	14 935	30 781	-10.0	4.6	18.4	17.7	15.3	22.9
Jefferson	176	496	2 611	8.4	41.0	27.7	10.8	5 884	18 250	41 506	-1.6	7.0	9.0	10.0	6.7	9.9
Judith Basin	0	1 278	556	8.8	42.8	23.6	3.9	8 704	14 291	29 241	-3.6	5.0	21.1	16.3	16.3	24.7
Lake	378	3 028	7 008	7.4	47.5	22.2	31.0	6 717	15 173	28 740	8.3	4.7	18.7	17.2	14.0	23.1
Lewis and Clark	NA	NA	14 412	15.7	37.9	31.6	59.5	6 012	18 763	37 360	5.3	6.0	10.9	11.4	7.3	11.5
Liberty	NA	NA	512	6.3	50.0	17.6	3.7	8 935	14 882	30 284	-9.7	4.5	20.3	15.8	19.0	27.6
Lincoln	356	3 362	4 528	7.3	57.8	13.7	21.0	6 190	13 923	26 754	-4.7	2.1	19.2	18.5	14.2	22.6
McCone	NA	NA	435	3.4	52.1	16.4	2.4	8 428	15 162	29 718	8.0	3.5	16.8	16.9	14.1	16.9
Madison	43	666	1 480	4.6	42.8	25.5	8.5	7 795	16 944	30 233	2.0	4.8	12.1	12.7	10.2	13.0
Meagher	359	2 207	428	5.8	53.8	18.7	2.2	7 045	15 019	29 375	15.5	2.9	18.9	18.3	16.4	25.9
Mineral	996	1 588	888	7.7	60.5	12.3	6.5	8 456	15 166	27 143	-3.5	4.9	15.8	15.4	12.8	17.1
Missoula	NA	NA	30 019	8.5	35.5	32.8	88.9	6 391	17 808	34 454	9.6	6.2	14.8	15.5	8.8	13.4
Musselshell	529	2 713	1 008	7.1	55.5	16.7	5.2	6 888	15 389	25 527	14.0	2.7	19.9	18.0	13.0	23.5
Park	NA	NA	3 349	13.7	44.7	23.1	15.5	6 759	17 704	31 739	4.3	5.4	11.4	13.0	7.2	9.8
Petroleum	NA	NA	113	0.0	52.9	17.4	0.9	11 476	15 986	24 107	-6.6	5.7	23.2	23.4	21.0	28.8
Phillips	108	1 272	1 174	5.6	53.1	17.1	8.4	8 725	15 058	28 702	-4.0	2.9	18.3	17.0	13.8	20.6
Pondera	293	973	1 825	8.7	53.4	19.8	12.0	8 857	14 276	30 464	-3.6	4.2	18.8	17.3	15.0	21.2
Powder River	NA	NA	437	6.9	48.0	16.0	2.8	7 310	15 351	28 398	-5.4	3.4	12.9	13.8	9.9	11.6
Powell	539	2 805	1 483	13.3	56.9	13.1	7.8	7 293	13 816	30 625	5.4	3.5	12.6	12.5	10.2	15.9
Prairie	0	828	215	2.8	53.6	14.8	1.7	9 276	14 422	25 451	13.5	1.9	17.2	15.6	13.3	23.4
Ravalli	305	894	8 361	14.1	44.1	22.5	35.5	5 653	17 993	31 992	12.8	6.7	13.8	12.1	9.6	17.2
Richland	NA	NA	2 399	4.3	51.9	17.2	14.5	7 139	16 006	32 110	2.7	3.3	12.2	12.5	8.1	12.4
Roosevelt	NA	NA	3 651	4.8	51.8	15.6	26.5	9 418	11 347	24 834	-4.9	3.6	32.4	27.7	27.6	35.9
Rosebud	317	878	2 924	10.3	51.5	17.6	22.8	10 516	15 032	35 898	-1.7	5.0	22.4	17.8	17.8	26.0
Sanders	601	2 144	2 280	9.7	56.0	15.5	13.2	7 185	14 593	26 852	7.4	4.0	17.2	16.8	13.3	22.2
Sheridan	NA	NA	852	7.7	50.3	18.4	6.9	9 750	16 038	29 518	6.0	4.6	14.7	13.1	10.6	16.1
Silver Bow	473	4 380	9 439	13.3	49.2	21.7	32.1	6 092	17 009	30 402	6.7	4.9	14.9	14.3	10.7	17.9
Stillwater	109	593	1 888	6.5	51.6	17.8	10.7	6 754	18 468	39 205	23.7	5.3	9.8	9.2	6.2	9.2
Sweet Grass	220	1 045	808	8.5	46.5	23.6	4.0	6 345	17 880	32 422	15.6	6.0	11.4	10.0	9.0	13.5
Teton	46	1 616	1 586	10.0	48.4	20.8	9.0	6 755	14 635	30 197	1.8	3.3	16.6	14.1	12.2	20.4
Toole	NA	NA	1 297	10.0	54.1	16.8	7.1	7 224	14 731	30 169	-10.6	3.3	12.9	11.2	9.7	14.1
Treasure	NA	NA	212	2.4	54.8	18.2	1.5	9 475	14 392	29 830	22.3	3.9	14.7	13.5	8.5	15.4
Valley	142	1 771	1 808	6.1	55.8	15.7	11.7	8 669	16 246	30 979	5.9	4.2	13.5	14.3	9.5	15.3
Wheatland	0	44	478	6.7	61.8	13.5	3.4	7 347	11 954	24 492	7.6	1.8	20.4	14.7	11.1	15.7
Wibaux	NA	NA	249	1.2	58.0	16.0	1.8	8 588	16 121	28 224	8.4	3.8	15.3	15.3	8.6	14.6
Yellowstone	247	4 370	33 876	11.6	42.6	26.4	132.3	6 050	19 303	36 727	5.4	7.3	11.1	11.1	8.5	13.6
NEBRASKA	314	3 943	480 705	17.2	44.7	23.7	1 987.9	6 966	19 613	39 250	12.3	8.1	9.7	9.7	6.7	10.2
Adams	168	4 737	8 746	26.9	46.8	19.9	38.4	7 862	18 308	37 160	13.4	6.0	9.3	9.9	5.5	9.6
Antelope	17	887	1 892	11.8	54.3	14.3	13.6	11 042	14 601	30 114	21.5	3.6	13.6	14.1	10.3	15.9
Arthur	0	0	116	2.6	42.5	15.7	1.0	12 638	15 810	27 375	7.0	4.9	13.8	14.6	7.9	20.0
Banner	NA	NA	205	4.4	38.8	19.6	1.6	7 660	17 149	31 339	5.2	4.8	13.6	12.7	12.3	16.3

1. Data for serious crimes have not been adjusted for underreporting; this may affect comparability between geographic areas and over time.   2. Per 100,000 population estimated by the FBI.   3. All persons 3 years old and over enrolled in nursery school through college.   4. Persons 25 years old and over.   5. Elementary and secondary education expenditures.   6. Based on population enumerated as of April 1, 2000.

Table B. States and Counties — Personal Income

	Personal income, 2002												
			Per capita[1]					Transfer payments					
									Government payments to individuals				
STATE County	Total (mil dol)	Percent change, 2001–2002	Dollars	Rank	Wages and salaries[2] (mil dol)	Proprietor's income (mil dol)	Dividends, interest, and rent (mil dol)	Total (mil dol)	Total (mil dol)	Social Security (mil dol)	Medical payments (mil dol)	Income mainte-nance (mil dol)	Unemploy-ment insurance (mil dol)
	62	63	64	65	66	67	68	69	70	71	72	73	74
MISSOURI—Cont'd													
St. Louis city	9 194	2.8	27 352	638	13 098	917	1 544	2 254	2 174	548	1 056	371	72
MONTANA	22 606	3.8	24 831	X	13 537	2 288	4 905	3 789	3 560	1 527	1 250	300	96
Beaverhead	211	3.4	23 524	1 558	111	21	55	41	39	15	15	3	1
Big Horn	207	1.6	16 187	3 045	148	3	36	54	51	12	21	11	3
Blaine	113	0.7	16 593	3 019	51	12	30	29	27	9	12	3	1
Broadwater	94	6.0	21 436	2 169	41	10	20	20	19	9	7	1	0
Carbon	251	2.8	25 792	934	66	20	75	39	37	18	13	2	1
Carter	24	-17.6	17 556	2 947	8	1	9	5	5	2	2	0	0
Cascade	2 113	3.9	26 546	778	1 316	179	445	362	343	142	125	27	7
Chouteau	125	6.8	22 081	1 994	38	12	40	25	23	12	9	1	0
Custer	261	0.1	22 837	1 768	149	17	64	54	51	23	18	4	1
Daniels	55	0.7	28 286	513	23	11	15	10	10	5	4	0	0
Dawson	195	1.3	22 320	1 927	125	11	39	41	38	17	13	2	0
Deer Lodge	192	2.8	21 163	2 247	87	11	39	53	51	23	19	4	1
Fallon	59	-4.6	21 838	2 055	39	4	13	12	12	6	5	0	0
Fergus	269	0.7	23 057	1 706	128	34	71	57	54	25	21	3	2
Flathead	1 981	4.3	25 583	982	1 151	207	480	316	296	134	98	22	10
Gallatin	1 914	4.9	26 890	720	1 220	260	436	183	165	80	44	10	4
Garfield	25	-12.1	20 617	2 399	9	3	10	5	4	2	2	0	0
Glacier	240	3.0	18 192	2 871	147	22	35	67	64	14	27	15	0
Golden Valley	19	-2.3	17 318	2 967	5	-1	7	4	4	2	1	0	0
Granite	65	5.8	22 704	1 819	24	13	15	13	12	6	4	1	0
Hill	399	4.2	24 437	1 279	233	29	97	80	76	23	27	8	2
Jefferson	267	5.5	25 696	956	86	28	48	37	34	16	10	2	1
Judith Basin	41	-6.1	18 404	2 844	14	-1	16	9	9	4	3	0	1
Lake	527	4.4	19 545	2 651	259	42	123	119	112	47	40	11	4
Lewis and Clark	1 550	4.4	27 453	622	1 123	138	310	221	207	94	66	16	5
Liberty	46	14.1	22 571	1 858	22	5	15	10	10	5	4	0	0
Lincoln	366	4.7	19 559	2 646	167	50	70	101	96	43	33	9	4
McCone	35	-5.4	19 202	2 715	18	2	9	7	6	3	2	0	0
Madison	157	3.2	22 533	1 869	61	22	50	29	27	14	9	1	1
Meagher	42	3.0	21 810	2 062	16	7	11	9	9	4	3	0	0
Mineral	79	5.3	20 619	2 396	31	9	16	22	21	9	7	2	1
Missoula	2 626	5.2	26 823	731	1 847	302	508	349	325	127	114	30	9
Musselshell	76	2.2	17 045	2 990	27	4	19	23	21	9	8	1	0
Park	365	3.9	23 005	1 720	150	41	94	65	61	23	20	4	2
Petroleum	8	-13.2	15 682	3 059	3	1	2	2	2	1	0	0	0
Phillips	89	-1.4	20 496	2 433	40	9	25	21	19	9	8	1	0
Pondera	137	7.7	21 871	2 046	61	14	37	31	29	12	11	3	1
Powder River	33	-6.7	18 102	2 880	13	3	11	6	5	3	2	0	0
Powell	135	3.2	19 211	2 711	76	15	30	28	27	11	10	2	1
Prairie	26	-8.1	22 030	2 009	9	2	9	7	6	3	2	0	0
Ravalli	837	5.0	22 194	1 960	316	100	214	160	150	72	51	10	5
Richland	219	1.1	23 590	1 539	128	21	47	42	40	18	16	2	1
Roosevelt	199	4.6	19 113	2 738	108	20	34	58	55	15	23	12	1
Rosebud	215	1.2	23 226	1 651	185	7	32	36	34	12	12	5	2
Sanders	195	5.3	18 679	2 801	85	21	44	53	51	24	16	4	2
Sheridan	95	-1.7	24 882	1 164	34	14	31	20	19	10	7	1	0
Silver Bow	857	4.3	25 624	973	496	107	159	173	165	74	60	14	3
Stillwater	227	0.5	26 877	721	182	13	50	31	29	14	10	2	1
Sweet Grass	82	-0.6	22 716	1 815	32	9	32	13	12	6	4	1	0
Teton	141	4.4	22 257	1 944	54	16	40	28	26	13	9	1	1
Toole	118	6.3	21 835	2 057	71	18	27	20	18	9	6	1	0
Treasure	16	4.0	20 525	2 422	6	2	4	3	3	2	1	0	0
Valley	193	1.6	26 050	878	91	25	48	41	39	16	15	3	1
Wheatland	37	-5.9	17 042	2 992	15	1	10	11	11	4	5	1	0
Wibaux	20	-7.6	20 024	2 544	7	2	5	5	5	2	2	0	0
Yellowstone	3 735	3.7	28 330	509	2 586	341	692	529	496	217	174	39	12
NEBRASKA	50 414	2.1	29 182	X	33 947	4 821	9 870	7 069	6 666	2 774	2 740	504	148
Adams	784	1.9	25 370	1 027	493	49	194	137	130	58	52	9	2
Antelope	176	-1.6	24 275	1 318	63	34	42	33	32	14	14	2	1
Arthur	5	17.4	12 238	3 102	3	-4	3	2	2	1	0	0	0
Banner	16	-0.8	21 223	2 232	6	2	4	2	2	1	1	0	0

1. Based on the resident population estimated as of July 1 of the year shown. 2. Includes other labor income.

Table B. States and Counties — Earnings, Social Security, and Housing

STATE County	Earnings, 2002									Social Security beneficiaries, December 2003		Housing units, 2003	
			Percent by selected industries										
			Goods-related[1]		Service-related and health								
	Total (mil dol)	Farm	Total	Manu-facturing	Infor-mation and profes-sional and technical services	Retail trade	Finance, insur-ance, and real estate	Health services	Govern-ment	Number	Rate[2]	Supple-mental Security Income recipients, December 2003	Total	Percent change, 2000–2003
	75	76	77	78	79	80	81	82	83	84	85	86	87	88
MISSOURI—Cont'd														
St. Louis city	14 015	0.0	D	12.4	13.2	2.2	6.2	10.2	17.0	58 395	176	17 645	173 875	-1.4
MONTANA	15 825	1.3	16.3	6.0	8.4	9.4	6.4	12.2	22.8	163 659	178	14 365	419 726	1.7
Beaverhead	132	8.6	D	2.0	6.5	7.8	7.9	10.1	29.8	1 620	182	91	4 554	-0.4
Big Horn	152	0.0	D	D	2.4	4.5	2.0	D	51.2	1 660	129	302	4 662	0.2
Blaine	63	7.3	D	D	D	6.8	2.0	D	49.5	1 070	159	151	2 936	-0.4
Broadwater	51	9.5	D	20.3	3.7	3.9	D	D	19.9	1 010	228	66	2 015	0.6
Carbon	86	4.1	16.6	4.4	5.7	11.5	5.8	D	22.9	1 965	201	99	5 478	-0.3
Carter	9	0.0	4.7	1.1	D	6.0	D	D	38.5	295	221	13	805	-0.7
Cascade	1 494	0.4	D	2.9	7.6	9.3	7.5	16.6	30.8	15 055	189	1 514	35 469	0.7
Chouteau	49	19.9	4.3	1.7	D	7.6	5.9	D	30.2	1 145	205	55	2 752	-0.9
Custer	166	-0.2	7.5	2.1	5.0	10.2	7.1	17.0	29.2	2 525	222	230	5 343	-0.3
Daniels	33	19.9	D	0.9	21.4	3.2	2.8	D	18.9	535	276	17	1 140	-1.2
Dawson	136	3.8	D	1.2	D	8.7	4.4	12.2	21.8	1 800	205	97	4 144	-0.6
Deer Lodge	98	0.0	D	2.8	7.7	7.9	3.6	16.9	35.2	2 295	256	254	4 924	-0.7
Fallon	43	-1.4	D	1.5	D	8.0	3.1	8.7	21.3	615	223	22	1 403	-0.5
Fergus	162	2.0	D	9.9	4.1	10.6	4.9	D	23.6	2 760	236	169	5 528	-0.5
Flathead	1 358	0.2	22.8	11.5	8.1	11.4	7.2	11.9	14.2	14 395	181	1 110	35 682	2.6
Gallatin	1 481	0.8	19.4	7.3	10.4	11.3	8.7	7.3	20.5	8 305	113	420	31 507	6.8
Garfield	12	15.8	D	D	D	6.9	D	D	28.8	270	219	8	950	-1.1
Glacier	169	5.0	7.1	0.7	D	7.3	2.0	D	51.0	1 700	128	428	5 219	-0.5
Golden Valley	4	-13.8	D	D	1.5	D	3.4	D	60.8	235	224	11	443	-1.6
Granite	37	7.1	D	9.0	D	4.4	D	D	24.2	665	230	31	2 049	-1.2
Hill	262	2.4	6.9	1.2	8.4	9.4	4.3	D	29.2	2 450	150	327	7 438	-0.2
Jefferson	115	0.5	37.2	7.8	3.4	4.3	D	D	26.8	1 775	169	102	4 176	-0.5
Judith Basin	13	-3.8	D	D	D	3.9	D	2.3	52.3	485	221	19	1 306	-1.4
Lake	301	1.2	17.5	9.4	5.7	10.1	4.0	11.7	32.2	5 380	198	523	13 755	1.1
Lewis and Clark	1 260	0.2	8.8	2.6	11.7	8.3	8.6	10.3	35.8	9 865	173	866	25 842	0.7
Liberty	27	23.3	D	D	D	3.9	3.2	16.4	21.1	420	204	12	1 059	-1.0
Lincoln	217	0.4	21.6	14.8	3.9	8.2	3.2	9.2	28.4	4 745	252	450	9 350	0.3
McCone	20	10.6	D	D	D	4.3	D	D	24.2	395	217	18	1 078	-0.8
Madison	83	0.0	25.4	4.4	4.3	7.5	17.2	D	21.4	1 525	219	29	4 633	-0.8
Meagher	23	19.8	D	D	D	6.3	D	D	23.8	460	234	20	1 342	-1.5
Mineral	40	0.8	17.9	13.2	D	13.3	D	6.9	31.3	995	256	19	1 973	0.6
Missoula	2 150	-0.1	D	6.2	10.2	10.0	6.4	15.6	18.7	13 345	135	1 637	43 515	5.3
Musselshell	32	2.4	20.4	3.5	5.6	8.0	3.8	D	25.3	1 050	235	79	2 300	-0.7
Park	190	4.6	16.5	6.5	7.2	11.6	6.6	11.0	15.4	2 610	165	179	8 279	0.4
Petroleum	3	15.2	4.6	0.0	D	D	2.4	D	43.0	90	183	7	289	-1.0
Phillips	49	4.1	D	1.9	2.9	7.6	D	D	28.4	1 045	245	99	2 474	-1.1
Pondera	75	13.5	21.6	2.5	2.3	8.7	4.1	10.1	22.3	1 300	211	113	2 814	-0.7
Powder River	15	1.6	D	D	D	8.5	D	D	39.3	335	183	14	1 003	-0.4
Powell	91	5.4	D	D	1.5	4.7	D	D	46.5	1 210	173	80	2 908	-0.8
Prairie	11	23.2	D	D	D	5.9	D	0.6	40.2	320	277	12	710	-1.1
Ravalli	416	0.5	D	13.2	7.0	10.6	5.7	8.4	20.8	8 050	208	474	16 125	1.1
Richland	149	5.4	25.7	8.4	5.5	8.4	3.0	D	18.5	1 920	210	118	4 551	-0.1
Roosevelt	127	9.9	D	2.0	D	9.1	1.9	8.2	51.5	1 705	163	289	4 022	-0.5
Rosebud	192	0.2	24.7	0.1	2.3	3.3	1.1	D	35.8	1 340	144	162	3 936	0.6
Sanders	106	-0.7	16.0	8.5	4.0	7.2	3.7	D	24.3	2 745	263	209	5 281	0.2
Sheridan	48	17.3	D	1.3	3.7	6.8	4.4	D	27.2	1 075	293	51	2 144	-1.1
Silver Bow	603	0.1	14.1	3.8	14.7	11.3	3.3	13.8	17.9	7 365	222	867	16 108	-0.4
Stillwater	195	-0.6	D	5.3	D	3.2	D	2.2	7.9	1 510	179	72	3 986	1.0
Sweet Grass	41	2.9	D	6.6	6.4	14.4	6.2	1.3	26.4	710	197	12	1 890	1.6
Teton	70	13.5	D	1.5	D	6.7	4.8	D	22.2	1 390	218	65	2 894	-0.5
Toole	89	6.5	D	1.0	D	6.2	3.1	D	25.6	915	171	62	2 287	-0.6
Treasure	8	27.2	2.8	0.0	D	2.6	D	D	24.4	195	265	5	419	-0.7
Valley	115	10.7	7.8	2.1	3.3	8.8	4.6	D	24.0	1 765	240	155	4 804	-0.9
Wheatland	16	0.3	D	D	D	6.7	4.7	13.5	39.4	470	223	22	1 135	-1.6
Wibaux	9	15.8	3.9	1.1	D	1.2	3.1	D	35.9	245	251	13	581	-1.0
Yellowstone	2 927	0.3	16.6	6.6	9.5	9.6	7.2	15.8	13.4	22 495	169	2 012	56 316	3.2
NEBRASKA	38 768	2.3	19.3	12.1	9.3	7.1	8.3	9.8	17.4	287 891	166	21 876	746 397	3.3
Adams	542	2.0	26.3	21.0	4.7	8.2	4.3	D	17.8	5 885	191	437	13 168	1.2
Antelope	97	21.0	D	4.0	D	7.9	5.0	7.6	18.6	1 635	227	67	3 335	-0.3
Arthur	-1	0.0	D	D	D	D	-15.0	0.0	0.0	115	289	6	279	2.2
Banner	7	38.1	D	5.2	1.9	0.0	D	0.0	30.4	135	174	1	380	1.3

1. Covers mining, construction, and manufacturing.   2. Per 1,000 resident population estimated as of July 1 of the year shown.

Table B. States and Counties — Housing, Labor Force, and Employment

STATE County	Housing units, 2000 Occupied units Total	Percent	Owner-occupied Median value[1]	With a mortgage	Without a mortgage	Renter-occupied Median rent[3]	Median rent as a percent of income	Substandard units[4] (percent)	Civilian labor force, 2003 Total	Percent change, 2002–2003	Unemployment Total	Rate[5]	Civilian employment,[6] 2000 Total	Percent Management, professional and related occupations	Production, transportation, and material moving occupations
	89	90	91	92	93	94	95	96	97	98	99	100	101	102	103
MISSOURI—Cont'd															
St. Louis city	147 076	46.9	63 900	20.1	11.4	442	26.1	5.5	161 963	2.4	16 347	10.1	143 850	29.7	15.4
MONTANA	358 667	69.1	99 500	22.2	10.4	447	25.3	3.8	474 910	2.5	22 494	4.7	425 977	33.1	11.2
Beaverhead	3 684	63.7	89 200	21.6	10.2	392	25.7	2.6	4 940	2.2	181	3.7	4 478	34.6	11.0
Big Horn	3 924	64.9	61 400	20.5	11.1	356	17.6	15.7	5 111	0.6	803	15.7	4 660	33.5	7.3
Blaine	2 501	61.0	56 800	19.7	12.0	295	19.1	9.2	2 607	0.6	142	5.4	2 789	41.4	6.8
Broadwater	1 752	79.3	85 500	22.4	10.2	409	22.1	4.6	2 185	3.8	108	4.9	2 032	32.5	13.5
Carbon	4 065	74.2	101 700	22.1	11.0	439	22.2	2.7	4 654	0.8	177	3.8	4 566	35.4	9.8
Carter	543	74.6	34 600	27.5	13.1	325	17.8	2.6	914	1.9	20	2.2	743	59.5	3.1
Cascade	32 547	64.9	92 500	22.1	10.1	414	25.2	3.5	36 527	0.8	1 674	4.6	34 792	30.5	10.4
Chouteau	2 226	68.6	69 000	24.6	11.5	287	17.3	3.9	2 542	2.1	64	2.5	2 600	45.3	8.0
Custer	4 768	70.1	63 100	19.3	11.7	373	22.0	2.9	5 715	0.6	179	3.1	5 554	32.1	7.7
Daniels	892	77.9	45 100	20.7	11.7	346	22.6	0.4	1 125	-5.2	25	2.2	903	43.3	6.1
Dawson	3 625	74.0	62 700	18.5	11.4	346	21.4	1.6	4 834	0.9	116	2.4	4 358	32.7	11.0
Deer Lodge	3 995	73.9	70 700	21.6	12.4	321	24.7	3.0	3 575	-6.9	232	6.5	3 790	27.7	9.5
Fallon	1 140	77.3	48 000	17.8	11.4	322	20.5	1.4	1 580	-0.6	42	2.7	1 429	34.5	13.7
Fergus	4 860	73.7	70 600	21.4	9.9	413	25.1	2.3	5 943	0.2	302	5.1	5 589	37.0	10.0
Flathead	29 588	73.3	125 600	24.8	9.9	484	25.5	4.5	41 633	3.2	2 672	6.4	34 680	28.2	15.3
Gallatin	26 323	62.4	143 000	23.2	9.9	555	26.0	3.0	46 035	3.3	1 309	2.8	37 611	35.4	10.8
Garfield	532	73.3	34 700	21.1	14.0	319	17.3	4.1	884	1.0	21	2.4	654	48.9	8.1
Glacier	4 304	62.0	60 900	18.1	13.9	351	19.7	11.8	5 372	4.2	627	11.7	4 750	37.8	8.1
Golden Valley	365	77.5	47 700	19.9	11.2	348	30.4	3.3	475	3.3	33	6.9	512	43.9	10.0
Granite	1 200	74.0	78 300	25.4	11.1	381	25.1	5.6	1 126	0.4	78	6.9	1 272	31.2	10.5
Hill	6 457	64.4	80 500	21.6	11.1	364	24.3	5.0	9 306	1.4	361	3.9	7 415	33.1	10.2
Jefferson	3 747	83.2	128 700	21.6	9.9	419	21.8	3.5	5 024	3.1	218	4.3	4 895	39.3	7.8
Judith Basin	951	77.2	56 700	19.6	11.6	340	18.3	3.8	1 112	2.6	49	4.4	1 068	50.0	7.5
Lake	10 192	71.5	117 200	24.3	11.0	403	24.9	4.5	11 642	0.8	784	6.7	11 069	31.4	14.1
Lewis and Clark	22 850	70.0	112 200	22.0	9.9	457	24.5	3.1	28 394	2.9	1 114	3.9	28 651	39.6	8.9
Liberty	833	71.9	58 800	25.6	9.9	340	20.4	5.2	1 062	2.3	32	3.0	893	40.9	6.6
Lincoln	7 764	76.5	82 600	22.0	11.4	374	26.4	7.2	7 018	4.7	1 117	15.9	6 814	27.1	17.4
McCone	810	77.7	42 600	21.4	12.1	406	21.8	1.4	1 138	-0.2	27	2.4	1 011	43.1	6.8
Madison	2 956	70.4	104 500	22.9	11.8	460	24.3	3.2	3 909	1.5	154	3.9	3 169	32.4	11.6
Meagher	803	73.2	72 100	23.2	11.5	373	27.7	4.2	963	3.4	52	5.4	904	34.4	5.1
Mineral	1 584	73.0	88 300	25.7	11.5	418	26.2	6.8	1 637	-0.2	148	9.0	1 678	24.2	16.0
Missoula	38 439	61.9	136 500	23.5	10.1	530	30.8	3.4	56 671	4.1	2 189	3.9	50 436	32.3	10.9
Musselshell	1 878	76.9	54 600	20.1	12.3	350	24.3	4.6	1 788	1.0	127	7.1	1 929	30.6	11.6
Park	6 828	66.4	97 900	23.1	11.9	443	24.6	3.5	9 622	0.4	440	4.6	7 857	31.1	11.2
Petroleum	211	74.4	58 300	20.0	16.9	330	30.0	0.9	292	3.9	14	4.8	232	51.7	2.6
Phillips	1 848	70.5	60 700	21.0	9.9	320	18.1	2.1	2 121	1.6	98	4.6	2 154	36.1	10.4
Pondera	2 410	70.2	70 500	21.1	12.7	367	20.1	6.8	3 134	1.3	160	5.1	2 699	41.6	10.0
Powder River	737	72.9	59 800	19.0	12.7	346	17.4	1.9	1 152	0.1	31	2.7	924	44.8	6.8
Powell	2 422	71.3	73 500	19.7	9.9	411	20.8	2.6	2 366	0.6	137	5.8	2 602	32.5	14.3
Prairie	537	77.7	36 500	16.7	10.7	283	18.1	2.6	604	-3.5	22	3.6	577	48.0	8.5
Ravalli	14 289	75.7	133 400	25.4	9.9	502	27.3	3.8	19 252	3.8	1 051	5.5	15 730	32.2	11.9
Richland	3 878	72.3	61 000	19.0	10.4	347	20.1	2.0	5 228	-1.7	239	4.6	4 465	32.7	13.3
Roosevelt	3 581	65.3	47 400	18.3	13.1	323	22.9	7.3	4 137	3.3	321	7.8	3 867	38.8	8.1
Rosebud	3 307	67.2	66 700	17.4	10.5	350	18.6	8.6	4 782	8.1	300	6.3	3 926	34.0	12.9
Sanders	4 273	76.5	82 900	24.7	11.4	390	25.1	5.1	4 465	3.6	367	8.2	3 952	30.1	17.5
Sheridan	1 741	80.1	45 800	19.7	10.9	290	22.5	2.0	1 928	0.9	68	3.5	1 877	37.8	13.1
Silver Bow	14 432	70.4	74 900	21.2	11.0	362	24.7	3.1	16 680	1.5	852	5.1	15 768	32.4	11.1
Stillwater	3 234	76.0	102 200	19.8	9.9	439	19.5	3.1	5 330	-0.8	161	3.0	3 907	27.9	14.9
Sweet Grass	1 476	74.1	97 800	21.7	11.3	429	20.9	2.9	1 839	0.4	47	2.6	1 772	35.2	8.4
Teton	2 538	75.7	74 700	22.9	10.7	362	22.6	4.5	3 202	1.4	108	3.4	2 719	39.4	9.7
Toole	1 962	71.5	60 700	20.9	10.7	372	23.1	2.9	2 922	8.6	80	2.7	2 280	30.4	9.5
Treasure	357	71.4	40 700	20.5	11.4	283	31.0	3.6	443	4.7	16	3.6	429	34.3	6.1
Valley	3 150	75.9	59 400	18.3	10.5	351	24.0	1.7	4 267	3.6	151	3.5	3 511	35.2	7.7
Wheatland	853	72.2	53 100	20.4	11.5	315	21.2	2.2	1 124	0.4	46	4.1	1 020	37.5	5.4
Wibaux	421	73.2	37 500	21.3	9.9	281	20.9	1.0	555	0.0	17	3.1	503	41.0	12.7
Yellowstone	52 084	69.2	101 900	21.2	9.9	474	25.2	2.8	72 034	3.0	2 596	3.6	65 512	31.0	11.8
NEBRASKA	666 184	67.4	88 000	19.7	10.5	491	23.0	3.0	976 034	2.1	39 370	4.0	877 237	33.0	15.1
Adams	12 141	66.8	77 200	19.7	9.9	445	22.3	2.8	15 329	-2.0	607	4.0	16 044	30.4	18.6
Antelope	2 953	76.4	44 600	18.3	11.9	327	19.7	2.2	3 116	2.6	122	3.9	3 690	35.4	11.8
Arthur	185	63.8	44 300	11.3	9.9	286	22.1	2.2	218	1.9	10	4.6	251	42.2	6.4
Banner	311	64.6	45 800	30.3	9.9	246	15.6	1.9	403	3.6	8	2.0	396	41.9	8.3

1. Specified owner-occupied units. 2. Median monthly owner costs is often in the minimum category—9.9 percent or less, which is indicated as 9.9 percent. 3. Specified renter-occupied units. 4. Overcrowded or lacking complete plumbing facilities. 5. Percent of civilian labor force. 6. Persons 16 years old and over.

Table B. States and Counties — Nonfarm Employment and Agriculture

STATE County	Private nonfarm establishments, employment and payroll, 2001									Agriculture, 2002			
	Number of establishments	Employment						Annual payroll		Farms			Farm operators whose principal occupation is farming (percent)
		Total	Health care and social assistance	Manufacturing	Retail trade	Finance and insurance	Professional, scientific, and technical services	Total (mil dol)	Average per employee (dollars)	Number	Percent with—		
											Less than 50 acres	500 acres and over	
	104	105	106	107	108	109	110	111	112	113	114	115	116
MISSOURI—Cont'd													
St. Louis city	9 493	270 043	36 099	27 957	17 269	20 694	17 537	10 755	39 827	NA	NA	NA	NA
MONTANA	32 294	301 460	49 761	20 759	52 917	13 987	16 191	7 227	23 973	27 870	23.3	46.4	63.5
Beaverhead	356	2 145	379	52	470	113	75	41	19 156	421	24.5	46.3	61.5
Big Horn	216	1 913	453	D	370	74	53	54	28 282	584	16.3	55.3	67.1
Blaine	167	1 025	329	D	232	43	11	23	22 654	588	8.2	66.2	70.2
Broadwater	111	758	106	221	110	26	20	18	24 197	279	19.7	41.2	66.3
Carbon	328	1 949	280	101	305	74	55	34	17 507	703	20.6	35.1	64.4
Carter	28	116	D	D	19	D	D	2	17 845	289	5.2	85.5	82.7
Cascade	2 519	27 540	5 594	937	5 281	2 064	1 007	607	22 026	1 037	26.8	37.0	56.8
Chouteau	152	715	211	38	152	47	D	12	16 957	787	4.3	76.5	84.6
Custer	393	3 752	1 104	73	744	181	103	84	22 441	425	20.0	48.7	69.6
Daniels	85	533	D	D	109	33	12	12	21 794	364	3.3	74.5	75.8
Dawson	304	2 468	622	D	484	92	45	44	17 771	522	8.4	66.9	71.1
Deer Lodge	237	2 400	924	91	289	63	36	48	20 011	109	24.8	45.9	53.2
Fallon	116	684	D	7	139	37	9	15	21 778	327	8.9	67.0	69.7
Fergus	446	3 133	746	277	526	155	81	63	20 202	830	14.1	62.4	68.8
Flathead	3 279	29 075	3 632	3 655	4 843	1 385	1 737	709	24 370	1 075	53.0	9.1	51.0
Gallatin	3 565	29 937	3 004	3 010	5 391	869	1 753	683	22 828	1 074	38.5	23.2	52.0
Garfield	23	129	D	D	42	D	0	2	13 628	268	6.3	86.2	83.6
Glacier	282	2 095	454	D	411	74	89	51	24 537	472	8.7	65.0	68.6
Golden Valley	16	53	D	D	D	0	D	0	8 000	140	7.1	68.6	69.3
Granite	87	432	53	D	75	D	6	8	19 410	140	9.3	61.4	59.3
Hill	505	4 706	1 135	49	876	105	171	92	19 546	836	6.1	66.3	66.9
Jefferson	209	1 446	192	115	190	42	30	37	25 308	372	29.8	26.1	48.4
Judith Basin	58	178	16	D	15	D	D	3	14 798	316	11.7	71.8	77.8
Lake	710	5 436	1 069	812	1 007	232	152	121	22 196	1 185	47.8	11.9	54.9
Lewis and Clark	1 970	20 980	4 048	646	3 624	1 770	1 461	508	24 216	635	47.9	20.9	52.6
Liberty	70	508	D	D	56	21	15	10	19 906	297	3.4	82.5	90.6
Lincoln	559	3 806	624	653	639	135	86	82	21 529	310	45.8	8.1	48.4
McCone	51	357	D	D	47	25	D	8	21 913	496	7.1	73.2	69.6
Madison	288	1 097	124	110	144	66	D	25	22 681	513	23.4	39.8	58.1
Meagher	65	275	80	0	57	D	D	4	16 298	136	16.2	66.2	76.5
Mineral	115	778	157	147	197	D	D	12	15 359	85	34.1	12.9	41.2
Missoula	3 674	42 622	6 724	2 892	7 785	1 607	2 248	1 071	25 136	641	55.5	11.4	44.6
Musselshell	121	593	158	D	119	24	16	11	17 808	319	12.9	53.0	69.0
Park	732	4 255	635	409	726	185	198	83	19 400	527	27.1	38.5	53.9
Petroleum	11	20	D	0	3	0	0	0	22 600	89	2.2	73.0	73.0
Phillips	142	837	204	7	198	75	27	14	16 848	525	6.9	66.7	71.6
Pondera	202	1 371	278	77	293	60	52	29	20 890	520	11.9	63.7	75.8
Powder River	72	201	D	D	75	17	15	3	13 711	301	9.0	80.4	78.1
Powell	157	1 087	287	D	133	43	14	21	19 600	274	23.0	44.2	64.6
Prairie	34	180	D	D	29	17	D	3	14 494	162	6.2	75.9	82.7
Ravalli	1 232	7 755	1 001	1 088	1 366	385	298	163	21 070	1 441	64.5	6.6	51.7
Richland	393	3 150	535	375	505	122	97	66	20 952	587	13.1	60.6	67.5
Roosevelt	240	1 841	387	110	460	68	47	30	16 090	683	6.3	64.1	66.6
Rosebud	199	2 637	161	D	321	48	52	88	33 511	412	11.7	58.7	67.2
Sanders	347	1 893	306	193	299	79	42	36	18 876	464	32.5	20.7	51.3
Sheridan	151	883	256	21	189	57	30	14	15 863	626	3.7	70.6	74.4
Silver Bow	1 126	11 948	2 479	416	2 262	282	988	294	24 636	155	32.3	22.6	53.5
Stillwater	228	2 792	205	314	300	54	D	113	40 546	552	21.7	47.1	61.4
Sweet Grass	143	615	20	63	188	31	28	12	19 725	357	16.2	53.8	57.4
Teton	202	1 155	239	29	208	87	31	21	18 127	700	13.0	53.7	72.7
Toole	217	1 533	191	40	261	55	38	32	20 623	405	4.4	75.8	70.1
Treasure	24	95	D	D	27	D	5	2	20 895	115	12.2	62.6	78.3
Valley	251	1 789	455	55	315	149	66	35	19 636	743	6.6	63.9	72.9
Wheatland	60	328	D	D	77	21	D	4	13 128	163	8.0	71.8	67.5
Wibaux	23	146	D	0	D	D	5	2	15 240	215	6.0	65.1	72.6
Yellowstone	4 963	60 587	9 070	3 294	9 922	2 642	4 752	1 634	26 978	1 279	37.1	25.6	50.3
NEBRASKA	49 710	746 168	102 838	108 539	109 468	53 136	35 738	20 831	27 917	49 355	14.8	41.6	73.0
Adams	946	13 947	2 681	3 433	2 137	357	286	322	23 120	561	11.4	47.6	80.9
Antelope	235	1 373	254	141	352	85	15	25	18 279	792	8.8	44.9	78.8
Arthur	13	56	0	D	9	D	D	1	13 446	76	10.5	81.6	89.5
Banner	6	21	0	0	0	D	0	0	21 810	226	1.8	65.9	72.6

STATE County	Agriculture, 2002 (cont'd)															
	Land in farms					Value of land and buildings (dollars)			Value of products sold				Percent of farms with sales of —		Government payments	
			Acres					Value of machinery and equipment average per farm (dollars)			Percent from —					
	Acreage (1,000)	Percent change, 1997–2002	Average size of farm	Total irrigated (1,000)	Total cropland (1,000)	Average per farm	Average per acre		Total (mil dol)	Average per farm (dollars)	Crops	Live-stock and poultry products	$10,000 or more	$100,000 or more	Total ($1,000)	Percent of farms
	117	118	119	120	121	122	123	124	125	126	127	128	129	130	131	132
MISSOURI—Cont'd	NA	NA	NA	NA	NA	NA	NA	NA	NA	NA	NA	NA	NA	NA	NA	NA
St. Louis city	NA	NA	NA	NA	NA	NA	NA	NA	NA	NA	39.0	61.0	49.6	18.0	210 749	44.5
MONTANA	59 612	1.7	2 139	1 976	18 316	835 250	386	83 976	1 882	67 532	39.0	61.0	49.6	18.0	210 749	44.5
Beaverhead........................	1 279	11.0	3 038	209	192	1 605 518	548	96 562	63	150 274	14.9	85.1	52.0	28.5	998	25.7
Big Horn............................	2 811	1.5	4 814	54	388	1 137 354	246	91 386	66	113 419	26.9	73.1	59.6	27.1	4 169	39.4
Blaine...............................	2 261	0.1	3 846	50	706	947 437	245	108 702	53	90 637	45.4	54.6	64.5	27.4	8 917	64.3
Broadwater........................	470	3.8	1 684	49	151	771 349	464	99 468	19	68 165	60.4	39.6	54.1	22.2	1 949	43.4
Carbon..............................	754	2.4	1 072	77	161	868 404	766	65 333	47	66 221	28.8	71.2	54.1	11.9	1 154	35.3
Carter...............................	1 667	4.9	5 768	2	230	1 131 648	197	109 296	30	105 302	3.7	96.3	78.5	42.2	1 954	55.0
Cascade............................	1 389	-3.6	1 339	42	507	603 928	425	58 769	51	49 160	36.8	63.2	42.9	13.1	6 100	43.7
Chouteau...........................	2 301	4.0	2 924	12	1 364	1 265 042	420	135 216	56	70 704	75.3	24.7	61.0	22.4	18 848	81.2
Custer...............................	1 904	0.3	4 480	28	169	899 121	194	70 665	41	95 735	14.8	85.2	56.5	26.4	2 003	38.1
Daniels.............................	815	6.5	2 240	1	539	636 668	292	117 776	27	74 733	77.7	22.3	57.1	24.7	5 683	86.5
Dawson............................	1 411	-0.4	2 703	18	467	559 258	219	106 914	36	69 247	53.8	46.2	43.1	10.1	5 496	65.3
Deer Lodge.......................	135	32.4	1 239	17	25	698 856	627	59 034	4	39 407	15.0	85.0	43.1	10.1	49	11.0
Fallon...............................	932	-2.2	2 851	1	241	756 861	262	85 786	22	68 622	9.7	90.3	58.7	20.8	2 677	64.5
Fergus..............................	2 282	1.5	2 749	13	677	1 018 176	301	97 016	61	73 743	30.8	69.2	61.4	26.3	6 125	51.0
Flathead...........................	235	8.8	218	32	108	465 200	2 344	42 663	31	28 384	63.5	36.5	28.6	6.4	508	14.0
Gallatin............................	709	-6.7	660	102	286	821 164	1 091	76 714	76	70 852	53.3	46.7	40.8	17.8	2 304	21.8
Garfield............................	2 182	0.9	8 141	4	378	1 350 434	165	111 938	32	119 400	20.0	80.0	74.6	37.7	4 888	66.4
Glacier.............................	1 645	1.4	3 486	22	536	1 201 891	336	110 183	39	83 179	52.1	47.9	58.5	20.8	6 354	50.2
Golden Valley...................	661	3.6	4 720	5	131	1 114 086	243	80 251	8	57 146	12.0	88.0	44.3	14.3	2 104	61.4
Granite.............................	283	5.6	2 021	35	39	1 439 578	700	77 608	11	79 133	10.8	89.2	60.7	28.6	184	21.4
Hill..................................	1 809	10.1	2 164	3	1 178	656 884	319	126 306	43	51 980	77.2	22.8	53.9	17.0	16 312	76.1
Jefferson..........................	387	6.3	1 041	26	71	633 451	603	40 670	10	26 085	12.7	87.3	23.7	8.9	593	15.9
Judith Basin	830	-0.6	2 626	8	307	1 284 006	526	116 997	32	102 031	26.2	73.8	72.2	32.9	3 079	60.8
Lake.................................	602	0.8	508	89	135	627 455	1 156	51 069	39	33 215	46.2	53.8	46.7	7.6	932	19.4
Lewis and Clark................	842	2.4	1 326	43	104	638 667	565	49 146	23	35 628	30.8	69.2	29.8	7.7	772	16.5
Liberty.............................	905	-1.1	3 048	6	652	1 000 240	335	161 659	26	87 209	66.8	33.2	68.4	24.6	8 421	89.6
Lincoln.............................	54	17.4	175	5	19	442 601	2 869	21 499	3	8 115	31.1	68.8	18.1	0.6	18	4.2
McCone............................	1 346	2.5	2 714	10	581	623 990	226	116 959	30	59 788	58.9	41.1	62.1	21.0	6 032	73.0
Madison............................	1 029	-4.7	2 005	99	149	1 209 397	648	74 770	37	72 279	18.5	81.5	49.7	22.0	829	24.4
Meagher...........................	857	-8.8	6 303	42	115	2 759 126	434	135 496	20	144 959	11.3	88.7	69.1	33.8	1 081	41.9
Mineral.............................	16	0.0	191	1	5	370 136	1 937	25 164	1	8 635	24.4	75.6	16.5	0.0	6	8.2
Missoula...........................	258	-1.5	403	19	44	608 634	1 438	37 745	8	13 044	33.3	66.7	20.0	2.5	142	10.0
Musselshell......................	1 034	8.5	3 240	12	162	841 756	242	60 477	16	49 381	13.8	86.2	39.2	13.2	2 126	34.5
Park.................................	847	13.1	1 607	58	156	1 265 450	713	73 642	21	39 787	20.1	79.9	41.2	11.4	1 013	21.6
Petroleum.........................	538	-0.6	6 045	5	89	1 685 561	277	118 205	9	101 877	11.3	88.7	71.9	37.1	908	48.3
Phillips.............................	1 897	-4.1	3 613	35	538	811 774	219	78 517	38	72 016	32.1	67.9	56.8	23.2	7 712	65.3
Pondera............................	900	2.5	1 731	78	609	762 640	453	115 028	48	92 657	64.4	35.6	66.0	28.7	8 694	70.2
Powder River.....................	1 522	-2.4	5 055	9	181	1 142 208	218	91 226	30	98 009	3.8	96.2	73.8	33.2	1 666	46.8
Powell..............................	619	-4.6	2 258	63	77	1 385 954	620	61 308	19	69 793	14.2	85.8	48.9	21.9	302	23.0
Prairie..............................	620	1.1	3 825	15	127	854 986	211	117 827	19	114 498	29.3	70.7	73.5	38.3	1 890	74.7
Ravalli.............................	245	33.2	170	76	101	503 888	2 676	35 434	29	19 876	36.0	64.0	24.4	4.2	408	10.1
Richland............................	1 201	-1.2	2 047	48	514	641 611	290	144 450	68	115 695	44.3	55.7	58.8	24.2	6 068	67.3
Roosevelt..........................	1 441	0.8	2 111	22	791	648 073	299	108 508	51	74 366	77.3	22.7	54.3	21.7	8 022	76.3
Rosebud...........................	2 541	-5.2	6 167	32	236	1 106 686	180	80 966	42	102 583	18.4	81.6	60.2	23.8	2 677	43.2
Sanders...........................	346	-15.6	745	17	53	967 266	1 096	42 640	14	30 342	47.3	52.7	34.1	5.0	200	15.7
Sheridan...........................	1 047	4.6	1 672	8	706	516 544	335	93 929	43	68 832	78.1	21.9	57.2	22.4	7 533	81.0
Silver Bow........................	74	-26.0	476	6	12	563 605	977	40 503	3	18 440	8.4	91.6	30.3	6.5	41	11.0
Stillwater..........................	890	-0.8	1 613	26	253	785 212	480	56 815	29	52 788	12.8	87.2	47.5	10.9	2 748	44.9
Sweet Grass.....................	867	3.3	2 429	44	100	1 375 446	556	73 595	17	46 718	10.1	89.9	47.9	12.6	623	23.2
Teton...............................	1 231	10.2	1 758	130	644	719 310	362	112 489	73	103 579	47.3	52.7	57.6	26.3	10 209	68.3
Toole................................	1 088	-0.3	2 686	4	690	931 265	350	138 509	34	84 977	74.3	25.7	58.0	26.2	8 947	78.5
Treasure...........................	607	0.2	5 277	19	35	1 304 805	239	105 541	20	170 108	24.7	75.3	66.1	31.3	515	50.4
Valley..............................	2 052	14.8	2 761	49	846	707 910	257	106 914	67	90 763	48.0	52.0	61.1	23.6	9 610	74.8
Wheatland........................	842	1.0	5 163	15	187	1 492 759	285	121 551	18	109 997	14.6	85.4	62.6	23.3	1 916	57.7
Wibaux.............................	536	12.8	2 492	1	176	594 584	241	66 566	12	57 493	38.6	61.4	56.3	19.1	1 931	78.1
Yellowstone......................	1 569	2.8	1 226	78	378	689 301	505	64 789	118	92 107	20.6	79.4	39.2	12.2	4 313	32.7
NEBRASKA.....................	45 903	0.8	930	7 625	22 521	723 863	776	111 776	9 704	196 609	34.9	65.1	69.5	32.0	347 517	64.9
Adams..............................	344	0.0	614	199	293	875 730	1 557	123 134	157	278 979	46.0	54.0	80.4	48.3	5 411	66.1
Antelope...........................	527	7.1	665	225	378	729 434	1 086	119 341	196	247 958	38.9	61.1	77.5	44.8	6 700	69.1
Arthur..............................	436	-6.2	5 740	8	50	1 133 195	195	92 524	14	183 509	7.7	92.3	89.5	52.6	449	53.9
Banner.............................	411	-7.8	1 819	20	185	586 582	306	164 575	56	247 915	14.9	85.1	57.5	19.9	2 861	79.2

Table B. States and Counties — Residential Construction, Wholesale Trade, Retail Trade, and Real Estate

STATE County	Value of residential construction authorized by building permits, 2003		Wholesale trade, 1997				Retail trade,[1] 1997				Real estate and rental and leasing, 1997			
	New construction ($1,000)	Number of housing units	Number of establish-ments	Number of employees	Sales (mil dol)	Annual payroll (mil dol)	Number of establish-ments	Number of employees	Sales (mil dol)	Annual payroll (mil dol)	Number of establish-ments	Number of employees	Receipts (mil dol)	Annual payroll (mil dol)
	133	134	135	136	137	138	139	140	141	142	143	144	145	146
MISSOURI—Cont'd														
St. Louis city	116 774	1 215	902	16 599	10 582.9	646.4	1 241	14 511	2 361.7	282.4	401	3 520	402.9	76.7
MONTANA	411 698	3 767	1 577	14 381	7 709.5	372.3	5 042	48 337	7 779.1	746.5	1 186	4 265	353.4	58.1
Beaverhead.........................	823	6	11	95	16.3	1.6	60	474	69.5	7.2	13	36	2.1	0.6
Big Horn	489	6	10	D	D	D	50	415	56.5	5.7	7	D	D	D
Blaine	0	0	13	81	58.2	1.2	36	204	30.5	2.7	3	4	0.4	0.0
Broadwater.........................	345	6	8	61	37.1	1.8	17	103	12.7	1.1	3	5	0.1	0.0
Carbon	3 585	47	13	55	9.9	1.0	45	267	32.8	3.2	14	28	1.4	0.2
Carter	0	0	1	D	D	D	4	18	2.6	0.2	NA	NA	NA	NA
Cascade	26 348	201	141	1 231	1 114.8	32.6	427	5 049	803.0	81.8	100	395	30.4	4.6
Chouteau............................	720	5	14	89	108.7	2.1	34	169	33.5	2.4	6	D	D	D
Custer	348	5	20	147	94.3	2.6	72	770	113.5	10.7	13	19	1.1	0.1
Daniels	180	2	7	29	23.7	0.7	17	125	30.9	2.7	NA	NA	NA	NA
Dawson	919	5	22	117	39.7	2.6	61	522	69.6	6.9	9	30	9.4	0.9
Deer Lodge	8 993	57	2	D	D	D	42	259	49.5	3.8	7	21	1.0	0.2
Fallon	468	6	7	52	15.1	0.5	20	120	22.5	1.6	2	D	D	D
Fergus	178	3	27	199	187.8	4.4	80	581	89.6	7.2	11	54	2.5	0.4
Flathead	69 910	448	102	784	347.1	19.7	475	4 285	696.4	70.0	132	467	34.0	5.9
Gallatin	88 911	761	129	1 126	476.1	31.9	472	4 594	710.3	73.6	142	516	50.6	6.9
Garfield	0	0	1	D	D	D	5	35	4.4	0.4	NA	NA	NA	NA
Glacier..............................	0	0	15	77	72.2	1.5	54	426	71.1	6.8	9	100	4.2	2.4
Golden Valley	0	0	2	D	D	D	2	D	D	D	NA	NA	NA	NA
Granite	0	0	3	12	3.6	0.3	11	73	13.2	0.9	1	D	D	D
Hill	1 042	7	28	218	145.2	4.9	90	907	140.7	13.0	22	69	4.6	0.7
Jefferson	0	0	10	18	6.9	0.5	25	148	17.8	1.9	10	D	D	D
Judith Basin	0	0	6	D	D	D	8	26	4.4	0.2	1	D	D	D
Lake	6 237	49	23	129	34.1	2.2	125	1 056	157.5	15.8	24	35	2.4	0.4
Lewis and Clark	13 469	129	76	772	217.0	18.2	304	3 196	529.4	49.7	80	377	27.1	5.1
Liberty	0	0	5	40	43.9	0.9	14	72	11.1	0.9	2	D	D	D
Lincoln..............................	402	5	10	30	4.9	0.7	94	602	91.5	8.7	18	47	2.5	0.4
McCone	0	0	5	55	25.1	1.3	8	58	8.0	0.7	NA	NA	NA	NA
Madison	2 073	16	6	17	5.7	0.4	40	165	24.6	2.3	10	14	0.5	0.2
Meagher	0	0	1	D	D	D	12	43	8.2	0.6	NA	NA	NA	NA
Mineral	908	6	NA	NA	NA	NA	19	164	20.3	2.5	3	D	D	D
Missoula	61 773	947	183	1 991	775.9	50.0	540	6 800	1 069.0	105.7	138	593	46.2	8.2
Musselshell	0	0	7	28	7.8	0.6	22	134	15.6	1.6	4	11	1.6	0.1
Park	1 846	14	23	138	33.9	3.3	111	588	102.7	8.5	28	39	6.2	0.5
Petroleum..........................	0	0	1	D	D	D	2	D	D	D	NA	NA	NA	NA
Phillips	195	2	5	37	15.7	0.8	29	209	31.1	2.8	2	D	D	D
Pondera.............................	164	2	21	132	55.3	2.4	32	260	51.8	4.2	7	15	1.0	0.2
Powder River	0	0	NA	NA	NA	NA	14	78	9.0	0.9	1	D	D	D
Powell...............................	0	0	6	D	D	D	24	131	15.8	1.9	5	5	0.6	0.1
Prairie	206	2	3	D	D	D	5	37	5.2	0.4	NA	NA	NA	NA
Ravalli	5 788	85	44	283	166.4	8.7	154	1 197	179.8	16.8	53	178	10.7	2.3
Richland	1 336	14	26	228	188.7	4.2	66	506	83.6	7.5	12	34	2.5	0.3
Roosevelt	360	3	10	42	57.5	1.1	53	367	53.0	5.2	7	16	1.0	0.1
Rosebud............................	90	1	NA	NA	NA	NA	39	392	42.4	4.6	6	66	2.3	1.2
Sanders............................	0	0	12	51	65.0	1.2	51	239	33.2	3.2	11	10	0.9	0.1
Sheridan	0	0	13	67	44.1	1.1	41	176	26.2	2.3	2	D	D	D
Silver Bow	3 609	37	55	534	192.0	10.7	220	2 147	333.1	32.0	39	134	11.3	2.0
Stillwater	1 420	9	6	14	6.1	0.3	37	339	47.7	4.0	4	1	0.7	0.1
Sweet Grass	789	5	2	D	D	D	26	177	36.4	2.9	6	11	0.5	0.1
Teton	570	7	10	66	31.2	1.6	33	247	50.1	3.6	7	13	0.5	0.1
Toole	245	3	18	99	71.5	2.8	30	181	24.2	2.5	8	32	1.4	0.2
Treasure	0	0	3	22	8.8	0.6	5	25	2.2	0.2	NA	NA	NA	NA
Valley	350	2	15	126	71.2	2.5	52	342	53.1	4.8	7	28	1.2	0.3
Wheatland	0	0	3	17	3.8	0.3	14	89	10.6	0.8	2	D	D	D
Wibaux	0	0	1	D	D	D	2	D	D	D	NA	NA	NA	NA
Yellowstone	106 609	864	389	4 915	2 648.9	143.4	717	8 736	1 575.6	144.9	195	770	85.9	12.3
NEBRASKA......................	1 250 209	10 339	3 157	41 002	38 015.4	1 170.2	8 295	102 684	16 529.3	1 554.6	1 587	8 240	891.1	160.8
Adams	26 103	227	60	D	D	D	180	2 204	289.5	30.4	39	97	10.9	1.3
Antelope	576	5	21	162	88.4	3.1	51	314	52.1	3.7	2	D	D	D
Arthur	NA	NA	NA	NA	NA	NA	3	5	0.3	0.0	NA	NA	NA	NA
Banner..............................	NA	NA	1	D	D	D	NA	NA	NA	NA	NA	NA	NA	NA

1. Establishments with payroll.

Table B. States and Counties — Professional Services, Manufacturing, and Accommodation and Foodservices

STATE County	Professional, scientific, and technical services,[1] 1997				Manufacturing, 1997				Accommodation and foodservices, 1997			
	Number of establishments	Number of employees	Receipts (mil dol)	Annual payroll (mil dol)	Number of establishments	Number of employees	Receipts (mil dol)	Annual payroll (mil dol)	Number of establishments	Number of employees	Sales (mil dol)	Annual payroll (mil dol)
	147	148	149	150	151	152	153	154	155	156	157	158
MISSOURI—Cont'd												
St. Louis city	963	13 915	1 819.8	663.7	802	33 836	8 605.5	1 243.6	954	18 843	686.6	195.8
MONTANA	2 082	10 735	769.4	297.7	1 160	19 611	4 866.3	560.1	3 278	38 533	1 198.9	325.4
Beaverhead	22	51	2.9	0.9	NA	NA	NA	NA	47	337	11.1	2.4
Big Horn	13	50	2.3	1.0	NA	NA	NA	NA	35	241	8.1	2.0
Blaine	8	12	0.6	0.3	NA	NA	NA	NA	18	101	2.5	0.7
Broadwater	4	7	0.6	0.2	NA	NA	NA	NA	17	128	3.3	0.8
Carbon	14	51	2.1	0.7	NA	NA	NA	NA	52	417	14.3	4.4
Carter	1	D	D	D	NA	NA	NA	NA	5	17	0.4	0.1
Cascade	176	994	69.3	28.6	80	925	228.5	23.9	267	3 592	109.7	29.4
Chouteau	4	10	0.5	0.1	NA	NA	NA	NA	22	71	1.7	0.4
Custer	26	117	5.7	2.4	NA	NA	NA	NA	43	629	17.2	4.9
Daniels	3	9	0.4	0.1	NA	NA	NA	NA	10	D	D	D
Dawson	12	50	1.5	0.5	NA	NA	NA	NA	29	415	9.4	2.6
Deer Lodge	10	25	2.7	0.4	NA	NA	NA	NA	39	420	12.2	3.3
Fallon	5	11	0.3	0.1	NA	NA	NA	NA	12	88	2.9	0.5
Fergus	27	77	4.2	1.0	NA	NA	NA	NA	49	652	16.5	4.2
Flathead	187	659	44.8	16.0	124	3 887	790.5	121.5	319	3 940	132.1	35.9
Gallatin	259	1 031	87.6	33.3	148	1 992	273.8	48.3	285	4 694	154.0	44.1
Garfield	1	D	D	D	NA	NA	NA	NA	5	D	D	D
Glacier	16	46	2.8	1.2	NA	NA	NA	NA	52	403	18.5	4.4
Golden Valley	NA	NA	NA	NA	NA	NA	NA	NA	4	13	0.5	0.1
Granite	4	2	0.5	0.1	NA	NA	NA	NA	15	85	1.8	0.4
Hill	32	156	9.0	3.6	NA	NA	NA	NA	53	679	18.6	4.9
Jefferson	11	21	1.5	0.5	NA	NA	NA	NA	27	205	5.1	1.2
Judith Basin	1	D	D	D	NA	NA	NA	NA	13	D	D	D
Lake	37	127	7.1	2.7	30	840	115.3	19.5	86	594	20.5	5.3
Lewis and Clark	159	1 174	104.9	39.3	46	D	D	D	182	2 343	67.7	18.1
Liberty	5	14	0.8	0.2	NA	NA	NA	NA	4	16	0.5	0.1
Lincoln	23	56	3.1	1.0	33	657	125.4	21.3	68	439	16.7	3.8
McCone	1	D	D	D	NA	NA	NA	NA	5	D	D	D
Madison	8	16	1.0	0.4	NA	NA	NA	NA	44	117	7.7	1.9
Meagher	3	3	0.3	0.1	NA	NA	NA	NA	16	57	2.6	0.6
Mineral	3	4	0.4	0.0	NA	NA	NA	NA	24	178	4.8	1.5
Missoula	276	1 617	109.7	45.2	136	2 690	562.3	89.4	329	4 782	145.6	40.4
Musselshell	11	20	1.1	0.3	NA	NA	NA	NA	20	D	D	D
Park	46	138	7.4	2.6	36	535	63.3	13.3	111	1 043	34.0	9.7
Petroleum	NA	NA	NA	NA	NA	NA	NA	NA	3	D	D	D
Phillips	5	14	0.8	0.3	NA	NA	NA	NA	23	140	4.0	0.9
Pondera	10	45	1.8	0.8	NA	NA	NA	NA	18	D	D	D
Powder River	2	D	D	D	NA	NA	NA	NA	7	D	D	D
Powell	4	5	0.3	0.1	NA	NA	NA	NA	25	D	D	D
Prairie	2	D	D	D	NA	NA	NA	NA	5	D	D	D
Ravalli	52	223	11.9	6.4	66	870	95.2	21.3	92	793	21.1	6.0
Richland	25	95	6.1	2.3	NA	NA	NA	NA	40	401	10.3	2.7
Roosevelt	11	36	1.8	0.8	NA	NA	NA	NA	29	210	5.9	1.5
Rosebud	7	14	0.7	0.2	NA	NA	NA	NA	29	301	7.5	1.8
Sanders	11	38	1.1	0.5	NA	NA	NA	NA	27	189	4.9	1.2
Sheridan	8	30	1.3	0.4	NA	NA	NA	NA	26	D	D	D
Silver Bow	88	861	60.2	25.7	NA	NA	NA	NA	130	1 354	47.8	12.3
Stillwater	11	20	1.7	0.4	NA	NA	NA	NA	24	D	D	D
Sweet Grass	4	25	1.2	0.5	NA	NA	NA	NA	15	170	6.2	1.7
Teton	4	8	0.3	0.1	NA	NA	NA	NA	26	122	3.3	0.8
Toole	10	32	1.7	0.5	NA	NA	NA	NA	27	135	4.8	1.0
Treasure	2	D	D	D	NA	NA	NA	NA	4	D	D	D
Valley	9	44	2.9	1.0	NA	NA	NA	NA	33	261	7.6	1.8
Wheatland	2	D	D	D	NA	NA	NA	NA	14	77	1.8	0.4
Wibaux	3	6	0.2	0.1	NA	NA	NA	NA	9	D	D	D
Yellowstone	404	2 664	199.7	74.9	182	3 223	1 797.9	110.1	365	6 691	205.3	58.7
NEBRASKA	3 076	25 720	2 273.4	838.0	1 960	106 690	27 859.2	3 040.5	4 070	61 048	1 726.6	488.2
Adams	41	188	12.2	5.2	63	3 526	593.0	88.9	82	1 230	29.1	8.4
Antelope	11	19	0.9	0.3	NA	NA	NA	NA	17	146	2.8	0.7
Arthur	NA	NA	NA	NA	NA	NA	NA	NA	NA	NA	NA	NA
Banner	NA	NA	NA	NA	NA	NA	NA	NA	NA	NA	NA	NA

1. Firms subject to federal tax.

Table B. States and Counties — **Health Care and Social Assistance, Other Services, and Federal Funds**

STATE County	Health care and social assistance,[1] 1997				Other services,[1] 1997				Federal funds and grants, 2002–2003 Expenditures (mil dol)			
									Total	Direct payments for individuals[2]		
	Number of establishments	Number of employees	Receipts (mil dol)	Annual payroll (mil dol)	Number of establishments	Number of employees	Receipts (mil dol)	Annual payroll (mil dol)		Social Security and government retirement	Medicare	Food stamps and Supplemental Security Income
	159	160	161	162	163	164	165	166	167	168	169	170
MISSOURI—Cont'd												
St. Louis city	581	9 806	612.5	263.9	673	4 693	334.1	101.2	9 142.0	719.3	606.6	196.7
MONTANA	2 034	15 673	928.6	412.6	1 612	6 986	449.1	117.0	7 092.4	2 246.9	697.8	137.0
Beaverhead..........................	29	194	9.8	3.6	18	45	3.3	0.6	66.8	22.9	9.4	0.8
Big Horn.............................	7	113	2.5	1.7	6	23	1.2	0.3	113.7	19.4	7.6	3.7
Blaine................................	5	25	1.2	0.4	8	17	1.3	0.3	87.0	14.6	4.4	1.5
Broadwater...........................	6	20	0.6	0.2	9	8	1.2	0.1	31.3	14.0	3.6	0.4
Carbon...............................	10	120	4.2	2.0	10	21	0.9	0.2	50.1	23.4	9.2	0.8
Carter................................	1	D	D	D	1	D	D	D	17.5	4.0	1.0	0.1
Cascade..............................	205	1 729	104.2	40.5	153	690	43.3	11.4	768.2	234.1	72.4	13.2
Chouteau.............................	6	44	1.1	0.5	6	8	0.7	0.1	73.3	14.1	5.1	1.3
Custer...............................	38	273	13.7	7.7	17	80	5.6	1.4	90.3	34.3	10.4	1.7
Daniels...............................	3	16	0.7	0.2	5	6	0.7	0.1	22.5	6.6	2.5	0.1
Dawson..............................	20	92	4.1	1.4	22	81	5.1	1.3	56.1	25.0	8.3	0.8
Deer Lodge	30	153	9.2	3.1	9	23	1.8	0.4	63.5	29.9	12.4	2.3
Fallon...............................	NA	NA	NA	NA	9	20	1.9	0.3	17.6	7.3	2.5	0.5
Fergus................................	36	239	11.1	3.9	21	64	4.3	0.7	92.1	34.7	14.4	1.4
Flathead..............................	195	1 213	77.8	32.0	163	710	50.7	12.0	435.4	200.0	48.6	9.2
Gallatin.............................	165	1 134	63.6	27.0	139	642	36.4	9.2	330.4	113.7	25.7	3.5
Garfield..............................	NA	NA	NA	NA	1	D	D	D	15.5	4.1	1.2	0.0
Glacier..............................	16	40	2.2	0.6	18	90	5.5	1.3	131.2	21.9	8.6	3.8
Golden Valley........................	1	D	D	D	NA	NA	NA	NA	10.8	3.1	1.0	0.1
Granite...............................	2	D	D	D	NA	NA	NA	NA	23.5	7.4	2.3	0.3
Hill..................................	25	107	6.3	3.0	52	167	8.8	2.2	158.5	39.6	14.6	3.1
Jefferson.............................	18	129	5.2	2.8	7	21	1.2	0.3	62.4	26.0	5.4	0.7
Judith Basin	1	D	D	D	1	D	D	D	22.5	6.8	1.8	0.1
Lake.................................	39	400	13.8	7.3	32	53	3.9	0.8	220.0	62.8	19.9	4.1
Lewis and Clark	159	1 257	70.4	27.3	88	412	24.0	6.5	698.4	168.3	38.6	18.2
Liberty...............................	2	D	D	D	5	5	0.6	0.1	38.4	9.4	2.3	0.1
Lincoln..............................	33	214	9.7	3.3	30	70	5.4	1.1	131.1	62.4	14.4	4.1
McCone..............................	3	D	D	D	1	D	D	D	20.1	4.6	2.2	0.3
Madison..............................	3	9	0.6	0.1	10	39	2.5	0.5	35.2	18.5	5.6	0.2
Meagher..............................	4	18	0.5	0.1	1	D	D	D	14.5	5.5	1.8	0.2
Mineral..............................	7	15	0.7	0.2	5	8	0.4	0.1	38.4	13.8	3.3	0.8
Missoula.............................	285	2 305	151.7	70.7	184	956	61.9	17.0	540.5	188.6	56.6	14.0
Musselshell..........................	3	9	0.4	0.1	4	9	0.8	0.2	39.8	13.2	4.9	0.5
Park.................................	31	342	13.8	6.1	35	147	9.1	2.2	84.7	40.1	14.0	1.6
Petroleum............................	NA	NA	NA	NA	NA	NA	NA	NA	6.0	1.2	0.4	0.0
Phillips..............................	6	19	0.7	0.4	11	31	2.6	0.4	48.1	12.2	5.2	0.7
Pondera..............................	12	46	2.2	0.5	10	25	2.0	0.4	61.5	15.9	7.5	0.8
Powder River	1	D	D	D	5	6	0.5	0.1	17.2	4.7	1.2	0.1
Powell...............................	9	96	1.9	1.0	6	9	0.5	0.1	38.2	16.8	5.4	0.7
Prairie...............................	NA	NA	NA	NA	2	D	D	D	11.2	4.4	1.6	0.1
Ravalli..............................	56	395	17.6	7.2	51	186	11.1	2.9	219.4	108.6	26.9	3.6
Richland.............................	21	86	5.8	1.5	23	61	4.6	1.1	61.9	22.6	10.3	1.3
Roosevelt............................	10	214	6.9	4.4	11	19	1.2	0.2	127.4	19.6	9.6	4.1
Rosebud..............................	11	40	2.0	0.5	6	22	2.0	0.4	78.9	17.3	5.2	1.9
Sanders..............................	19	110	6.8	3.0	10	26	1.6	0.3	67.9	35.9	9.3	1.7
Sheridan..............................	5	37	1.7	0.9	6	19	1.5	0.3	39.4	13.0	5.2	0.3
Silver Bow	114	1 055	53.4	24.7	71	282	16.6	4.3	244.4	94.6	40.8	8.6
Stillwater.............................	7	128	4.0	1.9	11	26	2.3	0.4	43.8	20.0	6.1	0.5
Sweet Grass	2	D	D	D	3	5	0.5	0.1	18.5	8.3	2.7	0.2
Teton................................	9	76	7.0	1.6	5	4	0.5	0.2	52.0	17.5	6.4	0.5
Toole................................	13	47	3.8	1.6	3	6	0.5	0.1	45.9	8.1	5.6	0.4
Treasure.............................	NA	NA	NA	NA	NA	NA	NA	NA	5.0	2.3	0.9	0.0
Valley	15	63	4.2	1.9	15	38	3.2	0.5	75.3	25.3	8.1	1.2
Wheatland............................	2	D	D	D	1	D	D	D	20.7	6.9	3.7	0.2
Wibaux...............................	NA	NA	NA	NA	1	D	D	D	8.7	2.9	0.8	0.1
Yellowstone..........................	334	2 942	228.1	114.5	291	1 788	114.1	34.1	731.2	294.8	99.3	16.6
NEBRASKA....................	3 057	34 763	2 027.7	970.3	3 288	16 940	1 039.2	297.1	10 999.9	3 853.8	1 296.8	191.5
Adams................................	71	598	49.0	23.2	50	229	16.4	4.3	163.0	73.1	25.2	3.5
Antelope..............................	9	127	3.9	2.2	18	36	2.3	0.4	56.4	17.8	7.8	0.5
Arthur................................	NA	NA	NA	NA	1	D	D	D	2.4	1.7	0.3	0.0
Banner...............................	NA	NA	NA	NA	NA	NA	NA	NA	8.0	1.4	0.4	0.0

1. Firms subject to federal tax.   2. State totals may include programs not allocated by county.

STATE County	Federal funds and grants, 2002–2003 (cont'd) Expenditures (mil dol) (cont'd)							Local government finances, 2002 General revenue				
	Procurement contract awards			Grants[1]						Taxes		
											Per capita[2] (dollars)	
	Salaries and wages	Defense	Other	Medicaid and other health-related	Nutrition and family welfare	Education	Other	Total (mil dol)	Intergovern-mental (mil dol)	Total (mil dol)	Total	Property
	171	172	173	174	175	176	177	178	179	180	181	182
MISSOURI—Cont'd												
St. Louis city	804.1	4 906.9	359.5	793.5	157.3	45.4	436.5	1 904.7	687.4	667.1	1 972	767
MONTANA	844.6	190.0	307.3	652.7	219.4	216.9	849.4	X	X	X	X	X
Beaverhead	10.6	0.0	2.8	5.4	1.1	1.0	9.8	29.1	8.3	7.1	787	783
Big Horn	21.9	0.0	3.7	11.1	2.9	10.0	19.1	36.5	22.0	10.1	781	778
Blaine	8.3	-0.1	2.3	11.0	2.7	11.9	15.2	27.6	19.0	4.7	687	681
Broadwater	2.1	0.1	0.8	2.1	0.4	0.1	5.1	14.4	5.6	3.3	754	746
Carbon	3.7	0.1	1.7	4.6	0.8	0.5	3.3	21.6	9.7	8.5	877	818
Carter	0.9	0.0	0.6	0.8	0.1	0.1	4.2	4.4	1.7	2.2	1 663	1 662
Cascade	215.1	72.6	10.8	78.0	12.6	6.3	34.7	167.8	72.0	54.5	686	671
Chouteau	1.6	0.0	3.1	1.3	0.4	0.7	8.7	19.6	7.2	6.9	1 241	1 238
Custer	12.8	0.0	6.9	11.8	1.9	1.5	4.5	29.2	13.2	8.0	708	691
Daniels	1.3	0.0	0.2	0.4	0.1	0.1	1.8	10.3	3.2	2.3	1 177	1 176
Dawson	2.7	0.0	0.6	4.7	2.1	1.3	3.2	28.3	11.6	8.6	988	981
Deer Lodge	4.3	0.0	0.5	8.8	3.3	0.9	0.5	17.2	9.1	4.5	501	485
Fallon	0.4	0.0	0.3	0.8	0.2	0.3	1.8	24.3	18.0	2.3	840	839
Fergus	8.7	0.4	3.5	8.8	1.9	1.4	5.7	27.8	13.7	9.2	789	778
Flathead	41.1	1.1	48.7	48.7	9.1	4.7	19.7	173.9	71.0	61.2	792	717
Gallatin	36.4	6.4	9.1	38.1	5.2	4.7	70.8	139.3	47.6	51.3	721	674
Garfield	0.9	0.0	0.1	0.4	0.1	0.2	3.3	3.9	1.7	1.6	1 275	1 272
Glacier	19.1	1.3	4.6	17.8	6.5	14.3	20.4	41.7	26.4	8.4	641	637
Golden Valley	0.2	0.0	0.2	0.0	0.1	0.1	1.7	3.1	1.5	1.4	1 306	1 305
Granite	1.5	0.0	0.2	1.3	0.4	0.2	9.8	8.8	3.3	2.9	1 001	999
Hill	6.7	0.0	1.9	23.8	5.8	12.7	15.7	45.7	28.2	10.7	656	651
Jefferson	12.7	0.0	0.6	5.1	0.7	0.8	10.0	20.6	10.3	6.7	644	641
Judith Basin	1.5	0.0	0.3	1.3	0.1	0.2	3.2	7.1	3.1	3.2	1 425	1 421
Lake	6.7	59.0	11.7	19.7	5.0	9.9	15.3	55.7	31.0	16.2	603	595
Lewis and Clark	77.3	2.3	20.5	66.0	54.8	61.7	177.6	139.1	57.1	45.2	799	783
Liberty	1.0	0.0	0.4	0.4	0.1	0.1	8.9	6.4	2.9	2.7	1 310	1 304
Lincoln	19.1	1.0	7.8	10.1	4.4	2.6	5.0	41.2	22.5	9.1	487	483
McCone	0.9	0.0	0.3	1.3	0.2	0.1	1.7	5.1	2.3	2.0	1 118	1 111
Madison	3.2	0.1	1.1	2.1	0.2	0.3	3.0	24.5	7.1	8.6	1 224	1 206
Meagher	1.3	0.0	0.2	2.1	0.2	0.1	2.2	4.8	2.0	2.2	1 156	1 152
Mineral	2.0	0.9	0.4	1.3	0.6	0.2	15.0	11.6	5.6	3.7	963	961
Missoula	85.5	3.8	51.5	66.4	13.0	9.7	35.1	192.6	77.4	79.4	810	788
Musselshell	1.0	0.0	0.5	2.5	0.5	0.2	13.5	9.4	4.6	2.9	647	646
Park	4.5	0.2	5.4	8.8	1.7	1.4	5.7	32.3	14.7	10.1	644	630
Petroleum	0.2	0.0	0.1	0.0	0.0	0.0	0.9	2.0	0.8	0.6	1 180	1 178
Phillips	2.9	0.0	1.1	6.6	0.5	0.7	7.0	17.3	9.1	4.7	1 092	1 082
Pondera	2.2	0.0	0.5	5.0	0.6	2.6	10.1	18.3	9.7	5.4	868	860
Powder River	0.9	0.0	0.2	0.4	0.1	0.4	3.2	6.6	2.6	2.0	1 073	1 072
Powell	3.4	0.0	0.9	2.9	0.9	1.6	5.3	13.9	6.5	4.5	640	624
Prairie	0.4	0.0	0.4	0.8	0.0	0.1	0.4	5.3	1.9	1.4	1 187	1 176
Ravalli	26.4	0.5	21.8	13.8	4.7	2.5	9.6	61.6	35.8	19.2	508	500
Richland	4.9	0.0	0.9	5.5	1.3	0.8	6.8	26.3	13.7	7.0	760	758
Roosevelt	11.3	22.4	3.1	11.6	3.9	12.9	15.9	42.6	27.1	8.9	852	848
Rosebud	9.8	0.0	2.2	10.6	3.0	5.1	17.3	63.7	20.5	12.0	1 290	1 287
Sanders	5.0	0.0	0.5	6.7	1.4	1.8	5.4	24.5	12.0	8.5	817	811
Sheridan	2.9	0.0	0.5	3.3	0.4	0.4	2.1	16.0	9.1	4.6	1 200	1 198
Silver Bow	17.0	5.8	18.6	33.1	8.5	2.9	10.7	74.8	32.7	25.6	767	748
Stillwater	1.8	0.0	0.4	1.3	0.4	0.7	7.3	20.6	8.0	8.1	960	957
Sweet Grass	1.5	0.0	0.2	0.9	0.2	0.3	3.6	13.4	3.7	3.4	943	942
Teton	2.5	0.4	1.8	3.7	0.5	1.0	1.4	23.9	9.9	5.4	851	837
Toole	3.8	0.2	3.2	2.5	0.5	0.2	7.6	23.2	6.9	4.2	818	808
Treasure	0.4	0.0	0.1	0.0	0.1	0.0	0.5	3.5	0.9	2.2	2 741	2 738
Valley	8.4	5.6	1.7	6.2	0.7	1.4	3.5	24.4	12.5	7.2	971	964
Wheatland	1.6	0.0	0.3	1.3	0.2	0.2	1.6	5.9	2.7	2.2	1 032	1 029
Wibaux	0.3	0.0	0.1	1.2	0.1	0.1	0.8	4.8	3.1	1.1	1 070	1 061
Yellowstone	119.9	5.8	45.1	68.4	17.9	10.8	31.5	301.9	118.2	92.5	703	668
NEBRASKA	1 192.0	312.2	296.1	1 065.7	346.9	236.7	862.6	X	X	X	X	X
Adams	6.7	2.5	1.0	21.7	7.1	2.1	8.8	122.7	41.0	47.7	1 527	1 292
Antelope	2.0	6.0	2.8	5.1	0.8	0.4	2.8	22.1	8.8	10.1	1 386	1 221
Arthur	0.1	0.0	0.0	0.0	0.0	0.1	0.0	1.9	0.6	1.1	2 731	2 625
Banner	0.2	0.0	0.0	0.0	0.0	0.1	0.5	3.0	1.0	1.8	2 325	2 171

1. State totals may include programs not allocated by county. 2. Based on the resident population estimated as of July 1 of the year shown.

Table B. States and Counties — Local Government Finances, Government Employment, and Elections

STATE County	Total (mil dol)	Per capita[1] (dollars)	Education	Health and hospitals	Police protection	Public welfare	Highways	Total (mil dol)	Per capita[1] (dollars)	Federal civilian	Federal military	State and local	Democratic	Republican	All other
	183	184	185	186	187	188	189	190	191	192	193	194	195	196	197
MISSOURI—Cont'd															
St. Louis city	1 828.7	5 405	38.0	1.8	7.5	0.0	0.9	1 902.1	5 622	16 156	1 832	26 935	80.4	19.1	0.5
MONTANA	X	X	X	X	X	X	X	X	X	13 379	8 107	68 923	38.6	59.1	2.4
Beaverhead	29.3	3 256	36.6	32.6	3.4	0.3	4.0	6.3	696	234	44	773	26.0	72.3	1.7
Big Horn	34.2	2 651	73.8	0.9	3.2	0.2	5.8	0.6	43	496	62	1 613	51.4	47.0	1.6
Blaine	25.7	3 722	66.5	0.9	5.0	0.2	7.2	3.0	442	193	33	591	46.0	52.5	1.6
Broadwater	14.8	3 387	54.0	1.4	4.0	0.5	2.8	5.8	1 318	60	21	225	22.7	75.6	1.8
Carbon	20.7	2 143	59.8	0.4	5.5	0.1	8.2	10.2	1 059	84	47	516	34.7	62.8	2.5
Carter	3.9	2 914	51.9	7.4	3.4	1.9	9.0	0.3	211	21	0	112	10.7	87.9	1.4
Cascade	164.5	2 071	53.5	2.1	8.1	1.1	6.4	59.6	750	1 496	3 997	3 874	40.9	56.9	2.2
Chouteau	18.3	3 283	44.9	19.7	3.4	1.1	7.5	3.7	673	39	27	446	32.2	65.7	2.1
Custer	31.0	2 729	59.1	3.1	9.0	0.1	2.9	2.6	230	230	55	834	32.3	65.3	2.4
Daniels	11.0	5 599	35.9	34.8	2.6	0.9	2.6	2.9	1 487	34	10	174	29.1	68.3	2.6
Dawson	28.3	3 253	56.7	2.5	12.4	1.0	5.9	8.0	922	40	43	820	33.3	64.3	2.4
Deer Lodge	18.0	1 980	50.8	2.7	7.6	0.1	4.7	12.3	1 359	82	44	842	59.4	38.0	2.6
Fallon	14.7	5 432	50.1	4.7	3.5	0.6	11.0	2.3	842	17	13	258	19.4	79.0	1.6
Fergus	26.1	2 237	63.0	1.7	5.9	0.5	4.7	6.2	530	166	57	865	25.8	72.2	2.0
Flathead	173.3	2 244	55.6	2.6	5.1	0.8	4.7	66.4	859	853	375	3 537	30.0	67.3	2.8
Gallatin	138.1	1 939	45.1	1.7	7.3	3.5	3.4	79.0	1 109	605	366	7 646	41.2	56.2	2.6
Garfield	3.8	3 115	53.9	9.1	3.5	1.7	7.3	0.0	37	28	0	96	7.9	90.1	2.0
Glacier	42.7	3 254	79.0	3.7	2.5	0.1	4.0	4.2	318	473	64	1 610	57.9	40.1	2.0
Golden Valley	3.0	2 788	61.8	0.6	3.1	0.7	5.8	1.2	1 143	10	0	73	22.8	75.9	1.3
Granite	10.4	3 623	51.5	2.5	4.6	14.8	6.8	4.6	1 611	40	14	228	25.2	71.3	3.6
Hill	45.5	2 777	69.2	2.1	5.0	0.2	3.8	15.7	958	122	83	1 874	45.0	52.7	2.3
Jefferson	21.1	2 025	59.5	1.4	7.2	0.4	5.5	11.2	1 072	65	54	769	32.0	65.5	2.4
Judith Basin	8.1	3 550	67.2	1.0	2.9	0.7	8.5	2.1	935	45	11	164	25.1	73.4	1.6
Lake	52.2	1 939	66.0	1.8	5.1	0.2	4.5	16.2	601	131	130	2 403	39.4	57.6	3.0
Lewis and Clark	132.7	2 347	47.9	2.1	6.6	3.3	4.6	74.8	1 323	1 427	285	7 365	42.6	55.3	2.1
Liberty	6.3	3 105	60.2	3.3	4.6	0.0	8.7	2.4	1 164	25	10	140	27.2	71.1	1.7
Lincoln	42.4	2 273	51.9	1.1	5.9	0.1	9.7	6.4	342	471	90	916	27.5	69.7	2.8
McCone	5.0	2 710	48.8	5.1	5.3	1.8	8.1	0.8	461	27	0	160	28.1	69.6	2.3
Madison	22.0	3 147	41.1	15.6	4.0	14.3	6.1	6.9	985	75	34	463	25.0	73.0	2.0
Meagher	4.3	2 217	54.7	4.2	6.1	0.1	10.9	0.3	132	36	0	133	25.4	71.7	2.9
Mineral	10.7	2 816	63.5	1.3	5.9	0.1	5.9	4.4	1 151	58	18	279	29.5	67.6	2.9
Missoula	192.9	1 967	53.2	2.7	9.0	0.3	3.7	119.6	1 219	1 475	482	8 142	51.4	45.7	2.8
Musselshell	9.5	2 144	59.6	2.5	7.2	0.7	4.3	1.2	270	17	21	243	24.0	74.0	2.0
Park	31.5	1 998	50.6	1.3	7.8	0.3	3.8	8.8	561	92	76	660	38.9	58.1	3.0
Petroleum	2.1	4 128	48.3	0.9	3.2	0.0	7.0	0.2	366	0	0	50	18.8	78.1	3.1
Phillips	17.6	4 065	56.5	1.4	3.8	0.8	6.8	5.5	1 274	62	21	358	21.0	77.3	1.7
Pondera	17.8	2 855	71.2	2.6	4.9	0.1	5.0	3.3	523	42	30	455	33.4	64.8	1.8
Powder River	6.9	2 360	40.1	1.4	5.2	23.4	7.8	0.0	17	19	0	203	15.0	83.3	1.8
Powell	13.9	1 980	55.9	1.0	7.8	0.5	6.1	0.2	33	72	34	1 037	26.9	70.5	2.6
Prairie	5.1	4 286	35.2	28.2	3.7	2.0	4.2	1.9	1 568	17	0	171	24.6	74.2	1.2
Ravalli	59.9	1 582	60.5	1.3	6.5	0.0	5.2	24.2	638	554	184	1 438	31.0	66.8	2.2
Richland	25.1	2 714	61.1	1.8	5.3	1.1	7.4	9.0	972	97	45	665	26.0	72.2	1.8
Roosevelt	41.6	3 962	71.7	8.5	4.3	0.0	3.4	3.6	343	233	51	1 633	54.5	43.7	1.8
Rosebud	65.6	7 078	37.3	0.6	3.0	0.1	2.4	422.5	45 567	236	45	1 638	42.4	55.3	2.3
Sanders	23.6	2 278	60.2	1.6	5.8	0.1	9.0	2.1	201	141	50	567	29.1	67.2	3.7
Sheridan	16.3	4 280	46.2	3.5	4.3	1.1	10.6	1.8	466	76	18	298	41.5	56.9	1.6
Silver Bow	71.7	2 147	46.1	3.9	7.7	0.1	4.3	69.6	2 084	322	178	2 241	57.9	39.7	2.5
Stillwater	19.9	2 360	58.2	0.4	4.8	0.4	10.2	7.5	891	36	41	434	25.1	72.7	2.2
Sweet Grass	12.7	3 508	37.2	3.0	4.5	34.3	2.9	0.3	81	38	18	337	22.5	76.1	1.4
Teton	23.1	3 660	43.4	14.4	3.0	5.3	3.2	6.5	1 034	72	31	436	31.2	66.4	2.4
Toole	24.8	4 864	33.7	40.3	4.3	0.0	4.1	13.1	2 573	96	25	525	29.9	68.5	1.6
Treasure	2.5	3 219	61.7	2.3	3.6	0.6	5.6	0.7	921	0	0	71	25.1	72.2	2.7
Valley	23.0	3 112	56.3	1.4	4.2	1.0	8.1	8.8	1 193	145	36	573	35.6	61.7	2.7
Wheatland	6.0	2 754	64.6	2.6	5.9	0.1	7.9	0.0	16	41	10	173	25.4	71.6	3.0
Wibaux	5.5	5 228	36.5	1.4	3.0	1.8	7.2	0.4	362	13	0	102	25.7	72.7	1.6
Yellowstone	296.8	2 255	47.3	5.4	9.0	0.0	3.6	79.8	606	1 787	662	6 674	36.4	61.7	1.9
NEBRASKA	X	X	X	X	X	X	X	X	X	15 850	14 150	135 251	32.1	66.6	1.3
Adams	115.8	3 708	70.9	0.0	4.0	0.1	5.8	82.8	2 653	123	108	2 557	28.6	69.6	1.8
Antelope	22.1	3 029	65.7	0.1	3.0	0.1	16.3	4.6	626	43	25	547	18.0	80.7	1.3
Arthur	2.3	5 555	50.0	0.2	1.2	0.0	15.2	0.0	0	0	0	41	9.1	90.2	0.8
Banner	2.9	3 746	67.3	0.1	1.4	0.0	22.2	0.0	0	0	0	73	13.0	86.5	0.5

1. Based on the resident population estimated as of July 1 of the year shown.

STATE/ County code	CBSA code[1]	County Type[2]	STATE County	Land area,[3] (sq km) 2000	Population and population characteristics, 2003			Race alone or in combination, not Hispanic or Latino (percent)					Age (percent)					
					Total persons	Rank	Per square kilometer	White	Black	Am. Indian, Alaska Native	Asian and Pacific Islander[4]	Percent Hispanic or Latino[4]	Under 5 years	5 to 17 years	18 to 24 years	25 to 34 years	35 to 44 years	45 to 54 years
				1	2	3	4	5	6	7	8	9	10	11	12	13	14	15
			NEBRASKA—Cont'd															
31 009	...	9	Blaine	1 841	533	3 135	0.3	99.2	0.0	0.6	0.0	0.2	5.3	17.8	7.5	9.2	15.6	14.1
31 011	...	9	Boone	1 779	5 923	2 778	3.3	98.8	0.1	0.1	0.1	1.1	5.1	21.1	7.6	7.5	15.1	14.5
31 013	...	7	Box Butte	2 785	11 669	2 317	4.2	88.6	0.6	3.7	0.9	7.7	6.6	19.2	9.2	10.4	14.2	17.4
31 015	...	9	Boyd	1 399	2 330	3 031	1.7	99.1	0.1	0.6	0.2	0.1	4.2	17.2	8.2	6.5	13.1	14.7
31 017	...	9	Brown	3 163	3 490	2 949	1.1	98.6	0.2	0.4	0.4	0.7	5.0	17.2	7.9	8.3	13.4	14.6
31 019	28260	5	Buffalo	2 507	43 043	1 060	17.2	93.5	0.8	0.5	0.9	5.0	6.7	17.3	16.1	14.0	12.7	12.7
31 021	...	8	Burt	1 276	7 562	2 631	5.9	97.1	0.3	1.2	0.5	1.4	6.1	18.2	8.1	7.7	13.6	15.0
31 023	...	6	Butler	1 511	8 899	2 535	5.9	97.7	0.1	0.3	0.2	1.9	6.7	19.2	9.0	9.6	14.9	13.8
31 025	36540	2	Cass	1 448	25 242	1 560	17.4	97.6	0.3	0.8	0.7	1.5	6.5	19.7	9.5	11.0	15.8	14.6
31 027	...	9	Cedar	1 917	9 242	2 505	4.8	99.2	0.2	0.3	0.1	0.5	5.5	21.1	8.7	8.5	13.9	13.7
31 029	...	9	Chase	2 317	4 041	2 907	1.7	95.8	0.2	0.1	0.2	3.7	6.0	17.1	8.6	9.1	12.8	15.6
31 031	...	7	Cherry	15 438	6 053	2 770	0.4	93.6	0.2	5.9	1.1	1.0	5.8	19.2	8.7	10.6	13.7	14.4
31 033	...	7	Cheyenne	3 099	9 940	2 447	3.2	93.7	0.1	0.7	1.1	4.5	6.3	17.9	9.6	11.7	14.1	14.6
31 035	25580	9	Clay	1 484	6 896	2 698	4.6	95.1	0.1	0.3	0.3	4.2	5.4	19.1	8.9	8.4	14.3	15.7
31 037	...	7	Colfax	1 070	10 497	2 399	9.8	71.1	0.2	0.2	0.2	28.4	7.7	19.7	9.9	11.1	14.7	12.4
31 039	...	7	Cuming	1 481	9 863	2 457	6.7	93.2	0.2	0.3	0.3	6.2	6.0	19.1	8.2	9.7	14.4	13.6
31 041	...	7	Custer	6 671	11 542	2 331	1.7	98.4	0.1	0.6	0.3	0.9	5.9	19.3	7.4	8.6	13.6	14.4
31 043	43580	3	Dakota	683	20 492	1 776	30.0	69.5	0.9	2.3	3.9	24.4	8.4	21.0	10.3	14.3	14.2	12.8
31 045	...	7	Dawes	3 616	8 985	2 525	2.5	92.9	1.0	4.0	0.7	2.5	5.4	14.8	22.1	11.1	10.2	11.9
31 047	30420	7	Dawson	2 623	24 598	1 597	9.4	71.0	0.4	0.8	0.6	27.5	8.3	20.6	9.2	12.0	14.1	13.2
31 049	...	9	Deuel	1 139	2 053	3 055	1.8	96.4	0.0	0.5	0.4	2.7	4.7	16.5	8.6	7.4	14.7	15.9
31 051	43580	3	Dixon	1 234	6 121	2 765	5.0	92.7	0.1	0.3	0.4	6.6	6.4	19.6	8.9	9.6	14.1	14.8
31 053	23340	4	Dodge	1 384	35 961	1 240	26.0	93.1	0.7	0.5	0.8	5.5	6.0	17.5	10.6	11.0	14.3	13.2
31 055	36540	2	Douglas	857	476 703	128	556.2	78.0	12.2	0.9	2.8	7.6	7.7	18.6	10.1	15.0	15.1	13.7
31 057	...	9	Dundy	2 382	2 225	3 040	0.9	95.3	0.1	1.0	0.6	3.2	4.4	15.7	8.4	8.0	13.1	17.3
31 059	...	9	Fillmore	1 493	6 425	2 737	4.3	97.3	0.3	0.7	0.1	2.0	5.3	19.3	7.3	8.2	14.3	14.2
31 061	...	9	Franklin	1 492	3 442	2 952	2.3	99.0	0.0	0.3	0.1	0.7	4.4	17.8	7.6	8.9	14.4	13.6
31 063	...	9	Frontier	2 524	2 904	2 991	1.2	98.4	0.1	0.4	0.4	1.0	4.6	16.9	14.8	8.3	12.5	15.1
31 065	...	9	Furnas	1 860	5 196	2 830	2.8	97.9	0.1	1.0	0.3	1.3	5.8	17.3	7.9	8.4	13.2	14.6
31 067	13100	6	Gage	2 215	23 363	1 648	10.5	97.7	0.5	1.1	0.5	1.0	5.8	16.8	9.6	10.8	14.4	14.1
31 069	...	9	Garden	4 414	2 193	3 041	0.5	97.8	0.1	0.3	0.3	1.6	3.2	15.7	7.6	6.7	13.8	15.2
31 071	...	9	Garfield	1 476	1 841	3 069	1.2	98.6	0.1	0.4	0.1	1.1	4.3	17.3	7.2	7.3	13.1	15.0
31 073	30420	9	Gosper	1 187	2 089	3 051	1.8	97.8	0.0	0.2	0.3	1.8	6.8	15.9	7.5	7.9	13.3	15.8
31 075	...	9	Grant	2 010	695	3 130	0.3	98.1	0.0	0.1	0.3	1.4	2.4	18.4	10.1	8.6	15.0	17.7
31 077	...	9	Greeley	1 476	2 603	3 013	1.8	98.2	0.8	0.1	0.1	1.0	5.4	17.5	7.6	7.8	12.8	14.3
31 079	24260	5	Hall	1 415	54 293	885	38.4	81.9	0.8	0.5	1.4	16.1	7.8	19.1	9.2	12.7	14.2	13.8
31 081	...	7	Hamilton	1 408	9 478	2 487	6.7	98.1	0.4	0.2	0.3	1.3	6.2	20.3	9.2	9.8	14.5	15.3
31 083	...	9	Harlan	1 432	3 664	2 935	2.6	98.9	0.2	0.2	0.1	0.8	4.4	17.4	8.1	7.5	12.7	15.6
31 085	...	9	Hayes	1 847	1 104	3 104	0.6	97.0	0.3	0.2	0.5	2.5	3.5	19.7	8.9	6.0	15.9	16.1
31 087	...	9	Hitchcock	1 839	3 031	2 983	1.6	98.0	0.2	0.5	0.1	1.6	4.3	16.1	9.9	7.4	13.7	14.5
31 089	...	7	Holt	6 249	11 078	2 365	1.8	98.6	0.1	0.3	0.3	0.8	5.5	19.2	8.1	8.0	14.6	15.0
31 091	...	9	Hooker	1 868	737	3 126	0.4	98.4	0.0	0.7	0.1	1.1	4.7	17.1	7.6	5.2	12.9	14.5
31 093	24260	9	Howard	1 475	6 632	2 720	4.5	98.1	0.3	0.4	0.2	1.1	5.2	19.5	9.5	9.6	14.4	13.9
31 095	...	7	Jefferson	1 484	8 082	2 589	5.4	98.0	0.1	0.4	0.2	1.4	5.1	16.6	8.0	9.3	13.8	15.4
31 097	...	8	Johnson	974	4 429	2 879	4.5	90.7	0.2	0.5	3.7	5.1	4.9	17.5	9.3	8.4	14.1	14.9
31 099	28260	7	Kearney	1 337	6 862	2 701	5.1	97.0	0.2	0.2	0.3	2.5	5.8	18.8	8.7	10.8	15.1	14.8
31 101	...	7	Keith	2 749	8 472	2 565	3.1	95.0	0.1	0.7	0.4	4.0	5.1	17.8	7.9	10.1	14.9	15.1
31 103	...	9	Keya Paha	2 003	953	3 111	0.5	95.1	0.0	0.4	0.0	4.7	6.0	18.4	6.5	9.1	13.2	12.3
31 105	...	6	Kimball	2 465	3 853	2 924	1.6	95.3	0.5	1.0	0.1	3.7	5.4	17.8	7.8	8.4	13.4	14.7
31 107	...	9	Knox	2 870	9 054	2 518	3.2	91.0	0.1	7.8	0.2	1.1	5.6	18.3	8.1	7.5	13.0	14.6
31 109	30700	2	Lancaster	2 173	260 995	228	120.1	89.4	3.6	1.0	3.9	3.7	7.0	16.3	13.8	15.7	14.1	13.4
31 111	35820	5	Lincoln	6 641	34 802	1 278	5.2	93.4	0.9	0.8	0.6	5.0	6.8	18.3	9.9	11.3	13.5	15.0
31 113	35820	9	Logan	1 478	710	3 128	0.5	97.6	0.1	1.3	0.0	1.0	5.5	16.2	9.2	8.3	14.6	18.6
31 115	...	9	Loup	1 476	744	3 125	0.5	98.0	0.0	0.3	0.1	1.6	3.9	18.7	9.1	8.5	11.8	14.8
31 117	...	9	McPherson	2 225	542	3 134	0.2	98.2	0.0	0.0	0.4	1.5	5.5	18.3	9.6	8.7	12.4	17.0
31 119	35740	5	Madison	1 483	35 777	1 234	24.1	86.0	2.0	1.5	0.7	10.6	7.2	18.6	12.5	11.7	14.5	13.3
31 121	24260	7	Merrick	1 256	8 134	2 586	6.5	97.2	0.3	0.1	0.2	2.2	5.4	19.6	8.5	9.3	14.2	13.9
31 123	...	9	Morrill	3 687	5 284	2 821	1.4	89.3	0.1	1.0	0.3	9.4	6.1	19.0	9.3	9.1	13.6	15.4
31 125	...	9	Nance	1 143	3 741	2 932	3.3	94.0	0.0	0.3	0.1	1.3	6.0	19.6	8.3	7.6	15.1	15.6
31 127	...	7	Nemaha	1 060	7 136	2 673	6.7	97.4	0.4	0.5	0.8	1.1	4.7	16.7	13.0	8.8	13.9	15.6
31 129	...	9	Nuckolls	1 490	4 841	2 852	3.2	98.7	0.1	0.1	0.2	1.1	5.0	16.1	8.8	7.5	13.1	14.2
31 131	...	6	Otoe	1 595	15 504	2 063	9.7	96.1	0.3	0.5	0.3	3.2	6.2	18.6	8.8	10.1	14.5	14.1
31 133	...	9	Pawnee	1 118	2 918	2 989	2.6	98.7	0.0	0.3	0.3	0.8	4.9	16.5	7.3	7.9	12.7	14.2
31 135	...	9	Perkins	2 287	3 057	2 979	1.3	96.5	0.3	0.4	0.3	2.8	5.4	18.8	8.6	10.0	12.3	15.7
31 137	...	7	Phelps	1 399	9 630	2 477	6.9	96.7	0.2	0.4	0.5	2.6	6.5	18.7	7.9	9.9	14.6	14.1
31 139	35740	9	Pierce	1 486	7 713	2 623	5.2	98.6	0.2	0.5	0.3	0.7	5.5	20.4	10.2	9.0	15.4	13.5

1. CBSA = Core Based Statistical Area. See Appendix A for explanation. See Appendix B for list of metropolitan areas with component counties.   2. County type code from the Economic Research Service of USDA Rural-Urban Continuum Codes. See Appendix A for definition.   3. Dry land or land partially or temporarily covered by water.   4. Hispanic or Latino persons may be of any race.

Table B. States and Counties — **Population and Households**

STATE County	55 to 64 years (16)	65 to 74 years (17)	75 years and over (18)	Percent female (19)	1990 (20)	2000 (21)	1990–2000 (22)	2000–2003 (23)	Births (24)	Deaths (25)	Net migration (26)	Number (27)	Percent change 1990–2000 (28)	Persons per household (29)	Female family householder[1] (30)	One person (31)
NEBRASKA—Cont'd																
Blaine	13.9	10.5	8.8	49.0	675	583	-13.6	-8.6	20	14	-54	238	-11.2	2.45	2.5	26.9
Boone	9.3	9.6	12.0	50.0	6 667	6 259	-6.1	-5.4	201	214	-323	2 454	-4.1	2.50	5.5	29.1
Box Butte	8.9	7.2	7.8	50.0	13 130	12 158	-7.4	-4.0	538	448	-587	4 780	-2.4	2.50	8.3	27.5
Boyd	11.5	10.9	14.2	51.5	2 835	2 438	-14.0	-4.4	60	110	-56	1 014	-11.7	2.36	3.7	32.0
Brown	11.2	9.9	12.5	50.6	3 657	3 525	-3.6	-1.0	110	152	14	1 530	2.1	2.27	5.9	31.6
Buffalo	7.5	5.2	6.2	50.8	37 447	42 259	12.9	1.9	1 893	1 023	-52	15 930	16.0	2.48	8.3	26.1
Burt	10.4	10.5	11.2	51.5	7 868	7 791	-1.0	-2.9	300	361	-160	3 155	0.5	2.43	6.2	26.5
Butler	10.0	8.1	9.0	49.0	8 601	8 767	1.9	1.5	396	347	-6	3 426	5.3	2.53	5.7	28.3
Cass	9.9	6.4	5.7	50.5	21 318	24 334	14.1	3.7	1 057	758	631	9 161	17.5	2.63	7.6	21.6
Cedar	8.7	9.0	11.6	49.9	10 131	9 615	-5.1	-3.9	315	324	-367	3 623	-0.8	2.60	4.3	27.0
Chase	10.0	9.8	10.9	51.0	4 381	4 068	-7.1	-0.7	160	164	-21	1 662	-2.5	2.39	5.5	27.3
Cherry	10.8	8.6	8.7	49.8	6 307	6 148	-2.5	-1.5	238	215	-112	2 508	2.9	2.42	6.9	28.9
Cheyenne	9.3	8.1	8.5	50.9	9 494	9 830	3.5	1.1	426	447	141	4 071	5.7	2.38	8.0	30.1
Clay	10.3	8.8	9.3	51.0	7 123	7 039	-1.2	-2.0	236	225	-154	2 756	0.5	2.52	5.5	25.7
Colfax	8.1	7.6	8.9	48.2	9 139	10 441	14.2	0.5	575	331	-191	3 682	3.4	2.80	7.1	25.7
Cuming	9.1	9.6	11.3	49.5	10 117	10 203	0.9	-3.3	388	367	-362	3 945	2.4	2.53	5.3	27.1
Custer	10.8	9.5	11.4	51.0	12 270	11 793	-3.9	-2.1	455	551	-149	4 826	-2.6	2.39	5.4	28.9
Dakota	8.2	5.3	4.9	50.3	16 742	20 253	21.0	1.2	1 135	499	-411	7 095	17.6	2.81	11.9	22.9
Dawes	8.5	7.0	7.8	51.1	9 021	9 060	0.4	-0.8	325	288	-103	3 512	5.6	2.28	7.9	31.0
Dawson	8.8	6.5	7.2	49.5	19 940	24 365	22.2	1.0	1 375	824	-334	8 824	12.7	2.71	7.9	24.6
Deuel	10.7	9.4	13.1	51.5	2 237	2 098	-6.2	-2.1	71	114	-2	908	-0.8	2.29	5.9	31.2
Dixon	10.1	7.9	9.8	49.8	6 143	6 339	3.2	-3.4	252	271	-205	2 413	3.2	2.58	6.5	25.9
Dodge	9.8	8.3	9.1	51.4	34 500	36 160	4.8	-0.6	1 445	1 429	-188	14 433	7.3	2.42	8.5	27.6
Douglas	8.2	5.5	5.2	50.8	416 444	463 585	11.3	2.8	25 157	12 129	445	182 194	13.1	2.48	12.1	29.8
Dundy	10.0	9.3	13.4	50.4	2 582	2 292	-11.2	-2.9	71	94	-41	961	-11.4	2.29	3.9	30.9
Fillmore	10.9	9.2	12.2	51.6	7 103	6 634	-6.6	-3.2	223	332	-94	2 689	-4.9	2.37	5.0	30.2
Franklin	10.2	10.4	13.6	51.7	3 938	3 574	-9.2	-3.7	93	170	-55	1 485	-10.3	2.34	6.0	29.2
Frontier	10.4	9.5	8.5	49.1	3 101	3 099	-0.1	-6.3	84	106	-166	1 192	-1.2	2.48	4.8	26.3
Furnas	10.8	10.2	13.1	52.1	5 553	5 324	-4.1	-2.4	205	307	-23	2 278	-2.4	2.28	5.9	32.5
Gage	9.5	8.6	10.2	51.1	22 794	22 993	0.9	1.6	859	914	437	9 316	3.3	2.36	7.1	29.2
Garden	12.8	13.2	12.5	51.1	2 460	2 292	-6.8	-4.3	45	111	-27	1 020	-1.9	2.19	6.0	32.5
Garfield	12.4	10.2	14.6	52.6	2 141	1 902	-11.2	-3.2	52	140	33	813	-5.9	2.27	3.6	32.7
Gosper	11.5	10.9	10.6	49.6	1 928	2 143	11.2	-2.5	107	100	-59	863	13.0	2.42	3.9	22.8
Grant	11.5	10.8	6.3	47.9	769	747	-2.9	-7.0	13	11	-53	292	-3.6	2.56	6.5	22.3
Greeley	9.7	10.8	13.3	50.3	3 006	2 714	-9.7	-4.1	95	110	-90	1 077	-4.9	2.46	6.4	30.5
Hall	9.0	6.7	7.1	50.3	48 925	53 534	9.4	1.4	2 872	1 673	-438	20 356	9.0	2.57	9.7	25.5
Hamilton	9.6	7.2	7.7	50.3	8 862	9 403	6.1	0.8	360	315	42	3 503	8.3	2.64	5.9	21.1
Harlan	11.4	11.2	12.4	50.8	3 810	3 786	-0.6	-3.2	100	146	-68	1 597	0.8	2.34	4.3	30.8
Hayes	10.0	11.5	8.9	50.0	1 222	1 068	-12.6	3.4	29	31	43	430	-10.4	2.48	2.6	26.5
Hitchcock	11.8	10.7	12.2	51.7	3 750	3 111	-17.0	-2.6	91	134	-34	1 287	-12.3	2.37	6.4	27.4
Holt	10.1	9.2	11.3	51.0	12 599	11 551	-8.3	-4.1	389	417	-447	4 608	-2.9	2.46	5.6	28.7
Hooker	10.6	11.0	17.0	54.3	793	783	-1.3	-5.9	25	27	-43	335	0.9	2.26	3.9	33.1
Howard	9.9	8.1	9.1	49.7	6 057	6 567	8.4	1.0	196	200	77	2 546	10.3	2.56	6.2	26.0
Jefferson	10.3	9.7	13.2	50.9	8 759	8 333	-4.9	-3.0	269	315	-192	3 527	-2.9	2.32	5.8	29.6
Johnson	10.4	9.0	11.8	52.2	4 673	4 488	-4.0	-1.3	122	154	-21	1 887	-2.7	2.35	5.5	29.9
Kearney	9.9	7.6	8.7	50.0	6 629	6 882	3.8	-0.3	242	247	-7	2 643	4.8	2.50	6.4	24.3
Keith	11.7	10.5	8.9	50.7	8 584	8 875	3.4	-4.5	293	312	-376	3 707	8.1	2.37	7.0	27.9
Keya Paha	12.9	10.7	11.3	48.6	1 029	983	-4.5	-3.1	45	23	-48	409	-2.4	2.40	4.4	26.2
Kimball	12.5	10.2	11.8	50.9	4 108	4 089	-0.5	-5.8	142	144	-232	1 727	4.7	2.33	6.7	30.5
Knox	10.5	10.4	12.8	51.2	9 564	9 374	-2.0	-3.4	341	482	-176	3 811	-0.2	2.40	6.0	29.9
Lancaster	7.7	5.1	5.1	50.0	213 641	250 291	17.2	4.3	11 986	5 567	4 515	99 187	19.9	2.40	9.1	29.1
Lincoln	9.8	7.6	7.6	51.0	32 508	34 632	6.5	0.5	1 561	1 175	-202	14 076	11.0	2.41	8.0	28.3
Logan	12.3	9.6	8.0	52.0	878	774	-11.8	-8.3	33	46	-53	316	-1.3	2.45	3.8	25.0
Loup	12.4	10.1	10.2	47.7	683	712	4.2	4.5	17	16	35	289	4.7	2.46	4.2	27.0
McPherson	9.6	8.3	10.9	50.2	546	533	-2.4	1.7	18	6	-1	202	-4.7	2.64	3.5	19.8
Madison	8.2	6.3	7.8	50.1	32 655	35 226	7.9	1.6	1 778	1 080	-129	13 436	9.4	2.52	8.4	27.9
Merrick	11.1	8.6	9.4	51.1	8 062	8 204	1.8	-0.9	272	258	-82	3 209	4.8	2.51	6.5	25.0
Morrill	10.8	8.9	8.3	51.5	5 423	5 440	0.3	-2.9	220	258	-115	2 138	2.6	2.49	6.5	26.9
Nance	9.0	10.1	10.7	48.5	4 275	4 038	-5.5	-7.4	151	197	-255	1 577	-0.5	2.49	5.6	27.4
Nemaha	9.6	7.8	10.8	51.4	7 980	7 576	-5.1	-5.8	227	344	-325	3 047	-1.0	2.32	7.2	30.5
Nuckolls	11.5	10.5	14.0	51.9	5 786	5 057	-12.6	-4.3	152	232	-134	2 218	-6.0	2.26	4.6	32.3
Otoe	9.9	7.9	10.2	51.0	14 252	15 396	8.0	0.7	614	568	77	6 060	7.1	2.48	7.2	26.4
Pawnee	11.9	11.4	15.4	51.6	3 317	3 087	-6.9	-5.5	95	164	-100	1 339	-4.9	2.27	5.6	32.9
Perkins	10.1	8.3	11.6	49.5	3 367	3 200	-5.0	-4.5	121	130	-137	1 275	-0.6	2.47	4.6	27.5
Phelps	10.3	8.8	9.6	50.5	9 715	9 747	0.3	-1.2	417	405	-117	3 844	2.0	2.47	5.8	26.7
Pierce	9.4	7.3	9.4	50.3	7 827	7 857	0.4	-1.8	285	324	-100	2 979	1.7	2.59	5.7	25.7

1. No spouse present.

Items 16—31

Table B. States and Counties — **Vital Statistics, Health Resources, and Crime**

STATE County	Births, average 1999–2001 Total	Rate[1]	Deaths, average 1999–2001 Number Total	Number Infant[2]	Rate Total[1]	Rate Infant[3]	Physicians,[4] 2000 Number	Rate[5]	Hospitals,[4] 1998 Number	Beds Number	Beds Rate[5]	Medicare enrollees, 2003	Serious crimes known to police,[6] 2002 Total Number	Rate[7]
	32	33	34	35	36	37	38	39	40	41	42	43	44	45
NEBRASKA—Cont'd														
Blaine	7	12.8	6	0	0.0	D	0	0	0	0	0	108	NA	NA
Boone	61	9.8	64	1	10.3	D	6	96	1	34	533	1 347	10	158
Box Butte	157	12.9	133	1	11.0	D	7	58	1	36	281	1 929	289	2 352
Boyd	18	7.6	34	0	14.2	D	4	164	1	29	1 131	657	21	852
Brown	38	10.7	44	0	12.5	D	5	142	1	23	647	818	80	2 246
Buffalo	593	14.1	319	4	7.6	D	113	267	1	183	451	5 541	1 752	4 103
Burt	81	10.5	110	0	14.2	D	6	77	1	23	288	1 753	71	1 191
Butler	119	13.5	103	0	11.7	D	4	46	1	34	392	1 687	86	971
Cass	326	13.4	210	2	8.6	D	6	25	0	0	0	3 416	NA	NA
Cedar	101	10.5	106	1	11.0	D	1	10	0	0	0	1 840	NA	NA
Chase	49	12.2	57	0	14.1	D	2	49	1	26	612	900	27	657
Cherry	71	11.6	65	0	10.6	D	4	65	1	36	569	1 233	63	1 014
Cheyenne	129	13.1	125	2	12.7	D	11	112	1	106	1 119	1 832	326	3 282
Clay	83	11.9	85	0	12.1	D	2	28	0	0	0	1 470	NA	NA
Colfax	167	15.9	103	1	9.8	D	5	48	1	49	457	3 926	142	1 346
Cuming	122	12.0	118	1	11.6	D	6	59	1	49	490	1 961	78	757
Custer	133	11.3	156	0	13.3	D	8	68	3	146	1 214	2 524	167	1 401
Dakota	366	18.1	158	4	7.8	D	6	30	0	0	0	2 519	516	2 521
Dawes	102	11.2	87	0	9.6	D	8	88	2	51	568	1 537	49	535
Dawson	422	17.3	239	3	9.8	D	16	66	3	118	509	3 547	866	3 517
Deuel	19	9.3	28	0	13.4	D	1	48	0	0	0	505	40	1 887
Dixon	80	12.7	66	0	10.4	D	1	16	0	0	0	1 140	104	1 623
Dodge	449	12.4	420	3	11.6	D	41	113	1	262	742	6 816	1 293	3 539
Douglas	7 469	16.1	3 618	57	7.8	7.6	1 609	347	8	2 604	587	60 442	30 675	6 548
Dundy	22	9.8	32	0	14.1	D	4	175	1	14	608	493	19	820
Fillmore	74	11.2	97	1	14.7	D	3	45	1	33	476	1 419	91	1 358
Franklin	34	9.4	56	0	15.6	D	4	112	1	20	536	902	34	942
Frontier	30	9.8	30	0	9.8	D	0	0	0	0	0	519	27	862
Furnas	62	11.6	101	0	18.9	D	4	75	1	65	1 208	1 449	97	1 803
Gage	269	11.7	292	3	12.7	D	28	122	1	143	631	4 997	1 005	4 326
Garden	17	7.3	40	0	17.6	D	4	175	1	56	2 619	666	39	1 684
Garfield	18	9.3	35	0	18.2	D	2	105	0	0	0	531	25	1 155
Gosper	27	12.6	27	0	12.7	D	0	0	0	0	0	493	0	0
Grant	6	8.1	4	0	0.0	D	1	134	0	0	0	166	22	802
Greeley	31	11.3	39	1	14.5	D	0	0	0	0	0	635		
Hall	869	16.2	507	7	9.5	8.1	85	159	1	197	380	8 240	3 235	5 980
Hamilton	111	11.8	99	1	10.6	D	10	106	1	82	866	1 500	138	1 452
Harlan	31	8.3	48	0	12.8	D	2	53	1	25	667	849	1	26
Hayes	8	7.1	8	0	7.7	D	0	0	0	0	0	131	NA	NA
Hitchcock	26	8.5	48	0	15.3	D	0	0	0	0	0	774	10	318
Holt	123	10.6	133	1	11.5	D	11	95	2	47	390	2 383	135	1 157
Hooker	9	11.6	11	0	13.8	D	1	128	0	0	0	214	3	379
Howard	71	10.8	73	0	11.1	D	3	46	1	37	573	1 247	134	2 019
Jefferson	92	11.0	111	0	13.4	D	6	72	1	73	871	2 002	223	2 648
Johnson	43	9.7	54	0	12.1	D	3	67	1	30	657	1 007	45	992
Kearney	82	11.9	77	1	11.1	D	6	87	1	80	1 167	1 179	172	2 473
Keith	90	10.2	99	1	11.2	D	3	34	1	41	473	1 705	208	2 319
Keya Paha	11	11.2	8	0	8.5	D	0	0	0	0	0	212	0	0
Kimball	42	10.3	49	0	11.9	D	1	24	1	30	735	921	NA	NA
Knox	102	10.9	136	1	14.6	D	4	43	1	77	836	2 279	67	707
Lancaster	3 687	14.7	1 672	23	6.7	6.3	488	195	3	702	298	30 383	15 956	6 309
Lincoln	466	13.5	334	3	9.7	D	50	144	1	105	313	5 952	NA	NA
Logan	10	12.9	10	0	12.9	D	0	0	0	0	0	155	NA	NA
Loup	6	8.9	5	0	0.0	D	0	0	0	0	0	99	0	0
McPherson	5	8.7	3	0	0.0	D	0	0	0	0	0	131	0	0
Madison	542	15.3	325	3	9.2	D	67	190	3	199	575	5 977	1 602	4 825
Merrick	87	10.7	86	1	10.5	D	2	24	1	79	981	1 515	135	1 628
Morrill	69	12.7	71	1	13.1	D	4	74	1	20	367	1 036	86	1 564
Nance	45	11.2	52	0	13.0	D	1	25	1	20	488	823	37	907
Nemaha	68	9.1	98	0	12.9	D	5	66	1	39	507	1 379	128	1 672
Nuckolls	47	9.4	78	0	15.4	D	4	79	1	49	938	1 301	NA	NA
Otoe	185	12.0	174	2	11.3	D	7	45	2	67	453	2 857	376	2 417
Pawnee	28	9.2	54	0	17.6	D	3	97	1	17	543	809	71	2 276
Perkins	32	10.1	42	0	13.0	D	5	156	1	76	2 397	621	23	711
Phelps	123	12.6	121	1	12.4	D	8	82	1	55	555	1 861	247	2 508
Pierce	91	11.6	96	0	12.2	D	1	13	2	59	746	1 337	53	862

1. Per 1,000 estimated resident population.   2. Deaths of infants under 1 year old.   3. Deaths of infants under 1 year old per 1,000 live births.   4. Data subject to copyright.   5. Per 100,000 resident population as of July 1 of the year shown.   6. Data for serious crimes have not been adjusted for underreporting; this may affect comparability between geographic areas and over time.   7. Per 100,000 population estimated by the FBI.

Table B. States and Counties — **Crime, Education, Money Income, and Poverty**

STATE County	Serious crimes known to police[1] 2002 (cont'd) Rate[2] Violent	Property	Education — School enrollment and attainment, 2000 — Enrollment[3] Total	Percent private	Attainment[4] (percent) High school graduate or less	Bachelor's degree or more	Local government expenditures,[5] 2000–2001 Total current expenditures (mil dol)	Current expenditures per student (dollars)	Money income, 1999 Per capita income[6] (dollars)	Households Median income Dollars	Percent change, 1989–1999 (constant 1999 dollars)	Percent with income of $100,000 or more	Percent below poverty level, 1999 Persons	Households	Families	Families with children
	46	47	48	49	50	51	52	53	54	55	56	57	58	59	60	61
NEBRASKA—Cont'd																
Blaine	NA	NA	136	0.7	45.2	12.3	1.5	10 193	12 323	25 278	-4.6	1.7	19.4	18.6	18.7	25.7
Boone	32	127	1 676	11.8	57.4	13.1	8.8	7 187	15 831	31 444	8.1	4.3	10.4	11.7	8.3	11.0
Box Butte	171	2 182	3 384	7.9	49.4	15.3	17.2	6 736	18 407	39 366	10.6	6.0	10.7	11.6	9.7	15.1
Boyd	41	812	568	2.1	59.9	12.8	4.2	8 273	13 840	26 075	18.9	2.8	15.2	15.1	12.9	18.8
Brown	197	2 049	810	7.8	54.0	17.2	6.3	9 696	15 924	28 356	23.7	3.0	11.1	11.2	8.5	14.3
Buffalo	211	3 892	14 318	8.6	37.5	30.2	52.5	7 373	17 510	36 782	14.1	5.7	11.2	11.7	6.3	9.8
Burt	67	1 124	1 891	4.1	56.5	14.2	10.4	6 290	16 654	33 954	20.0	3.4	8.9	9.2	6.6	10.9
Butler	0	971	2 263	28.7	58.2	13.6	8.3	6 494	16 394	36 331	16.2	3.7	8.2	8.5	4.8	7.2
Cass	NA	NA	6 664	12.4	47.6	18.7	25.6	6 937	20 156	46 515	21.5	8.4	5.2	5.4	4.2	7.0
Cedar	NA	NA	2 646	26.3	56.7	13.0	11.4	7 046	15 514	33 435	18.4	3.5	9.1	9.6	6.3	8.6
Chase	97	559	969	5.8	53.2	16.6	7.0	7 722	17 490	32 351	12.1	6.1	9.6	10.5	7.9	11.0
Cherry	48	966	1 524	9.6	46.1	19.4	8.4	8 206	15 943	29 268	14.9	4.6	12.3	12.9	9.6	13.3
Cheyenne	141	3 141	2 414	4.3	48.5	16.8	16.0	8 333	17 437	33 438	6.4	5.4	10.0	10.0	8.2	11.0
Clay	NA	NA	1 891	7.8	50.7	16.2	18.2	8 323	16 870	34 259	11.1	4.8	10.4	9.8	8.5	11.9
Colfax	28	1 317	2 799	9.1	65.0	11.5	13.0	6 087	15 148	35 849	20.5	4.5	10.8	9.9	7.2	11.2
Cuming	39	718	2 552	33.7	61.8	12.3	10.9	6 755	16 443	33 186	14.2	3.5	9.0	9.2	7.0	9.1
Custer	109	1 292	2 835	7.2	51.3	16.1	16.5	7 474	16 171	30 677	6.5	3.5	12.4	11.6	9.1	14.5
Dakota	83	2 438	5 524	11.5	62.8	12.4	21.5	5 864	16 125	38 834	13.8	6.0	11.4	10.9	9.2	13.0
Dawes	44	492	3 367	3.8	39.2	28.4	8.9	6 753	16 353	29 476	23.4	5.9	18.9	20.0	9.8	13.1
Dawson	138	3 379	6 269	4.0	61.9	14.4	29.6	5 823	15 973	36 132	20.0	5.4	10.8	10.0	8.6	12.4
Deuel	47	1 840	466	7.5	50.6	17.4	4.0	8 238	17 891	32 981	15.4	4.4	9.1	8.5	5.3	11.2
Dixon	62	1 561	1 670	5.8	57.4	14.1	5.1	6 292	15 350	34 201	27.0	3.0	10.0	10.9	7.5	10.2
Dodge	77	3 462	9 093	19.9	56.7	15.0	42.8	6 891	17 757	37 188	11.5	4.8	8.6	8.8	5.3	8.9
Douglas	646	5 902	132 512	24.2	38.9	30.6	519.6	6 722	22 879	43 209	7.7	11.9	9.8	9.3	6.7	10.3
Dundy	0	820	530	5.3	48.5	16.7	3.1	9 186	15 786	27 010	-5.5	4.5	13.6	14.2	11.0	16.7
Fillmore	90	1 268	1 609	7.7	54.5	15.7	10.7	8 697	17 465	35 162	12.7	3.8	7.8	8.8	4.8	7.1
Franklin	28	914	829	3.7	53.6	15.8	3.8	7 824	15 390	29 304	6.1	3.6	13.2	12.9	9.7	16.0
Frontier	0	862	947	3.4	46.4	17.9	7.1	9 042	16 648	33 038	20.8	4.9	12.2	13.8	9.3	11.7
Furnas	19	1 785	1 226	5.8	55.6	16.1	10.2	8 399	17 223	30 498	26.5	4.7	10.6	11.0	6.9	10.5
Gage	138	4 188	5 467	11.0	56.9	15.4	27.8	8 012	17 190	34 908	13.6	4.2	8.7	9.3	6.6	10.2
Garden	0	1 684	492	5.7	55.1	14.2	3.9	9 678	15 414	26 458	5.8	3.3	14.8	13.7	10.8	21.9
Garfield	NA	NA	437	5.0	55.5	13.4	2.8	7 774	14 368	27 407	17.9	2.9	12.6	15.3	9.7	10.9
Gosper	0	1 155	501	4.2	50.1	17.6	2.0	6 528	17 957	36 827	6.8	5.7	7.9	7.4	4.8	8.5
Grant	0	0	210	7.6	41.0	24.7	1.9	10 228	14 815	34 821	36.0	2.0	9.7	7.4	8.2	13.8
Greeley	0	802	725	17.4	56.1	13.5	5.1	8 398	13 731	28 375	15.7	2.8	14.6	13.4	11.9	17.3
Hall	253	5 727	12 912	10.6	53.3	15.9	57.3	6 350	17 386	36 972	7.7	6.0	12.0	11.5	9.2	14.5
Hamilton	42	1 410	2 594	8.2	45.5	18.6	10.4	6 201	17 590	40 277	19.8	6.3	7.5	7.1	5.9	8.8
Harlan	0	26	924	8.8	52.1	15.3	2.6	7 134	15 618	30 679	23.6	3.5	10.1	10.5	7.0	11.7
Hayes	NA	NA	289	2.8	51.4	11.6	1.7	10 266	14 099	26 667	-3.3	3.2	18.4	16.1	14.6	21.6
Hitchcock	32	286	764	4.7	52.0	13.8	6.7	14 587	14 804	28 287	6.7	3.8	14.9	13.9	10.9	17.7
Holt	17	1 139	2 924	13.2	56.4	14.5	14.8	7 356	15 256	30 738	14.1	3.7	13.0	14.0	9.8	12.6
Hooker	0	379	181	5.5	51.4	15.7	1.8	9 302	15 513	27 868	11.0	3.3	6.9	10.1	4.9	7.0
Howard	196	1 823	1 723	5.0	56.0	14.2	9.8	6 346	15 535	33 305	14.3	3.5	11.7	11.8	8.5	10.6
Jefferson	166	2 482	1 844	12.4	56.4	14.4	12.1	7 016	18 380	32 629	11.7	4.4	8.9	10.3	8.0	12.8
Johnson	0	992	1 028	7.4	63.0	14.7	6.7	7 767	16 437	32 460	21.3	4.2	8.9	10.2	6.7	10.1
Kearney	216	2 258	1 779	5.3	47.0	21.3	9.6	6 853	18 118	39 247	7.4	4.2	8.5	8.0	5.5	9.0
Keith	123	2 197	2 090	7.1	50.3	16.8	13.3	8 895	17 421	32 325	5.0	3.9	9.3	9.2	6.6	9.7
Keya Paha	0	0	196	3.6	53.9	15.7	1.4	9 610	11 860	24 911	7.8	2.2	26.9	24.7	22.4	35.1
Kimball	NA	NA	913	4.9	52.5	13.5	4.8	6 752	17 525	30 586	-2.0	4.7	11.1	11.3	9.1	13.7
Knox	42	665	2 258	8.9	57.6	14.4	13.7	8 064	13 971	27 564	14.8	2.5	15.6	14.8	12.5	18.1
Lancaster	515	5 794	76 553	16.9	34.7	32.6	249.4	6 938	21 265	41 850	7.7	9.4	9.5	9.7	5.5	8.7
Lincoln	NA	NA	8 777	10.2	46.0	16.2	37.5	6 458	18 696	36 568	5.0	6.5	9.7	9.8	7.2	11.4
Logan	NA	NA	201	2.0	47.1	10.5	1.7	7 976	14 937	33 125	16.0	3.8	10.5	11.1	6.5	12.9
Loup	0	0	168	10.7	50.9	13.3	1.1	8 656	12 427	26 250	8.9	2.1	17.7	16.0	14.2	23.3
McPherson	0	0	132	9.1	51.1	22.2	0.9	9 474	13 055	25 750	9.5	3.3	16.2	13.1	14.0	13.6
Madison	226	4 599	9 710	21.6	51.2	17.0	39.1	6 257	16 804	35 807	9.0	4.7	11.2	11.5	7.5	11.9
Merrick	97	1 532	2 058	13.5	56.3	14.9	9.0	6 387	15 958	34 961	15.6	2.9	8.9	9.6	7.0	10.2
Morrill	55	1 510	1 378	4.5	55.7	14.3	7.8	7 077	14 725	30 235	16.0	2.9	14.7	13.7	10.0	15.5
Nance	74	833	1 026	5.8	58.2	11.4	5.3	6 428	16 886	31 267	12.2	4.1	13.1	12.5	10.2	15.8
Nemaha	13	1 659	2 268	5.1	47.6	22.9	12.9	10 550	17 004	32 588	8.4	4.4	12.6	13.6	8.3	12.1
Nuckolls	NA	NA	1 187	7.8	55.5	13.1	4.0	7 855	15 608	28 958	6.4	3.0	11.2	11.1	6.5	11.9
Otoe	39	2 378	3 963	14.4	53.9	18.1	17.4	6 673	17 752	37 302	19.7	5.6	8.1	8.7	5.9	8.5
Pawnee	128	2 148	672	3.7	61.4	14.4	5.0	7 770	16 687	29 000	18.0	3.9	11.0	12.9	6.8	9.1
Perkins	0	711	779	11.9	47.7	17.6	4.9	9 417	17 830	34 205	10.1	6.3	13.6	12.4	9.5	14.3
Phelps	51	2 457	2 387	6.5	46.8	20.4	16.6	8 373	19 044	37 319	4.1	7.1	8.9	9.6	6.2	9.6
Pierce	33	830	2 264	13.6	57.6	13.3	10.1	6 582	15 980	32 239	7.6	4.8	11.8	12.1	8.8	11.5

1. Data for serious crimes have not been adjusted for underreporting; this may affect comparability between geographic areas and over time. 2. Per 100,000 population estimated by the FBI. 3. All persons 3 years old and over enrolled in nursery school through college. 4. Persons 25 years old and over. 5. Elementary and secondary education expenditures. 6. Based on population enumerated as of April 1, 2000.

Table B. States and Counties — **Personal Income**

STATE County	Total (mil dol)	Percent change, 2001– 2002	Per capita[1] Dollars	Per capita[1] Rank	Wages and salaries[2] (mil dol)	Proprietor's income (mil dol)	Dividends, interest, and rent (mil dol)	Transfer payments Total (mil dol)	Government payments to individuals Total (mil dol)	Social Security (mil dol)	Medical payments (mil dol)	Income mainte- nance (mil dol)	Unemploy- ment insurance (mil dol)
	62	63	64	65	66	67	68	69	70	71	72	73	74
NEBRASKA—Cont'd													
Blaine	6	10.5	10 655	3 107	5	-5	4	2	2	1	1	0	0
Boone	146	-1.1	24 042	1 392	52	24	39	29	28	13	12	1	1
Box Butte	316	3.2	26 685	753	238	36	54	53	50	18	18	4	1
Boyd	43	-11.7	18 095	2 882	16	-2	15	14	13	6	6	1	0
Brown	79	4.0	22 617	1 845	32	10	24	18	17	8	7	1	0
Buffalo	1 071	3.8	24 995	1 130	793	76	204	155	145	61	58	10	3
Burt	190	-0.2	25 025	1 121	55	19	39	42	41	18	19	2	1
Butler	206	-3.8	23 095	1 696	66	10	58	37	35	17	14	2	1
Cass	714	2.1	28 802	469	149	32	111	92	86	39	34	5	2
Cedar	236	-4.4	25 333	1 035	78	52	54	37	35	18	14	2	1
Chase	107	0.7	26 604	763	46	16	32	20	19	9	8	1	0
Cherry	144	5.4	23 620	1 527	59	14	44	27	26	12	10	2	1
Cheyenne	272	1.5	27 363	636	187	31	52	44	41	20	16	3	1
Clay	183	0.7	26 483	793	91	21	42	32	30	14	12	2	1
Colfax	264	-0.1	25 166	1 087	153	23	61	47	44	17	24	2	1
Cuming	301	2.1	30 082	343	118	84	62	44	41	22	16	2	1
Custer	291	-2.3	25 117	1 099	122	49	69	57	54	25	23	3	1
Dakota	452	2.3	22 194	1 960	432	24	62	74	70	27	31	7	2
Dawes	179	5.6	19 760	2 598	95	9	41	41	39	15	13	3	1
Dawson	550	2.2	22 522	1 872	348	50	109	94	88	39	37	7	2
Deuel	49	0.8	23 703	1 501	16	4	16	10	10	5	3	0	0
Dixon	160	-0.2	25 849	922	53	32	24	24	23	11	10	1	0
Dodge	943	1.7	26 234	847	529	59	199	176	167	76	71	9	3
Douglas	17 342	2.6	36 765	110	14 137	2 056	3 410	1 929	1 818	666	798	176	48
Dundy	67	-0.7	30 454	308	23	10	22	12	12	5	6	1	0
Fillmore	181	-1.3	28 068	538	74	21	57	30	28	15	10	2	1
Franklin	81	-4.6	23 189	1 666	23	6	25	20	19	9	8	1	0
Frontier	62	-11.5	20 727	2 361	25	6	14	12	11	5	4	1	0
Furnas	114	-9.5	21 669	2 099	51	0	35	31	29	13	13	2	2
Gage	622	-1.6	26 744	745	297	59	118	153	148	51	82	6	2
Garden	50	0.1	22 612	1 848	20	-1	18	14	13	6	5	1	0
Garfield	48	2.5	25 470	1 006	17	5	17	11	10	5	5	0	0
Gosper	54	-4.1	25 818	929	14	4	16	10	10	5	3	0	0
Grant	9	18.4	12 040	3 105	5	-5	5	3	3	2	1	0	0
Greeley	60	-5.0	22 655	1 836	19	9	19	13	12	6	5	1	0
Hall	1 431	3.3	26 582	769	1 022	134	293	231	219	87	86	19	5
Hamilton	232	2.0	24 612	1 234	93	30	55	36	34	18	12	2	1
Harlan	82	-2.9	22 442	1 895	24	10	19	19	18	9	7	1	0
Hayes	19	-12.7	16 880	3 003	7	2	6	4	4	2	1	0	0
Hitchcock	53	-13.3	17 405	2 958	22	-5	16	16	16	8	6	1	1
Holt	273	3.0	24 384	1 286	114	58	61	55	52	23	24	3	1
Hooker	14	15.5	18 576	2 818	8	-4	5	4	4	2	2	0	0
Howard	151	0.5	23 100	1 694	40	19	31	27	26	12	10	2	1
Jefferson	194	-3.5	23 576	1 541	89	14	49	43	41	19	16	2	1
Johnson	107	-1.0	24 362	1 289	56	1	24	21	20	10	8	1	0
Kearney	190	1.4	27 892	566	62	32	39	35	33	13	17	1	0
Keith	204	4.6	23 452	1 584	104	23	46	41	39	20	14	2	1
Keya Paha	17	-0.8	18 132	2 876	4	3	5	4	4	2	1	0	0
Kimball	91	-4.7	22 821	1 772	44	5	25	21	20	11	7	1	0
Knox	186	-6.0	20 445	2 445	69	14	48	50	48	20	22	3	1
Lancaster	7 766	4.2	30 192	333	5 890	634	1 402	898	838	344	327	69	19
Lincoln	885	2.7	25 621	976	596	70	165	167	159	52	57	12	4
Logan	16	-1.3	21 825	2 059	5	1	4	3	3	2	1	0	0
Loup	7	1.4	9 281	3 110	3	-3	4	3	3	1	1	0	0
McPherson	7	0.7	12 647	3 100	2	-1	2	2	1	1	1	0	0
Madison	886	3.3	24 614	1 233	662	75	177	152	143	60	59	11	5
Merrick	201	2.0	24 774	1 188	69	27	42	37	35	16	14	2	1
Morrill	113	3.6	21 293	2 210	42	15	24	25	24	10	10	2	1
Nance	82	-8.6	21 148	2 253	25	7	19	22	21	8	10	1	1
Nemaha	200	-8.3	27 567	605	153	13	44	37	35	15	15	2	1
Nuckolls	110	-9.0	22 692	1 826	41	6	30	29	28	14	12	1	0
Otoe	378	-0.7	24 471	1 271	187	15	87	70	67	32	26	3	2
Pawnee	71	-10.5	23 483	1 575	22	6	21	16	15	8	6	1	0
Perkins	78	-9.4	25 224	1 069	32	16	18	15	15	7	6	1	0
Phelps	281	1.0	28 920	456	154	46	59	49	46	22	20	2	1
Pierce	174	-5.1	22 511	1 874	51	18	38	31	29	14	12	2	1

1. Based on the resident population estimated as of July 1 of the year shown.   2. Includes other labor income.

Table B. States and Counties — Earnings, Social Security, and Housing

STATE County	Earnings, 2002									Social Security beneficiaries, December 2003			Housing units, 2003	
			Percent by selected industries											
			Goods-related[1]		Service-related and health							Supplemental Security Income recipients, December 2003		Percent change, 2000–2003
	Total (mil dol)	Farm	Total	Manufacturing	Information and professional and technical services	Retail trade	Finance, insurance, and real estate	Health services	Government	Number	Rate[2]		Total	
	75	76	77	78	79	80	81	82	83	84	85	86	87	88
NEBRASKA—Cont'd														
Blaine	0	-994.0	49.9	49.9	D	D	D	12.8	677.6	115	216	6	339	1.8
Boone	77	24.0	D	4.3	2.7	7.2	4.6	6.1	24.8	1 420	240	54	2 752	0.7
Box Butte	274	8.5	6.7	4.2	D	4.4	3.0	D	13.7	1 880	161	145	5 502	0.3
Boyd	14	-43.1	D	6.9	D	11.0	10.9	9.9	52.7	685	294	38	1 421	1.1
Brown	43	15.9	D	3.5	D	8.7	D	D	32.3	925	265	43	1 923	0.4
Buffalo	869	1.3	27.7	21.4	4.5	9.0	4.5	16.8	16.2	6 230	145	321	17 443	3.6
Burt	74	13.0	12.3	5.1	D	6.6	7.5	5.5	26.8	1 955	259	95	3 727	0.1
Butler	76	3.5	24.5	19.1	3.0	11.2	D	D	25.0	1 885	212	87	4 064	4.2
Cass	181	-2.6	D	15.0	3.9	9.1	8.6	6.3	23.1	3 910	155	127	10 603	4.2
Cedar	131	22.8	20.3	12.4	D	6.0	4.9	4.3	18.1	2 035	220	68	4 253	1.3
Chase	62	18.5	5.6	2.3	D	10.9	D	3.8	25.8	990	245	40	1 940	0.7
Cherry	73	5.3	D	4.7	D	14.2	5.6	6.5	25.6	1 345	222	91	3 252	1.0
Cheyenne	218	0.9	17.2	14.0	2.9	11.2	3.8	5.5	13.1	2 005	202	125	4 657	1.9
Clay	112	14.1	D	15.4	D	5.0	D	4.4	28.7	1 475	214	45	3 061	-0.2
Colfax	176	9.8	D	D	D	4.1	3.1	D	11.8	1 785	170	83	4 095	0.2
Cuming	202	37.3	D	13.3	3.4	4.4	4.2	7.4	10.9	2 345	238	62	4 309	0.6
Custer	171	21.8	17.6	13.1	3.0	7.4	2.9	9.9	17.8	2 790	242	154	5 599	0.3
Dakota	456	1.0	D	49.7	2.1	4.6	7.7	D	8.5	2 920	142	238	7 671	1.9
Dawes	103	-8.0	D	1.3	D	14.0	4.1	11.5	40.7	1 690	188	103	4 013	0.2
Dawson	398	8.6	D	34.9	3.0	7.8	3.7	D	17.6	4 080	166	270	9 824	0.2
Deuel	20	9.0	D	D	D	11.8	D	D	24.6	550	268	16	1 019	-1.3
Dixon	85	29.7	D	D	D	2.1	D	D	14.9	1 190	194	48	2 689	0.6
Dodge	588	2.1	D	22.3	D	11.1	5.5	D	18.0	7 690	214	371	15 744	1.8
Douglas	16 193	0.0	D	7.0	13.7	6.9	12.1	9.9	11.0	65 900	138	7 439	200 658	4.1
Dundy	33	29.3	D	D	D	D	D	7.4	24.8	565	254	26	1 197	0.1
Fillmore	95	16.9	22.0	4.4	D	5.3	D	4.8	23.2	1 575	245	68	2 986	-0.1
Franklin	29	12.2	D	D	D	9.2	7.4	5.4	34.9	1 005	292	45	1 721	-1.4
Frontier	32	9.4	D	D	D	10.5	D	5.3	34.7	590	203	28	1 551	0.5
Furnas	51	-2.2	9.0	2.5	9.8	7.7	D	13.5	33.8	1 485	286	91	2 717	-0.5
Gage	356	5.3	D	24.7	D	8.7	4.1	11.9	23.8	5 555	238	393	10 345	3.1
Garden	19	-1.2	D	D	D	17.2	9.2	0.9	48.2	700	319	25	1 296	-0.2
Garfield	22	12.6	D	12.3	D	8.9	D	8.9	22.6	555	301	26	1 023	0.2
Gosper	18	19.3	D	D	5.2	1.6	D	0.9	27.9	570	273	17	1 282	0.1
Grant	1	-831.3	D	0.0	D	66.8	D	0.0	428.4	190	273	5	455	1.3
Greeley	28	23.5	10.6	5.5	D	6.3	4.8	3.3	28.0	675	259	38	1 204	0.4
Hall	1 156	1.0	D	25.7	4.6	9.4	5.8	11.4	16.4	9 105	168	800	22 005	2.0
Hamilton	124	13.1	26.9	16.8	7.0	5.2	5.7	D	15.8	1 860	196	61	3 895	1.2
Harlan	35	7.5	D	8.5	D	9.0	9.6	D	23.5	955	261	37	2 360	1.4
Hayes	9	34.9	D	D	D	D	D	0.0	29.4	180	163	8	530	0.8
Hitchcock	17	-38.3	28.2	8.5	D	5.2	D	D	59.2	850	280	40	1 680	0.3
Holt	172	13.5	20.4	16.9	3.6	8.2	4.1	D	14.8	2 650	239	183	5 364	1.6
Hooker	4	-97.7	D	D	D	D	D	D	59.0	235	319	6	438	-0.5
Howard	59	26.4	D	0.8	D	8.6	D	2.8	31.1	1 380	208	48	2 869	3.1
Jefferson	102	6.0	D	17.4	4.7	9.9	3.9	D	16.9	2 120	262	142	3 940	-0.1
Johnson	57	-8.4	D	D	D	7.0	D	9.2	44.4	1 100	248	43	2 138	1.0
Kearney	93	30.7	10.9	5.9	4.4	3.8	4.5	D	17.8	1 275	186	65	2 836	-0.4
Keith	126	5.5	D	11.3	6.8	12.9	8.1	D	16.8	2 040	241	102	5 450	5.3
Keya Paha	7	37.8	D	4.4	D	5.3	2.9	D	23.4	255	268	5	555	1.3
Kimball	49	-5.0	28.4	14.8	D	12.2	D	D	26.7	1 040	270	48	1 976	0.2
Knox	83	9.6	D	4.7	5.0	9.4	D	D	37.9	2 410	266	140	4 780	0.1
Lancaster	6 524	0.0	19.6	13.1	10.2	6.2	8.3	12.9	21.4	34 015	130	3 413	109 196	4.8
Lincoln	666	1.5	D	1.8	4.6	8.8	4.3	14.7	17.5	5 740	165	633	15 799	2.3
Logan	6	19.2	D	0.0	D	D	D	3.9	31.2	175	246	12	390	1.0
Loup	-1	0.0	0.0	0.0	-9.6	D	0.0	0.0	0.0	155	208	7	378	0.3
McPherson	1	-95.4	D	0.0	D	D	D	D	115.0	115	212	6	288	1.8
Madison	736	2.6	D	20.2	4.5	9.2	4.7	12.1	17.6	6 455	180	556	14 639	1.4
Merrick	97	23.6	D	10.7	2.7	5.0	3.7	D	19.1	1 825	224	100	3 674	0.7
Morrill	57	19.6	D	1.6	D	6.1	3.6	4.7	28.0	1 110	210	88	2 467	0.3
Nance	31	5.7	D	D	D	5.5	D	11.3	38.9	940	251	71	1 760	-1.5
Nemaha	166	1.6	15.2	11.5	D	4.8	D	5.2	56.0	1 570	220	111	3 458	0.6
Nuckolls	47	-4.0	5.9	0.8	5.8	13.0	D	19.0	25.5	1 430	295	79	2 520	-0.4
Otoe	202	-4.2	36.2	28.3	D	7.9	5.8	D	21.5	3 325	214	131	6 744	2.7
Pawnee	28	11.6	D	17.6	D	6.8	3.6	9.1	29.4	905	310	41	1 594	0.4
Perkins	47	20.5	12.5	2.0	D	4.2	D	3.6	22.6	700	229	31	1 446	0.1
Phelps	200	19.0	D	20.9	D	5.9	3.6	D	13.7	2 105	219	98	4 215	0.6
Pierce	69	14.8	11.7	2.2	5.4	8.0	D	8.7	23.4	1 510	196	57	3 266	0.6

1. Covers mining, construction, and manufacturing.   2. Per 1,000 resident population estimated as of July 1 of the year shown.

STATE County	Housing units, 2000								Civilian labor force, 2003				Civilian employment,[6] 2000		
	Occupied units										Unemployment		Percent		
		Owner-occupied				Renter-occupied									
				Median owner cost as a percent of income											
	Total	Percent	Median value[1]	With a mortgage	Without a mortgage[2]	Median rent[3]	Median rent as a percent of income	Sub-standard units[4] (percent)	Total	Percent change, 2002–2003	Total	Rate[5]	Total	Management, professional and related occupations	Production, transportation, and material moving occupations
	89	90	91	92	93	94	95	96	97	98	99	100	101	102	103
NEBRASKA—Cont'd															
Blaine	238	65.1	22 500	28.8	11.8	365	14.3	2.9	365	1.1	8	2.2	278	42.4	8.6
Boone	2 454	75.2	50 700	18.7	11.8	310	18.1	1.1	2 953	2.0	101	3.4	2 979	36.5	13.9
Box Butte	4 780	70.1	71 700	17.1	10.4	411	19.2	3.4	5 802	2.3	282	4.9	5 839	23.6	23.9
Boyd	1 014	80.4	22 500	17.9	12.3	261	14.2	1.6	1 147	2.0	34	3.0	1 164	41.2	10.8
Brown	1 530	74.4	42 700	19.5	11.1	347	19.0	1.8	1 811	2.6	68	3.8	1 743	34.6	11.2
Buffalo	15 930	63.6	91 300	20.5	11.0	495	24.2	2.0	27 162	1.3	904	3.3	23 404	30.2	14.9
Burt	3 155	75.9	59 700	20.1	11.7	395	20.8	1.9	3 517	1.3	220	6.3	3 735	29.3	14.3
Butler	3 426	75.5	62 900	18.8	9.9	389	17.1	2.6	4 499	3.5	203	4.5	4 322	29.3	24.8
Cass	9 161	79.7	95 400	20.3	10.9	502	20.1	2.0	13 121	1.0	564	4.3	12 573	29.0	15.1
Cedar	3 623	80.3	55 200	19.7	11.6	350	18.9	1.7	4 961	4.2	152	3.1	4 615	32.2	16.4
Chase	1 662	77.1	56 900	17.8	10.6	335	19.5	1.6	2 070	10.2	49	2.4	1 962	32.9	11.6
Cherry	2 508	62.2	63 300	20.5	11.2	424	22.4	2.0	3 660	5.6	87	2.4	3 192	37.6	7.6
Cheyenne	4 071	72.8	56 500	19.2	10.5	388	20.0	2.9	6 017	6.2	147	2.4	5 033	27.9	15.1
Clay	2 756	77.8	50 900	18.6	11.0	363	20.3	2.6	3 078	-2.7	103	3.3	3 380	33.2	17.9
Colfax	3 682	75.4	57 800	17.2	9.9	410	17.6	6.7	5 770	7.3	177	3.1	5 268	22.3	35.7
Cuming	3 945	71.5	66 000	19.4	9.9	398	20.0	2.4	5 425	3.8	129	2.4	5 216	29.7	20.8
Custer	4 826	73.2	45 100	18.1	10.1	333	21.8	1.9	5 824	1.1	143	2.5	5 724	34.8	16.6
Dakota	7 095	67.5	81 200	19.1	10.4	516	23.7	8.6	10 414	-1.8	508	4.9	10 096	22.6	29.5
Dawes	3 512	62.6	55 200	17.9	9.9	394	26.5	2.6	4 634	-0.6	188	4.1	4 762	32.4	8.6
Dawson	8 824	69.1	64 100	19.0	10.9	453	20.6	7.6	14 169	5.2	501	3.5	11 361	22.2	30.4
Deuel	908	78.0	48 300	17.0	11.3	338	20.6	2.1	954	9.2	27	2.8	1 064	31.1	14.1
Dixon	2 413	76.3	58 100	19.3	10.5	401	19.0	3.1	2 785	8.5	112	4.0	3 145	27.9	20.9
Dodge	14 433	67.9	83 400	18.8	10.3	485	22.5	2.1	20 494	2.2	937	4.6	18 354	23.9	21.5
Douglas	182 194	63.2	100 800	19.8	10.5	541	23.6	3.6	275 380	0.8	12 832	4.7	239 418	36.5	11.9
Dundy	961	72.4	32 600	15.7	11.2	286	15.0	1.9	1 124	1.0	34	3.0	1 103	38.2	9.7
Fillmore	2 689	74.7	51 300	18.7	10.9	367	17.4	1.3	3 342	3.8	119	3.6	3 224	34.6	14.4
Franklin	1 485	81.3	33 100	19.9	12.0	361	19.0	2.2	1 791	5.8	54	3.0	1 648	35.9	13.4
Frontier	1 192	73.0	54 800	20.6	11.0	368	20.5	1.9	1 703	4.7	41	2.4	1 616	33.8	12.7
Furnas	2 278	76.6	37 300	18.8	10.8	314	19.5	2.4	2 495	3.2	64	2.6	2 411	33.9	17.4
Gage	9 316	71.4	68 600	19.3	10.3	421	20.7	1.1	13 217	3.2	533	4.0	11 728	29.3	19.9
Garden	1 020	70.8	44 300	20.4	11.5	325	19.9	0.9	1 045	7.5	39	3.7	1 137	36.2	10.6
Garfield	813	72.6	38 200	22.0	13.2	313	25.5	1.0	1 094	1.4	31	2.8	911	36.3	9.7
Gosper	863	75.6	67 900	18.2	11.3	406	18.3	1.5	1 226	5.4	33	2.7	1 058	34.4	13.8
Grant	292	67.8	27 500	16.0	9.9	369	15.3	3.8	371	1.1	8	2.2	410	31.7	7.1
Greeley	1 077	78.4	36 600	21.3	11.3	306	16.8	2.2	1 423	3.3	51	3.6	1 277	43.5	8.3
Hall	20 356	65.9	83 700	20.6	10.8	456	24.5	4.8	32 370	2.2	1 333	4.1	26 925	25.1	20.5
Hamilton	3 503	75.2	78 200	19.7	9.9	420	18.1	1.6	5 391	2.3	184	3.4	4 767	32.5	16.2
Harlan	1 597	80.2	43 100	17.4	12.1	370	20.1	1.8	1 741	1.6	50	2.9	1 767	32.0	15.6
Hayes	430	71.9	31 800	24.6	11.1	296	16.8	5.1	495	-0.2	17	3.4	523	43.4	10.1
Hitchcock	1 287	78.0	38 000	19.3	9.9	329	22.1	1.8	1 543	4.8	55	3.6	1 437	32.2	14.2
Holt	4 608	73.5	59 700	19.5	12.8	323	17.6	2.1	6 597	4.3	194	2.9	5 708	32.7	12.0
Hooker	335	74.0	41 300	14.9	10.1	284	15.7	0.6	402	-3.4	10	2.5	372	26.9	14.0
Howard	2 546	77.2	66 100	21.5	12.3	403	21.0	2.3	3 525	2.5	156	4.4	3 330	29.5	15.7
Jefferson	3 527	75.7	42 100	17.7	9.9	349	23.5	1.0	4 055	1.3	166	4.1	4 079	28.5	22.8
Johnson	1 887	75.0	51 300	17.6	11.7	378	20.1	2.4	2 685	4.8	85	3.2	2 141	34.3	16.9
Kearney	2 643	74.0	77 600	19.1	10.4	453	21.8	2.0	3 888	1.0	112	2.9	3 527	31.8	15.0
Keith	3 707	73.1	69 300	19.5	11.9	404	22.7	3.1	4 812	1.0	159	3.3	4 443	28.9	14.1
Keya Paha	409	71.4	28 200	25.0	12.9	277	23.1	1.7	519	4.4	10	1.9	468	51.1	5.6
Kimball	1 727	76.5	49 400	19.0	11.8	381	22.1	3.7	2 052	4.5	46	2.2	2 013	28.0	18.9
Knox	3 811	74.9	42 100	19.0	12.5	264	17.6	2.0	4 820	5.6	155	3.2	4 374	36.4	11.2
Lancaster	99 187	60.5	105 900	20.5	9.9	519	24.6	3.1	154 725	1.4	6 196	4.0	139 561	36.0	13.4
Lincoln	14 076	69.2	78 200	19.2	11.8	427	22.4	3.1	19 313	4.4	711	3.7	16 928	24.7	18.1
Logan	316	71.5	51 700	22.5	11.6	340	14.3	2.2	402	4.1	12	3.0	390	36.7	10.8
Loup	289	77.5	27 500	20.7	11.8	278	18.8	0.7	475	8.0	11	2.3	324	40.1	13.0
McPherson	202	67.3	40 900	17.5	9.9	269	14.1	1.5	328	6.1	8	2.4	256	65.2	2.3
Madison	13 436	65.8	80 100	20.0	10.4	434	23.1	3.5	22 443	11.8	893	4.0	17 798	25.7	21.9
Merrick	3 209	74.3	62 700	20.8	10.9	401	19.5	1.9	4 611	2.0	174	3.8	4 021	30.0	17.9
Morrill	2 138	71.4	49 500	17.8	11.0	370	20.4	4.1	2 806	0.6	109	3.9	2 541	31.8	14.7
Nance	1 577	74.8	45 500	17.8	10.6	352	22.8	2.2	1 896	5.3	124	6.5	1 892	30.6	16.7
Nemaha	3 047	72.5	58 200	17.4	9.9	360	20.1	1.3	4 293	7.5	163	3.8	3 687	33.5	16.6
Nuckolls	2 218	80.0	33 000	19.0	11.3	315	21.2	1.4	2 300	4.9	57	2.5	2 421	31.9	13.9
Otoe	6 060	74.0	78 000	19.5	11.0	434	20.3	1.7	8 529	5.1	353	4.1	7 693	30.2	19.3
Pawnee	1 339	81.0	30 300	18.1	11.8	309	18.7	1.7	1 753	2.9	68	3.9	1 477	36.2	14.3
Perkins	1 275	75.6	52 200	17.8	9.9	389	21.5	1.6	1 534	1.1	32	2.1	1 533	39.8	10.1
Phelps	3 844	73.2	71 400	17.9	11.3	378	18.9	1.5	4 975	-2.0	145	2.9	4 948	30.5	15.1
Pierce	2 979	77.8	59 900	19.1	12.1	372	19.3	1.5	4 305	11.6	157	3.6	3 916	29.5	20.0

1. Specified owner-occupied units.   2. Median monthly owner costs is often in the minimum category—9.9 percent or less, which is indicated as 9.9 percent.   3. Specified renter-occupied units.   4. Overcrowded or lacking complete plumbing facilities.   5. Percent of civilian labor force.   6. Persons 16 years old and over.

	Private nonfarm establishments, employment and payroll, 2001								Agriculture, 2002			
	Employment						Annual payroll		Farms			
										Percent with—		
STATE County	Number of establishments	Total	Health care and social assistance	Manufacturing	Retail trade	Finance and insurance	Professional, scientific, and technical services	Total (mil dol)	Average per employee (dollars)	Number	Less than 50 acres	500 acres and over	Farm operators whose principal occupation is farming (percent)
	104	105	106	107	108	109	110	111	112	113	114	115	116
NEBRASKA—Cont'd													
Blaine	13	29	0	0	5	D	D	1	19 379	106	4.7	67.0	82.1
Boone	199	1 441	388	22	322	76	17	27	18 752	692	7.5	42.5	75.0
Box Butte	377	3 435	563	469	688	156	90	69	20 105	476	6.9	54.4	74.2
Boyd	81	404	118	D	95	34	12	6	16 079	314	6.1	58.3	78.7
Brown	148	941	218	D	237	73	D	15	15 881	311	8.0	56.9	74.0
Buffalo	1 316	20 254	3 464	4 112	3 876	702	435	477	23 530	989	16.2	41.2	70.6
Burt	215	1 324	203	98	255	107	62	24	17 960	621	15.6	32.9	74.4
Butler	189	1 797	371	497	198	88	D	37	20 348	840	15.1	32.3	69.2
Cass	514	3 767	345	285	663	188	67	86	22 888	679	26.5	30.2	65.7
Cedar	300	1 800	108	273	331	110	55	36	19 960	949	15.0	33.7	77.7
Chase	135	965	161	D	230	62	20	20	21 177	326	9.5	63.5	75.5
Cherry	225	1 661	267	D	453	83	D	29	17 408	557	6.1	79.2	83.7
Cheyenne	316	4 866	398	756	1 629	393	41	120	24 576	616	5.4	62.2	75.0
Clay	190	1 285	133	65	227	74	25	26	20 291	503	15.7	50.3	77.5
Colfax	272	3 869	309	D	428	111	D	94	24 178	589	21.2	31.1	75.0
Cuming	350	3 305	438	837	495	177	56	69	20 963	904	18.1	27.1	76.0
Custer	375	2 607	647	457	548	135	81	51	19 638	1 149	11.1	57.0	76.1
Dakota	453	10 505	443	5 360	929	589	83	275	26 225	296	20.3	28.7	64.9
Dawes	292	2 203	327	D	615	72	D	34	15 657	406	9.6	60.3	72.4
Dawson	688	9 643	924	4 259	1 522	267	176	214	22 187	718	15.2	44.2	74.2
Deuel	79	459	17	D	205	42	D	9	19 115	252	6.3	61.1	76.2
Dixon	132	699	237	D	104	61	D	12	16 751	660	16.2	27.6	68.5
Dodge	1 068	14 964	2 108	3 378	2 956	471	300	353	23 563	734	21.3	32.0	71.7
Douglas	14 151	296 080	37 558	25 920	34 968	27 463	18 723	9 973	33 684	361	47.4	18.6	54.3
Dundy	73	446	189	D	60	16	23	9	20 466	262	3.4	61.8	80.9
Fillmore	232	1 797	347	267	248	130	14	40	22 137	499	7.6	55.5	85.6
Franklin	98	546	199	D	94	43	18	9	16 522	378	9.3	47.4	75.1
Frontier	77	468	90	0	50	D	D	9	19 447	318	7.2	65.7	85.8
Furnas	182	1 346	348	D	327	103	61	29	21 341	412	10.4	54.1	78.9
Gage	694	7 929	1 544	1 889	1 408	276	130	162	20 464	1 272	19.8	31.4	66.9
Garden	62	400	D	0	87	32	5	7	17 098	253	7.9	64.4	76.7
Garfield	91	532	113	53	141	D	D	8	15 329	190	10.0	56.3	74.7
Gosper	52	187	D	D	13	29	10	4	20 091	242	5.0	59.5	83.9
Grant	25	89	0	D	D	D	D	2	17 303	73	17.8	67.1	89.0
Greeley	76	419	56	D	123	36	D	7	17 053	361	7.2	47.1	80.3
Hall	1 860	28 455	3 569	6 384	5 322	1 634	581	681	23 937	595	19.0	36.8	72.6
Hamilton	271	2 487	296	687	313	79	51	61	24 359	603	13.3	45.8	83.3
Harlan	106	609	151	D	114	43	13	10	15 833	346	12.1	47.1	76.3
Hayes	24	78	D	D	D	D	D	1	17 397	260	3.5	60.0	79.2
Hitchcock	68	333	11	0	88	25	0	6	17 375	299	5.4	67.2	81.3
Holt	438	3 108	615	245	731	165	83	54	17 315	1 166	8.8	54.9	78.1
Hooker	31	156	60	D	40	D	0	3	17 276	81	3.7	79.0	75.3
Howard	146	804	177	D	219	81	20	14	17 781	600	17.2	32.3	74.0
Jefferson	246	2 536	319	597	405	93	52	52	20 603	631	13.0	40.1	74.6
Johnson	130	987	184	D	189	62	D	18	18 040	571	13.7	24.9	65.0
Kearney	189	1 460	446	117	181	90	17	28	19 520	412	7.0	60.2	87.9
Keith	366	3 001	371	413	665	153	87	58	19 348	363	11.3	49.9	70.0
Keya Paha	20	41	0	D	15	D	D	1	18 049	185	4.3	70.8	93.5
Kimball	150	1 509	104	D	246	54	63	27	18 099	362	5.2	57.7	70.4
Knox	274	1 451	329	D	435	103	42	22	15 471	1 016	9.3	41.6	76.7
Lancaster	7 128	127 601	18 868	16 216	17 237	10 504	8 232	3 553	27 842	1 607	39.2	17.1	52.7
Lincoln	980	10 448	1 978	329	2 914	472	316	214	20 466	959	15.3	51.0	67.4
Logan	18	63	0	D	20	D	0	1	15 841	119	6.7	62.2	83.2
Loup	10	15	0	0	1	D	0	0	13 467	120	2.5	65.8	81.7
McPherson	7	17	0	0	D	D	0	0	10 059	128	4.7	73.4	75.0
Madison	1 333	20 333	2 975	5 628	3 376	497	454	472	23 202	766	18.8	31.1	71.0
Merrick	231	1 863	296	309	377	91	25	39	20 743	513	16.2	39.6	77.0
Morrill	120	719	130	D	151	50	D	13	17 915	443	9.9	49.2	70.0
Nance	108	471	113	0	101	50	23	7	15 454	392	13.8	40.1	69.4
Nemaha	206	1 873	355	D	312	116	39	43	23 210	483	11.2	34.4	73.7
Nuckolls	185	1 237	385	D	285	71	35	20	16 091	476	9.7	49.4	73.9
Otoe	438	4 719	686	1 390	709	230	110	104	22 066	797	21.7	29.2	65.4
Pawnee	72	459	122	D	47	40	15	9	18 558	531	11.1	31.8	67.0
Perkins	105	791	188	20	100	47	9	17	21 699	438	4.3	57.5	78.1
Phelps	321	3 795	780	926	525	175	94	95	25 013	470	8.5	53.6	80.6
Pierce	212	1 567	318	64	367	84	25	27	17 422	697	16.5	32.3	74.9

Table B. States and Counties — **Agriculture**

STATE County	Land in farms — Acreage (1,000) [117]	Percent change, 1997–2002 [118]	Acres — Average size of farm [119]	Acres — Total irrigated (1,000) [120]	Acres — Total cropland (1,000) [121]	Value of land and buildings (dollars) — Average per farm [122]	Value of land and buildings (dollars) — Average per acre [123]	Value of machinery and equipment average per farm (dollars) [124]	Value of products sold — Total (mil dol) [125]	Value of products sold — Average per farm (dollars) [126]	Percent from — Crops [127]	Percent from — Livestock and poultry products [128]	Percent of farms with sales of — $10,000 or more [129]	Percent of farms with sales of — $100,000 or more [130]	Government payments — Total ($1,000) [131]	Government payments — Percent of farms [132]
NEBRASKA—Cont'd																
Blaine	441	-2.4	4 162	10	50	1 013 015	241	91 003	22	204 503	2.9	97.1	70.8	34.0	619	38.7
Boone	431	-3.8	622	162	313	688 887	1 152	121 636	197	284 796	27.3	72.7	77.3	38.2	5 935	71.1
Box Butte	675	-3.2	1 418	133	377	675 703	477	167 028	130	273 234	44.1	55.9	69.1	33.8	3 647	63.4
Boyd	308	3.7	981	6	122	438 884	436	76 014	30	96 830	14.7	85.3	74.2	23.2	1 336	56.7
Brown	686	-2.1	2 207	52	164	701 152	343	86 603	93	180 995	14.4	85.6	71.7	31.2	1 670	46.3
Buffalo	601	-3.2	608	234	374	787 773	1 312	128 090	179	180 995	43.8	56.2	69.8	34.9	7 484	57.6
Burt	310	6.2	499	51	281	929 958	1 700	116 982	95	153 384	54.6	45.4	71.7	32.9	5 069	71.0
Butler	375	5.9	446	110	311	850 209	1 902	87 145	95	112 513	56.2	43.8	63.9	25.6	5 528	76.0
Cass	320	6.3	472	2	272	1 036 681	2 075	114 833	46	68 159	81.7	18.3	60.8	24.2	3 451	62.9
Cedar	460	3.4	485	85	371	560 435	1 200	102 401	168	176 997	32.3	67.7	75.7	35.7	6 540	66.1
Chase	540	-3.1	1 655	169	285	1 088 912	667	215 466	142	436 281	47.6	52.4	74.2	48.5	5 325	70.6
Cherry	3 777	-2.7	6 781	35	426	1 519 677	225	106 917	119	214 158	9.3	90.7	78.6	46.1	3 334	40.2
Cheyenne	803	3.1	1 304	51	599	506 534	374	99 367	88	143 042	34.5	65.5	68.5	20.0	5 001	80.2
Clay	374	2.5	744	201	302	1 196 393	1 503	168 876	160	317 380	47.0	53.0	81.1	52.7	3 355	65.9
Colfax	244	6.1	415	59	214	627 679	1 629	121 938	170	287 946	22.8	77.2	74.5	36.5	4 967	64.7
Cuming	366	1.7	405	43	319	658 526	1 571	111 129	581	642 698	9.6	90.4	82.6	43.1	4 967	54.7
Custer	1 502	-3.2	1 307	207	487	696 003	535	104 469	282	245 368	21.8	78.2	75.0	31.9	7 945	54.7
Dakota	152	7.0	512	11	127	712 465	1 348	95 332	30	102 084	81.8	18.2	57.8	24.3	2 467	63.9
Dawes	786	-4.4	1 937	15	172	657 099	362	55 803	26	64 626	14.3	85.7	65.8	18.5	1 396	49.5
Dawson	623	-4.2	867	226	330	830 919	1 014	137 066	371	517 176	20.1	79.9	79.0	44.2	5 487	55.3
Deuel	294	4.3	1 167	17	258	479 906	430	110 574	30	117 484	48.5	51.5	70.6	22.2	2 352	79.0
Dixon	277	14.0	419	17	213	489 299	1 246	73 816	102	154 224	33.7	66.3	55.3	21.1	5 240	76.5
Dodge	339	5.0	462	111	308	953 974	1 955	126 664	132	179 195	50.1	49.9	74.9	35.4	3 983	66.5
Douglas	95	-15.9	262	13	83	991 875	3 900	79 578	36	98 441	61.8	38.2	47.4	20.5	1 326	41.0
Dundy	567	-4.1	2 164	89	220	1 037 720	478	157 471	92	350 528	43.0	57.0	73.7	44.7	4 172	74.8
Fillmore	364	2.0	729	202	323	1 178 604	1 685	191 054	128	256 519	61.9	38.1	87.2	55.5	5 145	70.9
Franklin	331	-5.7	876	93	181	702 072	768	115 077	54	143 257	62.5	37.6	74.9	36.5	3 375	70.1
Frontier	487	-8.3	1 530	63	221	798 177	529	119 930	65	204 034	36.0	64.0	78.3	43.4	3 126	70.1
Furnas	441	-2.0	1 070	68	299	665 988	604	142 197	84	203 872	36.8	63.2	73.1	31.3	4 204	81.6
Gage	552	6.4	434	54	430	459 046	1 093	102 305	102	80 089	51.1	48.9	58.7	21.9	8 326	73.6
Garden	1 072	-0.6	4 237	35	178	1 091 896	255	119 562	53	210 994	23.6	76.4	75.9	34.8	2 039	65.6
Garfield	293	-4.9	1 543	14	80	524 809	351	67 154	34	177 344	8.3	91.7	72.1	27.4	876	42.1
Gosper	262	12.0	1 084	83	145	806 413	836	151 941	48	197 062	59.6	40.4	80.6	43.0	2 493	74.0
Grant	490	2.7	6 711	1	42	1 438 314	213	93 210	14	197 725	D	D	79.5	50.7	388	31.5
Greeley	293	0.7	812	61	128	665 337	741	77 738	61	168 307	25.6	74.4	70.6	30.2	2 382	64.8
Hall	316	-7.6	531	187	234	806 081	1 661	151 296	132	222 452	48.7	51.3	73.3	41.0	4 829	57.0
Hamilton	348	1.2	577	268	313	1 100 103	1 841	158 065	158	261 744	60.3	39.7	86.2	56.2	5 479	66.3
Harlan	309	-4.9	893	72	194	637 251	714	117 827	59	171 673	46.3	53.7	73.4	30.6	2 857	69.4
Hayes	408	-4.2	1 570	50	189	609 051	415	111 665	71	271 221	24.5	75.5	73.8	37.3	2 525	76.5
Hitchcock	434	6.9	1 450	32	251	787 250	487	115 452	32	108 645	54.3	45.7	79.9	30.8	2 715	74.6
Holt	1 481	1.2	1 270	235	663	654 599	518	119 197	206	176 887	37.1	62.9	75.4	32.1	7 513	48.9
Hooker	424	14.3	5 233	5	19	1 076 296	202	57 374	11	141 441	4.8	95.2	75.3	38.3	318	44.4
Howard	294	-10.9	489	103	185	456 814	999	94 837	99	164 627	30.3	69.7	69.0	27.3	3 385	63.5
Jefferson	364	15.6	576	71	260	617 607	1 181	96 144	79	125 342	48.8	51.2	67.0	29.2	4 979	71.8
Johnson	205	4.1	360	13	145	379 888	967	66 240	23	39 898	42.6	57.4	46.8	8.9	4 281	80.2
Kearney	331	3.4	804	216	280	1 223 182	1 447	229 426	205	497 791	40.6	59.4	88.6	62.9	5 984	76.7
Keith	628	3.5	1 730	91	263	887 295	509	151 431	96	263 246	39.3	60.7	63.8	32.0	3 152	64.7
Keya Paha	463	-7.4	2 504	16	116	851 560	345	88 751	29	157 804	11.2	88.8	75.1	37.3	962	47.6
Kimball	550	-2.7	1 518	27	354	487 406	309	102 499	22	60 424	64.2	35.8	51.7	13.0	4 076	86.7
Knox	599	0.5	590	46	332	451 954	726	84 952	160	157 905	17.6	82.4	73.8	27.9	4 898	66.6
Lancaster	449	6.7	279	17	365	568 129	1 963	67 973	71	44 354	68.6	31.4	40.9	12.9	6 321	58.4
Lincoln	1 529	7.7	1 594	207	431	846 826	509	112 748	289	301 231	24.6	75.4	67.9	32.0	6 709	48.3
Logan	359	11.1	3 017	19	69	930 778	310	107 695	17	145 870	34.7	65.3	73.9	40.3	860	52.9
Loup	338	-0.3	2 813	10	49	794 672	279	72 692	18	152 237	5.8	94.2	72.5	28.3	544	45.8
McPherson	529	19.4	4 130	13	47	928 787	218	56 968	19	145 559	6.9	93.1	78.9	40.6	521	40.6
Madison	342	4.0	447	98	282	578 944	1 333	92 654	140	182 878	35.8	64.2	70.8	30.5	4 142	58.5
Merrick	283	3.3	552	176	217	684 366	1 339	117 971	113	219 468	48.7	51.3	78.4	44.2	3 498	61.2
Morrill	872	1.3	1 969	123	234	657 996	327	104 187	163	366 990	18.3	81.7	70.0	34.5	2 720	65.0
Nance	229	-6.1	584	54	149	505 315	917	135 423	55	140 958	38.4	61.6	67.6	28.3	2 765	70.7
Nemaha	255	6.7	529	4	208	675 249	1 271	85 786	38	78 206	54.9	45.1	62.7	17.8	3 636	78.5
Nuckolls	351	7.3	736	58	239	697 215	900	96 559	49	103 851	68.3	31.7	78.4	32.1	3 247	60.3
Otoe	343	-3.1	430	5	278	641 056	1 498	77 358	44	54 628	54.0	46.0	55.0	16.6	4 807	69.3
Pawnee	257	11.7	484	3	165	435 415	845	68 643	22	41 629	48.4	51.6	69.5	12.1	4 776	80.4
Perkins	548	-0.9	1 252	122	438	931 829	641	169 785	83	190 149	68.2	31.8	70.5	33.6	5 426	76.9
Phelps	366	-3.4	779	251	294	1 159 506	1 479	205 673	341	726 127	25.6	74.4	86.0	62.3	6 030	71.5
Pierce	333	7.8	477	115	271	614 586	1 246	108 128	122	174 550	37.2	62.8	75.5	34.4	3 913	62.8

Table B. States and Counties — Residential Construction, Wholesale Trade, Retail Trade, and Real Estate

STATE County	Value of residential construction authorized by building permits, 2003		Wholesale trade, 1997				Retail trade,[1] 1997				Real estate and rental and leasing, 1997			
	New construction ($1,000)	Number of housing units	Number of establishments	Number of employees	Sales (mil dol)	Annual payroll (mil dol)	Number of establishments	Number of employees	Sales (mil dol)	Annual payroll (mil dol)	Number of establishments	Number of employees	Receipts (mil dol)	Annual payroll (mil dol)
	133	134	135	136	137	138	139	140	141	142	143	144	145	146
NEBRASKA—Cont'd														
Blaine	NA	NA	3	D	D	D	4	7	0.9	0.1	NA	NA	NA	NA
Boone	520	4	21	200	164.8	4.2	49	334	60.5	5.2	4	8	0.6	0.1
Box Butte	466	4	24	250	84.0	6.1	72	698	107.3	9.7	16	31	1.4	0.3
Boyd	0	0	6	D	D	D	15	62	7.9	0.6	2	D	D	D
Brown	615	7	9	D	D	D	30	191	28.8	2.5	1	D	D	D
Buffalo	42 169	363	68	915	589.2	22.5	239	3 234	455.3	48.7	43	155	14.8	1.8
Burt	960	7	18	129	52.2	3.8	51	241	49.2	3.7	4	10	0.4	0.1
Butler	824	9	13	D	D	D	25	210	23.3	2.4	2	D	D	D
Cass	17 787	162	28	D	D	D	77	740	113.5	8.8	15	41	4.0	0.6
Cedar	1 408	11	24	154	79.8	3.2	51	308	62.9	4.3	6	15	0.7	0.2
Chase	1 277	14	19	222	118.5	5.4	35	240	44.8	3.7	1	D	D	D
Cherry	1 626	21	13	51	37.2	1.2	49	399	60.7	5.8	3	D	D	D
Cheyenne	10 848	77	18	D	D	D	61	964	649.8	22.2	7	34	0.9	0.2
Clay	1 277	10	19	185	100.2	4.1	40	202	43.9	2.9	4	8	0.2	0.1
Colfax	1 112	11	23	207	81.4	4.5	51	383	76.3	5.9	5	8	0.3	0.1
Cuming	780	4	24	D	D	D	60	466	97.8	6.7	7	17	1.8	0.2
Custer	474	5	19	142	74.3	2.7	83	534	81.2	6.7	8	16	1.6	0.1
Dakota	7 041	64	30	D	D	D	80	878	105.0	11.5	16	D	D	D
Dawes	1 034	15	16	D	D	D	61	663	81.4	6.7	12	26	1.2	0.1
Dawson	3 151	19	46	504	306.3	11.4	149	1 401	185.4	18.9	19	70	4.2	0.6
Deuel	125	1	5	D	D	D	15	136	24.6	1.6	1	D	D	D
Dixon	1 363	10	9	80	47.1	1.7	16	97	23.5	1.4	1	D	D	D
Dodge	13 385	124	71	748	587.7	21.1	185	2 313	479.8	37.8	37	172	13.5	2.4
Douglas	347 140	3 075	1 039	17 083	11 542.8	574.0	1 931	34 920	5 634.5	591.7	574	4 411	553.6	106.0
Dundy	0	0	5	D	D	D	17	84	15.7	1.4	3	5	0.3	0.0
Fillmore	502	5	21	170	83.0	4.5	38	229	30.5	2.5	4	9	0.2	0.1
Franklin	0	0	7	43	20.9	0.9	23	97	13.0	1.2	NA	NA	NA	NA
Frontier	0	0	7	D	D	D	17	78	6.3	0.6	NA	NA	NA	NA
Furnas	0	0	11	D	D	D	41	285	55.2	4.0	1	D	D	D
Gage	4 000	41	46	277	148.3	6.6	153	1 310	190.1	15.8	20	98	3.8	0.9
Garden	125	2	4	D	D	D	15	80	9.6	0.9	2	D	D	D
Garfield	130	1	3	D	D	D	26	135	33.0	1.8	NA	NA	NA	NA
Gosper	513	5	4	D	D	D	5	17	2.0	0.1	NA	NA	NA	NA
Grant	NA	NA	2	D	D	D	6	41	2.9	0.4	NA	NA	NA	NA
Greeley	0	0	7	D	D	D	19	111	32.8	1.9	1	D	D	D
Hall	22 671	177	116	1 534	690.4	41.5	347	4 646	722.1	69.2	61	178	22.4	3.3
Hamilton	3 002	26	26	376	208.8	8.1	35	302	39.9	4.2	10	21	0.9	0.3
Harlan	90	1	7	D	D	D	20	103	17.0	1.3	NA	NA	NA	NA
Hayes	0	0	2	D	D	D	1	D	D	D	1	D	D	D
Hitchcock	0	0	7	D	D	D	14	93	18.2	1.3	1	D	D	D
Holt	2 323	17	40	341	166.2	4.7	95	610	99.6	7.5	6	17	1.3	0.1
Hooker	0	0	1	D	D	D	8	43	4.1	0.5	NA	NA	NA	NA
Howard	3 965	46	7	54	30.7	1.7	38	210	25.1	2.8	2	D	D	D
Jefferson	198	2	22	246	144.3	5.7	51	448	60.6	6.1	7	34	0.8	0.2
Johnson	277	4	7	71	29.0	1.1	34	196	29.1	2.6	4	8	0.3	0.0
Kearney	1 046	6	11	131	135.3	3.8	28	166	24.2	2.1	3	5	0.2	0.0
Keith	5 087	48	24	213	190.6	4.8	75	669	97.8	9.6	8	11	0.9	0.2
Keya Paha	NA	NA	3	D	D	D	6	12	2.1	0.2	1	D	D	D
Kimball	568	3	10	D	D	D	30	183	21.1	2.1	2	D	D	D
Knox	646	5	17	D	D	D	73	373	61.3	4.5	4	12	0.3	0.1
Lancaster	299 464	2 426	304	D	D	D	996	15 734	2 270.4	232.0	267	1 480	150.3	25.4
Lincoln	21 074	190	56	461	259.7	11.9	198	2 107	314.5	28.9	31	100	7.7	1.3
Logan	NA	NA	NA	NA	NA	NA	2	D	D	D	NA	NA	NA	NA
Loup	35	1	NA	NA	NA	NA	3	D	D	D	NA	NA	NA	NA
McPherson	NA	NA	2	D	D	D	2	D	D	D	NA	NA	NA	NA
Madison	15 207	136	81	D	D	D	226	3 048	479.6	41.6	46	147	12.8	2.0
Merrick	2 243	33	20	137	109.4	3.7	39	250	31.5	3.2	4	5	0.2	0.1
Morrill	0	0	11	119	30.7	2.7	23	162	23.9	2.0	4	5	0.5	0.0
Nance	0	0	10	D	D	D	21	111	14.8	1.2	5	4	0.2	0.0
Nemaha	1 477	21	12	D	D	D	45	323	51.5	3.7	4	6	0.5	0.1
Nuckolls	0	0	13	109	44.9	1.7	40	284	43.2	3.7	2	D	D	D
Otoe	8 747	66	21	159	131.3	3.6	98	694	110.6	9.5	11	15	1.7	0.3
Pawnee	0	0	6	D	D	D	12	53	7.1	0.6	2	D	D	D
Perkins	232	2	20	125	136.7	2.8	18	92	12.4	1.2	2	D	D	D
Phelps	791	6	25	D	D	D	70	533	81.8	7.4	6	17	0.9	0.2
Pierce	3 734	29	18	97	40.0	1.9	51	312	45.1	3.6	2	D	D	D

1. Establishments with payroll.

STATE County	Professional, scientific, and technical services,[1] 1997				Manufacturing, 1997				Accommodation and foodservices, 1997			
	Number of establishments	Number of employees	Receipts (mil dol)	Annual payroll (mil dol)	Number of establishments	Number of employees	Receipts (mil dol)	Annual payroll (mil dol)	Number of establishments	Number of employees	Sales (mil dol)	Annual payroll (mil dol)
	147	148	149	150	151	152	153	154	155	156	157	158
NEBRASKA—Cont'd												
Blaine	1	D	D	D	NA	NA	NA	NA	1	D	D	D
Boone	2	D	D	D	NA	NA	NA	NA	14	60	1.8	0.4
Box Butte	21	63	3.7	1.3	NA	NA	NA	NA	35	441	10.3	3.1
Boyd	3	7	0.5	0.1	NA	NA	NA	NA	6	17	0.5	0.1
Brown	4	10	0.5	0.2	NA	NA	NA	NA	16	95	2.3	0.6
Buffalo	65	343	21.1	8.0	47	4 392	817.1	122.1	118	2 322	65.8	18.7
Burt	8	26	1.7	0.4	NA	NA	NA	NA	17	141	3.1	0.7
Butler	7	24	1.1	0.6	NA	NA	NA	NA	18	D	D	D
Cass	24	D	D	D	NA	NA	NA	NA	45	340	10.3	2.6
Cedar	9	17	1.0	0.3	NA	NA	NA	NA	21	D	D	D
Chase	3	7	0.3	0.1	NA	NA	NA	NA	12	75	1.8	0.5
Cherry	12	33	2.1	0.4	NA	NA	NA	NA	27	179	5.9	1.5
Cheyenne	15	50	2.3	0.8	NA	NA	NA	NA	37	456	12.5	3.4
Clay	10	22	0.9	0.2	NA	NA	NA	NA	21	D	D	D
Colfax	5	17	1.1	0.3	4	D	D	D	31	D	D	D
Cuming	16	57	2.7	0.8	30	803	522.2	18.0	33	265	6.2	1.5
Custer	15	42	2.5	0.5	NA	NA	NA	NA	32	206	5.0	1.0
Dakota	26	97	5.5	1.8	23	D	D	D	41	656	21.2	6.1
Dawes	14	46	2.5	1.0	NA	NA	NA	NA	37	398	9.4	2.5
Dawson	34	109	6.0	2.1	26	3 899	1 300.0	88.8	63	759	19.4	4.8
Deuel	2	D	D	D	NA	NA	NA	NA	10	50	1.1	0.4
Dixon	4	4	0.2	0.0	NA	NA	NA	NA	9	39	1.4	0.2
Dodge	48	285	13.2	5.8	67	3 437	1 009.7	87.5	99	1 490	41.3	10.2
Douglas	1 244	12 434	1 125.5	466.4	555	27 335	7 140.4	897.4	1 033	19 822	618.8	184.4
Dundy	8	8	0.6	0.1	NA	NA	NA	NA	8	D	D	D
Fillmore	5	13	0.9	0.3	NA	NA	NA	NA	23	121	3.7	0.7
Franklin	6	23	1.2	0.3	NA	NA	NA	NA	10	44	1.3	0.2
Frontier	2	D	D	D	NA	NA	NA	NA	4	D	D	D
Furnas	8	46	2.6	1.5	NA	NA	NA	NA	17	D	D	D
Gage	25	80	4.2	1.3	34	1 700	305.5	43.9	50	583	15.6	4.1
Garden	3	3	0.2	0.0	NA	NA	NA	NA	8	61	0.9	0.2
Garfield	2	D	D	D	NA	NA	NA	NA	5	16	0.6	0.1
Gosper	5	12	0.9	0.2	NA	NA	NA	NA	3	D	D	D
Grant	NA	NA	NA	NA	NA	NA	NA	NA	6	25	0.9	0.1
Greeley	1	D	D	D	NA	NA	NA	NA				
Hall	99	427	32.4	11.9	81	5 791	1 823.3	156.3	155	2 833	71.5	21.0
Hamilton	14	37	2.6	0.7	21	691	332.7	19.9	12	129	2.9	0.9
Harlan	4	7	0.9	0.1	NA	NA	NA	NA	15	D	D	D
Hayes	NA	NA	NA	NA	NA	NA	NA	NA	1	D	D	D
Hitchcock	1	D	D	D	NA	NA	NA	NA	4	D	D	D
Holt	14	56	2.7	0.8	NA	NA	NA	NA	30	313	7.3	1.6
Hooker	NA	NA	NA	NA	NA	NA	NA	NA	4	19	0.5	0.1
Howard	7	13	0.5	0.1	NA	NA	NA	NA	17	107	1.9	0.5
Jefferson	13	27	1.3	0.4	11	649	67.5	11.8	19	D	D	D
Johnson	3	9	0.4	0.1	NA	NA	NA	NA	10	73	1.4	0.4
Kearney	8	17	1.0	0.2	NA	NA	NA	NA	15	D	D	D
Keith	15	70	4.3	1.5	NA	NA	NA	NA	57	584	20.0	4.7
Keya Paha	1	D	D	D	NA	NA	NA	NA	2	D	D	D
Kimball	12	28	1.3	0.3	NA	NA	NA	NA	18	205	6.3	1.7
Knox	14	19	1.2	0.2	NA	NA	NA	NA	30	122	3.4	0.6
Lancaster	483	7 161	688.0	211.6	267	15 322	3 855.1	502.3	545	11 230	318.5	91.8
Lincoln	53	269	17.0	6.2	NA	NA	NA	NA	96	1 645	44.8	13.1
Logan	NA	NA	NA	NA	NA	NA	NA	NA	2	D	D	D
Loup	NA	NA	NA	NA	NA	NA	NA	NA	1	D	D	D
McPherson	1	D	D	D	NA	NA	NA	NA	1	D	D	D
Madison	66	262	16.1	7.1	52	4 908	1 402.4	154.3	101	1 541	40.2	11.3
Merrick	6	16	0.6	0.3	NA	NA	NA	NA	17	168	3.4	0.9
Morrill	NA	NA	NA	NA	NA	NA	NA	NA	16	109	2.3	0.7
Nance	3	10	0.3	0.1	NA	NA	NA	NA	4	12	0.4	0.1
Nemaha	8	14	0.6	0.2	NA	NA	NA	NA	21	221	4.8	1.4
Nuckolls	8	29	0.8	0.3	NA	NA	NA	NA	14	D	D	D
Otoe	20	57	4.3	1.3	17	1 354	212.3	35.0	47	658	17.4	4.7
Pawnee	3	D	D	D	NA	NA	NA	NA	8	36	0.9	0.2
Perkins	5	12	0.6	0.2	NA	NA	NA	NA	9	D	D	D
Phelps	21	79	6.6	1.8	8	D	D	D	20	221	5.7	1.5
Pierce	8	29	1.2	0.4	NA	NA	NA	NA	14	58	1.7	0.3

1. Firms subject to federal tax.

Table B. States and Counties — Health Care and Social Assistance, Other Services, and Federal Funds

STATE County	Health care and social assistance,[1] 1997				Other services,[1] 1997				Federal funds and grants, 2002–2003 Expenditures (mil dol)			
										Direct payments for individuals[2]		
	Number of establishments	Number of employees	Receipts (mil dol)	Annual payroll (mil dol)	Number of establishments	Number of employees	Receipts (mil dol)	Annual payroll (mil dol)	Total	Social Security and government retirement	Medicare	Food stamps and Supplemental Security Income
	159	160	161	162	163	164	165	166	167	168	169	170
NEBRASKA—Cont'd												
Blaine	NA	NA	NA	NA	NA	NA	NA	NA	3.5	1.8	0.4	0.0
Boone	9	90	2.6	1.2	13	22	2.1	0.4	41.0	16.2	6.5	0.5
Box Butte	20	180	8.1	3.1	25	117	6.1	1.5	63.3	30.3	7.9	1.1
Boyd	5	82	2.2	0.8	4	6	0.3	0.0	22.9	7.8	4.5	0.2
Brown	6	82	2.6	1.2	10	28	1.4	0.2	22.3	10.8	3.5	0.3
Buffalo	92	827	67.8	36.4	82	463	29.9	8.6	174.9	78.3	26.0	3.1
Burt	10	154	4.4	2.5	16	37	2.8	0.5	59.5	21.7	10.7	1.2
Butler	9	140	5.1	2.8	13	39	2.2	0.5	54.6	20.9	7.0	0.6
Cass	22	279	9.0	4.7	24	101	7.0	1.7	125.4	62.0	17.6	1.7
Cedar	13	165	5.4	2.7	17	58	3.6	0.9	55.6	21.7	8.1	0.4
Chase	7	77	2.4	1.1	8	23	2.2	0.4	30.9	11.5	4.8	0.3
Cherry	10	51	3.1	1.2	10	23	2.4	0.3	36.2	18.3	5.1	0.7
Cheyenne	17	146	6.3	3.1	21	71	4.4	1.1	63.6	25.0	10.3	0.9
Clay	7	130	3.1	1.9	12	23	1.6	0.2	56.8	19.8	6.3	0.5
Colfax	16	198	7.1	3.5	28	77	4.5	1.1	61.6	23.3	14.3	0.5
Cuming	12	126	4.6	1.9	30	104	9.3	1.6	56.8	24.4	9.6	0.5
Custer	17	245	10.4	4.8	24	58	3.7	0.7	82.8	32.8	12.4	1.2
Dakota	20	235	12.5	5.5	32	275	29.7	8.5	80.4	33.8	13.9	2.1
Dawes	19	131	6.5	3.0	22	41	2.5	0.5	58.5	23.3	6.4	1.3
Dawson	32	395	18.4	8.6	52	181	16.5	3.1	105.4	46.9	17.3	2.3
Deuel	3	10	0.7	0.1	5	22	0.7	0.2	18.6	6.6	2.5	0.0
Dixon	8	133	3.5	1.5	15	33	2.4	0.5	37.2	13.7	6.1	0.3
Dodge	77	852	42.7	19.4	96	360	19.3	5.1	179.9	90.7	35.9	3.7
Douglas	966	11 736	835.2	393.7	899	6 682	398.4	127.0	2 677.7	990.4	383.1	76.6
Dundy	3	9	0.6	0.1	3	6	0.5	0.1	23.0	6.6	3.6	0.1
Fillmore	12	152	5.1	2.7	20	53	2.6	0.6	51.9	18.4	6.6	0.5
Franklin	5	113	2.7	1.6	6	11	0.8	0.1	28.1	11.2	4.5	0.3
Frontier	2	D	D	D	9	28	1.5	0.4	30.5	7.3	2.7	0.1
Furnas	6	102	4.0	2.2	15	39	2.5	0.4	52.7	18.4	7.7	0.5
Gage	28	287	12.8	5.4	58	181	9.8	2.2	144.2	64.1	19.1	1.9
Garden	2	D	D	D	1	D	D	D	27.3	9.1	3.2	0.1
Garfield	2	D	D	D	3	5	0.4	0.1	12.8	6.4	2.6	0.1
Gosper	2	D	D	D	1	D	D	D	16.8	7.0	1.9	0.1
Grant	NA	NA	NA	NA	2	D	D	D	4.2	2.5	0.6	0.0
Greeley	3	D	D	D	7	16	1.4	0.3	19.8	7.9	2.7	0.3
Hall	109	1 263	75.6	38.6	118	858	50.2	15.6	307.0	123.0	39.8	6.9
Hamilton	14	84	4.0	1.6	19	53	4.3	0.9	50.4	20.8	6.8	0.5
Harlan	3	7	0.5	0.2	8	25	2.3	0.3	32.4	11.9	4.3	0.2
Hayes	NA	NA	NA	NA	1	D	D	D	12.6	2.1	1.1	0.0
Hitchcock	NA	NA	NA	NA	4	11	0.5	0.1	27.7	10.6	3.3	0.3
Holt	20	179	7.7	3.4	30	83	6.7	1.2	75.7	29.9	13.2	1.3
Hooker	2	D	D	D	3	5	0.2	0.0	4.6	2.7	1.0	0.0
Howard	6	74	2.5	1.3	9	21	1.6	0.3	37.9	17.1	6.6	0.4
Jefferson	9	136	4.8	2.5	16	35	1.9	0.4	62.7	24.9	8.3	0.7
Johnson	7	83	3.7	1.5	8	17	1.4	0.3	35.4	12.0	4.5	0.3
Kearney	10	30	1.6	0.4	14	43	3.2	0.6	39.3	15.7	6.8	0.3
Keith	15	130	6.1	2.5	28	112	6.7	1.5	50.0	23.4	6.8	0.5
Keya Paha	NA	NA	NA	NA	1	D	D	D	6.2	2.8	0.8	0.0
Kimball	6	23	1.4	0.4	10	34	2.1	0.3	32.7	12.8	3.4	0.3
Knox	12	97	4.1	1.8	15	29	2.4	0.4	78.9	26.4	11.5	1.0
Lancaster	548	6 380	376.7	184.1	418	2 512	134.2	42.0	1 624.1	509.1	135.0	28.5
Lincoln	80	813	49.0	18.5	70	335	19.7	5.6	197.0	96.5	27.7	5.2
Logan	NA	NA	NA	NA	1	D	D	D	6.5	2.6	0.8	0.1
Loup	1	D	D	D	2	D	D	D	3.7	1.8	0.8	0.0
McPherson	NA	NA	NA	NA	1	D	D	D	4.2	2.2	0.4	0.0
Madison	91	932	53.2	26.0	90	410	23.6	6.5	189.9	76.6	24.8	3.9
Merrick	12	164	4.6	2.5	19	41	2.8	0.6	46.9	20.0	8.4	0.4
Morrill	3	D	D	D	6	27	1.0	0.3	32.0	14.4	4.8	0.4
Nance	6	109	3.5	1.8	9	21	1.2	0.3	32.0	9.9	4.4	0.7
Nemaha	12	62	3.6	1.6	17	44	3.4	0.7	56.6	18.6	7.4	0.8
Nuckolls	9	65	3.5	1.5	12	32	2.6	0.5	44.2	16.2	6.5	0.6
Otoe	31	362	14.8	6.8	28	85	5.9	1.4	103.9	38.2	13.2	1.2
Pawnee	4	63	2.3	1.0	10	30	1.9	0.3	31.5	9.7	4.3	0.3
Perkins	4	24	1.0	0.3	10	24	3.3	0.6	31.1	9.0	3.6	0.1
Phelps	12	118	7.9	4.3	23	94	7.3	1.4	53.9	26.6	9.0	0.8
Pierce	8	104	3.2	1.2	14	38	6.1	0.6	42.7	16.8	6.9	0.5

1. Firms subject to federal tax. 2. State totals may include programs not allocated by county.

Items 159—170

NE(Blaine)—NE(Pierce) 447

	Federal funds and grants, 2002–2003 (cont'd)							Local government finances, 2002				
	Expenditures (mil dol) (cont'd)							General revenue				
		Procurement contract awards		Grants[1]							Taxes	
											Per capita[2] (dollars)	
STATE County	Salaries and wages	Defense	Other	Medicaid and other health-related	Nutrition and family welfare	Education	Other	Total (mil dol)	Intergovern-mental (mil dol)	Total (mil dol)	Total	Property
	171	172	173	174	175	176	177	178	179	180	181	182
NEBRASKA—Cont'd												
Blaine	0.4	0.0	0.1	0.4	0.1	0.0	0.0	2.3	0.6	1.6	2 955	2 822
Boone	1.9	0.0	0.4	3.4	0.6	0.4	1.9	25.8	5.2	8.5	1 390	1 189
Box Butte	3.6	0.0	1.0	4.7	1.2	1.1	2.4	47.1	14.4	15.0	1 261	895
Boyd	1.1	0.0	0.3	1.7	0.3	0.3	1.8	13.0	5.4	5.6	2 418	2 079
Brown	1.1	0.0	0.2	3.0	0.3	0.2	0.8	16.5	4.1	4.6	1 314	1 034
Buffalo	9.7	0.1	2.4	13.1	5.9	1.9	15.5	107.0	40.1	45.8	1 072	792
Burt	1.9	2.2	0.4	5.5	1.0	0.3	4.5	25.4	6.7	11.8	1 548	1 278
Butler	2.8	0.1	0.6	4.7	0.6	0.5	3.2	29.9	5.3	14.8	1 676	1 302
Cass	4.3	0.0	1.2	7.2	2.7	1.1	9.8	56.8	20.4	26.1	1 049	891
Cedar	3.9	0.2	0.6	4.7	0.8	0.6	1.7	25.6	7.9	12.1	1 305	1 049
Chase	1.3	0.0	0.2	1.7	0.4	0.3	1.6	17.2	3.4	6.9	1 735	1 583
Cherry	2.3	0.0	0.4	3.8	0.7	0.6	3.1	28.9	5.4	12.0	1 946	1 546
Cheyenne	2.9	0.2	0.7	5.9	0.7	0.6	4.2	35.7	11.1	17.1	1 720	1 148
Clay	10.6	0.0	1.6	2.1	0.6	0.8	4.2	29.8	12.3	12.9	1 857	1 428
Colfax	3.7	0.0	0.5	5.1	0.7	0.5	3.7	23.6	8.3	11.8	1 122	989
Cuming	2.7	0.0	0.5	3.0	3.0	0.7	2.3	26.4	6.4	14.1	1 405	1 123
Custer	3.4	0.0	0.8	9.3	1.2	0.8	3.6	33.9	12.4	15.2	1 323	1 088
Dakota	4.3	0.0	0.6	14.4	2.1	1.6	3.1	43.3	21.4	16.6	814	634
Dawes	7.0	0.0	1.8	4.9	2.8	1.4	4.7	23.8	10.7	8.7	967	691
Dawson	5.3	1.6	0.9	12.7	2.3	0.9	4.1	90.0	28.8	28.9	1 174	935
Deuel	0.6	0.0	0.1	2.1	0.2	0.2	2.0	8.5	1.7	4.7	2 295	1 697
Dixon	1.9	0.6	0.9	3.0	0.4	1.5	1.9	21.8	8.6	8.4	1 349	1 069
Dodge	8.6	1.2	5.9	15.3	3.9	1.7	3.0	155.8	35.4	47.9	1 330	852
Douglas	333.2	24.2	137.8	390.1	80.7	44.0	173.9	1 506.8	456.2	725.2	1 534	1 092
Dundy	0.7	0.0	0.2	1.7	0.2	0.1	1.5	10.4	2.1	3.4	1 527	1 451
Fillmore	2.0	0.0	0.5	3.8	0.5	0.3	5.9	28.5	5.1	11.7	1 786	1 477
Franklin	1.3	0.0	0.3	1.7	0.3	0.3	0.8	14.1	3.0	5.3	1 528	1 172
Frontier	1.1	0.0	0.3	1.7	0.2	0.2	5.4	16.1	4.6	6.1	2 049	1 858
Furnas	2.1	0.0	0.5	6.8	0.4	0.4	2.5	22.3	7.3	9.5	1 805	1 389
Gage	7.2	0.0	1.4	16.5	2.6	4.1	8.6	62.8	26.3	24.2	1 048	820
Garden	1.0	0.0	8.6	1.7	0.2	0.2	0.5	13.9	2.1	6.0	2 748	2 548
Garfield	0.5	0.0	0.3	1.3	0.2	0.2	0.2	6.7	2.6	2.2	1 164	923
Gosper	0.5	0.0	0.1	0.0	0.1	0.1	1.3	9.6	1.6	3.8	1 845	1 431
Grant	0.4	0.0	0.1	0.0	0.0	0.0	0.3	2.5	0.4	2.0	2 765	2 643
Greeley	1.1	0.0	0.3	1.3	0.4	0.2	0.9	11.4	4.1	4.1	1 555	1 406
Hall	35.4	6.3	17.6	31.0	6.1	4.2	24.3	148.9	53.9	63.0	1 174	869
Hamilton	1.9	0.0	0.7	5.1	0.7	0.5	3.9	27.1	8.7	12.7	1 358	1 146
Harlan	1.3	0.2	0.3	1.7	0.2	0.2	2.3	11.1	2.6	3.9	1 084	826
Hayes	0.2	0.0	0.0	0.4	0.0	0.1	0.7	3.6	1.5	1.7	1 541	1 432
Hitchcock	0.9	0.0	0.2	2.1	0.3	0.2	1.6	10.3	4.3	3.7	1 207	991
Holt	3.2	0.0	0.6	9.3	1.5	0.8	5.9	32.4	10.7	16.0	1 431	1 101
Hooker	0.2	0.0	0.0	0.4	0.1	0.0	0.0	4.3	0.6	2.1	2 875	2 643
Howard	1.7	0.0	0.4	3.0	0.6	0.4	1.4	28.5	7.7	8.0	1 235	1 042
Jefferson	2.5	0.0	0.5	6.8	3.1	0.4	3.8	24.2	8.0	12.0	1 449	1 185
Johnson	2.1	0.0	0.3	2.5	0.4	0.6	2.4	19.3	6.1	8.0	1 803	1 513
Kearney	1.7	0.2	0.4	2.1	0.3	0.3	2.9	24.9	4.4	11.7	1 707	1 426
Keith	2.2	0.0	0.4	3.4	0.7	0.4	4.6	27.0	10.9	12.6	1 441	1 075
Keya Paha	0.1	0.0	0.0	0.8	0.1	0.1	0.1	2.5	0.6	1.6	1 698	1 611
Kimball	0.8	0.0	1.2	1.7	0.3	0.1	3.1	22.0	3.6	6.7	1 691	1 156
Knox	2.8	0.0	0.7	8.6	1.8	1.9	10.5	25.0	10.9	10.1	1 107	902
Lancaster	172.8	47.7	33.6	179.1	102.0	92.4	278.3	764.9	246.2	336.3	1 306	986
Lincoln	14.4	1.4	2.6	20.8	3.9	2.2	6.5	120.0	37.8	54.5	1 586	948
Logan	0.1	0.0	0.1	0.8	0.1	0.1	0.4	2.8	1.1	1.4	1 873	1 594
Loup	0.1	0.0	0.0	0.0	0.1	0.0	0.2	1.8	0.6	1.1	1 447	1 365
McPherson	0.1	0.0	0.0	0.8	0.0	0.1	0.1	1.7	0.4	1.1	2 038	1 978
Madison	13.5	0.4	17.9	20.2	3.2	1.8	16.2	122.1	40.7	51.2	1 420	1 029
Merrick	1.8	0.0	0.5	4.2	0.7	0.7	4.6	31.9	6.9	10.5	1 312	1 025
Morrill	1.1	0.0	0.5	2.5	0.7	0.4	0.8	21.7	7.9	7.1	1 336	1 000
Nance	0.8	0.0	0.2	4.7	0.4	0.2	2.2	15.3	4.6	6.0	1 544	1 387
Nemaha	1.9	0.0	0.4	4.7	0.6	0.9	4.4	32.6	11.0	7.6	1 034	880
Nuckolls	1.8	0.0	0.4	4.2	0.5	0.2	1.8	6.8	2.4	2.8	573	390
Otoe	5.1	0.0	4.0	7.2	1.5	0.4	7.6	42.1	11.6	19.0	1 228	989
Pawnee	1.2	0.0	0.3	3.0	0.3	0.2	2.1	11.7	3.1	3.5	1 158	1 033
Perkins	0.9	0.0	0.2	0.0	0.2	0.3	2.9	16.4	2.6	5.4	1 772	1 526
Phelps	2.2	0.0	0.5	4.7	0.6	0.7	1.2	29.4	9.0	15.1	1 573	1 133
Pierce	1.6	0.0	0.3	2.5	0.5	0.4	1.3	27.8	7.6	10.6	1 347	969

1. State totals may include programs not allocated by county.   2. Based on the resident population estimated as of July 1 of the year shown.

Table B. States and Counties — Local Government Finances, Government Employment, and Elections

STATE County	Total (mil dol)	Per capita[1] (dollars)	Education	Health and hospitals	Police protection	Public welfare	Highways	Total (mil dol)	Per capita[1] (dollars)	Federal civilian	Federal military	State and local	Democratic	Republican	All other
	183	184	185	186	187	188	189	190	191	192	193	194	195	196	197
NEBRASKA—Cont'd															
Blaine	2.2	4 147	70.0	0.8	2.2	0.0	11.3	0.0	0	30	0	64	10.8	89.2	0.0
Boone	26.6	4 382	37.2	37.4	1.5	0.1	7.5	4.4	717	39	21	574	18.9	79.8	1.4
Box Butte	42.0	3 537	43.2	24.5	2.8	0.2	8.1	8.2	694	65	41	1 059	32.2	66.0	1.8
Boyd	10.4	4 470	61.8	0.6	1.6	0.7	13.6	0.9	382	23	0	267	19.6	79.6	0.8
Brown	18.2	5 167	38.3	20.0	2.1	0.4	10.5	14.3	4 056	26	12	402	15.5	82.4	2.2
Buffalo	97.2	2 272	61.0	0.1	5.6	0.2	7.4	35.8	836	166	149	3 411	22.1	76.4	1.4
Burt	22.2	2 918	51.1	12.0	2.4	0.1	12.7	5.8	764	42	26	614	34.7	64.1	1.2
Butler	26.5	2 995	37.7	19.6	2.1	0.2	12.3	13.0	1 474	56	31	548	25.6	72.5	1.9
Cass	62.4	2 513	51.4	3.5	3.1	0.5	11.9	60.1	2 421	78	86	1 152	31.4	67.5	1.2
Cedar	23.2	2 501	55.4	0.2	1.9	6.6	18.0	8.1	871	97	32	646	23.9	74.7	1.4
Chase	17.4	4 370	45.2	25.7	1.4	0.2	6.7	5.5	1 388	29	14	561	14.8	84.3	0.9
Cherry	26.3	4 259	35.6	26.5	2.2	0.6	13.0	1.5	245	50	21	534	15.9	82.5	1.6
Cheyenne	31.3	3 144	56.9	0.4	2.9	0.5	7.5	20.7	2 076	53	35	831	18.7	79.9	1.4
Clay	27.8	4 017	68.3	0.7	1.9	0.4	9.2	3.7	530	174	24	631	22.4	76.1	1.5
Colfax	22.7	2 155	66.5	0.0	3.0	0.4	11.8	12.3	1 170	79	37	584	27.3	71.3	1.4
Cuming	25.9	2 591	48.4	0.2	3.4	9.6	17.4	10.2	1 023	57	35	648	22.3	76.6	1.0
Custer	36.0	3 132	57.1	0.2	1.6	0.4	19.5	18.0	1 562	64	40	892	18.5	80.5	1.0
Dakota	43.8	2 155	64.6	0.2	5.2	0.3	8.0	23.7	1 166	84	71	982	45.6	53.6	0.8
Dawes	23.3	2 585	42.4	0.1	3.1	6.2	13.5	7.8	863	156	31	967	28.1	70.3	1.6
Dawson	84.7	3 440	48.5	20.9	2.7	0.1	7.2	55.3	2 246	104	85	1 845	21.9	77.1	1.0
Deuel	9.8	4 742	46.0	0.2	3.2	15.1	10.3	2.2	1 047	16	0	167	20.9	77.9	1.2
Dixon	22.7	3 634	58.8	0.1	2.2	10.2	10.6	1.4	232	42	22	382	31.3	67.4	1.3
Dodge	167.2	4 645	39.2	37.4	2.1	0.2	4.6	61.7	1 715	125	127	2 656	32.3	66.4	1.3
Douglas	1 566.6	3 314	45.1	2.9	5.6	0.5	4.3	2 061.7	4 361	5 430	2 190	30 931	39.9	58.8	1.3
Dundy	10.4	4 676	33.9	38.0	1.8	0.0	10.4	0.4	165	18	0	235	17.7	81.7	0.6
Fillmore	28.5	4 362	42.2	21.2	1.4	3.8	15.9	5.9	898	41	23	745	25.9	72.7	1.5
Franklin	12.6	3 638	37.0	26.1	2.1	0.4	12.0	0.7	188	33	12	340	24.0	74.5	1.5
Frontier	16.9	5 703	45.9	29.7	2.1	0.1	9.2	0.3	105	21	10	351	18.7	79.1	2.1
Furnas	21.1	4 021	55.2	0.3	0.6	0.4	9.5	19.0	3 618	41	18	563	20.0	79.0	1.0
Gage	61.8	2 673	54.0	0.1	4.0	0.3	11.7	50.0	2 164	123	80	2 277	35.2	63.4	1.4
Garden	13.8	6 278	30.9	30.5	1.6	0.0	9.1	0.4	179	24	0	306	17.0	82.1	0.9
Garfield	5.0	2 650	61.0	0.2	2.8	0.2	11.3	0.9	487	17	0	165	19.3	79.2	1.5
Gosper	7.2	3 492	31.3	0.1	3.6	24.0	12.6	1.6	765	17	0	162	19.8	79.5	0.6
Grant	3.1	4 327	68.7	0.5	2.6	1.8	9.2	0.8	1 062	0	0	87	10.4	88.9	0.8
Greeley	10.1	3 816	57.5	0.4	1.0	16.8	10.9	2.1	794	22	0	280	29.0	69.2	1.8
Hall	149.3	2 785	46.3	0.8	5.5	0.3	9.0	137.8	2 571	669	188	3 842	29.5	69.0	1.5
Hamilton	20.5	2 190	60.0	1.4	2.5	0.4	9.3	2.2	235	40	32	586	21.0	77.6	1.4
Harlan	9.6	2 635	31.2	29.3	2.4	0.3	13.1	1.0	263	37	13	254	21.1	77.3	1.6
Hayes	3.6	3 254	62.3	0.2	1.9	0.0	16.0	1.0	865	11	0	89	11.1	88.1	0.8
Hitchcock	10.0	3 313	71.3	0.0	1.3	0.0	10.7	5.1	1 675	21	10	354	19.9	78.8	1.3
Holt	30.1	2 686	52.6	0.2	2.2	0.7	16.3	10.4	929	55	39	814	17.4	81.5	1.1
Hooker	4.2	5 658	50.9	22.8	1.2	0.0	9.2	0.1	134	0	0	94	13.9	85.0	1.1
Howard	22.7	3 501	48.8	17.9	1.8	0.1	8.3	5.7	881	35	22	567	30.2	67.8	2.0
Jefferson	21.0	2 551	65.6	0.0	3.0	0.3	11.7	5.5	665	43	29	480	33.8	64.9	1.3
Johnson	19.3	4 343	35.6	16.1	1.3	0.0	9.7	13.8	3 108	47	15	710	37.2	61.2	1.6
Kearney	22.9	3 342	55.8	17.0	1.6	0.5	8.6	7.5	1 092	36	24	503	21.0	77.6	1.4
Keith	26.7	3 063	59.9	0.7	4.2	0.7	7.4	3.6	417	40	30	583	18.1	81.0	0.9
Keya Paha	2.7	2 850	51.8	0.0	0.8	0.1	17.3	0.3	334	0	0	70	17.6	80.8	1.6
Kimball	15.9	4 029	34.1	28.0	2.4	0.0	8.5	4.4	1 103	21	14	406	19.5	79.5	1.0
Knox	22.9	2 517	58.0	0.1	3.0	0.0	20.5	8.5	934	54	31	1 100	25.8	72.7	1.5
Lancaster	771.5	2 996	52.2	2.5	3.8	1.9	6.5	889.5	3 454	2 681	947	28 419	42.2	56.4	1.4
Lincoln	119.8	3 484	58.4	0.4	4.9	0.2	5.7	59.7	1 735	237	119	2 549	30.3	68.4	1.3
Logan	2.5	3 381	72.4	0.4	1.7	0.0	10.4	0.1	133	0	0	75	15.9	83.6	0.5
Loup	2.0	2 662	62.2	0.6	2.9	0.0	11.5	0.1	141	0	0	56	17.8	81.2	1.0
McPherson	1.7	3 057	64.0	0.1	1.6	0.0	18.6	0.4	766	0	0	37	15.8	83.0	1.3
Madison	116.5	3 234	59.9	1.4	3.7	3.9	8.4	45.9	1 273	228	126	3 460	20.7	78.2	1.1
Merrick	23.8	2 966	38.0	27.3	2.0	0.3	11.6	16.8	2 096	37	28	573	22.8	75.8	1.4
Morrill	19.4	3 663	43.5	14.2	2.3	8.4	8.0	9.2	1 738	24	18	471	21.8	76.5	1.7
Nance	14.2	3 641	58.3	21.3	2.5	0.0	6.6	2.7	703	25	14	399	27.0	71.3	1.8
Nemaha	27.3	3 741	56.5	16.5	2.3	0.0	8.2	1.7	233	40	25	1 545	28.7	69.9	1.4
Nuckolls	5.8	1 188	0.0	0.1	5.4	1.8	31.6	0.7	145	35	17	381	21.9	76.4	1.7
Otoe	40.7	2 633	48.1	11.3	2.9	0.6	10.8	18.9	1 222	64	54	1 053	30.8	68.0	1.1
Pawnee	11.4	3 754	39.4	30.1	1.0	0.3	8.5	2.4	782	27	11	248	32.4	66.5	1.1
Perkins	17.7	5 771	27.4	46.5	1.7	0.5	13.1	1.8	600	25	11	370	16.8	82.3	0.8
Phelps	30.1	3 133	62.0	0.6	2.8	0.1	12.0	7.3	760	45	33	776	17.7	81.5	0.8
Pierce	24.5	3 119	47.4	15.6	1.5	0.0	12.7	10.2	1 304	38	27	487	16.1	83.2	0.8

1. Based on the resident population estimated as of July 1 of the year shown.

Table B. States and Counties — Land Area and Population

STATE/County code	CBSA code[1]	County Type[2]	STATE County	Land area[3] (sq km) 2000	Population and population characteristics, 2003			Race alone or in combination, not Hispanic or Latino (percent)					Age (percent)					
					Total persons	Rank	Per square kilometer	White	Black	Am. Indian, Alaska Native	Asian and Pacific Islander	Percent Hispanic or Latino[4]	Under 5 years	5 to 17 years	18 to 24 years	25 to 34 years	35 to 44 years	45 to 54 years
				1	2	3	4	5	6	7	8	9	10	11	12	13	14	15
			NEBRASKA—Cont'd															
31 141	18100	5	Platte	1 756	31 197	1 376	17.8	90.6	0.6	0.6	0.7	8.2	7.1	20.7	10.0	10.8	15.2	14.4
31 143	...	9	Polk	1 137	5 478	2 811	4.8	98.2	0.2	0.1	0.3	1.6	5.4	17.2	8.6	9.5	13.0	15.5
31 145	...	7	Red Willow	1 856	11 252	2 349	6.1	96.1	0.3	0.7	0.4	3.0	6.1	17.3	10.7	9.4	13.4	14.4
31 147	...	7	Richardson	1 433	9 008	2 520	6.3	96.4	0.4	3.1	0.3	1.2	4.8	18.3	8.5	8.2	14.4	13.8
31 149	...	9	Rock	2 612	1 613	3 082	0.6	98.7	0.0	0.4	0.2	0.7	4.3	15.7	7.5	8.9	13.3	18.4
31 151	...	6	Saline	1 490	14 189	2 151	9.5	87.0	0.7	0.5	1.6	10.6	6.0	18.2	14.0	10.2	13.7	12.4
31 153	36540	2	Sarpy	623	132 476	432	212.6	88.9	4.7	0.8	3.0	4.3	8.1	20.9	10.7	14.9	16.6	12.8
31 155	36540	2	Saunders	1 953	20 008	1 804	10.2	98.2	0.2	0.5	0.3	1.2	6.2	19.8	9.0	9.5	16.3	14.2
31 157	42420	5	Scotts Bluff	1 915	36 954	1 211	19.3	80.3	0.5	2.1	0.8	16.9	7.0	18.0	9.8	10.9	13.3	14.3
31 159	30700	2	Seward	1 489	16 671	1 984	11.2	97.6	0.5	0.4	0.8	1.4	5.8	16.9	17.0	9.5	13.4	13.4
31 161	...	9	Sheridan	6 322	5 808	2 789	0.9	88.9	0.2	10.7	0.5	1.5	5.5	17.5	8.7	9.8	12.5	15.4
31 163	...	9	Sherman	1 466	3 127	2 974	2.1	98.4	0.1	0.3	0.4	1.1	5.2	16.9	7.1	8.2	13.6	15.0
31 165	...	9	Sioux	5 352	1 491	3 090	0.3	97.1	0.0	0.1	0.3	2.6	3.8	17.2	9.1	8.7	14.3	16.2
31 167	35740	9	Stanton	1 113	6 582	2 724	5.9	96.2	0.6	0.8	0.2	2.7	6.4	21.3	10.3	10.7	15.4	13.6
31 169	...	9	Thayer	1 488	5 662	2 796	3.8	98.5	0.1	0.4	0.2	1.1	5.3	17.0	6.9	7.6	12.9	15.2
31 171	...	9	Thomas	1 846	669	3 132	0.4	98.8	0.0	0.3	0.0	0.9	4.8	14.1	8.8	9.0	12.4	18.5
31 173	...	8	Thurston	1 020	7 142	2 672	7.0	45.4	0.6	52.2	0.1	2.9	10.6	25.6	10.7	9.6	13.1	10.4
31 175	...	9	Valley	1 471	4 572	2 867	3.1	97.7	0.3	0.4	0.2	1.8	4.8	18.0	8.0	8.3	13.0	14.0
31 177	36540	2	Washington	1 011	19 690	1 822	19.5	97.7	0.6	0.5	0.5	1.1	6.3	18.7	11.8	10.3	14.7	15.0
31 179	...	6	Wayne	1 148	9 474	2 488	8.3	96.0	1.0	0.4	0.8	2.1	5.2	14.8	24.6	9.8	11.5	11.8
31 181	...	9	Webster	1 489	3 867	2 923	2.6	98.2	0.2	0.6	0.7	0.6	4.7	17.3	6.9	7.1	13.9	14.1
31 183	...	9	Wheeler	1 490	821	3 118	0.6	99.1	0.0	0.2	0.0	0.6	6.2	20.6	8.9	8.5	13.3	16.2
31 185	...	7	York	1 491	14 363	2 140	9.6	95.5	1.5	0.7	0.7	2.2	5.7	17.8	10.5	10.0	14.1	14.8
32 000	...	X	NEVADA	284 448	2 241 154	X	7.9	65.3	7.1	1.7	6.2	21.9	7.3	18.6	8.9	15.3	15.3	13.3
32 001	21980	6	Churchill	12 766	24 773	1 585	1.9	82.4	1.0	6.6	3.1	9.2	11.6	21.0	8.2	11.5	14.0	12.5
32 003	29820	1	Clark	20 488	1 576 541	17	76.9	60.3	9.3	1.2	7.2	24.4	7.6	18.6	8.8	15.7	15.0	12.2
32 005	23820	4	Douglas	1 839	44 110	1 042	24.0	90.5	0.4	2.2	1.1	7.0	4.3	17.7	7.7	8.5	14.8	16.9
32 007	21220	5	Elko	44 493	44 094	1 044	1.0	74.2	0.6	5.8	0.7	19.8	7.5	24.4	9.9	13.0	16.1	14.4
32 009	...	9	Esmeralda	9 294	858	3 116	0.1	82.3	0.1	6.1	0.1	12.5	3.8	12.9	8.4	9.3	13.5	14.3
32 011	21220	9	Eureka	10 815	1 513	3 087	0.1	86.9	0.5	3.4	1.1	10.0	5.8	21.3	7.1	10.0	19.4	14.9
32 013	...	7	Humboldt	24 988	14 709	2 118	0.6	75.7	0.6	5.5	1.0	18.5	7.4	23.6	8.8	10.7	16.8	15.7
32 015	...	7	Lander	14 228	5 049	2 838	0.4	78.4	0.4	3.9	0.5	17.3	7.6	25.2	8.0	8.6	17.3	15.8
32 017	...	8	Lincoln	27 541	4 264	2 890	0.2	90.6	1.9	2.1	0.5	5.5	4.8	22.7	9.7	8.7	12.1	13.1
32 019	...	5	Lyon	5 164	40 126	1 133	7.8	85.5	0.8	3.1	1.2	11.2	5.7	19.9	9.0	10.7	14.1	13.2
32 021	...	7	Mineral	9 729	4 791	2 856	0.5	69.7	4.3	16.6	1.1	9.1	4.7	18.3	7.7	7.9	12.3	14.5
32 023	37220	6	Nye	47 000	35 717	1 253	0.8	86.3	1.6	3.1	1.4	9.4	5.2	17.8	7.5	8.6	12.9	13.3
32 027	...	8	Pershing	15 635	6 444	2 735	0.4	70.2	5.6	4.3	0.8	20.0	5.5	18.9	10.1	16.0	19.4	20.7
32 029	39900	2	Storey	682	3 511	2 944	5.1	92.1	0.3	2.3	1.2	5.1	2.9	14.5	8.0	8.6	15.7	20.7
32 031	39900	2	Washoe	16 426	370 853	167	22.6	73.5	2.1	2.3	5.5	18.6	6.9	18.1	9.6	14.1	15.2	14.3
32 033	...	9	White Pine	22 989	8 490	2 563	0.4	79.4	4.4	4.6	1.1	11.3	4.4	18.2	9.2	12.9	16.0	15.3
32 510	16180	3	Carson City city	371	55 311	871	149.1	79.3	1.7	2.8	1.9	15.6	6.7	16.9	8.6	12.3	14.8	14.3
33 000	...	X	NEW HAMPSHIRE	23 227	1 287 687	X	55.4	95.5	1.1	0.6	1.9	1.8	5.7	18.1	9.3	11.6	17.1	15.9
33 001	29060	4	Belknap	1 039	60 356	816	58.1	97.9	0.4	0.8	0.9	0.7	4.8	16.9	8.7	10.9	15.9	15.8
33 003	...	8	Carroll	2 419	46 134	1 002	19.1	98.4	0.4	0.7	0.6	0.5	4.2	16.5	7.3	9.4	15.1	16.3
33 005	28300	4	Cheshire	1 832	75 965	677	41.5	97.8	0.6	0.7	0.9	0.8	4.9	16.9	12.8	10.3	15.0	15.3
33 007	13620	7	Coos	4 663	33 019	1 333	7.1	98.6	0.2	0.7	0.5	0.6	4.6	16.5	7.9	10.0	15.3	16.0
33 009	30100	5	Grafton	4 438	84 038	637	18.9	96.1	0.8	0.9	2.2	1.1	4.8	15.5	14.3	11.0	14.1	15.5
33 011	31700	2	Hillsborough	2 270	394 663	155	173.9	92.1	1.8	0.6	2.9	3.6	6.3	19.1	8.2	12.9	18.2	15.1
33 013	18180	4	Merrimack	2 420	143 622	396	59.3	97.1	0.7	0.7	1.3	1.1	5.6	18.0	9.6	11.5	17.2	15.9
33 015	14460	1	Rockingham	1 800	290 104	202	161.2	96.5	0.8	0.4	1.7	1.3	5.8	19.2	7.4	11.4	19.1	16.5
33 017	14460	1	Strafford	955	117 740	477	123.3	96.4	1.0	0.6	1.9	1.1	5.9	16.8	13.4	12.8	16.4	13.7
33 019	...	7	Sullivan	1 392	42 048	1 079	30.2	98.3	0.5	0.8	0.5	0.6	5.6	17.1	7.8	11.0	15.5	15.8
34 000	...	X	NEW JERSEY	19 211	8 638 396	X	449.7	65.3	13.8	0.4	7.0	14.5	6.6	18.1	8.4	12.9	16.6	14.5
34 001	12100	2	Atlantic	1 453	263 410	224	181.3	64.2	17.1	0.6	6.1	13.3	6.5	18.6	8.7	12.4	16.6	13.8
34 003	35620	1	Bergen	607	897 569	49	1 478.7	70.2	5.6	0.3	12.8	12.1	5.8	17.1	7.2	12.2	17.0	15.1
34 005	37980	1	Burlington	2 084	444 381	141	213.2	75.9	16.6	0.6	3.9	4.7	6.0	18.2	8.6	12.7	17.1	14.4
34 007	37980	1	Camden	576	513 909	113	892.2	66.6	19.0	0.5	4.4	10.7	6.8	19.5	8.9	12.8	16.2	14.2
34 009	36140	3	Cape May	661	101 845	536	154.1	91.0	4.9	0.4	0.8	3.6	5.0	16.5	7.8	9.8	14.5	14.5
34 011	47220	3	Cumberland	1 267	149 306	379	117.8	57.5	20.3	1.2	1.2	21.0	6.8	18.5	9.2	14.4	15.7	13.3
34 013	35620	1	Essex	327	796 313	61	2 435.2	37.4	42.0	0.5	4.4	16.8	7.5	19.0	9.0	14.2	16.1	13.5
34 015	37980	1	Gloucester	841	266 962	217	317.4	85.9	9.8	0.4	1.9	2.9	6.7	16.3	8.9	11.9	16.8	14.6
34 017	35620	1	Hudson	121	607 419	94	5 020.0	36.0	13.0	0.4	10.6	41.1	6.7	16.3	8.9	19.0	16.6	12.6
34 019	35620	1	Hunterdon	1 114	128 265	442	115.1	91.9	2.5	0.3	2.6	3.4	5.8	18.6	7.5	9.9	18.3	17.4

1. CBSA = Core Based Statistical Area. See Appendix A for explanation. See Appendix B for list of metropolitan areas with component counties. 2. County type code from the Economic Research Service of USDA Rural-Urban Continuum Codes. See Appendix A for definition. 3. Dry land or land partially or temporarily covered by water. 4. Hispanic or Latino persons may be of any race.

Table B. States and Counties — **Population and Households**

STATE County	55 to 64 years	65 to 74 years	75 years and over	Percent female	1990	2000	1990–2000	2000–2003	Births	Deaths	Net migration	Number	Percent change, 1990–2000	Persons per household	Female family householder[1]	One person
	16	17	18	19	20	21	22	23	24	25	26	27	28	29	30	31
NEBRASKA—Cont'd																
Platte	9.0	6.3	6.9	50.4	29 820	31 662	6.2	-1.5	1 382	839	-878	12 076	10.2	2.59	7.6	25.9
Polk	9.1	9.3	12.6	49.8	5 655	5 639	-0.3	-2.9	174	185	-144	2 259	1.6	2.43	4.1	27.6
Red Willow	9.7	9.1	10.1	51.7	11 705	11 448	-2.2	-1.7	458	455	-191	4 710	-0.3	2.37	7.2	28.6
Richardson	11.1	9.4	12.7	51.6	9 937	9 531	-4.1	-5.5	260	514	-267	3 993	-3.1	2.34	7.4	32.2
Rock	10.8	9.6	13.7	52.6	2 019	1 756	-13.0	-8.1	45	67	-124	763	-4.4	2.26	6.4	31.3
Saline	8.6	6.8	9.6	50.1	12 715	13 843	8.9	2.5	538	529	348	5 188	7.4	2.50	7.2	27.5
Sarpy	7.3	4.4	2.6	50.3	102 583	122 595	19.5	8.1	7 120	2 020	4 793	43 426	27.9	2.79	9.6	18.4
Saunders	9.8	7.7	7.5	50.1	18 285	19 830	8.4	0.9	796	584	-16	7 498	10.1	2.61	6.7	23.6
Scotts Bluff	9.6	8.4	8.8	52.2	36 025	36 951	2.6	0.0	1 816	1 364	-445	14 887	5.9	2.44	10.7	27.8
Seward	8.7	7.2	8.1	49.0	15 450	16 496	6.8	1.1	633	492	49	6 013	10.7	2.53	5.6	24.9
Sheridan	10.1	10.1	12.1	50.9	6 750	6 198	-8.2	-6.3	221	253	-365	2 549	-2.6	2.38	8.0	29.6
Sherman	11.2	11.5	12.5	51.4	3 718	3 318	-10.8	-5.8	96	139	-143	1 394	-2.6	2.34	5.7	30.4
Sioux	11.8	11.1	6.0	47.5	1 549	1 475	-4.8	1.1	27	24	15	605	-1.1	2.44	5.1	23.6
Stanton	9.5	6.1	6.8	50.4	6 244	6 455	3.4	2.0	281	196	41	2 297	6.0	2.76	7.2	19.2
Thayer	11.5	10.8	14.4	51.0	6 635	6 055	-8.7	-6.5	193	299	-290	2 541	-4.8	2.31	5.0	31.5
Thomas	12.3	9.0	12.0	52.2	851	729	-14.3	-8.2	15	39	-36	325	2.8	2.24	4.3	31.4
Thurston	7.9	6.8	5.9	50.1	6 936	7 171	3.4	-0.4	520	245	-311	2 255	-1.4	3.14	19.1	21.3
Valley	11.0	10.2	13.4	52.1	5 169	4 647	-10.1	-1.6	136	201	-1	1 965	-8.2	2.32	5.1	31.0
Washington	9.3	6.6	6.1	50.0	16 607	18 780	13.1	4.8	784	503	633	6 940	15.3	2.63	7.0	21.8
Wayne	7.5	6.4	7.4	52.0	9 364	9 851	5.2	-3.8	300	204	-477	3 437	6.3	2.51	5.4	25.1
Webster	11.6	10.9	14.5	52.3	4 279	4 061	-5.1	-4.8	119	194	-118	1 708	-2.7	2.28	5.0	32.6
Wheeler	10.5	10.2	6.9	51.3	948	886	-6.5	-7.3	39	23	-76	352	0.6	2.52	3.1	29.0
York	9.8	7.9	9.6	52.3	14 428	14 598	1.2	-1.6	540	446	-327	5 722	4.7	2.42	6.0	27.5
NEVADA	10.0	6.6	4.6	49.0	1 201 675	1 998 257	66.3	12.2	102 521	53 711	190 642	751 165	61.1	2.62	11.1	24.9
Churchill	9.3	6.6	5.6	50.2	17 938	23 982	33.7	3.3	2 106	680	-634	8 912	33.7	2.64	10.4	22.5
Clark	9.2	6.2	4.1	49.1	741 368	1 375 765	85.6	14.6	74 427	36 304	159 627	512 253	78.5	2.65	11.8	24.5
Douglas	12.7	9.3	6.4	49.7	27 637	41 259	49.3	6.9	1 113	959	2 667	16 401	55.2	2.50	8.0	20.7
Elko	8.5	4.0	2.7	48.0	33 463	45 291	35.3	-2.6	1 973	721	-2 507	15 638	32.8	2.85	8.4	20.9
Esmeralda	17.0	12.9	7.8	43.9	1 344	971	-27.8	-11.6	24	33	-101	455	-22.6	2.12	6.4	36.0
Eureka	13.1	8.7	5.3	47.9	1 547	1 651	6.7	-8.4	64	44	-158	666	7.9	2.47	5.0	29.1
Humboldt	8.9	5.0	4.0	47.1	12 844	16 106	25.4	-8.7	687	343	-1 814	5 733	26.3	2.77	7.6	22.8
Lander	11.8	5.1	3.2	48.6	6 266	5 794	-7.5	-12.9	282	142	-919	2 093	-5.4	2.73	8.1	22.3
Lincoln	12.0	9.3	7.5	48.0	3 775	4 165	10.3	2.4	126	150	124	1 540	16.2	2.48	7.9	31.3
Lyon	10.8	7.9	5.3	49.4	20 001	34 501	72.5	16.3	1 309	1 175	5 376	13 007	69.4	2.61	9.1	21.4
Mineral	13.7	10.8	9.8	50.0	6 475	5 071	-21.7	-5.5	143	282	-147	2 197	-13.1	2.26	11.5	31.6
Nye	13.4	12.4	7.2	48.9	17 781	32 485	82.7	9.9	1 019	1 418	3 584	13 309	99.7	2.42	7.4	25.7
Pershing	10.2	4.3	3.7	38.6	4 336	6 693	54.4	-3.7	234	108	-376	1 962	21.6	2.69	7.3	24.3
Storey	16.0	7.6	4.5	47.5	2 526	3 399	34.6	3.3	24	50	141	1 462	45.3	2.32	7.5	25.6
Washoe	9.5	5.8	4.6	49.2	254 667	339 486	33.3	9.2	16 388	8 901	23 770	132 084	29.1	2.53	10.3	27.0
White Pine	10.6	7.9	7.0	43.4	9 264	9 181	-0.9	-7.5	233	283	-659	3 282	-0.4	2.42	9.3	29.6
Carson City city	10.6	7.6	7.3	48.7	40 443	52 457	29.7	5.4	2 369	2 118	2 668	20 171	26.9	2.44	11.0	27.8
NEW HAMPSHIRE	10.4	6.1	5.8	50.7	1 109 252	1 235 786	11.4	4.2	47 194	32 188	37 082	474 606	15.4	2.53	9.1	24.4
Belknap	11.0	7.5	7.2	51.0	49 216	56 325	14.4	7.2	1 838	1 886	4 014	22 459	19.2	2.45	9.2	24.4
Carroll	12.1	9.4	8.3	50.9	35 410	43 666	23.3	5.7	1 217	1 403	2 613	18 351	28.8	2.35	7.8	26.6
Cheshire	10.2	6.8	6.6	51.1	70 121	73 825	5.3	2.9	2 496	2 310	1 978	28 299	9.4	2.47	9.0	25.5
Coos	11.3	9.2	9.2	51.0	34 828	33 111	-4.9	-0.3	958	1 378	350	13 961	1.2	2.33	8.8	28.8
Grafton	10.3	6.7	6.7	50.8	74 929	81 743	9.1	2.8	2 528	2 207	2 028	31 598	14.7	2.38	8.3	27.4
Hillsborough	9.2	5.3	5.1	50.5	335 838	380 841	13.4	3.6	16 126	9 010	6 957	144 455	16.0	2.58	9.5	24.3
Merrimack	9.4	5.8	6.1	50.8	120 240	136 225	13.3	5.4	5 129	3 689	5 864	51 843	16.3	2.51	9.8	24.6
Rockingham	9.9	5.6	4.6	50.5	245 845	277 359	12.8	4.6	10 768	6 220	8 218	104 529	17.3	2.63	8.2	22.0
Strafford	8.4	5.7	5.3	51.5	104 233	112 233	7.7	4.3	4 610	2 747	3 665	42 581	12.8	2.50	10.0	24.8
Sullivan	11.0	8.1	7.3	50.5	38 592	40 458	4.8	3.9	1 524	1 338	1 395	16 530	11.1	2.41	8.6	25.7
NEW JERSEY	10.0	6.4	6.6	51.3	7 747 750	8 414 350	8.6	2.7	370 057	240 899	99 345	3 064 645	9.7	2.68	12.6	24.5
Atlantic	9.2	6.8	6.5	51.5	224 327	252 552	12.6	4.3	11 477	8 525	8 134	95 024	11.6	2.59	14.8	27.0
Bergen	10.6	7.4	7.6	51.7	825 380	884 118	7.1	1.5	32 140	24 380	6 645	330 817	7.1	2.64	9.7	24.7
Burlington	9.6	6.5	5.9	50.5	395 066	423 394	7.2	5.0	16 634	11 561	15 953	154 371	13.0	2.65	10.9	22.9
Camden	9.1	6.1	6.2	51.7	502 824	508 932	1.2	1.0	22 817	15 164	-2 285	185 744	3.9	2.68	15.4	25.1
Cape May	11.7	10.0	10.2	51.9	95 089	102 326	7.6	-0.5	3 318	4 308	620	42 148	11.3	2.36	10.9	30.2
Cumberland	9.0	6.3	6.4	48.8	138 053	146 438	6.1	2.0	6 933	5 059	1 123	49 143	4.3	2.73	17.3	23.6
Essex	9.1	5.9	5.7	52.2	777 964	793 633	2.0	0.3	40 370	23 603	-12 494	283 736	1.8	2.72	20.4	26.7
Gloucester	9.1	6.0	5.4	51.5	230 082	254 673	10.7	4.8	9 754	7 202	9 773	90 717	15.1	2.75	11.6	21.2
Hudson	8.6	5.8	5.4	50.7	553 099	608 975	10.1	-0.3	27 303	15 284	-14 047	230 546	10.4	2.60	16.6	29.5
Hunterdon	11.0	5.8	5.0	50.6	107 852	121 989	13.1	5.1	4 674	2 587	4 330	43 678	15.2	2.69	6.3	20.0

1. No spouse present.

Table B. States and Counties — Vital Statistics, Health Resources, and Crime

STATE County	Births, average 1999–2001 Total	Rate[1]	Deaths, average 1999–2001 Number Total	Infant[2]	Rate Total[1]	Infant[3]	Physicians,[4] 2000 Number	Rate[5]	Hospitals,[4] 1998 Number	Beds Number	Beds Rate[5]	Medicare enrollees, 2003	Serious crimes known to police,[6] 2002 Total Number	Rate[7]
	32	33	34	35	36	37	38	39	40	41	42	43	44	45
NEBRASKA—Cont'd														
Platte	440	14.0	257	4	8.1	D	23	73	1	81	264	2 899	755	2 360
Polk	63	11.3	61	0	10.9	D	1	18	1	21	373	1 088	82	1 439
Red Willow	143	12.5	134	1	11.7	D	14	122	1	44	391	2 391	300	2 593
Richardson	87	9.2	155	0	16.4	D	6	63	2	69	732	2 181	139	1 443
Rock	13	7.7	19	0	10.9	D	2	114	1	54	3 098	381	18	1 015
Saline	166	12.0	167	1	12.0	D	6	43	2	130	1 003	2 486	257	1 837
Sarpy	2 128	17.2	554	11	4.5	5.3	125	102	1	185	153	8 837	3 346	2 701
Saunders	250	12.6	172	2	8.6	D	5	25	1	30	156	3 243	287	1 432
Scotts Bluff	532	14.4	410	3	11.1	D	84	227	1	218	604	7 323	1 259	3 372
Seward	195	11.8	154	1	9.3	D	9	55	1	49	301	2 567	268	1 608
Sheridan	69	11.1	85	1	13.8	D	4	65	1	40	620	1 337	171	2 730
Sherman	35	10.5	41	0	12.3	D	3	90	0	0	0	766	51	1 521
Sioux	9	6.0	8	0	5.7	D	1	68	0	0	0	142	5	335
Stanton	76	11.8	52	0	8.0	D	0	0	0	0	0	587	59	905
Thayer	58	9.6	101	0	16.7	D	3	50	1	20	319	1 538	69	1 128
Thomas	8	10.7	11	0	14.8	D	0	0	0	0	0	127	NA	NA
Thurston	159	22.2	72	2	10.1	D	4	56	1	47	655	986	NA	NA
Valley	43	9.2	63	0	13.7	D	4	86	1	96	2 086	1 105	NA	NA
Washington	230	12.2	164	2	8.7	D	10	53	1	46	247	2 528	372	1 960
Wayne	101	10.3	67	1	6.8	D	5	51	1	31	330	1 327	146	1 467
Webster	41	10.2	61	1	15.1	D	2	49	1	16	398	1 069	70	1 706
Wheeler	11	12.4	7	1	8.3	D	0	0	0	0	0	140	1	112
York	161	11.0	149	1	10.2	D	9	62	2	108	744	2 674	274	1 858
NEVADA	30 524	15.2	15 543	191	7.7	6.3	2 983	149	23	3 716	213	273 724	97 752	4 498
Churchill	353	14.7	207	1	8.6	D	27	113	1	40	172	3 425	831	3 186
Clark	22 082	15.9	10 505	141	7.6	6.4	1 969	143	8	2 249	194	182 306	72 126	4 820
Douglas	349	8.5	300	2	7.3	D	46	111	0	0	0	6 647	963	2 146
Elko	695	15.4	208	4	4.6	D	37	82	1	50	108	3 598	1 202	2 440
Esmeralda	7	7.2	11	0	11.0	D	0	0	0	0	0	164	7	663
Eureka	17	10.0	11	0	6.6	D	1	61	0	0	0	230	24	1 336
Humboldt	255	15.9	103	1	6.4	D	11	68	1	30	165	1 697	414	2 363
Lander	95	16.5	38	0	6.5	D	3	52	1	6	86	521	121	1 920
Lincoln	48	11.5	45	0	10.7	D	4	96	1	19	450	850	47	1 038
Lyon	407	11.8	327	1	9.4	D	13	38	1	44	146	6 726	757	2 017
Mineral	48	9.5	76	1	14.9	D	2	39	1	35	641	1 132	51	925
Nye	320	9.8	387	3	11.9	D	10	31	1	45	156	8 351	1 219	3 450
Pershing	70	10.5	37	0	5.5	D	1	15	1	34	626	556	179	2 459
Storey	8	2.3	18	0	5.2	D	0	0	0	0	0	169	80	2 164
Washoe	4 950	14.5	2 602	31	7.6	6.3	735	217	4	1 009	322	45 151	17 477	4 733
White Pine	81	8.9	89	0	9.7	D	8	87	1	39	387	1 499	192	1 923
Carson City city	739	14.0	581	4	11.0	D	116	221	1	116	235	10 596	2 074	3 635
NEW HAMPSHIRE	14 435	11.6	9 683	74	7.8	5.1	2 603	211	26	3 179	268	179 564	28 306	2 220
Belknap	563	10.0	553	4	9.8	D	108	192	1	115	219	11 430	1 695	3 057
Carroll	392	9.0	421	2	9.6	D	59	135	2	128	325	9 202	987	2 603
Cheshire	745	10.1	678	3	9.2	D	113	153	1	177	246	11 811	1 275	1 721
Coos	316	9.6	425	2	12.9	D	62	187	3	172	523	7 420	365	1 291
Grafton	807	9.9	665	5	8.1	D	555	679	5	613	783	13 130	1 579	2 305
Hillsborough	4 983	13.0	2 708	23	7.1	4.7	732	192	5	938	258	48 117	NA	NA
Merrimack	1 527	11.2	1 136	9	8.3	6.1	318	233	3	347	272	19 872	NA	NA
Rockingham	3 320	11.9	1 850	13	6.6	4.0	405	146	3	405	149	35 183	4 262	1 900
Strafford	1 342	11.9	830	6	7.4	D	179	159	2	213	196	15 429	NA	NA
Sullivan	441	10.9	417	6	10.3	D	72	178	1	71	177	7 309	745	2 218
NEW JERSEY	115 177	13.7	74 497	749	8.8	6.5	20 834	248	94	30 258	373	1 219 935	259 789	3 024
Atlantic	3 436	13.6	2 527	31	10.0	8.9	493	195	4	1 043	438	39 508	12 711	4 930
Bergen	10 691	12.1	7 657	53	8.7	5.0	2 882	326	6	3 153	367	139 478	16 217	1 797
Burlington	5 202	12.2	3 564	29	8.4	5.5	891	210	3	922	219	61 140	9 832	2 275
Camden	7 102	13.9	4 745	67	9.3	9.5	1 529	300	8	2 067	409	72 843	18 825	3 623
Cape May	1 034	10.1	1 346	10	13.2	9.3	153	150	1	239	244	22 252	4 707	4 506
Cumberland	2 038	13.9	1 529	27	10.4	13.2	240	164	3	631	450	22 649	7 547	5 048
Essex	12 249	15.4	7 267	120	9.2	9.8	2 824	356	13	4 875	650	100 583	42 731	5 274
Gloucester	3 182	12.5	2 165	18	8.5	5.7	325	128	1	339	137	33 388	8 405	3 233
Hudson	8 818	14.5	4 788	64	7.9	7.3	1 206	198	9	2 435	437	70 397	23 140	3 722
Hunterdon	1 484	12.1	796	6	6.5	D	225	184	1	197	161	15 585	1 180	957

1. Per 1,000 estimated resident population. 2. Deaths of infants under 1 year old. 3. Deaths of infants under 1 year old per 1,000 live births. 4. Data subject to copyright. 5. Per 100,000 resident population as of July 1 of the year shown. 6. Data for serious crimes have not been adjusted for underreporting; this may affect comparability between geographic areas and over time. 7. Per 100,000 population estimated by the FBI.

STATE County	Serious crimes known to police,[1] 2002 (cont'd) Rate[2] Violent	Property	Education — School enrollment and attainment, 2000 — Enrollment[3] Total	Percent private	Attainment[4] (percent) High school graduate or less	Bachelor's degree or more	Local government expenditures,[5] 2000–2001 Total current expenditures (mil dol)	Current expenditures per student (dollars)	Money income, 1999 Per capita income[6] (dollars)	Households Median income Dollars	Percent change, 1989–1999 (constant 1999 dollars)	Percent with income of $100,000 or more	Percent below poverty level, 1999 Persons	Households	Families	Families with children
	46	47	48	49	50	51	52	53	54	55	56	57	58	59	60	61
NEBRASKA—Cont'd																
Platte	66	2 294	8 809	29.2	51.5	17.2	33.4	7 313	18 064	39 359	12.1	6.0	7.7	8.1	5.4	7.7
Polk	18	1 422	1 408	4.8	53.4	13.5	9.2	7 374	17 934	37 819	8.4	4.2	5.8	6.3	4.4	5.4
Red Willow	130	2 464	2 925	6.5	47.0	15.2	14.2	7 013	16 303	32 293	7.6	4.0	9.6	11.3	7.6	12.4
Richardson	62	1 381	2 298	9.1	60.1	13.6	11.7	6 864	16 460	29 884	13.9	3.1	10.1	11.1	6.3	9.8
Rock	0	1 015	363	8.0	54.6	12.2	2.5	9 314	14 350	25 795	1.2	3.6	21.8	19.5	17.7	30.7
Saline	57	1 780	3 929	22.5	58.2	14.0	16.4	6 112	16 287	35 914	9.3	3.9	9.4	10.5	6.4	9.6
Sarpy	85	2 616	38 813	16.7	31.4	30.2	120.6	6 215	21 985	53 804	12.6	12.3	4.2	4.0	3.1	4.6
Saunders	65	1 367	5 208	20.1	51.6	16.9	19.8	6 625	18 392	42 173	20.5	6.0	6.6	7.1	5.3	7.1
Scotts Bluff	158	3 214	9 375	11.6	50.0	17.3	41.8	6 480	17 355	32 016	11.5	5.9	14.5	13.2	11.0	17.9
Seward	84	1 524	5 376	32.8	44.4	22.6	22.1	8 344	18 379	42 700	16.8	7.6	7.0	8.4	4.1	6.5
Sheridan	335	2 395	1 549	4.9	50.3	17.2	8.2	7 289	14 844	29 484	14.1	3.1	13.2	11.9	11.0	17.3
Sherman	239	1 282	770	2.7	58.8	10.8	4.7	8 528	14 064	28 646	25.2	2.3	12.9	13.5	8.0	15.6
Sioux	67	268	360	9.2	45.5	21.5	1.6	11 896	15 999	29 851	18.1	5.7	15.4	11.5	11.1	18.7
Stanton	15	889	1 832	16.8	51.8	13.7	3.1	6 445	15 511	36 676	12.0	4.2	6.8	8.1	5.3	6.6
Thayer	49	1 079	1 356	10.0	56.4	15.0	8.9	8 634	17 043	30 740	12.7	3.9	10.7	10.8	7.6	10.2
Thomas	NA	NA	166	1.8	48.5	17.2	1.3	11 000	15 335	27 292	17.6	1.9	14.3	13.3	13.6	15.1
Thurston	NA	NA	2 352	8.3	56.7	12.0	16.2	8 772	10 951	28 170	12.8	1.8	25.6	20.1	19.3	27.0
Valley	NA	NA	1 095	10.0	53.4	16.4	5.7	7 706	14 996	27 926	8.3	3.3	12.8	13.5	10.1	15.2
Washington	11	1 950	5 340	18.4	45.9	22.7	20.6	6 094	21 055	48 500	21.1	11.5	6.0	6.2	4.1	6.3
Wayne	70	1 396	4 077	4.4	44.1	28.0	14.9	8 918	14 644	32 366	15.0	4.7	14.5	14.1	7.4	10.5
Webster	73	1 633	953	8.7	55.9	13.7	4.3	6 621	16 802	30 026	21.8	3.3	11.2	11.8	7.7	13.2
Wheeler	0	112	236	5.1	46.4	14.9	1.5	9 934	14 355	26 771	-11.8	4.7	20.9	19.3	15.4	21.0
York	20	1 837	4 000	23.4	50.4	17.0	15.2	7 206	17 670	37 093	7.3	4.6	8.5	7.9	6.0	9.0
NEVADA	638	3 860	492 885	9.1	48.7	18.2	1 975.7	5 798	21 989	44 581	7.0	11.3	10.5	9.4	7.5	11.4
Churchill	326	2 860	6 660	4.6	45.4	16.7	32.6	6 774	19 264	40 808	4.7	6.8	8.7	8.6	6.2	10.3
Clark	726	4 094	329 929	9.3	50.4	17.3	1 279.9	5 525	21 785	44 616	8.0	11.5	10.8	9.5	7.9	11.8
Douglas	129	2 017	10 499	9.7	35.0	23.2	49.0	6 967	27 288	51 849	9.6	14.6	7.3	7.3	5.8	9.4
Elko	189	2 251	13 237	6.4	51.3	14.8	68.7	6 806	18 482	48 383	6.8	8.6	8.9	8.5	7.0	8.8
Esmeralda	95	568	235	9.8	65.4	9.6	1.3	12 168	18 971	33 203	-3.4	5.5	15.3	18.1	7.5	7.9
Eureka	278	1 058	440	3.9	55.0	13.6	5.1	16 757	18 629	41 417	-0.7	6.9	12.6	14.2	8.9	10.1
Humboldt	365	1 998	4 563	4.3	53.0	14.2	27.2	7 140	19 539	47 147	5.5	8.0	9.7	8.8	7.7	9.6
Lander	524	1 396	1 755	3.6	57.6	10.8	10.7	7 386	16 998	46 067	0.9	4.0	12.5	10.8	8.6	12.2
Lincoln	88	949	1 192	2.0	54.7	15.1	9.4	9 185	17 326	31 979	14.0	3.7	16.5	17.9	11.5	15.3
Lyon	213	1 804	8 802	8.9	51.4	11.3	43.0	6 450	18 543	40 699	20.9	5.8	10.4	9.6	7.2	11.2
Mineral	109	816	1 176	6.5	59.1	10.1	7.8	8 953	16 952	32 891	-6.8	3.6	15.2	15.9	11.0	19.9
Nye	374	3 076	6 644	8.4	62.0	10.1	36.6	6 927	17 962	36 024	-11.2	5.6	10.7	10.7	7.3	12.1
Pershing	330	2 129	1 830	5.8	60.7	8.7	8.5	9 471	16 589	40 670	10.0	4.9	11.4	11.1	10.2	14.5
Storey	784	1 379	665	7.4	43.0	18.0	4.5	10 058	23 642	45 490	4.3	7.1	5.8	5.8	2.5	5.3
Washoe	554	4 179	89 970	9.6	41.2	23.7	323.6	5 751	24 277	45 815	6.9	12.9	10.0	9.1	6.7	10.3
White Pine	300	1 622	2 290	6.9	52.8	11.8	12.1	7 812	18 309	36 688	-0.4	4.8	11.0	12.0	10.3	16.0
Carson City city	533	3 102	12 998	8.7	45.4	18.5	55.7	6 606	20 943	41 809	-1.4	9.3	10.0	9.2	6.9	11.7
NEW HAMPSHIRE	161	2 059	332 888	20.6	42.7	28.7	1 472.8	7 194	23 844	49 467	1.3	13.8	6.5	6.9	4.3	6.5
Belknap	142	2 914	13 322	14.7	46.9	23.3	76.4	7 439	22 758	43 605	3.1	9.3	6.1	6.5	4.5	7.6
Carroll	195	2 408	9 809	12.2	44.0	26.5	59.0	7 988	21 931	39 990	5.8	9.4	7.9	7.9	5.5	8.9
Cheshire	109	1 611	21 073	19.0	48.2	26.6	84.7	7 872	20 685	42 382	-0.3	8.6	8.0	8.2	4.4	6.8
Coos	110	1 182	7 435	8.0	64.7	11.9	40.2	7 115	17 218	33 593	-3.5	4.1	10.0	11.7	6.8	10.6
Grafton	99	2 206	24 139	28.5	43.3	32.7	116.0	8 554	22 227	41 962	3.9	10.1	8.6	8.4	5.1	7.7
Hillsborough	NA	NA	103 468	23.9	40.5	30.1	430.8	6 518	25 198	53 384	-1.7	16.6	6.3	6.4	4.3	6.3
Merrimack	NA	NA	36 957	22.0	41.5	29.1	148.2	6 933	23 208	48 522	0.9	12.0	5.9	6.6	4.1	6.3
Rockingham	152	1 748	73 404	20.8	38.1	31.7	347.2	7 636	26 656	58 150	3.3	19.0	4.5	4.8	3.1	4.5
Strafford	NA	NA	34 333	13.7	44.1	26.4	114.3	6 742	20 479	44 803	1.6	9.3	9.2	8.8	5.0	8.2
Sullivan	179	2 039	8 948	11.2	55.5	19.7	56.0	7 773	21 319	40 938	4.9	7.7	8.5	8.9	5.2	8.6
NEW JERSEY	375	2 650	2 217 832	21.8	47.3	29.8	14 809.4	11 247	27 006	55 146	0.3	21.3	8.5	8.3	6.3	9.2
Atlantic	530	4 400	66 098	14.9	56.5	18.7	457.8	10 537	21 034	43 933	-3.0	10.6	10.5	10.1	7.6	10.9
Bergen	120	1 677	220 538	26.8	39.6	38.2	1 448.1	11 743	33 638	65 241	-1.4	28.6	5.0	5.3	3.4	4.6
Burlington	214	2 060	111 053	18.8	44.0	28.4	743.4	10 453	26 339	58 608	2.9	20.1	4.7	4.7	3.2	4.6
Camden	538	3 085	141 671	18.2	51.9	24.0	979.9	11 488	22 354	48 097	-1.1	14.7	10.4	10.0	8.1	12.0
Cape May	327	4 178	23 063	16.7	54.5	22.0	176.9	11 488	24 172	41 591	1.7	12.3	8.6	8.3	6.4	10.1
Cumberland	692	4 357	37 622	13.0	67.8	11.7	303.7	11 923	17 376	39 150	-2.8	8.2	15.0	13.7	11.3	16.7
Essex	967	4 307	221 424	22.8	51.6	27.5	1 564.6	12 888	24 943	44 944	-3.1	18.5	15.6	15.4	12.8	17.9
Gloucester	247	2 986	73 630	18.0	52.6	22.0	451.3	10 021	22 708	54 273	2.6	15.5	6.2	6.7	4.3	6.2
Hudson	669	3 053	157 624	25.6	56.3	25.3	971.3	12 201	21 154	40 293	-3.0	12.8	15.5	15.3	13.3	18.9
Hunterdon	32	925	31 562	17.2	34.0	41.8	242.9	11 216	36 370	79 888	8.8	37.0	2.6	2.8	1.6	2.1

1. Data for serious crimes have not been adjusted for underreporting; this may affect comparability between geographic areas and over time.   2. Per 100,000 population estimated by the FBI.   3. All persons 3 years old and over enrolled in nursery school through college.   4. Persons 25 years old and over.   5. Elementary and secondary education expenditures.   6. Based on population enumerated as of April 1, 2000.

Table B. States and Counties — **Personal Income**

	Personal income, 2002												
			Per capita[1]						Transfer payments				
										Government payments to individuals			
STATE County	Total (mil dol)	Percent change, 2001– 2002	Dollars	Rank	Wages and salaries[2] (mil dol)	Proprietor's income (mil dol)	Dividends, interest, and rent (mil dol)	Total (mil dol)	Total (mil dol)	Social Security (mil dol)	Medical payments (mil dol)	Income mainte- nance (mil dol)	Unemploy- ment insurance (mil dol)
	62	63	64	65	66	67	68	69	70	71	72	73	74
NEBRASKA—Cont'd													
Platte	812	0.9	25 937	901	590	80	172	106	98	53	30	7	4
Polk	142	-1.8	25 699	953	41	24	30	25	24	13	9	1	1
Red Willow	278	0.6	24 622	1 231	155	29	70	58	56	24	22	3	1
Richardson	216	-6.4	23 668	1 511	76	20	50	52	50	21	21	3	1
Rock	36	3.1	21 153	2 251	14	4	11	8	8	3	3	0	0
Saline	342	0.8	24 320	1 303	230	23	67	57	53	26	21	3	1
Sarpy	3 574	4.7	27 638	598	2 200	83	437	328	299	126	99	19	8
Saunders	543	1.0	27 263	658	144	46	85	78	74	34	31	3	2
Scotts Bluff	900	2.9	24 489	1 267	540	101	162	189	180	77	71	18	3
Seward	456	0.2	27 402	631	193	42	93	61	58	29	21	2	1
Sheridan	126	3.5	21 016	2 298	48	3	39	30	28	13	11	2	0
Sherman	62	-7.3	19 412	2 670	20	2	17	18	17	7	7	1	0
Sioux	23	13.0	15 663	3 060	6	-3	7	4	4	2	1	0	0
Stanton	137	-3.4	21 018	2 297	69	13	16	19	18	8	6	1	1
Thayer	156	-2.2	27 021	697	67	23	44	34	32	15	14	2	0
Thomas	13	18.5	19 411	2 672	9	-2	5	3	3	2	1	0	0
Thurston	142	-0.8	20 046	2 540	79	13	19	40	38	10	19	7	1
Valley	103	-0.5	22 618	1 844	45	9	29	24	23	11	10	1	0
Washington	572	4.0	29 616	379	321	24	91	68	63	30	25	3	1
Wayne	218	-1.9	22 841	1 766	115	29	41	36	33	14	13	2	1
Webster	96	-6.3	24 612	1 234	32	11	22	22	21	10	9	1	0
Wheeler	22	4.0	26 548	776	10	7	5	3	3	2	1	0	1
York	382	1.8	26 535	781	248	38	87	64	61	30	25	3	1
NEVADA	66 235	4.2	30 559	X	45 620	4 691	13 734	7 687	7 221	3 122	2 703	553	435
Churchill	665	4.4	27 234	662	378	70	108	101	96	36	38	11	4
Clark	44 572	5.0	29 396	404	31 915	3 219	8 188	5 305	4 979	2 104	1 896	401	312
Douglas	1 770	3.3	40 997	55	797	95	601	162	153	93	41	6	6
Elko	1 127	1.0	25 266	1 058	713	35	172	106	96	39	33	8	6
Esmeralda	25	0.9	28 018	552	11	0	5	4	4	2	2	0	0
Eureka	39	-2.8	23 927	1 429	286	2	9	5	5	2	2	0	2
Humboldt	385	1.5	25 917	904	292	26	72	46	43	18	15	4	1
Lander	136	0.3	26 300	830	90	9	22	16	15	6	6	1	1
Lincoln	90	7.1	21 135	2 254	69	5	18	19	19	8	7	1	0
Lyon	886	3.9	23 340	1 616	390	32	169	151	143	71	46	9	9
Mineral	112	4.0	23 495	1 570	68	6	21	28	27	10	12	2	1
Nye	894	6.9	25 833	925	455	44	179	189	182	96	58	10	7
Pershing	108	1.7	16 463	3 028	84	2	21	18	16	7	7	1	1
Storey	101	0.9	29 609	380	37	3	21	9	8	5	5	1	0
Washoe	13 324	2.2	36 831	108	8 577	1 024	3 658	1 249	1 171	510	433	82	70
White Pine	229	3.6	26 516	784	125	11	37	36	34	16	14	2	1
Carson City city	1 774	3.1	32 522	204	1 336	110	433	241	230	98	93	13	13
NEW HAMPSHIRE	43 310	1.9	33 985	X	27 195	3 609	7 118	5 022	4 717	2 084	1 977	265	153
Belknap	1 912	3.9	32 318	214	979	227	404	276	262	127	102	15	5
Carroll	1 457	4.0	32 185	217	640	165	398	234	223	103	95	11	4
Cheshire	2 236	3.4	29 842	362	1 275	167	427	317	299	138	125	16	4
Coos	870	2.2	26 337	824	455	78	154	214	206	82	97	12	6
Grafton	2 796	5.4	33 574	169	2 166	336	609	373	353	151	159	19	5
Hillsborough	13 914	0.6	35 496	128	9 764	987	1 929	1 418	1 324	570	567	83	40
Merrimack	4 548	3.5	32 121	219	3 161	326	784	568	534	236	224	30	13
Rockingham	11 098	1.1	38 592	75	6 322	1 035	1 670	978	909	420	346	37	63
Strafford	3 241	1.3	27 906	565	1 914	158	486	448	420	171	180	29	13
Sullivan	1 238	3.7	29 880	360	520	130	257	198	188	85	82	12	1
NEW JERSEY	338 388	1.8	39 461	X	216 021	28 306	56 150	42 280	40 179	14 836	18 214	2 423	2 879
Atlantic	8 210	4.1	31 702	237	6 147	1 112	1 186	1 428	1 365	455	642	98	108
Bergen	47 287	0.9	52 867	15	27 045	5 932	9 702	4 080	3 861	1 785	1 575	118	217
Burlington	15 985	4.0	36 513	112	10 125	1 026	2 340	1 919	1 813	761	763	71	102
Camden	16 430	4.0	32 108	222	9 751	1 107	2 203	2 712	2 586	839	1 255	218	154
Cape May	3 549	5.5	34 879	144	1 479	241	738	738	713	263	328	26	68
Cumberland	3 823	5.9	25 856	920	2 497	286	482	925	889	259	444	74	79
Essex	30 493	1.2	38 312	83	22 121	2 871	4 993	4 634	4 438	1 187	2 272	471	334
Gloucester	7 939	4.3	30 265	325	3 996	394	927	1 149	1 085	428	464	54	76
Hudson	18 456	0.7	30 259	328	15 276	1 299	2 185	3 206	3 056	735	1 583	313	301
Hunterdon	6 974	1.7	55 050	12	2 873	684	1 145	457	427	198	177	8	24

1. Based on the resident population estimated as of July 1 of the year shown.   2. Includes other labor income.

STATE County	Earnings, 2002 Total (mil dol)	Farm	Goods-related[1] Total	Manu-facturing	Service-related and health Information and professional and technical services	Retail trade	Finance, insurance, and real estate	Health services	Govern-ment	Social Security beneficiaries, December 2003 Number	Rate[2]	Supplemental Security Income recipients, December 2003	Housing units, 2003 Total	Percent change, 2000–2003
	75	76	77	78	79	80	81	82	83	84	85	86	87	88
NEBRASKA—Cont'd														
Platte	670	4.4	D	35.4	4.3	6.1	3.7	D	15.3	5 375	172	230	13 094	1.4
Polk	65	30.1	D	D	D	5.8	4.2	D	19.6	1 250	228	30	2 735	0.7
Red Willow	184	3.6	16.7	10.2	D	12.7	5.9	D	19.6	2 560	228	178	5 331	1.0
Richardson	96	7.4	D	7.7	D	10.4	4.4	11.1	21.8	2 415	268	149	4 532	-0.6
Rock	18	20.1	7.3	3.6	D	4.5	D	D	31.7	405	251	29	948	1.4
Saline	253	4.4	52.2	49.3	D	4.3	2.9	D	16.2	2 655	187	108	5 658	0.8
Sarpy	2 283	-0.2	D	4.6	6.6	5.9	2.7	2.8	38.3	13 170	99	702	50 309	11.8
Saunders	190	14.3	D	8.7	4.1	8.5	4.2	D	22.6	3 625	181	124	8 549	3.4
Scotts Bluff	641	4.6	13.6	6.7	7.8	9.1	7.1	16.9	17.5	8 195	222	898	16 308	1.2
Seward	235	7.8	27.7	20.9	7.1	5.0	4.9	D	16.8	2 955	177	92	6 589	2.5
Sheridan	51	-2.5	D	2.6	D	13.1	D	2.4	42.0	1 465	252	76	3 015	0.1
Sherman	22	0.0	D	D	D	7.0	7.2	2.5	38.1	865	277	42	1 816	-1.3
Sioux	4	-32.8	D	6.9	D	7.1	D	1.7	66.1	260	174	3	789	1.2
Stanton	81	12.8	D	D	D	1.7	1.7	D	12.0	990	150	29	2 472	0.8
Thayer	91	14.6	30.8	28.1	3.1	5.0	D	D	21.4	1 660	293	79	2 837	0.3
Thomas	7	-31.8	D	D	D	13.4	D	0.0	39.3	175	262	6	454	1.8
Thurston	92	9.5	13.8	7.8	1.6	4.9	D	6.4	49.3	1 135	159	181	2 469	0.1
Valley	54	10.5	D	1.4	D	8.1	6.9	4.3	37.0	1 210	265	60	2 262	-0.5
Washington	345	2.0	D	14.8	D	9.2	2.7	D	24.6	3 060	155	72	7 689	3.8
Wayne	144	15.5	21.2	15.1	D	5.4	4.8	6.3	28.4	1 515	160	71	3 681	0.5
Webster	43	17.0	D	1.2	D	5.0	9.1	7.2	22.4	1 135	294	59	1 962	-0.5
Wheeler	17	69.0	D	D	0.7	1.0	D	0.4	11.6	180	219	6	568	1.2
York	286	6.6	D	17.0	4.5	7.9	4.1	D	14.6	3 020	210	124	6 183	0.2
NEVADA	50 311	0.2	16.6	4.5	8.7	7.8	8.6	7.1	14.9	327 320	146	30 983	935 934	13.1
Churchill	448	2.6	D	5.5	4.7	7.6	4.6	D	37.3	4 035	163	326	9 998	2.7
Clark	35 134	0.0	14.8	3.1	8.8	7.8	9.1	6.7	13.4	218 970	139	23 009	648 682	15.9
Douglas	892	0.0	D	11.7	7.2	6.4	6.9	4.2	11.0	9 385	213	181	20 936	10.2
Elko	748	1.6	18.8	0.9	3.7	7.7	3.4	5.4	23.0	4 405	100	408	18 772	1.7
Esmeralda	11	6.7	D	0.5	D	D	0.0	0.0	30.1	230	268	19	846	1.6
Eureka	288	1.0	D	D	D	D	D	D	3.0	265	175	19	1 046	2.0
Humboldt	318	5.2	38.6	4.1	D	8.2	1.8	D	20.2	2 060	140	197	7 031	1.1
Lander	99	5.0	D	D	D	6.0	1.1	0.9	26.4	665	132	61	2 790	0.4
Lincoln	73	3.2	D	D	D	4.1	2.0	D	36.9	945	222	231	2 197	0.9
Lyon	422	3.5	32.1	20.5	D	12.8	2.4	D	17.3	8 050	201	452	15 307	7.2
Mineral	73	-0.8	D	D	D	5.1	D	1.7	35.0	1 285	268	119	2 876	0.3
Nye	498	2.3	19.2	1.2	30.4	6.1	2.5	D	16.0	10 590	296	450	16 210	1.7
Pershing	85	4.4	D	D	D	5.0	0.9	1.1	36.5	720	112	55	2 395	0.3
Storey	40	0.0	D	24.7	D	4.2	D	D	20.9	550	157	14	1 673	4.8
Washoe	9 601	0.1	18.0	8.1	9.0	7.7	9.0	9.8	14.6	52 970	143	4 646	158 453	10.1
White Pine	135	2.5	11.2	0.4	D	7.4	3.5	4.2	54.4	1 745	206	126	4 412	-0.6
Carson City city	1 446	0.0	D	10.8	6.9	9.3	7.0	7.6	36.4	10 440	189	626	22 310	4.8
NEW HAMPSHIRE	30 804	0.1	24.0	16.8	10.8	9.9	9.0	10.5	11.8	211 499	164	12 762	569 016	4.0
Belknap	1 206	0.1	D	20.5	D	13.7	D	11.2	12.4	12 625	209	707	33 595	4.6
Carroll	804	0.2	D	6.1	8.6	14.9	D	10.8	11.7	10 945	237	489	36 159	4.1
Cheshire	1 442	0.5	D	20.4	6.2	10.4	10.0	9.6	12.6	13 940	184	831	32 716	2.6
Coos	533	0.2	D	15.8	D	11.9	3.3	13.9	18.1	8 780	266	637	19 824	1.0
Grafton	2 502	0.0	19.1	14.9	9.1	8.5	3.8	19.0	10.4	15 200	181	842	45 059	3.0
Hillsborough	10 751	0.0	26.7	20.3	13.1	9.1	10.9	9.9	9.6	56 680	144	4 056	156 036	4.1
Merrimack	3 487	0.3	18.8	11.4	8.8	9.0	9.4	11.7	19.4	24 050	167	1 709	58 888	4.7
Rockingham	7 357	0.1	21.9	13.0	12.5	10.6	9.7	7.6	8.3	42 105	145	1 565	118 224	4.6
Strafford	2 072	0.1	23.0	17.9	8.4	9.2	7.1	11.5	21.2	18 320	156	1 257	47 749	4.9
Sullivan	650	0.5	D	34.4	D	10.6	5.8	8.6	14.1	8 675	206	655	20 766	3.0
NEW JERSEY	244 326	0.1	16.2	10.9	16.0	7.2	11.8	9.1	14.0	1 363 838	158	149 376	3 398 272	2.7
Atlantic	7 259	0.4	D	3.2	7.5	8.3	4.3	9.5	16.7	45 140	171	5 193	119 297	4.6
Bergen	32 977	0.0	15.9	11.8	17.3	7.7	11.8	10.4	7.6	150 290	167	8 867	345 413	1.6
Burlington	11 151	0.2	17.6	12.0	10.3	8.2	13.5	9.6	16.9	71 375	161	4 287	168 869	4.7
Camden	10 858	0.1	17.5	11.5	13.1	7.8	6.7	13.8	17.9	80 945	158	12 809	201 867	1.1
Cape May	1 720	0.3	D	1.9	6.1	11.7	9.2	9.5	26.1	25 265	248	1 498	94 624	3.9
Cumberland	2 783	1.8	25.0	19.4	5.0	9.2	4.3	11.7	25.8	25 955	174	4 663	53 692	1.6
Essex	24 992	0.0	12.5	8.8	15.3	4.5	13.1	10.3	18.7	111 735	140	25 483	304 123	1.0
Gloucester	4 390	0.6	25.8	15.9	7.4	11.1	3.9	9.1	18.0	41 770	156	3 149	99 922	5.1
Hudson	16 575	0.0	D	5.3	11.2	5.6	30.7	6.0	15.5	75 335	124	21 549	242 985	1.0
Hunterdon	3 557	0.3	D	6.9	19.7	15.6	5.9	7.6	12.3	17 335	135	618	46 866	4.1

1. Covers mining, construction, and manufacturing.   2. Per 1,000 resident population estimated as of July 1 of the year shown.

Table B. States and Counties — Housing, Labor Force, and Employment

STATE County	Housing units, 2000 Total	Percent	Median value[1]	With a mortgage	Without a mortgage[2]	Median rent[3]	Median rent as a percent of income	Substandard units[4] (percent)	Civilian labor force, 2003 Total	Percent change, 2002–2003	Unemployment Total	Rate[5]	Civilian employment,[6] 2000 Total	Management, professional and related occupations	Production, transportation, and material moving occupations
	89	90	91	92	93	94	95	96	97	98	99	100	101	102	103
NEBRASKA—Cont'd															
Platte	12 076	73.3	80 800	18.4	9.9	429	21.2	3.3	17 732	2.0	914	5.2	16 240	28.5	26.5
Polk	2 259	76.9	57 800	17.9	9.9	387	19.5	1.2	2 318	-3.1	100	4.3	2 806	31.6	16.2
Red Willow	4 710	70.6	58 900	18.6	12.0	393	22.5	1.4	6 491	4.3	188	2.9	5 758	28.5	16.4
Richardson	3 993	74.7	38 900	17.6	10.7	298	20.7	1.3	4 382	4.0	286	6.5	4 343	28.6	18.6
Rock	763	73.1	37 800	22.9	11.9	282	16.5	2.6	909	4.5	39	4.3	901	39.2	9.8
Saline	5 188	70.8	69 000	18.9	10.6	443	19.2	3.1	7 678	3.0	235	3.1	7 039	29.1	28.3
Sarpy	43 426	69.2	112 100	20.1	9.9	607	22.6	2.1	65 222	0.5	2 118	3.2	61 347	36.8	10.1
Saunders	7 498	79.6	87 800	20.0	10.7	474	21.4	2.2	11 670	4.5	438	3.8	10 276	28.5	18.6
Scotts Bluff	14 887	66.2	71 500	19.2	11.5	433	24.9	3.8	19 560	4.6	963	4.9	17 258	31.1	13.7
Seward	6 013	72.0	88 100	19.6	10.4	449	21.5	1.6	9 045	2.0	327	3.6	8 662	31.4	16.9
Sheridan	2 549	69.9	41 700	19.1	11.9	369	20.9	2.8	3 029	8.8	69	2.3	3 008	36.9	8.0
Sherman	1 394	80.6	38 000	19.6	12.4	350	20.7	3.4	1 571	2.5	50	3.2	1 636	33.4	15.5
Sioux	605	66.8	42 600	25.0	10.5	413	18.8	3.3	791	4.5	17	2.1	718	50.3	8.4
Stanton	2 297	80.1	67 200	21.0	10.6	411	18.9	2.2	3 785	11.9	130	3.4	3 295	30.2	19.3
Thayer	2 541	80.0	38 800	18.1	11.0	321	18.4	1.6	3 309	2.8	73	2.2	2 882	34.3	16.0
Thomas	325	73.5	34 300	12.8	9.9	300	14.1	0.6	461	3.6	17	3.7	383	34.7	12.8
Thurston	2 255	60.8	50 600	16.6	10.6	301	15.7	12.7	3 024	7.2	282	9.3	2 550	31.1	14.5
Valley	1 965	75.8	45 000	19.1	11.9	289	22.7	0.9	2 734	6.4	81	3.0	2 241	33.2	11.8
Washington	6 940	77.3	114 300	20.7	11.1	539	22.0	2.1	11 147	0.6	334	3.0	10 146	32.6	12.0
Wayne	3 437	64.8	76 700	17.8	11.8	404	24.8	1.3	6 379	3.5	211	3.3	5 437	30.0	14.3
Webster	1 708	78.3	38 300	19.2	11.3	301	17.6	0.8	1 625	-2.5	60	3.7	1 804	34.2	14.6
Wheeler	352	70.2	35 000	18.8	10.7	270	10.0	3.1	408	2.0	12	2.9	456	42.8	9.6
York	5 722	69.6	74 900	18.9	10.6	439	22.5	1.5	9 271	11.3	249	2.7	7 260	29.2	16.9
NEVADA	751 165	60.9	142 000	23.8	9.9	699	26.5	8.9	1 141 351	1.1	59 439	5.2	933 280	25.7	10.4
Churchill	8 912	65.8	117 100	20.6	9.9	595	23.0	5.9	9 709	-1.5	589	6.1	10 288	26.4	14.4
Clark	512 253	59.1	139 500	23.9	9.9	716	27.0	9.5	813 832	1.7	43 057	5.3	637 339	24.4	9.5
Douglas	16 401	74.2	181 800	24.2	9.9	780	26.1	3.5	20 332	-0.2	1 097	5.4	19 348	33.4	8.7
Elko	15 638	69.8	123 100	20.2	9.9	583	21.2	8.4	19 788	-2.3	1 097	5.5	21 613	23.6	10.9
Esmeralda	455	66.4	75 600	18.8	9.9	381	13.8	3.3	440	-4.1	17	3.9	443	24.2	13.5
Eureka	666	74.0	89 200	20.2	9.9	469	15.5	8.0	743	-1.5	42	5.7	720	31.7	4.7
Humboldt	5 733	73.0	117 400	19.1	9.9	531	19.0	10.2	7 183	-0.9	360	5.0	7 017	25.7	14.2
Lander	2 093	77.1	82 400	16.5	9.9	496	18.4	7.5	2 022	-8.5	143	7.1	2 528	24.4	19.1
Lincoln	1 540	74.7	80 300	18.9	10.7	328	26.6	4.3	1 028	-10.2	68	6.6	1 458	25.2	9.0
Lyon	13 007	75.9	119 200	23.7	9.9	591	24.1	5.4	15 500	-0.6	1 064	6.9	15 399	25.4	17.5
Mineral	2 197	72.7	59 500	18.4	9.9	398	17.9	3.8	1 909	-3.4	123	6.4	2 061	26.4	11.3
Nye	13 309	76.4	122 100	23.2	9.9	541	22.0	4.9	17 346	2.5	1 119	6.5	12 323	21.6	12.5
Pershing	1 962	69.4	82 200	18.7	11.5	498	20.9	9.1	2 178	-3.2	119	5.5	2 268	22.7	17.1
Storey	1 462	79.7	134 800	23.2	9.9	513	18.2	3.3	1 720	-1.3	55	3.2	1 782	25.9	12.8
Washoe	132 084	59.3	161 600	24.4	9.9	675	26.2	8.9	200 069	0.2	8 793	4.4	171 723	29.5	12.1
White Pine	3 282	76.5	70 000	19.6	13.1	452	19.6	4.4	2 877	-5.4	112	3.9	3 321	26.1	9.4
Carson City city	20 171	63.1	147 500	22.6	9.9	650	26.6	6.6	24 674	-0.3	1 584	6.4	23 649	30.2	13.8
NEW HAMPSHIRE	474 606	69.7	133 300	22.3	13.6	646	24.2	2.1	718 885	1.8	30 734	4.3	650 871	35.8	14.8
Belknap	22 459	74.1	109 600	22.6	13.2	588	24.5	1.8	30 628	-0.3	1 107	3.6	28 848	30.7	16.1
Carroll	18 351	77.7	119 900	23.3	13.4	552	24.1	2.1	23 859	0.5	743	3.1	21 418	30.0	10.5
Cheshire	28 299	70.9	105 300	23.1	14.5	596	25.8	1.9	40 168	0.1	1 270	3.2	38 065	32.4	17.7
Coos	13 961	71.1	70 500	19.6	14.7	399	24.1	1.8	16 994	0.2	836	4.9	15 686	24.3	22.0
Grafton	31 598	68.6	109 500	21.3	12.7	560	24.4	1.9	47 240	5.5	1 011	2.1	42 329	36.6	13.4
Hillsborough	144 455	64.9	139 100	22.1	13.7	694	24.2	2.4	224 213	2.4	10 745	4.8	202 366	37.8	14.8
Merrimack	51 843	69.5	117 900	21.9	13.0	613	24.1	1.9	83 923	2.7	2 591	3.1	70 851	36.0	13.1
Rockingham	104 529	75.6	164 900	22.8	13.4	717	23.3	1.6	166 754	0.8	9 360	5.6	151 291	38.4	13.1
Strafford	42 581	64.4	121 000	22.3	14.2	623	24.9	2.5	64 087	1.4	2 490	3.9	59 534	34.0	16.0
Sullivan	16 530	72.1	91 900	22.1	14.1	537	23.7	1.9	21 021	2.0	581	2.8	20 483	27.9	23.3
NEW JERSEY	3 064 645	65.6	170 800	23.7	15.3	751	25.5	5.4	4 375 020	0.5	256 983	5.9	3 950 029	38.0	12.0
Atlantic	95 024	66.3	122 000	24.7	15.7	677	26.7	5.8	134 273	2.8	9 321	6.9	116 051	25.6	9.1
Bergen	330 817	67.2	250 300	24.5	15.7	872	25.2	4.7	447 757	-0.1	22 048	4.9	435 277	43.1	9.1
Burlington	154 371	77.4	137 400	23.3	14.5	758	24.6	2.3	232 622	0.9	10 777	4.6	205 886	38.7	11.3
Camden	185 744	70.0	111 200	23.3	15.6	635	26.7	4.7	262 182	1.1	15 911	6.1	235 355	35.5	12.3
Cape May	42 148	74.3	137 600	24.8	16.1	650	27.7	2.0	46 070	2.7	4 575	9.9	44 503	31.5	8.0
Cumberland	49 143	67.9	91 200	22.8	14.0	616	28.7	5.8	66 369	2.3	5 739	8.6	59 129	24.8	20.9
Essex	283 736	45.6	208 400	24.2	16.1	675	26.3	8.6	388 814	1.0	28 255	7.3	336 390	35.6	12.9
Gloucester	90 717	79.9	120 100	23.1	14.5	645	26.4	2.0	137 393	1.2	7 568	5.5	124 786	33.3	13.6
Hudson	230 546	30.6	150 300	26.5	17.9	703	24.8	12.4	286 851	-2.7	22 967	8.0	271 770	32.3	17.0
Hunterdon	43 678	83.7	245 000	23.7	14.1	867	25.3	1.0	67 523	-1.3	2 640	3.9	63 448	49.0	7.5

1. Specified owner-occupied units.   2. Median monthly owner costs is often in the minimum category—9.9 percent or less, which is indicated as 9.9 percent.   3. Specified renter-occupied units.   4. Overcrowded or lacking complete plumbing facilities.   5. Percent of civilian labor force.   6. Persons 16 years old and over.

STATE County	Private nonfarm establishments, employment and payroll, 2001									Agriculture, 2002			
		Employment						Annual payroll		Farms			
											Percent with—		
	Number of establishments	Total	Health care and social assistance	Manufacturing	Retail trade	Finance and insurance	Professional, scientific, and technical services	Total (mil dol)	Average per employee (dollars)	Number	Less than 50 acres	500 acres and over	Farm operators whose principal occupation is farming (percent)
	104	105	106	107	108	109	110	111	112	113	114	115	116
NEBRASKA—Cont'd													
Platte	997	15 237	1 165	5 622	2 145	510	455	372	24 418	1 000	19.0	30.7	79.1
Polk	142	1 131	281	D	122	50	29	19	16 679	527	12.0	37.0	79.1
Red Willow	443	4 127	630	498	1 091	159	129	80	19 342	380	17.4	55.0	72.6
Richardson	288	2 184	433	404	382	122	62	41	18 922	732	10.9	29.5	60.1
Rock	63	348	D	D	71	16	D	5	15 486	271	8.1	64.2	82.3
Saline	303	5 729	535	2 736	505	139	43	148	25 750	728	13.5	34.6	75.4
Sarpy	2 325	29 278	3 106	2 187	5 339	2 176	2 102	778	26 561	355	41.4	20.8	53.0
Saunders	460	3 317	506	484	594	173	130	69	20 668	1 157	22.7	26.8	69.7
Scotts Bluff	1 198	13 149	2 470	1 245	2 565	526	694	305	23 177	780	17.9	26.2	65.0
Seward	422	5 703	698	1 041	526	234	88	115	20 196	862	22.2	30.0	67.4
Sheridan	194	1 140	224	D	339	67	38	17	15 010	613	7.7	57.3	75.5
Sherman	78	448	81	D	109	28	15	7	15 272	448	10.5	41.7	77.2
Sioux	14	37	0	0	18	D	D	0	10 703	318	3.8	65.4	78.9
Stanton	87	453	10	D	86	33	7	7	15 826	655	13.4	26.7	67.3
Thayer	217	1 786	412	407	227	123	28	41	22 733	558	9.9	45.7	77.8
Thomas	36	169	0	D	19	D	D	3	19 959	79	6.3	77.2	74.7
Thurston	126	1 367	387	240	214	D	30	31	23 012	438	18.5	31.5	71.5
Valley	172	1 087	304	D	215	62	58	20	18 631	419	11.7	47.5	77.3
Washington	500	5 646	654	1 019	870	172	144	162	28 751	760	31.1	22.5	64.3
Wayne	257	3 699	379	1 676	422	343	82	80	21 610	623	17.3	30.5	72.7
Webster	92	632	180	D	133	36	D	11	17 755	449	11.8	43.9	67.0
Wheeler	17	92	0	D	18	D	0	1	9 402	194	10.8	58.8	75.8
York	514	6 725	789	1 210	906	348	129	157	23 376	617	13.9	45.4	77.8
NEVADA	48 863	916 981	71 693	40 147	111 982	32 858	42 395	27 538	30 031	2 989	46.7	24.2	58.7
Churchill	489	5 479	729	509	1 040	145	640	135	24 649	498	53.6	9.6	59.4
Clark	30 365	650 239	46 806	18 985	76 824	24 093	30 059	19 522	30 023	253	79.8	3.2	42.7
Douglas	1 340	18 151	516	2 144	1 379	308	651	523	28 827	178	59.0	16.9	53.4
Elko	978	16 227	988	133	2 125	365	583	464	28 582	397	31.5	41.8	66.2
Esmeralda	13	112	0	D	D	0	D	4	38 696	18	2.8	61.1	83.3
Eureka	37	2 270	D	D	61	D	0	125	54 912	73	5.5	58.9	79.5
Humboldt	378	5 194	358	333	847	65	103	168	32 276	233	28.8	47.2	70.4
Lander	88	1 172	109	143	205	D	D	36	30 972	116	37.9	33.6	62.9
Lincoln	89	585	D	D	179	54	D	10	16 472	109	34.9	20.2	61.5
Lyon	522	6 820	503	1 341	1 558	65	310	176	25 832	330	47.6	18.8	64.2
Mineral	92	1 200	211	D	117	43	D	29	24 076	17	41.2	29.4	76.5
Nye	560	5 739	373	247	972	129	D	146	25 361	172	55.2	22.1	55.8
Pershing	93	1 227	111	39	216	D	10	39	31 665	115	17.4	41.7	64.3
Storey	76	438	D	D	D	D	D	9	20 311	6	100.0	0.0	33.3
Washoe	11 161	174 173	17 501	11 787	21 910	6 331	8 515	5 333	30 621	332	64.2	14.2	41.6
White Pine	205	1 699	363	21	347	D	D	44	26 026	121	24.8	34.7	55.4
Carson City city	2 333	24 411	3 010	4 236	4 126	1 152	1 388	712	29 171	21	52.4	19.0	61.9
NEW HAMPSHIRE	37 312	556 877	70 316	96 262	93 210	23 637	26 701	18 494	33 210	3 363	45.9	5.2	48.6
Belknap	1 868	21 388	3 016	4 521	4 702	695	552	606	28 353	231	48.1	3.5	43.7
Carroll	1 851	20 076	2 515	1 725	3 632	511	2 389	454	22 634	229	43.7	4.8	40.6
Cheshire	1 967	29 502	4 018	6 190	5 123	2 011	665	836	28 337	323	43.0	5.6	48.9
Coos	975	D	2 212	1 676	2 154	298	142	D	D	208	30.3	9.1	46.6
Grafton	2 917	50 038	8 153	6 124	7 073	910	1 395	1 401	28 001	421	28.7	10.5	51.1
Hillsborough	10 781	182 450	21 751	37 319	27 708	7 608	9 954	6 783	37 180	481	59.9	1.7	48.0
Merrimack	4 034	56 389	9 477	9 377	8 840	3 935	2 378	1 764	31 281	502	45.0	7.2	51.8
Rockingham	9 388	128 759	11 968	18 428	25 241	5 363	7 055	4 785	37 164	445	60.0	1.1	52.1
Strafford	2 478	35 523	5 467	6 927	6 265	1 912	1 950	1 126	31 701	281	47.0	3.2	56.9
Sullivan	1 052	12 349	1 739	3 975	2 472	394	221	324	26 276	242	39.3	6.6	36.8
NEW JERSEY	234 558	3 622 788	433 354	379 647	434 008	221 268	282 874	154 239	42 575	9 924	70.5	3.5	52.3
Atlantic	6 423	119 759	13 069	4 668	14 766	2 682	5 490	3 620	30 225	456	70.8	1.8	63.4
Bergen	33 205	474 632	52 658	50 692	53 043	27 071	30 732	21 591	45 491	91	93.4	0.0	53.8
Burlington	10 411	172 031	20 451	21 547	24 108	18 169	11 494	6 230	36 212	906	69.2	6.8	56.4
Camden	12 528	181 069	30 677	19 313	26 191	7 972	14 201	6 054	33 434	216	79.2	1.4	57.4
Cape May	4 012	26 099	3 716	915	5 452	917	1 239	736	28 215	197	77.2	1.0	64.0
Cumberland	2 997	44 657	6 954	10 778	7 013	1 308	1 351	1 347	30 157	616	62.8	5.4	61.9
Essex	19 748	334 071	52 807	33 232	28 437	20 593	26 339	13 856	41 476	15	100.0	0.0	53.3
Gloucester	5 742	79 874	9 439	10 580	14 068	2 051	2 967	2 528	31 652	692	69.4	3.2	52.7
Hudson	13 471	223 542	20 973	17 313	21 080	30 754	11 287	10 625	47 530	0	NA	NA	NA
Hunterdon	3 968	44 628	5 177	4 591	6 342	1 019	4 560	1 996	44 724	1 514	70.2	2.4	47.2

Table B. States and Counties — Agriculture

STATE County	Acreage (1,000)	Percent change, 1997-2002	Average size of farm	Total irrigated (1,000)	Total cropland (1,000)	Average per farm	Average per acre	Value of machinery and equipment average per farm (dollars)	Total (mil dol)	Average per farm (dollars)	Crops	Live-stock and poultry products	$10,000 or more	$100,000 or more	Total ($1,000)	Percent of farms
	117	118	119	120	121	122	123	124	125	126	127	128	129	130	131	132
NEBRASKA—Cont'd																
Platte	435	3.6	435	179	365	748 042	1 700	126 256	199	199 414	36.3	63.7	77.4	38.2	6 399	66.8
Polk	264	1.9	502	144	226	972 107	1 851	142 746	149	281 900	33.3	66.7	82.9	45.4	3 323	63.4
Red Willow	429	-1.6	1 129	45	252	670 406	569	138 978	96	251 374	24.7	75.3	73.7	30.8	2 683	60.3
Richardson	321	0.6	438	1	245	417 609	973	78 948	53	72 335	54.3	45.7	58.2	20.1	5 247	79.4
Rock	629	-0.3	2 320	34	178	753 385	319	85 990	55	203 484	16.3	83.7	70.5	38.4	1 956	52.0
Saline	345	8.5	474	94	282	621 676	1 317	104 244	66	90 268	71.6	28.4	69.2	28.2	5 165	69.5
Sarpy	105	2.9	296	10	91	1 065 732	3 567	70 567	47	131 778	34.2	65.8	48.7	17.7	1 129	51.0
Saunders	458	5.0	396	97	400	767 441	2 023	133 143	151	130 786	50.7	49.3	63.9	23.9	5 816	64.0
Scotts Bluff	427	-3.6	548	173	234	373 762	648	96 063	191	245 060	23.7	76.3	67.7	27.4	2 517	54.1
Seward	364	13.4	422	128	306	772 875	1 786	119 356	117	135 455	50.9	49.1	61.8	26.1	5 057	67.6
Sheridan	1 486	-0.1	2 424	51	317	574 154	253	87 741	70	114 830	25.7	74.3	67.4	28.9	3 197	58.2
Sherman	316	-2.5	706	61	143	492 988	621	82 974	43	97 073	42.3	57.7	72.1	27.7	2 828	67.9
Sioux	1 103	-1.1	3 469	40	118	973 961	277	100 373	67	211 224	12.5	87.5	77.4	34.3	1 162	55.0
Stanton	243	7.5	371	21	185	524 111	1 317	74 224	82	125 868	32.0	68.0	61.7	25.5	4 123	73.4
Thayer	380	3.3	682	133	296	862 079	1 333	131 894	101	181 474	59.3	40.7	74.6	42.1	4 928	72.9
Thomas	349	-5.4	4 415	2	13	895 711	205	56 452	11	133 712	D	D	70.9	34.2	315	35.4
Thurston	214	13.2	489	10	192	671 630	1 335	107 671	93	211 551	38.6	61.4	61.6	32.4	3 204	73.5
Valley	315	-5.4	751	78	152	487 500	674	104 771	71	168 541	30.2	69.8	76.1	30.8	2 497	62.8
Washington	242	10.5	319	20	211	726 531	2 252	93 469	86	112 808	46.1	53.9	59.2	24.5	3 133	58.2
Wayne	281	9.3	452	30	245	624 954	1 458	93 269	117	187 022	33.8	66.2	70.8	32.6	4 091	70.8
Webster	318	1.3	709	49	183	597 946	850	83 729	84	187 641	27.0	73.0	65.0	24.9	3 533	69.3
Wheeler	338	15.4	1 743	46	121	899 296	525	134 128	146	753 372	7.7	92.3	77.3	45.9	1 960	58.8
York	354	0.3	573	242	319	1 103 666	2 009	180 841	161	260 669	56.3	43.7	82.8	52.4	4 992	64.8
NEVADA	6 331	-1.2	2 118	747	940	953 619	446	110 619	447	149 545	35.3	64.7	44.6	19.4	4 322	14.7
Churchill	149	15.5	300	50	54	409 362	1 563	81 819	51	101 637	22.2	77.8	46.0	15.7	455	14.3
Clark	69	-2.8	272	D	10	962 798	3 567	54 791	17	67 207	39.0	61.0	19.4	6.3	34	5.1
Douglas	211	134.4	1 185	31	79	1 087 216	840	82 400	9	51 306	46.4	53.7	31.5	8.4	138	9.6
Elko	2 472	-13.4	6 227	183	203	1 001 634	164	71 802	45	114 133	3.7	96.3	47.4	21.9	1 581	21.9
Esmeralda	D	D	D	16	18	1 528 588	1 042	164 176	D	D	D	D	72.2	72.2	D	D
Eureka	266	23.7	3 650	42	53	815 230	230	152 656	13	173 412	70.7	29.3	82.2	52.1	120	23.3
Humboldt	761	3.8	3 267	138	174	1 212 650	380	202 630	55	235 832	68.4	31.6	63.1	40.8	707	29.2
Lander	620	27.6	5 347	45	60	1 273 980	247	144 158	21	177 715	49.8	50.2	58.6	30.2	123	17.2
Lincoln	D	D	D	21	26	517 501	1 058	126 743	11	105 051	62.0	38.0	48.6	17.4	31	9.2
Lyon	226	29.9	686	57	72	913 744	1 405	126 925	74	225 668	49.3	50.7	49.7	18.8	316	10.9
Mineral	D	NA	D	10	9	2 894 659	193	223 412	3	180 868	D	D	35.3	23.5	0	0.0
Nye	98	14.0	567	36	41	528 199	1 044	104 129	22	130 346	19.5	80.5	39.0	12.2	78	11.6
Pershing	131	10.1	1 140	29	53	805 471	680	138 432	26	223 544	33.5	66.5	69.6	31.3	218	25.2
Storey	0	NA	15	D	0	600 000	32 143	13 933	D	D	0.0	0.0	0.0	0.0	0	0.0
Washoe	802	3.9	2 416	45	50	1 748 915	595	113 293	18	53 556	55.7	44.3	22.6	8.1	222	6.0
White Pine	203	-17.8	1 679	34	37	887 634	544	145 253	76	628 302	5.2	94.8	57.0	28.1	242	20.7
Carson City city	4	-42.9	209	2	2	651 109	3 235	75 258	1	44 199	21.8	78.2	47.6	4.8	D	D
NEW HAMPSHIRE	445	7.2	132	2	129	400 943	3 131	40 868	145	43 067	57.4	42.6	26.2	7.5	3 823	10.7
Belknap	23	9.5	101	0	6	368 252	3 444	34 181	5	21 140	65.2	34.8	19.0	5.2	64	6.1
Carroll	30	25.0	130	0	7	402 315	2 833	41 214	4	18 035	68.4	31.6	17.9	3.5	92	4.8
Cheshire	41	-2.4	128	0	12	407 379	3 176	42 906	12	38 110	27.3	72.8	28.5	7.1	447	9.6
Coos	44	2.3	212	0	14	231 580	1 196	39 041	9	43 351	18.8	81.2	26.9	9.1	386	17.8
Grafton	86	13.2	204	0	25	370 970	2 147	44 631	20	47 033	17.3	82.7	30.9	10.2	1 063	20.2
Hillsborough	40	5.3	83	0	14	477 112	5 619	33 501	15	30 701	76.0	24.0	26.4	6.2	470	7.9
Merrimack	79	25.4	158	1	19	380 947	2 683	47 705	41	81 996	82.7	17.3	27.1	8.2	487	10.2
Rockingham	32	-8.6	71	0	11	459 477	6 824	35 995	17	38 101	78.2	21.8	26.3	7.6	290	5.6
Strafford	34	30.8	120	0	10	370 844	2 910	36 669	10	35 136	62.9	37.1	26.7	5.3	131	11.7
Sullivan	36	-23.4	149	0	12	435 887	2 559	53 408	12	49 328	32.8	67.2	25.6	11.6	393	14.0
NEW JERSEY	806	-3.2	81	97	548	741 808	9 245	53 954	750	75 561	87.7	12.3	29.0	10.7	4 441	5.9
Atlantic	30	-3.2	67	12	19	414 096	5 796	76 470	79	172 166	99.0	1.0	39.9	19.7	D	D
Bergen	1	-66.7	14	0	1	684 924	48 159	32 405	8	83 123	96.4	3.6	52.7	18.7	D	D
Burlington	111	6.7	123	14	67	867 945	6 778	65 531	83	91 891	87.5	12.5	36.6	14.2	629	5.8
Camden	10	11.1	47	2	7	519 176	11 446	34 859	14	63 141	99.1	1.0	29.6	10.6	D	D
Cape May	10	0.0	51	2	5	341 959	7 049	31 825	11	57 110	95.6	4.4	24.9	8.1	D	D
Cumberland	71	7.6	115	19	54	585 323	4 714	88 585	123	199 143	97.8	2.2	45.3	23.7	254	7.6
Essex	0	NA	10	0	0	495 369	45 867	28 048	1	49 116	98.8	1.2	46.7	20.0	0	0.0
Gloucester	51	-12.1	73	12	37	671 557	9 485	55 112	66	95 389	93.9	6.1	28.5	15.2	405	5.2
Hudson	0	NA	0	0	0	0	0	0	0	0	0.0	0.0	0.0	0.0	0	0.0
Hunterdon	109	3.8	72	1	78	882 975	11 994	41 567	42	27 917	82.1	17.9	20.5	3.7	427	6.7

Table B. States and Counties — Residential Construction, Wholesale Trade, Retail Trade, and Real Estate

STATE County	Value of residential construction authorized by building permits, 2003 — New construction ($1,000)	Number of housing units	Wholesale trade, 1997 — Number of establishments	Number of employees	Sales (mil dol)	Annual payroll (mil dol)	Retail trade,[1] 1997 — Number of establishments	Number of employees	Sales (mil dol)	Annual payroll (mil dol)	Real estate and rental and leasing, 1997 — Number of establishments	Number of employees	Receipts (mil dol)	Annual payroll (mil dol)
	133	134	135	136	137	138	139	140	141	142	143	144	145	146
NEBRASKA—Cont'd														
Platte	8 456	52	55	680	324.8	14.8	176	1 984	293.7	27.9	23	90	7.1	1.0
Polk	315	2	11	141	117.1	4.0	24	126	23.8	1.7	1	D	D	D
Red Willow	1 431	11	20	119	D	D	109	1 124	176.3	15.7	14	51	3.3	0.5
Richardson	549	4	25	119	74.0	2.6	66	387	59.4	4.6	7	11	1.0	0.1
Rock	0	0	7	D	D	D	10	57	6.4	0.6	NA	NA	NA	NA
Saline	4 339	31	15	109	72.7	2.8	62	584	95.6	8.9	6	24	1.1	0.4
Sarpy	291 824	2 236	84	D	D	D	291	4 663	695.6	63.7	72	D	D	D
Saunders	20 521	152	21	150	72.1	2.7	79	602	92.8	7.5	8	14	1.2	0.2
Scotts Bluff	6 391	53	79	826	225.8	19.0	239	2 624	391.9	38.8	40	136	9.2	1.9
Seward	11 156	72	25	235	94.2	5.9	63	564	80.7	6.8	10	45	1.6	0.3
Sheridan	0	0	17	245	117.2	3.6	58	397	56.9	4.4	4	D	D	D
Sherman	1 141	12	4	D	D	D	18	84	17.8	1.2	1	D	D	D
Sioux	NA	NA	2	D	D	D	5	17	2.2	0.2	NA	NA	NA	NA
Stanton	1 771	13	5	D	D	D	13	59	8.2	0.8	4	11	0.3	0.1
Thayer	366	3	16	112	96.0	2.1	45	285	44.2	3.5	3	D	D	D
Thomas	NA	NA	1	D	D	D	6	27	4.2	0.3	1	D	D	D
Thurston	665	5	9	54	31.4	1.2	29	239	42.4	3.1	1	D	D	D
Valley	300	3	13	151	101.4	3.1	38	226	27.3	2.9	3	8	0.4	0.1
Washington	17 050	112	22	D	D	D	72	675	233.9	14.3	14	D	D	D
Wayne	830	5	11	D	D	D	46	386	47.0	4.5	7	D	D	D
Webster	95	2	13	103	48.4	2.0	22	143	21.3	2.0	NA	NA	NA	NA
Wheeler	0	0	1	D	D	D	4	16	1.7	0.1	NA	NA	NA	NA
York	2 798	23	38	363	207.4	10.2	98	1 027	160.2	13.9	12	24	1.9	0.3
NEVADA	4 879 197	43 366	2 253	27 251	12 806.9	918.5	6 222	89 452	18 220.8	1 798.2	2 460	16 890	2 276.5	381.5
Churchill	16 022	121	17	123	29.3	2.3	87	1 023	177.6	16.9	21	80	4.1	0.8
Clark	3 888 554	36 732	1 298	15 824	6 366.0	526.9	3 803	58 477	12 321.5	1 201.7	1 521	12 437	1 672.5	291.4
Douglas	107 865	629	46	205	67.6	6.8	141	1 143	203.3	23.5	95	506	61.1	8.8
Elko	10 412	96	61	636	268.9	24.2	171	2 226	426.8	39.1	34	237	22.3	4.2
Esmeralda	NA	NA	1	D	D	D	2	D	D	D	NA	NA	NA	NA
Eureka	NA	NA	3	4	3.4	0.1	7	D	D	D	1	D	D	D
Humboldt	3 437	26	29	161	64.2	4.4	79	967	193.7	15.7	11	23	2.1	0.2
Lander	300	4	7	46	19.8	1.0	20	311	36.6	4.0	3	12	2.3	0.1
Lincoln	1 042	14	1	D	D	D	15	141	12.5	1.5	5	14	0.6	0.1
Lyon	70 040	487	26	145	46.0	4.5	81	723	140.6	13.9	22	63	6.9	0.8
Mineral	242	8	2	D	D	D	23	172	32.1	2.7	2	D	D	D
Nye	0	0	19	D	D	D	107	777	140.4	13.0	20	62	4.3	0.7
Pershing	115	1	2	D	D	D	21	177	36.4	2.4	2	D	D	D
Storey	4 407	36	2	D	D	D	24	82	7.5	1.4	1	D	D	D
Washoe	740 251	4 997	639	9 339	5 663.6	324.9	1 328	19 418	3 751.1	389.5	614	3 058	444.5	66.1
White Pine	1 750	12	12	64	17.6	1.6	51	376	55.5	6.1	6	27	3.2	0.6
Carson City city	34 761	203	88	557	222.4	18.7	262	3 383	678.4	66.1	102	343	51.2	7.4
NEW HAMPSHIRE	1 207 854	8 641	2 033	22 631	11 371.1	875.0	6 645	84 170	15 890.1	1 428.2	1 399	6 639	719.4	151.1
Belknap	91 651	672	74	628	181.7	25.9	414	4 073	713.8	69.2	75	241	26.6	4.9
Carroll	105 976	649	61	371	80.8	10.6	428	3 267	551.1	55.4	73	314	33.6	6.5
Cheshire	54 082	384	92	1 187	403.5	37.6	402	5 097	1 155.4	92.0	68	312	26.2	5.9
Coos	10 932	91	27	308	81.0	6.6	229	1 959	423.8	32.8	23	111	6.2	1.1
Grafton	84 591	576	112	944	333.4	31.6	589	6 164	1 031.6	110.2	122	432	38.8	7.9
Hillsborough	299 055	2 051	721	8 588	4 792.9	366.4	1 692	25 208	4 927.0	455.6	436	2 269	233.8	53.1
Merrimack	145 667	1 028	189	2 328	799.5	78.0	628	7 629	1 500.7	127.7	139	882	116.2	20.2
Rockingham	287 248	1 987	605	6 504	4 328.9	271.2	1 617	22 905	4 218.8	356.8	331	1 702	192.0	45.2
Strafford	90 424	934	109	1 508	281.0	39.9	436	5 807	1 020.0	92.8	91	279	34.8	4.9
Sullivan	38 227	269	43	265	88.4	7.4	210	2 061	347.8	35.8	41	97	11.2	1.4
NEW JERSEY	3 781 901	32 984	17 812	266 944	227 366.7	11 886.1	34 837	420 724	79 914.9	7 926.0	8 292	47 558	8 881.9	1 376.5
Atlantic	249 261	2 285	234	2 312	831.5	81.0	1 258	14 308	2 513.2	253.8	236	1 424	203.3	27.0
Bergen	263 954	1 289	3 876	55 657	62 435.3	2 713.6	4 284	52 065	10 766.1	1 052.8	1 360	8 772	1 821.6	278.9
Burlington	189 915	1 805	769	13 262	16 206.9	547.1	1 570	22 857	4 410.8	426.6	322	2 872	788.8	85.9
Camden	161 761	1 934	922	10 789	6 139.0	400.0	2 052	26 577	4 612.4	481.0	376	3 159	432.5	92.7
Cape May	233 617	1 693	74	907	201.0	21.6	784	4 990	961.1	102.7	208	589	126.5	18.9
Cumberland	39 439	374	189	2 230	989.4	69.4	578	7 157	1 226.5	130.1	115	486	52.0	9.4
Essex	202 680	2 235	1 478	23 082	17 599.5	1 025.5	2 819	27 068	4 518.1	512.9	915	6 280	1 084.7	165.4
Gloucester	188 439	1 859	381	6 268	6 023.1	218.8	989	14 030	2 441.7	231.3	152	663	81.8	14.2
Hudson	190 118	2 116	1 065	21 629	11 271.5	864.6	2 327	22 670	3 842.9	384.9	542	3 070	628.1	96.1
Hunterdon	128 795	814	208	1 595	1 201.5	74.9	600	6 415	1 454.5	143.7	98	270	57.2	6.2

1. Establishments with payroll.

Table B. States and Counties — Professional Services, Manufacturing, and Accommodation and Foodservices

STATE County	Professional, scientific, and technical services,[1] 1997				Manufacturing, 1997				Accommodation and foodservices, 1997			
	Number of establishments	Number of employees	Receipts (mil dol)	Annual payroll (mil dol)	Number of establishments	Number of employees	Receipts (mil dol)	Annual payroll (mil dol)	Number of establishments	Number of employees	Sales (mil dol)	Annual payroll (mil dol)
	147	148	149	150	151	152	153	154	155	156	157	158
NEBRASKA—Cont'd												
Platte	54	307	23.1	8.4	74	6 120	1 217.2	164.1	75	1 130	29.7	8.3
Polk	9	18	1.1	0.2	NA	NA	NA	NA	12	56	1.5	0.3
Red Willow	29	119	6.1	2.3	NA	NA	NA	NA	39	536	12.7	3.5
Richardson	16	41	2.0	0.6	NA	NA	NA	NA	26	214	4.7	1.3
Rock	2	D	D	D	NA	NA	NA	NA	9	33	0.7	0.2
Saline	16	36	1.7	0.6	19	2 512	659.9	64.7	39	442	10.0	2.7
Sarpy	141	1 410	146.1	55.8	55	D	D	D	155	2 462	72.2	20.5
Saunders	21	95	5.6	2.8	NA	NA	NA	NA	39	D	D	D
Scotts Bluff	68	379	19.3	9.1	54	1 732	357.5	46.2	100	1 207	33.1	9.2
Seward	21	48	3.7	0.7	18	1 039	111.7	30.1	37	589	12.6	3.2
Sheridan	8	20	1.0	0.3	NA	NA	NA	NA	24	D	D	D
Sherman	4	D	D	D	NA	NA	NA	NA	9	D	D	D
Sioux	1	D	D	D	NA	NA	NA	NA	2	D	D	D
Stanton	3	D	D	D	NA	NA	NA	NA	6	D	D	D
Thayer	9	21	1.0	0.2	NA	NA	NA	NA	14	124	2.4	0.5
Thomas	NA	NA	NA	NA	NA	NA	NA	NA	4	43	1.0	0.3
Thurston	4	13	0.9	0.1	NA	NA	NA	NA	8	95	3.0	1.3
Valley	12	46	1.6	0.8	NA	NA	NA	NA	20	D	D	D
Washington	21	D	D	D	21	861	372.1	25.1	45	489	11.8	3.0
Wayne	13	28	1.6	0.4	15	1 473	221.3	28.6	26	411	7.6	2.0
Webster	3	D	D	D	NA	NA	NA	NA	9	40	1.3	0.3
Wheeler	NA	NA	NA	NA	NA	NA	NA	NA	5	D	D	D
York	22	117	6.4	2.4	33	1 207	214.6	32.8	43	804	22.1	6.3
NEVADA	4 171	28 963	2 974.4	1 171.1	1 615	37 849	6 361.8	1 178.0	3 632	241 672	15 322.7	4 665.3
Churchill	28	120	6.2	2.8	NA	NA	NA	NA	53	706	26.0	8.0
Clark	2 405	20 281	2 105.8	832.7	814	D	D	D	2 164	185 322	12 412.3	3 771.0
Douglas	149	526	47.0	20.9	65	1 897	241.8	66.3	92	8 414	523.9	151.1
Elko	68	353	27.4	10.9	NA	NA	NA	NA	134	6 268	301.0	78.6
Esmeralda	1	D	D	D	NA	NA	NA	NA	5	12	0.5	0.1
Eureka	NA	NA	NA	NA	NA	NA	NA	NA	6	55	2.0	0.4
Humboldt	18	80	4.9	2.3	NA	NA	NA	NA	53	1 125	46.4	15.2
Lander	1	D	D	D	NA	NA	NA	NA	19	160	5.8	1.3
Lincoln	2	D	D	D	NA	NA	NA	NA	18	100	2.5	0.7
Lyon	31	240	18.4	6.8	50	1 561	280.4	47.9	43	465	15.8	4.4
Mineral	3	8	0.1	0.1	NA	NA	NA	NA	12	258	9.7	3.2
Nye	17	73	13.6	2.4	NA	NA	NA	NA	54	1 035	40.5	12.8
Pershing	4	5	0.3	0.1	NA	NA	NA	NA	21	289	7.6	2.2
Storey	5	16	1.3	0.5	NA	NA	NA	NA	10	49	2.4	0.7
Washoe	1 193	6 422	659.7	259.7	418	11 522	1 931.3	361.9	778	34 517	1 815.8	583.1
White Pine	13	23	3.0	1.7	NA	NA	NA	NA	37	493	17.4	4.8
Carson City city	233	806	86.2	30.2	186	4 157	514.5	120.8	133	2 404	93.1	27.7
NEW HAMPSHIRE	3 341	18 268	1 626.6	713.1	2 328	98 934	19 813.1	3 361.4	3 029	43 964	1 543.5	449.8
Belknap	110	479	36.6	16.4	133	4 658	497.4	133.4	213	2 237	89.1	26.1
Carroll	108	1 906	43.0	23.2	93	1 634	180.7	45.9	269	3 810	143.2	42.4
Cheshire	144	553	41.1	16.7	168	6 212	787.3	196.4	133	2 178	68.9	21.2
Coos	43	142	10.0	4.8	50	3 051	494.3	94.0	121	1 572	56.2	18.2
Grafton	227	1 024	87.9	39.0	148	6 886	881.5	205.6	325	4 761	156.3	47.3
Hillsborough	1 210	7 764	741.2	330.5	737	36 656	6 260.7	1 397.9	702	12 020	412.7	120.6
Merrimack	392	1 938	196.2	85.9	224	9 674	1 314.4	304.9	261	3 807	126.1	36.2
Rockingham	873	3 862	386.0	161.0	500	16 582	6 596.5	573.3	727	9 947	384.2	109.3
Strafford	167	949	68.7	29.0	159	9 080	2 106.2	281.5	209	2 830	84.3	22.1
Sullivan	67	251	15.9	6.6	116	4 501	694.2	128.6	69	780	22.6	6.3
NEW JERSEY	25 849	220 238	25 943.8	10 441.0	11 812	409 788	97 060.8	15 430.2	16 974	251 872	13 407.4	3 608.2
Atlantic	513	3 885	380.8	157.4	160	4 927	600.3	143.0	766	55 638	5 015.2	1 328.3
Bergen	4 134	24 327	3 087.0	1 149.8	1 806	59 877	10 419.7	2 223.7	1 910	24 315	1 116.9	304.0
Burlington	1 048	10 752	1 204.1	466.6	464	18 766	3 945.9	740.7	711	11 085	391.4	109.3
Camden	1 464	11 673	1 073.7	485.3	677	21 055	3 617.6	729.5	881	11 826	440.4	120.2
Cape May	211	795	69.1	26.7	82	813	110.4	19.1	961	4 642	368.1	95.0
Cumberland	200	1 061	88.9	34.1	210	12 985	1 896.1	398.3	218	2 554	78.8	21.1
Essex	2 232	23 080	3 055.9	1 213.8	1 206	35 578	8 416.4	1 359.9	1 320	16 915	853.8	234.2
Gloucester	404	2 099	213.9	71.8	290	11 013	6 882.8	416.5	386	6 419	201.6	53.6
Hudson	977	7 208	931.6	342.8	979	26 470	4 220.8	787.8	1 127	10 056	466.5	119.6
Hunterdon	493	3 163	709.5	183.4	175	5 064	1 104.4	194.8	237	2 439	102.5	28.9

1. Firms subject to federal tax.

Table B. States and Counties — Health Care and Social Assistance, Other Services, and Federal Funds

STATE County	Health care and social assistance,[1] 1997				Other services,[1] 1997				Federal funds and grants, 2002–2003 Expenditures (mil dol)	Direct payments for individuals[2]		
	Number of establishments	Number of employees	Receipts (mil dol)	Annual payroll (mil dol)	Number of establishments	Number of employees	Receipts (mil dol)	Annual payroll (mil dol)	Total	Social Security and government retirement	Medicare	Food stamps and Supplemental Security Income
	159	160	161	162	163	164	165	166	167	168	169	170
NEBRASKA—Cont'd												
Platte	49	561	30.8	14.2	79	309	18.6	5.4	124.2	63.9	15.5	2.4
Polk	7	21	0.9	0.3	10	25	1.7	0.3	36.2	14.2	6.0	0.2
Red Willow	28	185	9.5	3.8	24	93	4.9	1.2	75.0	33.0	11.4	1.3
Richardson	20	248	8.8	3.9	17	57	3.2	0.7	72.5	28.2	12.3	1.2
Rock	3	D	D	D	7	19	1.1	0.3	11.1	5.1	1.5	0.2
Saline	25	237	9.3	4.2	20	67	3.8	0.9	77.9	33.2	10.5	0.8
Sarpy	121	1 820	71.1	37.9	142	753	44.7	14.1	943.4	220.5	27.4	3.6
Saunders	21	234	6.6	3.3	26	57	5.0	0.9	89.3	43.4	16.8	1.0
Scotts Bluff	91	886	58.3	30.2	91	460	25.6	7.4	227.3	98.3	30.9	8.4
Seward	22	262	10.4	5.9	37	117	9.0	2.1	81.5	35.3	9.6	0.8
Sheridan	7	34	2.9	1.0	16	23	1.8	0.3	38.0	18.6	6.3	0.9
Sherman	4	D	D	D	7	9	0.8	0.1	30.3	10.4	3.6	0.2
Sioux	NA	NA	NA	NA	2	D	D	D	9.4	2.3	0.4	0.0
Stanton	4	D	D	D	6	11	1.3	0.2	23.6	8.3	2.7	0.2
Thayer	6	82	3.1	1.7	17	31	3.0	0.4	44.2	18.9	6.4	0.6
Thomas	NA	NA	NA	NA	2	D	D	D	6.4	1.9	1.0	0.1
Thurston	4	D	D	D	7	19	1.5	0.3	71.3	12.8	7.6	1.8
Valley	9	75	3.2	1.5	12	35	3.3	0.5	36.6	14.2	5.6	0.4
Washington	14	108	6.4	2.6	27	74	3.8	1.0	88.0	35.9	12.4	0.7
Wayne	11	228	7.6	3.8	20	65	3.0	0.9	45.1	16.3	5.5	0.6
Webster	8	132	3.3	1.7	4	17	1.6	0.2	37.5	13.0	5.4	0.3
Wheeler	NA	NA	NA	NA	NA	NA	NA	NA	6.6	2.1	0.8	0.1
York	27	154	8.2	3.6	49	205	11.9	3.4	89.1	35.0	12.2	1.2
NEVADA	3 226	39 476	3 406.5	1 358.9	2 175	16 185	1 061.7	328.0	11 637.4	4 561.5	1 352.3	258.8
Churchill	24	234	8.4	4.4	30	102	6.5	1.9	250.8	70.5	19.1	2.4
Clark	2 053	29 105	2 567.0	988.7	1 324	11 045	707.8	221.1	7 170.4	3 078.6	937.9	192.6
Douglas	67	358	28.2	11.3	44	177	11.5	3.2	163.1	104.2	25.3	2.0
Elko	52	459	34.6	13.7	57	422	38.4	9.6	150.2	57.7	12.1	2.0
Esmeralda	NA	NA	NA	NA	1	D	D	D	18.3	14.3	0.5	0.0
Eureka	NA	NA	NA	NA	2	D	D	D	6.4	3.4	1.2	0.0
Humboldt	19	122	8.7	2.7	28	115	6.1	1.7	67.4	26.6	7.5	2.0
Lander	2	D	D	D	4	D	D	D	25.6	8.7	3.0	0.1
Lincoln	2	D	D	D	2	D	D	D	32.7	13.5	3.9	0.4
Lyon	16	100	3.9	1.7	25	256	15.3	5.4	164.4	105.7	24.8	4.0
Mineral	6	135	5.3	2.5	6	15	1.6	0.3	81.4	21.3	5.9	1.7
Nye	19	118	6.8	3.1	22	88	9.6	1.4	205.0	134.4	26.0	4.7
Pershing	3	16	0.3	0.1	1	D	D	D	20.4	8.2	2.8	0.4
Storey	1	D	D	D	NA	NA	NA	NA	6.9	4.5	0.7	0.1
Washoe	779	7 430	649.9	288.0	518	3 269	217.6	68.7	1 736.0	713.8	224.9	38.1
White Pine	11	109	5.6	2.8	7	30	2.1	0.6	65.4	22.2	5.8	1.8
Carson City city	172	1 274	86.7	39.8	104	634	42.2	13.5	648.5	173.1	50.8	5.5
NEW HAMPSHIRE	2 373	28 889	1 734.1	836.3	2 159	11 379	794.5	236.6	7 349.2	2 775.9	898.5	102.0
Belknap	116	1 145	69.8	32.6	108	437	27.6	7.6	327.1	164.4	55.4	6.3
Carroll	82	920	41.2	17.3	67	204	13.6	3.3	253.5	135.8	39.6	4.3
Cheshire	106	1 454	71.2	34.8	126	690	50.7	13.6	355.9	168.2	56.8	6.7
Coos	43	340	16.6	7.7	52	210	18.7	3.8	249.4	101.3	45.0	4.1
Grafton	148	1 312	107.0	64.7	153	753	45.4	13.5	618.5	194.4	66.4	5.7
Hillsborough	742	9 268	587.4	284.8	640	4 143	286.7	93.3	2 137.2	760.3	248.0	33.4
Merrimack	260	3 170	208.9	109.2	265	1 218	96.4	25.4	996.2	296.2	102.2	11.8
Rockingham	580	8 259	465.7	205.7	537	2 853	186.5	58.2	1 243.9	583.4	173.1	13.1
Strafford	230	2 534	136.7	67.4	144	701	50.9	14.5	589.7	261.3	74.9	10.8
Sullivan	66	487	29.7	12.0	67	170	18.0	3.3	219.1	110.2	36.9	5.8
NEW JERSEY	18 905	172 723	13 702.4	5 900.2	15 077	78 644	5 434.8	1 665.1	53 678.8	17 678.1	9 337.8	1 049.1
Atlantic	540	5 024	376.4	175.3	429	2 485	130.7	42.1	1 601.4	566.0	308.7	34.9
Bergen	2 738	24 529	2 115.1	914.8	2 088	11 009	807.5	256.1	4 224.9	1 995.9	1 007.0	50.3
Burlington	747	8 697	624.8	287.6	656	3 844	265.5	87.6	3 712.3	1 053.0	382.9	27.4
Camden	1 144	11 362	836.3	391.6	846	5 239	332.6	100.1	2 935.4	1 087.1	609.2	110.1
Cape May	208	1 289	94.5	43.3	168	803	42.6	14.7	688.0	322.1	180.7	9.0
Cumberland	238	2 191	161.8	74.8	243	1 156	65.2	20.6	874.8	303.4	187.8	31.8
Essex	1 966	17 414	1 352.7	619.9	1 371	8 525	595.8	191.2	5 493.8	1 366.9	981.0	216.8
Gloucester	385	4 443	272.5	134.0	424	2 172	141.1	40.0	1 099.1	519.4	247.0	18.7
Hudson	1 003	6 962	521.4	213.4	915	4 477	264.3	77.8	3 483.3	803.9	628.1	151.4
Hunterdon	224	1 932	132.7	62.1	200	956	65.3	20.3	406.3	230.8	86.6	3.0

1. Firms subject to federal tax.   2. State totals may include programs not allocated by county.

Table B. States and Counties — Federal Funds and Local Government Finances

	Federal funds and grants, 2002–2003 (cont'd)							Local government finances, 2002				
	Expenditures (mil dol) (cont'd)							General revenue				
	Procurement contract awards		Grants[1]							Taxes		
STATE County	Salaries and wages	Defense	Other	Medicaid and other health-related	Nutrition and family welfare	Education	Other	Total (mil dol)	Intergovern-mental (mil dol)	Total (mil dol)	Per capita[2] (dollars) Total	Per capita[2] (dollars) Property
	171	172	173	174	175	176	177	178	179	180	181	182
NEBRASKA—Cont'd												
Platte	8.6	0.0	1.3	10.3	1.9	1.2	6.4	93.4	22.6	33.2	1 064	813
Polk	1.3	0.0	0.3	1.7	0.3	0.3	2.2	21.1	3.9	11.2	2 021	1 758
Red Willow	4.5	0.0	0.7	4.2	1.2	0.8	4.0	34.4	15.0	12.8	1 129	836
Richardson	2.3	0.0	0.8	7.2	2.3	0.5	4.0	23.1	10.4	9.9	1 091	931
Rock	0.4	0.0	0.3	0.8	0.2	0.2	0.4	5.9	1.6	3.3	1 935	1 543
Saline	3.7	0.0	4.0	5.5	0.7	1.2	3.3	51.1	13.0	17.6	1 249	957
Sarpy	403.3	209.7	4.3	14.4	6.2	18.8	23.5	281.3	112.2	116.0	897	680
Saunders	5.5	2.4	1.0	4.7	1.2	0.8	2.3	52.1	13.6	23.3	1 171	987
Scotts Bluff	10.8	0.0	9.2	31.0	10.5	3.3	12.7	124.1	53.1	44.5	1 211	776
Seward	3.4	0.1	1.2	3.4	0.9	0.9	10.1	44.3	12.7	22.7	1 360	1 135
Sheridan	1.3	0.0	0.5	3.0	1.0	0.6	0.9	27.6	7.6	8.1	1 332	1 020
Sherman	0.9	0.0	0.2	3.4	4.2	0.2	1.2	8.4	3.4	3.9	1 223	1 092
Sioux	0.5	0.0	0.1	0.4	0.0	0.1	4.4	4.1	0.9	3.0	2 077	1 954
Stanton	1.2	0.0	0.2	1.7	0.2	0.2	0.8	10.5	3.2	4.2	649	604
Thayer	1.8	0.0	0.5	4.2	0.6	0.2	1.9	26.5	6.0	10.7	1 874	1 583
Thomas	1.7	0.0	1.1	0.0	0.1	0.1	0.5	2.8	1.6	1.6	2 326	2 199
Thurston	6.8	0.5	6.1	12.4	5.3	6.2	5.4	26.9	14.6	4.6	633	533
Valley	1.8	0.0	0.6	7.2	0.4	0.3	1.4	23.6	5.4	5.9	1 290	1 081
Washington	3.0	4.3	0.7	5.9	0.7	0.9	16.3	45.5	15.3	24.0	1 247	1 011
Wayne	2.4	0.0	0.4	3.0	0.5	0.6	4.5	26.9	8.2	12.3	1 297	918
Webster	1.5	0.0	0.3	3.4	0.3	0.3	2.9	15.1	4.6	5.5	1 376	1 024
Wheeler	0.2	0.0	0.1	0.0	0.1	0.1	0.2	2.6	0.6	1.8	2 053	1 900
York	3.2	0.0	0.7	4.2	0.9	0.6	17.0	37.9	9.2	21.8	1 516	1 054
NEVADA	1 222.0	386.7	1 085.6	765.3	264.5	207.3	717.9	X	X	X	X	X
Churchill	61.4	61.2	2.1	21.0	1.9	3.1	5.6	91.8	45.4	12.7	531	451
Clark	861.3	187.1	942.8	450.5	112.1	73.8	258.4	5 571.3	1 975.7	1 770.4	1 163	726
Douglas	6.0	2.9	7.5	3.3	2.9	2.7	5.5	145.3	62.9	48.7	1 127	774
Elko	22.0	0.2	7.7	19.1	3.9	3.5	17.5	143.4	86.4	27.5	617	397
Esmeralda	0.3	0.0	0.7	0.5	0.6	0.3	0.1	5.4	2.9	1.8	2 016	1 946
Eureka	0.2	0.0	0.1	0.5	0.7	0.2	0.0	14.5	5.2	7.2	4 563	4 456
Humboldt	9.1	0.1	3.2	8.3	1.4	1.1	4.0	73.6	33.0	16.2	1 078	825
Lander	4.4	-0.1	1.3	3.0	0.8	0.9	3.0	29.1	14.5	11.7	2 223	1 819
Lincoln	2.1	5.2	3.0	1.6	1.1	0.4	1.3	22.5	15.6	4.2	980	916
Lyon	4.7	4.1	1.3	10.8	2.0	2.1	3.9	91.4	55.5	24.2	640	527
Mineral	3.6	36.8	0.6	7.4	1.1	1.1	1.8	25.6	11.3	3.5	725	578
Nye	9.4	6.4	2.1	5.5	1.7	2.6	9.2	112.5	62.7	26.9	780	686
Pershing	0.7	0.0	0.8	2.5	0.8	0.2	0.7	29.5	15.9	5.6	849	710
Storey	0.2	0.0	0.1	0.0	0.6	0.3	0.4	11.6	5.7	4.7	1 369	1 052
Washoe	195.0	72.3	100.5	167.8	32.5	24.3	134.0	1 378.0	553.9	478.5	1 321	839
White Pine	8.7	0.2	5.9	6.6	1.7	1.6	8.5	28.9	19.1	5.2	596	478
Carson City city	33.0	10.2	5.7	56.9	55.0	76.9	179.2	224.1	76.9	38.2	704	456
NEW HAMPSHIRE	571.2	531.1	207.2	801.4	176.9	133.4	753.6	X	X	X	X	X
Belknap	13.7	4.8	4.6	44.6	5.8	3.0	23.0	196.3	65.2	101.7	1 720	1 698
Carroll	8.8	0.6	2.5	22.5	3.8	2.4	32.1	137.9	50.9	73.2	1 614	1 597
Cheshire	11.8	2.7	3.5	51.9	10.8	5.4	30.7	205.5	85.0	102.4	1 362	1 347
Coos	8.9	0.0	3.2	36.9	8.8	2.5	36.2	103.8	48.1	45.1	1 362	1 354
Grafton	31.2	46.6	33.8	146.3	7.5	4.9	71.1	259.0	94.0	135.4	1 624	1 604
Hillsborough	279.7	380.3	46.4	198.9	30.1	18.2	116.9	1 031.6	419.4	467.3	1 191	1 154
Merrimack	51.6	9.5	19.1	113.3	58.2	64.0	246.6	363.3	142.7	181.7	1 287	1 268
Rockingham	135.4	71.5	78.1	86.9	16.8	10.9	69.4	750.0	268.6	403.7	1 402	1 383
Strafford	23.8	14.8	14.4	65.2	14.7	9.1	84.7	285.2	115.7	137.5	1 185	1 138
Sullivan	6.2	0.2	1.6	34.9	6.0	3.3	12.7	108.4	42.7	53.7	1 303	1 284
NEW JERSEY	4 158.6	3 873.1	1 587.9	5 007.2	1 408.0	892.8	4 172.9	X	X	X	X	X
Atlantic	250.4	35.5	86.9	168.8	35.5	10.6	78.5	1 129.0	413.9	549.7	2 119	2 078
Bergen	234.3	284.1	122.7	232.7	22.9	15.6	227.1	3 273.4	620.5	2 069.8	2 312	2 293
Burlington	538.5	1 242.5	93.4	132.2	27.8	23.7	161.1	1 598.1	580.8	850.3	1 942	1 908
Camden	194.0	153.8	167.1	331.2	92.7	25.3	131.2	2 375.8	974.9	796.8	1 556	1 540
Cape May	61.6	16.6	14.0	37.3	7.3	4.9	31.2	518.3	149.7	278.8	2 733	2 655
Cumberland	47.9	41.8	10.0	142.5	33.3	13.0	51.2	601.2	393.4	134.6	911	893
Essex	481.6	114.6	129.3	967.4	243.2	59.7	802.3	2 956.5	1 212.6	1 333.4	1 670	1 599
Gloucester	94.8	19.3	48.6	81.6	17.1	6.8	31.1	905.6	367.6	415.0	1 584	1 567
Hudson	448.4	64.1	135.7	704.4	124.3	35.0	311.6	1 973.4	859.4	755.8	1 236	1 207
Hunterdon	24.0	8.7	8.2	26.2	1.8	1.7	14.0	631.7	93.1	476.9	3 791	3 762

1. State totals may include programs not allocated by county.   2. Based on the resident population estimated as of July 1 of the year shown.

	Local government finances, 2002 (cont'd)								Government employment, 2002				Presidential election, 2004		
	Direct general expenditure							Debt outstanding					Percent of vote cast —		
			Percent of total for —												
STATE County	Total (mil dol)	Per capita[1] (dollars)	Educa-tion	Health and hospitals	Police protec-tion	Public welfare	High-ways	Total (mil dol)	Per capita[1] (dollars)	Federal civilian	Federal military	State and local	Demo-cratic	Republi-can	All other
	183	184	185	186	187	188	189	190	191	192	193	194	195	196	197
NEBRASKA—Cont'd															
Platte	76.9	2 462	57.2	0.3	4.9	0.3	9.1	1 350.9	43 278	127	108	2 431	18.9	79.8	1.2
Polk	21.1	3 822	56.4	14.5	1.7	0.1	9.8	2.9	528	26	19	433	19.2	79.6	1.2
Red Willow	32.5	2 856	48.9	0.6	2.8	14.9	5.8	10.0	876	74	39	1 024	20.1	78.5	1.4
Richardson	24.5	2 698	65.9	0.0	2.9	0.7	11.4	7.2	788	49	32	624	30.3	68.3	1.4
Rock	5.5	3 228	50.2	4.8	4.4	0.3	12.9	0.7	400	0	0	209	14.7	84.0	1.2
Saline	53.3	3 771	34.6	27.5	1.6	0.5	11.9	15.6	1 108	75	49	1 226	43.5	55.2	1.3
Sarpy	285.1	2 204	54.6	0.2	4.9	0.3	7.3	241.8	1 870	2 388	7 989	4 747	30.0	69.0	1.0
Saunders	52.9	2 661	50.7	14.8	2.5	0.7	11.0	22.5	1 131	105	69	1 243	30.6	67.9	1.5
Scotts Bluff	117.5	3 196	56.0	0.2	3.6	1.9	6.0	14.5	393	183	128	2 863	26.7	72.2	1.1
Seward	47.1	2 824	63.6	0.2	3.0	0.2	7.0	22.3	1 340	61	58	973	28.1	70.8	1.1
Sheridan	28.9	4 773	31.8	36.9	2.3	5.9	8.9	6.1	1 006	33	21	744	16.6	82.2	1.3
Sherman	8.9	2 791	59.3	0.1	3.1	1.1	14.2	5.7	1 806	20	11	290	32.9	65.3	1.8
Sioux	3.6	2 535	45.0	0.0	1.5	0.0	26.5	0.3	205	13	0	86	15.6	83.6	0.8
Stanton	9.5	1 457	36.6	0.2	4.2	0.0	20.5	23.0	3 515	29	23	304	20.3	78.7	1.0
Thayer	21.7	3 814	44.3	27.9	2.7	0.1	5.3	3.7	655	42	20	636	26.5	72.2	1.3
Thomas	2.6	3 664	55.1	0.0	1.2	0.0	13.2	0.2	332	13	0	100	13.5	85.1	1.4
Thurston	33.9	4 711	70.6	13.1	1.3	0.0	4.5	22.1	3 063	129	25	1 213	37.9	61.4	0.7
Valley	23.1	5 084	27.7	37.9	1.6	0.2	6.0	4.9	1 079	32	16	659	24.7	74.2	1.1
Washington	43.7	2 275	56.6	0.0	4.1	0.2	13.9	20.8	1 081	52	67	1 560	27.8	71.3	0.9
Wayne	24.5	2 579	60.5	0.1	2.2	0.6	10.3	9.3	980	40	33	1 063	26.0	72.9	1.2
Webster	14.3	3 608	46.6	15.3	1.8	0.4	10.1	3.3	824	33	14	303	28.0	70.5	1.5
Wheeler	2.8	3 151	60.7	0.0	2.5	0.5	16.1	0.0	26	0	0	71	17.9	80.8	1.3
York	36.6	2 551	43.1	0.7	4.6	0.7	16.3	23.0	1 606	63	50	1 021	19.2	79.4	1.3
NEVADA	X	X	X	X	X	X	X	X	X	15 391	11 967	112 945	47.9	50.5	1.6
Churchill	89.4	3 722	41.9	0.7	6.0	1.5	4.3	29.5	1 227	656	1 108	1 421	47.9	50.5	1.6
Clark	5 563.2	3 655	34.8	8.4	7.2	1.3	8.4	9 579.5	6 293	9 540	9 933	66 505	47.9	50.5	1.6
Douglas	145.1	3 361	36.4	2.8	8.3	1.4	3.3	49.6	1 149	106	61	2 029	47.9	50.5	1.6
Elko	148.7	3 337	49.3	1.3	8.9	0.7	5.9	35.1	787	440	64	3 258	47.9	50.5	1.6
Esmeralda	5.5	6 247	25.2	1.9	19.4	0.7	12.5	0.0	0	0	0	100	47.9	50.5	1.6
Eureka	13.6	8 563	39.5	5.6	7.1	1.1	10.9	1.2	781	0	0	200	47.9	50.5	1.6
Humboldt	73.6	4 902	38.0	19.9	5.4	0.9	4.3	104.9	6 994	195	21	1 155	47.9	50.5	1.6
Lander	30.5	5 815	37.5	21.8	7.7	1.4	8.8	11.5	2 196	93	0	492	47.9	50.5	1.6
Lincoln	19.8	4 659	53.0	0.7	5.8	1.5	10.4	6.1	1 435	49	0	542	47.9	50.5	1.6
Lyon	101.0	2 667	57.4	1.6	7.7	1.7	5.7	55.2	1 457	73	53	1 700	47.9	50.5	1.6
Mineral	27.5	5 680	29.4	26.8	6.6	1.2	4.9	5.2	1 080	82	0	521	47.9	50.5	1.6
Nye	126.1	3 654	42.0	11.9	8.2	1.0	6.6	57.7	1 672	172	59	1 511	47.9	50.5	1.6
Pershing	29.8	4 492	35.4	18.6	5.1	1.5	5.7	10.7	1 610	14	0	709	47.9	50.5	1.6
Storey	11.8	3 447	41.2	0.1	13.0	0.1	7.1	2.9	840	0	0	184	47.9	50.5	1.6
Washoe	1 334.5	3 683	30.1	0.9	8.2	2.5	13.6	2 023.3	5 584	3 185	538	21 625	47.9	50.5	1.6
White Pine	28.2	3 242	49.9	0.9	10.7	1.0	7.4	16.3	1 871	215	12	1 207	47.9	50.5	1.6
Carson City city	212.8	3 919	31.7	35.3	5.0	0.7	4.4	116.5	2 145	555	79	9 786	47.9	50.5	1.6
NEW HAMPSHIRE	X	X	X	X	X	X	X	X	X	7 823	3 729	78 524	50.3	49.0	0.7
Belknap	181.6	3 072	49.6	0.6	5.1	8.1	4.7	61.2	1 035	270	159	3 527	43.7	55.6	0.7
Carroll	130.2	2 872	53.2	1.0	4.1	6.2	6.5	29.8	657	126	121	2 494	47.4	51.8	0.8
Cheshire	216.8	2 883	56.7	0.6	4.2	7.5	5.1	63.2	840	200	202	5 107	59.3	40.0	0.7
Coos	105.4	3 184	46.6	1.8	3.0	14.7	5.2	53.0	1 600	159	89	2 675	50.9	48.4	0.8
Grafton	252.4	3 026	56.4	0.7	4.1	5.5	6.0	83.0	995	588	224	6 222	55.9	43.3	0.8
Hillsborough	1 067.0	2 719	51.4	0.6	5.3	4.4	4.5	822.8	2 097	3 944	1 095	16 769	48.2	51.2	0.6
Merrimack	348.5	2 467	53.7	0.5	5.1	8.8	5.3	220.9	1 564	851	381	15 360	52.3	47.1	0.6
Rockingham	721.7	2 507	57.1	0.6	6.3	5.0	3.7	259.1	900	1 253	1 024	12 566	47.6	51.8	0.6
Strafford	288.0	2 480	48.3	0.2	5.1	8.3	3.2	192.5	1 658	322	324	11 276	55.7	43.6	0.7
Sullivan	103.9	2 518	46.9	0.5	3.7	15.0	5.9	39.3	954	110	110	2 528	52.6	46.7	0.7
NEW JERSEY	X	X	X	X	X	X	X	X	X	61 698	21 846	532 057	52.7	46.5	0.9
Atlantic	1 146.3	4 419	50.9	0.9	7.6	1.8	2.6	965.0	3 720	2 744	596	18 374	52.6	46.6	0.8
Bergen	3 241.4	3 621	54.1	5.7	6.9	2.4	2.6	1 563.8	1 747	3 042	1 277	41 336	51.6	47.7	0.7
Burlington	1 484.3	3 390	61.3	2.0	5.8	1.6	3.4	1 192.2	2 723	5 699	5 812	23 852	53.2	46.1	0.8
Camden	2 212.2	4 321	51.4	2.2	5.3	3.7	7.2	3 173.3	6 198	3 048	729	32 697	62.2	36.8	1.0
Cape May	515.8	5 056	40.9	2.2	5.9	3.7	6.2	515.3	5 052	390	1 431	8 312	42.2	56.7	1.1
Cumberland	574.1	3 885	61.4	1.9	3.9	6.5	2.1	275.0	1 861	737	211	13 443	52.3	45.9	1.8
Essex	2 972.9	3 724	36.2	3.7	9.2	6.3	1.7	2 201.6	2 758	8 587	1 156	66 907	69.7	29.4	0.9
Gloucester	876.6	3 345	61.4	0.9	5.4	2.1	2.4	804.9	3 072	1 057	374	15 980	52.2	46.9	0.9
Hudson	1 898.1	3 104	33.2	3.7	10.0	4.2	1.5	1 545.9	2 528	6 891	969	35 448	66.7	32.6	0.7
Hunterdon	549.4	4 368	50.1	1.0	11.4	0.5	5.5	391.8	3 115	342	179	8 175	39.0	59.9	1.1

1. Based on the resident population estimated as of July 1 of the year shown.

STATE/ County code	CBSA code[1]	County Type[2]	STATE County	Land area[3] (sq km) 2000	Total persons	Rank	Per square kilometer	White	Black	Am. Indian, Alaska Native	Asian and Pacific Islander	Percent Hispanic or Latino[4]	Under 5 years	5 to 17 years	18 to 24 years	25 to 34 years	35 to 44 years	45 to 54 years
				(1)	1	2	3	4	5	6	7	8	9	10	11	12	13
			NEW JERSEY—Cont'd															
34 021	45940	2	Mercer	585	361 981	172	618.8	62.7	20.2	0.4	6.8	10.9	6.3	17.6	10.7	13.2	16.0	14.3
34 023	35620	1	Middlesex	802	780 995	63	973.8	58.9	9.5	0.4	17.1	15.3	6.6	17.2	9.2	14.8	16.8	13.8
34 025	35620	1	Monmouth	1 222	632 274	91	517.4	80.5	8.1	0.4	4.9	7.0	6.3	19.1	7.9	11.2	17.3	15.5
34 027	35620	1	Morris	1 215	483 150	125	397.7	81.1	2.9	0.3	7.7	8.9	6.6	18.1	7.1	11.8	17.9	15.5
34 029	35620	1	Ocean	1 648	546 081	108	331.4	89.7	3.2	0.3	1.6	5.8	6.1	16.8	7.5	11.2	14.5	12.4
34 031	35620	1	Passaic	480	498 357	119	1 038.2	50.8	12.8	0.3	4.3	32.5	7.8	18.9	9.4	13.8	16.1	13.1
34 033	37980	1	Salem	875	64 854	764	74.1	79.9	15.1	0.7	0.7	4.4	6.0	18.5	9.2	11.4	15.3	15.1
34 035	35620	1	Somerset	789	311 600	190	394.9	71.2	8.3	0.3	11.0	10.2	7.1	18.7	6.5	12.6	19.0	15.3
34 037	35620	1	Sussex	1 350	151 146	374	112.0	93.0	1.4	0.4	1.7	4.3	6.0	20.2	7.9	10.9	18.3	16.4
34 039	35620	1	Union	268	529 360	109	1 975.2	52.0	21.6	0.3	4.4	22.4	7.0	18.3	8.1	13.3	16.9	13.9
34 041	10900	2	Warren	927	109 219	506	117.8	90.9	2.6	0.3	1.9	4.9	6.2	18.7	7.8	11.7	17.9	14.8
35 000	...	X	NEW MEXICO	314 309	1 874 614	X	6.0	44.6	2.1	9.7	1.5	43.2	7.1	19.7	10.6	12.3	14.2	14.2
35 001	10740	2	Bernalillo	3 020	581 442	98	192.5	47.9	3.0	4.4	2.7	43.5	7.0	17.9	10.2	13.7	15.0	14.3
35 003	...	9	Catron	17 943	3 415	2 955	0.2	77.1	0.4	2.6	0.8	19.8	4.1	14.6	7.5	6.4	11.1	19.5
35 005	40740	5	Chaves	15 723	60 591	814	3.9	50.5	1.9	1.1	0.8	46.4	7.2	20.4	11.3	10.4	13.1	13.3
35 006	24380	6	Cibola	11 757	26 453	1 520	2.2	25.7	1.0	40.2	0.4	33.5	8.1	21.1	10.6	11.6	14.3	13.0
35 007	...	7	Colfax	9 730	14 051	2 162	1.4	51.0	0.4	1.3	0.4	47.4	5.4	18.3	8.5	9.1	13.7	15.5
35 009	17580	5	Curry	3 641	45 440	1 011	12.5	57.9	7.2	1.1	3.0	32.6	8.5	21.2	11.8	13.6	14.2	10.9
35 011	...	9	De Baca	6 021	2 091	3 050	0.3	62.7	0.0	0.5	0.4	36.4	4.2	16.5	9.0	7.3	12.8	12.9
35 013	29740	3	Dona Ana	9 861	182 165	314	18.5	31.9	1.6	1.1	1.2	64.9	7.9	20.6	13.2	13.0	13.1	11.8
35 015	16100	5	Eddy	10 831	51 470	913	4.8	57.1	1.5	1.1	0.6	40.2	7.3	20.1	10.3	10.2	13.6	14.5
35 017	43500	7	Grant	10 272	29 818	1 409	2.9	49.7	0.5	1.3	0.4	48.7	6.4	18.0	9.7	9.7	12.4	14.6
35 019	...	7	Guadalupe	7 849	4 574	2 866	0.6	17.6	1.2	0.8	0.8	79.6	6.0	16.2	11.0	10.6	18.1	13.9
35 021	...	9	Harding	5 505	747	3 123	0.1	54.8	0.4	0.5	0.0	44.4	2.4	13.7	9.1	6.4	11.2	15.9
35 023	...	7	Hidalgo	8 924	5 234	2 825	0.6	42.8	0.3	0.3	0.2	56.3	6.5	22.0	9.8	9.4	13.8	14.2
35 025	26020	5	Lea	11 378	55 504	868	4.9	51.6	4.7	1.0	0.5	42.9	7.8	20.9	11.7	12.1	14.1	13.0
35 027	...	7	Lincoln	12 512	20 322	1 784	1.6	71.3	0.5	2.3	0.3	26.3	5.1	16.5	8.1	8.4	12.5	15.8
35 028	31060	6	Los Alamos	283	18 802	1 870	66.4	82.2	0.7	1.0	5.2	12.4	4.9	18.8	7.3	8.1	15.8	17.5
35 029	19700	6	Luna	7 680	25 732	1 546	3.4	39.1	0.8	1.0	0.4	59.1	7.5	21.1	9.6	9.7	11.5	10.9
35 031	23700	4	McKinley	14 112	72 555	698	5.1	12.3	0.8	75.0	0.0	12.6	9.2	26.9	11.1	12.4	14.3	12.0
35 033	...	8	Mora	5 002	5 216	2 827	1.0	17.6	0.1	0.8	0.0	81.4	5.2	18.8	10.3	9.5	13.9	15.8
35 035	10460	4	Otero	17 163	62 371	795	3.6	56.0	4.1	6.0	2.0	33.4	7.2	21.1	10.4	12.2	14.9	12.4
35 037	...	7	Quay	7 446	9 605	2 479	1.3	58.5	0.9	1.0	1.1	38.7	5.4	17.3	9.1	8.5	12.9	14.8
35 039	21580	6	Rio Arriba	15 171	40 731	1 118	2.7	14.1	0.3	12.2	0.2	73.6	7.5	20.0	9.5	12.0	14.9	14.8
35 041	38780	7	Roosevelt	6 342	18 107	1 909	2.9	62.2	1.7	1.3	0.8	34.6	7.8	19.6	15.1	13.0	12.4	11.4
35 043	10740	2	Sandoval	9 607	98 786	548	10.3	50.6	2.2	16.1	1.5	31.2	6.8	21.0	9.6	11.6	15.7	14.2
35 045	22140	3	San Juan	14 281	122 272	464	8.6	45.0	0.7	39.8	0.6	15.4	8.1	22.7	12.0	12.0	14.3	12.9
35 047	29780	6	San Miguel	12 217	29 670	1 413	2.4	19.7	0.7	1.2	0.7	78.0	6.1	19.3	12.0	11.0	14.4	14.4
35 049	42140	3	Santa Fe	4 945	136 423	415	27.6	46.3	0.8	3.0	1.3	49.5	5.7	17.0	9.1	12.1	15.3	17.1
35 051	...	6	Sierra	10 827	13 125	2 230	1.2	70.3	0.4	1.9	0.2	27.7	4.3	14.7	7.2	7.0	11.0	13.1
35 053	...	6	Socorro	17 214	18 178	1 902	1.1	38.8	0.6	11.5	1.5	48.5	6.7	20.0	13.0	11.8	13.0	13.6
35 055	45340	7	Taos	5 706	31 269	1 373	5.5	36.4	0.5	6.5	0.6	56.8	5.9	17.1	8.4	10.7	14.5	17.4
35 057	10740	7	Torrance	8 663	16 802	1 975	1.9	57.7	1.7	2.7	0.6	38.4	5.9	22.2	9.5	11.0	15.6	14.9
35 059	...	9	Union	9 920	3 814	2 926	0.4	62.6	0.2	0.4	0.5	36.5	5.0	19.4	9.3	8.9	13.7	14.9
35 061	10740	2	Valencia	2 765	67 839	742	24.5	40.1	1.2	3.2	0.6	55.7	7.2	21.4	9.9	12.0	15.8	13.7
36 000	...	X	NEW YORK	122 283	19 190 115	X	156.9	61.3	16.0	0.6	6.9	16.3	6.3	17.3	9.5	13.9	15.8	14.2
36 001	10580	2	Albany	1 356	297 845	195	219.6	80.5	12.4	0.6	4.1	3.8	5.3	16.0	11.5	13.3	15.0	14.8
36 003	...	7	Allegany	2 668	50 562	929	19.0	96.7	1.1	0.6	1.1	1.2	5.1	16.6	17.5	10.2	13.0	13.4
36 005	35620	1	Bronx	109	1 363 198	26	12 506.4	13.6	32.0	0.6	3.6	51.3	8.4	20.8	10.5	15.2	15.2	11.5
36 007	13780	2	Broome	1 831	199 360	289	108.9	90.3	4.4	0.6	3.6	2.4	5.3	16.2	11.8	11.2	14.8	14.1
36 009	36460	4	Cattaraugus	3 393	83 354	639	24.6	94.5	1.4	2.8	0.7	1.3	5.7	18.0	11.0	10.8	14.5	14.9
36 011	12180	4	Cayuga	1 795	81 726	647	45.5	93.0	4.3	0.6	0.5	2.3	5.4	17.4	9.8	12.2	16.1	14.8
36 013	27460	4	Chautauqua	2 751	137 645	410	50.0	91.9	2.5	0.7	0.6	5.0	5.4	17.1	11.5	11.0	14.4	14.5
36 015	21300	3	Chemung	1 057	90 413	595	85.5	90.3	6.9	0.5	1.2	2.2	5.8	17.0	10.1	12.0	15.2	14.7
36 017	...	6	Chenango	2 316	51 659	912	22.3	96.6	1.1	0.6	0.4	1.7	5.4	18.3	9.0	10.9	15.3	14.8
36 019	38460	5	Clinton	2 691	81 366	649	30.2	92.6	3.5	0.6	1.0	2.8	4.5	15.9	13.3	13.2	16.5	14.0
36 021	26460	6	Columbia	1 647	63 405	782	38.5	90.9	5.0	0.4	1.4	3.2	4.7	17.4	8.2	10.7	15.2	15.6
36 023	18660	4	Cortland	1 294	48 691	959	37.6	96.4	1.6	0.7	0.7	1.5	5.5	16.3	15.4	11.8	14.2	13.6
36 025	...	6	Delaware	3 746	47 226	977	12.6	94.8	1.8	0.7	0.8	2.5	4.6	16.3	10.1	9.6	13.5	14.9
36 027	39100	2	Dutchess	2 076	290 885	201	140.1	79.0	10.2	0.5	3.6	7.9	5.5	17.8	10.7	12.0	17.0	14.4
36 029	15380	1	Erie	2 704	941 293	39	348.1	80.3	13.9	0.9	2.1	3.7	5.6	17.2	9.4	12.1	15.3	14.6
36 031	...	6	Essex	4 654	38 992	1 162	8.4	93.6	3.1	0.7	0.6	2.5	4.5	15.9	8.6	12.9	16.0	15.1
36 033	31660	5	Franklin	4 226	51 056	922	12.1	83.3	6.5	5.9	0.5	4.1	4.3	15.9	11.1	14.4	17.5	14.0
36 035	24100	4	Fulton	1 285	55 206	873	43.0	95.1	2.2	0.5	0.9	1.9	5.3	17.6	8.9	11.7	15.5	14.7

1. CBSA = Core Based Statistical Area. See Appendix A for explanation. See Appendix B for list of metropolitan areas with component counties.
2. County type code from the Economic Research Service of USDA Rural-Urban Continuum Codes. See Appendix A for definition.
3. Dry land or land partially or temporarily covered by water.
4. Hispanic or Latino persons may be of any race.

Table B. States and Counties — **Population and Households**

STATE County	\[16\] 55 to 64 years	\[17\] 65 to 74 years	\[18\] 75 years and over	\[19\] Percent female	\[20\] 1990	\[21\] 2000	\[22\] 1990–2000	\[23\] 2000–2003	\[24\] Births	\[25\] Deaths	\[26\] Net migration	\[27\] Number	\[28\] Percent change, 1990–2000	\[29\] Persons per household	\[30\] Female family householder[1]	\[31\] One person
NEW JERSEY—Cont'd																
Mercer	9.2	6.0	6.2	51.1	325 759	350 761	7.7	3.2	15 164	9 590	6 030	125 807	7.6	2.62	13.8	25.6
Middlesex	8.8	6.0	5.9	50.8	671 712	750 162	11.7	4.1	33 890	18 539	16 138	265 815	11.3	2.74	10.8	22.4
Monmouth	10.0	6.3	6.1	51.3	553 124	615 301	11.2	2.8	25 412	17 920	10 195	224 236	13.5	2.70	10.0	23.8
Morris	10.9	6.3	5.5	50.9	421 330	470 212	11.6	2.8	20 505	11 254	3 985	169 711	14.1	2.72	7.9	21.5
Ocean	9.4	9.5	11.7	52.4	433 203	510 916	17.9	6.9	21 538	22 647	36 121	200 402	19.2	2.51	9.2	27.0
Passaic	9.0	5.9	5.9	51.4	470 872	489 049	3.9	1.9	27 027	13 262	-5 856	163 856	5.5	2.92	16.0	22.2
Salem	10.4	6.9	7.4	51.6	65 294	64 285	-1.5	0.9	2 455	2 263	458	24 295	2.1	2.60	13.3	24.3
Somerset	9.5	5.6	5.1	51.0	240 222	297 490	23.8	4.7	14 082	6 602	7 035	108 984	23.4	2.69	8.2	22.8
Sussex	10.1	4.9	4.3	50.5	130 936	144 166	10.1	4.8	5 701	3 225	4 553	50 831	14.3	2.80	8.0	18.9
Union	9.4	6.3	7.0	51.7	493 819	522 541	5.8	1.3	24 583	15 284	-2 131	186 124	3.4	2.77	14.2	23.6
Warren	9.6	6.1	6.3	51.2	91 675	102 437	11.7	6.6	4 280	2 640	5 065	38 660	13.7	2.61	9.2	24.0
NEW MEXICO	9.9	6.5	5.5	50.8	1 515 069	1 819 046	20.1	3.1	87 305	45 302	13 805	677 971	24.9	2.63	13.2	25.4
Bernalillo	9.2	6.0	5.5	51.1	480 577	556 678	15.8	4.4	26 768	13 848	12 130	220 936	19.1	2.47	12.9	28.5
Catron	17.9	12.9	8.3	49.1	2 563	3 543	38.2	-3.6	84	119	-80	1 584	56.8	2.23	7.6	30.1
Chaves	9.3	7.4	7.3	51.1	57 849	61 382	6.1	-1.3	2 862	1 869	-1 801	22 561	9.6	2.66	13.7	24.8
Cibola	9.0	7.0	4.4	51.2	23 794	25 595	7.6	3.4	1 395	759	246	8 327	14.2	2.95	18.3	21.1
Colfax	12.8	9.1	8.2	49.2	12 925	14 189	9.8	-1.0	523	443	-204	5 821	17.4	2.37	10.3	27.7
Curry	7.5	6.1	5.3	50.5	42 207	45 044	6.7	0.9	2 488	1 220	-876	16 766	10.9	2.62	12.8	25.5
De Baca	11.4	12.9	14.2	51.3	2 252	2 240	-0.5	-6.7	63	101	-110	922	1.0	2.35	7.3	30.8
Dona Ana	7.9	6.2	4.7	50.8	135 510	174 682	28.9	4.3	9 701	3 449	1 308	59 556	32.2	2.85	14.7	21.3
Eddy	9.6	7.3	7.1	51.0	48 605	51 658	6.3	-0.4	2 473	1 748	-895	19 379	10.9	2.63	11.9	24.2
Grant	12.2	9.4	8.3	51.4	27 676	31 002	12.0	-3.8	1 265	1 031	-1 439	12 146	24.3	2.50	12.9	25.7
Guadalupe	9.6	8.1	6.4	45.1	4 156	4 680	12.6	-2.3	191	119	-175	1 655	8.9	2.51	14.3	27.9
Harding	12.6	14.3	14.7	49.8	987	810	-17.9	-7.8	6	29	-38	371	-6.3	2.18	7.5	35.3
Hidalgo	10.0	8.2	7.3	49.8	5 958	5 932	-0.4	-11.8	214	143	-796	2 152	7.4	2.72	13.6	25.3
Lea	8.4	6.7	5.5	49.9	55 765	55 511	-0.5	0.0	2 891	1 660	-1 248	19 699	2.0	2.73	12.2	25.1
Lincoln	13.9	11.2	6.9	51.0	12 219	19 411	58.9	4.7	670	514	761	8 202	71.3	2.34	9.3	26.7
Los Alamos	13.9	6.6	5.5	49.6	18 115	18 343	1.3	2.5	570	380	226	7 497	3.9	2.43	5.7	24.9
Luna	10.1	10.4	8.3	51.2	18 110	25 016	38.1	2.9	1 266	766	213	9 397	38.3	2.64	12.4	26.4
McKinley	7.4	4.5	2.9	51.8	60 686	74 798	23.3	-3.0	4 388	1 695	-5 019	21 476	29.5	3.44	22.7	19.5
Mora	11.9	8.9	6.3	49.8	4 264	5 180	21.5	0.7	164	155	34	2 017	32.8	2.54	11.9	26.9
Otero	9.0	7.4	4.9	50.4	51 928	62 298	20.0	0.1	2 778	1 458	-1 301	22 984	26.6	2.66	11.8	23.3
Quay	13.0	10.5	9.4	52.0	10 823	10 155	-6.2	-5.4	357	421	-499	4 201	-0.9	2.37	12.0	28.9
Rio Arriba	10.1	6.5	4.9	50.7	34 365	41 190	19.9	-1.1	2 228	1 076	-1 629	15 044	31.3	2.71	15.9	23.5
Roosevelt	8.0	6.1	5.7	50.8	16 702	18 018	7.9	0.5	965	457	-404	6 639	10.8	2.60	11.7	24.7
Sandoval	8.6	5.5	5.0	51.2	63 319	89 908	42.0	9.9	4 140	1 940	6 597	31 411	50.5	2.84	12.2	19.9
San Juan	7.9	5.2	3.8	50.4	91 605	113 801	24.2	7.4	6 376	2 679	4 738	37 711	31.2	2.99	14.7	19.3
San Miguel	10.5	6.6	5.5	51.0	25 743	30 126	17.0	-1.5	1 205	731	-925	11 134	28.0	2.58	16.4	26.6
Santa Fe	11.3	6.2	4.8	51.0	98 928	129 292	30.7	5.5	4 953	2 498	4 753	52 482	38.7	2.42	11.7	29.4
Sierra	14.3	14.5	13.5	50.2	9 912	13 270	33.9	-1.1	335	698	222	6 113	38.1	2.13	8.6	35.9
Socorro	10.0	6.3	4.8	49.3	14 764	18 078	22.4	0.6	792	457	-223	6 675	27.9	2.62	13.3	26.8
Taos	12.3	7.3	5.6	50.7	23 118	29 979	29.7	4.3	1 237	729	807	12 675	44.8	2.34	12.7	32.1
Torrance	10.0	6.0	4.2	48.5	10 285	16 911	64.4	-0.6	630	366	-375	6 024	64.1	2.72	12.3	23.2
Union	11.9	10.4	8.9	50.5	4 124	4 174	1.2	-8.6	131	190	-303	1 733	7.3	2.40	9.1	30.0
Valencia	9.3	6.0	4.4	49.7	45 235	66 152	46.2	2.6	3 196	1 554	110	22 681	49.5	2.86	13.1	18.8
NEW YORK	10.0	6.5	6.5	51.7	17 990 778	18 976 457	5.5	1.1	835 326	515 916	-108 872	7 056 860	6.3	2.61	14.7	28.1
Albany	9.3	6.6	7.5	52.0	292 812	294 565	0.6	1.1	10 510	9 315	2 359	120 512	4.0	2.32	12.2	33.0
Allegany	9.6	7.2	6.7	50.0	50 470	49 927	-1.1	1.3	1 704	1 546	517	18 009	5.9	2.53	9.0	26.0
Bronx	8.0	5.2	4.8	53.2	1 203 789	1 332 650	10.7	2.3	82 389	33 428	-18 827	463 212	9.2	2.78	30.4	27.4
Broome	10.0	7.7	8.6	51.6	212 160	200 536	-5.5	-0.6	6 881	6 964	-938	80 749	-1.3	2.37	10.8	31.0
Cattaraugus	10.1	7.5	7.2	50.9	84 234	83 955	-0.3	-0.7	3 168	2 728	-971	32 023	5.1	2.52	10.8	26.8
Cayuga	9.7	6.8	7.5	49.6	82 313	81 963	-0.4	-0.3	2 890	2 280	-792	30 558	5.1	2.53	11.0	26.2
Chautauqua	10.1	7.7	8.2	51.2	141 895	139 750	-1.5	-1.5	5 004	4 890	-2 133	54 515	1.5	2.45	10.8	28.1
Chemung	9.8	7.4	8.1	50.6	95 195	91 070	-4.3	-0.7	3 500	3 081	-1 027	35 049	-0.6	2.44	12.4	27.9
Chenango	11.1	7.4	7.4	50.7	51 768	51 401	-0.7	0.5	1 854	1 747	184	19 926	4.1	2.52	9.8	26.1
Clinton	9.2	6.7	5.3	48.9	85 969	79 894	-7.1	1.8	2 318	2 178	1 399	29 423	1.0	2.47	10.2	26.3
Columbia	11.9	8.0	8.1	50.2	62 982	63 094	0.2	0.5	1 953	2 264	678	24 796	4.6	2.43	10.3	27.1
Cortland	9.5	6.0	6.4	51.6	48 963	48 599	-0.7	0.2	1 767	1 459	-178	18 210	5.6	2.50	10.3	26.5
Delaware	12.4	9.5	9.2	50.7	47 352	48 055	1.5	-1.7	1 353	1 759	-362	19 270	9.2	2.39	9.0	28.3
Dutchess	9.7	6.3	5.6	50.0	259 462	280 150	8.0	3.8	10 404	7 349	7 786	99 536	11.1	2.63	10.3	24.6
Erie	9.8	7.6	8.2	52.0	968 584	950 265	-1.9	-0.9	35 182	32 879	-10 649	380 873	1.0	2.41	13.7	30.5
Essex	10.7	8.3	7.8	48.1	37 152	38 851	4.6	0.4	1 142	1 315	336	15 028	9.5	2.39	8.9	28.3
Franklin	9.2	6.6	6.2	45.3	46 540	51 134	9.9	-0.2	1 435	1 417	-44	17 931	10.1	2.46	11.1	28.2
Fulton	10.3	7.4	8.5	50.8	54 191	55 073	1.6	0.2	1 982	1 968	167	21 884	4.2	2.43	11.3	27.7

1. No spouse present.

STATE County	Births, average 1999–2001		Deaths, average 1999–2001				Physicians,[4] 2000		Hospitals,[4] 1998			Medicare enrollees, 2003	Serious crimes known to police,[6] 2002	
			Number		Rate					Beds			Total	
	Total	Rate[1]	Total	Infant[2]	Total[1]	Infant[3]	Number	Rate[5]	Number	Number	Rate[5]		Number	Rate[7]
	32	33	34	35	36	37	38	39	40	41	42	43	44	45
NEW JERSEY—Cont'd														
Mercer	4 595	13.1	3 027	35	8.6	7.6	1 046	298	5	1 674	505	52 272	13 186	3 682
Middlesex	10 349	13.7	5 786	60	7.7	5.8	1 998	266	6	1 907	266	97 921	19 872	2 595
Monmouth	8 125	13.2	5 437	40	8.8	4.9	1 504	244	5	1 857	308	89 357	14 760	2 350
Morris	6 474	13.8	3 511	20	7.5	3.1	1 305	278	4	1 909	415	61 978	7 158	1 491
Ocean	6 650	12.9	6 942	29	13.5	4.3	726	142	5	1 433	293	122 603	11 638	2 231
Passaic	7 829	16.0	4 061	49	8.3	6.3	991	203	6	1 947	401	64 890	17 135	3 432
Salem	793	12.3	715	5	11.1	D	90	140	2	243	374	10 690	1 684	2 566
Somerset	4 413	14.8	2 035	20	6.8	4.5	822	276	1	374	132	32 785	5 311	1 749
Sussex	1 786	12.4	1 005	7	7.0	4.1	168	117	2	271	189	16 608	1 646	1 118
Union	7 565	14.4	4 725	52	9.0	6.9	1 280	245	7	2 422	484	76 708	19 367	3 630
Warren	1 362	13.2	869	6	8.4	D	136	133	2	320	325	16 079	1 579	1 510
NEW MEXICO	27 181	14.9	13 743	181	7.6	6.6	3 602	198	36	4 015	231	250 113	94 196	5 078
Bernalillo	8 316	14.9	4 172	54	7.5	6.5	1 987	357	8	1 619	308	75 116	40 314	7 101
Catron	28	8.1	32	0	9.1	D	2	56	0	0	0	794	20	554
Chaves	905	14.7	626	7	10.2	7.7	82	134	2	277	443	10 095	4 107	6 561
Cibola	449	17.5	206	4	8.0	D	18	70	1	43	164	2 781	746	2 858
Colfax	159	11.2	140	0	9.9	D	27	190	1	46	338	2 610	282	2 307
Curry	790	17.6	376	7	8.4	8.4	55	122	1	106	234	6 096	2 431	5 380
De Baca	17	7.8	29	0	12.9	D	1	45	1	25	1 046	538	NA	NA
Dona Ana	3 001	17.1	1 077	16	6.1	5.4	240	137	1	221	131	22 166	NA	NA
Eddy	763	14.8	555	7	10.7	9.6	58	112	2	174	325	8 571	2 673	5 074
Grant	415	13.4	309	3	10.0	D	50	161	1	68	215	5 915	1 101	3 715
Guadalupe	58	12.6	44	1	9.5	D	8	171	1	20	494	811	NA	NA
Harding	4	4.5	9	0	11.6	D	0	0	0	0	0	233	11	1 565
Hidalgo	79	13.4	49	0	8.3	D	2	34	0	0	0	850	56	926
Lea	903	16.2	496	7	8.9	7.4	39	70	2	278	496	7 799	3 264	5 766
Lincoln	203	10.5	159	2	8.2	D	23	118	1	38	232	3 790	545	2 974
Los Alamos	183	10.1	112	1	6.1	D	45	245	1	53	289	2 232	257	1 374
Luna	398	15.9	259	4	10.3	D	22	88	1	119	494	5 056	1 216	4 766
McKinley	1 382	18.6	456	15	6.1	10.9	121	162	1	70	104	6 372	2 992	3 922
Mora	50	9.8	49	0	9.6	D	0	0	0	0	0	940	21	398
Otero	842	13.6	443	4	7.2	D	54	87	1	67	123	8 244	NA	NA
Quay	112	11.1	131	1	13.0	D	7	69	1	37	369	2 128	577	5 572
Rio Arriba	666	16.2	333	4	8.1	D	42	102	1	80	212	5 651	NA	NA
Roosevelt	288	15.9	140	2	7.7	D	23	128	1	151	830	2 566	743	4 044
Sandoval	1 279	14.2	560	7	6.2	5.7	72	80	0	0	0	11 821	1 883	2 067
San Juan	1 927	16.9	738	11	6.5	5.7	152	134	1	126	119	12 891	4 103	3 535
San Miguel	382	12.7	247	1	8.2	D	42	139	1	56	193	4 526	1 031	3 524
Santa Fe	1 612	12.4	798	11	6.2	6.6	329	254	1	208	169	16 964	6 339	4 965
Sierra	107	8.1	218	1	16.5	D	15	113	1	47	426	3 599	NA	NA
Socorro	254	14.1	132	0	7.3	D	10	55	1	32	196	2 171	706	3 829
Taos	368	12.3	220	2	7.3	D	43	143	1	29	108	4 678	NA	NA
Torrance	205	12.3	110	2	6.6	D	4	24	0	0	0	1 911	NA	NA
Union	42	10.1	53	1	13.0	D	3	72	1	25	627	891	NA	NA
Valencia	991	15.0	465	5	7.0	D	26	39	0	0	0	9 143	NA	NA
NEW YORK	256 125	13.5	159 123	1 588	8.4	6.2	58 453	308	235	73 682	405	2 763 299	537 121	2 804
Albany	3 209	10.9	2 908	25	9.9	7.7	1 384	470	3	1 322	452	44 866	12 288	4 132
Allegany	541	10.8	488	4	9.7	D	39	78	2	177	347	8 139	871	1 806
Bronx	22 725	17.1	10 496	154	7.9	6.8	3 122	234	12	5 509	461	149 665	(7)NA	(7)NA
Broome	2 229	11.1	2 176	18	10.8	7.9	473	236	3	802	408	38 389	6 278	3 101
Cattaraugus	986	11.8	849	8	10.1	8.5	129	154	3	353	415	14 788	2 131	2 571
Cayuga	914	11.2	724	6	8.8	D	102	124	1	266	327	13 006	1 844	2 229
Chautauqua	1 559	11.2	1 505	10	10.8	6.2	181	130	4	687	497	25 700	3 539	2 508
Chemung	1 093	12.0	967	6	10.6	D	216	237	2	495	538	16 716	3 035	3 301
Chenango	566	11.0	520	5	10.1	D	59	115	1	132	259	9 197	1 280	2 482
Clinton	783	9.8	660	5	8.2	D	143	179	1	409	511	11 625	1 540	1 938
Columbia	612	9.7	693	4	11.0	D	98	155	1	194	307	11 272	1 043	1 771
Cortland	562	11.5	440	4	9.0	D	58	119	1	260	541	7 216	1 500	3 057
Delaware	447	9.3	548	4	11.4	D	35	73	4	214	464	9 170	934	1 925
Dutchess	3 261	11.6	2 227	19	7.9	5.7	576	206	3	686	259	42 083	5 905	2 124
Erie	11 107	11.7	10 049	88	10.6	8.0	2 870	302	12	4 100	439	167 356	32 198	3 356
Essex	367	9.5	416	3	10.7	D	25	64	3	95	253	7 577	705	1 797
Franklin	454	8.9	448	2	8.8	D	78	153	2	245	504	7 907	1 026	1 988
Fulton	647	11.8	574	3	10.4	D	65	118	1	208	393	9 273	1 281	2 338

1. Per 1,000 estimated resident population. 2. Deaths of infants under 1 year old. 3. Deaths of infants under 1 year old per 1,000 live births. 4. Data subject to copyright. 5. Per 100,000 resident population as of July 1 of the year shown. 6. Data for serious crimes have not been adjusted for underreporting; this may affect comparability between geographic areas and over time. 7. Per 100,000 population estimated by the FBI. 7. Bronx, Kings, Queens, and Richmond Counties included with New York County.

Table B. States and Counties — Crime, Education, Money Income, and Poverty

STATE County	Violent	Property	Total	Percent private	High school graduate or less	Bachelor's degree or more	Total current expenditures (mil dol)	Current expenditures per student (dollars)	Per capita income[6] (dollars)	Dollars	Percent change, 1989–1999 (constant 1999 dollars)	Percent with income of $100,000 or more	Persons	Households	Families	Families with children
	46	47	48	49	50	51	52	53	54	55	56	57	58	59	60	61
NEW JERSEY—Cont'd																
Mercer	531	3 151	99 649	26.5	43.8	34.0	698.3	12 454	27 914	56 613	2.2	23.0	8.6	8.6	5.9	8.9
Middlesex	230	2 365	200 431	18.7	44.7	33.0	1 177.4	10 859	26 535	61 446	0.2	22.9	6.6	6.1	4.2	6.0
Monmouth	214	2 136	165 915	22.6	39.5	34.6	1 112.3	10 678	31 149	64 271	4.2	27.9	6.3	6.3	4.5	6.6
Morris	116	1 375	122 655	25.3	33.4	44.1	844.7	11 568	36 964	77 340	2.3	35.8	3.9	3.6	2.4	3.3
Ocean	188	2 043	118 859	22.4	54.7	19.5	715.7	9 565	23 054	46 443	4.4	13.2	7.0	6.5	4.8	7.9
Passaic	483	2 949	129 731	22.1	57.9	21.2	883.5	11 864	21 370	49 210	-2.6	17.3	12.3	11.0	9.4	14.1
Salem	337	2 229	16 618	13.1	59.8	15.2	125.0	10 535	20 874	45 573	2.3	10.7	9.5	9.1	7.2	10.9
Somerset	94	1 655	76 743	23.1	31.9	46.5	504.3	10 834	37 970	76 933	3.1	35.9	3.8	3.5	2.3	3.3
Sussex	82	1 036	40 610	16.4	43.6	27.2	290.6	10 589	26 992	65 266	-0.5	23.5	4.0	4.4	2.8	3.9
Union	404	3 226	136 230	21.7	50.4	28.5	925.8	11 513	26 992	55 339	-1.4	22.1	8.4	8.3	6.3	9.2
Warren	83	1 427	26 106	16.7	50.5	24.4	191.9	10 575	25 728	56 100	4.6	18.3	5.4	6.0	3.6	5.3
NEW MEXICO	740	4 338	533 786	10.8	47.7	23.5	1 964.4	6 133	17 261	34 133	5.5	7.6	18.4	16.8	14.5	20.8
Bernalillo	1 021	6 081	156 057	14.7	40.3	30.5	486.4	5 703	20 790	38 788	5.4	10.3	13.7	12.7	10.2	15.4
Catron	138	415	714	10.2	50.6	18.4	4.4	9 520	13 951	23 892	-3.7	2.6	24.5	22.2	17.4	32.7
Chaves	981	5 580	18 132	9.0	53.9	16.2	70.5	5 977	14 990	28 513	-2.5	4.9	21.3	19.1	17.6	26.1
Cibola	571	2 287	7 644	13.7	61.5	12.0	23.1	6 376	11 731	27 774	22.7	2.8	24.8	23.4	21.5	28.5
Colfax	360	1 947	3 353	6.8	53.4	18.5	18.9	7 496	16 418	30 744	10.0	4.9	14.8	14.1	12.0	19.7
Curry	511	4 869	14 012	5.5	49.5	15.3	54.0	5 834	15 049	28 917	1.0	4.6	19.0	17.9	15.5	22.3
De Baca	NA	NA	532	0.4	57.6	16.2	3.6	9 387	14 065	25 441	20.7	2.6	17.7	19.2	13.6	25.1
Dona Ana	NA	NA	60 034	6.1	52.4	22.3	219.2	5 952	13 999	29 808	1.5	5.3	25.4	22.3	20.2	28.9
Eddy	537	4 537	14 292	8.1	59.4	13.5	65.2	6 130	15 823	31 998	1.7	5.0	17.2	16.7	13.6	19.0
Grant	324	3 391	8 657	7.7	49.7	20.5	38.2	6 988	14 597	29 134	1.6	4.1	18.7	17.3	15.1	24.0
Guadalupe	NA	NA	1 279	8.0	69.2	10.3	8.6	9 360	11 241	24 783	38.2	1.2	21.6	25.2	18.1	23.5
Harding	711	853	174	10.3	59.6	18.1	2.2	13 156	16 240	26 111	2.2	4.1	16.3	16.9	12.9	30.7
Hidalgo	198	727	1 699	2.6	68.1	9.9	10.9	9 211	12 431	24 819	-21.4	3.8	27.3	25.4	23.9	31.5
Lea	813	4 953	16 534	7.0	60.8	11.6	71.9	5 983	14 184	29 799	-5.0	4.5	21.1	19.9	17.3	24.1
Lincoln	900	2 074	4 483	8.1	43.6	22.8	26.6	7 460	19 338	33 886	29.4	7.8	14.9	12.8	10.8	20.2
Los Alamos	53	1 320	5 057	12.5	15.7	60.5	30.3	8 346	34 646	78 993	7.3	34.1	2.9	3.9	1.9	2.0
Luna	647	4 120	6 401	2.7	70.1	10.4	28.8	5 401	11 218	20 784	-1.4	2.2	32.9	28.9	27.2	39.9
McKinley	691	3 232	28 043	9.3	62.7	11.8	106.8	6 797	9 872	25 005	6.5	3.6	36.1	33.1	31.9	36.7
Mora	303	95	1 418	9.9	61.9	15.5	9.0	10 804	12 340	24 518	40.5	3.7	25.4	27.4	20.9	27.5
Otero	NA	NA	18 135	7.4	48.1	15.4	51.5	5 684	14 345	30 861	1.5	3.3	19.3	17.1	15.6	22.7
Quay	1 777	3 795	2 619	2.1	62.9	13.7	14.9	7 607	14 938	24 894	-1.0	3.0	20.9	20.9	15.7	22.5
Rio Arriba	NA	NA	11 581	12.2	58.3	11.5	47.7	7 235	14 263	29 429	19.2	4.5	20.3	20.7	16.6	20.3
Roosevelt	376	3 668	6 636	5.7	48.5	22.6	23.0	6 693	14 185	26 586	5.8	4.3	22.7	23.8	17.3	22.1
Sandoval	250	1 817	26 442	12.9	42.6	24.8	88.2	5 851	19 174	44 949	15.6	9.2	12.1	10.2	9.0	12.4
San Juan	656	2 880	36 608	6.4	53.7	13.5	144.3	5 980	14 282	33 762	12.7	5.5	21.5	19.9	18.0	23.1
San Miguel	701	2 824	9 583	9.1	51.1	21.2	39.5	7 178	13 268	26 524	10.4	3.9	24.4	24.2	19.9	25.4
Santa Fe	530	4 434	33 486	20.6	35.2	36.9	83.8	5 459	23 594	42 207	6.8	13.0	12.0	11.5	9.4	13.4
Sierra	NA	NA	2 595	9.9	55.3	13.1	10.8	6 348	15 023	24 152	15.1	3.1	20.9	20.2	13.8	25.0
Socorro	900	2 929	5 817	5.7	56.9	19.4	18.1	7 202	12 826	23 439	-9.0	4.5	31.7	29.3	24.1	35.3
Taos	NA	NA	7 505	13.0	47.5	25.9	39.7	7 542	16 103	26 762	17.4	5.1	20.9	22.3	16.1	21.2
Torrance	NA	NA	4 660	6.5	55.9	14.4	37.7	6 356	14 134	30 446	15.5	4.1	19.0	18.1	15.2	21.6
Union	NA	NA	1 084	8.4	64.0	13.0	7.6	8 924	14 700	28 080	14.7	2.8	18.1	15.8	14.2	24.1
Valencia	NA	NA	18 520	9.3	56.2	14.8	79.0	5 930	14 747	34 099	4.4	4.5	16.8	15.0	13.5	18.7
NEW YORK	496	2 308	5 217 030	23.6	48.7	27.4	32 088.8	11 210	23 389	43 393	-2.0	15.3	14.6	13.9	11.5	16.9
Albany	560	3 572	83 713	23.0	40.7	33.3	422.0	10 273	23 345	42 935	-4.2	12.6	10.6	10.7	7.2	11.7
Allegany	240	1 565	16 263	23.4	56.4	17.2	89.5	10 597	14 975	32 106	-1.1	4.2	15.5	15.3	10.5	17.2
Bronx	[7]NA	[7]NA	419 114	21.5	63.5	14.6	[7]NA	[7]NA	13 959	27 611	-6.3	6.1	30.7	29.0	28.0	36.5
Broome	230	2 871	56 153	10.3	48.9	22.7	316.8	9 654	19 168	35 347	-8.5	7.8	12.8	12.8	8.8	14.4
Cattaraugus	259	2 312	22 211	17.4	60.0	14.9	171.3	10 385	15 959	33 404	6.2	4.6	13.7	12.3	10.0	16.0
Cayuga	199	2 029	20 377	11.5	56.9	15.5	110.4	8 979	18 003	37 487	1.2	6.1	11.1	10.8	7.8	12.5
Chautauqua	239	2 270	37 459	8.0	55.3	16.9	240.6	9 977	16 840	33 458	3.0	5.6	13.8	12.8	9.7	16.9
Chemung	335	2 966	22 739	20.1	54.0	18.6	133.0	9 873	18 264	36 415	3.7	6.6	13.0	12.8	9.1	15.5
Chenango	227	2 255	13 094	6.7	59.3	14.4	97.4	9 908	16 427	33 679	-3.7	5.1	14.4	12.9	10.7	17.4
Clinton	283	1 655	22 184	9.7	57.1	17.8	140.6	10 467	17 946	37 028	2.4	6.1	13.9	14.3	9.4	13.8
Columbia	192	1 579	15 183	14.9	51.7	22.5	105.8	10 693	22 265	41 915	4.7	10.5	9.0	8.9	6.4	10.6
Cortland	190	2 868	15 221	7.2	53.0	18.8	73.6	9 492	16 622	34 364	-4.5	5.6	15.5	15.3	9.3	14.1
Delaware	280	1 645	11 874	6.6	57.5	16.6	82.8	11 099	17 357	32 461	0.1	5.6	12.9	12.5	9.3	15.2
Dutchess	245	1 880	78 962	22.8	44.1	27.6	458.6	9 979	23 940	53 086	-6.5	17.2	7.5	7.5	5.0	7.6
Erie	482	2 874	256 351	21.1	47.0	24.5	1 514.6	10 572	20 357	38 567	2.5	9.4	12.2	12.3	9.2	15.2
Essex	181	1 616	8 857	10.8	57.7	18.3	55.9	11 139	18 194	34 823	3.7	5.2	11.6	11.4	7.8	12.6
Franklin	368	1 619	12 024	12.3	64.1	13.0	97.7	11 090	15 888	31 517	7.6	4.4	14.6	14.2	10.1	14.7
Fulton	139	2 199	13 249	6.3	60.8	13.5	90.4	9 218	16 844	33 663	5.0	4.7	12.5	11.6	9.2	14.8

1. Data for serious crimes have not been adjusted for underreporting; this may affect comparability between geographic areas and over time. 2. Per 100,000 population estimated by the FBI. 3. All persons 3 years old and over enrolled in nursery school through college. 4. Persons 25 years old and over. 5. Elementary and secondary education expenditures. 6. Based on population enumerated as of April 1, 2000. 7. Bronx, Kings, Queens, and Richmond Counties included with New York County.

Table B. States and Counties — **Personal Income**

STATE County	Personal income, 2002 Total (mil dol) [62]	Percent change, 2001–2002 [63]	Per capita[1] Dollars [64]	Per capita[1] Rank [65]	Wages and salaries[2] (mil dol) [66]	Proprietor's income (mil dol) [67]	Dividends, interest, and rent (mil dol) [68]	Transfer payments Total (mil dol) [69]	Government payments to individuals Total (mil dol) [70]	Social Security (mil dol) [71]	Medical payments (mil dol) [72]	Income maintenance (mil dol) [73]	Unemployment insurance (mil dol) [74]
NEW JERSEY—Cont'd													
Mercer	14 582	2.2	40 711	57	11 962	1 014	2 653	1 877	1 789	630	851	125	99
Middlesex	28 926	1.0	37 449	95	24 263	2 009	4 034	3 368	3 178	1 235	1 343	141	276
Monmouth	27 419	1.4	43 684	41	13 086	1 887	4 932	2 886	2 732	1 086	1 182	116	218
Morris	26 804	1.2	56 002	7	19 425	2 846	4 671	1 795	1 678	789	650	44	110
Ocean	16 907	3.7	31 497	248	5 762	960	3 485	3 348	3 217	1 492	1 365	89	143
Passaic	15 552	2.2	31 323	259	8 831	968	2 321	2 637	2 515	763	1 235	222	210
Salem	1 875	3.5	28 977	452	1 150	79	272	372	356	133	167	22	22
Somerset	16 942	0.6	55 057	11	12 540	1 456	2 776	1 085	1 009	468	373	36	80
Sussex	5 609	2.0	37 676	92	1 620	370	740	535	499	213	205	17	38
Union	21 098	0.9	39 889	61	14 304	1 619	3 855	2 638	2 508	926	1 135	144	191
Warren	3 529	3.0	32 824	195	1 767	145	509	491	465	191	208	18	28
NEW MEXICO	45 974	5.0	24 823	X	29 363	3 851	8 096	7 933	7 448	2 589	3 182	857	175
Bernalillo	17 295	4.4	30 204	332	13 274	1 424	3 051	2 373	2 223	800	934	222	59
Catron	55	2.3	15 769	3 057	20	-1	18	16	15	8	4	1	0
Chaves	1 367	2.3	22 727	1 811	649	259	233	301	285	105	127	36	5
Cibola	424	9.8	16 221	3 042	232	16	53	117	110	34	51	13	2
Colfax	312	4.9	21 961	2 027	172	23	73	73	69	28	28	6	2
Curry	1 077	5.9	23 984	1 415	674	108	169	208	198	58	86	24	3
De Baca	43	2.0	20 299	2 479	17	4	10	13	12	5	5	1	0
Dona Ana	3 674	7.3	20 573	2 411	2 023	310	606	753	706	209	315	109	14
Eddy	1 218	4.6	23 763	1 479	753	130	195	257	244	97	105	26	5
Grant	598	1.0	19 762	2 597	312	22	128	174	166	66	69	15	5
Guadalupe	66	2.5	14 415	3 087	40	0	10	26	25	7	13	3	1
Harding	13	-16.9	17 107	2 985	7	0	4	4	4	2	1	0	0
Hidalgo	93	0.5	17 471	2 953	47	6	15	27	26	8	12	3	0
Lea	1 251	0.0	22 503	1 876	786	145	160	264	250	88	120	26	4
Lincoln	420	7.7	21 289	2 213	182	31	119	96	91	42	35	7	1
Los Alamos	888	8.7	48 485	19	1 235	26	194	40	40	22	14	1	0
Luna	434	9.1	17 195	2 975	204	41	77	136	129	49	49	17	6
McKinley	1 127	5.1	15 299	3 068	734	23	129	300	280	51	126	63	4
Mora	79	6.2	15 028	3 076	27	-2	13	29	28	8	12	4	1
Otero	1 205	7.8	19 459	2 664	805	59	223	230	215	83	84	18	1
Quay	187	0.7	19 314	2 693	96	5	38	58	56	21	24	6	1
Rio Arriba	800	8.0	19 537	2 653	341	43	108	196	186	56	88	24	6
Roosevelt	429	5.8	23 792	1 474	179	87	57	94	90	25	39	9	1
Sandoval	2 412	2.8	25 211	1 073	1 108	102	353	349	324	129	129	28	11
San Juan	2 458	3.9	20 511	2 427	1 728	221	316	447	415	139	173	52	13
San Miguel	591	8.2	19 851	2 574	268	40	81	172	164	40	83	24	3
Santa Fe	4 417	6.5	32 932	187	2 332	518	1 177	476	440	190	168	38	9
Sierra	249	5.8	19 207	2 713	81	20	63	89	86	35	36	7	1
Socorro	335	8.6	18 577	2 817	187	20	52	79	74	21	33	13	1
Taos	645	7.9	20 912	2 322	301	85	137	144	136	46	60	16	5
Torrance	325	5.1	19 521	2 655	104	16	39	70	66	20	29	10	1
Union	98	-5.1	24 751	1 196	40	20	18	21	20	8	8	2	0
Valencia	1 390	6.1	20 598	2 404	404	51	175	295	278	88	120	35	6
NEW YORK	685 110	0.8	35 805	X	475 801	70 920	112 582	117 921	112 900	31 372	59 531	12 660	4 290
Albany	10 598	3.3	35 763	125	11 321	935	1 809	1 784	1 707	545	621	169	37
Allegany	1 005	2.2	19 925	2 560	497	66	148	257	244	92	101	28	10
Bronx	28 457	3.7	20 950	2 313	10 083	1 277	2 633	9 706	9 351	1 479	5 858	1 447	372
Broome	5 223	2.2	26 088	870	3 883	278	893	1 120	1 068	439	428	110	44
Cattaraugus	1 928	3.6	23 119	1 689	1 123	140	259	488	466	160	177	47	20
Cayuga	1 999	3.4	24 526	1 257	976	113	308	400	378	146	158	37	17
Chautauqua	3 079	2.4	22 263	1 942	1 862	181	467	797	760	289	313	97	30
Chemung	2 230	1.2	24 558	1 246	1 484	107	354	537	513	191	219	54	21
Chenango	1 180	3.1	22 960	1 735	603	88	188	269	256	102	103	27	12
Clinton	1 952	4.0	24 142	1 359	1 327	117	267	407	385	134	169	45	14
Columbia	1 832	1.5	28 980	450	758	141	370	347	331	134	140	28	10
Cortland	1 100	2.2	22 693	1 825	641	83	151	237	224	81	96	27	12
Delaware	1 118	3.7	23 609	1 532	609	121	215	263	251	105	106	21	8
Dutchess	9 379	1.1	32 604	200	5 489	497	1 473	1 330	1 254	514	532	94	41
Erie	27 537	2.9	29 208	421	19 204	1 853	4 469	5 408	5 160	1 945	2 148	571	191
Essex	921	4.1	23 687	1 504	533	66	176	213	203	78	90	18	8
Franklin	1 027	3.2	20 232	2 494	642	59	151	260	247	89	106	27	10
Fulton	1 395	3.7	25 311	1 042	636	104	225	323	309	110	142	31	9

1. Based on the resident population estimated as of July 1 of the year shown.   2. Includes other labor income.

Table B. States and Counties — Earnings, Social Security, and Housing

STATE County	Earnings, 2002									Social Security beneficiaries, December 2003		Supplemental Security Income recipients, December 2003	Housing units, 2003	
	Total (mil dol)	Percent by selected industries								Number	Rate[2]		Total	Percent change, 2000–2003
		Farm	Goods-related[1]		Service-related and health				Govern-ment					
			Total	Manu-facturing	Information and professional and technical services	Retail trade	Finance, insurance, and real estate	Health services						
	75	76	77	78	79	80	81	82	83	84	85	86	87	88
NEW JERSEY—Cont'd														
Mercer	12 977	0.0	D	4.4	18.9	4.9	12.3	8.3	24.0	56 975	157	7 958	136 986	2.8
Middlesex	26 272	0.0	19.6	15.4	20.3	6.2	9.8	6.4	12.0	110 275	141	9 919	279 914	2.3
Monmouth	14 973	0.2	12.7	4.7	20.9	8.2	10.6	11.9	16.7	98 405	156	6 765	249 553	3.6
Morris	22 271	0.1	14.9	10.3	21.5	6.1	14.9	6.3	8.0	68 410	142	3 404	180 590	3.6
Ocean	6 721	0.1	14.6	4.7	7.7	13.7	7.4	17.4	20.5	138 385	253	4 839	262 222	5.4
Passaic	9 800	0.0	22.9	15.1	9.1	8.9	8.9	10.7	16.4	72 650	146	13 902	171 065	0.6
Salem	1 229	1.4	D	19.4	3.8	5.7	3.0	9.3	15.6	12 895	199	1 132	26 643	1.9
Somerset	13 996	0.1	D	13.5	24.7	6.1	9.6	5.5	6.3	40 305	129	1 876	117 122	4.6
Sussex	1 990	0.1	14.9	5.4	12.8	9.8	8.5	12.8	19.4	20 080	133	1 379	58 678	3.8
Union	15 923	0.0	26.4	19.9	14.9	6.8	8.3	8.5	11.7	82 430	156	8 870	194 180	0.6
Warren	1 912	-0.1	D	26.1	5.4	13.1	3.8	10.2	14.7	17 875	164	1 092	43 661	6.1
NEW MEXICO	33 214	1.9	15.8	6.0	11.3	7.9	5.8	9.2	28.4	294 669	157	50 212	816 436	4.6
Bernalillo	14 697	0.1	13.3	6.2	17.7	7.8	7.7	9.7	22.6	86 920	149	12 646	254 217	6.3
Catron	19	-19.8	D	1.2	D	3.4	2.5	D	76.2	995	291	55	2 755	8.1
Chaves	908	14.6	22.5	9.6	4.6	6.6	3.5	10.4	20.1	11 790	195	2 156	26 035	1.5
Cibola	247	-0.1	12.2	7.0	D	9.4	1.9	D	47.1	3 935	149	662	10 642	3.0
Colfax	195	-1.1	17.0	3.3	4.2	9.6	4.8	D	30.6	3 155	225	350	9 073	1.3
Curry	781	10.1	D	1.5	D	6.6	3.0	D	43.5	6 790	149	1 426	19 598	2.0
De Baca	21	17.1	D	D	D	4.6	5.2	7.9	30.5	570	273	90	1 375	5.2
Dona Ana	2 332	5.9	D	4.9	8.3	7.5	3.7	12.2	35.6	25 490	140	5 753	69 241	6.2
Eddy	883	3.2	33.4	5.7	3.9	6.5	4.8	8.5	18.1	10 135	197	1 448	22 669	1.9
Grant	334	-1.4	D	D	D	7.8	3.4	D	36.4	7 125	239	775	14 428	2.6
Guadalupe	40	-11.7	D	0.1	D	12.1	D	6.3	35.8	935	204	263	2 252	4.3
Harding	6	-18.9	D	0.0	D	9.8	D	D	52.6	230	308	27	595	9.2
Hidalgo	54	11.6	D	D	D	7.4	D	6.8	38.6	990	189	174	2 993	5.1
Lea	931	3.6	36.2	1.3	2.9	6.7	4.6	D	14.1	9 230	166	1 554	23 788	1.6
Lincoln	213	-1.8	12.6	1.3	5.7	16.1	6.8	D	24.3	4 575	225	311	15 972	4.4
Los Alamos	1 261	0.0	D	D	8.7	1.3	1.8	2.9	69.7	2 365	126	34	8 477	6.8
Luna	245	8.3	D	10.7	2.2	11.7	2.8	D	29.2	5 940	231	940	11 670	3.4
McKinley	757	-0.3	12.6	2.7	D	11.8	1.8	9.3	44.1	7 730	107	3 975	27 471	2.8
Mora	26	-19.5	D	D	D	7.7	D	D	47.6	1 180	226	336	3 051	2.6
Otero	863	0.0	D	1.4	4.6	6.7	2.9	6.7	60.0	10 025	161	1 112	30 226	3.3
Quay	101	-1.4	6.2	1.1	2.3	11.4	4.7	9.9	35.0	2 450	255	368	5 820	2.8
Rio Arriba	384	-0.6	12.9	3.5	D	9.8	2.6	13.7	45.7	7 280	179	1 666	18 549	3.0
Roosevelt	267	31.4	D	3.8	2.1	6.0	1.9	5.3	26.0	2 955	163	564	7 945	2.6
Sandoval	1 209	0.1	51.6	41.0	D	5.7	3.2	3.1	18.4	14 405	146	1 649	37 592	7.8
San Juan	1 949	3.9	27.9	3.3	3.5	8.0	3.0	8.3	22.0	15 865	130	3 540	44 462	2.9
San Miguel	308	-2.1	9.1	1.0	D	8.0	3.4	14.6	48.3	5 200	175	1 861	14 610	2.5
Santa Fe	2 850	0.2	11.5	2.6	11.8	10.7	10.1	9.6	26.0	19 815	145	2 019	59 766	3.6
Sierra	102	7.2	D	D	3.9	8.8	3.9	D	34.1	4 015	306	468	9 047	3.7
Socorro	207	4.6	D	3.1	11.2	5.8	2.2	D	47.2	2 650	146	759	8 144	4.3
Taos	387	0.2	16.1	1.7	D	14.6	5.3	12.4	22.2	5 725	183	1 020	18 001	4.3
Torrance	120	5.7	9.2	2.5	D	11.3	2.4	D	37.3	2 590	154	387	7 567	4.3
Union	60	32.5	D	0.6	4.4	5.7	D	D	22.9	990	260	111	2 326	4.5
Valencia	454	1.7	D	7.1	3.3	10.7	4.1	7.7	32.5	10 610	156	1 664	26 079	5.8
NEW YORK	546 721	0.1	12.0	7.5	16.5	5.1	19.9	9.9	14.5	3 035 697	158	623 774	7 802 245	1.6
Albany	12 256	0.0	D	4.1	13.7	5.4	9.4	10.0	32.7	52 320	176	6 267	131 881	1.5
Allegany	563	2.5	29.9	23.0	D	6.3	2.0	8.6	28.6	9 780	193	1 445	24 882	1.5
Bronx	11 360	0.0	D	3.7	5.7	6.1	6.0	30.3	15.6	161 080	118	88 455	496 921	1.3
Broome	4 161	0.2	D	22.1	7.9	7.0	5.3	12.6	20.3	43 475	218	5 557	89 205	0.4
Cattaraugus	1 263	0.8	25.7	21.9	3.2	8.2	2.9	11.7	27.1	17 025	204	2 638	40 288	1.1
Cayuga	1 089	2.7	D	16.3	4.8	8.8	2.4	12.6	25.8	14 745	180	1 872	35 856	1.1
Chautauqua	2 043	1.3	31.6	26.6	5.1	8.0	3.3	12.5	20.4	29 550	215	4 088	65 373	0.7
Chemung	1 591	0.3	D	20.5	5.4	9.1	4.6	14.5	21.6	19 395	215	2 887	38 135	1.0
Chenango	692	1.7	33.1	27.3	6.0	7.1	7.8	8.4	24.2	11 040	214	1 536	24 206	1.3
Clinton	1 444	1.0	D	20.4	D	8.3	2.4	13.9	27.3	14 755	181	2 562	33 971	2.7
Columbia	898	3.7	D	10.8	9.7	9.4	4.9	15.5	22.1	13 455	212	1 646	30 915	2.3
Cortland	724	1.1	26.1	20.8	6.3	8.7	3.4	12.4	25.3	8 500	175	1 177	20 237	0.6
Delaware	730	1.9	36.2	28.8	4.6	9.1	4.0	D	24.3	10 975	232	1 252	29 311	1.2
Dutchess	5 986	0.2	31.9	26.1	7.0	6.9	5.6	12.6	17.8	48 495	167	4 920	109 326	3.0
Erie	21 057	0.1	23.1	18.2	10.0	6.4	9.0	10.9	17.6	188 430	200	25 194	420 832	1.2
Essex	599	0.5	20.0	10.9	5.1	9.2	3.0	9.0	34.2	8 190	210	989	23 651	2.3
Franklin	701	1.5	D	3.1	4.2	7.4	2.7	D	48.3	10 030	196	1 657	24 164	1.0
Fulton	741	0.6	D	15.1	8.1	9.7	3.7	15.4	23.7	11 480	208	1 698	27 987	0.7

1. Covers mining, construction, and manufacturing. 2. Per 1,000 resident population estimated as of July 1 of the year shown.

STATE County	Housing units, 2000								Civilian labor force, 2003				Civilian employment,[6] 2000		
	Occupied units										Unemployment			Percent	
			Owner-occupied			Renter-occupied									
				Median owner cost as a percent of income											
	Total	Percent	Median value[1]	With a mort-gage	Without a mort-gage[2]	Median rent[3]	Median rent as a per-cent of income	Sub-stand-ard units[4] (percent)	Total	Percent change, 2002–2003	Total	Rate[5]	Total	Management, professional and related occupations	Production, transpor-tation, and material moving occupations
	89	90	91	92	93	94	95	96	97	98	99	100	101	102	103
NEW JERSEY—Cont'd															
Mercer	125 807	67.0	147 400	22.5	14.7	727	24.9	4.4	191 314	2.2	9 158	4.8	166 647	43.2	9.7
Middlesex	265 815	66.7	168 500	23.2	14.8	845	23.6	6.4	418 292	-1.6	22 476	5.4	370 817	40.6	12.8
Monmouth	224 236	74.6	203 100	23.7	15.1	759	27.0	2.8	334 410	1.9	17 589	5.3	294 622	41.8	8.4
Morris	169 711	76.0	257 400	22.9	13.6	883	23.4	2.9	268 794	1.0	11 728	4.4	243 783	47.7	8.1
Ocean	200 402	83.2	131 300	24.7	16.6	819	29.3	2.4	241 166	2.3	13 740	5.7	213 336	31.6	11.1
Passaic	163 856	55.6	190 600	24.8	16.5	747	26.8	9.7	231 826	0.2	17 843	7.7	215 508	30.0	18.4
Salem	24 295	73.0	105 200	22.7	14.0	602	26.3	2.5	31 952	1.4	2 194	6.9	29 360	28.4	19.7
Somerset	108 984	77.2	235 000	22.5	14.4	898	23.7	3.8	175 258	-1.6	7 483	4.3	154 032	50.3	8.7
Sussex	50 831	82.7	157 700	24.2	14.6	790	25.7	1.3	78 238	1.4	4 272	5.5	73 913	37.0	11.4
Union	186 124	61.6	188 800	23.6	16.0	752	24.9	7.3	278 847	0.9	17 535	6.3	244 197	35.4	15.3
Warren	38 660	72.8	155 500	24.2	14.9	689	24.6	1.6	55 068	1.5	3 164	5.7	51 219	34.8	13.1
NEW MEXICO	677 971	70.0	108 100	22.2	9.9	503	26.6	8.7	896 867	2.5	57 200	6.4	763 116	34.0	10.7
Bernalillo	220 936	63.6	128 300	23.0	9.9	560	27.6	6.0	312 916	1.8	16 620	5.3	262 588	37.9	9.2
Catron	1 584	80.4	82 000	28.8	10.6	392	19.7	10.0	1 177	5.9	104	8.8	1 270	31.0	10.4
Chaves	22 561	70.9	61 000	19.8	9.9	402	25.0	8.0	26 014	3.0	2 238	8.6	23 028	27.6	15.8
Cibola	8 327	77.1	62 600	19.1	9.9	355	19.0	15.2	14 072	8.7	814	5.8	8 703	29.6	11.7
Colfax	5 821	72.7	76 600	20.6	10.0	414	22.3	3.4	7 060	3.9	490	6.9	6 045	29.6	11.6
Curry	16 766	59.4	64 700	20.3	9.9	427	24.9	6.1	20 928	2.6	823	3.9	16 983	27.4	13.2
De Baca	922	77.8	45 800	21.1	11.0	371	22.3	4.8	977	4.4	85	8.7	893	32.7	11.3
Dona Ana	59 556	67.5	90 900	21.0	9.9	445	28.3	11.4	78 324	4.0	5 866	7.5	67 685	32.3	11.6
Eddy	19 379	74.3	64 200	18.6	9.9	394	23.8	5.9	24 263	1.3	1 659	6.8	20 591	25.1	14.4
Grant	12 146	74.5	87 900	22.8	9.9	419	26.0	5.3	12 491	-4.2	1 746	14.0	11 413	29.9	11.6
Guadalupe	1 655	74.1	52 100	21.6	13.7	322	22.3	5.0	1 691	-1.9	135	8.0	1 598	26.3	10.1
Harding	371	75.2	27 300	37.5	10.0	367	33.3	4.9	458	4.8	27	5.9	364	39.6	5.2
Hidalgo	2 152	67.8	53 900	19.6	10.3	267	22.4	8.1	1 775	0.5	113	6.4	2 119	20.5	14.2
Lea	19 699	72.6	50 100	17.8	9.9	388	24.1	7.9	25 946	1.4	1 258	4.8	20 254	25.1	15.7
Lincoln	8 202	77.2	108 400	22.4	9.9	468	26.3	4.6	8 795	5.7	357	4.1	8 539	27.9	9.1
Los Alamos	7 497	78.6	228 300	19.4	9.9	666	19.7	1.9	10 412	3.3	177	1.7	9 656	68.4	3.4
Luna	9 397	75.0	66 000	20.5	9.9	337	27.3	11.5	12 674	9.2	2 814	22.2	7 161	22.7	16.0
McKinley	21 476	72.4	57 000	20.3	9.9	374	18.8	37.4	27 254	5.1	2 198	8.1	21 940	32.4	13.5
Mora	2 017	82.5	75 900	18.9	13.2	357	32.4	12.4	1 977	3.8	284	14.4	1 686	28.2	7.9
Otero	22 984	66.9	78 800	21.5	9.9	441	24.5	7.4	21 710	2.9	1 547	7.1	21 934	28.3	13.1
Quay	4 201	70.5	54 000	21.4	12.1	311	23.4	5.3	4 099	-1.1	249	6.1	4 044	29.7	8.9
Rio Arriba	15 044	81.7	107 500	23.5	10.8	394	22.0	8.8	22 537	4.9	1 742	7.7	16 563	29.9	9.4
Roosevelt	6 639	62.7	54 900	20.0	9.9	391	26.2	6.6	8 358	0.2	290	3.5	7 450	34.6	12.9
Sandoval	31 411	83.6	115 400	22.8	9.9	726	26.8	8.0	46 914	1.6	3 037	6.5	38 870	36.0	10.8
San Juan	37 711	75.3	91 300	19.6	9.9	459	22.8	16.4	52 687	0.9	4 313	8.2	44 541	25.2	14.5
San Miguel	11 134	73.2	90 100	27.1	12.3	430	31.6	6.6	13 801	2.8	995	7.2	11 372	34.1	7.1
Santa Fe	52 482	68.6	189 400	23.9	9.9	690	28.2	5.7	71 175	3.5	2 664	3.7	64 930	41.7	6.4
Sierra	6 113	74.8	77 800	23.4	9.9	348	27.5	6.3	4 233	-1.4	195	4.6	4 470	26.8	9.4
Socorro	6 675	71.0	80 900	21.9	12.3	362	28.5	9.1	7 297	2.9	422	5.8	7 127	36.6	8.8
Taos	12 675	75.5	150 400	26.5	11.3	531	32.1	8.7	14 448	3.3	1 575	10.9	13 556	31.5	7.2
Torrance	6 024	83.9	82 800	24.5	11.7	458	27.6	7.6	7 743	1.1	400	5.2	6 786	30.3	14.2
Union	1 733	72.9	49 800	20.6	10.5	376	29.7	3.2	2 066	1.8	65	3.1	1 894	32.3	11.0
Valencia	22 681	83.9	108 300	23.9	9.9	490	27.5	8.4	30 600	1.9	1 903	6.2	27 063	26.9	15.1
NEW YORK	7 056 860	53.0	148 700	23.2	13.6	672	26.8	8.4	9 315 319	-0.3	588 959	6.3	8 382 988	36.7	11.7
Albany	120 512	57.7	116 300	20.9	11.1	611	25.6	2.2	162 434	0.2	5 731	3.5	144 480	42.3	8.6
Allegany	18 009	73.9	50 400	19.8	12.1	423	28.1	2.6	23 945	1.0	1 876	7.8	21 494	31.3	18.0
Bronx	463 212	19.5	190 400	28.5	13.7	620	28.0	20.7	521 240	-0.4	54 372	10.4	428 654	26.6	12.3
Broome	80 749	65.1	75 800	19.9	11.7	462	26.8	1.9	97 879	-2.3	5 683	5.8	91 340	34.6	14.9
Cattaraugus	32 023	74.4	60 800	20.0	12.2	425	24.9	2.7	41 645	1.4	2 905	7.0	37 830	27.4	21.1
Cayuga	30 558	72.0	75 300	21.4	13.6	482	25.9	1.8	38 353	0.5	2 342	6.1	37 552	27.8	19.6
Chautauqua	54 515	69.3	64 000	20.6	13.1	438	27.0	1.8	65 809	-1.0	4 186	6.4	63 029	27.2	21.5
Chemung	35 049	68.9	67 200	20.7	12.7	493	27.7	1.5	42 900	-1.7	2 829	6.6	39 220	32.0	15.9
Chenango	19 926	75.3	62 700	20.4	12.1	439	26.3	2.1	23 838	-1.7	1 510	6.3	22 714	29.5	19.9
Clinton	29 423	68.5	84 200	20.1	11.1	479	26.1	2.4	41 470	1.0	2 567	6.2	35 162	28.9	15.8
Columbia	24 796	70.5	111 800	22.5	12.2	553	25.0	2.0	34 676	0.4	1 198	3.5	29 587	33.6	13.8
Cortland	18 210	64.3	74 700	21.3	12.8	471	27.1	1.9	22 872	-1.4	1 629	7.1	22 664	31.6	16.9
Delaware	19 270	75.7	74 200	21.7	12.7	451	27.6	2.3	21 877	0.9	1 076	4.9	20 840	31.6	17.9
Dutchess	99 536	68.9	154 200	22.9	12.4	707	25.9	2.8	130 442	0.7	4 949	3.8	130 793	38.4	10.2
Erie	380 873	65.3	90 800	21.7	13.6	516	28.1	2.2	466 610	0.0	28 409	6.1	431 174	34.7	14.6
Essex	15 028	73.8	77 100	20.7	14.8	452	24.7	2.5	17 656	-3.3	913	5.2	16 539	29.1	13.7
Franklin	17 931	70.3	62 600	19.4	13.1	409	25.8	2.6	22 471	1.2	1 558	6.9	20 104	29.1	13.1
Fulton	21 884	72.1	67 400	21.6	13.8	458	25.8	1.9	26 776	-1.3	1 571	5.9	24 261	26.5	22.1

1. Specified owner-occupied units.   2. Median monthly owner costs is often in the minimum category—9.9 percent or less, which is indicated as 9.9 percent.   3. Specified renter-occupied units.   4. Overcrowded or lacking complete plumbing facilities.   5. Percent of civilian labor force.   6. Persons 16 years old and over.

Table B. States and Counties — Nonfarm Employment and Agriculture

STATE County	Number of establishments	Employment — Total	Health care and social assistance	Manufacturing	Retail trade	Finance and insurance	Professional, scientific, and technical services	Annual payroll Total (mil dol)	Average per employee (dollars)	Farms — Number	Percent with— Less than 50 acres	500 acres and over	Farm operators whose principal occupation is farming (percent)
	104	105	106	107	108	109	110	111	112	113	114	115	116
NEW JERSEY—Cont'd													
Mercer	10 088	182 869	23 280	10 463	19 822	17 276	17 804	8 063	44 089	304	72.4	4.6	46.4
Middlesex	20 698	402 745	32 182	50 245	41 060	19 660	50 929	17 814	44 233	275	77.5	4.0	56.0
Monmouth	18 699	217 824	32 450	11 014	36 923	11 248	18 433	8 157	37 446	892	80.5	2.7	56.8
Morris	17 575	310 950	26 728	31 024	30 888	17 581	34 299	18 376	59 095	407	77.1	0.7	44.2
Ocean	11 226	113 947	24 961	6 731	24 661	4 368	5 736	3 225	28 303	217	79.7	2.3	51.6
Passaic	11 843	172 511	22 102	29 743	23 722	9 628	9 482	6 189	35 878	70	94.3	0.0	61.4
Salem	1 338	18 584	2 745	3 723	D	514	374	715	38 486	753	58.6	6.4	53.7
Somerset	9 545	180 012	16 087	19 211	16 883	15 602	21 488	10 125	56 248	442	73.8	4.1	43.2
Sussex	3 507	30 474	5 147	2 002	5 784	1 891	1 763	910	29 874	1 029	66.2	1.7	47.3
Union	14 709	236 325	26 637	35 244	25 106	10 188	11 577	10 225	43 268	18	100.0	0.0	66.7
Warren	2 768	31 400	4 932	6 618	5 998	732	1 054	1 159	36 897	814	63.8	4.4	48.4
NEW MEXICO	42 686	553 357	81 105	36 932	88 851	24 652	30 545	14 823	26 788	15 170	44.7	28.8	55.9
Bernalillo	15 576	249 523	34 595	18 371	34 391	14 091	18 309	7 225	28 956	618	83.2	3.9	43.0
Catron	73	281	D	D	D	D	4	4	15 117	206	15.0	49.5	71.4
Chaves	1 479	14 837	2 419	2 140	2 588	582	583	329	22 203	604	40.1	36.6	55.1
Cibola	351	6 273	780	457	917	111	174	134	21 429	155	29.0	54.2	55.5
Colfax	521	4 164	528	261	723	153	95	81	19 403	284	10.9	45.8	71.8
Curry	1 015	11 048	2 578	272	2 421	538	258	228	20 642	677	13.9	49.8	63.5
De Baca	60	361	87	D	68	D	D	6	16 767	188	32.4	52.1	63.8
Dona Ana	3 226	37 764	6 956	2 516	6 599	1 319	2 682	816	21 615	1 691	81.1	5.6	45.4
Eddy	1 204	14 955	2 246	1 086	2 281	590	283	410	27 429	510	44.7	31.6	52.2
Grant	671	7 937	1 255	304	1 235	216	782	178	22 486	272	26.5	46.7	52.2
Guadalupe	102	951	76	0	282	D	D	17	17 821	208	20.2	61.1	57.7
Harding	16	33	D	0	D	D	0	1	22 424	129	4.7	76.0	72.9
Hidalgo	101	794	133	D	236	D	2	14	17 091	144	17.4	54.2	54.9
Lea	1 361	15 205	2 111	582	2 324	488	381	389	25 604	554	28.5	38.8	58.1
Lincoln	724	4 704	505	99	988	197	162	94	20 008	343	36.2	40.2	56.6
Los Alamos	421	6 231	1 041	D	414	288	700	222	35 687	6	83.3	0.0	0.0
Luna	403	3 405	560	359	828	141	75	62	18 271	171	25.1	43.9	73.1
McKinley	1 034	14 633	3 019	692	3 923	360	258	335	22 874	150	16.7	48.0	60.0
Mora	54	366	155	D	72	7	D	8	20 801	410	19.0	33.7	60.5
Otero	1 030	12 182	1 965	419	2 355	423	669	237	19 485	622	60.5	15.4	50.8
Quay	273	1 994	369	107	497	96	60	35	17 512	594	14.5	51.7	63.1
Rio Arriba	682	6 536	1 270	244	1 461	147	107	141	21 558	988	55.8	16.4	53.2
Roosevelt	350	2 916	312	185	699	122	74	52	17 728	804	14.6	42.7	59.0
Sandoval	1 261	20 473	1 144	4 673	2 273	889	369	713	34 827	347	55.6	18.7	49.3
San Juan	2 558	36 218	4 649	1 347	5 929	873	944	1 074	29 650	808	71.2	5.3	50.0
San Miguel	495	5 083	1 988	52	1 083	175	105	101	19 914	565	21.6	38.4	63.2
Santa Fe	4 730	44 482	5 826	1 342	9 068	1 838	2 459	1 205	27 081	460	65.2	13.3	51.7
Sierra	279	1 956	358	60	365	72	D	31	15 762	223	41.3	28.7	64.6
Socorro	247	2 501	425	117	319	86	351	56	22 563	388	48.2	25.5	61.1
Taos	1 123	8 638	1 404	169	1 739	178	245	164	19 014	453	59.2	12.6	53.2
Torrance	213	1 838	85	45	509	85	D	32	17 657	461	20.4	46.2	61.8
Union	122	772	148	17	82	107	16	14	18 341	419	2.1	70.2	72.1
Valencia	836	9 443	2 072	865	2 133	365	283	192	20 331	718	85.7	3.6	52.5
NEW YORK	493 863	7 428 349	1 204 095	689 425	841 493	610 998	554 444	343 498	46 241	37 255	30.4	9.4	60.8
Albany	8 840	167 669	26 307	9 289	22 864	16 203	13 223	5 706	34 031	484	38.2	3.3	55.4
Allegany	825	11 426	1 821	2 467	1 554	186	192	253	22 141	867	14.9	8.9	51.3
Bronx	14 209	206 920	81 687	10 375	21 195	2 865	4 410	6 703	32 394	0	NA	NA	NA
Broome	4 298	85 376	12 650	20 078	12 315	3 530	3 321	2 473	28 961	588	23.6	5.4	53.9
Cattaraugus	1 930	24 813	3 333	5 765	4 234	598	408	614	24 727	1 157	22.3	5.8	54.3
Cayuga	1 546	18 604	3 595	3 944	3 427	362	708	485	26 070	881	26.2	13.1	62.0
Chautauqua	3 132	49 017	8 202	15 041	6 646	828	1 293	1 209	24 662	1 734	36.3	4.5	60.3
Chemung	1 871	35 224	6 467	7 563	5 908	1 111	991	928	26 357	427	26.9	6.8	48.2
Chenango	1 008	13 021	1 969	3 302	1 979	920	344	338	25 939	960	24.9	8.3	59.1
Clinton	1 850	24 543	4 407	4 561	4 580	480	543	648	26 404	604	21.4	13.9	65.6
Columbia	1 656	15 720	3 561	2 081	2 612	686	738	411	26 118	498	32.9	13.7	67.7
Cortland	1 073	16 325	3 298	3 808	2 540	414	833	379	23 244	569	21.6	9.5	58.7
Delaware	1 121	12 554	2 212	4 349	1 622	444	288	334	26 622	788	18.4	11.0	63.1
Dutchess	6 862	98 314	16 985	20 590	13 614	3 032	4 643	3 437	34 960	667	45.6	4.7	58.0
Erie	22 593	411 750	64 327	60 729	52 893	24 663	20 954	12 408	30 135	1 289	45.3	4.0	59.4
Essex	1 164	10 027	1 551	1 232	1 944	223	319	246	24 578	236	26.7	13.1	49.2
Franklin	1 086	10 031	2 826	760	1 765	314	234	227	22 630	532	18.6	14.5	68.2
Fulton	1 082	13 425	2 422	2 803	2 040	358	233	331	24 670	246	31.3	6.1	55.7

STATE County	Land in farms Acreage (1,000) [117]	Percent change, 1997–2002 [118]	Acres Average size of farm [119]	Total irrigated (1,000) [120]	Total cropland (1,000) [121]	Value of land and buildings (dollars) Average per farm [122]	Average per acre [123]	Value of machinery and equipment average per farm (dollars) [124]	Value of products sold Total (mil dol) [125]	Average per farm (dollars) [126]	Percent from — Crops [127]	Live-stock and poultry products [128]	Percent of farms with sales of — $10,000 or more [129]	$100,000 or more [130]	Government payments Total ($1,000) [131]	Percent of farms [132]
NEW JERSEY—Cont'd																
Mercer	25	-10.7	82	1	20	1 296 915	18 855	45 689	12	40 286	89.0	11.0	31.3	9.9	140	9.5
Middlesex	22	-21.4	79	3	17	1 060 696	14 664	87 190	23	82 555	93.8	6.2	33.8	13.1	177	4.0
Monmouth	47	-20.3	53	5	33	791 503	17 187	63 417	82	91 425	89.1	10.9	34.4	10.0	127	2.8
Morris	17	-22.7	42	1	10	1 025 669	26 419	36 572	42	102 897	97.5	2.5	23.6	8.4	53	2.2
Ocean	12	9.1	56	1	4	455 399	14 522	35 164	11	49 434	83.6	16.4	29.5	9.7	D	D
Passaic	2	0.0	22	0	0	707 097	32 161	22 793	6	86 768	98.5	1.5	25.7	7.1	0	0.0
Salem	96	4.3	128	19	77	593 464	4 572	78 473	73	96 310	76.9	23.1	31.6	14.1	699	13.1
Somerset	36	-21.7	82	0	23	911 321	14 440	50 486	15	34 081	54.9	45.1	24.9	6.6	210	5.7
Sussex	75	2.7	73	1	38	505 823	7 136	27 611	15	14 340	54.7	45.3	16.4	4.4	332	3.9
Union	0	NA	10	0	0	962 630	93 158	63 259	7	374 975	99.7	0.3	61.1	27.8	0	0.0
Warren	78	-6.0	96	3	56	773 777	7 428	46 112	40	48 772	46.4	53.6	25.9	9.1	623	10.8
NEW MEXICO	44 810	-2.1	2 954	845	2 575	698 908	234	58 262	1 700	112 065	23.4	76.6	31.7	10.5	50 201	21.4
Bernalillo	D	D	D	8	19	314 650	477	19 160	20	32 404	27.6	72.4	12.1	2.8	154	3.2
Catron	1 645	-8.4	7 985	2	17	1 079 512	136	37 470	8	40 568	3.8	96.2	41.3	10.7	211	12.6
Chaves	2 516	-14.5	4 165	70	101	906 296	212	93 665	284	470 115	10.6	89.4	50.3	27.8	3 024	26.2
Cibola	1 691	-0.5	10 909	10	22	1 706 618	153	23 467	4	26 474	D	D	38.1	3.9	126	19.4
Colfax	2 216	-0.5	7 804	23	50	1 724 949	224	54 774	21	72 303	4.3	95.7	46.1	15.5	363	21.5
Curry	916	-3.4	1 354	95	497	625 394	526	100 689	233	343 576	11.4	88.6	43.6	21.4	12 018	69.3
De Baca	1 409	-2.3	7 497	8	22	979 899	129	49 028	15	81 069	23.6	76.4	53.7	23.4	844	35.6
Dona Ana	581	0.0	343	83	95	593 335	1 565	65 938	252	148 934	48.9	51.1	27.5	9.5	2 420	7.5
Eddy	1 183	-7.3	2 320	45	71	552 919	255	68 893	82	161 198	30.2	69.8	40.6	16.1	811	20.0
Grant	1 218	3.7	4 478	4	13	893 388	186	22 975	8	27 733	1.9	98.1	36.8	6.3	159	14.0
Guadalupe	1 462	3.0	7 028	3	15	786 987	104	29 603	10	50 407	3.3	96.7	41.8	12.5	277	19.7
Harding	992	-21.0	7 689	D	34	D	D	41 823	11	88 436	D	D	61.2	14.7	680	56.6
Hidalgo	1 128	2.1	7 830	11	35	1 087 050	139	75 140	17	115 612	68.3	31.7	57.6	16.7	402	31.3
Lea	2 258	12.8	4 076	61	128	654 908	156	88 338	98	177 433	23.0	77.0	42.2	17.5	2 841	28.9
Lincoln	1 606	-18.7	4 681	5	19	887 798	184	42 066	11	32 407	2.1	97.9	33.2	11.1	675	16.3
Los Alamos	D	NA	D	D	0	D	D	9 090	0	2 625	D	D	0.0	0.0	0	0.0
Luna	710	17.7	4 149	23	37	921 812	228	142 308	47	277 419	70.0	30.0	59.6	31.0	1 106	33.3
McKinley	3 170	0.4	21 132	2	31	1 582 773	75	44 187	6	42 674	D	D	25.3	4.0	265	12.0
Mora	955	-2.1	2 328	14	69	756 417	309	38 780	15	35 684	6.6	93.4	25.2	6.1	215	16.6
Otero	1 208	11.7	1 941	8	21	490 368	241	24 891	11	16 952	53.1	46.9	25.2	3.7	203	4.8
Quay	1 652	-11.0	2 780	30	247	510 626	180	57 820	23	38 951	11.8	88.2	42.3	9.6	4 972	60.8
Rio Arriba	1 431	-2.2	1 449	20	87	451 225	328	48 037	11	10 679	16.6	83.4	18.6	1.3	544	10.3
Roosevelt	1 501	5.8	1 867	91	396	535 531	265	89 304	190	236 422	13.0	87.0	41.2	19.2	11 935	63.4
Sandoval	763	-2.2	2 199	11	40	460 877	196	23 780	6	16 255	47.3	52.7	21.3	4.0	D	D
San Juan	1 757	NA	2 174	67	99	705 781	324	92 036	37	45 829	72.9	27.1	15.1	2.1	D	D
San Miguel	2 092	-18.2	3 702	15	81	941 868	250	39 093	12	21 731	10.0	90.0	19.8	4.1	331	10.6
Santa Fe	684	4.9	1 486	19	38	764 738	485	27 412	12	25 615	74.1	25.9	13.5	3.5	387	6.7
Sierra	1 363	5.9	6 112	7	17	1 069 839	175	45 666	19	86 934	29.8	70.2	48.9	13.5	247	17.0
Socorro	1 523	-7.8	3 926	12	26	813 130	208	55 624	36	92 206	12.3	87.7	42.5	13.7	697	12.9
Taos	466	50.3	1 029	8	37	589 978	588	27 735	3	7 558	17.7	82.3	11.7	0.9	146	11.7
Torrance	1 697	14.9	3 681	26	68	726 937	193	56 126	36	78 920	26.1	73.9	38.0	12.1	937	25.4
Union	2 243	0.7	5 354	49	126	1 057 795	200	87 746	143	342 361	10.1	89.9	63.5	27.9	1 778	44.6
Valencia	369	-3.9	514	14	18	317 057	668	28 077	18	24 672	20.9	79.1	14.8	2.5	266	5.3
NEW YORK	7 661	5.6	206	75	4 841	345 504	1 708	96 252	3 118	83 689	36.4	63.6	44.1	17.3	110 234	26.6
Albany	69	21.1	143	0	41	506 093	3 185	58 939	19	39 990	48.4	51.6	31.6	7.9	650	21.9
Allegany	180	13.9	208	1	102	196 765	1 056	64 446	46	52 553	21.7	78.3	33.1	12.6	2 178	29.5
Bronx	0	NA	0	0	0	0	0	0	0	0	0.0	0.0	0.0	0.0	0	0.0
Broome	98	14.0	167	0	54	380 796	2 953	56 935	29	48 966	20.0	80.0	30.6	10.4	1 051	17.0
Cattaraugus	202	5.2	175	0	108	218 769	1 293	92 376	58	50 434	26.9	73.1	36.0	10.3	2 227	28.1
Cayuga	238	-5.6	270	1	178	383 708	1 523	139 374	128	145 334	26.6	73.4	54.3	24.2	3 744	40.3
Chautauqua	256	4.5	148	1	150	192 994	1 401	66 620	99	57 232	36.0	64.0	45.8	15.1	3 636	19.6
Chemung	69	16.9	162	0	37	221 352	1 380	75 945	12	28 253	32.6	67.4	23.9	7.3	644	19.7
Chenango	190	3.8	198	0	101	240 114	1 108	50 591	52	54 460	10.0	90.0	40.5	19.4	2 852	27.5
Clinton	169	13.4	279	0	82	301 399	1 081	143 861	78	129 862	21.7	78.3	43.9	22.5	2 984	26.8
Columbia	120	4.3	240	2	78	867 345	3 165	110 017	52	104 807	34.1	65.9	52.4	20.3	1 667	21.1
Cortland	127	5.0	223	0	70	246 280	1 074	144 158	40	69 786	8.8	91.2	43.6	19.0	1 949	33.7
Delaware	192	4.3	243	0	92	405 821	1 707	72 854	51	64 111	14.4	85.6	45.4	19.4	1 979	28.2
Dutchess	112	4.7	168	1	59	766 660	6 291	58 787	32	47 544	66.7	33.3	37.5	8.8	546	11.7
Erie	162	13.3	125	3	112	247 650	1 847	55 783	92	71 654	45.9	54.1	35.8	12.6	2 109	20.6
Essex	55	14.6	233	0	25	342 420	1 435	79 380	9	36 578	43.2	56.8	41.5	10.2	365	16.5
Franklin	138	-15.3	260	1	78	206 475	971	81 641	48	90 231	13.0	87.0	52.3	25.0	1 894	30.5
Fulton	38	11.8	153	0	23	264 970	1 622	60 232	8	34 241	15.6	84.4	33.7	12.6	469	17.9

Table B. States and Counties — Residential Construction, Wholesale Trade, Retail Trade, and Real Estate

STATE County	Value of residential construction authorized by building permits, 2003		Wholesale trade, 1997				Retail trade,[1] 1997				Real estate and rental and leasing, 1997			
	New construction ($1,000)	Number of housing units	Number of establishments	Number of employees	Sales (mil dol)	Annual payroll (mil dol)	Number of establishments	Number of employees	Sales (mil dol)	Annual payroll (mil dol)	Number of establishments	Number of employees	Receipts (mil dol)	Annual payroll (mil dol)
	133	134	135	136	137	138	139	140	141	142	143	144	145	146
NEW JERSEY—Cont'd														
Mercer	93 357	1 188	472	8 480	4 403.0	291.5	1 442	18 217	3 183.1	326.1	289	1 685	256.7	43.1
Middlesex	245 301	2 306	1 866	36 168	24 256.4	1 554.4	2 785	39 421	7 364.0	720.8	616	4 098	743.5	129.7
Monmouth	382 091	2 756	1 197	9 577	6 298.1	410.3	2 870	34 839	6 400.5	627.7	599	2 795	444.5	74.8
Morris	217 383	1 555	1 397	20 533	20 939.4	1 027.2	2 241	30 767	6 499.9	635.5	536	2 920	620.8	109.8
Ocean	453 554	4 009	429	2 903	937.2	95.4	1 923	23 431	4 728.3	431.5	386	1 345	190.3	30.2
Passaic	86 449	829	1 006	13 154	9 085.0	601.8	1 843	25 468	4 659.9	469.0	415	1 710	251.4	45.8
Salem	31 239	307	45	517	440.3	19.3	226	2 682	401.3	41.5	52	183	20.5	3.6
Somerset	163 840	1 260	672	12 018	18 285.3	643.4	1 178	15 351	3 305.8	306.7	271	1 555	249.8	45.8
Sussex	94 538	587	181	D	D	D	502	4 689	953.6	92.7	82	256	36.5	5.6
Union	92 774	1 198	1 222	22 744	15 712.5	1 085.7	2 100	22 616	4 809.2	464.9	648	3 184	756.1	88.6
Warren	73 396	585	129	D	D	D	466	5 106	862.2	90.1	74	242	35.2	4.7
NEW MEXICO	1 703 302	13 759	2 182	21 344	7 397.6	601.1	7 421	86 300	14 984.5	1 455.5	1 887	8 844	893.9	165.2
Bernalillo	688 047	6 569	1 037	12 824	4 594.3	388.2	2 307	34 361	6 497.7	623.6	751	4 519	504.2	85.0
Catron	NA	NA	NA	NA	NA	NA	12	37	3.1	0.3	3	22	1.6	0.4
Chaves	7 278	55	74	599	231.3	13.8	269	2 702	411.0	40.5	74	198	18.6	3.1
Cibola	0	0	17	82	21.8	1.4	77	809	149.3	11.3	13	80	4.0	1.2
Colfax	14 994	68	13	D	D	D	95	606	104.6	9.1	16	49	3.0	0.5
Curry	18 207	161	44	342	120.5	7.3	235	2 455	342.6	34.6	53	177	9.8	1.8
De Baca	NA	NA	1	D	D	D	13	59	8.7	0.8	2	D	D	D
Dona Ana	223 160	1 767	122	978	283.6	25.0	511	6 266	1 059.1	98.1	175	530	44.8	7.4
Eddy	6 578	67	69	384	274.7	10.3	232	2 312	372.7	38.9	58	217	15.6	3.8
Grant	NA	NA	32	198	56.6	4.1	125	1 165	190.4	17.9	31	89	6.7	1.2
Guadalupe	NA	NA	5	7	9.8	0.2	27	333	32.0	3.5	2	D	D	D
Harding	NA	NA	NA	NA	NA	NA	3	13	8.1	0.5	NA	NA	NA	NA
Hidalgo	NA	NA	3	D	D	D	36	238	49.3	3.7	1	D	D	D
Lea	5 744	38	121	964	308.7	27.2	248	2 375	405.3	42.6	58	360	43.0	10.5
Lincoln	31 680	195	16	35	7.7	0.6	148	1 079	149.1	15.1	53	129	11.4	1.7
Los Alamos	28 549	110	9	75	41.4	4.1	59	555	74.1	8.0	16	D	D	D
Luna	6 444	95	22	233	49.3	3.1	95	950	177.5	12.3	13	38	2.7	0.5
McKinley	3 083	24	74	761	191.9	13.5	269	3 670	585.5	59.6	36	156	11.7	2.1
Mora	NA	NA	NA	NA	NA	NA	12	57	7.3	0.7	2	D	D	D
Otero	28 198	168	22	121	29.7	2.5	215	2 281	326.5	32.3	47	170	11.8	2.1
Quay	NA	NA	10	33	4.5	0.4	71	594	99.6	8.5	12	44	1.7	0.4
Rio Arriba	1 480	10	19	84	40.2	1.6	104	1 149	189.0	18.2	15	33	2.4	0.4
Roosevelt	3 719	50	17	103	33.7	2.0	71	626	121.2	10.6	11	18	1.0	0.1
Sandoval	97 364	1 038	48	456	248.3	11.2	155	1 902	274.0	31.0	42	193	18.0	3.1
San Juan	44 360	367	158	1 278	381.9	35.7	494	5 896	990.8	96.7	87	495	35.1	15.3
San Miguel	NA	NA	16	62	19.4	1.3	114	1 087	168.4	15.1	14	53	2.8	0.5
Santa Fe	70 719	561	167	1 260	340.2	39.3	846	7 868	1 422.9	149.4	200	D	D	D
Sierra	320	3	7	21	7.5	0.8	60	379	62.6	5.2	15	47	1.8	0.4
Socorro	1 307	8	6	102	12.3	1.4	57	385	70.6	6.3	10	26	1.5	0.2
Taos	26 099	207	16	59	11.8	1.0	259	1 554	206.8	23.7	39	145	7.3	1.4
Torrance	NA	NA	10	57	10.4	1.2	44	441	73.2	5.6	6	6	0.5	0.1
Union	NA	NA	2	D	D	D	27	103	15.3	1.3	2	D	D	D
Valencia	34 994	329	25	104	38.1	1.7	131	1 993	336.2	30.4	30	96	8.5	1.2
NEW YORK	6 193 971	49 708	37 499	414 249	319 697.6	17 185.8	75 241	805 208	139 303.9	14 329.8	27 214	145 326	27 770.1	4 447.8
Albany	110 481	793	581	8 866	4 335.8	322.3	1 483	21 444	3 567.2	348.1	343	2 535	383.6	57.6
Allegany	7 857	100	26	235	54.8	3.9	181	1 646	210.6	20.4	18	57	3.4	0.6
Bronx	220 645	2 935	755	10 728	5 373.6	389.9	3 110	21 641	3 434.9	352.5	2 171	7 435	1 212.8	182.5
Broome	48 917	298	261	D	D	D	829	11 881	1 763.3	164.2	128	613	82.3	10.1
Cattaraugus	15 336	144	86	979	409.1	28.0	380	4 190	570.7	56.1	52	182	16.1	2.8
Cayuga	17 779	166	78	746	201.3	20.7	265	3 250	516.8	50.5	42	187	18.7	3.1
Chautauqua	46 363	373	159	2 171	748.6	57.6	591	7 096	1 011.1	96.6	86	395	41.9	7.0
Chemung	18 528	145	107	1 667	447.2	49.2	412	5 963	875.9	82.9	66	345	47.9	7.4
Chenango	4 273	78	30	332	64.3	6.7	204	1 793	293.8	27.3	32	66	7.4	1.1
Clinton	34 126	257	115	1 515	407.0	29.6	445	4 967	756.6	70.8	65	219	18.2	2.5
Columbia	55 644	322	81	686	250.6	20.2	260	2 647	424.1	42.0	49	128	11.6	2.4
Cortland	11 474	111	35	401	195.7	11.8	200	2 658	423.9	38.5	24	90	11.1	1.3
Delaware	19 034	155	40	278	150.8	7.4	243	1 810	307.8	29.2	38	118	13.1	1.6
Dutchess	212 609	1 144	274	D	D	D	1 097	13 506	2 259.5	225.7	256	1 502	165.9	28.5
Erie	362 615	2 312	1 680	25 712	14 962.5	884.6	3 628	55 286	8 036.3	797.2	738	5 325	719.1	126.1
Essex	30 950	199	22	178	49.7	5.2	251	1 611	283.8	25.9	34	89	10.1	2.2
Franklin	10 930	124	37	310	126.7	6.8	215	1 834	283.9	26.0	25	71	6.6	1.3
Fulton	12 801	112	78	763	336.1	22.7	195	2 019	331.8	30.1	26	72	7.8	1.1

1. Establishments with payroll.

STATE County	Professional, scientific, and technical services,[1] 1997				Manufacturing, 1997				Accommodation and foodservices, 1997			
	Number of establishments	Number of employees	Receipts (mil dol)	Annual payroll (mil dol)	Number of establishments	Number of employees	Receipts (mil dol)	Annual payroll (mil dol)	Number of establishments	Number of employees	Sales (mil dol)	Annual payroll (mil dol)
	147	148	149	150	151	152	153	154	155	156	157	158
NEW JERSEY—Cont'd												
Mercer	1 223	10 930	1 407.3	586.2	352	13 537	2 413.6	579.7	703	9 870	394.0	109.9
Middlesex	2 682	33 101	3 953.4	1 790.4	977	49 983	13 688.0	1 950.6	1 318	17 941	761.8	201.0
Monmouth	2 195	13 292	1 460.2	617.6	587	12 820	2 318.3	402.7	1 377	18 131	689.8	194.5
Morris	2 452	26 674	3 528.4	1 443.6	749	24 461	7 531.5	979.6	1 080	14 790	665.8	184.0
Ocean	831	4 325	347.8	151.1	309	7 174	939.8	201.1	946	10 569	420.2	108.7
Passaic	1 083	7 338	817.1	256.0	1 059	34 589	6 464.2	1 237.6	764	8 212	338.9	91.0
Salem	86	301	22.3	9.1	48	4 188	1 156.2	207.5	109	1 246	45.1	12.5
Somerset	1 501	23 781	2 218.9	898.2	376	16 289	5 148.4	856.7	618	8 092	356.6	102.2
Sussex	329	1 059	109.1	40.6	146	2 854	320.8	87.2	254	3 006	106.2	31.4
Union	1 554	10 502	1 178.1	480.0	996	40 157	13 883.3	1 619.7	1 064	11 982	513.2	138.3
Warren	237	892	86.8	36.4	164	7 188	1 982.3	294.4	224	2 144	80.6	20.8
NEW MEXICO	3 702	31 535	3 243.4	1 307.3	1 593	39 664	17 906.1	1 135.8	3 825	67 134	2 144.9	599.1
Bernalillo	1 881	23 092	2 578.3	1 040.4	703	D	D	D	1 202	26 744	878.1	248.1
Catron	2	D	D	D	NA	NA	NA	NA	11	45	1.7	0.4
Chaves	87	458	37.5	13.6	51	D	D	D	115	1 970	54.8	14.7
Cibola	18	62	3.1	1.1	NA	NA	NA	NA	46	642	21.4	5.3
Colfax	31	77	5.0	2.0	NA	NA	NA	NA	79	1 205	34.6	12.7
Curry	66	249	13.5	5.3	NA	NA	NA	NA	83	1 631	45.9	13.1
De Baca	2	D	D	D	NA	NA	NA	NA	8	44	1.2	0.3
Dona Ana	222	1 334	107.3	45.7	111	2 290	395.5	46.9	253	4 278	121.7	32.6
Eddy	53	231	20.3	9.0	41	1 057	641.4	43.9	102	1 761	52.5	14.3
Grant	37	173	8.7	3.3	NA	NA	NA	NA	72	823	25.1	6.2
Guadalupe	2	D	D	D	NA	NA	NA	NA	33	317	10.1	2.4
Harding	2	D	D	D	NA	NA	NA	NA	3	10	0.1	0.0
Hidalgo	2	D	D	D	2	D	D	D	24	301	7.9	2.6
Lea	67	338	19.9	8.4	45	524	379.7	14.8	109	1 510	42.0	11.3
Lincoln	53	154	10.4	3.8	NA	NA	NA	NA	99	866	30.1	7.6
Los Alamos	67	728	76.2	32.1	NA	NA	NA	NA	42	696	20.5	6.3
Luna	20	68	2.7	1.1	16	776	49.5	10.7	51	595	16.0	4.4
McKinley	38	219	10.6	3.7	NA	NA	NA	NA	133	2 061	69.3	17.5
Mora	3	D	D	D	NA	NA	NA	NA	4	12	0.2	0.1
Otero	53	240	12.3	5.3	26	593	93.8	10.5	99	1 324	37.0	9.9
Quay	12	48	1.8	0.8	NA	NA	NA	NA	46	526	16.2	3.9
Rio Arriba	35	87	5.9	1.6	NA	NA	NA	NA	89	1 059	33.9	9.5
Roosevelt	12	37	2.2	0.6	NA	NA	NA	NA	30	581	12.4	3.3
Sandoval	97	396	28.0	10.7	57	D	D	D	92	1 501	46.0	12.1
San Juan	166	919	50.9	19.9	71	1 147	257.8	30.3	173	3 478	100.0	27.3
San Miguel	30	87	4.0	1.3	NA	NA	NA	NA	69	796	24.0	5.8
Santa Fe	464	1 964	205.9	85.1	162	1 436	124.8	31.7	361	7 498	304.8	89.1
Sierra	18	41	1.9	0.6	NA	NA	NA	NA	47	437	13.0	3.2
Socorro	20	102	7.6	2.8	NA	NA	NA	NA	51	658	18.7	5.2
Taos	71	181	11.8	4.0	NA	NA	NA	NA	167	2 232	63.7	19.1
Torrance	10	24	1.6	0.4	NA	NA	NA	NA	32	361	8.9	2.5
Union	7	17	1.0	0.3	NA	NA	NA	NA	20	226	4.8	1.2
Valencia	54	180	12.7	3.8	40	967	110.3	22.3	80	946	28.3	7.0
NEW YORK	45 619	416 892	57 475.0	21 773.1	23 908	785 891	146 720.2	26 515.8	38 045	473 327	21 671.1	6 101.1
Albany	860	8 250	848.7	330.0	272	9 065	2 182.4	335.9	841	12 586	449.2	125.0
Allegany	49	148	11.4	3.7	57	2 919	542.8	102.4	87	961	29.1	7.8
Bronx	391	1 980	158.6	50.7	527	12 941	1 252.3	319.6	1 067	8 264	371.6	95.7
Broome	316	2 334	183.7	68.6	242	20 429	3 147.6	787.8	476	6 940	204.2	58.1
Cattaraugus	79	357	31.5	7.8	95	5 341	930.5	162.9	227	3 309	79.5	23.4
Cayuga	90	532	36.1	15.0	100	3 859	618.6	110.4	172	1 688	52.5	14.2
Chautauqua	168	815	48.5	19.2	222	13 084	2 973.6	409.1	368	4 323	124.9	35.4
Chemung	104	827	56.5	18.3	94	9 098	1 357.3	278.1	213	2 965	86.2	24.4
Chenango	65	267	19.9	6.7	86	3 829	790.4	120.3	97	848	24.0	6.0
Clinton	92	328	20.9	8.1	82	4 188	777.9	131.8	189	2 243	64.7	20.0
Columbia	132	538	43.8	16.1	86	2 531	331.1	62.2	142	1 130	41.9	11.1
Cortland	62	457	36.4	13.8	70	4 521	736.1	123.5	125	1 845	53.0	13.7
Delaware	75	224	10.1	3.6	60	4 386	783.7	147.9	124	740	31.1	7.3
Dutchess	591	3 149	284.3	113.6	210	11 848	3 032.9	521.3	558	6 243	252.1	64.4
Erie	1 790	15 551	1 413.9	527.1	1 251	63 234	14 054.5	2 422.1	2 143	31 916	935.4	271.6
Essex	59	145	11.9	3.5	40	1 474	285.2	50.4	219	1 942	86.9	28.1
Franklin	53	170	10.8	4.0	26	1 165	144.4	24.9	127	899	30.6	7.9
Fulton	59	183	12.4	4.0	116	3 548	443.6	86.6	112	957	28.2	7.3

1. Firms subject to federal tax.

Table B. States and Counties — Health Care and Social Assistance, Other Services, and Federal Funds

STATE County	Health care and social assistance,[1] 1997				Other services,[1] 1997				Federal funds and grants, 2002–2003 Expenditures (mil dol)			
										Direct payments for individuals[2]		
	Number of establishments	Number of employees	Receipts (mil dol)	Annual payroll (mil dol)	Number of establishments	Number of employees	Receipts (mil dol)	Annual payroll (mil dol)	Total	Social Security and government retirement	Medicare	Food stamps and Supplemental Security Income
	159	160	161	162	163	164	165	166	167	168	169	170
NEW JERSEY—Cont'd												
Mercer	792	6 837	576.4	260.0	538	2 985	210.3	62.1	3 730.2	967.5	448.5	51.0
Middlesex	1 429	13 628	1 231.2	469.8	1 261	6 628	511.4	145.4	3 983.4	1 331.6	733.4	60.4
Monmouth	1 695	13 866	1 057.5	462.7	1 177	5 961	382.6	119.5	4 120.3	1 393.3	664.6	43.5
Morris	1 330	11 147	930.5	387.8	1 031	5 308	403.3	119.0	2 020.0	923.5	383.2	17.7
Ocean	984	12 337	855.6	362.5	767	3 074	185.1	50.9	3 161.3	1 743.1	842.3	33.2
Passaic	1 033	8 552	840.7	306.5	823	3 926	287.8	89.5	2 444.3	831.3	512.0	90.8
Salem	108	744	56.1	22.9	102	285	20.0	4.5	389.7	152.6	88.3	8.6
Somerset	706	7 075	613.1	252.4	498	2 331	175.9	54.8	1 084.9	533.4	196.7	9.2
Sussex	244	2 849	151.9	67.9	250	886	61.8	16.6	521.0	262.0	108.7	7.5
Union	1 194	10 405	800.1	348.7	1 100	5 844	432.1	137.8	2 568.7	1 058.8	618.8	65.7
Warren	197	1 440	101.0	42.3	190	750	53.8	14.5	467.0	231.1	122.2	8.0
NEW MEXICO	2 923	32 824	2 057.3	864.3	2 318	13 448	759.1	227.2	18 735.9	4 151.2	1 190.5	420.2
Bernalillo	1 152	16 080	1 115.2	463.3	896	6 596	374.4	121.2	6 732.7	1 400.7	392.1	113.3
Catron	NA	NA	NA	NA	2	D	D	D	27.5	12.8	2.0	0.5
Chaves	121	826	48.5	22.8	79	335	19.5	5.0	352.4	143.2	46.9	17.7
Cibola	20	203	10.3	4.2	28	72	3.7	0.9	120.3	44.6	0.0	5.4
Colfax	18	154	8.0	3.3	22	54	2.8	0.8	83.6	40.2	13.6	2.6
Curry	96	738	41.0	16.5	76	334	17.7	4.7	422.2	112.3	31.8	6.1
De Baca	3	D	D	D	3	7	0.4	0.1	17.0	7.4	2.7	0.5
Dona Ana	272	3 149	177.9	75.3	169	1 025	43.9	13.2	1 241.1	347.6	95.4	56.5
Eddy	84	1 101	70.4	26.4	84	353	25.1	5.5	433.2	121.8	50.5	12.9
Grant	46	298	18.7	8.4	46	149	6.9	1.7	192.3	92.5	25.8	6.9
Guadalupe	4	37	0.9	0.6	5	22	1.4	0.3	56.3	9.5	4.5	1.8
Harding	1	D	D	D	1	D	D	D	8.1	3.0	0.9	0.1
Hidalgo	5	D	D	D	4	5	0.6	0.1	42.3	16.2	4.7	1.5
Lea	86	1 121	70.6	23.1	100	722	43.4	12.7	260.8	104.7	51.9	14.5
Lincoln	35	214	9.3	5.6	23	96	5.4	1.3	108.8	58.1	13.4	2.9
Los Alamos	48	352	20.1	10.0	16	68	4.3	1.5	2 087.4	30.0	9.9	0.2
Luna	34	155	8.3	3.1	18	78	4.3	1.0	141.9	66.4	20.6	7.6
McKinley	41	391	15.1	5.9	69	332	16.1	4.5	592.5	98.6	31.2	32.0
Mora	3	72	1.4	0.9	1	D	D	D	46.9	12.8	3.5	2.0
Otero	61	491	27.0	11.6	59	284	13.8	4.2	626.4	180.6	31.3	10.2
Quay	19	123	4.7	2.1	19	79	4.4	0.9	82.8	29.2	11.0	3.2
Rio Arriba	46	545	30.4	13.0	27	68	4.4	0.9	286.5	76.5	25.9	12.8
Roosevelt	12	44	2.9	1.4	27	82	5.2	1.1	134.3	36.4	16.7	5.2
Sandoval	57	610	37.7	15.5	55	302	13.7	4.0	370.3	185.2	46.7	13.0
San Juan	169	1 379	85.8	39.6	176	1 076	66.4	18.7	575.5	193.4	60.4	26.1
San Miguel	55	523	21.5	9.8	29	88	4.5	1.1	235.8	58.9	22.8	9.6
Santa Fe	298	2 831	164.1	74.0	170	854	54.5	15.8	1 173.4	316.7	69.7	13.0
Sierra	9	54	1.6	0.7	16	62	2.3	0.7	106.7	53.4	18.9	3.2
Socorro	12	81	5.5	2.2	12	24	2.1	0.4	150.6	33.4	9.2	7.3
Taos	53	397	23.0	8.4	31	86	5.5	1.2	197.0	66.8	17.8	11.2
Torrance	7	29	1.7	0.8	10	21	1.1	0.2	73.9	32.1	16.0	4.3
Union	4	57	3.3	1.0	5	16	1.0	0.2	32.0	12.4	4.7	0.8
Valencia	52	628	28.4	12.4	40	151	9.3	3.1	295.6	152.8	47.3	15.5
NEW YORK	36 054	358 075	26 008.3	10 970.9	30 104	146 365	10 014.6	2 858.7	137 898.0	37 462.4	21 967.6	4 719.9
Albany	601	7 195	516.5	239.9	513	3 599	270.1	79.1	9 170.5	1 265.5	271.3	45.7
Allegany	66	1 028	34.0	14.3	49	181	10.5	2.2	254.2	108.4	44.2	10.2
Bronx	1 050	15 530	1 014.2	448.1	1 254	4 612	319.1	93.3	(4)	(4)	(4)	(4)
Broome	343	3 912	286.7	131.3	296	1 407	93.2	24.7	1 295.7	503.3	214.0	40.2
Cattaraugus	112	1 266	87.1	25.9	94	400	27.0	6.1	596.2	195.4	80.1	16.4
Cayuga	136	969	60.5	25.6	85	411	31.5	7.1	404.6	173.7	75.5	12.0
Chautauqua	243	2 304	109.8	49.9	178	721	45.2	11.3	840.9	342.1	140.1	30.0
Chemung	162	1 675	123.1	60.7	108	553	36.1	9.8	539.2	228.8	92.2	19.3
Chenango	62	417	22.8	9.8	59	164	12.2	2.7	266.1	122.3	40.4	9.6
Clinton	146	1 302	79.3	33.9	115	466	29.7	8.3	412.7	176.2	61.2	16.6
Columbia	106	1 196	63.4	26.8	94	308	27.3	6.1	356.7	152.5	61.3	8.6
Cortland	82	967	44.5	20.5	71	484	45.9	15.9	219.9	96.6	36.5	8.2
Delaware	54	243	15.8	5.1	60	162	12.1	2.5	301.3	121.1	49.7	7.6
Dutchess	583	4 980	347.7	145.8	448	1 802	125.0	33.3	1 310.9	600.0	233.5	28.8
Erie	1 916	25 392	1 397.0	624.4	1 603	9 094	585.9	169.4	6 281.5	2 339.0	1 033.4	197.5
Essex	39	288	14.5	7.2	43	148	9.7	2.0	259.4	104.7	40.2	6.1
Franklin	71	354	30.1	11.0	49	129	7.0	1.6	287.2	105.8	41.8	9.4
Fulton	70	430	26.6	9.7	59	343	19.6	6.6	269.3	122.2	50.1	9.7

1. Firms subject to federal tax.   2. State totals may include programs not allocated by county.   4. Bronx, Kings, Queens, and Richmond Counties included with New York County.

Table B. States and Counties — Federal Funds and Local Government Finances

STATE County	Federal funds and grants, 2002–2003 (cont'd)							Local government finances, 2002				
	Expenditures (mil dol) (cont'd)							General revenue				
	Procurement contract awards			Grants[1]						Taxes		
											Per capita[2] (dollars)	
	Salaries and wages	Defense	Other	Medicaid and other health-related	Nutrition and family welfare	Education	Other	Total (mil dol)	Intergovern-mental (mil dol)	Total (mil dol)	Total	Property
	171	172	173	174	175	176	177	178	179	180	181	182
NEW JERSEY—Cont'd												
Mercer	183.0	107.7	115.3	472.8	306.2	294.9	737.3	1 637.7	606.7	796.6	2 216	2 190
Middlesex	254.1	104.0	213.6	384.8	40.2	18.7	774.4	2 481.1	769.1	1 396.3	1 800	1 767
Monmouth	469.8	948.1	138.7	269.6	40.0	20.2	110.6	2 453.7	722.3	1 335.2	2 120	2 091
Morris	244.0	203.0	74.2	90.7	9.4	6.6	55.4	1 755.1	306.8	1 171.7	2 447	2 425
Ocean	192.8	59.5	40.9	133.9	34.5	14.8	50.3	1 629.8	515.8	904.5	1 684	1 660
Passaic	89.6	283.0	29.3	376.1	79.5	22.7	98.6	1 452.1	549.3	753.7	1 517	1 507
Salem	13.7	4.5	3.6	39.7	7.8	3.1	61.8	282.4	118.4	99.4	1 543	1 520
Somerset	105.5	66.4	69.4	56.6	9.8	3.8	30.0	1 100.6	247.4	706.4	2 280	2 250
Sussex	24.3	21.5	10.2	34.2	4.0	3.3	42.6	531.2	175.9	297.8	2 003	1 985
Union	186.3	80.1	71.6	291.2	49.2	20.5	87.6	2 035.2	801.8	985.5	1 857	1 835
Warren	20.0	14.3	4.8	33.3	8.0	3.7	15.4	399.5	155.4	191.9	1 784	1 766
NEW MEXICO	1 925.9	955.4	4 863.6	1 887.2	502.3	519.7	1 413.1	X	X	X	X	X
Bernalillo	958.8	467.8	2 400.6	496.1	83.7	45.2	304.7	1 601.0	816.6	477.4	832	501
Catron	4.4	0.1	1.6	2.9	0.3	0.2	2.7	9.4	7.8	0.8	239	229
Chaves	21.6	4.6	8.9	72.0	10.0	6.9	15.2	161.8	103.0	33.3	554	264
Cibola	19.7	18.2	3.0	1.3	10.1	5.4	5.4	50.5	35.2	9.6	364	161
Colfax	3.2	1.5	0.6	14.1	2.3	0.9	3.9	54.7	26.2	10.0	707	397
Curry	134.8	37.3	4.6	46.5	9.9	4.1	8.9	121.1	87.3	20.3	451	194
De Baca	0.7	0.0	0.2	3.5	0.6	0.1	0.7	7.6	5.9	0.8	383	272
Dona Ana	146.6	219.1	78.6	139.6	29.9	15.6	77.7	459.5	284.2	110.7	620	305
Eddy	27.5	1.8	135.2	51.9	12.4	2.9	13.8	157.1	93.2	36.9	722	356
Grant	11.8	0.1	3.6	34.4	5.2	2.3	4.2	106.2	58.1	13.3	439	219
Guadalupe	1.9	0.2	0.3	18.6	1.1	0.3	17.8	23.7	15.0	4.2	913	578
Harding	0.6	0.0	0.2	0.7	0.1	0.1	1.6	5.1	4.2	0.5	640	534
Hidalgo	2.4	0.0	0.2	6.4	1.5	0.5	7.4	20.2	12.6	4.3	807	640
Lea	6.4	0.0	1.5	47.3	9.9	4.6	9.5	178.8	105.3	40.8	734	279
Lincoln	5.4	0.1	2.5	9.5	2.2	1.7	12.8	67.4	40.3	16.4	827	590
Los Alamos	15.1	13.0	1 994.1	17.3	0.2	0.6	6.9	128.6	95.1	18.7	1 020	490
Luna	7.7	3.1	1.4	22.7	4.2	2.1	4.1	63.8	43.5	8.6	340	187
McKinley	115.4	38.2	29.3	144.6	23.8	59.3	16.5	201.1	154.4	28.1	379	199
Mora	2.2	0.0	0.4	20.3	2.8	0.6	2.2	15.7	14.0	1.5	288	213
Otero	197.9	123.7	9.3	33.3	7.0	7.9	18.7	109.3	72.6	23.8	387	211
Quay	3.0	0.0	0.6	14.2	4.8	1.1	6.6	37.0	24.0	6.9	707	291
Rio Arriba	17.1	1.0	12.3	102.0	11.0	10.0	11.1	98.1	64.4	23.9	582	440
Roosevelt	3.1	0.7	0.9	22.9	3.5	3.8	7.5	43.1	29.2	6.6	366	177
Sandoval	16.1	1.5	3.3	55.9	10.9	14.1	20.3	210.3	125.4	51.0	531	318
San Juan	79.3	1.2	15.5	99.2	15.7	37.5	27.7	414.1	228.8	85.4	710	390
San Miguel	7.9	1.4	1.4	94.1	11.8	7.9	13.2	90.2	66.9	15.4	519	305
Santa Fe	71.0	14.2	130.2	148.8	103.4	118.3	174.4	355.1	162.6	129.0	959	524
Sierra	5.1	0.0	1.3	16.4	1.5	1.0	5.5	27.4	17.7	5.9	457	254
Socorro	9.7	5.7	9.2	25.2	4.1	3.8	38.1	42.9	27.6	10.2	563	391
Taos	16.1	0.6	9.2	58.1	6.6	2.1	7.2	79.4	54.1	16.7	542	286
Torrance	3.3	0.0	1.7	15.3	2.3	1.0	6.3	57.3	44.7	8.2	493	377
Union	2.9	0.0	0.5	6.6	0.6	0.5	0.7	17.2	13.2	2.6	663	408
Valencia	7.3	0.3	1.6	45.5	13.0	5.1	4.9	147.8	109.2	27.7	410	243
NEW YORK	8 535.2	4 252.8	3 505.4	26 018.6	5 892.8	2 772.6	12 890.7	X	X	X	X	X
Albany	326.3	57.9	85.7	571.0	121.7	933.7	5 311.9	1 195.8	377.1	596.1	2 013	1 274
Allegany	7.8	1.1	6.1	41.6	12.9	3.3	9.0	203.6	120.4	62.1	1 238	937
Bronx	(4)	(4)	(4)	(4)	(4)	(4)	(4)	(4)	(4)	(4)	(4)	(4)
Broome	50.7	172.1	17.0	154.4	28.3	17.4	83.0	813.4	377.4	307.0	1 533	1 050
Cattaraugus	28.4	6.0	25.0	74.4	18.4	77.4	12.6	401.7	220.4	123.7	1 485	954
Cayuga	12.3	4.9	4.5	72.0	12.6	6.4	19.2	304.7	146.3	104.1	1 277	885
Chautauqua	27.3	48.9	20.1	126.5	29.1	14.3	46.0	606.0	304.3	183.0	1 323	1 013
Chemung	25.9	4.4	6.1	94.9	17.8	6.0	38.1	333.9	168.0	109.7	1 210	797
Chenango	7.7	3.0	2.0	46.4	8.7	5.1	12.6	209.2	118.8	62.9	1 225	1 011
Clinton	28.1	4.5	7.8	71.5	12.3	6.4	16.8	316.7	158.8	103.4	1 275	883
Columbia	11.3	0.7	6.6	80.7	8.2	3.5	13.2	248.2	96.3	114.3	1 800	1 370
Cortland	8.4	1.5	2.3	35.6	9.1	4.1	12.5	184.8	95.0	62.2	1 273	873
Delaware	15.3	15.6	13.9	48.5	7.8	3.1	12.5	229.0	96.5	81.4	1 720	1 504
Dutchess	69.7	6.3	19.2	241.7	23.1	15.3	53.0	1 052.5	372.7	535.8	1 862	1 410
Erie	495.6	239.9	264.6	1 029.0	222.8	82.4	290.0	3 816.5	1 652.4	1 402.2	1 484	1 037
Essex	23.7	16.0	5.3	44.2	6.3	2.1	8.8	184.7	66.4	86.7	2 227	1 767
Franklin	10.4	0.1	3.1	75.8	9.7	5.8	15.7	222.8	125.3	61.8	1 213	974
Fulton	7.2	9.3	2.6	49.4	7.6	4.2	2.6	234.0	110.3	75.6	1 374	1 047

1. State totals may include programs not allocated by county.   2. Based on the resident population estimated as of July 1 of the year shown.   4. Bronx, Kings, Queens, and Richmond Counties included with New York County.

Table B. States and Counties — Local Government Finances, Government Employment, and Elections

STATE County	Local government finances, 2002 (cont'd) Direct general expenditure Total (mil dol)	Per capita[1] (dollars)	Percent of total for — Education	Health and hospitals	Police protection	Public welfare	High-ways	Debt outstanding Total (mil dol)	Per capita[1] (dollars)	Government employment, 2002 Federal civilian	Federal military	State and local	Presidential election, 2004 Percent of vote cast — Democratic	Republican	All other
	183	184	185	186	187	188	189	190	191	192	193	194	195	196	197
NEW JERSEY—Cont'd															
Mercer	1 554.6	4 325	53.8	1.1	5.5	4.3	1.6	1 564.9	4 353	2 894	551	48 450	61.0	38.1	0.9
Middlesex	2 511.0	3 238	55.0	1.3	6.4	2.6	2.1	2 413.0	3 111	3 513	1 260	52 524	56.2	42.9	0.9
Monmouth	2 510.9	3 987	55.1	1.1	5.5	2.9	3.6	2 068.5	3 284	8 219	2 589	31 901	44.5	54.6	0.9
Morris	1 668.0	3 484	57.8	1.6	5.9	1.0	3.8	1 255.4	2 622	5 008	941	24 468	41.3	57.9	0.8
Ocean	1 586.9	2 955	54.9	0.6	6.4	3.6	4.2	1 469.2	2 736	2 831	1 407	22 576	38.8	60.3	0.9
Passaic	1 466.6	2 953	45.7	3.0	7.7	5.6	2.7	897.8	1 808	1 836	708	26 796	55.2	44.1	0.7
Salem	283.6	4 401	49.6	1.9	3.2	6.0	3.9	521.7	8 096	181	92	3 937	46.1	52.8	1.0
Somerset	1 074.8	3 468	61.4	2.4	4.9	1.0	4.0	849.7	2 742	1 565	441	14 284	47.3	51.8	0.9
Sussex	522.8	3 516	66.2	1.2	4.0	1.4	5.2	342.2	2 302	375	212	7 014	34.2	64.5	1.3
Union	1 986.9	3 743	54.1	2.9	7.1	3.3	2.8	1 242.4	2 341	2 455	758	30 009	58.7	40.5	0.7
Warren	402.0	3 739	57.5	2.8	3.3	3.3	3.5	243.7	2 266	284	153	5 574	37.3	61.2	1.4
NEW MEXICO	X	X	X	X	X	X	X	X	X	29 043	16 796	164 116	48.9	50.0	1.1
Bernalillo	1 539.3	2 683	45.6	2.4	8.2	0.4	4.8	1 405.5	2 450	12 993	5 714	48 298	51.3	47.5	1.2
Catron	8.8	2 495	55.2	0.0	6.3	0.0	10.1	2.0	568	138	0	209	27.8	71.5	0.8
Chaves	165.1	2 743	49.8	0.1	6.9	1.7	2.6	94.5	1 570	358	168	4 288	31.0	68.1	0.9
Cibola	46.3	1 767	59.1	0.3	3.5	1.7	3.8	21.4	818	389	71	3 041	55.6	41.1	3.3
Colfax	53.7	3 785	43.4	29.0	5.1	0.3	4.8	13.6	959	58	38	1 543	47.3	51.6	1.0
Curry	119.0	2 644	67.9	0.3	5.4	0.4	3.9	34.4	764	859	3 564	2 636	24.8	74.6	0.6
De Baca	7.6	3 570	57.1	2.5	3.3	0.0	15.1	3.7	1 723	16	0	183	28.3	71.1	0.6
Dona Ana	437.1	2 447	62.4	0.5	5.4	1.3	4.0	268.6	1 503	3 394	538	16 323	50.7	48.2	1.0
Eddy	147.9	2 893	54.6	4.5	6.9	1.0	5.7	55.0	1 075	517	138	2 959	33.9	65.5	0.6
Grant	96.5	3 190	42.7	27.8	4.3	1.0	2.4	32.3	1 068	245	81	3 203	53.4	45.4	1.2
Guadalupe	22.7	4 990	60.6	11.5	1.8	0.5	4.6	6.0	1 312	34	12	386	59.2	40.3	0.5
Harding	5.3	7 013	50.4	0.2	3.7	0.0	12.2	1.2	1 541	16	0	100	40.5	58.7	0.8
Hidalgo	19.0	3 554	60.1	4.4	8.3	0.4	2.8	7.0	1 305	71	14	436	43.5	55.3	1.2
Lea	185.9	3 340	54.5	5.9	6.8	0.9	4.3	36.2	651	117	151	3 351	20.0	79.4	0.5
Lincoln	66.0	3 333	48.4	0.7	7.2	1.1	4.9	30.8	1 554	115	53	1 208	31.5	67.4	1.2
Los Alamos	109.4	5 976	33.0	0.0	5.1	0.7	4.2	113.8	6 219	239	51	10 466	46.5	51.9	1.6
Luna	58.2	2 306	58.7	0.4	5.5	0.8	6.8	13.5	535	210	68	1 524	44.0	54.9	1.2
McKinley	195.9	2 648	70.3	0.6	4.5	0.7	2.4	79.0	1 068	2 412	199	4 998	63.4	35.5	1.1
Mora	15.0	2 838	79.5	0.0	1.6	0.3	3.0	2.9	542	48	14	314	66.4	32.8	0.7
Otero	102.8	1 669	61.5	0.5	7.7	0.8	2.8	46.6	756	1 957	4 283	4 622	30.9	67.8	1.3
Quay	34.5	3 513	63.9	0.1	4.6	0.5	7.5	9.2	942	64	26	966	34.6	64.6	0.8
Rio Arriba	97.7	2 381	65.1	0.1	3.6	0.7	2.7	47.2	1 150	388	110	4 787	65.0	34.3	0.7
Roosevelt	44.3	2 445	69.5	0.1	6.7	0.4	4.4	17.0	940	62	49	2 125	29.2	69.9	0.9
Sandoval	212.4	2 211	63.1	0.6	8.3	1.8	4.2	102.3	1 065	385	258	5 677	48.0	50.9	1.1
San Juan	431.8	3 587	56.0	0.2	3.8	1.3	4.6	1 050.0	8 723	1 571	326	9 707	32.9	65.7	1.4
San Miguel	88.5	2 982	70.9	0.8	3.7	0.6	2.1	27.4	925	176	80	4 237	71.7	27.3	1.0
Santa Fe	346.1	2 572	42.4	0.6	8.3	2.4	6.9	435.6	3 238	1 260	368	15 885	71.0	28.0	1.0
Sierra	25.4	1 954	48.3	0.0	3.1	1.1	5.2	13.0	998	116	35	772	37.4	61.3	1.3
Socorro	42.3	2 345	53.7	1.0	6.8	1.5	4.5	6.2	342	239	49	2 490	51.2	47.2	1.7
Taos	73.2	2 379	64.7	0.1	4.2	2.0	2.9	29.5	959	328	83	1 924	74.0	24.8	1.2
Torrance	59.8	3 590	77.4	0.0	3.0	0.4	2.6	24.9	1 497	90	45	1 047	36.7	61.9	1.4
Union	16.3	4 150	62.9	0.2	4.9	1.3	8.7	0.7	189	64	11	318	21.9	77.2	0.9
Valencia	140.6	2 080	74.1	0.2	3.9	1.8	1.4	78.9	1 168	114	182	4 093	43.3	55.7	1.0
NEW YORK	X	X	X	X	X	X	X	X	X	133 079	49 540	1 309 933	57.8	40.5	1.8
Albany	1 235.9	4 173	40.2	2.7	5.0	17.1	4.5	945.3	3 192	5 690	984	63 657	60.1	37.7	2.2
Allegany	241.3	4 808	57.5	3.1	1.1	11.0	8.7	216.7	4 319	145	70	3 998	33.7	64.2	2.0
Bronx	(3)	(3)	(3)	(3)	(3)	(3)	(3)	(3)	(3)	10 470	1 922	15 424	82.3	16.7	1.0
Broome	863.9	4 312	48.3	2.0	2.8	13.8	4.1	540.2	2 697	801	292	19 232	50.0	47.8	2.3
Cattaraugus	441.6	5 304	54.5	3.3	1.8	11.4	7.4	286.7	3 443	250	123	8 586	39.1	58.8	2.1
Cayuga	326.4	4 002	50.2	3.6	3.1	10.3	6.4	202.9	2 487	185	114	5 959	49.8	47.8	2.4
Chautauqua	684.3	4 947	55.1	2.0	2.7	13.3	6.1	457.4	3 306	408	197	9 888	45.0	53.0	2.1
Chemung	367.7	4 058	46.7	2.3	3.0	18.5	7.0	230.6	2 544	434	138	6 818	43.3	54.2	2.5
Chenango	241.4	4 704	63.5	2.5	1.7	6.8	8.0	153.8	2 997	122	71	4 282	42.9	54.8	2.3
Clinton	335.9	4 143	55.5	3.9	1.5	12.3	7.2	193.8	2 391	539	113	7 573	52.2	45.4	2.4
Columbia	252.9	3 981	50.7	4.2	2.0	13.7	7.0	129.1	2 033	192	88	4 531	54.2	43.3	2.5
Cortland	193.4	3 962	46.8	4.0	2.5	10.5	7.8	153.8	3 151	127	69	3 875	46.9	50.7	2.3
Delaware	259.7	5 491	42.7	8.2	0.9	14.1	10.4	136.5	2 886	149	67	4 497	39.7	57.6	2.7
Dutchess	1 100.9	3 826	54.2	4.6	3.3	8.2	4.4	770.3	2 677	1 242	400	21 093	46.4	51.7	1.9
Erie	4 008.1	4 241	44.2	7.7	4.3	13.4	4.5	2 390.5	2 530	9 036	1 734	67 335	56.0	41.5	2.4
Essex	195.3	5 015	38.5	4.0	1.1	13.4	10.8	120.8	3 102	373	54	4 254	45.6	52.0	2.4
Franklin	268.5	5 268	54.1	2.7	1.1	11.4	5.9	194.2	3 811	167	71	7 493	51.3	46.6	2.1
Fulton	223.1	4 052	46.6	2.1	2.8	15.0	6.5	209.9	3 813	106	77	4 143	41.2	56.7	2.1

1. Based on the resident population estimated as of July 1 of the year shown.   3. Bronx, Kings, Queens, and Richmond Counties included with New York County.

STATE/ County code	CBSA code[1]	County Type[2]	STATE County	Land area,[3] (sq km) 2000	Total persons	Rank	Per square kilometer	White	Black	Am. Indian, Alaska Native	Asian and Pacific Islander	Percent Hispanic or Latino[4]	Under 5 years	5 to 17 years	18 to 24 years	25 to 34 years	35 to 44 years	45 to 54 years
					1	2	3	4	5	6	7	8	9	10	11	12	13	14	15
			NEW YORK—Cont'd															
36 037	12860	4	Genesee	1 280	60 020	822	46.9	94.4	2.7	1.0	0.7	2.0	5.6	18.2	9.1	11.5	16.5	14.5
36 039	...	6	Greene	1 678	48 865	958	29.1	88.7	5.7	0.6	0.9	4.8	4.6	16.5	11.1	11.1	14.9	14.5
36 041	...	8	Hamilton	4 456	5 278	2 823	1.2	97.4	1.2	0.2	0.2	1.1	4.2	13.5	7.7	9.6	13.0	17.2
36 043	46540	2	Herkimer	3 655	63 704	777	17.4	97.5	0.8	0.5	0.6	1.1	5.0	17.0	10.0	10.8	14.8	14.8
36 045	48060	4	Jefferson	3 295	114 651	484	34.8	82.0	9.7	0.9	1.5	7.3	7.0	17.9	12.5	15.2	15.4	11.9
36 047	35620	1	Kings	183	2 472 523	7	13 511.1	35.2	35.9	0.5	9.3	20.3	7.5	18.5	9.7	15.5	15.0	13.0
36 049	...	6	Lewis	3 303	26 636	1 517	8.1	97.5	1.0	0.5	0.3	1.0	5.7	19.2	9.6	10.9	15.8	14.8
36 051	40380	1	Livingston	1 637	64 658	770	39.5	93.3	3.1	0.6	1.1	2.6	4.8	15.9	15.7	11.4	16.0	14.8
36 053	45060	2	Madison	1 699	70 182	720	41.3	96.0	1.6	0.8	0.9	1.4	5.3	17.0	13.7	10.5	15.5	14.5
36 055	40380	1	Monroe	1 708	736 738	71	431.3	76.4	15.0	0.6	3.2	6.1	6.0	18.1	10.0	12.7	15.6	14.6
36 057	11220	4	Montgomery	1 048	49 371	943	47.1	88.9	1.6	0.5	0.7	8.9	5.9	17.1	8.6	11.2	14.2	14.4
36 059	35620	1	Nassau	743	1 339 463	27	1 802.8	71.1	11.3	0.3	6.5	11.7	5.9	17.6	8.2	11.3	16.3	15.3
36 061	35620	1	New York	59	1 564 798	18	26 522.0	47.0	15.4	0.5	11.0	27.4	5.9	11.8	8.0	21.0	17.3	13.4
36 063	15380	1	Niagara	1 354	218 150	268	161.1	89.9	7.1	1.3	0.9	1.7	5.6	17.3	9.7	11.2	15.8	15.1
36 065	46540	2	Oneida	3 141	234 373	251	74.6	88.6	6.2	0.5	1.7	3.8	5.3	17.0	10.0	12.0	15.3	14.3
36 067	45060	2	Onondaga	2 021	460 517	134	227.9	83.5	10.8	1.4	2.9	3.0	6.1	18.1	10.1	12.2	15.6	14.4
36 069	40380	1	Ontario	1 669	102 445	531	61.4	94.0	2.5	0.5	1.0	2.8	5.4	17.8	9.8	11.0	16.0	15.6
36 071	39100	2	Orange	2 114	363 153	170	171.8	74.3	9.5	0.6	2.4	14.5	6.7	20.2	10.3	12.4	16.4	14.0
36 073	45060	1	Orleans	1 014	43 629	1 053	43.0	88.6	7.0	0.8	0.4	3.9	5.4	18.4	9.8	12.6	17.0	14.2
36 075	45060	2	Oswego	2 469	123 495	458	50.0	96.9	0.8	0.7	0.6	1.6	5.6	18.5	12.3	11.6	16.0	14.2
36 077	36580	6	Otsego	2 597	62 196	798	23.9	95.1	1.9	0.5	0.9	2.2	4.2	15.8	15.4	10.4	13.3	14.3
36 079	35620	1	Putnam	599	99 550	543	166.2	87.9	2.1	0.3	1.8	8.5	5.9	18.6	7.9	11.5	18.6	16.5
36 081	35620	1	Queens	283	2 225 486	10	7 863.9	32.2	20.6	0.9	21.6	26.2	6.5	15.8	8.7	16.4	16.5	13.6
36 083	10580	2	Rensselaer	1 694	154 007	364	90.9	89.6	5.8	0.6	2.4	2.7	5.5	17.1	10.7	12.5	15.6	14.8
36 085	35620	1	Richmond	151	459 737	135	3 044.6	69.0	10.1	0.4	7.2	14.3	6.1	17.9	9.1	13.9	16.3	14.4
36 087	35620	1	Rockland	451	292 989	198	649.6	69.5	12.1	0.5	6.9	12.0	7.2	19.4	8.9	11.5	15.4	14.3
36 089	36300	5	St. Lawrence	6 956	111 655	496	16.1	93.6	2.6	1.2	0.9	2.2	5.2	16.0	15.1	11.7	14.7	13.8
36 091	10580	2	Saratoga	2 103	209 818	280	99.8	94.5	1.9	0.5	1.8	2.2	5.7	17.2	8.9	13.1	17.0	15.1
36 093	10580	2	Schenectady	534	147 289	387	275.8	85.4	8.2	0.6	3.2	4.0	5.8	17.3	8.9	11.5	15.6	14.7
36 095	10580	2	Schoharie	1 611	31 685	1 366	19.7	95.8	1.4	0.7	0.4	2.2	4.7	16.6	12.4	10.4	14.9	15.0
36 097	...	6	Schuyler	851	19 455	1 837	22.9	96.4	1.5	0.8	0.4	1.4	5.4	17.3	9.9	10.8	15.0	15.6
36 099	42900	6	Seneca	842	35 183	1 267	41.8	91.3	4.8	0.5	0.9	3.2	4.9	16.6	9.8	14.0	15.6	14.3
36 101	18500	4	Steuben	3 607	99 012	546	27.4	95.6	1.9	0.6	1.4	1.4	5.7	18.0	9.0	11.6	15.2	15.0
36 103	35620	1	Suffolk	2 363	1 468 037	23	621.3	76.7	7.8	0.5	3.5	12.5	6.5	18.3	8.6	12.5	17.3	14.2
36 105	...	4	Sullivan	2 512	74 948	684	29.8	79.2	9.0	0.6	1.5	10.5	5.5	17.7	9.1	11.0	15.8	14.9
36 107	13780	2	Tioga	1 343	51 746	910	38.5	97.0	0.8	0.5	0.9	1.4	5.6	18.6	8.8	10.5	16.7	15.4
36 109	27060	3	Tompkins	1 233	101 411	537	82.2	83.0	4.3	0.8	10.1	3.6	4.1	13.0	24.2	14.4	12.1	12.2
36 111	28740	3	Ulster	2 918	181 111	317	62.1	85.6	6.3	0.8	1.7	7.0	5.0	16.7	10.0	12.1	16.5	15.5
36 113	24020	3	Warren	2 251	64 715	768	28.7	97.0	0.9	0.5	0.7	1.5	4.9	16.7	9.0	11.6	15.1	15.1
36 115	24020	3	Washington	2 164	61 872	802	28.6	94.3	3.0	0.5	0.4	2.3	4.9	17.3	9.9	12.5	15.9	14.6
36 117	40380	1	Wayne	1 565	93 728	575	59.9	92.9	3.6	0.6	0.7	3.0	5.8	19.3	8.6	11.3	17.0	15.2
36 119	35620	1	Westchester	1 121	940 302	40	838.8	62.2	14.7	0.4	5.8	17.9	6.6	17.8	7.8	12.6	16.7	14.6
36 121	...	6	Wyoming	1 536	42 932	1 061	28.0	91.0	5.3	0.4	0.6	3.0	4.8	16.7	9.8	13.8	15.7	15.0
36 123	...	6	Yates	876	24 720	1 588	28.2	97.7	0.7	0.4	0.3	1.3	6.0	18.5	11.2	9.5	13.9	14.1
37 000		X	**NORTH CAROLINA**	126 161	8 407 248	X	66.6	69.8	22.0	1.5	2.0	5.6	7.0	17.8	9.8	14.6	15.2	13.7
37 001	15500	3	Alamance	1 114	136 773	414	122.8	71.1	18.9	0.8	1.4	8.8	6.8	17.6	10.1	13.8	14.9	13.1
37 003	25860	2	Alexander	674	34 784	1 279	51.6	91.4	4.7	0.4	1.4	2.7	6.5	17.7	8.5	13.9	15.4	13.9
37 005	...	9	Alleghany	608	10 874	2 375	17.9	91.9	1.3	0.3	0.2	6.4	4.9	14.4	8.3	11.9	13.4	14.6
37 007	16740	1	Anson	1 377	25 168	1 561	18.3	49.3	48.6	0.5	0.7	1.1	6.5	18.4	9.1	13.3	14.7	14.1
37 009	...	9	Ashe	1 104	25 071	1 567	22.7	96.1	0.7	0.3	0.2	2.8	5.5	14.2	8.1	11.8	14.3	14.9
37 011	...	8	Avery	640	17 700	1 930	27.7	92.8	4.0	0.5	0.3	2.7	4.8	14.1	10.8	15.1	15.0	13.2
37 013	47820	6	Beaufort	2 144	45 407	1 012	21.2	68.1	28.5	0.3	0.3	3.1	6.7	16.9	8.2	11.3	13.5	15.1
37 015	...	9	Bertie	1 811	19 544	1 833	10.8	36.1	62.4	0.4	0.1	1.1	6.6	19.1	8.7	10.4	14.6	14.9
37 017	...	6	Bladen	2 266	32 723	1 343	14.4	56.3	37.2	2.1	0.2	4.6	7.3	17.8	9.3	12.3	13.8	14.6
37 019	48900	2	Brunswick	2 214	81 592	648	36.9	82.6	13.5	1.0	0.4	3.1	5.7	15.7	8.3	11.7	13.1	13.1
37 021	11700	2	Buncombe	1 699	212 672	274	125.2	88.2	7.7	0.9	1.1	3.2	5.9	16.2	8.8	13.1	14.8	14.8
37 023	25860	2	Burke	1 312	89 657	601	68.3	85.3	6.6	0.5	4.0	4.2	5.9	18.1	9.0	13.1	15.1	14.0
37 025	16740	1	Cabarrus	944	142 740	400	151.2	78.2	14.0	0.6	1.3	6.6	7.4	18.9	8.8	14.9	16.1	13.1
37 027	25860	2	Caldwell	1 221	78 728	664	64.5	90.6	5.5	0.4	0.6	3.4	6.3	17.4	8.0	14.0	15.3	14.3
37 029	21020	8	Camden	623	7 863	2 608	12.6	81.6	16.0	0.7	0.8	1.2	5.3	18.2	9.3	11.6	16.1	13.4
37 031	33980	4	Carteret	1 346	60 865	811	45.2	90.2	7.1	0.8	0.8	1.9	5.0	15.1	7.7	11.0	14.7	15.5
37 033	...	8	Caswell	1 100	23 632	1 628	21.5	62.8	35.1	0.2	0.2	1.9	5.5	17.2	8.6	13.3	15.6	15.3
37 035	25860	2	Catawba	1 036	146 971	389	141.9	81.3	8.4	0.4	3.6	7.0	6.8	17.8	8.8	14.6	15.4	13.9
37 037	20500	2	Chatham	1 769	55 238	872	31.2	71.9	15.4	0.6	1.8	10.9	6.3	16.5	8.5	14.7	15.3	13.7
37 039	...	9	Cherokee	1 179	25 048	1 570	21.2	95.4	1.8	2.2	0.4	1.1	5.5	15.0	7.8	11.1	12.3	14.2

1. CBSA = Core Based Statistical Area. See Appendix A for explanation. See Appendix B for list of metropolitan areas with component counties.   2. County type code from the Economic Research Service of USDA Rural-Urban Continuum Codes. See Appendix A for definition.   3. Dry land or land partially or temporarily covered by water.   4. Hispanic or Latino persons may be of any race.

STATE County	55 to 64 years (16)	65 to 74 years (17)	75 years and over (18)	Percent female (19)	1990 (20)	2000 (21)	1990–2000 (22)	2000–2003 (23)	Births (24)	Deaths (25)	Net migration (26)	Number (27)	Percent change, 1990–2000 (28)	Persons per household (29)	Female family householder[1] (30)	One person (31)
NEW YORK—Cont'd																
Genesee	9.9	7.0	7.6	50.9	60 060	60 370	0.5	-0.6	2 226	1 872	-662	22 770	5.3	2.59	9.8	24.8
Greene	11.3	8.1	7.4	48.5	44 739	48 195	7.7	1.4	1 372	1 714	1 034	18 256	10.0	2.42	11.6	27.9
Hamilton	14.8	10.8	9.3	50.5	5 279	5 379	1.9	-1.9	164	247	-5	2 362	9.7	2.24	10.3	27.9
Herkimer	10.8	7.6	9.0	51.4	65 809	64 427	-2.1	-1.1	2 123	2 337	-457	25 734	3.2	2.46	6.7	29.6
Jefferson	8.0	5.8	5.6	48.0	110 943	111 738	0.7	2.6	5 483	2 861	-4 328	40 068	5.9	2.58	10.3	27.6
Kings	8.8	6.0	5.7	53.0	2 300 664	2 465 326	7.2	0.3	133 570	60 404	-69 158	880 727	6.3	2.75	22.3	24.4
Lewis	9.7	7.5	6.6	50.4	26 796	26 944	0.6	-1.1	1 088	736	-659	10 040	8.5	2.66	8.4	27.8
Livingston	9.1	6.1	5.5	50.0	62 372	64 328	3.1	0.5	2 059	1 680	18	22 150	4.5	2.60	10.0	23.1
Madison	10.2	6.5	6.0	50.9	69 166	69 441	0.4	1.1	2 453	1 802	166	25 368	7.6	2.55	9.7	24.5
Monroe	9.6	6.2	6.9	51.7	713 968	735 343	3.0	0.2	29 383	20 340	-7 432	286 512	5.4	2.47	13.4	28.6
Montgomery	9.8	7.8	10.8	52.0	51 981	49 708	-4.4	-0.7	1 963	2 072	-188	20 038	-0.7	2.42	11.6	29.5
Nassau	10.4	7.5	7.5	51.7	1 287 873	1 334 544	3.6	0.4	52 367	37 424	-8 784	447 387	3.7	2.93	10.9	18.8
New York	9.7	6.4	5.9	52.4	1 487 536	1 537 195	3.3	1.8	67 728	37 516	-2 777	738 644	3.1	2.00	12.6	48.0
Niagara	9.9	7.4	7.9	51.6	220 756	219 846	-0.4	-0.8	7 961	7 643	-1 885	87 846	3.6	2.45	12.3	28.6
Oneida	10.0	7.4	8.7	50.2	250 836	235 469	-6.1	-0.5	8 051	8 786	-219	90 496	-2.2	2.43	12.0	29.5
Onondaga	9.2	6.7	7.0	52.1	468 973	458 336	-2.3	0.5	18 784	13 323	-2 944	181 153	1.8	2.46	12.9	29.4
Ontario	10.5	6.6	6.7	51.1	95 101	100 224	5.4	2.2	3 624	2 945	1 647	38 370	9.9	2.53	9.9	24.7
Orange	8.7	5.1	4.8	49.8	307 571	341 367	11.0	6.4	15 836	8 206	14 095	114 788	13.1	2.85	11.4	21.5
Orleans	9.6	6.2	6.3	50.4	41 846	44 171	5.6	-1.2	1 531	1 290	-770	15 363	6.5	2.65	11.2	23.7
Oswego	9.4	5.9	5.5	50.6	121 785	122 377	0.5	0.9	4 589	3 303	-59	45 522	7.3	2.60	10.8	24.3
Otsego	10.5	7.2	7.7	51.7	60 390	61 676	2.1	0.8	1 719	1 774	623	23 291	7.2	2.43	9.5	27.0
Putnam	10.5	5.4	4.2	49.9	83 941	95 745	14.1	4.0	3 828	1 938	1 833	32 703	16.4	2.86	8.3	18.1
Queens	9.4	6.5	6.3	51.7	1 951 598	2 229 379	14.2	-0.2	100 874	52 817	-54 806	782 664	8.7	2.81	16.0	25.6
Rensselaer	9.7	6.6	6.7	50.8	154 429	152 538	-1.2	1.0	5 477	4 916	1 073	59 894	4.0	2.46	12.0	27.9
Richmond	10.0	6.1	5.5	51.5	378 977	443 728	17.1	3.6	18 414	11 924	9 974	156 341	19.8	2.78	13.9	23.2
Rockland	10.8	6.9	5.2	51.0	265 475	286 753	8.0	2.2	14 604	6 908	-1 356	92 675	9.2	3.01	10.3	19.3
St. Lawrence	9.6	7.0	6.2	49.3	111 974	111 931	0.0	-0.2	3 949	3 428	-709	40 506	6.7	2.49	10.3	26.5
Saratoga	10.1	5.9	5.5	50.7	181 276	200 635	10.7	4.6	7 784	4 873	6 368	78 165	17.7	2.51	9.0	24.5
Schenectady	9.7	7.2	9.0	51.8	149 285	146 555	-1.8	0.5	5 475	4 945	312	59 684	0.8	2.38	12.3	30.6
Schoharie	10.7	7.8	7.2	50.2	31 840	31 582	-0.8	0.3	957	1 010	184	11 991	6.5	2.49	9.3	25.8
Schuyler	11.2	7.4	7.3	49.9	18 662	19 224	3.0	1.2	682	581	152	7 374	8.2	2.52	9.7	23.6
Seneca	10.0	7.2	7.1	48.1	33 683	33 342	-1.0	5.5	1 179	1 042	1 657	12 630	2.8	2.51	10.3	25.3
Steuben	10.7	7.6	7.4	51.0	99 088	98 726	-0.4	0.3	3 735	3 412	36	39 071	4.8	2.49	10.6	27.2
Suffolk	10.1	6.4	5.5	50.9	1 321 339	1 419 369	7.4	3.4	64 276	37 141	23 003	469 299	10.5	2.96	10.8	18.3
Sullivan	11.2	7.4	6.7	49.3	69 277	73 966	6.8	1.3	2 727	2 463	799	27 661	12.6	2.50	11.4	27.9
Tioga	10.5	7.6	6.0	50.5	52 337	51 784	-1.1	-0.1	1 887	1 298	-574	19 725	4.7	2.60	9.8	22.4
Tompkins	7.5	4.6	4.7	50.3	94 097	96 501	2.6	5.1	2 753	1 979	4 219	36 420	9.2	2.32	8.2	32.5
Ulster	10.5	6.8	6.4	50.3	165 380	177 749	7.5	1.9	5 778	5 340	3 043	67 499	11.0	2.47	10.9	27.9
Warren	10.9	7.8	7.4	51.4	59 209	63 303	6.9	2.2	2 100	1 943	1 291	25 726	14.0	2.41	10.4	27.3
Washington	10.3	7.3	6.6	48.5	59 330	61 042	2.9	1.4	1 982	1 972	868	22 458	10.9	2.55	10.4	24.0
Wayne	10.2	6.5	5.9	50.7	89 123	93 765	5.2	0.0	3 561	2 586	-933	34 908	9.2	2.64	10.3	22.4
Westchester	10.1	6.9	6.9	51.9	874 866	923 459	5.6	1.8	41 473	24 625	506	337 142	5.3	2.67	12.2	25.7
Wyoming	9.7	6.2	6.2	45.9	42 507	43 424	2.2	-1.1	1 375	1 113	-722	14 906	7.3	2.62	9.2	23.2
Yates	10.9	8.1	7.3	51.3	22 810	24 621	7.9	0.4	946	875	44	9 029	7.2	2.59	9.4	24.6
NORTH CAROLINA	9.8	6.5	5.6	50.9	6 632 448	8 049 313	21.4	4.4	386 343	235 328	210 546	3 132 013	24.4	2.49	12.5	25.4
Alamance	9.3	7.1	6.7	51.8	108 213	130 800	20.9	4.6	6 184	4 321	4 177	51 584	20.9	2.46	12.7	26.0
Alexander	11.1	7.1	5.0	50.1	27 544	33 603	22.0	3.5	1 379	961	802	13 137	27.2	2.54	9.4	21.9
Alleghany	13.1	10.6	8.6	50.5	9 590	10 677	11.3	1.8	344	432	292	4 593	18.0	2.28	7.5	27.8
Anson	10.0	6.8	7.5	50.8	23 474	25 275	7.7	-0.4	1 073	970	-189	9 204	7.9	2.59	19.8	25.1
Ashe	12.8	9.5	8.6	50.8	22 209	24 384	9.8	2.8	852	952	786	10 411	17.7	2.31	8.4	25.8
Avery	10.9	8.4	7.5	46.8	14 867	17 167	15.5	3.1	587	554	507	6 532	18.3	2.34	9.1	26.6
Beaufort	12.3	8.9	7.1	52.4	42 283	44 958	6.3	1.0	2 138	1 878	242	18 319	13.4	2.42	13.3	25.7
Bertie	10.2	8.8	7.3	53.4	20 388	19 773	-3.0	-1.2	924	915	-207	7 743	4.5	2.53	20.1	27.0
Bladen	10.9	7.9	6.1	51.7	28 663	32 278	12.6	1.4	1 607	1 320	189	12 897	19.9	2.45	15.7	27.7
Brunswick	13.5	10.7	6.1	50.7	50 985	73 143	43.5	11.6	2 938	2 422	7 679	30 438	51.7	2.38	10.2	22.9
Buncombe	10.5	7.6	7.6	51.8	174 357	206 330	18.3	3.1	8 058	7 421	5 828	85 776	21.1	2.33	10.8	28.9
Burke	10.7	7.6	6.2	49.9	75 740	89 148	17.7	0.6	3 485	2 683	-258	34 528	18.3	2.48	11.0	25.5
Cabarrus	8.8	5.7	5.1	50.6	98 935	131 063	32.5	8.9	7 012	3 655	8 152	49 519	32.0	2.60	10.5	21.8
Caldwell	11.2	7.6	5.9	50.8	70 709	77 415	9.5	1.7	3 154	2 551	452	30 768	13.2	2.48	11.0	23.1
Camden	10.5	7.0	5.5	50.0	5 904	6 885	16.6	14.2	248	208	910	2 662	22.1	2.58	9.4	20.7
Carteret	13.0	10.0	7.4	50.8	52 407	59 383	13.3	2.5	1 895	2 276	1 856	25 204	18.7	2.31	9.6	26.1
Caswell	11.3	7.2	6.2	49.3	20 662	23 501	13.7	0.6	807	832	175	8 670	16.1	2.56	14.2	23.2
Catawba	10.1	6.7	5.6	50.6	118 412	141 685	19.7	3.7	6 626	4 367	3 077	55 533	21.5	2.51	10.9	24.6
Chatham	9.5	7.1	7.0	50.5	38 979	49 329	26.6	12.0	2 125	1 619	5 295	19 741	29.1	2.47	10.0	24.5
Cherokee	14.0	10.4	9.0	51.7	20 170	24 298	20.5	3.1	870	1 016	889	10 336	29.8	2.32	9.3	25.7

1. No spouse present.

STATE County	Births, average 1999–2001 Total	Births Rate[1]	Deaths, avg 1999–2001 Number Total	Number Infant[2]	Deaths Rate Total[1]	Rate Infant[3]	Physicians,[4] 2000 Number	Physicians Rate[5]	Hospitals,[4] 1998 Number	Beds Number	Beds Rate[5]	Medicare enrollees, 2003	Serious crimes known to police,[6] 2002 Total Number	Rate[7]
	32	33	34	35	36	37	38	39	40	41	42	43	44	45
NEW YORK—Cont'd														
Genesee	709	11.7	576	2	9.6	D	74	123	2	166	274	10 124	1 465	2 436
Greene	441	9.2	523	3	10.9	D	29	60	1	195	408	8 748	786	1 615
Hamilton	44	8.2	71	0	13.2	D	2	37	0	0	0	1 251	110	2 025
Herkimer	665	10.3	722	3	11.2	D	50	78	2	320	500	11 688	1 321	2 303
Jefferson	1 716	15.4	856	11	7.7	6.2	195	175	3	391	352	15 651	2 039	1 808
Kings	39 871	16.2	18 792	268	7.6	6.7	5 659	230	19	9 324	411	298 100	[7]NA	[7]NA
Lewis	336	12.5	227	2	8.4	D	24	89	1	189	687	4 211	336	1 235
Livingston	668	10.4	504	4	7.8	D	46	72	1	72	109	9 355	1 604	2 470
Madison	770	11.1	574	6	8.2	D	85	122	2	334	470	10 610	1 307	2 121
Monroe	9 253	12.6	6 272	65	8.5	7.1	2 493	339	7	2 481	346	111 240	30 544	4 114
Montgomery	607	12.2	627	4	12.6	D	79	159	2	381	751		752	1 499
Nassau	16 792	12.6	11 356	90	8.5	5.3	5 602	420	15	5 925	455	220 282	22 976	1 705
New York	19 981	13.0	11 943	114	7.7	5.7	14 006	911	18	11 672	753	218 544	[7]250 630	[7]3 100
Niagara	2 527	11.5	2 360	15	10.7	5.9	283	129	5	974	447	39 808	7 864	3 543
Oneida	2 560	10.9	2 631	22	11.2	8.6	485	206	4	959	416	44 617	6 768	2 876
Onondaga	5 948	13.0	4 111	59	9.0	9.9	1 583	345	4	1 674	365	73 209	17 582	3 800
Ontario	1 117	11.1	878	6	8.8	D	210	210	3	667	669	16 159	2 060	2 036
Orange	4 975	14.5	2 532	29	7.4	5.8	595	174	6	1 054	320	43 565	8 633	2 510
Orleans	508	11.5	401	2	9.1	D	40	91	1	101	227	6 398	589	1 321
Oswego	1 464	12.0	1 027	9	8.4	6.1	109	89	2	271	219	18 299	3 069	2 484
Otsego	558	9.0	578	2	9.4	D	220	357	2	438	721	10 762	906	1 505
Putnam	1 173	12.2	583	3	6.1	D	148	155	1	188	201	11 183	1 269	1 313
Queens	31 599	14.2	16 459	178	7.4	5.6	5 170	232	13	4 681	234	284 959	[7]NA	[7]NA
Rensselaer	1 728	11.3	1 505	14	9.9	8.3	242	159	2	616	403	23 825	4 953	3 216
Richmond	5 824	13.1	3 605	38	8.1	6.5	1 223	276	3	1 387	341	60 830	[7]NA	[7]NA
Rockland	4 637	16.1	2 131	21	7.4	4.5	866	302	5	745	265	41 458	5 003	1 728
St. Lawrence	1 204	10.8	1 052	7	9.4	5.8	148	132	5	372	327	18 817	2 477	2 284
Saratoga	2 542	12.6	1 439	8	7.1	3.3	217	108	1	227	115	28 443	2 859	1 412
Schenectady	1 748	11.9	1 553	12	10.6	7.1	371	253	2	619	425	29 101	5 066	3 424
Schoharie	304	9.6	301	2	9.5	D	26	82	1	70	216	5 382	641	2 010
Schuyler	214	11.1	190	2	9.9	D	19	99	1	173	905	3 122	310	1 597
Seneca	362	10.7	318	3	9.4	D	20	60	0	0	0	5 602	636	1 928
Steuben	1 180	11.9	1 030	10	10.4	8.2	137	139	3	651	665	17 452	1 413	1 428
Suffolk	20 052	14.1	11 162	101	7.8	5.0	3 324	234	13	4 236	309	206 795	35 960	2 545
Sullivan	847	11.5	794	9	10.8	10.2	92	124	2	295	427	13 170	1 808	2 421
Tioga	602	11.6	403	2	7.8	D	24	46	0	0	0	7 884	593	1 134
Tompkins	872	9.0	614	7	6.3	8.4	183	190	1	204	212	11 004	3 005	3 085
Ulster	1 780	10.0	1 604	9	9.0	5.1	300	169	3	413	248	27 798	4 069	2 328
Warren	649	10.2	603	5	9.5	D	166	262	1	440	718	11 805	1 889	2 956
Washington	631	10.3	598	4	9.8	D	52	85	1	113	187	15 544	1 971	2 164
Wayne	1 174	12.5	784	5	8.4	D	82	87	2	336	354	15 544	1 971	2 164
Westchester	12 705	13.7	7 510	59	8.1	4.6	4 057	439	14	3 695	412	140 083	19 434	2 141
Wyoming	426	9.8	364	4	8.4	D	37	85	1	262	595	6 275	1 128	2 573
Yates	302	12.3	271	3	11.0	D	27	110	1	217	897	4 590	388	1 561
NORTH CAROLINA	117 430	14.5	70 823	1 028	8.8	8.8	16 441	204	121	21 735	288	1 205 466	392 826	4 721
Alamance	1 859	14.2	1 308	22	10.0	11.7	172	131	1	220	184	22 534	6 477	4 862
Alexander	443	13.2	290	2	8.6	D	18	54	1	44	141	4 949	809	2 329
Alleghany	110	10.3	137	1	12.8	D	13	122	1	46	467	2 512	123	1 115
Anson	339	13.4	289	6	11.4	D	11	44	1	125	513	5 277	414	1 643
Ashe	274	11.2	292	3	11.9	D	21	86	1	115	479	3 577	190	1 085
Avery	176	10.2	173	0	10.0	D	11	64	2	115	731	9 092	1 725	3 712
Beaufort	643	14.3	548	7	12.2	11.4	64	142	2	146	328	4 398	421	2 060
Bertie	261	13.1	274	3	13.8	D	10	51	1	16	78	5 608	1 612	4 832
Bladen	475	14.7	390	5	12.1	D	19	59	1	62	202	5 608	1 612	4 832
Brunswick	858	11.7	718	6	9.8	D	53	72	2	100	146	16 207	3 508	4 714
Buncombe	2 520	12.2	2 227	26	10.8	10.3	620	300	2	714	366	37 852	8 108	3 813
Burke	1 114	12.5	822	9	9.2	8.4	131	147	2	228	276	14 132	2 233	2 462
Cabarrus	2 097	15.9	1 105	16	8.4	7.8	207	158	1	331	276	20 509	4 736	3 496
Caldwell	1 017	13.1	761	9	9.8	8.5	75	97	1	81	106	12 707	2 085	2 607
Camden	63	9.1	66	0	9.5	D	1	15	0	0	0	1 169	NA	NA
Carteret	609	10.2	674	6	11.3	D	92	155	1	117	195	10 949	2 010	3 275
Caswell	261	11.1	243	4	10.4	D	4	17	0	0	0	3 506	458	2 070
Catawba	2 052	14.4	1 299	18	9.1	8.8	274	193	2	459	346	21 870	6 584	4 509
Chatham	661	13.3	484	4	9.7	D	56	114	1	50	110	7 187	1 761	3 454
Cherokee	265	10.9	304	1	12.5	D	41	169	2	222	975	5 850	683	2 719

1. Per 1,000 estimated resident population.   2. Deaths of infants under 1 year old.   3. Deaths of infants under 1 year old per 1,000 live births.   4. Data subject to copyright.   5. Per 100,000 resident population as of July 1 of the year shown.   6. Data for serious crimes have not been adjusted for underreporting; this may affect comparability between geographic areas and over time.   7. Per 100,000 population estimated by the FBI.   7. Bronx, Kings, Queens, and Richmond Counties included with New York County.

Table B. States and Counties — Crime, Education, Money Income, and Poverty

STATE County	Serious crimes known to police,[1] 2002 (cont'd) Rate[2] Violent	Property	Education — School enrollment and attainment, 2000 — Enrollment[3] Total	Percent private	Attainment[4] (percent) High school graduate or less	Bachelor's degree or more	Local government expenditures,[5] 2000–2001 Total current expenditures (mil dol)	Current expenditures per student (dollars)	Money income, 1999 Per capita income[6] (dollars)	Households Median income Dollars	Percent change, 1989–1999 (constant 1999 dollars)	Percent with income of $100,000 or more	Percent below poverty level, 1999 Persons	Households	Families	Families with children
	46	47	48	49	50	51	52	53	54	55	56	57	58	59	60	61
NEW YORK—Cont'd																
Genesee	136	2 300	16 129	12.5	53.7	16.3	108.7	10 114	18 498	40 542	-2.5	6.0	7.6	7.8	5.6	8.9
Greene	300	1 315	10 810	11.1	57.9	16.4	75.1	9 710	18 931	36 493	-1.1	7.7	12.2	12.2	8.6	13.3
Hamilton	129	1 897	1 059	8.0	53.9	18.4	12.2	17 417	18 643	32 287	3.6	6.3	10.4	10.6	6.0	10.6
Herkimer	364	1 938	16 600	7.1	56.0	15.7	110.3	9 425	16 141	32 924	6.2	3.7	12.5	12.9	8.9	14.2
Jefferson	191	1 617	28 331	10.1	53.4	16.0	175.4	9 414	16 202	34 006	-2.4	4.9	13.3	13.3	10.0	14.9
Kings	[7]NA	[7]NA	731 672	26.2	57.9	21.8	[7]NA	[7]NA	16 775	32 135	-6.9	9.4	25.1	24.0	22.0	29.1
Lewis	147	1 088	6 915	7.6	67.1	11.7	47.6	9 518	14 971	34 361	-0.1	3.7	13.2	13.5	10.1	14.5
Livingston	117	2 353	19 552	11.6	51.5	19.2	97.4	9 560	18 062	42 066	1.1	7.3	10.4	9.8	5.8	9.0
Madison	117	2 004	20 630	21.0	49.8	21.6	117.7	9 572	19 105	40 184	1.2	9.1	9.8	10.1	6.3	9.8
Monroe	310	3 804	214 378	23.7	41.3	31.2	1 298.4	10 684	22 821	44 891	-5.4	13.1	11.2	10.8	8.2	13.1
Montgomery	171	1 327	11 609	10.8	61.1	13.6	79.0	9 947	17 005	32 128	-0.6	5.2	12.0	11.8	9.0	13.9
Nassau	198	1 507	357 675	26.3	40.1	35.4	2 798.3	11 553	32 151	72 030	-1.2	32.3	5.2	5.3	3.5	4.9
New York	[7]790	[7]2 310	358 066	39.8	34.8	49.4	[7]11 851.3	[7]11 112	42 922	47 030	8.5	23.9	20.0	16.6	17.6	26.8
Niagara	366	3 177	57 484	17.1	53.7	17.4	367.5	10 222	19 219	38 136	-0.1	7.8	10.6	11.1	8.2	13.5
Oneida	291	2 585	60 218	15.6	53.5	18.3	363.8	9 573	18 516	35 909	0.1	6.9	13.0	12.8	9.8	13.5
Onondaga	425	3 375	132 420	24.0	43.4	28.5	756.7	9 665	21 336	40 847	-4.3	11.0	12.2	12.3	8.6	16.5
Ontario	101	1 935	26 901	18.6	44.2	24.7	177.1	9 665	21 533	44 579	0.1	10.3	7.3	7.4	4.9	7.8
Orange	356	2 154	101 077	20.9	49.2	22.5	651.0	10 257	21 597	52 058	-1.2	16.1	10.5	9.1	7.6	11.1
Orleans	193	1 128	10 701	8.0	63.2	13.0	73.4	8 894	16 457	37 972	-0.3	5.2	10.8	9.1	7.7	12.4
Oswego	148	2 336	35 840	6.2	60.8	14.4	243.7	9 596	16 853	36 598	-6.3	6.2	14.0	13.4	9.7	14.6
Otsego	226	1 279	19 248	9.1	51.7	22.0	98.2	10 074	16 806	33 444	-0.8	6.0	14.9	14.2	8.8	14.3
Putnam	73	1 239	25 652	21.3	37.9	33.9	200.0	12 702	30 127	72 279	0.3	31.4	4.4	4.0	2.7	3.6
Queens	[7]NA	[7]NA	586 090	24.9	53.4	24.3	[7]NA	[7]NA	19 222	42 439	-7.6	12.2	14.6	14.1	11.9	16.5
Rensselaer	355	2 861	42 526	26.9	47.6	23.7	242.4	10 453	21 095	42 905	-0.1	10.0	9.5	9.9	6.7	10.4
Richmond	[7]NA	[7]NA	122 303	30.8	51.1	23.2	[7]NA	[7]NA	23 905	55 039	-6.6	19.3	10.0	10.1	7.9	11.4
Rockland	190	1 538	84 629	37.7	37.2	37.5	576.4	14 100	28 082	67 971	-4.1	30.8	9.5	7.5	6.3	9.5
St. Lawrence	242	2 042	32 990	19.6	58.5	16.4	185.5	10 343	15 728	32 356	1.2	4.6	16.9	16.0	12.3	18.9
Saratoga	129	1 282	51 400	18.0	40.8	30.9	334.7	9 616	23 945	49 460	0.5	13.3	5.7	6.0	3.8	6.0
Schenectady	380	3 044	37 662	19.0	46.1	26.3	213.7	9 572	21 992	41 739	-1.6	10.5	10.9	10.4	7.8	12.8
Schoharie	210	1 800	8 606	10.5	56.4	17.3	60.9	10 936	17 778	36 585	4.4	6.5	11.4	11.2	7.9	12.2
Schuyler	149	1 448	4 643	9.6	57.5	15.5	24.3	9 922	17 039	36 010	4.2	5.2	11.8	10.6	8.8	14.4
Seneca	167	1 762	8 433	16.8	56.6	17.5	49.9	9 419	17 630	37 140	-3.4	5.9	11.5	10.3	8.0	12.5
Steuben	123	1 305	24 686	9.7	54.5	17.9	191.4	9 939	18 197	35 479	4.3	6.8	13.2	12.0	9.9	15.8
Suffolk	218	2 327	387 491	17.2	45.1	27.5	3 151.7	12 592	26 577	65 288	-1.1	25.5	6.0	5.6	3.9	5.7
Sullivan	335	2 086	18 389	13.2	57.7	16.7	138.4	12 315	18 892	36 998	-0.2	8.7	16.3	13.7	11.6	18.6
Tioga	61	1 073	13 238	10.2	52.6	19.7	86.2	9 145	18 673	40 266	-4.8	7.9	8.4	8.0	6.0	8.8
Tompkins	135	2 949	42 942	52.3	30.9	47.5	141.2	10 069	19 659	37 272	0.0	10.8	17.6	17.1	6.8	10.6
Ulster	300	2 028	46 266	12.5	48.3	25.0	319.0	11 076	20 846	42 551	-6.9	10.8	11.4	10.5	7.2	11.2
Warren	192	2 763	15 874	11.2	49.0	23.2	111.0	9 832	20 727	39 198	-4.1	8.6	9.7	9.3	7.2	11.9
Washington	344	1 457	14 653	7.2	61.1	14.3	106.2	9 720	17 958	37 668	-2.2	6.1	9.4	9.3	6.8	10.3
Wayne	145	2 019	24 533	9.9	53.9	17.0	182.5	9 838	19 258	44 157	1.2	8.1	8.6	8.5	6.0	9.2
Westchester	281	1 860	244 926	28.7	38.5	40.9	1 986.6	13 915	36 726	63 582	-2.2	31.0	8.8	8.5	6.4	9.4
Wyoming	162	2 411	10 379	10.0	63.4	11.5	54.4	9 315	17 248	39 895	7.9	4.9	8.4	8.0	5.8	9.7
Yates	117	1 444	6 376	25.3	56.2	18.2	28.6	9 368	16 781	34 640	3.7	4.9	13.1	10.7	8.9	15.4
NORTH CAROLINA	470	4 251	2 043 225	13.8	50.3	22.5	8 330.5	6 445	20 307	39 184	9.4	9.4	12.3	12.4	9.0	13.3
Alamance	336	4 526	32 488	20.2	54.8	19.2	124.4	5 907	19 391	39 168	7.1	7.4	11.1	11.2	7.6	10.8
Alexander	193	2 136	7 232	7.6	66.9	9.3	31.0	5 711	18 507	38 684	8.5	5.3	8.5	9.8	5.9	8.5
Alleghany	100	1 015	2 029	6.4	63.8	11.7	11.8	8 175	17 691	29 244	17.8	5.1	17.2	18.5	11.3	15.0
Anson	223	2 859	6 464	5.9	68.2	9.2	30.1	6 660	14 853	29 849	1.7	4.3	17.8	19.0	15.5	20.8
Ashe	71	1 571	4 610	5.2	64.7	12.1	23.0	7 085	16 429	28 824	13.2	4.3	13.5	14.9	10.1	15.2
Avery	74	1 011	3 841	18.9	61.2	14.5	19.7	7 800	15 176	30 627	11.7	4.6	15.3	17.1	10.9	15.7
Beaufort	364	3 348	10 641	9.0	58.7	16.0	49.2	6 517	16 722	31 066	6.4	5.6	19.5	19.8	15.2	23.7
Bertie	83	1 977	4 939	11.1	72.9	8.8	27.5	7 405	14 096	25 177	5.3	4.3	23.5	24.7	19.3	26.0
Bladen	839	3 992	7 732	7.5	63.2	11.3	38.9	6 674	14 735	26 877	5.2	4.0	21.0	21.6	16.6	23.2
Brunswick	241	4 474	14 593	11.1	55.0	16.1	73.0	7 026	19 857	35 888	13.8	7.3	12.6	12.3	9.5	16.0
Buncombe	362	3 451	47 002	14.9	46.4	25.3	197.2	6 779	20 384	36 666	5.6	7.8	11.4	11.5	7.8	12.7
Burke	133	2 329	20 594	8.4	62.8	12.8	86.4	5 925	17 397	35 629	2.5	4.9	10.7	11.2	8.0	12.3
Cabarrus	249	3 246	32 182	12.8	51.9	19.1	140.3	5 994	21 121	46 140	14.0	11.4	7.1	7.0	4.8	7.4
Caldwell	215	2 392	16 808	8.5	65.9	10.4	76.2	6 014	17 353	35 739	3.5	5.1	10.7	11.1	7.6	11.5
Camden	NA	NA	1 720	6.7	51.9	16.2	9.2	7 183	18 681	39 493	10.1	8.9	10.1	11.1	7.9	11.1
Carteret	270	3 004	12 345	13.2	47.6	19.8	63.9	7 492	21 260	38 344	10.6	8.1	10.7	11.0	8.0	14.0
Caswell	271	1 798	5 432	8.3	67.5	8.3	24.5	6 733	16 470	35 018	14.6	3.9	14.4	15.1	10.9	14.8
Catawba	292	4 217	32 637	11.7	56.5	17.0	145.3	6 085	20 358	40 536	3.2	8.3	9.1	9.0	6.5	10.4
Chatham	241	3 212	10 643	11.1	48.8	27.6	49.8	6 829	23 355	42 851	11.8	11.2	9.7	10.1	7.1	11.8
Cherokee	231	2 489	4 813	5.5	61.5	11.0	26.0	6 909	15 814	27 992	6.2	3.9	15.3	16.8	11.7	16.7

1. Data for serious crimes have not been adjusted for underreporting; this may affect comparability between geographic areas and over time.   2. Per 100,000 population estimated by the FBI.   3. All persons 3 years old and over enrolled in nursery school through college.   4. Persons 25 years old and over.   5. Elementary and secondary education expenditures.   6. Based on population enumerated as of April 1, 2000.   7. Bronx, Kings, Queens, and Richmond Counties included with New York County.

Items 46—61

STATE County	Personal income, 2002 Total (mil dol)	Percent change, 2001–2002	Per capita[1] Dollars	Per capita[1] Rank	Wages and salaries[2] (mil dol)	Proprietor's income (mil dol)	Dividends, interest, and rent (mil dol)	Transfer payments Total (mil dol)	Government payments to individuals Total (mil dol)	Social Security (mil dol)	Medical payments (mil dol)	Income mainte- nance (mil dol)	Unemploy- ment insurance (mil dol)
	62	63	64	65	66	67	68	69	70	71	72	73	74
NEW YORK—Cont'd													
Genesee	1 500	2.0	25 024	1 122	778	86	221	303	287	118	112	22	17
Greene	1 226	3.7	25 294	1 049	489	47	206	258	245	102	98	24	8
Hamilton	136	4.2	25 822	928	49	10	36	32	30	14	12	2	1
Herkimer	1 453	2.3	22 807	1 776	590	80	214	354	338	131	143	31	13
Jefferson	2 734	5.1	23 999	1 406	2 052	115	360	512	486	168	200	61	25
Kings	62 232	1.9	25 138	1 094	18 843	2 684	7 149	17 733	17 081	2 712	10 842	2 478	691
Lewis	554	2.9	20 814	2 343	219	50	86	129	122	45	52	12	8
Livingston	1 522	1.8	23 512	1 565	689	87	223	291	274	110	109	29	15
Madison	1 839	3.0	26 357	818	747	123	303	318	300	116	128	25	14
Monroe	23 927	1.7	32 506	205	18 116	1 739	4 261	4 129	3 935	1 365	1 717	519	168
Montgomery	1 259	3.7	25 546	990	623	40	206	327	314	121	143	28	11
Nassau	66 351	0.4	49 543	18	31 058	5 846	14 208	7 279	6 927	2 842	3 137	362	216
New York	131 576	-2.8	84 591	1	202 519	36 775	24 713	12 522	12 116	2 360	7 019	1 376	534
Niagara	5 539	2.5	25 381	1 026	3 118	177	754	1 219	1 162	477	462	112	57
Oneida	5 895	2.9	25 174	1 084	4 046	314	970	1 367	1 305	478	574	145	43
Onondaga	13 839	4.0	30 119	342	11 157	919	2 088	2 447	2 326	871	970	277	83
Ontario	2 930	1.2	28 788	471	1 750	183	469	497	470	192	187	39	23
Orange	10 323	3.4	29 013	448	5 230	664	1 415	1 594	1 502	519	694	161	54
Orleans	942	3.3	21 623	2 118	442	47	131	211	199	78	78	24	11
Oswego	2 745	4.4	22 365	1 917	1 417	100	321	607	575	219	235	63	31
Otsego	1 439	3.3	23 240	1 646	800	100	282	314	298	119	127	24	10
Putnam	3 885	1.0	39 434	69	1 068	158	584	393	367	149	162	17	17
Queens	64 314	1.5	28 877	461	23 282	2 629	8 779	15 942	15 355	3 012	9 615	1 808	548
Rensselaer	4 441	2.6	28 978	451	2 137	206	650	826	786	292	340	77	27
Richmond	15 929	0.5	34 980	142	3 853	676	1 907	3 447	3 327	755	2 059	312	107
Rockland	12 031	1.8	41 311	51	5 478	908	1 895	1 540	1 463	519	720	110	47
St. Lawrence	2 300	1.6	20 629	2 392	1 430	126	340	587	558	201	237	64	27
Saratoga	6 500	2.5	31 420	253	2 775	350	1 002	804	750	323	296	54	27
Schenectady	4 678	3.9	31 845	229	3 184	304	939	839	800	310	355	76	21
Schoharie	751	1.6	23 733	1 485	315	33	112	158	149	56	65	13	7
Schuyler	429	1.4	22 099	1 992	142	31	61	104	99	39	40	9	6
Seneca	816	3.2	23 306	1 629	379	58	123	172	163	66	68	14	7
Steuben	2 590	-4.8	26 034	882	1 768	179	364	556	530	194	209	56	32
Suffolk	54 808	1.7	37 650	93	29 316	3 116	8 745	7 198	6 816	2 612	3 042	560	245
Sullivan	2 006	5.2	27 056	689	902	159	335	476	456	152	230	46	12
Tioga	1 281	1.6	24 732	1 203	615	48	173	237	223	96	82	24	11
Tompkins	2 521	4.1	25 242	1 060	2 057	134	531	358	332	133	122	38	10
Ulster	4 864	3.3	27 013	699	2 201	287	845	919	872	335	392	82	27
Warren	1 795	4.3	28 020	550	1 233	130	384	336	319	137	125	27	13
Washington	1 354	2.7	22 039	2 007	611	60	192	301	285	107	125	29	10
Wayne	2 395	1.3	25 551	989	1 042	75	316	462	437	177	175	40	28
Westchester	52 074	-0.5	55 522	8	24 899	4 763	10 908	5 367	5 121	1 794	2 405	487	149
Wyoming	916	3.0	21 278	2 218	519	53	132	186	175	73	68	14	11
Yates	513	1.1	20 926	2 317	190	24	96	126	120	50	47	10	6
NORTH CAROLINA	230 777	2.4	27 785	X	158 633	16 705	40 178	36 068	34 132	13 290	13 930	3 679	1 515
Alamance	3 587	1.8	26 459	804	2 209	275	651	604	572	255	221	46	32
Alexander	835	-0.3	24 299	1 310	312	73	123	142	134	54	56	12	8
Alleghany	263	-1.0	24 328	1 299	104	39	60	59	57	23	25	5	2
Anson	558	-1.9	22 066	2 000	265	50	84	145	139	45	64	19	5
Ashe	594	2.4	23 853	1 455	247	78	120	137	131	51	59	12	5
Avery	405	1.6	22 876	1 757	195	69	89	94	89	32	44	7	2
Beaufort	1 009	0.7	22 311	1 931	550	47	218	260	250	96	103	31	9
Bertie	418	2.6	21 293	2 210	193	26	64	135	130	41	62	21	3
Bladen	680	-1.8	20 936	2 314	393	30	104	201	193	60	89	28	7
Brunswick	1 885	3.3	23 908	1 439	758	201	404	436	418	189	165	36	13
Buncombe	5 739	2.3	27 288	654	3 824	382	1 371	1 027	978	408	402	82	26
Burke	2 131	1.3	23 890	1 443	1 198	211	336	410	389	158	162	36	20
Cabarrus	4 155	4.2	29 733	370	2 312	302	644	564	531	221	228	39	24
Caldwell	1 984	3.1	25 235	1 065	1 090	187	312	374	356	142	147	32	22
Camden	192	4.6	25 896	913	49	8	37	32	31	13	12	2	1
Carteret	1 668	3.8	27 713	586	629	129	416	300	286	124	110	22	7
Caswell	510	0.7	21 581	2 125	114	9	80	108	102	39	43	12	4
Catawba	3 936	-0.3	26 925	716	3 324	243	761	623	588	263	212	50	45
Chatham	1 890	1.6	35 151	138	529	212	502	218	205	97	79	15	8
Cherokee	487	1.8	19 752	2 601	253	49	89	155	149	60	62	12	8

1. Based on the resident population estimated as of July 1 of the year shown. 2. Includes other labor income.

STATE County	Earnings, 2002									Social Security beneficiaries, December 2003		Housing units, 2003		
		Percent by selected industries												
		Goods-related[1]			Service-related and health							Supplemental Security Income recipients, December 2003		
	Total (mil dol)	Farm	Total	Manufacturing	Information and professional and technical services	Retail trade	Finance, insurance, and real estate	Health services	Government	Number	Rate[2]		Total	Percent change, 2000–2003
	75	76	77	78	79	80	81	82	83	84	85	86	87	88
NEW YORK—Cont'd														
Genesee	864	3.3	23.5	17.4	3.5	7.9	3.2	9.1	26.5	11 725	195	1 066	24 407	0.9
Greene	536	0.7	D	8.0	7.0	9.0	3.5	D	37.3	10 545	216	1 127	27 027	1.8
Hamilton	59	0.0	D	1.1	D	11.0	D	D	39.3	1 440	273	103	8 071	1.3
Herkimer	670	1.4	27.3	20.7	6.9	9.2	3.5	9.3	25.1	13 755	216	1 596	32 288	0.8
Jefferson	2 168	0.7	10.3	6.3	3.6	7.0	2.9	10.5	52.2	18 365	160	2 899	54 537	0.9
Kings	21 528	0.0	13.7	6.7	8.9	7.4	9.3	26.9	10.7	288 855	117	143 679	940 176	1.0
Lewis	269	4.1	28.7	22.0	D	7.2	2.0	D	32.5	4 970	187	649	15 651	3.4
Livingston	776	1.9	18.9	12.2	3.7	9.6	2.9	8.3	40.8	10 880	168	1 016	24 640	2.6
Madison	871	1.7	19.5	14.1	8.9	8.6	5.9	D	20.9	11 970	171	1 249	29 098	1.6
Monroe	19 854	0.1	29.6	25.2	12.7	5.8	5.8	10.4	11.1	129 100	175	18 713	309 654	1.7
Montgomery	663	1.3	D	21.3	4.7	11.2	3.1	D	17.3	12 600	255	1 485	22 586	0.3
Nassau	36 904	0.0	D	5.6	15.6	8.2	14.0	14.5	13.7	239 915	179	16 486	460 334	0.5
New York	239 294	0.0	3.8	2.0	23.6	2.5	34.4	4.7	11.2	219 000	140	78 715	814 456	2.0
Niagara	3 295	0.5	D	31.7	4.6	7.5	2.7	10.4	18.8	46 275	212	4 956	97 031	1.4
Oneida	4 359	0.5	15.8	12.1	7.5	7.6	7.8	14.5	25.5	50 675	216	7 651	103 328	0.5
Onondaga	12 076	0.1	21.4	16.4	11.6	6.3	8.2	10.8	15.7	84 125	183	11 738	199 761	1.6
Ontario	1 933	1.0	29.2	19.6	5.2	11.2	4.6	12.4	19.1	19 275	188	1 745	43 995	3.2
Orange	5 894	0.5	13.2	7.2	9.9	10.0	4.8	11.6	27.7	51 840	143	6 174	128 785	4.9
Orleans	489	4.5	19.7	14.5	D	6.4	2.3	D	41.8	7 860	180	893	17 486	0.8
Oswego	1 517	1.0	D	17.0	4.1	7.2	2.7	9.5	25.8	22 250	180	2 950	53 755	1.7
Otsego	899	1.2	11.8	6.4	4.9	9.2	6.5	22.0	19.9	12 665	204	1 468	30 391	6.7
Putnam	1 226	0.2	19.1	7.1	10.5	6.9	7.0	15.2	20.5	13 545	136	784	35 989	2.7
Queens	25 911	0.0	D	7.3	5.8	6.3	8.1	16.0	9.0	291 125	131	72 652	825 099	1.0
Rensselaer	2 343	0.2	16.1	6.6	11.2	7.6	6.3	13.0	23.2	29 045	189	3 231	67 124	1.5
Richmond	4 529	0.0	D	D	15.8	8.5	D	25.6	10.4	71 060	155	11 838	170 000	3.7
Rockland	6 385	0.0	D	14.4	14.0	7.2	8.0	14.0	17.0	46 420	158	5 049	96 496	1.6
St. Lawrence	1 556	0.8	23.2	16.8	3.6	8.1	2.7	11.2	33.1	21 630	194	3 749	50 374	1.3
Saratoga	3 125	0.3	D	11.8	10.1	9.4	7.8	8.2	19.3	31 945	152	2 556	90 644	4.5
Schenectady	3 488	0.1	24.7	18.8	19.9	6.0	3.9	12.3	14.4	30 345	206	4 033	65 574	0.8
Schoharie	347	2.6	D	2.9	4.2	9.7	5.7	D	36.8	5 915	187	682	16 155	1.5
Schuyler	172	1.3	D	14.2	4.2	9.6	3.2	D	29.4	4 085	210	421	9 330	1.6
Seneca	438	2.1	D	D	3.6	10.5	2.6	9.6	23.5	6 970	198	727	14 907	0.8
Steuben	1 947	0.8	25.9	23.4	15.1	5.5	4.0	8.7	17.9	20 190	204	2 984	46 885	1.6
Suffolk	32 432	0.2	18.3	10.5	11.9	7.8	9.4	10.6	18.7	241 975	165	21 207	535 805	2.6
Sullivan	1 060	0.2	D	3.2	10.2	8.9	7.5	16.2	30.7	15 835	211	2 789	45 840	2.5
Tioga	663	1.4	57.6	53.4	2.9	5.4	1.6	4.5	15.2	9 930	192	983	21 760	1.6
Tompkins	2 191	0.5	13.0	10.1	8.1	5.4	3.7	D	12.5	12 790	126	1 571	39 917	3.3
Ulster	2 489	0.6	15.8	10.4	7.2	11.3	5.8	13.7	26.0	33 120	183	4 266	79 456	2.3
Warren	1 363	0.1	D	13.1	9.7	10.8	6.6	16.2	13.6	13 905	215	1 582	35 851	2.9
Washington	671	2.9	30.8	24.3	D	6.9	1.9	7.2	36.2	11 620	188	1 438	27 304	1.9
Wayne	1 117	2.8	D	25.4	6.2	8.0	2.6	7.0	29.4	18 160	194	2 016	39 584	2.1
Westchester	29 663	0.0	14.4	7.5	17.6	5.9	13.3	11.2	13.1	152 545	162	15 260	354 190	1.4
Wyoming	573	4.9	23.1	19.0	D	6.1	4.0	5.1	36.5	7 950	176	620	17 136	1.2
Yates	214	4.2	D	17.3	4.6	7.7	4.0	D	21.9	5 145	208	560	12 227	1.4
NORTH CAROLINA	175 339	1.0	24.9	18.2	9.2	7.2	7.7	8.6	18.4	1 436 124	171	194 611	3 779 034	7.2
Alamance	2 484	0.0	D	24.0	5.9	7.9	6.5	10.4	9.8	26 055	190	2 346	58 775	6.0
Alexander	386	4.1	D	46.4	3.6	6.7	3.3	D	12.8	6 025	173	553	14 754	4.7
Alleghany	143	15.5	D	23.1	2.9	6.0	4.0	D	15.6	2 730	251	339	6 717	4.8
Anson	315	7.4	D	23.5	D	5.0	1.9	5.0	25.0	5 195	206	1 048	10 399	1.7
Ashe	325	11.0	D	25.8	2.9	9.6	4.4	D	12.6	6 165	246	920	14 048	5.9
Avery	264	9.1	D	8.7	D	7.7	4.9	D	16.2	3 655	206	435	12 288	3.2
Beaufort	597	-2.1	34.7	26.8	D	8.7	3.5	12.0	17.9	10 965	241	1 806	22 788	2.9
Bertie	220	9.7	34.2	31.7	1.5	4.3	1.7	D	18.7	5 395	276	1 464	9 242	2.1
Bladen	424	2.0	47.5	44.1	D	5.4	2.0	4.8	19.6	7 360	225	1 848	15 691	2.4
Brunswick	959	-0.3	D	7.5	6.5	9.0	14.7	6.9	16.9	20 320	249	1 895	57 903	12.6
Buncombe	4 206	0.6	22.2	14.7	7.9	8.6	5.4	17.8	15.9	43 295	204	4 564	99 611	6.0
Burke	1 409	2.0	D	32.3	4.7	6.1	3.7	12.3	20.6	17 365	194	1 825	38 615	3.2
Cabarrus	2 614	0.3	31.9	23.5	4.9	9.1	4.9	6.3	16.7	22 615	158	1 819	58 682	11.0
Caldwell	1 277	2.2	42.2	37.8	D	7.0	3.5	7.4	11.2	15 420	196	1 375	34 858	4.3
Camden	58	3.6	14.2	6.8	11.6	11.6	3.6	D	24.4	1 510	192	130	3 267	9.9
Carteret	758	0.3	15.0	6.2	7.3	12.1	6.6	8.0	24.4	13 680	225	1 116	42 534	3.9
Caswell	122	-2.1	D	18.4	3.6	5.6	3.1	D	42.8	4 670	198	789	9 978	3.9
Catawba	3 567	0.4	42.3	37.9	3.1	8.0	3.4	9.3	10.4	26 680	182	2 191	63 999	6.8
Chatham	741	5.6	D	28.1	D	7.7	6.9	8.5	11.4	10 095	183	677	22 911	7.3
Cherokee	302	1.0	D	18.0	4.1	12.6	5.6	D	18.6	6 950	277	914	14 385	6.6

1. Covers mining, construction, and manufacturing.   2. Per 1,000 resident population estimated as of July 1 of the year shown.

Table B. States and Counties — Housing, Labor Force, and Employment

STATE County	Housing units, 2000 Occupied units Total	Owner-occupied Percent	Owner-occupied Median value[1]	Median owner cost as a percent of income With a mortgage	Median owner cost as a percent of income Without a mortgage[2]	Renter-occupied Median rent[3]	Renter-occupied Median rent as a percent of income	Sub-standard units[4] (percent)	Civilian labor force, 2003 Total	Percent change, 2002–2003	Unemployment Total	Unemployment Rate[5]	Civilian employment,[6] 2000 Total	Percent Management, professional and related occupations	Percent Production, transportation, and material moving occupations
	89	90	91	92	93	94	95	96	97	98	99	100	101	102	103
NEW YORK—Cont'd															
Genesee	22 770	72.9	83 200	21.8	12.5	517	26.4	1.8	31 022	0.1	2 116	6.8	29 690	28.6	19.6
Greene	18 256	72.2	92 400	22.4	13.4	508	27.8	2.0	23 361	1.0	1 103	4.7	20 355	30.5	13.3
Hamilton	2 362	79.3	86 700	21.9	12.0	457	26.6	1.3	2 757	4.0	156	5.7	2 324	30.2	11.1
Herkimer	25 734	71.2	67 500	19.9	13.0	420	25.8	1.4	30 891	0.0	1 826	5.9	29 223	28.1	17.8
Jefferson	40 068	59.8	68 200	20.0	13.1	486	25.3	2.6	44 639	0.7	3 435	7.7	40 482	29.9	13.9
Kings	880 727	27.1	224 100	27.2	12.9	672	28.0	16.6	1 039 735	-1.0	95 832	9.2	927 030	32.5	12.3
Lewis	10 040	77.0	63 600	19.1	11.6	444	25.9	2.5	11 794	-1.4	933	7.9	11 733	26.3	21.3
Livingston	22 150	74.5	88 800	21.7	12.6	541	28.2	1.8	33 382	0.0	2 099	6.3	30 550	32.0	16.5
Madison	25 368	74.9	81 500	21.2	12.7	509	24.3	1.8	35 469	0.2	2 088	5.9	32 663	31.9	16.2
Monroe	286 512	65.1	98 700	21.5	12.7	612	28.5	2.2	389 769	-0.3	21 835	5.6	351 605	40.0	13.7
Montgomery	20 038	67.1	67 600	21.3	14.5	464	25.7	2.3	23 520	0.8	1 667	7.1	21 724	28.1	20.5
Nassau	447 387	80.3	242 300	24.9	15.8	964	26.9	4.1	718 463	0.6	28 247	3.9	631 188	41.0	7.8
New York	738 644	20.1	1 000 001[7]	21.3	9.9	796	24.8	11.7	818 998	-1.8	66 952	8.2	770 283	55.8	6.0
Niagara	87 846	69.9	82 600	21.4	13.6	479	26.7	1.8	109 152	-0.1	8 232	7.5	100 810	28.6	19.1
Oneida	90 496	67.2	76 500	20.8	12.7	470	26.8	1.9	114 211	-0.3	5 898	5.2	102 740	31.8	15.3
Onondaga	181 153	64.5	85 400	20.9	13.2	550	27.4	2.1	239 431	0.0	12 096	5.1	215 714	37.5	12.6
Ontario	38 370	73.6	94 100	21.6	12.9	564	25.8	1.6	53 681	-0.4	2 983	5.6	50 822	35.0	15.5
Orange	114 788	67.0	144 500	23.2	13.8	714	26.8	4.5	169 915	2.0	8 013	4.7	151 744	33.2	12.1
Orleans	15 363	75.6	72 600	22.4	13.2	519	28.1	2.5	20 380	0.4	1 539	7.6	18 718	25.9	23.2
Oswego	45 522	72.8	74 200	20.4	12.7	507	27.8	2.1	58 200	1.2	5 096	8.8	54 139	25.1	21.0
Otsego	23 291	73.0	75 900	21.5	13.0	485	28.7	1.7	33 248	-1.2	1 465	4.4	27 601	35.3	12.9
Putnam	32 703	82.2	206 900	24.4	14.3	913	26.1	2.4	59 845	1.4	1 995	3.3	48 932	41.1	6.9
Queens	782 664	42.8	212 600	27.5	12.8	775	26.3	17.0	1 085 919	-1.3	74 754	6.9	956 784	30.5	13.2
Rensselaer	59 894	64.9	102 900	21.7	12.1	547	24.2	2.0	81 868	-0.2	3 552	4.3	75 214	35.9	12.7
Richmond	156 341	63.8	209 100	23.4	11.7	742	25.2	5.3	217 081	-0.8	16 165	7.4	195 074	35.0	8.8
Rockland	92 675	71.7	242 500	24.3	14.2	884	28.3	6.8	158 133	1.4	6 500	4.1	135 262	44.2	7.7
St. Lawrence	40 506	70.6	60 200	19.3	11.3	428	27.9	2.7	51 793	-0.2	4 196	8.1	45 406	29.8	14.2
Saratoga	78 165	72.0	120 400	21.5	11.8	638	23.6	1.2	111 023	0.0	3 964	3.6	102 898	39.9	11.4
Schenectady	59 684	65.4	94 500	21.8	12.7	572	26.9	1.9	74 959	0.3	2 953	3.9	67 713	36.5	11.2
Schoharie	11 991	75.3	82 500	22.4	13.1	506	26.8	2.2	15 226	-0.9	767	5.0	14 042	30.0	17.2
Schuyler	7 374	77.2	68 400	21.3	12.0	466	24.8	2.2	9 421	2.1	698	7.4	8 584	29.8	17.5
Seneca	12 630	73.7	72 400	20.8	13.2	521	27.5	2.0	16 641	0.3	958	5.8	14 697	30.4	18.6
Steuben	39 071	74.2	66 200	19.9	11.7	468	26.0	2.3	45 946	-5.8	3 849	8.4	44 141	32.5	18.7
Suffolk	469 299	79.8	185 200	25.3	16.2	945	28.3	3.5	767 336	0.7	34 101	4.4	683 062	35.7	10.7
Sullivan	27 661	68.1	93 300	23.8	14.6	545	27.7	4.2	32 708	0.3	1 685	5.2	30 244	31.0	12.0
Tioga	19 725	77.8	77 400	20.4	11.4	468	24.8	1.8	25 627	-2.0	1 538	6.0	24 701	34.2	18.6
Tompkins	36 420	53.8	101 600	21.6	11.5	611	32.0	2.6	55 119	1.6	1 687	3.1	48 192	50.2	7.5
Ulster	67 499	68.0	113 100	22.5	13.1	626	28.0	2.7	86 454	0.6	3 693	4.3	83 748	35.4	12.1
Warren	25 726	69.9	97 500	22.5	12.3	557	26.9	1.8	33 083	2.8	1 769	5.3	30 071	32.1	12.7
Washington	22 458	74.3	77 400	22.2	13.3	509	25.5	2.3	29 145	2.4	1 287	4.4	27 357	25.1	21.0
Wayne	34 908	77.6	85 700	21.8	13.1	527	26.4	1.9	48 480	-1.1	3 195	6.6	45 545	30.7	21.9
Westchester	337 142	60.1	325 800	24.1	15.4	839	26.3	6.6	467 754	0.3	18 716	4.0	432 600	45.6	6.6
Wyoming	14 906	76.9	74 000	21.7	12.3	482	24.9	1.8	21 968	1.3	1 379	6.3	18 955	26.1	18.5
Yates	9 029	77.0	75 600	22.9	13.5	467	27.7	3.2	14 886	1.5	646	4.3	11 191	28.5	17.7
NORTH CAROLINA	3 132 013	69.4	108 300	21.3	9.9	548	24.3	4.0	4 229 772	1.5	272 826	6.5	3 824 741	31.2	18.7
Alamance	51 584	70.1	107 200	21.7	9.9	557	23.5	4.0	73 110	1.0	5 235	7.2	64 895	28.2	23.0
Alexander	13 137	80.5	95 600	20.5	9.9	439	20.7	3.5	17 421	-1.2	1 395	8.0	18 223	19.6	39.5
Alleghany	4 593	79.0	89 700	21.6	10.3	363	23.2	2.0	4 936	-1.2	488	9.9	5 145	25.1	26.7
Anson	9 204	76.0	64 300	21.1	10.9	404	25.3	5.6	10 889	0.0	1 200	11.0	10 109	19.4	32.4
Ashe	10 411	81.0	91 600	22.4	9.9	375	23.8	2.6	11 975	0.2	853	7.1	11 390	22.4	25.5
Avery	6 532	80.5	88 000	20.9	9.9	430	24.9	2.1	8 651	3.9	369	4.3	7 196	25.7	16.3
Beaufort	18 319	75.1	81 900	21.6	11.3	405	24.8	3.6	18 892	0.2	1 838	9.7	18 913	28.1	19.3
Bertie	7 743	74.9	59 200	23.3	12.2	358	25.7	6.1	8 671	2.2	665	7.7	7 539	22.7	29.7
Bladen	12 897	77.8	65 200	21.1	11.6	350	23.5	4.1	20 107	-0.9	1 378	6.9	13 109	24.0	22.8
Brunswick	30 438	82.2	127 400	23.3	10.9	535	26.7	3.2	37 823	2.4	2 291	6.1	32 355	23.5	13.5
Buncombe	85 776	70.3	119 600	22.2	9.9	551	25.6	2.3	110 703	3.1	4 290	3.9	100 924	32.0	16.6
Burke	34 528	74.1	85 900	20.4	9.9	450	21.3	3.8	43 110	-1.5	3 504	8.1	43 194	22.3	32.3
Cabarrus	49 519	74.7	118 200	21.0	10.9	566	22.2	3.3	77 433	5.4	6 205	8.0	66 970	29.0	17.7
Caldwell	30 768	74.9	86 700	20.6	9.9	446	21.6	2.9	39 576	-0.5	3 869	9.8	39 806	20.1	38.1
Camden	2 662	83.5	103 100	21.6	11.2	514	26.0	1.0	3 833	4.4	112	2.9	3 099	29.1	15.1
Carteret	25 204	76.6	123 900	22.2	9.9	511	24.0	2.0	29 560	2.0	1 501	5.1	27 110	29.3	11.4
Caswell	8 670	79.4	80 800	19.6	9.9	390	22.5	3.6	11 592	-6.9	1 023	8.8	10 156	20.0	31.1
Catawba	55 533	72.6	103 000	20.6	9.9	525	21.5	4.0	77 121	-2.1	6 758	8.8	75 192	23.8	32.0
Chatham	19 741	77.2	127 200	21.2	9.9	579	23.1	5.2	29 934	2.4	1 340	4.5	25 095	35.1	20.4
Cherokee	10 336	82.1	86 000	22.7	9.9	350	23.2	3.3	10 345	-0.7	752	7.3	10 162	22.6	22.8

1. Specified owner-occupied units.   2. Median monthly owner costs is often in the minimum category—9.9 percent or less, which is indicated as 9.9 percent.   3. Specified renter-occupied units.   4. Overcrowded or lacking complete plumbing facilities.   5. Percent of civilian labor force.   6. Persons 16 years old and over.   7. $1,000,001 is the top code symbolizing a median value over one million.

Table B. States and Counties — Nonfarm Employment and Agriculture

STATE County	Private nonfarm establishments, employment and payroll, 2001									Agriculture, 2002			
	Number of establishments	Employment						Annual payroll		Farms			Farm operators whose principal occupation is farming (percent)
		Total	Health care and social assistance	Manufacturing	Retail trade	Finance and insurance	Professional, scientific, and technical services	Total (mil dol)	Average per employee (dollars)	Number	Percent with—		
											Less than 50 acres	500 acres and over	
	104	105	106	107	108	109	110	111	112	113	114	115	116
NEW YORK—Cont'd													
Genesee	1 339	16 482	2 618	3 706	2 578	337	340	425	25 768	580	39.0	12.6	63.3
Greene	1 131	9 688	907	795	2 155	307	376	214	22 081	342	38.6	9.5	56.1
Hamilton	209	792	37	24	D	D	D	17	21 710	24	54.2	0.0	33.3
Herkimer	1 175	13 594	2 235	4 148	2 392	385	193	319	23 485	690	17.2	9.1	66.4
Jefferson	2 297	26 445	5 505	3 399	5 701	810	660	641	24 237	1 028	14.7	18.0	64.5
Kings	38 732	437 905	136 570	38 876	49 211	15 874	14 335	13 509	30 849	1	100.0	0.0	0.0
Lewis	545	4 523	744	1 341	714	94	96	108	23 883	721	16.1	13.5	70.0
Livingston	1 253	12 142	1 480	2 335	2 637	278	497	287	23 664	801	32.5	12.9	55.8
Madison	1 372	20 268	2 739	3 046	2 859	525	675	499	24 602	734	25.2	11.7	66.2
Monroe	16 828	359 832	51 032	66 337	42 077	12 880	20 389	12 781	35 520	631	59.6	9.5	59.0
Montgomery	1 136	15 312	4 014	4 239	2 303	636	346	384	25 069	624	22.8	12.5	67.5
Nassau	47 591	564 164	90 121	36 330	82 312	44 424	44 299	21 525	38 154	65	87.7	0.0	46.2
New York	106 493	2 122 694	217 722	59 751	121 548	365 849	289 165	164 383	77 441	4	100.0	0.0	0.0
Niagara	4 484	63 877	9 475	15 772	10 480	1 314	1 492	1 882	29 465	801	43.2	7.7	60.3
Oneida	4 906	86 529	17 215	13 957	12 449	8 210	2 815	2 294	26 515	1 087	25.9	9.6	64.2
Onondaga	11 737	224 972	30 487	30 459	29 816	12 114	12 301	7 245	32 204	725	39.3	10.6	61.0
Ontario	2 600	39 508	6 534	7 292	8 154	900	1 367	1 108	28 033	896	41.5	11.7	61.9
Orange	8 220	95 978	15 904	8 843	19 020	4 010	4 177	2 768	28 838	706	40.2	6.9	67.7
Orleans	694	7 398	1 470	1 766	1 428	567	81	170	22 927	504	33.9	10.7	55.6
Oswego	2 020	25 098	3 852	4 990	4 278	679	676	774	30 850	682	30.5	4.8	59.5
Otsego	1 348	17 800	4 693	1 478	3 194	1 188	508	452	25 416	1 028	19.0	8.5	62.3
Putnam	2 624	19 612	3 910	1 938	2 791	609	1 102	666	33 953	52	61.5	5.8	53.8
Queens	36 976	477 041	89 158	42 642	51 197	12 248	12 301	16 500	34 588	2	100.0	0.0	0.0
Rensselaer	2 688	41 777	7 828	4 324	5 912	1 287	3 377	1 242	29 725	549	37.9	7.3	58.1
Richmond	7 506	85 897	25 143	1 583	13 842	3 105	4 079	2 663	30 998	16	100.0	0.0	6.3
Rockland	8 660	102 382	19 733	9 859	14 040	4 364	5 542	3 672	35 862	29	62.1	0.0	58.6
St. Lawrence	2 140	28 009	5 911	4 548	5 097	777	641	741	26 472	1 451	11.8	14.8	63.6
Saratoga	4 269	55 467	6 441	6 281	10 343	4 105	2 708	1 634	29 456	592	48.8	5.2	61.5
Schenectady	2 945	49 033	10 578	5 456	7 290	1 894	4 402	1 743	35 554	200	45.0	2.0	49.5
Schoharie	591	5 768	885	843	1 320	243	250	136	23 601	579	24.0	7.1	57.5
Schuyler	348	2 967	786	605	476	76	D	74	24 914	405	29.4	6.2	52.8
Seneca	655	7 728	1 201	1 804	1 824	172	91	205	26 551	466	29.4	14.6	65.5
Steuben	1 783	32 949	5 621	8 194	4 088	978	568	1 621	49 192	1 501	17.6	11.9	57.4
Suffolk	43 840	536 663	77 336	64 745	75 219	24 949	36 913	19 908	37 095	651	76.3	1.5	62.8
Sullivan	1 902	17 110	4 078	684	3 040	1 174	499	417	24 352	381	35.2	7.1	63.8
Tioga	804	8 709	899	2 661	1 347	224	559	196	22 542	604	22.8	9.3	57.0
Tompkins	2 143	43 074	3 672	4 045	4 801	991	2 122	1 128	26 198	563	38.9	8.9	55.1
Ulster	4 363	46 676	8 387	6 227	8 686	2 288	2 333	1 177	25 222	532	44.7	6.6	64.1
Warren	2 347	32 759	5 068	4 743	5 470	1 532	1 150	1 013	30 909	72	59.7	1.4	47.2
Washington	1 100	10 286	1 401	3 724	1 859	196	180	273	26 537	887	24.2	13.9	61.7
Wayne	1 728	19 822	2 614	6 639	3 408	498	616	539	27 188	904	37.8	8.4	66.9
Westchester	30 809	393 475	68 113	17 311	47 968	20 192	25 947	18 327	46 577	129	68.2	3.9	58.1
Wyoming	817	8 430	1 350	2 173	1 492	362	264	199	23 609	767	28.4	12.4	67.5
Yates	518	5 387	1 008	775	713	81	152	115	21 362	722	22.6	5.3	67.5
NORTH CAROLINA	204 075	3 431 554	410 872	690 686	441 460	186 767	158 447	103 027	30 023	53 930	45.6	7.2	58.7
Alamance	3 355	60 291	6 972	19 378	7 682	1 665	1 208	1 562	25 912	831	43.2	3.7	52.5
Alexander	587	9 035	581	5 327	1 013	132	131	201	22 231	661	54.8	2.3	58.9
Alleghany	289	2 959	462	1 029	369	74	37	59	19 902	544	47.4	5.0	49.6
Anson	463	6 095	332	2 507	651	105	72	143	23 504	539	33.4	8.2	56.2
Ashe	544	5 740	821	1 757	862	192	70	128	22 280	1 152	49.6	2.3	50.3
Avery	567	6 206	1 233	852	774	79	96	128	20 589	495	62.8	1.4	61.0
Beaufort	1 151	15 307	1 945	4 187	2 483	409	612	345	22 510	395	30.4	26.1	67.6
Bertie	371	5 175	936	2 229	469	82	78	100	19 413	330	28.5	21.5	74.8
Bladen	522	11 385	1 115	7 087	876	121	188	235	20 628	551	35.9	12.5	65.7
Brunswick	1 700	17 616	1 825	2 381	3 091	374	478	454	25 795	271	48.3	6.6	60.1
Buncombe	6 454	96 722	17 176	16 238	13 950	2 736	3 291	2 573	26 606	1 192	63.8	1.9	56.3
Burke	1 557	31 625	4 264	15 579	3 024	455	512	739	23 371	439	62.9	1.4	54.2
Cabarrus	3 253	51 858	6 227	11 706	8 818	1 022	1 601	1 526	29 436	658	43.9	3.0	52.9
Caldwell	1 559	30 193	2 411	15 629	3 146	488	387	710	23 526	411	54.0	2.4	51.8
Camden	107	525	D	D	D	D	D	10	18 768	70	24.3	45.7	78.6
Carteret	1 887	17 396	2 593	1 531	3 644	453	591	357	20 524	128	60.2	5.5	47.7
Caswell	230	1 697	397	319	276	62	D	28	16 787	517	22.8	9.1	62.9
Catawba	4 439	94 955	8 567	40 521	10 333	1 929	1 381	2 592	27 299	715	47.3	3.9	52.7
Chatham	933	13 238	1 530	6 268	1 592	174	323	320	24 144	1 128	48.0	2.4	61.0
Cherokee	618	7 490	1 257	1 811	1 484	205	189	158	21 127	262	55.0	1.9	51.5

STATE County	Acreage (1,000) 117	Percent change, 1997–2002 118	Average size of farm 119	Total irrigated (1,000) 120	Total cropland (1,000) 121	Average per farm 122	Average per acre 123	Value of machinery and equipment average per farm (dollars) 124	Total (mil dol) 125	Average per farm (dollars) 126	Crops 127	Livestock and poultry products 128	$10,000 or more 129	$100,000 or more 130	Total ($1,000) 131	Percent of farms 132
NEW YORK—Cont'd	177	3.5	306	7	142	412 369	1 395	120 121	125	215 410	38.2	61.8	47.9	18.6	3 199	41.0
Genesee	58	18.4	169	0	32	390 409	2 130	51 935	14	42 033	40.1	59.9	31.6	7.0	314	19.3
Greene	1	0.0	59	D	1	D	D	15 031	0	8 603	D	D	12.5	4.2	0	0.0
Hamilton	159	12.0	231	0	97	258 994	1 171	68 458	50	72 213	13.5	86.5	52.2	23.9	2 425	32.6
Herkimer	331	13.7	322	0	219	272 367	872	80 647	100	96 830	10.4	89.6	51.2	23.1	4 969	34.3
Jefferson	D	NA	D	D	D	D	D	D	D	D	D	D	100.0	0.0	D	D
Kings	197	9.4	273	0	114	219 952	820	103 351	72	100 108	9.8	90.2	58.8	32.3	3 765	36.5
Lewis	209	6.1	262	2	155	376 388	1 461	100 965	84	104 942	34.3	65.7	38.3	16.0	3 161	40.2
Livingston	168	-9.7	229	0	106	281 846	1 267	123 635	62	83 929	12.1	87.9	48.2	25.6	3 469	34.1
Madison	107	3.9	169	3	85	357 629	1 969	99 142	54	85 477	84.6	15.4	38.2	12.7	1 552	17.7
Monroe	152	12.6	244	0	112	363 550	1 493	109 550	52	83 010	19.5	80.5	53.5	21.2	2 586	36.1
Montgomery	1	0.0	17	0	0	572 913	30 396	97 143	8	126 935	D	D	44.6	15.4	0	0.0
Nassau	0	NA	1	0	0	7 500	7 500	35 000	0	97 549	100.0	0.0	100.0	0.0	0	0.0
New York	148	16.5	185	3	124	315 855	1 691	101 356	60	74 789	66.4	33.6	42.4	12.0	2 471	27.0
Niagara	220	1.9	203	0	146	225 598	1 181	74 100	78	72 098	28.9	71.1	47.9	20.7	3 540	30.4
Oneida	156	6.1	216	2	114	355 435	1 484	127 518	82	113 330	29.9	70.1	44.8	20.7	3 332	25.4
Onondaga	195	4.8	217	1	152	355 018	1 679	115 577	87	97 184	43.2	56.8	45.0	17.5	3 006	29.5
Ontario	108	13.7	153	4	71	664 668	4 339	158 435	66	93 802	61.7	38.3	52.7	19.1	1 890	20.3
Orange	133	-7.0	264	5	109	332 449	1 241	113 426	69	136 739	88.7	11.3	44.4	18.5	2 461	42.9
Orleans	103	0.0	151	1	58	343 023	2 275	45 411	32	46 226	56.3	43.7	36.1	12.6	786	21.7
Oswego	206	-0.5	201	0	112	326 860	1 683	85 124	51	49 322	13.0	87.0	41.8	17.0	2 658	26.4
Otsego	7	133.3	129	0	2	1 185 971	9 515	56 224	2	46 653	96.5	3.5	34.6	7.7	D	D
Putnam	D	NA	D	D	D	D	D	D	D	D	D	D	50.0	0.0	0	0.0
Queens	92	-7.1	168	1	54	357 354	2 595	55 105	28	51 224	42.7	57.3	37.7	10.6	1 480	26.4
Rensselaer	0	NA	3	0	D	273 578	98 954	40 508	2	107 511	D	D	25.0	18.8	0	0.0
Richmond	D	D	D	0	1	1 075 563	25 154	68 688	3	108 939	95.2	4.8	65.5	24.1	0	0.0
Rockland	403	1.8	278	0	221	198 182	746	91 853	100	68 722	8.9	91.1	45.1	17.0	4 680	26.7
St. Lawrence	75	2.7	127	0	48	360 607	2 818	69 189	33	56 128	30.0	70.0	33.3	9.5	1 164	16.7
Saratoga	22	22.2	109	0	12	283 611	2 133	121 203	4	20 041	60.0	40.0	31.5	5.0	62	6.5
Schenectady	113	1.8	195	1	71	285 003	1 717	57 276	27	46 596	27.7	72.3	43.2	13.1	1 630	28.3
Schoharie	74	13.8	182	0	38	267 332	1 555	42 317	18	44 225	25.4	74.6	38.0	9.4	569	19.3
Schuyler	127	8.5	273	0	101	423 149	1 505	163 660	45	97 089	40.8	59.2	60.9	24.5	1 408	31.5
Seneca	373	6.9	249	3	226	268 260	1 103	121 202	85	56 498	31.6	68.4	41.4	14.5	3 428	29.0
Steuben	34	-5.6	52	15	27	920 960	18 133	206 704	201	309 035	88.3	11.7	60.4	29.2	147	5.7
Suffolk	64	10.3	167	0	34	522 088	2 798	72 534	38	99 090	7.1	92.9	39.9	13.1	555	19.9
Sullivan	128	17.4	212	0	75	391 961	1 385	96 928	30	49 567	20.4	79.6	38.6	15.2	1 798	31.0
Tioga	101	6.3	179	0	67	304 567	1 686	252 933	42	74 438	21.1	78.9	36.4	13.0	1 492	24.5
Tompkins	83	20.3	157	4	39	534 962	3 539	81 821	34	64 692	83.5	16.5	39.5	10.7	777	12.8
Ulster	6	-33.3	89	0	2	293 339	3 136	27 841	3	34 942	90.3	9.7	34.7	6.9	D	D
Warren	206	5.6	232	1	131	298 920	1 356	94 903	82	92 413	14.5	85.5	50.4	22.1	4 468	29.9
Washington	165	-1.2	183	2	123	445 334	2 488	103 930	104	114 885	69.7	30.3	51.0	22.6	3 435	32.9
Wayne	10	25.0	77	0	2	1 087 369	15 094	64 567	9	68 637	95.4	4.6	36.4	15.5	D	D
Westchester	215	10.3	281	4	151	390 945	1 341	168 143	178	232 078	17.0	83.0	51.1	26.9	5 649	37.0
Wyoming	115	9.5	159	0	80	281 899	1 863	75 985	50	69 769	41.8	58.2	63.0	24.5	950	19.5
Yates																
NORTH CAROLINA	9 079	-0.5	168	264	5 472	518 719	3 088	63 902	6 962	129 087	28.9	71.1	36.3	16.3	97 696	22.8
Alamance	98	-9.3	118	2	45	412 829	3 867	48 571	29	34 552	36.5	63.5	29.5	7.0	400	18.3
Alexander	58	-3.3	88	1	31	365 857	4 629	36 883	67	101 170	5.0	95.0	42.5	29.0	455	16.0
Alleghany	73	-15.1	134	0	36	433 026	3 451	50 273	24	43 819	44.8	55.2	38.6	8.5	418	14.2
Anson	100	22.0	186	1	35	558 979	2 774	62 903	107	199 416	2.9	97.1	41.4	26.5	1 056	43.6
Ashe	108	2.9	94	1	50	379 042	4 163	36 210	29	25 331	79.9	20.1	34.3	4.2	167	9.8
Avery	31	14.8	62	0	14	264 169	4 363	32 853	28	32 853	98.8	1.2	51.5	8.3	41	5.5
Beaufort	170	9.7	430	3	153	825 179	1 923	129 985	74	187 050	66.0	34.0	62.0	35.4	2 403	44.3
Bertie	143	-7.1	432	6	93	877 015	2 014	150 526	85	257 652	34.6	65.4	70.3	42.4	2 155	41.2
Bladen	145	13.3	264	12	79	806 777	2 954	77 120	255	462 158	15.5	84.5	48.6	29.8	1 020	30.3
Brunswick	41	10.8	152	3	24	448 040	3 183	46 801	35	128 619	48.9	51.1	30.6	12.9	393	16.2
Buncombe	95	9.2	80	2	39	462 101	4 486	30 487	22	18 314	60.6	39.4	19.1	2.1	150	8.2
Burke	32	10.3	73	1	17	339 660	4 030	44 166	31	70 404	55.5	44.5	28.5	10.7	66	8.9
Cabarrus	73	15.9	111	1	43	453 688	4 902	32 596	31	46 464	19.1	80.9	20.5	4.6	476	20.2
Caldwell	35	-5.4	85	1	14	358 975	4 849	33 730	16	33 730	59.4	40.6	21.4	6.6	70	5.6
Camden	D	D	D	D	55	1 634 453	1 884	286 090	20	281 615	D	D	61.4	48.6	736	47.1
Carteret	60	0.0	467	0	47	985 552	2 100	102 803	16	123 994	97.5	2.5	39.1	10.9	58	12.5
Caswell	117	-15.2	226	2	40	648 780	2 594	61 871	24	46 546	54.2	45.8	38.5	8.9	285	22.4
Catawba	79	9.7	110	1	41	356 785	3 603	48 376	21	29 997	35.3	64.7	22.1	5.7	423	20.3
Chatham	119	5.3	105	1	46	325 326	3 387	48 806	122	108 045	4.7	95.3	34.4	15.8	475	17.1
Cherokee	22	-12.0	85	0	9	379 345	4 939	31 494	11	42 311	10.6	89.4	19.5	1.9	163	19.5

Table B. States and Counties — Residential Construction, Wholesale Trade, Retail Trade, and Real Estate

STATE County	Value of residential construction authorized by building permits, 2003		Wholesale trade, 1997				Retail trade,[1] 1997				Real estate and rental and leasing, 1997			
	New construction ($1,000)	Number of housing units	Number of establishments	Number of employees	Sales (mil dol)	Annual payroll (mil dol)	Number of establishments	Number of employees	Sales (mil dol)	Annual payroll (mil dol)	Number of establishments	Number of employees	Receipts (mil dol)	Annual payroll (mil dol)
	133	134	135	136	137	138	139	140	141	142	143	144	145	146
NEW YORK—Cont'd														
Genesee	16 053	118	99	1 140	385.6	31.5	231	2 649	366.4	35.6	42	136	15.3	2.5
Greene	55 892	330	39	516	222.6	14.8	230	1 673	278.3	27.1	33	122	12.2	1.8
Hamilton	7 816	48	2	D	D	D	35	140	23.7	2.6	3	D	D	D
Herkimer	15 494	143	33	D	D	D	254	2 183	313.4	29.7	45	96	9.8	1.1
Jefferson	21 731	255	93	958	280.7	26.0	514	5 679	1 016.3	90.8	94	407	56.9	7.5
Kings	457 970	6 054	2 953	25 838	11 371.6	742.8	6 994	45 941	7 983.6	821.8	3 230	10 872	1 924.2	256.5
Lewis	13 624	189	25	186	68.8	3.7	99	743	134.0	11.1	10	D	D	D
Livingston	23 557	215	68	633	212.6	18.7	245	2 676	411.3	38.4	34	132	13.0	2.3
Madison	21 551	164	63	473	159.8	13.4	260	2 935	463.3	43.2	48	134	10.4	2.1
Monroe	340 679	2 401	1 113	15 298	9 311.1	634.8	2 546	43 294	6 513.2	634.1	614	5 984	684.3	127.4
Montgomery	8 928	91	54	561	148.6	14.7	222	2 381	378.4	34.0	21	100	7.5	1.9
Nassau	195 435	978	4 124	36 401	23 793.6	1 597.9	6 751	81 902	16 483.6	1 615.9	2 157	9 913	1 894.6	287.4
New York	364 970	5 232	11 629	119 913	151 792.8	6 473.4	11 222	102 965	19 502.4	2 447.2	8 510	59 793	14 318.2	2 331.7
Niagara	75 461	613	237	2 573	656.6	64.4	886	11 500	1 607.6	159.9	111	509	50.8	8.1
Oneida	47 506	338	245	D	D	D	971	12 664	1 846.1	180.5	163	652	79.1	11.5
Onondaga	165 368	1 243	992	13 949	11 159.8	526.1	1 974	30 203	4 372.3	443.4	403	4 020	364.9	88.9
Ontario	72 597	510	152	1 092	471.6	36.4	520	7 791	1 118.6	106.3	62	226	22.5	4.3
Orange	231 980	1 765	448	D	D	D	1 438	17 131	3 047.7	290.4	278	1 075	156.1	22.6
Orleans	8 243	78	26	205	36.3	3.9	139	1 371	191.5	18.1	17	52	3.9	0.7
Oswego	28 314	296	73	443	140.0	11.0	396	4 609	747.1	69.5	60	264	34.2	6.3
Otsego	19 853	152	50	427	99.4	9.8	298	3 064	539.3	47.4	36	135	11.7	2.0
Putnam	60 872	368	126	729	278.2	27.0	320	2 707	497.6	49.9	107	251	37.8	6.8
Queens	348 621	4 399	2 787	27 165	12 942.0	952.6	5 933	48 425	8 756.0	890.1	2 385	11 853	1 919.0	297.2
Rensselaer	71 536	702	131	1 066	780.5	33.5	440	5 814	854.3	86.0	75	300	43.7	7.0
Richmond	304 118	2 598	358	1 763	627.1	55.5	1 197	13 522	2 235.3	219.4	234	842	152.1	18.8
Rockland	57 180	411	662	5 606	5 826.0	221.0	1 114	11 601	2 229.9	228.2	338	1 260	231.7	44.8
St. Lawrence	22 328	255	74	665	316.4	18.3	483	5 161	791.8	73.6	70	203	18.8	3.5
Saratoga	268 782	1 308	195	2 324	1 539.6	74.8	721	9 063	1 509.8	139.0	137	666	95.1	13.5
Schenectady	40 421	298	121	1 733	618.3	60.0	582	7 606	1 174.0	119.1	76	461	45.2	10.7
Schoharie	9 936	121	12	89	24.4	1.9	134	1 364	190.1	18.4	17	54	5.2	0.8
Schuyler	5 608	53	14	D	D	D	72	713	119.5	11.7	11	D	D	D
Seneca	3 092	35	28	311	53.9	6.0	174	1 560	250.3	22.6	17	D	D	D
Steuben	19 004	215	46	366	89.9	8.1	403	4 526	663.4	63.8	59	261	22.1	4.1
Suffolk	745 088	3 204	3 400	42 107	21 953.6	1 616.1	6 393	68 059	13 509.7	1 352.7	1 281	5 853	1 009.5	166.2
Sullivan	70 385	603	82	688	235.8	16.7	344	2 842	485.9	49.0	82	231	26.1	3.9
Tioga	8 135	80	31	D	D	D	145	1 205	218.1	20.0	13	55	4.1	0.6
Tompkins	41 486	336	71	432	239.6	13.8	373	4 367	616.3	65.7	81	450	42.1	8.2
Ulster	122 196	805	183	2 163	522.0	59.5	771	8 107	1 278.3	132.1	135	418	54.6	7.9
Warren	76 188	502	93	D	D	D	466	5 236	850.6	83.9	63	265	39.2	5.2
Washington	17 307	276	44	D	D	D	209	1 693	265.2	25.9	24	76	6.1	0.9
Wayne	31 013	218	78	745	327.1	26.0	296	3 569	576.4	54.2	46	148	15.2	2.3
Westchester	419 709	1 791	1 947	31 486	23 918.0	1 313.0	4 191	46 984	9 189.0	958.6	1 760	7 321	1 533.8	235.8
Wyoming	8 286	74	32	202	107.4	4.7	159	1 609	247.0	23.8	16	89	3.6	1.0
Yates	9 297	75	21	D	D	D	107	739	105.4	10.6	23	105	6.1	1.4
NORTH CAROLINA	10 267 977	79 226	12 284	157 774	98 080.1	5 574.1	35 563	416 287	72 356.8	6 697.4	7 346	39 349	5 026.0	900.6
Alamance	125 303	1 163	172	1 756	550.7	53.7	643	7 630	1 245.1	117.8	97	397	69.3	7.3
Alexander	31 583	167	24	91	23.1	1.9	100	900	142.5	11.6	8	21	1.2	0.2
Alleghany	11 712	82	3	D	D	D	53	317	59.0	4.7	7	13	0.8	0.1
Anson	5 897	39	17	208	86.2	6.5	96	771	105.4	9.8	11	26	1.8	0.4
Ashe	38 232	282	24	69	44.2	1.3	103	830	163.0	13.2	19	37	4.1	0.7
Avery	45 169	187	19	98	35.1	2.6	108	822	130.9	11.9	38	187	11.0	2.7
Beaufort	34 940	214	77	683	245.4	16.6	234	2 398	386.0	33.1	30	118	8.4	1.3
Bertie	4 799	43	21	268	158.6	4.8	69	458	70.8	6.5	7	14	1.1	0.2
Bladen	11 103	90	29	298	144.7	7.5	111	895	129.4	11.9	12	56	9.8	1.1
Brunswick	399 327	2 870	57	367	77.0	8.6	276	2 490	441.9	38.1	86	949	64.7	15.0
Buncombe	293 031	1 737	340	D	D	D	1 136	13 179	2 193.4	210.4	221	1 037	131.9	21.8
Burke	34 682	260	78	583	248.4	16.0	315	3 079	557.8	46.2	43	103	10.3	1.6
Cabarrus	221 250	1 909	157	1 480	953.9	45.4	468	6 467	1 131.8	103.6	98	497	60.0	11.1
Caldwell	42 765	340	77	842	791.3	31.6	330	3 329	515.1	45.8	39	116	11.3	1.9
Camden	23 092	188	5	D	D	D	24	128	14.9	1.6	1	D	D	D
Carteret	100 175	614	61	623	141.3	13.5	406	3 510	598.7	53.4	112	478	46.8	7.1
Caswell	10 910	83	5	75	4.5	1.1	49	267	44.0	3.9	3	4	0.5	0.0
Catawba	126 962	852	308	5 844	2 543.2	177.7	779	10 011	1 719.8	161.1	146	643	80.5	13.2
Chatham	147 171	769	58	523	262.9	12.8	177	1 451	226.1	21.3	20	61	3.6	0.6
Cherokee	44 218	413	24	186	51.1	3.1	139	1 266	217.0	18.3	17	89	11.2	2.0

1. Establishments with payroll.

Table B. States and Counties — Professional Services, Manufacturing, and Accommodation and Foodservices

STATE County	Professional, scientific, and technical services,[1] 1997				Manufacturing, 1997				Accommodation and foodservices, 1997			
	Number of establishments	Number of employees	Receipts (mil dol)	Annual payroll (mil dol)	Number of establishments	Number of employees	Receipts (mil dol)	Annual payroll (mil dol)	Number of establishments	Number of employees	Sales (mil dol)	Annual payroll (mil dol)
	147	148	149	150	151	152	153	154	155	156	157	158
NEW YORK—Cont'd												
Genesee	67	715	25.7	10.4	107	3 979	778.1	127.0	131	1 770	51.7	14.5
Greene	58	283	25.1	6.1	37	740	118.4	22.4	207	1 508	62.6	16.4
Hamilton	3	6	0.7	0.1	NA	NA	NA	NA	59	140	10.4	2.8
Herkimer	58	192	8.7	2.9	71	4 971	662.4	135.8	153	1 225	40.6	10.6
Jefferson	98	591	36.8	16.0	84	3 896	812.6	132.0	295	2 835	102.5	28.1
Kings	1 906	7 731	790.0	250.4	2 672	48 589	5 725.5	1 139.9	2 221	15 748	734.5	188.1
Lewis	20	58	3.1	1.0	24	1 560	505.3	53.1	67	314	10.9	2.4
Livingston	77	344	20.4	8.0	48	2 196	500.5	59.5	138	1 399	39.3	10.3
Madison	89	495	41.7	12.0	69	2 526	506.7	69.3	171	1 948	59.9	17.5
Monroe	1 623	15 316	1 643.0	622.2	1 007	82 459	21 774.7	3 521.8	1 439	22 914	760.6	219.4
Montgomery	55	237	21.1	7.0	84	4 790	637.7	123.6	115	910	36.9	8.5
Nassau	5 784	34 253	3 832.4	1 425.5	1 653	42 717	7 117.3	1 550.8	2 881	35 707	1 544.2	431.3
New York	15 163	230 278	38 237.5	14 755.2	5 165	93 784	14 028.9	2 551.8	7 219	127 621	8 318.2	2 423.4
Niagara	253	1 269	128.7	36.2	310	18 164	4 403.5	836.5	592	6 876	207.6	58.3
Oneida	344	2 312	177.2	62.8	280	15 079	2 485.3	447.1	528	5 931	180.1	50.8
Onondaga	1 057	10 334	935.4	370.6	510	33 289	6 614.4	1 296.3	1 062	16 009	509.8	151.5
Ontario	171	946	108.6	34.5	161	7 196	999.1	226.4	262	3 516	110.7	31.5
Orange	605	2 643	269.0	96.7	346	D	D	D	687	6 763	256.5	67.0
Orleans	27	66	5.5	1.1	48	2 269	496.0	71.2	66	598	15.2	4.1
Oswego	108	436	31.0	12.8	108	5 082	2 210.7	204.9	262	3 128	87.0	25.4
Otsego	84	299	27.5	8.1	68	1 481	225.0	38.0	165	1 675	62.8	16.7
Putnam	248	853	73.2	28.6	74	1 595	258.9	60.3	144	1 207	45.7	12.0
Queens	1 756	7 829	678.8	231.1	2 043	50 505	6 412.8	1 433.2	2 666	25 321	1 336.5	357.1
Rensselaer	226	1 546	125.6	53.3	110	5 023	767.2	169.1	269	3 092	92.0	25.8
Richmond	574	2 143	210.4	68.0	162	2 156	316.2	59.6	553	5 427	239.6	55.3
Rockland	923	4 197	526.9	177.3	309	10 739	3 649.8	413.3	558	5 553	246.6	64.4
St. Lawrence	109	445	26.2	10.5	85	5 311	1 602.2	201.4	259	2 497	74.9	20.3
Saratoga	369	2 011	132.0	47.3	139	6 400	1 513.9	263.2	380	5 431	197.3	58.4
Schenectady	227	3 994	484.7	196.4	119	5 134	1 687.8	212.2	313	3 126	106.6	29.8
Schoharie	31	116	5.5	2.1	28	1 024	180.8	24.0	51	547	14.4	4.1
Schuyler	21	38	3.2	0.6	17	574	88.8	18.3	49	281	11.4	3.1
Seneca	33	97	9.2	3.1	31	2 037	457.2	71.2	72	646	23.3	7.0
Steuben	113	550	35.4	13.2	74	8 070	1 338.5	264.2	211	2 332	74.7	21.4
Suffolk	3 680	21 383	2 149.9	773.5	2 535	70 317	12 009.2	2 433.5	2 795	29 208	1 266.9	336.3
Sullivan	140	407	33.4	9.1	54	D	D	D	246	3 607	148.1	43.4
Tioga	53	417	60.8	14.2	48	5 055	1 569.6	239.8	84	749	24.2	6.7
Tompkins	188	1 411	135.8	49.5	94	3 613	667.1	123.6	312	3 477	113.2	31.7
Ulster	321	2 013	183.7	69.3	215	6 449	785.0	183.7	468	5 662	215.7	63.1
Warren	151	1 114	127.8	40.2	84	4 014	820.7	144.0	407	4 078	179.5	51.6
Washington	59	125	8.5	2.5	99	3 852	642.0	122.7	100	584	19.8	4.8
Wayne	98	386	23.0	8.5	145	8 041	1 435.2	221.8	140	1 473	46.2	12.4
Westchester	3 550	20 530	2 818.2	1 016.6	869	18 797	3 012.0	626.3	1 833	19 829	1 018.1	285.1
Wyoming	37	143	8.0	3.0	55	3 011	371.9	79.1	73	544	16.4	4.1
Yates	27	85	6.1	2.3	27	522	225.2	15.6	55	322	13.0	3.1
NORTH CAROLINA	14 351	101 610	9 760.9	3 693.5	11 306	773 548	161 900.5	21 297.9	14 579	262 848	8 625.0	2 393.2
Alamance	173	878	66.5	29.8	282	21 490	3 324.8	588.2	246	5 028	145.1	39.9
Alexander	31	106	5.4	2.0	99	5 512	635.0	129.2	38	575	15.5	4.5
Alleghany	15	27	1.3	0.4	22	1 422	245.3	27.2	25	246	6.2	1.8
Anson	19	73	4.0	1.4	37	3 426	364.8	74.3	30	406	12.1	3.3
Ashe	17	46	2.8	0.8	37	2 093	242.1	42.2	43	464	12.5	3.8
Avery	20	59	8.2	1.5	11	802	85.4	14.6	47	468	22.1	5.6
Beaufort	60	569	24.3	9.7	65	5 772	927.8	139.8	68	924	29.1	7.2
Bertie	5	40	2.3	0.8	16	D	D	D	15	162	4.4	1.1
Bladen	25	147	10.1	3.0	36	6 559	1 040.9	127.4	50	544	17.9	4.7
Brunswick	89	281	20.8	6.4	57	2 340	1 013.3	86.9	155	1 843	67.4	16.7
Buncombe	466	2 386	174.1	77.3	332	D	D	D	506	9 130	334.3	98.9
Burke	91	447	25.9	10.3	171	17 279	2 126.9	416.7	118	2 451	63.1	16.7
Cabarrus	158	808	59.2	24.6	166	13 099	7 991.8	409.7	155	3 317	123.7	31.7
Caldwell	55	259	17.6	7.2	167	15 254	1 633.1	344.4	102	1 332	40.9	10.8
Camden	4	18	0.8	0.4	NA	NA	NA	NA	3	D	D	D
Carteret	93	319	30.8	9.0	69	1 576	173.1	29.4	202	3 010	106.0	28.7
Caswell	13	29	2.8	0.8	NA	NA	NA	NA	14	88	2.7	0.7
Catawba	238	1 109	86.6	30.8	575	40 469	5 512.8	1 035.2	315	6 274	179.7	52.0
Chatham	63	170	12.3	4.8	76	7 109	1 014.3	158.2	51	D	D	D
Cherokee	34	178	8.0	4.0	27	2 776	315.0	56.3	47	525	15.4	4.0

1. Firms subject to federal tax.

Table B. States and Counties — Health Care and Social Assistance, Other Services, and Federal Funds

STATE County	Health care and social assistance,[1] 1997				Other services,[1] 1997				Federal funds and grants, 2002–2003 Expenditures (mil dol)			
									Total	Direct payments for individuals[2]		
	Number of establishments	Number of employees	Receipts (mil dol)	Annual payroll (mil dol)	Number of establishments	Number of employees	Receipts (mil dol)	Annual payroll (mil dol)	Total	Social Security and government retirement	Medicare	Food stamps and Supplemental Security Income
	159	160	161	162	163	164	165	166	167	168	169	170
NEW YORK—Cont'd												
Genesee..................	90	912	44.9	18.3	90	559	31.0	8.5	327.5	143.2	58.4	6.2
Greene..................	63	444	25.2	9.9	61	191	16.7	3.8	259.0	121.4	47.2	7.0
Hamilton..................	1	D	D	D	9	17	1.6	0.3	31.6	17.0	6.8	0.6
Herkimer..................	63	454	24.5	9.9	86	512	61.8	15.2	352.4	151.7	69.9	9.9
Jefferson..................	157	1 324	89.2	47.9	129	482	33.6	9.0	1 239.9	233.0	76.3	20.0
Kings..................	3 102	28 475	2 029.6	781.4	2 747	10 809	715.0	212.2	(4)	(4)	(4)	(4)
Lewis..................	26	D	D	D	30	50	5.5	0.9	140.2	57.7	18.9	4.1
Livingston..................	79	449	26.6	10.3	75	300	16.3	4.1	259.8	128.8	50.3	7.5
Madison..................	87	669	46.2	19.8	81	206	17.2	3.7	302.1	149.2	49.3	7.7
Monroe..................	1 299	14 414	951.7	402.5	1 048	6 001	401.6	118.8	4 311.2	1 518.9	731.4	140.5
Montgomery..................	103	992	56.7	24.9	86	323	18.2	4.4	313.7	140.4	71.1	9.4
Nassau..................	4 486	45 327	3 665.3	1 504.1	3 201	17 088	1 105.6	342.1	7 694.7	3 223.9	1 832.7	94.1
New York..................	5 360	39 451	3 780.3	1 523.5	4 188	26 361	1 825.5	505.9	(4)56 291.1	(4)12 056.7	(4)10 595.1	(4)3 181.7
Niagara..................	359	3 906	182.8	78.7	305	1 279	78.8	20.4	1 250.4	556.1	238.8	35.7
Oneida..................	421	4 299	287.8	133.6	328	1 733	112.9	29.0	1 630.1	632.6	255.2	52.0
Onondaga..................	894	9 567	722.2	341.2	762	5 753	413.2	119.8	2 900.1	1 027.0	414.5	89.4
Ontario..................	142	1 391	86.3	33.6	133	495	31.5	8.5	548.4	241.1	86.2	11.3
Orange..................	651	5 619	366.9	158.9	548	2 588	189.5	50.7	2 076.9	662.3	287.0	45.4
Orleans..................	62	417	25.5	9.9	50	108	8.6	2.0	199.0	88.0	36.2	6.0
Oswego..................	119	1 103	58.1	25.8	133	426	32.8	7.6	547.5	262.3	91.8	19.4
Otsego..................	75	536	35.2	15.5	84	298	22.6	5.9	333.0	144.6	58.3	7.8
Putnam..................	189	1 999	132.1	58.2	168	670	50.3	12.6	321.3	170.9	75.9	3.9
Queens..................	2 966	32 874	2 271.0	935.6	2 834	12 307	766.9	235.7	(4)	(4)	(4)	(4)
Rensselaer..................	244	2 820	150.8	67.9	187	755	51.1	13.2	2 268.2	348.6	146.5	23.7
Richmond..................	732	8 746	651.7	299.6	600	2 398	153.3	41.5	(4)	(4)	(4)	(4)
Rockland..................	761	6 753	508.3	227.1	527	1 985	147.2	38.2	1 447.3	578.4	302.7	31.0
St. Lawrence..................	158	1 295	76.0	31.2	113	475	25.6	6.4	622.7	253.8	93.8	25.1
Saratoga..................	286	2 050	132.7	51.6	203	1 027	63.3	17.9	777.2	428.1	129.1	14.9
Schenectady..................	311	4 202	274.7	126.0	196	1 239	84.3	22.9	1 579.9	393.5	166.1	27.1
Schoharie..................	33	297	14.5	5.2	43	103	7.3	1.6	158.0	72.4	27.8	4.4
Schuyler..................	18	181	8.0	3.6	15	38	2.9	0.5	94.5	44.3	14.2	3.0
Seneca..................	38	372	19.7	7.5	31	96	7.1	1.3	171.1	83.4	28.8	4.1
Steuben..................	139	1 282	75.5	33.7	106	371	24.2	5.9	604.7	250.8	92.9	20.2
Suffolk..................	3 042	33 419	2 448.6	1 030.0	2 986	12 507	944.8	266.3	8 306.7	3 067.2	1 480.5	127.2
Sullivan..................	130	1 001	58.9	22.9	112	563	29.0	7.5	507.6	176.2	95.4	15.2
Tioga..................	46	322	14.1	6.0	50	166	10.7	2.8	594.1	105.0	34.0	7.2
Tompkins..................	157	1 307	85.1	35.3	108	555	32.4	8.8	607.2	152.8	49.6	10.5
Ulster..................	343	3 292	191.7	75.6	243	938	55.6	15.1	863.2	379.8	155.8	25.7
Warren..................	146	1 371	104.1	52.7	107	511	39.9	12.1	342.2	162.0	56.6	8.8
Washington..................	45	614	25.9	11.6	62	157	11.4	2.6	294.1	138.4	50.5	8.4
Wayne..................	99	761	40.6	17.2	106	317	24.3	5.9	518.1	206.8	80.6	12.4
Westchester..................	2 629	23 146	1 909.4	815.9	1 883	8 331	617.8	180.7	5 154.7	1 985.2	1 190.7	107.8
Wyoming..................	40	513	22.7	11.5	47	180	10.3	2.7	208.4	86.1	33.4	4.0
Yates..................	21	D	D	D	25	113	8.2	1.8	122.7	63.5	22.0	3.7
NORTH CAROLINA.........	12 582	173 770	10 708.8	4 859.6	11 483	64 802	4 060.6	1 204.0	51 766.4	17 961.4	6 230.4	1 489.7
Alamance..................	212	3 555	289.1	106.9	202	1 339	80.3	23.2	584.6	300.9	115.5	14.4
Alexander..................	31	317	14.0	7.1	41	176	10.9	2.7	118.1	64.4	23.8	4.0
Alleghany..................	12	200	5.7	2.5	11	20	1.6	0.2	68.5	30.5	12.3	2.0
Anson..................	23	261	10.8	5.5	28	106	6.8	1.8	150.1	55.4	29.5	8.3
Ashe..................	27	244	11.7	5.6	25	70	5.1	1.1	149.7	63.0	24.4	5.5
Avery..................	26	342	12.6	6.6	25	77	5.2	1.4	96.5	44.9	20.3	3.2
Beaufort..................	63	893	45.4	20.6	91	387	24.1	7.2	281.2	129.1	41.4	12.5
Bertie..................	20	355	13.7	5.0	20	76	5.0	1.0	185.5	51.5	23.6	12.5
Bladen..................	54	719	27.4	12.4	23	81	4.0	1.1	261.4	78.4	31.1	13.4
Brunswick..................	94	1 170	67.3	26.0	68	239	16.7	3.8	502.6	259.1	67.6	14.3
Buncombe..................	459	6 057	428.7	214.9	347	1 834	104.9	33.0	1 229.9	558.8	197.1	37.2
Burke..................	122	1 068	69.6	35.7	81	468	27.4	8.9	507.9	184.1	70.6	12.7
Cabarrus..................	163	2 348	148.2	73.7	216	965	57.8	17.5	553.8	287.6	122.2	13.0
Caldwell..................	94	1 492	62.5	28.6	98	433	26.8	7.2	315.4	167.8	64.2	9.7
Camden..................	2	D	D	D	5	25	2.2	0.8	47.3	25.4	6.2	0.9
Carteret..................	95	1 123	51.2	24.0	103	409	20.0	5.1	386.1	218.2	51.6	9.3
Caswell..................	20	303	8.7	3.8	10	18	0.9	0.2	112.7	45.7	17.6	5.9
Catawba..................	251	4 733	345.0	149.4	239	1 385	82.6	26.1	563.9	302.4	98.9	17.5
Chatham..................	43	525	25.3	9.4	56	209	12.9	4.3	196.7	102.3	38.9	4.6
Cherokee..................	43	285	16.7	6.6	19	63	5.3	1.2	155.3	78.8	25.4	5.7

1. Firms subject to federal tax. 2. State totals may include programs not allocated by county. 4. Bronx, Kings, Queens, and Richmond Counties included with New York County.

Table B. States and Counties — Federal Funds and Local Government Finances

STATE County	Federal funds and grants, 2002–2003 (cont'd) Expenditures (mil dol) (cont'd) Procurement contract awards — Salaries and wages (171)	Defense (172)	Other (173)	Grants[1] — Medicaid and other health-related (174)	Nutrition and family welfare (175)	Education (176)	Other (177)	Local government finances, 2002 — General revenue — Total (mil dol) (178)	Intergovernmental (mil dol) (179)	Taxes — Total (mil dol) (180)	Per capita[2] (dollars) Total (181)	Property (182)
NEW YORK—Cont'd												
Genesee	25.2	1.1	16.7	38.8	5.7	5.9	15.0	273.9	126.3	91.6	1 533	1 042
Greene	8.0	18.9	2.5	33.2	5.9	4.1	9.6	182.8	70.6	93.5	1 926	1 517
Hamilton	1.4	0.5	0.4	1.9	0.5	1.3	1.3	39.3	7.9	27.1	5 120	4 636
Herkimer	8.1	5.4	2.3	54.2	8.3	6.2	24.9	259.9	135.1	84.7	1 329	993
Jefferson	509.9	103.3	118.0	93.1	19.3	19.3	31.6	430.9	238.6	127.6	1 180	840
Kings	(4)	(4)	(4)	(4)	(4)	(4)	(4)	(4)	(4)	(4)	(4)	(4)
Lewis	4.6	3.6	1.2	26.9	4.4	1.5	9.2	135.7	60.5	32.0	1 201	967
Livingston	10.3	0.9	2.6	35.0	6.1	4.1	8.5	242.2	116.4	77.8	1 200	953
Madison	10.2	6.2	2.9	46.2	7.7	4.9	7.5	243.4	126.2	86.1	1 234	1 037
Monroe	211.5	219.6	87.7	710.3	145.2	86.6	264.3	3 103.4	1 357.5	1 241.4	1 681	1 264
Montgomery	7.2	7.0	2.7	42.9	7.7	3.5	15.2	214.6	99.9	68.6	1 389	1 044
Nassau	513.0	542.3	125.4	781.5	79.7	67.8	347.3	7 189.2	1 758.5	4 614.2	3 431	2 756
New York	(4)3 494.4	(4)323.1	(4)1 210.4	(4)16 454.6	(4)2 703.6	(4)825.2	(4)3 921.9	(4)55 539.9	(4)22 464.2	(4)22 235.2	(4)2 750	(4)1 100
Niagara	98.1	23.7	9.7	168.8	41.5	18.6	40.2	915.0	401.5	325.0	1 490	1 117
Oneida	143.3	71.0	19.7	272.8	35.4	20.3	89.1	889.8	453.9	306.2	1 303	872
Onondaga	260.2	231.5	161.4	364.1	72.5	39.5	188.4	1 831.6	852.4	668.8	1 451	993
Ontario	53.0	49.6	9.1	54.4	8.7	6.8	15.5	442.9	182.1	184.4	1 815	1 262
Orange	315.7	347.1	29.5	225.1	40.4	25.9	83.1	1 471.3	568.9	679.6	1 905	1 458
Orleans	5.7	0.0	9.3	25.4	8.2	4.6	9.2	161.4	87.1	51.8	1 179	896
Oswego	18.1	6.9	7.1	90.4	19.2	10.4	15.6	524.9	256.4	180.7	1 470	1 174
Otsego	11.1	4.3	11.5	62.6	9.2	4.5	10.5	223.6	105.0	82.4	1 327	981
Putnam	12.3	9.9	5.4	25.4	3.1	6.8	7.1	383.8	105.0	240.6	2 449	2 095
Queens	(4)	(4)	(4)	(4)	(4)	(4)	(4)	(4)	(4)	(4)	(4)	(4)
Rensselaer	33.8	7.1	9.2	455.7	1 044.2	11.5	145.4	630.3	285.1	222.0	1 448	1 097
Richmond	(4)	(4)	(4)	(4)	(4)	(4)	(4)	(4)	(4)	(4)	(4)	(4)
Rockland	48.5	84.1	31.1	239.5	34.5	19.1	65.3	1 386.5	370.7	805.8	2 761	2 299
St. Lawrence	32.8	4.2	7.6	135.0	24.2	11.5	17.0	458.3	236.1	132.2	1 189	846
Saratoga	77.6	6.5	7.9	68.8	13.3	7.7	16.4	690.4	274.1	323.1	1 560	1 137
Schenectady	81.8	400.2	287.8	118.2	20.8	11.6	61.2	596.6	251.8	251.9	1 712	1 245
Schoharie	5.6	0.1	1.4	30.5	4.4	2.4	5.5	132.7	72.5	48.7	1 529	1 234
Schuyler	3.5	0.0	0.9	18.2	2.5	2.0	4.8	65.2	34.1	21.6	1 116	833
Seneca	6.8	6.7	2.3	25.6	2.4	2.2	3.8	123.6	63.4	43.1	1 233	890
Steuben	49.2	10.6	11.8	81.8	14.8	10.1	48.5	456.5	237.0	144.4	1 454	1 062
Suffolk	849.7	595.4	614.7	997.1	154.2	86.2	290.0	6 963.2	2 208.2	3 968.8	2 721	2 085
Sullivan	14.5	0.5	19.3	136.0	10.4	6.5	28.1	384.7	137.8	173.5	2 336	2 004
Tioga	12.5	384.4	4.5	21.8	7.3	3.4	10.7	169.6	93.3	54.6	1 054	792
Tompkins	22.4	6.4	8.8	105.9	12.4	12.5	198.1	348.4	136.2	151.3	1 525	1 085
Ulster	34.6	15.8	13.2	173.9	21.4	11.7	23.0	735.6	259.1	370.5	2 058	1 591
Warren	18.0	2.7	4.2	54.6	7.7	4.0	19.4	280.2	94.8	138.8	2 173	1 565
Washington	9.7	5.4	2.4	43.9	9.8	5.6	12.4	247.0	120.7	81.3	1 329	1 087
Wayne	12.6	78.0	6.5	75.8	11.4	7.0	17.0	393.8	200.1	129.3	1 375	1 148
Westchester	332.4	69.0	111.5	733.9	125.8	64.2	367.3	5 455.0	1 477.9	2 899.9	3 094	2 525
Wyoming	6.7	7.6	31.7	21.0	3.1	2.5	3.3	176.9	77.4	47.2	1 094	794
Yates	5.1	0.0	1.2	15.6	2.4	1.7	3.3	80.2	32.8	36.6	1 491	1 229
NORTH CAROLINA	6 540.7	1 988.2	1 806.2	6 238.1	1 545.5	986.9	2 842.6	X	X	X	X	X
Alamance	15.9	9.2	6.6	68.1	9.6	7.8	28.0	289.6	152.7	83.3	613	468
Alexander	3.4	0.0	2.0	12.9	2.7	2.0	1.6	56.0	32.9	15.4	446	296
Alleghany	2.6	0.0	1.3	14.8	1.0	0.7	2.2	23.0	13.2	7.3	676	514
Anson	3.7	6.5	0.8	32.0	4.6	3.0	2.3	70.5	46.2	14.0	554	418
Ashe	4.4	0.0	1.0	37.2	2.4	1.6	9.4	46.9	27.2	15.3	618	446
Avery	2.7	0.1	0.7	18.1	2.1	1.5	1.7	39.8	18.1	14.4	816	614
Beaufort	7.2	0.8	1.7	50.9	6.6	5.3	9.4	151.1	89.5	30.7	674	505
Bertie	4.4	8.5	0.8	46.3	5.3	2.2	5.0	47.5	32.2	10.0	509	399
Bladen	6.6	44.3	12.4	48.8	6.6	4.8	5.8	122.8	53.9	22.1	680	536
Brunswick	16.8	85.8	2.5	39.2	6.2	3.1	5.0	245.0	84.7	101.8	1 296	1 033
Buncombe	150.1	19.8	49.0	125.3	21.6	15.7	39.3	538.6	251.4	185.5	878	645
Burke	8.0	143.5	9.0	48.4	7.4	13.3	4.6	208.3	113.7	50.8	567	496
Cabarrus	19.4	0.7	4.0	48.0	9.6	8.3	36.0	337.7	142.9	129.4	923	744
Caldwell	8.4	0.0	2.8	35.8	7.8	6.1	8.0	173.2	103.7	43.0	548	409
Camden	2.4	0.0	0.2	4.3	0.8	0.4	5.1	19.5	13.2	5.3	713	547
Carteret	26.5	3.9	19.8	24.9	9.7	3.8	14.3	220.2	72.6	62.8	1 043	767
Caswell	2.9	0.0	0.7	29.6	3.2	1.5	3.2	45.2	30.4	10.2	432	293
Catawba	38.4	5.6	9.1	40.6	9.3	9.0	22.5	585.6	173.1	118.1	805	616
Chatham	7.4	0.9	1.7	23.1	3.2	2.1	10.1	104.1	45.9	43.8	812	635
Cherokee	7.4	-1.3	1.4	27.4	4.1	2.0	2.1	61.8	29.7	14.6	586	381

1. State totals may include programs not allocated by county. 2. Based on the resident population estimated as of July 1 of the year shown. 4. Bronx, Kings, Queens, and Richmond Counties included with New York County.

STATE County	Local government finances, 2002 (cont'd)									Government employment, 2002			Presidential election, 2004		
	Direct general expenditure							Debt outstanding					Percent of vote cast —		
			Percent of total for —												
	Total (mil dol)	Per capita[1] (dollars)	Education	Health and hospitals	Police protection	Public welfare	Highways	Total (mil dol)	Per capita[1] (dollars)	Federal civilian	Federal military	State and local	Democratic	Republican	All other
	183	184	185	186	187	188	189	190	191	192	193	194	195	196	197
NEW YORK—Cont'd															
Genesee	306.6	5 128	54.1	5.4	2.4	11.6	6.1	184.4	3 084	684	84	4 869	37.1	61.0	1.8
Greene	196.1	4 039	47.8	3.2	1.6	10.4	10.1	98.4	2 027	113	67	4 062	39.1	58.7	2.2
Hamilton	41.9	7 908	42.2	5.7	1.3	2.9	14.4	14.6	2 759	22	0	659	32.1	65.9	2.0
Herkimer	314.1	4 927	61.4	2.6	1.5	7.9	9.2	200.4	3 143	136	91	4 723	40.8	56.8	2.3
Jefferson	479.3	4 432	53.5	2.6	2.1	9.4	7.1	354.9	3 282	2 533	11 779	8 434	43.3	54.7	2.0
Kings	(3)	(3)	(3)	(3)	(3)	(3)	(3)	(3)	(3)	7 790	3 936	26 367	74.1	24.8	1.1
Lewis	149.5	5 606	40.7	19.9	0.8	10.3	8.5	101.7	3 811	70	37	2 246	40.2	57.8	2.0
Livingston	281.5	4 342	51.9	3.3	1.9	18.5	7.1	213.2	3 289	156	90	7 168	38.0	59.5	2.5
Madison	249.6	3 576	55.6	3.0	1.9	7.8	7.9	168.2	2 411	152	97	4 302	42.9	55.0	2.1
Monroe	3 332.4	4 513	48.1	3.3	4.0	13.4	3.8	2 216.5	3 002	2 941	1 123	45 912	50.2	48.0	1.8
Montgomery	237.3	4 805	50.5	1.2	2.1	13.8	5.4	180.6	3 656	125	68	3 041	44.4	53.5	2.1
Nassau	7 527.9	5 597	46.5	6.2	8.8	7.3	2.7	6 410.3	4 766	5 959	2 642	76 208	52.2	46.6	1.2
New York	(3)56 436.4	(3)6 981	(3)25.5	(3)10.2	(3)6.7	(3)15.6	(3)2.1	(3)72 168.5	(3)8 927	28 900	2 363	436 404	81.7	16.6	1.7
Niagara	962.3	4 412	49.6	2.0	3.6	11.4	4.6	1 024.0	4 695	1 387	322	11 490	49.1	48.8	2.0
Oneida	957.9	4 077	50.8	2.0	3.0	12.3	5.6	745.2	3 171	2 006	439	20 345	42.2	55.3	2.5
Onondaga	2 032.0	4 410	46.1	2.9	3.7	12.9	4.8	1 437.3	3 119	4 395	996	35 873	53.9	44.0	2.0
Ontario	453.3	4 463	54.8	3.0	2.4	8.3	7.8	301.7	2 970	1 158	143	6 908	41.9	56.2	1.9
Orange	1 544.3	4 329	53.1	2.6	3.7	12.7	4.0	948.0	2 657	5 334	6 321	21 877	43.5	54.9	1.5
Orleans	183.7	4 185	55.9	3.1	1.9	13.4	5.6	125.9	2 869	92	61	4 398	35.4	62.8	1.8
Oswego	552.5	4 495	54.4	2.4	2.0	12.1	5.9	298.8	2 430	253	195	9 619	47.3	50.4	2.3
Otsego	240.3	3 872	51.3	3.1	1.4	15.5	8.7	139.3	2 245	168	87	4 661	46.7	51.1	2.2
Putnam	408.3	4 156	62.3	2.9	3.7	4.7	5.3	217.7	2 216	200	136	4 166	41.3	57.4	1.3
Queens	(3)	(3)	(3)	(3)	(3)	(3)	(3)	(3)	(3)	12 103	3 160	21 265	70.8	28.0	1.2
Rensselaer	656.5	4 283	51.9	2.8	2.7	13.2	5.4	502.0	3 275	442	233	10 778	49.3	48.3	2.4
Richmond	(3)	(3)	(3)	(3)	(3)	(3)	(3)	(3)	(3)	1 177	1 010	5 285	42.1	56.7	1.2
Rockland	1 419.8	4 865	48.3	7.9	5.1	8.3	3.9	615.7	2 110	649	407	19 514	48.6	49.7	1.6
St. Lawrence	447.6	4 026	47.4	8.5	2.1	9.9	7.7	302.3	2 719	503	174	10 574	54.4	43.4	2.2
Saratoga	706.4	3 410	58.8	2.5	2.1	9.9	6.3	428.3	2 068	393	1 758	11 735	45.1	52.9	2.1
Schenectady	622.9	4 234	45.7	1.8	3.7	19.1	4.8	387.5	2 634	676	243	10 664	51.4	46.5	2.1
Schoharie	143.0	4 489	56.3	3.3	1.1	8.7	9.2	92.2	2 894	97	44	2 691	38.4	59.2	2.4
Schuyler	84.1	4 342	56.9	3.5	1.3	8.6	8.2	60.2	3 107	55	27	1 098	39.9	58.0	2.1
Seneca	128.9	3 685	51.6	3.7	2.6	10.0	4.8	90.2	2 579	116	52	2 420	45.3	52.3	2.4
Steuben	515.1	5 187	59.8	2.7	1.4	10.5	9.5	274.9	2 768	984	139	7 272	33.9	64.3	1.9
Suffolk	7 159.0	4 908	56.0	2.4	6.1	6.0	2.8	4 734.2	3 246	13 559	2 306	89 268	49.0	48.7	2.3
Sullivan	400.2	5 388	45.6	4.3	2.2	13.8	7.9	186.1	2 506	234	103	6 162	48.4	49.4	2.1
Tioga	184.7	3 568	60.7	3.5	1.9	8.6	6.7	91.1	1 760	176	77	2 543	40.2	57.8	2.0
Tompkins	371.9	3 749	50.0	4.0	2.9	7.9	7.0	250.7	2 527	308	159	6 065	63.5	33.5	3.0
Ulster	776.1	4 312	50.6	3.2	3.0	15.3	5.2	358.1	1 989	461	268	13 975	54.1	43.3	2.6
Warren	286.4	4 481	46.5	3.5	2.7	10.6	6.8	126.7	1 982	263	97	4 464	42.7	54.9	2.3
Washington	269.5	4 404	57.3	2.5	1.6	13.9	6.0	149.7	2 446	154	85	5 287	41.9	55.4	2.7
Wayne	431.8	4 589	61.2	2.2	1.8	11.2	4.8	243.6	2 589	191	131	7 933	37.9	60.2	1.9
Westchester	5 656.3	6 035	42.7	11.3	4.8	7.8	2.2	3 371.0	3 597	5 332	1 305	59 018	57.8	40.6	1.7
Wyoming	197.6	4 577	43.6	20.4	2.3	8.5	8.7	119.4	2 766	116	60	4 363	33.6	64.8	1.6
Yates	99.8	4 068	34.2	3.8	2.6	7.8	9.1	73.2	2 984	80	34	1 189	38.7	59.4	1.9
NORTH CAROLINA	X	X	X	X	X	X	X	X	X	60 073	117 219	575 927	43.5	56.1	0.4
Alamance	295.9	2 177	48.9	9.6	6.3	6.3	1.8	133.0	979	254	235	6 106	38.1	61.6	0.3
Alexander	62.3	1 810	64.8	5.6	3.0	8.5	0.7	16.3	473	48	59	1 408	30.3	69.4	0.3
Alleghany	22.9	2 110	58.8	3.1	4.0	8.5	0.2	4.9	450	55	19	584	39.9	59.7	0.4
Anson	67.1	2 647	61.7	3.1	4.0	8.2	1.3	16.6	657	61	44	2 271	58.5	41.4	0.2
Ashe	42.6	1 717	61.5	1.4	3.5	10.9	1.3	17.1	689	67	43	1 163	37.9	61.7	0.5
Avery	36.3	2 061	58.4	2.6	4.3	7.9	1.5	15.4	876	58	30	1 227	24.0	75.6	0.4
Beaufort	151.8	3 330	40.9	9.4	3.0	6.9	1.0	100.2	2 199	126	79	2 865	35.8	63.9	0.3
Bertie	49.1	2 492	57.7	0.6	3.6	10.3	1.3	33.3	1 692	91	34	1 019	61.0	38.6	0.4
Bladen	132.6	4 080	43.5	15.5	2.4	5.6	0.6	40.2	1 238	122	56	2 253	49.3	50.4	0.2
Brunswick	265.0	3 373	42.3	10.7	5.5	4.8	1.9	114.7	1 460	345	193	3 813	39.2	60.4	0.3
Buncombe	593.4	2 810	43.7	8.7	4.6	5.8	1.7	363.7	1 722	2 542	440	12 552	49.4	50.1	0.5
Burke	205.6	2 293	52.9	12.8	4.9	9.3	0.9	58.5	652	131	154	7 886	38.6	61.1	0.4
Cabarrus	342.8	2 445	44.3	1.2	5.8	7.8	1.7	348.8	2 488	268	244	10 605	32.5	67.2	0.4
Caldwell	171.4	2 183	59.9	4.7	5.0	10.5	1.5	36.4	463	123	135	4 078	32.0	67.6	0.4
Camden	19.2	2 570	71.5	1.3	3.7	5.6	0.0	11.1	1 485	18	13	387	36.8	63.0	0.2
Carteret	224.1	3 720	35.6	28.2	4.1	4.0	1.3	99.3	1 648	259	339	4 191	30.2	69.4	0.4
Caswell	46.5	1 973	65.2	5.6	3.1	12.7	0.0	15.0	636	52	41	1 413	48.1	51.6	0.2
Catawba	489.6	3 338	35.6	30.4	3.5	7.0	1.5	224.7	1 532	520	255	8 799	32.1	67.6	0.3
Chatham	95.4	1 769	54.0	5.3	5.4	7.8	1.0	42.1	782	128	93	2 096	49.7	49.8	0.4
Cherokee	56.4	2 269	61.3	3.9	3.3	6.7	0.4	13.6	545	167	43	1 246	32.8	66.9	0.4

1. Based on the resident population estimated as of July 1 of the year shown.   3. Bronx, Kings, Queens, and Richmond Counties included with New York County.

Table B. States and Counties — Land Area and Population

STATE/ County code	CBSA code[1]	County Type[2]	STATE County	Land area,[3] (sq km) 2000	Population and population characteristics, 2003													
								Race alone or in combination, not Hispanic or Latino (percent)					Age (percent)					
					Total persons	Rank	Per square kilometer	White	Black	Am. Indian, Alaska Native	Asian and Pacific Islander	Percent Hispanic or Latino[4]	Under 5 years	5 to 17 years	18 to 24 years	25 to 34 years	35 to 44 years	45 to 54 years
				1	2	3	4	5	6	7	8	9	10	11	12	13	14	15
			NORTH CAROLINA—Cont'd															
37 041	...	7	Chowan	447	14 433	2 131	32.3	60.8	37.3	0.3	0.3	1.6	6.6	17.9	8.4	9.8	13.4	13.9
37 043	...	9	Clay	556	9 288	2 502	16.7	97.5	1.0	0.5	0.0	1.2	4.2	13.8	7.9	10.0	12.0	15.4
37 045	43140	4	Cleveland	1 203	98 249	551	81.7	76.9	21.1	0.3	0.9	1.3	6.6	18.9	9.0	12.8	14.7	13.8
37 047	...	6	Columbus	2 426	54 518	881	22.5	63.1	31.1	3.6	0.2	2.5	7.2	18.4	9.6	12.1	14.2	14.2
37 049	35100	5	Craven	1 835	91 754	587	50.0	70.5	25.6	0.8	1.7	2.7	8.5	17.4	11.5	12.6	13.7	13.0
37 051	22180	2	Cumberland	1 691	303 953	193	179.7	53.7	38.1	2.3	3.6	5.2	8.9	20.3	12.6	16.0	15.3	11.7
37 053	47260	1	Currituck	678	20 834	1 758	30.7	91.3	6.6	0.7	0.6	1.3	5.7	18.6	8.7	11.4	16.3	14.0
37 055	28620	5	Dare	993	33 116	1 327	33.3	94.3	2.7	0.7	0.6	2.4	5.3	15.9	7.4	12.4	16.2	16.0
37 057	30540	4	Davidson	1 430	152 178	370	106.4	85.5	9.2	0.7	1.1	4.2	6.5	17.9	8.4	13.6	16.1	13.9
37 059	49180	2	Davie	687	37 151	1 206	54.1	88.1	6.9	0.4	0.5	4.6	6.3	17.8	8.1	12.9	15.1	14.5
37 061	...	6	Duplin	2 118	51 181	918	24.2	54.3	27.9	0.3	0.3	17.5	7.6	18.8	9.5	14.3	14.2	12.9
37 063	20500	2	Durham	752	236 781	249	314.9	47.0	39.6	0.7	4.2	9.8	7.8	16.3	10.7	19.0	15.3	12.8
37 065	40580	3	Edgecombe	1 308	54 895	876	42.0	38.3	58.2	0.3	0.2	3.2	7.1	20.1	9.2	11.8	15.0	15.1
37 067	49180	2	Forsyth	1 061	317 810	186	299.5	64.8	25.8	0.6	1.5	8.3	7.1	17.5	9.4	14.3	15.4	14.0
37 069	39580	2	Franklin	1 274	52 006	906	40.8	65.1	28.5	0.6	0.4	5.9	6.6	18.4	9.7	14.4	16.5	13.4
37 071	16740	1	Gaston	923	193 097	298	209.2	80.7	14.2	0.6	1.1	4.1	6.8	18.2	8.4	14.5	15.4	14.2
37 073	...	8	Gates	882	10 754	2 382	12.2	60.5	38.1	0.5	0.5	0.7	5.5	20.2	8.0	10.9	16.9	13.5
37 075	...	9	Graham	756	7 994	2 595	10.6	91.3	0.5	7.4	0.3	0.8	5.7	15.8	8.1	11.5	13.8	14.5
37 077	...	6	Granville	1 376	51 852	909	37.7	60.0	34.3	0.8	0.6	5.0	6.2	18.1	9.4	14.9	16.9	13.6
37 079	24780	3	Greene	687	19 990	1 806	29.1	49.8	40.2	0.4	0.2	9.7	6.6	18.1	10.0	14.5	15.2	13.7
37 081	24660	2	Guilford	1 682	433 789	144	257.9	61.7	30.7	0.8	3.4	4.5	6.8	17.4	10.1	14.8	15.4	13.7
37 083	40260	4	Halifax	1 879	56 491	861	30.1	41.5	53.7	3.6	0.6	1.0	6.7	19.2	9.1	11.5	14.7	14.1
37 085	20380	4	Harnett	1 541	99 407	545	64.5	68.3	23.3	1.3	1.2	7.1	7.6	19.6	10.9	16.2	15.0	11.6
37 087	11700	2	Haywood	1 434	55 442	870	38.7	96.5	1.3	0.8	0.4	1.5	5.1	15.6	7.1	11.8	14.1	14.1
37 089	11700	2	Henderson	969	93 817	574	96.8	89.3	3.2	0.5	0.8	6.9	5.8	15.4	7.3	11.4	13.4	13.2
37 091	...	7	Hertford	915	22 310	1 690	24.4	36.5	60.7	1.3	0.6	1.2	6.0	18.1	11.0	9.8	14.2	15.1
37 093	22180	2	Hoke	1 013	37 643	1 191	37.2	41.7	38.4	11.4	1.7	8.5	9.4	21.2	10.5	17.2	15.0	10.9
37 095	...	9	Hyde	1 587	5 567	2 806	3.5	61.5	36.1	0.3	0.3	1.8	4.8	14.6	8.9	13.9	16.1	15.9
37 097	44380	4	Iredell	1 491	133 387	423	89.5	80.8	13.4	0.5	1.6	4.3	7.0	18.8	8.2	13.5	16.0	13.4
37 099	...	6	Jackson	1 271	34 304	1 299	27.0	85.1	1.8	11.5	0.6	2.0	5.3	13.6	17.0	12.2	12.1	13.0
37 101	39580	2	Johnston	2 051	136 802	412	66.7	74.0	16.0	0.6	0.5	9.4	7.8	18.9	8.6	16.3	16.4	12.5
37 103	35100	8	Jones	1 222	10 197	2 428	8.3	61.4	34.9	0.4	0.4	3.2	5.5	19.0	8.1	10.9	15.3	15.5
37 105	41820	4	Lee	666	49 138	949	73.8	66.0	20.0	0.6	0.7	13.2	7.9	18.7	8.6	12.1	15.3	14.5
37 107	28820	4	Lenoir	1 036	58 549	838	56.5	55.2	40.7	0.2	0.4	3.6	6.8	18.6	8.2	11.5	14.7	14.9
37 109	30740	4	Lincoln	774	67 275	750	86.9	86.0	6.4	0.5	0.5	2.4	6.7	18.5	8.2	13.6	16.0	14.1
37 111	...	6	McDowell	1 144	42 867	1 063	37.5	90.9	4.1	0.6	1.0	3.8	6.3	16.7	8.4	14.3	14.6	14.3
37 113	...	7	Macon	1 338	31 175	1 379	23.3	95.9	1.4	0.6	0.6	2.0	5.0	15.1	7.6	10.0	12.5	14.0
37 115	11700	2	Madison	1 164	19 858	1 813	17.1	97.1	0.9	0.5	0.3	1.5	5.7	15.6	10.5	12.1	13.9	14.4
37 117	...	6	Martin	1 194	25 070	1 568	21.0	52.8	44.3	0.5	0.3	2.4	6.5	18.5	8.4	10.7	14.4	15.3
37 119	16740	1	Mecklenburg	1 363	752 366	67	552.0	58.8	29.6	0.6	4.1	8.0	7.9	18.1	8.9	17.7	17.0	13.2
37 121	...	9	Mitchell	573	15 831	2 048	27.6	96.8	0.4	0.3	0.3	2.4	5.2	15.5	7.5	11.6	14.1	14.4
37 123	...	6	Montgomery	1 273	27 306	1 492	21.5	65.3	20.5	0.5	1.7	12.3	7.4	17.8	9.1	13.2	13.8	13.9
37 125	43860	4	Moore	1 807	79 267	659	43.9	79.0	15.3	1.0	0.7	4.6	5.7	16.5	7.7	11.3	13.5	12.3
37 127	40580	3	Nash	1 399	89 732	599	64.1	60.1	35.4	0.8	0.8	3.7	6.9	18.7	8.7	12.9	15.4	14.7
37 129	48900	2	New Hanover	515	168 088	336	326.4	80.1	16.7	0.7	1.2	2.2	6.0	15.2	10.8	15.2	14.5	13.8
37 131	40260	9	Northampton	1 389	21 782	1 716	15.7	39.8	59.5	0.4	0.2	0.7	6.0	17.7	8.0	10.6	14.3	14.3
37 133	27340	3	Onslow	1 986	147 524	386	74.3	73.9	19.4	1.4	3.7	4.8	10.8	17.5	22.0	15.6	13.0	9.1
37 135	20500	2	Orange	1 036	118 183	476	114.1	75.9	13.9	0.9	5.8	5.0	5.3	15.2	16.3	15.8	14.3	14.5
37 137	35100	9	Pamlico	873	12 783	2 257	14.6	74.1	23.8	0.7	0.4	1.2	4.3	15.3	7.7	10.8	14.2	15.4
37 139	21020	7	Pasquotank	588	36 071	1 235	61.3	56.7	41.0	0.8	1.2	1.3	6.5	18.1	12.3	11.9	14.8	12.9
37 141	48900	2	Pender	2 255	43 527	1 054	19.3	73.1	22.0	0.7	0.3	4.4	5.8	17.2	8.4	12.6	15.4	14.2
37 143	21020	9	Perquimans	640	11 644	2 319	18.2	72.5	26.6	0.2	0.3	0.6	5.6	16.6	8.4	9.7	13.7	13.3
37 145	20500	2	Person	1 016	36 864	1 216	36.3	68.6	28.8	0.7	0.2	2.2	6.4	17.9	8.0	13.0	15.7	14.8
37 147	24780	3	Pitt	1 688	138 690	408	82.2	60.6	34.6	0.5	1.4	3.7	7.0	16.9	15.3	16.0	13.5	12.6
37 149	...	8	Polk	616	18 824	1 869	30.6	90.9	5.5	0.3	0.3	3.3	5.1	15.2	6.6	10.6	13.1	14.6
37 151	24660	2	Randolph	2 039	135 151	417	66.3	85.2	5.6	0.7	0.9	8.3	7.0	18.4	8.3	13.9	15.7	13.8
37 153	40460	4	Richmond	1 228	46 643	985	38.0	63.8	30.6	2.3	0.9	3.3	7.1	19.2	10.5	12.8	13.9	13.1
37 155	31300	4	Robeson	2 457	125 756	451	51.2	30.2	24.9	39.2	0.7	6.1	8.2	20.6	10.8	14.3	14.1	12.9
37 157	24660	2	Rockingham	1 467	92 590	583	63.1	76.1	19.7	0.5	0.4	3.8	6.3	17.3	7.8	13.0	15.1	14.8
37 159	41580	4	Rowan	1 324	133 931	420	101.2	78.3	15.6	0.6	1.0	5.1	6.4	18.3	9.5	13.3	15.2	13.6
37 161	22580	4	Rutherford	1 461	63 540	779	43.5	86.5	11.4	0.5	0.4	1.7	6.5	17.8	8.3	12.6	14.0	13.8
37 163	...	6	Sampson	2 449	62 037	801	25.3	55.4	29.5	2.0	0.4	13.2	7.5	18.8	9.6	14.1	14.3	13.1
37 165	29900	6	Scotland	827	35 757	1 250	43.2	51.5	37.6	10.3	0.6	1.2	6.7	20.6	10.3	12.1	14.0	14.6
37 167	10620	6	Stanly	1 023	58 846	834	57.5	83.6	11.7	0.6	1.8	2.8	6.4	18.6	9.1	12.8	15.1	13.8
37 169	49180	2	Stokes	1 170	45 168	1 018	38.6	93.2	4.6	0.5	0.3	1.8	5.9	18.1	7.6	13.1	16.5	14.8
37 171	34340	4	Surry	1 390	72 278	702	52.0	88.0	4.0	0.5	0.5	7.5	6.5	17.5	7.9	13.1	14.7	13.8

1. CBSA = Core Based Statistical Area. See Appendix A for explanation. See Appendix B for list of metropolitan areas with component counties. 2. County type code from the Economic Research Service of USDA Rural-Urban Continuum Codes. See Appendix A for definition. 3. Dry land or land partially or temporarily covered by water. 4. Hispanic or Latino persons may be of any race.

Table B. States and Counties — **Population and Households**

STATE County	55 to 64 years (16)	65 to 74 years (17)	75 years and over (18)	Percent female (19)	1990 (20)	2000 (21)	1990–2000 (22)	2000–2003 (23)	Births (24)	Deaths (25)	Net migration (26)	Number (27)	Percent change, 1990–2000 (28)	Persons per household (29)	Female family householder[1] (30)	One person (31)
NORTH CAROLINA—Cont'd																
Chowan	11.1	9.5	8.8	52.9	13 506	14 526	7.6	-0.6	659	578	214	5 580	9.1	2.48	15.7	25.3
Clay	14.0	11.2	10.6	51.2	7 155	8 775	22.6	5.8	229	381	647	3 847	31.4	2.25	7.5	26.3
Cleveland	10.4	7.2	6.3	51.9	84 958	96 287	13.3	2.0	4 249	3 375	1 180	37 046	15.6	2.53	13.7	23.6
Columbus	10.8	7.8	6.1	52.1	49 587	54 749	10.4	-0.4	2 670	2 139	-715	21 308	15.4	2.50	15.8	26.5
Craven	9.1	8.0	5.8	49.6	81 812	91 436	11.8	0.3	5 188	2 782	-2 078	34 582	17.1	2.50	12.5	23.4
Cumberland	7.0	5.0	3.1	49.4	274 713	302 963	10.3	0.3	17 795	6 684	-10 251	107 358	17.3	2.65	15.5	22.4
Currituck	10.5	6.5	4.7	50.0	13 736	18 190	32.4	14.5	708	527	2 393	6 902	37.0	2.61	9.2	19.4
Dare	11.5	8.2	5.2	49.5	22 746	29 967	31.7	10.5	1 135	802	2 741	12 690	35.7	2.34	8.1	25.0
Davidson	10.5	7.0	5.7	51.0	126 688	147 246	16.2	3.3	6 155	4 495	3 373	58 156	18.8	2.50	10.8	22.9
Davie	10.9	7.4	6.2	50.7	27 859	34 835	25.0	6.6	1 484	1 120	1 925	13 750	27.5	2.51	9.2	22.2
Duplin	9.3	7.0	5.8	50.4	39 995	49 063	22.7	4.3	2 623	1 616	1 165	18 267	22.4	2.63	14.2	24.5
Durham	7.5	4.6	4.7	51.3	181 844	223 314	22.8	6.0	12 578	5 422	6 519	89 015	23.1	2.40	14.8	30.0
Edgecombe	9.8	6.7	5.7	53.5	56 692	55 606	-1.9	-1.3	2 769	2 034	-1 399	20 392	0.4	2.67	21.5	24.0
Forsyth	9.3	6.6	5.8	52.0	265 855	306 067	15.1	3.8	15 057	8 980	6 007	123 851	15.3	2.39	13.5	28.9
Franklin	8.8	5.6	4.7	50.6	36 414	47 260	29.8	10.0	2 106	1 449	4 002	17 843	23.2	2.58	13.1	23.5
Gaston	10.0	6.9	5.7	51.6	174 769	190 365	8.9	1.4	8 341	6 675	1 322	73 936	13.1	2.53	13.2	23.3
Gates	10.9	7.4	6.4	50.8	9 305	10 516	13.0	2.3	383	420	279	3 901	16.4	2.66	13.3	21.7
Graham	12.7	10.0	8.4	51.4	7 196	7 993	11.1	0.0	290	348	66	3 354	11.2	2.35	8.4	26.0
Granville	9.3	6.2	4.8	47.4	38 341	48 498	26.5	6.9	2 038	1 460	2 733	16 654	26.8	2.58	15.0	23.9
Greene	9.0	6.3	5.3	48.5	15 384	18 974	23.3	5.4	819	518	733	6 696	24.1	2.65	17.3	22.6
Guilford	9.1	6.1	5.6	51.9	347 431	421 048	21.2	3.0	19 523	11 283	4 938	168 667	22.5	2.41	13.4	27.9
Halifax	10.2	7.8	7.2	52.5	55 516	57 370	3.3	-1.5	2 582	2 252	-1 195	22 122	8.8	2.51	20.4	27.7
Harnett	7.8	5.4	4.3	50.6	67 833	91 025	34.2	9.2	4 838	2 460	5 887	33 800	34.4	2.61	13.5	23.3
Haywood	12.7	10.3	8.9	51.9	46 948	54 033	15.1	2.6	1 753	2 134	1 792	23 100	20.2	2.30	9.5	26.7
Henderson	11.4	10.4	10.8	51.4	69 747	89 173	27.9	5.2	3 490	3 543	4 646	37 414	30.3	2.33	8.4	25.7
Hertford	11.0	8.0	7.6	54.3	22 317	22 601	1.3	-1.3	934	977	-622	8 953	9.9	2.48	19.5	26.9
Hoke	6.3	4.2	2.9	49.4	22 856	33 646	47.2	11.9	2 224	779	2 508	11 373	53.6	2.86	18.2	19.0
Hyde	10.6	8.9	8.2	47.2	5 411	5 826	7.7	-4.4	204	225	-241	2 185	4.3	2.36	13.1	30.6
Iredell	9.7	6.6	5.4	50.7	93 205	122 660	31.6	8.7	6 071	3 597	8 148	47 360	33.1	2.56	11.3	22.7
Jackson	11.5	7.7	6.0	51.0	26 835	33 121	23.4	3.6	1 155	1 010	1 041	13 191	36.2	2.30	10.0	27.0
Johnston	8.6	5.1	4.1	50.1	81 306	121 965	50.0	12.2	6 706	3 202	11 100	46 595	47.6	2.58	10.6	23.1
Jones	10.6	8.4	7.4	51.7	9 361	10 381	10.9	-1.8	318	403	-126	4 061	16.3	2.53	15.2	24.5
Lee	10.2	7.2	6.1	50.9	41 370	49 040	18.5	0.2	2 647	1 585	-1 167	18 466	17.7	2.61	13.4	23.5
Lenoir	10.7	8.3	6.8	52.7	57 274	59 648	4.1	-1.8	2 706	2 382	-1 374	23 862	8.8	2.43	17.3	28.4
Lincoln	10.5	6.4	5.0	50.4	50 319	63 780	26.8	5.5	2 959	1 879	2 448	24 041	28.1	2.62	10.0	20.1
McDowell	11.0	7.8	6.6	50.2	35 681	42 151	18.1	1.7	1 698	1 448	505	16 604	21.4	2.45	10.2	24.3
Macon	13.3	11.5	10.5	52.0	23 504	29 811	26.8	4.6	1 012	1 190	1 507	12 828	30.4	2.28	8.0	27.0
Madison	11.8	8.3	7.7	50.6	16 953	19 635	15.8	1.4	704	682	214	8 000	23.3	2.34	8.9	26.3
Martin	10.9	8.4	7.3	53.6	25 078	25 593	2.1	-2.0	1 045	1 020	-488	10 020	7.5	2.53	17.6	25.7
Mecklenburg	7.6	4.4	3.9	50.6	511 211	695 454	36.0	8.2	39 331	14 997	32 835	273 416	36.6	2.49	12.4	27.6
Mitchell	13.0	10.0	8.6	51.0	14 433	15 687	8.7	0.9	533	660	279	6 551	13.4	2.37	8.1	25.2
Montgomery	10.6	7.1	6.5	49.3	23 359	26 822	14.8	1.8	1 346	843	-6	9 848	18.8	2.61	12.4	24.1
Moore	10.8	10.6	10.7	51.8	59 000	74 769	26.7	6.0	2 845	2 840	4 435	30 713	28.9	2.38	12.4	24.9
Nash	9.7	6.8	5.8	51.9	76 677	87 420	14.0	2.6	4 171	2 849	1 110	33 644	15.9	2.54	14.5	25.0
New Hanover	10.0	6.9	5.9	51.6	120 284	160 307	33.3	4.9	6 548	4 797	6 058	68 183	41.6	2.29	11.5	28.9
Northampton	11.8	9.1	8.8	52.2	21 004	22 086	5.2	-1.9	887	938	-236	8 691	14.5	2.44	18.3	28.4
Onslow	5.5	4.5	2.5	43.7	149 838	150 355	0.3	-1.9	10 298	2 596	-10 794	48 122	18.4	2.72	11.6	18.6
Orange	8.1	4.6	4.2	52.4	93 662	118 227	26.2	0.0	4 169	2 280	780	45 863	27.0	2.36	9.4	28.1
Pamlico	13.2	11.3	8.2	49.7	11 368	12 934	13.8	-1.2	320	485	22	5 178	14.5	2.38	11.5	25.0
Pasquotank	9.2	6.7	6.7	51.4	31 298	34 897	11.5	3.4	1 514	1 219	892	12 907	13.4	2.52	16.3	25.4
Pender	11.6	8.2	5.8	49.9	28 855	41 082	42.4	6.0	1 616	1 248	2 049	16 054	44.5	2.49	11.2	22.9
Perquimans	13.0	10.5	9.0	52.3	10 447	11 368	8.8	2.4	396	519	405	4 645	16.5	2.42	12.6	24.1
Person	10.3	7.2	6.3	51.8	30 180	35 623	18.0	3.5	1 557	1 309	1 011	14 085	23.3	2.50	13.8	24.2
Pitt	7.4	5.1	4.4	52.5	108 480	133 798	23.3	3.7	6 612	3 391	1 875	52 539	29.8	2.43	14.4	28.3
Polk	11.8	10.4	12.8	52.3	14 458	18 324	26.7	2.7	590	861	778	7 908	29.4	2.28	7.9	28.9
Randolph	10.3	6.7	5.4	50.5	106 546	130 454	22.4	3.6	6 054	3 758	2 537	50 659	23.3	2.55	10.2	22.5
Richmond	10.1	7.3	6.4	51.0	44 511	46 564	4.6	0.2	2 246	1 713	-411	17 873	6.4	2.51	17.0	26.3
Robeson	8.6	5.6	4.4	51.2	105 170	123 339	17.3	2.0	6 892	4 209	-86	43 677	20.8	2.75	20.6	22.7
Rockingham	10.8	7.8	7.2	51.6	86 064	91 928	6.8	0.7	3 761	3 261	255	36 989	10.6	2.45	12.8	25.7
Rowan	9.6	6.9	6.9	50.6	110 605	130 340	17.8	2.8	5 427	4 413	2 681	49 940	17.5	2.52	11.9	24.7
Rutherford	11.0	8.1	7.8	51.9	56 956	62 899	10.4	1.0	2 724	2 466	443	25 191	13.5	2.44	11.7	25.5
Sampson	9.4	6.9	5.7	50.5	47 297	60 161	27.2	3.1	3 051	2 090	969	22 273	27.1	2.64	14.3	23.7
Scotland	10.0	6.3	5.3	53.0	33 763	35 998	6.6	-0.7	1 548	1 194	-582	13 399	13.2	2.61	20.4	24.4
Stanly	10.2	7.4	6.7	50.3	51 765	58 100	12.2	1.3	2 434	1 884	262	22 223	12.5	2.53	10.5	24.3
Stokes	11.1	7.0	5.5	51.1	37 224	44 711	20.1	1.0	1 628	1 336	225	17 579	24.5	2.51	9.7	22.8
Surry	10.8	8.0	7.5	51.2	61 704	71 219	15.4	1.5	3 067	2 550	620	28 408	17.1	2.46	9.7	25.0

1. No spouse present.

Table B. States and Counties — Vital Statistics, Health Resources, and Crime

STATE County	Births, average 1999–2001 Total	Births, average 1999–2001 Rate[1]	Deaths, average 1999–2001 Number Total	Deaths, average 1999–2001 Number Infant[2]	Deaths, average 1999–2001 Rate Total[1]	Deaths, average 1999–2001 Rate Infant[3]	Physicians,[4] 2000 Number	Physicians,[4] 2000 Rate[5]	Hospitals,[4] 1998 Number	Hospitals,[4] 1998 Beds Number	Hospitals,[4] 1998 Beds Rate[5]	Medicare enrollees, 2003	Serious crimes known to police,[6] 2002 Total Number	Serious crimes known to police,[6] 2002 Total Rate[7]
	32	33	34	35	36	37	38	39	40	41	42	43	44	45
NORTH CAROLINA—Cont'd														
Chowan	200	13.7	184	1	12.6	D	27	186	1	111	782	3 017	532	3 543
Clay	71	8.0	110	0	12.5	D	2	23	0	0	0	2 281	136	1 499
Cleveland	1 289	13.4	1 003	15	10.4	11.6	116	120	3	421	454	17 241	4 725	4 849
Columbus	820	15.0	640	9	11.7	11.4	33	60	1	136	258	10 589	3 363	6 157
Craven	1 613	17.6	825	14	9.0	8.5	168	184	1	276	313	15 956	3 859	4 083
Cumberland	5 481	18.1	1 979	61	6.5	11.1	543	179	2	515	181	32 018	19 468	6 217
Currituck	217	11.8	168	2	9.2	D	9	49	0	0	0	2 726	574	3 053
Dare	342	11.4	245	3	8.1	D	20	67	0	0	0	4 780	2 004	6 470
Davidson	1 928	13.1	1 315	15	8.9	8.0	99	67	2	195	138	20 680	4 221	2 801
Davie	451	12.9	344	6	9.8	D	36	103	1	46	143	5 858	702	2 002
Duplin	793	16.1	517	7	10.5	8.8	31	63	1	80	186	7 615	1 716	3 412
Durham	3 737	16.6	1 707	29	7.6	7.8	1 736	777	2	1 187	586	26 302	16 792	7 275
Edgecombe	826	14.8	620	10	11.1	11.7	42	76	1	127	230	9 420	3 080	5 359
Forsyth	4 569	14.9	2 718	48	8.8	10.5	1 102	360	3	1 648	573	47 834	19 875	6 282
Franklin	638	13.4	428	6	9.0	D	32	68	1	67	150	6 214	1 300	2 681
Gaston	2 673	14.0	1 982	28	10.4	10.6	234	123	1	404	219	29 960	9 111	4 752
Gates	107	10.2	122	1	11.6	D	0	0	0	0	0	1 824	131	1 205
Graham	101	12.7	114	1	14.4	D	4	50	0	0	0	1 716	NA	NA
Granville	602	12.4	437	4	9.0	D	58	120	1	66	154	7 071	1 897	3 784
Greene	245	12.9	166	2	8.8	D	3	16	0	0	0	2 336	768	3 916
Guilford	5 916	14.0	3 467	51	8.2	8.7	857	204	3	1 155	298	59 659	24 787	5 695
Halifax	766	13.4	658	6	11.5	D	54	94	2	262	464	11 870	2 653	4 528
Harnett	1 450	15.9	720	10	7.9	7.1	53	58	1	134	163	10 414	5 206	5 533
Haywood	553	10.2	653	3	12.1	D	77	143	1	141	274	12 436	1 352	2 421
Henderson	1 063	11.9	1 065	8	11.9	7.2	179	201	2	281	348	22 244	1 940	2 105
Hertford	286	12.7	284	6	12.7	D	30	133	1	124	556	4 265	1 108	4 743
Hoke	667	19.7	233	4	6.9	D	11	33	0	0	0	2 760	1 796	5 164
Hyde	54	9.3	70	1	12.1	D	2	34	0	0	0	985	37	614
Iredell	1 907	15.4	1 098	15	8.9	7.9	186	152	3	442	390	19 119	4 725	3 727
Jackson	363	11.0	306	4	9.3	D	73	220	1	186	616	5 259	NA	NA
Johnston	2 025	16.5	956	14	7.8	6.7	63	52	1	127	119	15 332	5 810	4 609
Jones	102	9.9	118	0	11.4	D	5	48	0	0	0	1 880	190	1 771
Lee	834	16.9	483	6	9.8	D	85	173	1	137	278	9 069	3 442	6 934
Lenoir	834	14.0	711	12	11.9	14.0	109	183	1	252	427	11 749	3 916	6 407
Lincoln	897	14.0	548	9	8.6	10.4	53	83	1	75	129	9 704	1 767	2 680
McDowell	440	10.4	362	4	8.6	D	32	76	1	65	162	7 802	1 026	2 355
Macon	306	10.2	368	3	12.3	D	41	138	2	105	371	7 546	673	2 184
Madison	221	11.3	217	2	11.1	D	9	46	0	0	0	3 865	164	874
Martin	435	17.0	386	3	15.1	D	33	129	1	49	187	4 985	1 131	4 275
Mecklenburg	11 540	16.5	4 494	88	6.4	7.6	1 648	237	6	1 895	300	74 147	51 886	7 293
Mitchell	167	10.6	203	2	12.9	D	21	134	1	40	270	3 468	NA	NA
Montgomery	407	15.2	263	3	9.8	D	15	56	1	86	357	4 344	931	3 358
Moore	906	12.1	839	8	11.2	8.8	194	259	1	359	503	18 566	2 673	3 521
Nash	1 263	14.4	867	13	9.9	10.6	148	169	2	285	313	14 103	5 073	5 668
New Hanover	2 020	12.6	1 391	13	8.7	6.4	405	253	2	611	408	26 215	11 958	7 285
Northampton	265	12.1	293	4	13.3	D	7	32	0	0	0	4 845	289	1 491
Onslow	3 213	21.5	773	26	5.2	8.0	175	116	1	133	93	13 248	3 560	2 304
Orange	1 253	10.6	720	9	6.1	7.2	988	836	1	648	588	12 436	5 630	4 607
Pamlico	101	7.9	144	0	11.2	D	4	31	0	0	0	2 541	215	1 608
Pasquotank	450	12.9	377	3	10.8	D	81	232	1	130	366	5 644	1 425	3 951
Pender	479	11.6	372	4	9.0	D	18	44	1	66	167	6 889	1 121	2 640
Perquimans	119	10.5	147	2	12.9	D	2	18	0	0	0	2 603	203	1 728
Person	460	12.9	367	5	10.3	D	18	51	1	93	276	5 655	992	2 694
Pitt	1 966	14.7	1 025	22	7.7	11.4	511	382	1	571	451	17 276	8 451	6 111
Polk	187	10.2	278	1	15.2	D	31	169	1	26	154	4 686	367	1 938
Randolph	1 887	14.4	1 108	18	8.5	9.7	91	70	1	105	87	19 793	5 113	3 878
Richmond	681	14.6	527	5	11.3	D	37	79	2	193	418	8 782	2 309	4 797
Robeson	2 132	17.3	1 209	27	9.8	12.7	92	75	1	280	242	18 728	7 084	5 576
Rockingham	1 182	12.8	1 014	9	11.0	7.3	95	103	2	372	413	16 882	3 630	3 862
Rowan	1 696	13.0	1 339	12	10.2	7.3	178	137	1	238	190	19 374	3 944	2 927
Rutherford	841	13.4	744	10	11.8	11.5	68	108	1	114	187	11 814	2 066	3 178
Sampson	924	15.4	626	8	10.4	8.7	48	80	1	146	278	9 047	1 933	3 234
Scotland	502	14.0	356	7	9.9	14.6	49	136	1	174	486	5 586	1 927	5 179
Stanly	747	12.8	594	6	10.2	D	59	102	1	119	212	10 124	2 383	4 046
Stokes	516	11.6	402	4	9.0	D	20	45	1	93	215	6 192	1 332	2 882
Surry	952	13.4	774	7	10.9	7.7	75	105	2	253	377	14 145	2 730	3 708

1. Per 1,000 estimated resident population.   2. Deaths of infants under 1 year old.   3. Deaths of infants under 1 year old per 1,000 live births.   4. Data subject to copyright.   5. Per 100,000 resident population as of July 1 of the year shown.   6. Data for serious crimes have not been adjusted for underreporting; this may affect comparability between geographic areas and over time.   7. Per 100,000 population estimated by the FBI.

STATE County	Serious crimes known to police,[1] 2002 (cont'd) Rate[2] Violent	Property	Education School enrollment and attainment, 2000 Enrollment[3] Total	Percent private	Attainment[4] (percent) High school graduate or less	Bachelor's degree or more	Local government expenditures,[5] 2000–2001 Total current expenditures (mil dol)	Current expenditures per student (dollars)	Money income, 1999 Per capita income[6] (dollars)	Households Median income Dollars	Percent change, 1989–1999 (constant 1999 dollars)	Percent with income of $100,000 or more	Percent below poverty level, 1999 Persons	Households	Families	Families with children
	46	47	48	49	50	51	52	53	54	55	56	57	58	59	60	61
NORTH CAROLINA—Cont'd																
Chowan	360	3 183	3 709	18.1	60.5	16.4	17.9	7 149	15 027	30 928	12.9	3.2	17.6	17.8	13.7	19.9
Clay	44	1 455	1 774	4.3	57.3	15.4	9.4	7 473	18 221	31 397	26.1	5.3	11.4	13.6	7.8	13.6
Cleveland	364	4 485	23 444	12.8	61.9	13.3	112.5	6 469	17 395	35 283	-0.8	5.9	13.3	13.4	10.1	14.8
Columbus	851	5 306	13 690	6.4	65.1	10.1	64.0	6 282	14 415	26 805	8.0	3.9	22.7	22.3	17.6	24.8
Craven	451	3 632	22 182	12.2	47.9	19.3	90.6	6 111	18 423	35 966	4.5	6.3	13.1	13.1	9.9	15.6
Cumberland	638	5 579	88 163	12.7	43.4	19.1	315.2	6 181	17 376	37 466	9.5	6.3	12.8	12.6	10.4	14.2
Currituck	287	2 766	4 264	11.8	56.9	13.3	23.1	7 194	19 908	40 822	8.9	7.0	10.7	9.4	8.9	14.4
Dare	300	6 169	6 006	11.3	39.0	27.7	32.6	6 960	23 614	42 411	7.7	10.3	8.0	8.1	5.5	8.5
Davidson	230	2 571	32 736	10.8	61.2	12.8	143.7	5 786	18 703	38 640	3.0	6.1	10.1	10.3	7.0	10.8
Davie	185	1 816	8 108	12.4	56.6	17.6	35.1	6 120	21 359	40 174	0.8	10.1	8.6	9.7	6.4	9.1
Duplin	362	3 050	11 574	6.3	65.8	10.5	50.9	5 912	14 499	29 890	13.0	4.4	19.4	19.8	15.3	21.3
Durham	840	6 434	63 107	29.0	36.2	40.1	231.5	7 474	23 156	43 337	5.7	12.9	13.4	12.8	9.8	14.8
Edgecombe	471	4 887	14 634	6.4	71.3	8.5	50.5	6 495	14 435	30 983	7.8	4.2	19.6	19.4	16.0	22.5
Forsyth	599	5 683	78 172	21.5	45.0	28.7	309.3	6 693	23 023	42 097	2.9	11.5	11.0	10.8	7.9	12.3
Franklin	151	2 531	11 252	15.2	60.9	13.2	46.8	6 020	17 562	38 968	15.8	5.6	12.6	13.1	10.0	14.0
Gaston	587	4 165	44 264	14.3	58.2	14.2	185.1	5 991	19 225	39 482	4.5	7.7	10.9	10.9	8.3	12.5
Gates	101	1 104	2 709	5.8	63.9	10.5	15.1	7 378	15 963	35 647	13.3	4.8	17.0	18.0	14.5	15.5
Graham	NA	NA	1 474	4.6	67.6	11.2	9.9	7 999	14 237	26 645	18.4	3.4	19.5	20.7	14.4	21.4
Granville	373	3 411	11 186	10.5	61.1	13.0	48.4	5 956	17 118	39 965	12.3	7.3	11.7	12.2	9.0	13.0
Greene	581	3 335	4 652	10.2	69.3	8.2	20.5	6 669	15 452	32 074	5.2	3.4	20.2	21.0	16.0	23.1
Guilford	596	5 099	114 435	16.0	42.2	30.3	431.3	6 707	23 340	42 618	5.2	12.6	10.6	10.3	7.6	11.7
Halifax	403	4 126	14 896	8.5	67.7	11.1	73.6	7 069	13 810	26 459	4.0	4.3	23.9	23.7	19.4	27.6
Harnett	636	4 898	25 203	16.0	57.6	12.8	92.7	5 638	16 775	35 105	20.2	5.4	14.9	15.7	11.3	15.6
Haywood	202	2 218	11 291	9.3	54.4	16.0	51.7	6 614	18 554	33 922	12.4	4.9	11.5	11.6	8.1	14.1
Henderson	151	1 954	17 967	12.8	46.0	24.1	74.0	6 284	21 110	38 109	5.2	7.7	9.7	9.6	6.8	12.4
Hertford	449	4 293	5 716	12.2	65.3	11.1	27.0	6 600	15 641	26 422	8.2	4.4	18.3	19.9	15.9	19.7
Hoke	446	4 719	9 385	8.8	58.9	10.9	36.2	5 766	13 635	33 230	8.6	4.0	17.7	17.5	14.4	18.0
Hyde	33	581	1 255	11.6	67.9	10.6	8.1	11 566	13 164	28 444	19.8	3.8	15.4	16.9	10.3	14.6
Iredell	300	3 427	28 540	10.6	53.7	17.4	131.8	6 063	21 148	41 920	9.0	9.2	8.2	8.8	6.2	9.1
Jackson	NA	NA	10 089	6.0	46.9	25.5	25.5	6 797	17 582	32 552	12.6	5.9	15.1	17.1	9.5	15.1
Johnston	384	4 225	28 470	9.0	55.9	15.9	130.0	6 094	18 788	40 872	20.9	7.0	12.8	12.8	8.9	11.9
Jones	177	1 594	2 635	13.3	64.2	9.5	12.4	8 054	15 916	30 882	18.5	4.0	16.9	17.8	14.2	19.4
Lee	445	6 489	11 864	11.0	53.6	17.2	55.7	6 234	19 147	38 900	9.6	8.6	12.8	12.5	9.8	14.3
Lenoir	633	5 774	14 821	9.8	59.4	13.3	67.1	6 458	16 744	31 191	9.5	5.0	16.6	17.6	12.6	18.6
Lincoln	165	2 515	14 743	9.9	60.1	13.0	63.0	5 696	18 877	41 421	7.6	7.6	9.2	10.1	6.9	9.9
McDowell	202	2 153	9 182	6.3	65.9	9.0	39.8	6 156	16 109	32 396	6.9	4.4	11.6	12.6	9.0	13.2
Macon	52	2 132	6 010	9.9	54.9	16.2	27.2	6 776	18 642	32 139	17.0	5.7	12.6	12.6	8.8	14.2
Madison	75	800	4 542	25.5	62.5	16.1	18.2	7 132	16 076	30 985	21.7	4.5	15.4	17.6	10.9	16.0
Martin	601	3 674	6 555	6.7	63.9	11.6	33.3	6 835	15 102	28 793	7.2	4.4	20.2	20.8	16.3	22.4
Mecklenburg	1 091	6 201	183 309	20.4	33.7	37.1	733.3	7 010	27 352	50 579	11.3	17.2	9.2	8.2	6.6	9.3
Mitchell	NA	NA	3 102	8.8	64.3	12.2	16.4	6 892	15 933	30 508	10.5	4.0	13.8	15.0	10.7	14.6
Montgomery	198	3 160	6 120	6.8	67.9	10.0	30.0	6 582	16 504	32 903	8.0	5.7	15.4	15.8	10.9	15.9
Moore	234	3 286	16 320	8.6	43.3	26.8	73.4	6 505	23 377	41 240	9.4	10.9	11.4	10.8	8.0	14.2
Nash	434	5 235	22 221	13.7	58.3	17.2	112.7	5 906	18 863	37 147	7.0	8.2	13.4	13.8	10.3	15.2
New Hanover	695	6 591	42 293	12.2	38.2	31.0	148.1	6 800	23 123	40 172	9.4	10.7	13.1	13.3	8.3	13.6
Northampton	175	1 316	5 438	9.9	69.0	10.8	26.2	6 962	15 413	26 652	10.0	4.7	21.3	22.2	17.0	25.7
Onslow	162	2 141	37 631	8.8	48.5	14.8	124.2	5 875	14 853	33 756	7.4	4.1	12.9	12.2	10.8	14.8
Orange	329	4 278	44 716	9.9	28.3	51.5	132.3	8 146	24 873	42 372	5.2	17.4	14.1	14.8	6.2	8.4
Pamlico	150	1 459	2 810	7.2	56.1	14.7	16.4	7 655	18 005	34 084	20.5	6.0	15.3	15.2	11.8	20.1
Pasquotank	488	3 463	10 325	10.4	53.5	16.4	40.7	6 742	14 815	30 444	3.9	4.7	18.4	18.1	15.5	23.2
Pender	158	2 482	9 203	8.4	56.7	13.6	41.5	6 312	17 882	35 902	14.8	6.7	13.6	13.7	9.5	14.6
Perquimans	136	1 591	2 592	9.1	61.1	12.3	14.3	7 707	15 728	29 538	9.8	3.2	17.9	18.5	13.9	23.5
Person	416	2 279	8 423	9.4	63.2	10.3	37.8	6 347	18 709	37 159	7.9	5.0	12.0	13.0	9.4	11.8
Pitt	643	5 468	45 735	8.3	45.3	26.4	125.0	6 187	18 243	32 868	4.9	7.5	20.3	20.8	13.5	18.7
Polk	132	1 806	3 529	14.7	47.6	25.7	16.9	6 740	19 804	36 259	0.7	7.2	10.1	11.7	6.4	10.2
Randolph	129	3 749	29 217	10.4	65.7	11.1	120.4	5 585	18 236	38 348	5.2	5.8	9.1	9.7	6.8	10.4
Richmond	349	4 448	11 419	6.6	66.5	10.1	51.9	6 223	14 485	28 830	-2.3	4.3	19.6	19.9	15.9	23.2
Robeson	703	4 873	34 487	6.0	65.8	11.4	137.3	5 718	13 224	28 202	6.5	4.1	22.8	23.7	19.6	26.4
Rockingham	283	3 579	19 909	9.3	64.4	10.8	93.1	6 316	17 120	33 784	-1.0	5.3	12.8	13.9	10.2	14.1
Rowan	302	2 625	31 855	15.6	59.3	14.2	129.7	6 294	18 071	37 494	5.9	5.8	10.6	11.1	8.1	12.1
Rutherford	235	2 942	14 178	9.5	62.9	12.5	65.5	6 340	16 270	31 122	-2.8	4.6	13.9	15.1	10.4	16.7
Sampson	268	2 967	14 305	6.3	66.1	11.1	64.5	6 140	14 976	31 793	20.1	5.4	17.6	18.0	13.5	19.0
Scotland	425	4 754	10 267	9.9	58.1	15.9	49.4	6 776	15 693	31 010	2.3	5.4	20.6	20.7	17.4	25.8
Stanly	368	3 677	14 133	12.1	62.5	12.7	60.7	5 931	17 825	36 898	8.2	5.8	10.7	11.0	8.1	12.6
Stokes	407	2 475	9 914	11.3	66.9	9.3	47.6	6 418	18 130	38 808	3.4	5.2	9.1	10.5	6.9	8.6
Surry	418	3 290	15 791	6.3	62.5	12.0	79.0	6 842	17 722	33 046	4.9	5.5	12.4	13.4	9.1	12.4

1. Data for serious crimes have not been adjusted for underreporting; this may affect comparability between geographic areas and over time. 2. Per 100,000 population estimated by the FBI. 3. All persons 3 years old and over enrolled in nursery school through college. 4. Persons 25 years old and over. 5. Elementary and secondary education expenditures. 6. Based on population enumerated as of April 1, 2000.

Table B. States and Counties — **Personal Income**

STATE County	Personal income, 2002							Transfer payments					
			Per capita[1]						Government payments to individuals				
	Total (mil dol)	Percent change, 2001–2002	Dollars	Rank	Wages and salaries[2] (mil dol)	Proprietor's income (mil dol)	Dividends, interest, and rent (mil dol)	Total (mil dol)	Total (mil dol)	Social Security (mil dol)	Medical payments (mil dol)	Income maintenance (mil dol)	Unemployment insurance (mil dol)
	62	63	64	65	66	67	68	69	70	71	72	73	74
NORTH CAROLINA—Cont'd													
Chowan	351	1.1	24 743	1 200	167	28	84	83	80	30	34	11	1
Clay	198	2.6	21 625	2 116	52	17	46	53	51	23	21	4	1
Cleveland	2 248	1.2	23 020	1 716	1 207	102	370	506	483	191	192	51	32
Columbus	1 220	-0.6	22 273	1 938	571	120	186	370	357	106	176	51	10
Craven	2 459	3.1	26 917	717	1 979	126	477	432	412	158	172	44	9
Cumberland	7 985	6.9	26 323	826	6 819	317	1 057	1 195	1 134	333	423	166	37
Currituck	520	6.1	26 481	796	134	30	75	73	68	29	27	6	2
Dare	928	8.1	28 908	458	544	123	218	126	118	56	44	7	6
Davidson	3 907	1.5	25 914	907	1 589	236	756	633	598	264	227	57	30
Davie	1 056	2.2	28 827	465	351	67	234	156	147	68	59	10	6
Duplin	1 040	-4.6	20 578	2 409	548	114	158	248	236	75	107	32	8
Durham	7 211	2.6	30 813	285	9 825	515	1 185	890	835	300	353	96	43
Edgecombe	1 236	0.4	22 469	1 888	847	74	197	323	310	93	142	49	16
Forsyth	9 821	2.5	31 236	265	7 909	674	2 078	1 336	1 262	543	495	121	49
Franklin	1 214	1.0	24 043	1 391	367	75	173	208	196	66	90	24	9
Gaston	5 242	2.5	27 173	670	2 625	390	724	934	888	345	372	99	45
Gates	216	0.1	20 331	2 471	53	6	34	50	47	19	21	5	1
Graham	166	2.5	20 592	2 405	71	17	27	50	48	16	23	4	2
Granville	1 114	2.3	21 787	2 068	779	28	189	200	188	74	77	22	9
Greene	401	-3.6	20 567	2 413	127	29	57	84	79	24	37	13	3
Guilford	13 429	2.0	31 225	266	11 510	1 009	2 544	1 774	1 672	698	638	170	85
Halifax	1 143	0.3	20 197	2 503	556	56	177	369	356	115	151	65	11
Harnett	2 181	2.9	22 484	1 883	706	162	337	387	364	120	160	45	16
Haywood	1 334	3.6	24 261	1 324	549	109	264	312	299	137	114	25	10
Henderson	2 610	2.7	28 252	515	1 308	177	698	518	496	247	190	31	11
Hertford	472	3.2	21 044	2 286	299	14	72	141	136	42	62	22	2
Hoke	641	3.8	17 739	2 928	226	27	68	137	129	37	56	21	6
Hyde	111	-2.1	19 420	2 669	58	9	25	30	29	9	14	4	1
Iredell	3 504	2.7	26 863	726	2 055	176	602	541	510	218	214	38	25
Jackson	771	4.7	22 744	1 804	458	61	160	151	143	56	58	13	4
Johnston	3 387	1.4	25 502	999	1 277	264	426	497	466	168	204	55	19
Jones	223	-5.2	21 728	2 082	58	13	34	56	53	18	25	6	1
Lee	1 309	3.1	26 598	766	1 001	93	202	251	239	90	101	25	10
Lenoir	1 408	0.1	23 936	1 426	922	56	249	363	349	117	163	44	9
Lincoln	1 565	1.5	23 638	1 519	665	50	163	266	251	104	103	22	15
McDowell	896	0.9	20 951	2 312	556	71	111	197	187	81	76	17	3
Macon	736	4.7	23 874	1 450	345	64	199	173	166	79	66	11	3
Madison	419	0.5	21 097	2 270	127	29	70	102	98	35	43	10	3
Martin	554	4.2	22 000	2 017	353	19	85	161	155	47	67	20	11
Mecklenburg	28 332	3.9	38 556	78	27 641	3 182	4 527	2 431	2 257	879	862	271	138
Mitchell	317	0.3	20 028	2 542	172	17	53	91	87	34	37	7	5
Montgomery	611	1.5	22 606	1 849	350	60	95	128	121	42	53	15	6
Moore	2 503	2.0	32 107	223	1 043	233	823	439	421	209	152	28	10
Nash	2 313	0.5	25 998	888	1 519	146	368	415	394	143	155	52	18
New Hanover	4 873	2.9	29 408	402	3 329	438	1 131	775	736	299	294	68	33
Northampton	483	-1.0	22 084	1 993	158	48	68	143	138	46	62	22	3
Onslow	3 808	5.9	25 317	1 039	3 066	114	479	453	427	130	170	54	13
Orange	3 937	3.2	33 375	176	2 654	146	864	374	346	144	145	28	12
Pamlico	316	4.3	24 565	1 245	81	16	70	72	69	29	28	6	1
Pasquotank	769	3.6	21 576	2 128	537	40	144	178	170	56	74	21	3
Pender	930	1.6	21 720	2 084	267	53	158	208	198	77	82	21	9
Perquimans	250	0.9	21 603	2 121	56	19	50	66	63	27	25	7	1
Person	866	2.6	23 690	1 502	433	14	117	176	167	65	72	16	8
Pitt	3 388	3.1	24 731	1 204	2 402	147	580	568	536	180	236	85	20
Polk	597	2.5	31 719	235	136	39	229	102	98	52	36	5	2
Randolph	3 158	0.6	23 629	1 524	1 630	210	418	548	516	226	202	44	26
Richmond	991	0.1	21 163	2 247	529	82	128	297	285	88	120	36	12
Robeson	2 286	1.6	18 328	2 856	1 197	83	289	707	678	174	323	126	23
Rockingham	2 122	2.0	22 930	1 743	1 116	96	322	484	462	185	197	45	21
Rowan	3 325	3.7	24 910	1 158	1 896	123	555	588	557	234	218	47	21
Rutherford	1 415	2.4	22 355	1 921	754	143	208	331	316	133	122	34	16
Sampson	1 436	12.5	23 476	1 577	580	296	175	299	284	98	130	35	8
Scotland	759	1.0	21 284	2 215	563	23	105	208	200	66	86	32	9
Stanly	1 363	0.6	23 193	1 664	646	92	220	278	264	111	111	22	11
Stokes	1 035	0.7	23 040	1 709	242	40	154	177	167	73	66	14	8
Surry	1 729	-0.3	23 999	1 406	1 055	137	261	366	349	138	153	30	16

1. Based on the resident population estimated as of July 1 of the year shown. 2. Includes other labor income.

Table B. States and Counties — Earnings, Social Security, and Housing

STATE County	Earnings, 2002									Social Security beneficiaries, December 2003		Supplemental Security Income recipients, December 2003	Housing units, 2003	
	Total (mil dol)	Farm	Goods-related[1]		Service-related and health					Number	Rate[2]		Total	Percent change, 2000–2003
			Total	Manufacturing	Information and professional and technical services	Retail trade	Finance, insurance, and real estate	Health services	Government					
	75	76	77	78	79	80	81	82	83	84	85	86	87	88

NORTH CAROLINA—Cont'd

STATE County	75	76	77	78	79	80	81	82	83	84	85	86	87	88
Chowan	195	8.4	23.6	18.9	4.5	7.5	4.1	D	17.7	3 480	241	543	6 571	2.0
Clay	69	1.8	D	6.1	D	16.2	9.5	9.0	22.6	2 690	290	301	5 870	8.2
Cleveland	1 309	0.7	39.1	33.9	3.3	8.0	2.8	D	15.3	20 685	211	2 681	41 809	3.7
Columbus	691	6.5	27.0	22.6	D	7.8	6.1	D	18.3	12 940	237	3 777	24 595	2.2
Craven	2 105	-0.2	D	9.5	6.3	5.0	2.9	7.3	53.0	17 850	195	2 546	40 065	5.0
Cumberland	7 136	0.0	11.9	7.6	3.7	6.1	2.9	4.8	59.2	39 030	128	7 614	124 178	4.9
Currituck	164	1.3	17.9	2.6	4.6	15.0	D	D	23.7	3 330	160	259	11 924	11.6
Dare	668	0.0	D	3.6	D	14.0	15.7	4.1	16.7	5 720	173	253	29 450	10.4
Davidson	1 825	0.1	D	31.4	4.5	7.8	4.1	8.3	13.4	27 770	182	2 261	65 479	4.9
Davie	418	0.2	D	33.0	D	8.5	5.2	5.9	13.6	7 060	190	525	16 013	7.1
Duplin	663	10.0	33.8	29.4	D	6.2	2.4	5.0	18.0	9 325	182	1 932	21 154	3.1
Durham	10 339	0.0	D	33.0	13.6	3.8	4.3	13.1	9.1	30 455	129	4 539	105 087	10.1
Edgecombe	921	2.4	D	19.8	9.0	6.7	4.3	D	21.3	11 085	202	2 940	24 856	3.6
Forsyth	8 583	0.0	23.9	19.0	10.4	7.2	9.9	13.9	8.6	53 405	168	5 687	141 183	6.1
Franklin	442	2.7	D	25.0	4.5	8.8	2.7	8.0	19.2	7 895	152	1 487	21 888	7.5
Gaston	3 015	0.3	40.3	34.5	4.3	7.8	4.1	12.1	12.4	35 805	185	4 049	82 332	4.4
Gates	59	6.4	12.9	11.3	3.5	5.3	D	6.2	40.3	2 180	203	327	4 462	1.7
Graham	87	2.6	D	D	2.2	5.7	2.7	5.5	20.7	2 040	255	331	5 275	3.8
Granville	807	-0.7	39.9	36.1	D	4.4	1.6	D	39.9	8 795	170	1 386	19 375	8.3
Greene	156	9.2	21.4	11.5	2.7	5.7	2.5	8.8	32.5	2 935	147	706	7 572	2.2
Guilford	12 519	0.2	23.9	18.2	10.2	7.7	9.8	10.1	10.8	68 865	159	7 576	193 463	7.2
Halifax	613	3.0	D	19.9	2.9	10.2	3.4	7.9	29.8	14 000	248	4 468	25 715	1.6
Harnett	868	1.9	D	10.3	6.6	9.3	5.1	D	21.0	14 135	142	2 527	41 123	6.5
Haywood	658	2.3	D	17.0	6.2	12.4	4.8	D	21.2	14 620	264	1 458	29 913	4.4
Henderson	1 486	3.1	D	25.8	3.9	9.3	4.8	9.9	13.7	25 155	268	1 782	45 806	6.5
Hertford	313	1.3	25.1	20.3	2.6	8.1	3.2	D	19.9	5 055	227	1 486	9 892	1.7
Hoke	253	2.4	D	31.9	D	3.5	2.3	D	30.8	4 595	122	1 048	13 683	9.3
Hyde	67	3.1	9.2	3.1	D	5.9	D	3.8	41.6	1 095	197	250	3 326	0.7
Iredell	2 231	1.4	D	26.6	3.9	9.8	3.3	11.2	13.1	23 110	173	2 075	57 758	11.2
Jackson	519	1.1	D	4.2	D	7.6	5.4	13.0	36.9	6 285	183	663	20 982	8.8
Johnston	1 541	2.6	D	25.2	D	9.6	4.3	5.7	16.8	19 960	146	3 471	55 622	10.8
Jones	71	9.0	10.4	3.4	D	5.4	D	15.4	26.2	2 270	223	389	4 762	1.8
Lee	1 094	1.0	49.0	44.0	D	7.2	2.7	7.6	10.6	9 740	198	1 221	20 935	5.2
Lenoir	978	0.8	D	18.6	5.7	9.2	4.0	10.8	25.2	13 395	229	2 856	27 894	2.6
Lincoln	715	1.4	D	32.7	3.2	8.0	2.9	4.7	17.4	11 150	166	1 038	28 274	9.9
McDowell	626	5.1	51.5	45.6	D	7.5	2.1	D	14.2	9 140	213	1 064	18 964	3.2
Macon	409	1.6	D	9.6	7.6	11.9	7.3	12.2	14.4	8 820	283	748	21 566	4.0
Madison	156	3.1	D	17.3	2.3	5.1	4.3	D	20.8	4 450	224	806	10 137	4.3
Martin	372	0.9	47.7	42.6	4.0	7.2	2.0	D	16.7	5 620	224	1 281	11 087	1.4
Mecklenburg	30 823	0.2	D	9.7	14.3	5.8	16.9	5.2	8.7	85 910	114	10 470	335 547	14.6
Mitchell	189	2.9	26.9	12.4	D	10.8	2.6	12.8	23.3	3 955	250	612	8 100	2.3
Montgomery	409	7.6	D	40.8	D	5.7	1.8	D	15.6	5 015	184	794	14 486	2.4
Moore	1 276	3.5	18.1	10.7	6.1	8.3	6.8	23.5	11.9	20 920	264	1 406	37 186	5.8
Nash	1 665	0.9	D	26.8	4.3	8.4	9.5	8.1	14.1	16 395	183	3 047	38 996	5.2
New Hanover	3 766	0.2	20.9	12.1	10.5	9.7	7.7	10.3	19.4	30 690	183	3 745	86 111	8.2
Northampton	206	20.3	D	12.9	D	4.6	D	D	25.6	5 655	260	1 448	10 681	2.2
Onslow	3 181	0.1	4.6	1.2	2.3	4.7	1.9	3.1	75.2	16 075	109	2 385	59 356	6.5
Orange	2 800	0.3	7.4	4.2	9.0	6.7	8.2	4.9	51.9	13 805	117	1 276	51 379	4.2
Pamlico	97	3.3	14.9	3.8	2.6	10.1	2.8	D	31.7	3 330	261	325	6 961	2.7
Pasquotank	577	0.8	9.0	4.8	D	10.7	4.1	10.1	44.9	6 660	185	1 196	14 763	3.3
Pender	320	5.3	D	10.1	D	8.2	3.6	D	27.1	8 710	200	1 100	22 042	6.0
Perquimans	75	10.9	12.6	3.6	D	7.9	2.3	D	32.1	3 130	269	377	6 258	3.6
Person	447	-2.2	40.9	35.7	2.4	8.9	2.3	8.0	17.0	7 290	198	964	16 160	4.2
Pitt	2 549	-0.1	D	15.9	5.5	8.0	5.0	10.8	32.5	20 760	150	4 928	64 281	10.1
Polk	175	1.7	27.3	13.6	6.5	5.4	6.6	D	17.0	5 230	278	274	9 666	5.2
Randolph	1 841	4.7	41.8	34.5	2.9	6.6	3.1	6.4	12.2	23 765	176	2 028	57 296	5.3
Richmond	611	6.2	31.5	22.4	D	9.2	2.9	11.5	17.8	10 255	220	2 060	20 811	4.7
Robeson	1 280	0.4	26.6	19.8	3.1	9.2	3.9	14.8	23.4	22 045	175	7 277	49 468	3.5
Rockingham	1 212	0.4	D	38.5	2.9	7.6	2.8	D	14.2	20 155	218	2 803	41 310	2.7
Rowan	2 019	1.2	33.6	28.2	3.1	7.4	2.6	9.6	17.5	24 805	185	2 266	56 547	4.8
Rutherford	897	0.1	45.8	39.2	2.3	10.5	2.6	9.5	13.7	14 435	227	1 644	30 530	3.4
Sampson	876	33.4	D	15.4	2.8	6.1	1.8	D	16.2	12 000	193	2 242	25 816	2.7
Scotland	585	1.1	44.8	41.4	2.8	7.4	2.1	12.2	13.3	7 585	212	1 805	15 153	3.1
Stanly	737	2.7	D	29.2	2.5	9.0	3.1	11.5	16.7	11 825	201	1 063	25 575	4.0
Stokes	282	1.7	26.9	13.9	D	8.3	4.3	D	23.5	8 190	181	798	19 899	3.3
Surry	1 192	4.8	D	25.5	D	8.8	3.4	7.9	14.3	15 135	209	1 942	31 889	2.8

1. Covers mining, construction, and manufacturing.   2. Per 1,000 resident population estimated as of July 1 of the year shown.

Table B. States and Counties — Housing, Labor Force, and Employment

STATE County	Housing units, 2000								Civilian labor force, 2003				Civilian employment,[6] 2000		
	Occupied units							Sub-stand-ard units[4] (percent)			Unemployment			Percent	
	Owner-occupied					Renter-occupied									Management, professional and related occupations	Production, transportation, and material moving occupations
				Median owner cost as a percent of income											
	Total	Percent	Median value[1]	With a mortgage	Without a mortgage[2]	Median rent[3]	Median rent as a percent of income		Total	Percent change, 2002–2003	Total	Rate[5]	Total		
	89	90	91	92	93	94	95	96	97	98	99	100	101	102	103
NORTH CAROLINA—Cont'd															
Chowan	5 580	72.3	85 200	21.6	11.8	429	26.1	4.2	7 089	6.2	328	4.6	6 020	24.3	20.7
Clay	3 847	84.6	99 800	22.7	9.9	408	27.2	2.1	3 689	1.8	153	4.1	3 769	24.0	14.7
Cleveland	37 046	72.9	83 200	20.3	10.2	447	23.0	3.3	43 879	-2.4	4 548	10.4	44 961	22.8	31.4
Columbus	21 308	76.4	76 100	22.9	11.9	379	25.3	4.3	22 213	0.3	1 931	8.7	20 957	24.1	20.2
Craven	34 582	66.7	96 600	21.1	10.3	501	24.0	3.5	38 318	2.4	2 104	5.5	35 725	28.7	16.1
Cumberland	107 358	59.4	88 800	23.2	10.8	581	24.8	4.6	129 741	2.1	7 242	5.6	110 337	28.8	16.6
Currituck	6 902	81.5	115 500	23.4	9.9	590	26.9	2.8	10 631	4.4	301	2.8	8 528	26.1	11.9
Dare	12 690	74.5	137 200	24.7	9.9	638	24.8	1.6	22 275	4.8	1 126	5.1	15 696	29.8	7.6
Davidson	58 156	74.2	98 600	20.4	9.9	464	22.0	3.2	83 113	2.4	6 434	7.7	74 150	22.8	29.2
Davie	13 750	83.3	116 200	21.1	9.9	493	21.4	2.8	19 265	1.6	1 146	5.9	16 947	29.7	23.5
Duplin	18 267	74.9	74 800	21.7	11.9	399	21.3	7.6	23 484	1.2	1 717	7.3	21 642	23.7	24.8
Durham	89 015	54.2	129 000	21.3	9.9	658	25.7	5.5	129 285	2.1	6 675	5.2	114 375	45.8	9.0
Edgecombe	20 392	64.0	70 800	21.7	11.9	442	26.1	6.8	26 140	-1.2	2 911	11.1	22 720	19.4	28.4
Forsyth	123 851	65.6	114 000	20.2	9.9	523	23.6	3.7	160 291	0.8	8 566	5.3	150 831	35.6	15.9
Franklin	17 843	77.8	101 800	22.3	11.9	488	23.4	5.5	25 390	2.2	1 508	5.9	22 726	25.3	20.7
Gaston	73 936	68.9	90 300	20.8	11.0	535	23.2	3.5	103 478	1.6	7 769	7.5	91 354	24.6	25.7
Gates	3 901	82.0	77 200	19.2	12.0	448	24.8	5.2	4 549	0.0	132	2.9	4 330	25.5	23.2
Graham	3 354	82.7	76 100	19.4	11.2	319	21.3	3.2	4 392	0.8	348	7.9	3 298	19.9	23.6
Granville	16 654	75.1	100 400	21.1	9.9	481	23.6	4.7	26 167	1.0	1 933	7.4	20 875	29.8	20.5
Greene	6 696	74.7	74 300	22.5	10.3	405	23.9	8.3	9 632	1.9	567	5.9	7 893	22.6	25.0
Guilford	168 667	62.7	116 900	21.1	9.9	590	24.4	3.8	233 919	0.7	14 270	6.1	217 104	34.7	15.5
Halifax	22 122	67.0	68 300	21.3	12.9	399	26.0	6.0	22 567	2.5	2 153	9.5	20 859	21.5	23.7
Harnett	33 800	70.3	91 200	21.7	11.0	486	24.5	4.1	37 854	-0.1	2 778	7.3	39 096	24.9	21.0
Haywood	23 100	77.3	99 100	22.0	9.9	455	23.2	2.8	24 570	0.3	1 285	5.2	24 101	27.3	18.2
Henderson	37 414	78.8	130 100	21.1	9.9	513	24.0	3.0	43 213	4.3	1 651	3.8	39 531	28.6	18.6
Hertford	8 953	70.0	61 700	24.5	11.4	410	24.3	4.1	11 113	-4.5	500	4.5	8 699	26.2	23.5
Hoke	11 373	75.0	83 900	24.2	11.4	504	25.4	7.0	13 299	1.5	1 241	9.3	13 115	23.5	25.1
Hyde	2 185	78.4	76 500	23.7	13.4	383	18.8	5.4	3 105	0.6	229	7.4	2 236	19.1	13.5
Iredell	47 360	75.3	116 100	21.3	9.9	540	22.7	2.6	70 165	4.6	4 577	6.5	61 204	27.6	25.6
Jackson	13 191	72.5	106 700	19.6	9.9	430	25.0	2.9	17 675	1.9	752	4.3	15 688	31.3	11.6
Johnston	46 595	73.4	108 800	21.8	11.1	498	24.0	3.6	70 284	2.3	3 164	4.5	59 641	30.5	16.4
Jones	4 061	79.6	75 100	21.9	11.7	396	27.8	5.1	4 843	0.8	244	5.0	4 313	21.7	19.3
Lee	18 466	71.7	95 100	20.7	10.2	497	23.4	5.3	27 192	1.1	1 975	7.3	23 012	27.3	25.3
Lenoir	23 862	67.0	82 600	21.9	11.5	405	24.4	4.0	29 822	1.1	2 029	6.8	25 532	25.8	21.0
Lincoln	24 041	78.5	104 500	20.5	9.9	482	20.4	3.4	36 275	2.6	2 695	7.4	32 331	22.3	30.4
McDowell	16 604	77.2	72 000	19.4	9.9	411	20.7	3.3	20 290	1.2	1 627	8.0	19 581	19.4	35.0
Macon	12 828	81.3	103 700	21.5	9.9	485	24.6	2.5	15 749	3.0	584	3.7	12 865	26.7	13.5
Madison	8 000	76.5	94 600	20.7	9.9	367	23.7	3.2	9 609	2.4	403	4.2	8 731	27.9	21.3
Martin	10 020	71.8	68 400	21.4	12.2	400	27.0	4.9	11 070	0.5	925	8.4	10 649	22.7	25.0
Mecklenburg	273 416	62.3	141 800	21.4	9.9	693	24.3	4.9	417 880	2.5	24 215	5.8	369 275	39.5	11.1
Mitchell	6 551	80.9	78 800	21.4	9.9	379	21.5	2.4	7 185	-2.0	629	8.8	7 047	21.0	30.2
Montgomery	9 848	76.5	77 200	20.9	9.9	407	21.6	6.6	12 019	-2.3	1 223	10.2	11 830	23.2	32.7
Moore	30 713	78.6	131 100	21.9	9.9	528	23.6	2.8	31 440	1.3	2 153	6.8	32 051	31.2	15.5
Nash	33 644	67.7	95 800	20.3	10.7	494	24.3	5.1	44 258	-0.6	3 409	7.7	39 609	29.2	20.3
New Hanover	68 183	64.7	135 600	23.0	10.2	631	29.0	2.2	90 470	2.1	4 783	5.3	81 238	34.5	11.1
Northampton	8 691	76.8	57 500	20.6	13.4	386	27.5	5.3	8 435	3.0	721	8.5	7 954	22.3	22.6
Onslow	48 122	58.1	85 900	22.1	9.9	518	23.1	4.4	51 531	1.1	2 953	5.7	49 020	26.1	11.4
Orange	45 863	57.6	179 000	21.4	9.9	684	30.9	5.3	66 116	2.6	2 057	3.1	62 509	49.8	7.0
Pamlico	5 178	82.1	89 900	23.2	10.2	466	25.4	2.7	5 749	2.6	258	4.5	5 035	25.4	18.1
Pasquotank	12 907	65.7	85 500	23.0	13.7	493	27.4	2.9	16 602	4.2	696	4.2	14 401	28.0	12.3
Pender	16 054	82.6	113 400	23.5	9.9	491	25.9	3.1	19 572	5.7	1 425	7.3	17 896	23.7	18.3
Perquimans	4 645	78.6	82 800	23.9	13.2	419	29.2	2.8	5 337	4.0	195	3.7	4 432	23.6	17.2
Person	14 085	74.6	90 400	20.7	10.1	455	22.7	3.6	17 295	1.9	1 545	8.9	16 778	24.6	23.3
Pitt	52 539	58.1	96 800	20.5	11.3	471	27.8	4.6	72 983	0.0	4 889	6.7	64 565	33.7	14.5
Polk	7 908	78.6	112 000	22.2	9.9	515	23.9	2.8	8 584	2.8	309	3.6	7 922	28.9	19.3
Randolph	50 659	76.6	94 700	20.0	9.9	463	21.3	4.1	74 961	0.7	4 568	6.1	67 150	21.5	31.4
Richmond	17 873	72.0	59 300	20.0	12.6	404	24.5	3.7	19 022	-1.5	2 231	11.7	18 995	22.4	27.5
Robeson	43 677	72.8	66 100	21.3	11.6	389	25.8	7.1	50 623	-1.4	5 049	10.0	48 279	20.3	27.3
Rockingham	36 989	73.7	81 400	21.0	9.9	437	23.1	3.5	45 501	-0.9	4 390	9.6	42 413	22.3	28.5
Rowan	49 940	73.6	95 200	20.9	10.1	496	22.3	3.3	70 368	5.8	6 338	9.0	61 687	23.2	27.0
Rutherford	25 191	74.5	77 600	21.0	10.2	404	23.2	2.8	29 600	1.3	3 017	10.2	28 222	21.7	29.5
Sampson	22 273	73.5	76 700	20.5	11.8	387	22.4	5.6	25 698	1.3	1 690	6.6	26 472	23.9	25.3
Scotland	13 399	69.1	73 200	19.8	9.9	433	25.1	4.5	18 601	3.6	2 280	12.3	14 274	28.8	26.3
Stanly	22 223	76.2	87 700	21.4	10.7	463	21.2	3.6	26 608	2.3	2 303	8.7	27 977	23.4	25.5
Stokes	17 579	82.0	94 700	20.6	9.9	449	20.6	3.3	23 087	1.0	1 435	6.2	22 239	22.4	26.4
Surry	28 408	76.3	87 500	20.9	9.9	411	22.2	4.1	33 536	-0.7	2 918	8.7	34 201	24.0	27.3

1. Specified owner-occupied units.   2. Median monthly owner costs is often in the minimum category—9.9 percent or less, which is indicated as 9.9 percent.   3. Specified renter-occupied units.   4. Overcrowded or lacking complete plumbing facilities.   5. Percent of civilian labor force.   6. Persons 16 years old and over.

Table B. States and Counties — Nonfarm Employment and Agriculture

STATE County	Private nonfarm establishments, employment and payroll, 2001									Agriculture, 2002			
		Employment						Annual payroll		Farms			
												Percent with—	Farm operators whose principal occupation is farming (percent)
	Number of establishments	Total	Health care and social assistance	Manufacturing	Retail trade	Finance and insurance	Professional, scientific, and technical services	Total (mil dol)	Average per employee (dollars)	Number	Less than 50 acres	500 acres and over	
	104	105	106	107	108	109	110	111	112	113	114	115	116
NORTH CAROLINA—Cont'd													
Chowan	361	4 346	910	1 063	678	119	83	102	23 463	173	31.2	24.3	68.8
Clay	232	1 525	290	183	311	D	40	30	19 477	168	54.8	1.8	51.8
Cleveland	2 147	32 432	4 278	11 579	4 865	677	491	817	25 179	1 131	40.5	2.7	51.3
Columbus	1 181	14 083	2 366	3 028	2 570	820	251	318	22 558	828	40.5	10.4	60.1
Craven	2 160	27 298	5 080	4 384	4 321	808	1 425	722	26 448	275	33.1	16.7	67.6
Cumberland	5 250	86 042	13 856	12 175	15 642	2 643	3 040	2 096	24 357	478	46.4	10.9	57.3
Currituck	454	3 101	205	137	887	51	90	63	20 344	82	50.0	23.2	75.6
Dare	1 729	12 539	369	384	2 947	335	644	292	23 268	8	50.0	37.5	75.0
Davidson	2 700	42 878	3 906	18 176	5 243	875	649	1 071	24 985	1 138	46.7	2.7	53.8
Davie	697	8 954	741	3 243	1 028	214	134	217	24 244	705	46.7	2.8	54.5
Duplin	896	11 400	1 496	3 620	1 781	202	279	235	20 614	1 190	43.4	10.2	72.0
Durham	5 964	169 763	20 843	30 816	14 384	4 024	18 990	7 342	43 249	238	58.4	3.8	53.8
Edgecombe	957	19 200	2 238	6 125	1 697	377	278	494	25 739	281	30.6	27.4	73.0
Forsyth	8 493	177 802	24 383	23 844	20 783	16 820	8 800	5 782	32 519	783	61.2	1.1	54.3
Franklin	756	7 650	1 073	2 115	1 141	126	186	205	26 752	574	36.9	9.2	60.1
Gaston	4 105	63 443	7 362	20 503	9 289	1 698	1 468	1 650	26 003	450	47.3	1.6	51.1
Gates	129	940	D	192	239	D	45	18	18 895	129	30.2	24.8	65.1
Graham	187	1 851	167	675	220	D	D	42	22 439	143	60.1	1.4	45.5
Granville	776	14 195	2 530	5 928	1 319	193	233	386	27 183	674	30.4	10.5	53.1
Greene	216	1 945	600	284	277	D	21	34	17 486	271	29.5	24.4	81.2
Guilford	13 615	262 272	24 909	46 455	31 907	17 296	11 509	8 312	31 691	1 095	54.0	3.9	54.7
Halifax	1 113	14 361	2 711	2 835	2 970	366	311	336	23 412	380	31.1	23.9	58.4
Harnett	1 435	19 632	2 282	3 278	2 852	492	453	413	21 026	730	47.1	7.8	64.9
Haywood	1 411	14 469	2 549	2 457	2 809	410	471	342	23 610	795	58.9	2.1	55.2
Henderson	2 302	30 809	4 826	7 875	5 019	813	735	863	28 019	525	58.3	3.2	61.7
Hertford	547	7 466	1 512	1 390	1 559	169	124	171	22 843	136	30.1	30.1	75.0
Hoke	272	4 909	527	2 462	546	D	44	115	23 445	201	48.8	13.9	60.2
Hyde	177	1 079	55	165	175	D	30	19	17 703	144	41.0	39.6	62.5
Iredell	3 360	50 374	7 041	14 518	6 945	1 112	1 147	1 395	27 694	1 262	43.3	3.5	57.1
Jackson	906	8 497	2 058	599	1 520	211	278	191	22 432	248	67.3	1.6	50.0
Johnston	2 561	29 519	2 969	7 047	5 268	706	1 076	732	24 793	1 144	45.2	7.7	66.4
Jones	154	1 212	302	207	144	D	D	29	23 828	154	20.8	27.3	87.0
Lee	1 384	23 283	2 317	9 472	2 955	434	366	604	25 959	304	48.7	6.3	56.3
Lenoir	1 492	26 375	5 721	5 712	3 443	730	625	642	24 357	428	32.7	18.7	76.4
Lincoln	1 347	19 729	1 704	7 282	2 419	302	1 083	485	24 583	618	50.6	2.9	51.8
McDowell	776	15 091	1 263	8 336	1 644	182	183	335	22 230	282	48.9	2.5	53.5
Macon	1 087	8 840	1 530	963	1 805	333	188	215	24 282	347	53.3	0.3	45.2
Madison	309	3 194	430	829	405	50	38	65	20 314	973	47.9	1.5	54.5
Martin	530	5 758	814	1 029	1 212	152	107	118	20 494	305	25.9	23.3	73.4
Mecklenburg	24 341	537 703	41 676	38 891	47 968	75 646	36 940	21 068	39 182	300	60.0	2.0	48.3
Mitchell	386	4 561	659	1 398	875	107	48	101	22 049	358	61.7	1.7	49.7
Montgomery	537	9 448	394	5 523	991	228	79	207	21 905	292	38.0	7.5	58.2
Moore	2 088	27 132	6 429	3 903	4 127	698	868	698	25 711	820	47.8	3.4	60.6
Nash	2 271	38 680	5 112	8 582	5 761	2 230	1 062	1 096	28 327	478	41.4	16.9	64.4
New Hanover	6 055	79 611	11 476	8 983	13 607	3 036	4 883	2 162	27 163	77	70.1	0.0	39.0
Northampton	320	2 901	460	597	495	D	60	68	23 597	328	33.5	25.3	75.3
Onslow	2 562	29 978	4 142	1 564	6 841	945	928	559	18 654	404	44.3	5.7	59.4
Orange	2 930	39 354	10 522	1 160	6 439	3 463	2 345	1 176	29 878	627	43.2	4.3	56.8
Pamlico	218	1 717	217	97	309	D	29	36	20 737	68	35.3	35.3	77.9
Pasquotank	918	10 692	2 434	736	2 578	396	312	238	22 297	157	27.4	35.0	69.4
Pender	686	5 334	1 041	843	951	79	117	108	20 340	296	43.2	11.1	61.8
Perquimans	185	1 379	190	137	225	D	37	26	18 719	193	16.6	34.7	77.7
Person	726	9 901	980	3 889	1 405	216	142	258	26 048	374	34.8	11.2	66.0
Pitt	3 221	54 431	10 729	9 169	8 161	1 844	2 085	1 348	24 756	448	30.1	25.4	67.2
Polk	452	3 813	1 254	695	485	70	105	77	20 272	260	55.0	1.5	53.5
Randolph	2 740	45 241	3 439	21 998	5 189	868	562	1 061	23 455	1 583	45.5	2.6	60.2
Richmond	971	13 459	2 099	4 578	2 223	283	289	285	21 210	257	33.9	6.6	65.0
Robeson	1 994	32 315	5 534	9 323	5 319	1 068	696	679	21 009	873	43.6	17.2	62.3
Rockingham	1 794	27 766	3 208	11 632	3 577	680	395	703	25 303	871	36.6	6.0	52.9
Rowan	2 519	44 203	6 265	11 721	4 754	851	776	1 182	26 741	951	43.3	4.8	54.7
Rutherford	1 301	21 368	2 301	9 528	2 732	367	230	514	24 054	653	39.5	2.6	53.0
Sampson	1 025	13 663	1 889	4 094	2 397	298	203	303	22 206	1 178	37.1	12.1	70.2
Scotland	707	16 833	1 836	7 426	1 736	238	108	375	22 290	159	37.7	20.1	53.5
Stanly	1 400	17 754	2 578	6 291	2 802	431	274	426	24 009	719	44.9	6.3	53.1
Stokes	606	5 618	916	1 262	803	125	117	119	21 109	934	39.3	3.3	58.7
Surry	1 821	34 073	3 262	11 186	4 430	737	433	816	23 947	1 268	47.5	2.8	56.9

STATE County	Land in farms		Acres			Value of land and buildings (dollars)		Value of machinery and equipment average per farm (dollars)	Value of products sold		Percent from —		Percent of farms with sales of —		Government payments	
	Acreage (1,000)	Percent change, 1997–2002	Average size of farm	Total irrigated (1,000)	Total cropland (1,000)	Average per farm	Average per acre		Total (mil dol)	Average per farm (dollars)	Crops	Live-stock and poultry products	$10,000 or more	$100,000 or more	Total ($1,000)	Percent of farms
	117	118	119	120	121	122	123	124	125	126	127	128	129	130	131	132
NORTH CAROLINA—Cont'd																
Chowan	60	17.6	346	7	47	830 343	2 382	137 261	38	220 552	73.0	27.0	72.3	42.2	1 674	35.3
Clay	13	-27.8	80	0	6	396 351	5 168	40 570	1	7 942	34.6	65.4	18.5	0.6	61	20.8
Cleveland	117	12.5	104	1	66	341 012	3 052	31 676	41	36 072	26.3	73.7	22.0	6.5	1 250	39.5
Columbus	160	-5.9	193	4	109	447 861	2 210	69 291	106	128 320	39.0	61.0	43.8	17.4	1 683	29.6
Craven	79	-6.0	287	2	60	621 114	2 403	112 621	49	178 803	51.2	48.8	50.5	28.0	1 510	34.9
Cumberland	90	-12.6	189	3	53	433 526	2 530	62 238	58	120 513	25.0	75.0	33.1	13.8	627	27.2
Currituck	35	-12.5	424	0	30	1 324 800	3 010	100 534	9	112 294	96.9	3.2	53.7	24.4	479	35.4
Dare	D	D	D	0	5	1 098 170	1 268	100 232	1	114 470	100.0	0.0	62.5	50.0	252	50.0
Davidson	105	6.1	92	2	58	316 327	3 981	49 394	26	22 871	30.4	69.6	23.5	4.0	610	19.9
Davie	76	7.0	108	1	43	471 222	4 146	49 668	14	19 908	30.9	69.1	23.1	5.8	285	15.3
Duplin	235	-1.3	197	24	163	564 942	2 959	93 025	715	601 057	8.3	91.7	66.6	51.3	2 953	25.5
Durham	26	18.2	110	1	10	558 230	5 416	40 674	7	27 987	82.2	17.7	27.7	7.1	100	24.8
Edgecombe	164	-4.7	582	12	107	1 188 753	2 074	118 016	98	348 343	41.5	58.5	55.5	35.2	2 526	47.0
Forsyth	52	2.0	66	1	28	301 414	4 559	40 808	14	18 064	80.4	19.6	15.8	2.9	122	11.1
Franklin	128	-6.6	224	4	57	657 908	2 892	63 042	40	70 198	65.5	34.5	34.0	11.8	756	34.0
Gaston	42	20.0	93	0	21	408 594	4 218	40 571	12	26 539	23.8	76.2	20.9	5.6	365	25.8
Gates	64	3.2	496	2	51	937 669	1 839	167 361	32	249 000	45.9	54.1	67.4	39.5	1 155	52.7
Graham	8	14.3	56	0	3	212 859	3 731	25 478	2	12 340	27.3	72.7	19.6	2.1	6	9.8
Granville	147	-9.3	217	4	50	559 405	2 701	42 286	22	32 829	86.3	13.7	35.5	8.2	439	30.6
Greene	98	-4.9	361	5	76	1 047 812	2 995	130 482	159	586 396	18.5	81.5	72.7	51.7	1 621	50.9
Guilford	111	-0.9	102	3	55	473 643	5 071	48 138	45	41 509	67.8	32.2	26.1	7.9	504	12.3
Halifax	195	5.4	512	3	125	886 263	1 810	129 783	64	169 601	45.5	54.5	43.9	29.2	5 437	59.7
Harnett	114	-1.7	157	4	70	579 018	3 546	73 725	105	143 881	28.5	71.5	37.3	21.4	1 408	24.0
Haywood	65	0.0	81	0	27	364 616	4 646	30 984	12	15 420	45.9	54.1	20.0	2.8	293	11.8
Henderson	49	8.9	93	3	31	572 415	5 243	52 199	61	115 744	88.2	11.8	38.3	12.0	2 315	28.8
Hertford	80	5.3	587	7	54	1 162 572	1 934	181 222	96	708 924	22.0	78.0	75.0	46.3	1 582	46.3
Hoke	63	-6.0	315	2	45	867 176	2 690	114 924	45	221 436	23.7	76.3	38.3	20.4	808	21.9
Hyde	103	8.4	716	D	92	1 264 802	1 819	208 106	33	228 251	97.8	2.2	47.2	38.9	2 270	81.3
Iredell	147	-6.4	116	2	85	514 253	4 566	42 633	146	115 370	5.2	94.8	31.3	12.9	1 710	18.8
Jackson	16	-15.8	66	0	6	644 489	6 098	41 441	8	32 875	95.3	4.7	27.4	2.8	12	8.5
Johnston	194	-8.1	170	6	132	599 437	3 582	67 625	146	127 197	45.8	54.2	43.4	19.4	2 059	30.1
Jones	76	5.6	494	3	53	1 136 331	2 309	174 258	90	582 644	21.5	78.5	63.0	45.5	1 936	42.9
Lee	46	2.2	152	1	21	418 104	3 217	37 783	22	72 585	43.9	56.1	35.5	11.5	111	17.1
Lenoir	122	-18.7	284	4	92	942 742	3 326	137 483	141	330 315	29.5	70.5	63.1	44.9	2 229	33.4
Lincoln	58	-7.9	93	1	35	337 142	3 970	37 170	18	28 928	22.0	78.0	19.7	4.4	511	24.8
McDowell	24	14.3	87	0	9	265 697	3 355	31 578	23	80 681	68.1	31.9	27.7	10.3	167	13.8
Macon	22	-4.3	65	0	9	537 610	6 039	68 473	5	13 249	52.9	47.1	21.9	2.6	33	15.3
Madison	84	5.0	86	0	27	299 366	3 942	19 979	10	10 690	81.8	18.2	20.2	1.0	237	12.1
Martin	111	-3.5	363	2	78	781 589	2 128	139 267	40	130 792	63.1	36.9	67.9	31.8	2 186	44.9
Mecklenburg	25	-13.8	85	1	12	636 077	9 616	35 460	72	238 380	93.3	6.7	19.7	5.3	99	14.0
Mitchell	26	4.0	73	0	9	275 730	4 331	24 812	4	10 818	87.3	12.7	21.8	2.0	20	6.1
Montgomery	42	0.0	143	1	13	399 131	3 337	33 985	68	233 850	4.0	96.0	38.4	26.7	208	18.2
Moore	101	0.0	123	3	36	303 612	3 027	39 526	91	111 017	18.0	82.0	32.3	21.0	511	14.1
Nash	160	-8.6	335	8	103	888 020	2 503	111 972	108	226 852	50.6	49.4	50.8	33.5	2 290	39.3
New Hanover	D	D	D	0	2	449 401	9 976	33 007	3	43 447	96.4	3.6	39.0	6.5	44	7.8
Northampton	151	-5.6	459	4	96	858 573	2 011	120 728	61	187 090	29.0	71.0	56.1	31.7	2 837	48.2
Onslow	64	1.6	158	2	44	427 198	2 949	78 796	90	222 911	19.4	80.6	47.0	24.8	586	21.3
Orange	71	-2.7	113	1	35	517 706	4 874	27 302	22	35 270	50.9	49.1	30.5	8.5	551	19.0
Pamlico	52	4.0	770	2	45	1 503 045	1 956	227 253	16	242 338	93.0	7.0	60.3	39.7	1 428	64.7
Pasquotank	99	15.1	633	1	94	1 260 846	1 940	140 737	35	220 622	98.1	1.9	72.0	36.3	1 723	42.0
Pender	63	-8.7	212	4	39	669 994	3 118	86 886	102	343 451	22.0	78.0	48.0	28.4	417	20.9
Perquimans	94	22.1	489	3	87	1 106 437	2 285	143 434	38	199 192	61.1	38.9	78.2	47.2	2 588	51.3
Person	95	-20.8	254	2	42	744 566	2 463	77 882	18	48 454	82.2	17.8	39.8	11.8	469	29.7
Pitt	186	-3.6	415	5	137	1 004 236	2 389	122 004	120	268 088	47.8	52.2	58.3	35.7	3 987	34.6
Polk	27	-12.9	104	0	9	474 753	4 682	35 269	5	17 467	61.3	38.7	18.1	3.1	154	20.8
Randolph	157	6.1	99	1	75	359 572	3 814	59 055	148	93 477	9.5	90.5	33.7	19.2	998	17.5
Richmond	49	-9.3	192	1	20	471 183	2 482	51 670	66	256 943	7.8	92.2	42.8	31.1	188	28.0
Robeson	287	0.7	328	5	224	629 801	1 994	98 350	191	218 371	31.3	68.7	46.7	19.9	3 327	32.6
Rockingham	136	1.5	156	4	51	408 043	2 665	45 998	29	32 785	78.5	21.5	33.3	8.2	314	23.7
Rowan	115	6.5	121	1	69	453 671	3 595	52 993	36	38 120	59.4	40.6	22.5	5.3	651	20.6
Rutherford	68	11.5	104	0	31	258 688	3 035	35 195	9	14 096	19.9	80.1	20.5	2.5	183	18.7
Sampson	298	10.0	253	25	192	784 955	3 084	102 554	676	573 592	11.6	88.4	61.9	41.9	3 697	31.4
Scotland	58	7.4	367	3	40	825 124	2 219	77 629	47	293 099	11.4	88.6	45.9	23.3	1 213	35.8
Stanly	108	13.7	150	2	71	569 832	3 650	66 535	57	78 778	14.5	85.5	30.0	11.1	1 263	27.0
Stokes	107	-2.7	115	1	42	349 876	2 906	44 065	23	24 506	70.1	29.9	31.2	5.2	174	14.3
Surry	129	-0.8	102	2	64	447 193	3 646	71 433	89	70 275	24.1	75.9	31.6	12.1	457	15.1

Table B. States and Counties — Residential Construction, Wholesale Trade, Retail Trade, and Real Estate

STATE County	Value of residential construction authorized by building permits, 2003 — New construction ($1,000)	Number of housing units	Wholesale trade, 1997 — Number of establishments	Number of employees	Sales (mil dol)	Annual payroll (mil dol)	Retail trade,[1] 1997 — Number of establishments	Number of employees	Sales (mil dol)	Annual payroll (mil dol)	Real estate and rental and leasing, 1997 — Number of establishments	Number of employees	Receipts (mil dol)	Annual payroll (mil dol)
	133	134	135	136	137	138	139	140	141	142	143	144	145	146
NORTH CAROLINA—Cont'd														
Chowan	7 612	39	14	207	72.1	5.7	67	730	109.6	9.8	9	14	1.5	0.1
Clay	23 588	179	1	D	D	D	38	324	52.2	3.8	9	20	1.4	0.3
Cleveland	50 175	402	126	1 434	1 355.9	39.1	431	4 707	707.4	68.9	76	354	45.8	6.6
Columbus	11 558	112	62	463	241.3	10.6	296	2 565	387.7	37.4	28	97	8.7	1.4
Craven	80 898	765	76	746	307.6	23.2	443	4 560	772.6	71.3	74	325	28.1	5.2
Cumberland	205 316	1 744	205	2 454	845.3	66.5	1 061	14 929	2 563.3	239.3	272	1 182	137.5	23.4
Currituck	119 986	560	20	D	D	D	81	541	98.6	10.2	20	110	11.0	3.4
Dare	214 675	866	41	374	103.9	7.1	389	2 494	442.4	43.4	106	872	61.8	16.8
Davidson	85 347	667	193	1 972	791.9	67.8	494	5 131	892.0	88.7	100	371	29.4	7.2
Davie	52 137	329	33	406	109.2	8.3	107	902	166.2	14.4	10	15	2.6	0.4
Duplin	18 340	118	44	D	D	D	226	1 879	280.4	25.2	18	65	7.5	0.9
Durham	367 480	2 919	249	4 343	2 306.3	158.4	1 010	13 322	2 032.6	213.2	246	1 301	160.8	30.6
Edgecombe	7 397	77	47	602	454.3	19.9	196	1 631	214.2	21.5	43	354	45.6	7.8
Forsyth	289 259	2 752	478	6 706	3 625.1	219.9	1 489	20 888	3 731.2	344.9	350	1 819	276.6	38.7
Franklin	55 197	435	34	481	166.1	13.8	127	1 057	176.2	15.0	19	60	5.3	0.9
Gaston	164 977	1 317	269	2 047	958.5	67.6	767	9 662	1 587.9	146.5	119	423	37.0	6.8
Gates	3 234	18	6	51	16.7	1.1	29	248	41.8	3.1	3	10	0.5	0.1
Graham	8 240	56	2	D	D	D	36	278	44.6	3.5	5	5	0.7	0.1
Granville	56 619	447	32	222	219.0	8.2	151	1 334	217.1	19.9	24	60	4.2	0.6
Greene	6 503	27	13	122	34.8	2.7	38	302	47.7	4.2	4	8	0.5	0.1
Guilford	499 449	3 677	1 347	21 568	13 448.1	882.9	2 059	29 817	5 179.3	530.8	529	3 704	441.0	82.9
Halifax	13 150	98	36	424	101.7	11.1	306	3 255	462.0	43.7	29	210	17.6	3.7
Harnett	86 225	987	62	756	257.7	18.5	284	2 713	443.2	37.0	45	154	10.7	2.0
Haywood	75 332	468	49	349	127.3	9.4	266	2 847	569.8	46.5	48	119	11.3	1.8
Henderson	135 664	911	91	613	228.0	15.8	386	4 192	901.3	75.2	66	252	28.1	4.9
Hertford	5 797	63	27	264	126.0	5.7	134	1 313	176.9	17.7	14	51	2.7	1.0
Hoke	66 691	523	7	102	30.3	2.8	74	486	67.5	5.9	11	24	1.4	0.3
Hyde	2 976	22	9	61	21.8	1.3	36	164	26.8	2.5	5	D	D	D
Iredell	273 330	2 049	196	2 443	1 373.6	76.5	510	5 993	1 065.8	93.2	95	341	33.8	6.4
Jackson	96 372	559	16	66	18.2	1.6	178	1 472	220.6	20.1	44	112	9.8	2.2
Johnston	203 444	1 594	117	1 269	836.8	26.3	486	4 580	857.9	71.5	65	221	20.4	3.3
Jones	0	0	7	60	12.9	1.2	30	142	33.7	2.2	1	D	D	D
Lee	34 044	339	75	1 159	517.1	32.2	292	3 109	591.9	51.0	59	196	18.2	3.3
Lenoir	14 762	121	80	1 382	486.7	28.2	352	3 597	565.6	51.2	45	170	14.1	2.5
Lincoln	80 362	634	73	1 035	629.9	29.4	212	2 346	406.2	36.6	40	151	13.0	2.5
McDowell	22 596	197	30	293	59.0	6.1	167	1 557	273.4	22.0	22	50	5.0	0.8
Macon	58 499	332	30	101	16.5	1.7	241	1 750	308.1	27.5	38	80	10.6	1.5
Madison	17 766	153	9	D	D	D	51	327	49.0	4.0	8	16	0.6	0.1
Martin	3 958	28	32	220	76.1	5.3	117	1 263	195.1	17.1	10	33	1.7	0.4
Mecklenburg	1 138 633	9 854	2 638	38 333	35 019.8	1 574.3	2 971	44 557	8 517.2	815.7	994	9 430	1 449.2	292.7
Mitchell	7 865	62	11	D	D	D	81	486	97.3	7.3	15	38	3.2	0.6
Montgomery	15 894	92	22	110	58.6	3.0	100	825	137.0	11.7	10	150	5.2	3.1
Moore	113 781	869	92	579	297.6	16.5	360	4 003	616.7	60.5	70	240	19.8	4.7
Nash	60 968	685	125	2 204	1 038.8	67.9	524	5 885	1 035.5	93.0	80	404	50.2	7.3
New Hanover	410 707	2 904	324	3 528	1 216.9	95.4	1 026	12 352	2 461.1	210.9	252	1 140	117.7	22.4
Northampton	3 533	30	22	243	214.8	6.1	66	532	85.4	8.9	4	D	D	D
Onslow	113 629	1 048	69	D	D	D	564	6 542	1 090.1	96.7	129	497	53.0	7.5
Orange	194 615	1 169	78	428	312.3	12.0	387	5 549	837.2	95.0	126	414	60.0	9.3
Pamlico	12 410	71	12	144	19.0	2.4	49	364	53.8	5.0	9	16	2.4	0.2
Pasquotank	24 570	219	46	606	150.7	12.8	201	2 548	405.0	37.6	37	133	10.1	1.9
Pender	72 734	681	33	326	99.1	8.0	131	906	153.9	13.5	28	94	9.9	1.7
Perquimans	12 306	65	9	87	32.6	1.7	38	274	31.7	3.0	3	D	D	D
Person	39 901	246	30	273	81.1	6.4	160	1 556	250.2	22.7	13	76	4.3	0.9
Pitt	147 832	1 709	181	2 153	1 246.8	66.4	643	7 956	1 384.8	124.8	121	495	51.4	7.9
Polk	24 504	197	14	39	19.7	0.8	61	417	63.3	5.9	21	34	3.7	0.5
Randolph	72 699	715	174	1 637	582.0	44.5	457	4 821	845.0	77.1	58	211	22.3	3.2
Richmond	13 790	305	38	368	96.9	8.9	229	2 165	368.2	32.8	34	139	8.8	1.5
Robeson	37 526	306	82	843	349.6	22.0	450	4 844	1 011.7	79.8	46	260	14.0	4.5
Rockingham	45 832	424	59	394	177.6	10.0	421	3 974	619.8	55.4	59	224	17.6	2.8
Rowan	83 621	661	117	1 392	548.3	39.7	450	4 820	799.2	74.3	69	236	25.3	5.0
Rutherford	39 721	303	66	525	334.9	15.0	286	2 861	443.5	41.1	51	164	12.8	3.0
Sampson	18 943	137	52	587	231.1	17.6	246	2 125	373.8	31.1	25	85	5.3	1.2
Scotland	6 833	65	29	212	75.0	6.1	178	1 856	255.3	26.1	27	113	7.3	1.4
Stanly	38 878	416	61	474	228.3	15.8	265	2 722	472.3	44.5	32	123	12.2	1.9
Stokes	24 419	182	18	D	D	D	118	774	135.5	11.7	12	63	2.2	0.4
Surry	28 869	221	90	1 147	646.3	24.8	381	5 594	780.0	75.6	60	183	20.0	2.5

1. Establishments with payroll.

Table B. States and Counties — Professional Services, Manufacturing, and Accommodation and Foodservices

STATE County	Professional, scientific, and technical services,[1] 1997				Manufacturing, 1997				Accommodation and foodservices, 1997			
	Number of establishments	Number of employees	Receipts (mil dol)	Annual payroll (mil dol)	Number of establishments	Number of employees	Receipts (mil dol)	Annual payroll (mil dol)	Number of establishments	Number of employees	Sales (mil dol)	Annual payroll (mil dol)
	147	148	149	150	151	152	153	154	155	156	157	158
NORTH CAROLINA—Cont'd												
Chowan	13	65	4.7	1.9	18	1 061	114.2	23.8	27	364	10.1	2.5
Clay	12	25	2.1	0.7	NA	NA	NA	NA	13	D	D	D
Cleveland	110	425	26.4	9.9	173	14 655	2 497.0	399.9	131	2 422	60.5	17.6
Columbus	46	129	10.0	2.2	46	4 767	895.5	129.9	75	1 058	26.7	6.7
Craven	145	1 022	71.2	32.1	86	4 344	796.4	118.5	159	3 004	87.1	24.8
Cumberland	329	2 084	142.1	47.7	121	12 282	2 766.9	384.6	495	10 654	318.4	91.2
Currituck	19	36	2.7	0.8	NA	NA	NA	NA	45	339	13.7	4.0
Dare	76	345	20.7	7.7	NA	NA	NA	NA	274	2 854	140.0	37.6
Davidson	129	438	31.4	10.5	326	21 576	2 249.4	521.7	177	2 802	87.4	24.8
Davie	28	91	5.2	2.0	45	2 886	406.9	76.4	41	D	D	D
Duplin	47	121	7.2	2.4	48	4 688	675.9	95.2	65	976	28.6	7.6
Durham	614	7 922	1 119.6	369.6	181	31 489	11 223.8	1 027.2	468	9 414	378.5	105.7
Edgecombe	42	301	17.0	5.0	50	7 720	1 606.6	234.0	52	747	22.1	6.2
Forsyth	781	5 462	536.2	203.9	399	26 545	9 676.3	908.6	632	12 945	408.0	116.2
Franklin	35	131	8.9	3.4	55	2 259	444.6	67.3	37	D	D	D
Gaston	231	1 157	80.5	29.7	492	31 175	5 772.7	863.2	297	5 315	158.7	42.3
Gates	4	10	0.5	0.1	NA	NA	NA	NA	4	53	1.2	0.4
Graham	3	D	D	D	3	D	D	D	17	160	7.7	2.4
Granville	38	117	8.7	2.7	57	6 990	1 534.2	185.2	52	680	23.3	5.9
Greene	10	23	1.5	0.5	NA	NA	NA	NA	10	117	2.9	0.8
Guilford	1 155	8 157	762.2	273.6	862	47 158	10 546.4	1 431.2	924	19 991	637.5	185.4
Halifax	51	229	9.6	3.4	59	4 136	567.7	113.7	76	1 531	51.7	13.4
Harnett	90	292	23.9	8.5	82	5 959	633.7	149.2	88	1 289	37.1	10.0
Haywood	58	250	14.1	6.5	49	3 321	726.3	130.2	151	2 038	65.9	17.5
Henderson	120	429	28.8	11.6	132	8 361	1 745.8	260.1	167	3 146	97.2	28.6
Hertford	16	74	6.0	2.2	30	1 695	459.2	37.2	39	632	16.8	4.6
Hoke	13	30	1.9	0.5	11	3 151	414.8	72.8	19	189	5.4	1.3
Hyde	5	13	0.7	0.2	NA	NA	NA	NA	33	158	10.2	2.4
Iredell	176	872	88.0	26.3	263	16 978	3 172.6	476.5	195	3 470	117.5	31.9
Jackson	49	194	14.6	4.7	36	699	76.3	15.9	102	942	32.9	8.6
Johnston	133	506	33.9	13.2	114	6 588	1 622.3	192.1	151	2 548	90.9	23.7
Jones	4	7	0.4	0.1	NA	NA	NA	NA	6	41	1.3	0.3
Lee	63	271	17.5	6.5	108	12 130	2 167.9	319.4	83	1 390	40.5	11.4
Lenoir	65	424	28.5	13.9	82	7 120	1 596.1	201.4	95	1 678	51.5	14.6
Lincoln	69	236	14.0	5.9	112	8 047	990.9	196.4	73	962	26.8	7.1
McDowell	28	126	7.0	3.0	63	6 084	866.3	140.9	64	861	26.7	7.0
Macon	38	142	7.2	3.2	34	1 358	174.7	32.5	92	943	30.0	8.2
Madison	11	23	0.8	0.3	NA	NA	NA	NA	24	230	6.1	1.9
Martin	21	73	4.5	2.0	22	1 902	307.9	40.6	43	659	17.5	4.8
Mecklenburg	2 315	27 365	2 902.6	1 123.7	1 001	42 494	8 831.4	1 429.8	1 553	33 351	1 194.2	330.2
Mitchell	10	38	1.9	0.8	32	1 868	151.4	37.1	25	324	8.9	2.6
Montgomery	14	60	2.7	0.9	78	5 292	666.7	112.1	28	D	D	D
Moore	130	562	42.8	16.8	105	5 943	903.7	129.8	154	3 202	133.0	34.6
Nash	113	688	60.8	22.2	104	9 879	1 721.8	267.8	168	3 481	111.6	30.2
New Hanover	497	3 123	251.6	103.9	203	8 378	2 698.2	338.8	455	8 834	281.4	76.7
Northampton	18	42	2.4	0.6	13	749	233.0	20.5	12	D	D	D
Onslow	137	725	34.9	11.9	37	1 829	346.4	37.7	249	4 420	127.9	34.5
Orange	349	1 746	149.0	63.4	78	1 209	142.1	34.0	283	4 443	154.1	44.3
Pamlico	12	28	1.9	0.4	NA	NA	NA	NA	18	293	13.6	4.4
Pasquotank	52	231	15.8	5.1	31	884	148.6	18.5	74	1 183	31.7	9.3
Pender	36	65	4.7	1.3	39	1 123	135.8	24.3	48	499	15.2	4.5
Perquimans	8	28	1.6	0.5	NA	NA	NA	NA	11	D	D	D
Person	34	125	8.3	2.8	39	5 138	1 084.8	135.5	45	716	20.8	5.4
Pitt	219	1 303	88.0	35.3	119	9 305	2 741.9	280.8	237	5 342	153.5	41.8
Polk	28	65	4.4	1.4	25	904	150.9	19.9	36	431	10.9	3.3
Randolph	127	464	42.9	12.9	411	24 954	3 612.7	559.8	150	2 433	75.9	21.0
Richmond	47	186	11.1	3.8	58	4 814	719.7	114.5	69	1 140	28.6	7.1
Robeson	93	534	29.0	7.9	96	11 890	2 407.9	264.0	171	2 685	85.3	22.4
Rockingham	79	327	16.4	5.6	124	13 958	3 214.4	387.0	124	1 913	60.2	16.5
Rowan	120	451	45.0	15.0	201	14 324	3 677.9	413.8	158	2 891	82.4	22.4
Rutherford	52	177	12.7	3.3	97	11 480	1 514.2	278.6	93	1 280	37.4	10.2
Sampson	48	162	9.8	3.6	61	4 202	768.5	102.4	66	903	26.6	7.3
Scotland	27	86	6.7	2.9	59	8 534	1 533.3	234.0	52	1 134	28.9	7.0
Stanly	50	187	11.3	4.0	124	8 086	1 167.5	210.3	92	1 338	34.1	9.1
Stokes	29	72	4.3	1.3	33	1 218	167.7	37.0	39	D	D	D
Surry	101	371	23.5	7.4	149	14 915	1 697.3	300.1	149	1 899	56.6	15.4

1. Firms subject to federal tax.

STATE County	Health care and social assistance,[1] 1997				Other services,[1] 1997				Federal funds and grants, 2002–2003 Expenditures (mil dol)			
										Direct payments for individuals[2]		
	Number of establishments	Number of employees	Receipts (mil dol)	Annual payroll (mil dol)	Number of establishments	Number of employees	Receipts (mil dol)	Annual payroll (mil dol)	Total	Social Security and government retirement	Medicare	Food stamps and Supplemental Security Income
	159	160	161	162	163	164	165	166	167	168	169	170
NORTH CAROLINA—Cont'd												
Chowan	29	419	17.5	8.5	17	68	4.2	1.0	100.2	44.4	14.4	4.8
Clay	7	125	5.0	2.0	10	22	1.0	0.3	62.1	31.0	9.7	1.8
Cleveland	158	1 782	102.2	51.5	133	466	30.8	8.6	485.5	229.0	81.8	20.0
Columbus	89	1 544	62.7	32.4	77	310	18.8	4.7	392.4	141.6	72.8	24.2
Craven	158	1 872	128.5	55.6	124	679	35.1	10.6	1 103.8	308.8	74.4	18.1
Cumberland	407	6 135	366.5	159.9	402	2 631	145.7	45.1	4 175.0	849.2	143.0	73.0
Currituck	16	67	3.5	1.0	20	56	4.3	1.0	91.4	56.9	13.5	2.6
Dare	33	474	20.9	8.9	46	184	10.9	3.3	158.3	92.5	20.7	2.2
Davidson	136	1 834	87.1	41.6	147	603	38.3	10.6	574.2	273.8	107.1	18.4
Davie	33	521	21.9	8.7	27	102	4.9	1.5	148.0	81.9	28.0	2.9
Duplin	69	815	29.0	11.9	63	273	16.5	4.5	275.6	107.3	44.9	12.6
Durham	387	5 893	338.6	159.6	333	2 215	121.0	43.2	2 198.7	397.9	161.4	39.5
Edgecombe	55	1 370	75.8	32.7	75	340	16.9	4.8	364.7	86.1	73.5	25.1
Forsyth	538	7 866	624.0	257.2	511	3 492	188.9	65.2	1 577.6	683.7	254.8	50.1
Franklin	44	1 217	46.3	18.9	37	132	8.4	2.2	207.4	84.9	38.2	10.7
Gaston	268	3 601	222.2	106.3	293	1 736	108.7	31.1	810.9	413.5	172.8	34.2
Gates	4	D	D	D	8	44	2.8	0.6	67.2	28.1	10.1	2.4
Graham	3	106	4.1	1.8	11	25	1.7	0.4	48.3	21.9	8.2	1.9
Granville	53	782	26.6	11.7	39	138	9.2	2.6	376.7	93.3	37.0	8.7
Greene	15	271	10.0	4.7	10	37	3.3	0.9	88.5	30.6	14.7	5.1
Guilford	816	11 217	822.5	392.9	768	5 117	346.8	101.1	2 273.3	882.8	314.0	65.8
Halifax	73	1 286	57.4	27.3	93	442	23.0	6.7	448.8	149.9	65.6	32.4
Harnett	95	908	41.9	17.2	88	370	18.5	4.8	434.4	160.0	67.5	18.7
Haywood	97	1 131	55.1	24.3	85	391	16.8	5.4	354.1	170.4	53.7	11.3
Henderson	158	1 545	103.1	44.9	122	489	30.9	9.0	517.7	309.1	101.8	10.9
Hertford	52	569	21.7	9.4	48	225	12.4	3.0	159.5	54.8	22.1	7.8
Hoke	23	302	10.8	4.6	17	51	2.9	0.7	121.1	53.7	15.6	7.9
Hyde	4	18	1.0	0.2	3	15	0.8	0.2	44.6	12.6	6.3	2.1
Iredell	254	3 584	223.7	87.6	169	939	54.8	16.6	497.1	262.3	110.5	13.5
Jackson	55	560	41.8	19.2	48	189	10.6	2.5	155.6	72.9	23.8	5.9
Johnston	126	1 766	77.5	34.3	138	513	33.4	9.1	503.8	211.9	94.8	21.9
Jones	12	222	13.8	6.3	4	8	0.4	0.1	71.7	30.0	12.0	3.0
Lee	95	1 679	97.1	48.2	83	358	21.0	6.0	261.9	134.4	47.8	8.7
Lenoir	138	1 891	100.5	43.4	88	613	28.6	8.8	415.5	156.7	82.4	20.4
Lincoln	80	793	42.8	21.7	80	332	17.0	5.0	230.9	130.6	44.7	8.2
McDowell	47	615	27.5	13.0	35	148	8.1	2.3	192.4	101.9	30.9	7.8
Macon	52	509	27.1	12.5	61	218	12.7	3.5	192.9	103.3	34.0	4.9
Madison	19	253	12.2	5.6	14	39	3.4	0.9	141.2	45.6	18.6	5.0
Martin	35	435	17.9	8.0	28	99	4.4	1.3	192.9	66.9	27.4	11.5
Mecklenburg	1 223	17 239	1 346.8	597.4	1 297	10 102	675.5	215.0	3 095.7	1 106.2	377.5	99.0
Mitchell	22	216	10.5	4.5	19	82	6.2	1.5	105.5	42.9	16.3	3.4
Montgomery	31	333	11.9	5.6	33	91	3.9	1.1	143.6	56.8	24.4	6.4
Moore	136	2 037	147.2	78.6	98	393	27.4	7.7	465.5	289.6	80.4	10.6
Nash	150	3 089	204.2	82.6	136	907	57.7	16.0	466.6	228.9	58.2	17.2
New Hanover	402	5 653	372.8	157.1	331	1 889	116.3	35.2	946.4	417.6	129.8	34.3
Northampton	16	243	9.9	4.6	20	45	2.6	0.5	198.4	61.9	23.6	11.3
Onslow	188	2 489	127.1	57.5	195	914	45.5	13.4	2 079.2	366.3	55.7	22.2
Orange	217	2 446	122.8	60.3	144	738	40.4	13.0	831.2	191.0	71.1	9.5
Pamlico	15	183	7.4	3.1	15	54	3.9	1.0	79.3	43.8	10.4	3.7
Pasquotank	77	803	49.5	24.4	59	277	15.0	4.3	276.3	99.3	33.9	10.5
Pender	35	432	21.8	8.4	41	147	8.9	2.4	199.7	105.0	32.3	8.4
Perquimans	11	169	5.7	2.5	11	44	1.6	0.4	87.1	42.1	11.4	3.5
Person	42	344	16.4	7.7	53	147	10.2	2.2	164.6	71.4	30.4	5.6
Pitt	205	3 334	216.7	115.5	158	875	49.1	13.7	635.3	237.1	94.9	35.6
Polk	30	401	15.8	6.8	17	47	3.7	1.0	102.0	65.0	18.5	1.6
Randolph	144	1 747	87.5	39.0	188	1 064	70.9	15.7	432.4	231.4	89.2	11.6
Richmond	80	1 051	55.8	22.1	66	279	16.9	4.5	280.1	127.6	50.3	15.6
Robeson	154	2 076	95.9	47.2	120	437	27.6	7.2	709.4	244.1	111.9	51.8
Rockingham	141	1 697	84.6	36.4	126	480	26.9	8.0	478.4	218.4	97.0	18.6
Rowan	186	2 571	128.8	58.8	150	645	38.9	12.3	630.0	292.0	106.8	19.9
Rutherford	93	1 060	47.1	22.6	81	269	16.1	4.2	310.4	156.2	51.1	12.2
Sampson	66	758	34.7	17.2	70	332	22.7	6.2	314.9	120.2	51.8	12.8
Scotland	70	715	42.3	20.2	47	189	10.5	2.9	212.2	78.0	29.0	14.4
Stanly	98	1 115	44.2	21.9	81	410	34.5	11.9	260.8	133.5	51.6	7.7
Stokes	30	488	21.2	8.8	38	157	9.6	3.0	155.4	84.6	26.5	5.3
Surry	108	1 278	71.4	34.7	93	407	25.2	6.5	354.2	171.3	75.2	12.6

1. Firms subject to federal tax.   2. State totals may include programs not allocated by county.

Table B. States and Counties — Federal Funds and Local Government Finances

STATE County	Federal funds and grants, 2002–2003 (cont'd) Expenditures (mil dol) (cont'd)							Local government finances, 2002 General revenue				
	Salaries and wages	Procurement contract awards		Grants[1]						Taxes	Per capita[2] (dollars)	
		Defense	Other	Medicaid and other health-related	Nutrition and family welfare	Education	Other	Total (mil dol)	Intergovern- mental (mil dol)	Total (mil dol)	Total	Property
	171	172	173	174	175	176	177	178	179	180	181	182
NORTH CAROLINA—Cont'd												
Chowan	2.9	0.0	0.5	13.9	5.1	1.1	4.6	35.1	19.7	9.2	636	465
Clay	1.2	0.1	0.4	11.2	0.7	0.6	5.3	19.2	12.8	5.0	542	359
Cleveland	11.8	11.5	3.5	75.4	13.8	8.1	21.3	418.8	129.6	63.0	643	509
Columbus	8.5	0.4	3.4	92.5	12.2	5.8	10.6	152.1	103.5	29.9	543	418
Craven	470.1	109.0	6.0	70.9	9.9	8.8	14.3	377.1	122.6	53.5	582	415
Cumberland	2 163.2	555.1	42.6	160.4	51.3	31.8	57.4	1 036.6	387.6	210.0	692	533
Currituck	2.9	1.8	2.7	6.8	1.3	1.2	0.4	62.5	25.0	30.5	1 553	1 075
Dare	17.5	10.2	5.5	5.1	1.3	0.9	1.5	127.4	30.6	70.2	2 187	1 491
Davidson	11.8	12.3	63.2	49.6	10.0	9.9	11.7	297.5	169.1	90.4	598	452
Davie	3.9	4.5	1.1	16.2	1.8	2.2	4.4	71.9	35.0	23.7	645	504
Duplin	9.5	0.0	3.6	60.1	9.4	9.2	7.2	131.3	85.1	29.4	579	449
Durham	293.8	81.1	312.9	640.5	24.9	32.7	185.1	684.9	274.4	272.9	1 165	943
Edgecombe	32.6	0.2	8.1	72.4	14.9	6.2	15.2	156.7	103.1	32.6	593	474
Forsyth	77.4	24.7	39.7	286.0	33.9	21.8	74.2	793.0	370.9	296.9	943	751
Franklin	5.4	0.6	2.4	46.3	5.1	3.3	6.5	102.2	51.5	32.4	642	494
Gaston	23.7	1.5	5.9	91.4	23.5	13.1	21.9	489.6	258.4	148.7	769	627
Gates	1.5	0.0	0.4	12.1	1.8	0.8	1.0	22.0	14.8	5.3	498	372
Graham	2.2	0.0	1.1	10.2	1.1	1.2	0.4	21.5	13.4	4.4	542	380
Granville	64.3	0.1	111.6	37.9	5.3	3.8	11.5	110.9	47.4	26.1	513	370
Greene	2.2	0.0	0.5	17.2	5.6	1.9	4.2	43.6	29.8	9.1	470	350
Guilford	250.4	183.3	109.1	178.4	44.2	39.1	157.0	1 200.6	504.5	441.9	1 026	832
Halifax	7.7	0.2	2.6	106.1	18.6	14.4	10.5	166.6	105.6	36.8	651	503
Harnett	20.9	52.0	9.1	68.7	11.5	5.7	6.4	192.0	110.9	48.1	496	355
Haywood	11.0	32.5	1.8	43.1	6.3	3.0	17.7	153.8	75.6	40.6	741	555
Henderson	12.9	10.4	3.4	37.2	7.8	4.8	12.2	296.1	94.7	65.9	713	524
Hertford	4.9	0.0	1.5	36.3	5.6	2.9	1.8	83.2	50.1	15.5	701	533
Hoke	3.6	0.3	2.6	23.6	5.8	2.7	1.9	59.9	39.5	13.4	372	284
Hyde	2.1	0.1	1.2	9.6	1.2	0.5	0.8	22.2	13.4	5.6	979	726
Iredell	15.9	1.2	4.0	47.9	9.1	5.6	17.7	270.9	136.8	95.4	733	545
Jackson	3.6	0.0	0.9	27.3	2.7	6.2	4.7	72.7	40.1	25.5	757	526
Johnston	13.7	0.4	3.1	101.5	11.5	5.9	20.9	361.4	158.2	92.2	692	510
Jones	1.3	0.1	0.3	14.2	2.3	1.4	1.5	30.1	20.8	5.2	502	386
Lee	9.5	0.9	2.2	35.7	5.2	3.6	5.7	138.3	74.0	40.6	819	662
Lenoir	20.1	2.5	5.7	77.6	10.8	7.4	16.7	218.2	121.5	41.6	704	546
Lincoln	7.5	0.0	2.3	20.0	4.3	2.9	8.3	137.6	68.6	45.3	680	508
McDowell	5.0	0.2	1.4	29.9	5.0	5.0	3.2	81.4	50.6	21.2	494	334
Macon	10.6	2.2	2.8	23.2	5.9	1.7	4.1	66.8	29.2	27.4	891	666
Madison	2.9	0.7	7.7	34.5	2.6	2.3	17.2	48.1	30.1	9.9	497	380
Martin	5.0	0.0	0.8	35.4	9.1	2.0	6.4	99.9	48.6	18.6	741	582
Mecklenburg	347.5	51.2	537.2	232.8	61.9	48.5	175.0	3 753.1	894.1	1 089.0	1 476	1 135
Mitchell	2.8	0.2	0.5	24.4	4.6	6.0	2.5	42.6	28.0	9.2	583	404
Montgomery	3.2	18.3	1.4	22.5	3.3	1.8	3.0	67.0	40.8	15.3	559	430
Moore	10.7	0.2	2.5	42.0	5.7	5.7	10.1	178.0	91.6	58.3	746	576
Nash	5.6	6.6	2.1	74.3	16.4	7.2	33.6	438.1	187.0	65.2	730	572
New Hanover	57.5	19.8	51.4	113.2	18.2	12.3	72.1	935.4	203.5	209.8	1 266	998
Northampton	2.8	0.0	0.7	45.1	12.9	2.0	7.0	58.3	36.7	13.6	624	514
Onslow	1 269.5	257.1	8.5	48.0	12.8	9.7	17.1	370.2	164.1	72.8	488	341
Orange	24.0	2.4	40.4	342.6	12.6	24.1	100.7	332.2	144.4	145.7	1 210	1 009
Pamlico	2.5	0.0	1.7	10.8	1.6	0.9	1.7	35.8	23.0	8.6	671	525
Pasquotank	50.7	7.4	8.4	22.1	7.0	7.2	17.0	204.9	60.0	24.0	676	493
Pender	5.3	0.9	2.4	29.9	6.2	3.2	3.3	97.8	59.9	29.8	698	535
Perquimans	1.8	3.2	0.4	12.2	2.3	1.4	1.1	29.8	17.0	6.7	584	457
Person	4.0	0.5	0.8	35.2	5.1	3.2	2.7	99.0	48.6	29.6	809	643
Pitt	24.8	16.4	6.3	123.4	19.0	15.0	21.8	360.0	202.5	87.5	638	468
Polk	2.8	0.0	0.7	9.5	1.5	1.1	0.6	34.7	17.0	13.7	725	580
Randolph	13.8	1.8	5.8	41.1	8.5	7.0	15.2	258.0	141.9	78.8	587	447
Richmond	7.2	0.0	1.3	50.0	7.0	4.5	11.4	127.3	69.7	25.9	553	407
Robeson	15.7	1.2	5.6	176.6	31.9	15.2	24.1	292.1	188.9	63.0	503	361
Rockingham	10.9	12.1	9.3	75.9	10.6	7.0	14.1	221.6	118.3	61.9	667	534
Rowan	76.8	0.5	16.0	45.2	15.3	9.7	34.0	276.2	149.4	85.6	642	504
Rutherford	7.7	4.2	1.9	54.9	8.2	5.7	4.4	153.3	81.0	36.7	579	421
Sampson	8.6	0.0	3.6	69.6	10.4	5.4	10.2	143.7	94.7	31.5	515	380
Scotland	3.6	0.2	0.9	48.8	18.1	6.4	7.5	96.0	58.4	26.6	737	576
Stanly	14.0	2.8	1.7	24.3	3.9	4.3	10.0	135.4	74.1	40.2	686	536
Stokes	4.6	0.1	5.0	21.0	2.6	3.7	1.5	79.8	45.4	24.6	548	407
Surry	9.9	0.0	2.2	59.6	4.8	5.1	8.5	180.2	97.9	47.6	660	483

1. State totals may include programs not allocated by county.   2. Based on the resident population estimated as of July 1 of the year shown.

Table B. States and Counties — Local Government Finances, Government Employment, and Elections

STATE County	Direct general expenditure — Total (mil dol)	Per capita¹ (dollars)	Percent of total for — Education	Health and hospitals	Police protection	Public welfare	Highways	Debt outstanding — Total (mil dol)	Per capita¹ (dollars)	Federal civilian	Federal military	State and local	Democratic	Republican	All other
	183	184	185	186	187	188	189	190	191	192	193	194	195	196	197
NORTH CAROLINA—Cont'd															
Chowan	40.8	2 808	48.2	5.6	3.7	9.4	1.2	21.4	1 470	51	25	890	44.7	55.1	0.2
Clay	17.2	1 874	57.4	10.7	3.6	3.6	0.4	2.4	266	24	16	431	33.5	65.9	0.5
Cleveland	339.4	3 465	39.1	34.9	3.3	6.2	0.7	168.9	1 725	198	169	5 394	38.3	61.4	0.3
Columbus	152.9	2 783	55.0	4.6	3.0	7.9	0.8	90.8	1 653	154	95	3 479	48.7	51.0	0.3
Craven	390.4	4 247	30.4	39.6	3.1	4.5	1.0	142.0	1 545	5 677	9 316	7 484	39.1	60.6	0.3
Cumberland	1 045.1	3 445	38.1	34.0	4.8	5.5	1.2	657.8	2 168	9 903	47 815	20 916	47.9	51.9	0.3
Currituck	52.5	2 674	60.8	2.8	4.6	4.9	0.0	17.2	877	49	34	985	32.5	67.0	0.6
Dare	130.8	4 073	32.6	7.8	7.2	3.7	1.6	65.3	2 033	236	188	2 397	39.5	60.1	0.4
Davidson	290.2	1 919	58.3	6.8	5.5	7.4	1.1	79.9	528	182	261	6 390	28.8	70.9	0.3
Davie	69.4	1 891	54.3	7.1	3.8	5.9	1.3	17.7	482	61	63	1 441	25.4	74.2	0.4
Duplin	124.7	2 454	52.5	3.0	4.7	8.9	1.1	49.0	964	158	105	3 352	41.6	58.1	0.3
Durham	675.7	2 885	38.0	6.8	6.7	9.1	2.1	614.1	2 622	4 596	489	12 550	67.9	31.7	0.3
Edgecombe	147.0	2 673	44.6	6.2	3.7	12.0	0.6	23.9	435	470	97	4 439	60.9	39.0	0.2
Forsyth	860.8	2 733	42.0	6.3	6.2	6.2	2.9	666.7	2 117	1 137	551	16 846	45.3	54.3	0.3
Franklin	97.1	1 924	54.1	6.4	3.9	8.7	0.7	55.9	1 108	79	87	2 234	44.4	55.2	0.3
Gaston	508.7	2 629	41.0	14.8	5.8	6.4	1.8	306.4	1 584	386	335	9 047	30.5	69.2	0.3
Gates	25.0	2 354	65.8	0.2	2.3	6.6	0.0	47.9	4 505	33	18	630	52.3	47.5	0.2
Graham	20.2	2 514	52.9	14.4	2.1	7.2	0.6	4.4	552	67	14	450	31.4	66.5	2.1
Granville	115.3	2 263	49.2	21.6	4.0	5.8	1.0	48.1	944	1 050	88	6 442	48.6	51.2	0.2
Greene	38.7	1 991	56.5	2.7	3.9	9.4	0.4	6.0	309	49	33	1 383	50.1	49.5	0.4
Guilford	1 281.3	2 973	45.0	6.0	6.5	6.5	2.3	848.8	1 970	3 901	822	26 222	41.1	58.8	0.1
Halifax	165.3	2 920	51.4	9.0	3.6	9.7	1.5	89.1	1 575	135	99	5 023	58.5	41.3	0.1
Harnett	211.7	2 181	51.7	9.1	4.0	7.3	1.0	122.7	1 264	123	173	4 663	35.3	64.5	0.2
Haywood	155.7	2 840	44.9	20.3	3.9	6.0	2.0	112.4	2 051	144	94	3 675	43.3	56.3	0.4
Henderson	299.0	3 232	30.7	45.2	3.4	5.2	0.8	92.3	997	226	159	5 056	34.6	65.0	0.4
Hertford	81.5	3 698	44.5	6.2	3.0	21.7	0.9	89.9	4 078	82	38	1 777	63.1	36.4	0.5
Hoke	62.0	1 720	63.3	8.8	4.7	4.3	1.0	16.9	470	51	62	2 158	52.1	47.6	0.3
Hyde	19.6	3 433	45.7	10.6	2.7	7.0	0.0	3.8	664	43	11	776	45.8	53.8	0.4
Iredell	295.3	2 269	57.6	2.8	6.1	6.5	1.4	122.8	943	272	224	7 225	31.8	68.0	0.3
Jackson	78.4	2 323	55.6	4.3	2.7	5.7	0.5	24.2	718	66	58	5 524	47.7	51.8	0.5
Johnston	394.7	2 964	52.0	17.1	3.3	5.8	1.0	238.9	1 794	214	229	6 642	31.4	68.4	0.2
Jones	25.7	2 509	52.0	3.4	2.4	10.8	0.5	1.1	108	29	18	521	41.6	58.1	0.3
Lee	138.5	2 797	58.7	2.0	5.5	6.3	1.5	70.3	1 420	165	85	2 945	38.9	60.8	0.3
Lenoir	220.3	3 729	40.5	16.2	3.5	4.9	1.2	55.1	933	324	102	6 373	42.7	57.1	0.1
Lincoln	132.7	1 992	56.3	4.4	4.4	9.1	0.4	130.5	1 960	109	115	3 207	31.8	67.9	0.3
McDowell	80.1	1 867	64.0	1.7	4.3	8.5	1.5	27.9	651	110	74	2 519	33.3	66.3	0.4
Macon	67.4	2 192	50.3	6.4	4.8	5.3	1.5	28.3	920	226	53	1 384	36.6	63.0	0.4
Madison	44.4	2 221	48.2	3.4	3.0	9.9	1.0	6.7	337	71	34	908	44.7	54.7	0.6
Martin	90.9	3 626	44.9	6.9	3.7	7.4	0.7	368.1	14 686	83	43	1 745	48.7	51.1	0.1
Mecklenburg	3 704.4	5 020	27.4	33.6	4.5	5.0	2.8	4 197.1	5 687	4 947	1 385	50 483	51.8	47.9	0.3
Mitchell	43.8	2 767	64.1	1.3	2.4	8.2	1.0	4.5	285	59	27	1 347	22.1	77.6	0.3
Montgomery	65.8	2 411	59.3	3.3	5.0	7.4	1.6	36.3	1 331	85	47	1 701	42.8	57.0	0.2
Moore	180.6	2 310	55.1	3.6	5.3	6.6	2.0	77.3	988	162	134	4 279	35.2	64.5	0.2
Nash	426.1	4 772	35.8	33.3	3.3	3.7	1.4	49.0	548	80	154	6 108	42.5	57.3	0.2
New Hanover	984.1	5 939	23.4	44.6	5.4	3.7	0.7	705.0	4 254	887	485	15 480	43.8	55.9	0.4
Northampton	58.1	2 665	46.5	5.3	2.9	11.3	1.2	19.4	890	58	38	1 459	63.7	36.2	0.1
Onslow	380.3	2 552	40.5	30.6	3.7	5.5	0.6	105.9	711	5 357	39 788	7 098	30.1	69.6	0.3
Orange	345.9	2 872	49.5	8.4	5.7	4.4	1.2	241.6	2 005	320	264	29 656	67.0	32.5	0.5
Pamlico	35.3	2 739	53.2	3.4	2.4	8.7	1.3	11.6	902	32	46	881	38.7	60.9	0.3
Pasquotank	181.1	5 110	29.6	45.7	2.7	4.2	0.6	63.3	1 785	623	646	4 926	51.1	48.5	0.4
Pender	100.4	2 350	51.9	4.0	3.5	7.1	0.5	39.7	930	92	74	2 340	41.0	58.7	0.3
Perquimans	30.4	2 647	48.4	1.5	3.6	7.3	0.9	8.3	726	30	20	688	39.8	59.8	0.4
Person	94.8	2 591	53.2	4.4	4.0	7.7	1.3	134.0	3 659	63	63	2 168	40.7	59.0	0.3
Pitt	396.1	2 886	44.1	6.3	5.4	6.5	2.5	226.2	1 649	380	255	18 197	46.4	53.4	0.2
Polk	32.5	1 726	55.8	2.1	6.0	8.9	1.3	8.5	452	48	32	773	41.6	57.3	1.0
Randolph	272.4	2 030	57.9	6.4	4.6	6.0	1.2	136.8	1 019	212	231	6 041	25.2	74.5	0.3
Richmond	115.1	2 457	58.0	2.9	4.5	8.5	1.3	21.0	448	123	81	3 096	51.9	47.9	0.2
Robeson	298.4	2 380	58.0	4.3	4.6	9.7	1.0	87.8	700	274	219	8 151	52.5	47.3	0.3
Rockingham	221.3	2 385	53.6	6.6	5.7	7.4	1.9	95.6	1 030	176	160	4 492	38.4	61.3	0.2
Rowan	270.5	2 028	58.0	2.4	5.2	7.6	1.7	138.7	1 040	1 597	232	6 024	32.2	67.4	0.4
Rutherford	156.9	2 479	53.9	12.1	4.5	7.1	1.2	60.6	958	120	109	3 481	33.2	66.3	0.5
Sampson	145.4	2 374	57.3	9.2	3.7	7.7	0.8	92.5	1 510	136	105	3 855	43.1	56.8	0.2
Scotland	98.1	2 718	55.4	3.4	4.6	10.0	1.5	34.7	961	55	62	2 077	55.3	44.5	0.1
Stanly	150.1	2 564	62.9	3.1	4.4	6.0	1.7	56.3	961	158	102	3 211	29.8	69.9	0.3
Stokes	77.7	1 727	61.8	5.2	3.7	7.8	0.3	30.8	685	82	78	1 801	29.8	70.0	0.3
Surry	188.8	2 615	52.7	15.3	3.9	5.9	1.0	94.7	1 311	168	124	4 637	32.0	67.6	0.4

1. Based on the resident population estimated as of July 1 of the year shown.

Table B. States and Counties — Land Area and Population

STATE/County code	CBSA code[1]	County Type[2]	STATE County	Land area[3] (sq km) 2000	Total persons	Rank	Per square kilometer	White	Black	Am. Indian, Alaska Native	Asian and Pacific Islander	Percent Hispanic or Latino[4]	Under 5 years	5 to 17 years	18 to 24 years	25 to 34 years	35 to 44 years	45 to 54 years
					1	2	3	4	5	6	7	8	9	10	11	12	13	14	15

Columns below correspond to: Land area (1 not shown in numbering), Total persons (1), Rank (2), Per square kilometer (3), White (4), Black (5), Am. Indian (6), Asian (7), Pct Hispanic (8), Under 5 (9), 5–17 (10), 18–24 (11), 25–34 (12), 35–44 (13), 45–54 (14). The printed column numbers 1–15 count Land area as 1.

NORTH CAROLINA—Cont'd

STATE/County code	CBSA code	Type	County	Land area	Total persons	Rank	Per sq km	White	Black	Am. Ind.	Asian/PI	Pct Hisp.	Under 5	5–17	18–24	25–34	35–44	45–54
37 173	...	8	Swain	1 368	13 126	2 229	9.6	68.1	1.7	30.3	0.2	1.7	6.6	17.4	8.9	11.6	13.9	13.8
37 175	14820	6	Transylvania	980	29 406	1 419	30.0	94.0	4.4	0.8	0.6	1.1	4.7	15.2	8.9	9.8	12.6	13.4
37 177	...	9	Tyrrell	1 010	4 156	2 900	4.1	52.5	41.3	0.2	0.9	5.1	5.4	16.0	10.0	12.7	17.1	14.2
37 179	16740	1	Union	1 651	145 986	394	88.4	79.3	12.0	0.6	1.0	7.8	7.9	20.4	8.6	13.4	14.2	13.8
37 181	25780	4	Vance	657	43 736	1 050	66.6	44.8	49.9	0.3	0.5	4.7	7.9	18.2	9.7	17.1	17.4	13.4
37 183	39580	2	Wake	2 155	695 681	76	322.8	68.9	20.5	0.7	4.7	6.6	7.6	18.2	9.7	17.1	17.4	13.4
37 185	...	8	Warren	1 110	19 812	1 814	17.8	38.7	54.4	5.2	0.2	2.0	5.3	17.5	9.1	11.1	14.3	14.3
37 187	...	7	Washington	903	13 399	2 204	14.8	46.9	50.3	0.1	0.5	2.6	6.4	18.9	8.6	10.4	13.1	15.4
37 189	14380	6	Watauga	809	42 808	1 065	52.9	95.9	1.8	0.5	0.7	1.6	3.8	11.6	24.5	12.8	11.3	12.9
37 191	24140	3	Wayne	1 431	113 104	490	79.0	59.6	33.9	0.7	1.4	5.5	7.6	19.0	9.7	13.5	15.5	13.5
37 193	35900	6	Wilkes	1 961	67 055	753	34.2	91.0	4.2	0.3	0.6	4.4	6.4	16.5	8.3	13.3	15.0	14.5
37 195	48980	4	Wilson	961	75 338	681	78.4	53.0	39.5	0.3	0.7	7.0	7.2	18.5	9.3	13.1	14.5	14.5
37 197	49180	6	Yadkin	869	37 421	1 195	43.1	88.6	3.3	0.4	0.2	7.8	6.5	17.8	7.8	13.3	15.5	13.8
37 199	...	8	Yancey	809	18 069	1 913	22.3	94.8	0.8	0.4	0.2	4.0	5.5	15.7	7.7	11.6	13.3	15.4
38 000	...	X	**NORTH DAKOTA**	178 647	633 837	X	3.5	92.2	1.0	5.4	1.0	1.3	5.8	17.3	12.0	12.2	13.7	14.7
38 001	...	9	Adams	2 559	2 505	3 020	1.0	98.6	0.5	0.4	0.2	0.3	3.1	16.4	6.7	6.8	13.0	16.1
38 003	...	6	Barnes	3 863	11 083	2 364	2.9	97.7	0.7	1.0	0.3	0.6	4.9	15.7	11.5	9.0	12.8	15.7
38 005	...	9	Benson	3 576	6 881	2 699	1.9	50.7	0.2	48.9	0.0	0.7	9.0	25.0	10.2	9.1	12.8	12.1
38 007	19860	9	Billings	2 982	850	3 117	0.3	99.5	0.0	0.7	0.2	0.4	4.8	17.1	8.8	7.9	17.4	19.9
38 009	...	9	Bottineau	4 322	6 820	2 703	1.6	97.1	0.4	1.7	0.7	0.6	3.3	16.1	10.8	7.2	13.2	16.7
38 011	...	9	Bowman	3 010	3 045	2 982	1.0	99.0	0.0	0.2	0.0	0.9	4.5	16.6	7.9	8.3	14.1	16.3
38 013	...	9	Burke	2 858	2 098	3 049	0.7	99.1	0.1	0.2	0.2	0.4	4.0	14.7	6.6	6.4	14.2	16.3
38 015	13900	3	Burleigh	4 230	71 693	708	16.9	95.3	0.4	3.7	0.7	0.7	5.8	16.8	12.6	12.6	15.0	14.9
38 017	22020	3	Cass	4 572	127 138	448	27.8	94.7	1.6	1.3	2.0	1.4	6.4	16.1	13.9	16.7	14.3	13.5
38 019	...	9	Cavalier	3 855	4 484	2 874	1.2	98.4	0.3	1.4	0.2	0.6	4.1	18.0	6.4	5.6	13.7	16.7
38 021	...	9	Dickey	2 929	5 492	2 810	1.9	97.0	0.3	0.6	0.7	1.9	5.8	16.5	11.0	9.7	11.5	13.6
38 023	...	9	Divide	3 262	2 247	3 036	0.7	98.2	0.0	0.2	1.0	0.6	3.5	14.1	7.2	5.9	11.8	15.5
38 025	...	9	Dunn	5 205	3 539	2 940	0.7	85.9	0.1	13.1	0.2	0.8	5.0	19.7	8.7	8.0	14.0	17.2
38 027	...	9	Eddy	1 632	2 598	3 014	1.6	95.7	0.2	3.5	0.2	0.7	4.5	16.9	8.1	7.2	12.7	15.7
38 029	...	8	Emmons	3 911	4 005	2 909	1.0	98.1	0.1	0.1	0.5	1.3	4.5	18.3	5.9	6.6	13.7	14.3
38 031	...	9	Foster	1 645	3 495	2 948	2.1	98.6	0.3	0.5	0.2	0.8	4.5	19.5	7.2	9.3	15.0	14.0
38 033	...	9	Golden Valley	2 595	1 828	3 071	0.7	97.6	0.2	1.3	0.1	1.4	4.8	21.6	7.9	7.1	13.0	14.7
38 035	24220	3	Grand Forks	3 724	64 736	767	17.4	92.5	2.0	2.9	2.0	2.1	6.0	16.2	17.9	15.5	13.7	12.5
38 037	...	8	Grant	4 298	2 665	3 008	0.6	97.1	0.0	2.0	0.9	0.5	4.4	15.9	7.5	7.4	12.2	16.1
38 039	...	9	Griggs	1 835	2 578	3 015	1.4	99.2	0.1	0.2	0.2	0.4	3.2	15.7	8.3	6.8	12.4	16.8
38 041	...	9	Hettinger	2 933	2 548	3 018	0.9	98.9	0.2	0.4	0.2	0.3	3.6	16.4	6.8	6.6	12.7	16.6
38 043	...	8	Kidder	3 499	2 577	3 016	0.7	99.0	0.2	0.1	0.2	0.6	4.5	15.8	7.9	6.5	14.0	16.1
38 045	...	9	La Moure	2 971	4 512	2 871	1.5	99.0	0.1	0.2	0.1	0.6	4.0	16.9	8.4	7.3	14.1	14.9
38 047	...	9	Logan	2 571	2 157	3 045	0.8	98.9	0.2	0.1	0.4	0.6	5.1	16.2	5.2	6.4	13.5	13.2
38 049	33500	9	McHenry	4 854	5 722	2 795	1.2	98.3	0.1	0.9	0.2	1.0	4.8	16.7	8.6	7.8	13.4	16.1
38 051	...	9	McIntosh	2 526	3 178	2 968	1.3	98.5	0.0	0.4	0.5	1.0	3.7	13.9	6.9	6.2	12.4	12.0
38 053	...	9	McKenzie	7 102	5 615	2 801	0.8	78.2	0.3	21.1	0.2	1.0	5.6	21.7	9.0	7.4	14.1	16.2
38 055	...	8	McLean	5 465	8 935	2 530	1.6	93.0	0.1	6.9	0.2	0.9	4.1	16.4	8.0	7.3	12.9	18.0
38 057	...	6	Mercer	2 708	8 449	2 567	3.1	96.6	0.1	2.7	0.7	0.4	4.3	20.6	8.7	6.8	17.4	18.3
38 059	13900	3	Morton	4 989	25 135	1 563	5.0	96.5	0.2	2.8	0.5	0.8	5.7	18.9	9.7	10.8	15.4	15.7
38 061	...	8	Mountrail	4 724	6 480	2 733	1.4	68.4	0.2	30.8	0.3	1.2	7.0	19.2	8.8	8.8	12.7	15.4
38 063	...	8	Nelson	2 542	3 454	2 951	1.4	98.5	0.1	0.7	0.6	0.3	3.9	15.4	6.4	6.0	12.2	15.8
38 065	...	8	Oliver	1 874	1 905	3 067	1.0	97.3	0.2	2.2	0.2	0.6	3.8	19.3	8.7	5.8	13.5	22.5
38 067	...	9	Pembina	2 898	8 201	2 583	2.8	94.0	0.2	2.4	0.4	4.1	4.8	17.0	9.1	8.5	14.1	16.8
38 069	...	7	Pierce	2 636	4 480	2 875	1.7	97.7	0.1	1.2	0.4	0.6	5.4	16.5	7.9	7.8	14.4	14.2
38 071	...	7	Ramsey	3 069	11 616	2 324	3.8	90.4	0.4	7.5	0.5	0.7	6.2	17.7	9.5	9.3	15.1	14.6
38 073	...	8	Ransom	2 235	5 838	2 785	2.6	98.3	0.3	0.7	0.3	1.0	5.0	17.6	8.2	10.5	13.7	14.5
38 075	...	9	Renville	2 266	2 473	3 023	1.1	97.7	0.4	0.8	0.6	0.7	4.0	16.1	8.7	8.2	14.7	17.1
38 077	33500	6	Richland	3 721	17 598	1 933	4.7	96.1	0.6	2.4	0.6	1.1	5.3	17.1	16.3	10.0	13.9	13.9
38 079	47420	9	Rolette	2 337	13 732	2 185	5.9	27.4	0.1	72.8	0.2	0.9	9.6	24.7	11.1	10.5	14.4	12.1
38 081	...	9	Sargent	2 224	4 225	2 893	1.9	98.1	0.2	0.8	0.2	1.2	6.0	19.6	6.5	9.5	14.7	15.8
38 083	...	9	Sheridan	2 517	1 540	3 086	0.6	99.1	0.1	0.5	0.1	0.3	3.1	15.3	6.4	4.9	11.6	16.4
38 085	...	9	Sioux	2 834	4 070	2 906	1.4	17.2	0.2	81.3	0.3	1.5	9.9	26.8	13.2	12.6	14.2	10.6
38 087	...	9	Slope	3 154	746	3 124	0.2	99.7	0.0	0.1	0.0	0.1	4.4	15.8	8.7	7.0	15.4	17.8
38 089	19860	7	Stark	3 466	22 131	1 699	6.4	97.0	0.5	1.6	0.5	1.2	5.5	17.8	12.7	10.1	14.0	14.6
38 091	...	8	Steele	1 845	2 081	3 052	1.1	99.1	0.1	0.7	0.0	0.2	3.7	19.5	8.3	6.9	14.1	16.0
38 093	27420	7	Stutsman	5 753	21 255	1 739	3.7	96.9	0.5	1.5	0.6	1.0	5.0	15.9	11.8	9.6	14.6	15.8
38 095	...	9	Towner	2 654	2 667	3 005	1.0	97.5	0.1	2.1	0.1	0.3	3.0	17.7	6.9	5.6	15.5	16.7
38 097	...	8	Traill	2 232	8 278	2 577	3.7	96.7	0.1	0.8	0.2	2.2	4.8	17.2	11.5	9.2	14.2	14.1
38 099	...	6	Walsh	3 320	11 720	2 312	3.5	92.0	0.3	1.2	0.3	6.4	5.5	17.2	8.1	9.0	14.8	16.1

1. CBSA = Core Based Statistical Area. See Appendix A for explanation. See Appendix B for list of metropolitan areas with component counties.
2. County type code from the Economic Research Service of USDA Rural-Urban Continuum Codes. See Appendix A for definition.
3. Dry land or land partially or temporarily covered by water.
4. Hispanic or Latino persons may be of any race.

Table B. States and Counties — **Population and Households**

STATE County	55 to 64 years	65 to 74 years	75 years and over	Percent female	1990	2000	1990–2000	2000–2003	Births	Deaths	Net migration	Number	Percent change, 1990–2000	Persons per household	Female family householder[1]	One person
	16	17	18	19	20	21	22	23	24	25	26	27	28	29	30	31
NORTH CAROLINA—Cont'd																
Swain	11.6	8.8	7.1	51.1	11 268	12 968	15.1	1.2	586	549	140	5 137	23.1	2.44	13.9	25.8
Transylvania	13.5	11.8	10.3	51.6	25 520	29 334	14.9	0.2	839	1 124	388	12 320	24.1	2.30	8.7	26.1
Tyrrell	9.6	7.8	7.7	44.9	3 856	4 149	7.6	0.2	152	164	28	1 537	4.5	2.42	16.6	28.2
Union	8.2	4.8	3.5	49.9	84 210	123 677	46.9	18.0	7 439	2 764	17 067	43 390	48.1	2.81	9.8	17.0
Vance	9.7	6.7	5.6	52.7	38 892	42 954	10.4	1.8	2 484	1 626	-62	16 199	14.4	2.60	20.4	24.2
Wake	7.4	4.0	3.2	50.2	426 311	627 846	47.3	10.8	34 325	10 950	44 113	242 040	46.0	2.51	9.8	25.7
Warren	11.3	9.5	8.0	51.1	17 265	19 972	15.7	-0.8	700	796	-37	7 708	22.3	2.48	17.3	26.2
Washington	11.8	8.6	7.2	52.4	13 997	13 723	-2.0	-2.4	567	629	-255	5 367	6.2	2.52	18.8	24.7
Watauga	9.1	6.3	5.1	50.2	36 952	42 695	15.5	0.3	1 117	901	-59	16 540	20.8	2.26	6.8	28.6
Wayne	9.2	6.9	5.0	50.6	104 666	113 329	8.3	-0.2	5 748	3 449	-2 510	42 612	15.5	2.55	15.4	24.5
Wilkes	11.5	7.9	6.3	50.6	59 393	65 632	10.5	2.2	2 824	2 159	818	26 650	15.8	2.43	9.4	24.5
Wilson	9.7	7.0	5.9	52.2	66 061	73 814	11.7	2.1	3 652	2 474	424	28 613	14.0	2.51	16.5	26.4
Yadkin	10.8	7.9	6.4	51.0	30 488	36 348	19.2	3.0	1 558	1 225	776	14 505	20.2	2.47	9.0	24.0
Yancey	12.1	9.6	8.8	50.7	15 419	17 774	15.3	1.7	636	603	278	7 472	22.0	2.36	7.8	25.4
NORTH DAKOTA	9.4	6.9	7.9	50.0	638 800	642 200	0.5	-1.3	24 648	19 620	-13 288	257 152	6.8	2.41	7.8	29.3
Adams	12.0	11.8	14.4	52.9	3 174	2 593	-18.3	-3.4	54	140	4	1 121	-11.5	2.24	5.5	32.6
Barnes	10.6	8.8	11.5	51.0	12 545	11 775	-6.1	-5.9	333	515	-515	4 884	-1.8	2.29	6.8	31.5
Benson	8.9	6.6	6.8	49.9	7 198	6 964	-3.3	-1.2	408	198	-292	2 328	-5.4	2.97	16.6	24.5
Billings	11.2	7.3	8.4	46.6	1 108	888	-19.9	-4.3	31	19	-47	366	-5.4	2.43	4.4	26.8
Bottineau	12.4	9.4	11.9	49.5	8 011	7 149	-10.8	-4.6	146	308	-165	2 962	-4.6	2.30	4.3	31.5
Bowman	11.4	10.1	11.9	51.1	3 596	3 242	-9.8	-6.1	94	181	-108	1 358	-4.4	2.32	4.1	31.5
Burke	14.6	12.2	12.5	49.7	3 002	2 242	-25.3	-6.4	57	71	-124	1 013	-19.1	2.21	5.3	31.6
Burleigh	8.8	6.4	6.1	51.0	60 131	69 416	15.4	3.3	2 766	1 642	1 207	27 670	22.0	2.42	8.7	28.1
Cass	7.2	4.7	4.9	49.8	102 874	123 138	19.7	3.2	5 483	2 438	1 063	51 315	27.4	2.32	7.6	31.2
Cavalier	13.2	11.8	12.3	50.5	6 064	4 831	-20.3	-7.2	117	230	-235	2 017	-15.1	2.34	3.8	30.8
Dickey	10.5	9.5	12.8	50.5	6 107	5 757	-5.7	-4.6	223	229	-260	2 283	-0.7	2.36	4.9	32.0
Divide	12.9	10.9	17.6	49.4	2 899	2 283	-21.2	-1.6	54	140	53	1 005	-15.8	2.18	4.2	33.4
Dunn	11.3	8.3	8.5	49.6	4 005	3 600	-10.1	-1.7	114	144	-26	1 378	-3.8	2.57	7.2	25.3
Eddy	10.3	11.0	14.4	51.4	2 951	2 757	-6.6	-5.8	74	163	-69	1 164	-2.5	2.30	5.0	34.2
Emmons	11.9	12.7	14.0	49.6	4 830	4 331	-10.3	-7.5	116	213	-226	1 786	-3.4	2.38	4.4	28.4
Foster	10.5	11.2	10.6	50.1	3 983	3 759	-5.6	-7.0	97	202	-158	1 540	-0.1	2.39	6.4	30.6
Golden Valley	10.2	7.8	13.8	51.0	2 108	1 924	-8.7	-5.0	60	65	-88	761	-6.2	2.38	4.9	31.5
Grand Forks	7.2	4.8	5.0	49.1	70 683	66 109	-6.5	-2.1	2 646	1 469	-2 610	25 435	0.4	2.43	8.8	28.3
Grant	13.4	11.6	13.4	49.1	3 549	2 841	-19.9	-6.2	81	157	-98	1 195	-13.0	2.30	3.8	31.8
Griggs	11.7	10.4	15.7	49.8	3 303	2 754	-16.6	-6.4	50	114	-111	1 178	-9.0	2.29	4.7	31.6
Hettinger	12.3	13.0	13.3	50.4	3 445	2 715	-21.2	-6.2	59	142	-82	1 152	-14.1	2.30	3.8	31.2
Kidder	11.4	11.6	12.9	49.5	3 332	2 753	-17.4	-6.4	74	117	-132	1 158	-7.1	2.34	4.1	29.9
La Moure	10.9	11.1	13.0	49.1	5 383	4 701	-12.7	-4.0	123	164	-142	1 942	-6.4	2.38	4.0	30.8
Logan	13.5	13.6	14.9	50.2	2 847	2 308	-18.9	-6.5	70	101	-120	963	-12.1	2.32	3.1	29.2
McHenry	11.1	10.5	11.8	49.3	6 528	5 987	-8.3	-4.4	169	202	-228	2 526	-1.0	2.35	5.6	29.8
McIntosh	11.3	15.2	20.0	52.4	4 021	3 390	-15.7	-6.3	84	205	-83	1 467	-13.0	2.19	3.5	32.0
McKenzie	11.0	7.2	8.7	49.8	6 383	5 737	-10.1	-2.1	209	154	-177	2 151	-6.5	2.64	9.3	25.8
McLean	13.0	9.5	11.4	50.5	10 457	9 311	-11.0	-4.0	220	409	-183	3 815	-3.0	2.40	5.6	26.6
Mercer	10.0	6.9	7.6	49.5	9 808	8 644	-11.9	-2.3	252	297	-145	3 346	-6.0	2.55	5.1	24.8
Morton	9.3	7.3	7.4	50.1	23 700	25 303	6.8	-0.7	897	802	-245	9 889	14.0	2.51	8.5	25.7
Mountrail	10.8	8.1	9.7	50.8	7 021	6 631	-5.6	-2.3	308	349	-105	2 560	-1.0	2.53	11.8	28.5
Nelson	13.3	11.9	16.5	50.6	4 410	3 715	-15.8	-7.0	99	216	-145	1 628	-11.1	2.18	5.2	36.3
Oliver	12.5	7.7	7.2	48.0	2 381	2 065	-13.3	-7.7	53	47	-163	791	-2.2	2.61	3.9	21.0
Pembina	10.3	9.0	11.0	49.6	9 238	8 585	-7.1	-4.5	260	340	-306	3 535	-0.6	2.38	5.3	30.5
Pierce	10.6	10.1	14.3	51.3	5 052	4 675	-7.5	-4.2	176	261	-109	1 964	-0.5	2.31	6.3	32.0
Ramsey	10.1	8.3	10.4	50.1	12 681	12 066	-4.8	-3.7	493	551	-398	4 957	-0.4	2.34	8.5	31.1
Ransom	9.6	9.3	11.8	48.8	5 921	5 890	-0.5	-0.9	167	291	83	2 350	2.9	2.39	5.1	30.7
Renville	10.7	9.9	12.1	50.1	3 160	2 610	-17.4	-5.2	61	101	-92	1 085	-10.3	2.35	5.6	28.5
Richland	8.1	6.6	8.6	47.9	18 148	17 998	-0.8	-2.2	606	496	-518	6 885	5.6	2.43	6.5	29.4
Rolette	8.0	5.3	4.4	50.4	12 772	13 674	7.1	0.4	946	427	-458	4 556	9.8	2.97	22.7	22.6
Sargent	12.0	7.5	9.6	47.9	4 549	4 366	-4.0	-3.2	180	126	-187	1 786	1.3	2.43	3.9	27.7
Sheridan	15.0	14.2	15.4	49.0	2 148	1 710	-20.4	-9.9	34	64	-136	731	-14.8	2.31	4.4	27.5
Sioux	6.8	3.5	2.2	48.3	3 761	4 044	7.5	0.6	251	110	-117	1 095	7.1	3.63	29.1	16.6
Slope	10.9	11.0	8.4	46.5	907	767	-15.4	-2.7	21	13	-27	313	-6.0	2.45	3.8	27.2
Stark	9.0	7.7	8.4	50.6	22 832	22 636	-0.9	-2.2	797	683	-624	8 932	5.3	2.44	7.9	29.1
Steele	11.7	11.1	9.5	48.6	2 420	2 258	-6.7	-7.8	41	93	-124	923	-6.9	2.45	4.4	28.3
Stutsman	9.7	8.1	9.8	50.7	22 241	21 908	-1.5	-3.0	683	769	-564	8 954	3.4	2.28	7.5	32.7
Towner	11.8	10.0	14.1	50.7	3 627	2 876	-20.7	-7.3	49	113	-146	1 218	-15.0	2.31	4.6	33.6
Traill	9.7	8.2	11.1	49.6	8 752	8 477	-3.1	-2.3	236	314	-114	3 341	0.4	2.41	5.4	29.3
Walsh	10.8	8.6	11.3	49.8	13 840	12 389	-10.5	-5.4	439	515	-602	5 029	-3.8	2.39	7.5	31.3

1. No spouse present.

STATE County	Births, average 1999–2001		Deaths, average 1999–2001				Physicians,[4] 2000		Hospitals,[4] 1998			Medicare enrollees, 2003	Serious crimes known to police,[6] 2002	
			Number		Rate					Beds			Total	
	Total	Rate[1]	Total	Infant[2]	Total[1]	Infant[3]	Number	Rate[5]	Number	Number	Rate[5]		Number	Rate[7]
	32	33	34	35	36	37	38	39	40	41	42	43	44	45
NORTH CAROLINA—Cont'd														
Swain	178	13.7	154	1	11.9	D	16	123	1	24	195	2 632	NA	NA
Transylvania	277	9.5	342	2	11.7	D	49	167	1	90	316	7 284	479	1 580
Tyrrell	46	11.1	45	0	10.7	D	1	24	0	0	0	712	106	2 471
Union	2 200	17.6	825	15	6.6	6.8	78	63	1	226	205	12 898	4 209	3 292
Vance	727	16.8	467	9	10.8	12.4	44	102	1	87	206	7 562	3 423	7 709
Wake	10 067	15.9	3 259	65	5.2	6.4	1 235	197	7	1 295	227	63 470	28 004	4 356
Warren	207	10.3	224	2	11.2	D	11	55	0	0	0	3 589	NA	NA
Washington	177	12.9	183	2	13.4	D	8	58	1	49	360	2 666	355	2 503
Watauga	345	8.1	285	3	6.7	D	96	225	2	205	500	5 351	1 371	3 107
Wayne	1 750	15.4	1 072	19	9.5	10.7	152	134	1	267	238	17 762	5 777	4 932
Wilkes	883	13.4	656	6	10.0	D	55	84	1	130	207	11 204	1 637	2 413
Wilson	1 091	14.8	765	12	10.4	11.3	98	133	1	277	406	12 196	3 979	5 415
Yadkin	500	13.8	370	3	10.2	D	15	41	1	50	143	6 414	813	2 330
Yancey	203	11.4	196	1	11.0	D	10	56	0	0	0	3 868	99	593
NORTH DAKOTA	7 648	11.9	6 002	60	9.4	7.9	1 355	211	46	4 304	674	103 220	15 258	2 406
Adams	18	7.0	42	0	16.4	D	15	578	1	45	1 658	590	15	586
Barnes	106	9.1	153	0	13.1	D	7	59	1	50	418	2 478	110	946
Benson	130	18.7	63	1	9.0	D	1	14	0	0	0	1 024	NA	NA
Billings	7	8.2	7	0	8.2	D	0	0	0	0	0	71	NA	NA
Bottineau	49	6.9	95	1	13.4	D	3	42	1	67	927	1 535	53	751
Bowman	26	8.2	49	0	15.3	D	6	185	1	36	1 085	724	NA	NA
Burke	16	7.2	22	0	9.7	D	0	0	0	0	0	589	0	0
Burleigh	851	12.2	507	6	7.3	D	257	370	2	513	767	10 252	1 901	2 774
Cass	1 665	13.5	761	11	6.2	6.8	425	345	3	667	571	14 051	4 202	3 456
Cavalier	34	7.2	70	0	14.7	D	3	62	1	28	559	1 103	68	1 426
Dickey	65	11.4	79	0	13.9	D	6	104	1	30	532	1 168	36	633
Divide	14	6.0	45	0	20.0	D	0	0	1	25	1 057	539	NA	NA
Dunn	34	9.4	40	1	11.3	D	0	0	0	0	0	547	0	0
Eddy	25	9.0	49	0	17.9	D	0	0	0	0	0	671	19	698
Emmons	32	7.3	63	0	14.7	D	1	23	1	25	580	1 084	32	748
Foster	33	8.9	63	0	16.9	D	4	106	1	70	1 841	816	NA	NA
Golden Valley	16	8.6	18	0	9.6	D	2	104	0	0	0	444	11	579
Grand Forks	836	12.7	438	5	6.6	D	188	284	2	413	618	7 148	2 873	4 570
Grant	21	7.5	45	0	16.0	D	1	35	1	50	1 684	670	18	642
Griggs	17	6.2	41	0	14.9	D	3	109	1	69	2 428	644	NA	NA
Hettinger	21	7.9	40	0	14.8	D	0	0	0	0	0	743	4	149
Kidder	26	9.4	37	0	13.6	D	0	0	0	0	0	615	19	699
La Moure	35	7.4	53	1	11.3	D	0	0	0	0	0	1 165	NA	NA
Logan	19	8.3	32	0	14.0	D	0	0	0	0	0	585	NA	NA
McHenry	54	9.1	66	0	11.0	D	2	33	0	0	0	1 451	66	1 117
McIntosh	28	8.2	65	0	19.3	D	5	147	2	94	2 731	1 146	NA	NA
McKenzie	64	11.1	57	2	10.0	D	0	0	1	26	458	796	53	936
McLean	79	8.5	126	1	13.6	D	8	86	2	84	866	2 112	91	990
Mercer	75	8.6	81	0	9.4	D	7	81	1	32	340	1 377	59	720
Morton	290	11.5	242	3	9.6	D	12	47	1	36	146	4 306	519	2 077
Mountrail	93	14.0	90	2	13.5	D	5	75	1	25	377	1 277	49	748
Nelson	28	7.5	74	0	20.1	D	3	81	1	14	377	1 063	NA	NA
Oliver	16	7.8	13	0	6.4	D	0	0	0	0	0	225	21	1 030
Pembina	82	9.6	96	1	11.2	D	2	23	1	90	1 061	1 743	55	649
Pierce	47	10.1	75	0	16.0	D	11	235	1	220	4 759	1 023	42	910
Ramsey	144	11.9	157	2	13.0	D	28	232	1	55	454	2 395	NA	NA
Ransom	56	9.6	95	0	16.3	D	4	68	1	70	1 212	1 195	12	466
Renville	17	6.5	35	0	13.3	D	2	77	0	0	0	529	NA	NA
Richland	193	10.8	171	1	9.5	D	10	56	0	0	0	2 714	433	2 436
Rolette	272	19.8	117	4	8.6	D	13	95	1	101	710	1 633	52	385
Sargent	49	11.2	40	0	9.2	D	0	0	0	0	0	801	33	765
Sheridan	9	5.5	18	0	10.9	D	1	58	0	0	0	441	NA	NA
Sioux	90	22.5	28	1	6.9	D	1	25	0	0	0	292	NA	NA
Slope	7	9.0	4	0	0.0	D	0	0	0	0	0	93	NA	NA
Stark	255	11.3	210	3	9.3	D	38	168	2	135	593	4 151	459	2 082
Steele	15	6.9	27	0	11.9	D	0	0	0	0	0	418	NA	NA
Stutsman	216	9.9	237	1	10.9	D	42	192	1	56	267	4 194	450	2 080
Towner	15	5.2	38	0	13.2	D	0	0	1	32	1 060	614	11	387
Traill	82	9.7	103	2	12.2	D	3	35	2	52	609	1 631	NA	NA
Walsh	144	11.7	151	1	12.2	D	16	129	2	49	362	2 615	394	3 221

1. Per 1,000 estimated resident population.   2. Deaths of infants under 1 year old.   3. Deaths of infants under 1 year old per 1,000 live births.   4. Data subject to copyright.   5. Per 100,000 resident population as of July 1 of the year shown.   6. Data for serious crimes have not been adjusted for underreporting; this may affect comparability between geographic areas and over time.   7. Per 100,000 population estimated by the FBI.

Table B. States and Counties — Crime, Education, Money Income, and Poverty

STATE County	Serious crimes known to police,[1] 2002 (cont'd) Rate[2] — Violent	Property	Education — School enrollment and attainment, 2000 — Enrollment[3] Total	Percent private	Attainment[4] (percent) High school graduate or less	Bachelor's degree or more	Local government expenditures,[5] 2000–2001 Total current expenditures (mil dol)	Current expenditures per student (dollars)	Money income, 1999 Per capita income[6] (dollars)	Households Median income Dollars	Percent change, 1989–1999 (constant 1999 dollars)	Percent with income of $100,000 or more	Percent below poverty level, 1999 Persons	Households	Families	Families with children
	46	47	48	49	50	51	52	53	54	55	56	57	58	59	60	61
NORTH CAROLINA—Cont'd																
Swain	NA	NA	3 071	7.1	59.6	13.9	12.4	7 117	14 647	28 608	32.5	3.8	18.3	17.2	13.3	19.9
Transylvania	96	1 484	6 292	18.1	47.5	23.7	27.8	6 825	20 767	38 587	14.1	6.9	9.5	10.2	6.6	11.5
Tyrrell	233	2 238	994	6.1	67.5	10.6	7.2	9 608	13 326	25 684	16.8	3.3	23.3	24.0	19.1	27.3
Union	205	3 088	32 693	17.8	50.6	21.3	132.9	5 737	21 978	50 638	21.7	13.7	8.1	7.9	5.8	8.0
Vance	716	6 993	10 894	7.6	66.2	10.7	51.8	6 001	15 897	31 301	8.1	5.7	20.5	19.3	16.3	22.9
Wake	394	3 962	178 475	18.0	28.4	43.9	657.1	6 486	27 004	54 988	13.0	19.6	7.8	7.4	4.9	7.2
Warren	NA	NA	4 667	12.4	64.5	11.6	22.4	6 899	14 716	28 351	24.6	4.3	19.4	20.7	15.7	21.7
Washington	508	1 995	3 423	8.2	67.5	11.6	18.4	8 040	14 994	28 865	-1.6	5.3	21.8	21.1	17.6	27.7
Watauga	140	2 966	16 832	8.1	42.2	33.2	33.1	6 771	17 258	32 611	19.9	6.1	17.9	18.8	7.2	9.9
Wayne	442	4 489	29 896	13.3	55.3	15.0	118.7	6 090	17 010	33 942	7.2	5.4	13.8	13.8	10.2	15.2
Wilkes	178	2 235	13 770	6.8	65.5	11.3	66.6	6 311	17 516	34 258	14.5	5.1	11.9	13.7	8.8	12.5
Wilson	584	4 831	18 243	13.7	62.3	15.1	81.1	6 414	17 102	33 116	2.6	6.4	18.5	18.5	13.8	20.1
Yadkin	181	2 149	7 982	10.0	64.8	10.3	36.6	6 249	18 576	36 660	8.9	5.9	10.0	11.9	7.1	10.3
Yancey	84	509	3 307	8.9	65.7	13.1	17.9	7 120	16 335	29 674	13.8	3.7	15.8	16.7	10.9	17.7
NORTH DAKOTA	78	2 328	179 667	8.9	44.0	22.0	690.0	6 342	17 769	34 604	11.0	5.7	11.9	12.5	8.3	12.0
Adams	0	586	577	3.3	52.3	16.6	2.7	6 697	18 425	29 079	4.4	5.2	10.4	12.1	8.5	10.3
Barnes	34	912	3 096	5.2	47.5	22.1	12.3	6 838	16 566	31 166	13.6	4.2	10.8	12.8	6.4	9.6
Benson	NA	NA	2 216	1.9	56.4	10.9	9.0	8 791	11 509	26 688	17.4	2.6	29.1	24.2	24.4	33.1
Billings	NA	NA	210	3.3	54.2	18.8	1.5	19 127	16 186	32 667	7.4	5.0	12.8	13.0	10.7	8.4
Bottineau	0	751	1 786	1.6	48.4	14.9	8.6	7 250	16 227	29 853	-0.3	4.1	10.7	12.2	7.5	9.7
Bowman	NA	NA	752	2.3	49.9	17.9	5.0	6 697	17 662	31 906	10.6	4.2	8.2	9.3	5.9	8.8
Burke	0	0	438	5.7	56.1	12.0	3.0	8 384	14 026	25 330	-1.6	1.6	15.4	17.2	11.7	12.9
Burleigh	80	2 693	18 617	20.7	35.8	28.7	62.7	5 787	20 436	41 309	8.1	7.5	7.8	9.1	5.3	8.8
Cass	127	3 329	37 145	8.2	32.0	31.3	118.8	6 241	20 889	38 147	5.9	8.2	10.1	10.8	5.7	8.3
Cavalier	21	1 405	1 094	8.8	51.6	13.1	5.7	6 894	15 817	31 868	11.6	3.8	11.5	11.1	7.8	11.9
Dickey	53	581	1 531	21.3	52.3	16.6	5.6	5 953	15 846	29 231	7.5	4.7	14.8	14.5	11.6	17.7
Divide	NA	NA	436	0.5	54.5	13.3	2.5	7 529	16 225	30 089	4.1	3.4	14.6	17.1	9.5	16.1
Dunn	0	0	972	4.2	54.7	16.3	5.3	9 547	14 624	30 015	12.7	4.4	17.5	17.4	13.8	19.4
Eddy	37	661	597	2.5	52.5	15.9	3.7	7 115	15 941	28 642	10.4	5.8	9.7	10.9	6.9	9.3
Emmons	23	725	923	3.9	64.1	12.3	5.1	6 523	14 604	26 119	15.1	4.2	20.1	22.0	14.7	19.6
Foster	NA	NA	982	5.0	51.9	19.8	3.6	5 052	17 928	32 019	14.8	5.0	9.3	10.7	7.6	11.1
Golden Valley	0	579	505	5.3	46.6	19.8	2.9	6 548	14 173	29 967	10.0	3.2	15.3	15.0	10.8	17.3
Grand Forks	113	4 457	23 794	4.9	35.2	27.8	63.8	6 049	17 868	35 785	5.9	5.7	12.3	13.0	8.0	11.9
Grant	36	606	629	3.2	59.7	11.2	3.1	7 941	14 616	23 165	-0.7	2.8	20.3	20.2	14.7	20.5
Griggs	NA	NA	609	2.0	53.9	15.7	4.1	7 202	16 131	29 572	13.4	4.0	10.1	11.0	7.8	6.8
Hettinger	37	112	596	2.0	57.8	14.4	4.5	7 996	15 555	29 209	10.9	4.2	14.8	14.5	12.1	19.0
Kidder	74	625	539	2.6	63.0	11.0	3.6	7 290	14 270	25 389	8.7	3.4	19.8	20.4	17.6	19.2
La Moure	NA	NA	1 074	5.7	58.5	13.9	6.9	6 859	17 059	29 707	12.2	5.1	14.7	14.4	12.3	17.0
Logan	NA	NA	483	6.6	63.7	12.9	3.1	7 086	16 947	27 986	6.9	5.7	15.1	15.4	12.6	18.7
McHenry	17	1 100	1 351	1.0	57.9	13.2	7.1	6 279	15 140	27 274	11.1	3.5	15.8	16.7	12.0	17.0
McIntosh	NA	NA	654	5.7	66.6	9.9	3.5	6 495	15 018	26 389	10.4	4.3	15.4	17.8	10.6	13.1
McKenzie	0	936	1 675	6.0	53.5	15.7	10.5	9 548	14 732	29 342	-11.4	4.3	17.2	15.7	13.7	18.9
McLean	11	979	2 082	1.9	51.8	15.1	11.6	6 295	16 220	32 337	10.1	3.2	13.5	14.6	10.4	16.3
Mercer	12	708	2 442	4.9	52.0	14.4	12.6	6 323	18 256	42 269	-1.6	5.4	7.5	10.3	5.5	5.7
Morton	112	1 965	6 330	10.9	51.7	17.0	25.2	5 396	17 202	37 028	16.4	5.8	9.6	10.9	6.8	9.3
Mountrail	31	718	1 796	4.8	51.7	15.6	9.6	6 256	13 422	27 098	4.0	2.9	19.3	19.4	14.0	20.2
Nelson	NA	NA	823	6.8	49.5	17.5	4.4	6 388	16 320	28 892	11.1	2.9	10.3	12.1	7.2	9.2
Oliver	49	981	549	9.1	55.4	12.0	2.0	6 918	16 271	36 650	18.6	3.8	14.9	13.7	11.2	16.1
Pembina	12	637	1 954	2.5	52.1	16.4	12.1	6 921	18 692	36 430	16.6	5.5	9.2	9.8	7.4	9.2
Pierce	65	845	1 028	6.4	53.3	14.7	4.5	6 035	14 055	26 524	-2.3	3.4	12.5	14.3	9.3	12.7
Ramsey	NA	NA	3 016	8.9	45.1	18.8	14.7	6 548	18 060	35 600	21.7	5.6	12.6	12.3	8.7	14.2
Ransom	NA	NA	1 311	4.3	54.4	15.8	5.9	5 268	18 219	37 672	21.8	4.0	8.8	9.6	6.3	8.0
Renville	116	349	596	4.7	48.8	16.1	4.8	6 606	16 478	30 746	1.0	2.9	11.0	11.7	8.5	11.1
Richland	56	2 380	5 726	6.4	44.2	15.2	19.0	6 438	16 339	36 098	10.8	4.5	10.4	12.9	6.1	8.6
Rolette	0	385	4 863	2.9	52.9	14.7	21.8	6 885	10 873	26 232	28.8	3.0	31.0	30.1	28.0	35.5
Sargent	0	765	988	3.6	54.0	12.7	4.6	5 233	18 689	37 213	16.2	5.3	8.2	9.6	6.0	8.0
Sheridan	NA	NA	339	1.5	63.4	9.7	1.7	8 645	13 283	24 450	6.1	2.2	21.0	20.6	16.0	23.4
Sioux	NA	NA	1 566	8.7	53.5	11.2	5.8	12 368	7 731	22 483	12.8	1.4	39.2	34.7	33.6	38.9
Slope	NA	NA	180	3.9	53.9	16.0	0.3	8 371	14 513	24 667	0.0	4.5	16.9	20.8	15.4	19.2
Stark	50	2 032	6 347	18.4	47.9	22.3	21.2	5 526	15 929	32 526	9.8	4.5	12.3	15.2	7.9	10.6
Steele	NA	NA	585	2.2	42.2	19.8	2.6	7 750	17 601	35 757	14.2	5.5	7.1	7.9	5.0	8.3
Stutsman	134	1 946	5 399	23.6	52.9	19.7	19.1	5 846	17 706	33 848	12.4	4.4	10.4	11.0	6.8	9.7
Towner	35	352	679	2.7	51.9	16.1	3.3	6 525	17 605	32 740	31.0	5.4	8.9	10.5	6.3	9.2
Traill	NA	NA	2 369	1.4	42.2	21.8	10.8	6 273	18 014	37 445	26.4	5.0	9.2	10.3	6.4	9.3
Walsh	57	3 164	2 811	4.5	55.5	13.3	15.2	7 012	16 496	33 845	14.6	3.9	10.9	11.6	7.7	11.8

1. Data for serious crimes have not been adjusted for underreporting; this may affect comparability between geographic areas and over time.   2. Per 100,000 population estimated by the FBI.   3. All persons 3 years old and over enrolled in nursery school through college.   4. Persons 25 years old and over.   5. Elementary and secondary education expenditures.   6. Based on population enumerated as of April 1, 2000.

STATE County	Personal income, 2002							Transfer payments					
	Total (mil dol)	Percent change, 2001–2002	Per capita[1]		Wages and salaries[2] (mil dol)	Proprietor's income (mil dol)	Dividends, interest, and rent (mil dol)	Total (mil dol)	Government payments to individuals				
			Dollars	Rank					Total (mil dol)	Social Security (mil dol)	Medical payments (mil dol)	Income mainte-nance (mil dol)	Unemploy-ment insurance (mil dol)
	62	63	64	65	66	67	68	69	70	71	72	73	74
NORTH CAROLINA—Cont'd													
Swain	256	6.3	19 662	2 617	174	8	43	76	73	26	32	8	3
Transylvania	776	2.1	26 342	822	336	58	246	177	170	85	60	11	8
Tyrrell	78	-3.4	18 800	2 782	30	6	14	21	20	7	9	3	1
Union	3 654	1.4	26 227	850	1 770	211	471	419	386	169	146	35	20
Vance	960	2.1	21 880	2 043	540	47	150	251	241	79	99	41	10
Wake	24 012	1.2	35 515	127	18 116	1 699	3 869	1 970	1 811	722	686	168	140
Warren	356	-0.7	17 878	2 912	119	18	50	107	102	34	45	16	3
Washington	282	-0.4	20 969	2 307	98	-1	47	83	80	29	33	12	3
Watauga	1 042	3.9	24 265	1 322	642	121	227	151	141	60	53	12	3
Wayne	2 641	2.9	23 376	1 602	1 757	79	428	530	505	176	217	65	13
Wilkes	1 620	-3.6	24 266	1 321	942	130	265	330	314	121	134	30	15
Wilson	1 814	1.8	24 205	1 342	1 492	43	298	386	369	137	155	49	14
Yadkin	863	0.7	23 134	1 683	304	42	130	168	159	68	69	11	6
Yancey	354	0.7	19 680	2 614	122	36	72	97	93	38	38	9	4
NORTH DAKOTA	17 022	3.6	26 852	X	11 285	1 812	3 319	2 717	2 572	1 056	1 002	172	60
Adams	49	-9.1	19 658	2 620	27	-2	13	15	14	6	7	1	0
Barnes	286	3.7	25 493	1 001	129	42	67	57	55	25	21	3	1
Benson	135	11.5	19 678	2 615	66	18	28	36	34	10	14	5	1
Billings	17	-13.5	19 151	2 728	9	1	6	2	2	1	0	0	0
Bottineau	193	5.6	27 960	554	64	42	46	37	35	16	14	2	1
Bowman	75	-6.8	24 332	1 297	36	6	24	15	15	7	6	1	0
Burke	54	3.2	25 478	1 004	19	9	17	12	11	6	4	1	0
Burleigh	2 079	4.0	29 305	408	1 554	176	363	287	270	110	107	16	6
Cass	3 846	4.5	30 687	292	3 202	394	670	402	373	155	128	24	10
Cavalier	122	-2.7	26 636	758	49	15	41	24	23	12	9	1	0
Dickey	155	8.8	27 864	572	58	41	31	29	28	11	13	1	0
Divide	52	-5.7	23 635	1 521	19	4	21	12	12	6	4	0	0
Dunn	65	-8.1	18 373	2 847	27	4	17	13	13	5	6	1	0
Eddy	64	8.8	24 255	1 327	23	8	15	16	16	7	7	1	0
Emmons	75	-18.8	18 418	2 839	32	2	25	21	20	9	8	1	0
Foster	91	3.5	25 523	995	52	13	21	17	16	8	6	1	0
Golden Valley	33	-3.4	18 155	2 873	16	1	11	8	8	4	3	0	0
Grand Forks	1 725	5.9	26 563	771	1 384	136	291	222	207	79	74	15	6
Grant	47	-17.0	17 562	2 945	17	-2	16	14	13	6	6	1	0
Griggs	71	3.2	27 311	645	28	14	18	15	14	7	7	1	0
Hettinger	50	-25.0	19 171	2 721	20	-2	18	15	15	7	7	1	0
Kidder	59	-5.3	22 728	1 809	18	12	15	14	14	6	6	1	0
La Moure	122	1.4	26 684	754	36	32	30	23	22	11	8	1	0
Logan	52	-10.9	23 526	1 557	14	10	16	13	12	5	6	1	0
McHenry	124	-1.5	21 652	2 105	34	14	29	31	29	13	11	2	1
McIntosh	75	-7.2	23 349	1 611	29	5	25	23	23	9	12	1	0
McKenzie	125	0.7	22 139	1 977	78	13	30	23	22	9	9	2	0
McLean	224	-3.0	24 859	1 166	109	15	54	50	48	21	20	2	1
Mercer	240	1.3	28 084	534	218	14	39	34	32	14	13	1	1
Morton	579	1.2	22 983	1 730	300	19	93	111	105	41	43	7	3
Mountrail	155	1.7	23 821	1 465	68	18	32	36	35	12	15	3	1
Nelson	90	7.3	25 913	908	27	12	27	24	23	10	12	1	0
Oliver	43	-9.3	22 145	1 970	32	-2	10	7	6	4	2	0	0
Pembina	255	4.9	30 783	287	140	51	62	38	36	18	13	1	2
Pierce	95	2.5	20 981	2 303	49	5	25	24	23	10	10	1	0
Ramsey	306	4.8	26 037	881	165	40	65	63	60	24	25	4	1
Ransom	156	5.9	26 763	743	68	28	28	29	28	11	12	1	0
Renville	63	-0.9	25 125	1 096	23	6	17	14	14	6	6	0	0
Richland	475	11.8	27 288	654	280	97	88	67	63	29	21	3	1
Rolette	261	2.1	18 982	2 757	156	20	29	86	83	15	36	19	4
Sargent	134	-0.5	31 259	264	101	29	33	17	16	8	5	1	0
Sheridan	30	-6.3	19 066	2 746	8	2	10	9	9	4	4	1	0
Sioux	57	2.8	13 970	3 091	60	-2	5	21	20	2	10	4	0
Slope	4	-75.4	5 540	3 111	3	-6	4	3	3	2	1	0	0
Stark	541	2.1	24 396	1 285	336	56	99	101	96	39	39	6	2
Steele	61	13.9	29 064	441	18	17	17	9	9	5	3	0	0
Stutsman	550	1.8	25 716	948	330	67	116	101	96	41	37	6	2
Towner	75	13.9	27 482	619	26	13	23	16	15	7	7	1	0
Traill	234	12.4	28 181	522	99	42	44	40	38	17	15	1	1
Walsh	343	6.6	28 861	462	155	78	69	61	58	27	24	3	1

1. Based on the resident population estimated as of July 1 of the year shown.   2. Includes other labor income.

Table B. States and Counties — Earnings, Social Security, and Housing

STATE County	Earnings, 2002									Social Security beneficiaries, December 2003		Supplemental Security Income recipients, December 2003	Housing units, 2003	
			Percent by selected industries											
			Goods-related[1]		Service-related and health									
	Total (mil dol)	Farm	Total	Manufacturing	Information and professional and technical services	Retail trade	Finance, insurance, and real estate	Health services	Government	Number	Rate[2]	Total	Total	Percent change, 2000–2003
	75	76	77	78	79	80	81	82	83	84	85	86	87	88
NORTH CAROLINA—Cont'd														
Swain	182	0.2	D	5.2	1.8	8.5	1.7	16.1	43.0	3 195	243	372	7 514	5.8
Transylvania	394	1.8	D	23.8	D	8.1	6.3	D	13.9	8 485	289	556	16 264	4.6
Tyrrell	35	7.6	D	D	D	10.2	D	D	41.6	855	206	160	2 085	2.6
Union	1 982	2.3	D	26.3	4.8	6.9	2.9	4.6	13.3	17 955	123	1 349	53 772	17.7
Vance	587	-0.6	D	23.9	3.5	16.0	3.6	D	19.7	9 300	213	2 327	18 705	2.8
Wake	19 815	0.0	16.4	8.4	19.1	7.3	8.6	6.6	17.1	73 150	105	8 202	293 580	13.4
Warren	138	8.9	19.0	13.7	D	6.2	2.0	D	35.9	4 205	212	1 086	10 877	3.1
Washington	97	-8.3	12.4	7.6	2.7	10.4	3.5	D	43.3	3 200	239	663	6 228	0.9
Watauga	763	2.0	12.4	4.9	5.9	10.3	6.8	16.6	26.7	6 810	159	638	24 480	5.7
Wayne	1 836	0.6	D	14.7	2.9	7.8	3.9	10.7	35.1	20 995	186	4 359	48 951	3.5
Wilkes	1 073	4.3	D	18.9	D	8.3	4.9	4.5	15.0	14 595	218	1 946	30 094	2.8
Wilson	1 535	-0.5	D	30.6	D	6.7	3.1	6.4	15.3	15 460	205	2 812	32 362	5.3
Yadkin	347	3.4	37.3	28.5	D	8.9	2.8	6.5	16.2	7 525	201	724	16 384	3.6
Yancey	158	8.9	D	20.3	4.8	8.4	3.1	D	19.4	4 580	253	677	9 986	2.6
NORTH DAKOTA	13 097	4.7	16.3	8.6	6.6	7.8	6.3	12.5	22.4	114 047	180	8 101	296 959	2.5
Adams	25	-20.7	8.8	5.3	D	15.1	D	46.5	20.6	665	265	29	1 413	-0.2
Barnes	172	12.0	D	16.8	3.7	5.6	D	11.7	20.1	2 740	247	144	5 582	-0.3
Benson	84	11.9	D	D	D	2.9	2.6	1.1	60.7	1 240	180	188	2 959	0.9
Billings	10	0.9	D	0.0	D	3.3	0.9	0.8	43.9	160	188	3	527	-0.4
Bottineau	106	22.6	16.1	7.1	D	6.4	4.2	D	18.4	1 725	253	63	4 444	0.8
Bowman	43	-2.3	18.4	3.4	5.4	9.6	D	15.1	18.4	780	256	34	1 592	-0.3
Burke	28	14.5	11.3	3.8	D	D	4.9	D	30.8	640	305	17	1 407	-0.4
Burleigh	1 729	0.1	12.9	6.0	7.9	8.5	6.3	17.8	22.5	11 520	161	929	30 747	6.0
Cass	3 596	1.9	D	8.9	10.9	8.5	10.7	13.7	12.8	15 650	123	1 264	57 748	7.4
Cavalier	64	-1.5	D	D	D	5.2	D	11.2	16.1	1 285	287	38	2 732	0.3
Dickey	99	30.9	15.5	11.9	D	6.1	2.5	12.3	9.8	1 265	230	79	2 658	0.1
Divide	23	-0.5	D	D	4.9	6.3	6.3	D	22.6	635	283	18	1 460	-0.6
Dunn	31	2.0	D	D	D	5.2	D	D	26.4	670	189	40	1 961	-0.2
Eddy	32	15.1	D	D	D	5.0	D	15.4	19.5	725	279	33	1 422	0.3
Emmons	34	-14.2	D	D	D	8.5	D	15.4	25.1	1 170	292	52	2 174	0.3
Foster	65	10.4	25.7	20.7	5.5	7.9	3.7	13.3	14.2	895	256	28	1 785	-0.4
Golden Valley	17	-7.8	D	D	D	5.4	6.7	17.4	27.8	460	252	7	965	-0.8
Grand Forks	1 521	3.1	D	4.7	4.9	9.3	3.9	14.0	34.8	7 925	122	603	27 678	1.1
Grant	15	-45.9	D	15.1	D	6.0	D	31.4	39.0	745	280	48	1 733	0.6
Griggs	41	22.3	D	9.6	D	5.6	D	D	15.7	725	281	37	1 517	-0.3
Hettinger	18	-35.9	D	D	D	4.0	D	13.4	37.3	795	312	22	1 418	-0.1
Kidder	30	23.0	D	3.7	D	4.3	4.7	6.8	21.0	700	272	35	1 639	1.8
La Moure	68	37.1	6.0	4.4	1.5	2.5	D	D	15.6	1 275	283	35	2 293	1.0
Logan	24	14.8	D	4.4	D	7.3	D	9.8	19.6	670	311	45	1 195	1.0
McHenry	47	16.0	D	10.2	D	3.1	4.1	4.7	29.8	1 495	261	30	3 004	0.7
McIntosh	34	5.7	D	9.4	D	8.4	7.2	28.8	18.2	1 210	381	42	1 857	0.2
McKenzie	91	6.7	13.6	2.9	D	2.3	D	D	48.4	1 000	178	59	2 753	1.3
McLean	124	2.5	D	D	D	4.0	D	8.9	20.9	2 270	254	116	5 278	0.3
Mercer	233	-0.5	D	D	3.0	3.6	1.5	4.2	8.5	1 535	182	62	4 442	0.9
Morton	319	0.0	D	17.3	8.9	9.7	4.4	D	16.4	4 660	185	330	10 963	3.6
Mountrail	85	15.6	D	D	7.5	5.2	3.5	10.0	30.1	1 380	213	111	3 432	-0.2
Nelson	39	13.6	D	6.5	0.7	6.3	8.0	13.4	21.4	1 050	304	23	2 010	-0.2
Oliver	30	-12.2	D	D	D	D	D	D	12.4	400	210	9	896	-0.8
Pembina	191	19.2	D	23.5	D	5.2	D	4.4	15.6	1 900	232	72	4 086	-0.7
Pierce	55	-1.6	D	D	D	8.6	D	D	15.6	1 160	259	45	2 281	0.5
Ramsey	205	6.2	D	3.4	D	13.1	6.4	13.3	24.5	2 630	226	217	5 751	0.4
Ransom	96	23.8	15.6	11.3	2.7	5.4	4.5	10.7	14.4	1 245	213	49	2 699	3.6
Renville	29	8.8	D	D	D	4.5	D	8.6	24.8	625	253	13	1 422	0.6
Richland	377	20.4	D	25.7	D	4.4	2.1	D	17.6	3 015	171	125	7 596	0.3
Rolette	176	1.8	D	D	2.2	7.9	D	D	61.3	2 045	149	647	5 032	0.1
Sargent	129	20.2	D	D	D	1.4	1.8	0.9	6.7	880	208	39	2 025	0.4
Sheridan	10	14.3	D	D	D	1.0	0.0	D	29.7	510	331	31	922	-0.2
Sioux	57	-5.7	D	0.0	D	D	0.0	D	97.7	350	86	167	1 245	2.4
Slope	-3	0.0	D	0.0	-2.6	D	-2.4	0.0	0.0	150	201	4	453	0.4
Stark	391	-1.1	24.2	8.9	D	9.7	4.7	D	18.3	4 540	205	372	9 879	1.6
Steele	36	43.7	D	D	D	4.9	D	0.3	13.1	515	247	13	1 229	-0.2
Stutsman	397	4.2	D	15.6	5.1	8.3	5.4	D	19.1	4 420	208	444	9 852	0.4
Towner	39	21.1	15.8	12.9	D	5.2	7.5	D	14.9	700	262	15	1 556	-0.1
Traill	141	28.0	D	11.6	2.1	4.6	4.1	D	16.0	1 750	211	47	3 702	-0.2
Walsh	234	24.1	18.4	15.1	3.9	4.2	4.8	D	17.8	2 870	245	113	5 727	-0.5

1. Covers mining, construction, and manufacturing.   2. Per 1,000 resident population estimated as of July 1 of the year shown.

STATE County	Housing units, 2000 Occupied units Owner-occupied Total	Percent	Median value[1]	Median owner cost as a percent of income With a mortgage	Without a mortgage[2]	Renter-occupied Median rent[3]	Median rent as a percent of income	Sub-standard units[4] (percent)	Civilian labor force, 2003 Total	Percent change, 2002–2003	Unemployment Total	Rate[5]	Civilian employment,[6] 2000 Total	Percent Management, professional and related occupations	Production, transportation, and material moving occupations
	89	90	91	92	93	94	95	96	97	98	99	100	101	102	103
NORTH CAROLINA—Cont'd															
Swain	5 137	76.9	86 800	20.0	9.9	384	23.1	5.0	8 026	8.5	612	7.6	5 363	25.5	14.1
Transylvania	12 320	79.4	122 300	20.8	9.9	468	23.9	2.2	10 651	-5.0	1 122	10.5	12 607	27.3	18.6
Tyrrell	1 537	74.8	59 000	23.4	17.9	375	24.2	5.8	2 255	5.2	209	9.3	1 568	20.0	18.8
Union	43 390	80.6	128 500	21.7	9.9	587	22.5	4.2	73 928	2.5	3 653	4.9	62 261	30.7	16.5
Vance	16 199	66.2	82 200	21.9	11.5	441	26.8	5.8	19 138	-0.9	2 552	13.3	18 228	23.1	25.0
Wake	242 040	65.9	162 900	21.1	9.9	727	25.0	3.5	394 369	2.1	18 699	4.7	343 426	47.0	7.9
Warren	7 708	77.2	80 500	21.5	11.5	395	26.3	5.2	6 928	-2.4	681	9.8	7 299	25.2	23.7
Washington	5 367	73.5	69 400	21.4	11.4	403	29.5	4.9	6 105	1.6	541	8.9	5 417	22.5	22.4
Watauga	16 540	62.9	139 300	22.2	9.9	548	34.7	2.1	25 421	3.0	615	2.4	21 349	34.3	8.6
Wayne	42 612	65.3	87 600	20.8	10.3	455	23.1	4.1	51 492	-1.0	3 026	5.9	47 140	28.1	18.8
Wilkes	26 650	77.9	89 200	20.0	9.9	416	20.8	2.2	33 319	-0.2	2 574	7.7	31 632	22.4	29.1
Wilson	28 613	61.2	86 400	22.1	11.5	469	25.1	5.4	38 915	0.8	3 583	9.2	33 508	25.3	23.3
Yadkin	14 505	80.3	90 600	21.7	9.9	438	19.9	3.5	18 769	1.4	1 164	6.2	17 687	23.9	26.9
Yancey	7 472	80.2	93 000	19.9	9.9	371	21.4	2.8	6 094	-2.3	536	8.8	7 781	22.8	27.4
NORTH DAKOTA	257 152	66.6	74 400	19.4	10.2	412	22.3	2.5	346 471	0.8	13 746	4.0	316 632	33.3	12.4
Adams	1 121	70.9	37 500	17.8	12.1	295	16.5	2.5	1 293	1.6	34	2.6	1 217	38.3	10.0
Barnes	4 884	71.1	57 600	19.1	9.9	324	22.3	1.5	5 720	1.0	195	3.4	5 640	32.3	15.0
Benson	2 328	68.3	31 100	15.7	10.2	292	17.0	12.6	2 838	1.9	212	7.5	2 372	34.9	14.3
Billings	366	76.2	56 500	19.3	9.9	392	12.7	4.4	471	-1.5	26	5.5	447	38.7	8.5
Bottineau	2 962	80.0	43 600	18.7	10.9	365	21.1	2.2	3 393	-1.8	182	5.4	3 140	30.3	11.5
Bowman	1 358	79.5	53 600	17.3	9.9	316	14.0	0.4	1 763	2.0	31	1.8	1 661	37.3	14.6
Burke	1 013	84.6	24 700	18.4	10.9	285	20.0	1.8	908	-0.2	24	2.6	1 018	36.1	15.1
Burleigh	27 670	68.0	98 900	20.0	10.1	446	22.1	2.0	41 964	1.7	1 303	3.1	37 434	36.5	9.7
Cass	51 315	54.4	98 400	20.3	9.9	463	23.0	2.4	77 346	1.5	2 044	2.6	70 485	33.4	12.4
Cavalier	2 017	81.5	46 100	18.8	9.9	313	22.1	1.2	2 374	-0.5	87	3.7	2 136	34.6	11.2
Dickey	2 283	71.4	48 700	18.7	9.9	332	20.9	2.1	2 748	-2.0	80	2.9	2 857	33.0	14.7
Divide	1 005	81.9	31 000	19.4	10.8	293	21.0	1.2	1 085	3.7	28	2.6	984	40.9	10.1
Dunn	1 378	79.9	37 400	18.8	9.9	231	16.3	4.4	1 982	1.4	84	4.2	1 618	37.9	14.3
Eddy	1 164	75.3	34 000	16.2	10.7	294	18.2	1.1	1 244	0.4	82	6.6	1 221	39.1	14.1
Emmons	1 786	84.2	37 000	19.3	12.7	271	18.2	1.8	1 986	-0.9	140	7.0	1 870	40.9	9.0
Foster	1 540	74.3	55 300	18.3	11.2	342	22.0	0.6	1 976	-3.2	71	3.6	1 803	35.6	17.7
Golden Valley	761	77.8	40 600	18.1	9.9	323	21.0	1.4	897	4.4	19	2.1	846	43.6	10.0
Grand Forks	25 435	53.7	92 800	20.6	11.6	477	24.1	2.9	36 419	1.0	1 265	3.5	33 431	32.2	11.1
Grant	1 195	79.6	23 500	20.2	12.4	257	19.3	2.1	1 464	-0.7	56	3.8	1 256	46.7	9.5
Griggs	1 178	78.4	36 000	17.8	10.7	274	20.7	1.8	1 563	2.3	36	2.3	1 137	41.8	11.3
Hettinger	1 152	84.3	30 300	17.0	9.9	225	19.6	1.0	1 273	-0.5	49	3.8	1 172	40.9	12.1
Kidder	1 158	81.9	33 400	19.4	12.3	260	21.0	2.1	1 372	-0.9	90	6.6	1 172	40.9	12.1
La Moure	1 942	81.0	34 600	17.6	10.7	287	20.1	2.1	2 321	2.6	86	3.7	2 102	36.4	15.6
Logan	963	85.4	30 200	17.0	12.0	277	19.8	2.2	1 075	0.6	31	2.9	964	39.9	11.6
McHenry	2 526	81.5	32 600	18.3	10.0	267	21.5	2.5	2 803	1.0	233	8.3	2 589	33.2	11.4
McIntosh	1 467	82.8	28 100	17.9	12.7	280	18.2	1.0	1 620	0.9	39	2.4	1 430	37.2	11.9
McKenzie	2 151	73.9	51 100	16.5	9.9	274	14.9	5.1	3 214	1.8	131	4.1	2 444	37.5	11.9
McLean	3 815	82.3	48 400	15.9	9.9	291	19.5	2.1	4 329	-2.6	352	8.1	4 065	31.8	11.8
Mercer	3 346	84.4	62 500	14.9	10.1	325	22.0	0.9	4 863	1.7	309	6.4	4 120	27.2	17.9
Morton	9 889	75.6	74 800	19.8	9.9	405	24.8	2.6	13 977	1.9	623	4.5	12 846	30.5	12.2
Mountrail	2 560	72.6	39 700	18.4	12.4	337	20.5	4.5	3 074	1.8	200	6.5	2 743	36.8	8.4
Nelson	1 628	80.3	36 100	19.3	10.4	275	18.9	0.5	1 495	2.7	75	5.0	1 637	36.7	13.0
Oliver	791	85.6	59 600	16.5	10.1	280	13.3	1.5	1 150	13.3	64	5.6	991	35.2	15.7
Pembina	3 535	78.3	55 100	17.8	9.9	361	19.2	1.0	4 472	2.2	422	9.4	4 004	28.7	18.2
Pierce	1 964	73.1	62 300	19.3	12.8	374	22.8	1.8	2 324	1.1	109	4.7	2 085	37.0	10.6
Ramsey	4 957	64.9	63 500	18.1	9.9	324	20.2	2.2	6 156	-1.7	292	4.7	5 656	32.4	9.5
Ransom	2 350	75.5	56 100	17.5	10.0	304	19.7	2.4	2 653	-1.6	76	2.9	2 869	31.4	22.0
Renville	1 085	77.7	44 500	19.2	10.6	326	22.7	1.5	1 270	0.2	38	3.0	1 232	38.6	12.4
Richland	6 885	69.5	67 200	19.2	11.0	374	20.1	1.8	9 241	0.1	332	3.6	8 741	28.9	18.6
Rolette	4 556	67.4	55 200	15.8	9.9	281	22.1	9.6	5 844	-4.0	865	14.8	4 544	36.0	11.1
Sargent	1 786	79.6	44 800	16.1	9.9	340	17.6	1.6	2 382	1.8	49	2.1	2 136	29.3	30.3
Sheridan	731	84.8	23 900	21.4	11.1	264	20.3	2.1	678	6.6	50	7.4	669	43.0	10.2
Sioux	1 095	46.1	48 000	17.4	11.1	235	13.2	18.7	1 754	-1.0	101	5.8	1 160	33.3	7.3
Slope	313	87.2	23 900	12.5	9.9	325	12.5	1.0	420	4.2	16	3.8	399	56.1	9.0
Stark	8 932	70.3	70 400	19.3	11.0	342	23.6	1.8	12 905	1.1	481	3.7	11 151	32.2	14.6
Steele	923	76.9	34 600	19.3	9.9	271	17.3	1.4	1 089	-1.6	21	1.9	1 055	38.8	10.1
Stutsman	8 954	67.2	66 600	18.9	10.1	366	20.7	1.7	11 223	-1.3	416	3.7	11 003	31.8	13.1
Towner	1 218	74.9	42 200	16.6	10.3	309	20.9	1.0	1 236	-1.0	56	4.5	1 341	38.8	12.9
Traill	3 341	72.4	60 000	17.6	10.6	344	21.3	1.8	3 539	-0.7	149	4.2	3 932	30.3	15.7
Walsh	5 029	76.8	52 100	19.1	10.5	361	20.3	2.9	5 911	-1.5	303	5.1	5 834	29.1	15.6

1. Specified owner-occupied units.   2. Median monthly owner costs is often in the minimum category—9.9 percent or less, which is indicated as 9.9 percent.   3. Specified renter-occupied units.   4. Overcrowded or lacking complete plumbing facilities.   5. Percent of civilian labor force.   6. Persons 16 years old and over.

STATE County	Number of establish-ments	Employment Total	Health care and social assistance	Manufac-turing	Retail trade	Finance and insurance	Professional, scientific, and technical services	Annual payroll Total (mil dol)	Average per employee (dollars)	Farms Number	Percent with— Less than 50 acres	500 acres and over	Farm operators whose principal occu-pation is farming (percent)
	104	105	106	107	108	109	110	111	112	113	114	115	116
NORTH CAROLINA—Cont'd													
Swain	407	5 799	698	314	582	68	77	116	20 067	83	49.4	4.8	54.2
Transylvania	757	9 447	1 168	2 869	1 404	311	225	256	27 123	256	64.1	1.2	46.1
Tyrrell	78	335	D	D	124	D	D	7	20 693	91	19.8	39.6	80.2
Union	2 980	40 042	2 814	12 518	5 065	676	982	1 118	27 918	1 224	52.9	6.1	58.4
Vance	906	15 434	1 810	3 908	4 061	235	224	341	22 116	228	24.6	18.9	50.4
Wake	20 812	355 071	36 529	23 586	44 592	18 412	32 145	12 221	34 419	846	55.7	4.3	54.8
Warren	265	2 292	201	727	352	59	40	42	18 424	297	24.9	12.8	55.2
Washington	280	3 796	498	D	406	D	D	131	34 618	193	32.1	33.7	74.1
Watauga	1 565	16 295	2 606	1 181	3 187	407	561	327	20 045	731	54.9	1.0	49.2
Wayne	2 317	38 610	7 354	9 144	5 892	1 146	731	911	23 583	722	42.5	13.3	66.5
Wilkes	1 334	24 575	2 144	8 035	3 393	2 249	364	719	29 267	1 273	50.6	2.5	62.6
Wilson	1 784	35 132	3 541	9 336	3 882	2 963	1 107	945	26 890	315	38.1	21.9	68.6
Yadkin	659	8 622	1 068	3 249	896	89	232	189	21 933	1 044	50.1	3.7	58.7
Yancey	346	3 484	394	1 131	563	157	113	74	21 104	622	66.9	0.8	50.5
NORTH DAKOTA	20 206	257 335	47 003	24 321	41 415	13 503	9 200	6 436	25 012	30 619	6.7	56.8	70.7
Adams	106	696	305	D	159	24	15	15	21 960	394	6.1	61.4	68.8
Barnes	372	3 921	959	351	503	129	84	72	18 268	838	9.2	46.3	66.9
Benson	113	1 124	D	225	59	36	2	22	19 980	567	5.1	62.1	79.2
Billings	34	171	0	0	11	0	D	5	28 368	238	3.4	68.5	72.7
Bottineau	260	1 619	344	77	322	90	45	28	17 535	879	5.0	51.1	65.8
Bowman	162	1 033	D	D	195	70	58	19	18 201	360	3.1	63.1	68.3
Burke	88	275	D	0	53	33	4	6	18 201	455	—	—	—
Burleigh	2 343	35 298	7 512	1 528	5 548	1 784	2 307	910	21 487	946	14.3	41.1	52.1
Cass	4 235	74 635	10 883	7 017	10 243	5 889	3 065	2 102	28 166	961	14.5	54.8	73.6
Cavalier	186	1 287	266	D	203	98	12	28	21 882	607	3.1	65.2	81.2
Dickey	207	1 606	407	107	252	53	28	28	17 489	533	8.8	51.6	73.7
Divide	82	511	194	0	62	37	12	8	15 857	532	3.9	68.0	77.3
Dunn	80	720	D	D	106	33	D	14	20 099	582	4.6	68.2	75.6
Eddy	74	559	180	D	86	18	10	10	17 145	325	4.3	60.0	71.4
Emmons	136	1 246	225	D	188	50	16	34	27 215	699	2.9	61.1	72.7
Foster	155	1 426	305	D	274	D	D	30	21 184	309	7.1	58.6	76.4
Golden Valley	71	461	D	D	D	D	D	D	16 390	231	3.9	63.2	73.6
Grand Forks	1 749	28 149	5 664	2 105	5 994	863	815	688	24 450	863	11.7	42.3	68.6
Grant	78	461	185	D	73	31	6	8	16 299	548	5.7	70.1	75.7
Griggs	114	873	D	115	125	D	D	17	19 424	423	5.7	45.6	60.5
Hettinger	101	396	86	D	70	40	D	8	20 439	489	6.3	57.7	63.2
Kidder	62	375	D	D	62	30	16	7	17 755	584	4.8	63.7	71.6
La Moure	139	936	D	131	112	99	14	17	18 439	621	5.3	50.6	68.3
Logan	75	403	108	D	44	28	D	6	14 643	445	3.6	63.1	74.8
McHenry	138	616	111	D	91	53	12	13	20 326	901	5.0	59.6	70.1
McIntosh	125	885	348	74	154	56	4	16	18 190	526	5.9	54.9	64.6
McKenzie	163	1 087	190	86	148	80	21	23	21 326	632	5.2	66.5	75.3
McLean	241	1 877	405	D	250	148	17	57	30 435	918	6.0	58.0	69.1
Mercer	250	3 457	391	79	415	88	33	137	39 696	456	6.1	50.9	64.0
Morton	667	7 082	1 360	873	1 044	333	370	195	27 584	855	6.9	63.0	69.7
Mountrail	195	1 675	346	D	290	71	51	31	18 475	682	2.3	66.9	76.1
Nelson	135	840	312	D	134	79	6	14	16 076	598	5.4	41.0	63.4
Oliver	33	373	D	D	D	D	5	20	52 603	307	6.8	60.3	68.7
Pembina	315	2 997	365	863	615	142	21	71	23 593	524	5.9	52.3	76.0
Pierce	149	1 456	391	D	247	90	30	28	19 321	487	6.4	61.4	70.4
Ramsey	428	4 305	1 078	178	869	233	85	84	19 622	554	8.8	52.3	72.0
Ransom	203	1 599	364	256	278	63	37	33	20 772	528	5.9	42.4	64.2
Renville	91	564	D	D	111	30	5	10	18 098	353	3.4	70.8	77.9
Richland	531	6 761	613	2 196	717	165	109	167	24 684	813	10.7	56.3	80.2
Rolette	211	3 150	526	519	488	72	73	60	19 028	523	3.1	51.8	64.8
Sargent	133	2 175	99	D	145	D	D	82	37 575	469	7.5	52.9	75.5
Sheridan	46	182	D	D	D	18	D	4	22 599	393	1.8	62.8	68.4
Sioux	31	843	D	0	48	0	D	22	25 561	179	7.3	80.4	84.4
Slope	11	35	0	0	0	0	D	1	20 029	259	2.3	68.0	78.4
Stark	863	8 641	1 593	948	1 610	292	266	189	21 833	774	11.5	49.5	68.6
Steele	75	368	0	74	62	46	D	8	22 147	318	6.6	59.1	77.7
Stutsman	642	9 706	2 132	1 778	1 380	370	131	218	22 425	988	7.1	56.7	68.5
Towner	94	700	D	182	59	62	17	12	17 656	418	6.2	63.2	73.9
Traill	308	2 447	599	382	315	148	52	51	20 851	427	6.3	66.7	81.7
Walsh	438	4 102	695	857	748	147	85	86	20 890	905	7.1	42.3	66.5

Table B. States and Counties — **Agriculture**

Agriculture, 2002 (cont'd)

STATE County	Land in farms — Acres — Acreage (1,000)	Percent change, 1997–2002	Average size of farm	Total irrigated (1,000)	Total cropland (1,000)	Value of land and buildings (dollars) Average per farm	Average per acre	Value of machinery and equipment average per farm (dollars)	Value of products sold Total (mil dol)	Average per farm (dollars)	Percent from — Crops	Livestock and poultry products	Percent of farms with sales of — $10,000 or more	$100,000 or more	Government payments Total ($1,000)	Percent of farms
	117	118	119	120	121	122	123	124	125	126	127	128	129	130	131	132
NORTH CAROLINA—Cont'd																
Swain	7	0.0	86	0	3	373 303	4 461	57 059	1	13 768	D	D	24.1	1.2	4	18.1
Transylvania	18	38.5	71	0	10	433 673	6 417	38 538	17	64 909	75.4	24.6	30.1	7.8	52	7.8
Tyrrell	74	34.5	809	0	70	1 380 993	1 809	257 269	29	323 110	72.6	27.4	45.1	29.8	2 300	21.7
Union	191	7.3	156	1	136	574 022	3 688	78 917	261	213 482	10.8	89.2	33.8	18.0	287	36.4
Vance	75	11.9	329	2	25	718 057	2 142	74 278	14	60 717	96.3	3.7	33.8	18.0	287	36.4
Wake	93	-17.7	110	5	46	636 877	6 388	47 769	56	66 520	74.7	25.3	30.0	11.1	631	17.0
Warren	75	-6.3	254	2	35	711 770	2 146	155 543	27	90 902	32.6	67.4	42.4	19.9	455	50.8
Washington	114	6.5	593	4	100	1 124 786	1 954	157 276	46	239 113	73.7	26.3	62.2	42.0	1 705	51.8
Watauga	52	-8.8	71	0	22	272 128	4 026	31 665	12	15 889	56.7	43.3	30.0	2.0	60	9.7
Wayne	171	-25.3	237	7	127	722 503	3 162	124 792	318	440 063	13.7	86.3	61.2	38.5	2 524	33.8
Wilkes	124	-2.4	98	1	55	308 987	2 997	51 478	208	163 005	2.5	97.5	38.6	25.6	680	11.9
Wilson	115	-10.2	364	3	85	951 772	2 471	137 583	79	250 690	76.5	23.5	50.8	29.2	1 303	37.5
Yadkin	117	14.7	112	2	69	425 076	3 257	57 831	65	62 282	23.6	76.4	30.2	13.7	631	19.0
Yancey	39	-2.5	62	0	14	315 788	4 628	33 653	6	8 997	77.0	23.0	20.9	1.1	77	10.0
NORTH DAKOTA	39 295	-0.2	1 283	203	26 506	517 448	404	124 298	3 233	105 600	76.1	23.9	61.5	28.8	293 067	78.0
Adams	605	-4.0	1 535	0	358	407 212	250	103 691	24	61 396	27.3	72.7	55.8	18.3	3 559	81.0
Barnes	857	-1.5	1 023	2	738	477 097	448	115 902	94	112 428	91.7	8.3	58.8	33.3	10 014	85.4
Benson	733	-3.3	1 293	7	558	441 255	355	135 155	55	97 389	77.1	22.9	62.1	28.0	6 003	79.5
Billings	811	2.1	3 407	0	138	846 162	250	76 917	13	53 019	19.4	80.6	67.2	15.1	1 038	66.0
Bottineau	948	-1.3	1 079	D	822	437 812	409	116 743	72	82 198	89.8	10.2	56.7	24.9	8 725	85.3
Bowman	759	6.2	2 109	0	384	533 322	249	105 666	26	72 830	32.4	67.6	58.6	19.2	3 124	79.7
Burke	600	-2.4	1 319	D	448	405 377	295	118 168	32	70 071	87.4	12.6	61.5	25.1	3 829	79.1
Burleigh	866	-3.3	915	5	470	313 366	339	57 910	45	47 632	44.4	55.6	46.5	13.1	4 971	61.5
Cass	1 127	5.5	1 173	12	1 073	1 025 746	876	201 103	209	217 437	93.6	6.4	70.4	51.5	10 467	77.9
Cavalier	819	-6.4	1 349	0	764	713 947	542	177 912	91	149 141	98.3	1.7	71.7	47.1	11 064	83.2
Dickey	599	3.3	1 125	10	445	538 341	502	143 154	72	135 065	70.1	29.9	65.5	33.8	5 353	78.8
Divide	761	3.3	1 430	2	570	390 699	285	96 901	41	77 053	85.1	14.9	72.7	29.7	5 481	89.7
Dunn	1 106	-17.2	1 900	1	421	482 200	252	84 372	47	79 986	33.2	66.8	52.3	22.5	3 708	91.4
Eddy	349	1.5	1 073	D	243	335 751	315	93 245	21	65 196	69.6	30.4	64.2	20.7	5 272	73.8
Emmons	838	1.7	1 199	4	487	341 322	280	85 405	47	67 631	33.4	66.6	59.2	31.1	3 519	76.4
Foster	383	3.5	1 239	1	312	460 314	399	118 200	40	128 531	65.9	34.1	64.2	24.7	2 418	77.9
Golden Valley	580	0.2	2 513	0	183	591 971	246	93 659	19	84 112	43.1	56.9	61.5	24.7	1 887	77.9
Grand Forks	756	-2.5	876	14	699	705 045	793	173 016	145	167 833	89.1	10.9	51.6	32.2	9 729	84.9
Grant	1 057	9.0	1 928	2	503	587 279	309	87 384	42	76 712	22.7	77.3	68.1	26.5	3 591	75.2
Griggs	379	-2.8	896	3	298	339 186	354	96 265	30	70 296	83.5	16.5	46.3	20.3	4 542	83.7
Hettinger	681	-3.7	1 392	D	552	480 579	336	118 004	35	72 494	79.2	20.8	51.1	22.3	5 310	84.5
Kidder	794	9.5	1 360	14	403	400 538	281	88 955	44	76 074	44.1	55.9	56.2	22.1	4 022	77.2
La Moure	677	0.9	1 090	6	579	617 472	558	140 669	80	128 104	78.2	21.8	59.4	36.1	6 881	80.4
Logan	578	8.9	1 298	2	303	323 440	245	94 051	36	79 974	26.0	74.0	60.0	23.4	3 428	80.4
McHenry	1 126	5.5	1 250	7	693	369 001	329	81 683	67	74 880	54.0	46.0	61.0	23.1	6 768	75.2
McIntosh	569	12.0	1 081	D	369	273 772	287	87 743	39	74 790	43.9	56.1	57.2	20.5	3 865	81.2
McKenzie	1 193	2.0	1 888	23	469	603 918	304	121 341	56	88 409	58.9	41.1	71.4	27.7	2 904	68.0
McLean	1 095	-4.2	1 193	6	819	510 675	427	117 190	84	91 798	82.2	17.8	63.0	28.1	9 102	80.8
Mercer	536	-2.7	1 176	2	245	294 727	268	72 357	22	48 799	45.0	55.0	62.5	14.0	1 710	57.5
Morton	1 276	3.8	1 493	6	583	415 736	303	99 831	69	81 035	28.5	71.5	65.6	26.9	7 002	79.6
Mountrail	1 068	7.1	1 566	D	626	500 336	306	104 111	53	78 302	83.1	16.9	39.3	22.1	7 260	90.5
Nelson	532	-0.6	889	0	431	315 364	345	80 724	41	68 894	38.4	61.6	68.1	20.8	1 263	62.5
Oliver	404	1.0	1 315	4	181	347 968	242	100 976	23	73 546	38.4	61.6	66.3	20.8	983	62.5
Pembina	614	-3.0	1 171	0	569	983 362	765	221 713	142	271 213	96.3	3.7	67.2	44.1	7 261	77.1
Pierce	531	-6.3	1 090	D	399	354 889	346	86 204	36	74 528	71.0	29.0	58.7	27.3	5 134	84.6
Ramsey	636	-3.3	1 148	D	580	444 923	368	166 134	55	99 570	95.3	4.7	51.3	29.4	7 745	83.4
Ransom	501	-2.7	948	16	346	465 373	520	127 299	60	113 312	70.6	29.4	50.4	25.0	5 199	84.7
Renville	527	2.1	1 493	D	463	734 850	536	186 793	44	125 032	91.9	8.1	77.9	43.6	4 359	78.5
Richland	891	10.1	1 096	3	815	1 033 326	945	231 780	201	247 663	87.2	12.8	77.7	50.4	10 635	78.2
Rolette	508	3.0	971	0	351	317 673	329	80 197	32	61 278	68.0	32.0	52.0	18.0	4 282	72.7
Sargent	505	5.9	1 077	15	426	573 977	543	154 636	78	166 718	81.7	18.3	67.8	42.2	4 823	84.4
Sheridan	469	-4.7	1 193	0	311	343 318	281	114 151	25	62 790	72.3	27.7	56.7	21.6	3 311	84.7
Sioux	702	-0.4	3 925	D	136	817 686	201	97 940	13	73 670	13.3	86.7	73.7	28.5	1 037	56.4
Slope	763	0.8	2 944	0	254	743 097	244	98 048	20	78 274	41.2	58.8	68.3	24.3	1 937	77.6
Stark	777	-3.6	1 004	0	491	330 265	324	85 883	48	61 721	45.3	54.7	57.0	17.4	4 974	65.6
Steele	401	-2.9	1 261	3	362	735 288	577	183 704	52	164 148	96.6	3.4	68.6	45.6	3 757	85.2
Stutsman	1 215	-4.0	1 230	5	905	486 703	407	126 027	97	97 865	74.9	25.1	55.6	26.8	11 386	80.3
Towner	549	-3.7	1 313	0	483	462 591	359	121 743	45	107 226	92.1	7.9	66.0	34.7	5 617	82.8
Traill	530	7.3	1 240	D	515	1 007 758	842	275 874	101	236 444	98.3	1.7	81.0	58.5	5 316	80.1
Walsh	759	5.7	839	1	667	593 948	719	159 774	150	165 655	97.3	2.7	49.4	28.6	11 331	88.2

Table B. States and Counties — Residential Construction, Wholesale Trade, Retail Trade, and Real Estate

STATE County	Value of residential construction authorized by building permits, 2003		Wholesale trade, 1997				Retail trade,[1] 1997				Real estate and rental and leasing, 1997			
	New construction ($1,000)	Number of housing units	Number of establish-ments	Number of employees	Sales (mil dol)	Annual payroll (mil dol)	Number of establish-ments	Number of employees	Sales (mil dol)	Annual payroll (mil dol)	Number of establish-ments	Number of employees	Receipts (mil dol)	Annual payroll (mil dol)
	133	134	135	136	137	138	139	140	141	142	143	144	145	146
NORTH CAROLINA—Cont'd														
Swain	12 177	142	9	109	27.3	2.7	118	472	62.1	6.3	7	12	0.5	0.1
Transylvania	59 563	246	16	68	20.9	1.8	110	1 127	158.2	14.9	32	73	7.9	1.4
Tyrrell	1 302	8	4	14	16.0	0.3	19	107	18.1	1.4	1	D	D	D
Union	436 490	2 929	241	2 214	813.4	75.6	383	4 245	753.0	69.2	67	222	25.9	4.4
Vance	19 688	148	33	489	274.0	13.2	251	2 763	454.0	42.1	46	146	17.2	2.6
Wake	1 368 097	10 631	1 249	18 833	13 259.1	826.0	2 719	38 755	7 391.9	664.3	792	4 777	862.5	130.1
Warren	16 070	118	9	22	5.6	0.6	55	369	44.1	5.3	6	D	D	D
Washington	2 510	20	15	91	36.4	2.5	65	446	71.0	6.4	7	32	2.0	0.5
Watauga	105 992	823	47	422	166.1	12.0	342	3 207	519.8	44.3	69	231	18.4	3.1
Wayne	63 909	690	151	2 217	891.1	59.4	523	6 169	1 033.0	88.1	81	263	21.0	4.5
Wilkes	33 623	254	66	818	431.1	22.8	259	2 906	458.6	41.3	38	127	16.7	2.3
Wilson	43 507	423	121	1 264	471.1	33.6	393	4 416	735.4	66.2	63	192	19.3	3.0
Yadkin	22 107	143	32	D	D	D	144	851	167.9	13.6	15	46	5.1	0.5
Yancey	6 649	129	5	15	1.5	0.2	66	541	112.6	8.8	13	28	2.1	0.3
NORTH DAKOTA	397 521	3 721	1 604	16 992	8 618.4	454.4	3 569	40 685	6 702.1	616.1	657	3 325	287.0	46.3
Adams	55	1	10	67	51.0	1.4	21	169	34.3	2.7	2	D	D	D
Barnes	3 511	53	35	281	150.2	6.3	76	602	81.1	7.4	3	2	0.3	0.0
Benson	0	0	10	36	31.8	1.3	18	76	14.7	0.7	4	D	D	D
Billings	550	2	1	D	D	D	6	10	1.4	0.2	NA	NA	NA	NA
Bottineau	0	0	13	71	84.2	2.4	54	325	57.3	4.7	9	D	D	D
Bowman	85	1	5	97	56.1	2.2	27	196	43.5	2.8	2	D	D	D
Burke	0	0	7	41	33.4	0.7	16	89	14.5	0.9	4	6	0.1	0.0
Burleigh	107 530	761	143	1 574	619.8	43.5	366	5 114	814.6	82.5	92	563	48.9	6.9
Cass	163 089	1 727	366	5 945	2 755.5	182.6	572	9 697	1 669.2	161.3	163	1 067	111.5	17.3
Cavalier	320	2	20	113	93.6	3.2	33	241	48.7	3.4	2	D	D	D
Dickey	420	4	22	153	93.2	3.5	41	297	46.9	4.3	3	4	0.2	0.0
Divide	0	0	8	45	59.8	1.2	15	70	9.0	1.0	2	7	0.4	0.0
Dunn	100	2	9	35	9.5	0.8	19	110	29.3	1.6	4	D	D	D
Eddy	0	0	7	42	23.1	0.9	11	59	9.9	0.7	2	D	D	D
Emmons	140	1	9	64	34.3	0.8	34	174	35.1	2.4	2	D	D	D
Foster	355	3	17	109	68.0	2.7	30	222	38.7	3.2	5	D	D	D
Golden Valley	75	1	4	58	32.8	1.3	17	88	17.7	1.2	NA	NA	NA	NA
Grand Forks	46 294	512	130	1 511	552.4	41.3	351	5 596	934.7	81.4	70	524	33.9	7.0
Grant	0	0	10	51	19.4	0.9	15	77	14.0	1.1	2	D	D	D
Griggs	0	0	15	83	36.7	2.1	22	133	22.6	1.9	3	D	D	D
Hettinger	25	1	9	54	27.3	1.2	13	79	16.9	1.1	3	D	D	D
Kidder	210	4	5	23	9.8	0.4	11	62	13.9	0.6	1	D	D	D
La Moure	115	1	17	155	88.6	2.9	22	105	18.7	1.6	3	3	0.1	0.0
Logan	0	0	8	111	96.9	1.2	12	52	11.8	0.8	1	D	D	D
McHenry	0	0	19	92	64.7	2.3	23	109	14.3	1.1	7	13	0.5	0.0
McIntosh	319	2	8	43	22.2	0.9	27	146	29.0	2.1	2	D	D	D
McKenzie	190	2	11	62	18.3	1.6	27	179	23.8	2.2	2	D	D	D
McLean	2 524	28	22	124	114.3	3.2	46	343	47.0	3.9	4	13	0.4	0.1
Mercer	573	4	12	58	22.8	1.1	46	440	56.2	5.2	5	6	0.3	0.0
Morton	25 761	192	49	409	193.4	9.2	101	944	196.0	18.4	21	53	3.9	0.5
Mountrail	1 173	20	13	D	D	D	46	299	47.0	3.7	4	D	D	D
Nelson	300	3	20	188	92.1	3.4	22	114	15.5	1.2	5	11	0.2	0.0
Oliver	70	1	2	D	D	D	3	23	4.0	0.2	NA	NA	NA	NA
Pembina	445	4	28	211	113.7	4.4	77	620	103.0	8.4	4	9	0.2	0.0
Pierce	120	1	13	183	90.1	3.5	30	252	42.5	3.0	4	3	0.3	0.0
Ramsey	1 352	10	35	374	170.5	9.3	92	1 014	141.2	14.0	11	161	5.2	1.1
Ransom	483	26	9	154	130.2	4.6	39	275	39.4	3.3	4	8	0.4	0.0
Renville	192	3	15	56	57.8	1.4	14	105	27.7	1.9	1	D	D	D
Richland	3 212	25	54	479	208.3	8.7	91	797	137.9	11.9	18	73	5.7	0.7
Rolette	180	2	10	71	79.4	1.5	49	486	79.7	6.5	4	D	D	D
Sargent	943	8	11	80	48.5	1.6	28	161	25.5	2.0	3	7	0.2	0.0
Sheridan	0	0	5	25	7.5	0.4	8	33	6.1	0.5	3	7	0.1	0.0
Sioux	0	0	2	D	D	D	11	60	14.0	0.7	1	D	D	D
Slope	0	0	NA	NA	NA	NA	NA	NA	NA	NA	1	D	D	D
Stark	11 467	78	57	434	276.6	9.8	166	1 591	255.9	23.5	30	74	6.3	1.1
Steele	0	0	7	42	47.1	1.4	8	51	12.3	0.7	1	D	D	D
Stutsman	4 616	28	37	300	235.0	8.0	137	1 419	207.8	19.4	24	95	6.9	1.1
Towner	0	0	11	D	D	D	19	87	10.4	0.8	4	23	1.0	0.1
Traill	1 559	12	30	293	184.0	6.6	47	314	49.2	4.4	8	D	D	D
Walsh	797	5	42	383	151.7	8.2	91	706	116.1	10.2	10	18	0.5	0.2

1. Establishments with payroll.

Table B. States and Counties — Professional Services, Manufacturing, and Accommodation and Foodservices

STATE County	Professional, scientific, and technical services,[1] 1997				Manufacturing, 1997				Accommodation and foodservices, 1997			
	Number of establishments	Number of employees	Receipts (mil dol)	Annual payroll (mil dol)	Number of establishments	Number of employees	Receipts (mil dol)	Annual payroll (mil dol)	Number of establishments	Number of employees	Sales (mil dol)	Annual payroll (mil dol)
	147	148	149	150	151	152	153	154	155	156	157	158
NORTH CAROLINA—Cont'd												
Swain	6	46	2.1	1.1	NA	NA	NA	NA	79	796	38.1	10.4
Transylvania	50	150	11.6	3.9	28	3 071	715.1	119.3	72	798	34.0	10.7
Tyrrell	3	D	D	D	NA	NA	NA	NA	8	D	D	D
Union	141	744	65.2	19.9	228	13 113	2 543.5	356.9	151	2 618	73.0	18.6
Vance	34	208	10.2	4.1	53	5 085	1 218.0	119.2	66	1 532	38.6	10.7
Wake	2 366	18 158	2 000.3	798.8	639	23 789	10 420.0	784.7	1 229	24 776	896.6	251.0
Warren	15	36	2.1	0.7	13	813	95.5	15.3	13	D	D	D
Washington	8	20	0.8	0.3	15	D	D	D	22	334	9.6	2.5
Watauga	97	331	21.0	7.2	56	1 223	97.4	24.8	165	2 847	91.3	25.0
Wayne	129	596	43.4	16.0	101	9 495	1 417.5	231.1	158	2 953	84.4	23.1
Wilkes	73	336	19.9	6.5	108	8 082	1 081.2	168.1	97	1 436	42.9	10.8
Wilson	90	1 238	61.9	27.5	96	8 954	4 980.3	288.1	138	2 771	85.4	23.1
Yadkin	27	198	7.0	3.5	43	3 616	787.3	94.5	70	922	26.2	7.7
Yancey	21	115	4.3	1.8	21	1 645	373.4	39.3	26	268	7.4	2.2
NORTH DAKOTA	1 077	7 076	418.0	175.7	704	21 956	5 115.9	604.8	1 827	26 330	684.9	189.0
Adams	6	13	0.5	0.2	NA	NA	NA	NA	9	54	1.2	0.4
Barnes	15	58	4.3	1.5	NA	NA	NA	NA	36	318	8.1	2.1
Benson	3	2	0.3	0.1	NA	NA	NA	NA	12	D	D	D
Billings	NA	NA	NA	NA	NA	NA	NA	NA	30	151	4.8	1.3
Bottineau	12	33	2.4	0.9	NA	NA	NA	NA	18	128	3.2	0.7
Bowman	8	29	1.9	0.9	NA	NA	NA	NA	18	D	D	D
Burke	3	6	0.3	0.0	NA	NA	NA	NA				
Burleigh	176	1 604	87.5	37.2	54	1 310	99.7	47.3	156	3 485	96.8	27.8
Cass	272	2 318	164.1	65.9	183	6 757	1 512.2	173.5	294	7 184	195.0	55.2
Cavalier	10	17	0.7	0.2	NA	NA	NA	NA	23	D	D	D
Dickey	8	22	0.9	0.4	NA	NA	NA	NA	20	177	3.2	0.8
Divide	4	13	0.5	0.2	NA	NA	NA	NA	8	52	1.4	0.2
Dunn	2	D	D	D	NA	NA	NA	NA	10	D	D	D
Eddy	1	D	D	D	NA	NA	NA	NA	13	55	1.9	0.4
Emmons	7	11	0.5	0.1	NA	NA	NA	NA	15	D	D	D
Foster	7	13	0.7	0.2	NA	NA	NA	NA	14	D	D	D
Golden Valley	5	10	0.9	0.3	NA	NA	NA	NA	7	57	1.3	0.3
Grand Forks	109	771	51.3	24.1	52	1 737	251.5	39.0	180	4 126	93.8	27.1
Grant	3	4	0.2	0.0	NA	NA	NA	NA	8	37	1.0	0.2
Griggs	3	D	D	D	NA	NA	NA	NA	12	71	1.7	0.5
Hettinger	3	8	0.2	0.1	NA	NA	NA	NA	9	34	0.9	0.2
Kidder	2	D	D	D	NA	NA	NA	NA	5	49	1.3	0.4
La Moure	3	7	0.2	0.0	NA	NA	NA	NA	16	D	D	D
Logan	2	D	D	D	NA	NA	NA	NA	8	33	0.9	0.2
McHenry	5	10	0.7	0.1	NA	NA	NA	NA	14	D	D	D
McIntosh	2	D	D	D	NA	NA	NA	NA	16	67	1.5	0.3
McKenzie	5	23	0.7	0.4	NA	NA	NA	NA	21	75	2.3	0.5
McLean	7	14	0.8	0.2	NA	NA	NA	NA	35	155	4.2	0.9
Mercer	10	33	1.7	0.5	NA	NA	NA	NA	32	276	6.3	1.9
Morton	30	286	8.6	3.6	27	883	573.4	27.2	49	580	15.7	4.1
Mountrail	4	22	0.5	0.3	NA	NA	NA	NA	30	158	4.1	1.0
Nelson	5	14	0.3	0.1	NA	NA	NA	NA	5	D	D	D
Oliver	2	D	D	D	NA	NA	NA	NA	29	244	5.5	1.3
Pembina	13	25	1.8	0.7	16	D	D	D	17	104	3.2	0.9
Pierce	8	27	1.1	0.3	NA	NA	NA	NA				
Ramsey	19	51	3.3	1.1	NA	NA	NA	NA	43	551	15.2	4.2
Ransom	8	15	0.6	0.2	NA	NA	NA	NA	25	176	4.2	0.9
Renville	4	5	0.1	0.0	NA	NA	NA	NA	12	D	D	D
Richland	29	112	6.6	2.5	34	2 261	373.0	69.2	44	384	11.3	2.6
Rolette	4	8	0.4	0.1	5	D	D	D	21	109	3.6	0.7
Sargent	5	8	0.3	0.1	NA	NA	NA	NA	5	46	1.6	0.3
Sheridan	3	3	0.1	0.0	NA	NA	NA	NA	3	23	0.9	0.2
Sioux	NA	NA	NA	NA	NA	NA	NA	NA	3	D	D	D
Slope	NA	NA	NA	NA	NA	NA	NA	NA	2	D	D	D
Stark	46	214	12.0	6.0	30	718	75.8	17.6	64	1 059	26.6	7.2
Steele	2	D	D	D	NA	NA	NA	NA	8	21	0.8	0.1
Stutsman	26	119	6.4	3.4	28	1 446	250.3	41.0	61	850	22.1	6.3
Towner	5	12	0.7	0.3	NA	NA	NA	NA	9	40	1.5	0.3
Traill	12	31	1.8	0.8	NA	NA	NA	NA	36	363	6.9	1.8
Walsh	17	57	3.2	0.9	NA	NA	NA	NA	41	271	7.4	1.7

1. Firms subject to federal tax.

Table B. States and Counties — Health Care and Social Assistance, Other Services, and Federal Funds

STATE County	Health care and social assistance,[1] 1997				Other services,[1] 1997				Federal funds and grants, 2002–2003 Expenditures (mil dol)			
											Direct payments for individuals[2]	
	Number of establishments	Number of employees	Receipts (mil dol)	Annual payroll (mil dol)	Number of establishments	Number of employees	Receipts (mil dol)	Annual payroll (mil dol)	Total	Social Security and government retirement	Medicare	Food stamps and Supplemental Security Income
	159	160	161	162	163	164	165	166	167	168	169	170
NORTH CAROLINA—Cont'd												
Swain	17	430	14.8	7.5	18	70	3.5	1.0	113.7	36.4	12.9	4.6
Transylvania	51	543	25.7	11.5	33	85	5.2	1.3	188.4	106.1	30.0	4.7
Tyrrell	2	D	D	D	5	10	1.2	0.2	26.8	9.0	3.6	1.3
Union	114	1 263	75.0	36.2	158	788	46.4	12.8	354.7	187.6	57.1	12.3
Vance	69	1 252	49.6	24.2	41	147	9.4	2.4	255.7	96.7	37.2	17.0
Wake	1 202	16 538	1 124.1	514.0	1 005	7 036	559.0	152.3	4 184.1	1 155.5	319.5	63.7
Warren	13	237	8.3	4.0	15	53	2.5	0.5	124.1	44.7	17.4	7.7
Washington	15	147	4.1	1.8	18	61	4.5	0.9	90.0	36.6	13.7	4.8
Watauga	98	1 386	70.3	35.3	61	288	13.4	3.9	152.4	72.5	25.9	5.3
Wayne	181	2 357	114.4	56.0	151	998	58.5	18.5	903.9	288.5	96.3	28.8
Wilkes	81	966	48.9	21.7	66	302	18.9	5.5	313.5	140.4	53.7	11.6
Wilson	133	1 903	100.6	48.5	108	776	39.2	12.7	406.2	160.5	71.2	20.1
Yadkin	33	471	19.7	9.0	40	248	11.2	3.8	157.7	81.9	30.2	4.7
Yancey	16	243	8.5	3.5	14	30	1.9	0.6	103.0	47.3	15.6	4.9
NORTH DAKOTA	1 013	13 181	904.1	386.4	1 281	6 294	364.3	101.3	5 725.7	1 413.9	559.0	70.0
Adams	7	104	5.2	3.0	8	14	1.2	0.2	30.3	7.8	3.4	0.2
Barnes	17	106	4.2	2.3	28	99	5.8	1.5	88.5	30.9	12.1	1.2
Benson	2	D	D	D	3	D	D	D	103.4	13.5	6.7	2.1
Billings	NA	NA	NA	NA	2	D	D	D	7.9	1.4	0.4	0.0
Bottineau	6	15	1.1	0.2	12	29	2.0	0.4	60.4	19.9	9.6	0.7
Bowman	7	82	4.0	1.3	15	25	2.9	0.4	26.9	9.0	4.6	0.2
Burke	NA	NA	NA	NA	5	5	0.4	0.0	28.9	7.5	4.2	0.2
Burleigh	137	1 456	121.5	55.6	135	811	44.5	13.6	627.6	161.9	49.3	6.9
Cass	244	5 939	474.2	191.5	261	2 059	115.5	36.1	651.3	212.2	62.1	10.2
Cavalier	8	26	2.6	1.0	12	31	1.7	0.4	63.5	13.5	6.2	0.3
Dickey	10	43	3.8	2.2	13	32	1.8	0.4	57.3	14.1	7.5	0.6
Divide	3	8	0.8	0.4	6	12	1.1	0.1	28.9	7.2	3.7	0.2
Dunn	1	D	D	D	3	5	0.2	0.0	24.0	7.1	3.6	0.3
Eddy	2	D	D	D	8	15	1.3	0.2	26.3	8.3	4.1	0.2
Emmons	5	8	0.5	0.2	7	11	0.7	0.2	48.1	12.0	5.8	0.3
Foster	9	94	3.0	1.2	14	55	2.9	0.8	51.6	10.0	4.6	0.2
Golden Valley	4	D	D	D	6	13	0.9	0.2	17.3	5.9	2.5	0.1
Grand Forks	84	1 492	65.4	44.1	113	731	36.6	11.3	559.3	100.5	38.4	5.2
Grant	4	17	0.6	0.2	6	9	0.7	0.1	36.3	7.9	5.4	0.3
Griggs	3	D	D	D	5	15	0.7	0.2	27.7	7.9	3.9	0.3
Hettinger	4	D	D	D	6	11	1.0	0.2	46.2	8.5	4.6	0.2
Kidder	2	D	D	D	2	D	D	D	32.3	7.3	4.2	0.2
La Moure	4	16	0.6	0.3	9	13	0.9	0.1	56.2	13.5	6.3	0.3
Logan	5	53	1.1	0.5	4	9	0.7	0.1	27.4	6.6	3.4	0.2
McHenry	6	17	0.6	0.2	7	12	1.4	0.1	58.2	18.7	8.8	0.6
McIntosh	4	30	1.5	0.9	8	14	1.0	0.2	39.1	11.5	8.0	0.3
McKenzie	3	D	D	D	9	28	1.4	0.4	43.6	11.0	4.3	0.9
McLean	10	136	3.6	1.9	19	48	3.0	0.7	96.1	27.9	12.5	0.9
Mercer	10	57	3.5	1.3	15	59	2.7	0.6	41.2	17.7	8.2	0.5
Morton	24	133	7.1	3.7	49	219	15.2	4.3	161.8	56.5	23.3	3.1
Mountrail	7	12	0.6	0.1	10	16	1.2	0.3	190.5	16.7	7.9	1.0
Nelson	8	118	2.0	0.9	11	12	1.2	0.2	47.2	12.6	7.2	0.2
Oliver	2	D	D	D	1	D	D	D	11.4	3.5	1.6	0.1
Pembina	10	53	2.6	1.3	16	43	2.5	0.4	97.4	22.1	10.1	0.5
Pierce	8	80	4.9	2.2	9	31	1.1	0.4	46.8	12.3	6.3	0.4
Ramsey	24	209	11.7	5.4	22	91	5.1	1.4	149.0	32.0	14.2	1.8
Ransom	15	60	2.3	0.8	13	24	2.1	0.4	44.5	14.8	7.1	0.3
Renville	3	2	0.3	0.0	6	41	3.6	0.7	31.5	7.9	3.7	0.1
Richland	21	181	10.2	4.2	27	89	5.3	1.2	103.3	35.9	13.2	1.5
Rolette	9	52	3.4	1.7	9	26	1.3	0.3	147.6	23.8	9.9	7.4
Sargent	4	D	D	D	7	12	0.4	0.1	41.3	9.9	4.7	0.2
Sheridan	NA	NA	NA	NA	4	13	0.3	0.0	20.0	4.8	3.0	0.3
Sioux	1	D	D	D	NA	NA	NA	NA	67.1	5.1	2.2	2.1
Slope	NA	NA	NA	NA	1	D	D	D	14.5	1.5	0.4	0.0
Stark	43	284	15.7	7.3	64	257	18.4	4.4	135.0	49.9	22.1	3.0
Steele	1	D	D	D	8	16	1.0	0.2	28.6	6.1	2.9	0.2
Stutsman	39	509	21.0	7.4	44	192	10.7	2.6	175.0	52.4	19.6	3.0
Towner	3	D	D	D	6	11	1.2	0.2	42.0	8.0	4.4	0.2
Traill	11	73	4.0	2.5	20	39	4.2	0.7	69.8	21.6	9.3	0.6
Walsh	19	99	4.2	2.1	38	123	6.7	1.5	99.5	31.9	15.4	1.2

1. Firms subject to federal tax. 2. State totals may include programs not allocated by county.

STATE County	Federal funds and grants, 2002–2003 (cont'd)							Local government finances, 2002				
	Expenditures (mil dol) (cont'd)							General revenue				
	Procurement contract awards		Grants[1]								Taxes	
											Per capita[2] (dollars)	
	Salaries and wages	Defense	Other	Medicaid and other health-related	Nutrition and family welfare	Education	Other	Total (mil dol)	Intergovern-mental (mil dol)	Total (mil dol)	Total	Property
	171	172	173	174	175	176	177	178	179	180	181	182
NORTH CAROLINA—Cont'd												
Swain	12.2	0.0	3.6	19.4	4.7	2.6	8.7	26.4	16.2	5.5	421	251
Transylvania	7.5	0.1	19.4	13.5	2.1	1.6	2.2	63.1	28.2	25.6	867	664
Tyrrell	1.0	0.0	0.7	6.6	1.1	0.5	0.8	14.9	10.3	2.9	695	550
Union	15.3	10.3	3.9	30.6	12.4	6.2	10.4	278.0	130.4	90.4	648	483
Vance	6.2	0.1	7.9	55.2	11.9	4.8	11.8	137.8	81.3	28.7	647	470
Wake	315.7	60.3	126.3	372.9	406.5	339.1	950.3	1 895.9	699.2	728.4	1 078	833
Warren	2.4	0.4	0.6	36.9	5.1	1.4	5.6	48.5	29.0	13.3	668	537
Washington	2.2	0.3	0.4	17.1	3.9	1.8	1.3	41.2	22.4	8.0	595	463
Watauga	6.4	0.1	1.2	21.7	2.6	3.6	5.2	93.3	44.1	32.9	768	537
Wayne	202.7	76.1	11.4	109.6	24.9	11.4	26.0	285.6	184.2	57.3	508	361
Wilkes	11.3	2.0	2.4	66.4	6.6	4.1	8.8	149.1	85.9	42.6	638	463
Wilson	9.1	2.7	2.8	78.8	14.5	7.6	23.0	211.8	117.8	57.3	764	604
Yadkin	4.0	0.1	1.0	24.5	4.5	1.9	3.4	67.2	36.3	22.6	606	458
Yancey	2.8	0.0	0.7	26.1	2.2	1.3	0.5	39.3	21.2	10.4	580	413
NORTH DAKOTA	717.1	262.1	135.4	417.2	161.4	157.9	800.6	X	X	X	X	X
Adams	0.9	0.0	0.2	2.7	0.3	0.1	3.4	5.9	2.2	2.4	973	924
Barnes	5.1	1.3	1.2	6.9	1.5	0.4	6.4	29.6	12.8	9.4	838	799
Benson	6.8	0.9	11.4	9.8	4.5	4.9	16.9	20.0	13.1	3.9	567	564
Billings	1.6	0.0	0.3	0.0	0.0	0.1	2.5	5.0	2.8	0.9	1 040	637
Bottineau	3.4	0.0	0.6	3.8	1.0	0.2	3.0	15.1	6.6	5.5	800	788
Bowman	1.1	0.0	0.2	1.1	0.4	0.1	1.5	9.5	5.5	2.7	867	842
Burke	2.4	0.0	0.6	1.5	0.3	0.1	1.3	5.9	2.6	2.2	1 011	989
Burleigh	65.4	1.7	7.9	47.4	41.7	59.0	158.1	173.2	60.0	65.5	922	767
Cass	136.3	11.2	21.5	51.9	10.9	4.5	98.5	358.0	104.0	150.1	1 199	996
Cavalier	1.7	0.0	0.3	3.1	0.7	0.2	6.3	12.3	4.7	5.6	1 235	1 173
Dickey	1.7	0.0	0.4	4.2	0.8	0.2	5.3	12.4	4.8	5.0	905	854
Divide	1.1	0.0	2.2	3.1	0.2	0.1	1.3	8.0	3.1	2.9	1 325	1 204
Dunn	1.0	1.6	0.2	1.9	0.5	0.3	2.6	10.0	5.6	3.1	889	869
Eddy	1.3	0.0	0.3	1.9	0.4	0.3	2.0	8.5	3.1	4.3	1 637	1 607
Emmons	1.2	0.1	0.3	4.2	0.7	0.2	2.4	10.4	4.0	4.7	1 144	1 134
Foster	1.6	0.0	8.2	1.1	0.4	0.1	13.2	9.8	3.7	3.9	1 083	912
Golden Valley	0.6	0.0	0.1	1.1	0.2	0.2	2.0	6.6	3.3	2.1	1 123	1 077
Grand Forks	144.1	110.7	12.1	38.7	8.3	12.4	47.3	203.0	80.7	66.0	1 017	782
Grant	1.8	0.0	0.4	3.8	0.6	0.2	4.6	8.2	3.1	3.1	1 168	1 135
Griggs	1.3	0.0	0.3	1.1	0.4	0.1	2.3	9.8	3.5	4.0	1 519	1 514
Hettinger	1.3	0.0	0.2	5.0	0.4	0.1	4.8	7.8	3.4	3.0	1 139	1 127
Kidder	1.3	0.0	0.3	2.3	0.4	0.1	5.9	8.2	3.8	2.8	1 084	1 078
La Moure	2.4	0.3	0.9	3.8	0.7	0.2	5.9	24.0	14.7	6.3	1 395	1 354
Logan	0.8	0.0	0.2	2.7	0.3	0.1	2.0	5.2	2.2	2.1	981	941
McHenry	3.4	0.0	1.8	4.6	2.6	0.3	3.8	13.0	5.2	4.9	867	828
McIntosh	1.3	0.0	0.3	3.4	0.4	0.2	3.0	6.9	2.7	3.0	935	898
McKenzie	2.8	2.3	7.3	1.5	0.9	0.6	6.2	19.0	10.4	4.7	826	804
McLean	5.4	9.0	7.0	12.2	1.2	0.6	3.3	20.0	10.7	5.3	590	581
Mercer	2.4	0.0	0.5	5.2	0.7	0.2	2.4	32.7	12.7	6.1	720	679
Morton	6.1	20.1	5.4	12.2	4.4	0.8	13.1	60.8	24.2	22.0	872	805
Mountrail	5.5	1.4	1.5	5.8	3.0	3.3	131.5	24.0	15.0	5.3	818	784
Nelson	1.6	0.0	0.4	3.8	0.5	0.1	4.5	10.6	4.0	5.0	1 464	1 457
Oliver	0.2	0.0	0.0	1.5	0.1	0.1	0.7	10.4	2.7	1.2	646	612
Pembina	8.1	12.2	3.4	6.9	0.8	0.3	4.0	21.5	7.5	10.6	1 288	1 235
Pierce	1.7	0.2	0.2	4.6	0.7	0.2	8.3	9.6	4.0	4.2	935	855
Ramsey	10.5	0.4	4.5	9.6	1.8	1.0	43.1	29.2	11.4	11.2	954	783
Ransom	2.1	0.0	0.4	2.7	0.6	0.2	4.3	18.0	5.0	6.1	1 050	1 002
Renville	1.1	0.0	0.2	1.1	0.2	0.3	3.8	9.6	4.0	3.7	1 443	1 424
Richland	4.1	1.7	1.1	7.6	1.6	0.5	11.7	38.5	14.8	17.0	965	942
Rolette	28.3	3.2	1.9	24.8	10.4	9.7	11.4	32.3	25.4	3.8	276	253
Sargent	2.4	0.0	0.5	3.1	0.7	0.1	4.3	10.4	4.1	4.4	1 025	1 016
Sheridan	0.5	0.0	0.1	3.8	0.3	0.1	0.5	3.7	1.5	1.6	995	971
Sioux	8.1	0.1	1.0	5.8	6.2	9.1	18.3	11.1	9.4	0.8	191	190
Slope	0.1	0.0	0.0	0.4	0.0	0.0	2.7	1.9	0.9	0.6	743	738
Stark	8.6	0.1	1.2	12.2	4.0	1.5	16.5	47.5	21.5	16.5	747	619
Steele	0.9	0.0	2.3	0.4	0.2	0.1	5.0	6.0	1.9	2.9	1 404	1 392
Stutsman	11.7	0.3	6.7	25.6	4.2	0.6	17.8	48.6	18.7	19.6	924	789
Towner	1.2	0.0	0.2	1.5	0.5	0.1	2.5	7.4	2.6	3.1	1 152	1 128
Traill	2.6	0.0	0.9	3.4	1.9	0.2	6.2	20.7	7.4	9.7	1 178	1 153
Walsh	4.1	1.0	1.3	6.5	1.5	1.3	6.5	25.8	10.9	10.4	871	817

1. State totals may include programs not allocated by county. 2. Based on the resident population estimated as of July 1 of the year shown.

Table B. States and Counties — Local Government Finances, Government Employment, and Elections

STATE County	Local government finances, 2002 (cont'd) Direct general expenditure — Total (mil dol)	Per capita[1] (dollars)	Percent of total for — Education	Health and hospitals	Police protection	Public welfare	Highways	Debt outstanding — Total (mil dol)	Per capita[1] (dollars)	Government employment, 2002 — Federal civilian	Federal military	State and local	Presidential election, 2004 Percent of vote cast — Democratic	Republican	All other
	183	184	185	186	187	188	189	190	191	192	193	194	195	196	197
NORTH CAROLINA—Cont'd															
Swain	26.3	2 004	54.1	11.0	3.6	7.9	0.5	7.2	544	297	23	1 733	48.0	51.5	0.5
Transylvania	59.4	2 015	45.3	4.9	7.3	11.3	0.8	29.4	995	171	51	1 249	38.1	61.3	0.6
Tyrrell	13.5	3 230	51.6	0.7	3.6	8.6	0.4	0.8	197	16	0	421	46.0	53.8	0.3
Union	299.1	2 142	56.0	2.8	4.6	6.4	0.8	248.6	1 780	239	241	6 764	29.4	70.4	0.3
Vance	149.1	3 362	50.6	14.1	3.8	7.4	0.9	65.5	1 477	105	76	3 401	55.9	43.9	0.2
Wake	1 965.4	2 909	44.8	4.8	5.0	4.1	3.7	7 620.4	11 281	4 551	1 919	67 423	48.3	51.3	0.4
Warren	44.3	2 226	52.6	6.8	3.3	12.8	0.5	21.9	1 102	38	34	1 398	64.4	35.5	0.1
Washington	40.4	2 988	45.6	15.4	3.9	9.9	1.4	16.9	1 249	45	23	1 164	54.2	45.6	0.2
Watauga	90.4	2 110	39.7	6.7	6.2	4.9	2.8	39.3	917	104	80	5 118	46.7	52.7	0.6
Wayne	281.2	2 489	52.9	5.7	3.8	6.8	1.5	95.0	841	1 260	4 624	8 535	37.4	62.4	0.2
Wilkes	163.9	2 454	68.8	3.7	2.8	6.3	0.5	52.2	781	196	115	4 410	37.4	62.4	0.2
Wilson	213.5	2 848	45.0	9.2	5.2	9.1	1.4	108.0	1 441	204	129	6 011	29.0	70.7	0.3
Yadkin	65.9	1 766	57.5	5.1	5.9	10.6	1.4	7.3	196	77	64	1 551	46.0	53.8	0.2
Yancey	38.6	2 150	49.6	19.8	3.4	9.3	0.4	2.2	122	77	31	814	22.4	77.3	0.3
NORTH DAKOTA	X	X	X	X	X	X	X	X	X	9 626	12 057	56 364	35.5	62.9	1.6
Adams	6.1	2 454	48.2	0.5	2.6	4.6	11.6	0.3	126	23	17	156	27.3	70.9	1.8
Barnes	28.4	2 525	38.5	2.4	6.0	2.7	16.2	17.4	1 547	91	76	967	37.6	60.9	1.5
Benson	20.0	2 898	52.9	1.2	1.0	2.6	18.3	0.2	23	171	47	1 377	53.3	44.6	2.1
Billings	4.5	5 355	33.8	0.5	5.4	0.0	26.7	0.0	0	40	0	80	17.6	79.6	2.8
Bottineau	14.1	2 053	60.8	0.0	3.5	0.8	15.4	2.4	350	67	46	506	31.7	67.0	1.3
Bowman	9.7	3 085	57.1	0.4	2.7	2.3	16.7	0.0	14	24	21	241	23.1	74.6	2.2
Burke	5.9	2 731	53.4	0.5	2.5	2.3	17.3	0.4	189	63	14	164	28.7	69.4	1.8
Burleigh	159.4	2 242	46.9	1.1	5.5	3.1	11.3	109.3	1 538	998	483	8 246	29.9	68.5	1.6
Cass	363.9	2 908	37.8	1.1	3.5	2.1	4.8	409.7	3 274	2 066	881	8 666	39.0	59.4	1.6
Cavalier	10.5	2 304	55.9	1.4	3.6	2.0	16.7	2.1	454	45	31	277	36.1	62.6	1.4
Dickey	12.0	2 179	45.1	0.6	2.1	4.8	18.7	2.5	451	31	37	290	31.3	67.0	1.7
Divide	7.9	3 618	35.3	0.9	1.6	2.1	14.5	1.0	459	29	15	123	38.3	59.4	2.3
Dunn	9.8	2 760	60.3	0.0	2.3	1.2	19.6	0.0	0	30	24	233	32.1	66.4	1.4
Eddy	7.7	2 915	45.0	0.0	2.7	2.4	32.8	2.1	809	29	18	178	44.0	54.0	2.0
Emmons	9.6	2 346	53.7	1.1	1.7	2.8	17.0	1.4	344	33	28	236	28.8	68.7	2.5
Foster	9.2	2 562	41.2	1.0	3.4	2.5	17.6	1.5	404	29	24	230	29.4	69.0	1.6
Golden Valley	6.2	3 370	53.6	1.5	3.4	3.2	15.4	0.6	336	14	12	165	21.0	77.5	1.4
Grand Forks	220.7	3 399	32.3	0.9	4.0	1.7	4.5	255.0	3 928	1 260	3 263	8 125	41.5	56.8	1.7
Grant	8.1	3 006	41.9	14.2	1.2	2.9	10.1	1.3	483	33	18	162	21.3	76.6	2.1
Griggs	9.8	3 767	45.5	5.5	1.9	2.5	21.2	2.4	924	28	18	171	35.1	63.0	1.9
Hettinger	6.9	2 638	62.7	0.0	3.3	1.5	15.2	1.8	695	26	18	185	27.0	69.9	3.0
Kidder	8.6	3 321	49.2	3.2	2.0	3.4	17.5	1.4	532	33	17	170	31.7	65.9	2.5
La Moure	23.4	5 196	29.2	0.0	1.6	1.4	6.1	1.5	334	48	30	281	30.5	68.1	1.3
Logan	5.5	2 514	61.1	0.7	1.8	3.0	13.4	1.1	507	22	15	126	23.5	74.7	1.9
McHenry	12.4	2 183	61.4	0.0	2.3	2.6	13.5	1.8	315	78	38	405	36.5	61.9	1.6
McIntosh	6.8	2 076	57.5	0.1	1.7	1.8	11.7	0.3	99	29	22	181	25.4	72.8	1.9
McKenzie	20.2	3 538	57.1	5.8	2.7	2.3	13.6	0.3	51	82	38	1 265	30.6	68.7	0.6
McLean	19.3	2 141	65.7	0.5	4.9	0.5	10.7	6.8	760	138	61	642	35.0	63.5	1.5
Mercer	32.5	3 806	37.6	0.7	5.2	1.6	12.3	96.4	11 285	49	58	613	27.0	71.1	1.9
Morton	58.2	2 305	46.2	2.8	4.7	3.5	11.9	42.6	1 686	115	170	1 372	32.2	65.9	1.9
Mountrail	23.9	3 671	48.3	1.6	2.1	1.8	6.2	2.5	387	119	44	596	48.4	50.3	1.3
Nelson	9.8	2 887	47.9	0.0	2.7	0.3	16.6	6.3	1 846	37	23	223	40.5	57.6	1.9
Oliver	10.7	5 585	19.5	1.7	1.8	1.2	7.8	77.3	40 462	0	13	126	27.7	70.6	1.7
Pembina	21.7	2 621	57.2	1.5	2.9	3.3	10.1	5.3	640	152	91	516	34.3	63.9	1.8
Pierce	9.0	1 995	55.6	1.4	3.0	3.7	18.4	1.1	248	34	31	218	31.3	67.1	1.6
Ramsey	28.0	2 380	51.8	1.3	3.5	1.8	13.3	11.6	984	186	79	1 239	38.5	60.1	1.5
Ransom	15.3	2 647	41.9	1.2	2.8	2.1	11.1	5.1	876	48	39	432	46.1	52.0	2.0
Renville	10.0	3 926	51.7	0.2	2.4	13.6	10.6	1.0	383	25	17	200	33.9	64.8	1.3
Richland	36.6	2 081	48.0	1.8	4.7	2.5	11.1	16.8	956	81	119	1 994	34.4	64.0	1.6
Rolette	33.0	2 393	80.9	0.5	2.0	2.7	5.6	5.5	400	862	93	1 951	63.4	34.4	2.2
Sargent	9.6	2 251	53.9	1.5	2.6	2.8	11.1	5.2	1 223	50	29	243	46.4	52.2	1.5
Sheridan	3.3	2 082	54.9	0.9	2.9	1.8	21.6	0.0	10	18	11	99	21.1	77.0	1.8
Sioux	10.7	2 580	60.6	0.1	0.3	0.7	2.9	0.0	5	230	28	1 251	70.5	28.0	1.5
Slope	1.5	1 972	21.3	5.4	3.1	0.5	35.1	0.0	20	0	0	36	20.2	78.2	1.6
Stark	44.5	2 008	53.3	2.5	4.9	5.1	9.8	7.3	327	191	149	1 806	29.0	69.4	1.6
Steele	5.4	2 558	46.2	1.2	3.2	4.4	23.3	0.1	62	21	14	137	50.8	48.3	0.9
Stutsman	47.3	2 228	42.2	2.1	4.4	3.6	7.2	50.4	2 371	261	143	1 673	34.0	64.4	1.6
Towner	7.1	2 618	49.6	2.2	1.7	4.0	15.6	2.5	934	25	18	151	43.6	54.2	2.2
Traill	21.2	2 561	52.3	0.8	2.4	3.1	15.1	4.5	551	46	56	670	38.9	59.8	1.3
Walsh	23.9	1 994	52.0	2.3	3.5	4.0	9.6	6.9	576	81	81	1 390	36.8	61.6	1.7

1. Based on the resident population estimated as of July 1 of the year shown.

STATE/County code	CBSA code[1]	County Type[2]	STATE County	Land area[3] (sq km) 2000	Total persons	Rank	Per square kilometer	White	Black	Am. Indian, Alaska Native	Asian and Pacific Islander	Percent Hispanic or Latino[4]	Under 5 years	5 to 17 years	18 to 24 years	25 to 34 years	35 to 44 years	45 to 54 years
					1	2	3	4	5	6	7	8	9	10	11	12	13	14	15
			NORTH DAKOTA—Cont'd															
38 101	33500	5	Ward	5 213	56 721	858	10.9	92.2	3.6	2.7	1.7	1.9	7.2	18.0	12.1	14.2	14.4	12.7
38 103	...	9	Wells	3 293	4 702	2 859	1.4	98.9	0.2	0.3	0.3	0.3	3.8	16.4	6.7	5.9	14.5	15.3
38 105	48780	7	Williams	5 362	19 319	1 848	3.6	94.2	0.3	6.1	0.3	1.1	5.4	17.9	10.7	9.2	14.3	16.4
39 000	...	X	OHIO	106 056	11 435 798	X	107.8	84.7	12.1	0.6	1.7	2.0	6.5	18.1	9.8	12.8	14.9	14.7
39 001	...	6	Adams	1 512	28 026	1 463	18.5	98.2	0.3	1.5	0.2	0.8	6.4	18.8	9.9	12.8	14.5	13.6
39 003	30620	3	Allen	1 047	108 241	509	103.4	85.4	13.1	0.6	0.9	1.5	7.0	18.3	10.8	11.7	14.5	14.3
39 005	11740	4	Ashland	1 099	53 749	892	48.9	97.9	1.0	0.4	0.7	0.6	6.5	18.0	12.0	11.4	13.7	14.1
39 007	11780	4	Ashtabula	1 819	103 120	527	56.7	93.9	3.6	0.5	0.5	2.5	6.2	18.8	9.0	11.7	15.0	14.7
39 009	11900	4	Athens	1 312	64 380	774	49.1	94.3	2.7	0.9	2.5	1.0	4.8	12.6	26.9	13.5	10.9	11.0
39 011	47540	4	Auglaize	1 039	46 740	984	45.0	98.4	0.5	0.5	0.6	0.7	6.5	19.5	9.3	11.4	15.4	14.5
39 013	48540	3	Belmont	1 392	69 636	726	50.0	95.3	4.1	0.4	0.4	0.4	4.9	15.5	9.2	11.7	14.7	15.7
39 015	17140	1	Brown	1 274	43 807	1 047	34.4	98.4	1.1	0.5	0.2	0.3	6.2	19.7	9.4	12.8	16.1	13.7
39 017	17140	1	Butler	1 210	343 207	176	283.6	90.4	6.2	0.5	2.3	1.7	6.8	18.3	12.1	12.9	15.5	14.1
39 019	15940	2	Carroll	1 022	29 599	1 415	29.0	98.4	0.6	0.6	0.2	0.6	5.7	17.9	8.9	11.2	14.9	15.5
39 021	46500	6	Champaign	1 110	39 544	1 140	35.6	96.2	2.8	0.6	0.4	0.8	6.3	18.5	9.5	11.9	15.2	14.5
39 023	44220	3	Clark	1 036	143 351	398	138.4	88.9	9.6	0.9	0.8	1.3	6.6	17.9	9.9	11.5	14.0	14.6
39 025	17140	1	Clermont	1 171	185 799	307	158.7	97.1	1.2	0.5	1.1	0.9	7.1	19.3	9.4	13.2	16.7	14.5
39 027	48940	6	Clinton	1 064	41 756	1 090	39.2	96.4	2.5	0.6	0.6	0.8	6.8	18.6	11.0	12.5	15.2	14.1
39 029	20620	4	Columbiana	1 379	111 523	497	80.9	96.1	2.4	0.5	0.4	1.2	5.7	17.4	9.0	12.2	15.1	15.3
39 031	18740	6	Coshocton	1 461	37 132	1 207	25.4	97.7	1.5	0.5	0.4	0.7	6.3	18.5	9.6	11.3	14.8	14.4
39 033	15340	4	Crawford	1 041	46 091	1 004	44.3	98.0	0.7	0.5	0.4	0.9	6.3	17.6	8.7	12.0	14.5	14.8
39 035	17460	1	Cuyahoga	1 187	1 363 888	25	1 149.0	66.0	28.6	0.5	2.6	3.5	6.4	18.1	8.2	12.9	15.5	14.6
39 037	24820	6	Darke	1 553	52 960	898	34.1	98.3	0.6	0.4	0.4	0.9	6.1	18.7	9.0	11.5	14.8	14.2
39 039	19580	4	Defiance	1 065	39 054	1 158	36.7	90.8	1.8	0.5	0.4	7.1	6.3	18.2	10.4	11.8	14.1	15.6
39 041	18140	1	Delaware	1 146	132 797	430	115.9	92.5	3.4	0.6	3.7	1.1	6.9	18.9	10.8	14.2	16.5	13.8
39 043	41780	3	Erie	660	78 709	665	119.3	88.6	9.4	0.6	0.6	2.2	5.8	17.8	8.5	10.6	14.9	15.5
39 045	18140	1	Fairfield	1 308	132 549	431	101.3	93.4	5.0	0.6	1.1	1.0	6.3	18.9	9.9	12.8	15.8	14.3
39 047	47860	6	Fayette	1 053	28 158	1 456	26.7	95.8	2.5	0.5	0.6	1.4	6.6	18.1	8.7	12.3	14.7	14.9
39 049	18140	1	Franklin	1 398	1 088 944	33	778.9	74.1	20.0	0.8	4.4	2.7	7.5	17.8	10.1	17.0	15.8	13.4
39 051	45780	2	Fulton	1 054	42 446	1 071	40.3	93.0	0.4	0.5	0.6	6.0	6.6	19.9	9.4	11.4	15.5	15.2
39 053	38580	1	Gallia	1 214	31 398	1 371	25.9	95.8	2.9	0.9	0.6	0.6	6.2	17.5	10.6	11.7	14.7	14.4
39 055	17460	1	Geauga	1 045	93 941	572	89.9	97.7	1.4	0.3	0.7	0.5	5.8	20.3	8.7	9.0	15.2	16.3
39 057	19380	2	Greene	1 075	151 257	373	140.7	89.8	6.9	0.8	2.9	1.3	5.6	16.8	14.7	11.5	14.3	14.6
39 059	15740	6	Guernsey	1 352	41 362	1 100	30.6	97.1	2.1	0.9	0.4	0.8	6.4	18.6	9.3	11.6	14.6	14.2
39 061	17140	1	Hamilton	1 055	823 472	57	780.5	72.6	24.6	0.6	2.2	1.2	6.8	18.3	9.5	13.5	15.4	14.4
39 063	22300	4	Hancock	1 376	73 133	697	53.1	94.1	1.5	0.5	1.7	3.0	6.4	18.1	10.5	12.7	14.9	14.1
39 065	...	6	Hardin	1 218	31 608	1 368	26.0	97.8	1.0	0.6	0.5	0.8	5.8	17.2	15.0	12.5	13.4	12.9
39 067	...	6	Harrison	1 045	15 967	2 033	15.3	97.5	2.5	0.1	0.1	0.5	5.4	16.5	8.4	10.9	14.3	15.6
39 069	...	6	Henry	1 079	29 318	1 424	27.2	93.6	0.5	0.3	0.6	5.3	6.4	19.2	9.7	11.9	15.1	14.4
39 071	...	6	Highland	1 433	41 963	1 081	29.3	97.3	1.8	0.6	0.5	0.6	7.0	19.3	9.5	12.7	14.4	13.5
39 073	...	6	Hocking	1 095	28 644	1 438	26.2	98.1	1.1	0.9	0.4	0.5	6.4	18.1	9.3	12.0	15.3	14.9
39 075	...	7	Holmes	1 096	40 681	1 121	37.1	98.8	0.5	0.2	0.1	0.8	9.8	24.7	10.9	12.7	12.5	11.0
39 077	35940	4	Huron	1 276	60 231	819	47.2	94.7	1.2	0.5	0.4	3.9	7.1	20.1	9.3	12.5	15.0	14.0
39 079	...	7	Jackson	1 089	33 074	1 329	30.4	98.1	0.8	0.7	0.2	0.8	6.3	18.4	9.6	13.1	14.7	14.3
39 081	48260	3	Jefferson	1 061	71 888	706	67.8	93.0	6.1	0.5	0.5	0.7	5.1	15.5	9.5	10.6	13.8	15.9
39 083	34540	4	Knox	1 365	56 930	854	41.7	97.9	0.9	0.6	0.5	0.7	6.1	17.4	13.0	11.3	14.4	13.9
39 085	17460	1	Lake	591	228 878	256	387.3	94.5	2.5	0.4	1.4	2.1	5.7	17.5	8.2	12.0	16.1	15.5
39 087	26580	2	Lawrence	1 178	62 550	791	53.1	97.1	2.3	0.5	0.3	0.5	5.9	17.4	9.7	12.6	14.4	14.2
39 089	18140	1	Licking	1 778	150 634	376	84.7	96.1	2.6	0.7	0.9	0.7	6.5	18.4	10.2	11.7	15.8	14.5
39 091	13340	4	Logan	1 187	46 411	991	39.1	97.1	2.2	0.5	0.6	0.7	6.6	19.0	9.1	11.9	15.0	14.4
39 093	17460	1	Lorain	1 276	291 164	200	228.2	83.8	9.0	0.8	1.0	7.0	6.4	18.9	9.7	11.9	15.6	14.6
39 095	45780	2	Lucas	882	454 216	138	515.0	76.4	18.0	0.7	1.8	4.8	6.9	18.8	9.9	13.7	14.6	14.2
39 097	18140	1	Madison	1 205	40 624	1 122	33.7	92.1	6.6	0.4	0.8	0.7	6.1	17.6	10.1	13.7	17.5	14.4
39 099	49660	2	Mahoning	1 075	251 660	234	234.1	80.6	16.2	0.6	0.8	3.0	5.7	17.8	9.0	11.1	14.1	15.4
39 101	32020	4	Marion	1 046	66 396	757	63.5	92.0	6.2	0.5	0.7	1.3	5.9	17.8	9.4	13.0	15.9	14.7
39 103	17460	1	Medina	1 092	161 641	344	148.0	97.2	1.1	0.4	1.0	1.0	6.4	19.3	9.0	11.9	16.7	15.2
39 105	...	6	Meigs	1 112	23 242	1 654	20.9	98.3	1.0	0.8	0.2	0.5	6.0	16.9	9.4	11.8	14.8	15.1
39 107	16380	7	Mercer	1 200	40 933	1 111	34.1	98.0	0.2	0.5	0.4	1.2	6.6	20.9	9.6	10.8	14.3	14.9
39 109	19380	2	Miami	1 054	100 230	540	95.1	96.1	2.4	0.5	1.2	0.8	6.3	18.4	9.1	11.7	15.1	14.9
39 111	...	8	Monroe	1 180	14 927	2 105	12.7	99.1	0.3	0.5	0.1	0.4	5.1	16.9	8.8	10.5	14.3	15.4
39 113	19380	2	Montgomery	1 196	552 187	104	461.7	76.6	20.9	0.7	2.0	1.3	6.7	17.6	9.8	13.0	14.9	14.3
39 115	...	6	Morgan	1 082	14 843	2 112	13.7	95.8	4.9	1.8	0.1	0.4	5.9	18.2	9.6	10.4	14.9	14.2
39 117	18140	1	Morrow	1 052	33 568	1 313	31.9	98.4	0.4	0.8	0.3	0.6	6.3	19.4	9.5	12.0	15.7	14.8
39 119	49780	4	Muskingum	1 721	85 423	622	49.6	94.9	5.1	0.8	0.4	0.5	6.2	18.6	10.5	11.8	14.6	14.0
39 121	...	6	Noble	1 033	14 054	2 161	13.6	92.5	6.7	0.3	0.1	0.5	4.3	16.0	13.4	14.0	16.5	13.4

1. CBSA = Core Based Statistical Area. See Appendix A for explanation. See Appendix B for list of metropolitan areas with component counties. 2. County type code from the Economic Research Service of USDA Rural-Urban Continuum Codes. See Appendix A for definition. 3. Dry land or land partially or temporarily covered by water. 4. Hispanic or Latino persons may be of any race.

Table B. States and Counties — **Population and Households**

STATE County	55 to 64 years	65 to 74 years	75 years and over	Percent female	Total persons 1990	Total persons 2000	Percent change 1990–2000	Percent change 2000–2003	Births	Deaths	Net migration	Households 2000 Number	Percent change, 1990–2000	Persons per household	Female family householder[1]	One person
	16	17	18	19	20	21	22	23	24	25	26	27	28	29	30	31
NORTH DAKOTA—Cont'd																
Ward	7.9	6.3	6.7	50.3	57 921	58 795	1.5	-3.5	2 802	1 601	-3 371	23 041	7.2	2.46	8.4	27.2
Wells	12.0	11.9	15.2	51.2	5 864	5 102	-13.0	-7.8	122	243	-282	2 215	-7.9	2.25	4.8	32.6
Williams	9.7	7.9	9.1	51.1	21 129	19 761	-6.5	-2.3	663	666	-441	8 095	0.7	2.38	8.8	30.9
OHIO	9.9	6.7	6.6	51.3	10 847 115	11 353 140	4.7	0.7	493 802	354 822	-53 041	4 445 773	8.8	2.49	12.1	27.3
Adams	10.2	7.3	5.9	50.8	25 371	27 330	7.7	2.5	1 217	994	488	10 501	14.2	2.57	10.4	24.0
Allen	9.4	6.9	7.1	50.0	109 755	108 473	-1.2	-0.2	4 991	3 698	-1 466	40 646	3.1	2.52	12.4	26.3
Ashland	9.8	7.0	6.9	50.8	47 507	52 523	10.6	2.3	2 296	1 506	497	19 524	14.2	2.58	8.5	24.0
Ashtabula	10.0	7.3	7.2	51.0	99 880	102 728	2.9	0.4	4 203	3 871	190	39 397	7.2	2.56	11.4	24.8
Athens	7.4	4.7	4.3	50.9	59 549	62 223	4.5	3.5	2 093	1 581	1 680	22 501	11.7	2.40	9.2	28.3
Auglaize	8.9	6.8	7.7	50.8	44 585	46 611	4.5	0.3	1 919	1 445	-295	17 376	8.8	2.62	7.8	23.3
Belmont	10.5	8.5	9.6	50.8	71 074	70 226	-1.2	-0.8	2 189	2 920	188	28 309	0.5	2.37	11.2	28.7
Brown	9.6	6.6	5.2	50.7	34 966	42 285	20.9	3.6	1 782	1 224	993	15 555	25.7	2.69	10.0	20.2
Butler	8.7	5.9	4.8	51.1	291 479	332 807	14.2	3.1	15 528	8 689	3 982	123 082	17.7	2.61	10.7	22.7
Carroll	11.0	7.6	6.6	50.8	26 521	28 836	8.7	2.6	1 101	860	545	11 126	15.1	2.56	7.7	22.9
Champaign	10.8	6.6	6.3	50.9	36 019	38 890	8.0	1.7	1 609	1 210	302	14 952	12.8	2.56	9.2	23.5
Clark	10.8	7.4	7.4	51.8	147 538	144 742	-1.9	-1.0	6 113	5 371	-2 055	56 648	2.6	2.49	12.8	26.0
Clermont	9.1	5.4	4.2	50.8	150 094	177 977	18.6	4.4	8 775	4 312	3 546	66 013	25.2	2.67	10.0	21.0
Clinton	9.1	6.2	5.8	50.9	35 444	40 543	14.4	3.0	1 869	1 281	666	15 416	18.2	2.56	10.1	23.7
Columbiana	10.3	7.6	7.4	50.2	108 276	112 075	3.5	-0.5	4 197	4 063	-585	42 973	5.4	2.52	10.3	24.8
Coshocton	10.3	7.4	7.2	51.1	35 427	36 655	3.5	1.3	1 545	1 222	194	14 356	6.9	2.52	9.2	25.4
Crawford	10.9	7.9	7.8	51.8	47 870	46 966	-1.9	-1.9	1 905	1 679	-1 080	18 957	3.1	2.45	10.5	26.3
Cuyahoga	9.5	7.3	8.2	52.7	1 412 140	1 393 978	-1.3	-2.2	60 209	50 158	-39 958	571 457	1.5	2.39	15.7	32.8
Darke	10.2	7.4	8.1	50.8	53 617	53 309	-0.6	-0.7	2 030	1 731	-617	20 419	4.9	2.56	8.0	23.5
Defiance	10.2	6.9	6.5	50.7	39 350	39 500	0.4	-1.1	1 585	1 028	-988	15 138	7.6	2.57	9.6	23.0
Delaware	7.9	4.3	3.3	50.5	66 929	109 989	64.3	20.7	6 040	2 103	18 318	39 674	71.6	2.70	6.7	18.1
Erie	11.3	8.0	7.9	51.3	76 781	79 551	3.6	-1.1	3 008	2 648	-1 165	31 727	9.7	2.45	11.2	27.0
Fairfield	9.4	5.9	5.0	50.3	103 468	122 759	18.6	8.0	5 335	3 504	7 729	45 425	23.4	2.65	9.1	20.7
Fayette	10.3	7.5	6.9	50.6	27 466	28 433	3.5	-1.0	1 203	1 117	-344	11 054	8.1	2.51	11.5	24.5
Franklin	8.0	5.1	4.5	51.2	961 437	1 068 978	11.2	1.9	56 110	26 596	-8 950	438 778	15.9	2.39	13.0	30.9
Fulton	9.3	6.2	6.3	51.1	38 498	42 084	9.3	0.9	1 858	1 223	-228	15 480	14.6	2.69	8.2	21.1
Gallia	10.7	7.7	6.2	51.1	30 954	31 069	0.4	1.1	1 298	1 065	139	12 060	6.1	2.50	11.0	25.2
Geauga	11.5	6.7	5.8	50.8	81 087	90 895	12.1	3.4	3 512	2 071	1 699	31 630	17.6	2.84	7.2	17.6
Greene	9.8	6.6	5.3	51.3	136 731	147 886	8.2	2.3	5 593	3 873	1 793	55 312	14.4	2.53	9.6	23.0
Guernsey	10.4	7.8	6.8	51.3	39 024	40 792	4.5	1.4	1 706	1 353	258	16 094	8.1	2.38	11.4	26.1
Hamilton	9.0	6.7	6.9	52.2	866 228	845 303	-2.4	-2.6	38 818	27 347	-33 738	346 790	2.3	2.38	14.3	32.9
Hancock	9.5	6.3	6.8	51.4	65 536	71 295	8.8	2.6	3 008	2 003	899	27 898	13.2	2.49	8.7	26.0
Hardin	9.4	6.6	6.4	50.6	31 111	31 945	2.7	-1.1	1 180	937	-564	11 963	6.3	2.51	8.9	26.5
Harrison	11.2	8.6	8.8	51.2	16 085	15 856	-1.4	0.7	532	693	284	6 398	4.7	2.44	8.8	25.6
Henry	9.4	6.8	7.1	50.8	29 108	29 210	0.4	0.4	1 285	877	-286	10 935	5.1	2.62	8.1	23.5
Highland	9.9	7.2	6.3	51.2	35 728	40 875	14.4	2.7	1 920	1 495	685	15 587	17.8	2.60	10.3	23.2
Hocking	10.9	7.3	5.7	50.2	25 533	28 241	10.6	1.4	1 199	994	236	10 843	16.0	2.54	9.5	23.7
Holmes	7.4	5.7	4.8	50.0	32 849	38 943	18.6	4.5	2 747	846	-125	11 337	21.7	3.35	6.5	16.1
Huron	9.1	6.5	6.0	51.0	56 238	59 487	5.8	1.3	2 909	1 785	-329	22 307	10.2	2.64	10.4	23.1
Jackson	9.4	7.2	6.5	51.6	30 230	32 641	8.0	1.3	1 329	1 241	375	12 619	12.1	2.55	12.0	24.0
Jefferson	11.3	9.3	9.4	52.3	80 298	73 894	-8.0	-2.7	2 417	3 375	-1 015	30 417	-2.9	2.36	11.6	28.5
Knox	9.6	7.0	6.5	51.3	47 473	54 500	14.8	4.5	2 266	1 720	1 880	19 975	15.9	2.56	8.5	23.9
Lake	10.7	7.3	7.0	51.3	215 500	227 511	5.6	0.6	8 586	6 692	-332	89 700	11.5	2.50	10.0	25.6
Lawrence	11.0	7.9	6.5	52.0	61 834	62 319	0.8	0.4	2 429	2 375	227	24 732	8.0	2.49	11.9	24.9
Licking	10.2	6.6	5.3	51.2	128 300	145 491	13.4	3.5	6 341	4 207	2 956	55 609	17.7	2.56	10.0	23.1
Logan	10.0	7.4	6.4	50.8	42 310	46 005	8.7	0.9	1 967	1 450	-67	17 956	12.6	2.53	9.5	24.8
Lorain	9.6	6.4	6.1	50.9	271 126	284 664	5.0	2.3	12 080	7 884	2 543	105 836	10.2	2.61	12.6	23.6
Lucas	8.9	6.3	6.6	51.7	462 361	455 054	-1.6	-0.2	21 152	15 233	-6 562	182 847	3.0	2.44	14.7	30.1
Madison	9.2	6.1	5.1	45.9	37 078	40 213	8.5	1.0	1 640	1 189	9	13 672	14.0	2.62	9.9	22.3
Mahoning	10.0	8.3	9.4	52.2	264 806	257 555	-2.7	-2.3	9 661	10 334	-5 103	102 587	1.4	2.44	14.1	29.1
Marion	9.8	6.9	6.5	48.1	64 274	66 217	3.0	0.3	2 653	2 025	-371	24 578	4.7	2.50	11.4	25.1
Medina	9.8	5.6	4.9	50.7	122 354	151 095	23.5	7.0	6 666	3 404	7 244	54 542	30.5	2.74	7.8	18.9
Meigs	10.9	7.8	7.0	51.4	22 987	23 072	0.4	0.7	937	902	160	9 234	6.6	2.47	10.0	25.0
Mercer	8.8	7.2	7.4	50.1	39 443	40 924	3.8	0.0	1 699	1 205	-457	14 756	10.1	2.74	7.4	22.7
Miami	10.9	7.0	6.3	50.9	93 184	98 868	6.1	1.4	4 169	3 234	560	38 437	11.2	2.54	9.7	23.2
Monroe	12.7	8.8	7.9	50.5	15 497	15 180	-2.0	-1.7	515	584	-169	6 021	4.6	2.50	8.1	24.0
Montgomery	9.9	7.2	6.8	51.9	573 809	559 062	-2.6	-1.2	25 050	18 277	-13 580	229 229	1.3	2.37	13.8	30.4
Morgan	11.1	8.7	7.0	50.9	14 194	14 897	5.0	-0.4	552	551	-33	5 890	13.9	2.50	9.9	25.5
Morrow	10.1	6.3	5.0	50.1	27 749	31 628	14.0	6.1	1 408	816	1 327	11 499	19.1	2.72	8.1	19.0
Muskingum	9.7	7.3	7.1	52.0	82 068	84 585	3.1	1.0	3 387	2 697	255	32 518	5.7	2.53	12.0	24.9
Noble	8.4	7.4	6.1	43.3	11 336	14 058	24.0	0.0	393	376	-16	4 546	9.9	2.61	7.7	24.3

1. No spouse present.

Table B. States and Counties — Vital Statistics, Health Resources, and Crime

STATE County	Births, average 1999–2001		Deaths, average 1999–2001				Physicians,[4] 2000		Hospitals,[4] 1998			Medicare enrollees, 2003	Serious crimes known to police,[6] 2002 Total	
			Number		Rate					Beds			Total	
	Total	Rate[1]	Total	Infant[2]	Total[1]	Infant[3]	Number	Rate[5]	Number	Number	Rate[5]		Number	Rate[7]
	32	33	34	35	36	37	38	39	40	41	42	43	44	45
NORTH DAKOTA—Cont'd														
Ward	869	14.8	490	7	8.4	8.4	172	293	3	768	1 309	8 444	1 150	1 981
Wells	42	8.2	85	0	16.8	D	5	98	1	149	2 865	1 366	NA	NA
Williams	221	11.2	198	1	10.0	D	43	218	2	128	635	3 815	289	1 481
OHIO	153 209	13.5	108 223	1 197	9.5	7.8	23 939	211	188	39 924	356	1 727 096	469 104	4 107
Adams	393	14.3	302	3	11.0	D	18	66	1	64	224	5 189	148	629
Allen	1 579	14.6	1 113	14	10.3	8.7	203	187	3	581	542	16 855	4 956	4 703
Ashland	706	13.4	490	4	9.3	D	49	93	1	65	124	7 863	NA	NA
Ashtabula	1 329	12.9	1 117	9	10.9	6.8	99	96	3	280	271	17 600	NA	NA
Athens	638	10.2	478	6	7.7	D	89	143	2	150	244	7 644	NA	NA
Auglaize	602	12.9	472	3	10.1	D	32	69	1	122	259	8 340	836	1 349
Belmont	705	10.1	934	6	13.3	D	82	117	3	391	565	13 998	293	716
Brown	574	13.6	385	6	9.1	D	37	88	1	58	142	6 040		
Butler	4 814	14.4	2 654	41	8.0	8.5	381	114	5	792	240	42 945	16 139	5 161
Carroll	326	11.3	258	1	8.9	D	18	62	0	0	0	3 509	141	547
Champaign	511	13.2	371	4	9.6	D	17	44	1	73	191	5 665	1 070	2 735
Clark	1 934	13.4	1 666	15	11.5	7.9	202	140	2	464	319	24 374	7 784	5 357
Clermont	2 712	15.2	1 273	16	7.1	6.0	134	75	1	151	86	17 803	3 236	1 878
Clinton	588	14.5	371	3	9.2	D	56	138	1	81	203	6 315	624	1 530
Columbiana	1 311	11.7	1 208	12	10.8	9.4	118	105	2	361	324	19 879	1 230	1 197
Coshocton	480	13.1	388	1	10.6	D	30	82	1	151	418	6 080	705	1 912
Crawford	598	12.8	516	6	11.0	D	53	113	3	242	513	8 466	NA	NA
Cuyahoga	18 510	13.3	15 233	176	10.9	9.5	5 559	399	23	7 398	536	230 176	46 734	3 509
Darke	664	12.5	548	3	10.3	D	31	58	1	92	170	8 677	716	1 412
Defiance	527	13.3	331	3	8.4	D	60	152	2	111	279	6 083	NA	NA
Delaware	1 648	14.8	627	12	5.6	7.5	124	113	1	110	119	10 191	3 244	2 932
Erie	937	11.8	822	7	10.3	7.8	157	197	2	444	567	13 908	3 296	4 138
Fairfield	1 666	13.5	1 027	10	8.3	5.8	158	129	1	219	177	16 403	3 018	2 444
Fayette	372	13.1	333	1	11.7	D	22	77	1	44	154	4 367	1 062	3 713
Franklin	17 072	15.9	8 188	145	7.6	8.5	2 891	270	11	3 872	379	125 180	80 417	7 829
Fulton	587	13.9	368	2	8.7	D	24	57	1	86	205	6 637	723	1 708
Gallia	404	13.0	318	5	10.2	D	86	277	1	269	805	5 656	799	2 954
Geauga	1 135	12.5	651	4	7.2	D	137	151	1	122	137	10 617	483	572
Greene	1 716	11.6	1 140	9	7.7	5.2	293	198	1	210	143	15 717	5 556	3 735
Guernsey	537	13.2	420	3	10.3	D	64	157	1	141	344	7 550	NA	NA
Hamilton	12 170	14.4	8 383	126	9.9	10.4	3 066	363	12	4 114	485	132 278	45 563	5 682
Hancock	935	13.1	608	7	8.5	7.8	109	153	1	150	218	9 691	NA	NA
Hardin	389	12.2	294	2	9.2	D	19	59	1	51	161	4 811	NA	NA
Harrison	161	10.2	200	2	12.6	D	13	82	1	48	298	3 291	132	828
Henry	395	13.5	270	3	9.2	D	15	51	1	44	147	4 669	422	1 577
Highland	598	14.6	464	6	11.3	D	35	86	2	95	235	6 705	1 281	3 214
Hocking	360	12.7	293	2	10.4	D	20	71	1	91	314	4 168	719	2 531
Holmes	869	22.2	269	7	6.9	8.4	25	64	1	55	145	3 181	236	660
Huron	866	14.6	532	7	9.0	8.5	60	101	3	212	352	10 211	1 339	2 237
Jackson	441	13.5	363	2	11.1	D	25	77	1	49	150	5 381	480	1 462
Jefferson	771	10.4	1 022	5	13.8	D	95	129	2	374	502	15 953	1 822	2 451
Knox	709	13.0	534	2	9.8	D	45	83	1	117	219	8 835	NA	NA
Lake	2 650	11.6	2 077	14	9.1	5.3	347	153	2	339	151	36 930	NA	NA
Lawrence	774	12.4	729	9	11.7	11.2	41	66	1	183	284	11 619	297	578
Licking	1 982	13.6	1 259	15	8.7	7.6	138	95	1	185	135	20 001	4 302	3 050
Logan	635	13.8	461	6	10.0	D	47	102	1	87	188	7 382	1 084	2 342
Lorain	3 774	13.3	2 442	25	8.6	6.5	392	138	5	970	344	41 144	NA	NA
Lucas	6 486	14.3	4 599	56	10.1	8.7	1 455	320	8	2 676	597	66 964	32 560	7 189
Madison	513	12.7	361	5	9.0	D	23	57	1	107	257	5 830	NA	NA
Mahoning	2 979	11.6	3 176	29	12.3	9.8	598	232	4	1 284	503	50 229	NA	NA
Marion	824	12.4	650	5	9.8	D	126	190	2	233	360	10 751	2 952	4 431
Medina	1 993	13.1	1 053	10	6.9	4.9	157	104	3	198	137	19 111	NA	NA
Meigs	292	12.6	264	1	11.4	D	15	65	1	69	287	3 896	23	111
Mercer	567	13.9	355	4	8.7	D	53	130	1	87	211	6 648	521	1 266
Miami	1 293	13.1	916	7	9.3	5.7	138	140	2	287	292	15 687	3 015	3 031
Monroe	172	11.3	187	1	12.3	D	6	40	0	0	0	2 864	112	733
Montgomery	7 674	13.7	5 607	60	10.0	7.8	1 548	277	8	2 957	530	94 617	28 208	5 552
Morgan	174	11.7	167	2	11.2	D	3	20	0	0	0	2 286	243	1 622
Morrow	401	12.6	254	2	8.0	D	8	25	1	66	210	3 768	390	1 226
Muskingum	1 090	12.9	859	9	10.2	8.3	141	167	2	511	605	15 138	3 794	4 523
Noble	134	9.5	109	0	7.8	D	4	28	0	0	0	1 730	73	516

1. Per 1,000 estimated resident population.   2. Deaths of infants under 1 year old.   3. Deaths of infants under 1 year old per 1,000 live births.   4. Data subject to copyright.   5. Per 100,000 resident population as of July 1 of the year shown.   6. Data for serious crimes have not been adjusted for underreporting; this may affect comparability between geographic areas and over time.   7. Per 100,000 population estimated by the FBI.

Table B. States and Counties — Crime, Education, Money Income, and Poverty

STATE County	Serious crimes known to police,[1] 2002 (cont'd) Rate[2] Violent	Property	Education School enrollment and attainment, 2000 Enrollment[3] Total	Percent private	Attainment[4] (percent) High school graduate or less	Bachelor's degree or more	Local government expenditures,[5] 2000–2001 Total current expenditures (mil dol)	Current expenditures per student (dollars)	Money income, 1999 Per capita income[6] (dollars)	Households Median income Dollars	Percent change, 1989–1999 (constant 1999 dollars)	Percent with income of $100,000 or more	Percent below poverty level, 1999 Persons	Households	Families	Families with children
	46	47	48	49	50	51	52	53	54	55	56	57	58	59	60	61
NORTH DAKOTA—Cont'd																
Ward	65	1 915	16 316	8.5	41.6	22.1	58.8	6 016	16 926	33 670	9.0	4.9	10.8	11.5	7.9	11.5
Wells	NA	NA	1 158	4.7	58.3	13.7	7.0	7 572	17 932	31 894	27.8	4.6	13.5	16.0	10.3	9.8
Williams	72	1 409	5 133	8.6	49.2	16.5	23.0	6 437	16 763	31 491	0.8	4.8	11.9	12.0	9.6	16.0
OHIO	351	3 756	3 014 460	17.9	53.1	21.1	13 822.5	7 515	21 003	40 956	6.2	9.8	10.6	10.7	7.8	12.2
Adams	68	561	6 202	6.4	75.8	7.2	33.4	6 364	14 515	29 315	33.7	3.6	17.4	18.0	12.8	19.8
Allen	480	4 223	28 722	19.3	60.1	13.4	126.7	6 816	17 511	37 048	1.5	6.7	12.1	12.5	9.6	14.9
Ashland	NA	NA	14 026	22.9	63.7	15.9	53.2	6 947	17 308	39 179	9.3	6.2	9.5	9.1	7.1	10.7
Ashtabula	NA	NA	24 547	9.8	65.9	11.1	124.4	6 897	16 814	35 607	9.8	4.9	12.1	11.6	9.2	14.5
Athens	NA	NA	28 058	3.8	51.2	25.7	70.0	7 924	14 171	27 322	6.1	5.8	27.4	27.7	14.0	19.7
Auglaize	NA	NA	12 239	10.0	61.9	13.4	56.9	6 261	19 593	43 367	7.3	7.8	6.2	6.2	4.9	6.9
Belmont	74	1 275	15 628	14.6	65.5	11.1	67.8	6 970	16 221	29 714	5.4	3.7	14.6	15.3	11.7	18.4
Brown	24	691	10 406	7.1	70.5	8.8	55.6	6 493	17 100	38 303	12.7	5.1	11.6	11.4	8.8	13.0
Butler	435	4 725	95 720	14.4	50.3	23.5	372.4	6 714	22 076	47 885	9.9	12.9	8.7	8.9	5.4	7.9
Carroll	47	500	6 740	8.8	72.9	9.1	21.2	5 226	16 701	35 509	2.5	4.3	11.4	11.4	8.5	14.0
Champaign	115	2 620	9 309	12.7	65.8	10.6	53.7	7 056	19 542	43 139	2.9	6.8	7.6	7.5	5.1	8.6
Clark	409	4 948	36 734	15.9	58.4	14.9	183.7	7 390	19 501	40 340	8.2	7.9	10.7	10.1	7.9	12.9
Clermont	129	1 749	46 454	17.9	53.3	20.8	190.1	6 649	22 370	49 386	13.2	13.1	7.1	7.6	5.3	7.8
Clinton	103	1 427	10 521	15.9	59.0	14.1	59.0	7 066	18 462	40 467	10.9	5.8	8.6	9.3	6.4	8.7
Columbiana	149	1 048	26 376	9.1	67.1	10.8	122.7	6 852	16 655	34 226	9.0	4.3	11.5	11.3	9.0	14.5
Coshocton	8	1 904	8 641	11.8	72.4	9.8	41.2	6 521	16 364	34 701	9.4	4.3	9.1	9.6	7.0	8.9
Crawford	NA	NA	10 769	13.0	69.2	9.7	52.7	6 512	17 466	36 227	7.9	4.3	10.4	10.5	7.8	12.6
Cuyahoga	556	2 953	365 498	24.3	48.4	25.1	1 838.8	9 006	22 272	39 168	2.0	10.7	13.1	12.7	10.3	16.2
Darke	120	1 292	13 068	10.1	67.6	10.1	58.4	6 329	18 670	39 307	5.8	6.1	8.0	7.8	6.0	9.3
Defiance	NA	NA	10 009	14.4	61.1	14.3	43.1	6 044	19 667	44 938	6.2	6.9	5.6	6.3	4.5	6.8
Delaware	138	2 794	30 948	25.4	32.1	41.0	117.5	8 123	31 600	67 258	32.1	27.4	3.8	3.9	2.9	4.1
Erie	222	3 915	19 104	14.2	57.0	16.6	130.0	9 100	21 530	42 746	4.4	9.1	8.3	8.3	6.0	9.7
Fairfield	150	2 294	31 818	14.6	50.8	20.8	146.7	6 765	21 671	47 962	14.1	12.9	5.9	6.5	4.5	6.9
Fayette	122	3 590	6 481	5.5	68.9	10.7	31.5	6 005	18 063	36 735	20.4	5.0	10.1	10.9	7.7	11.1
Franklin	696	7 133	307 823	17.0	41.4	31.8	1 389.7	8 172	23 059	42 734	4.7	11.5	11.6	11.3	8.2	12.1
Fulton	83	1 625	11 406	11.0	58.8	13.2	74.1	7 945	18 999	44 074	2.9	7.0	5.4	5.8	4.0	5.7
Gallia	78	2 876	7 742	16.0	67.9	11.6	39.2	7 390	15 183	30 191	7.1	4.9	18.1	17.4	13.5	20.6
Geauga	26	546	24 286	26.3	41.8	31.7	99.6	7 730	27 944	60 200	9.0	22.7	4.6	4.1	2.8	4.3
Greene	135	3 599	46 402	21.7	41.1	31.1	171.6	7 359	23 057	48 656	3.1	13.7	8.5	9.3	5.2	8.0
Guernsey	NA	NA	9 866	9.9	67.8	10.0	44.1	7 004	15 542	30 110	6.0	3.7	16.0	15.8	12.9	18.6
Hamilton	640	5 043	233 939	26.5	45.0	29.2	1 015.0	8 117	24 053	40 964	3.4	12.8	11.8	12.0	8.8	13.8
Hancock	NA	NA	19 271	21.5	52.2	21.7	84.0	7 120	20 991	43 856	2.3	9.0	7.5	7.7	5.2	8.3
Hardin	NA	NA	9 275	31.9	69.9	11.4	41.7	6 692	16 200	34 440	4.2	4.4	13.2	14.6	8.9	13.3
Harrison	19	809	3 343	8.4	70.1	9.0	16.9	6 434	16 479	30 318	13.2	4.1	13.3	13.9	11.0	15.5
Henry	116	1 461	7 621	14.2	66.4	11.1	43.0	8 245	18 667	42 657	2.3	5.9	7.0	6.7	5.3	8.9
Highland	449	2 765	9 963	7.1	68.5	9.7	48.1	5 921	16 521	35 313	22.2	4.7	11.8	12.5	9.0	13.2
Hocking	77	2 453	6 737	9.0	68.2	9.8	24.8	6 056	16 095	34 261	12.2	4.6	13.5	15.2	10.3	14.6
Holmes	31	629	8 965	34.8	80.6	8.3	27.5	5 943	14 197	36 944	8.1	7.0	12.9	11.6	10.5	13.5
Huron	55	2 182	15 240	17.2	67.7	10.9	70.2	6 080	18 133	40 558	10.2	5.7	8.5	8.3	6.5	9.5
Jackson	55	1 407	7 870	9.6	69.6	11.0	34.0	5 786	14 789	30 661	24.7	2.7	16.5	17.8	13.6	18.6
Jefferson	313	2 138	17 543	20.8	64.8	11.8	81.8	7 128	16 476	30 853	3.7	4.3	15.1	15.3	11.4	19.2
Knox	NA	NA	14 679	25.9	60.3	16.7	59.7	7 076	17 695	38 877	17.1	6.5	10.1	9.6	7.4	10.9
Lake	NA	NA	56 308	19.0	48.0	21.5	282.3	8 078	23 160	48 763	1.9	11.5	5.1	5.3	3.5	6.0
Lawrence	35	543	15 147	5.8	67.8	10.3	75.7	6 738	14 678	29 127	11.4	3.7	18.9	18.5	15.1	23.7
Licking	103	2 947	37 916	17.8	56.0	18.4	163.3	6 800	20 581	44 124	10.9	9.4	7.5	8.0	5.5	8.3
Logan	95	2 247	10 951	8.7	68.2	11.5	55.1	7 041	18 984	41 479	15.0	7.2	9.3	9.3	7.1	10.3
Lorain	NA	NA	75 017	20.4	54.0	16.6	338.3	7 457	21 054	45 042	7.8	10.7	9.0	8.8	6.7	10.9
Lucas	747	6 442	129 500	20.3	49.4	21.3	539.8	7 808	20 518	38 004	0.1	9.3	13.9	13.6	10.7	17.0
Madison	NA	NA	9 790	17.0	62.7	13.0	47.4	6 663	18 721	44 212	9.9	8.3	7.8	8.4	6.2	9.3
Mahoning	NA	NA	64 677	15.3	57.7	17.5	290.6	7 370	18 818	35 248	9.0	7.1	12.5	12.5	9.6	16.1
Marion	153	4 278	16 180	10.4	64.7	11.1	84.9	7 175	18 255	38 709	9.4	5.5	9.7	9.7	7.4	11.3
Medina	NA	NA	40 364	16.7	47.6	24.8	201.1	7 221	24 251	55 811	9.1	15.0	4.6	4.3	3.5	5.2
Meigs	10	102	5 161	6.0	73.4	7.4	25.8	6 566	13 848	27 287	14.7	2.7	19.8	19.9	14.3	22.7
Mercer	44	1 222	11 195	7.2	65.8	12.7	64.6	6 585	18 531	42 742	7.4	6.7	6.4	7.3	4.6	6.7
Miami	98	2 934	24 416	13.0	57.1	16.3	126.8	7 144	21 669	44 109	4.5	9.5	6.7	7.1	5.1	8.4
Monroe	46	688	3 438	11.5	71.3	8.4	18.9	6 468	15 096	30 467	11.1	2.3	13.9	14.5	11.0	16.4
Montgomery	528	5 025	150 213	21.7	46.9	22.8	640.1	7 659	21 743	40 156	-0.7	9.8	11.3	11.2	8.3	13.2
Morgan	87	1 535	3 555	6.8	69.9	9.1	17.1	6 919	13 967	28 868	0.4	2.5	18.4	18.7	15.7	24.1
Morrow	57	1 169	7 830	10.1	68.7	9.5	34.8	6 171	17 830	40 882	11.4	5.6	9.0	8.8	6.6	9.6
Muskingum	216	4 307	21 558	16.1	63.7	12.6	114.2	7 018	17 533	35 185	9.3	5.0	12.9	12.3	9.9	15.4
Noble	14	502	3 540	10.3	69.3	8.1	14.0	5 687	14 100	32 940	13.4	2.8	11.4	12.6	8.3	11.4

1. Data for serious crimes have not been adjusted for underreporting; this may affect comparability between geographic areas and over time.   2. Per 100,000 population estimated by the FBI.   3. All persons 3 years old and over enrolled in nursery school through college.   4. Persons 25 years old and over.   5. Elementary and secondary education expenditures.   6. Based on population enumerated as of April 1, 2000.

Table B. States and Counties — **Personal Income**

STATE County	Personal income, 2002 Total (mil dol)	Percent change, 2001–2002	Per capita[1] Dollars	Rank	Wages and salaries[2] (mil dol)	Proprietor's income (mil dol)	Dividends, interest, and rent (mil dol)	Transfer payments Total (mil dol)	Government payments to individuals Total (mil dol)	Social Security (mil dol)	Medical payments (mil dol)	Income maintenance (mil dol)	Unemployment insurance (mil dol)
	62	63	64	65	66	67	68	69	70	71	72	73	74
NORTH DAKOTA—Cont'd													
Ward	1 592	5.0	27 946	560	1 129	125	285	234	222	85	83	15	5
Wells	131	12.6	27 308	647	52	22	37	29	28	12	12	1	0
Williams	486	2.2	24 917	1 156	292	39	107	96	91	42	34	6	2
OHIO	333 079	2.2	29 195	X	229 962	22 294	55 617	53 869	50 637	19 360	20 880	4 619	1 826
Adams	546	1.0	19 660	2 619	192	48	93	157	149	46	69	19	7
Allen	2 728	2.0	25 237	1 064	2 185	190	491	497	466	198	173	42	17
Ashland	1 209	1.2	22 744	1 804	666	67	220	211	196	91	70	12	9
Ashtabula	2 403	2.1	23 335	1 617	1 160	107	341	580	551	186	252	47	21
Athens	1 267	3.1	19 885	2 569	763	73	212	269	252	67	105	33	7
Auglaize	1 291	1.2	27 652	595	716	46	248	195	182	79	75	9	7
Belmont	1 632	3.2	23 390	1 597	724	94	293	421	402	159	170	34	10
Brown	990	2.0	22 815	1 775	228	61	135	197	184	67	80	15	10
Butler	9 996	2.5	29 415	401	5 351	531	1 524	1 357	1 260	514	494	104	41
Carroll	669	2.7	22 878	1 756	205	90	102	127	119	53	44	9	6
Champaign	1 011	-1.5	25 743	942	415	63	156	166	155	65	61	11	6
Clark	3 762	0.0	26 159	859	2 013	161	575	771	730	262	322	68	28
Clermont	5 431	3.0	29 638	375	2 153	340	672	683	631	260	235	45	32
Clinton	1 051	0.9	25 441	1 012	991	33	170	176	165	65	69	12	5
Columbiana	2 541	2.4	22 771	1 793	1 124	142	382	578	547	218	232	46	17
Coshocton	858	1.3	23 206	1 660	464	69	147	182	172	69	72	15	6
Crawford	1 100	1.1	23 721	1 492	581	46	198	240	227	95	88	18	10
Cuyahoga	45 866	1.1	33 382	175	37 476	4 512	8 760	7 739	7 348	2 588	3 275	755	252
Darke	1 379	-0.2	26 042	880	655	88	237	227	212	102	75	13	8
Defiance	1 030	0.9	26 259	841	760	51	162	164	152	72	53	11	6
Delaware	5 336	4.5	42 419	46	2 050	331	988	354	318	144	106	18	12
Erie	2 378	1.6	30 155	336	1 567	200	428	385	363	156	138	24	13
Fairfield	3 716	2.9	28 786	472	1 222	175	576	488	452	192	168	34	17
Fayette	702	1.0	24 964	1 143	362	44	109	141	133	47	61	12	5
Franklin	35 729	3.3	32 947	186	32 833	3 296	4 854	4 425	4 117	1 322	1 735	484	159
Fulton	1 147	1.1	27 097	681	783	82	196	174	162	73	62	9	6
Gallia	751	2.2	23 973	1 417	456	31	127	211	202	55	104	24	5
Geauga	3 507	0.9	37 868	90	1 252	217	663	329	303	152	101	11	12
Greene	4 500	3.1	29 951	356	3 207	227	784	536	494	207	176	39	14
Guernsey	893	5.2	21 705	2 087	487	61	137	229	217	77	100	20	8
Hamilton	29 845	2.9	35 883	124	27 686	2 266	6 318	4 127	3 891	1 417	1 672	395	112
Hancock	2 140	2.8	29 425	398	1 742	113	375	271	250	121	83	16	8
Hardin	671	0.8	21 134	2 256	307	30	104	132	123	53	48	9	4
Harrison	354	2.8	22 312	1 930	124	13	54	88	84	33	35	7	3
Henry	743	0.3	25 343	1 032	427	23	128	128	119	53	47	6	6
Highland	897	2.4	21 476	2 156	384	52	133	196	184	67	80	16	6
Hocking	610	3.7	21 376	2 188	221	25	79	138	130	47	55	14	4
Holmes	792	2.7	19 647	2 622	523	157	125	108	97	36	45	7	2
Huron	1 452	0.7	24 234	1 331	982	66	233	264	247	98	89	18	13
Jackson	675	3.9	20 449	2 444	359	34	95	173	164	55	67	22	6
Jefferson	1 707	3.1	23 622	1 526	925	68	303	462	441	176	183	41	9
Knox	1 345	2.9	23 925	1 432	679	97	219	263	248	96	114	17	7
Lake	7 059	1.0	30 860	280	3 911	323	1 135	1 040	976	441	369	44	45
Lawrence	1 272	2.9	20 472	2 439	357	45	155	387	369	119	163	50	6
Licking	4 108	1.9	27 631	599	1 949	220	602	608	566	230	217	44	23
Logan	1 216	2.9	26 293	834	887	46	153	200	187	77	74	14	6
Lorain	7 768	0.2	26 964	703	4 150	399	1 161	1 316	1 235	492	477	108	63
Lucas	13 093	2.5	28 959	470	10 030	867	2 073	2 387	2 258	757	990	261	86
Madison	1 062	2.1	26 313	827	532	91	141	157	146	58	63	11	4
Mahoning	6 553	2.2	25 924	903	3 788	387	1 141	1 494	1 422	553	598	133	49
Marion	1 574	2.7	23 759	1 481	1 075	73	235	313	294	113	117	29	9
Medina	4 859	1.8	30 685	293	2 070	224	734	571	526	232	198	24	25
Meigs	458	-1.1	19 760	2 598	132	38	58	128	121	40	52	16	5
Mercer	1 053	-0.5	25 760	938	526	73	208	165	154	75	55	8	7
Miami	2 797	0.8	28 076	536	1 612	97	452	421	392	179	143	26	15
Monroe	309	3.5	20 615	2 400	169	17	48	79	74	31	31	7	3
Montgomery	16 884	2.0	30 528	303	13 466	1 005	3 161	2 758	2 602	986	1 072	249	78
Morgan	297	1.6	20 052	2 538	127	22	48	77	73	27	30	7	5
Morrow	741	1.6	22 484	1 883	194	39	89	125	116	48	44	10	6
Muskingum	2 090	2.6	24 540	1 252	1 383	103	305	433	409	159	161	46	15
Noble	238	5.6	17 055	2 987	120	11	38	56	52	22	20	4	3

1. Based on the resident population estimated as of July 1 of the year shown.   2. Includes other labor income.

STATE County	Earnings, 2002									Social Security beneficiaries, December 2003		Supple- mental Security Income recipients, December 2003	Housing units, 2003	
	Total (mil dol)	Farm	Goods-related[1]		Service-related and health				Govern- ment	Number	Rate[2]		Total	Percent change, 2000– 2003
			Total	Manu- facturing	Infor- mation and profes- sional and technical services	Retail trade	Finance, insur- ance, and real estate	Health services						
	75	76	77	78	79	80	81	82	83	84	85	86	87	88
NORTH DAKOTA—Cont'd														
Ward	1 254	1.9	8.6	1.7	D	8.4	5.4	13.0	38.7	8 980	158	685	25 472	1.5
Wells	74	20.1	D	2.3	1.5	8.6	D	14.1	13.8	1 360	289	77	2 644	0.0
Williams	331	2.0	23.4	2.7	5.3	9.2	5.3	D	16.5	4 210	218	293	9 702	0.2
OHIO	252 256	0.1	26.3	20.3	9.6	7.3	7.9	10.5	15.0	1 932 026	169	243 679	4 918 787	2.8
Adams	241	-1.7	D	10.8	D	13.5	4.9	9.5	23.4	5 615	200	1 610	12 100	2.4
Allen	2 375	-0.5	35.4	29.5	3.9	8.0	3.8	16.2	14.2	19 635	181	2 466	44 601	0.8
Ashland	732	-0.1	37.5	31.2	5.4	7.2	3.2	D	16.3	9 140	170	472	21 297	2.2
Ashtabula	1 268	0.2	38.1	32.5	D	8.1	3.8	11.7	17.1	19 295	187	2 402	44 800	2.3
Athens	836	0.2	8.4	4.1	4.2	8.4	4.1	11.2	52.3	7 990	124	2 073	25 134	0.9
Auglaize	762	0.1	51.5	44.4	3.3	6.0	3.6	5.1	14.9	7 865	168	357	18 832	2.0
Belmont	819	-0.1	19.8	8.0	5.4	14.3	5.5	15.3	19.9	16 060	231	2 050	31 209	-0.1
Brown	289	-4.1	D	12.0	4.7	10.2	5.6	D	30.0	7 510	171	868	17 752	3.3
Butler	5 882	-0.1	28.8	20.2	4.9	7.4	9.8	9.8	15.1	50 925	148	5 525	134 774	3.8
Carroll	295	13.5	35.9	27.8	D	7.5	D	D	12.5	5 455	184	309	13 071	0.4
Champaign	478	0.4	D	43.0	D	7.0	5.0	D	16.7	6 680	169	446	16 296	2.6
Clark	2 174	0.3	30.3	25.3	3.9	10.2	4.0	14.0	16.0	27 120	189	3 606	61 840	1.3
Clermont	2 493	-0.3	29.8	20.8	D	9.8	10.7	8.0	12.5	26 125	141	2 225	73 823	6.6
Clinton	1 024	-0.9	D	19.9	2.7	5.5	4.3	D	13.3	7 010	168	650	17 190	3.7
Columbiana	1 266	1.2	30.5	24.0	4.1	8.5	4.0	12.8	17.8	22 125	198	2 681	46 855	1.7
Coshocton	533	1.1	39.1	33.5	4.3	6.5	3.2	D	12.1	7 215	194	709	16 255	0.9
Crawford	627	-1.4	D	39.1	4.3	6.4	6.0	D	14.1	9 275	201	866	20 365	0.9
Cuyahoga	41 989	0.0	20.1	15.3	13.8	5.6	11.6	11.1	13.6	246 390	181	40 325	617 323	0.1
Darke	744	-1.1	D	28.1	D	7.8	5.8	D	12.1	10 350	195	621	21 930	1.6
Defiance	811	-0.8	D	48.4	3.5	9.1	4.1	D	10.0	7 130	183	658	16 386	2.2
Delaware	2 381	0.0	17.2	10.3	14.1	8.9	22.0	5.5	10.5	13 980	105	629	52 409	23.7
Erie	1 766	0.2	37.0	32.1	3.4	6.4	3.7	9.5	13.9	15 095	192	1 245	36 403	1.4
Fairfield	1 397	-0.4	27.7	18.3	5.7	9.4	5.9	9.9	23.7	19 735	149	1 751	51 977	8.5
Fayette	406	-2.1	D	33.1	2.6	15.3	5.7	D	15.8	5 120	182	706	12 162	2.2
Franklin	36 129	0.0	14.2	8.7	14.0	8.3	11.9	9.3	16.2	135 685	125	23 437	498 787	5.9
Fulton	865	0.3	D	47.9	D	5.4	3.7	D	10.8	7 185	169	378	16 719	3.0
Gallia	487	-0.5	14.7	10.3	1.9	8.3	4.4	D	16.9	6 340	202	1 702	13 555	0.4
Geauga	1 469	0.2	D	30.3	5.4	6.3	4.8	7.4	11.1	14 145	151	438	34 173	4.2
Greene	3 434	-0.1	D	6.6	12.8	6.8	4.1	5.5	48.5	22 505	149	1 631	61 616	5.8
Guernsey	549	-0.1	28.2	19.6	4.4	9.8	3.4	13.9	20.5	8 460	205	1 332	19 210	2.3
Hamilton	29 952	0.0	20.4	15.0	13.0	5.7	8.7	10.8	10.9	138 315	168	20 886	378 254	1.3
Hancock	1 855	-0.5	D	34.1	3.5	7.9	4.0	8.9	7.8	11 805	161	749	30 633	2.8
Hardin	337	0.4	36.5	33.0	2.8	7.5	3.3	D	17.9	5 440	172	538	13 012	0.8
Harrison	137	1.4	38.6	18.6	2.5	5.9	2.4	D	21.1	3 470	217	406	7 734	0.7
Henry	450	-2.3	D	D	D	7.3	5.1	7.0	17.2	5 265	180	286	11 842	1.9
Highland	436	-1.6	D	28.0	5.0	10.0	9.3	8.0	20.9	7 620	182	996	17 815	1.3
Hocking	246	-1.3	D	22.4	3.0	11.5	4.2	6.6	28.0	5 200	182	777	12 166	0.2
Holmes	679	1.6	50.3	37.0	2.5	6.9	2.7	D	8.7	3 840	94	283	12 309	0.2
Huron	1 048	1.2	48.1	38.6	3.9	6.0	2.8	D	11.1	9 765	162	878	24 070	2.0
Jackson	393	0.5	43.4	34.0	2.8	10.3	3.8	D	15.6	6 335	192	1 462	14 376	3.4
Jefferson	993	0.2	29.8	18.6	4.8	8.1	3.5	15.3	15.1	17 420	242	2 499	33 565	0.8
Knox	776	1.6	39.7	28.8	D	6.8	3.6	9.6	14.6	10 070	177	863	22 720	4.3
Lake	4 233	1.5	D	30.3	7.0	8.7	3.9	9.0	12.9	41 085	180	1 799	95 743	2.4
Lawrence	401	-0.1	D	5.8	D	12.8	4.6	10.9	29.0	13 180	211	3 821	27 553	1.3
Licking	2 169	0.7	27.3	19.1	D	11.6	8.7	9.9	15.5	24 385	162	2 318	62 071	5.6
Logan	934	0.1	53.8	49.4	3.8	5.2	3.7	6.0	9.7	7 960	172	587	22 359	3.7
Lorain	4 549	1.0	38.3	31.8	4.2	7.7	3.9	10.3	17.2	48 205	166	4 946	116 930	5.0
Lucas	10 898	0.2	26.2	19.8	8.1	7.7	6.4	14.4	15.1	74 655	164	14 099	199 997	1.9
Madison	623	-1.5	D	32.2	4.9	6.5	2.6	D	22.5	5 960	147	462	14 952	3.8
Mahoning	4 176	0.1	18.8	11.0	6.8	11.3	6.7	17.1	16.4	54 660	217	7 275	112 934	1.0
Marion	1 148	-1.0	D	28.6	9.7	7.9	3.7	9.3	22.4	11 760	177	1 941	26 754	1.7
Medina	2 294	0.4	29.0	20.7	7.8	9.3	5.2	8.6	13.0	22 480	139	876	61 221	7.8
Meigs	170	11.1	D	D	D	10.2	3.3	D	23.2	4 550	196	1 003	10 896	1.1
Mercer	599	4.0	D	27.6	D	7.6	6.3	5.8	17.7	7 520	184	337	16 248	2.3
Miami	1 709	-0.2	40.9	34.8	3.7	8.7	3.8	9.4	12.5	17 930	179	1 341	41 134	1.4
Monroe	186	-1.1	59.2	53.5	2.0	4.4	D	D	16.7	3 405	228	407	7 217	0.1
Montgomery	14 471	0.0	25.9	21.5	12.4	5.7	6.2	12.7	14.7	99 285	180	13 425	251 053	1.1
Morgan	149	2.4	D	18.8	2.0	5.7	4.1	5.7	17.9	3 065	206	441	7 798	0.3
Morrow	234	0.1	31.7	24.3	D	7.6	3.9	D	25.8	5 225	156	396	12 375	2.0
Muskingum	1 486	0.1	27.5	21.1	3.0	12.0	3.8	D	14.2	16 815	197	2 637	35 529	1.0
Noble	132	-1.6	31.9	25.2	1.4	5.9	D	7.7	35.3	2 390	170	220	5 560	1.5

1. Covers mining, construction, and manufacturing.　2. Per 1,000 resident population estimated as of July 1 of the year shown.

Table B. States and Counties — Housing, Labor Force, and Employment

STATE County	Housing units, 2000								Civilian labor force, 2003				Civilian employment,[6] 2000		
	Occupied units										Unemployment		Percent		
			Owner-occupied			Renter-occupied									
				Median owner cost as a percent of income											Production, transportation, and material moving occupations
	Total	Percent	Median value[1]	With a mortgage	Without a mortgage[2]	Median rent[3]	Median rent as a percent of income	Sub-standard units[4] (percent)	Total	Percent change, 2002–2003	Total	Rate[5]	Total	Management, professional and related occupations	
	89	90	91	92	93	94	95	96	97	98	99	100	101	102	103
NORTH DAKOTA—Cont'd															
Ward	23 041	62.7	79 500	19.0	9.9	408	23.5	2.2	29 119	0.4	1 200	4.1	26 102	32.0	10.3
Wells	2 215	76.5	38 700	19.2	9.9	267	19.4	1.0	2 431	-0.3	120	4.9	2 159	33.6	13.6
Williams	8 095	71.6	56 100	18.5	10.4	331	19.8	2.0	9 830	-0.1	375	3.8	9 606	27.4	13.0
OHIO	4 445 773	69.1	103 700	20.6	10.6	515	24.2	2.1	5 915 176	1.2	363 385	6.1	5 402 175	31.0	19.0
Adams	10 501	73.9	67 400	20.5	11.4	381	22.7	5.2	11 451	1.1	1 375	12.0	11 297	20.4	27.6
Allen	40 646	72.1	81 800	18.9	9.9	446	23.1	1.7	52 574	1.9	3 703	7.0	47 919	25.0	25.6
Ashland	19 524	75.6	95 900	20.1	10.7	471	22.4	2.4	26 221	0.6	1 882	7.2	25 182	24.8	28.1
Ashtabula	39 397	74.1	85 300	20.9	11.2	473	23.5	2.4	47 067	1.9	4 172	8.9	46 701	22.1	27.7
Athens	22 501	60.4	84 300	20.2	9.9	469	36.5	3.3	29 633	3.2	1 429	4.8	26 341	34.6	11.1
Auglaize	17 376	77.9	90 600	18.7	9.9	457	19.2	1.5	24 339	0.2	1 166	4.8	23 631	26.4	27.8
Belmont	28 309	75.0	64 600	19.0	10.3	362	24.4	1.5	33 432	0.9	1 833	5.5	28 450	24.5	18.6
Brown	15 555	79.5	89 900	20.6	9.9	433	22.7	3.2	21 451	2.1	1 615	7.5	19 056	21.6	25.8
Butler	123 082	71.6	123 200	20.4	10.1	569	24.0	1.8	203 732	2.7	9 077	4.5	163 468	33.4	16.7
Carroll	11 126	80.0	89 700	20.4	9.9	411	22.6	1.9	13 788	0.2	1 123	8.1	13 216	20.6	30.3
Champaign	14 952	76.0	95 500	20.6	10.6	469	21.8	1.8	20 331	2.2	1 369	6.7	19 299	23.0	31.6
Clark	56 648	71.5	90 500	19.7	10.1	487	24.0	1.7	69 490	-0.2	5 065	7.3	67 204	27.0	22.8
Clermont	66 013	74.8	122 900	21.0	10.2	552	23.5	1.7	100 012	1.9	5 469	5.5	90 030	30.5	16.0
Clinton	15 416	68.9	96 800	21.0	9.9	494	22.7	2.3	25 912	2.3	1 185	4.6	20 421	24.2	25.9
Columbiana	42 973	76.0	79 800	20.3	10.7	421	23.7	1.6	51 855	1.6	4 082	7.9	50 310	21.3	27.7
Coshocton	14 356	76.0	79 300	19.5	9.9	385	20.7	2.2	17 180	2.3	1 393	8.1	16 846	22.0	33.3
Crawford	18 957	72.5	79 200	18.7	9.9	418	22.8	1.7	21 848	0.9	1 860	8.5	21 773	21.9	32.3
Cuyahoga	571 457	63.2	113 800	22.1	12.4	541	25.6	2.2	675 380	1.1	45 763	6.8	634 419	34.8	14.9
Darke	20 419	76.6	91 100	19.1	9.9	447	21.4	1.4	30 895	3.5	2 006	6.5	25 808	23.6	28.7
Defiance	15 138	79.6	86 800	19.1	9.9	472	19.6	1.6	21 131	-0.4	1 334	6.3	19 917	22.2	34.2
Delaware	39 674	80.4	190 400	20.9	9.9	639	23.1	1.0	70 548	0.7	2 535	3.6	58 580	45.6	9.4
Erie	31 727	72.0	109 800	20.2	10.3	498	23.2	1.5	44 123	1.4	2 629	6.0	37 750	26.9	23.5
Fairfield	45 425	76.2	129 500	21.0	9.9	550	23.1	1.1	68 571	0.8	3 550	5.2	61 476	32.2	15.3
Fayette	11 054	66.6	85 800	20.5	10.5	489	23.0	1.4	16 510	3.4	858	5.2	13 690	22.1	28.6
Franklin	438 778	56.9	116 200	21.2	10.9	595	24.3	2.7	631 795	0.8	30 811	4.9	559 129	37.5	11.9
Fulton	15 480	80.1	108 300	20.9	9.9	484	20.5	1.8	23 549	0.3	1 553	6.6	21 242	23.2	27.4
Gallia	12 060	74.8	77 600	19.4	11.9	391	27.4	2.5	16 364	2.7	1 279	7.8	12 129	25.8	20.3
Geauga	31 630	87.3	182 400	21.5	10.9	592	22.8	2.0	49 141	1.6	2 407	4.9	45 124	38.8	12.8
Greene	55 312	69.6	121 200	20.5	9.9	587	25.4	1.8	73 881	0.3	3 671	5.0	71 603	38.7	13.1
Guernsey	16 094	73.4	65 500	19.6	10.4	385	24.4	3.2	20 601	2.5	1 621	7.9	16 975	22.6	25.5
Hamilton	346 790	59.8	111 400	20.7	11.2	485	24.2	2.5	437 918	1.6	22 376	5.1	405 192	36.9	12.8
Hancock	27 898	73.1	100 400	18.6	9.9	487	22.6	1.4	43 299	-0.7	1 900	4.4	36 393	29.3	25.6
Hardin	11 963	73.0	73 800	19.3	10.1	405	23.6	2.4	15 351	1.5	866	5.6	14 705	23.2	31.1
Harrison	6 398	77.5	58 400	18.6	9.9	385	25.5	2.3	6 903	-1.7	534	7.7	6 690	21.7	25.8
Henry	10 935	80.5	86 800	19.1	10.5	480	21.1	1.8	17 394	6.1	1 174	6.7	14 096	21.6	32.1
Highland	15 587	75.3	82 100	20.1	10.2	434	22.8	2.6	19 889	3.2	1 262	6.3	17 994	21.5	30.9
Hocking	10 843	75.6	83 300	19.9	10.1	386	22.5	3.2	12 188	0.1	976	8.0	12 113	22.4	24.9
Holmes	11 337	76.9	107 700	22.2	9.9	422	18.5	6.8	20 277	2.9	689	3.4	16 677	20.9	32.0
Huron	22 307	72.2	95 100	19.7	10.0	474	21.2	2.6	29 336	0.8	2 674	9.1	28 095	21.2	33.4
Jackson	12 619	73.8	70 400	21.0	11.5	408	26.4	2.8	15 340	2.9	1 350	8.8	13 281	24.1	25.9
Jefferson	30 417	74.3	65 400	19.1	9.9	378	23.9	1.4	30 578	2.0	2 116	6.9	29 381	22.3	20.1
Knox	19 975	75.7	92 100	20.7	10.5	446	22.0	2.4	27 600	1.2	1 601	5.8	25 571	27.6	22.1
Lake	89 700	77.5	127 900	21.7	11.1	623	23.8	1.3	126 971	1.3	8 036	6.3	118 749	32.1	17.7
Lawrence	24 732	74.8	69 400	20.1	10.4	421	26.6	2.6	26 467	3.2	1 681	6.4	23 760	24.3	17.9
Licking	55 609	74.4	110 700	20.6	9.9	504	23.3	1.5	78 830	1.7	4 734	6.0	72 422	29.2	17.7
Logan	17 956	75.6	88 300	19.1	10.9	489	22.0	1.8	28 436	1.0	1 224	4.3	22 544	22.6	32.2
Lorain	105 836	74.1	115 100	21.1	10.6	518	24.3	2.0	143 704	1.3	10 451	7.3	135 582	27.4	21.6
Lucas	182 847	65.3	90 700	19.9	11.6	484	24.8	2.2	232 866	0.2	18 168	7.8	212 019	30.0	19.1
Madison	13 672	72.3	104 300	21.4	11.3	510	22.3	2.2	20 240	1.0	975	4.8	18 205	25.9	21.7
Mahoning	102 587	72.8	79 700	20.5	11.6	446	25.0	1.8	115 082	1.1	8 949	7.8	111 374	26.9	20.2
Marion	24 578	72.9	78 500	19.4	10.6	500	24.9	1.7	31 932	-0.6	1 893	5.9	29 750	22.7	27.7
Medina	54 542	81.2	144 400	21.8	10.0	625	24.0	1.4	84 921	1.4	4 764	5.6	77 827	33.0	15.5
Meigs	9 234	79.4	59 600	21.6	9.9	351	23.2	3.2	7 112	-4.7	1 115	15.7	8 953	22.0	20.6
Mercer	14 756	80.2	94 000	19.7	9.9	433	20.8	2.1	19 964	1.9	979	4.9	20 003	25.2	29.0
Miami	38 437	72.3	109 600	20.2	9.9	522	23.0	1.1	52 153	0.3	3 156	6.1	50 739	29.1	24.1
Monroe	6 021	80.7	62 500	18.9	9.9	352	24.7	3.9	5 366	1.0	471	8.8	5 891	21.4	27.1
Montgomery	229 229	64.7	95 900	20.9	11.4	525	24.4	2.0	279 450	0.4	17 618	6.3	262 274	33.5	17.1
Morgan	5 890	78.2	66 800	18.8	9.9	347	23.8	4.2	4 343	-0.3	714	16.4	5 939	23.8	23.9
Morrow	11 499	82.2	97 400	21.6	11.0	455	22.3	2.6	15 521	2.0	1 030	6.6	15 333	22.1	25.5
Muskingum	32 518	73.5	83 300	19.2	10.1	406	23.1	2.3	44 807	0.4	3 299	7.4	38 536	25.7	25.4
Noble	4 546	79.8	63 700	18.8	10.3	368	21.8	4.5	5 768	3.1	511	8.9	5 104	23.4	29.1

1. Specified owner-occupied units. 2. Median monthly owner costs is often in the minimum category—9.9 percent or less, which is indicated as 9.9 percent. 3. Specified renter-occupied units. 4. Overcrowded or lacking complete plumbing facilities. 5. Percent of civilian labor force. 6. Persons 16 years old and over.

Table B. States and Counties — Nonfarm Employment and Agriculture

STATE County	Private nonfarm establishments, employment and payroll, 2001									Agriculture, 2002			
	Employment						Annual payroll		Farms			
											Percent with—		
	Number of establishments	Total	Health care and social assistance	Manufacturing	Retail trade	Finance and insurance	Professional, scientific, and technical services	Total (mil dol)	Average per employee (dollars)	Number	Less than 50 acres	500 acres and over	Farm operators whose principal occupation is farming (percent)
	104	105	106	107	108	109	110	111	112	113	114	115	116
NORTH DAKOTA—Cont'd													
Ward	1 629	21 643	4 483	580	4 735	667	969	492	22 714	966	11.1	58.7	72.8
Wells	200	1 331	402	34	269	92	25	24	17 829	579	3.8	57.9	70.5
Williams	798	6 977	1 256	127	1 318	305	154	148	21 166	858	6.6	60.4	70.7
OHIO	269 944	4 932 943	666 671	936 161	637 766	252 318	236 447	156 868	31 800	77 797	39.5	9.0	55.9
Adams	435	4 435	893	954	963	159	96	99	22 430	1 320	33.9	5.8	56.1
Allen	2 861	50 220	9 059	10 106	7 660	1 268	1 074	1 383	27 544	968	36.9	11.3	54.8
Ashland	1 058	17 251	1 822	6 310	2 248	338	592	443	25 708	1 089	34.3	5.9	55.5
Ashtabula	2 232	29 035	4 631	9 362	4 816	632	415	710	24 470	1 283	37.9	4.1	56.4
Athens	1 157	13 572	2 161	1 368	2 578	426	462	308	22 722	673	26.7	4.8	47.5
Auglaize	1 043	17 611	1 833	7 387	2 104	427	295	526	29 865	1 020	31.3	11.0	59.3
Belmont	1 610	19 698	3 915	1 886	5 250	870	386	444	22 550	753	26.4	6.6	53.0
Brown	603	5 883	1 274	700	1 057	203	132	138	23 445	1 400	38.7	7.0	54.7
Butler	6 220	114 752	15 782	19 318	15 244	6 999	5 042	3 483	30 354	1 060	53.7	5.1	51.8
Carroll	489	5 469	640	1 799	799	94	87	121	22 072	749	28.4	4.5	53.7
Champaign	685	9 991	1 951	3 316	1 241	268	136	263	26 358	937	45.9	11.8	60.7
Clark	2 694	49 568	7 688	11 540	7 245	1 662	966	1 317	26 570	756	52.1	12.8	56.9
Clermont	3 256	47 365	4 545	7 654	9 444	2 283	2 242	1 565	33 042	973	59.0	5.1	49.0
Clinton	799	22 374	1 717	4 527	1 884	731	200	706	31 545	811	37.4	18.4	57.5
Columbiana	2 313	28 896	5 191	7 604	4 779	888	620	673	23 304	1 184	45.1	3.3	51.7
Coshocton	747	13 165	1 815	4 207	1 393	265	361	368	27 972	1 043	28.0	7.2	57.8
Crawford	949	16 109	2 098	6 687	1 567	483	911	417	25 875	693	29.1	18.0	68.7
Cuyahoga	37 897	774 716	116 180	107 812	75 951	56 661	52 702	27 515	35 516	159	86.2	0.0	47.8
Darke	1 268	16 941	2 023	5 206	2 663	589	259	436	25 746	1 764	41.8	10.2	58.3
Defiance	855	16 540	1 580	6 225	2 718	630	294	553	33 450	982	37.7	11.8	53.1
Delaware	2 804	41 760	3 120	5 337	6 802	2 235	2 737	1 452	34 779	785	54.9	14.0	55.5
Erie	2 026	31 521	3 734	8 816	4 788	699	713	1 022	32 424	392	41.6	16.3	55.9
Fairfield	2 578	31 266	4 950	5 388	5 663	830	879	728	23 297	1 173	50.3	8.6	53.1
Fayette	664	9 395	913	2 762	2 726	233	85	223	23 729	480	33.8	28.1	65.8
Franklin	28 098	629 360	70 962	51 234	81 699	60 783	41 048	22 010	34 972	561	62.4	7.8	51.3
Fulton	1 122	19 561	1 944	9 599	1 826	417	568	550	28 099	783	39.8	14.4	58.2
Gallia	642	9 697	2 602	1 003	1 713	346	131	270	27 810	936	32.5	2.8	48.3
Geauga	2 647	29 994	3 094	10 488	3 547	576	945	878	29 278	975	56.7	1.4	53.8
Greene	2 835	46 016	5 386	4 635	9 118	1 132	6 054	1 244	27 040	819	53.7	10.5	52.9
Guernsey	951	12 855	2 232	3 170	1 657	325	209	328	25 520	910	28.8	3.7	51.5
Hamilton	24 703	543 407	74 352	72 796	59 875	32 122	37 324	19 782	36 405	399	67.9	2.8	46.4
Hancock	1 795	39 942	3 518	12 538	5 214	896	787	1 218	30 491	976	35.0	16.0	58.4
Hardin	505	8 039	805	2 426	1 118	197	86	197	24 498	842	29.6	16.6	64.7
Harrison	328	3 395	507	1 067	345	D	64	82	24 264	450	18.4	12.4	54.4
Henry	612	9 024	1 082	3 683	1 018	292	104	255	28 248	844	29.3	14.9	63.9
Highland	746	9 812	1 452	3 282	1 697	417	134	231	23 518	1 381	35.8	9.8	54.2
Hocking	559	5 674	977	1 434	884	174	147	125	21 993	434	32.5	1.8	44.0
Holmes	993	13 632	1 280	4 907	1 854	325	265	318	23 363	1 809	31.1	2.2	65.7
Huron	1 248	22 478	2 072	9 558	2 631	584	335	631	28 074	865	34.0	13.4	54.5
Jackson	656	10 138	1 014	3 213	1 587	1 662	187	220	21 689	458	27.9	6.1	49.1
Jefferson	1 553	22 812	4 090	4 609	3 559	748	418	608	26 643	461	29.1	5.4	49.9
Knox	1 105	17 615	2 188	4 323	2 132	436	310	479	27 215	1 258	39.3	7.2	50.1
Lake	6 417	97 270	10 318	26 677	16 305	2 600	3 474	2 925	30 073	333	70.6	1.5	55.0
Lawrence	883	9 593	1 971	1 240	2 277	389	185	200	20 829	644	34.8	1.2	51.7
Licking	2 857	48 302	5 146	9 253	7 009	3 867	1 589	1 355	28 055	1 482	47.4	5.9	51.3
Logan	953	18 291	1 515	6 695	2 008	354	835	562	30 734	1 055	41.5	11.5	50.7
Lorain	5 873	94 341	12 069	25 262	14 244	2 176	2 557	2 759	29 248	975	52.5	8.6	53.1
Lucas	11 082	218 849	41 847	28 734	29 688	7 448	10 947	6 962	31 813	405	62.5	12.1	60.7
Madison	736	10 943	986	3 510	1 404	187	446	292	26 696	730	37.8	22.5	63.8
Mahoning	6 365	94 025	17 223	12 226	13 796	3 611	3 540	2 474	26 310	652	45.1	2.6	52.8
Marion	1 397	24 614	4 086	6 415	3 540	603	550	662	26 910	520	29.8	23.3	62.3
Medina	3 971	52 320	5 763	10 783	8 873	2 557	1 852	1 445	27 624	1 188	59.6	4.3	54.1
Meigs	346	3 228	672	D	687	156	58	84	25 984	552	24.8	5.6	52.9
Mercer	996	12 631	1 521	2 940	1 915	584	251	304	24 052	1 268	33.0	10.6	65.7
Miami	2 227	39 118	4 010	14 117	5 498	792	705	1 111	28 403	1 071	53.1	10.0	59.1
Monroe	278	3 576	D	D	389	112	D	107	29 913	654	17.6	4.1	58.4
Montgomery	13 084	283 943	41 272	50 292	33 676	10 669	14 706	9 488	33 415	832	63.5	5.8	50.1
Morgan	190	2 116	280	573	332	108	40	57	27 090	508	16.3	6.5	56.5
Morrow	406	4 553	793	1 370	680	92	134	104	22 914	863	41.1	9.7	56.9
Muskingum	1 986	34 815	5 589	9 342	5 152	860	541	868	24 933	1 222	30.9	6.6	52.3
Noble	208	2 511	418	723	398	86	20	56	22 250	602	22.4	4.8	46.8

Table B. States and Counties — **Agriculture**

	Land in farms		Acres			Value of land and buildings (dollars)		Value of machinery and equipment average per farm (dollars)	Value of products sold		Percent from —		Percent of farms with sales of —		Government payments	
STATE County	Acreage (1,000)	Percent change, 1997–2002	Average size of farm	Total irrigated (1,000)	Total cropland (1,000)	Average per farm	Average per acre		Total (mil dol)	Average per farm (dollars)	Crops	Live-stock and poultry products	$10,000 or more	$100,000 or more	Total ($1,000)	Percent of farms
	117	118	119	120	121	122	123	124	125	126	127	128	129	130	131	132
NORTH DAKOTA—Cont'd																
Ward	1 109	-8.2	1 148	1	862	499 311	419	121 374	91	94 127	83.0	17.0	69.6	31.4	9 373	70.3
Wells	668	-10.2	1 154	D	560	414 378	375	159 854	61	105 828	82.9	17.1	59.2	32.3	6 081	81.0
Williams	1 181	-2.0	1 376	21	845	456 077	323	113 135	66	76 873	83.7	16.3	65.3	25.9	6 551	73.0
OHIO	14 583	3.4	187	41	11 424	509 307	2 732	68 119	4 264	54 804	54.1	45.9	40.0	11.4	197 425	37.1
Adams	198	1.5	150	0	107	239 479	1 890	35 465	20	15 501	50.8	49.2	28.7	3.4	1 320	38.3
Allen	188	-1.1	194	0	168	576 950	3 031	72 666	41	42 628	73.3	26.7	48.8	12.3	2 859	56.9
Ashland	161	-1.8	148	0	119	464 749	2 890	67 764	50	46 126	30.9	69.1	43.2	10.4	2 304	39.6
Ashtabula	170	14.1	133	0	112	292 427	2 399	47 257	40	31 126	49.8	50.2	33.5	7.0	1 928	27.1
Athens	105	26.5	156	0	44	226 787	1 780	40 665	8	11 826	44.0	56.0	20.2	2.4	304	21.5
Auglaize	218	2.3	214	0	199	608 027	2 932	139 817	70	69 044	43.4	56.6	59.8	18.9	4 493	61.6
Belmont	142	-4.1	188	0	68	310 286	1 644	58 902	15	19 622	29.7	70.3	26.8	5.7	531	18.5
Brown	221	12.8	158	0	159	386 449	2 367	51 088	31	22 270	82.4	17.6	34.9	6.5	2 019	32.3
Butler	138	2.2	130	0	106	493 643	4 111	53 320	35	33 258	68.4	31.6	25.5	7.0	1 973	24.4
Carroll	124	9.7	165	0	75	367 438	2 091	36 689	23	31 085	52.1	47.9	29.8	6.4	903	26.6
Champaign	208	-6.3	222	D	180	626 706	2 842	73 946	50	53 839	74.1	25.9	41.6	12.6	3 686	47.3
Clark	165	-4.1	219	2	143	724 496	3 539	78 700	71	93 796	78.3	21.7	38.4	13.5	2 866	39.0
Clermont	116	31.8	119	0	85	450 268	3 611	49 546	18	18 661	87.5	12.5	20.3	5.1	584	11.9
Clinton	239	7.2	294	0	213	835 802	2 900	97 213	53	65 183	89.0	11.0	51.0	19.4	4 404	56.2
Columbiana	136	-1.4	115	0	93	345 270	2 896	62 850	44	36 789	30.1	69.9	32.1	10.7	2 084	21.7
Coshocton	180	5.9	172	0	103	394 453	2 278	79 106	35	33 133	35.3	64.7	32.5	7.7	2 192	33.0
Crawford	234	3.1	338	0	214	863 236	2 438	121 839	69	99 358	56.2	43.8	62.2	20.8	3 664	58.2
Cuyahoga	4	0.0	26	0	2	541 920	21 742	79 448	19	117 116	96.5	3.5	34.0	14.5	D	D
Darke	339	3.0	192	1	308	617 607	3 170	95 332	304	172 452	17.3	82.7	53.2	19.9	5 562	46.0
Defiance	209	12.4	213	0	183	456 584	2 069	54 088	43	43 995	75.3	24.7	41.6	12.3	3 126	68.3
Delaware	163	1.2	207	0	139	714 762	3 793	62 094	50	64 270	77.8	22.2	39.4	13.8	2 282	35.0
Erie	95	5.6	242	0	83	819 142	3 118	82 603	33	83 180	90.0	10.0	55.1	18.6	1 090	45.4
Fairfield	196	-0.5	167	0	154	505 863	3 324	66 480	41	35 020	70.6	29.4	34.0	9.3	2 880	39.9
Fayette	203	-16.5	423	0	185	1 028 723	2 423	171 321	46	96 524	87.8	12.2	57.3	30.4	2 938	52.3
Franklin	82	2.5	145	1	64	643 692	4 684	57 608	32	56 154	91.1	8.9	32.1	10.3	1 051	25.5
Fulton	197	0.0	252	3	180	651 679	2 654	98 867	70	89 539	62.1	37.9	56.2	21.5	3 665	54.9
Gallia	118	0.9	126	0	51	195 117	1 799	26 612	14	15 272	37.1	62.9	22.6	2.7	325	14.4
Geauga	66	11.9	68	0	37	384 254	6 207	23 082	23	23 318	58.6	41.4	29.7	4.7	395	5.9
Greene	169	-5.1	206	1	146	595 720	3 082	67 634	51	61 731	83.1	16.9	40.0	12.8	2 089	38.8
Guernsey	137	-0.7	151	0	63	224 428	1 915	33 657	13	14 126	26.8	73.2	25.6	3.4	410	20.7
Hamilton	30	3.4	74	1	19	356 530	5 138	37 600	24	59 235	81.6	18.4	26.8	11.3	132	7.8
Hancock	262	-5.4	269	0	240	680 969	2 424	75 371	46	47 318	77.5	22.5	55.9	13.9	3 346	54.3
Hardin	246	-0.4	293	D	224	665 100	2 194	88 055	96	113 479	35.9	64.1	51.8	16.6	4 294	58.1
Harrison	138	25.5	308	0	57	354 993	1 157	34 933	17	37 399	12.8	87.2	31.3	5.1	594	20.9
Henry	236	-3.3	280	0	222	737 870	2 522	77 963	59	69 808	90.5	9.5	66.5	18.2	3 621	60.5
Highland	273	12.8	198	0	207	486 006	2 452	66 332	44	31 560	72.7	27.3	36.0	8.6	4 809	57.1
Hocking	50	4.2	115	0	23	232 684	2 516	34 537	4	8 189	58.5	41.5	17.3	1.6	179	20.5
Holmes	207	20.3	114	0	132	381 197	3 484	49 897	97	53 645	10.6	89.4	54.9	13.4	2 100	14.2
Huron	228	-1.7	264	4	199	735 890	2 771	85 037	66	76 759	80.3	19.7	49.4	15.8	3 405	51.9
Jackson	74	0.0	161	0	41	250 606	1 367	44 515	6	13 892	37.8	62.2	23.8	2.2	301	30.1
Jefferson	67	-5.6	146	0	35	206 595	1 866	49 333	7	14 674	39.2	60.8	25.4	3.7	333	23.6
Knox	209	1.5	166	0	150	440 415	2 878	53 830	55	43 575	44.0	56.0	38.0	9.5	2 597	35.9
Lake	20	5.3	59	2	12	388 816	8 039	65 035	72	217 695	98.9	1.1	39.9	15.0	D	D
Lawrence	65	10.2	101	0	25	161 919	1 785	19 688	4	5 793	47.8	52.2	10.9	0.9	153	13.0
Licking	237	0.0	160	0	173	583 951	3 517	52 525	106	71 338	37.3	62.7	30.6	7.0	3 477	24.9
Logan	225	2.7	213	0	189	538 384	2 148	93 552	49	46 417	56.7	43.3	34.9	11.3	3 947	51.6
Lorain	162	23.7	166	2	137	548 493	3 164	79 050	98	100 295	86.8	13.2	43.1	11.8	1 844	27.2
Lucas	78	-2.5	192	2	74	639 642	3 365	102 135	41	102 350	92.9	7.1	48.9	20.5	1 313	33.6
Madison	246	-6.1	337	0	225	1 068 829	3 099	115 994	61	83 248	76.8	23.2	55.2	24.9	4 037	47.4
Mahoning	77	5.5	117	1	58	379 707	3 110	51 881	28	42 179	45.8	54.2	38.0	10.4	730	18.9
Marion	206	-6.8	395	0	190	904 764	2 229	121 072	48	91 545	74.3	25.7	60.8	21.9	3 812	63.3
Medina	123	18.3	103	0	93	431 717	4 851	64 602	40	34 069	59.0	41.0	31.7	6.9	1 239	15.6
Meigs	90	5.9	164	1	41	300 965	1 731	41 497	19	34 661	75.6	24.4	28.3	6.9	382	24.8
Mercer	269	3.1	212	0	243	692 702	3 257	103 725	277	218 747	12.7	87.3	69.6	34.5	7 060	58.9
Miami	184	-4.2	172	1	164	524 193	3 275	61 680	40	37 170	78.4	21.6	37.6	10.2	2 906	38.4
Monroe	107	-2.7	164	0	43	214 402	1 408	30 163	7	10 897	19.8	80.2	18.8	2.6	310	21.1
Montgomery	102	-3.8	122	0	87	490 185	3 876	54 480	33	39 591	87.5	12.5	30.6	7.3	1 228	27.4
Morgan	100	2.0	197	D	43	289 384	1 467	41 806	9	18 294	26.3	73.7	25.8	4.1	465	29.5
Morrow	179	11.2	207	0	147	546 657	2 464	59 184	36	41 421	65.4	34.6	39.4	10.2	2 485	39.4
Muskingum	193	7.2	158	0	102	270 530	1 924	47 145	26	20 961	38.6	61.4	26.8	4.9	1 569	27.2
Noble	107	8.1	178	0	50	273 779	1 611	37 796	5	8 755	40.2	59.9	16.8	1.3	152	13.0

Table B. States and Counties — Residential Construction, Wholesale Trade, Retail Trade, and Real Estate

STATE County	New construction ($1,000)	Number of housing units	Number of establishments	Number of employees	Sales (mil dol)	Annual payroll (mil dol)	Number of establishments	Number of employees	Sales (mil dol)	Annual payroll (mil dol)	Number of establishments	Number of employees	Receipts (mil dol)	Annual payroll (mil dol)
	133	134	135	136	137	138	139	140	141	142	143	144	145	146
NORTH DAKOTA—Cont'd														
Ward	14 864	158	95	1 203	701.6	32.9	339	4 819	753.7	74.3	60	234	27.1	3.6
Wells	150	1	18	148	91.2	3.7	42	238	41.4	3.4	7	12	0.7	0.1
Williams	3 357	32	89	693	331.0	17.4	138	1 417	207.5	19.7	27	109	12.9	3.0
OHIO	7 502 920	53 041	17 322	254 226	158 310.2	9 192.2	44 521	630 098	102 938.8	9 924.5	9 692	62 628	7 243.7	1 334.6
Adams	120	1	9	50	32.1	1.2	105	913	134.5	12.0	9	25	1.3	0.3
Allen	44 094	284	190	D	D	D	542	7 908	1 291.4	116.0	107	454	37.7	6.8
Ashland	17 391	150	47	282	121.3	7.3	183	2 242	311.1	33.0	34	124	10.0	2.0
Ashtabula	6 844	331	86	572	152.0	12.9	429	4 962	711.1	68.9	78	249	22.9	3.9
Athens	3 187	40	37	298	72.5	7.7	232	2 609	345.7	36.3	61	252	16.6	3.4
Auglaize	27 423	200	46	D	D	D	192	2 114	341.5	30.1	32	97	10.0	1.3
Belmont	2 604	23	58	D	D	D	383	5 359	737.6	68.3	48	226	11.5	2.8
Brown	16 013	115	15	239	73.7	5.6	114	922	141.7	12.4	18	56	3.2	0.5
Butler	400 353	2 635	454	D	D	D	922	13 529	2 188.6	208.5	235	1 324	149.7	25.7
Carroll	909	6	25	180	83.6	5.2	79	819	129.6	11.3	7	23	1.5	0.1
Champaign	22 178	202	31	427	160.8	11.4	124	1 254	204.1	18.3	27	83	6.2	0.8
Clark	33 033	273	124	1 704	1 035.2	49.6	528	7 439	1 102.9	107.9	82	317	32.4	5.0
Clermont	208 435	1 436	186	2 602	1 935.9	96.5	540	8 901	1 656.2	141.0	112	525	62.7	8.8
Clinton	24 065	209	39	360	192.2	11.1	154	2 101	434.7	33.4	23	200	56.1	5.7
Columbiana	7 889	83	111	866	278.0	24.5	468	4 934	823.4	68.7	65	303	22.5	4.7
Coshocton	695	4	31	203	70.5	4.7	146	1 538	209.8	20.1	13	73	7.1	2.3
Crawford	6 715	45	52	520	175.4	13.3	173	1 726	251.8	23.6	27	83	6.6	1.1
Cuyahoga	382 990	2 108	3 292	52 577	31 169.4	2 131.0	5 700	78 658	12 662.9	1 310.3	1 516	16 216	1 939.1	351.0
Darke	12 573	105	65	985	491.2	30.1	206	2 398	385.4	37.4	30	133	15.5	3.6
Defiance	17 520	146	46	568	306.7	16.4	195	2 580	424.8	39.7	24	123	11.0	2.2
Delaware	560 558	2 864	173	1 596	828.4	62.2	258	4 080	792.9	70.2	86	230	29.0	4.5
Erie	41 265	334	94	1 123	397.0	31.0	382	4 784	732.0	71.4	77	292	27.2	5.1
Fairfield	247 132	1 553	104	649	209.1	18.6	405	5 430	841.7	81.9	87	418	38.6	7.2
Fayette	13 114	100	44	329	749.2	10.8	246	2 154	329.8	30.6	14	48	7.0	0.9
Franklin	1 130 494	9 580	1 843	36 442	22 320.0	1 411.7	4 276	76 175	13 622.2	1 355.4	1 262	10 255	1 089.3	237.6
Fulton	23 557	170	68	603	365.4	16.9	179	1 715	294.2	26.3	32	171	15.6	2.5
Gallia	415	4	27	187	45.2	2.6	172	1 665	281.5	24.0	25	74	4.4	0.9
Geauga	92 386	394	194	1 425	691.5	53.9	317	3 311	565.0	55.6	68	194	30.0	3.8
Greene	160 579	1 158	110	1 316	1 540.4	47.0	564	8 922	1 321.9	125.0	104	386	52.6	6.9
Guernsey	6 846	61	42	390	97.3	10.8	167	1 722	294.0	24.9	30	160	11.3	1.8
Hamilton	281 980	2 346	2 047	37 207	32 788.6	1 413.1	3 774	59 154	9 310.4	938.2	1 076	7 783	1 197.0	207.2
Hancock	39 553	221	103	1 053	507.6	30.5	323	4 557	767.9	67.6	63	389	39.4	7.4
Hardin	3 730	38	19	D	D	D	111	1 089	160.7	14.5	13	47	2.9	0.4
Harrison	665	3	18	185	63.1	6.0	60	379	55.2	5.0	8	103	2.9	0.9
Henry	12 924	98	43	283	216.7	7.8	106	1 060	191.5	16.3	15	74	7.4	1.3
Highland	7 349	107	45	424	218.2	7.8	160	1 698	258.5	22.9	24	112	7.5	1.1
Hocking	8 123	108	14	D	D	D	92	880	145.1	14.3	16	45	3.5	0.4
Holmes	1 417	14	38	418	92.5	9.4	159	1 495	242.0	24.0	11	28	1.9	0.5
Huron	21 662	192	54	573	204.4	16.0	234	2 616	445.0	38.1	45	144	12.8	2.6
Jackson	12 605	124	27	304	72.5	7.2	162	1 542	234.8	21.5	13	42	2.9	0.5
Jefferson	5 609	33	69	D	D	D	335	3 969	531.4	52.9	50	198	15.9	3.2
Knox	41 956	394	58	362	168.3	9.0	183	2 076	313.4	28.8	39	147	9.8	1.5
Lake	178 475	895	425	4 392	1 590.9	148.8	975	15 509	2 831.2	260.7	180	801	87.0	13.9
Lawrence	1 475	16	37	D	D	D	206	2 503	360.7	31.7	24	D	D	D
Licking	203 606	1 325	144	1 600	623.1	45.1	502	6 392	1 105.2	104.2	100	493	37.4	8.4
Logan	24 398	191	45	1 671	844.2	47.2	187	1 919	309.0	26.9	29	79	6.9	1.2
Lorain	359 657	2 262	245	2 627	997.6	74.8	929	13 595	2 379.8	210.1	204	868	76.6	13.7
Lucas	240 742	1 681	751	10 580	6 302.2	377.3	1 860	29 585	4 842.2	473.7	403	2 530	289.8	55.5
Madison	23 701	250	38	904	355.4	26.2	122	1 423	276.8	22.5	19	75	5.5	0.8
Mahoning	76 554	574	407	5 559	2 132.4	177.3	1 187	16 420	2 547.9	235.5	173	1 028	102.8	19.4
Marion	17 788	158	61	559	219.3	17.5	237	3 549	548.9	53.8	55	202	17.5	3.9
Medina	264 941	1 381	295	2 724	1 155.8	93.5	524	7 764	1 346.0	123.4	99	378	46.0	7.0
Meigs	738	8	12	70	21.7	1.5	98	798	113.9	11.0	8	26	1.6	0.3
Mercer	26 880	170	57	952	384.7	24.1	192	2 151	330.0	32.3	29	116	16.4	3.0
Miami	64 025	342	110	1 832	3 072.8	56.2	371	5 018	845.4	72.4	82	332	33.2	5.5
Monroe	0	0	8	D	D	D	58	445	50.5	5.3	7	D	D	D
Montgomery	297 201	2 418	888	12 913	7 638.5	508.0	2 143	35 936	5 603.5	549.9	533	3 336	393.4	75.4
Morgan	50	1	10	D	D	D	35	345	45.4	3.8	4	D	D	D
Morrow	5 350	56	8	D	D	D	65	670	113.5	8.6	18	43	2.6	0.3
Muskingum	4 024	70	79	1 114	415.6	30.0	428	4 690	787.9	68.1	67	214	23.1	4.4
Noble	2 883	34	8	109	28.2	2.1	47	393	54.0	4.9	3	D	D	D

1. Establishments with payroll.

Table B. States and Counties — Professional Services, Manufacturing, and Accommodation and Foodservices

STATE County	Professional, scientific, and technical services,[1] 1997				Manufacturing, 1997				Accommodation and foodservices, 1997			
	Number of establish-ments	Number of employees	Receipts (mil dol)	Annual payroll (mil dol)	Number of establish-ments	Number of employees	Receipts (mil dol)	Annual payroll (mil dol)	Number of establish-ments	Number of employees	Sales (mil dol)	Annual payroll (mil dol)
	147	148	149	150	151	152	153	154	155	156	157	158
NORTH DAKOTA—Cont'd												
Ward	86	818	38.0	17.4	58	770	281.6	18.0	158	2 896	72.1	20.9
Wells	14	31	1.1	0.3	NA	NA	NA	NA	21	164	2.9	0.7
Williams	42	171	8.5	4.0	NA	NA	NA	NA	63	819	20.8	6.0
OHIO	21 182	182 805	18 294.7	6 948.0	17 974	984 201	241 902.9	35 950.5	22 631	401 206	12 411.0	3 444.2
Adams	23	82	4.9	1.1	31	D	D	D	37	508	13.9	3.7
Allen	171	951	59.8	21.9	132	9 529	6 631.7	407.8	231	4 260	127.5	33.1
Ashland	48	396	28.5	10.2	98	7 135	1 157.5	215.7	102	1 440	40.7	11.4
Ashtabula	105	340	23.8	7.8	175	9 984	1 794.3	302.6	235	2 759	83.8	21.7
Athens	61	333	18.7	8.1	43	1 351	222.1	32.5	141	2 364	57.4	16.2
Auglaize	46	207	18.1	4.7	93	8 236	1 737.6	288.7	102	1 533	37.9	10.4
Belmont	81	327	23.7	7.3	55	1 523	272.5	36.9	152	2 281	67.6	18.0
Brown	28	84	5.4	1.7	25	1 110	280.8	33.4	60	531	15.6	3.8
Butler	444	3 148	291.9	89.2	396	20 391	6 567.8	819.2	519	9 919	286.3	79.6
Carroll	20	52	3.8	1.1	40	1 782	302.3	56.7	45	459	10.5	2.7
Champaign	26	93	5.4	1.5	55	3 452	946.8	101.3	64	776	20.0	5.2
Clark	146	738	43.5	16.7	230	13 231	4 071.5	520.0	248	4 662	132.8	36.6
Clermont	258	1 541	183.0	58.8	167	7 892	1 544.3	305.5	224	4 370	133.9	37.7
Clinton	34	166	8.5	3.8	50	4 969	809.6	135.5	74	1 268	36.3	10.1
Columbiana	127	850	51.5	22.3	209	8 616	1 109.3	246.3	210	2 526	70.1	19.2
Coshocton	31	321	26.5	6.4	55	4 814	1 191.3	162.9	52	719	19.2	5.7
Crawford	41	159	9.2	3.1	90	6 575	1 194.7	211.6	94	1 160	30.5	7.8
Cuyahoga	3 936	40 008	4 384.1	1 769.9	2 712	116 680	23 382.3	4 640.6	3 031	55 025	1 846.3	493.4
Darke	50	166	11.7	4.7	92	5 811	1 147.4	172.4	91	1 143	32.4	8.5
Defiance	42	221	19.2	5.9	48	7 150	1 338.9	329.2	72	1 281	33.4	8.9
Delaware	211	1 435	304.2	79.3	117	5 131	1 285.7	187.6	160	2 623	79.3	23.9
Erie	107	470	38.4	17.2	154	6 251	833.7	188.2	185	3 478	106.8	30.4
Fairfield	159	587	45.5	17.0	45	2 959	572.8	83.5	56	1 002	32.4	9.2
Fayette	26	75	5.7	1.5	45	2 959	572.8	83.5	56	1 002	32.4	9.2
Franklin	2 934	30 270	3 163.8	1 195.7	1 061	48 265	11 837.7	1 754.6	2 330	49 486	1 669.9	483.2
Fulton	43	204	17.9	5.2	110	9 108	1 673.4	276.5	78	1 002	27.8	7.3
Gallia	31	314	12.4	7.0	18	948	117.6	26.9	59	970	30.9	7.9
Geauga	236	716	66.9	24.6	233	9 851	1 380.2	306.2	146	1 977	58.6	16.8
Greene	328	5 471	628.3	231.4	141	4 952	738.0	166.2	248	5 129	157.3	44.3
Guernsey	49	203	17.2	5.3	59	3 773	899.9	113.7	91	1 459	49.3	14.1
Hamilton	2 527	29 765	3 162.6	1 244.3	1 450	76 053	20 077.9	3 027.9	1 967	40 513	1 365.9	387.4
Hancock	104	508	35.5	14.2	97	11 964	2 792.4	422.5	172	3 184	87.5	25.8
Hardin	22	61	3.3	0.8	38	2 412	484.3	84.6	58	647	17.2	5.0
Harrison	19	72	2.0	0.6	24	678	105.8	14.2	37	225	5.7	1.4
Henry	26	87	4.7	1.4	54	3 947	1 721.1	148.6	60	D	D	D
Highland	38	107	5.2	1.4	41	3 851	653.8	94.4	58	743	22.9	5.8
Hocking	22	142	6.1	2.8	26	2 102	341.2	60.4	51	619	20.4	5.5
Holmes	32	180	10.1	3.7	164	4 621	710.1	100.2	58	845	26.0	7.5
Huron	61	488	24.6	10.0	110	11 114	2 152.7	326.0	110	1 696	43.6	12.5
Jackson	29	139	9.4	2.3	37	3 631	780.5	83.4	49	694	21.7	5.6
Jefferson	88	352	17.6	6.9	45	2 244	463.3	78.7	166	1 724	48.6	13.6
Knox	46	211	14.2	5.1	72	4 924	972.3	174.4	96	1 418	36.9	10.5
Lake	499	3 214	235.8	103.3	769	25 423	4 661.0	893.2	482	9 435	257.2	68.6
Lawrence	40	140	8.4	3.2	44	1 969	998.1	65.0	73	1 078	32.1	8.3
Licking	162	1 433	76.2	32.9	150	9 489	2 455.1	321.1	266	4 206	124.4	35.8
Logan	54	658	38.6	13.9	58	6 295	3 766.0	238.9	101	1 502	37.0	10.5
Lorain	329	1 766	119.0	53.4	437	27 252	11 225.5	1 054.4	489	7 639	215.9	56.2
Lucas	932	9 186	895.0	329.7	652	33 116	12 071.0	1 404.8	1 034	18 683	602.0	161.6
Madison	35	264	19.3	7.2	51	3 401	606.5	102.8	61	1 219	39.6	11.0
Mahoning	426	2 485	189.4	76.5	405	13 001	2 110.0	398.6	536	8 653	255.8	69.3
Marion	81	399	23.0	8.2	86	6 842	1 924.7	229.8	116	1 947	57.7	15.4
Medina	276	1 157	89.1	33.2	306	10 672	1 744.7	346.7	229	4 400	117.6	33.6
Meigs	21	63	2.9	0.9	NA	NA	NA	NA	26	313	10.1	2.3
Mercer	27	179	14.9	4.8	62	4 473	775.7	130.8	79	1 027	27.5	7.4
Miami	135	534	36.5	16.6	265	13 848	2 611.8	454.9	178	3 231	91.4	26.2
Monroe	16	54	2.6	0.7	21	D	D	D	18	D	D	D
Montgomery	1 206	12 424	1 232.1	442.6	927	56 299	15 734.7	2 337.3	1 129	23 022	717.5	202.7
Morgan	13	53	3.5	0.6	10	921	135.5	27.5	15	178	4.2	1.2
Morrow	13	46	1.8	0.6	27	1 778	366.2	57.5	39	370	10.2	2.5
Muskingum	79	397	31.4	11.0	113	10 096	1 214.6	248.8	189	3 177	91.6	25.2
Noble	6	22	1.1	0.4	12	D	D	D	18	204	6.1	1.7

1. Firms subject to federal tax.

Table B. States and Counties — **Health Care and Social Assistance, Other Services, and Federal Funds**

STATE County	Health care and social assistance,[1] 1997				Other services,[1] 1997				Federal funds and grants, 2002–2003 Expenditures (mil dol)			
										Direct payments for individuals[2]		
	Number of establishments	Number of employees	Receipts (mil dol)	Annual payroll (mil dol)	Number of establishments	Number of employees	Receipts (mil dol)	Annual payroll (mil dol)	Total	Social Security and government retirement	Medicare	Food stamps and Supplemental Security Income
	159	160	161	162	163	164	165	166	167	168	169	170
NORTH DAKOTA—Cont'd												
Ward...............	105	1 081	92.6	29.7	110	592	28.7	8.7	576.7	136.0	44.8	6.0
Wells...............	6	29	1.8	0.6	13	23	2.0	0.4	50.5	16.0	7.4	0.5
Williams............	49	251	14.3	5.2	52	234	16.4	3.9	112.8	51.1	20.0	2.6
OHIO	20 399	261 520	15 440.1	7 477.0	17 314	116 165	7 087.5	2 165.7	69 901.6	24 062.5	11 382.7	2 165.3
Adams................	31	393	15.2	6.1	18	47	2.3	0.4	198.9	62.7	28.2	11.5
Allen................	201	2 625	161.8	86.0	182	1 071	61.2	17.0	711.3	379.1	101.4	25.2
Ashland..............	83	851	37.4	18.6	75	350	19.7	5.8	193.1	103.9	36.7	4.5
Ashtabula............	149	2 319	122.5	53.6	140	585	27.0	7.6	557.8	239.9	127.9	21.4
Athens...............	77	891	49.5	21.9	53	266	10.7	3.4	322.6	92.3	47.3	16.9
Auglaize.............	67	815	41.3	17.8	74	431	25.4	8.7	197.0	87.9	48.4	2.5
Belmont..............	121	1 643	66.0	29.6	93	418	21.5	6.3	422.3	196.1	96.2	18.4
Brown................	28	646	22.5	10.8	37	106	7.4	1.5	179.9	79.8	33.9	7.2
Butler...............	464	5 629	329.1	164.6	422	2 924	192.6	59.6	1 319.5	596.8	241.2	43.8
Carroll..............	24	277	13.4	5.5	25	152	8.9	3.0	102.1	49.7	18.1	3.4
Champaign............	37	328	16.7	6.4	59	236	13.9	3.6	193.3	80.0	29.3	2.9
Clark................	240	2 758	159.6	78.1	202	1 384	72.8	21.4	837.3	377.7	158.7	31.9
Clermont.............	187	2 554	127.9	62.1	220	1 177	71.5	21.9	519.1	261.7	89.9	17.6
Clinton..............	52	634	35.3	16.7	55	266	12.0	4.6	192.8	88.2	36.6	5.2
Columbiana...........	182	2 229	106.7	49.7	164	737	37.8	12.9	571.6	267.8	128.4	22.9
Coshocton............	52	679	30.1	13.1	46	178	9.5	2.5	162.4	78.9	32.5	5.7
Crawford.............	77	810	36.0	16.2	53	326	19.8	6.1	258.7	112.3	53.5	8.1
Cuyahoga.............	3 042	36 747	2 409.7	1 137.5	2 511	19 147	1 466.9	396.0	9 755.3	3 151.2	2 000.1	396.0
Darke................	61	729	32.3	15.6	88	348	21.4	5.6	235.7	111.5	46.4	4.6
Defiance.............	59	736	47.0	18.9	59	275	16.5	4.5	167.0	80.7	31.9	5.5
Delaware.............	132	1 349	71.2	30.6	98	459	29.9	7.9	534.9	152.4	43.3	5.2
Erie.................	168	1 369	87.3	45.4	123	647	29.0	9.2	420.5	192.4	89.4	10.9
Fairfield............	226	2 544	137.0	62.5	157	811	44.3	14.5	431.8	236.1	87.4	12.6
Fayette..............	41	547	22.6	10.5	37	159	6.8	1.8	171.1	56.4	24.5	5.4
Franklin.............	2 171	28 471	1 920.5	962.2	1 579	12 799	783.6	249.5	8 107.1	2 010.5	793.1	214.8
Fulton...............	62	717	37.4	15.7	63	258	16.1	4.3	166.9	87.4	39.8	1.8
Gallia...............	45	885	62.1	30.0	34	127	6.6	1.8	194.2	71.4	33.7	13.1
Geauga...............	158	1 490	73.1	33.8	140	695	44.3	13.5	235.8	144.6	50.2	3.1
Greene...............	212	2 290	138.0	67.2	217	1 318	69.4	24.8	2 189.3	310.8	75.6	13.9
Guernsey.............	81	946	44.5	21.9	65	293	12.8	3.8	228.9	95.6	44.4	10.4
Hamilton.............	1 956	27 934	1 781.5	898.4	1 591	11 379	724.4	232.3	6 957.4	1 803.3	961.7	188.8
Hancock..............	130	1 505	90.6	45.0	107	656	36.8	11.6	251.9	118.7	46.5	5.7
Hardin...............	28	383	14.0	5.5	32	111	6.0	1.7	129.5	39.8	29.9	3.5
Harrison.............	14	280	10.5	4.7	19	42	2.4	0.6	96.0	44.4	19.7	3.4
Henry................	30	451	17.0	7.9	37	165	12.6	3.1	120.5	61.1	25.7	2.2
Highland.............	49	624	25.4	11.9	39	240	15.0	4.4	205.1	87.0	37.9	7.1
Hocking..............	38	442	19.8	8.4	37	130	6.0	1.5	124.4	56.1	25.4	6.8
Holmes...............	41	1 047	45.7	20.1	34	120	10.6	2.2	80.0	39.3	11.5	1.7
Huron................	77	997	52.7	25.2	67	388	20.2	5.8	272.6	142.6	55.0	8.3
Jackson..............	28	415	17.8	6.9	44	168	10.3	2.1	191.7	70.8	27.9	10.8
Jefferson............	135	1 788	87.0	39.1	121	820	38.7	12.4	503.4	224.0	121.9	23.4
Knox.................	98	1 237	56.2	23.2	60	511	17.2	5.5	239.3	113.8	49.7	6.3
Lake.................	429	4 882	258.6	119.2	464	2 577	166.6	52.4	929.0	505.1	224.4	15.5
Lawrence.............	54	1 013	36.8	16.6	63	217	11.9	3.4	404.9	162.1	68.2	31.1
Licking..............	185	3 415	147.2	75.7	176	1 191	62.0	24.2	757.3	301.2	104.0	19.1
Logan................	73	605	32.5	14.1	55	394	29.3	6.6	211.3	97.2	45.7	5.4
Lorain...............	444	5 189	310.7	162.5	379	2 474	131.6	40.4	1 302.4	573.3	271.5	45.7
Lucas................	944	13 899	900.9	461.4	798	5 289	332.8	100.2	2 528.5	893.2	559.4	135.6
Madison..............	54	457	25.9	9.4	31	159	9.9	2.5	162.1	76.2	33.5	3.3
Mahoning.............	629	7 696	434.1	203.3	415	2 852	162.8	49.9	1 610.6	679.3	367.5	69.4
Marion...............	116	1 754	99.9	50.3	95	389	20.5	6.0	313.1	141.8	66.4	14.8
Medina...............	265	3 147	151.0	71.5	239	1 347	75.0	22.7	485.4	279.7	103.5	7.3
Meigs................	16	336	13.0	4.7	19	45	3.1	0.7	160.3	52.0	22.8	9.0
Mercer...............	63	816	36.1	16.7	71	298	22.3	5.6	117.0	27.2	35.2	1.2
Miami................	151	1 606	99.0	45.2	154	824	44.1	13.5	441.3	218.1	83.2	10.1
Monroe...............	9	140	5.1	1.7	21	60	2.9	0.6	89.6	36.7	16.5	3.2
Montgomery	1 167	15 974	1 017.3	491.6	914	9 895	499.5	183.9	4 086.9	1 460.3	606.2	111.8
Morgan...............	10	129	5.4	2.6	13	33	2.1	0.6	78.4	31.0	13.1	3.1
Morrow...............	28	368	12.6	5.9	20	61	3.1	0.7	95.8	50.0	15.0	3.1
Muskingum............	159	1 935	124.7	58.6	141	999	56.4	17.8	445.6	195.9	78.6	21.0
Noble................	17	353	10.7	5.0	14	28	1.7	0.4	50.3	21.5	9.0	2.0

1. Firms subject to federal tax.   2. State totals may include programs not allocated by county.

STATE County	Salaries and wages	Defense	Other	Medicaid and other health-related	Nutrition and family welfare	Education	Other	Total (mil dol)	Intergovern-mental (mil dol)	Total (mil dol)	Total	Property
	171	172	173	174	175	176	177	178	179	180	181	182
NORTH DAKOTA—Cont'd												
Ward	198.6	82.1	11.2	24.8	10.2	13.0	25.7	119.5	53.9	43.6	764	590
Wells	1.5	0.0	0.6	4.2	0.5	0.2	3.1	12.8	4.7	5.1	1 054	1 015
Williams	5.9	0.1	2.9	9.6	3.2	0.9	4.0	44.7	19.8	17.2	878	781
OHIO	5 361.9	4 271.2	2 276.4	7 841.1	2 614.5	1 268.8	3 963.0	X	X	X	X	X
Adams	4.7	1.7	1.3	72.2	7.4	2.7	2.6	88.8	42.3	22.7	817	782
Allen	33.4	36.8	6.8	61.1	16.1	8.5	26.5	334.0	164.7	111.3	1 029	695
Ashland	6.6	1.7	1.6	13.4	4.0	3.1	9.4	131.2	55.9	50.1	947	639
Ashtabula	15.5	3.8	16.8	47.7	17.9	7.5	52.5	311.7	164.4	103.9	1 013	813
Athens	16.4	1.7	11.8	63.8	13.6	6.3	25.1	183.7	97.4	51.8	819	569
Auglaize	5.8	8.6	1.5	11.3	6.2	2.3	10.3	129.9	52.3	51.0	1 098	674
Belmont	12.5	1.0	6.9	47.8	14.5	5.7	17.6	181.5	105.1	52.6	757	540
Brown	5.1	0.8	2.3	28.8	7.2	2.7	5.8	135.6	69.5	25.5	587	472
Butler	36.1	73.8	28.7	145.7	33.0	14.8	83.5	1 017.6	422.4	388.6	1 141	868
Carroll	3.1	0.6	0.8	15.7	3.3	1.8	2.2	52.1	29.2	14.5	497	407
Champaign	4.9	30.5	1.2	19.5	3.5	2.4	6.7	125.9	59.9	39.2	1 002	675
Clark	58.1	16.8	6.1	108.6	22.8	10.8	31.8	414.5	208.8	144.9	1 010	692
Clermont	20.1	1.2	5.4	65.0	14.7	8.3	29.2	501.2	225.0	170.0	927	761
Clinton	8.8	0.3	2.1	24.4	4.5	4.6	9.5	224.3	72.9	39.0	949	733
Columbiana	36.5	4.9	5.0	61.3	20.2	7.3	9.9	262.9	155.0	73.5	658	486
Coshocton	6.0	1.9	1.3	18.9	7.4	2.3	4.7	102.8	53.7	33.8	916	688
Crawford	4.6	0.8	2.6	22.4	6.4	3.4	36.4	118.1	50.8	44.0	948	639
Cuyahoga	1 039.1	262.1	449.9	1 446.9	298.0	119.1	446.5	6 728.5	2 368.7	2 953.4	2 142	1 261
Darke	7.1	0.3	2.8	20.6	14.8	2.9	6.6	136.8	71.7	46.8	883	598
Defiance	6.0	1.5	4.7	14.3	6.0	2.3	7.5	115.6	43.4	39.0	991	629
Delaware	20.4	7.8	5.3	17.2	3.0	4.3	265.1	307.1	78.3	163.0	1 300	931
Erie	15.1	30.3	10.9	27.1	9.8	5.1	24.8	287.5	98.8	118.8	1 500	1 128
Fairfield	17.0	0.2	3.9	37.6	9.6	5.3	16.4	322.8	142.7	128.3	993	662
Fayette	3.2	0.0	1.1	23.0	5.3	1.8	44.9	104.2	36.4	28.7	1 020	707
Franklin	814.8	522.8	264.1	1 037.8	823.3	505.9	1 009.5	4 631.7	1 665.0	2 150.9	1 979	1 216
Fulton	6.0	1.8	1.4	8.7	2.6	2.2	5.8	120.0	41.8	56.9	1 338	886
Gallia	4.9	0.0	1.2	48.0	7.2	2.9	6.2	97.7	56.4	24.1	772	576
Geauga	8.6	3.4	2.2	9.9	2.4	3.8	5.5	236.4	77.5	123.2	1 325	1 174
Greene	960.8	537.0	146.4	60.7	10.3	12.3	40.7	427.4	157.8	182.7	1 218	914
Guernsey	6.5	0.7	1.6	37.8	6.8	3.5	20.3	129.2	81.3	31.2	762	540
Hamilton	645.1	1 258.2	615.2	893.7	152.0	65.2	280.2	3 405.4	1 140.2	1 585.6	1 902	1 254
Hancock	10.1	0.0	2.2	21.8	6.1	4.1	21.6	198.3	75.4	80.7	1 116	771
Hardin	4.9	4.0	1.2	12.7	4.1	4.4	7.7	101.9	57.8	26.6	838	480
Harrison	4.2	1.0	0.9	10.5	3.2	1.4	6.4	41.7	25.2	10.6	667	566
Henry	4.5	0.0	1.1	8.4	2.0	2.0	2.5	97.9	42.9	36.6	1 243	922
Highland	6.4	1.1	1.4	38.8	7.0	2.5	5.5	137.6	62.0	26.8	640	409
Hocking	3.3	0.1	1.1	17.7	4.4	1.7	6.9	86.8	36.7	18.4	644	503
Holmes	4.3	0.3	3.0	9.3	1.4	2.2	1.5	93.0	33.9	27.1	672	551
Huron	9.2	6.0	2.2	21.8	5.9	4.1	8.6	180.4	88.8	64.5	1 074	638
Jackson	4.0	0.0	1.1	53.2	8.3	2.5	11.7	97.1	61.8	17.9	544	405
Jefferson	16.3	2.0	4.7	66.3	15.9	6.2	15.0	182.9	101.2	62.7	866	679
Knox	6.8	0.0	1.8	30.0	6.2	5.8	9.5	152.4	77.9	54.3	969	710
Lake	31.3	12.8	13.0	45.1	13.7	12.6	46.2	781.6	229.4	402.4	1 757	1 257
Lawrence	8.4	0.1	2.6	84.6	19.4	8.3	16.7	204.3	127.3	28.5	458	300
Licking	29.5	157.7	5.6	61.8	16.2	7.6	42.1	377.7	146.1	169.7	1 141	723
Logan	10.2	1.0	2.0	23.3	4.6	2.7	8.4	149.8	68.1	55.4	1 196	994
Lorain	132.4	20.6	10.9	119.6	42.9	19.8	43.9	922.6	409.3	331.4	1 149	817
Lucas	156.4	28.8	90.3	376.8	89.5	37.6	118.1	1 722.9	683.5	714.5	1 575	943
Madison	5.3	0.6	1.5	22.4	3.1	2.3	4.7	104.6	45.1	41.0	1 016	794
Mahoning	88.2	7.3	20.3	225.2	58.3	22.8	48.8	797.5	393.0	264.5	1 044	767
Marion	9.6	0.9	5.1	37.1	15.9	3.8	8.7	248.6	133.9	68.2	1 033	744
Medina	20.8	16.2	5.4	22.4	5.8	6.7	12.5	474.2	193.9	194.1	1 225	1 038
Meigs	3.8	2.9	1.2	27.3	6.0	2.2	30.8	79.7	61.2	11.6	503	404
Mercer	5.6	0.1	2.5	9.6	3.9	2.3	8.9	150.6	65.8	38.4	940	624
Miami	14.5	29.7	4.8	34.0	7.8	4.9	23.8	298.9	113.9	120.3	1 208	850
Monroe	3.4	1.6	0.9	18.0	2.8	1.5	4.4	49.0	27.3	14.2	948	746
Montgomery	289.4	627.6	236.6	404.5	104.9	50.3	136.5	2 230.4	843.5	869.2	1 568	952
Morgan	4.7	1.2	0.5	12.5	2.9	1.2	7.4	56.0	29.8	19.8	1 345	1 009
Morrow	3.2	0.0	0.9	9.9	3.3	2.0	2.6	93.3	42.1	22.1	670	477
Muskingum	20.8	3.0	4.2	70.4	13.9	7.6	21.4	274.6	150.9	81.8	959	640
Noble	1.7	0.0	0.5	8.4	4.3	0.9	0.9	32.7	20.9	7.2	511	434

1. State totals may include programs not allocated by county. 2. Based on the resident population estimated as of July 1 of the year shown.

	Local government finances, 2002 (cont'd)										Government employment, 2002			Presidential election, 2004		
	Direct general expenditure							Debt outstanding						Percent of vote cast —		
			Percent of total for —													
STATE County	Total (mil dol)	Per capita[1] (dollars)	Educa-tion	Health and hospitals	Police protec-tion	Public welfare	High-ways	Total (mil dol)	Per capita[1] (dollars)	Federal civilian	Federal military	State and local	Demo-cratic	Republi-can	All other
	183	184	185	186	187	188	189	190	191	192	193	194	195	196	197
NORTH DAKOTA—Cont'd															
Ward	122.3	2 141	52.8	1.8	4.9	2.5	5.2	52.7	922	1 264	5 263	3 748	32.2	66.4	1.4
Wells	12.4	2 569	53.7	0.0	1.7	5.8	18.8	0.0	4	40	33	289	33.6	64.6	1.8
Williams	44.3	2 265	53.2	4.0	4.9	3.1	10.2	6.1	312	113	132	1 543	28.2	70.3	1.6
OHIO	X	X	X	X	X	X	X	X	X	78 642	33 726	727 225	48.7	50.8	0.5
Adams	87.7	3 154	43.4	22.3	3.1	7.2	6.7	48.2	1 734	79	64	1 528	35.7	63.7	0.6
Allen	338.5	3 131	53.0	3.4	5.0	5.5	5.7	113.9	1 053	442	254	7 251	33.5	66.1	0.4
Ashland	125.9	2 379	48.6	5.7	6.0	4.3	6.6	28.5	539	111	121	2 934	34.3	65.0	0.8
Ashtabula	302.8	2 954	45.4	5.2	4.6	11.9	5.5	74.3	724	251	246	5 318	53.0	46.4	0.7
Athens	178.2	2 817	46.1	7.0	3.0	14.2	5.5	90.4	1 428	272	158	9 826	63.2	36.1	0.7
Auglaize	128.3	2 762	52.3	1.3	3.0	5.3	8.4	63.6	1 368	96	106	2 909	25.7	73.8	0.5
Belmont	176.1	2 536	53.7	0.7	3.2	13.3	7.5	89.1	1 283	172	160	4 180	52.8	46.7	0.5
Brown	133.5	3 071	51.8	22.8	3.5	4.2	4.8	30.5	702	97	100	2 173	35.9	63.5	0.5
Butler	1 104.5	3 243	43.6	4.4	6.3	5.6	6.5	1 275.9	3 747	551	807	20 589	33.5	66.1	0.4
Carroll	53.5	1 836	44.9	5.9	5.1	9.8	10.3	7.8	268	55	67	958	44.7	54.4	1.0
Champaign	138.3	3 536	49.9	11.8	4.3	5.1	6.8	25.7	657	83	90	1 975	37.0	62.6	0.5
Clark	401.8	2 802	50.9	5.6	6.0	8.4	4.5	160.0	1 116	624	338	7 464	48.6	51.0	0.5
Clermont	501.7	2 736	49.6	2.6	4.0	8.2	3.5	442.5	2 414	323	420	7 003	29.0	70.7	0.3
Clinton	223.3	5 435	31.6	35.0	1.6	5.2	3.4	394.9	9 611	155	94	3 290	29.3	70.4	0.3
Columbiana	267.8	2 395	54.9	9.3	4.5	6.3	5.0	92.8	830	581	257	5 049	47.3	52.1	0.6
Coshocton	109.4	2 969	53.6	5.3	3.6	10.0	7.9	67.2	1 824	100	84	1 685	42.4	57.1	0.5
Crawford	124.6	2 683	47.0	3.3	5.6	8.1	7.4	39.9	860	83	106	2 245	35.6	63.8	0.7
Cuyahoga	6 510.3	4 721	35.0	12.4	5.9	6.5	3.3	7 385.3	5 355	15 958	3 779	89 674	66.4	33.1	0.5
Darke	143.9	2 718	57.8	3.8	5.1	5.5	6.7	26.5	500	120	121	2 247	29.8	69.6	0.6
Defiance	126.1	3 205	46.3	9.6	4.5	5.3	5.9	38.2	971	117	91	2 061	37.5	61.8	0.8
Delaware	328.3	2 618	47.6	2.8	2.6	2.4	6.6	356.0	2 839	270	287	5 251	33.5	66.1	0.3
Erie	291.7	3 683	46.3	2.1	5.4	8.3	3.9	135.3	1 708	195	182	5 659	53.3	46.5	0.2
Fairfield	357.0	2 764	55.0	4.1	4.1	5.0	5.1	319.7	2 475	266	297	7 547	36.4	63.0	0.6
Fayette	108.6	3 856	32.6	23.8	4.1	5.5	7.4	27.8	986	61	65	1 570	36.9	62.7	0.4
Franklin	4 629.4	4 260	37.1	7.2	6.4	5.9	4.1	5 013.5	4 613	12 018	3 150	111 009	54.4	45.1	0.5
Fulton	132.3	3 107	62.3	1.1	3.9	2.1	9.7	94.1	2 210	102	98	2 293	37.4	62.2	0.4
Gallia	93.5	2 988	55.9	3.8	5.5	9.7	8.6	9.1	292	98	72	1 899	38.3	61.4	0.4
Geauga	239.3	2 573	46.6	7.3	4.5	4.8	8.3	84.7	911	132	213	3 856	39.4	60.2	0.4
Greene	427.8	2 853	49.2	3.6	7.4	6.2	4.4	322.7	2 152	11 035	3 033	11 320	38.3	61.2	0.5
Guernsey	110.5	2 695	47.5	4.6	4.7	11.2	6.8	44.8	1 093	120	94	2 583	43.5	55.9	0.6
Hamilton	3 301.4	3 960	35.9	7.6	7.0	6.7	3.0	3 321.2	3 984	10 031	2 019	54 851	47.1	52.5	0.4
Hancock	201.7	2 790	44.8	7.2	4.8	3.6	5.6	105.4	1 458	179	167	3 314	28.9	70.7	0.4
Hardin	91.4	2 879	58.2	1.5	4.5	11.6	6.8	25.8	813	87	73	1 660	36.4	63.1	0.5
Harrison	42.0	2 641	43.9	1.2	2.8	16.2	10.8	9.4	592	65	36	882	46.6	52.6	0.8
Henry	94.6	3 209	54.8	1.7	2.6	11.5	5.9	44.4	1 506	80	68	2 025	33.8	65.6	0.6
Highland	150.9	3 606	43.5	23.2	3.0	4.6	2.5	53.1	1 269	121	96	2 307	33.5	66.1	0.4
Hocking	85.0	2 985	33.5	30.4	4.0	8.9	6.3	38.8	1 362	51	65	1 627	46.8	52.6	0.7
Holmes	94.3	2 335	35.4	25.5	2.0	6.1	7.7	37.0	916	76	93	1 524	23.9	75.6	0.5
Huron	178.7	2 977	55.3	1.8	4.7	6.1	5.7	70.1	1 168	146	139	2 802	41.3	58.1	0.6
Jackson	105.5	3 213	60.8	1.6	4.2	7.6	5.2	75.2	2 289	78	75	1 507	39.6	60.1	0.3
Jefferson	185.0	2 555	47.0	8.1	3.1	10.3	6.2	70.7	976	251	167	3 813	52.3	47.3	0.4
Knox	146.9	2 621	49.1	4.2	3.5	6.6	7.6	71.9	1 283	119	128	2 802	36.4	63.1	0.5
Lake	879.9	3 842	48.2	5.8	5.8	4.1	5.5	267.7	1 169	470	551	12 029	48.4	51.1	0.5
Lawrence	219.5	3 530	57.2	17.8	1.7	6.9	3.3	31.3	504	146	142	3 427	43.7	55.8	0.5
Licking	427.3	2 873	52.8	2.8	4.5	5.1	4.6	221.1	1 486	496	355	7 141	37.7	61.8	0.4
Logan	150.8	3 260	49.0	0.9	6.0	7.5	6.7	77.4	1 673	148	110	2 292	31.9	67.6	0.5
Lorain	941.6	3 265	51.3	5.5	4.3	4.8	2.8	785.0	2 722	1 177	683	14 292	55.9	43.7	0.4
Lucas	1 654.6	3 648	37.4	4.9	6.0	6.9	3.5	1 506.2	3 321	2 050	1 117	31 666	60.0	39.8	0.2
Madison	99.0	2 453	55.0	5.1	3.7	6.4	5.9	39.6	982	83	92	2 970	35.6	64.0	0.4
Mahoning	756.1	2 985	47.8	6.1	5.8	6.2	4.8	373.9	1 476	1 443	606	14 894	62.5	36.8	0.7
Marion	248.6	3 765	51.3	4.1	4.4	5.7	3.1	271.9	4 117	154	152	5 954	40.8	58.7	0.5
Medina	509.0	3 213	55.2	4.1	4.5	2.9	3.4	330.4	2 085	317	363	6 672	42.7	56.8	0.5
Meigs	69.1	2 989	61.5	0.9	1.7	5.3	18.4	36.7	1 587	81	53	1 091	41.1	58.4	0.6
Mercer	157.7	3 863	54.6	18.4	2.4	3.0	7.9	57.9	1 420	105	94	2 746	24.5	74.9	0.6
Miami	297.7	2 989	49.3	3.7	6.7	3.6	7.1	188.4	1 892	222	229	4 811	33.9	65.8	0.3
Monroe	46.6	3 113	45.9	3.2	4.7	17.8	9.3	5.5	370	60	34	897	54.8	44.4	0.8
Montgomery	2 099.3	3 786	38.1	3.7	7.0	8.5	4.9	1 612.7	2 909	5 784	4 358	30 051	50.4	49.1	0.4
Morgan	57.3	3 883	52.9	0.8	3.5	10.5	8.0	9.2	626	40	34	736	42.7	56.2	1.0
Morrow	117.7	3 570	41.6	25.0	1.6	6.1	4.6	83.4	2 528	59	76	1 585	35.2	64.3	0.5
Muskingum	266.6	3 124	53.3	2.2	4.9	11.3	4.7	130.7	1 532	298	197	5 237	42.1	57.4	0.5
Noble	30.3	2 153	50.6	2.4	6.1	11.3	12.3	3.7	265	28	32	1 116	40.5	58.8	0.7

1. Based on the resident population estimated as of July 1 of the year shown.

Table B. States and Counties — Land Area and Population

STATE/ County code	CBSA code[1]	County Type[2]	STATE County	Land area[3] (sq km) 2000	Total persons	Rank	Per square kilometer	White	Black	Am. Indian, Alaska Native	Asian and Pacific Islander		Percent Hispanic or Latino[4]	Under 5 years	5 to 17 years	18 to 24 years	25 to 34 years	35 to 44 years	45 to 54 years
					1	2	3	4	5	6	7	8	9	10	11	12	13	14	15
			OHIO—Cont'd																
39 123	45780	2	Ottawa	660	41 192	1 103	62.4	95.2	0.7	0.3	0.3		3.8	5.0	16.5	8.7	10.2	15.0	16.0
39 125	...	6	Paulding	1 078	19 665	1 827	18.2	95.5	1.3	0.6	0.2		3.0	5.5	19.2	9.7	11.5	15.5	15.2
39 127	...	6	Perry	1 061	35 074	1 273	33.1	98.9	0.4	0.7	0.2		0.5	6.8	19.9	9.7	12.3	15.1	14.0
39 129	18140	1	Pickaway	1 300	51 723	911	39.8	93.7	5.2	0.8	0.3		0.7	5.8	18.2	9.7	13.6	16.7	14.4
39 131	...	7	Pike	1 143	28 194	1 454	24.7	97.6	1.0	1.7	0.3		0.6	6.6	19.2	9.8	13.0	15.1	13.0
39 133	10420	2	Portage	1 275	154 870	358	121.5	94.6	3.9	0.6	1.3		0.7	5.5	16.9	14.0	12.8	15.0	14.2
39 135	19380	2	Preble	1 100	42 417	1 073	38.6	98.6	0.5	0.5	0.4		0.5	5.5	18.5	9.3	11.8	15.7	15.1
39 137	...	6	Putnam	1 253	34 754	1 280	27.7	95.1	0.2	0.2	0.2		4.4	6.6	21.1	10.0	10.8	15.6	13.9
39 139	31900	3	Richland	1 287	128 267	441	99.7	88.7	10.1	0.7	0.8		0.9	6.2	17.8	9.1	12.2	15.0	14.8
39 141	17060	4	Ross	1 783	74 424	688	41.7	92.6	6.5	0.8	0.5		0.6	5.9	17.1	9.4	13.8	16.7	14.8
39 143	23380	4	Sandusky	1 060	61 753	804	58.3	89.7	3.3	0.3	0.4		7.2	6.7	18.6	9.2	11.6	14.9	14.9
39 145	39020	4	Scioto	1 586	77 453	671	48.8	95.6	3.0	1.4	0.5		0.7	6.2	17.3	10.3	13.3	14.4	13.8
39 147	45660	4	Seneca	1 426	57 734	848	40.5	94.1	2.3	0.3	0.6		3.6	6.1	18.5	11.3	11.2	14.7	13.9
39 149	43380	4	Shelby	1 060	48 566	960	45.8	96.1	2.2	0.4	1.3		1.0	7.5	20.2	9.2	12.5	15.5	13.9
39 151	15940	2	Stark	1 492	377 519	164	253.0	90.9	8.0	0.7	0.9		0.9	6.1	18.0	9.1	11.5	14.8	15.1
39 153	10420	2	Summit	1 069	546 774	107	511.5	83.7	14.1	0.6	2.0		0.9	6.4	18.1	8.6	12.8	15.6	15.0
39 155	49660	2	Trumbull	1 597	221 785	263	138.9	90.6	8.4	0.5	0.6		0.8	5.8	17.5	8.7	11.6	14.6	15.3
39 157	35420	4	Tuscarawas	1 470	91 706	588	62.4	97.9	1.0	0.5	0.4		0.9	6.3	18.0	9.0	11.8	15.0	14.7
39 159	18140	1	Union	1 131	43 750	1 049	38.7	95.4	3.0	0.5	0.5		0.9	7.0	19.6	8.8	14.6	17.4	13.8
39 161	46780	6	Van Wert	1 062	29 277	1 427	27.6	97.1	1.1	0.2	0.3		1.7	5.8	18.7	9.5	11.4	14.5	14.5
39 163	...	9	Vinton	1 072	13 231	2 218	12.3	98.7	0.3	1.1	0.1		0.5	6.4	19.4	9.5	13.0	15.1	14.5
39 165	17140	1	Warren	1 035	181 743	315	175.6	93.5	3.0	0.5	2.7		1.2	7.0	19.3	9.3	13.8	17.5	13.6
39 167	37620	3	Washington	1 645	62 505	793	38.0	97.7	1.2	0.7	0.7		0.5	5.4	16.8	10.0	11.1	15.0	15.3
39 169	49300	2	Wayne	1 438	113 121	489	78.7	96.7	1.8	0.5	0.9		0.9	6.8	19.3	10.9	11.7	14.8	14.3
39 171	...	7	Williams	1 092	38 802	1 168	35.5	95.5	0.9	0.5	0.7		2.9	5.8	18.4	9.6	12.0	15.5	14.5
39 173	45780	2	Wood	1 599	123 020	460	76.9	93.9	1.4	0.5	1.4		3.5	5.5	16.6	16.5	12.4	13.9	14.1
39 175	...	7	Wyandot	1 051	22 826	1 671	21.7	97.6	0.3	0.2	0.6		1.5	6.0	18.2	9.2	11.6	14.9	14.5
40 000	...	X	OKLAHOMA	177 847	3 511 532	X	19.7	76.9	8.4	10.9	2.1		5.7	7.0	18.1	10.9	13.1	14.1	13.8
40 001	...	6	Adair	1 491	21 614	1 722	14.5	54.4	0.2	48.1	0.2		3.6	8.2	21.4	10.2	12.8	13.6	12.4
40 003	...	9	Alfalfa	2 245	5 910	2 780	2.6	89.8	4.3	3.8	0.2		3.1	3.6	13.7	8.4	10.2	17.7	14.9
40 005	...	7	Atoka	2 534	14 142	2 157	5.6	81.2	5.9	16.3	0.3		1.6	5.9	16.7	10.0	13.1	15.2	13.8
40 007	...	9	Beaver	4 699	5 582	2 804	1.2	85.5	0.4	1.8	0.2		12.6	5.6	18.8	9.3	9.3	14.8	14.6
40 009	...	7	Beckham	2 336	19 894	1 812	8.5	86.3	5.4	3.5	0.6		5.6	6.7	16.4	10.9	13.9	14.8	13.6
40 011	...	6	Blaine	2 405	11 678	2 316	4.9	74.7	6.4	11.5	3.6		7.1	5.9	17.0	10.9	12.6	14.8	13.1
40 013	20460	6	Bryan	2 354	37 306	1 198	15.8	83.2	1.8	15.7	0.7		2.9	6.6	17.3	11.8	12.5	12.6	12.7
40 015	...	6	Caddo	3 311	30 070	1 401	9.1	66.9	3.8	25.8	0.2		6.7	6.8	20.3	10.3	11.0	14.2	12.9
40 017	36420	1	Canadian	2 330	92 904	579	39.9	86.9	2.4	5.8	3.0		4.2	6.2	19.5	10.4	12.4	16.1	14.9
40 019	11620	5	Carter	2 134	46 396	992	21.7	80.0	8.4	11.8	1.0		2.9	6.8	18.3	9.0	11.5	13.9	14.2
40 021	45140	2	Cherokee	1 945	43 783	1 048	22.5	61.8	1.5	38.2	0.9		4.5	7.0	18.1	14.8	12.5	12.7	12.1
40 023	...	7	Choctaw	2 004	15 431	2 066	7.7	71.3	12.1	19.3	0.2		1.4	7.2	18.1	9.3	11.1	13.0	13.0
40 025	...	9	Cimarron	4 753	2 961	2 986	0.6	81.1	0.6	1.6	0.2		17.1	6.0	19.6	8.3	8.6	13.2	14.3
40 027	36420	1	Cleveland	1 389	219 966	265	158.4	84.0	4.5	6.8	4.4		4.2	6.0	16.9	14.0	15.1	14.9	13.8
40 029	...	9	Coal	1 342	5 946	2 775	4.4	79.3	0.5	23.1	0.4		2.1	6.4	19.3	9.0	11.3	13.4	13.6
40 031	30020	3	Comanche	2 770	113 890	487	41.1	64.3	21.8	6.9	4.1		7.3	8.1	19.4	13.7	15.0	14.6	11.3
40 033	...	6	Cotton	1 649	6 582	2 724	4.0	85.0	3.1	9.3	0.2		4.6	6.1	18.2	9.2	11.1	14.1	12.9
40 035	...	6	Craig	1 971	14 880	2 108	7.5	78.8	3.8	26.1	0.5		1.3	6.5	16.9	9.2	10.6	15.7	13.4
40 037	46140	2	Creek	2 475	68 794	730	27.8	85.9	3.0	13.2	0.6		2.2	6.5	19.3	9.6	11.4	14.5	14.3
40 039	...	7	Custer	2 555	24 962	1 576	9.8	80.7	3.4	7.3	1.2		9.5	6.7	16.1	16.5	11.1	13.1	12.6
40 041	...	6	Delaware	1 918	38 709	1 170	20.2	75.8	0.4	27.7	0.4		1.7	5.8	17.6	8.9	10.7	12.7	13.0
40 043	...	9	Dewey	2 590	4 549	2 868	1.8	92.0	0.1	6.1	0.1		3.1	4.9	16.0	9.5	8.2	13.8	14.9
40 045	...	9	Ellis	3 183	3 996	2 911	1.3	95.6	0.2	1.7	0.2		3.1	5.0	15.4	8.0	8.5	12.5	16.6
40 047	21420	6	Garfield	2 741	57 105	852	20.8	88.4	3.6	3.5	2.1		4.7	7.0	17.5	9.6	12.0	14.3	14.0
40 049	...	6	Garvin	2 091	27 218	1 495	13.0	86.4	2.7	9.7	0.3		3.6	6.8	17.2	9.7	11.5	13.5	13.4
40 051	36420	1	Grady	2 851	47 439	971	16.6	88.7	3.3	7.2	0.7		3.0	6.3	18.8	11.3	11.6	14.7	13.7
40 053	...	9	Grant	2 591	4 973	2 847	1.9	94.8	0.1	2.9	0.2		2.4	4.9	17.5	9.4	9.4	14.0	14.3
40 055	...	7	Greer	1 656	5 888	2 782	3.6	80.1	9.8	3.9	0.3		7.2	4.6	13.1	10.6	13.4	15.4	13.1
40 057	...	9	Harmon	1 393	3 053	2 981	2.2	67.3	8.5	1.3	0.3		22.7	6.7	17.7	10.3	8.8	13.9	14.2
40 059	...	9	Harper	2 691	3 398	2 956	1.3	91.1	0.0	1.0	0.1		7.8	5.2	15.8	8.5	8.5	13.8	15.9
40 061	...	6	Haskell	1 495	12 044	2 290	8.1	82.7	0.8	19.5	0.4		1.8	7.2	18.0	9.7	10.7	12.4	12.8
40 063	...	7	Hughes	2 089	13 898	2 174	6.7	76.9	4.7	19.9	0.3		2.6	5.5	16.4	9.3	12.8	14.4	13.3
40 065	11060	5	Jackson	2 079	27 338	1 489	13.1	72.0	8.7	2.3	2.4		16.2	8.0	20.6	10.5	12.5	15.6	12.2
40 067	...	8	Jefferson	1 965	6 535	2 730	3.3	85.2	0.6	7.5	1.6		7.4	6.0	16.7	8.9	10.9	13.6	13.1
40 069	...	7	Johnston	1 669	10 522	2 395	6.3	80.3	2.2	19.5	0.3		2.5	6.1	17.8	11.6	10.5	13.0	14.1
40 071	38620	5	Kay	2 379	47 260	974	19.9	85.5	1.9	10.2	1.2		4.5	6.8	18.4	9.9	10.4	13.9	14.1
40 073	...	6	Kingfisher	2 339	14 072	2 160	6.0	86.9	1.9	4.5	0.3		8.4	6.8	18.2	10.4	9.8	15.2	14.1

1. CBSA = Core Based Statistical Area. See Appendix A for explanation. See Appendix B for list of metropolitan areas with component counties. 2. County type code from the Economic Research Service of USDA Rural-Urban Continuum Codes. See Appendix A for definition. 3. Dry land or land partially or temporarily covered by water. 4. Hispanic or Latino persons may be of any race.

Table B. States and Counties — **Population and Households**

STATE County	55 to 64 years (16)	65 to 74 years (17)	75 years and over (18)	Percent female (19)	Total persons 1990 (20)	Total persons 2000 (21)	Percent change 1990–2000 (22)	Percent change 2000–2003 (23)	Births (24)	Deaths (25)	Net migration (26)	Households 2000 Number (27)	Percent change, 1990–2000 (28)	Persons per household (29)	Female family householder[1] (30)	One person (31)
OHIO—Cont'd																
Ottawa	12.0	8.6	7.8	50.6	40 029	40 985	2.4	0.5	1 337	1 363	281	16 474	8.6	2.45	8.5	25.0
Paulding	10.8	6.7	6.4	50.8	20 488	20 293	-1.0	-3.1	675	540	-765	7 773	7.2	2.59	8.1	23.0
Perry	9.2	6.4	5.7	50.1	31 557	34 078	8.0	2.9	1 573	1 034	505	12 500	11.0	2.70	9.8	21.4
Pickaway	10.2	6.4	5.0	46.5	48 248	52 727	9.3	-1.9	2 035	1 500	-1 543	17 599	12.8	2.63	9.8	20.6
Pike	9.3	6.8	6.7	51.3	24 249	27 695	14.2	1.8	1 215	993	302	10 444	18.6	2.61	11.9	22.8
Portage	9.3	6.1	5.0	51.2	142 585	152 061	6.6	1.8	5 401	3 496	1 078	56 449	14.7	2.56	10.1	23.3
Preble	10.5	7.2	6.3	50.2	40 113	42 337	5.5	0.2	1 512	1 303	-78	16 001	11.5	2.62	8.5	20.6
Putnam	8.4	6.5	7.0	50.3	33 819	34 726	2.7	0.1	1 459	934	-475	12 200	10.1	2.81	7.4	21.3
Richland	10.4	7.7	6.9	49.7	126 137	128 852	2.2	-0.5	5 231	3 978	-1 782	49 534	4.1	2.47	11.4	26.5
Ross	9.9	6.6	5.7	48.0	69 330	73 345	5.8	1.5	2 896	2 326	572	27 136	11.6	2.50	11.1	24.9
Sandusky	9.8	7.2	7.3	51.0	61 963	61 792	-0.3	-0.1	2 795	1 962	-825	23 717	5.6	2.56	10.5	24.1
Scioto	10.0	7.9	7.2	51.0	80 327	79 195	-1.4	-2.2	3 221	3 173	-1 766	30 871	3.6	2.45	13.1	26.9
Seneca	9.2	7.1	7.0	50.5	59 733	58 683	-1.8	-1.6	2 277	1 942	-1 272	22 292	4.8	2.56	10.2	24.7
Shelby	9.0	6.1	5.9	50.2	44 915	47 910	6.7	1.4	2 404	1 375	-330	17 636	12.9	2.68	9.3	22.0
Stark	10.2	7.4	7.7	51.9	367 585	378 098	2.9	-0.2	15 050	12 761	-2 559	148 316	6.3	2.49	11.5	26.1
Summit	9.5	6.9	7.1	51.7	514 990	542 899	5.4	0.7	22 889	17 500	-2 144	217 788	8.9	2.45	12.6	28.0
Trumbull	10.9	8.0	8.0	51.5	227 795	225 116	-1.2	-1.5	8 564	7 927	-3 849	89 020	3.4	2.48	12.5	26.9
Tuscarawas	10.1	7.5	7.6	51.1	84 090	90 914	8.1	0.9	3 777	3 138	266	35 653	11.5	2.52	9.3	24.9
Union	8.4	5.0	4.3	51.8	31 969	40 909	28.0	6.9	1 999	975	1 791	14 346	30.0	2.70	8.0	19.9
Van Wert	10.0	7.5	8.0	51.2	30 464	29 659	-2.6	-1.3	1 095	1 011	-452	11 587	2.8	2.52	8.5	24.7
Vinton	9.9	6.7	5.1	50.2	11 098	12 806	15.4	3.3	567	415	277	4 892	20.2	2.59	10.2	23.6
Warren	8.2	5.0	3.9	49.4	113 973	158 383	39.0	14.7	8 069	3 499	18 225	55 966	43.0	2.72	8.0	18.9
Washington	11.0	8.1	7.3	51.3	62 254	63 251	1.6	-1.2	2 202	2 234	-680	25 137	6.4	2.45	9.1	25.4
Wayne	9.5	6.6	5.9	50.5	101 461	111 564	10.0	1.4	5 071	3 142	-242	40 445	13.5	2.68	8.7	22.7
Williams	10.1	6.8	7.3	50.2	36 956	39 188	6.0	-1.0	1 444	1 278	-527	15 105	9.4	2.52	9.0	24.9
Wood	8.5	5.6	5.4	51.4	113 269	121 065	6.9	1.6	4 420	3 082	755	45 172	13.8	2.51	8.5	25.8
Wyandot	9.5	7.8	7.9	51.2	22 254	22 908	2.9	-0.4	910	797	-173	8 882	8.7	2.53	9.2	25.4
OKLAHOMA	10.0	6.9	6.2	50.7	3 145 576	3 450 654	9.7	1.8	162 253	115 649	15 639	1 342 293	11.3	2.49	11.4	26.7
Adair	9.2	6.6	5.3	50.5	18 421	21 038	14.2	2.7	1 242	766	127	7 471	17.0	2.76	12.9	22.8
Alfalfa	11.8	9.5	10.9	43.1	6 416	6 105	-4.8	-3.2	127	180	-131	2 199	-10.9	2.29	5.7	31.0
Atoka	10.9	7.6	6.5	45.7	12 778	13 879	8.6	1.9	519	568	320	4 964	10.4	2.48	10.2	27.1
Beaver	10.7	9.2	8.0	49.6	6 023	5 857	-2.8	-4.7	196	179	-290	2 245	-3.5	2.57	6.1	22.0
Beckham	8.8	7.5	7.8	47.7	18 812	19 799	5.2	0.5	902	812	19	7 356	0.1	2.44	10.4	28.5
Blaine	9.5	7.9	8.6	45.9	11 470	11 976	4.4	-2.5	447	526	-226	4 159	-5.9	2.50	8.6	29.0
Bryan	10.0	7.9	7.3	51.0	32 089	36 534	13.9	2.1	1 641	1 306	459	14 422	15.2	2.47	10.8	26.6
Caddo	10.0	7.6	7.0	50.3	29 550	30 150	2.0	-0.3	1 373	1 284	-139	10 957	0.7	2.62	13.0	24.8
Canadian	9.5	5.6	4.1	50.1	74 409	87 697	17.9	5.9	3 659	2 117	3 662	31 484	23.0	2.71	9.7	19.2
Carter	10.0	8.1	7.7	51.7	42 919	45 621	6.3	1.7	2 006	1 878	702	17 992	8.4	2.47	12.0	26.6
Cherokee	9.5	6.7	5.1	50.7	34 049	42 521	24.9	3.0	1 966	1 326	650	16 175	27.8	2.52	11.9	25.3
Choctaw	11.3	8.6	8.5	52.5	15 302	15 342	0.3	0.6	791	662	-36	6 220	4.5	2.43	14.4	28.3
Cimarron	11.4	9.3	10.5	50.8	3 301	3 148	-4.6	-5.9	113	117	-190	1 257	-3.3	2.47	6.0	29.3
Cleveland	8.6	5.0	3.6	49.7	174 253	208 016	19.4	5.7	8 027	4 247	8 158	79 186	23.7	2.51	10.0	24.4
Coal	9.8	8.9	8.7	51.0	5 780	6 031	4.3	-1.4	226	279	-27	2 373	4.1	2.51	10.6	27.3
Comanche	7.3	5.7	4.3	48.3	111 486	114 996	3.1	-1.0	6 149	2 765	-4 569	39 808	6.0	2.63	14.1	23.4
Cotton	11.1	8.1	8.7	50.2	6 651	6 614	-0.6	-0.5	259	270	-18	2 614	0.2	2.46	9.7	27.3
Craig	11.4	8.3	7.9	49.6	14 104	14 950	6.0	-0.5	658	587	-134	5 620	6.6	2.46	9.7	27.0
Creek	11.0	7.4	5.9	50.8	60 915	67 367	10.6	2.1	2 886	2 268	879	25 289	12.5	2.64	10.9	21.6
Custer	9.0	7.1	7.1	51.4	26 897	26 142	-2.8	-4.5	1 140	941	-1 421	10 136	2.2	2.45	9.5	27.8
Delaware	12.9	10.0	7.5	50.7	28 070	37 077	32.1	4.4	1 415	1 453	1 649	14 838	34.9	2.46	8.9	24.0
Dewey	12.7	8.9	11.8	51.0	5 551	4 743	-14.6	-4.1	151	294	-48	1 962	-11.7	2.35	5.0	30.0
Ellis	12.4	10.4	11.7	50.2	4 497	4 075	-9.4	-1.9	122	214	14	1 769	-3.1	2.27	6.0	29.2
Garfield	9.6	7.8	8.2	51.4	56 735	57 813	1.9	-1.2	2 734	2 264	-1 172	23 175	3.2	2.42	10.5	27.7
Garvin	10.6	8.9	8.9	51.8	26 605	27 210	2.3	0.0	1 240	1 233	14	10 865	4.3	2.45	10.1	26.9
Grady	10.1	6.7	5.9	51.1	41 747	45 516	9.0	4.2	1 842	1 536	1 606	17 341	11.6	2.58	9.7	22.9
Grant	11.0	10.4	10.4	51.5	5 689	5 144	-9.6	-3.3	142	249	-57	2 089	-10.2	2.42	6.3	28.4
Greer	10.0	9.2	11.0	43.4	6 559	6 061	-7.6	-2.9	186	271	-97	2 237	-12.3	2.27	9.6	33.4
Harmon	10.1	8.9	11.6	52.0	3 793	3 283	-13.4	-7.0	136	209	-158	1 266	-14.8	2.47	9.2	29.0
Harper	11.6	11.2	10.7	51.4	4 063	3 562	-12.3	-4.6	122	169	-121	1 509	-8.3	2.33	6.5	29.2
Haskell	11.4	8.6	8.4	50.8	10 940	11 792	7.8	2.1	565	543	231	4 624	7.1	2.52	9.1	24.7
Hughes	10.7	9.0	9.1	48.5	13 014	14 154	8.8	-1.8	512	676	-91	5 319	1.8	2.42	11.3	28.6
Jackson	8.4	6.6	5.7	50.1	28 764	28 439	-1.1	-3.9	1 464	863	-1 743	10 590	1.3	2.61	10.7	24.2
Jefferson	11.3	9.5	10.4	51.0	7 010	6 818	-2.7	-4.2	243	366	-157	2 716	-4.5	2.38	9.2	28.8
Johnston	10.7	8.4	7.3	51.3	10 032	10 513	4.8	0.1	401	454	70	4 057	7.2	2.53	10.7	25.2
Kay	10.1	8.1	8.7	51.5	48 056	48 080	0.0	-1.7	2 149	1 893	-1 075	19 157	0.4	2.45	10.2	27.9
Kingfisher	9.8	7.9	7.3	50.9	13 212	13 926	5.4	1.0	612	524	72	5 247	6.4	2.60	8.0	23.5

1. No spouse present.

Table B. States and Counties — **Vital Statistics, Health Resources, and Crime**

STATE County	Births, average 1999–2001 Total	Rate[1]	Deaths, average 1999–2001 Number Total	Infant[2]	Rate Total[1]	Infant[3]	Physicians,[4] 2000 Number	Rate[5]	Hospitals,[4] 1998 Number	Beds Number	Rate[5]	Medicare enrollees, 2003	Serious crimes known to police,[6] 2002 Total Number	Rate[7]
	32	33	34	35	36	37	38	39	40	41	42	43	44	45
OHIO—Cont'd														
Ottawa	426	10.4	442	2	10.8	D	37	90	1	41	100	8 057	NA	NA
Paulding	244	12.0	181	2	8.9	D	5	25	1	51	254	2 967	280	1 667
Perry	488	14.3	309	4	9.1	D	6	18	0	0	0	5 593	505	1 626
Pickaway	616	11.7	442	5	8.4	D	28	53	2	131	244	6 730	1 836	3 461
Pike	355	12.8	305	3	11.0	D	25	90	1	40	144	4 373	NA	NA
Portage	1 701	11.2	1 087	8	7.1	4.7	145	95	1	285	188	19 379	NA	NA
Preble	491	11.6	368	1	8.7	D	16	38	0	0	0	6 466	925	2 221
Putnam	486	14.0	284	3	8.2	D	14	40	0	0	0	5 243	160	566
Richland	1 644	12.8	1 276	12	9.9	7.3	185	144	3	411	323	21 933	6 728	5 190
Ross	906	12.3	707	5	9.6	D	117	160	1	212	281	11 258	4 140	5 611
Sandusky	863	14.0	613	5	9.9	D	65	105	1	130	209	8 923	NA	NA
Scioto	1 050	13.3	981	9	12.4	8.9	93	117	2	281	350	14 980	2 502	3 236
Seneca	709	12.1	561	3	9.6	D	44	75	2	134	223	10 962	NA	NA
Shelby	765	15.9	417	5	8.7	D	37	77	1	106	223	6 290	NA	NA
Stark	4 820	12.8	3 879	37	10.3	7.7	734	194	5	1 710	458	67 546	12 421	4 025
Summit	7 052	13.0	5 336	57	9.8	8.0	1 339	247	6	1 936	360	84 655	22 052	4 306
Trumbull	2 696	12.0	2 398	20	10.7	7.4	369	164	2	660	293	38 834	8 184	4 118
Tuscarawas	1 194	13.1	929	6	10.2	D	99	109	2	273	308	15 570	1 106	1 209
Union	631	15.3	269	4	6.5	D	42	103	1	56	142	4 084	658	2 205
Van Wert	345	11.6	298	2	10.1	D	26	88	1	99	328	4 432	250	1 941
Vinton	174	13.5	122	1	9.5	D	1	8	0	0	0	1 862	2 801	1 932
Warren	2 432	15.2	1 080	12	6.8	4.8	122	77	0	0	0	18 046	1 145	1 856
Washington	712	11.3	686	4	10.9	D	97	153	2	250	394	11 242	NA	NA
Wayne	1 595	14.3	947	11	8.5	7.1	126	113	2	128	116	16 715	581	1 474
Williams	503	12.9	376	5	9.6	D	30	77	1	78	205	6 235	NA	NA
Wood	1 383	11.4	935	7	7.7	4.8	134	111	1	98	82	15 101	359	1 878
Wyandot	282	12.3	234	2	10.3	D	12	52	1	31	136	3 975		
OKLAHOMA	49 637	14.4	34 820	403	10.1	8.1	5 448	158	110	11 495	343	521 286	165 715	4 743
Adair	375	17.8	228	4	10.8	D	8	38	1	34	167	3 294	711	3 338
Alfalfa	40	6.7	73	0	12.0	D	2	33	0	0	0	1 308	67	1 084
Atoka	162	11.7	167	2	12.0	D	6	43	1	45	340	2 164	445	3 167
Beaver	62	10.6	62	0	10.6	D	2	34	1	24	396	976	126	2 125
Beckham	267	13.4	265	1	13.3	D	27	136	2	128	654	3 204	452	2 255
Blaine	146	12.2	165	1	13.8	D	8	67	2	97	923	2 031	226	1 864
Bryan	505	13.9	427	4	11.7	D	30	82	1	103	297	6 691	1 393	3 766
Caddo	416	13.8	376	4	12.5	D	15	50	2	87	281	5 277	838	2 745
Canadian	1 099	12.5	625	9	7.1	8.5	36	41	1	54	63	9 561	4 444	5 005
Carter	647	14.2	579	4	12.7	D	70	153	2	206	463	9 066	2 463	5 332
Cherokee	594	14.0	383	4	9.0	D	40	94	1	61	156	5 771	1 081	2 511
Choctaw	220	14.4	212	1	13.9	D	12	78	1	66	438	3 319	514	3 309
Cimarron	32	10.4	38	1	12.3	D	3	95	1	20	676	602	21	659
Cleveland	2 437	11.7	1 240	15	5.9	6.2	239	115	1	236	117	18 473	11 088	5 265
Coal	73	12.0	81	1	13.4	D	2	33	1	20	333	1 163	176	2 882
Comanche	1 914	16.7	842	12	7.3	6.4	186	162	2	339	299	13 205	5 919	5 084
Cotton	73	11.1	85	0	13.0	D	2	30	0	0	0	1 166	87	1 299
Craig	199	13.4	191	3	12.8	D	21	140	1	28	194	3 275	372	2 458
Creek	891	13.2	693	7	10.3	7.5	30	45	3	220	328	9 808	2 117	3 104
Custer	343	13.2	287	2	11.0	D	29	111	2	96	377	3 784	790	2 985
Delaware	451	12.2	439	3	11.8	D	20	54	1	62	182	6 212	860	2 291
Dewey	49	10.3	97	1	20.4	D	2	42	1	18	365	1 025	73	1 520
Ellis	40	10.0	61	0	15.0	D	7	172	1	59	1 375	922	14	339
Garfield	833	14.4	673	10	11.6	12.0	115	199	2	298	524	10 225	3 171	5 417
Garvin	377	13.9	375	3	13.8	D	24	88	2	75	277	5 967	771	2 799
Grady	572	12.6	470	4	10.3	D	45	99	1	156	340	6 278	1 750	3 797
Grant	52	10.1	77	1	15.0	D	1	19	0	0	0	1 088	97	1 863
Greer	62	10.3	91	0	15.1	D	10	165	1	40	628	1 341	130	2 119
Harmon	38	11.6	63	0	19.3	D	2	61	1	24	690	632	113	3 400
Harper	37	10.6	53	0	14.9	D	2	56	1	25	695	815	76	2 107
Haskell	167	14.2	164	1	13.9	D	6	51	1	41	361	2 551	125	1 047
Hughes	162	11.5	200	3	14.2	D	14	99	2	72	511	2 904	336	2 345
Jackson	470	16.5	271	2	9.5	D	47	165	1	103	358	3 763	1 263	4 386
Jefferson	80	11.8	112	0	16.5	D	5	73	1	41	623	1 557	171	2 477
Johnston	119	11.4	125	1	11.9	D	5	48	1	36	348	2 019	183	1 719
Kay	700	13.4	593	5	12.3	D	57	119	2	168	360	9 188	2 475	5 084
Kingfisher	186	13.4	164	1	11.8	D	9	65	1	28	207	2 356	240	1 702

1. Per 1,000 estimated resident population.   2. Deaths of infants under 1 year old.   3. Deaths of infants under 1 year old per 1,000 live births.   4. Data subject to copyright.   5. Per 100,000 resident population as of July 1 of the year shown.   6. Data for serious crimes have not been adjusted for underreporting; this may affect comparability between geographic areas and over time.   7. Per 100,000 population estimated by the FBI.

STATE County	Serious crimes known to police,[1] 2002 (cont'd) Rate[2] Violent	Serious crimes known to police,[1] 2002 (cont'd) Rate[2] Property	Education School enrollment and attainment, 2000 Enrollment[3] Total	Education School enrollment and attainment, 2000 Enrollment[3] Percent private	Education Attainment[4] (percent) High school graduate or less	Education Attainment[4] (percent) Bachelor's degree or more	Education Local government expenditures,[5] 2000–2001 Total current expenditures (mil dol)	Education Local government expenditures,[5] 2000–2001 Current expenditures per student (dollars)	Money income, 1999 Per capita income[6] (dollars)	Money income, 1999 Households Median income Dollars	Money income, 1999 Households Median income Percent change, 1989–1999 (constant 1999 dollars)	Money income, 1999 Households Percent with income of $100,000 or more	Percent below poverty level, 1999 Persons	Percent below poverty level, 1999 Households	Percent below poverty level, 1999 Families	Percent below poverty level, 1999 Families with children
	46	47	48	49	50	51	52	53	54	55	56	57	58	59	60	61
OHIO—Cont'd																
Ottawa	NA	NA	9 895	9.4	56.3	16.0	50.9	7 637	21 973	44 224	5.0	9.1	5.9	6.3	4.2	6.9
Paulding	48	1 619	5 172	9.7	70.9	7.8	24.9	6 213	18 062	40 327	5.9	5.0	7.7	7.7	4.9	7.8
Perry	39	1 588	8 928	8.6	72.2	6.9	43.6	6 691	15 674	34 383	18.9	3.2	11.8	12.8	9.4	13.6
Pickaway	107	3 354	12 644	10.2	65.5	11.4	61.0	6 294	17 478	42 832	12.2	7.6	9.5	9.6	7.6	11.9
Pike	NA	NA	6 897	7.1	71.4	9.7	40.5	7 026	16 093	31 649	20.9	4.8	18.6	18.7	15.1	21.7
Portage	NA	NA	46 475	10.5	54.0	21.0	180.5	7 406	20 428	44 347	9.1	9.8	9.3	9.9	5.9	9.5
Preble	175	2 046	10 416	8.3	67.8	10.1	51.0	6 435	18 444	42 093	13.6	5.7	6.1	6.1	4.5	6.6
Putnam	7	558	9 685	12.2	61.6	12.9	48.0	6 476	18 680	46 426	6.3	7.2	5.6	5.9	4.0	4.9
Richland	174	5 017	31 084	13.4	62.8	12.6	172.8	7 939	18 582	37 397	1.8	6.9	10.6	10.3	8.2	13.7
Ross	145	5 466	17 385	7.9	66.1	11.3	90.9	7 388	17 569	37 117	13.8	5.8	12.0	12.0	9.1	13.4
Sandusky	NA	NA	16 006	14.0	61.6	11.9	82.3	7 336	19 239	40 584	3.9	6.7	7.5	7.6	5.7	8.6
Scioto	270	2 966	18 990	7.2	65.8	10.1	106.6	7 715	15 408	28 008	18.5	4.2	19.3	19.9	15.2	23.2
Seneca	NA	NA	16 006	22.7	63.2	12.5	67.0	7 063	17 027	38 037	4.9	4.1	9.0	8.9	6.1	9.2
Shelby	NA	NA	12 315	11.4	63.8	12.8	56.0	6 174	20 255	44 507	7.1	8.0	6.7	6.9	5.3	7.7
Stark	337	3 688	94 779	17.8	57.8	17.9	452.1	6 970	20 417	39 824	6.4	8.6	9.2	9.3	6.8	11.3
Summit	310	3 996	142 049	15.8	47.9	25.1	653.6	7 588	22 842	42 304	8.6	11.3	9.9	9.9	7.5	12.2
Trumbull	355	3 763	53 297	13.5	61.8	14.5	275.0	7 504	19 188	38 298	1.1	7.3	10.3	10.4	7.9	13.4
Tuscarawas	85	1 124	21 272	10.6	67.9	12.2	103.8	6 686	17 276	35 489	6.6	4.9	9.4	9.8	7.2	10.3
Union	NA	NA	10 216	12.9	57.9	15.9	43.7	6 946	20 577	51 743	15.8	10.8	4.6	5.8	3.6	4.6
Van Wert	84	2 122	7 501	13.3	65.0	12.0	36.8	8 311	18 293	39 497	2.6	4.5	5.5	5.8	4.2	5.5
Vinton	0	1 941	3 146	4.5	76.9	6.0	15.5	6 098	13 731	29 465	15.0	3.0	20.0	18.9	15.1	21.3
Warren	67	1 865	41 655	18.6	45.0	28.4	182.1	6 946	25 517	57 952	17.4	19.3	4.2	4.6	3.0	4.4
Washington	126	1 729	15 573	16.3	58.5	15.0	71.3	6 707	18 082	34 275	4.3	5.8	11.4	11.6	8.6	14.6
Wayne	NA	NA	29 064	19.7	62.0	17.2	141.8	7 504	18 330	41 538	5.9	7.3	8.0	8.0	5.4	8.4
Williams	58	1 415	9 356	8.7	65.6	10.7	43.5	6 022	18 441	40 735	6.6	4.7	6.0	6.5	3.9	5.3
Wood	NA	NA	42 352	9.6	46.2	26.2	154.1	8 227	21 284	44 442	6.0	11.1	9.6	10.1	4.7	7.2
Wyandot	16	1 862	5 557	15.0	66.5	9.8	23.4	5 837	17 170	38 839	5.3	3.6	5.5	6.0	3.8	5.2
OKLAHOMA	503	4 240	930 865	10.6	50.9	20.3	3 654.4	5 869	17 646	33 400	5.4	6.6	14.7	14.6	11.2	16.5
Adair	582	2 756	5 702	5.9	71.4	9.8	35.3	7 372	11 185	24 881	9.7	2.0	23.2	24.3	19.4	26.9
Alfalfa	146	938	1 228	4.3	59.4	14.9	6.4	7 254	14 704	30 259	22.4	4.2	13.7	14.1	11.8	17.0
Atoka	605	2 562	3 231	4.0	70.5	10.1	14.6	6 353	12 919	24 752	32.6	3.1	19.8	20.9	15.7	21.4
Beaver	135	1 990	1 434	2.4	55.1	17.6	10.1	8 051	17 905	36 715	-0.2	5.5	11.7	10.9	8.8	13.8
Beckham	85	2 170	4 648	4.5	58.8	15.5	22.0	5 995	14 488	27 402	6.5	4.5	18.2	17.8	14.3	22.1
Blaine	115	1 748	2 801	3.4	65.7	14.0	15.2	6 943	13 546	28 356	3.5	3.2	16.9	16.6	12.8	19.4
Bryan	324	3 441	9 959	5.7	56.9	17.9	40.6	6 002	14 217	27 888	25.0	3.5	18.4	20.5	14.0	19.4
Caddo	462	2 283	8 304	4.5	64.6	14.2	44.4	6 738	13 298	27 347	14.0	2.9	21.7	20.1	16.7	23.5
Canadian	407	4 598	24 386	10.2	44.7	20.9	90.8	5 146	19 691	45 439	-0.1	9.0	7.9	8.1	5.8	8.3
Carter	894	4 438	11 129	6.1	59.8	15.1	53.8	6 025	15 511	29 405	0.4	4.2	16.6	17.0	12.7	19.3
Cherokee	307	2 204	13 564	6.0	53.5	22.1	47.5	6 348	13 436	26 536	12.8	3.2	22.9	22.2	17.0	24.4
Choctaw	605	2 704	3 715	3.1	67.7	9.9	17.9	6 371	12 296	22 743	36.0	1.8	24.3	25.2	20.4	30.5
Cimarron	94	565	780	4.6	55.0	17.7	5.3	8 407	15 744	30 625	18.9	4.4	17.6	16.5	13.9	19.8
Cleveland	396	4 869	67 969	9.2	38.6	28.0	188.6	5 252	20 114	41 846	3.9	9.3	10.6	11.5	6.4	9.0
Coal	475	2 407	1 519	4.2	68.4	12.4	9.3	7 430	12 013	23 705	24.5	2.5	23.1	22.9	18.5	23.7
Comanche	637	4 446	32 582	7.0	46.3	19.1	126.2	5 663	15 728	33 867	3.4	5.2	15.6	15.4	13.2	18.6
Cotton	224	1 075	1 557	2.6	62.2	14.0	7.3	5 907	14 626	27 210	6.7	3.8	18.2	19.1	13.7	21.8
Craig	198	2 259	3 336	3.6	63.8	10.5	19.4	6 247	16 539	30 997	21.5	3.7	13.7	14.2	10.9	15.3
Creek	378	2 726	17 579	8.1	62.4	11.7	72.2	5 364	16 191	33 168	3.7	4.8	13.5	13.7	10.8	14.6
Custer	280	2 705	8 868	3.5	50.2	22.8	30.8	6 195	18 524	28 524	-6.0	4.8	18.5	19.8	12.4	18.8
Delaware	139	2 152	7 983	5.6	61.7	13.3	40.4	6 127	15 424	27 996	11.5	4.6	18.3	17.1	14.1	22.4
Dewey	187	1 333	1 121	3.2	61.0	16.6	7.0	8 603	15 806	28 172	10.5	4.3	15.0	16.6	11.4	15.4
Ellis	48	291	848	4.0	57.1	19.2	6.0	8 321	16 472	27 951	3.9	4.0	12.5	12.8	9.2	18.3
Garfield	436	4 982	14 004	10.2	53.4	19.6	57.7	5 951	17 457	33 006	5.7	5.1	13.9	13.1	10.5	16.7
Garvin	287	2 512	6 197	3.4	67.4	12.0	31.6	5 804	14 856	28 070	12.0	3.7	15.9	16.0	11.4	15.9
Grady	616	3 181	12 198	6.3	58.8	14.4	47.0	5 628	15 846	32 625	11.0	4.4	13.9	15.1	10.4	15.1
Grant	19	1 843	1 322	4.4	53.3	16.2	7.7	7 315	15 709	28 977	-0.4	3.7	13.7	12.7	10.5	15.2
Greer	65	2 053	1 265	5.1	59.6	12.6	6.4	6 899	14 053	25 793	12.9	3.5	19.6	19.3	15.0	25.4
Harmon	181	3 219	793	2.3	69.0	12.1	4.5	7 185	13 464	22 365	19.9	3.1	29.7	26.9	23.5	33.3
Harper	277	1 830	829	2.4	54.2	19.2	5.7	8 349	18 011	33 705	10.0	5.4	10.2	9.2	7.1	12.7
Haskell	184	863	2 759	1.2	65.7	10.3	14.5	6 128	13 775	24 553	17.2	3.8	20.5	22.0	16.1	22.1
Hughes	216	2 128	3 242	5.8	68.3	9.7	16.4	6 570	12 687	22 621	11.0	2.8	21.9	21.4	16.7	23.8
Jackson	233	4 154	8 036	4.0	47.8	18.5	34.1	5 738	15 454	30 737	5.4	4.6	16.2	15.6	13.6	19.8
Jefferson	608	1 869	1 494	2.1	68.1	10.6	8.5	6 682	12 899	23 674	13.3	2.8	19.2	20.6	16.3	23.2
Johnston	310	1 409	2 768	3.8	61.4	13.3	12.6	6 473	13 747	24 592	19.9	3.3	22.0	21.8	17.8	22.4
Kay	616	4 468	12 077	8.2	52.3	18.3	50.4	5 462	16 643	30 762	-5.8	5.7	16.0	14.8	12.4	18.8
Kingfisher	85	1 617	3 504	8.7	57.6	16.1	20.6	6 442	18 167	36 676	7.6	7.5	10.8	10.4	8.5	13.5

1. Data for serious crimes have not been adjusted for underreporting; this may affect comparability between geographic areas and over time. 2. Per 100,000 population estimated by the FBI. 3. All persons 3 years old and over enrolled in nursery school through college. 4. Persons 25 years old and over. 5. Elementary and secondary education expenditures. 6. Based on population enumerated as of April 1, 2000.

Table B. States and Counties — Personal Income

	Personal income, 2002												
			Per capita[1]					Transfer payments					
									Government payments to individuals				
STATE County	Total (mil dol)	Percent change, 2001–2002	Dollars	Rank	Wages and salaries[2] (mil dol)	Proprietor's income (mil dol)	Dividends, interest, and rent (mil dol)	Total (mil dol)	Total (mil dol)	Social Security (mil dol)	Medical payments (mil dol)	Income maintenance (mil dol)	Unemployment insurance (mil dol)
	62	63	64	65	66	67	68	69	70	71	72	73	74
OHIO—Cont'd													
Ottawa	1 220	1.6	29 768	367	532	56	229	223	211	91	86	9	10
Paulding	450	-1.1	22 613	1 846	176	12	69	80	75	36	26	6	3
Perry	667	4.1	19 277	2 700	238	19	70	165	156	56	68	16	6
Pickaway	1 194	0.4	23 110	1 692	631	37	167	202	187	76	71	18	8
Pike	584	2.2	20 845	2 333	409	31	94	162	154	47	69	21	8
Portage	4 131	2.9	26 834	729	2 151	217	596	622	578	230	217	39	24
Preble	1 009	0.8	23 751	1 484	409	25	143	179	167	73	65	11	6
Putnam	921	1.2	26 547	777	407	40	166	133	124	58	46	6	4
Richland	3 222	3.3	25 098	1 106	2 380	135	473	619	583	246	228	49	23
Ross	1 717	3.5	23 123	1 688	1 141	63	235	347	326	117	128	41	13
Sandusky	1 536	1.9	24 831	1 170	987	61	234	280	263	115	101	17	12
Scioto	1 633	2.8	20 914	2 320	829	70	214	515	492	140	225	68	16
Seneca	1 380	0.7	23 822	1 464	754	45	219	299	282	108	126	17	12
Shelby	1 297	2.9	26 801	736	1 295	53	200	181	167	76	60	12	7
Stark	10 392	2.5	27 519	614	6 546	679	1 738	1 869	1 762	739	691	148	58
Summit	17 016	2.6	31 155	268	11 448	993	2 825	2 715	2 560	992	1 060	232	90
Trumbull	5 614	2.0	25 156	1 089	3 802	233	934	1 203	1 140	475	470	89	40
Tuscarawas	2 109	2.2	23 029	1 714	1 157	122	353	414	388	168	146	30	16
Union	1 175	4.2	27 349	639	1 553	48	135	136	123	53	47	9	4
Van Wert	711	-1.7	24 277	1 317	380	28	117	123	114	57	38	6	4
Vinton	245	3.7	18 677	2 802	90	7	42	64	60	18	27	8	3
Warren	5 402	2.7	30 956	271	2 407	293	669	574	525	233	193	26	21
Washington	1 577	5.8	25 230	1 068	1 004	94	248	315	297	121	121	24	9
Wayne	2 820	2.7	25 002	1 126	1 841	213	513	452	420	182	166	30	13
Williams	985	1.6	25 288	1 052	668	50	167	169	158	69	60	10	7
Wood	3 432	2.5	28 055	541	2 476	159	590	455	421	172	150	23	15
Wyandot	556	0.6	24 419	1 282	373	10	93	101	94	41	37	5	4
OKLAHOMA	90 508	2.6	25 936	X	54 656	11 187	15 477	15 179	14 367	5 715	5 718	1 394	336
Adair	383	5.3	17 948	2 903	166	45	48	101	96	30	45	13	1
Alfalfa	118	-6.3	19 752	2 601	41	17	32	28	26	14	10	1	0
Atoka	242	6.3	17 296	2 968	99	38	37	63	60	24	25	7	1
Beaver	126	-1.2	22 533	1 869	42	15	32	22	21	10	8	1	0
Beckham	392	3.5	19 599	2 635	216	42	90	89	85	34	37	9	1
Blaine	221	5.1	18 940	2 768	95	27	54	53	50	21	21	5	1
Bryan	766	3.2	20 733	2 359	377	58	110	183	175	65	73	18	1
Caddo	595	6.5	19 832	2 580	247	65	118	141	134	50	54	18	2
Canadian	2 326	3.4	25 527	993	815	144	329	286	265	113	95	18	10
Carter	1 066	3.5	23 145	1 679	706	92	206	236	225	90	96	21	5
Cherokee	822	7.7	18 945	2 765	405	72	118	201	191	60	81	19	2
Choctaw	282	4.3	18 323	2 858	118	27	41	95	91	30	40	13	1
Cimarron	63	-2.7	21 025	2 291	25	7	19	13	12	7	4	1	0
Cleveland	5 660	4.8	26 240	844	2 133	404	806	641	591	246	203	49	15
Coal	102	8.2	17 033	2 993	34	7	16	33	32	10	15	3	1
Comanche	2 686	3.9	23 725	1 490	2 006	134	384	439	416	135	142	50	4
Cotton	139	3.0	21 453	2 165	29	14	23	30	29	12	12	2	0
Craig	315	5.0	21 357	2 193	183	28	57	87	84	30	41	6	1
Creek	1 510	1.3	22 003	2 015	610	92	224	298	282	120	111	21	9
Custer	555	2.6	22 104	1 988	307	52	131	116	110	40	43	11	2
Delaware	851	4.0	22 391	1 912	214	90	150	179	170	74	68	14	2
Dewey	106	3.0	23 224	1 653	35	12	30	23	22	10	10	1	0
Ellis	89	-1.4	22 140	1 975	29	8	26	21	20	9	8	1	0
Garfield	1 454	2.9	25 444	1 011	876	110	297	306	293	114	137	22	3
Garvin	621	3.3	22 835	1 769	279	58	112	189	182	61	97	14	3
Grady	1 047	5.3	22 407	1 905	424	93	159	178	167	73	59	18	3
Grant	121	1.4	24 097	1 373	40	13	34	26	25	12	10	1	0
Greer	133	3.4	22 434	1 898	55	12	21	36	35	13	16	3	0
Harmon	63	-2.4	20 385	2 464	22	9	12	19	18	6	9	2	0
Harper	92	-0.2	26 791	737	32	14	28	18	17	9	7	1	0
Haskell	253	3.4	21 535	2 139	101	23	39	69	66	24	28	7	1
Hughes	247	3.3	17 660	2 935	80	33	39	82	79	27	37	7	1
Jackson	645	4.7	23 566	1 543	471	36	115	122	116	37	51	12	1
Jefferson	118	1.8	18 095	2 882	40	10	25	39	37	15	17	3	1
Johnston	188	6.3	18 032	2 893	84	15	26	56	54	20	21	6	1
Kay	1 186	2.5	24 890	1 163	802	101	245	227	216	102	73	19	6
Kingfisher	351	-0.3	25 219	1 071	189	39	73	56	52	25	21	3	1

1. Based on the resident population estimated as of July 1 of the year shown.　2. Includes other labor income.

Table B. States and Counties — Earnings, Social Security, and Housing

STATE County	Earnings, 2002									Social Security beneficiaries, December 2003		Supplemental Security Income recipients, December 2003	Housing units, 2003	
	Total (mil dol)	Farm	Goods-related[1]		Service-related and health				Govern-ment					
			Total	Manu-facturing	Information and profes-sional and technical services	Retail trade	Finance, insur-ance, and real estate	Health services		Number	Rate[2]		Total	Percent change, 2000–2003
	75	76	77	78	79	80	81	82	83	84	85	86	87	88
OHIO—Cont'd														
Ottawa	589	0.0	27.3	20.5	D	9.1	5.2	D	16.8	8 975	218	290	26 118	2.3
Paulding	188	-3.4	D	31.0	3.1	7.9	3.5	D	24.8	3 635	185	277	8 775	3.5
Perry	257	0.9	43.8	23.5	3.4	5.8	3.4	D	23.3	6 145	175	849	13 807	1.1
Pickaway	668	-1.0	D	35.4	D	6.4	3.4	D	28.1	8 165	158	837	19 153	3.0
Pike	440	-0.4	D	49.5	3.5	6.0	2.6	6.9	15.7	5 525	196	1 422	11 893	2.5
Portage	2 368	0.4	34.3	27.6	4.5	7.3	3.1	4.7	27.3	22 600	146	1 898	62 686	4.3
Preble	434	-1.4	D	42.5	D	7.3	3.3	4.5	17.8	7 525	177	410	17 645	2.7
Putnam	448	0.5	D	44.2	2.2	6.1	4.0	4.7	14.3	5 825	168	300	13 128	2.9
Richland	2 514	0.2	38.9	34.5	5.5	8.0	3.8	11.3	16.6	24 675	192	2 755	54 332	2.4
Ross	1 205	-0.4	D	25.3	4.3	8.4	2.9	11.8	27.3	12 595	169	2 742	30 166	2.4
Sandusky	1 047	0.6	D	44.3	3.0	7.5	2.9	D	13.4	11 280	183	820	25 592	1.3
Scioto	898	-0.2	17.2	10.6	3.7	9.2	3.8	21.5	25.5	15 770	204	5 581	34 813	2.2
Seneca	798	-1.7	41.0	33.3	4.0	7.6	5.1	9.8	15.3	10 930	189	894	24 116	1.8
Shelby	1 348	-0.1	D	56.1	D	5.0	2.2	D	8.5	7 570	156	555	19 212	2.8
Stark	7 224	0.3	D	26.5	5.9	8.9	6.0	13.3	12.0	71 895	190	6 805	159 871	1.8
Summit	12 441	0.0	D	17.1	8.4	7.9	6.8	12.2	12.6	94 790	173	10 939	236 682	2.5
Trumbull	4 034	0.0	48.0	44.4	3.5	7.4	4.4	9.6	11.7	45 615	206	4 530	96 126	1.1
Tuscarawas	1 279	1.6	34.8	27.1	3.8	9.8	4.2	10.3	15.1	17 270	188	1 453	38 501	1.0
Union	1 601	0.9	D	58.6	D	2.8	1.7	1.9	8.4	5 470	125	315	16 791	10.3
Van Wert	407	-2.4	D	40.0	2.2	6.8	9.0	D	12.9	5 670	194	310	12 517	1.2
Vinton	97	-0.1	40.7	18.6	D	4.9	4.4	5.6	29.3	2 110	159	470	5 750	1.7
Warren	2 700	-0.3	28.8	22.8	8.3	10.4	9.8	5.5	13.4	22 920	126	1 167	67 163	14.4
Washington	1 098	0.6	43.0	22.8	4.1	7.8	4.1	11.6	12.4	12 425	199	1 694	28 074	1.1
Wayne	2 054	2.3	44.8	36.6	4.2	6.4	4.3	6.6	14.6	18 285	162	1 420	44 144	4.3
Williams	718	0.1	56.7	52.3	2.4	5.0	3.0	8.6	11.7	6 905	178	403	16 550	2.5
Wood	2 635	0.0	D	31.4	5.5	5.8	3.6	6.0	18.7	16 955	138	956	50 038	5.4
Wyandot	383	-2.0	60.5	51.3	D	4.4	2.4	D	13.1	4 260	187	234	9 480	1.7
OKLAHOMA	65 843	0.9	24.9	15.7	8.6	7.7	6.1	8.9	21.3	613 515	175	75 262	1 552 599	2.5
Adair	211	10.0	D	29.3	2.4	8.7	1.8	5.8	23.2	3 930	182	886	8 562	2.6
Alfalfa	58	19.7	D	D	D	6.2	D	5.9	29.3	1 400	237	46	2 788	-1.6
Atoka	137	3.0	D	15.9	3.1	8.9	3.7	D	34.8	3 035	215	551	5 762	1.6
Beaver	57	8.4	D	D	D	3.3	D	D	30.0	1 065	191	44	2 722	0.1
Beckham	257	2.2	24.8	1.9	D	12.8	6.9	12.7	14.5	3 815	192	511	8 915	1.4
Blaine	122	6.8	25.1	17.8	3.3	7.3	4.4	5.9	25.6	2 355	202	235	5 190	-0.3
Bryan	434	1.9	D	10.5	3.8	7.7	4.4	10.8	32.1	7 460	200	1 328	17 147	2.6
Caddo	312	12.8	6.0	0.8	3.8	7.0	3.5	D	33.5	5 825	194	808	13 142	0.4
Canadian	959	0.5	33.6	21.2	4.9	8.4	6.6	4.6	24.3	12 150	131	527	36 277	6.8
Carter	798	0.0	31.0	19.6	6.2	8.4	4.0	11.5	13.2	9 620	207	1 415	20 919	1.7
Cherokee	477	5.7	6.9	0.9	2.6	8.5	3.3	6.3	54.3	7 215	165	1 148	20 181	3.5
Choctaw	145	1.7	D	3.6	3.1	10.2	3.0	D	26.3	3 730	242	1 030	7 638	1.3
Cimarron	32	18.6	D	0.6	D	13.4	6.3	1.1	33.9	705	238	38	1 574	-0.6
Cleveland	2 537	-0.1	12.9	5.4	9.0	10.2	6.7	8.5	32.4	26 390	120	2 272	89 625	5.6
Coal	41	2.9	D	D	D	11.3	3.5	12.0	31.8	1 305	219	259	2 752	0.3
Comanche	2 140	0.3	D	9.6	4.3	6.1	3.6	5.8	56.5	15 795	139	2 547	45 787	0.8
Cotton	43	15.6	D	1.1	D	8.9	4.9	5.2	31.3	1 410	214	127	3 088	0.1
Craig	210	2.5	D	13.9	3.7	8.2	5.0	6.6	33.4	3 420	230	487	6 497	0.6
Creek	702	0.0	35.7	23.0	3.9	8.3	4.2	11.4	15.9	12 625	184	981	28 600	2.2
Custer	359	0.8	21.8	13.0	5.7	10.8	5.9	D	27.2	4 335	174	602	11 759	0.7
Delaware	304	10.6	D	12.1	4.9	11.5	5.0	D	20.4	8 280	214	862	22 959	3.0
Dewey	46	5.4	13.6	3.3	6.4	9.0	6.2	2.0	36.2	1 135	250	71	2 425	0.0
Ellis	36	7.9	D	2.0	D	9.9	3.8	8.0	36.2	990	248	52	2 124	-1.0
Garfield	986	0.8	19.6	10.9	D	8.3	5.1	13.2	24.5	11 580	203	1 236	26 164	0.4
Garvin	337	1.8	27.3	10.9	3.6	16.5	4.2	D	23.3	6 650	244	874	12 727	0.7
Grady	517	3.1	37.0	26.2	D	8.2	4.0	6.5	19.1	8 185	173	1 062	19 886	2.3
Grant	53	11.0	9.4	0.8	D	6.7	8.7	4.9	25.3	1 260	253	51	2 595	-1.0
Greer	66	12.8	D	D	D	4.9	2.5	3.7	50.9	1 480	251	182	2 769	-0.7
Harmon	31	18.5	D	D	D	8.8	D	2.0	37.8	745	244	133	1 647	0.0
Harper	46	18.6	D	D	D	6.0	D	4.5	31.3	900	265	40	1 852	-0.6
Haskell	124	5.4	23.3	10.8	D	9.7	D	17.2	24.8	3 005	250	468	5 676	1.8
Hughes	113	15.0	12.5	2.1	D	10.5	4.2	3.7	29.5	3 265	235	472	6 249	0.2
Jackson	506	1.8	D	5.7	2.0	7.4	2.3	4.1	59.2	4 285	157	602	12 379	0.0
Jefferson	49	10.0	13.8	6.6	D	7.9	7.4	5.0	36.7	1 710	262	179	3 378	0.1
Johnston	99	6.1	D	27.5	D	4.5	D	9.9	27.3	2 440	232	366	4 867	1.8
Kay	903	0.5	44.5	20.6	5.1	6.8	4.1	7.9	13.4	10 295	218	758	21 727	-0.4
Kingfisher	228	7.6	26.9	9.9	D	7.6	5.1	4.1	13.4	2 605	185	146	5 958	1.3

1. Covers mining, construction, and manufacturing.   2. Per 1,000 resident population estimated as of July 1 of the year shown.

Table B. States and Counties — Housing, Labor Force, and Employment

STATE County	Housing units, 2000 Total	Percent	Owner-occupied Median value[1]	Median owner cost as a percent of income With a mortgage	Without a mortgage[2]	Renter-occupied Median rent[3]	Median rent as a percent of income	Sub-standard units[4] (percent)	Civilian labor force, 2003 Total	Percent change, 2002–2003	Unemployment Total	Rate[5]	Civilian employment,[6] 2000 Total	Percent Management, professional and related occupations	Production, transportation, and material moving occupations
	89	90	91	92	93	94	95	96	97	98	99	100	101	102	103
OHIO—Cont'd															
Ottawa	16 474	80.7	113 000	19.9	10.1	496	20.4	1.7	21 430	2.8	1 814	8.5	19 830	26.2	21.7
Paulding	7 773	83.9	73 800	18.1	9.9	393	19.1	2.7	9 908	0.3	686	6.9	9 839	20.7	35.5
Perry	12 500	79.4	72 500	19.2	9.9	415	20.9	2.2	14 968	0.2	1 465	9.8	14 664	20.2	29.2
Pickaway	17 599	74.6	112 400	20.7	9.9	494	24.0	2.1	24 943	1.0	1 475	5.9	22 281	26.2	21.4
Pike	10 444	70.1	77 400	18.5	9.9	544	25.4	1.6	85 954	1.6	4 708	5.5	79 709	28.4	20.9
Portage	56 449	71.3	123 000	20.9	10.0	492	22.2	1.9	22 183	-0.6	1 326	6.0	20 560	24.2	27.1
Preble	16 001	78.9	93 500	20.4	9.9	492	22.2	1.9	20 615	1.4	1 309	6.3	17 095	24.3	30.6
Putnam	12 200	84.1	93 300	18.3	9.9	446	17.2	2.1							
Richland	49 534	71.6	88 100	19.9	10.1	451	23.3	1.9	61 365	1.1	4 790	7.8	58 219	23.9	26.0
Ross	27 136	73.5	87 000	19.3	9.9	430	22.2	2.9	35 613	1.4	2 604	7.3	30 994	23.9	25.3
Sandusky	23 717	75.3	90 100	19.0	9.9	462	20.5	1.6	31 740	0.8	2 310	7.3	30 489	22.9	32.9
Scioto	30 871	70.1	63 400	19.7	10.4	378	25.8	2.4	33 859	-1.5	2 905	8.6	28 966	26.1	18.7
Seneca	22 292	75.1	81 300	18.6	9.9	433	21.4	1.8	28 691	3.8	2 074	7.2	28 825	21.7	31.7
Shelby	17 636	74.4	97 000	19.2	9.9	499	21.7	1.5	30 360	2.1	1 568	5.2	23 949	25.0	32.2
Stark	148 316	72.4	100 300	20.0	9.9	486	23.3	1.4	191 662	-0.2	12 820	6.7	180 590	28.7	21.5
Summit	217 788	70.2	109 100	21.0	11.2	546	25.0	1.7	290 722	1.4	16 711	5.7	263 097	33.1	16.1
Trumbull	89 020	74.3	85 500	18.9	9.9	461	23.7	1.9	109 354	1.4	8 295	7.6	99 546	24.5	26.2
Tuscarawas	35 653	75.0	88 100	20.3	9.9	443	22.7	1.5	46 727	4.6	2 966	6.3	42 874	22.7	28.2
Union	14 346	77.5	128 800	20.8	10.9	574	22.7	1.9	21 461	4.4	884	4.1	20 826	27.1	23.4
Van Wert	11 587	81.7	76 000	18.4	9.9	412	19.4	1.4	15 560	-3.4	880	5.7	14 583	22.4	33.0
Vinton	4 892	77.8	64 400	19.1	9.9	391	26.7	5.9	3 907	-5.2	542	13.9	4 892	16.6	33.0
Warren	55 966	78.5	142 200	20.2	10.1	613	22.9	1.4	93 908	2.2	4 160	4.4	77 718	37.7	15.6
Washington	25 137	76.2	80 400	19.0	9.9	400	23.7	1.9	33 395	1.5	1 995	6.0	28 607	27.5	20.1
Wayne	40 445	73.3	108 100	20.1	9.9	492	22.2	2.7	60 105	1.7	2 869	4.8	55 500	26.4	25.6
Williams	15 105	76.8	85 700	19.3	9.9	476	20.8	1.6	19 710	-1.2	1 460	7.4	20 039	20.6	38.8
Wood	45 172	70.6	120 000	19.7	10.2	508	24.9	1.6	67 963	-0.2	3 649	5.4	62 448	32.9	20.1
Wyandot	8 882	74.7	82 300	17.9	9.9	408	18.0	1.5	14 128	6.9	762	5.4	11 501	20.7	33.8
OKLAHOMA	1 342 293	68.4	70 700	19.2	9.9	456	24.3	4.2	1 696 060	0.1	96 034	5.7	1 545 296	30.3	15.4
Adair	7 471	73.3	45 400	21.6	11.4	342	20.6	6.9	9 497	7.1	958	10.1	8 421	22.1	31.8
Alfalfa	2 199	81.7	29 000	18.6	9.9	282	17.7	1.8	2 463	0.1	57	2.3	2 367	33.8	12.3
Atoka	4 964	76.4	43 800	19.1	12.4	327	23.3	5.0	5 502	5.8	400	7.3	4 850	24.9	22.9
Beaver	2 245	79.1	58 200	18.0	9.9	389	14.4	3.6	2 602	0.0	94	3.6	2 719	31.2	16.3
Beckham	7 356	71.1	51 700	17.8	9.9	353	22.0	3.4	10 888	2.4	298	2.7	7 885	27.2	12.4
Blaine	4 159	76.9	41 900	17.9	10.5	332	22.1	4.8	4 742	2.2	212	4.5	4 525	29.9	17.1
Bryan	14 422	69.3	55 900	19.0	9.9	375	23.7	3.9	18 861	0.2	731	3.9	15 643	27.8	19.8
Caddo	10 957	73.5	44 300	18.6	10.0	329	19.2	6.2	12 056	1.0	642	5.3	11 342	29.1	16.7
Canadian	31 484	78.9	84 600	19.6	9.9	510	23.3	3.2	48 741	-0.1	2 243	4.6	43 694	31.6	15.2
Carter	17 992	71.1	58 400	19.2	10.4	416	24.5	3.6	22 437	4.9	1 056	4.7	19 319	25.6	19.6
Cherokee	16 175	66.8	67 100	19.9	9.9	389	26.1	6.1	19 878	1.5	1 063	5.3	17 870	29.7	14.6
Choctaw	6 220	70.9	41 500	18.4	9.9	302	23.5	3.8	5 875	-1.4	564	9.6	5 690	26.6	17.8
Cimarron	1 257	72.6	37 000	15.1	9.9	284	18.2	4.9	1 613	0.2	49	3.0	1 417	35.3	13.0
Cleveland	79 186	67.0	88 500	19.2	9.9	526	26.9	3.3	117 245	-0.1	4 435	3.8	104 978	35.3	10.8
Coal	2 373	75.3	33 800	19.7	11.0	287	25.1	4.7	2 306	-2.1	399	17.3	2 275	28.1	21.4
Comanche	39 808	60.3	71 600	19.7	9.9	452	24.3	4.7	42 878	1.4	1 553	3.6	40 436	29.5	14.3
Cotton	2 614	76.4	47 200	18.1	11.3	328	23.0	3.8	2 333	12.7	115	4.9	2 667	29.0	18.7
Craig	5 620	74.9	52 100	19.2	9.9	396	21.5	3.4	6 451	0.4	341	5.3	6 366	24.0	23.4
Creek	25 289	78.0	67 400	19.2	9.9	428	21.9	3.8	33 121	-1.0	2 477	7.5	29 525	23.6	21.8
Custer	10 136	63.7	67 800	19.0	9.9	371	24.9	3.9	11 891	0.3	392	3.3	12 389	29.5	13.9
Delaware	14 838	79.2	81 900	22.7	10.7	390	23.7	4.9	17 860	-0.1	875	4.9	14 745	23.4	23.4
Dewey	1 962	79.0	38 000	18.0	11.0	303	17.7	3.0	2 023	1.5	66	3.3	2 121	32.9	14.3
Ellis	1 769	80.7	34 000	17.5	10.3	339	19.4	1.6	1 608	2.7	36	2.2	1 950	33.7	13.2
Garfield	23 175	70.2	58 800	18.9	9.9	436	23.9	2.7	26 535	0.7	945	3.6	26 012	27.2	14.8
Garvin	10 865	73.9	45 400	18.9	11.0	388	22.4	3.6	11 851	0.8	581	4.9	11 618	23.1	20.8
Grady	17 341	75.7	62 500	18.9	9.9	396	22.6	3.2	20 871	0.3	1 005	4.8	20 584	26.2	19.5
Grant	2 089	78.8	36 300	19.9	9.9	391	22.3	2.2	2 227	0.3	78	3.5	2 345	34.3	11.8
Greer	2 237	74.8	32 300	17.7	11.2	290	20.7	3.5	2 394	-1.0	139	5.8	2 057	31.8	12.7
Harmon	1 266	77.2	28 000	17.5	11.6	274	22.4	4.4	1 220	-2.6	48	3.9	1 278	30.6	13.5
Harper	1 509	78.7	37 900	14.0	9.9	315	17.6	2.5	1 716	0.1	53	3.1	1 711	33.5	11.2
Haskell	4 624	77.3	44 500	18.4	10.5	301	23.5	6.3	5 622	-0.9	394	7.0	4 601	26.5	20.8
Hughes	5 319	75.8	32 600	20.8	11.6	309	23.3	4.3	5 832	1.6	537	9.2	4 982	26.1	17.2
Jackson	10 590	60.3	59 600	19.5	11.5	429	22.9	3.8	13 482	4.1	425	3.2	11 080	28.5	13.2
Jefferson	2 716	74.1	33 300	19.0	12.2	261	22.7	3.4	2 406	-3.1	141	5.9	2 604	26.6	19.3
Johnston	4 057	73.7	40 000	18.4	11.0	321	23.1	5.5	5 273	9.2	253	4.8	4 151	25.7	22.5
Kay	19 157	71.7	53 400	18.4	10.4	414	23.9	3.2	21 800	-4.1	1 718	7.9	20 375	29.3	18.2
Kingfisher	5 247	78.2	67 900	17.7	9.9	384	20.6	3.0	6 691	0.5	204	3.0	6 644	27.8	17.8

1. Specified owner-occupied units. 2. Median monthly owner costs is often in the minimum category—9.9 percent or less, which is indicated as 9.9 percent. 3. Specified renter-occupied units. 4. Overcrowded or lacking complete plumbing facilities. 5. Percent of civilian labor force. 6. Persons 16 years old and over.

Table B. States and Counties — Nonfarm Employment and Agriculture

STATE County	Private nonfarm establishments, employment and payroll, 2001									Agriculture, 2002			
	Number of establishments	Employment						Annual payroll		Farms			Farm operators whose principal occupation is farming (percent)
		Total	Health care and social assistance	Manufacturing	Retail trade	Finance and insurance	Professional, scientific, and technical services	Total (mil dol)	Average per employee (dollars)	Number	Percent with— Less than 50 acres	500 acres and over	
	104	105	106	107	108	109	110	111	112	113	114	115	116
OHIO—Cont'd													
Ottawa	1 128	11 838	1 184	2 894	1 715	285	213	350	29 528	517	39.1	11.4	55.9
Paulding	339	4 188	470	1 553	591	131	51	101	24 132	651	32.4	22.6	64.2
Perry	495	4 924	673	1 608	686	202	113	117	23 694	639	36.0	3.9	53.5
Pickaway	800	11 877	1 725	3 782	1 626	339	384	335	28 188	791	42.5	20.0	58.7
Pike	464	10 054	1 439	5 291	1 184	209	105	292	29 018	505	28.1	4.4	50.9
Portage	3 128	44 616	4 769	13 096	5 587	680	1 235	1 241	27 819	962	56.2	2.9	52.1
Preble	725	9 871	701	3 855	1 488	259	222	264	26 731	1 065	45.2	10.0	57.7
Putnam	729	10 179	672	4 341	1 199	270	123	257	25 235	1 348	25.5	12.9	58.6
Richland	3 010	50 976	6 630	14 003	7 925	1 277	1 036	1 388	27 220	1 086	37.0	4.9	57.9
Ross	1 352	20 787	4 268	4 000	3 534	387	378	646	31 092	952	31.7	12.1	52.8
Sandusky	1 441	24 643	2 909	10 175	2 756	531	461	670	27 202	802	38.8	15.1	58.9
Scioto	1 466	18 639	5 305	2 210	3 538	647	325	412	22 084	709	36.7	4.2	51.1
Seneca	1 340	20 785	2 718	6 631	2 316	578	332	533	25 659	1 185	29.4	14.0	60.2
Shelby	1 075	25 144	1 823	13 494	2 085	329	383	861	34 225	1 022	31.2	10.2	54.7
Stark	9 413	165 225	25 335	40 459	22 833	5 682	4 641	4 601	27 848	1 337	53.9	4.2	53.2
Summit	14 476	254 029	34 952	37 384	33 582	10 754	11 659	8 120	31 963	377	73.7	1.9	48.8
Trumbull	4 631	81 006	10 403	25 513	11 952	2 108	1 882	2 578	31 827	1 016	40.4	4.2	53.3
Tuscarawas	2 392	33 575	4 242	9 511	5 225	789	706	784	23 337	1 076	32.4	5.5	57.0
Union	816	20 734	1 438	8 679	1 621	229	1 451	1 005	48 460	1 021	45.2	14.5	60.4
Van Wert	607	10 859	1 752	4 148	1 297	734	169	263	24 265	681	28.6	25.0	63.7
Vinton	153	1 682	264	D	D	D	D	42	25 214	237	25.3	5.9	48.5
Warren	2 968	58 326	3 780	13 039	6 638	3 338	2 873	1 887	32 350	1 036	63.3	5.9	49.2
Washington	1 563	22 981	3 447	5 889	2 924	736	582	616	26 793	952	22.7	4.2	53.6
Wayne	2 635	43 420	4 448	15 176	5 301	1 403	898	1 196	27 552	1 894	40.5	5.9	65.6
Williams	921	16 710	1 764	8 579	1 721	364	228	452	27 021	1 099	37.9	9.8	53.0
Wood	2 658	46 925	3 951	13 739	6 450	908	2 363	1 394	29 714	1 066	37.5	19.0	59.1
Wyandot	552	8 828	828	4 120	791	270	134	217	24 556	607	31.6	21.3	64.7
OKLAHOMA	85 276	1 212 230	173 678	163 256	168 790	55 565	53 702	33 404	27 556	83 300	24.2	18.0	55.3
Adair	207	3 532	477	1 855	510	117	D	75	21 225	1 130	27.9	8.1	54.8
Alfalfa	139	912	228	D	144	67	38	15	16 788	666	8.1	37.8	67.1
Atoka	238	2 013	401	391	451	82	55	36	17 806	1 206	18.3	14.5	56.1
Beaver	170	857	64	D	108	58	D	18	21 265	960	5.7	42.3	58.2
Beckham	646	6 076	1 120	183	1 263	257	146	116	19 040	1 012	15.4	25.4	58.1
Blaine	304	2 565	641	386	293	120	81	51	19 961	825	9.6	36.0	58.2
Bryan	585	9 892	1 477	1 303	1 437	228	354	218	22 069	1 673	24.0	12.9	56.7
Caddo	527	4 340	609	80	998	228	123	99	22 754	1 504	13.0	27.7	60.7
Canadian	1 765	19 209	1 699	3 139	2 876	571	422	466	24 237	1 360	29.3	21.2	58.2
Carter	1 340	16 241	2 399	2 980	2 410	551	537	445	27 407	1 353	24.3	13.5	51.4
Cherokee	674	7 333	1 691	159	1 723	250	238	136	18 592	1 221	29.1	7.4	55.9
Choctaw	262	3 011	595	187	655	104	54	51	16 872	1 095	18.9	15.5	58.4
Cimarron	95	470	122	0	95	47	D	8	16 430	545	4.0	56.3	68.8
Cleveland	4 271	48 328	7 580	3 486	8 976	1 416	2 340	1 108	22 928	1 294	50.5	5.3	52.1
Coal	72	1 095	258	380	230	7	D	15	14 009	617	13.8	19.4	57.5
Comanche	2 169	27 466	5 162	3 437	4 777	1 162	1 318	645	23 478	1 188	23.7	16.8	53.1
Cotton	93	621	87	49	141	45	12	10	15 968	488	6.8	34.0	65.6
Craig	357	5 254	1 444	865	673	157	129	117	22 315	1 289	24.0	12.9	57.3
Creek	1 275	15 610	2 374	4 243	1 945	570	253	388	24 836	1 838	36.0	6.9	45.8
Custer	832	8 044	1 306	1 194	1 628	335	324	167	20 728	802	16.5	34.7	60.0
Delaware	626	5 616	1 292	697	1 160	258	171	102	18 189	1 393	26.7	8.5	57.0
Dewey	136	712	76	D	177	73	22	16	22 052	774	7.6	35.7	55.8
Ellis	119	620	175	16	108	41	29	14	21 942	727	5.6	37.7	59.4
Garfield	1 664	19 700	3 748	1 430	3 327	672	507	464	23 577	1 083	17.9	30.8	61.2
Garvin	618	6 803	1 012	986	1 057	226	115	161	23 656	1 637	25.0	13.9	53.0
Grady	910	10 312	1 319	2 834	1 454	385	234	241	23 413	1 804	25.2	17.0	57.3
Grant	125	787	116	D	108	70	D	20	25 685	744	10.2	42.7	66.8
Greer	100	842	212	D	127	52	16	16	18 956	515	8.3	31.7	51.1
Harmon	75	397	82	D	107	71	11	7	18 436	397	5.8	41.6	68.8
Harper	117	614	129	D	106	D	23	12	18 733	517	5.2	44.5	64.8
Haskell	223	2 357	803	93	419	57	D	43	18 057	901	20.1	15.4	59.2
Hughes	240	2 076	508	68	406	69	43	33	16 074	955	14.3	18.3	59.3
Jackson	570	7 516	1 553	992	1 432	307	387	154	20 447	732	17.1	33.3	53.8
Jefferson	124	896	129	266	138	68	24	14	15 412	483	11.8	34.6	64.4
Johnston	161	2 393	545	845	210	39	11	47	19 734	682	20.7	16.0	58.9
Kay	1 260	18 268	1 847	3 901	2 576	560	1 114	529	28 975	1 003	21.7	26.1	58.7
Kingfisher	414	4 436	475	404	613	279	101	120	27 012	1 063	12.8	29.4	60.8

Table B. States and Counties — **Agriculture**

STATE County	Acreage (1,000)	Percent change, 1997–2002	Average size of farm	Total irrigated (1,000)	Total cropland (1,000)	Average per farm	Average per acre	Value of machinery and equipment average per farm (dollars)	Total (mil dol)	Average per farm (dollars)	Crops	Live-stock and poultry products	$10,000 or more	$100,000 or more	Total ($1,000)	Percent of farms
	117	118	119	120	121	122	123	124	125	126	127	128	129	130	131	132
OHIO—Cont'd																
Ottawa	114	7.5	221	1	105	479 253	2 177	73 202	24	46 241	92.0	8.0	50.3	8.7	1 560	55.7
Paulding	238	13.3	366	D	222	774 192	2 090	91 709	67	102 416	52.0	48.0	47.2	16.7	3 670	67.6
Perry	92	-5.2	144	0	61	393 040	2 261	36 488	14	22 278	60.1	39.9	25.5	5.5	768	25.7
Pickaway	275	3.0	348	1	248	997 805	2 983	110 790	59	74 062	82.1	17.9	48.0	19.1	4 483	46.6
Pike	84	7.7	166	0	45	310 127	1 652	42 531	8	16 415	55.6	44.4	25.0	1.6	765	35.2
Portage	97	11.5	101	1	67	477 528	4 245	59 839	25	25 670	66.5	33.5	28.9	5.9	918	15.8
Preble	198	0.5	186	0	174	479 555	2 510	70 035	58	54 611	55.7	44.3	39.9	13.1	3 781	40.9
Putnam	332	13.7	246	1	304	560 242	2 386	75 759	88	65 524	61.4	38.6	66.2	14.5	4 535	59.9
Richland	159	1.9	146	0	120	403 516	2 734	50 742	46	42 683	42.6	57.4	42.2	13.8	2 057	34.4
Ross	247	-2.0	259	D	172	583 033	2 065	59 014	37	39 357	77.4	22.6	31.7	10.0	3 010	44.2
Sandusky	196	-1.5	245	0	180	593 891	2 300	98 998	51	63 647	88.9	11.1	55.5	17.1	3 085	52.0
Scioto	96	-6.8	136	0	54	238 818	1 619	46 215	15	20 968	40.3	59.6	22.1	3.1	684	23.3
Seneca	280	-4.4	237	1	249	546 260	2 346	46 919	56	46 919	78.5	21.5	54.6	11.9	3 721	58.6
Shelby	207	2.5	203	0	185	517 487	2 742	77 582	65	63 848	41.5	58.5	57.0	17.2	3 986	57.8
Stark	145	5.8	109	1	109	443 936	4 039	70 527	69	51 643	41.1	58.9	36.0	10.2	2 222	19.7
Summit	21	23.5	56	0	14	364 001	5 723	37 552	11	29 294	90.6	9.4	27.6	6.6	115	6.6
Trumbull	126	12.5	124	0	86	373 675	3 017	54 798	31	30 086	50.7	49.3	35.1	8.0	1 379	26.2
Tuscarawas	160	13.5	148	0	96	374 127	2 856	60 830	52	48 394	19.3	80.7	36.1	10.5	1 568	21.9
Union	256	24.9	251	0	230	672 903	2 563	102 427	89	86 945	46.3	53.7	44.5	14.1	4 818	50.8
Van Wert	250	5.5	367	D	237	917 663	2 599	126 817	59	86 721	81.7	18.3	70.6	25.6	3 468	62.7
Vinton	44	18.9	184	D	23	370 473	2 064	30 643	4	16 004	78.9	21.1	16.9	3.0	93	26.2
Warren	126	6.8	122	1	97	561 267	4 851	52 988	30	28 589	88.3	11.7	25.2	5.5	1 619	20.5
Washington	141	-4.1	149	0	65	307 857	1 970	72 963	18	19 380	42.0	58.0	27.1	4.3	673	21.5
Wayne	267	10.8	141	1	210	641 421	4 460	74 880	159	83 758	20.3	79.7	55.6	18.9	5 342	29.8
Williams	213	4.9	194	D	178	455 783	2 249	60 737	45	40 588	58.6	41.4	32.2	8.6	4 886	70.4
Wood	306	0.7	287	1	285	783 863	2 764	106 348	81	76 151	76.2	23.8	54.7	17.5	4 178	60.6
Wyandot	201	-3.8	331	0	182	911 051	2 784	88 814	72	118 854	35.7	64.3	50.2	17.5	3 278	59.8
OKLAHOMA	33 662	1.3	404	518	14 843	285 730	699	42 155	4 456	53 498	18.4	81.6	37.2	7.7	149 942	29.2
Adair	238	5.8	211	1	91	240 360	1 179	35 214	80	71 183	1.7	98.3	36.0	12.5	977	21.1
Alfalfa	461	-8.2	693	1	322	506 346	706	95 720	71	107 325	21.2	78.8	62.3	19.4	4 084	63.7
Atoka	492	16.9	408	1	157	244 215	627	29 216	22	18 517	7.9	92.1	34.2	2.9	412	16.6
Beaver	1 019	-2.8	1 061	23	395	385 069	365	72 663	120	124 835	6.4	93.6	40.8	9.4	6 213	73.5
Beckham	533	6.8	527	6	239	298 798	575	42 007	35	34 762	24.5	75.5	60.0	13.6	3 548	53.8
Blaine	537	-1.8	651	5	303	414 208	613	79 644	77	93 594	24.3	75.7	56.3	13.6	1 311	20.4
Bryan	458	9.0	274	7	198	244 223	868	30 947	55	32 581	21.8	78.2	34.5	3.4	5 191	47.1
Caddo	711	-2.2	473	38	385	305 001	619	57 133	89	59 106	37.4	62.6	52.8	12.8	2 813	33.0
Canadian	501	7.3	368	5	308	378 972	1 000	68 301	85	62 352	26.6	73.4	48.4	13.8	481	13.8
Carter	431	12.8	318	0	150	282 551	763	27 806	24	17 625	7.3	92.7	28.0	3.5	470	16.1
Cherokee	221	-7.1	181	1	92	229 729	1 156	29 573	94	77 042	70.2	29.8	29.5	5.7	203	5.4
Choctaw	337	-0.3	308	0	127	189 222	607	23 006	29	26 501	10.3	89.7	39.2	3.8	5 602	79.8
Cimarron	1 122	4.2	2 058	50	469	633 682	301	102 811	182	334 021	9.2	90.8	47.3	23.9	325	13.1
Cleveland	165	1.9	128	2	78	229 123	1 862	28 805	13	10 218	31.7	68.3	19.9	1.5	236	17.3
Coal	263	-3.7	426	0	89	297 735	634	32 643	14	22 568	6.4	93.5	42.0	3.7	2 198	32.1
Comanche	425	-2.3	358	0	178	280 816	768	46 020	33	27 687	25.2	74.8	36.9	6.5	2 275	53.9
Cotton	334	-4.6	685	0	195	364 626	522	53 247	38	77 642	21.7	78.3	53.3	16.2	939	25.7
Craig	436	4.3	338	1	154	259 987	770	40 570	58	44 717	12.6	87.4	41.1	6.7	227	11.0
Creek	366	4.3	199	1	131	190 122	906	22 235	17	9 420	19.6	80.4	16.6	1.6	4 095	56.4
Custer	545	-12.8	679	4	284	397 565	579	79 033	44	55 432	33.1	66.9	54.6	13.2	778	19.7
Delaware	282	6.4	203	0	124	276 410	1 508	30 518	132	94 478	2.9	97.1	39.7	13.9	2 997	55.7
Dewey	584	-5.7	755	2	204	444 682	521	65 243	26	33 768	25.9	74.1	47.3	7.9	3 277	67.8
Ellis	673	0.4	925	12	183	316 997	328	47 661	43	58 550	9.7	90.3	41.4	8.0	4 942	54.8
Garfield	632	2.8	584	D	448	386 358	684	73 041	75	68 985	43.7	56.3	62.4	17.1	1 156	20.9
Garvin	469	4.5	286	2	180	237 777	823	44 896	38	23 395	22.8	77.2	32.8	4.2	2 825	29.5
Grady	602	-1.1	333	8	267	264 348	789	43 723	96	53 011	14.0	86.0	42.3	9.1	5 015	69.1
Grant	595	1.7	799	1	437	480 482	583	103 213	58	78 022	54.8	45.2	59.0	20.2	2 677	71.3
Greer	325	3.5	631	6	175	252 535	396	48 086	18	34 839	41.3	58.7	43.5	7.4	3 415	76.3
Harmon	296	-2.6	747	19	158	292 725	365	60 115	27	69 038	39.0	61.0	48.6	14.9	3 206	67.1
Harper	601	3.6	1 163	7	205	383 214	330	55 146	142	274 752	2.3	97.7	43.1	13.5	380	16.1
Haskell	275	2.6	305	2	108	262 153	880	35 578	67	73 992	2.5	97.5	41.5	11.7	874	24.3
Hughes	374	5.4	392	3	125	231 446	606	37 681	55	57 241	4.1	95.9	35.4	6.1	5 019	57.8
Jackson	454	-4.8	620	51	309	341 860	523	80 313	68	92 667	54.1	45.9	48.1	18.7	1 238	41.8
Jefferson	407	-7.7	843	0	127	450 202	501	39 904	50	103 686	7.6	92.4	55.9	17.2	575	18.6
Johnston	326	-2.4	478	2	96	351 167	751	35 074	26	38 428	7.2	92.8	35.9	5.9	3 467	48.3
Kay	480	2.3	478	2	324	317 375	737	64 236	47	47 302	58.6	41.4	48.2	13.6	3 678	52.4
Kingfisher	553	-0.4	520	5	372	403 050	754	75 576	88	82 965	22.7	77.3	61.3	20.5	3 678	52.4

Table B. States and Counties — Residential Construction, Wholesale Trade, Retail Trade, and Real Estate

STATE County	Value of residential construction authorized by building permits, 2003		Wholesale trade, 1997				Retail trade,[1] 1997				Real estate and rental and leasing, 1997			
	New construction ($1,000)	Number of housing units	Number of establishments	Number of employees	Sales (mil dol)	Annual payroll (mil dol)	Number of establishments	Number of employees	Sales (mil dol)	Annual payroll (mil dol)	Number of establishments	Number of employees	Receipts (mil dol)	Annual payroll (mil dol)
	133	134	135	136	137	138	139	140	141	142	143	144	145	146
OHIO—Cont'd														
Ottawa	21 389	259	42	184	85.8	5.1	171	1 648	353.3	29.3	60	364	21.4	4.1
Paulding	1 574	12	19	155	69.8	4.0	62	638	102.4	8.9	6	32	1.8	0.3
Perry	5 755	78	15	D	D	D	83	648	105.2	8.9	14	44	2.7	1.7
Pickaway	31 801	216	38	326	141.8	9.1	147	1 630	284.0	23.8	34	82	7.8	1.0
Pike	23 253	204	16	103	26.1	2.8	98	1 105	153.5	12.9	8	52	3.8	0.4
Portage	106 586	836	183	2 648	1 180.5	96.5	465	5 828	1 117.9	92.8	104	409	39.4	6.3
Preble	22 454	191	32	586	249.6	20.2	112	1 334	218.3	18.7	17	83	5.0	1.0
Putnam	10 776	82	51	330	162.0	7.7	115	1 344	181.2	17.2	14	103	4.4	1.1
Richland	63 167	490	157	1 902	633.2	53.8	590	8 848	1 297.7	127.7	98	407	43.3	6.3
Ross	4 923	48	63	531	147.5	12.8	279	3 882	581.9	52.7	51	167	22.4	3.9
Sandusky	23 595	239	64	880	213.7	24.2	241	2 945	470.3	43.2	32	129	9.8	2.0
Scioto	2 501	66	68	550	219.3	12.3	321	3 629	543.0	53.4	40	185	17.5	2.6
Seneca	12 706	156	63	756	359.2	20.7	231	2 447	407.9	38.9	39	101	7.9	1.1
Shelby	26 483	204	51	666	276.3	18.6	167	2 126	309.4	28.4	32	186	16.9	4.1
Stark	250 473	1 550	517	8 242	4 151.7	275.8	1 618	23 170	3 671.2	357.2	274	1 273	126.1	22.9
Summit	360 772	2 354	1 070	13 375	8 443.7	501.6	2 172	32 463	5 515.7	546.7	476	2 994	373.8	68.4
Trumbull	58 910	480	231	2 867	1 212.0	80.4	913	12 617	1 943.2	192.9	175	1 139	123.5	21.8
Tuscarawas	25 873	195	109	1 096	300.2	26.4	439	5 240	758.8	75.6	73	285	29.8	5.1
Union	104 639	579	38	280	165.6	11.5	103	1 291	279.1	22.0	28	105	16.1	2.7
Van Wert	10 604	95	40	D	D	D	110	1 279	207.6	17.9	14	34	10.0	0.9
Vinton	0	0	4	D	D	D	28	201	27.1	2.3	4	D	D	D
Warren	376 899	2 666	181	2 324	6 034.5	91.2	455	6 709	1 111.7	106.3	95	414	48.4	8.0
Washington	6 151	54	74	826	166.6	19.3	279	3 063	501.0	45.8	48	146	17.7	2.7
Wayne	70 972	532	144	1 489	654.1	41.5	393	5 250	801.4	79.5	80	345	26.7	6.1
Williams	20 153	162	49	557	344.7	17.4	153	1 573	227.7	21.4	25	80	6.5	1.1
Wood	108 648	1 095	169	2 731	1 496.8	82.5	436	5 864	947.2	83.4	97	597	77.3	14.3
Wyandot	10 424	74	28	296	129.6	7.4	94	842	109.4	11.2	11	44	2.3	0.5
OKLAHOMA	1 861 185	14 968	5 191	59 641	32 132.3	1 756.1	14 352	161 613	27 065.6	2 406.9	3 344	15 354	1 576.0	284.5
Adair	466	5	4	31	5.6	0.4	54	482	67.0	5.1	5	11	0.6	0.1
Alfalfa	0	0	19	129	52.0	2.1	25	136	18.4	1.5	4	5	0.3	0.1
Atoka	435	11	19	124	48.8	2.2	49	530	71.9	6.2	4	6	0.4	0.1
Beaver	60	1	10	30	10.3	0.7	25	116	14.4	1.1	2	D	D	D
Beckham	2 672	29	31	163	58.0	3.5	130	1 036	204.1	13.6	24	151	15.1	3.4
Blaine	0	0	17	D	D	D	69	357	42.6	3.7	6	6	0.2	0.0
Bryan	8 492	81	44	597	287.4	12.3	127	1 243	206.8	17.6	27	83	4.4	0.9
Caddo	1 931	23	26	284	111.4	5.8	142	998	128.7	11.7	10	D	D	D
Canadian	67 019	496	87	670	819.0	17.5	212	2 957	620.1	46.6	69	309	29.7	5.6
Carter	19 082	186	78	835	244.7	23.7	275	2 594	413.3	35.5	50	166	13.5	2.4
Cherokee	17 713	227	21	201	44.5	2.7	144	1 843	235.0	20.2	26	62	6.7	1.3
Choctaw	450	7	14	D	D	D	71	551	75.4	5.9	5	D	D	D
Cimarron	0	0	7	36	13.7	0.6	19	116	24.4	1.5	2	D	D	D
Cleveland	183 390	1 623	159	1 462	528.6	37.2	616	7 679	1 318.6	115.2	205	764	68.7	11.6
Coal	200	4	2	D	D	D	18	150	17.1	1.4	NA	NA	NA	NA
Comanche	18 666	162	84	766	200.6	16.4	436	5 216	691.8	67.8	133	523	48.7	8.1
Cotton	257	3	7	40	10.7	0.6	20	114	21.7	1.3	3	3	0.2	0.0
Craig	207	3	24	208	74.9	3.7	67	571	99.2	8.6	10	34	3.7	0.5
Creek	13 530	120	77	914	255.9	25.4	186	1 854	284.4	23.7	28	87	6.2	1.1
Custer	2 651	32	45	367	211.8	9.9	172	1 472	235.0	18.9	38	111	11.3	2.1
Delaware	8 760	83	15	82	27.1	1.1	132	1 067	148.9	13.8	24	67	4.9	0.9
Dewey	0	0	7	D	D	D	32	174	20.8	1.8	5	19	2.0	0.6
Ellis	0	0	7	34	14.9	0.8	28	143	20.1	1.7	2	D	D	D
Garfield	16 860	179	122	1 967	570.1	48.9	302	3 423	501.7	47.8	70	287	24.6	4.8
Garvin	1 761	25	26	287	67.8	5.3	127	1 097	172.0	13.4	18	48	6.4	1.3
Grady	13 132	88	63	576	173.4	14.7	162	1 512	241.3	19.7	32	93	8.8	1.7
Grant	34	1	18	D	D	D	18	92	12.8	0.9	1	D	D	D
Greer	0	0	5	49	13.4	0.4	26	129	15.4	1.5	3	6	0.5	0.0
Harmon	0	0	3	D	D	D	25	154	20.2	1.9	3	6	0.5	0.1
Harper	333	4	9	42	13.4	0.9	17	90	10.8	0.9	3	4	0.1	0.0
Haskell	780	15	7	90	41.5	1.2	42	395	57.9	5.2	7	12	0.1	0.1
Hughes	0	0	14	222	35.7	2.8	64	431	58.6	4.8	3	6	0.2	0.0
Jackson	3 237	30	34	161	66.7	3.9	125	1 420	241.2	19.8	23	57	4.4	0.7
Jefferson	142	1	5	D	D	D	30	164	25.5	1.8	6	17	0.9	0.2
Johnston	2 410	36	7	54	14.4	1.1	37	167	22.1	1.9	5	D	D	D
Kay	6 498	37	61	444	210.2	12.0	263	2 718	397.6	36.5	53	134	11.5	1.7
Kingfisher	2 196	14	33	234	159.3	7.3	60	576	90.0	7.3	10	22	1.2	0.2

1. Establishments with payroll.

Table B. States and Counties — Professional Services, Manufacturing, and Accommodation and Foodservices

STATE County	Professional, scientific, and technical services,[1] 1997				Manufacturing, 1997				Accommodation and foodservices, 1997			
	Number of establishments	Number of employees	Receipts (mil dol)	Annual payroll (mil dol)	Number of establishments	Number of employees	Receipts (mil dol)	Annual payroll (mil dol)	Number of establishments	Number of employees	Sales (mil dol)	Annual payroll (mil dol)
	147	148	149	150	151	152	153	154	155	156	157	158
OHIO—Cont'd												
Ottawa	51	156	11.7	4.1	56	2 886	634.2	100.8	168	1 346	62.6	15.7
Paulding	13	62	3.9	1.5	39	1 628	256.5	46.4	32	332	10.1	2.6
Perry	20	107	5.1	2.2	35	1 763	238.9	50.8	38	294	8.3	2.0
Pickaway	51	168	10.4	4.0	44	4 726	1 134.4	188.6	72	1 069	31.7	9.2
Pike	13	44	2.3	0.5	28	4 953	1 202.3	190.2	51	643	21.2	5.6
Portage	194	635	55.4	18.9	298	12 984	2 154.2	417.8	267	4 761	124.6	35.1
Preble	42	158	7.7	2.3	61	3 274	698.0	109.2	67	689	22.1	6.0
Putnam	25	89	5.2	1.5	42	4 005	1 237.1	129.9	54	D	D	D
Richland	168	933	73.3	23.5	220	15 212	2 444.7	567.1	272	4 613	140.1	38.6
Ross	66	263	22.8	7.1	48	D	D	D	119	2 225	61.3	16.8
Sandusky	80	383	23.8	8.9	124	10 156	2 533.6	307.1	110	1 699	50.0	12.9
Scioto	68	368	19.3	7.4	63	1 942	290.8	55.0	151	2 199	65.4	17.9
Seneca	63	234	13.2	4.1	101	6 882	1 124.6	231.2	128	1 325	33.9	9.7
Shelby	55	363	22.9	13.4	136	13 278	5 129.2	470.5	95	1 554	48.6	12.4
Stark	640	3 610	312.3	109.0	629	39 352	8 222.5	1 324.1	761	14 302	389.8	107.6
Summit	1 305	9 742	996.9	382.8	1 091	42 312	6 846.7	1 506.1	1 156	20 197	612.2	173.1
Trumbull	278	2 058	129.6	58.2	282	34 101	11 235.6	1 622.1	449	7 323	203.5	55.7
Tuscarawas	113	1 212	46.0	27.1	226	9 823	2 054.6	304.1	212	3 365	90.6	25.7
Union	45	1 079	231.5	69.4	40	8 462	7 467.2	370.7	57	766	23.1	6.8
Van Wert	30	102	7.5	2.5	50	4 553	942.1	140.8	58	878	21.9	5.6
Vinton	6	21	1.1	0.3	17	624	91.2	15.4	15	D	D	D
Warren	215	1 557	180.8	56.4	198	12 145	2 186.4	407.3	243	4 694	154.7	44.6
Washington	77	385	29.8	10.9	104	5 242	1 900.9	187.8	122	2 023	65.4	18.6
Wayne	126	671	43.9	14.7	252	16 172	3 105.0	521.5	178	3 206	79.0	23.9
Williams	30	136	9.2	2.4	131	9 132	1 831.5	267.1	84	1 197	30.3	9.1
Wood	177	1 674	187.3	50.2	192	13 357	2 602.3	512.7	270	4 905	134.4	37.0
Wyandot	25	81	4.3	1.1	53	4 188	573.1	112.1	57	656	16.3	4.5
OKLAHOMA	7 009	40 633	3 543.0	1 323.7	4 087	164 060	37 453.2	4 963.2	6 534	105 934	3 151.3	856.8
Adair	13	39	1.6	0.5	14	1 626	312.6	33.9	15	D	D	D
Alfalfa	8	18	1.0	0.2	NA	NA	NA	NA	6	D	D	D
Atoka	13	32	1.5	0.4	NA	NA	NA	NA	15	D	D	D
Beaver	10	28	1.8	0.3	NA	NA	NA	NA	8	D	D	D
Beckham	30	127	6.7	1.6	15	622	98.0	17.1	56	721	19.7	5.1
Blaine	18	55	2.5	0.8					24	236	5.0	1.5
Bryan	35	128	6.0	2.3	31	949	122.5	19.3	50	733	23.5	5.8
Caddo	26	92	3.7	1.3	NA	NA	NA	NA	48	277	8.0	2.0
Canadian	139	336	24.0	7.3	64	3 003	1 024.4	82.3	122	1 704	49.4	12.7
Carter	86	288	16.9	5.8	45	2 801	1 012.6	105.4	97	1 466	44.3	12.5
Cherokee	39	146	6.7	2.1	NA	NA	NA	NA	78	930	26.6	7.0
Choctaw	14	29	2.0	0.4	NA	NA	NA	NA	25	D	D	D
Cimarron	5	11	0.4	0.1	NA	NA	NA	NA	11	91	1.8	0.4
Cleveland	395	1 656	138.9	47.5	151	4 287	902.3	116.4	330	6 474	188.1	51.6
Coal	2	D	D	D	NA	NA	NA	NA	3	D	D	D
Comanche	127	1 062	63.0	30.5	51	3 325	900.8	119.8	203	3 660	96.9	28.9
Cotton	7	14	0.5	0.2	NA	NA	NA	NA	7	D	D	D
Craig	13	41	3.6	0.7	18	978	128.1	21.7	39	409	14.1	3.9
Creek	78	246	19.0	6.3	96	4 032	703.3	116.4	86	991	31.2	7.8
Custer	53	259	14.2	4.6	23	D	D	D	65	1 110	27.7	7.8
Delaware	38	115	7.1	2.8	30	673	45.2	12.1	67	808	24.1	6.7
Dewey	6	13	0.8	0.3	NA	NA	NA	NA	5	D	D	D
Ellis	9	19	0.7	0.3	NA	NA	NA	NA	7	D	D	D
Garfield	92	432	33.6	12.1	66	2 389	506.2	62.7	123	1 896	51.9	14.7
Garvin	35	94	4.8	1.4	26	1 153	615.4	29.4	44	458	13.3	3.5
Grady	69	202	16.6	4.9	64	2 792	747.0	70.0	63	983	24.5	6.5
Grant	6	14	0.9	0.2	NA	NA	NA	NA	7	30	0.8	0.2
Greer	6	7	0.3	0.1	NA	NA	NA	NA	8	55	1.4	0.4
Harmon	3	7	0.3	0.1	NA	NA	NA	NA	3	D	D	D
Harper	7	19	0.7	0.2	NA	NA	NA	NA	8	34	0.7	0.2
Haskell	11	29	1.3	0.4	NA	NA	NA	NA	16	D	D	D
Hughes	11	33	1.6	0.5	NA	NA	NA	NA	21	D	D	D
Jackson	29	404	15.3	6.5	12	896	205.1	16.3	56	841	24.2	6.3
Jefferson	8	16	0.5	0.1	NA	NA	NA	NA	13	D	D	D
Johnston	6	10	0.6	0.2	10	678	98.4	17.1	12	142	2.8	0.9
Kay	73	829	36.4	14.9	74	4 019	2 001.2	126.5	102	1 446	40.3	10.8
Kingfisher	18	77	3.1	1.3	NA	NA	NA	NA	27	D	D	D

1. Firms subject to federal tax.

Table B. States and Counties — Health Care and Social Assistance, Other Services, and Federal Funds

STATE County	Health care and social assistance,[1] 1997				Other services,[1] 1997				Federal funds and grants, 2002–2003			
										Expenditures (mil dol)		
											Direct payments for individuals[2]	
	Number of establishments	Number of employees	Receipts (mil dol)	Annual payroll (mil dol)	Number of establishments	Number of employees	Receipts (mil dol)	Annual payroll (mil dol)	Total	Social Security and government retirement	Medicare	Food stamps and Supplemental Security Income
	159	160	161	162	163	164	165	166	167	168	169	170
OHIO—Cont'd												
Ottawa	48	538	26.8	13.5	67	344	18.7	5.4	213.1	113.5	48.3	2.9
Paulding	23	193	6.8	2.9	16	96	4.2	1.3	77.0	27.0	16.3	1.8
Perry	24	400	13.4	6.7	22	64	4.0	0.8	167.0	74.3	32.6	8.6
Pickaway	52	953	37.2	19.2	50	175	10.9	2.9	194.4	92.3	35.0	7.0
Pike	30	522	18.9	8.4	20	61	4.0	1.0	229.7	58.0	22.7	12.1
Portage	174	1 715	100.7	46.4	182	984	49.4	16.3	585.4	259.6	111.1	17.5
Preble	39	585	23.1	9.0	57	262	13.5	4.0	166.1	88.1	34.9	3.8
Putnam	34	516	17.9	8.0	36	137	8.6	2.5	99.1	39.9	25.9	1.8
Richland	256	2 797	156.8	72.6	199	1 512	81.1	31.0	635.3	288.1	120.9	22.5
Ross	107	1 218	60.6	28.6	92	554	26.4	8.4	434.2	162.3	56.1	19.9
Sandusky	116	966	50.8	22.5	96	620	30.8	10.6	256.6	118.7	58.3	7.7
Scioto	151	2 448	105.9	52.2	82	347	17.8	4.4	541.1	191.5	98.9	42.7
Seneca	108	927	50.5	22.4	80	382	17.4	5.2	278.1	139.6	62.6	7.5
Shelby	62	643	36.7	17.1	52	249	19.0	4.8	173.5	78.9	36.5	4.8
Stark	732	9 505	603.8	291.3	685	4 541	265.0	82.0	1 892.0	910.7	395.8	62.7
Summit	1 130	14 026	863.9	438.0	977	6 761	368.7	117.2	3 120.2	1 116.7	637.8	104.9
Trumbull	476	5 373	297.3	135.8	310	1 805	98.9	26.8	1 204.2	564.4	286.1	45.2
Tuscarawas	159	2 663	103.8	48.7	161	917	66.3	18.5	394.8	202.9	76.4	11.6
Union	47	435	26.2	12.5	51	226	11.6	4.0	115.8	54.8	23.6	2.9
Van Wert	51	529	30.2	13.2	38	233	10.2	3.0	107.8	50.5	23.3	2.1
Vinton	6	179	4.2	2.3	4	13	1.8	0.2	60.1	23.8	9.6	4.0
Warren	156	2 400	94.2	43.0	161	1 201	72.7	28.1	471.7	263.9	77.1	8.4
Washington	101	1 419	81.8	36.0	113	509	31.8	8.3	325.2	149.9	63.9	13.3
Wayne	135	1 906	93.7	44.8	141	665	50.2	10.9	426.0	214.8	79.5	11.2
Williams	48	762	46.3	17.6	51	291	22.7	4.7	153.8	80.9	36.3	2.8
Wood	143	1 915	83.5	37.8	169	1 187	70.3	21.3	420.1	188.4	87.3	7.8
Wyandot	24	269	11.4	5.1	43	177	12.1	3.5	106.5	49.5	21.5	1.8
OKLAHOMA	6 991	91 803	5 061.4	2 244.0	4 572	26 308	1 599.4	458.5	25 253.9	8 421.6	3 365.9	713.3
Adair	21	373	11.1	5.3	9	23	1.2	0.2	159.4	42.9	23.2	5.1
Alfalfa	8	55	1.7	0.8	10	18	1.1	0.2	60.2	17.9	8.8	0.5
Atoka	19	257	6.9	3.1	16	42	2.8	0.5	83.8	30.8	16.0	4.1
Beaver	6	26	1.3	0.5	9	33	1.8	0.3	37.8	13.0	4.6	0.5
Beckham	62	589	23.3	10.6	29	121	15.8	2.0	124.0	41.4	22.3	4.9
Blaine	16	237	7.9	3.4	14	36	1.7	0.4	73.8	27.8	15.2	2.4
Bryan	54	1 038	61.3	23.5	30	176	9.4	3.0	296.6	94.1	44.6	9.5
Caddo	44	420	12.1	5.6	29	79	4.9	1.0	274.2	79.4	35.4	8.8
Canadian	93	1 101	39.9	16.5	84	384	21.8	6.4	374.9	186.2	47.2	7.8
Carter	128	1 418	76.0	35.2	70	325	17.2	4.5	280.0	116.8	58.3	11.9
Cherokee	54	535	22.3	8.0	30	115	6.7	1.7	319.3	89.9	37.6	11.5
Choctaw	22	289	10.7	5.3	15	66	2.7	0.7	162.1	43.6	24.5	8.0
Cimarron	3	D	D	D	10	30	1.3	0.2	34.7	8.6	3.0	0.3
Cleveland	361	3 856	203.4	91.1	198	1 123	60.7	16.7	899.8	463.7	97.3	81.7
Coal	6	31	1.4	0.6	2	D	D	D	42.4	16.5	8.4	1.1
Comanche	208	2 349	141.5	52.8	146	778	36.3	10.9	1 286.5	350.2	68.6	26.6
Cotton	8	122	3.4	1.7	8	26	1.8	0.4	48.1	19.2	9.1	1.1
Craig	21	102	5.2	1.8	18	44	3.7	1.0	94.1	44.4	19.1	2.0
Creek	86	1 358	49.0	22.6	70	301	22.8	6.6	284.3	150.8	54.5	12.2
Custer	64	632	26.6	10.9	38	201	11.8	3.0	119.7	35.3	30.5	3.5
Delaware	46	555	21.6	8.6	25	94	4.5	1.2	203.1	93.5	38.0	8.2
Dewey	5	24	0.9	0.3	4	16	1.0	0.2	35.4	14.1	8.5	0.6
Ellis	8	96	3.0	1.5	8	22	1.0	0.2	29.0	12.1	7.1	0.4
Garfield	145	1 487	90.8	40.6	104	476	26.0	7.0	443.7	154.9	65.2	11.6
Garvin	42	842	28.5	14.9	24	117	7.7	1.7	239.7	81.6	47.9	7.0
Grady	67	997	45.4	22.2	49	213	13.9	3.8	208.7	100.1	35.9	10.5
Grant	3	D	D	D	9	12	1.4	0.2	42.2	15.1	8.8	0.5
Greer	12	188	7.8	4.1	4	13	0.7	0.2	55.7	18.2	13.2	1.5
Harmon	3	D	D	D	4	15	0.7	0.1	35.2	8.4	7.3	1.4
Harper	8	74	2.0	0.8	10	17	1.5	0.3	30.0	10.8	5.4	0.3
Haskell	20	256	9.6	4.5	13	49	2.5	0.7	90.6	38.5	17.5	3.5
Hughes	18	271	9.0	4.4	5	19	1.4	0.2	111.1	41.0	21.5	3.8
Jackson	48	489	19.0	7.8	26	131	9.3	2.3	360.9	80.9	31.3	7.2
Jefferson	13	273	7.5	4.3	9	23	1.5	0.3	56.7	21.6	11.5	1.4
Johnston	15	232	7.0	3.7	7	14	0.9	0.2	75.7	27.7	12.2	2.8
Kay	110	864	44.9	19.0	80	304	18.5	4.8	363.7	130.3	48.9	9.2
Kingfisher	14	224	7.7	3.1	26	95	6.1	1.4	98.7	33.0	14.7	1.5

1. Firms subject to federal tax.   2. State totals may include programs not allocated by county.

Table B. States and Counties — Federal Funds and Local Government Finances

STATE County	Federal funds and grants, 2002–2003 (cont'd) Expenditures (mil dol) (cont'd)							Local government finances, 2002 General revenue				
	Procurement contract awards			Grants[1]						Taxes	Per capita[2] (dollars)	
	Salaries and wages	Defense	Other	Medicaid and other health-related	Nutrition and family welfare	Education	Other	Total (mil dol)	Intergovernmental (mil dol)	Total (mil dol)	Total	Property
	171	172	173	174	175	176	177	178	179	180	181	182
OHIO—Cont'd												
Ottawa	16.8	0.2	2.1	7.3	2.6	2.0	12.6	133.9	37.3	59.4	1 447	1 192
Paulding	3.1	2.3	0.9	7.6	1.8	1.3	7.5	79.2	39.3	15.9	803	564
Perry	4.4	0.1	1.2	27.6	5.9	2.6	6.1	119.1	91.5	16.2	470	383
Pickaway	6.0	0.4	1.6	31.7	6.7	2.8	0.8	180.3	68.1	45.5	851	624
Pike	4.2	0.4	70.5	40.8	9.2	2.7	7.3	105.2	69.9	19.2	688	624
Portage	19.7	20.7	4.6	44.1	15.6	16.9	37.6	528.2	176.2	166.3	1 080	813
Preble	5.6	0.0	1.3	13.4	4.2	2.0	5.1	107.3	48.3	39.0	913	566
Putnam	4.7	0.5	1.9	9.3	2.1	2.3	2.3	110.9	62.2	28.6	824	538
Richland	62.0	2.5	7.8	68.3	16.2	9.6	26.8	426.9	208.6	146.5	1 144	776
Ross	67.5	0.1	12.5	69.1	12.2	5.1	21.8	251.6	153.2	68.3	918	563
Sandusky	7.3	0.5	2.9	20.9	11.9	4.2	16.4	183.0	85.3	62.8	1 018	678
Scioto	11.3	0.3	5.3	135.6	24.7	10.3	10.5	256.3	165.0	43.2	554	364
Seneca	8.8	2.4	2.1	23.3	5.9	4.5	9.3	150.2	74.8	54.4	936	610
Shelby	5.4	0.4	1.4	15.4	4.7	2.6	10.8	140.8	49.5	61.8	1 274	777
Stark	82.4	42.5	26.0	188.7	50.2	30.3	72.5	1 099.1	536.6	394.1	1 043	779
Summit	174.2	427.9	47.1	309.2	82.7	38.0	130.4	1 880.5	636.5	868.9	1 590	1 031
Trumbull	33.3	10.1	7.6	97.8	35.5	18.8	94.8	624.5	303.3	216.9	970	724
Tuscarawas	14.0	2.6	3.3	41.3	12.0	8.7	17.8	243.0	113.1	86.7	948	708
Union	4.5	0.2	1.3	11.9	2.4	1.7	4.8	161.6	40.1	56.5	1 313	839
Van Wert	3.9	0.3	4.0	8.7	2.2	1.5	5.4	82.2	38.7	28.6	973	631
Vinton	1.5	0.0	0.6	14.3	2.9	1.3	1.2	43.4	32.5	5.9	448	340
Warren	19.5	7.1	9.0	40.1	9.6	4.6	25.6	443.2	143.0	210.4	1 202	854
Washington	12.1	3.3	5.1	42.7	9.9	7.5	11.0	188.5	97.7	63.5	1 015	726
Wayne	16.6	5.1	6.0	39.6	11.7	6.7	20.6	397.8	145.1	115.6	1 025	766
Williams	5.6	0.4	1.6	9.6	2.4	2.1	4.4	101.9	43.3	38.9	996	682
Wood	17.4	1.2	5.2	30.3	6.0	12.6	25.7	386.0	137.5	173.8	1 420	990
Wyandot	3.8	0.0	0.9	10.8	1.5	1.1	5.3	75.0	23.5	19.0	833	513
OKLAHOMA	3 352.6	1 470.5	1 017.3	2 259.8	784.4	570.0	1 521.4	X	X	X	X	X
Adair	2.9	18.5	0.6	48.4	4.2	8.7	2.4	47.0	34.5	6.8	320	159
Alfalfa	2.4	0.0	0.5	2.8	0.3	0.3	20.4	9.5	4.7	3.3	552	392
Atoka	3.6	0.0	0.5	20.7	2.8	1.9	2.5	29.8	17.4	5.0	356	235
Beaver	1.6	0.0	0.4	1.0	0.4	0.3	7.2	23.0	9.2	9.9	1 773	1 555
Beckham	3.1	0.2	0.7	15.9	2.4	1.9	22.9	53.0	21.1	22.3	1 124	680
Blaine	3.5	2.2	0.6	7.2	6.0	1.7	2.9	32.2	16.1	5.3	442	327
Bryan	7.8	36.4	3.8	49.5	15.6	9.7	14.2	68.5	39.8	16.8	453	258
Caddo	22.3	4.3	22.3	31.1	8.2	7.7	9.0	75.6	47.6	14.4	479	295
Canadian	72.2	0.2	5.3	12.4	6.0	7.6	22.3	183.1	79.1	59.6	652	442
Carter	8.4	1.9	1.6	36.8	6.7	5.0	31.7	103.3	48.1	34.5	747	416
Cherokee	27.3	0.1	7.2	57.9	19.7	13.5	39.8	96.7	49.0	14.3	330	143
Choctaw	3.3	10.9	0.9	40.7	6.4	3.3	19.2	28.4	19.1	5.8	383	147
Cimarron	1.0	0.0	0.2	1.4	0.3	0.3	5.6	9.8	4.0	2.5	847	709
Cleveland	54.1	1.4	37.6	33.7	14.2	14.8	76.1	508.6	155.8	141.8	658	382
Coal	1.1	0.0	0.3	12.2	1.2	1.3	0.2	15.3	10.6	2.8	480	346
Comanche	583.2	121.1	10.5	48.3	20.1	16.8	25.2	321.8	123.2	61.2	539	266
Cotton	1.9	0.0	0.4	6.5	0.9	0.5	3.0	12.9	9.2	2.1	324	211
Craig	3.7	0.0	0.9	18.1	1.6	2.1	1.2	35.3	18.0	12.8	878	694
Creek	8.8	1.6	1.8	32.8	8.1	4.5	7.6	130.1	71.2	37.3	543	326
Custer	9.9	0.0	1.3	10.5	3.2	2.7	11.2	70.6	27.6	20.0	793	385
Delaware	4.3	1.1	1.1	29.7	6.2	5.3	14.0	57.9	35.2	17.4	460	310
Dewey	2.0	0.0	0.5	2.9	0.3	0.5	2.3	18.2	9.3	3.9	841	657
Ellis	1.3	0.0	0.3	1.4	0.3	0.5	1.4	11.1	6.3	3.3	822	630
Garfield	74.5	86.9	3.1	21.3	5.4	4.6	8.7	118.4	50.7	46.3	809	418
Garvin	5.7	52.0	1.4	28.9	3.3	3.4	6.3	69.6	28.8	20.2	745	495
Grady	6.6	1.1	2.8	28.9	6.8	3.7	4.7	107.7	46.9	21.9	470	269
Grant	2.0	0.0	0.5	2.0	0.4	0.3	3.4	14.8	7.8	4.9	979	852
Greer	1.5	0.3	0.3	9.0	0.7	0.8	4.0	16.3	7.3	2.1	365	258
Harmon	1.2	0.3	0.2	5.3	0.8	0.3	3.8	7.0	4.6	1.4	450	315
Harper	1.3	0.0	0.3	1.0	0.2	0.1	6.5	9.0	3.8	2.9	841	680
Haskell	2.8	0.1	0.5	19.1	6.1	1.6	0.3	23.6	15.1	4.9	416	211
Hughes	2.6	0.0	0.6	24.8	2.3	2.2	7.2	35.1	18.3	6.8	485	316
Jackson	121.0	52.0	10.2	22.6	6.4	4.1	10.8	112.4	34.3	13.2	483	253
Jefferson	1.8	0.1	0.4	11.4	0.6	0.7	4.9	17.1	9.5	2.6	394	228
Johnston	2.9	0.0	0.7	17.3	3.8	2.6	1.2	16.8	11.2	3.4	330	253
Kay	9.2	103.3	2.6	21.2	4.9	4.5	18.7	102.2	49.7	32.1	673	444
Kingfisher	3.7	0.5	29.8	2.6	1.2	1.9	5.4	35.5	18.0	12.2	885	616

1. State totals may include programs not allocated by county.   2. Based on the resident population estimated as of July 1 of the year shown.

Table B. States and Counties — Local Government Finances, Government Employment, and Elections

STATE County	Local government finances, 2002 (cont'd) Direct general expenditure — Total (mil dol)	Per capita[1] (dollars)	Percent of total for — Education	Health and hospitals	Police protection	Public welfare	High- ways	Debt outstanding Total (mil dol)	Per capita[1] (dollars)	Government employment, 2002 Federal civilian	Federal military	State and local	Presidential election, 2004 Percent of vote cast — Demo- cratic	Republi- can	All other
	183	184	185	186	187	188	189	190	191	192	193	194	195	196	197
OHIO—Cont'd															
Ottawa	132.6	3 230	44.2	7.9	5.5	8.2	7.4	69.1	1 682	165	140	2 111	47.9	51.8	0.3
Paulding	68.9	3 472	46.1	25.3	3.5	4.4	6.7	37.1	1 868	56	45	1 234	36.6	62.8	0.6
Perry	104.4	3 035	59.0	2.8	2.6	8.3	4.7	40.9	1 188	75	79	1 760	47.9	51.6	0.5
Pickaway	176.0	3 294	44.9	23.2	2.5	4.9	5.2	50.8	951	92	122	4 076	37.5	62.0	0.5
Pike	98.4	3 525	66.7	3.3	1.9	4.5	5.6	18.1	647	74	64	1 797	47.6	51.8	0.5
Portage	551.9	3 586	39.7	26.0	4.3	4.5	3.5	287.9	1 871	311	370	14 771	53.0	46.5	0.5
Preble	103.9	2 435	52.1	3.5	6.3	7.1	8.3	57.6	1 349	93	98	2 090	34.5	65.0	0.6
Putnam	99.7	2 871	64.7	3.5	3.8	3.7	6.7	53.1	1 528	85	80	1 723	23.3	76.2	0.5
Richland	406.3	3 174	48.9	7.1	4.7	6.8	6.0	176.8	1 381	655	295	9 056	39.7	59.8	0.5
Ross	260.8	3 502	55.3	9.1	2.9	6.1	4.0	119.1	1 599	1 384	173	5 178	44.1	54.5	1.5
Sandusky	173.6	2 814	51.0	0.6	7.0	14.2	4.9	72.0	1 167	120	141	3 553	43.7	56.0	0.4
Scioto	225.8	2 894	57.2	3.6	3.6	11.1	3.5	161.8	2 074	181	180	5 799	47.6	52.0	0.4
Seneca	151.5	2 608	52.6	5.1	6.2	5.8	6.5	47.6	820	142	134	3 009	40.6	58.9	0.6
Shelby	145.0	2 989	45.5	1.1	4.6	7.2	9.2	96.2	1 982	100	111	2 754	28.5	71.0	0.5
Stark	1 067.2	2 824	52.2	6.8	5.2	6.9	3.9	417.1	1 104	1 198	869	18 971	50.4	49.1	0.5
Summit	1 893.0	3 465	39.5	8.5	5.6	5.3	6.2	1 273.3	2 330	2 808	1 294	31 152	56.6	43.0	0.4
Trumbull	616.0	2 756	51.6	6.1	4.7	6.5	3.8	229.6	1 027	494	515	11 016	61.6	37.9	0.5
Tuscarawas	230.7	2 521	51.3	3.8	3.1	6.1	5.4	97.3	1 063	228	211	4 872	43.9	55.6	0.5
Union	173.7	4 038	39.1	30.0	5.2	3.6	3.5	131.7	3 063	77	99	3 095	29.4	70.1	0.4
Van Wert	74.0	2 519	48.3	0.4	5.5	11.4	7.1	44.8	1 523	70	67	1 420	27.6	72.0	0.4
Vinton	42.8	3 259	41.4	2.8	2.7	11.3	10.4	9.7	740	26	30	848	44.8	54.8	0.5
Warren	478.1	2 730	54.7	3.7	4.5	2.1	4.9	548.4	3 131	297	401	7 907	27.5	72.1	0.4
Washington	178.7	2 856	50.7	7.6	5.1	11.8	8.3	86.7	1 387	232	143	3 223	41.4	58.1	0.5
Wayne	385.5	3 420	39.7	27.2	3.2	5.1	4.6	114.9	1 019	265	259	7 291	38.1	61.6	0.3
Williams	99.6	2 552	50.3	2.2	3.8	11.2	7.4	32.9	842	96	89	2 186	34.8	64.6	0.6
Wood	386.1	3 154	51.0	7.5	5.0	3.4	4.5	194.5	1 589	232	307	12 922	46.4	53.0	0.6
Wyandot	69.2	3 039	39.0	28.9	4.2	4.1	7.4	7.4	327	74	52	1 344	33.6	65.7	0.7
OKLAHOMA	X	X	X	X	X	X	X	X	X	44 903	37 835	250 743	34.4	65.6	0.0
Adair	48.2	2 255	82.0	1.3	2.6	0.0	4.4	15.1	708	45	79	1 351	34.0	66.0	0.0
Alfalfa	9.7	1 651	69.3	1.1	3.8	0.1	6.1	2.1	349	50	22	471	17.6	82.4	0.0
Atoka	27.7	1 983	57.1	17.0	3.3	0.0	8.7	4.5	320	68	52	1 196	38.3	61.7	0.0
Beaver	20.8	3 735	48.3	12.1	2.2	0.0	27.8	2.7	493	35	21	502	11.6	88.4	0.0
Beckham	45.0	2 267	52.4	0.5	6.3	0.0	16.2	7.8	395	52	74	1 026	26.1	73.9	0.0
Blaine	34.4	2 843	47.3	20.8	2.8	1.4	10.5	4.1	337	72	45	872	27.6	72.4	0.0
Bryan	71.3	1 925	63.3	1.3	4.4	0.0	5.8	23.4	633	125	142	3 898	40.0	60.0	0.0
Caddo	77.6	2 586	69.5	4.1	3.2	0.0	9.5	9.0	301	516	111	2 343	37.6	62.4	0.0
Canadian	187.5	2 051	62.6	9.0	4.5	0.0	5.6	120.1	1 313	605	792	4 580	22.6	77.4	0.0
Carter	105.0	2 273	61.2	2.4	6.3	0.5	7.0	25.2	545	118	172	2 793	34.7	65.3	0.0
Cherokee	95.0	2 188	58.6	24.8	1.8	0.0	3.6	20.0	461	553	161	6 423	47.4	52.6	0.0
Choctaw	28.5	1 883	68.2	5.1	2.7	0.0	6.9	6.0	396	65	56	1 076	45.4	54.6	0.0
Cimarron	10.2	3 392	55.0	25.4	2.4	0.0	5.1	0.9	314	21	15	342	12.9	87.1	0.0
Cleveland	526.5	2 441	43.1	29.8	5.0	0.0	4.4	205.8	954	690	875	20 184	34.1	65.9	0.0
Coal	14.7	2 487	68.3	5.5	1.0	0.0	10.4	3.4	571	17	22	385	46.3	53.7	0.0
Comanche	311.8	2 749	48.9	29.3	3.9	0.0	3.0	119.5	1 054	3 203	14 034	8 386	36.2	63.8	0.0
Cotton	13.7	2 125	60.5	0.3	1.4	0.0	17.2	3.2	494	33	24	383	34.0	66.0	0.0
Craig	32.9	2 251	62.5	0.0	3.2	0.0	15.8	8.8	604	63	54	1 755	39.1	60.9	0.0
Creek	137.6	1 998	70.0	0.1	4.4	0.0	4.0	75.7	1 099	120	257	2 886	34.5	65.5	0.0
Custer	72.2	2 868	52.3	15.6	3.6	0.1	8.6	38.3	1 522	167	93	2 747	26.3	73.7	0.0
Delaware	59.2	1 566	73.6	1.3	4.0	0.0	4.4	22.1	585	76	140	1 663	35.8	64.2	0.0
Dewey	18.4	3 999	52.5	17.0	1.6	0.0	15.7	4.2	903	38	17	514	18.1	81.9	0.0
Ellis	12.2	3 066	51.6	1.3	2.3	0.0	25.0	1.7	426	27	15	366	19.0	81.0	0.0
Garfield	105.0	1 834	63.9	1.8	5.7	0.0	8.5	57.4	1 003	386	1 444	3 291	24.0	76.0	0.0
Garvin	65.0	2 392	52.5	18.2	3.6	0.1	10.4	18.8	691	93	101	2 246	32.8	67.2	0.0
Grady	112.5	2 410	43.4	25.8	3.7	0.0	13.0	26.2	561	99	173	2 609	29.7	70.3	0.0
Grant	16.0	3 177	54.8	1.9	3.1	0.0	25.7	3.0	594	42	19	353	22.6	77.4	0.0
Greer	17.7	3 059	41.6	31.3	3.5	0.0	9.7	2.3	398	31	21	902	32.0	68.0	0.0
Harmon	7.7	2 502	57.4	1.1	5.9	0.0	16.7	1.0	321	27	11	345	29.7	70.3	0.0
Harper	9.8	2 819	62.3	2.9	2.7	0.0	9.4	0.0	4	28	13	399	16.1	83.9	0.0
Haskell	23.0	1 958	67.7	2.4	2.6	0.0	5.8	1.3	108	63	43	923	44.7	55.3	0.0
Hughes	34.5	2 459	58.6	18.3	2.1	0.0	7.7	17.3	1 238	47	52	990	42.7	57.3	0.0
Jackson	110.3	4 036	34.4	46.7	2.8	0.0	3.1	39.9	1 460	1 626	1 962	2 484	24.1	75.9	0.0
Jefferson	14.9	2 267	61.0	1.1	2.0	0.0	5.2	42.1	6 397	44	24	491	40.6	59.4	0.0
Johnston	16.9	1 612	79.5	2.1	3.7	0.0	3.0	4.7	454	51	39	783	39.4	60.6	0.0
Kay	110.5	2 318	57.6	1.9	5.2	0.0	7.0	64.6	1 355	150	176	3 395	29.7	70.3	0.0
Kingfisher	37.9	2 761	65.1	0.4	3.5	0.0	5.8	9.7	705	59	51	803	15.4	84.6	0.0

1. Based on the resident population estimated as of July 1 of the year shown.

Table B. States and Counties — **Land Area and Population**

STATE/County code	CBSA code[1]	County Type[2]	STATE County	Land area,[3] (sq km) 2000	Total persons	Rank	Per square kilometer	White	Black	Am. Indian, Alaska Native	Asian and Pacific Islander	Percent Hispanic or Latino[4]	Under 5 years	5 to 17 years	18 to 24 years	25 to 34 years	35 to 44 years	45 to 54 years
				1	2	3	4	5	6	7	8	9	10	11	12	13	14	15
			OKLAHOMA—Cont'd															
40 075	...	6	Kiowa	2 628	9 977	2 444	3.8	81.6	4.5	7.8	0.5	7.2	6.1	16.8	9.4	9.1	14.0	13.9
40 077	...	7	Latimer	1 870	10 575	2 394	5.7	78.8	1.1	23.4	0.2	1.6	6.3	17.6	13.3	9.9	13.7	12.3
40 079	22900	2	Le Flore	4 107	48 896	957	11.9	82.1	2.6	14.6	0.6	4.7	7.3	18.2	10.8	12.2	13.8	13.1
40 081	36420	1	Lincoln	2 481	32 262	1 354	13.0	89.4	2.9	9.0	0.4	1.6	6.4	19.3	9.7	10.9	14.6	14.3
40 083	36420	1	Logan	1 928	35 420	1 260	18.4	82.3	11.8	4.8	0.7	2.8	5.8	17.6	14.8	11.0	14.0	14.3
40 085	11620	9	Love	1 335	8 905	2 533	6.7	83.9	2.1	8.4	0.3	7.6	5.8	18.0	9.2	10.6	14.0	14.1
40 087	36420	1	McClain	1 475	28 595	1 440	19.4	88.3	0.7	8.7	0.3	5.3	6.3	18.6	10.0	11.1	15.7	14.0
40 089	...	7	McCurtain	4 797	34 006	1 302	7.1	73.9	9.6	17.2	0.3	3.4	7.2	19.9	9.4	11.8	13.6	13.4
40 091	...	6	McIntosh	1 606	19 735	1 818	12.3	77.5	5.0	22.0	0.4	1.4	5.6	16.5	8.5	9.3	12.3	13.1
40 093	...	9	Major	2 478	7 422	2 645	3.0	94.2	0.2	1.4	0.1	4.7	5.1	17.1	8.7	9.3	14.0	15.2
40 095	...	6	Marshall	961	13 652	2 187	14.2	79.9	2.1	11.5	0.2	9.7	6.5	16.4	9.4	10.8	12.8	13.1
40 097	...	6	Mayes	1 699	38 870	1 164	22.9	77.9	0.4	26.4	0.5	1.8	6.5	19.0	9.7	11.7	13.3	13.5
40 099	...	7	Murray	1 083	12 718	2 259	11.7	82.4	2.1	15.0	0.4	3.8	6.4	16.5	9.9	10.9	13.3	13.4
40 101	34780	4	Muskogee	2 108	70 255	718	33.3	68.1	13.9	20.5	0.9	3.0	7.0	18.2	10.4	11.9	13.9	13.5
40 103	...	6	Noble	1 896	11 251	2 351	5.9	86.7	2.0	11.9	0.6	1.9	6.4	18.0	9.1	11.6	14.8	14.1
40 105	...	6	Nowata	1 463	10 836	2 379	7.4	80.7	3.0	21.9	0.2	1.3	5.9	18.8	9.7	10.2	13.9	13.5
40 107	...	6	Okfuskee	1 618	11 679	2 315	7.2	70.3	10.3	22.1	0.1	1.5	5.8	17.2	10.2	11.5	14.5	13.5
40 109	36420	1	Oklahoma	1 837	676 066	80	368.0	67.8	16.5	5.1	4.0	9.8	7.8	17.7	10.4	14.7	14.4	13.4
40 111	46140	2	Okmulgee	1 805	39 681	1 137	22.0	74.0	11.0	18.5	0.3	2.1	6.6	19.3	10.9	10.9	13.5	13.6
40 113	46140	2	Osage	5 830	45 249	1 016	7.8	72.7	11.4	19.8	0.4	2.2	5.7	18.6	9.6	10.5	15.2	15.5
40 115	33060	6	Ottawa	1 221	32 761	1 341	26.8	78.7	1.0	22.3	0.7	3.6	6.6	18.3	10.8	11.3	12.8	12.8
40 117	46140	2	Pawnee	1 475	16 789	1 976	11.4	86.5	0.8	15.2	0.3	1.1	5.9	19.1	9.2	10.8	14.1	14.5
40 119	44660	4	Payne	1 778	71 059	714	40.0	86.3	3.9	6.9	4.1	2.0	5.7	12.8	22.3	15.9	11.5	13.8
40 121	32540	6	Pittsburg	3 382	44 168	1 041	13.1	81.0	4.2	17.0	0.4	2.0	5.7	16.7	9.4	11.8	13.5	12.4
40 123	10220	7	Pontotoc	1 864	35 174	1 268	18.9	78.6	2.8	20.2	0.7	2.7	6.7	17.3	12.7	11.8	13.5	12.4
40 125	43060	4	Pottawatomie	2 040	67 348	749	33.0	82.0	3.5	15.3	1.1	2.6	6.9	18.1	12.1	12.0	14.0	12.9
40 127	...	9	Pushmataha	3 619	11 750	2 308	3.2	81.7	0.7	20.3	0.1	1.6	5.9	18.7	9.0	9.5	14.0	13.0
40 129	...	9	Roger Mills	2 957	3 201	2 965	1.1	90.9	0.2	6.3	0.1	2.9	5.9	14.9	9.2	8.2	14.3	16.0
40 131	46140	2	Rogers	1 748	77 193	674	44.2	84.8	1.0	17.2	0.7	2.3	6.1	20.3	10.3	11.6	15.2	13.7
40 133	...	7	Seminole	1 638	24 489	1 601	15.0	74.2	6.2	21.9	0.5	2.1	7.2	18.5	10.6	10.2	13.3	13.6
40 135	22900	2	Sequoyah	1 745	39 979	1 135	22.9	76.3	2.2	27.4	0.4	2.2	6.6	19.7	9.5	12.0	14.0	13.0
40 137	20340	4	Stephens	2 264	42 474	1 070	18.8	88.0	2.6	7.0	0.6	4.1	6.0	17.4	9.3	10.1	13.9	14.6
40 139	25100	7	Texas	5 276	19 935	1 808	3.8	65.6	0.6	1.5	1.2	31.8	8.8	18.9	12.0	14.9	14.2	12.7
40 141	...	6	Tillman	2 258	8 835	2 538	3.9	71.3	8.5	3.4	0.5	17.6	6.2	19.3	9.0	9.5	13.5	13.2
40 143	46140	2	Tulsa	1 477	570 313	99	386.1	74.4	12.1	7.9	2.5	7.0	7.8	18.4	9.7	14.5	15.0	14.4
40 145	46140	2	Wagoner	1 458	61 827	803	42.4	83.6	4.6	13.3	0.9	2.6	6.4	19.6	10.1	11.7	15.0	14.4
40 147	12780	4	Washington	1 080	49 121	950	45.5	84.9	2.9	13.6	1.1	3.0	5.9	17.8	9.6	10.5	13.0	14.9
40 149	...	7	Washita	2 599	11 247	2 352	4.3	91.6	0.6	3.5	0.3	5.1	5.6	18.2	9.7	10.1	14.4	13.7
40 151	...	7	Woods	3 332	8 670	2 556	2.6	92.8	2.2	2.2	0.7	2.7	4.7	13.3	16.5	11.3	12.1	12.2
40 153	49260	7	Woodward	3 218	18 461	1 883	5.7	91.3	1.1	2.9	0.5	5.2	6.5	17.3	10.7	11.0	15.2	14.2
41 000	...	X	**OREGON**	248 631	3 559 596	X	14.3	84.3	2.1	2.2	4.5	9.2	6.3	17.6	9.8	14.1	14.4	15.0
41 001	...	7	Baker	7 946	16 375	2 006	2.1	95.7	0.3	2.1	0.6	2.4	4.8	17.5	8.2	8.2	13.5	16.2
41 003	18700	3	Benton	1 752	79 335	658	45.3	87.9	1.1	1.3	6.6	5.1	5.0	14.2	17.6	14.4	12.6	14.7
41 005	38900	1	Clackamas	4 839	357 435	173	73.9	89.8	1.1	1.4	4.2	5.7	5.8	18.7	9.2	12.1	15.0	16.5
41 007	11820	4	Clatsop	2 143	35 820	1 247	16.7	91.9	0.7	1.8	2.1	5.0	5.3	17.1	10.2	10.3	13.6	16.8
41 009	38900	1	Columbia	1 701	46 261	997	27.2	94.6	0.6	2.6	1.2	3.0	5.9	19.3	9.3	11.4	15.1	15.8
41 011	18300	5	Coos	4 145	63 019	784	15.2	92.7	0.5	4.2	1.4	3.7	4.7	15.8	9.0	9.2	13.2	15.3
41 013	39260	6	Crook	7 717	20 600	1 771	2.7	92.3	0.1	1.8	0.5	6.2	5.7	18.8	9.0	11.6	13.2	14.1
41 015	15060	7	Curry	4 215	21 813	1 713	5.2	93.1	0.2	3.5	1.0	4.0	3.9	14.4	6.9	7.2	11.4	15.2
41 017	13460	3	Deschutes	7 817	129 492	436	16.6	93.9	0.5	1.5	1.5	4.2	5.8	17.5	9.1	12.9	14.4	15.2
41 019	40700	4	Douglas	13 045	102 332	532	7.8	94.1	0.3	3.2	1.2	3.5	5.3	17.1	9.1	9.8	13.0	15.2
41 021	...	9	Gilliam	3 119	1 778	3 074	0.6	96.7	0.2	0.9	0.2	2.1	4.6	16.4	7.3	8.3	15.9	18.1
41 023	...	9	Grant	11 729	7 454	2 641	0.6	95.9	0.1	2.6	0.2	2.2	4.4	18.5	8.5	7.4	13.4	17.2
41 025	...	7	Harney	26 248	7 184	2 666	0.3	92.0	0.2	4.3	1.0	3.8	5.6	19.6	6.6	9.2	15.3	16.8
41 027	26220	6	Hood River	1 353	20 760	1 763	15.3	71.2	0.5	1.1	2.1	25.9	7.4	19.7	9.1	12.2	15.3	14.8
41 029	32780	3	Jackson	7 214	190 077	301	26.3	90.0	0.7	2.1	1.9	7.4	5.6	17.6	9.6	11.3	13.1	15.2
41 031	...	6	Jefferson	4 612	19 667	1 826	4.3	66.2	0.4	15.7	0.5	18.5	7.4	21.2	9.0	12.4	13.8	13.1
41 033	24420	4	Josephine	4 247	79 030	661	18.6	93.4	0.5	2.6	1.2	4.3	5.0	16.8	8.2	9.5	12.6	14.8
41 035	28900	5	Klamath	15 395	64 769	765	4.2	86.1	0.9	5.5	1.4	8.5	6.3	18.8	9.2	11.0	13.2	15.0
41 037	...	7	Lake	21 072	7 440	2 644	0.4	91.2	0.2	3.3	0.8	5.9	4.7	17.6	7.7	9.4	13.2	16.7
41 039	21660	2	Lane	11 795	330 527	181	28.0	90.4	1.4	2.4	3.6	5.1	5.5	16.1	11.5	13.4	13.6	15.3
41 041	...	4	Lincoln	2 537	44 667	1 030	17.6	90.1	0.5	4.7	1.3	5.7	4.7	15.7	8.3	9.2	12.9	16.8
41 043	10540	4	Linn	5 937	106 121	514	17.9	92.8	0.4	2.4	1.6	4.7	6.4	18.3	9.5	12.1	13.8	14.4
41 045	36620	6	Malheur	25 607	31 239	1 375	1.2	68.5	1.3	1.5	2.4	27.2	7.6	19.7	11.5	12.2	13.7	12.8
41 047	41420	2	Marion	3 066	296 995	196	96.9	75.9	1.2	2.1	2.9	19.7	7.4	19.4	10.7	14.2	13.9	13.1

1. CBSA = Core Based Statistical Area. See Appendix A for explanation. See Appendix B for list of metropolitan areas with component counties. 2. County type code from the Economic Research Service of USDA Rural-Urban Continuum Codes. See Appendix A for definition. 3. Dry land or land partially or temporarily covered by water. 4. Hispanic or Latino persons may be of any race.

Table B. States and Counties — Population and Households

STATE County	Population, 2003 (cont'd) Age (percent) (cont'd)				Population — change and components of change, 1990–2003							Households, 2000			Percent	
	55 to 64 years	65 to 74 years	75 years and over	Percent female	Total persons 1990	2000	1990–2000	2000–2003	Births	Deaths	Net migration	Number	Percent change, 1990–2000	Persons per house-hold	Female family house-holder[1]	One person
	16	17	18	19	20	21	22	23	24	25	26	27	28	29	30	31
OKLAHOMA—Cont'd																
Kiowa	11.2	9.1	10.8	50.9	11 347	10 227	-9.9	-2.4	400	537	-107	4 208	-7.5	2.35	10.4	30.6
Latimer	11.0	8.5	7.6	50.7	10 333	10 692	3.5	-1.1	415	403	-118	3 951	7.0	2.54	11.5	24.9
Le Flore	10.4	7.4	6.3	50.0	43 270	48 109	11.2	1.6	2 451	1 839	222	17 861	12.1	2.61	11.0	23.1
Lincoln	11.0	7.7	6.2	50.7	29 216	32 080	9.8	0.6	1 328	1 107	10	12 178	12.4	2.59	9.2	22.4
Logan	9.8	6.5	5.2	50.3	29 011	33 924	16.9	4.4	1 310	1 055	1 236	12 389	21.7	2.57	9.8	23.7
Love	12.3	8.6	7.5	50.4	7 788	8 831	13.4	0.8	332	357	105	3 442	15.0	2.54	10.0	22.9
McClain	11.0	7.2	5.1	50.4	22 795	27 740	21.7	3.1	1 197	868	544	10 331	24.0	2.66	9.0	19.4
McCurtain	10.9	7.6	6.3	51.5	33 433	34 402	2.9	-1.2	1 619	1 450	-541	13 216	8.0	2.56	14.6	25.4
McIntosh	13.7	11.8	9.6	52.2	16 779	19 456	16.0	1.4	731	866	427	8 085	19.1	2.37	10.4	26.7
Major	11.6	9.8	10.1	51.1	8 055	7 545	-6.3	-1.6	250	351	-13	3 046	-2.4	2.44	6.0	25.2
Marshall	12.3	10.6	8.3	50.3	10 829	13 184	21.7	3.5	546	590	514	5 371	23.5	2.40	8.8	26.4
Mayes	10.9	8.1	6.9	50.3	33 366	38 369	15.0	1.3	1 667	1 399	274	14 823	17.0	2.55	9.0	23.8
Murray	11.5	9.3	8.9	50.7	12 042	12 623	4.8	0.8	508	516	119	5 003	7.6	2.45	10.2	25.2
Muskogee	9.8	7.4	7.6	51.6	68 078	69 451	2.0	1.2	3 301	2 631	207	26 458	5.1	2.51	13.3	26.7
Noble	11.0	8.3	7.2	50.5	11 045	11 411	3.3	-1.4	485	424	-214	4 504	6.6	2.47	8.4	25.5
Nowata	10.8	8.6	8.1	50.7	9 992	10 569	5.8	2.5	399	470	346	4 147	3.8	2.50	9.8	25.5
Okfuskee	11.2	8.6	7.6	48.4	11 551	11 814	2.3	-1.1	454	524	-56	4 270	2.5	2.52	11.2	27.8
Oklahoma	8.8	6.2	5.8	51.3	599 611	660 448	10.1	2.4	36 225	21 319	1 157	266 834	12.2	2.41	13.5	30.2
Okmulgee	10.5	7.7	7.1	51.1	36 490	39 685	8.8	0.0	1 717	1 571	-91	15 300	8.9	2.53	13.1	27.1
Osage	11.2	7.6	6.0	49.3	41 645	44 437	6.7	1.8	1 602	1 269	530	16 617	8.0	2.58	10.3	23.3
Ottawa	10.9	8.7	8.2	51.2	30 561	33 194	8.6	-1.3	1 433	1 483	-369	12 984	7.1	2.48	10.7	26.6
Pawnee	12.1	7.7	6.7	50.5	15 575	16 612	6.7	1.1	642	653	200	6 383	6.3	2.58	9.0	22.8
Payne	7.2	5.0	5.4	49.0	61 507	68 190	10.9	4.2	2 726	1 741	1 917	26 680	11.9	2.29	8.3	30.1
Pittsburg	11.4	8.7	8.2	49.5	40 950	43 953	7.3	0.5	1 685	1 893	443	17 157	7.8	2.40	11.2	27.7
Pontotoc	10.0	7.6	7.1	51.3	34 119	35 143	3.0	0.1	1 588	1 438	-101	13 978	5.0	2.44	10.8	28.1
Pottawatomie	9.8	7.3	6.1	51.5	58 760	65 521	11.5	2.8	3 002	2 519	1 381	24 540	12.6	2.55	11.8	24.0
Pushmataha	12.1	9.7	8.3	51.8	10 997	11 667	6.1	0.7	437	500	151	4 739	8.4	2.42	10.8	27.9
Roger Mills	12.5	9.7	10.1	49.5	4 147	3 436	-17.1	-6.8	128	163	-207	1 428	-10.0	2.38	6.8	28.6
Rogers	10.1	6.5	4.7	50.7	55 170	70 641	28.0	9.3	2 942	1 929	5 445	25 724	29.5	2.71	8.9	19.0
Seminole	10.8	8.4	8.0	51.5	25 412	24 894	-2.0	-1.6	1 207	1 211	-372	9 575	-0.9	2.54	13.3	25.9
Sequoyah	11.1	7.7	5.8	50.8	33 828	38 972	15.2	2.6	1 761	1 295	569	14 761	19.7	2.61	11.9	22.4
Stephens	10.8	9.5	8.5	51.4	42 299	43 182	2.1	-1.6	1 647	2 003	-289	17 463	4.2	2.44	9.2	25.3
Texas	8.4	5.4	4.7	48.2	16 419	20 107	22.5	-0.9	1 214	474	-950	7 153	15.1	2.75	7.5	21.2
Tillman	11.1	9.0	10.6	50.8	10 384	9 287	-10.6	-4.9	381	421	-399	3 594	-8.6	2.48	10.7	28.8
Tulsa	8.9	6.0	5.7	51.2	503 341	563 299	11.9	1.2	30 364	17 398	-5 733	226 892	12.0	2.43	12.1	29.6
Wagoner	11.0	6.3	4.1	50.4	47 883	57 491	20.1	7.5	2 400	1 258	3 141	21 010	24.0	2.73	9.8	17.7
Washington	10.9	8.7	9.0	51.8	48 066	48 996	1.9	0.3	1 928	1 927	169	20 179	4.9	2.40	9.3	27.5
Washita	10.3	8.6	9.9	51.8	11 441	11 508	0.6	-2.3	391	496	-143	4 506	1.9	2.50	8.5	25.3
Woods	10.2	8.6	11.0	48.5	9 103	9 089	-0.2	-4.6	278	457	-240	3 684	-3.1	2.20	7.3	33.4
Woodward	10.3	7.5	7.0	49.8	18 976	18 486	-2.6	-0.1	799	555	-257	7 141	0.8	2.48	8.4	25.4
OREGON	10.2	6.2	6.5	50.3	2 842 337	3 421 399	20.4	4.0	145 101	100 483	95 743	1 333 723	20.9	2.51	9.8	26.1
Baker	12.8	10.0	9.6	50.4	15 317	16 741	9.3	-2.2	499	694	-157	6 883	12.5	2.37	8.6	27.8
Benton	8.2	5.0	5.4	50.0	70 811	78 153	10.4	1.5	2 547	1 485	177	30 145	15.4	2.43	7.2	26.1
Clackamas	10.4	5.6	5.5	50.6	278 850	338 391	21.4	5.6	13 199	8 815	14 958	128 201	23.8	2.62	9.0	22.0
Clatsop	11.0	7.7	7.7	50.5	33 301	35 630	7.0	0.5	1 234	1 328	318	14 703	9.9	2.35	9.7	29.5
Columbia	10.7	5.9	5.3	50.1	37 557	43 560	16.0	6.2	1 655	1 320	2 346	16 375	17.7	2.65	8.7	21.1
Coos	12.7	9.8	9.4	51.1	60 273	62 779	4.2	0.4	1 894	2 799	1 151	26 213	8.6	2.34	9.9	27.2
Crook	11.0	8.0	6.8	50.2	14 111	19 182	35.9	7.4	760	675	1 321	7 354	34.8	2.57	8.2	21.3
Curry	13.9	13.4	13.0	51.1	19 327	21 137	9.4	3.2	542	1 032	1 146	9 543	14.8	2.19	7.2	29.7
Deschutes	10.1	6.8	5.9	50.3	74 976	115 367	53.9	12.2	4 719	3 178	12 334	45 595	56.1	2.50	8.5	22.0
Douglas	11.7	9.4	8.0	50.9	94 649	100 399	6.1	1.9	3 490	3 790	2 329	39 821	11.0	2.48	9.6	23.9
Gilliam	12.0	10.0	10.7	49.6	1 717	1 915	11.5	-7.2	59	77	-119	819	17.7	2.31	5.9	29.5
Grant	13.0	9.5	8.3	49.8	7 853	7 935	1.0	-6.1	213	321	-385	3 246	5.0	2.39	7.9	27.1
Harney	12.0	9.0	7.0	48.8	7 060	7 609	7.8	-5.6	270	266	-435	3 036	10.0	2.45	6.8	25.9
Hood River	8.4	6.2	6.5	50.7	16 903	20 411	20.8	1.7	1 007	583	-71	7 248	12.8	2.70	8.8	22.7
Jackson	10.6	7.5	8.2	51.4	146 387	181 269	23.8	4.9	6 727	6 322	8 454	71 532	25.0	2.48	10.5	25.1
Jefferson	10.5	7.7	5.1	49.7	13 676	19 009	39.0	3.5	999	631	304	6 727	41.8	2.80	10.5	18.6
Josephine	12.2	9.8	10.0	51.6	62 649	75 726	20.9	4.4	2 380	3 288	4 191	31 000	23.6	2.41	10.4	25.4
Klamath	10.9	8.0	7.1	49.9	57 702	63 775	10.5	1.6	2 661	2 270	694	25 205	12.8	2.49	10.0	25.3
Lake	12.5	10.1	8.0	49.8	7 186	7 422	3.3	0.2	238	236	20	3 084	11.5	2.39	7.5	26.2
Lane	9.8	6.4	6.9	50.8	282 912	322 959	14.2	2.3	11 549	9 446	5 818	130 453	17.7	2.42	10.0	26.6
Lincoln	13.2	10.1	9.1	50.6	38 889	44 479	14.4	0.4	1 337	1 901	772	19 296	17.3	2.27	10.0	29.3
Linn	10.3	7.0	7.4	50.6	91 227	103 069	13.0	3.0	4 333	3 335	2 156	39 541	13.9	2.58	10.0	23.8
Malheur	8.9	6.6	7.2	46.6	26 038	31 615	21.4	-1.2	1 556	845	-1 111	10 221	8.1	2.77	10.4	23.7
Marion	8.5	5.7	6.2	49.4	228 483	284 834	24.7	4.3	14 529	8 184	6 073	101 641	21.7	2.70	11.0	24.0

1. No spouse present.

Table B. States and Counties — Vital Statistics, Health Resources, and Crime

STATE County	Births, average 1999-2001 Total	Rate[1]	Deaths, average 1999-2001 Number Total	Infant[2]	Rate Total[1]	Infant[3]	Physicians,[4] 2000 Number	Rate[5]	Hospitals,[4] 1998 Number	Beds Number	Rate[5]	Medicare enrollees, 2003	Serious crimes known to police,[6] 2002 Total Number	Rate[7]
	32	33	34	35	36	37	38	39	40	41	42	43	44	45
OKLAHOMA—Cont'd														
Kiowa	130	12.8	181	3	17.8	D	5	49	1	50	471	2 194	302	2 916
Latimer	129	12.1	125	1	11.8	D	2	19	1	33	320	1 489	186	1 718
Le Flore	728	15.1	559	6	11.6	D	37	77	2	84	180	8 665	1 072	2 201
Lincoln	386	12.1	335	2	10.5	D	9	28	2	44	140	4 930	653	2 010
Logan	369	10.9	318	3	9.4	D	20	59	1	32	103	3 912	777	2 262
Love	105	11.9	105	1	12.0	D	1	11	1	40	469	1 567	185	2 069
McClain	376	13.5	259	5	9.3	D	11	40	1	32	122	4 218	756	2 692
McCurtain	528	15.4	438	4	12.8	D	17	49	1	89	256	5 835	1 258	3 612
McIntosh	208	10.7	267	2	13.7	D	8	41	1	33	173	4 812	719	3 650
Major	76	10.1	98	2	12.9	D	5	66	1	24	307	1 474	167	2 186
Marshall	170	12.9	181	1	13.7	D	5	38	1	25	203	2 830	302	2 263
Mayes	534	13.9	416	4	10.8	D	17	44	1	43	114	6 407	1 106	2 847
Murray	159	12.6	170	1	13.4	D	11	87	1	48	389	2 396	355	2 778
Muskogee	1 009	14.5	811	6	11.6	D	116	167	1	225	321	12 814	2 870	4 081
Noble	139	12.2	124	0	10.8	D	5	44	1	42	368	1 945	204	1 766
Nowata	132	12.5	130	1	12.3	D	8	76	1	32	321	2 068	293	2 738
Okfuskee	151	12.8	163	1	13.8	D	7	59	1	20	175	2 260	360	3 010
Oklahoma	10 958	16.6	6 410	108	9.7	9.8	1 929	292	13	3 325	525	92 985	51 219	7 660
Okmulgee	523	13.2	478	5	12.0	D	34	86	2	118	304	6 791	1 319	3 283
Osage	476	10.7	384	2	8.6	D	16	36	3	411	959	3 945	1 461	3 247
Ottawa	454	13.7	436	3	13.2	D	25	75	1	119	385	7 260	1 076	3 202
Pawnee	200	12.1	200	1	12.0	D	8	48	2	43	262	2 827	464	2 759
Payne	826	12.0	513	3	7.5	D	85	125	2	177	272	8 357	2 516	3 644
Pittsburg	506	11.6	564	7	12.9	13.2	49	111	1	171	400	8 105	1 542	3 465
Pontotoc	490	14.0	446	5	12.7	D	51	145	1	144	416	6 363	1 205	3 387
Pottawatomie	917	14.0	734	8	11.2	8.7	62	95	2	160	257	10 223	2 646	3 989
Pushmataha	140	12.0	164	2	14.0	D	5	43	1	46	397	2 446	434	3 674
Roger Mills	41	12.1	46	0	13.3	D	3	87	1	15	419	683	38	1 092
Rogers	903	12.7	559	5	7.9	D	65	92	1	86	126	8 874	1 254	1 753
Seminole	369	14.8	357	5	14.3	D	16	64	1	39	157	4 814	699	2 773
Sequoyah	550	14.1	395	4	10.1	D	14	36	1	41	109	6 733	1 106	2 803
Stephens	511	11.8	588	3	13.6	D	31	72	1	100	230	7 969	1 463	3 346
Texas	387	19.3	149	6	7.4	D	12	60	1	49	263	2 167	477	2 343
Tillman	120	12.9	124	2	13.3	D	6	65	1	58	610	1 825	193	2 053
Tulsa	9 273	16.4	5 149	72	9.1	7.7	1 493	265	6	1 898	349	83 995	35 660	6 253
Wagoner	720	12.5	372	6	6.4	D	25	43	1	100	181	5 151	1 257	2 159
Washington	584	11.9	572	2	11.7	D	69	141	1	233	490	9 895	1 972	3 975
Washita	128	11.1	144	1	12.5	D	2	17	1	38	322	2 289	119	1 021
Woods	86	9.5	140	1	15.5	D	3	33	1	50	598	1 751	128	1 391
Woodward	250	13.5	174	2	9.4	D	22	119	1	68	367	2 975	724	3 868
OREGON	45 443	13.2	29 711	254	8.7	5.6	7 338	214	62	7 352	224	513 253	171 443	4 868
Baker	165	9.9	203	0	12.2	D	22	131	1	129	784	3 628	505	2 931
Benton	800	10.2	448	3	5.7	D	179	229	1	124	159	8 656	2 860	3 555
Clackamas	4 137	12.2	2 575	19	7.6	4.7	597	176	3	339	101	43 287	14 149	4 062
Clatsop	381	10.7	388	3	10.9	D	57	160	2	69	195	6 374	1 624	4 428
Columbia	540	12.4	390	2	8.9	D	14	32	0	0	0	6 287	933	2 081
Coos	616	9.8	831	5	13.2	D	117	186	3	178	286	13 920	1 439	2 253
Crook	224	11.6	190	2	9.9	D	15	78	1	35	203	3 585	678	3 434
Curry	159	7.5	330	1	15.6	D	21	99	1	24	113	6 522	373	1 714
Deschutes	1 411	12.2	904	10	7.8	7.3	208	180	2	223	211	18 952	5 444	4 585
Douglas	1 088	10.8	1 150	8	11.5	7.7	181	180	3	284	279	21 733	2 897	2 803
Gilliam	18	9.3	21	0	11.0	D	1	52	0	0	0	417	21	1 065
Grant	70	8.9	95	1	12.2	D	5	63	1	75	929	1 543	136	1 665
Harney	90	11.9	80	0	10.6	D	8	105	1	52	722	1 339	109	1 392
Hood River	333	16.3	171	3	8.4	D	43	211	1	54	276	2 825	389	1 852
Jackson	2 089	11.5	1 867	10	10.3	4.9	400	221	3	471	272	33 915	8 344	4 472
Jefferson	305	16.1	167	2	8.8	D	16	84	1	109	656	3 263	573	2 929
Josephine	779	10.3	966	6	12.7	D	111	147	2	146	196	18 173	2 411	3 093
Klamath	823	12.9	666	6	10.4	D	109	171	1	256	405	11 278	1 855	2 826
Lake	73	9.8	84	1	11.2	D	8	108	1	67	937	1 634	87	1 139
Lane	3 681	11.4	2 829	24	8.8	6.5	636	197	4	620	197	51 244	16 667	5 014
Lincoln	426	9.6	552	5	12.4	D	71	160	2	75	165	9 859	2 136	4 666
Linn	1 397	13.5	986	9	9.5	6.2	129	125	2	120	115	18 110	5 114	4 821
Malheur	498	15.8	260	3	8.2	D	45	142	1	74	259	4 856	1 101	3 384
Marion	4 547	15.9	2 438	26	8.5	5.8	498	175	3	466	174	41 567	19 521	6 659

1. Per 1,000 estimated resident population.   2. Deaths of infants under 1 year old.   3. Deaths of infants under 1 year old per 1,000 live births.   4. Data subject to copyright.   5. Per 100,000 resident population as of July 1 of the year shown.   6. Data for serious crimes have not been adjusted for underreporting; this may affect comparability between geographic areas and over time.   7. Per 100,000 population estimated by the FBI.

Table B. States and Counties — **Crime, Education, Money Income, and Poverty**

	Serious crimes known to police,[1] 2002 (cont'd) Rate[2]		Education — School enrollment and attainment, 2000						Money income, 1999				Percent below poverty level, 1999			
			Enrollment[3]		Attainment[4] (percent)		Local government expenditures,[5] 2000–2001			Households — Median income							
STATE County	Violent	Property	Total	Percent private	High school graduate or less	Bachelor's degree or more	Total current expenditures (mil dol)	Current expenditures per student (dollars)	Per capita income[6] (dollars)	Dollars	Percent change, 1989–1999 (constant 1999 dollars)	Percent with income of $100,000 or more	Persons	Households	Families	Families with children
	46	47	48	49	50	51	52	53	54	55	56	57	58	59	60	61
OKLAHOMA—Cont'd																
Kiowa	406	2 511	2 390	1.9	58.9	14.8	12.7	6 783	14 231	26 053	18.8	3.5	19.3	20.6	15.0	23.2
Latimer	360	1 358	2 953	2.8	61.1	12.0	11.5	6 261	12 842	23 962	2.0	3.3	22.7	22.4	19.0	26.9
Le Flore	331	1 870	11 821	3.9	64.7	11.3	58.5	6 127	13 737	27 278	7.8	3.4	19.1	19.0	15.4	21.7
Lincoln	345	1 666	8 108	7.5	64.5	11.1	31.4	5 317	14 890	31 187	7.9	4.0	14.5	14.3	11.2	15.1
Logan	326	1 936	10 009	10.3	53.1	19.1	25.4	5 903	17 872	36 784	13.8	7.1	12.9	12.4	11.1	15.1
Love	291	1 778	2 124	5.0	67.8	10.8	9.5	5 740	16 648	32 558	19.3	4.9	11.8	12.9	8.7	13.0
McClain	374	2 318	7 367	8.2	57.4	15.7	28.5	5 195	18 158	37 275	9.1	7.5	10.5	10.4	8.3	10.9
McCurtain	603	3 009	8 723	2.5	66.9	10.8	49.8	6 495	13 693	24 162	9.6	3.5	24.7	24.8	21.0	11.8
McIntosh	279	3 371	4 197	5.7	62.6	13.1	20.8	6 304	16 410	25 964	8.9	5.4	18.2	18.2	13.5	29.8
Major	249	1 937	1 762	9.6	61.8	14.4	11.1	6 692	17 272	30 949	-2.3	4.5	12.0	12.7	9.3	21.7
Marshall	187	2 075	2 820	3.2	63.3	11.4	13.9	5 752	14 982	26 437	20.8	3.6	17.9	18.1	13.5	12.7
Mayes	404	2 443	9 429	5.2	62.0	12.1	42.6	5 825	15 350	31 125	9.2	4.0	14.3	14.3	11.2	20.4
Murray	477	2 300	2 765	2.5	61.5	14.9	12.6	5 521	16 084	30 294	23.1	3.8	14.1	14.7	11.1	16.9
Muskogee	557	3 524	17 289	4.9	56.8	15.4	79.7	5 881	14 828	28 438	3.7	4.4	17.9	17.6	14.1	13.9
Noble	61	1 705	2 796	3.8	58.6	15.8	16.2	7 040	17 022	33 968	8.8	5.4	12.8	13.2	9.6	20.5
Nowata	271	2 467	2 578	3.6	66.5	9.5	11.9	5 950	14 244	29 470	20.0	3.2	14.1	15.1	9.0	14.8
Okfuskee	485	2 525	2 678	5.0	70.2	9.2	15.2	6 686	12 746	24 324	15.0	3.1	23.0	22.0	17.3	13.7
Oklahoma	630	7 029	177 872	15.4	43.5	25.4	643.8	5 953	19 551	35 063	-0.1	8.0	15.3	14.1	11.7	25.5
Okmulgee	299	2 984	10 580	4.6	60.5	11.4	42.9	5 839	14 065	27 652	18.5	3.5	18.9	19.7	14.9	18.1
Osage	469	2 778	11 443	7.8	56.2	14.6	31.0	6 780	17 014	34 477	4.2	5.8	13.2	13.6	10.3	22.1
Ottawa	238	2 964	8 325	4.3	58.9	12.2	35.9	5 726	14 478	27 507	15.6	3.0	16.6	16.0	13.6	15.0
Pawnee	309	2 450	4 117	3.8	61.4	12.1	14.6	5 306	15 261	31 661	11.2	4.0	13.0	13.5	13.0	20.1
Payne	256	3 388	28 426	3.4	40.0	34.2	61.9	6 193	15 983	28 733	9.2	6.4	20.3	22.8	9.6	13.7
Pittsburg	229	3 236	10 214	4.9	60.3	12.9	50.8	6 225	15 494	28 679	12.9	4.0	17.2	17.7	10.8	14.6
Pontotoc	287	3 100	10 199	4.2	53.5	21.8	41.8	6 143	14 664	26 955	11.8	4.3	16.5	17.7	13.6	20.4
Pottawatomie	503	3 485	17 776	14.9	56.4	15.5	70.5	5 685	15 972	31 573	7.2	4.8	14.6	14.8	11.8	17.4
Pushmataha	491	3 183	2 777	2.0	66.3	12.4	17.0	7 054	12 864	22 127	21.0	2.8	23.2	24.8	18.8	17.0
Roger Mills	115	977	758	3.2	59.3	15.8	9.1	10 850	16 821	30 078	11.3	5.1	16.3	16.5	11.5	26.9
Rogers	137	1 616	19 354	9.6	49.4	16.9	71.9	5 287	19 073	44 471	12.6	8.3	8.6	9.4	6.6	18.2
Seminole	290	2 484	6 499	4.5	61.6	12.1	31.6	6 437	13 956	25 568	11.9	3.0	20.8	20.3	16.7	10.0
Sequoyah	707	2 096	9 537	3.5	64.7	10.9	50.6	5 983	13 405	27 615	11.5	3.3	19.8	20.3	16.1	24.3
Stephens	224	3 122	10 155	5.5	60.3	16.6	48.1	5 851	16 357	30 709	0.9	4.6	14.6	15.2	11.6	22.0
Texas	128	2 215	5 517	6.5	56.7	17.7	25.7	6 650	15 692	35 872	13.2	5.5	14.1	13.1	10.2	17.1
Tillman	234	1 819	2 304	3.2	67.0	12.5	13.1	6 874	14 270	24 828	3.8	4.4	21.9	21.6	17.3	15.4
Tulsa	841	5 411	152 977	20.3	41.5	26.9	590.1	5 586	21 115	38 213	4.5	9.8	11.6	11.3	8.7	24.5
Wagoner	158	2 001	15 269	10.5	54.5	15.4	33.3	5 540	18 272	41 744	8.8	7.4	8.9	8.9	6.7	13.4
Washington	347	3 628	12 166	11.7	46.9	25.8	49.8	5 658	20 250	35 816	-7.6	9.7	11.9	12.5	8.7	10.1
Washita	154	867	3 007	5.2	59.3	15.1	13.2	6 112	15 528	29 563	19.7	4.6	15.5	15.1	13.1	14.3
Woods	174	1 217	2 625	2.1	49.2	23.7	10.3	7 167	17 487	28 927	8.9	5.5	15.0	15.5	8.7	19.7
Woodward	630	3 238	4 392	4.4	58.2	15.2	20.2	5 676	16 734	33 581	5.0	4.8	12.5	12.1	8.7	13.4
OREGON	292	4 576	876 092	14.0	41.1	25.1	4 124.5	7 571	20 940	40 916	11.8	10.0	11.6	10.8	7.9	11.8
Baker	168	2 762	3 629	6.8	64.1	16.4	21.9	7 753	15 612	30 367	2.0	3.7	14.7	14.1	10.1	12.4
Benton	163	3 393	30 859	7.3	22.2	47.4	70.5	7 057	21 868	41 897	14.2	12.5	14.6	14.6	6.8	16.6
Clackamas	141	3 921	87 642	16.1	35.2	28.4	396.9	7 272	25 973	52 080	9.4	17.5	6.6	6.1	4.6	9.9
Clatsop	166	4 262	8 478	10.6	43.5	19.1	40.8	7 340	19 515	36 301	7.5	6.4	13.2	11.7	9.1	7.1
Columbia	45	2 036	10 694	8.8	49.6	14.0	58.5	6 800	20 078	45 797	15.5	8.7	9.1	9.0	6.7	14.6
Coos	77	2 177	14 249	6.4	49.2	15.0	79.9	8 499	17 547	31 542	6.0	4.8	15.0	14.8	11.1	10.4
Crook	547	2 887	4 562	8.9	58.4	12.6	23.2	7 263	16 899	35 186	7.9	4.7	11.3	11.0	8.1	17.8
Curry	78	1 636	3 801	6.6	50.4	16.4	22.2	7 221	18 138	30 117	-0.7	4.9	12.2	13.2	9.7	14.4
Deschutes	161	4 424	27 802	12.1	38.8	25.0	143.5	7 186	21 767	41 847	14.0	10.3	9.3	8.9	6.3	13.6
Douglas	78	2 725	22 732	10.1	53.7	13.3	130.1	7 807	16 581	33 223	4.4	4.6	13.1	12.8	9.6	9.3
Gilliam	51	1 015	438	4.1	45.8	13.4	6.6	18 660	17 659	33 611	4.1	5.2	9.1	9.9	6.7	15.5
Grant	73	1 592	1 888	11.9	52.8	15.7	14.0	10 357	16 794	32 560	-1.6	4.9	13.7	12.4	11.2	10.2
Harney	115	1 277	1 713	5.5	57.1	11.9	15.1	10 601	16 159	30 957	3.2	5.0	11.8	12.4	8.6	16.3
Hood River	76	1 776	5 124	11.9	48.5	23.1	29.0	7 685	17 877	38 326	13.0	7.4	14.2	10.7	9.8	11.0
Jackson	264	4 209	44 630	10.6	45.1	22.3	210.3	7 204	19 498	36 461	8.3	8.0	12.5	11.9	8.9	14.1
Jefferson	460	2 469	4 882	5.6	55.2	13.7	31.5	8 476	15 675	35 853	13.4	5.9	14.6	12.1	10.4	14.7
Josephine	122	2 971	16 787	13.4	49.3	14.1	78.6	6 831	17 234	31 229	11.0	5.4	15.0	14.3	11.3	17.4
Klamath	215	2 611	16 355	9.4	52.6	15.9	82.2	7 444	16 719	31 537	1.8	5.0	16.8	15.1	12.0	19.7
Lake	118	1 021	1 669	5.0	53.7	15.5	12.6	9 100	16 136	29 506	-10.9	3.3	16.1	15.7	13.4	19.9
Lane	246	4 768	90 503	9.4	38.3	25.5	367.3	7 632	19 681	36 942	8.8	7.9	14.4	14.1	9.0	19.9
Lincoln	321	4 345	9 074	8.5	44.1	20.8	44.9	6 908	18 692	32 769	6.6	5.5	13.9	12.1	9.8	14.8
Linn	139	4 682	25 835	13.7	51.1	13.4	134.5	7 539	17 633	37 518	10.8	6.0	11.4	10.6	8.9	17.9
Malheur	230	3 153	8 244	9.1	59.5	11.1	45.9	8 187	13 895	30 241	11.2	4.9	18.6	16.7	14.6	13.6
Marion	248	6 411	73 702	14.8	47.0	19.8	389.2	7 446	18 408	40 314	11.6	7.8	13.5	11.4	9.6	22.1

1. Data for serious crimes have not been adjusted for underreporting; this may affect comparability between geographic areas and over time.   2. Per 100,000 population estimated by the FBI.   3. All persons 3 years old and over enrolled in nursery school through college.   4. Persons 25 years old and over.   5. Elementary and secondary education expenditures.   6. Based on population enumerated as of April 1, 2000.

Table B. States and Counties — **Personal Income**

STATE County	Personal income, 2002 Total (mil dol)	Percent change, 2001-2002	Per capita[1] Dollars	Per capita[1] Rank	Wages and salaries[2] (mil dol)	Proprietor's income (mil dol)	Dividends, interest, and rent (mil dol)	Transfer payments Total (mil dol)	Govt payments to individuals Total (mil dol)	Social Security (mil dol)	Medical payments (mil dol)	Income maintenance (mil dol)	Unemployment insurance (mil dol)
	62	63	64	65	66	67	68	69	70	71	72	73	74
OKLAHOMA—Cont'd													
Kiowa	220	3.3	22 108	1 985	83	21	46	60	58	22	26	5	1
Latimer	223	-0.7	21 126	2 260	132	17	38	60	58	22	21	5	1
Le Flore	961	2.4	19 776	2 594	319	101	136	258	246	82	106	29	3
Lincoln	671	3.5	20 813	2 344	200	44	115	127	120	53	44	11	3
Logan	837	4.3	24 004	1 404	194	87	128	129	121	51	45	10	2
Love	181	4.2	20 394	2 460	62	10	27	40	38	17	15	3	1
McClain	664	5.0	23 677	1 509	217	40	83	108	101	44	39	7	3
McCurtain	684	-1.9	20 081	2 528	357	108	88	181	173	57	79	24	3
McIntosh	394	5.4	19 999	2 549	107	35	72	121	116	47	47	10	2
Major	162	-0.8	21 484	2 152	63	19	41	33	31	16	11	2	0
Marshall	273	7.4	20 088	2 526	122	23	51	73	70	30	29	6	1
Mayes	831	2.3	21 458	2 162	346	65	141	184	175	74	68	15	5
Murray	257	4.2	20 369	2 466	103	25	42	67	64	26	26	5	2
Muskogee	1 531	6.1	21 926	2 034	1 102	98	254	380	363	129	151	36	7
Noble	241	-3.0	21 269	2 224	134	14	59	53	50	21	22	4	1
Nowata	196	3.5	18 417	2 840	55	14	36	52	50	23	19	4	1
Okfuskee	202	7.2	17 348	2 965	74	26	28	67	64	21	31	7	1
Oklahoma	20 015	1.5	29 818	363	17 223	2 840	3 516	2 801	2 645	991	1 046	325	78
Okmulgee	761	4.0	19 178	2 718	301	36	109	207	198	74	84	21	4
Osage	1 012	4.1	22 420	1 903	200	79	145	159	148	75	47	11	6
Ottawa	654	2.7	19 880	2 570	275	65	102	194	187	75	80	15	4
Pawnee	361	3.6	21 482	2 153	107	25	59	80	76	35	30	5	2
Payne	1 517	2.2	21 627	2 114	1 002	108	285	243	227	91	86	19	3
Pittsburg	911	3.8	20 636	2 388	504	68	175	224	214	86	85	20	4
Pontotoc	755	2.5	21 638	2 110	455	50	143	191	183	67	76	17	3
Pottawatomie	1 436	4.2	21 522	2 142	594	109	225	282	267	106	99	33	5
Pushmataha	217	6.7	18 504	2 830	74	29	31	73	70	23	33	7	1
Roger Mills	75	1.6	23 518	1 562	26	7	26	15	14	7	6	1	0
Rogers	1 880	2.9	24 998	1 129	800	136	274	275	258	117	93	17	8
Seminole	466	4.4	18 961	2 760	221	20	80	149	143	48	63	18	3
Sequoyah	759	4.5	19 144	2 729	234	76	96	200	191	71	82	22	3
Stephens	988	2.1	23 207	1 658	472	122	200	218	208	96	71	16	6
Texas	489	-12.0	24 344	1 292	325	60	79	62	57	27	21	5	1
Tillman	167	6.4	18 703	2 799	73	16	28	48	45	18	20	5	0
Tulsa	19 965	1.6	35 030	141	14 336	4 257	3 436	2 341	2 207	918	881	189	73
Wagoner	1 337	2.5	22 106	1 987	199	43	171	201	187	89	62	15	6
Washington	1 476	5.4	30 028	350	727	173	431	245	233	117	85	15	5
Washita	218	5.5	19 163	2 724	75	15	44	56	54	22	23	5	1
Woods	194	1.0	22 079	1 996	86	19	54	44	42	19	15	2	1
Woodward	392	-0.9	21 257	2 226	254	35	77	77	73	34	27	6	2
OREGON	101 359	2.4	28 792	X	67 854	8 890	19 889	15 960	15 158	5 850	5 434	1 243	1 249
Baker	353	3.2	21 424	2 173	172	13	95	92	88	38	31	7	6
Benton	2 399	2.8	30 421	310	1 662	166	578	248	230	109	57	17	8
Clackamas	12 526	1.7	35 543	126	5 922	989	2 374	1 335	1 255	545	389	70	117
Clatsop	898	3.1	25 196	1 079	532	87	194	175	167	73	56	13	11
Columbia	1 238	1.8	27 234	662	393	74	190	210	200	80	70	12	22
Coos	1 499	5.0	23 937	1 425	764	107	342	391	377	158	132	31	25
Crook	441	3.6	21 859	2 050	225	46	100	103	98	41	38	6	8
Curry	530	4.6	24 679	1 218	202	42	175	145	140	74	45	8	6
Deschutes	3 540	5.1	28 193	521	1 935	453	857	558	529	228	172	36	49
Douglas	2 493	5.6	24 644	1 225	1 405	144	505	621	598	245	219	45	42
Gilliam	34	12.1	18 416	2 841	29	-10	15	8	8	5	2	0	0
Grant	186	3.6	24 967	1 140	100	8	49	41	39	16	14	3	4
Harney	164	2.3	22 382	1 913	92	9	38	37	36	14	12	3	4
Hood River	499	3.6	24 151	1 356	317	34	114	84	79	32	26	6	10
Jackson	4 942	4.3	26 477	798	2 714	532	1 168	911	869	383	284	72	60
Jefferson	402	3.8	20 510	2 428	224	3	85	95	91	34	39	9	5
Josephine	1 774	4.3	22 791	1 785	732	174	420	497	480	197	182	43	24
Klamath	1 479	5.5	23 002	1 721	849	109	282	370	355	126	141	29	22
Lake	162	-1.1	21 854	2 052	84	11	41	40	38	17	12	3	3
Lane	8 647	2.5	26 416	810	5 311	625	1 894	1 525	1 450	587	492	130	99
Lincoln	1 158	3.5	26 029	883	552	110	283	274	264	112	97	20	16
Linn	2 525	3.4	24 067	1 380	1 567	174	457	544	520	203	185	47	44
Malheur	582	2.8	18 608	2 810	418	28	141	140	133	51	52	14	8
Marion	7 398	3.2	25 208	1 075	4 893	622	1 352	1 352	1 285	460	509	126	86

1. Based on the resident population estimated as of July 1 of the year shown. 2. Includes other labor income.

Table B. States and Counties — Earnings, Social Security, and Housing

STATE County	Earnings, 2002 Total (mil dol)	Farm	Goods-related[1] Total	Manu-facturing	Service-related and health — Information and profes-sional and technical services	Retail trade	Finance, insur-ance, and real estate	Health services	Govern-ment	Social Security beneficiaries, December 2003 Number	Rate[2]	Supple-mental Security Income recipients, December 2003	Housing units, 2003 Total	Percent change, 2000–2003
	75	76	77	78	79	80	81	82	83	84	85	86	87	88
OKLAHOMA—Cont'd														
Kiowa	104	9.1	16.7	11.1	4.2	7.7	D	9.9	32.7	2 505	251	345	5 260	-0.8
Latimer	149	0.5	D	D	1.4	5.7	D	2.9	35.7	2 630	249	264	4 776	1.4
Le Flore	420	8.2	22.9	13.8	D	11.2	4.2	D	28.0	9 850	201	2 101	20 547	2.0
Lincoln	244	0.8	D	7.6	3.6	8.2	12.7	4.5	24.8	6 275	195	601	13 933	1.6
Logan	281	1.2	14.3	3.5	9.7	9.3	10.6	D	26.6	5 620	159	348	14 057	1.1
Love	72	1.5	D	27.7	2.8	10.4	4.5	3.9	28.9	1 875	211	181	4 131	1.6
McClain	257	2.2	23.7	5.1	3.5	14.4	5.5	3.9	21.7	4 895	171	306	11 723	4.8
McCurtain	465	7.9	D	30.4	3.7	6.2	1.9	5.4	18.5	7 045	207	1 568	15 693	1.7
McIntosh	142	1.9	D	8.9	3.6	16.3	5.6	D	26.0	5 405	274	618	12 930	2.3
Major	82	6.1	D	7.4	5.0	9.3	D	6.5	20.7	1 815	245	64	3 544	0.1
Marshall	145	-1.5	D	31.6	2.5	9.8	6.0	7.7	18.4	3 345	245	360	8 676	1.9
Mayes	412	2.1	D	27.8	D	11.5	2.6	D	24.6	8 055	207	813	17 885	2.7
Murray	128	2.8	19.3	6.4	7.5	12.5	4.1	7.9	32.5	2 850	224	256	6 544	1.0
Muskogee	1 200	0.3	29.9	19.3	3.8	8.2	4.4	D	27.7	14 545	207	2 440	30 041	1.6
Noble	148	2.5	D	D	D	5.0	D	6.1	23.7	2 320	206	167	5 108	0.5
Nowata	68	3.9	26.0	15.2	D	7.2	4.3	9.4	26.8	2 520	233	191	4 750	1.0
Okfuskee	100	4.6	19.7	11.2	D	10.4	D	10.6	38.7	2 610	223	500	5 172	1.1
Oklahoma	20 063	0.0	21.9	14.0	9.4	6.7	7.2	9.8	23.4	102 515	152	14 464	303 891	3.0
Okmulgee	337	-0.2	24.5	19.8	3.3	10.4	4.6	D	32.7	8 505	214	1 349	17 402	0.5
Osage	280	-0.1	31.6	10.9	D	5.7	5.1	4.9	30.3	8 435	186	433	19 211	2.0
Ottawa	340	5.0	D	16.3	3.9	8.9	4.6	D	23.0	8 125	248	1 097	14 969	0.9
Pawnee	132	0.2	16.5	4.8	D	11.6	6.0	12.4	28.4	3 690	220	271	7 521	0.8
Payne	1 110	0.1	13.5	5.8	5.9	8.8	4.1	5.7	46.0	9 525	134	1 123	29 968	2.2
Pittsburg	572	0.1	15.8	10.1	4.6	10.4	3.9	D	39.6	10 155	230	1 467	21 869	1.6
Pontotoc	505	0.3	19.2	13.0	5.0	8.3	10.1	12.7	30.7	7 565	215	1 226	15 723	1.0
Pottawatomie	703	1.2	25.6	17.7	8.0	9.7	3.9	11.0	19.9	12 270	182	1 653	27 700	1.5
Pushmataha	103	-0.3	D	6.4	5.4	9.7	2.7	15.7	33.2	2 985	254	601	5 870	1.3
Roger Mills	33	6.4	D	D	D	10.1	D	D	40.4	790	247	51	1 748	-0.1
Rogers	936	-0.2	39.2	29.1	D	7.3	4.3	6.1	18.1	12 190	158	625	28 963	5.4
Seminole	242	-0.3	31.7	17.8	2.6	7.9	3.5	D	28.9	5 495	224	924	11 232	0.8
Sequoyah	310	-0.7	D	10.7	6.8	12.0	3.9	15.8	29.4	8 560	214	1 567	17 531	3.5
Stephens	594	0.5	42.6	16.4	D	13.4	4.8	D	13.0	10 185	240	884	19 978	0.6
Texas	385	13.1	D	D	D	6.9	3.1	3.7	16.9	2 640	132	174	8 248	2.9
Tillman	89	11.6	D	D	D	5.3	D	4.1	30.8	2 080	235	286	4 295	-1.1
Tulsa	18 592	0.0	29.7	20.8	13.1	7.3	6.7	9.2	7.9	88 635	155	10 467	251 347	3.0
Wagoner	242	0.8	31.5	20.0	4.0	9.6	4.3	D	23.2	9 410	152	604	25 413	9.7
Washington	900	0.4	35.2	3.8	6.0	7.9	5.3	D	9.6	11 130	227	849	22 358	0.5
Washita	90	1.2	20.7	3.5	6.9	8.2	4.6	5.7	31.2	2 580	229	221	5 472	0.4
Woods	105	2.6	12.8	6.5	3.8	13.0	7.0	D	36.8	1 890	218	88	4 445	-1.0
Woodward	288	2.5	24.7	6.0	3.3	9.9	9.3	6.0	23.8	3 605	195	270	8 368	0.3
OREGON	76 744	1.1	21.9	15.0	9.6	7.6	7.3	9.9	17.0	591 461	166	57 506	1 515 354	4.3
Baker	185	-4.4	17.0	11.6	5.9	9.8	3.9	D	31.3	4 085	249	349	8 551	1.8
Benton	1 828	1.7	D	26.3	9.5	4.7	3.0	10.7	27.0	10 600	134	627	33 576	5.0
Clackamas	6 911	2.3	24.4	15.3	9.3	7.9	9.1	9.9	11.8	52 525	147	3 094	143 418	4.7
Clatsop	619	0.1	25.9	19.3	D	9.9	4.9	10.1	21.4	7 435	208	718	19 931	1.2
Columbia	466	2.2	30.4	24.2	4.0	8.2	4.1	5.2	20.1	7 895	171	421	18 567	5.7
Coos	871	1.1	14.3	8.6	5.0	9.3	3.6	8.9	30.0	16 430	261	1 814	29 493	0.8
Crook	271	-3.3	20.6	15.4	2.2	18.7	2.7	D	22.2	4 320	210	234	8 948	8.3
Curry	243	0.7	D	13.2	4.8	12.0	5.1	6.7	22.0	7 425	340	406	11 822	3.6
Deschutes	2 388	-0.4	21.4	9.5	10.5	11.0	9.4	13.3	14.3	23 350	180	1 366	61 723	13.1
Douglas	1 549	0.1	24.3	18.8	4.8	7.6	3.5	11.2	24.8	25 585	250	2 013	44 572	3.0
Gilliam	18	-52.4	8.1	0.0	D	5.4	D	7.4	46.0	465	262	34	1 035	-0.8
Grant	108	-3.5	16.1	9.3	D	6.5	2.5	D	42.6	1 775	238	137	4 140	3.4
Harney	101	3.7	13.8	9.4	D	8.8	3.2	D	45.4	1 570	219	142	3 558	0.7
Hood River	351	7.8	16.8	11.4	5.4	9.7	2.3	11.3	16.9	3 245	156	207	8 165	4.4
Jackson	3 246	0.3	18.8	9.2	6.7	13.0	6.1	14.0	16.2	39 415	207	3 100	80 476	6.3
Jefferson	226	-1.5	D	26.8	1.5	6.6	2.3	D	41.9	3 610	184	315	8 861	6.5
Josephine	907	0.0	19.9	12.4	5.6	12.9	6.1	13.7	18.8	20 890	264	1 732	34 740	4.5
Klamath	958	2.1	D	11.3	6.1	8.3	5.2	10.8	25.0	13 335	206	1 461	29 448	2.0
Lake	95	-1.4	17.7	11.2	4.3	6.8	3.0	D	44.1	1 910	257	125	4 063	1.6
Lane	5 936	0.4	21.9	14.8	9.4	8.9	5.6	12.6	19.3	59 135	179	5 611	143 484	3.3
Lincoln	661	-0.2	D	9.2	4.9	11.5	3.8	9.5	24.5	11 640	261	763	27 521	2.4
Linn	1 741	2.1	34.5	28.5	3.5	7.2	3.2	7.9	15.6	20 925	197	2 238	44 070	3.6
Malheur	446	4.9	D	9.2	3.5	10.2	3.1	D	31.8	5 565	178	709	11 385	1.4
Marion	5 515	3.4	15.1	8.6	5.5	7.6	5.7	13.3	30.1	47 315	159	4 976	112 702	4.2

1. Covers mining, construction, and manufacturing.   2. Per 1,000 resident population estimated as of July 1 of the year shown.

Table B. States and Counties — Housing, Labor Force, and Employment

STATE County	Total	Percent	Median value[1]	With a mortgage	Without a mortgage[2]	Median rent[3]	Median rent as a percent of income	Sub-standard units[4] (percent)	Total	Percent change, 2002–2003	Total	Rate[5]	Total	Management, professional and related occupations	Production, transportation, and material moving occupations
	89	90	91	92	93	94	95	96	97	98	99	100	101	102	103
OKLAHOMA—Cont'd															
Kiowa	4 208	75.2	34 600	17.5	11.1	312	23.8	2.9	4 533	-4.3	207	4.6	4 166	30.3	16.6
Latimer	3 951	74.5	46 800	19.8	10.5	327	23.7	4.2	4 093	-3.1	250	6.1	3 959	26.9	17.6
Le Flore	17 861	75.1	51 600	19.0	11.0	372	24.7	4.8	20 118	1.0	1 347	6.7	19 205	24.3	27.2
Lincoln	12 178	80.1	53 200	19.2	10.3	397	22.2	3.9	13 143	-8.6	795	6.0	13 927	22.9	20.6
Logan	12 389	78.4	74 100	19.0	10.2	417	22.8	3.6	16 143	0.5	688	4.3	15 994	29.7	12.6
Love	3 442	81.8	49 400	20.1	9.9	388	21.8	4.4	4 278	5.9	226	5.3	3 901	23.7	27.2
McClain	10 331	81.3	77 200	18.9	9.9	446	21.4	3.7	13 897	-0.2	645	4.6	12 980	27.4	15.2
McCurtain	13 216	73.3	44 500	19.2	10.5	302	23.7	4.8	14 890	-2.6	1 581	10.6	13 236	21.9	23.1
McIntosh	8 085	78.9	60 700	20.2	11.5	375	24.7	5.3	7 983	-3.3	634	7.9	7 281	27.9	17.6
Major	3 046	81.0	50 400	16.9	9.9	345	19.5	2.1	3 577	0.1	104	2.9	3 621	29.0	16.4
Marshall	5 371	79.2	49 400	19.8	11.2	354	23.1	4.6	5 471	2.2	224	4.1	5 295	22.2	25.7
Mayes	14 823	77.0	66 500	18.2	9.9	394	20.9	4.5	15 011	-2.6	1 403	9.3	16 520	22.8	24.4
Murray	5 003	74.2	51 800	17.4	10.7	377	20.2	3.1	5 444	1.4	280	5.1	5 575	26.5	19.3
Muskogee	26 458	69.6	57 700	19.6	10.1	396	25.5	4.5	31 258	-2.9	2 268	7.3	27 265	26.0	21.3
Noble	4 504	75.2	54 400	18.0	9.9	388	20.0	2.9	5 315	-1.9	202	3.8	5 336	23.1	22.4
Nowata	4 147	77.7	41 100	18.6	9.9	354	22.3	4.0	4 091	4.7	312	7.6	4 521	27.4	22.9
Okfuskee	4 270	76.0	39 100	19.4	11.3	316	21.9	5.3	3 994	-4.5	426	10.7	4 133	25.8	22.9
Oklahoma	266 834	60.4	75 800	19.8	9.9	483	24.5	4.9	347 866	0.4	19 166	5.5	305 829	32.2	12.7
Okmulgee	15 300	72.6	46 000	19.4	10.5	369	23.8	4.3	15 636	5.7	1 522	9.7	15 661	22.9	18.7
Osage	16 617	80.5	63 500	18.7	9.9	359	22.0	3.6	20 648	-1.5	1 393	6.7	19 262	28.4	17.0
Ottawa	12 984	73.9	47 200	18.5	9.9	355	23.3	3.8	13 312	-0.9	1 199	9.0	14 172	25.8	20.9
Pawnee	6 383	80.0	56 300	19.3	11.9	419	21.1	4.4	7 562	1.5	600	7.9	7 268	25.7	20.4
Payne	26 680	55.9	79 700	18.7	9.9	459	33.1	3.0	36 369	-0.1	932	2.6	34 495	37.5	12.2
Pittsburg	17 157	76.0	53 400	18.3	10.1	386	25.6	3.4	19 396	5.8	1 215	6.3	16 607	27.9	15.4
Pontotoc	13 978	67.0	58 000	20.1	11.1	377	25.5	3.3	18 993	7.4	882	4.6	15 687	29.1	16.6
Pottawatomie	24 540	72.2	60 500	18.8	10.2	431	24.2	3.8	30 380	0.9	1 847	6.1	28 247	27.8	17.5
Pushmataha	4 739	77.8	42 600	19.8	10.5	276	22.1	5.8	5 482	12.2	428	7.8	4 261	26.4	17.9
Roger Mills	1 428	78.8	39 000	20.6	9.9	314	21.1	1.8	2 050	3.1	40	2.0	1 635	34.6	10.1
Rogers	25 724	81.1	94 100	18.8	9.9	480	23.6	3.0	38 088	-1.2	2 342	6.1	33 314	29.7	17.0
Seminole	9 575	72.3	39 300	19.7	11.2	375	24.7	5.5	10 552	0.6	1 120	10.6	9 600	25.4	21.4
Sequoyah	14 761	75.2	59 800	19.9	10.7	354	24.6	5.2	17 349	1.5	1 200	6.9	15 902	22.1	22.4
Stephens	17 463	75.6	54 500	19.1	9.9	391	22.7	3.3	18 476	0.7	889	4.8	17 783	29.2	17.1
Texas	7 153	67.1	67 500	18.4	9.9	450	19.4	9.1	14 040	-1.8	310	2.2	9 596	27.4	19.7
Tillman	3 594	77.2	29 100	19.0	11.6	335	21.2	5.0	3 403	-3.4	139	4.1	3 483	27.4	19.7
Tulsa	226 892	61.8	87 000	19.2	9.9	520	24.1	4.4	303 475	-1.5	19 490	6.4	275 856	34.3	12.2
Wagoner	21 010	81.0	89 800	19.0	9.9	469	22.8	4.1	30 219	-1.1	1 822	6.0	27 369	26.2	16.5
Washington	20 179	74.0	63 000	17.0	9.9	406	22.5	2.3	20 141	5.5	1 231	6.1	21 349	33.9	14.1
Washita	4 506	74.7	39 800	17.9	9.9	373	21.1	2.7	4 835	0.1	159	3.3	5 057	30.2	16.8
Woods	3 684	69.6	46 300	16.8	9.9	359	26.3	1.4	4 748	0.7	542	11.4	4 263	30.9	10.5
Woodward	7 141	72.0	61 100	19.0	9.9	396	20.5	2.8	9 019	-0.4	402	4.5	8 449	26.6	16.3
OREGON	1 333 723	64.2	152 100	23.2	10.5	620	26.9	5.3	1 858 879	1.0	152 151	8.2	1 627 769	33.1	14.7
Baker	6 883	70.0	84 700	24.9	11.6	453	26.4	3.8	7 406	-0.8	703	9.5	6 717	30.5	16.1
Benton	30 145	57.3	169 800	21.4	9.9	597	30.3	3.5	41 672	1.1	1 739	4.2	38 356	46.9	9.7
Clackamas	128 201	71.1	199 000	23.2	10.2	702	25.7	3.8	193 889	0.1	14 305	7.4	169 648	34.8	13.1
Clatsop	14 703	64.2	143 400	24.0	10.8	543	26.6	3.7	18 272	3.4	1 291	7.1	16 497	26.6	13.3
Columbia	16 375	76.1	150 700	22.5	9.9	581	24.7	4.4	22 576	0.8	2 640	11.7	20 034	26.4	22.0
Coos	26 213	68.2	98 900	21.8	11.8	499	27.7	4.5	28 146	2.1	2 477	8.8	25 187	28.5	14.1
Crook	7 354	74.2	100 000	22.5	11.1	538	24.6	5.4	7 789	-0.9	845	10.8	8 090	24.5	23.4
Curry	9 543	72.9	148 000	25.7	10.2	550	26.2	4.2	8 991	5.7	654	7.3	7 981	26.9	14.0
Deschutes	45 595	72.3	148 800	23.4	10.6	644	27.4	3.6	68 771	4.1	5 316	7.7	55 754	31.3	12.8
Douglas	39 821	71.7	104 800	22.1	10.1	489	25.8	4.2	48 015	1.9	4 868	10.1	41 670	25.5	20.5
Gilliam	819	69.6	71 000	19.1	13.5	484	23.0	1.2	1 100	-0.6	73	6.6	941	27.8	17.4
Grant	3 246	73.3	79 700	21.4	9.9	432	19.8	4.4	3 836	1.8	433	11.3	3 341	32.5	15.5
Harney	3 036	72.6	73 300	19.7	12.1	453	23.4	4.3	3 743	-1.0	423	11.3	3 412	32.6	16.3
Hood River	7 248	64.9	152 400	24.4	9.9	538	24.7	8.6	11 910	2.1	1 159	9.7	9 525	32.5	12.2
Jackson	71 532	66.5	140 000	23.5	10.3	597	28.8	4.9	97 407	3.4	7 150	7.3	80 714	30.6	14.4
Jefferson	6 727	71.3	105 500	22.9	11.7	501	23.3	10.6	8 020	0.1	632	7.9	8 149	25.0	23.6
Josephine	31 000	70.0	128 700	24.3	9.9	534	28.4	5.5	31 897	4.2	2 819	8.8	28 264	26.5	15.2
Klamath	25 205	68.0	91 100	19.9	9.9	475	27.4	5.8	29 752	2.0	3 021	10.2	26 177	28.3	16.3
Lake	3 084	68.8	65 700	18.4	9.9	401	22.5	4.3	3 461	2.5	361	10.4	3 081	30.2	14.4
Lane	130 653	62.3	141 000	23.3	9.9	604	29.7	3.9	171 406	1.2	13 438	7.8	155 460	31.9	15.5
Lincoln	19 296	65.7	148 800	25.9	12.1	575	28.0	4.3	22 095	2.4	1 903	8.6	19 263	27.3	9.9
Linn	39 541	67.9	124 100	23.1	11.4	580	28.3	5.2	52 429	1.0	5 740	10.9	46 140	25.1	21.9
Malheur	10 221	63.8	86 900	20.5	9.9	443	24.9	8.8	15 539	4.5	1 518	9.8	11 302	26.7	16.5
Marion	101 641	62.9	132 600	23.5	10.1	574	25.9	8.1	151 111	1.9	11 938	7.9	126 682	29.1	15.4

1. Specified owner-occupied units. 2. Median monthly owner costs is often in the minimum category—9.9 percent or less, which is indicated as 9.9 percent. 3. Specified renter-occupied units. 4. Overcrowded or lacking complete plumbing facilities. 5. Percent of civilian labor force. 6. Persons 16 years old and over.

STATE County	Private nonfarm establishments, employment and payroll, 2001								Agriculture, 2002			
	Number of establish-ments	Employment					Annual payroll		Farms			Farm operators whose principal occu-pation is farming (percent)
		Total	Health care and social assistance	Manufac-turing	Retail trade	Finance and insurance	Professional, scientific, and technical services	Total (mil dol)	Average per employee (dollars)	Number	Percent with—		
											Less than 50 acres	500 acres and over	
	104	105	106	107	108	109	110	111	112	113	114	115	116
OKLAHOMA—Cont'd													
Kiowa	232	2 199	865	D	296	96	47	40	18 247	662	11.9	43.4	68.3
Latimer	159	1 558	396	D	204	59	27	32	20 469	738	24.8	10.8	51.1
Le Flore	739	7 838	1 685	882	2 094	350	329	155	19 836	1 927	31.8	8.8	54.2
Lincoln	524	4 901	623	513	795	657	113	100	20 346	2 218	23.3	9.3	49.5
Logan	547	4 916	1 185	309	824	168	178	88	17 830	1 205	24.9	14.4	54.1
Love	137	1 454	135	448	222	37	38	30	20 326	725	23.4	17.0	51.4
McClain	602	4 547	552	305	1 028	259	142	89	19 558	1 273	36.1	12.5	51.7
McCurtain	595	8 169	1 172	2 907	1 110	227	377	184	22 467	1 855	30.8	7.5	56.2
McIntosh	399	3 111	690	359	790	132	119	56	18 014	944	21.1	11.7	57.7
Major	219	1 678	333	202	329	79	39	36	21 210	879	13.7	31.7	60.1
Marshall	260	3 440	346	1 482	488	150	46	74	21 390	477	26.2	11.9	53.5
Mayes	753	9 561	970	3 032	1 485	252	232	238	24 863	1 552	31.8	8.2	58.0
Murray	268	2 470	298	D	602	103	84	46	18 640	525	22.3	17.7	55.8
Muskogee	1 615	24 444	5 433	5 193	3 481	616	622	597	24 428	1 740	32.6	7.7	53.3
Noble	209	3 693	477	D	383	132	76	95	25 667	776	13.3	26.9	61.9
Nowata	166	1 348	265	273	166	73	40	27	20 085	887	21.2	16.0	56.3
Okfuskee	160	1 935	624	291	224	60	D	36	18 363	901	18.5	15.3	54.6
Oklahoma	21 258	345 801	48 797	37 313	43 230	18 391	18 810	9 818	28 391	1 268	52.1	5.3	43.0
Okmulgee	674	6 878	1 614	1 235	1 318	297	171	154	22 413	1 268	26.3	9.0	50.5
Osage	540	4 117	647	635	695	151	118	84	20 458	1 420	26.1	23.6	53.7
Ottawa	698	7 619	1 599	1 763	1 320	290	143	151	19 852	1 137	32.9	7.4	53.0
Pawnee	300	2 792	483	253	505	154	72	62	22 060	826	23.2	18.0	51.5
Payne	1 582	19 791	2 868	2 670	3 597	688	898	434	21 941	1 445	30.4	10.9	45.4
Pittsburg	910	10 215	2 427	831	2 069	419	202	211	20 637	1 687	26.3	13.8	57.3
Pontotoc	911	12 166	2 460	2 057	1 915	1 015	693	247	20 309	1 368	25.4	11.6	50.4
Pottawatomie	1 351	18 615	3 262	3 591	2 983	526	344	381	20 465	1 663	28.0	7.5	50.8
Pushmataha	187	1 722	597	192	337	42	34	30	17 617	780	19.5	15.9	55.1
Roger Mills	75	534	96	D	145	D	D	9	17 013	677	7.2	47.6	61.2
Rogers	1 310	16 654	1 997	5 266	2 285	554	314	454	27 232	1 803	45.7	6.3	49.0
Seminole	508	6 224	979	1 637	830	183	103	119	19 074	1 167	23.5	10.9	50.1
Sequoyah	609	6 295	1 456	474	1 486	264	157	111	17 712	1 259	32.4	7.5	53.9
Stephens	1 027	13 492	1 814	2 427	2 217	720	292	342	25 365	1 359	23.5	14.8	50.7
Texas	515	6 847	644	2 466	857	261	119	169	24 661	1 002	7.5	44.7	58.1
Tillman	173	1 528	300	D	216	91	D	31	20 009	592	9.1	38.7	66.7
Tulsa	18 260	328 130	37 156	40 210	37 570	16 691	17 755	10 952	33 377	1 146	54.5	5.4	47.6
Wagoner	768	6 474	547	1 484	1 027	219	208	138	21 338	1 217	40.7	8.2	48.3
Washington	1 204	16 744	2 312	1 694	2 738	607	1 077	651	38 906	847	39.2	10.2	50.4
Washita	247	1 668	345	121	333	101	42	30	18 221	1 006	13.3	34.3	65.3
Woods	286	2 230	380	D	507	190	52	39	17 522	761	9.6	41.5	63.2
Woodward	682	7 564	1 094	534	1 231	586	149	174	23 040	842	13.2	34.6	54.8
OREGON	101 003	1 364 924	162 009	197 897	194 479	60 654	69 510	44 082	32 296	40 033	62.5	10.2	53.9
Baker	540	3 856	557	648	871	181	121	81	21 004	703	34.7	27.0	63.7
Benton	1 936	28 257	3 767	7 681	3 132	556	1 618	949	33 568	912	71.2	5.5	49.9
Clackamas	9 669	117 234	11 966	17 198	17 654	4 232	5 148	3 768	32 143	4 676	82.2	1.3	48.6
Clatsop	1 395	11 398	1 569	808	2 396	257	268	246	21 541	248	55.2	2.4	46.0
Columbia	831	9 011	926	2 717	1 380	233	250	267	29 598	878	72.2	1.6	46.4
Coos	1 699	18 033	3 464	1 657	3 100	542	486	425	23 564	748	47.7	6.4	58.2
Crook	433	4 967	405	1 405	521	90	75	132	26 654	685	56.1	19.9	52.1
Curry	696	5 153	606	716	1 152	159	132	112	21 798	207	43.5	18.4	62.3
Deschutes	4 692	44 117	5 377	4 932	8 621	1 533	2 096	1 148	26 016	1 632	78.6	2.8	48.3
Douglas	2 686	30 107	4 303	6 260	4 787	707	754	775	25 735	2 110	53.7	7.5	56.2
Gilliam	62	626	79	D	88	D	D	14	22 316	156	5.8	73.1	69.9
Grant	273	1 543	239	186	262	58	54	35	22 640	394	26.1	39.1	59.1
Harney	196	1 522	217	D	326	44	D	35	22 841	524	22.3	43.7	64.1
Hood River	790	7 360	1 025	954	1 202	92	275	159	21 554	562	70.5	0.5	58.0
Jackson	5 442	62 806	9 306	7 033	11 089	1 809	1 817	1 653	26 314	1 953	70.3	3.6	53.0
Jefferson	287	4 129	314	1 795	746	79	65	107	25 804	428	34.1	24.3	59.6
Josephine	1 954	18 254	3 025	3 212	3 630	591	459	425	23 277	728	78.4	1.0	63.3
Klamath	1 600	17 020	2 588	2 654	3 124	640	1 000	448	26 333	1 228	42.8	19.5	57.2
Lake	209	1 276	241	231	255	34	31	27	20 997	462	19.0	40.0	68.6
Lane	9 561	117 509	16 453	20 005	19 102	4 106	6 117	3 220	27 399	2 577	71.8	3.6	49.9
Lincoln	1 630	13 406	1 650	930	2 840	323	277	298	22 247	374	64.2	3.5	52.9
Linn	2 550	33 707	3 618	8 572	5 084	917	997	954	28 316	2 346	63.8	7.7	56.3
Malheur	750	8 656	1 150	1 375	2 122	236	221	188	21 672	1 272	34.7	21.1	69.3
Marion	7 495	94 980	15 780	10 789	15 300	6 034	3 132	2 559	26 946	3 203	72.0	4.3	53.3

STATE County	Land in farms — Acreage (1,000) [117]	Percent change, 1997–2002 [118]	Acres — Average size of farm [119]	Acres — Total irrigated (1,000) [120]	Acres — Total cropland (1,000) [121]	Value of land and buildings (dollars) — Average per farm [122]	Average per acre [123]	Value of machinery and equipment average per farm (dollars) [124]	Value of products sold — Total (mil dol) [125]	Average per farm (dollars) [126]	Percent from — Crops [127]	Percent from — Livestock and poultry products [128]	Percent of farms with sales of — $10,000 or more [129]	$100,000 or more [130]	Government payments — Total ($1,000) [131]	Percent of farms [132]
OKLAHOMA—Cont'd																
Kiowa	580	-2.5	877	3	341	447 393	503	81 882	50	75 496	42.3	57.7	66.5	19.3	4 808	63.6
Latimer	206	2.0	279	1	60	179 508	640	33 290	14	19 063	3.0	97.0	26.4	3.4	241	13.4
Le Flore	411	1.0	213	8	185	255 559	1 220	32 624	169	87 790	5.1	94.9	36.3	14.8	660	15.6
Lincoln	472	9.5	213	0	194	191 380	872	26 071	25	11 385	14.0	86.0	25.7	1.5	731	17.3
Logan	366	-3.9	303	1	179	273 479	975	32 628	41	34 408	24.0	76.0	36.8	5.2	1 256	32.6
Love	244	-8.3	337	2	94	255 698	794	33 164	17	22 883	16.6	83.4	34.5	4.3	556	21.5
McClain	307	14.6	241	1	133	278 074	1 149	41 339	35	27 379	26.8	73.2	32.9	5.1	885	21.0
McCurtain	358	9.1	193	1	146	184 860	954	29 275	149	80 410	3.0	97.0	37.3	15.3	690	6.4
McIntosh	266	4.7	282	0	106	225 400	773	29 110	18	18 601	12.1	87.9	38.2	3.4	679	21.4
Major	509	3.7	579	8	255	334 736	558	56 708	72	82 398	14.1	85.9	49.9	11.1	3 148	49.8
Marshall	164	0.0	344	1	46	300 303	674	35 187	12	24 631	33.7	66.3	35.2	5.5	331	19.7
Mayes	302	6.3	195	1	151	254 562	1 243	35 960	45	29 228	9.4	90.6	34.3	7.1	819	17.5
Murray	202	-0.5	385	D	54	274 648	693	34 520	20	38 884	4.4	95.6	36.4	5.1	457	22.7
Muskogee	352	5.7	202	5	171	194 000	905	31 818	36	20 794	30.9	69.1	32.4	3.4	925	17.8
Noble	395	-4.4	509	0	206	369 974	718	49 057	35	44 526	38.5	61.5	51.4	11.6	2 208	48.2
Nowata	311	0.6	351	1	95	279 698	761	26 793	29	32 893	6.5	93.5	36.6	4.7	424	22.1
Okfuskee	290	2.8	322	1	96	216 469	771	25 058	24	26 335	6.8	93.2	31.6	4.7	435	19.5
Oklahoma	172	7.5	136	2	85	218 709	1 927	27 191	21	16 859	57.7	42.3	22.9	3.7	517	13.8
Okmulgee	289	-4.3	228	0	114	209 622	906	30 462	15	11 520	19.4	80.6	24.7	1.6	601	18.8
Osage	1 186	-1.7	835	0	170	436 004	542	32 903	63	44 049	6.9	93.1	35.8	6.8	1 159	17.0
Ottawa	226	5.1	199	1	125	255 217	1 267	34 172	71	62 727	40.3	59.7	34.0	7.5	663	21.6
Pawnee	281	6.8	340	0	81	196 517	595	28 971	25	29 807	9.4	90.6	34.0	4.8	578	27.2
Payne	341	0.6	236	1	136	238 676	1 005	25 234	29	19 906	11.5	88.5	27.4	2.8	1 013	23.5
Pittsburg	505	2.9	299	1	160	215 913	756	23 726	30	17 724	15.4	84.6	33.1	3.0	564	16.6
Pontotoc	368	9.9	269	1	142	232 059	808	25 016	26	19 014	8.1	91.9	28.3	2.9	448	16.7
Pottawatomie	343	2.1	206	1	145	209 333	991	25 494	22	13 134	21.5	78.5	23.3	1.9	506	15.6
Pushmataha	310	21.1	397	1	88	216 870	555	33 906	10	12 225	9.5	90.5	29.0	1.4	211	14.7
Roger Mills	739	6.9	1 091	5	182	457 260	390	48 263	27	40 316	8.5	91.5	54.2	9.0	2 282	55.2
Rogers	310	-1.0	172	1	132	251 616	1 405	25 542	26	14 397	17.6	82.4	21.9	2.6	549	12.4
Seminole	279	0.4	239	1	117	173 897	742	23 644	18	15 838	13.4	86.6	24.8	2.6	337	19.1
Sequoyah	222	-24.2	177	2	103	186 643	1 286	32 755	25	20 026	19.0	81.0	28.4	3.0	256	11.2
Stephens	420	-1.6	309	1	160	197 625	676	35 577	34	25 006	9.7	90.3	31.3	5.2	1 162	27.2
Texas	1 181	8.6	1 179	162	698	605 676	519	133 712	663	661 186	8.1	91.9	42.6	18.0	10 600	72.1
Tillman	485	4.1	818	9	332	481 095	547	78 319	53	90 319	43.0	57.0	58.1	18.2	4 034	62.3
Tulsa	151	5.6	132	5	86	307 208	2 122	25 803	23	20 447	73.4	26.6	21.4	3.2	203	10.0
Wagoner	260	7.9	214	5	132	306 061	1 344	32 481	35	29 105	64.4	35.6	28.8	5.0	958	19.7
Washington	223	-6.3	263	1	75	256 022	1 030	23 972	20	23 289	20.8	79.2	28.5	3.9	468	20.2
Washita	568	-3.1	565	6	361	328 640	590	72 088	69	68 997	29.3	70.7	59.3	15.6	5 365	55.9
Woods	816	1.4	1 073	2	316	521 764	486	76 646	56	72 997	16.1	83.9	53.0	12.7	4 246	63.6
Woodward	726	0.6	863	5	206	390 806	455	47 262	67	79 885	5.5	94.5	45.7	8.6	2 708	51.7
OREGON	17 080	-2.1	427	1 908	5 417	508 882	1 202	63 462	3 195	79 822	68.7	31.3	30.9	10.5	52 085	11.1
Baker	870	-13.7	1 237	127	147	662 738	546	63 215	47	67 453	23.9	76.1	48.6	15.9	834	24.3
Benton	130	-0.8	143	21	93	507 363	3 854	62 936	85	92 746	87.7	12.3	25.7	8.7	285	5.6
Clackamas	215	19.4	46	27	121	418 469	9 600	44 015	332	71 002	82.3	17.7	26.4	6.6	299	2.1
Clatsop	22	-4.3	90	1	10	285 734	2 776	35 520	7	29 745	18.3	81.7	18.1	6.5	119	2.4
Columbia	62	-6.1	71	3	26	376 831	3 813	34 404	29	32 757	82.5	17.5	13.2	2.4	119	2.7
Coos	144	-11.7	193	11	38	376 831	3 364	37 710	22	29 357	38.0	62.0	33.7	7.5	367	5.3
Crook	938	2.4	1 369	78	86	699 605	531	59 914	33	47 990	30.8	69.2	30.8	10.1	172	6.4
Curry	70	-17.6	340	3	11	790 974	1 949	51 513	12	56 679	66.2	33.8	37.7	12.6	171	5.3
Deschutes	138	11.3	85	44	50	423 461	5 172	23 540	21	12 857	42.7	57.3	18.0	2.5	91	1.7
Douglas	390	-3.0	185	16	108	346 175	2 060	36 772	37	17 615	36.5	63.5	19.7	3.1	192	4.7
Gilliam	643	-13.5	4 122	7	295	1 288 176	305	167 689	17	111 348	70.2	29.8	56.4	30.1	4 138	80.8
Grant	892	-17.5	2 265	42	108	776 913	306	64 512	17	43 335	17.9	82.1	35.8	9.6	1 002	23.9
Harney	1 575	15.9	3 006	133	207	815 042	289	69 141	36	67 846	20.6	79.4	45.4	17.4	1 002	23.9
Hood River	29	3.6	52	20	21	521 070	9 364	49 621	60	106 047	97.4	2.6	53.4	27.8	203	7.5
Jackson	252	2.4	129	50	68	428 469	2 824	43 963	54	27 748	69.8	30.2	18.5	2.9	278	5.9
Jefferson	701	-10.5	1 639	57	96	830 129	561	123 348	41	95 292	84.4	15.6	48.4	21.3	980	36.0
Josephine	32	-8.6	44	9	16	211 540	4 153	28 095	13	17 867	49.2	50.8	17.9	2.7	257	4.3
Klamath	703	-1.5	572	242	233	527 619	1 012	97 123	105	85 567	56.9	43.1	42.7	15.5	2 031	16.9
Lake	748	1.5	1 619	194	231	773 588	487	136 503	57	123 350	47.3	52.7	58.0	28.4	274	11.5
Lane	235	4.9	91	22	132	363 136	4 572	38 602	88	34 080	66.7	33.3	21.6	5.0	674	3.5
Lincoln	33	3.1	88	1	9	318 161	2 607	23 618	6	16 874	53.5	46.5	18.2	2.7	D	D
Linn	386	-1.8	164	31	288	516 273	2 849	65 318	152	64 713	72.7	27.3	27.2	10.3	1 006	6.0
Malheur	1 175	-6.5	924	223	269	550 305	537	106 943	232	182 134	47.9	52.1	58.5	26.1	1 872	24.7
Marion	341	11.4	106	100	251	510 810	5 107	87 306	431	134 457	84.6	15.4	35.3	14.8	908	6.2

Items 117—132

Table B. States and Counties — Residential Construction, Wholesale Trade, Retail Trade, and Real Estate

STATE County	Value of residential construction authorized by building permits, 2003		Wholesale trade, 1997				Retail trade,[1] 1997				Real estate and rental and leasing, 1997			
	New construction ($1,000)	Number of housing units	Number of establishments	Number of employees	Sales (mil dol)	Annual payroll (mil dol)	Number of establishments	Number of employees	Sales (mil dol)	Annual payroll (mil dol)	Number of establishments	Number of employees	Receipts (mil dol)	Annual payroll (mil dol)
	133	134	135	136	137	138	139	140	141	142	143	144	145	146
OKLAHOMA—Cont'd														
Kiowa	270	3	18	123	44.7	2.4	56	353	37.5	3.3	8	13	1.6	0.3
Latimer	0	0	6	D	D	D	31	237	26.1	2.9	4	29	2.5	0.8
Le Flore	5 427	70	27	120	42.4	2.3	162	1 578	247.2	20.0	25	55	3.6	0.5
Lincoln	4 080	41	21	D	D	D	154	1 011	136.3	12.6	11	13	0.7	0.1
Logan	1 876	17	18	D	D	D	96	816	133.3	10.5	21	37	3.4	0.5
Love	1 200	24	6	79	28.7	1.9	35	290	51.7	3.5	1	D	D	D
McClain	21 127	192	19	D	D	D	96	940	192.0	14.6	13	27	2.2	0.5
McCurtain	3 157	47	30	239	69.8	4.8	138	1 119	167.2	15.1	11	46	2.1	0.5
McIntosh	3 695	51	10	17	6.7	0.3	94	650	140.1	9.2	11	22	1.4	0.2
Major	1 138	7	17	151	69.4	2.3	48	323	59.6	4.1	3	7	0.6	0.1
Marshall	342	4	12	124	48.7	3.5	56	416	56.6	5.3	11	26	1.0	0.2
Mayes	2 620	25	36	216	71.5	5.2	135	1 313	191.8	16.5	15	69	3.4	0.5
Murray	2 143	23	10	73	25.5	1.1	49	492	93.1	7.3	3	17	1.2	0.2
Muskogee	18 782	156	91	1 185	313.2	30.4	349	3 613	561.7	52.8	56	218	16.7	3.3
Noble	175	1	9	50	17.2	0.9	57	478	72.3	6.4	10	22	2.1	0.2
Nowata	320	8	9	107	28.4	1.6	33	180	27.3	2.1	7	22	1.6	0.6
Okfuskee	1 221	21	2	D	D	D	33	235	37.5	2.7	3	6	0.5	0.1
Oklahoma	753 000	5 625	1 517	21 108	15 144.3	638.9	3 098	41 034	7 479.8	681.3	913	5 379	612.2	107.7
Okmulgee	1 458	23	30	150	42.7	3.2	142	1 324	207.3	17.8	14	36	2.0	0.4
Osage	9 447	127	23	147	29.5	3.2	112	748	95.8	8.8	13	35	1.9	0.4
Ottawa	2 128	37	30	D	D	D	138	1 136	180.8	15.2	23	67	5.9	0.7
Pawnee	13	1	9	D	D	D	55	484	69.9	6.2	10	17	0.8	0.2
Payne	28 407	194	62	664	211.2	13.1	299	3 336	466.1	43.4	70	278	16.2	3.3
Pittsburg	6 547	59	51	333	114.2	8.2	185	2 059	326.3	26.7	39	150	8.3	1.9
Pontotoc	2 232	33	53	492	257.6	10.4	180	1 859	266.9	23.5	27	73	7.2	1.2
Pottawatomie	13 872	178	44	D	D	D	276	2 847	397.8	37.0	55	200	18.5	2.5
Pushmataha	316	3	10	130	11.1	1.4	56	294	42.0	3.3	5	3	0.4	0.0
Roger Mills	170	1	3	6	4.6	0.1	22	110	14.8	1.4	1	D	D	D
Rogers	55 547	473	65	518	357.8	16.7	192	1 994	353.2	28.6	38	243	15.8	3.2
Seminole	4 194	72	28	169	53.8	4.6	104	813	116.1	10.6	17	73	4.2	0.7
Sequoyah	9 965	112	15	110	47.6	1.4	159	1 387	218.9	17.0	16	44	2.1	0.5
Stephens	8 260	64	53	441	90.6	10.0	221	2 074	314.1	27.7	29	115	11.3	2.5
Texas	1 998	15	40	D	D	D	99	936	130.2	11.6	21	57	3.9	0.6
Tillman	0	0	13	155	33.4	3.0	43	346	31.4	2.6	2	D	D	D
Tulsa	418 889	2 997	1 438	18 675	9 427.0	658.2	2 440	35 520	6 410.4	590.8	802	4 358	506.2	92.5
Wagoner	65 085	613	34	209	98.3	4.3	109	971	149.2	12.0	33	113	10.1	2.0
Washington	16 490	96	34	284	52.0	7.1	216	2 613	425.8	38.7	42	161	10.2	2.5
Washita	0	0	16	118	33.2	2.0	51	310	46.2	3.8	12	46	2.0	0.5
Woods	543	16	21	170	48.0	3.2	58	533	65.4	6.8	8	10	0.6	0.2
Woodward	1 690	13	50	342	68.9	6.7	128	1 074	179.2	15.3	22	107	10.6	2.6
OREGON	3 770 948	25 015	5 943	74 790	53 679.1	2 578.7	14 467	178 349	33 396.8	3 308.8	4 556	23 058	2 704.0	470.9
Baker	7 292	39	19	90	13.2	2.0	93	805	121.3	11.7	23	55	5.0	0.6
Benton	65 414	439	63	681	112.6	15.9	294	3 175	473.9	53.2	111	379	38.9	5.5
Clackamas	405 455	1 722	685	8 723	6 383.3	314.7	1 092	16 098	3 448.3	312.3	422	2 231	240.5	44.9
Clatsop	36 140	218	39	383	88.4	7.0	274	2 173	332.4	36.8	57	181	14.3	2.1
Columbia	45 803	293	26	161	61.5	4.4	137	1 360	199.8	22.1	28	83	7.6	1.2
Coos	6 450	45	60	496	233.2	14.6	289	3 040	505.2	52.1	64	208	18.5	3.4
Crook	31 653	224	16	72	21.5	1.5	57	494	89.3	8.4	14	24	3.6	0.4
Curry	34 113	180	20	62	14.2	1.1	121	1 041	148.4	16.8	31	76	8.3	1.4
Deschutes	485 150	3 145	191	1 303	571.0	39.7	687	7 130	1 297.1	128.7	198	1 028	140.5	16.9
Douglas	55 401	348	84	1 152	404.1	27.0	457	4 416	669.0	71.2	126	391	34.9	5.1
Gilliam	0	0	3	D	D	D	13	72	8.7	1.1	NA	NA	NA	NA
Grant	NA	NA	4	28	5.9	0.8	45	316	42.4	4.4	7	7	0.6	0.1
Harney	1 066	10	6	31	9.7	0.7	41	299	51.5	5.4	7	15	1.1	0.2
Hood River	23 689	166	27	181	92.2	9.9	129	1 286	170.3	19.8	23	72	7.2	0.8
Jackson	275 725	2 138	284	2 678	1 022.7	69.8	835	9 564	2 075.3	172.2	248	1 003	95.9	15.2
Jefferson	14 563	111	18	221	78.0	5.3	57	647	109.9	11.4	17	34	2.8	0.4
Josephine	97 455	624	59	441	175.6	9.2	326	3 322	590.3	57.9	71	313	20.6	3.6
Klamath	57 398	305	66	954	293.1	22.1	290	3 116	544.8	55.5	67	200	20.7	2.8
Lake	1 836	15	7	D	D	D	48	266	39.4	4.3	9	D	D	D
Lane	254 145	1 534	535	6 144	2 498.6	179.6	1 462	18 145	3 322.6	328.3	463	2 042	226.5	35.0
Lincoln	40 779	254	39	296	72.5	7.0	372	2 794	415.2	43.8	77	183	22.7	2.6
Linn	90 582	677	131	1 534	766.0	44.5	391	4 662	800.9	78.7	97	361	31.5	5.2
Malheur	9 789	47	50	951	171.0	18.0	163	1 903	302.9	30.7	26	68	6.0	1.0
Marion	233 229	1 588	326	3 247	1 184.0	91.9	1 081	14 637	2 672.5	266.3	380	1 748	194.5	36.3

1. Establishments with payroll.

STATE County	Professional, scientific, and technical services,[1] 1997				Manufacturing, 1997				Accommodation and foodservices, 1997			
	Number of establishments	Number of employees	Receipts (mil dol)	Annual payroll (mil dol)	Number of establishments	Number of employees	Receipts (mil dol)	Annual payroll (mil dol)	Number of establishments	Number of employees	Sales (mil dol)	Annual payroll (mil dol)
	147	148	149	150	151	152	153	154	155	156	157	158
OKLAHOMA—Cont'd												
Kiowa	14	41	1.6	0.4	NA	NA	NA	NA	15	D	D	D
Latimer	5	14	0.5	0.1	NA	NA	NA	NA	14	107	2.8	0.8
Le Flore	48	314	13.4	6.8	32	1 104	137.0	24.4	55	616	18.2	4.7
Lincoln	35	123	5.5	1.5	21	737	132.0	14.1	46	570	12.4	3.3
Logan	30	101	7.4	2.6	NA	NA	NA	NA	43	D	D	D
Love	7	21	0.7	0.2	19	D	D	D	17	157	5.3	1.3
McClain	34	81	3.8	1.3	19	D	D	D	38	D	D	D
McCurtain	29	388	10.7	6.0	25	2 758	794.7	79.6	51	537	14.9	3.7
McIntosh	19	84	4.5	1.7	NA	NA	NA	NA	46	439	12.6	3.4
Major	9	20	1.5	0.3	NA	NA	NA	NA	16	D	D	D
Marshall	15	43	2.1	0.6	20	1 196	130.5	24.3	27	222	7.3	1.8
Mayes	30	97	5.8	2.7	68	3 357	731.5	102.4	72	755	19.7	5.0
Murray	18	64	4.5	1.1	NA	NA	NA	NA	24	266	8.4	2.3
Muskogee	72	363	25.4	8.1	87	4 780	990.3	155.3	135	2 097	58.8	15.2
Noble	12	22	1.7	0.6	13	D	D	D	20	316	7.2	2.0
Nowata	11	20	1.2	0.3	NA	NA	NA	NA	12	139	3.1	0.9
Okfuskee	7	17	1.1	0.3	NA	NA	NA	NA	12	96	2.9	0.7
Oklahoma	2 262	14 060	1 266.2	502.1	851	39 462	9 922.1	1 281.5	1 493	29 780	918.6	255.9
Okmulgee	30	114	5.8	2.2	35	1 120	295.4	38.5	59	664	20.7	5.5
Osage	34	116	4.1	1.1	21	939	137.1	31.2	42	389	9.5	2.5
Ottawa	35	104	5.5	1.9	67	1 819	276.4	41.4	59	676	18.1	5.1
Pawnee	22	74	22.7	2.0	NA	NA	NA	NA	28	199	5.7	1.4
Payne	116	694	59.3	20.6	60	2 584	846.8	76.5	149	2 867	66.5	18.3
Pittsburg	61	203	14.1	4.0	27	875	217.1	20.7	75	1 275	37.3	10.2
Pontotoc	61	293	20.1	7.3	47	1 743	209.7	36.6	59	1 151	29.3	8.2
Pottawatomie	72	288	22.2	6.5	72	3 673	654.9	119.7	135	2 726	76.3	21.1
Pushmataha	14	36	2.6	0.6	NA	NA	NA	NA	17	96	3.3	0.8
Roger Mills	4	D	D	D	NA	NA	NA	NA	9	57	1.3	0.3
Rogers	67	237	16.8	6.3	122	4 562	822.9	147.4	89	1 324	38.0	10.0
Seminole	26	77	4.0	1.2	30	1 689	252.3	33.4	33	413	11.7	2.9
Sequoyah	31	93	7.5	2.4	NA	NA	NA	NA	74	900	24.0	6.3
Stephens	56	216	15.3	4.6	58	1 941	470.4	49.8	85	1 159	30.9	8.3
Texas	25	112	6.5	2.7	13	D	D	D	55	617	16.7	4.4
Tillman	13	38	1.8	0.7	NA	NA	NA	NA	14	D	D	D
Tulsa	1 953	13 985	1 437.7	533.5	1 136	39 402	7 858.1	1 310.7	1 316	23 663	771.3	207.7
Wagoner	45	104	11.5	2.5	66	1 924	432.7	50.8	60	786	23.1	5.1
Washington	76	827	76.2	24.4	48	1 327	183.8	50.0	92	1 595	51.6	14.0
Washita	16	51	2.7	0.8	NA	NA	NA	NA	9	37	0.9	0.1
Woods	21	45	2.9	0.5	NA	NA	NA	NA	23	317	6.3	1.8
Woodward	36	116	6.8	2.1	30	591	260.5	21.5	46	613	18.3	4.6
OREGON	8 117	52 514	4 734.6	1 925.0	5 768	213 111	47 666.0	7 095.3	8 363	124 425	4 385.7	1 236.6
Baker	27	105	7.4	2.4	NA	NA	NA	NA	62	540	19.0	4.7
Benton	210	1 367	116.7	50.1	106	8 547	1 391.9	494.5	205	2 807	85.9	24.0
Clackamas	745	3 526	348.4	129.8	589	18 655	3 667.4	632.2	571	10 002	331.1	94.6
Clatsop	60	212	12.6	4.0	49	858	142.4	21.2	200	2 250	89.4	25.5
Columbia	36	208	10.2	3.6	57	3 079	1 008.5	128.4	75	782	24.3	7.2
Coos	96	377	26.8	9.2	104	1 937	391.2	57.6	186	2 004	61.4	17.0
Crook	18	62	3.7	1.3	21	1 506	225.3	39.4	34	383	12.7	3.4
Curry	38	94	6.1	2.0	32	727	116.2	26.2	112	785	30.5	8.1
Deschutes	295	1 206	105.1	37.4	202	4 884	698.6	129.5	305	4 722	194.2	55.6
Douglas	140	550	30.9	13.2	157	7 141	1 494.7	226.4	274	3 635	138.1	37.9
Gilliam	4	D	D	D	NA	NA	NA	NA	8	67	1.7	0.4
Grant	16	49	2.4	1.1	NA	NA	NA	NA	32	179	5.8	1.4
Harney	7	25	1.7	0.5	NA	NA	NA	NA	25	170	5.2	1.5
Hood River	53	180	12.4	5.2	58	1 128	157.5	27.2	76	1 107	36.2	10.8
Jackson	341	1 917	99.5	35.4	301	7 428	1 424.0	201.7	474	6 253	205.3	60.3
Jefferson	12	35	3.0	0.7	21	1 793	351.3	52.2	31	371	11.9	3.2
Josephine	106	280	17.0	5.2	117	2 812	439.6	76.8	168	1 928	66.9	18.0
Klamath	88	775	35.2	13.7	72	3 013	562.6	86.1	156	1 899	73.1	17.2
Lake	7	20	1.2	0.4	NA	NA	NA	NA	26	196	6.1	1.5
Lane	797	4 682	374.3	138.8	624	19 262	3 881.8	589.8	809	12 022	387.8	110.5
Lincoln	74	297	21.2	7.0	59	1 060	255.2	34.4	274	3 644	134.7	37.8
Linn	142	861	48.9	21.5	184	9 794	1 918.8	347.8	183	2 400	73.1	20.3
Malheur	38	171	10.4	3.5	28	D	D	D	73	947	33.3	9.1
Marion	519	2 708	210.3	82.7	402	12 651	2 232.8	354.4	529	8 872	281.6	78.1

1. Firms subject to federal tax.

Table B. States and Counties — Health Care and Social Assistance, Other Services, and Federal Funds

STATE County	Health care and social assistance,[1] 1997				Other services,[1] 1997				Federal funds and grants, 2002–2003 Expenditures (mil dol)			
										Direct payments for individuals[2]		
	Number of establishments	Number of employees	Receipts (mil dol)	Annual payroll (mil dol)	Number of establishments	Number of employees	Receipts (mil dol)	Annual payroll (mil dol)	Total	Social Security and government retirement	Medicare	Food stamps and Supplemental Security Income
	159	160	161	162	163	164	165	166	167	168	169	170
OKLAHOMA—Cont'd												
Kiowa	19	200	6.2	2.6	12	39	2.2	0.5	86.6	32.2	18.1	2.7
Latimer	24	426	12.5	7.6	9	26	1.3	0.3	64.8	25.6	13.2	2.6
Le Flore	63	1 000	32.2	16.2	39	117	9.9	1.9	310.2	125.7	59.6	15.6
Lincoln	36	510	14.3	6.0	15	56	2.4	0.9	165.0	86.8	26.9	5.7
Logan	40	1 045	22.9	11.2	28	99	5.5	1.7	176.3	64.8	27.4	4.6
Love	9	152	4.7	2.3	3	D	D	D	56.0	22.5	10.4	1.5
McClain	32	365	11.8	5.1	25	83	5.6	1.4	118.9	65.6	23.8	3.3
McCurtain	47	669	19.1	9.0	32	140	8.1	1.5	270.4	80.2	49.4	14.1
McIntosh	39	908	29.1	14.3	19	46	3.0	0.7	154.4	73.2	29.1	4.7
Major	6	28	1.5	0.5	3	D	D	D	43.1	20.0	8.6	0.6
Marshall	18	265	10.3	5.1	14	33	3.1	0.6	81.3	41.0	19.0	2.5
Mayes	48	462	15.9	6.4	39	117	7.3	1.7	185.4	93.5	37.0	8.3
Murray	22	341	11.2	5.2	13	33	2.3	0.4	78.9	36.1	16.3	2.8
Muskogee	175	2 633	111.4	49.5	76	399	24.2	7.3	570.2	203.8	86.0	21.0
Noble	17	327	9.5	4.6	9	12	1.3	0.3	68.2	27.1	12.2	2.0
Nowata	13	212	4.7	2.7	11	29	2.0	0.5	60.3	28.6	11.7	1.8
Okfuskee	17	435	10.5	4.5	3	11	0.5	0.1	88.7	35.0	16.4	3.8
Oklahoma	1 916	25 018	1 706.7	750.5	1 209	9 534	541.1	166.5	6 818.9	1 688.8	628.5	93.4
Okmulgee	63	921	33.0	15.5	37	108	7.3	1.5	276.6	99.2	50.8	12.8
Osage	41	471	14.9	7.1	21	44	2.5	0.5	189.4	65.0	26.5	5.6
Ottawa	57	695	22.7	11.7	34	118	7.1	1.9	259.4	97.8	51.4	9.6
Pawnee	23	262	8.9	4.2	16	35	2.8	0.6	95.0	41.8	18.9	2.6
Payne	113	1 283	60.8	28.2	92	441	19.6	5.6	394.2	122.5	54.4	8.5
Pittsburg	71	1 391	62.8	31.6	38	190	10.8	2.9	369.3	136.1	52.7	12.4
Pontotoc	82	1 037	48.4	22.0	57	325	18.3	5.7	273.7	94.2	44.1	10.5
Pottawatomie	105	1 694	74.2	32.8	65	272	15.7	4.1	386.5	180.8	53.7	15.5
Pushmataha	19	339	12.0	5.1	11	29	1.8	0.3	96.9	34.5	19.0	4.1
Roger Mills	3	D	D	D	3	D	D	D	23.6	8.7	5.5	0.5
Rogers	83	1 388	69.8	26.3	63	307	21.0	6.9	297.6	143.2	43.3	5.6
Seminole	33	792	22.9	10.8	21	43	3.9	0.7	190.5	70.4	35.5	10.5
Sequoyah	52	812	30.5	12.6	34	107	5.8	1.4	226.2	96.5	40.6	11.3
Stephens	83	979	44.1	19.4	56	214	12.4	2.8	272.5	132.4	51.4	8.3
Texas	34	192	13.4	4.2	32	103	6.5	1.3	93.5	30.2	16.7	1.8
Tillman	10	182	3.5	1.8	9	25	1.3	0.3	78.5	24.6	14.6	2.6
Tulsa	1 489	20 172	1 369.8	608.8	1 006	6 871	473.8	138.7	2 792.9	1 217.3	538.2	105.2
Wagoner	48	877	34.1	16.3	42	103	6.4	1.4	166.8	84.3	33.8	5.9
Washington	108	947	63.5	31.7	68	369	20.5	6.8	240.5	138.8	51.6	8.2
Washita	10	68	2.9	1.2	16	49	3.4	0.9	81.4	31.3	16.4	2.0
Woods	21	200	6.6	2.6	16	56	2.6	0.6	59.1	24.5	16.4	0.9
Woodward	41	357	16.1	6.4	34	134	10.0	2.3	99.9	41.9	18.1	3.0
OREGON	7 328	68 285	4 431.4	1 899.6	4 794	28 185	1 897.5	561.9	21 253.4	7 739.6	2 604.0	665.5
Baker	31	124	7.8	2.3	33	148	6.7	1.4	122.3	53.2	14.9	4.0
Benton	148	1 994	140.5	52.6	88	461	26.3	7.9	393.4	135.8	38.7	8.2
Clackamas	638	5 206	377.7	161.5	417	2 263	158.1	44.8	1 450.0	616.9	209.7	109.4
Clatsop	79	685	39.6	15.1	44	175	11.9	3.5	231.4	99.2	34.5	7.6
Columbia	59	340	20.0	8.6	33	119	6.3	1.8	190.7	96.9	34.0	5.0
Coos	156	1 328	85.3	30.9	79	298	23.2	5.9	424.4	211.0	65.5	20.7
Crook	36	202	9.3	3.1	14	49	3.2	0.9	107.2	53.7	16.4	3.0
Curry	45	237	11.9	3.8	28	65	4.3	0.8	170.0	96.7	31.0	4.5
Deschutes	253	2 073	147.7	57.1	159	904	56.1	18.4	532.1	305.4	73.2	15.0
Douglas	233	1 999	126.3	60.1	132	669	38.5	11.0	685.0	334.5	93.5	25.6
Gilliam	3	27	0.7	0.3	1	D	D	D	23.8	6.3	1.7	0.2
Grant	13	72	3.1	1.1	8	16	1.9	0.3	59.3	23.6	7.0	1.8
Harney	16	111	4.2	2.0	13	48	2.1	0.6	53.4	21.1	5.4	1.5
Hood River	55	367	18.2	7.0	24	160	6.5	1.6	110.1	40.4	12.6	2.7
Jackson	384	3 810	244.3	110.5	222	1 192	80.6	21.6	1 013.2	505.8	142.3	37.7
Jefferson	15	76	4.6	2.0	17	69	3.1	0.8	94.1	44.5	11.9	4.2
Josephine	164	1 555	81.9	30.7	94	369	23.7	5.6	494.6	262.5	73.4	26.9
Klamath	158	881	58.3	25.3	83	343	25.1	6.5	423.5	180.8	55.3	18.4
Lake	9	42	2.6	1.1	10	9	1.5	0.2	70.7	25.1	6.8	1.9
Lane	751	7 176	492.8	217.7	473	3 210	194.0	57.1	1 741.0	758.5	247.0	75.8
Lincoln	99	677	37.9	15.2	53	251	16.1	4.2	289.5	148.2	49.3	9.7
Linn	154	1 466	89.1	44.8	123	611	37.6	11.6	556.7	264.8	84.2	25.2
Malheur	70	381	23.5	8.3	52	188	13.6	3.4	152.8	64.3	21.1	8.6
Marion	629	5 965	354.9	156.3	373	2 003	116.9	37.4	2 054.2	729.3	208.1	62.2

1. Firms subject to federal tax. 2. State totals may include programs not allocated by county.

	Federal funds and grants, 2002–2003 (cont'd)							Local government finances, 2002				
	Expenditures (mil dol) (cont'd)							General revenue				
		Procurement contract awards		Grants[1]							Taxes	
												Per capita[2] (dollars)
STATE County	Salaries and wages	Defense	Other	Medicaid and other health-related	Nutrition and family welfare	Education	Other	Total (mil dol)	Intergovern-mental (mil dol)	Total (mil dol)	Total	Property
	171	172	173	174	175	176	177	178	179	180	181	182
OKLAHOMA—Cont'd												
Kiowa	3.7	0.1	0.6	14.3	2.1	1.1	4.4	25.3	15.2	7.1	718	547
Latimer	1.4	0.0	0.6	9.3	1.9	1.9	3.4	38.6	20.5	14.0	1 332	1 122
Le Flore	10.4	0.6	1.9	60.6	7.4	10.4	11.7	96.9	57.6	17.1	352	194
Lincoln	6.0	1.1	1.3	20.0	3.6	1.8	9.5	51.6	30.1	14.0	435	238
Logan	5.1	0.3	22.6	14.7	3.5	6.5	17.8	53.4	25.9	10.6	307	189
Love	1.4	0.2	0.3	8.3	0.8	0.7	7.4	14.4	9.2	3.3	374	225
McClain	4.1	0.0	1.0	11.2	1.8	2.1	3.2	63.5	28.4	26.0	920	673
McCurtain	7.7	0.2	1.6	69.3	7.9	21.0	14.7	71.7	50.9	13.5	395	247
McIntosh	2.7	1.3	0.8	26.5	2.9	2.7	9.9	41.8	29.0	8.5	429	181
Major	2.1	0.0	3.1	2.4	0.6	0.3	1.8	20.1	8.6	4.6	619	501
Marshall	1.8	0.0	0.3	10.8	1.3	2.9	0.4	28.2	19.4	5.8	431	232
Mayes	4.6	0.0	1.2	25.2	3.6	5.7	3.5	65.1	37.5	19.3	495	243
Murray	4.2	0.0	0.8	14.4	1.7	0.9	0.7	23.5	12.6	5.6	444	218
Muskogee	77.4	3.3	26.6	87.2	14.0	10.4	26.2	246.7	70.8	63.6	909	496
Noble	2.9	0.0	0.8	5.0	1.8	1.6	11.2	34.2	12.9	9.1	801	647
Nowata	2.2	1.4	0.4	8.5	1.0	1.4	2.3	18.3	12.4	3.6	332	222
Okfuskee	2.8	0.0	0.5	20.1	3.4	1.9	3.9	28.2	20.6	4.6	391	249
Oklahoma	1 679.5	740.4	619.8	420.9	236.2	193.8	450.3	1 758.4	585.6	696.4	1 036	459
Okmulgee	7.8	2.9	1.2	54.3	14.3	6.9	20.7	83.6	43.3	16.7	420	189
Osage	45.7	0.0	5.5	16.1	6.4	6.8	9.8	51.8	31.9	11.0	243	151
Ottawa	7.7	4.6	27.5	32.3	7.9	6.3	9.1	77.6	40.6	21.7	657	481
Pawnee	5.7	1.5	0.8	8.8	11.0	1.6	1.6	29.1	16.3	5.9	350	198
Payne	22.1	32.2	5.0	22.5	4.7	28.1	75.9	152.4	58.5	50.6	723	374
Pittsburg	52.1	39.0	11.8	44.9	6.0	7.4	5.0	126.9	49.1	33.4	760	249
Pontotoc	14.5	0.4	28.9	42.4	6.6	10.5	13.7	71.7	38.9	22.6	648	262
Pottawatomie	12.1	2.9	2.7	48.6	11.8	8.4	42.2	155.4	71.1	42.6	638	285
Pushmataha	2.2	0.1	0.4	22.2	2.2	2.0	9.5	24.4	18.3	3.4	293	150
Roger Mills	2.1	0.0	0.5	3.1	0.5	0.4	0.4	14.1	7.4	3.2	1 012	546
Rogers	22.9	0.4	1.9	20.7	8.8	7.2	38.2	122.6	63.0	39.9	528	368
Seminole	7.8	0.6	1.0	36.2	7.2	6.2	10.6	61.7	31.2	12.9	520	306
Sequoyah	8.9	6.7	1.2	48.6	5.8	5.9	-0.5	71.9	50.7	12.1	305	154
Stephens	6.7	1.8	1.6	25.4	5.5	2.9	33.0	80.9	42.4	26.3	617	349
Texas	3.8	0.0	-5.3	4.6	1.4	2.1	8.3	67.8	25.9	15.4	762	508
Tillman	2.5	-0.1	0.5	12.6	4.1	1.1	3.4	25.9	14.0	3.5	385	244
Tulsa	223.5	119.4	83.1	201.7	63.4	43.3	153.7	1 667.2	511.0	709.7	1 242	705
Wagoner	4.5	0.0	0.9	22.3	4.5	3.4	5.8	58.2	31.1	19.1	317	160
Washington	2.3	2.3	1.6	14.1	3.3	4.3	12.1	100.1	42.1	39.2	796	429
Washita	2.6	9.7	0.6	5.1	1.2	2.0	3.5	31.8	18.0	8.6	753	610
Woods	2.7	0.0	0.5	2.4	0.6	3.2	5.2	25.2	11.4	10.0	1 144	824
Woodward	6.2	0.4	8.7	5.3	1.5	1.3	10.4	47.6	22.2	16.5	896	442
OREGON	1 780.9	474.4	723.8	2 364.0	694.4	444.6	1 600.3	X	X	X	X	X
Baker	14.8	0.1	6.4	22.0	1.9	1.2	2.7	45.2	27.9	11.2	678	625
Benton	42.2	4.4	10.3	41.5	6.0	6.2	83.4	202.6	95.2	68.5	872	782
Clackamas	136.8	17.0	22.6	150.6	55.8	20.4	95.8	1 010.5	421.9	370.5	1 053	943
Clatsop	25.8	6.2	14.4	23.1	3.7	3.6	11.1	143.0	62.5	49.7	1 389	1 186
Columbia	5.3	17.1	1.4	17.2	5.8	2.4	4.0	126.7	62.3	39.8	879	801
Coos	32.7	1.7	9.0	44.2	11.7	5.7	17.1	292.8	113.0	49.5	789	666
Crook	15.3	0.0	4.1	9.0	1.7	1.0	2.7	74.0	40.7	22.2	1 111	949
Curry	7.4	0.9	9.7	9.3	2.2	1.4	6.2	63.1	27.4	21.1	989	872
Deschutes	43.9	7.5	15.6	31.6	9.2	6.4	19.0	391.2	160.7	152.3	1 215	1 010
Douglas	74.7	0.5	45.8	64.4	15.9	9.1	16.0	335.7	208.4	61.4	608	563
Gilliam	0.4	0.0	0.1	0.4	0.3	0.2	2.2	15.2	8.0	3.2	1 744	1 637
Grant	11.5	1.4	6.2	4.0	1.0	0.8	1.8	42.9	25.6	4.7	622	593
Harney	11.0	0.0	5.3	4.1	1.2	0.6	2.6	35.5	18.8	4.7	636	622
Hood River	6.2	15.2	4.4	10.2	5.5	2.1	8.8	73.2	46.4	14.7	708	605
Jackson	94.6	0.9	35.8	95.3	24.5	13.8	50.4	506.9	268.2	166.2	892	731
Jefferson	7.3	0.0	1.4	8.5	4.5	5.4	4.6	74.5	35.4	15.7	793	679
Josephine	19.1	2.4	14.9	54.8	11.0	5.3	16.3	241.6	162.9	47.5	613	505
Klamath	64.4	5.4	17.0	39.2	10.4	6.2	17.5	198.2	125.4	35.8	557	515
Lake	13.1	0.0	16.0	3.6	1.0	0.7	2.1	37.4	20.5	5.8	784	723
Lane	112.0	16.7	47.7	254.2	53.2	41.9	97.7	1 081.6	520.8	301.5	923	793
Lincoln	16.7	0.4	3.8	29.1	6.7	2.9	19.7	188.1	55.8	72.6	1 627	1 437
Linn	24.2	2.8	11.9	67.8	17.5	7.7	42.1	332.1	184.3	92.3	880	766
Malheur	11.6	0.0	3.9	20.6	5.9	3.6	6.6	115.7	71.4	20.3	648	556
Marion	91.3	2.8	23.7	235.0	174.7	158.5	343.3	980.9	531.8	257.5	878	779

1. State totals may include programs not allocated by county.   2. Based on the resident population estimated as of July 1 of the year shown.

Table B. States and Counties — Local Government Finances, Government Employment, and Elections

STATE County	Local government finances, 2002 (cont'd)									Government employment, 2002			Presidential election, 2004		
	Direct general expenditure							Debt outstanding					Percent of vote cast —		
	Total (mil dol)	Per capita[1] (dollars)	Education	Health and hospitals	Police protection	Public welfare	Highways	Total (mil dol)	Per capita[1] (dollars)	Federal civilian	Federal military	State and local	Democratic	Republican	All other
	183	184	185	186	187	188	189	190	191	192	193	194	195	196	197
OKLAHOMA—Cont'd															
Kiowa	24.8	2 494	55.2	1.9	4.2	0.1	18.0	4.7	477	61	37	1 010	35.1	64.9	0.0
Latimer	40.3	3 821	80.2	0.0	0.9	0.3	12.7	3.9	368	23	39	1 737	43.4	56.6	0.0
Le Flore	100.3	2 071	65.9	8.9	3.7	0.2	6.9	19.2	396	205	179	3 181	38.7	61.3	0.0
Lincoln	50.7	1 572	67.0	2.3	4.8	0.0	9.6	20.4	633	84	124	1 687	28.5	71.5	0.0
Logan	57.0	1 652	47.7	19.5	5.1	0.0	5.6	21.5	624	94	128	1 971	29.8	70.2	0.0
Love	13.8	1 553	75.7	0.0	3.6	0.0	7.6	3.8	422	32	33	707	40.1	59.9	0.0
McClain	58.8	2 082	63.9	1.0	9.9	0.0	6.3	26.2	926	70	105	1 384	27.2	72.8	0.0
McCurtain	71.6	2 095	73.6	2.1	2.6	0.6	4.9	18.3	534	164	127	2 272	33.0	67.0	0.0
McIntosh	42.7	2 165	54.8	0.7	4.1	0.1	24.5	13.1	664	37	73	1 035	48.9	51.1	0.0
Major	22.8	3 037	44.7	23.9	2.7	0.0	17.0	3.8	504	41	28	437	14.7	85.3	0.0
Marshall	27.7	2 042	57.9	2.1	2.2	0.0	16.7	5.5	409	30	50	724	38.3	61.7	0.0
Mayes	62.3	1 603	71.8	2.4	4.9	0.0	8.9	15.7	403	78	144	2 374	41.1	58.9	0.0
Murray	22.7	1 798	57.8	2.9	4.5	0.0	12.3	6.4	507	87	47	1 242	38.7	61.3	0.0
Muskogee	254.5	3 637	41.3	29.7	3.3	0.0	5.1	178.5	2 551	1 560	261	5 677	45.4	54.6	0.0
Noble	36.0	3 186	51.5	22.8	3.3	0.1	8.6	17.8	1 576	50	42	1 059	25.1	74.9	0.0
Nowata	18.3	1 700	78.8	0.0	2.5	0.0	8.3	6.6	612	39	40	492	37.2	62.8	0.0
Okfuskee	28.5	2 447	56.5	0.0	3.6	0.0	26.9	9.0	773	42	43	1 003	40.7	59.3	0.0
Oklahoma	1 832.3	2 725	42.1	1.1	8.2	0.1	6.2	1 838.8	2 734	24 723	10 029	50 720	35.8	64.2	0.0
Okmulgee	85.6	2 149	56.2	13.0	4.9	0.0	5.2	18.5	464	148	147	2 812	46.8	53.2	0.0
Osage	52.7	1 168	60.9	6.9	4.0	0.1	10.9	12.4	274	216	195	2 020	41.3	58.7	0.0
Ottawa	76.7	2 323	67.6	0.6	4.8	0.0	5.1	13.4	406	135	122	2 282	40.6	59.4	0.0
Pawnee	30.9	1 839	49.4	16.6	3.8	0.0	12.5	14.3	850	190	62	785	36.7	63.3	0.0
Payne	159.2	2 277	45.6	13.0	6.1	0.0	4.8	90.7	1 297	360	276	15 151	34.1	65.9	0.0
Pittsburg	133.6	3 037	40.4	35.3	2.5	0.1	4.8	89.9	2 042	1 424	170	3 379	40.1	59.9	0.0
Pontotoc	78.7	2 256	63.0	0.6	3.5	0.0	2.7	31.7	910	235	129	4 071	34.9	65.1	0.0
Pottawatomie	153.2	2 296	55.4	16.6	4.2	0.3	7.8	45.2	678	184	249	3 687	33.4	66.6	0.0
Pushmataha	23.5	2 010	73.8	1.6	2.9	0.0	12.5	1.7	141	46	43	939	40.3	59.7	0.0
Roger Mills	15.8	4 924	25.2	16.5	3.2	0.0	39.0	1.1	347	43	12	381	21.6	78.4	0.0
Rogers	131.0	1 734	60.7	1.0	4.0	0.0	8.1	54.0	715	401	280	4 008	32.3	67.7	0.0
Seminole	62.7	2 533	55.8	16.9	3.2	0.0	6.8	21.8	882	139	92	2 124	39.3	60.7	0.0
Sequoyah	71.8	1 801	73.8	1.1	3.7	0.0	5.7	27.4	686	145	165	2 363	40.0	60.0	0.0
Stephens	82.1	1 925	63.7	0.6	4.4	0.0	4.0	41.9	983	103	158	1 997	28.8	71.2	0.0
Texas	66.7	3 308	40.0	27.3	2.7	0.0	10.7	8.3	411	80	75	1 776	15.7	84.3	0.0
Tillman	28.2	3 139	47.6	17.8	3.6	0.0	10.6	10.8	1 197	47	33	766	34.1	65.9	0.0
Tulsa	1 703.2	2 981	46.0	2.5	6.9	1.7	2.6	2 196.5	3 844	3 688	2 149	30 030	35.6	64.4	0.0
Wagoner	58.2	964	61.7	3.0	4.5	0.0	9.3	46.9	777	79	223	1 395	32.4	67.6	0.0
Washington	102.6	2 086	58.9	0.4	5.8	0.1	7.0	45.4	924	106	182	2 137	29.3	70.7	0.0
Washita	33.9	2 959	60.5	0.2	2.7	0.0	20.0	6.1	536	56	42	772	26.6	73.4	0.0
Woods	25.4	2 897	58.4	0.9	2.4	0.0	12.3	9.3	1 062	45	32	1 298	22.7	77.3	0.0
Woodward	44.8	2 425	57.2	4.5	5.4	0.5	9.5	18.5	1 000	108	68	1 702	19.1	80.9	0.0
OREGON	X	X	X	X	X	X	X	X	X	28 901	11 373	235 891	51.5	47.6	1.0
Baker	41.7	2 530	51.4	6.1	5.8	2.1	5.5	7.8	471	306	45	926	29.2	69.5	1.3
Benton	229.2	2 916	36.1	7.0	7.1	1.6	4.8	125.3	1 594	685	282	11 432	58.2	40.6	1.1
Clackamas	1 049.9	2 984	51.6	5.0	5.5	1.3	4.0	848.0	2 410	1 983	1 192	14 246	48.8	50.5	0.7
Clatsop	138.6	3 872	41.5	7.9	5.8	0.3	6.0	82.1	2 294	156	459	2 488	54.7	44.2	1.1
Columbia	129.5	2 859	53.6	4.6	4.2	0.1	3.3	159.1	3 511	80	124	1 859	50.6	47.9	1.5
Coos	282.3	4 505	37.3	36.6	3.2	0.3	2.7	86.3	1 377	379	391	5 297	43.7	55.0	1.3
Crook	51.4	2 572	50.6	2.4	5.9	0.5	7.0	26.9	1 344	337	55	899	30.3	68.4	1.3
Curry	58.6	2 753	42.8	15.5	6.5	0.5	4.2	48.9	2 295	124	103	1 064	41.0	57.6	1.4
Deschutes	410.0	3 273	49.8	4.6	6.4	0.7	6.2	341.6	2 728	837	345	6 176	42.3	56.7	1.0
Douglas	330.1	3 271	49.9	9.7	4.2	0.5	7.0	93.5	926	1 506	337	6 597	33.1	65.6	1.2
Gilliam	13.2	7 155	53.7	1.3	2.6	0.0	4.2	1.1	601	11	0	213	32.6	66.5	0.9
Grant	46.1	6 160	31.3	30.2	2.2	3.0	16.2	12.3	1 650	278	20	764	19.2	79.1	1.6
Harney	35.4	4 825	47.5	30.7	2.3	0.5	5.9	3.1	426	266	20	815	22.7	76.5	0.8
Hood River	72.7	3 496	51.6	13.0	3.9	1.0	3.8	31.9	1 536	136	57	1 209	57.0	42.2	0.9
Jackson	517.0	2 773	46.1	6.4	5.5	0.0	5.9	303.4	1 628	1 671	522	9 351	43.5	55.5	0.9
Jefferson	68.5	3 467	46.7	22.7	3.9	0.4	4.6	73.1	3 699	154	54	2 220	40.0	59.0	1.0
Josephine	249.3	3 217	47.4	14.1	4.8	1.1	3.9	94.6	1 221	330	213	3 421	36.1	62.4	1.6
Klamath	190.4	2 958	50.0	7.5	3.3	0.3	6.9	386.6	6 006	903	183	4 438	26.4	72.5	1.1
Lake	37.5	5 044	33.6	26.1	3.5	0.0	12.0	7.9	1 058	315	20	614	20.6	78.3	1.1
Lane	1 105.1	3 383	46.6	4.5	5.8	3.5	6.2	844.0	2 584	1 879	957	23 798	58.3	40.8	1.0
Lincoln	208.9	4 680	24.6	25.3	4.6	1.0	5.4	116.1	2 600	257	194	3 366	56.8	42.0	1.2
Linn	359.3	3 424	57.9	2.3	4.4	2.0	4.8	175.1	1 668	327	288	6 314	38.4	60.4	1.2
Malheur	108.9	3 484	56.1	5.6	3.4	0.0	4.4	86.2	2 758	249	87	3 018	23.8	75.2	1.0
Marion	1 043.7	3 560	54.9	6.2	4.7	0.0	4.0	684.8	2 336	1 393	809	30 797	44.7	54.4	0.9

1. Based on the resident population estimated as of July 1 of the year shown.

Table B. States and Counties — Land Area and Population

STATE/ County code	CBSA code[1]	County Type[2]	STATE County	Land area,[3] (sq km) 2000	Population and population characteristics, 2003			Race alone or in combination, not Hispanic or Latino (percent)					Age (percent)					
					Total persons	Rank	Per square kilometer	White	Black	Am. Indian, Alaska Native	Asian and Pacific Islander	Percent Hispanic or Latino[4]	Under 5 years	5 to 17 years	18 to 24 years	25 to 34 years	35 to 44 years	45 to 54 years
				1	2	3	4	5	6	7	8	9	10	11	12	13	14	15
			OREGON—Cont'd															
41 049	37820	6	Morrow	5 264	11 627	2 322	2.2	70.5	0.2	1.8	0.6	27.6	8.0	21.7	10.2	12.9	13.9	14.0
41 051	38900	1	Multnomah	1 127	677 813	79	601.4	77.6	6.7	1.9	7.9	8.9	6.6	15.8	8.9	17.7	15.9	15.2
41 053	41420	2	Polk	1 919	65 995	759	34.4	86.9	0.8	2.9	2.2	9.3	5.7	17.8	12.0	11.6	12.5	14.3
41 055	...	9	Sherman	2 132	1 754	3 075	0.8	91.4	0.2	1.7	0.5	6.5	3.6	19.6	8.0	5.6	15.8	16.6
41 057	...	6	Tillamook	2 855	24 590	1 598	8.6	91.1	0.3	2.3	1.1	6.6	4.7	16.2	8.4	9.6	13.1	15.6
41 059	37820	5	Umatilla	8 327	72 008	704	8.6	77.6	1.0	3.8	1.1	17.5	7.1	19.8	10.4	12.8	14.3	13.8
41 061	29260	7	Union	5 275	24 561	1 599	4.7	94.3	0.7	1.2	2.0	2.8	6.0	17.2	12.4	10.5	12.0	15.8
41 063	...	9	Wallowa	8 146	7 082	2 678	0.9	97.3	0.2	1.5	0.4	1.7	4.6	17.3	7.5	6.7	12.8	19.0
41 065	17180	6	Wasco	6 167	23 591	1 631	3.8	84.7	0.6	4.2	1.7	10.1	6.3	18.0	8.6	10.3	13.5	15.6
41 067	38900	1	Washington	1 874	479 496	127	255.9	76.8	1.8	1.2	9.8	13.0	7.7	18.8	8.7	16.9	16.2	13.9
41 069	...	9	Wheeler	4 442	1 505	3 089	0.3	94.2	0.1	0.9	0.2	5.1	3.6	15.5	8.2	6.6	12.9	14.0
41 071	38900	1	Yamhill	1 853	89 384	602	48.2	84.4	0.9	2.1	1.7	12.4	6.6	18.8	12.4	12.9	14.5	13.7
42 000	...	X	PENNSYLVANIA	116 074	12 365 455	X	106.5	84.2	10.4	0.4	2.4	3.4	5.7	17.2	9.5	11.9	15.0	14.9
42 001	23900	4	Adams	1 347	96 456	559	71.6	94.0	1.5	0.4	0.7	4.0	5.5	17.7	10.7	11.7	15.5	14.1
42 003	38300	1	Allegheny	1 891	1 261 303	29	667.0	84.2	13.2	0.4	2.4	0.9	5.4	16.0	8.7	12.0	15.3	15.3
42 005	38300	1	Armstrong	1 694	71 659	709	42.3	98.4	1.0	0.2	0.2	0.5	4.9	16.5	8.3	10.9	15.4	15.5
42 007	38300	1	Beaver	1 125	178 697	319	158.8	92.8	6.5	0.4	0.4	0.8	5.0	16.6	8.5	10.2	15.5	15.4
42 009	...	6	Bedford	2 628	49 941	933	19.0	98.9	0.4	0.4	0.4	0.5	5.5	16.8	8.2	11.6	15.0	14.5
42 011	39740	2	Berks	2 224	385 307	161	173.2	84.6	4.0	0.3	1.3	10.6	6.0	17.9	9.8	11.9	15.6	14.1
42 013	11020	3	Blair	1 362	127 175	446	93.4	97.9	1.4	0.3	0.6	0.5	5.5	16.2	9.8	11.3	14.5	15.1
42 015	42380	6	Bradford	2 980	62 643	789	21.0	98.1	0.6	0.6	0.6	0.6	5.7	18.2	8.3	10.9	15.0	14.9
42 017	37980	1	Bucks	1 573	613 110	93	389.8	91.4	3.4	0.3	3.3	2.4	5.8	18.3	8.1	11.6	17.2	15.7
42 019	38300	1	Butler	2 042	180 040	318	88.2	97.8	1.0	0.2	0.9	0.5	5.9	17.5	9.6	11.5	16.2	14.8
42 021	27780	3	Cambria	1 782	149 453	378	83.9	95.6	3.3	0.2	0.5	1.0	4.9	15.1	9.8	11.0	14.1	15.5
42 023	...	7	Cameron	1 029	5 777	2 792	5.6	98.5	0.7	0.2	0.1	0.6	4.2	17.6	8.4	9.8	14.1	15.0
42 025	10900	2	Carbon	987	60 131	821	60.9	97.0	1.0	0.4	0.5	1.6	4.8	16.0	8.3	11.8	15.6	14.6
42 027	44300	3	Centre	2 868	141 636	401	49.4	91.3	2.8	0.3	4.9	1.5	4.2	12.6	23.3	14.5	12.4	11.3
42 029	37980	1	Chester	1 958	457 393	136	233.6	87.7	6.3	0.4	2.9	3.6	6.2	18.6	9.1	11.7	16.7	15.1
42 031	...	6	Clarion	1 560	41 208	1 102	26.4	98.3	0.9	0.3	0.4	0.4	4.7	15.5	15.0	11.0	13.5	13.7
42 033	20180	4	Clearfield	2 972	82 874	642	27.9	97.2	1.8	0.3	0.3	0.6	4.7	16.4	8.6	12.2	15.7	14.6
42 035	30820	6	Clinton	2 307	37 435	1 194	16.2	98.1	0.7	0.3	0.6	0.6	5.3	15.4	13.6	11.0	13.4	13.7
42 037	14100	4	Columbia	1 258	64 605	772	51.4	97.3	1.0	0.4	0.7	1.1	4.3	14.8	14.9	11.0	13.8	14.0
42 039	32740	4	Crawford	2 623	89 846	598	34.3	97.2	1.9	0.5	0.4	0.6	5.8	17.6	10.5	11.0	14.4	14.7
42 041	25420	2	Cumberland	1 425	219 892	266	154.3	93.9	2.8	0.3	2.4	1.4	5.0	15.8	11.2	12.0	15.1	15.1
42 043	25420	2	Dauphin	1 360	253 388	232	186.3	76.3	17.9	0.5	2.7	4.2	6.2	17.7	7.9	12.8	15.7	15.6
42 045	37980	1	Delaware	477	554 432	103	1 162.3	78.2	16.6	0.4	4.3	1.6	6.0	18.1	9.9	11.7	15.6	14.4
42 047	41260	7	Elk	2 146	34 310	1 297	16.0	98.9	0.2	0.2	0.4	0.5	5.2	17.3	7.9	11.1	15.8	15.0
42 049	21500	2	Erie	2 077	279 966	210	134.8	90.7	6.8	0.4	0.9	2.2	6.0	17.9	11.6	11.9	14.4	14.5
42 051	38300	1	Fayette	2 046	146 121	393	71.4	95.6	4.0	0.3	0.4	0.4	5.2	16.5	8.4	11.6	14.6	15.3
42 053	...	9	Forest	1 109	4 989	2 846	4.5	95.0	3.1	0.4	0.3	1.4	3.5	18.7	7.9	7.2	13.1	14.3
42 055	16540	4	Franklin	1 999	133 155	426	66.6	95.0	2.7	0.3	0.8	1.9	6.1	17.0	8.6	12.3	14.5	14.0
42 057	...	8	Fulton	1 133	14 534	2 125	12.8	98.7	0.6	0.4	0.2	0.4	5.7	17.7	8.4	12.2	14.6	13.9
42 059	...	6	Greene	1 491	40 398	1 127	27.1	94.7	4.0	0.4	0.4	0.9	4.9	15.9	10.4	13.1	14.7	15.8
42 061	26500	6	Huntingdon	2 264	45 865	1 007	20.3	93.2	5.4	0.4	0.3	1.2	5.3	15.5	11.0	13.2	15.1	14.2
42 063	26860	4	Indiana	2 148	89 054	603	41.5	97.1	1.7	0.2	0.9	0.5	4.7	14.7	16.3	10.9	13.2	14.3
42 065	...	7	Jefferson	1 698	45 945	1 006	27.1	99.0	0.3	0.3	0.3	0.5	5.4	16.8	9.1	10.9	14.8	14.6
42 067	...	6	Juniata	1 014	23 065	1 663	22.7	97.0	0.4	0.2	0.2	2.3	6.1	17.8	8.7	12.0	14.8	14.0
42 069	42540	2	Lackawanna	1 188	210 458	279	177.2	96.1	1.7	0.2	0.9	1.6	5.1	15.9	9.8	11.1	14.4	14.3
42 071	29540	2	Lancaster	2 458	482 775	126	196.4	89.6	3.2	0.3	1.8	6.0	6.7	19.1	9.8	11.7	14.9	13.8
42 073	35260	4	Lawrence	934	93 408	576	100.0	95.3	4.2	0.3	0.4	0.6	5.3	16.9	9.4	10.3	14.0	15.0
42 075	30140	3	Lebanon	937	122 652	463	130.9	92.6	1.4	0.3	1.0	5.2	5.6	17.0	9.1	11.5	15.0	14.4
42 077	10900	2	Lehigh	898	320 517	185	356.9	82.3	4.1	0.3	2.9	11.4	5.8	17.5	8.6	12.0	15.7	14.5
42 079	42540	2	Luzerne	2 307	313 528	189	135.9	95.9	2.0	0.2	0.8	1.5	4.7	15.5	9.0	11.5	14.8	14.7
42 081	48700	3	Lycoming	3 198	118 438	475	37.0	94.5	4.6	0.4	0.6	0.6	5.3	16.7	10.8	11.2	14.9	14.9
42 083	14620	7	McKean	2 542	45 236	1 017	17.8	96.0	2.2	0.4	0.4	1.2	5.3	16.9	9.0	12.5	15.0	14.5
42 085	49660	2	Mercer	1 740	119 895	470	68.9	93.6	5.6	0.4	0.6	0.7	5.5	17.0	10.2	10.6	14.2	14.4
42 087	30380	4	Mifflin	1 067	46 335	995	43.4	98.4	0.7	0.2	0.4	0.6	5.9	17.8	7.8	11.6	14.5	13.8
42 089	20700	4	Monroe	1 576	154 495	362	98.0	82.2	8.9	0.6	1.9	7.7	5.3	19.5	10.6	10.7	16.3	14.4
42 091	37980	1	Montgomery	1 251	770 747	66	616.1	85.0	8.1	0.4	5.3	2.2	6.1	17.4	7.7	12.5	16.4	14.8
42 093	14100	6	Montour	339	18 083	1 911	53.3	96.4	1.5	0.1	1.3	1.0	5.8	17.8	7.6	10.8	15.9	14.9
42 095	10900	2	Northampton	968	278 169	212	287.4	88.3	3.3	0.3	1.8	6.9	5.2	16.9	10.5	11.2	15.5	14.6
42 097	44980	4	Northumberland	1 191	93 323	578	78.4	96.8	1.8	0.3	0.2	1.2	5.2	15.7	8.2	11.4	15.1	14.8
42 099	25420	2	Perry	1 434	44 188	1 040	30.8	98.4	0.8	0.3	0.2	0.7	5.8	18.4	8.6	11.7	16.3	16.0
42 101	37980	1	Philadelphia	350	1 479 339	20	4 226.7	41.6	44.4	0.6	5.6	9.1	6.8	18.4	10.4	14.5	14.6	12.9
42 103	35620	1	Pike	1 416	52 163	904	36.8	90.1	4.5	0.7	0.7	4.8	4.5	19.4	8.4	9.7	16.2	14.2

1. CBSA = Core Based Statistical Area. See Appendix A for explanation. See Appendix B for list of metropolitan areas with component counties. 2. County type code from the Economic Research Service of USDA Rural-Urban Continuum Codes. See Appendix A for definition. 3. Dry land or land partially or temporarily covered by water. 4. Hispanic or Latino persons may be of any race.

Table B. States and Counties — Population and Households

STATE County	Population, 2003 (cont'd) Age (percent) (cont'd)				Population — change and components of change, 1990–2003							Households, 2000				
					Total persons		Percent change		Components of change, 2000–2003						Percent	
	55 to 64 years	65 to 74 years	75 years and over	Percent female	1990	2000	1990–2000	2000–2003	Births	Deaths	Net migration	Number	Percent change, 1990–2000	Persons per house-hold	Female family house-holder[1]	One person
	16	17	18	19	20	21	22	23	24	25	26	27	28	29	30	31
OREGON—Cont'd																
Morrow	9.2	5.9	4.3	48.5	7 625	10 995	44.2	5.7	548	277	364	3 776	34.7	2.90	8.8	18.1
Multnomah	8.5	4.9	5.8	50.3	583 887	660 486	13.1	2.6	29 801	19 106	7 167	272 098	12.4	2.37	10.8	32.5
Polk	9.4	6.6	8.2	51.5	49 541	62 380	25.9	5.8	2 391	1 765	3 049	23 058	26.9	2.62	9.2	22.3
Sherman	12.4	9.5	9.9	48.3	1 918	1 934	0.8	-9.3	31	53	-157	797	1.7	2.43	6.5	28.7
Tillamook	12.9	10.2	9.1	49.8	21 570	24 262	12.5	1.4	754	949	543	10 200	15.3	2.33	7.7	27.9
Umatilla	9.1	6.0	6.2	49.0	59 249	70 548	19.1	2.1	3 328	2 042	210	25 195	14.4	2.67	10.6	23.7
Union	10.5	7.2	7.5	51.1	23 598	24 530	3.9	0.1	993	862	-72	9 740	7.8	2.45	8.5	26.1
Wallowa	12.8	10.2	9.5	49.9	6 911	7 226	4.6	-2.0	209	257	-89	3 029	8.3	2.35	6.9	27.1
Wasco	11.0	8.1	8.5	50.7	21 683	23 791	9.7	-0.8	933	989	-125	9 401	9.2	2.47	9.9	26.1
Washington	7.9	4.2	4.4	50.0	311 554	445 342	42.9	7.7	23 892	8 985	19 568	169 162	42.2	2.61	9.0	24.7
Wheeler	17.1	13.5	10.4	50.0	1 396	1 547	10.8	-2.7	34	52	-23	653	11.8	2.32	4.0	27.4
Yamhill	8.4	5.5	5.9	49.3	65 551	84 992	29.7	5.2	3 790	2 325	3 024	28 732	28.1	2.78	9.9	19.7
PENNSYLVANIA	10.3	7.3	8.0	51.6	11 882 842	12 281 054	3.4	0.7	464 646	424 782	52 463	4 777 003	6.3	2.48	11.6	27.7
Adams	9.6	6.9	6.7	50.8	78 274	91 292	16.6	5.7	3 471	2 712	4 403	33 652	19.9	2.61	8.5	21.3
Allegheny	10.0	8.1	9.4	52.5	1 336 449	1 281 666	-4.1	-1.6	45 214	50 405	-14 228	537 150	-0.8	2.31	12.4	32.7
Armstrong	10.5	8.6	9.4	51.4	73 478	72 392	-1.5	-1.0	2 208	2 818	-52	29 005	2.5	2.46	9.0	25.9
Beaver	10.6	9.1	9.4	52.0	186 093	181 412	-2.5	-1.5	5 727	6 914	-1 398	72 576	0.9	2.44	11.4	26.9
Bedford	11.5	8.9	7.9	50.6	47 919	49 984	4.3	-0.1	1 762	1 615	-143	19 768	9.6	2.50	7.7	23.5
Berks	9.5	7.1	7.4	50.9	336 523	373 638	11.0	3.1	15 068	11 887	8 647	141 570	10.9	2.55	9.9	24.6
Blair	10.5	8.3	9.1	52.0	130 542	129 144	-1.1	-1.5	4 576	5 425	-1 021	51 518	2.4	2.43	11.2	27.8
Bradford	11.2	8.1	7.7	51.1	60 967	62 761	2.9	-0.2	2 343	2 064	-339	24 453	8.7	2.52	8.9	24.7
Bucks	10.1	6.6	6.0	50.8	541 174	597 635	10.4	2.6	23 057	16 401	9 611	218 725	14.8	2.69	8.8	21.5
Butler	9.5	6.7	7.4	51.1	152 013	174 083	14.5	3.4	6 861	5 483	4 751	65 862	19.0	2.55	8.1	24.2
Cambria	10.4	8.9	10.6	51.3	163 062	152 598	-6.4	-2.1	4 816	6 427	-1 404	60 531	-2.4	2.38	10.4	29.8
Cameron	11.6	9.1	10.7	50.8	5 913	5 974	1.0	-3.3	160	243	-111	2 465	2.9	2.39	9.2	30.1
Carbon	10.5	8.8	9.1	51.3	56 803	58 802	3.5	2.3	1 865	2 551	1 990	23 701	7.8	2.44	9.9	26.0
Centre	7.5	5.4	4.8	48.8	124 812	135 758	8.8	4.3	3 887	2 935	5 000	49 323	15.6	2.45	6.1	26.6
Chester	9.8	6.1	5.6	50.8	376 389	433 501	15.2	5.5	18 411	10 636	16 351	157 905	18.5	2.65	8.1	22.6
Clarion	10.1	7.9	7.6	51.8	41 699	41 765	0.2	-1.3	1 288	1 428	-377	16 052	7.1	2.46	8.4	26.0
Clearfield	10.8	8.4	8.8	49.8	78 097	83 382	6.8	-0.6	2 543	2 964	-8	32 785	10.0	2.44	9.3	26.3
Clinton	10.4	8.4	8.4	51.6	37 182	37 914	2.0	-1.3	1 351	1 393	-414	14 773	6.7	2.42	9.4	26.6
Columbia	10.0	7.8	8.3	52.4	63 202	64 151	1.5	0.7	1 774	1 997	736	24 915	6.1	2.42	8.7	26.6
Crawford	10.6	7.7	7.8	51.2	86 166	90 366	4.9	-0.6	3 439	3 110	-754	34 678	7.7	2.50	9.2	26.2
Cumberland	10.0	7.3	7.5	51.0	195 257	213 674	9.4	2.9	7 151	6 498	5 753	83 015	13.0	2.41	8.0	26.7
Dauphin	9.7	7.2	7.0	52.0	237 813	251 798	5.9	0.6	10 388	8 083	-515	102 670	7.8	2.39	12.9	30.0
Delaware	9.1	7.0	8.1	52.1	547 658	550 864	0.6	0.6	22 034	18 763	-230	206 320	2.5	2.56	12.9	27.6
Elk	10.2	8.8	9.0	50.5	34 878	35 112	0.7	-2.3	1 183	1 223	-744	14 124	7.6	2.45	8.7	27.3
Erie	9.2	6.7	7.5	51.1	275 575	280 843	1.9	-0.5	10 892	8 756	-2 852	106 507	4.9	2.51	12.1	27.6
Fayette	10.6	8.5	9.6	52.2	145 351	148 644	2.3	-1.7	4 854	6 079	-1 184	59 969	6.9	2.43	12.4	28.0
Forest	13.9	11.5	9.8	47.4	4 802	4 946	3.0	0.9	133	220	129	2 000	4.8	2.29	6.7	29.1
Franklin	10.4	8.1	8.1	51.3	121 082	129 313	6.8	3.0	5 204	4 136	2 924	50 633	10.9	2.49	8.2	23.7
Fulton	11.9	8.2	6.4	50.2	13 837	14 261	3.1	1.9	520	466	234	5 660	10.1	2.50	8.2	24.0
Greene	9.8	7.2	7.9	48.2	39 550	40 672	2.8	-0.7	1 344	1 440	-133	15 060	3.0	2.48	10.9	25.7
Huntingdon	10.7	7.8	7.1	47.8	44 164	45 586	3.2	0.6	1 594	1 341	77	16 759	7.9	2.44	8.3	25.8
Indiana	9.7	7.2	7.8	51.6	89 994	89 605	-0.4	-0.6	2 787	2 976	-290	34 123	7.6	2.47	8.2	26.5
Jefferson	10.5	8.5	9.3	50.9	46 083	45 932	-0.3	0.0	1 684	1 814	191	18 375	4.4	2.45	9.1	26.6
Juniata	10.5	8.1	7.4	50.4	20 625	22 821	10.6	1.1	891	702	68	8 584	13.0	2.60	6.3	21.1
Lackawanna	10.4	8.6	10.5	52.7	219 097	213 295	-2.6	-1.3	7 049	9 635	-34	86 218	2.0	2.38	11.8	31.3
Lancaster	9.2	6.8	7.2	51.1	422 822	470 658	11.3	2.6	21 472	13 791	5 098	172 560	14.3	2.64	8.6	23.1
Lawrence	10.2	8.7	10.3	52.4	96 246	94 643	-1.7	-1.3	3 268	3 839	-588	37 091	2.0	2.47	11.5	27.0
Lebanon	10.2	8.0	8.4	51.2	113 744	120 327	5.8	1.9	4 453	4 047	2 042	46 551	9.0	2.49	9.2	25.2
Lehigh	9.6	7.3	8.1	51.6	291 130	312 090	7.2	2.7	11 963	10 370	7 078	121 906	8.0	2.48	10.5	27.1
Luzerne	10.8	8.8	10.5	51.6	328 149	319 250	-2.7	-1.8	9 485	14 627	-291	130 687	1.7	2.34	11.5	31.3
Lycoming	10.1	7.9	8.2	50.9	118 710	120 044	1.1	-1.3	4 153	3 988	-1 702	47 003	4.6	2.44	10.3	26.9
McKean	10.1	8.3	8.5	49.5	47 131	45 936	-2.5	-1.5	1 558	1 783	-461	18 024	1.0	2.40	10.1	28.3
Mercer	10.4	8.5	9.4	51.4	121 003	120 293	-0.6	-0.3	4 272	4 665	109	46 712	2.5	2.44	10.9	27.0
Mifflin	11.2	8.8	8.6	51.7	46 197	46 486	0.6	-0.3	1 768	1 686	-176	18 413	4.0	2.49	8.5	26.0
Monroe	9.2	6.5	5.1	50.6	95 681	138 687	44.9	11.4	5 010	3 799	14 130	49 454	44.6	2.73	8.8	20.2
Montgomery	9.8	7.1	7.6	51.4	678 193	750 097	10.6	2.8	30 464	23 020	15 026	286 098	12.2	2.54	8.8	25.6
Montour	10.4	8.4	9.0	52.0	17 735	18 236	2.8	-0.8	722	739	-108	7 085	8.3	2.43	8.9	28.0
Northampton	9.7	7.1	8.0	51.2	247 110	267 066	8.1	4.2	9 315	8 174	9 916	101 541	11.6	2.53	9.8	24.7
Northumberland	11.0	8.7	10.1	50.8	96 771	94 556	-2.3	-1.3	3 239	3 940	-435	38 835	0.3	2.34	9.6	30.2
Perry	10.5	6.7	5.5	50.4	41 172	43 602	5.9	1.3	1 683	1 245	200	16 695	11.7	2.58	7.8	21.7
Philadelphia	8.9	6.7	7.1	53.4	1 585 577	1 517 550	-4.3	-2.5	71 097	56 771	-52 556	590 071	-2.2	2.48	22.3	33.8
Pike	10.5	8.3	5.9	50.2	28 032	46 302	65.2	12.7	1 275	1 140	5 531	17 433	65.5	2.63	7.6	20.7

1. No spouse present.

Table B. States and Counties — **Vital Statistics, Health Resources, and Crime**

STATE County	Births, average 1999–2001 Total	Births, average 1999–2001 Rate[1]	Deaths, average 1999–2001 Number Total	Deaths, average 1999–2001 Number Infant[2]	Deaths, average 1999–2001 Rate Total[1]	Deaths, average 1999–2001 Rate Infant[3]	Physicians,[4] 2000 Number	Physicians,[4] 2000 Rate[5]	Hospitals,[4] 1998 Number	Hospitals,[4] 1998 Beds Number	Hospitals,[4] 1998 Beds Rate[5]	Medicare enrollees, 2003	Serious crimes known to police,[6] 2002 Total Number	Serious crimes known to police,[6] 2002 Total Rate[7]
	32	33	34	35	36	37	38	39	40	41	42	43	44	45
OREGON—Cont'd														
Morrow	170	15.4	77	1	7.0	D	3	27	1	44	441	1 364	373	3 296
Multnomah	9 314	14.1	5 716	50	8.6	5.3	2 595	393	8	2 130	338	88 643	51 336	7 552
Polk	714	11.4	511	3	8.2	D	65	104	1	51	83	9 624	3 086	4 882
Sherman	14	7.1	18	0	9.2	D	0	0	0	0	0	413	35	1 759
Tillamook	231	9.5	285	1	11.7	D	35	144	1	45	185	5 468	798	3 319
Umatilla	1 075	15.3	599	6	8.5	D	88	125	2	98	150	10 083	2 344	3 321
Union	307	12.5	245	2	10.0	D	48	196	1	69	278	4 260	530	2 278
Wallowa	63	8.7	80	1	11.2	D	4	55	1	32	434	1 613	115	1 546
Wasco	293	12.4	291	2	12.3	D	40	168	1	49	212	4 515	1 009	4 121
Washington	7 390	16.5	2 605	31	5.8	4.2	856	192	4	742	186	42 211	17 120	3 735
Wheeler	11	7.2	18	0	11.9	D	0	0	0	0	0	384	21	1 318
Yamhill	1 211	14.2	674	8	7.9	6.3	113	133	2	102	124	11 588	2 525	2 886
PENNSYLVANIA	145 041	11.8	130 275	1 043	10.6	7.2	31 671	258	214	46 466	387	2 110 470	350 446	2 841
Adams	1 049	11.5	825	7	9.0	6.7	75	82	1	102	118	13 748	1 309	1 528
Allegheny	14 220	11.1	15 358	115	12.0	8.1	5 380	420	22	7 470	589	236 649	38 474	3 361
Armstrong	737	10.2	873	6	12.1	D	57	79	1	187	256	15 725	611	1 020
Beaver	1 811	10.0	2 141	10	11.8	5.3	241	133	2	558	303	35 807	NA	NA
Bedford	572	11.5	503	7	10.1	12.2	39	78	1	78	158	9 477	840	1 700
Berks	4 623	12.4	3 633	34	9.7	7.3	637	170	3	874	246	61 325	10 891	3 212
Blair	1 472	11.4	1 610	8	12.5	5.2	271	210	4	593	454	25 027	3 067	2 978
Bradford	748	11.9	633	4	10.1	D	185	295	3	404	647	11 568	1 009	1 648
Bucks	7 294	12.2	5 031	31	8.4	4.3	1 215	203	7	1 254	213	84 893	12 955	2 208
Butler	2 130	12.2	1 683	12	9.6	5.6	191	110	1	286	167	28 318	3 402	2 058
Cambria	1 531	10.0	1 971	12	12.9	8.1	342	224	4	872	559	32 844	2 423	1 957
Cameron	58	9.8	75	0	12.5	D	5	84	0	0	0	1 257	153	2 550
Carbon	586	9.9	753	3	12.8	D	52	88	2	270	459	12 417	NA	NA
Centre	1 242	9.1	852	6	6.3	D	244	180	2	232	175	16 231	2 831	2 076
Chester	5 807	13.4	3 182	32	7.3	5.5	942	217	5	745	177	54 623	7 864	1 862
Clarion	413	9.9	424	2	10.2	D	51	122	1	88	210	7 063	745	1 827
Clearfield	824	9.9	911	7	10.9	8.5	118	142	2	286	354	15 296	1 353	1 833
Clinton	423	11.2	417	4	11.0	D	48	127	2	315	851	6 749	936	3 118
Columbia	594	9.3	650	3	10.1	D	88	137	2	391	610	12 318	NA	NA
Crawford	1 105	12.2	984	8	10.9	7.5	126	139	2	248	277	16 299	1 630	1 930
Cumberland	2 236	10.4	2 006	9	9.4	4.0	486	227	3	552	265	36 367	3 945	1 838
Dauphin	3 163	12.6	2 481	19	9.9	6.0	998	396	4	1 435	584	39 398	7 243	3 264
Delaware	6 826	12.4	5 770	39	10.5	5.8	1 636	297	9	2 112	389	89 771	12 770	2 436
Elk	376	10.7	378	1	10.8	D	51	145	2	304	880	6 749	773	2 192
Erie	3 460	12.3	2 735	28	9.7	8.1	616	219	6	1 167	422	45 799	7 084	2 544
Fayette	1 559	10.5	1 853	14	12.5	9.2	146	98	3	440	304	31 047	3 355	2 712
Forest	38	7.7	76	0	15.2	D	1	20	0	0	0	1 478	193	3 885
Franklin	1 648	12.7	1 269	11	9.8	6.5	157	121	2	297	232	22 675	2 561	1 972
Fulton	162	11.3	131	0	9.2	D	7	49	1	96	662	2 500	226	1 706
Greene	403	9.9	459	5	11.3	D	37	91	1	107	263	7 198	609	1 807
Huntingdon	507	11.1	416	2	9.1	D	44	97	1	104	233	7 847	597	1 304
Indiana	880	9.8	908	7	10.1	7.6	108	121	1	150	169	15 160	1 278	1 491
Jefferson	510	11.1	553	4	12.0	D	64	139	2	127	275	9 385	599	1 667
Juniata	291	12.8	234	3	10.3	D	6	26	0	0	0	3 770	226	1 055
Lackawanna	2 171	10.2	2 942	13	13.8	6.1	498	233	5	1 143	548	43 798	NA	NA
Lancaster	6 763	14.3	4 235	48	9.0	7.0	756	161	5	1 118	245	73 091	12 033	2 833
Lawrence	1 038	11.0	1 169	10	12.4	9.6	114	120	3	526	554	21 238	2 786	3 163
Lebanon	1 417	11.8	1 256	9	10.4	6.1	208	173	2	216	184	21 824	2 850	2 468
Lehigh	3 753	12.0	3 154	31	10.1	8.3	1 006	322	4	1 077	360	53 249	10 647	3 470
Luzerne	2 992	9.4	4 465	18	14.0	6.1	717	225	6	1 337	426	66 650	7 493	2 722
Lycoming	1 327	11.1	1 249	10	10.4	7.8	248	207	4	612	522	21 787	2 789	2 485
McKean	506	11.0	571	3	12.4	D	58	126	2	269	578	8 675	540	1 214
Mercer	1 353	11.2	1 481	12	12.3	9.1	245	204	4	638	523	24 345	2 493	2 478
Mifflin	589	12.7	518	4	11.1	D	73	157	1	232	494	8 714	NA	NA
Monroe	1 464	10.5	1 133	9	8.1	5.9	163	118	1	228	182	21 150	3 486	2 516
Montgomery	9 421	12.5	7 050	54	9.4	5.7	3 182	424	9	2 062	287	128 399	15 781	2 186
Montour	214	11.8	233	3	12.8	D	310	1 700	1	460	2 594	3 595	NA	NA
Northampton	2 886	10.8	2 480	16	9.3	5.5	397	149	3	880	340	47 446	NA	NA
Northumberland	992	10.5	1 208	7	12.8	7.4	75	79	2	193	205	19 762	NA	NA
Perry	524	12.0	383	5	8.8	D	24	55	0	0	0	6 369	780	1 881
Philadelphia	21 607	14.3	17 613	239	11.6	11.1	6 593	434	31	8 778	611	228 243	83 402	5 472
Pike	410	8.8	368	0	7.9	D	17	37	0	0	0	6 977	547	1 352

1. Per 1,000 estimated resident population. 2. Deaths of infants under 1 year old. 3. Deaths of infants under 1 year old per 1,000 live births. 4. Data subject to copyright. 5. Per 100,000 resident population as of July 1 of the year shown. 6. Data for serious crimes have not been adjusted for underreporting; this may affect comparability between geographic areas and over time. 7. Per 100,000 population estimated by the FBI.

Table B. States and Counties — Crime, Education, Money Income, and Poverty

STATE County	Serious crimes known to police,[1] 2002 (cont'd) Rate[2] Violent	Property	Education School enrollment and attainment, 2000 Enrollment[3] Total	Percent private	Attainment[4] (percent) High school graduate or less	Bachelor's degree or more	Local government expenditures,[5] 2000–2001 Total current expenditures (mil dol)	Current expenditures per student (dollars)	Money income, 1999 Per capita income[6] (dollars)	Households Median income Dollars	Percent change, 1989–1999 (constant 1999 dollars)	Percent with income of $100,000 or more	Percent below poverty level, 1999 Persons	House-holds	Families	Families with children
	46	47	48	49	50	51	52	53	54	55	56	57	58	59	60	61
OREGON—Cont'd																
Morrow	362	2 934	2 868	3.6	57.9	11.0	16.0	7 117	15 802	37 521	16.5	5.3	14.8	11.3	11.3	17.2
Multnomah	745	6 806	162 670	19.3	37.4	30.7	771.0	8 297	22 606	41 278	14.1	10.5	12.7	11.4	8.2	12.9
Polk	209	4 673	17 391	12.4	40.4	25.3	43.6	6 698	19 282	42 311	19.8	8.4	11.5	10.9	6.3	11.2
Sherman	50	1 709	465	6.0	48.6	19.0	4.2	11 473	17 448	35 142	4.5	5.6	14.6	14.5	12.3	17.6
Tillamook	166	3 152	5 039	9.0	52.9	17.6	29.9	7 938	19 052	34 269	16.1	5.4	11.4	10.9	8.1	14.1
Umatilla	69	3 252	18 290	8.0	51.9	16.0	100.2	7 779	16 410	36 249	18.4	5.5	12.7	11.6	9.8	14.1
Union	77	2 201	7 032	6.4	45.3	21.8	41.6	9 958	16 907	33 738	11.7	5.3	13.8	15.0	8.5	12.3
Wallowa	13	1 533	1 677	10.8	49.2	20.3	10.1	8 453	17 276	32 129	12.3	5.9	14.0	14.5	9.8	17.2
Wasco	127	3 994	5 507	12.2	51.9	15.7	33.0	9 014	17 195	35 959	7.5	5.8	12.9	12.0	10.3	15.9
Washington	162	3 573	116 491	17.5	31.2	34.5	515.1	7 025	24 969	52 122	9.1	16.1	7.4	6.4	4.9	7.4
Wheeler	0	1 318	358	14.0	57.8	14.3	3.5	13 659	15 884	28 750	40.6	4.2	15.6	13.9	12.7	22.7
Yamhill	157	2 730	23 412	22.7	48.1	20.6	106.9	6 908	18 951	44 111	16.0	8.9	9.2	9.0	6.0	8.9
PENNSYLVANIA	402	2 439	3 135 934	23.5	56.2	22.4	14 506.9	8 105	20 880	40 106	2.7	10.3	11.0	11.0	7.8	12.1
Adams	135	1 392	23 246	22.4	64.1	16.7	154.2	10 531	18 577	42 704	4.9	7.0	7.1	7.1	4.9	7.5
Allegheny	523	2 838	322 016	24.3	47.5	28.3	1 563.7	9 086	22 491	38 329	1.4	10.5	11.2	11.5	7.9	13.1
Armstrong	99	922	15 812	8.1	71.1	10.4	96.8	8 625	15 709	31 557	4.1	4.1	11.7	12.0	9.3	14.0
Beaver	NA	NA	41 572	15.9	58.8	15.8	218.1	7 722	18 402	36 995	13.4	6.1	9.4	9.7	7.2	12.1
Bedford	105	1 595	10 487	8.5	72.4	10.2	58.3	7 047	16 316	32 731	12.7	3.9	10.3	11.1	7.7	10.7
Berks	421	2 791	94 301	17.3	61.3	18.5	493.0	7 656	21 232	44 714	3.8	10.2	9.4	8.8	6.3	10.3
Blair	293	2 685	29 585	14.1	66.2	13.9	139.7	7 053	16 743	32 861	5.1	4.6	12.6	12.8	9.1	14.8
Bradford	93	1 555	14 740	12.0	65.4	14.8	88.6	7 731	17 148	35 038	8.8	5.5	11.8	11.7	9.0	13.5
Bucks	152	2 057	157 810	27.6	43.6	31.2	858.5	9 620	27 430	59 727	2.6	21.6	4.5	4.8	3.1	4.2
Butler	234	1 825	45 627	12.4	52.2	23.5	186.6	6 701	20 794	42 308	7.3	10.5	9.1	9.4	6.1	8.4
Cambria	263	1 694	34 592	18.5	67.3	13.7	177.4	9 100	16 058	30 179	4.7	4.1	12.5	13.2	9.4	15.7
Cameron	200	2 350	1 384	9.0	70.2	12.1	6.9	6 208	15 968	32 212	15.1	3.0	9.4	10.3	6.6	9.8
Carbon	NA	NA	12 781	13.7	68.9	11.0	64.1	7 777	17 064	35 113	2.5	4.2	9.5	9.8	6.8	11.7
Centre	120	1 956	56 564	7.1	45.6	36.3	132.2	9 155	18 020	36 165	3.3	8.5	18.8	17.7	6.1	8.7
Chester	204	1 658	119 787	27.0	36.7	42.5	603.5	9 361	31 627	65 295	6.5	27.4	5.2	5.0	3.1	4.4
Clarion	110	1 717	12 036	7.7	68.7	15.3	70.6	9 431	15 243	30 770	6.0	3.9	15.4	16.1	10.4	16.2
Clearfield	217	1 617	18 092	10.7	71.9	11.1	107.7	6 915	16 010	31 357	7.2	4.0	12.5	12.7	9.1	15.4
Clinton	143	2 975	9 857	9.8	67.6	13.4	43.2	8 449	15 750	31 064	4.5	4.4	14.2	13.5	9.0	15.5
Columbia	NA	NA	17 963	7.8	65.8	15.8	80.1	7 525	16 973	34 094	4.8	5.3	13.1	12.4	7.1	11.1
Crawford	143	1 787	22 134	19.4	66.6	14.7	89.1	7 502	16 870	33 560	8.2	5.5	12.8	12.2	8.7	14.0
Cumberland	114	1 724	54 249	22.2	49.7	27.9	293.3	8 021	23 610	46 707	0.8	12.0	6.6	6.6	3.8	6.2
Dauphin	450	2 814	60 052	17.1	54.0	23.5	293.8	7 857	22 134	41 507	-0.3	9.8	9.7	9.4	7.5	12.0
Delaware	414	2 023	154 448	37.1	46.5	30.0	666.3	9 284	25 040	50 092	-0.1	16.8	8.0	7.9	5.8	8.6
Elk	218	1 974	7 993	23.6	66.8	12.3	33.3	7 243	18 174	37 550	12.4	3.9	7.0	7.4	5.0	8.3
Erie	272	2 272	77 763	25.8	57.1	20.9	327.7	7 713	17 932	36 627	2.6	6.4	12.0	11.7	8.2	13.5
Fayette	229	2 483	32 185	11.6	71.8	11.5	152.9	7 314	15 274	27 451	6.4	4.2	18.0	18.2	13.8	22.6
Forest	101	3 784	1 101	24.0	73.8	8.9	7.1	9 401	14 341	27 581	7.1	2.8	16.4	12.7	10.0	12.4
Franklin	306	1 666	28 494	15.7	66.0	14.8	119.4	6 657	19 339	40 476	4.6	6.5	7.6	7.9	5.4	8.3
Fulton	257	1 449	2 996	5.9	75.1	9.3	18.2	7 446	16 409	34 882	9.4	3.6	10.8	11.3	8.2	12.9
Greene	98	1 709	9 468	13.1	71.8	12.2	55.4	8 643	14 959	30 352	13.5	4.4	15.9	15.9	13.1	19.6
Huntingdon	175	1 129	10 515	16.6	72.7	11.9	44.0	6 823	15 379	33 313	7.5	4.1	11.3	11.7	8.2	12.1
Indiana	138	1 354	27 443	7.2	65.4	17.0	114.0	9 178	15 312	30 233	-2.0	4.8	17.3	16.8	9.8	14.9
Jefferson	245	1 422	10 163	10.3	70.4	11.7	51.3	8 158	16 186	31 722	7.0	3.9	11.8	11.8	8.5	13.9
Juniata	79	975	4 798	13.4	77.2	8.8	19.1	5 652	16 142	34 698	1.8	4.0	9.5	9.5	6.7	9.7
Lackawanna	NA	NA	52 278	31.5	58.5	19.6	234.4	8 573	18 710	34 438	3.3	7.0	10.6	11.6	7.0	11.4
Lancaster	216	2 617	115 931	23.7	61.5	20.5	536.9	7 861	20 398	45 507	1.9	9.7	7.8	7.0	5.3	8.0
Lawrence	370	2 793	21 804	13.7	64.1	15.1	103.4	6 882	16 835	33 152	10.6	5.6	12.1	12.2	8.9	15.4
Lebanon	288	2 179	26 552	19.6	68.0	15.4	121.3	6 786	19 773	40 838	3.1	7.7	7.5	7.4	5.4	8.9
Lehigh	320	3 150	77 729	23.2	53.8	23.3	367.4	8 041	21 897	43 449	-0.4	11.9	9.3	8.6	6.6	10.9
Luzerne	313	2 409	73 449	25.8	60.4	16.4	320.8	8 063	18 228	33 771	6.5	6.1	11.1	11.9	8.1	12.9
Lycoming	184	2 301	29 073	15.5	61.3	15.1	150.3	7 870	17 224	34 016	-0.9	5.7	11.5	11.9	7.9	13.0
McKean	130	1 084	10 674	11.9	65.7	14.0	71.7	9 298	16 777	33 040	6.4	4.1	13.1	12.5	10.6	16.9
Mercer	263	2 215	29 564	21.2	62.2	17.3	173.3	9 055	17 636	34 666	4.9	5.4	11.5	11.0	8.8	14.9
Mifflin	NA	NA	9 564	17.9	74.8	10.9	59.1	9 505	15 553	32 175	5.1	3.8	12.5	13.8	8.6	12.7
Monroe	157	2 359	39 478	12.9	54.8	20.5	197.9	7 032	20 011	46 257	6.0	10.9	9.0	8.7	6.2	8.5
Montgomery	197	1 990	194 722	33.4	38.8	38.7	1 021.5	10 254	30 898	60 829	3.6	23.5	4.4	4.7	2.8	4.1
Montour	NA	NA	4 244	16.7	59.8	22.1	19.4	7 005	19 302	38 075	4.0	8.9	8.7	7.5	4.5	7.5
Northampton	NA	NA	70 501	28.5	55.8	21.2	336.6	8 110	21 399	45 234	2.4	11.1	7.9	8.1	5.7	8.6
Northumberland	NA	NA	19 600	15.4	72.3	11.1	90.5	6 445	16 489	31 314	5.3	3.5	11.9	12.7	8.7	13.9
Perry	251	1 630	9 718	10.0	69.7	11.3	50.3	6 771	18 551	41 909	5.6	6.2	7.7	7.5	5.4	8.2
Philadelphia	1 316	4 156	440 307	33.1	62.1	17.9	1 397.6	6 571	16 509	30 746	-7.0	6.3	22.9	21.8	18.4	26.0
Pike	79	1 273	11 944	11.8	54.5	19.0	32.8	6 676	20 315	44 608	9.5	9.2	6.9	6.9	5.1	7.6

1. Data for serious crimes have not been adjusted for underreporting; this may affect comparability between geographic areas and over time. 2. Per 100,000 population estimated by the FBI. 3. All persons 3 years old and over enrolled in nursery school through college. 4. Persons 25 years old and over. 5. Elementary and secondary education expenditures. 6. Based on population enumerated as of April 1, 2000.

Table B. States and Counties — **Personal Income**

								Personal income, 2002					
									Transfer payments				
										Government payments to individuals			
STATE County	Total (mil dol)	Percent change, 2001–2002	Per capita¹ Dollars	Per capita¹ Rank	Wages and salaries² (mil dol)	Proprietor's income (mil dol)	Dividends, interest, and rent (mil dol)	Total (mil dol)	Total (mil dol)	Social Security (mil dol)	Medical payments (mil dol)	Income maintenance (mil dol)	Unemployment insurance (mil dol)
	62	63	64	65	66	67	68	69	70	71	72	73	74
OREGON—Cont'd													
Morrow	242	10.9	20 826	2 340	142	31	40	38	36	16	9	2	5
Multnomah	22 857	1.6	33 840	165	21 058	3 050	4 167	3 232	3 078	926	1 260	304	300
Polk	1 634	4.3	25 241	1 061	579	91	371	262	247	113	78	16	16
Sherman	32	22.2	17 647	2 936	24	-11	11	11	10	5	4	1	1
Tillamook	630	4.1	25 734	944	276	74	150	140	135	64	46	9	6
Umatilla	1 627	3.3	22 789	1 786	1 092	101	283	334	318	108	126	28	27
Union	587	4.0	24 007	1 403	363	28	117	128	123	46	44	9	7
Wallowa	178	9.8	25 076	1 110	83	19	49	39	37	17	11	2	4
Wasco	566	1.6	24 008	1 402	330	24	130	128	123	49	44	9	10
Washington	14 904	0.0	31 578	242	11 752	802	2 408	1 502	1 394	542	440	92	164
Wheeler	30	-1.0	19 736	2 607	9	-1	12	8	8	4	2	0	0
Yamhill	2 206	2.1	25 088	1 109	1 055	135	402	343	323	133	114	23	26
PENNSYLVANIA	383 618	2.9	31 116	X	248 949	32 338	65 145	66 755	63 602	24 248	27 903	4 791	3 484
Adams	2 548	3.5	26 957	706	1 143	203	494	381	357	166	144	18	13
Allegheny	46 303	2.3	36 500	113	35 002	6 241	7 934	7 460	7 135	2 749	3 172	491	360
Armstrong	1 789	1.7	24 929	1 153	650	178	294	426	408	162	170	29	26
Beaver	4 720	1.9	26 357	818	2 224	259	632	1 104	1 059	430	447	65	64
Bedford	1 109	2.6	22 254	1 946	540	104	179	257	244	100	92	16	22
Berks	11 262	2.8	29 531	390	7 112	681	1 939	1 830	1 732	732	695	117	111
Blair	3 165	3.4	24 815	1 171	2 142	224	475	774	741	237	317	59	38
Bradford	1 461	2.9	23 290	1 633	857	120	243	303	287	126	110	25	12
Bucks	24 199	2.2	39 717	65	11 342	1 798	4 011	2 624	2 468	1 094	1 004	103	161
Butler	5 308	2.5	29 780	366	2 771	301	811	868	822	332	352	46	50
Cambria	3 590	2.6	23 885	1 444	1 967	230	587	1 017	979	351	447	65	45
Cameron	137	2.0	23 465	1 580	89	7	28	35	34	14	12	2	4
Carbon	1 511	3.5	25 320	1 038	500	114	255	350	335	138	134	17	24
Centre	3 560	4.9	25 394	1 025	2 749	273	628	495	460	189	154	26	22
Chester	21 012	2.6	46 737	27	12 724	1 808	4 269	1 690	1 575	738	590	68	92
Clarion	1 001	3.6	24 250	1 328	523	133	162	231	221	86	94	16	9
Clearfield	1 927	4.7	23 131	1 685	1 070	142	303	502	481	173	207	35	40
Clinton	860	5.2	22 888	1 755	470	61	117	205	196	77	75	14	16
Columbia	1 617	4.7	25 101	1 104	896	183	267	324	307	129	124	18	24
Crawford	2 020	2.1	22 433	1 899	1 071	175	319	488	465	180	189	38	29
Cumberland	7 152	3.8	32 854	193	5 738	449	1 372	896	841	384	325	33	33
Dauphin	8 075	4.5	31 955	226	8 128	558	1 234	1 223	1 159	442	492	90	57
Delaware	21 327	3.2	38 508	79	10 818	2 067	3 868	2 945	2 804	1 094	1 263	163	145
Elk	927	2.6	26 873	724	576	69	175	193	185	82	70	10	16
Erie	7 095	2.1	25 301	1 046	4 842	461	1 161	1 441	1 369	527	547	132	95
Fayette	3 519	4.1	23 988	1 413	1 305	269	527	1 011	973	323	440	102	50
Forest	113	5.6	22 710	1 818	49	9	24	43	42	16	19	2	4
Franklin	3 371	2.4	25 622	975	1 784	199	681	580	546	246	220	34	20
Fulton	354	2.8	24 705	1 209	183	59	54	65	61	26	24	5	4
Greene	860	3.5	21 234	2 231	545	43	123	240	230	77	106	23	9
Huntingdon	941	2.4	20 519	2 424	429	67	145	228	216	82	85	15	23
Indiana	2 117	4.2	23 802	1 471	1 171	226	380	475	453	171	179	33	29
Jefferson	1 067	3.8	23 302	1 631	504	102	191	275	264	98	112	18	17
Juniata	554	2.8	24 214	1 339	197	76	101	105	99	40	40	6	7
Lackawanna	6 090	2.3	28 846	463	3 562	550	1 090	1 325	1 271	475	576	76	61
Lancaster	14 001	2.9	29 266	413	9 083	1 174	2 607	1 952	1 830	862	707	119	72
Lawrence	2 195	2.7	23 413	1 591	1 116	137	357	596	572	224	246	44	28
Lebanon	3 380	2.6	27 836	575	1 621	227	557	577	546	248	222	26	25
Lehigh	10 257	3.2	32 374	209	7 983	851	1 779	1 687	1 606	642	697	104	107
Luzerne	8 529	2.6	27 120	674	5 325	598	1 445	1 975	1 895	730	816	110	107
Lycoming	2 980	1.6	25 096	1 107	1 881	274	503	619	588	238	225	46	49
McKean	1 122	2.4	24 705	1 209	637	83	175	266	254	100	109	21	14
Mercer	2 940	3.8	24 541	1 250	1 733	187	488	726	696	281	310	52	24
Mifflin	1 012	2.1	21 772	2 072	531	102	145	254	242	98	103	18	16
Monroe	3 761	4.4	25 223	1 070	1 953	223	576	621	583	264	217	38	37
Montgomery	36 298	2.6	47 461	22	27 739	3 647	7 532	3 607	3 412	1 549	1 409	121	211
Montour	504	3.4	27 757	580	549	35	75	102	97	37	49	5	3
Northampton	8 245	3.9	30 133	340	3 815	465	1 373	1 358	1 288	560	543	65	68
Northumberland	2 236	2.3	23 919	1 435	1 067	125	382	535	512	213	208	30	28
Perry	1 139	3.5	25 932	902	252	65	159	181	170	64	68	11	10
Philadelphia	39 257	3.6	26 369	816	35 633	3 078	4 787	10 688	10 306	2 416	5 552	1 484	483
Pike	1 266	4.3	25 292	1 050	289	99	232	200	187	104	58	10	5

1. Based on the resident population estimated as of July 1 of the year shown.   2. Includes other labor income.

Table B. States and Counties — Earnings, Social Security, and Housing

STATE County	Earnings, 2002									Social Security beneficiaries, December 2003		Supplemental Security Income recipients, December 2003	Housing units, 2003	
			Percent by selected industries											
			Goods-related[1]		Service-related and health									
	Total (mil dol)	Farm	Total	Manu-facturing	Infor-mation and profes-sional and technical services	Retail trade	Finance, insur-ance, and real estate	Health services	Govern-ment	Number	Rate[2]		Total	Percent change, 2000–2003
	75	76	77	78	79	80	81	82	83	84	85	86	87	88
OREGON—Cont'd														
Morrow	173	21.3	D	17.1	D	3.4	2.8	0.9	19.6	1 660	143	111	4 381	2.5
Multnomah	24 107	0.1	D	9.3	13.7	5.7	10.1	9.5	15.6	91 185	135	15 716	295 031	2.2
Polk	670	5.5	20.9	14.0	3.3	5.6	2.4	8.4	33.3	11 650	177	1 091	25 530	4.4
Sherman	13	-97.8	D	D	D	26.3	D	D	109.7	445	254	22	941	0.6
Tillamook	350	8.1	23.2	16.1	D	7.5	4.0	8.6	22.5	6 470	263	391	16 388	3.0
Umatilla	1 193	1.7	D	12.0	D	7.4	3.6	8.4	27.2	11 420	159	1 262	28 549	3.2
Union	391	-1.8	D	15.7	D	9.0	3.7	11.7	27.1	4 845	197	497	10 655	0.5
Wallowa	102	-6.8	31.2	13.9	3.8	11.6	4.5	4.7	28.8	1 865	263	117	3 966	1.7
Wasco	354	-0.1	D	11.7	4.2	10.9	4.3	15.9	30.5	5 080	215	510	10 711	0.6
Washington	12 553	0.8	35.1	28.1	10.2	7.2	7.0	6.6	7.1	52 270	109	4 249	191 574	7.1
Wheeler	8	-21.9	D	D	D	9.0	D	3.0	66.6	465	309	12	842	0.0
Yamhill	1 190	8.0	29.5	22.5	4.1	7.3	4.5	10.1	16.6	13 650	153	872	32 537	7.5
PENNSYLVANIA	281 286	0.3	22.3	15.9	12.4	7.1	9.0	12.0	13.2	2 386 426	193	310 485	5 365 486	2.2
Adams	1 346	2.1	33.8	22.8	4.5	7.8	3.7	9.4	16.0	17 145	178	795	37 771	5.4
Allegheny	41 243	0.0	18.2	11.7	15.6	5.8	10.7	12.6	10.2	260 245	206	31 381	589 916	1.1
Armstrong	829	2.5	26.7	13.1	4.8	11.2	3.8	12.3	15.6	16 830	235	2 217	32 875	1.5
Beaver	2 483	0.1	D	18.5	7.8	7.9	3.2	13.6	14.2	41 775	234	4 066	78 955	1.5
Bedford	644	1.4	D	23.4	2.5	9.6	2.7	7.4	14.6	10 925	219	1 093	24 077	2.3
Berks	7 793	0.9	31.2	24.4	8.5	7.7	6.8	10.0	11.3	71 085	184	6 824	155 828	3.7
Blair	2 366	0.2	D	16.1	7.1	10.5	4.0	15.3	15.8	25 500	201	4 519	55 696	1.2
Bradford	977	1.6	34.1	29.9	3.5	8.1	3.9	20.1	13.3	13 655	218	1 950	29 185	1.8
Bucks	13 139	0.2	26.1	15.9	12.7	9.8	7.3	10.5	9.3	99 750	163	5 369	233 541	3.6
Butler	3 072	0.2	32.6	23.9	5.6	10.4	4.0	8.8	13.9	32 805	182	3 185	73 421	5.1
Cambria	2 197	0.5	14.3	9.0	9.1	9.7	7.0	18.0	19.5	36 215	242	4 715	66 182	0.6
Cameron	96	0.1	61.6	58.5	D	5.4	D	D	16.9	1 420	246	126	4 620	0.6
Carbon	615	0.3	22.6	15.4	8.9	10.2	5.0	14.9	17.8	14 305	238	1 069	31 149	2.2
Centre	3 022	0.2	16.1	10.5	9.4	6.5	4.4	7.8	42.4	18 695	132	1 655	55 667	4.7
Chester	14 532	1.0	21.1	15.2	15.5	7.8	18.0	8.6	7.2	66 560	146	3 317	173 285	5.8
Clarion	656	0.6	32.6	25.2	D	9.9	3.3	8.5	23.7	8 770	213	1 089	19 803	1.9
Clearfield	1 212	0.1	20.4	12.6	D	10.1	4.0	15.7	17.2	18 085	218	2 478	38 445	1.6
Clinton	531	0.6	37.8	33.4	3.3	9.8	3.7	8.7	21.9	7 925	212	954	18 605	2.4
Columbia	1 079	0.8	D	32.3	5.4	8.5	3.2	9.2	17.2	13 395	207	1 358	28 412	2.4
Crawford	1 247	0.3	34.6	28.4	4.7	8.1	3.3	13.6	15.5	18 660	208	2 725	43 261	2.0
Cumberland	6 187	0.1	D	8.5	D	8.5	11.8	10.4	17.3	38 025	173	1 749	90 445	4.0
Dauphin	8 686	0.1	15.3	9.9	9.0	5.3	9.6	10.7	25.5	44 080	174	5 529	113 462	2.1
Delaware	12 885	0.0	20.3	13.9	15.1	7.4	11.1	13.1	9.5	99 400	179	9 112	219 883	1.3
Elk	646	-0.1	57.0	52.9	3.1	5.0	2.3	10.1	8.6	7 875	230	608	18 317	1.1
Erie	5 303	0.4	31.8	26.4	6.2	8.3	7.4	14.4	13.9	52 525	188	8 610	116 272	1.7
Fayette	1 574	0.3	19.7	12.0	6.9	12.6	3.8	13.9	16.4	34 010	233	8 485	67 400	1.4
Forest	58	0.0	D	11.0	D	7.1	D	D	29.1	1 620	325	148	8 882	2.1
Franklin	1 983	1.2	D	21.6	5.3	9.0	3.8	13.2	17.5	26 690	200	2 168	56 296	4.6
Fulton	242	1.7	D	46.5	1.4	5.7	2.2	D	12.4	2 985	205	341	7 059	4.0
Greene	587	0.1	44.3	3.8	2.2	6.4	2.3	D	21.6	8 055	199	1 781	17 024	2.1
Huntingdon	496	1.8	D	17.2	2.6	6.9	4.6	D	27.3	9 070	198	1 101	21 621	2.7
Indiana	1 397	1.0	22.3	10.8	5.9	9.2	6.3	9.7	23.7	17 310	194	2 566	38 090	2.3
Jefferson	607	0.6	38.2	29.2	3.9	8.5	3.3	D	13.0	10 250	223	1 370	22 503	1.8
Juniata	273	1.7	43.0	33.6	2.9	9.1	4.2	D	10.3	4 380	190	392	10 251	2.2
Lackawanna	4 112	0.1	23.4	18.4	8.3	9.8	7.9	16.0	13.2	49 685	236	5 649	96 219	0.9
Lancaster	10 257	0.7	36.2	25.6	8.2	8.9	6.1	10.0	8.8	83 225	172	7 288	186 695	3.7
Lawrence	1 253	0.1	26.0	16.2	6.3	9.6	6.7	14.6	16.9	22 415	240	3 072	40 318	1.7
Lebanon	1 848	0.7	D	24.5	D	9.2	D	14.2	17.9	24 980	204	1 724	51 164	3.7
Lehigh	8 834	0.1	D	21.3	8.5	6.6	7.4	15.5	8.4	62 510	195	7 054	133 070	3.2
Luzerne	5 922	0.1	21.5	15.8	8.8	7.9	6.8	13.8	15.3	75 930	242	8 423	146 026	0.9
Lycoming	2 155	0.3	34.0	29.1	5.7	8.6	4.8	12.8	16.8	24 690	208	3 232	53 380	1.7
McKean	720	0.3	37.8	29.2	D	7.1	3.9	11.6	17.3	10 155	224	1 552	21 807	0.8
Mercer	1 919	0.6	30.9	26.4	4.2	9.1	4.7	17.1	12.5	27 895	233	3 782	51 072	2.4
Mifflin	633	0.7	40.3	35.1	2.8	9.5	4.1	12.7	12.2	10 370	224	1 363	21 094	1.7
Monroe	2 175	0.0	D	14.0	6.0	11.1	5.8	8.4	24.2	26 620	172	2 058	72 310	7.0
Montgomery	31 387	0.0	23.4	16.5	19.6	6.1	13.4	10.7	6.2	133 005	173	6 756	305 601	2.7
Montour	584	1.2	7.3	5.8	2.4	3.2	3.9	D	10.2	3 935	218	467	7 806	2.3
Northampton	4 280	0.1	28.9	20.0	7.6	8.2	6.1	8.8	14.0	53 835	194	4 363	111 167	4.2
Northumberland	1 192	0.6	34.8	29.0	5.0	8.1	3.1	8.3	15.1	22 840	245	2 581	43 482	0.7
Perry	316	3.8	D	11.5	4.3	12.1	3.9	4.7	24.7	7 065	160	555	19 514	3.0
Philadelphia	38 710	0.0	D	5.7	18.6	3.7	10.7	13.7	18.5	251 755	170	91 882	659 260	-0.4
Pike	389	0.2	D	6.2	9.2	9.5	12.4	6.2	24.0	10 340	198	574	36 399	5.0

1. Covers mining, construction, and manufacturing.   2. Per 1,000 resident population estimated as of July 1 of the year shown.

Table B. States and Counties — Housing, Labor Force, and Employment

STATE County	Housing units, 2000 Occupied units — Owner-occupied Total	Percent	Median value[1]	Median owner cost as a percent of income — With a mortgage	Without a mortgage[2]	Renter-occupied — Median rent[3]	Median rent as a percent of income	Substandard units[4] (percent)	Civilian labor force, 2003 Total	Percent change, 2002–2003	Unemployment Total	Rate[5]	Civilian employment,[6] 2000 Total	Percent — Management, professional and related occupations	Production, transportation, and material moving occupations
	89	90	91	92	93	94	95	96	97	98	99	100	101	102	103
OREGON—Cont'd															
Morrow	3 776	73.1	89 000	19.8	9.9	473	21.0	12.8	5 050	6.0	518	10.3	4 635	24.9	23.5
Multnomah	272 098	56.9	157 900	23.8	11.9	633	27.3	6.0	376 655	-0.1	33 812	9.0	341 522	35.7	14.1
Polk	23 058	68.4	142 700	23.4	9.9	565	28.1	5.4	31 953	1.7	2 217	6.9	29 247	33.8	14.3
Sherman	797	70.4	77 400	18.9	9.9	390	23.0	3.8	949	1.9	113	11.9	827	34.1	16.0
Tillamook	10 200	71.9	143 900	23.3	9.9	532	25.4	4.1	11 921	1.2	788	6.6	10 956	27.3	17.2
Umatilla	25 195	64.9	98 100	20.7	9.9	481	22.9	7.1	38 356	-0.4	3 268	8.5	31 068	25.4	19.3
Union	9 740	66.6	93 600	20.5	12.0	487	27.6	2.9	12 675	0.1	829	6.5	10 883	30.7	17.0
Wallowa	3 029	71.8	111 300	22.7	11.3	451	24.8	3.4	3 411	-1.6	372	10.9	3 043	32.9	14.1
Wasco	9 401	68.4	105 500	21.9	11.4	488	26.8	4.9	12 887	0.8	1 377	10.7	10 302	27.1	16.0
Washington	169 162	66.5	184 800	22.7	9.9	720	25.3	5.6	272 309	0.0	19 776	7.3	233 091	40.0	12.3
Wheeler	653	72.1	66 300	23.6	10.6	410	23.5	3.4	599	-0.8	50	8.3	614	34.7	12.9
Yamhill	28 732	69.6	146 200	23.6	10.5	623	26.1	5.3	42 881	0.4	3 587	8.4	39 196	27.6	18.7
PENNSYLVANIA	4 777 003	71.3	97 000	21.6	12.2	531	25.0	2.4	6 170 013	-1.8	343 884	5.6	5 653 500	32.6	16.3
Adams	33 652	76.8	110 100	23.3	10.9	509	22.1	2.6	47 330	-0.2	1 902	4.0	46 188	24.9	23.0
Allegheny	537 150	67.0	84 200	20.9	12.9	516	25.5	1.5	665 241	-2.2	34 235	5.1	591 905	37.8	10.1
Armstrong	29 005	77.3	64 500	20.5	12.4	395	23.7	1.9	31 186	-1.8	2 193	7.0	30 308	22.1	25.2
Beaver	72 576	74.9	85 000	21.1	13.0	438	23.2	1.5	85 646	-2.6	5 342	6.2	82 493	26.2	18.1
Bedford	19 768	80.2	80 200	21.9	11.2	401	22.1	2.0	25 434	-3.5	2 130	8.4	22 458	23.0	26.8
Berks	141 570	74.0	104 900	21.4	12.0	545	24.3	2.8	184 361	-1.7	11 479	6.2	180 881	29.3	21.3
Blair	51 518	72.9	73 600	20.4	11.5	411	25.7	1.4	65 274	-1.7	3 322	5.1	57 756	25.6	19.5
Bradford	24 453	75.5	73 900	20.5	11.2	414	23.8	1.8	29 730	-2.0	1 709	5.7	27 985	27.6	25.9
Bucks	218 725	77.3	163 200	23.0	13.0	736	24.2	1.9	337 285	-1.6	15 673	4.6	308 281	38.4	12.0
Butler	65 862	77.8	114 100	21.0	10.7	487	24.3	1.4	93 371	-2.3	4 923	5.3	82 534	32.0	17.0
Cambria	60 531	74.7	62 700	20.2	12.3	361	23.5	1.2	64 914	-1.7	4 402	6.8	61 115	27.9	17.2
Cameron	2 465	75.0	61 300	20.4	12.1	368	20.9	1.5	2 708	1.7	214	7.9	2 541	20.0	38.0
Carbon	23 701	78.2	82 100	23.1	12.6	458	25.4	1.4	27 715	-0.8	2 276	8.2	26 458	22.8	24.5
Centre	49 323	60.2	114 900	22.2	9.9	565	31.3	4.1	68 746	-2.5	2 331	3.4	64 663	41.6	11.1
Chester	157 905	76.3	182 500	21.8	11.9	754	23.5	2.0	248 019	-1.3	9 448	3.8	221 255	45.2	9.7
Clarion	16 052	72.2	68 800	18.9	10.1	383	25.0	2.6	19 452	-1.4	1 022	5.3	17 969	25.8	20.7
Clearfield	32 785	79.2	62 600	21.3	12.0	376	23.8	1.6	38 488	-1.9	3 095	8.0	35 659	23.1	24.1
Clinton	14 773	73.0	78 000	21.1	13.0	411	26.3	1.6	18 844	-2.5	1 351	7.2	16 895	23.6	24.9
Columbia	24 915	72.2	87 300	20.8	11.0	448	25.1	1.8	33 629	-0.7	2 283	6.8	30 006	23.7	24.4
Crawford	34 678	75.4	72 800	19.8	12.0	406	24.1	3.0	41 072	-3.6	2 964	7.2	39 514	26.4	25.9
Cumberland	83 015	73.0	120 500	21.1	9.9	576	23.5	1.3	126 107	-1.5	4 010	3.2	106 711	34.6	14.5
Dauphin	102 670	65.4	99 900	20.9	11.5	557	23.6	2.5	143 686	-1.5	5 987	4.2	122 805	34.9	14.2
Delaware	206 320	71.9	128 800	22.3	13.8	662	26.3	2.3	284 494	-1.3	14 395	5.1	258 782	39.3	9.7
Elk	14 124	79.4	78 000	19.8	10.1	418	22.3	1.2	16 594	-4.0	1 197	7.2	16 745	22.5	36.2
Erie	106 507	69.2	85 300	20.4	11.6	445	25.0	2.0	140 261	-3.1	9 678	6.9	129 325	29.2	20.5
Fayette	59 969	73.1	63 900	20.8	11.1	367	25.0	1.8	59 508	-1.9	4 990	8.4	59 017	23.9	20.7
Forest	2 000	82.6	57 300	18.8	11.9	337	24.9	2.1	2 175	-1.8	355	16.3	1 830	23.6	26.8
Franklin	50 633	74.0	97 800	20.6	9.9	455	20.6	1.9	64 537	-0.5	2 736	4.2	62 780	27.5	21.6
Fulton	5 660	79.0	83 900	21.0	10.4	389	21.2	2.0	6 481	-1.2	407	6.3	6 709	21.3	26.8
Greene	15 060	74.1	56 900	19.1	12.2	367	24.3	2.5	16 468	-2.8	1 093	6.6	15 168	24.9	16.4
Huntingdon	16 759	77.6	72 800	20.5	11.2	380	20.9	1.8	18 886	-3.7	1 652	8.7	18 887	24.8	24.2
Indiana	34 123	71.8	72 700	21.2	11.2	426	29.2	2.7	37 532	-2.0	2 526	6.7	37 758	26.0	17.3
Jefferson	18 375	77.2	59 100	19.8	10.8	377	25.0	1.6	21 080	-1.5	1 418	6.7	19 846	21.9	28.2
Juniata	8 584	77.7	87 000	20.7	9.9	395	19.1	2.4	11 008	0.3	607	5.5	10 584	23.1	26.8
Lackawanna	86 218	67.6	93 400	21.8	13.5	440	24.3	0.9	105 906	-1.7	5 713	5.4	96 290	29.6	17.4
Lancaster	172 560	70.9	119 300	22.0	9.9	572	23.6	2.7	255 433	-1.9	10 090	4.0	235 686	28.1	22.0
Lawrence	37 091	77.3	72 200	20.3	12.4	424	26.9	1.9	40 051	-1.8	2 641	6.6	41 035	26.6	20.7
Lebanon	46 551	72.7	100 700	21.4	10.7	470	22.5	2.1	67 620	-1.4	2 553	3.8	59 767	25.4	23.2
Lehigh	121 906	68.8	113 600	21.8	12.4	586	25.2	2.5	166 551	-1.5	9 278	5.6	150 424	33.5	16.9
Luzerne	130 687	70.3	84 800	21.1	13.2	434	24.4	1.2	156 401	-1.5	9 706	6.2	143 492	27.7	19.0
Lycoming	47 003	69.5	86 200	20.9	12.1	449	24.9	1.4	56 982	-2.0	3 601	6.3	54 817	24.4	22.6
McKean	18 024	74.8	53 500	18.9	11.3	416	25.7	1.4	20 880	-2.9	1 305	6.3	20 085	25.9	27.5
Mercer	46 712	76.2	76 000	20.1	11.7	443	24.6	1.9	58 302	-2.3	3 000	5.1	52 142	27.6	21.0
Mifflin	18 413	74.1	73 300	21.1	11.6	384	25.1	2.9	20 919	-3.1	1 565	7.5	20 466	21.8	31.2
Monroe	49 454	78.3	125 200	24.3	13.4	658	26.7	1.9	60 994	0.2	4 460	7.3	63 598	29.5	16.1
Montgomery	286 098	73.5	160 700	22.1	12.4	757	23.8	1.8	425 767	-1.5	18 676	4.4	384 688	44.5	9.9
Montour	7 085	72.8	93 400	21.5	9.9	459	21.1	2.3	8 862	-3.0	361	4.1	8 212	34.3	19.2
Northampton	101 541	73.3	120 000	22.4	12.6	576	25.2	1.7	138 022	-1.2	7 593	5.5	127 810	31.4	18.1
Northumberland	38 835	73.6	69 300	20.7	11.3	389	23.2	1.4	43 346	-2.7	3 082	7.1	41 814	22.9	26.5
Perry	16 695	79.6	96 500	21.7	9.9	473	20.9	2.1	24 167	-1.4	1 131	4.7	21 740	23.9	21.4
Philadelphia	590 071	59.3	59 700	21.5	13.4	569	28.4	6.0	666 933	-1.4	50 903	7.6	584 957	31.5	12.5
Pike	17 433	84.8	118 300	24.5	13.7	701	28.2	1.6	22 763	-0.1	1 131	5.0	19 639	28.6	14.3

1. Specified owner-occupied units.   2. Median monthly owner costs is often in the minimum category—9.9 percent or less, which is indicated as 9.9 percent.   3. Specified renter-occupied units.   4. Overcrowded or lacking complete plumbing facilities.   5. Percent of civilian labor force.   6. Persons 16 years old and over.

Table B. States and Counties — Nonfarm Employment and Agriculture

	Private nonfarm establishments, employment and payroll, 2001									Agriculture, 2002			
	Employment						Annual payroll		Farms			
											Percent with—		
STATE County	Number of establishments	Total	Health care and social assistance	Manufacturing	Retail trade	Finance and insurance	Professional, scientific, and technical services	Total (mil dol)	Average per employee (dollars)	Number	Less than 50 acres	500 acres and over	Farm operators whose principal occupation is farming (percent)
	104	105	106	107	108	109	110	111	112	113	114	115	116
OREGON—Cont'd													
Morrow	153	1 630	117	D	154	79	D	46	27 951	375	21.9	54.7	69.9
Multnomah	23 593	406 053	46 087	43 652	43 384	23 623	28 873	14 696	36 194	710	83.2	1.5	47.0
Polk	1 147	12 767	1 530	2 115	1 559	229	304	293	22 980	1 324	64.4	5.2	51.7
Sherman	47	274	D	0	D	D	D	4	15 464	210	10.5	65.2	67.1
Tillamook	702	6 288	714	1 219	996	132	130	153	24 293	333	37.8	3.3	70.0
Umatilla	1 608	20 571	2 826	3 774	4 447	584	1 021	494	24 022	1 648	53.9	23.1	53.5
Union	729	7 083	1 081	1 311	1 486	186	203	157	22 189	993	49.3	19.4	48.0
Wallowa	338	1 463	253	D	287	82	51	34	22 909	503	37.8	32.4	59.8
Wasco	715	7 495	1 537	772	1 344	235	185	178	23 758	538	34.0	30.5	62.6
Washington	12 512	221 760	16 335	36 395	28 690	11 352	12 701	9 344	42 135	1 900	74.4	2.6	48.1
Wheeler	36	107	D	D	D	6	D	2	14 280	164	17.7	47.6	68.9
Yamhill	2 017	24 097	2 886	5 964	3 258	666	557	638	26 497	2 329	73.8	4.2	49.1
PENNSYLVANIA	295 096	5 123 111	758 225	780 266	670 446	307 930	302 487	169 850	33 154	58 105	37.8	4.2	56.7
Adams	1 911	29 685	3 672	8 880	3 546	577	396	725	24 420	1 261	49.2	6.5	55.3
Allegheny	34 819	691 041	110 204	52 469	75 771	48 037	55 953	24 678	35 711	464	61.6	1.3	47.0
Armstrong	1 496	16 317	3 046	2 737	3 221	526	751	392	24 022	739	21.5	6.6	50.9
Beaver	3 476	48 497	7 982	10 150	7 726	1 402	1 976	1 324	27 302	645	39.1	1.6	54.7
Bedford	1 081	14 476	1 352	4 156	3 061	343	179	346	23 915	1 093	22.3	5.9	61.1
Berks	8 210	151 116	17 147	39 293	20 413	8 360	7 470	4 701	31 109	1 791	48.4	4.5	63.5
Blair	3 235	49 572	8 640	8 487	8 560	1 517	2 154	1 256	25 340	504	31.0	6.7	64.9
Bradford	1 321	19 022	4 399	6 131	2 983	544	441	515	27 057	1 495	22.3	8.4	59.5
Bucks	18 032	252 054	28 514	36 192	40 236	11 050	14 918	8 206	32 557	917	70.1	3.4	55.0
Butler	4 294	62 054	8 283	14 691	10 251	1 432	1 976	1 860	29 979	1 174	33.8	3.5	53.7
Cambria	3 520	49 418	10 115	6 010	7 866	3 371	2 672	1 160	23 472	634	34.4	5.8	48.9
Cameron	140	1 997	178	1 114	260	23	18	46	23 197	35	17.1	0.0	45.7
Carbon	1 114	14 384	2 111	2 959	2 120	401	196	320	22 260	206	49.5	2.4	43.7
Centre	3 163	46 374	5 667	8 176	8 038	1 835	3 227	1 158	24 971	1 213	37.6	4.2	48.2
Chester	12 399	194 895	25 102	19 314	25 852	10 953	23 470	8 386	43 030	1 918	59.6	2.9	57.3
Clarion	1 067	12 387	1 815	2 683	2 313	378	263	296	23 878	591	18.3	6.9	52.3
Clearfield	1 922	26 263	4 783	4 542	4 420	788	561	611	23 269	468	33.5	3.2	50.6
Clinton	742	10 160	1 144	2 998	2 329	188	177	222	21 857	420	36.0	4.5	57.9
Columbia	1 499	24 541	3 257	7 460	3 564	776	788	671	27 325	884	32.6	4.6	52.0
Crawford	2 152	28 294	4 526	8 890	3 976	539	629	675	23 871	1 416	29.1	4.8	57.0
Cumberland	5 587	116 606	13 850	12 425	15 943	9 905	5 581	3 562	30 545	1 116	38.0	4.6	60.7
Dauphin	6 573	138 623	19 031	12 122	15 829	10 620	7 406	4 443	32 053	852	47.2	2.9	53.9
Delaware	13 214	214 183	34 475	18 776	28 948	12 677	13 251	8 470	39 544	76	82.9	0.0	42.1
Elk	990	14 405	2 018	7 255	1 586	246	208	379	26 345	226	38.9	0.4	42.9
Erie	6 994	122 308	17 695	35 139	16 472	4 617	3 304	3 348	27 375	1 283	37.7	3.9	55.5
Fayette	2 753	34 269	6 516	4 341	6 507	855	984	744	21 696	978	36.2	3.7	47.9
Forest	146	1 187	D	190	D	D	D	26	22 141	59	40.7	1.7	59.3
Franklin	2 804	42 437	7 009	9 906	6 510	997	1 459	1 098	25 883	1 418	31.1	6.1	68.9
Fulton	290	5 449	492	3 010	336	129	71	146	26 815	561	18.0	6.2	54.7
Greene	668	8 615	1 336	700	1 191	249	123	275	31 870	881	19.4	3.5	47.0
Huntingdon	826	10 132	1 604	2 686	1 536	415	229	224	22 059	848	28.4	6.1	59.4
Indiana	1 984	27 017	3 345	3 117	4 407	1 265	1 497	639	23 648	903	25.2	5.4	48.5
Jefferson	1 185	13 242	2 093	4 321	1 713	332	277	304	22 929	548	22.4	4.0	50.5
Juniata	501	5 961	673	2 354	744	223	63	138	23 123	644	34.9	3.1	67.4
Lackawanna	5 397	94 447	17 201	16 649	13 476	4 710	2 644	2 380	25 199	289	33.2	1.4	57.1
Lancaster	11 524	214 803	27 559	50 760	32 915	7 202	7 634	6 340	29 516	5 293	44.5	1.2	74.3
Lawrence	2 163	29 351	4 778	5 581	4 002	1 667	1 184	735	25 051	703	35.3	3.8	58.3
Lebanon	2 597	38 962	6 654	9 981	6 526	878	949	1 031	26 458	1 104	46.4	1.5	63.0
Lehigh	8 190	165 692	26 911	24 418	19 239	8 676	5 655	6 018	36 318	618	62.1	5.5	55.2
Luzerne	7 580	127 970	19 795	21 032	18 681	5 646	4 422	3 287	25 685	548	40.5	3.5	46.2
Lycoming	2 825	47 378	7 968	12 858	7 295	1 724	1 329	1 209	25 509	1 323	30.7	3.3	52.5
McKean	1 116	15 261	2 427	5 030	1 985	330	280	384	25 161	265	30.6	4.9	55.5
Mercer	2 938	45 108	9 110	9 867	7 742	1 218	837	1 091	24 188	1 239	28.1	3.2	55.4
Mifflin	924	14 528	2 527	5 161	2 463	323	193	347	23 893	752	29.8	2.8	70.5
Monroe	3 312	41 183	4 491	5 369	8 728	966	1 401	996	24 191	324	52.8	2.5	45.7
Montgomery	26 051	515 433	59 651	61 535	60 361	58 013	40 383	22 306	43 277	729	67.6	1.6	52.0
Montour	355	11 474	D	1 496	755	603	235	413	35 963	304	29.6	4.6	49.7
Northampton	5 667	80 747	9 145	15 972	10 561	5 633	2 496	2 416	29 916	487	56.3	9.9	61.8
Northumberland	1 765	23 907	3 152	6 994	3 652	570	478	570	23 858	719	39.9	6.0	52.9
Perry	753	6 138	646	922	1 513	216	149	123	20 075	752	27.0	5.3	60.9
Philadelphia	25 621	609 775	116 414	39 454	49 489	59 140	64 030	23 590	38 687	9	88.9	0.0	66.7
Pike	732	5 556	484	284	1 225	160	191	118	21 194	51	37.3	11.8	54.9

Table B. States and Counties — Agriculture

STATE County	Acreage (1,000) [117]	Percent change, 1997-2002 [118]	Average size of farm [119]	Total irrigated (1,000) [120]	Total cropland (1,000) [121]	Average per farm (dollars) [122]	Average per acre [123]	Value of machinery and equipment average per farm (dollars) [124]	Total (mil dol) [125]	Average per farm (dollars) [126]	Crops [127]	Live-stock and poultry products [128]	$10,000 or more [129]	$100,000 or more [130]	Total ($1,000) [131]	Percent of farms [132]
OREGON—Cont'd																
Morrow	1 125	0.6	2 999	95	465	1 127 290	365	144 885	237	632 815	43.9	56.1	54.9	22.9	7 556	61.6
Multnomah	34	0.0	48	8	24	505 733	10 876	46 930	68	95 143	97.8	2.2	33.5	10.1	59	2.5
Polk	169	-1.2	128	13	125	548 559	4 948	56 604	90	67 663	74.9	25.1	27.2	9.3	605	11.3
Sherman	508	19.5	2 418	2	335	889 122	368	138 674	15	71 359	88.9	11.1	51.4	27.1	4 865	75.2
Tillamook	40	11.1	119	6	22	557 675	5 259	81 089	89	267 110	1.1	98.9	54.1	44.1	1 881	23.7
Umatilla	1 331	-1.0	808	122	750	605 831	765	82 533	206	124 803	76.2	23.8	36.2	15.5	11 461	32.0
Union	478	-10.2	482	65	158	510 520	1 044	193 196	48	48 352	63.7	36.3	28.9	7.8	1 656	22.6
Wallowa	518	-16.6	1 030	40	118	596 339	614	50 768	21	41 303	34.1	65.9	41.7	10.7	1 588	40.0
Wasco	1 087	-4.2	2 020	32	241	782 204	394	79 336	43	80 340	77.9	22.1	45.5	18.8	3 721	34.6
Washington	131	0.0	69	25	96	537 825	7 294	47 656	232	122 010	93.4	6.6	34.8	11.4	1 092	9.1
Wheeler	738	8.5	4 501	14	38	1 217 864	274	54 371	6	38 152	9.9	90.1	40.2	11.0	226	13.4
Yamhill	196	5.4	84	25	132	541 936	6 885	58 874	209	89 548	82.4	17.6	26.0	7.6	1 035	10.9
PENNSYLVANIA	7 745	8.0	133	43	5 121	452 874	3 419	59 995	4 257	73 263	31.0	69.0	39.1	16.5	85 794	20.6
Adams	181	1.1	144	3	135	594 491	3 781	74 562	140	110 871	38.2	61.8	40.5	16.8	2 595	22.7
Allegheny	34	25.9	73	0	19	364 958	4 763	38 100	9	20 239	87.3	12.7	23.7	5.6	62	7.1
Armstrong	131	9.2	177	0	83	429 378	2 333	60 428	46	62 687	76.1	23.9	31.7	6.9	659	20.8
Beaver	63	16.7	97	0	39	267 155	2 976	37 071	11	16 788	36.2	63.9	22.0	4.5	345	15.2
Bedford	193	-3.0	176	0	113	373 068	1 980	51 997	57	52 595	15.3	84.7	38.7	17.6	2 632	24.8
Berks	216	-2.7	120	2	173	661 305	5 527	63 509	287	160 233	41.8	58.2	50.1	24.5	3 805	22.8
Blair	86	2.4	170	0	60	512 958	3 126	79 549	63	125 699	9.4	90.6	51.8	27.4	1 987	28.0
Bradford	302	-1.6	202	0	185	351 386	1 790	63 670	100	66 753	7.2	92.8	40.9	19.9	3 607	30.6
Bucks	77	-8.3	84	1	59	768 909	9 418	61 622	62	67 219	80.7	19.3	34.8	12.5	773	12.4
Butler	144	21.0	123	1	96	491 784	3 950	56 795	32	27 648	51.1	48.9	29.3	7.0	789	21.0
Cambria	88	0.0	139	0	58	421 590	2 687	48 999	18	28 773	43.1	56.9	25.9	6.2	819	26.5
Cameron	4	0.0	122	0	1	228 370	1 878	28 678	0	9 574	54.9	45.1	20.0	0.0	D	D
Carbon	19	-5.0	93	0	14	419 182	4 436	46 452	8	39 551	87.0	13.0	33.0	7.3	105	25.7
Centre	165	21.3	136	1	104	447 167	3 400	47 969	53	44 010	27.8	72.2	38.0	13.8	1 654	18.3
Chester	168	-4.0	88	2	124	889 836	10 358	53 782	377	196 440	76.5	23.5	40.1	22.7	2 191	12.7
Clarion	109	16.0	184	0	67	364 272	1 837	62 906	18	29 843	27.7	72.3	29.3	8.0	749	26.4
Clearfield	61	15.1	130	0	37	190 830	1 650	28 376	11	23 910	45.5	54.5	29.1	7.1	389	20.7
Clinton	53	29.3	127	1	34	340 487	2 804	48 436	27	63 596	22.7	77.3	43.8	22.9	595	20.5
Columbia	124	12.7	140	1	89	448 782	3 137	80 984	35	39 732	55.0	45.0	32.8	8.5	1 616	44.2
Crawford	222	7.2	157	0	133	288 743	1 738	67 748	58	41 026	21.4	78.6	35.2	11.1	1 820	18.1
Cumberland	143	0.0	128	1	115	484 967	3 826	64 693	90	80 351	19.2	80.8	49.3	25.1	2 460	26.6
Dauphin	95	9.2	111	1	77	556 467	5 291	48 991	46	54 562	21.2	78.8	35.4	13.5	948	24.8
Delaware	D	D	D	0	1	764 965	22 852	30 887	7	94 131	98.7	1.3	35.5	14.5	D	D
Elk	22	29.4	98	0	11	346 849	3 104	55 219	3	12 757	36.3	63.7	21.2	4.9	51	9.3
Erie	166	-1.2	129	2	106	299 506	2 320	72 463	64	50 187	65.2	34.8	42.6	12.6	1 488	19.6
Fayette	125	14.7	128	0	71	268 741	1 844	53 543	21	21 824	41.2	58.8	21.4	4.7	738	11.7
Forest	6	20.0	96	D	3	196 661	2 008	27 019	1	11 283	32.9	67.1	27.1	1.7	D	D
Franklin	245	2.9	173	3	191	641 792	3 879	82 598	218	153 986	10.6	89.4	57.9	37.1	6 098	29.2
Fulton	101	7.4	179	0	54	414 929	2 318	84 981	26	45 771	10.4	89.6	30.8	10.9	1 184	36.2
Greene	142	8.4	161	0	75	152 750	1 184	33 740	7	8 169	30.9	69.1	16.2	1.4	148	6.6
Huntingdon	143	14.4	169	0	78	456 492	2 436	55 752	43	51 238	14.4	85.6	30.4	11.4	1 593	24.3
Indiana	157	12.9	174	1	91	315 708	1 879	63 115	56	62 004	65.3	34.7	34.8	11.0	1 052	18.8
Jefferson	87	8.8	159	0	58	359 097	1 856	56 218	12	22 036	31.5	68.5	27.7	7.7	468	16.1
Juniata	86	-1.1	134	0	55	369 626	3 059	62 032	68	104 999	6.8	93.2	52.3	26.1	1 482	37.6
Lackawanna	33	10.0	114	0	22	333 285	3 205	65 040	14	46 820	65.7	34.3	37.4	11.4	164	13.8
Lancaster	412	5.1	78	6	333	610 359	7 955	68 923	798	150 831	11.1	88.9	68.3	39.6	6 846	11.4
Lawrence	87	0.0	124	0	59	308 650	2 441	145 126	22	31 808	24.5	75.5	40.0	8.5	817	18.8
Lebanon	125	12.6	113	2	103	592 004	5 349	74 969	191	173 101	9.0	91.0	57.3	37.6	2 921	20.1
Lehigh	91	-1.1	148	1	73	610 357	4 504	79 161	50	80 694	73.0	27.0	34.6	11.2	1 294	20.6
Luzerne	73	28.1	134	1	39	551 229	3 541	50 259	22	40 887	81.0	19.0	28.6	10.4	403	19.3
Lycoming	177	30.1	134	2	104	315 040	2 318	48 714	49	37 188	32.9	67.1	29.2	10.8	1 370	22.2
McKean	42	7.7	157	0	19	195 407	1 179	34 523	5	18 084	21.8	78.2	24.2	4.9	106	17.7
Mercer	164	-1.8	133	0	109	256 427	2 070	46 184	44	35 300	31.9	68.1	38.6	9.4	1 753	24.5
Mifflin	90	13.9	120	0	61	381 165	3 189	51 401	55	73 788	8.6	91.4	57.7	23.1	1 748	22.9
Monroe	33	26.9	102	0	19	567 011	5 191	48 045	7	20 305	71.2	28.8	18.5	5.2	136	13.9
Montgomery	48	14.3	66	0	34	698 038	12 748	50 921	35	48 608	71.5	28.5	30.5	10.0	443	12.3
Montour	40	0.0	131	0	28	385 870	2 996	60 460	27	90 178	71.2	28.8	37.5	12.2	549	39.1
Northampton	78	0.0	159	0	66	720 687	4 862	89 116	22	44 870	63.2	36.8	37.4	14.2	1 136	23.8
Northumberland	119	3.5	166	1	94	494 522	3 099	62 032	99	138 009	26.8	73.2	46.0	19.7	1 751	37.7
Perry	129	12.2	172	0	90	473 540	3 203	57 438	70	92 784	13.3	86.7	41.2	21.0	1 886	34.4
Philadelphia	D	NA	D	D	0	629 052	26 090	16 482	0	40 350	100.0	0.0	77.8	11.1	0	0.0
Pike	10	66.7	198	0	3	506 258	2 878	43 009	2	35 211	70.3	29.7	19.6	11.8	D	D

STATE County	New construction ($1,000)	Number of housing units	Number of establishments	Number of employees	Sales (mil dol)	Annual payroll (mil dol)	Number of establishments	Number of employees	Sales (mil dol)	Annual payroll (mil dol)	Number of establishments	Number of employees	Receipts (mil dol)	Annual payroll (mil dol)
	Value of residential construction authorized by building permits, 2003		Wholesale trade, 1997				Retail trade,¹ 1997				Real estate and rental and leasing, 1997			
	133	134	135	136	137	138	139	140	141	142	143	144	145	146
OREGON—Cont'd														
Morrow	1 837	9	12	73	103.1	2.1	30	217	38.8	3.2	4	D	D	D
Multnomah	514 172	4 871	1 850	28 384	25 188.5	1 017.7	3 025	39 841	7 334.5	791.4	1 118	8 335	1 053.2	208.9
Polk	58 055	391	41	425	87.3	8.7	143	1 592	232.4	24.3	54	145	14.5	1.9
Sherman	150	1	2	D	D	D	13	91	12.9	1.3	NA	NA	NA	NA
Tillamook	38 896	281	22	114	18.8	2.0	123	1 044	144.1	15.0	28	104	6.7	1.3
Umatilla	27 521	190	75	954	331.6	22.8	290	3 188	567.2	53.7	61	164	14.5	2.2
Union	6 192	31	34	301	96.2	7.4	129	1 355	227.7	23.5	22	61	6.2	0.7
Wallowa	NA	NA	4	11	5.1	0.2	52	336	61.8	6.2	13	29	2.6	0.4
Wasco	2 780	17	36	550	115.7	11.3	134	1 468	256.9	26.1	28	81	7.0	1.3
Washington	729 661	4 196	1 035	13 622	13 153.8	603.2	1 499	25 124	5 453.5	512.3	579	3 098	418.9	64.6
Wheeler	0	0	1	D	D	D	6	19	8.5	0.5	1	D	D	D
Yamhill	101 385	784	73	485	259.1	14.8	269	3 313	627.2	58.4	82	306	36.1	4.6
PENNSYLVANIA	6 051 793	47 356	17 138	237 567	159 354.2	8 588.2	50 208	650 144	109 948.5	10 561.9	8 684	57 519	7 668.6	1 360.5
Adams	76 542	532	88	1 211	909.7	33.2	330	3 072	472.7	45.6	45	139	12.6	1.8
Allegheny	396 911	2 451	2 490	33 034	28 256.0	1 269.4	5 353	78 841	12 929.7	1 218.0	1 274	9 616	1 645.6	239.8
Armstrong	15 722	157	48	285	65.1	5.9	310	3 255	487.1	43.3	31	116	12.1	2.7
Beaver	54 501	412	148	1 515	570.5	46.5	668	8 513	1 180.5	113.7	80	374	35.1	7.2
Bedford	17 576	172	44	451	207.7	11.7	216	2 298	438.9	35.6	18	41	4.1	0.5
Berks	263 911	1 991	439	7 051	3 121.7	253.0	1 468	19 302	3 330.7	326.2	215	1 324	191.3	28.1
Blair	39 309	362	160	2 836	1 641.3	82.3	639	8 310	1 331.2	117.7	90	419	34.8	6.9
Bradford	17 639	180	55	512	175.1	10.7	296	3 315	521.2	46.4	31	92	10.0	1.5
Bucks	331 905	3 215	1 433	16 257	8 415.9	684.2	2 549	36 195	7 217.4	701.3	506	3 166	420.4	82.5
Butler	145 646	1 146	272	4 732	4 540.8	140.5	709	9 317	1 480.2	137.0	112	492	76.0	10.6
Cambria	29 753	237	144	2 115	580.7	57.5	693	8 555	1 244.8	111.5	77	347	32.4	5.1
Cameron	630	10	2	D	D	D	27	287	31.0	3.8	NA	NA	NA	NA
Carbon	63 431	420	34	240	91.4	7.0	219	2 102	316.7	30.9	27	81	5.5	1.3
Centre	113 521	1 022	100	D	D	D	617	7 861	1 153.9	108.7	111	704	83.1	14.0
Chester	436 139	2 961	1 013	10 955	15 420.9	459.6	1 517	22 625	5 879.6	490.8	328	2 052	319.1	55.0
Clarion	10 664	118	47	470	568.5	13.8	226	2 100	330.5	32.3	17	74	5.9	1.7
Clearfield	22 559	225	80	713	280.5	17.7	397	4 935	768.4	68.8	42	294	23.9	6.0
Clinton	16 017	159	28	D	D	D	176	1 877	296.2	24.6	19	74	7.9	1.1
Columbia	22 457	191	50	D	D	D	317	3 462	533.9	45.1	46	178	18.6	3.3
Crawford	21 975	254	81	652	175.5	14.6	360	3 970	628.8	58.6	49	165	15.3	1.9
Cumberland	180 289	1 378	260	3 589	2 439.6	122.7	955	15 697	2 759.5	268.2	177	1 390	195.7	35.7
Dauphin	146 212	1 262	341	9 844	8 700.1	320.2	1 125	15 204	2 532.8	246.1	196	1 369	198.2	29.3
Delaware	191 513	1 149	807	9 947	9 506.8	438.9	2 080	28 710	5 003.6	516.4	411	4 236	574.0	100.6
Elk	5 693	55	40	335	89.7	8.7	163	1 668	219.9	20.4	15	49	6.1	0.9
Erie	77 850	769	334	4 069	1 277.8	131.9	1 225	16 323	2 562.1	239.0	180	834	75.5	13.8
Fayette	29 453	249	123	1 566	406.8	29.3	599	7 056	1 110.2	96.3	77	296	28.4	4.7
Forest	2 452	31	4	D	D	D	35	162	28.6	2.3	5	6	0.4	0.2
Franklin	109 724	992	102	1 862	610.3	49.0	566	6 249	1 035.7	94.4	77	296	29.3	4.6
Fulton	7 366	89	7	32	6.6	6.9	55	402	70.7	5.3	5	37	2.8	0.7
Greene	9 020	85	34	364	78.9	6.9	136	1 240	259.2	18.4	15	40	4.1	0.4
Huntingdon	17 007	185	24	D	D	D	169	1 495	252.8	22.5	17	36	3.2	0.5
Indiana	30 154	289	80	870	418.8	19.6	391	4 986	723.6	64.3	58	223	15.7	2.8
Jefferson	10 284	139	62	515	121.4	12.0	209	1 828	299.2	24.6	26	87	5.1	1.0
Juniata	7 320	76	24	D	D	D	71	649	123.6	9.0	12	15	1.3	0.2
Lackawanna	68 551	497	286	3 636	1 126.0	95.7	1 039	13 167	1 966.3	189.8	145	747	72.7	12.8
Lancaster	336 665	2 690	663	11 020	10 936.6	341.6	2 012	29 237	4 671.7	480.8	281	1 906	247.2	41.9
Lawrence	25 332	201	90	1 070	430.2	29.0	370	4 286	627.1	61.4	58	264	27.6	5.2
Lebanon	87 551	744	118	D	D	D	490	6 480	1 209.1	106.8	59	270	29.2	4.0
Lehigh	204 601	1 424	560	7 469	4 668.7	255.6	1 376	18 976	3 509.2	333.2	264	1 659	207.1	33.1
Luzerne	123 197	935	388	5 697	2 149.6	152.3	1 406	18 945	2 856.4	269.2	208	1 240	113.0	26.5
Lycoming	36 215	289	137	2 195	481.9	51.4	605	7 600	1 149.3	108.4	78	299	32.2	4.7
McKean	5 169	63	44	426	229.2	12.7	200	1 969	280.5	26.8	21	58	4.5	0.5
Mercer	47 958	377	124	1 692	656.3	41.9	618	7 852	1 285.0	112.8	84	281	29.6	5.0
Mifflin	15 743	154	53	552	111.7	12.4	195	2 427	368.4	34.8	27	88	8.7	1.3
Monroe	290 949	1 724	93	1 012	345.3	28.5	658	7 621	1 160.6	111.7	111	808	60.9	12.4
Montgomery	346 546	2 598	2 004	29 378	22 878.2	1 395.6	3 689	54 728	9 607.4	1 025.8	876	6 649	1 019.2	199.7
Montour	11 088	90	15	209	65.8	5.2	76	797	131.3	10.0	10	24	2.7	0.3
Northampton	262 936	1 947	312	4 465	2 066.2	167.7	832	10 051	1 831.8	168.1	115	648	79.3	16.6
Northumberland	28 485	261	72	1 016	582.6	26.5	367	3 689	658.7	58.9	58	231	15.5	3.5
Perry	20 232	191	17	D	D	D	141	1 280	205.3	17.5	7	D	D	D
Philadelphia	133 705	1 754	1 403	22 298	12 004.0	848.4	4 782	51 398	8 118.2	887.1	964	9 550	1 158.1	253.5
Pike	152 447	888	23	D	D	D	107	1 203	182.6	16.9	27	274	40.9	3.0

1. Establishments with payroll.

Table B. States and Counties — Professional Services, Manufacturing, and Accommodation and Foodservices

STATE County	Professional, scientific, and technical services,[1] 1997				Manufacturing, 1997				Accommodation and foodservices, 1997			
	Number of establishments	Number of employees	Receipts (mil dol)	Annual payroll (mil dol)	Number of establishments	Number of employees	Receipts (mil dol)	Annual payroll (mil dol)	Number of establishments	Number of employees	Sales (mil dol)	Annual payroll (mil dol)
	147	148	149	150	151	152	153	154	155	156	157	158
OREGON—Cont'd												
Morrow	3	D	D	D	10	741	183.4	20.9	18	123	4.2	0.9
Multnomah	2 682	23 427	2 336.0	967.7	1 309	47 763	8 715.4	1 600.4	1 937	33 949	1 315.1	373.6
Polk	63	200	14.2	5.6	63	2 358	357.4	63.4	77	997	30.7	7.8
Sherman	NA	NA	NA	NA	NA	NA	NA	NA	9	D	D	D
Tillamook	32	96	5.8	2.4	31	1 227	317.8	32.5	128	1 086	35.5	10.1
Umatilla	67	235	16.7	5.4	75	4 623	790.6	107.2	159	1 950	66.4	17.2
Union	35	163	10.4	3.8	28	1 250	273.9	37.2	77	773	23.6	6.3
Wallowa	14	31	1.8	0.6	NA	NA	NA	NA	47	198	5.8	1.4
Wasco	38	154	9.7	4.0	26	751	374.7	28.1	73	925	34.3	11.8
Washington	1 203	8 082	800.5	354.2	828	38 997	14 360.2	1 413.2	798	14 299	495.8	140.6
Wheeler	NA	NA	NA	NA	NA	NA	NA	NA	6	D	D	D
Yamhill	111	408	32.6	12.4	159	6 092	1 268.3	194.9	146	1 997	58.3	17.0
PENNSYLVANIA	23 184	235 025	26 240.3	10 448.3	17 128	826 521	172 193.2	27 641.3	24 465	365 158	12 227.2	3 364.1
Adams	81	341	22.2	7.6	127	8 209	1 401.3	214.1	190	2 789	89.3	25.5
Allegheny	3 432	44 926	5 155.6	1 988.1	1 500	55 620	10 576.1	2 130.8	2 912	52 581	1 711.4	477.5
Armstrong	77	421	28.6	8.5	92	3 617	409.2	94.9	135	1 133	32.8	8.2
Beaver	208	1 760	108.0	45.3	221	10 311	3 161.9	383.1	307	3 796	108.3	28.1
Bedford	34	123	6.6	2.2	61	3 231	472.8	76.6	108	1 674	49.5	14.4
Berks	546	5 520	476.6	215.2	587	41 614	7 729.4	1 510.7	706	10 091	330.4	90.9
Blair	181	1 838	151.6	53.5	157	8 966	1 592.4	251.7	254	4 003	108.8	29.6
Bradford	67	318	17.9	5.2	73	6 405	1 273.7	191.5	117	1 185	35.3	9.7
Bucks	1 729	11 075	1 155.1	489.6	1 236	41 592	7 593.0	1 518.9	1 047	15 741	569.3	147.8
Butler	262	1 519	132.2	51.3	276	14 891	2 990.0	533.0	317	5 439	156.6	42.8
Cambria	184	1 619	98.6	42.3	153	7 403	1 349.5	186.3	314	4 143	111.4	30.6
Cameron	7	27	1.4	0.4	20	1 259	151.4	34.6	14	106	2.6	0.7
Carbon	63	182	11.2	3.9	63	3 646	311.9	76.2	97	1 200	41.8	11.3
Centre	211	2 332	167.5	85.9	159	8 546	1 409.3	255.4	287	5 241	154.8	41.2
Chester	1 567	18 172	2 446.6	972.8	629	20 791	4 332.2	771.1	642	10 790	365.4	102.7
Clarion	42	180	17.7	6.8	49	2 711	441.7	76.4	108	1 331	38.7	9.9
Clearfield	91	428	26.1	8.2	107	4 864	791.0	120.2	153	1 840	56.1	14.5
Clinton	30	139	8.3	2.5	54	3 212	677.1	89.2	79	932	28.6	6.9
Columbia	67	629	29.4	14.1	100	D	D	D	154	2 218	59.3	15.9
Crawford	97	442	31.2	11.0	301	8 714	1 263.4	289.4	180	2 357	67.3	19.0
Cumberland	404	3 989	326.3	155.4	221	13 804	3 307.3	444.8	415	7 623	235.2	65.6
Dauphin	560	5 277	559.2	198.0	222	14 871	3 590.9	522.4	611	10 456	394.4	107.3
Delaware	1 417	13 750	1 876.1	669.2	522	19 341	7 315.2	867.0	1 025	13 991	514.1	134.1
Elk	41	130	7.2	2.2	130	8 338	1 393.3	288.0	82	617	18.5	4.4
Erie	379	2 330	177.7	62.4	570	32 813	5 779.3	1 142.3	614	9 599	265.2	73.3
Fayette	115	700	49.4	14.7	128	3 842	656.7	106.0	278	4 886	157.3	47.7
Forest	3	D	D	D	NA	NA	NA	NA	20	142	4.9	1.2
Franklin	158	948	61.7	25.2	191	12 763	2 212.0	379.5	217	3 274	105.8	28.1
Fulton	12	31	1.6	0.4	22	D	D	D	24	278	10.0	2.7
Greene	27	99	5.9	1.9	27	630	81.5	15.1	56	620	19.4	4.7
Huntingdon	36	233	10.2	4.4	44	2 300	493.0	59.5	84	778	22.9	6.3
Indiana	89	601	62.6	20.2	88	4 634	344.1	98.9	167	2 707	64.8	17.5
Jefferson	56	253	14.4	5.5	88	4 634	680.9	132.0	89	928	23.9	6.4
Juniata	18	34	2.2	0.5	57	2 443	290.6	61.1	33	312	8.5	2.0
Lackawanna	358	2 585	230.1	88.2	306	16 052	2 562.7	463.0	520	7 421	219.3	59.4
Lancaster	639	5 130	439.8	165.6	918	52 908	10 585.4	1 752.0	877	15 724	506.4	145.6
Lawrence	103	553	37.7	14.8	169	5 092	1 076.6	156.4	196	2 488	67.3	17.2
Lebanon	113	608	42.2	17.9	199	9 376	1 710.3	254.3	209	2 687	76.0	22.3
Lehigh	651	4 837	410.7	164.1	504	23 277	7 690.0	877.2	648	11 892	412.7	114.7
Luzerne	466	3 666	251.7	98.7	408	24 362	4 501.1	700.8	694	9 780	292.7	79.8
Lycoming	137	1 014	68.8	27.1	208	12 982	2 460.4	370.2	283	3 571	106.1	28.5
McKean	57	226	11.4	3.3	67	5 346	875.7	158.7	118	1 057	30.0	7.8
Mercer	130	679	49.4	22.0	198	10 457	2 440.8	326.8	270	3 953	113.3	32.6
Mifflin	24	117	7.0	2.2	72	5 373	922.7	163.1	83	989	26.0	7.0
Monroe	235	1 110	77.4	31.5	113	4 744	812.9	171.0	345	6 179	241.8	67.7
Montgomery	2 934	29 664	3 693.5	1 488.4	1 398	67 234	20 666.6	2 649.5	1 504	23 896	915.4	254.0
Montour	17	D	D	D	22	1 530	820.4	65.8	39	586	15.8	4.5
Northampton	422	2 211	255.1	80.9	353	18 244	2 638.4	546.1	513	5 497	195.0	50.0
Northumberland	79	351	25.4	6.9	115	7 812	1 526.7	217.3	180	1 641	43.7	11.7
Perry	29	92	6.6	1.5	32	845	82.7	19.1	61	467	14.8	3.4
Philadelphia	2 444	49 894	6 317.4	2 690.5	1 342	47 928	11 098.1	1 582.4	2 989	38 521	1 691.6	461.1
Pike	53	137	11.9	3.7	NA	NA	NA	NA	91	1 221	49.0	15.2

1. Firms subject to federal tax.

STATE County	Health care and social assistance,[1] 1997				Other services,[1] 1997				Federal funds and grants, 2002–2003			
									Expenditures (mil dol)			
										Direct payments for individuals[2]		
	Number of establish-ments	Number of employees	Receipts (mil dol)	Annual payroll (mil dol)	Number of establish-ments	Number of employees	Receipts (mil dol)	Annual payroll (mil dol)	Total	Social Security and government retirement	Medicare	Food stamps and Supplemental Security Income
	159	160	161	162	163	164	165	166	167	168	169	170
OREGON—Cont'd												
Morrow	4	20	0.6	0.3	8	29	1.6	0.5	74.8	21.3	7.6	0.9
Multnomah	1 649	17 599	1 221.2	535.8	1 268	9 706	688.9	211.7	4 768.0	1 438.1	603.1	98.3
Polk	92	510	24.7	10.2	58	229	14.3	3.6	277.2	94.9	38.6	6.4
Sherman	1	D	D	D	2	D	D	D	37.0	5.7	2.4	0.5
Tillamook	32	252	12.1	5.2	26	102	7.7	1.8	149.3	81.7	27.6	4.1
Umatilla	141	1 047	56.9	21.7	87	303	21.1	5.9	547.1	150.9	51.5	15.4
Union	71	517	26.4	10.0	34	112	7.9	2.0	150.4	64.6	23.2	5.7
Wallowa	14	85	4.3	1.6	18	41	3.3	0.7	51.5	23.8	7.2	1.2
Wasco	58	387	27.9	11.3	32	95	7.0	1.6	153.3	67.6	20.0	4.9
Washington	915	9 348	572.9	246.9	593	3 512	257.1	78.3	1 119.8	541.3	219.5	36.7
Wheeler	2	D	D	D	3	D	D	D	10.1	5.5	2.1	0.1
Yamhill	151	1 716	102.3	39.4	92	429	30.6	8.3	368.5	165.4	63.7	11.8
PENNSYLVANIA	24 888	262 603	17 633.5	7 994.9	19 754	107 502	7 085.7	2 049.0	90 350.4	30 528.5	16 802.6	2 329.1
Adams	109	807	44.7	22.0	106	496	33.0	9.6	429.3	217.4	67.0	4.8
Allegheny	3 230	39 435	2 895.2	1 276.4	2 570	15 947	1 084.0	308.5	11 441.5	3 538.5	2 310.7	245.7
Armstrong	125	1 089	50.7	21.4	97	307	20.0	4.4	457.3	215.3	120.0	14.4
Beaver	310	2 700	186.7	87.5	255	1 360	67.6	20.3	1 062.8	527.8	280.1	32.3
Bedford	88	465	27.8	11.1	73	195	12.4	2.8	283.1	128.2	57.6	6.9
Berks	601	6 387	412.6	200.5	559	3 102	183.2	56.4	1 670.8	832.0	373.4	49.2
Blair	284	2 816	200.5	83.6	251	1 319	72.7	18.9	824.8	366.8	172.3	30.5
Bradford	81	1 044	40.3	21.6	68	225	14.1	3.4	350.2	153.1	57.9	13.5
Bucks	1 329	13 239	859.9	379.8	1 132	6 494	450.6	145.0	2 544.8	1 297.6	605.1	38.4
Butler	311	2 751	160.1	71.3	296	1 456	95.1	28.2	992.7	413.0	211.6	21.2
Cambria	351	2 749	180.8	92.5	220	1 097	69.8	19.0	1 203.8	454.5	264.2	35.1
Cameron	10	40	2.0	1.0	9	12	1.2	0.2	38.5	16.8	8.4	0.8
Carbon	101	616	37.2	14.4	59	183	13.4	3.0	331.4	175.6	92.6	7.3
Centre	212	2 520	169.1	72.4	159	958	52.2	14.5	961.1	228.5	89.5	10.9
Chester	893	10 268	660.5	321.3	672	4 641	414.5	117.1	1 946.9	843.1	357.0	23.0
Clarion	71	685	38.0	18.2	58	252	20.5	4.5	239.0	99.1	60.5	8.7
Clearfield	159	1 397	81.0	30.1	103	509	34.9	8.6	464.9	210.7	111.0	17.2
Clinton	49	254	15.5	5.7	42	136	9.8	2.1	195.4	89.2	43.9	7.2
Columbia	113	1 185	57.7	24.3	89	320	18.8	4.2	321.7	158.0	76.5	6.6
Crawford	167	1 530	85.4	40.1	126	527	38.1	10.1	465.3	222.8	106.6	17.2
Cumberland	425	5 511	392.2	192.7	389	2 333	136.9	44.6	1 397.2	626.4	192.0	11.0
Dauphin	545	5 434	343.1	155.6	417	2 535	171.0	52.1	4 390.9	994.4	266.8	40.7
Delaware	1 280	14 634	995.3	454.5	985	5 017	332.8	104.5	3 111.4	1 336.7	822.9	66.9
Elk	66	329	21.1	10.0	49	192	11.8	2.9	173.2	91.7	45.5	3.8
Erie	560	5 498	423.4	190.6	476	2 174	135.0	39.6	1 512.9	625.8	299.4	64.5
Fayette	269	3 290	153.4	65.3	209	867	47.7	11.7	1 144.7	436.9	286.9	65.3
Forest	6	105	7.1	3.5	6	27	0.9	0.3	43.9	20.6	10.0	0.9
Franklin	181	1 666	109.9	50.1	219	938	52.9	14.4	790.3	381.9	110.4	12.8
Fulton	15	98	4.1	1.3	21	53	4.2	0.7	86.1	37.2	13.0	2.2
Greene	61	450	24.9	10.9	46	190	12.3	3.5	305.4	103.4	63.9	12.7
Huntingdon	65	325	19.5	8.0	55	130	8.6	1.8	229.7	107.5	47.6	7.0
Indiana	200	1 402	77.0	30.2	126	573	42.3	9.2	541.7	211.6	116.7	18.1
Jefferson	112	663	43.9	14.9	81	290	20.5	4.4	265.6	128.1	66.2	9.6
Juniata	22	208	9.5	3.7	22	72	5.6	1.1	102.0	51.8	21.7	2.3
Lackawanna	536	5 276	351.1	158.7	349	2 096	109.4	33.1	1 545.1	607.4	373.9	35.4
Lancaster	710	8 212	523.8	252.0	808	4 429	276.4	81.6	1 972.5	994.7	368.8	46.6
Lawrence	183	1 709	100.0	45.6	139	648	32.5	8.6	631.8	288.8	164.1	22.6
Lebanon	194	1 655	107.1	49.7	192	785	52.1	13.6	746.9	318.8	113.0	9.6
Lehigh	845	8 416	625.6	307.6	583	4 350	295.2	91.8	1 513.1	592.9	374.2	56.5
Luzerne	736	8 132	501.2	218.3	499	2 288	136.0	34.6	2 338.1	949.1	542.0	57.4
Lycoming	218	2 050	134.4	58.6	176	887	57.5	15.2	652.4	286.8	131.4	22.7
McKean	89	598	37.3	15.0	69	222	12.2	3.1	280.2	117.3	57.9	11.0
Mercer	303	2 686	162.7	72.5	203	876	44.3	12.9	718.1	342.7	184.7	28.4
Mifflin	79	550	40.2	19.3	53	198	14.2	3.0	325.8	115.5	60.1	8.1
Monroe	226	1 759	108.5	48.9	191	733	54.3	12.8	706.8	325.0	126.8	15.8
Montgomery	2 171	27 990	2 082.6	949.7	1 524	9 822	622.2	209.1	3 996.0	1 857.2	921.5	43.4
Montour	26	573	31.5	10.6	20	75	3.9	0.8	94.7	46.1	25.1	2.5
Northampton	515	4 607	284.1	115.7	409	2 186	139.2	42.8	1 410.5	708.3	366.7	16.5
Northumberland	147	1 673	68.6	28.3	121	553	34.3	8.5	578.1	264.8	138.1	13.7
Perry	45	326	13.5	5.4	42	93	5.8	1.1	183.8	101.1	39.3	3.8
Philadelphia	2 574	27 295	1 931.1	899.0	1 913	10 971	737.4	199.6	16 215.5	3 142.5	2 916.1	796.1
Pike	46	307	16.4	5.6	29	91	6.9	1.4	174.7	105.9	32.4	3.7

1. Firms subject to federal tax.   2. State totals may include programs not allocated by county.

STATE County	Federal funds and grants, 2002–2003 (cont'd)							Local government finances, 2002				
	Expenditures (mil dol) (cont'd)							General revenue				
	Procurement contract awards			Grants[1]						Taxes		
											Per capita[2] (dollars)	
	Salaries and wages	Defense	Other	Medicaid and other health-related	Nutrition and family welfare	Education	Other	Total (mil dol)	Intergovern-mental (mil dol)	Total (mil dol)	Total	Property
	171	172	173	174	175	176	177	178	179	180	181	182
OREGON—Cont'd												
Morrow	3.2	2.5	3.3	1.8	0.9	0.7	7.3	49.5	18.9	15.0	1 292	1 170
Multnomah	706.0	158.4	331.3	863.1	97.3	58.4	333.1	3 309.8	1 227.8	1 211.2	1 787	1 206
Polk	7.6	0.5	2.4	43.1	5.4	9.2	60.7	115.0	68.5	27.8	431	364
Sherman	4.2	4.1	0.6	1.3	0.1	0.2	8.0	10.4	5.2	3.7	2 086	1 999
Tillamook	8.7	0.1	2.2	11.7	2.4	2.0	1.7	84.8	37.6	27.0	1 095	989
Umatilla	38.3	150.2	8.6	42.3	14.9	6.0	30.7	224.3	133.4	54.1	758	689
Union	11.1	0.1	7.5	13.7	3.9	2.2	11.5	80.8	52.5	15.6	637	574
Wallowa	4.9	0.1	1.9	7.1	0.8	0.5	1.9	30.1	13.0	5.8	826	775
Wasco	17.2	8.0	1.6	13.3	3.0	1.7	5.9	99.4	56.9	23.1	976	929
Washington	61.8	40.1	18.8	92.7	19.4	18.8	60.5	1 258.6	482.8	501.0	1 059	926
Wheeler	0.5	0.0	0.1	0.4	0.1	0.2	0.9	7.3	5.4	1.0	674	666
Yamhill	35.0	6.9	13.9	32.8	11.7	7.8	11.9	239.7	128.0	65.4	743	643
PENNSYLVANIA	6 362.5	5 606.6	2 530.1	9 647.4	2 512.6	1 272.3	5 191.1	X	X	X	X	X
Adams	33.2	12.3	12.4	47.9	5.9	2.1	11.7	196.3	61.3	100.1	1 060	765
Allegheny	983.3	1 015.7	714.7	1 428.3	202.3	50.6	802.3	5 308.6	2 137.9	2 023.5	1 593	1 152
Armstrong	13.8	4.7	13.0	54.0	9.5	2.1	7.5	184.3	90.7	64.7	902	768
Beaver	24.0	9.8	9.5	101.0	27.9	5.3	35.4	593.7	225.4	173.5	967	781
Bedford	8.6	1.4	2.1	38.3	4.8	1.5	25.3	104.2	55.5	31.8	637	496
Berks	77.8	31.2	28.5	137.9	29.2	11.6	64.3	1 128.6	412.3	493.7	1 292	1 024
Blair	53.6	0.7	15.7	103.8	22.4	4.3	42.9	298.0	157.5	96.2	753	537
Bradford	14.0	7.5	8.9	47.9	8.5	2.1	26.0	197.3	102.8	50.0	796	601
Bucks	90.0	161.1	86.2	125.3	28.0	7.5	87.4	1 732.5	470.3	946.6	1 551	1 245
Butler	74.4	4.7	117.9	84.9	14.6	4.6	32.7	446.9	184.5	164.4	923	702
Cambria	96.1	110.5	23.1	109.9	21.4	7.2	63.3	415.8	210.2	105.7	702	545
Cameron	1.2	0.0	0.3	5.5	2.7	0.3	2.4	15.0	6.9	5.3	902	753
Carbon	7.9	5.4	2.7	25.3	4.1	1.5	7.4	152.6	56.5	64.5	1 080	848
Centre	35.6	160.7	14.1	88.0	12.2	10.0	253.0	280.2	82.7	125.5	906	641
Chester	186.1	125.9	181.3	106.4	20.7	8.7	70.1	1 265.2	311.5	712.9	1 584	1 303
Clarion	9.9	1.7	6.2	26.7	4.9	2.4	9.7	96.0	54.9	29.3	709	552
Clearfield	20.1	3.9	7.4	54.2	9.7	3.2	24.1	185.0	100.8	63.2	759	608
Clinton	10.1	0.0	1.8	23.2	5.1	2.5	5.1	88.2	37.5	30.9	819	625
Columbia	11.1	0.2	2.5	30.9	6.3	2.7	13.9	138.8	60.2	58.8	917	666
Crawford	16.1	0.5	3.8	51.7	14.8	3.9	18.3	202.7	107.4	67.0	746	612
Cumberland	347.4	96.0	17.0	49.3	7.3	4.0	26.6	508.1	138.1	264.6	1 215	830
Dauphin	200.1	214.9	53.9	416.3	619.5	364.3	1 120.4	971.5	316.6	339.9	1 344	952
Delaware	170.0	212.8	37.0	246.4	50.2	19.1	111.3	1 720.0	510.9	760.7	1 374	1 244
Elk	6.4	0.1	1.8	12.5	3.0	1.6	5.7	79.6	32.4	30.2	877	660
Erie	93.4	29.4	22.5	161.9	47.4	12.9	122.3	763.7	375.9	250.4	893	716
Fayette	29.5	6.5	19.6	208.0	30.0	7.7	45.3	284.5	181.6	70.6	482	360
Forest	2.6	0.6	0.8	4.3	0.6	0.4	2.0	14.4	6.7	6.4	1 316	1 137
Franklin	69.6	106.8	10.4	55.1	9.1	3.8	8.5	259.5	106.4	98.1	746	567
Fulton	2.1	0.9	1.1	11.8	1.7	0.4	11.4	33.1	19.2	11.0	768	626
Greene	9.0	0.8	41.3	52.2	6.3	2.7	10.3	103.9	49.7	40.5	999	857
Huntingdon	7.7	1.8	1.9	34.0	6.1	1.8	5.5	79.2	43.6	24.4	533	406
Indiana	15.2	5.6	16.4	78.8	11.8	3.6	42.1	192.4	100.4	65.2	734	570
Jefferson	9.3	0.2	2.2	31.1	6.4	1.6	7.7	94.7	51.2	29.9	653	497
Juniata	4.8	0.1	1.0	11.3	2.3	0.4	2.1	28.6	15.0	11.0	485	332
Lackawanna	63.0	160.3	22.6	152.8	27.8	6.4	73.2	533.7	198.6	229.0	1 087	774
Lancaster	97.2	82.8	50.9	146.5	36.7	15.1	92.5	1 089.3	348.2	504.6	1 054	831
Lawrence	27.6	4.3	8.0	66.8	16.9	3.8	21.3	219.1	116.7	69.8	742	567
Lebanon	115.8	27.6	21.6	37.4	6.2	2.3	84.4	294.8	95.7	112.4	927	705
Lehigh	69.6	221.5	12.6	123.0	22.1	9.2	7.7	1 003.0	347.4	409.6	1 290	1 011
Luzerne	184.2	26.0	64.9	212.5	38.9	9.6	93.2	718.7	254.2	308.6	981	709
Lycoming	38.7	32.1	12.2	65.3	17.0	4.0	29.0	307.2	138.0	108.0	907	633
McKean	30.2	0.3	4.4	32.4	6.6	1.7	15.9	123.1	59.6	34.3	764	592
Mercer	20.2	1.8	4.4	70.4	18.7	4.3	31.5	275.9	138.0	92.8	777	577
Mifflin	7.9	0.5	1.6	37.2	5.0	1.7	81.9	86.3	33.9	31.2	671	509
Monroe	98.5	63.4	14.2	27.5	7.0	3.9	19.0	371.9	105.4	227.9	1 531	1 344
Montgomery	294.9	298.8	182.3	189.6	27.9	11.1	147.0	2 302.0	522.6	1 312.7	1 713	1 403
Montour	2.5	0.1	0.8	11.3	1.4	0.3	2.4	52.2	14.6	17.5	962	659
Northampton	82.9	4.3	21.7	111.8	24.4	7.8	45.4	844.8	288.9	371.7	1 360	1 071
Northumberland	17.0	1.2	5.7	74.8	8.1	3.5	42.3	219.2	110.8	58.3	624	393
Perry	6.0	0.6	1.6	17.1	2.7	0.9	5.5	89.1	41.0	38.2	871	574
Philadelphia	1 985.6	1 786.2	489.4	3 368.9	554.3	136.6	774.9	7 925.2	4 087.6	2 643.5	1 772	555
Pike	11.9	0.0	1.6	4.4	1.2	0.9	12.5	81.3	17.5	46.3	925	879

1. State totals may include programs not allocated by county.   2. Based on the resident population estimated as of July 1 of the year shown.

STATE County	Total (mil dol)	Per capita¹ (dollars)	Education	Health and hospitals	Police protection	Public welfare	Highways	Total (mil dol)	Per capita¹ (dollars)	Federal civilian	Federal military	State and local	Democratic	Republican	All other
	183	184	185	186	187	188	189	190	191	192	193	194	195	196	197
OREGON—Cont'd															
Morrow	50.0	4 315	38.9	16.8	3.3	0.0	9.3	38.3	3 307	71	37	709	32.9	66.0	1.1
Multnomah	3 278.5	4 838	33.2	2.8	5.2	4.8	3.9	4 597.0	6 784	10 997	2 375	55 098	71.9	27.3	0.8
Polk	122.6	1 896	45.6	16.1	7.4	0.2	4.0	80.1	1 239	118	177	5 696	43.8	55.3	0.9
Sherman	11.3	6 337	38.4	2.0	4.5	0.4	7.4	0.7	388	95	0	164	35.6	63.1	1.4
Tillamook	72.5	2 945	47.0	6.9	4.2	0.7	5.6	49.1	1 994	129	113	1 604	48.5	50.4	1.0
Umatilla	234.1	3 278	60.5	4.8	3.4	0.8	3.4	153.1	2 143	819	199	5 989	33.9	65.1	1.1
Union	84.1	3 435	53.6	0.4	3.0	0.6	4.3	18.7	762	232	72	2 460	32.8	66.0	1.2
Wallowa	30.9	4 395	36.5	40.9	2.5	1.7	2.9	22.1	3 139	133	19	557	28.5	70.3	1.2
Wasco	102.3	4 323	49.5	7.3	4.2	6.3	8.2	101.0	4 269	385	66	1 907	47.6	51.2	1.2
Washington	1 323.7	2 797	49.1	3.4	5.6	0.1	6.5	1 285.8	2 717	801	1 302	16 657	52.5	46.7	0.9
Wheeler	6.3	4 138	61.5	3.8	3.1	0.0	12.7	0.4	230	0	0	151	28.0	70.0	2.0
Yamhill	225.2	2 557	52.6	6.5	5.4	0.3	5.8	173.4	1 969	550	242	3 577	42.6	56.2	1.2
PENNSYLVANIA	X	X	X	X	X	X	X	X	X	105 200	37 776	652 697	50.8	48.6	0.6
Adams	195.9	2 074	54.5	0.4	1.9	9.0	4.2	259.1	2 744	561	254	4 664	32.6	66.9	0.5
Allegheny	5 232.5	4 120	36.5	7.2	4.3	5.6	3.5	11 163.9	8 791	14 989	4 120	61 774	57.1	42.1	0.7
Armstrong	184.6	2 576	57.3	0.1	1.0	8.2	5.5	152.0	2 120	209	192	2 862	38.7	60.8	0.5
Beaver	611.0	3 407	44.3	5.7	2.9	8.9	2.9	1 453.1	8 102	382	481	8 402	51.0	48.4	0.6
Bedford	100.2	2 007	62.9	0.2	0.5	1.7	6.6	78.0	1 561	114	134	2 257	26.5	73.2	0.3
Berks	1 161.3	3 039	51.7	4.3	3.6	5.4	2.7	1 879.8	4 920	1 081	1 047	19 736	46.5	52.9	0.6
Blair	269.0	2 104	57.4	0.2	3.5	3.9	4.2	310.9	2 432	920	343	8 198	33.5	65.9	0.6
Bradford	215.8	3 436	52.2	2.4	1.4	10.8	3.6	645.2	10 273	171	169	3 136	33.3	66.2	0.5
Bucks	1 860.8	3 048	52.7	4.2	4.3	4.0	4.2	2 022.4	3 313	1 334	1 636	21 487	51.1	48.3	0.6
Butler	478.3	2 686	56.8	5.8	1.9	4.7	4.5	750.1	4 212	1 401	478	8 145	35.2	64.3	0.4
Cambria	429.7	2 856	43.7	6.2	3.2	10.4	4.1	608.9	4 047	1 241	573	8 602	48.7	50.8	0.5
Cameron	19.9	3 400	63.0	0.0	0.5	2.9	3.8	15.4	2 630	15	16	436	33.0	66.5	0.5
Carbon	154.0	2 580	49.0	1.3	2.1	9.9	2.7	193.2	3 237	120	161	2 769	48.8	50.0	1.2
Centre	305.9	2 208	44.2	4.2	2.8	6.3	3.5	312.4	2 255	437	461	37 562	47.8	51.6	0.6
Chester	1 397.8	3 105	54.3	6.0	3.6	4.3	2.4	1 979.0	4 396	1 829	1 209	18 793	47.5	52.0	0.5
Clarion	96.4	2 333	62.6	0.2	1.2	3.8	6.1	78.4	1 898	101	111	3 869	35.4	64.1	0.4
Clearfield	170.0	2 044	69.5	0.7	2.1	2.8	4.8	178.1	2 141	234	224	4 921	39.5	60.0	0.5
Clinton	93.1	2 472	59.7	0.1	1.4	2.8	3.7	78.4	2 080	142	101	2 786	41.8	57.5	0.7
Columbia	138.4	2 157	65.2	0.0	2.9	1.1	4.7	143.5	2 237	145	173	4 713	39.8	59.7	0.5
Crawford	200.8	2 235	46.6	6.4	1.7	7.9	5.9	187.9	2 091	281	241	4 381	41.7	57.3	1.0
Cumberland	619.5	2 845	61.8	1.2	2.4	4.8	4.3	721.7	3 315	5 685	1 391	11 692	35.7	63.8	0.5
Dauphin	1 038.7	4 107	44.3	5.2	3.1	6.5	2.4	2 183.5	8 633	2 821	879	42 382	45.5	54.0	0.5
Delaware	1 819.2	3 287	43.9	6.6	4.3	5.1	2.8	3 678.7	6 647	2 364	1 533	22 956	57.2	42.4	0.5
Elk	86.0	2 497	41.4	0.1	1.7	2.6	6.3	78.5	2 277	86	93	1 395	45.5	54.0	0.5
Erie	782.7	2 792	44.3	0.7	2.6	18.1	3.0	1 188.5	4 239	1 416	811	15 403	53.8	45.7	0.5
Fayette	285.1	1 944	59.4	7.1	1.2	3.3	3.9	237.5	1 620	435	393	5 601	53.1	45.9	1.0
Forest	13.6	2 777	59.0	0.2	0.0	4.6	7.1	10.8	2 206	57	13	362	38.5	61.0	0.5
Franklin	259.3	1 970	49.9	5.3	1.9	7.0	4.3	176.1	1 338	1 679	357	5 811	28.3	71.4	0.3
Fulton	29.0	2 020	68.4	0.2	0.6	3.1	4.8	34.3	2 387	31	38	773	23.5	76.1	0.4
Greene	101.0	2 491	60.0	4.9	0.5	4.4	6.4	134.8	3 327	115	108	2 826	49.3	50.0	0.7
Huntingdon	81.1	1 774	63.0	1.4	1.3	3.0	4.8	98.1	2 147	113	122	3 031	32.6	67.2	0.3
Indiana	181.8	2 048	58.1	4.7	1.3	5.9	4.2	182.6	2 056	218	253	7 604	43.7	55.9	0.4
Jefferson	95.2	2 092	63.4	0.1	2.0	2.1	5.5	87.5	1 909	111	123	1 846	31.1	68.3	0.6
Juniata	29.1	1 277	68.1	0.2	4.6	2.9	6.7	2.0	88	70	61	641	27.9	71.5	0.6
Lackawanna	569.7	2 704	42.8	0.7	3.9	5.6	4.7	724.1	3 436	1 108	576	10 660	56.3	42.3	1.4
Lancaster	1 180.7	2 467	48.5	3.8	4.0	4.8	3.3	1 962.3	4 100	1 470	1 284	18 780	33.5	65.9	0.6
Lawrence	211.7	2 249	54.2	6.7	2.2	4.9	4.5	173.5	1 844	453	253	4 268	49.4	50.3	0.3
Lebanon	276.8	2 284	48.1	9.7	2.9	9.7	3.3	349.9	2 887	1 976	339	5 101	32.5	66.7	0.8
Lehigh	1 041.3	3 279	40.8	5.0	3.0	8.0	2.7	2 324.6	7 321	1 345	899	15 299	50.8	48.5	0.7
Luzerne	723.5	2 299	51.2	0.5	3.2	2.1	3.8	939.7	2 987	3 429	888	15 336	50.9	48.0	1.1
Lycoming	323.5	2 719	55.1	0.0	2.3	4.8	3.8	457.1	3 841	593	320	8 201	31.8	67.4	0.8
McKean	126.1	2 809	51.8	0.2	1.8	8.5	4.0	132.9	2 961	484	120	2 332	36.1	62.8	1.1
Mercer	292.0	2 443	56.9	5.4	3.0	2.4	4.9	363.1	3 038	270	320	5 698	47.7	51.4	0.8
Mifflin	86.6	1 865	54.5	0.0	2.6	0.3	3.8	93.5	2 014	96	125	1 737	29.2	69.7	1.1
Monroe	377.3	2 535	67.6	0.1	2.7	4.1	4.0	566.2	3 804	3 130	414	7 563	49.6	49.7	0.7
Montgomery	2 414.9	3 150	49.1	2.0	4.5	6.2	3.2	3 368.1	4 394	4 413	3 289	31 651	55.5	44.0	0.5
Montour	49.4	2 711	44.3	1.0	2.4	3.1	4.0	243.0	13 342	33	49	1 333	34.9	64.4	0.7
Northampton	851.8	3 117	47.6	4.2	3.4	8.6	3.5	1 396.9	5 111	1 250	732	12 189	50.1	49.0	1.0
Northumberland	227.4	2 436	49.0	5.8	2.7	14.2	3.8	198.8	2 130	197	250	4 492	39.5	60.2	0.3
Perry	97.2	2 216	73.9	0.0	0.9	0.6	4.4	99.9	2 278	79	117	1 981	27.9	71.6	0.4
Philadelphia	7 341.8	4 920	23.4	13.6	6.7	5.9	1.3	13 085.2	8 769	35 338	4 714	81 914	80.5	19.3	0.3
Pike	73.5	1 468	50.6	0.5	2.2	0.7	4.4	67.6	1 349	211	134	1 936	40.6	58.4	0.9

1. Based on the resident population estimated as of July 1 of the year shown.

Table B. States and Counties — Land Area and Population

STATE/ County code	CBSA code[1]	County Type[2]	STATE County	Land area,[3] (sq km) 2000	Population and population characteristics, 2003													
								Race alone or in combination, not Hispanic or Latino (percent)					Age (percent)					
					Total persons	Rank	Per square kilometer	White	Black	Am. Indian, Alaska Native	Asian and Pacific Islander	Percent Hispanic or Latino[4]	Under 5 years	5 to 17 years	18 to 24 years	25 to 34 years	35 to 44 years	45 to 54 years
				1	2	3	4	5	6	7	8	9	10	11	12	13	14	15
			PENNSYLVANIA—Cont'd															
42 105	...	9	Potter	2 800	18 141	1 905	6.5	98.0	0.9	0.4	0.4	0.6	6.0	18.8	8.5	10.6	14.3	14.7
42 107	39060	4	Schuylkill	2 016	147 944	383	73.4	95.9	2.5	0.2	0.6	1.2	4.7	15.1	8.2	12.3	15.2	14.9
42 109	42780	7	Snyder	858	38 015	1 183	44.3	97.6	1.0	0.1	0.6	0.9	5.7	17.3	12.2	11.3	14.8	14.0
42 111	43740	4	Somerset	2 783	79 365	657	28.5	96.9	2.0	0.2	0.3	0.7	4.9	15.9	8.7	11.7	15.0	15.2
42 113	...	8	Sullivan	1 165	6 427	2 736	5.5	94.5	3.4	0.8	0.2	1.3	3.9	16.2	10.3	8.5	14.3	13.3
42 115	...	6	Susquehanna	2 131	41 812	1 085	19.6	98.6	0.6	0.4	0.3	0.6	5.4	18.3	8.7	10.0	15.5	15.2
42 117	...	6	Tioga	2 936	41 557	1 095	14.2	98.1	0.8	0.5	0.4	0.6	5.1	16.8	12.0	10.7	13.7	14.3
42 119	30260	4	Union	820	42 552	1 068	51.9	87.4	7.1	0.4	1.6	4.2	4.5	14.2	14.5	14.2	15.8	13.4
42 121	36340	4	Venango	1 748	56 600	860	32.4	97.8	1.4	0.4	0.3	0.5	5.2	17.6	8.4	10.4	14.8	15.8
42 123	47620	6	Warren	2 288	42 820	1 064	18.7	98.8	0.4	0.4	0.4	0.4	5.2	17.3	7.9	10.2	15.1	15.8
42 125	38300	1	Washington	2 220	204 286	286	92.0	95.6	3.7	0.3	0.6	0.6	5.1	16.2	8.8	10.8	15.0	15.7
42 127	...	6	Wayne	1 889	49 092	952	26.0	96.1	1.6	0.5	0.4	1.7	5.0	17.2	8.2	10.3	15.0	14.7
42 129	38300	1	Westmoreland	2 656	368 224	168	138.6	96.7	2.4	0.3	0.4	0.7	4.7	16.1	8.0	10.5	15.4	16.0
42 131	42540	2	Wyoming	1 029	28 153	1 457	27.4	98.3	0.6	0.3	0.4	0.7	5.5	18.0	9.7	11.3	15.0	15.2
42 133	49620	2	York	2 343	394 919	154	168.6	92.0	4.2	0.4	1.2	3.2	5.8	17.7	8.7	12.0	16.3	15.1
44 000	...	X	RHODE ISLAND	2 706	1 076 164	X	397.7	82.4	5.3	0.9	3.1	9.5	5.7	17.0	10.6	12.7	15.7	14.5
44 001	39300	1	Bristol	64	50 989	923	796.7	96.7	0.8	0.4	1.5	1.2	4.7	16.7	10.6	10.1	15.9	15.4
44 003	39300	1	Kent	441	171 297	330	388.4	94.9	1.5	0.6	2.1	1.9	5.3	16.8	7.9	12.1	17.0	15.6
44 005	39300	1	Newport	269	85 934	620	319.5	92.4	4.1	0.7	2.0	2.2	5.2	16.3	8.4	11.4	16.6	16.0
44 007	39300	1	Providence	1 070	639 444	87	597.6	74.7	7.7	0.9	3.9	14.9	6.1	17.2	11.4	13.6	15.4	13.1
44 009	39300	1	Washington	862	128 502	439	149.1	95.0	1.3	1.4	2.0	1.4	5.1	16.5	12.0	10.7	15.9	15.5
45 000	...	X	SOUTH CAROLINA	77 983	4 147 152	X	53.2	65.9	30.2	0.6	1.3	2.8	6.7	18.0	10.3	13.5	14.7	14.1
45 001	...	6	Abbeville	1 316	26 381	1 522	20.0	68.9	30.0	0.2	0.3	0.9	6.3	18.0	10.5	11.7	14.0	14.3
45 003	12260	2	Aiken	2 778	146 736	391	52.8	70.4	26.4	0.9	1.0	2.4	6.3	18.8	9.5	12.1	15.1	14.3
45 005	...	6	Allendale	1 057	10 934	2 372	10.3	25.4	72.5	0.1	0.2	1.9	7.5	18.5	10.7	12.8	14.3	14.8
45 007	11340	3	Anderson	1 860	171 510	328	92.2	80.9	17.3	0.5	0.7	1.3	6.5	17.8	8.8	12.9	14.8	14.1
45 009	...	7	Bamberg	1 019	16 040	2 027	15.7	36.5	62.5	0.2	0.2	0.8	7.0	17.7	13.4	10.9	13.1	14.3
45 011	...	6	Barnwell	1 420	23 369	1 646	16.5	54.9	43.2	0.4	0.6	1.3	7.0	20.1	9.3	11.7	14.8	14.5
45 013	25940	5	Beaufort	1 520	132 889	429	87.4	67.0	24.4	0.5	1.5	7.6	7.1	16.6	12.2	13.3	12.8	11.1
45 015	16700	2	Berkeley	2 843	146 449	392	51.5	66.3	28.9	1.0	2.9	2.5	7.3	19.9	11.9	13.7	15.6	13.4
45 017	17900	2	Calhoun	985	15 367	2 070	15.6	50.9	47.3	0.3	0.2	1.6	6.0	17.8	8.5	11.2	14.0	16.0
45 019	16700	2	Charleston	2 379	321 014	184	134.9	61.1	35.1	0.6	1.8	2.5	7.0	16.8	11.2	14.7	14.7	13.5
45 021	23500	4	Cherokee	1 017	53 555	894	52.7	76.2	21.0	0.5	0.5	2.4	7.2	18.5	9.1	14.0	14.6	13.9
45 023	16900	6	Chester	1 504	33 906	1 307	22.5	59.6	39.2	0.4	0.3	0.8	7.2	19.3	8.9	12.2	14.8	14.6
45 025	...	6	Chesterfield	2 068	43 251	1 057	20.9	63.1	33.8	0.7	0.6	2.6	6.8	19.4	8.8	12.9	14.8	14.7
45 027	...	6	Clarendon	1 573	32 871	1 337	20.9	44.8	52.8	0.3	0.4	1.9	6.4	18.2	11.8	11.1	12.9	14.2
45 029	47500	6	Colleton	2 736	39 173	1 149	14.3	56.1	41.6	0.8	0.3	1.7	7.3	19.4	9.3	11.5	14.0	14.2
45 031	22500	3	Darlington	1 453	67 956	741	46.8	56.3	42.5	0.3	0.2	0.9	6.8	19.0	9.0	12.6	14.3	15.1
45 033	19900	6	Dillon	1 049	31 027	1 383	29.6	50.1	45.5	2.4	0.4	2.1	7.8	20.5	10.0	12.2	14.3	14.0
45 035	16700	2	Dorchester	1 489	104 168	521	70.0	70.1	26.2	1.2	1.7	2.1	6.1	20.9	9.5	12.7	16.7	13.9
45 037	12260	2	Edgefield	1 300	24 703	1 591	19.0	56.4	41.0	0.4	0.4	2.1	5.8	17.4	10.6	14.1	16.6	14.8
45 039	17900	2	Fairfield	1 778	23 840	1 621	13.4	39.1	59.3	0.2	0.4	1.2	7.1	18.5	8.9	12.2	14.4	15.5
45 041	22500	3	Florence	2 072	128 335	440	61.9	57.5	40.4	0.5	1.0	1.1	7.0	18.3	10.1	13.0	14.5	14.5
45 043	23860	4	Georgetown	2 110	58 924	830	27.9	60.6	37.1	0.3	0.5	1.9	6.3	17.7	8.4	11.3	13.3	14.3
45 045	24860	2	Greenville	2 046	395 357	153	193.2	74.6	19.2	0.4	1.9	4.8	6.8	17.7	9.4	14.3	15.6	14.0
45 047	24940	4	Greenwood	1 180	67 503	745	57.2	63.7	32.0	0.3	1.0	3.5	7.0	18.2	10.4	13.3	14.0	13.2
45 049	...	6	Hampton	1 450	21 391	1 734	14.8	40.3	56.6	0.4	0.3	2.8	6.9	19.7	9.7	13.3	14.6	14.1
45 051	34820	3	Horry	2 936	210 757	278	71.8	79.7	16.2	0.8	1.2	3.1	6.1	15.3	9.0	13.8	14.5	13.4
45 053	25940	6	Jasper	1 699	20 998	1 752	12.4	39.1	52.0	0.4	0.5	8.1	6.7	19.2	10.7	14.1	15.4	12.7
45 055	17900	2	Kershaw	1 881	54 481	883	29.0	71.2	26.4	0.6	0.4	1.9	6.6	18.5	9.0	11.6	15.3	15.0
45 057	29580	4	Lancaster	1 422	62 520	792	44.0	70.4	27.3	0.5	0.4	2.0	6.6	18.3	9.1	13.7	15.2	14.2
45 059	24860	2	Laurens	1 852	70 269	717	37.9	70.7	26.3	0.5	0.3	2.7	6.1	18.3	9.9	12.9	14.7	13.9
45 061	...	6	Lee	1 063	20 331	1 783	19.1	33.9	63.9	0.2	0.3	2.0	6.6	17.9	11.1	13.0	15.2	14.7
45 063	17900	2	Lexington	1 811	226 528	258	125.1	82.6	13.9	0.7	1.3	2.3	6.7	18.6	8.7	13.4	16.1	14.9
45 065	...	8	McCormick	931	10 233	2 423	11.0	46.0	52.8	0.1	0.6	0.9	4.5	14.1	9.1	12.7	14.1	14.1
45 067	...	6	Marion	1 267	35 113	1 271	27.7	40.8	56.4	0.4	0.3	2.2	7.2	19.3	10.2	12.2	13.2	15.3
45 069	13500	6	Marlboro	1 242	28 411	1 444	22.9	44.1	51.7	3.9	0.3	0.7	7.2	18.5	9.8	13.5	15.2	14.2
45 071	35140	6	Newberry	1 634	36 840	1 217	22.5	61.1	32.7	0.4	0.3	5.8	6.5	17.0	10.6	12.5	14.1	14.0
45 073	42860	6	Oconee	1 620	68 523	733	42.3	88.2	8.7	0.5	0.4	2.7	5.7	16.5	8.3	12.5	13.8	14.1
45 075	36700	4	Orangeburg	2 865	91 028	594	31.8	35.6	62.5	0.8	0.6	1.0	6.9	18.1	12.3	11.5	13.6	13.8
45 077	24860	2	Pickens	1 287	112 859	491	87.7	90.0	6.9	0.5	1.3	2.0	5.8	16.0	15.2	13.6	13.9	12.7
45 079	17900	2	Richland	1 959	332 104	180	169.5	47.8	47.6	0.6	2.6	2.7	6.7	17.5	13.1	15.3	15.2	13.6
45 081	17900	2	Saluda	1 172	19 087	1 857	16.3	60.5	29.3	0.2	0.0	10.2	6.5	17.4	10.2	12.5	14.2	13.9
45 083	43900	2	Spartanburg	2 100	261 281	227	124.4	73.4	21.5	0.5	2.0	3.4	6.4	18.0	9.4	13.6	15.1	14.2

1. CBSA = Core Based Statistical Area. See Appendix A for explanation. See Appendix B for list of metropolitan areas with component counties. 2. County type code from the Economic Research Service of USDA Rural-Urban Continuum Codes. See Appendix A for definition. 3. Dry land or land partially or temporarily covered by water. 4. Hispanic or Latino persons may be of any race.

Table B. States and Counties — **Population and Households**

STATE County	Population, 2003 (cont'd) Age (percent) (cont'd)				Population — change and components of change, 1990–2003							Households, 2000				
					Total persons		Percent change		Components of change, 2000–2003						Percent	
	55 to 64 years	65 to 74 years	75 years and over	Percent female	1990	2000	1990–2000	2000–2003	Births	Deaths	Net migration	Number	Percent change, 1990–2000	Persons per house-hold	Female family house-holder[1]	One person
	16	17	18	19	20	21	22	23	24	25	26	27	28	29	30	31
PENNSYLVANIA—Cont'd																
Potter	10.8	8.4	8.1	50.4	16 717	18 080	8.2	0.3	737	617	-39	7 005	12.2	2.54	7.6	24.7
Schuylkill	10.4	9.0	10.5	49.9	152 585	150 336	-1.5	-1.6	4 659	6 962	55	60 530	-0.4	2.36	10.2	29.9
Snyder	10.2	7.3	6.7	51.2	36 680	37 546	2.4	1.2	1 503	1 049	54	13 654	7.0	2.58	7.4	22.4
Somerset	10.5	8.7	9.5	49.7	78 218	80 023	2.3	-0.8	2 570	2 936	-237	31 222	5.6	2.45	8.5	26.1
Sullivan	12.6	11.2	11.0	49.9	6 104	6 556	7.4	-2.0	157	338	56	2 660	16.7	2.30	6.8	29.3
Susquehanna	11.5	8.3	7.4	50.2	40 380	42 238	4.6	-1.0	1 450	1 533	-278	16 529	10.9	2.53	8.6	24.3
Tioga	11.2	8.3	7.9	51.2	41 126	41 373	0.6	0.4	1 421	1 360	160	15 925	6.4	2.48	8.6	24.4
Union	9.1	6.3	7.1	44.0	36 176	41 624	15.1	2.2	1 269	1 137	833	13 178	12.7	2.50	6.9	25.3
Venango	11.0	8.8	8.1	51.2	59 381	57 565	-3.1	-1.7	1 898	2 137	-672	22 747	1.5	2.45	9.9	26.2
Warren	11.9	8.8	8.3	50.9	45 050	43 863	-2.6	-2.4	1 443	1 604	-867	17 696	2.6	2.42	8.4	27.2
Washington	10.7	8.3	9.1	51.8	204 584	202 897	-0.8	0.7	6 588	8 359	3 238	81 130	3.3	2.44	10.3	27.0
Wayne	11.2	9.2	8.3	50.0	39 944	47 722	19.5	2.9	1 548	1 802	1 638	18 350	25.4	2.50	8.9	25.2
Westmoreland	11.1	8.8	9.4	51.7	370 321	369 993	-0.1	-0.5	10 894	14 098	1 760	149 813	4.0	2.41	9.6	26.9
Wyoming	11.2	7.0	6.7	50.4	28 076	28 080	0.0	0.3	992	875	-23	10 762	7.6	2.55	9.3	24.1
York	10.1	6.9	6.5	50.8	339 574	381 751	12.4	3.4	14 791	10 811	9 338	148 219	15.2	2.52	9.0	23.3
RHODE ISLAND	9.8	6.4	7.7	51.8	1 003 464	1 048 319	4.5	2.7	40 114	31 964	20 573	408 424	8.1	2.47	12.9	28.6
Bristol	10.1	7.7	8.8	51.8	48 859	50 648	3.7	0.7	1 501	1 674	549	19 033	8.4	2.52	9.9	25.1
Kent	10.1	7.0	7.7	51.9	161 143	167 090	3.7	2.5	5 970	5 598	3 876	67 320	8.5	2.45	10.5	27.6
Newport	11.3	7.1	7.5	51.1	87 194	85 433	-2.0	0.6	2 752	2 153	-38	35 228	7.8	2.45	10.3	29.9
Providence	8.5	6.2	7.7	52.0	596 270	621 602	4.2	2.9	25 746	19 534	12 319	239 936	6.0	2.35	14.9	29.8
Washington	10.2	6.3	6.5	51.4	109 998	123 546	12.3	4.0	4 145	3 005	3 867	46 907	19.3	2.52	9.4	24.1
SOUTH CAROLINA	10.4	6.7	5.6	51.3	3 486 310	4 012 012	15.1	3.4	182 193	122 447	77 775	1 533 854	21.9	2.53	14.8	25.0
Abbeville	10.6	7.4	7.0	51.9	23 862	26 167	9.7	0.8	1 087	795	-33	10 131	15.4	2.51	15.3	25.3
Aiken	9.9	7.2	5.9	51.8	120 991	142 552	17.8	2.9	5 977	4 680	3 062	55 587	23.8	2.53	13.8	25.2
Allendale	9.3	6.2	6.8	47.4	11 727	11 211	-4.4	-2.5	592	392	-484	3 915	3.3	2.56	25.8	30.0
Anderson	10.9	7.3	6.2	51.6	145 177	165 740	14.2	3.5	7 106	5 846	4 526	65 649	18.3	2.48	12.8	24.3
Bamberg	10.6	7.4	6.9	53.0	16 902	16 658	-1.4	-3.7	769	571	-812	6 123	9.6	2.55	21.3	27.8
Barnwell	9.7	6.8	5.9	52.1	20 293	23 478	15.7	-0.5	1 095	831	-360	9 021	27.1	2.57	19.3	26.4
Beaufort	9.7	9.1	6.5	49.0	86 425	120 937	39.9	9.9	6 145	3 179	8 882	45 532	48.3	2.51	11.0	21.5
Berkeley	8.8	5.2	3.3	49.4	128 658	142 651	10.9	2.7	6 839	3 157	312	49 922	17.8	2.75	14.2	19.4
Calhoun	12.2	7.3	6.4	52.5	12 753	15 185	19.1	1.2	639	503	59	5 917	31.9	2.54	15.8	24.5
Charleston	9.3	6.2	5.5	51.6	295 159	309 969	5.0	3.6	15 030	9 114	5 345	123 326	15.2	2.42	15.9	28.3
Cherokee	10.3	6.6	5.7	51.6	44 506	52 537	18.0	1.9	2 524	1 869	403	20 495	24.5	2.53	15.4	25.0
Chester	10.6	6.8	5.9	51.8	32 170	34 068	5.9	-0.5	1 674	1 103	-680	12 880	12.5	2.62	18.6	24.2
Chesterfield	10.5	6.7	5.3	51.8	38 575	42 768	10.9	1.1	2 011	1 311	-160	16 557	17.9	2.54	16.3	25.9
Clarendon	11.3	8.0	6.0	50.6	28 450	32 502	14.2	1.1	1 465	1 085	33	11 812	23.8	2.62	19.8	24.6
Colleton	11.2	7.1	5.7	52.0	34 377	38 264	11.3	2.4	1 925	1 307	337	14 470	20.2	2.62	16.8	24.0
Darlington	10.6	6.7	5.6	52.6	61 851	67 394	9.0	0.8	3 103	2 411	-50	25 793	17.2	2.57	16.8	24.0
Dillon	9.5	6.1	5.5	53.4	29 114	30 722	5.5	1.0	1 705	1 087	-277	11 199	13.3	2.71	22.3	25.1
Dorchester	9.1	5.3	3.9	51.0	83 060	96 413	16.1	8.0	3 961	2 292	6 070	34 709	23.0	2.72	14.6	20.2
Edgefield	9.9	5.9	5.0	46.8	18 360	24 595	34.0	0.4	942	759	-50	8 270	28.7	2.66	15.5	22.4
Fairfield	10.3	7.0	6.1	52.4	22 295	23 454	5.2	1.6	1 151	880	135	8 774	17.5	2.63	20.0	24.4
Florence	10.0	6.4	5.6	52.9	114 344	125 761	10.0	2.0	6 127	4 312	892	47 147	17.2	2.59	18.1	24.5
Georgetown	11.9	8.9	6.7	52.1	46 302	55 797	20.5	5.6	2 560	1 814	2 403	21 659	33.1	2.55	15.1	23.3
Greenville	9.7	6.1	5.5	51.1	320 127	379 616	18.6	4.1	17 276	11 167	9 882	149 556	21.7	2.47	12.3	26.8
Greenwood	9.9	7.1	6.6	52.9	59 567	66 271	11.3	1.9	3 108	2 226	424	25 729	13.2	2.49	16.1	26.3
Hampton	9.2	6.7	5.6	49.3	18 186	21 386	17.6	0.0	998	723	-264	7 444	17.7	2.64	18.8	25.8
Horry	11.1	9.1	5.9	50.8	144 053	196 629	36.5	7.2	8 364	6 326	11 866	81 800	46.7	2.37	11.5	25.8
Jasper	9.7	6.0	5.0	47.2	15 487	20 678	33.5	1.5	944	496	-105	7 042	32.9	2.75	18.2	23.2
Kershaw	10.6	7.0	5.7	51.8	43 599	52 647	20.8	3.5	2 333	1 742	1 261	20 188	27.7	2.58	13.6	22.6
Lancaster	10.5	6.7	5.4	50.4	54 516	61 351	12.5	1.9	2 669	1 938	503	23 178	17.2	2.56	15.5	23.7
Laurens	11.0	7.0	6.0	51.4	58 132	69 567	19.7	1.0	2 692	2 406	526	26 290	27.3	2.55	15.6	24.6
Lee	9.0	6.4	5.7	49.5	18 437	20 119	9.1	1.1	890	703	54	6 886	13.7	2.68	23.8	25.9
Lexington	10.0	5.8	4.6	51.3	167 526	216 014	28.9	4.9	9 645	5 757	6 799	83 240	35.1	2.56	11.6	22.5
McCormick	13.6	10.2	7.3	46.7	8 868	9 958	12.3	2.8	319	362	328	3 558	30.3	2.39	17.6	24.4
Marion	10.1	6.6	5.8	53.5	33 899	35 466	4.6	-1.0	1 763	1 245	-864	13 301	13.0	2.64	23.6	25.4
Marlboro	9.9	6.5	5.8	51.0	29 716	28 818	-3.0	-1.4	1 424	1 191	-612	10 478	3.1	2.59	22.2	26.9
Newberry	10.7	7.2	7.1	51.3	33 172	36 108	8.9	2.0	1 596	1 333	496	14 026	13.9	2.50	16.1	26.5
Oconee	12.3	9.6	6.5	50.8	57 494	66 215	15.2	3.5	2 449	2 041	1 905	27 283	22.0	2.40	10.1	24.7
Orangeburg	10.3	7.1	6.4	53.6	84 804	91 582	8.0	-0.6	4 361	3 144	-1 631	34 118	18.0	2.58	20.3	26.0
Pickens	9.5	6.2	5.5	49.9	93 896	110 757	18.0	1.9	4 255	2 890	853	41 306	23.6	2.50	9.4	23.3
Richland	8.0	5.1	4.5	51.7	286 321	320 677	12.0	3.6	14 765	8 462	5 400	120 101	18.2	2.44	16.3	29.1
Saluda	11.0	7.6	6.7	50.1	16 441	19 181	16.7	-0.5	853	626	-303	7 127	22.4	2.65	14.5	22.5
Spartanburg	10.2	6.6	5.8	51.3	226 793	253 791	11.9	3.0	10 800	8 634	5 524	97 735	15.7	2.52	13.8	24.8

1. No spouse present.

Items 16—31

Table B. States and Counties — Vital Statistics, Health Resources, and Crime

STATE County	Births, average 1999–2001 Total	Rate[1]	Deaths, average 1999–2001 Number Total	Number Infant[2]	Rate Total[1]	Rate Infant[3]	Physicians,[4] 2000 Number	Rate[5]	Hospitals,[4] 1998 Number	Beds Number	Beds Rate[5]	Medicare enrollees, 2003	Serious crimes known to police,[6] 2002 Total Number	Rate[7]
	32	33	34	35	36	37	38	39	40	41	42	43	44	45
PENNSYLVANIA—Cont'd														
Potter	221	12.3	193	1	10.7	D	29	160	1	120	698	3 426	245	1 729
Schuylkill	1 446	9.6	2 094	9	13.9	6.5	188	125	4	605	408	31 576	2 266	1 967
Snyder	449	11.9	317	5	8.4	D	34	91	0	0	0	6 148	564	1 620
Somerset	819	10.3	920	6	11.5	D	86	107	3	230	287	15 770	1 011	1 466
Sullivan	51	7.9	109	0	16.7	D	3	46	0	0	0	1 510	147	2 232
Susquehanna	462	10.9	470	4	11.1	D	33	78	2	139	330	7 587	599	1 586
Tioga	435	10.5	439	2	10.6	D	49	118	1	103	248	7 855	431	1 126
Union	385	9.2	336	3	8.1	D	86	207	1	135	330	6 234	403	1 118
Venango	625	10.9	657	5	11.4	D	100	174	2	308	532	11 250	1 237	2 139
Warren	475	10.8	503	4	11.5	D	73	166	1	105	239	8 182	619	1 513
Washington	2 077	10.2	2 490	15	12.3	7.1	292	144	3	713	347	40 747	845	1 826
Wayne	494	10.3	546	1	11.5	D	63	132	1	95	210	11 711	396	1 779
Westmoreland	3 510	9.5	4 338	19	11.7	5.5	621	168	6	1 169	314	72 357	6 307	1 512
Wyoming	316	11.2	263	2	9.4	D	25	89	1	63	216	4 825	396	2 396
York	4 548	11.9	3 313	20	8.7	4.5	641	168	3	768	206	58 951	7 312	
RHODE ISLAND	12 528	11.9	9 919	79	9.4	6.3	2 859	273	10	2 814	285	172 474	38 393	3 589
Bristol	490	9.7	525	3	10.4	D	74	146	0	0	0	8 913	1 145	2 215
Kent	1 863	11.1	1 676	9	10.0	4.8	334	200	1	359	222	29 539	4 729	2 774
Newport	939	11.0	736	3	8.6	D	153	179	1	200	241	14 171	2 746	3 150
Providence	7 913	12.7	6 031	60	9.7	7.6	2 078	334	6	2 030	354	101 294	27 217	4 291
Washington	1 322	10.7	950	4	7.7	D	220	178	2	225	186	18 475	2 458	1 950
SOUTH CAROLINA	55 606	13.8	36 538	516	9.1	9.3	6 704	167	64	11 249	293	606 323	217 569	5 297
Abbeville	349	13.3	234	4	9.0	D	20	76	0	0	0	3 899	992	3 703
Aiken	1 887	13.2	1 345	18	9.4	9.5	132	93	2	273	204	22 135	5 504	3 772
Allendale	176	15.7	116	3	10.4	D	18	161	1	78	681	1 636	452	3 938
Anderson	2 219	13.4	1 723	20	10.4	8.9	256	154	1	445	277	28 369	9 096	5 361
Bamberg	222	13.4	183	3	11.1	D	13	78	1	84	509	2 561	485	2 844
Barnwell	340	14.5	244	6	10.4	D	14	60	1	35	161	3 588	939	3 907
Beaufort	1 863	15.4	935	11	7.7	5.7	233	193	3	234	215	21 697	6 190	5 000
Berkeley	2 166	15.2	893	18	6.2	8.5	40	28	0	0	0	13 457	6 278	4 299
Calhoun	174	11.5	157	2	10.3	D	2	13	0	0	0	1 832	303	2 008
Charleston	4 551	14.6	2 718	45	8.7	10.0	1 414	456	7	1 760	556	44 638	22 455	7 076
Cherokee	734	14.0	538	9	10.2	12.3	42	80	1	125	254	7 833	2 570	4 778
Chester	471	13.8	337	4	9.9	D	20	59	1	163	474	5 632	1 886	5 408
Chesterfield	600	14.0	420	6	9.8	D	26	61	1	66	161	6 603	1 906	4 353
Clarendon	433	13.3	325	6	10.0	D	17	52	1	56	182	5 340	1 191	3 579
Colleton	583	15.2	389	4	10.2	D	34	89	1	116	310	6 169	2 163	5 522
Darlington	949	14.1	736	13	10.9	14.0	59	88	2	150	226	9 968	4 195	6 080
Dillon	484	15.7	317	5	10.3	D	22	72	1	90	303	4 751	2 052	6 524
Dorchester	1 193	12.4	703	13	7.3	10.6	66	68	1	111	126	12 411	4 184	4 315
Edgefield	299	12.2	216	5	8.8	D	5	20	0	0	0	2 614	615	2 443
Fairfield	323	13.8	279	2	11.9	D	10	43	1	41	183	3 661	1 463	6 093
Florence	1 887	15.0	1 297	24	10.3	12.9	290	231	4	765	612	20 013	8 503	6 605
Georgetown	797	14.2	542	9	9.7	11.3	72	129	1	141	262	13 875	2 947	5 159
Greenville	5 426	14.3	3 318	32	8.7	6.0	817	215	4	1 314	371	56 817	18 199	4 683
Greenwood	934	14.1	673	10	10.1	10.7	161	243	1	355	558	11 550	3 289	4 848
Hampton	303	14.2	206	3	9.7	D	10	47	1	36	188	3 831	777	3 650
Horry	2 502	12.7	1 876	21	9.5	8.5	272	138	3	480	275	33 827	16 397	8 165
Jasper	298	14.4	163	3	7.9	D	20	97	0	0	0	2 356	1 378	6 510
Kershaw	713	13.6	510	5	9.7	D	52	99	1	198	407	8 731	2 056	3 815
Lancaster	820	13.4	612	9	10.0	11.4	51	83	1	166	282	9 188	3 562	5 828
Laurens	831	12.0	721	8	10.4	10.0	42	60	1	80	126	10 296	3 318	4 659
Laurens	270	13.4	204	4	10.1	D	3	15	0	0	0	2 841	817	3 967
Lee														
Lexington	2 971	13.7	1 677	23	7.7	7.9	221	102	1	287	140	27 354	9 113	4 121
McCormick	86	8.6	110	1	11.1	D	8	80	0	0	0	2 135	290	2 845
Marion	508	14.4	394	7	11.1	14.4	32	90	2	190	549	6 042	2 195	6 093
Marlboro	428	14.8	357	5	12.4	D	19	66	1	108	365	4 757	1 776	6 020
Newberry	499	13.8	384	6	10.6	D	32	89	1	64	186	6 535	1 162	3 144
Oconee	783	11.8	630	5	9.5	D	66	100	1	195	304	13 509	2 283	3 368
Orangeburg	1 314	14.4	941	17	10.3	13.2	125	136	2	292	332	15 015	5 795	6 181
Pickens	1 344	12.1	899	7	8.1	5.2	91	82	2	132	123	17 023	3 437	3 031
Richland	4 359	13.6	2 554	40	7.9	9.1	1 099	343	4	1 267	413	38 799	23 992	7 308
Saluda	262	13.7	199	2	10.4	D	8	42	0	0	0	2 478	369	1 879
Spartanburg	3 350	13.2	2 551	23	10.0	7.0	418	165	3	681	275	41 603	13 903	5 351

1. Per 1,000 estimated resident population.   2. Deaths of infants under 1 year old.   3. Deaths of infants under 1 year old per 1,000 live births.   4. Data subject to copyright.   5. Per 100,000 resident population as of July 1 of the year shown.   6. Data for serious crimes have not been adjusted for underreporting; this may affect comparability between geographic areas and over time.   7. Per 100,000 population estimated by the FBI.

Table B. States and Counties — Crime, Education, Money Income, and Poverty

STATE County	Serious crimes known to police,[1] 2002 (cont'd) Rate[2] Violent	Property	Education — School enrollment and attainment, 2000 — Enrollment[3] Total	Percent private	Attainment[4] (percent) High school graduate or less	Bachelor's degree or more	Local government expenditures,[5] 2000–2001 Total current expenditures (mil dol)	Current expenditures per student (dollars)	Money income, 1999 Per capita income[6] (dollars)	Households — Median income Dollars	Percent change, 1989–1999 (constant 1999 dollars)	Percent with income of $100,000 or more	Percent below poverty level, 1999 Persons	House-holds	Families	Families with children
	46	47	48	49	50	51	52	53	54	55	56	57	58	59	60	61
PENNSYLVANIA—Cont'd																
Potter	127	1 602	4 194	7.9	66.7	12.3	22.9	7 064	16 070	32 253	12.3	4.0	12.7	11.9	9.3	15.7
Schuylkill	401	1 566	30 760	15.7	71.1	10.7	154.8	7 687	17 230	32 699	5.7	4.4	9.5	10.7	6.7	10.4
Snyder	350	1 270	9 512	29.9	73.2	12.5	37.2	6 640	16 756	35 981	3.5	5.3	9.9	9.8	6.7	9.7
Somerset	122	1 344	16 927	9.3	72.9	10.8	86.4	7 030	15 178	30 911	6.2	3.3	11.8	12.1	9.1	13.7
Sullivan	106	2 126	1 347	8.9	67.6	12.8	7.9	8 749	16 438	30 279	12.1	4.9	14.5	12.8	7.4	12.1
Susquehanna	154	1 432	10 047	10.2	64.7	13.2	60.9	7 243	16 435	33 622	1.2	4.8	12.3	11.9	8.9	13.7
Tioga	57	1 068	10 811	8.4	64.2	14.2	49.8	7 314	15 549	32 020	5.6	4.0	13.5	13.2	9.3	14.0
Union	136	982	10 801	37.6	65.9	18.0	80.5	17 995	17 918	40 336	8.7	8.1	8.8	9.6	5.1	7.5
Venango	161	1 979	13 090	11.9	68.4	13.1	76.3	7 300	16 252	32 257	6.3	4.5	13.4	13.2	10.4	17.3
Warren	147	1 367	10 028	11.1	63.7	14.2	45.1	6 890	17 862	36 083	1.9	4.9	9.9	8.8	6.8	10.7
Washington	194	1 631	46 477	15.3	60.0	18.8	259.9	8 455	19 935	37 607	9.9	8.4	9.8	10.6	6.9	11.6
Wayne	194	1 615	10 913	11.7	62.8	14.6	77.2	8 009	16 977	34 082	1.8	5.4	11.3	11.5	8.4	12.9
Westmoreland	164	1 615	84 043	16.5	55.6	20.2	419.6	7 425	19 674	37 106	7.3	7.8	8.6	9.4	6.2	10.3
Wyoming	248	1 264	7 072	15.1	61.6	15.4	36.5	7 605	17 452	36 365	-0.5	6.4	10.2	10.5	7.8	12.0
York	186	2 210	90 912	17.9	60.9	18.4	378.3	6 717	21 086	45 268	3.3	8.8	6.7	6.7	4.6	7.1
RHODE ISLAND	285	3 304	290 605	24.4	49.8	25.6	1 423.0	9 104	21 688	42 090	-2.7	11.5	11.9	12.4	8.9	14.2
Bristol	104	2 111	14 156	35.5	42.7	34.3	64.9	9 234	26 503	50 737	0.6	19.0	6.3	7.8	4.4	5.9
Kent	167	2 606	40 874	20.0	47.2	24.8	250.1	9 518	23 833	47 617	-1.7	11.8	6.6	7.5	4.8	7.2
Newport	227	2 923	22 211	26.0	36.4	38.3	112.3	9 422	26 779	50 448	4.8	16.0	7.1	7.9	5.4	9.0
Providence	374	3 917	176 038	26.6	55.6	21.3	821.6	8 857	19 255	36 950	-7.0	9.2	15.5	15.7	11.9	19.0
Washington	86	1 863	37 326	13.8	37.4	35.5	174.2	9 523	25 530	53 103	7.0	16.7	7.3	7.5	4.2	6.7
SOUTH CAROLINA	822	4 475	1 053 152	14.1	53.6	20.4	4 452.9	6 577	18 795	37 082	5.1	8.1	14.1	14.1	10.7	15.7
Abbeville	847	2 856	6 687	18.2	65.8	12.8	25.9	6 696	15 370	32 635	4.8	3.4	13.7	14.8	10.1	15.2
Aiken	370	3 402	37 855	13.1	54.0	19.9	141.1	5 609	18 772	37 889	-6.0	8.6	13.8	14.0	10.6	16.1
Allendale	967	2 971	3 132	5.7	71.3	9.3	18.3	9 342	11 293	20 898	3.6	3.9	34.5	33.6	28.4	40.0
Anderson	720	4 641	39 271	13.7	59.3	15.9	174.8	6 315	18 365	36 807	6.4	6.9	12.0	13.0	9.1	13.1
Bamberg	768	2 076	4 940	15.5	63.6	15.4	22.2	7 651	12 584	24 007	2.1	3.5	27.8	26.9	23.9	30.8
Barnwell	820	3 087	6 391	6.9	67.2	11.6	33.5	6 379	15 870	28 591	-9.4	5.5	20.9	22.5	17.9	23.6
Beaufort	738	4 262	27 897	17.2	36.3	33.2	125.0	7 473	25 377	46 992	14.9	15.6	10.7	9.5	8.0	13.9
Berkeley	627	3 672	39 541	12.9	54.1	14.4	166.4	6 247	16 879	39 908	2.1	6.3	11.8	11.8	9.7	13.5
Calhoun	504	1 505	3 652	16.1	62.5	14.2	16.3	7 367	17 446	32 736	2.6	6.6	16.2	17.0	13.2	17.8
Charleston	1 004	6 073	87 355	19.9	41.4	30.7	276.2	6 169	21 393	37 810	4.7	11.0	16.4	15.5	12.4	18.7
Cherokee	608	4 170	12 165	10.1	69.9	11.8	59.5	6 390	16 421	33 787	2.0	4.8	13.9	14.8	11.0	15.0
Chester	1 035	4 373	8 226	7.0	69.0	9.6	43.6	6 386	14 709	32 425	4.7	3.9	15.3	16.8	11.9	17.3
Chesterfield	724	3 629	10 526	10.0	69.4	9.7	51.4	6 294	14 233	29 483	4.2	3.5	20.3	21.0	16.7	21.4
Clarendon	718	2 861	8 452	10.1	69.2	11.4	39.7	6 467	13 998	27 131	14.4	4.5	23.1	23.8	18.7	24.7
Colleton	978	4 544	9 704	12.1	67.3	11.5	45.6	6 590	14 831	29 733	7.3	4.2	21.1	20.9	17.3	24.5
Darlington	1 012	5 069	17 661	13.7	63.2	13.5	77.7	6 709	16 283	31 087	2.2	5.9	20.3	20.4	16.4	22.9
Dillon	1 110	5 415	8 481	8.2	72.9	9.2	38.5	5 954	13 272	26 630	7.9	3.5	24.2	24.5	19.4	26.8
Dorchester	708	3 606	28 267	15.7	47.5	21.4	119.9	6 232	18 840	43 316	4.8	8.7	9.7	10.0	7.1	9.8
Edgefield	310	2 133	6 110	10.3	64.0	12.5	27.3	6 730	15 415	35 146	13.6	6.5	15.5	16.1	13.0	17.4
Fairfield	1 395	4 698	5 873	11.0	68.7	11.7	32.8	8 702	14 911	30 376	5.2	5.2	19.6	21.0	17.2	23.4
Florence	877	5 728	33 873	13.3	57.8	18.7	140.5	6 325	17 876	35 144	7.8	7.3	16.4	16.3	13.5	18.4
Georgetown	758	4 401	13 450	7.5	55.0	20.0	77.0	7 364	19 805	35 312	9.6	8.7	17.1	15.9	13.4	21.6
Greenville	772	3 911	96 798	23.8	46.8	26.2	361.1	6 030	22 081	41 149	5.3	11.7	10.5	10.6	7.9	11.7
Greenwood	999	3 849	17 843	11.1	56.6	18.9	74.9	6 092	17 446	34 702	9.5	6.1	14.2	14.1	9.9	14.2
Hampton	672	2 978	5 899	11.1	70.8	10.1	31.1	6 498	13 129	28 771	15.0	4.0	21.8	22.4	17.8	24.4
Horry	973	7 193	42 752	10.8	51.0	18.7	204.1	6 829	19 949	36 470	8.8	7.1	12.0	11.2	8.4	14.4
Jasper	794	5 716	5 407	21.1	70.8	8.7	19.3	6 484	14 161	30 727	26.6	5.5	20.7	19.9	15.4	21.6
Kershaw	759	3 056	12 532	9.5	60.1	16.3	64.0	6 521	18 360	38 804	2.1	5.9	12.8	13.0	9.7	13.5
Lancaster	1 003	4 825	14 891	7.8	65.8	10.2	69.6	6 133	16 276	34 688	2.0	4.9	12.8	13.0	9.7	14.0
Laurens	1 012	3 647	17 251	15.2	67.3	11.7	60.3	5 979	15 761	33 933	1.4	4.4	14.3	13.8	11.6	17.1
Lee	908	3 059	5 138	16.0	73.7	9.2	22.9	7 475	13 896	26 907	10.2	4.3	21.8	25.3	17.7	22.5
Lexington	580	3 541	55 402	10.2	46.5	24.6	323.4	6 866	21 063	44 659	1.0	9.9	9.0	8.9	6.4	9.4
McCormick	863	1 982	2 139	11.7	64.4	16.0	9.4	7 930	14 770	31 577	22.2	5.1	17.9	19.3	15.1	24.0
Marion	1 038	5 055	9 764	6.9	70.5	10.2	43.9	6 480	13 878	26 526	10.8	3.9	23.2	23.1	19.1	26.4
Marlboro	1 444	4 576	7 049	8.4	74.1	8.3	31.3	5 612	13 385	26 598	9.6	3.0	21.7	22.9	17.7	23.9
Newberry	703	2 440	8 802	17.0	64.4	14.8	41.6	7 154	16 045	32 867	4.5	5.1	17.0	17.0	13.6	20.7
Oconee	562	2 806	14 546	10.0	59.3	18.2	77.2	6 908	18 965	36 666	6.1	6.7	10.8	12.0	7.6	12.6
Orangeburg	1 202	4 979	27 308	14.7	60.1	16.3	118.5	7 184	15 057	29 567	8.9	4.7	21.4	21.9	17.0	22.9
Pickens	346	2 686	34 574	9.3	57.1	19.1	96.5	6 053	17 434	36 214	2.3	6.5	13.7	14.4	7.8	10.6
Richland	1 111	6 197	97 237	14.4	37.7	32.5	340.3	7 653	20 794	39 961	3.1	10.8	13.7	13.1	10.1	14.5
Saluda	525	1 355	4 394	5.8	69.3	11.9	14.9	6 784	16 328	35 774	20.1	4.8	15.6	15.4	12.0	18.3
Spartanburg	848	4 504	61 998	13.8	56.8	18.2	295.0	6 900	18 738	37 579	3.8	7.5	12.3	12.8	9.2	13.4

1. Data for serious crimes have not been adjusted for underreporting; this may affect comparability between geographic areas and over time.   2. Per 100,000 population estimated by the FBI.   3. All persons 3 years old and over enrolled in nursery school through college.   4. Persons 25 years old and over.   5. Elementary and secondary education expenditures.   6. Based on population enumerated as of April 1, 2000.

Table B. States and Counties — **Personal Income**

	Personal income, 2002												
			Per capita[1]					Transfer payments					
									Government payments to individuals				
STATE County	Total (mil dol)	Percent change, 2001–2002	Dollars	Rank	Wages and salaries[2] (mil dol)	Proprietor's income (mil dol)	Dividends, interest, and rent (mil dol)	Total (mil dol)	Total (mil dol)	Social Security (mil dol)	Medical payments (mil dol)	Income mainte- nance (mil dol)	Unemploy- ment insurance (mil dol)
	62	63	64	65	66	67	68	69	70	71	72	73	74
PENNSYLVANIA—Cont'd													
Potter	449	1.3	24 684	1 215	284	56	62	96	91	37	37	7	6
Schuylkill	3 563	2.6	23 947	1 421	1 730	183	615	900	862	343	346	44	59
Snyder	977	1.8	25 758	939	558	74	170	243	233	68	142	8	8
Somerset	1 763	2.4	22 148	1 969	858	152	302	456	436	166	185	29	30
Sullivan	156	4.2	23 839	1 459	50	13	36	43	42	20	17	2	2
Susquehanna	1 008	2.0	24 024	1 398	260	82	176	212	201	88	76	15	13
Tioga	876	2.2	21 050	2 281	441	64	152	214	203	88	77	16	11
Union	975	2.0	23 091	1 698	681	75	188	161	150	68	58	9	8
Venango	1 351	1.3	23 767	1 478	721	63	220	419	405	132	217	28	15
Warren	1 040	0.8	24 099	1 372	567	69	174	239	228	99	93	14	14
Washington	6 057	2.9	29 740	369	2 998	455	903	1 234	1 181	486	500	71	65
Wayne	1 194	4.4	24 650	1 224	474	66	245	277	264	120	104	16	13
Westmoreland	10 545	2.6	28 635	480	5 079	594	1 692	2 165	2 071	858	873	114	127
Wyoming	660	4.2	23 618	1 529	428	39	106	133	126	52	51	9	9
York	11 222	3.0	28 810	466	6 938	543	1 859	1 605	1 506	707	556	97	86
RHODE ISLAND	32 967	3.4	30 859	X	20 817	2 207	5 703	5 877	5 623	1 893	2 612	495	259
Bristol	1 953	3.1	38 252	86	515	83	473	236	224	105	82	10	11
Kent	5 533	3.9	32 555	203	3 277	244	849	908	867	337	351	51	64
Newport	3 172	4.2	36 908	107	2 119	156	706	407	387	153	164	25	16
Providence	17 949	3.0	28 301	511	12 981	1 485	2 817	3 770	3 619	1 080	1 804	382	146
Washington	4 360	4.0	34 289	154	1 925	239	859	556	525	219	212	28	23
SOUTH CAROLINA	104 653	2.8	25 502	X	69 337	6 632	17 651	18 327	17 312	6 767	7 046	1 878	575
Abbeville	591	-5.9	22 437	1 896	272	52	74	153	147	48	72	12	5
Aiken	3 922	3.3	27 019	698	2 693	273	672	673	637	262	259	67	10
Allendale	190	0.9	17 156	2 977	145	5	26	62	59	16	27	13	1
Anderson	4 252	1.3	24 983	1 132	2 209	355	648	777	734	337	273	63	27
Bamberg	310	0.9	18 973	2 759	152	16	42	94	90	27	39	13	2
Barnwell	512	-4.4	21 978	2 020	365	13	66	123	117	35	55	18	6
Beaufort	4 536	4.1	34 935	143	2 565	362	1 514	551	522	266	184	35	8
Berkeley	3 223	5.8	22 225	1 953	1 434	176	378	500	464	168	181	55	12
Calhoun	360	1.3	23 632	1 523	163	24	57	67	63	23	27	8	2
Charleston	9 613	4.9	30 361	313	8 025	927	1 943	1 365	1 288	453	577	146	35
Cherokee	1 107	1.4	20 669	2 378	707	40	164	242	228	97	88	24	9
Chester	716	1.9	21 019	2 295	415	34	89	177	168	62	69	20	10
Chesterfield	878	1.7	20 332	2 470	528	55	121	213	202	72	88	27	7
Clarendon	626	1.9	19 015	2 752	247	26	107	182	174	56	76	29	6
Colleton	790	2.9	20 298	2 480	336	50	115	212	202	67	92	28	6
Darlington	1 591	2.1	23 455	1 582	906	58	73	351	334	116	144	47	13
Dillon	569	-1.1	18 333	2 854	285	20	73	172	164	46	76	31	5
Dorchester	2 340	5.4	23 134	1 683	994	29	294	390	365	130	165	35	8
Edgefield	517	3.7	20 930	2 316	221	19	65	89	83	33	33	11	2
Fairfield	503	3.2	21 078	2 274	300	19	66	121	115	38	52	15	5
Florence	3 272	2.8	25 738	943	2 483	246	461	672	640	195	290	87	22
Georgetown	1 536	4.3	26 460	803	728	145	390	353	338	127	152	34	14
Greenville	11 547	1.4	29 544	386	9 666	799	2 016	1 568	1 470	649	582	126	42
Greenwood	1 582	0.9	23 552	1 547	1 174	96	265	317	300	129	104	31	13
Hampton	423	2.7	19 920	2 561	225	20	68	112	107	34	47	16	4
Horry	5 059	3.5	24 584	1 241	3 216	337	1 056	961	910	417	335	83	31
Jasper	402	5.5	19 171	2 721	167	21	42	80	75	21	34	14	2
Kershaw	1 353	4.5	25 171	1 085	655	96	217	237	223	96	87	21	7
Lancaster	1 338	2.1	21 513	2 146	695	78	194	291	276	112	114	28	12
Laurens	1 506	1.3	21 490	2 150	678	48	223	355	337	128	149	33	15
Lee	360	0.3	17 744	2 927	131	12	46	108	102	29	48	17	3
Lexington	6 452	2.9	28 981	449	3 064	449	950	807	752	323	294	67	19
McCormick	188	3.9	18 373	2 847	67	10	40	56	54	24	20	6	2
Marion	653	1.1	18 603	2 813	338	25	65	212	204	55	97	33	8
Marlboro	514	1.0	17 956	2 902	281	13	65	156	148	48	65	25	5
Newberry	787	1.3	21 397	2 181	430	28	129	178	169	69	67	18	7
Oconee	1 712	1.9	25 209	1 074	996	90	374	335	318	153	118	21	13
Orangeburg	1 956	3.0	21 418	2 175	1 167	85	280	486	463	153	186	72	19
Pickens	2 520	2.3	22 486	1 882	1 243	131	394	436	408	186	153	30	11
Richland	9 301	3.1	28 318	510	9 051	643	1 490	1 344	1 264	423	529	133	24
Saluda	416	0.1	21 816	2 060	137	15	52	80	75	31	28	10	2
Spartanburg	6 523	3.1	25 182	1 082	5 076	313	938	1 144	1 079	468	400	99	53

1. Based on the resident population estimated as of July 1 of the year shown.   2. Includes other labor income.

Table B. States and Counties — Earnings, Social Security, and Housing

STATE County	Total (mil dol)	Farm	Goods-related[1] Total	Manufacturing	Information and professional and technical services	Retail trade	Finance, insurance, and real estate	Health services	Government	Social Security beneficiaries, December 2003 Number	Rate[2]	Supplemental Security Income recipients, December 2003	Housing units, 2003 Total	Percent change, 2000–2003
	75	76	77	78	79	80	81	82	83	84	85	86	87	88
PENNSYLVANIA—Cont'd														
Potter	340	3.0	18.4	9.0	D	5.0	2.0	D	12.2	4 075	225	499	12 448	2.4
Schuylkill	1 913	0.4	32.4	26.6	4.6	10.3	4.1	13.0	17.4	35 875	242	3 166	68 484	1.0
Snyder	632	1.0	D	34.4	2.9	10.2	3.4	D	16.9	7 220	190	502	15 267	2.5
Somerset	1 010	1.3	28.4	18.0	3.9	10.4	4.3	10.1	18.7	17 860	225	2 250	37 882	1.9
Sullivan	63	0.8	D	12.9	3.0	9.0	4.2	D	23.5	1 825	284	117	6 069	0.9
Susquehanna	342	1.9	21.2	7.5	5.8	12.0	3.8	11.2	22.5	9 395	225	893	22 245	1.9
Tioga	505	1.7	D	26.1	D	9.3	4.4	D	24.4	9 415	227	1 207	20 484	3.0
Union	757	0.5	D	15.7	D	5.7	2.9	D	26.2	7 045	166	491	15 108	2.9
Venango	784	0.1	28.5	24.4	D	9.8	4.4	15.5	20.6	13 640	241	2 094	27 248	1.3
Warren	636	0.8	27.2	23.2	7.6	16.6	4.6	10.7	17.5	9 825	229	875	23 316	1.1
Washington	3 453	0.1	31.0	16.8	8.6	7.4	D	12.3	12.1	47 480	232	5 404	89 794	2.9
Wayne	540	1.4	16.3	4.9	D	12.3	5.7	11.9	21.5	12 395	252	884	31 339	2.4
Westmoreland	5 673	0.1	29.5	21.2	7.1	10.8	4.2	11.5	13.1	83 860	228	8 010	164 177	1.9
Wyoming	467	1.7	47.9	38.7	2.6	5.8	1.9	7.6	10.3	5 585	198	531	13 061	2.7
York	7 481	0.1	37.7	29.5	5.8	8.0	4.4	10.6	11.4	69 645	176	6 037	163 981	4.6
RHODE ISLAND	23 024	0.1	D	13.8	10.3	6.9	9.2	13.1	17.9	192 662	179	29 143	445 783	1.4
Bristol	598	0.0	D	17.9	D	7.4	4.1	10.6	17.1	10 170	199	428	20 082	1.0
Kent	3 521	0.0	D	16.9	10.1	10.2	9.6	11.2	13.3	33 515	196	3 052	71 580	1.7
Newport	2 274	0.2	D	9.9	11.7	6.4	3.4	6.9	38.5	15 740	183	1 328	40 263	1.8
Providence	14 466	0.0	18.6	12.9	10.8	5.7	10.9	14.9	15.2	111 920	175	23 089	254 931	0.7
Washington	2 164	0.3	24.0	17.5	D	10.4	4.9	10.9	22.3	21 315	166	1 214	58 927	3.7
SOUTH CAROLINA	75 968	0.3	25.9	18.7	7.7	8.2	7.2	7.8	20.5	735 084	177	105 693	1 854 624	5.8
Abbeville	325	1.1	52.7	47.3	2.3	4.2	2.0	D	16.6	5 350	203	582	11 804	1.3
Aiken	2 966	0.2	26.0	14.1	4.9	6.7	5.6	5.6	12.2	27 120	185	3 618	64 639	4.3
Allendale	150	1.9	34.2	31.5	D	3.7	D	D	33.1	1 955	179	752	4 640	1.6
Anderson	2 564	0.5	D	31.6	3.6	10.1	3.8	7.1	17.9	35 690	208	3 428	77 081	5.3
Bamberg	169	1.6	27.0	22.9	2.2	9.2	4.4	7.0	28.7	3 155	197	738	7 225	1.3
Barnwell	378	0.4	31.1	28.5	34.9	5.0	2.0	D	15.3	4 065	174	1 110	10 310	1.2
Beaufort	2 927	0.1	D	2.1	8.7	8.4	10.9	5.5	32.2	27 345	206	1 845	67 981	12.3
Berkeley	1 610	0.9	D	28.0	3.6	6.6	4.4	3.7	20.4	20 185	138	2 421	58 070	6.1
Calhoun	187	-0.3	52.9	41.9	2.6	5.1	2.0	D	16.4	2 815	183	464	7 156	4.3
Charleston	8 952	0.1	12.4	5.5	10.7	8.4	8.7	9.6	28.5	49 690	155	8 138	151 113	7.1
Cherokee	747	0.3	D	40.4	2.4	6.3	2.7	D	12.2	10 575	197	1 179	22 977	2.6
Chester	450	0.8	49.1	42.4	2.7	5.0	2.0	D	20.0	6 905	204	948	14 685	2.2
Chesterfield	582	2.3	D	43.4	1.8	5.7	3.6	7.6	13.5	8 370	194	1 633	19 431	3.3
Clarendon	273	1.3	22.7	17.4	3.4	10.1	3.4	5.9	30.4	6 825	208	1 689	15 716	2.7
Colleton	385	0.6	D	15.4	4.1	9.9	5.4	9.7	20.7	8 065	206	1 922	18 629	2.8
Darlington	963	-0.1	46.3	39.0	2.8	6.7	2.6	D	12.8	12 800	188	2 640	29 646	2.4
Dillon	305	-0.9	33.8	29.9	D	13.3	3.2	D	19.7	5 770	186	1 843	12 889	1.7
Dorchester	1 023	0.1	34.0	26.3	6.3	9.6	2.6	7.4	18.0	15 140	145	1 979	40 105	7.7
Edgefield	240	4.7	24.3	20.6	1.3	4.9	2.0	D	32.1	3 980	161	684	9 499	3.0
Fairfield	319	0.6	D	30.2	D	8.6	1.8	D	18.6	4 505	189	842	10 605	2.1
Florence	2 728	-0.1	D	20.6	6.4	8.7	10.3	11.9	19.0	22 405	175	5 753	53 259	2.7
Georgetown	873	0.7	23.5	15.1	D	8.9	9.0	10.3	20.1	13 705	233	1 665	30 181	6.7
Greenville	10 465	0.1	26.9	20.1	12.1	8.6	7.9	6.9	10.9	66 030	167	7 520	172 427	5.9
Greenwood	1 270	0.7	D	34.0	4.1	7.9	4.2	7.8	21.3	13 360	198	1 610	29 108	3.1
Hampton	245	1.1	22.8	18.9	10.3	6.5	2.1	5.3	28.9	4 125	193	1 066	8 710	1.5
Horry	3 553	-0.7	15.7	5.4	8.2	13.0	12.5	8.1	13.9	45 520	216	4 399	134 761	10.4
Jasper	188	0.8	D	7.8	D	10.1	2.5	D	26.3	1 605	76	592	8 220	3.7
Kershaw	751	0.4	D	35.6	D	6.9	6.0	4.9	16.0	10 455	192	1 404	23 818	5.0
Lancaster	774	0.2	41.6	35.5	D	8.0	7.7	8.8	16.7	11 875	190	1 314	26 108	4.6
Laurens	726	1.4	D	30.2	D	5.8	2.0	D	21.5	14 060	200	1 937	31 105	2.9
Lee	143	1.0	19.1	15.9	1.7	7.4	3.5	D	34.7	3 680	181	997	7 817	1.9
Lexington	3 512	0.3	D	16.3	D	10.5	6.8	6.5	16.5	33 700	149	3 011	96 119	5.7
McCormick	76	6.1	18.9	16.3	1.2	3.8	D	D	44.6	2 475	242	326	4 678	4.9
Marion	363	0.3	D	31.2	D	9.0	3.9	D	24.9	6 720	191	1 837	15 417	1.8
Marlboro	294	0.5	D	43.2	2.0	5.6	1.9	D	21.9	5 880	207	1 718	12 001	0.9
Newberry	458	2.0	39.8	33.0	3.6	6.8	2.1	6.6	18.8	7 485	203	1 000	17 139	2.0
Oconee	1 086	1.0	42.6	33.7	D	6.3	2.8	D	15.1	16 255	237	1 150	33 996	5.0
Orangeburg	1 252	1.0	D	25.7	2.9	10.0	3.4	6.7	24.6	17 840	196	4 353	40 565	3.2
Pickens	1 374	0.5	D	23.4	D	8.1	4.5	8.0	29.9	19 665	174	1 496	48 350	5.1
Richland	9 694	0.0	10.9	6.1	11.5	6.7	11.9	10.2	30.0	45 125	136	7 388	138 373	6.6
Saluda	153	7.3	36.3	31.5	D	6.1	4.7	D	22.3	3 565	187	522	8 696	1.8
Spartanburg	5 389	0.2	39.2	32.9	4.9	7.7	4.3	7.2	13.9	49 690	190	6 129	112 636	5.3

1. Covers mining, construction, and manufacturing.   2. Per 1,000 resident population estimated as of July 1 of the year shown.

Table B. States and Counties — Housing, Labor Force, and Employment

STATE County	Housing units, 2000 — Occupied units — Total	Owner-occupied Percent	Median value[1]	Median owner cost as a percent of income — With a mortgage	Without a mortgage[2]	Median rent[3]	Median rent as a percent of income	Substandard units[4] (percent)	Civilian labor force, 2003 Total	Percent change, 2002–2003	Unemployment Total	Rate[5]	Civilian employment,[6] 2000 Total	Percent — Management, professional and related occupations	Production, transportation, and material moving occupations
	89	90	91	92	93	94	95	96	97	98	99	100	101	102	103
PENNSYLVANIA—Cont'd															
Potter	7 005	77.4	68 700	20.4	11.9	432	23.1	3.0	9 833	-7.9	691	7.0	7 800	26.3	25.6
Schuylkill	60 530	77.9	63 300	20.4	12.5	379	22.6	1.4	65 997	-2.1	4 902	7.4	63 902	23.7	26.9
Snyder	13 654	76.5	87 900	21.5	10.7	439	22.6	3.4	18 567	-2.8	867	4.7	17 809	22.8	27.5
Somerset	31 222	78.0	70 200	21.6	10.8	366	23.3	1.7	37 564	-1.5	2 700	7.2	34 541	24.7	22.2
Sullivan	2 660	80.4	74 900	20.9	12.1	346	21.9	2.7	2 458	-2.8	165	6.7	2 732	23.2	23.0
Susquehanna	16 529	79.5	81 800	22.5	12.5	427	24.7	2.0	19 344	-4.2	1 324	6.8	19 072	26.3	23.2
Tioga	15 925	76.1	72 000	21.4	11.2	421	24.7	1.8	20 675	-1.1	1 268	6.1	18 324	25.9	25.2
Union	13 178	73.4	97 800	20.7	9.9	473	24.5	1.7	19 020	-3.1	807	4.2	16 266	31.0	22.5
Venango	22 747	76.4	55 900	19.0	11.0	382	23.9	1.3	25 655	-1.2	1 553	6.1	24 487	25.5	23.7
Warren	17 696	78.2	64 300	18.8	11.0	401	21.5	1.6	19 452	-3.9	1 373	7.1	20 408	26.0	25.4
Washington	81 130	77.1	87 500	20.2	11.0	423	24.9	1.6	97 518	-2.5	5 874	6.0	90 861	29.3	15.9
Wayne	18 350	80.5	102 100	24.1	12.1	481	26.3	1.5	21 083	1.0	1 117	5.3	20 222	26.8	16.8
Westmoreland	149 813	78.0	90 600	20.9	11.7	432	23.5	1.1	183 644	-2.4	10 459	5.7	167 853	30.8	17.1
Wyoming	10 762	79.0	93 900	22.6	12.5	470	23.9	1.6	14 285	-1.3	805	5.6	12 788	25.9	20.9
York	148 219	76.1	110 500	22.0	10.5	531	23.0	1.6	197 758	-2.3	9 841	5.0	195 962	28.4	22.7
RHODE ISLAND	408 424	60.0	133 000	22.7	13.4	553	25.7	3.3	572 956	3.6	30 158	5.3	500 731	33.9	15.2
Bristol	19 033	71.2	164 600	22.9	14.7	578	24.2	1.5	27 722	3.4	1 172	4.2	24 894	41.6	10.9
Kent	67 320	71.6	118 100	22.9	14.1	613	24.9	1.9	95 355	3.5	4 778	5.0	85 788	33.4	14.0
Newport	35 228	61.6	164 100	23.2	13.0	689	24.5	1.9	46 869	3.8	2 024	4.3	41 644	41.2	8.1
Providence	239 936	53.2	123 900	22.7	13.5	527	26.0	4.4	331 721	3.6	19 359	5.8	284 618	31.2	18.1
Washington	46 907	72.9	158 600	22.5	12.2	645	25.5	1.6	71 288	3.7	2 824	4.0	63 787	39.4	10.4
SOUTH CAROLINA	1 533 854	72.2	94 900	20.5	9.9	510	24.4	3.8	2 002 520	3.0	136 297	6.8	1 824 700	29.1	19.0
Abbeville	10 131	80.4	70 600	19.4	11.0	367	25.2	3.8	11 976	2.9	1 182	9.9	11 567	21.8	35.3
Aiken	55 587	75.7	87 600	19.5	9.9	475	23.9	3.2	65 540	4.3	3 888	5.9	63 756	30.8	18.7
Allendale	3 915	72.5	46 900	24.6	14.5	305	24.2	8.2	4 097	-2.9	253	6.2	3 425	22.2	29.3
Anderson	65 649	76.3	88 200	19.8	9.9	454	24.2	2.3	85 620	3.1	5 911	6.9	77 732	26.2	24.2
Bamberg	6 123	74.8	61 800	20.0	10.9	299	25.9	7.4	8 325	10.9	473	5.7	5 913	28.0	23.0
Barnwell	9 021	75.5	66 600	18.4	10.5	384	24.1	5.9	10 030	-1.1	1 083	10.8	9 410	22.2	29.0
Beaufort	45 532	73.3	213 900	23.4	9.9	690	24.9	4.6	58 122	6.7	1 747	3.0	47 862	32.3	8.1
Berkeley	49 922	74.2	91 300	20.4	9.9	562	23.1	4.3	69 979	4.0	3 262	4.7	61 248	25.2	18.0
Calhoun	5 917	84.3	72 500	18.9	10.9	370	21.3	4.7	7 012	1.8	490	7.0	6 544	24.2	26.1
Charleston	123 326	61.1	130 200	22.1	11.0	605	27.7	3.7	168 790	3.5	7 804	4.6	142 550	35.9	9.9
Cherokee	20 495	73.9	74 100	19.5	9.9	401	22.2	3.6	26 980	3.4	2 475	9.2	23 559	18.3	32.3
Chester	12 880	78.3	62 800	18.6	9.9	409	23.1	5.1	14 667	0.1	2 213	15.1	14 771	19.8	31.3
Chesterfield	16 557	76.2	65 900	19.8	9.9	391	25.1	4.9	19 638	4.1	2 239	11.4	17 691	20.3	31.9
Clarendon	11 812	79.1	77 700	19.3	10.8	320	24.7	5.8	12 982	0.1	1 171	9.0	11 963	22.5	25.7
Colleton	14 470	80.2	73 200	22.3	10.9	405	24.9	6.1	15 045	0.6	1 193	7.9	14 874	22.1	19.9
Darlington	25 793	77.0	74 100	19.2	9.9	374	24.0	4.1	29 189	0.1	2 739	9.4	28 779	24.6	24.6
Dillon	11 199	72.0	60 700	19.7	10.9	335	24.9	6.5	12 573	0.6	1 535	12.2	12 427	18.8	29.2
Dorchester	34 709	75.0	104 600	20.9	9.9	568	22.8	3.7	52 041	3.8	2 296	4.4	44 081	31.5	16.4
Edgefield	8 270	80.4	83 400	20.9	9.9	361	23.0	4.5	10 943	3.9	468	4.3	9 596	24.3	25.4
Fairfield	8 774	77.5	69 900	21.9	9.9	395	22.4	6.1	9 179	-5.0	1 516	16.5	10 074	19.8	29.8
Florence	47 147	73.0	85 200	19.6	9.9	452	23.9	4.2	64 329	2.7	5 401	8.4	55 619	30.2	18.4
Georgetown	21 659	81.3	114 700	21.4	10.4	489	24.6	4.0	26 778	4.6	3 335	12.5	23 630	25.4	18.0
Greenville	149 556	68.2	111 800	20.3	9.9	544	23.5	3.0	200 329	2.8	9 459	4.7	188 489	33.2	17.1
Greenwood	25 729	69.3	81 200	19.5	9.9	440	22.5	4.2	32 053	2.4	3 391	10.6	30 201	27.5	25.8
Hampton	7 444	78.1	62 300	20.1	11.8	370	23.4	5.6	7 859	-2.8	853	10.9	7 787	21.3	25.1
Horry	81 800	73.0	119 700	21.9	9.9	594	25.0	3.3	110 408	6.3	5 671	5.1	97 577	26.2	10.1
Jasper	7 042	77.8	77 600	23.0	10.5	493	24.9	7.7	9 901	7.2	514	5.2	8 628	17.1	14.4
Kershaw	20 188	82.0	88 000	19.3	9.9	455	22.5	3.5	24 122	4.5	1 867	7.7	25 005	26.8	21.3
Lancaster	23 178	75.2	77 100	19.8	9.9	427	22.0	3.5	27 776	-1.5	3 103	11.2	28 110	19.6	28.9
Laurens	26 290	77.4	74 800	19.8	9.9	448	25.3	3.4	26 483	-2.7	2 748	10.4	31 278	21.1	31.3
Lee	6 886	79.3	56 400	20.6	11.6	330	25.3	5.5	8 766	4.9	794	9.1	7 480	19.3	32.0
Lexington	83 240	77.2	106 300	19.6	9.9	548	23.6	2.6	122 988	1.7	4 109	3.3	110 330	35.1	12.0
McCormick	3 558	81.1	70 700	22.6	10.2	304	22.1	4.8	3 962	4.8	569	14.4	3 392	22.6	28.3
Marion	13 301	73.4	63 500	19.4	11.4	386	24.9	5.1	14 029	3.9	2 415	17.2	14 100	21.8	29.8
Marlboro	10 478	70.8	54 900	20.7	10.1	342	25.3	5.8	12 233	9.4	2 189	17.9	11 042	17.7	38.0
Newberry	14 026	76.7	78 000	20.8	9.9	385	22.1	4.9	18 826	7.3	1 392	7.4	15 857	23.7	24.6
Oconee	27 283	78.4	97 500	19.3	9.9	424	21.8	2.7	27 496	-1.5	2 434	8.9	30 147	25.1	26.9
Orangeburg	34 118	75.6	72 600	20.3	9.9	389	23.8	5.6	41 497	2.8	4 827	11.6	36 785	25.3	22.7
Pickens	41 306	73.4	96 100	19.6	9.9	479	27.4	2.8	56 568	3.1	3 611	6.4	53 229	28.2	20.8
Richland	120 101	61.4	98 700	20.9	9.9	570	25.4	3.8	164 911	2.1	7 605	4.6	150 195	38.9	10.5
Saluda	7 127	80.6	74 000	19.4	9.9	394	22.4	5.4	9 457	0.0	536	5.7	8 699	21.0	29.6
Spartanburg	97 735	72.0	91 100	20.5	9.9	485	23.8	3.6	132 272	2.9	9 548	7.2	119 910	26.6	24.5

1. Specified owner-occupied units. 2. Median monthly owner costs is often in the minimum category—9.9 percent or less, which is indicated as 9.9 percent. 3. Specified renter-occupied units. 4. Overcrowded or lacking complete plumbing facilities. 5. Percent of civilian labor force. 6. Persons 16 years old and over.

Table B. States and Counties — **Nonfarm Employment and Agriculture**

| | Private nonfarm establishments, employment and payroll, 2001 | | | | | | | | Agriculture, 2002 | | | |
STATE County	Number of establishments	Total	Health care and social assistance	Manufacturing	Retail trade	Finance and insurance	Professional, scientific, and technical services	Total (mil dol)	Average per employee (dollars)	Number	Less than 50 acres	500 acres and over	Farm operators whose principal occupation is farming (percent)
	104	105	106	107	108	109	110	111	112	113	114	115	116
PENNSYLVANIA—Cont'd													
Potter........................	438	5 438	1 046	1 210	600	99	108	133	24 404	343	16.3	10.5	53.4
Schuylkill	3 086	43 440	7 215	13 146	7 765	1 332	839	1 108	25 496	838	43.2	5.4	49.2
Snyder.......................	840	13 871	826	4 885	2 681	348	244	310	22 328	784	35.6	3.8	61.4
Somerset..................	1 935	21 503	2 997	5 305	3 389	758	561	497	23 097	1 194	22.0	7.3	59.2
Sullivan.....................	170	1 191	373	D	160	D	D	26	21 565	170	18.8	7.1	64.7
Susquehanna	817	6 554	1 193	1 015	1 243	234	189	130	19 809	1 116	28.9	5.6	48.3
Tioga........................	859	10 832	1 635	3 117	2 120	364	216	229	21 098	973	13.9	7.9	55.6
Union	853	16 910	3 503	3 811	1 582	336	217	403	23 829	521	27.4	4.0	67.2
Venango....................	1 291	17 217	3 101	4 411	3 183	595	222	434	25 197	473	30.9	4.0	47.6
Warren	982	15 557	2 476	4 248	2 877	464	282	429	27 605	499	27.5	4.2	55.5
Washington	4 912	75 433	9 060	11 561	9 672	1 827	2 874	2 300	30 486	2 506	41.1	2.0	43.4
Wayne	1 428	13 470	2 279	986	2 686	548	445	294	21 843	661	20.3	5.0	64.3
Westmoreland...........	8 921	127 438	17 725	23 249	19 884	3 320	4 264	3 596	28 220	1 353	36.7	2.4	48.0
Wyoming	635	9 400	883	D	1 210	215	156	300	31 905	358	21.5	5.3	62.8
York	8 234	156 588	18 502	42 979	22 368	4 129	4 454	4 761	30 407	2 546	61.5	3.9	48.5
RHODE ISLAND	28 539	414 638	69 900	66 630	54 355	24 332	19 490	13 158	31 734	858	59.8	1.3	51.5
Bristol........................	1 162	D	1 638	2 835	1 428	296	277	D	D	37	73.0	0.0	62.2
Kent...........................	4 941	70 417	9 540	10 913	12 298	5 935	2 552	2 143	30 429	100	63.0	1.0	50.0
Newport.....................	2 705	28 727	5 039	2 863	4 001	1 009	2 351	839	29 210	166	63.3	1.2	48.8
Providence	16 213	263 206	47 619	43 223	30 150	16 117	11 357	8 636	32 811	290	59.3	0.7	53.1
Washington	3 517	36 302	6 064	6 796	6 478	975	2 953	1 113	30 663	265	55.1	2.3	50.6
SOUTH CAROLINA	97 030	1 596 385	185 465	325 619	218 946	62 996	65 784	43 840	27 462	24 541	41.7	8.3	46.4
Abbeville....................	335	6 647	665	4 132	505	128	95	168	25 219	538	35.1	8.7	46.7
Aiken.........................	2 620	52 432	4 390	21 367	6 628	987	3 781	1 906	36 357	929	43.5	4.6	50.3
Allendale...................	146	2 146	242	1 205	292	D	30	49	23 013	156	20.5	24.4	46.2
Anderson...................	3 674	58 439	7 785	18 853	8 588	1 368	1 161	1 537	26 295	1 644	49.9	3.5	45.9
Bamberg....................	305	3 818	735	1 278	506	125	63	81	21 299	340	17.9	16.8	47.4
Barnwell....................	395	6 159	479	3 216	969	127	223	150	24 357	370	33.2	10.8	44.3
Beaufort....................	4 397	48 382	5 146	1 026	9 081	1 411	2 279	1 254	25 925	116	61.2	12.1	44.0
Berkeley....................	1 858	26 704	1 639	6 124	4 161	508	1 130	721	26 987	398	56.3	5.3	46.7
Calhoun.....................	198	2 218	402	790	187	D	D	45	20 410	281	27.0	19.9	49.5
Charleston.................	10 520	175 646	32 380	10 533	24 674	5 681	10 443	4 800	27 326	417	64.5	5.3	42.0
Cherokee...................	1 012	19 817	1 159	8 155	2 556	317	169	491	24 779	430	39.3	4.2	44.7
Chester.....................	570	9 794	927	4 869	1 077	158	101	259	26 446	430	30.2	8.4	50.5
Chesterfield...............	731	13 257	1 126	6 612	1 571	225	71	320	24 164	595	27.6	10.3	42.9
Clarendon..................	509	6 341	1 330	1 404	1 235	192	99	129	20 368	390	31.5	20.3	46.7
Colleton	806	8 516	928	1 592	1 750	323	265	191	22 454	495	36.8	10.3	47.5
Darlington.................	1 266	21 286	2 007	6 089	2 892	464	297	645	30 324	361	33.0	18.8	52.9
Dillon	529	8 209	1 390	2 769	1 559	148	84	163	19 903	197	15.7	27.9	70.1
Dorchester................	1 820	23 045	2 086	4 011	3 879	642	731	568	24 666	365	51.0	5.8	46.6
Edgefield	333	4 940	451	2 068	473	61	69	142	28 766	325	35.1	11.4	44.9
Fairfield	309	5 934	580	2 220	605	109	67	194	32 723	237	33.3	13.5	37.6
Florence	3 256	56 726	10 143	11 532	9 125	4 672	1 610	1 474	25 983	612	37.3	13.7	56.9
Georgetown...............	1 836	23 227	3 038	4 015	3 279	521	539	543	23 361	226	44.7	13.3	45.6
Greenville..................	11 468	241 202	19 347	41 388	24 848	9 074	11 499	7 739	32 087	909	56.9	3.2	42.7
Greenwood................	1 528	29 518	4 537	9 846	4 179	820	805	750	25 411	501	43.3	5.2	46.3
Hampton....................	446	4 591	333	1 243	926	129	82	115	24 950	248	19.4	23.0	39.9
Horry	7 211	86 594	7 425	6 233	16 570	3 292	2 927	1 902	21 970	988	40.9	8.9	54.0
Jasper.......................	419	3 498	239	D	980	66	63	73	20 843	163	37.4	12.9	41.7
Kershaw....................	1 185	15 306	1 535	4 747	2 275	623	386	361	23 573	479	47.0	5.6	46.3
Lancaster..................	1 151	16 063	1 893	4 862	2 416	865	255	432	26 902	637	43.5	4.6	48.2
Laurens....................	889	17 104	1 809	6 196	1 825	488	377	390	22 818	931	38.8	6.6	46.9
Lee	240	2 558	258	455	517	66	59	50	19 663	324	25.3	18.2	42.0
Lexington	4 952	67 560	6 970	9 240	11 107	2 362	2 279	1 771	26 220	1 086	56.4	2.8	43.9
McCormick.................	125	1 100	81	D	152	57	D	20	17 887	97	34.0	14.4	38.1
Marion	647	9 077	1 098	3 683	1 416	280	79	207	22 772	213	38.0	16.9	59.6
Marlboro	416	6 292	903	3 385	681	137	D	160	25 371	222	23.4	26.1	50.5
Newberry...................	725	11 785	1 154	4 822	1 401	209	343	270	22 887	633	34.0	6.6	45.3
Oconee.....................	1 526	21 909	2 357	7 287	2 921	411	430	587	26 807	878	54.0	2.5	40.4
Orangeburg...............	1 929	28 090	3 640	8 342	4 615	863	633	653	23 257	968	28.2	13.4	44.8
Pickens.....................	2 168	30 922	3 067	8 962	4 627	667	621	694	22 438	622	61.3	1.3	36.8
Richland....................	9 265	183 420	24 807	14 192	22 920	18 573	15 171	5 225	28 484	429	48.3	5.4	42.9
Saluda......................	248	3 972	502	2 253	343	51	D	86	21 646	574	28.2	8.7	53.7
Spartanburg	6 266	119 590	13 745	32 668	14 083	2 657	3 349	3 525	29 475	1 412	55.7	2.3	45.5

STATE County	Acreage (1,000)	Percent change, 1997–2002	Average size of farm	Total irrigated (1,000)	Total cropland (1,000)	Value of land and buildings (dollars) Average per farm	Average per acre	Value of machinery and equipment average per farm (dollars)	Total (mil dol)	Average per farm (dollars)	Percent from — Crops	Livestock and poultry products	Percent of farms with sales of — $10,000 or more	$100,000 or more	Government payments Total ($1,000)	Percent of farms
	117	118	119	120	121	122	123	124	125	126	127	128	129	130	131	132
PENNSYLVANIA—Cont'd																
Potter	94	13.3	275	D	44	427 674	1 678	64 651	26	77 090	35.4	64.6	34.4	15.5	807	21.6
Schuylkill	111	23.3	132	2	78	398 309	3 383	63 602	70	83 879	45.0	55.0	34.8	14.4	1 356	32.1
Snyder	100	7.5	128	1	72	426 932	3 558	118 461	81	102 807	9.6	90.4	55.0	24.9	1 101	20.7
Somerset	223	8.3	187	1	135	359 375	1 895	59 206	66	55 112	13.5	86.5	44.8	14.3	2 646	28.6
Sullivan	31	14.8	183	0	17	285 700	1 878	49 082	7	41 531	10.2	89.8	34.7	11.2	278	26.5
Susquehanna	189	11.8	170	0	105	355 776	2 162	55 679	43	38 658	6.5	93.5	27.3	12.8	1 514	17.7
Tioga	200	-1.0	206	0	114	454 735	2 328	52 561	49	49 958	13.1	86.9	38.6	14.9	1 570	21.4
Union	69	9.5	133	0	57	498 509	4 156	68 947	55	105 597	10.2	89.8	63.7	36.7	954	29.6
Venango	65	41.3	136	0	32	188 302	1 489	29 244	8	16 463	33.2	66.8	23.7	4.4	250	15.9
Warren	78	21.9	156	0	37	224 296	1 287	48 377	15	30 347	14.1	85.9	26.7	9.6	624	17.0
Washington	261	40.3	104	1	143	229 196	2 095	35 303	30	12 037	45.7	54.3	15.4	2.1	872	13.6
Wayne	113	2.7	171	0	57	356 704	2 111	49 847	21	32 487	14.3	85.7	33.3	13.2	913	16.3
Westmoreland	151	2.0	112	0	104	314 444	2 814	45 928	35	26 211	44.1	55.9	28.4	5.9	1 169	19.2
Wyoming	62	1.6	173	0	35	357 773	2 276	57 735	12	34 650	21.7	78.3	33.2	10.9	404	26.3
York	285	9.2	112	2	223	542 750	4 805	51 153	148	57 985	38.1	61.9	30.9	10.9	3 070	17.6
RHODE ISLAND	61	10.9	71	4	24	658 290	9 225	57 882	56	64 740	84.9	15.1	42.3	13.1	528	6.1
Bristol	1	-50.0	34	0	1	762 064	22 431	55 054	4	100 134	99.1	0.9	48.6	13.5	D	D
Kent	8	33.3	78	0	2	511 268	6 553	47 553	4	37 554	90.1	9.9	39.0	9.0	D	D
Newport	11	10.0	65	1	6	870 132	13 362	60 485	15	90 917	87.3	12.7	57.8	18.7	161	7.2
Providence	17	13.3	58	1	5	521 024	8 982	45 286	12	40 849	70.6	29.4	33.8	9.7	D	D
Washington	25	13.6	93	2	9	716 794	7 743	74 772	21	79 802	87.7	12.3	42.3	14.7	144	6.8
SOUTH CAROLINA	4 846	5.5	197	96	2 270	410 897	2 067	53 108	1 490	60 705	39.8	60.2	21.6	6.8	38 384	24.9
Abbeville	95	17.3	177	1	35	353 021	2 029	40 932	11	20 735	25.5	74.5	19.5	3.0	251	21.4
Aiken	144	7.5	155	2	57	355 660	2 219	49 446	50	54 306	15.8	84.2	21.2	8.0	640	16.7
Allendale	108	17.4	690	8	51	871 703	1 252	82 469	10	66 534	80.2	19.8	19.9	10.3	1 174	67.3
Anderson	177	6.6	108	1	87	349 436	3 314	33 010	37	22 534	40.3	59.7	17.8	2.6	789	16.2
Bamberg	105	4.0	310	5	48	438 855	1 314	49 441	15	44 297	67.8	32.2	20.9	7.9	1 281	56.8
Barnwell	85	-12.4	230	1	35	346 228	1 306	63 207	7	19 102	66.4	33.6	23.2	5.4	981	39.2
Beaufort	44	12.8	383	1	7	989 887	2 473	53 514	10	85 179	96.0	4.0	26.7	4.3	24	3.4
Berkeley	57	11.8	143	1	17	363 253	2 745	45 446	26	65 241	95.8	4.2	14.8	1.5	131	15.1
Calhoun	95	-6.9	337	5	56	433 470	1 478	96 248	12	41 212	68.8	31.2	26.7	8.5	1 643	48.4
Charleston	48	9.1	114	2	12	617 928	4 967	38 954	18	43 329	88.5	11.5	23.0	7.4	58	6.5
Cherokee	64	-1.5	149	0	25	299 445	2 030	31 167	24	55 791	7.9	92.1	16.7	2.3	126	20.2
Chester	97	19.8	226	0	32	443 089	1 997	36 809	18	40 877	8.6	91.4	18.6	3.7	250	14.9
Chesterfield	129	4.0	216	1	51	291 783	1 408	29 234	62	104 902	12.4	87.6	22.7	10.1	882	51.4
Clarendon	148	4.2	379	2	92	509 182	1 415	107 221	62	157 999	45.6	54.4	31.8	19.5	2 284	55.1
Colleton	137	-11.6	278	1	36	467 374	1 750	43 754	13	26 661	78.2	21.8	17.2	2.6	386	25.5
Darlington	161	1.9	447	1	97	472 581	996	124 187	40	109 636	47.7	52.3	39.3	16.1	1 841	39.9
Dillon	112	23.1	570	2	90	768 990	1 391	179 402	69	351 508	32.9	67.1	58.9	35.0	1 816	55.8
Dorchester	58	-10.8	158	0	31	352 639	1 985	53 131	13	34 684	20.8	79.2	17.8	6.3	533	21.6
Edgefield	74	4.2	229	5	26	491 871	2 032	76 731	49	149 396	91.8	8.2	23.1	6.8	397	30.5
Fairfield	56	19.1	238	0	17	464 227	1 493	38 120	16	68 804	4.6	95.4	19.0	5.5	74	9.7
Florence	171	1.2	280	3	104	437 720	1 570	93 787	35	57 280	84.9	15.1	34.6	13.7	1 611	33.8
Georgetown	55	3.8	242	1	15	485 959	2 122	57 955	24	105 939	91.8	8.2	23.5	8.4	211	32.3
Greenville	87	24.3	96	1	38	394 871	3 402	32 817	18	19 972	81.9	18.1	12.7	2.8	130	8.5
Greenwood	81	19.1	161	2	25	293 815	1 858	20 228	6	11 415	21.2	78.8	16.6	1.6	133	17.4
Hampton	128	9.4	516	3	44	810 055	1 498	73 127	6	24 906	89.3	10.7	24.6	7.7	937	48.4
Horry	188	2.2	191	1	101	439 723	2 171	75 665	54	55 112	70.8	29.2	31.5	11.9	1 777	27.8
Jasper	79	16.2	485	3	15	709 122	1 454	81 353	9	52 421	96.4	3.5	14.1	3.1	152	19.0
Kershaw	70	-4.1	146	1	24	319 777	2 116	43 702	84	176 356	2.5	97.5	20.9	9.8	325	17.1
Lancaster	81	8.0	128	0	31	219 240	2 204	26 090	46	71 759	3.6	96.4	16.5	5.2	220	13.7
Laurens	143	12.6	153	1	59	427 315	2 236	45 709	16	16 808	13.2	86.8	18.8	2.5	562	17.6
Lee	123	2.5	378	1	85	555 478	1 381	92 994	34	103 934	30.9	69.1	28.1	13.0	2 373	65.1
Lexington	103	10.8	95	7	49	272 996	2 780	60 134	96	88 133	36.2	63.8	20.7	8.7	273	10.8
McCormick	23	15.0	240	0	5	602 895	2 626	24 460	2	15 770	8.6	91.3	21.6	2.1	35	21.6
Marion	93	16.3	438	1	58	617 759	1 503	108 845	24	113 412	67.7	32.3	33.8	16.9	438	40.8
Marlboro	115	-1.7	518	2	74	658 729	1 204	92 125	23	101 431	48.2	51.8	34.2	14.9	2 581	59.0
Newberry	104	9.5	164	1	43	345 156	2 052	45 049	57	89 866	D	D	20.4	7.4	908	23.4
Oconee	78	18.2	89	1	32	365 293	4 792	28 820	56	64 234	D	D	18.8	5.9	288	9.3
Orangeburg	274	0.7	283	17	157	356 273	1 371	82 778	69	71 414	46.8	53.2	24.9	9.1	4 099	48.8
Pickens	47	0.0	75	1	23	395 488	4 652	25 022	7	10 731	78.2	21.8	10.5	0.6	56	7.1
Richland	63	10.5	148	1	25	510 722	3 296	37 741	7	15 631	D	D	15.6	2.6	238	11.4
Saluda	107	-3.6	186	4	45	377 660	2 016	62 705	64	111 565	8.6	91.4	30.1	11.7	528	29.3
Spartanburg	126	17.8	90	2	59	346 877	4 029	35 260	25	17 893	64.5	35.5	16.8	2.5	388	9.7

STATE County	Value of residential construction authorized by building permits, 2003		Wholesale trade, 1997				Retail trade,[1] 1997				Real estate and rental and leasing, 1997			
	New construction ($1,000)	Number of housing units	Number of establish-ments	Number of employees	Sales (mil dol)	Annual payroll (mil dol)	Number of establish-ments	Number of employees	Sales (mil dol)	Annual payroll (mil dol)	Number of establish-ments	Number of employees	Receipts (mil dol)	Annual payroll (mil dol)
	133	134	135	136	137	138	139	140	141	142	143	144	145	146
PENNSYLVANIA—Cont'd														
Potter	6 621	101	13	58	17.4	1.0	77	611	88.3	8.3	5	45	1.6	0.3
Schuylkill	47 327	498	134	1 798	632.2	42.0	659	7 129	1 062.5	106.3	76	255	21.9	5.4
Snyder	19 435	182	29	444	160.4	11.8	190	2 558	365.6	33.5	16	59	6.4	0.9
Somerset	29 791	230	87	840	274.5	21.8	367	3 361	543.1	46.2	38	136	16.0	2.3
Sullivan	5 679	59	5	D	D	D	29	186	24.7	2.3	5	15	2.9	0.1
Susquehanna	16 822	164	34	D	D	D	161	1 221	217.8	17.3	10	26	5.6	0.5
Tioga	13 436	160	28	293	93.3	6.8	170	1 924	287.9	26.3	18	43	3.2	0.5
Union	21 674	142	33	313	89.9	10.0	140	1 492	225.3	19.6	29	149	19.7	2.8
Venango	11 146	130	53	530	128.3	12.1	247	2 792	417.4	37.8	37	119	14.9	1.6
Warren	6 297	73	36	285	67.1	8.4	185	2 742	718.6	52.9	18	91	4.8	1.2
Washington	159 271	998	305	3 803	1 481.0	132.5	778	9 187	1 531.6	152.6	129	551	72.1	9.9
Wayne	48 423	468	35	262	67.5	5.9	246	2 444	397.0	38.4	37	150	10.6	1.8
Westmoreland	167 092	1 100	473	6 482	3 967.1	221.0	1 557	19 333	3 230.2	280.5	237	1 015	114.5	20.2
Wyoming	11 017	98	23	D	D	D	126	1 241	214.3	17.4	11	32	1.8	0.4
York	367 185	3 148	450	9 498	3 428.1	275.9	1 447	20 356	3 250.6	315.4	236	1 138	128.3	21.5
RHODE ISLAND	338 012	2 286	1 590	18 762	7 602.7	635.2	4 169	45 747	7 505.8	752.1	922	4 649	573.4	105.4
Bristol	17 011	120	55	324	108.4	9.4	168	1 311	211.6	20.6	43	77	13.2	1.7
Kent	47 977	325	312	3 491	1 778.6	128.9	804	11 839	1 985.9	187.9	164	1 228	179.9	31.2
Newport	55 431	271	102	561	242.3	18.6	485	3 844	626.2	66.1	97	351	47.3	9.9
Providence	112 628	906	1 003	13 417	5 094.4	450.9	2 163	22 850	3 663.7	374.6	510	2 765	291.3	57.1
Washington	104 964	664	118	969	378.9	27.2	549	5 903	1 018.3	103.0	108	228	41.7	5.6
SOUTH CAROLINA	4 616 026	38 191	5 035	58 910	34 179.8	1 866.8	18 481	209 256	33 634.3	3 107.2	3 541	18 760	2 012.6	377.1
Abbeville	5 455	56	10	36	12.1	0.9	65	469	58.6	5.2	5	16	0.6	0.2
Aiken	114 131	978	97	D	D	D	533	6 455	936.6	87.1	101	277	28.2	4.8
Allendale	352	3	11	44	17.9	0.9	46	311	53.6	3.8	7	15	0.7	0.2
Anderson	152 306	1 384	186	1 704	873.0	46.4	743	8 860	1 349.1	124.7	113	418	50.3	6.6
Bamberg	1 086	13	10	D	D	D	78	524	68.4	6.4	6	24	1.0	0.2
Barnwell	3 572	35	8	D	D	D	107	1 020	116.2	11.6	12	27	2.9	0.3
Beaufort	542 877	2 802	118	548	169.4	15.2	751	7 444	1 340.9	129.2	273	1 886	231.0	44.3
Berkeley	165 912	1 344	75	926	577.6	25.7	292	3 347	537.5	47.1	67	547	66.2	10.2
Calhoun	6 761	91	10	114	24.1	2.9	37	267	31.1	2.9	2	D	D	D
Charleston	568 236	4 635	472	5 296	3 727.1	175.5	1 850	22 298	3 483.7	347.7	466	2 618	269.0	48.9
Cherokee	17 646	172	42	D	D	D	232	2 137	366.7	30.3	35	107	12.3	1.5
Chester	10 561	80	27	905	331.5	24.2	129	1 142	186.1	14.4	12	38	5.6	0.9
Chesterfield	13 860	120	33	330	91.8	8.6	182	1 632	240.9	21.4	19	45	2.1	0.6
Clarendon	9 828	103	22	187	56.2	4.2	130	1 120	165.6	14.9	9	30	1.8	0.4
Colleton	14 110	136	44	487	212.5	11.9	188	1 890	259.4	23.5	36	152	14.3	2.7
Darlington	18 265	204	81	858	728.0	19.1	310	2 715	423.4	36.3	29	93	7.4	1.2
Dillon	5 598	52	29	292	177.3	9.4	151	1 612	196.0	19.6	22	59	5.9	0.7
Dorchester	166 209	1 415	59	422	97.3	7.9	282	3 450	516.9	46.3	57	187	31.1	3.5
Edgefield	13 959	163	10	D	D	D	79	455	78.8	6.5	11	31	1.4	0.3
Fairfield	9 600	84	8	94	29.5	2.6	70	764	82.8	7.1	7	24	1.0	0.3
Florence	6 500	47	206	2 847	1 017.6	81.6	759	8 935	1 467.3	138.4	114	387	40.7	7.3
Georgetown	111 730	727	56	363	119.6	9.6	346	3 178	481.9	47.6	55	220	16.5	5.0
Greenville	335 149	3 551	930	12 025	10 685.9	451.4	1 852	24 775	4 496.4	380.2	415	2 158	288.9	48.3
Greenwood	21 222	192	52	760	148.1	13.6	339	4 601	606.1	60.7	56	206	22.0	3.5
Hampton	3 119	31	11	D	D	D	131	952	114.1	10.8	9	22	1.7	0.4
Horry	624 543	5 130	230	1 824	481.5	49.5	1 522	14 457	2 505.2	230.7	360	3 026	259.6	59.7
Jasper	6 497	68	12	177	65.5	4.7	79	531	76.9	6.8	9	37	2.9	0.7
Kershaw	38 558	391	24	113	36.9	3.1	221	2 150	296.5	27.2	29	83	6.8	1.0
Lancaster	47 720	362	48	353	136.3	9.2	264	2 608	401.3	36.3	35	108	9.3	1.9
Laurens	21 889	166	40	351	86.5	9.5	200	1 743	296.2	24.4	33	101	6.3	1.3
Lee	1 719	17	15	124	38.5	2.7	74	576	72.4	6.6	5	D	D	D
Lexington	219 388	2 047	301	4 749	2 282.6	152.0	803	10 332	1 803.7	156.6	141	684	86.4	13.6
McCormick	9 532	53	5	D	D	D	41	204	23.5	2.0	2	D	D	D
Marion	3 000	53	31	235	91.6	5.3	178	1 609	215.7	20.9	13	39	3.5	0.8
Marlboro	1 686	19	16	133	54.3	3.8	115	796	122.3	10.6	13	37	2.6	0.5
Newberry	15 627	104	22	D	D	D	152	1 388	198.1	19.4	12	64	3.2	0.9
Oconee	121 413	905	57	D	D	D	276	2 738	403.9	35.1	41	143	12.8	3.1
Orangeburg	21 278	263	103	933	380.9	25.4	461	4 793	704.3	65.2	46	224	15.1	2.9
Pickens	110 471	752	86	D	D	D	372	4 237	655.2	58.1	53	237	22.4	3.9
Richland	397 594	3 768	540	7 346	2 989.4	251.7	1 558	22 311	3 475.6	350.7	392	2 614	310.4	61.3
Saluda	7 704	58	11	102	38.7	1.7	67	415	76.4	5.4	4	12	0.7	0.2
Spartanburg	178 007	2 081	484	6 234	3 965.3	214.8	1 117	13 785	2 311.6	213.5	198	898	90.4	17.9

1. Establishments with payroll.

STATE County	Professional, scientific, and technical services,[1] 1997				Manufacturing, 1997				Accommodation and foodservices, 1997			
	Number of establish-ments	Number of employees	Receipts (mil dol)	Annual payroll (mil dol)	Number of establish-ments	Number of employees	Receipts (mil dol)	Annual payroll (mil dol)	Number of establish-ments	Number of employees	Sales (mil dol)	Annual payroll (mil dol)
	147	148	149	150	151	152	153	154	155	156	157	158
PENNSYLVANIA—Cont'd												
Potter	23	51	4.6	1.0	29	1 166	117.6	28.8	49	270	9.1	1.8
Schuylkill	127	628	44.5	15.6	226	14 370	2 625.1	393.7	297	2 931	85.2	22.8
Snyder	31	130	8.4	3.0	65	4 413	414.2	111.3	78	1 218	36.9	10.3
Somerset	85	471	27.0	8.9	118	4 828	644.1	117.1	168	1 902	54.4	15.4
Sullivan	6	D	D	D	NA	NA	NA	NA	24	105	3.9	0.9
Susquehanna	35	167	8.1	2.6	51	1 160	132.6	22.1	79	693	22.2	5.3
Tioga	45	170	8.6	3.9	46	2 930	415.9	69.4	89	1 091	31.8	7.9
Union	40	146	10.3	4.0	36	3 394	434.5	86.0	90	1 501	46.3	12.1
Venango	45	185	9.3	2.8	89	3 950	1 084.6	137.8	99	1 143	31.5	9.2
Warren	45	162	10.3	4.0	81	4 670	1 116.3	147.8	112	984	27.9	6.7
Washington	297	1 729	197.2	68.1	278	11 725	2 788.4	402.3	351	4 812	133.0	38.8
Wayne	78	329	21.7	8.5	68	1 039	182.3	24.5	172	2 459	106.7	32.2
Westmoreland	611	3 878	398.3	129.6	597	24 404	4 000.2	800.2	710	12 235	320.9	93.5
Wyoming	32	105	8.0	3.3	35	D	D	D	56	722	19.0	4.9
York	502	3 457	268.4	105.2	661	45 754	8 156.9	1 557.5	635	10 721	318.7	91.1
RHODE ISLAND	2 349	14 866	1 418.1	541.5	2 535	75 599	10 482.0	2 288.6	2 617	34 162	1 220.9	340.6
Bristol	59	141	13.5	3.5	100	2 634	267.0	73.0	104	1 386	38.9	10.7
Kent	392	1 573	151.5	52.3	411	12 933	2 115.3	417.1	409	6 904	221.4	61.5
Newport	235	2 401	256.1	92.4	98	2 304	296.1	100.0	328	4 643	207.1	59.8
Providence	1 419	8 957	888.0	345.9	1 774	49 910	6 435.0	1 440.9	1 338	17 307	581.4	162.6
Washington	244	1 794	109.0	47.4	152	7 818	1 368.6	257.6	438	3 922	172.1	45.9
SOUTH CAROLINA	6 576	47 679	6 820.9	1 850.5	4 450	346 142	70 797.0	10 369.4	7 775	150 621	4 835.8	1 313.8
Abbeville	10	30	2.5	1.0	36	3 978	607.5	101.4	26	368	8.3	2.5
Aiken	176	3 782	439.6	166.2	99	19 999	4 256.3	896.7	212	3 618	99.4	26.3
Allendale	7	24	2.3	0.7	14	1 440	310.3	33.6	6	50	1.7	0.4
Anderson	199	777	55.2	16.2	240	20 589	4 180.1	611.4	283	4 919	144.6	37.1
Bamberg	10	35	2.2	0.6	24	1 175	180.4	28.5	24	310	6.5	1.7
Barnwell	19	256	30.9	15.0	22	3 376	450.3	75.9	33	327	10.6	2.6
Beaufort	367	2 006	193.0	85.2	94	1 087	137.5	28.7	353	7 838	337.6	93.2
Berkeley	79	365	24.0	10.2	75	6 396	2 811.2	210.6	135	2 304	63.8	17.4
Calhoun	16	24	2.0	0.5	18	809	97.6	22.9	7	D	D	D
Charleston	950	7 688	732.4	293.3	261	10 530	3 039.4	366.3	847	19 759	710.6	198.0
Cherokee	40	158	9.1	4.0	76	8 195	1 767.1	231.4	85	1 771	40.6	10.8
Chester	22	60	3.4	1.2	54	5 260	964.1	145.8	46	660	19.2	5.0
Chesterfield	29	78	3.6	0.8	58	7 450	1 408.2	196.4	65	882	23.3	6.4
Clarendon	20	89	5.7	3.1	24	1 396	122.4	26.1	50	617	16.2	4.3
Colleton	57	245	18.2	4.4	26	1 779	196.0	46.9	57	856	26.2	7.6
Darlington	60	300	22.1	6.2	63	6 002	2 054.6	185.9	91	964	31.4	8.3
Dillon	21	86	4.8	1.7	25	3 613	394.3	62.9	54	929	26.0	7.1
Dorchester	81	486	27.6	11.1	79	3 669	738.3	110.6	115	2 188	61.8	17.4
Edgefield	17	37	2.0	0.5	28	2 041	333.3	44.6	23	289	6.0	1.7
Fairfield	21	69	3.4	1.2	20	2 239	1 001.9	79.8	21	297	7.8	1.8
Florence	179	1 194	83.8	33.0	139	11 011	2 114.2	328.2	245	4 857	147.1	40.5
Georgetown	103	362	40.3	14.9	78	4 974	1 057.6	141.6	151	2 804	86.9	25.8
Greenville	1 040	11 157	3 374.0	547.5	672	45 372	9 507.5	1 431.8	818	17 006	506.6	141.8
Greenwood	87	467	34.0	12.2	93	11 612	1 875.1	339.6	122	2 320	64.5	17.5
Hampton	18	88	15.5	1.9	20	1 307	196.7	44.2	30	393	10.4	2.9
Horry	400	1 766	135.5	53.8	160	6 687	927.8	173.4	1 044	20 246	881.7	228.5
Jasper	20	55	3.5	0.9	NA	NA	NA	NA	35	769	21.7	5.8
Kershaw	69	266	17.2	5.2	62	4 916	1 637.9	151.8	80	1 197	31.0	8.0
Lancaster	42	128	7.2	2.6	54	5 341	1 561.6	145.5	76	1 112	33.2	8.2
Laurens	33	128	7.8	2.0	72	6 447	834.1	171.7	68	1 218	31.3	8.6
Lee	10	42	2.0	0.9	9	641	172.4	18.3	14	D	D	D
Lexington	330	1 535	115.6	47.2	225	9 964	2 080.7	324.2	338	7 502	203.3	55.4
McCormick	5	12	0.3	0.2	NA	NA	NA	NA	8	127	2.2	0.6
Marion	25	64	4.1	1.5	32	5 007	727.0	112.5	45	610	14.2	3.6
Marlboro	21	58	3.2	0.9	22	2 935	755.2	82.1	36	403	10.5	2.6
Newberry	36	132	8.5	2.0	49	5 553	735.4	130.5	43	697	16.7	4.2
Oconee	77	299	29.0	7.7	80	7 487	1 136.0	202.8	101	1 845	42.2	11.0
Orangeburg	84	459	29.9	12.2	90	9 370	1 700.3	222.9	149	2 583	72.1	18.6
Pickens	110	466	24.5	9.1	134	11 790	1 916.3	305.7	193	3 985	97.9	27.3
Richland	913	7 920	944.2	323.7	235	13 558	3 220.7	460.8	695	13 674	418.6	117.0
Saluda	11	27	0.8	0.3	14	2 565	375.2	46.9	18	D	D	D
Spartanburg	330	2 445	215.8	95.7	481	35 102	7 534.6	1 108.6	465	9 520	244.2	68.7

1. Firms subject to federal tax.

Table B. States and Counties — Health Care and Social Assistance, Other Services, and Federal Funds

STATE County	Health care and social assistance,[1] 1997				Other services,[1] 1997				Federal funds and grants, 2002–2003 Expenditures (mil dol)			
										Direct payments for individuals[2]		
	Number of establishments	Number of employees	Receipts (mil dol)	Annual payroll (mil dol)	Number of establishments	Number of employees	Receipts (mil dol)	Annual payroll (mil dol)	Total	Social Security and government retirement	Medicare	Food stamps and Supplemental Security Income
	159	160	161	162	163	164	165	166	167	168	169	170
PENNSYLVANIA—Cont'd												
Potter....	27	242	13.3	4.8	18	74	5.1	1.0	94.5	45.5	18.1	3.6
Schuylkill	234	3 154	170.2	76.2	203	797	47.0	11.4	905.5	441.3	242.7	20.9
Snyder................	51	308	18.2	7.5	50	200	14.2	3.2	151.1	79.0	33.8	3.1
Somerset............	133	983	52.9	22.2	125	395	26.3	5.7	493.6	210.2	115.1	13.6
Sullivan..............	6	116	7.4	3.1	5	8	0.5	0.1	40.7	20.3	8.0	0.7
Susquehanna	47	564	25.1	9.7	53	109	10.7	2.1	215.0	103.4	42.5	6.5
Tioga.................	70	408	21.2	9.3	48	142	12.8	3.0	240.7	104.4	43.2	7.6
Union.................	84	704	47.1	20.2	38	105	6.4	1.5	269.0	85.9	31.2	2.9
Venango.............	112	730	49.0	23.7	94	442	41.1	12.1	335.4	153.9	78.9	14.8
Warren...............	61	641	37.9	18.5	69	207	12.5	2.6	233.4	111.5	53.4	6.0
Washington	462	4 547	285.1	130.5	331	2 213	167.2	44.3	1 275.7	581.5	360.5	39.6
Wayne................	74	710	39.0	17.3	85	260	16.7	4.4	287.2	164.0	59.7	5.9
Westmoreland	851	6 910	432.2	183.6	642	3 158	191.3	52.4	2 210.1	1 000.1	624.3	59.1
Wyoming............	46	340	15.9	7.1	43	124	9.6	2.3	130.1	66.6	29.6	3.3
York..................	586	6 842	469.4	214.2	585	3 058	202.4	58.0	2 074.9	852.0	296.5	38.9
RHODE ISLAND	2 074	25 368	1 459.3	647.4	1 949	8 602	546.2	167.8	8 035.8	2 402.7	1 183.2	200.7
Bristol................	76	977	49.7	26.1	72	257	15.2	4.0	254.7	124.9	55.1	4.5
Kent..................	375	4 650	285.3	112.5	341	1 447	87.5	25.8	933.0	428.2	199.9	24.0
Newport.............	151	1 726	79.3	33.8	156	782	46.1	17.5	1 303.5	252.0	82.7	11.2
Providence	1 223	15 312	909.9	414.2	1 157	5 106	345.3	103.1	4 377.1	1 312.4	737.7	148.4
Washington	249	2 703	135.1	60.8	223	1 010	52.2	17.3	673.2	285.0	107.7	12.6
SOUTH CAROLINA	6 261	78 888	5 318.5	2 361.3	5 672	32 166	1 901.0	563.8	28 038.2	9 626.6	3 124.6	922.5
Abbeville............	29	223	8.8	4.3	19	64	3.7	0.9	129.4	56.3	16.4	5.2
Aiken.................	201	3 163	222.5	87.8	160	937	45.7	12.3	2 335.9	350.8	119.7	30.8
Allendale............	5	44	3.6	1.0	10	25	1.2	0.3	80.9	20.3	11.3	7.5
Anderson............	244	2 970	183.4	95.2	220	1 123	65.4	22.4	770.0	401.9	137.2	24.4
Bamberg............	28	268	13.6	6.0	17	51	3.1	0.9	115.5	33.3	17.7	7.4
Barnwell.............	36	285	13.1	5.4	28	60	4.8	1.0	144.2	47.0	24.6	10.5
Beaufort.............	206	1 814	134.8	50.4	181	1 060	58.9	18.3	1 094.0	386.7	88.4	20.6
Berkeley	87	986	39.6	16.3	111	473	23.6	5.8	562.8	298.2	58.1	24.1
Calhoun..............	10	138	4.6	2.2	13	56	2.4	0.8	71.2	25.6	8.4	4.8
Charleston..........	841	9 962	678.6	280.8	628	4 622	268.8	88.5	3 328.4	877.1	282.8	81.4
Cherokee............	59	688	50.2	19.6	64	325	18.8	6.3	224.5	107.5	39.6	9.2
Chester..............	34	187	12.8	6.2	36	154	8.0	1.9	167.1	77.8	34.3	10.2
Chesterfield	46	709	39.8	15.7	35	135	7.6	2.1	237.3	86.7	35.9	13.0
Clarendon...........	36	468	19.5	8.6	29	135	9.6	2.1	217.4	74.8	29.6	15.0
Colleton.............	48	829	57.2	19.8	39	201	12.5	3.2	244.2	98.2	45.1	14.0
Darlington...........	75	1 008	66.8	27.0	80	351	22.7	5.7	354.7	138.2	57.3	24.8
Dillon.................	56	784	38.4	15.9	36	158	8.2	2.1	192.6	59.6	34.3	16.4
Dorchester..........	122	1 530	93.9	32.5	124	541	28.6	8.6	476.9	261.9	56.4	18.5
Edgefield	21	206	7.7	3.2	16	46	2.4	0.6	117.5	37.1	14.2	5.4
Fairfield.............	16	292	9.9	4.5	14	50	2.9	0.8	123.3	51.5	22.0	8.3
Florence	276	5 558	399.9	193.5	191	1 268	73.1	21.7	765.4	280.2	121.6	46.3
Georgetown.........	125	991	67.4	28.4	97	386	24.0	6.6	369.7	206.7	70.4	14.3
Greenville...........	673	7 746	575.5	285.4	674	4 537	290.3	86.2	1 994.5	801.0	286.1	63.1
Greenwood..........	105	1 370	88.1	44.1	96	431	23.8	7.3	332.8	164.8	50.7	13.7
Hampton.............	22	210	14.4	3.5	25	154	7.0	2.1	156.6	51.2	21.9	7.9
Horry.................	326	4 036	295.9	117.8	336	1 477	91.5	25.5	1 023.4	525.3	147.6	38.1
Jasper................	21	123	5.8	2.5	22	130	6.0	1.3	103.7	33.7	14.3	5.1
Kershaw	55	588	40.9	18.4	87	308	16.1	4.7	258.9	134.4	43.0	8.9
Lancaster	90	1 530	109.5	40.0	87	344	23.5	4.8	272.4	129.4	52.2	12.2
Laurens	54	532	27.2	13.0	58	217	12.3	3.2	309.3	143.2	48.8	16.1
Lee....................	14	93	3.0	1.6	16	70	2.8	0.6	121.9	40.2	16.5	10.8
Lexington	281	3 405	193.8	89.3	346	2 257	145.4	41.8	947.6	468.1	122.0	22.2
McCormick	5	47	3.2	1.6	6	20	0.7	0.1	66.8	32.6	7.4	2.6
Marion...............	65	564	27.6	13.8	38	134	6.9	1.8	338.0	79.2	45.3	15.9
Marlboro.............	33	507	38.1	13.8	20	73	2.9	0.7	189.8	61.1	33.3	11.7
Newberry............	41	441	17.1	8.2	55	252	17.8	4.7	212.6	94.5	32.3	8.7
Oconee..............	99	777	48.8	24.1	84	362	18.2	5.3	323.0	190.3	58.9	8.4
Orangeburg.........	146	1 161	73.0	31.2	135	603	27.6	8.7	589.8	212.0	83.3	38.9
Pickens..............	133	2 019	117.3	61.0	114	441	26.1	7.2	487.6	244.8	72.5	11.3
Richland	686	9 381	723.4	331.4	509	3 641	199.5	62.5	3 363.8	877.7	212.9	73.1
Saluda...............	17	220	5.7	2.6	14	53	3.5	0.7	78.9	34.1	10.8	4.8
Spartanburg	377	4 899	364.5	167.8	377	2 038	153.4	41.2	1 115.6	579.9	192.6	47.1

1. Firms subject to federal tax.   2. State totals may include programs not allocated by county.

Table B. States and Counties — Federal Funds and Local Government Finances

	Federal funds and grants, 2002–2003 (cont'd)							Local government finances, 2002				
	Expenditures (mil dol) (cont'd)							General revenue				
	Procurement contract awards			Grants[1]						Taxes		
											Per capita[2] (dollars)	
STATE County	Salaries and wages	Defense	Other	Medicaid and other health-related	Nutrition and family welfare	Education	Other	Total (mil dol)	Intergovern-mental (mil dol)	Total (mil dol)	Total	Property
	171	172	173	174	175	176	177	178	179	180	181	182
PENNSYLVANIA—Cont'd												
Potter	3.4	0.4	0.9	15.6	2.4	0.8	1.7	46.3	23.8	16.8	922	757
Schuylkill	44.8	1.9	12.3	89.2	14.2	3.7	23.5	350.7	171.0	111.1	748	545
Snyder	5.7	0.1	1.7	15.0	2.1	1.0	4.3	70.8	27.6	30.9	816	537
Somerset	15.0	32.2	3.4	62.5	9.7	2.7	22.4	155.5	80.1	53.0	1 140	1 001
Sullivan	1.7	0.1	0.5	4.4	0.5	0.2	3.3	15.5	6.7	7.4	892	808
Susquehanna	9.6	1.3	2.0	21.8	4.0	1.4	17.8	98.9	53.0	37.5	892	808
Tioga	10.3	0.6	2.6	31.9	7.4	1.5	22.3	101.0	56.5	31.7	764	600
Union	94.7	2.7	15.8	13.1	7.4	0.8	9.4	72.5	25.0	28.8	686	454
Venango	9.1	0.2	2.2	45.2	8.6	2.6	17.9	164.9	85.8	45.4	799	617
Warren	12.0	10.9	3.1	21.2	5.4	1.4	5.4	86.7	38.0	38.9	899	713
Washington	38.6	9.7	11.1	142.8	27.9	7.1	43.0	526.5	238.4	190.2	932	735
Wayne	10.7	0.2	5.8	19.1	4.0	1.7	12.5	132.7	40.7	69.1	1 414	1 348
Westmoreland	72.8	44.0	29.5	208.2	48.5	10.0	91.5	916.3	399.3	358.6	973	779
Wyoming	4.7	0.0	1.4	13.3	3.3	1.1	5.1	69.0	31.2	28.7	1 031	851
York	141.7	456.3	38.1	130.3	22.9	7.7	70.2	994.2	306.8	416.4	1 070	823
RHODE ISLAND	816.8	498.8	160.3	1 119.4	249.0	147.4	718.5	X	X	X	X	X
Bristol	9.1	2.7	1.7	27.1	3.6	2.9	19.0	122.1	38.0	72.6	1 415	1 403
Kent	64.4	5.2	37.7	89.9	18.6	13.9	32.0	422.8	113.5	266.1	1 561	1 507
Newport	406.7	430.0	19.8	53.4	11.9	11.1	18.2	245.4	68.6	149.5	1 739	1 655
Providence	273.8	43.6	82.1	894.0	183.7	111.9	518.7	1 582.1	650.1	789.5	1 244	1 224
Washington	62.8	17.2	19.0	54.5	10.5	7.6	84.8	334.5	82.4	217.0	1 707	1 675
SOUTH CAROLINA	2 862.7	1 486.5	2 127.9	3 127.8	661.9	564.4	1 614.9	X	X	X	X	X
Abbeville	2.9	0.3	1.3	22.6	2.4	1.8	18.5	48.9	26.4	17.5	661	586
Aiken	59.6	13.6	1 598.4	95.6	11.6	8.6	34.1	280.8	137.2	92.9	639	551
Allendale	1.7	0.0	0.4	28.4	2.9	1.4	4.5	35.1	16.5	9.8	894	758
Anderson	29.6	2.8	15.4	86.4	9.4	18.0	34.7	332.3	163.7	126.0	739	636
Bamberg	2.6	0.0	1.7	27.1	4.1	6.7	4.3	33.1	21.0	9.5	585	556
Barnwell	2.9	9.2	0.6	34.2	3.5	2.4	4.2	68.3	39.1	14.3	609	498
Beaufort	404.9	99.7	5.3	45.4	11.9	7.6	18.7	419.6	87.1	175.0	1 367	1 207
Berkeley	36.3	19.4	3.3	51.6	19.8	13.3	20.3	264.1	145.3	75.7	521	418
Calhoun	1.8	0.0	0.5	15.4	1.8	1.1	5.9	25.4	12.4	10.3	672	643
Charleston	794.8	604.8	135.8	331.9	31.9	26.5	137.6	1 009.4	311.0	440.0	1 390	1 046
Cherokee	6.1	0.0	5.2	31.9	4.3	3.8	11.2	125.5	46.4	37.8	706	584
Chester	4.5	0.0	0.9	26.6	4.2	3.9	2.7	109.2	40.7	28.1	822	730
Chesterfield	5.6	0.1	1.5	64.9	7.6	3.2	14.6	82.5	49.7	24.3	562	406
Clarendon	4.1	0.0	0.8	57.1	5.7	4.9	15.2	86.8	40.3	17.4	529	436
Colleton	6.2	1.1	1.7	50.9	8.1	3.3	13.5	81.7	46.3	29.8	767	630
Darlington	7.6	0.1	1.8	83.5	10.2	6.7	10.9	130.2	67.7	47.1	693	591
Dillon	4.6	0.0	0.8	55.1	5.5	3.5	7.3	61.2	41.5	11.6	375	232
Dorchester	15.9	38.7	3.2	53.6	6.5	5.0	11.5	194.3	103.6	64.0	635	564
Edgefield	25.7	0.2	2.6	21.5	2.3	1.8	3.9	45.6	27.8	14.4	578	525
Fairfield	3.2	0.2	3.0	25.9	3.2	2.4	3.5	56.7	19.0	33.6	1 399	1 359
Florence	44.8	2.7	11.4	158.4	20.0	17.6	36.0	270.0	134.4	91.0	715	531
Georgetown	8.6	3.4	2.4	43.7	6.2	4.3	7.8	181.6	74.5	73.3	1 257	1 099
Greenville	107.2	254.1	145.6	167.8	31.4	25.4	88.1	1 573.2	341.4	379.2	969	846
Greenwood	11.1	0.2	2.2	46.1	19.1	5.3	8.0	293.6	67.9	46.6	690	627
Hampton	21.4	0.0	3.7	35.4	3.6	1.7	5.1	45.7	27.4	14.1	660	590
Horry	31.6	5.1	7.6	99.0	17.2	11.3	117.4	655.9	175.2	271.3	1 317	957
Jasper	2.3	13.9	0.7	28.3	2.7	1.6	0.4	37.8	19.0	14.4	689	540
Kershaw	7.2	0.2	1.5	39.8	4.0	3.5	15.3	143.6	54.3	35.1	654	565
Lancaster	7.3	0.1	6.0	38.7	5.7	4.9	13.7	120.0	70.8	36.1	580	512
Laurens	6.9	0.0	1.7	45.2	4.9	3.8	33.4	154.9	61.4	33.7	478	414
Lee	2.3	0.0	0.4	33.1	3.9	2.0	3.7	35.4	19.8	11.6	569	491
Lexington	41.2	35.6	8.3	61.1	9.4	13.8	161.7	760.3	279.0	220.2	988	928
McCormick	3.8	1.8	0.5	13.6	1.2	2.1	1.1	25.3	17.8	5.7	561	511
Marion	6.4	108.5	1.1	57.1	6.0	7.6	4.7	122.8	54.6	17.1	490	393
Marlboro	5.2	0.1	3.1	55.1	5.0	2.4	5.8	54.8	35.4	12.6	438	382
Newberry	8.5	0.4	1.4	32.5	3.1	2.6	25.1	79.5	38.2	27.8	753	681
Oconee	9.4	0.5	2.4	37.5	3.0	3.9	7.8	130.3	50.5	65.5	964	911
Orangeburg	13.6	0.4	2.8	134.2	19.9	18.1	35.4	289.0	109.0	81.6	895	717
Pickens	18.0	10.1	3.7	40.8	5.2	8.1	63.4	171.2	81.0	69.0	610	427
Richland	772.6	214.0	102.8	311.0	168.9	206.3	344.7	765.1	276.5	326.1	991	879
Saluda	3.3	0.0	1.0	17.6	1.4	1.4	1.2	26.6	15.4	7.7	400	367
Spartanburg	34.9	1.2	10.3	153.8	21.5	15.8	37.2	703.2	239.3	242.1	934	831

1. State totals may include programs not allocated by county. 2. Based on the resident population estimated as of July 1 of the year shown.

Table B. States and Counties — Local Government Finances, Government Employment, and Elections

STATE County	Direct general expenditure — Total (mil dol)	Per capita[1] (dollars)	Education	Health and hospitals	Police protection	Public welfare	Highways	Debt outstanding — Total (mil dol)	Per capita[1] (dollars)	Federal civilian	Federal military	State and local	Democratic	Republican	All other
	183	184	185	186	187	188	189	190	191	192	193	194	195	196	197
PENNSYLVANIA—Cont'd															
Potter	55.6	3 054	58.9	0.0	1.0	0.4	5.3	51.3	2 813	45	49	1 087	28.4	70.9	0.7
Schuylkill	340.3	2 292	43.8	5.6	2.5	7.9	4.0	332.1	2 236	649	398	7 090	44.8	54.6	0.6
Snyder	66.2	1 750	60.9	0.1	1.3	2.7	5.5	55.2	1 458	84	102	2 544	29.0	70.6	0.5
Somerset	150.7	1 897	60.4	0.2	1.8	3.3	6.8	172.4	2 169	183	213	4 438	35.0	64.7	0.4
Sullivan	15.5	2 391	56.5	0.4	0.8	3.8	11.4	4.2	654	20	17	369	37.1	62.4	0.5
Susquehanna	98.1	2 332	74.6	0.6	0.5	1.8	4.9	60.5	1 437	101	114	1 832	38.6	60.8	0.6
Tioga	110.3	2 661	54.7	4.9	1.0	8.8	5.3	112.5	2 713	144	112	3 132	30.9	68.5	0.6
Union	64.7	1 540	48.6	2.2	2.9	2.8	5.6	115.4	2 748	1 484	115	2 090	35.3	64.2	0.5
Venango	154.0	2 710	52.1	5.2	1.9	3.7	4.3	231.7	4 079	144	152	3 501	38.2	61.1	0.7
Warren	88.0	2 034	58.2	0.1	2.4	1.0	6.1	51.9	1 200	229	116	2 317	41.8	57.1	1.1
Washington	554.2	2 715	48.2	2.9	2.6	11.3	3.7	731.9	3 586	531	571	9 330	50.1	49.6	0.3
Wayne	132.6	2 712	69.0	0.9	0.9	2.7	2.9	165.8	3 391	108	131	2 387	36.7	62.4	0.9
Westmoreland	998.8	2 711	54.1	6.6	2.4	6.3	3.5	1 364.9	3 705	993	990	15 464	43.5	55.9	0.6
Wyoming	72.4	2 605	64.9	1.1	1.4	5.3	4.2	60.3	2 170	59	74	1 134	38.7	60.8	0.5
York	1 052.0	2 703	46.5	6.8	3.5	4.1	2.8	1 465.8	3 766	3 643	1 500	13 695	35.4	63.8	0.7
RHODE ISLAND	X	X	X	X	X	X	X	X	X	9 954	8 258	58 555	59.5	38.9	1.6
Bristol	121.8	2 374	68.3	0.2	4.8	0.1	2.8	85.2	1 662	104	249	1 881	58.3	40.0	1.7
Kent	420.2	2 464	59.6	0.0	7.0	0.6	3.1	255.2	1 497	714	745	8 428	55.0	43.4	1.6
Newport	241.3	2 807	59.4	0.1	7.3	0.3	2.8	93.5	1 087	4 030	3 799	3 364	57.1	41.2	1.7
Providence	1 519.4	2 393	52.3	0.1	7.8	0.2	2.5	834.3	1 314	4 580	2 874	34 157	62.6	35.9	1.5
Washington	360.7	2 837	65.9	0.4	5.6	0.4	3.0	221.0	1 738	526	591	10 725	55.6	42.6	1.8
SOUTH CAROLINA	X	X	X	X	X	X	X	X	X	27 571	54 044	295 791	40.8	58.0	1.1
Abbeville	52.9	2 001	66.3	1.6	4.5	0.1	2.7	20.9	791	48	98	1 473	44.2	54.8	1.0
Aiken	319.7	2 200	58.9	1.3	5.0	0.1	2.1	124.2	855	820	541	6 614	33.2	65.7	1.0
Allendale	35.4	3 233	54.2	24.3	3.4	0.1	0.5	8.8	804	26	41	1 411	71.4	27.4	1.1
Anderson	363.2	2 129	68.1	1.7	5.2	0.2	2.8	193.7	1 136	366	637	11 083	32.0	67.0	1.0
Bamberg	35.9	2 198	68.3	1.3	4.3	0.0	0.7	12.8	786	42	61	1 355	63.6	35.4	0.9
Barnwell	63.8	2 725	59.2	16.2	4.1	0.0	1.1	31.1	1 330	48	87	1 680	45.9	53.0	1.1
Beaufort	421.2	3 291	37.9	19.1	4.8	1.0	2.0	594.3	4 644	1 936	12 351	6 717	39.0	60.3	0.7
Berkeley	335.7	2 311	75.1	1.4	3.8	0.3	1.8	462.1	3 181	447	538	7 014	38.0	60.6	1.3
Calhoun	26.9	1 748	70.4	4.5	5.1	0.1	0.1	4.8	311	31	57	956	49.0	49.8	1.1
Charleston	985.1	3 112	40.0	2.2	7.2	0.3	2.3	1 422.3	4 493	7 164	11 695	33 435	47.1	51.1	1.8
Cherokee	98.4	1 838	65.8	1.6	5.3	0.2	2.1	1 364.8	25 498	94	199	2 354	34.5	64.6	0.8
Chester	106.3	3 108	44.9	28.6	3.4	0.1	1.6	65.7	1 919	70	127	2 340	49.4	49.4	1.2
Chesterfield	100.1	2 318	78.3	0.8	4.0	0.2	1.7	49.7	1 150	101	161	2 046	47.8	51.7	0.5
Clarendon	80.2	2 438	58.6	20.2	4.1	0.1	2.1	49.3	1 497	65	122	2 350	53.7	45.9	0.4
Colleton	81.5	2 100	69.3	2.5	6.0	0.2	3.0	20.6	530	114	146	2 146	47.5	51.5	1.0
Darlington	132.0	1 944	67.9	1.5	5.0	0.5	1.7	70.5	1 038	102	252	3 202	46.5	52.7	0.8
Dillon	61.6	1 992	69.4	1.3	5.1	0.2	3.6	13.0	422	83	115	1 525	52.4	46.5	1.1
Dorchester	193.6	1 920	70.4	2.0	4.2	0.3	3.2	103.2	1 023	187	370	4 844	35.7	62.9	1.4
Edgefield	45.3	1 821	72.2	1.1	2.2	0.1	4.1	16.5	662	455	92	1 199	41.6	57.6	0.9
Fairfield	52.4	2 184	66.3	0.2	6.8	0.0	2.2	26.2	1 091	49	89	1 524	61.1	37.4	1.5
Florence	280.5	2 204	59.6	1.6	5.4	0.3	2.2	298.9	2 349	685	475	12 220	43.3	55.9	0.8
Georgetown	176.1	3 023	57.5	1.5	5.5	0.2	2.7	266.3	4 571	111	258	3 985	45.0	53.4	1.6
Greenville	1 553.3	3 969	31.1	41.8	3.2	0.2	1.4	1 763.4	4 506	1 700	1 492	23 651	32.8	66.0	1.2
Greenwood	292.2	4 332	29.2	52.5	2.2	0.1	0.7	188.4	2 793	183	251	7 072	38.2	60.9	1.0
Hampton	48.2	2 263	69.4	2.9	5.8	0.5	2.7	8.9	417	358	79	1 317	60.2	38.7	1.1
Horry	694.1	3 369	41.1	11.7	5.1	0.3	5.9	575.6	2 794	461	767	10 980	36.3	62.0	1.7
Jasper	38.6	1 841	58.6	2.6	7.6	0.3	3.8	14.0	670	37	78	1 318	56.1	42.9	1.1
Kershaw	160.6	2 995	56.9	28.3	2.8	0.1	0.4	92.9	1 733	110	199	3 110	37.0	61.5	1.5
Lancaster	134.6	2 163	72.9	2.3	4.7	0.1	1.6	129.6	2 083	119	232	3 526	36.7	62.1	1.3
Laurens	159.0	2 255	48.9	24.3	3.9	0.1	1.9	90.1	1 277	101	266	4 318	38.5	60.8	0.7
Lee	37.5	1 833	69.4	0.0	4.8	0.0	2.2	17.6	862	41	76	1 384	62.6	36.9	0.5
Lexington	764.5	3 430	50.2	30.3	3.1	0.1	0.2	493.1	2 212	514	828	13 777	27.2	71.9	1.0
McCormick	17.0	1 667	61.3	3.3	4.6	0.1	0.4	27.6	2 698	91	38	841	51.7	47.8	0.5
Marion	114.5	3 274	43.7	32.9	3.8	0.2	1.9	62.3	1 783	80	135	2 396	57.0	41.8	1.2
Marlboro	54.9	1 913	68.1	0.8	5.4	0.1	2.0	29.6	1 033	88	107	1 650	58.2	40.0	1.9
Newberry	71.4	1 936	67.2	0.7	4.6	0.3	2.9	31.9	865	136	137	2 234	36.1	61.7	2.2
Oconee	126.3	1 859	70.2	0.4	5.8	0.2	3.2	125.3	1 844	166	252	3 949	30.4	68.4	1.2
Orangeburg	295.1	3 236	52.0	29.5	3.8	0.2	0.8	122.9	1 348	207	345	7 602	65.7	33.8	0.5
Pickens	169.0	1 494	64.7	2.1	8.0	0.1	3.4	96.6	854	227	436	9 424	25.4	73.5	1.1
Richland	793.0	2 410	51.9	1.4	6.1	0.0	0.8	797.0	2 422	7 725	11 893	47 699	57.0	42.0	1.0
Saluda	30.7	1 597	67.9	2.0	5.4	0.0	2.6	22.4	1 165	45	72	932	39.7	59.8	0.5
Spartanburg	690.7	2 663	53.6	0.8	4.3	0.2	1.9	2 168.9	8 364	498	968	16 757	34.7	64.1	1.2

1. Based on the resident population estimated as of July 1 of the year shown.

Table B. States and Counties — **Land Area and Population**

STATE/ County code	CBSA code[1]	County Type[2]	STATE County	Land area[3] (sq km) 2000	Total persons	Rank	Per square kilometer	White	Black	Am. Indian, Alaska Native	Asian and Pacific Islander	Percent Hispanic or Latino[4]	Under 5 years	5 to 17 years	18 to 24 years	25 to 34 years	35 to 44 years	45 to 54 years
				1	2	3	4	5	6	7	8	9	10	11	12	13	14	15
			SOUTH CAROLINA—Cont'd															
45 085	44940	3	Sumter	1 723	105 958	517	61.5	48.1	49.2	0.6	1.5	1.6	8.0	20.0	10.6	12.5	15.1	13.0
45 087	46420	6	Union	1 332	29 105	1 431	21.9	67.6	31.5	0.3	0.4	0.7	6.1	17.3	8.2	11.9	14.7	14.7
45 089	...	6	Williamsburg	2 419	36 008	1 237	14.9	32.3	66.7	0.3	0.2	0.8	7.3	20.1	9.8	11.2	13.2	15.6
45 091	16740	1	York	1 768	178 070	321	100.7	75.9	20.0	1.1	1.3	2.4	6.6	18.9	10.1	13.5	15.7	14.0
46 000	...	X	SOUTH DAKOTA	196 540	764 309	X	3.9	88.6	1.1	9.0	1.0	1.5	6.8	18.8	11.1	11.8	14.0	14.1
46 003	...	9	Aurora	1 834	2 926	2 988	1.6	94.2	0.4	2.8	0.2	2.5	5.1	21.2	8.7	7.6	13.0	12.7
46 005	26700	7	Beadle	3 260	16 269	2 016	5.0	96.6	1.2	1.3	0.5	1.0	5.9	17.5	9.1	9.1	14.4	15.1
46 007	...	9	Bennett	3 070	3 530	2 941	1.1	47.0	0.3	56.6	0.4	2.0	9.2	25.7	11.6	9.9	13.7	11.1
46 009	...	9	Bon Homme	1 459	7 104	2 677	4.9	95.3	0.8	3.3	0.1	0.6	4.4	16.4	10.0	10.1	15.5	14.2
46 011	15100	7	Brookings	2 058	28 265	1 450	13.7	96.1	0.6	1.1	1.9	1.0	5.7	14.1	22.7	13.7	11.6	11.6
46 013	10100	5	Brown	4 437	34 666	1 286	7.8	95.3	0.5	3.6	0.9	0.7	6.1	16.5	11.2	11.7	14.0	14.4
46 015	...	9	Brule	2 121	5 205	2 829	2.5	90.2	0.3	8.9	0.6	0.5	5.4	23.0	9.0	8.5	13.8	14.0
46 017	...	9	Buffalo	1 219	1 994	3 061	1.6	16.5	0.1	82.9	0.2	0.9	11.2	28.8	13.1	11.2	12.6	9.8
46 019	...	6	Butte	5 824	9 212	2 508	1.6	95.9	0.3	2.3	0.2	2.5	6.2	20.0	10.0	8.8	14.1	15.3
46 021	...	9	Campbell	1 906	1 679	3 079	0.9	99.2	0.0	0.4	0.2	0.2	4.9	18.0	6.8	5.6	17.0	13.1
46 023	...	9	Charles Mix	2 843	9 178	2 512	3.2	69.4	0.3	29.6	0.3	1.7	8.4	22.4	8.6	9.4	12.5	11.9
46 025	...	9	Clark	2 481	3 915	2 916	1.6	98.7	0.2	0.7	0.1	0.4	4.9	18.7	9.1	7.6	13.2	15.1
46 027	46820	6	Clay	1 066	13 191	2 223	12.4	92.9	1.3	3.2	2.7	0.9	5.7	13.1	25.2	16.5	10.3	10.4
46 029	47980	7	Codington	1 781	25 929	1 539	14.6	96.9	0.3	2.0	0.6	1.0	6.8	18.5	11.4	11.8	14.7	13.9
46 031	...	8	Corson	4 034	4 288	2 887	0.7	36.1	0.2	62.5	0.2	2.2	9.5	26.4	11.3	9.5	13.6	10.9
46 033	...	8	Custer	6 405	7 585	2 628	1.9	94.6	0.4	4.7	0.4	1.5	4.3	17.6	9.7	8.7	12.6	17.0
46 035	33580	7	Davison	1 128	18 744	1 873	16.6	96.2	0.5	2.2	0.5	1.2	6.4	17.8	12.6	10.9	13.7	13.4
46 037	...	9	Day	2 664	5 891	2 781	2.2	91.7	0.2	8.1	0.1	0.4	5.7	18.1	7.2	7.4	13.5	15.0
46 039	...	9	Deuel	1 615	4 364	2 882	2.7	98.4	0.2	0.6	0.3	0.8	5.1	18.3	8.0	9.5	15.0	13.8
46 041	...	9	Dewey	5 964	6 133	2 761	1.0	24.6	0.1	75.2	0.2	1.0	10.8	26.7	11.6	10.6	14.9	10.3
46 043	...	9	Douglas	1 123	3 310	2 961	2.9	98.3	0.3	1.3	0.1	0.4	4.8	19.5	7.9	7.7	13.1	14.4
46 045	10100	9	Edmunds	2 967	4 221	2 895	1.4	99.0	0.2	0.4	0.2	0.5	5.7	19.5	7.7	7.6	14.4	14.4
46 047	...	7	Fall River	4 506	7 305	2 658	1.6	90.8	0.4	8.8	0.4	2.0	4.4	16.4	8.4	7.5	11.1	16.7
46 049	...	9	Faulk	2 590	2 469	3 024	1.0	99.3	0.1	0.4	0.1	0.2	4.7	18.8	8.7	6.9	14.3	14.0
46 051	...	7	Grant	1 768	7 625	2 625	4.3	98.6	0.0	0.6	0.4	0.6	5.3	18.7	8.6	8.4	15.0	14.9
46 053	...	9	Gregory	2 631	4 500	2 873	1.7	92.5	0.0	6.3	0.5	0.9	4.7	16.9	7.6	6.3	13.0	15.3
46 055	...	8	Haakon	4 696	2 007	3 060	0.4	96.9	0.0	2.4	0.1	0.7	4.4	16.4	10.4	7.2	14.6	17.8
46 057	47980	9	Hamlin	1 313	5 615	2 801	4.3	98.4	0.1	0.6	0.3	0.6	7.3	19.8	9.9	9.1	13.7	12.4
46 059	...	9	Hand	3 721	3 520	2 942	0.9	99.4	0.0	0.1	0.1	0.3	4.8	17.4	7.3	6.4	14.1	15.3
46 061	33580	8	Hanson	1 126	3 510	2 945	3.1	99.7	0.0	0.1	0.1	0.1	8.0	19.8	9.6	10.8	13.8	12.1
46 063	...	9	Harding	6 917	1 288	3 100	0.2	97.4	0.0	1.3	0.2	1.1	5.4	20.4	9.2	8.1	15.2	18.9
46 065	38180	7	Hughes	1 919	16 684	1 982	8.7	88.6	0.4	10.3	0.8	1.4	6.1	19.7	8.5	10.8	15.7	15.6
46 067	...	9	Hutchinson	2 105	7 731	2 619	3.7	98.7	0.2	0.7	0.1	0.5	5.6	18.0	7.5	8.5	12.7	13.4
46 069	...	9	Hyde	2 230	1 573	3 083	0.7	91.4	0.3	7.9	0.1	0.5	5.8	18.9	6.9	8.1	13.2	14.3
46 071	...	8	Jackson	4 841	2 853	2 995	0.6	49.0	0.1	51.6	0.1	0.5	8.7	25.3	11.4	8.8	13.4	12.4
46 073	...	9	Jerauld	1 372	2 180	3 043	1.6	98.9	0.1	0.6	0.1	0.3	5.0	14.1	8.9	7.9	12.0	15.7
46 075	...	9	Jones	2 514	1 087	3 106	0.4	96.6	0.1	3.1	0.1	0.6	5.3	16.7	8.9	7.5	15.5	17.0
46 077	...	9	Kingsbury	2 171	5 555	2 808	2.6	98.3	0.2	0.5	0.5	0.7	5.1	17.5	8.0	7.1	14.4	14.7
46 079	...	6	Lake	1 459	11 040	2 367	7.6	97.1	0.4	0.9	0.8	1.0	5.4	16.3	15.0	9.6	13.2	14.6
46 081	43940	6	Lawrence	2 072	21 880	1 707	10.6	95.3	0.5	2.8	0.5	1.9	4.9	16.4	14.0	10.8	13.2	15.1
46 083	43620	3	Lincoln	1 497	29 302	1 425	19.6	97.1	0.9	1.0	1.4	0.7	7.5	19.9	11.4	14.2	15.2	13.0
46 085	...	9	Lyman	4 247	3 916	2 915	0.9	63.8	0.1	36.1	0.5	0.6	8.5	22.7	9.2	10.7	13.8	13.4
46 087	43620	9	McCook	1 488	5 864	2 784	3.9	98.6	0.1	0.4	0.2	0.8	6.7	20.5	8.5	9.2	14.4	12.9
46 089	...	9	McPherson	2 945	2 723	3 002	0.9	99.3	0.0	0.3	0.1	0.2	4.5	16.9	6.8	7.4	12.3	13.4
46 091	...	9	Marshall	2 170	4 272	2 888	2.0	92.4	0.3	6.3	0.2	1.0	4.7	19.2	7.6	7.9	13.6	14.7
46 093	39660	3	Meade	8 989	24 715	1 590	2.7	92.8	2.5	3.3	1.8	2.1	8.0	19.4	11.5	13.0	15.2	14.0
46 095	...	9	Mellette	3 384	2 118	3 047	0.6	45.1	0.0	54.5	0.2	1.5	8.8	25.8	9.2	9.1	12.9	12.1
46 097	...	8	Miner	1 477	2 717	3 003	1.8	98.2	0.7	0.3	0.1	0.8	4.7	17.5	8.5	7.5	14.2	15.6
46 099	43620	3	Minnehaha	2 097	154 617	361	73.7	92.3	2.5	2.4	1.6	2.4	7.4	18.3	10.6	14.6	15.8	13.5
46 101	...	8	Moody	1 346	6 511	2 731	4.8	86.0	0.5	13.8	0.9	0.9	6.4	20.3	9.6	10.5	14.7	14.8
46 103	39660	3	Pennington	7 190	91 881	586	12.8	88.0	1.5	8.7	1.6	2.6	7.2	18.4	11.0	12.7	14.7	14.3
46 105	...	9	Perkins	7 437	3 187	2 967	0.4	97.3	0.2	1.6	0.2	0.8	4.1	17.4	8.0	8.2	14.2	15.4
46 107	...	9	Potter	2 244	2 508	3 019	1.1	98.4	0.0	1.2	0.4	0.2	4.9	16.4	6.7	5.5	14.4	15.4
46 109	...	9	Roberts	2 852	10 128	2 433	3.6	67.9	0.3	32.6	0.4	0.5	7.0	21.5	9.7	9.0	12.8	13.2
46 111	...	9	Sanborn	1 474	2 612	3 012	1.8	98.0	0.2	0.4	0.5	1.1	5.3	17.5	11.3	7.5	12.9	16.4
46 113	...	7	Shannon	5 423	13 209	2 219	2.4	6.1	0.1	93.3	0.1	1.3	12.1	31.2	12.8	12.3	12.2	8.7
46 115	...	7	Spink	3 895	6 972	2 687	1.8	97.8	0.2	1.4	0.2	0.4	5.0	18.6	8.7	8.6	15.1	15.5
46 117	38180	9	Stanley	3 738	2 752	3 000	0.7	92.3	0.5	7.5	0.4	0.5	5.4	20.4	9.1	10.1	15.2	16.0
46 119	...	9	Sully	2 608	1 456	3 091	0.6	98.2	0.1	1.0	0.4	0.8	5.8	17.7	7.6	8.3	16.7	15.5
46 121	...	9	Todd	3 595	9 468	2 489	2.6	14.2	0.5	85.0	0.3	1.6	13.1	30.4	11.6	11.9	11.9	10.1

1. CBSA = Core Based Statistical Area. See Appendix A for explanation. See Appendix B for list of metropolitan areas with component counties.   2. County type code from the Economic Research Service of USDA Rural-Urban Continuum Codes. See Appendix A for definition.   3. Dry land or land partially or temporarily covered by water.   4. Hispanic or Latino persons may be of any race.

Table B. States and Counties — **Population and Households**

STATE County	55 to 64 years	65 to 74 years	75 years and over	Percent female	1990	2000	1990–2000	2000–2003	Births	Deaths	Net migration	Number	Percent change, 1990–2000	Persons per household	Female family householder[1]	One person
	16	17	18	19	20	21	22	23	24	25	26	27	28	29	30	31
SOUTH CAROLINA—Cont'd																
Sumter	8.6	6.4	5.2	51.8	101 276	104 646	3.3	1.3	5 736	3 074	-1 294	37 728	15.3	2.68	18.3	23.2
Union	11.3	8.4	7.7	53.2	30 337	29 881	-1.5	-2.6	1 205	1 132	-824	12 087	6.0	2.44	16.8	26.8
Williamsburg	10.0	7.3	6.1	53.2	36 815	37 217	1.1	-3.2	1 829	1 251	-1 772	13 714	13.3	2.69	22.4	24.9
York	9.2	5.7	4.5	51.4	131 497	164 614	25.2	8.2	7 492	4 280	10 070	61 051	29.9	2.63	13.3	21.3
SOUTH DAKOTA	9.1	6.8	7.4	50.3	696 004	754 844	8.5	1.3	33 914	22 917	-1 114	290 245	12.0	2.50	9.0	27.6
Aurora	10.9	10.3	11.6	48.1	3 135	3 058	-2.5	-4.3	90	158	-62	1 165	1.7	2.45	5.0	28.2
Beadle	10.0	8.8	11.0	50.6	18 253	17 023	-6.7	-4.4	627	633	-755	7 210	-1.8	2.30	7.4	33.1
Bennett	7.6	6.3	5.6	50.7	3 206	3 574	11.5	-1.2	224	101	-160	1 123	9.0	3.14	17.5	23.3
Bon Homme	9.6	9.0	11.6	43.9	7 089	7 260	2.4	-2.1	184	304	-29	2 635	-0.5	2.38	5.1	29.5
Brookings	7.0	5.0	5.9	49.3	25 207	28 220	12.0	0.2	1 095	589	-445	10 665	19.7	2.38	6.6	29.6
Brown	9.4	7.6	8.9	51.8	35 580	35 460	-0.3	-2.2	1 379	1 192	-989	14 638	5.6	2.32	7.9	30.8
Brule	9.0	7.4	9.9	51.6	5 485	5 364	-2.2	-3.0	197	166	-192	1 998	0.1	2.49	7.2	29.9
Buffalo	7.2	3.7	3.1	49.4	1 759	2 032	15.5	-1.9	141	98	-77	526	17.9	3.83	31.4	16.0
Butte	9.4	8.1	7.3	50.5	7 914	9 094	14.9	1.3	396	282	8	3 516	15.9	2.55	9.0	25.6
Campbell	12.2	11.6	12.3	50.6	1 965	1 782	-9.3	-5.8	54	59	-98	725	-5.5	2.43	2.6	28.6
Charles Mix	9.8	8.1	9.4	50.6	9 131	9 350	2.4	-1.8	510	330	-351	3 343	3.4	2.74	11.7	28.3
Clark	10.0	10.3	12.7	51.2	4 403	4 143	-5.9	-5.5	130	157	-194	1 598	-6.0	2.54	4.7	28.1
Clay	6.3	4.6	5.5	51.4	13 186	13 537	2.7	-2.6	500	318	-538	4 878	10.0	2.32	8.1	31.0
Codington	8.2	6.7	7.6	50.4	22 698	25 897	14.1	0.1	1 120	784	-283	10 357	18.5	2.46	8.1	27.9
Corson	8.1	6.1	4.5	50.3	4 195	4 181	-0.3	2.6	266	140	-17	1 271	-2.5	3.29	19.7	22.1
Custer	13.6	9.3	6.8	48.9	6 179	7 275	17.7	4.3	190	276	392	2 970	26.3	2.35	6.6	25.9
Davison	8.5	7.2	8.9	51.1	17 503	18 741	7.1	0.0	787	561	-204	7 585	9.2	2.38	8.2	30.8
Day	10.7	10.4	13.5	51.0	6 978	6 267	-10.2	-6.0	210	314	-273	2 586	-5.3	2.36	6.8	31.8
Deuel	10.4	10.4	10.6	50.3	4 522	4 498	-0.5	-3.0	140	145	-120	1 843	4.3	2.40	4.9	28.6
Dewey	6.7	5.2	3.3	51.4	5 523	5 972	8.1	2.7	460	159	-128	1 863	8.3	3.15	22.3	22.1
Douglas	10.4	9.7	13.7	51.3	3 746	3 458	-7.7	-4.3	114	140	-120	1 321	-2.3	2.54	3.6	26.8
Edmunds	11.7	9.9	11.5	50.0	4 356	4 367	0.3	-3.3	155	197	-97	1 681	0.7	2.52	4.8	25.6
Fall River	12.4	11.6	11.8	48.2	7 353	7 453	1.4	-2.0	188	376	48	3 127	9.2	2.23	8.5	32.7
Faulk	10.1	11.9	12.2	51.2	2 744	2 640	-3.8	-6.5	75	108	-136	1 014	-4.1	2.56	3.4	29.1
Grant	10.3	8.5	10.7	50.4	8 372	7 847	-6.3	-2.8	264	314	-169	3 116	-1.2	2.44	5.2	28.6
Gregory	11.3	10.5	15.0	51.2	5 359	4 792	-10.6	-6.1	139	237	-199	2 022	-5.5	2.32	5.7	33.9
Haakon	10.8	8.5	11.5	51.4	2 624	2 196	-16.3	-8.6	58	77	-172	870	-6.0	2.47	4.8	26.0
Hamlin	9.3	8.0	10.4	50.9	4 974	5 540	11.4	1.4	284	205	3	2 048	10.5	2.62	4.8	27.0
Hand	10.7	12.0	13.5	50.8	4 272	3 741	-12.4	-5.9	107	146	-179	1 543	-5.0	2.38	4.4	30.2
Hanson	9.5	7.6	6.7	49.9	2 994	3 139	4.8	11.8	208	88	251	1 115	4.0	2.82	3.7	21.7
Harding	9.6	6.7	7.7	48.2	1 669	1 353	-18.9	-4.8	51	24	-89	525	-11.3	2.50	5.3	31.0
Hughes	10.0	6.7	6.8	51.7	14 817	16 481	11.2	1.2	642	495	66	6 512	12.7	2.41	8.9	29.8
Hutchinson	9.8	10.7	15.3	50.8	8 262	8 075	-2.3	-4.3	290	455	-178	3 190	-1.0	2.43	4.4	29.6
Hyde	10.9	10.7	12.0	48.6	1 696	1 671	-1.5	-5.9	48	79	-66	679	-0.1	2.41	6.0	30.3
Jackson	8.6	6.1	5.9	50.5	2 811	2 930	4.2	-2.6	163	72	-166	945	4.7	3.08	14.7	25.2
Jerauld	11.6	10.6	15.5	50.4	2 425	2 295	-5.4	-5.0	73	107	-80	987	2.2	2.28	6.3	31.3
Jones	11.3	10.7	9.3	48.3	1 324	1 193	-9.9	-8.9	36	21	-121	509	-1.9	2.34	7.5	33.2
Kingsbury	10.1	10.7	13.4	51.2	5 925	5 815	-1.9	-4.5	177	301	-136	2 406	2.1	2.34	4.4	31.5
Lake	9.0	7.5	8.9	50.0	10 550	11 276	6.9	-2.1	382	395	-216	4 372	8.5	2.41	5.9	29.2
Lawrence	9.2	7.2	7.7	50.7	20 655	21 802	5.6	0.4	748	608	-56	8 881	12.0	2.33	8.5	29.6
Lincoln	6.9	4.1	4.7	50.0	15 427	24 131	56.4	21.4	1 415	494	4 074	8 782	60.8	2.72	6.7	19.5
Lyman	9.2	7.1	5.9	48.9	3 638	3 895	7.1	0.5	220	118	-75	1 400	10.4	2.77	13.8	24.6
McCook	9.5	7.8	10.9	50.7	5 688	5 832	2.5	0.5	248	211	2	2 204	2.8	2.58	5.1	26.8
McPherson	12.5	13.0	15.6	51.4	3 228	2 904	-10.0	-6.2	73	125	-113	1 227	-7.9	2.31	2.7	31.1
Marshall	12.0	9.6	12.0	49.4	4 844	4 576	-5.5	-6.6	121	207	-218	1 844	-3.9	2.43	6.5	30.1
Meade	7.9	5.5	4.9	49.5	21 878	24 253	10.9	1.9	1 323	584	-251	8 805	24.3	2.66	8.3	19.9
Mellette	8.1	6.9	6.6	50.6	2 137	2 083	-2.5	1.7	105	64	-8	694	1.9	2.94	16.7	24.2
Miner	9.3	10.6	13.8	49.6	3 272	2 884	-11.9	-5.8	78	124	-122	1 212	-5.0	2.33	5.4	32.3
Minnehaha	7.7	5.5	5.5	50.3	123 809	148 281	19.8	4.3	7 482	3 632	2 707	57 996	21.6	2.46	9.5	27.8
Moody	9.8	6.0	8.7	50.5	6 507	6 595	1.4	-1.3	274	195	-155	2 526	5.3	2.58	8.5	26.4
Pennington	8.5	6.5	5.6	50.3	81 343	88 565	8.9	3.7	4 402	2 185	1 217	34 641	13.4	2.49	11.7	26.1
Perkins	10.4	10.4	13.5	50.8	3 932	3 363	-14.5	-5.2	76	142	-109	1 429	-9.9	2.31	5.2	32.9
Potter	11.6	12.1	14.5	51.2	3 190	2 693	-15.6	-6.9	97	122	-158	1 145	-8.3	2.29	4.9	31.3
Roberts	10.1	7.8	8.5	50.1	9 914	10 016	1.0	1.1	493	374	-11	3 683	1.8	2.66	11.8	26.8
Sanborn	10.0	9.6	9.1	48.0	2 833	2 675	-5.6	-2.4	87	97	-54	1 043	-1.5	2.53	4.9	25.4
Shannon	5.3	3.2	1.5	50.4	9 902	12 466	25.9	6.0	1 111	412	60	2 785	26.3	4.36	36.4	13.2
Spink	9.7	9.6	10.3	48.2	7 981	7 454	-6.6	-6.5	243	248	-485	2 847	-5.8	2.45	6.1	29.3
Stanley	12.4	6.2	4.4	49.9	2 453	2 772	13.0	-0.7	112	65	-61	1 111	20.6	2.49	10.1	25.2
Sully	12.3	9.1	9.2	49.7	1 589	1 556	-2.1	-6.4	61	27	-127	630	1.4	2.47	4.3	25.7
Todd	5.5	3.3	2.3	51.3	8 352	9 050	8.4	4.6	850	252	-170	2 462	11.4	3.62	31.8	18.9

1. No spouse present.

STATE County	Births, average 1999–2001 Total	Rate[1]	Deaths, average 1999–2001 Number Total	Infant[2]	Rate Total[1]	Infant[3]	Physicians,[4] 2000 Number	Rate[5]	Hospitals,[4] 1998 Number	Beds Number	Rate[5]	Medicare enrollees, 2003	Serious crimes known to police,[6] 2002 Total Number	Rate[7]
	32	33	34	35	36	37	38	39	40	41	42	43	44	45
SOUTH CAROLINA—Cont'd														
Sumter	1 675	16.0	921	16	8.8	9.6	127	121	1	230	215	14 509	6 521	6 087
Union	380	12.7	349	3	11.7	D	26	87	2	117	384	6 070	1 300	4 322
Williamsburg	546	14.7	377	10	10.1	17.7	18	48	1	48	129	5 724	1 294	3 396
York	2 304	13.9	1 265	23	7.7	9.8	181	110	1	276	179	22 501	9 485	5 628
SOUTH DAKOTA	10 451	13.8	6 966	76	9.2	7.3	1 307	173	51	4 195	568	121 777	17 342	2 279
Aurora	31	10.3	43	0	14.1	D	0	0	0	0	0	623	3	97
Beadle	186	10.9	197	1	11.6	D	30	176	1	95	553	3 576	76	443
Bennett	64	17.9	32	0	9.0	D	3	84	1	68	2 006	429	2	27
Bon Homme	61	8.4	89	0	12.3	D	5	69	2	47	611	1 533	NA	NA
Brookings	329	11.7	184	1	6.6	D	16	57	1	140	539	3 305	551	1 937
Brown	460	13.0	368	3	10.4	D	68	192	1	203	573	6 349	676	1 891
Brule	63	11.8	53	0	10.0	D	9	168	1	54	972	1 008	NA	NA
Buffalo	40	19.5	24	1	11.8	D	1	49	0	0	0	139	NA	NA
Butte	122	13.4	87	1	9.6	D	9	99	1	128	1 419	1 680	NA	NA
Campbell	16	9.1	15	0	8.6	D	0	0	0	0	0	695	NA	NA
Charles Mix	158	17.0	111	2	12.0	D	5	53	2	87	932	1 679	13	151
Clark	43	10.3	49	0	11.7	D	0	0	0	0	0	949	19	455
Clay	158	11.7	95	1	7.0	D	7	52	1	95	626	1 463	376	2 755
Codington	361	13.9	234	1	9.0	D	51	197	1	119	467	4 370	801	3 068
Corson	84	20.0	39	1	9.3	D	0	0	0	0	0	976	30	712
Custer	57	7.8	79	0	10.9	D	6	82	1	11	159	1 436	NA	NA
Davison	247	13.2	184	1	9.8	D	37	197	1	99	550	3 553	525	2 779
Day	66	10.6	92	0	14.8	D	1	16	1	28	438	1 477	NA	NA
Deuel	45	10.1	49	0	11.0	D	2	44	1	20	443	944	43	948
Dewey	136	22.7	50	1	8.4	D	3	50	0	0	0	662	22	365
Douglas	34	9.8	42	0	12.2	D	2	58	1	9	253	802	0	0
Edmunds	47	10.9	62	0	14.2	D	2	46	1	58	1 375	912	3	68
Fall River	64	8.6	109	0	14.6	D	20	268	1	74	1 037	2 008	NA	NA
Faulk	23	8.8	30	0	11.6	D	0	0	1	12	476	674	10	376
Grant	83	10.6	98	1	12.6	D	2	25	1	115	1 426	1 629	NA	NA
Gregory	41	8.6	76	1	16.0	D	2	42	2	113	2 284	1 226	11	316
Haakon	22	10.1	28	0	13.0	D	1	46	1	50	2 125	445	NA	NA
Hamlin	83	14.9	65	0	11.8	D	0	0	0	0	0	1 051	NA	NA
Hand	33	8.8	44	0	11.8	D	3	80	1	30	724	780	29	769
Hanson	60	18.8	21	0	6.6	D	0	0	0	0	0	561	NA	NA
Harding	13	9.9	9	0	6.4	D	0	0	0	0	0	203	1	73
Hughes	205	12.4	136	1	8.3	D	24	146	1	86	559	2 356	639	3 845
Hutchinson	91	11.3	130	0	16.1	D	12	149	2	210	2 610	2 003	16	216
Hyde	19	11.3	24	0	14.3	D	0	0	0	0	0	359	2	119
Jackson	55	19.0	22	1	7.7	D	2	68	0	0	0	372	NA	NA
Jerauld	22	9.4	29	0	12.8	D	3	131	1	28	1 260	568	6	259
Jones	9	8.0	8	0	7.1	D	0	0	0	0	0	233	NA	NA
Kingsbury	54	9.3	90	0	15.5	D	4	69	1	17	298	1 504	2	34
Lake	117	10.4	111	0	9.8	D	7	62	1	49	440	2 005	NA	NA
Lawrence	219	10.1	181	3	8.3	D	30	138	2	64	284	3 725	559	2 543
Lincoln	397	16.3	154	2	6.3	D	13	54	1	28	137	1 916	NA	NA
Lyman	69	17.8	36	1	9.1	D	2	51	0	0	0	557	11	280
McCook	73	12.6	64	0	11.1	D	1	17	0	0	0	1 140	62	1 054
McPherson	26	9.0	43	0	15.0	D	2	69	1	25	913	537	NA	NA
Marshall	38	8.4	56	0	12.3	D	2	44	1	25	548	989	38	824
Meade	370	15.3	168	4	6.9	D	35	144	1	114	520	3 387	434	1 775
Mellette	31	15.2	23	0	11.0	D	0	0	0	0	0	279	19	904
Miner	32	11.2	38	0	13.2	D	1	35	0	0	0	661	24	826
Minnehaha	2 317	15.6	1 104	17	7.4	7.2	500	337	3	821	574	20 640	4 350	2 910
Moody	81	12.3	67	1	10.1	D	4	61	1	20	307	934	NA	NA
Pennington	1 356	15.2	670	11	7.5	8.1	241	272	1	328	374	13 099	4 405	4 933
Perkins	27	7.9	48	0	14.2	D	0	0	1	56	1 598	818	39	1 150
Potter	27	10.1	41	0	15.2	D	5	186	2	104	3 640	748	29	1 068
Roberts	141	14.0	120	1	11.9	D	4	40	1	31	317	1 749	108	1 070
Sanborn	28	10.7	27	0	10.0	D	0	0	0	0	0	585	29	1 075
Shannon	339	27.1	113	6	9.0	D	8	64	0	0	0	889	NA	NA
Spink	79	10.6	83	0	11.2	D	8	107	1	35	462	1 684	53	705
Stanley	32	11.7	19	0	6.7	D	2	72	0	0	0	373	70	2 504
Sully	16	10.5	10	0	6.7	D	0	0	0	0	0	239	12	765
Todd	242	26.6	76	3	8.4	D	6	66	0	0	0	549	NA	NA

1. Per 1,000 estimated resident population.   2. Deaths of infants under 1 year old.   3. Deaths of infants under 1 year old per 1,000 live births.   4. Data subject to copyright.   5. Per 100,000 resident population as of July 1 of the year shown.   6. Data for serious crimes have not been adjusted for underreporting; this may affect comparability between geographic areas and over time.   7. Per 100,000 population estimated by the FBI.

Table B. States and Counties — Crime, Education, Money Income, and Poverty

STATE County	Serious crimes known to police,[1] 2002 (cont'd) Rate[2]		School enrollment and attainment, 2000				Local government expenditures,[5] 2000–2001		Money income, 1999				Percent below poverty level, 1999			
			Enrollment[3]		Attainment[4] (percent)				Per capita income[6] (dollars)	Households Median income						
	Violent	Property	Total	Percent private	High school graduate or less	Bachelor's degree or more	Total current expenditures (mil dol)	Current expenditures per student (dollars)		Dollars	Percent change, 1989–1999 (constant 1999 dollars)	Percent with income of $100,000 or more	Persons	Households	Families	Families with children
	46	47	48	49	50	51	52	53	54	55	56	57	58	59	60	61
SOUTH CAROLINA—Cont'd																
Sumter	1 030	5 058	30 345	15.0	55.4	15.8	119.8	6 283	15 657	33 278	10.6	5.3	16.2	16.3	13.1	18.2
Union	635	3 687	6 799	5.9	69.5	9.8	34.6	6 637	15 877	31 441	8.7	3.7	14.3	16.0	11.1	17.3
Williamsburg	816	2 580	10 681	7.6	69.6	11.5	42.6	6 657	12 794	24 214	-2.1	3.4	27.9	29.0	23.7	32.4
York	1 026	4 602	44 094	11.0	51.2	20.9	203.8	6 763	20 536	44 539	6.0	10.2	10.0	10.1	7.3	10.6
SOUTH DAKOTA	177	2 101	208 229	11.4	48.3	21.5	779.7	6 092	17 562	35 282	16.7	5.9	13.2	12.5	9.3	13.9
Aurora	65	32	759	5.5	56.5	12.7	4.3	8 130	13 887	29 783	34.4	2.3	11.4	12.3	7.8	10.5
Beadle	23	420	4 139	18.9	51.9	18.3	18.4	6 197	17 832	30 510	1.3	3.4	11.9	14.3	7.9	13.7
Bennett	NA	NA	1 257	5.1	56.4	12.7	4.8	7 865	10 106	25 313	11.7	2.0	39.2	29.2	30.3	39.4
Bon Homme	0	27	1 529	7.1	57.1	15.3	8.9	6 401	13 892	30 644	28.3	2.4	12.9	13.6	9.4	13.8
Brookings	39	1 898	11 458	3.2	38.0	32.2	22.3	5 305	17 586	35 438	21.0	5.5	14.0	15.1	6.2	9.5
Brown	123	1 768	9 554	14.5	45.8	23.6	28.9	5 792	18 464	35 017	13.5	5.3	9.9	11.3	7.0	10.6
Brule	NA	NA	1 475	6.2	50.5	20.6	8.0	6 555	14 874	32 370	13.7	3.8	14.3	10.9	8.1	9.8
Buffalo	NA	NA	779	10.3	69.7	5.4	NA	NA	5 213	12 692	-35.1	1.3	56.9	56.2	55.7	61.2
Butte	NA	NA	2 361	10.8	57.2	12.2	10.1	5 482	13 997	29 040	9.1	3.2	12.8	13.4	9.4	14.6
Campbell	NA	NA	410	3.4	54.1	14.8	2.2	7 235	14 117	28 793	24.6	2.6	14.1	18.4	11.2	9.3
Charles Mix	47	105	2 522	12.5	59.9	14.1	11.9	6 629	11 502	26 060	17.3	1.9	26.9	23.4	20.8	29.3
Clark	0	455	974	2.9	63.3	11.4	4.7	6 048	15 597	30 208	18.1	3.2	14.8	13.0	10.9	14.4
Clay	110	2 645	6 399	3.3	33.6	38.7	9.7	6 102	14 452	27 535	5.7	5.4	21.2	21.6	12.8	17.2
Codington	176	2 892	6 730	12.7	52.8	18.8	25.0	5 329	18 761	36 257	23.7	6.2	9.0	10.7	5.6	8.4
Corson	142	569	1 410	3.3	61.9	11.3	7.4	9 148	8 615	20 654	7.3	1.3	41.0	34.5	32.8	41.2
Custer	NA	NA	1 731	10.9	44.4	24.4	6.6	6 435	17 945	36 303	19.2	4.9	9.4	9.3	6.2	12.2
Davison	212	2 567	5 217	22.1	50.0	20.2	18.1	5 776	17 879	33 476	20.2	5.1	11.5	13.6	8.2	12.1
Day	NA	NA	1 449	4.0	58.3	15.4	7.6	6 773	15 856	30 227	19.9	3.0	14.3	15.4	11.4	17.0
Deuel	22	926	1 079	4.3	60.3	13.3	3.6	5 669	15 977	31 788	33.0	3.1	10.3	11.8	6.9	9.3
Dewey	83	282	2 154	2.9	54.8	12.2	6.7	8 956	9 251	23 272	18.6	1.8	33.6	31.5	29.8	36.9
Douglas	0	0	842	23.4	58.9	14.5	3.1	6 784	13 827	28 478	24.2	2.7	14.6	15.4	12.2	14.6
Edmunds	23	45	1 050	11.2	59.7	15.5	4.8	6 306	16 149	32 205	16.5	4.4	13.8	14.4	10.4	14.2
Fall River	NA	NA	1 418	9.8	51.9	19.2	7.9	6 463	17 048	29 631	7.7	4.5	13.6	13.2	7.8	14.6
Faulk	0	376	606	14.4	60.4	13.1	3.3	6 703	14 660	30 237	20.3	3.3	18.1	14.3	12.6	18.9
Grant	NA	NA	1 871	9.6	63.1	14.8	8.4	5 840	16 543	33 088	5.1	4.5	9.9	11.3	7.5	8.6
Gregory	58	259	1 051	2.2	61.3	12.0	6.5	6 977	13 656	22 732	0.4	2.1	20.1	20.6	15.1	22.3
Haakon	NA	NA	517	2.5	54.4	15.4	3.1	6 404	16 780	29 894	5.1	6.7	13.9	14.2	12.0	16.0
Hamlin	NA	NA	1 477	7.7	62.9	12.8	7.3	5 685	16 982	33 851	26.3	4.7	12.1	9.9	7.2	10.2
Hand	0	769	825	3.8	58.1	15.6	4.0	6 800	18 735	32 377	24.8	5.8	9.2	12.2	6.1	8.7
Hanson	NA	NA	763	4.3	61.1	14.0	3.6	6 739	14 778	33 049	12.2	5.1	16.6	13.5	12.5	16.7
Harding	73	0	395	8.1	46.6	17.8	2.1	6 850	12 794	25 000	-8.0	3.4	21.1	21.8	19.4	23.5
Hughes	427	3 418	4 081	8.8	38.1	32.0	16.1	5 598	20 689	42 970	18.2	7.3	8.0	9.1	6.0	7.6
Hutchinson	13	202	1 797	10.7	56.4	14.1	11.1	6 478	15 922	30 026	18.7	3.0	13.0	12.2	9.6	12.4
Hyde	0	119	357	5.9	56.2	16.0	2.1	7 535	16 356	31 103	16.3	4.3	12.3	14.3	7.8	10.7
Jackson	NA	NA	964	2.1	51.6	16.2	2.8	7 110	9 981	23 945	3.3	2.2	36.5	29.9	29.5	40.8
Jerauld	43	216	473	3.4	61.0	12.3	3.5	8 097	16 856	30 690	22.9	4.0	20.6	16.8	15.2	25.1
Jones	NA	NA	303	2.0	53.3	17.8	1.6	7 259	15 896	30 288	6.3	4.0	15.8	12.7	11.9	21.1
Kingsbury	0	34	1 360	5.5	59.6	16.2	6.0	6 651	16 522	31 262	14.7	4.5	10.0	10.1	7.0	10.2
Lake	NA	NA	3 471	5.9	50.9	21.1	12.2	5 907	16 446	34 087	7.2	4.2	9.7	10.4	5.4	8.0
Lawrence	127	2 416	6 595	6.7	44.2	24.0	19.5	6 067	17 195	31 755	-4.8	5.5	14.8	14.3	9.5	15.1
Lincoln	NA	NA	6 784	13.2	41.4	25.5	17.9	5 325	22 304	48 338	26.0	11.6	4.4	5.3	3.2	4.0
Lyman	0	280	1 128	3.5	59.7	15.9	3.1	7 230	13 862	28 509	-3.5	3.8	24.3	20.5	19.4	26.9
McCook	119	935	1 493	10.6	55.8	16.3	6.8	6 514	16 374	35 396	26.9	4.2	8.1	8.4	5.5	7.2
McPherson	NA	NA	546	5.9	68.7	10.7	3.2	6 396	12 748	22 380	8.6	3.0	22.6	22.8	17.0	22.5
Marshall	43	780	1 110	5.4	57.8	16.2	5.6	6 237	15 462	30 567	24.3	3.3	13.9	14.0	10.4	14.8
Meade	217	1 558	6 506	11.0	46.1	16.8	17.6	5 760	17 680	36 992	11.6	5.0	9.4	9.6	7.9	11.1
Mellette	238	666	647	2.0	56.3	16.6	4.5	8 519	10 362	23 219	18.9	2.2	35.8	33.7	30.4	40.5
Miner	0	826	678	3.1	60.8	13.5	3.3	6 124	15 155	29 519	17.2	2.9	11.8	13.1	8.2	12.9
Minnehaha	270	2 640	38 766	20.4	43.2	26.0	142.6	5 635	20 713	42 566	14.1	8.4	7.5	7.5	5.0	7.8
Moody	NA	NA	1 788	5.3	51.8	17.4	7.0	6 137	16 541	35 467	10.3	4.9	9.6	9.7	7.3	10.7
Pennington	335	4 598	24 276	11.7	41.5	25.0	96.7	5 672	18 938	37 485	10.1	7.1	11.5	10.8	8.6	14.3
Perkins	59	1 091	732	4.1	56.9	14.6	4.6	7 456	15 734	27 750	4.0	4.5	16.9	16.3	12.4	18.7
Potter	37	1 031	583	8.1	56.6	16.2	3.5	6 729	17 417	30 086	8.3	4.5	12.6	12.6	8.9	15.4
Roberts	218	852	2 692	2.2	61.4	13.4	12.3	6 545	13 428	28 322	20.6	3.3	22.1	19.6	16.6	24.6
Sanborn	222	853	653	4.6	56.2	14.8	3.6	7 064	18 301	33 375	25.3	5.5	14.9	14.5	11.0	14.2
Shannon	NA	NA	4 956	5.8	56.4	12.1	12.9	13 241	6 286	20 916	40.2	2.3	52.3	45.5	45.1	51.8
Spink	93	612	1 700	7.4	57.5	14.4	9.7	6 654	15 728	31 717	21.7	5.1	12.8	12.2	10.2	16.4
Stanley	36	2 469	698	6.7	47.3	22.1	3.3	5 614	20 300	41 170	37.3	6.8	8.7	9.2	6.6	9.8
Sully	64	701	358	3.4	53.2	16.4	2.7	7 670	17 407	32 500	2.5	5.1	12.1	11.6	10.6	15.3
Todd	NA	NA	3 548	1.4	57.2	12.1	19.5	9 527	7 714	20 035	11.9	2.8	48.3	42.7	44.0	49.9

1. Data for serious crimes have not been adjusted for underreporting; this may affect comparability between geographic areas and over time. 2. Per 100,000 population estimated by the FBI. 3. All persons 3 years old and over enrolled in nursery school through college. 4. Persons 25 years old and over. 5. Elementary and secondary education expenditures. 6. Based on population enumerated as of April 1, 2000.

Table B. States and Counties — **Personal Income**

STATE County	Personal income, 2002 Total (mil dol)	Percent change, 2001–2002	Per capita[1] Dollars	Per capita[1] Rank	Wages and salaries[2] (mil dol)	Proprietor's income (mil dol)	Dividends, interest, and rent (mil dol)	Transfer payments Total (mil dol)	Government payments to individuals Total (mil dol)	Social Security (mil dol)	Medical payments (mil dol)	Income mainte- nance (mil dol)	Unemploy- ment insurance (mil dol)
	62	63	64	65	66	67	68	69	70	71	72	73	74
SOUTH CAROLINA—Cont'd													
Sumter	2 270	4.3	21 577	2 126	1 631	84	338	482	457	149	182	70	16
Union	645	2.0	22 002	2 016	307	32	83	171	164	69	64	16	9
Williamsburg	622	-1.9	17 066	2 986	310	13	84	205	196	58	85	36	9
York	4 570	3.3	26 300	830	2 461	249	624	668	624	265	237	57	33
SOUTH DAKOTA	20 507	0.6	26 967	X	12 562	2 248	4 502	3 085	2 923	1 243	1 190	221	36
Aurora	65	-13.5	22 115	1 983	20	5	22	13	12	6	5	1	0
Beadle	455	-2.5	27 501	616	245	44	112	86	82	35	37	4	1
Bennett	57	-13.5	16 208	3 043	25	-4	13	19	18	4	8	3	0
Bon Homme	157	-6.2	21 955	2 030	59	18	46	31	30	14	12	1	1
Brookings	684	0.0	24 094	1 374	491	41	149	84	78	35	28	4	1
Brown	1 079	2.5	30 925	273	628	147	266	152	145	64	60	7	1
Brule	115	-8.2	22 179	1 964	51	10	32	22	21	9	10	1	0
Buffalo	24	-12.3	12 159	3 103	21	-1	4	10	10	2	5	2	0
Butte	193	1.0	21 344	2 196	69	28	46	38	36	17	13	3	0
Campbell	37	-21.8	21 467	2 158	11	5	12	9	8	4	4	0	0
Charles Mix	209	-8.4	22 674	1 828	96	29	54	48	46	16	21	5	1
Clark	103	-3.5	25 753	940	26	32	25	18	17	9	6	1	0
Clay	322	-1.6	24 338	1 295	163	49	59	45	42	16	16	3	0
Codington	699	1.4	27 091	685	450	82	160	97	92	45	34	5	2
Corson	67	-7.0	15 819	3 056	25	1	15	23	22	4	11	4	1
Custer	182	2.9	24 279	1 316	69	17	49	32	30	15	10	2	1
Davison	545	1.6	29 101	432	351	57	141	85	81	34	37	5	1
Day	154	1.1	25 528	992	55	30	42	32	30	14	12	2	1
Deuel	116	-0.8	26 196	855	45	25	25	19	18	9	7	1	0
Dewey	103	-2.2	16 928	3 001	67	1	18	32	30	6	14	7	1
Douglas	72	-14.0	21 343	2 197	27	12	18	16	15	7	7	1	0
Edmunds	120	-10.7	28 035	545	28	29	32	18	17	8	8	1	0
Fall River	163	0.8	22 200	1 958	91	5	42	43	41	17	14	2	0
Faulk	63	-4.5	25 302	1 045	16	17	18	12	11	6	5	0	0
Grant	209	3.3	27 341	640	116	36	48	34	33	16	14	1	1
Gregory	104	-13.3	22 913	1 748	37	12	36	25	24	11	10	2	0
Haakon	43	-26.8	20 843	2 336	22	-2	17	9	8	4	3	0	0
Hamlin	128	-0.2	22 801	1 783	43	18	28	22	21	10	9	1	0
Hand	80	-18.4	22 447	1 894	33	0	32	17	16	8	6	1	0
Hanson	68	-2.9	20 070	2 532	13	9	19	10	9	6	3	0	0
Harding	23	-17.2	18 107	2 878	11	1	9	4	3	2	1	0	0
Hughes	475	2.1	28 646	479	344	39	106	61	57	26	23	4	1
Hutchinson	193	-7.4	24 596	1 238	67	24	66	37	36	19	14	1	0
Hyde	26	-30.1	16 783	3 007	18	-7	12	7	7	3	3	0	0
Jackson	40	-7.3	14 128	3 090	21	-3	11	14	13	4	5	2	0
Jerauld	56	-12.3	24 926	1 155	29	10	15	12	11	6	5	0	0
Jones	26	-17.6	23 009	1 719	13	3	7	4	4	2	1	0	0
Kingsbury	147	-4.5	26 102	867	52	26	37	29	28	13	12	1	0
Lake	286	1.7	25 825	927	145	38	60	46	43	21	17	2	1
Lawrence	567	5.4	26 252	842	297	93	141	92	87	41	31	4	1
Lincoln	817	4.9	29 428	397	202	96	113	60	54	32	16	2	1
Lyman	73	-16.7	18 628	2 808	38	-3	21	18	17	6	7	2	0
McCook	163	0.4	27 916	563	39	31	33	24	23	11	10	1	1
McPherson	56	-14.0	19 908	2 566	17	6	19	13	12	7	4	1	0
Marshall	116	0.4	26 599	765	37	33	32	20	19	9	7	1	0
Meade	644	3.0	26 210	853	222	91	124	82	77	32	27	6	1
Mellette	33	0.3	16 357	3 037	10	0	7	11	11	2	6	2	0
Miner	58	-7.0	20 638	2 387	20	9	13	13	12	6	5	1	0
Minnehaha	5 001	4.4	32 776	196	4 120	637	882	533	500	224	206	31	7
Moody	181	2.6	27 639	596	70	36	32	23	21	10	8	1	1
Pennington	2 526	4.4	27 759	579	1 892	114	569	373	354	145	139	28	4
Perkins	68	-17.5	20 686	2 375	34	0	25	16	16	7	6	1	0
Potter	66	-16.5	26 145	863	24	0	32	14	13	7	6	0	0
Roberts	223	4.3	22 487	1 881	84	45	43	44	42	17	16	4	1
Sanborn	76	-1.7	29 647	373	20	12	25	11	11	5	4	1	0
Shannon	181	4.8	13 874	3 092	140	3	15	74	71	7	30	19	0
Spink	191	-5.8	26 939	713	65	28	48	55	53	16	34	2	0
Stanley	72	-8.1	26 459	804	31	-2	22	8	8	4	2	1	0
Sully	25	-51.5	16 955	2 998	14	-10	13	5	5	3	2	0	0
Todd	124	5.0	13 243	3 099	93	-3	10	50	48	4	22	13	1

1. Based on the resident population estimated as of July 1 of the year shown.   2. Includes other labor income.

STATE County	Earnings, 2002									Social Security beneficiaries, December 2003		Housing units, 2003	
		Percent by selected industries											
			Goods-related[1]		Service-related and health								
	Total (mil dol)	Farm	Total	Manu-facturing	Infor-mation and profes-sional and technical services	Retail trade	Finance, insur-ance, and real estate	Health services	Govern-ment	Number	Rate[2]	Supple-mental Security Income recipients, December 2003	Total	Percent change, 2000–2003
	75	76	77	78	79	80	81	82	83	84	85	86	87	88
SOUTH CAROLINA—Cont'd														
Sumter	1 715	0.3	D	21.3	3.0	6.5	3.5	8.5	36.4	17 620	166	4 106	42 968	2.9
Union	339	0.5	D	39.3	1.9	8.3	3.2	3.6	25.1	7 550	259	918	13 436	0.6
Williamsburg	323	0.3	D	26.9	D	6.5	4.3	D	24.6	7 170	199	2 184	15 840	1.9
York	2 710	0.6	26.0	20.2	D	8.2	5.9	9.2	14.4	27 220	153	2 748	74 695	13.1
SOUTH DAKOTA	14 810	3.4	17.7	11.1	5.5	8.3	9.7	13.0	19.5	137 880	180	12 574	337 100	4.3
Aurora	26	-0.2	D	D	D	9.7	D	9.9	32.9	725	248	30	1 300	0.2
Beadle	289	2.8	D	10.1	3.6	8.8	7.2	D	21.6	3 825	235	360	8 222	0.2
Bennett	20	-29.9	D	D	D	10.8	D	D	50.0	535	152	145	1 300	1.7
Bon Homme	77	5.8	18.6	11.7	2.5	9.2	4.5	13.7	26.9	1 665	234	73	3 020	0.4
Brookings	532	4.0	D	29.8	3.4	5.4	4.1	4.7	30.2	3 695	131	219	12 122	4.7
Brown	775	4.8	D	12.2	5.5	9.0	7.2	D	15.3	6 945	200	519	16 116	1.6
Brule	62	-2.1	D	0.8	5.7	13.7	5.3	17.4	20.3	990	190	89	2 303	1.4
Buffalo	21	-4.7	D	0.5	D	D	D	D	93.6	235	118	91	625	3.8
Butte	97	-0.7	D	7.1	6.4	11.7	5.0	D	19.0	1 875	204	164	4 156	2.4
Campbell	16	15.2	D	D	D	7.0	D	2.0	21.3	465	277	24	969	0.7
Charles Mix	125	5.5	7.9	2.8	D	8.6	4.5	D	36.4	1 940	211	256	3 885	0.8
Clark	58	45.0	12.4	4.7	2.8	6.2	D	4.1	13.1	1 010	258	77	1 866	-0.7
Clay	212	5.3	4.8	1.4	D	6.3	4.2	9.7	45.2	1 655	125	115	5 578	2.6
Codington	532	3.5	29.7	22.6	D	11.3	7.8	D	13.7	4 875	188	368	11 669	3.0
Corson	26	-1.1	D	D	D	3.9	D	D	74.8	565	132	223	1 564	1.8
Custer	86	-3.3	11.7	2.9	D	9.1	4.3	D	37.4	1 680	221	107	3 871	6.8
Davison	409	0.3	D	18.9	8.2	12.8	4.8	D	10.9	3 850	205	365	8 354	3.2
Day	85	23.9	20.3	10.0	D	7.0	5.2	8.4	16.9	1 655	281	110	3 631	0.4
Deuel	70	22.6	21.6	14.9	D	6.2	3.3	6.9	11.4	1 070	245	56	2 217	2.1
Dewey	68	-7.6	D	D	D	4.2	D	2.2	79.1	830	135	311	2 197	3.0
Douglas	39	16.8	13.9	6.7	D	4.1	D	10.1	14.8	855	258	56	1 457	0.3
Edmunds	57	33.2	D	D	D	8.9	D	3.5	17.4	1 010	239	38	2 044	1.1
Fall River	97	-2.6	4.9	1.3	3.6	7.0	3.6	D	49.7	2 125	291	189	3 902	2.4
Faulk	33	48.1	D	D	D	1.6	2.3	6.3	15.6	625	253	42	1 254	1.5
Grant	151	15.7	D	13.0	2.7	11.3	11.4	7.1	8.5	1 745	229	85	3 507	1.5
Gregory	48	-3.5	D	1.7	5.6	14.7	D	17.7	20.3	1 315	292	114	2 430	1.0
Haakon	20	-38.6	D	D	D	18.8	9.3	D	26.4	470	234	18	1 020	1.8
Hamlin	61	21.1	D	D	D	6.0	D	4.5	24.0	1 145	204	49	2 659	1.3
Hand	34	-10.1	13.0	4.6	D	11.3	D	D	23.7	930	264	51	1 847	0.4
Hanson	22	25.6	D	6.6	D	4.1	D	D	21.2	760	217	25	1 234	1.3
Harding	13	-9.3	D	5.1	D	7.5	D	D	34.9	210	163	7	797	-0.9
Hughes	382	-1.4	D	0.9	6.0	9.4	7.6	11.9	45.0	2 760	165	261	7 260	2.9
Hutchinson	91	15.6	13.5	8.8	D	8.9	D	D	15.7	2 155	279	82	3 533	0.5
Hyde	11	-65.2	D	D	D	22.8	D	D	62.9	400	254	28	769	0.0
Jackson	18	-27.1	6.4	1.2	D	18.1	D	D	68.9	470	165	103	1 201	2.4
Jerauld	39	9.5	D	D	1.3	9.3	4.7	8.1	12.8	700	321	39	1 172	0.4
Jones	16	2.9	D	0.0	D	12.3	8.2	D	31.2	255	235	7	619	0.8
Kingsbury	78	24.0	19.9	14.3	2.9	6.3	7.4	8.8	11.9	1 495	269	71	2 760	1.3
Lake	183	8.7	D	19.3	3.6	7.7	4.6	8.8	19.0	2 245	203	132	5 454	3.3
Lawrence	390	-0.2	29.0	18.4	3.2	8.0	6.8	10.5	15.9	4 355	199	291	10 900	4.5
Lincoln	297	10.9	28.0	13.6	4.7	7.8	6.2	D	9.2	3 450	118	85	11 997	31.4
Lyman	35	-16.7	D	D	D	17.9	D	D	60.9	660	169	70	1 663	1.7
McCook	70	31.3	10.0	5.2	4.8	9.3	3.4	D	14.1	1 230	210	63	2 462	3.3
McPherson	23	15.6	D	4.9	D	3.8	D	10.6	23.5	840	308	36	1 455	-0.7
Marshall	69	39.4	16.1	12.4	D	4.3	D	5.3	15.1	1 105	259	48	2 594	1.2
Meade	313	-1.2	12.0	5.1	5.2	6.0	9.6	D	37.6	3 800	154	250	10 659	5.0
Mellette	10	-1.4	D	1.8	D	9.0	D	D	63.8	315	149	104	845	2.5
Miner	29	20.8	D	D	D	8.0	D	D	20.1	700	258	29	1 399	-0.6
Minnehaha	4 758	0.6	D	10.2	6.8	8.2	17.9	16.8	9.3	22 840	148	2 014	64 215	6.6
Moody	106	28.0	16.5	8.3	D	3.2	D	5.3	28.5	1 155	177	55	2 753	0.3
Pennington	2 005	-0.1	15.6	7.5	6.6	9.5	6.4	16.1	24.6	15 625	170	1 622	39 217	5.3
Perkins	34	-16.8	D	D	3.3	11.3	D	11.3	25.3	815	256	69	1 875	1.1
Potter	24	-10.2	19.0	9.8	D	8.4	6.8	13.8	24.6	745	297	28	1 807	2.7
Roberts	129	26.5	D	3.5	D	6.3	2.9	6.6	34.3	2 000	197	227	4 788	1.1
Sanborn	32	26.1	D	D	D	3.6	D	D	16.9	580	222	42	1 214	-0.5
Shannon	143	0.0	D	0.0	D	D	D	D	84.1	1 195	90	969	3 253	4.2
Spink	93	25.1	4.2	0.7	D	4.5	4.9	3.6	34.7	1 720	247	159	3 330	-0.7
Stanley	28	-20.9	50.4	0.4	D	11.1	2.2	0.8	19.4	455	165	8	1 342	5.1
Sully	4	-247.8	D	2.5	D	45.3	D	D	89.4	320	220	6	866	2.6
Todd	90	-3.8	0.8	0.1	1.7	3.1	D	3.9	86.3	730	77	486	2 845	2.9

1. Covers mining, construction, and manufacturing.   2. Per 1,000 resident population estimated as of July 1 of the year shown.

STATE County	Housing units, 2000 Total	Owner-occupied Percent	Median value[1]	Median owner cost as a percent of income With a mortgage	Without a mortgage[2]	Renter-occupied Median rent[3]	Median rent as a percent of income	Substandard units[4] (percent)	Civilian labor force, 2003 Total	Percent change, 2002–2003	Unemployment Total	Rate[5]	Civilian employment,[6] 2000 Total	Percent Management, professional and related occupations	Production, transportation, and material moving occupations
	89	90	91	92	93	94	95	96	97	98	99	100	101	102	103
SOUTH CAROLINA—Cont'd															
Sumter	37 728	69.5	78 700	19.5	9.9	461	23.6	4.2	46 235	4.0	3 641	7.9	41 372	24.9	23.1
Union	12 087	76.7	61 900	19.7	10.6	373	23.0	3.4	13 440	-2.9	1 833	13.6	12 896	19.3	32.9
Williamsburg	13 714	80.7	63 300	20.9	10.9	291	28.2	6.1	14 762	6.6	2 672	18.1	13 644	22.6	26.6
York	61 051	73.1	119 600	20.7	9.9	581	23.6	3.5	92 316	3.8	7 845	8.5	81 476	29.6	19.6
SOUTH DAKOTA	290 245	68.2	79 600	19.7	10.5	426	22.9	3.6	424 876	1.4	15 270	3.6	374 373	32.6	14.2
Aurora	1 165	76.1	32 600	16.6	10.9	309	20.3	4.0	1 102	-8.2	39	3.5	1 447	39.7	13.7
Beadle	7 210	67.7	56 000	18.1	12.0	366	23.5	2.0	8 782	-0.9	419	4.8	8 417	32.0	20.1
Bennett	1 123	59.5	36 500	18.2	10.2	358	28.3	14.1	1 091	-0.5	58	5.3	1 238	40.5	7.7
Bon Homme	2 635	76.1	46 100	17.9	12.3	300	17.0	2.6	3 150	1.3	83	2.6	3 088	38.5	15.5
Brookings	10 665	58.2	88 500	19.2	9.9	396	23.4	1.7	17 615	4.2	360	2.0	16 369	32.1	18.6
Brown	14 638	66.3	72 700	18.7	10.8	375	22.0	1.7	21 595	0.9	578	2.7	18 917	30.1	13.7
Brule	1 998	71.2	64 900	19.7	12.1	378	18.7	3.3	2 681	0.0	74	2.8	2 501	40.5	7.4
Buffalo	526	43.2	26 300	17.5	25.0	319	21.3	21.1	884	4.4	64	7.2	433	31.6	7.2
Butte	3 516	73.4	60 200	21.1	14.4	401	21.8	2.9	4 003	1.4	171	4.3	4 415	27.0	15.7
Campbell	725	82.1	27 400	19.1	11.7	279	15.2	0.8	902	4.8	61	6.8	838	42.6	10.5
Charles Mix	3 343	68.3	49 100	20.2	12.8	307	21.4	6.8	4 855	0.5	171	3.5	3 656	37.7	8.8
Clark	1 598	80.7	36 700	20.8	12.0	334	23.3	2.4	1 766	-2.9	115	6.5	1 882	36.3	13.1
Clay	4 878	54.4	79 500	18.6	9.9	440	31.8	1.9	7 811	3.1	120	1.5	6 872	35.1	8.1
Codington	10 357	70.1	84 200	19.8	10.5	401	24.2	1.6	15 224	1.4	693	4.6	13 951	26.4	24.0
Corson	1 271	59.2	21 600	18.7	11.2	266	17.3	16.8	1 574	2.7	115	7.3	1 248	41.4	7.7
Custer	2 970	77.0	89 100	21.2	10.0	349	20.2	2.8	3 832	1.8	149	3.9	3 409	34.6	12.9
Davison	7 585	61.8	71 600	18.4	11.3	388	23.9	2.8	10 936	1.8	301	2.8	9 562	29.9	16.7
Day	2 586	76.1	33 100	17.5	10.3	303	20.9	2.3	3 073	0.4	227	7.4	2 701	35.6	13.9
Deuel	1 843	80.0	44 400	19.4	10.8	303	20.3	2.0	2 613	3.4	122	4.7	2 223	35.0	19.4
Dewey	1 863	55.3	36 000	18.1	14.9	308	21.7	14.4	2 738	5.8	380	13.9	1 978	35.4	10.3
Douglas	1 321	81.0	34 600	18.6	12.6	300	18.5	3.9	1 656	2.5	44	2.7	1 596	41.9	12.6
Edmunds	1 681	82.0	42 000	17.8	12.7	270	20.5	2.3	2 333	0.6	51	2.2	1 976	37.8	11.5
Fall River	3 127	69.5	54 300	19.9	13.1	369	24.0	4.7	3 436	1.3	155	4.5	3 167	34.7	13.2
Faulk	1 014	81.5	31 600	17.1	10.1	270	17.6	3.8	1 113	1.5	30	2.7	1 164	40.6	8.7
Grant	3 116	77.4	60 400	17.5	9.9	350	27.6	1.7	4 568	1.9	196	4.3	3 763	31.1	15.5
Gregory	2 022	74.7	32 700	18.9	11.9	264	19.0	2.4	2 667	2.3	89	3.3	2 186	39.2	9.1
Haakon	870	76.9	46 200	17.8	11.8	364	17.8	3.8	1 094	-0.4	28	2.6	1 139	37.4	14.7
Hamlin	2 048	81.8	49 300	19.7	12.5	329	18.9	4.5	2 692	1.8	116	4.3	2 500	30.9	20.8
Hand	1 543	74.1	45 700	19.0	10.0	306	22.4	1.2	2 018	-1.7	48	2.4	1 853	40.9	7.9
Hanson	1 115	79.2	45 900	18.4	11.9	322	17.3	5.6	1 989	2.3	56	2.8	1 466	33.0	17.3
Harding	525	73.7	47 100	23.6	17.8	318	18.6	2.9	779	1.3	27	3.5	681	54.3	4.4
Hughes	6 512	66.2	94 400	18.2	9.9	404	21.3	2.9	10 241	-0.7	247	2.4	8 887	40.7	6.8
Hutchinson	3 190	78.8	42 000	18.1	12.1	314	21.0	2.9	3 852	-0.3	134	3.5	3 623	37.0	13.6
Hyde	679	71.6	33 800	21.0	12.2	310	18.1	0.9	842	4.9	25	3.0	788	47.0	5.7
Jackson	945	63.6	31 500	18.3	12.2	335	19.1	16.3	1 169	6.5	95	8.1	955	42.7	8.6
Jerauld	987	72.1	39 000	17.7	10.6	317	19.8	2.8	1 619	5.1	33	2.0	1 109	35.4	15.0
Jones	509	72.5	38 700	17.1	12.3	338	22.7	1.0	863	9.7	13	1.5	642	37.7	8.7
Kingsbury	2 406	76.1	42 900	17.2	9.9	315	21.3	1.7	2 740	-1.1	120	4.4	2 706	34.9	22.2
Lake	4 372	70.5	73 800	20.2	9.9	382	22.3	1.5	6 318	-1.8	264	4.2	5 933	29.5	17.0
Lawrence	8 881	64.8	87 700	21.4	11.8	416	24.7	2.7	11 876	1.2	353	3.0	10 487	28.8	11.5
Lincoln	8 782	79.7	104 100	20.3	9.9	559	21.8	1.7	16 496	1.6	322	2.0	13 371	33.8	14.0
Lyman	1 400	68.8	44 100	17.6	11.8	288	18.5	8.9	2 517	2.1	102	4.1	1 692	42.7	7.7
McCook	2 204	78.9	57 400	18.5	11.6	375	20.1	3.1	2 427	-0.4	95	3.9	2 777	34.5	15.2
McPherson	1 227	83.2	20 100	18.2	13.9	253	18.3	1.6	1 316	-2.4	54	4.1	1 190	38.9	10.7
Marshall	1 844	77.9	41 300	18.3	11.4	302	19.5	2.9	2 098	2.8	124	5.9	1 986	36.5	17.3
Meade	8 805	68.2	82 200	20.9	11.3	468	22.0	3.2	14 433	2.9	480	3.3	11 172	27.4	14.8
Mellette	694	65.0	25 800	12.2	11.8	279	28.1	11.1	798	3.5	61	7.6	768	43.8	6.3
Miner	1 212	76.4	26 500	21.2	10.2	333	18.5	1.4	1 193	-1.2	57	4.8	1 396	36.5	22.0
Minnehaha	57 996	64.7	101 200	20.2	9.9	516	23.1	2.5	96 149	1.8	2 943	3.1	82 806	30.7	14.7
Moody	2 526	72.5	58 500	19.3	9.9	381	19.7	3.0	3 590	0.1	267	7.4	3 380	30.8	16.6
Pennington	34 641	66.2	90 900	20.9	9.9	497	25.5	3.3	50 979	1.6	1 702	3.3	44 384	31.8	12.1
Perkins	1 429	76.6	33 200	19.5	12.6	293	20.5	2.4	1 940	-1.8	54	2.8	1 612	43.8	13.0
Potter	1 145	79.1	42 800	19.9	10.5	318	20.3	1.2	1 372	-1.3	34	2.5	1 291	37.3	9.6
Roberts	3 683	68.9	43 500	18.8	10.1	305	18.8	4.9	4 961	2.7	296	6.0	4 223	34.8	12.0
Sanborn	1 043	77.7	30 300	16.1	9.9	301	19.5	2.8	1 617	1.1	49	3.0	1 341	35.9	17.6
Shannon	2 785	49.6	25 900	18.6	10.1	304	18.0	49.0	4 187	4.0	581	13.9	2 601	37.8	9.0
Spink	2 847	73.8	34 500	18.5	10.9	325	22.0	2.8	3 278	1.0	96	2.9	3 184	34.0	10.7
Stanley	1 111	76.6	83 900	18.4	9.9	440	20.2	2.5	1 708	-0.5	55	3.2	1 706	34.8	11.5
Sully	630	75.9	55 600	19.2	10.6	343	17.5	1.4	928	4.5	13	1.4	787	41.7	9.4
Todd	2 462	45.0	27 500	19.9	11.9	272	17.7	24.0	3 341	0.0	278	8.3	2 612	36.9	9.4

1. Specified owner-occupied units. 2. Median monthly owner costs is often in the minimum category—9.9 percent or less, which is indicated as 9.9 percent. 3. Specified renter-occupied units. 4. Overcrowded or lacking complete plumbing facilities. 5. Percent of civilian labor force. 6. Persons 16 years old and over.

	Private nonfarm establishments, employment and payroll, 2001								Agriculture, 2002			
	Employment						Annual payroll		Farms			
										Percent with—		Farm operators whose principal occupation is farming (percent)
STATE County	Number of establishments	Total	Health care and social assistance	Manufacturing	Retail trade	Finance and insurance	Professional, scientific, and technical services	Total (mil dol)	Average per employee (dollars)	Number	Less than 50 acres	500 acres and over	
	104	105	106	107	108	109	110	111	112	113	114	115	116
SOUTH CAROLINA—Cont'd													
Sumter	1 875	35 830	3 774	12 719	4 759	1 024	712	867	24 197	537	42.8	12.5	46.0
Union	511	7 940	849	3 848	1 185	248	112	176	22 215	299	31.8	6.0	49.2
Williamsburg	526	7 155	439	2 540	937	202	126	156	21 775	681	27.0	15.9	43.6
York	3 852	54 529	5 675	12 501	7 671	1 511	1 881	1 594	29 229	858	42.8	5.0	44.6
SOUTH DAKOTA	24 032	310 035	51 759	47 077	49 835	24 303	8 108	7 613	24 556	31 736	13.6	49.0	72.6
Aurora	99	437	D	D	104	36	25	7	16 602	401	9.5	49.1	70.6
Beadle	596	6 324	1 177	828	1 015	487	91	140	22 193	728	15.5	51.4	72.5
Bennett	71	594	122	D	119	D	D	11	17 998	231	2.6	71.4	85.7
Bon Homme	207	1 657	450	345	267	80	12	30	17 965	665	11.0	39.8	76.7
Brookings	751	12 201	1 319	4 622	1 622	504	239	266	21 821	962	22.6	28.3	58.7
Brown	1 320	17 285	2 912	2 268	3 114	734	419	388	22 463	1 155	18.1	46.4	70.0
Brule	217	1 715	427	D	297	68	37	30	17 567	365	9.6	60.0	76.4
Buffalo	9	171	D	0	D	0	D	3	16 988	73	4.1	74.0	68.5
Butte	282	1 932	226	163	521	81	110	39	19 971	639	12.2	46.9	71.2
Campbell	51	313	D	D	26	D	7	5	17 256	293	6.8	60.8	72.4
Charles Mix	291	2 480	537	94	471	108	50	44	17 771	755	10.6	52.3	83.4
Clark	127	701	99	158	95	D	19	12	16 632	588	11.1	47.4	68.9
Clay	306	3 279	537	101	1 151	103	46	46	13 880	536	15.1	52.4	78.9
Codington	1 000	13 154	1 414	3 961	2 379	882	190	297	22 607	694	25.8	32.4	60.5
Corson	48	250	11	D	50	D	D	3	13 652	344	4.1	80.5	85.8
Custer	210	1 006	126	25	177	40	24	22	21 699	303	15.5	42.6	63.7
Davison	745	10 871	1 671	1 736	2 740	359	396	241	22 135	481	26.0	31.6	61.7
Day	195	1 454	330	210	238	68	23	26	18 182	704	9.7	39.2	64.5
Deuel	136	929	205	166	133	57	20	22	23 350	583	13.0	34.8	67.9
Dewey	98	1 329	604	D	212	25	8	32	23 734	358	3.6	72.9	77.7
Douglas	118	784	D	87	121	33	14	13	16 425	394	14.5	44.4	76.9
Edmunds	121	758	130	D	190	47	13	16	21 005	386	7.3	62.2	77.2
Fall River	205	2 268	D	15	334	48	48	70	31 033	278	9.4	68.0	77.7
Faulk	76	356	D	D	98	19	8	6	16 478	265	3.8	77.0	86.8
Grant	264	3 087	342	381	441	325	56	71	22 993	548	13.0	38.1	72.1
Gregory	191	1 096	264	23	243	80	34	18	16 601	587	8.9	58.4	80.4
Haakon	93	612	D	D	78	46	12	12	19 243	268	3.0	77.6	85.1
Hamlin	144	865	168	149	209	63	6	17	19 743	451	17.3	41.2	69.4
Hand	132	933	205	D	150	D	23	17	18 029	480	7.1	67.1	79.4
Hanson	52	227	D	D	D	31	D	6	25 485	319	17.6	48.6	74.3
Harding	37	167	82	0	D	D	4	3	16 192	223	4.0	87.4	91.0
Hughes	634	6 151	1 198	81	1 254	409	195	127	20 595	258	14.3	53.1	66.7
Hutchinson	251	2 220	609	474	352	114	35	44	19 981	768	12.4	48.4	78.9
Hyde	45	523	D	D	23	10	8	11	21 231	187	4.8	70.6	80.7
Jackson	52	268	D	D	136	D	D	4	15 925	308	2.9	76.9	84.1
Jerauld	70	393	67	D	126	D	7	7	17 450	272	8.1	47.1	71.3
Jones	49	265	D	D	111	23	D	6	22 170	163	3.7	74.8	88.3
Kingsbury	209	1 344	255	281	233	108	32	27	20 304	599	14.9	48.1	76.8
Lake	342	3 646	688	988	560	120	57	78	21 374	513	18.7	42.3	66.1
Lawrence	841	8 365	1 091	592	1 289	201	169	172	20 547	239	18.4	28.5	54.4
Lincoln	666	6 236	888	859	986	291	109	174	27 856	841	27.2	25.3	64.2
Lyman	80	608	D	0	311	25	D	10	15 666	420	7.6	64.3	70.7
McCook	177	1 132	271	173	218	53	48	21	18 934	539	17.8	44.2	75.3
McPherson	92	445	132	41	53	60	D	7	15 672	413	5.3	62.2	69.0
Marshall	147	1 413	256	371	170	203	26	30	21 490	529	10.4	52.7	78.8
Meade	544	4 455	1 391	228	669	194	136	110	24 637	895	12.4	58.3	73.3
Mellette	33	155	D	0	45	D	6	2	14 942	200	4.5	78.5	84.5
Miner	69	613	141	D	90	D	D	12	19 328	370	7.6	44.9	71.4
Minnehaha	5 173	99 375	17 231	11 913	13 236	13 506	2 979	2 720	27 367	1 209	32.1	24.2	61.9
Moody	174	1 509	120	225	184	44	63	35	22 929	580	21.6	30.5	69.1
Pennington	3 282	42 953	7 061	4 615	6 876	2 602	1 480	1 050	24 449	696	18.8	41.8	65.2
Perkins	135	1 029	154	182	344	60	17	17	16 787	452	2.9	81.6	83.2
Potter	135	856	182	D	210	72	11	14	16 266	256	9.4	57.4	80.5
Roberts	255	1 883	502	97	400	93	32	30	16 007	936	12.7	39.9	77.1
Sanborn	62	556	D	D	70	23	17	9	16 424	394	8.1	46.7	67.0
Shannon	61	1 678	301	D	206	D	11	36	21 583	200	6.0	60.0	67.5
Spink	173	1 092	265	33	234	86	24	21	19 042	682	8.1	61.9	76.1
Stanley	93	847	0	D	116	D	26	18	21 651	166	8.4	72.9	71.7
Sully	59	240	D	D	86	30	6	5	19 229	228	5.3	68.4	70.2
Todd	65	1 159	254	0	178	D	D	27	22 956	249	2.8	73.5	79.9

STATE County	Agriculture, 2002 (cont'd)															
	Land in farms					Value of land and buildings (dollars)		Value of machinery and equipment average per farm (dollars)	Value of products sold				Percent of farms with sales of —		Government payments	
			Acres								Percent from —					
	Acreage (1,000)	Percent change, 1997–2002	Average size of farm	Total irrigated (1,000)	Total cropland (1,000)	Average per farm	Average per acre		Total (mil dol)	Average per farm (dollars)	Crops	Live-stock and poultry products	$10,000 or more	$100,000 or more	Total ($1,000)	Percent of farms
	117	118	119	120	121	122	123	124	125	126	127	128	129	130	131	132
SOUTH CAROLINA—Cont'd																
Sumter	136	-2.2	253	6	85	511 947	1 958	62 688	55	102 692	27.7	72.3	25.1	10.4	1 378	39.3
Union	51	-3.8	170	0	16	253 665	1 747	24 437	2	5 763	D	D	14.0	0.7	67	15.4
Williamsburg	206	9.0	302	1	101	473 907	1 655	61 329	28	40 594	80.9	19.1	25.7	8.8	2 734	60.1
York	119	3.5	139	1	54	501 077	4 067	42 844	83	96 588	D	D	19.1	3.3	382	13.5
SOUTH DAKOTA	43 785	-1.3	1 380	401	20 318	618 651	442	107 376	3 835	120 829	41.1	58.9	68.1	30.5	215 084	63.8
Aurora	351	2.3	875	0	226	531 725	592	76 345	52	129 315	22.7	77.3	71.6	23.9	2 294	68.1
Beadle	810	14.6	1 112	15	587	579 803	537	126 196	97	133 774	36.6	63.4	67.3	30.6	6 282	65.1
Bennett	727	-8.8	3 148	7	233	756 355	241	107 213	23	100 621	27.5	72.5	83.1	36.4	1 775	62.3
Bon Homme	345	10.9	518	7	272	450 616	787	96 869	67	100 095	36.0	64.0	78.6	25.7	3 097	63.8
Brookings	418	2.5	435	16	329	410 408	871	84 061	98	101 449	43.8	56.2	55.1	24.2	5 369	66.9
Brown	1 155	7.9	1 000	6	897	753 590	737	163 102	169	146 469	66.0	34.0	60.3	35.2	11 567	67.7
Brule	447	-3.0	1 225	3	265	558 852	493	115 520	51	139 627	24.2	75.8	74.0	31.5	2 878	64.9
Buffalo	285	-5.6	3 903	2	77	1 071 568	272	146 393	13	181 073	15.3	84.7	67.1	32.9	780	50.7
Butte	1 262	8.2	1 976	81	226	507 408	263	69 720	57	88 857	21.9	78.1	68.5	26.3	2 659	44.0
Campbell	391	-1.3	1 335	3	212	396 745	314	89 456	25	86 518	41.7	58.3	60.4	25.6	2 309	80.9
Charles Mix	736	8.2	975	12	516	663 908	596	118 757	97	128 002	37.9	62.1	75.0	30.7	5 453	71.8
Clark	526	2.3	894	5	365	548 288	633	116 886	102	174 250	31.1	68.9	63.6	31.3	4 875	78.2
Clay	373	65.0	695	16	342	808 682	1 276	138 760	75	140 047	87.6	12.4	80.6	50.4	3 202	66.6
Codington	387	0.5	557	10	290	391 851	738	97 822	74	106 069	46.4	53.6	59.1	26.8	3 937	60.8
Corson	1 389	-13.5	4 038	1	369	709 312	172	102 886	38	109 330	10.6	89.4	78.5	36.9	2 566	68.3
Custer	589	23.7	1 944	4	95	751 595	387	58 119	12	41 156	7.5	92.5	49.5	12.9	477	30.4
Davison	279	1.8	579	2	223	424 175	709	94 460	43	88 860	43.7	56.3	56.8	23.9	2 155	51.6
Day	531	-0.9	754	2	375	453 756	601	84 535	57	80 613	62.8	37.2	54.3	20.2	6 415	78.8
Deuel	328	5.5	562	1	220	391 810	708	80 157	66	112 751	34.0	66.0	58.8	24.4	4 714	73.4
Dewey	1 368	-26.1	3 821	D	256	837 805	213	103 857	29	80 811	4.4	95.6	70.7	27.4	2 209	58.7
Douglas	237	-4.0	601	1	183	451 676	656	115 440	62	157 793	22.8	77.2	77.4	38.1	1 726	62.2
Edmunds	585	-7.9	1 516	D	380	699 849	465	134 918	75	194 441	41.6	58.4	69.4	37.6	3 368	72.8
Fall River	982	0.4	3 533	14	144	902 622	254	70 349	51	184 541	4.5	95.5	69.1	21.6	990	44.2
Faulk	535	-6.3	2 018	D	338	769 011	391	155 254	64	240 178	52.7	47.3	83.4	51.3	2 539	76.6
Grant	350	-2.5	639	5	273	487 085	728	108 022	82	149 956	47.8	52.2	68.4	34.3	4 355	73.2
Gregory	651	15.0	1 109	1	330	466 571	396	77 074	44	74 364	22.9	77.1	78.2	24.2	2 600	56.9
Haakon	1 222	-7.8	4 558	D	473	992 949	218	128 157	39	145 042	15.8	84.2	77.2	44.0	3 269	67.9
Hamlin	307	10.0	681	7	252	558 248	792	112 320	58	128 817	62.3	37.7	67.8	37.3	3 363	76.1
Hand	868	7.0	1 809	4	509	585 596	347	129 414	77	160 294	34.2	65.8	74.6	36.7	4 907	72.5
Hanson	249	7.8	780	1	203	662 725	770	165 090	49	152 243	48.8	51.2	72.4	32.6	1 818	72.7
Harding	1 674	-1.6	7 507	1	212	1 120 983	149	133 182	31	137 508	D	D	84.3	48.9	2 094	62.8
Hughes	368	-5.9	1 425	8	225	662 079	441	116 980	21	82 993	49.0	51.0	62.4	24.4	2 248	65.5
Hutchinson	506	5.6	658	2	413	527 261	800	130 154	99	128 954	44.7	55.3	76.8	34.8	3 943	69.8
Hyde	469	-11.8	2 507	D	189	742 297	302	122 996	23	122 032	21.2	78.8	78.6	41.2	1 759	64.7
Jackson	1 191	-12.0	3 866	2	246	785 834	200	84 070	23	76 157	8.7	91.3	76.3	26.3	1 776	56.2
Jerauld	336	-2.9	1 237	1	192	515 545	401	96 024	34	125 282	28.7	71.3	61.4	26.5	1 678	70.6
Jones	516	-12.4	3 169	1	191	866 379	267	112 212	19	113 797	25.9	74.1	71.2	39.3	2 123	75.5
Kingsbury	519	7.9	866	1	426	659 838	743	108 708	86	143 913	45.1	54.9	73.1	33.4	4 915	66.4
Lake	325	5.9	634	1	263	686 682	982	111 814	67	129 664	54.4	45.6	68.0	35.1	3 328	64.5
Lawrence	141	-17.5	589	4	40	544 288	724	38 251	10	41 804	9.9	90.1	47.3	10.0	247	24.3
Lincoln	310	-2.8	368	1	277	689 097	1 673	105 197	88	104 599	62.8	37.2	70.4	29.5	3 448	55.6
Lyman	885	-6.3	2 108	9	392	737 503	344	122 712	42	100 431	33.5	66.5	61.7	29.3	5 302	75.5
McCook	345	10.6	640	D	284	555 569	860	103 440	73	134 932	57.6	42.4	69.8	38.4	3 310	67.5
McPherson	537	-5.6	1 300	1	290	476 620	346	92 230	60	146 208	10.8	89.2	60.3	23.7	2 978	78.0
Marshall	525	4.0	992	2	340	577 637	603	120 780	101	191 829	35.9	64.1	63.7	31.9	5 081	77.7
Meade	2 229	7.5	2 490	6	538	704 033	268	83 831	66	74 160	9.5	90.5	64.6	22.1	3 210	41.7
Mellette	660	0.8	3 302	1	125	680 640	208	79 489	31	153 053	D	D	81.5	33.0	919	50.0
Miner	291	3.9	787	D	210	486 794	695	89 173	41	111 144	48.3	51.7	71.9	29.2	2 229	67.0
Minnehaha	422	3.9	349	1	365	490 218	1 461	96 702	120	99 184	56.0	44.0	60.5	25.4	5 229	53.6
Moody	283	-0.4	488	2	237	630 638	1 205	106 472	78	134 267	49.6	50.4	66.6	30.5	3 760	66.4
Pennington	1 210	15.9	1 738	12	332	602 796	351	59 655	43	61 981	24.5	75.5	53.9	16.2	2 097	33.6
Perkins	1 782	4.5	3 942	0	491	737 409	189	99 756	46	100 782	6.3	93.7	78.8	34.7	3 727	65.9
Potter	453	-14.5	1 769	D	314	813 069	442	167 668	29	113 718	57.4	42.6	64.5	29.7	3 286	73.0
Roberts	593	3.9	633	4	449	410 297	700	84 690	88	94 021	64.1	35.9	62.7	28.0	5 290	73.7
Sanborn	380	9.5	965	0	264	487 531	487	108 430	43	108 351	37.5	62.5	71.1	25.6	2 685	65.5
Shannon	1 267	-14.0	6 333	D	164	1 047 724	168	63 339	13	64 898	6.6	93.4	54.5	18.0	984	39.0
Spink	911	7.3	1 336	18	722	828 950	564	143 176	134	196 792	61.3	38.7	74.6	46.8	7 783	76.0
Stanley	866	-3.3	5 219	D	223	1 081 307	208	157 889	18	107 000	33.6	66.4	64.5	28.9	2 049	54.8
Sully	573	-4.3	2 515	19	456	1 202 997	482	186 002	36	157 122	72.0	28.0	68.4	39.0	4 590	81.6
Todd	917	-15.4	3 681	4	187	782 287	208	76 150	27	107 410	14.7	85.3	77.5	32.5	890	41.4

Table B. States and Counties — Residential Construction, Wholesale Trade, Retail Trade, and Real Estate

STATE County	Value of residential construction authorized by building permits, 2003		Wholesale trade, 1997				Retail trade,[1] 1997				Real estate and rental and leasing, 1997			
	New construction ($1,000)	Number of housing units	Number of establishments	Number of employees	Sales (mil dol)	Annual payroll (mil dol)	Number of establishments	Number of employees	Sales (mil dol)	Annual payroll (mil dol)	Number of establishments	Number of employees	Receipts (mil dol)	Annual payroll (mil dol)
	133	134	135	136	137	138	139	140	141	142	143	144	145	146
SOUTH CAROLINA—Cont'd														
Sumter	55 151	653	84	671	208.6	18.1	425	4 841	782.0	72.8	74	277	26.6	4.3
Union	5 955	47	13	38	14.2	1.1	113	1 228	155.2	15.0	17	51	3.1	0.7
Williamsburg	1 092	51	39	367	98.0	7.0	146	1 006	155.6	13.3	6	31	1.0	0.3
York	409 159	2 785	267	3 598	3 001.9	124.2	615	7 155	1 244.4	112.7	120	486	46.0	9.8
SOUTH DAKOTA	540 686	4 986	1 402	15 509	7 874.2	389.8	4 311	45 867	11 707.1	689.6	719	2 951	245.7	45.1
Aurora	381	7	4	38	13.4	1.1	18	D	D	D	3	3	0.1	0.0
Beadle	3 689	26	27	279	183.9	5.8	120	1 082	152.9	15.5	24	99	4.0	1.0
Bennett	0	0	4	59	44.9	0.5	21	D	D	D	1	D	D	D
Bon Homme	35	1	17	129	51.4	1.8	43	D	D	D	5	17	0.6	0.0
Brookings	11 284	145	29	505	265.8	8.3	139	1 513	169.2	17.5	28	80	5.7	0.8
Brown	8 479	109	83	897	637.3	21.5	237	3 128	497.4	47.9	50	123	11.6	2.0
Brule	1 826	17	9	94	36.5	1.7	51	D	D	D	2	D	D	D
Buffalo	NA	NA	NA	NA	NA	NA	2	D	D	D	2	D	D	D
Butte	1 607	20	19	139	83.1	2.4	59	402	66.7	6.5	10	D	D	D
Campbell	0	0	6	D	D	D	10	D	D	D	1	D	D	D
Charles Mix	233	3	16	120	63.6	2.3	73	497	63.9	5.7	4	5	0.4	0.0
Clark	333	4	7	76	80.6	1.4	16	D	D	D	3	4	0.1	0.0
Clay	3 099	24	9	44	18.3	1.2	52	493	75.4	6.8	12	24	2.0	0.3
Codington	19 975	151	74	560	320.7	15.8	191	2 382	347.2	32.8	33	94	7.5	1.3
Corson	0	0	5	D	D	D	14	D	D	D	NA	NA	NA	NA
Custer	10 150	115	2	D	D	D	32	D	D	D	9	19	2.6	0.5
Davison	6 828	90	36	504	216.7	12.6	153	1 747	230.7	21.8	27	64	4.0	0.5
Day	1 717	22	7	85	53.2	1.8	42	D	D	D	5	9	0.7	0.1
Deuel	3 940	24	6	19	7.6	0.2	26	D	D	D	1	D	D	D
Dewey	0	0	6	33	12.6	0.7	27	D	D	D	2	D	D	D
Douglas	0	0	9	60	17.4	1.2	18	D	D	D	1	D	D	D
Edmunds	157	2	11	147	101.5	3.3	21	D	D	D	4	8	0.3	0.1
Fall River	988	8	6	31	5.5	0.5	45	D	D	D	5	6	0.9	0.1
Faulk	3 820	23	6	25	10.6	0.4	11	D	D	D	1	D	D	D
Grant	2 866	28	18	413	106.2	7.4	55	451	68.1	5.3	2	D	D	D
Gregory	267	4	14	88	39.2	1.3	44	D	D	D	3	6	0.2	0.1
Haakon	0	0	10	124	62.4	1.6	20	D	D	D	1	D	D	D
Hamlin	4 840	35	10	60	38.3	1.4	29	D	D	D	3	3	0.1	0.0
Hand	905	14	12	156	58.5	3.0	22	D	D	D	2	D	D	D
Hanson	NA	NA	9	30	34.3	0.5	10	D	D	D	1	D	D	D
Harding	50	1	2	D	D	D	6	28	4.9	0.5	NA	NA	NA	NA
Hughes	10 421	68	22	159	85.8	4.2	121	1 221	194.7	17.4	19	102	4.0	0.9
Hutchinson	966	8	23	245	147.3	5.3	53	D	D	D	2	D	D	D
Hyde	0	0	3	D	D	D	11	D	D	D	NA	NA	NA	NA
Jackson	0	0	2	D	D	D	17	D	D	D	1	D	D	D
Jerauld	180	2	6	D	D	D	16	D	D	D	2	D	D	D
Jones	0	0	3	9	7.5	0.3	13	D	D	D	1	D	D	D
Kingsbury	1 810	16	10	94	69.3	2.4	40	D	D	D	3	7	0.3	0.0
Lake	7 342	61	12	125	81.0	3.5	67	581	115.0	10.4	14	25	1.8	0.3
Lawrence	32 921	246	21	59	12.1	0.9	147	1 334	226.1	18.6	35	134	8.9	1.2
Lincoln	34 719	335	39	305	200.4	8.0	72	625	150.5	11.1	7	65	2.8	1.6
Lyman	420	7	5	D	D	D	18	D	D	D	NA	NA	NA	NA
McCook	2 935	28	13	53	33.5	1.0	31	D	D	D	2	D	D	D
McPherson	460	4	2	D	D	D	16	D	D	D	3	4	0.2	0.0
Marshall	892	18	10	82	43.0	1.2	23	D	D	D	NA	NA	NA	NA
Meade	26 398	213	22	134	94.8	2.4	81	630	115.9	9.8	16	77	4.1	0.8
Mellette	0	0	NA	NA	NA	NA	9	58	5.1	0.5	1	D	D	D
Miner	1 190	10	8	39	19.9	0.7	15	D	D	D	NA	NA	NA	NA
Minnehaha	208 677	2 135	356	5 412	2 145.1	163.3	770	12 238	1 999.4	191.7	185	947	97.5	17.4
Moody	285	2	6	32	13.1	0.8	23	D	D	D	5	D	D	D
Pennington	82 240	645	173	2 027	675.7	57.8	581	6 870	1 132.0	112.2	126	530	52.7	9.0
Perkins	109	1	8	62	49.4	0.8	26	159	15.8	1.8	1	D	D	D
Potter	170	1	11	98	57.3	2.3	28	D	D	D	2	D	D	D
Roberts	5 042	49	19	144	202.6	2.6	49	D	D	D	1	D	D	D
Sanborn	806	8	9	39	15.6	0.7	8	D	D	D	1	D	D	D
Shannon	NA	NA	NA	NA	NA	NA	15	D	D	D	1	D	D	D
Spink	164	3	16	146	133.0	3.8	39	261	51.7	4.0	3	6	0.2	0.0
Stanley	2 998	21	5	D	D	D	19	D	D	D	1	D	D	D
Sully	716	6	4	D	D	D	14	D	D	D	1	D	D	D
Todd	0	0	1	D	D	D	17	D	D	D	1	D	D	D

1. Establishments with payroll.

STATE County	Professional, scientific, and technical services,[1] 1997				Manufacturing, 1997				Accommodation and foodservices, 1997			
	Number of establish- ments	Number of employees	Receipts (mil dol)	Annual payroll (mil dol)	Number of establish- ments	Number of employees	Receipts (mil dol)	Annual payroll (mil dol)	Number of establish- ments	Number of employees	Sales (mil dol)	Annual payroll (mil dol)
	147	148	149	150	151	152	153	154	155	156	157	158
SOUTH CAROLINA—Cont'd												
Sumter	116	471	29.1	8.9	84	12 655	2 050.4	303.0	133	2 311	70.0	19.1
Union	21	50	3.3	1.2	43	5 355	679.6	129.2	36	646	13.5	3.6
Williamsburg	27	131	10.1	2.6	34	3 392	533.4	86.8	35	334	10.1	3.1
York	268	1 362	97.5	39.5	222	11 731	2 325.7	391.8	264	5 073	152.9	39.0
SOUTH DAKOTA	1 282	6 228	450.4	161.7	888	46 539	12 305.5	1 162.6	2 258	30 131	888.0	234.4
Aurora	3	10	0.2	0.1	NA	NA	NA	NA	15	49	1.3	0.3
Beadle	25	85	6.0	1.6	21	1 134	263.5	25.7	66	671	17.2	4.8
Bennett	4	5	0.1	0.0	NA	NA	NA	NA	6	47	1.3	0.2
Bon Homme	5	22	5.2	0.7	NA	NA	NA	NA	22	D	D	D
Brookings	41	173	11.3	4.1	31	3 449	902.0	92.4	62	1 236	26.9	7.2
Brown	72	374	22.4	8.0	38	2 492	397.5	61.0	105	1 616	47.4	13.3
Brule	13	31	1.2	0.4	NA	NA	NA	NA	30	276	10.2	2.8
Buffalo	NA	NA	NA	NA	NA	NA	NA	NA	NA	NA	NA	NA
Butte	14	59	4.4	1.1	NA	NA	NA	NA	23	D	D	D
Campbell	2	D	D	D	NA	NA	NA	NA	8	20	0.7	0.1
Charles Mix	12	31	1.7	0.6	NA	NA	NA	NA	27	592	38.8	6.8
Clark	4	7	0.3	0.1	NA	NA	NA	NA	11	56	1.4	0.3
Clay	12	31	1.6	0.3	NA	NA	NA	NA	46	812	15.5	3.8
Codington	53	261	13.7	6.4	63	4 115	395.8	102.6	78	1 185	33.1	9.1
Corson	2	D	D	D	NA	NA	NA	NA	3	5	0.2	0.0
Custer	17	33	1.6	0.6	NA	NA	NA	NA	46	243	14.8	3.9
Davison	33	294	21.3	6.9	36	1 719	365.9	47.2	79	1 190	33.2	9.4
Day	5	17	1.2	0.4	NA	NA	NA	NA	20	125	2.7	0.7
Deuel	4	18	0.7	0.2	NA	NA	NA	NA	12	65	1.6	0.3
Dewey	3	9	0.4	0.1	NA	NA	NA	NA	7	64	1.7	0.5
Douglas	3	2	0.3	0.0	NA	NA	NA	NA	9	28	0.6	0.1
Edmunds	4	2	0.2	0.1	NA	NA	NA	NA	10	61	1.4	0.3
Fall River	11	27	1.2	0.3	NA	NA	NA	NA	35	278	12.4	1.7
Faulk	3	6	0.2	0.1	NA	NA	NA	NA	6	14	0.5	0.1
Grant	12	37	1.6	0.6	6	D	D	D	21	216	5.6	1.5
Gregory	6	20	1.5	0.3	NA	NA	NA	NA	19	91	2.3	0.5
Haakon	3	6	0.3	0.1	NA	NA	NA	NA	9	44	1.3	0.3
Hamlin	5	4	0.3	0.1	NA	NA	NA	NA	13	D	D	D
Hand	5	11	0.5	0.1	NA	NA	NA	NA	9	46	1.2	0.2
Hanson	3	3	0.1	0.0	NA	NA	NA	NA	4	25	0.5	0.1
Harding	2	D	D	D	NA	NA	NA	NA	7	77	1.0	0.2
Hughes	39	197	15.5	5.2	NA	NA	NA	NA	55	894	25.7	7.7
Hutchinson	10	25	1.3	0.5	NA	NA	NA	NA	16	D	D	D
Hyde	2	D	D	D	NA	NA	NA	NA	4	D	D	D
Jackson	NA	NA	NA	NA	NA	NA	NA	NA	17	66	3.8	0.8
Jerauld	3	3	0.2	0.0	NA	NA	NA	NA	7	38	0.8	0.2
Jones	2	D	D	D	NA	NA	NA	NA	12	41	2.4	0.7
Kingsbury	4	12	0.7	0.2	NA	NA	NA	NA	22	98	3.3	0.5
Lake	15	51	3.1	0.8	23	950	167.2	19.7	34	353	8.1	2.2
Lawrence	42	145	8.8	3.5	30	502	88.2	13.1	111	1 728	59.2	15.7
Lincoln	15	56	3.9	1.8	30	D	D	D	33	344	7.8	2.0
Lyman	1	D	D	D	NA	NA	NA	NA	15	96	3.2	0.7
McCook	6	15	0.7	0.3	NA	NA	NA	NA	23	132	2.7	0.6
McPherson	3	8	0.1	0.1	NA	NA	NA	NA	10	D	D	D
Marshall	9	25	1.2	0.4	NA	NA	NA	NA	18	71	1.9	0.5
Meade	21	57	4.9	1.1	NA	NA	NA	NA	54	517	15.7	4.1
Mellette	2	D	D	D	NA	NA	NA	NA	4	14	0.6	0.1
Miner	3	9	0.3	0.1	NA	NA	NA	NA	8	43	1.0	0.2
Minnehaha	366	2 381	182.7	72.6	168	D	D	D	386	8 074	223.4	64.0
Moody	7	54	3.3	1.2	NA	NA	NA	NA	17	D	D	D
Pennington	207	1 119	91.0	30.6	134	4 263	867.3	100.8	326	5 125	163.7	44.3
Perkins	3	10	0.3	0.1	NA	NA	NA	NA	15	91	1.6	0.4
Potter	5	D	D	D	NA	NA	NA	NA	12	79	3.2	0.6
Roberts	10	16	0.6	0.3	NA	NA	NA	NA	29	187	4.6	1.1
Sanborn	6	10	0.6	0.2	NA	NA	NA	NA	6	D	D	D
Shannon	2	D	D	D	NA	NA	NA	NA	6	39	1.2	0.4
Spink	6	17	1.2	0.2	NA	NA	NA	NA	18	191	4.2	1.0
Stanley	4	4	0.4	0.1	NA	NA	NA	NA	8	55	1.5	0.4
Sully	3	2	0.3	0.1	NA	NA	NA	NA	6	87	1.9	0.3
Todd	1	D	D	D	NA	NA	NA	NA	5	40	1.2	0.3

1. Firms subject to federal tax.

Table B. States and Counties — **Health Care and Social Assistance, Other Services, and Federal Funds**

STATE County	Health care and social assistance,[1] 1997				Other services,[1] 1997				Federal funds and grants, 2002–2003 Expenditures (mil dol)		Direct payments for individuals[2]	
	Number of establish-ments	Number of employees	Receipts (mil dol)	Annual payroll (mil dol)	Number of establish-ments	Number of employees	Receipts (mil dol)	Annual payroll (mil dol)	Total	Social Security and government retirement	Medicare	Food stamps and Supplemental Security Income
	159	160	161	162	163	164	165	166	167	168	169	170
SOUTH CAROLINA—Cont'd												
Sumter	128	1 347	81.0	40.6	123	827	47.5	14.1	877.5	267.8	72.2	37.3
Union	35	325	17.0	7.4	34	130	5.7	1.5	157.5	79.7	30.7	7.4
Williamsburg	42	342	18.6	7.7	45	220	10.1	3.2	239.2	71.9	33.9	20.6
York	212	4 122	263.1	110.3	223	1 226	66.6	21.9	614.6	331.6	110.5	24.3
SOUTH DAKOTA	1 314	14 080	881.6	414.3	1 356	5 828	344.7	90.7	6 201.6	1 753.3	604.4	106.2
Aurora	4	D	D	D	5	15	1.2	0.1	34.9	7.9	3.6	0.2
Beadle	40	394	19.8	7.9	35	148	6.6	1.9	157.4	47.9	19.5	2.0
Bennett	2	D	D	D	3	7	0.4	0.1	33.3	6.8	2.3	1.8
Bon Homme	7	35	2.0	1.1	7	17	1.4	0.3	50.9	18.1	9.1	0.8
Brookings	37	274	15.8	7.4	40	171	8.2	2.3	126.3	45.5	16.3	1.9
Brown	105	749	54.0	20.8	79	383	21.6	5.5	312.8	83.7	36.4	3.6
Brule	22	239	10.1	3.9	12	36	4.3	0.6	47.5	13.2	6.1	0.9
Buffalo	1	D	D	D	NA	NA	NA	NA	30.1	2.0	1.4	0.5
Butte	17	80	3.3	1.1	20	65	4.0	0.8	53.2	24.5	6.1	1.4
Campbell	1	D	D	D	2	D	D	D	23.6	7.7	3.2	0.1
Charles Mix	15	117	3.3	1.2	22	51	5.0	0.7	105.5	22.1	10.2	2.0
Clark	5	95	2.7	1.4	9	14	0.9	0.1	38.9	11.2	4.6	0.4
Clay	14	120	4.9	2.2	18	70	2.8	0.7	79.8	20.4	8.0	1.2
Codington	46	408	26.0	12.6	63	265	13.9	3.4	132.9	55.4	16.3	2.7
Corson	2	D	D	D	1	D	D	D	47.0	12.7	5.1	1.9
Custer	9	21	1.2	0.3	7	7	0.4	0.1	58.9	24.5	4.7	0.7
Davison	58	507	29.6	12.5	44	158	10.3	2.3	108.8	43.4	20.7	2.2
Day	11	80	3.7	1.1	12	21	2.0	0.4	79.8	18.0	8.9	1.0
Deuel	2	D	D	D	7	11	1.4	0.2	38.3	11.5	4.7	0.3
Dewey	3	D	D	D	1	D	D	D	68.8	9.9	3.0	3.3
Douglas	2	D	D	D	7	38	1.8	0.4	28.6	9.3	4.3	0.3
Edmunds	4	86	2.7	1.5	7	11	0.9	0.1	38.6	11.0	5.7	0.2
Fall River	11	44	1.8	0.7	11	28	2.2	0.3	88.0	36.4	7.3	1.0
Faulk	1	D	D	D	7	14	2.1	0.2	24.0	7.6	3.6	0.2
Grant	13	149	6.5	2.9	19	51	4.0	0.8	57.4	19.9	8.5	0.7
Gregory	8	29	2.1	1.1	9	20	1.4	0.2	46.2	14.7	6.8	0.9
Haakon	2	D	D	D	6	14	1.4	0.2	22.9	6.8	2.1	0.1
Hamlin	5	153	3.5	1.9	7	8	1.0	0.2	31.4	12.5	4.4	0.3
Hand	5	33	2.0	1.0	13	18	1.0	0.2	74.6	9.4	4.1	0.3
Hanson	NA	NA	NA	NA	NA	NA	NA	NA	28.1	8.3	1.8	0.2
Harding	1	D	D	D	NA	NA	NA	NA	13.1	4.1	1.0	0.1
Hughes	41	485	23.9	7.2	33	140	7.8	2.0	319.5	52.9	10.9	2.0
Hutchinson	12	77	3.7	1.3	16	41	3.1	0.6	65.3	21.8	10.3	0.5
Hyde	3	D	D	D	3	6	0.4	0.0	22.1	4.8	1.8	0.2
Jackson	2	D	D	D	NA	NA	NA	NA	23.4	5.7	1.1	1.0
Jerauld	3	5	0.3	0.0	7	9	1.2	0.1	24.0	6.6	3.8	0.2
Jones	1	D	D	D	NA	NA	NA	NA	15.3	3.2	1.2	0.1
Kingsbury	11	172	5.0	2.3	11	44	2.5	0.5	56.4	18.6	8.1	0.4
Lake	12	156	6.3	3.1	19	50	3.5	0.7	65.6	26.3	11.3	1.0
Lawrence	49	255	16.4	5.8	50	154	9.4	2.5	126.1	58.0	16.4	2.3
Lincoln	19	300	17.6	6.2	33	135	10.9	2.5	64.6	28.8	9.4	0.7
Lyman	3	8	0.5	0.3	2	D	D	D	53.4	8.7	2.9	0.8
McCook	14	202	6.0	3.2	9	30	2.2	0.4	35.2	14.1	6.3	0.5
McPherson	5	13	0.6	0.1	4	7	0.7	0.1	23.1	6.1	3.2	0.3
Marshall	7	176	4.3	2.2	11	38	2.5	0.6	41.0	12.6	5.6	0.4
Meade	19	134	6.2	1.8	34	65	5.5	1.1	198.9	59.4	14.8	1.8
Mellette	1	D	D	D	2	D	D	D	17.9	3.7	1.9	1.0
Miner	1	D	D	D	8	22	2.3	0.4	32.3	7.6	4.5	0.3
Minnehaha	284	4 344	347.2	194.3	283	1 858	101.3	31.5	842.5	306.1	91.6	15.4
Moody	7	46	1.2	0.5	8	27	1.7	0.3	40.5	13.1	6.1	0.4
Pennington	226	2 315	163.6	65.6	191	1 049	55.5	17.4	698.5	241.1	55.4	15.6
Perkins	6	8	0.6	0.2	11	22	2.2	0.4	48.0	11.1	4.7	0.4
Potter	5	19	0.6	0.3	6	17	1.9	0.2	44.1	8.9	4.4	0.1
Roberts	11	157	4.9	1.9	15	28	1.8	0.3	80.0	21.7	9.3	2.1
Sanborn	2	D	D	D	7	11	1.1	0.1	30.9	7.0	3.7	0.2
Shannon	1	D	D	D	1	D	D	D	182.5	15.4	6.1	10.6
Spink	8	111	4.1	1.8	9	20	1.8	0.5	79.5	20.8	10.7	0.7
Stanley	NA	NA	NA	NA	6	14	0.7	0.2	26.0	6.2	1.7	0.1
Sully	NA	NA	NA	NA	1	D	D	D	31.0	3.3	1.3	0.1
Todd	2	D	D	D	1	D	D	D	111.0	10.1	4.5	6.8

1. Firms subject to federal tax.   2. State totals may include programs not allocated by county.

Table B. States and Counties — **Federal Funds and Local Government Finances**

	Federal funds and grants, 2002–2003 (cont'd)							Local government finances, 2002				
	Expenditures (mil dol) (cont'd)							General revenue				
	Procurement contract awards		Grants[1]								Taxes	
											Per capita[2] (dollars)	
STATE County	Salaries and wages	Defense	Other	Medicaid and other health-related	Nutrition and family welfare	Education	Other	Total (mil dol)	Intergovern-mental (mil dol)	Total (mil dol)	Total	Property
	171	172	173	174	175	176	177	178	179	180	181	182
SOUTH CAROLINA—Cont'd												
Sumter	240.0	40.2	14.4	117.0	21.1	13.7	34.2	214.6	127.0	67.2	639	496
Union	5.1	0.1	1.0	24.1	3.3	2.0	3.4	96.3	35.8	19.8	672	627
Williamsburg	6.1	0.1	1.4	70.6	7.2	4.9	8.1	71.1	48.6	17.5	480	409
York	23.5	3.8	6.1	56.8	14.6	9.7	20.0	398.7	149.7	198.7	1 143	977
SOUTH DAKOTA	673.2	196.3	184.7	468.6	176.3	181.9	870.8	X	X	X	X	X
Aurora	1.0	0.0	0.2	1.0	0.3	0.1	6.5	7.4	2.3	3.8	1 288	1 053
Beadle	24.1	0.0	5.4	15.3	1.2	0.4	13.9	34.6	11.4	17.1	1 031	879
Bennett	1.2	0.0	2.4	3.2	0.6	2.4	6.6	13.2	5.3	2.7	768	595
Bon Homme	1.9	0.0	0.8	3.9	0.5	0.3	4.3	18.3	6.1	7.2	1 011	847
Brookings	9.8	0.3	2.6	8.4	1.4	0.9	20.9	92.3	14.2	27.7	976	727
Brown	33.2	13.3	20.5	22.1	5.0	4.1	49.4	73.4	18.7	42.7	1 221	856
Brule	1.9	0.2	0.8	4.2	0.4	0.5	4.9	13.6	5.2	6.9	1 342	1 020
Buffalo	5.8	1.4	0.8	2.1	2.1	0.4	4.5	0.6	0.1	0.4	197	160
Butte	2.8	0.0	0.4	3.6	2.3	0.3	8.2	20.0	8.5	7.6	846	674
Campbell	0.5	0.0	0.1	2.3	0.1	0.2	2.1	4.2	1.3	2.4	1 375	1 176
Charles Mix	8.6	1.5	1.0	9.9	4.2	6.2	15.3	27.1	15.1	8.6	936	785
Clark	1.4	0.0	0.3	3.6	0.4	0.2	4.8	9.4	3.0	5.3	1 318	1 175
Clay	4.1	0.0	1.2	15.8	3.0	1.6	12.1	21.8	6.1	11.1	842	704
Codington	12.7	0.0	4.6	11.7	1.6	0.5	8.0	65.8	23.2	27.7	1 069	686
Corson	4.1	0.0	0.6	4.9	1.2	4.4	5.6	12.8	10.0	1.9	440	332
Custer	9.8	0.1	3.6	2.9	0.4	0.2	11.4	14.0	3.8	8.9	1 197	922
Davison	5.8	0.1	1.7	11.4	1.6	2.2	5.7	51.0	19.5	21.5	1 143	752
Day	3.0	0.0	0.6	7.1	0.8	0.4	27.2	14.7	5.9	7.0	1 159	873
Deuel	1.7	0.0	0.4	2.9	0.3	0.1	9.5	7.9	2.6	4.4	995	852
Dewey	15.9	0.0	1.8	6.9	4.0	7.5	9.4	9.5	6.6	2.2	360	286
Douglas	1.3	0.0	0.3	1.3	0.3	0.1	2.0	6.6	1.9	3.7	1 086	853
Edmunds	1.1	0.0	0.2	2.4	0.3	0.1	6.0	12.4	5.9	5.0	1 187	1 085
Fall River	23.5	1.7	5.0	5.2	0.8	0.8	5.5	15.9	5.2	8.0	1 089	887
Faulk	1.1	0.0	0.2	1.3	0.1	0.1	2.1	7.6	2.0	3.1	1 229	1 134
Grant	2.6	0.0	0.6	4.9	0.5	0.2	2.0	18.5	4.3	10.1	1 321	1 065
Gregory	1.9	1.2	0.5	3.6	0.7	3.0	4.7	11.7	5.4	5.2	1 147	884
Haakon	0.9	0.0	0.1	0.0	0.2	1.2	3.4	8.2	1.8	3.1	1 501	1 124
Hamlin	1.6	0.0	0.4	1.9	0.5	0.2	3.3	15.5	4.9	7.0	1 262	1 101
Hand	0.9	0.0	0.2	1.9	0.2	0.1	36.8	7.9	2.3	4.7	1 323	1 096
Hanson	0.7	0.0	0.2	0.6	0.2	0.1	8.2	6.2	2.8	2.7	810	729
Harding	1.3	0.1	0.5	0.0	0.1	0.1	1.7	4.5	1.5	2.4	1 902	1 524
Hughes	13.7	0.7	6.2	31.8	32.4	49.3	103.3	38.5	13.3	18.5	1 103	817
Hutchinson	2.5	0.0	0.5	5.2	0.5	0.3	5.2	19.4	7.4	9.8	1 230	1 063
Hyde	0.2	0.0	0.1	0.6	0.1	0.1	3.9	3.5	0.9	2.3	1 441	1 239
Jackson	4.2	0.0	0.5	0.6	0.4	0.6	3.0	4.7	2.7	1.7	582	494
Jerauld	0.7	0.0	0.2	1.0	0.2	0.1	3.4	5.7	1.8	2.8	1 247	1 048
Jones	0.4	0.0	0.3	0.6	0.0	0.1	5.0	2.6	0.7	1.6	1 427	1 213
Kingsbury	2.4	0.0	0.5	1.9	0.4	0.2	5.1	13.4	5.1	6.6	1 159	1 023
Lake	3.6	0.0	0.5	4.9	3.7	1.1	2.5	25.1	8.2	11.6	1 031	831
Lawrence	8.8	0.1	5.2	10.1	1.7	1.0	16.3	57.9	16.4	28.4	1 316	1 009
Lincoln	3.2	0.0	0.7	4.2	0.7	0.3	9.5	41.9	12.3	25.8	934	776
Lyman	3.7	0.2	0.3	3.0	1.3	1.1	14.6	6.1	2.1	3.4	848	674
McCook	2.1	0.0	0.4	2.6	0.4	0.2	1.6	13.1	3.8	7.8	1 356	1 178
McPherson	0.7	0.0	0.1	2.6	0.2	0.1	1.3	5.7	1.8	3.2	1 125	994
Marshall	1.4	0.0	0.4	3.2	0.5	0.2	7.0	10.3	3.6	5.4	1 221	987
Meade	34.0	50.1	3.6	5.8	1.3	3.4	17.1	43.2	16.4	17.0	696	577
Mellette	0.6	0.0	0.1	3.2	0.6	1.4	3.0	8.0	5.8	1.5	791	658
Miner	1.1	0.0	0.2	5.0	0.2	0.1	4.8	7.2	2.3	4.0	1 415	1 218
Minnehaha	125.4	15.0	55.3	65.4	9.3	3.1	80.5	387.5	103.2	216.2	1 417	1 117
Moody	6.6	0.0	0.7	2.2	0.6	1.9	2.3	13.6	5.1	5.7	882	775
Pennington	196.2	11.9	21.3	42.5	13.6	11.6	73.3	231.1	76.9	115.0	1 265	866
Perkins	1.5	0.0	0.3	3.9	0.3	0.2	15.6	8.7	3.5	3.8	1 165	1 000
Potter	1.1	0.0	0.5	1.6	0.2	0.1	8.7	6.3	1.6	4.1	1 651	1 423
Roberts	6.8	0.0	1.6	12.1	3.1	3.9	7.7	19.9	10.1	7.5	746	619
Sanborn	1.0	0.0	0.2	1.6	0.2	0.1	8.8	5.1	2.6	2.1	797	711
Shannon	26.0	2.0	4.0	25.8	13.3	12.3	50.2	17.3	16.1	0.7	54	27
Spink	3.0	0.0	0.6	5.2	0.5	0.2	15.8	22.1	6.0	9.3	1 307	1 068
Stanley	0.1	0.2	0.1	0.3	0.2	0.4	8.9	7.3	2.6	3.7	1 326	1 025
Sully	0.3	0.1	0.1	0.0	0.1	0.0	5.0	4.2	1.0	2.7	1 781	1 555
Todd	14.7	0.0	3.6	16.3	6.1	14.4	23.6	24.1	21.0	1.9	206	138

1. State totals may include programs not allocated by county.   2. Based on the resident population estimated as of July 1 of the year shown.

Table B. States and Counties — Local Government Finances, Government Employment, and Elections

| STATE County | Local government finances, 2002 (cont'd) | | | | | | | | | Government employment, 2002 | | | Presidential election, 2004 | | |
| | Direct general expenditure | | | | | | | Debt outstanding | | | | | Percent of vote cast — | | |
	Total (mil dol)	Per capita[1] (dollars)	Education	Health and hospitals	Police protection	Public welfare	Highways	Total (mil dol)	Per capita[1] (dollars)	Federal civilian	Federal military	State and local	Democratic	Republican	All other
	183	184	185	186	187	188	189	190	191	192	193	194	195	196	197
SOUTH CAROLINA—Cont'd															
Sumter	196.6	1 869	68.1	1.1	6.4	0.6	1.8	117.4	1 116	1 091	5 988	6 048	50.5	48.9	0.6
Union	102.6	3 479	38.4	40.2	4.1	0.1	1.7	42.8	1 453	88	110	2 279	42.9	56.2	0.9
Williamsburg	66.2	1 814	69.7	2.9	3.4	0.2	2.0	25.1	688	88	136	2 191	65.0	34.5	0.6
York	390.5	2 248	65.7	0.3	4.8	0.2	1.3	493.6	2 841	373	647	9 863	34.5	64.4	1.0
SOUTH DAKOTA	X	X	X	X	X	X	X	X	X	10 923	7 689	60 377	38.4	59.9	1.6
Aurora	10.0	3 388	68.5	0.2	2.3	0.2	13.1	2.4	802	27	16	243	37.6	61.2	1.2
Beadle	36.3	2 193	49.0	0.1	5.3	0.8	9.5	21.8	1 316	384	91	1 078	40.6	58.0	1.4
Bennett	13.3	3 761	49.7	29.3	3.3	0.2	4.4	0.1	14	38	19	249	46.6	51.1	2.3
Bon Homme	17.2	2 408	54.2	0.3	2.9	0.2	13.0	20.9	2 917	40	39	591	37.9	60.5	1.5
Brookings	90.4	3 186	28.0	20.8	3.3	0.2	6.2	39.8	1 403	152	165	4 832	40.7	57.3	2.0
Brown	80.2	2 290	49.6	0.7	4.4	1.5	11.8	31.4	896	552	194	2 387	42.7	55.8	1.5
Brule	12.7	2 470	69.0	0.2	4.3	0.3	9.4	5.4	1 051	43	28	345	39.6	58.7	1.7
Buffalo	0.5	230	0.0	0.0	9.0	0.4	52.5	0.0	0	141	11	336	71.7	26.5	1.8
Butte	21.2	2 347	52.5	0.7	5.6	0.2	5.4	15.7	1 736	55	50	512	23.6	74.1	2.2
Campbell	4.1	2 349	54.7	0.8	3.2	0.8	15.9	0.2	137	17	10	114	24.9	73.8	1.3
Charles Mix	25.7	2 796	68.4	0.3	2.5	0.2	8.9	10.3	1 118	189	51	1 227	44.9	53.3	1.8
Clark	9.3	2 331	53.4	1.7	2.6	0.5	19.2	4.3	1 079	33	22	237	37.6	61.7	0.7
Clay	23.4	1 772	52.1	0.5	6.3	0.4	13.3	16.8	1 269	57	77	2 873	54.0	43.9	2.1
Codington	61.4	2 371	62.1	0.2	4.0	0.4	7.8	21.2	818	180	143	1 724	37.7	61.0	1.3
Corson	17.4	3 990	88.3	0.0	1.8	0.0	5.6	0.1	23	91	24	547	56.4	41.8	1.9
Custer	13.1	1 751	53.8	0.0	7.9	0.0	8.1	7.2	966	221	41	544	29.6	67.9	2.6
Davison	56.1	2 990	56.8	0.1	6.8	0.9	6.1	30.8	1 641	113	103	1 139	36.4	62.1	1.4
Day	13.5	2 220	58.8	1.1	3.2	0.5	18.1	2.2	360	66	33	432	51.3	47.2	1.5
Deuel	8.1	1 835	48.5	3.6	4.4	0.6	23.6	0.8	188	36	24	272	39.8	58.3	1.9
Dewey	11.2	1 854	83.4	0.5	1.7	0.1	7.1	0.8	127	363	33	1 141	62.6	35.9	1.4
Douglas	6.5	1 930	53.1	0.6	3.0	0.2	20.6	1.6	461	31	19	167	19.5	79.3	1.1
Edmunds	12.4	2 916	41.3	14.0	1.9	10.3	15.5	2.6	605	27	23	362	34.2	64.2	1.6
Fall River	15.6	2 131	55.6	1.0	4.6	0.1	9.7	4.1	561	517	40	511	34.5	62.8	2.8
Faulk	8.3	3 327	42.0	22.7	3.7	0.6	19.7	0.0	14	25	14	166	30.5	68.9	0.6
Grant	18.8	2 447	49.5	0.9	2.9	0.4	18.0	33.9	4 411	45	42	360	39.9	58.5	1.6
Gregory	11.7	2 597	62.2	0.1	3.4	0.0	16.9	3.0	663	39	25	313	31.9	66.2	1.9
Haakon	8.8	4 288	40.2	0.0	2.2	0.0	14.3	1.0	469	19	11	144	17.7	81.2	1.1
Hamlin	14.9	2 688	52.4	2.7	1.7	11.9	12.8	10.1	1 821	37	31	478	33.7	64.6	1.7
Hand	7.7	2 180	52.6	0.0	4.9	0.7	17.8	5.5	1 561	25	20	226	30.5	67.8	1.7
Hanson	6.3	1 876	64.7	0.5	1.5	0.3	18.1	2.2	640	11	19	154	34.7	64.1	1.2
Harding	4.5	3 547	51.6	0.6	2.4	0.0	26.6	0.0	0	33	0	107	11.5	86.4	2.1
Hughes	47.7	2 851	53.8	0.2	5.0	0.1	6.5	40.5	2 418	278	94	3 546	30.5	68.1	1.4
Hutchinson	20.6	2 587	62.5	0.2	2.3	0.6	18.6	9.7	1 224	46	44	465	28.4	69.9	1.7
Hyde	5.8	3 676	69.2	0.1	0.3	0.1	16.0	1.9	1 175	0	0	223	28.8	70.1	1.1
Jackson	5.2	1 827	68.5	0.4	2.3	0.1	11.9	1.1	377	106	16	235	40.0	57.1	2.9
Jerauld	5.5	2 485	62.3	1.8	3.2	0.3	13.0	0.2	96	19	12	165	39.0	59.5	1.5
Jones	2.6	2 367	64.4	0.3	3.6	0.0	14.2	0.0	28	11	0	182	18.7	78.8	2.5
Kingsbury	14.0	2 469	63.7	0.5	2.6	0.4	15.7	4.7	833	46	31	269	38.6	59.9	1.6
Lake	23.2	2 069	57.4	0.4	4.8	0.6	11.0	64.1	5 702	64	62	1 062	41.8	55.9	2.3
Lawrence	51.0	2 362	41.4	0.6	6.5	0.1	9.2	84.0	3 888	191	119	1 554	33.2	64.5	2.3
Lincoln	46.9	1 695	57.6	0.1	4.2	0.8	17.3	26.8	970	51	152	802	33.4	65.4	1.2
Lyman	6.5	1 627	50.6	1.8	3.1	0.7	20.6	0.6	160	79	22	607	44.9	53.1	2.0
McCook	15.5	2 676	61.8	1.1	2.4	0.3	19.3	10.5	1 816	39	32	286	36.7	61.7	1.6
McPherson	6.1	2 156	64.6	0.1	1.9	0.4	11.4	0.5	193	21	16	173	23.4	74.7	1.9
Marshall	10.0	2 267	57.4	1.0	3.7	0.4	22.0	2.5	564	32	24	325	46.5	52.5	1.0
Meade	43.6	1 782	58.7	0.5	5.3	0.1	7.4	16.1	658	1 152	129	1 399	25.6	72.6	1.9
Mellette	7.6	3 945	79.0	0.7	3.4	0.0	5.0	0.4	219	16	11	228	38.8	59.4	1.8
Miner	8.0	2 838	50.0	0.9	4.7	0.3	24.2	0.4	129	24	15	170	43.6	55.1	1.3
Minnehaha	375.0	2 458	50.3	1.3	5.7	0.9	8.3	326.5	2 140	2 099	890	7 135	41.6	56.9	1.5
Moody	16.1	2 469	64.5	3.4	5.1	0.4	11.5	13.8	2 116	152	36	785	46.6	51.9	1.5
Pennington	231.7	2 550	49.3	1.2	5.4	0.4	9.9	115.0	1 265	1 339	3 939	5 354	31.6	66.7	1.7
Perkins	10.3	3 143	45.3	0.4	3.9	1.9	17.7	1.6	490	35	18	286	23.1	73.3	3.6
Potter	6.3	2 503	56.3	0.5	2.9	0.0	19.9	1.0	403	24	14	166	28.6	70.6	0.7
Roberts	19.9	1 988	67.0	0.9	3.1	0.5	12.8	3.0	304	142	55	1 217	50.7	48.1	1.2
Sanborn	5.5	2 105	71.7	0.3	2.0	0.1	8.6	0.0	5	22	14	186	40.7	57.3	2.0
Shannon	17.1	1 294	97.2	0.1	0.4	0.0	1.3	0.0	0	568	73	2 728	84.6	12.5	2.9
Spink	22.5	3 159	48.5	22.2	3.5	0.3	11.4	3.8	533	59	39	969	39.2	59.9	1.0
Stanley	7.2	2 614	54.8	0.9	7.4	0.6	10.9	1.4	508	0	15	168	28.6	69.6	1.8
Sully	4.3	2 824	69.6	0.0	1.8	0.5	15.0	0.2	133	12	0	120	21.8	76.3	1.8
Todd	26.7	2 826	96.3	0.0	0.3	0.1	1.4	0.0	0	295	52	2 019	72.2	25.2	2.6

1. Based on the resident population estimated as of July 1 of the year shown.

Table B. States and Counties — Land Area and Population

STATE/ County code	CBSA code[1]	County Type[2]	STATE County	Land area,[3] (sq km) 2000	Population and population characteristics, 2003													
					Total persons	Rank	Per square kilometer	Race alone or in combination, not Hispanic or Latino (percent)				Percent Hispanic or Latino[4]	Age (percent)					
								White	Black	Am. Indian, Alaska Native	Asian and Pacific Islander		Under 5 years	5 to 17 years	18 to 24 years	25 to 34 years	35 to 44 years	45 to 54 years
				1	2	3	4	5	6	7	8	9	10	11	12	13	14	15
			SOUTH DAKOTA—Cont'd															
46 123	...	7	Tripp	4 179	6 177	2 757	1.5	88.1	0.3	11.7	0.1	0.7	5.9	20.0	8.4	8.5	14.5	13.6
46 125	43620	3	Turner	1 598	8 594	2 558	5.4	98.9	0.2	0.5	0.3	0.4	5.1	19.0	8.1	9.2	14.2	15.1
46 127	43580	7	Union	1 192	13 024	2 237	10.9	95.4	0.9	0.3	2.4	1.5	6.3	18.7	9.4	12.6	14.7	15.1
46 129	...	7	Walworth	1 833	5 562	2 807	3.0	88.3	0.1	11.8	0.2	0.6	6.1	16.6	7.7	8.2	12.7	14.8
46 135	49460	7	Yankton	1 351	21 452	1 729	15.9	94.9	1.4	1.8	0.6	1.9	5.6	18.4	9.8	12.1	15.5	14.8
46 137	...	9	Ziebach	5 082	2 551	3 017	0.5	25.2	0.0	73.5	0.2	1.1	10.5	27.9	13.1	10.7	13.7	10.4
47 000	...	X	TENNESSEE	106 752	5 841 748	X	54.7	79.3	17.0	0.6	1.5	2.5	6.6	17.3	9.8	14.0	15.2	14.3
47 001	28940	2	Anderson	874	71 904	705	82.3	93.8	4.1	0.8	1.2	1.2	5.4	16.6	8.4	11.6	14.7	15.2
47 003	43180	6	Bedford	1 227	40 253	1 130	32.8	81.0	8.4	0.5	0.7	10.0	7.4	17.8	10.3	14.3	14.5	12.5
47 005	...	7	Benton	1 023	16 500	1 996	16.1	96.4	1.9	0.7	0.3	1.0	4.9	15.9	8.1	11.4	14.0	14.5
47 007	...	8	Bledsoe	1 052	12 556	2 265	11.9	94.8	3.6	1.0	0.1	1.2	5.0	17.0	8.7	13.8	16.6	15.0
47 009	28940	2	Blount	1 447	111 510	498	77.1	94.9	2.9	0.8	1.2	1.1	5.6	16.4	9.1	12.9	15.3	14.7
47 011	17420	3	Bradley	851	90 264	596	106.1	92.6	4.3	0.8	0.9	2.3	6.4	16.6	11.0	13.9	15.1	13.6
47 013	29220	6	Campbell	1 243	40 125	1 134	32.3	98.4	0.4	0.9	0.2	0.8	6.0	16.2	9.0	13.1	14.0	14.0
47 015	34980	1	Cannon	688	13 204	2 220	19.2	96.3	1.4	0.7	0.2	1.8	5.9	18.0	9.3	12.5	15.6	13.3
47 017	...	6	Carroll	1 551	29 342	1 422	18.9	88.0	10.8	0.6	0.3	1.1	5.9	16.5	9.4	11.9	14.1	13.6
47 019	27740	3	Carter	883	58 394	840	66.1	97.0	1.7	0.6	0.4	1.0	5.0	14.8	9.8	13.3	14.4	14.0
47 021	34980	1	Cheatham	784	37 364	1 196	47.7	96.6	1.4	0.6	0.5	1.4	6.7	19.3	8.6	13.3	18.4	14.8
47 023	27180	3	Chester	747	15 842	2 043	21.2	89.3	9.1	0.5	0.5	1.2	5.8	16.9	15.2	12.8	13.8	12.7
47 025	...	6	Claiborne	1 125	30 415	1 397	27.0	97.9	0.8	0.6	0.7	0.7	5.7	17.2	9.4	13.0	14.8	14.4
47 027	...	8	Clay	612	7 947	2 597	13.0	96.1	1.6	0.4	0.3	1.8	5.3	15.5	8.4	12.5	15.3	14.1
47 029	35460	6	Cocke	1 125	34 329	1 295	30.5	96.4	2.1	0.9	0.2	1.1	5.8	16.3	8.8	13.1	14.7	14.9
47 031	46100	4	Coffee	1 111	49 643	936	44.7	92.7	4.0	0.7	0.8	2.7	6.4	17.8	9.3	12.4	14.8	13.4
47 033	...	8	Crockett	687	14 491	2 127	21.1	80.1	13.8	0.3	0.1	5.9	6.6	17.7	9.0	12.4	15.2	12.9
47 035	18900	7	Cumberland	1 765	49 391	942	28.0	98.1	0.3	0.7	0.5	1.1	5.2	15.3	7.7	11.5	13.1	12.1
47 037	34980	1	Davidson	1 301	569 842	100	438.0	64.1	27.6	0.7	3.4	5.6	7.3	15.3	9.8	17.4	16.1	14.0
47 039	...	9	Decatur	865	11 610	2 325	13.4	93.9	3.5	0.5	0.2	2.4	5.5	15.0	8.4	12.2	13.9	13.8
47 041	...	9	De Kalb	789	18 037	1 914	22.9	93.8	1.6	0.7	0.3	4.2	6.1	16.3	9.3	13.3	15.2	13.7
47 043	34980	1	Dickson	1 269	44 935	1 027	35.4	93.7	4.8	0.8	0.4	1.2	6.9	18.8	9.1	13.3	15.8	13.6
47 045	20540	5	Dyer	1 322	37 308	1 197	28.2	84.8	13.5	0.4	0.5	1.5	6.8	18.1	9.3	12.8	14.8	14.2
47 047	32820	1	Fayette	1 825	32 289	1 352	17.7	67.1	30.8	0.6	1.1	1.2	6.3	17.7	10.3	12.4	14.4	14.2
47 049	...	9	Fentress	1 291	16 935	1 964	13.1	99.0	0.2	0.4	0.1	0.6	5.8	17.0	9.1	12.8	14.5	14.3
47 051	46100	6	Franklin	1 436	40 512	1 123	28.2	92.0	5.5	0.8	0.7	1.9	5.7	16.0	12.4	11.3	14.0	14.1
47 053	...	4	Gibson	1 561	47 922	964	30.7	79.2	19.4	0.6	0.3	1.1	6.2	17.0	8.9	11.9	14.5	13.7
47 055	...	6	Giles	1 582	29 390	1 420	18.6	87.5	11.3	0.7	0.4	0.8	6.0	17.2	9.5	11.8	15.0	14.4
47 057	34100	3	Grainger	726	21 445	1 730	29.5	98.1	0.4	0.5	0.1	1.2	5.8	16.2	8.6	14.1	15.5	14.5
47 059	24620	6	Greene	1 610	63 991	775	39.7	96.1	2.2	0.5	0.4	1.3	5.4	15.9	9.1	12.9	14.8	14.4
47 061	...	8	Grundy	934	14 389	2 136	15.4	98.4	0.3	0.8	0.2	0.9	6.5	17.6	9.6	13.1	14.0	13.4
47 063	34100	3	Hamblen	417	58 851	832	141.1	87.1	4.5	0.5	0.9	7.8	6.7	16.2	9.3	13.9	14.6	13.6
47 065	16860	2	Hamilton	1 405	309 510	192	220.3	75.7	20.9	0.7	1.8	2.0	6.1	16.5	9.8	13.3	14.7	15.1
47 067	...	8	Hancock	576	6 702	2 714	11.6	98.9	0.5	0.6	0.1	0.4	5.2	16.3	10.2	11.7	14.6	15.5
47 069	...	6	Hardeman	1 729	28 174	1 455	16.3	57.6	40.8	0.5	0.4	1.2	5.9	17.0	10.5	14.5	16.4	13.8
47 071	...	6	Hardin	1 497	25 927	1 540	17.3	94.7	3.9	0.6	0.2	1.2	5.4	16.4	8.6	12.1	13.9	14.3
47 073	28700	3	Hawkins	1 260	55 037	875	43.7	97.2	1.7	0.4	0.3	0.8	5.9	16.4	8.2	14.0	15.2	14.3
47 075	15140	6	Haywood	1 381	19 626	1 828	14.2	46.1	50.5	0.1	0.2	3.3	7.1	19.1	10.0	12.4	14.2	14.7
47 077	...	6	Henderson	1 347	25 900	1 541	19.2	90.9	8.1	0.6	0.2	1.1	6.4	17.4	9.2	13.0	15.0	14.0
47 079	37540	7	Henry	1 455	31 185	1 378	21.4	89.9	8.9	0.6	0.4	1.0	6.0	15.6	8.4	11.3	14.3	14.3
47 081	34980	1	Hickman	1 586	23 352	1 649	14.7	94.2	4.2	1.1	0.1	1.0	6.4	17.8	9.4	14.2	16.0	13.7
47 083	...	8	Houston	519	8 085	2 588	15.6	94.7	3.8	0.3	0.2	1.6	6.7	17.5	7.7	11.8	13.0	13.8
47 085	...	8	Humphreys	1 378	18 123	1 908	13.2	95.5	3.3	0.5	0.4	0.8	6.0	17.0	8.5	12.2	14.4	14.6
47 087	18260	8	Jackson	800	11 208	2 353	14.0	98.4	0.3	0.6	0.1	0.9	4.8	15.9	8.6	13.1	14.8	14.7
47 089	34100	3	Jefferson	709	46 919	982	66.2	95.4	2.4	0.7	0.5	1.7	5.6	16.4	10.7	13.4	14.8	12.8
47 091	...	6	Johnson	773	17 948	1 918	23.2	95.9	2.7	0.6	0.2	0.8	4.5	14.0	8.1	14.4	14.6	14.7
47 093	28940	2	Knox	1 317	392 995	156	298.4	88.2	9.0	0.7	1.8	1.4	6.0	15.8	10.8	14.3	15.3	14.3
47 095	...	9	Lake	423	7 824	2 612	18.5	66.0	32.0	0.8	0.3	1.3	4.7	12.3	14.6	17.5	16.5	13.0
47 097	...	6	Lauderdale	1 218	27 077	1 503	22.2	63.4	34.8	0.9	0.3	1.2	7.4	17.0	10.7	14.8	15.9	13.1
47 099	29980	6	Lawrence	1 598	40 704	1 119	25.5	96.8	1.7	0.7	0.3	1.1	6.7	18.6	9.2	12.7	14.5	12.9
47 101	...	6	Lewis	731	11 438	2 338	15.6	96.7	1.8	0.4	0.3	1.1	5.8	18.2	9.6	12.0	15.0	14.4
47 103	...	6	Lincoln	1 477	31 773	1 362	21.5	91.1	7.1	1.1	0.4	1.2	5.7	17.0	9.1	11.7	15.2	14.3
47 105	28940	2	Loudon	593	41 624	1 094	70.2	95.7	1.3	0.9	0.4	2.6	5.7	15.6	7.7	12.1	14.3	14.0
47 107	11940	4	McMinn	1 114	50 662	928	45.5	93.4	4.6	0.8	0.7	1.9	6.2	17.0	9.1	12.7	14.8	13.9
47 109	...	6	McNairy	1 451	24 938	1 578	17.2	92.6	6.3	0.6	0.4	0.9	6.4	16.9	8.4	11.9	13.8	14.3
47 111	34980	1	Macon	795	21 023	1 751	26.4	96.6	0.3	0.5	0.3	2.5	6.6	18.1	9.6	14.3	14.6	13.6
47 113	27180	3	Madison	1 443	93 873	573	65.1	63.7	33.7	0.5	0.9	1.9	7.0	18.0	11.4	13.4	14.8	13.9
47 115	16860	2	Marion	1 291	27 880	1 471	21.6	94.5	4.3	0.7	0.2	0.8	6.0	16.8	9.1	12.8	14.6	15.3

1. CBSA = Core Based Statistical Area. See Appendix A for explanation. See Appendix B for list of metropolitan areas with component counties.   2. County type code from the Economic Research Service of USDA Rural-Urban Continuum Codes. See Appendix A for definition.   3. Dry land or land partially or temporarily covered by water.   4. Hispanic or Latino persons may be of any race.

Table B. States and Counties — **Population and Households**

	Population, 2003 (cont'd)				Population — change and components of change, 1990–2003							Households, 2000				
	Age (percent) (cont'd)				Total persons		Percent change		Components of change, 2000–2003						Percent	
STATE County	55 to 64 years	65 to 74 years	75 years and over	Percent female	1990	2000	1990–2000	2000–2003	Births	Deaths	Net migration	Number	Percent change, 1990–2000	Persons per house-hold	Female family house-holder[1]	One person
	16	17	18	19	20	21	22	23	24	25	26	27	28	29	30	31
SOUTH DAKOTA—Cont'd																
Tripp	10.3	8.9	11.1	51.1	6 924	6 430	-7.1	-3.9	228	305	-175	2 550	-0.9	2.48	6.6	29.6
Turner	10.0	8.8	11.1	50.4	8 576	8 849	3.2	-2.9	274	391	-129	3 510	5.3	2.46	5.6	26.5
Union	9.2	6.3	6.7	50.3	10 189	12 584	23.5	3.5	507	378	325	4 927	27.7	2.53	6.3	24.2
Walworth	12.1	11.6	11.7	51.4	6 087	5 974	-1.9	-6.9	213	315	-317	2 506	2.4	2.31	8.9	31.4
Yankton	8.9	6.9	8.0	49.4	19 252	21 652	12.5	-0.9	763	594	-354	8 187	15.2	2.43	8.3	29.3
Ziebach	7.4	4.3	2.9	50.4	2 220	2 519	13.5	1.3	156	45	-80	741	17.6	3.40	23.8	17.4
TENNESSEE	10.3	6.7	5.7	51.2	4 877 203	5 689 283	16.7	2.7	255 980	181 364	79 587	2 232 905	20.5	2.48	12.9	25.8
Anderson	11.3	8.0	8.5	52.2	68 250	71 330	4.5	0.8	2 500	2 605	734	29 780	8.7	2.37	11.5	27.7
Bedford	9.5	6.4	5.6	50.1	30 411	37 586	23.6	7.1	1 943	1 209	1 933	13 905	19.8	2.67	11.9	21.5
Benton	13.3	9.9	8.4	51.7	14 524	16 537	13.9	-0.2	539	751	191	6 863	18.7	2.37	9.5	25.7
Bledsoe	11.7	6.8	4.9	45.7	9 669	12 367	27.9	1.5	406	401	189	4 430	35.8	2.53	9.1	22.1
Blount	11.0	7.3	6.6	51.5	85 962	105 823	23.1	5.4	4 070	3 573	5 122	42 667	26.9	2.43	10.0	24.4
Bradley	10.5	6.9	5.1	51.0	73 712	87 965	19.3	2.6	3 798	2 542	1 121	34 281	24.2	2.50	10.9	23.4
Campbell	11.9	8.6	6.8	51.7	35 079	39 854	13.6	0.7	1 592	1 490	216	16 125	22.6	2.44	12.6	25.4
Cannon	11.0	7.8	5.7	51.3	10 467	12 826	22.5	2.9	495	469	354	4 998	25.6	2.53	9.9	24.3
Carroll	11.3	8.8	8.4	51.9	27 514	29 475	7.1	-0.5	1 184	1 409	109	11 779	9.8	2.42	11.5	25.8
Carter	11.6	7.7	6.9	50.0	51 505	56 742	10.2	2.9	1 828	2 082	1 912	23 486	16.3	2.35	11.0	26.5
Cheatham	9.4	5.2	3.7	50.0	27 140	35 912	32.3	4.0	1 582	884	780	12 878	35.3	2.76	9.6	16.9
Chester	9.3	7.0	6.3	51.2	12 819	15 540	21.2	1.9	570	508	251	5 660	24.2	2.55	11.5	22.6
Claiborne	11.3	7.6	5.9	51.8	26 137	29 862	14.3	1.9	1 166	1 214	615	11 799	22.5	2.48	11.0	23.4
Clay	13.4	8.7	7.0	50.6	7 238	7 976	10.2	-0.4	272	309	19	3 379	18.4	2.33	9.7	27.6
Cocke	11.9	8.1	5.6	51.4	29 141	33 565	15.2	2.3	1 298	1 388	869	13 762	23.0	2.41	13.0	25.7
Coffee	10.4	8.2	6.5	51.1	40 343	48 014	19.0	3.4	2 102	1 759	1 301	18 885	21.8	2.50	11.1	24.3
Crockett	10.9	7.6	8.1	51.8	13 378	14 532	8.6	-0.3	640	625	-38	5 632	8.7	2.53	11.8	25.3
Cumberland	12.7	12.7	8.7	51.5	34 736	46 802	34.7	5.5	1 660	1 782	2 676	19 508	45.3	2.37	9.6	22.4
Davidson	8.5	5.8	5.4	51.4	510 786	569 891	11.6	0.0	28 866	16 726	-12 262	237 405	14.4	2.30	14.3	33.4
Decatur	13.0	9.8	8.7	51.1	10 472	11 731	12.0	-1.0	403	494	-6	4 908	16.4	2.34	9.0	27.6
De Kalb	11.0	7.7	6.5	50.6	14 360	17 423	21.3	3.5	698	589	517	6 984	22.6	2.45	11.1	25.5
Dickson	9.8	6.5	5.2	50.9	35 061	43 156	23.1	4.1	2 059	1 364	1 095	16 473	26.5	2.59	11.5	22.3
Dyer	10.5	6.9	6.4	52.0	34 854	37 279	7.0	0.1	1 711	1 436	-222	14 751	8.3	2.49	13.6	25.3
Fayette	10.1	6.6	5.5	50.8	25 559	28 806	12.7	12.1	1 315	920	2 998	10 467	23.8	2.71	14.0	20.5
Fentress	12.2	7.7	6.1	50.9	14 669	16 625	13.3	1.9	648	677	349	6 693	21.4	2.46	11.3	25.5
Franklin	10.8	8.2	6.7	51.1	34 923	39 270	12.4	3.2	1 441	1 431	1 242	15 003	18.5	2.51	10.4	22.6
Gibson	10.6	8.6	8.9	52.7	46 315	48 152	4.0	-0.5	2 086	2 338	80	19 518	6.3	2.41	13.6	27.4
Giles	11.6	7.5	7.1	51.5	25 741	29 447	14.4	-0.2	1 085	1 121	5	11 713	19.1	2.47	11.9	25.7
Grainger	11.7	7.7	5.1	50.3	17 095	20 659	20.8	3.8	820	711	676	8 270	29.3	2.48	8.8	22.5
Greene	11.9	8.7	6.5	51.3	55 832	62 909	12.7	1.7	2 293	2 441	1 255	25 756	19.9	2.38	10.8	25.8
Grundy	11.5	7.6	6.5	50.9	13 362	14 332	7.3	0.4	627	591	29	5 562	16.3	2.54	12.0	24.0
Hamblen	11.6	7.9	5.8	50.4	50 480	58 128	15.2	1.2	2 678	1 987	80	23 211	19.5	2.47	11.3	24.7
Hamilton	10.3	7.3	6.6	52.1	285 536	307 896	7.8	0.5	13 112	10 344	-854	124 444	11.3	2.41	13.5	27.9
Hancock	11.5	8.6	6.9	51.0	6 739	6 786	0.7	-1.2	251	290	-29	2 769	11.5	2.39	11.0	27.7
Hardeman	9.6	6.6	5.8	46.1	23 377	28 105	20.2	0.2	1 160	952	-111	9 412	13.7	2.56	17.6	25.1
Hardin	12.4	9.0	7.3	51.0	22 633	25 578	13.0	1.4	889	1 128	614	10 426	19.5	2.41	10.1	25.5
Hawkins	12.2	7.5	5.9	51.3	44 565	53 563	20.2	2.8	2 036	1 810	1 259	21 936	27.8	2.42	9.8	24.4
Haywood	9.0	6.8	6.7	53.2	19 437	19 797	1.9	-0.9	1 001	713	-446	7 558	7.8	2.59	22.0	25.4
Henderson	10.7	7.5	6.5	51.8	21 844	25 522	16.8	1.5	1 118	976	261	10 306	20.9	2.44	11.7	24.9
Henry	12.1	9.6	8.6	51.7	27 888	31 115	11.6	0.2	1 220	1 373	256	13 019	14.6	2.35	11.2	27.0
Hickman	10.3	6.5	5.4	47.3	16 754	22 295	33.1	4.7	1 006	782	824	8 081	35.2	2.59	9.6	22.6
Houston	11.9	9.0	7.9	50.6	7 018	8 088	15.2	0.0	340	312	-22	3 216	19.9	2.46	10.4	25.3
Humphreys	12.1	8.6	6.6	50.9	15 813	17 929	13.4	1.1	724	651	136	7 238	19.4	2.44	10.2	25.0
Jackson	12.3	8.7	6.6	50.6	9 297	10 984	18.1	2.0	333	451	341	4 466	22.6	2.43	10.3	25.5
Jefferson	11.4	7.6	5.4	50.6	33 016	44 294	34.2	5.9	1 653	1 475	2 443	17 155	39.1	2.49	9.8	22.5
Johnson	12.7	8.0	7.0	46.0	13 766	17 499	27.1	2.6	487	679	635	6 827	26.3	2.35	10.0	26.4
Knox	9.6	6.6	6.0	51.5	335 749	382 032	13.8	2.9	15 574	11 782	7 461	157 872	18.1	2.34	10.9	29.6
Lake	9.3	6.6	6.2	38.1	7 129	7 954	11.6	-1.6	227	366	21	2 410	-0.3	2.36	16.3	30.0
Lauderdale	9.5	5.9	5.9	47.7	23 491	27 101	15.4	-0.1	1 372	991	-378	9 567	13.6	2.55	17.6	25.6
Lawrence	10.5	7.7	6.8	51.5	35 303	39 926	13.1	1.9	1 903	1 370	272	15 480	16.1	2.56	10.6	23.7
Lewis	11.2	7.3	6.0	50.6	9 247	11 367	22.9	0.6	396	414	101	4 381	24.0	2.54	10.7	23.5
Lincoln	11.0	8.4	7.2	51.6	28 157	31 340	11.3	1.4	1 182	1 325	604	12 503	14.9	2.47	10.9	24.6
Loudon	12.8	9.8	6.7	51.1	31 255	39 086	25.1	6.5	1 532	1 446	2 439	15 944	31.2	2.42	8.9	22.8
McMinn	11.3	7.5	6.7	51.5	42 383	49 015	15.6	3.3	2 053	1 606	1 184	19 721	20.6	2.45	10.6	24.4
McNairy	12.1	8.5	7.4	51.6	22 422	24 653	10.0	1.2	1 124	997	169	9 980	13.0	2.42	9.9	25.9
Macon	10.2	6.7	5.7	50.2	15 906	20 386	28.2	3.1	873	694	462	7 916	28.5	2.55	8.8	23.8
Madison	8.9	6.0	6.1	51.9	77 982	91 837	17.8	2.2	4 388	2 780	515	35 552	20.1	2.49	15.9	26.2
Marion	12.0	7.8	5.5	51.2	24 683	27 776	12.5	0.4	1 091	1 000	47	11 037	19.8	2.49	11.6	23.6

1. No spouse present.

Table B. States and Counties — Vital Statistics, Health Resources, and Crime

STATE County	Births, average 1999–2001 Total	Births Rate¹	Deaths, average 1999–2001 Number Total	Number Infant²	Rate Total¹	Rate Infant³	Physicians, 2000 Number	Physicians Rate⁵	Hospitals, 1998 Number	Beds Number	Beds Rate⁵	Medicare enrollees, 2003	Serious crimes known to police, 2002 Total Number	Total Rate⁷
	32	33	34	35	36	37	38	39	40	41	42	43	44	45
SOUTH DAKOTA—Cont'd														
Tripp	74	11.5	76	1	11.9	D	6	93	1	116	1 722	1 287	NA	NA
Turner	92	10.4	121	1	13.7	D	5	57	1	77	892	1 757	24	269
Union	170	13.5	116	1	9.2	D	12	95	0	0	0	2 098	62	525
Walworth	70	11.8	95	1	16.1	D	5	84	1	35	627	860	181	3 427
Yankton	261	12.1	193	3	8.9	D	78	360	1	271	1 287	3 552	443	2 029
Ziebach	43	17.0	14	0	5.4	D	0	0	0	0	0	151	8	315
TENNESSEE	78 585	13.8	54 721	668	9.6	8.5	11 281	198	135	21 953	404	871 938	290 961	5 019
Anderson	783	11.0	779	3	10.9	D	182	255	1	305	429	13 679	3 335	4 588
Bedford	587	15.6	372	4	9.9	D	24	64	1	182	527	5 791	1 009	2 635
Benton	172	10.4	218	1	13.2	D	13	79	1	47	288	3 627	390	2 314
Bledsoe	131	10.6	117	0	9.5	D	2	16	1	26	241	1 545	147	1 166
Blount	1 257	11.8	1 054	8	9.9	6.1	145	137	1	203	200	17 809	3 671	3 404
Bradley	1 188	13.5	789	8	9.0	6.7	126	143	2	266	319	13 317	3 777	4 214
Campbell	500	12.6	453	4	11.4	D	25	63	2	200	523	8 437	1 642	4 043
Cannon	151	11.8	142	2	11.1	D	7	55	1	55	453	2 114	264	2 020
Carroll	374	12.6	436	6	14.8	D	23	78	2	92	316	6 556	732	2 437
Carter	585	10.3	623	5	11.0	D	46	81	1	100	188	9 096	1 809	3 129
Cheatham	501	13.9	256	2	7.1	D	9	25	1	19	54	3 855	909	2 484
Chester	182	11.7	148	2	9.5	D	3	19	0	0	0	2 132	337	2 128
Claiborne	358	12.0	346	2	11.6	D	18	60	1	110	373	6 292	639	2 100
Clay	90	11.3	89	1	11.2	D	5	63	1	28	386	1 216	165	2 030
Cocke	410	12.2	396	2	11.8	D	20	60	1	109	341	6 403	1 453	4 248
Coffee	661	13.8	514	5	10.7	D	81	169	3	286	625	9 023	2 230	4 558
Crockett	192	13.2	178	1	12.3	D	5	34	0	0	0	2 724	381	2 573
Cumberland	503	10.7	512	3	10.9	D	65	139	1	160	361	11 637	1 783	3 739
Davidson	8 760	15.4	5 074	82	8.9	9.4	2 499	439	10	3 405	638	73 765	48 470	8 347
Decatur	137	11.7	154	2	13.2	D	7	60	1	40	370	2 186	262	2 192
De Kalb	219	12.5	195	1	11.2	D	13	75	1	58	364	3 175	631	3 554
Dickson	629	14.6	395	3	9.1	D	35	81	1	114	270	6 498	1 772	4 030
Dyer	504	13.6	448	5	12.1	D	56	150	1	125	340	6 341	1 836	4 833
Fayette	405	13.9	273	2	9.4	D	12	42	1	38	125	3 559	910	3 100
Fentress	208	12.5	198	2	11.9	D	9	54	1	71	439	3 504	467	2 757
Franklin	463	11.8	422	2	10.7	D	56	143	2	72	192	6 759	1 259	3 146
Gibson	634	13.2	720	10	15.0	15.2	29	60	3	218	452	9 842	1 605	3 271
Giles	360	12.2	326	3	11.1	D	20	68	1	109	377	5 107	827	2 756
Grainger	245	11.8	212	2	10.2	D	5	24	0	0	0	3 927	512	2 432
Greene	735	11.7	712	8	11.3	10.4	77	122	2	285	471	12 641	2 362	3 685
Grundy	196	13.7	184	1	12.8	D	4	28	0	0	0	2 762	147	1 007
Hamblen	831	14.3	591	5	10.1	D	78	134	2	302	559	9 578	2 622	4 427
Hamilton	3 959	12.9	3 166	41	10.3	10.3	927	301	8	1 589	539	51 069	20 919	6 668
Hancock	74	10.9	87	1	12.9	D	4	59	0	0	0	1 132	150	2 169
Hardeman	355	12.4	291	5	10.2	D	22	78	1	48	193	4 620	1 325	4 627
Hardin	280	10.9	323	4	12.6	D	17	66	1	121	485	4 758	980	3 760
Hawkins	646	12.0	527	5	9.8	D	30	56	1	50	101	9 328	1 431	2 622
Haywood	291	14.7	213	2	10.8	D	11	56	1	54	277	2 836	1 018	5 046
Henderson	348	13.7	301	3	11.8	D	11	43	1	25	102	4 774	998	3 837
Henry	379	12.2	437	3	14.1	D	32	103	1	101	336	6 735	1 082	3 413
Hickman	306	13.7	227	1	10.2	D	10	45	1	18	88	3 517	608	2 676
Houston	104	12.8	93	0	11.5	D	8	99	1	35	446	1 544	166	2 014
Humphreys	220	12.3	194	3	10.8	D	12	67	1	42	246	3 282	467	2 556
Jackson	109	9.9	146	1	13.3	D	6	55	1	32	332	1 738	111	992
Jefferson	535	12.1	427	2	9.6	D	29	65	1	67	153	9 083	1 635	3 622
Johnson	168	9.5	191	1	10.8	D	12	69	1	51	304	3 716	283	1 587
Knox	4 784	12.5	3 582	25	9.4	5.2	1 215	318	6	1 897	517	58 827	18 733	4 812
Lake	74	9.4	112	1	14.2	D	4	50	0	0	0	1 245	140	1 727
Lauderdale	415	15.1	303	5	11.1	D	10	37	1	70	289	4 311	1 189	4 306
Lawrence	565	14.1	412	5	10.3	D	23	58	1	83	211	7 939	1 605	3 945
Lewis	137	12.1	126	1	11.1	D	5	44	0	0	0	1 746	261	2 253
Lincoln	378	12.1	386	4	12.3	D	18	57	1	63	212	5 710	882	2 762
Loudon	483	12.3	431	3	11.0	D	38	97	1	30	77	8 939	1 362	3 420
McMinn	619	12.6	506	3	10.3	D	50	102	2	169	365	8 657	2 435	4 875
McNairy	342	13.9	304	3	12.3	D	10	41	1	48	200	5 502	652	2 678
Macon	270	13.2	210	2	10.3	D	12	59	1	43	237	3 069	398	1 916
Madison	1 347	14.6	867	15	9.4	10.9	288	314	2	710	826	13 660	5 718	6 110
Marion	350	12.6	307	2	11.1	D	26	94	2	92	343	4 428	982	3 470

1. Per 1,000 estimated resident population. 2. Deaths of infants under 1 year old. 3. Deaths of infants under 1 year old per 1,000 live births. 4. Data subject to copyright. 5. Per 100,000 resident population as of July 1 of the year shown. 6. Data for serious crimes have not been adjusted for underreporting; this may affect comparability between geographic areas and over time. 7. Per 100,000 population estimated by the FBI.

— # Crime, Education, Money Income, and Poverty

STATE County	Serious crimes known to police,[1] 2002 (cont'd) Rate[2] Violent	Property	Education — Enrollment[3] Total	Percent private	Attainment[4] (percent) High school graduate or less	Bachelor's degree or more	Local government expenditures,[5] 2000–2001 Total current expenditures (mil dol)	Current expenditures per student (dollars)	Money income, 1999 Per capita income[6] (dollars)	Households Median income Dollars	Percent change, 1989–1999 (constant 1999 dollars)	Percent with income of $100,000 or more	Percent below poverty level, 1999 Persons	House-holds	Families	Families with children
	46	47	48	49	50	51	52	53	54	55	56	57	58	59	60	61
SOUTH DAKOTA—Cont'd																
Tripp	NA	NA	1 609	4.7	58.7	13.5	7.4	5 988	13 776	28 333	5.0	3.4	19.9	21.3	15.9	17.6
Turner	45	224	2 149	8.1	54.1	17.0	9.5	6 171	17 343	36 059	34.7	4.9	7.2	8.7	5.7	5.9
Union	25	500	3 301	12.7	45.6	26.3	15.7	6 015	24 355	44 790	49.7	11.6	5.5	6.5	3.7	4.9
Walworth	170	3 256	1 323	7.6	58.7	15.8	6.3	6 805	15 492	27 834	6.2	3.3	18.2	17.2	14.7	23.2
Yankton	156	1 873	5 720	17.7	47.9	23.0	19.8	5 407	17 312	35 374	20.8	5.1	9.6	9.6	6.6	10.1
Ziebach	0	315	883	7.4	64.3	12.0	2.6	10 200	7 463	18 063	-4.8	2.0	49.9	45.1	45.2	55.0
TENNESSEE	717	4 302	1 415 105	14.9	55.7	19.6	5 112.7	5 707	19 393	36 360	9.1	8.3	13.5	14.0	10.3	15.0
Anderson	358	4 231	16 224	7.7	54.0	20.8	83.6	6 763	19 009	35 483	-0.3	7.4	13.1	13.4	10.2	15.9
Bedford	295	2 339	8 678	9.8	69.3	11.1	30.0	4 828	16 698	36 729	15.8	6.0	13.1	13.6	9.7	13.8
Benton	309	2 006	3 320	8.5	76.6	6.3	13.7	5 405	14 646	28 679	4.7	2.6	15.6	15.4	11.9	19.4
Bledsoe	246	920	2 571	8.2	75.1	7.1	9.7	5 536	13 889	28 982	18.2	3.8	18.1	19.7	14.9	18.0
Blount	484	2 920	23 856	12.5	56.0	17.9	97.9	6 034	19 416	37 862	10.2	7.3	9.7	10.9	7.3	11.4
Bradley	519	3 695	22 171	20.9	56.0	15.9	72.3	5 397	18 108	35 034	1.5	6.2	12.2	13.3	9.0	14.2
Campbell	497	3 546	7 939	4.9	76.8	7.0	32.1	5 167	13 301	25 285	14.4	2.9	22.8	23.5	18.4	27.6
Cannon	436	1 584	2 831	9.8	76.0	8.4	10.3	4 967	16 405	32 809	6.9	3.8	12.8	15.1	9.6	13.6
Carroll	283	2 154	6 547	10.3	70.5	11.1	26.8	5 324	16 251	30 463	9.2	4.3	13.9	15.1	10.9	16.4
Carter	323	2 805	12 454	8.7	64.4	12.8	46.8	5 651	14 678	27 371	6.4	3.0	16.9	18.1	12.8	19.8
Cheatham	350	2 134	8 906	12.6	61.7	15.1	34.7	5 058	18 882	45 836	10.8	7.7	7.4	7.7	5.3	7.4
Chester	335	1 793	4 531	32.2	65.3	11.2	11.3	4 585	15 756	34 349	31.7	3.7	14.4	15.6	11.1	16.0
Claiborne	223	1 876	6 863	11.9	74.2	8.9	26.5	5 686	13 032	25 782	12.0	2.6	22.6	24.5	18.4	23.9
Clay	320	1 710	1 712	0.9	80.2	6.8	6.6	5 512	13 320	23 958	0.2	3.3	19.1	20.8	14.3	21.0
Cocke	544	3 704	6 849	4.9	76.9	6.2	28.0	5 270	13 881	25 553	13.1	3.2	22.5	23.6	18.7	28.7
Coffee	307	4 251	11 485	8.8	59.2	17.5	49.1	5 473	18 137	34 898	4.7	6.0	14.3	15.2	10.9	16.0
Crockett	446	2 127	3 233	8.9	72.1	9.1	13.0	4 838	14 600	30 015	10.1	3.6	16.9	18.3	13.2	17.6
Cumberland	277	3 462	9 432	7.7	63.1	13.7	32.2	4 900	16 808	30 901	12.3	4.6	14.7	14.9	11.1	19.1
Davidson	1 529	6 818	141 200	29.2	43.1	30.5	449.8	6 648	23 069	39 797	4.4	10.6	13.0	11.9	10.0	15.7
Decatur	268	1 924	2 284	5.8	76.3	7.3	9.4	5 339	17 285	28 741	19.3	4.0	16.0	18.9	13.8	18.5
De Kalb	394	3 160	3 693	7.7	72.9	11.3	12.8	6 082	17 217	30 359	16.5	4.9	17.0	19.0	11.8	16.7
Dickson	453	3 577	10 311	10.1	67.1	11.3	42.0	5 277	18 043	39 056	19.0	6.0	10.2	11.1	8.1	11.7
Dyer	769	4 065	8 964	8.7	67.3	12.0	39.8	5 869	16 451	32 788	10.4	4.9	15.9	17.0	13.0	18.4
Fayette	344	2 756	6 736	26.1	64.3	12.8	20.0	5 635	17 969	40 279	35.0	9.5	14.3	15.9	10.9	15.8
Fentress	195	2 562	3 601	4.4	79.9	8.3	12.1	5 103	12 999	23 238	24.2	3.0	23.1	25.4	19.5	23.6
Franklin	437	2 709	9 706	21.9	61.7	15.3	31.9	5 499	17 987	36 044	14.5	6.1	13.2	14.5	9.6	14.9
Gibson	430	2 841	10 813	7.2	68.4	10.1	43.3	5 130	16 320	31 105	10.6	4.1	12.8	14.6	9.4	14.6
Giles	383	2 373	6 974	12.0	70.1	10.6	25.1	5 424	17 543	34 824	17.4	5.4	11.7	12.8	9.0	12.7
Grainger	271	2 161	4 193	4.6	77.1	7.8	15.5	4 666	14 505	27 997	9.1	3.8	18.7	20.3	15.1	18.6
Greene	509	3 176	13 201	11.4	67.8	12.8	52.9	5 571	15 746	30 382	5.1	3.7	14.5	15.9	11.2	17.0
Grundy	219	787	3 040	5.9	80.3	7.1	12.7	5 175	12 039	22 959	4.0	2.5	25.8	25.9	22.6	29.5
Hamblen	442	3 984	11 928	7.4	63.7	13.3	52.3	5 394	17 743	32 350	0.9	5.9	14.4	15.1	10.5	15.7
Hamilton	972	5 696	77 307	21.9	46.5	23.9	259.7	6 505	21 593	38 930	9.2	9.9	12.1	12.3	9.2	14.1
Hancock	145	2 025	1 401	5.9	76.0	10.2	6.5	5 497	11 986	19 760	24.4	1.9	29.4	31.2	25.3	32.9
Hardeman	733	3 893	6 246	10.8	71.3	7.8	23.3	5 081	13 349	29 111	13.3	2.9	19.7	20.4	16.9	22.7
Hardin	426	3 334	5 325	10.8	72.1	9.8	20.6	5 446	15 598	27 819	16.9	4.5	18.8	19.3	14.6	20.8
Hawkins	220	2 402	11 234	8.0	69.3	10.0	40.2	5 210	16 073	31 300	6.1	3.7	15.8	17.3	12.7	18.8
Haywood	1 170	3 876	4 975	6.2	71.8	11.1	20.2	5 698	14 669	27 671	18.5	4.5	19.5	21.7	16.3	21.7
Henderson	527	3 311	5 456	8.9	70.5	9.3	21.4	5 014	17 019	32 057	13.1	4.0	12.4	13.8	9.2	12.3
Henry	508	2 905	6 506	6.2	69.6	12.1	25.2	5 381	15 855	30 169	18.9	3.9	14.3	14.1	10.6	17.1
Hickman	440	2 236	4 976	14.8	73.1	6.7	18.8	5 094	14 446	31 013	7.0	3.6	14.3	16.0	11.6	15.0
Houston	158	1 857	1 742	6.1	71.0	10.3	6.7	4 642	15 614	29 968	10.9	3.7	18.1	19.5	14.3	18.9
Humphreys	356	2 200	3 901	10.0	71.2	9.3	15.7	5 262	17 757	35 786	19.7	4.5	10.8	12.6	7.6	12.0
Jackson	116	876	2 188	5.4	77.2	8.4	8.2	4 890	15 020	26 502	9.1	3.8	18.1	21.2	15.1	15.3
Jefferson	348	3 275	10 701	19.3	64.6	12.8	35.1	5 157	16 841	32 824	10.0	5.1	13.4	14.3	9.6	14.5
Johnson	359	1 228	3 316	6.5	76.1	6.9	13.3	5 963	13 388	23 067	14.7	2.6	22.6	24.2	18.7	25.7
Knox	655	4 157	102 622	14.4	44.6	29.0	296.1	5 701	21 875	37 454	7.2	10.4	12.6	13.7	8.4	12.9
Lake	308	1 419	1 424	6.3	79.3	5.4	5.1	5 219	10 794	21 995	-2.6	1.9	23.6	23.6	19.9	29.5
Lauderdale	681	3 625	6 156	8.7	75.9	7.7	23.9	5 249	13 682	29 751	16.7	3.4	19.2	21.0	16.2	21.4
Lawrence	659	3 286	9 223	9.1	72.8	8.7	35.5	5 165	15 848	30 498	8.9	3.6	14.6	15.1	10.7	15.3
Lewis	302	1 951	2 649	13.5	70.7	8.5	8.8	4 569	14 664	30 444	30.5	2.9	13.4	14.3	10.3	14.8
Lincoln	338	2 424	7 089	7.3	67.1	11.9	25.9	4 996	18 837	33 434	13.1	7.7	13.6	15.6	10.0	14.8
Loudon	404	3 015	7 829	7.7	57.6	17.0	36.7	5 473	21 061	40 401	24.0	9.0	10.0	10.5	6.9	10.4
McMinn	895	3 980	10 614	10.3	66.9	10.8	40.7	5 133	16 725	31 919	8.5	4.6	14.5	16.0	10.9	15.7
McNairy	288	2 391	5 328	10.4	71.7	8.8	20.7	5 054	16 385	30 154	19.9	3.7	15.9	17.8	11.8	16.1
Macon	351	1 565	4 610	3.4	78.8	5.6	17.7	4 723	15 286	29 867	16.1	3.3	15.1	17.5	11.3	14.0
Madison	902	5 208	24 814	27.9	52.1	21.5	84.7	6 209	19 389	36 982	16.1	8.7	14.0	14.2	10.8	15.4
Marion	654	2 816	6 125	7.1	69.8	9.5	23.1	5 191	16 419	31 419	16.7	5.3	14.1	14.7	10.8	16.6

1. Data for serious crimes have not been adjusted for underreporting; this may affect comparability between geographic areas and over time. 2. Per 100,000 population estimated by the FBI. 3. All persons 3 years old and over enrolled in nursery school through college. 4. Persons 25 years old and over. 5. Elementary and secondary education expenditures. 6. Based on population enumerated as of April 1, 2000.

STATE County	Total (mil dol)	Percent change, 2001–2002	Per capita[1] Dollars	Rank	Wages and salaries[2] (mil dol)	Proprietor's income (mil dol)	Dividends, interest, and rent (mil dol)	Transfer payments Total (mil dol)	Government payments to individuals Total (mil dol)	Social Security (mil dol)	Medical payments (mil dol)	Income maintenance (mil dol)	Unemployment insurance (mil dol)
	62	63	64	65	66	67	68	69	70	71	72	73	74
SOUTH DAKOTA—Cont'd													
Tripp	140	-10.2	22 404	1 906	59	20	39	30	29	13	12	2	0
Turner	242	-0.7	28 109	531	51	35	46	35	33	17	13	1	0
Union	480	-2.6	37 416	97	449	49	125	42	40	21	14	2	1
Walworth	127	-4.7	22 257	1 944	57	11	37	30	29	13	11	2	0
Yankton	540	0.7	25 147	1 091	376	36	127	87	83	37	35	5	1
Ziebach	27	-11.9	10 303	3 109	11	-3	5	10	9	1	4	3	0
TENNESSEE	159 865	3.4	27 611	X	107 194	18 301	22 372	27 009	25 725	9 657	11 266	2 704	818
Anderson	1 942	4.8	27 100	680	1 846	144	360	389	373	163	155	34	8
Bedford	927	2.2	23 635	1 521	526	91	132	162	153	63	62	14	7
Benton	339	3.5	20 470	2 441	127	27	63	100	97	39	43	8	2
Bledsoe	240	1.9	19 262	2 702	69	36	23	55	52	17	26	6	1
Blount	2 784	5.3	25 353	1 031	1 694	219	449	486	461	211	185	34	11
Bradley	2 302	2.8	25 733	945	1 400	386	298	395	375	156	159	33	10
Campbell	815	5.7	20 409	2 457	298	64	106	273	264	84	125	32	5
Cannon	313	4.6	23 924	1 433	55	29	46	69	66	23	34	5	2
Carroll	652	3.1	22 231	1 951	244	49	112	184	178	65	80	15	9
Carter	1 151	3.8	20 233	2 493	344	76	152	301	289	111	123	28	11
Cheatham	962	2.9	25 956	895	258	119	98	126	118	47	52	9	4
Chester	340	2.2	21 366	2 191	109	40	47	70	66	27	28	6	2
Claiborne	634	4.3	21 082	2 273	257	40	102	194	188	61	91	23	2
Clay	161	4.3	20 220	2 497	59	20	24	48	46	14	23	5	2
Cocke	639	4.8	18 777	2 786	261	36	84	201	193	63	89	24	8
Coffee	1 219	4.8	24 780	1 184	921	115	177	256	245	97	109	21	7
Crockett	328	2.1	22 613	1 846	134	27	60	82	79	27	39	7	3
Cumberland	1 088	4.2	22 339	1 924	499	128	209	294	283	138	110	19	7
Davidson	20 476	2.8	35 959	121	19 273	3 989	2 987	2 490	2 363	843	1 068	256	85
Decatur	255	1.9	21 749	2 077	115	24	36	76	74	23	40	5	3
De Kalb	387	4.4	21 739	2 080	152	49	66	93	89	31	44	9	3
Dickson	1 057	2.2	23 893	1 441	496	93	131	195	185	71	83	16	7
Dyer	896	1.5	24 124	1 364	575	98	125	200	192	70	86	21	7
Fayette	813	2.6	26 073	873	211	75	124	131	124	51	48	15	5
Fentress	343	4.0	20 388	2 463	107	55	44	120	116	32	61	14	3
Franklin	885	3.1	22 048	2 005	325	83	137	200	191	80	83	15	5
Gibson	1 109	1.6	23 063	1 704	541	112	164	292	281	105	132	24	11
Giles	699	1.5	23 705	1 499	359	50	115	147	140	55	61	11	7
Grainger	432	5.9	20 363	2 467	111	31	48	114	109	37	53	11	4
Greene	1 545	3.4	24 275	1 318	929	129	213	412	397	131	214	29	11
Grundy	281	2.3	19 611	2 627	55	39	27	94	91	27	46	12	2
Hamblen	1 446	3.8	24 747	1 197	1 239	141	195	298	285	113	120	26	10
Hamilton	9 454	2.3	30 572	299	7 770	951	1 499	1 540	1 471	586	626	145	32
Hancock	100	4.1	14 758	3 083	27	3	12	41	40	10	21	7	1
Hardeman	509	2.9	18 010	2 897	229	44	67	147	141	45	66	21	4
Hardin	581	2.0	22 431	1 900	276	65	89	160	154	54	75	15	5
Hawkins	1 180	4.2	21 564	2 133	482	53	163	271	259	107	111	25	7
Haywood	397	-0.1	20 292	2 481	210	21	51	104	100	30	47	16	5
Henderson	571	3.4	22 138	1 978	321	38	83	135	129	48	59	11	7
Henry	728	2.4	23 279	1 634	388	90	123	181	174	74	73	14	5
Hickman	420	3.3	18 083	2 885	100	25	54	103	98	37	45	9	4
Houston	166	3.9	20 743	2 357	39	12	23	48	46	15	24	3	1
Humphreys	405	2.5	22 396	1 911	243	25	63	94	90	37	40	7	3
Jackson	230	5.0	20 578	2 409	61	28	38	66	64	21	31	8	2
Jefferson	996	2.9	21 742	2 079	393	87	152	236	226	87	101	19	8
Johnson	290	5.3	16 269	3 038	105	17	47	105	101	34	47	11	5
Knox	11 792	4.2	30 327	318	8 649	1 416	1 773	1 683	1 596	661	660	150	32
Lake	106	-1.6	13 369	3 097	47	-1	17	43	42	12	22	5	1
Lauderdale	483	-0.6	17 784	2 920	244	32	65	135	129	41	62	18	6
Lawrence	861	3.1	21 200	2 236	393	81	115	225	216	79	94	20	17
Lewis	219	4.8	19 138	2 731	74	20	25	62	60	20	29	5	3
Lincoln	745	3.9	23 521	1 560	273	72	114	147	140	57	60	13	4
Loudon	1 069	4.3	26 212	852	392	52	189	223	214	99	90	13	4
McMinn	1 074	2.6	21 407	2 178	659	78	149	260	249	96	108	22	9
McNairy	544	1.8	22 040	2 006	235	56	62	152	146	50	72	15	4
Macon	443	1.5	21 262	2 225	123	46	59	100	96	33	46	9	5
Madison	2 425	3.2	25 983	890	2 109	212	323	445	424	148	185	50	14
Marion	625	2.1	22 496	1 879	205	43	66	155	149	52	71	14	5

1. Based on the resident population estimated as of July 1 of the year shown.   2. Includes other labor income.

Table B. States and Counties — Earnings, Social Security, and Housing

STATE County	Total (mil dol)	Farm	Goods-related[1] Total	Manu-facturing	Information and professional and technical services	Retail trade	Finance, insurance, and real estate	Health services	Govern-ment	Social Security beneficiaries, December 2003 Number	Rate[2]	Supplemental Security Income recipients, December 2003	Housing units, 2003 Total	Percent change, 2000–2003
	75	76	77	78	79	80	81	82	83	84	85	86	87	88
SOUTH DAKOTA—Cont'd														
Tripp	79	9.6	7.2	2.2	5.3	14.0	D	15.5	17.6	1 435	232	134	3 083	1.5
Turner	86	26.6	D	4.1	3.8	6.8	5.0	9.9	16.6	1 935	225	76	3 886	0.9
Union	499	5.0	20.6	18.3	4.8	1.4	4.6	7.1	4.7	2 160	166	88	5 621	5.2
Walworth	68	-2.3	D	D	D	14.6	6.7	13.8	19.2	1 480	266	119	3 168	0.8
Yankton	412	2.8	D	23.8	D	8.4	5.3	D	17.0	4 045	189	301	9 065	2.5
Ziebach	7	-38.0	D	D	D	7.1	D	0.9	80.6	185	73	88	914	4.0
TENNESSEE	125 495	0.1	23.5	17.7	8.7	8.4	8.0	11.1	13.9	1 041 360	178	161 361	2 552 506	4.6
Anderson	1 989	0.0	D	29.8	19.8	5.2	3.2	8.2	13.3	16 485	229	2 341	33 275	2.5
Bedford	617	1.2	D	40.7	D	7.5	4.9	D	12.5	7 040	175	771	15 605	4.1
Benton	155	-0.1	D	22.2	2.8	12.1	4.3	D	19.3	4 350	264	499	8 837	2.8
Bledsoe	104	17.4	D	16.2	D	D	3.9	3.1	29.0	2 280	182	362	5 290	2.9
Blount	1 914	-0.1	D	25.9	3.7	12.1	6.2	5.7	12.6	22 015	197	2 242	48 664	3.4
Bradley	1 786	0.4	D	31.5	4.0	6.6	8.3	D	10.9	16 915	187	2 308	38 545	4.7
Campbell	362	0.4	32.4	16.6	3.4	11.7	5.9	D	21.1	10 105	252	2 999	18 807	1.5
Cannon	84	-0.9	D	13.7	3.2	13.5	3.4	D	18.5	2 715	206	266	5 569	2.7
Carroll	293	1.3	30.3	25.3	D	10.9	5.6	D	16.4	7 240	247	861	13 343	2.2
Carter	420	0.1	D	14.7	4.2	11.4	5.0	D	19.0	12 920	221	1 849	26 503	2.2
Cheatham	377	0.1	D	39.4	D	7.3	5.0	2.8	14.1	5 215	140	385	14 437	6.9
Chester	149	-1.1	D	15.2	D	13.8	4.7	D	18.1	2 985	188	301	6 457	4.5
Claiborne	297	0.1	20.7	12.0	3.1	8.8	4.3	D	19.4	7 460	245	2 104	14 257	7.5
Clay	79	0.9	D	24.9	D	13.5	2.3	10.8	16.1	1 925	242	401	4 085	3.2
Cocke	297	0.9	D	29.4	D	10.9	3.9	10.4	18.6	7 820	228	1 808	16 261	2.6
Coffee	1 036	0.5	D	22.9	16.5	9.9	3.7	7.4	13.4	10 360	209	1 443	21 514	3.7
Crockett	162	-2.6	43.3	35.7	D	9.1	4.6	D	13.3	3 205	221	454	6 247	1.8
Cumberland	626	2.7	27.7	14.1	D	12.5	5.0	13.3	11.7	14 770	299	1 330	23 210	3.4
Davidson	23 262	0.0	12.9	8.0	13.0	7.0	9.2	17.3	10.6	81 885	144	12 057	262 261	3.7
Decatur	139	-1.4	31.7	22.3	4.8	9.2	D	13.0	15.1	2 695	232	341	6 611	2.5
De Kalb	201	1.5	30.5	27.3	D	8.4	3.1	11.3	12.8	3 655	203	621	8 559	1.8
Dickson	589	0.2	D	28.9	4.8	12.5	4.5	9.8	14.7	7 650	170	938	18 825	6.9
Dyer	673	0.4	43.6	37.8	D	7.0	6.2	8.7	13.2	7 735	207	1 511	16 690	3.5
Fayette	285	-0.6	34.1	26.7	4.5	5.6	12.8	D	16.3	5 965	185	1 024	11 758	4.9
Fentress	162	3.3	D	12.9	3.9	15.4	D	D	16.0	4 195	248	1 121	7 807	2.8
Franklin	408	3.4	D	20.7	6.6	11.7	4.1	D	14.1	8 600	212	922	17 772	5.7
Gibson	653	0.8	42.4	37.4	3.8	8.5	5.9	D	14.7	11 480	240	1 430	21 571	2.4
Giles	409	-0.4	D	43.3	D	10.2	5.0	D	11.2	6 205	211	730	13 421	2.3
Grainger	142	1.3	D	38.0	3.1	7.7	D	4.3	18.0	4 615	215	983	10 054	3.3
Greene	1 058	-0.3	D	39.1	D	9.6	4.8	D	13.0	15 280	239	2 432	29 190	3.8
Grundy	94	6.5	D	12.2	D	13.6	3.4	D	21.6	3 360	234	833	6 441	2.5
Hamblen	1 380	0.0	D	43.5	D	8.1	5.0	8.1	9.3	12 320	209	1 909	25 575	3.6
Hamilton	8 721	0.0	20.6	15.1	8.0	9.2	12.2	8.7	16.2	58 070	188	7 739	139 020	3.2
Hancock	30	-1.0	28.9	20.2	D	D	1.7	7.7	36.8	1 400	209	615	3 328	1.5
Hardeman	273	0.0	32.7	29.0	D	7.9	3.9	D	24.0	5 450	193	1 625	11 049	3.3
Hardin	341	0.0	D	30.0	2.7	10.0	4.8	5.1	15.7	6 335	244	1 018	13 190	3.0
Hawkins	535	-0.9	D	44.5	D	9.9	2.1	4.2	16.3	12 255	223	1 772	25 258	3.4
Haywood	231	-1.9	38.1	33.4	2.7	8.5	9.7	5.7	16.4	3 635	185	1 063	8 337	3.1
Henderson	359	-0.6	51.7	46.7	D	8.4	4.7	D	11.9	5 590	216	737	11 825	3.3
Henry	478	1.1	D	29.3	4.2	15.0	4.0	D	17.4	8 030	257	876	16 178	2.5
Hickman	125	-1.8	30.4	19.6	D	10.2	4.1	6.9	26.1	4 320	185	578	9 148	2.7
Houston	51	-0.5	23.8	15.5	D	12.9	2.6	D	26.3	1 710	212	297	4 012	2.8
Humphreys	268	-0.8	45.7	39.7	1.6	7.9	2.9	5.4	23.0	3 925	217	447	8 756	3.2
Jackson	88	-0.8	32.3	25.1	D	5.8	D	7.8	15.3	2 650	236	493	5 289	2.4
Jefferson	479	-0.4	D	23.6	D	9.4	3.6	D	14.9	9 820	209	1 240	20 536	6.3
Johnson	122	-0.8	D	19.8	D	13.1	4.1	5.0	22.6	4 295	239	872	8 226	4.4
Knox	10 065	0.0	15.0	8.6	12.1	10.8	7.1	13.4	15.8	66 735	170	9 495	179 945	5.0
Lake	45	-4.8	10.2	9.6	D	10.6	2.3	D	52.2	1 435	183	365	2 722	0.2
Lauderdale	276	1.9	41.2	37.6	D	9.9	4.8	4.9	22.5	4 855	179	1 241	10 969	3.8
Lawrence	474	-0.3	D	35.2	D	11.8	4.0	D	14.2	8 990	221	1 316	17 140	1.9
Lewis	94	-1.3	D	22.4	2.9	14.6	2.9	D	18.9	2 350	205	276	4 959	2.9
Lincoln	346	5.2	36.0	30.6	3.9	11.6	4.5	4.6	21.1	6 665	210	807	14 236	1.7
Loudon	444	4.3	D	28.2	3.7	9.8	4.9	6.2	16.9	10 210	245	789	18 004	4.2
McMinn	737	0.2	D	39.8	D	9.4	4.4	6.6	12.1	10 860	214	1 617	22 113	2.3
McNairy	291	-0.9	51.8	48.6	D	8.7	2.4	7.9	12.4	6 090	244	1 235	11 502	2.5
Macon	169	3.2	20.9	15.0	11.0	13.5	7.3	D	18.0	4 115	196	655	9 184	3.3
Madison	2 321	0.0	D	24.2	4.8	9.4	4.3	11.9	18.7	15 940	170	2 898	40 245	5.3
Marion	248	0.2	D	24.6	D	15.1	5.3	D	15.9	5 740	206	905	12 898	6.2

1. Covers mining, construction, and manufacturing.   2. Per 1,000 resident population estimated as of July 1 of the year shown.

Table B. States and Counties — Housing, Labor Force, and Employment

STATE County	Housing units, 2000 Total	Percent	Median value[1]	Median owner cost as a percent of income With a mortgage	Median owner cost as a percent of income Without a mortgage[2]	Median rent[3]	Median rent as a percent of income	Substandard units[4] (percent)	Civilian labor force, 2003 Total	Percent change, 2002–2003	Unemployment Total	Rate[5]	Civilian employment[6] 2000 Total	Percent Management, professional and related occupations	Production, transportation, and material moving occupations
	89	90	91	92	93	94	95	96	97	98	99	100	101	102	103
SOUTH DAKOTA—Cont'd															
Tripp	2 550	75.0	50 300	20.0	11.6	302	22.1	4.7	3 438	1.2	115	3.3	3 005	39.5	9.3
Turner	3 510	77.4	57 600	20.4	11.5	363	19.7	0.8	4 016	1.6	145	3.6	4 456	34.1	15.3
Union	4 927	74.5	89 600	19.9	11.1	505	18.6	1.2	6 713	-4.1	341	5.1	6 748	37.7	15.1
Walworth	2 506	71.2	40 300	20.8	11.5	381	22.6	4.7	3 048	-0.7	151	5.0	2 640	34.5	8.7
Yankton	8 187	69.1	77 900	19.5	9.9	396	21.5	2.4	11 488	-0.1	370	3.2	10 800	29.0	18.5
Ziebach	741	59.6	38 300	24.1	12.6	331	35.0	19.6	760	8.6	64	8.4	679	49.3	6.6
TENNESSEE	2 232 905	69.9	93 000	21.1	9.9	505	24.8	3.3	2 909 445	-0.6	168 954	5.8	2 651 638	29.5	19.9
Anderson	29 780	72.5	87 500	19.9	9.9	450	24.3	1.9	36 950	0.1	1 706	4.6	31 309	31.6	15.9
Bedford	13 905	73.5	79 000	20.8	9.9	488	23.7	5.5	19 820	5.8	1 645	8.3	18 522	21.2	30.3
Benton	6 863	80.6	67 000	20.6	9.9	367	22.9	3.0	7 391	0.9	775	10.5	6 694	20.7	28.5
Bledsoe	4 430	81.7	67 200	25.2	9.9	343	22.3	4.7	3 795	-1.7	382	10.1	4 957	18.2	33.6
Blount	42 667	75.9	103 900	20.9	9.9	450	23.0	1.8	56 454	-0.2	2 268	4.0	50 065	28.9	19.1
Bradley	34 281	68.6	91 700	20.9	9.9	455	24.5	2.5	42 511	-0.9	2 340	5.5	42 469	25.4	26.2
Campbell	16 125	73.4	65 600	23.3	10.1	356	26.5	3.8	17 439	-0.4	1 132	6.5	14 599	19.2	28.1
Cannon	4 998	78.5	79 600	20.9	9.9	382	23.9	2.9	5 456	-0.1	326	6.0	5 927	18.2	29.4
Carroll	11 779	79.0	60 900	19.9	9.9	384	22.3	2.7	12 250	0.9	1 523	12.4	12 772	22.8	31.6
Carter	23 486	74.9	77 300	20.7	9.9	393	24.3	2.2	26 811	-1.7	1 764	6.6	25 628	23.9	21.5
Cheatham	12 878	83.6	109 100	21.5	9.9	588	23.3	2.4	19 411	-0.9	797	4.1	18 356	27.4	17.0
Chester	5 660	77.3	78 900	19.4	9.9	401	26.3	4.3	8 322	-3.1	463	5.6	7 094	22.8	23.0
Claiborne	11 799	78.5	72 000	20.4	9.9	353	24.1	3.4	13 196	-0.3	669	5.1	11 754	22.1	30.6
Clay	3 379	80.0	56 400	20.0	13.6	252	21.3	2.8	2 993	8.2	397	13.3	3 434	19.1	35.0
Cocke	13 762	75.5	73 600	22.1	9.9	334	23.7	4.4	16 788	-0.8	1 519	9.0	14 041	18.1	28.0
Coffee	18 885	71.5	82 200	19.9	9.9	445	24.6	2.4	25 541	2.3	1 245	4.9	21 968	27.9	23.7
Crockett	5 632	74.9	65 200	20.5	9.9	393	23.0	3.2	7 609	1.4	786	10.3	6 318	21.0	30.8
Cumberland	19 508	80.6	91 400	22.7	9.9	418	25.1	2.0	25 109	3.3	1 536	6.1	18 818	23.8	22.2
Davidson	237 405	55.3	115 800	21.9	9.9	615	25.2	4.1	314 434	-0.9	14 050	4.5	291 283	37.2	11.9
Decatur	4 908	80.1	58 300	18.8	9.9	346	22.9	3.4	5 209	-2.0	517	9.9	5 173	19.7	31.8
De Kalb	6 984	75.0	82 600	20.7	9.9	389	25.4	3.3	9 451	5.0	464	4.9	7 988	25.4	30.7
Dickson	16 473	76.1	96 200	20.8	9.9	506	25.8	2.8	21 715	-0.9	1 152	5.3	20 664	23.0	20.7
Dyer	14 751	65.6	74 900	19.5	10.0	424	23.5	3.5	17 937	-0.9	1 353	7.5	16 615	24.6	27.8
Fayette	10 467	80.3	100 100	22.9	9.9	383	25.0	4.4	14 309	-1.2	1 015	7.1	12 783	26.4	19.3
Fentress	6 693	79.1	56 500	22.3	10.5	322	23.3	3.4	6 336	0.5	606	9.6	6 323	21.2	30.2
Franklin	15 003	78.5	82 600	19.8	9.9	439	23.6	2.6	20 435	2.7	1 016	5.0	17 529	26.4	26.1
Gibson	19 518	72.1	66 300	19.8	9.9	398	21.7	2.9	20 275	-1.0	2 249	11.1	21 405	22.0	33.3
Giles	11 713	75.4	72 900	19.4	9.9	427	22.0	2.4	15 770	-2.9	1 587	10.1	13 800	21.5	34.4
Grainger	8 270	83.6	74 000	21.3	9.9	348	21.8	4.7	10 323	-2.9	759	7.4	8 937	18.0	33.7
Greene	25 756	76.7	80 400	20.0	9.9	377	22.8	2.6	37 401	2.3	2 673	7.1	28 882	23.8	30.0
Grundy	5 562	82.1	52 300	22.7	11.6	339	26.9	4.3	5 385	1.3	349	6.5	5 383	17.6	34.3
Hamblen	23 211	72.5	85 300	20.3	9.9	418	21.8	3.4	31 105	-2.1	1 883	6.1	27 430	22.3	32.6
Hamilton	124 444	65.9	94 700	19.9	9.9	510	24.3	2.6	155 433	-2.0	6 314	4.1	149 166	33.5	17.1
Hancock	2 769	78.7	53 900	21.1	9.9	206	25.5	9.5	2 667	4.2	182	6.8	2 489	23.2	32.7
Hardeman	9 412	74.1	59 900	20.9	10.6	387	24.1	5.4	9 924	0.7	1 036	10.4	10 157	21.7	28.8
Hardin	10 426	77.3	69 200	20.9	10.5	371	23.3	2.8	12 147	-0.8	1 258	10.4	10 805	20.0	28.7
Hawkins	21 936	78.7	82 500	20.3	9.9	395	22.5	2.7	25 841	0.0	1 843	7.1	22 728	21.1	33.0
Haywood	7 558	65.9	68 400	21.6	10.8	400	24.5	5.6	9 226	3.2	1 143	12.4	8 473	21.4	32.6
Henderson	10 306	79.2	74 000	21.3	9.9	412	24.9	2.2	14 663	1.6	1 212	8.3	11 703	21.5	33.7
Henry	13 019	77.4	75 800	21.6	9.9	403	22.9	2.5	14 444	-1.2	1 406	9.7	13 634	23.2	27.4
Hickman	8 081	80.2	79 600	22.4	9.9	430	22.6	4.8	8 491	0.7	611	7.2	9 075	19.4	26.2
Houston	3 216	77.0	63 300	19.6	9.9	394	24.5	3.9	2 692	-0.4	313	11.6	3 308	21.7	30.7
Humphreys	7 238	77.9	76 000	18.6	9.9	398	22.3	2.6	8 356	0.2	645	7.7	8 153	20.3	27.7
Jackson	4 466	80.8	68 800	21.6	11.3	314	22.4	3.6	5 044	1.0	467	9.3	4 632	19.1	32.6
Jefferson	17 155	77.9	88 800	21.3	9.9	420	24.1	2.6	23 476	-2.7	1 435	6.1	20 664	22.9	24.2
Johnson	6 827	79.7	72 200	23.9	10.4	344	24.9	3.8	6 751	-1.3	634	9.4	6 311	20.6	25.7
Knox	157 872	66.9	98 500	20.7	9.9	493	26.1	1.8	213 791	-0.2	6 684	3.1	187 717	36.7	11.7
Lake	2 410	60.0	53 000	20.4	11.4	287	23.9	2.9	2 729	2.2	169	6.2	2 334	17.0	26.1
Lauderdale	9 567	65.0	59 900	19.7	10.9	407	22.7	4.2	9 520	-0.4	1 382	14.5	10 245	21.4	34.7
Lawrence	15 480	77.1	72 400	20.5	10.5	395	22.7	3.6	19 529	0.8	2 167	11.1	17 139	21.4	31.9
Lewis	4 381	79.5	66 700	19.2	9.9	357	22.9	4.4	4 297	-0.4	501	11.7	4 841	20.9	28.3
Lincoln	12 503	76.2	73 900	19.8	10.2	388	22.3	3.2	15 253	0.9	859	5.6	14 762	25.6	26.7
Loudon	15 944	79.1	97 300	20.1	9.9	462	21.5	2.2	21 855	-0.6	922	4.2	18 072	25.6	22.7
McMinn	19 721	75.7	80 300	20.3	9.9	409	22.7	2.5	21 911	-1.0	1 905	8.7	21 947	21.8	33.1
McNairy	9 980	80.0	61 400	20.1	9.9	356	22.7	2.5	11 485	-0.6	923	8.0	10 797	21.8	32.5
Macon	7 916	78.6	67 700	20.0	9.9	364	24.9	4.9	9 320	3.1	916	9.8	9 510	17.0	34.1
Madison	35 552	67.0	85 100	19.9	9.9	510	24.6	2.8	50 892	-2.4	2 948	5.8	43 558	30.9	19.7
Marion	11 037	80.5	76 100	20.8	9.9	420	22.1	2.8	12 806	-3.0	729	5.7	12 056	21.6	30.3

1. Specified owner-occupied units. 2. Median monthly owner costs is often in the minimum category—9.9 percent or less, which is indicated as 9.9 percent. 3. Specified renter-occupied units. 4. Overcrowded or lacking complete plumbing facilities. 5. Percent of civilian labor force. 6. Persons 16 years old and over.

Table B. States and Counties — Nonfarm Employment and Agriculture

	Private nonfarm establishments, employment and payroll, 2001									Agriculture, 2002			
		Employment						Annual payroll		Farms			
												Percent with—		
STATE County	Number of establishments	Total	Health care and social assistance	Manufacturing	Retail trade	Finance and insurance	Professional, scientific, and technical services	Total (mil dol)	Average per employee (dollars)	Number	Less than 50 acres	500 acres and over	Farm operators whose principal occupation is farming (percent)
	104	105	106	107	108	109	110	111	112	113	114	115	116

SOUTH DAKOTA—Cont'd													
Tripp	223	1 720	363	D	400	83	54	32	18 519	666	8.7	63.4	75.2
Turner	271	1 706	373	101	303	103	34	30	17 758	713	16.0	35.5	73.6
Union	403	13 768	524	7 134	1 627	460	160	546	39 632	522	18.0	37.7	73.8
Walworth	243	1 877	371	D	433	75	104	33	17 356	299	12.0	54.8	70.6
Yankton	700	9 921	1 731	2 508	1 610	650	191	226	22 763	690	17.8	35.5	72.3
Ziebach	15	159	D	0	15	D	0	3	20 761	227	4.8	79.7	79.3
TENNESSEE	129 659	2 378 510	291 760	448 948	310 202	107 781	96 986	70 722	29 734	87 595	43.6	4.3	50.3
Anderson	1 676	39 369	3 837	9 792	3 971	788	9 908	1 501	38 127	596	53.2	1.3	40.3
Bedford	755	12 849	1 041	5 546	1 243	266	152	309	24 062	1 667	42.7	5.0	47.3
Benton	321	3 453	524	896	699	140	D	71	20 493	595	37.5	3.5	47.2
Bledsoe	135	1 363	181	581	156	31	D	28	20 634	560	27.1	6.3	52.5
Blount	2 212	40 058	4 069	8 811	5 529	1 753	1 006	1 177	29 385	1 302	54.6	1.5	47.5
Bradley	1 872	38 740	5 611	11 894	4 435	1 320	787	1 030	26 585	921	48.0	3.3	56.7
Campbell	628	7 378	1 294	2 050	1 503	304	116	160	21 623	419	45.1	1.7	49.9
Cannon	156	1 329	212	296	248	53	54	25	18 658	974	38.9	3.3	50.4
Carroll	521	6 775	1 038	2 604	969	298	98	148	21 783	973	33.6	5.7	52.1
Carter	729	10 396	1 748	2 668	1 551	354	119	227	21 876	573	63.2	1.6	52.5
Cheatham	515	6 432	358	2 679	829	126	164	164	25 562	669	38.4	2.4	48.9
Chester	242	3 335	361	691	547	77	61	68	20 306	512	28.1	4.9	48.4
Claiborne	468	7 958	904	3 295	775	282	91	167	20 925	1 388	47.6	2.2	58.1
Clay	121	1 377	300	469	137	33	13	31	22 399	514	37.7	5.3	51.6
Cocke	491	6 760	828	2 487	1 318	182	67	154	22 816	880	43.4	1.1	52.4
Coffee	1 222	21 312	2 121	5 946	3 414	467	2 044	622	29 188	1 069	48.0	5.8	50.9
Crockett	277	2 875	360	1 075	304	149	D	77	26 655	420	37.4	16.2	63.6
Cumberland	961	12 099	2 024	2 459	2 496	359	217	272	22 447	854	41.7	4.7	47.1
Davidson	18 155	395 387	52 136	26 039	44 261	22 502	18 367	13 572	34 326	560	53.6	2.5	43.6
Decatur	252	3 333	701	996	447	162	72	76	22 793	438	19.4	6.4	51.1
De Kalb	311	4 570	460	2 199	461	118	72	126	27 528	887	44.6	3.2	50.5
Dickson	883	12 762	1 479	4 075	2 185	456	133	328	25 684	1 448	40.0	2.0	45.2
Dyer	922	15 292	1 489	6 120	2 123	526	207	369	24 134	534	36.0	18.5	60.1
Fayette	431	4 304	385	1 713	410	205	87	108	25 048	894	34.7	11.2	48.0
Fentress	272	2 949	792	490	674	157	D	57	19 272	573	41.2	5.4	58.6
Franklin	655	8 117	1 253	2 149	1 538	222	149	190	23 444	1 135	48.5	5.8	55.5
Gibson	1 059	14 598	1 834	6 380	2 017	475	244	370	25 326	1 092	42.4	11.5	51.1
Giles	573	8 524	755	3 538	1 337	294	255	194	22 778	1 922	30.1	3.9	45.8
Grainger	249	2 725	169	1 412	366	D	D	56	20 566	1 216	46.3	1.2	50.4
Greene	1 188	21 948	2 674	7 827	3 065	537	315	538	24 506	3 367	56.9	1.2	53.4
Grundy	195	1 437	265	238	419	45	D	23	16 102	409	49.1	2.4	53.3
Hamblen	1 390	31 436	3 360	14 250	3 586	597	288	857	27 258	736	55.6	1.8	50.8
Hamilton	8 810	174 484	20 631	33 255	19 714	12 804	8 088	5 052	28 955	700	54.1	2.7	47.4
Hancock	63	581	D	D	116	D	D	9	16 100	568	38.4	2.5	58.6
Hardeman	410	6 345	1 318	1 824	749	230	D	143	22 491	602	23.3	10.8	44.9
Hardin	520	6 131	756	2 132	952	178	102	145	23 688	634	31.9	6.9	52.7
Hawkins	588	11 750	711	6 160	1 457	218	79	303	25 776	2 014	49.4	1.3	53.1
Haywood	370	4 805	351	1 948	801	283	47	111	23 106	408	23.0	22.8	53.4
Henderson	527	7 570	588	3 052	1 071	294	121	171	22 649	1 084	27.1	6.8	46.9
Henry	743	10 248	1 417	3 021	1 386	314	216	229	22 363	965	33.5	7.5	50.7
Hickman	331	2 464	464	629	370	88	D	54	22 058	756	29.4	5.7	46.3
Houston	115	1 051	319	210	181	41	6	21	19 547	336	26.5	4.8	41.4
Humphreys	316	4 440	443	1 984	671	65	62	135	30 481	718	29.7	8.1	45.4
Jackson	104	1 332	150	654	125	61	13	31	23 327	609	37.3	4.8	51.4
Jefferson	656	10 320	832	3 151	1 549	227	159	223	21 601	1 311	52.6	1.3	52.7
Johnson	245	2 692	288	801	495	86	D	59	22 084	666	55.1	1.1	49.4
Knox	11 099	188 129	29 199	16 988	29 118	8 941	10 349	5 425	28 838	1 410	60.3	1.1	47.3
Lake	91	660	105	D	158	21	11	12	18 400	64	15.6	54.7	82.8
Lauderdale	381	6 597	502	3 205	843	217	51	149	22 605	624	38.0	15.9	52.4
Lawrence	799	11 198	972	4 286	1 816	262	167	248	22 113	1 869	38.7	3.4	50.0
Lewis	211	2 008	390	539	380	34	D	40	19 671	251	26.3	6.8	47.4
Lincoln	607	7 852	785	3 504	1 488	172	122	148	18 800	1 926	35.5	5.7	49.6
Loudon	744	10 219	946	3 217	1 596	322	198	265	25 951	954	56.4	2.3	49.9
McMinn	898	17 032	1 579	8 238	2 226	512	221	443	26 005	1 204	46.3	3.1	45.5
McNairy	444	9 413	721	2 713	849	111	43	161	17 143	822	23.7	5.1	42.8
Macon	320	3 795	455	1 451	785	191	58	70	18 375	1 317	40.7	3.0	50.8
Madison	2 592	52 389	8 058	12 393	7 272	1 294	1 200	1 416	27 026	740	38.6	9.7	46.5
Marion	433	5 695	684	1 691	1 168	190	321	119	20 847	298	35.2	8.4	50.0

Table B. States and Counties — **Agriculture**

| | Land in farms | | | | | Value of land and buildings (dollars) | | Value of machinery and equipment average per farm (dollars) | Value of products sold | | | | Percent of farms with sales of — | | Government payments | |
STATE County	Acreage (1,000)	Percent change, 1997–2002	Acres Average size of farm	Total irrigated (1,000)	Total cropland (1,000)	Average per farm	Average per acre		Total (mil dol)	Average per farm (dollars)	Percent from — Crops	Percent from — Livestock and poultry products	$10,000 or more	$100,000 or more	Total ($1,000)	Percent of farms
	117	118	119	120	121	122	123	124	125	126	127	128	129	130	131	132
SOUTH DAKOTA—Cont'd																
Tripp	1 054	13.3	1 582	5	503	562 356	338	89 214	91	136 933	15.8	84.2	73.6	33.3	4 332	62.2
Turner	348	-1.1	487	18	304	647 670	1 291	119 974	99	139 343	45.7	54.3	77.4	32.5	3 185	65.2
Union	277	9.1	530	33	250	1 050 300	1 923	129 305	80	153 055	61.1	38.9	76.2	39.3	3 470	67.2
Walworth	427	-2.3	1 429	1	233	458 517	340	131 265	31	102 413	45.9	54.1	61.5	27.1	2 122	66.6
Yankton	342	31.0	496	13	289	545 556	1 049	117 219	78	113 458	58.3	41.7	71.7	31.2	2 686	59.0
Ziebach	1 173	-21.7	5 167	0	225	916 111	173	115 050	21	93 710	5.7	94.3	75.8	32.6	2 383	56.8
TENNESSEE	11 682	5.0	133	61	6 993	325 783	2 405	45 263	2 200	25 113	48.8	51.2	22.5	4.4	59 231	18.3
Anderson	48	17.1	80	0	25	318 874	4 033	31 191	4	6 655	34.3	65.7	12.8	1.0	72	13.3
Bedford	219	5.8	132	0	115	335 231	2 494	44 808	86	51 366	6.6	93.4	29.3	9.4	1 120	20.5
Benton	78	13.0	131	0	40	195 174	1 580	37 065	5	8 718	30.5	69.5	14.1	1.7	394	28.2
Bledsoe	93	-3.1	166	1	52	348 552	2 174	59 905	26	45 797	25.7	74.3	36.1	8.6	187	14.3
Blount	105	12.9	81	1	68	428 810	5 304	44 464	24	18 806	61.8	38.2	19.8	2.8	304	4.1
Bradley	95	5.6	103	0	46	353 023	3 804	44 797	59	64 244	7.3	92.7	26.9	11.9	449	12.5
Campbell	34	9.7	82	D	19	169 425	1 970	31 950	3	8 135	33.9	66.0	16.7	1.4	59	12.2
Cannon	122	18.4	125	0	59	334 799	2 768	34 176	14	14 348	42.0	58.0	19.4	3.5	418	16.4
Carroll	183	6.4	188	D	122	311 912	1 675	48 781	25	25 350	82.4	17.6	20.0	3.6	1 512	46.9
Carter	37	-5.1	65	0	19	236 611	3 033	74 886	7	12 908	35.2	64.8	20.6	1.6	128	11.0
Cheatham	72	5.9	108	0	43	320 153	3 109	30 278	8	11 299	76.8	23.2	22.4	2.1	98	17.9
Chester	79	8.2	154	0	43	240 110	1 644	29 251	5	9 402	66.8	33.2	18.4	1.6	566	45.1
Claiborne	135	-6.3	97	0	64	188 169	1 840	40 184	17	12 483	32.7	67.3	21.1	1.0	217	10.3
Clay	70	-2.8	137	0	33	277 583	1 515	38 034	21	40 362	10.5	89.5	28.2	4.7	148	18.5
Cocke	73	-2.7	83	0	41	235 750	2 809	45 737	15	16 527	44.1	55.9	17.3	2.5	293	4.7
Coffee	145	6.6	136	2	95	354 002	2 581	54 132	30	28 210	41.6	58.4	23.6	6.5	827	16.2
Crockett	145	-4.0	345	D	126	696 981	2 048	108 978	35	83 595	95.6	4.4	44.3	18.3	1 974	51.7
Cumberland	110	10.0	129	0	60	418 582	2 570	52 559	36	41 778	15.6	84.4	20.1	3.2	432	17.1
Davidson	51	-1.9	90	0	23	479 284	6 559	63 425	11	19 579	79.8	20.2	15.7	1.3	77	6.1
Decatur	88	0.0	202	0	40	280 028	1 326	48 105	4	9 932	35.2	64.8	23.7	1.1	346	34.7
De Kalb	100	1.0	113	1	50	265 020	2 544	29 459	37	41 879	85.2	14.8	25.3	2.5	296	18.6
Dickson	158	6.0	109	0	74	256 785	2 612	31 990	12	8 346	36.9	63.1	17.7	0.6	183	11.0
Dyer	213	-9.0	398	5	194	781 615	1 896	102 917	45	84 434	92.2	7.8	43.8	16.9	1 933	42.3
Fayette	274	1.1	306	1	173	650 266	2 031	62 943	38	42 543	77.1	22.9	21.0	8.8	2 837	38.1
Fentress	80	14.3	139	0	40	329 687	2 253	60 728	33	57 221	D	D	31.4	11.7	160	17.5
Franklin	153	15.9	135	1	109	335 508	2 681	58 151	59	52 110	42.0	58.0	33.3	13.7	914	21.5
Gibson	311	11.9	285	3	272	459 366	1 594	87 545	64	58 984	85.5	14.5	30.1	11.2	3 876	51.1
Giles	271	8.8	141	1	130	250 396	2 093	31 711	29	14 925	17.6	82.4	19.1	2.6	1 142	25.5
Grainger	103	6.2	85	1	51	211 602	2 064	31 899	16	13 308	56.0	44.0	22.5	2.4	120	9.0
Greene	247	9.3	73	0	159	223 653	2 941	38 979	55	16 285	21.8	78.2	19.8	2.8	786	12.6
Grundy	42	16.7	103	1	20	204 017	2 136	56 085	42	103 090	20.5	79.5	46.7	21.5	54	4.2
Hamblen	58	11.5	79	1	38	270 088	3 852	40 720	20	27 785	45.4	54.6	19.0	3.1	214	10.5
Hamilton	63	10.5	91	0	32	365 055	3 074	43 898	11	16 008	20.3	79.7	17.1	2.9	133	6.6
Hancock	64	-5.9	113	0	27	215 382	1 954	40 427	6	11 118	38.6	61.4	21.7	1.1	58	10.4
Hardeman	154	-7.2	255	0	80	363 952	1 236	75 715	13	21 249	77.0	23.0	20.8	3.8	952	43.2
Hardin	112	-3.4	177	1	67	287 955	1 476	74 447	9	13 843	71.8	28.2	18.9	2.5	745	39.3
Hawkins	168	14.3	83	0	83	238 610	2 716	39 324	22	10 879	48.0	52.0	17.6	1.5	178	4.8
Haywood	211	-0.5	517	2	180	838 311	1 621	138 160	45	109 135	97.5	2.5	42.9	19.4	3 216	58.6
Henderson	173	13.8	160	0	91	225 948	1 394	37 061	18	16 749	31.7	68.3	22.8	4.3	1 027	47.0
Henry	194	4.9	201	1	127	314 525	1 536	53 803	46	47 888	51.6	48.4	29.7	8.8	1 608	41.7
Hickman	129	0.8	170	0	59	308 789	1 519	40 077	9	11 291	28.1	71.9	19.7	2.2	173	11.8
Houston	49	0.0	145	0	24	229 397	1 457	34 984	5	13 485	14.4	85.6	18.2	2.7	63	9.8
Humphreys	135	10.7	188	0	63	326 138	1 599	50 011	10	13 710	37.1	62.9	20.8	3.6	163	10.2
Jackson	79	-4.8	130	0	33	246 239	1 731	26 404	4	7 185	46.3	53.7	18.4	0.5	55	8.7
Jefferson	108	10.2	82	D	67	287 860	3 853	40 755	23	17 573	16.6	83.4	18.8	2.1	383	13.7
Johnson	49	0.0	74	0	25	243 083	3 744	29 567	7	10 504	44.4	55.6	18.2	1.7	96	11.6
Knox	94	6.8	66	1	53	358 556	5 170	33 849	20	14 353	67.5	32.5	14.5	1.6	89	5.5
Lake	90	0.0	1 409	4	88	2 094 192	1 509	320 380	18	276 280	99.9	0.1	76.6	48.4	848	60.9
Lauderdale	215	12.0	345	2	189	541 763	1 420	82 335	38	61 125	94.7	5.3	34.1	13.3	2 804	53.4
Lawrence	236	10.3	126	1	128	221 103	1 808	39 991	30	15 858	31.1	68.9	21.3	2.5	1 611	34.7
Lewis	37	0.0	147	0	15	272 848	1 906	36 939	3	10 183	59.0	41.0	15.1	1.2	25	8.0
Lincoln	284	2.9	148	2	149	333 963	2 024	40 450	46	24 065	37.8	62.2	23.9	3.9	1 479	26.5
Loudon	83	12.2	87	0	49	345 996	3 938	53 257	51	53 069	D	D	16.4	3.0	479	12.4
McMinn	128	0.8	106	0	72	271 489	2 814	39 856	33	27 452	9.4	90.6	20.3	5.1	849	8.7
McNairy	134	3.1	163	1	75	184 754	1 061	56 951	9	10 806	68.9	31.1	16.2	2.7	893	47.2
Macon	145	7.4	110	0	74	305 082	2 648	54 649	26	19 370	68.1	31.9	28.2	4.1	326	16.0
Madison	162	11.0	219	3	120	539 067	2 530	70 456	27	36 657	80.2	19.8	22.6	7.0	1 862	45.4
Marion	51	0.0	171	0	26	357 306	2 009	49 964	14	48 509	11.1	88.9	32.6	8.7	68	7.0

Table B. States and Counties — **Residential Construction, Wholesale Trade, Retail Trade, and Real Estate**

STATE County	Value of residential construction authorized by building permits, 2003 — New construction ($1,000)	Number of housing units	Wholesale trade, 1997 — Number of establishments	Number of employees	Sales (mil dol)	Annual payroll (mil dol)	Retail trade,[1] 1997 — Number of establishments	Number of employees	Sales (mil dol)	Annual payroll (mil dol)	Real estate and rental and leasing, 1997 — Number of establishments	Number of employees	Receipts (mil dol)	Annual payroll (mil dol)
	133	134	135	136	137	138	139	140	141	142	143	144	145	146
SOUTH DAKOTA—Cont'd														
Tripp	240	2	17	175	82.4	3.1	52	364	52.1	4.5	3	11	0.3	0.1
Turner	2 054	22	14	76	99.5	1.8	42	D	D	D	5	D	D	D
Union	21 584	153	26	210	225.0	6.1	45	D	D	D	7	15	1.6	0.1
Walworth	153	2	11	69	34.2	1.5	61	398	54.3	4.9	6	8	0.4	0.1
Yankton	7 327	47	50	428	290.1	8.6	162	1 988	229.6	25.2	19	72	6.4	1.2
Ziebach	NA	NA	2	D	D	D	3	D	D	D	NA	NA	NA	NA
TENNESSEE	4 478 748	37 530	8 234	120 228	82 626.4	3 975.4	24 808	304 452	50 813.2	4 810.3	4 999	29 626	3 732.0	667.3
Anderson	43 180	308	51	342	105.9	9.9	331	3 923	700.9	60.8	74	336	39.2	6.4
Bedford	8 288	159	43	284	72.3	7.7	145	1 298	207.4	18.1	29	70	9.7	1.3
Benton	722	6	14	99	35.2	2.5	78	746	92.5	9.4	11	28	2.1	0.3
Bledsoe	NA	NA	2	D	D	D	31	162	23.6	1.8	2	D	D	D
Blount	36 826	290	97	1 347	655.2	38.2	385	5 590	1 189.1	99.3	80	443	48.3	7.4
Bradley	52 401	614	93	2 328	1 651.3	51.0	392	4 103	745.7	66.1	72	278	29.4	4.9
Campbell	3 170	43	26	477	117.6	15.0	159	1 551	228.9	21.3	18	106	8.9	1.5
Cannon	908	9	8	D	D	D	30	213	33.3	2.9	4	D	D	D
Carroll	1 943	37	26	210	48.2	4.6	121	950	127.4	11.6	14	30	3.1	0.2
Carter	2 448	20	28	D	D	D	156	1 602	265.1	23.2	19	71	5.8	0.8
Cheatham	29 909	296	20	119	29.3	3.1	75	729	130.0	10.5	14	D	D	D
Chester	3 179	39	10	62	34.4	1.3	65	481	99.8	7.8	5	20	0.8	0.3
Claiborne	16 755	184	17	D	D	D	97	736	111.5	10.2	15	78	5.5	0.9
Clay	NA	NA	2	D	D	D	23	127	19.0	1.7	2	D	D	D
Cocke	270	4	19	167	68.9	5.3	126	1 361	191.3	16.3	22	96	4.1	0.9
Coffee	16 149	173	50	482	127.4	10.7	283	3 127	490.6	43.8	46	134	13.0	2.2
Crockett	255	2	15	D	D	D	58	339	58.4	4.4	3	3	0.5	0.0
Cumberland	11 808	102	35	276	130.5	7.7	222	2 171	368.6	32.4	44	512	43.9	11.2
Davidson	595 894	4 313	1 445	26 012	17 005.2	962.7	3 017	44 452	7 737.6	782.7	866	6 603	1 119.8	173.2
Decatur	482	10	7	36	3.3	0.5	50	371	65.1	5.2	4	7	0.6	0.1
De Kalb	1 443	23	8	271	96.3	6.6	65	419	67.3	5.7	14	26	1.4	0.3
Dickson	30 397	242	27	471	274.7	11.5	185	2 158	412.9	35.2	32	D	D	D
Dyer	10 158	125	47	572	221.2	15.7	220	2 237	362.4	30.4	33	92	8.0	1.9
Fayette	59 607	341	21	163	102.8	5.1	69	459	77.4	7.0	10	26	2.1	0.4
Fentress	50	4	8	20	4.3	0.4	64	570	77.2	7.1	5	54	3.3	0.8
Franklin	24 384	261	23	145	46.9	3.4	164	1 555	231.0	21.9	20	73	4.2	0.7
Gibson	11 801	104	51	520	333.2	14.4	248	2 221	358.4	33.0	30	76	5.4	0.8
Giles	1 303	16	34	302	93.1	9.5	137	1 218	201.7	16.9	16	78	3.0	0.8
Grainger	0	0	9	46	18.6	1.0	59	385	57.2	4.5	4	11	0.4	0.1
Greene	26 752	348	44	679	283.5	12.4	253	2 871	440.2	39.9	35	97	11.2	1.6
Grundy	NA	NA	4	20	2.1	0.4	57	414	51.5	5.4	8	33	1.1	0.2
Hamblen	22 489	211	70	1 199	460.2	35.1	323	3 595	645.9	54.7	52	184	29.4	3.2
Hamilton	260 725	2 011	694	D	D	D	1 531	20 122	3 269.6	325.8	347	2 045	236.7	58.5
Hancock	35	2	4	25	3.2	0.2	20	100	13.4	1.4	NA	NA	NA	NA
Hardeman	8 767	72	22	D	D	D	103	860	120.7	11.2	10	32	2.6	0.3
Hardin	1 560	34	18	92	35.9	3.0	131	1 079	183.3	15.4	18	50	3.4	0.6
Hawkins	8 873	92	11	D	D	D	138	1 230	194.9	16.0	19	56	4.0	0.7
Haywood	1 238	21	12	135	114.6	3.4	100	830	146.4	12.0	13	33	2.3	0.4
Henderson	4 052	32	20	150	44.1	3.1	124	1 090	177.7	16.0	8	22	1.4	0.2
Henry	8 519	123	41	625	198.0	16.1	167	1 608	244.6	21.9	20	55	5.0	0.5
Hickman	630	8	8	35	9.2	0.5	66	360	48.8	4.5	8	18	1.0	0.2
Houston	127	1	4	D	D	D	29	164	23.7	2.0	2	D	D	D
Humphreys	2 256	26	11	142	52.0	3.0	77	657	110.8	9.5	3	16	0.7	0.2
Jackson	0	0	1	D	D	D	27	145	20.5	1.4	3	5	0.3	0.1
Jefferson	46 106	387	42	246	73.8	6.2	120	1 415	249.5	21.1	18	53	2.6	0.6
Johnson	4 865	102	3	D	D	D	57	417	67.5	6.3	8	D	D	D
Knox	348 825	2 961	950	12 580	7 507.7	449.4	1 946	28 344	5 029.7	478.9	464	2 822	326.5	65.7
Lake	336	7	9	D	D	D	26	172	20.1	2.0	4	13	1.0	0.1
Lauderdale	11 632	183	26	548	364.9	18.4	100	867	123.9	11.4	10	21	2.6	0.5
Lawrence	700	11	42	296	174.6	8.7	200	1 822	315.2	27.1	22	77	8.6	1.2
Lewis	333	4	8	67	11.6	1.3	59	367	66.3	5.4	6	5	0.4	0.1
Lincoln	819	4	29	211	102.6	3.9	138	1 360	205.6	18.0	25	92	9.8	1.6
Loudon	37 328	243	41	232	93.1	6.0	137	1 407	271.7	21.0	23	46	7.5	1.2
McMinn	4 893	62	32	D	D	D	209	2 119	361.7	30.3	35	120	12.5	2.2
McNairy	2 723	27	21	D	D	D	100	728	117.2	9.9	14	69	6.8	1.1
Macon	2 205	21	12	84	19.2	1.2	81	582	89.3	7.8	9	37	1.8	0.4
Madison	66 256	722	161	2 186	756.4	60.5	582	8 169	1 196.5	114.9	90	423	43.2	7.4
Marion	15 906	142	15	D	D	D	111	1 232	186.5	15.2	13	68	3.3	0.7

1. Establishments with payroll.

STATE County	Professional, scientific, and technical services,[1] 1997				Manufacturing, 1997				Accommodation and foodservices, 1997			
	Number of establishments	Number of employees	Receipts (mil dol)	Annual payroll (mil dol)	Number of establishments	Number of employees	Receipts (mil dol)	Annual payroll (mil dol)	Number of establishments	Number of employees	Sales (mil dol)	Annual payroll (mil dol)
	147	148	149	150	151	152	153	154	155	156	157	158
SOUTH DAKOTA—Cont'd												
Tripp	12	29	1.9	0.5	NA	NA	NA	NA	19	184	4.9	1.4
Turner	10	22	1.2	0.3	NA	NA	NA	NA	17	92	2.2	0.4
Union	31	80	5.7	2.1	26	D	D	D	37	473	15.7	3.8
Walworth	10	63	3.4	1.1	NA	NA	NA	NA	31	218	6.4	1.5
Yankton	41	203	12.9	4.7	30	2 517	452.2	62.3	67	989	23.6	6.2
Ziebach	NA	NA	NA	NA	NA	NA	NA	NA	2	D	D	D
TENNESSEE	8 812	72 225	6 911.8	2 686.6	7 407	483 823	98 503.1	14 351.9	9 604	197 881	6 790.2	1 880.3
Anderson	180	7 960	934.5	384.6	107	8 559	1 336.2	328.0	129	2 384	71.6	19.9
Bedford	36	233	10.9	3.2	64	5 582	1 302.7	146.6	49	727	19.8	4.9
Benton	11	44	2.0	0.5	17	1 150	97.5	23.7	39	339	10.7	2.1
Bledsoe	5	D	D	D	NA	NA	NA	NA	8	82	1.8	0.5
Blount	122	646	55.4	22.5	126	7 027	2 806.9	251.9	167	3 223	97.3	26.5
Bradley	116	699	48.8	17.8	142	12 974	2 931.7	363.8	138	2 533	81.8	21.8
Campbell	27	108	7.6	2.1	53	1 945	243.7	49.1	60	910	26.6	6.7
Cannon	7	19	2.5	0.2	NA	NA	NA	NA	10	119	2.9	0.8
Carroll	24	66	3.8	1.1	50	3 103	456.7	64.1	45	532	12.0	2.9
Carter	36	130	6.8	2.0	48	1 960	273.4	50.7	47	846	21.9	5.8
Cheatham	20	104	23.2	4.1	42	3 060	579.7	81.9	29	348	11.0	2.8
Chester	6	16	1.3	0.2	24	853	76.0	18.7	19	306	6.6	2.1
Claiborne	23	81	3.0	1.2	34	3 584	317.1	67.1	22	412	12.1	3.2
Clay	4	D	D	D	8	771	85.7	13.7	20	73	3.4	0.8
Cocke	20	43	2.7	0.7	40	2 627	382.8	64.6	52	978	30.5	8.3
Coffee	59	D	D	D	67	5 595	1 082.9	178.4	106	1 949	56.5	15.7
Crockett	10	D	D	D	16	1 241	160.8	26.6	16	82	4.8	0.7
Cumberland	42	168	9.7	3.8	47	2 437	442.9	58.9	75	1 300	39.6	11.4
Davidson	1 694	15 055	1 636.8	605.8	752	31 716	6 721.8	1 100.0	1 407	37 523	1 511.7	426.3
Decatur	11	D	D	D	35	1 113	137.0	21.8	21	175	3.9	0.9
De Kalb	14	54	2.4	0.7	28	2 740	333.9	65.7	22	317	6.6	1.7
Dickson	37	120	8.4	2.9	51	3 574	710.3	102.5	70	1 116	37.7	10.6
Dyer	45	179	12.2	3.2	42	6 404	1 121.4	183.5	67	998	30.2	7.6
Fayette	21	50	4.9	1.4	39	1 193	271.6	33.3	18	196	5.0	1.5
Fentress	12	64	3.7	2.1	31	1 471	141.4	22.5	18	225	6.0	1.5
Franklin	38	142	10.7	3.5	43	1 872	438.2	53.1	50	592	16.9	4.4
Gibson	41	176	9.2	2.9	90	7 607	1 085.6	200.7	62	815	22.1	5.9
Giles	28	127	11.5	5.1	48	3 515	679.7	104.6	38	615	14.7	3.7
Grainger	5	D	D	D	35	1 321	180.9	30.6	10	D	D	D
Greene	49	171	13.4	5.5	107	7 990	1 296.7	198.0	102	1 622	42.1	11.9
Grundy	3	D	D	D	NA	NA	NA	NA	8	60	1.9	0.5
Hamblen	68	309	20.2	7.1	129	14 586	2 039.2	369.6	100	2 269	58.3	15.6
Hamilton	664	4 570	401.5	162.7	515	32 559	5 493.2	991.4	711	13 376	453.2	128.2
Hancock	2	D	D	D	NA	NA	NA	NA	2	D	D	D
Hardeman	11	40	2.2	0.7	37	1 957	274.7	51.4	30	291	8.2	1.8
Hardin	26	78	3.5	1.1	52	2 628	530.2	70.0	49	576	17.2	4.4
Hawkins	32	123	7.1	1.9	50	6 534	1 040.9	219.4	45	788	18.0	4.9
Haywood	12	22	1.8	0.6	23	2 477	425.5	64.1	26	350	11.4	2.9
Henderson	24	48	4.2	0.9	47	4 302	710.9	101.6	36	568	13.5	3.7
Henry	32	191	14.5	4.9	66	3 483	506.1	79.7	61	890	22.1	6.0
Hickman	12	66	3.0	1.3	31	1 017	139.5	22.2	23	D	D	D
Houston	4	D	D	D	NA	NA	NA	NA	12	59	1.9	0.4
Humphreys	11	42	2.1	0.8	29	1 976	854.1	75.4	35	358	13.4	3.2
Jackson	5	D	D	D	8	681	104.9	11.8	7	41	1.4	0.3
Jefferson	31	79	5.1	1.3	56	2 880	434.0	59.7	51	790	24.6	6.4
Johnson	7	D	D	D	19	1 392	206.4	29.2	16	197	5.3	1.5
Knox	937	8 000	724.2	280.7	493	20 782	3 245.5	550.3	769	17 252	550.9	157.6
Lake	4	D	D	D	NA	NA	NA	NA	15	140	3.9	1.2
Lauderdale	15	57	2.1	0.6	22	3 525	353.8	74.4	22	283	7.5	1.8
Lawrence	36	110	6.2	1.9	56	5 501	1 063.8	145.8	45	740	21.6	5.8
Lewis	8	27	2.5	0.5	22	600	101.1	16.4	19	D	D	D
Lincoln	34	92	9.4	2.2	43	2 381	455.0	62.9	44	D	D	D
Loudon	43	132	10.2	2.8	45	3 150	806.7	93.0	56	825	26.3	7.3
McMinn	40	160	11.5	3.9	74	8 791	1 572.2	279.4	84	1 303	41.6	10.2
McNairy	14	29	2.1	0.7	48	2 632	328.1	58.2	28	360	6.8	1.7
Macon	12	26	2.6	0.3	38	1 403	80.1	25.9	19	253	6.2	1.5
Madison	142	993	77.8	36.9	138	12 429	3 473.4	382.5	183	4 110	137.7	37.1
Marion	22	53	2.9	0.8	29	1 726	212.8	38.5	41	673	20.4	5.4

1. Firms subject to federal tax.

Table B. States and Counties — Health Care and Social Assistance, Other Services, and Federal Funds

STATE County	Health care and social assistance,[1] 1997				Other services,[1] 1997				Federal funds and grants, 2002–2003 Expenditures (mil dol)			
										Direct payments for individuals[2]		
	Number of establishments	Number of employees	Receipts (mil dol)	Annual payroll (mil dol)	Number of establishments	Number of employees	Receipts (mil dol)	Annual payroll (mil dol)	Total	Social Security and government retirement	Medicare	Food stamps and Supplemental Security Income
	159	160	161	162	163	164	165	166	167	168	169	170
SOUTH DAKOTA—Cont'd												
Tripp	19	86	4.6	1.9	11	27	1.8	0.4	48.5	16.6	6.1	1.2
Turner	12	84	2.3	1.3	13	24	1.3	0.2	52.0	20.6	8.6	0.5
Union	17	191	9.9	3.3	19	60	4.9	1.3	166.8	26.7	12.2	0.8
Walworth	12	194	7.6	3.9	15	68	4.0	1.1	38.5	11.7	4.7	0.7
Yankton	46	530	37.7	17.8	43	200	11.2	2.8	120.4	44.7	19.4	2.5
Ziebach	NA	NA	NA	NA	1	D	D	D	23.1	3.0	0.8	1.3
TENNESSEE	10 113	155 667	10 753.0	4 659.9	7 767	49 204	2 996.7	918.7	42 602.4	13 004.3	5 658.0	1 461.9
Anderson	156	1 801	117.4	61.3	104	530	26.9	9.4	2 933.3	209.9	83.2	20.6
Bedford	50	439	21.5	8.2	40	378	18.1	5.4	157.5	80.7	30.9	5.4
Benton	20	270	10.7	4.1	15	53	3.4	0.9	107.9	55.6	23.4	3.4
Bledsoe	9	394	19.0	9.3	4	10	0.4	0.1	59.6	20.7	12.5	4.1
Blount	140	1 604	94.2	43.5	140	703	38.6	12.8	519.8	272.9	93.7	20.4
Bradley	201	10 357	442.3	201.0	101	1 304	69.6	26.1	379.5	184.7	81.2	17.9
Campbell	53	590	28.7	11.4	41	144	9.6	2.3	381.0	115.3	55.6	23.0
Cannon	10	192	15.7	6.0	12	33	1.8	0.7	68.2	30.6	19.2	1.5
Carroll	44	687	30.9	12.6	36	112	5.9	1.4	294.0	86.4	43.6	7.8
Carter	68	1 103	58.0	21.4	55	236	14.7	3.4	282.0	132.9	49.8	16.7
Cheatham	26	401	16.0	6.2	17	43	2.9	0.8	113.9	60.4	22.4	4.0
Chester	9	162	6.5	2.7	12	44	2.8	0.6	75.5	28.3	13.8	3.4
Claiborne	30	474	21.5	8.8	27	98	6.1	1.4	204.7	82.2	37.9	15.4
Clay	9	D	D	D	6	18	1.3	0.3	50.9	15.1	10.9	1.8
Cocke	26	324	20.7	6.8	30	103	5.2	1.4	210.9	81.6	36.2	12.7
Coffee	124	2 058	116.4	46.0	83	666	52.0	14.4	629.2	127.9	56.1	12.7
Crockett	15	284	10.2	5.1	22	59	5.4	1.0	94.5	33.4	19.7	3.1
Cumberland	87	764	45.6	18.0	49	179	8.8	2.4	203.9	164.2	54.0	8.7
Davidson	1 462	27 389	2 174.0	925.5	1 092	8 627	530.2	163.9	4 848.2	1 240.2	572.8	135.8
Decatur	18	527	22.5	10.3	20	98	6.5	1.7	73.9	27.8	23.3	2.6
De Kalb	33	426	24.6	10.8	15	90	3.4	1.0	109.2	40.3	24.8	4.7
Dickson	47	1 305	72.4	29.1	51	233	17.5	4.9	193.1	95.2	40.1	7.5
Dyer	85	746	49.5	19.6	64	324	14.1	4.4	228.9	84.2	43.6	11.9
Fayette	15	222	10.6	4.8	17	63	5.7	1.1	171.5	50.9	23.6	9.2
Fentress	26	886	45.8	17.7	20	52	3.5	0.7	123.5	44.8	29.1	8.0
Franklin	53	911	66.7	22.4	38	121	8.3	1.9	222.9	105.5	47.9	6.4
Gibson	81	1 068	45.6	19.4	64	313	15.6	4.9	314.0	126.4	74.0	9.3
Giles	38	561	27.0	10.6	35	115	8.4	1.6	166.4	71.8	34.9	6.1
Grainger	13	345	9.0	3.5	12	30	2.8	0.6	116.1	49.4	23.1	6.5
Greene	93	996	63.5	24.4	75	271	15.3	4.7	373.5	161.6	59.6	15.4
Grundy	10	44	1.9	0.6	9	20	1.8	0.3	87.3	35.7	19.7	7.3
Hamblen	129	1 760	108.8	41.2	76	429	24.3	8.1	307.2	129.8	58.5	16.9
Hamilton	756	10 787	832.6	371.4	546	3 752	221.0	68.0	2 693.9	812.4	369.1	79.0
Hancock	6	106	3.4	1.6	4	9	0.9	0.2	55.6	12.9	9.6	5.6
Hardeman	23	359	15.7	6.5	26	80	6.4	0.9	207.3	58.6	34.0	13.0
Hardin	35	280	14.7	4.7	29	75	6.0	1.3	169.3	62.4	33.2	8.9
Hawkins	38	402	18.2	7.9	36	120	7.7	2.1	298.0	130.6	46.8	13.2
Haywood	18	245	14.8	5.4	23	140	8.7	2.6	144.3	33.5	26.5	9.3
Henderson	30	375	16.9	6.7	38	102	7.5	1.6	168.9	61.1	34.1	6.4
Henry	62	779	36.8	17.2	46	215	10.7	3.1	201.7	94.8	40.7	6.1
Hickman	13	440	15.2	7.9	20	82	6.7	2.0	102.2	47.5	19.6	4.5
Houston	8	281	14.8	5.6	5	7	0.5	0.1	50.9	23.4	10.2	1.4
Humphreys	18	297	14.6	5.7	16	54	4.0	1.0	352.5	46.0	20.8	3.0
Jackson	8	172	7.4	3.0	5	18	1.2	0.3	62.8	21.8	14.5	3.2
Jefferson	39	581	22.5	9.1	39	119	7.5	1.8	243.2	127.1	44.3	9.2
Johnson	15	139	4.1	1.9	14	47	3.0	0.8	112.7	47.4	22.2	5.9
Knox	925	10 391	963.0	451.7	669	4 539	241.1	76.1	2 762.3	909.9	363.5	85.4
Lake	6	D	D	D	4	D	D	D	52.9	15.0	10.9	2.9
Lauderdale	13	209	11.0	4.1	24	78	6.6	1.6	175.4	52.9	32.4	10.8
Lawrence	59	889	48.9	17.4	36	122	7.6	1.8	235.4	105.0	48.2	10.0
Lewis	15	402	13.7	7.1	9	17	1.9	0.5	59.8	23.5	14.7	2.8
Lincoln	41	369	19.6	7.6	38	126	8.7	1.8	170.4	80.9	29.4	5.8
Loudon	43	622	29.5	12.2	41	211	11.9	3.4	241.5	135.4	46.2	6.5
McMinn	77	1 080	61.3	24.7	48	200	10.0	2.9	256.7	121.9	52.6	11.1
McNairy	34	516	23.4	9.4	33	89	6.4	1.4	186.1	67.5	36.9	8.6
Macon	17	221	11.9	3.9	13	34	2.8	0.6	108.8	36.7	23.0	5.2
Madison	205	3 755	293.3	150.0	170	1 062	57.5	18.4	502.2	190.5	92.2	25.0
Marion	33	658	35.8	13.3	21	101	5.9	1.6	155.1	66.8	38.9	7.5

1. Firms subject to federal tax.　　2. State totals may include programs not allocated by county.

Table B. States and Counties — Federal Funds and Local Government Finances

	Federal funds and grants, 2002–2003 (cont'd)							Local government finances, 2002				
	Expenditures (mil dol) (cont'd)							General revenue				
	Procurement contract awards		Grants[1]							Taxes		
											Per capita[2] (dollars)	
STATE County	Salaries and wages	Defense	Other	Medicaid and other health-related	Nutrition and family welfare	Education	Other	Total (mil dol)	Intergovern-mental (mil dol)	Total (mil dol)	Total	Property
	171	172	173	174	175	176	177	178	179	180	181	182
SOUTH DAKOTA—Cont'd												
Tripp	2.1	0.0	0.5	4.5	0.7	0.7	2.8	14.1	5.0	7.1	1 132	822
Turner	2.3	0.0	0.6	4.5	0.5	0.3	2.1	17.5	6.5	8.8	1 015	816
Union	2.8	95.2	14.6	5.2	0.9	0.3	0.2	34.0	7.2	20.3	1 578	1 308
Walworth	2.2	0.1	0.3	4.2	0.7	0.3	4.8	12.1	4.9	5.7	1 003	754
Yankton	11.6	0.8	2.1	12.0	1.4	0.4	14.0	50.0	13.3	25.7	1 200	905
Ziebach	0.3	0.0	0.3	2.3	0.6	1.4	7.4	4.1	2.8	1.0	381	297
TENNESSEE	3 357.2	2 161.0	5 361.0	5 306.6	994.5	659.1	2 096.8	X	X	X	X	X
Anderson	83.4	19.3	2 421.0	65.5	9.7	5.4	14.2	170.0	68.5	69.3	967	694
Bedford	5.6	0.3	1.0	24.7	2.7	2.7	0.7	96.2	29.9	24.1	612	406
Benton	2.9	0.9	0.8	16.1	1.7	1.6	1.1	23.0	13.0	5.6	338	200
Bledsoe	1.1	0.0	0.3	13.8	4.0	1.0	1.3	19.8	14.4	3.4	268	201
Blount	20.2	21.2	5.6	57.6	6.6	7.0	11.4	314.9	75.8	71.6	652	501
Bradley	15.0	0.0	2.7	47.7	8.4	6.1	6.1	211.2	63.1	48.9	546	391
Campbell	5.2	95.6	2.4	55.1	6.1	3.7	16.1	61.3	34.4	16.7	417	272
Cannon	1.7	0.1	0.4	11.3	1.0	0.9	0.3	19.3	12.3	4.4	335	229
Carroll	5.9	95.8	2.2	39.5	3.0	2.2	2.1	47.6	30.6	8.2	279	138
Carter	6.2	0.1	2.3	52.4	5.2	4.3	9.1	74.0	44.4	18.1	319	223
Cheatham	5.9	0.4	1.2	11.7	1.9	1.7	4.2	64.8	29.9	23.9	645	401
Chester	2.5	0.0	0.4	15.7	4.6	0.9	3.3	22.6	12.8	6.6	416	217
Claiborne	3.9	0.0	1.2	45.6	7.6	4.4	3.4	65.1	28.7	10.9	361	244
Clay	2.0	0.7	0.2	18.0	0.9	0.7	0.3	14.0	8.2	3.8	469	330
Cocke	4.5	0.0	1.2	58.7	5.1	2.8	5.8	57.3	31.2	16.0	470	315
Coffee	34.7	333.5	7.6	33.3	3.5	3.9	9.4	90.6	40.2	34.7	701	414
Crockett	3.0	0.8	0.6	22.4	1.9	1.2	2.5	26.2	15.7	6.6	452	307
Cumberland	5.9	0.0	-71.8	32.5	3.6	2.7	2.5	67.4	31.9	23.1	476	269
Davidson	514.4	64.8	316.0	759.3	258.5	262.9	639.8	1 664.3	447.1	686.1	1 202	1 034
Decatur	2.5	0.0	0.7	14.1	1.0	0.9	0.6	17.8	10.8	3.9	339	190
De Kalb	2.6	5.2	0.7	18.9	1.5	1.4	3.9	27.3	16.5	6.0	337	239
Dickson	6.9	0.2	1.5	26.0	3.4	2.7	8.4	93.3	37.1	37.9	856	495
Dyer	7.8	5.1	1.2	49.5	3.6	4.5	5.8	68.7	33.5	17.5	474	342
Fayette	3.7	0.1	1.4	51.3	5.7	2.0	18.2	41.4	22.1	14.2	456	291
Fentress	2.8	0.2	1.4	31.7	2.5	1.2	0.9	24.9	15.2	6.2	370	178
Franklin	9.3	5.5	2.0	30.5	3.0	2.9	4.7	61.5	29.9	21.5	537	348
Gibson	10.8	3.4	1.8	59.8	5.7	3.7	6.3	101.1	51.5	28.5	590	374
Giles	4.5	0.9	1.3	33.2	2.4	2.4	5.4	53.2	23.3	19.2	655	441
Grainger	3.3	0.3	0.6	30.7	2.0	1.7	-2.0	27.3	18.5	5.8	273	176
Greene	12.5	31.5	5.9	61.6	5.1	6.7	6.4	97.8	47.1	30.1	472	313
Grundy	1.7	0.0	0.4	16.7	2.1	1.5	1.5	24.1	15.7	5.0	349	274
Hamblen	10.7	0.9	1.6	51.8	12.9	6.4	5.8	99.6	38.1	45.3	773	401
Hamilton	506.5	14.4	507.6	237.2	39.8	28.5	61.3	1 197.7	247.3	337.4	1 091	796
Hancock	0.6	0.0	0.4	22.9	1.7	0.8	0.9	15.5	12.3	1.6	234	172
Hardeman	3.6	24.3	1.0	51.7	5.2	2.2	10.5	44.0	25.8	11.3	378	220
Hardin	6.7	0.4	2.0	41.8	2.5	2.2	6.2	54.5	20.4	13.1	508	295
Hawkins	19.3	-0.3	12.8	58.2	4.4	3.6	6.6	76.9	39.3	26.6	486	319
Haywood	4.1	0.0	0.7	47.3	4.9	1.7	6.9	38.9	21.6	11.1	563	389
Henderson	4.1	19.1	1.1	31.4	2.0	1.8	6.5	42.5	22.8	13.1	509	232
Henry	10.4	0.6	2.4	30.8	2.8	2.7	6.3	100.6	26.5	18.4	590	292
Hickman	4.3	4.6	0.8	16.3	1.5	1.3	1.5	34.4	19.8	8.3	360	237
Houston	1.9	0.0	0.6	9.3	2.5	0.6	0.3	14.7	8.9	3.4	423	298
Humphreys	28.1	0.1	231.4	17.2	1.5	1.3	2.3	35.1	16.0	9.5	525	359
Jackson	1.5	0.0	0.4	17.8	1.0	0.8	1.2	17.2	11.7	3.6	324	241
Jefferson	7.8	0.0	1.7	33.7	3.1	2.6	9.7	64.7	31.7	19.8	431	291
Johnson	2.3	0.3	0.6	27.3	2.1	1.8	1.5	25.8	14.9	6.4	359	249
Knox	273.6	117.2	358.6	277.1	38.7	33.0	224.1	902.5	249.1	480.6	1 234	732
Lake	1.5	0.6	0.4	14.8	1.5	0.7	1.3	11.7	7.3	3.0	379	226
Lauderdale	5.6	2.4	0.9	48.4	4.9	2.3	4.8	45.3	24.9	12.7	453	280
Lawrence	7.2	0.0	1.5	40.8	3.2	2.9	12.9	69.8	33.4	24.4	602	340
Lewis	1.6	0.1	0.2	11.3	1.1	0.9	1.8	19.0	11.0	4.7	413	226
Lincoln	3.9	0.1	1.0	31.9	8.5	2.2	2.8	95.3	46.1	15.1	474	255
Loudon	10.5	0.2	1.6	27.5	2.9	3.1	5.2	77.7	32.2	25.2	619	362
McMinn	6.9	0.9	1.5	38.9	2.8	3.4	12.4	105.4	38.9	28.7	574	371
McNairy	5.1	0.0	1.1	50.3	6.6	3.2	5.2	37.4	22.9	8.6	348	237
Macon	2.5	6.7	0.5	20.7	5.4	1.7	1.8	31.2	18.7	8.7	417	281
Madison	34.1	0.5	7.2	95.6	5.9	8.7	21.4	590.4	75.0	109.1	1 169	585
Marion	6.0	0.0	1.1	25.0	4.0	2.4	2.1	45.4	24.5	13.7	495	247

1. State totals may include programs not allocated by county. 2. Based on the resident population estimated as of July 1 of the year shown.

	Local government finances, 2002 (cont'd)									Government employment, 2002			Presidential election, 2004		
	Direct general expenditure							Debt outstanding					Percent of vote cast —		
			Percent of total for —												
STATE County	Total (mil dol)	Per capita[1] (dollars)	Education	Health and hospitals	Police protection	Public welfare	High-ways	Total (mil dol)	Per capita[1] (dollars)	Federal civilian	Federal military	State and local	Demo-cratic	Republi-can	All other
	183	184	185	186	187	188	189	190	191	192	193	194	195	196	197
SOUTH DAKOTA—Cont'd															
Tripp	14.9	2 363	56.3	1.2	5.1	0.2	16.8	10.0	1 590	40	35	419	30.0	68.7	1.3
Turner	17.3	1 992	59.7	0.5	3.4	0.2	17.5	13.8	1 595	46	48	462	34.1	63.8	2.1
Union	32.7	2 535	54.5	0.4	4.1	0.2	13.2	36.8	2 853	52	71	671	42.6	56.6	0.9
Walworth	11.6	2 034	52.9	0.5	5.2	0.2	12.0	2.6	455	38	31	393	30.7	68.1	1.2
Yankton	53.6	2 500	44.0	1.7	4.5	0.2	9.1	53.8	2 506	197	118	1 621	40.6	57.5	1.8
Ziebach	4.2	1 602	70.8	0.6	2.9	0.0	14.2	0.0	0	10	14	176	57.5	40.1	2.4
TENNESSEE	X	X	X	X	X	X	X	X	X	50 233	21 610	357 680	42.5	56.8	0.7
Anderson	155.2	2 167	58.6	2.1	5.7	0.1	4.2	192.5	2 688	1 114	234	3 922	40.7	58.4	0.9
Bedford	94.2	2 391	36.5	33.4	3.3	0.3	3.8	47.1	1 196	100	128	2 292	38.4	61.0	0.6
Benton	25.4	1 542	58.2	1.1	7.7	0.0	10.2	17.3	1 051	73	53	824	54.6	44.6	0.8
Bledsoe	21.7	1 740	58.0	1.7	2.9	1.0	8.9	17.5	1 404	22	40	1 002	40.1	59.4	0.5
Blount	310.0	2 822	35.0	38.6	4.0	0.1	3.5	308.0	2 804	262	358	6 166	30.9	68.2	0.9
Bradley	209.5	2 336	39.7	31.7	4.7	0.0	3.4	160.7	1 792	254	293	4 794	26.5	72.8	0.7
Campbell	65.9	1 646	50.6	1.4	5.3	0.3	7.8	54.4	1 359	81	130	2 108	43.7	55.7	0.7
Cannon	20.5	1 573	56.4	2.6	4.5	0.1	9.6	15.9	1 215	43	42	488	45.9	53.5	0.6
Carroll	52.1	1 777	57.9	0.3	5.4	0.0	8.0	35.9	1 225	90	95	1 410	43.1	56.2	0.7
Carter	82.5	1 454	67.9	1.0	5.6	0.2	6.5	37.3	658	107	184	2 139	28.8	71.0	0.3
Cheatham	62.1	1 678	60.4	8.7	3.5	0.0	5.2	56.1	1 517	90	120	1 491	37.7	61.6	0.7
Chester	19.8	1 244	62.1	0.1	7.5	0.5	8.4	13.4	843	34	52	964	34.7	64.9	0.5
Claiborne	76.1	2 522	56.5	25.3	3.0	0.1	5.9	31.9	1 058	66	98	1 984	38.3	61.2	0.6
Clay	12.4	1 541	61.7	1.9	4.1	0.0	13.5	2.1	265	46	26	387	49.9	49.1	1.0
Cocke	66.8	1 958	58.2	0.3	3.6	0.1	8.5	27.0	790	72	111	1 599	32.0	67.4	0.6
Coffee	96.5	1 952	57.8	2.6	4.8	0.3	4.6	63.1	1 277	370	273	2 934	40.9	58.5	0.6
Crockett	25.9	1 784	59.5	2.5	4.0	2.4	10.3	29.2	2 009	48	47	648	43.0	56.7	0.4
Cumberland	73.2	1 506	52.3	3.1	3.9	0.0	6.6	59.6	1 226	100	158	1 910	35.2	64.1	0.7
Davidson	1 850.4	3 242	30.4	8.0	6.5	1.2	1.8	3 992.3	6 994	8 914	2 506	38 501	54.8	44.5	0.7
Decatur	17.9	1 538	54.5	0.3	6.2	1.4	11.5	20.5	1 760	32	38	654	48.0	51.4	0.6
De Kalb	25.3	1 431	58.0	0.8	5.7	2.2	6.3	37.1	2 096	44	57	805	46.5	52.6	0.9
Dickson	106.9	2 416	54.2	1.5	5.1	2.6	4.8	148.4	3 356	106	144	2 371	44.6	54.7	0.7
Dyer	94.4	2 551	57.7	2.3	6.3	0.0	5.7	90.4	2 443	115	120	2 490	38.3	61.2	0.5
Fayette	40.5	1 298	60.4	1.5	5.8	0.0	10.9	17.7	566	59	101	1 492	38.6	60.8	0.5
Fentress	22.8	1 349	62.7	3.8	3.2	0.0	10.2	17.8	1 056	40	55	842	35.4	64.1	0.5
Franklin	67.5	1 686	60.8	1.0	5.6	0.8	6.0	48.8	1 219	154	130	1 619	45.7	53.5	0.9
Gibson	115.3	2 389	55.2	1.5	6.7	0.1	5.4	65.9	1 365	164	158	2 567	44.3	55.1	0.6
Giles	60.4	2 059	58.9	2.3	4.9	0.0	8.9	35.7	1 215	81	95	1 241	45.7	53.4	0.9
Grainger	25.7	1 216	67.1	2.2	4.6	0.0	10.3	17.0	808	52	68	718	34.1	65.2	0.7
Greene	124.6	1 954	59.0	2.0	3.9	0.3	5.3	82.3	1 291	257	207	3 678	31.5	67.7	0.7
Grundy	22.3	1 556	60.7	1.2	3.1	0.5	15.9	14.1	981	23	47	703	56.6	42.7	0.7
Hamblen	105.0	1 790	57.0	0.3	6.2	0.1	4.1	79.1	1 349	173	191	3 276	33.3	66.1	0.6
Hamilton	1 110.0	3 589	25.1	31.9	5.7	2.1	2.9	1 197.6	3 872	6 387	1 049	21 861	41.8	57.4	0.8
Hancock	16.8	2 466	62.7	3.9	2.1	0.3	7.5	14.5	2 140	10	22	416	30.4	68.9	0.7
Hardeman	44.1	1 479	58.1	3.0	6.9	0.0	6.7	21.3	715	60	97	1 968	54.3	44.9	0.7
Hardin	52.0	2 012	43.6	24.9	3.4	0.0	6.8	18.1	699	139	84	1 441	38.5	61.2	0.3
Hawkins	73.1	1 335	62.8	1.3	4.7	0.0	7.5	44.1	804	283	178	2 075	33.0	66.5	0.5
Haywood	38.9	1 980	57.5	2.7	4.7	0.0	10.8	1.3	65	63	64	1 006	57.8	41.6	0.6
Henderson	43.8	1 701	63.7	0.1	4.7	0.3	7.4	46.4	1 802	64	83	1 073	34.2	65.2	0.6
Henry	103.2	3 310	35.9	41.2	3.6	0.0	5.0	42.0	1 347	138	131	2 258	43.5	55.7	0.8
Hickman	31.0	1 341	67.3	3.3	3.9	0.0	6.7	16.7	723	55	75	1 047	49.1	50.3	0.6
Houston	17.8	2 234	55.7	2.6	2.8	0.0	10.4	14.6	1 836	17	26	500	59.2	40.0	0.8
Humphreys	33.8	1 872	53.5	0.7	3.7	0.4	7.3	82.4	4 556	398	59	874	57.6	41.8	0.6
Jackson	20.5	1 840	68.5	2.5	3.2	0.1	9.4	6.6	597	33	36	417	59.3	40.1	0.6
Jefferson	63.5	1 386	63.6	3.1	5.2	0.1	5.5	43.6	952	134	149	2 006	31.8	67.5	0.7
Johnson	25.2	1 403	62.6	1.0	4.3	0.2	9.2	18.0	1 002	45	58	868	27.9	71.5	0.5
Knox	877.2	2 253	39.6	3.3	6.5	2.1	3.2	1 172.8	3 012	3 643	1 414	34 227	37.0	62.1	0.9
Lake	10.5	1 351	50.7	3.6	6.2	0.0	13.0	7.1	911	19	25	744	55.6	43.8	0.6
Lauderdale	43.6	1 557	57.7	0.9	5.6	0.3	8.4	26.6	949	62	91	1 825	51.8	48.2	0.0
Lawrence	67.3	1 664	54.3	2.1	5.0	0.2	9.2	63.8	1 576	116	131	1 859	39.6	59.8	0.6
Lewis	19.9	1 737	48.6	4.0	5.0	0.0	9.2	10.9	955	25	37	578	43.4	55.8	0.9
Lincoln	119.3	3 753	34.3	19.8	2.1	28.4	3.4	82.0	2 581	70	103	2 521	36.5	62.8	0.7
Loudon	74.9	1 843	51.1	0.5	5.8	0.0	5.6	132.1	3 251	158	132	1 789	28.7	70.7	0.6
McMinn	103.9	2 076	43.6	16.7	3.6	3.9	5.4	56.9	1 136	122	162	2 315	32.7	66.6	0.7
McNairy	38.8	1 571	60.8	1.0	5.2	0.0	9.7	44.4	1 795	89	80	1 097	41.3	58.3	0.4
Macon	32.3	1 550	61.8	1.1	6.3	0.3	8.5	26.8	1 285	37	68	981	36.8	62.8	0.3
Madison	571.9	6 125	17.9	60.7	2.4	0.0	2.2	358.6	3 841	535	306	10 372	43.5	56.1	0.4
Marion	50.7	1 835	58.6	2.2	6.0	0.0	6.3	37.9	1 370	80	90	1 123	48.3	51.0	0.7

1. Based on the resident population estimated as of July 1 of the year shown.

Table B. States and Counties — **Land Area and Population**

					Population and population characteristics, 2003													
									Race alone or in combination, not Hispanic or Latino (percent)						Age (percent)				
STATE/ County code	CBSA code[1]	County Type[2]	STATE County	Land area,[3] (sq km) 2000	Total persons	Rank	Per square kilometer	White	Black	Am. Indian, Alaska Native	Asian and Pacific Islander[4]	Percent Hispanic or Latino[4]	Under 5 years	5 to 17 years	18 to 24 years	25 to 34 years	35 to 44 years	45 to 54 years
				1	2	3	4	5	6	7	8	9	10	11	12	13	14	15
			TENNESSEE—Cont'd															
47 117	...	6	Marshall	972	27 537	1 483	28.3	88.9	7.6	0.6	0.3	3.3	6.6	17.9	9.5	13.1	15.7	14.6
47 119	17940	4	Maury	1 587	73 198	696	46.1	81.9	13.9	0.6	0.6	4.0	6.9	18.3	9.8	12.4	15.5	14.8
47 121	...	8	Meigs	505	11 430	2 340	22.6	97.5	1.5	0.4	0.2	0.5	6.8	17.3	8.8	13.6	14.5	13.8
47 123	...	6	Monroe	1 644	41 051	1 109	25.0	94.9	2.3	1.1	0.7	2.2	6.4	17.6	9.5	13.2	14.3	13.4
47 125	17300	3	Montgomery	1 397	141 064	404	101.0	73.3	20.8	1.2	3.3	4.1	8.7	20.2	10.6	16.9	16.0	11.4
47 127	46100	9	Moore	335	5 911	2 779	17.6	96.0	3.0	0.3	0.1	0.7	5.3	16.8	9.2	12.6	14.3	14.6
47 129	...	6	Morgan	1 352	20 080	1 801	14.9	96.5	2.6	0.5	0.2	0.7	5.5	16.2	9.8	14.7	16.3	14.4
47 131	46460	7	Obion	1 411	32 386	1 351	23.0	87.4	10.2	0.4	0.2	2.3	6.5	16.3	8.8	12.8	13.8	14.7
47 133	18260	7	Overton	1 122	20 151	1 797	18.0	98.4	0.4	0.7	0.2	0.7	5.4	16.5	8.9	13.1	14.3	14.2
47 135	...	8	Perry	1 075	7 627	2 624	7.1	96.4	2.1	0.9	0.1	1.1	5.8	17.7	8.3	11.4	13.0	14.5
47 137	...	9	Pickett	422	5 006	2 844	11.9	98.4	0.6	0.3	0.0	0.9	5.7	14.7	9.1	11.4	13.6	13.6
47 139	17420	3	Polk	1 127	16 171	2 022	14.3	98.2	0.5	1.1	0.2	0.9	6.2	16.1	8.2	13.3	14.5	14.1
47 141	18260	3	Putnam	1 039	64 973	762	62.5	93.1	2.0	0.6	1.3	3.7	5.9	15.5	13.4	14.4	13.5	12.3
47 143	...	6	Rhea	818	29 286	1 426	35.8	95.6	2.2	0.9	0.5	1.6	6.4	16.6	10.7	12.4	14.0	14.0
47 145	25340	4	Roane	935	52 424	902	56.1	96.1	2.8	1.0	0.5	0.7	5.5	15.8	8.4	11.5	14.3	15.5
47 147	34980	1	Robertson	1 234	58 181	843	47.1	87.2	8.3	0.7	0.5	3.9	6.8	18.9	9.7	13.4	16.6	13.9
47 149	34980	1	Rutherford	1 603	202 310	288	126.2	83.6	10.7	0.6	2.8	3.5	7.3	18.3	12.6	16.1	16.1	12.4
47 151	...	6	Scott	1 378	21 675	1 720	15.7	98.9	0.2	1.0	0.2	0.5	6.8	18.2	10.1	14.2	14.3	13.7
47 153	16860	2	Sequatchie	689	11 958	2 293	17.4	97.8	0.8	0.6	0.3	0.8	6.3	17.5	8.9	14.3	14.9	13.9
47 155	42940	4	Sevier	1 534	75 503	679	49.2	97.0	0.7	0.9	0.8	1.5	5.8	16.3	8.8	13.3	15.3	14.9
47 157	32820	1	Shelby	1 954	906 178	46	463.8	44.3	50.9	0.5	2.3	2.9	7.6	19.9	9.6	14.6	15.5	14.3
47 159	34980	1	Smith	814	18 225	1 896	22.4	95.4	2.9	0.8	0.2	1.3	5.9	18.1	9.5	12.7	16.4	14.2
47 161	17300	3	Stewart	1 187	12 847	2 252	10.8	94.8	2.0	1.2	1.5	1.1	6.1	17.2	8.7	11.8	15.7	14.3
47 163	28700	3	Sullivan	1 070	153 050	367	143.0	96.5	2.2	0.5	0.6	0.7	5.4	15.7	7.8	12.4	14.8	15.1
47 165	34980	1	Sumner	1 371	138 752	407	101.2	90.8	6.3	0.7	1.1	2.1	6.5	18.2	9.6	13.0	16.1	14.5
47 167	32820	1	Tipton	1 190	54 184	887	45.5	78.9	19.2	0.9	0.7	1.3	6.7	20.7	10.2	12.5	16.5	13.6
47 169	34980	1	Trousdale	296	7 447	2 642	25.2	85.9	11.8	0.4	0.2	2.0	6.1	17.4	9.8	12.0	15.0	14.6
47 171	27740	3	Unicoi	482	17 709	1 929	36.7	96.7	0.6	0.3	0.2	2.5	5.0	14.7	7.8	12.1	14.5	15.1
47 173	28940	2	Union	579	18 830	1 868	32.5	98.4	0.5	0.9	0.2	0.8	6.2	18.1	9.7	13.5	16.4	13.6
47 175	...	9	Van Buren	708	5 478	2 811	7.7	98.6	0.9	0.3	0.1	0.3	5.5	16.6	9.5	12.7	14.4	15.4
47 177	32660	6	Warren	1 121	39 129	1 154	34.9	90.4	3.4	0.5	0.5	5.7	6.9	16.9	9.4	13.7	14.7	13.6
47 179	27740	3	Washington	845	110 078	502	130.3	93.5	4.2	0.6	1.0	1.6	5.7	15.0	10.4	14.6	14.7	14.1
47 181	...	8	Wayne	1 901	16 947	1 959	8.9	91.3	7.4	0.5	0.3	0.8	4.9	15.1	9.4	15.7	16.2	13.2
47 183	...	7	Weakley	1 503	34 314	1 296	22.8	90.1	6.9	0.4	1.8	1.3	5.7	15.3	14.7	13.1	13.1	13.2
47 185	...	7	White	975	23 584	1 633	24.2	97.0	1.8	0.6	0.3	0.9	6.0	16.6	8.8	12.2	14.7	14.1
47 187	34980	1	Williamson	1 509	141 301	402	93.6	90.3	5.0	0.4	2.1	2.9	6.3	20.7	8.7	11.4	17.2	16.9
47 189	34980	1	Wilson	1 478	95 366	565	64.5	91.3	6.6	0.7	0.7	1.5	6.7	18.4	9.3	12.8	16.9	14.9
48 000		X	TEXAS	678 051	22 118 509	X	32.6	51.3	11.4	0.7	3.4	34.2	8.2	20.0	10.6	14.8	15.0	13.1
48 001	37300	5	Anderson	2 773	54 790	877	19.8	64.4	22.3	0.6	0.6	12.6	6.1	15.0	10.2	17.7	18.2	12.8
48 003	11380	6	Andrews	3 887	12 868	2 251	3.3	54.7	1.7	0.7	0.8	42.4	7.7	21.9	10.7	10.6	14.9	13.1
48 005	31260	5	Angelina	2 076	80 935	651	39.0	69.1	14.7	0.6	0.8	15.6	7.8	19.8	9.9	13.3	14.0	12.9
48 007	18580	2	Aransas	652	23 574	1 636	36.2	73.9	1.5	1.3	2.6	21.7	5.4	17.4	8.6	9.1	12.6	13.4
48 009	48660	3	Archer	2 356	9 189	2 509	3.9	93.6	0.2	1.7	0.2	5.4	5.8	20.2	10.1	9.3	15.8	14.8
48 011	11100	3	Armstrong	2 366	2 056	3 053	0.9	93.5	0.3	0.3	0.0	5.8	5.5	19.3	8.1	8.9	13.7	14.6
48 013	41700	1	Atascosa	3 191	41 867	1 084	13.1	38.8	0.6	0.7	0.4	59.8	8.1	22.3	10.8	12.7	13.9	12.1
48 015	26420	1	Austin	1 690	25 057	1 569	14.8	72.0	10.2	0.4	0.3	17.6	6.7	19.2	10.1	10.9	14.0	14.0
48 017	...	7	Bailey	2 141	6 660	2 717	3.1	48.6	1.3	0.4	0.2	49.6	9.6	21.1	9.9	10.0	12.2	12.3
48 019	41700	1	Bandera	2 051	19 347	1 846	9.4	84.3	0.4	1.5	0.3	14.5	5.3	18.4	8.5	9.7	14.5	14.9
48 021	12420	1	Bastrop	2 301	67 077	752	29.2	64.1	8.6	1.0	0.7	26.5	7.4	19.9	9.8	13.4	15.5	13.8
48 023	...	6	Baylor	2 255	3 909	2 918	1.7	85.1	3.5	0.6	0.6	10.2	5.3	18.0	7.9	7.3	12.2	13.6
48 025	13300	4	Bee	2 280	32 431	1 349	14.2	33.8	9.6	0.3	0.5	55.9	6.2	16.6	14.3	19.2	15.1	11.1
48 027	28660	2	Bell	2 745	248 727	240	90.6	59.0	20.2	1.2	4.2	18.3	10.7	20.3	11.2	16.0	14.1	11.0
48 029	41700	1	Bexar	3 229	1 471 644	22	455.8	34.9	6.9	0.5	2.1	56.5	8.1	20.3	10.8	14.5	14.7	12.5
48 031	...	8	Blanco	1 842	8 809	2 541	4.8	82.7	0.7	1.2	0.2	16.1	6.3	18.0	8.9	11.0	14.3	15.5
48 033	...	9	Borden	2 328	682	3 131	0.3	84.9	0.1	0.7	0.3	15.0	3.7	17.7	11.6	9.8	16.1	16.0
48 035	...	6	Bosque	2 562	17 696	1 931	6.9	84.6	1.9	1.2	0.2	12.9	6.1	17.8	8.7	9.6	13.3	13.1
48 037	45500	3	Bowie	2 300	89 699	600	39.0	71.0	23.5	1.2	0.7	4.8	6.6	17.9	10.1	13.4	14.8	13.9
48 039	26420	1	Brazoria	3 591	263 149	225	73.3	63.5	9.2	0.8	3.4	24.1	7.9	20.3	9.9	13.7	16.6	13.7
48 041	17780	3	Brazos	1 517	159 830	346	105.4	65.7	10.8	0.6	4.4	19.4	6.8	14.7	25.8	16.7	10.6	8.7
48 043	...	7	Brewster	16 039	9 247	2 504	0.6	53.3	1.2	1.0	0.5	44.7	6.1	15.6	14.7	12.8	10.9	13.9
48 045	...	9	Briscoe	2 332	1 663	3 080	0.7	71.1	3.3	0.4	0.4	25.6	7.8	19.8	9.1	8.5	12.2	13.8
48 047	...	6	Brooks	2 443	7 720	2 622	3.2	7.8	0.1	0.1	0.2	91.7	8.0	22.8	10.4	9.2	12.5	12.5
48 049	15220	5	Brown	2 445	38 103	1 182	15.6	78.8	4.0	0.9	0.5	16.5	6.4	18.8	11.4	11.1	12.8	13.2
48 051	17780	3	Burleson	1 724	16 941	1 962	9.8	69.5	14.4	0.8	0.2	15.8	6.6	19.3	9.5	10.8	13.9	13.6
48 053	...	6	Burnet	2 580	38 809	1 167	15.0	82.2	1.5	1.1	0.5	15.7	6.4	17.2	8.8	10.6	13.7	12.7

1. CBSA = Core Based Statistical Area. See Appendix A for explanation. See Appendix B for list of metropolitan areas with component counties.   2. County type code from the Economic Research Service of USDA Rural-Urban Continuum Codes. See Appendix A for definition.   3. Dry land or land partially or temporarily covered by water.   4. Hispanic or Latino persons may be of any race.

Table B. States and Counties — Population and Households

| | Population, 2003 (cont'd) | | | | Population — change and components of change, 1990–2003 | | | | | | | | Households, 2000 | | | | |
| | Age (percent) (cont'd) | | | | Total persons | | Percent change | | Components of change, 2000–2003 | | | | | | | Percent | |
STATE County	55 to 64 years	65 to 74 years	75 years and over	Percent female	1990	2000	1990–2000	2000–2003	Births	Deaths	Net migration	Number	Percent change, 1990–2000	Persons per house-hold	Female family house-holder[1]	One person
	16	17	18	19	20	21	22	23	24	25	26	27	28	29	30	31
TENNESSEE—Cont'd																
Marshall	9.9	6.2	6.0	50.9	21 539	26 767	24.3	2.9	1 240	871	426	10 307	24.7	2.56	11.6	23.9
Maury	9.2	6.4	5.4	51.3	54 812	69 498	26.8	5.3	3 327	2 283	2 701	26 444	28.3	2.58	12.9	23.2
Meigs	12.5	7.1	4.8	50.1	8 033	11 086	38.0	3.1	509	379	228	4 304	43.7	2.55	9.9	20.8
Monroe	11.3	7.2	5.9	50.6	30 541	38 961	27.6	5.4	1 656	1 366	1 780	15 329	34.9	2.51	10.0	23.3
Montgomery	6.5	4.7	3.3	49.9	100 498	134 768	34.1	4.7	7 742	2 725	1 359	48 330	40.7	2.70	12.2	20.2
Moore	12.9	7.9	6.8	50.3	4 696	5 740	22.2	3.0	186	182	167	2 211	27.5	2.55	7.6	21.4
Morgan	10.7	6.9	5.2	46.8	17 300	19 757	14.2	1.6	719	612	240	6 990	19.7	2.58	10.3	22.1
Obion	11.7	7.9	7.4	51.4	31 717	32 450	2.3	-0.2	1 445	1 229	-242	13 182	6.2	2.42	11.1	25.7
Overton	12.2	8.6	6.8	51.0	17 636	20 118	14.1	0.2	728	755	85	8 110	20.4	2.46	9.9	24.1
Perry	12.4	9.2	7.1	50.2	6 612	7 631	15.4	-0.1	283	284	-1	3 023	20.3	2.48	8.8	25.2
Pickett	13.4	11.5	7.3	50.3	4 548	4 945	8.7	1.2	167	205	98	2 091	17.1	2.33	7.8	27.2
Polk	12.7	8.4	6.3	50.2	13 643	16 050	17.6	0.8	690	631	72	6 448	26.6	2.46	9.0	23.3
Putnam	9.7	7.0	6.1	50.1	51 373	62 315	21.3	4.3	2 624	1 962	2 038	24 865	25.9	2.40	9.8	27.1
Rhea	11.3	7.4	6.3	51.4	24 344	28 400	16.7	3.1	1 242	992	649	11 184	21.8	2.46	11.2	23.8
Roane	12.5	8.6	7.6	51.4	47 227	51 910	9.9	1.0	1 877	2 061	728	21 200	14.9	2.42	10.1	25.0
Robertson	9.0	6.0	4.6	50.0	41 492	54 433	31.2	6.9	2 750	1 500	2 469	19 906	34.5	2.71	11.2	18.6
Rutherford	7.2	4.2	3.2	50.1	118 570	182 023	53.5	11.1	9 636	3 776	14 193	66 443	57.8	2.65	11.2	20.8
Scott	10.8	6.4	5.0	50.5	18 358	21 127	15.1	2.6	1 023	663	201	8 203	25.5	2.55	11.8	24.3
Sequatchie	11.1	7.0	5.0	50.5	8 863	11 370	28.3	5.2	440	339	481	4 463	35.8	2.52	11.2	22.4
Sevier	11.5	7.7	5.3	51.0	51 050	71 170	39.4	6.1	2 942	2 184	3 527	28 467	45.8	2.48	10.1	22.0
Shelby	8.2	5.1	4.7	52.1	826 330	897 472	8.6	1.0	48 522	25 989	-13 317	338 366	11.5	2.60	20.1	27.0
Smith	9.9	6.7	6.2	50.8	14 143	17 712	25.2	2.9	654	556	424	6 878	28.4	2.55	9.8	23.4
Stewart	11.3	8.2	6.3	50.4	9 479	12 370	30.5	3.9	490	497	478	4 930	34.0	2.49	8.1	23.1
Sullivan	12.3	8.7	7.6	51.7	143 596	153 048	6.6	0.0	5 486	5 728	342	63 556	12.0	2.36	10.2	26.4
Sumner	10.2	5.9	4.8	50.8	103 281	130 449	26.3	6.4	5 754	3 481	5 993	48 941	32.8	2.64	10.8	20.3
Tipton	9.0	5.6	4.2	50.7	37 568	51 271	36.5	5.7	2 428	1 490	1 950	18 106	38.9	2.78	13.9	18.7
Trousdale	10.9	7.0	6.7	50.0	5 920	7 259	22.6	2.6	283	285	193	2 780	23.0	2.55	11.3	23.0
Unicoi	12.3	9.3	8.7	51.4	16 549	17 667	6.8	0.2	563	799	298	7 516	13.5	2.31	9.5	27.5
Union	10.3	6.7	4.4	50.5	13 694	17 808	30.0	5.7	751	524	782	6 742	36.7	2.62	10.5	19.8
Van Buren	12.5	7.8	6.1	50.2	4 846	5 508	13.7	-0.5	197	154	-60	2 180	21.2	2.49	11.0	21.9
Warren	10.4	7.4	6.3	50.6	32 992	38 276	16.0	2.2	1 794	1 294	388	15 181	19.7	2.47	11.2	25.0
Washington	10.4	7.2	6.8	51.4	92 336	107 198	16.1	2.7	4 045	3 705	2 603	44 195	23.4	2.33	10.5	27.8
Wayne	11.2	7.5	6.3	44.6	13 935	16 842	20.9	0.6	562	555	111	5 936	14.7	2.47	10.1	24.4
Weakley	9.8	7.1	7.3	51.4	31 972	34 895	9.1	-1.7	1 287	1 246	-613	13 599	13.4	2.38	9.5	27.0
White	11.8	8.7	6.8	50.8	20 090	23 102	15.0	2.1	946	919	463	9 229	19.5	2.47	10.8	23.4
Williamson	8.9	4.5	3.2	50.6	81 021	126 638	56.3	11.6	5 494	2 232	11 172	44 725	60.1	2.81	7.8	16.6
Wilson	10.2	5.5	4.1	50.5	67 675	88 809	31.2	7.4	4 078	2 378	4 787	32 798	36.3	2.67	10.1	18.1
TEXAS	8.4	5.3	4.5	50.2	16 986 335	20 851 820	22.8	6.1	1 190 484	475 020	546 729	7 393 354	21.8	2.74	12.7	23.7
Anderson	8.1	6.0	5.8	40.3	48 024	55 109	14.8	-0.6	2 176	1 844	-651	15 678	10.2	2.58	13.2	24.8
Andrews	8.6	7.2	5.8	50.8	14 338	13 004	-9.3	-1.0	675	305	-503	4 601	-3.3	2.81	9.5	21.8
Angelina	9.3	6.7	5.9	50.9	69 884	80 130	14.7	1.0	4 176	2 538	-786	28 685	14.7	2.70	12.3	22.8
Aransas	12.8	11.2	8.5	50.2	17 892	22 497	25.7	4.8	775	848	1 142	9 132	31.6	2.43	9.4	25.3
Archer	10.0	7.4	5.9	49.8	7 973	8 854	11.0	3.8	303	205	239	3 345	13.1	2.63	7.2	21.9
Armstrong	11.3	9.3	10.9	51.8	2 021	2 148	6.3	-4.3	75	63	-103	802	4.4	2.58	6.1	21.4
Atascosa	8.5	5.8	4.7	50.8	30 533	38 628	26.5	8.4	2 165	921	1 976	12 816	28.9	2.99	13.0	18.9
Austin	10.0	7.1	7.2	50.7	19 832	23 590	18.9	6.2	1 066	895	1 303	8 747	17.0	2.67	9.6	22.8
Bailey	9.3	8.0	7.1	50.8	7 064	6 594	-6.7	1.0	435	167	-202	2 348	-4.3	2.78	7.5	22.3
Bandera	12.1	9.4	6.2	50.2	10 562	17 645	67.1	9.6	630	477	1 510	7 010	67.7	2.49	7.3	23.2
Bastrop	8.3	5.3	4.1	48.8	38 263	57 733	50.9	16.2	3 003	1 419	7 549	20 097	50.2	2.77	10.5	21.5
Baylor	12.7	11.0	12.8	51.9	4 385	4 093	-6.7	-4.5	134	247	-71	1 791	-6.0	2.26	8.2	33.3
Bee	7.2	5.5	4.8	40.3	25 135	32 359	28.7	0.2	1 283	733	-450	9 061	5.5	2.74	14.8	23.7
Bell	6.8	4.7	4.1	49.8	191 073	237 974	24.5	4.5	17 696	4 915	-1 850	85 507	27.2	2.68	12.3	22.3
Bexar	7.8	5.4	4.8	51.2	1 185 394	1 392 931	17.5	5.7	77 187	30 482	33 115	488 942	19.5	2.78	15.5	24.0
Blanco	11.8	7.3	7.8	50.4	5 972	8 418	41.0	4.6	328	336	406	3 303	41.3	2.50	7.2	24.0
Borden	12.0	10.4	5.1	48.2	799	729	-8.8	-6.4	10	13	-41	292	-0.7	2.50	6.2	22.6
Bosque	11.9	9.2	10.2	51.1	15 125	17 204	13.7	2.9	698	869	657	6 726	12.3	2.48	8.2	25.4
Bowie	9.8	6.7	6.8	49.6	81 665	89 306	9.4	0.4	3 774	3 106	-185	33 058	8.1	2.50	15.0	26.0
Brazoria	8.1	4.9	3.5	48.4	191 707	241 767	26.1	8.8	13 419	5 362	13 169	81 954	28.0	2.82	10.4	19.1
Brazos	5.4	3.6	3.2	49.4	121 862	152 415	25.1	4.9	7 134	2 326	2 702	55 202	26.2	2.52	10.0	25.5
Brewster	10.0	7.5	6.7	50.3	8 653	8 866	2.5	4.3	364	240	265	3 669	9.5	2.31	10.0	32.8
Briscoe	12.6	9.4	9.7	50.3	1 971	1 790	-9.2	-7.1	73	65	-131	724	-8.2	2.47	7.6	27.9
Brooks	10.0	8.5	6.7	52.1	8 204	7 976	-2.8	-3.2	422	197	-483	2 711	1.4	2.92	19.1	21.4
Brown	10.2	7.9	8.1	50.7	34 371	37 674	9.6	1.1	1 544	1 408	336	14 306	9.2	2.48	10.9	26.5
Burleson	10.1	8.5	7.4	51.3	13 625	16 470	20.9	2.9	722	467	232	6 363	22.9	2.57	11.4	24.9
Burnet	10.4	9.9	8.2	51.7	22 677	34 147	50.6	13.7	1 598	1 300	4 393	13 133	45.0	2.53	8.6	22.5

1. No spouse present.

TN(Marshall)—TX(Burnet) 619

STATE County	Births, average 1999–2001		Deaths, average 1999–2001				Physicians,[4] 2000		Hospitals,[4] 1998			Medicare enrollees, 2003	Serious crimes known to police,[6] 2002	
			Number		Rate					Beds			Total	
	Total	Rate[1]	Total	Infant[2]	Total[1]	Infant[3]	Number	Rate[5]	Number	Number	Rate[5]		Number	Rate[7]
	32	33	34	35	36	37	38	39	40	41	42	43	44	45
TENNESSEE—Cont'd														
Marshall	362	13.5	272	3	10.1	D	13	49	1	96	365	4 009	727	2 665
Maury	1 010	14.5	697	6	10.0	D	132	190	1	302	434	10 751	3 572	5 044
Meigs	157	14.2	98	0	8.9	D	3	27	0	0	0	1 893	258	2 284
Monroe	526	13.5	396	6	10.2	D	25	64	1	59	169	6 854	1 749	4 405
Montgomery	2 421	18.0	828	18	6.2	7.3	169	125	1	164	129	13 019	6 937	5 051
Moore	60	10.5	48	0	8.3	D	0	0	0	0	0	569	97	1 658
Morgan	220	11.2	186	3	9.4	D	5	25	0	0	0	2 757	252	1 252
Obion	431	13.3	370	3	11.4	D	42	129	1	133	413	6 352	1 534	4 639
Overton	223	11.1	236	2	11.8	D	13	65	1	79	404	3 738	301	1 468
Perry	95	12.5	97	0	12.7	D	4	52	1	74	986	1 485	180	2 315
Pickett	59	11.9	66	1	13.4	D	2	40	0	0	0	899	22	437
Polk	206	12.9	195	1	12.2	D	11	69	1	40	269	3 388	213	1 302
Putnam	828	13.2	611	7	9.8	8.0	108	173	1	116	196	12 090	2 458	3 871
Rhea	392	13.8	290	4	10.2	D	10	35	1	131	471	5 291	780	2 695
Roane	592	11.4	611	2	11.8	D	39	75	2	165	330	10 805	1 934	3 656
Robertson	832	15.2	473	3	8.6	D	37	68	1	115	217	7 751	1 934	3 487
Rutherford	2 849	15.6	1 111	16	6.1	5.6	226	124	1	221	133	17 788	7 080	3 817
Scott	304	14.3	200	1	9.4	D	16	76	1	97	484	3 675	680	3 159
Sequatchie	143	12.6	115	0	10.1	D	8	70	0	0	0	1 640	388	3 349
Sevier	914	12.8	640	6	9.0	D	61	86	1	46	71	12 179	3 680	5 074
Shelby	14 634	16.3	7 964	186	8.9	12.7	2 290	255	13	4 940	569	106 637	74 246	8 119
Smith	224	12.7	183	0	10.4	D	17	96	2	78	477	2 883	362	2 006
Stewart	143	11.5	148	0	12.0	D	4	32	0	0	0	2 307	111	881
Sullivan	1 718	11.2	1 705	19	11.1	11.1	469	306	3	802	532	31 077	6 556	4 204
Sumner	1 805	13.8	1 063	8	8.1	4.2	126	97	3	242	195	16 906	4 065	3 058
Tipton	723	14.1	425	7	8.3	9.7	32	62	1	100	211	6 452	2 132	4 081
Trousdale	94	13.0	87	0	12.0	D	8	110	1	26	380	1 077	260	3 515
Unicoi	172	9.8	227	1	12.9	D	16	91	1	48	279	4 086	563	3 127
Union	228	12.8	156	0	8.7	D	1	6	0	0	0	2 377	445	2 452
Van Buren	57	10.4	59	0	10.8	D	1	18	0	0	0	730	71	1 265
Warren	549	14.3	382	2	10.0	D	37	97	1	142	393	7 023	1 222	3 133
Washington	1 303	12.2	1 110	11	10.4	8.7	448	418	3	591	578	19 767	5 258	4 814
Wayne	173	10.2	164	1	9.6	D	10	59	1	54	327	2 599	314	1 830
Weakley	401	11.6	374	3	10.8	D	31	89	1	65	197	5 477	807	2 270
White	290	12.5	282	1	12.2	D	15	65	1	60	264	4 720	874	3 713
Williamson	1 704	13.4	669	8	5.3	4.7	237	187	1	109	93	13 253	2 619	2 030
Wilson	1 252	14.0	685	6	7.7	D	86	97	2	395	471	10 470	2 971	3 283
TEXAS	359 356	17.2	149 859	2 133	7.2	5.9	35 952	172	406	55 695	282	2 390 053	1 130 292	5 190
Anderson	658	12.0	602	4	11.0	D	61	111	2	225	430	7 691	1 709	2 969
Andrews	204	15.6	104	3	8.0	D	10	77	1	72	515	1 841	357	2 628
Angelina	1 281	16.0	804	9	10.0	6.8	111	139	3	346	447	12 666	3 244	3 876
Aransas	240	10.7	283	3	12.6	D	21	93	0	0	0	4 349	1 564	6 656
Archer	95	10.9	71	1	8.1	D	0	0	0	0	0	1 072	132	1 427
Armstrong	24	11.2	25	0	11.6	D	0	0	0	0	0	396	34	1 516
Atascosa	625	16.1	308	3	7.9	D	21	54	1	30	82	4 632	846	2 097
Austin	331	14.0	270	2	11.4	D	16	68	1	30	128	4 158	478	1 940
Bailey	128	19.5	57	1	8.6	D	3	45	1	31	449	1 108	150	2 178
Bandera	184	10.4	151	2	8.5	D	7	40	0	0	0	2 981	542	2 941
Bastrop	878	15.1	423	2	7.2	D	21	36	1	28	56	7 314	2 089	3 464
Baylor	39	9.7	70	0	17.4	D	2	49	1	39	939	1 045	69	1 614
Bee	403	12.5	226	3	7.0	D	17	53	1	59	213	3 581	642	1 899
Bell	5 242	22.0	1 520	39	6.4	7.4	665	279	4	755	338	24 285	12 378	5 003
Bexar	23 795	17.0	10 106	141	7.2	5.9	3 899	280	16	4 128	305	170 645	105 316	7 239
Blanco	107	12.7	98	0	11.6	D	3	36	0	0	0	2 999	104	1 183
Borden	4	5.5	4	0	0.0	D	0	0	0	0	0	40	13	1 708
Bosque	203	11.8	270	1	15.6	D	24	140	1	72	435	3 651	171	952
Bowie	1 161	13.0	968	8	10.8	6.9	193	216	4	711	851	13 869	4 211	4 514
Brazoria	4 001	16.5	1 615	19	6.6	4.8	179	74	4	310	135	25 645	7 588	3 015
Brazos	2 184	14.4	723	11	4.7	5.0	254	167	2	256	192	11 985	8 539	5 364
Brewster	116	13.1	76	2	8.6	D	9	102	1	34	382	1 402	200	2 160
Briscoe	24	13.4	22	0	12.2	D	0	0	0	0	0	377	18	963
Brooks	131	16.5	81	0	10.2	D	3	38	0	0	0	1 380	339	4 069
Brown	497	13.2	460	4	12.2	D	51	135	1	164	443	6 889	2 089	5 309
Burleson	229	13.9	149	1	9.0	D	6	36	1	33	211	2 961	254	1 476
Burnet	467	13.6	379	3	11.0	D	29	85	1	42	130	6 194	853	2 392

1. Per 1,000 estimated resident population.   2. Deaths of infants under 1 year old.   3. Deaths of infants under 1 year old per 1,000 live births.   4. Data subject to copyright.   5. Per 100,000 resident population as of July 1 of the year shown.   6. Data for serious crimes have not been adjusted for underreporting; this may affect comparability between geographic areas and over time.   7. Per 100,000 population estimated by the FBI.

Table B. States and Counties — Crime, Education, Money Income, and Poverty

	Serious crimes known to police,[1] 2002 (cont'd) Rate[2]		Education School enrollment and attainment, 2000 Enrollment[3]		Attainment[4] (percent)		Local government expenditures,[5] 2000–2001		Money income, 1999	Households Median income			Percent below poverty level, 1999			
STATE County	Violent	Property	Total	Percent private	High school graduate or less	Bachelor's degree or more	Total current expenditures (mil dol)	Current expenditures per student (dollars)	Per capita income[6] (dollars)	Dollars	Percent change, 1989–1999 (constant 1999 dollars)	Percent with income of $100,000 or more	Persons	Households	Families	Families with children
	46	47	48	49	50	51	52	53	54	55	56	57	58	59	60	61
TENNESSEE—Cont'd																
Marshall	363	2 302	6 342	5.7	67.6	10.6	26.6	5 489	17 749	38 457	20.0	6.3	10.0	11.5	7.3	10.8
Maury	750	4 294	16 743	16.9	58.4	13.6	64.6	5 799	19 365	41 591	18.0	9.1	10.9	11.1	8.3	12.2
Meigs	80	2 204	2 335	11.6	73.2	7.0	9.0	5 069	14 551	29 354	8.3	2.8	18.3	18.5	15.8	22.6
Monroe	776	3 630	8 665	10.3	70.5	10.1	32.1	4 577	14 951	30 337	13.3	4.1	15.5	16.4	12.0	16.5
Montgomery	531	4 521	38 242	9.8	46.1	19.3	119.8	5 134	17 265	38 981	13.5	6.3	10.0	10.5	7.9	11.2
Moore	205	1 453	1 312	7.2	63.4	11.8	5.6	5 577	19 040	36 591	-2.9	7.6	9.6	11.3	7.8	10.2
Morgan	154	1 098	4 260	5.2	77.1	6.0	16.6	5 108	12 925	27 712	7.0	2.6	16.0	17.7	13.5	15.5
Obion	532	4 107	7 182	5.0	70.3	10.3	30.1	5 543	17 409	32 764	9.1	5.3	13.3	13.7	10.1	15.6
Overton	78	1 390	4 459	4.4	78.9	8.3	15.3	4 973	13 910	26 915	9.5	2.0	16.0	17.9	12.3	17.5
Perry	257	2 058	1 594	6.3	74.6	7.1	6.8	5 783	16 969	28 061	9.7	4.2	15.4	17.8	12.6	14.9
Pickett	60	377	1 021	4.0	76.5	9.1	4.5	6 058	14 681	24 673	22.5	3.6	15.6	16.8	12.0	20.2
Polk	147	1 156	3 089	8.6	75.4	7.5	13.0	5 342	16 025	29 643	1.8	5.0	13.0	15.3	9.7	10.9
Putnam	243	3 628	17 803	7.1	59.5	20.2	47.5	5 062	16 927	30 914	6.1	5.6	16.4	17.7	10.3	14.7
Rhea	335	2 360	6 583	8.9	68.9	9.1	22.5	4 895	15 672	30 418	13.7	4.9	14.7	16.5	11.4	16.6
Roane	329	3 327	10 736	8.3	61.3	14.8	41.6	5 835	18 456	33 226	2.1	6.5	13.9	15.3	10.3	16.0
Robertson	707	2 780	12 851	12.7	64.2	11.9	49.0	4 775	19 054	43 174	12.0	7.6	9.0	9.6	6.4	9.4
Rutherford	518	3 299	53 906	9.6	50.0	22.9	168.4	5 429	19 938	46 312	11.6	9.2	9.0	10.0	5.8	7.6
Scott	687	2 471	4 995	2.7	77.4	7.5	22.1	5 700	12 927	24 093	13.1	2.5	20.2	22.0	17.6	22.2
Sequatchie	475	2 874	2 422	11.4	71.8	10.2	9.1	4 634	16 468	30 959	19.9	4.9	16.5	17.3	13.5	19.7
Sevier	301	4 774	15 086	9.3	61.8	13.5	70.4	5 573	18 064	34 719	12.1	5.5	10.7	11.8	8.2	11.5
Shelby	1 216	6 903	259 171	16.5	45.4	25.3	956.6	5 953	20 856	39 593	8.6	11.6	16.0	14.9	12.9	18.3
Smith	416	1 590	3 995	5.8	73.0	9.3	13.7	4 389	17 473	35 625	14.0	5.2	12.2	13.7	10.3	13.2
Stewart	103	777	2 710	5.5	67.7	10.2	10.7	4 783	16 302	32 316	15.6	3.8	12.4	14.9	10.6	11.5
Sullivan	525	3 679	32 281	11.7	57.2	18.1	159.4	6 855	19 202	33 529	-0.5	6.7	12.9	13.9	9.7	15.4
Sumner	388	2 670	32 250	14.6	52.4	18.6	120.8	5 405	21 164	46 030	7.8	10.8	8.1	8.5	6.2	9.1
Tipton	570	3 510	14 163	10.1	62.1	10.8	54.2	5 027	17 952	41 856	30.6	7.4	12.1	13.0	10.3	14.0
Trousdale	473	3 042	1 609	9.1	73.8	8.9	6.1	4 438	15 838	32 212	19.1	3.9	13.4	14.5	9.7	12.5
Unicoi	367	2 761	3 316	4.1	68.3	10.6	14.1	5 763	15 612	29 863	8.2	3.7	13.1	14.2	8.7	14.6
Union	325	2 127	3 890	4.2	79.2	5.8	17.2	5 803	13 375	27 335	3.8	4.0	19.6	20.2	16.8	22.9
Van Buren	143	1 123	1 203	3.9	80.4	7.8	4.5	5 355	17 497	28 165	1.4	3.2	15.2	16.5	13.7	17.3
Warren	308	2 825	7 910	6.1	72.0	9.1	32.7	5 142	15 759	30 920	9.5	4.5	16.6	17.4	13.0	19.9
Washington	508	4 305	26 774	8.3	51.8	22.9	85.6	5 785	19 085	33 116	4.0	7.0	13.9	15.2	10.2	15.5
Wayne	338	1 492	3 539	4.9	76.7	8.0	13.8	5 256	14 472	26 576	7.3	2.8	16.3	17.5	12.9	17.9
Weakley	228	2 042	10 280	4.7	65.6	15.3	24.1	4 934	15 408	30 008	6.3	3.8	16.0	18.5	11.1	15.9
White	446	3 267	4 904	5.6	74.3	7.9	18.3	4 564	14 791	29 383	10.0	3.5	14.3	15.5	11.2	15.2
Williamson	126	1 903	35 558	22.9	29.8	44.4	150.4	6 415	32 496	69 104	17.9	30.2	4.7	4.9	3.5	4.5
Wilson	449	2 834	21 923	19.2	53.0	19.6	78.0	5 488	22 739	50 140	13.6	12.4	6.7	7.3	4.6	6.4
TEXAS	579	4 611	5 948 260	11.4	49.2	23.2	26 432.9	6 511	19 617	39 927	10.0	11.5	15.4	14.0	12.0	16.6
Anderson	250	2 719	11 231	7.6	63.8	11.1	52.3	6 161	13 838	31 957	4.6	4.4	16.5	16.8	12.7	18.2
Andrews	250	2 378	3 864	4.2	64.6	12.4	25.9	8 194	15 916	34 036	-4.2	4.7	16.4	16.7	13.9	17.8
Angelina	609	3 267	21 101	7.4	58.1	14.7	96.5	5 984	15 876	33 806	9.5	6.0	15.8	15.2	12.4	18.5
Aransas	302	6 354	5 072	9.5	54.5	16.7	24.3	7 247	18 560	30 702	7.2	7.5	19.9	17.5	15.5	26.0
Archer	173	1 254	2 406	6.5	54.9	15.9	13.9	6 927	19 300	38 514	14.1	7.0	9.0	10.0	6.8	9.3
Armstrong	178	1 337	546	4.4	45.4	20.5	2.8	7 152	17 151	38 194	23.2	6.3	10.6	10.0	7.9	10.4
Atascosa	154	1 943	11 272	5.5	66.8	10.5	57.4	6 879	14 276	33 081	22.8	5.6	20.2	19.3	16.1	21.3
Austin	179	1 761	5 952	8.8	57.8	17.3	33.5	6 203	18 140	38 615	14.8	8.4	12.1	12.5	8.8	12.7
Bailey	247	1 931	1 775	3.7	70.0	9.3	12.3	8 090	12 979	27 901	4.5	3.7	16.7	16.5	13.5	16.9
Bandera	174	2 767	4 107	9.3	47.1	19.4	20.1	6 886	19 635	39 013	17.7	7.9	10.8	11.3	7.7	11.3
Bastrop	297	3 167	14 375	8.9	54.8	17.0	77.2	6 750	18 146	43 578	35.3	8.9	11.6	11.3	8.4	12.5
Baylor	374	1 240	878	3.2	62.6	12.1	5.4	7 486	16 384	24 627	6.4	3.1	16.1	15.7	12.9	20.8
Bee	189	1 710	7 807	7.9	61.1	12.2	33.9	6 584	10 625	28 392	2.5	3.2	24.0	21.6	19.7	27.5
Bell	466	4 537	65 774	11.7	42.8	19.8	316.3	6 323	17 219	36 872	15.5	6.5	12.1	11.6	9.7	13.8
Bexar	727	6 512	407 384	14.1	47.4	22.7	1 753.1	6 685	18 363	38 328	10.0	9.9	15.9	14.3	12.7	18.0
Blanco	45	1 137	1 847	8.4	49.4	22.2	11.6	7 444	19 721	39 369	31.4	9.5	11.2	11.4	8.1	13.3
Borden	131	1 577	201	5.5	49.0	21.4	3.1	20 812	18 364	29 205	-26.0	9.6	14.0	13.7	11.8	13.1
Bosque	78	874	3 846	4.4	56.2	15.4	23.3	7 280	17 455	34 181	18.8	6.2	12.7	14.0	8.9	14.4
Bowie	523	3 991	22 200	6.3	54.6	16.1	102.6	6 285	17 357	33 001	1.3	6.5	17.7	17.1	13.8	21.7
Brazoria	269	2 746	68 391	11.4	47.7	19.6	289.2	6 065	20 021	48 632	5.2	13.6	10.2	9.7	8.1	11.1
Brazos	440	4 924	73 264	5.8	38.8	37.0	134.8	6 402	16 212	29 104	6.1	8.3	26.9	27.7	14.0	18.1
Brewster	194	1 965	2 971	4.9	54.5	27.7	11.9	8 117	15 183	27 386	15.9	4.2	18.2	19.9	12.6	19.2
Briscoe	160	802	436	5.5	55.6	17.5	2.1	8 141	14 218	29 917	25.8	3.6	16.0	16.0	11.5	16.8
Brooks	468	3 601	2 428	2.1	73.5	6.8	13.7	7 377	10 234	18 622	2.6	3.1	40.2	37.7	36.9	42.9
Brown	651	4 658	9 963	14.4	60.4	15.0	46.6	6 443	15 624	30 974	19.5	4.9	17.2	17.5	14.0	21.2
Burleson	326	1 151	3 971	8.8	66.4	13.2	22.3	6 941	16 616	33 026	24.2	5.5	17.2	16.2	13.2	18.9
Burnet	252	2 139	7 243	8.8	54.7	17.4	42.9	6 682	18 850	37 921	31.8	8.4	10.9	10.3	7.9	12.8

1. Data for serious crimes have not been adjusted for underreporting; this may affect comparability between geographic areas and over time.   2. Per 100,000 population estimated by the FBI.   3. All persons 3 years old and over enrolled in nursery school through college.   4. Persons 25 years old and over.   5. Elementary and secondary education expenditures.   6. Based on population enumerated as of April 1, 2000.

Table B. States and Counties — Personal Income

STATE County	Total (mil dol) 62	Percent change, 2001–2002 63	Per capita[1] Dollars 64	Per capita[1] Rank 65	Wages and salaries[2] (mil dol) 66	Proprietor's income (mil dol) 67	Dividends, interest, and rent (mil dol) 68	Transfer payments Total (mil dol) 69	Government payments to individuals Total (mil dol) 70	Social Security (mil dol) 71	Medical payments (mil dol) 72	Income maintenance (mil dol) 73	Unemployment insurance (mil dol) 74
TENNESSEE—Cont'd													
Marshall	699	5.2	25 524	994	474	54	105	118	112	46	50	10	4
Maury	1 899	4.5	26 562	772	1 697	156	247	320	304	114	140	28	9
Meigs	223	5.6	19 711	2 610	57	23	27	60	57	20	25	6	2
Monroe	761	3.3	18 833	2 775	392	60	108	202	193	74	81	21	8
Montgomery	3 548	5.1	25 689	959	1 401	224	438	474	446	143	165	46	14
Moore	131	1.7	21 959	2 028	57	5	21	22	20	10	8	1	1
Morgan	380	5.1	18 976	2 758	100	34	43	106	101	39	42	11	4
Obion	805	1.8	24 837	1 168	600	64	131	162	154	64	65	14	4
Overton	408	4.1	20 172	2 505	140	46	59	115	111	38	54	10	3
Perry	166	2.1	22 076	1 997	77	16	25	47	46	16	24	3	1
Pickett	89	3.1	17 541	2 949	26	8	15	32	31	11	15	3	1
Polk	353	1.8	21 902	2 038	83	22	43	92	89	34	42	7	3
Putnam	1 521	3.6	23 705	1 499	1 078	157	249	317	303	115	137	26	8
Rhea	593	6.3	20 492	2 436	402	32	76	158	152	55	70	16	4
Roane	1 247	5.7	23 878	1 447	808	50	146	308	297	120	130	25	6
Robertson	1 453	3.3	25 413	1 023	537	140	167	235	222	88	98	17	10
Rutherford	5 270	4.9	26 946	711	3 543	677	549	572	529	209	213	46	26
Scott	374	1.7	17 270	2 970	169	26	45	138	133	36	65	19	5
Sequatchie	236	2.0	20 026	2 543	74	12	27	58	56	19	27	5	1
Sevier	1 828	5.4	24 603	1 237	951	217	288	330	313	132	130	26	14
Shelby	29 704	3.3	32 914	189	24 060	3 919	3 748	3 910	3 709	1 179	1 599	642	111
Smith	427	2.8	23 533	1 552	196	33	66	89	85	29	43	7	4
Stewart	263	3.8	20 560	2 417	102	15	42	65	62	24	25	5	2
Sullivan	4 018	2.8	26 306	829	2 914	334	680	818	784	355	312	63	15
Sumner	3 738	2.4	27 410	629	1 440	334	463	526	495	208	208	38	21
Tipton	1 252	2.4	23 468	1 579	384	57	121	213	201	71	88	23	7
Trousdale	156	2.3	21 129	2 258	44	16	22	40	38	12	19	4	1
Unicoi	400	5.0	22 671	1 830	205	14	55	114	110	36	50	8	3
Union	335	3.6	18 096	2 881	77	11	36	84	80	30	36	10	2
Van Buren	114	3.8	20 565	2 414	41	10	11	28	26	9	13	2	1
Warren	871	5.2	22 510	1 875	584	89	126	215	207	70	105	18	8
Washington	2 654	3.0	24 323	1 302	2 028	203	424	545	521	202	223	42	14
Wayne	277	4.8	16 256	3 041	113	16	43	87	84	29	39	8	4
Weakley	742	1.7	21 625	2 116	375	58	116	165	158	63	67	12	5
White	456	2.9	19 411	2 672	216	42	58	132	127	48	59	12	4
Williamson	5 790	3.1	42 370	47	2 948	703	820	349	318	161	119	14	12
Wilson	2 811	2.8	30 120	341	1 168	244	356	357	336	137	141	21	15
TEXAS	631 208	2.2	29 039	X	426 590	90 425	88 160	78 142	73 288	25 819	31 853	8 298	2 950
Anderson	1 033	2.2	18 950	2 764	641	95	166	233	220	74	103	20	5
Andrews	279	1.4	21 564	2 133	167	16	43	56	53	22	24	6	2
Angelina	1 991	3.2	24 775	1 187	1 228	213	349	406	388	138	181	39	10
Aransas	579	3.8	25 094	1 108	171	39	153	120	115	50	47	10	3
Archer	245	2.0	27 107	676	58	24	46	31	29	15	9	2	0
Armstrong	52	-0.1	24 596	1 238	17	3	12	11	10	4	5	0	0
Atascosa	809	3.8	19 654	2 621	293	78	100	161	152	49	71	20	4
Austin	686	3.7	27 918	562	366	48	142	107	101	42	46	7	2
Bailey	152	0.4	23 244	1 644	77	22	29	32	31	11	15	4	0
Bandera	486	4.5	25 625	972	73	28	100	73	69	33	23	5	2
Bastrop	1 417	1.6	22 057	2 004	381	81	186	199	185	72	75	18	8
Baylor	81	-4.2	20 698	2 371	29	5	19	26	25	10	12	2	0
Bee	508	2.9	15 701	3 058	265	34	73	127	119	34	59	15	2
Bell	6 274	5.3	25 581	984	5 633	319	852	837	788	242	285	83	25
Bexar	40 373	3.1	27 910	564	28 659	5 840	6 018	5 604	5 287	1 625	2 346	655	142
Blanco	236	3.8	26 817	732	76	28	50	44	42	16	21	2	1
Borden	14	7.0	20 878	2 327	6	-1	5	2	2	1	0	0	0
Bosque	402	2.6	22 902	1 752	114	39	88	89	85	38	34	6	2
Bowie	2 168	4.4	24 233	1 332	1 390	159	429	414	394	134	182	42	8
Brazoria	7 099	2.7	27 639	596	3 509	346	874	817	759	307	324	61	39
Brazos	3 255	3.6	20 806	2 346	2 545	238	552	377	342	133	130	43	4
Brewster	217	4.6	23 991	1 412	139	6	53	38	36	14	11	4	0
Briscoe	37	-5.1	21 518	2 143	14	2	8	9	9	4	4	1	0
Brooks	129	3.9	16 599	3 018	67	5	22	50	48	11	26	9	1
Brown	806	3.5	21 221	2 233	492	57	120	215	206	71	101	17	4
Burleson	368	3.3	21 957	2 029	121	15	73	77	73	30	29	7	1
Burnet	968	4.0	25 765	937	346	100	285	170	162	82	56	10	4

1. Based on the resident population estimated as of July 1 of the year shown.   2. Includes other labor income.

Table B. States and Counties — Earnings, Social Security, and Housing

STATE County	Earnings, 2002									Social Security beneficiaries, December 2003		Supplemental Security Income recipients, December 2003	Housing units, 2003	
	Total (mil dol)	Farm	Goods-related[1] Total	Manu-facturing	Information and professional and technical services	Retail trade	Finance, insurance, and real estate	Health services	Govern-ment	Number	Rate[2]		Total	Percent change, 2000–2003
	75	76	77	78	79	80	81	82	83	84	85	86	87	88
TENNESSEE—Cont'd														
Marshall	528	-0.1	D	56.9	D	6.0	3.1	2.2	10.1	4 900	178	499	11 866	6.1
Maury	1 852	-0.2	D	46.5	5.2	6.4	4.7	6.7	13.0	12 205	167	1 642	30 792	7.4
Meigs	80	-0.2	36.7	32.1	3.6	6.8	D	4.6	16.8	2 240	196	408	5 364	3.4
Monroe	452	-0.1	D	44.5	1.7	8.3	3.7	D	11.7	8 730	213	1 592	17 915	3.6
Montgomery	1 625	0.3	D	20.5	D	11.6	5.4	10.4	19.4	16 535	117	2 365	56 759	8.8
Moore	61	2.2	D	D	D	2.9	D	5.2	37.2	1 045	177	74	2 689	6.9
Morgan	134	0.3	D	20.7	3.2	7.5	D	5.9	29.0	4 585	228	610	7 955	3.1
Obion	663	0.8	55.3	50.0	2.6	8.2	3.6	D	9.7	7 030	217	989	14 742	1.7
Overton	186	1.0	33.0	28.0	2.6	11.0	7.0	D	18.8	4 775	237	816	9 411	2.7
Perry	93	-0.8	D	48.2	D	5.0	4.8	17.4	12.0	1 825	239	211	4 224	2.6
Pickett	34	3.8	D	12.5	D	19.6	D	8.8	21.7	1 355	271	211	3 024	2.3
Polk	105	3.9	D	13.8	2.2	17.0	5.9	8.5	25.4	3 710	229	533	7 564	2.6
Putnam	1 234	-0.1	31.7	25.9	6.2	9.8	4.9	8.3	20.9	12 865	198	1 972	27 992	4.0
Rhea	434	0.6	45.4	41.6	2.1	5.1	2.6	D	30.9	6 085	208	1 050	13 108	4.3
Roane	859	-0.3	D	8.0	42.5	8.1	2.0	D	18.6	12 580	240	1 764	23 950	2.5
Robertson	676	1.6	D	37.4	3.1	9.7	4.2	D	16.0	9 510	163	903	22 877	9.0
Rutherford	4 220	-0.1	D	30.1	6.8	7.7	6.6	10.9	11.2	22 600	112	2 339	81 163	14.9
Scott	195	0.3	37.0	29.9	2.1	9.4	2.9	11.4	20.2	4 690	216	1 604	9 152	2.7
Sequatchie	86	-0.1	D	27.1	3.4	8.0	7.5	7.2	19.4	2 345	196	349	5 089	3.5
Sevier	1 168	-0.4	D	7.6	4.3	16.6	8.5	4.2	13.5	14 880	197	1 263	39 365	5.7
Shelby	27 978	0.0	14.4	9.5	7.3	7.3	9.9	9.5	14.2	124 695	138	31 002	379 174	4.5
Smith	229	0.1	D	32.0	2.4	11.0	5.0	11.1	11.6	3 415	187	486	7 879	2.8
Stewart	117	0.8	19.5	15.7	D	8.2	4.3	3.2	52.5	2 840	221	362	6 135	2.6
Sullivan	3 248	-0.1	D	31.0	6.7	7.8	4.4	15.2	8.6	36 740	240	4 446	71 039	2.9
Sumner	1 774	-0.1	35.6	23.6	6.0	8.3	7.1	8.8	13.6	21 685	156	2 235	55 531	7.5
Tipton	441	0.9	D	26.4	2.4	8.8	4.5	D	19.0	8 285	153	1 196	20 836	9.3
Trousdale	60	-0.8	24.8	22.4	D	7.2	D	5.6	24.5	1 510	203	231	3 205	3.6
Unicoi	219	0.0	D	38.2	D	3.7	2.0	4.8	15.8	4 300	243	661	8 356	1.7
Union	88	0.3	D	31.8	D	7.9	4.4	6.2	24.4	3 680	195	641	8 435	6.6
Van Buren	51	1.2	D	D	D	3.1	D	D	20.2	1 135	207	175	2 531	3.2
Warren	673	3.9	D	49.6	D	8.1	3.0	6.7	9.7	8 090	207	1 377	17 072	2.3
Washington	2 231	0.5	D	17.9	8.0	8.9	6.5	15.0	20.8	21 945	199	2 929	49 330	3.2
Wayne	129	0.4	D	26.2	1.6	10.8	4.1	4.0	28.5	3 465	204	490	6 914	3.2
Weakley	432	2.5	23.6	18.8	D	8.4	5.5	D	27.0	6 845	199	713	15 370	3.0
White	258	-0.3	D	41.6	D	9.8	3.4	D	13.6	5 635	239	830	10 476	2.8
Williamson	3 651	-0.1	D	4.4	18.9	7.8	20.8	14.1	7.7	15 540	110	602	52 025	10.7
Wilson	1 411	-0.2	37.1	27.2	D	8.7	5.8	8.5	9.1	14 100	148	1 143	37 687	7.9
TEXAS	517 015	0.5	23.1	12.5	12.6	7.1	9.8	8.1	14.8	2 792 148	126	455 232	8 658 290	6.1
Anderson	736	0.4	10.1	2.8	5.4	18.1	4.7	13.6	30.2	8 200	150	1 213	18 873	2.4
Andrews	183	-0.5	40.6	6.5	D	5.8	4.9	D	21.7	2 180	169	268	5 506	2.0
Angelina	1 441	0.2	27.5	22.3	D	13.3	4.4	13.8	16.1	14 905	184	2 596	33 360	2.9
Aransas	210	-0.1	14.5	3.8	D	13.5	6.1	5.4	17.0	5 355	227	458	13 362	4.0
Archer	83	13.9	20.8	1.4	D	5.4	2.9	3.8	21.0	1 605	175	100	3 900	0.7
Armstrong	20	4.7	D	D	D	3.4	D	D	21.6	430	209	20	919	-0.1
Atascosa	371	4.9	15.9	3.3	5.4	10.5	4.4	D	20.9	6 345	152	925	15 358	3.2
Austin	415	1.6	35.8	23.6	11.4	6.4	6.6	3.4	12.9	4 535	181	364	10 533	3.2
Bailey	98	10.2	9.8	6.2	4.9	6.9	D	2.5	21.3	1 260	189	152	2 733	-0.2
Bandera	101	-0.4	D	1.3	5.9	10.6	8.3	6.2	24.8	3 640	188	249	9 704	2.1
Bastrop	462	1.5	15.3	7.2	6.6	13.5	5.2	6.0	32.8	8 225	123	927	23 354	4.9
Baylor	34	-3.1	D	D	D	9.4	6.1	16.7	27.7	1 150	294	120	2 780	-1.4
Bee	299	0.8	12.7	3.2	4.2	8.3	3.6	D	46.0	4 245	131	930	11 052	1.0
Bell	5 952	0.1	D	5.8	4.0	6.1	3.3	8.6	56.1	28 715	115	4 366	100 397	8.2
Bexar	34 499	0.2	12.7	5.5	11.1	7.4	11.6	9.8	23.3	195 565	133	39 492	551 428	5.8
Blanco	105	5.2	D	1.5	D	8.4	10.0	D	17.2	1 765	200	97	4 110	2.0
Borden	5	-15.2	D	0.0	D	D	D	0.0	64.0	110	161	1	439	0.9
Bosque	152	9.4	23.2	13.6	3.7	9.2	4.6	12.3	21.0	4 070	230	285	8 720	0.9
Bowie	1 549	1.2	12.3	7.7	D	10.8	6.1	20.3	27.0	15 865	177	2 832	37 390	2.5
Brazoria	3 855	0.2	46.5	28.7	6.1	7.3	4.3	5.0	14.7	30 575	116	3 314	98 504	8.7
Brazos	2 783	0.2	14.5	7.0	8.8	7.8	5.9	10.9	39.2	13 725	86	1 963	64 101	8.6
Brewster	145	-4.7	6.2	1.1	10.7	9.0	5.1	D	35.1	1 615	175	195	4 715	2.2
Briscoe	16	-0.9	D	7.1	D	5.3	D	D	25.1	410	247	45	1 012	0.6
Brooks	71	3.2	D	D	D	8.6	D	D	40.5	1 585	205	629	3 230	0.8
Brown	549	1.0	32.6	28.1	3.0	10.1	4.0	D	19.0	7 925	208	1 122	18 075	1.0
Burleson	136	-1.2	29.0	8.1	D	9.8	5.8	D	22.2	3 340	197	413	8 409	2.6
Burnet	447	-0.4	20.9	7.4	7.9	11.6	13.1	8.7	17.0	8 520	220	472	17 352	8.9

1. Covers mining, construction, and manufacturing.   2. Per 1,000 resident population estimated as of July 1 of the year shown.

Table B. States and Counties — Housing, Labor Force, and Employment

STATE County	Housing units, 2000 Total	Percent	Median value[1]	With a mortgage	Without a mortgage[2]	Median rent[3]	Median rent as a percent of income	Substandard units[4] (percent)	Civilian labor force, 2003 Total	Percent change, 2002–2003	Unemployment Total	Rate[5]	Civilian employment,[6] 2000 Total	Management, professional and related occupations	Production, transportation, and material moving occupations
	89	90	91	92	93	94	95	96	97	98	99	100	101	102	103
TENNESSEE—Cont'd															
Marshall	10 307	73.0	83 800	19.5	9.9	444	22.7	2.3	11 896	-7.6	1 621	13.6	13 086	21.5	35.2
Maury	26 444	72.8	96 800	19.7	9.9	514	22.9	3.4	37 886	-1.3	2 486	6.6	34 164	24.8	25.1
Meigs	4 304	81.9	87 200	21.4	9.9	365	23.0	3.3	4 754	-1.9	394	8.3	4 463	16.6	34.2
Monroe	15 329	78.3	79 400	20.9	9.9	396	22.3	3.4	18 831	-0.1	1 510	8.0	16 219	19.0	34.3
Montgomery	48 330	63.5	85 100	21.8	9.9	549	24.0	4.0	63 319	-0.8	2 996	4.7	54 703	27.3	18.9
Moore	2 211	83.7	85 600	21.3	10.2	402	20.5	1.9	3 503	2.4	99	2.8	2 741	24.7	25.1
Morgan	6 990	82.8	60 200	22.8	9.9	397	23.2	3.2	6 652	-4.2	697	10.5	7 420	17.7	28.1
Obion	13 182	71.5	67 500	18.9	10.7	393	21.8	2.9	15 973	-2.3	1 297	8.1	14 774	19.3	32.7
Overton	8 110	80.8	71 600	21.4	10.6	345	21.3	2.9	9 497	-1.0	628	6.6	8 874	20.1	32.4
Perry	3 023	85.8	62 600	21.2	9.9	365	23.6	4.3	3 357	-0.9	233	6.9	3 230	21.4	37.0
Pickett	2 091	84.3	66 900	22.1	10.9	241	17.9	2.9	2 196	-2.6	152	6.9	2 129	20.1	29.0
Polk	6 448	80.8	72 100	19.3	9.9	345	19.7	3.8	6 760	-0.9	466	6.9	6 938	16.5	35.8
Putnam	24 865	65.6	92 600	21.6	9.9	441	26.3	2.6	31 619	-1.7	1 524	4.8	29 694	28.7	22.1
Rhea	11 184	75.4	76 700	19.9	9.9	384	24.2	2.7	12 126	-0.9	756	6.2	12 489	18.5	34.8
Roane	21 200	77.5	86 500	20.0	9.9	398	24.1	2.0	24 305	-1.3	1 333	5.5	22 773	26.7	22.7
Robertson	19 906	76.5	107 300	21.5	9.9	502	24.2	3.4	29 678	-0.9	1 660	5.6	27 534	24.7	21.1
Rutherford	66 443	69.8	113 500	20.9	9.9	601	26.9	2.9	106 489	-0.9	4 660	4.4	95 968	30.5	18.4
Scott	8 203	76.5	60 300	23.1	12.5	347	24.6	4.1	8 832	-4.0	965	10.9	7 899	21.0	33.6
Sequatchie	4 463	76.2	80 300	23.8	9.9	382	22.4	4.0	4 821	2.1	271	5.6	4 939	21.9	29.3
Sevier	28 467	73.3	112 500	21.6	9.9	513	23.4	2.8	41 382	0.1	2 668	6.4	35 212	23.0	14.6
Shelby	338 366	63.1	92 200	21.7	10.4	566	25.9	5.5	454 817	-0.6	29 158	6.4	408 221	33.4	14.6
Smith	6 878	78.8	87 100	21.6	9.9	401	21.6	3.0	10 639	2.7	809	7.6	8 236	22.3	29.6
Stewart	4 930	79.3	76 800	21.2	9.9	420	22.7	3.5	4 256	0.1	396	9.3	4 998	23.1	24.7
Sullivan	63 556	75.8	88 000	20.3	9.9	419	24.4	1.6	74 763	-0.8	4 295	5.7	68 098	28.6	18.9
Sumner	48 941	75.5	125 800	21.5	9.9	594	25.7	2.9	72 297	-1.0	3 395	4.7	65 926	30.2	17.7
Tipton	18 106	76.2	91 500	21.0	9.9	470	23.2	3.6	24 957	-0.1	1 835	7.4	23 280	23.6	20.9
Trousdale	2 780	76.3	76 800	19.7	10.5	452	23.2	2.6	2 161	5.4	215	9.9	3 306	18.7	29.3
Unicoi	7 516	76.6	82 400	19.6	9.9	380	24.3	2.6	7 968	-1.7	548	6.9	7 538	22.3	27.2
Union	6 742	80.9	79 000	23.1	9.9	388	26.0	4.1	9 064	-0.1	389	4.3	7 467	15.9	27.0
Van Buren	2 180	85.6	55 800	21.3	9.9	346	22.9	4.1	2 533	3.1	220	8.7	2 520	15.5	41.0
Warren	15 181	72.9	72 800	20.7	9.9	416	24.1	3.0	19 674	1.0	1 198	6.1	17 847	20.2	30.8
Washington	44 195	68.2	96 700	20.9	9.9	446	26.0	2.0	54 068	-1.9	2 656	4.9	51 358	31.3	16.6
Wayne	5 936	82.9	56 600	21.7	9.9	322	22.8	3.0	7 118	-2.9	767	10.8	6 009	19.5	35.2
Weakley	13 599	68.8	67 900	19.7	9.9	391	25.0	1.8	16 988	-2.7	1 528	9.0	15 828	22.9	28.0
White	9 229	79.7	76 300	22.0	9.9	392	22.2	2.8	10 861	0.6	931	8.6	10 378	18.8	34.9
Williamson	44 725	81.5	208 400	21.3	9.9	744	24.1	1.8	72 919	-1.1	2 212	3.0	65 562	46.0	9.3
Wilson	32 798	81.4	136 600	21.0	9.9	567	24.9	2.3	50 022	-0.6	2 441	4.9	46 621	31.7	17.0
TEXAS	7 393 354	63.8	82 500	20.1	10.9	574	24.4	10.0	10 910 344	2.1	737 516	6.8	9 234 372	33.3	13.2
Anderson	15 678	73.9	58 900	20.0	12.7	456	24.3	5.5	19 845	2.9	1 111	5.6	17 046	24.9	14.9
Andrews	4 601	79.7	42 500	19.0	9.9	397	19.1	5.6	5 531	7.1	300	5.4	5 064	25.5	19.6
Angelina	28 685	72.4	63 600	19.0	10.2	461	25.7	7.7	37 753	2.6	2 512	6.7	33 857	26.8	20.7
Aransas	9 132	75.1	79 000	20.8	12.4	475	23.1	7.1	10 431	4.0	750	7.2	8 578	25.9	10.8
Archer	3 345	81.2	61 200	19.4	11.4	424	19.6	3.2	4 418	1.3	140	3.2	4 341	30.4	16.7
Armstrong	802	79.1	60 500	15.0	11.9	436	18.8	2.9	1 063	-3.6	33	3.1	975	33.7	13.8
Atascosa	12 816	78.5	52 900	19.5	10.9	398	24.4	12.4	18 651	2.0	1 231	6.6	15 430	23.8	16.3
Austin	8 747	77.2	85 000	18.8	10.2	475	20.1	7.2	14 341	1.4	692	4.8	10 768	30.0	17.0
Bailey	2 348	71.3	37 300	19.3	11.5	383	19.6	11.7	3 813	4.5	211	5.5	2 724	24.0	19.7
Bandera	7 010	82.9	99 000	20.2	9.9	477	22.0	5.8	7 924	-0.3	306	3.9	7 810	35.0	9.1
Bastrop	20 097	80.3	93 400	19.9	10.1	549	23.7	8.5	31 851	1.8	2 066	6.5	26 529	30.5	14.8
Baylor	1 791	72.6	34 200	22.5	12.5	271	20.0	4.1	1 776	7.5	95	5.3	1 571	36.3	8.5
Bee	9 061	65.5	47 200	19.2	10.2	416	22.7	9.5	10 686	4.2	747	7.0	9 944	25.3	12.0
Bell	85 507	55.7	78 100	20.6	9.9	543	23.8	7.1	102 049	2.1	5 663	5.5	90 230	30.7	14.3
Bexar	488 942	61.2	74 100	20.5	9.9	556	24.8	10.0	716 483	2.3	40 791	5.7	595 911	32.9	10.6
Blanco	3 303	78.6	93 000	20.5	9.9	479	19.9	7.0	4 131	4.6	155	3.8	3 941	30.9	9.9
Borden	292	73.3	43 100	34.0	43.0	225	9.9	6.8	363	2.3	14	3.9	343	49.6	9.0
Bosque	6 726	77.5	57 900	19.5	12.2	432	21.6	4.6	6 938	2.1	426	6.1	7 101	29.5	16.6
Bowie	33 058	70.9	66 600	18.9	10.4	459	26.4	4.7	40 610	1.7	2 358	5.8	35 947	27.6	16.7
Brazoria	81 954	74.0	88 500	18.5	9.9	542	22.1	8.0	114 206	2.6	10 182	8.9	106 662	32.7	15.0
Brazos	55 202	45.6	96 000	19.7	10.6	584	38.0	7.8	82 861	3.5	1 896	2.3	72 096	39.3	9.5
Brewster	3 669	59.4	67 000	19.1	12.4	370	25.0	7.2	5 895	4.4	143	2.4	4 054	31.9	7.6
Briscoe	724	77.1	30 000	17.0	10.1	301	26.0	5.2	711	-9.4	34	4.8	784	34.9	8.5
Brooks	2 711	73.1	34 600	19.1	15.4	250	27.5	15.3	3 547	0.7	299	8.4	2 454	22.6	13.5
Brown	14 306	72.2	47 800	19.0	11.8	441	25.3	4.5	17 414	0.4	784	4.5	15 536	25.8	19.1
Burleson	6 363	79.6	55 900	19.2	11.5	443	24.3	6.9	8 027	4.6	434	5.4	7 024	26.6	17.6
Burnet	13 133	78.4	93 600	21.2	11.3	509	25.4	6.4	17 615	7.8	877	5.0	14 974	28.2	12.7

1. Specified owner-occupied units. 2. Median monthly owner costs is often in the minimum category—9.9 percent or less, which is indicated as 9.9 percent. 3. Specified renter-occupied units. 4. Overcrowded or lacking complete plumbing facilities. 5. Percent of civilian labor force. 6. Persons 16 years old and over.

Table B. States and Counties — **Nonfarm Employment and Agriculture**

STATE County	Private nonfarm establishments, employment and payroll, 2001									Agriculture, 2002			
	Number of establishments	Employment						Annual payroll		Farms			
		Total	Health care and social assistance	Manufacturing	Retail trade	Finance and insurance	Professional, scientific, and technical services	Total (mil dol)	Average per employee (dollars)	Number	Percent with—		Farm operators whose principal occupation is farming (percent)
											Less than 50 acres	500 acres and over	
	104	105	106	107	108	109	110	111	112	113	114	115	116

STATE County	104	105	106	107	108	109	110	111	112	113	114	115	116
TENNESSEE—Cont'd													
Marshall	505	12 245	584	7 637	1 117	198	104	297	24 294	1 312	36.5	4.2	50.6
Maury	1 502	29 872	4 167	10 725	3 305	1 453	828	1 080	36 159	1 754	38.4	4.7	48.7
Meigs	94	1 374	91	744	144	D	D	34	24 678	340	30.9	4.4	51.5
Monroe	678	11 280	950	5 396	1 756	261	211	268	23 795	955	45.2	2.6	47.4
Montgomery	2 256	34 998	3 789	7 869	6 969	985	1 858	801	22 887	1 090	39.8	6.6	50.3
Moore	56	789	86	D	D	D	D	25	32 309	387	27.9	7.2	51.7
Morgan	161	1 687	259	638	229	57	11	36	21 074	403	33.0	3.0	47.1
Obion	729	14 857	1 073	7 173	1 868	463	111	412	27 706	701	33.2	15.4	58.1
Overton	291	3 438	704	1 217	472	119	60	73	21 271	1 106	44.1	2.9	52.9
Perry	105	2 115	385	1 313	134	29	D	51	24 127	266	27.4	7.9	57.5
Pickett	78	1 001	108	521	92	35	4	19	18 604	401	45.9	2.2	49.1
Polk	250	1 962	320	406	323	186	23	40	20 274	274	50.7	4.7	49.6
Putnam	1 709	27 766	3 356	8 333	4 345	740	730	663	23 881	1 302	49.2	2.4	47.5
Rhea	486	8 329	749	4 428	920	159	91	182	21 832	455	42.0	4.4	48.8
Roane	720	8 765	1 667	1 823	1 895	315	156	180	20 563	722	47.9	1.2	50.1
Robertson	955	14 046	1 211	5 440	1 792	275	345	334	23 772	1 621	47.8	5.6	53.3
Rutherford	3 498	69 972	7 835	17 787	9 833	3 472	1 723	2 143	30 621	2 088	49.8	2.9	48.9
Scott	339	6 005	595	2 951	810	154	D	123	20 401	296	39.9	3.4	43.6
Sequatchie	173	2 313	358	897	294	97	D	42	17 978	208	38.5	6.3	47.6
Sevier	2 489	28 193	1 389	2 267	6 360	782	520	606	21 483	907	49.6	1.2	52.6
Shelby	21 134	477 968	54 245	35 124	54 744	21 144	20 138	16 018	33 513	716	59.2	6.6	47.1
Smith	294	4 581	711	1 679	588	154	D	129	28 106	1 126	33.0	3.3	52.8
Stewart	150	1 266	184	423	254	51	10	25	19 847	367	28.9	5.2	46.3
Sullivan	3 574	64 586	10 520	15 543	8 540	1 716	1 517	1 994	30 871	1 453	61.3	1.3	51.0
Sumner	2 491	33 391	3 983	9 625	4 320	1 152	1 081	870	26 043	1 957	50.2	2.5	50.0
Tipton	686	9 456	1 041	2 980	1 484	264	181	221	23 339	627	46.4	9.7	55.2
Trousdale	119	1 152	236	324	211	52	32	22	18 663	360	33.9	3.3	53.9
Unicoi	248	3 797	507	1 394	353	98	D	107	28 185	166	60.8	1.8	58.4
Union	184	1 996	104	976	231	71	23	40	20 251	585	43.9	1.2	47.9
Van Buren	48	704	99	D	27	D	3	23	32 632	230	35.7	4.3	41.3
Warren	791	12 761	962	6 403	1 780	293	128	318	24 939	1 594	49.6	3.9	54.1
Washington	2 740	49 630	8 461	8 434	7 245	2 948	1 372	1 203	24 238	1 913	63.1	2.0	52.5
Wayne	239	2 775	280	1 061	380	151	26	49	17 568	713	25.5	7.2	53.6
Weakley	633	9 231	1 759	2 990	1 146	275	152	201	21 734	1 231	42.2	7.9	50.3
White	399	6 400	659	3 093	840	96	47	145	22 679	1 168	41.6	2.9	49.4
Williamson	4 457	74 614	8 806	4 588	10 682	8 006	7 509	2 608	34 951	1 712	46.7	3.2	47.5
Wilson	2 086	28 168	2 090	6 887	4 324	857	794	950	33 734	2 142	44.3	2.7	49.4
TEXAS	473 868	8 161 321	950 030	948 284	1 049 439	407 005	479 969	282 315	34 592	228 926	32.6	18.0	53.6
Anderson	948	11 172	1 971	772	1 825	642	228	275	24 591	1 735	33.0	8.3	51.9
Andrews	270	2 762	361	357	357	105	D	70	25 207	169	30.8	39.6	56.8
Angelina	1 839	30 820	6 424	6 630	4 286	937	828	800	25 946	931	47.0	4.2	47.4
Aransas	488	3 632	372	104	889	107	154	70	19 214	62	51.6	11.3	41.9
Archer	160	702	64	33	117	23	D	18	25 640	495	13.9	42.8	63.2
Armstrong	32	272	D	D	21	0	D	7	26 059	269	5.9	53.5	60.6
Atascosa	567	6 183	1 208	429	1 438	216	281	135	21 894	1 539	24.6	19.9	56.3
Austin	541	5 864	503	1 595	1 037	334	219	153	26 101	2 086	35.0	8.1	48.9
Bailey	171	1 425	259	D	246	58	38	30	20 855	436	9.4	45.2	63.1
Bandera	322	1 666	127	76	276	72	54	30	17 963	780	29.4	20.8	55.9
Bastrop	815	7 646	1 166	1 135	1 648	340	347	169	22 153	2 187	40.8	8.0	53.2
Baylor	141	1 129	541	40	132	37	20	16	14 365	253	13.8	46.6	64.4
Bee	449	4 396	864	282	928	190	128	90	20 419	866	24.4	22.6	57.2
Bell	4 115	74 594	18 656	7 583	10 930	3 372	3 034	1 871	25 143	2 080	44.1	8.6	50.8
Bexar	29 726	585 667	81 343	38 623	71 025	40 645	34 439	17 903	30 568	2 385	51.4	6.1	50.4
Blanco	216	1 830	159	93	338	104	44	44	23 889	784	21.0	25.3	52.0
Borden	3	D	0	0	D	0	0	D	D	132	1.5	70.5	75.8
Bosque	317	2 554	596	507	434	131	69	58	22 682	1 285	22.5	18.0	49.2
Bowie	2 090	30 846	6 802	3 834	5 539	1 006	642	780	25 279	1 337	33.5	8.2	55.7
Brazoria	3 834	60 367	4 925	13 071	9 522	1 397	1 860	2 120	35 114	2 455	51.1	11.5	48.1
Brazos	3 191	47 681	6 679	4 874	8 150	1 881	2 592	1 148	24 076	1 350	40.3	10.5	47.0
Brewster	292	2 219	441	37	404	189	56	38	17 273	136	16.2	63.2	69.1
Briscoe	48	201	D	15	29	26	D	3	17 209	264	8.3	48.1	58.0
Brooks	136	1 290	D	6	299	81	21	19	14 968	351	15.7	21.7	53.8
Brown	885	12 066	2 272	3 506	1 925	403	151	286	23 728	1 347	23.8	19.3	51.3
Burleson	283	2 317	240	208	496	139	45	53	22 991	1 550	27.6	11.6	55.8
Burnet	934	7 251	762	869	1 695	240	245	170	23 426	1 370	30.1	17.4	52.0

Items 104—116

Table B. States and Counties — Agriculture

STATE County	Land in farms Acreage (1,000)	Percent change, 1997–2002	Average size of farm	Total irrigated (1,000)	Total cropland (1,000)	Value of land and buildings Average per farm	Average per acre	Value of machinery and equipment average per farm (dollars)	Value of products sold Total (mil dol)	Average per farm (dollars)	Percent from — Crops	Livestock and poultry products	Percent of farms with sales of — $10,000 or more	$100,000 or more	Government payments Total ($1,000)	Percent of farms
	117	118	119	120	121	122	123	124	125	126	127	128	129	130	131	132
TENNESSEE—Cont'd																
Marshall	175	4.8	133	0	85	296 304	2 255	36 913	22	16 753	11.0	89.0	20.0	3.2	702	15.1
Maury	241	-0.8	137	0	124	389 898	2 579	33 306	21	11 820	25.2	74.8	19.1	2.4	871	18.3
Meigs	49	0.0	144	0	23	360 395	2 813	42 285	6	16 593	14.9	85.1	24.4	3.5	140	12.1
Monroe	99	2.1	104	0	56	310 606	2 926	37 582	22	22 712	11.7	88.3	18.8	5.3	406	5.3
Montgomery	167	1.2	153	1	103	365 001	2 412	44 706	28	25 623	69.3	30.7	30.5	5.9	546	21.0
Moore	63	21.2	162	0	32	331 078	2 091	35 133	10	24 908	6.5	93.6	27.4	5.7	154	15.0
Morgan	57	23.9	140	0	26	258 565	2 322	66 303	10	25 193	9.2	90.8	20.8	5.2	72	16.9
Obion	264	9.1	376	4	219	631 498	1 666	121 093	63	89 678	68.0	32.0	40.7	16.0	2 266	52.2
Overton	124	13.8	112	0	67	258 369	2 480	27 968	16	14 817	14.6	85.4	20.7	2.4	174	7.3
Perry	50	-7.4	187	0	18	287 428	1 484	43 862	3	9 584	35.7	64.4	19.2	2.3	101	21.4
Pickett	42	13.5	104	D	23	226 846	2 364	27 761	11	26 310	22.9	77.2	32.9	4.2	168	20.2
Polk	32	0.0	115	0	18	422 315	4 136	63 943	22	78 640	8.8	91.2	28.8	19.0	288	17.9
Putnam	119	6.3	91	0	60	259 001	2 979	32 111	11	8 779	31.3	68.7	15.9	1.0	271	11.7
Rhea	61	8.9	134	1	33	339 576	2 705	37 755	18	39 140	44.4	55.6	26.6	5.7	242	9.9
Roane	63	18.9	88	0	28	271 247	3 568	35 404	6	7 839	31.5	68.5	12.3	0.7	143	11.6
Robertson	233	-1.3	144	1	168	363 949	2 548	55 587	65	40 025	76.5	23.5	36.3	8.8	1 573	21.4
Rutherford	211	8.2	101	0	106	321 875	2 959	27 240	19	9 299	23.7	76.3	14.8	1.8	517	13.7
Scott	35	16.7	117	0	15	239 668	2 024	43 541	6	19 759	4.5	95.5	12.5	5.1	173	12.2
Sequatchie	28	7.7	136	0	14	258 528	2 263	36 544	5	23 068	14.8	85.2	27.9	4.8	93	14.4
Sevier	75	4.2	83	0	38	384 242	3 770	32 938	10	10 878	24.2	75.8	17.5	1.7	75	9.4
Shelby	116	-9.4	162	3	81	660 831	3 821	65 607	24	33 143	92.3	7.7	17.7	5.4	964	14.7
Smith	141	2.2	126	0	64	267 441	2 085	34 697	11	9 879	39.7	60.3	20.9	1.3	119	6.7
Stewart	55	-3.5	151	0	24	240 348	2 069	31 899	5	13 456	65.3	34.7	26.2	3.0	54	7.6
Sullivan	101	17.4	69	0	59	266 256	3 485	34 608	23	15 557	25.5	74.5	16.9	2.4	114	3.4
Sumner	193	6.0	99	0	112	329 935	3 296	35 243	26	13 372	54.1	45.9	19.6	2.3	511	13.8
Tipton	169	-0.6	269	2	147	522 452	1 948	79 422	32	50 430	93.1	6.9	26.8	9.3	1 496	31.6
Trousdale	47	-9.6	129	0	26	329 257	2 629	39 749	7	18 488	67.2	32.8	35.3	3.6	131	5.3
Unicoi	9	12.5	56	0	4	344 722	6 288	33 336	4	24 837	D	D	0.0	3.6	19	5.4
Union	48	-5.9	82	0	24	207 518	2 687	27 867	3	5 013	39.2	60.8	10.8	0.2	60	11.8
Van Buren	32	0.0	137	0	13	278 917	1 982	33 041	3	11 966	15.2	84.8	27.0	2.6	102	22.6
Warren	173	6.8	108	4	106	275 735	2 448	59 700	94	58 901	86.6	13.4	40.5	9.6	416	8.8
Washington	134	11.7	70	1	87	299 430	4 056	46 468	38	20 018	33.2	66.8	21.0	2.9	399	7.7
Wayne	125	-3.8	175	D	54	229 640	1 288	46 064	10	13 740	13.6	86.4	23.0	2.5	330	26.8
Weakley	240	7.6	195	D	188	313 638	1 524	54 165	59	47 722	57.2	42.8	25.5	8.9	2 264	46.7
White	137	15.1	118	0	74	297 118	2 508	35 879	19	16 506	13.3	86.7	25.9	2.3	585	21.5
Williamson	202	2.0	118	1	109	518 566	5 166	39 875	26	15 144	41.6	58.4	19.2	2.5	176	6.3
Wilson	235	11.4	110	0	123	372 004	3 307	27 828	19	8 684	21.8	78.2	16.5	1.2	198	3.6
TEXAS	129 878	-1.1	567	5 075	38 658	439 066	768	40 553	14 135	61 744	26.4	73.6	28.5	6.4	528 979	18.4
Anderson	365	3.1	210	1	135	218 359	1 038	25 800	23	13 293	28.6	71.4	22.8	1.6	205	1.9
Andrews	804	-3.0	4 757	5	102	776 928	164	49 063	9	51 310	25.8	74.2	27.2	10.1	1 342	37.3
Angelina	117	-0.8	125	0	48	217 631	2 320	31 319	18	19 801	4.1	95.9	15.3	1.9	39	1.6
Aransas	50	163.2	807	0	1	814 587	1 008	14 392	D	D	D	D	9.7	3.2	D	D
Archer	536	-12.3	1 083	1	113	539 348	529	53 030	58	117 147	2.6	97.4	49.3	20.2	1 989	39.4
Armstrong	506	-9.6	1 882	8	163	683 284	374	60 277	27	98 980	15.7	84.3	45.0	15.2	2 130	74.0
Atascosa	670	-5.4	435	22	223	379 448	950	38 613	52	33 663	33.3	66.7	28.7	4.4	3 583	13.9
Austin	367	0.0	176	4	135	369 864	2 176	31 625	24	11 524	23.6	76.4	25.3	2.2	590	3.7
Bailey	394	-3.7	905	66	288	410 966	440	89 715	128	293 198	18.2	81.8	46.1	25.7	6 273	70.9
Bandera	367	0.8	470	1	40	810 346	1 738	25 991	7	8 925	12.6	87.4	16.3	1.0	209	8.7
Bastrop	423	7.9	193	3	142	381 735	1 859	28 138	28	12 722	15.4	84.6	21.5	1.6	183	4.5
Baylor	328	-13.2	1 295	2	149	651 040	517	81 764	43	168 209	7.4	92.6	60.1	20.9	1 472	51.8
Bee	510	21.1	588	2	144	562 971	826	33 485	19	22 484	38.2	61.8	28.4	5.4	1 064	18.9
Bell	451	10.8	217	3	233	248 894	1 293	36 173	41	19 631	42.7	57.3	22.0	3.4	1 271	14.0
Bexar	441	-1.6	185	19	156	457 197	2 000	25 886	81	33 844	73.5	26.5	15.2	2.5	915	10.6
Blanco	389	2.1	497	3	63	1 127 932	2 441	17 524	12	15 370	53.9	46.1	22.2	0.9	120	8.5
Borden	480	-6.8	3 636	1	71	1 329 713	347	80 602	8	59 370	49.5	50.5	59.1	20.5	1 233	56.1
Bosque	563	2.7	438	2	137	634 453	1 477	22 018	38	29 533	31.0	69.0	25.3	3.0	1 453	17.8
Bowie	308	9.6	230	4	127	368 185	1 626	36 549	37	27 929	18.5	81.5	25.8	4.7	1 087	9.1
Brazoria	614	8.3	250	17	225	396 372	1 516	27 555	47	19 317	52.3	47.7	19.4	3.4	3 163	6.0
Brazos	309	16.6	229	14	117	439 909	1 712	30 550	47	34 859	18.8	81.2	26.0	4.1	628	2.7
Brewster	1 676	-30.1	12 320	1	38	1 453 218	115	41 414	5	38 293	9.6	90.4	42.6	10.3	429	21.3
Briscoe	426	-20.1	1 612	30	140	470 484	274	79 377	15	55 222	54.0	46.0	44.7	16.7	2 748	79.9
Brooks	440	-3.9	1 253	1	54	690 594	576	30 620	8	21 575	3.6	96.3	17.9	3.7	374	30.2
Brown	482	-6.6	358	5	131	340 038	897	23 667	26	19 101	13.5	86.5	21.0	2.2	942	20.3
Burleson	389	20.8	251	17	131	353 352	1 402	30 444	36	23 386	28.8	71.2	31.2	4.6	1 407	5.9
Burnet	565	5.2	413	1	104	863 202	1 815	16 787	10	7 487	7.9	92.1	18.8	0.8	254	8.0

Table B. States and Counties — **Residential Construction, Wholesale Trade, Retail Trade, and Real Estate**

STATE County	Value of residential construction authorized by building permits, 2003		Wholesale trade, 1997				Retail trade,[1] 1997				Real estate and rental and leasing, 1997			
	New construction ($1,000)	Number of housing units	Number of establishments	Number of employees	Sales (mil dol)	Annual payroll (mil dol)	Number of establishments	Number of employees	Sales (mil dol)	Annual payroll (mil dol)	Number of establishments	Number of employees	Receipts (mil dol)	Annual payroll (mil dol)
	133	134	135	136	137	138	139	140	141	142	143	144	145	146
TENNESSEE—Cont'd														
Marshall	13 079	197	17	104	21.4	2.4	122	1 153	180.9	16.7	17	46	3.9	0.7
Maury	126 204	1 387	54	631	251.3	17.9	306	3 451	572.9	55.7	70	301	31.2	5.9
Meigs	229	3	3	D	D	D	21	163	24.2	2.3	1	D	D	D
Monroe	10 642	184	22	171	48.3	2.8	165	1 505	234.5	19.9	17	38	2.7	0.4
Montgomery	140 498	1 991	93	716	281.8	19.0	523	6 895	1 175.8	108.1	105	378	49.8	5.9
Moore	5 525	44	1	D	D	D	12	51	5.6	0.5	NA	NA	NA	NA
Morgan	0	0	9	D	D	D	41	209	31.2	2.8	2	D	D	D
Obion	6 605	66	43	768	243.7	19.1	183	1 834	296.5	26.8	32	107	6.2	1.5
Overton	118	1	10	D	D	D	64	439	77.1	5.9	8	38	3.2	0.9
Perry	0	0	2	D	D	D	27	145	21.5	1.7	7	10	0.6	0.1
Pickett	NA	NA	2	D	D	D	20	109	17.0	1.3	4	47	1.9	0.5
Polk	14 412	111	9	D	D	D	53	366	47.0	4.4	6	34	2.0	0.5
Putnam	49 768	615	88	1 188	425.9	31.6	379	3 925	648.6	60.2	56	180	20.7	3.2
Rhea	25 579	197	15	98	26.8	2.7	100	903	137.8	12.3	16	44	3.8	0.4
Roane	7 729	68	22	345	139.8	10.2	176	1 832	308.9	25.9	29	62	5.6	1.2
Robertson	53 334	617	68	785	233.0	19.0	178	1 823	331.4	29.1	28	78	9.2	1.3
Rutherford	369 140	3 550	189	3 908	2 177.0	129.4	594	8 766	1 515.6	144.4	142	725	142.4	17.0
Scott	710	10	20	158	50.1	2.9	74	555	88.0	7.3	7	22	1.4	0.2
Sequatchie	513	9	10	D	D	D	42	288	56.1	4.2	7	13	1.2	0.1
Sevier	56 931	580	50	D	D	D	683	5 554	857.5	86.3	140	727	70.0	14.1
Shelby	753 953	5 510	1 851	34 481	35 419.2	1 214.8	3 574	56 612	8 959.2	891.3	813	7 077	853.1	168.9
Smith	8 358	70	15	105	55.7	2.4	62	642	100.8	8.9	14	34	4.1	0.4
Stewart	320	4	NA	NA	NA	NA	35	260	43.5	3.4	5	26	2.4	0.2
Sullivan	62 379	664	236	2 971	1 268.6	78.9	754	8 945	1 515.6	141.2	127	555	62.5	9.3
Sumner	139 948	1 209	141	1 369	500.2	37.9	403	4 252	665.2	64.4	100	552	60.0	11.9
Tipton	53 086	512	36	229	101.7	4.2	169	1 571	279.7	23.0	21	59	5.1	0.7
Trousdale	5 440	59	8	224	38.6	3.3	28	190	23.4	2.3	2	D	D	D
Unicoi	2 766	74	9	121	70.3	5.0	50	342	59.1	4.9	11	35	2.1	0.4
Union	9 650	97	9	D	D	D	36	204	28.2	2.3	7	16	0.6	0.1
Van Buren	NA	NA	2	D	D	D	10	30	7.4	0.4	2	D	D	D
Warren	2 465	31	45	339	101.5	8.6	177	1 803	267.0	26.2	28	102	8.1	1.3
Washington	110 181	850	162	2 131	1 192.8	55.5	540	6 873	1 123.1	103.1	118	510	48.3	8.6
Wayne	470	7	8	D	D	D	67	370	45.8	4.2	4	D	D	D
Weakley	5 054	71	49	680	320.2	19.9	153	1 211	171.8	16.1	21	76	5.0	1.0
White	587	5	22	190	62.8	4.3	90	856	183.5	13.2	11	20	3.2	0.2
Williamson	414 734	1 771	228	1 749	2 559.9	95.7	540	7 729	1 421.4	142.1	156	1 505	168.7	35.8
Wilson	175 663	1 384	95	1 075	605.8	29.4	290	3 216	566.5	49.6	70	243	42.1	4.5
TEXAS	19 551 763	177 194	33 346	425 744	323 111.7	15 504.9	74 105	950 848	182 516.1	16 197.1	20 753	128 915	15 957.4	3 119.2
Anderson	1 426	24	46	338	166.1	9.7	194	1 877	316.1	27.2	28	111	13.3	2.2
Andrews	1 800	11	20	103	24.6	2.3	52	356	59.7	5.7	10	33	1.9	0.5
Angelina	17 960	181	81	1 237	288.2	31.1	343	4 238	688.8	62.7	77	275	20.7	4.8
Aransas	12 613	101	16	63	24.8	1.7	90	771	124.8	11.8	28	67	7.6	1.1
Archer	1 250	9	18	142	41.5	2.3	27	111	23.4	2.0	1	D	D	D
Armstrong	438	3	2	D	D	D	6	19	2.9	0.2	1	D	D	D
Atascosa	6 111	81	30	227	89.6	6.6	108	1 246	177.2	16.3	19	61	4.1	0.9
Austin	5 054	45	22	390	212.8	11.3	123	1 114	211.4	16.7	19	53	5.9	0.6
Bailey	375	3	20	203	112.1	4.3	36	271	33.9	3.1	2	D	D	D
Bandera	221	2	5	7	0.9	0.1	54	275	50.9	3.9	13	28	2.7	0.4
Bastrop	23 991	379	28	205	69.0	3.4	135	1 450	397.0	20.8	27	64	6.1	1.0
Baylor	0	0	14	D	D	D	21	126	21.4	1.5	2	D	D	D
Bee	279	4	18	128	92.3	3.2	92	1 008	141.8	15.5	22	60	7.0	1.1
Bell	247 367	2 315	150	D	D	D	829	10 409	1 733.5	163.4	240	1 089	93.2	15.9
Bexar	1 179 374	9 747	1 829	25 191	12 639.2	810.7	4 505	64 928	11 657.5	1 111.1	1 342	8 770	1 115.1	203.5
Blanco	2 109	21	7	D	D	D	46	231	35.2	3.4	9	25	1.8	0.3
Borden	NA	NA	1	D	D	D	1	D	D	D	NA	NA	NA	NA
Bosque	339	4	11	105	63.3	1.6	73	443	73.2	6.0	10	16	2.2	0.4
Bowie	29 349	354	134	D	D	D	445	5 222	940.7	83.0	88	510	60.2	8.5
Brazoria	514 723	3 191	220	2 524	840.2	102.1	629	8 945	1 534.4	136.0	196	1 231	142.8	29.3
Brazos	174 334	1 848	130	1 655	426.5	41.9	569	7 994	1 336.2	122.2	181	1 090	78.5	17.2
Brewster	1 684	18	12	62	18.3	1.1	56	460	58.1	6.1	10	26	1.3	0.2
Briscoe	NA	NA	6	D	D	D	9	29	4.3	0.3	1	D	D	D
Brooks	170	2	5	14	3.8	0.2	32	287	38.4	3.8	NA	NA	NA	NA
Brown	3 640	90	42	337	95.7	8.5	194	1 843	302.0	24.6	32	73	7.8	1.2
Burleson	2 289	22	26	136	133.1	4.3	66	477	81.4	6.5	5	8	1.1	0.1
Burnet	64 720	677	27	163	34.9	4.2	159	1 534	281.0	24.6	52	90	8.6	1.0

1. Establishments with payroll.

STATE County	Professional, scientific, and technical services,[1] 1997				Manufacturing, 1997				Accommodation and foodservices, 1997			
	Number of establishments	Number of employees	Receipts (mil dol)	Annual payroll (mil dol)	Number of establishments	Number of employees	Receipts (mil dol)	Annual payroll (mil dol)	Number of establishments	Number of employees	Sales (mil dol)	Annual payroll (mil dol)
	147	148	149	150	151	152	153	154	155	156	157	158
TENNESSEE—Cont'd												
Marshall	23	72	3.9	1.2	45	7 552	1 349.1	169.4	34	446	12.9	3.2
Maury	87	396	33.4	11.5	75	11 361	4 431.7	532.6	96	2 152	58.3	16.5
Meigs	6	D	D	D	13	764	125.1	14.2	7	83	1.9	0.6
Monroe	26	72	4.0	1.0	84	5 488	834.9	144.8	55	770	27.7	7.0
Montgomery	120	756	41.0	12.3	83	6 519	1 271.6	182.7	237	4 699	132.3	37.3
Moore	1	D	D	D	NA	NA	NA	NA	5	D	D	D
Morgan	5	D	D	D	24	925	98.8	20.1	8	289	3.8	1.1
Obion	25	74	7.0	1.5	46	5 656	1 140.0	195.5	51	927	19.9	5.3
Overton	21	34	2.4	0.7	29	1 249	126.4	23.7	21	263	7.6	1.9
Perry	5	D	D	D	15	1 689	169.8	34.9	6	19	0.7	0.1
Pickett	2	D	D	D	NA	NA	NA	NA	7	D	D	D
Polk	6	D	D	D	22	1 061	72.1	18.3	18	160	4.8	1.2
Putnam	104	554	43.9	14.4	141	9 927	1 757.7	232.3	119	2 960	82.2	22.6
Rhea	18	46	4.6	1.0	40	4 674	434.7	105.6	46	531	17.3	4.3
Roane	34	87	9.2	1.9	42	2 075	256.0	47.1	60	1 083	27.2	7.6
Robertson	48	140	9.2	2.8	74	5 019	730.9	127.2	54	1 213	28.4	7.4
Rutherford	211	888	70.9	24.6	191	19 096	8 851.9	754.7	244	6 157	191.5	56.0
Scott	15	48	3.1	1.5	40	2 915	330.0	56.5	22	292	9.3	2.7
Sequatchie	6	D	D	D	11	948	223.8	18.3	16	D	D	D
Sevier	108	392	25.5	9.1	103	2 611	272.4	64.5	453	8 176	384.1	105.5
Shelby	1 675	15 189	1 503.4	565.4	902	44 145	11 758.7	1 476.9	1 429	35 241	1 362.6	371.5
Smith	11	33	2.1	0.6	23	1 710	396.6	44.9	19	D	D	D
Stewart	4	D	D	D	NA	NA	NA	NA	12	97	3.2	0.7
Sullivan	232	1 319	123.9	59.0	182	18 602	4 245.2	816.7	266	5 599	169.5	48.7
Sumner	157	1 200	54.3	21.3	205	11 852	1 932.0	333.8	144	2 207	67.1	18.6
Tipton	35	160	8.8	2.8	39	3 327	604.8	88.6	44	581	18.2	4.6
Trousdale	5	D	D	D	12	693	63.8	14.4	10	115	2.2	0.6
Unicoi	12	21	1.3	0.4	22	1 518	202.5	36.3	19	337	7.1	1.8
Union	7	18	0.6	0.1	20	1 099	141.1	23.6	10	101	3.0	0.8
Van Buren	2	D	D	D	NA	NA	NA	NA	2	D	D	D
Warren	32	105	7.3	1.9	73	6 610	1 133.3	192.5	56	880	24.0	6.6
Washington	196	1 340	75.9	26.0	151	10 370	1 300.9	257.6	190	4 858	140.6	41.1
Wayne	11	D	D	D	28	1 487	99.6	23.0	19	D	D	D
Weakley	30	73	4.0	1.1	45	3 287	574.0	74.9	55	797	18.7	4.7
White	23	72	5.6	1.5	49	3 442	457.3	81.0	17	D	D	D
Williamson	411	3 425	387.2	161.1	115	4 723	846.6	130.7	189	4 711	160.6	44.9
Wilson	104	346	29.5	9.3	114	5 533	1 122.9	161.1	111	2 225	68.7	19.8
TEXAS	42 492	351 422	42 044.1	15 906.7	21 808	959 665	297 657.0	32 760.8	34 160	638 333	22 698.8	6 175.4
Anderson	61	240	19.4	7.6	41	1 419	287.4	36.1	58	1 031	29.7	8.1
Andrews	14	37	3.0	0.8	NA	NA	NA	NA	20	D	D	D
Angelina	108	508	44.1	14.6	88	7 536	1 363.6	212.8	119	1 908	60.7	17.4
Aransas	32	436	17.6	12.2	NA	NA	NA	NA	72	823	24.9	6.8
Archer	5	16	0.6	0.2	NA	NA	NA	NA	5	31	1.0	0.2
Armstrong	NA	NA	NA	NA	NA	NA	NA	NA	4	21	0.4	0.1
Atascosa	30	312	13.2	4.1	NA	NA	NA	NA	44	450	13.4	3.6
Austin	37	145	8.3	3.4	32	947	153.6	26.8	46	425	15.4	3.8
Bailey	14	31	1.6	0.3	NA	NA	NA	NA	17	D	D	D
Bandera	17	30	4.0	1.0	NA	NA	NA	NA	36	288	10.0	3.0
Bastrop	48	146	10.8	4.1	52	801	78.3	18.5	68	889	25.7	7.3
Baylor	8	22	0.9	0.3	NA	NA	NA	NA	9	74	1.9	0.4
Bee	32	112	6.0	1.7	NA	NA	NA	NA	47	503	14.1	3.7
Bell	193	1 901	166.5	48.2	135	7 365	1 351.3	224.5	376	6 673	202.9	53.5
Bexar	2 841	21 741	2 052.4	805.6	1 101	35 919	5 565.5	986.5	2 558	56 118	2 027.8	563.1
Blanco	11	35	3.1	1.2	NA	NA	NA	NA	22	239	6.2	1.9
Borden	NA	NA	NA	NA	NA	NA	NA	NA	NA	NA	NA	NA
Bosque	15	28	1.6	0.6	18	548	74.9	13.4	19	99	2.8	0.7
Bowie	124	566	53.3	16.0	75	4 056	975.5	128.0	142	2 456	82.9	20.0
Brazoria	246	1 212	93.4	38.8	199	14 149	10 761.0	682.9	295	4 787	148.4	41.8
Brazos	279	2 086	200.9	74.8	101	3 126	382.2	79.6	275	5 668	170.7	48.2
Brewster	17	30	2.0	0.4	NA	NA	NA	NA	45	579	15.1	4.0
Briscoe	4	7	0.2	0.1	NA	NA	NA	NA	2	D	D	D
Brooks	8	25	2.2	0.3	NA	NA	NA	NA	21	201	7.2	2.0
Brown	38	130	7.7	1.8	39	3 055	848.5	98.7	77	1 048	31.7	8.3
Burleson	11	38	1.5	0.4	NA	NA	NA	NA	25	234	6.2	1.6
Burnet	49	125	7.8	3.0	42	714	72.5	16.7	63	878	33.9	10.5

1. Firms subject to federal tax.

Table B. States and Counties — **Health Care and Social Assistance, Other Services, and Federal Funds**

STATE County	Health care and social assistance,[1] 1997				Other services,[1] 1997				Federal funds and grants, 2002–2003 Expenditures (mil dol)			
									Total	Direct payments for individuals[2]		
	Number of establish-ments	Number of employees	Receipts (mil dol)	Annual payroll (mil dol)	Number of establish-ments	Number of employees	Receipts (mil dol)	Annual payroll (mil dol)		Social Security and government retirement	Medicare	Food stamps and Supplemental Security Income
	159	160	161	162	163	164	165	166	167	168	169	170
TENNESSEE—Cont'd												
Marshall	38	368	16.0	6.4	27	82	5.2	1.3	124.7	54.2	29.5	4.5
Maury	132	1 526	107.5	38.9	98	579	34.1	10.8	319.9	147.8	67.6	16.1
Meigs	5	148	4.2	1.6	4	4	0.7	0.1	62.2	29.3	10.0	4.0
Monroe	42	508	20.8	8.5	33	116	6.0	1.9	202.0	95.9	34.5	12.7
Montgomery	153	2 191	123.6	51.0	172	821	43.1	11.7	671.1	347.0	66.1	24.8
Moore	4	D	D	D	4	2	0.3	0.0	19.0	9.1	4.7	0.6
Morgan	5	38	2.3	0.9	4	D	D	D	101.7	39.6	18.4	6.0
Obion	55	593	34.6	13.8	46	375	18.5	6.2	198.9	85.4	40.1	7.4
Overton	22	524	33.0	13.1	17	71	4.3	0.8	125.4	47.1	30.2	5.3
Perry	12	287	15.3	5.7	6	10	0.7	0.2	51.6	19.6	13.5	1.4
Pickett	4	76	3.6	1.1	4	5	0.4	0.1	32.4	10.9	7.7	1.4
Polk	18	69	6.1	2.2	10	37	2.1	0.5	114.3	47.4	23.5	4.3
Putnam	134	1 325	84.4	34.9	107	451	29.4	7.3	399.7	160.0	69.3	14.2
Rhea	34	208	11.3	5.0	29	90	4.5	1.3	229.2	76.1	33.5	10.7
Roane	65	577	32.7	12.1	40	149	10.3	2.9	399.5	152.2	67.3	15.0
Robertson	60	639	31.8	13.0	69	219	15.1	3.1	216.6	111.8	45.9	6.7
Rutherford	250	3 668	197.6	93.2	203	1 001	67.1	19.6	684.6	294.7	92.0	20.1
Scott	30	637	30.1	14.1	17	408	12.4	6.3	223.8	47.2	29.7	12.9
Sequatchie	16	179	7.6	3.4	11	30	1.6	0.3	73.2	23.0	11.1	3.2
Sevier	76	674	34.7	13.7	110	415	25.4	7.3	302.8	174.2	49.1	11.0
Shelby	1 739	22 689	1 984.1	837.5	1 362	10 783	684.5	219.4	6 944.5	1 665.9	779.9	340.2
Smith	29	568	27.0	9.5	21	61	3.7	1.0	94.1	36.6	27.4	3.4
Stewart	7	115	5.4	2.0	7	29	2.2	0.6	122.0	43.9	12.3	3.0
Sullivan	352	5 392	403.3	190.0	239	1 608	88.0	26.9	907.8	444.0	165.8	39.5
Sumner	210	2 658	162.7	63.9	169	774	39.2	11.6	612.3	252.7	105.7	20.2
Tipton	53	618	28.3	11.9	44	190	12.0	2.6	252.7	113.8	39.6	13.2
Trousdale	14	143	6.4	2.2	5	15	1.2	0.2	37.9	13.5	11.2	1.1
Unicoi	21	259	11.9	5.1	16	55	3.7	0.7	293.9	58.8	23.5	5.0
Union	8	90	3.1	0.9	7	39	2.9	0.6	66.7	30.7	11.3	5.5
Van Buren	5	88	2.6	1.1	NA	NA	NA	NA	24.7	8.9	5.9	1.1
Warren	63	920	67.1	23.7	42	137	10.1	2.5	213.6	87.0	59.4	9.7
Washington	240	3 536	262.5	121.0	178	1 217	54.7	21.5	1 144.3	298.6	110.5	24.6
Wayne	15	323	13.5	5.6	12	16	1.9	0.3	86.2	33.5	17.1	4.4
Weakley	41	995	60.6	23.1	40	155	11.9	3.7	194.7	70.9	40.4	6.3
White	31	486	28.3	10.3	22	65	4.0	1.1	133.2	60.8	28.3	5.9
Williamson	268	5 184	312.7	154.3	158	1 806	188.3	57.2	402.0	210.2	63.5	6.7
Wilson	145	3 170	205.2	85.3	99	504	22.2	6.5	356.1	169.5	78.8	9.5
TEXAS	37 974	557 007	35 620.9	14 725.4	29 162	197 113	12 477.7	3 785.0	140 451.0	37 151.2	16 282.6	3 878.5
Anderson	112	1 568	90.0	39.4	55	209	14.1	3.6	262.5	114.1	62.6	8.3
Andrews	15	124	9.9	2.5	29	174	11.1	3.1	54.5	24.8	12.6	2.7
Angelina	187	3 211	176.1	76.9	141	692	46.9	13.1	409.1	177.8	93.7	17.4
Aransas	31	362	17.2	6.4	21	76	4.0	1.0	122.2	67.8	23.1	4.3
Archer	5	D	D	D	10	34	2.4	0.5	57.8	18.8	6.6	10.8
Armstrong	1	D	D	D	1	D	D	D	22.4	5.5	2.6	0.1
Atascosa	37	733	34.8	14.9	34	152	7.5	2.2	179.3	76.1	29.6	8.2
Austin	30	484	16.1	8.4	33	84	4.8	1.1	657.8	55.4	28.0	2.5
Bailey	6	27	1.3	0.4	20	78	3.6	0.9	52.0	13.1	8.6	1.2
Bandera	12	144	4.1	2.0	13	33	1.7	0.4	82.9	58.3	11.8	1.4
Bastrop	33	383	15.1	6.1	45	183	12.4	3.7	247.3	119.1	38.5	7.1
Baylor	8	794	6.5	3.6	16	27	3.3	0.3	33.1	13.7	8.4	0.5
Bee	46	493	23.0	10.5	38	164	8.0	2.2	155.9	53.4	32.5	8.0
Bell	292	5 985	414.0	140.2	323	1 765	82.8	26.7	3 556.4	631.3	129.9	34.1
Bexar	2 900	51 908	3 052.9	1 251.8	2 167	15 346	841.4	272.7	12 747.6	3 614.9	1 205.9	329.8
Blanco	10	158	4.6	3.0	10	30	2.5	0.5	67.7	42.5	16.2	0.6
Borden	NA	NA	NA	NA	NA	NA	NA	NA	7.0	0.7	0.5	0.0
Bosque	11	164	8.4	3.7	12	29	1.9	0.4	97.6	52.9	22.4	2.1
Bowie	233	3 731	231.1	110.2	138	872	55.1	15.5	719.5	258.9	109.2	20.9
Brazoria	306	2 905	155.5	65.8	298	1 312	88.5	24.1	750.6	393.5	156.2	27.7
Brazos	263	2 838	212.1	84.9	196	1 244	64.8	18.4	1 826.9	189.9	61.0	16.6
Brewster	10	42	2.4	0.9	12	35	1.8	0.3	61.0	20.9	6.9	1.5
Briscoe	NA	NA	NA	NA	3	9	0.2	0.0	23.6	5.1	3.8	0.3
Brooks	9	389	6.0	2.4	10	60	3.1	0.8	67.8	14.7	10.7	4.9
Brown	96	2 526	115.5	44.1	63	292	14.5	4.2	228.2	96.4	56.2	7.9
Burleson	10	136	5.5	2.3	21	90	5.2	1.3	91.1	40.7	17.0	4.1
Burnet	61	454	20.4	7.3	51	126	9.5	2.2	165.3	104.5	28.4	4.3

1. Firms subject to federal tax.   2. State totals may include programs not allocated by county.

Table B. States and Counties — Federal Funds and Local Government Finances

	Federal funds and grants, 2002–2003 (cont'd)							Local government finances, 2002				
	Expenditures (mil dol) (cont'd)							General revenue				
	Procurement contract awards			Grants[1]						Taxes		
											Per capita[2] (dollars)	
STATE County	Salaries and wages	Defense	Other	Medicaid and other health-related	Nutrition and family welfare	Education	Other	Total (mil dol)	Intergovern-mental (mil dol)	Total (mil dol)	Total	Property
	171	172	173	174	175	176	177	178	179	180	181	182
TENNESSEE—Cont'd												
Marshall	4.0	3.2	1.4	20.3	1.4	2.5	1.8	53.1	21.3	22.7	830	574
Maury	12.2	0.0	5.2	48.1	4.3	4.6	7.8	296.2	51.3	53.7	750	424
Meigs	2.4	0.0	0.4	9.3	3.1	0.8	2.6	16.6	11.1	3.4	298	219
Monroe	5.4	0.7	1.7	40.4	2.4	3.8	2.3	59.7	33.3	18.6	464	248
Montgomery	90.6	5.7	24.6	51.5	10.4	10.5	14.9	265.6	104.9	111.5	807	487
Moore	0.4	0.0	0.1	1.5	1.8	0.3	0.4	11.1	6.8	2.7	449	414
Morgan	2.2	0.0	0.9	21.3	3.9	1.3	7.0	28.1	18.2	6.8	341	277
Obion	7.5	0.6	1.1	31.9	3.3	2.8	13.2	56.4	26.0	20.4	631	350
Overton	3.4	0.0	0.7	33.2	1.9	1.6	0.8	30.0	17.3	7.3	362	210
Perry	1.5	0.0	0.3	10.2	0.6	0.6	3.5	15.9	8.4	3.9	510	379
Pickett	0.5	0.0	0.2	10.4	0.5	0.4	0.3	10.7	6.8	2.5	499	284
Polk	4.6	0.0	4.1	19.7	1.3	1.1	7.4	24.0	14.7	6.5	405	266
Putnam	15.0	1.9	56.9	52.7	10.0	4.4	6.5	218.1	40.6	42.8	666	402
Rhea	66.6	0.0	4.0	30.2	3.1	2.2	1.2	59.5	24.6	12.5	431	275
Roane	32.3	0.2	44.5	51.4	6.4	4.0	17.3	105.6	39.2	31.5	603	371
Robertson	6.5	0.1	1.9	30.2	3.8	2.9	3.1	97.8	41.6	39.3	684	412
Rutherford	97.5	9.3	38.3	57.0	7.7	13.6	27.8	363.3	132.0	146.7	753	501
Scott	5.7	51.4	25.0	42.1	3.9	1.9	3.4	40.0	27.4	6.7	310	220
Sequatchie	1.1	0.0	20.0	8.9	1.2	1.0	3.5	18.0	10.1	5.7	482	338
Sevier	19.0	1.0	3.4	34.0	4.3	3.6	2.3	191.8	50.5	95.1	1 278	380
Shelby	945.9	1 137.2	471.6	968.1	169.2	65.8	318.1	2 976.0	923.0	1 309.3	1 446	963
Smith	5.0	0.4	1.0	16.3	1.3	0.9	0.7	30.7	15.6	9.4	518	284
Stewart	33.4	0.1	13.9	12.3	0.9	0.9	0.9	23.4	15.0	5.0	397	285
Sullivan	32.1	42.3	5.9	119.5	18.7	10.7	20.2	289.8	99.8	125.7	821	566
Sumner	28.9	2.7	117.1	54.6	5.7	5.8	11.6	254.6	105.9	101.7	747	492
Tipton	7.4	8.3	1.4	46.8	6.2	2.9	4.9	93.0	52.7	26.0	487	339
Trousdale	2.6	0.0	0.3	7.1	0.6	0.4	0.2	12.4	7.7	3.3	443	405
Unicoi	5.2	7.5	169.2	20.5	1.7	1.3	0.9	48.2	14.2	8.2	464	321
Union	1.4	0.0	0.3	16.5	1.9	1.3	-2.6	26.8	17.5	4.6	247	168
Van Buren	0.3	0.7	0.5	5.3	0.5	0.4	0.8	8.8	5.7	2.0	365	232
Warren	7.8	1.4	1.3	34.2	2.9	2.9	2.5	67.1	32.9	23.1	595	384
Washington	96.1	5.5	461.6	80.9	8.2	9.2	32.0	206.4	74.2	88.0	807	492
Wayne	1.9	0.0	0.5	21.2	1.3	1.1	4.8	29.6	16.7	6.6	380	237
Weakley	8.0	0.0	17.0	24.4	12.1	2.6	2.6	57.2	27.6	18.7	548	311
White	3.7	0.0	0.8	26.6	1.7	1.6	2.7	34.7	19.7	9.9	421	260
Williamson	22.6	1.6	6.9	29.1	3.5	4.5	51.4	407.0	91.3	181.2	1 324	827
Wilson	13.9	0.0	2.4	37.3	10.2	4.8	25.4	164.8	57.4	72.0	774	479
TEXAS	13 939.2	20 821.0	9 002.4	12 679.1	3 982.0	3 108.6	8 652.9	X	X	X	X	X
Anderson	8.5	0.1	2.3	53.5	2.9	1.8	7.7	86.0	34.6	40.7	745	596
Andrews	1.2	0.0	0.2	5.5	0.8	0.6	1.9	63.1	5.3	37.0	2 855	2 711
Angelina	23.9	0.4	3.8	65.1	7.1	3.1	7.9	223.3	107.2	72.6	901	666
Aransas	1.5	0.0	0.4	7.9	1.9	1.4	13.1	44.0	8.6	27.8	1 213	1 030
Archer	11.6	0.0	0.2	4.0	0.3	0.3	0.7	21.6	10.0	8.9	994	832
Armstrong	0.4	0.0	0.1	1.5	0.1	0.1	8.7	4.3	2.2	1.5	703	607
Atascosa	3.2	0.0	0.8	34.1	4.5	2.2	6.2	84.5	47.8	26.1	636	529
Austin	7.3	537.7	2.0	17.5	1.4	0.7	3.4	53.8	19.0	26.6	1 081	910
Bailey	1.4	0.0	0.7	5.7	0.9	0.4	1.4	23.9	8.7	5.9	909	760
Bandera	4.7	0.0	0.3	4.4	0.5	0.6	0.2	32.1	11.1	16.6	869	762
Bastrop	22.9	0.5	3.2	37.5	5.4	2.0	10.1	140.8	52.1	54.5	853	751
Baylor	1.1	0.0	0.2	5.2	0.5	0.2	0.5	10.7	5.4	3.5	891	765
Bee	2.4	0.0	0.9	30.2	7.9	2.9	6.8	77.7	38.7	19.1	590	449
Bell	1 895.6	579.8	32.0	48.7	18.7	49.3	73.9	709.1	351.2	206.2	843	637
Bexar	2 540.9	1 931.1	1 079.7	1 114.3	211.2	108.5	446.0	4 489.6	1 703.7	1 652.9	1 143	937
Blanco	3.5	0.0	1.3	2.6	0.1	0.3	0.2	18.2	4.4	10.6	1 201	1 064
Borden	0.9	0.1	0.0	0.0	0.1	0.1	2.6	6.5	0.3	5.7	8 074	8 001
Bosque	3.7	0.0	0.8	11.7	0.8	0.8	1.1	38.5	18.0	15.4	878	763
Bowie	110.4	77.5	9.0	81.9	11.4	4.8	26.8	219.8	102.5	73.2	814	609
Brazoria	31.6	3.1	11.5	58.5	9.6	7.9	21.2	649.1	153.3	372.4	1 447	1 255
Brazos	62.5	19.8	25.0	106.9	12.2	10.4	1 284.2	332.4	81.8	174.4	1 118	859
Brewster	8.5	4.9	2.6	6.0	0.8	3.1	1.3	35.8	10.8	8.8	974	695
Briscoe	0.5	0.0	0.1	3.4	0.1	0.1	1.4	3.9	1.5	1.8	1 026	910
Brooks	4.0	2.0	0.2	25.8	2.2	0.8	1.8	25.3	10.9	10.7	1 375	1 269
Brown	7.5	6.8	1.5	30.4	3.5	1.8	10.1	92.8	43.5	33.7	888	689
Burleson	2.8	0.3	0.7	19.5	1.8	0.7	1.0	37.4	15.4	17.2	1 018	885
Burnet	6.7	0.5	1.9	13.9	0.8	0.9	2.8	83.0	21.8	50.3	1 365	1 184

1. State totals may include programs not allocated by county.   2. Based on the resident population estimated as of July 1 of the year shown.

Table B. States and Counties — Local Government Finances, Government Employment, and Elections

STATE County	\<--- Direct general expenditure ---\> Total (mil dol)	Per capita[1] (dollars)	Percent of total for — Education	Health and hospitals	Police protection	Public welfare	Highways	Debt outstanding Total (mil dol)	Per capita[1] (dollars)	Government employment, 2002 Federal civilian	Federal military	State and local	Presidential election, 2004 Percent of vote cast — Democratic	Republican	All other
	183	184	185	186	187	188	189	190	191	192	193	194	195	196	197
TENNESSEE—Cont'd															
Marshall	49.8	1 818	57.2	3.4	5.3	0.2	7.1	78.0	2 848	66	89	1 451	44.5	54.9	0.6
Maury	300.5	4 197	24.4	50.9	3.3	0.0	2.9	200.8	2 805	200	233	5 896	41.2	58.3	0.5
Meigs	16.7	1 480	59.6	1.3	3.9	0.0	10.9	8.9	789	31	37	396	38.6	60.5	0.9
Monroe	64.5	1 606	67.2	2.2	3.5	0.1	5.3	30.0	747	110	130	1 518	34.4	65.0	0.6
Montgomery	309.3	2 237	48.0	1.5	5.6	1.4	4.6	408.7	2 956	823	421	7 495	41.0	58.4	0.6
Moore	10.5	1 773	57.0	3.5	4.3	0.0	10.9	2.4	404	0	19	755	39.1	60.1	0.8
Morgan	30.1	1 517	77.0	1.7	2.2	0.1	5.5	10.5	529	46	64	1 373	39.9	60.1	0.0
Obion	61.2	1 889	61.3	0.2	5.8	0.0	6.6	18.0	556	126	106	1 697	41.0	58.1	0.9
Overton	38.0	1 874	66.9	2.2	3.4	0.1	5.6	33.3	1 641	57	66	1 109	53.1	46.3	0.6
Perry	15.1	1 999	46.4	1.9	8.2	0.0	11.9	8.7	1 156	17	24	345	50.2	48.3	1.6
Pickett	10.3	2 056	49.1	7.8	2.9	0.0	11.3	7.9	1 578	0	16	250	39.1	60.5	0.5
Polk	29.6	1 835	70.0	2.9	3.9	0.0	6.4	13.1	810	83	52	733	40.7	58.6	0.8
Putnam	220.3	3 426	30.8	45.9	3.7	0.0	3.1	153.8	2 391	252	215	7 089	39.9	59.1	0.9
Rhea	54.1	1 869	41.3	25.0	4.3	0.0	4.9	33.0	1 142	822	94	1 476	33.2	66.0	0.8
Roane	115.8	2 214	41.6	27.7	3.5	0.0	4.7	81.6	1 559	483	170	3 734	37.3	62.0	0.7
Robertson	88.2	1 536	57.0	2.0	8.8	0.0	6.0	100.4	1 749	106	186	2 962	39.0	60.5	0.5
Rutherford	432.7	2 220	52.7	2.5	6.1	1.2	3.5	515.7	2 645	590	656	11 144	37.5	61.8	0.7
Scott	37.1	1 721	64.6	2.9	5.5	0.2	6.2	45.2	2 098	97	70	1 181	40.5	59.1	0.4
Sequatchie	16.9	1 431	62.0	0.8	4.5	0.0	11.3	18.1	1 535	11	38	556	39.9	59.2	0.9
Sevier	206.4	2 773	38.1	1.4	6.2	0.1	8.8	271.8	3 651	366	242	4 053	27.8	71.5	0.7
Shelby	3 233.0	3 570	36.1	12.3	7.4	0.2	1.5	4 242.0	4 684	15 463	4 708	61 668	57.5	42.0	0.6
Smith	42.7	2 347	69.2	1.9	4.6	0.0	5.8	27.9	1 532	105	59	655	51.6	47.8	0.6
Stewart	21.6	1 703	62.7	3.1	4.7	0.1	9.7	22.7	1 787	518	41	569	51.2	47.9	0.8
Sullivan	337.9	2 208	55.2	1.7	5.3	0.0	4.4	268.6	1 755	504	500	6 812	31.4	67.9	0.7
Sumner	246.7	1 812	52.8	2.6	6.0	0.1	6.5	180.3	1 324	465	442	5 829	34.6	64.8	0.5
Tipton	90.4	1 692	66.7	0.3	3.2	0.0	6.0	61.0	1 141	111	173	2 300	34.0	65.4	0.5
Trousdale	11.9	1 622	55.5	1.6	6.4	0.0	11.1	5.2	709	49	24	376	58.0	41.2	0.8
Unicoi	47.6	2 681	31.3	48.0	2.6	0.2	6.3	28.0	1 576	82	58	974	31.8	67.4	0.8
Union	24.8	1 338	69.7	1.1	3.3	0.0	6.6	15.0	808	22	60	674	37.6	61.8	0.6
Van Buren	8.4	1 524	63.1	3.3	4.6	0.0	16.0	4.1	735	0	18	322	51.5	47.7	0.8
Warren	63.4	1 630	57.1	3.1	5.4	0.1	5.3	47.6	1 224	119	126	1 652	47.3	52.1	0.6
Washington	202.2	1 855	44.2	1.1	7.2	0.1	6.5	359.4	3 297	1 805	369	9 669	33.2	66.1	0.7
Wayne	33.2	1 916	49.9	0.1	2.7	20.5	9.3	21.8	1 261	27	56	1 292	32.6	66.8	0.5
Weakley	57.3	1 674	45.9	0.7	6.5	7.3	9.1	42.7	1 249	139	116	3 511	41.4	57.9	0.7
White	34.1	1 457	56.3	1.8	4.8	0.0	7.9	27.0	1 151	63	76	1 075	43.7	55.5	0.8
Williamson	423.9	3 096	48.4	17.8	3.0	0.0	4.0	517.8	3 783	315	444	6 454	27.3	72.1	0.6
Wilson	161.0	1 730	56.4	0.5	6.5	0.1	6.4	166.3	1 787	171	303	3 375	34.4	65.1	0.6
TEXAS	X	X	X	X	X	X	X	X	X	173 581	164 212	1 430 075	38.3	61.2	0.5
Anderson	84.7	1 552	63.9	0.4	5.8	0.0	5.1	22.9	419	124	101	5 539	28.8	70.9	0.3
Andrews	57.0	4 404	44.1	30.8	5.2	0.0	3.3	33.6	2 597	22	24	1 052	14.9	84.7	0.4
Angelina	230.5	2 861	53.7	10.5	4.7	0.0	4.6	161.8	2 008	376	150	6 379	32.8	66.8	0.3
Aransas	45.9	2 001	52.4	2.1	6.4	1.4	7.0	23.5	1 027	21	42	982	28.5	71.0	0.4
Archer	21.2	2 358	69.7	0.6	3.6	0.0	6.7	17.8	1 980	25	20	482	19.8	80.0	0.2
Armstrong	4.5	2 079	64.2	0.0	4.2	0.0	12.4	0.0	0	0	0	128	17.1	82.9	0.0
Atascosa	91.1	2 225	74.4	0.2	3.1	0.8	3.3	36.2	883	56	76	2 243	36.5	63.1	0.4
Austin	54.9	2 232	66.0	1.6	6.1	0.1	4.2	47.5	1 931	107	47	1 359	24.2	75.5	0.3
Bailey	23.6	3 648	47.3	35.7	3.5	0.2	3.6	4.9	753	32	12	620	22.8	77.1	0.1
Bandera	28.8	1 505	69.2	1.3	4.4	5.2	5.1	8.0	419	17	35	750	19.9	79.5	0.6
Bastrop	142.6	2 230	61.5	14.9	6.2	0.4	3.5	149.8	2 343	364	118	3 411	41.9	56.9	1.2
Baylor	10.9	2 779	62.6	2.6	2.9	0.0	8.2	2.2	568	21	0	261	28.5	71.3	0.2
Bee	75.6	2 341	72.9	0.5	3.3	0.0	3.1	23.5	728	46	60	3 784	42.5	57.1	0.3
Bell	686.4	2 805	65.1	2.7	3.9	0.4	2.0	817.9	3 343	7 443	43 628	15 558	34.1	65.5	0.5
Bexar	4 704.9	3 253	52.3	10.4	4.8	2.8	2.4	8 836.4	6 110	27 088	40 173	94 763	44.5	54.9	0.6
Blanco	16.7	1 884	71.2	0.0	4.7	0.6	3.4	12.7	1 428	76	16	408	27.7	71.6	0.7
Borden	5.5	7 783	80.2	0.0	1.0	0.0	11.9	0.0	0	0	0	87	15.3	84.4	0.3
Bosque	36.7	2 093	66.7	10.7	3.0	1.1	4.6	23.4	1 332	79	32	915	23.9	75.7	0.3
Bowie	223.4	2 485	61.8	2.9	9.2	0.4	4.0	126.1	1 402	3 170	186	5 684	35.2	64.6	0.2
Brazoria	712.1	2 768	62.9	5.1	4.2	0.3	4.1	858.2	3 336	470	522	14 687	31.0	68.3	0.6
Brazos	343.0	2 197	39.3	3.9	5.9	0.6	8.1	388.7	2 490	970	403	28 341	29.8	69.4	0.8
Brewster	33.1	3 669	34.5	33.9	3.9	0.1	2.9	11.3	1 254	211	18	1 177	46.2	52.9	0.9
Briscoe	3.3	1 932	63.5	0.2	3.0	0.0	5.8	8.9	5 167	16	0	115	23.6	76.4	0.0
Brooks	24.3	3 130	59.8	1.1	5.2	1.0	3.5	4.4	567	127	14	585	68.2	31.6	0.2
Brown	93.3	2 459	51.0	9.2	4.3	0.5	3.9	52.7	1 388	113	71	2 810	17.7	81.8	0.4
Burleson	36.7	2 172	66.4	1.7	4.3	0.1	9.5	16.1	955	59	31	837	33.9	65.6	0.4
Burnet	84.2	2 284	58.7	2.2	6.7	0.3	4.0	68.4	1 854	72	68	2 030	26.4	72.9	0.7

1. Based on the resident population estimated as of July 1 of the year shown.

Table B. States and Counties — **Land Area and Population**

STATE/County code	CBSA code[1]	County Type[2]	STATE County	Land area[3] (sq km) 2000	Total persons	Rank	Per square kilometer	White	Black	Am. Indian, Alaska Native	Asian and Pacific Islander[4]	Percent Hispanic or Latino[4]	Under 5 years	5 to 17 years	18 to 24 years	25 to 34 years	35 to 44 years	45 to 54 years
				1	2	3	4	5	6	7	8	9	10	11	12	13	14	15
			TEXAS—Cont'd															
48 055	12420	1	Caldwell	1 413	35 572	1 255	25.2	48.4	8.2	0.4	0.4	43.1	7.5	20.4	10.2	14.2	14.8	12.6
48 057	47020	3	Calhoun	1 327	20 454	1 779	15.4	50.2	2.4	0.5	3.3	43.9	7.7	20.8	9.1	11.1	14.4	13.4
48 059	10180	3	Callahan	2 327	13 110	2 231	5.6	91.2	0.6	1.0	0.6	7.5	5.4	19.0	9.3	9.3	14.1	13.7
48 061	15180	3	Cameron	2 346	363 092	171	154.8	13.5	0.3	0.1	0.5	85.7	10.7	23.5	10.9	13.3	12.2	10.5
48 063	...	6	Camp	512	11 756	2 307	23.0	63.6	17.6	0.5	0.4	18.4	7.4	19.9	9.2	11.5	12.8	12.7
48 065	11100	3	Carson	2 391	6 507	2 732	2.7	89.9	0.9	1.3	0.1	8.3	6.1	20.2	9.4	9.5	15.3	14.9
48 067	...	6	Cass	2 428	29 995	1 404	12.4	78.1	19.3	0.9	0.2	2.3	5.8	17.9	9.3	10.2	13.4	13.8
48 069	...	6	Castro	2 327	7 900	2 601	3.4	44.2	2.6	0.4	0.0	52.9	8.5	23.4	10.7	9.9	12.6	13.2
48 071	26420	1	Chambers	1 552	27 581	1 481	17.8	76.2	9.9	0.9	1.0	12.6	6.1	20.7	10.5	12.6	15.7	15.3
48 073	27380	6	Cherokee	2 725	47 568	969	17.5	69.0	15.4	0.7	0.4	15.2	7.6	19.0	9.9	12.7	13.7	12.7
48 075	...	7	Childress	1 840	7 563	2 630	4.1	63.0	14.4	0.3	0.4	22.2	7.0	15.7	13.5	13.2	16.0	11.5
48 077	48660	3	Clay	2 843	11 207	2 354	3.9	94.6	0.4	2.0	0.0	4.1	4.5	18.7	9.4	10.3	15.5	15.0
48 079	...	9	Cochran	2 008	3 486	2 950	1.7	47.6	5.1	0.6	0.2	46.5	7.9	23.0	11.0	8.4	13.9	12.0
48 081	...	6	Coke	2 328	3 725	2 933	1.6	78.7	2.1	0.8	0.1	18.5	4.4	18.6	10.1	7.6	12.0	13.0
48 083	...	6	Coleman	3 264	8 777	2 544	2.7	83.4	2.5	0.8	0.3	13.5	6.4	17.2	7.8	9.1	12.4	13.4
48 085	19100	1	Collin	2 195	597 147	95	272.0	73.4	6.2	0.9	9.5	11.6	8.2	20.2	8.5	16.4	18.3	13.1
48 087	...	9	Collingsworth	2 380	3 023	2 984	1.3	69.2	5.7	1.9	0.3	23.5	5.5	19.6	9.0	8.3	12.6	13.8
48 089	...	6	Colorado	2 494	20 643	1 766	8.3	64.4	14.1	0.4	0.3	21.3	6.4	18.7	11.2	9.6	12.8	13.0
48 091	41700	1	Comal	1 454	87 785	610	60.4	75.2	1.1	0.7	0.6	23.1	6.4	18.4	9.2	11.3	14.3	14.4
48 093	...	7	Comanche	2 429	13 541	2 195	5.6	76.8	0.5	1.0	0.2	22.0	6.2	18.6	8.5	9.4	12.6	11.9
48 095	...	8	Concho	2 568	3 774	2 929	1.5	55.4	1.1	0.1	0.2	43.2	3.2	11.0	12.6	21.5	16.6	12.6
48 097	23620	6	Cooke	2 263	37 996	1 184	16.8	84.8	2.9	1.3	0.6	11.4	6.7	19.8	10.3	11.5	13.6	13.2
48 099	28660	2	Coryell	2 724	75 195	683	27.6	63.5	20.9	1.5	3.2	13.6	7.6	19.4	16.6	19.0	16.1	9.0
48 101	...	9	Cottle	2 334	1 752	3 076	0.8	67.4	10.9	0.6	0.0	21.8	5.1	17.4	7.6	6.1	13.5	13.5
48 103	...	6	Crane	2 035	3 885	2 920	1.9	49.3	3.1	0.4	0.4	46.9	6.0	22.6	10.7	9.1	14.7	14.9
48 105	...	7	Crockett	7 271	3 934	2 913	0.5	43.0	0.7	0.4	0.3	55.6	6.8	20.4	9.4	9.0	14.2	14.9
48 107	31180	3	Crosby	2 330	6 742	2 709	2.9	46.8	4.0	0.2	0.1	48.9	7.8	22.1	9.3	10.9	12.1	12.1
48 109	...	9	Culberson	9 874	2 760	2 999	0.3	26.3	0.7	0.4	0.9	71.7	7.8	23.0	10.2	10.7	13.4	13.9
48 111	...	7	Dallam	3 897	6 100	2 768	1.6	67.6	1.8	0.7	0.4	29.7	8.2	22.8	9.1	13.8	14.5	13.1
48 113	19100	1	Dallas	2 278	2 284 096	9	1 002.7	40.7	20.6	0.7	4.6	34.3	9.0	19.7	9.8	17.4	16.0	12.4
48 115	29500	7	Dawson	2 336	14 411	2 132	6.2	41.4	8.6	0.3	0.4	49.5	6.7	18.3	10.5	13.9	15.5	13.3
48 117	25820	6	Deaf Smith	3 878	18 415	1 885	4.7	37.9	1.1	0.4	0.2	60.4	9.6	23.8	10.6	11.8	12.3	11.7
48 119	19100	1	Delta	718	5 451	2 813	7.6	87.8	8.4	1.2	0.2	3.4	5.5	18.3	9.9	11.1	13.7	12.0
48 121	19100	1	Denton	2 301	510 795	114	222.0	73.8	6.6	1.0	5.8	14.3	8.0	19.6	10.6	17.4	17.3	12.5
48 123	...	6	De Witt	2 355	20 100	1 799	8.5	60.8	10.5	0.5	0.2	28.2	5.7	17.1	9.0	10.5	15.8	13.8
48 125	...	8	Dickens	2 342	2 705	3 004	1.2	64.8	8.2	0.2	0.1	26.8	5.0	12.9	13.1	14.9	14.3	11.9
48 127	...	6	Dimmit	3 447	10 341	2 413	3.0	13.5	0.9	0.2	0.5	85.0	8.5	24.0	10.5	11.7	12.3	12.4
48 129	...	8	Donley	2 408	3 877	2 922	1.6	87.9	4.9	0.8	0.2	6.7	5.0	17.1	12.2	8.9	11.5	12.6
48 131	...	7	Duval	4 643	12 616	2 263	2.7	10.6	0.5	0.3	0.1	88.6	7.6	21.2	10.2	12.3	14.0	11.7
48 133	...	6	Eastland	2 398	18 300	1 887	7.6	84.9	2.1	0.9	0.3	12.4	5.8	16.7	11.7	9.0	12.3	12.8
48 135	36220	3	Ector	2 334	122 692	462	52.6	48.9	4.5	0.7	0.7	45.7	8.6	21.4	11.2	12.6	14.0	13.0
48 137	...	9	Edwards	5 490	2 031	3 057	0.4	52.0	1.0	0.5	0.0	46.5	5.8	22.5	10.1	8.9	13.4	13.8
48 139	19100	1	Ellis	2 434	124 411	455	51.1	70.9	8.3	0.8	0.5	20.2	7.4	21.4	11.2	12.6	15.1	13.4
48 141	21340	2	El Paso	2 624	705 436	73	268.8	15.4	2.3	0.4	1.1	81.3	9.4	22.6	10.8	13.5	14.0	11.7
48 143	44500	7	Erath	2 814	33 370	1 319	11.9	82.9	0.8	0.8	0.5	15.6	6.5	17.6	15.4	13.6	12.3	11.5
48 145	...	6	Falls	1 992	17 860	1 924	9.0	55.5	26.8	0.3	0.2	17.4	5.7	21.3	9.4	11.4	13.9	12.6
48 147	...	6	Fannin	2 309	32 276	1 353	14.0	84.8	7.9	1.6	0.4	6.3	5.6	16.9	10.5	12.5	14.9	14.9
48 149	...	6	Fayette	2 461	22 370	1 688	9.1	79.0	6.7	0.4	0.2	13.8	5.7	16.9	9.1	9.3	13.3	14.2
48 151	...	8	Fisher	2 334	4 142	2 901	1.8	75.5	2.8	0.7	0.1	21.2	4.5	17.6	8.5	9.2	13.3	13.7
48 153	...	6	Floyd	2 570	7 446	2 643	2.9	46.6	3.8	0.6	0.2	48.9	7.8	22.6	9.4	10.1	12.8	12.0
48 155	...	9	Foard	1 830	1 541	3 085	0.8	77.4	4.0	0.7	0.2	17.8	4.7	19.4	8.6	9.8	11.9	13.2
48 157	26420	1	Fort Bend	2 265	419 772	146	185.3	43.9	20.3	0.5	14.7	21.7	6.9	22.4	10.4	12.6	16.6	15.2
48 159	...	8	Franklin	740	9 906	2 451	13.4	85.6	4.0	0.6	0.3	9.8	6.0	17.3	9.2	11.0	12.9	13.0
48 161	...	7	Freestone	2 273	18 605	1 878	8.2	72.3	18.3	0.5	0.3	9.1	6.1	16.7	10.7	13.3	14.0	12.9
48 163	...	6	Frio	2 935	16 345	2 010	5.6	20.0	4.7	0.1	0.5	74.7	8.1	20.1	12.1	15.9	13.7	11.3
48 165	...	7	Gaines	3 891	14 438	2 130	3.7	60.2	2.3	0.4	0.3	37.0	8.6	24.9	11.5	11.0	13.7	11.8
48 167	26420	1	Galveston	1 032	266 775	219	258.5	63.2	15.2	0.8	2.8	19.1	7.1	19.2	9.6	12.7	15.7	14.5
48 169	...	6	Garza	2 319	5 011	2 843	2.2	54.8	5.2	0.4	0.3	39.8	7.0	21.9	9.1	13.9	13.8	12.0
48 171	...	7	Gillespie	2 748	22 226	1 696	8.1	83.4	0.2	0.6	0.2	16.0	5.1	15.5	7.9	8.8	11.5	13.0
48 173	...	8	Glasscock	2 333	1 355	3 096	0.6	72.0	0.7	0.1	0.0	27.2	6.3	23.1	11.1	8.5	16.1	14.7
48 175	47020	3	Goliad	2 211	7 116	2 675	3.2	59.1	5.3	0.2	0.2	35.3	6.0	18.0	9.7	9.7	14.3	14.2
48 177	...	6	Gonzales	2 765	19 057	1 859	6.9	50.2	8.4	0.2	0.3	41.3	7.9	19.6	10.2	11.5	13.2	12.1
48 179	37420	6	Gray	2 404	21 496	1 726	8.9	78.1	5.8	2.2	0.5	15.0	6.0	17.7	9.7	11.7	14.1	13.6
48 181	43300	3	Grayson	2 418	115 153	483	47.6	84.6	6.0	2.4	0.8	8.0	6.9	18.2	10.3	11.8	14.1	13.4
48 183	30980	3	Gregg	710	113 941	486	160.5	68.0	20.3	1.0	0.9	10.8	7.6	19.1	10.8	12.8	14.0	13.3
48 185	...	6	Grimes	2 055	24 963	1 575	12.1	64.1	18.8	0.5	0.3	16.8	6.5	17.7	9.4	12.4	16.2	14.5

1. CBSA = Core Based Statistical Area. See Appendix A for explanation. See Appendix B for list of metropolitan areas with component counties. 2. County type code from the Economic Research Service of USDA Rural-Urban Continuum Codes. See Appendix A for definition. 3. Dry land or land partially or temporarily covered by water. 4. Hispanic or Latino persons may be of any race.

STATE County	55 to 64 years	65 to 74 years	75 years and over	Percent female	1990	2000	1990–2000	2000–2003	Births	Deaths	Net migration	Number	Percent change, 1990–2000	Persons per house-hold	Female family house-holder[1]	One person
	16	17	18	19	20	21	22	23	24	25	26	27	28	29	30	31
TEXAS—Cont'd																
Caldwell	7.8	5.8	5.5	50.4	26 392	32 194	22.0	10.5	1 693	861	2 470	10 816	23.7	2.82	13.3	21.2
Calhoun	10.1	8.3	5.7	49.8	19 053	20 647	8.4	-0.9	1 050	502	-757	7 442	9.8	2.75	11.0	21.3
Callahan	11.3	9.3	7.9	51.9	11 859	12 905	8.8	1.6	431	454	233	5 061	10.9	2.53	9.3	23.3
Cameron	6.9	5.8	5.0	52.1	260 120	335 227	28.9	8.3	27 210	5 759	6 846	97 267	32.7	3.40	17.4	15.4
Camp	10.3	8.4	7.5	51.0	9 904	11 549	16.6	1.8	563	423	67	4 336	14.9	2.62	12.5	24.2
Carson	10.5	8.2	7.4	51.4	6 576	6 516	-0.9	-0.1	239	207	-48	2 470	2.8	2.60	8.1	22.3
Cass	12.4	9.0	8.8	51.9	29 982	30 438	1.5	-1.5	1 084	1 227	-275	12 190	7.7	2.46	12.2	26.4
Castro	9.1	8.0	5.6	49.9	9 070	8 285	-8.7	-4.6	422	216	-611	2 761	-4.0	2.98	8.7	20.5
Chambers	9.3	5.0	3.6	49.9	20 088	26 031	29.6	6.0	1 034	625	1 131	9 139	31.9	2.82	9.0	17.8
Cherokee	9.4	7.3	7.2	49.7	41 049	46 659	13.7	1.9	2 372	1 685	273	16 651	11.1	2.63	12.8	24.2
Childress	9.1	7.6	7.3	40.9	5 953	7 688	29.1	-1.6	347	276	-188	2 474	1.6	2.40	11.4	30.8
Clay	12.0	8.4	6.6	51.2	10 024	11 006	9.8	1.8	265	309	262	4 323	13.5	2.52	7.3	23.5
Cochran	10.0	9.2	6.7	52.5	4 377	3 730	-14.8	-6.5	200	141	-300	1 309	-8.5	2.79	9.9	20.9
Coke	11.3	13.3	10.7	49.4	3 424	3 864	12.9	-3.6	96	176	-56	1 544	12.4	2.31	8.1	29.0
Coleman	12.1	10.8	12.1	52.2	9 710	9 235	-4.9	-5.0	348	459	-327	3 889	-3.4	2.33	9.3	30.2
Collin	7.3	3.1	2.1	49.9	264 036	491 675	86.2	21.5	29 877	6 090	79 377	181 970	89.9	2.68	7.5	23.2
Collingsworth	10.9	9.6	12.4	51.4	3 573	3 206	-10.3	-5.7	94	168	-109	1 294	-10.6	2.44	9.8	27.8
Colorado	10.3	9.1	8.8	51.0	18 383	20 390	10.9	1.2	875	882	271	7 641	8.8	2.56	10.9	26.2
Comal	10.0	7.4	6.5	50.7	51 832	78 021	50.5	12.5	3 540	2 078	8 045	29 066	50.5	2.64	9.0	20.6
Comanche	12.4	10.5	10.1	50.9	13 381	14 026	4.8	-3.5	491	630	-350	5 522	3.8	2.48	8.1	26.3
Concho	9.3	6.6	7.0	34.5	3 044	3 966	30.3	-4.8	67	126	-124	1 058	-0.5	2.45	9.7	26.6
Cooke	10.0	7.5	7.0	50.4	30 777	36 363	18.1	4.5	1 652	1 218	1 221	13 643	18.2	2.60	9.9	23.3
Coryell	5.4	3.4	2.6	48.7	64 226	74 978	16.7	0.3	3 247	1 059	-1 963	19 950	19.6	2.91	11.0	16.9
Cottle	11.9	10.7	14.8	53.5	2 247	1 904	-15.3	-8.0	68	84	-136	820	-10.4	2.28	10.6	32.0
Crane	9.8	6.4	6.1	51.6	4 652	3 996	-14.1	-2.8	126	98	-139	1 360	-11.5	2.91	7.9	18.8
Crockett	11.4	7.7	6.4	50.7	4 078	4 099	0.5	-4.0	174	102	-238	1 524	5.2	2.65	9.3	24.7
Crosby	10.9	8.3	7.7	52.4	7 304	7 072	-3.2	-4.7	339	231	-446	2 512	-0.2	2.78	11.4	23.8
Culberson	11.1	8.0	4.7	49.5	3 407	2 975	-12.7	-7.2	144	61	-302	1 052	-2.2	2.82	13.5	21.5
Dallam	8.5	5.9	4.7	49.6	5 461	6 222	13.9	-2.0	275	137	-265	2 317	9.2	2.68	9.7	26.2
Dallas	7.4	4.4	3.6	49.7	1 852 691	2 218 899	19.8	2.9	140 468	44 501	-32 227	807 621	15.1	2.71	14.1	27.3
Dawson	8.5	7.2	7.1	44.4	14 349	14 985	4.4	-3.8	661	455	-786	4 726	-7.0	2.69	11.0	23.9
Deaf Smith	8.2	6.5	5.8	51.3	19 153	18 561	-3.1	-0.8	1 154	474	-838	6 180	0.0	2.96	12.6	19.7
Delta	12.2	7.9	9.1	51.5	4 857	5 327	9.7	2.3	189	194	137	2 094	10.2	2.49	10.0	27.5
Denton	6.7	2.8	2.0	50.0	273 664	432 976	58.2	18.0	25 227	5 672	56 725	158 903	55.8	2.67	8.6	22.2
De Witt	10.0	8.8	9.5	48.2	18 840	20 013	6.2	0.4	724	797	175	7 207	0.2	2.53	11.8	26.4
Dickens	9.5	8.8	9.6	43.2	2 571	2 762	7.4	-2.1	84	131	-7	980	-8.7	2.29	7.9	32.4
Dimmit	8.8	6.0	5.9	51.0	10 433	10 248	-1.8	0.9	590	278	-207	3 308	7.7	3.06	17.2	18.0
Donley	11.9	11.6	10.0	52.2	3 696	3 828	3.6	1.3	114	161	98	1 578	4.2	2.30	7.5	31.4
Duval	9.6	7.5	7.0	49.9	12 918	13 120	1.6	-3.8	613	382	-732	4 350	4.6	2.88	16.8	22.9
Eastland	11.4	10.1	10.3	51.2	18 488	18 297	-1.0	0.0	643	974	338	7 321	-0.4	2.39	9.5	28.6
Ector	8.1	6.2	4.8	51.3	118 934	121 123	1.8	1.3	7 061	3 038	-2 416	43 846	3.6	2.72	13.7	24.0
Edwards	13.2	8.5	5.6	49.2	2 266	2 162	-4.6	-6.1	76	48	-148	801	0.8	2.66	8.9	24.7
Ellis	8.2	4.8	3.9	50.2	85 167	111 360	30.8	11.7	5 890	2 909	9 885	37 020	29.5	2.96	11.0	16.6
El Paso	7.3	5.6	4.3	52.0	591 610	679 622	14.9	3.8	46 068	11 831	-8 448	210 022	17.7	3.18	18.0	17.8
Erath	8.1	6.6	6.6	50.6	27 991	33 001	17.9	1.1	1 418	1 050	18	12 568	15.5	2.48	7.2	27.7
Falls	9.3	8.1	8.7	53.5	17 712	18 576	4.9	-3.9	634	753	-604	6 496	0.1	2.54	15.6	29.4
Fannin	10.1	8.0	8.0	46.9	24 804	31 242	26.0	3.3	1 104	1 346	1 301	11 105	14.6	2.51	10.3	25.2
Fayette	10.4	9.3	11.8	51.2	20 095	21 804	8.5	2.6	879	995	685	8 722	7.7	2.44	7.8	28.0
Fisher	11.7	11.2	11.8	51.5	4 842	4 344	-10.3	-4.7	89	189	-102	1 785	-5.7	2.39	8.1	28.3
Floyd	9.4	8.4	7.8	51.2	8 497	7 771	-8.5	-4.2	362	288	-409	2 730	-8.5	2.79	9.7	21.3
Foard	11.1	10.0	12.9	53.2	1 794	1 622	-9.6	-5.0	45	49	-76	664	-10.1	2.38	9.5	31.8
Fort Bend	7.1	3.4	2.2	50.1	225 421	354 452	57.2	18.4	17 311	4 738	51 357	110 915	57.5	3.14	11.4	13.5
Franklin	11.5	10.1	8.1	51.1	7 802	9 458	21.2	4.7	369	339	419	3 754	24.4	2.48	8.4	24.6
Freestone	10.1	7.8	8.0	47.3	15 818	17 867	13.0	4.1	732	659	669	6 588	8.7	2.48	10.7	26.4
Frio	7.8	6.2	5.0	45.5	13 472	16 252	20.6	0.6	870	383	-392	4 743	14.9	2.98	16.0	20.6
Gaines	7.3	6.4	4.3	50.6	14 123	14 467	2.4	-0.2	818	264	-589	4 681	4.0	3.07	8.8	18.2
Galveston	9.2	5.9	4.8	51.0	217 396	250 158	15.1	6.6	12 205	6 886	11 259	94 782	16.4	2.60	13.1	25.1
Garza	9.3	7.3	6.2	47.1	5 143	4 872	-5.3	2.9	216	180	95	1 663	-8.7	2.65	11.2	23.8
Gillespie	12.2	11.8	12.9	52.2	17 204	20 814	21.0	6.8	726	865	1 534	8 521	27.0	2.38	7.0	25.8
Glasscock	10.4	6.3	3.9	47.3	1 447	1 406	-2.8	-3.6	57	14	-95	483	5.9	2.91	2.9	23.8
Goliad	11.2	8.5	8.3	50.5	5 980	6 928	15.9	2.7	267	216	146	2 644	19.7	2.57	8.7	22.8
Gonzales	9.1	8.0	8.0	50.2	17 205	18 628	8.3	2.3	1 000	665	113	6 782	8.8	2.69	12.3	25.2
Gray	10.2	9.2	9.2	49.3	23 967	22 744	-5.1	-5.5	841	896	-1 187	8 793	-7.9	2.39	9.0	28.7
Grayson	9.9	7.4	7.2	51.3	95 019	110 595	16.4	4.1	5 232	4 066	3 445	42 849	16.3	2.51	11.4	25.5
Gregg	8.8	6.9	6.1	51.4	104 948	111 379	6.1	2.3	5 817	3 890	723	42 687	6.6	2.54	13.5	26.1
Grimes	9.5	7.3	5.9	46.8	18 843	23 552	25.0	6.0	1 069	802	1 134	7 753	28.4	2.69	12.6	23.8

1. No spouse present.

Table B. States and Counties — Vital Statistics, Health Resources, and Crime

STATE County	Births, average 1999–2001		Deaths, average 1999–2001				Physicians,[4] 2000		Hospitals,[4] 1998			Medicare enrollees, 2003	Serious crimes known to police,[6] 2002	
				Number		Rate				Beds			Total	
	Total	Rate[1]	Total	Infant[2]	Total[1]	Infant[3]	Number	Rate[5]	Number	Number	Rate[5]		Number	Rate[7]
	32	33	34	35	36	37	38	39	40	41	42	43	44	45

TEXAS—Cont'd

STATE County	32	33	34	35	36	37	38	39	40	41	42	43	44	45
Caldwell	514	15.8	277	4	8.5	D	11	34	1	21	65	4 325	964	2 867
Calhoun	329	15.9	166	1	8.0	D	15	73	1	75	364	3 035	733	3 399
Callahan	132	10.3	147	0	11.4	D	1	8	0	0	0	2 441	105	779
Cameron	8 246	24.4	1 855	34	5.5	4.2	385	115	5	951	291	38 107	22 627	6 462
Camp	170	14.8	150	1	13.1	D	2	17	1	41	374	2 366	369	3 059
Carson	72	11.1	64	0	9.8	D	0	0	0	0	0	1 045	43	632
Cass	335	11.0	387	5	12.8	D	12	39	3	114	370	6 249	763	2 400
Castro	146	17.6	64	1	7.8	D	4	48	1	30	359	1 051	169	1 953
Chambers	317	12.2	187	2	7.2	D	13	50	2	60	253	2 153	979	3 601
Cherokee	705	15.1	535	4	11.4	D	66	141	2	148	345	6 717	1 579	3 253
Childress	95	12.4	89	0	11.6	D	6	78	1	35	465	1 187	184	2 291
Clay	90	8.2	103	1	9.5	D	2	18	1	32	303	1 479	188	1 635
Cochran	55	14.7	43	1	11.5	D	2	54	1	30	759	605	87	2 233
Coke	36	9.3	57	0	14.7	D	2	52	0	0	0	777	66	1 635
Coleman	114	12.3	155	0	16.8	D	8	87	1	25	262	2 227	199	2 063
Collin	8 726	17.5	1 805	34	3.6	3.9	565	115	4	498	116	31 024	21 056	4 100
Collingsworth	32	10.1	50	0	15.7	D	3	94	1	20	608	650	106	3 165
Colorado	263	12.9	278	2	13.6	D	22	108	3	98	515	3 775	569	2 672
Comal	1 081	13.7	655	6	8.3	D	93	119	1	77	105	13 862	3 677	4 512
Comanche	166	11.9	209	1	15.0	D	9	64	2	35	258	2 786	245	1 672
Concho	25	6.4	36	0	9.1	D	3	76	1	20	641	544	35	845
Cooke	489	13.4	382	5	10.5	D	19	52	2	80	244	5 616	1 314	3 460
Coryell	995	13.4	338	7	4.5	7.0	65	87	1	48	62	5 450	1 679	2 144
Cottle	22	11.7	31	1	16.1	D	1	53	0	0	0	452	6	302
Crane	53	13.2	34	0	8.6	D	4	100	1	28	621	507	77	1 845
Crockett	53	12.9	41	0	10.1	D	2	49	1	20	435	567	85	1 986
Crosby	110	15.6	81	1	11.6	D	1	14	1	35	485	1 140	27	366
Culberson	43	14.4	22	0	7.4	D	1	34	1	25	820	344	10	322
Dallam	101	16.2	50	1	8.1	D	1	16	1	130	1 969	1 268	277	4 262
Dallas	42 024	18.8	13 870	255	6.2	6.1	5 076	229	27	6 052	295	212 737	161 124	6 952
Dawson	218	14.5	150	1	10.0	D	8	53	1	40	272	2 268	346	2 211
Deaf Smith	368	19.9	159	4	8.6	D	12	65	1	39	205	2 432	735	3 791
Delta	60	11.2	73	0	13.8	D	1	19	0	0	0	995	140	2 516
Denton	7 378	16.8	1 742	34	4.0	4.6	386	89	4	605	158	25 279	17 034	3 798
De Witt	239	11.9	264	1	13.2	D	14	70	1	49	249	3 365	546	2 612
Dickens	23	8.4	41	1	14.8	D	0	0	0	0	0	558	23	797
Dimmit	164	16.0	99	1	9.6	D	7	68	1	26	251	1 429	342	3 195
Donley	38	9.8	58	1	15.2	D	0	0	0	0	0	881	59	1 476
Duval	198	15.1	116	1	8.9	D	0	0	0	0	0	2 061	361	2 634
Eastland	217	11.9	307	2	16.9	D	4	22	1	36	205	4 140	534	2 794
Ector	2 196	18.0	979	15	8.0	7.0	189	156	2	401	319	15 937	7 498	5 927
Edwards	21	9.4	15	0	6.8	D	2	93	0	0	0	1 423	52	2 303
Ellis	1 779	15.9	886	13	7.9	7.1	63	57	2	65	63	13 288	4 401	3 784
El Paso	14 154	20.7	3 976	67	5.8	4.8	1 047	154	6	1 829	260	79 128	30 012	4 228
Erath	450	13.7	325	2	9.9	D	35	106	1	75	238	4 992	928	2 692
Falls	205	11.1	239	1	12.9	D	24	129	1	29	166	2 878	383	1 974
Fannin	355	11.4	424	2	13.6	D	18	58	1	65	231	5 574	854	2 617
Fayette	256	11.7	311	1	14.2	D	27	124	1	43	201	5 083	304	1 335
Fisher	36	8.4	59	0	13.8	D	1	23	1	23	542	919	61	1 345
Floyd	123	15.9	92	2	11.9	D	4	51	1	27	330	1 220	126	1 552
Foard	15	9.2	20	0	12.5	D	0	0	0	0	0	377	21	1 240
Fort Bend	5 140	14.3	1 431	24	4.0	4.7	362	102	2	209	62	22 138	12 529	3 389
Franklin	104	10.9	104	1	10.9	D	6	63	1	30	310	1 455	164	1 660
Freestone	218	12.2	201	2	11.2	D	10	56	1	16	91	2 958	254	1 361
Frio	276	17.0	125	1	7.7	D	10	62	2	40	254	1 913	568	3 346
Gaines	268	18.5	90	1	6.2	D	6	41	1	33	220	1 636	214	1 416
Galveston	3 745	14.9	2 145	24	8.5	6.3	914	365	2	927	378	32 702	9 355	4 643
Garza	67	13.6	57	0	11.5	D	3	62	1	13	282	772	59	1 159
Gillespie	225	10.8	287	1	13.8	D	48	231	1	58	289	5 302	379	1 743
Glasscock	17	12.2	4	0	0.0	D	0	0	0	0	0	109	1	68
Goliad	79	11.5	69	0	9.9	D	4	58	0	0	0	1 133	55	760
Gonzales	293	15.7	222	1	11.9	D	17	91	1	34	194	3 370	295	1 516
Gray	265	11.7	287	2	12.6	D	32	141	1	92	390	4 242	1 656	6 971
Grayson	1 538	13.9	1 282	12	11.6	8.0	190	172	3	540	525	19 015	4 889	4 232
Gregg	1 772	15.8	1 196	17	10.7	9.8	207	186	3	460	406	20 021	7 597	6 530
Grimes	325	13.7	250	2	10.5	D	8	34	1	18	77	3 318	674	2 740

1. Per 1,000 estimated resident population. 2. Deaths of infants under 1 year old. 3. Deaths of infants under 1 year old per 1,000 live births. 4. Data subject to copyright. 5. Per 100,000 resident population as of July 1 of the year shown. 6. Data for serious crimes have not been adjusted for underreporting; this may affect comparability between geographic areas and over time. 7. Per 100,000 population estimated by the FBI.

Table B. States and Counties — Crime, Education, Money Income, and Poverty

	Serious crimes known to police,[1] 2002 (cont'd) Rate[2]		Education School enrollment and attainment, 2000				Local government expenditures,[5] 2000–2001		Money income, 1999	Households			Percent below poverty level, 1999			
			Enrollment[3]		Attainment[4] (percent)					Median income						
STATE County	Violent	Property	Total	Percent private	High school graduate or less	Bachelor's degree or more	Total current expenditures (mil dol)	Current expenditures per student (dollars)	Per capita income[6] (dollars)	Dollars	Percent change, 1989–1999 (constant 1999 dollars)	Percent with income of $100,000 or more	Persons	House-holds	Families	Families with children
	46	47	48	49	50	51	52	53	54	55	56	57	58	59	60	61

TEXAS—Cont'd

	46	47	48	49	50	51	52	53	54	55	56	57	58	59	60	61
Caldwell	396	2 471	8 294	8.5	63.5	13.3	38.4	6 150	15 099	36 573	35.0	5.6	13.1	12.4	10.4	12.5
Calhoun	320	3 079	5 469	9.3	64.1	12.1	29.4	7 118	17 125	35 849	17.5	6.3	16.4	15.1	12.7	17.5
Callahan	59	720	3 130	4.2	58.8	12.3	19.9	6 889	15 204	32 463	16.7	3.9	12.2	12.9	9.0	13.7
Cameron	431	6 031	109 790	6.1	64.9	13.4	567.0	6 771	10 960	26 155	12.3	4.8	33.1	29.3	28.2	36.5
Camp	373	2 686	3 000	9.8	63.1	12.2	13.3	5 945	16 500	31 164	17.9	7.0	20.9	17.7	15.9	25.5
Carson	176	455	1 779	5.0	48.4	15.5	10.4	8 155	19 368	40 285	12.0	6.4	7.3	7.7	5.4	7.0
Cass	277	2 123	7 138	6.4	63.2	12.0	40.2	6 692	15 777	28 441	6.4	4.0	17.7	18.8	14.7	20.3
Castro	220	1 734	2 425	5.4	64.3	14.7	14.6	7 597	14 457	30 619	27.8	6.6	19.0	17.2	15.7	21.7
Chambers	320	3 281	7 139	6.4	55.5	12.1	35.8	6 828	19 863	47 964	12.7	12.8	11.0	10.6	8.3	11.3
Cherokee	505	2 748	11 603	11.2	63.6	11.4	50.6	6 419	13 980	29 313	13.1	4.4	17.9	17.6	13.7	19.8
Childress	237	2 055	1 691	8.6	66.0	8.6	8.3	6 841	12 452	27 457	27.0	2.6	17.6	16.5	13.7	24.5
Clay	122	1 514	2 661	4.8	59.2	13.9	14.6	7 180	16 361	35 738	12.1	4.8	10.3	10.8	8.1	10.3
Cochran	180	2 053	1 081	1.6	65.6	10.2	10.9	11 214	13 125	27 525	6.1	5.4	27.0	21.7	21.4	31.3
Coke	124	1 511	937	2.8	59.8	14.7	7.0	8 526	16 734	29 085	12.6	6.0	13.0	14.2	9.7	15.5
Coleman	52	2 011	2 018	5.7	67.2	11.7	13.2	8 104	14 911	25 658	23.1	5.0	19.9	20.6	15.5	24.4
Collin	363	3 737	136 630	17.3	23.2	47.3	592.3	6 494	33 345	70 835	14.6	30.4	4.9	4.2	3.3	4.3
Collingsworth	299	2 867	797	4.4	54.2	15.3	5.8	8 174	15 318	25 438	22.8	5.7	18.7	17.9	14.8	21.8
Colorado	211	2 460	5 113	13.4	64.3	14.4	25.1	6 659	16 910	32 425	16.1	6.4	16.2	16.5	12.3	17.2
Comal	470	4 042	19 006	12.6	44.6	26.2	101.5	6 084	21 914	46 147	16.6	12.3	8.6	8.1	6.4	10.4
Comanche	198	1 474	3 192	4.0	64.4	13.0	16.2	6 514	14 677	28 422	20.9	3.9	17.3	18.5	13.9	21.4
Concho	97	748	740	7.8	67.9	14.1	4.2	8 697	15 727	31 313	46.2	6.1	11.9	12.9	7.5	11.1
Cooke	379	3 080	9 620	11.5	52.3	15.7	39.8	6 479	17 889	37 649	14.3	7.3	14.1	13.6	10.9	18.4
Coryell	267	1 877	19 217	9.9	51.0	12.4	66.2	6 307	14 410	35 999	14.0	4.5	9.5	9.2	7.8	10.6
Cottle	101	201	399	1.5	64.5	15.3	2.7	8 401	16 212	25 446	21.5	3.7	18.4	18.0	13.7	23.8
Crane	72	1 773	1 256	2.7	64.2	12.8	9.9	9 750	15 374	32 194	-21.8	7.3	13.4	14.4	12.4	15.2
Crockett	93	1 892	1 129	1.2	66.8	10.4	7.9	9 498	14 414	29 355	14.5	3.8	19.4	18.9	14.9	21.8
Crosby	27	338	1 992	3.6	68.8	10.5	13.9	8 736	14 445	25 769	11.8	5.4	28.1	24.9	22.6	29.0
Culberson	161	161	888	3.6	71.5	13.9	5.6	8 089	11 493	25 882	16.3	1.7	25.1	25.5	21.5	27.5
Dallam	523	3 739	1 650	7.0	67.1	9.6	11.3	6 627	13 653	27 946	5.2	4.0	14.1	16.5	11.3	14.4
Dallas	862	6 090	591 553	15.3	46.7	27.0	2 586.1	6 307	22 603	43 324	2.0	13.7	13.4	11.3	10.6	14.8
Dawson	319	1 891	3 867	5.4	69.6	10.5	21.3	7 075	15 011	28 211	11.0	5.7	19.7	17.0	16.4	26.1
Deaf Smith	444	3 348	5 645	7.6	65.6	11.8	26.5	6 351	13 119	29 601	4.0	4.5	20.6	19.9	19.3	24.3
Delta	162	2 354	1 344	6.2	60.6	13.9	7.8	6 510	15 080	29 094	7.2	3.9	17.6	18.3	14.6	19.2
Denton	305	3 493	130 034	12.8	30.5	36.6	458.6	6 505	26 895	58 216	17.4	21.7	6.6	7.1	4.1	5.4
De Witt	225	2 387	4 753	7.1	65.0	11.8	33.7	7 419	14 780	28 714	18.5	5.1	19.6	19.1	15.3	20.3
Dickens	173	624	545	4.0	67.9	8.4	4.3	10 175	13 156	25 898	33.1	3.0	17.4	17.1	14.1	21.6
Dimmit	336	2 859	3 249	4.2	72.0	10.1	18.3	7 453	9 765	21 917	33.5	0.5	33.2	32.6	29.7	38.1
Donley	75	1 401	1 031	3.1	48.3	15.8	6.3	9 471	15 958	29 006	28.9	4.6	15.9	16.8	10.5	18.9
Duval	445	2 189	3 856	3.3	70.0	8.9	23.6	7 446	11 324	22 416	22.7	3.5	27.2	27.1	23.0	28.3
Eastland	256	2 538	4 568	5.5	60.9	12.7	22.6	7 079	14 870	26 832	26.6	4.3	16.8	18.1	12.1	20.3
Ector	526	5 400	36 067	5.9	58.8	12.0	164.4	6 126	15 031	31 152	-2.6	5.2	18.7	18.4	16.1	21.8
Edwards	531	1 771	598	2.2	62.3	17.3	6.9	9 162	12 691	25 298	28.6	3.5	31.6	24.5	24.6	38.7
Ellis	288	3 496	32 112	11.4	53.0	17.1	150.3	6 056	20 212	50 350	22.7	12.4	8.6	8.3	6.8	9.6
El Paso	606	3 622	226 320	8.1	56.8	16.6	986.0	6 302	13 421	31 051	2.1	6.3	23.8	21.6	20.5	26.6
Erath	142	2 550	11 111	7.0	49.5	25.0	32.7	6 020	16 655	30 708	15.0	7.0	16.0	17.6	10.3	14.7
Falls	299	1 675	5 024	8.3	67.9	9.6	20.8	6 566	14 311	26 589	14.9	4.1	22.6	22.6	18.8	25.9
Fannin	282	2 335	7 106	8.3	63.2	12.6	34.7	6 541	16 066	34 501	24.2	5.2	13.9	15.3	9.9	15.6
Fayette	44	1 291	4 935	13.3	64.5	14.6	24.2	6 608	18 888	34 526	28.7	7.1	11.4	13.4	8.1	12.0
Fisher	88	1 256	971	2.4	65.1	12.4	6.2	8 592	15 120	27 659	6.3	3.4	17.5	15.8	13.5	22.6
Floyd	74	1 479	2 161	4.5	67.5	12.3	14.2	7 754	14 206	26 851	4.2	6.3	21.5	20.4	19.5	26.4
Foard	59	1 181	402	1.7	65.1	10.5	2.7	7 917	14 799	25 813	2.7	3.1	14.3	17.3	9.9	12.4
Fort Bend	411	2 978	114 365	14.3	35.1	36.9	455.0	6 101	24 985	63 831	11.0	25.5	7.1	6.4	5.5	6.8
Franklin	233	1 427	2 230	4.6	58.2	16.2	9.1	6 231	17 563	31 955	2.9	8.0	15.6	15.0	12.5	20.4
Freestone	139	1 222	4 486	8.0	60.9	10.9	22.5	7 080	16 338	31 283	8.0	4.9	14.2	14.9	9.8	15.1
Frio	230	3 116	4 659	3.8	70.7	8.4	23.1	7 342	16 069	24 504	29.7	3.3	29.0	27.6	24.5	31.5
Gaines	126	1 290	4 369	11.2	70.2	10.5	27.9	9 361	13 088	30 432	1.4	5.3	21.7	19.1	17.3	23.7
Galveston	529	4 114	69 639	11.0	45.5	22.7	406.3	6 128	21 568	42 419	7.1	13.0	13.2	12.7	10.1	15.0
Garza	59	1 100	1 384	5.6	68.3	10.0	8.7	7 291	12 704	27 206	6.6	5.2	22.3	23.5	17.5	25.9
Gillespie	32	1 711	4 229	15.5	49.4	22.9	21.1	6 587	20 423	38 109	19.6	7.8	10.2	10.5	7.1	9.9
Glasscock	0	68	458	1.7	54.3	18.7	3.2	9 197	18 279	35 655	-9.4	9.9	14.7	11.2	11.5	13.0
Goliad	124	636	1 652	7.6	57.2	12.3	10.8	7 695	17 126	34 201	18.9	5.8	16.4	15.0	11.9	22.5
Gonzales	396	1 120	4 671	5.0	71.8	10.7	26.0	6 667	14 269	28 368	20.7	4.6	18.6	19.6	13.8	19.9
Gray	551	6 419	5 609	8.6	58.3	11.9	25.0	6 286	16 702	31 368	-3.2	6.1	13.8	14.9	11.2	16.2
Grayson	275	3 957	27 885	12.0	49.8	17.2	126.0	6 357	18 862	37 178	9.6	7.5	11.3	12.1	8.4	13.2
Gregg	583	5 947	29 686	11.8	48.6	19.5	153.3	6 580	18 449	35 006	2.2	7.9	15.1	14.7	12.0	17.7
Grimes	207	2 533	5 846	5.8	65.5	10.3	27.9	6 482	14 368	32 280	16.5	5.8	16.6	17.3	13.8	18.7

1. Data for serious crimes have not been adjusted for underreporting; this may affect comparability between geographic areas and over time.   2. Per 100,000 population estimated by the FBI.   3. All persons 3 years old and over enrolled in nursery school through college.   4. Persons 25 years old and over.   5. Elementary and secondary education expenditures.   6. Based on population enumerated as of April 1, 2000.

STATE County	Total (mil dol)	Percent change, 2001–2002	Per capita[1]		Wages and salaries[2] (mil dol)	Proprietor's income (mil dol)	Dividends, interest, and rent (mil dol)	Total (mil dol)	Transfer payments				
									Government payments to individuals				
			Dollars	Rank					Total (mil dol)	Social Security (mil dol)	Medical payments (mil dol)	Income maintenance (mil dol)	Unemployment insurance (mil dol)
	62	63	64	65	66	67	68	69	70	71	72	73	74
TEXAS—Cont'd													
Caldwell	706	1.9	20 223	2 496	199	39	100	137	129	44	59	15	4
Calhoun	434	-0.9	21 251	2 227	500	33	75	91	86	35	37	8	3
Callahan	288	4.9	22 337	1 926	67	21	49	64	61	27	25	5	2
Cameron	5 697	6.7	16 126	3 046	3 409	445	743	1 500	1 421	322	697	301	37
Camp	310	1.3	26 614	762	115	57	57	63	61	23	27	7	2
Carson	171	-0.4	25 879	915	308	11	29	26	24	12	9	1	1
Cass	664	2.0	22 007	2 012	278	90	111	179	172	64	79	16	5
Castro	221	-9.1	27 538	611	81	81	24	34	32	11	15	5	0
Chambers	760	2.1	28 026	547	339	23	122	88	82	36	34	7	2
Cherokee	1 136	4.0	24 165	1 352	489	222	187	237	226	82	107	22	4
Childress	126	5.2	16 616	3 015	77	11	25	32	31	11	14	3	0
Clay	271	2.3	24 113	1 366	69	36	46	44	41	20	15	3	1
Cochran	84	-5.8	23 732	1 486	36	17	18	18	18	6	8	2	0
Coke	76	1.5	20 052	2 538	32	1	18	20	19	9	9	1	0
Coleman	189	2.5	21 283	2 216	57	17	38	66	64	23	31	5	1
Collin	23 231	0.7	40 831	56	9 640	1 874	2 786	1 050	923	423	307	53	101
Collingsworth	78	-3.1	25 255	1 059	30	11	16	18	17	7	9	2	0
Colorado	502	2.4	24 577	1 243	196	45	124	103	99	42	44	8	2
Comal	2 471	4.5	29 171	425	1 068	196	476	333	314	145	121	18	9
Comanche	326	3.8	24 036	1 395	115	53	66	80	77	30	36	6	1
Concho	63	-2.5	16 537	3 022	26	5	14	16	15	5	8	1	0
Cooke	935	0.2	24 778	1 186	415	116	194	159	151	65	60	10	4
Coryell	1 513	5.2	20 235	2 491	400	59	186	160	146	55	66	15	5
Cottle	47	1.8	26 602	764	22	4	9	11	11	5	5	1	0
Crane	76	4.9	19 339	2 687	54	3	11	16	15	6	7	2	0
Crockett	74	6.4	19 123	2 734	40	1	21	15	14	6	6	1	0
Crosby	162	6.3	23 594	1 538	57	12	25	42	41	12	23	5	0
Culberson	45	11.3	16 096	3 047	28	3	6	12	12	3	5	2	0
Dallam	163	-14.5	26 490	790	107	52	28	29	28	8	14	2	0
Dallas	82 527	1.5	36 289	116	84 038	17 414	11 235	7 211	6 700	2 381	2 774	752	509
Dawson	279	3.6	19 208	2 712	143	29	55	78	74	23	40	8	1
Deaf Smith	413	-9.0	22 498	1 878	177	100	73	80	76	25	37	11	1
Delta	106	2.6	19 553	2 647	37	5	15	29	28	10	13	3	1
Denton	15 444	1.0	31 603	241	5 014	677	1 618	967	858	351	333	51	63
De Witt	434	3.3	21 661	2 101	211	39	91	107	103	37	52	9	2
Dickens	45	2.2	16 855	3 004	19	3	8	17	16	5	9	1	0
Dimmit	158	5.0	15 420	3 064	86	11	19	52	50	12	26	10	1
Donley	93	2.6	24 223	1 336	27	10	18	21	20	9	8	1	0
Duval	227	2.2	17 664	2 934	103	4	28	82	79	18	46	12	2
Eastland	428	3.8	23 528	1 554	209	42	78	117	112	41	52	9	2
Ector	2 732	2.8	22 342	1 923	1 869	220	386	531	503	179	219	64	22
Edwards	38	6.9	18 442	2 836	14	3	13	10	10	4	4	1	0
Ellis	3 276	3.1	27 294	651	1 222	226	350	487	460	148	156	32	104
El Paso	13 992	5.1	20 129	2 514	9 254	1 924	1 743	2 708	2 554	674	1 100	492	20
Erath	809	3.8	24 431	1 280	419	117	141	146	138	48	63	10	2
Falls	342	5.7	19 074	2 745	140	28	53	91	87	27	41	10	1
Fannin	664	2.0	20 847	2 332	264	53	107	160	152	58	70	10	4
Fayette	616	2.7	27 662	594	277	54	161	122	117	51	53	6	2
Fisher	90	-1.0	21 380	2 186	33	4	17	25	24	10	11	2	0
Floyd	179	-1.3	24 365	1 288	66	42	30	38	36	13	17	5	1
Foard	35	-2.8	22 236	1 949	10	3	9	11	10	4	5	1	0
Fort Bend	13 160	2.2	33 000	185	4 523	904	1 624	793	703	302	271	64	37
Franklin	252	2.6	25 854	921	84	39	53	49	47	23	19	3	1
Freestone	360	1.8	19 551	2 649	175	28	67	82	77	32	31	7	2
Frio	268	5.0	16 382	3 036	113	37	31	71	67	16	36	12	2
Gaines	312	6.1	21 904	2 037	165	69	39	57	54	17	28	7	1
Galveston	7 971	3.2	30 541	301	3 613	437	1 126	1 043	984	378	438	85	38
Garza	99	4.6	19 594	2 638	48	16	19	26	25	8	13	3	0
Gillespie	594	4.0	27 410	629	220	54	204	117	112	55	47	5	1
Glasscock	26	-10.1	18 892	2 772	14	0	8	3	3	2	1	0	0
Goliad	151	2.1	21 449	2 167	42	9	34	33	32	12	15	2	1
Gonzales	460	1.0	24 349	1 291	176	105	77	97	92	32	40	12	2
Gray	565	0.8	25 860	918	304	77	99	122	117	49	53	8	4
Grayson	2 644	1.3	23 274	1 636	1 612	154	440	538	513	202	219	34	17
Gregg	3 213	2.6	28 418	501	2 234	421	620	585	559	210	253	50	18
Grimes	459	0.7	18 598	2 814	229	33	78	92	87	34	37	10	3

1. Based on the resident population estimated as of July 1 of the year shown.   2. Includes other labor income.

Table B. States and Counties — **Earnings, Social Security, and Housing**

STATE County	Earnings, 2002									Social Security beneficiaries, December 2003		Supplemental Security Income recipients, December 2003	Housing units, 2003	
	Total (mil dol)	Goods-related[1]			Service-related and health				Government	Number	Rate[2]		Total	Percent change, 2000–2003
		Farm	Total	Manu-facturing	Infor-mation and profes-sional and technical services	Retail trade	Finance, insur-ance, and real estate	Health services						
	75	76	77	78	79	80	81	82	83	84	85	86	87	88
TEXAS—Cont'd														
Caldwell	238	1.8	14.6	4.0	3.6	9.2	4.1	D	24.4	5 155	145	757	12 611	6.0
Calhoun	533	-0.4	69.1	56.2	4.5	3.8	2.3	D	9.9	3 635	178	384	10 467	2.2
Callahan	88	4.4	25.8	5.8	D	10.2	5.8	D	27.9	2 985	228	237	6 015	1.5
Cameron	3 854	1.0	13.6	9.8	5.1	9.0	4.9	17.3	27.0	44 335	122	17 229	130 222	8.8
Camp	172	25.0	D	11.1	D	6.4	6.2	D	10.1	2 505	213	394	5 309	1.5
Carson	319	1.4	D	D	D	1.4	D	D	8.4	1 200	184	65	2 849	1.2
Cass	369	5.7	30.7	24.4	2.6	10.0	3.2	D	19.3	7 235	241	1 007	14 184	2.1
Castro	163	55.1	D	4.3	1.7	3.8	2.2	1.2	14.1	1 275	161	165	3 200	0.1
Chambers	362	1.3	49.6	35.8	1.9	4.8	3.7	2.5	16.0	3 740	136	334	11 417	10.5
Cherokee	710	18.9	18.0	14.3	D	10.2	6.8	8.6	21.0	9 130	192	1 184	19 603	2.2
Childress	89	5.9	D	5.5	D	9.6	4.0	4.8	47.5	1 235	163	148	3 019	-1.3
Clay	105	5.5	D	8.0	D	8.5	D	7.5	17.6	2 230	199	124	5 063	1.4
Cochran	52	23.3	D	D	D	2.9	D	D	25.8	685	197	112	1 593	0.4
Coke	33	-8.3	21.9	0.7	D	9.5	D	1.4	37.4	925	248	49	2 876	1.2
Coleman	74	0.4	13.8	3.5	D	12.1	6.1	9.3	32.8	2 560	292	269	5 234	-0.3
Collin	11 514	0.1	21.4	14.6	23.1	8.8	13.0	6.9	9.8	41 920	70	3 369	228 421	17.2
Collingsworth	41	23.9	D	D	D	8.1	5.2	3.5	24.2	755	250	93	1 690	-1.9
Colorado	241	3.1	25.0	12.8	D	12.9	5.0	D	15.8	4 475	217	404	9 523	1.0
Comal	1 264	-0.1	29.5	16.3	6.0	15.2	5.4	9.4	12.8	15 520	177	860	36 728	12.3
Comanche	169	18.3	10.5	4.3	4.6	9.1	4.7	7.4	18.7	3 365	249	306	7 168	0.9
Concho	31	8.1	D	D	D	2.9	D	8.3	27.0	605	160	83	1 494	0.4
Cooke	531	0.5	31.7	20.6	D	10.0	5.8	4.5	18.2	6 665	175	455	15 346	1.9
Coryell	460	0.1	D	3.2	D	9.8	6.5	4.4	50.1	6 755	90	625	22 208	2.0
Cottle	26	7.3	D	8.2	5.8	8.5	5.1	D	17.5	510	291	59	1 068	-1.8
Crane	57	-3.1	D	D	D	4.7	2.4	6.4	22.7	610	157	87	1 592	-0.3
Crockett	41	-4.7	28.1	0.0	3.1	10.2	D	2.0	32.3	650	165	93	2 076	1.3
Crosby	70	14.9	D	2.6	D	5.8	D	7.9	24.7	1 340	199	186	3 186	-0.5
Culberson	32	5.9	D	D	0.6	13.4	D	D	44.4	460	167	86	1 344	1.7
Dallam	159	21.9	6.5	1.5	5.7	5.7	5.1	2.1	15.4	940	154	110	2 727	1.1
Dallas	101 452	0.0	18.9	11.6	18.7	6.3	15.3	7.1	7.9	236 210	103	36 792	891 436	4.4
Dawson	172	10.7	9.9	2.5	2.9	8.0	5.7	4.3	31.7	2 580	179	496	5 498	0.0
Deaf Smith	277	32.4	D	8.5	2.9	5.1	3.2	2.9	15.4	2 800	152	493	6 919	0.1
Delta	42	5.1	D	D	D	6.0	D	10.1	27.3	1 170	215	173	2 436	1.1
Denton	5 692	0.1	20.8	12.4	10.6	11.0	6.4	8.7	19.0	35 895	70	2 596	192 285	14.4
De Witt	249	1.3	23.9	17.0	3.6	8.5	8.3	D	32.2	4 315	215	624	8 827	0.8
Dickens	21	7.3	D	0.2	D	7.3	D	2.8	27.6	605	224	76	1 367	-0.1
Dimmit	97	4.0	D	D	D	8.7	D	7.8	46.2	1 740	168	664	4 150	0.9
Donley	37	17.1	4.3	1.7	D	11.4	D	6.6	36.5	975	251	86	2 392	0.6
Duval	107	-2.2	39.6	0.1	D	3.7	2.4	4.3	38.1	2 450	194	791	5 647	1.9
Eastland	251	4.1	40.6	17.2	D	8.0	4.4	7.0	18.2	4 555	249	484	9 527	-0.2
Ector	2 089	-0.3	28.1	10.3	D	10.8	6.1	8.5	17.3	18 630	152	3 388	50 923	2.9
Edwards	16	-8.7	D	0.3	D	13.1	5.8	D	47.3	500	246	92	1 218	0.1
Ellis	1 447	0.5	44.6	36.8	D	8.5	4.3	6.3	14.8	15 765	127	1 827	42 937	9.9
El Paso	11 178	0.1	17.4	12.2	5.9	8.2	9.9	10.2	27.6	88 945	126	23 611	235 592	5.0
Erath	536	14.6	21.1	16.7	5.5	7.8	4.2	10.5	18.9	5 355	160	433	14 691	1.9
Falls	168	4.1	D	6.9	D	7.9	2.5	D	45.7	3 375	189	692	7 703	0.6
Fannin	318	1.3	D	12.4	3.8	11.2	7.3	D	32.4	6 475	201	696	13 155	2.1
Fayette	331	3.0	23.7	11.2	4.7	9.1	8.9	D	20.1	5 595	250	394	11 134	0.2
Fisher	37	4.3	D	D	D	5.7	D	4.3	32.4	1 090	263	87	2 277	0.0
Floyd	108	33.9	6.6	2.6	D	5.6	5.9	3.6	18.0	1 410	189	182	3 201	-0.6
Foard	13	9.5	D	D	D	4.4	8.7	12.7	32.6	405	263	47	847	-0.4
Fort Bend	5 427	1.2	35.4	14.1	9.4	7.0	7.6	6.3	14.4	31 410	75	3 311	127 642	10.0
Franklin	123	14.7	13.3	3.8	4.1	23.0	5.8	12.1	11.6	2 365	239	140	5 188	1.1
Freestone	204	-1.8	29.6	4.4	D	9.6	4.6	D	21.7	3 630	195	358	8 369	2.8
Frio	151	20.5	6.8	1.7	D	6.1	3.6	D	28.7	2 355	144	572	5 751	1.6
Gaines	234	25.2	21.2	1.8	D	4.6	2.7	1.4	16.7	1 925	133	316	5 501	1.7
Galveston	4 050	0.0	21.5	14.8	6.3	7.2	8.2	6.6	31.7	37 810	142	4 587	119 227	6.7
Garza	63	-0.7	29.9	0.8	D	5.6	D	1.9	21.2	860	172	88	1 929	0.1
Gillespie	274	0.1	20.4	7.9	5.7	12.9	6.8	18.7	14.4	5 730	258	215	10 212	3.1
Glasscock	13	4.3	D	0.0	D	D	D	D	32.8	155	114	11	667	1.1
Goliad	50	4.1	D	D	D	8.6	D	4.4	31.9	1 420	200	167	3 485	1.7
Gonzales	281	32.6	15.2	9.4	D	6.8	3.4	D	16.0	3 845	202	655	8 287	1.1
Gray	381	3.5	39.7	23.8	D	8.5	5.2	D	14.5	4 790	223	456	10 518	-0.5
Grayson	1 766	0.2	32.2	24.3	4.7	9.9	8.2	16.0	12.5	21 415	186	2 176	49 360	2.2
Gregg	2 655	0.0	28.1	13.8	9.0	11.0	5.7	14.5	10.2	20 785	182	3 382	47 152	1.7
Grimes	262	2.6	34.6	25.7	6.0	5.8	3.3	4.5	28.6	3 830	153	589	9 681	2.0

1. Covers mining, construction, and manufacturing.   2. Per 1,000 resident population estimated as of July 1 of the year shown.

Table B. States and Counties — Housing, Labor Force, and Employment

STATE County	Housing units, 2000 Occupied units Total	Percent	Owner-occupied Median value[1]	Median owner cost as a percent of income With a mortgage	Without a mortgage[2]	Renter-occupied Median rent[3]	Median rent as a percent of income	Sub-standard units[4] (percent)	Civilian labor force, 2003 Total	Percent change, 2002–2003	Unemployment Total	Rate[5]	Civilian employment,[6] 2000 Total	Percent Management, professional and related occupations	Production, transportation, and material moving occupations
	89	90	91	92	93	94	95	96	97	98	99	100	101	102	103
TEXAS—Cont'd															
Caldwell	10 816	69.6	68 000	20.4	10.6	472	22.6	9.7	16 108	2.0	1 205	7.5	13 403	24.1	16.6
Calhoun	7 442	72.8	56 400	17.2	9.9	440	21.1	10.1	8 634	0.5	724	8.4	8 246	25.6	20.7
Callahan	5 061	80.8	49 800	20.3	10.6	394	22.9	2.8	6 637	2.6	302	4.6	5 593	27.0	15.8
Cameron	97 267	67.7	53 000	22.2	12.1	413	26.6	22.8	144 354	3.3	15 890	11.0	108 904	27.7	15.8
Camp	4 336	74.8	61 000	18.8	12.4	402	20.1	8.8	5 905	3.4	416	7.0	4 615	23.7	18.1
Carson	2 470	83.6	52 400	16.3	9.9	398	16.5	3.3	3 370	3.5	123	3.6	3 031	29.9	18.9
Cass	12 190	78.6	53 300	19.1	10.9	356	23.9	5.2	14 499	-1.6	1 059	7.3	11 875	23.5	22.0
Castro	2 761	71.0	51 000	18.1	11.3	363	20.3	14.6	3 319	3.5	171	5.2	3 353	31.4	18.0
Chambers	9 139	83.6	85 000	18.0	9.9	487	18.7	6.5	13 010	2.7	810	6.2	11 736	26.9	22.0
Cherokee	16 651	73.8	53 700	20.7	11.9	412	22.3	8.0	20 319	2.8	922	4.5	18 691	23.3	19.3
Childress	2 474	70.7	44 900	18.0	11.3	347	22.2	5.0	3 263	1.7	111	3.4	2 569	28.8	8.6
Clay	4 323	83.0	48 100	18.6	12.2	394	19.4	2.5	5 503	-2.2	208	3.8	5 307	28.7	17.3
Cochran	1 309	74.1	25 700	18.8	10.3	381	16.9	10.2	1 426	3.9	148	10.4	1 334	31.3	11.8
Coke	1 544	78.8	48 100	18.7	9.9	280	23.8	5.1	1 430	-2.6	35	2.4	1 450	30.8	15.0
Coleman	3 889	74.6	32 300	19.3	12.4	310	21.6	3.7	3 151	-2.1	225	7.1	3 655	28.1	18.9
Collin	181 970	68.7	155 500	20.5	10.8	798	22.9	4.0	323 154	0.5	20 091	6.2	266 999	51.8	5.8
Collingsworth	1 294	78.9	35 400	17.6	13.2	293	24.2	4.3	1 754	3.5	67	3.8	1 271	34.5	8.9
Colorado	7 641	76.7	59 200	19.3	10.3	375	21.2	7.5	8 446	4.3	409	4.8	8 721	26.6	19.8
Comal	29 066	77.2	117 000	20.3	9.9	626	24.4	4.9	44 593	1.8	2 165	4.9	36 319	35.4	12.4
Comanche	5 522	76.2	43 600	17.8	12.1	353	22.7	7.3	6 809	2.1	258	3.8	5 887	26.4	17.3
Concho	1 058	75.0	43 600	19.1	10.3	373	23.8	5.0	1 478	1.7	38	2.6	1 185	40.7	8.5
Cooke	13 643	72.1	73 100	19.2	10.8	458	21.6	5.7	17 776	5.1	850	4.8	16 443	25.2	22.8
Coryell	19 950	54.8	69 500	19.8	10.8	548	23.7	6.1	21 432	1.8	1 281	6.0	21 078	27.8	11.8
Cottle	820	71.6	26 900	15.8	11.4	218	19.2	2.9	886	5.9	54	6.1	808	30.2	8.5
Crane	1 360	85.3	39 100	17.2	12.0	403	19.1	9.4	1 828	5.8	124	6.8	1 449	25.5	18.3
Crockett	1 524	71.5	52 400	16.8	11.6	315	18.9	9.1	1 829	1.7	53	2.9	1 794	21.7	13.3
Crosby	2 512	69.3	35 600	18.9	10.7	334	23.1	11.5	2 928	3.4	201	6.9	2 649	30.7	14.1
Culberson	1 052	70.4	32 500	20.4	13.5	323	19.2	6.6	1 095	-3.6	92	8.4	1 293	23.6	11.5
Dallam	2 317	63.0	44 600	18.3	9.9	426	22.1	6.9	3 602	3.4	104	2.9	2 774	26.9	14.4
Dallas	807 621	52.6	92 700	20.5	11.3	647	24.0	13.4	1 245 374	0.5	97 810	7.9	1 060 458	33.8	13.1
Dawson	4 726	73.4	39 300	18.9	12.0	341	25.2	10.3	5 805	2.6	378	6.5	4 951	23.7	10.7
Deaf Smith	6 180	67.4	46 600	19.0	10.4	371	22.1	13.1	6 941	-2.9	415	6.0	7 122	26.5	21.4
Delta	2 094	77.1	39 400	21.4	13.8	392	24.5	4.5	2 824	-0.4	125	4.4	2 265	25.2	20.0
Denton	158 903	64.5	133 200	20.6	10.8	725	25.1	4.7	278 937	1.0	13 980	5.0	239 154	41.3	9.2
De Witt	7 207	76.6	47 100	17.8	10.4	344	23.4	5.5	8 710	2.5	399	4.6	7 893	27.7	18.7
Dickens	980	77.7	22 900	18.3	13.8	312	20.8	4.0	835	2.0	41	4.9	979	30.1	7.9
Dimmit	3 308	73.9	29 000	20.8	12.5	337	29.8	18.2	3 937	5.5	456	11.6	3 342	22.6	17.3
Donley	1 578	74.4	46 100	18.4	10.9	321	22.6	2.4	1 632	0.7	57	3.5	1 655	33.8	10.2
Duval	4 350	80.8	28 600	19.4	11.4	292	22.9	11.5	5 015	4.1	443	8.8	4 276	23.4	18.2
Eastland	7 321	76.7	33 100	18.8	12.1	360	23.7	4.6	9 168	-3.7	399	4.4	7 620	27.7	19.1
Ector	43 846	68.6	47 700	19.0	10.1	400	23.4	9.0	63 234	3.8	4 482	7.1	50 029	23.8	16.4
Edwards	801	79.7	38 200	25.0	12.7	400	17.3	12.9	815	-0.7	31	3.8	809	38.4	7.7
Ellis	37 020	76.2	91 400	19.6	11.0	584	22.2	8.2	57 667	1.5	3 972	6.9	53 528	29.1	18.1
El Paso	210 022	63.6	69 600	21.7	10.1	468	27.2	14.9	298 163	2.7	28 806	9.7	240 723	29.1	16.8
Erath	12 568	63.1	67 600	19.8	11.7	450	27.1	5.8	17 406	1.5	512	2.9	14 926	32.9	15.6
Falls	6 496	71.7	38 800	19.7	10.2	343	24.0	7.6	7 930	2.1	419	5.3	6 359	26.3	18.7
Fannin	11 105	74.7	54 500	18.7	11.5	432	23.4	4.3	12 436	-3.4	845	6.8	12 327	26.7	19.9
Fayette	8 722	78.2	71 600	18.6	9.9	400	20.4	6.5	11 172	-0.2	360	3.2	10 039	28.5	17.0
Fisher	1 785	76.8	31 300	16.7	12.3	274	19.9	4.9	1 820	-1.5	92	5.1	1 844	30.4	14.9
Floyd	2 730	74.0	37 900	18.8	11.0	366	22.5	13.2	3 123	0.8	280	9.0	2 945	30.2	13.6
Foard	664	75.0	26 100	18.0	12.7	268	22.5	2.7	731	-1.9	61	8.3	678	32.6	16.7
Fort Bend	110 915	80.8	115 100	20.3	10.3	730	23.8	7.9	208 885	2.8	12 291	5.9	166 172	44.4	8.9
Franklin	3 754	79.0	66 100	19.7	13.1	404	24.3	6.1	4 528	2.4	159	3.5	3 874	28.4	16.9
Freestone	6 588	78.6	56 000	18.7	11.3	378	19.5	4.9	8 779	1.9	469	5.3	6 967	25.3	15.7
Frio	4 743	69.0	35 100	21.1	12.8	335	24.0	16.1	6 131	6.0	508	8.3	5 257	21.3	12.8
Gaines	4 681	78.6	48 000	18.7	9.9	343	19.0	12.2	6 959	2.6	302	4.3	5 460	27.2	16.1
Galveston	94 782	66.2	85 200	20.4	11.8	571	25.4	6.3	126 304	3.5	10 376	8.2	114 221	35.9	11.3
Garza	1 663	70.9	38 700	22.9	10.9	315	21.4	6.0	2 459	8.2	115	4.7	1 834	28.0	11.0
Gillespie	8 521	77.5	106 400	22.7	9.9	529	23.9	4.6	10 855	1.7	261	2.4	9 301	33.9	9.0
Glasscock	483	67.3	56 400	19.6	9.9	331	9.9	7.0	606	-2.7	23	3.8	599	40.7	12.4
Goliad	2 644	80.3	57 400	18.8	9.9	357	21.5	5.1	2 630	-2.2	129	4.9	2 949	27.5	13.6
Gonzales	6 782	69.2	48 500	19.1	10.2	313	19.4	11.0	8 477	5.4	416	4.9	7 906	25.3	17.8
Gray	8 793	77.4	36 700	17.3	9.9	403	21.1	2.5	9 148	0.0	478	5.2	8 750	24.0	17.3
Grayson	42 849	70.5	69 100	19.3	11.8	518	23.8	4.4	52 208	2.4	3 839	7.4	50 801	29.6	17.5
Gregg	42 687	64.1	76 800	19.1	10.0	474	23.7	6.0	60 419	2.5	4 175	6.9	49 089	29.2	17.7
Grimes	7 753	77.8	56 700	19.3	12.2	428	21.2	9.9	8 410	3.4	746	8.9	8 905	23.8	19.1

1. Specified owner-occupied units.   2. Median monthly owner costs is often in the minimum category—9.9 percent or less, which is indicated as 9.9 percent.   3. Specified renter-occupied units.   4. Overcrowded or lacking complete plumbing facilities.   5. Percent of civilian labor force.   6. Persons 16 years old and over.

	Private nonfarm establishments, employment and payroll, 2001								Agriculture, 2002			
	Employment						Annual payroll		Farms			
											Percent with—	
STATE County	Number of establishments	Total	Health care and social assistance	Manufacturing	Retail trade	Finance and insurance	Professional, scientific, and technical services	Total (mil dol)	Average per employee (dollars)	Number	Less than 50 acres	500 acres and over	Farm operators whose principal occupation is farming (percent)
	104	105	106	107	108	109	110	111	112	113	114	115	116
TEXAS—Cont'd													
Caldwell	515	4 113	745	433	735	184	118	80	19 527	1 402	37.5	9.9	54.0
Calhoun	415	8 041	430	3 995	713	217	303	328	40 818	328	26.5	29.6	59.8
Callahan	195	1 025	93	77	267	88	D	21	20 832	893	25.0	20.8	54.3
Cameron	5 847	86 874	20 302	10 820	14 195	2 533	2 847	1 701	19 578	1 120	59.0	14.9	59.5
Camp	240	2 833	420	369	516	70	D	77	27 005	399	36.6	4.0	54.6
Carson	125	795	185	D	142	46	20	15	19 165	363	12.4	57.6	61.7
Cass	569	4 973	1 047	562	975	226	102	96	19 324	956	28.9	9.0	52.7
Castro	197	1 350	268	131	285	104	18	28	21 096	535	7.1	55.1	71.8
Chambers	377	6 323	436	2 364	578	172	111	231	36 587	610	41.1	21.3	52.3
Cherokee	789	12 510	2 983	3 249	1 642	317	166	254	20 285	1 508	32.7	7.0	51.4
Childress	160	1 162	227	D	321	50	D	24	21 054	300	8.3	40.3	57.7
Clay	118	969	72	D	228	46	D	21	22 062	892	17.7	28.8	62.6
Cochran	62	399	159	D	64	D	D	8	19 669	292	3.4	58.2	64.7
Coke	65	603	D	D	86	D	8	15	25 526	335	6.6	44.8	52.2
Coleman	214	1 549	395	52	282	96	D	28	18 052	829	6.8	38.0	57.8
Collin	11 855	207 894	15 082	25 870	32 414	16 534	13 910	9 127	43 904	2 135	58.5	5.4	43.9
Collingsworth	72	468	147	D	110	37	D	10	21 207	449	12.9	35.2	62.1
Colorado	557	5 162	869	643	936	154	84	120	23 238	1 770	26.8	14.6	55.1
Comal	2 108	26 530	3 147	4 514	4 078	532	765	672	25 343	852	35.9	11.6	48.0
Comanche	300	2 498	541	241	508	138	47	49	19 711	1 352	19.2	19.0	59.4
Concho	54	563	D	D	50	D	D	10	18 027	411	8.8	51.8	65.9
Cooke	852	12 671	904	4 994	1 915	275	175	295	23 303	1 765	38.4	12.0	49.5
Coryell	711	8 278	995	469	1 668	422	1 143	176	21 239	1 221	22.7	21.8	49.8
Cottle	54	341	44	D	55	D	0	6	17 355	233	2.6	46.4	57.5
Crane	84	861	86	D	83	20	6	41	47 957	44	31.8	59.1	50.0
Crockett	124	1 045	22	0	271	D	14	19	18 411	198	3.5	71.7	55.1
Crosby	128	984	277	76	221	62	D	21	21 409	373	5.9	54.7	74.3
Culberson	62	487	84	D	160	D	D	9	17 649	74	4.1	68.9	60.8
Dallam	240	1 653	30	51	314	89	35	35	21 045	412	3.4	62.9	68.2
Dallas	63 613	1 505 640	114 956	164 136	132 142	99 111	117 264	63 999	42 506	730	61.2	4.9	45.8
Dawson	352	2 523	371	173	541	151	82	53	21 021	581	7.7	55.4	74.9
Deaf Smith	438	4 255	475	1 098	576	131	89	93	21 855	703	13.1	54.1	65.7
Delta	68	611	273	D	57	25	D	10	16 342	507	32.0	11.8	55.8
Denton	8 277	113 375	11 785	11 123	21 094	4 706	4 516	3 372	29 740	2 358	62.4	5.3	46.3
De Witt	370	3 625	809	795	577	188	107	75	20 597	1 786	21.7	16.3	54.8
Dickens	53	408	62	0	54	D	D	7	17 752	396	4.0	37.9	59.1
Dimmit	188	1 479	306	D	317	62	23	29	19 864	268	22.4	38.8	58.2
Donley	91	394	37	28	147	25	D	6	16 018	440	5.9	34.5	59.3
Duval	137	1 130	133	D	202	117	D	24	21 076	1 228	8.2	25.8	49.3
Eastland	477	4 957	745	859	707	138	76	119	24 052	1 166	15.7	20.5	52.9
Ector	2 983	40 725	6 006	3 827	6 449	989	1 110	1 115	27 367	287	65.9	16.4	46.7
Edwards	39	139	8	0	D	D	6	3	20 065	349	6.9	53.9	61.6
Ellis	2 062	28 669	2 201	10 053	3 947	712	494	770	26 850	2 089	45.0	9.0	48.3
El Paso	12 214	199 453	28 399	30 930	28 710	7 069	7 120	4 585	22 990	600	74.2	7.7	53.5
Erath	842	9 493	1 224	1 496	2 002	313	587	190	20 067	1 977	25.1	14.2	52.8
Falls	280	2 410	780	274	473	138	60	54	22 349	1 199	24.9	17.2	58.4
Fannin	508	5 505	1 006	1 173	970	452	83	141	25 615	1 976	31.2	11.8	50.7
Fayette	740	6 636	902	1 187	1 091	337	199	144	21 637	2 973	27.9	7.6	53.2
Fisher	77	740	163	D	97	53	16	17	22 932	595	10.3	37.0	57.5
Floyd	185	1 173	252	76	197	77	40	22	19 034	551	5.1	47.9	71.7
Foard	39	329	71	D	21	D	8	4	13 146	203	6.4	45.8	70.0
Fort Bend	6 291	80 899	6 705	11 486	16 317	2 174	5 491	2 744	33 923	1 560	48.2	11.4	53.2
Franklin	186	5 094	3 361	159	242	79	51	66	12 943	549	29.7	12.0	57.0
Freestone	354	3 139	446	120	643	127	66	82	26 275	1 468	27.3	12.9	51.3
Frio	256	2 063	468	59	508	81	24	41	19 860	537	13.8	38.4	60.3
Gaines	325	2 352	312	91	439	89	37	53	22 528	724	8.1	49.4	73.8
Galveston	4 808	68 155	12 037	6 858	11 002	4 119	1 934	1 889	27 715	664	60.1	8.3	53.9
Garza	122	1 227	112	D	114	35	D	25	20 720	246	13.0	48.8	67.5
Gillespie	832	6 428	1 345	456	1 450	235	210	136	21 125	1 812	26.5	19.9	51.3
Glasscock	19	142	0	0	D	10	D	4	24 944	199	5.5	72.9	74.4
Goliad	110	776	96	D	131	33	16	17	21 686	984	19.2	18.1	52.8
Gonzales	390	4 068	652	992	645	148	86	91	22 438	1 816	20.3	19.3	58.4
Gray	669	6 393	947	1 120	1 138	165	177	179	28 071	351	12.5	43.3	63.8
Grayson	2 560	39 252	7 590	9 235	6 142	2 413	968	1 062	27 047	2 597	46.9	6.6	49.4
Gregg	3 907	59 240	8 279	11 191	8 807	1 787	2 134	1 611	27 193	444	52.5	3.4	43.5
Grimes	336	4 370	205	1 663	749	153	175	131	30 069	1 704	34.6	10.0	52.6

STATE County	Land in farms					Value of land and buildings (dollars)		Value of machinery and equipment average per farm (dollars)	Value of products sold				Percent of farms with sales of —		Government payments	
			Acres								Percent from —					
	Acreage (1,000)	Percent change, 1997–2002	Average size of farm	Total irrigated (1,000)	Total cropland (1,000)	Average per farm	Average per acre		Total (mil dol)	Average per farm (dollars)	Crops	Live-stock and poultry products	$10,000 or more	$100,000 or more	Total ($1,000)	Percent of farms
	117	118	119	120	121	122	123	124	125	126	127	128	129	130	131	132
TEXAS—Cont'd																
Caldwell	305	15.1	217	2	107	345 037	1 676	25 529	35	25 029	11.9	88.1	24.7	2.1	300	5.1
Calhoun	248	16.4	756	5	95	578 008	868	62 054	19	57 600	48.6	51.4	44.8	14.9	1 940	25.3
Callahan	515	5.3	577	1	129	337 230	592	26 661	17	18 906	12.0	88.0	24.0	3.6	930	21.4
Cameron	350	-5.1	313	105	254	543 412	1 549	60 969	75	66 640	83.5	16.5	37.5	12.6	2 685	27.7
Camp	69	9.5	174	D	34	313 853	1 890	37 160	82	204 691	1.1	98.9	33.8	11.3	30	2.0
Carson	452	-3.4	1 244	47	249	542 179	444	88 518	44	121 360	32.2	67.8	48.8	19.6	3 483	56.2
Cass	193	12.9	202	0	78	257 062	1 254	31 762	32	33 753	9.8	90.2	24.4	5.2	126	1.4
Castro	564	0.9	1 053	207	444	661 867	665	157 311	593	1 107 742	12.7	87.3	62.6	45.4	8 959	68.2
Chambers	275	13.6	451	16	134	388 428	906	41 509	13	21 924	41.0	59.0	29.2	7.2	2 438	14.4
Cherokee	286	1.1	190	1	120	313 135	1 357	36 106	123	81 684	70.1	29.9	29.3	5.5	211	0.9
Childress	369	-6.1	1 229	4	156	499 851	322	90 402	14	45 308	53.4	46.6	38.3	13.3	2 629	65.3
Clay	654	8.3	734	1	186	458 162	636	46 556	39	43 906	10.0	90.0	42.9	9.4	1 635	32.2
Cochran	439	9.2	1 504	84	300	534 786	369	125 119	40	135 397	94.2	5.8	49.7	28.4	6 453	81.2
Coke	485	0.6	1 449	0	59	707 490	522	35 373	13	38 041	4.5	95.5	25.4	3.3	606	34.0
Coleman	642	-12.9	775	0	188	502 209	612	41 130	16	18 983	21.8	78.2	35.6	3.7	1 348	37.3
Collin	310	14.8	145	1	194	383 393	2 534	31 648	38	17 855	67.2	32.8	13.0	2.9	1 108	8.0
Collingsworth	507	3.9	1 129	25	200	506 619	456	71 677	34	76 224	72.9	27.1	43.4	16.5	4 764	65.5
Colorado	539	3.5	304	31	207	440 707	1 513	34 963	42	23 495	44.8	55.2	32.1	5.5	3 871	9.4
Comal	203	10.9	239	0	37	563 883	2 102	19 915	6	6 609	26.5	73.5	12.8	0.7	125	10.4
Comanche	543	1.5	402	21	225	436 729	977	49 280	103	75 823	14.3	85.7	40.8	8.1	2 145	24.0
Concho	544	-14.5	1 324	4	142	765 866	514	53 269	14	34 815	48.0	52.0	49.6	11.4	2 531	65.9
Cooke	459	-4.2	260	1	182	322 632	1 413	32 917	46	26 215	16.0	84.0	28.0	4.6	724	11.2
Coryell	493	-23.7	404	1	165	458 848	1 063	27 165	35	28 412	14.8	85.2	31.5	3.4	787	22.3
Cottle	574	13.2	2 464	4	149	587 636	234	55 925	13	55 920	31.2	68.8	40.8	10.3	2 552	75.1
Crane	D	D	D	0	1	1 117 129	112	40 814	1	29 605	0.2	99.7	45.5	9.1	271	25.0
Crockett	1 735	-10.3	8 765	D	1	1 779 196	202	46 129	10	51 706	D	D	49.5	16.2	1 188	32.8
Crosby	490	-13.0	1 313	121	294	582 138	466	128 225	40	105 998	91.0	9.0	59.2	33.0	6 414	78.8
Culberson	1 695	8.0	22 899	5	59	1 932 204	83	58 314	7	100 963	46.7	53.3	48.6	21.6	446	27.0
Dallam	884	-5.2	2 146	230	470	1 232 703	601	181 034	370	897 376	22.5	77.5	64.1	42.7	6 710	72.6
Dallas	89	-40.3	122	1	48	254 263	2 969	23 414	19	26 009	88.4	11.6	15.3	3.3	299	6.6
Dawson	572	-5.5	985	53	471	550 928	531	129 892	55	95 332	94.7	5.3	52.8	27.4	10 279	80.2
Deaf Smith	964	9.5	1 372	143	568	644 463	440	144 455	842	1 197 464	4.6	95.4	53.8	28.6	11 068	66.9
Delta	142	18.3	280	1	90	222 752	942	47 647	11	21 055	44.8	55.2	27.4	4.1	732	25.4
Denton	349	-3.9	148	1	160	454 653	2 898	31 612	49	20 824	24.0	76.0	18.3	2.4	893	7.0
De Witt	577	3.0	323	3	166	370 658	1 199	25 125	30	16 530	7.7	92.3	35.0	2.5	707	14.7
Dickens	567	6.4	1 432	7	135	424 696	286	42 503	12	29 741	41.8	58.2	35.9	7.1	2 413	66.7
Dimmit	571	10.2	2 129	3	42	1 088 490	493	23 446	27	102 569	9.2	90.8	30.6	5.2	239	16.4
Donley	584	-9.2	1 328	24	89	473 900	360	40 133	74	167 304	12.1	87.9	43.4	12.7	2 104	54.1
Duval	850	0.7	692	4	162	490 753	725	25 333	13	10 546	14.0	86.0	15.1	1.1	1 299	29.9
Eastland	498	0.2	427	15	192	295 011	729	26 613	30	26 036	30.0	70.0	30.0	3.3	3 137	25.0
Ector	504	9.1	1 755	1	4	261 924	141	18 504	2	6 525	14.9	85.1	13.9	1.4	236	5.9
Edwards	974	-14.7	2 789	0	19	1 127 482	418	34 182	7	21 413	2.3	97.7	36.4	3.4	874	19.2
Ellis	464	8.9	222	1	264	395 983	1 588	37 287	43	20 793	62.0	38.0	19.1	4.2	2 584	15.2
El Paso	114	-53.3	190	37	51	399 653	2 187	66 508	68	113 140	42.8	57.2	29.5	11.2	421	6.8
Erath	581	-5.2	294	15	212	398 442	1 332	43 820	208	105 065	4.8	95.2	29.4	7.5	3 102	19.0
Falls	409	13.0	341	1	261	318 101	868	53 342	68	56 709	25.7	74.3	39.4	11.3	1 243	19.3
Fannin	483	8.5	245	7	273	299 810	1 150	30 266	57	29 030	34.3	65.7	26.9	4.0	1 417	15.5
Fayette	552	7.2	186	1	221	353 597	1 879	26 558	52	17 389	10.2	89.8	25.4	1.7	498	5.3
Fisher	479	-16.7	805	3	229	297 987	427	59 347	19	31 789	52.1	47.9	38.7	7.9	4 012	65.4
Floyd	574	3.2	1 041	135	388	499 265	484	114 933	159	288 132	D	D	47.2	26.0	8 768	77.7
Foard	286	-7.1	1 411	2	113	472 664	343	69 643	9	46 630	43.9	56.1	47.3	12.8	1 158	65.0
Fort Bend	415	-3.9	266	16	194	465 595	1 926	45 762	50	31 956	73.3	26.7	27.9	7.1	4 211	17.0
Franklin	132	-2.2	241	1	59	309 234	1 228	37 010	64	116 363	2.0	98.0	39.9	15.7	347	4.6
Freestone	429	1.4	292	1	127	251 674	900	20 018	33	22 176	6.4	93.6	30.1	3.0	73	1.7
Frio	603	-8.9	1 123	33	152	856 965	782	59 255	71	132 153	45.1	54.9	42.1	11.0	6 424	24.8
Gaines	759	-1.7	1 048	221	565	609 909	602	142 036	145	199 744	73.0	27.0	52.2	33.7	27 082	72.7
Galveston	127	21.0	192	2	46	207 830	1 576	22 498	6	8 508	40.8	59.2	15.1	1.4	379	2.6
Garza	500	-2.7	2 031	11	88	517 465	266	61 429	10	39 585	64.6	35.4	40.7	14.2	1 398	57.7
Gillespie	645	-7.1	356	4	112	690 744	1 994	33 933	24	13 223	20.6	79.4	24.9	1.5	653	18.7
Glasscock	493	12.8	2 477	30	170	870 073	353	134 772	14	68 526	83.7	16.3	59.3	24.6	2 293	51.3
Goliad	506	16.6	514	1	113	480 885	908	24 007	17	17 209	10.2	89.8	31.0	2.6	485	16.1
Gonzales	696	-2.0	383	5	184	442 022	1 174	36 562	278	152 849	7.8	92.2	44.5	9.8	942	22.0
Gray	453	-19.3	1 290	18	158	491 149	428	89 312	95	270 276	7.9	92.1	40.7	10.5	2 044	48.1
Grayson	441	5.8	170	2	232	342 282	1 921	28 228	42	16 121	47.8	52.2	20.3	2.8	1 315	11.1
Gregg	47	-7.8	105	0	21	200 883	1 454	30 057	2	5 441	22.8	77.2	0.0	0.0	D	D
Grimes	415	12.2	243	3	131	440 901	1 798	28 559	32	18 659	14.2	85.8	27.5	3.3	116	0.9

STATE County	Value of residential construction authorized by building permits, 2003		Wholesale trade, 1997				Retail trade,[1] 1997				Real estate and rental and leasing, 1997			
	New construction ($1,000)	Number of housing units	Number of establishments	Number of employees	Sales (mil dol)	Annual payroll (mil dol)	Number of establishments	Number of employees	Sales (mil dol)	Annual payroll (mil dol)	Number of establishments	Number of employees	Receipts (mil dol)	Annual payroll (mil dol)
	133	134	135	136	137	138	139	140	141	142	143	144	145	146
TEXAS—Cont'd														
Caldwell	12 351	122	25	166	63.1	2.9	92	806	128.4	10.1	19	55	4.9	0.7
Calhoun	10 554	127	29	135	51.9	3.7	77	725	111.1	10.3	16	81	12.7	1.9
Callahan	420	5	8	38	7.2	0.8	36	266	65.4	4.3	3	11	0.5	0.1
Cameron	262 230	3 444	387	3 772	1 218.9	81.6	1 117	13 089	1 904.0	179.3	283	1 208	98.5	18.1
Camp	898	12	11	80	13.2	0.9	58	532	109.6	9.1	7	19	2.2	0.2
Carson	1 746	11	6	37	20.4	0.8	29	233	25.2	2.3	4	28	0.3	0.1
Cass	2 419	38	30	222	106.8	6.1	137	1 261	161.5	16.8	18	64	3.5	0.5
Castro	0	0	20	D	D	D	41	208	47.7	3.2	5	D	D	D
Chambers	53 773	419	22	D	D	D	83	648	133.8	9.4	15	84	9.8	2.1
Cherokee	2 190	32	39	250	75.5	8.4	146	1 542	262.6	21.5	32	94	8.2	1.5
Childress	670	49	14	101	51.7	2.3	38	309	43.7	3.8	3	7	0.2	0.1
Clay	349	5	7	51	17.3	1.2	34	267	53.3	4.1	2	D	D	D
Cochran	0	0	7	26	7.9	0.5	15	87	15.6	1.5	NA	NA	NA	NA
Coke	0	0	3	D	D	D	21	98	24.2	1.3	1	D	D	D
Coleman	0	0	18	102	29.9	1.2	53	324	57.1	4.2	8	15	2.0	0.2
Collin	1 884 948	11 083	737	7 373	7 169.8	326.9	1 301	20 311	4 220.4	407.2	430	1 982	349.3	58.0
Collingsworth	0	0	5	18	7.4	0.4	17	113	17.4	2.1	1	D	D	D
Colorado	1 461	17	40	235	84.9	4.3	113	879	163.3	13.3	12	D	D	D
Comal	248 051	1 747	99	653	320.1	20.0	317	3 242	633.3	55.7	84	339	28.7	5.0
Comanche	520	6	29	370	124.5	8.5	77	456	79.6	6.4	4	D	D	D
Concho	NA	NA	4	20	2.7	0.4	14	82	14.1	1.2	NA	NA	NA	NA
Cooke	8 655	60	45	354	102.5	6.6	240	2 013	355.6	28.9	18	68	11.7	1.1
Coryell	22 491	335	17	D	D	D	144	1 781	268.7	22.0	44	139	7.4	1.6
Cottle	50	1	1	D	D	D	10	40	10.3	0.6	1	D	D	D
Crane	0	0	6	D	D	D	17	129	21.7	1.8	2	D	D	D
Crockett	NA	NA	6	15	6.7	0.4	31	263	26.6	3.2	2	D	D	D
Crosby	0	0	12	171	65.4	4.8	33	226	41.8	3.2	3	6	0.4	0.1
Culberson	242	2	1	D	D	D	25	162	28.2	1.7	NA	NA	NA	NA
Dallam	648	3	22	275	191.7	10.0	43	250	65.3	4.3	7	11	1.3	0.1
Dallas	1 989 539	15 448	6 054	108 131	100 787.3	4 621.7	7 878	117 812	24 538.2	2 400.4	3 352	30 049	4 268.4	932.5
Dawson	0	0	25	122	91.4	2.8	68	553	95.8	8.6	10	39	1.8	0.5
Deaf Smith	595	3	46	368	120.8	10.0	88	595	113.9	8.9	14	37	3.6	0.6
Delta	779	6	2	D	D	D	19	94	16.2	1.2	1	D	D	D
Denton	832 815	5 987	423	3 935	2 762.2	141.4	1 143	16 966	3 180.1	284.9	324	1 540	177.5	29.7
De Witt	753	8	22	155	86.4	2.6	81	663	93.0	9.1	14	73	5.0	1.4
Dickens	NA	NA	1	D	D	D	12	54	7.4	0.5	NA	NA	NA	NA
Dimmit	721	14	7	17	6.2	0.4	34	328	50.3	4.5	3	D	D	D
Donley	0	0	2	D	D	D	20	114	23.6	1.7	3	6	0.7	0.1
Duval	NA	NA	6	D	D	D	36	203	35.2	2.6	5	11	1.0	0.2
Eastland	50	1	29	368	255.7	9.1	113	682	116.5	8.8	10	22	3.4	0.4
Ector	25 924	173	355	3 518	1 047.6	117.9	538	6 060	1 139.9	104.4	136	853	87.8	18.1
Edwards	NA	NA	2	D	D	D	9	47	5.8	0.4	1	D	D	D
Ellis	101 520	920	94	751	375.7	19.6	310	3 054	572.7	47.5	86	321	35.2	5.5
El Paso	307 811	5 271	1 000	11 129	6 089.3	309.6	2 134	28 986	4 698.9	430.5	550	2 458	285.3	48.1
Erath	8 299	129	43	378	118.9	6.8	157	1 674	274.1	24.6	26	80	7.8	1.0
Falls	797	12	14	D	D	D	68	435	65.4	5.4	9	31	1.3	0.3
Fannin	4 841	52	26	321	187.8	7.7	101	929	193.8	14.8	15	29	2.4	0.3
Fayette	1 361	15	39	411	318.6	10.6	141	1 063	185.9	15.2	17	63	3.7	0.7
Fisher	0	0	3	D	D	D	17	96	12.4	1.3	2	D	D	D
Floyd	100	1	19	181	58.0	2.7	32	206	47.7	3.2	6	12	0.4	0.1
Foard	0	0	2	D	D	D	6	22	4.3	0.3	1	D	D	D
Fort Bend	245 289	1 950	405	3 793	2 972.1	143.0	825	11 992	2 229.9	196.4	220	763	93.3	17.7
Franklin	9 047	105	5	19	2.6	0.4	32	220	37.2	3.3	7	18	1.1	0.3
Freestone	3 174	44	15	61	26.4	1.2	63	481	105.9	7.7	6	21	0.9	0.2
Frio	406	7	23	D	D	D	52	461	82.1	6.2	7	10	0.8	0.1
Gaines	374	4	22	182	135.6	5.2	62	470	88.9	7.4	10	24	1.3	0.4
Galveston	403 830	3 193	198	1 522	561.3	46.6	921	10 591	1 786.9	165.8	224	1 160	128.5	25.4
Garza	0	0	8	32	18.7	0.8	29	123	18.3	1.5	3	20	0.8	0.1
Gillespie	13 178	83	36	334	89.8	5.8	153	1 361	172.9	18.6	25	82	5.5	1.0
Glasscock	NA	NA	1	D	D	D	5	D	D	D	NA	NA	NA	NA
Goliad	NA	NA	4	12	2.8	0.2	20	100	17.4	1.3	2	D	NA	NA
Gonzales	604	9	38	353	153.3	6.0	82	728	99.2	8.4	14	41	2.1	0.3
Gray	0	0	42	309	178.7	9.6	130	1 068	169.1	16.0	24	98	18.2	4.2
Grayson	31 528	337	132	958	406.1	25.1	474	6 213	1 092.0	98.5	104	351	32.0	5.8
Gregg	40 841	303	342	3 564	1 863.5	114.0	734	8 825	1 549.7	145.1	134	649	74.8	17.0
Grimes	952	14	19	187	137.0	4.1	73	663	120.5	9.9	12	93	5.7	1.0

1. Establishments with payroll.

Table B. States and Counties — Professional Services, Manufacturing, and Accommodation and Foodservices

STATE County	Professional, scientific, and technical services,[1] 1997				Manufacturing, 1997				Accommodation and foodservices, 1997			
	Number of establishments	Number of employees	Receipts (mil dol)	Annual payroll (mil dol)	Number of establishments	Number of employees	Receipts (mil dol)	Annual payroll (mil dol)	Number of establishments	Number of employees	Sales (mil dol)	Annual payroll (mil dol)
	147	148	149	150	151	152	153	154	155	156	157	158
TEXAS—Cont'd												
Caldwell	28	68	4.3	1.2	18	556	39.2	9.7	36	370	14.1	3.7
Calhoun	30	270	16.6	9.2	20	3 815	2 689.3	208.8	53	524	15.2	4.2
Callahan	9	18	1.5	0.4	NA	NA	NA	NA	15	130	2.9	0.8
Cameron	339	2 278	126.5	42.7	235	12 694	1 732.8	242.4	513	8 349	278.2	71.7
Camp	14	27	3.7	1.2	NA	NA	NA	NA	17	96	3.5	0.9
Carson	3	9	0.6	0.1	NA	NA	NA	NA	10	D	D	D
Cass	26	86	4.8	1.5	26	546	63.9	11.4	47	548	14.7	4.0
Castro	9	28	1.9	0.7	NA	NA	NA	NA	14	D	D	D
Chambers	20	80	6.3	1.9	15	1 499	1 989.7	83.5	31	577	14.9	3.9
Cherokee	47	153	9.5	2.6	91	3 178	327.4	67.0	47	632	20.3	4.9
Childress	9	32	1.6	0.4	NA	NA	NA	NA	24	256	7.2	1.8
Clay	8	12	1.0	0.2	NA	NA	NA	NA	11	61	1.5	0.4
Cochran	4	8	0.3	0.1	NA	NA	NA	NA	5	16	0.5	0.1
Coke	2	D	D	D	NA	NA	NA	NA	7	D	D	D
Coleman	13	34	1.4	0.4	NA	NA	NA	NA	21	173	4.2	1.2
Collin	1 161	6 165	783.9	285.6	318	21 326	6 235.9	972.3	563	11 830	430.9	119.6
Collingsworth	5	25	1.6	0.9	NA	NA	NA	NA	7	43	1.0	0.2
Colorado	28	65	4.0	1.3	29	825	76.0	17.4	48	569	15.3	3.7
Comal	121	382	30.6	11.3	84	4 016	558.6	101.2	172	2 468	80.4	22.8
Comanche	12	28	2.6	0.7	NA	NA	NA	NA	22	165	4.8	1.3
Concho	3	5	0.3	0.1	NA	NA	NA	NA	9	81	2.8	0.6
Cooke	37	112	7.4	2.7	68	3 318	437.7	88.2	64	965	29.0	7.6
Coryell	35	265	16.0	8.2	25	556	52.3	12.0	60	1 201	30.4	9.9
Cottle	NA	NA	NA	NA	NA	NA	NA	NA	5	D	D	D
Crane	4	3	0.4	0.0	NA	NA	NA	NA	7	83	1.9	0.5
Crockett	8	32	2.3	0.8	NA	NA	NA	NA	24	218	6.4	1.7
Crosby	4	6	0.4	0.1	NA	NA	NA	NA	5	34	1.1	0.3
Culberson	2	D	D	D	NA	NA	NA	NA	21	224	6.0	1.5
Dallam	14	D	D	D	NA	NA	NA	NA	27	264	8.7	1.9
Dallas	8 030	90 234	11 406.1	4 676.3	3 383	151 686	29 962.5	5 499.4	4 194	98 652	4 045.9	1 102.7
Dawson	15	60	4.2	1.2	NA	NA	NA	NA	30	283	9.8	2.7
Deaf Smith	16	60	3.5	1.4	32	1 128	376.7	28.9	29	D	D	D
Delta	4	4	0.2	0.1	NA	NA	NA	NA	2	D	D	D
Denton	624	5 359	319.1	237.8	305	13 556	2 741.8	459.8	488	9 742	325.0	90.4
De Witt	20	71	3.8	1.2	24	721	87.9	16.4	37	290	8.9	2.6
Dickens	2	D	D	D	NA	NA	NA	NA	7	38	1.5	0.3
Dimmit	10	24	1.7	0.8	NA	NA	NA	NA	12	125	4.0	1.0
Donley	7	11	0.6	0.1	NA	NA	NA	NA	14	79	2.2	0.5
Duval	4	10	0.4	0.1	NA	NA	NA	NA	16	88	2.8	0.7
Eastland	30	86	3.7	1.1	25	713	98.3	17.4	43	382	9.3	2.6
Ector	192	1 005	69.1	26.5	203	3 526	1 286.2	115.6	234	3 806	119.9	32.9
Edwards	2	D	D	D	NA	NA	NA	NA	3	D	D	D
Ellis	96	298	25.2	8.6	174	9 635	2 397.9	285.0	113	1 652	52.5	14.7
El Paso	927	5 777	398.1	161.7	652	36 723	7 966.5	773.9	1 094	19 292	703.3	194.0
Erath	42	320	16.8	7.2	37	2 186	387.7	53.3	68	1 029	30.2	7.9
Falls	10	28	1.4	0.6	NA	NA	NA	NA	20	92	3.7	0.9
Fannin	27	70	4.6	1.8	40	1 784	340.6	43.6	33	281	9.9	2.7
Fayette	34	127	7.1	2.3	39	1 056	148.6	23.2	55	780	20.9	6.0
Fisher	6	8	0.4	0.1	NA	NA	NA	NA	6	D	D	D
Floyd	8	21	1.3	0.3	NA	NA	NA	NA	16	75	2.0	0.6
Foard	3	8	0.2	0.1	NA	NA	NA	NA	3	8	0.2	0.1
Fort Bend	517	4 843	1 024.3	303.6	270	11 923	2 704.9	452.7	319	5 889	205.4	56.2
Franklin	11	31	1.8	0.6	NA	NA	NA	NA	18	198	5.1	1.3
Freestone	23	87	4.8	1.6	NA	NA	NA	NA	24	297	9.2	2.6
Frio	8	28	0.8	0.2	NA	NA	NA	NA	23	168	5.7	1.5
Gaines	9	33	1.9	1.1	NA	NA	NA	NA	21	D	D	D
Galveston	333	1 375	131.6	52.5	160	7 279	9 182.6	392.5	485	9 156	301.5	82.4
Garza	1	D	D	D	NA	NA	NA	NA	13	115	2.7	0.7
Gillespie	48	125	8.2	2.8	45	721	70.7	13.1	67	815	25.9	7.6
Glasscock	1	D	D	D	NA	NA	NA	NA	1	D	D	D
Goliad	7	16	0.9	0.3	NA	NA	NA	NA	13	114	2.6	0.7
Gonzales	26	69	4.3	1.2	19	747	173.6	16.8	26	242	7.1	1.9
Gray	41	181	11.9	3.9	20	1 082	419.9	53.2	55	658	19.0	5.0
Grayson	162	715	52.6	19.6	140	10 223	3 557.3	365.4	200	3 312	104.8	30.7
Gregg	277	1 516	113.5	44.0	205	13 008	3 408.6	447.6	274	4 575	D	D
Grimes	22	52	4.3	1.1	21	1 910	386.9	63.3	25	D	D	D

1. Firms subject to federal tax.

Table B. States and Counties — Health Care and Social Assistance, Other Services, and Federal Funds

STATE County	Health care and social assistance,[1] 1997				Other services,[1] 1997				Federal funds and grants, 2002–2003 Expenditures (mil dol)			
										Direct payments for individuals[2]		
	Number of establishments	Number of employees	Receipts (mil dol)	Annual payroll (mil dol)	Number of establishments	Number of employees	Receipts (mil dol)	Annual payroll (mil dol)	Total	Social Security and government retirement	Medicare	Food stamps and Supplemental Security Income
	159	160	161	162	163	164	165	166	167	168	169	170
TEXAS—Cont'd												
Caldwell	33	506	19.2	8.2	29	88	4.9	1.1	147.3	63.4	31.1	5.2
Calhoun	25	288	11.9	4.9	31	106	5.7	1.6	111.3	42.9	17.2	3.6
Callahan	8	108	3.6	1.6	8	17	1.4	0.3	70.4	36.2	14.1	1.3
Cameron	509	11 065	498.3	216.2	338	2 279	96.3	30.0	1 665.3	423.2	248.0	142.4
Camp	19	174	6.9	2.9	10	28	1.9	0.4	79.3	33.7	17.9	2.9
Carson	2	D	D	D	9	22	2.0	0.3	46.0	14.5	7.8	0.8
Cass	39	723	28.5	11.6	33	144	10.6	3.5	203.8	92.4	43.5	7.6
Castro	6	58	1.8	0.6	18	55	4.7	1.0	59.6	13.1	7.3	1.4
Chambers	13	135	3.5	1.5	20	78	6.8	2.2	146.2	33.2	22.3	2.7
Cherokee	81	1 155	43.3	20.0	51	105	8.1	1.7	223.9	93.4	56.8	8.2
Childress	10	149	6.5	2.9	5	26	1.1	0.3	47.8	15.4	8.7	1.2
Clay	6	114	4.1	1.8	5	19	1.9	0.3	52.6	24.5	10.6	0.9
Cochran	1	D	D	D	1	D	D	D	38.4	7.4	4.3	1.0
Coke	NA	NA	NA	NA	5	14	0.8	0.1	20.8	10.1	4.6	0.3
Coleman	17	193	7.9	3.0	14	40	5.5	0.5	76.7	29.6	21.9	2.1
Collin	903	9 790	793.9	309.0	480	2 868	169.6	54.3	1 398.2	548.3	144.9	22.3
Collingsworth	5	133	3.8	2.2	3	7	0.7	0.1	49.7	8.3	5.9	0.7
Colorado	28	349	16.4	6.7	31	91	5.4	1.4	125.9	48.8	25.5	3.0
Comal	151	1 335	69.3	28.7	126	645	37.9	11.5	374.3	237.4	62.3	6.4
Comanche	25	357	13.2	6.0	11	53	3.0	0.8	99.7	37.0	24.5	2.3
Concho	4	D	D	D	2	D	D	D	23.2	8.0	5.0	1.0
Cooke	51	553	24.5	9.7	45	220	11.4	2.9	163.7	80.6	37.0	4.5
Coryell	33	439	18.3	7.9	55	200	11.3	2.9	216.7	122.7	27.6	6.1
Cottle	4	58	1.4	0.6	3	D	D	D	26.7	5.6	3.3	0.4
Crane	8	133	7.0	4.1	4	10	1.1	0.1	14.6	7.0	4.8	0.7
Crockett	2	D	D	D	7	66	2.9	1.0	18.0	7.8	2.8	0.6
Crosby	6	D	D	D	7	11	1.2	0.1	67.4	13.9	14.0	2.0
Culberson	1	D	D	D	1	D	D	D	14.2	4.1	3.1	0.7
Dallam	5	18	1.3	0.6	14	D	D	D	49.7	17.3	8.5	0.8
Dallas	5 123	69 423	5 748.0	2 306.3	3 683	30 022	2 019.0	651.6	11 483.7	3 097.3	1 575.0	348.1
Dawson	20	169	7.6	2.8	27	116	5.3	1.4	124.3	26.3	27.4	4.1
Deaf Smith	17	245	9.5	3.9	36	141	9.5	2.3	108.7	29.3	16.5	4.8
Delta	6	172	5.5	2.5	4	D	D	D	37.8	14.3	8.6	0.8
Denton	599	7 690	531.4	215.6	421	2 850	212.3	58.0	1 154.0	436.4	141.6	20.3
De Witt	26	407	19.0	6.9	28	83	5.3	1.3	114.5	42.2	27.9	4.4
Dickens	4	54	1.1	0.4	3	5	0.7	0.1	24.5	6.9	8.2	0.6
Dimmit	19	141	6.5	2.6	12	95	5.2	1.4	74.9	14.5	11.3	5.4
Donley	2	D	D	D	4	9	0.7	0.2	31.6	11.5	5.8	0.5
Duval	10	498	21.9	11.3	8	63	2.9	0.9	110.2	24.2	23.2	5.9
Eastland	39	447	19.3	8.5	33	111	6.7	1.7	140.0	56.1	32.2	2.9
Ector	227	3 674	163.7	68.9	233	1 777	194.4	40.8	500.9	212.4	116.0	30.0
Edwards	1	D	D	D	4	D	D	D	18.7	6.1	6.9	0.8
Ellis	113	1 385	73.2	31.0	108	488	31.1	7.9	407.9	199.5	88.5	12.7
El Paso	984	16 524	1 165.3	455.8	824	5 779	265.7	87.6	4 317.6	1 203.5	469.7	216.6
Erath	56	911	46.3	19.3	61	300	14.0	4.1	172.0	72.1	33.2	3.6
Falls	19	395	14.0	6.3	25	61	3.6	0.8	119.3	42.8	22.4	4.8
Fannin	34	699	24.5	12.4	24	82	5.9	1.2	205.0	82.2	39.4	4.4
Fayette	44	589	25.4	9.8	49	168	8.4	2.3	140.1	64.8	33.0	2.4
Fisher	5	57	2.3	0.9	6	16	1.1	0.2	37.9	11.7	7.6	0.6
Floyd	11	103	4.5	1.6	12	44	3.5	0.9	84.3	15.2	10.4	1.7
Foard	3	49	1.7	0.9	2	D	D	D	16.6	5.3	3.0	0.3
Fort Bend	441	4 969	297.4	122.0	337	2 296	141.9	44.5	724.8	355.0	96.9	27.2
Franklin	13	2 632	29.5	18.5	14	31	2.5	0.7	51.0	23.2	11.1	0.9
Freestone	26	310	11.3	4.6	20	83	5.4	1.2	90.9	41.7	16.3	2.8
Frio	22	288	12.7	4.6	13	54	1.9	0.6	94.0	22.2	13.1	4.5
Gaines	11	111	7.5	2.4	31	115	9.1	2.1	137.5	19.7	14.4	2.4
Galveston	360	4 424	215.2	97.2	358	2 159	134.4	39.7	1 642.4	500.5	252.4	46.0
Garza	3	84	2.3	1.1	4	12	0.9	0.2	49.8	9.3	8.2	1.0
Gillespie	56	587	29.5	10.2	47	144	9.7	2.2	122.5	79.1	26.7	1.3
Glasscock	NA	NA	NA	NA	2	D	D	D	18.3	1.9	0.6	0.0
Goliad	5	110	4.7	2.0	4	8	0.4	0.1	39.8	16.3	8.5	1.2
Gonzales	20	202	7.6	3.1	26	119	5.0	1.4	139.3	47.3	21.4	5.2
Gray	47	1 147	58.5	24.1	44	160	10.4	2.7	125.6	57.1	41.0	3.7
Grayson	278	4 362	225.0	104.6	123	649	32.9	9.6	561.4	294.3	126.7	15.5
Gregg	330	5 135	305.2	129.6	232	1 637	105.3	29.9	593.9	284.6	131.9	23.3
Grimes	17	363	13.4	5.8	16	46	3.6	0.7	113.7	44.9	22.1	4.7

1. Firms subject to federal tax. 2. State totals may include programs not allocated by county.

Table B. States and Counties — **Federal Funds and Local Government Finances**

STATE County	Federal funds and grants, 2002–2003 (cont'd)							Local government finances, 2002				
	Expenditures (mil dol) (cont'd)							General revenue				
	Procurement contract awards			Grants[1]						Taxes		
											Per capita[2] (dollars)	
	Salaries and wages	Defense	Other	Medicaid and other health-related	Nutrition and family welfare	Education	Other	Total (mil dol)	Intergovern-mental (mil dol)	Total (mil dol)	Total	Property
	171	172	173	174	175	176	177	178	179	180	181	182
TEXAS—Cont'd												
Caldwell	3.4	0.0	0.9	33.4	1.8	1.4	4.7	68.2	32.9	20.2	575	485
Calhoun	4.2	15.5	0.9	12.4	2.1	0.8	5.3	103.0	5.1	62.5	3 035	2 828
Callahan	2.1	0.5	1.1	7.6	0.6	0.5	4.6	28.4	15.6	10.0	781	574
Cameron	99.8	13.5	20.0	399.3	87.0	36.5	148.5	995.9	580.1	247.6	700	524
Camp	1.7	0.0	0.4	17.3	0.8	0.6	3.5	22.5	10.9	8.9	760	633
Carson	0.9	0.0	0.2	1.8	0.2	0.3	12.5	18.3	2.3	13.0	1 975	1 867
Cass	4.7	0.1	1.2	38.4	7.5	1.4	6.1	88.5	28.0	24.5	814	715
Castro	0.9	0.0	0.2	4.5	1.9	0.6	2.8	29.6	12.4	8.1	1 004	888
Chambers	3.2	46.6	3.8	8.7	1.5	0.8	16.4	102.6	17.3	70.8	2 600	2 409
Cherokee	4.9	0.1	1.3	43.1	4.3	2.0	7.0	90.1	50.2	27.4	577	482
Childress	1.8	0.0	0.6	6.0	0.8	0.4	6.9	24.2	7.2	4.3	570	429
Clay	1.4	0.0	0.4	4.1	0.4	0.4	7.1	40.2	11.4	8.7	763	718
Cochran	0.8	0.0	0.2	3.2	0.4	0.4	0.7	16.9	5.1	9.1	2 611	2 447
Coke	0.9	0.0	0.2	1.4	0.2	0.3	1.7	15.5	8.3	4.8	1 253	1 161
Coleman	2.5	0.0	0.5	11.6	4.0	0.5	2.5	30.9	9.2	5.7	644	520
Collin	74.7	444.9	51.2	50.1	9.7	7.1	33.9	1 562.0	177.7	1 071.2	1 890	1 644
Collingsworth	1.9	0.0	0.2	4.5	0.4	0.2	6.7	11.8	5.1	2.8	908	787
Colorado	3.3	0.0	1.7	23.6	2.1	0.8	3.6	48.9	14.3	22.5	1 103	959
Comal	27.6	1.0	2.4	19.7	3.4	2.2	6.9	239.9	40.5	161.8	1 901	1 643
Comanche	2.8	0.1	0.6	15.3	0.8	0.7	0.6	43.5	13.4	8.8	645	560
Concho	0.9	0.0	0.2	3.5	0.3	0.1	0.3	12.7	3.6	4.3	1 103	1 016
Cooke	4.6	2.0	1.2	11.9	1.8	1.5	12.6	122.9	40.1	38.2	1 014	800
Coryell	10.7	9.8	1.4	16.3	3.4	11.7	2.1	122.7	59.5	31.3	420	327
Cottle	0.6	0.1	0.1	2.6	0.3	0.1	9.6	5.2	1.9	2.4	1 351	1 200
Crane	0.4	0.1	0.1	1.1	0.1	0.2	0.2	24.0	1.2	19.3	4 986	4 818
Crockett	0.3	0.0	0.1	3.2	0.5	0.2	1.5	25.4	2.1	22.4	5 876	5 779
Crosby	1.1	0.0	0.2	6.6	1.1	0.5	2.2	21.3	12.7	6.1	890	777
Culberson	2.4	0.0	0.3	1.9	0.2	0.2	0.4	9.3	2.7	5.3	1 854	1 644
Dallam	1.2	0.0	0.3	2.1	0.6	0.3	0.5	18.1	6.9	9.1	1 473	1 163
Dallas	1 606.0	1 512.7	1 269.9	998.3	191.3	82.2	710.5	8 243.9	1 493.9	4 567.6	2 000	1 507
Dawson	2.8	0.0	0.4	14.2	5.7	1.1	9.5	48.6	15.5	18.5	1 259	1 086
Deaf Smith	2.2	0.0	1.7	12.9	3.1	1.2	5.7	54.0	20.7	16.6	902	790
Delta	1.2	0.0	0.3	8.6	0.9	0.2	1.3	13.5	8.1	4.0	744	638
Denton	213.7	84.3	22.5	38.5	7.8	13.9	144.9	979.0	162.7	633.0	1 296	1 127
De Witt	3.1	0.0	0.7	28.4	3.2	0.9	2.3	77.9	25.8	15.4	767	665
Dickens	0.7	0.0	0.1	3.4	0.4	0.2	0.4	6.9	3.0	3.1	1 134	890
Dimmit	6.2	0.2	0.3	23.5	8.2	1.1	3.5	35.5	22.4	7.9	774	591
Donley	0.8	0.0	0.1	2.9	0.4	0.2	5.0	15.8	7.8	3.4	868	696
Duval	3.0	0.0	0.2	39.7	3.1	1.2	7.6	46.1	19.1	15.7	1 223	1 073
Eastland	3.7	0.0	1.0	18.4	1.1	0.9	10.9	59.7	26.4	12.9	706	573
Ector	11.7	0.2	2.9	49.0	17.6	8.9	43.8	487.3	161.7	136.1	1 113	884
Edwards	0.7	0.0	0.1	2.1	0.3	0.2	1.1	9.9	3.3	5.4	2 602	2 522
Ellis	14.3	2.0	3.5	44.6	4.3	3.0	26.8	264.7	94.6	133.7	1 114	928
El Paso	744.3	643.3	125.2	473.6	110.7	63.9	143.0	2 086.8	1 013.5	639.8	917	721
Erath	4.5	1.8	8.1	17.0	1.4	1.5	8.6	65.7	26.0	29.9	905	721
Falls	3.8	0.0	0.7	35.2	2.3	1.0	1.9	33.4	19.2	9.9	545	396
Fannin	23.7	0.8	2.3	35.2	3.2	1.0	6.8	60.1	29.1	20.5	649	556
Fayette	4.8	0.0	1.3	27.1	1.2	0.6	3.3	47.8	10.5	28.5	1 279	1 135
Fisher	1.1	0.0	0.2	5.6	0.4	0.3	2.3	19.5	5.6	6.2	1 459	1 360
Floyd	1.7	0.0	0.9	8.6	1.6	0.6	4.6	22.7	11.3	5.9	789	702
Foard	0.3	0.0	0.1	2.4	1.8	0.1	0.8	4.9	2.3	2.0	1 320	1 213
Fort Bend	54.5	13.6	10.5	42.3	10.4	7.4	50.8	914.9	251.7	545.3	1 365	1 205
Franklin	7.8	0.1	0.3	5.0	0.4	0.3	0.8	17.8	2.8	11.5	1 188	1 081
Freestone	2.2	0.2	0.6	18.1	1.4	0.6	6.8	47.5	6.0	30.5	1 638	1 532
Frio	1.3	0.0	0.3	23.2	4.4	1.2	4.2	45.9	22.4	9.6	589	481
Gaines	1.4	0.0	0.3	6.3	1.3	1.0	5.0	69.0	7.8	38.3	2 676	2 588
Galveston	69.6	257.4	74.8	332.1	22.1	10.2	61.5	917.1	209.9	531.5	2 035	1 791
Garza	0.8	0.0	0.2	3.7	0.8	0.3	21.8	19.1	6.3	9.1	1 834	1 655
Gillespie	3.7	0.3	0.9	4.5	1.6	0.6	1.9	44.2	8.1	27.3	1 264	1 032
Glasscock	0.1	0.0	0.0	0.8	0.1	0.1	6.8	9.2	0.9	7.9	5 795	5 658
Goliad	1.0	0.0	0.2	8.4	0.7	0.3	1.8	19.8	5.5	11.5	1 622	1 524
Gonzales	22.0	0.1	0.8	29.8	2.8	1.1	6.4	60.1	20.9	15.0	793	655
Gray	3.7	0.0	0.9	13.2	0.9	0.8	0.9	46.8	12.8	26.0	1 176	1 018
Grayson	18.3	2.6	5.7	64.6	8.1	3.3	11.9	278.2	110.1	114.4	1 005	802
Gregg	23.5	1.3	4.7	75.8	22.2	4.3	11.9	349.9	112.6	157.7	1 392	1 044
Grimes	3.2	1.5	1.2	27.9	2.4	1.0	4.4	44.3	15.6	22.8	923	813

1. State totals may include programs not allocated by county.   2. Based on the resident population estimated as of July 1 of the year shown.

— # Local Government Finances, Government Employment, and Elections

STATE County	Local government finances, 2002 (cont'd)									Government employment, 2002			Presidential election, 2004		
	Direct general expenditure							Debt outstanding					Percent of vote cast —		
			Percent of total for —												
	Total (mil dol)	Per capita[1] (dollars)	Education	Health and hospitals	Police protection	Public welfare	Highways	Total (mil dol)	Per capita[1] (dollars)	Federal civilian	Federal military	State and local	Democratic	Republican	All other
	183	184	185	186	187	188	189	190	191	192	193	194	195	196	197
TEXAS—Cont'd															
Caldwell	63.4	1 810	65.1	1.8	4.5	0.4	3.1	39.8	1 135	61	65	1 598	43.7	55.7	0.7
Calhoun	103.3	5 015	53.0	19.0	3.3	0.8	3.7	62.9	3 053	43	86	1 407	37.0	62.7	0.3
Callahan	33.8	2 650	77.8	0.0	2.5	0.1	4.0	18.5	1 449	32	24	658	19.0	80.5	0.4
Cameron	1 051.5	2 974	64.8	1.3	4.2	0.4	2.4	1 007.2	2 849	2 209	772	23 787	49.2	50.4	0.4
Camp	22.0	1 888	71.3	0.5	3.0	0.0	5.2	22.0	1 886	31	22	514	40.1	59.5	0.4
Carson	18.0	2 734	72.3	1.3	4.8	0.2	7.2	0.8	119	182	12	409	16.5	83.2	0.3
Cass	79.6	2 642	53.1	24.8	4.1	0.2	4.1	24.6	817	76	56	2 058	38.1	61.6	0.3
Castro	30.3	3 748	46.7	36.3	4.1	0.0	3.3	3.7	457	24	15	734	25.9	73.9	0.2
Chambers	94.1	3 455	58.9	3.3	4.6	0.4	4.4	116.6	4 281	51	50	1 521	25.4	74.1	0.5
Cherokee	90.2	1 900	60.8	11.5	4.2	0.2	4.0	42.6	898	87	88	4 112	28.1	71.6	0.4
Childress	21.9	2 886	41.0	41.8	3.0	0.0	0.0	4.5	597	37	14	1 124	23.8	76.0	0.2
Clay	44.0	3 858	44.4	11.4	2.5	0.0	4.6	189.6	16 637	28	21	539	24.6	75.1	0.2
Cochran	19.5	5 605	69.1	13.5	2.5	0.1	4.4	0.5	132	18	0	368	22.5	77.3	0.3
Coke	14.5	3 774	57.4	0.0	2.6	25.7	3.0	0.9	238	18	0	430	16.5	83.2	0.3
Coleman	26.9	3 023	49.5	27.5	2.4	0.0	3.5	10.5	1 179	48	16	772	20.4	79.4	0.3
Collin	1 813.8	3 200	65.2	0.8	3.7	0.0	3.3	2 917.3	5 147	955	1 055	25 877	28.1	71.3	0.6
Collingsworth	12.1	3 914	48.2	24.6	3.0	0.0	5.2	0.4	139	23	0	301	24.8	75.2	0.0
Colorado	47.6	2 337	54.3	14.7	4.8	0.7	5.5	23.1	1 135	61	38	1 063	28.1	71.5	0.4
Comal	263.4	3 095	59.8	0.8	3.8	0.4	2.0	289.8	3 405	169	158	4 127	22.3	77.1	0.6
Comanche	39.0	2 876	42.6	35.0	2.6	0.0	4.1	10.4	765	57	25	973	27.7	71.9	0.4
Concho	11.6	3 001	39.4	31.5	3.0	0.0	3.6	2.2	570	28	0	253	22.3	76.7	1.1
Cooke	119.6	3 179	50.5	21.0	4.5	0.1	3.0	64.5	1 714	79	70	2 602	20.8	78.9	0.3
Coryell	122.3	1 642	59.4	16.3	4.8	0.0	2.9	97.0	1 302	285	112	5 821	29.0	70.6	0.4
Cottle	3.9	2 174	60.1	2.1	2.6	0.2	7.8	0.8	421	19	0	134	27.9	71.7	0.4
Crane	19.0	4 913	54.3	15.1	4.7	0.2	2.5	4.2	1 071	0	0	375	16.1	83.5	0.3
Crockett	22.3	5 845	71.7	0.5	1.9	0.3	6.2	2.1	549	0	0	427	27.4	72.2	0.5
Crosby	21.0	3 058	77.4	0.9	3.7	0.0	3.6	0.3	46	26	13	513	27.3	72.4	0.3
Culberson	9.6	3 375	61.4	2.2	2.0	0.1	1.8	5.8	2 041	62	0	308	47.9	52.0	0.1
Dallam	17.8	2 882	63.1	0.5	5.3	0.1	5.1	5.8	930	27	11	643	18.2	81.6	0.2
Dallas	8 330.3	3 647	40.7	10.5	5.6	0.3	3.5	11 419.3	5 000	26 742	5 971	127 125	49.0	50.4	0.5
Dawson	47.0	3 197	57.6	17.8	3.1	0.1	4.5	70.6	4 798	61	27	1 501	24.5	75.2	0.2
Deaf Smith	52.2	2 836	48.3	21.9	4.8	0.1	3.1	23.9	1 299	49	34	1 245	21.4	78.3	0.3
Delta	12.2	2 270	66.7	0.0	2.4	0.5	6.4	13.0	2 425	24	10	329	30.1	69.5	0.3
Denton	1 151.9	2 358	60.9	2.0	4.5	0.2	3.2	2 167.9	4 438	1 317	915	25 950	29.5	70.0	0.5
De Witt	80.0	3 984	45.8	38.7	2.2	0.0	2.6	22.2	1 107	49	37	2 274	24.0	75.8	0.2
Dickens	6.7	2 466	65.7	0.1	1.5	0.5	4.9	1.4	518	17	0	182	23.0	76.7	0.3
Dimmit	38.2	3 749	55.2	21.5	2.3	0.0	2.0	14.8	1 446	192	19	953	66.3	33.3	0.4
Donley	16.7	4 297	71.1	0.1	2.3	9.8	5.1	17.7	4 552	17	0	459	19.3	80.5	0.3
Duval	51.6	4 027	57.1	21.2	4.2	0.9	3.0	22.2	1 734	85	24	1 180	71.3	28.4	0.4
Eastland	59.5	3 266	67.0	15.7	2.1	0.1	2.4	23.0	1 265	68	34	1 387	23.1	76.6	0.4
Ector	478.2	3 910	41.3	33.8	3.9	0.0	1.6	261.0	2 134	200	229	9 055	23.7	75.9	0.4
Edwards	8.5	4 078	74.5	1.5	2.5	0.0	5.1	0.9	432	19	0	221	22.5	77.4	0.1
Ellis	288.9	2 406	70.4	0.2	5.5	0.6	3.8	390.4	3 252	214	222	5 624	25.1	74.6	0.3
El Paso	2 124.7	3 046	57.0	12.0	5.1	0.1	1.1	1 755.4	2 516	8 445	12 179	48 528	56.2	43.3	0.5
Erath	63.4	1 916	51.6	12.7	7.0	0.4	5.0	57.5	1 739	85	61	3 153	20.1	79.4	0.4
Falls	33.0	1 825	66.1	0.1	4.2	0.7	7.3	16.3	900	397	34	1 657	38.6	61.3	0.1
Fannin	61.8	1 951	63.0	1.3	4.1	0.1	6.4	45.7	1 444	538	59	1 842	33.5	66.1	0.3
Fayette	46.5	2 084	60.1	2.7	4.8	0.1	10.5	11.0	492	81	41	1 503	27.0	72.5	0.5
Fisher	15.8	3 729	42.5	35.4	2.2	0.4	4.1	12.6	2 971	29	0	362	39.4	60.4	0.2
Floyd	20.2	2 712	63.1	19.4	3.6	0.0	1.6	0.3	45	34	14	570	22.0	77.8	0.2
Foard	4.2	2 700	63.7	1.9	3.8	0.0	9.4	1.0	665	12	0	123	40.1	59.2	0.7
Fort Bend	889.8	2 227	61.8	0.7	4.8	0.5	3.4	1 606.4	4 021	532	740	18 823	42.2	57.5	0.4
Franklin	17.1	1 762	56.3	0.1	4.3	0.0	9.9	14.9	1 534	19	18	400	23.6	75.9	0.5
Freestone	56.5	3 041	74.0	8.7	4.3	0.0	4.7	21.8	1 174	41	34	1 171	29.0	70.7	0.3
Frio	46.7	2 872	47.9	1.6	3.7	0.2	4.5	233.7	14 382	28	30	1 234	49.2	50.6	0.2
Gaines	67.6	4 723	63.0	20.1	2.4	0.0	2.3	2.2	152	31	27	1 214	14.6	85.1	0.3
Galveston	889.1	3 404	57.6	6.7	5.1	0.2	2.7	1 220.8	4 673	865	886	27 978	41.5	58.0	0.5
Garza	17.3	3 480	59.0	8.2	5.7	1.0	4.1	0.2	42	18	0	382	18.0	81.7	0.3
Gillespie	47.4	2 194	55.5	5.4	8.0	0.0	5.2	33.4	1 547	70	40	1 021	18.3	80.9	0.8
Glasscock	8.4	6 166	68.7	0.0	1.7	0.0	11.1	0.0	0	0	0	133	8.3	91.6	0.2
Goliad	19.2	2 716	60.9	2.7	6.7	0.3	9.4	3.7	529	18	13	461	34.9	64.8	0.3
Gonzales	59.0	3 123	43.9	31.6	3.1	0.0	5.6	19.7	1 043	76	35	1 314	28.4	71.3	0.4
Gray	44.0	1 992	57.3	0.2	6.1	0.0	6.2	24.0	1 086	65	41	1 452	15.0	84.7	0.2
Grayson	279.5	2 455	57.3	3.9	4.5	0.7	3.8	297.7	2 615	344	213	5 551	30.2	69.4	0.4
Gregg	348.9	3 081	51.6	11.0	5.7	0.0	3.8	360.0	3 179	315	212	7 227	29.1	70.7	0.2
Grimes	43.3	1 749	64.3	0.6	7.1	0.0	6.1	24.2	979	49	46	1 860	33.9	65.7	0.5

1. Based on the resident population estimated as of July 1 of the year shown.

Table B. States and Counties — **Land Area and Population**

STATE/ County code	CBSA code[1]	County Type[2]	STATE County	Land area[3] (sq km) 2000	Total persons	Rank	Per square kilometer	White	Black	Am. Indian, Alaska Native	Asian and Pacific Islander	Percent Hispanic or Latino[4]	Under 5 years	5 to 17 years	18 to 24 years	25 to 34 years	35 to 44 years	45 to 54 years
					1	2	3	4	5	6	7	8	9	10	11	12	13	14	15
			TEXAS—Cont'd															
48 187	41700	1	Guadalupe	1 842	97 101	556	52.7	60.2	5.0	0.6	1.1	33.8	6.7	20.4	10.7	11.9	15.1	13.3
48 189	38380	4	Hale	2 602	35 874	1 244	13.8	44.2	5.1	0.5	0.4	50.1	8.8	21.5	12.3	11.8	13.6	11.1
48 191	...	9	Hall	2 339	3 833	2 925	1.6	62.1	8.1	0.3	0.2	29.5	7.7	19.7	8.5	9.1	11.6	11.1
48 193	...	6	Hamilton	2 164	8 118	2 587	3.8	90.7	0.2	0.8	0.2	8.5	5.6	17.8	8.1	9.1	12.5	12.3
48 195	...	7	Hansford	2 382	5 210	2 828	2.2	64.0	0.2	0.4	0.5	35.0	7.1	20.5	9.2	10.3	14.4	13.6
48 197	...	7	Hardeman	1 801	4 440	2 877	2.5	79.8	5.0	0.9	0.3	14.4	5.5	17.8	9.4	9.5	12.4	14.1
48 199	13140	2	Hardin	2 316	49 634	937	21.4	90.0	6.6	0.9	0.4	2.9	6.7	19.6	10.2	11.7	14.8	14.3
48 201	26420	1	Harris	4 478	3 596 086	3	803.1	40.3	18.2	0.5	5.8	36.0	8.7	20.5	9.9	16.2	15.7	13.2
48 203	32220	4	Harrison	2 328	62 708	787	26.9	69.4	23.6	0.6	0.5	6.5	6.5	19.1	12.0	11.0	14.4	14.2
48 205	...	9	Hartley	3 787	5 223	2 826	1.4	78.1	6.6	0.3	0.3	14.7	6.8	15.8	5.8	13.6	18.7	15.9
48 207	...	6	Haskell	2 339	5 739	2 793	2.5	72.6	3.4	0.5	0.3	23.5	6.0	17.3	8.4	7.9	13.0	13.8
48 209	12420	1	Hays	1 756	114 193	485	65.0	64.1	3.8	0.7	1.1	31.1	6.7	17.7	16.9	15.1	13.4	12.2
48 211	...	9	Hemphill	2 356	3 333	2 958	1.4	79.7	1.6	0.9	0.3	17.7	6.3	20.9	8.4	9.7	14.1	15.5
48 213	11980	4	Henderson	2 264	77 277	673	34.1	85.2	6.4	1.0	0.4	7.8	6.4	17.6	9.5	10.9	12.9	12.9
48 215	32580	2	Hidalgo	4 066	635 540	89	156.3	9.7	0.3	0.1	0.7	89.2	11.3	24.4	11.5	14.3	12.0	9.5
48 217	...	6	Hill	2 493	34 444	1 292	13.8	77.3	7.2	1.0	0.4	15.1	7.2	18.3	10.2	11.2	12.8	12.5
48 219	30220	6	Hockley	2 352	22 807	1 675	9.7	56.5	3.6	0.5	0.2	39.6	7.5	20.3	13.7	10.5	13.9	12.5
48 221	24180	4	Hood	1 092	45 046	1 024	41.3	90.8	0.6	1.3	0.5	7.7	5.5	17.3	8.6	10.5	13.7	13.6
48 223	44860	6	Hopkins	2 026	32 681	1 345	16.1	81.0	7.7	0.9	0.2	10.8	7.0	18.8	9.7	12.4	13.7	13.2
48 225	...	7	Houston	3 188	23 109	1 660	7.2	64.5	26.5	0.4	0.3	8.5	5.5	17.0	8.7	11.0	15.7	14.2
48 227	13700	5	Howard	2 338	32 849	1 339	14.1	56.0	3.9	0.8	0.8	39.2	6.4	17.6	10.3	14.2	15.7	13.3
48 229	...	8	Hudspeth	11 839	3 193	2 966	0.3	19.5	0.8	1.1	0.2	78.5	6.8	25.6	11.2	13.8	13.0	11.7
48 231	19100	1	Hunt	2 179	81 024	650	37.2	80.3	9.3	1.3	0.8	9.5	6.9	18.9	11.7	12.5	14.2	13.0
48 233	14420	6	Hutchinson	2 298	22 959	1 667	10.0	79.5	2.7	2.3	0.4	16.5	7.1	19.5	10.5	10.2	13.2	15.1
48 235	41660	3	Irion	2 723	1 742	3 077	0.6	72.7	1.6	0.3	0.0	25.5	4.1	19.2	8.3	10.9	15.4	14.2
48 237	...	6	Jack	2 374	8 949	2 528	3.8	85.0	5.4	1.1	0.3	8.7	5.7	17.0	11.9	12.9	15.6	12.3
48 239	...	6	Jackson	2 148	14 247	2 149	6.6	65.3	7.5	0.5	0.4	26.6	6.7	19.5	10.3	10.6	14.2	14.0
48 241	...	6	Jasper	2 428	35 509	1 257	14.6	77.4	17.7	0.9	0.4	4.4	6.7	19.0	9.4	11.8	14.0	13.5
48 243	...	9	Jeff Davis	5 865	2 236	3 038	0.4	63.3	0.8	0.6	0.1	35.5	4.1	18.8	7.8	7.6	14.2	17.8
48 245	13140	2	Jefferson	2 340	248 605	241	106.2	50.5	34.9	0.6	3.2	11.7	6.9	18.7	10.5	13.1	14.8	13.8
48 247	...	6	Jim Hogg	2 943	5 024	2 841	1.7	22.2	0.5	0.4	0.1	89.3	7.6	22.8	9.5	10.2	13.5	11.7
48 249	10860	4	Jim Wells	2 239	40 469	1 124	18.1	22.2	0.5	0.2	0.5	76.7	7.9	22.5	10.6	11.9	13.5	12.2
48 251	19100	1	Johnson	1 889	139 068	405	73.6	82.7	2.6	1.1	0.9	13.6	7.1	20.5	10.7	13.1	15.5	13.3
48 253	10180	3	Jones	2 411	20 039	1 802	8.3	66.0	11.9	0.7	0.5	21.4	4.8	16.6	13.0	14.1	16.6	12.7
48 255	...	6	Karnes	1 943	15 276	2 079	7.9	39.3	10.4	0.3	0.4	49.5	5.4	15.7	12.9	17.9	15.5	11.4
48 257	19100	1	Kaufman	2 036	81 955	646	40.3	76.3	10.3	1.0	0.7	12.7	7.1	20.6	10.6	12.3	15.0	13.1
48 259	41700	1	Kendall	1 716	26 178	1 532	15.3	80.7	0.3	0.7	0.3	18.5	6.0	20.1	9.0	9.6	14.9	15.0
48 261	28780	9	Kenedy	3 773	408	3 137	0.1	22.3	0.0	0.2	0.5	77.0	9.1	18.1	12.3	10.8	14.2	10.8
48 263	...	9	Kent	2 337	770	3 121	0.3	90.1	0.6	0.1	0.0	9.1	4.2	16.2	6.9	5.3	14.0	14.3
48 265	28500	4	Kerr	2 865	45 311	1 014	15.8	76.9	1.7	0.9	0.6	20.6	5.6	16.7	8.6	9.0	12.3	12.2
48 267	...	7	Kimble	3 239	4 535	2 870	1.4	77.5	0.3	0.5	0.6	21.4	6.1	17.0	8.5	9.4	12.3	14.2
48 269	...	9	King	2 363	319	3 139	0.1	85.3	0.0	1.3	0.0	13.5	2.8	26.0	9.4	7.8	17.6	16.3
48 271	...	9	Kinney	3 531	3 311	2 960	0.9	47.0	1.8	0.3	0.3	50.9	5.7	18.2	8.2	10.1	11.4	11.9
48 273	28780	4	Kleberg	2 256	31 308	1 372	13.9	26.1	3.3	0.5	1.5	69.0	8.1	19.0	14.9	15.3	11.8	11.2
48 275	...	9	Knox	2 199	3 928	2 914	1.8	65.3	8.1	0.3	0.5	26.1	6.3	20.5	8.2	7.5	13.0	12.1
48 277	37580	4	Lamar	2 375	49 464	941	20.8	81.7	13.4	1.8	0.6	3.8	6.9	18.9	9.5	11.9	13.6	12.7
48 279	...	6	Lamb	2 632	14 637	2 121	5.6	49.8	4.1	0.4	0.1	45.8	7.6	20.8	10.4	10.5	12.7	12.1
48 281	28660	2	Lampasas	1 844	19 407	1 841	10.5	80.4	3.2	1.2	0.4	15.4	6.5	19.9	10.0	11.7	14.3	12.6
48 283	...	6	La Salle	3 856	5 822	2 787	1.5	18.8	3.1	0.1	0.3	77.7	8.6	20.5	11.3	12.5	13.8	12.0
48 285	...	6	Lavaca	2 512	19 063	1 858	7.6	80.2	6.6	0.3	0.2	12.9	6.4	17.1	9.0	9.0	13.0	13.6
48 287	...	6	Lee	1 628	16 530	1 995	10.2	68.1	11.6	0.5	0.3	19.9	6.7	21.0	10.5	11.0	14.0	13.1
48 289	...	8	Leon	2 777	16 017	2 030	5.8	80.6	9.8	0.5	0.3	9.2	6.1	17.2	9.2	9.5	12.9	13.4
48 291	26420	1	Liberty	3 004	74 117	691	24.7	75.1	12.3	0.9	0.4	12.1	7.0	20.0	10.4	14.5	15.9	13.2
48 293	...	6	Limestone	2 354	22 621	1 679	9.6	65.7	18.9	0.7	0.2	15.3	6.8	18.5	10.2	12.4	13.3	12.9
48 295	...	9	Lipscomb	2 414	3 092	2 978	1.3	74.2	0.5	1.6	0.1	24.0	6.0	19.9	9.3	8.4	14.7	13.9
48 297	...	6	Live Oak	2 684	11 902	2 298	4.4	57.4	2.4	0.5	0.3	39.7	5.4	15.8	11.2	11.2	14.5	14.8
48 299	...	7	Llano	2 421	18 034	1 915	7.4	92.6	0.4	1.0	0.3	6.4	4.3	12.4	6.3	7.8	10.6	13.5
48 301	...	9	Loving	1 743	62	3 141	0.0	88.7	0.0	0.0	0.0	11.3	8.1	12.9	6.5	3.2	12.9	25.8
48 303	31180	3	Lubbock	2 330	250 446	236	107.5	61.9	7.7	0.6	1.4	29.1	7.6	18.0	14.4	14.6	13.0	12.0
48 305	...	6	Lynn	2 310	6 182	2 756	2.7	51.8	3.1	0.6	0.2	44.5	6.7	22.6	10.3	9.4	15.2	12.6
48 307	...	7	McCulloch	2 769	7 896	2 603	2.9	69.7	1.7	0.5	0.2	28.1	6.5	19.4	8.3	8.7	12.2	14.3
48 309	47380	3	McLennan	2 698	219 807	267	81.5	63.9	15.2	0.7	1.4	19.8	7.5	18.9	14.3	12.5	13.0	12.0
48 311	...	8	McMullen	2 883	868	3 115	0.3	63.8	1.2	0.2	0.0	34.8	4.6	16.5	9.8	7.9	15.1	15.3
48 313	...	6	Madison	1 216	12 821	2 254	10.5	60.0	22.2	0.3	0.6	17.3	6.2	15.5	13.3	17.6	13.4	11.1
48 315	...	8	Marion	987	11 028	2 368	11.2	73.4	23.0	1.8	0.3	2.9	5.7	16.7	8.1	9.7	13.4	14.3
48 317	...	6	Martin	2 369	4 600	2 863	1.9	55.6	1.3	0.5	0.5	42.5	8.2	24.3	9.0	11.8	14.0	11.7

1. CBSA = Core Based Statistical Area. See Appendix A for explanation. See Appendix B for list of metropolitan areas with component counties.
2. County type code from the Economic Research Service of USDA Rural-Urban Continuum Codes. See Appendix A for definition.
3. Dry land or land partially or temporarily covered by water.
4. Hispanic or Latino persons may be of any race.

Table B. States and Counties — Population and Households

STATE County	Population, 2003 (cont'd) Age (percent) (cont'd)				Population — change and components of change, 1990–2003							Households, 2000				
					Total persons		Percent change		Components of change, 2000–2003						Percent	
	55 to 64 years	65 to 74 years	75 years and over	Percent female	1990	2000	1990–2000	2000–2003	Births	Deaths	Net migration	Number	Percent change, 1990–2000	Persons per house-hold	Female family house-holder[1]	One person
	16	17	18	19	20	21	22	23	24	25	26	27	28	29	30	31
TEXAS—Cont'd																
Guadalupe	8.8	6.3	5.0	50.8	64 873	89 023	37.2	9.1	3 758	1 898	6 107	30 900	36.3	2.83	11.2	18.9
Hale	8.4	6.7	6.1	49.5	34 671	36 602	5.6	-2.0	2 104	961	-1 913	11 975	2.3	2.86	11.6	21.0
Hall	10.8	9.8	11.2	52.8	3 905	3 782	-3.1	1.3	203	185	32	1 548	-7.2	2.42	9.0	32.4
Hamilton	11.6	11.1	11.5	51.4	7 733	8 229	6.4	-1.3	297	440	42	3 374	3.8	2.37	7.7	28.4
Hansford	10.1	8.2	7.5	50.5	5 848	5 369	-8.2	-3.0	253	180	-240	2 005	-5.1	2.63	5.9	24.0
Hardeman	11.1	9.6	11.0	52.7	5 283	4 724	-10.6	-6.0	154	195	-236	1 943	-7.5	2.40	10.4	29.5
Hardin	9.8	6.9	5.3	50.8	41 320	48 073	16.3	3.2	2 153	1 505	951	17 805	21.2	2.68	10.2	20.7
Harris	7.6	4.2	3.1	50.0	2 818 101	3 400 578	20.7	5.7	207 740	64 745	54 841	1 205 516	17.4	2.79	13.7	25.1
Harrison	10.0	6.9	5.9	51.5	57 483	62 110	8.0	1.0	2 638	2 043	92	23 087	11.5	2.62	13.6	23.7
Hartley	10.8	6.7	6.0	41.3	3 634	5 537	52.4	-5.7	224	107	-437	1 604	20.4	2.56	4.7	21.6
Haskell	10.7	12.1	13.5	53.4	6 820	6 093	-10.7	-5.8	241	286	-301	2 569	-6.7	2.33	8.8	29.4
Hays	6.7	4.1	3.2	49.6	65 614	97 589	48.7	17.0	4 970	1 668	12 921	33 410	50.4	2.69	9.0	21.0
Hemphill	11.0	8.1	7.1	49.2	3 720	3 351	-9.9	-0.5	132	108	-39	1 280	-5.0	2.50	5.9	24.4
Henderson	11.3	9.7	7.7	50.8	58 543	73 277	25.2	5.5	3 044	2 972	3 874	28 804	25.5	2.50	10.4	23.7
Hidalgo	6.0	4.9	4.3	51.4	383 545	569 463	48.5	11.6	49 286	8 565	25 815	156 824	51.6	3.60	15.7	13.1
Hill	10.4	8.4	7.9	50.6	27 146	32 321	19.1	6.6	1 641	1 344	1 831	12 204	18.9	2.58	10.1	24.8
Hockley	8.7	6.6	5.9	51.2	24 199	22 716	-6.1	0.4	1 080	619	-344	7 994	0.1	2.77	11.5	21.2
Hood	12.0	9.9	7.3	50.9	28 981	41 100	41.8	9.6	1 485	1 570	3 921	16 176	45.2	2.50	7.8	21.6
Hopkins	10.2	7.4	7.2	50.7	28 833	31 960	10.8	2.3	1 544	1 152	371	12 286	12.0	2.56	10.0	24.1
Houston	10.4	8.9	9.0	46.9	21 375	23 185	8.5	-0.3	813	1 030	168	8 259	6.0	2.44	14.2	27.9
Howard	8.8	7.8	6.8	45.6	32 343	33 627	4.0	-2.3	1 437	1 190	-1 017	11 389	-0.8	2.53	12.2	26.8
Hudspeth	10.6	6.6	4.0	50.5	2 915	3 344	14.7	-4.5	127	46	-237	1 092	15.4	3.03	11.4	21.1
Hunt	9.9	6.6	5.5	50.2	64 343	76 596	19.0	5.8	3 560	2 237	3 111	28 742	19.4	2.60	11.0	24.1
Hutchinson	9.4	8.1	7.7	50.8	25 689	23 857	-7.1	-3.8	1 069	877	-1 108	9 283	-3.7	2.54	9.1	23.9
Irion	12.0	8.7	6.3	49.4	1 629	1 771	8.7	-1.6	33	36	-24	694	15.5	2.55	6.6	21.8
Jack	9.7	8.0	6.9	45.2	6 981	8 763	25.5	2.1	321	300	166	3 047	11.8	2.52	9.2	24.5
Jackson	9.6	8.0	7.7	50.8	13 039	14 391	10.4	-1.0	605	446	-288	5 336	10.4	2.65	10.5	24.2
Jasper	10.8	8.4	6.8	51.2	31 102	35 604	14.5	-0.3	1 562	1 181	-414	13 450	17.7	2.58	12.5	23.3
Jeff Davis	13.1	9.0	7.3	49.2	1 946	2 207	13.4	1.3	62	70	40	896	15.0	2.39	6.9	26.3
Jefferson	8.7	6.8	6.8	49.6	239 389	252 051	5.3	-1.4	11 244	8 195	-6 481	92 880	2.6	2.55	16.2	27.3
Jim Hogg	10.7	8.0	7.6	51.1	5 109	5 281	3.4	-4.9	263	162	-359	1 815	8.4	2.89	14.6	23.4
Jim Wells	8.8	6.5	5.6	51.2	37 679	39 326	4.4	2.9	2 006	1 026	217	12 961	8.2	2.99	15.2	19.7
Johnson	9.0	5.5	3.9	49.9	97 165	126 811	30.5	9.7	6 175	3 292	9 197	43 636	30.4	2.85	10.0	17.3
Jones	9.4	7.2	6.5	39.8	16 490	20 785	26.0	-3.6	627	786	-557	6 140	-0.6	2.58	10.1	24.1
Karnes	7.5	6.7	7.6	40.6	12 455	15 446	24.0	-1.1	553	535	-172	4 454	2.7	2.66	13.7	24.4
Kaufman	8.7	5.4	4.3	50.5	52 220	71 313	36.6	14.9	3 586	2 236	9 050	24 367	36.7	2.87	11.3	17.8
Kendall	10.9	7.0	6.0	50.6	14 589	23 743	62.7	10.3	964	770	2 197	8 613	61.2	2.70	7.9	19.2
Kenedy	13.5	7.8	4.4	49.0	460	414	-10.0	-1.4	24	10	-17	138	-4.8	2.97	10.9	18.8
Kent	15.8	12.5	14.7	53.2	1 010	859	-15.0	-10.4	20	57	-50	353	-11.5	2.33	5.9	28.0
Kerr	10.7	11.6	12.9	52.0	36 304	43 653	20.2	3.8	1 639	1 998	2 026	17 813	23.8	2.35	9.2	27.5
Kimble	12.3	10.8	9.7	51.3	4 122	4 468	8.4	1.5	176	222	118	1 866	14.9	2.37	8.6	28.6
King	9.1	5.3	5.0	43.9	354	356	0.6	-10.4	10	9	-39	108	-12.9	2.77	1.9	16.7
Kinney	11.9	14.1	10.7	49.9	3 119	3 379	8.3	-2.0	119	127	-58	1 314	10.7	2.55	6.4	26.6
Kleberg	8.4	5.9	4.8	49.5	30 274	31 549	4.2	-0.8	1 679	774	-1 163	10 896	8.3	2.78	13.9	22.3
Knox	10.2	10.5	12.6	53.0	4 837	4 253	-12.1	-7.6	146	222	-254	1 690	-10.4	2.44	9.9	29.6
Lamar	10.5	7.4	8.1	52.1	43 949	48 499	10.4	2.0	2 107	1 793	690	19 077	13.6	2.48	13.2	26.1
Lamb	9.5	8.4	8.6	51.6	15 072	14 709	-2.4	-0.5	729	542	-238	5 360	-2.3	2.69	10.2	23.7
Lampasas	9.7	7.3	6.4	50.9	13 521	17 762	31.4	9.3	775	604	1 437	6 554	29.6	2.66	9.5	21.9
La Salle	9.8	6.2	5.4	46.7	5 254	5 866	11.6	-0.8	321	138	-221	1 819	6.9	2.89	15.4	22.9
Lavaca	10.4	9.4	12.2	51.8	18 690	19 210	2.8	-0.8	815	847	-107	7 669	4.4	2.44	9.3	27.6
Lee	8.9	7.2	6.8	49.5	12 854	15 657	21.8	5.6	721	417	575	5 663	20.3	2.65	8.8	23.8
Leon	11.7	11.1	8.6	51.1	12 665	15 335	21.1	4.4	620	634	691	6 189	23.6	2.46	9.2	24.8
Liberty	8.7	5.6	4.3	51.0	52 726	70 154	33.1	5.6	3 351	2 183	2 765	23 242	25.4	2.80	11.4	20.4
Limestone	9.7	8.0	7.6	48.8	20 946	22 051	5.3	2.6	993	904	502	7 906	2.4	2.55	13.5	25.6
Lipscomb	10.3	8.1	9.3	51.4	3 143	3 057	-2.7	1.1	115	104	24	1 205	-2.0	2.50	5.9	28.0
Live Oak	11.3	9.1	7.9	44.6	9 556	12 309	28.8	-3.3	428	313	-518	4 230	19.2	2.53	8.7	23.9
Llano	15.5	15.7	14.0	51.4	11 631	17 044	46.5	5.8	496	839	1 291	7 879	49.3	2.13	5.9	28.3
Loving	16.1	17.7	3.2	45.2	107	67	-37.4	-7.5	3	0	-7	31	-26.2	2.16	6.5	32.3
Lubbock	7.7	5.8	5.2	51.0	222 636	242 628	9.0	3.2	12 487	6 064	1 420	92 516	13.5	2.52	12.6	26.9
Lynn	10.2	8.0	6.7	50.5	6 758	6 550	-3.1	-5.6	258	184	-445	2 354	-1.2	2.76	11.1	23.1
McCulloch	11.7	9.7	9.8	52.3	8 778	8 205	-6.5	-3.8	298	388	-223	3 277	-3.9	2.47	10.2	28.2
McLennan	8.0	6.2	6.3	51.4	189 123	213 517	12.9	2.9	10 680	6 189	2 014	78 859	12.3	2.59	13.6	26.0
McMullen	13.2	9.2	8.3	49.5	817	851	4.2	2.0	19	15	17	355	11.3	2.40	5.6	30.7
Madison	9.1	6.8	7.0	41.5	10 931	12 940	18.4	-0.9	528	460	-258	3 914	16.9	2.57	11.7	24.5
Marion	13.7	10.9	8.2	51.2	9 984	10 941	9.6	0.8	409	477	174	4 610	13.9	2.35	11.9	28.8
Martin	8.5	7.2	6.3	51.3	4 956	4 746	-4.2	-3.1	223	166	-206	1 624	-0.5	2.87	9.5	21.7

1. No spouse present.

Table B. States and Counties — **Vital Statistics, Health Resources, and Crime**

STATE County	Births, average 1999–2001 Total	Rate[1]	Deaths, average 1999–2001 Number Total	Infant[2]	Rate Total[1]	Infant[3]	Physicians,[4] 2000 Number	Rate[5]	Hospitals,[4] 1998 Number	Beds Number	Rate[5]	Medicare enrollees, 2003	Serious crimes known to police,[6] 2002 Total Number	Rate[7]
	32	33	34	35	36	37	38	39	40	41	42	43	44	45
TEXAS—Cont'd														
Guadalupe	1 174	13.2	610	7	6.8	5.7	61	69	1	77	96	11 159	3 294	3 543
Hale	659	18.1	305	6	8.4	D	38	104	2	174	474	5 274	1 528	3 997
Hall	54	14.3	62	0	16.5	D	4	106	1	28	768	824	79	2 000
Hamilton	90	11.0	146	0	17.9	D	7	85	1	28	368	1 594	73	849
Hansford	89	16.6	59	0	11.0	D	1	19	1	113	2 113	863	51	909
Hardeman	52	11.1	69	1	14.8	D	9	191	2	44	958	991	87	1 763
Hardin	640	13.3	479	4	10.0	D	19	40	1	57	117	7 121	1 239	2 467
Harris	62 624	18.3	19 846	342	5.8	5.5	8 070	237	43	10 917	341	297 637	211 891	5 966
Harrison	792	12.7	632	8	10.2	9.7	42	68	1	108	181	8 073	2 666	4 110
Hartley	77	14.0	35	1	6.3	D	6	108	0	0	0	156	163	2 818
Haskell	68	11.1	91	0	15.0	D	6	98	1	32	520	1 460	78	1 384
Hays	1 448	14.7	512	5	5.2	D	107	110	1	113	128	9 618	3 283	3 221
Hemphill	46	13.6	36	0	10.7	D	4	119	1	19	538	464	29	829
Henderson	966	13.2	902	7	12.3	7.2	52	71	1	102	148	10 229	2 970	3 880
Hidalgo	14 846	25.8	2 799	63	4.9	4.2	513	90	5	1 036	198	58 418	34 075	5 742
Hill	479	14.8	410	1	12.7	D	17	53	2	140	459	6 326	1 033	3 060
Hockley	359	15.8	199	1	8.7	D	12	53	1	44	185	3 113	513	2 162
Hood	459	11.1	479	3	11.6	D	43	105	1	55	148	8 841	1 398	3 257
Hopkins	458	14.3	366	4	11.5	D	27	84	1	77	252	5 294	807	2 417
Houston	247	10.7	325	1	14.1	D	12	52	1	50	228	4 569	437	1 805
Howard	445	13.3	379	2	11.3	D	67	199	1	153	477	5 276	1 235	3 516
Hudspeth	38	11.3	17	0	5.1	D	0	0	0	0	0	354	35	1 002
Hunt	1 057	13.8	729	5	9.5	D	65	85	2	138	195	11 247	4 595	5 743
Hutchinson	327	13.8	270	3	11.4	D	22	92	1	40	166	4 028	962	4 201
Irion	11	6.1	11	0	6.1	D	0	0	0	0	0	254	28	1 514
Jack	102	11.7	91	1	10.4	D	4	46	1	18	242	1 281	124	1 355
Jackson	201	14.0	158	1	11.0	D	14	97	1	31	227	2 233	287	1 909
Jasper	498	14.0	390	2	11.0	D	31	87	2	96	287	5 794	1 121	3 014
Jeff Davis	18	8.3	24	0	10.7	D	1	45	0	0	0	393	19	824
Jefferson	3 458	13.8	2 569	30	10.2	8.8	526	209	7	1 589	657	38 007	16 223	6 162
Jim Hogg	77	14.7	47	1	8.9	D	1	19	0	0	0	840	69	1 251
Jim Wells	643	16.3	339	2	8.6	D	25	64	1	123	307	6 024	2 182	5 312
Johnson	1 862	14.6	1 024	11	8.0	5.7	75	59	1	102	86	16 409	4 825	3 643
Jones	198	9.6	233	1	11.3	D	11	53	3	85	455	2 711	503	2 317
Karnes	178	11.5	164	2	10.6	D	6	39	1	34	275	2 540	188	1 165
Kaufman	1 055	14.7	671	8	9.3	7.3	52	73	2	173	263	13 901	3 527	4 735
Kendall	306	12.9	231	1	9.7	D	28	118	0	0	0	4 310	449	1 810
Kenedy	8	18.7	4	0	0.0	D	0	0	0	0	0	59	12	2 778
Kent	5	5.9	16	0	19.2	D	0	0	0	0	0	206	12	1 338
Kerr	501	11.5	614	1	14.0	D	137	314	1	123	284	11 621	1 143	2 507
Kimble	52	11.7	63	0	14.2	D	4	90	1	18	436	873	121	2 593
King	2	6.8	2	0	0.0	D	0	0	0	0	0	31	2	57
Kinney	38	11.1	39	1	11.5	D	2	59	0	0	0	751	0	0
Kleberg	525	16.7	242	4	7.7	D	27	86	1	90	298	3 703	2 172	6 591
Knox	51	12.1	70	0	16.7	D	2	47	1	14	329	922	84	1 891
Lamar	672	13.9	586	3	12.1	D	99	204	2	355	771	8 618	3 893	7 685
Lamb	223	15.2	181	3	12.3	D	14	95	1	42	285	2 613	173	1 218
Lampasas	234	13.2	175	2	9.8	D	8	45	1	22	124	2 921	463	2 496
La Salle	102	17.5	51	1	8.7	D	1	17	0	0	0	807	127	2 073
Lavaca	233	12.2	267	2	14.0	D	21	109	2	56	298	4 941	211	1 052
Lee	214	13.6	152	1	9.7	D	4	26	0	0	0	3 984	322	1 969
Leon	187	12.2	199	1	13.0	D	5	33	0	0	0	3 984	259	1 617
Liberty	1 040	14.8	659	12	9.4	11.2	39	56	2	133	204	9 651	2 617	3 571
Limestone	290	13.2	302	1	13.7	D	12	54	2	74	354	4 175	951	4 129
Lipscomb	35	11.6	36	0	11.8	D	0	0	0	0	0	575	8	251
Live Oak	125	10.3	111	1	9.1	D	2	16	0	0	0	1 388	81	630
Llano	145	8.5	259	1	15.2	D	13	76	1	27	200	4 767	505	2 959
Loving	0	4.8	0	0	0.0	D	0	0	0	0	0	21	0	0
Lubbock	3 822	15.7	1 957	29	8.0	7.5	746	307	6	1 551	676	30 738	16 001	6 314
Lynn	87	13.3	66	1	10.2	D	3	46	1	24	358	1 007	124	1 813
McCulloch	100	12.3	132	0	16.1	D	8	98	1	27	309	1 760	197	2 299
McLennan	3 227	15.1	1 989	26	9.3	8.0	359	168	3	638	314	31 068	14 889	6 676
McMullen	4	5.1	6	0	0.0	D	0	0	0	0	0	139	9	1 012
Madison	160	12.4	143	1	11.1	D	14	108	1	28	236	1 744	303	2 242
Marion	120	11.0	148	1	13.5	D	4	37	0	0	0	1 877	360	3 150
Martin	75	15.7	53	1	11.1	D	4	84	1	26	516	625	53	1 069

1. Per 1,000 estimated resident population.   2. Deaths of infants under 1 year old.   3. Deaths of infants under 1 year old per 1,000 live births.   4. Data subject to copyright.   5. Per 100,000 resident population as of July 1 of the year shown.   6. Data for serious crimes have not been adjusted for underreporting; this may affect comparability between geographic areas and over time.   7. Per 100,000 population estimated by the FBI.

Table B. States and Counties — Crime, Education, Money Income, and Poverty

STATE County	Serious crimes known to police,[1] 2002 (cont'd) Rate[2] Violent	Property	Education School enrollment and attainment, 2000 Enrollment[3] Total	Percent private	Attainment[4] (percent) High school graduate or less	Bachelor's degree or more	Local government expenditures,[5] 2000–2001 Total current expenditures (mil dol)	Current expenditures per student (dollars)	Money income, 1999 Per capita income[6] (dollars)	Households Median income Dollars	Percent change, 1989–1999 (constant 1999 dollars)	Percent with income of $100,000 or more	Percent below poverty level, 1999 Persons	Households	Families	Families with children
	46	47	48	49	50	51	52	53	54	55	56	57	58	59	60	61
TEXAS—Cont'd																
Guadalupe	274	3 268	25 322	14.3	52.0	19.1	98.5	6 026	18 430	43 949	22.1	9.1	9.8	9.3	7.3	10.4
Hale	309	3 688	10 891	11.4	62.8	14.4	51.1	6 356	13 655	31 280	9.9	5.0	18.0	17.1	14.3	19.0
Hall	127	1 873	880	5.1	71.1	10.3	7.1	8 492	13 210	23 016	22.5	1.6	26.3	23.7	21.6	36.0
Hamilton	116	733	1 863	4.6	59.2	16.8	12.7	8 028	16 800	31 150	27.7	5.8	14.2	13.9	10.6	17.5
Hansford	125	785	1 408	4.4	59.9	18.6	10.6	8 183	17 408	35 438	2.3	6.3	16.4	14.9	12.0	18.4
Hardeman	223	1 540	1 135	2.3	62.6	12.8	7.6	8 675	16 824	28 312	12.9	5.2	17.8	16.6	14.6	23.3
Hardin	257	2 211	12 456	6.8	60.8	13.0	70.5	6 603	17 962	37 612	10.7	7.1	11.2	12.2	8.8	11.7
Harris	912	5 054	973 905	12.2	47.0	26.9	4 304.1	6 504	21 435	42 598	2.4	14.4	15.0	13.1	12.1	16.3
Harrison	358	3 752	17 187	16.3	55.8	15.4	76.3	6 027	16 702	33 520	10.3	5.3	16.7	16.4	12.9	17.9
Hartley	311	2 507	1 190	20.6	56.6	17.6	3.1	9 534	18 067	46 327	19.6	11.4	6.6	6.3	3.7	6.7
Haskell	124	1 260	1 375	2.2	65.4	14.4	10.1	9 233	14 918	23 690	-9.0	4.4	22.8	21.4	16.9	29.0
Hays	239	2 981	35 718	7.5	38.2	31.3	126.0	6 451	19 931	45 006	31.4	12.9	14.3	14.4	6.4	8.3
Hemphill	143	686	908	2.8	49.3	17.9	7.3	9 428	16 929	35 456	-8.0	5.1	12.6	12.3	10.9	15.0
Henderson	587	3 294	16 770	8.0	58.9	12.1	62.8	6 234	17 772	32 533	16.7	6.9	15.1	15.4	11.7	17.3
Hidalgo	487	5 255	188 181	3.8	69.8	12.9	1 003.7	6 952	9 899	24 863	10.8	4.7	35.9	31.9	31.3	39.1
Hill	198	2 861	7 820	6.9	61.5	12.5	42.8	7 051	15 514	31 600	17.2	4.8	15.7	15.5	11.9	16.9
Hockley	244	1 918	6 942	4.0	58.0	13.6	39.9	8 100	15 022	31 085	-2.4	4.9	18.9	17.1	14.8	20.3
Hood	135	3 121	9 233	9.3	46.1	20.5	43.2	6 064	22 261	43 668	2.8	11.5	8.5	9.0	6.0	9.3
Hopkins	216	2 202	7 986	7.1	62.1	15.1	38.2	6 245	17 182	32 136	15.2	6.5	14.6	15.4	11.3	16.0
Houston	157	1 648	5 478	12.4	64.7	12.2	26.1	6 939	14 525	28 119	15.4	4.2	21.0	20.9	15.6	23.3
Howard	239	3 277	8 543	6.3	60.7	11.1	37.2	6 622	15 027	30 805	-0.9	5.7	18.6	18.2	14.5	20.2
Hudspeth	344	658	1 000	4.0	74.5	9.7	6.4	7 355	9 549	21 045	1.7	3.1	35.8	32.9	32.6	36.9
Hunt	584	5 160	21 088	9.0	57.4	16.8	87.5	6 202	17 554	36 752	8.0	6.8	12.8	13.0	8.6	12.9
Hutchinson	218	3 983	6 379	6.5	54.5	14.3	31.1	6 484	17 317	36 588	1.9	6.1	11.1	11.4	8.8	12.9
Irion	378	1 135	474	5.5	52.2	21.5	3.5	9 677	20 515	37 500	15.0	9.4	8.4	10.0	8.3	8.2
Jack	131	1 224	2 103	10.8	60.8	12.8	11.7	7 151	15 210	32 500	11.8	4.5	12.9	13.5	10.1	12.2
Jackson	180	1 730	3 738	3.7	61.6	12.8	23.5	7 118	16 693	35 254	26.8	5.6	14.7	15.9	12.2	16.0
Jasper	280	2 735	8 698	6.7	66.6	10.5	49.8	6 933	15 636	30 902	12.5	4.3	18.1	18.6	15.0	20.5
Jeff Davis	87	738	555	10.1	44.3	35.1	4.2	10 415	18 846	32 212	26.2	6.3	15.0	15.2	14.1	16.1
Jefferson	636	5 526	67 831	10.3	54.7	16.3	306.2	6 904	17 571	34 706	2.8	8.3	17.4	16.9	14.6	21.3
Jim Hogg	435	816	1 506	3.3	70.3	9.5	9.4	7 996	12 185	25 833	30.8	3.7	25.9	28.5	24.2	27.5
Jim Wells	694	4 618	11 609	4.1	67.5	10.9	56.9	6 455	12 252	28 843	17.2	4.3	24.1	23.1	20.1	27.3
Johnson	263	3 379	34 577	13.3	55.7	13.8	152.2	5 891	18 400	44 621	8.5	8.8	8.8	9.3	6.9	9.2
Jones	235	2 082	5 352	8.8	70.3	8.2	24.4	7 700	13 656	29 572	14.2	5.4	16.8	17.5	13.1	18.8
Karnes	192	973	3 494	4.5	73.2	9.4	19.2	7 488	13 603	26 526	22.2	4.1	21.9	21.0	18.5	25.2
Kaufman	679	4 056	19 166	11.3	59.3	12.3	105.6	6 135	18 827	44 783	22.2	10.4	10.5	10.5	7.8	10.8
Kendall	121	1 690	6 471	11.6	37.6	31.4	37.0	6 122	24 619	49 521	34.4	17.0	10.5	9.6	7.9	11.1
Kenedy	926	1 852	104	2.9	64.0	20.3	0.9	13 456	17 959	25 000	12.8	3.6	15.3	13.8	9.9	11.0
Kent	111	1 226	179	1.1	58.9	15.1	2.5	17 396	17 626	30 433	16.1	5.4	10.4	10.8	9.2	11.1
Kerr	105	2 402	9 399	14.9	48.0	23.3	44.6	6 471	19 767	34 283	10.0	7.8	14.5	13.2	10.3	17.6
Kimble	214	2 378	1 035	4.3	62.1	17.3	5.8	7 770	17 127	29 396	24.6	5.1	18.8	18.0	13.4	21.3
King	0	0	84	2.4	47.8	24.6	1.6	18 547	12 321	35 625	-4.0	0.0	20.7	17.1	17.9	21.3
Kinney	0	57	807	2.0	60.4	17.7	4.7	7 134	15 350	28 320	33.8	4.9	24.0	21.8	19.2	26.9
Kleberg	889	5 702	11 650	7.6	54.8	20.4	44.6	7 331	13 542	29 313	-0.3	5.8	26.7	25.5	21.2	30.1
Knox	113	1 778	1 129	3.5	66.9	11.8	8.2	9 225	13 443	25 453	9.1	3.2	22.9	20.8	17.1	28.2
Lamar	1 005	6 680	12 054	8.8	56.9	14.5	57.4	6 382	17 000	31 609	9.2	5.1	16.4	16.4	12.8	18.8
Lamb	239	979	3 793	3.9	64.7	11.1	26.1	7 669	15 169	27 898	9.3	4.9	20.9	18.6	18.0	23.2
Lampasas	183	2 312	4 706	6.8	61.7	16.2	21.4	6 037	17 184	36 176	19.3	7.1	14.1	13.8	10.7	15.0
La Salle	245	1 828	1 545	2.3	75.6	6.4	10.2	7 862	9 692	21 857	4.2	2.1	29.8	30.2	28.2	34.6
Lavaca	60	992	4 471	16.1	68.1	11.4	14.6	6 746	16 398	29 132	8.7	5.1	13.2	15.4	10.2	14.5
Lee	300	1 669	3 941	11.7	65.0	13.1	18.9	6 339	17 163	36 280	25.3	6.2	11.9	13.6	9.7	12.0
Leon	287	1 330	3 454	5.3	64.1	12.1	20.1	6 743	17 599	30 981	14.4	6.4	15.6	16.2	12.6	18.3
Liberty	351	3 221	17 632	7.0	66.6	8.1	87.2	6 050	15 539	38 361	26.1	6.4	14.3	14.3	11.1	14.9
Limestone	391	3 738	5 437	4.5	62.6	11.1	31.0	7 454	14 352	29 366	11.4	4.1	17.8	18.0	14.4	20.0
Lipscomb	31	219	737	1.6	54.8	18.9	6.8	9 463	16 328	31 964	-3.5	5.8	16.7	13.9	12.9	17.7
Live Oak	54	576	2 803	8.2	61.2	12.0	14.7	7 531	15 886	32 057	14.2	5.4	16.5	15.6	14.1	18.9
Llano	176	2 783	2 364	7.6	49.1	21.0	13.8	8 211	23 547	34 830	36.1	9.1	10.3	9.2	7.2	13.8
Loving	0	0	27	14.8	51.0	5.9	NA	NA	24 084	40 000	12.1	13.3	0.0	0.0	0.0	0.0
Lubbock	1 052	5 262	80 919	9.2	46.9	24.4	279.1	6 608	17 323	32 198	-1.5	7.0	17.8	18.1	12.0	17.9
Lynn	73	1 740	1 884	4.7	66.1	13.4	12.8	8 328	14 090	26 694	11.5	6.1	22.6	23.0	19.3	24.5
McCulloch	513	1 785	1 813	2.9	64.5	14.0	12.7	7 676	14 579	25 705	15.6	2.8	22.5	23.2	17.3	26.5
McLennan	581	6 095	68 392	24.0	51.3	19.1	263.8	6 726	17 174	33 560	10.2	7.5	17.6	17.6	12.4	17.6
McMullen	0	1 012	191	5.2	60.5	16.2	2.4	14 149	22 258	32 500	-17.2	8.4	20.7	17.9	15.9	21.6
Madison	303	1 938	2 887	6.8	71.1	11.5	15.6	6 616	14 056	29 418	22.7	5.9	15.8	16.1	12.3	17.8
Marion	481	2 669	2 167	9.2	65.7	8.5	9.5	6 253	14 535	25 347	23.4	4.0	22.4	22.3	17.8	28.4
Martin	182	888	1 383	3.8	65.6	11.8	9.2	8 756	15 647	31 836	15.0	6.3	18.7	18.7	14.9	21.1

1. Data for serious crimes have not been adjusted for underreporting; this may affect comparability between geographic areas and over time.   2. Per 100,000 population estimated by the FBI.   3. All persons 3 years old and over enrolled in nursery school through college.   4. Persons 25 years old and over.   5. Elementary and secondary education expenditures.   6. Based on population enumerated as of April 1, 2000.

Table B. States and Counties — **Personal Income**

STATE County	Total (mil dol)	Percent change, 2001–2002	Per capita[1] Dollars	Per capita[1] Rank	Wages and salaries[2] (mil dol)	Proprietor's income (mil dol)	Dividends, interest, and rent (mil dol)	Transfer payments Total (mil dol)	Government payments to individuals Total (mil dol)	Social Security (mil dol)	Medical payments (mil dol)	Income maintenance (mil dol)	Unemployment insurance (mil dol)
	62	63	64	65	66	67	68	69	70	71	72	73	74
TEXAS—Cont'd													
Guadalupe	2 257	4.1	23 919	1 435	832	78	318	332	311	129	118	27	7
Hale	786	1.1	21 965	2 025	464	122	121	163	155	53	73	19	3
Hall	72	4.9	19 058	2 747	34	8	15	22	22	9	10	2	0
Hamilton	196	2.8	24 497	1 264	76	20	44	49	47	19	22	3	0
Hansford	103	-11.7	30 853	281	67	53	30	21	20	9	8	1	0
Hardeman	162	-0.2	22 854	1 762	42	8	23	26	25	10	12	2	0
Hardin	1 159	3.1	23 596	1 536	335	46	163	234	223	85	104	14	8
Harris	130 404	1.7	36 825	109	101 872	31 567	15 301	11 087	10 290	3 404	4 695	1 225	518
Harrison	1 424	2.7	22 806	1 778	849	119	233	259	245	92	100	28	7
Hartley	147	-6.4	28 436	498	35	46	25	9	8	6	1	1	0
Haskell	128	-3.8	21 900	2 039	50	14	27	37	36	15	16	3	0
Hays	2 623	2.2	23 910	1 438	1 178	219	400	293	269	107	101	24	10
Hemphill	112	1.4	33 435	174	54	24	29	13	12	6	5	1	0
Henderson	1 796	2.8	23 796	1 472	487	150	299	373	356	164	138	26	8
Hidalgo	9 056	7.3	14 769	3 082	5 171	1 009	1 084	2 404	2 266	460	1 076	558	63
Hill	729	3.5	21 634	2 112	257	77	119	175	168	67	71	13	4
Hockley	501	1.1	22 100	1 990	260	40	72	111	106	35	49	10	2
Hood	1 275	5.0	29 039	443	331	62	251	214	204	102	75	9	6
Hopkins	746	0.5	23 071	1 703	353	102	129	149	142	57	64	11	3
Houston	526	-0.1	22 703	1 820	310	40	88	131	126	47	60	13	2
Howard	712	2.6	21 501	2 148	438	46	125	167	160	54	75	15	3
Hudspeth	55	9.5	16 432	3 034	29	8	8	12	11	3	4	3	0
Hunt	1 875	2.1	23 424	1 588	914	113	233	346	328	133	133	29	11
Hutchinson	556	1.0	24 026	1 397	387	31	90	107	102	48	38	8	4
Irion	44	3.9	25 241	1 061	17	0	9	6	6	3	2	0	1
Jack	176	8.0	19 777	2 593	77	17	34	36	34	15	15	2	1
Jackson	318	-1.2	22 279	1 937	167	16	68	69	66	25	32	5	2
Jasper	776	4.4	21 765	2 076	374	82	120	201	193	70	91	20	7
Jeff Davis	48	11.4	21 852	2 053	29	-2	11	8	8	4	2	1	0
Jefferson	6 491	3.5	26 096	869	5 006	690	1 046	1 323	1 268	445	609	124	39
Jim Hogg	101	5.2	19 745	2 605	45	1	23	28	27	7	14	4	1
Jim Wells	810	3.7	20 242	2 489	446	54	103	226	217	57	119	30	5
Johnson	3 348	2.6	24 677	1 219	1 132	221	393	490	460	172	196	35	19
Jones	360	1.4	17 746	2 926	161	25	56	92	87	32	43	7	2
Karnes	249	2.9	16 260	3 040	118	15	45	71	68	22	35	8	1
Kaufman	1 941	1.8	24 892	1 162	739	119	229	327	310	116	143	25	15
Kendall	841	5.2	33 206	181	301	68	185	100	94	46	36	4	2
Kenedy	11	-3.7	25 650	966	10	1	4	1	1	0	0	0	0
Kent	17	-2.5	21 457	2 163	8	0	6	5	5	2	2	0	0
Kerr	1 318	5.0	29 416	400	522	163	464	250	240	123	81	14	3
Kimble	86	4.2	19 157	2 726	41	4	23	23	22	9	9	2	0
King	8	1.0	25 303	1 044	5	1	2	1	1	0	0	0	0
Kinney	63	6.2	18 368	2 849	24	-1	19	17	16	7	6	2	0
Kleberg	622	3.9	19 901	2 568	376	25	84	138	131	35	59	19	3
Knox	84	2.5	21 120	2 262	42	5	15	27	26	9	13	2	0
Lamar	1 108	2.3	22 598	1 852	690	116	185	245	234	91	105	25	1
Lamb	303	0.0	20 719	2 364	141	37	45	83	80	26	37	8	7
Lampasas	444	4.5	23 524	1 558	134	19	80	86	81	28	40	6	1
La Salle	93	-4.0	15 960	3 052	45	10	15	28	26	7	12	4	2
Lavaca	465	2.8	24 508	1 259	153	47	106	114	110	45	53	6	1
Lee	373	2.1	22 838	1 767	167	24	68	63	59	26	26	4	1
Leon	370	0.9	23 332	1 618	200	24	79	90	87	39	36	6	2
Liberty	1 694	2.8	23 015	1 718	512	196	170	328	312	102	159	28	13
Limestone	471	4.3	21 045	2 284	254	41	68	126	121	42	59	11	2
Lipscomb	82	4.5	26 632	759	38	14	20	12	12	6	5	1	0
Live Oak	211	0.1	17 584	2 943	108	8	43	46	44	17	21	4	1
Llano	422	3.7	23 608	1 533	131	26	112	101	97	49	37	4	1
Loving	4	0.3	65 922	5	1	0	2	0	0	0	0	0	0
Lubbock	6 203	4.1	25 067	1 113	4 093	623	992	1 061	1 005	338	490	103	12
Lynn	128	6.2	20 076	2 530	53	15	22	31	30	11	14	3	0
McCulloch	185	1.9	23 519	1 561	83	18	43	50	48	18	24	4	1
McLennan	5 212	4.1	24 003	1 405	3 553	457	825	893	844	328	310	92	18
McMullen	25	-1.0	29 107	429	9	3	9	3	3	1	1	0	0
Madison	283	6.4	22 118	1 982	117	61	53	55	52	21	23	6	1
Marion	199	3.2	18 054	2 887	49	19	34	60	58	23	22	6	1
Martin	90	-5.7	19 346	2 685	47	-4	20	21	20	7	10	2	0

1. Based on the resident population estimated as of July 1 of the year shown.   2. Includes other labor income.

STATE County	Earnings, 2002 Total (mil dol)	Farm	Goods-related[1] Total	Manu-facturing	Information and professional and technical services	Retail trade	Finance, insurance, and real estate	Health services	Govern-ment	Social Security beneficiaries, December 2003 Number	Rate[2]	Supplemental Security Income recipients, December 2003	Housing units, 2003 Total	Percent change, 2000–2003
	75	76	77	78	79	80	81	82	83	84	85	86	87	88
TEXAS—Cont'd														
Guadalupe	910	0.9	38.7	29.4	D	8.8	4.5	D	19.6	14 875	153	1 523	35 820	6.7
Hale	586	12.4	20.4	16.8	D	18.1	3.1	D	15.5	5 765	161	897	13 711	1.4
Hall	41	8.3	6.5	4.4	D	9.6	14.4	3.1	23.9	950	248	123	1 958	-1.5
Hamilton	96	10.7	D	7.3	4.9	12.4	3.8	D	21.7	2 185	269	137	4 459	0.1
Hansford	121	44.2	15.7	1.6	2.5	4.0	D	0.8	14.9	930	179	69	2 323	-0.3
Hardeman	50	4.1	D	D	2.3	8.9	4.1	5.9	28.9	1 130	255	146	2 331	-1.1
Hardin	381	-0.1	31.9	11.3	5.7	12.0	5.0	D	20.3	8 570	173	894	20 460	3.1
Harris	133 439	0.0	28.9	12.6	14.3	5.3	8.9	6.1	8.5	341 605	95	67 146	1 384 012	6.6
Harrison	967	0.6	43.1	31.2	7.4	7.8	5.2	D	12.0	10 730	171	1 806	26 741	1.8
Hartley	81	54.4	D	D	D	3.2	2.0	D	17.1	570	109	16	1 783	1.3
Haskell	65	12.1	8.0	0.8	D	13.1	5.8	6.7	25.1	1 635	285	167	3 537	-0.5
Hays	1 398	-0.3	23.4	11.6	8.5	12.7	5.5	8.5	24.4	11 565	101	1 309	40 733	14.3
Hemphill	77	20.7	27.8	0.4	3.0	5.5	D	D	15.2	565	170	29	1 535	-0.8
Henderson	637	1.6	22.3	11.0	D	13.9	7.3	12.3	16.6	17 140	222	1 174	37 016	3.0
Hidalgo	6 180	1.0	12.0	4.9	5.2	11.1	5.1	18.3	26.7	68 910	108	29 368	214 555	11.4
Hill	335	3.8	30.2	12.9	D	13.1	3.9	D	20.6	7 390	215	670	14 792	1.1
Hockley	300	6.0	30.4	1.7	2.8	6.7	4.1	5.9	21.4	3 790	166	505	9 276	1.4
Hood	393	2.9	17.5	4.6	10.3	14.3	8.0	11.2	16.0	10 225	227	432	19 706	3.1
Hopkins	454	9.4	22.4	12.4	D	10.6	5.0	D	16.5	6 290	192	733	14 309	2.1
Houston	350	2.2	17.3	11.4	15.2	7.5	5.1	6.8	22.0	5 220	226	872	10 848	1.1
Howard	485	0.3	24.2	11.3	3.4	8.5	4.7	D	32.7	5 950	181	937	13 704	0.8
Hudspeth	37	23.2	D	0.8	D	1.6	D	0.9	48.7	460	144	100	1 511	2.7
Hunt	1 027	0.3	36.6	29.8	4.9	9.0	4.2	5.9	23.2	14 340	177	1 830	33 109	1.9
Hutchinson	418	-0.1	61.0	33.9	2.2	5.8	2.1	D	14.3	4 605	201	348	10 921	0.5
Irion	17	-15.9	D	1.9	D	D	D	1.5	24.2	320	184	29	917	0.3
Jack	94	-1.3	40.3	2.2	D	5.1	6.3	3.6	18.5	1 665	186	120	3 687	0.5
Jackson	183	0.8	D	D	4.6	6.0	2.9	2.8	19.3	2 660	187	265	6 600	0.8
Jasper	456	0.0	32.7	27.3	5.1	10.3	4.8	9.8	16.7	7 505	211	1 156	16 931	2.1
Jeff Davis	27	-13.4	D	D	D	4.2	D	D	39.7	465	208	54	1 420	0.0
Jefferson	5 696	0.0	28.4	18.6	14.1	7.7	4.4	11.8	15.1	44 570	179	7 530	103 655	1.5
Jim Hogg	46	-4.7	14.6	1.7	D	10.9	D	4.4	47.7	1 000	199	243	2 344	1.6
Jim Wells	501	1.0	30.3	2.1	4.6	8.2	7.2	D	15.9	6 950	172	1 998	15 028	1.4
Johnson	1 353	0.6	32.7	21.3	D	12.0	5.3	8.8	15.8	18 280	131	1 773	48 870	5.6
Jones	186	1.6	9.4	2.8	2.3	6.5	4.7	5.6	50.5	3 475	173	389	7 327	1.3
Karnes	133	-0.5	15.0	7.5	D	6.6	4.4	7.1	43.1	2 745	180	606	5 519	0.7
Kaufman	858	0.4	D	20.0	D	11.6	4.9	8.0	21.1	12 385	151	1 578	27 967	7.0
Kendall	370	-1.2	20.7	8.9	8.7	19.0	14.0	5.9	15.1	5 005	191	167	10 648	10.8
Kenedy	11	13.5	D	0.0	2.2	0.0	0.0	D	16.7	50	123	7	282	0.4
Kent	8	-4.7	D	0.0	D	D	D	D	66.4	240	312	14	557	1.1
Kerr	685	-0.5	16.6	6.1	9.8	11.4	10.0	15.8	20.3	12 760	282	745	20 855	3.1
Kimble	45	-8.9	D	21.7	D	11.9	D	4.3	27.2	1 070	236	89	2 986	-0.3
King	7	28.4	D	0.0	D	0.0	1.3	0.0	34.1	25	78	NA	175	0.6
Kinney	23	-7.2	D	D	D	2.1	D	1.8	73.1	885	267	136	1 917	0.5
Kleberg	400	1.8	9.6	1.5	D	8.8	3.6	D	49.1	4 315	138	915	12 763	0.2
Knox	47	6.5	22.1	2.1	D	4.9	D	D	30.7	1 040	265	134	2 135	0.3
Lamar	807	0.6	D	29.5	D	10.5	5.0	14.4	14.0	10 160	205	1 707	21 564	2.1
Lamb	178	19.1	12.3	9.7	D	7.1	D	3.5	20.4	2 935	201	394	6 294	0.0
Lampasas	153	-0.8	D	14.4	4.0	12.1	7.5	7.5	21.8	3 415	176	349	7 754	2.0
La Salle	56	9.6	D	0.1	D	4.7	D	3.4	42.1	1 025	176	291	2 442	0.2
Lavaca	200	2.1	39.7	32.9	2.9	9.6	4.9	D	14.9	5 095	267	495	9 698	0.4
Lee	191	3.2	28.7	7.5	5.5	9.3	5.7	D	23.6	2 725	165	220	7 035	2.7
Leon	223	0.8	56.7	16.6	5.8	5.7	4.3	1.6	11.8	4 085	255	425	8 490	2.3
Liberty	708	0.4	31.1	20.6	3.7	11.1	6.0	D	19.0	10 730	145	1 694	27 378	3.9
Limestone	295	1.7	17.0	10.4	2.9	7.9	3.3	D	32.2	4 980	220	701	9 816	0.9
Lipscomb	52	17.4	D	D	D	3.3	D	0.4	19.7	610	197	37	1 528	-0.8
Live Oak	116	-5.3	D	D	D	7.9	3.9	2.8	38.3	1 810	152	261	6 268	1.2
Llano	157	-0.9	15.3	2.6	4.0	10.1	9.9	D	25.7	5 190	288	224	12 414	4.9
Loving	1	4.9	D	0.0	D	0.0	0.0	0.0	37.7	20	323	NA	70	0.0
Lubbock	4 716	0.6	11.4	5.9	9.2	10.3	8.0	15.4	22.2	35 420	141	4 994	105 501	4.9
Lynn	68	19.3	3.5	2.1	8.2	2.8	7.7	2.3	24.9	1 190	192	174	2 675	0.1
McCulloch	101	1.5	D	12.4	4.0	22.1	5.1	6.3	22.3	2 030	257	264	4 234	1.2
McLennan	4 010	0.5	24.7	18.0	5.9	7.7	10.1	10.5	17.3	35 450	161	5 278	87 375	3.0
McMullen	12	10.7	D	0.0	D	3.2	D	D	32.4	160	184	13	600	2.2
Madison	178	27.7	D	1.0	4.8	9.3	8.6	8.4	24.2	2 200	172	252	4 910	2.4
Marion	68	1.1	D	12.7	D	13.7	D	6.9	23.9	2 580	234	383	6 518	2.1
Martin	43	-12.5	D	D	D	12.5	3.9	8.2	31.9	735	160	84	1 966	3.6

1. Covers mining, construction, and manufacturing.   2. Per 1,000 resident population estimated as of July 1 of the year shown.

Table B. States and Counties — Housing, Labor Force, and Employment

STATE County	Housing units, 2000								Civilian labor force, 2003				Civilian employment,[6] 2000		
	Occupied units										Unemployment		Percent		
	Owner-occupied					Renter-occupied									
				Median owner cost as a percent of income											
	Total	Percent	Median value[1]	With a mortgage	Without a mortgage[2]	Median rent[3]	Median rent as a percent of income	Substandard units[4] (percent)	Total	Percent change, 2002–2003	Total	Rate[5]	Total	Management, professional and related occupations	Production, transportation, and material moving occupations
	89	90	91	92	93	94	95	96	97	98	99	100	101	102	103
TEXAS—Cont'd															
Guadalupe	30 900	77.0	91 400	19.8	9.9	508	21.8	8.1	49 439	1.6	2 053	4.2	40 845	28.8	16.5
Hale	11 975	64.8	53 800	19.2	9.9	408	22.0	11.1	17 162	3.5	1 100	6.4	14 646	28.0	19.8
Hall	1 548	74.3	24 100	19.3	13.3	310	20.0	9.0	1 770	-0.7	77	4.4	1 422	29.4	11.7
Hamilton	3 374	77.8	47 300	19.0	12.8	388	20.5	3.7	4 438	1.9	149	3.4	3 422	30.5	15.4
Hansford	2 005	74.4	49 900	17.2	11.3	375	20.2	6.6	2 481	1.5	76	3.1	2 419	29.8	16.2
Hardeman	1 943	73.2	29 300	17.1	12.1	327	22.6	3.5	1 838	5.8	141	7.7	2 121	27.2	18.0
Hardin	17 805	82.5	75 800	18.1	10.4	480	22.1	5.3	23 140	2.5	2 022	8.7	20 631	25.1	18.7
Harris	1 205 516	55.3	87 000	19.7	10.6	590	23.8	13.5	1 891 103	2.3	132 911	7.0	1 545 933	34.8	12.6
Harrison	23 087	77.2	68 400	19.1	10.7	442	24.6	5.6	29 549	2.6	1 911	6.5	26 290	26.1	20.8
Hartley	1 604	76.4	94 000	18.2	9.9	478	25.4	4.1	3 280	3.3	41	1.3	2 055	34.9	12.2
Haskell	2 569	78.9	30 600	21.4	12.9	329	24.1	4.0	2 898	6.8	138	4.8	2 417	34.7	14.1
Hays	33 410	64.9	129 400	21.0	10.5	628	31.1	7.1	57 473	1.6	3 236	5.6	50 484	36.0	9.6
Hemphill	1 280	77.3	56 800	18.3	12.2	453	21.4	4.7	2 154	9.5	29	1.3	1 571	30.7	13.0
Henderson	28 804	80.0	75 300	19.7	11.1	464	24.7	6.3	29 851	1.4	1 892	6.3	29 594	24.5	16.6
Hidalgo	156 824	73.1	52 400	23.0	12.1	401	26.0	25.5	232 358	6.4	31 580	13.6	180 121	26.3	14.4
Hill	12 204	75.0	54 700	20.7	12.7	436	25.0	6.4	15 448	-1.5	1 063	6.9	13 365	24.5	19.4
Hockley	7 994	74.4	50 400	19.1	10.3	410	23.6	7.4	11 493	6.3	514	4.5	9 572	27.5	14.0
Hood	16 176	81.2	112 100	19.9	10.6	541	23.3	5.0	19 103	1.9	1 285	6.7	18 203	30.9	12.4
Hopkins	12 286	71.4	61 000	19.3	12.8	430	21.7	6.3	15 182	0.5	869	5.7	14 451	25.5	20.7
Houston	8 259	76.1	49 300	22.8	13.1	376	26.1	6.2	10 018	6.3	532	5.3	7 958	25.2	16.4
Howard	11 389	69.5	39 000	17.8	10.4	414	25.1	5.7	14 155	0.0	699	4.9	12 092	30.8	14.1
Hudspeth	1 092	81.0	30 500	20.5	13.5	317	17.9	15.9	1 472	4.4	112	7.6	1 127	20.3	19.5
Hunt	28 742	71.4	62 000	19.4	11.2	476	23.9	5.7	37 043	1.3	2 621	7.1	34 539	28.3	16.8
Hutchinson	9 283	78.9	45 300	16.3	9.9	379	22.1	4.3	8 695	-1.4	642	7.4	9 849	24.8	18.3
Irion	694	77.7	60 800	19.3	9.9	491	14.9	4.3	771	0.4	30	3.9	849	29.9	17.9
Jack	3 047	76.8	44 100	19.3	13.0	360	18.8	4.4	4 080	4.2	131	3.2	3 331	25.4	15.0
Jackson	5 336	73.7	52 700	17.7	11.1	406	20.3	7.3	7 962	0.9	326	4.1	6 034	27.0	20.1
Jasper	13 450	80.6	59 900	20.0	9.9	392	22.7	5.5	14 713	1.3	1 774	12.1	13 327	22.4	19.3
Jeff Davis	896	70.2	59 800	22.8	10.9	354	16.6	4.4	1 611	6.8	26	1.6	1 031	39.0	5.9
Jefferson	92 880	65.9	59 400	18.5	10.8	477	24.5	6.6	119 222	2.9	10 739	9.0	99 640	28.8	14.9
Jim Hogg	1 815	77.6	32 400	20.5	9.9	366	22.3	11.8	2 348	2.8	156	6.6	1 877	22.7	12.8
Jim Wells	12 961	76.5	41 300	19.5	11.6	420	22.9	11.0	18 656	6.0	1 436	7.7	14 352	24.2	14.1
Johnson	43 636	78.9	81 900	18.9	11.3	540	22.5	5.8	67 032	1.6	4 493	6.7	59 464	26.2	18.8
Jones	6 140	79.2	34 600	19.8	11.7	376	23.9	4.6	10 040	2.8	342	3.4	6 849	27.7	14.9
Karnes	4 454	74.0	41 600	19.4	10.2	326	19.9	8.1	5 911	0.5	316	5.3	4 705	28.7	14.0
Kaufman	24 367	79.2	85 700	20.5	10.8	533	23.5	6.6	36 206	1.4	3 470	9.6	33 242	26.9	17.1
Kendall	8 613	79.6	139 900	21.7	9.9	659	29.3	6.0	18 072	7.7	549	3.0	10 902	39.9	7.4
Kenedy	138	40.6	22 500	16.3	9.9	425	14.2	12.3	224	7.2	4	1.8	187	38.0	2.1
Kent	353	78.5	24 200	18.4	9.9	247	14.7	3.1	488	16.5	22	4.5	382	41.6	9.4
Kerr	17 813	73.3	96 600	21.5	10.7	536	25.4	4.5	19 039	5.7	620	3.3	17 328	31.5	10.5
Kimble	1 866	73.6	50 700	23.2	12.6	365	25.5	6.2	2 299	3.0	61	2.7	1 954	28.8	13.6
King	108	38.9	13 800	0.0	10.8	217	9.9	8.3	152	-9.0	6	3.9	149	32.9	6.0
Kinney	1 314	77.9	45 800	19.4	11.4	369	23.6	10.4	1 273	4.0	90	7.1	1 005	34.7	8.3
Kleberg	10 896	58.6	51 800	19.6	11.9	447	27.1	10.4	13 971	9.0	845	6.0	12 361	31.3	11.5
Knox	1 690	75.4	27 800	18.8	12.7	250	19.5	5.1	1 997	6.8	88	4.4	1 587	31.1	9.6
Lamar	19 077	67.2	57 300	18.9	12.2	430	23.7	4.0	22 503	2.9	1 706	7.6	20 416	27.0	19.1
Lamb	5 360	75.6	34 300	18.7	10.3	342	21.5	7.4	6 854	2.9	427	6.2	5 728	28.2	17.9
Lampasas	6 554	74.0	72 400	19.9	9.9	439	22.1	5.9	10 215	5.1	399	3.9	7 679	30.3	11.9
La Salle	1 819	74.7	22 700	19.9	12.2	276	19.7	15.6	2 898	3.1	179	6.2	1 826	19.6	13.5
Lavaca	7 669	78.4	55 800	18.8	10.0	366	23.0	4.6	9 504	8.6	201	2.1	8 677	26.3	23.2
Lee	5 663	79.4	75 000	18.9	12.1	436	20.6	7.0	7 108	2.5	352	5.0	7 309	27.0	16.3
Leon	6 189	82.8	64 200	19.5	12.1	410	23.2	5.3	6 935	-2.3	524	7.6	6 012	24.5	16.1
Liberty	23 242	79.0	63 900	18.7	10.4	450	22.7	8.0	31 972	3.0	3 341	10.4	26 574	20.4	20.9
Limestone	7 906	74.9	46 300	19.3	10.9	426	24.5	6.1	10 210	3.6	466	4.6	8 533	29.0	17.1
Lipscomb	1 205	77.9	39 700	17.0	9.9	366	17.9	5.1	1 743	6.8	54	3.1	1 287	31.7	14.3
Live Oak	4 230	81.4	55 200	18.5	9.9	366	19.1	6.8	4 567	4.8	159	3.5	4 244	29.0	14.7
Llano	7 879	80.9	102 100	23.3	10.9	547	22.8	3.5	5 911	4.1	296	5.0	6 561	30.3	9.9
Loving	31	80.6	0.0	0.0	9.9	575	22.5	9.7	54	0.0	5	9.3	42	26.2	14.3
Lubbock	92 516	59.2	69 100	19.6	10.1	507	28.2	6.4	130 645	2.0	4 676	3.6	114 711	33.2	10.8
Lynn	2 354	74.6	38 500	17.5	10.8	289	20.9	10.2	2 777	-0.6	146	5.3	2 528	33.5	10.1
McCulloch	3 277	72.7	34 000	18.6	13.1	386	24.2	5.9	3 794	7.9	153	4.0	3 204	29.2	17.6
McLennan	78 859	60.2	67 700	19.6	11.1	499	26.3	6.6	105 310	2.3	5 398	5.1	94 076	30.0	15.5
McMullen	355	80.8	46 800	38.0	9.9	420	19.0	9.3	323	12.2	14	4.3	347	34.0	16.4
Madison	3 914	77.0	55 900	18.6	10.2	436	21.9	7.7	4 562	2.9	187	4.1	4 186	21.4	13.0
Marion	4 610	82.1	48 700	20.4	12.8	399	24.8	6.4	3 718	7.2	310	8.3	4 082	23.6	20.9
Martin	1 624	74.3	53 800	21.7	11.0	311	19.6	8.7	2 054	10.3	81	3.9	1 803	31.8	12.1

1. Specified owner-occupied units.   2. Median monthly owner costs is often in the minimum category—9.9 percent or less, which is indicated as 9.9 percent.   3. Specified renter-occupied units.   4. Overcrowded or lacking complete plumbing facilities.   5. Percent of civilian labor force.   6. Persons 16 years old and over.

Table B. States and Counties — Nonfarm Employment and Agriculture

STATE County	Private nonfarm establishments, employment and payroll, 2001									Agriculture, 2002			
	Number of establishments	Employment						Annual payroll		Farms			Farm operators whose principal occupation is farming (percent)
		Total	Health care and social assistance	Manufacturing	Retail trade	Finance and insurance	Professional, scientific, and technical services	Total (mil dol)	Average per employee (dollars)	Number	Percent with—		
											Less than 50 acres	500 acres and over	
	104	105	106	107	108	109	110	111	112	113	114	115	116

STATE County	104	105	106	107	108	109	110	111	112	113	114	115	116
TEXAS—Cont'd													
Guadalupe	1 411	20 033	2 196	5 945	3 077	500	339	499	24 906	2 442	43.8	6.3	48.1
Hale	825	11 864	1 293	2 747	1 623	371	252	273	22 994	915	10.1	44.0	68.7
Hall	91	749	122	62	179	42	D	13	17 150	311	5.1	45.7	61.7
Hamilton	214	1 785	395	235	284	69	47	38	21 069	996	11.1	23.6	55.6
Hansford	174	1 078	176	D	222	105	39	27	25 297	290	9.0	65.5	64.8
Hardeman	98	808	169	D	110	49	D	19	24 054	344	5.8	41.6	60.8
Hardin	697	8 391	1 055	941	1 620	165	221	178	21 197	517	64.0	3.7	49.9
Harris	85 205	1 682 264	158 091	155 770	176 413	78 819	128 183	70 422	41 861	2 452	61.7	4.7	45.1
Harrison	1 162	16 115	1 588	3 753	2 174	1 116	588	402	24 954	1 116	37.8	10.8	48.4
Hartley	80	716	308	D	144	0	16	16	21 985	253	8.6	73.1	48.4
Haskell	146	905	211	D	197	64	28	16	17 790	579	7.1	63.6	73.1
Hays	2 260	25 908	3 825	3 101	5 467	596	983	633	24 428	1 106	43.0	11.3	47.2
Hemphill	148	996	147	11	130	78	16	24	24 266	239	7.9	53.6	67.8
Henderson	1 190	12 976	1 773	1 924	2 737	428	360	283	21 808	1 798	38.7	7.1	53.9
Hidalgo	8 382	120 612	23 271	10 373	23 568	4 380	4 735	2 462	20 412	2 104	59.8	12.1	53.0
Hill	682	7 876	1 938	1 124	1 859	216	104	149	18 913	2 014	32.4	11.0	52.6
Hockley	494	5 402	1 338	314	685	185	150	123	22 806	767	15.0	40.4	63.6
Hood	951	8 019	1 020	464	1 857	369	289	176	21 972	935	48.8	8.8	49.2
Hopkins	730	8 541	1 103	1 325	1 684	390	210	201	23 585	1 923	28.5	10.0	56.6
Houston	380	3 328	521	526	693	130	96	66	19 815	1 514	25.5	13.8	56.6
Howard	738	10 043	2 327	1 290	1 382	313	140	239	23 832	466	18.7	39.9	57.1
Hudspeth	41	195	D	0	57	D	D	4	21 456	131	7.6	62.6	83.2
Hunt	1 297	16 387	2 929	2 613	3 239	541	707	365	22 264	2 784	47.1	5.6	50.7
Hutchinson	491	6 043	581	1 731	903	152	132	211	34 964	262	23.7	42.0	58.4
Irion	47	312	D	D	D	D	9	8	25 753	151	23.8	51.7	51.0
Jack	182	1 347	188	D	182	96	D	30	22 319	884	13.2	24.2	52.6
Jackson	277	4 111	357	D	522	89	D	110	26 862	917	23.1	26.0	63.5
Jasper	690	8 755	1 530	1 941	1 672	269	143	195	22 275	763	59.9	2.9	48.9
Jeff Davis	55	388	D	0	36	D	4	7	17 080	79	12.7	74.7	53.2
Jefferson	5 848	100 224	16 879	14 171	14 827	3 046	4 282	3 056	30 491	775	47.5	17.0	55.6
Jim Hogg	105	804	83	26	225	48	20	15	18 555	234	4.3	50.0	57.7
Jim Wells	769	10 552	3 622	269	1 537	348	237	223	21 100	912	23.1	20.6	55.5
Johnson	2 216	26 955	2 848	5 701	4 539	691	629	652	24 177	2 579	56.1	4.7	43.2
Jones	312	3 000	532	108	458	112	51	62	20 569	918	16.9	28.0	56.5
Karnes	264	1 971	341	152	418	97	52	41	20 620	1 157	13.8	19.6	56.1
Kaufman	1 462	18 551	2 440	4 821	2 793	588	507	454	24 448	2 438	51.9	5.7	50.4
Kendall	757	6 690	509	743	1 150	598	453	169	25 319	967	34.1	17.3	48.6
Kenedy	4	D	0	0	0	0	0	D	D	28	10.7	75.0	89.3
Kent	16	94	0	0	D	D	0	11	120 138	182	5.5	51.6	51.1
Kerr	1 348	14 612	4 065	943	2 367	390	578	354	24 207	977	27.2	19.2	50.1
Kimble	137	1 222	119	265	248	40	24	24	19 309	528	16.5	43.0	57.4
King	NA	NA	NA	NA	NA	NA	NA	NA	NA	41	4.9	56.1	61.5
Kinney	35	235	D	0	45	D	0	4	15 962	148	5.4	72.3	61.5
Kleberg	551	5 333	878	180	1 344	272	148	109	20 455	348	46.6	14.7	53.2
Knox	122	728	211	0	101	62	11	15	20 092	271	12.9	48.7	65.3
Lamar	1 165	16 834	2 886	4 420	2 621	519	338	428	25 445	1 725	28.5	12.8	54.5
Lamb	311	3 001	563	D	506	161	D	67	22 397	931	6.0	41.8	63.5
Lampasas	387	3 789	402	481	636	143	93	74	19 598	861	25.1	21.5	53.8
La Salle	81	709	D	0	170	25	D	17	23 433	315	6.7	54.9	57.8
Lavaca	507	6 020	830	2 321	788	293	83	124	20 613	2 861	29.1	8.5	50.5
Lee	387	3 541	350	417	685	182	79	88	24 870	1 848	29.9	8.7	49.7
Leon	331	3 569	178	364	590	97	64	122	34 179	1 908	25.5	13.7	54.0
Liberty	1 030	11 377	1 732	1 201	2 689	328	389	273	23 956	1 596	50.3	7.1	46.8
Limestone	404	4 805	1 073	905	985	197	70	99	20 639	1 430	20.3	18.5	55.0
Lipscomb	91	360	D	D	73	34	18	7	18 381	307	3.9	55.7	69.7
Live Oak	214	1 717	169	D	391	102	31	41	23 994	845	14.7	29.1	54.7
Llano	453	3 497	634	105	540	188	63	74	21 074	692	18.8	34.8	55.1
Loving	1	D	0	0	0	0	0	D	D	14	0.0	100.0	50.0
Lubbock	6 508	96 497	16 974	6 684	15 865	4 579	3 320	2 277	23 594	1 142	32.0	29.4	61.3
Lynn	103	875	181	34	126	110	D	20	22 688	478	9.6	56.7	75.7
McCulloch	232	2 182	434	319	491	96	D	47	21 688	621	10.0	32.2	58.8
McLennan	4 780	85 175	13 644	14 270	10 571	4 081	2 352	2 128	24 980	2 571	46.7	8.8	49.3
McMullen	17	80	D	0	7	D	D	2	28 275	223	4.5	71.3	56.5
Madison	204	1 755	241	37	523	105	65	36	20 290	890	24.6	12.2	54.4
Marion	188	1 107	128	269	270	33	11	23	20 671	252	28.2	9.9	50.4
Martin	89	559	164	0	119	35	10	14	25 542	379	10.6	54.1	70.4

						Agriculture, 2002 (cont'd)									
		Land in farms				Value of land and buildings (dollars)			Value of products sold				Percent of farms with sales of —		Government payments
			Acres								Percent from —				
STATE County	Acreage (1,000)	Percent change, 1997–2002	Average size of farm (acres)	Total irrigated (1,000)	Total cropland (1,000)	Average per farm	Average per acre	Value of machinery and equipment average per farm (dollars)	Total (mil dol)	Average per farm (dollars)	Crops	Live-stock and poultry products	$10,000 or more	$100,000 or more	Total ($1,000)	Percent of farms
	117	118	119	120	121	122	123	124	125	126	127	128	129	130	131	132
TEXAS—Cont'd																
Guadalupe	385	10.6	158	3	184	282 965	2 021	22 367	37	15 236	44.0	56.0	19.9	2.0	696	10.9
Hale	605	3.1	661	291	527	374 046	591	108 456	225	246 171	45.7	54.3	54.2	34.2	15 998	78.1
Hall	432	-3.6	1 388	21	196	403 176	289	72 075	21	66 364	78.3	21.7	47.6	18.6	4 656	78.8
Hamilton	450	-3.4	451	1	125	395 334	900	29 160	42	41 770	6.3	93.7	34.2	5.4	1 028	27.8
Hansford	593	1.9	2 045	86	319	759 133	369	164 402	367	1 265 144	6.5	93.5	58.6	40.0	4 240	59.0
Hardeman	346	7.1	1 006	9	175	303 100	349	44 772	17	48 979	40.6	59.4	40.4	11.0	1 961	66.6
Hardin	69	6.2	133	1	19	177 393	1 260	21 037	D	D	D	D	13.0	0.6	D	D
Harris	305	-1.9	124	7	124	429 678	2 622	25 697	53	21 565	66.2	33.8	18.3	2.8	1 387	3.7
Harrison	229	7.0	205	1	81	272 822	1 199	20 647	12	11 036	13.8	86.2	17.7	1.7	137	2.0
Hartley	789	-4.1	3 120	123	276	1 170 274	376	185 216	447	1 767 886	15.3	84.7	65.6	46.2	3 606	66.8
Haskell	492	4.9	850	31	332	369 384	422	74 962	41	70 460	65.0	35.0	52.2	17.6	4 589	63.9
Hays	278	-6.7	252	0	58	754 577	2 877	25 074	15	13 213	27.3	72.7	13.1	1.7	137	5.8
Hemphill	546	-12.5	2 286	3	82	623 754	266	47 390	92	386 988	0.5	99.5	54.0	19.2	902	40.6
Henderson	341	-7.1	190	1	156	285 480	1 636	32 933	43	24 037	31.5	68.5	25.1	2.6	114	1.4
Hidalgo	593	-6.8	282	170	405	483 683	2 015	48 731	202	96 042	90.3	9.7	44.2	12.0	6 509	18.2
Hill	504	8.6	250	4	294	315 967	1 198	42 506	54	26 822	55.2	44.8	24.6	5.0	3 469	20.4
Hockley	491	-14.2	641	144	413	330 725	488	132 126	90	117 623	D	D	43.0	22.8	8 434	73.5
Hood	202	-10.2	216	3	76	441 083	2 321	36 330	22	23 240	19.0	81.0	19.3	2.5	301	9.9
Hopkins	431	11.7	224	6	231	314 118	1 405	42 476	134	69 797	3.0	97.0	36.2	11.1	2 357	7.1
Houston	465	5.7	307	5	163	326 850	1 080	34 366	34	22 776	18.4	81.6	31.7	4.2	714	2.8
Howard	518	-4.8	1 112	2	248	500 514	444	55 252	15	32 416	77.9	22.1	27.7	8.8	4 369	56.7
Hudspeth	2 122	-15.2	16 196	35	81	2 463 311	151	154 278	27	207 458	79.7	20.3	64.9	35.1	738	32.1
Hunt	400	13.3	144	1	226	228 154	1 585	23 768	28	10 081	41.7	58.3	15.2	1.5	1 059	9.1
Hutchinson	553	38.3	2 111	28	132	525 613	253	66 569	29	111 880	20.0	80.0	34.4	13.0	1 989	29.4
Irion	536	-17.8	3 552	1	10	838 032	234	33 412	3	23 096	3.3	96.7	39.7	5.3	590	25.2
Jack	596	12.0	674	D	114	493 959	713	22 911	16	17 593	5.1	94.9	26.0	2.7	410	14.3
Jackson	471	1.7	513	15	252	495 094	1 089	64 594	42	45 649	73.1	26.9	39.8	13.1	4 453	21.5
Jasper	96	10.3	126	0	26	188 997	1 536	26 449	5	6 307	31.2	68.8	13.9	1.0	3	1.0
Jeff Davis	1 489	0.5	18 845	1	25	2 509 624	131	44 024	6	80 574	2.3	97.7	53.2	20.3	131	13.9
Jefferson	388	-10.6	501	22	182	412 902	860	42 318	17	29 659	45.2	54.8	25.0	6.7	3 703	16.0
Jim Hogg	604	-21.4	2 579	2	43	1 136 549	447	31 294	7	29 659	2.1	97.9	32.5	3.0	326	16.2
Jim Wells	498	0.4	546	6	198	324 217	625	29 779	47	51 912	28.1	71.9	24.8	4.8	1 685	25.0
Johnson	362	8.7	140	1	167	282 853	2 185	23 935	44	16 906	15.5	84.5	15.9	1.9	1 575	11.4
Jones	517	12.6	563	4	352	333 379	520	55 393	39	42 728	49.3	50.7	34.7	10.0	4 746	51.3
Karnes	475	13.9	410	2	165	336 839	817	25 310	18	15 769	14.7	85.3	33.5	2.7	943	26.6
Kaufman	420	8.0	172	1	202	285 879	1 556	28 259	30	12 321	21.7	78.3	16.8	1.8	437	1.8
Kendall	327	0.6	338	1	42	643 715	2 168	19 411	7	7 262	13.8	86.2	16.3	1.2	185	11.7
Kenedy	474	-15.8	16 931	D	6	5 686 104	353	79 148	9	320 785	0.0	100.0	75.0	14.3	64	35.7
Kent	561	0.0	3 081	1	75	622 700	207	31 158	5	29 016	12.9	87.1	34.6	7.1	933	68.1
Kerr	564	2.9	578	2	57	599 955	1 134	21 058	12	12 276	9.4	90.6	18.3	1.7	210	8.7
Kimble	616	-20.3	1 166	2	31	866 517	651	21 427	7	13 933	8.9	91.1	25.0	2.7	405	21.2
King	547	NA	13 334	D	26	2 881 914	213	67 289	12	286 733	11.0	89.0	48.8	19.5	391	63.4
Kinney	614	-2.4	4 146	3	22	1 763 740	397	27 312	5	32 086	14.3	85.7	40.5	8.1	699	26.4
Kleberg	D	NA	D	D	103	1 672 084	598	45 415	58	166 054	17.0	83.0	24.1	7.2	2 628	26.4
Knox	564	-14.3	2 082	23	219	616 023	298	90 037	46	170 406	31.8	68.2	57.6	26.6	2 466	60.5
Lamar	470	9.0	273	4	234	225 611	880	33 738	39	22 600	30.2	69.8	29.7	4.6	1 754	16.1
Lamb	629	16.7	675	239	498	379 901	523	112 319	260	279 504	36.7	63.3	51.0	31.1	13 063	80.0
Lampasas	412	-5.3	479	0	80	667 020	1 215	26 179	13	15 534	10.1	89.9	28.7	1.6	354	17.2
La Salle	559	6.1	1 773	6	89	1 003 238	593	32 880	23	73 564	12.1	87.9	33.0	6.7	1 254	25.1
Lavaca	602	14.4	210	4	204	277 132	1 280	27 650	46	15 959	7.7	92.3	27.3	1.6	910	6.4
Lee	366	6.4	198	2	113	290 149	1 445	23 006	23	12 417	18.6	81.4	27.3	1.0	348	5.9
Leon	563	9.3	295	1	185	311 280	1 067	33 584	51	26 883	5.8	94.2	27.1	2.8	149	1.4
Liberty	305	-0.7	191	12	156	330 569	1 506	32 412	21	13 119	53.8	46.3	17.7	2.7	3 151	5.6
Limestone	530	19.6	371	1	205	251 383	743	33 592	33	22 922	12.6	87.4	32.5	4.0	701	9.0
Lipscomb	578	9.3	1 883	24	162	676 129	367	87 684	42	137 908	8.0	92.0	47.6	18.9	2 103	70.4
Live Oak	525	1.0	622	2	130	419 296	710	33 401	12	16 559	13.1	86.9	30.5	3.3	707	18.7
Llano	533	0.2	771	1	49	1 157 512	1 426	19 570	12	16 965	4.8	95.2	36.6	2.5	246	9.8
Loving	515	46.3	36 799	D	1	2 965 356	80	22 645	1	37 392	0.0	100.0	42.9	7.1	109	42.9
Lubbock	557	3.0	488	177	467	367 991	811	89 656	144	125 783	45.7	54.3	43.3	17.7	9 601	54.4
Lynn	530	-5.9	1 110	79	421	520 954	471	139 661	49	102 180	96.6	3.4	63.4	35.6	8 547	69.7
McCulloch	546	-14.8	880	1	145	622 689	724	33 224	13	20 878	22.5	77.5	32.0	4.3	1 393	35.4
McLennan	538	9.1	209	3	298	273 080	1 248	30 959	61	23 746	35.6	64.4	20.4	3.9	1 846	10.5
McMullen	597	14.6	2 677	D	29	1 820 052	707	41 900	6	28 692	2.8	97.2	43.0	3.1	230	17.9
Madison	245	9.4	275	0	92	304 147	1 137	37 776	61	68 064	D	D	32.2	3.1	232	0.8
Marion	60	-3.2	237	1	17	184 525	976	24 792	4	16 218	18.2	81.8	13.5	2.8	4	1.2
Martin	526	-2.4	1 388	10	281	596 871	434	107 860	14	37 134	91.7	8.3	43.3	11.3	4 825	71.5

Table B. States and Counties — **Residential Construction, Wholesale Trade, Retail Trade, and Real Estate**

STATE County	Value of residential construction authorized by building permits, 2003		Wholesale trade, 1997				Retail trade,[1] 1997				Real estate and rental and leasing, 1997			
	New construction ($1,000)	Number of housing units	Number of establish-ments	Number of employees	Sales (mil dol)	Annual payroll (mil dol)	Number of establish-ments	Number of employees	Sales (mil dol)	Annual payroll (mil dol)	Number of establish-ments	Number of employees	Receipts (mil dol)	Annual payroll (mil dol)
	133	134	135	136	137	138	139	140	141	142	143	144	145	146
TEXAS—Cont'd														
Guadalupe	136 183	1 127	82	681	366.1	20.6	215	2 665	498.1	41.7	58	205	21.4	3.5
Hale	2 440	17	74	540	294.5	13.3	164	1 566	264.7	23.6	31	111	6.2	1.4
Hall	0	0	6	25	10.1	0.5	22	137	43.1	2.1	NA	NA	NA	NA
Hamilton	60	1	10	118	42.1	2.2	57	301	45.4	4.0	4	D	D	D
Hansford	0	0	23	139	116.1	4.3	38	233	39.0	3.6	3	8	0.5	0.0
Hardeman	67	1	9	41	12.2	0.6	21	115	16.3	1.5	1	D	D	D
Hardin	3 611	32	28	150	33.4	3.3	152	1 630	350.6	24.5	24	90	6.8	0.8
Harris	3 853 866	40 983	7 564	101 357	110 399.7	4 129.7	11 596	168 038	31 045.1	2 921.9	4 039	33 808	4 154.7	829.5
Harrison	4 756	37	65	747	321.2	20.8	220	2 270	378.6	33.2	36	181	13.3	4.0
Hartley	NA	NA	5	D	D	D	10	84	14.4	1.2	7	D	D	D
Haskell	0	0	8	40	23.3	0.6	41	238	58.9	3.3	5	13	1.0	0.3
Hays	114 813	1 465	75	559	174.1	15.9	382	4 056	698.0	61.0	91	312	40.8	7.5
Hemphill	0	0	7	33	10.5	0.8	22	132	19.7	2.0	2	D	D	D
Henderson	14 571	142	42	215	98.3	4.6	221	2 586	381.1	34.3	52	191	18.3	2.8
Hidalgo	445 581	8 060	600	6 395	1 981.7	124.6	1 582	20 862	3 337.6	313.1	346	1 347	116.3	18.5
Hill	1 446	20	26	119	46.8	2.5	229	1 800	331.1	26.4	20	44	4.1	0.4
Hockley	1 416	12	40	255	81.5	6.3	86	725	150.6	11.3	21	42	3.6	0.6
Hood	8 975	85	29	83	32.5	2.0	159	1 702	346.6	30.3	44	274	14.5	3.6
Hopkins	4 429	84	48	1 088	607.1	27.0	174	1 753	357.2	27.8	23	123	9.2	1.6
Houston	713	8	16	136	49.4	2.4	91	772	122.4	10.6	10	17	1.2	0.2
Howard	361	3	50	559	215.5	22.0	149	1 509	248.6	21.1	37	121	9.5	2.0
Hudspeth	NA	NA	4	7	1.9	0.1	9	52	6.1	0.5	1	D	D	D
Hunt	8 385	122	54	447	263.6	10.1	258	3 013	479.9	41.7	56	214	14.3	3.8
Hutchinson	0	0	31	192	163.9	5.5	104	1 028	151.0	13.8	16	47	4.7	0.8
Irion	NA	NA	3	19	5.1	0.4	4	19	1.5	0.1	1	D	D	D
Jack	286	2	7	64	13.0	1.8	35	181	21.3	2.3	6	11	0.5	0.1
Jackson	2 650	24	22	177	58.4	3.3	63	479	90.6	7.6	11	25	1.6	0.2
Jasper	452	6	49	247	103.4	6.5	190	1 658	301.0	23.7	23	71	11.7	1.4
Jeff Davis	NA	NA	NA	NA	NA	NA	8	37	3.7	0.5	1	D	D	D
Jefferson	103 911	1 075	368	4 827	2 081.2	163.7	1 084	14 964	2 570.9	230.1	260	1 597	194.2	34.2
Jim Hogg	NA	NA	5	40	25.3	0.8	34	207	31.4	2.5	1	D	D	D
Jim Wells	3 383	42	56	522	139.8	14.1	160	1 531	258.1	23.4	41	258	35.3	7.5
Johnson	92 333	898	87	762	261.8	18.2	358	3 995	706.8	62.2	69	239	22.7	3.1
Jones	322	4	24	140	145.1	3.4	58	498	163.1	8.0	9	19	0.9	0.2
Karnes	868	15	14	168	45.8	2.4	54	434	59.8	5.1	5	19	1.1	0.1
Kaufman	82 911	864	77	665	189.3	16.8	286	2 693	573.3	43.0	34	103	8.2	1.3
Kendall	79 355	544	31	378	141.1	8.5	93	1 012	305.8	20.1	30	66	7.7	0.8
Kenedy	NA	NA	NA	NA	NA	NA	NA	NA	NA	NA	NA	NA	NA	NA
Kent	NA	NA	1	D	D	D	4	D	D	D	NA	NA	NA	NA
Kerr	13 897	88	48	271	65.6	6.4	210	2 467	436.1	38.4	63	180	18.2	3.2
Kimble	0	0	5	D	D	D	33	201	31.4	2.8	4	7	0.2	0.0
King	NA	NA	NA	NA	NA	NA	NA	NA	NA	NA	NA	NA	NA	NA
Kinney	244	2	2	D	D	D	9	41	4.2	0.4	3	4	0.4	0.0
Kleberg	737	9	10	42	8.2	0.9	113	1 414	214.3	20.0	24	65	7.0	0.8
Knox	NA	NA	13	79	29.8	1.7	31	163	24.7	2.0	1	D	D	D
Lamar	11 030	171	68	519	152.4	12.7	242	2 591	482.5	40.0	46	134	15.3	1.8
Lamb	0	0	25	146	72.6	3.1	63	450	75.4	5.9	5	11	0.5	0.1
Lampasas	2 779	25	16	79	36.3	0.7	65	562	94.4	7.8	12	32	2.1	0.3
La Salle	0	0	3	D	D	D	27	142	20.0	1.8	3	4	0.2	0.0
Lavaca	605	10	30	818	202.6	14.6	108	797	118.1	10.7	11	19	1.3	0.1
Lee	1 527	16	35	324	322.4	7.1	59	665	79.9	9.0	7	16	2.9	0.4
Leon	NA	NA	15	149	56.2	3.2	72	494	77.4	6.0	8	43	2.3	0.5
Liberty	21 907	258	53	D	D	D	204	2 472	441.7	36.5	45	179	17.7	4.2
Limestone	2 090	21	15	D	D	D	91	831	137.6	11.3	10	16	0.8	0.2
Lipscomb	0	0	11	32	12.5	0.6	17	82	10.6	0.8	1	D	D	D
Live Oak	166	3	9	77	25.4	0.9	45	397	75.0	5.1	7	14	1.3	0.2
Llano	32 183	325	15	222	85.5	5.4	77	380	69.1	5.3	17	56	6.0	1.0
Loving	NA	NA	1	D	D	D	NA	NA	NA	NA	NA	NA	NA	NA
Lubbock	278 963	2 956	505	6 628	3 867.8	181.3	1 084	14 538	2 673.0	238.0	296	1 905	133.8	30.7
Lynn	294	2	7	D	D	D	24	122	30.6	2.1	1	D	D	D
McCulloch	395	3	14	91	14.9	1.4	55	473	75.5	5.9	8	40	3.1	0.7
McLennan	100 476	891	315	3 755	1 716.3	102.1	862	10 227	1 797.8	162.7	212	1 086	131.4	21.4
McMullen	NA	NA	NA	NA	NA	NA	5	13	1.9	0.2	NA	NA	NA	NA
Madison	970	14	5	23	12.1	0.8	46	462	137.0	7.5	11	16	1.4	0.2
Marion	115	1	9	31	19.1	1.0	41	246	37.4	2.8	3	2	0.2	0.0
Martin	0	0	10	53	22.2	1.4	17	116	27.9	2.1	NA	NA	NA	NA

1. Establishments with payroll.

STATE County	Professional, scientific, and technical services,[1] 1997				Manufacturing, 1997				Accommodation and foodservices, 1997			
	Number of establish-ments	Number of employees	Receipts (mil dol)	Annual payroll (mil dol)	Number of establish-ments	Number of employees	Receipts (mil dol)	Annual payroll (mil dol)	Number of establish-ments	Number of employees	Sales (mil dol)	Annual payroll (mil dol)
	147	148	149	150	151	152	153	154	155	156	157	158
TEXAS—Cont'd												
Guadalupe	64	204	13.8	4.8	90	5 592	1 320.3	150.4	127	D	D	D
Hale	38	151	9.7	2.7	32	D	D	D	67	923	25.9	6.9
Hall	3	3	0.2	0.0	NA	NA	NA	NA	10	D	D	D
Hamilton	17	37	2.3	0.5	NA	NA	NA	NA	13	103	2.6	0.7
Hansford	6	19	1.3	0.5	NA	NA	NA	NA	11	D	D	D
Hardeman	7	10	0.4	0.1	NA	NA	NA	NA	10	D	D	D
Hardin	38	245	15.3	4.8	37	1 016	173.1	30.0	50	538	16.4	4.5
Harris	9 944	106 124	15 512.9	5 478.2	4 374	158 572	73 227.7	5 991.2	5 470	111 869	4 379.0	1 160.7
Harrison	86	506	83.6	27.3	90	3 128	600.4	83.2	75	1 017	35.1	9.3
Hartley	4	D	D	D	NA	NA	NA	NA	4	15	0.3	0.1
Haskell	7	13	0.6	0.1	NA	NA	NA	NA	8	97	2.3	0.7
Hays	140	459	42.9	14.1	108	3 389	477.0	96.2	177	2 890	88.4	25.4
Hemphill	7	14	1.4	0.2	NA	NA	NA	NA	12	69	1.4	0.3
Henderson	70	220	17.9	6.0	49	1 880	214.3	38.3	95	1 389	40.7	10.3
Hidalgo	482	2 682	193.4	62.7	261	10 284	1 428.2	178.3	626	10 871	352.1	90.1
Hill	29	89	6.2	1.5	37	1 237	174.4	30.7	67	785	25.3	6.4
Hockley	23	148	9.9	3.2	NA	NA	NA	NA	38	544	13.3	3.5
Hood	48	136	11.6	3.0	NA	NA	NA	NA	74	966	28.1	7.6
Hopkins	36	148	11.2	4.2	43	1 463	526.1	41.4	56	747	25.5	7.4
Houston	27	112	4.8	1.5	24	618	131.8	13.3	27	231	7.2	2.0
Howard	41	125	9.3	3.1	27	1 124	726.2	34.6	73	981	24.2	6.7
Hudspeth	NA	NA	NA	NA	NA	NA	NA	NA	5	35	1.4	0.2
Hunt	67	422	24.2	8.4	58	7 223	1 478.9	256.0	117	1 729	50.9	15.1
Hutchinson	24	115	7.4	2.7	30	1 718	1 949.1	89.1	48	578	15.1	4.0
Irion	1	D	D	D	NA	NA	NA	NA	5	D	D	D
Jack	12	27	1.2	0.5	NA	NA	NA	NA	11	D	D	D
Jackson	13	50	2.7	1.2	11	D	D	D	18	205	7.0	1.5
Jasper	32	126	10.3	1.9	29	1 911	543.2	76.6	49	714	21.6	5.6
Jeff Davis	1	D	D	D	NA	NA	NA	NA	12	138	4.5	1.3
Jefferson	469	4 143	490.9	204.3	230	14 471	15 920.2	727.0	426	8 206	261.9	69.9
Jim Hogg	3	14	0.7	0.3	NA	NA	NA	NA	14	106	3.0	0.9
Jim Wells	44	321	23.1	9.9	NA	NA	NA	NA	68	823	25.6	6.6
Johnson	113	499	39.3	12.2	170	5 942	981.4	161.3	134	1 885	60.2	16.6
Jones	13	46	2.2	0.8	NA	NA	NA	NA	24	119	3.7	1.0
Karnes	13	48	2.5	0.6	NA	NA	NA	NA	23	192	5.1	1.3
Kaufman	68	206	14.1	4.8	109	4 274	521.3	120.4	91	1 342	39.9	10.7
Kendall	57	158	11.6	3.9	NA	NA	NA	NA	50	858	27.7	8.5
Kenedy	1	D	D	D	NA	NA	NA	NA	1	D	D	D
Kent	NA	NA	NA	NA	NA	NA	NA	NA	1	D	D	D
Kerr	104	390	35.4	11.6	49	960	92.9	24.9	100	1 417	54.3	15.3
Kimble	7	43	1.7	0.5	NA	NA	NA	NA	27	212	6.7	1.9
King	NA	NA	NA	NA	NA	NA	NA	NA	1	D	D	D
Kinney	1	D	D	D	NA	NA	NA	NA	3	18	0.4	0.1
Kleberg	23	80	4.9	1.4	NA	NA	NA	NA	74	1 048	31.6	8.5
Knox	3	15	0.6	0.2	NA	NA	NA	NA	13	D	D	D
Lamar	52	243	13.6	4.3	60	4 809	2 056.3	161.0	96	1 466	45.9	13.0
Lamb	13	18	1.1	0.2	14	678	123.6	16.7	27	D	D	D
Lampasas	17	65	2.8	1.0	NA	NA	NA	NA	28	D	D	D
La Salle	3	8	0.7	0.1	NA	NA	NA	NA	8	93	3.4	0.9
Lavaca	28	100	19.9	2.2	46	2 127	192.5	37.2	32	375	9.2	2.6
Lee	24	87	6.4	2.5	NA	NA	NA	NA	24	252	8.2	2.1
Leon	15	42	2.4	0.7	NA	NA	NA	NA	24	385	9.3	2.6
Liberty	70	274	24.0	6.9	41	1 220	209.8	36.1	65	984	32.9	8.5
Limestone	22	48	3.4	0.9	17	790	80.1	15.4	33	290	9.7	2.4
Lipscomb	9	18	1.3	0.3	NA	NA	NA	NA	4	D	D	D
Live Oak	13	37	1.9	0.6	NA	NA	NA	NA	29	278	9.5	2.2
Llano	21	72	4.2	1.8	NA	NA	NA	NA	47	298	10.5	2.8
Loving	NA	NA	NA	NA	NA	NA	NA	NA	NA	NA	NA	NA
Lubbock	483	2 516	198.6	67.7	258	7 286	1 566.4	203.8	522	11 154	332.1	87.6
Lynn	4	13	0.4	0.2	NA	NA	NA	NA	7	48	1.0	0.3
McCulloch	17	95	6.7	2.4	NA	NA	NA	NA	23	181	7.1	1.6
McLennan	292	2 039	133.0	57.4	261	16 474	3 855.6	481.7	400	6 900	220.7	59.8
McMullen	1	D	D	D	NA	NA	NA	NA	2	D	D	D
Madison	15	60	4.5	1.3	NA	NA	NA	NA	19	213	7.9	2.1
Marion	4	8	0.8	0.1	NA	NA	NA	NA	35	185	5.0	1.3
Martin	4	11	0.7	0.3	NA	NA	NA	NA	4	28	0.6	0.2

1. Firms subject to federal tax.

Table B. States and Counties — **Health Care and Social Assistance, Other Services, and Federal Funds**

STATE County	Health care and social assistance,[1] 1997				Other services,[1] 1997				Federal funds and grants, 2002–2003 Expenditures (mil dol)			
										Direct payments for individuals[2]		
	Number of establishments	Number of employees	Receipts (mil dol)	Annual payroll (mil dol)	Number of establishments	Number of employees	Receipts (mil dol)	Annual payroll (mil dol)	Total	Social Security and government retirement	Medicare	Food stamps and Supplemental Security Income
	159	160	161	162	163	164	165	166	167	168	169	170
TEXAS—Cont'd												
Guadalupe	109	1 150	55.9	23.4	76	453	25.7	7.5	417.6	259.0	55.0	11.6
Hale	51	496	26.1	9.1	67	234	13.6	3.5	241.6	64.6	43.4	8.0
Hall	5	89	2.4	0.8	1	D	D	D	40.2	10.2	7.1	1.0
Hamilton	18	306	12.7	6.3	13	27	3.1	0.6	50.3	22.4	15.8	0.8
Hansford	4	D	D	D	14	53	3.6	1.2	40.0	11.5	5.1	0.4
Hardeman	11	83	3.3	1.0	8	22	2.2	0.4	40.1	13.3	8.0	0.8
Hardin	66	1 589	49.3	22.7	46	248	12.9	2.9	219.6	108.3	55.3	8.3
Harris	6 996	92 982	6 784.1	2 802.4	5 209	45 636	3 189.5	978.4	18 719.1	4 292.8	2 299.2	671.1
Harrison	89	946	46.6	19.0	74	369	28.9	7.1	317.3	118.7	57.7	14.2
Hartley	9	42	2.6	0.9	7	42	4.3	0.7	15.5	2.7	0.9	0.1
Haskell	12	163	6.0	2.3	14	65	3.2	0.7	55.8	18.1	11.0	1.1
Hays	135	1 412	77.9	32.7	93	434	22.2	5.9	413.5	165.1	44.2	9.5
Hemphill	3	17	1.1	0.5	6	12	1.5	0.3	14.2	6.7	4.0	0.2
Henderson	86	1 201	63.7	31.8	68	255	13.9	3.7	300.4	150.4	70.9	10.0
Hidalgo	833	15 858	1 167.0	431.0	479	2 465	114.3	30.6	2 608.3	588.1	370.1	243.2
Hill	29	533	30.0	10.4	44	172	9.5	2.5	205.5	91.6	40.3	5.4
Hockley	28	331	14.3	5.9	29	87	5.9	1.3	146.8	42.0	25.6	3.5
Hood	70	595	31.8	14.1	56	319	13.3	4.3	211.5	145.1	39.6	3.5
Hopkins	63	692	35.5	12.0	56	244	13.8	3.5	168.1	73.0	38.5	4.1
Houston	29	880	23.7	11.2	27	126	8.9	2.1	160.4	60.9	33.5	5.6
Howard	60	1 000	63.6	24.7	55	265	11.9	3.4	268.8	81.1	48.0	8.1
Hudspeth	NA	NA	NA	NA	3	5	0.3	0.1	34.4	4.8	2.3	0.5
Hunt	111	1 607	79.5	34.2	90	320	20.4	4.7	1 000.3	169.6	81.0	13.9
Hutchinson	39	769	31.5	12.5	33	219	17.3	3.8	115.9	56.0	26.7	3.1
Irion	NA	NA	NA	NA	NA	NA	NA	NA	7.7	3.9	1.6	0.2
Jack	7	74	2.8	1.1	9	12	1.1	0.2	33.6	16.9	9.1	1.0
Jackson	13	237	8.5	3.2	20	70	4.4	1.4	86.5	29.3	19.9	2.2
Jasper	65	1 412	42.3	21.7	47	238	12.1	3.6	206.1	81.6	51.9	7.8
Jeff Davis	5	15	0.8	0.2	NA	NA	NA	NA	13.2	6.0	1.9	0.3
Jefferson	707	11 019	681.3	287.9	471	3 318	188.7	56.0	1 678.1	528.7	370.2	65.3
Jim Hogg	3	73	1.4	0.9	3	6	0.5	0.1	42.2	9.1	8.6	1.7
Jim Wells	72	2 680	95.2	42.9	60	320	16.0	4.4	237.8	77.6	53.4	9.5
Johnson	135	1 711	82.7	38.2	145	633	43.2	10.7	465.2	261.9	100.4	14.1
Jones	17	362	13.4	4.9	15	35	2.6	0.5	101.4	40.8	23.3	2.7
Karnes	17	214	7.2	3.0	17	61	3.4	0.7	99.3	29.7	19.4	3.9
Kaufman	120	1 868	91.8	37.5	96	671	56.1	14.7	378.0	196.0	93.3	11.8
Kendall	40	527	19.8	9.2	37	153	8.2	2.7	146.7	94.3	20.3	1.4
Kenedy	NA	NA	NA	NA	NA	NA	NA	NA	2.2	0.6	0.3	0.0
Kent	NA	NA	NA	NA	NA	NA	NA	NA	12.2	2.9	1.3	0.1
Kerr	106	1 446	79.0	31.7	90	458	28.8	8.5	316.6	186.1	57.6	6.2
Kimble	3	D	D	D	7	29	1.6	0.4	27.0	12.3	5.4	0.6
King	NA	NA	NA	NA	NA	NA	NA	NA	2.2	0.4	0.2	0.0
Kinney	1	D	D	D	NA	NA	NA	NA	26.6	12.3	4.2	1.0
Kleberg	52	503	26.4	11.1	48	212	9.8	2.6	374.1	55.5	27.9	9.5
Knox	8	161	5.7	3.0	10	41	3.5	0.8	36.1	11.0	8.2	0.9
Lamar	148	2 772	101.2	46.8	84	394	18.9	5.2	301.5	123.0	55.8	12.2
Lamb	13	178	5.3	2.3	27	62	4.0	0.9	127.6	31.3	22.1	3.3
Lampasas	20	407	15.2	8.5	16	81	4.4	1.3	108.4	68.2	21.7	2.2
La Salle	5	D	D	D	7	24	1.4	0.2	46.8	10.2	6.4	1.8
Lavaca	34	354	15.4	6.2	32	107	6.9	1.7	142.7	61.1	34.1	2.0
Lee	21	178	8.1	2.8	24	75	6.0	1.2	59.8	30.6	12.8	1.1
Leon	16	192	7.8	3.5	20	59	3.2	0.7	121.0	54.1	24.0	2.6
Liberty	87	1 635	90.7	33.2	61	317	15.9	4.5	329.3	142.2	90.5	12.2
Limestone	31	456	17.0	6.6	25	65	4.9	1.2	135.9	55.5	26.4	5.0
Lipscomb	2	D	D	D	5	30	0.7	0.4	16.9	6.9	3.6	0.2
Live Oak	9	170	6.9	2.3	18	49	3.2	0.6	83.5	19.9	11.7	1.8
Llano	21	322	13.5	6.6	13	35	1.6	0.6	108.5	70.2	25.0	1.5
Loving	NA	NA	NA	NA	1	D	D	D	0.6	0.3	0.0	0.0
Lubbock	622	8 383	566.2	239.1	405	3 053	178.4	53.2	1 216.4	446.3	272.1	45.5
Lynn	4	9	0.5	0.2	7	20	1.3	0.3	67.1	12.7	9.2	1.4
McCulloch	12	261	8.9	4.8	17	63	2.8	0.6	58.3	22.9	14.0	2.2
McLennan	353	4 861	265.9	126.4	329	2 065	114.1	34.4	1 236.2	499.9	150.6	44.3
McMullen	NA	NA	NA	NA	NA	NA	NA	NA	3.7	1.9	0.6	0.0
Madison	13	235	6.8	3.5	10	78	12.4	1.7	52.0	23.9	10.4	2.2
Marion	10	177	4.9	2.4	16	43	2.1	0.5	75.4	27.9	11.4	2.5
Martin	7	92	4.5	1.6	5	D	D	D	39.1	8.1	5.2	0.6

1. Firms subject to federal tax.   2. State totals may include programs not allocated by county.

Table B. States and Counties — Federal Funds and Local Government Finances

	Federal funds and grants, 2002–2003 (cont'd)							Local government finances, 2002				
	Expenditures (mil dol) (cont'd)							General revenue				
	Procurement contract awards			Grants[1]						Taxes		
STATE County											Per capita[2] (dollars)	
	Salaries and wages	Defense	Other	Medicaid and other health-related	Nutrition and family welfare	Education	Other	Total (mil dol)	Intergovern-mental (mil dol)	Total (mil dol)	Total	Property
	171	172	173	174	175	176	177	178	179	180	181	182
TEXAS—Cont'd												
Guadalupe	13.3	1.8	2.7	42.6	6.1	3.0	13.7	166.6	64.1	81.6	866	731
Hale	6.8	0.0	1.8	35.4	5.4	2.0	15.9	85.2	43.8	28.6	796	578
Hall	1.1	0.0	0.2	5.8	0.6	0.3	2.7	16.3	5.5	4.2	1 139	948
Hamilton	1.7	0.1	0.5	6.6	0.3	0.3	0.8	25.6	9.0	7.4	917	757
Hansford	0.9	0.0	0.2	1.3	0.2	0.3	2.1	29.0	5.3	15.0	2 843	2 693
Hardeman	0.9	0.0	0.2	5.8	0.6	0.2	7.5	18.3	4.9	7.9	1 762	1 586
Hardin	4.0	0.0	1.2	26.7	6.2	1.4	7.0	97.8	49.4	38.2	780	693
Harris	1 664.4	1 785.9	4 480.4	1 745.2	354.9	187.9	1 011.4	11 939.6	2 950.4	6 124.7	1 722	1 379
Harrison	8.3	8.4	1.8	74.4	8.1	4.8	16.4	122.6	38.3	69.6	1 113	970
Hartley	0.3	0.0	0.0	0.3	0.1	0.1	0.2	4.6	1.0	3.2	583	512
Haskell	1.7	0.0	0.4	6.6	0.6	0.4	4.8	18.8	8.3	5.9	993	871
Hays	12.6	3.1	85.5	39.4	9.8	11.9	12.7	283.4	92.6	127.8	1 167	888
Hemphill	0.6	0.8	0.1	0.5	0.2	0.2	0.3	19.7	0.8	14.8	4 450	4 205
Henderson	6.5	0.0	1.7	45.2	3.5	2.7	4.4	140.7	55.8	63.4	836	682
Hidalgo	127.9	219.6	26.2	538.9	123.2	69.7	190.2	1 786.3	1 109.4	426.0	693	546
Hill	5.6	1.4	3.7	31.0	2.2	1.7	13.2	82.1	41.4	28.9	858	669
Hockley	2.9	0.0	0.8	13.8	12.8	2.0	6.5	106.0	40.5	37.3	1 632	1 525
Hood	6.3	5.8	1.7	7.4	1.3	0.9	-1.2	76.5	19.8	47.2	1 069	915
Hopkins	5.4	0.0	1.3	27.6	3.2	1.2	6.2	98.5	31.2	29.4	909	722
Houston	4.3	0.9	2.4	40.5	2.6	1.5	6.5	39.6	19.4	15.4	663	550
Howard	46.7	20.0	5.2	29.2	3.7	1.7	12.9	148.8	46.6	34.2	1 031	830
Hudspeth	3.5	0.4	0.1	0.5	0.5	0.4	19.2	15.9	5.3	5.2	1 560	1 478
Hunt	21.2	604.9	27.5	56.1	6.2	3.4	6.4	210.4	79.6	65.3	822	651
Hutchinson	4.0	0.1	0.7	8.7	0.8	0.9	9.6	94.8	21.8	35.0	1 518	1 293
Irion	0.3	0.0	0.1	0.8	0.0	0.1	0.4	5.8	0.7	4.8	2 713	2 614
Jack	1.2	0.0	0.3	3.4	0.3	0.3	0.7	22.9	7.7	9.2	1 031	882
Jackson	1.7	0.0	0.8	11.6	1.7	0.6	3.5	50.1	11.8	20.7	1 442	1 288
Jasper	4.5	0.2	0.9	38.1	4.5	1.6	14.1	77.9	36.8	32.3	904	787
Jeff Davis	1.2	0.0	0.5	1.6	0.1	0.2	1.4	7.4	3.6	3.0	1 359	1 223
Jefferson	205.5	33.9	110.8	188.6	34.4	11.6	91.6	728.9	177.6	388.8	1 562	1 273
Jim Hogg	3.3	1.7	0.1	14.3	1.0	0.4	1.5	16.3	7.2	8.2	1 582	1 486
Jim Wells	6.8	0.1	1.0	64.4	12.7	2.7	5.1	97.3	53.0	33.8	845	580
Johnson	15.9	0.2	3.9	38.3	4.4	3.3	17.9	271.8	116.4	115.2	845	728
Jones	3.7	0.0	0.6	14.7	1.7	0.9	2.0	46.5	21.8	12.7	625	479
Karnes	2.1	0.0	0.6	30.2	4.6	2.6	3.3	35.6	17.3	10.0	648	543
Kaufman	12.9	0.0	4.0	33.9	5.9	2.7	15.1	177.1	81.5	72.1	925	798
Kendall	3.7	18.7	2.1	3.4	1.0	0.7	0.5	72.9	11.4	51.8	2 041	1 891
Kenedy	0.1	0.0	0.3	0.3	0.0	0.0	0.5	4.6	0.1	4.4	10 511	10 451
Kent	0.5	0.0	0.1	1.0	0.2	0.0	4.2	4.9	0.1	4.3	5 307	5 276
Kerr	28.3	13.5	2.0	12.1	2.4	2.1	4.2	90.5	22.4	50.1	1 117	936
Kimble	0.8	0.0	0.2	2.4	0.4	0.2	4.4	17.2	6.2	4.8	1 061	872
King	0.1	0.0	0.0	0.3	0.0	0.0	0.1	3.8	0.1	3.4	10 333	10 069
Kinney	3.2	0.0	0.0	3.4	0.4	0.2	0.4	10.0	5.7	2.9	833	717
Kleberg	45.0	156.0	0.8	31.6	5.7	4.3	20.1	83.7	39.3	31.0	996	824
Knox	1.5	0.1	0.3	6.3	0.7	0.3	1.1	17.4	7.5	4.7	1 161	949
Lamar	9.3	0.4	2.5	69.4	5.9	3.0	10.3	124.9	51.3	51.6	1 052	819
Lamb	2.4	0.0	0.8	15.0	1.6	1.0	3.6	56.9	26.3	19.1	1 304	1 194
Lampasas	2.4	0.1	0.6	8.9	1.5	0.9	0.6	33.5	16.1	11.9	631	533
La Salle	3.5	0.0	0.1	15.6	1.6	0.4	5.2	21.0	10.1	5.6	951	819
Lavaca	3.2	0.0	0.8	32.6	1.3	0.7	5.1	39.2	6.3	18.2	960	829
Lee	1.8	0.0	0.5	10.3	0.8	0.5	-0.3	33.2	11.3	15.8	965	822
Leon	3.2	0.0	0.9	26.6	1.0	0.6	7.5	34.3	12.4	18.4	1 161	1 031
Liberty	8.1	0.0	2.2	42.9	6.0	2.6	12.1	142.6	62.1	60.7	823	733
Limestone	3.9	0.8	0.9	31.6	2.1	1.0	7.1	58.6	21.6	27.4	1 232	1 094
Lipscomb	1.4	0.0	0.2	1.1	0.1	0.2	0.8	12.6	2.8	7.8	2 522	2 344
Live Oak	18.9	0.0	9.8	7.6	0.6	0.4	9.6	24.4	5.6	16.1	1 344	1 239
Llano	2.1	0.0	0.6	5.8	0.1	0.4	2.4	33.5	3.3	25.4	1 431	1 366
Loving	0.1	0.0	0.0	0.0	0.0	0.0	0.2	1.2	0.0	1.1	16 250	16 250
Lubbock	85.0	16.4	12.7	128.6	24.5	12.4	116.9	751.3	261.7	230.5	931	706
Lynn	1.2	0.0	0.7	6.8	1.1	0.5	17.8	23.0	12.2	6.4	1 011	912
McCulloch	1.8	0.1	0.4	11.3	0.9	0.5	1.1	27.9	12.4	6.8	864	661
McLennan	119.5	76.5	15.6	157.8	22.5	11.8	61.3	739.1	240.8	217.0	997	732
McMullen	0.2	0.0	0.0	0.3	0.1	0.1	0.3	6.3	0.1	5.7	6 627	6 451
Madison	1.5	0.3	0.4	11.0	1.1	0.5	0.1	25.7	13.8	8.9	683	542
Marion	4.2	2.8	0.4	19.7	1.9	0.6	3.7	16.2	5.4	9.1	821	715
Martin	0.8	0.0	0.2	5.0	1.1	0.3	5.1	18.4	5.5	8.6	1 837	1 749

1. State totals may include programs not allocated by county.   2. Based on the resident population estimated as of July 1 of the year shown.

Table B. States and Counties — Local Government Finances, Government Employment, and Elections

STATE County	Total (mil dol) [183]	Per capita[1] (dollars) [184]	Education [185]	Health and hospitals [186]	Police protection [187]	Public welfare [188]	Highways [189]	Total (mil dol) [190]	Per capita[1] (dollars) [191]	Federal civilian [192]	Federal military [193]	State and local [194]	Democratic [195]	Republican [196]	All other [197]
TEXAS—Cont'd															
Guadalupe	191.6	2 033	67.0	1.0	4.3	0.0	3.1	200.9	2 132	187	173	4 800	26.6	72.9	0.5
Hale	82.4	2 294	61.6	8.8	6.6	0.6	3.9	18.8	524	128	67	2 438	20.5	79.2	0.3
Hall	14.8	4 053	49.5	30.4	3.2	0.1	3.3	0.7	191	27	0	304	32.4	67.5	0.2
Hamilton	24.3	3 013	51.8	29.9	2.2	0.0	1.6	13.4	1 664	37	15	591	22.8	77.1	0.1
Hansford	21.4	4 041	54.5	21.3	1.7	0.0	6.1	24.8	4 680	21	10	564	11.4	88.5	0.2
Hardeman	17.9	3 995	44.4	34.7	2.6	0.1	4.3	0.7	153	21	0	435	28.3	71.5	0.2
Hardin	97.8	1 997	75.3	0.0	3.1	0.7	3.2	80.0	1 633	56	91	2 303	27.0	72.6	0.4
Harris	13 130.8	3 691	44.7	8.1	5.1	0.2	3.9	24 414.9	6 864	23 647	7 853	213 070	44.6	54.9	0.5
Harrison	116.0	1 855	72.0	0.1	3.4	0.7	3.0	114.4	1 830	122	116	3 161	36.8	62.9	0.2
Hartley	4.7	867	65.4	0.2	4.7	0.0	5.3	0.6	118	12	10	481	15.3	84.4	0.2
Haskell	19.6	3 310	52.2	22.3	2.3	0.2	7.9	2.7	451	39	11	504	34.9	64.9	0.3
Hays	292.7	2 672	54.5	8.8	5.4	0.8	4.3	520.3	4 748	164	213	9 905	42.1	56.6	1.3
Hemphill	18.3	5 498	48.7	21.4	4.1	0.0	9.9	4.8	1 454	16	0	326	15.7	84.0	0.3
Henderson	141.1	1 862	70.7	0.2	6.5	0.0	4.3	98.5	1 299	104	141	2 996	29.5	70.1	0.4
Hidalgo	1 904.3	3 099	68.3	2.5	3.6	2.0	2.2	1 396.9	2 273	2 599	1 148	40 942	54.9	44.8	0.3
Hill	96.2	2 854	77.3	0.5	2.9	0.0	2.8	72.1	2 138	94	62	2 090	28.8	70.8	0.5
Hockley	111.5	4 883	78.5	0.4	1.7	0.3	2.1	131.0	5 737	53	42	1 839	18.3	81.3	0.4
Hood	75.8	1 717	60.6	0.2	4.5	0.1	3.8	127.5	2 889	102	82	1 678	22.9	76.6	0.6
Hopkins	96.6	2 990	43.7	26.0	4.3	0.1	4.3	48.0	1 487	94	60	2 071	28.6	71.2	0.2
Houston	37.1	1 596	70.4	0.2	5.0	0.0	6.4	17.2	739	85	43	2 055	33.2	66.5	0.3
Howard	145.8	4 388	40.7	13.4	2.7	0.2	2.2	193.6	5 829	829	62	2 870	26.1	73.3	0.5
Hudspeth	14.5	4 343	55.1	0.1	4.0	0.1	5.6	5.2	1 544	96	0	319	34.1	65.1	0.8
Hunt	241.0	3 037	51.7	18.8	3.9	0.0	2.8	242.4	3 054	281	209	6 270	28.3	71.3	0.4
Hutchinson	92.3	4 003	52.0	23.6	3.4	0.3	3.0	25.5	1 106	71	43	1 738	16.1	83.8	0.1
Irion	4.9	2 769	70.9	0.0	4.7	0.3	4.0	0.1	28	0	0	117	17.0	82.6	0.4
Jack	21.0	2 344	55.7	23.1	4.7	0.0	3.4	10.6	1 187	19	17	483	20.6	79.1	0.3
Jackson	47.3	3 291	56.2	18.9	3.5	0.1	5.3	58.1	4 043	38	27	1 082	25.6	74.2	0.2
Jasper	87.9	2 457	72.3	1.4	3.7	0.5	3.7	77.6	2 169	91	66	2 108	34.8	64.9	0.3
Jeff Davis	6.1	2 763	83.1	1.5	2.4	1.0	1.3	1.1	488	31	0	257	32.7	66.1	1.1
Jefferson	724.3	2 910	43.7	5.6	6.3	0.5	4.2	1 239.0	4 978	2 928	615	16 765	51.3	48.4	0.4
Jim Hogg	15.1	2 913	62.8	0.8	8.1	0.9	10.9	5.3	1 026	94	10	455	65.1	34.5	0.3
Jim Wells	102.4	2 564	68.9	0.1	3.6	0.7	3.5	131.3	3 286	91	113	2 193	53.9	45.8	0.3
Johnson	310.1	2 275	65.6	4.4	4.2	0.3	3.3	374.2	2 745	249	254	5 768	26.1	73.5	0.4
Jones	44.6	2 200	57.1	17.0	4.6	0.0	4.6	10.7	529	93	42	2 589	28.0	71.5	0.5
Karnes	32.6	2 113	59.4	12.0	4.5	0.0	6.8	9.7	632	40	29	1 596	33.0	66.7	0.3
Kaufman	206.1	2 644	75.7	0.1	3.2	0.4	3.0	206.8	2 653	177	145	4 791	29.5	70.2	0.3
Kendall	73.3	2 889	57.2	1.9	5.1	0.0	5.9	73.5	2 893	56	47	1 477	18.0	81.5	0.5
Kenedy	3.8	9 155	88.8	0.1	1.2	0.2	2.3	0.0	0	0	0	76	50.3	48.5	1.2
Kent	4.7	5 819	92.5	0.4	1.3	0.0	0.0	2.3	2 903	10	0	191	26.4	73.2	0.4
Kerr	96.1	2 143	66.3	0.4	5.9	0.6	3.4	66.3	1 479	537	83	2 748	21.5	78.0	0.5
Kimble	14.3	3 187	39.3	27.3	5.8	0.1	4.7	1.7	369	18	0	365	17.9	81.8	0.3
King	3.5	10 471	70.9	0.0	1.3	0.0	11.1	0.5	1 526	0	0	70	11.6	88.4	0.0
Kinney	8.5	2 452	62.9	2.7	11.2	0.0	5.9	2.0	567	107	0	233	33.9	65.6	0.5
Kleberg	80.4	2 581	55.5	1.2	9.1	2.7	5.9	15.0	480	611	547	3 756	45.6	53.9	0.5
Knox	16.7	4 112	52.4	22.8	4.7	1.0	3.9	2.4	581	37	0	422	30.0	69.7	0.3
Lamar	127.6	2 601	63.0	1.9	5.5	1.0	6.7	102.6	2 090	159	92	3 007	30.6	69.1	0.3
Lamb	54.9	3 745	57.8	13.6	4.6	0.1	3.4	20.2	1 377	49	27	1 044	20.1	79.8	0.1
Lampasas	33.6	1 785	65.3	2.3	7.0	0.2	5.9	13.7	729	49	35	920	22.6	77.0	0.4
La Salle	18.4	3 132	52.6	2.5	4.2	0.0	6.9	5.0	854	71	11	490	55.1	44.4	0.5
Lavaca	41.0	2 166	44.4	19.5	4.8	0.3	6.3	13.8	730	57	35	871	26.3	73.1	0.6
Lee	36.0	2 205	65.7	0.6	4.9	0.1	7.9	20.9	1 279	38	30	1 226	31.2	68.3	0.4
Leon	31.1	1 961	72.0	0.0	2.4	0.4	6.7	13.3	835	52	29	736	25.8	73.9	0.2
Liberty	164.0	2 224	67.7	0.7	3.9	0.2	3.8	95.1	1 290	126	137	3 593	31.3	68.3	0.4
Limestone	52.5	2 357	62.9	8.8	6.2	0.3	6.9	18.5	829	61	41	2 841	35.2	64.4	0.4
Lipscomb	12.1	3 904	56.2	11.5	2.9	0.1	6.7	0.0	9	25	0	326	13.8	86.0	0.2
Live Oak	23.8	1 984	58.3	1.8	9.6	0.5	13.3	4.5	371	309	22	612	24.7	75.0	0.3
Llano	38.5	2 169	62.0	0.7	5.0	0.5	4.7	25.4	1 430	35	33	1 088	23.7	75.9	0.5
Loving	1.1	16 422	0.0	0.0	6.9	0.0	11.1	0.0	0	0	0	16	15.0	81.3	3.8
Lubbock	742.6	2 999	39.8	27.7	4.9	0.1	2.2	485.0	1 959	1 225	513	22 314	24.2	75.4	0.4
Lynn	22.4	3 546	58.2	19.4	3.4	0.1	3.2	4.5	707	29	12	547	21.0	78.8	0.2
McCulloch	26.1	3 313	50.3	19.1	3.2	0.0	2.9	9.1	1 150	33	15	699	23.2	76.7	0.2
McLennan	768.0	3 528	44.5	3.7	4.4	0.2	2.2	3 092.5	14 205	2 886	441	13 566	33.8	65.8	0.3
McMullen	7.0	8 123	72.3	0.0	2.2	0.4	11.8	3.6	4 230	0	0	115	16.9	82.9	0.2
Madison	23.3	1 777	70.7	0.3	4.6	0.3	4.1	22.4	1 708	25	24	1 164	30.2	69.3	0.5
Marion	15.0	1 358	67.8	0.6	8.3	0.0	7.4	0.7	65	34	21	443	43.4	56.3	0.4
Martin	18.2	3 889	52.3	25.7	2.7	0.1	4.2	0.4	91	20	0	368	16.2	83.6	0.2

1. Based on the resident population estimated as of July 1 of the year shown.

STATE/ County code	CBSA code[1]	County Type[2]	STATE County	Land area,[3] (sq km) 2000	Population and population characteristics, 2003													
								Race alone or in combination, not Hispanic or Latino (percent)					Age (percent)					
					Total persons	Rank	Per square kilometer	White	Black	Am. Indian, Alaska Native	Asian and Pacific Islander[4]	Percent Hispanic or Latino[4]	Under 5 years	5 to 17 years	18 to 24 years	25 to 34 years	35 to 44 years	45 to 54 years
				1	2	3	4	5	6	7	8	9	10	11	12	13	14	15
			TEXAS—Cont'd															
48 319	...	9	Mason	2 414	3 777	2 928	1.6	77.5	0.1	0.6	0.0	21.9	4.9	16.0	7.6	8.4	11.9	14.1
48 321	13060	4	Matagorda	2 886	38 290	1 178	13.3	51.2	12.1	0.7	2.4	34.2	7.5	21.6	10.4	10.6	14.3	13.7
48 323	20580	5	Maverick	3 315	50 178	932	15.1	3.3	0.1	0.8	0.3	95.5	10.4	26.0	10.4	12.4	12.2	10.9
48 325	41700	1	Medina	3 439	41 553	1 096	12.1	51.1	2.1	0.7	0.4	46.2	7.1	20.6	10.5	12.8	14.2	12.8
48 327	...	8	Menard	2 336	2 354	3 029	1.0	65.9	0.5	0.7	0.3	32.5	5.6	16.5	9.3	7.7	13.0	14.2
48 329	33260	3	Midland	2 332	118 624	474	50.9	60.4	6.7	0.6	1.1	31.8	7.6	21.5	10.4	11.5	14.6	14.3
48 331	...	6	Milam	2 633	25 103	1 564	9.5	69.1	10.2	0.7	0.2	20.3	7.2	19.9	9.4	11.0	12.9	12.8
48 333	...	9	Mills	1 938	5 038	2 839	2.6	82.7	1.3	0.3	0.0	15.9	5.1	19.5	7.7	8.2	12.1	13.9
48 335	...	7	Mitchell	2 357	9 316	2 500	4.0	53.7	13.4	0.3	0.4	32.2	4.6	14.1	13.2	14.1	16.5	14.5
48 337	...	6	Montague	2 410	19 416	1 839	8.1	92.5	0.3	1.6	0.4	6.1	6.1	17.6	8.5	10.0	13.1	12.9
48 339	26420	1	Montgomery	2 704	344 700	175	127.5	80.3	3.7	0.9	1.5	14.6	7.4	20.8	10.0	12.9	15.3	13.9
48 341	20300	6	Moore	2 330	20 234	1 788	8.7	48.8	0.7	0.8	0.9	49.1	9.4	24.1	10.1	12.7	14.0	11.8
48 343	...	6	Morris	659	13 167	2 226	20.0	71.7	23.9	1.2	0.3	3.9	5.7	18.5	9.2	10.4	13.0	14.4
48 345	...	8	Motley	2 562	1 304	3 099	0.5	81.7	3.8	0.5	0.1	14.0	5.8	17.7	8.3	6.5	11.2	14.5
48 347	34860	5	Nacogdoches	2 452	59 584	825	24.3	69.4	16.8	0.7	0.8	13.0	6.8	17.2	17.5	12.9	11.7	11.7
48 349	18620	4	Navarro	2 610	47 331	972	18.1	64.4	16.0	0.7	0.8	18.8	7.4	19.7	11.6	12.3	13.5	12.2
48 351	...	8	Newton	2 416	14 869	2 109	6.2	75.0	20.1	1.0	0.4	4.0	5.7	18.8	10.5	11.7	14.0	13.9
48 353	45020	6	Nolan	2 362	15 110	2 095	6.4	66.1	4.7	0.2	0.2	29.1	7.1	19.8	9.9	10.1	13.0	13.8
48 355	18580	2	Nueces	2 165	315 206	187	145.6	36.5	3.8	0.5	1.4	58.4	8.1	20.1	10.5	12.9	14.5	13.8
48 357	...	7	Ochiltree	2 376	8 986	2 524	3.8	62.4	0.2	1.2	0.5	36.2	8.8	21.3	9.9	12.3	15.2	13.2
48 359	...	8	Oldham	3 887	2 159	3 044	0.6	85.4	2.7	1.2	0.6	10.4	5.2	28.4	8.1	9.4	11.8	15.0
48 361	13140	2	Orange	923	84 390	633	91.4	86.5	8.4	0.9	0.9	4.0	6.5	19.7	10.1	11.5	14.9	14.3
48 363	33420	6	Palo Pinto	2 468	27 325	1 490	11.1	82.2	2.3	1.3	0.7	14.5	6.8	18.9	9.3	11.3	13.3	13.5
48 365	...	6	Panola	2 074	22 606	1 680	10.9	77.4	17.6	0.9	0.4	4.4	6.4	18.0	10.5	10.5	13.4	14.9
48 367	19100	1	Parker	2 340	97 480	554	41.7	89.7	2.0	1.1	0.6	7.6	6.0	19.9	10.4	11.7	16.0	14.4
48 369	...	7	Parmer	2 283	9 896	2 454	4.3	45.0	1.0	0.3	0.4	53.3	8.0	24.1	10.2	10.9	13.4	12.0
48 371	...	7	Pecos	12 338	16 039	2 028	1.3	32.7	4.5	0.5	0.6	62.0	6.6	19.4	15.2	12.4	13.6	13.1
48 373	...	6	Polk	2 738	45 323	1 013	16.6	76.8	11.9	2.0	0.5	9.5	5.7	16.7	9.6	12.8	12.9	11.8
48 375	11100	3	Potter	2 355	117 335	480	49.8	56.6	10.2	1.1	2.4	30.8	9.0	19.9	10.6	14.3	14.3	12.0
48 377	...	7	Presidio	9 986	7 591	2 627	0.8	14.7	0.2	0.2	0.1	84.9	8.6	23.6	10.4	9.8	12.6	11.6
48 379	...	8	Rains	601	10 857	2 377	18.1	89.2	2.6	1.2	0.4	7.1	5.1	17.1	10.2	11.2	13.2	13.0
48 381	11100	3	Randall	2 368	107 333	512	45.3	85.5	1.6	1.0	1.4	11.3	6.3	18.8	11.2	13.1	14.4	14.4
48 383	...	6	Reagan	3 044	3 054	2 980	1.0	45.6	3.4	0.4	0.3	50.4	6.7	24.1	11.0	9.8	16.4	14.3
48 385	...	9	Real	1 813	3 020	2 985	1.7	77.7	0.3	1.0	0.2	21.4	4.3	18.0	8.5	8.2	12.7	13.0
48 387	...	6	Red River	2 720	13 812	2 181	5.1	77.3	17.2	1.2	0.1	5.0	6.0	17.1	8.9	10.9	12.8	13.5
48 389	37780	7	Reeves	6 827	12 238	2 281	1.8	23.1	2.0	0.3	0.4	74.3	7.6	21.0	13.2	10.7	13.0	12.9
48 391	...	6	Refugio	1 995	7 625	2 625	3.8	47.0	6.9	0.4	0.4	45.3	6.7	18.6	9.2	9.9	14.2	13.9
48 393	37420	9	Roberts	2 393	820	3 119	0.3	96.5	0.4	0.0	0.5	3.2	4.0	19.4	7.4	6.6	16.1	19.6
48 395	17780	3	Robertson	2 213	15 832	2 047	7.2	60.8	23.8	0.8	0.3	15.0	7.2	20.8	9.1	10.0	13.0	13.1
48 397	19100	1	Rockwall	334	54 630	879	163.6	81.5	4.2	0.8	1.8	12.5	6.9	21.2	10.1	12.0	16.1	13.6
48 399	...	6	Runnels	2 721	10 911	2 373	4.0	66.5	1.6	0.4	0.4	31.2	6.6	19.7	8.9	9.4	12.8	13.3
48 401	30980	3	Rusk	2 392	47 255	975	19.8	71.5	18.7	0.6	0.3	9.5	6.3	17.7	10.0	11.7	15.0	14.0
48 403	...	9	Sabine	1 270	10 379	2 410	8.2	87.4	9.9	0.8	0.2	2.3	5.1	15.9	7.3	9.2	11.8	11.9
48 405	...	9	San Augustine	1 367	8 913	2 532	6.5	68.6	26.6	0.4	0.2	4.5	6.4	16.7	8.2	9.2	12.4	12.8
48 407	26420	1	San Jacinto	1 478	23 917	1 617	16.2	81.0	12.3	1.1	0.6	6.1	6.2	18.6	9.4	10.3	13.5	13.4
48 409	18580	2	San Patricio	1 791	68 050	738	38.0	45.9	1.7	0.6	0.8	51.6	8.5	22.3	10.5	11.9	14.6	12.6
48 411	...	7	San Saba	2 938	6 053	2 770	2.1	73.4	2.8	0.4	0.2	23.3	5.5	21.2	10.8	8.1	11.9	12.7
48 413	...	8	Schleicher	3 394	2 816	2 997	0.8	52.5	1.5	0.1	0.3	45.7	6.9	19.9	10.3	9.4	13.7	15.5
48 415	43660	7	Scurry	2 337	16 081	2 026	6.9	62.9	6.2	0.5	0.3	30.4	6.7	17.9	12.7	10.9	13.6	14.1
48 417	...	8	Shackelford	2 367	3 305	2 962	1.4	91.0	0.4	0.5	0.0	8.3	5.9	18.7	9.1	9.2	14.4	15.5
48 419	...	6	Shelby	2 057	25 882	1 543	12.6	67.2	18.2	0.6	0.4	14.2	7.7	18.9	9.9	12.3	12.8	12.0
48 421	...	9	Sherman	2 391	3 158	2 970	1.3	69.5	0.6	0.5	0.0	29.4	5.8	23.8	9.0	11.3	14.6	12.8
48 423	46340	3	Smith	2 405	184 015	310	76.5	67.4	18.8	0.8	0.9	13.0	7.3	19.0	10.7	12.6	13.5	13.2
48 425	24180	8	Somervell	485	7 331	2 655	15.1	84.6	0.4	1.0	0.3	14.2	6.2	20.0	10.1	10.6	14.7	15.0
48 427	40100	4	Starr	3 168	57 678	849	18.2	2.0	0.0	0.1	0.3	97.6	11.4	26.0	11.7	13.3	12.2	9.4
48 429	...	7	Stephens	2 317	9 449	2 491	4.1	80.4	3.0	0.4	0.4	16.1	6.9	17.2	10.6	10.5	13.6	13.2
48 431	...	8	Sterling	2 391	1 342	3 097	0.6	65.9	0.1	0.4	0.1	33.5	5.0	21.0	9.5	8.9	18.3	13.9
48 433	...	8	Stonewall	2 379	1 448	3 092	0.6	84.5	3.7	0.6	0.3	11.6	6.4	14.5	9.3	7.1	13.9	14.0
48 435	...	7	Sutton	3 765	4 110	2 903	1.1	45.5	0.2	0.3	0.2	53.8	7.8	19.8	8.8	11.7	13.9	15.9
48 437	...	6	Swisher	2 332	8 015	2 592	3.4	56.3	6.2	0.7	0.1	37.1	8.3	20.1	11.1	11.2	12.2	12.0
48 439	19100	1	Tarrant	2 236	1 559 148	19	697.3	59.9	13.5	0.9	4.6	22.5	8.4	20.0	9.9	15.5	16.1	13.0
48 441	10180	3	Taylor	2 371	125 339	452	52.9	72.7	6.6	0.9	1.7	19.5	8.0	18.8	13.1	12.8	13.8	12.2
48 443	...	9	Terrell	6 106	1 034	3 109	0.2	50.0	0.0	1.5	0.9	47.6	3.6	19.5	7.1	8.2	12.3	14.8
48 445	...	6	Terry	2 305	12 453	2 271	5.4	49.0	5.1	0.4	0.2	45.4	7.7	20.0	11.3	11.5	14.6	12.2
48 447	...	9	Throckmorton	2 363	1 697	3 078	0.7	91.2	0.1	0.9	0.1	8.2	5.1	18.4	7.2	6.7	14.8	12.1
48 449	34420	7	Titus	1 063	28 603	1 439	26.9	56.3	10.6	0.4	0.4	32.6	8.8	22.1	10.3	13.6	13.4	11.3

1. CBSA = Core Based Statistical Area. See Appendix A for explanation. See Appendix B for list of metropolitan areas with component counties. 2. County type code from the Economic Research Service of USDA Rural-Urban Continuum Codes. See Appendix A for definition. 3. Dry land or land partially or temporarily covered by water. 4. Hispanic or Latino persons may be of any race.

Table B. States and Counties — **Population and Households**

STATE County	Population, 2003 (cont'd) Age (percent) (cont'd)				Population — change and components of change, 1990–2003							Households, 2000				
					Total persons		Percent change		Components of change, 2000–2003						Percent	
	55 to 64 years	65 to 74 years	75 years and over	Percent female	1990	2000	1990–2000	2000–2003	Births	Deaths	Net migration	Number	Percent change, 1990–2000	Persons per house-hold	Female family house-holder[1]	One person
	16	17	18	19	20	21	22	23	24	25	26	27	28	29	30	31
TEXAS—Cont'd																
Mason	14.0	11.3	11.9	51.9	3 423	3 738	9.2	1.0	111	172	106	1 607	12.0	2.31	7.7	29.2
Matagorda	8.9	6.8	5.5	50.3	36 928	37 957	2.8	0.9	1 809	1 140	-320	13 901	5.6	2.70	12.7	25.1
Maverick	7.0	5.4	4.1	52.2	36 378	47 297	30.0	6.1	3 555	752	89	13 089	34.2	3.60	16.0	12.9
Medina	9.0	6.5	5.6	48.8	27 312	39 304	43.9	5.7	1 817	975	1 405	12 880	41.4	2.91	11.1	18.2
Menard	13.0	10.2	11.6	49.6	2 252	2 360	4.8	-0.3	83	99	13	990	5.7	2.34	8.8	30.4
Midland	7.9	6.4	5.4	51.6	106 611	116 009	8.8	2.3	5 863	2 881	-321	42 745	9.8	2.68	11.4	24.2
Milam	10.4	8.1	8.3	50.7	22 946	24 238	5.6	3.6	1 192	968	645	9 199	5.9	2.59	11.3	25.9
Mills	12.8	9.9	12.3	50.1	4 531	5 151	13.7	-2.2	137	272	22	2 001	12.3	2.43	7.0	27.8
Mitchell	9.1	7.4	7.6	37.6	8 016	9 698	21.0	-3.9	271	319	-320	2 837	-7.1	2.48	11.4	27.5
Montague	11.9	10.3	9.2	51.7	17 274	19 117	10.7	1.6	763	879	432	7 770	13.3	2.41	8.8	27.1
Montgomery	8.7	4.9	3.3	50.2	182 201	293 768	61.2	17.3	15 510	6 684	41 101	103 296	62.5	2.83	9.5	18.3
Moore	7.5	5.7	4.7	49.8	17 865	20 121	12.6	0.6	1 281	424	-754	6 774	11.0	2.94	9.0	18.2
Morris	10.4	10.1	8.4	52.1	13 200	13 048	-1.2	0.9	489	598	234	5 215	4.6	2.47	14.1	25.8
Motley	14.1	10.4	12.0	49.3	1 532	1 426	-6.9	-8.6	43	59	-111	606	-6.3	2.35	8.7	25.7
Nacogdoches	8.0	6.2	5.9	52.0	54 753	59 203	8.1	0.6	2 685	1 656	-638	22 006	9.4	2.49	11.8	27.6
Navarro	9.3	6.7	6.8	50.4	39 926	45 124	13.0	4.9	2 315	1 720	1 655	16 491	10.9	2.65	12.2	24.1
Newton	11.0	8.1	6.2	48.9	13 569	15 072	11.1	-1.3	515	457	-245	5 583	13.7	2.59	11.5	24.1
Nolan	10.0	8.6	8.4	51.2	16 594	15 802	-4.8	-4.4	698	569	-836	6 170	-0.2	2.48	12.6	27.1
Nueces	8.6	6.0	5.2	51.1	291 145	313 645	7.7	0.5	16 967	7 594	-7 739	110 365	10.7	2.79	15.3	22.6
Ochiltree	8.9	6.4	5.2	50.0	9 128	9 006	-1.3	-0.2	519	231	-313	3 261	-2.0	2.74	7.9	21.0
Oldham	9.5	6.6	5.1	48.2	2 278	2 185	-4.1	-1.2	60	64	-21	735	7.9	2.61	8.8	21.0
Orange	10.0	7.4	5.6	51.0	80 509	84 966	5.5	-0.7	3 500	2 819	-1 205	31 642	9.0	2.65	12.1	21.7
Palo Pinto	10.8	8.4	7.5	50.8	25 055	27 026	7.9	1.1	1 192	1 223	362	10 594	11.2	2.52	10.4	26.2
Panola	10.9	8.4	7.6	51.6	22 035	22 756	3.3	-0.7	941	771	-297	8 821	7.0	2.53	11.3	25.1
Parker	9.7	5.9	4.3	49.1	64 785	88 495	36.6	10.2	3 564	2 372	7 591	31 131	35.1	2.75	8.7	18.3
Parmer	8.6	6.6	6.4	50.5	9 863	10 016	1.6	-1.2	510	256	-378	3 322	2.5	2.97	8.3	19.3
Pecos	9.2	6.5	5.0	44.9	14 675	16 809	14.5	-4.6	735	361	-1 166	5 153	9.4	2.86	11.6	19.6
Polk	10.8	10.3	8.1	48.6	30 687	41 133	34.0	10.2	1 655	1 714	4 198	15 119	27.5	2.50	10.8	24.6
Potter	7.6	5.8	5.8	49.5	97 841	113 546	16.1	3.3	7 163	3 756	482	40 760	9.1	2.61	15.0	27.6
Presidio	9.4	7.2	6.8	52.2	6 637	7 304	10.0	3.9	496	96	-113	2 530	12.2	2.85	13.6	24.2
Rains	12.1	9.0	6.4	49.8	6 715	9 139	36.1	18.8	340	341	1 672	3 617	38.6	2.51	9.1	22.3
Randall	9.1	6.6	5.2	51.2	89 673	104 312	16.3	2.9	4 078	2 249	1 320	41 240	19.4	2.49	9.2	25.4
Reagan	7.9	6.4	4.9	50.0	4 514	3 326	-26.3	-8.2	132	71	-336	1 107	-18.5	2.96	7.2	19.8
Real	14.3	11.9	9.0	51.2	2 412	3 047	26.3	-0.9	82	119	14	1 245	34.7	2.38	7.6	28.2
Red River	11.8	9.5	10.4	51.8	14 317	14 314	0.0	-3.5	548	717	-335	5 827	2.4	2.41	11.8	27.7
Reeves	9.6	7.7	6.1	47.1	15 852	13 137	-17.1	-6.8	691	307	-1 303	4 091	-15.4	2.93	12.4	21.6
Refugio	11.3	8.9	8.1	51.1	7 976	7 828	-1.9	-2.6	356	283	-277	2 985	1.6	2.59	12.8	24.6
Roberts	14.4	9.4	7.0	50.0	1 025	887	-13.5	-7.6	21	13	-77	362	-7.4	2.45	3.9	23.8
Robertson	10.9	8.0	8.4	52.4	15 511	16 000	3.2	-1.1	773	674	-255	6 179	6.7	2.55	15.5	26.9
Rockwall	8.3	4.4	3.3	49.6	25 604	43 080	68.3	26.8	2 268	967	9 929	14 530	64.4	2.92	8.0	14.4
Runnels	11.2	9.2	10.6	51.8	11 294	11 495	1.8	-5.1	478	443	-618	4 428	1.9	2.53	9.6	26.7
Rusk	10.4	7.5	7.5	48.8	43 735	47 372	8.3	-0.2	1 929	1 735	-235	17 364	6.4	2.57	11.2	24.2
Sabine	14.7	14.0	10.8	52.0	9 586	10 469	9.2	-0.9	330	559	151	4 485	12.5	2.31	8.7	27.0
San Augustine	12.3	11.1	11.0	52.4	7 999	8 946	11.8	-0.4	381	366	-39	3 575	16.3	2.43	13.5	27.0
San Jacinto	12.5	9.0	5.8	49.9	16 372	22 246	35.9	7.5	919	675	1 405	8 651	38.5	2.55	9.7	22.6
San Patricio	8.6	6.1	4.6	50.5	58 749	67 138	14.3	1.4	3 825	1 581	-1 314	22 093	17.7	2.97	12.7	18.7
San Saba	11.0	9.2	10.4	47.5	5 401	6 186	14.5	-2.2	227	287	-64	2 289	7.9	2.45	8.4	27.5
Schleicher	10.5	8.2	8.3	51.2	2 990	2 935	-1.8	-4.1	152	95	-170	1 115	6.1	2.59	7.5	25.4
Scurry	9.1	7.9	7.2	47.9	18 634	16 361	-12.2	-1.7	730	546	-469	5 756	-9.6	2.55	10.4	25.1
Shackelford	10.2	9.7	8.6	52.3	3 316	3 302	-0.4	0.1	134	105	-24	1 300	-2.7	2.49	8.7	26.2
Shelby	9.6	8.1	7.8	51.4	22 034	25 224	14.5	2.6	1 311	944	321	9 595	13.2	2.59	12.9	25.4
Sherman	10.1	6.5	6.6	49.4	2 858	3 186	11.5	-0.9	130	87	-73	1 124	6.7	2.76	6.0	21.5
Smith	9.2	7.3	6.5	51.9	151 309	174 706	15.5	5.3	8 786	5 629	6 267	65 692	15.7	2.59	12.3	24.7
Somervell	8.9	7.0	6.1	49.8	5 360	6 809	27.0	7.7	302	253	480	2 438	28.2	2.73	9.6	21.3
Starr	6.7	4.7	3.6	51.8	40 518	53 597	32.3	7.6	4 712	741	121	14 410	39.5	3.69	17.4	11.3
Stephens	10.9	9.1	8.6	48.7	9 010	9 674	7.4	-2.3	473	349	-357	3 661	3.0	2.47	9.9	26.4
Sterling	8.6	8.0	7.9	51.5	1 438	1 393	-3.1	-3.7	47	31	-71	513	3.8	2.67	7.0	23.2
Stonewall	12.2	12.5	12.8	52.6	2 013	1 693	-15.9	-14.5	74	79	-243	713	-11.5	2.32	8.8	29.0
Sutton	9.4	7.1	5.7	50.1	4 135	4 077	-1.4	-3.7	222	81	-106	1 515	3.3	2.67	7.7	22.6
Swisher	9.7	8.5	7.8	47.9	8 133	8 378	3.0	-4.3	475	236	-601	2 925	-2.3	2.65	9.5	24.1
Tarrant	7.7	4.5	3.6	50.3	1 170 103	1 446 219	23.6	7.8	85 501	30 514	58 834	533 864	21.7	2.67	12.2	24.9
Taylor	8.0	6.7	6.0	51.6	119 655	126 555	5.8	-1.0	6 593	3 670	-4 185	47 274	9.2	2.54	11.5	25.7
Terrell	12.4	12.2	8.1	49.8	1 410	1 081	-23.3	-4.3	22	19	-49	443	-15.5	2.44	7.4	31.8
Terry	9.2	7.9	6.9	48.3	13 218	12 761	-3.5	-2.4	614	370	-567	4 278	-4.5	2.76	11.9	22.1
Throckmorton	14.0	11.1	11.9	51.7	1 880	1 850	-1.6	-8.3	61	77	-141	765	-3.2	2.39	8.2	28.0
Titus	8.2	5.9	5.9	49.9	24 009	28 118	17.1	1.7	1 695	888	-316	9 552	12.3	2.88	11.4	22.1

1. No spouse present.

Table B. States and Counties — Vital Statistics, Health Resources, and Crime

STATE County	Births, average 1999–2001 Total	Rate[1]	Deaths, average 1999–2001 Number Total	Infant[2]	Rate Total[1]	Infant[3]	Physicians,[4] 2000 Number	Rate[5]	Hospitals,[4] 1998 Number	Beds Number	Rate[5]	Medicare enrollees, 2003	Serious crimes known to police,[6] 2002 Total Number	Rate[7]
	32	33	34	35	36	37	38	39	40	41	42	43	44	45
TEXAS—Cont'd														
Mason	32	8.6	54	1	14.5	D	2	54	0	0	0	897	58	1 486
Matagorda	563	14.8	369	3	9.7	D	31	82	2	68	179	5 299	1 838	4 636
Maverick	1 048	22.1	268	5	5.6	D	33	70	1	60	125	6 212	1 460	2 955
Medina	554	14.1	312	3	7.9	D	18	46	1	27	72	5 018	968	2 358
Menard	25	10.7	36	0	15.4	D	0	0	0	0	0	544	15	609
Midland	1 831	15.7	888	13	7.6	7.3	179	154	2	318	266	14 662	4 730	3 904
Milam	349	14.4	304	2	12.5	D	12	50	2	81	334	4 484	779	3 077
Mills	47	9.2	78	0	15.2	D	2	39	0	0	0	1 120	33	613
Mitchell	91	9.4	113	1	11.7	D	7	72	1	37	381	1 478	184	1 817
Montague	239	12.5	298	1	15.6	D	14	73	2	80	432	4 317	719	3 795
Montgomery	4 620	15.5	2 032	29	6.8	6.3	346	118	2	211	78	32 032	11 187	3 646
Moore	388	19.2	131	3	6.5	D	13	65	1	111	564	2 143	640	3 045
Morris	157	12.0	183	1	14.0	D	4	31	0	0	0	2 971	341	2 805
Motley	12	8.4	21	0	15.1	D	1	70	0	0	0	316	6	403
Nacogdoches	829	14.0	538	5	9.1	D	105	177	2	293	521	8 348	1 922	3 108
Navarro	677	15.0	543	5	12.0	D	54	120	1	134	321	7 388	2 131	4 521
Newton	156	10.4	143	0	9.5	D	3	20	0	0	0	2 142	177	1 124
Nolan	222	14.1	197	2	12.5	D	10	63	1	54	327	3 024	474	2 872
Nueces	5 233	16.7	2 496	35	8.0	6.7	747	238	8	1 549	490	40 149	23 259	7 100
Ochiltree	158	17.4	74	0	8.1	D	3	33	1	44	498	1 119	265	2 817
Oldham	22	10.2	20	0	9.1	D	0	0	0	0	0	365	26	1 139
Orange	1 096	12.9	858	10	10.1	8.8	48	56	1	136	160	13 041	3 987	4 493
Palo Pinto	373	13.8	350	4	13.0	D	20	74	1	44	171	4 495	871	3 085
Panola	290	12.8	250	4	11.0	D	7	31	1	30	130	3 798	663	2 789
Parker	1 074	12.1	733	5	8.2	D	45	51	1	80	98	10 578	2 493	2 697
Parmer	157	15.8	85	1	8.6	D	4	40	1	26	252	1 273	125	1 195
Pecos	222	13.3	115	1	6.9	D	8	48	2	37	231	1 881	384	2 187
Polk	493	11.9	527	3	12.7	D	21	51	1	28	56	14 314	1 146	2 667
Potter	2 200	19.3	1 186	25	10.4	11.2	387	341	3	927	851	23 398	8 087	6 819
Presidio	149	20.2	43	0	5.8	D	1	14	0	0	0	1 392	58	760
Rains	94	10.1	110	1	11.9	D	2	22	0	0	0	1 638	198	2 074
Randall	1 239	11.9	705	9	6.8	7.0	100	96	2	99	99	4 991	6 489	5 956
Reagan	49	14.8	25	0	7.6	D	3	90	1	61	1 451	367	32	921
Real	28	9.2	39	0	12.9	D	2	66	0	0	0	810	14	440
Red River	169	11.8	224	1	15.7	D	6	42	1	36	262	2 995	322	2 154
Reeves	208	15.9	108	1	8.2	D	7	53	1	46	318	1 850	449	3 272
Refugio	110	14.1	93	1	11.9	D	3	38	1	20	253	1 475	151	1 847
Roberts	9	9.8	6	0	0.0	D	1	113	0	0	0	130	18	1 944
Robertson	235	14.7	214	1	13.4	D	3	19	0	0	0	2 847	354	2 118
Rockwall	674	15.4	287	4	6.6	D	54	125	0	0	0	4 508	1 269	2 820
Runnels	153	13.4	143	1	12.5	D	9	78	2	38	330	2 356	257	2 141
Rusk	600	12.7	542	5	11.5	D	31	65	1	96	209	6 661	1 919	3 878
Sabine	110	10.5	176	2	16.8	D	4	38	1	36	341	3 262	261	2 387
San Augustine	114	12.8	125	0	14.0	D	4	45	1	16	198	1 952	324	3 467
San Jacinto	256	11.5	208	2	9.4	D	1	4	0	0	0	3 043	508	2 186
San Patricio	1 196	17.8	539	9	8.0	7.5	41	61	1	68	95	9 089	2 136	3 046
San Saba	68	11.0	78	0	12.6	D	1	16	0	0	0	1 147	78	1 207
Schleicher	39	13.3	30	0	10.2	D	2	68	1	17	570	463	20	652
Scurry	215	13.2	180	1	11.0	D	13	79	1	72	398	2 707	347	2 031
Shackelford	38	11.5	39	1	11.7	D	2	61	1	24	727	637	17	493
Shelby	390	15.5	317	3	12.6	D	8	32	1	48	211	4 646	770	2 923
Sherman	39	12.4	25	0	7.8	D	1	31	0	0	0	413	63	1 894
Smith	2 639	15.1	1 722	20	9.8	7.7	492	282	3	558	331	28 959	9 062	5 021
Somervell	88	12.8	73	1	10.7	D	5	73	1	58	903	946	170	2 390
Starr	1 440	26.6	250	9	4.6	6.5	8	15	1	44	79	6 196	1 111	1 985
Stephens	133	13.8	112	0	11.6	D	5	52	1	35	357	1 777	144	1 425
Sterling	14	9.8	10	0	6.9	D	0	0	0	0	0	182	6	412
Stonewall	18	11.0	28	0	17.0	D	1	59	1	16	897	384	11	622
Sutton	62	15.1	35	0	8.6	D	4	98	1	52	1 165	546	71	1 667
Swisher	134	16.1	79	2	9.5	D	4	48	1	30	361	1 495	217	2 480
Tarrant	25 413	17.5	9 448	183	6.5	7.2	2 312	160	16	3 465	256	141 146	93 787	6 209
Taylor	2 051	16.2	1 179	11	9.3	5.4	253	200	2	494	405	18 845	5 471	4 139
Terrell	7	6.2	12	0	10.8	D	0	0	0	0	0	234	0	0
Terry	207	16.2	124	0	9.7	D	10	78	1	42	326	2 057	281	2 108
Throckmorton	19	10.4	23	0	12.7	D	3	162	1	20	1 158	370	10	518
Titus	502	17.9	278	3	9.9	D	35	124	1	145	570	3 741	1 050	3 575

1. Per 1,000 estimated resident population. 2. Deaths of infants under 1 year old. 3. Deaths of infants under 1 year old per 1,000 live births. 4. Data subject to copyright. 5. Per 100,000 resident population as of July 1 of the year shown. 6. Data for serious crimes have not been adjusted for underreporting; this may affect comparability between geographic areas and over time. 7. Per 100,000 population estimated by the FBI.

Table B. States and Counties — Crime, Education, Money Income, and Poverty

STATE County	Serious crimes known to police,[1] 2002 (cont'd) Rate[2] Violent	Property	Education — School enrollment and attainment, 2000 Enrollment[3] Total	Percent private	Attainment[4] (percent) High school graduate or less	Bachelor's degree or more	Local government expenditures,[5] 2000–2001 Total current expenditures (mil dol)	Current expenditures per student (dollars)	Money income, 1999 Per capita income[6] (dollars)	Households Median income Dollars	Percent change, 1989–1999 (constant 1999 dollars)	Percent with income of $100,000 or more	Percent below poverty level, 1999 Persons	Households	Families	Families with children
	46	47	48	49	50	51	52	53	54	55	56	57	58	59	60	61
TEXAS—Cont'd																
Mason	77	1 409	756	4.6	49.7	18.7	4.6	7 527	20 931	30 921	49.8	6.7	13.2	13.8	10.1	20.4
Matagorda	424	4 212	10 524	7.8	60.9	12.5	55.1	6 831	15 709	32 174	-5.6	7.7	18.5	18.3	14.9	21.3
Maverick	215	2 741	15 541	3.5	76.7	9.1	76.4	6 102	8 758	21 232	28.9	3.4	34.8	35.4	32.0	35.4
Medina	263	2 095	10 809	7.6	61.2	13.3	52.9	6 306	15 210	36 063	19.5	6.5	15.4	15.0	12.0	16.1
Menard	41	568	544	1.5	61.6	17.2	5.1	10 838	15 987	24 762	29.1	4.2	25.8	23.1	20.0	31.7
Midland	495	3 408	34 805	13.3	43.8	24.8	151.9	6 590	20 369	39 082	-6.7	11.9	12.9	12.1	10.3	14.6
Milam	249	2 828	6 297	6.1	66.1	11.6	31.3	6 453	16 920	33 186	34.6	5.3	15.9	16.4	12.2	17.3
Mills	37	576	1 128	2.7	59.2	20.2	8.8	8 614	15 915	30 579	29.6	5.9	18.4	18.3	12.7	16.9
Mitchell	109	1 708	2 012	4.8	69.3	10.4	11.7	8 103	14 043	25 399	7.4	3.1	17.7	20.5	15.0	22.4
Montague	248	3 547	4 192	4.8	62.4	11.3	24.9	7 698	17 115	31 048	21.3	5.3	14.0	14.5	10.0	15.1
Montgomery	387	3 259	81 114	12.3	45.8	25.3	356.0	5 969	24 544	50 864	17.4	19.0	9.4	9.4	7.1	9.5
Moore	305	2 741	5 772	3.2	66.4	11.0	27.8	5 871	15 214	34 852	-5.6	4.9	13.5	12.4	10.1	14.3
Morris	321	2 484	3 217	4.4	60.7	11.2	18.9	7 211	15 612	29 011	8.5	4.4	18.3	18.3	14.9	22.7
Motley	201	201	294	15.0	60.2	14.7	2.3	11 171	16 584	28 348	25.7	5.2	19.4	18.4	13.9	23.4
Nacogdoches	469	2 639	21 373	6.2	53.6	22.8	63.2	6 301	15 437	28 301	8.9	6.8	23.3	23.8	15.5	23.0
Navarro	236	4 286	12 175	6.6	61.0	12.2	57.0	6 468	15 266	31 268	8.4	5.7	18.2	17.8	13.9	19.5
Newton	184	940	3 518	6.7	76.7	5.5	18.1	7 067	13 381	28 500	27.4	3.0	19.1	19.8	15.5	22.0
Nolan	297	2 575	4 262	4.4	62.2	13.2	23.9	7 444	14 077	26 209	-4.1	3.9	21.7	22.2	18.3	26.8
Nueces	700	6 399	91 444	8.6	50.7	18.8	396.5	6 460	17 036	35 959	5.6	7.8	18.2	16.8	14.7	20.2
Ochiltree	351	2 466	2 357	5.6	58.2	16.1	12.4	6 220	16 707	38 013	7.4	6.7	13.0	11.1	9.8	14.5
Oldham	88	1 052	715	3.2	46.6	19.4	10.7	12 308	14 806	33 713	-10.9	5.9	19.8	13.2	10.5	19.1
Orange	581	3 911	22 128	8.6	59.7	11.0	108.1	6 410	17 554	37 586	5.3	7.7	13.8	14.1	11.4	15.6
Palo Pinto	181	2 905	6 254	4.8	60.5	12.1	34.5	6 862	15 454	31 203	13.9	3.7	15.9	15.7	12.3	18.0
Panola	345	2 444	5 765	6.1	58.9	13.4	30.0	7 789	15 439	31 909	12.9	5.4	14.1	16.5	11.6	15.3
Parker	149	2 548	23 189	10.0	49.9	18.6	100.5	6 163	20 305	45 497	10.7	11.2	8.3	8.9	5.9	8.1
Parmer	96	1 099	3 082	3.8	64.7	13.4	17.7	7 152	14 184	30 813	16.2	5.5	17.0	16.8	14.2	18.7
Pecos	165	2 022	4 947	5.1	66.9	12.9	27.8	9 022	12 212	28 033	-1.4	3.5	20.4	19.9	18.1	24.9
Polk	284	2 383	9 215	6.6	66.5	10.4	45.6	6 771	15 834	30 495	19.7	5.1	17.4	16.7	13.3	20.1
Potter	727	6 092	31 113	7.9	58.2	13.5	207.4	6 528	14 947	29 492	7.2	5.1	19.2	18.3	15.2	22.1
Presidio	131	629	2 151	1.4	75.2	11.7	13.1	6 707	9 558	19 860	13.6	2.2	36.4	35.0	32.5	38.2
Rains	73	2 001	2 022	5.0	64.5	11.5	9.1	5 809	16 442	33 712	15.4	4.8	14.9	13.7	11.4	14.6
Randall	636	5 320	30 922	10.8	33.8	28.9	37.1	4 991	21 840	42 712	1.0	9.9	8.1	9.2	5.7	8.2
Reagan	58	864	1 036	0.9	66.9	9.2	7.8	8 832	13 174	33 231	-13.5	3.0	11.8	12.7	9.3	9.2
Real	0	440	742	3.5	55.3	17.3	2.3	7 709	14 321	25 118	7.3	2.5	21.2	19.3	17.4	24.6
Red River	247	1 906	3 114	5.3	68.0	9.0	19.4	7 022	15 058	27 558	26.5	4.1	17.3	17.7	13.1	20.2
Reeves	262	3 010	3 606	1.5	78.2	8.0	19.3	6 436	10 811	23 306	-3.4	2.6	28.9	27.5	25.4	30.5
Refugio	147	1 700	1 906	4.0	64.4	11.6	12.4	7 725	15 481	29 986	7.6	5.0	17.8	18.0	14.3	21.7
Roberts	108	1 836	217	7.4	38.5	25.4	1.8	11 133	20 923	44 792	10.4	8.5	7.2	7.9	5.0	3.9
Robertson	479	1 640	4 049	5.8	67.8	12.7	26.0	7 915	14 714	28 886	25.0	5.0	20.6	21.4	17.3	25.4
Rockwall	236	2 585	12 565	13.4	36.2	32.7	60.4	5 848	28 573	65 164	14.3	25.1	4.7	4.2	3.8	4.9
Runnels	283	1 857	2 833	4.4	66.3	13.1	18.9	7 655	13 577	27 806	7.0	2.8	19.2	19.3	14.9	21.3
Rusk	618	3 260	11 399	8.8	58.9	12.8	50.8	6 771	16 674	32 898	10.2	5.7	14.6	14.7	10.9	17.6
Sabine	137	2 250	2 043	6.5	65.2	10.6	12.3	7 624	15 821	27 198	15.6	3.7	15.9	17.2	11.8	21.2
San Augustine	610	2 857	1 961	4.2	68.7	11.8	11.1	7 696	15 548	27 025	32.9	4.6	21.2	21.8	15.6	25.8
San Jacinto	211	1 975	5 092	7.2	66.0	9.6	24.3	6 021	16 144	32 220	20.7	4.8	18.8	19.5	15.1	19.2
San Patricio	211	2 835	19 646	5.6	58.4	13.0	103.6	6 643	15 425	34 836	13.4	6.5	18.0	17.1	14.6	19.8
San Saba	108	1 099	1 514	3.3	61.2	15.8	8.9	7 811	15 309	30 104	54.9	5.2	16.6	15.3	13.3	21.0
Schleicher	33	620	798	0.5	60.2	17.6	5.3	7 940	15 969	29 746	2.0	5.6	21.5	20.0	16.0	24.9
Scurry	123	1 908	4 259	4.4	59.6	11.8	24.1	7 919	15 871	31 646	-2.0	5.5	16.0	16.0	12.6	18.6
Shackelford	29	464	882	4.3	64.4	20.8	5.8	8 201	16 341	30 479	20.8	4.2	13.6	15.3	10.9	14.9
Shelby	319	2 604	6 145	6.0	66.6	12.2	31.7	6 595	15 186	29 112	24.2	5.1	19.4	19.7	14.9	20.5
Sherman	180	1 713	927	6.1	53.8	20.4	6.0	7 594	17 210	33 179	7.3	6.3	16.1	12.8	11.9	17.2
Smith	506	4 514	46 077	11.9	44.6	22.5	179.8	5 836	19 072	37 148	7.3	9.1	13.8	13.2	10.2	15.0
Somervell	211	2 179	1 907	7.6	54.4	17.2	16.8	10 075	18 367	39 404	-0.7	8.4	8.6	9.0	6.1	8.9
Starr	298	1 686	18 163	2.2	82.2	6.9	100.5	6 803	7 069	16 504	20.6	2.2	50.9	48.5	47.4	53.8
Stephens	79	1 346	2 381	6.9	57.0	13.4	10.6	5 910	15 475	29 583	14.7	5.8	15.6	14.4	12.6	20.0
Sterling	137	275	395	5.6	57.5	17.1	3.0	9 893	16 972	35 129	3.7	6.4	16.8	16.7	13.9	21.4
Stonewall	0	622	363	7.4	66.7	12.6	2.6	9 831	16 094	27 935	-2.0	4.4	19.3	19.4	14.8	25.1
Sutton	117	1 550	1 085	3.5	65.4	13.0	7.5	8 016	17 105	34 385	22.3	8.7	18.0	16.9	14.1	20.4
Swisher	263	2 217	2 196	6.1	61.3	16.2	13.8	7 654	14 326	29 846	13.5	4.0	17.4	16.5	14.2	22.3
Tarrant	534	5 675	399 208	15.8	42.2	26.6	1 658.2	6 138	22 548	46 179	6.3	13.9	10.6	9.6	8.0	11.3
Taylor	342	3 797	37 937	25.0	47.2	22.5	159.0	6 764	17 176	34 035	2.7	6.1	14.5	14.2	10.4	15.3
Terrell	0	0	277	9.0	56.5	19.0	2.7	13 275	13 721	24 219	-15.0	4.3	25.2	25.6	21.2	23.1
Terry	308	1 801	3 351	2.6	69.3	9.5	19.1	7 230	13 860	28 090	-6.6	4.7	23.3	20.5	19.2	27.4
Throckmorton	414	104	443	0.9	56.1	18.2	3.7	9 992	17 719	28 277	11.7	4.3	13.5	12.7	11.4	16.5
Titus	392	3 184	7 916	5.3	63.9	13.2	48.0	8 038	15 501	32 452	8.9	6.3	18.5	16.4	14.9	20.6

1. Data for serious crimes have not been adjusted for underreporting; this may affect comparability between geographic areas and over time. 2. Per 100,000 population estimated by the FBI. 3. All persons 3 years old and over enrolled in nursery school through college. 4. Persons 25 years old and over. 5. Elementary and secondary education expenditures. 6. Based on population enumerated as of April 1, 2000.

STATE County	Total (mil dol)	Percent change, 2001–2002	Per capita[1] Dollars	Per capita[1] Rank	Wages and salaries[2] (mil dol)	Proprietor's income (mil dol)	Dividends, interest, and rent (mil dol)	Transfer payments Total (mil dol)	Government payments to individuals Total (mil dol)	Social Security (mil dol)	Medical payments (mil dol)	Income maintenance (mil dol)	Unemployment insurance (mil dol)
	62	63	64	65	66	67	68	69	70	71	72	73	74
TEXAS—Cont'd													
Mason	83	12.2	21 966	2 024	28	12	22	19	19	9	8	1	0
Matagorda	808	-0.3	21 277	2 220	458	77	125	168	160	62	67	17	9
Maverick	606	5.0	12 432	3 101	336	48	51	221	210	41	108	48	8
Medina	842	4.0	20 672	2 377	249	42	124	159	150	50	74	14	3
Menard	43	6.1	18 311	2 860	14	0	13	13	13	5	6	1	0
Midland	3 956	0.8	33 728	167	2 193	750	803	450	424	177	175	43	14
Milam	541	2.0	21 591	2 123	279	40	98	122	116	46	49	11	3
Mills	116	3.5	22 644	1 838	43	12	25	30	29	11	15	2	0
Mitchell	147	1.1	15 577	3 062	78	8	30	43	41	16	19	4	1
Montague	442	2.7	23 020	1 716	119	50	82	111	107	46	48	7	2
Montgomery	10 736	2.0	32 688	199	3 481	756	1 473	1 029	955	409	402	70	32
Moore	451	-1.7	22 403	1 907	302	60	65	65	60	25	26	7	1
Morris	303	2.2	22 990	1 727	184	29	53	82	79	30	35	7	3
Motley	28	3.1	21 559	2 137	10	2	7	7	7	3	3	0	0
Nacogdoches	1 278	5.1	21 577	2 126	720	131	232	260	247	87	114	23	4
Navarro	1 002	3.2	21 397	2 181	514	63	173	222	212	77	93	21	5
Newton	255	3.7	17 146	2 979	63	17	31	69	66	22	30	8	3
Nolan	332	2.9	21 895	2 040	187	31	56	90	87	31	40	8	1
Nueces	8 152	3.8	25 961	893	5 695	871	1 251	1 408	1 338	412	636	178	39
Ochiltree	240	-8.7	26 484	792	128	58	41	30	28	13	11	3	1
Oldham	50	1.2	23 201	1 661	29	7	8	8	7	4	3	1	0
Orange	2 038	3.2	24 182	1 348	997	89	291	446	427	160	197	33	19
Palo Pinto	633	1.9	23 316	1 624	245	54	105	129	123	50	54	10	3
Panola	515	1.8	22 665	1 831	217	60	104	113	108	42	46	10	3
Parker	2 666	3.3	28 180	523	646	210	388	309	288	135	102	18	10
Parmer	233	-8.3	23 720	1 493	158	45	43	35	33	14	14	4	0
Pecos	250	3.2	15 346	3 066	155	18	38	59	55	18	27	8	1
Polk	1 138	4.4	25 632	970	335	74	332	359	349	174	137	20	5
Potter	2 790	4.6	24 125	1 363	2 769	489	463	564	538	158	266	60	17
Presidio	109	6.3	14 435	3 086	57	5	19	33	31	9	11	9	2
Rains	199	3.1	19 115	2 736	41	20	33	47	44	21	17	3	1
Randall	2 815	2.9	26 456	806	704	130	485	282	258	155	54	17	4
Reagan	57	1.7	17 913	2 907	41	1	10	12	11	4	5	1	0
Real	60	6.9	20 187	2 504	15	2	19	20	20	9	8	2	0
Red River	271	0.5	19 385	2 679	82	17	47	86	83	28	42	9	2
Reeves	215	2.5	17 139	2 980	122	19	27	61	59	18	27	9	4
Refugio	195	-1.3	25 291	1 051	60	9	68	42	40	16	19	4	0
Roberts	21	-1.3	24 324	1 300	6	2	4	3	3	1	1	0	0
Robertson	353	3.0	22 236	1 949	123	22	60	84	81	29	35	10	2
Rockwall	1 775	1.2	34 825	146	494	121	243	134	122	57	47	6	7
Runnels	232	-0.1	20 843	2 336	106	27	42	60	57	23	27	5	1
Rusk	1 057	2.7	22 399	1 908	483	98	194	212	201	84	85	17	5
Sabine	232	3.0	22 348	1 922	90	19	51	82	80	33	35	5	2
San Augustine	188	3.3	21 050	2 281	54	23	33	62	60	21	29	6	1
San Jacinto	490	2.9	21 044	2 286	66	25	65	106	101	44	40	10	2
San Patricio	1 433	5.1	21 215	2 234	799	50	177	297	283	94	131	38	8
San Saba	125	1.9	20 666	2 383	55	10	27	32	31	11	15	3	0
Schleicher	55	-0.7	18 746	2 790	25	2	13	13	12	5	5	1	0
Scurry	373	7.5	23 305	1 630	237	21	63	77	73	29	33	6	2
Shackelford	88	1.1	26 383	812	29	15	21	18	17	8	7	1	0
Shelby	580	2.0	22 762	1 798	231	118	88	142	136	46	67	14	3
Sherman	118	-12.4	37 118	103	31	57	14	9	9	4	4	1	0
Smith	5 144	4.0	28 466	494	3 275	708	997	819	779	320	327	65	19
Somervell	192	4.5	26 808	734	195	16	28	29	27	11	13	2	1
Starr	589	7.6	10 480	3 108	275	39	52	235	222	36	116	62	5
Stephens	215	1.4	22 743	1 806	89	30	51	52	50	20	24	4	1
Sterling	29	10.5	21 298	2 208	19	-1	9	5	5	2	2	0	0
Stonewall	43	-1.0	28 634	481	15	5	12	10	10	4	5	1	0
Sutton	94	9.6	22 925	1 744	71	0	22	16	15	6	8	2	0
Swisher	202	-4.2	25 067	1 113	74	54	35	37	35	15	14	4	1
Tarrant	47 785	2.1	31 307	261	33 880	5 618	5 788	4 615	4 273	1 640	1 710	413	258
Taylor	3 189	4.8	25 505	997	2 078	348	569	562	535	198	236	50	10
Terrell	31	3.8	30 623	297	18	-1	9	6	6	2	2	0	0
Terry	278	1.6	22 100	1 990	126	39	48	69	66	22	35	7	1
Throckmorton	46	-3.5	26 592	768	13	6	13	10	10	4	4	1	0
Titus	647	5.6	22 957	1 736	555	55	87	123	116	40	55	12	3

1. Based on the resident population estimated as of July 1 of the year shown.   2. Includes other labor income.

STATE County	Earnings, 2002 Total (mil dol)	Farm	Goods-related[1] Total	Manu-facturing	Service-related and health Infor-mation and profes-sional and technical services	Retail trade	Finance, insur-ance, and real estate	Health services	Govern-ment	Social Security beneficiaries, December 2003 Number	Rate[2]	Supple-mental Security Income recipients, December 2003	Housing units, 2003 Total	Percent change, 2000–2003
	75	76	77	78	79	80	81	82	83	84	85	86	87	88
TEXAS—Cont'd														
Mason	40	11.7	D	11.5	D	7.2	D	10.3	20.1	1 015	269	80	2 349	-1.0
Matagorda	535	4.6	15.1	6.9	5.3	6.2	3.4	D	16.5	6 475	169	874	18 826	1.2
Maverick	384	1.2	5.6	2.7	3.9	11.6	4.5	D	41.3	7 145	142	3 597	15 672	5.3
Medina	292	2.6	12.6	4.9	4.6	9.9	7.5	D	32.9	6 285	151	640	15 198	2.5
Menard	14	-13.7	D	D	D	17.0	D	4.4	48.1	615	261	77	1 607	0.0
Midland	2 944	-0.1	44.4	3.4	8.0	6.2	6.5	6.3	11.7	17 410	147	2 102	48 854	1.7
Milam	319	2.8	46.9	35.6	3.5	6.4	4.5	4.8	13.8	5 115	204	624	11 038	1.6
Mills	55	5.0	9.4	6.0	D	13.9	D	15.4	22.8	1 275	253	144	2 707	0.6
Mitchell	86	-0.1	13.0	0.7	D	7.0	D	D	51.7	1 645	177	216	4 171	0.1
Montague	169	2.1	23.2	5.6	5.3	11.0	7.4	D	25.9	4 860	250	423	10 000	1.4
Montgomery	4 237	0.3	23.3	8.6	11.0	9.8	12.2	9.2	12.2	41 305	120	4 135	127 684	13.2
Moore	362	6.1	45.6	36.7	2.7	7.1	3.5	2.8	14.4	2 515	124	198	7 610	1.8
Morris	213	4.5	D	49.9	7.3	4.0	3.5	3.1	11.7	3 365	256	437	6 112	1.6
Motley	12	14.0	D	D	D	9.4	4.6	D	29.7	365	280	35	833	-0.7
Nacogdoches	851	2.7	24.2	18.5	5.2	10.5	4.0	15.8	23.7	9 265	155	1 693	26 008	3.8
Navarro	577	1.5	25.6	18.8	D	14.2	6.0	10.4	19.4	8 710	184	1 416	18 660	1.1
Newton	81	-0.6	26.5	23.2	D	4.8	D	4.4	28.1	2 595	175	492	7 511	2.5
Nolan	218	0.9	23.3	16.6	5.0	9.1	4.0	7.4	27.9	3 265	216	440	7 064	-0.7
Nueces	6 566	0.3	22.1	9.5	9.0	8.0	6.0	13.0	21.4	46 835	149	9 499	126 190	2.6
Ochiltree	186	18.2	35.1	0.9	2.9	6.3	3.8	D	12.6	1 290	144	108	3 807	1.0
Oldham	36	22.6	D	D	D	3.7	D	D	30.9	360	167	24	820	0.6
Orange	1 086	0.0	43.1	33.6	D	7.6	5.1	7.1	14.9	16 010	190	1 797	35 603	2.4
Palo Pinto	299	-0.2	29.7	19.0	3.0	10.1	4.4	D	22.0	5 430	199	433	14 186	0.6
Panola	276	6.9	32.6	14.0	4.4	6.8	4.2	7.4	16.7	4 620	204	574	10 766	2.3
Parker	857	1.3	23.7	8.5	8.0	12.9	6.5	5.6	20.1	14 170	145	592	35 787	5.0
Parmer	204	25.2	D	D	1.4	1.8	1.6	1.5	13.3	1 490	151	155	3 761	0.8
Pecos	173	3.0	19.1	1.8	D	8.5	3.6	4.6	38.5	2 165	135	449	6 393	0.9
Polk	409	0.1	24.4	16.3	5.3	13.7	4.6	5.9	25.0	17 740	391	1 299	21 573	1.9
Potter	3 258	0.1	15.7	8.0	10.3	9.7	8.3	16.3	17.1	16 695	142	3 079	46 034	3.2
Presidio	62	5.2	D	0.7	1.6	6.7	D	D	57.1	1 470	194	672	3 506	6.3
Rains	62	11.8	21.5	6.8	D	11.8	D	1.7	21.1	2 160	199	156	4 633	2.4
Randall	834	4.3	D	8.8	5.6	10.6	7.0	6.3	20.4	15 250	142	495	44 489	2.8
Reagan	42	-4.7	D	D	D	5.2	4.1	D	28.5	460	151	37	1 475	1.6
Real	17	-11.5	D	D	D	4.4	D	D	36.4	940	311	112	2 059	2.6
Red River	100	6.0	D	21.5	D	11.0	3.5	13.4	25.2	3 330	241	534	7 007	1.3
Reeves	141	7.5	20.4	11.9	D	8.8	3.8	3.4	36.0	2 150	176	554	5 032	-0.2
Refugio	69	-4.2	27.1	1.0	4.0	10.3	8.0	D	31.5	1 705	224	226	3 678	0.2
Roberts	7	17.5	D	D	D	D	D	D	39.5	150	183	9	445	-0.9
Robertson	146	0.7	35.4	14.6	D	5.2	4.2	6.5	23.8	3 335	211	620	8 005	1.7
Rockwall	615	0.2	D	8.8	D	11.5	9.3	13.7	12.7	5 760	105	277	19 256	25.4
Runnels	133	6.3	35.4	30.1	2.4	7.4	6.1	5.0	20.4	2 605	239	291	5 358	-0.8
Rusk	581	4.2	37.0	10.9	D	7.3	4.6	6.2	13.8	8 850	187	1 000	20 171	1.5
Sabine	109	4.1	43.1	30.4	D	6.0	D	3.9	17.7	3 475	335	408	7 837	2.3
San Augustine	76	14.4	D	4.7	D	8.3	4.0	13.8	20.0	2 425	272	452	5 463	2.0
San Jacinto	91	2.0	D	5.8	D	7.0	4.4	D	30.4	4 775	200	529	11 792	2.4
San Patricio	849	1.2	31.0	18.3	D	5.1	2.2	4.7	37.2	10 610	156	2 406	26 089	4.9
San Saba	66	2.5	D	1.7	D	11.9	4.4	5.7	38.3	1 340	221	160	2 978	0.9
Schleicher	27	-2.5	D	D	D	2.0	3.7	5.4	34.0	545	194	53	1 380	0.7
Scurry	259	-0.4	29.4	2.2	1.9	6.2	19.2	2.7	22.3	3 000	187	309	7 136	0.3
Shackelford	44	-0.9	56.3	1.0	D	4.8	D	D	17.7	755	228	56	1 615	0.1
Shelby	348	18.2	D	21.9	6.6	8.4	3.9	4.8	12.4	5 340	206	921	12 224	2.3
Sherman	88	66.2	D	1.1	D	2.5	D	D	10.8	360	114	18	1 334	4.6
Smith	3 984	1.0	21.1	13.2	9.6	12.1	9.4	17.9	12.5	32 965	179	4 103	74 211	3.5
Somervell	212	0.0	D	2.4	D	2.5	1.7	D	9.7	1 170	160	91	2 880	4.7
Starr	314	3.6	4.1	0.8	2.5	12.9	2.0	D	48.9	7 185	125	3 773	17 859	1.5
Stephens	119	-1.8	44.1	12.3	3.4	7.5	4.4	7.0	22.1	2 135	226	232	4 892	0.0
Sterling	18	-8.8	D	0.0	D	17.6	6.3	D	26.8	200	149	22	639	0.9
Stonewall	21	11.7	D	0.0	1.7	6.8	D	D	27.0	440	304	33	941	0.5
Sutton	71	-8.2	49.4	0.6	D	5.5	4.2	1.9	18.0	615	150	96	2 000	0.1
Swisher	129	43.0	D	2.8	D	5.5	2.5	D	20.3	1 645	205	147	3 319	0.1
Tarrant	39 497	0.0	24.3	16.2	9.1	8.0	10.1	8.4	11.2	165 360	106	20 106	607 974	7.4
Taylor	2 426	0.1	12.2	4.6	6.6	8.5	7.4	14.5	28.6	21 155	169	2 927	53 104	2.0
Terrell	17	-9.0	D	D	D	0.8	D	D	59.4	230	222	29	1 002	1.1
Terry	165	17.7	14.6	1.1	D	11.3	4.1	D	23.3	2 330	187	338	5 095	0.2
Throckmorton	19	14.2	D	D	D	3.3	5.4	D	29.1	425	250	33	1 068	0.2
Titus	611	0.7	D	40.7	2.5	8.8	2.5	D	17.0	4 235	148	618	10 906	2.2

1. Covers mining, construction, and manufacturing.   2. Per 1,000 resident population estimated as of July 1 of the year shown.

STATE County	Housing units, 2000 Total	Percent	Owner-occupied Median value[1]	Median owner cost as a percent of income With a mortgage	Without a mortgage[2]	Renter-occupied Median rent[3]	Median rent as a percent of income	Sub-standard units[4] (percent)	Civilian labor force, 2003 Total	Percent change, 2002–2003	Unemployment Total	Rate[5]	Civilian employment,[6] 2000 Total	Percent Management, professional and related occupations	Production, transportation and material moving occupations
	89	90	91	92	93	94	95	96	97	98	99	100	101	102	103
TEXAS—Cont'd															
Mason	1 607	80.5	53 900	20.4	10.5	306	24.0	4.8	1 681	3.4	39	2.3	1 701	35.6	8.9
Matagorda	13 901	66.8	61 500	17.8	10.7	411	22.4	9.3	15 073	1.7	2 172	14.4	15 054	26.5	15.2
Maverick	13 089	69.5	50 200	21.0	12.0	323	27.8	26.2	20 714	8.2	4 706	22.7	13 161	21.5	20.5
Medina	12 880	79.7	68 100	20.6	10.6	453	22.3	7.7	16 484	2.8	878	5.3	16 168	27.2	13.2
Menard	990	75.4	28 900	19.0	14.1	339	23.3	4.7	912	-3.8	45	4.9	999	31.0	15.7
Midland	42 745	69.5	73 400	19.3	11.1	464	23.6	6.5	64 381	3.9	2 886	4.5	51 628	34.9	10.4
Milam	9 199	73.0	49 300	17.9	10.7	390	20.0	6.9	9 966	1.5	693	7.0	10 305	23.3	19.0
Mills	2 001	80.9	48 800	16.7	11.7	369	23.6	4.7	2 601	6.6	51	2.0	2 152	32.1	13.0
Mitchell	2 837	76.0	31 000	20.3	14.1	389	23.0	4.1	3 359	4.6	163	4.9	2 938	26.0	13.6
Montague	7 770	78.7	53 200	19.1	12.0	419	22.8	4.3	7 402	5.3	470	6.3	8 090	25.7	20.4
Montgomery	103 296	78.2	114 800	19.5	9.9	617	23.8	6.4	160 205	2.2	8 577	5.4	136 618	33.9	12.4
Moore	6 774	70.5	60 400	18.3	9.9	406	19.5	12.4	9 499	0.1	437	4.6	8 599	19.6	29.5
Morris	5 215	77.8	45 600	19.4	11.5	364	23.5	4.3	6 382	1.5	561	8.8	5 118	23.4	24.5
Motley	606	77.4	30 100	15.7	10.8	354	15.1	5.4	637	2.1	11	1.7	627	34.0	10.0
Nacogdoches	22 006	61.5	73 900	19.1	9.9	465	31.2	6.8	26 750	2.8	1 264	4.7	25 637	29.7	15.2
Navarro	16 491	70.7	56 700	18.9	12.7	454	24.1	7.9	22 138	-0.1	1 660	7.5	18 477	24.7	22.9
Newton	5 583	84.5	48 200	18.5	9.9	363	22.2	6.6	5 764	0.8	851	14.8	5 222	17.2	19.8
Nolan	6 170	67.4	35 300	17.1	11.2	340	23.1	4.7	7 167	4.5	393	5.5	6 430	29.7	18.7
Nueces	110 365	61.3	70 100	21.7	12.0	548	25.6	10.3	153 168	3.1	10 142	6.6	131 718	30.0	11.7
Ochiltree	3 261	72.5	48 800	18.5	9.9	431	19.6	9.3	4 868	3.0	134	2.8	4 146	24.3	17.1
Oldham	735	66.3	50 000	19.3	13.3	422	16.5	3.0	1 253	-0.3	33	2.6	978	29.9	9.6
Orange	31 642	77.2	66 100	18.0	9.9	472	23.9	5.6	41 019	3.3	4 649	11.3	35 693	25.1	18.0
Palo Pinto	10 594	71.9	46 700	19.1	12.5	455	23.2	5.9	11 803	1.6	689	5.8	11 988	24.8	21.6
Panola	8 821	80.8	60 600	19.4	9.9	368	23.9	5.4	8 417	7.2	678	8.1	9 075	24.9	20.4
Parker	31 131	80.6	99 400	19.4	11.5	548	24.4	4.3	45 367	1.3	2 290	5.0	41 587	31.0	14.7
Parmer	3 322	72.3	49 400	17.6	10.9	395	22.4	12.6	4 590	4.5	138	3.0	3 855	28.4	23.4
Pecos	5 153	74.2	40 200	18.5	10.3	367	18.3	9.6	6 518	3.5	360	5.5	6 094	23.5	13.5
Polk	15 119	81.6	60 000	20.4	10.7	421	24.9	6.5	15 702	4.4	1 066	6.8	14 006	24.7	16.7
Potter	40 760	60.1	54 400	20.2	10.2	451	25.1	9.2	58 182	4.2	3 751	6.4	46 722	22.4	17.8
Presidio	2 530	70.1	35 500	19.6	13.3	276	21.3	14.2	3 768	6.4	828	22.0	2 400	23.0	9.3
Rains	3 617	82.7	60 500	19.5	12.6	454	23.1	6.1	4 070	7.4	267	6.6	3 920	24.1	16.9
Randall	41 240	70.3	93 500	18.9	9.9	504	23.9	3.2	60 797	3.8	927	1.5	54 681	35.7	10.5
Reagan	1 107	78.4	50 500	19.6	11.7	369	22.2	12.5	1 603	0.4	48	3.0	1 406	24.2	19.6
Real	1 245	77.0	56 700	22.6	11.0	433	22.2	5.8	1 285	1.7	51	4.0	1 166	31.1	9.3
Red River	5 827	75.0	34 400	17.9	11.0	328	22.5	5.6	5 224	-1.2	396	7.6	5 942	20.4	28.7
Reeves	4 091	77.6	24 900	20.3	13.1	337	21.2	11.9	5 888	-11.7	664	11.3	4 231	19.2	22.4
Refugio	2 985	74.7	42 600	18.2	9.9	366	20.3	6.1	2 667	-1.0	102	3.8	3 239	24.4	15.7
Roberts	362	79.6	48 800	17.3	9.9	380	13.3	1.1	406	0.5	9	2.2	460	39.6	12.2
Robertson	6 179	71.6	53 000	20.3	13.5	344	23.9	7.6	6 704	3.9	427	6.4	6 318	24.5	18.2
Rockwall	14 530	82.7	147 100	20.9	11.2	699	22.9	3.6	26 924	0.9	1 482	5.5	21 585	43.0	8.8
Runnels	4 428	77.4	37 800	18.1	12.1	356	21.3	6.8	4 575	-8.4	183	4.0	4 606	28.7	21.9
Rusk	17 364	79.9	60 900	18.8	10.1	419	23.8	5.7	22 306	1.5	1 275	5.7	18 825	23.2	20.1
Sabine	4 485	86.2	57 600	19.3	11.5	319	18.6	3.7	3 921	0.1	513	13.1	3 258	24.1	19.0
San Augustine	3 575	81.6	52 000	21.2	10.9	317	23.7	6.6	3 190	0.9	208	6.5	3 210	25.4	21.2
San Jacinto	8 651	87.9	59 400	19.5	11.4	380	24.2	8.2	9 328	2.0	515	5.5	8 345	25.2	17.9
San Patricio	22 093	68.2	66 000	20.3	11.8	518	24.6	10.2	29 928	3.9	2 056	6.9	24 212	27.4	14.6
San Saba	2 289	75.6	47 000	18.0	12.0	402	20.6	6.1	2 744	10.8	73	2.7	2 426	30.5	13.0
Schleicher	1 115	75.7	45 700	19.9	10.9	321	16.1	8.5	1 483	7.1	42	2.8	1 280	35.5	8.5
Scurry	5 756	73.9	42 500	18.8	12.3	392	20.2	5.4	7 098	3.3	315	4.4	6 437	28.3	16.5
Shackelford	1 300	78.7	42 800	18.6	13.3	380	21.1	3.7	1 470	0.9	44	3.0	1 433	29.8	14.0
Shelby	9 595	78.2	55 600	18.0	9.9	327	22.5	7.7	9 697	2.0	784	8.1	9 801	24.8	23.4
Sherman	1 124	74.2	48 800	15.7	11.1	418	18.6	7.6	1 388	-7.7	22	1.6	1 373	36.3	12.1
Smith	65 692	69.7	82 600	19.8	10.4	517	25.1	6.3	97 127	2.8	4 800	4.9	77 518	30.3	16.1
Somervell	2 438	74.7	91 300	18.9	11.6	402	20.7	7.0	2 125	-2.1	231	10.9	3 115	29.1	15.8
Starr	14 410	79.4	37 800	22.9	13.0	281	28.6	28.8	23 967	5.4	4 536	18.9	13 385	22.7	13.2
Stephens	3 661	72.4	45 800	19.0	12.4	400	19.9	4.3	3 638	-6.3	251	6.9	3 923	25.8	16.2
Sterling	513	76.2	53 000	18.4	11.3	392	21.9	4.3	786	11.8	28	3.6	634	30.4	15.8
Stonewall	713	78.5	30 100	17.8	10.8	290	19.2	3.6	729	2.7	23	3.2	717	30.5	12.4
Sutton	1 515	72.0	49 900	17.6	12.0	362	19.0	9.6	2 177	3.0	46	2.1	1 855	26.0	17.8
Swisher	2 925	70.4	38 200	19.1	10.4	387	19.8	7.4	3 582	-1.9	169	4.7	3 332	33.9	17.0
Tarrant	533 864	60.8	90 300	20.3	11.2	612	23.7	8.2	831 474	1.3	53 670	6.5	715 387	34.5	13.3
Taylor	47 274	61.5	61 700	19.4	10.4	472	24.1	5.2	61 450	3.6	2 608	4.2	55 290	32.1	11.1
Terrell	443	77.7	26 500	16.2	13.9	446	20.0	6.1	665	-2.8	32	4.8	466	33.0	8.6
Terry	4 278	71.1	43 800	17.9	13.0	388	26.9	8.3	5 402	3.8	373	6.9	4 759	24.8	14.4
Throckmorton	765	77.3	34 200	17.2	12.0	327	17.1	1.4	838	1.6	27	3.2	848	34.9	13.9
Titus	9 552	72.4	63 800	20.5	12.4	462	22.9	12.6	14 446	3.0	744	5.2	11 265	23.5	23.0

1. Specified owner-occupied units.   2. Median monthly owner costs is often in the minimum category—9.9 percent or less, which is indicated as 9.9 percent.   3. Specified renter-occupied units.   4. Overcrowded or lacking complete plumbing facilities.   5. Percent of civilian labor force.   6. Persons 16 years old and over.

	Private nonfarm establishments, employment and payroll, 2001								Agriculture, 2002			
STATE County	Number of establishments	Employment						Annual payroll		Farms		Farm operators whose principal occupation is farming (percent)
		Total	Health care and social assistance	Manufacturing	Retail trade	Finance and insurance	Professional, scientific, and technical services	Total (mil dol)	Average per employee (dollars)	Number	Percent with—	
											Less than 50 acres	500 acres and over	
	104	105	106	107	108	109	110	111	112	113	114	115	116
TEXAS—Cont'd													
Mason	124	547	46	D	97	40	14	10	19 186	633	10.4	43.4	53.7
Matagorda	773	7 798	1 365	583	1 479	229	155	258	33 068	991	26.2	24.9	59.6
Maverick	796	7 217	944	910	1 935	342	165	125	17 334	214	34.6	26.2	50.5
Medina	585	4 785	722	534	1 113	214	282	95	19 758	1 951	27.8	18.7	53.6
Menard	49	266	D	D	67	24	3	4	13 658	336	10.7	44.3	64.9
Midland	4 038	48 396	5 384	2 199	6 318	1 734	2 240	1 508	31 159	477	48.6	16.6	36.9
Milam	421	5 340	683	1 860	721	205	115	168	31 506	1 991	26.2	12.5	55.0
Mills	125	875	265	69	179	53	14	18	20 423	768	16.1	25.9	56.9
Mitchell	137	1 152	337	D	225	56	38	24	21 191	451	12.0	33.0	55.7
Montague	433	3 121	702	289	614	177	94	63	20 213	1 399	19.4	17.1	51.4
Montgomery	5 995	83 064	6 826	7 768	14 939	2 503	5 652	2 617	31 505	1 701	61.8	4.8	42.9
Moore	440	6 977	562	3 333	747	150	95	183	26 243	276	10.9	63.4	76.1
Morris	250	4 285	262	2 229	388	121	89	134	31 260	403	33.3	10.9	51.4
Motley	51	191	D	D	28	16	1	3	17 827	201	2.5	57.2	62.7
Nacogdoches	1 264	18 405	3 143	4 156	3 167	518	1 124	404	21 951	1 290	32.2	6.3	58.7
Navarro	914	13 568	1 649	2 994	2 256	347	375	315	23 187	1 864	29.9	11.9	53.0
Newton	150	1 426	95	D	160	D	12	31	21 568	385	56.6	2.1	48.3
Nolan	391	4 402	774	892	664	174	152	100	22 682	516	14.0	34.3	48.1
Nueces	7 849	114 937	22 104	7 782	15 956	3 894	5 077	3 186	27 724	649	36.7	29.4	59.2
Ochiltree	297	2 669	265	D	413	107	99	64	24 152	367	11.2	61.3	70.6
Oldham	44	516	D	D	58	D	D	11	20 684	136	5.9	65.4	65.4
Orange	1 401	19 324	2 032	5 209	3 291	519	757	579	29 961	496	70.2	6.0	46.2
Palo Pinto	619	6 340	980	1 496	1 062	204	112	153	24 096	965	31.2	19.8	51.6
Panola	484	4 796	641	1 078	740	161	149	114	23 728	948	21.6	13.0	53.0
Parker	1 562	15 083	1 569	1 895	3 602	450	559	367	24 301	3 215	59.3	5.0	44.3
Parmer	214	3 445	94	D	248	56	D	85	24 575	660	8.6	52.9	76.8
Pecos	304	2 788	382	74	531	132	43	63	22 433	270	10.7	68.9	64.8
Polk	679	7 235	853	1 385	1 739	233	258	162	22 341	689	38.9	7.4	50.7
Potter	3 615	64 695	11 745	10 023	7 472	3 340	5 362	1 915	29 604	305	34.1	24.3	48.9
Presidio	116	579	D	D	184	41	14	10	17 271	123	9.8	67.5	58.5
Rains	138	950	21	109	178	46	30	18	18 494	584	42.8	7.7	50.9
Randall	1 978	21 628	1 841	1 082	4 514	1 207	468	506	23 405	748	29.4	29.7	48.0
Reagan	91	808	82	D	89	D	D	21	26 184	123	1.6	70.7	68.3
Real	68	349	67	48	50	D	9	6	17 590	301	16.6	45.8	54.5
Red River	223	2 415	439	868	425	76	17	42	17 223	1 217	21.9	16.1	57.6
Reeves	212	2 693	236	D	575	86	98	54	20 110	166	10.8	48.2	57.2
Refugio	145	1 081	157	D	222	94	D	25	23 203	274	24.1	29.9	56.9
Roberts	12	58	0	0	25	D	0	1	17 310	94	2.1	74.5	80.9
Robertson	236	2 192	371	327	375	141	25	50	22 599	1 555	23.9	14.5	55.7
Rockwall	1 076	11 640	1 218	1 550	2 390	285	591	286	24 604	385	60.5	4.2	44.2
Runnels	279	2 815	403	1 240	376	107	D	63	22 256	897	13.2	32.6	57.1
Rusk	748	9 544	1 042	1 238	1 274	348	299	257	26 894	1 391	29.3	8.4	52.8
Sabine	158	1 394	107	267	389	70	12	32	23 077	219	36.5	5.5	51.1
San Augustine	143	1 162	311	102	235	42	17	22	19 163	308	27.6	6.5	65.3
San Jacinto	158	865	79	31	227	23	61	16	18 973	598	49.8	5.0	53.2
San Patricio	1 016	10 421	1 296	2 018	2 138	316	455	269	25 830	575	38.8	28.3	62.6
San Saba	172	1 265	259	32	292	27	D	26	20 280	706	10.9	39.0	60.3
Schleicher	65	700	D	D	D	D	7	14	20 126	307	5.9	64.2	56.4
Scurry	394	4 147	460	285	724	123	54	101	24 333	674	16.2	30.9	55.5
Shackelford	101	539	D	13	65	42	16	12	23 169	252	13.5	45.6	56.0
Shelby	503	5 909	471	2 061	1 039	245	133	125	21 211	1 100	26.4	6.8	64.7
Sherman	70	459	8	D	65	D	D	13	27 954	322	7.8	64.9	66.1
Smith	4 919	75 564	14 203	11 052	11 459	2 773	3 464	2 236	29 594	2 264	47.8	4.5	47.9
Somervell	157	3 281	396	D	185	D	D	126	38 449	339	35.7	13.3	44.5
Starr	404	5 233	2 312	39	1 435	181	85	75	14 354	870	6.3	30.6	56.6
Stephens	272	2 176	334	448	407	89	53	48	22 105	435	7.4	37.9	51.5
Sterling	35	159	13	0	34	D	D	3	19 201	66	12.1	65.2	69.7
Stonewall	55	369	129	0	45	D	D	8	20 794	316	5.4	50.6	58.5
Sutton	145	1 116	61	D	197	23	24	30	26 635	191	5.2	75.4	68.1
Swisher	164	1 128	209	138	248	51	28	21	18 746	578	16.4	47.9	71.3
Tarrant	33 748	635 894	63 842	86 716	86 039	32 179	30 998	21 095	33 174	1 227	65.9	6.1	42.6
Taylor	3 476	48 664	10 033	3 281	7 489	2 429	1 305	1 131	23 244	1 183	30.3	20.2	45.6
Terrell	19	50	0	0	21	D	D	1	14 500	76	6.6	89.5	59.2
Terry	251	2 066	351	20	422	129	43	48	23 281	620	12.9	46.5	67.6
Throckmorton	64	362	69	D	D	36	3	7	19 224	257	5.1	48.6	61.1
Titus	664	11 916	1 931	4 467	1 503	269	170	302	25 350	776	32.7	8.5	52.4

STATE County	Land in farms — Acreage (1,000) [117]	Percent change, 1997–2002 [118]	Average size of farm [119]	Total irrigated (1,000) [120]	Total cropland (1,000) [121]	Value of land and buildings (dollars) Average per farm [122]	Average per acre [123]	Value of machinery and equipment average per farm (dollars) [124]	Value of products sold Total (mil dol) [125]	Average per farm (dollars) [126]	Percent from — Crops [127]	Livestock and poultry products [128]	Percent of farms with sales of — $10,000 or more [129]	$100,000 or more [130]	Government payments Total ($1,000) [131]	Percent of farms [132]
TEXAS—Cont'd																
Mason	556	-6.6	878	7	67	882 815	971	26 079	45	70 771	5.3	94.7	41.5	6.2	651	22.3
Matagorda	619	12.3	625	43	255	631 729	1 014	68 272	116	116 781	75.5	24.5	45.0	15.2	7 445	28.6
Maverick	476	1.3	2 225	8	45	610 130	292	30 948	35	162 241	12.0	88.0	35.0	9.8	82	4.2
Medina	805	7.3	413	56	236	490 542	1 127	30 612	61	31 134	38.1	61.9	25.1	4.3	2 042	16.8
Menard	549	10.7	1 633	2	25	812 564	494	29 552	7	22 099	10.5	89.5	40.5	4.8	943	34.5
Midland	362	-58.1	758	7	73	281 759	384	22 642	7	15 516	54.0	46.0	15.9	3.4	1 308	28.5
Milam	577	5.9	290	3	247	344 506	1 186	34 531	72	36 338	24.4	75.6	32.4	5.1	2 034	12.4
Mills	427	0.5	556	1	95	490 159	972	24 470	22	28 629	8.0	92.0	33.1	4.2	592	26.0
Mitchell	488	-9.8	1 082	3	171	365 892	341	55 944	12	27 371	57.2	42.8	29.9	6.4	3 367	70.1
Montague	504	2.0	360	1	180	506 373	1 260	33 400	32	22 782	11.8	88.2	30.3	4.5	759	17.9
Montgomery	198	2.6	116	1	58	404 839	2 809	26 397	20	11 798	57.5	42.5	15.4	1.1	39	1.6
Moore	550	-0.9	1 991	113	275	1 121 030	574	138 328	303	1 098 815	14.0	86.0	63.8	36.6	3 762	60.1
Morris	100	51.5	247	1	39	181 306	833	40 405	20	49 966	2.0	98.0	30.0	9.4	43	3.5
Motley	487	-17.5	2 423	6	113	655 772	268	60 195	10	49 224	32.4	67.6	51.2	13.9	1 835	64.7
Nacogdoches	274	-26.3	212	0	86	350 037	1 368	40 479	198	153 466	1.2	98.8	37.7	15.4	100	1.7
Navarro	537	4.1	288	0	223	252 480	868	35 536	37	19 598	32.4	67.6	26.8	3.6	1 450	11.2
Newton	69	11.3	180	0	15	204 941	957	22 010	1	3 414	28.7	71.3	6.8	0.3	36	1.3
Nolan	481	-7.5	933	3	152	540 893	475	58 798	13	25 956	53.1	46.9	28.5	5.6	2 535	51.4
Nueces	524	19.6	807	2	354	802 645	946	98 852	63	96 503	94.9	5.1	41.0	19.9	5 085	32.4
Ochiltree	559	-0.9	1 524	53	353	670 848	432	131 759	242	658 998	D	D	53.7	19.1	3 798	61.3
Oldham	936	11.2	6 885	8	123	1 438 650	213	65 171	66	484 917	3.5	96.5	53.7	17.6	1 444	55.1
Orange	73	-17.0	148	1	29	191 311	1 704	21 560	4	7 638	27.6	72.4	10.9	1.6	114	1.0
Palo Pinto	485	-7.4	503	2	111	392 494	800	29 306	15	15 890	15.5	84.5	22.1	3.1	476	12.5
Panola	223	10.4	235	0	84	240 993	1 007	43 961	46	48 756	3.0	97.0	32.4	6.5	102	2.1
Parker	487	1.5	151	1	167	399 193	2 287	21 572	48	14 806	26.9	73.1	15.2	1.9	263	4.6
Parmer	576	5.3	873	189	455	525 201	599	134 876	604	915 015	11.9	88.1	65.8	39.8	10 246	71.5
Pecos	2 916	-0.9	10 800	34	110	1 511 275	139	82 144	38	141 547	61.8	38.2	44.4	16.3	1 478	30.7
Polk	130	-4.4	189	0	45	244 206	1 359	35 092	6	8 388	20.6	79.4	19.7	0.7	6	0.7
Potter	522	16.0	1 711	5	70	641 480	371	32 622	19	63 900	6.7	93.3	21.3	5.6	1 606	25.6
Presidio	1 504	-11.0	12 225	3	51	3 989 305	324	35 856	51	415 870	D	D	48.0	16.3	255	22.8
Rains	94	0.0	160	0	43	264 199	1 565	31 161	12	20 189	19.4	80.6	27.7	4.3	287	6.3
Randall	512	11.3	685	27	272	415 311	555	54 368	261	349 112	4.2	95.8	28.3	8.0	5 031	42.2
Reagan	538	-13.8	4 376	10	67	889 200	204	82 095	7	53 399	67.0	33.0	55.3	18.7	2 032	62.6
Real	400	5.8	1 329	0	13	825 471	615	16 993	3	8 967	10.0	90.0	18.9	1.7	138	10.3
Red River	423	-4.9	347	3	138	356 892	879	26 116	31	25 352	14.1	85.9	31.4	5.1	1 381	15.3
Reeves	1 010	-0.4	6 084	11	89	829 482	139	78 520	19	111 824	39.5	60.5	31.9	11.4	1 162	47.6
Refugio	506	-8.0	1 847	3	107	806 492	430	66 429	21	78 172	58.6	41.4	42.7	14.2	1 473	27.4
Roberts	495	-12.5	5 262	7	50	1 205 215	218	74 521	13	140 767	16.8	83.2	62.8	36.2	848	70.2
Robertson	515	21.2	331	19	171	410 498	1 064	45 523	75	48 058	15.4	84.6	34.8	5.3	1 037	4.4
Rockwall	46	0.0	121	0	25	323 221	3 129	38 090	3	7 790	35.1	64.9	14.0	1.3	140	8.1
Runnels	585	0.7	652	3	299	350 768	598	55 156	27	30 540	54.1	45.9	38.9	7.0	4 070	57.6
Rusk	272	1.9	196	1	118	234 457	1 287	23 949	39	28 288	35.5	64.5	26.5	2.6	62	3.0
Sabine	31	24.0	141	0	12	318 432	1 906	39 108	7	31 291	5.5	94.5	23.7	1.4	D	D
San Augustine	59	-9.2	191	0	20	279 946	1 326	42 458	25	81 103	4.0	96.0	31.5	8.1	51	2.6
San Jacinto	93	9.4	156	0	35	247 220	2 118	18 330	6	9 227	26.0	74.0	15.2	1.0	7	1.7
San Patricio	345	-15.0	601	8	259	554 999	888	93 153	69	119 761	77.0	23.0	37.6	22.4	3 457	29.7
San Saba	709	-3.3	1 005	3	101	867 824	768	38 137	23	32 490	17.0	83.0	44.6	7.8	805	28.0
Schleicher	778	5.3	2 535	1	41	867 221	339	27 472	9	30 023	9.9	90.1	49.5	7.8	1 417	40.1
Scurry	565	18.0	838	3	240	317 251	380	33 922	23	34 164	39.5	60.5	28.2	5.8	3 534	57.7
Shackelford	557	7.9	2 211	1	56	913 303	437	38 030	15	59 725	8.4	91.6	37.3	9.1	976	43.7
Shelby	192	-4.5	175	0	68	267 600	1 855	51 388	241	218 763	0.8	99.2	41.8	21.5	91	2.5
Sherman	546	-10.0	1 696	149	380	919 130	560	176 442	295	916 366	16.1	83.9	58.1	36.6	6 174	76.4
Smith	287	14.3	127	2	129	213 780	1 566	27 419	64	28 051	75.0	25.0	20.4	2.4	106	1.3
Somervell	84	16.7	249	0	22	351 964	1 731	15 661	2	5 975	25.6	74.4	13.9	0.3	37	4.7
Starr	570	-10.4	656	6	194	412 455	662	33 769	67	76 717	16.1	83.9	21.3	2.4	2 412	36.0
Stephens	428	-8.0	984	0	70	408 878	480	24 455	9	20 132	5.7	94.3	28.3	2.8	361	28.0
Sterling	633	-10.3	9 591	0	11	1 880 225	200	49 911	6	87 703	1.0	99.0	50.0	18.2	562	28.8
Stonewall	524	8.3	1 659	1	121	455 194	293	47 935	9	28 574	33.8	66.2	39.9	6.3	1 823	67.4
Sutton	880	-4.9	4 606	1	9	1 707 662	362	32 194	6	33 593	3.7	96.3	51.3	7.9	597	27.2
Swisher	566	9.7	980	100	388	458 818	460	121 450	296	512 610	10.4	89.6	49.1	25.3	9 207	76.0
Tarrant	173	-6.0	141	1	57	526 850	3 011	32 019	29	23 701	74.7	25.3	13.0	2.9	148	4.1
Taylor	534	8.5	451	2	227	313 680	661	33 838	55	46 840	11.8	88.2	18.1	3.4	3 146	36.7
Terrell	1 413	9.5	18 593	D	8	1 982 058	107	43 870	4	51 256	D	D	57.9	7.9	458	30.3
Terry	445	-4.9	718	142	399	471 161	610	122 203	63	102 178	93.8	6.2	53.4	28.7	11 790	74.5
Throckmorton	561	-0.2	2 184	D	93	764 293	364	60 930	16	63 888	14.8	85.2	47.9	9.3	944	43.6
Titus	178	2.3	230	0	69	351 314	1 586	33 927	56	72 666	1.5	98.5	29.8	6.1	78	1.9

STATE County	Value of residential construction authorized by building permits, 2003		Wholesale trade, 1997				Retail trade,[1] 1997				Real estate and rental and leasing, 1997			
	New construction ($1,000)	Number of housing units	Number of establish-ments	Number of employees	Sales (mil dol)	Annual payroll (mil dol)	Number of establish-ments	Number of employees	Sales (mil dol)	Annual payroll (mil dol)	Number of establish-ments	Number of employees	Receipts (mil dol)	Annual payroll (mil dol)
	133	134	135	136	137	138	139	140	141	142	143	144	145	146
TEXAS—Cont'd														
Mason	95	1	9	56	38.3	1.1	20	107	10.9	1.0	2	D	D	D
Matagorda	10 442	115	33	D	D	D	152	1 443	224.7	21.7	30	109	6.6	1.6
Maverick	11 801	212	35	165	85.3	3.7	184	1 716	233.3	21.1	29	184	10.3	2.0
Medina	4 284	104	28	241	75.7	4.4	117	955	215.2	18.0	16	37	2.9	0.4
Menard	NA	NA	4	34	13.9	1.0	11	60	10.2	0.7	1	D	D	D
Midland	30 268	260	297	2 708	1 938.6	93.9	549	6 649	1 226.3	108.5	185	899	90.0	17.8
Milam	1 858	12	22	177	119.8	3.2	82	701	106.8	9.8	16	31	1.7	0.3
Mills	NA	NA	7	75	28.2	0.4	36	159	32.3	2.4	3	3	0.1	0.0
Mitchell	0	0	9	93	5.2	0.8	38	226	35.8	3.5	4	11	1.2	0.2
Montague	995	14	30	118	53.7	1.9	86	640	97.9	8.0	11	16	0.9	0.2
Montgomery	833 196	6 313	337	3 271	2 129.7	118.8	835	11 926	2 224.8	187.4	184	861	140.5	24.9
Moore	4 331	34	26	187	137.7	6.0	83	724	127.5	11.0	19	43	3.3	0.5
Morris	864	12	15	230	100.2	6.9	53	342	38.9	4.2	6	7	2.3	0.3
Motley	0	0	3	24	2.4	0.4	11	37	6.1	0.5	1	D	D	D
Nacogdoches	5 286	62	57	593	161.6	14.1	279	3 036	501.2	45.0	59	174	18.5	3.0
Navarro	2 010	21	45	409	227.5	10.7	196	2 007	347.9	29.4	34	99	9.9	1.6
Newton	0	0	3	22	9.4	0.5	36	185	26.8	2.1	4	13	0.3	0.1
Nolan	130	2	24	171	48.7	4.5	83	786	121.1	10.2	11	32	2.3	0.3
Nueces	140 534	1 523	493	5 029	1 803.1	154.0	1 286	17 018	2 783.5	265.9	388	2 526	334.1	63.2
Ochiltree	740	6	33	175	78.3	4.3	44	377	63.3	5.5	6	15	1.2	0.1
Oldham	419	3	5	27	5.2	0.5	11	60	8.0	0.8	NA	NA	NA	NA
Orange	33 693	277	49	316	61.6	7.4	290	3 310	546.1	44.8	61	337	20.2	4.9
Palo Pinto	571	6	30	223	62.4	4.7	132	1 072	171.9	14.5	23	87	8.8	1.4
Panola	314	20	25	161	135.3	3.9	90	696	97.1	8.1	13	37	2.6	0.4
Parker	42 718	389	75	579	231.6	15.6	236	2 657	602.3	49.3	58	144	17.9	2.4
Parmer	240	3	28	186	122.0	4.1	42	279	48.3	3.8	6	5	0.4	0.1
Pecos	368	3	15	101	28.2	2.8	75	576	84.1	8.3	7	28	2.2	0.3
Polk	21 167	165	26	214	114.6	3.7	132	1 701	272.1	24.8	21	79	3.9	1.2
Potter	130 629	1 007	247	3 204	1 209.8	105.5	641	7 939	1 531.3	137.3	159	803	96.0	14.4
Presidio	6 929	78	6	14	4.1	0.2	27	152	21.4	1.6	2	D	D	D
Rains	2 067	26	5	D	D	D	33	186	22.3	2.4	1	D	D	D
Randall	5 352	29	110	1 620	1 180.9	47.5	346	4 299	838.3	72.4	97	370	34.8	6.9
Reagan	51	4	4	D	D	D	16	84	19.5	1.3	NA	NA	NA	NA
Real	770	11	3	D	D	D	19	57	6.3	0.6	2	D	D	D
Red River	90	2	4	D	D	D	59	482	61.2	4.8	4	7	1.8	0.1
Reeves	180	1	13	138	12.0	1.7	43	383	64.2	5.7	6	7	0.3	0.1
Refugio	695	5	12	60	19.3	1.3	38	258	49.6	4.0	6	18	1.2	0.3
Roberts	NA	NA	2	D	D	D	4	20	1.7	0.2	NA	NA	NA	NA
Robertson	1 577	14	11	49	84.2	0.7	55	364	52.0	4.5	9	47	3.2	0.3
Rockwall	205 439	1 219	58	343	133.2	7.8	112	1 488	266.9	24.1	39	256	17.8	3.9
Runnels	0	0	17	614	64.8	12.6	57	413	69.5	5.5	6	10	0.3	0.1
Rusk	1 473	16	41	516	137.0	11.9	144	1 305	188.0	17.0	21	64	5.0	0.7
Sabine	70	1	5	18	4.0	0.4	47	284	40.6	4.0	6	7	0.7	0.1
San Augustine	105	2	11	67	13.3	1.1	42	312	45.0	3.6	2	D	D	D
San Jacinto	512	13	6	31	4.8	0.5	33	235	29.7	2.9	3	3	0.2	0.0
San Patricio	31 884	373	42	262	105.9	6.8	200	1 988	348.7	29.6	46	150	10.9	1.6
San Saba	41	1	15	105	48.2	1.2	38	254	51.1	3.6	NA	NA	NA	NA
Schleicher	0	0	2	D	D	D	11	45	7.7	0.7	2	D	D	D
Scurry	246	1	27	215	50.0	5.9	80	762	135.3	10.9	15	51	3.2	0.7
Shackelford	NA	NA	6	13	2.7	0.3	22	86	14.8	1.0	NA	NA	NA	NA
Shelby	0	0	27	168	99.7	4.3	103	984	155.0	12.4	14	27	4.2	0.3
Sherman	1 950	19	9	40	35.1	0.9	12	47	8.1	0.8	1	D	D	D
Smith	97 151	657	297	3 103	1 237.7	93.9	805	9 773	1 868.6	170.2	189	895	93.2	20.7
Somervell	6 492	50	4	D	D	D	29	220	29.1	2.5	5	10	0.5	0.1
Starr	0	0	21	105	37.2	2.3	131	1 379	201.2	16.3	10	51	2.7	0.5
Stephens	0	0	16	45	10.9	1.2	47	421	56.1	5.8	7	22	0.9	0.2
Sterling	NA	NA	3	8	1.5	0.2	5	38	5.8	0.4	NA	NA	NA	NA
Stonewall	NA	NA	2	D	D	D	10	39	5.7	0.5	1	D	D	D
Sutton	120	1	14	63	18.9	1.7	31	206	56.3	4.0	5	9	0.5	0.1
Swisher	0	0	15	94	42.2	2.1	39	255	41.2	3.2	5	10	0.9	0.1
Tarrant	1 855 812	15 746	2 399	33 372	22 102.4	1 219.5	5 015	71 758	14 097.9	1 326.3	1 384	8 249	1 132.8	196.3
Taylor	30 524	212	219	1 996	933.9	54.1	635	7 211	1 297.7	116.7	168	876	88.4	16.7
Terrell	NA	NA	1	D	D	D	7	26	2.7	0.3	3	3	0.1	0.0
Terry	100	1	22	216	108.6	5.2	46	458	81.3	7.3	6	26	2.3	0.6
Throckmorton	NA	NA	5	8	2.1	0.2	11	37	4.9	0.4	NA	NA	NA	NA
Titus	4 182	52	48	539	203.3	14.2	147	1 483	271.1	23.7	24	85	6.9	1.2

1. Establishments with payroll.

Table B. States and Counties — Professional Services, Manufacturing, and Accommodation and Foodservices

STATE County	Professional, scientific, and technical services,[1] 1997				Manufacturing, 1997				Accommodation and foodservices, 1997			
	Number of establish-ments	Number of employees	Receipts (mil dol)	Annual payroll (mil dol)	Number of establish-ments	Number of employees	Receipts (mil dol)	Annual payroll (mil dol)	Number of establish-ments	Number of employees	Sales (mil dol)	Annual payroll (mil dol)
	147	148	149	150	151	152	153	154	155	156	157	158
TEXAS—Cont'd												
Mason	6	10	0.7	0.1	NA	NA	NA	NA	8	46	1.3	0.3
Matagorda	47	144	8.2	3.4	29	D	D	D	77	804	26.6	7.0
Maverick	28	158	11.7	3.6	19	1 091	78.0	13.2	46	670	23.7	6.1
Medina	34	281	12.1	4.8	23	556	50.5	13.8	46	413	12.9	3.2
Menard	1	D	D	D	NA	NA	NA	NA	9	42	1.9	0.4
Midland	350	2 088	245.0	75.6	135	2 435	326.1	76.5	231	3 814	123.9	34.2
Milam	27	114	8.8	3.7	9	1 559	456.0	65.3	43	342	10.7	2.9
Mills	6	13	1.0	0.1	NA	NA	NA	NA	6	55	1.4	0.4
Mitchell	9	31	1.6	0.4	NA	NA	NA	NA	17	146	3.9	0.9
Montague	30	85	4.9	1.5	21	505	44.1	8.9	38	360	10.4	2.2
Montgomery	498	2 279	251.0	96.4	285	6 706	1 540.8	219.1	284	6 044	230.2	62.6
Moore	20	84	6.0	1.9	19	2 865	2 663.2	72.5	46	630	20.3	5.2
Morris	16	155	18.5	3.4	16	2 224	688.0	95.7	21	D	D	D
Motley	1	D	D	D	NA	NA	NA	NA	3	15	0.3	0.1
Nacogdoches	69	240	18.7	4.6	60	3 475	771.3	99.3	87	1 897	57.1	15.6
Navarro	45	270	13.3	6.2	49	2 191	336.0	58.5	54	878	25.5	6.7
Newton	5	9	0.4	0.1	10	620	133.2	15.8	15	87	3.0	0.8
Nolan	32	104	8.5	3.3	17	1 043	176.7	27.7	35	426	11.7	2.9
Nueces	690	4 415	415.4	150.1	223	8 925	9 988.5	373.8	730	12 846	418.6	111.6
Ochiltree	20	89	5.3	2.4	NA	NA	NA	NA	20	254	7.0	1.8
Oldham	2	D	D	D	NA	NA	NA	NA	3	60	1.2	0.4
Orange	93	442	37.2	14.6	82	6 137	2 893.4	302.4	115	2 096	58.6	16.2
Palo Pinto	29	78	5.4	1.5	37	1 183	134.2	32.6	66	657	21.3	5.6
Panola	35	110	10.2	2.1	12	1 092	125.0	19.7	26	342	10.9	3.2
Parker	104	407	52.2	19.8	101	2 538	310.8	63.5	93	1 316	41.5	10.8
Parmer	10	33	1.7	0.5	6	D	D	D	15	D	D	D
Pecos	15	61	3.1	0.9	NA	NA	NA	NA	32	392	12.7	3.1
Polk	45	248	11.9	4.1	25	1 693	295.8	54.6	55	732	21.5	6.2
Potter	271	2 556	180.1	78.2	145	D	D	D	337	5 864	191.0	51.3
Presidio	5	7	1.3	0.1	NA	NA	NA	NA	15	130	3.3	1.0
Rains	8	19	1.2	0.3	NA	NA	NA	NA	14	87	2.9	0.7
Randall	92	323	19.6	7.1	58	D	D	D	143	2 428	71.6	19.6
Reagan	4	38	1.0	0.8	NA	NA	NA	NA	9	D	D	D
Real	5	10	0.3	0.1	NA	NA	NA	NA	6	42	2.1	0.5
Red River	6	11	1.1	0.3	18	1 171	127.0	24.4	15	D	D	D
Reeves	12	147	6.2	2.2	4	D	D	D	28	285	8.4	2.3
Refugio	7	32	3.1	0.9	NA	NA	NA	NA	23	215	6.1	1.7
Roberts	NA	NA	NA	NA	NA	NA	NA	NA	1	D	D	D
Robertson	9	25	1.5	0.3	NA	NA	NA	NA	18	211	5.9	2.1
Rockwall	72	254	24.1	8.5	56	927	114.8	24.0	44	831	26.7	8.1
Runnels	13	31	1.1	0.3	15	1 453	151.1	28.1	21	119	3.2	0.7
Rusk	40	204	38.7	4.5	51	1 302	170.3	29.4	45	518	15.3	4.3
Sabine	6	14	0.8	0.2	NA	NA	NA	NA	19	166	4.3	1.2
San Augustine	7	15	0.6	0.2	NA	NA	NA	NA	8	57	1.9	0.4
San Jacinto	11	17	1.3	0.5	NA	NA	NA	NA	9	126	4.6	1.1
San Patricio	46	260	20.1	8.6	45	2 510	1 235.3	103.2	109	1 037	31.8	8.3
San Saba	10	19	0.9	0.3	NA	NA	NA	NA	12	D	D	D
Schleicher	2	D	D	D	NA	NA	NA	NA	6	D	D	D
Scurry	18	44	2.5	0.6	NA	NA	NA	NA	36	418	9.5	3.0
Shackelford	9	17	1.4	0.2	NA	NA	NA	NA	8	65	1.8	0.5
Shelby	24	132	10.3	2.0	29	1 989	303.2	39.3	23	243	8.5	2.0
Sherman	2	D	D	D	NA	NA	NA	NA	9	46	0.8	0.2
Smith	392	2 464	284.0	93.0	213	10 969	2 299.1	381.1	294	5 834	175.1	47.8
Somervell	6	15	1.3	0.3	NA	NA	NA	NA	21	197	6.1	1.9
Starr	19	80	5.0	1.4	NA	NA	NA	NA	35	326	10.9	2.4
Stephens	18	36	7.5	0.7	18	562	94.3	13.0	20	158	5.6	1.3
Sterling	4	6	0.3	0.1	NA	NA	NA	NA	4	19	0.7	0.2
Stonewall	1	D	D	D	NA	NA	NA	NA	6	23	0.6	0.1
Sutton	5	11	0.9	0.2	NA	NA	NA	NA	11	151	4.7	1.4
Swisher	4	24	1.2	0.6	NA	NA	NA	NA	12	D	D	D
Tarrant	2 965	19 656	1 912.7	734.6	2 009	95 970	18 621.6	3 583.2	2 330	49 749	1 821.5	499.8
Taylor	229	1 123	93.2	30.4	118	3 062	1 010.7	79.9	269	5 497	151.6	41.8
Terrell	3	3	0.2	0.0	NA	NA	NA	NA	2	D	D	D
Terry	15	43	2.5	0.9	NA	NA	NA	NA	24	272	7.9	2.1
Throckmorton	3	7	0.2	0.1	NA	NA	NA	NA	2	D	D	D
Titus	33	132	7.1	2.6	42	4 792	845.3	102.4	41	689	21.1	5.5

1. Firms subject to federal tax.

Table B. States and Counties — **Health Care and Social Assistance, Other Services, and Federal Funds**

STATE County	Health care and social assistance,[1] 1997				Other services,[1] 1997				Federal funds and grants, 2002–2003 Expenditures (mil dol)			
									Total	Direct payments for individuals[2]		
	Number of establish-ments	Number of employees	Receipts (mil dol)	Annual payroll (mil dol)	Number of establish-ments	Number of employees	Receipts (mil dol)	Annual payroll (mil dol)	Total	Social Security and government retirement	Medicare	Food stamps and Supplemental Security Income
	159	160	161	162	163	164	165	166	167	168	169	170
TEXAS—Cont'd												
Mason	2	D	D	D	3	D	D	D	29.7	11.7	5.5	0.5
Matagorda	50	434	21.7	8.1	63	288	20.9	7.5	207.0	75.3	34.0	8.1
Maverick	45	358	28.1	8.7	29	83	3.8	0.8	242.2	52.1	39.3	28.0
Medina	41	455	16.8	7.1	34	68	5.1	1.3	169.6	87.7	30.0	5.5
Menard	1	D	D	D	1	D	D	D	16.7	7.1	4.1	0.5
Midland	245	2 971	251.9	102.6	228	1 509	112.2	29.3	427.6	205.1	93.8	18.1
Milam	26	360	12.5	6.2	22	68	4.8	1.1	139.5	61.9	23.6	5.2
Mills	8	153	4.8	2.2	9	15	1.8	0.2	31.7	14.7	8.5	0.8
Mitchell	6	116	3.6	1.6	9	17	2.1	0.3	52.7	18.6	11.9	1.4
Montague	21	438	16.5	8.2	30	88	5.9	1.2	114.9	61.4	28.4	2.6
Montgomery	365	4 857	354.2	139.3	293	2 439	129.1	42.5	945.7	513.3	205.3	32.9
Moore	22	229	11.4	4.8	36	130	12.0	2.5	65.9	30.0	11.8	1.8
Morris	23	392	12.1	5.9	23	91	6.8	2.1	87.7	41.6	20.1	3.2
Motley	NA	NA	NA	NA	4	4	0.1	0.0	14.5	4.5	2.8	0.3
Nacogdoches	159	2 348	133.0	50.1	86	499	23.7	7.2	315.5	114.7	62.3	12.4
Navarro	59	1 510	99.8	34.8	57	278	15.0	3.9	250.3	103.3	47.6	9.6
Newton	3	D	D	D	5	14	1.3	0.2	84.2	29.5	16.3	3.9
Nolan	32	320	15.1	5.7	24	144	7.6	2.4	95.5	39.6	22.3	3.2
Nueces	853	14 979	795.0	357.7	545	3 669	216.3	66.8	2 139.1	642.1	301.7	83.7
Ochiltree	13	59	3.3	1.2	19	103	7.3	2.4	42.9	14.8	6.4	0.9
Oldham	1	D	D	D	4	9	0.3	0.1	26.8	5.2	2.2	0.1
Orange	148	1 622	82.6	35.8	97	509	34.9	10.6	444.5	195.7	111.1	16.3
Palo Pinto	48	406	18.7	7.0	49	190	17.4	3.7	151.6	67.3	32.8	4.6
Panola	33	525	16.9	7.3	28	107	6.1	1.5	122.2	52.4	27.3	4.1
Parker	101	969	46.0	18.4	100	498	30.5	8.9	323.6	188.2	55.7	6.4
Parmer	6	29	1.7	1.0	20	45	4.1	0.8	71.7	16.5	8.0	1.3
Pecos	14	191	6.9	3.2	29	214	9.5	3.4	59.1	21.3	10.5	3.5
Polk	41	590	22.3	8.5	37	128	12.4	2.5	344.5	217.0	66.9	10.5
Potter	357	5 450	440.6	191.7	232	1 524	95.5	27.7	1 239.9	367.0	136.5	29.8
Presidio	1	D	D	D	5	9	0.7	0.1	47.7	11.8	5.2	4.8
Rains	4	70	0.7	0.3	11	50	3.6	0.4	42.1	24.9	8.5	1.0
Randall	146	1 056	72.4	25.7	147	964	51.1	14.9	159.8	62.0	35.5	3.1
Reagan	5	29	1.2	0.7	11	29	2.9	0.7	15.8	5.0	2.4	0.3
Real	2	D	D	D	1	D	D	D	24.8	11.1	3.9	1.0
Red River	12	372	15.1	6.7	12	63	3.2	1.1	121.6	40.0	23.7	3.0
Reeves	17	163	5.7	1.8	16	36	2.4	0.7	68.6	20.9	12.8	4.3
Refugio	8	124	2.5	1.1	5	17	0.9	0.2	53.9	19.8	11.6	1.5
Roberts	1	D	D	D	NA	NA	NA	NA	5.5	2.0	1.0	0.0
Robertson	14	274	9.9	4.2	16	37	2.7	0.5	111.3	38.5	18.5	4.6
Rockwall	82	736	45.2	19.4	48	211	12.2	3.6	187.0	76.1	20.6	2.5
Runnels	26	242	11.5	5.7	16	38	2.7	0.7	72.9	29.7	16.2	1.7
Rusk	62	756	29.0	11.9	44	201	11.2	3.3	213.8	91.0	47.7	7.1
Sabine	9	338	5.6	2.7	10	19	1.7	0.4	93.1	46.3	22.8	2.4
San Augustine	13	280	11.5	5.3	9	41	1.9	0.4	66.9	25.1	14.3	2.7
San Jacinto	10	50	3.8	1.7	6	25	1.1	0.3	118.8	44.8	21.9	5.7
San Patricio	75	1 085	57.0	23.8	66	229	12.7	3.3	461.2	132.8	65.7	19.1
San Saba	7	165	5.0	2.6	8	21	1.1	0.3	49.5	14.8	10.1	0.8
Schleicher	3	D	D	D	5	10	0.8	0.1	16.6	6.6	3.3	0.4
Scurry	21	236	8.9	3.8	37	174	9.7	2.7	93.0	36.7	20.3	2.4
Shackelford	4	43	1.8	0.8	7	15	1.0	0.2	19.7	9.9	4.1	0.4
Shelby	34	697	32.7	12.8	35	115	7.7	1.8	176.8	61.6	37.3	6.1
Sherman	NA	NA	NA	NA	5	8	0.9	0.1	25.0	5.5	2.9	0.1
Smith	430	5 047	396.8	186.2	288	2 032	116.3	35.4	921.7	413.6	181.0	29.1
Somervell	11	115	5.1	2.6	6	19	0.9	0.3	26.6	13.4	6.0	1.4
Starr	41	1 150	28.2	13.6	32	98	4.2	0.9	238.2	45.8	32.5	33.8
Stephens	15	154	6.1	2.8	12	35	2.1	0.5	49.2	21.8	14.5	1.6
Sterling	2	D	D	D	2	D	D	D	6.6	2.2	1.3	0.1
Stonewall	3	D	D	D	3	13	1.0	0.4	13.7	5.0	2.8	0.2
Sutton	6	30	2.0	0.6	5	38	1.7	0.5	17.5	7.1	3.3	0.6
Swisher	5	61	2.5	1.0	13	34	2.4	0.4	66.6	18.4	10.1	1.4
Tarrant	2 847	35 845	2 381.1	1 039.4	2 145	14 698	948.3	296.2	15 523.7	2 319.6	943.2	172.1
Taylor	314	5 225	310.4	123.2	225	1 892	109.5	34.6	926.3	307.2	115.6	25.0
Terrell	NA	NA	NA	NA	1	D	D	D	8.2	3.4	1.3	0.2
Terry	11	152	7.0	2.7	20	58	4.4	1.2	114.1	25.6	19.0	3.2
Throckmorton	4	46	1.8	0.7	NA	NA	NA	NA	13.5	5.3	2.9	0.2
Titus	76	1 048	48.4	24.4	34	172	9.7	2.2	130.7	52.1	31.8	4.1

1. Firms subject to federal tax.   2. State totals may include programs not allocated by county.

	Federal funds and grants, 2002–2003 (cont'd)							Local government finances, 2002				
	Expenditures (mil dol) (cont'd)							General revenue				
	Procurement contract awards			Grants[1]						Taxes		
STATE County	Salaries and wages	Defense	Other	Medicaid and other health-related	Nutrition and family welfare	Education	Other	Total (mil dol)	Intergovern-mental (mil dol)	Total (mil dol)	Per capita[2] (dollars) Total	Property
	171	172	173	174	175	176	177	178	179	180	181	182
TEXAS—Cont'd												
Mason	0.7	0.1	1.2	3.7	0.2	0.1	0.2	8.4	4.2	3.4	901	790
Matagorda	4.9	4.3	1.3	25.3	14.8	1.7	17.5	134.6	28.4	64.8	1 709	1 538
Maverick	19.3	0.0	1.1	70.2	8.4	4.7	17.9	150.5	76.2	22.0	452	321
Medina	4.8	0.1	0.9	26.8	3.6	1.7	4.1	84.4	46.4	26.7	653	516
Menard	0.5	0.0	0.1	3.2	0.1	0.2	0.5	7.7	3.6	2.3	1 004	903
Midland	37.8	1.5	6.4	27.5	5.8	7.5	15.0	449.9	130.5	161.3	1 371	1 084
Milam	3.4	-0.3	0.9	32.4	2.3	1.2	4.9	57.4	23.4	23.9	962	814
Mills	1.0	0.0	0.3	4.7	0.2	0.6	0.4	12.8	8.6	3.5	688	588
Mitchell	1.1	0.0	0.3	8.9	0.4	0.4	3.8	30.9	7.0	11.2	1 198	1 054
Montague	3.6	0.1	0.9	14.5	1.0	0.7	0.4	63.9	19.4	15.4	800	681
Montgomery	42.4	4.6	12.3	60.5	11.2	6.4	48.3	713.3	231.5	386.6	1 177	1 049
Moore	3.5	0.0	0.3	3.4	0.3	0.8	4.0	67.4	9.8	30.4	1 496	1 377
Morris	1.8	0.0	0.6	16.6	1.9	0.6	0.3	26.0	7.0	16.1	1 216	1 081
Motley	0.3	0.0	0.0	1.8	0.0	0.1	0.4	3.1	1.3	1.5	1 095	972
Nacogdoches	11.3	0.2	2.2	57.9	8.6	3.7	22.0	190.2	57.9	45.4	763	622
Navarro	6.6	1.0	2.2	50.6	4.2	2.4	11.4	132.7	60.9	42.4	906	690
Newton	1.6	0.0	0.4	17.1	2.2	0.9	12.1	25.7	13.6	9.1	609	564
Nolan	2.5	0.1	0.5	13.8	2.1	0.9	3.0	55.6	15.0	18.1	1 196	1 004
Nueces	335.7	231.7	31.2	254.7	53.1	19.2	144.1	928.8	310.7	402.8	1 280	1 017
Ochiltree	1.3	0.0	0.3	1.3	0.1	0.3	6.7	31.3	8.3	14.4	1 591	1 309
Oldham	0.5	0.0	0.1	0.5	0.1	0.4	13.8	13.6	5.2	3.3	1 529	1 286
Orange	8.9	12.9	2.2	44.4	8.0	2.9	32.9	238.2	74.6	96.4	1 143	948
Palo Pinto	3.4	0.8	1.0	17.6	8.7	1.2	13.7	90.7	27.5	30.4	1 113	926
Panola	3.9	0.0	0.8	23.4	1.5	0.9	5.6	73.8	14.8	49.9	2 195	2 068
Parker	11.1	1.7	25.1	17.8	2.2	3.4	7.1	236.5	84.3	86.4	913	780
Parmer	3.2	0.0	0.3	4.2	0.7	0.6	0.3	25.4	13.5	8.9	905	757
Pecos	2.2	0.3	0.4	8.9	2.9	1.1	5.2	71.9	8.1	44.7	2 722	2 548
Polk	4.8	0.1	1.2	31.7	4.2	2.2	4.7	81.9	30.9	36.8	829	705
Potter	109.8	106.0	384.5	54.3	19.9	5.6	23.2	516.3	177.6	203.4	1 752	1 224
Presidio	6.4	1.2	0.7	13.9	1.0	0.9	1.4	24.2	16.7	5.0	651	518
Rains	1.0	0.0	0.3	5.3	0.3	0.3	0.0	16.6	5.8	7.3	710	602
Randall	3.0	0.0	0.6	7.7	0.8	4.9	19.7	68.8	19.3	39.7	371	345
Reagan	0.4	0.0	0.1	0.5	0.4	0.1	2.6	16.6	1.4	10.8	3 382	3 235
Real	0.5	0.0	1.5	3.7	0.3	0.2	2.5	9.9	1.6	4.8	1 587	1 482
Red River	2.6	0.3	0.8	39.7	2.7	0.7	4.7	32.3	20.5	8.9	637	535
Reeves	2.3	0.3	1.0	17.6	2.4	1.0	3.1	74.5	16.9	14.4	1 154	989
Refugio	1.8	0.0	0.3	7.6	1.0	0.4	3.6	29.9	7.0	15.5	2 002	1 850
Roberts	0.3	0.0	0.1	0.3	0.0	0.0	0.9	5.7	0.2	5.1	5 914	5 777
Robertson	2.7	0.0	0.6	35.0	2.4	0.9	4.5	49.2	17.4	25.7	1 600	1 472
Rockwall	5.9	42.8	6.1	4.2	0.5	0.5	26.4	118.3	24.1	79.3	1 559	1 339
Runnels	2.3	0.0	1.1	13.2	1.0	0.6	0.2	36.4	15.9	9.7	869	748
Rusk	6.0	0.1	1.4	41.6	3.5	1.8	10.6	98.7	33.8	52.7	1 109	1 007
Sabine	2.6	-0.1	0.4	13.9	0.9	1.3	2.3	22.2	5.7	6.6	634	506
San Augustine	1.2	0.0	0.5	19.2	1.0	0.8	2.0	15.0	8.9	4.4	489	386
San Jacinto	7.9	0.0	0.4	16.6	1.3	0.9	19.2	34.1	16.5	14.8	635	589
San Patricio	89.7	45.3	1.7	61.3	15.4	4.6	8.8	182.5	88.0	73.3	1 087	973
San Saba	1.2	0.2	0.3	10.0	8.1	0.4	2.3	14.5	8.4	4.4	718	581
Schleicher	0.5	0.0	0.1	2.1	0.3	0.2	0.9	11.9	2.9	5.4	1 833	1 671
Scurry	2.0	0.0	0.5	11.3	2.8	1.1	9.6	48.0	17.5	21.5	1 352	1 110
Shackelford	0.6	0.0	0.2	1.3	0.2	0.2	1.5	11.0	5.9	3.9	1 174	1 049
Shelby	4.6	0.7	0.9	47.3	6.2	1.2	10.1	49.9	29.0	15.3	601	501
Sherman	0.3	0.0	0.2	0.3	0.1	0.2	0.8	12.6	2.1	7.8	2 369	2 246
Smith	54.6	46.0	12.7	114.8	14.9	8.7	29.3	405.1	159.9	175.8	969	743
Somervell	1.1	0.0	0.2	3.4	0.1	0.2	0.2	42.5	1.8	36.6	5 064	4 946
Starr	13.2	0.2	2.5	73.8	17.9	8.2	3.9	164.3	107.5	27.8	491	432
Stephens	1.2	0.1	0.4	6.6	0.6	0.4	1.7	26.6	7.4	10.4	1 100	914
Sterling	0.2	0.0	0.0	0.5	0.1	0.1	1.7	6.3	0.4	5.5	4 090	3 981
Stonewall	0.4	0.0	0.1	1.1	0.1	0.1	0.6	7.6	1.0	3.5	2 376	2 208
Sutton	0.4	0.0	0.1	2.1	0.2	0.2	2.5	15.3	2.0	10.6	2 566	2 290
Swisher	1.3	0.0	0.3	5.4	1.9	0.4	1.5	27.5	11.0	7.1	880	748
Tarrant	1 009.9	9 968.1	230.8	419.7	77.2	48.8	239.6	4 536.4	1 116.2	2 450.2	1 604	1 271
Taylor	239.7	76.4	18.8	66.5	14.5	6.0	40.9	296.4	125.3	128.2	1 020	777
Terrell	0.6	0.0	0.0	1.6	0.1	0.1	0.6	6.7	0.5	5.5	5 557	5 328
Terry	1.6	0.0	0.4	13.4	2.2	0.8	9.2	47.5	17.9	15.8	1 239	1 102
Throckmorton	0.5	0.4	0.1	1.6	0.0	0.1	0.0	6.2	1.9	3.1	1 810	1 718
Titus	6.3	0.1	0.8	22.4	4.4	3.1	2.0	140.6	34.5	34.9	1 229	989

1. State totals may include programs not allocated by county. 2. Based on the resident population estimated as of July 1 of the year shown.

Table B. States and Counties — Local Government Finances, Government Employment, and Elections

STATE County	Total (mil dol) [183]	Per capita[1] (dollars) [184]	Percent of total for — Education [185]	Health and hospitals [186]	Police protection [187]	Public welfare [188]	Highways [189]	Debt outstanding Total (mil dol) [190]	Per capita[1] (dollars) [191]	Federal civilian [192]	Federal military [193]	State and local [194]	Demo-cratic [195]	Republican [196]	All other [197]
TEXAS—Cont'd															
Mason	11.1	2 940	43.1	1.1	2.1	0.4	4.4	1.8	471	17	0	266	22.2	77.3	0.5
Matagorda	129.6	3 415	58.1	13.9	3.6	0.1	4.4	91.1	2 400	90	70	2 574	34.8	64.9	0.3
Maverick	156.9	3 225	56.2	21.6	3.5	0.3	2.8	85.5	1 758	527	90	3 626	59.4	40.2	0.4
Medina	82.2	2 009	72.3	1.0	2.7	1.2	3.7	55.8	1 364	58	77	2 834	29.2	70.3	0.5
Menard	7.9	3 401	67.4	0.0	2.6	17.2	2.5	1.5	659	12	0	211	30.0	69.1	0.9
Midland	447.1	3 799	38.4	31.7	4.9	0.0	1.7	243.9	2 073	553	218	7 886	17.9	81.7	0.4
Milam	54.7	2 198	61.0	9.4	3.4	0.0	5.7	24.3	977	61	46	1 284	39.2	60.3	0.5
Mills	12.2	2 377	71.9	2.4	2.2	0.4	4.8	2.5	488	22	10	383	19.3	80.0	0.7
Mitchell	30.1	3 222	41.3	36.4	3.0	0.2	6.3	13.8	1 478	26	17	1 233	25.0	74.8	0.2
Montague	56.6	2 942	44.4	34.8	3.9	0.3	4.4	33.1	1 722	57	36	1 265	24.7	74.9	0.4
Montgomery	774.6	2 358	60.4	5.5	4.6	0.1	2.4	1 370.1	4 173	529	611	12 734	21.4	78.2	0.4
Moore	63.2	3 107	45.6	32.9	5.5	0.1	0.5	18.4	903	83	39	1 403	18.0	81.8	0.2
Morris	32.2	2 428	76.7	0.0	5.6	0.5	3.9	11.2	843	29	26	673	46.2	53.4	0.3
Motley	3.2	2 386	69.7	0.0	2.1	0.0	10.4	0.3	209	12	0	103	16.6	82.8	0.6
Nacogdoches	206.1	3 463	36.8	40.7	2.6	0.2	1.3	135.7	2 280	180	116	4 785	33.5	66.0	0.5
Navarro	135.9	2 903	65.4	0.9	6.2	0.4	4.4	101.6	2 170	108	87	3 281	32.8	66.9	0.3
Newton	28.4	1 900	78.8	0.0	2.8	0.4	3.3	23.7	1 589	27	28	706	44.2	55.5	0.3
Nolan	55.4	3 648	43.6	27.6	4.8	0.1	3.2	26.8	1 768	49	28	1 759	29.2	70.4	0.4
Nueces	880.8	2 799	53.9	6.3	5.8	0.2	2.9	950.2	3 019	5 354	3 479	21 221	42.6	57.0	0.4
Ochiltree	30.1	3 329	43.1	25.7	4.4	0.3	5.7	9.6	1 057	33	17	667	7.9	92.0	0.1
Oldham	13.9	6 442	81.3	1.2	3.0	0.0	2.3	0.4	191	0	0	292	12.8	87.1	0.1
Orange	232.1	2 751	52.3	0.3	5.4	0.2	2.9	615.0	7 290	124	173	4 264	36.0	63.7	0.3
Palo Pinto	88.6	3 245	44.7	29.7	2.4	0.0	4.9	68.0	2 491	57	52	1 799	28.2	71.4	0.4
Panola	67.3	2 958	74.5	0.0	3.3	0.3	6.4	27.3	1 201	80	42	1 194	29.6	70.2	0.2
Parker	298.9	3 159	62.0	17.3	3.0	0.0	3.0	279.0	2 949	169	175	4 536	21.9	77.7	0.4
Parmer	23.4	2 366	77.3	2.7	3.3	0.0	4.6	3.3	331	69	18	832	13.9	85.8	0.3
Pecos	76.0	4 628	47.2	23.6	2.9	0.1	2.4	40.4	2 458	49	30	1 837	28.1	71.5	0.4
Polk	80.6	1 813	66.6	3.4	4.4	0.8	5.0	264.3	5 947	80	82	2 901	33.4	66.2	0.4
Potter	479.9	4 133	53.8	7.9	6.2	0.0	3.3	340.6	2 934	1 760	261	10 884	26.2	73.5	0.4
Presidio	28.7	3 733	61.3	0.2	2.7	0.0	5.1	19.3	2 510	209	14	568	61.5	37.9	0.5
Rains	19.8	1 938	76.8	0.0	1.4	0.1	3.4	7.7	753	17	19	386	28.7	71.0	0.3
Randall	79.5	744	55.6	1.4	8.8	0.1	2.6	47.2	442	49	198	4 636	16.2	83.5	0.3
Reagan	15.8	4 955	46.6	18.6	3.4	0.0	6.0	5.7	1 807	14	0	340	16.1	83.7	0.2
Real	8.5	2 845	32.0	0.2	3.7	32.8	6.2	10.5	3 509	0	0	219	19.5	80.1	0.4
Red River	33.6	2 411	74.0	0.0	1.9	0.3	4.6	15.1	1 084	42	26	774	38.3	61.6	0.1
Reeves	74.9	6 005	30.6	11.3	3.2	0.0	1.9	106.0	8 492	82	23	1 517	47.2	52.4	0.3
Refugio	26.9	3 485	45.7	21.8	4.4	1.0	6.3	11.9	1 545	44	14	624	35.7	64.1	0.3
Roberts	6.3	7 396	67.8	0.2	4.8	0.1	10.4	0.7	861	12	0	92	8.4	91.6	0.0
Robertson	47.8	2 978	60.1	0.9	6.5	1.4	6.9	9.2	575	49	30	1 011	43.9	55.8	0.3
Rockwall	161.5	3 176	66.7	0.2	4.0	0.0	3.0	204.3	4 017	83	94	1 977	20.8	78.8	0.4
Runnels	32.4	2 914	59.1	20.8	2.7	0.1	3.9	14.1	1 264	46	21	808	19.5	80.2	0.3
Rusk	88.3	1 858	69.1	0.1	5.3	0.5	6.1	67.2	1 413	101	88	2 215	26.7	73.1	0.2
Sabine	19.7	1 896	69.0	8.4	3.0	0.0	4.7	2.4	229	61	19	484	31.9	67.8	0.3
San Augustine	16.5	1 845	68.1	0.0	5.2	0.1	4.8	9.1	1 018	24	17	453	40.2	59.5	0.3
San Jacinto	32.2	1 383	73.0	0.0	3.4	0.8	8.1	18.4	793	32	43	851	33.1	66.4	0.5
San Patricio	197.4	2 925	67.3	7.9	4.1	0.9	3.5	139.8	2 071	379	2 897	3 805	36.4	63.2	0.3
San Saba	14.4	2 339	68.9	1.1	2.5	0.9	5.7	3.3	543	24	11	674	19.7	80.0	0.3
Schleicher	11.2	3 806	44.5	26.8	4.1	0.7	7.1	0.8	288	15	0	282	23.5	76.2	0.3
Scurry	45.1	2 840	71.3	0.4	3.5	0.4	3.9	12.4	782	44	29	1 669	17.6	82.2	0.2
Shackelford	10.6	3 184	57.1	0.0	3.3	0.0	3.4	2.5	758	15	0	224	14.7	85.0	0.3
Shelby	50.0	1 964	72.6	0.0	3.1	0.5	4.9	28.9	1 136	93	47	1 192	31.8	67.9	0.3
Sherman	12.2	3 700	53.4	20.4	4.4	0.1	7.5	4.7	1 441	13	0	302	11.4	88.6	0.0
Smith	396.4	2 185	60.3	6.6	5.5	1.4	2.7	305.6	1 684	965	340	11 269	27.1	72.5	0.4
Somervell	39.7	5 501	63.7	9.1	2.7	0.0	7.4	1.4	194	15	13	543	23.4	76.3	0.2
Starr	169.6	2 991	76.1	7.5	1.9	0.0	3.3	76.5	1 349	327	105	4 337	73.6	26.1	0.3
Stephens	24.4	2 582	44.4	27.9	5.1	0.7	3.7	6.7	707	26	18	737	20.0	79.8	0.2
Sterling	5.7	4 265	61.3	3.0	2.8	8.8	3.6	0.0	0	0	0	151	12.3	87.7	0.0
Stonewall	8.0	5 376	30.8	29.6	4.1	0.0	3.9	0.4	273	14	0	194	41.3	58.2	0.5
Sutton	13.6	3 302	55.6	16.1	5.4	0.0	5.2	0.1	16	0	0	389	19.3	80.7	0.0
Swisher	25.1	3 104	52.5	17.0	3.1	0.0	2.0	3.0	367	33	15	750	30.7	69.1	0.2
Tarrant	4 466.2	2 924	49.7	8.7	6.4	0.2	4.0	8 248.7	5 401	13 544	4 160	77 370	37.0	62.5	0.5
Taylor	284.1	2 261	52.0	5.2	7.7	1.0	4.4	157.8	1 256	1 192	5 541	8 301	22.1	77.4	0.5
Terrell	6.6	6 583	74.6	2.6	2.3	0.0	5.1	0.2	168	16	0	259	34.0	65.4	0.6
Terry	47.4	3 729	47.3	25.0	3.5	0.2	4.0	16.5	1 298	35	24	1 104	20.0	79.8	0.2
Throckmorton	6.2	3 617	54.6	18.7	0.9	0.0	7.3	0.2	116	14	0	179	23.4	76.0	0.6
Titus	161.2	5 675	46.3	37.7	2.2	0.2	2.1	122.8	4 324	117	53	2 860	35.6	64.1	0.3

1. Based on the resident population estimated as of July 1 of the year shown.

Table B. States and Counties — Land Area and Population

STATE/ County code	CBSA code[1]	County Type[2]	STATE County	Land area,[3] (sq km) 2000	Population and population characteristics, 2003													
								Race alone or in combination, not Hispanic or Latino (percent)					Age (percent)					
					Total persons	Rank	Per square kilometer	White	Black	Am. Indian, Alaska Native	Asian and Pacific Islander	Percent Hispanic or Latino[4]	Under 5 years	5 to 17 years	18 to 24 years	25 to 34 years	35 to 44 years	45 to 54 years
					1	2	3	4	5	6	7	8	9	10	11	12	13	14	15
			TEXAS—Cont'd															
48 451	41660	3	Tom Green	3 942	103 528	525	26.3	62.2	3.7	0.8	1.1	33.0	7.3	18.5	12.8	12.2	13.6	12.7
48 453	12420	1	Travis	2 562	857 204	53	334.6	55.3	8.9	0.7	5.5	30.9	8.2	16.5	11.5	20.2	16.1	12.8
48 455	...	8	Trinity	1 794	14 151	2 156	7.9	82.3	11.5	0.7	0.3	5.7	6.0	16.6	8.7	9.9	11.9	12.4
48 457	...	6	Tyler	2 390	20 651	1 765	8.6	83.7	11.5	1.3	0.3	4.4	5.5	16.8	9.4	13.0	13.6	12.5
48 459	30980	3	Upshur	1 522	36 959	1 210	24.3	85.4	9.7	1.2	0.3	4.3	6.7	19.1	9.9	10.7	14.5	13.6
48 461	...	8	Upton	3 216	3 153	2 972	1.0	52.9	1.8	0.9	0.0	44.3	6.2	20.4	11.0	8.7	14.2	15.3
48 463	46620	7	Uvalde	4 031	26 787	1 513	6.6	31.4	0.4	0.3	0.4	67.6	9.1	22.1	10.9	11.8	12.3	11.6
48 465	19620	5	Val Verde	8 211	46 569	986	5.7	19.6	1.0	0.3	0.5	78.6	9.0	22.7	9.9	13.3	13.0	10.8
48 467	...	6	Van Zandt	2 198	50 664	926	23.1	88.8	3.1	1.1	0.3	7.5	6.0	18.5	9.4	10.9	13.6	13.4
48 469	47020	3	Victoria	2 286	85 395	623	37.4	52.4	6.1	0.4	0.9	40.7	8.0	20.6	10.0	12.2	14.5	13.6
48 471	26660	4	Walker	2 039	62 038	800	30.4	60.9	23.7	0.6	0.9	14.6	5.0	12.8	20.4	16.5	15.1	11.9
48 473	26420	1	Waller	1 330	34 579	1 290	26.0	51.3	27.2	0.6	0.5	21.1	7.5	18.0	17.6	12.6	13.1	12.6
48 475	...	6	Ward	2 164	10 293	2 418	4.8	50.4	4.6	0.8	0.3	44.2	6.8	22.1	10.2	8.9	14.3	14.1
48 477	14780	4	Washington	1 578	30 950	1 384	19.6	70.4	18.2	0.4	1.4	10.1	6.3	17.6	13.0	10.5	13.1	13.4
48 479	29700	3	Webb	8 694	213 615	271	24.6	4.3	0.1	0.1	0.4	95.1	12.5	24.8	11.1	14.9	12.7	9.6
48 481	20900	1	Wharton	2 823	41 144	1 106	14.6	51.9	14.4	0.2	0.4	33.2	7.3	20.4	11.0	11.1	14.0	13.5
48 483	...	9	Wheeler	2 368	4 809	2 854	2.0	81.6	3.0	0.7	0.7	14.0	4.9	18.0	8.4	9.1	13.0	15.2
48 485	48660	3	Wichita	1 626	129 257	437	79.5	74.3	10.2	1.5	2.6	13.2	7.3	18.0	14.3	12.7	14.5	12.3
48 487	46900	6	Wilbarger	2 515	13 858	2 176	5.5	68.4	8.2	0.9	0.7	22.3	7.3	20.8	10.5	10.5	12.9	12.7
48 489	39700	6	Willacy	1 545	20 094	1 800	13.0	11.0	2.0	0.1	0.1	86.7	9.2	22.3	12.7	12.5	13.1	11.1
48 491	12420	1	Williamson	2 908	303 587	194	104.4	71.7	6.0	0.7	4.1	18.9	8.2	21.1	9.5	15.6	17.2	12.4
48 493	41700	1	Wilson	2 090	35 244	1 262	16.9	60.7	1.4	0.5	0.5	37.3	6.6	21.0	10.3	11.3	15.5	14.1
48 495	...	6	Winkler	2 178	6 780	2 707	3.1	51.4	1.9	0.3	0.2	46.2	7.1	21.0	10.6	10.7	14.1	13.8
48 497	19100	3	Wise	2 343	54 465	884	23.2	86.1	1.1	1.4	0.5	12.0	6.5	20.5	10.1	12.5	15.9	13.3
48 499	...	6	Wood	1 684	39 286	1 145	23.3	87.7	5.6	1.0	0.3	6.2	5.6	15.8	9.7	9.6	12.1	12.7
48 501	...	7	Yoakum	2 071	7 249	2 660	3.5	49.2	1.3	0.6	0.1	48.8	7.8	22.5	11.0	9.3	15.4	13.2
48 503	...	6	Young	2 389	17 901	1 920	7.5	86.0	1.6	1.2	0.3	11.7	6.2	18.1	8.8	9.5	13.4	13.8
48 505	...	6	Zapata	2 582	12 905	2 247	5.0	12.8	0.2	0.1	0.2	86.8	9.9	23.2	10.8	12.4	11.6	10.5
48 507	...	7	Zavala	3 363	11 593	2 327	3.4	8.5	0.4	0.2	0.1	90.9	8.7	24.3	11.7	12.9	12.1	11.8
49 000	...	X	UTAH	212 751	2 351 467	X	11.1	85.4	1.1	1.6	3.3	9.9	9.8	21.8	13.3	16.2	12.3	11.1
49 001	...	9	Beaver	6 708	6 105	2 767	0.9	91.0	0.2	1.4	1.1	6.8	9.3	23.4	11.1	11.6	11.4	12.1
49 003	14940	4	Box Elder	14 823	44 504	1 035	3.0	91.1	0.4	1.1	1.4	6.8	9.0	24.7	12.8	11.8	12.5	10.8
49 005	30860	3	Cache	3 016	95 664	564	31.7	89.2	0.7	0.8	2.6	7.5	10.8	20.3	17.8	17.6	10.1	8.8
49 007	39220	7	Carbon	3 829	19 764	1 816	5.2	88.5	0.4	1.3	0.5	9.8	7.3	19.8	13.7	10.1	12.6	14.3
49 009	...	8	Daggett	1 809	889	3 113	0.5	92.9	0.4	0.8	0.1	5.8	7.6	14.3	10.7	12.8	12.4	14.3
49 011	36260	2	Davis	789	255 597	231	324.0	90.3	1.6	0.8	3.0	5.9	9.7	23.8	13.0	14.1	13.0	11.0
49 013	...	8	Duchesne	8 387	14 846	2 111	1.8	90.6	0.2	6.9	0.4	3.5	9.0	25.2	12.3	11.3	12.4	11.3
49 015	...	9	Emery	11 530	10 651	2 390	0.9	93.3	0.3	1.0	0.6	5.4	7.8	24.4	12.7	9.1	12.6	13.6
49 017	...	9	Garfield	13 401	4 542	2 869	0.3	94.3	0.2	2.1	0.6	3.2	7.5	22.4	10.9	10.9	11.5	13.8
49 019	...	7	Grand	9 535	8 759	2 549	0.9	88.5	0.3	5.9	0.3	5.7	6.7	19.0	10.0	13.0	13.8	15.7
49 021	16260	4	Iron	8 542	35 811	1 252	4.2	91.7	0.6	2.7	1.7	4.4	10.4	20.3	17.2	15.2	10.1	9.6
49 023	39340	4	Juab	8 785	8 792	2 542	1.0	96.1	0.2	1.0	0.4	2.5	10.5	26.0	12.0	12.6	11.1	10.5
49 025	...	6	Kane	10 339	6 039	2 772	0.6	95.8	0.1	2.0	0.3	2.3	6.5	20.7	10.3	9.6	10.9	14.1
49 027	...	7	Millard	17 066	12 455	2 270	0.7	89.1	0.1	1.7	0.8	8.6	7.6	25.9	13.0	8.7	12.3	12.1
49 029	36260	2	Morgan	1 578	7 518	2 634	4.8	98.3	0.1	0.5	0.4	1.3	7.0	25.4	14.4	9.7	12.8	12.1
49 031	...	8	Piute	1 963	1 380	3 095	0.7	93.8	0.1	0.9	0.1	5.0	7.6	20.2	9.6	8.0	10.1	12.8
49 033	...	8	Rich	2 664	2 019	3 058	0.8	97.6	0.0	0.0	0.5	1.9	6.1	23.6	13.0	8.2	11.6	12.5
49 035	41620	2	Salt Lake	1 910	924 247	44	483.9	80.5	1.4	1.1	5.0	13.4	9.3	20.9	11.9	16.3	13.7	12.0
49 037	...	7	San Juan	20 254	13 901	2 173	0.7	38.7	0.2	58.2	0.4	3.3	8.7	27.1	12.6	12.0	12.2	10.5
49 039	...	6	Sanpete	4 113	23 689	1 624	5.8	90.3	0.4	1.3	1.3	7.5	8.5	22.4	18.6	10.9	10.7	10.4
49 041	...	7	Sevier	4 948	19 103	1 856	3.9	94.6	0.4	2.2	0.4	3.0	8.7	24.1	12.5	10.2	11.9	11.3
49 043	41620	2	Summit	4 846	33 020	1 332	6.8	89.3	0.3	0.5	1.3	9.0	7.5	20.7	10.4	14.2	16.6	15.8
49 045	41620	2	Tooele	17 950	47 965	963	2.7	87.1	1.5	2.2	1.4	9.1	10.4	23.8	13.0	15.8	12.4	9.9
49 047	46860	7	Uintah	11 596	26 296	1 526	2.3	86.4	0.2	10.1	0.5	3.8	9.0	23.2	13.1	12.0	12.6	12.1
49 049	39340	2	Utah	5 176	398 059	152	76.9	89.6	0.6	0.9	2.7	7.7	12.1	22.4	16.4	17.7	10.0	7.9
49 051	...	6	Wasatch	3 049	17 509	1 935	5.7	92.5	0.2	0.9	0.8	6.5	9.1	23.3	12.4	13.9	13.4	11.5
49 053	41100	3	Washington	6 285	104 132	522	16.6	91.6	0.5	1.9	1.6	5.7	8.8	20.8	13.1	12.5	9.9	8.7
49 055	...	9	Wayne	6 372	2 454	3 025	0.4	96.9	0.3	0.4	0.3	2.4	7.7	22.5	9.1	11.4	11.1	13.6
49 057	36260	2	Weber	1 491	205 827	285	138.0	82.6	1.7	1.0	2.0	13.9	9.3	21.3	12.3	14.4	13.0	11.5
50 000	...	X	VERMONT	23 956	619 107	X	25.8	97.0	0.8	1.0	1.3	0.9	5.0	17.2	10.3	11.4	15.6	16.4
50 001	...	6	Addison	1 995	36 835	1 218	18.5	97.1	0.8	0.9	1.2	1.1	4.9	17.9	14.0	9.9	15.4	16.2
50 003	13540	6	Bennington	1 752	37 178	1 204	21.2	97.2	0.8	0.5	1.0	1.2	4.8	16.9	9.2	9.7	15.0	15.8
50 005	...	7	Caledonia	1 685	29 940	1 407	17.8	97.9	0.4	1.3	0.5	0.8	4.8	17.9	10.7	10.4	14.7	16.3

1. CBSA = Core Based Statistical Area. See Appendix A for explanation. See Appendix B for list of metropolitan areas with component counties. 2. County type code from the Economic Research Service of USDA Rural-Urban Continuum Codes. See Appendix A for definition. 3. Dry land or land partially or temporarily covered by water. 4. Hispanic or Latino persons may be of any race.

Table B. States and Counties — **Population and Households**

STATE County	55 to 64 years	65 to 74 years	75 years and over	Percent female	1990	2000	1990–2000	2000–2003	Births	Deaths	Net migration	Number	Percent change, 1990–2000	Persons per house-hold	Female family house-holder[1]	One person
	16	17	18	19	20	21	22	23	24	25	26	27	28	29	30	31
TEXAS—Cont'd																
Tom Green	8.7	6.9	6.8	51.6	98 458	104 010	5.6	-0.5	5 015	3 088	-2 412	39 503	11.6	2.52	11.9	27.2
Travis	6.6	3.6	3.0	48.5	576 407	812 280	40.9	5.5	47 465	12 607	9 776	320 766	37.7	2.47	10.4	30.1
Trinity	12.7	12.0	9.7	51.6	11 445	13 779	20.4	2.7	541	623	452	5 723	23.2	2.38	11.2	26.8
Tyler	11.3	10.1	7.9	48.0	16 646	20 871	25.4	-1.1	730	772	-153	7 775	20.4	2.48	10.0	24.3
Upshur	10.5	8.0	6.2	51.1	31 370	35 291	12.5	4.7	1 604	1 348	1 425	13 290	17.0	2.62	11.0	21.8
Upton	10.9	8.8	6.4	50.9	4 447	3 404	-23.5	-7.4	144	130	-272	1 256	-14.7	2.68	9.1	23.5
Uvalde	8.5	6.8	6.8	51.5	23 340	25 926	11.1	3.3	1 610	756	26	8 559	13.3	2.96	13.7	19.9
Val Verde	8.6	6.8	5.1	51.1	38 721	44 856	15.8	3.8	2 796	917	-150	14 151	19.5	3.11	13.9	17.5
Van Zandt	11.2	8.9	7.5	50.5	37 944	48 140	26.9	5.2	1 880	1 814	2 417	18 195	26.8	2.59	8.7	22.0
Victoria	8.9	6.5	5.6	51.3	74 361	84 088	13.1	1.6	4 481	2 083	-1 028	30 071	14.7	2.75	12.7	22.4
Walker	7.4	5.1	4.0	39.9	50 917	61 758	21.3	0.5	2 017	1 352	-328	18 303	22.7	2.44	11.7	27.0
Waller	8.4	5.0	4.1	50.2	23 374	32 663	39.7	5.9	1 654	741	1 018	10 557	42.6	2.79	13.0	21.0
Ward	10.0	8.2	7.0	50.2	13 115	10 909	-16.8	-5.6	502	276	-852	3 964	-10.8	2.66	11.6	23.6
Washington	9.2	8.1	8.4	51.1	26 154	30 373	16.1	1.9	1 284	1 082	398	11 322	17.7	2.53	11.4	25.7
Webb	5.9	4.1	3.3	51.8	133 239	193 117	44.9	10.6	19 319	2 817	4 219	50 740	47.3	3.75	18.3	12.4
Wharton	9.2	6.9	6.8	50.7	39 955	41 188	3.1	-0.1	1 978	1 274	-716	14 799	4.1	2.73	12.5	24.4
Wheeler	12.1	11.0	10.5	52.2	5 879	5 284	-10.1	-9.0	138	276	-340	2 152	-8.4	2.39	7.7	29.1
Wichita	8.1	6.9	6.0	48.8	122 378	131 664	7.6	-1.8	6 211	4 075	-4 594	48 441	7.0	2.49	11.9	27.2
Wilbarger	10.2	7.2	8.9	50.8	15 121	14 676	-2.9	-5.6	677	555	-945	5 537	-3.6	2.48	10.8	29.0
Willacy	7.9	6.2	5.3	48.7	17 705	20 082	13.4	0.1	1 300	293	-992	5 584	10.6	3.40	16.1	16.5
Williamson	6.6	3.8	3.1	50.1	139 551	249 967	79.1	21.5	15 291	3 681	40 674	86 766	77.8	2.82	9.6	17.6
Wilson	9.3	6.0	4.8	50.0	22 650	32 408	43.1	8.8	1 441	747	2 093	11 038	47.5	2.89	9.2	17.1
Winkler	9.4	7.8	7.3	51.3	8 626	7 173	-16.8	-5.5	323	240	-482	2 584	-12.1	2.72	10.1	21.7
Wise	9.5	5.8	4.1	49.6	34 679	48 793	40.7	11.6	2 234	1 256	4 567	17 178	41.1	2.77	8.2	18.3
Wood	12.5	11.3	9.1	50.8	29 380	36 752	25.1	6.9	1 435	1 651	2 708	14 583	27.6	2.42	8.2	24.1
Yoakum	9.2	6.3	5.4	51.5	8 786	7 322	-16.7	-1.0	370	171	-273	2 469	-13.0	2.95	8.5	17.3
Young	10.2	9.9	9.7	52.2	18 126	17 943	-1.0	-0.2	736	828	57	7 167	0.9	2.45	9.4	26.3
Zapata	7.8	6.8	6.3	50.8	9 279	12 182	31.3	5.9	857	250	142	3 921	37.0	3.10	13.0	17.5
Zavala	7.5	6.1	5.3	50.6	12 162	11 600	-4.6	-0.1	640	287	-363	3 428	2.1	3.28	21.8	16.6
UTAH	6.9	4.5	4.1	49.8	1 722 850	2 233 169	29.6	5.3	154 257	42 133	3 623	701 281	30.5	3.13	9.4	17.8
Beaver	7.5	7.2	6.5	48.4	4 765	6 005	26.0	1.7	370	164	-101	1 982	24.3	2.93	7.0	20.5
Box Elder	7.2	5.9	4.6	49.5	36 485	42 745	17.2	4.1	2 561	990	240	13 144	20.0	3.22	7.9	16.0
Cache	5.1	3.5	3.7	50.7	70 183	91 391	30.2	4.7	7 043	1 345	-1 430	27 543	31.0	3.24	7.2	14.5
Carbon	8.7	6.5	7.0	51.4	20 228	20 422	1.0	-3.2	946	656	-971	7 413	7.3	2.68	10.0	23.8
Daggett	12.5	11.0	4.9	43.4	690	921	33.5	-3.5	38	23	-46	340	34.4	2.48	4.4	25.9
Davis	6.4	4.2	3.2	49.7	187 941	238 994	27.2	6.9	16 166	3 689	4 384	71 201	32.8	3.31	9.2	13.6
Duchesne	8.5	6.0	3.8	49.5	12 645	14 371	13.6	3.3	871	386	-3	4 559	23.0	3.11	8.9	16.8
Emery	9.0	5.8	5.0	49.3	10 332	10 860	5.1	-1.9	549	239	-529	3 468	15.7	3.10	7.2	17.6
Garfield	9.3	8.2	6.5	48.8	3 980	4 735	19.0	-4.1	209	146	-259	1 576	19.3	2.92	6.8	20.5
Grand	9.0	6.9	5.6	50.5	6 620	8 485	28.2	3.2	373	244	152	3 434	38.0	2.44	10.7	29.5
Iron	6.4	4.9	3.8	50.3	20 789	33 779	62.5	5.8	2 516	524	1	10 627	69.5	3.11	8.5	15.9
Juab	6.5	4.6	5.2	49.5	5 817	8 238	41.6	6.7	561	169	170	2 456	36.4	3.31	7.9	17.5
Kane	11.0	9.5	7.5	50.0	5 169	6 046	17.0	-0.1	254	196	-66	2 237	29.8	2.67	6.0	23.3
Millard	8.1	6.5	5.9	48.7	11 333	12 405	9.5	0.4	619	365	-208	3 840	14.7	3.19	7.1	18.3
Morgan	8.5	5.5	3.6	49.2	5 528	7 129	29.0	5.5	329	90	154	2 046	31.6	3.48	5.6	11.7
Piute	13.3	10.1	8.5	48.7	1 277	1 435	12.4	-3.8	63	52	-67	509	13.4	2.79	5.7	22.4
Rich	10.0	7.3	6.5	49.8	1 725	1 961	13.7	3.0	71	30	19	645	23.8	3.01	3.7	17.1
Salt Lake	6.9	4.2	3.9	49.4	725 956	898 387	23.8	2.9	58 471	17 160	-15 877	295 141	22.6	3.00	10.4	20.8
San Juan	7.4	5.0	3.9	50.2	12 621	14 413	14.2	-3.6	768	301	-1 015	4 089	21.2	3.46	14.1	18.7
Sanpete	7.0	5.7	5.0	49.2	16 259	22 763	40.0	4.1	1 303	558	204	6 547	34.7	3.27	7.2	17.8
Sevier	8.7	6.6	6.2	50.1	15 431	18 842	22.1	1.4	1 093	537	-263	6 081	24.7	3.03	7.8	17.6
Summit	7.7	3.2	1.8	48.1	15 518	29 736	91.6	11.0	1 631	337	1 970	10 332	96.0	2.87	6.2	18.4
Tooele	6.0	3.7	2.8	50.6	26 601	40 735	53.1	17.7	3 222	696	4 563	12 677	47.7	3.11	9.5	16.8
Uintah	7.6	5.6	4.5	50.0	22 211	25 224	13.6	4.2	1 613	583	53	8 187	22.7	3.05	10.6	17.2
Utah	4.8	3.3	3.0	50.5	263 590	368 536	39.8	8.0	32 745	5 316	-283	99 937	42.4	3.59	8.0	11.2
Wasatch	6.7	4.4	3.2	49.3	10 089	15 215	50.8	15.1	1 020	296	1 526	4 743	54.3	3.18	7.5	14.3
Washington	7.1	8.2	8.0	50.6	48 560	90 354	86.1	15.2	5 904	2 274	10 037	29 939	96.2	2.97	8.0	17.5
Wayne	10.4	7.2	7.9	48.8	2 177	2 509	15.3	-2.2	116	65	-107	890	27.3	2.81	5.3	21.5
Weber	7.2	5.1	4.9	49.8	158 330	196 533	24.1	4.7	12 832	4 702	1 375	65 698	23.4	2.95	10.7	20.0
VERMONT	11.1	6.6	6.3	50.9	562 758	608 827	8.2	1.7	20 066	16 774	7 514	240 634	14.2	2.44	9.3	26.2
Addison	9.9	5.8	5.5	50.5	32 953	35 974	9.2	2.4	1 155	847	585	13 068	14.5	2.55	8.3	23.4
Bennington	11.5	8.4	8.5	51.8	35 845	36 994	3.2	0.5	1 161	1 252	311	14 846	9.2	2.41	10.1	26.8
Caledonia	10.5	7.1	7.2	50.5	27 846	29 702	6.7	0.8	954	998	299	11 663	12.5	2.46	10.4	25.6

1. No spouse present.

Table B. States and Counties — Vital Statistics, Health Resources, and Crime

STATE County	Births, average 1999–2001		Deaths, average 1999–2001				Physicians,[4] 2000		Hospitals,[4] 1998			Medicare enrollees, 2003	Serious crimes known to police,[6] 2002	
			Number		Rate					Beds			Total	
	Total	Rate[1]	Total	Infant[2]	Total[1]	Infant[3]	Number	Rate[5]	Number	Number	Rate[5]		Number	Rate[7]
	32	33	34	35	36	37	38	39	40	41	42	43	44	45

TEXAS—Cont'd														
Tom Green	1 578	15.2	1 011	14	9.7	9.1	213	205	3	478	465	16 133	6 149	5 660
Travis	14 116	17.3	3 960	70	4.9	5.0	1 771	218	7	1 517	213	65 178	49 126	5 790
Trinity	163	11.8	202	2	14.7	D	4	29	1	22	174	3 336	342	2 376
Tyler	232	11.2	242	2	11.7	D	11	53	1	36	176	3 920	309	1 417
Upshur	464	13.1	418	3	11.8	D	8	23	0	0	0	6 500	1 065	2 983
Upton	44	13.1	36	1	10.7	D	3	88	2	66	1 760	530	45	1 265
Uvalde	489	18.8	227	2	8.7	D	28	108	1	64	250	3 922	1 245	4 598
Val Verde	906	20.2	318	5	7.1	D	42	94	1	78	178	4 779	1 379	2 943
Van Zandt	595	12.4	588	3	12.2	D	15	31	1	26	59	8 562	1 470	3 008
Victoria	1 363	16.2	680	8	8.1	5.6	183	218	3	588	711	11 967	4 582	5 217
Walker	614	9.9	433	4	7.0	D	44	71	1	119	216	6 116	1 617	2 507
Waller	486	14.9	227	1	7.0	D	12	37	0	0	0	3 221	1 018	2 984
Ward	155	14.3	104	1	9.6	D	9	83	1	41	347	1 778	142	1 246
Washington	387	12.7	339	2	11.2	D	40	132	1	60	206	5 584	1 142	3 600
Webb	5 721	29.3	926	32	4.7	5.6	167	86	2	377	200	18 329	13 468	6 677
Wharton	612	14.9	393	2	9.6	D	69	168	2	221	551	6 315	1 858	4 319
Wheeler	51	9.6	84	0	16.0	D	6	114	2	63	1 190	1 152	72	1 304
Wichita	1 896	14.4	1 287	20	9.8	10.4	279	212	3	423	328	19 463	9 240	6 719
Wilbarger	198	13.7	179	2	12.3	D	28	191	1	52	379	2 536	792	5 167
Willacy	396	19.8	107	1	5.3	D	8	40	0	0	0	2 621	749	3 960
Williamson	4 388	17.2	1 162	20	4.6	4.5	211	84	3	213	95	22 195	6 699	2 566
Wilson	441	13.5	248	3	7.6	D	9	28	1	30	95	3 906	412	1 217
Winkler	97	13.4	82	1	11.4	D	6	84	1	16	201	1 089	117	1 561
Wise	685	14.0	415	4	8.4	D	18	37	1	50	113	5 772	1 130	2 217
Wood	416	11.3	504	3	13.7	D	25	68	2	78	227	8 558	825	2 149
Yoakum	124	16.8	55	1	7.5	D	3	41	1	24	300	976	143	1 870
Young	223	12.4	268	1	15.0	D	14	78	2	83	469	3 847	518	2 764
Zapata	250	20.4	87	1	7.1	D	3	25	0	0	0	1 373	455	3 576
Zavala	207	17.9	103	2	8.9	D	4	34	0	0	0	1 622	225	1 857
UTAH	47 201	21.1	12 361	235	5.5	5.0	3 665	164	39	4 269	203	220 221	103 129	4 452
Beaver	121	20.1	55	1	9.2	D	5	83	2	70	1 187	932	83	1 543
Box Elder	785	18.3	281	3	6.6	D	34	80	2	57	136	5 258	1 183	2 851
Cache	2 172	23.8	418	9	4.6	4.3	114	125	1	139	160	7 539	2 101	2 216
Carbon	307	15.1	190	2	9.4	D	21	103	1	88	420	3 293	846	3 994
Daggett	14	15.2	4	0	0.0	D	0	0	0	0	0	147	39	4 084
Davis	4 888	20.4	1 075	22	4.5	4.5	214	90	2	248	106	20 569	7 541	3 042
Duchesne	281	19.5	98	1	6.8	D	18	125	1	42	290	1 976	359	2 408
Emery	168	15.5	71	1	6.6	D	0	0	0	0	0	1 353	207	1 838
Garfield	65	13.8	45	1	9.6	D	3	63	1	20	468	779	NA	NA
Grand	115	13.6	64	0	7.5	D	9	106	1	34	421	1 211	520	5 908
Iron	771	22.8	160	5	4.7	D	17	50	1	47	164	3 947	916	2 829
Juab	174	21.1	55	2	6.7	D	4	49	1	20	264	967	NA	NA
Kane	84	14.0	60	1	10.0	D	6	99	1	33	532	1 178	NA	NA
Millard	187	15.1	105	2	8.5	D	5	40	2	40	327	1 604	391	3 039
Morgan	96	13.5	26	1	3.7	D	4	56	0	0	0	764	114	1 542
Piute	21	14.9	13	0	9.4	D	0	0	0	0	0	304	20	1 344
Rich	24	12.1	13	0	6.5	D	0	0	0	0	0	282	52	2 557
Salt Lake	18 024	20.0	5 055	95	5.6	5.3	2 264	252	9	1 924	226	83 291	57 943	6 221
San Juan	249	17.6	77	1	5.5	D	5	35	1	25	182	1 264	136	910
Sanpete	395	17.3	160	2	7.0	D	15	66	2	41	191	2 806	447	2 121
Sevier	336	17.8	162	1	8.6	D	12	64	1	27	146	2 863	780	3 991
Summit	472	15.8	94	1	3.2	D	47	158	0	0	0	1 825	1 308	4 431
Tooele	952	23.2	216	4	5.3	D	19	47	1	38	114	3 487	1 218	2 883
Uintah	466	18.3	170	3	6.7	D	18	71	1	39	152	2 919	788	3 012
Utah	9 983	26.9	1 546	46	4.2	4.6	398	108	4	610	182	28 248	13 497	3 531
Wasatch	299	19.5	82	1	5.4	D	9	59	1	40	301	1 512	187	1 185
Washington	1 809	19.9	678	8	7.4	4.6	115	127	1	103	125	16 219	2 386	2 546
Wayne	40	16.2	21	0	8.3	D	0	0	0	0	0	402	50	1 922
Weber	3 902	19.8	1 365	21	6.9	5.3	309	157	2	584	317	23 159	9 423	4 623
VERMONT	6 478	10.6	5 107	37	8.4	5.8	1 535	252	15	1 566	265	92 724	15 600	2 530
Addison	381	10.6	260	2	7.2	D	59	164	1	45	128	4 594	690	1 894
Bennington	358	9.7	395	3	10.7	D	105	284	1	140	389	6 921	876	2 338
Caledonia	284	9.6	285	2	9.6	D	40	135	1	37	130	4 970	790	2 233

1. Per 1,000 estimated resident population.   2. Deaths of infants under 1 year old.   3. Deaths of infants under 1 year old per 1,000 live births.   4. Data subject to copyright.   5. Per 100,000 resident population as of July 1 of the year shown.   6. Data for serious crimes have not been adjusted for underreporting; this may affect comparability between geographic areas and over time.   7. Per 100,000 population estimated by the FBI.

Table B. States and Counties — Crime, Education, Money Income, and Poverty

STATE County	Serious crimes known to police,[1] 2002 (cont'd) Rate[2] Violent	Property	Education — School enrollment and attainment, 2000 Enrollment[3] Total	Percent private	Attainment[4] (percent) High school graduate or less	Bachelor's degree or more	Local government expenditures,[5] 2000–2001 Total current expenditures (mil dol)	Current expenditures per student (dollars)	Money income, 1999 Per capita income[6] (dollars)	Households Median income Dollars	Percent change, 1989–1999 (constant 1999 dollars)	Percent with income of $100,000 or more	Percent below poverty level, 1999 Persons	Households	Families	Families with children
	46	47	48	49	50	51	52	53	54	55	56	57	58	59	60	61
TEXAS—Cont'd																
Tom Green	376	5 284	29 720	5.8	52.3	19.5	127.3	6 652	17 325	33 148	1.3	5.8	15.2	14.9	11.2	16.5
Travis	428	5 362	235 906	11.5	32.7	40.6	815.5	7 049	25 883	46 761	26.6	16.1	12.5	11.3	7.7	11.0
Trinity	327	2 050	2 836	4.0	66.4	9.4	17.5	7 320	15 472	27 070	18.8	3.7	17.6	18.2	13.2	20.0
Tyler	161	1 257	4 466	6.8	69.6	9.7	26.5	7 127	15 367	29 808	7.5	4.9	15.8	15.5	12.6	19.0
Upshur	151	2 831	8 817	8.0	60.0	11.1	42.7	6 426	16 358	33 347	13.4	5.0	14.9	15.2	12.3	16.6
Upton	112	1 153	959	0.7	67.1	11.8	9.6	11 719	14 274	28 977	-11.4	3.8	19.9	17.5	18.1	24.2
Uvalde	462	4 136	7 779	6.5	62.8	13.8	43.2	6 811	12 557	27 164	12.3	4.7	24.3	23.3	19.9	26.8
Val Verde	149	2 794	12 850	7.6	66.1	14.1	63.7	6 283	12 096	28 376	17.1	4.8	26.1	24.5	22.1	28.9
Van Zandt	254	2 754	11 226	8.6	62.4	11.6	54.9	5 925	16 930	35 029	23.7	6.0	13.3	13.8	10.3	14.9
Victoria	669	4 547	24 141	12.1	52.8	16.2	111.7	7 199	18 379	38 732	7.0	8.7	12.9	12.7	10.5	15.0
Walker	367	2 139	20 291	9.8	58.6	18.3	54.5	7 128	14 508	31 468	8.3	6.7	18.4	19.6	10.6	15.7
Waller	284	2 700	11 274	6.0	57.6	16.8	46.7	6 527	16 338	38 136	27.1	10.9	16.0	15.5	11.5	16.2
Ward	140	1 106	3 113	5.2	64.4	12.4	16.6	7 456	14 393	29 386	-1.8	4.8	17.9	19.2	15.8	21.5
Washington	482	3 117	8 413	13.3	56.5	19.0	32.8	6 357	17 384	36 760	18.7	7.2	12.9	14.6	9.8	13.2
Webb	588	6 089	67 101	6.8	65.0	13.9	309.0	6 084	10 759	28 100	15.7	6.2	31.2	28.1	26.7	32.8
Wharton	565	3 754	11 527	8.0	59.5	14.3	56.8	6 621	15 388	32 208	0.3	6.4	16.5	17.5	13.3	17.1
Wheeler	199	1 105	1 214	5.6	58.6	13.0	10.8	11 403	16 083	31 029	14.9	4.0	13.0	16.0	11.6	15.2
Wichita	773	5 946	35 683	9.5	49.9	20.0	146.7	6 526	16 965	33 780	5.2	5.8	13.2	13.3	10.3	14.9
Wilbarger	300	4 867	3 816	5.8	57.3	17.1	17.9	6 538	16 520	29 500	5.1	6.5	13.1	14.0	9.0	14.2
Willacy	497	3 463	6 058	2.1	75.6	7.5	35.4	7 450	9 421	22 114	12.8	2.5	33.2	32.9	29.2	36.2
Williamson	250	2 316	70 940	14.2	33.4	33.6	399.0	6 378	24 547	60 642	34.0	18.6	4.8	4.6	3.4	4.6
Wilson	127	1 090	8 879	7.5	60.3	12.8	43.2	6 212	17 253	40 006	28.4	7.9	11.3	12.2	9.2	10.7
Winkler	320	1 241	1 938	0.5	67.0	10.5	15.4	8 909	13 725	30 591	1.8	3.0	18.7	18.6	14.4	21.0
Wise	286	1 931	12 621	7.1	58.7	13.0	53.7	6 430	17 729	41 933	20.6	8.0	9.9	10.1	7.5	9.9
Wood	162	1 988	7 855	10.5	56.5	14.5	37.7	6 400	17 702	32 885	17.0	5.7	14.3	14.1	10.8	16.9
Yoakum	183	1 687	2 286	1.0	67.1	10.2	16.9	8 744	14 504	32 672	-8.0	6.2	19.6	18.2	17.6	21.8
Young	261	2 502	4 167	6.1	60.0	14.4	21.7	6 353	16 710	30 499	4.6	5.9	15.7	15.3	12.0	19.2
Zapata	472	3 104	3 703	2.9	74.6	8.7	18.9	6 507	10 486	24 635	22.8	3.3	35.8	29.6	29.3	40.7
Zavala	198	1 659	3 883	3.3	76.9	7.6	19.6	7 999	10 034	16 844	6.0	1.6	41.8	41.5	37.4	42.3
UTAH	237	4 216	741 524	12.9	36.9	26.1	2 230.9	4 673	18 185	45 726	15.5	11.2	9.4	8.9	6.5	8.7
Beaver	167	1 375	1 757	4.5	55.2	12.1	8.0	5 600	14 957	34 544	21.9	3.6	8.3	10.7	6.2	8.5
Box Elder	104	2 747	13 949	4.3	43.6	19.5	49.0	4 485	15 625	44 630	-0.7	6.4	7.1	7.3	5.8	7.6
Cache	107	2 110	37 654	4.2	32.2	31.9	84.9	4 478	15 094	39 730	9.7	7.7	13.5	13.1	8.0	9.4
Carbon	288	3 706	6 264	5.2	50.3	12.3	26.8	6 263	15 325	34 036	-0.9	4.8	13.4	14.0	10.0	12.4
Daggett	209	3 874	192	0.0	51.6	11.9	2.1	12 994	15 511	30 833	0.0	4.7	5.5	7.6	4.4	5.1
Davis	127	2 915	80 293	7.8	31.1	28.8	270.2	4 536	19 506	53 726	13.9	14.1	5.1	5.1	4.0	5.5
Duchesne	161	2 247	4 687	4.0	56.7	12.7	21.7	5 245	12 326	31 298	-1.5	3.3	16.8	17.4	14.2	18.7
Emery	62	1 776	3 518	3.1	51.1	11.6	15.2	5 594	14 243	39 850	-2.8	4.3	11.5	10.9	9.4	11.9
Garfield	NA	NA	1 301	3.2	46.7	20.3	7.6	6 823	13 439	35 180	23.7	2.3	8.1	8.8	6.1	8.2
Grand	261	5 647	2 054	6.9	44.3	22.9	8.0	5 130	17 356	32 387	11.1	5.7	14.8	13.0	10.9	19.3
Iron	130	2 700	13 246	3.8	35.5	23.8	37.2	5 185	13 568	33 114	6.3	5.3	19.2	16.8	13.1	18.0
Juab	NA	NA	2 607	6.8	52.4	12.2	11.6	5 468	12 790	38 139	20.4	4.5	10.4	11.2	7.9	9.5
Kane	NA	NA	1 688	6.2	39.8	21.1	8.4	6 266	15 455	34 247	20.6	3.3	7.9	8.5	5.5	7.3
Millard	132	2 907	4 187	3.5	43.9	16.8	20.2	6 014	13 408	36 178	2.1	3.5	13.1	11.5	9.4	13.2
Morgan	68	1 474	2 628	6.2	37.0	23.3	9.5	4 682	17 684	50 273	12.5	13.4	5.2	5.3	3.7	4.8
Piute	202	1 142	392	2.6	51.1	14.4	3.0	7 403	12 697	29 625	15.3	3.0	16.2	15.1	11.7	19.1
Rich	197	2 360	640	4.7	42.5	22.0	3.5	7 402	16 267	39 766	18.7	7.2	10.2	9.5	6.5	8.2
Salt Lake	351	5 870	275 773	11.3	37.2	27.4	801.0	4 543	20 190	48 373	19.4	13.0	8.0	7.7	5.7	8.0
San Juan	167	743	5 470	2.0	54.0	13.9	27.8	8 774	10 229	28 137	21.1	3.4	31.4	29.1	26.9	30.3
Sanpete	199	1 921	8 638	4.8	44.3	17.3	27.9	5 261	12 442	33 042	21.8	4.1	15.9	15.1	10.4	13.2
Sevier	164	3 827	5 971	5.5	48.5	15.2	23.0	5 087	14 180	35 822	14.4	3.9	10.8	11.1	8.3	11.9
Summit	58	4 373	8 606	12.9	24.6	45.5	35.7	5 727	33 767	64 962	31.5	28.7	5.4	4.6	3.0	4.3
Tooele	289	2 594	12 109	7.5	47.4	15.9	39.2	4 270	16 321	45 773	12.9	6.6	6.7	7.2	5.2	7.0
Uintah	199	2 813	7 936	4.8	56.2	13.2	31.7	5 278	13 571	34 518	7.2	4.5	14.5	13.6	12.0	16.2
Utah	104	3 427	148 809	29.6	28.3	31.5	360.4	4 421	15 557	45 833	24.4	11.1	12.0	10.7	6.8	7.8
Wasatch	57	1 128	4 874	8.5	35.7	26.3	17.8	4 849	19 869	49 612	32.0	11.3	5.2	5.3	4.2	5.7
Washington	226	2 320	26 270	8.6	39.1	21.0	82.1	4 467	15 873	37 212	12.6	6.9	11.2	9.7	7.7	13.0
Wayne	231	1 691	719	2.2	37.8	20.9	4.1	7 400	15 392	32 000	19.1	4.1	15.4	14.4	12.7	20.4
Weber	320	4 303	59 292	6.9	42.6	19.9	193.3	4 743	18 246	44 014	8.7	9.2	9.3	9.1	6.9	10.3
VERMONT	107	2 423	164 156	18.1	45.9	29.4	924.0	9 456	20 625	40 856	2.1	8.7	9.4	9.7	6.3	9.7
Addison	96	1 798	10 568	31.2	47.4	29.8	53.9	9 835	19 539	43 142	6.6	8.3	8.6	8.4	5.1	7.5
Bennington	115	2 223	9 380	22.6	48.2	27.1	55.0	10 716	21 193	39 926	4.3	9.6	10.0	10.2	7.0	11.6
Caledonia	76	2 157	7 986	20.0	55.0	22.5	47.2	11 985	16 976	34 800	2.2	5.1	12.3	12.4	9.0	14.5

1. Data for serious crimes have not been adjusted for underreporting; this may affect comparability between geographic areas and over time.   2. Per 100,000 population estimated by the FBI.   3. All persons 3 years old and over enrolled in nursery school through college.   4. Persons 25 years old and over.   5. Elementary and secondary education expenditures.   6. Based on population enumerated as of April 1, 2000.

STATE County	Total (mil dol)	Percent change, 2001–2002	Per capita[1] Dollars	Per capita[1] Rank	Wages and salaries[2] (mil dol)	Proprietor's income (mil dol)	Dividends, interest, and rent (mil dol)	Transfer payments Total (mil dol)	Government payments to individuals Total (mil dol)	Social Security (mil dol)	Medical payments (mil dol)	Income mainte-nance (mil dol)	Unemploy-ment insurance (mil dol)
	62	63	64	65	66	67	68	69	70	71	72	73	74
TEXAS—Cont'd													
Tom Green	2 640	2.2	25 562	987	1 664	177	540	458	436	168	188	42	7
Travis	30 091	-0.6	35 492	129	26 825	4 061	4 683	2 171	1 981	737	758	207	125
Trinity	287	3.9	20 415	2 456	65	21	52	86	83	38	33	7	1
Tyler	413	3.9	19 947	2 555	123	34	60	113	108	45	48	8	3
Upshur	791	2.5	21 693	2 091	191	62	120	186	178	74	76	15	5
Upton	67	-0.1	20 653	2 384	44	-1	13	15	14	6	6	1	0
Uvalde	528	3.8	19 839	2 579	267	48	110	132	126	36	58	20	2
Val Verde	847	7.0	18 503	2 831	586	45	107	174	164	44	75	31	3
Van Zandt	1 243	3.0	24 787	1 181	273	66	156	243	232	96	106	15	5
Victoria	2 323	1.6	27 310	646	1 361	204	455	371	352	132	159	36	10
Walker	1 105	4.5	17 899	2 909	786	58	188	192	178	67	72	17	2
Waller	757	3.7	22 258	1 943	368	44	83	124	116	39	48	11	3
Ward	215	2.3	20 506	2 431	111	13	41	51	49	20	20	6	1
Washington	904	3.3	29 443	396	449	69	278	154	147	59	65	11	1
Webb	3 437	6.9	16 593	3 019	2 359	352	346	720	674	140	329	149	14
Wharton	999	1.6	24 304	1 308	454	127	180	191	182	67	82	16	5
Wheeler	145	-9.6	29 114	428	48	43	23	33	32	12	17	2	1
Wichita	3 466	4.5	26 761	744	2 388	346	656	556	530	200	225	48	14
Wilbarger	342	2.8	24 455	1 277	211	23	72	76	73	26	35	6	1
Willacy	300	2.5	14 982	3 078	97	7	34	104	99	21	51	21	4
Williamson	7 833	-4.7	26 979	701	3 802	436	921	651	586	268	210	38	36
Wilson	805	6.5	23 421	1 590	173	36	95	121	114	41	52	10	2
Winkler	136	-1.0	19 484	2 662	74	9	22	36	34	12	16	3	2
Wise	1 193	4.0	22 563	1 861	503	98	172	163	151	70	57	11	6
Wood	800	4.0	21 015	2 299	266	77	150	217	209	91	88	12	4
Yoakum	168	3.5	23 200	1 662	113	23	27	30	29	11	13	3	1
Young	446	1.6	25 194	1 080	199	62	102	103	99	42	46	7	3
Zapata	174	6.7	13 659	3 094	96	7	36	53	50	12	25	10	1
Zavala	140	3.2	12 047	3 104	65	15	14	58	56	12	27	14	1
UTAH	57 134	2.8	24 639	X	41 816	4 695	9 126	6 652	6 130	2 440	2 109	639	316
Beaver	147	-0.5	24 111	1 368	65	45	20	25	24	9	10	2	1
Box Elder	948	1.8	21 563	2 135	764	56	148	132	122	58	40	11	4
Cache	1 868	3.7	19 792	2 591	1 293	94	326	238	217	86	70	20	8
Carbon	463	3.4	23 365	1 606	311	20	66	105	101	38	37	11	3
Daggett	15	1.8	17 330	2 966	14	0	4	3	3	2	1	0	0
Davis	6 471	4.1	25 947	897	3 911	353	931	579	524	219	171	50	22
Duchesne	310	1.8	20 854	2 331	181	14	44	62	58	21	23	8	4
Emery	199	0.9	18 776	2 787	160	8	25	40	38	16	13	4	2
Garfield	91	1.1	19 688	2 612	57	3	15	19	18	8	6	2	1
Grand	180	4.1	20 678	2 376	112	12	44	33	31	14	9	5	2
Iron	635	5.3	17 939	2 905	403	49	102	119	111	42	39	13	3
Juab	166	7.0	19 224	2 708	88	10	21	31	29	11	12	2	2
Kane	142	4.0	23 513	1 564	69	8	34	27	26	13	9	2	0
Millard	255	5.6	20 620	2 395	155	36	42	43	40	17	15	4	1
Morgan	167	0.1	22 397	1 910	61	6	32	16	15	8	4	1	0
Piute	25	3.3	18 043	2 890	8	4	4	6	6	3	2	0	0
Rich	45	3.8	22 963	1 734	16	3	13	6	5	3	1	0	0
Salt Lake	26 184	2.0	28 539	485	22 452	2 628	4 231	2 634	2 427	974	819	258	146
San Juan	198	4.9	14 297	3 088	123	2	30	51	48	12	18	15	1
Sanpete	386	6.0	16 501	3 023	184	43	60	80	75	31	26	8	2
Sevier	360	2.9	18 828	2 777	226	24	56	78	73	32	28	8	2
Summit	1 439	2.7	45 121	33	577	163	294	62	54	25	12	3	8
Tooele	917	4.6	19 947	2 555	528	34	103	101	91	32	33	11	6
Uintah	481	0.8	18 341	2 851	347	25	72	93	87	34	32	12	5
Utah	7 684	1.8	19 603	2 631	5 234	677	1 030	977	889	327	329	83	49
Wasatch	366	4.9	21 627	2 114	157	25	71	42	38	18	11	3	4
Washington	1 994	6.2	20 059	2 537	1 113	161	465	382	359	181	118	28	7
Wayne	50	-0.3	19 788	2 592	30	4	9	10	9	4	4	1	0
Weber	4 949	4.0	24 315	1 305	3 178	187	836	659	613	205	215	76	30
VERMONT	18 347	3.3	29 764	X	11 614	1 559	3 595	2 871	2 688	1 022	1 168	255	112
Addison	998	2.8	27 281	657	537	89	213	131	120	51	45	11	8
Bennington	1 189	2.7	32 024	225	654	130	307	193	182	80	70	18	7
Caledonia	752	3.8	25 163	1 088	370	105	136	144	135	53	50	15	10

1. Based on the resident population estimated as of July 1 of the year shown. 2. Includes other labor income.

STATE County	Earnings, 2002 Total (mil dol)	Farm	Goods-related[1] Total	Manu-facturing	Service-related and health Infor-mation and profes-sional and technical services	Retail trade	Finance, insur-ance, and real estate	Health services	Govern-ment	Social Security beneficiaries, December 2003 Number	Rate[2]	Supple-mental Security Income recipients, December 2003	Housing units, 2003 Total	Percent change, 2000–2003
	75	76	77	78	79	80	81	82	83	84	85	86	87	88
TEXAS—Cont'd														
Tom Green	1 841	0.3	18.2	10.1	10.3	7.6	5.6	14.9	27.5	18 315	177	2 370	44 651	1.7
Travis	30 886	0.0	21.6	15.7	18.8	5.7	10.1	7.4	18.0	75 080	88	10 759	373 424	11.2
Trinity	85	4.1	13.2	6.7	D	9.4	4.8	7.0	25.1	4 000	283	454	8 316	2.1
Tyler	157	-0.1	12.5	6.5	3.3	7.4	4.7	4.9	39.1	4 720	229	516	10 612	1.9
Upshur	253	2.8	19.9	7.6	8.8	9.9	5.2	D	22.1	7 475	202	790	15 289	2.4
Upton	43	-8.7	D	D	D	3.4	D	3.7	32.5	645	205	69	1 612	0.2
Uvalde	315	2.6	11.5	5.5	6.2	10.4	4.4	9.2	30.4	4 450	166	1 095	10 326	1.6
Val Verde	631	-0.7	D	3.6	D	8.7	3.2	8.1	51.5	6 460	139	2 275	16 809	3.2
Van Zandt	339	6.6	22.1	4.4	4.6	11.4	4.1	D	21.3	10 300	203	898	21 433	2.6
Victoria	1 565	-0.2	27.1	11.0	D	11.5	6.5	13.1	15.4	14 020	164	2 141	33 685	2.2
Walker	844	0.2	7.3	4.9	3.0	7.1	2.8	8.1	61.8	7 030	113	875	21 814	3.4
Waller	412	0.5	D	22.3	4.3	14.5	3.5	D	31.2	4 185	121	500	12 992	8.7
Ward	125	-2.7	31.1	1.4	3.0	8.2	7.9	3.7	29.9	2 090	203	317	4 863	0.6
Washington	518	1.4	31.7	23.4	D	9.0	8.9	D	19.7	6 280	203	811	13 551	2.3
Webb	2 711	-0.2	9.4	1.4	5.3	10.3	7.5	10.2	26.4	21 105	99	8 740	61 127	10.7
Wharton	581	9.2	23.6	13.2	3.9	9.4	5.0	D	17.8	7 295	177	1 002	16 903	1.8
Wheeler	91	37.7	8.4	0.4	7.9	7.7	3.1	D	17.9	1 250	260	99	2 662	-0.9
Wichita	2 734	0.1	22.6	14.6	5.6	7.5	4.1	11.6	35.6	21 245	164	2 888	54 113	1.5
Wilbarger	234	2.5	D	D	3.6	7.4	4.2	D	41.7	2 835	205	413	6 327	-0.7
Willacy	104	-2.2	D	0.4	D	11.3	4.0	9.5	39.0	3 100	154	1 210	6 960	3.5
Williamson	4 238	0.0	18.5	8.4	5.6	7.7	5.8	8.1	12.9	28 605	94	2 167	108 215	19.8
Wilson	209	6.0	15.7	5.4	3.7	10.3	3.4	D	32.5	4 960	141	588	12 553	3.7
Winkler	84	-1.1	42.2	0.3	D	5.4	3.2	2.7	23.6	1 280	189	204	3 202	-0.4
Wise	600	0.7	35.7	11.9	D	10.9	4.1	D	16.0	7 430	136	492	19 971	3.8
Wood	343	11.5	18.0	8.9	7.4	9.6	5.7	D	18.2	10 220	260	793	18 235	1.7
Yoakum	136	9.5	37.8	1.6	1.6	3.9	2.1	1.3	18.6	1 200	166	119	3 016	1.4
Young	261	0.0	37.7	13.3	6.8	8.6	D	5.3	17.5	4 325	242	394	8 535	0.4
Zapata	103	-1.3	36.6	0.6	3.2	6.7	3.6	4.4	32.3	1 585	123	482	6 348	2.9
Zavala	80	15.9	D	D	D	4.8	D	15.6	31.5	1 935	167	869	4 127	1.3
UTAH	46 511	0.5	20.2	11.9	11.2	7.9	8.0	7.5	19.3	256 551	109	21 394	826 551	7.5
Beaver	110	41.4	7.7	2.9	D	4.7	D	1.9	19.6	1 000	164	54	2 723	2.4
Box Elder	820	2.8	D	53.4	1.7	6.5	2.1	3.6	11.3	6 065	136	300	15 055	6.0
Cache	1 387	1.6	D	21.3	7.3	7.4	3.2	7.0	25.2	8 875	93	454	31 152	7.3
Carbon	331	-0.7	D	4.3	2.9	9.4	2.5	D	23.8	3 870	196	332	8 934	2.2
Daggett	14	-0.6	D	D	D	D	D	0.0	65.2	175	197	2	1 131	4.3
Davis	4 264	0.2	D	11.0	7.1	7.3	4.2	5.9	38.6	24 245	95	1 221	81 099	9.4
Duchesne	195	0.4	29.0	2.2	4.1	6.9	2.4	7.6	28.2	2 400	162	239	7 374	5.5
Emery	168	0.3	D	0.6	3.9	4.0	D	D	18.0	1 690	159	123	4 199	2.6
Garfield	60	-3.3	D	3.2	D	5.7	D	D	38.0	900	198	42	2 950	6.6
Grand	124	-0.2	D	1.3	4.1	13.2	3.3	5.4	27.7	1 460	167	116	4 380	7.8
Iron	452	5.2	D	11.3	D	9.7	6.8	5.9	30.4	4 645	130	389	14 869	9.2
Juab	98	3.4	D	15.4	7.0	7.5	1.9	3.9	19.8	1 200	136	74	3 042	8.3
Kane	78	-0.1	D	D	D	9.2	3.0	1.5	33.1	1 390	230	67	4 069	8.0
Millard	191	16.7	12.8	3.2	D	6.0	D	4.0	21.1	1 855	149	114	4 654	2.9
Morgan	67	0.3	D	16.0	D	7.9	2.7	1.3	19.0	860	114	17	2 324	7.7
Piute	12	35.6	D	0.0	0.5	D	D	D	36.5	360	261	15	753	1.1
Rich	19	13.9	D	D	0.0	6.1	D	D	34.0	330	163	5	2 685	11.5
Salt Lake	25 080	0.0	17.7	10.2	13.3	7.5	10.6	7.4	15.3	97 000	105	9 338	326 288	4.9
San Juan	125	-3.3	17.4	6.1	D	4.8	1.6	D	49.5	1 525	110	642	5 558	2.0
Sanpete	226	13.7	D	10.9	3.6	7.8	3.6	D	33.8	3 420	144	221	8 210	4.2
Sevier	250	4.4	19.4	6.6	D	11.0	2.7	D	24.9	3 465	181	219	7 301	4.1
Summit	739	0.6	16.8	4.0	9.0	8.3	15.1	3.9	11.4	2 445	74	62	18 989	8.6
Tooele	562	1.0	18.8	12.2	D	5.8	2.2	D	36.1	4 180	87	256	16 009	15.9
Uintah	372	-0.4	30.1	1.5	D	7.8	4.0	4.8	26.8	3 675	140	304	9 430	4.3
Utah	5 911	0.4	21.3	12.5	16.2	8.4	5.4	8.8	14.5	33 780	85	3 217	116 856	12.0
Wasatch	182	-0.2	D	7.4	8.8	8.2	6.6	6.1	23.7	1 865	107	74	7 513	14.5
Washington	1 273	-0.1	D	6.0	6.4	13.1	7.7	12.6	14.8	19 550	188	779	42 129	15.5
Wayne	34	10.6	D	D	D	4.4	D	D	31.4	450	183	18	1 372	3.2
Weber	3 365	0.0	25.7	19.2	D	8.4	5.5	10.1	26.1	23 875	116	2 650	75 503	7.2
VERMONT	13 173	0.9	24.4	17.4	D	8.8	6.6	11.8	16.7	108 248	175	12 819	302 106	2.6
Addison	626	3.8	D	17.4	D	9.0	4.5	11.1	12.1	5 490	149	568	15 848	3.5
Bennington	783	0.3	D	25.7	6.9	11.5	5.5	14.1	11.9	8 150	219	884	19 934	2.7
Caledonia	475	1.7	27.6	17.2	7.3	9.4	4.6	13.1	15.1	5 800	194	759	14 855	2.4

1. Covers mining, construction, and manufacturing.   2. Per 1,000 resident population estimated as of July 1 of the year shown.

Table B. States and Counties — Housing, Labor Force, and Employment

STATE County	Housing units, 2000 Total	Occupied units Percent	Owner-occupied Median value[1]	Median owner cost as a percent of income With a mortgage	Without a mortgage[2]	Renter-occupied Median rent[3]	Median rent as a percent of income	Sub-standard units[4] (percent)	Civilian labor force, 2003 Total	Percent change, 2002–2003	Unemployment Total	Rate[5]	Civilian employment,[6] 2000 Total	Percent Management, professional and related occupations	Production, transportation, and material moving occupations
	89	90	91	92	93	94	95	96	97	98	99	100	101	102	103
TEXAS—Cont'd															
Tom Green	39 503	64.1	63 600	19.7	10.4	457	24.6	5.7	51 628	1.8	1 989	3.9	45 418	27.9	13.2
Travis	320 766	51.5	134 700	21.2	9.9	727	27.0	8.5	501 220	1.1	29 351	5.9	441 161	43.7	8.6
Trinity	5 723	80.8	53 400	21.0	13.0	403	21.5	4.7	5 098	5.5	320	6.3	5 016	24.7	15.7
Tyler	7 775	84.0	50 600	19.6	10.7	432	21.5	5.4	7 801	12.3	774	9.9	6 827	22.5	17.7
Upshur	13 290	81.7	59 600	19.9	10.5	415	22.2	5.2	17 426	2.7	1 031	5.9	14 710	23.5	20.2
Upton	1 256	75.6	31 100	16.3	9.9	309	16.0	7.0	1 414	-1.4	71	5.0	1 305	28.8	18.2
Uvalde	8 559	72.0	46 000	18.8	10.8	414	24.6	14.1	11 579	3.6	1 008	8.7	9 896	25.9	16.4
Val Verde	14 151	66.0	58 600	19.7	12.3	408	22.4	15.2	20 171	4.3	1 619	8.0	15 097	25.2	14.8
Van Zandt	18 195	80.9	66 400	20.3	11.7	461	22.9	5.4	23 508	3.5	1 201	5.1	19 942	25.0	17.0
Victoria	30 071	67.4	73 300	18.5	10.5	507	22.9	7.1	45 200	0.2	2 359	5.2	38 464	28.5	15.1
Walker	18 303	59.9	80 400	19.8	10.9	509	28.6	6.5	23 973	3.9	803	3.3	22 554	29.8	10.9
Waller	10 557	72.5	84 700	20.1	11.5	473	24.3	9.1	15 177	2.2	1 033	6.8	13 699	28.6	14.9
Ward	3 964	78.2	34 400	17.1	10.0	349	22.1	7.1	3 798	0.1	293	7.7	3 966	29.0	18.4
Washington	11 322	73.5	84 200	19.6	9.9	479	23.8	5.3	16 078	4.4	571	3.6	13 497	27.3	18.4
Webb	50 740	65.7	74 600	24.0	12.5	449	27.3	27.8	84 173	4.7	6 177	7.3	62 558	26.7	14.6
Wharton	14 799	68.8	59 100	18.5	10.9	415	21.8	8.6	19 695	2.9	1 353	6.9	17 563	27.3	21.1
Wheeler	2 152	78.0	37 000	19.4	10.8	348	19.7	3.0	2 547	-2.7	65	2.6	2 402	27.9	12.1
Wichita	48 441	62.3	61 500	19.6	10.9	486	24.5	3.9	60 953	1.0	3 093	5.1	54 394	28.9	15.6
Wilbarger	5 537	66.3	46 800	19.4	13.0	377	22.3	3.8	7 501	0.7	267	3.6	6 468	28.3	16.8
Willacy	5 584	77.3	34 600	21.8	14.3	301	24.2	22.7	6 448	3.4	1 083	16.8	6 018	24.1	14.0
Williamson	86 766	74.2	125 800	20.8	9.9	787	24.3	4.5	164 676	1.2	8 277	5.0	129 192	42.4	9.8
Wilson	11 038	85.0	85 100	18.5	10.1	421	22.7	7.3	16 804	2.3	755	4.5	13 939	27.6	14.9
Winkler	2 584	83.2	29 600	17.0	11.5	370	20.6	6.3	2 911	1.9	244	8.4	2 561	21.3	20.9
Wise	17 178	81.3	89 100	20.0	11.0	484	23.0	5.9	28 656	5.3	1 333	4.7	22 665	26.2	19.0
Wood	14 583	81.4	69 800	20.3	11.7	436	22.4	4.0	14 804	2.2	814	5.5	14 431	26.6	17.0
Yoakum	2 469	78.2	40 400	17.8	10.7	394	18.6	10.2	3 035	3.3	152	5.0	2 861	25.9	17.7
Young	7 167	73.8	45 200	18.5	11.7	389	21.9	4.4	8 015	-0.7	429	5.4	7 875	26.3	18.3
Zapata	3 921	81.9	46 500	23.2	9.9	267	26.0	21.7	5 256	5.8	442	8.4	3 384	22.2	18.1
Zavala	3 428	73.0	25 300	21.3	12.6	217	22.7	30.1	4 733	8.3	736	15.6	3 034	24.3	17.4
UTAH	701 281	71.5	146 100	22.9	9.9	597	24.9	6.3	1 184 385	1.7	66 653	5.6	1 044 362	32.5	13.5
Beaver	1 982	78.9	89 200	20.9	10.0	490	23.7	5.0	2 497	-0.2	137	5.5	2 490	26.2	15.2
Box Elder	13 144	80.0	118 900	21.7	9.9	514	22.6	4.6	18 299	1.3	1 149	6.3	18 298	27.9	23.5
Cache	27 543	64.6	131 800	22.3	9.9	509	24.6	6.8	49 050	3.8	1 809	3.7	44 481	32.7	18.9
Carbon	7 413	77.4	86 100	18.6	10.9	433	23.5	3.4	9 474	0.1	743	7.8	8 625	24.1	15.5
Daggett	340	70.6	76 400	17.5	9.9	500	20.6	2.9	469	-0.2	22	4.7	381	26.8	7.9
Davis	71 201	77.6	156 400	22.1	9.9	637	24.0	3.7	124 837	1.7	6 532	5.2	111 038	34.5	11.9
Duchesne	4 559	80.8	81 800	22.8	9.9	452	24.0	5.7	6 381	-1.4	516	8.1	5 468	27.5	17.9
Emery	3 468	82.0	84 200	18.8	9.9	397	21.7	5.0	4 027	4.5	444	11.0	4 362	23.0	15.9
Garfield	1 576	79.0	90 500	20.9	9.9	435	18.0	4.3	2 806	-0.2	304	10.8	2 003	32.0	8.6
Grand	3 434	70.9	112 700	22.5	9.9	498	28.8	6.0	5 632	4.1	411	7.3	4 097	30.0	9.0
Iron	10 627	66.3	112 000	24.3	9.9	468	25.2	7.2	15 971	1.7	792	5.0	15 484	27.5	13.1
Juab	2 456	79.6	115 900	22.6	10.9	501	21.3	5.9	3 933	-2.4	286	7.3	3 421	22.5	20.4
Kane	2 237	78.1	103 900	22.1	9.9	406	18.5	4.0	2 857	1.6	132	4.6	2 666	29.2	11.8
Millard	3 840	79.6	84 700	19.5	9.9	388	20.9	6.0	4 801	-0.8	270	5.6	4 876	29.1	15.2
Morgan	2 046	88.3	174 500	22.3	9.9	580	22.2	2.8	4 027	6.4	169	4.2	3 150	32.9	13.5
Piute	509	87.2	80 900	20.6	9.9	395	26.8	3.9	633	9.0	38	6.0	541	33.5	12.8
Rich	645	83.7	84 300	19.5	9.9	354	16.9	4.8	1 102	2.3	49	4.4	804	38.8	9.6
Salt Lake	295 141	69.0	157 000	23.0	9.9	638	25.3	6.3	512 293	1.0	29 205	5.7	445 128	32.8	13.0
San Juan	4 089	79.3	68 400	23.2	9.9	383	18.8	32.6	4 645	0.4	472	10.2	4 235	32.9	13.7
Sanpete	6 547	78.8	104 800	24.5	10.2	432	22.9	8.1	9 413	2.6	671	7.1	8 596	28.3	16.3
Sevier	6 081	82.0	95 700	21.9	9.9	477	24.0	4.9	8 607	-1.1	462	5.4	7 539	24.1	16.8
Summit	10 332	75.5	296 000	24.3	9.9	909	24.6	3.8	16 599	1.4	1 298	7.8	16 557	39.4	8.1
Tooele	12 677	78.3	127 800	23.4	9.9	532	23.2	5.0	14 536	4.1	1 317	9.1	18 073	25.7	17.2
Uintah	8 187	77.0	84 800	20.4	9.9	422	21.6	6.7	13 013	4.4	798	6.1	10 258	24.9	15.4
Utah	99 937	66.8	156 400	23.5	9.9	580	25.5	8.3	181 831	1.6	8 421	4.6	166 107	36.5	11.4
Wasatch	4 743	80.6	185 300	24.9	9.9	731	25.0	4.9	7 725	1.8	549	7.1	6 989	30.9	12.1
Washington	29 939	74.0	139 800	25.8	9.9	594	26.7	6.9	47 927	6.4	2 110	4.4	35 646	26.9	13.2
Wayne	890	77.6	97 600	21.1	9.9	463	18.6	4.9	1 504	-4.8	109	7.2	1 111	34.2	10.0
Weber	65 698	74.9	125 600	22.5	9.9	544	24.8	5.7	109 497	2.0	7 439	6.8	91 938	29.8	16.6
VERMONT	240 634	70.6	111 500	22.4	13.9	553	26.2	2.0	350 684	0.6	16 013	4.6	317 134	36.3	14.0
Addison	13 068	75.0	111 300	23.3	14.0	565	23.8	2.1	21 758	2.2	859	3.9	18 896	36.6	13.6
Bennington	14 846	71.4	115 700	22.9	14.1	538	27.3	1.3	20 447	-1.0	1 066	5.2	18 680	32.4	16.6
Caledonia	11 663	72.9	83 100	21.9	14.4	428	26.4	2.0	15 911	1.5	958	6.0	14 556	31.0	17.0

1. Specified owner-occupied units.   2. Median monthly owner costs is often in the minimum category—9.9 percent or less, which is indicated as 9.9 percent.   3. Specified renter-occupied units.   4. Overcrowded or lacking complete plumbing facilities.   5. Percent of civilian labor force.   6. Persons 16 years old and over.

	Private nonfarm establishments, employment and payroll, 2001								Agriculture, 2002			
		Employment					Annual payroll		Farms			
										Percent with—		
STATE County	Number of establish-ments	Total	Health care and social assistance	Manufac-turing	Retail trade	Finance and insurance	Professional, scientific, and technical services	Total (mil dol)	Average per employee (dollars)	Number	Less than 50 acres	500 acres and over	Farm operators whose principal occu-pation is farming (percent)
	104	105	106	107	108	109	110	111	112	113	114	115	116
TEXAS—Cont'd													
Tom Green	2 520	35 561	6 140	3 866	5 532	1 661	1 267	862	24 246	1 024	43.1	28.4	54.2
Travis	23 785	470 071	44 004	57 133	54 755	22 277	43 660	19 639	41 779	1 306	46.4	9.9	51.3
Trinity	205	1 727	261	192	325	68	85	32	18 695	555	29.5	8.1	55.5
Tyler	290	4 330	402	386	548	82	63	78	17 967	615	54.5	4.9	48.6
Upshur	443	3 958	440	508	817	199	170	79	19 911	1 236	40.9	6.2	46.3
Upton	64	634	176	0	80	D	D	21	33 065	83	6.0	71.1	68.7
Uvalde	594	6 116	1 242	738	1 124	231	108	116	18 914	686	20.6	38.0	65.5
Val Verde	804	8 699	2 204	239	1 852	394	189	161	18 458	285	31.9	47.0	57.9
Van Zandt	743	7 089	975	643	1 456	232	185	147	20 699	2 842	46.0	6.0	52.6
Victoria	2 194	29 746	5 651	2 662	5 011	1 181	837	778	26 158	1 286	34.8	16.2	54.4
Walker	845	9 941	1 872	749	2 135	318	253	207	20 819	1 043	43.3	8.6	54.0
Waller	542	6 853	320	1 726	1 677	177	187	194	28 243	1 453	49.1	8.6	49.2
Ward	234	2 139	228	23	283	134	40	55	25 493	86	23.3	36.0	47.7
Washington	796	10 875	1 471	2 897	1 572	587	270	268	24 657	2 303	38.1	5.3	49.9
Webb	4 150	53 255	8 398	1 282	10 055	2 471	1 410	1 110	20 837	568	7.9	49.1	52.1
Wharton	962	11 428	2 028	2 194	1 908	438	184	256	22 408	1 538	31.7	22.1	64.0
Wheeler	169	1 231	374	29	193	53	19	20	16 227	565	9.9	38.8	52.2
Wichita	3 287	46 886	9 984	7 461	7 589	1 872	1 175	1 142	24 357	606	38.0	17.7	52.5
Wilbarger	331	4 066	491	991	869	308	70	91	22 378	502	18.7	34.7	63.3
Willacy	209	1 755	298	38	364	70	26	36	20 272	334	27.8	33.5	67.7
Williamson	5 024	72 747	6 678	9 259	12 295	5 969	3 677	2 304	31 668	2 510	45.0	11.2	49.6
Wilson	414	3 223	879	246	664	117	82	60	18 551	2 157	32.4	8.8	51.2
Winkler	145	1 055	151	0	205	53	18	27	25 761	44	13.6	45.5	54.5
Wise	931	10 967	1 169	1 384	1 803	317	248	316	28 807	2 696	49.9	6.8	49.3
Wood	779	6 440	1 246	627	1 315	340	168	130	20 211	1 495	41.0	5.9	54.3
Yoakum	176	1 657	88	86	202	35	D	57	34 441	298	9.4	53.0	60.7
Young	575	5 141	834	807	715	326	104	128	24 836	755	13.8	29.4	51.1
Zapata	144	1 446	118	D	263	66	14	35	23 948	388	4.6	49.5	56.4
Zavala	108	2 274	1 437	D	161	39	18	26	11 389	257	4.7	59.9	61.5
UTAH	56 851	914 829	92 153	120 445	126 475	44 759	58 516	26 064	28 491	15 282	54.8	14.0	48.7
Beaver	148	1 174	241	80	215	40	15	19	16 549	256	30.9	23.8	61.7
Box Elder	790	14 979	1 023	8 242	1 522	421	185	534	35 641	1 113	47.4	21.7	54.1
Cache	2 511	32 581	3 478	9 907	4 874	749	1 488	724	22 215	1 194	51.1	9.4	45.5
Carbon	506	6 373	985	407	1 194	129	303	159	25 018	243	66.3	15.2	41.2
Daggett	22	112	D	0	15	0	3	3	24 813	28	10.7	39.3	67.9
Davis	4 728	63 343	8 279	9 374	11 515	2 435	2 881	1 599	25 241	582	80.4	2.4	50.0
Duchesne	391	3 146	630	92	627	82	57	76	24 260	932	42.9	16.1	50.6
Emery	180	2 852	56	D	377	D	110	106	37 179	459	39.2	14.8	55.1
Garfield	138	1 044	D	106	110	21	10	22	21 440	225	37.3	17.8	56.4
Grand	389	2 866	189	D	580	57	90	53	18 381	94	59.6	11.7	54.3
Iron	887	9 276	817	1 360	1 736	384	1 022	172	18 574	438	40.6	28.8	51.4
Juab	152	1 795	260	259	274	27	D	43	23 794	236	32.2	33.5	51.7
Kane	186	1 532	161	131	390	D	20	26	17 146	131	29.0	37.4	54.2
Millard	228	2 616	262	414	572	68	94	78	29 872	646	29.9	31.1	56.5
Morgan	152	1 153	D	229	201	27	D	30	26 345	255	61.2	12.5	45.9
Piute	24	87	0	D	D	D	D	2	22 839	108	32.4	20.4	75.0
Rich	61	367	1	D	D	D	D	7	19 886	135	21.5	51.9	57.8
Salt Lake	26 175	481 260	46 102	53 596	58 061	32 484	33 083	15 231	31 649	712	82.3	3.1	40.7
San Juan	245	1 668	287	110	317	D	92	34	20 090	231	23.4	44.2	60.6
Sanpete	389	3 932	626	888	804	143	21	69	17 454	759	42.7	18.3	52.6
Sevier	490	5 301	643	481	1 101	108	124	117	21 997	568	52.1	11.4	52.6
Summit	1 539	16 512	456	645	2 684	424	608	366	22 136	557	53.5	15.8	49.7
Tooele	496	6 963	881	1 212	1 282	342	400	210	30 218	380	48.7	18.4	44.5
Uintah	791	6 852	529	220	1 354	136	381	179	26 149	908	56.8	11.1	42.5
Utah	7 640	141 351	13 034	16 260	18 656	3 045	11 618	3 566	25 231	2 046	73.6	5.2	44.3
Wasatch	481	3 356	364	228	560	101	181	70	20 880	380	69.7	3.7	41.8
Washington	2 633	28 038	3 845	2 398	5 870	776	918	615	21 949	481	53.2	14.3	46.6
Wayne	67	489	D	D	103	D	D	8	16 603	173	30.6	8.7	57.2
Weber	4 350	66 682	8 761	13 664	11 401	2 601	4 469	1 731	25 964	1 012	74.7	2.8	41.9
VERMONT	21 449	260 227	37 801	48 374	39 331	10 167	11 533	7 286	28 000	6 571	33.7	8.4	53.1
Addison	1 111	11 538	1 873	2 094	1 834	289	474	309	26 756	676	31.8	16.4	59.9
Bennington	1 584	16 767	2 723	3 190	3 436	382	408	433	25 834	228	44.7	8.8	57.0
Caledonia	943	9 627	1 629	2 081	1 760	358	322	234	24 330	505	30.7	7.5	49.5

STATE County	Acreage (1,000)	Percent change, 1997–2002	Average size of farm	Total irrigated (1,000)	Total cropland (1,000)	Value of land and buildings — Average per farm	Average per acre	Value of machinery and equipment average per farm (dollars)	Total (mil dol)	Average per farm (dollars)	Crops	Live-stock and poultry products	$10,000 or more	$100,000 or more	Total ($1,000)	Percent of farms
	117	118	119	120	121	122	123	124	125	126	127	128	129	130	131	132
TEXAS—Cont'd																
Tom Green	845	-11.9	825	27	212	495 874	628	62 755	97	94 945	19.4	80.6	30.0	10.0	4 287	28.2
Travis	298	-24.7	229	2	102	442 400	1 801	23 555	17	13 106	58.5	41.5	18.5	2.9	721	12.0
Trinity	105	6.1	189	0	43	268 567	1 248	33 299	9	16 131	3.9	96.1	28.1	1.3	D	D
Tyler	80	50.9	129	1	32	223 026	1 951	25 830	5	7 645	33.9	66.1	16.6	1.1	9	1.0
Upshur	196	12.0	159	1	80	224 701	1 556	36 222	41	33 024	5.3	94.7	20.8	4.7	194	1.6
Upton	723	-3.1	8 716	8	36	1 440 048	137	63 880	5	57 998	57.8	42.2	55.4	16.9	1 293	41.0
Uvalde	969	2.8	1 412	55	154	955 118	645	58 543	69	100 633	39.6	60.4	35.6	13.1	2 089	23.8
Val Verde	1 661	-5.0	5 829	2	14	1 244 259	211	42 374	11	38 264	6.3	93.7	32.3	7.4	959	14.0
Van Zandt	422	16.9	149	4	199	260 003	1 615	37 113	73	25 696	45.5	54.5	23.9	3.1	619	1.7
Victoria	514	12.2	400	5	166	345 189	898	46 531	29	22 600	48.0	52.0	28.9	4.5	1 909	10.6
Walker	206	12.0	198	1	62	397 766	2 453	30 512	25	24 326	54.5	45.5	19.5	1.3	6	1.2
Waller	277	16.4	191	12	124	452 948	2 805	36 038	38	26 073	57.9	42.1	26.6	3.6	1 578	8.4
Ward	466	28.4	5 414	1	10	747 330	138	20 006	2	19 545	D	D	20.9	3.5	321	24.4
Washington	355	5.7	154	1	151	388 413	2 459	34 100	37	15 927	18.2	81.8	23.0	1.7	139	3.2
Webb	2 043	-6.1	3 596	7	90	1 622 339	446	32 621	24	41 619	5.4	94.6	25.0	5.1	343	7.9
Wharton	638	-6.0	415	90	429	501 106	1 164	67 452	146	95 169	67.8	32.2	46.4	17.2	15 171	42.7
Wheeler	534	3.9	944	8	186	368 941	390	45 602	94	166 410	3.5	96.5	40.5	7.3	2 698	55.4
Wichita	302	-10.9	498	5	133	338 516	653	31 002	16	26 121	51.4	48.6	30.0	5.6	1 187	27.1
Wilbarger	872	-1.4	1 738	15	231	610 554	342	80 562	32	63 893	57.8	42.2	46.2	12.7	2 281	51.2
Willacy	370	29.4	1 107	10	230	1 157 601	1 066	124 651	19	56 608	77.5	22.5	43.4	13.5	2 817	43.7
Williamson	583	8.4	232	4	305	527 586	2 345	36 796	46	18 484	65.9	34.1	23.1	4.5	3 097	19.6
Wilson	446	0.0	207	13	197	286 625	1 315	36 919	43	19 799	17.8	82.2	23.0	2.0	2 008	20.7
Winkler	492	0.8	11 175	2	1	1 167 089	102	27 792	2	43 774	D	D	40.9	9.1	110	13.6
Wise	493	19.7	183	1	214	314 487	1 885	25 863	33	12 352	22.7	77.3	20.9	2.1	910	9.7
Wood	228	6.0	153	1	108	242 887	1 497	31 647	58	38 662	6.4	93.6	25.8	6.0	830	3.9
Yoakum	455	32.7	1 527	101	258	857 382	579	148 142	50	167 427	83.7	16.3	47.3	29.9	5 413	73.5
Young	510	-7.8	675	0	143	396 856	569	25 450	24	31 690	7.2	92.8	32.5	5.3	1 058	27.8
Zapata	398	-1.2	1 025	3	64	744 396	665	20 639	10	25 369	D	D	29.9	1.5	131	14.4
Zavala	707	19.6	2 752	27	97	1 904 123	652	72 504	49	189 471	22.2	77.8	42.0	18.7	1 369	31.1
UTAH	11 731	-2.4	768	1 091	2 067	586 310	756	62 600	1 116	73 020	23.1	76.9	33.6	10.4	26 669	19.5
Beaver	139	6.1	544	36	52	1 108 109	1 994	108 617	161	630 253	6.5	93.5	56.6	29.3	647	25.0
Box Elder	1 401	3.2	1 259	113	335	647 446	527	129 368	114	102 286	25.9	74.1	43.7	17.2	5 721	36.0
Cache	247	-7.1	207	84	146	464 945	1 878	76 957	97	80 925	15.2	84.8	38.4	15.1	2 866	31.9
Carbon	199	-1.5	821	11	18	365 700	439	35 795	3	13 707	17.5	82.5	21.8	4.1	414	15.2
Daggett	D	D	D	8	11	618 249	700	60 896	2	60 111	D	D	71.4	21.4	116	28.6
Davis	66	-2.9	113	21	27	476 068	3 802	50 577	30	52 211	87.1	12.9	24.2	5.8	182	9.6
Duchesne	1 305	-1.7	1 400	95	134	535 609	369	65 921	46	49 407	10.6	89.4	40.1	10.0	1 643	21.6
Emery	D	D	D	33	58	289 625	861	45 261	11	24 950	13.1	86.9	32.7	3.9	560	21.4
Garfield	80	-33.9	355	15	23	425 981	1 341	58 876	6	26 829	8.1	91.9	40.0	5.8	141	19.1
Grand	53	-30.3	561	3	12	587 003	1 057	35 281	2	23 145	34.0	66.0	26.6	8.5	106	7.4
Iron	479	18.3	1 094	69	90	953 569	808	93 672	77	176 718	48.2	51.8	39.3	18.5	945	21.2
Juab	270	-2.2	1 146	22	63	669 618	569	69 748	12	51 751	33.4	66.6	43.2	11.0	835	41.5
Kane	156	-10.9	1 190	3	9	646 706	581	43 600	3	25 841	D	D	35.1	3.8	211	18.3
Millard	445	-2.8	689	92	162	581 778	814	116 438	113	175 168	25.5	74.5	60.2	20.6	1 766	32.5
Morgan	D	D	D	11	19	780 392	1 060	38 667	7	29 340	10.2	89.7	29.4	9.8	269	11.8
Piute	D	D	D	13	18	447 141	1 331	95 998	9	83 588	8.4	91.6	48.1	16.7	240	23.1
Rich	509	-2.9	3 772	49	84	1 169 854	315	106 390	13	97 415	2.4	97.6	62.2	23.0	727	40.7
Salt Lake	82	-28.1	116	10	29	536 920	4 743	26 214	19	27 231	71.2	28.8	15.2	4.1	211	4.8
San Juan	1 559	-6.8	6 747	3	151	1 839 690	271	104 150	8	32 538	21.2	78.8	35.5	8.2	1 627	42.0
Sanpete	357	-0.8	471	65	114	562 102	1 220	72 026	94	123 412	5.1	94.9	41.2	16.5	1 760	22.0
Sevier	165	12.2	290	59	66	335 535	1 330	73 650	52	92 119	26.2	73.8	39.1	14.3	629	21.0
Summit	376	-36.3	674	28	38	948 457	1 250	49 399	20	35 023	5.8	94.2	31.8	9.5	440	12.7
Tooele	415	42.1	1 092	23	71	509 176	478	49 212	18	47 735	14.2	85.8	29.5	9.2	437	13.7
Uintah	D	D	D	61	80	568 934	232	38 291	30	32 522	11.2	88.8	26.2	4.7	831	15.2
Utah	343	-8.5	168	85	143	545 966	2 785	38 630	117	57 187	37.5	62.5	23.7	6.9	1 942	12.0
Wasatch	70	-34.0	183	14	15	519 809	2 936	30 665	6	14 965	16.1	83.9	17.4	3.2	163	6.8
Washington	217	33.1	451	15	41	781 922	1 659	39 157	7	15 085	41.6	58.4	27.7	3.5	332	11.9
Wayne	42	-30.0	245	18	20	441 685	1 678	56 861	11	60 827	7.1	92.9	59.5	11.0	329	28.9
Weber	87	7.4	86	31	39	361 597	5 772	41 578	27	26 292	25.4	74.6	23.2	6.4	580	9.8
VERMONT	1 245	-1.3	189	2	568	386 695	2 051	66 094	473	71 993	15.1	84.9	39.4	17.8	24 377	19.7
Addison	193	-5.9	286	0	124	474 864	1 795	104 007	106	156 691	10.7	89.3	51.3	32.0	6 308	33.0
Bennington	41	28.1	180	0	13	372 842	1 718	52 184	8	34 292	30.6	69.4	30.3	6.6	367	12.7
Caledonia	84	-10.6	167	0	36	307 705	2 013	57 188	24	47 107	17.0	83.0	37.6	14.3	1 238	17.4

STATE County	Value of residential construction authorized by building permits, 2003		Wholesale trade, 1997				Retail trade,[1] 1997				Real estate and rental and leasing, 1997			
	New construction ($1,000)	Number of housing units	Number of establish-ments	Number of employees	Sales (mil dol)	Annual payroll (mil dol)	Number of establish-ments	Number of employees	Sales (mil dol)	Annual payroll (mil dol)	Number of establish-ments	Number of employees	Receipts (mil dol)	Annual payroll (mil dol)
	133	134	135	136	137	138	139	140	141	142	143	144	145	146
TEXAS—Cont'd														
Tom Green	30 985	265	159	D	D	D	471	5 404	890.7	84.3	134	550	51.7	8.3
Travis	926 824	8 565	1 268	18 345	8 991.9	717.9	2 925	45 335	16 072.8	916.0	1 212	6 484	820.3	159.0
Trinity	0	0	5	D	D	D	60	365	56.1	4.5	4	7	0.9	0.1
Tyler	240	1	5	D	D	D	72	612	85.2	7.5	5	10	1.2	0.1
Upshur	1 486	13	17	49	104.5	2.3	101	895	145.1	11.7	9	29	1.5	0.2
Upton	0	0	8	41	24.7	0.9	16	94	14.7	1.1	NA	NA	NA	NA
Uvalde	2 631	41	40	318	165.3	6.2	124	1 054	178.0	15.5	26	85	6.2	0.9
Val Verde	8 012	142	30	291	54.5	5.1	173	1 798	278.1	25.3	31	105	8.5	1.4
Van Zandt	4 498	60	31	179	70.8	4.1	145	1 339	245.2	20.2	23	46	4.6	0.5
Victoria	12 827	117	141	1 665	422.1	46.0	398	5 052	868.7	80.1	91	455	60.5	10.5
Walker	9 567	98	36	247	89.5	4.4	174	2 245	386.7	32.0	47	218	39.1	4.1
Waller	6 942	206	38	D	D	D	80	1 280	480.4	25.6	9	91	3.9	1.3
Ward	216	6	15	103	74.4	2.9	49	381	54.0	5.5	12	83	7.1	2.1
Washington	5 727	38	36	543	289.2	14.6	143	1 565	270.3	22.8	32	155	13.4	2.7
Webb	136 485	1 671	339	2 453	1 105.4	51.1	730	9 051	1 524.6	138.8	155	574	64.3	10.0
Wharton	2 019	37	69	1 005	326.6	23.7	217	1 799	301.0	27.4	34	174	12.8	3.0
Wheeler	0	0	11	80	30.8	1.6	45	226	33.1	2.7	2	D	D	D
Wichita	50 094	520	211	1 906	434.6	44.8	598	7 268	1 198.7	107.3	151	D	D	D
Wilbarger	248	4	21	81	30.6	1.9	76	737	111.5	8.9	13	38	3.6	0.6
Willacy	8 754	136	10	68	16.9	1.6	43	386	61.8	4.6	4	28	1.8	0.3
Williamson	529 391	4 786	217	1 723	750.3	57.6	623	8 402	1 582.1	152.9	183	639	73.6	12.8
Wilson	1 952	23	16	82	36.7	1.6	68	625	109.5	8.9	8	46	3.7	0.6
Winkler	722	5	6	26	7.6	0.9	32	225	43.6	3.3	8	32	3.8	0.9
Wise	11 347	131	38	343	197.2	6.8	122	1 692	689.2	31.3	29	80	13.0	1.7
Wood	1 442	13	47	364	189.5	10.0	146	1 173	211.1	17.3	26	60	3.8	0.9
Yoakum	0	0	22	119	73.4	2.9	42	246	34.0	3.2	7	19	0.7	0.2
Young	519	8	39	194	83.9	3.3	100	737	113.5	10.1	21	53	12.4	1.2
Zapata	NA	NA	3	D	D	D	37	221	26.8	2.3	2	D	D	D
Zavala	140	3	3	42	6.8	0.7	20	178	22.5	2.3	1	D	D	D
UTAH	3 081 981	22 525	3 278	44 319	21 115.5	1 420.5	7 656	114 474	19 964.6	1 856.9	2 169	12 318	1 342.6	236.0
Beaver	4 532	38	3	19	4.0	0.3	30	205	29.4	2.1	1	D	D	D
Box Elder	41 302	392	28	245	73.4	6.1	126	1 452	250.1	19.5	21	67	7.9	1.1
Cache	117 267	926	85	696	146.4	12.4	349	5 242	682.7	70.7	67	439	24.5	6.7
Carbon	5 841	40	46	348	175.3	9.4	94	1 310	174.9	17.6	16	65	5.1	0.9
Daggett	790	15	NA	NA	NA	NA	6	16	1.6	0.3	1	D	D	D
Davis	422 865	2 853	241	2 868	1 184.9	70.7	582	9 488	1 809.7	157.6	165	784	96.1	13.0
Duchesne	10 533	120	20	103	31.1	1.9	62	541	96.3	8.4	9	40	3.8	0.6
Emery	1 294	13	7	15	5.8	0.3	37	359	48.4	3.7	4	8	0.2	0.0
Garfield	6 156	74	3	D	D	D	23	122	16.9	1.4	NA	NA	NA	NA
Grand	7 921	73	11	46	8.8	1.2	74	528	77.0	8.4	20	85	5.8	1.4
Iron	45 172	352	32	266	113.6	6.1	135	1 663	286.9	24.2	43	151	17.0	1.7
Juab	9 262	70	8	52	10.7	0.7	29	267	40.3	3.0	2	D	D	D
Kane	11 893	124	5	D	D	D	42	308	35.0	4.0	9	18	2.0	0.5
Millard	4 930	43	16	82	28.8	1.4	58	495	82.2	6.4	NA	NA	NA	NA
Morgan	14 839	89	7	D	D	D	20	151	24.7	1.9	1	D	D	D
Piute	580	8	1	D	D	D	7	25	2.0	0.2	NA	NA	NA	NA
Rich	14 151	115	1	D	D	D	13	43	6.0	0.6	2	D	D	D
Salt Lake	901 264	7 102	2 013	29 521	15 365.4	1 018.0	3 230	53 236	10 139.4	937.0	1 114	7 528	878.2	158.8
San Juan	4 188	28	11	105	12.6	1.2	41	304	33.7	3.4	3	3	0.3	0.0
Sanpete	5 473	53	8	36	15.1	0.6	73	688	90.1	7.3	10	29	1.9	0.3
Sevier	12 681	83	19	238	78.1	3.9	102	1 067	167.5	14.1	9	47	3.8	1.0
Summit	121 858	628	47	147	116.9	6.0	242	2 520	307.9	32.0	94	634	56.6	11.0
Tooele	48 922	415	9	120	10.3	1.4	74	1 170	182.8	16.7	12	51	4.7	0.8
Uintah	13 230	103	49	291	77.6	7.4	104	1 190	180.4	16.9	23	115	15.4	3.3
Utah	677 019	4 271	320	6 272	2 763.6	190.4	978	15 868	2 486.4	245.1	239	1 085	108.0	16.9
Wasatch	61 535	269	14	65	14.3	2.5	56	454	69.1	6.3	17	29	3.4	0.2
Washington	330 082	2 729	85	641	238.5	18.0	406	4 829	879.4	77.3	102	332	31.8	4.6
Wayne	2 588	19	1	D	D	D	16	86	9.9	0.8	NA	NA	NA	NA
Weber	183 814	1 480	187	2 025	640.6	57.3	647	10 847	1 753.5	170.3	185	781	74.7	12.7
VERMONT	405 980	2 843	941	10 987	4 731.4	330.6	4 093	36 306	5 898.6	603.3	701	2 362	240.6	42.2
Addison	24 259	171	41	296	90.2	7.7	186	1 523	316.1	30.3	34	87	8.0	1.0
Bennington	27 028	191	49	250	87.0	6.2	359	3 160	553.4	53.0	48	135	13.6	2.3
Caledonia	16 462	133	34	431	179.4	10.2	199	1 644	232.8	24.3	32	81	6.2	1.0

1. Establishments with payroll.

Table B. States and Counties — Professional Services, Manufacturing, and Accommodation and Foodservices

STATE County	Professional, scientific, and technical services,[1] 1997				Manufacturing, 1997				Accommodation and foodservices, 1997			
	Number of establishments	Number of employees	Receipts (mil dol)	Annual payroll (mil dol)	Number of establishments	Number of employees	Receipts (mil dol)	Annual payroll (mil dol)	Number of establishments	Number of employees	Sales (mil dol)	Annual payroll (mil dol)
	147	148	149	150	151	152	153	154	155	156	157	158
TEXAS—Cont'd												
Tom Green	154	767	60.2	17.2	100	4 452	827.6	105.1	192	3 763	110.8	32.7
Travis	3 128	27 621	3 169.1	1 299.3	774	52 353	14 692.9	1 986.2	1 643	36 951	1 322.6	375.5
Trinity	9	49	3.4	0.9	NA	NA	NA	NA	15	213	7.5	2.5
Tyler	17	41	3.8	0.9	13	565	42.1	8.9	17	D	D	D
Upshur	20	118	9.4	3.1	31	603	81.1	13.2	28	371	11.4	2.9
Upton	2	D	D	D	NA	NA	NA	NA	8	D	D	D
Uvalde	31	70	6.1	1.7	17	710	50.7	9.4	54	636	20.6	5.7
Val Verde	39	122	8.3	2.3	24	522	125.4	10.2	88	1 046	33.3	8.5
Van Zandt	37	120	10.5	3.0	38	622	68.2	16.2	54	586	19.4	5.3
Victoria	141	712	59.5	21.1	71	3 064	1 245.3	119.5	155	2 711	79.6	21.7
Walker	54	208	33.4	4.9	38	677	90.8	14.7	77	1 545	45.4	12.9
Waller	22	45	3.1	0.9	43	1 283	245.6	43.3	40	722	18.0	4.5
Ward	16	69	3.5	1.2	NA	NA	NA	NA	23	198	5.8	1.7
Washington	41	176	12.5	5.0	41	2 982	529.2	81.9	60	767	23.4	6.1
Webb	210	1 029	69.6	23.1	87	1 402	258.6	28.1	253	4 350	144.7	37.4
Wharton	47	169	12.4	4.0	46	2 152	372.3	51.9	59	780	24.8	6.0
Wheeler	10	18	1.5	0.4	NA	NA	NA	NA	17	D	D	D
Wichita	212	1 071	87.6	32.8	153	7 927	1 435.9	254.9	277	5 225	159.6	47.1
Wilbarger	15	46	3.0	0.8	9	681	236.7	19.8	37	444	10.8	3.4
Willacy	10	25	1.3	0.4	NA	NA	NA	NA	20	194	5.7	1.4
Williamson	355	1 874	233.4	73.6	240	11 727	9 637.4	418.8	287	4 499	155.0	41.9
Wilson	20	43	2.1	0.4	NA	NA	NA	NA	26	D	D	D
Winkler	8	19	4.1	0.4	NA	NA	NA	NA	13	100	2.4	0.7
Wise	36	130	8.8	2.7	54	1 340	180.3	37.8	53	861	23.4	6.7
Wood	40	113	7.1	2.0	45	649	143.4	13.5	59	599	16.8	4.3
Yoakum	8	18	1.0	0.3	NA	NA	NA	NA	19	D	D	D
Young	30	87	6.2	2.3	28	1 043	248.4	28.3	38	353	10.0	2.7
Zapata	5	9	0.5	0.1	NA	NA	NA	NA	21	188	7.2	1.6
Zavala	7	19	1.4	0.2	NA	NA	NA	NA	12	66	2.7	0.5
UTAH	4 282	36 468	3 306.1	1 303.1	2 860	119 140	24 014.4	3 726.1	3 780	74 390	2 309.0	648.8
Beaver	4	5	0.1	0.0	NA	NA	NA	NA	34	462	10.3	3.2
Box Elder	33	128	7.4	2.1	51	5 725	1 271.6	270.7	61	1 063	26.0	8.5
Cache	152	905	51.1	20.3	149	8 355	1 785.6	195.0	112	1 991	50.5	13.2
Carbon	27	217	6.8	2.1	NA	NA	NA	NA	54	641	16.9	4.3
Daggett	2	D	D	D	NA	NA	NA	NA	5	72	4.0	1.6
Davis	321	2 158	127.8	56.1	227	7 170	1 592.1	202.8	267	5 752	151.6	42.9
Duchesne	14	97	3.1	1.1	NA	NA	NA	NA	30	274	8.5	1.9
Emery	5	37	1.9	0.9	NA	NA	NA	NA	19	108	4.7	1.3
Garfield	3	5	0.1	0.0	NA	NA	NA	NA	46	425	22.4	7.6
Grand	22	72	4.2	1.3	NA	NA	NA	NA	82	1 141	38.3	9.9
Iron	40	332	10.5	4.2	50	1 520	206.4	37.9	82	1 349	42.0	12.6
Juab	10	D	D	D	NA	NA	NA	NA	22	292	6.8	2.0
Kane	6	18	1.0	0.2	NA	NA	NA	NA	34	328	14.0	3.7
Millard	5	D	D	D	NA	NA	NA	NA	24	328	6.0	1.8
Morgan	7	13	0.7	0.3	NA	NA	NA	NA	9	89	1.9	0.5
Piute	NA	NA	NA	NA	NA	NA	NA	NA	3	38	0.5	0.2
Rich	NA	NA	NA	NA	NA	NA	NA	NA	14	42	2.2	0.6
Salt Lake	2 367	21 993	2 312.1	887.6	1 441	53 424	10 012.2	1 706.4	1 570	35 480	1 200.5	333.7
San Juan	9	67	2.7	2.3	NA	NA	NA	NA	38	382	20.0	3.9
Sanpete	11	24	1.9	0.4	18	908	116.7	16.9	40	439	7.1	1.8
Sevier	25	91	4.9	2.5	NA	NA	NA	NA	43	628	15.7	4.4
Summit	131	479	55.9	22.7	40	861	86.2	21.4	131	3 481	105.1	33.8
Tooele	22	300	25.6	12.8	27	1 737	342.8	56.8	43	475	16.0	3.8
Uintah	43	171	11.7	3.9	NA	NA	NA	NA	52	657	18.1	4.8
Utah	582	6 094	463.3	195.3	390	15 949	2 667.3	461.0	392	8 270	228.0	64.3
Wasatch	31	95	6.4	2.4	NA	NA	NA	NA	36	682	19.7	6.7
Washington	131	605	38.8	15.4	92	1 949	243.4	48.4	195	3 580	113.2	31.6
Wayne	1	D	D	D	NA	NA	NA	NA	22	113	4.0	0.8
Weber	278	2 307	150.3	61.6	210	18 446	5 242.4	635.0	320	5 808	155.1	43.4
VERMONT	1 622	7 792	719.1	279.0	1 226	42 533	7 803.0	1 459.6	1 932	27 088	910.2	277.2
Addison	77	244	17.9	7.4	61	1 871	321.9	59.4	88	948	32.4	11.0
Bennington	86	237	17.2	6.4	88	3 090	504.8	94.1	163	2 044	76.6	21.3
Caledonia	58	229	14.4	7.6	55	1 950	198.0	54.0	72	767	24.4	6.9

1. Firms subject to federal tax.

Table B. States and Counties — Health Care and Social Assistance, Other Services, and Federal Funds

STATE County	Health care and social assistance,[1] 1997				Other services,[1] 1997				Federal funds and grants, 2002–2003 Expenditures (mil dol)			
										Direct payments for individuals[2]		
	Number of establishments	Number of employees	Receipts (mil dol)	Annual payroll (mil dol)	Number of establishments	Number of employees	Receipts (mil dol)	Annual payroll (mil dol)	Total	Social Security and government retirement	Medicare	Food stamps and Supplemental Security Income
	159	160	161	162	163	164	165	166	167	168	169	170
TEXAS—Cont'd												
Tom Green	186	3 404	208.9	91.7	180	961	58.3	16.1	670.7	249.6	88.1	18.0
Travis	1 705	29 036	1 985.2	805.8	1 336	9 356	590.9	192.2	7 399.4	1 454.7	365.9	95.6
Trinity	5	125	5.1	1.7	18	48	3.1	0.6	101.6	46.2	25.2	3.4
Tyler	22	389	15.5	6.9	10	24	1.8	0.4	110.1	54.4	29.8	3.6
Upshur	22	430	14.6	6.8	24	86	7.5	1.4	184.3	95.3	41.2	6.3
Upton	3	72	2.4	1.5	NA	NA	NA	NA	21.7	7.1	4.4	0.7
Uvalde	43	452	20.4	8.7	39	204	10.4	3.4	139.6	45.9	21.9	9.4
Val Verde	55	2 055	36.6	17.7	49	220	11.4	3.2	385.8	82.8	25.1	16.6
Van Zandt	53	1 004	31.0	15.0	41	238	16.1	4.7	271.6	161.3	61.5	5.8
Victoria	230	3 383	230.0	93.5	151	973	61.8	17.8	381.0	163.8	79.0	15.9
Walker	72	763	31.6	14.0	47	279	13.3	4.2	212.7	89.8	38.0	7.1
Waller	24	442	12.2	6.9	35	125	9.9	2.6	149.4	45.3	22.2	4.9
Ward	11	110	4.3	2.0	16	101	6.1	1.9	51.9	23.3	11.8	2.7
Washington	42	898	30.3	14.8	48	179	11.7	2.7	165.7	71.7	28.8	4.4
Webb	227	4 330	207.1	94.8	190	951	48.0	13.3	896.2	192.2	116.6	70.2
Wharton	55	1 645	84.7	30.6	71	273	17.6	4.4	249.9	84.9	48.8	8.8
Wheeler	13	174	6.1	3.4	7	23	1.3	0.2	39.1	15.2	12.0	0.6
Wichita	273	D	D	D	223	1 518	85.1	28.5	1 185.3	365.1	124.4	14.5
Wilbarger	29	402	19.8	7.8	18	60	4.0	1.1	91.9	33.3	22.8	2.6
Willacy	17	203	8.8	4.1	13	40	1.8	0.5	136.7	26.2	18.7	9.1
Williamson	293	3 179	180.9	72.2	269	1 508	95.9	29.7	1 309.3	384.4	85.7	13.6
Wilson	25	327	10.7	4.8	24	91	6.1	1.8	137.2	72.1	20.2	3.9
Winkler	10	108	4.1	1.7	10	37	2.5	0.5	32.7	14.4	10.7	1.6
Wise	51	615	24.2	10.8	51	243	16.5	4.3	168.9	89.3	30.5	3.6
Wood	54	660	25.0	11.2	38	141	7.5	2.1	222.6	122.4	50.0	5.3
Yoakum	5	24	1.2	0.4	12	44	3.5	0.9	57.7	13.2	7.0	1.1
Young	30	364	16.8	6.4	40	107	7.4	1.8	111.9	49.7	27.0	2.8
Zapata	6	75	2.1	1.0	6	15	1.1	0.2	57.0	15.9	14.5	4.2
Zavala	4	689	9.1	6.2	5	10	0.4	0.1	67.0	14.8	11.5	6.1
UTAH	3 851	46 989	2 988.8	1 226.7	2 728	17 612	1 090.5	312.6	13 499.8	3 786.6	1 040.4	207.5
Beaver	6	20	2.2	0.8	7	13	0.8	0.2	49.5	13.6	5.3	0.5
Box Elder	57	678	39.6	15.4	39	147	7.9	1.5	598.7	93.5	21.5	3.1
Cache	166	1 293	82.5	29.1	125	628	35.4	9.5	363.0	116.2	33.6	5.2
Carbon	53	829	55.8	18.8	34	220	19.3	4.9	103.2	52.4	20.3	4.0
Daggett	NA	NA	NA	NA	NA	NA	NA	NA	8.5	2.6	0.6	0.0
Davis	329	4 717	292.4	127.9	243	1 501	90.6	27.8	2 603.0	470.0	79.0	14.0
Duchesne	21	154	6.6	2.5	19	76	4.9	1.1	69.2	29.3	9.4	3.1
Emery	7	67	3.1	1.3	13	92	11.0	2.9	50.2	21.3	6.2	1.6
Garfield	1	D	D	D	2	D	D	D	32.5	11.8	3.5	0.5
Grand	10	36	2.2	0.7	13	21	1.9	0.3	50.7	17.9	4.1	1.4
Iron	47	343	15.9	5.7	42	136	9.1	2.0	136.4	60.9	14.5	3.7
Juab	8	145	4.6	1.5	7	27	2.6	0.6	34.7	15.3	5.9	1.1
Kane	7	35	1.5	0.7	12	52	2.8	0.7	47.5	17.5	5.2	0.7
Millard	16	70	3.4	1.2	9	28	3.0	0.6	52.3	22.7	8.5	1.5
Morgan	1	D	D	D	1	D	D	D	46.5	16.8	2.8	0.1
Piute	NA	NA	NA	NA	NA	NA	NA	NA	10.9	4.4	1.6	0.1
Rich	1	D	D	D	3	D	D	D	13.4	4.9	0.9	0.1
Salt Lake	1 766	23 094	1 579.6	652.7	1 285	9 616	622.4	185.2	4 686.5	1 334.7	434.9	86.4
San Juan	12	198	8.3	3.1	9	24	1.8	0.4	113.4	16.3	5.7	6.1
Sanpete	23	138	6.5	2.6	23	67	5.9	1.0	92.4	40.2	13.0	2.4
Sevier	33	299	12.2	5.1	28	141	13.1	2.1	100.2	41.9	16.0	2.3
Summit	41	285	14.9	5.4	34	157	8.7	2.2	89.2	33.4	5.7	0.5
Tooele	28	138	6.6	2.4	18	84	4.8	1.5	336.8	93.5	16.7	3.2
Uintah	47	412	26.6	9.3	42	134	16.0	2.6	129.0	43.8	13.1	3.2
Utah	596	7 371	421.0	178.8	340	2 256	103.9	29.1	1 029.2	427.2	138.1	27.1
Wasatch	17	183	6.6	2.8	15	43	3.7	0.9	41.6	22.4	5.5	0.7
Washington	193	1 722	114.0	41.2	98	433	32.9	8.4	406.5	245.8	55.7	7.4
Wayne	3	D	D	D	3	12	0.7	0.1	14.9	5.6	1.8	0.1
Weber	362	4 431	277.0	113.2	264	1 687	86.2	27.0	1 262.7	510.5	111.2	27.2
VERMONT	1 262	11 481	631.6	273.9	1 171	4 490	304.7	76.4	4 443.0	1 304.5	459.9	90.8
Addison	65	380	19.6	6.7	61	160	11.5	2.2	168.0	62.7	22.5	4.3
Bennington	107	1 132	56.3	26.5	78	282	18.2	4.9	225.8	92.7	34.7	6.3
Caledonia	48	459	21.9	9.8	53	160	11.6	2.7	167.0	68.4	24.5	5.1

1. Firms subject to federal tax.   2. State totals may include programs not allocated by county.

Table B. States and Counties — Federal Funds and Local Government Finances

	Federal funds and grants, 2002–2003 (cont'd)							Local government finances, 2002				
	Expenditures (mil dol) (cont'd)							General revenue				
	Procurement contract awards		Grants[1]								Taxes	
											Per capita[2] (dollars)	
STATE County	Salaries and wages	Defense	Other	Medicaid and other health-related	Nutrition and family welfare	Education	Other	Total (mil dol)	Intergovern-mental (mil dol)	Total (mil dol)	Total	Property
	171	172	173	174	175	176	177	178	179	180	181	182
TEXAS—Cont'd												
Tom Green	155.4	31.3	4.4	61.4	9.3	4.4	29.5	219.6	89.3	93.6	909	669
Travis	548.3	356.4	202.2	715.0	778.2	1 078.2	1 710.0	2 858.8	410.2	1 722.8	2 025	1 598
Trinity	2.3	0.0	0.6	18.0	1.2	0.7	3.8	25.6	14.1	9.4	666	585
Tyler	2.3	0.1	0.6	16.0	1.7	0.9	0.4	50.1	20.6	16.6	801	739
Upshur	3.9	0.0	1.1	27.6	2.1	1.5	4.1	67.0	32.8	27.4	750	670
Upton	0.4	0.0	0.1	1.8	0.3	0.2	4.8	28.2	2.3	22.1	6 719	6 584
Uvalde	5.7	0.1	0.6	28.8	8.9	2.7	3.5	109.0	48.7	18.5	696	478
Val Verde	117.0	73.0	5.0	43.8	10.6	3.3	7.0	112.4	68.6	26.7	581	406
Van Zandt	5.9	0.1	1.7	24.7	2.2	1.8	4.7	90.4	43.5	32.4	647	553
Victoria	16.8	0.7	3.3	51.5	11.8	6.0	20.1	321.8	84.7	107.3	1 263	1 001
Walker	11.4	0.1	2.1	31.3	3.8	4.4	14.5	198.0	38.5	42.0	673	513
Waller	4.3	9.2	0.9	14.7	2.7	4.9	22.7	78.4	33.5	37.8	1 110	1 001
Ward	1.4	0.2	0.3	9.7	0.6	0.6	1.0	38.5	7.2	20.5	1 948	1 819
Washington	4.6	0.6	1.0	38.7	1.6	0.9	5.4	117.2	40.4	38.5	1 258	1 047
Webb	74.0	10.6	29.5	219.0	98.5	23.4	40.2	693.7	352.4	196.7	948	714
Wharton	6.6	0.0	3.8	44.7	4.2	1.6	9.9	132.8	51.2	47.7	1 154	982
Wheeler	1.4	0.0	0.4	4.2	0.4	0.2	0.1	26.4	5.8	13.7	2 737	2 601
Wichita	342.4	144.1	51.4	68.6	15.1	8.3	40.4	293.3	100.3	135.4	1 042	771
Wilbarger	3.1	0.0	0.5	11.8	1.3	0.9	6.5	60.5	21.1	21.3	1 517	1 322
Willacy	1.6	0.0	0.4	35.8	3.9	2.0	23.8	55.8	35.2	15.2	762	631
Williamson	26.6	449.3	273.7	45.8	8.4	7.0	2.4	822.8	174.1	517.0	1 783	1 555
Wilson	3.9	0.0	0.8	21.6	1.1	1.1	4.1	69.7	35.0	22.5	653	593
Winkler	0.7	0.0	0.2	4.2	0.3	0.4	0.2	31.0	7.5	17.7	2 569	2 349
Wise	6.7	1.3	5.8	11.8	1.1	1.1	15.6	100.7	38.1	51.0	964	865
Wood	6.5	0.0	1.5	25.3	1.9	3.2	2.4	65.6	24.2	33.5	880	766
Yoakum	0.7	0.0	0.1	2.9	1.0	0.4	5.5	47.1	2.9	33.5	4 586	4 450
Young	3.8	0.0	0.7	13.4	1.1	0.7	10.3	49.1	17.2	15.0	849	673
Zapata	2.1	0.0	0.2	15.8	1.0	1.0	1.9	40.7	9.7	29.1	2 278	2 278
Zavala	0.7	0.0	0.2	25.1	2.2	1.2	2.7	29.8	22.3	4.6	402	362
UTAH	2 046.8	1 871.1	793.8	1 130.0	392.9	293.2	1 028.8	X	X	X	X	X
Beaver	1.9	0.0	0.9	7.8	0.6	0.1	17.7	24.0	9.6	5.9	975	750
Box Elder	13.3	27.1	400.8	12.8	3.8	1.0	13.8	104.2	50.3	31.5	716	535
Cache	21.3	40.5	34.0	32.3	11.5	9.2	29.1	189.8	95.0	49.4	527	324
Carbon	9.3	0.0	-15.6	13.1	7.1	3.2	5.5	60.1	25.8	20.1	1 011	738
Daggett	3.2	0.0	0.6	0.6	0.1	0.1	0.6	7.0	2.9	1.5	1 726	1 410
Davis	759.4	1 104.5	85.1	41.4	18.9	5.9	21.3	587.8	269.0	181.9	730	501
Duchesne	4.1	0.4	1.5	7.9	2.4	0.9	7.7	67.9	29.2	11.9	804	594
Emery	2.6	0.0	1.0	4.9	1.6	0.2	9.4	60.5	16.2	19.2	1 808	1 642
Garfield	6.2	0.0	3.4	3.0	0.6	0.1	3.1	22.7	10.1	4.6	1 009	655
Grand	11.0	0.0	4.7	3.9	1.6	0.2	5.3	28.6	12.1	11.4	1 303	747
Iron	19.1	1.1	6.4	6.9	6.2	1.9	6.9	90.6	39.3	28.0	796	551
Juab	1.4	2.5	0.4	3.1	0.7	0.2	3.0	25.9	15.2	6.5	757	567
Kane	5.2	0.3	6.8	0.6	0.6	0.2	10.4	28.9	12.4	7.4	1 213	900
Millard	5.3	1.9	0.9	4.9	1.8	0.4	2.0	48.1	17.6	21.7	1 743	1 593
Morgan	0.7	0.0	0.6	1.3	0.4	0.1	23.5	17.2	8.1	5.4	737	574
Piute	0.4	0.0	0.1	3.0	0.3	0.1	0.4	5.3	3.9	0.8	611	447
Rich	0.6	0.0	0.1	1.0	0.2	0.1	5.2	8.3	4.7	2.8	1 411	1 195
Salt Lake	649.5	485.2	155.2	607.1	190.5	120.8	537.0	2 477.5	903.9	970.8	1 056	698
San Juan	7.5	0.0	1.8	43.1	4.7	14.4	10.0	52.9	34.6	10.1	731	560
Sanpete	4.9	0.0	1.4	13.4	2.9	2.1	6.7	62.4	32.2	11.8	506	324
Sevier	11.1	0.0	2.9	9.8	2.9	0.5	11.6	53.2	28.7	14.1	740	505
Summit	8.4	12.2	3.4	1.6	0.8	0.3	22.0	142.0	22.2	86.7	2 722	2 001
Tooele	55.8	112.0	22.7	10.6	4.3	0.9	16.3	116.8	53.0	27.9	607	450
Uintah	19.6	0.0	4.6	9.9	5.9	3.2	24.2	89.1	44.7	26.0	993	595
Utah	69.1	40.3	34.3	128.0	34.8	12.9	58.5	872.5	411.1	277.5	716	470
Wasatch	3.2	0.5	1.6	4.3	1.0	0.2	1.9	65.3	21.7	17.9	1 055	744
Washington	51.0	1.3	4.7	15.6	5.7	3.7	8.8	226.9	88.9	83.6	840	536
Wayne	3.8	0.0	0.3	1.6	0.3	0.1	0.8	7.6	5.1	1.7	678	450
Weber	297.9	41.2	29.3	136.4	32.2	6.3	46.6	474.3	208.1	162.4	795	548
VERMONT	360.0	454.9	111.1	615.3	161.6	115.8	438.6	X	X	X	X	X
Addison	8.4	18.1	7.6	23.8	5.1	1.1	3.6	88.6	53.0	28.2	772	763
Bennington	8.2	0.2	2.0	26.6	6.9	2.2	41.4	85.9	50.4	26.3	709	682
Caledonia	7.3	5.0	2.4	31.1	6.0	2.7	9.8	68.2	44.1	18.2	607	578

1. State totals may include programs not allocated by county.   2. Based on the resident population estimated as of July 1 of the year shown.

STATE County	Local government finances, 2002 (cont'd) Direct general expenditure							Debt outstanding		Government employment, 2002			Presidential election, 2004 Percent of vote cast —		
	Total (mil dol)	Per capita¹ (dollars)	Percent of total for — Educa-tion	Health and hospitals	Police protec-tion	Public welfare	High-ways	Total (mil dol)	Per capita¹ (dollars)	Federal civilian	Federal military	State and local	Demo-cratic	Republi-can	All other
	183	184	185	186	187	188	189	190	191	192	193	194	195	196	197
TEXAS—Cont'd															
Tom Green	209.6	2 035	53.2	3.5	6.4	0.0	4.2	211.4	2 053	1 322	3 432	7 555	24.1	75.5	0.4
Travis	2 844.5	3 343	43.2	4.8	5.9	0.9	2.0	8 574.2	10 078	9 292	1 839	105 010	56.3	42.2	1.5
Trinity	23.7	1 681	78.4	0.0	4.1	0.4	4.9	4.2	297	43	26	654	35.5	64.2	0.3
Tyler	56.3	2 712	60.9	15.3	3.0	0.0	2.8	23.2	1 117	52	38	1 748	34.4	65.2	0.4
Upshur	63.2	1 730	75.6	0.1	4.6	0.1	3.7	17.7	485	66	68	1 613	29.1	70.6	0.3
Upton	26.6	8 106	53.6	21.3	2.7	0.0	5.4	0.8	251	0	0	417	15.5	84.5	0.0
Uvalde	114.4	4 316	65.1	21.9	1.9	0.2	1.2	55.5	2 094	151	49	2 527	38.9	60.8	0.3
Val Verde	119.7	2 607	61.4	0.6	4.8	1.3	2.8	88.2	1 922	1 868	1 526	2 644	40.5	59.1	0.4
Van Zandt	83.6	1 667	71.1	0.1	5.4	0.4	5.7	46.3	924	102	93	2 178	24.3	75.4	0.3
Victoria	331.2	3 900	38.7	32.9	5.2	0.1	3.3	270.3	3 182	225	158	6 482	28.9	70.6	0.5
Walker	192.5	3 086	26.8	2.0	3.9	0.2	6.5	845.3	13 549	181	121	12 473	33.6	65.8	0.6
Waller	97.1	2 851	74.7	0.1	3.7	0.4	4.0	83.4	2 450	60	76	3 546	44.3	55.4	0.3
Ward	35.0	3 327	45.0	22.9	3.7	0.2	4.2	0.7	69	21	19	1 061	23.9	75.9	0.2
Washington	126.6	4 133	75.9	1.1	3.2	0.1	3.6	74.4	2 428	67	57	2 920	26.0	73.6	0.4
Webb	733.4	3 533	60.3	1.7	5.3	1.2	5.6	827.9	3 988	2 082	387	14 979	57.0	42.7	0.3
Wharton	128.7	3 115	64.7	11.7	4.0	0.7	6.1	44.1	1 068	104	78	2 958	33.5	66.2	0.2
Wheeler	24.6	4 907	52.8	29.7	2.1	0.0	3.3	7.9	1 566	28	0	527	17.2	82.3	0.5
Wichita	291.4	2 242	50.9	3.7	6.1	0.9	3.6	281.3	2 164	2 557	10 578	9 614	28.1	71.3	0.6
Wilbarger	60.9	4 338	55.1	22.8	2.5	0.1	3.2	15.4	1 097	60	26	2 639	25.7	73.9	0.4
Willacy	52.0	2 599	70.2	1.2	3.7	0.1	4.7	34.5	1 724	33	41	1 211	61.4	37.8	0.7
Williamson	964.2	3 326	59.4	4.8	3.0	0.1	5.1	1 629.3	5 620	416	538	14 020	33.7	65.2	1.1
Wilson	71.5	2 069	70.3	9.2	3.2	0.0	3.8	57.4	1 661	63	64	1 984	29.7	69.9	0.4
Winkler	28.6	4 149	57.6	14.2	2.5	0.5	1.4	5.6	816	12	13	606	19.6	80.1	0.3
Wise	97.8	1 849	62.1	1.3	6.2	0.0	7.1	76.7	1 449	117	98	2 716	23.9	75.8	0.3
Wood	64.8	1 703	66.5	0.3	4.2	0.1	5.9	28.8	756	88	70	1 778	23.8	75.8	0.3
Yoakum	45.7	6 262	56.8	19.1	3.1	0.3	3.6	4.0	543	19	14	769	14.4	85.3	0.3
Young	44.2	2 494	52.5	16.9	5.7	0.2	4.7	13.9	782	70	33	1 381	20.4	79.3	0.3
Zapata	40.4	3 160	67.6	0.9	4.0	0.9	3.7	11.7	916	45	24	1 079	57.4	42.4	0.2
Zavala	30.4	2 631	81.4	0.8	3.4	0.0	0.0	16.0	1 384	11	21	850	74.8	24.9	0.3
UTAH	X	X	X	X	X	X	X	X	X	34 618	14 861	162 996	26.4	71.1	2.5
Beaver	24.7	4 044	40.1	9.1	5.0	0.0	11.2	34.2	5 602	41	24	630	19.5	79.3	1.1
Box Elder	116.9	2 656	48.4	1.1	5.0	0.0	5.1	72.0	1 634	203	175	2 195	12.2	85.7	2.1
Cache	181.0	1 932	54.4	4.6	4.7	0.0	4.6	159.8	1 705	360	382	9 103	16.0	81.8	2.2
Carbon	73.4	3 695	51.0	4.7	5.2	1.2	9.7	83.5	4 202	172	79	2 084	40.3	58.0	1.7
Daggett	6.0	6 728	40.5	0.8	7.1	0.0	6.2	7.0	7 950	68	0	161	21.5	76.4	2.0
Davis	576.6	2 314	57.4	2.1	5.6	0.4	3.7	302.7	1 215	12 548	6 030	10 474	19.1	78.9	2.0
Duchesne	64.6	4 354	39.9	33.6	3.1	0.1	5.6	30.9	2 082	87	59	1 479	13.2	85.5	1.3
Emery	58.7	5 526	33.8	0.9	4.3	0.0	5.7	291.4	27 419	66	42	780	17.8	80.8	1.5
Garfield	23.4	5 099	55.2	1.6	3.0	0.0	9.6	21.8	4 748	180	18	397	12.1	85.7	2.2
Grand	27.6	3 162	37.8	4.3	7.5	0.5	11.7	23.2	2 654	243	34	580	44.3	51.6	4.1
Iron	97.7	2 776	44.7	0.4	5.0	0.0	6.8	111.0	3 152	349	139	3 480	14.7	83.0	2.3
Juab	23.9	2 789	55.8	0.0	6.1	0.0	7.8	25.8	3 012	30	34	504	17.7	78.4	3.9
Kane	27.0	4 415	41.7	24.8	5.2	0.0	5.4	16.8	2 745	112	24	609	18.5	79.6	1.9
Millard	45.2	3 633	53.9	3.5	4.5	0.0	8.3	11.4	917	108	49	921	12.7	84.0	3.3
Morgan	17.2	2 326	65.1	0.0	5.1	0.0	4.0	5.2	709	12	29	339	12.4	85.9	1.8
Piute	5.6	4 079	66.0	0.4	4.8	0.1	10.9	2.0	1 470	0	0	129	16.0	83.5	0.5
Rich	7.2	3 659	61.9	1.3	3.2	0.9	7.5	3.0	1 529	14	0	173	10.5	88.9	0.6
Salt Lake	2 404.5	2 616	43.0	2.6	6.0	0.0	4.7	5 091.4	5 538	8 600	4 113	76 989	37.4	59.7	2.9
San Juan	48.1	3 487	63.5	2.1	2.8	0.0	10.2	25.5	1 851	176	54	1 624	38.2	60.4	1.4
Sanpete	59.5	2 543	55.5	15.7	5.0	0.0	4.2	42.6	1 820	78	92	2 279	13.9	82.4	3.7
Sevier	60.5	3 166	46.3	7.7	5.3	0.0	3.5	51.6	2 700	208	75	1 492	12.1	86.3	1.6
Summit	129.8	4 074	37.9	2.3	5.0	0.0	7.6	115.1	3 612	87	203	1 943	45.4	52.0	2.6
Tooele	147.0	3 193	53.5	2.1	7.2	0.0	6.3	153.6	3 336	1 705	237	1 742	24.9	73.0	2.1
Uintah	82.5	3 153	46.4	5.0	3.8	4.0	8.4	121.1	4 631	418	103	2 149	12.8	85.5	1.7
Utah	835.3	2 154	56.3	2.3	6.0	0.2	4.0	1 025.7	2 645	1 073	1 553	21 615	10.8	86.3	2.9
Wasatch	61.7	3 628	36.4	2.5	4.8	0.0	7.3	84.7	4 985	73	67	966	24.8	73.1	2.1
Washington	210.3	2 115	52.4	0.4	5.0	0.0	6.9	331.7	3 335	479	394	4 557	16.4	81.6	2.0
Wayne	7.7	3 012	55.9	0.4	5.4	0.0	16.6	4.0	1 570	105	10	182	20.5	78.1	1.4
Weber	468.4	2 294	49.0	1.1	6.4	2.8	3.5	272.0	1 332	7 017	826	13 420	27.2	70.6	2.3
VERMONT	X	X	X	X	X	X	X	X	X	5 764	4 059	43 633	59.1	38.9	2.0
Addison	85.0	2 327	74.6	0.3	1.5	0.1	9.7	33.9	927	141	235	1 762	59.9	38.5	1.6
Bennington	73.1	1 968	63.5	0.1	4.2	0.0	9.4	15.9	428	127	239	2 107	58.2	40.0	1.8
Caledonia	69.9	2 325	70.6	0.3	2.0	0.0	11.0	30.2	1 004	107	194	1 841	50.6	46.8	2.6

1. Based on the resident population estimated as of July 1 of the year shown.

Table B. States and Counties — Land Area and Population

STATE/ County code	CBSA code[1]	County Type[2]	STATE County	Land area[3] (sq km) 2000	Total persons	Rank	Per square kilometer	White	Black	Am. Indian, Alaska Native	Asian and Pacific Islander	Percent Hispanic or Latino[4]	Under 5 years	5 to 17 years	18 to 24 years	25 to 34 years	35 to 44 years	45 to 54 years
				1	2	3	4	5	6	7	8	9	10	11	12	13	14	15
			VERMONT—Cont'd															
50 007	15540	3	Chittenden	1 396	148 990	381	106.7	95.2	1.4	0.7	2.8	1.1	5.3	16.8	12.5	13.8	16.8	15.2
50 009	13620	9	Essex	1 723	6 569	2 727	3.8	98.2	0.3	1.9	0.4	0.6	5.3	18.0	8.6	10.2	15.6	15.5
50 011	15540	3	Franklin	1 650	47 023	979	28.5	97.2	0.5	2.7	0.5	0.6	5.9	19.9	8.7	12.3	17.5	14.8
50 013	15540	3	Grand Isle	214	7 490	2 638	35.0	98.4	0.2	1.4	0.2	0.4	4.6	17.1	8.4	10.4	17.0	17.2
50 015	...	8	Lamoille	1 194	24 284	1 609	20.3	97.9	0.6	1.2	0.7	0.8	5.0	17.3	10.3	13.0	15.8	15.4
50 017	30100	9	Orange	1 783	29 081	1 432	16.3	98.4	0.4	0.7	0.6	0.7	4.6	18.0	10.0	10.2	16.0	16.7
50 019	...	7	Orleans	1 807	27 103	1 502	15.0	97.8	0.4	1.5	0.4	0.8	5.1	17.5	9.0	10.7	14.6	15.7
50 021	40860	5	Rutland	2 415	63 504	780	26.3	98.2	0.5	0.6	0.6	0.7	4.8	16.5	9.7	10.2	15.7	16.6
50 023	12740	4	Washington	1 785	58 836	835	33.0	97.2	0.8	1.1	1.0	1.2	5.0	16.5	10.1	11.3	16.1	17.4
50 025	...	6	Windham	2 043	44 379	1 036	21.7	97.0	0.9	0.8	1.4	1.1	4.8	16.7	8.9	10.2	15.9	17.9
50 027	30100	7	Windsor	2 515	57 904	847	23.0	97.8	0.6	0.6	1.0	0.9	4.5	16.6	7.6	10.2	15.5	17.5
51 000	...	X	VIRGINIA	102 548	7 386 330	X	72.0	70.4	20.3	0.7	4.8	5.3	6.7	17.7	10.0	13.8	16.0	14.5
51 001	...	7	Accomack	1 179	39 025	1 159	33.1	62.2	30.6	0.5	0.3	6.9	6.1	17.4	9.6	11.2	14.2	13.9
51 003	16820	3	Albemarle	1 872	87 670	611	46.8	83.5	9.9	0.5	4.3	3.0	5.8	17.3	12.4	12.8	15.0	14.8
51 005	...	6	Alleghany	1 168	16 816	1 972	14.4	93.4	5.7	0.4	0.3	0.7	5.7	16.5	7.8	10.0	14.7	15.1
51 007	40060	1	Amelia	924	11 742	2 310	12.7	73.4	25.4	0.6	0.2	0.8	6.0	17.6	8.6	11.8	15.9	14.7
51 009	31340	3	Amherst	1 231	31 891	1 360	25.9	77.5	20.5	1.2	0.4	1.0	5.2	17.5	11.0	11.4	15.0	14.6
51 011	31340	3	Appomattox	864	13 710	2 186	15.9	76.6	22.8	0.1	0.2	0.5	5.7	17.7	8.6	11.5	15.2	13.8
51 013	47900	1	Arlington	67	187 873	304	2 804.1	64.2	9.2	0.6	9.4	18.1	6.7	10.6	6.0	25.2	18.2	14.3
51 015	44420	4	Augusta	2 513	67 427	747	26.8	94.8	3.7	0.4	0.4	1.2	5.1	17.3	9.0	11.7	16.3	15.6
51 017	...	9	Bath	1 378	5 013	2 842	3.6	91.5	7.4	0.4	0.6	0.4	3.9	15.4	7.7	11.6	15.9	15.0
51 019	31340	3	Bedford	1 954	62 661	788	32.1	92.5	6.2	0.5	0.6	0.7	4.9	17.9	7.8	11.3	16.3	16.3
51 021	...	8	Bland	929	6 965	2 690	7.5	95.1	4.4	0.2	0.1	0.5	4.0	14.3	8.5	13.9	15.7	16.2
51 023	40220	2	Botetourt	1 405	31 448	1 370	22.4	94.6	4.0	0.5	0.7	0.7	4.8	17.0	8.4	10.1	16.6	17.3
51 025	...	6	Brunswick	1 466	18 199	1 899	12.4	41.4	57.0	0.1	0.3	1.3	5.1	14.5	11.3	14.3	15.7	14.8
51 027	...	9	Buchanan	1 305	25 598	1 548	19.6	96.3	3.0	0.2	0.2	0.5	4.7	15.4	9.7	12.7	17.1	16.9
51 029	...	8	Buckingham	1 504	15 839	2 045	10.5	60.9	38.0	0.5	0.2	1.0	4.2	17.0	9.1	13.7	17.3	14.9
51 031	31340	3	Campbell	1 307	51 322	917	39.3	83.2	15.5	0.5	0.7	0.9	5.8	17.6	8.6	12.7	15.4	14.9
51 033	40060	1	Caroline	1 379	23 190	1 656	16.8	64.9	32.8	1.3	0.5	1.6	6.0	17.8	9.2	12.2	15.9	14.1
51 035	...	6	Carroll	1 234	29 336	1 423	23.8	97.8	0.5	0.3	0.1	1.5	5.0	15.4	8.0	12.3	14.6	15.0
51 036	40060	1	Charles City County	473	7 118	2 674	15.0	40.4	51.4	7.5	0.1	0.6	4.9	15.4	8.9	11.1	16.6	17.0
51 037	...	8	Charlotte	1 230	12 452	2 272	10.1	66.1	31.9	0.1	0.2	1.8	5.9	17.5	8.8	10.8	14.3	14.2
51 041	40060	1	Chesterfield	1 103	276 840	213	251.0	73.6	20.2	0.7	2.9	3.8	6.2	20.6	10.1	11.8	16.7	16.4
51 043	47900	1	Clarke	457	13 364	2 208	29.2	91.1	6.7	0.3	0.6	1.7	4.7	17.5	8.4	10.0	17.1	15.7
51 045	40220	2	Craig	856	5 159	2 832	6.0	98.8	0.5	0.2	0.3	0.3	5.8	17.2	8.0	10.4	17.0	15.5
51 047	...	6	Culpeper	987	38 555	1 172	39.1	79.0	17.0	0.7	1.0	3.6	6.4	18.3	9.9	13.2	16.1	13.3
51 049	40060	1	Cumberland	773	9 189	2 509	11.9	61.7	36.1	0.3	0.5	2.0	5.9	18.0	8.5	11.4	15.1	13.7
51 051	...	9	Dickenson	859	16 119	2 024	18.8	98.8	0.6	0.2	0.1	0.5	4.7	15.8	10.4	11.5	15.1	16.4
51 053	40060	1	Dinwiddie	1 305	24 853	1 579	19.0	65.1	33.2	0.5	0.5	1.2	4.9	18.2	8.7	11.6	17.7	15.2
51 057	...	8	Essex	668	10 260	2 421	15.4	58.2	39.7	0.8	1.0	0.9	5.3	17.2	8.1	11.1	14.5	14.9
51 059	47900	1	Fairfax	1 023	1 000 405	37	977.9	64.0	9.0	0.5	16.4	12.3	7.2	18.4	7.4	14.0	17.5	16.5
51 061	47900	1	Fauquier	1 683	61 137	808	36.3	87.9	8.9	0.7	1.1	2.7	6.0	19.2	9.2	10.9	17.0	15.4
51 063	...	9	Floyd	987	14 350	2 142	14.5	96.2	2.1	0.3	0.1	1.7	5.2	16.1	8.5	12.2	14.4	15.2
51 065	16820	3	Fluvanna	744	23 078	1 662	31.0	80.6	17.9	0.3	0.5	1.5	5.4	17.5	8.3	13.5	16.9	13.3
51 067	40220	2	Franklin	1 792	49 095	951	27.4	89.4	9.0	0.3	0.3	1.3	5.6	16.2	9.4	11.2	15.3	15.0
51 069	49020	3	Frederick	1 074	64 565	773	60.1	93.6	3.3	0.5	0.9	2.7	5.8	19.1	9.2	12.6	17.2	14.2
51 071	13980	3	Giles	925	16 956	1 957	18.3	97.5	1.6	0.2	0.2	0.6	6.0	15.9	7.9	12.3	15.0	14.3
51 073	47260	1	Gloucester	561	36 698	1 222	65.4	87.5	10.1	0.9	1.0	1.6	5.5	19.0	9.1	10.8	16.9	14.9
51 075	40060	1	Goochland	737	18 138	1 907	24.6	74.2	24.0	0.3	0.7	1.1	5.3	15.7	7.4	12.3	18.1	16.0
51 077	...	9	Grayson	1 146	16 557	1 993	14.4	95.6	2.3	0.5	0.0	2.0	4.8	15.3	7.2	11.6	14.6	15.5
51 079	16820	3	Greene	406	16 779	1 978	41.3	91.2	7.1	0.5	0.6	1.6	7.3	19.9	8.1	13.2	17.3	13.9
51 081	...	6	Greensville	765	11 581	2 328	15.1	37.5	61.0	0.1	0.5	1.0	4.4	12.8	8.7	17.4	20.4	15.5
51 083	...	6	Halifax	2 122	36 632	1 225	17.3	60.1	38.3	0.4	0.3	1.4	5.8	16.9	8.0	10.6	14.1	15.4
51 085	40060	1	Hanover	1 224	94 081	570	76.9	88.1	9.7	0.6	1.2	1.1	5.9	19.6	9.3	10.7	17.2	15.3
51 087	40060	1	Henrico	617	271 083	214	439.4	66.5	26.8	0.7	4.7	2.6	6.7	18.0	7.7	14.8	16.4	14.7
51 089	32300	4	Henry	990	57 090	853	57.7	72.4	22.6	0.4	0.4	4.7	5.4	16.3	8.5	12.1	15.6	14.6
51 091	...	9	Highland	1 077	2 504	3 021	2.3	99.1	0.0	0.2	0.2	0.6	3.9	14.6	6.5	7.1	13.9	17.2
51 093	47260	1	Isle of Wight	818	31 925	1 359	39.0	72.9	25.6	0.6	0.5	1.1	5.7	18.3	8.9	10.4	16.8	15.3
51 095	47260	1	James City County	370	53 487	895	144.6	83.0	13.6	0.7	1.8	2.0	5.2	16.6	8.4	10.8	14.9	13.9
51 097	40060	1	King and Queen	819	6 588	2 723	8.0	64.0	33.3	1.5	0.3	1.1	5.5	16.2	8.1	10.0	15.6	15.5
51 099	...	8	King George	466	18 213	1 898	39.1	79.0	18.1	0.9	1.5	1.8	6.7	19.9	10.0	12.6	16.8	13.6
51 101	40060	1	King William	713	14 131	2 158	19.8	76.1	21.2	1.9	0.3	1.2	6.7	18.6	8.2	13.0	16.4	14.5
51 103	...	9	Lancaster	345	12 074	2 288	35.0	70.3	28.5	0.2	0.4	0.7	4.4	13.2	7.4	8.1	12.2	13.4
51 105	...	8	Lee	1 132	23 734	1 623	21.0	98.5	0.6	0.8	0.2	0.5	5.3	16.7	9.2	12.2	14.2	15.0
51 107	47900	1	Loudoun	1 346	221 746	264	164.7	76.6	7.7	0.6	9.8	7.6	8.9	20.5	8.0	15.4	18.8	12.0

1. CBSA = Core Based Statistical Area. See Appendix A for explanation. See Appendix B for list of metropolitan areas with component counties.   2. County type code from the Economic Research Service of USDA Rural-Urban Continuum Codes. See Appendix A for definition.   3. Dry land or land partially or temporarily covered by water.   4. Hispanic or Latino persons may be of any race.

Table B. States and Counties — **Population and Households**

STATE County	Age (percent) (cont'd) 55 to 64 years	65 to 74 years	75 years and over	Percent female	Total persons 1990	2000	Percent change 1990–2000	2000–2003	Components of change, 2000–2003 Births	Deaths	Net migration	Households, 2000 Number	Percent change, 1990–2000	Persons per house-hold	Percent Female family house-holder[1]	One person
	16	17	18	19	20	21	22	23	24	25	26	27	28	29	30	31
VERMONT—Cont'd																
Chittenden	8.8	5.1	4.6	51.1	131 761	146 571	11.2	1.7	5 132	3 070	519	56 452	16.5	2.47	8.7	26.1
Essex	11.9	8.3	6.7	50.0	6 405	6 459	0.8	1.7	218	178	77	2 602	11.0	2.47	8.3	24.1
Franklin	9.4	5.8	5.0	50.4	39 980	45 417	13.6	3.5	1 780	1 212	1 078	16 765	17.0	2.67	9.9	20.6
Grand Isle	11.8	7.0	4.7	49.8	5 318	6 901	29.8	8.5	216	166	527	2 761	36.8	2.50	7.1	22.2
Lamoille	10.4	6.1	5.4	49.8	19 735	23 233	17.7	4.5	820	612	865	9 221	24.7	2.45	8.9	25.0
Orange	10.8	7.1	5.9	50.1	26 149	28 226	7.9	3.0	850	754	769	10 936	15.7	2.52	8.9	23.4
Orleans	11.3	7.5	7.5	50.4	24 053	26 277	9.2	3.1	907	913	848	10 446	17.7	2.45	9.6	25.2
Rutland	11.3	7.4	7.5	51.2	62 142	63 400	2.0	0.2	1 990	2 081	257	25 678	8.4	2.39	10.1	27.9
Washington	10.6	6.6	6.3	51.0	54 928	58 039	5.7	1.4	1 906	1 599	539	23 659	12.9	2.36	9.2	28.5
Windham	11.7	7.2	6.7	51.2	41 588	44 216	6.3	0.4	1 359	1 359	197	18 375	13.0	2.35	9.6	29.7
Windsor	12.2	8.0	8.0	51.2	54 055	57 418	6.2	0.8	1 618	1 733	643	24 162	12.3	2.35	9.0	28.1
VIRGINIA	10.1	6.0	5.3	50.8	6 189 197	7 078 515	14.4	4.3	321 528	184 285	168 252	2 699 173	17.8	2.54	11.9	25.1
Accomack	11.2	8.9	7.5	51.3	31 703	38 305	20.8	1.9	1 499	1 483	750	15 299	20.9	2.45	14.4	27.7
Albemarle	9.5	6.2	5.5	51.8	68 177	79 236	16.2	10.6	3 189	1 889	2 250	31 876	30.5	2.44	9.1	27.0
Alleghany	13.4	8.8	8.9	51.3	17 494	17 215	-1.6	-2.3	635	688	-325	6 983	NA	2.47	9.0	25.4
Amelia	11.4	7.4	6.2	50.4	8 787	11 400	29.7	3.0	481	389	262	4 240	35.4	2.66	11.4	20.7
Amherst	11.2	8.0	6.2	52.2	28 578	31 894	11.6	0.0	1 059	1 049	24	11 941	21.5	2.51	12.4	24.0
Appomattox	12.6	8.4	6.8	51.0	12 300	13 705	11.4	0.0	477	411	-45	5 322	17.5	2.55	11.5	21.3
Arlington	9.4	4.4	5.0	49.6	170 895	189 453	10.9	-0.8	8 947	3 584	-7 387	86 352	10.0	2.15	7.0	40.8
Augusta	11.7	7.2	5.6	49.7	54 557	65 615	20.3	2.8	2 137	1 689	1 404	24 818	25.5	2.56	8.6	20.1
Bath	13.7	10.5	6.7	49.7	4 799	5 048	5.2	-0.7	130	188	27	2 053	8.3	2.34	7.8	26.3
Bedford	12.1	7.5	5.2	50.2	45 553	60 371	32.5	3.8	1 850	1 489	1 939	23 838	37.9	2.52	7.5	20.2
Bland	12.3	8.2	6.4	44.8	6 514	6 871	5.5	1.4	198	209	106	2 568	14.4	2.43	8.7	23.3
Botetourt	12.1	7.9	5.5	50.0	24 992	30 496	22.0	3.1	869	818	906	11 700	27.9	2.56	7.0	19.2
Brunswick	10.2	8.3	6.4	46.4	15 987	18 419	15.2	-1.2	636	613	-211	6 277	14.1	2.47	16.6	27.6
Buchanan	12.6	7.6	4.9	49.1	31 333	26 978	-13.9	-5.1	814	984	-1 215	10 464	-5.4	2.46	10.6	22.5
Buckingham	10.3	7.3	6.1	44.8	12 873	15 623	21.4	1.4	402	524	342	5 324	22.6	2.52	14.2	25.1
Campbell	11.5	8.0	5.8	51.3	47 499	51 078	7.5	0.5	1 948	1 476	-162	20 639	15.0	2.45	11.4	24.6
Caroline	10.7	6.8	5.9	50.3	19 217	22 121	15.1	4.8	889	728	916	8 021	21.0	2.69	13.2	20.5
Carroll	12.3	9.4	7.9	50.5	26 519	29 245	10.3	0.3	869	958	200	12 186	16.5	2.36	8.6	25.4
Charles City County	12.3	8.1	4.9	51.1	6 282	6 926	10.3	2.8	223	198	168	2 670	23.6	2.59	15.2	22.5
Charlotte	11.1	9.5	8.2	52.1	11 688	12 472	6.7	-0.2	519	536	10	4 951	14.8	2.47	13.0	27.4
Chesterfield	9.5	4.5	3.2	51.0	209 599	259 903	24.0	6.5	10 947	4 910	10 892	93 772	27.7	2.73	11.2	18.5
Clarke	11.9	7.8	6.4	50.4	12 101	12 652	4.6	5.6	388	405	713	4 942	16.7	2.50	8.9	24.1
Craig	12.1	7.7	5.7	49.6	4 372	5 091	16.4	1.3	192	136	20	2 060	22.9	2.45	7.0	23.9
Culpeper	9.1	6.1	4.9	49.1	27 791	34 262	23.3	12.5	1 578	1 100	3 731	12 141	24.4	2.68	11.3	20.6
Cumberland	11.5	8.2	7.0	52.2	7 825	9 017	15.2	1.9	331	235	89	3 528	25.4	2.55	14.3	24.8
Dickenson	11.8	8.1	6.7	51.1	17 620	16 395	-7.0	-1.7	444	585	-110	6 732	4.3	2.42	10.6	25.3
Dinwiddie	11.4	6.6	5.3	50.3	22 279	24 533	10.1	1.3	754	626	223	9 107	21.6	2.58	13.9	22.2
Essex	11.1	8.7	8.1	52.1	8 689	9 989	15.0	2.7	355	410	331	3 995	22.6	2.46	14.0	26.1
Fairfax	10.6	4.8	3.5	50.4	818 310	969 749	18.5	3.2	47 266	13 931	-2 663	350 714	20.0	2.74	8.6	21.4
Fauquier	10.5	5.8	4.4	50.5	48 700	55 139	13.2	10.9	2 282	1 390	4 995	19 842	20.2	2.75	8.6	18.7
Floyd	12.3	7.9	7.8	50.5	11 965	13 874	16.0	3.4	458	463	481	5 791	21.6	2.39	8.1	24.7
Fluvanna	9.7	8.3	4.9	53.7	12 429	20 047	61.3	15.1	745	537	2 726	7 387	63.5	2.59	9.9	18.8
Franklin	12.3	8.3	6.2	50.8	39 549	47 286	19.6	3.8	1 797	1 451	1 456	18 963	29.4	2.44	9.4	22.6
Frederick	9.8	6.0	4.5	49.9	45 723	59 209	29.5	9.0	2 312	1 434	4 386	22 097	34.2	2.64	8.8	19.2
Giles	12.5	8.1	8.1	51.0	16 366	16 657	1.8	1.8	704	640	242	6 994	8.2	2.37	9.7	26.6
Gloucester	10.6	6.5	5.4	50.9	30 131	34 780	15.4	5.5	1 323	995	1 611	13 127	19.7	2.62	9.9	20.3
Goochland	12.1	7.2	4.8	50.0	14 163	16 863	19.1	7.6	662	500	1 098	6 158	26.2	2.51	8.4	19.9
Grayson	12.8	10.3	8.4	51.0	16 278	17 917	10.1	-7.6	509	685	-137	7 259	12.2	2.31	8.5	26.8
Greene	9.2	5.4	4.2	49.9	10 297	15 244	48.0	10.1	786	353	1 091	5 574	48.7	2.71	10.4	18.0
Greensville	9.6	6.4	5.0	37.9	8 553	11 560	35.2	0.2	368	320	-10	3 375	7.1	2.51	16.0	25.4
Halifax	11.9	9.0	8.7	52.5	36 030	37 355	3.7	-1.9	1 443	1 515	-617	15 018	40.0	2.43	14.8	27.4
Hanover	9.8	5.9	4.8	50.7	63 306	86 320	36.4	9.0	3 473	2 053	6 279	31 121	37.5	2.71	9.3	17.7
Henrico	8.8	5.9	6.3	52.8	217 878	262 300	20.4	3.3	11 706	7 560	4 938	108 121	21.3	2.39	13.1	28.9
Henry	12.5	8.7	6.8	51.0	56 942	57 930	1.7	-1.5	2 036	1 841	-984	23 910	9.8	2.40	12.2	25.8
Highland	15.1	10.3	11.1	50.1	2 635	2 536	-3.8	-1.3	60	119	27	1 131	4.6	2.24	7.1	29.1
Isle of Wight	10.8	7.1	5.0	51.1	25 053	29 728	18.7	7.4	1 141	949	1 972	11 319	25.3	2.61	12.2	20.0
James City County	10.9	9.3	7.6	51.3	34 779	48 102	38.3	11.2	1 615	1 186	4 879	19 003	46.5	2.47	8.9	21.4
King and Queen	12.5	8.7	7.9	51.5	6 289	6 630	5.4	-0.6	216	276	29	2 673	14.3	2.48	13.5	24.6
King George	9.4	5.2	4.1	49.4	13 527	16 803	24.2	8.4	745	442	1 088	6 091	28.6	2.70	10.5	20.4
King William	10.2	6.2	5.0	50.7	10 913	13 146	20.5	7.5	600	430	810	4 846	26.4	2.69	10.2	18.3
Lancaster	13.4	14.1	13.9	51.2	10 896	11 567	6.2	4.4	373	700	823	5 004	9.6	2.23	11.1	28.7
Lee	11.8	8.2	7.2	51.3	24 496	23 589	-3.7	0.6	774	989	370	9 706	5.1	2.41	11.7	27.0
Loudoun	6.8	2.9	2.1	50.4	86 185	169 599	96.8	30.7	12 254	2 394	40 907	59 900	96.5	2.82	7.8	18.4

1. No spouse present.

Table B. States and Counties — Vital Statistics, Health Resources, and Crime

STATE County	Births, average 1999–2001 Total	Rate[1]	Deaths, average 1999–2001 Number Total	Number Infant[2]	Rate Total[1]	Rate Infant[3]	Physicians,[4] 2000 Number	Rate[5]	Hospitals,[4] 1998 Number	Beds Number	Beds Rate[5]	Medicare enrollees, 2003	Serious crimes known to police,[6] 2002 Total Number	Rate[7]
	32	33	34	35	36	37	38	39	40	41	42	43	44	45
VERMONT—Cont'd														
Chittenden	1 668	11.4	922	11	6.3	6.8	656	448	2	582	408	17 078	5 148	3 468
Essex	53	8.3	61	0	9.4	D	3	46	0	0	0	1 322	NA	NA
Franklin	581	12.8	368	3	8.1	D	61	134	1	70	159	5 831	1 219	2 650
Grand Isle	288	40.3	52	1	7.2	D	6	87	0	0	0	1 062	60	858
Lamoille	258	11.1	186	1	8.0	D	52	224	1	49	227	3 313	618	2 627
Orange	237	8.4	223	1	7.9	D	40	142	1	42	150	4 244	268	938
Orleans	279	10.6	268	1	10.2	D	34	129	1	46	182	4 883	549	2 063
Rutland	632	10.0	624	4	9.8	D	131	207	1	188	301	11 638	1 731	2 696
Washington	605	10.4	498	4	8.6	D	123	212	1	122	217	9 225	1 630	2 773
Windham	426	9.7	426	1	9.7	D	98	222	2	81	190	7 178	1 217	2 718
Windsor	426	7.4	540	2	9.4	D	127	221	2	164	296	10 414	836	1 438
VIRGINIA	97 764	13.8	55 961	707	7.9	7.2	14 280	202	92	18 211	268	946 470	229 039	3 140
Accomack	445	11.7	451	4	11.8	D	24	63	0	0	0	6 904	736	1 906
Albemarle	1 017	12.8	577	6	7.2	D	426	538	0	0	0	9 000	2 274	2 785
Alleghany	129	9.0	158	0	11.0	D	35	NA	1	174	NA	1 956	232	1 308
Amelia	142	12.5	124	1	10.9	D	2	18	0	0	0	1 771	144	1 226
Amherst	341	10.7	302	1	9.5	D	14	44	0	0	0	5 210	389	1 184
Appomattox	152	11.1	136	1	9.9	D	6	44	0	0	0	2 242	112	793
Arlington	2 750	14.5	1 097	12	5.8	4.4	569	300	3	690	389	17 383	6 470	3 314
Augusta	666	10.2	490	5	7.5	D	86	131	1	131	212	6 821	798	1 180
Bath	45	9.0	62	0	12.3	D	6	119	1	25	511	1 108	15	288
Bedford	577	9.6	440	3	7.3	D	31	51	0	0	0	9 985	942	1 514
Bland	65	9.4	76	0	11.1	D	5	73	0	0	0	1 352	68	960
Botetourt	297	9.8	235	2	7.7	D	12	39	0	0	0	4 791	357	1 136
Brunswick	185	10.1	202	1	11.0	D	2	11	0	0	0	3 121	119	627
Buchanan	261	9.7	282	2	10.5	D	17	63	1	99	342	6 890	666	2 396
Buckingham	110	7.0	152	2	9.7	D	6	38	0	0	0	2 074	235	1 460
Campbell	637	12.5	448	3	8.8	D	19	37	0	0	0	6 618	1 129	2 145
Caroline	274	12.4	211	3	9.5	D	9	41	0	0	0	3 255	232	1 063
Carroll	280	9.6	307	1	10.5	D	14	48	0	0	0	4 826	404	1 472
Charles City County	72	10.3	67	1	9.7	D	3	43	0	0	0	898	70	981
Charlotte	160	12.9	169	0	13.6	D	5	40	0	0	0	3 223	104	809
Chesterfield	3 322	12.7	1 451	20	5.6	6.1	337	130	1	284	115	24 672	8 366	3 124
Clarke	117	9.2	128	1	10.0	D	9	71	0	0	0	1 890	270	2 071
Craig	58	11.4	40	1	7.8	D	4	79	0	0	0	790	32	610
Culpeper	456	13.2	320	1	9.3	D	47	137	1	70	212	5 111	671	1 901
Cumberland	93	10.4	89	1	10.0	D	5	55	0	0	0	1 038	111	1 195
Dickenson	150	9.2	177	1	10.8	D	13	79	1	50	296	3 904	217	1 285
Dinwiddie	237	9.7	195	2	8.0	D	26	106	0	0	0	3 134	676	2 723
Essex	112	11.2	132	2	13.3	D	21	210	1	100	1 096	1 845	235	2 283
Fairfax	14 165	14.6	4 177	65	4.3	4.6	2 292	236	3	507	55	66 660	19 154	1 917
Fauquier	683	12.3	405	2	7.3	D	75	136	1	106	196	6 641	862	1 517
Floyd	150	10.8	146	1	10.5	D	5	36	0	0	0	2 395	166	1 161
Fluvanna	221	10.9	147	2	7.3	D	13	65	0	0	0	3 502	247	1 196
Franklin	536	11.3	423	5	8.9	D	35	74	1	37	83	7 679	747	1 533
Frederick	753	12.7	410	4	6.9	D	12	20	0	0	0	7 045	1 297	2 126
Giles	221	13.2	197	2	11.8	D	13	78	1	53	326	3 667	66	401
Gloucester	395	11.3	308	4	8.8	D	35	101	1	71	202	4 939	628	1 752
Goochland	190	11.2	152	2	9.0	D	16	95	0	0	0	2 151	220	1 266
Grayson	176	10.1	221	1	12.7	D	8	45	0	0	0	3 080	168	910
Greene	238	15.5	115	1	7.5	D	4	26	0	0	0	1 831	158	1 006
Greensville	109	9.4	104	1	9.0	D	1	9	0	0	0	844	198	1 662
Halifax	451	12.1	475	3	12.7	D	9	24	1	192	521	7 667	672	1 746
Hanover	1 092	12.6	631	5	7.3	D	87	101	0	0	0	13 675	1 453	1 634
Henrico	3 635	13.9	2 306	31	8.8	8.5	831	317	4	1 231	500	29 701	10 966	4 057
Henry	647	11.2	567	4	9.8	D	13	22	0	0	0	9 458	1 832	3 069
Highland	18	7.0	35	0	13.7	D	3	118	0	0	0	572	21	804
Isle of Wight	346	11.6	268	2	9.0	D	10	34	0	0	0	4 496	793	2 589
James City County	492	10.2	345	2	7.2	D	96	200	0	0	0	2 567	1 062	2 143
King and Queen	65	9.8	78	1	11.8	D	0	0	0	0	0	1 117	NA	NA
King George	231	13.7	125	2	7.4	D	7	42	0	0	0	1 930	442	2 553
King William	188	14.2	116	1	8.8	D	6	46	0	0	0	1 965	173	1 277
Lancaster	108	9.3	213	0	18.5	D	42	363	1	76	668	3 711	155	1 450
Lee	240	10.2	307	2	13.0	D	24	102	1	80	336	5 294	568	2 337
Loudoun	3 513	20.3	696	14	4.0	3.9	194	114	1	119	83	11 980	4 067	2 327

1. Per 1,000 estimated resident population.   2. Deaths of infants under 1 year old.   3. Deaths of infants under 1 year old per 1,000 live births.   4. Data subject to copyright.   5. Per 100,000 resident population as of July 1 of the year shown.   6. Data for serious crimes have not been adjusted for underreporting; this may affect comparability between geographic areas and over time.   7. Per 100,000 population estimated by the FBI.

STATE County	Serious crimes known to police,[1] 2002 (cont'd) Rate[2] Violent	Property	Education — School enrollment and attainment, 2000 Enrollment[3] Total	Percent private	Attainment[4] (percent) High school graduate or less	Bachelor's degree or more	Local government expenditures,[5] 2000–2001 Total current expenditures (mil dol)	Current expenditures per student (dollars)	Money income, 1999 Per capita income[6] (dollars)	Households Median income Dollars	Percent change, 1989–1999 (constant 1999 dollars)	Percent with income of $100,000 or more	Percent below poverty level, 1999 Persons	Households	Families	Families with children
	46	47	48	49	50	51	52	53	54	55	56	57	58	59	60	61
VERMONT—Cont'd																
Chittenden	141	3 327	45 835	20.6	32.9	41.2	203.4	8 721	23 501	47 673	-3.8	13.1	8.8	8.9	4.9	7.3
Essex	NA	NA	1 543	7.5	71.0	10.8	15.0	10 279	14 388	30 490	1.5	2.3	13.7	13.9	9.9	15.2
Franklin	126	2 524	11 338	6.2	58.5	16.6	70.5	9 012	17 816	41 659	9.2	5.7	9.0	8.9	7.0	9.8
Grand Isle	14	844	1 629	10.4	49.6	25.0	7.8	10 271	22 207	43 033	4.9	9.8	7.6	8.1	5.9	8.6
Lamoille	85	2 542	6 279	10.5	43.6	31.2	32.5	8 232	20 972	39 356	7.2	8.8	9.6	9.4	6.4	9.6
Orange	35	903	7 349	14.1	53.4	23.9	51.2	9 716	18 784	39 855	5.9	6.1	9.1	8.9	6.1	9.9
Orleans	113	1 950	6 344	11.0	62.5	16.1	39.6	8 914	16 518	31 084	1.4	4.2	14.1	14.2	10.6	16.5
Rutland	112	2 584	16 135	13.6	51.5	23.2	91.7	9 044	18 874	36 743	-3.1	6.1	10.9	11.2	7.1	11.9
Washington	90	2 683	15 111	20.9	43.1	32.2	86.3	8 807	21 113	40 972	2.9	8.5	8.0	8.9	5.5	8.7
Windham	154	2 564	10 936	23.0	45.4	30.5	74.8	11 220	20 533	38 204	2.4	7.7	9.4	9.5	6.1	10.2
Windsor	65	1 372	13 723	15.2	44.2	30.2	95.1	9 972	22 369	40 688	3.5	9.5	7.7	8.9	5.2	7.8
VIRGINIA	291	2 849	1 868 101	16.2	44.5	29.5	8 334.6	7 286	23 975	46 677	4.2	15.1	9.6	9.6	7.0	10.2
Accomack	243	1 663	8 559	10.8	66.2	13.5	36.6	6 846	16 309	30 250	10.2	4.7	18.0	16.6	13.0	19.8
Albemarle	209	2 576	21 699	17.6	30.4	47.7	94.1	7 693	28 852	50 749	2.4	17.3	6.7	7.0	4.2	5.9
Alleghany	169	1 139	3 617	6.6	61.7	12.6	[7]28.5	[7]7 409	18 525	NA	NA	5.4	10.1	10.5	7.2	12.5
Amelia	111	1 115	2 734	15.5	67.9	9.8	11.3	6 333	18 858	40 252	12.6	7.5	8.4	9.1	6.7	8.5
Amherst	97	1 086	7 838	25.1	62.8	13.1	28.2	6 081	16 952	37 393	0.2	5.3	10.7	11.0	8.0	12.3
Appomattox	85	708	3 174	12.6	67.6	10.5	14.7	6 130	18 086	36 507	6.1	5.0	11.4	13.3	8.7	12.3
Arlington	224	3 090	40 996	33.3	23.9	60.2	214.9	11 388	37 706	63 001	5.1	26.7	7.8	6.4	5.0	7.5
Augusta	117	1 063	14 577	14.5	62.1	15.4	68.6	6 380	19 744	43 045	8.7	8.0	5.8	6.2	4.2	5.8
Bath	19	269	1 034	6.7	65.1	11.1	7.9	9 661	23 092	35 013	7.7	6.4	7.8	9.0	5.8	6.6
Bedford	96	1 418	13 656	17.8	52.6	20.9	[8]57.9	[8]5 411	21 582	43 136	4.5	9.6	7.1	7.7	5.2	7.3
Bland	56	904	1 436	12.3	67.2	9.2	6.0	6 658	17 744	30 397	-4.1	5.9	12.4	13.9	9.1	9.5
Botetourt	64	1 072	6 949	15.1	52.5	19.6	31.6	6 887	22 218	48 731	9.6	10.8	5.2	5.8	3.6	5.1
Brunswick	58	569	4 414	18.2	67.8	10.8	19.0	7 847	14 890	31 288	19.9	3.8	16.5	18.5	13.2	19.4
Buchanan	209	2 187	5 598	4.6	74.7	8.0	29.7	7 320	12 788	22 213	-16.7	2.4	23.2	23.9	19.8	26.4
Buckingham	174	1 286	3 417	7.3	75.3	8.5	15.3	6 769	13 669	29 882	-1.9	4.4	20.0	18.2	16.0	23.2
Campbell	188	1 957	12 058	15.4	59.9	14.6	53.5	6 188	18 134	37 280	2.0	5.7	10.6	11.1	7.9	11.5
Caroline	307	756	4 940	7.7	66.3	12.1	23.6	6 075	18 342	39 845	2.5	7.1	9.4	9.9	7.2	9.8
Carroll	124	1 348	5 729	5.6	69.6	9.5	27.1	6 781	16 475	30 597	5.6	3.5	12.5	14.3	8.7	13.3
Charles City County	182	799	1 543	15.5	68.9	10.5	8.4	8 962	19 182	42 745	7.7	7.1	10.6	11.7	8.0	12.2
Charlotte	218	591	2 876	8.0	71.6	10.3	14.7	6 641	14 717	28 929	5.1	3.4	18.1	18.5	12.7	16.6
Chesterfield	212	2 912	76 024	13.2	36.7	32.6	319.7	6 243	25 286	58 537	-0.1	17.8	4.5	4.2	3.3	4.8
Clarke	338	1 734	2 927	17.4	50.8	23.9	14.4	7 385	24 844	51 601	10.9	15.1	6.6	6.8	4.2	6.1
Craig	343	267	1 057	12.9	64.2	10.8	4.9	6 921	17 322	37 314	10.6	5.0	10.3	9.1	6.6	10.3
Culpeper	224	1 677	8 160	13.3	62.0	15.7	37.3	6 624	20 162	45 290	0.6	10.4	9.2	8.9	7.0	9.8
Cumberland	183	1 012	2 035	21.3	69.8	11.8	9.3	7 103	15 103	31 816	7.1	3.6	15.1	16.1	11.9	16.9
Dickenson	89	1 196	3 605	2.1	76.0	6.7	19.5	7 199	12 822	23 431	7.0	2.1	21.3	22.4	16.9	24.2
Dinwiddie	145	2 578	5 586	10.9	68.0	11.0	27.1	6 287	19 122	41 582	5.3	7.3	9.3	10.1	6.6	9.3
Essex	204	2 079	2 300	11.8	61.3	17.4	11.0	6 730	17 994	37 395	6.7	6.2	11.2	11.5	7.7	11.1
Fairfax	59	1 858	265 920	21.2	23.1	54.8	[9]1 414.3	[9]9 038	36 888	81 050	1.8	37.6	4.5	3.6	3.0	4.3
Fauquier	180	1 338	14 403	19.7	43.4	27.1	67.5	7 019	28 757	61 999	2.0	23.8	5.4	5.9	3.7	4.6
Floyd	28	1 133	2 800	9.7	68.2	12.5	12.6	6 447	16 345	31 585	2.4	3.3	11.7	14.8	8.5	11.6
Fluvanna	160	1 036	4 657	14.2	52.5	24.5	19.4	6 381	20 338	46 372	10.0	9.1	5.9	6.8	3.9	4.5
Franklin	121	1 412	10 503	15.2	60.4	14.8	45.6	6 390	19 605	38 056	7.5	7.8	9.7	10.4	7.3	10.7
Frederick	126	2 000	14 489	11.3	57.1	18.6	73.1	6 876	21 080	46 941	6.5	9.4	6.4	6.4	4.0	5.8
Giles	97	303	3 462	5.9	64.9	12.4	17.2	6 766	18 396	34 927	7.8	4.6	9.5	10.7	6.6	11.3
Gloucester	140	1 613	9 365	10.9	49.9	17.6	41.4	6 418	19 990	45 421	7.0	7.7	7.7	8.1	6.8	9.8
Goochland	196	1 070	3 725	30.4	50.6	29.4	15.2	7 656	29 105	56 307	15.6	22.8	6.9	7.1	4.3	6.2
Grayson	54	856	3 280	8.8	73.6	8.0	15.8	6 998	16 768	28 676	10.5	3.5	13.6	15.1	10.0	16.0
Greene	146	859	3 751	15.1	56.3	19.8	18.7	7 171	19 478	45 931	14.7	7.8	6.6	5.8	4.8	6.1
Greensville	512	1 150	2 619	13.6	77.1	11.0	[10]18.7	[10]6 748	14 632	32 000	7.7	3.9	14.7	17.2	12.4	15.0
Halifax	234	1 512	8 208	7.2	69.9	9.5	41.2	6 826	16 353	29 929	-0.1	4.0	15.7	17.3	11.5	15.8
Hanover	115	1 519	23 954	15.7	42.2	28.7	98.9	5 955	25 120	59 223	8.3	17.8	3.6	4.1	2.5	3.3
Henrico	222	3 835	65 953	16.2	37.1	34.9	267.2	6 414	26 410	49 185	2.8	14.5	6.2	6.1	4.5	6.9
Henry	337	2 732	12 980	10.0	67.8	9.4	58.6	6 658	17 110	31 816	-8.3	4.4	11.7	12.5	8.8	13.3
Highland	153	651	483	7.0	65.4	13.2	2.7	8 144	15 976	29 732	5.9	3.4	12.6	14.7	9.3	10.3
Isle of Wight	144	2 445	7 272	19.0	54.3	17.5	34.0	6 832	20 235	45 387	15.8	10.1	8.3	9.7	6.6	9.0
James City County	145	1 997	11 808	15.0	31.6	41.5	[11]66.2	[11]8 084	29 256	55 594	4.0	20.6	6.4	6.5	4.1	6.9
King and Queen	NA	NA	1 339	11.4	69.0	10.3	8.2	8 666	17 236	35 941	3.9	5.7	10.9	12.6	7.8	7.0
King George	254	2 299	4 551	13.9	52.0	23.6	19.7	6 710	21 562	49 882	4.4	12.0	5.6	5.6	4.4	5.3
King William	96	1 181	3 138	10.4	59.1	14.8	19.5	7 507	21 928	49 876	10.2	10.0	5.5	6.1	4.4	5.9
Lancaster	131	1 319	2 169	13.5	53.5	24.5	10.7	7 055	24 663	33 239	-9.3	11.8	12.5	13.4	9.9	16.1
Lee	144	2 193	5 068	6.9	71.2	9.5	27.6	7 246	13 625	22 972	17.0	3.7	23.9	25.4	20.2	26.8
Loudoun	207	2 121	46 444	20.1	25.1	47.2	248.8	7 822	33 530	80 648	15.3	35.3	2.8	2.6	1.7	2.3

1. Data for serious crimes have not been adjusted for underreporting; this may affect comparability between geographic areas and over time. 2. Per 100,000 population estimated by the FBI. 3. All persons 3 years old and over enrolled in nursery school through college. 4. Persons 25 years old and over. 5. Elementary and secondary education expenditures. 6. Based on population enumerated as of April 1, 2000. 7. Covington included with Alleghany County. 8. Bedford City included with Bedford County. 9. Fairfax City included with Fairfax County. 10. Emporia included with Greensville County. 11. Williamsburg included with James City County.

Table B. States and Counties — **Personal Income**

STATE County	Personal income, 2002 Total (mil dol)	Percent change, 2001–2002	Per capita[1] Dollars	Per capita[1] Rank	Wages and salaries[2] (mil dol)	Proprietor's income (mil dol)	Dividends, interest, and rent (mil dol)	Transfer payments Total (mil dol)	Government payments to individuals Total (mil dol)	Social Security (mil dol)	Medical payments (mil dol)	Income maintenance (mil dol)	Unemployment insurance (mil dol)
	62	63	64	65	66	67	68	69	70	71	72	73	74
VERMONT—Cont'd													
Chittenden	5 066	2.2	34 103	160	4 342	382	927	569	525	202	236	48	17
Essex	126	2.1	19 214	2 710	53	14	18	32	30	13	7	4	4
Franklin	1 195	2.8	25 663	963	579	94	155	183	169	56	69	23	11
Grand Isle	213	2.4	29 105	430	31	12	41	27	25	12	6	2	4
Lamoille	686	4.5	28 551	484	337	71	148	104	97	35	41	9	8
Orange	747	4.4	25 913	908	270	66	149	116	107	46	41	11	4
Orleans	642	3.4	24 090	1 375	305	81	122	151	143	48	64	16	8
Rutland	1 801	3.9	28 423	500	1 068	85	333	421	402	126	220	33	11
Washington	1 815	3.4	30 831	283	1 258	176	311	309	291	102	138	23	11
Windham	1 328	5.1	30 041	348	934	119	279	223	210	82	87	19	7
Windsor	1 788	4.0	30 905	274	875	137	456	267	250	118	93	21	4
VIRGINIA	238 991	2.8	32 793	X	170 511	15 848	39 960	25 611	23 883	10 290	8 865	2 070	927
Accomack	783	4.2	20 172	2 505	427	51	166	172	162	70	62	19	5
Albemarle	(3)4 452	(3)3.1	(3)35 254	(3)135	(3)3 379	(3)480	(3)1 218	(3)443	(3)413	(3)190	(3)161	(3)33	(3)11
Alleghany	(4)552	(4)2.0	(4)23 670	(4)1 510	(4)396	(4)22	(4)92	(4)132	(4)126	(4)50	(4)46	(4)9	(4)4
Amelia	288	0.0	24 635	1 227	78	24	41	45	42	21	15	4	1
Amherst	695	1.7	21 841	2 054	344	36	95	125	118	60	38	9	4
Appomattox	329	1.3	23 997	1 409	113	29	47	59	56	27	18	5	3
Arlington	10 428	2.1	55 148	9	12 994	816	1 904	462	417	171	173	33	12
Augusta	(5)2 844	(5)2.1	(5)25 680	(5)961	(5)1 699	(5)243	(5)547	(5)470	(5)443	(5)224	(5)156	(5)30	(5)14
Bath	140	2.6	27 663	593	77	6	37	26	25	11	10	1	1
Bedford	(6)1 992	(6)2.0	(6)29 228	(6)419	(6)570	(6)130	(6)441	(6)279	(6)262	(6)126	(6)82	(6)15	(6)8
Bland	137	3.5	19 867	2 572	66	8	20	34	32	14	12	2	2
Botetourt	980	3.6	31 482	250	314	80	161	114	106	54	30	4	3
Brunswick	341	1.8	18 573	2 819	155	18	53	90	86	32	34	9	2
Buchanan	550	2.4	21 116	2 263	303	35	110	195	189	85	65	18	5
Buckingham	281	1.8	17 809	2 916	103	32	44	65	61	25	25	7	2
Campbell	(7)2 833	(7)0.8	(7)24 340	(7)1 294	(7)2 615	(7)147	(7)492	(7)594	(7)566	(7)234	(7)237	(7)46	(7)20
Caroline	603	6.2	26 689	752	203	43	82	88	83	37	32	7	2
Carroll	(8)766	(8)2.8	(8)21 361	(8)2 192	(8)418	(8)57	(8)114	(8)207	(8)198	(8)78	(8)88	(8)14	(8)12
Charles City County	185	2.0	26 273	838	53	9	33	28	26	12	9	2	1
Charlotte	264	3.3	21 130	2 257	101	28	45	69	66	27	26	6	4
Chesterfield	9 096	2.7	33 586	168	4 723	583	1 301	705	639	351	191	45	20
Clarke	419	2.5	31 723	234	157	21	97	43	40	20	15	2	1
Craig	116	2.9	22 763	1 797	19	7	17	20	18	10	6	1	1
Culpeper	1 015	3.3	27 545	608	521	71	169	128	119	54	48	9	4
Cumberland	185	2.1	20 480	2 438	41	8	26	36	34	16	12	4	1
Dickenson	299	3.2	18 491	2 832	104	15	40	118	114	47	40	11	7
Dinwiddie	(9)1 945	(9)2.6	(9)25 958	(9)894	(9)1 189	(9)46	(9)281	(9)472	(9)454	(9)148	(9)221	(9)42	(9)10
Essex	237	1.5	23 391	1 596	114	13	43	53	50	21	21	4	2
Fairfax	(10)53 588	(10)2.1	(10)52 199	(10)16	(10)38 988	(10)5 188	(10)8 896	(10)2 262	(10)2 016	(10)929	(10)717	(10)134	(10)64
Fauquier	2 369	2.5	39 881	62	733	156	482	161	147	75	56	8	3
Floyd	307	3.5	21 527	2 141	76	33	57	59	56	27	19	4	2
Fluvanna	530	3.5	23 845	1 458	125	18	90	81	75	39	27	4	2
Franklin	1 192	3.4	24 582	1 242	412	47	223	204	192	96	59	14	11
Frederick	(11)2 536	(11)4.0	(11)29 063	(11)442	(11)1 857	(11)217	(11)443	(11)293	(11)272	(11)136	(11)93	(11)19	(11)10
Giles	363	2.9	21 463	2 159	189	16	53	88	84	39	32	6	3
Gloucester	941	3.6	26 260	840	271	39	159	123	114	54	42	8	2
Goochland	779	1.9	44 028	40	251	64	203	66	61	32	16	3	1
Grayson	335	2.5	20 102	2 523	73	16	62	84	80	37	27	7	6
Greene	385	4.0	23 603	1 534	122	22	45	50	46	20	17	4	3
Greensville	(12)313	(12)2.9	(12)18 154	(12)2 874	(12)288	(12)13	(12)48	(12)81	(12)76	(12)31	(12)33	(12)9	(12)2
Halifax	772	2.4	20 968	2 308	434	39	127	200	191	77	67	20	19
Hanover	3 063	2.4	33 366	177	1 549	133	471	293	270	140	99	10	6
Henrico	9 623	2.1	35 928	122	8 094	441	1 891	860	795	442	249	51	25
Henry	(13)1 677	(13)3.6	(13)23 144	(13)1 680	(13)978	(13)76	(13)347	(13)432	(13)414	(13)177	(13)121	(13)29	(13)73
Highland	61	-0.5	24 753	1 195	15	8	21	12	12	6	5	1	0
Isle of Wight	871	2.5	28 150	525	505	37	120	124	117	53	46	9	3
James City County	(14)2 357	(14)4.2	(14)37 322	(14)99	(14)1 401	(14)176	(14)650	(14)269	(14)254	(14)130	(14)94	(14)11	(14)4
King and Queen	163	2.3	24 747	1 197	44	10	24	29	27	12	10	2	1
King George	529	3.6	30 031	349	696	34	99	46	42	17	17	2	1
King William	394	2.3	28 594	482	146	16	63	50	47	23	18	3	1
Lancaster	394	3.3	32 861	192	147	24	165	78	75	39	28	4	3
Lee	471	6.6	19 956	2 553	181	28	65	159	154	54	64	19	5
Loudoun	7 438	-2.8	36 455	114	5 950	355	1 063	327	278	141	99	14	15

1. Based on the resident population estimated as of July 1 of the year shown.   2. Includes other labor income.   3. Charlottesville included with Albemarle County.   4. Covington included with Alleghany County.   5. Staunton and Waynesboro included with Augusta County.   6. Bedford City included with Bedford County.   7. Lynchburg included with Campbell County.   8. Galax included with Carroll County.   9. Petersburg and Colonial Heights included with Dinwiddie County.   10. Fairfax City and Falls Church included with Fairfax County.   11. Winchester included with Frederick County.   12. Emporia included with Greensville County.   13. Martinsville included with Henry County.   14. Williamsburg included with James City County.

STATE County	Earnings, 2002									Social Security beneficiaries, December 2003		Housing units, 2003	
		Percent by selected industries											
			Goods-related[1]		Service-related and health							Supplemental Security Income recipients, December 2003	
	Total (mil dol)	Farm	Total	Manufacturing	Information and professional and technical services	Retail trade	Finance, insurance, and real estate	Health services	Government	Number	Rate[2]	Total	Percent change, 2000–2003
	75	76	77	78	79	80	81	82	83	84	85	86	87	88

VERMONT—Cont'd													
Chittenden	4 724	0.2	28.1	21.8	12.2	7.9	7.4	12.2	14.6	20 370	137	2 107	61 042	3.7
Essex	67	2.4	45.5	40.6	D	3.8	D	D	21.1	1 545	235	181	4 794	0.7
Franklin	674	3.5	D	19.3	5.9	10.2	3.4	11.2	23.2	6 410	136	1 104	19 953	4.0
Grand Isle	43	7.1	D	2.8	D	8.4	D	D	26.6	1 280	171	118	4 780	2.5
Lamoille	408	1.3	19.8	10.7	6.7	10.4	4.6	13.3	14.8	3 745	154	416	11 485	4.3
Orange	336	2.4	21.7	11.0	7.4	8.3	4.0	12.3	21.4	5 045	173	493	13 562	1.3
Orleans	386	4.4	D	16.1	3.4	9.2	5.7	14.3	19.1	5 710	211	875	14 944	1.8
Rutland	1 153	0.5	25.2	16.6	6.6	10.0	4.3	13.5	15.9	13 525	213	1 938	32 589	0.9
Washington	1 434	0.3	15.2	10.2	9.1	8.0	13.2	9.9	25.0	10 725	182	1 444	28 320	2.4
Windham	1 052	0.8	D	12.3	D	8.4	4.8	9.5	10.2	8 460	191	900	27 642	2.2
Windsor	1 012	0.5	19.1	10.3	11.6	9.0	5.3	10.4	22.8	11 990	207	1 021	32 358	2.3
VIRGINIA	186 359	0.2	15.4	8.6	18.4	6.1	7.8	7.1	23.7	1 093 694	148	133 731	3 058 766	5.3
Accomack	478	2.2	25.2	20.8	8.0	6.5	4.2	D	29.2	8 000	205	1 280	19 869	1.6
Albemarle	[4]3 859	[4]0.2	[4]D	[4]D	[4]11.6	[4]7.0	[4]7.1	[4]8.5	[4]33.5	12 760	146	709	36 782	9.1
Alleghany	[5]418	[5]0.2	[5]D	[5]38.0	[5]D	[5]7.1	[5]D	[5]D	[5]14.2	3 535	210	435	7 958	36.9
Amelia	102	8.5	D	9.6	3.5	6.1	3.0	D	19.1	2 475	211	270	4 827	4.7
Amherst	379	0.2	33.8	23.2	3.6	6.8	2.7	D	27.5	6 360	199	659	13 273	2.4
Appomattox	142	1.1	D	18.4	D	9.6	7.6	3.6	20.8	3 050	222	366	6 030	3.5
Arlington	13 810	0.0	D	D	27.2	2.4	6.7	3.1	37.8	16 620	88	1 884	91 651	1.4
Augusta	[6]1 942	[6]0.7	[6]D	[6]D	[6]5.6	[6]6.9	[6]4.8	[6]D	[6]17.0	13 145	195	662	28 102	5.1
Bath	84	1.5	8.1	3.0	D	2.1	D	D	16.4	1 215	242	95	2 958	2.1
Bedford	[7]700	[7]0.5	[7]D	[7]21.2	[7]D	[7]7.1	[7]7.4	[7]8.0	[7]14.3	11 625	186	708	28 290	5.4
Bland	75	1.4	D	D	D	4.0	D	3.9	28.7	1 650	237	178	3 301	4.4
Botetourt	394	0.6	41.0	28.3	6.5	4.7	4.5	D	12.6	5 610	178	254	13 080	4.0
Brunswick	172	2.7	D	11.6	D	5.4	D	D	28.8	3 750	206	658	7 674	1.8
Buchanan	338	0.1	44.1	4.3	2.8	6.4	2.3	D	16.9	9 275	362	1 763	12 029	1.2
Buckingham	135	3.2	D	5.8	4.5	7.2	3.4	D	29.0	2 980	188	444	6 465	2.8
Campbell	[8]2 762	[8]0.1	[8]D	[8]31.3	[8]4.8	[8]9.3	[8]7.2	[8]12.2	[8]10.4	10 850	211	1 010	23 050	4.4
Caroline	246	0.7	D	6.8	D	8.6	6.4	2.5	24.1	4 110	177	347	9 404	5.8
Carroll	[9]476	[9]1.1	[9]D	[9]30.4	[9]D	[9]11.2	[9]3.0	[9]D	[9]16.8	7 115	243	809	15 199	3.5
Charles City County	62	1.7	D	17.2	D	D	3.8	D	19.4	1 390	195	146	3 019	4.3
Charlotte	128	6.9	32.0	26.8	D	6.6	D	D	21.3	3 225	259	572	5 997	4.6
Chesterfield	5 306	0.0	D	14.4	9.4	9.2	10.4	6.7	16.0	34 755	126	2 779	106 118	8.6
Clarke	178	1.3	D	26.7	D	4.9	5.6	D	14.4	2 205	165	137	5 675	5.3
Craig	26	2.2	D	D	D	7.0	7.4	D	34.0	1 125	218	106	2 654	3.9
Culpeper	592	0.9	19.2	10.3	13.2	7.7	5.8	D	19.1	6 045	157	678	13 987	8.7
Cumberland	49	7.4	D	D	D	11.3	D	3.7	26.0	1 790	195	251	4 227	3.5
Dickenson	119	0.4	24.6	0.3	3.9	9.3	D	9.8	25.0	5 275	327	1 025	7 781	1.3
Dinwiddie	[10]1 234	[10]0.5	[10]D	[10]14.2	[10]D	[10]11.0	[10]D	[10]D	[10]32.0	4 725	190	684	10 224	5.3
Essex	126	0.9	25.0	19.9	D	14.3	4.9	D	15.0	2 315	226	240	5 103	3.6
Fairfax	[11]44 177	[11]0.0	[11]8.2	[11]2.0	[11]36.6	[11]5.0	[11]9.3	[11]5.7	[11]14.3	87 725	88	8 098	377 901	5.1
Fauquier	889	1.0	23.0	5.2	11.5	8.7	7.4	10.1	15.0	7 785	127	448	22 998	9.3
Floyd	109	6.7	D	12.5	D	7.2	9.0	D	18.0	3 075	214	243	7 025	3.9
Fluvanna	143	1.5	D	D	D	4.6	3.5	D	29.8	4 070	176	228	9 173	14.4
Franklin	459	2.3	D	24.9	3.5	9.1	4.1	D	15.5	10 580	216	827	24 083	6.0
Frederick	[12]2 074	[12]0.3	[12]D	[12]28.0	[12]4.8	[12]9.2	[12]4.4	[12]14.1	[12]10.2	9 725	151	568	25 275	8.4
Giles	205	0.8	D	38.6	D	8.5	2.5	D	13.3	4 150	245	530	7 923	2.5
Gloucester	311	0.2	D	3.8	5.8	12.9	5.2	11.2	29.0	5 925	161	503	15 087	4.1
Goochland	314	0.6	D	4.0	D	4.6	D	D	16.2	3 180	175	170	7 262	10.8
Grayson	89	4.6	28.1	23.7	2.0	6.7	6.3	D	26.6	4 545	275	528	9 486	4.0
Greene	144	0.8	D	D	D	8.1	3.3	D	19.2	2 300	137	204	6 606	10.4
Greensville	[13]301	[13]0.9	[13]D	[13]28.1	[13]D	[13]6.3	[13]D	[13]13.7	[13]23.3	2 075	179	268	3 912	3.9
Halifax	473	1.6	D	28.5	2.5	7.7	3.4	12.4	15.9	9 215	252	1 740	17 149	1.2
Hanover	1 682	0.3	D	10.0	7.1	8.6	5.6	8.4	11.3	13 570	144	614	35 032	8.8
Henrico	8 534	0.1	12.7	7.2	12.4	7.6	24.0	9.7	7.1	42 055	155	2 300	119 230	5.9
Henry	[14]1 054	[14]0.4	[14]D	[14]31.8	[14]D	[14]9.9	[14]3.5	[14]D	[14]14.2	14 430	253	1 055	26 313	1.5
Highland	22	12.3	D	5.3	D	4.5	6.2	D	20.0	670	268	37	1 833	0.6
Isle of Wight	542	0.7	D	50.1	D	3.8	2.8	D	9.5	5 635	177	555	12 958	7.4
James City County	[15]1 577	[15]0.0	[15]D	[15]D	[15]7.0	[15]7.5	[15]10.0	[15]7.9	[15]22.3	10 385	194	277	23 754	14.4
King and Queen	54	-0.5	22.2	12.5	D	4.3	D	D	36.1	1 285	195	144	3 092	2.7
King George	731	0.0	3.5	1.2	23.8	1.6	1.5	1.1	60.8	2 130	117	171	7 400	8.5
King William	161	0.9	D	35.9	D	7.7	5.1	D	15.6	2 450	173	183	5 484	5.7
Lancaster	172	0.4	11.9	3.0	9.0	10.3	11.4	D	10.8	3 885	322	213	6 650	2.3
Lee	209	1.7	22.0	6.4	3.3	8.4	3.4	10.8	34.7	6 795	286	1 900	11 302	1.9
Loudoun	6 305	0.1	13.7	4.1	33.0	5.5	4.1	3.8	15.0	14 495	65	762	80 067	28.8

1. Covers mining, construction, and manufacturing.　2. Per 1,000 resident population estimated as of July 1 of the year shown.　4. Charlottesville included with Albemarle County.　5. Covington included with Alleghany County.　6. Staunton and Waynesboro included with Augusta County.　7. Bedford City included with Bedford County.　8. Lynchburg included with Campbell County.　9. Galax included with Carroll County.　10. Petersburg and Colonial Heights included with Dinwiddie County.　11. Fairfax City and Falls Church included with Fairfax County.　12. Winchester included with Frederick County.　13. Emporia included with Greensville County.　14. Martinsville included with Henry County.　15. Williamsburg included with James City County.

Table B. States and Counties — Housing, Labor Force, and Employment

	Housing units, 2000								Civilian labor force, 2003				Civilian employment,[6] 2000		
	Occupied units										Unemployment			Percent	
			Owner-occupied			Renter-occupied									
				Median owner cost as a percent of income											
STATE County	Total	Percent	Median value[1]	With a mortgage	Without a mortgage[2]	Median rent[3]	Median rent as a percent of income	Substandard units[4] (percent)	Total	Percent change, 2002–2003	Total	Rate[5]	Total	Management, professional and related occupations	Production, transportation, and material moving occupations
	89	90	91	92	93	94	95	96	97	98	99	100	101	102	103
VERMONT—Cont'd															
Chittenden	56 452	66.1	139 000	22.1	12.3	662	27.5	2.0	93 983	0.1	3 367	3.6	80 787	43.8	10.5
Essex	2 602	79.7	68 700	20.2	15.1	420	25.2	3.3	2 950	0.8	212	7.2	2 964	22.9	29.7
Franklin	16 765	75.0	99 300	22.3	14.3	539	24.2	2.1	25 808	0.1	1 345	5.2	23 065	30.6	19.6
Grand Isle	2 761	81.3	127 600	23.5	15.2	619	25.3	2.0	4 048	0.5	254	6.3	3 519	33.9	13.4
Lamoille	9 221	70.8	114 900	23.4	13.7	543	26.2	2.6	13 045	1.9	782	6.0	12 371	35.0	11.5
Orange	10 936	78.1	94 300	22.6	13.8	511	22.8	3.1	16 658	1.7	642	3.9	14 718	33.2	15.1
Orleans	10 446	74.1	78 800	21.6	15.2	420	26.7	2.1	13 507	2.8	1 031	7.6	12 018	28.9	20.0
Rutland	25 678	69.8	96 000	22.9	14.2	517	27.1	1.6	32 287	-0.2	1 770	5.5	31 629	30.6	16.6
Washington	23 659	68.5	102 500	22.0	14.4	519	25.5	1.9	34 256	0.2	1 628	4.8	31 276	39.2	10.3
Windham	18 375	67.9	109 500	22.7	14.3	552	25.6	2.4	23 292	-2.0	874	3.8	23 301	34.1	14.4
Windsor	24 162	71.5	108 500	22.9	14.4	539	25.8	1.8	32 735	2.6	1 227	3.7	29 354	36.8	13.3
VIRGINIA	2 699 173	68.1	125 400	21.4	9.9	650	24.5	3.9	3 773 263	1.1	153 522	4.1	3 412 647	38.2	12.5
Accomack	15 299	75.0	79 300	22.1	12.0	446	23.3	5.1	16 148	-0.1	809	5.0	16 618	24.2	20.0
Albemarle	31 876	65.8	161 100	20.4	9.9	712	25.7	3.0	38 864	0.8	1 041	2.7	39 584	51.9	6.2
Alleghany	6 990	79.0	NA	NA	NA	NA	NA	2.0	8 519	0.1	351	4.1	7 275	23.1	27.5
Amelia	4 240	82.0	92 400	20.9	9.9	480	20.2	4.2	5 461	-1.2	227	4.2	5 566	20.8	18.2
Amherst	11 941	78.1	88 800	19.6	9.9	427	21.4	2.9	15 042	-1.6	758	5.0	14 634	24.9	20.7
Appomattox	5 322	81.0	81 600	19.4	9.9	437	21.7	2.2	5 327	2.6	417	7.8	6 404	21.9	25.8
Arlington	86 352	43.3	262 400	19.7	9.9	897	23.3	8.4	116 043	1.3	2 620	2.3	114 040	61.3	3.4
Augusta	24 818	83.2	110 900	20.4	9.9	506	21.6	2.3	33 182	-0.5	1 020	3.1	32 962	25.6	23.1
Bath	2 053	79.8	79 700	18.8	9.9	367	14.5	2.6	2 554	3.1	136	5.3	2 506	24.4	14.6
Bedford	23 838	86.6	127 000	20.2	9.9	444	18.4	1.9	31 538	-1.6	1 265	4.0	30 426	29.3	18.0
Bland	2 568	86.1	71 500	18.4	9.9	349	16.4	2.1	3 583	-0.1	141	3.9	2 693	25.9	25.2
Botetourt	11 700	87.7	130 500	19.8	9.9	475	23.0	1.8	17 361	-2.3	490	2.8	15 719	30.3	15.6
Brunswick	6 277	77.7	73 000	20.8	10.4	349	19.0	5.9	8 194	0.1	533	6.5	6 467	24.3	21.5
Buchanan	10 464	82.9	55 400	22.8	9.9	336	30.3	2.5	7 728	-0.5	617	8.0	8 024	24.8	17.9
Buckingham	5 324	77.9	74 900	21.6	9.9	370	23.8	4.5	6 436	2.2	256	4.0	5 800	20.9	20.9
Campbell	20 639	77.3	96 900	19.0	9.9	427	22.0	2.3	26 287	-1.9	1 407	5.4	25 095	25.8	23.2
Caroline	8 021	82.0	88 900	22.1	9.9	587	23.9	5.8	10 903	-11.8	520	4.8	10 484	23.8	18.7
Carroll	12 186	81.7	68 900	19.7	9.9	366	22.4	3.4	13 529	0.4	922	6.8	13 702	19.9	31.9
Charles City County	2 670	84.9	86 700	20.4	10.2	420	14.8	4.4	3 760	-0.2	209	5.6	3 436	20.8	28.6
Charlotte	4 951	77.4	72 700	21.6	10.3	339	21.2	6.7	6 338	2.7	413	6.5	5 176	23.1	29.0
Chesterfield	93 772	80.9	120 500	20.1	9.9	717	23.9	1.9	148 849	0.0	4 834	3.2	135 700	39.5	11.0
Clarke	4 942	75.5	139 500	22.0	9.9	625	21.7	1.3	6 746	1.8	180	2.7	6 563	34.3	11.7
Craig	2 060	81.4	85 400	22.0	9.9	404	21.1	4.6	2 504	11.6	81	3.2	2 375	24.4	18.7
Culpeper	12 141	70.5	123 300	21.9	10.1	603	24.1	4.6	18 019	2.2	647	3.6	16 285	27.7	14.3
Cumberland	3 528	77.2	79 300	22.2	9.9	456	27.1	3.5	4 156	2.1	144	3.5	4 044	21.9	16.8
Dickenson	6 732	82.1	55 900	23.1	9.9	347	27.6	3.2	5 632	1.5	817	14.5	5 138	16.6	17.7
Dinwiddie	9 107	79.2	86 900	21.4	9.9	566	24.5	4.2	11 565	0.0	481	4.2	11 452	25.3	21.6
Essex	3 995	77.2	98 700	21.0	9.9	539	21.6	4.5	4 598	2.0	324	7.0	4 824	27.5	19.4
Fairfax	350 714	71.0	233 300	20.5	9.9	998	23.4	5.8	567 995	1.3	14 413	2.5	522 398	55.7	4.6
Fauquier	19 842	76.2	162 700	21.4	10.1	705	23.7	3.1	30 763	1.8	799	2.6	28 622	39.5	8.3
Floyd	5 791	81.8	79 700	20.9	9.9	407	21.8	4.1	7 041	6.4	241	3.4	6 612	23.3	22.9
Fluvanna	7 387	85.3	111 300	21.9	9.9	669	21.7	2.4	10 427	1.0	318	3.0	9 812	33.3	10.3
Franklin	18 963	81.2	105 000	21.0	9.9	395	20.8	2.4	24 747	0.6	1 187	4.8	22 944	24.4	22.5
Frederick	22 097	80.3	118 300	21.1	9.9	620	22.5	2.5	36 117	2.0	1 211	3.4	30 930	29.9	18.5
Giles	6 994	79.0	69 200	18.7	9.9	375	20.8	1.7	8 538	6.0	452	5.3	7 367	24.7	24.4
Gloucester	13 127	81.4	111 600	21.7	9.9	527	23.7	2.6	18 837	1.9	530	2.8	16 703	31.3	12.6
Goochland	6 158	86.7	149 800	21.0	9.9	589	23.9	2.5	8 915	-0.1	293	3.3	8 502	35.9	9.8
Grayson	7 259	81.3	65 800	18.5	9.9	318	21.1	3.9	7 866	-0.6	582	7.4	7 899	19.4	35.3
Greene	5 574	81.5	111 400	20.6	9.9	622	23.8	2.7	8 249	1.6	356	4.3	8 085	31.5	13.2
Greensville	3 375	78.3	69 000	19.4	9.9	395	18.5	3.5	5 657	-0.4	251	4.4	3 796	20.8	25.1
Halifax	15 018	76.0	73 300	20.4	10.3	360	21.8	5.9	18 383	-2.0	2 171	11.8	15 078	23.4	29.5
Hanover	31 121	84.3	143 300	20.8	9.9	686	24.8	1.6	50 403	-0.2	1 379	2.7	45 165	38.5	9.9
Henrico	108 121	65.7	121 300	21.0	9.9	676	23.7	2.4	150 656	0.0	5 531	3.7	138 815	40.2	9.9
Henry	23 910	76.9	75 500	19.2	9.9	389	21.6	2.7	26 098	0.3	3 650	14.0	26 838	18.9	34.5
Highland	1 131	83.7	83 700	25.0	9.9	339	20.2	3.3	1 237	-1.7	43	3.5	1 117	29.4	14.9
Isle of Wight	11 319	80.9	129 300	21.9	9.9	502	24.2	2.1	16 488	2.1	554	3.4	14 085	31.3	18.9
James City County	19 003	77.0	167 300	21.6	9.9	703	27.6	1.4	29 189	1.9	726	2.5	21 990	41.1	8.8
King and Queen	2 673	82.3	84 400	20.6	10.5	473	18.7	3.1	2 899	0.0	147	5.1	3 007	22.3	23.0
King George	6 091	71.8	123 200	20.9	9.9	622	21.4	3.3	8 632	2.0	238	2.8	7 851	38.0	13.1
King William	4 846	85.1	100 200	20.6	9.9	550	21.0	3.4	6 573	-0.2	262	4.0	6 694	28.1	16.1
Lancaster	5 004	83.0	131 600	22.7	10.4	508	23.6	4.0	4 985	0.4	294	5.9	4 381	27.6	13.7
Lee	9 706	74.4	56 900	18.9	9.9	341	29.4	3.9	9 990	0.7	574	5.7	8 337	26.3	19.4
Loudoun	59 900	79.4	200 500	22.0	9.9	954	23.7	2.7	119 248	1.1	3 399	2.9	93 258	52.7	5.8

1. Specified owner-occupied units.   2. Median monthly owner costs is often in the minimum category—9.9 percent or less, which is indicated as 9.9 percent.   3. Specified renter-occupied units.   4. Overcrowded or lacking complete plumbing facilities.   5. Percent of civilian labor force.   6. Persons 16 years old and over.

Table B. States and Counties — Nonfarm Employment and Agriculture

STATE County	Private nonfarm establishments, employment and payroll, 2001									Agriculture, 2002			
	Number of establishments	Employment						Annual payroll		Farms			
		Total	Health care and social assistance	Manufacturing	Retail trade	Finance and insurance	Professional, scientific, and technical services	Total (mil dol)	Average per employee (dollars)	Number	Percent with—		Farm operators whose principal occupation is farming (percent)
											Less than 50 acres	500 acres and over	
	104	105	106	107	108	109	110	111	112	113	114	115	116
VERMONT—Cont'd													
Chittenden	5 291	88 625	11 575	19 358	12 089	4 046	5 918	2 900	32 717	473	40.2	7.6	46.9
Essex	130	1 494	D	1 003	78	D	15	37	24 928	98	31.6	12.2	52.0
Franklin	1 056	11 928	2 434	2 976	2 128	297	284	299	25 061	770	25.2	11.8	65.5
Grand Isle	166	D	D	28	140	D	16	D	D	99	35.4	6.1	52.5
Lamoille	954	9 478	1 288	659	1 397	197	216	201	21 156	317	29.7	6.0	47.3
Orange	782	6 366	1 338	1 305	1 057	178	245	156	24 535	680	30.6	4.9	44.7
Orleans	847	7 426	1 366	1 662	1 338	230	124	170	22 886	583	23.8	10.8	67.8
Rutland	2 314	27 785	4 335	4 569	4 297	669	753	713	25 677	623	33.7	9.8	50.1
Washington	2 248	26 341	3 532	3 761	4 049	2 399	994	713	27 079	425	37.9	2.6	49.4
Windham	1 824	22 026	2 527	2 725	2 860	633	577	577	26 205	397	45.8	8.6	47.9
Windsor	2 198	19 974	3 061	2 963	2 868	470	1 187	525	26 271	697	42.9	2.7	44.6
VIRGINIA	176 532	2 943 854	311 022	343 849	399 336	165 930	305 927	102 538	34 831	47 606	35.9	7.5	53.6
Accomack	815	9 013	825	3 263	1 242	231	530	183	20 318	318	46.9	14.5	66.0
Albemarle	1 763	22 062	2 243	1 506	4 114	850	1 323	573	25 960	919	34.4	9.4	50.2
Alleghany	NA	NA	NA	NA	NA	NA	NA	NA	NA	202	28.7	4.5	49.0
Amelia	256	1 750	165	342	222	48	38	38	21 906	456	29.2	9.9	52.6
Amherst	586	7 129	403	1 832	1 298	92	178	182	25 564	460	19.8	8.7	50.7
Appomattox	275	2 855	178	1 044	581	80	52	58	20 436	389	19.3	8.0	51.9
Arlington	5 233	114 282	7 423	507	10 073	2 957	27 296	5 515	48 256	2	100.0	0.0	0.0
Augusta	1 148	17 241	3 065	4 910	1 720	253	309	489	28 345	1 691	39.9	8.3	57.4
Bath	140	776	119	D	114	19	19	24	30 805	124	15.3	21.8	58.1
Bedford	965	8 899	353	2 505	890	194	445	238	26 712	1 289	30.2	4.7	51.2
Bland	93	1 231	40	558	110	17	D	32	26 167	417	23.3	10.8	57.1
Botetourt	599	6 457	232	857	921	170	162	186	28 771	610	34.9	7.4	47.5
Brunswick	314	3 455	170	550	371	61	D	71	20 596	333	27.9	10.5	52.6
Buchanan	562	6 244	828	213	884	229	287	194	31 024	94	37.2	0.0	47.9
Buckingham	213	1 842	343	224	316	32	98	41	22 185	389	27.8	9.3	54.2
Campbell	934	11 921	535	3 013	1 841	247	376	287	24 092	664	19.3	9.8	55.3
Caroline	380	3 041	171	405	714	104	43	68	22 230	237	37.1	12.7	59.9
Carroll	461	4 665	493	1 486	841	D	98	93	19 911	953	30.8	3.3	56.0
Charles City County	135	1 409	D	209	D	D	D	31	22 004	88	45.5	18.2	61.4
Charlotte	247	2 436	163	1 021	293	58	51	51	20 753	535	18.7	9.2	56.4
Chesterfield	5 558	84 265	5 905	10 753	15 536	4 517	3 324	2 550	30 264	214	52.8	4.7	42.5
Clarke	305	3 317	235	1 186	288	81	69	88	26 617	472	43.9	6.4	53.0
Craig	58	331	D	D	66	D	D	6	19 360	228	25.4	9.2	49.6
Culpeper	814	10 530	1 205	1 519	1 916	659	668	323	30 660	669	39.3	8.1	49.2
Cumberland	130	828	D	67	231	D	18	16	19 562	283	21.2	10.6	58.3
Dickenson	283	2 009	372	52	429	64	69	54	27 045	117	32.5	2.6	48.7
Dinwiddie	254	4 684	D	571	356	131	D	123	26 276	361	28.0	10.5	62.3
Essex	331	3 739	556	889	848	164	81	74	19 690	127	22.8	26.0	55.1
Fairfax	25 811	533 482	31 551	12 271	50 699	26 847	136 601	28 836	54 053	151	66.9	0.7	41.1
Fauquier	1 542	14 173	2 180	1 049	2 377	570	1 215	425	29 998	1 344	43.4	6.2	53.6
Floyd	245	1 569	145	295	302	86	53	30	19 015	829	25.2	5.5	60.8
Fluvanna	336	2 137	228	73	249	33	93	48	22 375	328	26.8	6.4	42.4
Franklin	966	10 840	913	3 839	1 798	237	211	247	22 791	1 012	24.2	6.4	57.1
Frederick	1 213	19 731	1 262	4 597	2 876	270	994	518	26 269	720	39.2	5.6	51.8
Giles	323	4 192	426	1 765	746	D	89	119	28 361	407	27.5	6.4	52.6
Gloucester	803	6 424	981	235	1 498	243	271	124	19 290	153	57.5	9.2	41.8
Goochland	453	3 436	318	D	427	D	207	104	30 134	315	42.9	6.7	48.9
Grayson	186	1 519	188	616	156	73	19	34	22 685	939	36.0	6.4	51.8
Greene	279	1 827	171	101	371	29	100	41	22 616	214	28.5	3.7	44.9
Greensville	116	1 796	152	779	106	0	D	40	22 070	113	20.4	18.6	63.7
Halifax	769	12 213	1 311	4 575	1 480	205	128	299	24 478	905	19.7	11.7	58.9
Hanover	2 699	32 651	2 721	4 264	4 610	893	1 102	957	29 305	682	48.2	6.2	53.2
Henrico	7 367	155 149	16 683	11 575	19 444	31 219	8 565	5 530	35 643	185	50.8	4.9	50.8
Henry	849	12 874	534	5 882	1 927	475	127	284	22 044	305	27.2	4.6	49.2
Highland	98	458	15	D	D	D	8	7	16 017	293	10.6	17.4	54.6
Isle of Wight	535	11 080	558	4 644	1 053	142	222	356	32 169	204	35.8	24.5	65.2
James City County	1 039	13 205	913	1 262	2 215	288	897	334	25 323	64	54.7	4.7	50.0
King and Queen	110	707	D	220	69	D	D	15	20 533	154	21.4	14.3	52.6
King George	377	3 850	239	191	416	91	1 451	137	35 477	169	29.0	5.3	53.3
King William	328	3 149	254	999	510	130	96	100	31 614	135	28.1	21.5	45.2
Lancaster	504	3 714	950	108	610	282	142	91	24 373	61	44.3	11.5	54.1
Lee	356	3 621	629	435	615	192	82	89	24 496	1 103	37.4	2.6	47.7
Loudoun	4 724	74 593	4 502	5 466	10 520	1 964	7 752	2 975	39 884	1 516	64.4	4.5	45.1

Table B. States and Counties — **Agriculture**

	Agriculture, 2002 (cont'd)														
STATE County	Land in farms					Value of land and buildings (dollars)		Value of machinery and equipment average per farm (dollars)	Value of products sold				Percent of farms with sales of —		Government payments	
			Acres								Percent from —					
	Acreage (1,000)	Percent change, 1997–2002	Average size of farm	Total irrigated (1,000)	Total cropland (1,000)	Average per farm	Average per acre		Total (mil dol)	Average per farm (dollars)	Crops	Live-stock and poultry products	$10,000 or more	$100,000 or more	Total ($1,000)	Percent of farms
	117	118	119	120	121	122	123	124	125	126	127	128	129	130	131	132
VERMONT—Cont'd																
Chittenden	77	-7.2	162	0	35	335 682	2 466	56 069	28	59 427	36.9	63.1	37.6	14.2	1 234	16.1
Essex	20	-20.0	202	D	8	278 089	1 417	52 340	7	69 283	14.3	85.7	31.6	16.3	281	18.4
Franklin	190	0.0	247	0	98	391 243	1 521	102 269	115	149 915	6.0	94.0	56.4	35.1	6 401	30.9
Grand Isle	16	-23.8	165	0	12	504 156	3 182	101 040	9	93 292	15.9	84.1	39.4	23.2	362	29.3
Lamoille	54	10.2	170	0	18	331 173	2 045	46 418	14	43 319	27.5	72.5	37.2	12.3	705	17.4
Orange	110	12.2	162	0	44	318 322	1 838	41 066	32	47 070	19.0	81.0	34.7	14.0	1 398	15.4
Orleans	132	-8.3	227	D	66	390 921	1 536	84 936	57	98 354	5.7	94.3	51.5	24.5	2 712	24.4
Rutland	121	-4.0	195	0	46	488 173	2 632	56 757	24	38 503	17.2	82.8	33.4	12.5	1 527	20.9
Washington	54	-3.6	127	0	21	302 318	2 384	38 080	15	34 680	26.3	73.7	33.2	7.8	597	11.3
Windham	62	31.9	155	0	18	397 796	2 442	61 718	18	46 150	41.8	58.2	33.2	13.1	854	13.1
Windsor	90	0.0	129	0	29	433 007	3 544	49 394	16	22 723	34.1	65.9	23.8	6.9	395	9.0
VIRGINIA	8 625	4.8	181	99	4 194	490 064	2 675	43 303	2 361	49 593	30.4	69.6	32.7	8.2	54 677	19.3
Accomack	91	-1.1	286	10	73	580 120	1 962	110 795	109	343 184	43.5	56.5	67.3	38.1	964	29.2
Albemarle	177	2.9	193	1	69	788 736	4 446	43 764	19	20 857	35.3	64.7	24.7	3.3	274	8.1
Alleghany	33	6.5	163	0	12	313 802	2 197	35 575	2	9 839	14.4	85.7	16.8	0.5	21	8.4
Amelia	91	16.7	200	1	39	429 855	2 245	33 056	52	113 163	6.5	93.5	31.1	14.0	764	44.7
Amherst	100	7.5	217	0	32	499 862	2 402	31 436	6	13 844	15.9	84.1	26.7	1.5	61	7.6
Appomattox	85	10.4	218	1	39	328 095	1 533	33 498	7	17 177	21.7	78.3	29.0	4.1	256	35.0
Arlington	D	NA	D	0	0	D	D	D	D	D	0.0	0.0	0.0	0.0	0	0.0
Augusta	306	8.5	181	3	140	512 426	2 959	45 365	144	85 106	9.9	90.1	42.1	14.4	2 656	22.4
Bath	52	-10.3	422	0	17	851 934	2 115	34 823	3	20 319	4.0	96.0	28.2	3.2	37	17.7
Bedford	199	2.1	155	1	96	429 657	2 920	38 030	19	15 031	18.4	81.6	24.6	2.5	798	19.5
Bland	94	13.3	226	0	32	319 409	1 452	30 470	9	20 536	5.6	94.4	35.3	4.8	189	24.7
Botetourt	97	6.6	159	0	44	496 590	2 732	35 055	10	16 365	18.5	81.5	25.4	3.3	564	24.4
Brunswick	79	0.0	237	1	31	337 537	1 371	36 071	13	37 935	58.2	41.8	32.4	9.0	386	41.1
Buchanan	9	50.0	97	D	3	D	D	26 643	D	D	D	D	19.1	0.0	0	6.4
Buckingham	81	6.6	209	0	38	403 305	1 905	28 861	20	52 066	9.4	90.6	31.1	8.0	264	26.7
Campbell	139	-1.4	209	1	62	406 057	1 874	44 233	16	23 476	28.5	71.5	27.0	4.1	614	33.3
Caroline	59	7.3	250	2	39	667 381	2 286	69 594	12	48 600	83.3	16.7	30.0	9.7	639	28.7
Carroll	122	10.9	128	1	62	351 796	2 587	40 390	26	27 190	25.3	74.7	34.1	4.3	297	7.9
Charles City County	29	NA	326	1	18	904 640	2 689	85 628	6	71 343	78.4	21.6	25.0	18.2	475	28.4
Charlotte	134	1.5	250	1	52	329 107	1 323	38 751	16	29 542	41.7	58.3	34.4	7.5	352	24.5
Chesterfield	23	15.0	109	1	10	527 546	5 257	45 542	9	40 555	59.0	41.0	18.7	6.5	72	14.0
Clarke	74	4.2	157	0	48	848 149	4 781	38 786	16	33 086	33.8	66.2	32.4	7.6	422	12.3
Craig	48	4.3	212	0	19	418 814	1 902	41 669	4	15 830	14.1	85.9	36.0	1.8	100	28.9
Culpeper	125	8.7	187	1	71	711 009	4 162	46 260	37	54 877	51.3	48.7	30.9	6.0	694	17.3
Cumberland	63	3.3	221	0	23	506 968	2 218	44 544	28	100 016	9.0	91.0	35.3	15.5	405	30.7
Dickenson	12	33.3	101	D	4	146 353	1 556	19 248	1	6 294	28.0	72.0	0.0	0.9	0	3.4
Dinwiddie	92	3.4	256	1	46	426 650	1 635	43 146	15	40 707	64.3	35.7	29.4	10.2	782	36.8
Essex	58	-6.5	459	0	37	866 586	1 911	100 335	8	63 759	95.2	4.8	44.1	22.0	1 025	49.6
Fairfax	10	-16.7	66	0	4	635 657	8 361	37 067	5	35 551	82.1	17.9	19.9	6.6	19	7.3
Fauquier	238	-0.4	177	1	118	1 082 382	6 000	45 803	45	33 810	21.0	79.0	28.3	5.0	829	8.8
Floyd	135	9.8	163	1	58	308 517	2 113	32 136	33	39 567	31.7	68.3	33.8	4.1	481	14.5
Fluvanna	60	1.7	184	0	25	508 452	2 324	44 052	4	12 606	21.7	78.3	21.3	3.0	166	16.8
Franklin	173	8.8	170	1	82	338 976	2 183	47 019	37	36 068	17.3	82.7	30.8	8.9	1 547	21.0
Frederick	113	13.0	156	1	59	489 205	3 676	38 203	22	30 059	67.0	33.0	26.8	5.6	609	6.5
Giles	68	1.5	168	0	25	354 303	2 088	41 748	5	13 123	22.0	78.0	31.4	2.5	53	7.1
Gloucester	26	13.0	168	0	18	536 718	3 296	54 938	5	30 056	82.1	17.9	36.6	9.8	161	15.7
Goochland	52	10.6	166	0	26	574 669	3 001	41 842	6	18 254	25.8	74.2	20.0	4.8	277	14.0
Grayson	151	11.0	160	1	62	448 765	2 618	32 205	28	29 636	24.5	75.5	37.4	6.2	216	8.0
Greene	33	-2.9	152	0	15	560 192	3 875	39 735	6	27 172	14.3	85.7	38.8	3.3	153	29.4
Greensville	42	-27.6	376	1	24	515 163	1 399	91 069	6	49 223	90.3	9.7	40.7	14.2	1 079	42.5
Halifax	222	-2.6	245	3	89	384 446	1 588	43 601	28	30 635	65.2	34.8	37.1	7.4	726	26.3
Hanover	101	3.1	147	2	59	639 513	3 812	43 281	32	46 627	78.4	21.6	27.0	7.2	1 099	16.1
Henrico	28	7.7	152	D	16	586 125	4 021	31 859	8	41 137	88.6	11.4	19.5	5.9	245	13.5
Henry	53	10.4	174	0	22	292 138	1 582	27 782	4	14 705	32.7	67.3	19.7	2.0	74	12.5
Highland	96	5.5	328	D	29	758 308	2 298	40 836	13	43 476	2.9	97.1	53.6	5.8	49	12.6
Isle of Wight	87	-1.1	424	1	57	849 658	1 887	109 000	32	157 147	42.0	58.0	52.5	24.5	1 745	39.2
James City County	9	0.0	140	0	6	695 759	5 167	50 312	2	36 579	86.8	13.2	31.3	7.8	66	26.6
King and Queen	59	15.7	382	1	33	700 221	1 983	58 347	7	45 795	76.0	24.0	41.6	10.4	759	39.0
King George	32	-5.9	189	D	15	539 839	2 867	37 840	3	17 573	78.7	21.2	26.6	2.4	292	32.5
King William	61	8.9	455	2	37	880 107	2 018	101 200	14	106 628	88.2	11.8	43.7	13.3	989	48.9
Lancaster	12	-29.4	204	D	10	476 349	2 493	71 005	2	37 125	96.8	3.1	42.6	13.1	164	47.5
Lee	128	0.8	116	1	57	222 467	1 726	33 109	12	10 986	45.0	55.0	24.8	1.3	233	13.1
Loudoun	165	-10.8	109	4	104	871 905	10 807	38 864	39	25 515	49.4	50.6	24.3	4.0	668	10.4

STATE County	Value of residential construction authorized by building permits, 2003		Wholesale trade, 1997				Retail trade,[1] 1997				Real estate and rental and leasing, 1997			
	New construction ($1,000)	Number of housing units	Number of establishments	Number of employees	Sales (mil dol)	Annual payroll (mil dol)	Number of establishments	Number of employees	Sales (mil dol)	Annual payroll (mil dol)	Number of establishments	Number of employees	Receipts (mil dol)	Annual payroll (mil dol)
	133	134	135	136	137	138	139	140	141	142	143	144	145	146
VERMONT—Cont'd														
Chittenden	94 798	591	303	4 167	1 834.9	140.4	958	11 254	1 863.7	189.6	208	913	118.7	19.4
Essex	1 593	20	3	D	D	D	18	D	D	D	3	10	0.3	0.1
Franklin	38 513	301	49	582	381.6	15.8	237	1 734	324.4	28.6	37	102	7.8	1.3
Grand Isle	7 030	64	7	D	D	D	33	D	D	D	3	3	0.5	0.1
Lamoille	26 917	150	30	270	57.7	8.3	183	1 380	169.6	19.8	25	61	5.8	1.0
Orange	17 316	117	33	D	D	D	109	798	145.8	15.6	19	58	2.6	0.7
Orleans	13 404	126	36	D	D	D	174	1 161	220.4	19.9	18	27	2.7	0.3
Rutland	18 739	138	97	934	218.3	22.0	502	4 344	646.3	66.6	71	243	21.8	4.5
Washington	44 132	314	99	D	D	D	421	3 614	542.4	58.9	66	213	14.0	3.3
Windham	29 465	189	73	1 920	1 244.0	62.5	342	2 950	444.8	50.0	61	210	21.1	3.5
Windsor	46 325	338	87	704	242.9	19.1	372	2 559	415.5	44.7	76	219	17.5	3.7
VIRGINIA	6 876 972	55 936	7 868	106 365	61 046.7	3 784.4	29 032	379 039	62 569.9	6 202.6	6 717	43 976	5 749.2	1 028.4
Accomack	36 984	275	36	250	47.1	5.5	208	1 335	180.5	18.6	31	76	7.8	1.2
Albemarle	146 213	993	64	547	181.6	20.5	314	4 270	718.0	67.4	86	389	38.0	8.2
Alleghany	2 323	29	NA	NA	NA	NA	NA	NA	NA	NA	NA	NA	NA	NA
Amelia	16 517	116	9	167	41.1	4.8	36	226	41.0	4.0	3	6	0.9	0.1
Amherst	14 521	121	18	D	D	D	104	1 082	190.2	18.0	15	49	2.7	0.6
Appomattox	7 651	70	9	50	5.7	0.9	60	536	75.5	8.3	9	17	1.0	0.2
Arlington	900	7	110	1 208	819.8	57.2	665	10 098	1 819.4	188.7	257	3 137	690.6	84.2
Augusta	78 933	622	54	622	153.8	16.8	214	1 925	310.8	29.4	48	200	16.0	4.0
Bath	3 385	30	2	D	D	D	25	105	10.8	1.2	5	9	2.0	0.3
Bedford	102 221	615	34	170	281.9	4.8	92	604	83.9	10.0	28	55	6.9	0.9
Bland	3 491	50	6	D	D	D	18	145	19.8	1.4	NA	NA	NA	NA
Botetourt	39 444	247	34	464	213.9	12.5	81	796	130.2	11.0	17	47	2.6	0.5
Brunswick	5 283	43	7	54	27.6	1.3	60	455	49.6	5.3	4	D	D	D
Buchanan	2 065	25	34	296	140.3	8.7	130	1 018	135.2	13.7	14	32	2.4	0.9
Buckingham	6 596	74	5	16	6.6	0.3	42	254	34.4	3.7	7	D	D	D
Campbell	29 639	201	53	D	D	D	209	2 169	338.0	31.3	33	88	9.1	1.2
Caroline	48 259	365	16	74	27.8	2.0	69	608	118.4	8.5	10	26	2.0	0.3
Carroll	16 722	169	25	164	42.9	3.2	114	957	162.6	13.8	14	42	2.3	0.5
Charles City County	3 911	35	1	D	D	D	6	24	3.3	0.3	5	16	2.7	0.3
Charlotte	4 429	56	10	108	18.4	2.4	46	286	42.2	3.7	3	6	0.2	0.1
Chesterfield	316 637	2 933	372	3 154	1 447.5	116.3	938	15 275	2 412.6	230.7	201	1 151	183.9	27.9
Clarke	22 963	129	13	D	D	D	44	297	44.8	3.7	8	D	D	D
Craig	4 467	36	3	5	0.5	0.1	8	25	3.7	0.3	6	8	0.4	0.1
Culpeper	109 423	749	24	287	122.5	7.6	153	1 812	307.0	28.4	28	84	10.2	2.0
Cumberland	4 716	49	6	22	2.1	0.3	29	230	31.4	3.6	1	D	D	D
Dickenson	2 367	29	6	30	4.7	1.2	71	447	64.2	6.1	2	D	D	D
Dinwiddie	21 785	213	9	D	D	D	44	514	64.5	6.0	4	4	0.9	0.1
Essex	11 761	100	7	46	21.4	1.2	68	787	126.0	12.1	13	44	2.6	0.6
Fairfax	509 259	4 020	1 142	18 462	15 659.4	944.7	3 025	48 037	9 261.0	980.6	1 050	9 310	1 481.0	273.7
Fauquier	131 924	800	45	434	171.6	13.8	223	2 052	353.1	36.6	46	150	14.8	3.0
Floyd	10 808	90	6	18	10.7	0.4	45	364	55.3	4.3	7	8	0.8	0.1
Fluvanna	49 402	330	10	D	D	D	33	196	24.5	2.6	9	D	D	D
Franklin	87 052	476	33	186	85.4	5.2	180	1 707	257.7	23.4	20	99	9.8	1.8
Frederick	118 660	844	82	1 246	302.0	33.2	211	2 574	464.7	46.1	35	160	14.6	3.2
Giles	7 656	65	6	D	D	D	71	563	91.2	8.2	10	18	1.7	0.2
Gloucester	35 824	267	30	360	42.5	5.6	134	1 505	228.1	20.7	33	102	8.1	1.5
Goochland	81 779	286	25	168	72.8	4.9	50	391	72.5	6.7	11	15	2.7	0.4
Grayson	800	9	3	5	0.9	0.1	38	176	33.4	2.3	3	9	0.3	0.1
Greene	23 773	160	5	D	D	D	37	254	33.8	4.1	7	D	D	D
Greensville	2 059	39	10	45	18.4	0.9	26	179	23.0	1.9	4	21	1.1	0.2
Halifax	8 410	80	24	262	76.9	5.3	164	1 570	215.9	20.6	26	74	7.1	1.0
Hanover	128 358	896	240	4 199	3 044.5	150.2	309	4 693	830.0	80.6	72	249	33.0	5.2
Henrico	289 304	2 167	474	7 602	5 902.5	310.0	1 148	19 119	2 974.4	302.4	323	2 167	285.9	54.1
Henry	11 875	88	45	408	136.4	9.8	240	2 263	346.3	30.7	21	67	6.0	1.1
Highland	1 898	19	5	D	D	D	18	36	4.1	0.3	NA	NA	NA	NA
Isle of Wight	44 211	330	28	D	D	D	97	1 049	141.9	12.4	27	141	12.6	2.5
James City County	204 663	997	27	71	27.0	2.2	190	2 064	303.8	31.0	50	517	29.6	8.8
King and Queen	4 234	40	1	D	D	D	9	40	5.2	0.5	1	D	D	D
King George	55 211	428	7	46	7.3	0.9	48	306	53.2	4.8	15	D	D	D
King William	14 289	138	7	D	D	D	58	485	88.8	8.9	5	7	0.7	0.3
Lancaster	15 887	137	26	171	38.4	3.4	89	687	98.5	10.9	14	24	3.1	0.4
Lee	4 752	63	18	171	47.0	1.5	90	578	86.4	7.7	9	16	0.8	0.1
Loudoun	727 621	6 770	177	1 773	1 301.3	70.8	478	6 933	1 282.0	129.0	143	770	241.5	20.9

1. Establishments with payroll.

STATE County	Professional, scientific, and technical services,[1] 1997				Manufacturing, 1997				Accommodation and foodservices, 1997			
	Number of establish-ments	Number of employees	Receipts (mil dol)	Annual payroll (mil dol)	Number of establish-ments	Number of employees	Receipts (mil dol)	Annual payroll (mil dol)	Number of establish-ments	Number of employees	Sales (mil dol)	Annual payroll (mil dol)
	147	148	149	150	151	152	153	154	155	156	157	158
VERMONT—Cont'd												
Chittenden	514	3 854	429.4	157.5	234	14 302	3 942.1	624.0	392	6 211	207.7	61.1
Essex	4	3	0.7	0.3	11	883	86.0	25.7	21	D	D	D
Franklin	50	174	11.7	5.1	68	2 603	546.6	78.8	93	854	25.1	7.1
Grand Isle	9	16	0.9	0.3	NA	NA	NA	NA	21	D	D	D
Lamoille	78	166	11.3	4.3	51	697	85.2	18.0	112	3 415	122.2	36.5
Orange	56	164	12.0	5.0	58	1 220	128.5	29.3	58	626	20.8	6.4
Orleans	39	105	5.9	2.5	45	1 565	138.1	37.2	68	867	23.8	7.4
Rutland	155	580	42.7	19.8	123	4 635	542.2	150.5	234	3 358	108.6	31.7
Washington	191	729	54.3	21.9	152	2 901	446.2	84.7	176	2 200	63.0	20.2
Windham	124	442	29.1	10.8	120	3 473	442.8	99.5	218	3 194	106.1	36.6
Windsor	181	849	71.7	30.1	155	3 300	417.1	103.2	216	2 458	92.6	28.9
VIRGINIA	17 539	212 632	24 151.7	9 729.8	5 986	370 595	83 814.0	11 557.8	12 343	233 639	8 281.2	2 320.7
Accomack	42	476	49.7	16.0	32	3 209	244.5	52.6	100	892	32.9	9.0
Albemarle	178	1 030	80.9	32.2	54	D	D	D	140	3 054	114.8	35.1
Alleghany	NA	NA	NA	NA	NA	NA	NA	NA	NA	NA	NA	NA
Amelia	7	24	0.8	0.3	NA	NA	NA	NA	7	78	2.2	0.6
Amherst	27	80	4.7	2.0	44	1 678	395.1	53.8	44	615	19.3	4.9
Appomattox	10	34	2.3	0.5	18	1 216	112.7	28.5	19	185	5.6	1.5
Arlington	1 197	25 914	3 024.7	1 298.8	57	509	59.5	16.3	473	11 365	617.7	164.6
Augusta	56	280	15.6	6.0	66	5 372	1 312.4	175.1	66	1 112	33.0	10.0
Bath	7	13	1.3	0.2	3	D	D	D	16	81	2.6	0.9
Bedford	53	270	24.5	9.2	45	1 489	262.0	49.7	27	D	D	D
Bland	3	8	0.3	0.1	7	656	85.5	15.8	3	D	D	D
Botetourt	28	101	5.9	2.7	23	1 422	210.4	39.3	34	723	27.6	7.6
Brunswick	13	34	1.5	0.7	19	937	84.3	18.7	12	D	D	D
Buchanan	32	310	9.4	3.4	NA	NA	NA	NA	25	304	9.8	2.6
Buckingham	10	116	4.2	2.0	NA	NA	NA	NA	4	D	D	D
Campbell	51	243	29.5	9.4	62	5 098	1 383.7	123.5	55	D	D	D
Caroline	12	24	1.7	0.5	NA	NA	NA	NA	28	292	11.9	3.2
Carroll	20	64	3.3	1.0	35	2 430	286.3	45.3	41	498	15.6	4.0
Charles City County	2	D	D	D	10	680	62.2	16.0	6	D	D	D
Charlotte	8	33	1.2	0.3	15	1 178	143.6	25.4	13	117	3.1	1.0
Chesterfield	499	2 644	218.8	93.0	164	10 166	2 671.2	412.6	326	6 966	222.5	61.7
Clarke	18	47	4.4	1.5	13	1 167	190.3	33.7	20	D	D	D
Craig	2	D	D	D	NA	NA	NA	NA	4	D	D	D
Culpeper	50	620	46.6	17.0	28	1 484	278.9	45.3	52	629	22.0	5.9
Cumberland	7	14	0.6	0.2	NA	NA	NA	NA	4	19	0.4	0.1
Dickenson	11	65	2.8	1.6	NA	NA	NA	NA	13	99	3.0	0.8
Dinwiddie	7	D	D	D	NA	NA	NA	NA	16	154	5.9	1.3
Essex	17	66	2.9	1.2	18	1 140	119.4	24.8	23	356	12.4	3.8
Fairfax	4 748	88 929	11 813.4	4 743.6	478	13 181	2 594.5	551.9	1 523	31 596	1 368.8	382.6
Fauquier	131	561	53.4	23.7	36	867	107.8	25.7	70	1 415	47.6	13.9
Floyd	13	23	1.8	0.6	22	547	48.0	11.2	14	D	D	D
Fluvanna	22	47	2.3	0.9	NA	NA	NA	NA	9	107	5.0	1.5
Franklin	43	128	7.4	2.2	66	4 677	519.6	113.0	52	560	16.4	4.8
Frederick	50	441	13.1	5.9	69	3 416	741.1	97.0	72	1 317	45.6	12.8
Giles	11	65	2.8	1.6	15	2 731	538.6	90.5	17	187	6.1	1.7
Gloucester	46	172	9.7	3.8	NA	NA	NA	NA	43	686	19.3	5.1
Goochland	30	49	3.4	1.3	NA	NA	NA	NA	15	173	3.9	1.1
Grayson	7	34	0.8	0.4	18	1 085	123.4	25.8	14	65	1.8	0.6
Greene	9	37	4.7	1.7	NA	NA	NA	NA	10	134	4.5	1.3
Greensville	3	D	D	D	5	733	120.3	15.0	14	221	6.6	1.8
Halifax	32	102	5.6	1.9	42	4 707	652.9	113.8	61	773	23.7	5.9
Hanover	194	769	69.7	24.6	150	3 803	579.7	111.8	110	2 053	69.0	19.2
Henrico	726	5 767	519.4	238.5	216	10 857	2 432.3	379.0	458	9 892	350.6	96.8
Henry	29	97	4.5	1.2	70	7 970	858.4	189.1	73	1 105	31.6	8.4
Highland	3	3	0.1	0.0	NA	NA	NA	NA	6	50	1.0	0.3
Isle of Wight	22	145	8.6	4.0	17	4 698	1 546.8	106.6	34	D	D	D
James City County	106	541	40.2	16.7	26	D	D	D	77	1 715	74.6	21.0
King and Queen	1	D	D	D	NA	NA	NA	NA	2	D	D	D
King George	66	1 401	159.2	56.9	NA	NA	NA	NA	18	D	D	D
King William	17	55	2.5	0.9	13	1 114	357.2	56.5	10	136	3.9	1.1
Lancaster	36	117	9.5	4.0	NA	NA	NA	NA	25	452	17.4	6.2
Lee	20	49	2.6	0.8	17	784	70.8	10.8	18	200	5.7	1.5
Loudoun	530	3 624	618.6	187.5	128	3 459	480.8	132.8	212	3 877	154.8	45.8

1. Firms subject to federal tax.

STATE County	Health care and social assistance,[1] 1997				Other services,[1] 1997				Federal funds and grants, 2002–2003 Expenditures (mil dol)			
									Total	Direct payments for individuals[2]		
	Number of establishments	Number of employees	Receipts (mil dol)	Annual payroll (mil dol)	Number of establishments	Number of employees	Receipts (mil dol)	Annual payroll (mil dol)		Social Security and government retirement	Medicare	Food stamps and Supplemental Security Income
	159	160	161	162	163	164	165	166	167	168	169	170
VERMONT—Cont'd												
Chittenden	372	3 978	242.3	105.6	284	1 439	96.3	28.3	1 232.0	251.6	82.3	15.0
Essex	3	D	D	D	4	D	D	D	40.2	18.6	6.2	1.3
Franklin	72	746	32.1	14.4	73	219	13.6	3.7	251.4	83.5	31.2	8.4
Grand Isle	6	D	D	D	5	D	D	D	54.9	15.1	4.8	0.8
Lamoille	49	468	23.5	8.9	53	143	10.1	2.4	104.0	44.0	16.0	3.1
Orange	34	D	D	D	46	134	11.4	2.5	141.5	60.9	20.0	4.3
Orleans	30	390	14.2	7.0	60	131	10.7	2.1	198.3	64.2	22.3	6.3
Rutland	147	1 376	77.7	34.7	132	737	30.3	9.0	374.2	154.3	61.1	12.0
Washington	134	1 062	60.6	27.0	124	354	26.3	5.8	575.9	139.8	44.5	10.1
Windham	103	591	34.1	14.1	84	345	33.9	6.3	231.2	97.5	37.6	7.1
Windsor	92	621	36.5	13.9	114	365	26.9	6.4	379.0	151.2	52.1	6.9
VIRGINIA	12 014	150 797	9 859.6	4 417.9	11 301	68 807	4 397.2	1 360.3	82 454.0	18 936.8	5 067.3	982.7
Accomack	29	160	7.7	2.7	49	133	7.9	1.8	376.9	101.7	38.9	8.5
Albemarle	130	1 393	79.6	35.6	90	572	35.7	12.4	252.3	144.2	55.0	4.6
Alleghany	NA	NA	NA	NA	NA	NA	NA	NA	72.8	32.3	13.9	2.9
Amelia	8	110	3.5	1.8	23	44	2.6	0.6	49.7	27.0	7.0	1.6
Amherst	27	462	16.0	5.5	54	169	9.7	2.6	159.4	74.8	20.9	4.1
Appomattox	15	129	3.9	1.5	19	47	2.8	0.7	59.8	31.5	8.9	1.7
Arlington	321	5 064	393.6	160.4	355	1 996	141.4	40.0	8 836.6	450.3	129.2	14.8
Augusta	70	756	61.4	24.9	62	235	15.3	4.5	214.1	119.7	36.5	4.1
Bath	5	16	1.2	0.6	2	D	D	D	31.3	16.0	7.8	0.4
Bedford	28	224	11.3	5.4	25	111	5.4	1.9	247.2	172.8	33.3	4.9
Bland	7	89	4.4	1.7	5	26	3.6	0.7	34.5	18.8	7.8	0.8
Botetourt	28	280	10.0	4.1	49	175	10.5	2.5	117.2	77.8	19.7	1.5
Brunswick	9	120	4.1	1.9	23	94	3.7	1.2	125.3	49.7	18.3	4.4
Buchanan	35	470	22.1	8.7	40	140	8.8	2.3	270.5	107.5	36.9	14.4
Buckingham	10	332	12.8	5.3	14	34	2.4	0.5	72.1	28.4	12.9	2.8
Campbell	46	330	15.1	5.2	72	321	16.8	5.6	174.1	99.5	26.2	5.2
Caroline	11	118	4.3	1.9	27	130	10.2	2.5	125.9	58.4	18.1	2.9
Carroll	29	435	17.5	8.3	26	100	8.5	1.9	128.8	61.1	24.2	5.2
Charles City County	1	D	D	D	5	22	0.9	0.2	31.6	16.0	5.4	0.9
Charlotte	4	99	3.1	1.2	13	40	1.8	0.4	95.2	41.3	14.7	3.4
Chesterfield	383	4 392	241.1	118.4	342	2 383	175.8	50.1	558.6	358.1	85.7	14.8
Clarke	14	192	6.9	3.6	17	58	3.6	1.2	56.1	32.4	9.1	0.9
Craig	4	D	D	D	2	D	D	D	101.8	12.0	3.5	0.5
Culpeper	43	456	29.6	12.7	40	436	24.5	8.7	156.8	87.0	27.9	4.2
Cumberland	4	58	1.2	0.7	9	25	1.1	0.3	43.9	18.2	5.5	1.5
Dickenson	14	389	24.1	8.2	24	65	4.5	1.1	118.2	60.9	22.2	7.4
Dinwiddie	10	73	4.2	1.9	18	54	3.6	0.6	111.2	53.4	18.0	3.4
Essex	25	274	13.4	4.5	24	63	3.0	0.9	74.5	28.7	14.7	1.5
Fairfax	1 867	19 772	1 643.6	709.8	1 329	9 204	772.7	225.8	14 791.3	2 157.6	270.6	60.3
Fauquier	93	890	46.8	20.4	89	450	30.2	9.3	303.1	152.1	32.8	3.2
Floyd	15	155	5.0	2.2	13	34	2.3	0.4	59.1	33.2	11.7	1.4
Fluvanna	8	72	2.4	1.2	13	48	3.0	0.7	88.4	57.8	14.9	1.4
Franklin	35	503	21.9	9.8	75	224	13.0	3.3	189.5	108.6	32.4	5.1
Frederick	47	766	42.7	23.8	74	367	25.5	7.4	171.9	121.6	21.8	2.8
Giles	24	226	9.2	4.0	28	96	5.7	1.4	94.1	51.0	20.5	2.9
Gloucester	44	552	21.8	10.2	52	247	11.8	3.7	172.5	109.1	25.4	8.4
Goochland	18	100	4.5	2.4	18	43	3.4	0.8	75.2	33.0	9.7	1.1
Grayson	10	71	3.2	1.6	16	87	3.1	1.2	83.9	37.6	16.0	3.6
Greene	7	171	4.5	2.5	22	71	3.3	1.2	51.5	28.4	9.1	1.3
Greensville	4	D	D	D	5	11	1.3	0.3	37.3	12.4	3.7	1.0
Halifax	59	558	33.1	18.0	62	230	11.6	3.1	370.2	246.7	39.3	9.1
Hanover	124	1 273	70.8	35.3	180	1 032	64.0	20.6	329.5	207.1	56.6	3.8
Henrico	565	8 260	559.3	280.5	411	3 156	199.2	64.6	673.8	289.5	164.4	18.8
Henry	48	591	24.8	12.9	62	229	11.2	3.6	220.0	126.9	43.3	11.1
Highland	3	D	D	D	5	16	0.8	0.1	17.0	8.8	3.9	0.2
Isle of Wight	20	218	12.1	6.2	49	194	10.6	3.1	158.7	93.9	24.2	3.6
James City County	66	556	28.4	13.3	43	288	14.1	6.5	123.0	89.5	13.5	4.6
King and Queen	2	D	D	D	8	14	0.9	0.3	34.0	17.1	6.3	0.9
King George	16	188	10.2	3.4	24	91	6.2	1.5	639.2	52.3	9.8	1.8
King William	16	118	4.0	1.8	26	64	5.6	1.2	59.1	30.5	11.4	1.2
Lancaster	37	358	19.5	10.1	26	125	7.3	2.6	98.2	63.6	20.3	1.7
Lee	31	560	37.3	14.1	22	82	3.7	1.0	409.8	71.7	35.0	11.4
Loudoun	245	2 035	140.4	54.9	200	1 341	105.5	32.6	2 293.7	307.5	44.7	5.9

1. Firms subject to federal tax.   2. State totals may include programs not allocated by county.

Table B. States and Counties — **Federal Funds and Local Government Finances**

	Federal funds and grants, 2002–2003 (cont'd)							Local government finances, 2002				
	Expenditures (mil dol) (cont'd)							General revenue				
		Procurement contract awards		Grants[1]							Taxes	
STATE County											Per capita[2] (dollars)	
	Salaries and wages	Defense	Other	Medicaid and other health-related	Nutrition and family welfare	Education	Other	Total (mil dol)	Intergovern-mental (mil dol)	Total (mil dol)	Total	Property
	171	172	173	174	175	176	177	178	179	180	181	182
VERMONT—Cont'd												
Chittenden	144.5	382.8	21.6	159.2	19.9	12.7	111.5	373.2	196.2	111.0	745	694
Essex	3.3	0.0	0.9	6.7	1.5	0.3	0.8	14.6	10.0	3.8	579	559
Franklin	34.7	0.6	9.7	47.9	8.8	1.8	13.0	100.3	68.9	22.9	489	475
Grand Isle	1.2	0.0	26.0	4.2	0.8	0.2	0.9	15.6	9.1	5.3	723	716
Lamoille	4.8	0.0	1.2	20.8	3.3	2.6	4.6	58.6	33.6	17.6	734	724
Orange	6.8	2.3	1.9	24.7	4.3	1.5	10.2	75.0	48.9	21.7	758	756
Orleans	10.5	29.3	4.0	32.2	8.5	2.2	11.0	57.2	39.0	13.5	508	505
Rutland	21.9	4.3	7.1	76.0	11.9	3.3	14.6	162.7	101.8	45.5	720	698
Washington	24.7	5.7	4.5	85.0	52.4	54.1	143.6	140.7	82.5	40.6	690	687
Windham	10.3	0.9	3.2	28.9	9.4	2.2	22.8	117.6	62.3	42.9	970	960
Windsor	73.7	5.7	19.0	43.3	7.9	1.5	14.5	152.5	83.0	49.1	849	837
VIRGINIA	14 755.6	19 493.0	11 345.7	3 056.7	983.9	813.0	3 032.3	X	X	X	X	X
Accomack	46.4	49.8	79.3	30.0	6.4	2.1	7.0	74.1	43.0	26.0	667	484
Albemarle	7.1	0.9	13.4	18.5	2.4	3.8	0.2	201.6	69.4	104.0	1 270	858
Alleghany	1.5	0.0	0.3	9.8	2.2	1.8	6.8	45.6	22.3	14.4	849	713
Amelia	1.5	0.1	0.4	7.4	0.9	0.8	1.4	19.0	11.1	5.5	472	344
Amherst	3.6	0.1	9.6	14.3	1.7	1.8	26.5	55.4	30.8	18.1	564	377
Appomattox	2.9	0.1	0.9	9.3	1.1	0.8	1.5	26.6	16.3	8.2	596	447
Arlington	3 184.6	2 347.7	2 415.2	40.1	12.0	20.5	206.4	1 250.3	308.4	471.2	2 481	1 783
Augusta	7.3	0.1	2.2	18.7	4.5	3.0	11.1	139.6	76.4	44.1	657	436
Bath	2.0	0.7	0.3	3.1	0.4	0.3	-0.1	15.5	3.7	11.0	2 171	1 994
Bedford	7.8	2.7	1.8	13.7	2.8	2.3	3.6	138.0	69.9	43.5	702	585
Bland	1.6	0.1	0.5	4.2	0.5	0.4	-0.6	15.2	7.4	2.7	394	295
Botetourt	3.8	0.0	1.6	6.9	0.9	1.2	2.5	53.6	24.2	24.3	778	599
Brunswick	2.7	17.9	0.7	17.2	2.6	2.5	0.7	32.3	21.1	7.7	424	316
Buchanan	3.6	13.1	2.9	26.6	6.1	2.7	56.1	63.7	37.7	22.6	868	444
Buckingham	1.6	0.3	0.4	17.7	2.1	1.0	4.4	28.1	19.2	7.2	459	352
Campbell	8.2	0.6	1.4	20.8	3.6	3.4	3.2	94.4	51.3	31.5	613	463
Caroline	15.5	11.0	1.5	8.9	2.1	1.8	2.0	44.2	25.0	16.9	745	572
Carroll	3.0	0.1	4.6	21.4	2.3	2.2	3.0	47.6	27.1	14.5	497	362
Charles City County	1.1	-0.2	0.2	4.5	1.0	0.5	1.3	17.8	7.7	5.3	729	622
Charlotte	3.0	0.9	13.2	12.4	2.1	1.0	2.3	25.1	17.5	6.0	494	392
Chesterfield	28.4	14.7	6.1	14.8	7.2	11.6	12.5	658.5	272.0	300.9	1 110	820
Clarke	2.6	0.1	4.8	4.5	0.4	0.5	0.3	26.2	9.3	14.3	1 073	922
Craig	1.3	11.0	70.8	1.7	0.3	0.3	0.0	9.8	5.7	2.7	521	420
Culpeper	8.1	1.5	2.6	15.8	2.7	1.8	3.3	82.9	38.7	34.7	941	662
Cumberland	1.0	4.5	0.2	7.9	3.6	0.6	0.3	17.6	10.4	6.1	683	564
Dickenson	2.2	0.5	1.0	15.7	2.4	1.5	4.0	47.1	25.3	12.8	788	422
Dinwiddie	2.4	6.8	2.0	15.3	2.5	1.4	1.1	51.5	28.7	19.2	777	623
Essex	1.6	13.6	0.6	6.0	0.7	0.7	4.0	21.6	11.7	9.0	901	617
Fairfax	1 222.6	6 555.1	3 772.8	131.1	33.5	42.8	292.3	3 362.1	865.4	1 963.8	1 969	1 540
Fauquier	48.5	17.5	21.6	10.9	3.1	3.1	7.8	161.4	50.8	83.5	1 409	1 113
Floyd	2.7	0.0	0.6	6.7	0.8	0.8	0.2	22.3	13.3	7.5	530	388
Fluvanna	2.5	0.0	0.6	7.9	1.0	0.8	1.1	31.1	16.0	12.2	550	465
Franklin	7.1	0.2	1.4	19.7	3.4	3.1	3.0	81.9	44.7	31.1	641	448
Frederick	4.4	0.2	0.8	10.3	1.9	2.6	1.8	146.5	48.8	69.0	1 096	889
Giles	2.8	0.1	0.8	11.3	1.2	1.1	2.3	33.7	18.3	11.7	686	527
Gloucester	6.1	1.5	2.1	7.0	1.7	1.6	8.3	70.3	37.8	29.6	828	613
Goochland	2.5	0.1	1.8	5.2	0.8	1.1	14.1	44.5	12.7	28.0	1 601	1 371
Grayson	2.2	1.8	0.8	16.1	1.3	1.1	2.4	26.4	18.0	7.0	422	327
Greene	2.2	0.0	1.4	5.7	0.6	0.9	1.5	35.5	18.8	11.0	678	517
Greensville	0.1	0.0	0.0	5.7	2.3	1.0	0.7	33.3	22.0	5.7	493	371
Halifax	5.9	0.1	7.7	46.9	5.9	2.5	1.9	72.9	44.6	21.8	590	385
Hanover	11.0	3.5	4.0	10.6	2.0	2.8	23.3	217.9	92.1	100.0	1 086	812
Henrico	62.9	54.1	11.4	25.9	8.5	9.1	26.9	718.8	259.8	331.2	1 235	843
Henry	4.2	2.4	3.2	19.0	3.8	3.6	2.1	98.0	55.9	33.4	582	343
Highland	0.8	0.0	0.6	2.1	0.2	0.3	0.1	6.0	3.4	2.0	832	713
Isle of Wight	5.6	0.5	1.0	13.2	3.0	1.3	2.6	65.2	26.8	35.3	1 137	899
James City County	2.1	2.6	0.8	6.0	2.6	0.6	0.0	133.2	34.4	80.9	1 573	1 181
King and Queen	2.1	0.0	0.3	2.9	0.9	0.5	0.3	19.4	10.8	4.5	688	572
King George	275.3	283.5	9.3	3.9	0.9	0.8	0.2	45.4	16.2	13.8	784	608
King William	2.1	1.2	1.1	3.8	1.6	0.7	1.9	36.5	16.0	16.7	1 211	1 041
Lancaster	3.0	0.2	1.2	5.5	1.3	0.6	0.1	20.2	6.8	10.2	891	760
Lee	26.4	1.2	207.7	43.2	6.0	2.6	2.6	48.4	32.9	9.6	411	291
Loudoun	308.0	1 429.8	153.7	11.6	5.6	4.1	20.5	695.8	161.7	414.2	2 030	1 593

1. State totals may include programs not allocated by county. 2. Based on the resident population estimated as of July 1 of the year shown.

STATE County	Direct general expenditure Total (mil dol)	Per capita[1] (dollars)	Education	Health and hospitals	Police protection	Public welfare	Highways	Debt outstanding Total (mil dol)	Per capita[1] (dollars)	Government employment, 2002 Federal civilian	Federal military	State and local	Presidential election, 2004 Percent of vote cast — Democratic	Republican	All other
	183	184	185	186	187	188	189	190	191	192	193	194	195	196	197
VERMONT—Cont'd															
Chittenden	361.9	2 430	58.1	0.1	4.7	0.0	5.3	305.2	2 050	1 845	998	12 106	63.9	34.0	2.1
Essex	11.4	1 741	69.1	0.5	0.6	0.1	11.1	3.3	498	68	42	295	42.5	53.0	4.5
Franklin	92.1	1 972	74.4	0.4	1.8	0.0	8.1	66.2	1 418	893	300	2 330	54.9	43.4	1.7
Grand Isle	10.6	1 452	64.1	0.1	0.8	0.0	11.6	5.8	794	24	47	272	55.2	43.1	1.8
Lamoille	62.8	2 624	64.8	1.1	3.4	0.0	9.4	35.1	1 466	78	154	1 461	62.8	35.1	2.1
Orange	75.3	2 624	76.1	0.8	1.0	0.0	10.2	30.0	1 047	96	184	1 888	54.9	43.2	1.8
Orleans	51.5	1 936	74.8	0.2	1.3	0.0	11.3	22.2	833	199	171	1 660	51.8	46.4	1.8
Rutland	144.8	2 290	65.0	0.1	2.9	0.0	8.2	53.6	847	381	408	4 171	51.5	46.7	1.7
Washington	140.0	2 380	64.3	1.2	2.6	0.0	8.8	90.0	1 529	306	425	7 677	61.2	36.7	2.2
Windham	109.8	2 482	67.0	0.6	2.6	0.2	11.4	18.2	412	179	284	2 635	66.7	31.3	2.0
Windsor	144.6	2 500	62.1	0.4	3.3	0.1	10.8	34.4	595	1 320	378	3 428	60.6	37.5	2.0
VIRGINIA	X	X	X	X	X	X	X	X	X	157 936	168 433	493 577	45.3	54.0	0.7
Accomack	74.5	1 911	56.5	1.0	3.2	8.7	1.6	35.5	911	632	358	2 052	41.4	57.9	0.7
Albemarle	204.2	2 493	59.2	3.2	3.9	4.8	0.8	198.1	2 419	[3]1 304	[3]582	[3]25 303	50.7	48.6	0.7
Alleghany	50.4	2 970	54.6	8.5	2.6	6.6	0.0	47.7	2 810	[4]98	[4]61	[4]1 613	44.6	55.1	0.4
Amelia	18.6	1 586	66.9	0.5	5.3	5.6	0.0	15.6	1 336	33	31	514	34.5	64.9	0.6
Amherst	52.3	1 635	61.5	0.3	4.7	5.3	0.0	30.9	968	61	83	2 940	38.4	61.2	0.5
Appomattox	29.4	2 144	72.4	0.3	5.9	3.9	0.3	18.0	1 312	60	36	780	32.7	65.7	1.6
Arlington	1 439.3	7 578	24.8	1.9	2.5	3.6	2.5	2 311.3	12 169	28 048	14 906	10 170	67.8	31.5	0.7
Augusta	139.4	2 078	53.7	8.0	3.2	5.0	0.5	87.5	1 306	[5]329	[5]291	[5]8 673	23.7	74.5	1.9
Bath	13.4	2 639	60.2	1.2	5.7	4.5	0.0	8.5	1 669	45	13	376	36.4	63.0	0.6
Bedford	140.2	2 266	51.4	10.1	3.0	8.0	0.0	106.2	1 717	[6]160	[6]177	[6]2 652	28.9	70.0	1.1
Bland	10.2	1 481	60.8	0.8	5.2	7.9	0.0	4.0	575	19	18	562	29.6	68.6	1.9
Botetourt	51.7	1 654	64.1	1.3	6.0	4.3	1.2	43.5	1 391	58	82	1 164	30.4	68.9	0.7
Brunswick	30.9	1 694	64.2	0.5	4.9	7.0	0.2	4.4	242	54	48	1 457	58.7	41.2	0.1
Buchanan	60.9	2 343	57.3	0.7	3.5	9.4	7.5	30.7	1 182	58	68	1 744	54.3	45.4	0.3
Buckingham	29.9	1 897	59.6	0.8	3.5	6.8	0.0	12.1	766	33	41	1 047	46.3	52.6	1.1
Campbell	88.6	1 721	64.7	2.0	4.4	5.4	0.5	78.7	1 528	[7]554	[7]321	[7]7 046	29.9	69.1	1.0
Caroline	41.2	1 822	63.8	0.3	0.7	6.2	0.0	19.0	838	291	78	1 105	49.1	50.4	0.5
Carroll	43.7	1 500	65.2	0.5	5.0	6.8	0.6	44.7	1 535	[8]106	[8]93	[8]2 461	31.9	67.6	0.5
Charles City County	16.6	2 292	53.2	1.0	3.2	7.5	0.0	23.8	3 289	15	19	347	62.7	36.5	0.8
Charlotte	23.6	1 932	64.1	0.4	4.9	8.9	0.2	4.1	333	55	32	837	41.0	58.4	0.6
Chesterfield	672.6	2 481	58.1	4.1	5.2	4.0	0.2	552.8	2 039	3 140	713	15 133	36.9	62.7	0.4
Clarke	24.3	1 825	62.9	1.6	5.2	3.4	0.8	8.2	615	33	35	661	41.5	57.5	1.0
Craig	9.3	1 821	52.0	0.5	7.1	8.3	0.0	4.5	884	28	13	217	34.5	65.1	0.5
Culpeper	85.6	2 321	59.9	0.3	7.9	8.3	1.4	47.6	1 290	109	96	2 748	35.0	64.5	0.5
Cumberland	17.0	1 912	59.8	0.8	5.2	6.7	0.0	14.4	1 614	13	23	404	41.7	57.6	0.7
Dickenson	45.4	2 800	45.4	6.2	4.3	8.2	3.2	12.4	765	43	42	919	50.8	48.5	0.7
Dinwiddie	47.2	1 907	64.0	0.5	6.2	5.6	0.1	36.9	1 493	[9]308	[9]199	[9]9 925	42.2	57.2	0.7
Essex	24.9	2 494	54.1	0.0	4.5	4.2	0.0	15.0	1 506	29	26	438	46.2	53.1	0.7
Fairfax	3 428.9	3 437	50.7	4.2	4.3	5.8	1.5	3 258.8	3 267	[10]36 442	[10]6 341	[10]54 116	52.9	46.6	0.5
Fauquier	137.6	2 322	57.6	0.0	7.0	3.6	1.5	71.0	1 198	193	154	3 044	35.5	64.0	0.4
Floyd	25.0	1 755	59.7	0.9	2.9	6.4	0.0	9.8	684	51	37	505	37.0	62.0	1.0
Fluvanna	29.1	1 310	72.5	1.1	3.4	5.0	0.0	6.7	300	39	58	1 074	40.3	59.0	0.7
Franklin	79.1	1 631	66.8	0.2	5.0	6.6	0.7	39.1	807	112	126	1 755	36.0	63.3	0.7
Frederick	135.3	2 149	69.5	0.1	4.3	2.6	0.1	88.0	1 397	[11]421	[11]233	[11]4 732	31.1	68.1	0.8
Giles	32.8	1 922	55.0	1.1	6.4	4.4	2.0	26.8	1 566	44	45	843	40.6	57.6	1.7
Gloucester	71.2	1 990	63.2	0.6	4.9	3.5	0.0	61.2	1 713	102	92	2 387	31.4	68.1	0.6
Goochland	44.5	2 540	57.8	9.3	2.8	3.2	1.4	30.2	1 726	31	46	1 321	34.8	64.7	0.6
Grayson	26.4	1 588	66.5	0.9	5.5	9.1	0.2	1.8	108	35	43	662	34.0	65.2	0.7
Greene	34.8	2 140	59.8	1.0	4.3	7.3	0.0	15.8	973	42	42	759	32.3	65.9	1.8
Greensville	34.8	3 006	55.7	0.3	5.5	8.1	0.4	27.3	2 357	[12]32	[12]45	[12]1 859	60.1	39.6	0.3
Halifax	75.7	2 047	62.1	0.3	6.7	5.4	1.1	26.3	713	106	96	2 037	42.5	57.1	0.4
Hanover	219.6	2 386	58.2	5.7	5.8	2.1	1.6	154.9	1 683	158	240	4 605	28.1	71.4	0.5
Henrico	749.2	2 793	45.7	3.0	6.0	2.6	4.5	689.3	2 569	612	699	13 318	45.9	53.7	0.4
Henry	91.9	1 601	65.7	0.4	4.5	7.2	0.0	22.7	396	[13]148	[13]190	[13]3 843	42.0	57.0	1.0
Highland	5.6	2 327	55.4	0.1	9.7	7.9	1.9	2.1	850	12	0	152	34.4	64.7	0.9
Isle of Wight	59.4	1 912	59.9	0.8	5.0	5.5	2.5	7.1	228	102	81	1 421	37.0	62.6	0.4
James City County	81.8	1 591	0.0	13.3	6.0	5.6	0.0	167.3	3 253	[14]229	[14]511	[14]8 172	38.4	61.1	0.5
King and Queen	20.2	3 073	44.7	1.6	3.0	4.2	0.0	11.8	1 799	17	179	282	34.5	64.9	0.6
King George	42.8	2 424	49.1	0.6	5.1	4.0	0.0	48.6	2 755	3 518	1 018	764	35.5	64.1	0.5
King William	35.6	2 578	58.8	0.4	5.7	3.3	0.7	21.4	1 551	21	36	696	46.0	53.0	1.0
Lancaster	21.4	1 866	51.5	0.2	5.2	7.4	0.0	29.7	2 591	42	30	487	39.8	59.8	0.4
Lee	46.0	1 967	65.2	0.4	4.3	9.5	2.7	9.5	405	430	61	1 310	41.0	58.0	1.0
Loudoun	726.6	3 561	59.4	2.9	3.7	3.6	2.0	712.6	3 492	4 183	542	10 940	43.4	56.1	0.5

1. Based on the resident population estimated as of July 1 of the year shown.   3. Charlottesville included with Albemarle County.   4. Clifton Forge and Covington included with Alleghany County.   5. Staunton and Waynesboro included with Augusta County.   6. Bedford City included with Bedford County.   7. Lynchburg included with Campbell County.   8. Galax included with Carroll County.   9. Petersburg and Colonial Heights included with Dinwiddie County.   10. Fairfax City and Falls Church included with Fairfax County.   11. Winchester included with Frederick County.   12. Emporia included with Greensville County.   13. Martinsville included with Henry County.   14. Williamsburg included with James City County.

					Population and population characteristics, 2003												
								Race alone or in combination, not Hispanic or Latino (percent)					Age (percent)					
STATE/ County code	CBSA code[1]	County Type[2]	STATE County	Land area,[3] (sq km) 2000	Total persons	Rank	Per square kilometer	White	Black	Am. Indian, Alaska Native	Asian and Pacific Islander[4]	Percent Hispanic or Latino[4]	Under 5 years	5 to 17 years	18 to 24 years	25 to 34 years	35 to 44 years	45 to 54 years
				1	2	3	4	5	6	7	8	9	10	11	12	13	14	15
			VIRGINIA—Cont'd															
51 109	40060	1	Louisa	1 288	28 031	1 462	21.8	78.0	20.8	0.8	0.3	0.8	5.9	17.5	8.9	10.9	16.5	14.8
51 111	...	9	Lunenburg	1 118	13 167	2 226	11.8	58.9	38.6	0.3	0.2	2.3	4.6	15.5	9.6	11.8	15.9	15.1
51 113	...	8	Madison	832	13 036	2 236	15.7	87.3	11.4	0.2	0.7	1.0	5.1	17.5	9.1	10.7	15.3	15.4
51 115	47260	1	Mathews	222	9 216	2 507	41.5	88.0	10.7	0.2	0.2	0.9	3.7	14.7	7.5	9.1	13.7	14.6
51 117	...	7	Mecklenburg	1 616	32 551	1 348	20.1	59.8	38.3	0.4	0.4	1.5	5.3	15.6	8.3	11.5	14.8	14.5
51 119	...	8	Middlesex	337	10 211	2 426	30.3	79.4	19.3	0.3	0.1	0.9	3.8	14.8	7.6	8.6	13.2	14.5
51 121	13980	3	Montgomery	1 005	85 614	621	85.2	90.6	3.9	0.5	4.5	1.6	4.5	11.8	26.9	15.5	11.0	10.4
51 125	16820	3	Nelson	1 223	14 942	2 104	12.2	83.4	14.4	0.6	0.3	2.2	5.2	15.6	8.5	9.6	14.1	16.8
51 127	40060	1	New Kent	543	14 843	2 112	27.3	81.6	15.3	1.5	0.7	1.5	5.1	18.3	9.0	11.4	17.5	16.8
51 131	...	9	Northampton	537	13 285	2 216	24.7	53.6	41.7	0.2	0.3	4.5	6.5	16.9	9.0	8.9	13.2	14.0
51 133	...	9	Northumberland	498	12 742	2 258	25.6	72.7	25.9	0.2	0.3	1.2	4.7	13.6	7.0	7.6	12.0	12.7
51 135	...	6	Nottoway	815	15 603	2 057	19.1	57.1	40.3	0.2	0.5	2.2	5.4	16.9	9.5	12.6	15.3	13.5
51 137	...	6	Orange	885	28 018	1 465	31.7	84.2	14.0	0.4	0.4	1.6	5.7	16.4	8.5	11.2	15.1	14.0
51 139	...	8	Page	806	23 589	1 632	29.3	96.1	2.4	0.4	0.3	1.2	5.5	16.7	9.0	12.0	15.0	14.1
51 141	...	8	Patrick	1 251	19 182	1 854	15.3	91.3	6.4	0.3	0.2	2.1	4.8	15.6	7.8	12.3	14.8	14.6
51 143	19260	3	Pittsylvania	2 514	61 640	805	24.5	74.7	23.7	0.3	0.2	1.4	5.8	16.5	8.9	11.0	16.0	15.9
51 145	40060	1	Powhatan	677	24 649	1 592	36.4	83.5	15.3	0.5	0.2	1.0	5.5	16.9	9.1	14.1	18.6	15.2
51 147	...	6	Prince Edward	914	20 180	1 794	22.1	62.4	36.0	0.3	0.8	1.0	5.3	14.6	24.6	9.8	11.7	11.6
51 149	40060	1	Prince George	688	34 305	1 298	49.9	59.9	33.1	0.7	2.5	5.2	5.8	18.3	14.6	15.3	16.5	13.6
51 153	47900	1	Prince William	875	325 324	182	371.8	61.0	20.0	0.9	6.4	14.5	8.6	21.3	10.0	15.0	17.3	13.1
51 155	13980	3	Pulaski	830	35 030	1 274	42.2	92.4	6.1	0.6	0.5	1.1	5.4	15.0	8.0	13.4	14.5	15.8
51 157	...	8	Rappahannock	690	7 110	2 676	10.3	92.8	5.5	0.4	0.4	1.5	5.4	16.4	7.4	9.5	15.4	18.0
51 159	...	9	Richmond	496	9 006	2 521	18.2	63.5	33.7	0.1	0.4	2.5	4.2	12.5	9.8	13.9	17.6	14.0
51 161	40220	2	Roanoke	650	87 329	615	134.4	92.8	4.3	0.4	1.9	1.3	5.6	16.8	8.2	10.6	14.9	16.7
51 163	...	6	Rockbridge	1 553	20 973	1 753	13.5	95.5	3.3	0.6	0.6	0.6	4.8	16.1	9.1	11.0	14.5	15.1
51 165	25500	3	Rockingham	2 204	69 365	729	31.5	94.4	1.7	0.3	0.5	3.6	6.1	18.0	10.0	11.7	15.4	14.7
51 167	...	6	Russell	1 229	28 861	1 435	23.5	98.3	1.0	0.2	0.1	0.6	5.2	15.7	9.5	12.8	15.1	16.6
51 169	28700	3	Scott	1 390	23 005	1 664	16.6	98.5	0.8	0.5	0.1	0.5	4.9	15.1	8.3	11.9	14.2	14.9
51 171	...	6	Shenandoah	1 327	37 199	1 202	28.0	94.6	1.4	0.5	0.5	3.6	5.9	16.2	8.3	11.3	14.4	14.1
51 173	...	6	Smyth	1 171	32 700	1 344	27.9	96.9	2.0	0.4	0.3	0.9	5.4	16.1	8.8	12.2	14.7	14.8
51 175	...	6	Southampton	1 553	17 453	1 938	11.2	57.1	41.7	0.3	0.2	0.8	5.5	16.4	10.7	11.3	16.3	14.9
51 177	47900	1	Spotsylvania	1 038	107 838	511	103.9	80.7	14.3	0.8	2.1	3.9	7.0	21.2	9.8	13.5	16.5	13.4
51 179	47900	1	Stafford	700	111 021	500	158.6	77.8	15.9	1.1	2.8	4.9	6.9	22.4	10.6	12.9	17.6	13.4
51 181	47260	1	Surry	723	7 009	2 685	9.7	47.5	51.3	0.3	0.2	0.9	6.0	18.3	9.1	9.4	16.8	15.2
51 183	40060	1	Sussex	1 271	11 956	2 294	9.4	36.5	62.1	0.3	0.2	1.1	5.2	14.0	10.2	15.4	17.5	15.1
51 185	14140	7	Tazewell	1 346	44 362	1 037	33.0	96.3	2.3	0.4	0.8	0.6	4.9	15.6	9.6	11.5	13.9	16.6
51 187	47900	1	Warren	553	33 871	1 309	61.2	92.7	5.2	0.7	0.8	1.8	6.4	18.7	9.3	11.8	16.7	14.0
51 191	28700	3	Washington	1 458	51 405	915	35.3	97.6	1.4	0.4	0.4	0.7	5.1	15.0	9.6	11.8	15.1	15.6
51 193	...	7	Westmoreland	594	16 946	1 960	28.5	64.9	31.3	0.4	0.4	3.4	5.5	16.8	8.2	9.2	13.4	14.2
51 195	...	7	Wise	1 046	41 803	1 086	40.0	93.6	5.2	0.4	0.4	0.9	5.8	15.6	12.0	13.8	14.4	15.2
51 197	...	6	Wythe	1 200	27 941	1 467	23.3	95.9	2.9	0.3	0.4	0.8	5.8	15.7	8.6	13.1	14.6	14.9
51 199	47260	1	York	274	60 948	810	222.4	79.7	13.8	0.8	4.6	3.0	5.6	21.2	9.1	10.4	17.6	15.2
	...		Independent Cities															
51 510	47900	1	Alexandria City	39	128 923	438	3 305.7	58.7	21.8	0.6	6.0	14.5	8.3	10.0	5.0	24.3	19.3	14.3
51 515	31340	3	Bedford City	18	6 339	2 741	352.2	75.2	23.5	0.2	0.7	0.7	8.5	15.3	8.0	11.0	14.1	12.0
51 520	28700	3	Bristol City	33	17 206	1 946	521.4	92.4	5.9	0.7	0.6	1.2	5.5	15.0	9.3	11.6	13.0	13.4
51 530	...	6	Buena Vista City	18	6 320	2 743	351.1	92.7	5.7	0.3	0.5	1.0	6.7	16.1	10.8	11.9	13.2	13.0
51 540	16820	3	Charlottesville City	27	39 162	1 150	1 450.4	70.8	23.7	0.4	4.2	2.6	5.8	11.3	22.1	17.0	12.1	10.7
51 550	47260	1	Chesapeake City	882	210 834	277	239.0	66.0	30.0	0.8	2.5	2.2	6.8	20.8	9.7	12.0	17.5	14.4
51 570	40060	1	Colonial Heights City	19	17 286	1 944	909.8	87.3	8.2	0.2	3.2	1.7	5.8	16.8	9.3	11.6	13.8	13.3
51 580	...	6	Covington City	15	6 284	2 748	418.9	84.0	14.7	0.5	0.8	0.7	6.6	15.8	8.5	12.6	13.3	12.8
51 590	19260	3	Danville City	112	46 988	981	419.5	52.7	45.1	0.4	0.7	1.6	6.2	16.7	9.0	10.9	13.1	14.3
51 595	...	6	Emporia City	18	5 656	2 798	314.2	40.7	56.2	0.0	0.6	2.4	6.8	18.2	9.5	11.1	13.8	11.7
51 600	47900	1	Fairfax City	16	22 031	1 703	1 376.9	68.2	5.3	0.5	14.2	13.2	5.9	14.5	8.0	15.6	16.9	14.1
51 610	47900	1	Falls Church City	5	10 485	2 401	2 097.0	80.5	4.5	0.4	7.9	8.1	4.9	16.8	6.5	12.1	16.9	19.6
51 620	...	6	Franklin City	22	8 254	2 578	375.2	43.6	54.8	0.1	0.8	0.8	6.6	18.1	9.1	9.6	13.1	14.1
51 630	47900	1	Fredericksburg City	27	20 189	1 793	747.7	71.9	21.4	0.5	1.7	5.8	7.8	12.2	20.2	15.1	11.6	10.6
51 640	...	6	Galax City	21	6 655	2 719	316.9	80.0	6.7	0.4	0.8	12.4	7.6	15.9	8.4	11.8	12.7	12.9
51 650	47260	1	Hampton City	134	146 878	390	1 096.1	47.5	48.2	1.1	2.6	2.8	6.6	17.6	12.4	13.8	16.7	13.1
51 660	25500	3	Harrisonburg City	45	41 170	1 104	914.9	79.7	6.5	0.3	4.4	10.9	5.4	10.2	36.4	12.6	9.2	8.0
51 670	40060	1	Hopewell City	27	22 391	1 686	829.3	59.7	36.4	0.8	1.3	3.1	8.0	19.4	9.5	13.4	14.0	12.2
51 678	...	6	Lexington City	6	7 076	2 681	1 179.3	85.8	10.3	0.3	2.4	1.6	3.4	7.4	41.0	8.0	6.7	8.3
51 680	31340	3	Lynchburg City	128	65 113	761	508.7	66.6	30.9	0.8	1.6	1.5	6.2	15.9	15.6	11.8	12.1	12.6
51 683	47900	1	Manassas City	26	37 166	1 205	1 429.5	62.8	13.5	0.6	4.2	20.4	9.0	20.7	10.0	15.8	17.7	13.0

1. CBSA = Core Based Statistical Area. See Appendix A for explanation. See Appendix B for list of metropolitan areas with component counties. 2. County type code from the Economic Research Service of USDA Rural-Urban Continuum Codes. See Appendix A for definition. 3. Dry land or land partially or temporarily covered by water. 4. Hispanic or Latino persons may be of any race.

STATE County	Population, 2003 (cont'd) Age (percent) (cont'd)				Population — change and components of change, 1990–2003							Households, 2000				
	55 to 64 years	65 to 74 years	75 years and over	Percent female	Total persons 1990	Total persons 2000	1990–2000	2000–2003	Births	Deaths	Net migration	Number	Percent change, 1990–2000	Persons per house-hold	Female family house-holder[1]	One person
	16	17	18	19	20	21	22	23	24	25	26	27	28	29	30	31
VIRGINIA—Cont'd																
Louisa	10.7	7.4	5.4	50.8	20 325	25 627	26.1	9.4	1 056	861	2 173	9 945	33.9	2.56	10.8	22.1
Lunenburg	10.8	8.6	8.3	46.5	11 419	13 146	15.1	0.2	369	450	118	4 998	13.0	2.39	13.3	28.7
Madison	11.4	8.2	6.9	51.4	11 949	12 520	4.8	4.1	408	409	514	4 739	14.4	2.60	8.8	21.8
Mathews	15.2	11.6	10.3	51.6	8 348	9 207	10.3	0.1	218	456	251	3 932	11.4	2.32	7.9	24.9
Mecklenburg	11.7	10.2	8.2	50.5	29 241	32 380	10.7	0.5	1 167	1 322	358	12 951	15.2	2.38	14.1	27.2
Middlesex	15.4	11.9	10.1	51.8	8 653	9 932	14.8	2.8	246	493	518	4 253	20.5	2.27	9.5	27.1
Montgomery	7.4	4.6	3.9	47.2	73 913	83 629	13.1	2.4	2 520	1 748	1 243	30 997	18.1	2.40	7.6	25.5
Nelson	12.9	9.4	7.4	51.2	12 778	14 445	13.0	3.4	497	518	514	5 887	22.5	2.42	10.7	25.0
New Kent	10.7	5.5	3.6	49.3	10 466	13 462	28.6	10.3	466	357	1 238	4 925	32.5	2.65	9.0	16.6
Northampton	10.8	10.9	9.7	52.9	13 061	13 093	0.2	1.5	604	683	285	5 321	3.7	2.39	17.5	29.4
Northumberland	15.6	14.8	11.7	52.5	10 524	12 259	16.5	3.9	399	555	615	5 470	21.8	2.24	8.7	27.7
Nottoway	10.1	8.6	8.5	48.4	14 993	15 725	4.9	-0.8	567	663	-13	5 664	8.0	2.48	15.4	27.6
Orange	11.1	9.5	7.4	51.3	21 421	25 881	20.8	8.3	996	1 015	2 135	10 150	28.0	2.50	10.7	22.1
Page	11.4	8.6	7.2	50.8	21 690	23 177	6.9	1.8	871	798	351	9 305	15.5	2.46	10.5	24.4
Patrick	12.9	9.2	8.1	50.8	17 473	19 407	11.1	-1.2	509	625	-77	8 141	17.8	2.36	8.6	25.8
Pittsylvania	12.1	7.8	6.5	51.0	55 672	61 745	10.9	-0.2	2 318	2 046	-277	24 684	19.7	2.49	11.7	23.4
Powhatan	10.1	5.2	3.3	45.8	15 328	22 377	46.0	10.2	859	477	1 838	7 258	55.4	2.74	8.1	14.6
Prince Edward	8.1	6.6	7.1	50.8	17 320	19 720	13.9	2.3	758	725	433	6 561	22.1	2.43	14.9	28.9
Prince George	8.4	4.2	2.8	45.9	27 390	33 047	20.7	3.8	1 266	479	422	10 159	23.1	2.76	12.2	17.2
Prince William	7.4	3.1	1.8	49.9	214 954	280 813	30.6	15.9	17 542	3 742	30 010	94 570	35.7	2.94	11.2	17.1
Pulaski	12.6	8.2	7.2	50.4	34 496	35 127	1.8	-0.3	1 186	1 357	104	14 643	9.7	2.32	10.5	27.0
Rappahannock	14.3	8.4	5.7	50.8	6 622	6 983	5.5	1.8	252	235	112	2 788	11.7	2.50	7.1	23.4
Richmond	10.2	8.5	9.4	43.5	7 273	8 809	21.1	2.2	270	352	301	2 937	11.0	2.40	11.8	28.3
Roanoke	11.5	8.0	7.5	52.3	79 278	85 778	8.2	1.8	3 248	2 697	1 146	34 686	14.3	2.41	8.5	25.1
Rockbridge	12.6	9.4	6.9	49.9	18 350	20 808	13.4	0.8	595	569	159	8 486	17.8	2.43	9.5	23.9
Rockingham	10.1	7.3	6.5	50.5	57 482	67 725	17.8	2.4	2 713	1 806	686	25 355	22.2	2.61	7.9	21.2
Russell	11.9	8.1	6.1	51.3	28 667	30 308	5.7	-4.8	979	1 089	-257	11 789	10.8	2.44	10.1	23.1
Scott	12.8	9.6	8.6	51.6	23 204	23 403	0.9	-1.7	721	979	-116	9 795	9.2	2.35	9.0	26.1
Shenandoah	11.8	9.0	7.9	51.3	31 636	35 075	10.9	6.1	1 450	1 200	1 862	14 296	14.8	2.42	9.3	25.1
Smyth	11.8	9.1	7.6	51.5	32 370	33 081	2.2	-1.2	1 156	1 333	-164	13 493	10.3	2.37	11.2	26.0
Southampton	11.0	7.6	6.6	47.0	17 022	17 482	2.7	-0.2	654	628	-26	6 279	4.5	2.53	13.5	24.9
Spotsylvania	8.0	4.3	3.3	50.4	57 397	90 395	57.5	19.3	4 705	1 737	13 972	31 308	65.3	2.87	9.9	16.4
Stafford	7.3	3.2	2.2	49.6	62 255	92 446	48.5	20.1	4 642	1 390	14 801	30 187	55.5	3.01	9.3	13.8
Surry	11.3	7.4	6.1	51.9	6 145	6 829	11.1	2.6	256	222	150	2 619	14.7	2.61	14.1	23.7
Sussex	9.9	7.3	6.6	42.8	10 248	12 504	22.0	-4.4	401	455	-492	4 126	8.7	2.41	18.9	28.2
Tazewell	12.0	8.5	7.2	52.0	45 960	44 598	-3.0	-0.5	1 408	1 783	170	18 277	5.6	2.40	10.8	25.2
Warren	10.0	6.4	5.4	50.7	26 142	31 584	20.8	7.2	1 392	869	1 729	12 087	22.4	2.57	10.0	24.0
Washington	12.1	8.6	7.0	51.4	45 887	51 103	11.4	0.6	1 695	1 662	327	21 056	20.4	2.36	8.7	25.8
Westmoreland	13.5	10.2	8.6	51.9	15 480	16 718	8.0	1.4	593	685	333	6 846	13.0	2.43	13.5	26.9
Wise	9.9	7.1	6.4	49.1	39 573	40 123	1.4	4.2	1 629	1 524	-486	16 013	10.3	2.44	12.0	25.5
Wythe	11.4	8.5	7.2	52.1	25 471	27 599	8.4	1.2	1 031	1 112	452	11 511	16.8	2.36	10.5	26.3
York	10.1	5.7	3.7	50.7	42 434	56 297	32.7	8.3	2 099	1 071	3 572	20 000	38.2	2.78	9.4	16.7
Independent Cities																
Alexandria City	9.3	4.7	4.9	51.7	111 183	128 283	15.4	0.5	7 940	2 676	-4 922	61 889	16.2	2.04	9.2	43.4
Bedford City	8.3	9.9	12.4	52.6	6 176	6 299	2.0	0.6	420	450	89	2 519	1.8	2.26	17.2	33.0
Bristol City	10.9	10.2	10.9	54.5	18 426	17 367	-5.7	-0.9	623	874	99	7 678	1.1	2.18	13.6	34.3
Buena Vista City	11.1	9.0	8.1	53.3	6 406	6 349	-0.9	-0.5	273	231	-68	2 547	5.9	2.38	14.3	27.6
Charlottesville City	6.9	5.8	6.1	53.8	40 470	45 049	11.3	-13.1	1 667	1 129	-1 503	16 851	5.3	2.27	13.1	34.9
Chesapeake City	8.4	5.1	3.9	51.4	151 982	199 184	31.1	5.8	9 115	4 530	7 095	69 900	34.5	2.79	14.0	18.0
Colonial Heights City	10.5	9.2	9.5	52.9	16 064	16 897	5.2	2.3	684	698	437	7 027	10.4	2.37	13.0	27.6
Covington City	11.3	9.2	10.6	52.0	7 352	6 303	-14.3	-0.3	263	320	43	2 835	-5.4	2.22	12.5	34.0
Danville City	10.4	9.4	10.6	54.5	53 056	48 411	-8.8	-2.9	1 987	2 452	-949	20 607	-5.1	2.27	19.6	33.9
Emporia City	9.5	8.7	11.5	54.6	5 556	5 665	2.0	-0.2	270	378	113	2 226	9.6	2.43	21.0	32.2
Fairfax City	10.8	6.9	6.3	51.1	19 945	21 498	7.8	2.5	803	587	321	8 035	9.1	2.61	9.3	23.4
Falls Church City	11.1	5.2	7.5	51.3	9 464	10 377	9.6	1.0	320	231	32	4 471	6.6	2.31	8.6	33.8
Franklin City	10.8	8.9	9.4	54.9	8 392	8 346	-0.5	-1.1	403	476	-13	3 384	12.6	2.39	21.9	28.9
Fredericksburg City	7.5	6.4	6.9	55.3	19 033	19 279	1.3	4.7	1 181	739	519	8 102	8.8	2.09	13.1	39.2
Galax City	10.5	9.8	10.0	52.1	6 745	6 837	1.4	-2.7	365	374	-174	2 950	7.3	2.27	12.7	34.2
Hampton City	8.5	5.9	4.8	50.4	133 773	146 437	9.5	0.3	6 480	3 703	-2 291	53 887	8.5	2.49	16.4	26.6
Harrisonburg City	5.2	4.1	5.0	52.7	30 707	40 468	31.8	1.7	1 543	896	98	13 133	27.4	2.53	9.3	28.3
Hopewell City	9.2	7.4	7.2	53.3	23 101	22 354	-3.2	0.2	1 206	909	-167	9 055	0.5	2.43	21.2	27.6
Lexington City	7.1	7.6	8.9	44.4	6 959	6 867	-1.3	3.0	181	254	295	2 232	2.8	2.06	8.8	41.0
Lynchburg City	8.8	7.4	9.3	54.2	66 120	65 269	-1.3	-0.2	2 770	2 753	-92	25 477	1.3	2.30	16.0	32.7
Manassas City	7.0	3.5	2.4	49.0	27 757	35 135	26.6	5.8	2 239	602	447	11 757	24.0	2.92	11.3	21.1

1. No spouse present.

STATE County	Births, average 1999–2001 Total	Rate[1]	Deaths, average 1999–2001 Number Total	Infant[2]	Rate Total[1]	Infant[3]	Physicians,[4] 2000 Number	Rate[5]	Hospitals,[4] 1998 Number	Beds Number	Rate[5]	Medicare enrollees, 2003	Serious crimes known to police,[6] 2002 Total Number	Rate[7]
	32	33	34	35	36	37	38	39	40	41	42	43	44	45
VIRGINIA—Cont'd														
Louisa............	321	12.5	251	3	9.7	D	9	35	0	0	0	4 198	405	1 622
Lunenburg.........	106	8.0	140	1	10.6	D	5	38	0	0	0	1 994	153	1 129
Madison............	117	9.3	128	1	10.2	D	9	72	0	0	0	1 891	63	488
Mathews............	65	7.0	133	0	14.4	D	7	76	0	0	0	2 188	100	1 054
Mecklenburg......	352	10.9	406	3	12.5	D	32	99	1	138	444	7 018	791	2 371
Middlesex..........	81	8.2	147	0	14.8	D	14	141	0	0	0	2 523	162	1 583
Montgomery.......	809	9.6	509	5	6.1	D	89	106	1	90	119	8 864	1 582	1 836
Nelson.............	158	11.0	160	1	11.0	D	13	90	0	0	0	3 206	266	1 787
New Kent..........	143	10.6	101	1	7.5	D	4	30	0	0	0	2 040	282	2 033
Northampton......	176	13.4	197	1	15.0	D	41	313	1	158	1 243	2 943	292	2 164
Northumberland...	114	9.3	180	1	14.7	D	9	73	0	0	0	3 102	276	2 194
Nottoway..........	181	11.5	220	3	14.0	D	22	140	0	0	0	3 121	287	1 828
Orange............	322	12.4	297	1	11.4	D	25	97	0	0	0	6 066	352	1 320
Page..............	265	11.4	245	3	10.6	D	32	138	1	54	235	4 265	323	1 353
Patrick...........	178	9.2	206	1	10.6	D	15	77	1	61	331	3 846	434	2 170
Pittsylvania......	752	12.2	609	5	9.9	D	11	18	0	0	0	8 404	535	841
Powhatan..........	264	11.8	135	2	6.0	D	8	36	0	0	0	2 680	243	1 054
Prince Edward.....	220	11.1	219	4	11.1	D	36	183	1	108	568	3 651	271	1 334
Prince George.....	388	11.7	160	4	4.8	D	19	57	0	0	0	2 356	571	1 677
Prince William....	5 057	17.8	1 068	31	3.8	6.1	203	72	1	153	59	14 670	8 336	2 881
Pulaski...........	389	11.1	420	1	12.0	D	52	148	1	77	223	6 525	927	2 561
Rappahannock......	94	13.3	68	1	9.5	D	2	29	0	0	0	1 405	46	639
Richmond..........	83	9.3	114	1	12.9	D	2	23	0	0	0	1 656	43	474
Roanoke...........	919	10.7	839	5	9.8	D	159	185	0	0	0	6 477	1 550	1 754
Rockbridge........	183	8.8	175	2	8.5	D	8	38	0	0	0	2 390	92	452
Rockingham........	876	12.9	543	4	8.0	D	25	37	0	0	0	9 241	571	818
Russell...........	309	10.4	324	2	10.9	D	21	69	1	78	269	5 649	480	1 537
Scott.............	242	10.4	311	3	13.3	D	11	47	0	0	0	5 318	446	1 850
Shenandoah........	409	11.6	379	1	10.8	D	30	86	1	129	372	7 043	498	1 378
Smyth.............	360	10.9	396	2	12.0	D	53	160	1	176	537	7 159	655	1 922
Southampton.......	182	10.4	183	1	10.5	D	11	63	0	0	0	2 297	302	1 880
Spotsylvania......	1 306	14.3	526	7	5.7	5.6	53	59	0	0	0	5 195	2 218	2 381
Stafford..........	1 349	14.4	403	5	4.3	D	36	39	0	0	0	4 951	1 862	1 955
Surry.............	75	10.9	64	0	9.3	D	0	0	0	0	0	1 007	159	2 260
Sussex............	127	10.2	138	1	11.1	D	4	32	0	0	0	2 253	291	2 259
Tazewell..........	461	10.3	550	6	12.3	D	93	209	2	243	520	10 924	1 377	2 997
Warren............	431	13.6	284	1	9.0	D	30	95	1	87	289	4 343	831	2 553
Washington........	547	10.7	522	3	10.2	D	65	127	1	138	281	8 709	1 176	2 233
Westmoreland......	184	11.0	220	4	13.2	D	8	48	0	0	0	3 415	256	1 486
Wise..............	499	12.2	466	4	11.4	D	38	95	2	127	329	8 846	822	1 988
Wythe.............	331	12.0	340	3	12.3	D	31	112	1	106	404	6 030	637	2 355
York..............	668	11.8	320	4	5.6	D	59	105	0	0	0	8 910	1 186	2 045
Independent Cities............														
Alexandria City.....	2 560	19.9	841	15	6.5	5.9	409	319	1	347	293	19 696	5 233	3 959
Bedford City........	115	18.1	130	0	20.6	D	17	270	1	166	2 628	3 535	233	3 590
Bristol City........	175	10.0	253	1	14.5	D	6	35	0	0	0	5 623	765	4 275
Buena Vista City....	89	14.0	81	0	12.8	D	3	47	0	0	0	1 528	87	1 330
Charlottesville City.	510	11.5	359	6	8.1	D	515	1 143	2	734	1 920	7 515	1 745	3 759
Chesapeake City.....	2 792	14.0	1 367	29	6.8	10.5	377	189	1	260	130	21 879	8 773	4 275
Colonial Heights City	205	12.1	208	0	12.3	D	46	272	0	0	0	3 940	969	5 566
Covington City......	99	15.5	105	0	16.5	D	6	95	0	0	0	3 057	296	4 558
Danville City.......	574	11.9	757	8	15.7	13.9	155	320	1	336	661	13 256	2 266	4 543
Emporia City........	78	13.8	112	0	19.8	D	16	282	1	182	3 325	1 954	457	7 829
Fairfax City........	356	16.4	181	4	8.4	D	67	312	0	0	0	10 471	NA	NA
Falls Church City...	245	23.3	81	0	7.7	D	79	761	1	656	6 533	2 976	453	4 237
Franklin City.......	114	13.6	141	0	16.8	D	25	300	1	208	2 395	2 462	436	5 070
Fredericksburg City..	386	19.7	226	3	11.6	D	147	762	1	288	1 328	9 124	984	4 953
Galax City..........	115	17.0	121	0	17.8	D	40	585	1	149	2 171	3 423	307	4 358
Hampton City........	1 991	13.6	1 117	19	7.7	9.5	240	164	1	289	211	18 581	6 235	4 132
Harrisonburg City...	448	11.2	279	3	6.9	D	116	287	1	264	790	4 509	1 242	2 979
Hopewell City.......	352	15.8	275	3	12.3	D	49	219	1	140	621	4 133	1 106	4 802
Lexington City......	70	10.1	92	0	13.3	D	24	349	1	98	1 332	2 827	123	1 738
Lynchburg City......	824	12.7	841	9	12.9	10.9	214	328	2	529	808	14 966	2 648	3 937
Manassas City.......	722	20.5	190	4	5.4	D	19	54	1	152	430	6 482	1 261	3 483

1. Per 1,000 estimated resident population.   2. Deaths of infants under 1 year old.   3. Deaths of infants under 1 year old per 1,000 live births.   4. Data subject to copyright.   5. Per 100,000 resident population as of July 1 of the year shown.   6. Data for serious crimes have not been adjusted for underreporting; this may affect comparability between geographic areas and over time.   7. Per 100,000 population estimated by the FBI.

Table B. States and Counties — Crime, Education, Money Income, and Poverty

STATE County	Serious crimes known to police,[1] 2002 (cont'd) Rate[2] Violent	Property	Education: Enrollment[3] Total	Percent private	Attainment[4] (percent) High school graduate or less	Bachelor's degree or more	Local government expenditures,[5] 2000–2001 Total current expenditures (mil dol)	Current expenditures per student (dollars)	Money income, 1999 Per capita income[6] (dollars)	Households Median income Dollars	Percent change, 1989–1999 (constant 1999 dollars)	Percent with income of $100,000 or more	Percent below poverty level, 1999 Persons	Households	Families	Families with children
	46	47	48	49	50	51	52	53	54	55	56	57	58	59	60	61
VIRGINIA—Cont'd																
Louisa	108	1 514	5 754	10.1	63.1	14.0	27.4	6 490	19 479	39 402	12.1	7.6	10.2	11.2	7.1	10.7
Lunenburg	170	960	2 602	9.3	68.2	9.2	13.0	7 076	14 951	27 899	6.7	2.8	20.0	19.0	14.9	23.0
Madison	31	457	2 711	20.3	61.2	19.4	12.7	6 887	18 636	39 856	11.3	7.4	9.6	8.8	6.9	10.6
Mathews	63	991	1 744	10.5	53.0	19.2	8.2	6 311	23 610	43 222	17.3	7.1	6.0	6.8	4.3	7.4
Mecklenburg	276	2 095	6 732	6.8	66.3	12.1	31.3	6 273	17 171	31 380	11.7	5.6	15.5	16.1	11.6	16.4
Middlesex	29	1 554	1 929	9.0	56.2	18.9	8.8	6 516	22 708	36 875	9.1	8.4	13.0	12.1	9.7	14.4
Montgomery	137	1 699	37 615	5.2	41.0	35.9	65.3	7 162	17 077	32 330	4.9	7.3	23.2	22.1	8.8	12.8
Nelson	128	1 660	2 892	10.8	57.6	20.8	15.2	7 401	22 230	36 769	15.4	9.4	12.1	12.5	8.5	12.3
New Kent	144	1 889	3 026	7.4	54.1	16.3	14.5	6 199	22 893	53 595	3.9	12.7	4.9	4.8	3.4	5.3
Northampton	215	1 949	3 230	12.8	61.8	15.7	16.4	7 456	16 591	28 276	16.2	5.9	20.5	19.5	15.8	24.2
Northumberland	191	2 003	2 114	13.0	55.0	21.7	10.5	7 087	22 917	38 129	23.0	10.3	12.3	14.2	8.1	15.5
Nottoway	185	1 643	3 322	8.5	67.4	11.1	16.7	6 667	15 552	30 866	5.5	4.5	20.1	18.1	15.5	21.9
Orange	109	1 211	5 494	13.7	58.8	18.5	27.6	6 990	21 107	42 889	0.4	9.5	9.2	10.2	7.1	11.2
Page	113	1 239	4 692	7.3	74.9	9.8	21.7	6 130	16 321	33 359	-0.6	4.4	12.5	13.4	10.1	14.2
Patrick	175	1 995	3 770	6.6	72.2	8.6	17.0	6 428	15 574	28 705	-4.1	3.1	13.4	15.2	9.6	12.5
Pittsylvania	130	710	13 858	12.5	67.9	9.3	56.0	6 062	16 991	35 153	2.3	4.0	11.8	13.6	8.6	13.1
Powhatan	56	998	5 353	14.4	53.3	19.1	24.5	6 859	24 104	53 992	7.5	15.4	5.7	5.7	4.8	8.0
Prince Edward	212	1 122	7 257	19.3	58.5	19.2	16.8	6 416	14 510	31 301	8.9	5.8	18.9	18.1	14.6	21.6
Prince George	126	1 551	8 720	11.5	50.1	19.4	35.8	6 113	20 196	49 877	6.6	11.3	8.0	8.0	6.5	8.6
Prince William	223	2 658	83 548	16.5	36.1	31.5	379.8	6 950	25 641	65 960	-0.6	23.6	4.4	3.9	3.3	4.6
Pulaski	152	2 409	6 831	4.0	59.6	12.5	33.1	6 604	18 973	33 873	8.1	4.7	13.1	13.7	10.6	15.9
Rappahannock	83	556	1 453	19.8	54.1	22.9	7.7	7 578	23 863	45 943	5.6	12.8	7.6	6.9	5.2	7.4
Richmond	99	375	1 743	11.0	71.3	9.9	7.8	6 240	16 675	33 026	0.0	6.0	15.4	17.0	11.9	17.3
Roanoke	258	1 496	20 624	18.4	42.1	28.2	96.5	6 958	24 637	47 689	-3.8	12.1	4.5	4.8	2.7	3.9
Rockbridge	44	408	4 498	15.4	61.4	18.7	21.4	7 002	18 356	36 035	7.5	5.9	9.6	10.9	6.6	9.5
Rockingham	57	761	16 106	18.1	63.0	17.6	70.5	6 587	18 795	40 748	2.3	6.9	8.2	8.4	5.3	8.0
Russell	45	1 492	6 333	6.3	69.9	9.4	26.3	6 161	14 863	26 834	11.9	3.7	16.3	17.6	13.0	18.1
Scott	145	1 704	4 540	3.0	71.9	8.3	24.0	6 535	15 073	27 339	10.9	2.9	16.8	19.3	13.0	16.5
Shenandoah	89	1 289	7 076	13.5	63.1	14.7	36.3	6 660	19 755	39 173	9.9	6.6	8.2	8.7	5.8	10.9
Smyth	153	1 769	6 761	4.8	66.9	10.6	32.9	6 347	16 105	30 083	7.1	4.0	13.3	14.3	9.9	14.1
Southampton	100	1 780	3 963	14.8	63.3	11.7	19.7	6 893	16 930	33 995	-4.1	4.4	14.6	15.1	11.7	18.1
Spotsylvania	172	2 210	25 581	14.3	47.8	22.8	124.6	6 600	22 536	57 525	3.6	15.1	4.7	4.4	3.4	5.0
Stafford	173	1 782	29 156	12.5	39.3	29.6	137.4	6 503	24 762	66 809	11.3	20.9	3.5	3.4	2.4	3.0
Surry	355	1 904	1 750	16.6	62.6	12.8	12.3	9 992	16 682	37 558	11.7	3.9	10.8	12.8	9.7	12.7
Sussex	241	2 018	2 713	16.4	75.6	10.0	13.1	9 167	14 670	31 007	10.8	5.0	16.1	17.9	12.8	20.2
Tazewell	220	2 777	9 714	9.4	65.0	11.0	45.7	6 424	15 282	27 304	3.3	4.2	15.3	16.2	11.7	16.7
Warren	154	2 400	7 320	20.4	62.2	15.0	29.0	5 871	19 841	42 422	1.7	8.0	8.5	9.0	6.0	8.1
Washington	188	2 045	10 974	14.8	58.9	16.1	49.3	6 696	18 350	32 742	9.9	5.8	10.9	12.5	8.1	12.6
Westmoreland	145	1 341	3 622	8.9	64.1	13.3	16.5	6 276	19 473	35 797	8.1	5.7	14.7	15.3	11.2	19.0
Wise	213	1 775	9 569	5.7	67.4	10.8	46.5	6 696	14 271	26 149	-0.7	3.3	20.0	19.9	16.1	24.5
Wythe	144	2 211	5 862	7.3	62.2	12.1	26.2	6 057	17 639	32 235	14.4	4.9	11.0	13.9	8.5	12.6
York	193	1 852	17 228	14.9	29.5	37.4	73.6	6 260	24 560	57 956	6.9	18.5	3.5	3.6	2.7	3.8
Independent Cities																
Alexandria City	317	3 642	26 509	27.9	25.8	54.3	126.2	11 305	37 645	56 054	0.6	22.0	8.9	6.8	6.8	11.2
Bedford City	493	3 097	1 345	11.0	61.5	15.2	[7]NA	[7]NA	15 423	28 792	-6.0	5.2	19.7	19.4	15.4	28.0
Bristol City	525	3 750	3 677	19.7	56.9	17.0	17.7	7 360	17 311	27 389	6.0	3.9	16.2	16.4	13.2	22.8
Buena Vista City	245	1 085	1 501	17.8	65.0	10.5	7.6	6 779	16 377	32 410	0.8	4.2	10.4	12.5	8.2	14.4
Charlottesville City	754	3 005	20 969	6.4	40.6	40.8	44.4	9 962	16 973	31 007	-4.6	7.6	25.9	22.7	12.0	19.2
Chesapeake City	665	3 610	58 385	15.3	42.6	24.7	257.6	6 842	20 949	50 743	5.7	11.9	7.3	7.4	6.1	8.7
Colonial Heights City	253	5 313	3 884	9.8	50.8	19.0	21.0	7 572	23 659	43 224	-6.7	9.7	5.5	5.6	3.4	5.2
Covington City	277	4 281	1 202	5.5	68.4	6.4	[8]NA	[8]NA	16 758	30 325	7.9	2.2	12.9	12.0	10.7	17.1
Danville City	603	3 939	11 141	11.3	62.2	13.9	52.2	6 812	17 151	26 900	-1.9	5.2	20.0	18.6	15.9	27.1
Emporia City	1 131	6 699	1 282	7.3	70.3	14.2	[9]NA	[9]NA	15 377	30 333	7.5	4.1	16.0	14.4	11.4	16.9
Fairfax City	NA	NA	5 133	19.3	30.9	45.7	[10]NA	[10]NA	31 247	67 642	-1.1	26.5	5.7	4.6	2.4	3.6
Falls Church City	150	4 087	2 683	27.2	16.7	63.7	19.3	11 207	41 051	74 924	9.3	35.9	4.2	3.9	2.8	4.5
Franklin City	314	4 756	2 175	11.2	56.6	16.4	11.5	8 067	18 573	31 687	15.9	9.4	19.8	18.9	16.8	29.7
Fredericksburg City	720	4 234	6 061	9.9	47.3	30.5	20.2	9 414	21 527	34 585	-3.3	10.1	15.5	13.1	10.4	16.7
Galax City	355	4 003	1 446	3.0	68.2	11.1	8.3	6 279	17 447	28 236	3.7	4.4	18.6	20.4	13.6	22.3
Hampton City	403	3 729	42 305	22.4	42.5	21.8	155.4	6 670	19 774	39 532	-2.4	6.9	11.3	10.8	8.8	13.4
Harrisonburg City	309	2 669	19 504	9.3	46.7	31.2	30.0	8 017	14 898	29 949	-11.9	7.0	30.1	26.5	11.5	17.7
Hopewell City	729	4 072	5 474	8.7	64.1	10.2	28.7	7 225	16 338	33 196	-8.3	4.6	14.9	14.3	12.5	19.6
Lexington City	127	1 611	3 467	46.4	40.2	42.6	3.3	7 002	16 497	28 982	1.0	11.6	21.6	22.5	8.4	13.0
Lynchburg City	458	3 480	19 578	38.2	49.7	25.2	66.0	7 160	18 263	32 234	1.1	7.3	15.9	15.6	12.3	19.5
Manassas City	287	3 196	9 941	17.9	42.7	28.1	46.8	7 296	24 453	60 409	-3.7	19.5	6.3	4.8	3.7	5.0

1. Data for serious crimes have not been adjusted for underreporting; this may affect comparability between geographic areas and over time. 2. Per 100,000 population estimated by the FBI. 3. All persons 3 years old and over enrolled in nursery school through college. 4. Persons 25 years old and over. 5. Elementary and secondary education expenditures. 6. Based on population enumerated as of April 1, 2000. 7. Bedford City included with Bedford County. 8. Covington included with Alleghany County. 9. Emporia included with Greensville County. 10. Fairfax City included with Fairfax County.

Table B. States and Counties — **Personal Income**

STATE County	Personal income, 2002 Total (mil dol) [62]	Percent change, 2001–2002 [63]	Per capita[1] Dollars [64]	Per capita[1] Rank [65]	Wages and salaries[2] (mil dol) [66]	Proprietor's income (mil dol) [67]	Dividends, interest, and rent (mil dol) [68]	Transfer payments Total (mil dol) [69]	Government payments to individuals Total (mil dol) [70]	Social Security (mil dol) [71]	Medical payments (mil dol) [72]	Income maintenance (mil dol) [73]	Unemployment insurance (mil dol) [74]
VIRGINIA—Cont'd													
Louisa	732	3.8	27 039	692	275	91	96	108	101	44	41	8	3
Lunenburg	252	1.2	19 092	2 743	97	13	44	57	54	22	20	6	2
Madison	325	3.3	25 110	1 100	105	25	64	50	47	22	17	3	3
Mathews	319	2.6	34 588	149	45	17	84	49	47	23	17	2	1
Mecklenburg	707	2.4	21 771	2 073	375	47	136	178	170	72	64	15	14
Middlesex	284	3.0	28 089	533	95	12	83	55	53	27	20	3	1
Montgomery	(3)2 050	(3)4.0	(3)20 392	(3)2 461	(3)1 691	(3)120	(3)364	(3)280	(3)256	(3)118	(3)89	(3)21	(3)4
Nelson	388	3.3	26 344	821	99	22	75	70	66	30	26	4	2
New Kent	410	2.4	28 757	474	94	18	53	45	42	21	16	2	1
Northampton	307	4.2	23 453	1 583	173	24	69	73	69	29	27	8	2
Northumberland	340	2.7	26 976	702	78	18	126	74	71	37	25	4	3
Nottoway	353	1.7	22 546	1 865	195	20	60	91	88	28	42	7	2
Orange	724	5.4	26 543	779	253	27	158	132	125	60	48	7	4
Page	500	0.1	21 416	2 176	198	30	86	104	98	45	36	7	5
Patrick	387	3.3	20 062	2 536	162	26	60	106	101	39	34	7	18
Pittsylvania	(4)2 470	(4)3.3	(4)22 660	(4)1 832	(4)1 477	(4)97	(4)411	(4)561	(4)535	(4)234	(4)182	(4)53	(4)47
Powhatan	676	2.8	27 867	571	197	30	81	64	59	31	20	3	1
Prince Edward	341	2.3	17 043	2 991	253	14	65	84	80	31	31	9	2
Prince George	(5)1 325	(5)3.1	(5)23 474	(5)1 578	(5)1 230	(5)35	(5)191	(5)196	(5)184	(5)80	(5)65	(5)19	(5)6
Prince William	(6)11 294	3.7	(6)31 436	(6)252	(6)5 249	(6)484	(6)1 213	(6)687	(6)602	(6)241	(6)228	(6)59	(6)24
Pulaski	849	3.4	24 258	1 325	550	31	106	178	170	75	66	12	7
Rappahannock	207	2.7	28 923	455	52	20	63	28	26	13	11	1	0
Richmond	168	2.6	18 746	2 790	93	11	38	41	39	17	16	3	1
Roanoke	(7)3 654	(7)3.2	(7)32 911	(7)190	(7)2 328	(7)237	(7)818	(7)415	(7)388	(7)221	(7)100	(7)19	(7)12
Rockbridge	(8)798	(8)3.7	(8)23 383	(8)1 599	(8)467	(8)41	(8)179	(8)149	(8)141	(8)72	(8)50	(8)9	(8)3
Rockingham	(9)2 562	(9)1.1	(9)23 270	(9)1 637	(9)2 010	(9)179	(9)470	(9)340	(9)313	(9)163	(9)105	(9)23	(9)6
Russell	585	2.9	20 205	2 502	293	23	80	179	172	67	69	17	6
Scott	455	2.5	19 715	2 609	131	21	72	132	126	54	52	12	2
Shenandoah	896	2.7	24 618	1 232	449	66	176	149	140	74	49	8	4
Smyth	683	2.4	20 817	2 341	442	39	104	175	167	74	60	14	12
Southampton	(10)621	(10)1.9	(10)24 335	(10)1 296	(10)279	(10)19	(10)118	(10)129	(10)123	(10)50	(10)52	(10)13	(10)2
Spotsylvania	(11)3 566	(11)5.3	(11)29 072	(11)439	(11)1 818	(11)206	(11)506	(11)352	(11)322	(11)141	(11)124	(11)24	(11)9
Stafford	3 068	4.9	29 278	410	1 177	71	350	190	166	77	55	13	6
Surry	156	2.1	22 448	1 893	123	7	23	27	26	11	10	3	1
Sussex	257	2.1	21 199	2 237	119	10	38	60	57	21	27	6	2
Tazewell	985	4.2	22 269	1 941	502	38	163	290	279	110	103	24	5
Warren	883	3.6	26 701	751	342	41	129	113	105	51	36	9	4
Washington	(12)1 664	(12)1.6	(12)24 343	(12)1 293	(12)1 111	(12)104	(12)313	(12)345	(12)328	(12)154	(12)113	(12)26	(12)12
Westmoreland	418	3.3	24 970	1 137	92	22	81	85	81	35	33	7	3
Wise	(13)922	(13)2.4	(13)20 170	(13)2 507	(13)645	(13)39	(13)122	(13)302	(13)291	(13)107	(13)113	(13)31	(13)8
Wythe	576	2.9	20 716	2 366	322	31	88	142	135	59	52	11	6
York	(14)2 261	(14)5.0	(14)31 673	(14)239	(14)726	(14)90	(14)369	(14)205	(14)188	(14)93	(14)64	(14)8	(14)4
Independent Cities													
Alexandria City	7 156	2.7	55 071	10	5 798	374	1 189	415	384	119	183	39	13
Bedford City	(15)	(15)	(15)	(15)	(15)	(15)	(15)	(15)	(15)	(15)	(15)	(15)	(15)
Bristol City	(12)	(12)	(12)	(12)	(12)	(12)	(12)	(12)	(12)	(12)	(12)	(12)	(12)
Buena Vista City	(8)	(8)	(8)	(8)	(8)	(8)	(8)	(8)	(8)	(8)	(8)	(8)	(8)
Charlottesville City	(16)	(16)	(16)	(16)	(16)	(16)	(16)	(16)	(16)	(16)	(16)	(16)	(16)
Chesapeake City	5 956	5.1	28 910	457	3 159	243	651	627	578	237	212	54	23
Colonial Heights City	(17)	(17)	(17)	(17)	(17)	(17)	(17)	(17)	(17)	(17)	(17)	(17)	(17)
Covington City	(18)	(18)	(18)	(18)	(18)	(18)	(18)	(18)	(18)	(18)	(18)	(18)	(18)
Danville City	(4)	(4)	(4)	(4)	(4)	(4)	(4)	(4)	(4)	(4)	(4)	(4)	(4)
Emporia City	(19)	(19)	(19)	(19)	(19)	(19)	(19)	(19)	(19)	(19)	(19)	(19)	(19)
Fairfax City	(20)	(20)	(20)	(20)	(20)	(20)	(20)	(20)	(20)	(20)	(20)	(20)	(20)
Falls Church City	(20)	(20)	(20)	(20)	(20)	(20)	(20)	(20)	(20)	(20)	(20)	(20)	(20)
Franklin City	(10)	(10)	(10)	(10)	(10)	(10)	(10)	(10)	(10)	(10)	(10)	(10)	(10)
Fredericksburg City	(11)	(11)	(11)	(11)	(11)	(11)	(11)	(11)	(11)	(11)	(11)	(11)	(11)
Galax City	(21)	(21)	(21)	(21)	(21)	(21)	(21)	(21)	(21)	(21)	(21)	(21)	(21)
Hampton City	3 831	3.8	26 280	835	3 374	102	479	543	510	191	180	55	19
Harrisonburg City	(9)	(9)	(9)	(9)	(9)	(9)	(9)	(9)	(9)	(9)	(9)	(9)	(9)
Hopewell City	(5)	(5)	(5)	(5)	(5)	(5)	(5)	(5)	(5)	(5)	(5)	(5)	(5)
Lexington City	(8)	(8)	(8)	(8)	(8)	(8)	(8)	(8)	(8)	(8)	(8)	(8)	(8)
Lynchburg City	(22)	(22)	(22)	(22)	(22)	(22)	(22)	(22)	(22)	(22)	(22)	(22)	(22)
Manassas City	(6)	(6)	(6)	(6)	(6)	(6)	(6)	(6)	(6)	(6)	(6)	(6)	(6)

1. Based on the resident population estimated as of July 1 of the year shown.   2. Includes other labor income.   3. Radford included with Montgomery County.   4. Danville included with Pittsylvania County.   5. Hopewell included with Prince George County.   6. Manassas and Manassas Park included with Prince William County.   7. Salem included with Roanoke County.   8. Buena Vista and Lexington included with Rockbridge County.   9. Harrisonburg included with Rockingham County.   10. Franklin included with Southhampton County.   11. Fredericksburg included with Spotsylvania County.   12. Bristol included with Washington County.   13. Norton included with Wise County.   14. Poquoson included with York County.   15. Bedford City included with Bedford County.   16. Charlottesville included with Albemarle County.   17. Petersburg and Colonial Heights included with Dinwiddie County.   18. Covington included with Alleghany County.   19. Emporia included with Greensville County.   20. Fairfax City and Falls Church included with Fairfax County.   21. Galax included with Carroll County.   22. Lynchburg included with Campbell County.

STATE County	Earnings, 2002 Total (mil dol)	Farm	Goods-related[1] Total	Manu-facturing	Infor-mation and profes-sional and technical services	Retail trade	Finance, insur-ance, and real estate	Health services	Govern-ment	Social Security beneficiaries, December 2003 Number	Rate[2]	Supple-mental Security Income recipients, December 2003	Housing units, 2003 Total	Percent change, 2000–2003
	75	76	77	78	79	80	81	82	83	84	85	86	87	88
VIRGINIA—Cont'd														
Louisa	366	0.2	D	17.9	D	4.7	D	D	12.5	5 000	178	572	12 781	7.8
Lunenburg	110	4.2	27.2	15.6	D	6.8	D	4.2	27.9	2 670	203	470	5 783	0.8
Madison	130	1.7	22.8	11.3	4.1	20.4	2.6	D	15.4	2 295	176	222	5 509	5.2
Mathews	62	2.7	22.5	7.4	D	9.6	D	4.4	22.7	2 450	176	97	5 403	1.3
Mecklenburg	422	3.5	D	16.5	4.0	8.8	4.1	D	20.3	8 325	256	1 309	17 847	2.6
Middlesex	107	1.0	17.4	8.1	5.1	9.0	6.8	5.7	27.5	2 880	282	215	6 533	2.7
Montgomery	(4)1 811	(4)0.2	(4)D	(4)19.6	(4)D	(4)7.4	(4)4.9	(4)7.8	(4)35.7	10 195	119	1 027	33 985	4.5
Nelson	121	2.3	D	4.6	7.8	6.4	5.6	4.4	19.0	3 265	219	366	8 745	2.2
New Kent	112	0.4	24.7	5.0	D	10.2	D	D	21.5	2 185	147	124	5 767	10.8
Northampton	197	7.0	11.6	7.8	D	7.0	D	D	18.5	3 375	254	691	6 752	3.1
Northumberland	96	1.5	32.5	19.0	6.0	9.3	6.1	2.0	18.1	3 810	299	196	8 348	3.6
Nottoway	214	2.4	D	12.7	2.0	8.8	2.6	D	42.1	3 355	215	559	6 509	2.1
Orange	280	2.8	25.8	15.9	D	8.5	5.1	1.9	21.4	6 530	233	506	12 250	7.9
Page	227	2.4	39.1	30.2	D	7.8	2.4	D	19.4	5 200	220	551	10 717	1.5
Patrick	188	1.9	45.1	40.4	3.7	5.3	2.6	7.7	13.7	4 565	238	483	10 083	2.6
Pittsylvania	(5)1 574	(5)0.9	(5)D	(5)33.6	(5)3.2	(5)8.8	(5)3.3	(5)12.1	(5)15.5	13 750	223	1 645	28 810	2.9
Powhatan	227	0.6	D	1.8	5.7	5.7	5.3	D	38.4	3 245	132	216	8 370	11.5
Prince Edward	267	1.3	D	6.9	D	12.4	4.6	D	27.3	3 630	180	892	7 982	6.0
Prince George	(6)1 265	(6)0.1	(6)D	(6)15.9	(6)D	(6)D	(6)1.6	(6)D	(6)53.7	4 025	117	270	11 364	5.9
Prince William	(7)5 733	(7)0.0	(7)D	(7)D	(7)10.5	(7)D	(7)D	(7)D	(7)25.6	22 180	68	1 873	113 832	16.1
Pulaski	581	0.3	D	42.7	3.4	5.5	2.7	D	13.9	8 150	233	970	16 610	1.7
Rappahannock	72	1.0	19.0	5.2	23.6	7.9	D	D	17.2	1 430	201	98	3 404	3.1
Richmond	104	2.7	11.5	5.7	10.9	9.1	3.3	D	34.4	1 895	210	182	3 576	1.8
Roanoke	(8)2 564	(8)0.0	(8)D	(8)21.0	(8)7.8	(8)7.8	(8)8.3	(8)D	(8)15.3	16 820	193	490	37 715	4.4
Rockbridge	(9)507	(9)0.6	(9)D	(9)D	(9)7.6	(9)7.6	(9)D	(9)D	(9)21.1	4 605	220	280	10 162	6.4
Rockingham	(10)2 189	(10)1.4	(10)D	(10)28.1	(10)6.1	(10)9.1	(10)4.3	(10)9.4	(10)15.2	12 800	185	826	28 494	4.3
Russell	317	0.6	31.5	18.7	3.2	8.7	3.4	D	20.5	7 865	273	1 698	13 416	1.7
Scott	151	2.7	18.0	13.6	4.8	13.7	2.7	9.7	25.2	6 430	280	1 485	11 559	1.8
Shenandoah	514	1.8	43.6	36.8	5.4	8.6	3.5	D	13.1	8 105	218	504	17 512	4.8
Smyth	481	1.0	D	36.7	7.1	6.3	2.1	D	20.0	8 630	264	1 268	15 298	1.2
Southampton	(11)298	(11)3.6	(11)D	(11)9.9	(11)3.1	(11)9.2	(11)5.3	(11)D	(11)30.4	3 530	202	482	7 243	2.6
Spotsylvania	(12)2 024	(12)0.0	(12)D	(12)D	(12)8.7	(12)12.6	(12)7.3	(12)13.8	(12)16.3	11 775	109	623	38 719	16.2
Stafford	1 249	0.1	D	2.7	6.9	5.0	D	3.4	26.1	8 745	79	522	36 920	17.6
Surry	130	3.2	D	D	2.3	1.0	D	D	13.0	1 185	169	152	3 415	3.7
Sussex	130	5.4	D	7.9	D	6.9	D	D	41.3	2 335	195	455	4 683	0.6
Tazewell	540	0.6	20.3	11.0	5.8	12.7	4.5	D	19.7	12 065	272	2 175	20 637	1.2
Warren	383	0.5	D	D	5.3	8.8	4.6	10.0	17.1	5 345	158	436	13 991	5.2
Washington	(13)1 215	(13)0.7	(13)D	(13)25.3	(13)D	(13)9.9	(13)5.0	(13)8.1	(13)15.5	12 450	242	1 673	23 832	3.7
Westmoreland	114	4.6	D	16.4	5.5	10.2	5.9	D	24.5	3 915	231	350	9 515	2.5
Wise	(14)684	(14)0.0	(14)28.3	(14)2.6	(14)6.7	(14)8.6	(14)2.1	(14)D	(14)22.0	10 795	258	2 529	18 025	1.3
Wythe	353	1.0	22.0	17.8	D	14.6	3.5	D	21.4	6 750	242	882	12 990	1.9
York	(15)816	(15)0.1	(15)D	(15)D	(15)5.7	(15)7.1	(15)5.7	(15)5.2	(15)38.1	8 090	133	289	22 894	10.6
Independent Cities														
Alexandria City	6 172	0.0	D	D	26.5	5.1	7.3	4.9	26.7	11 520	89	2 059	67 702	5.4
Bedford City	(16)	(16)	(16)	(16)	(16)	(16)	(16)	(16)	(16)	1 890	298	283	2 728	1.0
Bristol City	(13)	(13)	(13)	(13)	(13)	(13)	(13)	(13)	(13)	4 730	275	877	8 571	1.2
Buena Vista City	(9)	(9)	(9)	(9)	(9)	(9)	(9)	(9)	(9)	1 460	231	194	2 777	2.2
Charlottesville City	(17)	(17)	(17)	(17)	(17)	(17)	(17)	(17)	(17)	5 815	148	1 120	17 618	0.2
Chesapeake City	3 403	0.3	22.8	7.4	10.7	9.6	5.9	5.8	19.6	26 350	125	2 664	76 373	5.1
Colonial Heights City	(18)	(18)	(18)	(18)	(18)	(18)	(18)	(18)	(18)	3 915	226	255	7 550	2.9
Covington City	(19)	(19)	(19)	(19)	(19)	(19)	(19)	(19)	(19)	1 780	283	322	3 172	-0.7
Danville City	(5)	(5)	(5)	(5)	(5)	(5)	(5)	(5)	(5)	12 320	262	2 326	23 036	-0.3
Emporia City	(20)	(20)	(20)	(20)	(20)	(20)	(20)	(20)	(20)	1 400	248	438	2 607	8.1
Fairfax City	(21)	(21)	(21)	(21)	(21)	(21)	(21)	(21)	(21)	2 610	118	912	8 611	5.0
Falls Church City	(21)	(21)	(21)	(21)	(21)	(21)	(21)	(21)	(21)	1 380	132	248	4 696	-0.6
Franklin City	(11)	(11)	(11)	(11)	(11)	(11)	(11)	(11)	(11)	1 960	237	557	3 816	1.3
Fredericksburg City	(12)	(12)	(12)	(12)	(12)	(12)	(12)	(12)	(12)	3 485	173	658	8 993	1.2
Galax City	(22)	(22)	(22)	(22)	(22)	(22)	(22)	(22)	(22)	2 040	307	412	3 230	0.4
Hampton City	3 476	0.0	9.7	6.4	13.9	6.0	2.5	5.8	50.9	20 875	142	2 605	58 031	1.3
Harrisonburg City	(10)	(10)	(10)	(10)	(10)	(10)	(10)	(10)	(10)	4 425	107	510	14 314	4.6
Hopewell City	(6)	(6)	(6)	(6)	(6)	(6)	(6)	(6)	(6)	4 465	199	802	9 870	1.2
Lexington City	(9)	(9)	(9)	(9)	(9)	(9)	(9)	(9)	(9)	1 580	223	194	2 365	-0.5
Lynchburg City	(23)	(23)	(23)	(23)	(23)	(23)	(23)	(23)	(23)	13 565	208	2 084	28 351	2.6
Manassas City	(7)	(7)	(7)	(7)	(7)	(7)	(7)	(7)	(7)	3 020	81	813	12 447	2.7

1. Covers mining, construction, and manufacturing.   2. Per 1,000 resident population estimated as of July 1 of the year shown.   4. Radford included with Montgomery County.   5. Danville included with Pittsylvania County.   6. Hopewell included with Prince George County.   7. Manassas and Manassas Park included with Prince William County.   8. Salem included with Roanoke County.   9. Buena Vista and Lexington included with Rockbridge County.   10. Harrisonburg included with Rockingham County.   11. Franklin included with Southhampton County.   12. Fredericksburg included with Spotsylvania County.   13. Bristol included with Washington County.   14. Norton included with Wise County.   15. Poquoson included with York County.   16. Bedford City included with Bedford County.   17. Charlottesville included with Albemarle County.   18. Petersburg and Colonial Heights included with Dinwiddie County.   19. Covington included with Alleghany County.   20. Emporia included with Greensville County.   21. Fairfax City and Falls Church included with Fairfax County.   22. Galax included with Carroll County.   23. Lynchburg included with Campbell County.

Table B. States and Counties — Housing, Labor Force, and Employment

STATE County	Housing units, 2000								Civilian labor force, 2003				Civilian employment,[6] 2000		
	Occupied units										Unemployment			Percent	
			Owner-occupied			Renter-occupied									Production, transportation, and material moving occupations
				Median owner cost as a percent of income										Management, professional and related occupations	
	Total	Percent	Median value[1]	With a mortgage	Without a mortgage[2]	Median rent[3]	Median rent as a percent of income	Sub-standard units[4] (percent)	Total	Percent change, 2002–2003	Total	Rate[5]	Total		
	89	90	91	92	93	94	95	96	97	98	99	100	101	102	103
VIRGINIA—Cont'd															
Louisa	9 945	81.4	96 400	22.3	9.9	504	22.7	4.1	10 961	1.0	598	5.5	12 204	24.1	18.0
Lunenburg	4 998	77.8	60 200	22.1	11.0	394	21.6	4.8	4 934	3.2	350	7.1	5 140	23.2	23.9
Madison	4 739	76.9	100 600	21.0	9.9	494	20.9	4.3	10 159	0.4	287	2.8	6 170	31.6	17.8
Mathews	3 932	84.7	118 000	21.0	10.1	506	22.0	3.0	4 792	0.7	113	2.4	4 046	27.3	15.7
Mecklenburg	12 951	74.3	80 200	21.7	9.9	375	20.9	4.8	14 237	-3.3	1 601	11.2	13 545	21.8	23.6
Middlesex	4 253	83.0	124 300	22.1	9.9	544	23.4	2.1	5 649	0.9	120	2.1	4 287	30.1	14.9
Montgomery	30 997	55.1	114 600	19.9	9.9	535	30.7	2.1	41 086	6.3	999	2.4	39 369	40.2	12.7
Nelson	5 887	80.8	95 100	20.5	9.9	440	20.6	5.0	7 080	-4.0	218	3.1	6 774	28.0	16.3
New Kent	4 925	88.8	128 100	21.2	9.9	636	22.2	1.4	7 362	0.1	278	3.8	6 948	30.7	13.9
Northampton	5 321	68.7	78 700	23.4	10.6	382	23.0	7.2	4 919	-0.8	286	5.8	5 177	27.1	16.4
Northumberland	5 470	87.4	129 100	22.9	9.9	478	19.3	4.9	5 523	0.9	315	5.7	4 894	30.0	14.0
Nottoway	5 664	70.9	73 200	21.7	10.5	438	24.4	4.0	6 610	0.5	254	3.8	5 973	23.5	21.2
Orange	10 150	77.1	115 000	22.6	9.9	583	23.6	2.6	11 913	4.0	527	4.4	12 117	27.3	14.9
Page	9 305	73.9	86 300	23.1	9.9	441	23.0	3.5	11 939	1.9	932	7.8	11 061	18.7	27.3
Patrick	8 141	80.2	75 300	19.2	9.9	333	20.2	3.8	8 491	-1.2	978	11.5	9 024	19.4	35.9
Pittsylvania	24 684	80.1	80 300	19.6	9.9	398	20.9	3.4	33 808	-0.8	2 588	7.7	29 593	19.9	30.4
Powhatan	7 258	88.9	132 500	20.5	9.9	623	25.7	1.6	11 797	-0.2	318	2.7	10 644	33.0	10.4
Prince Edward	6 561	68.5	93 000	22.5	9.9	459	23.6	5.2	8 220	1.6	403	4.9	7 674	31.4	15.1
Prince George	10 159	73.1	118 200	20.3	9.9	609	22.2	2.6	14 526	0.4	582	4.0	12 490	29.8	14.9
Prince William	94 570	71.7	149 600	22.1	9.9	862	24.3	4.4	165 405	1.8	5 243	3.2	144 748	41.1	7.2
Pulaski	14 643	73.6	80 000	18.5	9.9	382	22.3	2.1	17 353	6.7	1 241	7.2	16 425	24.0	27.4
Rappahannock	2 788	75.4	129 300	22.1	10.9	599	23.0	3.3	4 276	4.7	89	2.1	3 591	35.8	9.6
Richmond	2 937	77.2	86 700	20.8	9.9	457	22.4	4.7	3 885	1.0	249	6.4	3 201	23.1	17.0
Roanoke	34 686	77.1	118 100	20.1	9.9	575	21.6	1.1	49 310	-2.0	1 232	2.5	44 041	38.3	12.1
Rockbridge	8 486	77.6	92 400	20.9	9.9	442	22.4	3.1	11 348	2.2	354	3.1	10 116	24.1	24.1
Rockingham	25 355	78.0	107 700	21.3	9.9	485	21.0	3.5	39 329	0.8	984	2.5	34 650	26.6	23.9
Russell	11 789	81.1	69 800	20.7	9.9	355	23.4	2.9	13 694	0.5	812	5.9	10 869	24.4	28.0
Scott	9 795	78.3	69 100	19.4	9.9	335	21.7	4.0	9 225	3.0	538	5.8	9 246	21.3	23.4
Shenandoah	14 296	73.1	99 400	20.9	9.9	468	21.0	3.8	17 709	-1.0	666	3.8	17 710	22.5	23.8
Smyth	13 493	74.1	67 900	18.8	9.9	353	19.7	2.0	15 260	0.2	1 459	9.6	14 906	21.8	31.1
Southampton	6 279	74.3	82 500	21.2	9.9	409	23.0	5.8	8 112	1.2	315	3.9	7 109	23.2	24.3
Spotsylvania	31 308	82.2	128 500	22.0	9.9	805	24.9	2.7	52 284	2.0	1 254	2.4	45 651	34.9	12.2
Stafford	30 187	80.6	156 400	22.0	9.9	842	23.5	1.7	52 799	1.9	1 310	2.5	45 588	41.1	8.0
Surry	2 619	77.0	88 100	22.3	9.9	402	20.6	4.7	2 477	2.4	157	6.3	3 195	22.2	17.1
Sussex	4 126	69.5	71 600	21.0	10.5	434	24.1	6.1	6 030	1.3	377	6.3	4 263	21.7	24.0
Tazewell	18 277	77.3	67 900	20.5	9.9	376	22.3	2.2	20 403	0.9	1 075	5.3	17 593	25.5	17.7
Warren	12 087	74.1	108 800	21.0	9.9	531	22.0	3.5	16 279	1.9	656	4.0	15 687	26.9	13.7
Washington	21 056	77.3	90 400	19.9	9.9	412	21.9	2.1	25 407	1.6	1 507	5.9	23 803	27.6	23.0
Westmoreland	6 846	79.2	95 300	21.8	10.1	537	23.4	5.4	7 753	4.3	400	5.2	7 129	26.5	16.1
Wise	16 013	75.2	65 700	20.7	9.9	353	25.5	2.0	15 590	2.6	892	5.7	14 912	26.8	15.4
Wythe	11 511	77.4	77 300	19.4	9.9	401	21.4	2.6	14 721	1.2	848	5.8	13 222	20.9	28.0
York	20 000	75.8	152 700	21.7	9.9	708	23.0	1.6	30 495	1.9	788	2.6	25 433	45.9	9.1
Independent Cities															
Alexandria City	61 889	40.0	252 800	20.7	9.9	861	23.5	8.6	82 877	1.2	2 252	2.7	76 584	56.2	5.2
Bedford City	2 519	60.3	90 400	20.9	9.9	436	24.5	2.7	2 556	-1.4	109	4.3	2 465	22.7	25.6
Bristol City	7 678	65.0	71 400	19.7	10.4	409	25.8	0.8	7 935	4.9	541	6.8	7 179	26.6	21.2
Buena Vista City	2 547	70.6	72 900	21.1	9.9	403	21.1	1.8	3 450	1.8	148	4.3	3 054	17.4	29.5
Charlottesville City	16 851	40.9	119 000	21.6	9.9	596	30.4	3.2	20 676	0.9	685	3.3	20 943	44.0	7.4
Chesapeake City	69 900	74.9	122 300	23.5	10.6	642	25.8	3.2	112 832	2.2	4 112	3.6	92 376	35.6	11.5
Colonial Heights City	7 027	69.4	94 800	20.3	9.9	619	24.6	1.9	8 799	0.2	420	4.8	8 207	31.9	13.3
Covington City	2 835	69.8	52 500	19.3	10.4	404	24.4	1.9	3 115	0.1	181	5.8	2 696	14.2	28.2
Danville City	20 607	58.0	71 900	19.5	9.9	404	25.7	2.8	24 089	1.5	2 710	11.2	19 668	23.9	26.0
Emporia City	2 226	52.1	68 700	19.7	10.9	437	23.9	4.9	2 649	2.1	216	8.2	2 244	26.1	26.6
Fairfax City	8 035	69.1	192 100	20.1	9.9	945	24.1	7.1	13 157	2.5	263	2.0	11 924	50.0	5.5
Falls Church City	4 471	60.5	277 100	20.8	10.7	965	23.5	5.5	6 281	1.6	173	2.8	5 857	65.5	3.4
Franklin City	3 384	53.6	94 900	24.5	9.9	493	28.7	1.4	3 822	1.2	174	4.6	3 400	27.2	19.4
Fredericksburg City	8 102	35.5	135 800	21.7	9.9	651	26.8	2.2	10 410	1.5	613	5.9	9 766	37.4	9.5
Galax City	2 950	66.1	70 300	18.5	9.9	346	24.9	6.6	3 152	-0.4	244	7.7	3 072	18.3	39.3
Hampton City	53 887	58.6	91 100	22.8	10.7	603	26.4	3.6	73 879	2.0	3 766	5.1	60 810	32.1	13.7
Harrisonburg City	13 133	39.1	122 700	19.5	9.9	480	26.0	4.4	21 587	1.4	527	2.4	18 834	31.2	16.4
Hopewell City	9 055	55.9	77 300	21.7	10.5	512	24.3	3.7	10 639	0.3	764	7.2	9 377	19.6	22.5
Lexington City	2 232	55.2	131 900	23.8	9.9	434	32.6	0.8	2 926	1.4	58	2.0	2 113	45.8	7.0
Lynchburg City	25 477	58.5	85 300	20.8	9.9	469	24.5	2.4	29 302	-1.2	1 790	6.1	29 160	33.3	16.1
Manassas City	11 757	69.8	154 500	21.2	9.9	801	24.4	4.3	21 081	0.5	624	3.0	18 238	38.5	8.3

1. Specified owner-occupied units.   2. Median monthly owner costs is often in the minimum category—9.9 percent or less, which is indicated as 9.9 percent.   3. Specified renter-occupied units.   4. Overcrowded or lacking complete plumbing facilities.   5. Percent of civilian labor force.   6. Persons 16 years old and over.

Table B. States and Counties — Nonfarm Employment and Agriculture

STATE County	Private nonfarm establishments, employment and payroll, 2001									Agriculture, 2002			
	Number of establishments	Employment						Annual payroll		Farms			
		Total	Health care and social assistance	Manufacturing	Retail trade	Finance and insurance	Professional, scientific, and technical services	Total (mil dol)	Average per employee (dollars)	Number	Percent with—		Farm operators whose principal occupation is farming (percent)
											Less than 50 acres	500 acres and over	
	104	105	106	107	108	109	110	111	112	113	114	115	116
VIRGINIA—Cont'd													
Louisa	498	4 162	225	711	612	115	144	143	34 353	474	29.7	8.0	55.7
Lunenburg	196	1 822	137	621	312	81	D	47	25 975	375	18.9	12.0	57.1
Madison	256	2 381	249	526	705	D	D	53	22 464	531	36.3	8.1	55.6
Mathews	221	1 176	118	D	252	D	27	22	19 024	47	55.3	8.5	36.2
Mecklenburg	833	12 044	1 335	3 870	1 966	355	320	236	19 581	581	20.8	15.1	62.3
Middlesex	373	2 328	367	223	406	87	94	45	19 195	101	53.5	8.9	54.5
Montgomery	1 790	25 596	2 114	5 390	5 171	791	1 792	626	24 467	650	40.2	6.6	51.8
Nelson	372	3 183	184	195	327	55	179	54	17 067	456	28.5	7.0	49.6
New Kent	267	2 322	464	167	408	D	66	53	22 923	100	29.0	7.0	47.0
Northampton	335	3 206	879	528	571	68	38	76	23 597	187	43.3	19.3	57.2
Northumberland	343	2 101	50	263	338	70	76	52	24 931	128	38.3	18.0	64.8
Nottoway	346	3 902	804	539	793	124	62	75	19 244	408	25.7	6.4	56.4
Orange	626	7 541	270	2 465	928	102	206	193	25 580	486	31.1	8.8	47.5
Page	467	5 986	560	2 528	795	154	69	126	21 026	549	46.4	4.0	59.2
Patrick	321	4 491	551	2 198	459	77	66	107	23 839	629	34.8	3.5	49.3
Pittsylvania	946	11 775	1 283	4 236	1 520	171	106	260	22 104	1 304	22.1	9.7	57.4
Powhatan	489	4 808	202	77	521	110	158	85	17 670	229	35.8	10.0	52.0
Prince Edward	543	7 710	1 963	525	1 517	297	106	146	18 872	395	20.3	7.6	55.9
Prince George	345	5 151	378	321	743	79	126	133	25 758	218	32.6	9.6	60.6
Prince William	4 447	61 690	5 371	3 573	13 961	1 300	3 215	1 695	27 479	350	59.1	2.0	50.6
Pulaski	649	12 251	1 120	5 936	1 395	162	151	302	24 653	448	36.8	8.3	44.4
Rappahannock	214	1 357	41	92	235	16	102	35	25 566	443	40.2	6.8	52.4
Richmond	230	1 687	312	136	415	58	D	40	23 565	141	20.6	19.9	57.4
Roanoke	1 392	22 431	1 991	2 859	2 591	2 679	491	601	26 793	342	51.5	1.5	53.8
Rockbridge	283	4 492	144	2 105	733	22	54	100	22 207	789	31.9	8.9	49.0
Rockingham	1 153	22 470	1 283	9 968	1 909	278	282	625	27 823	2 043	40.7	3.9	62.9
Russell	557	6 431	748	1 763	851	198	317	166	25 768	1 128	36.6	5.5	50.7
Scott	341	3 312	871	286	889	71	257	70	21 109	1 490	38.3	2.1	50.5
Shenandoah	887	12 903	1 134	5 001	1 997	320	254	283	21 944	989	41.3	4.6	55.5
Smyth	669	11 057	1 902	4 901	1 448	224	252	267	24 177	877	48.6	6.3	49.6
Southampton	269	4 077	210	2 334	332	73	51	137	33 686	275	17.8	33.1	69.1
Spotsylvania	1 346	17 604	1 095	1 477	3 672	1 828	746	515	29 282	369	46.1	7.0	47.2
Stafford	1 474	19 133	1 137	898	2 488	4 487	815	571	29 833	236	50.8	3.8	50.4
Surry	91	1 438	D	152	85	D	D	79	54 861	121	24.0	24.0	52.9
Sussex	196	2 735	347	908	429	58	10	68	24 774	130	16.9	30.8	69.2
Tazewell	1 197	13 091	2 013	1 482	3 042	439	531	293	22 404	551	31.6	13.6	47.5
Warren	759	7 893	626	1 044	1 300	252	185	184	23 349	361	44.0	5.0	46.3
Washington	1 174	14 499	2 049	2 112	2 477	516	531	345	23 801	1 821	49.8	3.5	52.6
Westmoreland	409	2 513	157	529	526	88	131	49	19 396	165	25.5	27.3	64.8
Wise	900	9 492	1 208	623	1 855	238	369	252	26 499	140	44.3	6.4	32.1
Wythe	716	8 922	1 209	1 692	1 904	195	128	190	21 332	876	31.5	6.4	57.1
York	1 183	13 769	721	419	2 336	183	823	276	20 040	44	88.6	0.0	47.7
Independent Cities													
Alexandria City	4 449	79 901	6 121	1 507	8 378	5 041	15 463	3 322	41 574	NA	NA	NA	NA
Bedford City	489	5 769	836	1 840	912	133	144	136	23 509	NA	NA	NA	NA
Bristol City	689	15 573	428	6 086	2 388	431	281	405	25 981	NA	NA	NA	NA
Buena Vista City	125	1 963	162	1 025	220	31	19	51	26 155	NA	NA	NA	NA
Charlottesville City	2 397	41 564	9 408	4 129	5 095	4 067	2 546	1 392	33 490	NA	NA	NA	NA
Chesapeake City	4 490	75 696	6 241	4 940	13 134	2 053	6 586	1 968	25 996	268	64.2	10.4	66.4
Colonial Heights City	663	10 794	916	873	3 842	317	375	203	18 832	NA	NA	NA	NA
Covington City	272	4 939	162	2 523	715	127	55	174	35 302	NA	NA	NA	NA
Danville City	1 484	26 857	4 215	8 993	4 153	1 129	625	690	25 683	NA	NA	NA	NA
Emporia City	262	4 346	617	1 109	1 026	92	68	97	22 364	NA	NA	NA	NA
Fairfax City	2 208	31 981	2 449	245	6 468	1 721	8 757	1 423	44 501	NA	NA	NA	NA
Falls Church City	899	15 325	5 669	86	2 084	282	1 827	617	40 263	NA	NA	NA	NA
Franklin City	243	2 952	781	50	743	157	186	59	20 086	NA	NA	NA	NA
Fredericksburg City	1 750	25 034	5 084	1 165	5 569	898	1 168	652	26 057	NA	NA	NA	NA
Galax City	325	7 857	1 222	3 851	1 321	187	105	165	20 962	NA	NA	NA	NA
Hampton City	2 406	46 772	5 762	6 323	8 162	1 460	4 194	1 163	24 870	NA	NA	NA	NA
Harrisonburg City	1 585	25 790	4 342	4 112	5 041	883	1 172	650	25 214	NA	NA	NA	NA
Hopewell City	456	7 877	1 551	2 576	580	184	202	293	37 185	NA	NA	NA	NA
Lexington City	452	5 151	901	D	1 011	224	154	111	21 462	NA	NA	NA	NA
Lynchburg City	2 531	57 678	8 690	13 827	7 331	3 951	3 113	1 810	31 373	NA	NA	NA	NA
Manassas City	2 119	27 555	3 396	2 185	4 312	789	2 313	963	34 934	NA	NA	NA	NA

Table B. States and Counties — Agriculture

	Agriculture, 2002 (cont'd)															
	Land in farms					Value of land and buildings (dollars)			Value of products sold				Percent of farms with sales of —		Government payments	
			Acres								Percent from —					
STATE County	Acreage (1,000)	Percent change, 1997–2002	Average size of farm	Total irrigated (1,000)	Total cropland (1,000)	Average per farm	Average per acre	Value of machinery and equipment average per farm (dollars)	Total (mil dol)	Average per farm (dollars)	Crops	Live-stock and poultry products	$10,000 or more	$100,000 or more	Total ($1,000)	Percent of farms
	117	118	119	120	121	122	123	124	125	126	127	128	129	130	131	132
VIRGINIA—Cont'd																
Louisa	87	10.1	184	0	39	523 881	2 372	41 385	10	21 335	23.5	76.5	26.8	4.6	433	26.4
Lunenburg	92	17.9	244	1	41	341 400	1 332	39 150	14	37 132	56.8	43.2	30.9	6.9	368	35.2
Madison	103	3.0	194	0	48	617 452	3 098	44 763	18	33 954	18.4	81.6	34.1	7.3	749	23.9
Mathews	D	D	D	0	5	422 443	2 691	39 665	4	92 460	92.6	7.4	42.6	8.5	23	8.5
Mecklenburg	168	0.6	289	4	74	539 182	1 582	58 756	27	45 850	69.1	30.9	39.4	9.6	481	25.5
Middlesex	21	16.7	210	1	15	571 912	2 726	53 489	5	51 556	89.2	10.8	35.6	8.9	358	32.7
Montgomery	100	7.5	153	0	43	478 797	3 131	38 283	18	27 560	32.4	67.6	30.9	6.0	548	15.5
Nelson	85	16.4	186	1	39	442 150	2 103	27 229	8	16 590	64.3	35.7	28.5	2.2	224	17.8
New Kent	19	18.8	193	0	14	530 067	2 827	56 118	3	30 858	90.7	9.3	32.0	6.0	294	30.0
Northampton	52	-7.1	281	9	43	673 957	2 394	99 056	44	236 320	74.6	25.4	61.0	21.9	478	25.7
Northumberland	40	5.3	314	0	32	608 303	1 922	112 190	7	57 876	95.3	4.7	53.1	14.1	711	57.8
Nottoway	71	2.9	175	0	36	350 766	2 110	33 097	27	67 343	9.1	90.9	33.8	9.6	287	30.4
Orange	105	4.0	216	2	56	655 631	3 138	52 261	37	75 693	52.3	47.7	36.8	8.4	636	26.7
Page	64	-5.9	117	0	33	407 298	3 915	47 675	109	198 033	1.2	98.8	46.3	27.7	351	16.8
Patrick	91	23.0	144	0	35	275 767	1 645	37 735	15	24 209	44.3	55.7	28.3	2.7	156	12.7
Pittsylvania	289	8.2	221	6	125	377 897	1 582	51 993	55	41 866	56.2	43.8	32.4	8.5	1 281	32.2
Powhatan	55	27.9	239	0	21	690 419	3 027	39 786	8	35 376	19.3	80.7	28.8	6.1	211	19.2
Prince Edward	79	8.2	200	1	34	388 120	1 718	34 336	12	29 914	22.4	77.6	25.8	5.1	343	45.6
Prince George	55	22.2	253	D	26	492 183	1 964	44 675	4	19 682	88.6	11.4	27.1	4.6	590	32.1
Prince William	33	-8.3	93	1	22	607 838	6 604	34 838	10	27 203	39.9	60.1	24.6	3.4	240	11.1
Pulaski	81	1.3	181	0	37	460 397	2 244	46 580	14	32 202	6.1	93.9	32.4	5.1	215	9.4
Rappahannock	78	8.3	177	0	36	740 667	3 690	31 735	7	16 002	29.5	70.5	26.6	3.8	75	7.9
Richmond	45	25.0	318	D	30	609 286	1 738	82 639	7	47 195	87.5	12.5	49.6	12.8	695	56.0
Roanoke	31	14.8	90	0	11	297 820	3 336	32 314	4	11 201	50.6	49.4	23.1	1.8	44	5.3
Rockbridge	157	12.1	199	1	64	562 144	2 874	29 624	19	23 505	13.6	86.4	29.9	3.8	759	23.4
Rockingham	249	8.3	122	4	148	498 534	4 043	56 927	447	218 631	3.0	97.0	55.8	38.1	4 811	17.5
Russell	169	10.5	150	0	72	252 906	1 603	27 599	21	18 615	16.1	83.9	27.2	3.5	162	7.3
Scott	158	14.5	106	1	62	164 175	1 563	27 307	13	8 518	53.7	46.3	20.7	1.1	161	8.9
Shenandoah	133	4.7	135	1	70	481 467	3 280	34 993	70	70 432	9.2	90.8	34.7	9.9	564	11.6
Smyth	125	0.0	142	0	45	223 007	1 565	37 882	22	24 941	13.4	86.6	34.9	5.4	557	14.8
Southampton	169	-8.6	613	2	91	1 227 005	1 969	133 200	35	127 279	62.6	37.4	63.6	32.7	2 920	50.2
Spotsylvania	56	16.7	153	0	27	532 446	4 288	36 238	6	16 090	29.3	70.7	22.0	2.4	370	24.1
Stafford	26	30.0	111	0	14	572 687	4 880	39 315	2	10 530	46.4	53.6	19.9	2.1	90	17.8
Surry	48	6.7	394	1	39	761 535	1 905	86 615	19	156 006	D	D	52.1	18.2	1 265	61.2
Sussex	74	-9.8	571	1	38	969 902	1 554	97 757	25	192 878	D	D	58.5	22.3	1 206	60.0
Tazewell	139	3.7	252	0	47	416 471	1 561	34 753	18	32 182	6.5	93.5	39.9	5.8	252	10.0
Warren	49	8.9	136	0	24	545 878	3 827	31 456	6	15 376	18.8	81.2	21.9	2.5	17	3.6
Washington	197	10.7	108	1	88	249 686	2 428	35 003	51	27 784	19.7	80.3	27.7	4.3	804	12.6
Westmoreland	68	7.9	410	1	46	873 510	2 016	86 939	20	121 879	95.0	5.0	58.8	18.8	829	58.8
Wise	19	18.8	136	0	9	264 862	2 366	23 009	1	6 728	32.0	68.0	15.7	0.7	2	2.9
Wythe	151	7.9	172	1	69	355 209	2 158	44 083	31	34 849	7.6	92.4	40.4	7.5	1 206	28.0
York	1	-50.0	17	0	0	866 709	48 875	D	3	66 413	89.2	10.8	45.5	6.8	3	6.8
Independent Cities																
Alexandria City	NA	NA	NA	NA	NA	NA	NA	NA	NA	NA	NA	NA	NA	NA	NA	NA
Bedford City	NA	NA	NA	NA	NA	NA	NA	NA	NA	NA	NA	NA	NA	NA	NA	NA
Bristol City	NA	NA	NA	NA	NA	NA	NA	NA	NA	NA	NA	NA	NA	NA	NA	NA
Buena Vista City	NA	NA	NA	NA	NA	NA	NA	NA	NA	NA	NA	NA	NA	NA	NA	NA
Charlottesville City	NA	NA	NA	NA	NA	NA	NA	NA	NA	NA	NA	NA	NA	NA	NA	NA
Chesapeake City	61	0.0	228	0	55	807 303	3 500	61 002	36	133 952	92.1	7.9	34.0	13.4	831	20.9
Colonial Heights City	NA	NA	NA	NA	NA	NA	NA	NA	NA	NA	NA	NA	NA	NA	NA	NA
Covington City	NA	NA	NA	NA	NA	NA	NA	NA	NA	NA	NA	NA	NA	NA	NA	NA
Danville City	NA	NA	NA	NA	NA	NA	NA	NA	NA	NA	NA	NA	NA	NA	NA	NA
Emporia City	NA	NA	NA	NA	NA	NA	NA	NA	NA	NA	NA	NA	NA	NA	NA	NA
Fairfax City	NA	NA	NA	NA	NA	NA	NA	NA	NA	NA	NA	NA	NA	NA	NA	NA
Falls Church City	NA	NA	NA	NA	NA	NA	NA	NA	NA	NA	NA	NA	NA	NA	NA	NA
Franklin City	NA	NA	NA	NA	NA	NA	NA	NA	NA	NA	NA	NA	NA	NA	NA	NA
Fredericksburg City	NA	NA	NA	NA	NA	NA	NA	NA	NA	NA	NA	NA	NA	NA	NA	NA
Galax City	NA	NA	NA	NA	NA	NA	NA	NA	NA	NA	NA	NA	NA	NA	NA	NA
Hampton City	NA	NA	NA	NA	NA	NA	NA	NA	NA	NA	NA	NA	NA	NA	NA	NA
Harrisonburg City	NA	NA	NA	NA	NA	NA	NA	NA	NA	NA	NA	NA	NA	NA	NA	NA
Hopewell City	NA	NA	NA	NA	NA	NA	NA	NA	NA	NA	NA	NA	NA	NA	NA	NA
Lexington City	NA	NA	NA	NA	NA	NA	NA	NA	NA	NA	NA	NA	NA	NA	NA	NA
Lynchburg City	NA	NA	NA	NA	NA	NA	NA	NA	NA	NA	NA	NA	NA	NA	NA	NA
Manassas City	NA	NA	NA	NA	NA	NA	NA	NA	NA	NA	NA	NA	NA	NA	NA	NA

STATE County	Value of residential construction authorized by building permits, 2003		Wholesale trade, 1997				Retail trade,[1] 1997				Real estate and rental and leasing, 1997			
	New construction ($1,000)	Number of housing units	Number of establishments	Number of employees	Sales (mil dol)	Annual payroll (mil dol)	Number of establishments	Number of employees	Sales (mil dol)	Annual payroll (mil dol)	Number of establishments	Number of employees	Receipts (mil dol)	Annual payroll (mil dol)
	133	134	135	136	137	138	139	140	141	142	143	144	145	146
VIRGINIA—Cont'd														
Louisa	67 083	510	14	105	29.1	2.9	73	530	77.7	7.4	12	24	2.7	0.3
Lunenburg	3 541	26	11	55	25.9	1.3	56	368	39.7	4.9	2	D	D	D
Madison	20 876	140	9	30	7.6	0.6	48	418	86.9	7.4	4	6	0.3	0.1
Mathews	10 191	73	9	D	D	D	42	287	33.5	3.6	6	13	1.2	0.2
Mecklenburg	24 338	176	38	230	71.1	4.9	200	2 109	272.5	26.3	25	78	6.6	1.3
Middlesex	21 748	119	17	121	26.2	2.7	53	358	48.4	5.4	21	95	3.7	0.8
Montgomery	63 556	531	39	581	169.8	16.6	355	4 976	749.7	74.4	70	497	53.1	10.5
Nelson	29 892	169	7	13	6.1	0.3	51	225	27.6	2.6	11	76	5.9	2.2
New Kent	36 529	255	9	D	D	D	39	412	53.7	4.9	5	11	0.7	0.1
Northampton	20 370	158	22	D	D	D	79	594	73.0	7.5	6	D	D	D
Northumberland	28 152	176	13	D	D	D	54	338	42.4	5.0	10	51	3.2	0.8
Nottoway	6 719	55	14	D	D	D	80	676	86.3	8.8	4	9	0.4	0.2
Orange	63 406	386	23	163	68.4	4.1	104	946	160.1	15.8	20	44	3.1	0.5
Page	12 262	121	13	49	4.5	0.7	83	645	97.2	8.9	8	27	1.9	0.5
Patrick	8 166	83	11	194	24.5	3.7	59	432	66.1	6.1	10	16	1.4	0.2
Pittsylvania	28 002	246	46	D	D	D	213	2 170	300.5	27.9	23	91	11.1	1.8
Powhatan	51 559	337	21	D	D	D	55	391	78.8	7.3	11	45	2.1	0.4
Prince Edward	10 890	102	20	143	30.9	3.4	125	1 703	267.4	24.4	19	80	5.3	1.3
Prince George	25 947	222	16	189	62.4	5.8	66	632	91.8	8.4	14	30	2.8	0.5
Prince William	670 998	6 572	150	1 736	1 191.2	61.7	915	13 936	2 563.1	240.5	160	767	84.0	15.5
Pulaski	16 031	113	21	299	152.0	7.9	133	1 541	250.9	21.6	22	63	4.5	1.0
Rappahannock	14 168	60	6	D	D	D	33	244	49.0	4.3	5	11	1.3	0.2
Richmond	6 192	40	17	89	18.7	2.2	49	460	62.6	5.8	7	25	1.1	0.3
Roanoke	36 760	564	95	796	399.4	24.5	202	2 559	461.8	41.7	52	231	25.2	3.7
Rockbridge	20 848	118	10	D	D	D	79	961	165.3	13.9	11	19	1.8	0.2
Rockingham	63 822	447	57	1 140	539.7	30.6	242	2 075	356.2	35.4	34	452	65.5	12.3
Russell	6 534	70	15	98	93.9	2.6	102	910	154.2	14.5	11	29	3.1	0.7
Scott	8 967	90	11	D	D	D	91	788	143.0	11.0	11	44	11.0	1.1
Shenandoah	49 782	419	24	241	85.9	4.9	158	1 574	279.3	23.6	24	98	16.0	1.3
Smyth	6 317	52	25	237	65.7	6.8	170	1 560	232.1	20.8	16	78	4.3	1.1
Southampton	7 358	80	17	D	D	D	56	378	41.3	4.6	10	19	1.0	0.2
Spotsylvania	281 030	1 816	67	821	686.0	19.5	261	4 038	737.6	66.6	52	455	33.4	7.9
Stafford	244 823	1 509	47	D	D	D	202	2 336	413.5	39.7	42	193	19.8	3.2
Surry	7 238	75	3	52	8.6	0.8	17	84	8.9	1.0	NA	NA	NA	NA
Sussex	487	9	14	106	30.7	2.1	47	358	71.5	5.6	5	16	1.9	0.5
Tazewell	9 395	100	81	781	215.1	15.8	267	3 193	565.5	47.2	72	199	29.9	3.4
Warren	50 801	318	18	D	D	D	142	1 354	199.7	19.6	20	44	4.6	0.8
Washington	19 825	315	51	1 125	847.5	29.3	253	2 609	408.9	40.8	41	159	11.9	2.7
Westmoreland	15 234	131	17	64	35.9	1.6	71	546	83.4	8.0	9	18	1.9	0.3
Wise	5 383	73	46	354	177.5	9.7	183	1 961	310.9	28.3	25	89	5.4	1.3
Wythe	10 535	99	21	184	73.0	4.9	204	1 933	346.1	27.2	16	30	3.5	0.5
York	73 604	595	45	415	137.9	10.5	255	2 681	326.9	32.6	41	158	20.8	2.7
Independent Cities														
Alexandria City	13 811	72	137	1 830	899.6	75.1	593	7 746	1 507.6	160.0	202	2 023	354.1	57.9
Bedford City	1 497	19	19	D	D	D	81	975	136.3	13.5	15	34	2.2	0.5
Bristol City	5 587	89	40	D	D	D	155	2 266	331.7	29.2	23	104	11.4	2.2
Buena Vista City	1 479	15	2	D	D	D	32	257	33.2	3.5	6	12	0.8	0.1
Charlottesville City	18 708	356	81	954	265.9	29.7	360	4 345	730.3	73.2	97	458	50.1	9.8
Chesapeake City	212 408	1 660	246	3 833	1 768.2	115.7	779	12 554	1 993.3	184.5	144	704	98.0	15.9
Colonial Heights City	7 659	57	12	D	D	D	205	3 776	496.4	46.5	35	146	15.4	2.8
Covington City	463	7	9	44	15.3	1.1	61	539	90.4	7.9	13	27	1.7	0.3
Danville City	9 466	82	55	964	211.8	22.6	334	3 787	585.5	56.9	59	242	18.1	3.5
Emporia City	1 165	13	8	D	D	D	81	714	97.3	9.7	9	28	2.5	0.4
Fairfax City	3 461	16	48	519	515.2	22.3	305	5 870	1 288.0	115.5	68	345	48.3	9.4
Falls Church City	562	3	22	D	D	D	120	1 536	355.6	34.7	38	137	20.4	3.7
Franklin City	3 138	34	7	121	48.9	2.3	57	635	95.0	9.3	10	39	3.4	0.6
Fredericksburg City	9 383	46	53	723	427.3	23.3	317	3 701	567.3	60.7	57	297	43.2	6.5
Galax City	918	18	6	42	6.0	1.0	71	906	134.6	12.6	10	22	2.0	0.4
Hampton City	36 499	630	94	1 073	370.7	31.3	514	9 930	1 638.9	150.5	113	1 241	89.2	20.6
Harrisonburg City	22 384	281	62	971	749.2	25.5	308	4 161	690.8	64.0	48	263	30.8	5.5
Hopewell City	2 777	44	18	268	92.7	9.5	83	754	100.9	10.6	28	121	10.7	1.8
Lexington City	2 284	15	5	27	16.9	1.4	68	686	108.9	9.6	20	62	7.4	1.1
Lynchburg City	49 558	395	100	1 292	504.6	43.8	446	7 209	1 228.5	115.8	95	390	37.4	8.2
Manassas City	14 215	132	59	1 008	626.3	41.0	230	3 355	647.5	64.9	51	302	41.1	5.5

1. Establishments with payroll.

STATE County	Professional, scientific, and technical services,[1] 1997				Manufacturing, 1997				Accommodation and foodservices, 1997			
	Number of establishments	Number of employees	Receipts (mil dol)	Annual payroll (mil dol)	Number of establishments	Number of employees	Receipts (mil dol)	Annual payroll (mil dol)	Number of establishments	Number of employees	Sales (mil dol)	Annual payroll (mil dol)
	147	148	149	150	151	152	153	154	155	156	157	158
VIRGINIA—Cont'd												
Louisa	33	89	5.7	2.4	29	633	89.3	16.4	20	320	8.9	2.6
Lunenburg	7	27	1.1	0.6	16	900	76.3	16.2	5	41	1.0	0.3
Madison	18	32	1.5	0.5	NA	NA	NA	NA	12	126	5.7	1.7
Mathews	9	21	0.9	0.4	NA	NA	NA	NA	8	D	D	D
Mecklenburg	30	218	7.4	3.0	41	4 589	859.1	102.7	66	1 086	29.1	8.3
Middlesex	21	59	3.7	1.4	NA	NA	NA	NA	22	265	8.8	2.3
Montgomery	150	1 231	115.3	41.9	68	4 836	699.1	153.9	150	3 446	96.1	26.1
Nelson	25	81	5.0	2.2	14	621	41.2	8.7	21	708	23.6	8.3
New Kent	20	34	2.3	0.9	NA	NA	NA	NA	14	121	4.8	1.5
Northampton	14	39	1.6	0.4	NA	NA	NA	NA	29	408	15.6	4.0
Northumberland	11	30	1.7	0.7	19	575	59.6	12.9	16	115	3.1	1.1
Nottoway	15	69	2.2	0.8	18	681	139.9	11.3	29	391	9.7	2.5
Orange	42	145	9.7	3.8	35	2 529	445.6	68.8	34	478	14.6	3.9
Page	20	65	3.1	1.0	16	2 883	461.8	47.5	49	543	21.9	5.8
Patrick	10	37	1.4	0.5	38	2 610	249.7	55.7	22	D	D	D
Pittsylvania	26	182	4.1	1.2	59	D	D	D	56	608	19.7	5.6
Powhatan	30	55	3.8	1.6	NA	NA	NA	NA	9	124	3.9	0.9
Prince Edward	23	83	3.8	1.7	18	D	D	D	44	1 056	27.9	7.6
Prince George	36	277	31.7	13.1	NA	NA	NA	NA	27	674	20.9	5.2
Prince William	403	2 322	189.6	81.8	109	2 974	378.1	115.9	364	7 882	266.0	72.6
Pulaski	30	91	5.7	1.8	41	6 509	1 655.8	169.6	54	749	21.5	5.4
Rappahannock	18	58	6.4	2.3	NA	NA	NA	NA	13	206	8.7	2.9
Richmond	13	30	1.6	0.7	NA	NA	NA	NA	11	D	D	D
Roanoke	117	461	34.2	14.9	64	3 450	598.7	107.6	89	1 302	43.6	12.4
Rockbridge	14	31	2.0	0.7	24	2 090	335.4	50.0	44	525	19.9	5.7
Rockingham	46	214	13.5	5.4	74	9 272	4 112.5	269.7	79	1 706	54.2	14.4
Russell	28	339	9.1	4.6	26	1 614	129.2	28.8	29	339	9.7	2.7
Scott	20	D	D	D	NA	NA	NA	NA	18	D	D	D
Shenandoah	47	176	6.2	2.4	47	5 436	840.5	139.4	72	1 160	30.7	9.3
Smyth	34	165	11.2	4.6	53	4 913	692.6	109.2	47	526	16.5	4.4
Southampton	14	39	3.3	0.9	16	2 874	710.0	131.1	13	147	4.1	1.2
Spotsylvania	80	569	55.7	15.7	40	1 698	304.9	60.4	89	1 741	61.9	16.8
Stafford	96	351	37.9	12.8	47	711	99.2	17.2	95	1 809	57.3	14.9
Surry	5	14	1.0	0.3	NA	NA	NA	NA	5	D	D	D
Sussex	5	7	0.4	0.1	9	1 138	283.5	26.5	14	236	6.8	2.0
Tazewell	64	517	44.7	14.8	58	1 517	161.2	30.6	66	1 091	32.5	8.7
Warren	52	232	28.2	12.1	27	1 540	511.0	37.7	61	763	25.6	7.0
Washington	81	395	26.7	11.1	65	2 031	315.8	53.2	84	1 680	48.5	14.3
Westmoreland	28	73	5.3	1.6	16	694	124.6	13.5	37	253	9.7	2.6
Wise	53	299	18.5	8.6	24	556	64.2	10.1	49	688	20.5	5.6
Wythe	31	159	8.4	3.1	45	2 129	276.9	51.6	65	1 275	38.4	10.1
York	76	241	15.0	5.9	28	D	D	D	93	2 303	77.9	20.7
Independent Cities												
Alexandria City	894	12 710	1 456.2	634.2	114	1 907	328.1	59.4	310	6 616	308.3	92.3
Bedford City	38	114	6.9	2.4	30	2 278	254.3	62.2	24	D	D	D
Bristol City	54	D	D	D	41	6 954	1 222.9	184.4	52	D	D	D
Buena Vista City	8	19	0.6	0.2	10	D	D	D	11	162	4.4	1.4
Charlottesville City	206	1 448	118.7	49.7	67	D	D	D	179	3 521	121.5	34.7
Chesapeake City	263	2 653	198.1	84.5	132	4 558	1 085.0	147.0	305	6 321	187.4	51.6
Colonial Heights City	35	219	8.3	3.5	14	838	215.4	20.4	63	1 431	40.8	10.9
Covington City	13	39	2.8	0.9	11	2 615	1 004.9	113.4	16	209	6.7	1.8
Danville City	76	577	27.3	11.6	47	D	D	D	114	2 159	65.7	18.8
Emporia City	13	49	3.1	1.2	13	1 055	158.7	29.0	24	490	16.2	4.4
Fairfax City	504	4 979	887.1	240.3	NA	NA	NA	NA	150	3 029	108.0	29.4
Falls Church City	127	1 600	157.7	68.0	NA	NA	NA	NA	68	D	D	D
Franklin City	12	79	2.6	1.1	NA	NA	NA	NA	18	321	10.1	2.5
Fredericksburg City	134	658	44.7	17.4	41	1 059	240.7	28.6	141	2 748	92.0	24.4
Galax City	13	62	3.3	1.2	24	4 460	380.2	86.8	28	D	D	D
Hampton City	211	3 190	270.9	120.4	80	4 636	971.0	123.4	229	5 002	149.9	41.1
Harrisonburg City	95	618	50.9	19.6	38	3 687	725.8	102.6	109	2 318	70.2	19.0
Hopewell City	25	153	11.5	5.4	19	2 907	1 328.1	147.4	46	D	D	D
Lexington City	34	102	5.1	2.1	NA	NA	NA	NA	57	787	27.4	6.9
Lynchburg City	182	2 715	260.3	107.1	117	12 535	3 096.4	481.1	173	3 808	110.8	30.9
Manassas City	153	1 058	126.9	44.8	34	2 822	791.6	188.5	74	D	D	D

1. Firms subject to federal tax.

STATE County	Health care and social assistance,[1] 1997				Other services,[1] 1997				Federal funds and grants, 2002–2003			
									Expenditures (mil dol)			
										Direct payments for individuals[2]		
	Number of establishments	Number of employees	Receipts (mil dol)	Annual payroll (mil dol)	Number of establishments	Number of employees	Receipts (mil dol)	Annual payroll (mil dol)	Total	Social Security and government retirement	Medicare	Food stamps and Supplemental Security Income
	159	160	161	162	163	164	165	166	167	168	169	170
VIRGINIA—Cont'd												
Louisa	20	277	14.8	5.1	31	97	5.9	1.6	120.2	69.5	22.1	3.3
Lunenburg	5	13	1.1	0.4	18	57	2.3	0.6	61.2	28.9	11.9	2.2
Madison	10	155	4.9	2.3	9	23	2.3	0.5	81.9	42.3	11.4	1.2
Mathews	9	48	1.6	0.4	11	60	3.9	1.2	69.7	42.3	13.5	0.7
Mecklenburg	50	330	20.1	10.4	74	238	12.7	2.7	196.9	95.9	38.0	6.7
Middlesex	12	140	5.4	2.8	14	41	2.2	0.5	65.6	39.7	12.5	1.5
Montgomery	122	1 973	115.9	47.3	116	655	32.5	10.7	384.2	131.3	43.4	8.0
Nelson	13	131	7.1	2.5	13	30	2.3	0.6	58.6	51.5	16.0	2.2
New Kent	10	315	17.4	9.0	13	22	1.4	0.3	59.3	36.4	10.5	0.9
Northampton	26	286	17.0	7.8	16	49	2.5	0.6	243.7	39.7	15.4	4.6
Northumberland	8	68	3.1	1.3	29	108	6.8	1.8	86.9	54.2	17.1	1.4
Nottoway	17	316	10.8	4.2	36	87	5.8	1.5	138.9	49.9	18.1	4.3
Orange	31	240	17.3	5.6	38	147	10.0	2.4	164.8	106.9	28.3	3.0
Page	26	285	13.2	5.1	36	78	4.6	1.3	143.1	64.3	22.7	3.1
Patrick	21	300	10.6	5.4	16	56	3.8	0.9	89.2	47.9	16.7	2.7
Pittsylvania	46	472	30.8	13.8	81	293	14.2	4.0	275.1	112.0	42.5	8.7
Powhatan	13	99	4.2	2.0	15	42	2.9	0.9	67.5	44.6	10.3	1.5
Prince Edward	62	886	33.7	16.1	42	142	6.8	1.9	128.5	75.4	18.1	5.1
Prince George	11	D	D	D	24	103	6.0	2.2	557.4	96.1	10.5	1.8
Prince William	321	3 036	176.6	85.9	341	2 085	127.7	44.7	1 601.5	589.9	53.0	20.2
Pulaski	55	888	50.5	21.2	45	221	11.2	3.3	171.9	89.9	41.7	6.1
Rappahannock	4	15	1.0	0.2	9	25	2.4	0.5	42.9	27.0	7.5	0.6
Richmond	6	282	9.0	4.1	9	27	2.4	0.8	52.4	24.6	11.5	0.6
Roanoke	102	868	59.2	30.1	90	573	28.9	10.8	177.5	120.6	29.5	3.3
Rockbridge	14	156	5.5	2.9	16	54	3.9	1.0	184.0	37.3	11.6	1.9
Rockingham	51	375	20.7	10.6	95	483	33.1	9.6	275.0	168.4	42.6	5.5
Russell	39	650	28.8	12.8	32	136	6.7	2.3	183.3	92.7	38.7	9.0
Scott	24	506	29.7	10.5	20	88	3.4	1.2	156.2	67.1	30.9	8.6
Shenandoah	62	486	18.3	8.6	62	209	11.5	3.4	180.0	114.8	30.9	3.5
Smyth	48	448	25.6	13.1	45	185	12.6	2.8	218.8	92.2	35.1	7.1
Southampton	18	182	9.3	4.7	22	83	7.9	2.2	129.7	49.8	16.9	3.7
Spotsylvania	67	886	37.2	16.8	108	526	32.5	10.1	220.7	160.3	18.8	4.2
Stafford	89	982	47.1	21.2	120	581	35.1	10.3	335.1	206.8	21.9	4.2
Surry	4	20	1.5	0.7	2	D	D	D	41.7	16.5	6.4	1.4
Sussex	7	247	6.2	3.2	16	57	4.7	0.9	90.7	30.3	16.3	2.1
Tazewell	113	1 454	107.8	40.6	93	709	44.1	13.2	318.1	166.1	63.5	14.2
Warren	46	414	19.8	8.2	52	404	23.8	7.3	134.2	77.3	21.4	4.0
Washington	90	971	49.9	26.7	75	304	15.2	4.7	259.9	123.3	38.6	7.9
Westmoreland	11	63	2.1	1.3	19	62	3.6	0.8	117.6	67.4	23.8	2.7
Wise	58	601	33.1	13.1	72	212	15.2	3.6	346.0	134.7	54.4	21.2
Wythe	42	455	24.0	11.7	46	147	8.0	1.9	189.3	79.2	31.5	5.0
York	53	533	20.9	8.9	98	519	31.9	9.6	462.6	228.1	24.6	2.0
Independent Cities												
Alexandria City	323	2 788	216.5	105.2	267	1 919	122.4	42.9	3 545.9	570.3	138.8	18.2
Bedford City	30	206	10.4	5.0	44	219	14.8	4.4	63.9	44.0	10.2	1.1
Bristol City	26	344	13.6	6.2	44	195	12.0	3.2	153.9	71.3	30.5	5.0
Buena Vista City	5	28	1.5	0.7	9	16	0.9	0.2	37.8	19.3	7.5	0.9
Charlottesville City	162	2 092	138.9	54.6	133	827	41.6	14.5	655.6	114.0	44.1	8.4
Chesapeake City	338	3 228	195.7	87.9	305	2 846	241.4	53.0	1 103.5	540.8	117.5	22.7
Colonial Heights City	64	629	39.1	17.1	50	390	19.3	6.7	236.6	65.6	20.2	2.2
Covington City	12	63	3.4	1.7	15	59	5.6	1.1	73.5	40.7	18.5	2.4
Danville City	126	1 459	89.6	42.0	123	735	36.0	10.2	336.3	159.7	65.2	13.6
Emporia City	18	191	13.2	6.1	21	59	2.6	0.7	56.0	23.2	14.9	3.8
Fairfax City	149	1 180	86.4	39.6	126	686	49.5	16.6	3 281.5	304.4	42.1	5.4
Falls Church City	73	915	84.2	35.9	64	323	25.0	8.3	1 549.0	71.1	40.2	0.9
Franklin City	24	160	13.9	6.8	16	75	4.3	1.2	74.5	32.5	14.9	3.3
Fredericksburg City	140	1 805	132.1	67.2	93	633	37.2	12.3	268.0	160.7	24.5	4.6
Galax City	33	469	24.2	12.0	16	73	4.5	1.3	72.3	38.0	15.8	1.3
Hampton City	192	1 976	106.4	51.9	178	1 129	64.8	20.9	2 313.6	463.5	103.7	23.8
Harrisonburg City	116	1 538	90.7	41.6	84	434	28.1	7.5	123.7	58.7	24.6	3.5
Hopewell City	50	1 444	92.7	40.0	36	409	12.7	4.8	233.7	66.6	26.2	6.4
Lexington City	35	213	11.6	5.0	22	100	3.4	1.1	67.1	37.0	9.2	1.3
Lynchburg City	177	2 893	171.0	86.8	152	933	51.6	15.6	1 061.7	214.9	74.6	13.7
Manassas City	106	1 161	67.1	34.9	108	832	60.2	22.2	765.6	122.8	27.2	2.6

1. Firms subject to federal tax.   2. State totals may include programs not allocated by county.

Table B. States and Counties — Federal Funds and Local Government Finances

	Federal funds and grants, 2002–2003 (cont'd)							Local government finances, 2002				
	Expenditures (mil dol) (cont'd)							General revenue				
	Procurement contract awards			Grants[1]						Taxes		
STATE County											Per capita[2] (dollars)	
	Salaries and wages	Defense	Other	Medicaid and other health-related	Nutrition and family welfare	Education	Other	Total (mil dol)	Intergovern-mental (mil dol)	Total (mil dol)	Total	Property
	171	172	173	174	175	176	177	178	179	180	181	182
VIRGINIA—Cont'd												
Louisa	3.3	0.0	1.1	14.4	2.0	1.3	2.1	53.6	18.9	29.1	1 078	966
Lunenburg	1.5	2.3	0.4	11.0	1.5	0.7	0.3	20.8	12.6	6.5	490	383
Madison	3.7	0.2	10.9	7.9	1.8	0.7	0.4	21.5	10.8	9.5	734	550
Mathews	3.3	3.0	1.0	2.9	0.5	0.5	1.1	16.3	7.4	8.0	861	741
Mecklenburg	6.8	6.6	1.3	33.3	2.6	1.7	2.0	63.9	34.7	24.2	749	544
Middlesex	1.7	1.6	0.7	3.1	0.7	0.9	0.8	18.4	7.9	9.4	926	744
Montgomery	17.0	32.7	13.3	28.6	4.4	5.5	88.4	156.1	67.3	58.6	686	457
Nelson	3.8	-32.2	1.9	12.0	1.2	0.7	1.2	29.2	14.2	13.4	907	688
New Kent	2.0	0.4	0.5	3.3	1.7	0.7	2.2	29.2	14.8	12.2	859	703
Northampton	5.6	61.9	84.2	19.3	3.1	1.1	2.0	75.6	20.5	9.6	740	548
Northumberland	1.9	1.1	0.6	4.5	1.0	0.7	2.4	22.3	10.1	10.6	850	735
Nottoway	21.3	5.8	0.7	11.2	2.2	1.4	22.2	30.3	19.3	7.9	496	318
Orange	4.1	0.3	1.0	13.7	2.6	1.3	1.1	48.0	21.7	22.7	832	661
Page	8.9	0.7	22.4	11.7	1.4	1.3	6.0	44.1	26.9	12.7	546	397
Patrick	2.8	3.7	0.8	11.0	1.3	1.3	0.2	29.3	19.4	8.4	430	322
Pittsylvania	5.9	22.8	7.5	52.4	7.4	3.7	7.2	102.8	64.5	27.6	447	332
Powhatan	4.4	0.0	0.8	3.3	0.5	0.7	1.0	34.8	15.9	17.7	738	506
Prince Edward	4.4	1.1	0.9	14.1	2.3	1.1	2.0	37.0	20.0	12.6	632	351
Prince George	346.5	74.5	14.6	4.3	1.4	4.0	0.6	77.2	46.8	22.5	659	544
Prince William	547.5	218.0	64.8	16.5	8.9	10.6	65.5	1 053.1	451.7	414.6	1 329	970
Pulaski	4.5	0.7	1.0	17.9	3.1	2.4	-0.3	80.4	36.7	23.7	676	470
Rappahannock	2.3	0.0	0.3	3.9	0.3	0.5	0.1	13.4	5.1	7.4	1 033	899
Richmond	1.8	3.9	1.1	4.8	0.8	0.8	1.1	22.1	12.9	6.9	784	581
Roanoke	3.8	1.1	0.6	10.0	2.5	3.4	1.5	222.2	82.3	96.7	1 126	808
Rockbridge	51.2	10.5	25.1	8.9	1.4	1.1	33.5	45.5	20.7	16.2	780	541
Rockingham	12.2	0.4	7.8	19.6	2.1	3.1	3.6	135.1	68.8	48.5	706	566
Russell	3.9	0.0	1.1	27.3	3.5	3.0	1.7	58.9	32.7	14.9	513	345
Scott	5.2	0.0	0.9	32.6	3.9	1.8	1.9	52.5	34.0	12.0	521	334
Shenandoah	9.0	0.4	2.3	11.3	1.5	1.9	2.1	74.2	34.6	31.4	864	619
Smyth	6.5	22.6	7.1	30.3	6.0	1.9	6.4	65.3	41.4	17.1	521	350
Southampton	2.5	0.1	1.3	16.3	2.3	1.2	0.7	37.8	21.1	12.9	737	621
Spotsylvania	13.4	1.0	3.2	7.6	2.2	3.1	3.0	232.3	100.0	108.6	1 058	771
Stafford	53.0	7.3	3.5	6.4	3.5	5.1	21.1	252.7	109.8	104.4	996	794
Surry	1.3	0.0	0.3	3.6	0.9	0.4	2.1	22.5	5.8	15.5	2 181	2 118
Sussex	3.6	3.1	0.5	11.8	3.4	0.8	1.9	26.4	14.1	7.2	590	485
Tazewell	15.2	0.0	6.0	28.2	5.9	5.0	5.3	99.3	56.2	26.1	594	390
Warren	9.9	3.5	5.1	8.1	1.6	1.7	1.6	59.0	25.9	26.3	800	589
Washington	6.4	21.1	3.6	39.0	6.7	3.7	2.8	88.5	43.4	33.6	654	440
Westmoreland	4.5	0.5	1.1	6.9	2.8	1.2	4.5	31.6	16.8	11.9	711	586
Wise	9.8	0.2	65.6	36.1	6.2	4.7	5.4	99.7	62.4	26.4	634	381
Wythe	7.5	0.0	1.2	19.9	2.6	3.0	35.0	66.5	36.6	20.7	745	440
York	103.9	44.4	33.6	5.7	3.2	10.5	4.9	154.1	60.6	71.6	1 199	898
Independent Cities												
Alexandria City	642.8	1 298.4	505.7	52.1	12.8	36.8	258.5	471.0	109.8	293.3	2 242	1 568
Bedford City	2.3	0.1	0.5	2.2	0.0	0.5	2.9	13.8	6.1	5.6	904	561
Bristol City	16.1	0.5	3.6	19.4	1.9	1.3	1.7	53.4	22.2	18.5	1 080	577
Buena Vista City	1.7	0.0	1.1	5.3	0.6	0.4	0.3	16.5	9.5	4.8	760	521
Charlottesville City	78.1	61.6	21.3	186.9	7.1	8.2	117.9	127.2	51.2	59.2	1 351	761
Chesapeake City	62.3	203.8	35.1	42.8	12.9	10.3	47.9	758.9	261.0	264.1	1 278	859
Colonial Heights City	2.8	139.4	0.8	3.1	0.6	1.0	0.3	45.1	13.6	28.8	1 690	937
Covington City	3.6	0.2	0.8	5.2	0.8	0.6	0.8	20.4	8.5	9.3	1 462	993
Danville City	12.0	0.0	4.8	41.5	8.3	7.9	17.4	141.8	67.3	40.0	841	472
Emporia City	1.5	0.0	0.4	10.1	0.4	0.3	1.4	8.0	1.2	4.7	822	576
Fairfax City	75.6	1 408.3	1 349.6	10.2	6.3	10.5	57.0	75.4	11.4	56.2	2 550	1 449
Falls Church City	330.9	523.6	404.7	14.6	0.3	0.7	158.5	45.4	8.5	30.9	2 897	1 986
Franklin City	1.2	0.5	0.3	13.0	2.9	1.1	2.9	35.6	21.7	9.6	1 174	650
Fredericksburg City	16.0	9.7	5.9	8.5	3.8	1.1	11.0	101.9	33.4	39.7	1 978	962
Galax City	2.7	3.4	0.5	6.4	2.4	0.5	1.3	20.6	9.6	7.2	1 090	547
Hampton City	793.4	359.1	383.2	38.3	13.8	16.4	99.5	374.5	161.8	158.4	1 086	722
Harrisonburg City	9.7	2.7	2.9	7.0	1.8	2.2	6.8	88.6	20.4	40.4	988	438
Hopewell City	2.2	34.8	76.0	11.3	4.3	2.2	2.3	76.3	29.7	25.2	1 119	830
Lexington City	5.6	3.7	0.5	5.7	0.4	1.5	1.2	17.9	5.0	5.7	818	442
Lynchburg City	28.0	19.1	623.1	37.3	9.7	4.6	21.8	206.7	80.2	80.7	1 249	759
Manassas City	44.2	417.7	102.2	18.1	3.0	2.6	20.5	115.0	37.0	57.1	1 532	1 162

1. State totals may include programs not allocated by county.   2. Based on the resident population estimated as of July 1 of the year shown.

Table B. States and Counties — Local Government Finances, Government Employment, and Elections

STATE County	Local government finances, 2002 (cont'd)									Government employment, 2002			Presidential election, 2004		
	Direct general expenditure							Debt outstanding					Percent of vote cast —		
			Percent of total for —												
	Total (mil dol)	Per capita1 (dollars)	Education	Health and hospitals	Police protection	Public welfare	Highways	Total (mil dol)	Per capita1 (dollars)	Federal civilian	Federal military	State and local	Democratic	Republican	All other
	183	184	185	186	187	188	189	190	191	192	193	194	195	196	197
VIRGINIA—Cont'd															
Louisa	66.4	2 458	66.0	0.8	4.0	5.1	0.2	81.7	3 026	48	70	1 270	40.1	59.2	0.7
Lunenburg	19.7	1 477	70.1	1.0	6.4	3.9	0.4	12.0	899	28	35	839	45.1	54.5	0.4
Madison	20.3	1 569	66.2	2.5	5.8	5.7	0.0	9.3	721	74	34	488	37.7	54.5	0.4
Mathews	16.2	1 754	63.9	0.6	5.1	0.2	0.8	21.6	2 329	31	56	367	31.0	68.2	0.8
Mecklenburg	59.3	1 836	55.7	0.7	7.3	5.0	2.4	15.2	472	146	84	2 354	41.5	57.2	1.3
Middlesex	26.8	2 637	71.7	0.3	3.7	4.5	0.0	26.0	2 553	21	27	888	35.7	62.2	2.1
Montgomery	178.8	2 095	53.0	7.2	5.9	3.4	2.7	144.0	1 686	[3]384	[3]313	[3]15 206	44.3	54.8	0.9
Nelson	34.1	2 316	77.3	0.2	1.6	3.9	0.0	37.2	2 523	57	38	569	49.7	49.6	0.7
New Kent	25.1	1 771	62.2	0.7	6.6	4.8	0.0	5.4	381	40	37	606	30.7	68.2	1.0
Northampton	57.3	4 434	31.0	0.4	2.7	4.6	23.6	243.9	18 861	45	57	1 108	50.5	48.6	0.9
Northumberland	19.9	1 603	55.5	0.4	4.0	6.6	0.1	3.6	291	28	32	471	39.8	59.9	0.3
Nottoway	29.1	1 834	60.8	0.5	6.8	5.4	3.4	16.3	1 027	391	43	1 966	43.7	54.8	1.5
Orange	46.6	1 708	64.5	0.9	5.5	6.0	1.8	15.7	576	64	71	1 818	38.8	60.0	1.2
Page	41.0	1 760	56.8	1.2	6.9	7.3	1.9	11.1	477	174	61	959	34.7	64.9	0.4
Patrick	27.0	1 389	67.3	1.7	4.9	7.3	0.0	5.2	266	50	51	782	31.4	67.1	1.5
Pittsylvania	95.6	1 548	60.7	9.7	5.7	6.9	1.0	68.9	1 116	[4]266	[4]287	[4]6 242	34.0	64.3	1.7
Powhatan	38.3	1 596	75.7	0.6	4.9	4.0	0.0	56.7	2 361	50	63	2 178	25.6	73.7	0.6
Prince Edward	38.1	1 905	52.6	0.7	7.2	4.7	3.8	26.8	1 343	79	52	1 923	49.7	48.9	1.3
Prince George	81.9	2 399	50.9	0.2	3.8	2.5	0.0	87.5	2 563	[5]3 496	[5]5 936	[5]2 658	38.2	61.5	0.3
Prince William	1 034.2	3 316	51.7	2.1	5.9	3.0	1.8	1 029.1	3 300	[6]4 481	[6]6 820	[6]17 268	46.5	52.9	0.7
Pulaski	76.8	2 192	45.1	0.3	6.1	6.6	1.6	50.4	1 439	64	91	2 205	37.3	61.6	1.1
Rappahannock	12.9	1 786	65.3	1.2	3.3	7.2	1.6	0.0	0	36	19	308	45.5	53.7	0.8
Richmond	20.4	2 307	44.3	1.4	4.7	4.6	0.0	13.8	1 561	35	23	881	37.0	61.9	1.1
Roanoke	236.8	2 756	45.3	8.7	5.4	3.5	0.3	251.4	2 926	[7]1 638	[7]289	[7]6 645	34.3	65.2	0.5
Rockbridge	48.8	2 347	55.7	12.7	3.3	3.9	0.2	34.0	1 634	[8]150	[8]124	[8]2 572	39.6	59.0	1.4
Rockingham	138.1	2 012	58.3	4.8	3.8	7.2	1.0	71.5	1 042	[9]367	[9]293	[9]8 726	24.4	75.1	0.5
Russell	55.5	1 914	50.9	0.0	4.0	9.0	2.0	87.6	3 022	71	76	1 659	45.2	53.2	1.5
Scott	50.4	2 179	66.1	1.1	5.4	6.7	1.2	14.6	633	72	60	1 000	33.4	65.1	1.5
Shenandoah	73.6	2 027	54.1	0.5	5.0	6.3	2.0	68.3	1 880	152	95	1 734	30.3	69.1	0.6
Smyth	63.9	1 945	59.6	0.5	6.5	6.3	3.5	36.1	1 099	103	86	2 824	34.6	63.3	2.2
Southampton	39.2	2 247	59.9	0.5	4.4	4.5	0.4	24.4	1 398	[10]71	[10]66	[10]2 385	45.9	53.7	0.4
Spotsylvania	213.6	2 083	70.6	0.6	3.6	3.8	0.5	268.1	2 614	[11]295	[11]320	[11]7 706	36.6	62.9	0.4
Stafford	254.1	2 424	68.5	0.6	2.9	2.7	0.7	223.2	2 129	154	1 941	4 569	37.4	62.1	0.4
Surry	18.9	2 657	65.9	1.9	4.3	8.8	0.0	5.5	771	18	19	460	55.5	43.8	0.7
Sussex	28.2	2 309	67.2	0.3	7.1	6.5	0.1	28.5	2 332	61	32	1 267	55.7	43.5	0.8
Tazewell	95.6	2 172	47.9	15.5	4.5	5.5	2.3	40.9	929	109	115	3 203	41.1	57.5	1.4
Warren	55.2	1 676	55.8	0.0	8.4	5.6	2.9	25.5	776	183	88	1 412	37.3	61.2	1.6
Washington	92.6	1 805	57.6	0.3	5.4	4.9	1.9	46.9	914	[12]422	[12]182	[12]4 414	32.6	65.6	1.8
Westmoreland	30.9	1 851	57.8	0.7	6.2	6.8	0.6	18.3	1 098	66	43	765	49.2	50.4	0.4
Wise	88.1	2 113	57.6	0.3	5.8	4.9	2.5	30.9	741	[13]274	[13]119	[13]3 796	40.5	58.3	1.2
Wythe	75.4	2 713	55.9	0.7	5.0	5.5	1.8	79.7	2 868	119	72	2 062	31.0	68.6	0.4
York	144.4	2 418	56.1	0.6	3.0	2.8	0.2	114.3	1 914	[14]876	[14]2 107	[14]3 510	34.3	65.2	0.5
Independent Cities															
Alexandria City	465.7	3 560	34.8	5.9	7.4	8.5	4.1	286.8	2 192	7 836	5 029	8 987	67.0	32.4	0.6
Bedford City	9.4	1 512	6.8	0.7	15.7	0.3	13.0	34.2	5 495	[15]	[15]	[15]	41.0	57.9	1.1
Bristol City	52.9	3 090	35.7	1.0	8.8	7.4	4.2	67.0	3 914	[12]	[12]	[12]	35.8	63.7	0.5
Buena Vista City	19.2	3 043	61.2	0.4	5.6	2.2	4.0	6.0	949	[8]	[8]	[8]	38.7	59.8	1.5
Charlottesville City	129.1	2 946	37.3	1.4	7.8	7.9	2.9	59.8	1 364	[16]	[16]	[16]	72.1	27.2	0.7
Chesapeake City	771.0	3 731	38.0	24.5	5.1	2.8	4.9	828.9	4 011	1 095	1 275	13 971	42.4	57.2	0.4
Colonial Heights City	40.3	2 360	56.4	0.8	7.7	0.9	3.8	20.1	1 179	[17]	[17]	[17]	25.1	74.5	0.4
Covington City	21.4	3 365	41.9	0.3	7.0	3.1	6.3	16.3	2 569	[18]	[18]	[18]	51.4	48.1	0.6
Danville City	150.6	3 163	37.8	0.5	5.6	4.9	4.9	192.9	4 053	[4]	[4]	[4]	49.4	49.2	1.4
Emporia City	6.2	1 081	0.0	0.0	11.4	0.0	10.2	9.8	1 715	[19]	[19]	[19]	56.1	43.7	0.2
Fairfax City	43.5	1 974	7.2	0.0	17.3	0.5	16.9	31.3	1 420	[20]	[20]	[20]	51.3	47.9	0.8
Falls Church City	48.1	4 511	51.4	0.4	7.8	4.0	2.3	27.2	2 550	[20]	[20]	[20]	65.0	34.2	0.7
Franklin City	44.0	5 384	29.8	0.5	10.8	3.7	5.7	21.3	2 609	[10]	[10]	[10]	54.0	45.6	0.3
Fredericksburg City	110.5	5 504	19.8	13.6	4.9	3.3	7.3	202.6	10 092	[11]	[11]	[11]	54.3	45.1	0.5
Galax City	19.4	2 941	44.7	1.0	7.0	6.9	7.1	6.9	1 048	[21]	[21]	[21]	42.4	57.4	0.3
Hampton City	433.9	2 974	50.5	0.8	5.5	4.9	0.5	218.7	1 499	7 844	9 961	9 101	57.7	41.8	0.4
Harrisonburg City	89.6	2 189	40.9	0.4	5.5	0.0	6.6	310.8	7 598	[9]	[9]	[9]	42.7	56.5	0.8
Hopewell City	85.5	3 794	44.5	0.2	5.3	4.3	3.8	74.7	3 318	[5]	[5]	[5]	45.1	53.6	1.3
Lexington City	21.8	3 149	23.8	0.6	6.2	1.6	5.5	26.7	3 857	[8]	[8]	[8]	57.2	41.9	0.9
Lynchburg City	199.5	3 088	40.4	6.0	5.5	1.6	6.8	274.3	4 245	[22]	[22]	[22]	44.5	54.9	0.6
Manassas City	109.6	2 938	49.6	1.9	8.3	2.7	7.4	75.2	2 016	[6]	[6]	[6]	43.2	56.2	0.5

1. Based on the resident population estimated as of July 1 of the year shown.   3. Radford included with Montgomery County.   4. Danville included with Pittsylvania County.   5. Hopewell included with Prince George County.   6. Manassas and Manassas Park included with Prince William County.   7. Salem included with Roanoke County.   8. Buena Vista and Lexington included with Rockbridge County.   9. Harrisonburg included with Rockingham County.   10. Franklin included with Southhampton County.   11. Fredericksburg included with Spotsylvania County.   12. Bristol included with Washington County.   13. Norton included with Wise County.   14. Poquoson included with York County.   15. Bedford City included with Bedford County.   16. Charlottesville included with Albemarle County.   17. Petersburg and Colonial Heights included with Dinwiddie County.   18. Covington included with Alleghany County.   19. Emporia included with Greensville County.   20. Fairfax City and Falls Church included with Fairfax County.   21. Galax included with Carroll County.   22. Lynchburg included with Campbell County.

STATE/ County code	CBSA code[1]	County Type[2]	STATE County	Land area,[3] (sq km) 2000	Population and population characteristics, 2003													
								Race alone or in combination, not Hispanic or Latino (percent)					Age (percent)					
					Total persons	Rank	Per square kilometer	White	Black	Am. Indian, Alaska Native	Asian and Pacific Islander	Percent Hispanic or Latino[4]	Under 5 years	5 to 17 years	18 to 24 years	25 to 34 years	35 to 44 years	45 to 54 years
				1	2	3	4	5	6	7	8	9	10	11	12	13	14	15
			VIRGINIA—Cont'd															
51 685	47900	1	Manassas Park City	6	10 990	2 369	1 831.7	61.0	10.4	0.4	5.4	24.1	9.9	21.9	8.3	18.6	19.6	10.8
51 690	32300	4	Martinsville City	28	15 121	2 093	540.0	53.5	43.1	0.1	0.5	3.2	6.2	16.4	7.8	10.5	14.6	13.6
51 700	47260	1	Newport News City	177	181 647	316	1 026.3	51.4	42.5	1.1	3.5	4.1	8.7	20.2	9.6	14.7	15.9	12.4
51 710	47260	1	Norfolk City	139	241 727	247	1 739.0	48.0	45.7	1.1	3.8	3.8	8.0	16.8	17.6	15.7	13.5	11.2
51 720	...	7	Norton City	20	3 909	2 918	195.5	91.8	6.1	0.1	1.4	0.9	5.0	16.0	10.1	12.7	14.0	15.0
51 730	40060	1	Petersburg City	59	33 091	1 328	560.9	17.2	80.6	0.4	0.7	1.6	7.7	18.1	8.9	12.1	14.1	13.7
51 735	47260	1	Poquoson City	40	11 844	2 302	296.1	95.7	1.1	0.5	2.2	1.2	4.1	19.6	9.2	8.2	16.0	16.6
51 740	47260	1	Portsmouth City	86	99 617	542	1 158.3	44.6	53.1	1.1	1.1	1.6	7.7	18.5	11.1	13.3	14.7	12.9
51 750	13980	3	Radford City	25	15 006	2 099	600.2	89.2	8.2	0.5	1.8	1.3	3.9	8.2	38.9	13.7	7.9	8.4
51 760	40060	1	Richmond City	156	194 729	295	1 248.3	37.9	57.9	0.7	1.5	3.1	7.3	15.4	11.5	16.5	14.8	13.2
51 770	40220	2	Roanoke City	111	92 863	580	836.6	69.2	28.2	0.7	1.5	1.9	6.8	16.7	7.5	14.4	14.9	14.3
51 775	40220	2	Salem City	38	24 603	1 595	647.4	91.5	6.6	0.4	1.0	1.1	4.8	15.6	12.6	11.5	14.0	14.6
51 790	44420	4	Staunton City	51	23 848	1 620	467.6	84.7	14.0	0.5	0.7	1.2	5.3	14.4	10.5	12.6	13.9	14.1
51 800	47260	1	Suffolk City	1 036	73 515	693	71.0	54.6	43.0	0.7	1.3	1.5	6.9	19.9	9.6	12.6	16.2	12.9
51 810	47260	1	Virginia Beach City	643	439 467	143	683.5	70.4	20.5	1.0	6.6	4.3	7.3	19.9	9.7	15.0	17.2	13.3
51 820	44420	4	Waynesboro City	40	20 388	1 781	509.7	85.4	10.7	0.6	0.7	3.8	6.9	17.4	8.5	12.4	13.6	12.6
51 830	47260	1	Williamsburg City	22	11 605	2 326	527.5	80.1	12.6	0.4	5.2	2.5	3.2	6.0	44.7	9.9	7.6	7.6
51 840	49020	3	Winchester City	24	24 434	1 602	1 018.1	79.4	11.6	0.6	1.7	8.1	7.1	15.3	11.5	15.2	14.3	12.7
53 000	...	X	WASHINGTON	172 348	6 131 445	X	35.6	80.3	4.1	2.4	7.8	8.3	6.4	18.1	10.1	13.9	15.6	15.0
53 001	...	6	Adams	4 986	16 602	1 989	3.3	49.5	0.2	0.6	0.4	49.4	9.5	23.2	11.2	12.7	12.6	12.0
53 003	30300	3	Asotin	1 646	20 625	1 768	12.5	96.0	0.4	2.1	0.6	2.1	6.0	17.5	9.3	11.0	13.8	14.5
53 005	28420	3	Benton	4 411	153 660	365	34.8	82.2	1.4	1.2	2.9	13.7	7.0	20.5	10.5	12.2	14.8	14.5
53 007	48300	3	Chelan	7 566	67 973	740	9.0	78.1	0.3	1.3	1.1	20.1	6.9	19.3	10.0	11.2	14.3	14.5
53 009	38820	5	Clallam	4 505	66 892	754	14.8	89.5	0.9	5.7	1.8	3.8	4.7	15.5	9.3	9.3	12.3	15.0
53 011	38900	1	Clark	1 627	379 577	163	233.3	88.1	2.6	1.6	4.8	5.5	7.1	20.1	9.6	13.6	15.6	14.2
53 013	...	6	Columbia	2 250	4 093	2 904	1.8	91.3	0.3	1.2	0.7	6.9	4.4	16.9	9.4	9.5	13.5	16.4
53 015	31020	3	Cowlitz	2 949	95 146	566	32.3	91.4	0.9	2.8	1.8	5.2	6.2	19.0	9.7	11.9	14.4	14.7
53 017	48300	3	Douglas	4 715	33 753	1 310	7.2	77.2	0.4	1.6	0.8	21.0	6.5	20.7	10.0	11.0	14.5	14.4
53 019	...	9	Ferry	5 708	7 417	2 648	1.3	79.2	0.3	20.0	0.4	2.5	4.7	18.6	10.3	9.0	12.6	17.3
53 021	28420	3	Franklin	3 218	56 126	866	17.4	46.7	2.3	0.8	1.9	48.9	9.7	22.9	12.5	14.1	12.6	10.8
53 023	...	8	Garfield	1 840	2 371	3 028	1.3	96.5	0.0	0.5	0.8	2.6	4.7	16.8	10.0	6.4	12.8	17.1
53 025	34180	4	Grant	6 944	78 691	666	11.3	64.8	1.1	1.3	1.3	32.3	8.1	22.2	11.3	13.0	13.1	12.0
53 027	10140	4	Grays Harbor	4 965	69 406	727	14.0	88.1	0.7	6.1	1.8	5.6	5.6	17.5	10.4	11.4	14.1	14.8
53 029	36020	4	Island	540	76 384	675	141.5	88.9	2.7	1.7	5.9	3.7	6.1	18.0	9.5	12.9	14.4	13.3
53 031	...	6	Jefferson	4 699	27 716	1 474	5.9	93.7	0.9	3.5	1.7	2.1	3.8	14.1	7.8	8.1	12.5	17.7
53 033	42660	1	King	5 506	1 761 411	14	319.9	74.1	6.7	1.7	14.5	6.3	5.9	15.8	8.6	16.4	17.4	15.6
53 035	14740	3	Kitsap	1 026	240 719	248	234.6	85.7	3.6	2.9	7.4	4.6	6.2	19.0	10.6	12.3	15.6	15.4
53 037	21260	6	Kittitas	5 950	35 206	1 266	5.9	90.0	0.9	1.6	3.3	5.6	5.1	13.8	19.7	13.4	11.9	12.4
53 039	...	6	Klickitat	4 849	19 547	1 832	4.0	88.1	0.3	4.2	1.0	8.0	5.8	18.9	8.8	9.6	14.1	16.4
53 041	16500	4	Lewis	6 236	70 404	716	11.3	91.5	0.6	2.0	1.1	6.1	6.0	18.4	10.4	10.7	13.4	14.5
53 043	...	8	Lincoln	5 986	10 201	2 427	1.7	95.6	0.5	2.8	0.4	1.9	4.8	17.7	8.1	8.0	13.4	15.7
53 045	43220	6	Mason	2 489	52 129	905	20.9	88.8	1.2	4.8	2.0	5.3	5.1	16.6	10.0	11.2	13.9	14.6
53 047	...	6	Okanogan	13 644	39 134	1 152	2.9	74.3	0.4	11.9	0.9	14.2	6.2	19.3	9.5	10.4	13.3	15.8
53 049	...	7	Pacific	2 416	21 103	1 748	8.7	90.3	0.5	3.6	2.0	5.5	4.4	15.7	8.2	8.2	11.7	15.3
53 051	...	8	Pend Oreille	3 627	12 254	2 280	3.4	94.5	0.3	3.4	1.0	2.0	4.7	18.3	9.2	8.0	14.0	16.9
53 053	42660	1	Pierce	4 348	740 957	69	170.4	78.8	8.6	2.6	8.4	6.3	6.8	19.4	10.8	13.9	16.0	13.8
53 055	...	9	San Juan	453	14 761	2 117	32.6	95.4	0.4	1.3	1.6	2.3	3.5	14.3	6.8	7.5	12.6	19.5
53 057	34580	3	Skagit	4 494	109 234	505	24.3	83.4	0.7	2.4	2.4	12.5	6.1	18.4	10.5	11.6	13.9	14.3
53 059	38900	1	Skamania	4 290	10 292	2 419	2.4	92.1	0.4	3.3	0.7	4.8	5.7	18.2	9.5	9.9	16.3	17.0
53 061	42660	1	Snohomish	5 411	639 409	88	118.2	83.9	2.6	2.2	8.7	5.6	6.6	19.4	9.6	13.9	17.4	14.9
53 063	44060	2	Spokane	4 568	431 027	145	94.4	91.7	2.3	2.3	3.0	3.1	6.3	18.1	11.2	13.1	14.8	14.6
53 065	...	6	Stevens	6 419	40 776	1 115	6.4	92.1	0.5	6.7	1.0	1.8	5.2	20.0	9.8	8.7	14.0	16.9
53 067	36500	3	Thurston	1 883	221 950	262	117.9	85.9	3.2	2.6	6.9	4.8	5.8	17.7	10.4	13.0	15.0	15.6
53 069	...	8	Wahkiakum	684	3 748	2 930	5.5	95.3	0.3	2.6	0.6	2.6	3.8	15.9	8.1	8.3	13.2	16.4
53 071	47460	4	Walla Walla	3 291	56 751	857	17.2	79.9	1.7	1.4	1.8	16.4	6.0	17.2	14.2	12.0	13.4	13.2
53 073	13380	3	Whatcom	5 490	176 571	322	32.2	87.7	1.1	3.5	4.3	5.5	5.6	16.9	13.5	13.5	13.7	14.4
53 075	39420	4	Whitman	5 593	40 702	1 120	7.3	88.2	1.9	1.2	7.5	3.1	4.5	12.3	26.1	16.0	10.5	10.0
53 077	49420	3	Yakima	11 127	226 727	257	20.4	55.7	1.1	4.8	1.3	38.3	8.7	22.1	10.8	12.8	13.5	12.4
54 000	...	X	WEST VIRGINIA	62 361	1 810 354	X	29.0	95.2	3.6	0.6	0.8	0.7	5.6	16.0	9.6	12.4	14.0	15.6
54 001	...	7	Barbour	883	15 653	2 055	17.7	97.9	0.8	1.5	0.4	0.5	5.1	16.6	10.1	11.7	14.1	14.9
54 003	25180	3	Berkeley	832	85 272	624	102.5	92.1	5.9	0.7	1.0	1.7	6.5	18.6	9.2	13.6	15.4	14.0
54 005	16620	2	Boone	1 303	25 785	1 545	19.8	98.7	0.8	0.4	0.2	0.5	6.3	16.5	8.8	12.8	13.8	17.4
54 007	...	8	Braxton	1 330	14 771	2 116	11.1	98.3	0.7	0.9	0.2	0.4	5.2	16.4	8.5	12.5	15.1	15.3

1. CBSA = Core Based Statistical Area. See Appendix A for explanation. See Appendix B for list of metropolitan areas with component counties. 2. County type code from the Economic Research Service of USDA Rural-Urban Continuum Codes. See Appendix A for definition. 3. Dry land or land partially or temporarily covered by water. 4. Hispanic or Latino persons may be of any race.

STATE County	Population, 2003 (cont'd) Age (percent) (cont'd)				Population — change and components of change, 1990–2003 Total persons		Percent change		Components of change, 2000–2003			Households, 2000			Percent	
	55 to 64 years	65 to 74 years	75 years and over	Percent female	1990	2000	1990–2000	2000–2003	Births	Deaths	Net migration	Number	Percent change, 1990–2000	Persons per household	Female family householder[1]	One person
	16	17	18	19	20	21	22	23	24	25	26	27	28	29	30	31
VIRGINIA—Cont'd																
Manassas Park City	5.7	3.3	1.4	48.8	6 798	10 290	51.4	6.8	664	104	138	3 254	49.1	3.16	12.1	14.4
Martinsville City	10.0	9.7	11.6	54.8	16 162	15 416	-4.6	-1.9	676	886	-70	6 498	-5.0	2.27	19.1	34.2
Newport News City	7.8	5.3	4.8	52.1	171 477	180 150	5.1	0.8	10 586	4 723	-4 406	69 686	9.0	2.50	17.9	27.0
Norfolk City	6.7	4.8	5.3	48.1	261 250	234 403	-10.3	3.1	13 404	6 731	668	86 210	-3.7	2.45	18.8	30.2
Norton City	11.4	7.9	7.3	55.2	4 247	3 904	-8.1	0.1	136	178	49	1 730	1.9	2.23	15.7	34.9
Petersburg City	10.0	7.9	7.9	54.1	37 071	33 740	-9.0	-1.9	1 889	1 635	-906	13 799	-6.3	2.38	26.1	32.2
Poquoson City	12.9	7.3	5.1	49.8	11 005	11 566	5.1	2.4	276	228	230	4 166	10.5	2.75	8.4	15.9
Portsmouth City	8.6	6.4	7.2	51.6	103 910	100 565	-3.2	-0.9	5 276	3 538	-2 641	38 170	-1.5	2.51	20.9	27.5
Radford City	6.3	4.9	5.0	55.0	15 940	15 859	-0.5	-5.4	459	328	-1 010	5 809	11.6	2.25	8.9	32.0
Richmond City	8.1	6.4	7.2	53.5	202 713	197 790	-2.4	-1.5	10 536	7 642	-5 982	84 549	-0.9	2.21	20.4	37.6
Roanoke City	9.3	7.5	9.1	53.1	96 487	94 911	-1.6	-2.2	4 125	4 077	-2 083	42 003	2.4	2.20	16.5	35.9
Salem City	10.6	8.6	8.1	52.6	23 835	24 747	3.8	-0.6	796	1 057	135	9 954	8.7	2.32	11.5	29.0
Staunton City	10.5	8.7	9.7	52.8	24 581	23 853	-3.0	0.0	783	1 001	236	9 676	2.6	2.19	11.7	34.7
Suffolk City	8.9	5.6	4.7	51.8	52 143	63 677	22.1	15.4	3 233	2 026	8 368	23 283	25.7	2.69	16.8	20.2
Virginia Beach City	7.8	5.0	3.8	50.5	393 089	425 257	8.2	3.3	20 468	8 084	2 297	154 455	13.9	2.70	12.4	20.4
Waynesboro City	10.7	8.3	8.9	53.0	18 549	19 520	5.2	4.4	877	844	860	8 332	10.1	2.31	14.5	30.1
Williamsburg City	6.8	6.8	6.5	55.6	11 600	11 998	3.4	-3.3	295	452	-218	3 619	4.4	2.07	9.6	35.9
Winchester City	8.4	7.4	7.5	51.2	21 947	23 585	7.5	3.6	1 197	849	549	10 001	10.1	2.28	11.7	34.4
WASHINGTON	9.8	5.6	5.6	50.1	4 866 669	5 894 121	21.1	4.0	255 338	144 509	128 164	2 271 398	21.3	2.53	9.9	26.2
Adams	8.4	5.3	5.0	49.1	13 603	16 428	20.8	1.1	1 065	292	-613	5 229	14.0	3.09	10.1	18.7
Asotin	10.9	8.1	8.8	52.0	17 605	20 551	16.7	0.4	774	633	-47	8 364	19.4	2.42	11.9	27.0
Benton	9.0	5.3	4.8	50.1	112 560	142 475	26.6	7.9	6 955	3 172	7 383	52 866	25.2	2.68	10.2	23.2
Chelan	9.4	6.8	7.1	50.2	52 250	66 616	27.5	2.0	3 104	1 790	72	25 021	21.2	2.62	8.7	25.1
Clallam	11.9	10.3	11.1	50.7	56 210	64 525	14.8	3.7	1 964	2 522	3 274	27 164	18.9	2.31	9.0	28.1
Clark	8.8	4.7	4.5	50.2	238 053	345 238	45.0	9.9	17 130	7 559	24 553	127 208	43.8	2.69	10.3	21.8
Columbia	12.5	8.5	9.4	50.7	4 024	4 064	1.0	0.7	117	162	79	1 687	6.6	2.36	8.5	29.0
Cowlitz	10.4	6.7	6.6	50.5	82 119	92 948	13.2	2.4	3 971	2 906	1 257	35 850	13.3	2.55	10.7	24.3
Douglas	9.2	6.7	6.1	50.5	26 205	32 603	24.4	3.5	1 404	728	503	11 726	21.0	2.76	9.7	20.0
Ferry	13.2	7.8	5.5	48.1	6 295	7 260	15.3	2.2	227	165	103	2 823	25.6	2.49	10.2	24.8
Franklin	6.6	4.1	3.5	47.3	37 473	49 347	31.7	13.7	3 662	889	3 977	14 840	21.7	3.26	11.4	17.8
Garfield	10.2	10.1	10.8	50.5	2 248	2 397	6.6	-1.1	72	101	5	987	7.0	2.39	6.7	28.3
Grant	8.1	5.9	5.4	48.8	54 798	74 698	36.3	5.3	4 275	1 661	1 432	25 204	27.6	2.92	9.8	21.2
Grays Harbor	10.6	7.6	7.3	49.3	64 175	67 194	4.7	3.3	2 483	2 674	2 419	26 808	5.1	2.48	11.1	26.7
Island	10.3	7.3	6.7	50.1	60 195	71 558	18.9	6.7	2 944	1 841	3 680	27 784	27.5	2.52	7.8	21.5
Jefferson	14.4	10.9	10.0	50.6	20 406	25 953	27.2	6.8	671	857	1 568	11 645	35.0	2.21	8.2	28.5
King	9.3	5.0	5.4	50.2	1 507 305	1 737 034	15.2	1.4	69 965	37 590	-7 389	710 916	15.4	2.39	9.0	30.5
Kitsap	9.6	5.4	5.2	49.1	189 731	231 969	22.3	3.8	9 571	5 973	5 319	86 416	24.8	2.60	9.5	22.6
Kittitas	9.2	5.8	5.5	50.4	26 725	33 362	24.8	5.5	1 195	805	1 457	13 382	27.9	2.33	7.2	28.4
Klickitat	11.8	7.6	6.5	50.4	16 616	19 161	15.3	2.0	738	563	232	7 473	20.3	2.54	9.1	23.8
Lewis	10.7	7.6	7.7	50.3	59 358	68 600	15.6	2.6	2 722	2 365	1 487	26 306	17.0	2.57	9.9	24.0
Lincoln	12.8	9.8	9.5	50.3	8 864	10 184	14.9	0.2	296	361	92	4 151	15.1	2.42	6.4	26.0
Mason	11.1	9.0	7.3	48.4	38 341	49 405	28.9	5.5	1 718	1 732	2 700	18 912	29.8	2.49	9.2	23.3
Okanogan	11.0	8.1	6.7	50.3	33 350	39 564	18.6	-1.1	1 639	1 204	-865	15 027	18.8	2.58	11.0	24.5
Pacific	13.3	11.7	10.7	50.6	18 882	20 984	11.1	0.6	632	1 042	539	9 096	15.2	2.27	7.9	29.5
Pend Oreille	13.0	8.7	6.6	49.9	8 915	11 732	31.6	4.4	380	378	526	4 639	36.6	2.51	8.4	25.0
Pierce	8.5	5.3	4.7	50.2	586 203	700 820	19.6	5.7	32 373	17 473	25 326	260 800	21.5	2.60	11.8	24.3
San Juan	16.2	10.1	9.1	50.9	10 035	14 077	40.3	4.9	325	413	755	6 466	47.2	2.16	6.9	30.6
Skagit	9.6	6.8	7.3	50.5	79 545	102 979	29.5	6.1	4 456	3 164	4 985	38 852	27.1	2.60	9.7	23.3
Skamania	11.4	5.9	4.9	49.5	8 289	9 872	19.1	4.3	345	222	296	3 755	22.5	2.61	8.2	21.1
Snohomish	8.5	4.7	4.4	49.9	465 628	606 024	30.2	5.5	27 649	12 844	18 837	224 852	30.9	2.65	9.8	22.6
Spokane	8.9	5.9	6.4	50.8	361 333	417 939	15.7	3.1	17 573	12 002	7 987	163 611	15.5	2.46	11.0	28.1
Stevens	11.7	7.4	5.9	50.4	30 948	40 066	29.5	1.8	1 367	1 132	508	15 017	33.6	2.64	8.7	22.0
Thurston	9.7	5.6	5.6	51.0	161 238	207 355	28.6	7.0	8 192	5 351	11 735	81 625	31.3	2.50	10.3	25.1
Wahkiakum	15.1	11.1	9.1	49.6	3 327	3 824	14.9	-2.0	83	168	12	1 553	17.6	2.42	6.3	24.4
Walla Walla	8.5	6.2	8.3	49.3	48 439	55 180	13.9	2.8	2 253	1 603	953	19 647	11.5	2.54	9.5	27.1
Whatcom	8.8	5.8	5.8	50.7	127 780	166 814	30.5	5.8	6 390	4 019	7 490	64 446	32.8	2.51	8.8	25.6
Whitman	6.9	4.3	4.9	49.4	38 775	40 740	5.1	-0.1	1 208	732	-527	15 257	12.6	2.31	6.2	29.4
Yakima	8.2	5.4	5.7	50.1	188 823	222 581	17.9	1.9	13 450	5 421	-3 936	73 993	12.1	2.96	12.5	21.5
WEST VIRGINIA	11.4	8.0	7.3	51.2	1 793 477	1 808 344	0.8	0.1	66 283	68 098	4 504	736 481	7.0	2.40	10.7	27.1
Barbour	11.5	8.0	7.4	50.7	15 699	15 557	-0.9	0.6	507	594	197	6 123	4.9	2.47	10.3	25.1
Berkeley	9.2	6.0	4.4	50.2	59 253	75 905	28.1	12.3	3 455	2 159	7 868	29 569	32.3	2.53	10.7	24.2
Boone	10.7	7.1	6.1	51.0	25 870	25 535	-1.3	1.0	1 099	939	113	10 291	6.6	2.47	10.5	24.6
Braxton	11.7	7.7	7.7	49.3	12 998	14 702	13.1	0.5	474	541	147	5 771	16.6	2.46	9.2	25.2

1. No spouse present.

Table B. States and Counties — Vital Statistics, Health Resources, and Crime

STATE County	Births, average 1999–2001		Deaths, average 1999–2001				Physicians,[4] 2000		Hospitals,[4] 1998			Medicare enrollees, 2003	Serious crimes known to police,[6] 2002	
			Number		Rate					Beds			Total	
	Total	Rate[1]	Total	Infant[2]	Total[1]	Infant[3]	Number	Rate[5]	Number	Number	Rate[5]		Number	Rate[7]
	32	33	34	35	36	37	38	39	40	41	42	43	44	45
VIRGINIA—Cont'd														
Manassas Park City	210	20.3	38	0	3.6	D	13	126	0	0	0	11	247	2 330
Martinsville City	209	13.5	252	0	16.3	D	75	487	1	182	1 162	6 521	670	4 218
Newport News City	3 176	17.6	1 450	36	8.1	11.4	373	207	3	794	445	21 502	9 971	5 372
Norfolk City	3 965	16.9	2 056	46	8.8	11.5	852	363	5	1 321	614	27 685	15 501	6 418
Norton City	49	12.5	52	0	13.2	D	50	1 281	2	121	2 912	1 402	248	6 166
Petersburg City	545	16.1	500	7	14.8	13.5	94	279	1	296	852	7 916	2 574	7 404
Poquoson City	93	8.0	79	0	6.9	D	10	86	0	0	0	824	133	1 116
Portsmouth City	1 580	15.7	1 111	18	11.1	11.4	251	250	2	505	510	15 742	7 029	6 783
Radford City	147	9.3	111	0	7.0	D	62	391	1	159	1 011	2 218	NA	NA
Richmond City	3 038	15.3	2 363	45	11.9	14.7	1 160	586	7	1 853	954	36 435	18 234	8 947
Roanoke City	1 336	14.1	1 258	14	13.2	10.2	341	359	2	744	794	23 890	4 361	4 459
Salem City	240	9.7	314	2	12.7	D	179	723	1	335	1 357	6 512	637	2 498
Staunton City	251	10.6	299	0	12.6	D	71	298	0	0	0	6 757	921	3 747
Suffolk City	971	15.1	629	10	9.8	10.6	130	204	1	185	295	9 706	3 379	5 150
Virginia Beach City	6 280	14.8	2 417	47	5.7	7.5	751	177	2	430	99	43 060	16 087	3 671
Waynesboro City	291	14.9	239	0	12.2	D	33	169	0	0	0	5 592	883	4 390
Williamsburg City	77	6.4	137	0	11.4	D	94	783	1	105	877	6 519	313	2 532
Winchester City	339	14.3	264	2	11.1	D	193	818	1	365	1 611	5 226	1 478	6 082
WASHINGTON	80 064	13.5	44 149	427	7.5	5.3	16 660	283	92	12 093	213	775 358	309 931	5 107
Adams	328	20.1	112	4	6.9	D	13	79	2	61	398	1 511	822	4 859
Asotin	251	12.2	214	2	10.5	D	23	112	1	41	193	4 100	859	4 059
Benton	2 138	14.9	930	14	6.5	6.4	246	173	3	290	213	17 760	5 406	3 683
Chelan	974	14.7	556	4	8.4	D	199	299	3	246	410	7 970	3 212	4 683
Clallam	615	9.5	773	3	11.9	D	136	211	2	198	309	16 680	2 114	3 182
Clark	5 318	15.3	2 301	23	6.6	4.4	430	125	1	310	95	41 311	13 731	3 863
Columbia	32	8.0	55	0	13.6	D	4	98	1	18	433	824	180	4 302
Cowlitz	1 267	13.6	909	9	9.7	7.4	159	171	1	209	228	15 448	5 984	6 253
Douglas	448	13.7	232	1	7.1	D	15	46	0	0	0	7 361	1 338	3 986
Ferry	72	10.0	54	0	7.5	D	2	28	1	25	349	1 144	76	1 017
Franklin	1 116	22.5	298	7	6.0	6.3	54	109	1	140	301	4 829	1 976	3 889
Garfield	24	10.2	29	0	12.3	D	0	0	1	54	2 318	558	76	3 079
Grant	1 378	18.3	529	5	7.0	D	66	88	4	201	285	10 696	4 033	5 632
Grays Harbor	796	11.8	797	5	11.8	D	83	124	2	188	278	12 829	3 528	5 151
Island	923	12.9	539	4	7.5	D	109	152	1	51	73	9 499	NA	NA
Jefferson	211	8.1	270	0	10.4	D	47	181	1	43	164	6 372	748	2 799
King	22 105	12.7	11 683	108	6.7	4.9	6 018	346	19	4 155	251	201 881	102 094	5 708
Kitsap	2 986	12.9	1 756	18	7.6	6.1	435	188	1	252	108	29 277	9 147	3 830
Kittitas	368	11.0	244	2	7.3	D	39	117	1	39	123	4 541	1 939	5 645
Klickitat	237	12.4	178	1	9.3	D	11	57	2	58	301	3 357	597	3 026
Lewis	892	13.0	736	7	10.7	8.2	68	99	2	204	299	13 150	3 113	4 407
Lincoln	101	10.0	117	0	11.5	D	8	79	2	139	1 428	2 237	243	2 317
Mason	538	10.9	516	4	10.4	D	42	85	1	58	116	10 057	2 856	5 697
Okanogan	527	13.4	357	3	9.1	D	47	119	3	171	447	6 820	933	2 825
Pacific	187	8.9	299	1	14.3	D	22	105	2	43	207	5 283	672	3 110
Pend Oreille	122	10.4	108	1	9.2	D	7	60	1	96	833	2 309	405	3 353
Pierce	10 051	14.3	5 241	66	7.4	6.5	1 392	199	7	1 058	156	86 587	44 304	6 142
San Juan	98	7.0	118	0	8.4	D	42	298	0	0	0	2 811	214	1 476
Skagit	1 382	13.4	942	9	9.1	6.3	211	205	3	307	309	17 462	6 727	6 344
Skamania	110	11.2	74	1	7.5	D	4	41	0	0	0	1 032	346	3 404
Snohomish	8 580	14.1	3 877	42	6.4	4.9	777	128	5	621	106	65 660	23 890	3 924
Spokane	5 535	13.2	3 641	27	8.7	4.9	993	238	4	1 274	312	61 613	24 322	5 766
Stevens	443	11.1	345	2	8.6	D	34	85	2	100	253	6 330	978	2 388
Thurston	2 541	12.2	1 580	11	7.6	4.5	446	215	2	437	216	29 554	8 901	4 169
Wahkiakum	32	8.4	47	1	12.5	D	2	52	0	0	0	812	44	1 118
Walla Walla	696	12.6	521	2	9.4	D	169	306	2	207	385	8 946	2 322	4 087
Whatcom	2 011	12.0	1 206	8	7.2	4.0	298	179	1	228	145	23 740	8 879	5 169
Whitman	404	9.9	230	2	5.7	D	46	113	2	90	228	4 159	NA	NA
Yakima	4 226	19.0	1 734	28	7.8	6.5	370	166	4	481	221	28 709	14 319	6 248
WEST VIRGINIA	20 674	11.4	21 043	153	11.6	7.4	3 593	199	56	8 397	464	347 459	45 320	2 515
Barbour	163	10.5	195	2	12.6	D	8	51	1	72	446	2 935	134	864
Berkeley	1 043	13.7	642	9	8.4	8.6	108	142	1	209	294	11 308	2 463	3 256
Boone	338	13.2	297	1	11.6	D	12	47	1	38	145	4 925	323	1 296
Braxton	153	10.4	155	1	10.5	D	11	75	1	30	228	2 678	219	1 592

1. Per 1,000 estimated resident population. 2. Deaths of infants under 1 year old. 3. Deaths of infants under 1 year old per 1,000 live births. 4. Data subject to copyright. 5. Per 100,000 resident population as of July 1 of the year shown. 6. Data for serious crimes have not been adjusted for underreporting; this may affect comparability between geographic areas and over time. 7. Per 100,000 population estimated by the FBI.

Table B. States and Counties — Crime, Education, Money Income, and Poverty

	Serious crimes known to police,[1] 2002 (cont'd)		Education						Money income, 1999				Percent below poverty level, 1999			
	Rate[2]		School enrollment and attainment, 2000				Local government expenditures,[5] 2000–2001			Households						
			Enrollment[3]		Attainment[4] (percent)					Median income						
STATE County	Violent	Property	Total	Percent private	High school graduate or less	Bachelor's degree or more	Total current expenditures (mil dol)	Current expenditures per student (dollars)	Per capita income[6] (dollars)	Dollars	Percent change, 1989–1999 (constant 1999 dollars)	Percent with income of $100,000 or more	Persons	Households	Families	Families with children
	46	47	48	49	50	51	52	53	54	55	56	57	58	59	60	61
VIRGINIA—Cont'd																
Manassas Park City	113	2 216	2 862	15.1	51.0	20.3	14.7	7 319	21 048	60 794	15.8	13.8	5.2	4.8	4.7	5.3
Martinsville City	403	3 815	3 540	6.4	60.8	16.6	20.4	7 520	17 251	27 441	-9.0	5.9	19.2	19.8	14.0	23.7
Newport News City	730	4 642	50 215	12.8	45.6	19.9	219.7	6 657	17 843	36 597	-0.8	5.9	13.8	13.0	11.3	17.0
Norfolk City	559	5 859	63 867	14.5	51.2	19.6	266.7	7 141	17 372	31 815	0.5	6.3	19.4	18.1	15.5	23.2
Norton City	423	5 743	906	5.3	60.3	14.0	4.9	6 882	16 024	22 788	9.7	5.3	22.8	23.3	19.1	32.0
Petersburg City	765	6 639	8 191	9.1	61.7	14.8	43.7	7 301	15 989	28 851	0.8	4.4	19.6	19.1	16.7	24.4
Poquoson City	59	1 057	3 260	12.1	38.5	31.6	14.8	5 993	25 336	60 920	4.9	18.7	4.5	4.3	3.0	4.9
Portsmouth City	967	5 816	26 135	13.7	54.2	13.8	121.0	7 346	16 507	33 742	2.1	4.8	16.2	14.9	13.3	20.6
Radford City	NA	NA	8 502	4.2	36.3	34.1	10.4	6 566	14 289	24 654	-5.8	5.3	31.4	30.6	6.9	9.8
Richmond City	1 304	7 643	54 048	19.2	48.4	29.5	245.4	9 008	20 337	31 121	-1.6	8.3	21.4	19.3	17.1	26.9
Roanoke City	523	3 937	20 600	11.3	54.4	18.7	105.9	7 675	18 468	30 719	1.2	5.0	15.9	15.3	12.9	21.7
Salem City	98	2 400	6 792	26.8	50.2	19.8	27.2	6 878	20 091	38 997	-0.1	8.5	6.7	7.5	4.3	6.6
Staunton City	208	3 540	5 314	29.7	55.5	20.4	22.3	7 995	19 161	32 941	-3.3	6.6	11.7	13.2	7.7	13.1
Suffolk City	655	4 495	17 697	15.7	52.8	17.3	73.8	6 161	18 836	41 115	17.1	9.0	13.2	13.4	10.8	15.6
Virginia Beach City	219	3 452	121 415	15.5	35.5	28.1	509.0	6 647	22 365	48 705	-0.1	12.1	6.5	6.3	5.1	7.4
Waynesboro City	746	3 644	4 309	9.4	56.0	20.6	21.8	7 181	17 932	32 686	-8.8	5.4	12.8	12.4	11.0	19.7
Williamsburg City	186	2 346	6 365	9.9	31.2	45.0	(7)NA	(7)NA	18 483	37 093	8.7	13.2	18.3	15.7	9.3	22.5
Winchester City	370	5 711	5 762	24.0	51.3	23.7	29.4	8 653	20 500	34 335	-2.0	8.4	13.2	12.9	8.1	12.5
WASHINGTON	345	4 761	1 584 701	13.7	37.8	27.7	6 644.7	6 612	22 973	45 776	9.3	12.6	10.6	9.8	7.3	11.2
Adams	148	4 712	4 945	6.1	62.9	12.2	26.4	6 957	13 534	33 888	2.5	3.8	18.2	14.5	13.6	19.5
Asotin	232	3 828	5 037	6.7	46.9	18.0	23.8	6 791	17 748	33 524	9.0	6.4	15.4	13.4	11.6	19.5
Benton	232	3 453	40 139	10.1	38.9	26.3	187.5	6 510	21 301	47 044	7.4	11.3	10.3	9.1	7.8	11.7
Chelan	227	4 455	18 093	11.3	46.7	21.9	84.3	6 474	19 273	37 316	14.2	9.4	12.4	11.3	8.8	13.4
Clallam	154	3 028	14 410	10.9	42.3	20.8	68.6	6 808	19 517	36 449	6.7	5.9	12.5	12.2	8.9	16.0
Clark	244	3 619	92 185	11.9	39.2	22.1	415.4	6 307	21 448	48 376	13.2	11.8	9.1	8.2	6.9	10.3
Columbia	120	4 183	918	9.5	47.8	17.5	5.1	7 812	17 374	33 500	11.2	5.1	12.6	12.0	8.6	13.6
Cowlitz	373	5 880	23 679	9.6	49.6	13.3	113.6	6 416	18 583	39 797	6.3	7.3	14.0	12.7	10.3	16.5
Douglas	110	3 875	8 929	6.2	51.0	16.2	43.9	6 489	17 148	38 464	5.8	5.9	14.4	12.1	11.2	17.8
Ferry	120	896	1 875	7.9	51.7	13.5	10.1	8 499	15 019	30 388	-10.1	3.4	19.0	18.1	13.3	21.3
Franklin	325	3 564	14 657	6.2	60.3	13.6	76.1	6 986	15 459	38 991	18.0	9.0	19.2	16.8	15.5	22.3
Garfield	284	2 796	586	2.9	45.1	17.0	3.6	7 680	16 992	33 398	-1.2	4.7	14.2	12.9	12.0	15.4
Grant	316	5 316	21 570	5.2	55.6	13.7	103.4	6 496	15 037	35 276	17.4	6.1	17.4	15.2	13.1	19.3
Grays Harbor	172	4 979	16 737	5.8	53.2	12.7	88.0	6 839	16 799	34 160	10.3	5.1	16.1	15.1	11.9	19.0
Island	NA	NA	17 742	12.0	32.2	27.0	59.0	5 979	21 472	45 513	16.2	9.9	7.0	7.1	5.1	8.4
Jefferson	161	2 638	5 042	12.6	35.6	28.4	24.3	6 734	22 211	37 869	11.9	8.3	11.3	11.3	7.2	15.4
King	396	5 312	444 560	18.1	28.9	40.0	1 696.1	6 738	29 521	53 157	9.4	18.7	8.4	7.8	5.3	8.0
Kitsap	387	3 443	62 794	12.9	34.7	25.3	264.1	6 347	22 317	46 840	8.8	11.6	8.8	8.2	6.3	9.4
Kittitas	169	5 476	12 277	4.5	43.8	26.2	32.4	6 788	18 928	32 546	18.2	7.2	19.6	21.5	10.5	15.9
Klickitat	218	2 808	4 850	9.4	52.6	16.4	27.5	7 193	16 502	34 267	10.8	4.7	17.0	15.7	12.6	19.2
Lewis	311	4 096	17 267	9.3	52.4	12.9	87.3	6 787	17 082	35 511	8.3	5.2	14.0	13.2	10.4	16.5
Lincoln	133	2 184	2 355	10.7	44.7	18.8	20.6	9 786	17 888	35 255	6.6	5.6	12.6	11.8	8.4	14.4
Mason	349	5 348	11 233	7.6	48.7	15.6	55.4	6 547	18 056	39 586	12.0	6.1	12.2	11.7	8.8	15.3
Okanogan	254	2 570	10 277	6.5	54.1	15.9	61.0	7 209	14 900	29 726	9.0	4.1	21.3	19.3	16.0	24.3
Pacific	259	2 851	4 621	6.5	52.6	15.2	26.6	7 912	17 322	31 209	16.0	4.4	14.4	14.0	9.1	16.4
Pend Oreille	174	3 179	2 986	10.9	52.4	12.3	15.5	7 590	15 731	31 677	13.3	5.2	18.1	16.8	13.6	25.7
Pierce	555	5 587	191 320	14.3	42.9	20.6	837.2	6 545	20 948	45 204	10.6	10.4	10.5	9.6	7.5	11.3
San Juan	55	1 421	2 789	16.2	24.3	40.2	13.9	7 537	30 603	43 491	3.5	13.7	9.2	9.6	6.0	11.1
Skagit	186	6 158	26 225	8.9	42.4	20.8	131.8	6 975	21 256	42 381	11.1	9.5	11.1	9.5	7.9	11.6
Skamania	118	3 286	2 385	8.8	47.6	16.8	9.8	7 590	18 002	39 317	1.7	6.3	13.1	12.2	10.0	16.5
Snohomish	242	3 682	163 166	12.5	36.7	24.4	656.5	6 299	23 417	53 060	7.2	14.3	6.9	6.5	4.9	6.7
Spokane	418	5 348	117 842	15.5	37.7	25.0	493.6	6 799	19 233	37 308	7.8	7.9	12.3	12.2	8.3	12.9
Stevens	54	2 334	10 414	9.8	50.1	15.3	45.9	7 099	15 895	34 673	5.6	4.3	15.9	15.2	11.5	16.5
Thurston	293	3 876	56 997	12.6	34.3	29.8	249.4	6 604	22 415	46 975	12.9	10.8	8.8	8.8	5.8	9.4
Wahkiakum	102	1 016	912	12.6	48.0	14.8	3.3	6 503	19 063	39 444	8.9	4.7	8.1	7.5	5.9	11.5
Walla Walla	308	3 779	16 905	28.9	43.0	23.3	61.3	6 834	16 509	35 900	9.4	6.5	15.1	13.7	10.2	16.6
Whatcom	238	4 931	51 210	11.3	40.1	27.2	167.0	6 416	20 025	40 005	5.0	8.9	14.2	13.6	7.8	11.9
Whitman	NA	NA	20 964	4.3	26.4	44.0	40.3	8 335	15 298	28 584	-1.8	6.3	25.6	25.4	11.0	15.8
Yakima	271	5 977	63 808	8.8	58.7	15.3	315.3	6 595	15 606	34 828	9.8	7.0	19.7	16.4	14.8	21.9
WEST VIRGINIA	234	2 281	418 553	9.0	64.2	14.8	2 133.4	7 465	16 477	29 696	6.3	5.0	17.9	18.0	13.9	21.4
Barbour	168	697	3 687	14.9	73.4	11.8	18.1	6 818	12 440	24 729	17.9	2.3	22.6	22.2	18.4	27.1
Berkeley	294	2 963	17 453	9.8	62.8	15.1	93.5	7 148	17 982	38 763	5.3	6.0	11.5	11.4	8.7	13.1
Boone	104	1 192	5 551	4.1	77.0	7.2	38.9	8 689	14 453	25 669	11.9	2.8	22.0	21.9	18.3	25.7
Braxton	247	1 345	3 065	3.4	75.0	9.2	18.7	7 036	13 349	24 412	11.1	3.0	22.0	21.5	17.9	26.6

1. Data for serious crimes have not been adjusted for underreporting; this may affect comparability between geographic areas and over time.　2. Per 100,000 population estimated by the FBI.　3. All persons 3 years old and over enrolled in nursery school through college.　4. Persons 25 years old and over.　5. Elementary and secondary education expenditures.　6. Based on population enumerated as of April 1, 2000.　7. Williamsburg included with James City County.

Table B. States and Counties — **Personal Income**

STATE County	Personal income, 2002 Total (mil dol)	Percent change, 2001–2002	Per capita[1] Dollars	Per capita[1] Rank	Wages and salaries[2] (mil dol)	Proprietor's income (mil dol)	Dividends, interest, and rent (mil dol)	Transfer payments Total (mil dol)	Government payments to individuals Total (mil dol)	Social Security (mil dol)	Medical payments (mil dol)	Income maintenance (mil dol)	Unemployment insurance (mil dol)
	62	63	64	65	66	67	68	69	70	71	72	73	74
VIRGINIA—Cont'd													
Manassas Park City	(3)	(3)	(3)	(3)	(3)	(3)	(3)	(3)	(3)	(3)	(3)	(3)	(3)
Martinsville City	(4)	(4)	(4)	(4)	(4)	(4)	(4)	(4)	(4)	(4)	(4)	(4)	(4)
Newport News City	4 315	3.1	23 986	1 414	4 361	131	623	673	631	230	232	83	25
Norfolk City	6 015	4.5	24 873	1 165	10 387	288	1 012	939	892	276	373	126	35
Norton City	(5)	(5)	(5)	(5)	(5)	(5)	(5)	(5)	(5)	(5)	(5)	(5)	(5)
Petersburg City	(6)	(6)	(6)	(6)	(6)	(6)	(6)	(6)	(6)	(6)	(6)	(6)	(6)
Poquoson City	(7)	(7)	(7)	(7)	(7)	(7)	(7)	(7)	(7)	(7)	(7)	(7)	(7)
Portsmouth City	2 376	5.3	23 835	1 461	2 359	58	326	477	454	145	183	62	19
Radford City	(8)	(8)	(8)	(8)	(8)	(8)	(8)	(8)	(8)	(8)	(8)	(8)	(8)
Richmond City	6 337	2.1	32 237	216	8 681	631	1 317	1 092	1 044	315	474	148	38
Roanoke City	2 526	3.9	27 033	694	3 099	184	392	553	530	174	212	51	17
Salem City	(9)	(9)	(9)	(9)	(9)	(9)	(9)	(9)	(9)	(9)	(9)	(9)	(9)
Staunton City	(10)	(10)	(10)	(10)	(10)	(10)	(10)	(10)	(10)	(10)	(10)	(10)	(10)
Suffolk City	1 822	4.0	26 059	876	798	72	261	264	248	101	92	30	10
Virginia Beach City	14 032	4.6	32 374	209	7 288	987	2 203	1 235	1 140	488	387	92	38
Waynesboro City	(10)	(10)	(10)	(10)	(10)	(10)	(10)	(10)	(10)	(10)	(10)	(10)	(10)
Williamsburg City	(11)	(11)	(11)	(11)	(11)	(11)	(11)	(11)	(11)	(11)	(11)	(11)	(11)
Winchester City	(12)	(12)	(12)	(12)	(12)	(12)	(12)	(12)	(12)	(12)	(12)	(12)	(12)
WASHINGTON	198 018	2.4	32 638	X	135 757	16 497	35 003	26 989	25 358	8 911	9 029	2 201	2 439
Adams	376	5.8	22 907	1 750	215	29	85	83	79	21	36	8	9
Asotin	527	3.0	25 647	968	169	40	108	122	117	46	46	11	6
Benton	4 372	6.6	29 086	437	3 255	209	629	624	584	219	212	52	48
Chelan	1 869	4.6	27 812	576	1 270	228	365	333	315	119	113	30	30
Clallam	1 782	3.8	26 959	704	739	159	547	424	406	185	141	27	22
Clark	10 797	2.2	29 191	423	5 152	779	1 960	1 537	1 437	477	484	134	198
Columbia	111	-2.6	27 033	694	50	8	27	24	23	9	9	2	2
Cowlitz	2 373	1.5	25 104	1 102	1 534	172	401	530	504	188	179	52	52
Douglas	775	5.2	23 309	1 626	281	31	156	161	152	53	67	10	13
Ferry	140	3.9	19 258	2 704	58	10	32	40	38	13	15	4	3
Franklin	1 097	5.9	20 715	2 367	783	89	161	248	233	53	110	30	21
Garfield	57	2.7	24 469	1 274	33	-2	17	13	12	6	4	1	1
Grant	1 685	4.7	21 721	2 083	1 013	151	303	385	364	112	148	41	40
Grays Harbor	1 578	3.3	22 986	1 728	895	101	278	414	396	148	156	40	26
Island	2 181	5.2	29 031	444	1 056	149	530	306	288	135	86	15	20
Jefferson	859	4.5	31 545	247	280	53	287	164	157	75	53	9	9
King	77 524	0.7	44 135	38	68 110	8 613	13 887	7 240	6 763	2 376	2 260	517	723
Kitsap	7 570	5.7	31 740	233	4 292	397	1 425	938	878	296	321	70	75
Kittitas	837	5.3	24 188	1 346	409	75	178	150	140	54	46	10	10
Klickitat	481	4.9	24 790	1 179	222	39	110	111	106	37	38	10	13
Lewis	1 660	3.6	23 836	1 460	944	104	294	408	389	147	153	36	27
Lincoln	248	4.7	24 528	1 256	101	14	71	56	54	24	18	3	3
Mason	1 251	5.5	24 471	1 271	457	74	275	294	280	117	104	23	16
Okanogan	915	5.1	23 308	1 628	446	123	163	227	216	74	86	23	20
Pacific	482	3.7	23 217	1 657	195	33	120	141	136	60	49	10	8
Pend Oreille	265	3.3	21 912	2 035	107	22	55	69	66	22	27	8	4
Pierce	21 368	3.6	29 221	420	11 754	1 249	3 130	3 205	3 012	981	1 075	295	277
San Juan	582	3.4	39 812	64	170	56	281	68	64	34	20	3	4
Skagit	3 135	3.8	29 377	406	1 728	334	682	552	523	202	193	42	45
Skamania	229	1.5	22 728	1 809	68	6	45	40	38	14	12	4	4
Snohomish	19 848	1.9	31 312	260	10 587	884	2 791	2 369	2 198	786	736	158	269
Spokane	11 382	2.8	26 637	757	7 874	791	2 048	2 128	2 013	674	761	192	158
Stevens	834	2.6	20 610	2 401	350	62	148	217	206	74	76	20	18
Thurston	6 719	4.0	30 828	284	3 776	399	1 069	976	917	342	307	69	71
Wahkiakum	92	2.6	24 198	1 344	29	6	24	22	21	10	7	1	2
Walla Walla	1 354	4.6	24 159	1 354	909	106	281	268	253	96	94	22	16
Whatcom	4 509	3.9	25 902	911	2 682	369	966	753	706	268	245	61	56
Whitman	831	4.8	20 302	2 477	603	47	179	143	132	49	42	9	8
Yakima	5 324	4.0	23 714	1 497	3 165	489	895	1 202	1 141	311	500	148	112
WEST VIRGINIA	42 945	3.3	23 794	X	26 032	2 876	6 741	10 718	10 301	3 876	3 796	1 027	232
Barbour	292	5.9	18 798	2 784	92	20	43	94	90	31	32	11	4
Berkeley	1 979	4.8	24 310	1 306	1 098	126	261	329	310	125	91	29	7
Boone	506	4.8	19 705	2 611	397	28	64	163	157	60	48	19	8
Braxton	252	5.0	17 046	2 989	123	18	35	79	76	27	27	11	3

1. Based on the resident population estimated as of July 1 of the year shown. 2. Includes other labor income. 3. Manassas and Manassas Park included with Prince William County. 4. Martinsville included with Henry County. 5. Norton included with Wise County. 6. Petersburg and Colonial Heights included with Dinwiddie County. 7. Poquoson included with York County. 8. Radford included with Montgomery County. 9. Salem included with Roanoke County. 10. Staunton and Waynesboro included with Augusta County. 11. Williamsburg included with James City County. 12. Winchester included with Frederick County.

Table B. States and Counties — Earnings, Social Security, and Housing

STATE County	Earnings, 2002									Social Security beneficiaries, December 2003		Supplemental Security Income recipients, December 2003	Housing units, 2003	
			Percent by selected industries											
			Goods-related[1]		Service-related and health									
	Total (mil dol)	Farm	Total	Manu-facturing	Information and profes-sional and technical services	Retail trade	Finance, insur-ance, and real estate	Health services	Govern-ment	Number	Rate[2]		Total	Percent change, 2000–2003
	75	76	77	78	79	80	81	82	83	84	85	86	87	88
VIRGINIA—Cont'd														
Manassas Park City	[4]	[4]	[4]	[4]	[4]	[4]	[4]	[4]	[4]	765	70	NA	3 852	14.5
Martinsville City	[5]	[5]	[5]	[5]	[5]	[5]	[5]	[5]	[5]	4 395	291	644	7 281	0.4
Newport News City	4 492	0.0	D	28.5	9.9	5.6	4.0	8.0	26.2	24 620	136	4 307	76 193	2.8
Norfolk City	10 675	0.0	D	5.3	7.1	3.3	5.0	7.2	52.8	31 250	129	7 305	95 657	1.3
Norton City	[6]	[6]	[6]	[6]	[6]	[6]	[6]	[6]	[6]	1 200	307	303	1 951	0.3
Petersburg City	[7]	[7]	[7]	[7]	[7]	[7]	[7]	[7]	[7]	7 530	228	2 093	15 821	-0.8
Poquoson City	[8]	[8]	[8]	[8]	[8]	[8]	[8]	[8]	[8]	1 725	146	NA	4 403	2.4
Portsmouth City	2 417	0.0	D	4.5	3.1	3.1	2.5	8.5	58.4	17 475	175	3 915	41 907	0.7
Radford City	[9]	[9]	[9]	[9]	[9]	[9]	[9]	[9]	[9]	2 035	136	196	6 214	1.3
Richmond City	9 312	0.0	D	9.6	15.6	3.1	7.3	6.2	27.3	32 140	165	8 741	91 827	-0.5
Roanoke City	3 283	0.0	D	6.8	12.2	8.7	10.1	16.7	12.1	18 780	202	4 063	45 729	1.0
Salem City	[10]	[10]	[10]	[10]	[10]	[10]	[10]	[10]	[10]	5 300	215	364	10 546	1.4
Staunton City	[11]	[11]	[11]	[11]	[11]	[11]	[11]	[11]	[11]	5 470	229	652	10 472	0.4
Suffolk City	870	1.1	D	12.4	7.5	8.9	4.1	D	24.5	11 700	159	2 119	28 023	13.4
Virginia Beach City	8 274	0.0	D	2.8	D	7.1	12.2	6.8	30.1	50 835	116	4 533	167 900	3.5
Waynesboro City	[11]	[11]	[11]	[11]	[11]	[11]	[11]	[11]	[11]	4 850	238	517	9 083	2.5
Williamsburg City	[12]	[12]	[12]	[12]	[12]	[12]	[12]	[12]	[12]	2 405	207	150	4 333	11.7
Winchester City	[13]	[13]	[13]	[13]	[13]	[13]	[13]	[13]	[13]	4 735	194	624	11 014	4.0
WASHINGTON	152 254	1.1	19.5	12.7	16.2	7.1	7.4	8.6	18.6	890 466	145	109 056	2 567 328	4.7
Adams	244	15.6	15.9	13.6	1.6	7.0	2.6	D	21.4	2 240	135	269	5 875	1.8
Asotin	210	-1.2	D	9.0	5.6	10.8	7.1	15.9	19.4	4 870	236	594	9 236	1.4
Benton	3 464	2.5	12.1	6.2	24.5	6.3	3.6	7.2	16.8	21 165	138	2 116	59 431	6.2
Chelan	1 498	6.4	D	6.5	5.2	9.7	4.3	16.6	19.6	12 215	180	1 189	31 053	2.1
Clallam	898	0.3	14.0	5.9	5.5	10.8	4.9	9.4	32.9	18 985	284	1 480	31 795	3.6
Clark	5 930	0.2	24.7	12.4	12.6	7.3	6.4	11.3	17.2	49 220	130	6 123	145 125	8.3
Columbia	58	11.8	D	D	2.0	D	2.2	D	34.2	990	242	107	2 052	1.7
Cowlitz	1 706	0.5	D	25.5	3.6	8.0	3.8	11.5	14.5	18 790	197	2 555	39 996	3.6
Douglas	312	13.4	10.6	3.4	3.0	10.4	2.3	6.5	29.1	5 455	162	399	13 517	4.4
Ferry	68	0.5	D	D	D	6.2	1.9	1.7	48.6	1 480	200	201	3 862	2.3
Franklin	871	13.2	15.3	8.8	2.7	8.3	2.8	9.7	22.0	5 690	101	965	17 679	9.9
Garfield	31	-6.6	D	D	D	7.1	2.8	D	68.9	620	261	44	1 271	-1.3
Grant	1 164	16.1	D	15.0	D	7.6	2.5	6.9	26.5	12 090	154	1 606	30 057	3.4
Grays Harbor	996	0.8	D	17.4	4.8	9.4	4.0	8.4	25.5	14 970	216	2 200	32 905	1.3
Island	1 206	0.3	D	2.3	4.4	6.6	4.1	4.2	60.1	13 905	182	639	34 064	5.2
Jefferson	333	0.7	20.9	10.9	7.0	8.6	6.4	7.3	25.9	7 560	273	396	14 856	5.0
King	76 723	0.1	18.6	12.7	24.9	6.0	8.9	6.7	11.2	217 525	123	28 740	773 126	4.2
Kitsap	4 689	0.1	7.0	1.5	7.3	7.1	4.1	8.1	54.5	33 375	139	3 879	96 022	3.6
Kittitas	484	4.7	D	5.3	5.5	10.4	3.8	6.9	35.1	5 400	153	382	17 406	5.7
Klickitat	261	9.1	15.9	9.8	D	7.2	3.4	D	25.6	3 975	203	449	8 882	2.9
Lewis	1 049	1.8	24.0	13.8	3.4	9.8	2.9	10.6	19.2	15 245	217	1 747	30 052	1.6
Lincoln	115	5.9	5.8	1.9	5.2	9.1	6.1	D	42.5	2 550	250	130	5 338	0.8
Mason	531	-0.1	D	14.5	3.1	8.3	4.3	6.8	34.0	12 155	233	989	26 656	4.5
Okanogan	569	13.6	5.6	0.9	3.1	12.2	2.9	7.0	36.1	8 200	210	993	19 586	2.6
Pacific	228	4.1	15.7	11.3	2.7	8.2	4.9	5.4	33.9	6 170	292	563	14 095	0.7
Pend Oreille	130	0.4	D	32.8	2.9	4.4	2.5	D	37.5	2 425	198	412	6 772	2.5
Pierce	13 003	0.2	16.2	8.4	5.5	7.8	7.5	12.6	30.6	101 260	137	15 046	293 199	5.8
San Juan	226	0.1	D	4.4	8.7	10.2	9.4	4.3	16.5	3 230	219	96	10 472	7.4
Skagit	2 061	4.4	23.2	13.5	8.0	10.4	7.2	8.8	19.2	20 175	185	1 801	44 880	5.2
Skamania	74	-0.2	D	10.8	5.9	3.7	D	1.4	45.7	1 585	154	148	4 678	2.2
Snohomish	11 470	0.2	39.0	30.0	6.3	7.9	6.8	7.9	17.6	77 120	121	8 163	253 441	7.3
Spokane	8 664	0.2	16.6	10.1	8.2	9.6	8.6	14.6	20.3	69 715	162	10 083	180 977	3.4
Stevens	412	1.0	23.3	17.8	3.1	7.2	3.1	11.5	28.3	8 280	203	892	17 971	2.1
Thurston	4 176	0.8	10.0	4.0	6.5	9.0	5.4	10.8	42.2	35 160	158	3 628	91 349	5.4
Wahkiakum	35	-0.4	10.3	4.7	D	D	D	5.3	26.0	965	257	47	1 825	1.8
Walla Walla	1 015	7.2	D	16.7	D	7.0	4.9	D	23.3	9 795	173	1 005	21 602	2.2
Whatcom	3 051	2.3	D	13.8	8.2	8.6	6.0	10.3	18.4	27 825	158	3 128	78 327	6.0
Whitman	649	1.9	D	6.9	3.9	4.7	3.4	6.0	55.7	4 695	115	339	17 204	3.2
Yakima	3 654	12.2	15.7	11.4	4.6	7.9	4.0	13.2	19.3	33 365	147	5 469	80 694	1.9
WEST VIRGINIA	28 907	0.0	24.6	12.9	7.3	7.8	4.6	13.3	22.1	405 444	224	75 257	854 817	1.2
Barbour	112	-0.5	17.3	5.6	D	8.0	4.7	D	29.1	3 575	228	829	7 400	0.7
Berkeley	1 223	0.3	15.9	9.8	11.0	7.3	4.2	10.0	31.9	13 670	160	1 668	36 065	9.6
Boone	425	0.0	60.0	0.8	3.4	5.3	1.3	D	14.9	6 170	239	1 310	11 650	0.6
Braxton	141	-0.6	D	13.6	2.9	11.3	2.7	13.1	23.5	3 200	217	801	7 441	0.9

1. Covers mining, construction, and manufacturing. 2. Per 1,000 resident population estimated as of July 1 of the year shown. 4. Manassas and Manassas Park included with Prince William County. 5. Martinsville included with Henry County. 6. Norton included with Wise County. 7. Petersburg and Colonial Heights included with Dinwiddie County. 8. Poquoson included with York County. 9. Radford included with Montgomery County. 10. Salem included with Roanoke County. 11. Staunton and Waynesboro included with Augusta County. 12. Williamsburg included with James City County. 13. Winchester included with Frederick County.

Table B. States and Counties — Housing, Labor Force, and Employment

	Housing units, 2000								Civilian labor force, 2003		Unemployment		Civilian employment,[6] 2000		
	Occupied units													Percent	
		Owner-occupied				Renter-occupied									
				Median owner cost as a percent of income											
STATE County	Total	Percent	Median value[1]	With a mortgage	Without a mortgage[2]	Median rent[3]	Median rent as a percent of income	Sub-standard units[4] (percent)	Total	Percent change, 2002–2003	Total	Rate[5]	Total	Management, professional and related occupations	Production, transportation, and material moving occupations
	89	90	91	92	93	94	95	96	97	98	99	100	101	102	103
VIRGINIA—Cont'd															
Manassas Park City	3 254	78.7	116 000	24.3	12.9	930	22.4	5.0	5 883	1.5	118	2.0	5 513	30.5	10.9
Martinsville City	6 498	60.2	69 100	20.3	9.9	401	24.1	2.4	6 121	-3.1	849	13.9	6 086	26.0	30.8
Newport News City	69 686	52.4	96 400	22.9	10.5	559	25.7	4.5	88 753	2.3	4 775	5.4	78 194	30.5	13.6
Norfolk City	86 210	45.6	88 400	24.0	12.2	538	27.1	6.3	93 714	2.2	6 138	6.5	87 490	29.1	13.2
Norton City	1 730	56.0	62 800	19.6	9.9	347	25.0	1.9	1 473	3.6	79	5.4	1 455	27.0	14.4
Petersburg City	13 799	51.5	68 600	23.1	11.5	495	25.1	4.8	15 384	2.1	1 580	10.3	13 170	24.9	24.4
Poquoson City	4 166	84.1	153 400	22.1	10.9	697	23.4	1.3	6 398	2.4	176	2.8	5 550	44.1	9.9
Portsmouth City	38 170	58.5	81 300	23.5	12.6	540	27.7	4.4	46 807	2.2	2 855	6.1	40 353	27.7	14.7
Radford City	5 809	44.5	95 100	17.8	9.9	437	31.8	1.9	6 589	6.6	302	4.6	7 169	35.5	12.6
Richmond City	84 549	46.1	87 300	22.3	12.4	540	27.4	4.2	97 888	0.1	6 397	6.5	90 745	35.5	12.5
Roanoke City	42 003	56.3	80 300	21.2	9.9	448	24.3	2.7	48 439	-1.7	2 518	5.2	44 455	26.7	17.2
Salem City	9 954	67.6	104 200	20.0	9.9	550	24.3	0.9	13 538	-2.2	414	3.1	12 377	29.5	14.2
Staunton City	9 676	61.4	87 500	20.4	9.9	466	24.5	1.5	10 540	-0.5	388	3.7	11 107	27.4	18.9
Suffolk City	23 283	72.2	107 300	24.0	11.0	506	27.1	3.4	34 577	2.1	1 547	4.5	27 519	30.9	18.5
Virginia Beach City	154 455	65.6	123 200	23.9	10.1	734	26.4	3.2	220 878	2.1	8 229	3.7	194 923	35.9	9.0
Waynesboro City	8 332	61.2	89 300	21.1	9.9	469	24.6	2.5	9 264	-0.6	425	4.6	8 647	26.4	20.7
Williamsburg City	3 619	44.3	212 000	20.4	9.9	616	26.5	2.6	6 016	2.6	454	7.5	4 284	41.7	5.5
Winchester City	10 001	45.7	108 900	21.3	9.9	547	24.1	3.4	13 851	1.3	459	3.3	12 147	29.2	20.0
WASHINGTON	2 271 398	64.6	168 300	23.8	10.4	663	26.5	5.5	3 139 877	1.0	236 965	7.5	2 793 722	35.6	12.7
Adams	5 229	68.4	84 300	23.0	10.6	430	22.9	14.6	8 133	-0.4	787	9.7	6 490	25.2	18.1
Asotin	8 364	67.1	100 500	20.8	9.9	494	27.1	3.4	12 569	0.3	760	6.0	9 211	28.4	15.7
Benton	52 866	68.8	119 900	19.8	9.9	566	23.9	6.4	79 023	3.9	5 716	7.2	66 233	37.9	11.5
Chelan	25 021	64.6	148 400	24.1	10.8	535	27.0	9.2	35 657	1.4	3 234	9.1	28 507	30.5	11.5
Clallam	27 164	72.8	133 400	23.7	9.9	532	28.1	3.7	25 701	2.0	1 915	7.5	24 455	28.7	13.0
Clark	127 208	67.3	156 600	24.4	9.9	684	26.2	4.7	187 469	-0.1	18 526	9.9	163 623	30.9	16.6
Columbia	1 687	69.6	85 000	21.1	10.4	467	23.7	3.9	1 339	-0.9	136	10.2	1 720	31.6	12.7
Cowlitz	35 850	67.6	129 900	22.1	9.9	518	26.9	4.7	40 499	-0.6	4 152	10.3	39 888	23.6	21.1
Douglas	11 726	71.0	134 600	23.3	9.9	545	24.3	8.4	17 793	1.8	1 459	8.2	14 158	28.2	13.9
Ferry	2 823	73.0	92 400	20.8	9.9	380	22.6	10.2	2 516	-0.2	417	16.6	2 655	33.1	13.0
Franklin	14 840	65.7	102 000	20.8	9.9	464	25.4	18.7	25 511	3.7	2 406	9.4	19 513	24.7	17.5
Garfield	987	73.8	68 100	20.5	10.8	390	23.6	2.2	1 183	0.5	55	4.6	976	39.5	11.8
Grant	25 204	66.7	99 500	21.7	9.9	476	24.1	13.0	38 496	0.7	3 694	9.6	29 364	26.1	16.2
Grays Harbor	26 808	69.1	96 400	22.2	11.1	500	26.9	4.0	26 843	2.4	2 600	9.7	27 556	24.3	16.9
Island	27 784	70.1	174 800	25.1	9.9	684	27.2	3.5	28 254	-0.1	1 932	6.8	27 023	33.8	12.9
Jefferson	11 645	76.1	171 900	25.3	11.9	595	29.7	4.4	11 989	3.0	738	6.2	10 865	33.3	12.1
King	710 916	59.8	236 900	23.9	10.9	758	26.1	5.3	1 018 444	-0.5	68 750	6.8	929 205	43.4	10.1
Kitsap	86 416	67.4	152 100	23.8	10.5	667	26.5	3.9	102 110	1.9	6 531	6.4	98 146	34.9	10.4
Kittitas	13 382	58.3	133 400	22.2	10.9	497	35.6	3.8	16 287	4.8	1 175	7.2	15 509	30.7	11.1
Klickitat	7 473	68.8	110 400	24.1	10.4	498	26.4	6.7	8 649	-0.4	1 298	15.0	7 848	29.8	17.8
Lewis	26 306	71.4	117 800	23.3	11.1	551	28.9	5.2	30 097	4.4	2 718	9.0	26 881	23.9	17.5
Lincoln	4 151	76.6	83 500	22.5	9.9	438	24.6	2.1	4 806	2.4	270	5.6	4 152	37.0	8.8
Mason	18 912	79.0	132 300	23.3	9.9	579	24.3	5.3	20 832	5.8	1 712	8.2	19 314	25.9	15.1
Okanogan	15 027	68.6	91 400	22.0	9.9	423	25.1	9.2	19 289	2.7	1 910	9.9	15 368	29.8	12.0
Pacific	9 096	74.7	102 700	24.8	10.8	483	26.8	4.8	8 156	4.1	728	8.9	7 989	26.6	15.3
Pend Oreille	4 639	77.4	101 100	23.3	9.9	422	26.4	8.2	4 498	4.2	467	10.4	4 044	26.8	19.2
Pierce	260 800	63.5	149 600	24.4	11.1	624	26.4	5.2	355 694	2.4	27 716	7.8	314 158	30.1	15.1
San Juan	6 466	73.6	291 800	28.8	11.9	607	26.7	7.3	6 903	3.0	314	4.5	6 606	33.4	9.7
Skagit	38 852	69.7	158 100	24.9	11.2	668	27.9	6.4	54 054	2.4	4 178	7.8	45 729	28.5	15.5
Skamania	3 755	73.9	150 200	23.2	10.8	579	24.7	6.0	3 961	0.3	437	11.0	4 340	28.2	18.3
Snohomish	224 852	67.7	196 500	24.6	10.5	766	26.1	5.0	346 835	-0.4	27 745	8.0	302 051	33.7	13.2
Spokane	163 611	65.5	113 200	23.0	10.0	532	27.5	3.6	217 808	1.4	14 828	6.8	191 295	33.0	12.7
Stevens	15 017	78.1	112 000	23.7	10.1	453	27.2	6.4	17 046	1.0	1 638	9.6	15 568	29.9	16.8
Thurston	81 625	66.6	145 200	23.2	9.9	655	26.5	4.0	110 328	5.1	6 327	5.7	100 487	37.4	10.0
Wahkiakum	1 553	79.7	147 500	20.9	10.4	519	22.3	4.1	1 772	-0.4	140	7.9	1 554	29.5	14.2
Walla Walla	19 647	65.2	114 300	22.2	10.1	487	28.3	6.4	27 810	2.1	1 709	6.1	23 524	35.4	9.6
Whatcom	64 446	63.4	155 700	24.3	10.9	622	29.8	4.4	89 793	3.4	5 477	6.1	80 773	31.5	13.5
Whitman	15 257	47.8	119 600	20.5	9.9	482	35.9	3.1	19 579	1.7	523	2.7	18 870	45.5	6.3
Yakima	73 993	64.4	113 800	23.1	9.9	534	27.6	14.7	112 155	2.2	11 849	10.6	88 074	27.4	16.5
WEST VIRGINIA	736 481	75.2	72 800	19.5	9.9	401	25.8	2.3	787 286	-2.0	48 210	6.1	732 673	27.9	16.4
Barbour	6 123	78.5	56 100	19.9	9.9	330	28.6	3.4	5 706	-5.8	527	9.2	6 048	24.6	17.2
Berkeley	29 569	74.1	99 700	20.7	9.9	506	23.7	2.4	37 948	0.2	1 790	4.7	36 229	25.9	22.4
Boone	10 291	78.9	63 700	19.8	9.9	353	24.9	3.1	8 079	-0.9	613	7.6	8 788	21.7	16.0
Braxton	5 771	78.1	59 300	19.5	9.9	332	24.9	5.0	5 465	2.8	512	9.4	5 107	19.6	20.7

1. Specified owner-occupied units.   2. Median monthly owner costs is often in the minimum category—9.9 percent or less, which is indicated as 9.9 percent.   3. Specified renter-occupied units.   4. Overcrowded or lacking complete plumbing facilities.   5. Percent of civilian labor force.   6. Persons 16 years old and over.

Table B. States and Counties — **Nonfarm Employment and Agriculture**

	Private nonfarm establishments, employment and payroll, 2001								Agriculture, 2002			
	Employment						Annual payroll		Farms			
										Percent with—		
STATE County	Number of establishments	Total	Health care and social assistance	Manufacturing	Retail trade	Finance and insurance	Professional, scientific, and technical services	Total (mil dol)	Average per employee (dollars)	Number	Less than 50 acres	500 acres and over	Farm operators whose principal occupation is farming (percent)
	104	105	106	107	108	109	110	111	112	113	114	115	116
VIRGINIA—Cont'd													
Manassas Park City	182	2 962	0	143	306	D	84	108	36 421	NA	NA	NA	NA
Martinsville City	774	16 191	1 749	5 812	2 011	390	290	384	23 703	NA	NA	NA	NA
Newport News City	3 603	82 286	9 888	21 811	9 510	1 996	5 350	2 628	31 935	NA	NA	NA	NA
Norfolk City	5 437	114 613	17 298	9 150	14 075	8 650	7 695	3 639	31 747	NA	NA	NA	NA
Norton City	286	5 168	1 237	449	938	98	166	144	27 861	NA	NA	NA	NA
Petersburg City	846	14 081	2 757	2 981	2 028	318	591	399	28 326	NA	NA	NA	NA
Poquoson City	191	1 410	221	D	315	27	75	25	17 906	NA	NA	NA	NA
Portsmouth City	1 671	25 889	6 327	2 231	3 186	881	1 622	688	26 562	NA	NA	NA	NA
Radford City	357	6 267	1 199	2 215	838	191	145	174	27 699	NA	NA	NA	NA
Richmond City	7 454	165 500	25 328	17 354	12 627	16 443	10 451	5 976	36 108	NA	NA	NA	NA
Roanoke City	4 230	81 382	10 880	7 627	13 260	8 823	3 728	2 167	26 625	NA	NA	NA	NA
Salem City	953	22 377	5 133	4 780	3 560	428	504	682	30 477	NA	NA	NA	NA
Staunton City	904	12 052	2 011	541	2 268	501	364	273	22 675	NA	NA	NA	NA
Suffolk City	1 165	16 899	2 706	2 449	2 937	326	650	451	26 688	247	52.2	15.4	61.5
Virginia Beach City	10 188	143 359	13 079	6 459	23 459	8 753	12 853	3 676	25 640	172	58.1	5.2	52.3
Waynesboro City	625	10 299	592	3 279	1 438	296	199	323	31 361	NA	NA	NA	NA
Williamsburg City	827	17 955	3 272	1 193	2 811	278	460	468	26 056	NA	NA	NA	NA
Winchester City	1 239	23 980	4 638	6 492	4 027	906	600	739	30 801	NA	NA	NA	NA
WASHINGTON	164 072	2 294 285	287 251	316 227	317 052	101 117	141 642	86 533	37 717	35 939	57.5	12.8	58.5
Adams	399	4 133	549	1 294	560	151	59	100	24 159	717	15.9	50.2	70.6
Asotin	426	4 108	853	310	781	92	D	102	24 875	180	30.0	51.1	55.0
Benton	3 325	49 545	6 139	3 558	7 918	1 264	6 552	1 696	34 235	1 313	73.4	7.8	52.0
Chelan	2 282	24 589	4 493	2 302	4 111	773	699	671	27 275	1 193	69.1	2.6	69.2
Clallam	2 099	15 311	2 503	1 190	3 258	562	594	349	22 770	455	74.3	0.7	47.9
Clark	8 163	99 218	13 710	16 207	15 008	3 374	4 065	3 047	30 706	1 596	79.2	1.1	46.4
Columbia	130	904	201	D	143	34	D	26	29 208	255	24.7	42.4	69.8
Cowlitz	2 274	32 336	4 587	7 962	4 631	822	779	1 041	32 193	532	66.0	1.7	53.4
Douglas	526	4 100	302	140	1 127	199	128	98	23 892	947	49.9	24.9	70.2
Ferry	143	870	116	120	195	17	D	23	26 617	207	21.7	22.7	51.7
Franklin	1 126	14 094	1 533	3 538	2 280	258	188	365	25 924	943	36.3	29.0	74.8
Garfield	55	357	86	0	70	20	D	8	22 616	198	18.2	61.1	59.6
Grant	1 663	17 669	2 385	4 294	3 034	437	432	443	25 078	1 801	32.4	27.0	71.2
Grays Harbor	1 864	17 465	2 375	3 043	2 842	615	449	470	26 897	510	55.9	3.5	50.2
Island	1 643	11 105	1 859	672	2 423	773	386	256	23 064	348	77.3	0.6	60.9
Jefferson	1 035	6 713	1 162	984	998	169	156	159	23 612	207	71.5	0.5	57.5
King	59 548	1 053 579	103 704	133 536	115 145	52 072	88 430	49 305	46 798	1 548	88.2	0.3	53.2
Kitsap	5 377	49 570	9 376	1 946	11 113	2 067	2 987	1 279	25 804	587	89.6	0.5	53.8
Kittitas	1 014	7 658	1 072	529	1 559	147	149	169	22 126	931	51.2	9.2	51.9
Klickitat	551	3 980	437	1 170	786	93	153	104	26 039	702	36.2	25.4	53.7
Lewis	1 924	18 590	2 724	2 895	3 612	464	363	504	27 120	1 402	57.9	2.3	57.8
Lincoln	290	1 806	412	23	339	99	105	42	23 410	747	12.6	61.2	76.3
Mason	1 013	8 901	1 095	1 535	1 551	304	251	227	25 556	320	78.8	2.2	47.8
Okanogan	1 064	8 030	1 461	371	1 504	212	221	182	22 672	1 486	49.4	14.9	59.4
Pacific	666	4 256	582	728	544	177	102	84	19 805	341	56.6	5.0	55.7
Pend Oreille	237	1 642	325	348	208	33	D	50	30 374	263	38.4	9.5	55.5
Pierce	15 573	207 984	34 604	21 293	32 677	8 773	7 522	6 293	30 258	1 474	80.7	0.7	52.8
San Juan	896	3 751	228	143	621	111	212	102	27 087	225	67.1	1.8	51.1
Skagit	3 278	35 392	5 149	5 295	7 092	926	1 188	998	28 207	872	59.7	4.9	60.9
Skamania	158	1 006	D	261	106	25	151	26	25 706	99	60.6	0.0	54.5
Snohomish	15 355	209 047	21 160	55 627	31 256	8 937	7 879	7 644	36 565	1 574	80.8	1.3	52.2
Spokane	11 632	169 945	28 568	19 722	24 914	9 646	8 240	5 036	29 631	2 225	52.2	12.1	50.2
Stevens	872	7 214	1 313	1 673	1 167	157	158	173	24 047	1 269	34.5	12.6	57.7
Thurston	5 068	53 827	9 665	3 166	9 654	2 533	3 303	1 517	28 182	1 155	76.0	2.1	50.6
Wahkiakum	98	543	112	D	58	17	D	13	24 549	125	43.2	2.4	46.4
Walla Walla	1 278	17 220	3 783	1 883	2 593	701	376	437	25 387	890	47.4	28.2	56.6
Whatcom	5 423	58 667	6 615	8 473	9 841	2 054	2 826	1 677	28 583	1 485	62.2	2.4	54.2
Whitman	863	7 291	1 352	D	1 385	344	251	171	23 472	1 087	14.4	58.3	76.2
Yakima	4 698	60 204	10 574	9 182	9 948	1 621	1 655	1 571	26 096	3 730	66.5	5.7	62.7
WEST VIRGINIA	40 439	555 613	104 492	72 454	87 622	21 788	20 679	14 481	26 064	20 812	27.3	6.3	50.5
Barbour	253	2 520	515	110	424	85	62	36	14 448	445	24.5	7.9	48.8
Berkeley	1 447	20 721	4 165	3 741	3 599	561	729	541	26 090	676	51.8	3.0	50.0
Boone	373	5 408	549	51	851	125	182	208	38 438	24	16.7	0.0	62.5
Braxton	328	3 092	505	386	740	73	80	62	19 946	314	13.1	9.2	45.2

Table B. States and Counties — Agriculture

STATE County	Agriculture, 2002 (cont'd)														
	Land in farms					Value of land and buildings (dollars)		Value of machinery and equipment average per farm (dollars)	Value of products sold				Percent of farms with sales of —		Government payments	
			Acres								Percent from —					
	Acreage (1,000)	Percent change, 1997–2002	Average size of farm	Total irrigated (1,000)	Total cropland (1,000)	Average per farm	Average per acre		Total (mil dol)	Average per farm (dollars)	Crops	Live-stock and poultry products	$10,000 or more	$100,000 or more	Total ($1,000)	Percent of farms
	117	118	119	120	121	122	123	124	125	126	127	128	129	130	131	132
VIRGINIA—Cont'd																
Manassas Park City	NA	NA	NA	NA	NA	NA	NA	NA	NA	NA	NA	NA	NA	NA	NA	NA
Martinsville City	NA	NA	NA	NA	NA	NA	NA	NA	NA	NA	NA	NA	NA	NA	NA	NA
Newport News City	NA	NA	NA	NA	NA	NA	NA	NA	NA	NA	NA	NA	NA	NA	NA	NA
Norfolk City	NA	NA	NA	NA	NA	NA	NA	NA	NA	NA	NA	NA	NA	NA	NA	NA
Norton City	NA	NA	NA	NA	NA	NA	NA	NA	NA	NA	NA	NA	NA	NA	NA	NA
Petersburg City	NA	NA	NA	NA	NA	NA	NA	NA	NA	NA	NA	NA	NA	NA	NA	NA
Poquoson City	NA	NA	NA	NA	NA	NA	NA	NA	NA	NA	NA	NA	NA	NA	NA	NA
Portsmouth City	NA	NA	NA	NA	NA	NA	NA	NA	NA	NA	NA	NA	NA	NA	NA	NA
Radford City	NA	NA	NA	NA	NA	NA	NA	NA	NA	NA	NA	NA	NA	NA	NA	NA
Richmond City	NA	NA	NA	NA	NA	NA	NA	NA	NA	NA	NA	NA	NA	NA	NA	NA
Roanoke City	NA	NA	NA	NA	NA	NA	NA	NA	NA	NA	NA	NA	NA	NA	NA	NA
Salem City	NA	NA	NA	NA	NA	NA	NA	NA	NA	NA	NA	NA	NA	NA	NA	NA
Staunton City	NA	NA	NA	NA	NA	NA	NA	NA	NA	NA	NA	NA	NA	NA	NA	NA
Suffolk City	71	-6.6	286	1	57	681 587	2 339	108 078	41	165 746	87.3	12.7	49.0	27.1	1 839	36.4
Virginia Beach City	28	-6.7	165	0	24	649 775	3 645	47 521	10	56 168	79.9	20.1	45.9	8.1	422	25.0
Waynesboro City	NA	NA	NA	NA	NA	NA	NA	NA	NA	NA	NA	NA	NA	NA	NA	NA
Williamsburg City	NA	NA	NA	NA	NA	NA	NA	NA	NA	NA	NA	NA	NA	NA	NA	NA
Winchester City	NA	NA	NA	NA	NA	NA	NA	NA	NA	NA	NA	NA	NA	NA	NA	NA
WASHINGTON	15 318	0.9	426	1 823	8 038	623 333	1 486	80 212	5 331	148 327	67.2	32.8	40.6	18.4	133 763	20.4
Adams	1 067	-2.6	1 488	121	808	1 114 407	745	170 126	203	282 920	77.3	22.7	60.5	35.3	12 992	66.1
Asotin	280	-7.9	1 558	2	96	800 513	510	66 519	9	50 479	64.0	36.0	43.3	17.2	2 373	52.8
Benton	608	-0.7	463	188	471	782 342	1 701	106 823	401	305 080	91.5	8.5	38.0	18.6	5 400	15.0
Chelan	112	-9.7	94	35	52	527 519	6 563	52 320	169	142 000	97.1	2.9	72.5	35.0	2 181	19.3
Clallam	22	4.8	49	5	13	554 371	11 050	43 578	18	39 050	D	D	22.6	7.3	167	3.5
Clark	71	-2.7	44	5	38	422 339	10 011	33 199	54	34 091	52.3	47.7	19.1	5.9	205	1.8
Columbia	295	-4.8	1 156	3	192	799 402	708	145 706	27	103 985	85.6	14.4	48.2	24.7	3 643	65.1
Cowlitz	40	29.0	74	3	14	410 960	5 118	37 772	31	57 443	35.5	64.5	17.1	7.7	66	1.5
Douglas	879	-3.0	928	24	550	715 119	805	84 704	124	131 308	95.0	5.0	61.8	28.7	10 224	44.7
Ferry	799	-1.4	3 862	4	24	1 530 109	392	32 160	4	20 997	21.2	78.9	27.1	5.8	127	18.4
Franklin	665	17.9	705	241	476	962 716	1 448	215 237	350	371 668	84.9	15.1	63.3	44.0	9 369	41.5
Garfield	312	-4.0	1 578	1	189	850 214	529	135 321	20	99 887	79.3	20.7	59.6	29.3	3 472	71.2
Grant	1 074	-1.9	596	485	805	1 115 289	1 923	193 480	882	489 592	71.1	28.9	67.7	43.4	11 884	36.0
Grays Harbor	54	28.6	105	5	22	317 879	2 317	66 061	30	58 853	46.4	53.6	28.0	6.9	154	3.9
Island	15	-6.3	43	1	10	446 243	9 468	29 355	10	28 165	22.1	77.9	20.1	4.6	138	2.9
Jefferson	12	-7.7	59	1	6	340 617	5 441	24 513	7	32 232	14.6	85.4	28.5	6.8	163	6.3
King	42	0.0	27	4	22	459 385	21 338	27 224	120	77 555	60.5	39.5	24.5	8.4	803	4.8
Kitsap	16	-15.8	27	1	7	353 586	12 869	41 280	31	52 322	43.4	56.6	15.2	4.6	105	4.3
Kittitas	231	29.8	248	92	98	604 263	2 702	78 896	56	60 542	68.2	31.8	41.7	13.5	539	12.1
Klickitat	607	3.1	864	25	213	733 514	907	56 660	52	74 680	76.7	23.3	35.2	10.8	4 406	33.8
Lewis	131	11.0	93	9	63	307 961	3 023	34 544	89	63 802	24.0	76.0	24.1	8.5	718	5.3
Lincoln	1 233	-10.4	1 651	53	855	1 023 866	606	149 181	94	125 241	91.1	8.9	66.4	38.0	9 987	71.1
Mason	22	10.0	68	1	7	379 939	4 958	45 072	52	162 524	9.7	90.3	32.2	7.8	D	D
Okanogan	1 241	5.3	835	48	140	754 965	843	47 761	137	92 475	84.8	15.2	46.1	18.0	2 746	19.0
Pacific	52	30.0	152	3	17	347 338	2 076	102 766	31	89 932	14.1	85.9	44.9	9.4	238	6.7
Pend Oreille	61	-3.2	233	1	24	462 492	1 834	33 262	3	12 798	46.9	53.1	22.1	3.4	80	4.2
Pierce	57	11.8	39	6	28	425 050	9 655	34 726	94	63 887	37.1	62.9	19.8	6.0	212	2.4
San Juan	17	0.0	76	0	9	555 035	6 308	20 411	3	13 838	36.8	63.2	31.6	1.8	D	D
Skagit	114	22.6	131	18	76	613 134	5 113	99 671	217	249 294	70.1	29.9	43.5	21.1	1 835	14.7
Skamania	6	50.0	58	0	2	285 359	4 566	89 038	12	116 446	13.9	86.1	29.3	6.1	0	5.1
Snohomish	69	13.1	44	6	39	439 666	9 654	35 633	127	80 653	45.7	54.3	26.7	8.6	1 070	4.4
Spokane	643	9.0	289	12	422	566 929	2 114	56 915	94	42 181	82.3	17.7	28.3	9.8	4 279	23.0
Stevens	528	0.6	416	12	116	486 020	1 170	42 266	28	22 258	40.9	59.1	28.2	4.3	912	16.5
Thurston	74	32.1	64	7	30	400 151	8 458	37 299	115	99 286	43.0	57.0	20.6	6.1	243	2.8
Wahkiakum	12	-7.7	99	0	7	257 411	2 690	29 422	3	23 830	2.8	97.2	24.0	5.6	122	13.6
Walla Walla	701	-2.0	787	94	559	989 427	1 330	113 872	339	381 004	D	D	47.3	28.4	9 165	37.3
Whatcom	148	42.3	100	32	90	579 356	5 959	112 458	288	193 845	26.4	73.6	43.8	24.7	4 029	14.8
Whitman	1 328	2.1	1 222	6	1 088	957 243	859	161 794	163	149 614	95.5	4.5	67.4	43.7	19 215	70.4
Yakima	1 679	-0.2	450	269	361	577 843	1 271	84 172	844	226 239	60.2	39.8	55.0	23.0	10 501	19.7
WEST VIRGINIA	3 585	3.7	172	2	1 173	231 999	1 315	26 188	483	23 199	14.4	85.6	17.5	3.3	5 180	8.0
Barbour	79	-9.2	176	0	31	180 903	1 023	27 403	4	8 715	16.9	83.1	19.8	1.8	95	5.2
Berkeley	76	4.1	113	0	44	368 758	3 222	30 779	18	27 264	66.4	33.7	21.4	4.7	765	14.5
Boone	3	50.0	134	0	1	144 051	1 083	14 629	0	2 458	66.1	33.9	0.0	0.0	0	12.5
Braxton	66	-1.5	212	D	20	197 719	846	20 914	2	5 417	15.1	84.9	14.3	0.3	26	7.6

STATE County	New construction ($1,000)	Number of housing units	Number of establishments	Number of employees	Sales (mil dol)	Annual payroll (mil dol)	Number of establishments	Number of employees	Sales (mil dol)	Annual payroll (mil dol)	Number of establishments	Number of employees	Receipts (mil dol)	Annual payroll (mil dol)
	Value of residential construction authorized by building permits, 2003		Wholesale trade, 1997				Retail trade,[1] 1997				Real estate and rental and leasing, 1997			
	133	134	135	136	137	138	139	140	141	142	143	144	145	146
VIRGINIA—Cont'd														
Manassas Park City	12 349	162	13	180	36.7	6.4	16	142	28.7	2.9	2	D	D	D
Martinsville City	300	6	23	202	143.7	6.9	142	1 927	248.8	25.3	36	151	18.1	2.5
Newport News City	35 175	472	132	1 634	604.2	50.3	681	9 284	1 488.6	143.6	226	1 720	169.9	35.8
Norfolk City	81 768	771	324	5 845	2 914.6	183.9	918	12 628	1 900.4	207.3	273	2 128	203.8	44.2
Norton City	193	6	15	292	174.9	9.9	66	921	127.8	11.9	9	12	2.3	0.2
Petersburg City	481	10	35	538	139.2	16.8	189	1 764	290.0	29.5	28	131	11.1	2.2
Poquoson City	12 067	56	11	D	D	D	28	247	29.8	3.0	6	30	2.8	0.6
Portsmouth City	32 129	378	63	712	167.3	23.6	295	3 291	468.4	51.2	84	457	37.8	7.4
Radford City	4 261	64	8	296	51.7	3.3	58	561	79.2	8.6	21	108	11.3	1.4
Richmond City	44 671	495	464	7 572	5 979.5	283.5	1 013	11 579	1 738.1	193.5	265	2 166	213.5	54.8
Roanoke City	20 774	247	299	3 768	1 292.7	121.0	792	12 425	1 843.7	191.3	158	1 861	114.5	31.8
Salem City	6 772	57	86	1 809	635.8	58.6	174	3 089	452.5	51.8	26	179	13.9	4.0
Staunton City	4 651	52	33	327	132.0	7.4	168	2 213	330.5	32.0	43	214	15.9	3.3
Suffolk City	131 824	1 404	61	1 305	822.5	43.7	212	2 697	380.0	38.0	43	210	24.1	3.4
Virginia Beach City	238 877	1 941	479	5 642	1 922.8	159.4	1 621	21 987	3 342.7	337.2	472	3 101	333.0	66.8
Waynesboro City	7 444	95	21	D	D	D	115	1 512	216.6	22.2	29	131	9.4	1.9
Williamsburg City	18 292	144	16	D	D	D	163	2 262	330.2	33.7	32	201	40.9	8.3
Winchester City	14 847	122	39	569	301.1	16.4	283	3 667	571.3	58.7	55	208	24.5	5.3
WASHINGTON	6 346 021	42 825	10 039	118 810	75 397.8	4 376.0	22 841	283 653	52 472.9	5 385.9	7 544	41 899	5 352.8	935.3
Adams	5 466	57	36	408	158.5	11.2	71	526	100.2	9.7	11	25	1.8	0.2
Asotin	5 854	46	15	D	D	D	66	714	160.1	13.7	20	80	7.2	1.4
Benton	198 809	1 103	106	1 050	305.3	22.7	574	7 091	1 208.8	115.6	153	907	102.3	18.9
Chelan	58 819	416	115	1 760	782.5	53.1	415	4 030	697.7	73.3	121	526	38.9	9.2
Clallam	69 389	554	51	358	299.8	11.0	292	2 990	453.6	50.3	70	251	21.9	3.2
Clark	524 704	4 067	458	3 751	2 138.8	137.3	868	12 284	2 214.7	230.9	344	1 910	209.8	39.8
Columbia	955	6	14	D	D	D	29	147	23.2	2.5	2	D	D	D
Cowlitz	60 241	436	81	D	D	D	414	4 744	811.5	82.1	98	396	49.8	7.2
Douglas	33 527	247	31	188	81.8	5.6	91	1 109	184.9	17.4	18	99	9.9	1.5
Ferry	1 728	19	2	D	D	D	32	212	33.9	2.9	1	D	D	D
Franklin	141 505	1 146	93	1 111	550.7	33.0	196	2 205	487.4	45.9	40	219	23.1	4.6
Garfield	0	0	5	D	D	D	12	75	10.9	1.2	1	D	D	D
Grant	38 764	314	109	1 089	365.5	28.5	326	3 291	576.4	58.0	63	178	18.4	2.5
Grays Harbor	47 370	329	68	566	139.0	15.9	324	3 005	473.4	52.0	69	233	16.0	2.9
Island	97 832	656	33	126	40.9	3.2	231	2 000	311.9	33.5	80	226	23.6	3.5
Jefferson	44 770	300	23	D	D	D	149	974	146.0	14.3	34	100	7.9	1.1
King	1 852 660	9 857	4 937	63 696	50 226.1	2 641.6	7 031	99 542	19 399.8	2 025.3	3 119	20 887	3 219.0	560.3
Kitsap	229 865	1 460	135	925	330.9	29.9	773	10 338	1 722.1	179.5	240	1 053	103.4	16.3
Kittitas	54 417	431	36	350	129.9	9.2	178	1 427	230.8	23.0	40	135	12.1	1.7
Klickitat	14 724	115	22	120	33.9	2.2	69	346	47.4	5.4	24	58	5.4	0.6
Lewis	41 473	374	90	D	D	D	388	3 699	597.7	63.5	64	261	19.9	3.9
Lincoln	4 154	39	37	272	131.4	7.3	54	305	57.2	4.9	3	9	0.4	0.1
Mason	38 671	482	35	271	105.1	8.8	148	1 530	233.5	21.9	54	249	15.8	3.4
Okanogan	16 190	138	44	1 472	368.7	20.5	204	1 657	263.2	25.9	39	120	5.1	0.9
Pacific	7 408	75	14	D	D	D	115	680	87.1	11.0	21	37	3.6	0.3
Pend Oreille	6 539	58	5	D	D	D	44	247	35.8	3.3	7	16	0.9	0.2
Pierce	703 713	5 152	781	9 324	4 618.9	327.0	2 289	28 956	5 468.2	550.1	707	4 407	395.8	81.2
San Juan	40 790	180	17	D	D	D	115	561	81.7	10.1	48	92	13.0	1.8
Skagit	124 682	904	122	1 018	344.4	30.2	614	6 096	1 070.7	107.0	114	406	48.3	7.3
Skamania	10 537	70	2	D	D	D	15	137	14.2	1.7	5	10	0.9	0.1
Snohomish	752 280	5 592	755	6 808	3 561.6	232.3	2 027	26 302	5 303.0	524.2	670	3 061	366.2	65.2
Spokane	304 404	2 550	788	11 268	4 878.5	360.9	1 730	22 246	4 122.6	433.9	503	2 674	289.1	47.4
Stevens	17 094	152	28	133	39.8	3.2	141	1 239	184.0	18.6	26	96	10.2	1.3
Thurston	326 704	2 014	201	1 805	580.3	57.5	730	9 008	1 616.8	166.3	218	884	89.7	13.5
Wahkiakum	3 798	21	NA	NA	NA	NA	14	62	7.3	0.9	1	D	D	D
Walla Walla	37 808	285	78	726	318.1	16.4	222	2 426	376.4	41.9	45	187	17.0	2.6
Whatcom	320 530	2 320	308	2 451	1 042.7	76.0	840	9 758	1 673.3	165.7	220	877	91.8	12.3
Whitman	25 711	254	73	D	D	D	156	1 520	243.9	24.0	39	196	13.9	1.9
Yakima	82 139	606	291	4 871	1 853.8	141.9	854	10 174	1 741.6	174.9	212	1 018	99.9	17.0
WEST VIRGINIA	645 988	5 133	1 956	23 805	10 290.4	681.1	8 082	90 087	14 057.9	1 309.3	1 449	5 812	665.0	100.8
Barbour	824	10	9	75	12.7	1.2	57	509	69.3	6.7	4	6	1.9	0.0
Berkeley	187 058	1 530	52	D	D	D	335	4 000	546.7	52.2	67	241	18.9	3.4
Boone	634	8	19	121	52.9	3.5	110	984	146.3	14.4	15	26	4.4	0.3
Braxton	45	1	17	119	38.8	3.5	87	678	111.1	10.2	6	20	1.7	0.4

1. Establishments with payroll.

STATE County	Professional, scientific, and technical services,[1] 1997				Manufacturing, 1997				Accommodation and foodservices, 1997			
	Number of establish- ments	Number of employees	Receipts (mil dol)	Annual payroll (mil dol)	Number of establish- ments	Number of employees	Receipts (mil dol)	Annual payroll (mil dol)	Number of establish- ments	Number of employees	Sales (mil dol)	Annual payroll (mil dol)
	147	148	149	150	151	152	153	154	155	156	157	158
VIRGINIA—Cont'd												
Manassas Park City	7	74	4.9	2.0	NA	NA	NA	NA	5	136	3.2	1.2
Martinsville City	54	223	16.6	7.7	39	8 726	724.1	203.0	46	768	25.1	6.6
Newport News City	286	3 023	218.8	88.6	131	24 707	3 300.5	898.4	312	5 464	170.1	47.7
Norfolk City	439	6 582	468.7	207.0	199	10 996	5 737.3	402.2	539	9 980	299.4	85.1
Norton City	19	188	8.9	4.0	NA	NA	NA	NA	23	D	D	D
Petersburg City	45	1 122	79.8	42.1	43	2 553	409.6	72.4	83	1 194	34.2	10.1
Poquoson City	13	79	5.6	2.8	NA	NA	NA	NA	20	193	4.3	1.2
Portsmouth City	105	1 023	82.1	31.5	71	1 812	368.7	52.0	137	2 040	58.7	15.8
Radford City	31	151	13.9	4.9	21	2 838	393.4	84.6	34	567	14.3	3.6
Richmond City	732	8 113	853.7	356.0	325	21 879	11 748.3	941.2	551	9 087	304.2	91.4
Roanoke City	331	2 632	211.6	88.7	152	8 489	2 156.3	242.9	325	6 380	203.4	58.7
Salem City	65	325	28.8	8.7	73	6 478	1 035.6	202.3	86	1 751	45.2	13.2
Staunton City	45	199	12.5	6.1	NA	NA	NA	NA	72	1 029	34.4	9.4
Suffolk City	59	273	21.4	9.2	52	2 257	1 103.5	63.8	62	1 027	32.8	8.9
Virginia Beach City	895	8 910	726.1	302.6	236	5 806	967.2	139.2	888	18 145	576.3	163.3
Waynesboro City	26	100	5.2	2.4	31	4 558	802.5	160.2	51	838	26.1	7.7
Williamsburg City	34	281	28.5	10.0	14	D	D	D	140	4 581	204.8	55.5
Winchester City	97	479	34.0	15.6	43	6 047	1 431.3	196.1	99	1 713	58.0	18.4
WASHINGTON	13 411	101 848	10 564.8	4 247.3	7 801	328 511	78 852.5	13 004.1	13 105	194 955	6 995.1	1 962.9
Adams	16	54	5.7	1.0	13	1 088	274.7	25.9	37	387	12.2	3.0
Asotin	30	106	7.4	2.7	NA	NA	NA	NA	40	516	16.1	4.9
Benton	274	7 403	926.0	364.4	121	3 672	885.5	139.5	256	4 223	136.1	36.8
Chelan	118	593	45.2	18.6	88	2 535	552.2	76.2	240	2 946	98.8	27.1
Clallam	105	434	33.5	12.0	75	1 481	359.2	49.0	214	2 104	75.9	19.6
Clark	564	2 929	234.2	98.3	421	19 537	3 854.3	715.2	506	8 570	271.7	76.8
Columbia	1	D	D	D	NA	NA	NA	NA	12	D	D	D
Cowlitz	116	677	43.7	18.9	125	8 309	2 496.5	364.4	214	3 208	97.1	28.7
Douglas	23	83	5.1	2.3	NA	NA	NA	NA	46	733	21.6	6.3
Ferry	7	27	1.9	0.8	NA	NA	NA	NA	21	126	5.1	1.1
Franklin	44	134	12.9	4.6	47	3 092	1 160.5	69.1	87	1 105	34.6	9.3
Garfield	1	D	D	D	NA	NA	NA	NA	3	D	D	D
Grant	93	407	25.6	9.5	56	4 090	806.9	111.3	170	1 930	58.8	15.3
Grays Harbor	84	320	22.3	11.1	97	3 792	822.9	125.7	238	2 150	74.2	20.3
Island	98	261	20.0	6.5	49	625	62.5	17.0	122	1 410	44.3	11.9
Jefferson	62	118	7.2	2.3	56	D	D	D	98	1 105	35.1	10.3
King	6 767	61 617	6 900.4	2 784.9	2 993	134 028	26 480.3	5 682.6	4 456	76 070	3 161.2	896.4
Kitsap	443	2 226	169.0	65.5	143	1 441	142.7	36.8	399	5 998	180.2	50.6
Kittitas	37	116	9.5	3.1	32	662	102.4	15.6	125	1 431	45.6	13.0
Klickitat	32	77	5.3	1.9	25	D	D	D	48	297	9.5	2.9
Lewis	81	301	19.9	7.0	115	3 630	648.0	97.1	196	1 919	62.9	17.5
Lincoln	10	78	4.6	2.4	NA	NA	NA	NA	33	154	4.2	1.1
Mason	58	284	17.1	5.9	52	1 664	343.9	51.7	98	953	29.9	7.8
Okanogan	46	150	9.7	3.4	28	794	123.6	20.9	122	1 192	42.4	12.4
Pacific	33	56	4.2	1.6	36	848	112.8	19.0	110	818	26.9	7.6
Pend Oreille	11	56	3.5	1.4	NA	NA	NA	NA	27	167	4.8	1.4
Pierce	974	4 965	444.3	174.0	680	22 283	4 275.9	705.2	1 218	18 808	603.6	169.3
San Juan	53	135	11.8	5.2	NA	NA	NA	NA	99	778	40.1	13.1
Skagit	209	732	55.7	20.6	185	5 026	2 917.7	148.9	277	3 614	118.1	31.5
Skamania	9	13	1.1	0.3	NA	NA	NA	NA	17	221	4.4	1.2
Snohomish	958	4 690	472.5	177.7	837	58 170	19 903.2	2 918.1	1 108	16 699	558.4	153.9
Spokane	886	5 738	444.5	186.9	572	20 892	3 994.6	681.4	904	14 456	453.2	128.5
Stevens	31	93	5.4	2.1	40	1 546	363.6	53.6	82	689	23.5	5.4
Thurston	401	2 571	198.1	86.2	156	3 218	761.0	100.7	406	6 076	193.0	56.6
Wahkiakum	4	D	D	D	NA	NA	NA	NA	13	50	1.5	0.4
Walla Walla	76	314	20.5	8.0	66	2 400	544.7	89.4	113	1 482	42.8	12.0
Whatcom	390	2 615	246.5	109.0	314	9 184	3 947.0	281.4	429	5 926	195.5	52.8
Whitman	43	156	10.3	3.5	NA	NA	NA	NA	110	1 196	30.9	7.6
Yakima	223	1 298	119.4	43.2	239	10 163	2 090.5	264.6	411	5 371	178.6	47.8
WEST VIRGINIA	2 517	15 714	1 166.9	395.2	1 505	72 813	18 293.3	2 460.7	3 290	51 529	1 633.2	462.3
Barbour	15	53	1.8	0.7	NA	NA	NA	NA	22	D	D	D
Berkeley	81	610	55.2	18.1	38	3 093	470.4	85.1	129	1 947	67.6	17.0
Boone	17	104	7.5	2.9	NA	NA	NA	NA	22	259	8.3	2.4
Braxton	17	49	2.4	0.6	NA	NA	NA	NA	32	444	14.3	4.0

1. Firms subject to federal tax.

Table B. States and Counties — Health Care and Social Assistance, Other Services, and Federal Funds

STATE County	Health care and social assistance,[1] 1997				Other services,[1] 1997				Federal funds and grants, 2002–2003 Expenditures (mil dol)			
										Direct payments for individuals[2]		
	Number of establishments	Number of employees	Receipts (mil dol)	Annual payroll (mil dol)	Number of establishments	Number of employees	Receipts (mil dol)	Annual payroll (mil dol)	Total	Social Security and government retirement	Medicare	Food stamps and Supplemental Security Income
	159	160	161	162	163	164	165	166	167	168	169	170
VIRGINIA—Cont'd												
Manassas Park City	NA	NA	NA	NA	6	72	4.6	1.5	16.6	2.9	0.0	0.4
Martinsville City	78	712	46.8	21.4	40	196	8.8	2.5	145.8	78.6	28.9	1.6
Newport News City	324	3 878	217.6	122.3	306	2 234	116.3	41.1	1 732.3	472.6	129.7	40.9
Norfolk City	400	6 583	451.7	219.1	388	2 569	147.8	49.7	6 211.0	570.9	211.1	67.2
Norton City	35	248	23.3	13.0	19	73	3.6	1.3	51.1	20.5	8.3	1.2
Petersburg City	89	1 438	64.1	32.6	76	620	32.6	12.0	312.4	118.3	63.1	17.6
Poquoson City	10	150	6.0	3.0	16	74	3.1	1.2	31.1	22.6	4.7	0.4
Portsmouth City	170	2 393	134.8	71.8	163	1 364	74.6	27.2	1 758.0	311.4	121.3	38.4
Radford City	47	360	22.1	12.7	19	102	3.5	1.2	139.4	31.5	13.9	1.9
Richmond City	540	14 788	1 111.6	414.8	504	3 887	256.6	82.0	3 777.1	1 007.8	326.8	81.4
Roanoke City	274	3 623	274.3	127.4	337	2 403	123.8	43.2	964.7	352.6	142.7	27.4
Salem City	64	2 817	224.2	72.7	81	349	19.0	6.2	230.8	94.2	30.7	1.8
Staunton City	63	646	38.4	17.3	53	404	19.7	6.9	160.9	87.0	36.4	4.1
Suffolk City	89	1 334	69.9	34.9	85	453	22.2	6.7	522.9	179.5	55.1	10.7
Virginia Beach City	809	8 315	473.4	223.9	716	4 870	254.7	89.2	3 197.6	1 210.8	198.0	41.6
Waynesboro City	47	446	26.6	10.6	51	311	19.3	5.2	119.0	75.3	24.5	3.4
Williamsburg City	61	697	45.1	23.5	35	184	7.1	2.6	224.1	117.8	36.6	0.8
Winchester City	126	1 018	98.2	53.5	77	400	21.2	7.3	169.3	77.8	31.0	4.9
WASHINGTON	12 310	122 813	7 797.7	3 390.2	8 771	49 756	3 492.0	1 033.0	43 368.0	13 018.7	4 172.8	962.8
Adams	15	205	8.3	4.2	22	45	4.2	0.8	98.7	22.9	9.1	3.2
Asotin	41	459	18.6	6.7	21	68	3.7	1.1	121.4	58.9	20.4	5.5
Benton	335	2 841	183.0	74.1	178	1 008	55.3	17.2	2 970.2	284.5	82.6	17.8
Chelan	134	1 984	162.8	65.7	118	396	29.1	7.7	359.9	155.3	47.5	9.3
Clallam	173	1 335	72.2	28.6	99	394	27.2	6.8	493.9	268.3	76.3	11.1
Clark	475	6 155	369.2	170.5	414	2 117	141.8	43.3	1 468.8	689.3	190.0	53.7
Columbia	6	21	0.8	0.4	13	33	2.3	0.6	37.2	12.3	4.5	0.9
Cowlitz	168	1 933	110.4	48.6	138	706	43.7	13.4	487.3	229.6	80.8	22.8
Douglas	33	367	23.6	7.8	36	122	9.5	2.5	153.8	62.9	29.6	3.3
Ferry	9	30	0.9	0.2	3	D	D	D	44.3	19.6	4.6	1.5
Franklin	81	669	40.5	15.7	67	343	28.5	7.7	254.8	71.6	29.0	10.3
Garfield	4	9	0.6	0.2	5	8	0.7	0.1	33.6	8.0	2.9	0.3
Grant	84	781	53.0	19.4	88	371	28.8	7.2	380.8	148.8	46.3	12.6
Grays Harbor	147	1 201	69.5	33.2	98	347	22.1	6.0	424.8	189.8	80.0	19.6
Island	115	796	38.3	14.6	62	266	14.8	4.7	742.8	227.8	42.1	5.9
Jefferson	61	715	28.3	13.0	58	220	12.2	3.2	188.2	106.7	29.1	3.5
King	4 360	41 887	2 913.7	1 247.1	3 244	20 986	1 642.9	474.2	11 313.0	3 094.1	1 263.1	253.2
Kitsap	473	4 466	245.3	104.1	264	1 300	77.7	23.9	2 809.5	715.0	138.9	32.3
Kittitas	51	468	25.4	9.5	55	261	12.6	3.2	158.9	71.2	23.0	3.9
Klickitat	22	165	8.1	3.5	18	64	5.7	1.0	113.4	52.1	14.6	4.7
Lewis	138	1 451	84.3	35.4	84	443	40.2	10.2	405.0	196.6	74.8	15.6
Lincoln	14	60	4.0	1.9	17	24	2.0	0.4	74.4	34.8	11.5	1.0
Mason	60	458	27.2	9.5	51	194	10.5	3.1	285.2	175.9	49.6	10.6
Okanogan	69	594	33.3	14.1	51	138	10.7	2.2	262.7	102.6	30.3	9.7
Pacific	33	209	10.1	3.9	26	72	4.3	1.2	155.5	78.5	28.4	4.9
Pend Oreille	11	70	3.8	1.6	9	28	1.4	0.4	68.2	36.1	8.8	4.0
Pierce	1 439	14 037	865.7	384.0	908	5 430	354.7	114.5	5 052.6	1 761.5	438.7	136.8
San Juan	20	62	3.8	0.9	20	41	3.2	0.8	69.4	43.2	11.1	0.8
Skagit	219	2 291	142.9	67.5	151	880	60.6	18.6	539.0	270.3	95.4	17.3
Skamania	6	23	1.2	0.3	5	9	0.6	0.2	75.4	17.4	4.0	1.5
Snohomish	1 067	10 785	623.5	293.5	827	4 502	292.6	93.7	2 364.2	1 035.8	337.1	69.8
Spokane	991	11 137	681.4	306.8	699	4 355	258.4	78.5	2 554.2	1 014.6	368.1	83.9
Stevens	41	475	20.5	9.7	44	189	12.2	3.8	212.5	101.2	27.8	7.6
Thurston	459	4 551	322.8	137.0	264	1 356	79.0	24.2	2 283.3	688.1	139.8	32.5
Wahkiakum	4	72	2.7	1.2	2	D	D	D	22.1	12.3	4.7	0.4
Walla Walla	96	1 183	67.7	29.4	54	256	17.3	4.8	344.1	133.7	46.3	9.1
Whatcom	406	3 627	201.2	82.1	225	1 161	81.3	22.1	878.8	354.6	99.0	24.9
Whitman	59	647	30.7	14.4	56	207	11.4	3.0	259.8	61.3	23.8	2.9
Yakima	391	4 594	298.6	129.8	277	1 408	87.6	26.8	1 171.5	410.3	159.5	54.4
WEST VIRGINIA	3 266	40 085	2 575.0	1 056.9	2 512	14 805	867.4	255.9	14 226.4	5 287.8	2 076.6	591.5
Barbour	15	124	5.4	1.8	12	29	1.5	0.3	116.6	40.7	18.5	7.3
Berkeley	114	863	55.4	19.8	94	410	22.6	6.8	546.1	208.4	52.4	11.1
Boone	22	209	9.9	4.0	23	101	6.3	1.8	156.6	77.8	27.1	10.5
Braxton	12	140	4.4	1.8	14	43	3.1	1.0	94.3	36.7	13.6	5.4

1. Firms subject to federal tax.   2. State totals may include programs not allocated by county.

	Federal funds and grants, 2002–2003 (cont'd)							Local government finances, 2002				
	Expenditures (mil dol) (cont'd)							General revenue				
	Procurement contract awards			Grants[1]						Taxes		
STATE County	Salaries and wages	Defense	Other	Medicaid and other health-related	Nutrition and family welfare	Education	Other	Total (mil dol)	Intergovernmental (mil dol)	Total (mil dol)	Per capita[2] (dollars) Total	Property
	171	172	173	174	175	176	177	178	179	180	181	182
VIRGINIA—Cont'd												
Manassas Park City	2.2	0.1	0.4	8.2	0.5	0.7	1.2	29.1	11.9	13.3	1 218	872
Martinsville City	4.0	1.6	5.3	13.2	1.6	1.7	5.4	44.7	23.5	12.9	846	418
Newport News City	356.8	415.5	134.4	68.2	26.0	16.1	53.6	580.2	265.7	216.9	1 203	807
Norfolk City	2 982.9	1 856.0	142.0	168.2	57.7	32.2	76.0	1 149.3	493.7	288.2	1 206	673
Norton City	6.3	4.9	0.2	4.3	4.5	0.4	0.0	13.0	6.7	5.0	1 257	426
Petersburg City	10.8	3.5	6.7	41.7	9.2	7.2	20.0	217.8	60.6	32.7	989	661
Poquoson City	1.4	0.2	0.2	0.5	0.1	0.8	0.0	28.9	12.8	12.3	1 050	834
Portsmouth City	672.9	397.4	51.9	82.4	20.0	10.2	29.5	327.7	186.0	94.1	943	600
Radford City	7.2	65.7	0.6	5.5	3.2	1.6	2.6	25.8	12.4	8.6	549	327
Richmond City	562.5	98.4	122.7	418.6	288.4	256.8	549.6	924.1	374.6	332.3	1 683	1 157
Roanoke City	102.2	146.0	23.9	75.7	23.7	7.9	42.8	356.6	168.8	131.0	1 395	757
Salem City	72.3	0.2	6.7	9.4	0.8	1.4	0.8	73.8	21.7	40.6	1 636	1 074
Staunton City	7.9	0.1	1.4	15.1	2.0	2.8	2.2	54.1	23.9	22.7	961	536
Suffolk City	31.4	150.1	7.3	47.4	8.7	3.9	12.4	181.3	84.3	77.1	1 103	773
Virginia Beach City	1 059.8	467.3	52.6	40.8	17.4	34.8	40.2	1 213.4	410.4	582.7	1 343	905
Waynesboro City	2.8	1.0	1.1	6.2	1.7	0.9	1.6	55.4	23.0	23.9	1 187	796
Williamsburg City	22.5	17.8	5.8	2.9	1.9	2.2	13.6	118.2	29.8	82.5	7 051	5 625
Winchester City	20.0	1.1	12.9	12.7	2.2	2.4	3.0	94.5	29.0	37.8	1 561	700
WASHINGTON	5 758.2	3 196.0	3 432.5	4 200.4	1 257.9	715.4	2 707.2	X	X	X	X	X
Adams	2.6	0.0	2.8	29.2	3.7	0.9	4.4	83.1	35.5	15.3	930	690
Asotin	2.8	7.3	1.3	13.2	4.5	1.6	2.2	49.9	29.8	11.4	557	426
Benton	59.8	8.6	2 390.7	44.2	15.6	6.2	44.4	724.0	223.9	132.8	883	544
Chelan	36.9	0.1	20.4	42.1	11.6	5.8	18.5	238.7	98.5	67.9	1 012	696
Clallam	36.5	1.5	13.8	35.6	12.8	5.5	26.1	249.9	82.6	55.1	831	536
Clark	206.4	10.4	47.1	132.5	43.5	20.7	54.7	1 016.0	471.4	329.1	889	661
Columbia	2.5	0.6	3.4	4.9	0.9	0.1	1.9	20.0	8.9	3.3	804	657
Cowlitz	15.2	1.6	13.4	57.7	20.2	17.6	23.0	303.7	134.8	86.8	918	636
Douglas	7.0	11.0	0.5	11.5	3.5	1.1	7.0	103.9	57.2	27.1	811	663
Ferry	5.9	0.0	4.2	2.9	1.8	1.7	1.7	31.7	20.5	3.1	422	327
Franklin	27.8	23.6	6.7	24.0	13.8	8.0	14.9	170.2	88.3	41.8	792	494
Garfield	4.5	4.6	0.5	0.7	0.3	0.1	5.1	13.1	7.0	2.0	881	671
Grant	37.1	6.1	22.5	38.0	13.6	6.0	24.5	325.9	133.4	62.3	799	582
Grays Harbor	13.6	6.3	6.5	59.0	17.1	7.7	17.0	236.9	116.2	63.6	928	561
Island	351.3	79.5	2.4	12.0	4.0	6.6	8.5	178.7	75.2	48.1	641	460
Jefferson	7.2	9.1	2.4	11.6	5.0	1.8	10.3	99.9	28.3	31.5	1 178	832
King	1 359.2	1 810.4	452.5	1 827.4	205.0	94.3	815.4	7 865.6	2 479.7	2 992.7	1 701	933
Kitsap	1 151.0	456.5	83.9	86.2	28.0	33.4	69.2	622.1	310.0	202.1	856	622
Kittitas	9.1	0.1	8.8	13.5	4.9	6.0	9.3	107.0	39.3	28.2	819	507
Klickitat	5.1	0.3	4.9	10.9	3.9	1.2	9.5	89.8	40.9	14.6	755	496
Lewis	13.6	0.4	9.4	53.0	13.9	9.1	13.7	197.9	101.6	55.7	799	495
Lincoln	3.7	0.0	0.7	2.6	1.2	1.1	5.4	61.2	27.9	10.5	1 043	901
Mason	5.1	0.2	1.3	22.5	8.2	4.0	5.4	169.2	64.9	41.0	803	626
Okanogan	21.5	0.7	19.8	27.1	13.3	6.1	12.1	140.2	70.2	24.6	627	442
Pacific	7.7	-0.1	10.8	15.9	4.1	1.2	2.9	87.7	37.5	22.2	1 067	749
Pend Oreille	4.2	0.4	1.2	8.8	2.3	0.7	1.7	44.8	20.2	8.8	729	597
Pierce	1 363.0	412.2	73.9	450.9	115.7	52.0	202.3	2 159.8	967.6	724.0	989	699
San Juan	3.7	0.1	2.3	1.5	0.7	0.4	5.5	46.9	17.1	20.2	1 384	984
Skagit	21.6	8.2	15.5	46.3	17.8	14.7	21.1	486.8	171.9	114.6	1 072	729
Skamania	8.9	35.7	1.5	2.9	1.5	0.3	1.7	34.0	21.3	5.1	511	367
Snohomish	325.0	58.0	74.2	227.8	55.7	23.4	128.8	1 979.1	742.7	638.7	1 008	671
Spokane	375.0	73.2	67.2	305.5	73.1	36.3	106.1	1 212.2	598.5	361.8	846	577
Stevens	18.4	1.2	3.6	21.3	8.4	4.1	17.2	92.9	58.3	22.4	553	409
Thurston	67.6	10.7	12.5	197.4	253.1	236.1	612.2	622.7	284.7	218.0	1 002	701
Wahkiakum	0.8	0.0	0.8	1.7	0.4	0.1	0.5	15.4	6.2	2.5	653	433
Walla Walla	39.5	8.1	6.9	30.2	9.7	4.9	29.3	153.4	77.0	47.1	839	611
Whatcom	48.2	122.2	17.8	85.7	23.3	10.1	61.7	451.2	189.6	167.0	958	622
Whitman	17.2	4.6	7.5	34.9	4.1	7.2	55.6	122.9	45.9	32.3	796	576
Yakima	72.1	23.0	17.1	207.2	87.5	34.5	61.2	653.3	400.4	149.8	666	445
WEST VIRGINIA	1 288.9	184.8	480.1	1 664.8	424.7	283.1	1 189.3	X	X	X	X	X
Barbour	7.3	0.1	2.2	22.1	2.5	1.4	11.9	30.8	18.9	4.6	297	272
Berkeley	173.6	5.8	34.9	27.3	6.3	3.6	16.9	148.7	85.1	40.4	497	467
Boone	5.9	0.0	1.2	21.4	4.3	2.3	2.9	77.8	28.7	24.1	945	918
Braxton	3.4	0.6	1.2	23.7	2.6	1.5	5.3	28.2	16.4	4.6	312	287

1. State totals may include programs not allocated by county. 2. Based on the resident population estimated as of July 1 of the year shown.

STATE County	Total (mil dol) 183	Per capita[1] (dollars) 184	Educa-tion 185	Health and hospitals 186	Police protec-tion 187	Public welfare 188	High-ways 189	Total (mil dol) 190	Per capita[1] (dollars) 191	Federal civilian 192	Federal military 193	State and local 194	Demo-cratic 195	Republi-can 196	All other 197
VIRGINIA—Cont'd															
Manassas Park City	32.2	2 954	48.4	1.1	4.4	5.9	12.5	21.6	1 977	(3)	(3)	(3)	45.0	54.3	0.7
Martinsville City	50.8	3 327	41.9	0.7	7.2	0.5	5.7	23.8	1 562	(4)	(4)	(4)	54.3	45.4	0.3
Newport News City	591.3	3 280	40.7	5.5	5.6	7.0	3.5	753.2	4 178	4 606	8 099	11 287	52.5	47.0	0.5
Norfolk City	1 130.7	4 730	37.6	5.5	4.1	5.1	3.2	1 479.7	6 190	14 404	63 841	20 950	61.7	37.6	0.7
Norton City	13.0	3 263	43.7	0.4	8.9	8.3	9.6	4.9	1 245	(5)	(5)	(5)	48.3	51.2	0.5
Petersburg City	220.3	6 651	20.1	53.4	3.2	5.3	1.4	59.0	1 781	(6)	(6)	(6)	81.7	18.1	0.2
Poquoson City	28.3	2 423	55.1	1.1	5.7	0.6	4.2	28.5	2 442	(7)	(7)	(7)	22.0	77.3	0.7
Portsmouth City	338.2	3 389	35.6	3.2	5.5	6.5	1.4	282.9	2 835	9 984	5 121	6 195	61.1	38.5	0.4
Radford City	30.2	1 928	39.4	0.5	5.9	4.8	7.6	6.5	412	(8)	(8)	(8)	45.7	53.9	0.4
Richmond City	898.7	4 551	29.8	6.4	6.5	7.8	4.1	1 171.0	5 930	6 859	1 169	42 568	70.3	29.1	0.6
Roanoke City	360.5	3 840	30.9	0.5	4.2	7.3	3.3	433.9	4 623	1 807	280	6 507	52.4	46.4	1.2
Salem City	71.7	2 888	42.3	0.4	7.5	1.1	6.8	46.7	1 882	(9)	(9)	(9)	37.0	62.1	0.9
Staunton City	55.1	2 332	42.2	0.5	6.8	6.1	7.3	36.7	1 554	(10)	(10)	(10)	39.0	60.3	0.7
Suffolk City	185.8	2 656	45.3	0.7	4.8	6.1	2.4	259.4	3 708	286	296	4 355	46.5	52.9	0.6
Virginia Beach City	1 359.0	3 132	58.8	2.7	4.5	2.2	1.7	1 114.3	2 568	5 088	23 499	21 221	40.3	59.2	0.5
Waynesboro City	61.8	3 068	46.6	0.7	6.3	9.2	5.7	15.1	751	(10)	(10)	(10)	35.1	64.1	0.8
Williamsburg City	107.7	9 213	62.8	0.3	2.8	1.1	2.0	132.3	11 314	(11)	(11)	(11)	52.7	46.7	0.6
Winchester City	95.3	3 932	34.6	2.4	4.5	3.2	9.3	169.2	6 984	(12)	(12)	(12)	42.6	56.7	0.7
WASHINGTON	X	X	X	X	X	X	X	X	X	67 097	74 506	440 300	53.0	45.5	1.4
Adams	75.5	4 592	39.0	19.8	3.4	0.0	12.4	36.2	2 205	57	49	1 435	25.3	73.5	1.2
Asotin	47.5	2 321	51.6	4.7	3.8	0.0	11.1	31.3	1 531	67	61	1 031	37.9	60.4	1.6
Benton	469.1	3 119	45.4	15.6	3.9	0.0	4.9	6 775.4	45 060	823	461	9 856	32.3	66.3	1.4
Chelan	207.0	3 087	43.3	11.8	4.3	0.0	5.7	1 057.2	15 767	749	201	5 433	35.9	62.8	1.3
Clallam	251.9	3 800	31.3	36.2	3.1	0.0	4.7	98.3	1 482	490	491	6 022	47.1	50.8	2.2
Clark	1 013.1	2 736	51.2	2.5	4.0	0.3	7.9	1 688.8	4 561	2 660	1 118	18 091	46.8	51.9	1.3
Columbia	19.9	4 851	26.8	34.1	4.0	0.0	17.2	7.9	1 925	64	12	422	29.0	69.6	1.5
Cowlitz	324.8	3 437	42.3	3.3	4.6	0.0	4.0	335.6	3 550	250	282	5 451	52.9	45.7	1.4
Douglas	110.6	3 309	59.9	6.1	3.2	0.0	7.2	269.3	8 061	176	108	1 800	33.0	66.0	1.0
Ferry	25.7	3 532	42.9	22.6	3.3	0.0	7.3	5.7	784	146	22	769	35.7	60.7	3.6
Franklin	173.5	3 290	54.0	0.6	4.0	0.0	4.0	209.2	3 966	500	158	3 878	34.0	64.6	1.4
Garfield	12.9	5 550	28.1	26.8	3.9	0.0	14.2	4.2	1 792	131	0	356	28.2	70.6	1.2
Grant	295.7	3 792	41.8	24.0	3.3	0.6	5.2	691.7	8 870	611	234	6 373	29.9	68.5	1.6
Grays Harbor	245.8	3 589	45.0	6.5	5.1	0.0	5.8	196.2	2 865	209	251	6 080	51.9	46.4	1.6
Island	171.2	2 281	39.8	22.6	3.9	0.0	7.2	115.3	1 536	1 418	8 643	3 098	47.3	51.3	1.4
Jefferson	86.9	3 248	30.6	27.6	3.2	0.0	6.4	56.9	2 125	151	90	1 872	62.6	35.6	1.8
King	7 568.1	4 301	28.6	9.6	4.9	0.1	5.2	11 910.5	6 769	21 247	6 690	139 253	64.6	34.1	1.3
Kitsap	593.5	2 513	50.3	4.2	3.9	0.7	4.5	475.9	2 015	14 399	13 915	12 739	51.5	46.9	1.6
Kittitas	115.6	3 364	32.9	27.1	4.4	0.0	6.0	97.3	2 831	179	116	4 091	41.6	56.7	1.7
Klickitat	80.3	4 141	38.6	20.3	3.9	0.3	11.3	75.4	3 889	107	58	1 561	43.5	54.5	2.0
Lewis	186.6	2 677	50.0	5.9	4.8	0.0	8.3	239.1	3 429	267	208	4 732	34.1	64.2	1.8
Lincoln	58.9	5 837	39.3	31.6	2.8	0.0	8.5	20.1	1 995	81	30	1 334	29.3	69.2	1.5
Mason	160.5	3 147	39.1	27.3	3.1	0.0	4.3	111.3	2 182	97	152	4 359	51.4	46.7	1.9
Okanogan	130.8	3 338	42.9	23.1	4.4	0.1	5.1	61.0	1 557	487	117	4 841	39.4	58.7	1.9
Pacific	84.6	4 074	40.1	23.3	3.5	0.0	7.2	50.2	2 417	63	159	1 747	54.1	43.9	2.0
Pend Oreille	44.0	3 668	37.5	31.8	3.0	0.0	7.5	30.5	2 543	120	36	1 100	37.2	59.6	3.2
Pierce	2 173.5	2 968	47.7	4.3	4.1	0.3	4.8	2 275.1	3 107	9 467	25 579	42 987	50.6	48.2	1.2
San Juan	45.3	3 108	33.6	9.9	3.0	0.5	10.9	26.3	1 803	64	44	879	65.6	32.5	1.8
Skagit	454.2	4 249	33.7	29.1	4.0	0.0	6.2	335.5	3 138	414	319	9 358	48.5	49.9	1.6
Skamania	34.1	3 390	38.4	2.5	4.8	0.1	12.6	3.5	350	214	30	618	46.1	52.2	1.7
Snohomish	1 831.0	2 888	42.1	11.8	4.5	0.6	5.6	2 525.7	3 984	2 139	7 515	32 898	53.1	45.6	1.3
Spokane	1 134.0	2 653	52.4	2.9	5.0	0.0	4.2	804.5	1 882	4 417	4 901	28 423	43.7	54.8	1.6
Stevens	92.3	2 275	54.8	3.3	4.1	0.0	8.4	41.9	1 034	402	121	2 576	33.9	63.7	2.4
Thurston	591.1	2 716	50.9	4.8	4.2	0.0	6.5	432.7	1 988	986	694	34 373	55.5	42.6	1.9
Wahkiakum	14.3	3 770	32.9	12.2	4.6	0.2	17.1	4.4	1 154	13	11	233	45.5	52.5	2.0
Walla Walla	150.3	2 678	47.4	5.3	7.5	0.0	7.2	158.4	2 821	898	171	4 033	36.1	62.5	1.4
Whatcom	454.5	2 607	44.5	2.4	4.8	0.0	5.7	374.7	2 149	908	562	12 733	53.5	44.7	1.9
Whitman	118.2	2 910	36.9	26.5	4.3	0.0	7.7	44.4	1 092	283	135	8 693	44.7	53.6	1.7
Yakima	645.9	2 873	56.9	1.8	4.4	1.2	5.2	331.0	1 472	1 343	755	14 772	38.9	59.9	1.2
WEST VIRGINIA	X	X	X	X	X	X	X	X	X	21 280	7 963	119 013	43.2	56.1	0.7
Barbour	31.1	2 008	67.0	5.0	1.7	0.0	1.0	39.5	2 546	47	64	785	39.6	59.8	0.6
Berkeley	148.8	1 832	74.0	1.2	3.4	0.0	0.7	170.4	2 097	2 857	359	3 350	36.2	63.1	0.7
Boone	74.2	2 903	53.9	26.4	2.4	0.1	0.5	4.9	191	88	104	1 470	58.3	41.2	0.6
Braxton	30.1	2 037	69.7	1.2	1.0	0.0	0.4	86.4	5 840	68	60	794	50.2	49.3	0.5

1. Based on the resident population estimated as of July 1 of the year shown. 3. Manassas and Manassas Park included with Prince William County. 4. Martinsville included with Henry County. 5. Norton included with Wise County. 6. Petersburg and Colonial Heights included with Dinwiddie County. 7. Poquoson included with York County. 8. Radford included with Montgomery County. 9. Salem included with Roanoke County. 10. Staunton and Waynesboro included with Augusta County. 11. Williamsburg included with James City County. 12. Winchester included with Frederick County.

Table B. States and Counties — **Land Area and Population**

					Population and population characteristics, 2003				Race alone or in combination, not Hispanic or Latino (percent)					Age (percent)					
STATE/ County code	CBSA code[1]	County Type[2]	STATE County	Land area,[3] (sq km) 2000	Total persons	Rank	Per square kilometer	White	Black	Am. Indian, Alaska Native	Asian and Pacific Islander	Percent Hispanic or Latino[4]	Under 5 years	5 to 17 years	18 to 24 years	25 to 34 years	35 to 44 years	45 to 54 years
				1	2	3	4	5	6	7	8	9	10	11	12	13	14	15
			WEST VIRGINIA—Cont'd															
54 009	48260	3	Brooke	230	24 939	1 577	108.4	98.1	1.2	0.3	0.5	0.4	4.8	14.9	9.9	11.0	14.0	16.3
54 011	26580	2	Cabell	729	95 043	567	130.4	93.8	4.9	0.7	1.2	0.6	5.9	14.2	11.9	13.6	13.1	14.3
54 013	...	8	Calhoun	727	7 294	2 659	10.0	98.8	0.1	0.5	0.1	0.7	4.9	15.7	9.4	9.7	15.0	17.2
54 015	16620	2	Clay	887	10 352	2 411	11.7	98.7	0.2	1.5	0.1	0.4	6.3	18.3	9.4	12.0	14.6	14.9
54 017	17220	9	Doddridge	830	7 491	2 637	9.0	98.8	0.3	0.7	0.2	0.6	5.1	17.8	10.4	11.1	15.0	14.8
54 019	36060	6	Fayette	1 720	47 270	973	27.5	93.3	5.6	0.8	0.5	0.6	5.7	15.4	9.9	12.0	13.8	16.1
54 021	...	9	Gilmer	881	7 037	2 683	8.0	97.2	1.2	0.5	0.9	0.8	4.4	13.8	16.4	10.6	13.0	13.9
54 023	...	6	Grant	1 236	11 434	2 339	9.3	98.1	1.1	0.3	0.2	0.7	5.9	16.3	7.7	12.6	13.9	14.8
54 025	...	7	Greenbrier	2 645	34 656	1 287	13.1	95.5	3.6	1.0	0.3	0.7	5.4	15.6	8.5	10.8	14.0	15.6
54 027	49020	3	Hampshire	1 662	21 247	1 740	12.8	98.0	1.0	0.6	0.3	0.6	5.3	18.5	8.6	11.8	14.6	14.4
54 029	48260	3	Hancock	215	31 742	1 363	147.6	96.4	2.7	0.3	0.5	0.8	5.1	15.1	7.4	11.6	14.7	16.7
54 031	...	8	Hardy	1 511	12 990	2 242	8.6	97.2	2.0	0.4	0.2	0.7	5.6	17.4	8.0	11.8	15.4	14.7
54 033	17220	5	Harrison	1 078	68 032	739	63.1	96.4	2.0	0.5	1.0	0.9	5.8	16.7	8.8	11.7	14.5	15.1
54 035	...	6	Jackson	1 206	28 285	1 448	23.5	99.1	0.3	0.5	0.4	0.3	5.9	17.4	8.5	11.8	14.7	14.6
54 037	47900	1	Jefferson	543	46 270	996	85.2	90.9	6.7	0.7	1.1	2.0	6.3	17.1	10.5	12.4	15.9	14.9
54 039	16620	2	Kanawha	2 339	195 413	294	83.5	90.9	7.9	0.7	1.4	0.5	5.9	15.3	8.1	12.3	14.4	16.4
54 041	...	7	Lewis	990	17 148	1 950	17.3	98.8	0.2	0.6	0.4	0.5	5.6	16.0	8.0	11.8	14.4	15.1
54 043	16620	2	Lincoln	1 133	22 251	1 695	19.6	99.2	0.2	0.5	0.2	0.6	5.7	16.8	9.5	13.4	14.9	15.3
54 045	...	6	Logan	1 176	36 745	1 219	31.2	96.5	2.7	0.4	0.4	0.6	5.9	15.6	9.0	12.9	14.0	17.3
54 047	...	7	McDowell	1 385	25 348	1 555	18.3	88.3	11.2	0.6	0.1	0.5	5.3	16.7	8.5	10.9	14.7	17.7
54 049	21900	4	Marion	802	56 484	862	70.4	95.3	3.7	0.6	0.6	0.7	5.3	14.9	10.3	12.5	13.3	14.8
54 051	48540	3	Marshall	795	34 897	1 277	43.9	98.4	0.7	0.5	0.4	0.7	5.2	16.7	8.1	11.2	14.5	16.6
54 053	38580	6	Mason	1 118	26 079	1 536	23.3	98.6	0.5	0.5	0.3	0.5	5.5	16.1	9.0	11.8	14.5	15.6
54 055	14140	5	Mercer	1 089	62 113	799	57.0	92.8	6.3	0.6	0.7	0.4	5.8	15.0	9.3	12.4	13.0	15.4
54 057	19060	3	Mineral	849	27 147	1 499	32.0	96.0	3.3	0.3	0.5	0.6	5.9	17.0	9.4	11.7	14.2	15.0
54 059	...	6	Mingo	1 095	27 585	1 480	25.2	96.6	2.5	0.7	0.3	0.5	6.3	17.0	9.6	12.5	15.2	16.8
54 061	34060	3	Monongalia	935	84 370	634	90.2	92.3	3.9	0.6	3.6	1.0	5.0	12.7	19.7	15.9	12.6	12.7
54 063	...	3	Monroe	1 226	13 503	2 198	11.0	98.2	1.3	0.5	0.2	0.3	5.2	16.1	8.3	11.4	13.7	14.8
54 065	25180	3	Morgan	593	15 514	2 062	26.2	98.0	0.7	0.3	0.4	0.9	5.3	16.4	7.4	11.4	14.8	15.4
54 067	...	6	Nicholas	1 680	26 243	1 529	15.6	99.0	0.1	0.6	0.3	0.5	5.0	16.7	8.8	11.7	14.8	16.1
54 069	48540	3	Ohio	275	45 828	1 008	166.6	94.9	4.3	0.2	1.1	0.4	5.3	15.4	10.7	10.4	13.6	15.9
54 071	...	8	Pendleton	1 807	7 896	2 603	4.4	96.7	2.2	0.3	0.3	0.9	5.1	16.0	7.2	10.8	15.0	15.6
54 073	37620	3	Pleasants	339	7 521	2 633	22.2	98.2	0.6	0.6	0.3	0.4	5.9	16.6	8.7	12.0	15.7	15.7
54 075	...	9	Pocahontas	2 435	8 944	2 529	3.7	98.6	0.8	0.4	0.2	0.4	4.5	15.3	7.4	11.0	15.4	15.7
54 077	34060	3	Preston	1 679	29 705	1 412	17.7	98.8	0.5	0.3	0.2	0.6	4.9	17.0	9.2	11.8	14.9	15.4
54 079	16620	2	Putnam	897	53 035	897	59.1	97.7	1.1	0.4	0.8	0.5	6.1	17.9	8.5	12.1	16.0	16.0
54 081	13220	4	Raleigh	1 572	79 254	660	50.4	89.5	8.9	0.6	1.1	0.9	5.4	15.4	9.2	13.5	14.1	16.2
54 083	...	7	Randolph	2 693	28 254	1 451	10.5	97.6	1.2	0.3	0.5	0.7	5.2	16.3	9.2	12.6	15.1	14.8
54 085	...	8	Ritchie	1 175	10 515	2 396	8.9	98.9	0.2	0.6	0.2	0.5	5.2	16.4	8.8	11.2	15.1	15.2
54 087	...	6	Roane	1 252	15 362	2 071	12.3	98.5	0.3	0.5	0.4	0.8	5.5	16.3	9.7	11.4	14.1	15.7
54 089	...	7	Summers	935	13 917	2 170	14.9	91.7	7.5	0.6	0.3	0.7	3.8	13.4	8.5	13.0	15.2	16.5
54 091	17220	3	Taylor	448	16 127	2 023	36.0	98.0	1.0	0.5	0.3	0.6	4.9	16.5	8.7	12.2	15.6	15.5
54 093	...	9	Tucker	1 085	7 162	2 668	6.6	99.3	0.4	0.3	0.3	0.2	4.7	15.5	7.6	10.6	15.0	15.1
54 095	...	6	Tyler	667	9 439	2 492	14.2	99.4	0.1	0.2	0.1	0.4	5.1	17.0	7.8	10.6	14.5	16.1
54 097	...	7	Upshur	919	23 668	1 625	25.8	98.2	0.8	0.4	0.4	0.6	5.6	16.1	13.3	11.0	13.2	14.6
54 099	26580	2	Wayne	1 310	42 418	1 072	32.4	98.9	0.3	0.6	0.3	0.5	5.9	16.8	9.1	12.5	14.0	14.8
54 101	...	9	Webster	1 440	9 790	2 460	6.8	99.5	0.2	0.4	0.2	0.4	4.9	16.7	8.7	11.4	14.0	16.5
54 103	...	6	Wetzel	930	17 160	1 949	18.5	99.0	0.2	0.4	0.4	0.4	5.3	17.1	7.8	10.6	14.4	15.5
54 105	37620	3	Wirt	603	5 790	2 791	9.6	98.7	0.4	0.6	0.4	0.3	4.5	17.9	9.0	11.3	17.4	14.4
54 107	37620	3	Wood	951	87 339	614	91.8	97.5	1.4	0.6	0.8	0.5	5.8	16.7	8.5	11.8	14.8	15.3
54 109	...	7	Wyoming	1 297	24 830	1 582	19.1	98.5	0.8	0.4	0.1	0.6	5.5	15.7	8.8	11.6	14.3	18.4
55 000	...	X	WISCONSIN	140 663	5 472 299	X	38.9	87.4	6.2	1.2	2.2	3.9	6.2	18.2	10.3	12.5	15.5	14.7
55 001	...	8	Adams	1 678	20 567	1 772	12.3	93.4	2.6	1.5	0.4	2.5	4.1	14.2	8.3	11.5	15.3	13.9
55 003	...	7	Ashland	2 703	16 651	1 986	6.2	87.5	0.5	11.8	0.5	1.2	5.9	17.9	12.3	10.8	14.4	14.0
55 005	...	6	Barron	2 235	45 514	1 009	20.4	97.7	0.2	1.1	0.5	0.9	5.2	17.6	10.3	10.6	15.0	14.4
55 007	...	8	Bayfield	3 823	15 114	2 094	4.0	90.0	0.3	9.8	0.4	0.8	4.8	17.5	8.2	8.7	15.0	17.0
55 009	24580	2	Brown	1 369	233 888	252	170.8	89.5	1.8	2.7	2.7	4.5	6.8	18.6	10.5	13.9	16.6	14.1
55 011	...	8	Buffalo	1 773	13 814	2 180	7.8	98.5	0.2	0.4	0.4	0.7	5.3	17.7	8.9	10.5	15.6	15.0
55 013	...	8	Burnett	2 128	16 242	2 017	7.6	94.4	0.6	5.0	0.4	0.8	4.7	15.7	8.7	9.2	13.2	14.9
55 015	11540	3	Calumet	828	43 383	1 055	52.4	95.6	0.7	0.6	2.2	1.5	6.6	20.0	9.7	12.4	17.3	14.3
55 017	20740	3	Chippewa	2 617	56 773	855	21.7	97.7	0.4	0.6	1.2	0.7	6.0	18.5	9.7	11.1	15.8	14.7
55 019	...	6	Clark	3 148	33 969	1 303	10.8	97.7	0.2	0.7	0.3	1.4	7.3	20.8	10.0	10.2	14.3	13.1
55 021	31540	2	Columbia	2 004	54 076	889	27.0	96.9	1.0	0.6	0.5	1.5	5.8	17.7	9.0	11.8	16.5	14.7
55 023	...	7	Crawford	1 483	16 949	1 958	11.4	97.4	1.5	0.4	0.3	0.7	5.6	18.2	10.5	9.4	14.0	14.5
55 025	31540	2	Dane	3 113	449 378	140	144.4	87.4	4.9	0.7	4.9	3.7	6.1	16.0	12.6	16.0	15.8	14.4

1. CBSA = Core Based Statistical Area. See Appendix A for explanation. See Appendix B for list of metropolitan areas with component counties. 2. County type code from the Economic Research Service of USDA Rural-Urban Continuum Codes. See Appendix A for definition. 3. Dry land or land partially or temporarily covered by water. 4. Hispanic or Latino persons may be of any race.

Table B. States and Counties — **Population and Households**

	Population, 2003 (cont'd)				Population — change and components of change, 1990–2003							Households, 2000				
	Age (percent) (cont'd)				Total persons		Percent change		Components of change, 2000–2003						Percent	
STATE County	55 to 64 years	65 to 74 years	75 years and over	Percent female	1990	2000	1990–2000	2000–2003	Births	Deaths	Net migration	Number	Percent change, 1990–2000	Persons per house-hold	Female family house-holder[1]	One person
	16	17	18	19	20	21	22	23	24	25	26	27	28	29	30	31
WEST VIRGINIA—Cont'd																
Brooke	11.0	9.5	9.0	51.8	26 992	25 447	-5.7	-2.0	799	1 051	-230	10 396	2.6	2.36	9.9	27.9
Cabell	10.4	8.2	8.0	52.0	96 827	96 784	0.0	-1.8	3 820	3 798	-1 739	41 180	5.2	2.27	11.6	31.3
Calhoun	12.1	8.9	7.6	50.0	7 885	7 582	-3.8	-3.8	257	310	-225	3 071	3.1	2.46	10.3	24.9
Clay	10.5	7.9	6.0	50.6	9 983	10 330	3.5	0.2	440	378	-33	4 020	10.8	2.55	10.4	24.3
Doddridge	10.9	8.1	6.3	49.5	6 994	7 403	5.8	1.2	229	276	140	2 845	8.5	2.56	10.3	22.5
Fayette	10.6	8.2	8.0	50.2	47 952	47 579	-0.8	-0.6	1 815	2 159	70	18 945	3.6	2.41	13.2	26.9
Gilmer	11.2	8.2	7.3	49.4	7 669	7 160	-6.6	-1.7	197	223	-91	2 768	1.9	2.43	8.6	25.5
Grant	12.5	8.4	7.1	50.4	10 428	11 299	8.4	1.2	437	418	124	4 591	17.0	2.43	8.2	24.5
Greenbrier	12.1	9.5	8.4	51.5	34 693	34 453	-0.7	0.6	1 188	1 505	545	14 571	5.8	2.32	10.7	28.6
Hampshire	11.4	8.2	6.2	50.1	16 498	20 203	22.5	5.2	690	603	944	7 955	28.7	2.49	9.5	24.6
Hancock	11.0	9.9	9.0	51.9	35 233	32 667	-7.3	-2.8	1 067	1 429	-540	13 678	-0.7	2.36	10.7	26.6
Hardy	11.6	7.9	6.7	50.7	10 977	12 669	15.4	2.5	445	476	353	5 204	21.4	2.42	8.6	27.0
Harrison	10.9	8.0	8.3	52.0	69 371	68 652	-1.0	-0.9	2 536	2 844	-271	27 867	3.2	2.42	11.4	27.7
Jackson	11.1	9.3	6.6	51.3	25 938	28 000	7.9	1.0	1 099	984	190	11 061	14.7	2.50	9.4	22.7
Jefferson	10.1	5.9	4.7	50.4	35 926	42 190	17.4	9.7	1 868	1 198	3 340	16 165	25.2	2.54	10.0	23.2
Kanawha	11.0	8.5	8.2	52.3	207 619	200 073	-3.6	-2.3	7 549	8 236	-3 931	86 226	1.8	2.28	12.3	30.8
Lewis	11.3	8.8	7.9	51.8	17 223	16 919	-1.8	1.4	640	683	289	6 946	5.0	2.40	10.5	26.9
Lincoln	10.8	7.7	5.4	50.8	21 382	22 108	3.4	0.6	848	872	191	8 664	13.3	2.54	10.8	22.2
Logan	10.7	8.2	6.5	51.4	43 032	37 710	-12.4	-2.6	1 500	1 588	-885	14 880	-3.5	2.50	12.6	24.0
McDowell	11.7	8.5	7.8	52.4	35 233	27 329	-22.4	-7.2	957	1 306	-1 631	11 169	-13.3	2.42	14.9	27.3
Marion	11.0	8.1	9.2	52.2	57 249	56 598	-1.1	-0.2	1 943	2 513	508	23 652	4.3	2.34	10.7	28.9
Marshall	11.5	8.5	8.0	51.3	37 356	35 519	-4.9	-1.8	1 174	1 172	-577	14 207	1.1	2.44	10.8	25.6
Mason	11.7	8.9	6.6	51.0	25 178	25 957	3.1	0.5	908	894	131	10 587	10.2	2.42	10.1	25.5
Mercer	11.3	8.8	8.7	52.5	64 980	62 980	-3.1	-1.4	2 414	2 689	-571	26 509	4.4	2.33	11.2	28.7
Mineral	11.9	7.8	7.2	51.0	26 697	27 078	1.4	0.3	1 050	1 031	79	10 784	8.0	2.46	9.7	25.0
Mingo	10.1	7.1	5.6	51.6	33 739	28 253	-16.3	-2.4	1 192	1 074	-801	11 303	-4.5	2.49	12.7	25.2
Monongalia	8.0	5.3	5.1	49.3	75 509	81 866	8.4	3.1	2 751	2 159	1 972	33 446	15.0	2.28	8.3	31.3
Monroe	12.7	8.8	7.9	50.7	12 406	14 583	17.5	-7.4	455	451	311	5 447	14.7	2.41	7.9	25.8
Morgan	11.9	9.5	7.0	50.8	12 128	14 943	23.2	3.8	473	539	630	6 145	29.9	2.40	8.2	24.5
Nicholas	11.5	8.4	6.9	51.0	26 775	26 562	-0.8	-1.2	861	935	-220	10 722	7.5	2.46	10.0	24.8
Ohio	10.3	8.9	10.0	53.0	50 871	47 427	-6.8	-3.4	1 618	2 026	-1 195	19 733	-4.4	2.27	11.2	33.7
Pendleton	12.1	9.7	8.9	49.7	8 054	8 196	1.8	-3.7	257	237	-313	3 350	9.4	2.40	8.1	25.8
Pleasants	10.9	7.4	7.5	49.7	7 546	7 514	-0.4	0.1	282	279	8	2 887	4.3	2.51	10.4	22.9
Pocahontas	12.9	9.7	7.8	48.6	9 008	9 131	1.4	-2.0	254	407	-32	3 835	5.7	2.30	7.9	29.6
Preston	11.1	7.9	7.0	50.4	29 037	29 334	1.0	1.3	905	1 013	488	11 544	8.7	2.50	9.1	23.7
Putnam	10.7	6.7	5.1	50.5	42 835	51 589	20.4	2.8	2 027	1 361	802	20 028	27.6	2.56	8.9	20.6
Raleigh	10.6	7.9	7.4	50.8	76 819	79 220	3.1	0.0	2 828	3 068	303	31 793	7.8	2.38	11.9	27.1
Randolph	11.7	7.6	7.5	49.4	27 803	28 262	1.7	0.0	984	1 123	151	11 072	6.8	2.41	9.8	26.3
Ritchie	12.0	8.0	7.2	50.4	10 233	10 343	1.1	1.7	375	383	193	4 184	6.5	2.45	9.7	25.0
Roane	12.0	8.4	6.6	50.3	15 120	15 446	2.2	-0.5	509	625	47	6 161	7.3	2.49	9.3	23.5
Summers	11.2	9.8	8.7	55.9	14 204	12 999	-8.5	7.1	343	565	-236	5 530	5.5	2.32	10.0	29.1
Taylor	10.8	8.0	7.6	50.7	15 144	16 089	6.2	0.2	489	670	242	6 320	10.1	2.47	10.9	25.5
Tucker	13.7	9.7	8.9	51.3	7 728	7 321	-5.3	-2.2	205	234	-119	3 052	1.2	2.35	7.8	27.2
Tyler	12.5	9.0	7.5	51.3	9 796	9 592	-2.1	-1.6	323	352	-112	3 836	3.4	2.47	8.6	23.1
Upshur	10.9	7.6	7.0	51.4	22 867	23 404	2.3	1.1	899	869	263	8 972	8.8	2.45	9.1	25.2
Wayne	11.6	8.6	6.5	51.0	41 636	42 903	3.0	-1.1	1 606	1 474	-564	17 239	10.3	2.48	10.8	24.1
Webster	11.8	8.1	7.3	50.8	10 729	9 719	-9.4	0.7	300	375	155	4 010	0.4	2.41	10.6	26.5
Wetzel	12.8	9.2	7.7	51.6	19 258	17 693	-8.1	-3.0	593	674	-453	7 164	-1.9	2.45	9.3	25.7
Wirt	11.6	8.0	5.7	49.6	5 192	5 873	13.1	-1.4	152	156	-72	2 284	17.6	2.56	8.9	22.2
Wood	11.6	8.1	7.5	51.7	86 915	87 986	1.2	-0.7	3 298	3 270	-596	36 275	6.2	2.39	10.8	27.1
Wyoming	11.5	8.2	5.9	50.8	28 990	25 708	-11.3	-3.4	899	910	-853	10 454	-0.2	2.45	10.5	24.4
WISCONSIN	9.6	6.4	6.6	50.5	4 891 954	5 363 675	9.6	2.0	220 988	153 446	44 586	2 084 544	14.4	2.50	9.6	26.8
Adams	12.9	11.8	7.9	46.4	15 682	18 643	18.9	10.3	551	815	900	7 900	32.3	2.33	6.7	25.5
Ashland	9.3	7.0	8.6	50.5	16 307	16 866	3.4	-1.3	630	671	-159	6 718	7.4	2.39	10.9	30.8
Barron	10.3	7.9	8.5	50.4	40 750	44 963	10.3	1.2	1 518	1 557	637	17 851	15.7	2.48	8.2	25.4
Bayfield	12.6	9.0	7.5	49.5	14 008	15 013	7.2	0.7	439	534	211	6 207	12.5	2.40	7.8	26.4
Brown	8.2	5.3	5.3	50.2	194 594	226 778	16.5	3.1	10 322	5 316	2 501	87 295	20.8	2.51	8.9	26.5
Buffalo	10.4	8.6	8.1	49.8	13 584	13 804	1.6	0.1	462	434	-1	5 511	7.6	2.47	6.2	27.1
Burnett	13.0	11.5	8.6	50.1	13 084	15 674	19.8	3.6	497	636	699	6 613	26.2	2.33	7.5	26.9
Calumet	8.2	5.4	5.0	50.1	34 291	40 631	18.5	6.8	1 836	801	1 699	14 910	26.7	2.70	6.5	20.4
Chippewa	9.4	7.1	7.2	50.3	52 360	55 195	5.4	2.9	2 126	1 733	1 203	21 356	11.9	2.53	8.0	24.7
Clark	8.5	7.3	8.5	50.0	31 647	33 557	6.0	1.2	1 619	1 001	-174	12 047	7.5	2.73	6.5	23.8
Columbia	9.7	6.9	7.2	49.5	45 088	52 468	16.4	3.1	2 035	1 789	1 371	20 439	21.2	2.49	7.4	25.5
Crawford	10.9	8.0	8.3	49.5	15 940	17 243	8.2	-1.7	612	577	-326	6 677	12.9	2.48	8.4	26.7
Dane	8.0	4.6	4.6	50.4	367 085	426 526	16.2	5.4	17 717	8 651	14 039	173 484	21.5	2.37	7.9	29.4

1. No spouse present.

STATE County	Births, average 1999–2001 Total	Rate[1]	Deaths, average 1999–2001 Number Total	Number Infant[2]	Rate Total[1]	Rate Infant[3]	Physicians,[4] 2000 Number	Rate[5]	Hospitals,[4] 1998 Number	Beds Number	Beds Rate[5]	Medicare enrollees, 2003	Serious crimes known to police,[6] 2002 Total Number	Rate[7]
	32	33	34	35	36	37	38	39	40	41	42	43	44	45
WEST VIRGINIA—Cont'd														
Brooke	237	9.3	325	2	12.8	D	38	149	0	0	0	4 377	245	966
Cabell	1 175	12.2	1 180	9	12.2	7.9	384	397	2	738	783	20 289	4 631	4 802
Calhoun	79	10.5	99	0	13.1	D	5	66	0	0	0	1 570	75	993
Clay	131	12.7	122	1	11.8	D	6	58	0	0	0	1 993	98	1 010
Doddridge	76	10.3	85	0	11.5	D	1	14	0	0	0	965	NA	NA
Fayette	566	11.9	636	4	13.4	D	66	139	2	181	378	10 299	732	1 837
Gilmer	65	9.1	86	0	12.1	D	1	14	0	0	0	1 367	104	1 458
Grant	135	11.9	131	2	11.6	D	10	89	1	65	586	2 162	89	812
Greenbrier	375	10.9	448	2	13.0	D	86	250	1	132	373	7 799	377	1 098
Hampshire	233	11.5	192	2	9.5	D	12	59	1	47	247	3 495	330	1 639
Hancock	350	10.7	412	3	12.6	D	25	77	1	269	792	7 558	NA	NA
Hardy	144	11.4	141	0	11.1	D	6	47	0	0	0	2 234	165	1 307
Harrison	802	11.7	895	4	13.0	D	147	214	1	309	436	13 969	1 045	1 543
Jackson	335	12.0	312	4	11.1	D	17	61	1	72	257	5 550	406	1 455
Jefferson	562	13.3	372	3	8.8	D	38	90	1	56	135	5 977	498	1 348
Kanawha	2 410	12.1	2 524	15	12.6	6.1	641	320	5	1 278	633	40 285	8 279	4 428
Lewis	193	11.4	213	2	12.6	D	21	124	1	77	442	3 829	119	706
Lincoln	262	11.9	260	6	11.7	D	8	36	0	0	0	4 184	307	1 394
Logan	470	12.5	495	6	13.1	D	80	212	3	209	509	8 461	1 123	2 989
McDowell	316	11.6	413	4	15.1	D	24	88	1	124	414	6 918	404	1 627
Marion	595	10.5	735	5	13.0	D	105	186	1	217	385	11 837	924	1 723
Marshall	361	10.2	385	2	10.8	D	41	115	1	143	403	5 966	583	1 761
Mason	297	11.4	302	1	11.6	D	29	112	1	201	777	5 015	379	1 473
Mercer	752	12.0	832	4	13.2	D	163	259	3	555	870	14 269	2 351	3 746
Mineral	307	11.3	299	2	11.0	D	22	81	1	63	236	4 882	487	1 857
Mingo	381	13.5	322	3	11.4	D	36	127	1	76	238	6 378	380	1 373
Monongalia	849	10.4	649	4	7.9	D	472	577	2	562	725	9 709	2 486	3 048
Monroe	136	9.4	151	1	10.4	D	6	41	0	0	0	3 122	157	1 080
Morgan	155	10.4	157	1	10.5	D	13	87	1	44	323	2 857	251	1 831
Nicholas	269	10.1	300	2	11.3	D	36	136	2	170	616	5 486	746	2 819
Ohio	503	10.6	638	5	13.5	D	238	502	2	664	1 375	10 338	NA	NA
Pendleton	81	10.0	83	0	10.2	D	5	61	0	0	0	1 675	54	661
Pleasants	90	11.9	92	0	12.2	D	2	27	0	0	0	1 363	51	681
Pocahontas	85	9.3	113	1	12.4	D	12	131	1	40	432	1 901	204	2 242
Preston	283	9.7	340	3	11.6	D	29	99	1	58	195	5 317	257	916
Putnam	612	11.9	434	5	8.4	D	50	97	1	68	133	7 240	1 176	2 334
Raleigh	874	11.1	927	6	11.7	D	193	244	3	486	615	15 873	1 450	1 870
Randolph	324	11.4	344	3	12.1	D	55	195	1	131	457	5 617	699	2 482
Ritchie	102	9.9	136	1	13.1	D	7	68	0	0	0	1 984	NA	NA
Roane	167	10.8	182	1	11.8	D	19	123	1	73	476	2 910	292	1 897
Summers	111	8.5	184	2	14.2	D	9	69	1	95	723	2 829	145	1 120
Taylor	157	9.8	196	2	12.2	D	10	62	1	131	855	2 683	86	536
Tucker	69	9.4	85	0	11.6	D	3	41	0	0	0	1 508	83	1 422
Tyler	102	10.7	114	1	11.9	D	5	52	1	18	183	1 642	93	973
Upshur	265	11.3	273	2	11.7	D	28	120	1	95	404	4 180	278	1 192
Wayne	506	11.8	451	3	10.5	D	40	93	0	0	0	6 454	1 072	2 556
Webster	95	9.8	115	0	11.9	D	8	82	1	35	342	2 185	NA	NA
Wetzel	190	10.8	219	1	12.4	D	18	102	1	58	318	3 964	143	827
Wirt	54	9.1	45	0	7.7	D	1	17	0	0	0	1 061	NA	NA
Wood	1 005	11.4	1 022	7	11.6	7.0	176	200	2	508	585	16 429	2 338	2 667
Wyoming	282	11.0	289	3	11.3	D	7	27	0	0	0	5 598	256	999
WISCONSIN	68 869	12.8	46 587	469	8.7	6.8	10 763	201	126	17 111	328	803 678	176 987	3 253
Adams	172	9.0	231	1	12.1	D	9	48	1	58	314	3 000	50	264
Ashland	203	12.1	199	2	11.8	D	47	279	1	101	613	3 280	513	2 998
Barron	482	10.7	468	1	10.4	D	59	131	3	252	574	8 393	1 226	2 825
Bayfield	143	9.5	158	0	10.5	D	16	107	0	0	0	2 670	241	1 582
Brown	3 181	14.0	1 589	22	7.0	6.9	392	173	3	632	293	28 295	6 647	2 889
Buffalo	157	11.4	139	2	10.1	D	3	22	0	0	0	2 643	143	1 021
Burnett	145	9.3	188	1	12.0	D	6	38	1	84	574	3 366	425	2 673
Calumet	538	13.2	254	2	6.2	D	22	54	1	47	122	3 822	685	1 662
Chippewa	678	12.3	537	3	9.7	D	60	109	3	358	656	9 270	1 144	2 043
Clark	503	15.0	303	2	9.0	D	22	66	1	199	600	6 028	380	1 116
Columbia	630	12.0	537	7	10.2	10.6	65	124	2	213	416	9 696	1 494	2 807
Crawford	194	11.3	185	1	10.8	D	16	93	1	62	374	3 020	209	1 195
Dane	5 425	12.7	2 589	33	6.0	6.1	1 625	381	4	1 246	293	47 695	13 845	3 836

1. Per 1,000 estimated resident population. 2. Deaths of infants under 1 year old. 3. Deaths of infants under 1 year old per 1,000 live births. 4. Data subject to copyright. 5. Per 100,000 resident population as of July 1 of the year shown. 6. Data for serious crimes have not been adjusted for underreporting; this may affect comparability between geographic areas and over time. 7. Per 100,000 population estimated by the FBI.

	Serious crimes known to police,[1] 2002 (cont'd)		Education						Money income, 1999				Percent below poverty level, 1999			
	Rate[2]		School enrollment and attainment, 2000				Local government expenditures,[5] 2000–2001			Households						
			Enrollment[3]		Attainment[4] (percent)					Median income						
STATE County	Violent	Property	Total	Percent private	High school graduate or less	Bachelor's degree or more	Total current expenditures (mil dol)	Current expenditures per student (dollars)	Per capita income[6] (dollars)	Dollars	Percent change, 1989–1999 (constant 1999 dollars)	Percent with income of $100,000 or more	Persons	Households	Families	Families with children
	46	47	48	49	50	51	52	53	54	55	56	57	58	59	60	61
WEST VIRGINIA—Cont'd																
Brooke	103	864	5 883	18.4	63.9	13.4	28.6	7 632	17 131	32 981	-7.4	4.8	11.7	11.5	9.5	15.2
Cabell	303	4 499	25 315	8.6	54.0	20.9	95.5	7 593	17 638	28 479	-0.3	5.6	19.2	20.0	13.7	22.1
Calhoun	53	940	1 642	7.6	77.4	9.3	10.3	7 841	11 491	21 578	10.8	1.5	25.1	27.1	19.1	28.2
Clay	93	917	2 430	3.3	80.8	7.3	16.2	7 656	12 021	22 120	28.1	2.3	27.5	28.2	24.4	33.3
Doddridge	NA	NA	1 737	5.5	71.9	10.2	9.8	7 825	13 507	26 744	16.0	2.4	19.8	20.6	15.3	22.8
Fayette	146	1 691	10 243	7.9	71.2	10.7	55.7	7 660	13 809	24 788	10.0	3.0	21.7	21.7	18.2	27.7
Gilmer	182	1 275	2 212	1.5	66.9	17.1	8.9	7 859	12 498	22 857	17.0	2.9	25.9	26.1	20.2	27.3
Grant	64	748	2 273	5.7	72.3	11.4	14.0	7 089	15 696	28 916	2.9	2.9	16.3	16.8	12.6	17.5
Greenbrier	90	1 008	7 168	8.3	67.8	13.6	40.3	7 128	16 247	26 927	3.2	4.6	18.2	19.6	14.5	22.4
Hampshire	288	1 351	4 501	6.3	72.9	11.3	23.9	6 921	14 851	31 666	13.6	2.7	16.3	16.1	12.9	19.6
Hancock	NA	NA	6 671	13.6	64.7	11.5	32.9	7 325	17 724	33 759	-3.5	4.6	11.1	12.1	9.0	15.6
Hardy	254	1 054	2 840	4.2	74.3	9.4	13.6	6 065	15 859	31 846	14.3	4.0	13.1	15.1	10.5	13.8
Harrison	210	1 333	15 737	10.1	62.0	16.3	83.3	7 249	16 810	30 562	11.7	5.0	17.2	16.5	13.6	21.6
Jackson	97	1 358	6 340	5.0	62.3	12.4	36.3	7 173	16 205	32 434	11.5	4.3	15.2	15.3	12.2	20.2
Jefferson	143	1 204	10 289	11.2	55.6	21.6	50.4	7 328	20 441	44 374	6.7	10.1	10.3	10.7	7.2	10.9
Kanawha	470	3 958	42 554	11.9	56.2	20.6	223.1	7 629	20 354	33 766	4.7	7.7	14.4	14.3	11.2	18.2
Lewis	125	581	3 644	9.2	70.4	11.2	19.7	7 121	13 933	27 066	12.1	2.7	19.9	20.1	16.3	24.8
Lincoln	182	1 212	4 652	2.7	79.5	5.9	30.9	7 935	13 073	22 662	15.1	2.6	27.9	28.2	22.8	33.3
Logan	381	2 608	7 911	5.1	71.7	8.8	45.5	7 189	14 102	24 603	2.1	3.7	24.1	23.5	20.8	29.5
McDowell	181	1 446	5 746	3.3	83.1	5.6	41.1	8 522	10 174	16 931	-4.1	1.6	37.7	35.9	33.8	47.5
Marion	177	1 546	13 612	6.7	60.1	16.0	66.5	7 753	16 246	28 626	4.5	4.5	16.3	16.5	11.7	19.5
Marshall	76	1 686	7 980	9.2	66.8	10.7	44.8	8 050	16 472	30 989	1.7	4.5	16.6	15.5	12.4	20.4
Mason	124	1 348	5 443	3.8	73.8	8.8	32.0	7 405	14 804	27 134	0.3	3.7	19.9	20.5	16.6	23.7
Mercer	411	3 335	13 744	5.9	64.5	13.8	71.1	7 468	15 566	26 628	2.3	3.8	19.7	19.2	14.7	24.4
Mineral	229	1 628	6 308	5.5	66.1	11.7	33.4	7 247	15 384	31 149	5.2	3.3	14.7	15.1	11.5	19.3
Mingo	206	1 167	6 305	3.9	76.1	7.3	43.2	8 322	12 445	21 347	-1.1	2.8	29.7	29.8	25.9	36.5
Monongalia	275	2 773	30 286	6.3	46.9	32.4	75.8	7 394	17 106	28 625	-4.0	7.1	22.8	24.1	11.3	16.9
Monroe	138	943	2 971	4.0	73.1	8.2	14.8	7 038	17 435	27 575	12.7	4.0	16.2	16.8	12.6	19.7
Morgan	146	1 685	2 831	7.2	70.2	11.2	16.4	6 585	18 109	35 016	6.9	4.8	10.4	10.9	8.0	11.0
Nicholas	310	2 509	5 967	4.9	73.6	9.8	34.8	7 643	15 207	26 974	10.8	3.9	19.2	19.9	15.0	22.2
Ohio	NA	NA	12 425	25.1	53.1	23.1	45.9	7 790	17 734	30 836	2.1	5.9	15.8	16.6	11.5	19.1
Pendleton	61	600	1 718	7.6	70.6	10.8	9.3	7 226	15 805	30 429	15.8	3.6	11.4	13.2	8.0	9.8
Pleasants	40	641	1 690	5.6	69.6	9.7	14.6	10 202	16 920	32 736	16.5	5.2	13.7	13.2	10.9	17.3
Pocahontas	330	1 912	1 801	8.7	71.7	11.8	10.5	7 441	14 384	26 401	14.0	3.3	17.1	18.4	12.7	19.0
Preston	139	777	6 362	4.3	73.1	10.8	32.5	6 695	13 596	27 927	4.2	2.9	18.3	18.1	14.7	21.0
Putnam	151	2 183	12 580	11.7	55.0	19.7	62.4	7 131	20 471	41 892	13.8	10.1	9.3	9.9	7.1	10.5
Raleigh	177	1 693	17 797	13.4	64.3	12.7	92.1	7 679	16 233	28 181	7.2	5.0	18.5	17.7	14.6	23.8
Randolph	241	2 241	6 028	13.1	69.4	13.6	32.0	6 719	14 918	27 299	11.2	3.2	18.0	18.0	13.4	20.7
Ritchie	NA	NA	2 222	4.5	70.3	7.1	13.6	7 749	15 175	27 332	17.4	2.6	19.1	20.0	14.3	22.0
Roane	247	1 650	3 248	3.1	74.9	9.0	18.9	6 785	13 195	24 511	18.7	3.7	22.6	22.3	17.8	27.5
Summers	201	919	2 513	8.6	74.9	10.1	11.8	7 187	12 419	21 147	-4.4	2.4	24.4	24.2	20.3	32.2
Taylor	50	487	3 632	7.3	69.4	11.3	18.2	7 295	13 681	27 124	12.4	3.0	20.3	20.4	15.3	23.9
Tucker	308	1 114	1 449	6.7	73.0	10.6	8.7	7 007	16 349	26 250	8.9	4.0	18.1	17.6	14.9	22.9
Tyler	157	816	2 073	4.3	69.4	8.5	12.1	7 810	15 216	29 290	7.1	4.0	16.6	16.4	12.2	19.6
Upshur	64	1 128	6 164	26.3	68.8	13.8	28.6	7 266	13 559	26 973	7.1	3.1	20.0	20.9	16.0	25.5
Wayne	320	2 237	9 488	4.8	67.9	11.9	54.2	7 258	14 906	27 352	3.4	3.7	19.6	20.0	16.2	22.4
Webster	NA	NA	2 084	2.8	78.2	8.7	12.9	7 377	12 284	21 055	17.2	1.9	31.8	30.6	26.6	40.5
Wetzel	81	746	3 967	2.8	69.9	10.4	25.3	7 210	16 818	30 935	6.9	4.4	19.8	18.8	15.3	23.5
Wirt	NA	NA	1 473	2.4	72.6	9.9	7.9	6 793	14 000	30 748	35.0	2.8	19.6	17.8	17.0	22.0
Wood	172	2 495	19 616	10.2	56.9	15.2	103.7	7 404	18 073	33 285	-1.5	6.3	13.9	13.6	10.6	18.2
Wyoming	109	890	5 232	3.3	77.5	7.1	36.3	8 340	14 220	23 932	3.3	3.5	25.1	24.0	20.2	31.1
WISCONSIN	225	3 028	1 463 038	17.3	49.5	22.4	7 175.2	8 194	21 271	43 791	10.7	9.4	8.7	8.4	5.6	8.8
Adams	63	201	3 616	6.3	65.2	10.0	17.6	8 582	17 777	33 408	15.4	4.1	10.4	10.4	6.7	12.2
Ashland	88	2 911	4 768	21.7	56.4	16.5	28.3	9 142	16 069	31 628	23.8	3.0	11.9	14.3	7.8	12.5
Barron	212	2 613	10 864	8.4	57.1	14.9	65.2	7 747	18 091	37 275	22.9	5.6	8.8	9.4	6.0	9.5
Bayfield	118	1 464	3 665	10.1	47.2	21.6	19.4	9 070	16 407	33 390	20.3	4.2	12.5	13.3	9.2	14.1
Brown	200	2 690	61 176	20.3	48.6	22.5	299.4	7 811	21 784	46 447	10.4	9.7	6.9	7.0	4.6	7.1
Buffalo	57	964	3 261	9.5	59.7	14.0	19.7	7 678	18 123	37 200	17.5	4.7	7.5	8.7	5.3	6.2
Burnett	82	2 591	3 169	8.3	59.9	14.0	18.2	8 066	17 712	34 218	26.4	4.7	8.8	9.3	5.7	10.1
Calumet	73	1 589	11 173	17.7	53.2	20.8	30.0	6 968	21 919	52 569	14.9	9.8	3.5	3.8	2.6	3.7
Chippewa	73	1 970	14 029	16.5	56.7	14.7	70.3	7 828	18 243	39 596	14.0	5.5	8.2	8.4	5.9	9.1
Clark	62	1 055	8 564	18.7	67.3	10.3	45.9	7 884	15 100	34 577	16.0	4.3	12.7	11.3	8.6	12.2
Columbia	79	2 728	12 494	11.1	53.5	16.7	72.0	7 567	21 014	45 064	18.3	7.5	5.2	5.9	3.3	4.6
Crawford	51	1 143	4 180	13.6	61.2	13.2	21.9	8 187	16 833	34 135	18.5	4.9	10.2	10.5	7.2	11.3
Dane	268	3 567	132 595	11.1	30.1	40.6	566.9	8 872	24 985	49 223	12.0	13.0	9.4	9.2	4.0	6.1

1. Data for serious crimes have not been adjusted for underreporting; this may affect comparability between geographic areas and over time. 2. Per 100,000 population estimated by the FBI. 3. All persons 3 years old and over enrolled in nursery school through college. 4. Persons 25 years old and over. 5. Elementary and secondary education expenditures. 6. Based on population enumerated as of April 1, 2000.

STATE County	Personal income, 2002												
			Per capita[1]					Transfer payments					
									Government payments to individuals				
	Total (mil dol)	Percent change, 2001–2002	Dollars	Rank	Wages and salaries[2] (mil dol)	Proprietor's income (mil dol)	Dividends, interest, and rent (mil dol)	Total (mil dol)	Total (mil dol)	Social Security (mil dol)	Medical payments (mil dol)	Income mainte-nance (mil dol)	Unemploy-ment insurance (mil dol)
	62	63	64	65	66	67	68	69	70	71	72	73	74
WEST VIRGINIA—Cont'd													
Brooke	592	2.2	23 614	1 531	313	45	107	138	132	62	48	8	2
Cabell	2 444	3.2	25 588	979	1 937	136	442	604	582	202	221	53	9
Calhoun	121	3.7	16 451	3 031	45	10	18	45	44	16	16	6	2
Clay	158	3.5	15 202	3 069	83	10	19	55	52	20	15	9	2
Doddridge	137	6.0	18 437	2 837	36	9	26	33	31	15	6	4	1
Fayette	953	3.9	20 218	2 499	422	53	116	333	322	113	129	34	7
Gilmer	133	1.3	18 942	2 767	59	8	26	45	43	14	16	4	1
Grant	259	-2.8	22 786	1 787	161	22	43	63	60	21	24	5	2
Greenbrier	803	4.1	23 249	1 643	430	73	147	222	214	76	91	18	6
Hampshire	419	4.8	20 000	2 548	124	32	65	92	87	38	29	9	1
Hancock	773	3.5	24 147	1 358	611	30	114	208	201	86	84	12	2
Hardy	263	2.0	20 514	2 425	197	11	40	52	49	23	12	6	1
Harrison	1 754	4.2	25 817	930	1 268	142	310	422	406	153	148	41	12
Jackson	599	2.2	21 213	2 235	335	39	89	151	144	62	50	15	5
Jefferson	1 255	3.7	27 957	555	444	63	190	170	159	64	48	12	1
Kanawha	6 233	2.8	31 821	231	4 740	639	1 019	1 303	1 257	468	512	98	26
Lewis	357	4.1	21 135	2 254	186	30	64	96	93	37	33	12	2
Lincoln	370	4.4	16 611	3 017	86	13	44	118	112	44	29	22	4
Logan	813	4.9	21 975	2 021	434	24	91	314	305	97	117	30	5
McDowell	430	1.9	16 480	3 025	187	12	60	213	207	74	63	44	4
Marion	1 367	3.1	24 258	1 325	752	95	215	339	326	135	109	27	7
Marshall	789	1.9	22 541	1 867	485	55	115	185	177	72	64	16	6
Mason	516	1.9	19 814	2 583	280	16	75	154	148	56	57	16	5
Mercer	1 473	3.9	23 718	1 495	803	89	246	470	456	149	185	47	6
Mineral	583	3.5	21 487	2 151	245	27	79	156	149	52	58	11	3
Mingo	562	1.6	20 284	2 483	361	27	79	210	203	73	67	33	5
Monongalia	2 171	4.3	26 022	884	1 729	167	372	390	371	115	164	24	4
Monroe	261	2.4	19 588	2 640	73	20	39	71	68	29	22	7	1
Morgan	406	4.7	26 508	787	102	35	57	83	79	32	30	5	2
Nicholas	546	3.3	20 726	2 362	287	33	77	162	156	62	57	16	4
Ohio	1 354	2.3	29 265	414	986	55	376	309	299	120	122	20	4
Pendleton	175	-2.9	21 929	2 033	66	14	34	40	39	16	16	3	1
Pleasants	174	4.3	22 892	1 754	124	12	24	49	48	15	24	3	1
Pocahontas	202	3.6	22 581	1 855	106	19	34	65	63	20	32	4	2
Preston	606	4.4	20 496	2 433	236	45	83	155	148	58	52	15	5
Putnam	1 387	2.3	26 501	788	783	64	174	223	211	92	61	15	7
Raleigh	1 904	3.3	24 050	1 387	1 167	135	258	521	502	185	184	47	12
Randolph	646	4.0	22 768	1 795	356	62	98	185	178	56	81	16	5
Ritchie	206	3.7	19 772	2 596	98	12	32	57	54	22	19	6	2
Roane	271	1.5	17 713	2 930	96	20	42	87	83	33	31	11	2
Summers	237	4.1	16 932	3 000	79	6	35	95	92	25	39	11	2
Taylor	301	4.6	18 704	2 798	111	11	37	83	79	27	28	8	2
Tucker	154	3.6	21 238	2 229	78	10	25	46	44	17	19	3	1
Tyler	181	3.1	19 207	2 713	100	9	36	46	44	22	14	4	1
Upshur	457	4.6	19 516	2 656	274	33	71	122	117	45	36	15	5
Wayne	794	3.0	18 718	2 794	375	24	99	201	191	83	39	31	6
Webster	158	3.9	16 204	3 044	77	9	20	61	59	22	18	10	1
Wetzel	392	4.3	22 741	1 807	147	17	62	111	107	43	42	10	3
Wirt	101	2.8	17 379	2 960	21	6	14	27	26	11	7	4	1
Wood	2 200	2.8	25 105	1 101	1 602	141	353	508	488	191	181	48	11
Wyoming	476	3.5	19 110	2 739	228	13	52	165	159	68	44	24	3
WISCONSIN	163 464	3.0	30 050	X	111 429	10 657	29 190	23 353	21 983	9 244	8 899	1 743	1 183
Adams	465	6.2	22 698	1 824	150	46	89	107	102	53	35	6	3
Ashland	390	3.3	23 228	1 650	284	32	69	93	89	32	41	6	4
Barron	1 110	-0.2	24 420	1 281	678	100	201	214	202	88	85	12	9
Bayfield	348	3.6	23 085	1 701	108	33	72	77	73	33	28	5	3
Brown	7 210	4.1	31 095	269	6 107	452	1 346	798	740	330	268	47	53
Buffalo	402	1.5	29 087	436	207	43	74	61	57	26	24	3	2
Burnett	377	4.8	23 482	1 576	143	39	78	85	81	40	30	4	2
Calumet	1 277	2.4	30 050	347	415	105	214	124	114	60	34	4	12
Chippewa	1 441	2.2	25 655	965	773	113	254	258	244	100	105	14	16
Clark	734	2.1	21 691	2 092	315	67	146	150	142	58	65	7	7
Columbia	1 631	3.6	30 528	303	704	131	275	222	208	97	83	9	11
Crawford	384	4.1	22 595	1 853	232	28	78	75	71	31	29	5	3
Dane	15 687	4.6	35 414	130	12 717	1 097	2 997	1 458	1 347	573	536	98	65

1. Based on the resident population estimated as of July 1 of the year shown.   2. Includes other labor income.

Table B. States and Counties — Earnings, Social Security, and Housing

STATE County	Earnings, 2002									Social Security beneficiaries, December 2003		Supplemental Security Income recipients, December 2003	Housing units, 2003	
			Percent by selected industries											
			Goods-related[1]		Service-related and health									
	Total (mil dol)	Farm	Total	Manu-facturing	Information and professional and technical services	Retail trade	Finance, insurance, and real estate	Health services	Govern-ment	Number	Rate[2]		Total	Percent change, 2000–2003
	75	76	77	78	79	80	81	82	83	84	85	86	87	88
WEST VIRGINIA—Cont'd														
Brooke	359	0.0	D	39.7	D	6.7	3.0	D	11.4	5 885	236	450	11 069	-0.7
Cabell	2 073	0.0	D	12.1	7.2	8.2	6.3	21.8	17.3	20 460	215	4 219	45 569	-0.1
Calhoun	55	-0.9	33.7	2.6	D	7.8	D	D	26.0	1 910	262	601	3 887	1.0
Clay	93	0.0	D	D	D	5.4	2.3	6.6	24.7	2 420	234	715	4 876	0.8
Doddridge	45	-2.1	D	D	D	9.3	D	9.1	38.7	1 195	160	262	3 661	0.0
Fayette	475	0.0	21.8	9.9	5.1	9.1	4.9	D	26.9	12 230	259	2 498	21 831	1.0
Gilmer	67	-1.6	37.0	9.4	D	5.2	D	6.2	38.1	1 630	232	378	3 644	0.6
Grant	183	0.4	36.1	12.4	1.4	5.3	3.6	7.2	21.3	2 515	220	495	6 266	2.6
Greenbrier	503	0.4	15.6	8.3	4.4	9.9	3.5	D	18.4	8 435	243	1 463	17 872	1.3
Hampshire	156	0.3	D	5.2	D	8.2	4.7	D	30.9	4 380	206	707	11 460	2.5
Hancock	641	0.0	D	50.4	2.8	4.0	2.2	D	9.1	7 910	249	695	14 699	-0.2
Hardy	208	1.6	D	53.2	D	7.2	3.6	D	12.3	2 735	211	439	7 352	3.3
Harrison	1 410	-0.2	17.9	7.0	8.4	8.5	3.5	12.5	30.3	16 035	236	2 859	31 128	0.1
Jackson	374	-0.9	D	36.4	3.7	10.2	3.2	D	15.3	6 565	232	1 062	12 421	1.4
Jefferson	507	0.7	D	11.4	6.7	10.4	4.2	7.8	27.0	6 850	148	657	19 197	8.9
Kanawha	5 379	0.0	19.0	9.8	13.0	7.0	6.9	14.9	18.9	45 530	233	6 984	94 237	0.5
Lewis	216	-0.1	27.1	8.8	4.0	8.4	3.2	D	27.2	4 215	246	968	7 947	0.0
Lincoln	100	0.5	23.8	1.0	4.7	8.2	2.2	10.0	38.3	5 065	228	1 860	10 024	1.8
Logan	458	0.0	30.7	5.8	D	10.7	3.2	D	18.7	9 955	271	2 426	17 048	1.4
McDowell	199	0.0	28.8	1.1	4.8	7.4	3.3	7.5	35.3	8 335	329	3 559	13 468	-0.8
Marion	847	-0.1	26.6	7.6	D	8.0	4.4	9.6	20.2	13 150	233	1 935	26 569	-0.3
Marshall	540	-0.2	D	34.6	D	4.6	2.6	D	15.1	7 225	207	805	15 708	-0.7
Mason	295	-0.1	D	12.4	2.0	5.5	2.3	12.1	21.0	5 960	229	1 160	12 228	1.4
Mercer	892	-0.1	D	7.4	6.8	10.4	4.3	19.2	23.7	16 055	258	3 586	30 077	-0.2
Mineral	271	0.2	D	26.4	D	9.4	2.6	D	22.3	5 445	201	648	12 534	3.6
Mingo	388	0.0	44.5	3.2	3.3	4.2	1.8	D	15.6	7 745	281	2 776	13 162	2.0
Monongalia	1 896	-0.1	16.2	8.6	7.1	5.8	3.5	16.4	37.0	11 495	136	1 597	37 059	1.0
Monroe	93	-0.6	24.3	16.0	D	5.6	4.1	5.2	40.7	3 310	245	630	7 338	1.0
Morgan	136	-0.3	D	21.6	3.5	10.0	3.9	D	22.8	3 380	218	300	8 508	5.3
Nicholas	320	-0.1	29.6	11.7	4.0	10.9	2.4	8.1	24.4	6 680	255	1 205	12 650	2.0
Ohio	1 040	0.0	11.3	5.8	10.2	6.7	6.4	23.4	15.7	11 590	253	1 435	21 780	-1.7
Pendleton	80	2.7	D	D	3.4	6.1	D	8.6	43.1	1 940	246	267	5 152	1.0
Pleasants	136	-0.1	D	31.8	D	3.6	D	D	17.9	1 610	214	234	3 210	-0.1
Pocahontas	125	-0.7	D	11.0	8.5	7.1	3.9	D	22.7	2 240	250	337	7 560	-0.4
Preston	281	0.1	34.7	15.2	4.0	8.7	2.9	D	23.2	6 365	214	1 157	13 538	0.7
Putnam	848	0.0	33.1	19.0	8.9	6.2	4.2	D	12.1	9 410	177	943	22 402	3.6
Raleigh	1 301	0.0	19.2	2.7	7.0	10.2	5.7	14.3	21.3	19 070	241	3 515	35 908	0.6
Randolph	419	0.1	D	13.8	D	10.8	5.5	D	21.6	6 450	228	1 403	13 573	0.7
Ritchie	110	-1.7	57.6	49.0	D	6.5	D	D	17.8	2 625	250	487	5 496	-0.3
Roane	116	-1.4	28.9	11.4	4.0	12.4	6.0	16.2	22.9	3 850	251	882	7 413	0.7
Summers	85	-2.4	8.3	1.4	D	9.1	D	D	30.9	3 000	216	863	7 294	-0.5
Taylor	122	1.3	D	22.3	2.0	10.4	D	6.3	35.9	3 225	200	604	7 118	-0.1
Tucker	88	-0.1	29.8	15.7	D	6.5	4.0	D	24.9	1 860	260	215	4 624	-0.2
Tyler	109	0.7	D	52.4	D	4.6	2.0	D	18.9	2 265	240	251	4 765	-0.3
Upshur	307	-0.7	35.3	15.3	4.5	10.4	2.6	D	17.2	5 000	211	1 020	10 936	1.7
Wayne	399	-0.1	23.9	9.7	D	6.2	1.4	D	38.7	9 275	219	2 250	19 255	0.8
Webster	87	0.1	D	8.5	2.5	4.5	D	6.7	29.8	2 570	263	803	5 316	0.8
Wetzel	164	-0.2	18.9	2.1	3.4	16.8	4.1	D	30.1	4 240	247	794	8 304	-0.1
Wirt	26	-0.3	D	D	D	8.8	3.1	10.8	41.0	1 195	206	294	3 288	0.7
Wood	1 743	0.0	28.5	21.3	4.9	10.1	5.7	14.7	18.0	19 265	221	3 090	40 127	0.9
Wyoming	241	0.0	41.5	2.2	1.7	7.6	1.9	D	20.7	7 085	285	1 794	11 713	0.1
WISCONSIN	122 086	0.7	29.6	23.1	7.6	7.0	7.9	10.8	14.5	928 505	170	88 750	2 417 364	4.1
Adams	196	6.6	17.3	11.3	D	6.1	3.5	D	28.0	5 490	267	331	14 954	5.9
Ashland	316	-0.2	22.9	15.1	3.3	7.9	3.5	D	23.6	3 580	215	405	8 988	1.2
Barron	778	3.3	D	29.6	3.3	9.8	3.4	9.1	19.8	9 750	214	858	21 937	4.6
Bayfield	141	0.4	13.2	3.7	D	8.5	5.0	D	33.0	3 630	240	224	11 896	2.2
Brown	6 558	0.5	28.3	21.0	6.7	6.9	8.5	11.9	11.2	33 030	141	3 156	95 846	6.3
Buffalo	250	4.1	9.2	4.2	2.9	4.2	3.8	6.0	14.8	2 970	215	203	6 316	3.6
Burnett	182	1.3	D	23.4	3.9	7.0	4.6	D	23.2	4 355	268	267	13 113	4.2
Calumet	520	2.7	D	39.0	D	5.7	6.9	5.8	10.1	6 015	139	179	17 368	10.2
Chippewa	886	1.5	41.4	33.5	3.4	8.9	2.9	9.9	16.1	10 840	191	905	24 377	6.8
Clark	382	5.3	D	26.7	2.7	7.9	3.3	5.9	18.7	6 565	193	519	13 745	1.6
Columbia	835	0.4	37.7	29.2	3.3	8.6	3.9	9.6	17.0	9 955	184	567	23 668	4.3
Crawford	260	0.9	D	23.6	D	17.6	4.0	11.5	14.7	3 535	209	322	8 695	2.5
Dane	13 814	0.3	17.7	10.8	11.8	6.5	11.4	8.6	25.1	55 005	122	5 643	193 049	7.0

1. Covers mining, construction, and manufacturing.   2. Per 1,000 resident population estimated as of July 1 of the year shown.

STATE County	Housing units, 2000								Civilian labor force, 2003				Civilian employment,[6] 2000		
	Occupied units										Unemployment		Percent		
			Owner-occupied			Renter-occupied									
				Median owner cost as a percent of income											
	Total	Percent	Median value[1]	With a mortgage	Without a mortgage[2]	Median rent[3]	Median rent as a percent of income	Substandard units[4] (percent)	Total	Percent change, 2002–2003	Total	Rate[5]	Total	Management, professional and related occupations	Production, transportation, and material moving occupations
	89	90	91	92	93	94	95	96	97	98	99	100	101	102	103
WEST VIRGINIA—Cont'd															
Brooke	10 396	76.6	67 000	19.2	9.9	379	23.0	1.7	10 844	-2.3	696	6.4	10 904	24.4	22.4
Cabell	41 180	64.6	76 200	19.4	9.9	420	28.6	1.2	41 642	-1.6	1 972	4.7	41 258	30.8	12.2
Calhoun	3 071	79.0	46 000	20.8	9.9	302	22.3	6.2	2 752	1.5	447	16.2	2 541	25.9	23.7
Clay	4 020	79.1	55 600	21.2	9.9	278	25.1	5.2	3 964	-4.1	396	10.0	3 199	19.1	19.9
Doddridge	2 845	81.3	57 000	18.4	9.9	350	24.0	5.1	3 334	-1.7	152	4.6	2 605	22.0	19.3
Fayette	18 945	77.2	50 800	19.4	10.4	357	25.9	3.1	16 603	-3.3	1 379	8.3	16 152	23.3	14.3
Gilmer	2 768	72.3	63 900	20.2	10.0	373	28.3	1.9	2 722	3.7	183	6.7	2 470	28.4	14.2
Grant	4 591	80.8	78 400	21.7	9.9	361	22.8	2.7	4 185	-1.3	483	11.5	5 016	21.4	30.2
Greenbrier	14 571	76.5	71 300	20.6	9.9	372	28.4	2.5	14 124	2.1	1 021	7.2	13 495	26.0	14.4
Hampshire	7 955	81.1	78 300	19.5	9.9	389	22.2	4.1	8 997	-1.6	496	5.5	8 586	21.4	26.4
Hancock	13 678	77.0	70 500	18.9	9.9	451	23.1	1.3	14 016	-1.9	858	6.1	14 477	21.4	23.1
Hardy	5 204	80.5	74 700	19.5	9.9	375	20.8	3.9	8 066	1.7	300	3.7	6 129	19.4	32.9
Harrison	27 867	74.8	67 600	19.9	10.2	398	25.0	1.6	33 838	-0.8	1 886	5.6	28 167	29.6	13.4
Jackson	11 061	79.5	78 500	18.5	9.9	390	24.2	2.7	11 924	-3.8	1 179	9.9	11 468	28.5	20.1
Jefferson	16 165	75.9	116 700	20.4	9.9	496	24.3	2.6	21 899	0.1	722	3.3	21 581	33.4	13.4
Kanawha	86 226	70.3	80 700	18.3	9.9	444	23.9	1.6	100 687	-3.4	4 877	4.8	88 982	33.6	11.5
Lewis	6 946	73.0	63 400	20.9	9.9	340	23.0	2.5	6 983	-1.6	577	8.3	6 737	24.6	17.3
Lincoln	8 664	79.0	60 000	19.7	9.9	322	28.6	4.4	6 795	-1.9	605	8.9	7 231	19.2	19.6
Logan	14 880	76.8	62 500	21.4	10.2	368	27.3	2.1	11 934	-4.1	970	8.1	12 283	23.9	15.4
McDowell	11 169	79.8	22 600	22.9	11.7	260	29.1	3.5	6 933	-2.6	907	13.1	6 054	22.4	19.1
Marion	23 652	74.7	63 600	19.0	9.9	401	28.4	1.6	23 184	-2.6	1 417	6.1	23 809	30.1	12.7
Marshall	14 207	77.5	62 600	17.6	9.9	347	23.7	1.5	15 934	-3.5	952	6.0	14 442	22.7	19.6
Mason	10 587	80.9	65 100	19.1	9.9	316	27.2	2.5	9 068	1.1	1 185	13.1	9 363	22.3	22.6
Mercer	26 509	76.9	63 900	19.1	9.9	372	26.9	1.9	27 057	-2.4	1 537	5.7	23 451	28.0	15.5
Mineral	10 784	77.8	73 500	19.8	9.9	378	23.0	1.8	11 772	-3.1	905	7.7	11 788	22.2	22.9
Mingo	11 303	77.8	61 100	21.5	11.1	329	30.5	2.9	7 416	-5.7	815	11.0	8 046	23.8	15.0
Monongalia	33 446	61.0	95 500	19.6	9.9	453	36.6	2.1	41 283	-0.6	1 303	3.2	37 534	39.1	9.6
Monroe	5 447	84.4	64 700	20.4	9.9	388	22.3	3.3	5 530	3.3	250	4.5	5 272	21.6	23.8
Morgan	6 145	83.3	89 200	21.5	9.9	447	21.8	2.9	6 577	0.7	253	3.8	6 659	21.4	24.4
Nicholas	10 722	82.9	60 100	20.5	9.9	360	26.7	3.2	10 447	-2.7	822	7.9	9 883	23.8	17.5
Ohio	19 733	68.6	71 400	18.9	9.9	374	24.2	1.4	23 479	-2.6	996	4.2	20 654	33.7	12.0
Pendleton	3 350	79.2	76 600	19.3	9.9	376	19.6	3.7	3 588	-1.8	162	4.5	3 523	24.8	23.9
Pleasants	2 887	80.5	75 300	18.4	9.9	335	24.6	3.3	3 071	5.0	282	9.2	2 982	21.6	20.9
Pocahontas	3 835	80.3	64 000	21.8	10.2	355	22.1	3.6	4 215	0.4	300	7.1	3 640	25.1	14.4
Preston	11 544	83.1	63 100	19.4	9.9	336	25.2	2.6	12 672	-0.6	897	7.1	12 042	21.6	21.1
Putnam	20 028	84.0	102 900	18.8	9.9	496	23.4	1.7	26 634	-3.3	1 248	4.7	23 885	32.8	13.8
Raleigh	31 793	76.5	69 800	20.3	9.9	385	25.1	2.7	33 628	-3.1	2 013	6.0	29 343	26.8	12.2
Randolph	11 072	75.8	71 800	20.8	9.9	370	24.5	2.2	13 286	-1.9	875	6.6	11 579	26.1	19.1
Ritchie	4 184	81.7	51 100	18.0	9.9	323	21.7	4.2	4 261	-1.9	407	9.6	4 009	17.5	30.1
Roane	6 161	79.6	56 600	19.1	9.9	338	24.8	4.4	5 287	-4.1	538	10.2	5 475	23.9	19.7
Summers	5 530	79.1	56 100	22.7	11.5	284	27.3	3.3	4 183	-3.7	309	7.4	4 214	23.3	19.5
Taylor	6 320	79.6	61 400	20.9	11.3	330	25.2	2.8	7 411	-0.6	406	5.5	6 277	25.1	18.5
Tucker	3 052	82.5	61 100	23.0	9.9	370	22.6	2.1	3 341	-5.9	257	7.7	3 003	25.8	16.5
Tyler	3 836	83.7	61 500	19.2	9.9	343	23.6	3.2	4 206	-2.3	297	7.1	3 482	21.9	22.5
Upshur	8 972	76.7	70 000	20.9	9.9	362	25.9	2.9	10 365	-3.9	734	7.1	9 254	27.9	17.6
Wayne	17 239	78.1	70 900	19.7	9.9	382	26.7	2.5	16 399	-2.1	968	5.9	16 184	25.0	19.6
Webster	4 010	79.1	47 500	24.1	10.8	285	29.1	6.0	2 954	-1.7	233	7.9	2 906	22.2	19.8
Wetzel	7 164	78.5	66 000	19.0	9.9	335	26.0	2.3	7 400	-3.4	599	8.1	6 280	22.8	20.8
Wirt	2 284	83.1	62 300	15.7	9.9	313	24.5	4.4	2 154	4.8	315	14.6	2 263	21.9	24.2
Wood	36 275	73.4	77 500	19.1	9.9	429	25.6	1.3	43 460	-2.7	2 749	6.3	38 324	28.8	18.4
Wyoming	10 454	83.3	47 400	21.0	9.9	318	26.3	2.7	7 586	-7.9	640	8.4	7 600	24.6	15.6
WISCONSIN	2 084 544	68.4	112 200	20.9	11.2	540	23.4	2.8	3 078 254	1.8	173 533	5.6	2 734 925	31.3	19.8
Adams	7 900	85.4	83 600	22.3	12.2	443	23.6	3.2	8 403	0.4	436	5.2	7 859	21.7	23.0
Ashland	6 718	70.6	60 400	20.2	11.3	372	23.9	3.7	8 429	0.0	711	8.4	7 810	26.2	19.6
Barron	17 851	75.9	74 000	19.4	10.5	417	24.1	2.6	24 878	2.5	1 642	6.6	22 583	26.4	23.0
Bayfield	6 207	82.6	86 100	20.4	12.9	369	24.3	4.4	7 641	0.7	539	7.1	6 749	31.5	12.7
Brown	87 295	65.4	116 100	20.6	11.1	520	21.9	3.0	146 265	3.2	7 311	5.0	120 530	30.6	18.7
Buffalo	5 511	76.5	78 600	19.9	10.2	399	20.0	2.1	7 659	0.0	386	5.0	7 207	29.9	22.1
Burnett	6 613	84.5	87 500	21.5	11.2	398	21.5	3.5	7 992	3.8	416	5.2	6 893	25.6	22.0
Calumet	14 910	80.4	109 300	19.9	10.5	491	19.6	1.9	27 381	0.6	1 256	4.6	22 242	29.1	25.7
Chippewa	21 356	75.6	88 100	19.4	9.9	446	22.4	2.4	32 094	2.4	2 059	6.4	27 582	26.8	22.6
Clark	12 047	81.3	64 700	19.4	11.9	366	21.2	4.5	16 451	4.3	1 184	7.2	15 869	28.1	26.0
Columbia	20 439	74.9	115 000	22.7	10.9	507	21.3	1.9	28 609	1.1	1 802	6.3	27 324	28.2	20.8
Crawford	6 677	76.9	75 100	19.8	10.0	394	20.8	3.1	10 193	0.0	606	5.9	8 250	23.5	25.5
Dane	173 484	57.6	146 900	22.2	10.5	641	25.8	3.1	287 128	2.7	8 179	2.8	246 064	43.6	10.1

1. Specified owner-occupied units.   2. Median monthly owner costs is often in the minimum category—9.9 percent or less, which is indicated as 9.9 percent.   3. Specified renter-occupied units.   4. Overcrowded or lacking complete plumbing facilities.   5. Percent of civilian labor force.   6. Persons 16 years old and over.

Table B. States and Counties — Nonfarm Employment and Agriculture

STATE County	Private nonfarm establishments, employment and payroll, 2001									Agriculture, 2002			
	Number of establishments	Employment						Annual payroll		Farms			
		Total	Health care and social assistance	Manufacturing	Retail trade	Finance and insurance	Professional, scientific, and technical services	Total (mil dol)	Average per employee (dollars)	Number	Percent with—		Farm operators whose principal occupation is farming (percent)
											Less than 50 acres	500 acres and over	
	104	105	106	107	108	109	110	111	112	113	114	115	116
WEST VIRGINIA—Cont'd													
Brooke	432	6 987	1 883	1 469	566	149	73	161	22 997	98	32.7	5.1	53.1
Cabell	2 796	44 603	10 096	5 454	6 649	2 252	2 214	1 152	25 818	438	31.5	1.6	52.7
Calhoun	134	1 046	228	217	93	D	19	21	19 982	244	14.3	7.4	47.5
Clay	127	1 243	278	D	188	44	D	38	30 849	117	7.7	3.4	63.2
Doddridge	75	590	154	88	135	D	7	9	14 580	455	20.0	7.0	50.8
Fayette	914	9 010	1 744	793	2 203	296	226	201	22 362	240	38.3	2.1	45.4
Gilmer	124	889	157	173	121	30	39	18	20 045	249	9.6	16.1	51.0
Grant	287	3 284	504	922	370	103	54	90	27 435	357	23.8	17.6	61.9
Greenbrier	989	9 949	2 332	1 219	1 987	261	208	232	23 315	783	25.0	11.0	49.0
Hampshire	346	2 694	664	226	448	146	55	52	19 428	635	29.6	9.9	49.9
Hancock	659	13 849	1 031	7 354	1 375	345	212	415	29 969	85	48.2	1.2	67.1
Hardy	267	5 114	403	3 116	607	126	35	110	21 427	468	29.7	13.7	64.1
Harrison	1 864	25 143	4 956	2 061	5 013	700	1 077	647	25 732	798	28.2	4.5	44.7
Jackson	528	7 362	890	2 435	1 308	252	138	208	28 286	842	20.7	3.8	49.8
Jefferson	806	10 424	919	1 765	1 844	368	650	232	22 227	474	58.6	7.2	50.8
Kanawha	5 835	96 705	15 936	6 008	13 635	6 623	5 338	2 820	29 156	210	44.3	0.0	38.6
Lewis	394	4 270	1 118	577	810	112	82	92	21 633	372	15.1	9.1	50.8
Lincoln	230	1 888	416	16	407	55	74	47	24 933	242	30.6	3.3	59.1
Logan	781	9 211	1 692	653	2 019	231	252	245	26 628	21	42.9	0.0	38.1
McDowell	388	3 693	1 020	D	755	146	82	98	26 582	7	28.6	0.0	85.7
Marion	1 297	16 434	2 701	1 414	2 356	485	1 002	417	25 349	464	32.8	1.9	51.5
Marshall	534	6 951	1 397	630	1 248	160	148	175	25 130	706	21.0	1.4	46.2
Mason	348	4 867	1 014	815	735	113	84	143	29 481	939	28.0	4.8	49.6
Mercer	1 429	20 445	4 711	2 037	3 831	671	616	488	23 866	393	28.5	3.8	49.4
Mineral	464	5 176	958	1 147	952	141	107	120	23 249	465	30.5	7.3	54.2
Mingo	592	6 465	821	243	780	164	184	184	28 399	35	88.6	5.7	40.0
Monongalia	1 963	31 760	9 082	2 241	4 680	655	1 229	832	26 194	478	28.2	2.7	47.7
Monroe	183	1 173	165	D	178	62	D	27	22 636	682	20.7	10.1	51.3
Morgan	261	2 349	484	239	395	113	70	55	23 538	178	27.5	3.9	47.2
Nicholas	612	6 951	1 384	1 048	1 352	135	226	152	21 891	332	28.9	3.9	46.1
Ohio	1 578	27 444	6 915	1 354	2 544	1 373	1 173	675	24 589	166	22.3	2.4	48.8
Pendleton	162	1 135	307	81	240	48	13	20	17 931	546	19.0	17.6	62.8
Pleasants	125	1 852	189	562	295	64	36	66	35 530	203	29.6	1.0	49.3
Pocahontas	253	3 339	350	437	292	55	D	57	16 990	376	17.6	18.4	55.6
Preston	612	5 224	1 033	982	889	187	131	113	21 702	917	22.9	4.5	53.9
Putnam	1 073	12 818	1 451	1 665	1 921	454	703	373	29 130	505	34.9	1.8	49.1
Raleigh	1 983	24 550	4 822	1 165	4 370	915	968	632	25 745	230	39.6	4.8	44.8
Randolph	758	9 197	1 757	1 712	1 471	239	216	192	20 859	446	28.3	11.9	49.1
Ritchie	216	2 490	159	1 387	253	69	27	58	23 385	363	16.8	7.2	50.7
Roane	294	2 568	542	393	605	148	69	52	20 406	538	15.6	6.1	49.4
Summers	205	1 522	450	D	289	50	51	27	17 631	313	18.8	7.0	48.9
Taylor	218	2 108	698	372	422	59	11	40	19 134	348	39.9	3.7	52.0
Tucker	209	2 475	306	301	267	63	12	42	16 999	198	25.8	8.6	49.0
Tyler	139	1 711	283	901	181	78	11	59	34 402	300	21.7	4.7	51.0
Upshur	541	6 922	1 148	1 028	1 132	126	128	141	20 319	480	33.3	4.6	45.0
Wayne	599	7 526	1 474	1 213	1 149	154	181	215	28 621	217	17.1	5.5	49.3
Webster	195	1 962	441	238	182	32	26	52	26 664	110	45.5	0.9	42.7
Wetzel	413	4 954	518	D	1 106	168	92	162	32 769	336	22.6	2.4	52.7
Wirt	75	394	D	D	D	19	D	6	14 132	223	21.1	6.3	47.5
Wood	2 277	37 037	5 842	7 589	6 573	1 489	1 005	986	26 635	696	29.5	1.4	47.6
Wyoming	406	4 135	890	115	720	94	76	113	27 315	35	40.0	2.9	31.4
WISCONSIN	140 540	2 400 575	317 889	543 531	315 694	132 936	92 118	74 307	30 954	77 131	27.6	8.2	59.4
Adams	273	2 303	384	474	318	60	51	55	23 879	414	25.8	11.8	59.2
Ashland	568	7 266	1 457	1 661	980	187	144	171	23 485	227	12.3	11.5	48.0
Barron	1 315	16 727	2 160	5 552	2 909	418	293	417	24 926	1 647	22.8	9.4	60.4
Bayfield	420	2 444	219	194	377	84	27	44	17 976	468	16.9	11.1	45.9
Brown	6 348	131 468	15 230	26 624	16 653	9 972	4 782	4 143	31 517	1 117	14.0	6.4	62.8
Buffalo	372	4 044	401	322	359	140	79	121	30 021	1 128	16.6	14.6	65.2
Burnett	445	3 415	626	983	479	56	66	76	22 340	451	16.9	9.8	47.0
Calumet	773	11 405	642	5 222	1 405	313	163	302	26 464	733	33.8	8.6	70.1
Chippewa	1 227	17 281	2 691	5 457	2 846	390	315	429	24 852	1 621	18.6	9.1	68.6
Clark	788	8 438	1 441	3 177	1 123	270	132	184	21 835	2 200	14.6	6.3	73.2
Columbia	1 465	17 471	1 918	5 043	2 673	482	315	449	25 689	1 526	20.9	11.3	60.9
Crawford	381	6 741	1 260	1 979	1 585	139	66	144	21 405	1 278	19.1	7.3	54.8
Dane	12 537	229 323	30 990	27 166	31 371	19 838	15 890	7 412	32 323	2 887	40.4	7.6	55.8

Table B. States and Counties — Agriculture

STATE County	Land in farms		Acres			Value of land and buildings (dollars)		Value of machinery and equipment average per farm (dollars)	Value of products sold		Percent from —		Percent of farms with sales of —		Government payments	
	Acreage (1,000)	Percent change, 1997–2002	Average size of farm	Total irrigated (1,000)	Total cropland (1,000)	Average per farm	Average per acre		Total (mil dol)	Average per farm (dollars)	Crops	Live-stock and poultry products	$10,000 or more	$100,000 or more	Total ($1,000)	Percent of farms
	117	118	119	120	121	122	123	124	125	126	127	128	129	130	131	132
WEST VIRGINIA—Cont'd																
Brooke	14	0.0	141	0	5	171 765	1 206	29 948	1	7 429	25.5	74.5	12.2	2.0	32	12.2
Cabell	42	31.3	97	0	11	123 022	1 320	17 583	3	6 782	79.0	21.1	10.3	0.5	25	3.0
Calhoun	50	31.6	206	D	13	146 666	728	18 327	1	4 989	10.8	89.2	11.9	0.0	4	3.3
Clay	19	11.8	160	0	5	173 375	1 104	17 886	0	3 094	14.1	85.9	7.7	0.0	9	6.0
Doddridge	95	33.8	208	0	24	191 329	830	14 817	1	3 241	24.8	75.2	7.9	0.2	6	1.5
Fayette	24	4.3	101	D	8	132 862	1 317	19 126	2	6 478	41.5	58.5	10.8	0.8	14	8.3
Gilmer	66	4.8	265	D	19	205 064	793	24 795	3	10 237	5.6	94.4	20.9	0.8	31	5.6
Grant	108	-11.5	302	0	27	467 426	1 638	40 608	39	109 948	1.0	99.0	34.2	17.4	97	7.3
Greenbrier	193	4.9	246	0	51	355 114	1 490	34 510	35	44 667	3.0	97.0	34.2	6.6	332	10.2
Hampshire	139	-0.7	218	0	46	477 761	1 624	40 094	20	30 932	14.6	85.4	26.0	4.9	229	15.0
Hancock	7	0.0	83	0	3	195 719	2 373	25 996	1	7 006	77.2	22.8	11.8	1.2	D	D
Hardy	128	-10.5	274	0	40	431 143	1 724	55 217	124	264 161	0.8	99.2	47.0	32.9	290	11.5
Harrison	120	16.5	150	0	43	178 829	1 248	20 646	5	6 419	19.2	80.8	11.2	1.3	78	3.6
Jackson	129	10.3	153	0	45	191 617	1 264	24 087	5	5 576	23.5	76.5	10.5	0.7	96	6.2
Jefferson	72	-1.4	152	0	47	456 068	2 963	45 349	17	36 584	41.0	59.0	25.7	8.0	787	19.4
Kanawha	20	5.3	95	0	6	142 053	1 411	15 772	1	3 101	33.5	66.5	5.7	0.5	12	7.1
Lewis	79	0.0	212	0	26	237 506	1 069	27 075	3	7 175	13.5	86.5	21.2	0.5	19	5.9
Lincoln	35	29.6	144	0	7	150 508	1 097	14 724	1	4 001	75.8	24.2	11.6	0.0	19	4.5
Logan	2	NA	112	D	0	180 437	1 916	D	0	13 664	D	D	9.5	4.8	1	28.6
McDowell	1	NA	122	0	0	109 816	901	41 664	0	6 553	D	D	14.3	0.0	D	D
Marion	50	28.2	108	0	19	139 664	1 462	17 741	2	3 633	40.9	59.1	5.8	0.2	17	3.7
Marshall	91	16.7	128	0	37	128 580	950	17 881	3	4 171	32.9	67.1	8.1	0.7	45	4.1
Mason	142	17.4	151	0	49	191 174	1 276	25 120	17	17 972	59.9	40.1	17.3	2.3	339	9.4
Mercer	56	5.7	142	0	18	166 375	1 414	22 921	3	7 022	24.9	75.1	12.7	1.0	5	4.1
Mineral	81	1.3	174	D	25	268 838	1 303	22 181	14	30 528	6.7	93.3	15.5	4.5	79	8.6
Mingo	2	NA	45	D	0	33 722	828	D	0	802	D	D	2.9	0.0	0	0.0
Monongalia	60	3.4	126	0	26	184 892	1 376	27 673	2	5 136	16.9	83.1	12.8	0.4	32	4.6
Monroe	145	4.3	213	0	41	280 329	1 358	33 102	17	25 273	5.9	94.1	31.8	6.7	347	14.7
Morgan	23	-17.9	129	D	9	301 332	2 324	21 924	1	7 150	53.6	46.4	9.6	1.1	105	18.0
Nicholas	44	10.0	132	0	17	181 715	1 446	24 258	2	7 480	11.2	88.8	16.6	0.9	78	11.7
Ohio	22	4.8	134	0	10	162 213	1 222	23 891	2	10 504	23.3	76.7	18.7	4.2	58	17.5
Pendleton	171	-2.3	313	0	41	384 131	1 168	38 518	74	135 553	1.1	98.9	44.7	18.1	158	15.9
Pleasants	23	9.5	113	D	6	126 170	1 057	17 953	1	2 742	45.6	54.2	4.4	0.5	D	D
Pocahontas	123	-4.7	327	0	30	391 465	1 119	32 141	5	12 556	7.6	92.3	30.1	1.6	122	21.5
Preston	142	-6.6	155	0	52	232 063	1 415	26 182	10	11 161	16.8	83.2	22.0	1.5	238	8.2
Putnam	57	0.0	112	0	18	191 724	1 764	16 529	6	12 634	81.7	18.3	8.9	0.6	57	8.9
Raleigh	33	-5.7	142	0	12	196 736	1 371	27 822	2	8 601	22.0	78.0	19.1	0.4	12	5.7
Randolph	101	-2.9	227	0	30	230 614	1 033	29 685	6	13 833	10.3	89.7	19.3	3.6	90	7.6
Ritchie	81	-6.9	223	D	29	212 421	906	23 790	3	7 377	19.0	81.0	12.9	0.6	21	3.6
Roane	99	6.5	184	0	32	166 897	846	21 039	3	5 928	14.0	86.0	12.6	0.4	46	5.0
Summers	55	-3.5	175	0	17	223 805	1 187	27 418	5	16 418	43.7	56.3	14.4	1.3	64	7.0
Taylor	43	-2.3	125	D	19	186 539	1 367	22 967	4	11 555	47.2	52.8	10.6	2.6	48	5.5
Tucker	35	0.0	178	D	10	181 343	989	23 561	1	5 971	15.1	84.9	16.7	0.0	24	7.1
Tyler	53	10.4	177	0	18	164 561	930	23 370	1	4 841	21.6	78.4	10.7	0.3	28	8.3
Upshur	69	7.8	145	0	22	166 260	1 048	23 398	3	5 794	18.2	81.8	14.4	0.2	72	5.2
Wayne	36	24.1	166	0	7	184 540	1 048	16 653	1	6 409	59.2	40.8	6.5	0.9	51	8.3
Webster	11	37.5	102	0	3	104 382	1 099	17 317	0	1 356	33.6	66.4	0.9	0.0	7	10.0
Wetzel	49	2.1	146	D	12	120 017	808	20 497	1	2 137	26.0	74.0	2.4	0.3	D	D
Wirt	40	8.1	181	0	12	211 179	1 164	28 074	4	18 037	55.5	44.5	18.8	2.2	12	4.0
Wood	77	14.9	111	0	30	124 391	1 260	16 101	3	4 885	31.3	68.7	9.3	0.9	25	2.9
Wyoming	4	0.0	104	D	1	126 109	1 194	15 060	0	4 710	79.4	20.6	2.9	2.9	D	D
WISCONSIN	15 742	5.7	204	386	10 729	464 127	2 272	72 300	5 623	72 906	30.1	69.9	46.0	18.1	247 942	48.3
Adams	124	1.6	298	44	91	639 933	2 130	109 518	53	127 309	85.5	14.5	38.6	14.3	1 446	46.6
Ashland	59	25.5	259	0	29	297 017	1 129	45 528	6	27 455	14.7	85.3	21.6	7.5	249	10.6
Barron	352	8.3	214	10	234	332 765	1 629	73 329	150	91 025	20.8	79.2	48.1	19.7	5 287	47.7
Bayfield	112	33.3	239	0	60	270 969	1 061	42 317	12	25 075	31.4	68.6	28.4	8.3	401	12.2
Brown	197	0.5	176	0	171	507 662	2 942	81 893	150	134 070	11.1	88.9	52.3	25.7	4 557	47.3
Buffalo	316	2.3	280	2	167	405 616	1 501	76 187	96	84 997	13.7	86.3	52.4	20.8	3 970	59.0
Burnett	98	18.1	218	0	52	449 694	1 848	59 223	16	34 626	28.2	71.8	32.6	8.9	689	41.5
Calumet	150	4.2	205	0	130	518 429	2 749	95 762	82	111 674	18.2	81.8	58.3	28.4	3 242	48.8
Chippewa	374	0.3	231	0	239	336 964	1 527	76 125	106	65 588	18.5	81.5	52.2	21.5	5 101	45.5
Clark	461	11.4	210	3	315	304 762	1 492	71 450	174	79 289	8.8	91.2	63.2	27.5	6 668	39.9
Columbia	348	6.7	228	2	265	576 455	2 525	80 777	105	68 881	44.3	55.7	49.0	19.4	5 896	53.1
Crawford	255	9.4	199	0	130	324 768	1 737	40 850	42	32 649	31.6	68.4	37.6	9.0	3 181	55.9
Dane	515	0.4	179	5	415	580 806	3 264	79 725	288	99 632	29.7	70.3	45.4	18.7	12 111	53.3

Table B. States and Counties — Residential Construction, Wholesale Trade, Retail Trade, and Real Estate

STATE County	Value of residential construction authorized by building permits, 2003		Wholesale trade, 1997				Retail trade,[1] 1997				Real estate and rental and leasing, 1997			
	New construction ($1,000)	Number of housing units	Number of establishments	Number of employees	Sales (mil dol)	Annual payroll (mil dol)	Number of establishments	Number of employees	Sales (mil dol)	Annual payroll (mil dol)	Number of establishments	Number of employees	Receipts (mil dol)	Annual payroll (mil dol)
	133	134	135	136	137	138	139	140	141	142	143	144	145	146
WEST VIRGINIA—Cont'd														
Brooke	2 583	23	10	D	D	D	86	684	91.3	8.7	9	27	2.5	0.4
Cabell	3 923	41	169	D	D	D	553	7 592	1 120.1	113.1	113	D	D	D
Calhoun	NA	NA	1	D	D	D	29	168	20.7	1.9	4	5	0.2	0.0
Clay	1 605	26	1	D	D	D	33	208	37.9	2.6	2	D	D	D
Doddridge	NA	NA	2	D	D	D	15	47	7.0	0.6	1	D	D	D
Fayette	8 405	148	29	402	84.6	11.4	206	2 103	328.6	31.3	25	53	6.3	0.6
Gilmer	0	0	5	16	5.7	0.3	25	164	23.4	2.3	2	D	D	D
Grant	14 051	128	8	D	D	D	54	349	53.0	4.9	7	31	2.0	0.5
Greenbrier	31 914	111	32	211	47.0	5.0	217	2 176	329.0	31.1	33	175	10.2	2.7
Hampshire	16 813	171	14	67	11.5	1.2	59	440	67.8	5.9	5	17	0.7	0.1
Hancock	8 636	100	21	133	42.6	3.5	135	1 682	206.0	20.2	27	85	6.5	1.4
Hardy	10 186	118	5	D	D	D	50	426	53.2	6.0	11	19	1.3	0.3
Harrison	17 540	129	91	1 434	452.2	43.2	391	4 956	766.7	70.2	53	154	15.0	2.3
Jackson	4 506	56	28	394	145.5	8.9	115	1 442	293.5	23.2	13	31	3.3	0.3
Jefferson	163 894	810	19	D	D	D	142	1 291	197.7	21.0	32	73	13.2	1.4
Kanawha	12 577	139	388	4 807	2 162.1	146.8	976	14 450	2 428.6	217.7	285	1 575	204.1	32.0
Lewis	43	4	15	125	26.8	2.9	89	946	143.6	12.7	12	29	3.6	1.0
Lincoln	2 480	33	5	D	D	D	51	358	52.3	4.7	5	12	0.6	0.3
Logan	400	9	46	398	158.7	11.4	204	1 996	335.7	31.0	23	87	7.4	1.7
McDowell	965	23	14	102	157.6	3.0	97	860	108.3	11.9	18	55	5.6	1.0
Marion	1 481	22	67	695	154.8	18.3	236	2 567	421.5	35.7	43	144	9.1	1.6
Marshall	987	9	21	D	D	D	114	1 523	204.3	18.3	14	D	D	D
Mason	1 968	14	6	75	47.9	1.9	80	557	79.5	7.2	15	45	4.8	0.7
Mercer	1 724	17	72	1 265	354.4	31.1	321	3 683	588.2	53.0	42	134	76.7	3.2
Mineral	14 878	110	18	D	D	D	103	982	142.7	12.6	12	34	2.6	0.3
Mingo	271	5	30	234	54.0	5.7	122	1 006	176.1	15.9	16	38	3.1	0.4
Monongalia	9 152	89	81	688	439.0	19.7	373	4 750	677.2	70.5	108	442	41.8	6.2
Monroe	65	1	10	56	14.1	0.9	37	192	27.7	2.1	3	3	0.2	0.0
Morgan	22 327	197	7	D	D	D	53	355	59.7	6.2	5	11	0.7	0.2
Nicholas	4 147	40	31	255	64.1	5.9	139	1 333	213.7	18.6	20	35	4.0	0.6
Ohio	2 978	23	110	D	D	D	247	2 706	387.0	43.2	59	D	D	D
Pendleton	3 770	43	5	24	2.9	0.3	33	210	29.4	2.8	2	D	D	D
Pleasants	531	7	3	D	D	D	28	248	41.8	3.5	5	18	1.3	0.2
Pocahontas	5 116	42	4	25	8.7	0.4	55	373	46.4	4.5	8	41	3.1	0.7
Preston	61	1	26	199	97.3	4.7	87	828	147.0	11.6	20	61	3.5	0.8
Putnam	30 644	255	60	1 255	423.2	43.4	201	2 119	365.0	30.1	27	83	9.2	1.0
Raleigh	22 049	211	131	1 146	378.1	32.8	390	4 889	826.8	75.9	92	335	37.0	6.4
Randolph	2 604	34	37	355	152.5	8.6	149	1 343	201.1	18.4	20	80	4.2	0.8
Ritchie	0	0	8	52	11.2	1.2	48	282	42.0	3.7	4	D	D	D
Roane	0	0	10	D	D	D	58	475	75.1	7.1	4	D	D	D
Summers	2 257	40	10	121	29.5	2.4	45	247	36.0	3.9	2	D	D	D
Taylor	392	6	5	D	D	D	47	318	55.7	4.5	4	14	0.4	0.1
Tucker	843	10	3	D	D	D	38	266	40.9	3.8	8	77	3.1	0.8
Tyler	80	2	2	D	D	D	32	191	25.6	2.1	1	D	D	D
Upshur	7 633	106	20	310	75.7	3.6	101	837	155.2	14.0	14	33	2.5	0.4
Wayne	2 680	56	31	D	D	D	111	1 127	168.5	15.4	21	D	D	D
Webster	0	0	7	D	D	D	32	212	31.2	2.8	2	D	D	D
Wetzel	273	6	14	69	32.7	1.4	112	1 070	145.5	14.1	17	36	5.2	0.8
Wirt	75	1	2	D	D	D	14	72	10.6	0.7	3	4	0.4	0.1
Wood	17 905	167	116	1 357	489.8	34.0	462	6 058	990.2	91.0	76	400	42.1	7.9
Wyoming	20	1	9	53	47.9	1.7	98	759	108.4	11.3	10	62	3.8	1.0
WISCONSIN	5 504 609	40 884	8 025	110 309	57 192.9	3 764.9	21 717	305 255	50 520.5	4 826.2	4 598	23 924	2 637.5	464.1
Adams	37 080	318	11	146	28.0	2.8	37	327	64.7	5.5	9	D	D	D
Ashland	9 055	72	18	130	40.5	3.3	113	1 041	149.7	13.4	11	36	2.1	0.4
Barron	51 146	492	66	763	153.8	17.6	254	2 812	451.6	41.9	30	84	8.6	1.3
Bayfield	12 950	154	7	36	5.6	0.8	66	328	51.0	4.2	8	25	1.7	0.3
Brown	306 736	2 541	461	6 480	2 848.1	212.1	950	14 976	2 569.1	239.7	197	1 048	116.3	18.7
Buffalo	11 393	122	17	180	47.6	4.2	46	305	45.7	3.8	6	17	0.7	0.1
Burnett	22 726	206	9	20	10.2	0.5	71	530	77.1	7.6	10	D	D	D
Calumet	65 783	463	45	474	98.6	12.1	106	1 615	232.7	20.1	18	56	3.2	0.3
Chippewa	59 478	552	49	654	237.4	21.7	205	2 475	481.3	39.9	26	87	5.2	0.8
Clark	14 469	141	51	278	71.3	6.6	137	1 071	198.0	16.1	13	27	1.9	0.4
Columbia	62 227	470	64	735	352.5	18.5	228	2 434	407.4	37.7	32	55	7.1	1.0
Crawford	4 097	44	19	118	220.9	3.9	88	915	133.6	12.3	16	D	D	D
Dane	750 901	5 402	675	10 048	4 350.1	342.7	1 845	30 150	4 860.9	507.2	520	3 519	371.4	71.1

1. Establishments with payroll.

Table B. States and Counties — Professional Services, Manufacturing, and Accommodation and Foodservices

STATE County	Professional, scientific, and technical services,[1] 1997				Manufacturing, 1997				Accommodation and foodservices, 1997			
	Number of establishments	Number of employees	Receipts (mil dol)	Annual payroll (mil dol)	Number of establishments	Number of employees	Receipts (mil dol)	Annual payroll (mil dol)	Number of establishments	Number of employees	Sales (mil dol)	Annual payroll (mil dol)
	147	148	149	150	151	152	153	154	155	156	157	158
WEST VIRGINIA—Cont'd												
Brooke	18	85	4.5	1.5	22	1 275	637.6	49.6	58	D	D	D
Cabell	179	1 206	76.3	27.7	112	5 766	1 199.5	199.9	253	4 933	140.9	39.3
Calhoun	5	16	0.6	0.2	NA	NA	NA	NA	5	12	3.9	0.7
Clay	3	D	D	D	NA	NA	NA	NA	7	12	0.5	0.1
Doddridge	3	3	0.1	0.0	NA	NA	NA	NA	4	D	D	D
Fayette	46	200	11.9	4.2	34	807	169.4	27.5	65	918	27.9	8.5
Gilmer	6	37	2.1	0.5	NA	NA	NA	NA	11	92	2.5	0.6
Grant	14	34	2.1	0.7	18	929	106.2	15.6	21	166	4.4	1.0
Greenbrier	48	123	8.1	2.4	38	923	99.7	26.2	78	2 098	118.4	41.8
Hampshire	15	48	2.0	0.7	NA	NA	NA	NA	32	311	11.2	3.3
Hancock	47	190	20.1	4.6	37	8 011	2 105.3	330.3	84	D	D	D
Hardy	10	24	1.8	0.3	20	2 940	435.6	57.7	21	341	7.5	2.0
Harrison	115	836	61.4	21.7	68	2 022	394.0	72.7	151	2 340	73.0	20.6
Jackson	25	90	5.8	2.3	16	D	D	D	36	637	20.1	5.2
Jefferson	53	283	16.1	8.4	26	2 172	444.1	60.1	82	1 114	37.6	10.2
Kanawha	525	4 387	384.5	125.5	141	6 590	3 071.3	273.3	420	8 287	280.7	75.9
Lewis	14	77	5.0	1.2	18	538	52.6	13.5	30	341	12.4	3.3
Lincoln	15	78	4.4	2.0	NA	NA	NA	NA	11	D	D	D
Logan	45	341	16.2	7.0	39	853	82.6	20.2	63	751	24.0	6.1
McDowell	22	128	6.4	2.0	NA	NA	NA	NA	17	176	5.6	1.4
Marion	80	581	48.0	17.8	62	1 501	347.0	42.0	96	1 295	36.9	10.5
Marshall	24	100	9.6	3.4	NA	NA	NA	NA	61	661	19.6	5.5
Mason	22	68	3.8	1.1	16	1 173	466.3	47.1	30	307	7.6	2.1
Mercer	81	543	37.7	11.0	56	1 908	298.5	61.8	100	2 010	64.3	17.1
Mineral	20	66	3.1	0.7	16	1 138	136.3	40.4	48	486	13.2	3.4
Mingo	56	248	12.0	4.0	NA	NA	NA	NA	42	346	10.8	3.1
Monongalia	143	902	70.8	23.0	58	2 055	598.0	77.8	207	3 795	95.5	28.4
Monroe	9	10	0.8	0.1	NA	NA	NA	NA	13	D	11.8	D
Morgan	10	20	1.5	0.4	NA	NA	NA	NA	20	375	11.8	4.2
Nicholas	45	197	9.9	3.4	27	768	123.1	18.2	45	590	18.6	5.3
Ohio	115	923	81.0	23.4	58	D	D	D	148	2 136	60.3	17.5
Pendleton	6	7	0.5	0.1	7	595	47.3	10.4	11	105	2.7	0.7
Pleasants	7	20	0.5	0.1	6	D	D	D	11	127	3.6	1.1
Pocahontas	4	7	0.5	0.1	NA	NA	NA	NA	29	1 011	40.3	11.0
Preston	33	112	5.5	1.9	28	664	69.0	14.1	30	244	6.7	1.7
Putnam	66	414	26.1	9.9	35	1 091	234.0	38.5	67	1 050	32.2	8.5
Raleigh	116	765	53.4	23.2	56	999	164.9	32.6	140	2 489	84.4	23.3
Randolph	47	185	9.2	3.7	29	1 397	169.4	27.3	62	876	23.6	6.6
Ritchie	10	32	1.7	0.3	21	1 035	116.6	27.2	10	97	2.2	0.5
Roane	16	76	3.7	1.3	18	790	170.4	12.9	14	133	4.5	1.3
Summers	8	53	3.2	0.5	NA	NA	NA	NA	18	202	7.4	2.2
Taylor	7	10	0.5	0.1	NA	NA	NA	NA	15	119	3.6	0.9
Tucker	7	17	0.9	0.3	NA	NA	NA	NA	28	326	11.8	3.5
Tyler	7	13	0.6	0.2	12	D	D	D	15	D	D	D
Upshur	32	119	6.9	2.5	26	947	152.5	22.5	42	552	13.7	4.2
Wayne	23	132	8.1	3.3	33	1 770	325.0	47.3	49	443	12.4	3.4
Webster	7	25	1.3	0.3	NA	NA	NA	NA	12	D	D	D
Wetzel	17	87	4.8	1.5	18	D	D	D	42	420	12.3	3.6
Wirt	4	D	D	D	NA	NA	NA	NA	4	13	0.6	0.1
Wood	134	885	59.0	20.6	78	7 010	2 301.9	293.3	198	3 767	110.7	32.1
Wyoming	23	83	4.6	1.6	NA	NA	NA	NA	29	267	8.2	1.8
WISCONSIN	9 281	70 689	6 398.9	2 542.3	9 936	562 479	117 383.0	18 766.4	13 252	190 411	5 641.0	1 548.5
Adams	16	38	1.7	0.7	NA	NA	NA	NA	42	416	14.6	4.0
Ashland	30	102	5.9	2.3	28	1 661	150.7	44.8	73	753	20.8	5.7
Barron	46	230	13.8	5.8	96	5 430	891.5	133.9	146	1 395	39.5	10.4
Bayfield	13	22	1.9	0.5	NA	NA	NA	NA	92	620	22.2	5.5
Brown	373	3 348	270.8	118.7	396	25 825	6 457.4	1 015.7	533	10 183	283.4	81.9
Buffalo	19	39	1.6	0.6	NA	NA	NA	NA	45	D	D	D
Burnett	15	48	2.4	0.9	32	1 106	176.7	30.3	66	D	D	D
Calumet	33	258	18.3	10.2	64	6 078	1 018.9	190.9	75	932	24.9	6.4
Chippewa	54	230	17.0	7.1	112	6 442	989.8	203.7	132	1 322	34.3	8.5
Clark	30	78	4.1	1.5	87	2 863	799.6	70.7	66	D	D	D
Columbia	70	247	20.2	6.0	108	5 311	1 262.4	159.1	190	1 717	62.3	15.1
Crawford	11	38	1.9	1.2	20	2 252	509.1	50.8	54	614	15.7	4.3
Dane	1 132	10 748	943.4	412.4	564	26 568	4 840.5	864.4	993	18 607	554.1	156.9

1. Firms subject to federal tax.

Table B. States and Counties — Health Care and Social Assistance, Other Services, and Federal Funds

STATE County	Health care and social assistance,[1] 1997				Other services,[1] 1997				Federal funds and grants, 2002–2003 Expenditures (mil dol)			
									Total	Direct payments for individuals[2]		
	Number of establishments	Number of employees	Receipts (mil dol)	Annual payroll (mil dol)	Number of establishments	Number of employees	Receipts (mil dol)	Annual payroll (mil dol)		Social Security and government retirement	Medicare	Food stamps and Supplemental Security Income
	159	160	161	162	163	164	165	166	167	168	169	170
WEST VIRGINIA—Cont'd												
Brooke	50	713	30.7	13.6	30	128	4.8	1.5	167.5	62.3	32.8	6.2
Cabell	238	3 609	273.0	129.9	166	1 249	58.1	20.3	727.8	304.2	112.7	34.5
Calhoun	4	18	1.0	0.3	8	32	1.0	0.3	58.9	19.5	9.7	5.1
Clay	4	75	3.5	1.0	7	45	3.5	1.4	68.9	26.7	11.1	5.7
Doddridge	2	D	D	D	3	D	D	D	35.1	14.7	5.4	2.0
Fayette	64	1 298	62.5	22.6	53	244	17.5	4.6	357.9	157.0	74.9	19.2
Gilmer	6	95	3.9	1.1	6	14	0.8	0.1	63.2	17.8	7.8	2.9
Grant	15	77	4.1	1.3	18	59	3.1	0.9	71.5	31.5	9.9	3.4
Greenbrier	82	1 659	106.4	44.2	65	178	8.5	2.1	240.9	112.6	43.8	10.3
Hampshire	19	327	13.6	5.1	20	49	3.0	0.7	100.4	51.9	17.1	4.7
Hancock	71	814	36.7	16.6	46	218	10.9	2.9	199.1	106.3	60.0	4.3
Hardy	12	104	4.4	1.7	16	40	2.4	0.5	186.5	30.9	9.4	2.3
Harrison	169	1 976	101.3	39.1	115	527	28.0	8.4	570.1	205.4	87.7	24.6
Jackson	35	411	17.7	5.8	34	83	4.5	1.3	152.9	74.5	26.4	7.8
Jefferson	46	297	13.5	5.8	42	187	8.3	2.5	267.7	114.9	28.6	4.9
Kanawha	555	6 286	513.0	210.2	340	2 361	129.6	39.8	2 069.3	691.1	260.7	56.5
Lewis	27	412	29.3	9.4	34	88	5.3	1.3	124.0	50.1	21.7	6.9
Lincoln	8	122	5.5	2.4	20	71	3.7	1.4	150.7	57.8	21.5	13.9
Logan	51	551	31.1	13.4	68	493	43.3	11.9	307.5	134.5	57.6	20.5
McDowell	24	213	10.4	3.9	21	70	5.2	1.4	285.8	103.8	48.0	27.4
Marion	101	1 028	73.3	30.7	105	564	32.2	9.3	473.6	177.0	71.0	16.5
Marshall	57	790	34.0	14.3	31	178	8.8	3.0	169.0	86.0	38.0	7.6
Mason	31	220	13.8	5.1	27	98	5.5	1.6	170.6	70.6	27.4	8.2
Mercer	174	1 620	126.4	55.8	105	997	57.2	19.9	466.9	211.6	94.5	28.0
Mineral	37	548	28.4	10.1	38	128	7.1	2.0	164.2	74.3	36.3	5.0
Mingo	48	574	44.6	14.9	30	149	8.5	2.7	251.8	100.5	36.2	22.4
Monongalia	146	2 716	186.2	92.2	138	1 163	71.2	21.8	534.6	151.8	63.4	13.8
Monroe	5	103	3.6	1.5	8	12	1.4	0.3	100.7	42.4	17.5	4.3
Morgan	11	253	8.8	3.7	12	27	2.1	0.5	89.2	47.9	12.5	2.6
Nicholas	41	365	20.7	6.7	36	167	9.2	2.8	184.9	81.4	29.3	10.7
Ohio	179	1 592	107.0	45.0	104	855	44.7	15.1	382.8	142.6	69.7	11.7
Pendleton	9	56	1.6	0.5	7	19	1.0	0.2	62.2	22.2	8.8	1.5
Pleasants	11	207	5.0	2.2	6	52	4.7	1.1	37.6	18.8	7.9	1.9
Pocahontas	16	174	6.0	2.0	10	19	1.2	0.2	59.5	25.9	12.5	2.1
Preston	25	320	13.6	5.3	40	130	9.0	1.8	249.3	79.8	29.7	9.3
Putnam	63	918	63.5	20.7	49	243	12.9	4.2	199.2	109.2	33.3	7.6
Raleigh	209	3 068	227.3	79.9	120	697	42.8	13.3	635.2	260.9	98.2	28.9
Randolph	71	685	33.7	11.9	35	127	6.2	1.5	200.0	80.4	33.5	8.6
Ritchie	8	156	5.6	2.3	9	24	1.6	0.3	61.9	27.0	10.8	3.7
Roane	13	167	7.1	3.0	7	17	1.5	0.4	90.7	38.2	16.4	6.8
Summers	15	171	7.3	2.5	13	38	2.1	0.7	109.2	41.6	16.3	5.4
Taylor	15	183	7.2	3.8	16	64	3.3	0.8	91.4	40.1	14.8	4.8
Tucker	5	16	0.9	0.2	10	24	1.7	0.3	54.7	22.2	7.2	1.4
Tyler	7	96	2.5	0.8	10	28	1.7	0.4	45.1	22.7	8.8	2.3
Upshur	35	404	18.4	7.2	19	98	4.7	1.6	136.4	59.6	19.4	8.5
Wayne	27	229	10.1	4.3	51	296	20.5	5.3	285.3	91.9	32.7	15.3
Webster	9	108	3.3	1.3	6	18	1.3	0.2	82.0	30.3	12.5	6.4
Wetzel	32	306	13.8	5.0	28	97	4.0	1.0	114.5	55.8	20.0	7.0
Wirt	2	D	D	D	3	D	D	D	34.1	14.6	5.4	2.4
Wood	194	2 376	152.9	64.5	165	1 656	119.1	28.9	662.0	239.5	102.3	24.1
Wyoming	25	220	10.9	4.5	19	86	4.4	1.3	188.6	89.4	32.0	15.6
WISCONSIN	9 315	114 562	6 917.4	3 447.3	8 648	49 101	2 991.3	886.4	30 236.7	11 194.0	4 239.2	657.8
Adams	13	71	3.4	1.4	12	38	2.2	0.6	108.6	43.5	15.6	2.9
Ashland	41	778	33.6	19.7	31	91	5.7	1.4	121.8	43.9	18.9	2.7
Barron	73	879	37.9	17.7	89	303	17.2	4.5	235.7	107.8	35.6	4.6
Bayfield	13	D	D	D	12	28	1.5	0.4	92.9	38.7	13.4	1.5
Brown	380	5 467	359.7	190.1	391	2 650	143.4	46.4	900.0	399.4	124.0	21.7
Buffalo	15	169	10.6	5.1	21	38	3.0	0.5	85.4	34.2	11.1	1.2
Burnett	13	83	3.8	2.1	23	57	4.4	0.9	89.4	46.0	13.3	1.8
Calumet	50	450	21.5	10.2	48	130	8.1	2.1	130.9	53.2	18.9	1.2
Chippewa	77	1 130	46.0	21.5	74	283	20.1	5.0	287.6	121.5	45.5	5.5
Clark	39	364	12.2	5.5	51	127	9.3	1.4	171.1	71.0	34.0	2.6
Columbia	89	846	42.7	17.8	86	320	20.6	5.6	312.3	132.2	49.6	2.8
Crawford	28	590	19.2	9.9	22	87	4.9	1.1	104.3	39.0	13.7	1.6
Dane	785	9 899	735.9	320.2	664	4 412	258.5	88.8	3 388.6	836.2	230.3	36.7

1. Firms subject to federal tax.   2. State totals may include programs not allocated by county.

Items 159—170

STATE County	Federal funds and grants, 2002–2003 (cont'd) Expenditures (mil dol) (cont'd) Procurement contract awards			Grants[1]				Local government finances, 2002 General revenue		Taxes	Per capita[2] (dollars)	
	Salaries and wages	Defense	Other	Medicaid and other health-related	Nutrition and family welfare	Education	Other	Total (mil dol)	Intergovernmental (mil dol)	Total (mil dol)	Total	Property
	171	172	173	174	175	176	177	178	179	180	181	182
WEST VIRGINIA—Cont'd												
Brooke	3.2	0.0	0.7	10.0	2.1	1.6	45.6	43.5	19.9	17.0	676	599
Cabell	56.8	7.8	21.6	101.5	16.7	8.6	42.7	210.5	96.2	77.5	814	604
Calhoun	2.5	0.0	0.4	17.4	1.1	1.6	1.4	13.1	9.8	2.1	285	277
Clay	1.8	0.0	0.4	18.8	2.7	1.2	0.0	18.4	14.3	3.0	289	272
Doddridge	2.0	0.0	0.2	7.7	0.9	0.6	0.2	13.3	9.5	3.5	468	464
Fayette	18.7	0.3	3.6	56.0	9.5	4.3	11.5	81.6	45.9	23.0	489	417
Gilmer	13.2	0.0	0.9	11.9	1.0	1.0	2.6	18.0	6.5	3.7	529	511
Grant	3.1	0.3	0.9	13.2	2.5	0.7	4.6	54.8	11.0	7.5	664	651
Greenbrier	6.6	1.2	11.5	39.2	4.3	2.2	7.3	66.8	36.2	14.7	426	388
Hampshire	4.7	0.0	0.6	16.4	1.5	1.4	1.2	31.0	19.4	8.6	408	395
Hancock	4.6	0.1	1.9	11.1	3.1	1.6	5.8	66.7	24.6	23.4	730	610
Hardy	2.9	0.0	8.6	16.6	0.8	0.8	113.4	26.1	17.8	5.8	454	415
Harrison	128.0	13.7	17.8	48.5	10.3	6.3	19.0	147.8	64.7	55.8	822	586
Jackson	5.1	0.0	2.8	19.6	2.7	1.9	11.1	55.8	30.4	18.2	644	577
Jefferson	44.9	0.6	24.4	14.1	2.1	1.6	26.4	69.1	32.0	28.5	635	577
Kanawha	167.4	59.1	58.6	199.3	113.6	112.5	319.2	473.1	175.4	181.9	929	655
Lewis	11.5	0.1	0.7	23.5	2.0	1.3	5.5	27.3	16.5	7.9	474	423
Lincoln	3.0	0.0	0.8	41.0	5.0	2.4	4.5	36.3	27.1	7.3	330	294
Logan	7.8	0.8	1.6	44.0	8.8	4.5	4.0	114.2	82.6	26.9	727	698
McDowell	5.3	1.6	2.4	66.4	13.1	4.2	12.7	50.6	36.2	10.8	462	411
Marion	43.3	8.4	27.3	35.5	12.2	8.9	64.4	128.3	54.9	25.6	733	606
Marshall	7.3	0.0	1.1	17.5	3.9	3.1	3.6	83.8	32.6	25.6	554	514
Mason	8.5	5.9	1.0	22.2	3.2	2.1	20.6	49.0	25.9	14.4	554	514
Mercer	17.2	0.3	3.9	64.7	11.5	9.4	15.0	197.6	60.0	28.9	464	374
Mineral	3.7	15.8	1.0	15.4	3.3	3.0	4.4	45.3	30.4	11.3	415	378
Mingo	5.5	0.8	3.5	47.8	11.3	3.0	19.2	62.7	40.2	18.6	676	557
Monongalia	99.8	6.8	61.3	50.1	5.8	5.4	57.3	139.5	56.7	54.3	655	513
Monroe	13.7	0.0	0.6	18.9	1.6	1.0	0.0	20.6	14.1	3.0	203	188
Morgan	1.6	16.5	0.5	5.5	0.7	0.9	0.2	37.6	15.1	7.7	504	478
Nicholas	6.3	2.7	1.8	21.8	4.5	2.2	24.1	77.1	35.2	14.5	550	457
Ohio	29.9	8.4	5.0	31.6	9.0	8.6	55.8	94.3	36.3	34.5	748	489
Pendleton	11.7	0.4	2.2	11.3	0.6	0.8	2.6	12.1	8.9	2.3	296	265
Pleasants	0.9	0.0	0.2	4.7	0.8	0.5	1.6	33.4	6.6	9.2	1 209	1 153
Pocahontas	3.1	0.0	2.3	10.3	0.9	1.1	1.1	24.1	11.7	4.8	532	415
Preston	17.8	2.6	73.3	25.2	3.5	2.5	4.3	44.4	28.6	7.9	268	254
Putnam	9.3	1.0	2.2	20.2	3.1	2.3	9.8	96.6	42.6	30.0	575	545
Raleigh	93.2	0.5	20.3	63.5	11.7	4.9	44.0	157.4	77.9	49.1	622	508
Randolph	15.2	0.2	8.5	33.9	3.4	3.6	9.9	70.0	36.1	15.4	545	206
Ritchie	2.7	0.0	1.3	11.5	1.0	1.0	2.5	16.4	10.9	4.2	411	406
Roane	2.5	0.0	0.5	18.5	2.1	1.5	3.5	24.6	18.6	4.1	268	231
Summers	2.6	10.2	0.8	24.6	2.3	1.2	3.8	17.4	11.5	3.9	314	224
Taylor	9.9	0.5	0.6	13.7	2.1	1.6	2.1	24.2	14.9	5.8	363	311
Tucker	3.4	0.0	0.9	9.6	0.6	0.7	8.5	16.8	9.8	3.8	530	445
Tyler	1.4	0.0	0.3	6.2	1.1	0.8	0.7	26.0	10.2	5.7	609	593
Upshur	12.3	0.4	1.4	18.6	3.9	2.6	6.6	40.4	24.9	9.6	410	373
Wayne	55.4	0.7	2.8	52.9	4.9	2.9	22.9	66.5	42.4	18.2	429	402
Webster	1.3	0.0	0.4	21.9	2.2	3.3	3.3	16.0	11.2	3.1	315	275
Wetzel	3.8	0.0	0.8	18.8	2.5	1.4	4.0	60.2	20.5	11.0	634	508
Wirt	0.9	2.0	0.2	6.8	0.7	0.5	0.4	9.3	6.9	1.8	299	291
Wood	116.2	7.4	52.6	52.3	11.2	6.0	40.1	136.4	72.6	46.3	530	481
Wyoming	5.3	1.1	2.0	29.7	7.6	2.8	2.3	50.7	30.9	13.5	544	485
WISCONSIN	1 785.1	1 243.7	763.9	3 725.1	1 099.4	635.7	2 083.6	X	X	X	X	X
Adams	21.0	0.0	0.8	16.7	2.5	1.3	0.3	55.1	25.7	21.8	1 064	982
Ashland	9.2	9.1	1.4	20.4	4.2	4.5	4.8	66.6	42.3	15.9	945	861
Barron	9.1	0.0	2.4	42.0	11.8	2.8	8.6	153.5	82.3	46.2	1 017	928
Bayfield	7.1	0.1	5.3	14.7	3.9	1.7	5.5	59.4	29.2	22.6	1 493	1 393
Brown	69.0	15.2	58.5	96.4	24.3	14.4	50.8	940.7	375.3	289.5	1 247	1 221
Buffalo	6.2	2.1	4.9	10.8	1.9	0.7	3.5	46.2	29.2	12.1	879	826
Burnett	2.2	3.9	0.8	14.4	2.9	1.1	0.8	54.2	27.7	19.5	1 220	1 149
Calumet	10.3	0.1	1.9	7.8	1.9	1.2	4.4	84.9	41.5	27.4	648	630
Chippewa	11.9	10.2	3.0	37.2	7.8	4.2	21.5	168.0	95.2	48.8	871	793
Clark	6.9	0.6	4.6	26.4	3.9	2.3	2.0	117.8	66.6	25.1	741	727
Columbia	12.2	0.3	54.5	26.6	8.5	3.0	11.2	192.4	93.9	70.4	1 319	1 217
Crawford	4.1	4.6	4.9	17.9	2.5	1.1	9.9	55.8	33.3	15.0	888	800
Dane	283.8	30.6	75.8	543.8	239.5	243.2	802.7	1 645.6	655.0	699.7	1 579	1 445

1. State totals may include programs not allocated by county.   2. Based on the resident population estimated as of July 1 of the year shown.

Table B. States and Counties — Local Government Finances, Government Employment, and Elections

STATE County	Direct general expenditure — Total (mil dol)	Direct general expenditure — Per capita[1] (dollars)	Education	Health and hospitals	Police protection	Public welfare	Highways	Debt outstanding — Total (mil dol)	Debt outstanding — Per capita[1] (dollars)	Federal civilian	Federal military	State and local	Democratic	Republican	All other
	183	184	185	186	187	188	189	190	191	192	193	194	195	196	197
WEST VIRGINIA—Cont'd															
Brooke	45.9	1 825	69.4	2.2	4.3	0.1	2.4	30.0	1 193	43	102	1 008	51.1	48.1	0.8
Cabell	198.6	2 085	51.1	2.7	5.7	0.0	1.3	79.4	834	1 085	428	6 196	43.6	55.5	0.9
Calhoun	12.9	1 730	83.9	0.2	1.4	0.0	0.5	3.2	423	22	30	351	43.9	54.9	1.2
Clay	19.0	1 839	89.9	0.1	1.2	0.0	0.2	1.0	101	26	42	568	45.1	54.0	1.0
Doddridge	13.7	1 851	87.9	3.3	1.4	0.0	0.3	0.0	0	14	30	458	25.0	74.0	1.0
Fayette	80.8	1 715	68.1	0.5	3.9	0.0	1.8	92.2	1 956	292	192	2 770	52.9	46.4	0.7
Gilmer	14.8	2 123	56.7	0.1	3.2	0.0	0.5	1.9	278	65	28	589	40.6	58.4	1.0
Grant	49.7	4 373	29.8	41.8	1.7	0.0	0.2	131.2	11 542	53	46	924	19.0	80.6	0.4
Greenbrier	66.6	1 933	62.8	3.0	3.3	0.0	1.2	74.8	2 172	124	140	2 047	41.9	57.4	0.7
Hampshire	31.6	1 504	82.9	0.2	1.8	0.3	0.4	13.1	624	49	85	1 267	30.7	68.7	0.6
Hancock	65.0	2 027	49.8	0.7	6.3	0.0	4.0	111.7	3 480	69	130	1 313	48.2	51.0	0.8
Hardy	21.9	1 714	68.8	1.8	4.7	0.0	1.0	7.7	604	61	52	580	30.7	68.8	0.5
Harrison	139.5	2 056	63.1	1.7	4.3	0.0	1.9	142.8	2 104	3 810	278	3 705	43.3	55.9	0.8
Jackson	56.5	2 002	69.9	0.2	4.8	0.1	0.9	27.8	987	81	115	1 327	41.0	58.4	0.6
Jefferson	73.5	1 635	73.2	1.2	7.1	0.1	0.7	39.7	884	727	182	2 385	46.5	52.8	0.7
Kanawha	460.2	2 351	52.5	0.1	5.5	0.3	2.7	452.5	2 311	2 433	910	19 491	48.9	50.6	0.5
Lewis	26.7	1 598	77.1	2.0	2.9	0.0	1.5	3.5	213	62	68	1 453	34.3	64.5	1.2
Lincoln	36.4	1 636	88.2	0.7	0.9	0.2	0.0	3.9	175	49	90	869	49.4	50.0	0.6
Logan	115.1	3 110	89.4	0.0	1.6	0.0	0.4	28.6	772	121	150	1 968	54.1	45.4	0.4
McDowell	52.8	2 019	83.9	0.5	1.8	0.0	0.6	2.9	112	83	106	1 839	61.8	37.8	0.5
Marion	131.8	2 335	52.5	0.2	3.0	0.0	1.1	421.5	7 469	181	229	3 999	48.2	50.7	1.1
Marshall	83.0	2 379	54.7	0.2	4.3	0.0	1.5	258.8	7 417	69	160	1 958	42.7	56.5	0.8
Mason	47.8	1 837	71.3	0.4	2.6	0.1	1.0	64.3	2 475	185	112	1 319	45.1	54.1	0.8
Mercer	195.0	3 134	37.2	43.5	2.2	0.0	1.5	138.1	2 220	288	253	4 417	40.9	58.4	0.6
Mineral	45.8	1 692	76.7	0.4	2.3	0.0	1.2	13.0	481	70	110	1 448	30.8	68.4	0.7
Mingo	62.8	2 278	73.2	1.4	2.3	0.0	0.6	3.1	112	95	112	1 323	56.2	43.2	0.6
Monongalia	136.4	1 645	60.1	0.4	4.4	0.2	2.1	183.1	2 209	1 412	359	14 479	47.6	51.5	0.9
Monroe	20.7	1 417	77.1	0.0	1.9	0.0	0.2	7.2	491	219	59	560	38.9	60.2	0.9
Morgan	36.6	2 395	56.7	28.7	2.5	0.0	0.1	7.7	502	26	62	837	33.3	65.8	0.9
Nicholas	70.1	2 654	52.1	31.0	3.3	0.0	1.1	16.5	625	119	107	1 860	46.3	52.9	0.7
Ohio	93.5	2 028	46.9	1.1	7.2	0.1	3.7	97.5	2 115	485	188	3 467	41.8	57.4	0.8
Pendleton	12.1	1 524	79.1	0.9	0.7	1.1	0.1	1.0	122	168	236	366	39.0	60.5	0.5
Pleasants	30.4	4 017	42.0	0.2	1.7	0.2	0.6	216.4	28 556	16	31	609	39.4	59.9	0.7
Pocahontas	23.1	2 578	51.6	23.1	1.9	0.0	0.4	4.6	514	76	36	742	40.2	58.6	1.3
Preston	42.9	1 456	72.3	0.8	2.3	0.0	0.9	24.0	813	113	120	1 584	33.2	65.9	0.9
Putnam	98.4	1 884	66.4	1.8	2.4	0.0	0.5	208.5	3 992	148	213	2 224	37.0	62.5	0.5
Raleigh	164.0	2 078	66.9	0.4	5.3	0.4	1.6	84.9	1 076	1 602	524	3 625	38.8	60.6	0.6
Randolph	68.9	2 439	48.5	0.1	7.9	0.0	2.7	30.8	1 088	286	115	1 883	42.6	56.7	0.7
Ritchie	15.9	1 551	81.3	0.1	1.9	0.0	1.1	3.3	323	31	42	499	25.5	73.6	0.9
Roane	22.7	1 487	82.3	0.1	1.9	0.0	0.8	12.3	808	39	62	611	42.8	56.4	0.8
Summers	17.4	1 392	76.0	1.5	5.5	0.1	1.2	2.9	233	43	51	763	45.3	53.9	0.7
Taylor	25.1	1 561	75.7	0.0	1.9	0.0	1.7	6.6	414	44	65	1 130	40.0	59.3	0.6
Tucker	16.8	2 351	71.8	0.7	2.6	0.0	1.2	1.9	260	68	29	661	38.9	60.5	0.6
Tyler	20.5	2 177	60.4	21.6	1.7	0.0	0.9	16.5	1 752	27	38	510	33.0	66.0	1.0
Upshur	39.6	1 699	73.7	0.0	1.8	0.3	1.0	13.8	590	113	95	1 241	32.6	66.7	0.7
Wayne	67.7	1 596	83.0	1.5	2.3	0.0	0.5	12.1	284	924	172	2 025	45.2	54.1	0.7
Webster	17.3	1 788	77.9	0.4	1.2	0.0	0.7	1.6	170	20	39	654	52.9	46.4	0.7
Wetzel	57.2	3 296	44.3	38.2	2.8	0.0	2.1	32.0	1 844	50	71	1 158	47.4	51.9	0.7
Wirt	9.3	1 569	91.4	0.0	0.4	0.0	0.5	0.3	52	14	24	260	33.8	64.9	1.2
Wood	142.6	1 634	75.9	2.6	2.6	0.0	1.4	93.8	1 074	1 932	357	4 139	35.7	63.6	0.6
Wyoming	64.5	2 593	80.3	0.1	1.5	0.0	0.5	19.9	800	88	101	1 155	42.5	57.1	0.5
WISCONSIN	X	X	X	X	X	X	X	X	X	29 033	15 656	375 375	49.8	49.4	0.9
Adams	54.8	2 672	35.2	5.2	5.7	6.4	15.8	42.1	2 054	327	56	848	52.2	46.8	1.0
Ashland	69.5	4 128	42.8	2.4	4.6	9.8	15.4	42.4	2 520	203	46	1 901	62.7	36.4	0.9
Barron	161.4	3 551	43.7	4.1	3.7	7.1	19.1	113.3	2 494	151	123	4 359	48.9	50.3	0.7
Bayfield	63.5	4 190	40.7	9.6	3.7	0.4	20.9	32.1	2 115	146	53	1 228	60.3	38.7	1.0
Brown	1 016.5	4 378	45.0	4.7	4.4	3.6	7.0	881.0	3 794	974	679	15 661	44.6	54.5	0.9
Buffalo	49.2	3 582	43.7	0.9	2.4	8.2	21.9	26.4	1 924	163	37	783	52.7	46.2	1.2
Burnett	63.7	3 983	45.5	6.9	2.5	2.7	18.1	48.6	3 041	38	43	1 180	48.3	51.0	0.7
Calumet	92.3	2 178	41.0	0.4	4.8	4.7	9.6	87.8	2 073	110	115	1 284	40.8	58.3	0.9
Chippewa	187.1	3 336	46.8	6.8	7.4	2.5	14.2	120.6	2 151	216	153	3 340	48.4	50.7	1.0
Clark	116.6	3 447	41.7	7.8	3.4	15.1	13.0	59.3	1 754	112	92	1 903	46.1	52.7	1.1
Columbia	198.4	3 717	47.5	1.9	4.6	9.5	12.7	155.3	2 909	195	144	3 469	48.5	50.7	0.8
Crawford	57.5	3 404	40.9	1.8	4.4	11.3	16.1	47.8	2 828	74	46	974	55.3	43.7	1.0
Dane	1 672.5	3 774	46.9	2.2	5.5	9.8	5.0	1 466.5	3 309	4 359	1 276	67 743	66.1	33.0	0.9

1. Based on the resident population estimated as of July 1 of the year shown.

Table B. States and Counties — **Land Area and Population**

STATE/ County code	CBSA code[1]	County Type[2]	STATE County	Land area,[3] (sq km) 2000	Population and population characteristics, 2003			Race alone or in combination, not Hispanic or Latino (percent)					Age (percent)					
					Total persons	Rank	Per square kilometer	White	Black	Am. Indian, Alaska Native	Asian and Pacific Islander	Percent Hispanic or Latino[4]	Under 5 years	5 to 17 years	18 to 24 years	25 to 34 years	35 to 44 years	45 to 54 years
				1	2	3	4	5	6	7	8	9	10	11	12	13	14	15
			WISCONSIN—Cont'd															
55 027	13180	4	Dodge	2 285	87 115	616	38.1	94.2	2.6	0.6	0.5	2.6	5.5	17.4	10.0	12.9	17.0	14.2
55 029	...	6	Door	1 250	28 402	1 446	22.7	97.7	0.3	1.0	0.4	1.0	4.4	15.8	8.1	9.2	14.7	16.3
55 031	20260	2	Douglas	3 391	44 093	1 045	13.0	95.9	0.9	2.7	0.9	0.8	5.7	16.8	11.0	11.9	14.8	15.3
55 033	32860	6	Dunn	2 207	41 114	1 108	18.6	96.1	0.6	0.5	2.7	0.8	5.4	16.3	18.0	13.0	13.1	12.9
55 035	20740	3	Eau Claire	1 651	94 186	569	57.0	95.1	0.8	0.9	3.4	0.9	5.8	16.6	15.4	13.3	13.5	13.4
55 037	27020	9	Florence	1 264	5 081	2 836	4.0	98.6	0.5	0.5	0.3	0.5	4.1	16.0	8.3	9.3	16.5	15.2
55 039	22540	3	Fond du Lac	1 872	97 833	552	52.3	95.3	1.2	0.7	1.0	2.5	5.6	17.9	10.6	11.7	15.7	14.7
55 041	...	9	Forest	2 626	9 938	2 448	3.8	86.4	1.3	11.5	0.3	1.1	5.4	18.4	9.9	9.5	13.3	12.9
55 043	38420	6	Grant	2 973	49 368	945	16.6	98.1	0.8	0.2	0.7	0.6	5.2	16.7	14.9	10.4	13.7	13.5
55 045	33820	6	Green	1 513	34 280	1 300	22.7	98.4	0.5	0.4	0.4	0.8	5.8	19.0	8.7	11.2	16.5	14.9
55 047	...	6	Green Lake	918	19 204	1 850	20.9	97.6	0.3	0.3	0.5	1.6	5.6	16.6	9.0	9.7	15.1	15.2
55 049	31540	6	Iowa	1 975	23 288	1 651	11.8	98.9	0.4	0.3	0.4	0.4	6.4	19.0	8.7	11.2	17.2	15.1
55 051	...	9	Iron	1 961	6 727	2 711	3.4	98.3	0.1	1.0	0.2	0.8	3.3	14.2	7.9	9.2	15.2	15.0
55 053	...	6	Jackson	2 557	19 538	1 835	7.6	89.3	2.3	6.6	0.2	2.1	5.1	17.4	10.7	12.3	15.6	14.1
55 055	48020	4	Jefferson	1 443	77 421	672	53.7	94.4	0.4	0.6	0.7	4.5	5.9	17.4	11.7	12.5	16.0	14.4
55 057	...	7	Juneau	1 988	25 029	1 573	12.6	95.9	0.7	1.8	0.6	1.6	5.4	18.0	9.3	10.2	15.2	14.1
55 059	16980	2	Kenosha	707	156 209	354	220.9	85.3	6.1	0.8	1.6	7.7	6.8	19.5	10.1	12.9	16.8	13.6
55 061	24580	2	Kewaunee	887	20 455	1 778	23.1	98.7	0.2	0.5	0.2	0.7	5.7	18.2	9.6	11.1	16.1	14.7
55 063	29100	3	La Crosse	1 173	108 612	507	92.6	94.1	1.3	0.7	3.9	0.9	5.7	16.8	14.5	13.0	14.0	13.8
55 065	...	8	Lafayette	1 641	16 341	2 011	10.0	98.9	0.2	0.2	0.3	0.6	5.8	18.8	10.1	9.9	15.9	14.4
55 067	...	6	Langlade	2 260	20 788	1 760	9.2	97.7	0.5	1.2	0.4	1.0	5.2	17.6	8.4	9.9	14.9	14.5
55 069	32980	6	Lincoln	2 288	30 076	1 400	13.1	97.8	0.6	0.8	0.5	0.8	5.2	18.3	8.9	10.8	15.8	14.2
55 071	31820	4	Manitowoc	1 532	82 065	644	53.6	95.3	0.5	0.7	2.4	1.8	5.4	18.3	9.1	10.7	16.1	15.2
55 073	48140	3	Marathon	4 001	127 168	447	31.8	93.3	0.5	0.6	5.4	0.9	5.9	19.3	9.5	11.9	16.1	14.7
55 075	31940	6	Marinette	3 631	43 237	1 058	11.9	98.1	0.4	0.8	0.4	0.8	4.6	16.8	10.3	9.3	15.1	14.9
55 077	...	8	Marquette	1 180	14 853	2 110	12.6	97.4	0.5	0.6	0.3	1.5	5.1	16.0	8.7	9.5	14.8	14.4
55 078	...	8	Menominee	927	4 623	2 862	5.0	13.3	0.8	83.0	0.3	3.2	9.6	26.6	10.9	10.5	14.0	10.4
55 079	33340	1	Milwaukee	626	933 221	41	1 490.8	60.7	26.5	1.1	3.4	9.8	7.6	18.9	9.8	14.5	15.1	13.5
55 081	...	6	Monroe	2 333	41 796	1 088	17.9	96.2	0.6	1.3	0.7	1.8	6.7	19.5	9.8	10.6	15.3	14.6
55 083	24580	2	Oconto	2 585	36 904	1 215	14.3	97.9	0.4	1.4	0.3	0.8	5.3	18.4	9.1	10.4	17.0	14.5
55 085	...	7	Oneida	2 912	37 187	1 203	12.8	97.7	0.4	1.2	0.5	0.7	4.1	16.2	8.2	9.4	15.5	15.4
55 087	11540	3	Outagamie	1 658	167 411	338	101.0	93.1	0.8	1.9	2.9	2.1	6.6	19.6	9.8	13.3	17.2	13.8
55 089	33340	1	Ozaukee	601	84 772	627	141.1	96.0	1.2	0.4	1.5	1.4	5.3	19.2	9.1	9.2	16.4	16.6
55 091	...	6	Pepin	602	7 383	2 649	12.3	99.1	0.3	0.3	0.2	0.4	5.7	18.0	10.6	9.8	14.8	14.2
55 093	33460	1	Pierce	1 493	37 872	1 186	25.4	97.9	0.5	0.6	0.9	0.8	5.2	17.2	16.7	12.1	14.9	14.0
55 095	...	6	Polk	2 376	43 270	1 056	18.2	97.6	0.4	1.3	0.4	0.9	5.6	18.5	9.1	10.7	15.6	14.9
55 097	44620	4	Portage	2 088	67 386	748	32.3	94.5	0.6	0.6	2.8	1.4	5.5	16.9	15.0	12.5	14.7	14.1
55 099	...	9	Price	3 244	15 401	2 069	4.7	98.2	0.2	0.8	0.3	0.8	4.3	17.3	8.1	8.8	15.2	16.3
55 101	39540	3	Racine	863	192 284	299	222.8	79.6	11.2	0.7	1.1	8.6	6.8	19.2	9.5	11.8	16.3	14.6
55 103	...	6	Richland	1 518	18 193	1 900	12.0	98.3	0.5	0.3	0.4	1.0	5.5	17.9	10.5	9.8	14.1	15.0
55 105	27500	3	Rock	1 866	154 794	360	83.0	89.7	5.2	0.6	1.3	4.5	6.6	19.1	9.5	12.5	15.7	14.2
55 107	...	6	Rusk	2 365	15 268	2 080	6.5	97.6	0.7	0.5	0.5	0.8	5.3	17.7	10.1	9.6	14.2	14.5
55 109	33460	1	St. Croix	1 870	71 155	712	38.1	97.4	0.7	0.6	1.1	0.8	6.4	19.1	10.0	13.4	16.8	14.2
55 111	12660	4	Sauk	2 169	56 432	863	26.0	96.8	0.4	1.1	0.4	1.8	5.8	18.6	9.1	11.9	15.7	14.5
55 113	...	9	Sawyer	3 254	16 713	1 981	5.1	82.4	0.4	16.9	0.3	1.0	5.3	17.2	8.6	9.5	13.9	15.3
55 115	...	6	Shawano	2 312	41 050	1 110	17.8	91.6	0.4	7.2	0.6	1.2	5.7	18.3	8.7	11.0	15.7	13.4
55 117	43100	3	Sheboygan	1 330	113 376	488	85.2	90.5	1.2	0.6	4.4	3.9	5.7	18.3	9.6	12.2	16.3	14.8
55 119	...	6	Taylor	2 525	19 539	1 834	7.7	98.6	0.1	0.4	0.4	0.8	5.9	19.1	9.5	10.6	16.2	14.7
55 121	...	8	Trempealeau	1 901	27 306	1 492	14.4	96.4	0.3	0.3	0.2	1.1	5.9	18.2	8.5	11.2	15.5	14.3
55 123	...	6	Vernon	2 059	28 496	1 442	13.8	98.7	0.2	0.4	0.3	0.8	6.4	19.5	9.2	9.3	14.3	14.7
55 125	...	9	Vilas	2 263	22 041	1 702	9.7	89.9	0.3	9.1	0.3	0.7	4.1	14.9	7.9	8.8	13.6	13.9
55 127	48580	4	Walworth	1 438	96 812	558	67.3	91.0	0.9	0.4	0.9	7.4	5.7	17.5	12.2	12.1	15.0	13.7
55 129	...	6	Washburn	2 097	16 466	1 998	7.9	97.8	0.4	1.6	0.3	0.9	4.7	16.8	8.8	8.9	14.6	15.1
55 131	33340	1	Washington	1 116	122 241	465	109.5	97.1	0.7	0.4	1.0	1.4	6.2	18.8	8.9	11.8	17.8	15.0
55 133	33340	1	Waukesha	1 439	374 079	165	260.0	94.1	1.1	0.4	2.4	2.7	5.9	18.7	8.6	10.7	16.9	16.2
55 135	...	6	Waupaca	1 945	52 564	901	27.0	97.5	0.3	0.7	0.4	1.6	5.6	18.4	8.9	10.8	15.7	14.2
55 137	...	8	Waushara	1 621	23 623	1 629	14.6	94.7	0.4	0.9	0.5	4.2	4.7	17.2	8.6	9.2	14.8	14.7
55 139	36780	3	Winnebago	1 136	158 500	349	139.5	94.2	1.3	0.8	2.3	2.1	5.8	17.1	11.5	13.3	16.3	14.2
55 141	49220	4	Wood	2 053	75 402	680	36.7	96.5	0.5	0.9	1.7	0.9	5.7	18.1	9.1	10.8	15.7	14.9
56 000	...	X	**WYOMING**	251 489	501 242	X	2.0	89.5	1.1	2.8	1.0	6.8	6.2	18.0	11.1	11.9	14.0	16.2
56 001	29660	4	Albany	11 066	31 887	1 361	2.9	88.4	1.5	1.6	2.4	7.6	5.6	12.3	21.8	17.1	10.8	12.7
56 003	...	9	Big Horn	8 125	11 199	2 355	1.4	92.2	0.1	1.1	0.4	6.7	6.1	20.1	9.5	8.7	12.6	14.5
56 005	23940	5	Campbell	12 424	36 240	1 232	2.9	94.0	0.3	1.6	0.8	4.3	7.0	20.9	11.4	13.2	16.9	17.2
56 007	...	7	Carbon	20 451	15 302	2 074	0.7	83.1	1.1	1.6	0.9	14.0	5.8	16.4	10.2	10.6	15.7	17.8
56 009	...	6	Converse	11 020	12 330	2 276	1.1	93.1	0.3	1.5	0.5	5.6	5.8	19.5	9.5	10.4	15.2	18.0

1. CBSA = Core Based Statistical Area. See Appendix A for explanation. See Appendix B for list of metropolitan areas with component counties. 2. County type code from the Economic Research Service of USDA Rural-Urban Continuum Codes. See Appendix A for definition. 3. Dry land or land partially or temporarily covered by water. 4. Hispanic or Latino persons may be of any race.

STATE County	55 to 64 years	65 to 74 years	75 years and over	Percent female	Total persons 1990	Total persons 2000	Percent change 1990–2000	Percent change 2000–2003	Births	Deaths	Net migration	Households 2000 Number	Percent change 1990–2000	Persons per household	Female family householder[1]	One person
	16	17	18	19	20	21	22	23	24	25	26	27	28	29	30	31
WISCONSIN—Cont'd																
Dodge	9.0	6.6	7.2	47.7	76 559	85 897	12.2	1.4	3 026	2 798	1 072	31 417	17.0	2.56	7.5	24.1
Door	12.2	9.7	9.4	50.8	25 690	27 961	8.8	1.6	812	1 058	706	11 828	17.5	2.33	6.5	28.1
Douglas	9.7	6.8	7.5	50.8	41 758	43 287	3.7	1.9	1 620	1 388	607	17 808	8.8	2.36	10.1	29.8
Dunn	7.9	5.4	5.8	49.7	35 909	39 858	11.0	3.2	1 440	849	693	14 337	17.0	2.57	6.9	24.4
Eau Claire	8.3	5.7	6.5	51.4	85 183	93 142	9.3	1.1	3 602	2 343	-98	35 822	14.5	2.46	8.6	27.1
Florence	13.0	9.7	8.7	48.9	4 590	5 088	10.8	-0.1	124	181	57	2 133	21.5	2.35	6.0	27.9
Fond du Lac	9.3	6.7	7.6	51.0	90 083	97 296	8.0	0.6	3 498	3 062	219	36 931	13.1	2.52	7.8	25.4
Forest	11.2	10.9	8.8	50.2	8 776	10 024	14.2	-0.2	341	369	-45	4 043	22.9	2.39	9.8	28.2
Grant	9.3	7.6	8.0	48.9	49 266	49 597	0.7	-0.5	1 719	1 715	-171	18 465	7.5	2.51	7.5	26.0
Green	9.4	6.8	7.5	50.7	30 339	33 647	10.9	1.9	1 263	1 059	461	13 212	14.5	2.51	7.5	25.0
Green Lake	10.6	8.8	9.9	50.5	18 651	19 105	2.4	0.5	727	749	136	7 703	7.1	2.43	6.9	27.0
Iowa	9.0	6.6	6.5	50.1	20 150	22 780	13.1	2.2	971	672	231	8 764	18.3	2.56	7.6	24.3
Iron	12.9	11.6	11.7	50.9	6 153	6 861	11.5	-2.0	146	277	9	3 083	18.5	2.19	7.0	32.0
Jackson	9.8	7.3	7.1	46.9	16 588	19 100	15.1	2.3	675	688	456	7 070	17.3	2.49	8.6	26.2
Jefferson	9.4	6.0	6.2	50.4	67 783	74 021	9.2	4.6	2 914	1 914	738	28 205	17.4	2.55	8.2	23.6
Juneau	10.8	8.5	8.1	50.2	21 650	24 316	12.3	2.9	848	909	777	9 696	17.3	2.47	8.8	26.0
Kenosha	8.4	5.5	5.5	50.3	128 181	149 577	16.7	4.4	6 822	4 066	3 936	56 057	19.2	2.60	11.5	25.5
Kewaunee	9.7	6.8	8.0	49.9	18 878	20 187	6.9	1.3	760	672	191	7 623	12.8	2.61	6.6	23.5
La Crosse	8.4	6.0	6.4	51.4	97 904	107 120	9.4	1.4	3 980	3 073	747	41 599	13.5	2.45	8.4	28.4
Lafayette	9.2	7.7	7.9	50.1	16 074	16 137	0.4	1.3	624	431	37	6 211	5.7	2.57	7.6	25.4
Langlade	10.8	9.1	9.8	50.5	19 505	20 740	6.3	0.2	680	773	157	8 452	11.8	2.42	8.2	26.7
Lincoln	10.4	8.0	8.3	50.0	26 993	29 641	9.8	1.5	996	1 056	517	11 721	13.1	2.46	8.1	25.5
Manitowoc	9.9	7.4	8.2	50.4	80 421	82 887	3.1	-1.0	2 857	2 710	-910	32 721	8.7	2.49	7.5	26.8
Marathon	9.3	6.2	6.8	50.1	115 400	125 834	9.0	1.1	4 848	3 187	-196	47 702	14.8	2.60	7.4	23.6
Marinette	11.4	8.7	9.0	50.6	40 548	43 384	7.0	-0.3	1 268	1 707	334	17 585	13.1	2.38	7.4	28.3
Marquette	11.3	11.1	8.5	49.5	12 321	15 832	28.5	-6.2	490	580	394	5 986	23.9	2.41	6.7	25.4
Menominee	9.3	6.3	2.8	50.3	4 075	4 562	12.0	1.3	320	145	-111	1 345	24.7	3.35	26.6	16.5
Milwaukee	8.0	5.9	6.6	51.9	959 212	940 164	-2.0	-0.7	48 393	29 413	-25 834	377 729	1.3	2.43	16.3	33.0
Monroe	9.5	6.7	7.1	49.7	36 633	40 899	11.6	2.2	1 912	1 244	283	15 399	17.2	2.60	8.8	25.0
Oconto	10.5	7.6	6.9	49.7	30 226	35 634	17.9	3.6	1 231	1 162	1 189	13 979	23.9	2.52	6.9	23.5
Oneida	12.0	10.5	8.5	50.2	31 679	36 776	16.1	1.1	925	1 249	749	15 333	21.1	2.34	7.1	26.4
Outagamie	8.2	5.4	5.5	50.0	140 510	160 971	14.6	4.0	7 177	3 585	2 864	60 530	19.8	2.61	7.6	24.2
Ozaukee	10.8	6.8	6.1	50.7	72 894	82 317	12.9	3.0	2 788	1 994	1 746	30 857	20.0	2.61	6.5	21.4
Pepin	9.9	7.6	9.0	49.7	7 107	7 213	1.5	2.4	276	217	116	2 759	5.6	2.57	6.8	26.1
Pierce	8.3	4.7	4.7	50.7	32 765	36 804	12.3	2.9	1 247	713	570	13 015	18.2	2.65	7.5	21.3
Polk	10.4	7.2	7.5	49.9	34 773	41 319	18.8	4.7	1 563	1 317	1 679	16 254	24.5	2.51	7.4	25.2
Portage	8.5	5.6	5.6	50.2	61 405	67 182	9.4	0.3	2 391	1 464	-682	25 040	17.5	2.54	7.3	24.5
Price	11.3	9.1	10.0	49.7	15 600	15 822	1.4	-2.7	431	632	-211	6 564	8.4	2.37	6.6	28.5
Racine	9.3	6.1	6.0	50.5	175 034	188 831	7.9	1.8	8 441	5 264	467	70 819	11.1	2.59	12.3	24.5
Richland	10.2	7.6	9.1	50.4	17 521	17 924	2.3	1.5	654	613	238	7 118	8.0	2.48	7.7	27.2
Rock	9.4	6.5	6.2	50.6	139 510	152 307	9.2	1.6	6 537	4 380	505	58 617	12.2	2.54	10.9	25.1
Rusk	10.7	8.8	9.4	50.7	15 079	15 347	1.8	-0.5	562	669	50	6 095	7.1	2.45	7.9	27.0
St. Croix	8.3	4.7	4.5	49.9	50 251	63 155	25.7	12.7	2 786	1 433	6 506	23 410	32.7	2.66	7.0	21.2
Sauk	9.6	6.8	7.6	50.6	46 975	55 225	17.6	2.2	2 067	1 723	905	21 644	22.3	2.51	8.1	25.2
Sawyer	12.5	9.8	7.8	49.6	14 181	16 196	14.2	3.2	579	685	616	6 640	19.2	2.39	10.0	26.2
Shawano	10.6	8.2	8.6	50.1	37 157	40 664	9.4	0.9	1 455	1 457	418	15 815	14.8	2.51	8.0	24.9
Sheboygan	9.2	6.6	7.3	49.7	103 897	112 646	8.4	0.6	3 941	3 370	271	43 545	12.8	2.50	7.3	26.1
Taylor	9.0	7.2	8.2	49.4	18 901	19 680	4.1	-0.7	797	617	-308	7 529	12.5	2.58	7.1	24.7
Trempealeau	10.1	7.2	9.0	50.0	25 263	27 010	6.9	1.1	1 060	1 062	328	10 747	13.2	2.45	7.4	27.6
Vernon	10.1	7.9	8.6	50.5	25 617	28 056	9.5	1.6	1 218	1 090	338	10 825	11.3	2.55	6.8	26.7
Vilas	13.5	12.5	10.4	50.3	17 707	21 033	18.8	4.8	609	876	1 246	9 066	24.3	2.29	7.5	26.0
Walworth	9.2	6.4	6.3	50.1	75 000	93 759	25.0	3.3	3 630	2 619	3 819	34 522	25.0	2.57	8.2	24.7
Washburn	12.3	9.8	8.8	49.5	13 772	16 036	16.4	2.7	502	639	567	6 604	21.0	2.39	7.0	26.7
Washington	9.6	5.8	5.5	50.0	95 328	117 493	23.3	4.0	4 747	2 716	2 780	43 842	32.9	2.65	7.2	20.3
Waukesha	10.2	6.5	5.7	50.7	304 715	360 767	18.4	3.7	14 016	8 905	8 548	135 229	27.6	2.63	6.8	20.9
Waupaca	9.6	7.8	8.8	50.0	46 104	51 731	12.2	1.6	1 877	2 213	1 159	19 863	16.6	2.51	7.4	25.2
Waushara	11.7	10.3	8.4	49.2	19 385	23 154	19.4	2.0	723	917	754	9 336	22.6	2.43	6.7	24.9
Winnebago	8.9	6.2	6.3	50.1	140 320	156 763	11.7	1.1	5 940	4 100	80	61 157	14.9	2.43	8.3	25.0
Wood	9.7	7.4	8.5	50.9	73 605	75 555	2.6	-0.2	2 778	2 162	-714	30 135	9.7	2.47	8.0	27.2
WYOMING	10.6	6.4	5.5	49.7	453 589	493 782	8.9	1.5	20 306	13 398	700	193 608	14.7	2.48	8.7	26.3
Albany	7.8	4.5	3.9	48.4	30 797	32 014	4.0	-0.4	1 243	641	-723	13 269	11.0	2.23	7.5	31.4
Big Horn	11.4	8.8	8.3	49.7	10 525	11 461	8.9	-2.3	420	447	-235	4 312	10.4	2.60	6.8	25.0
Campbell	7.4	3.1	2.0	48.5	29 370	33 698	14.7	7.5	1 604	536	1 441	12 207	22.5	2.73	8.8	20.2
Carbon	11.5	6.9	5.5	46.9	16 659	15 639	-6.1	-2.2	583	466	-463	6 129	2.1	2.39	8.3	27.5
Converse	10.2	6.5	5.0	50.4	11 128	12 052	8.3	2.3	484	281	75	4 694	16.0	2.55	8.4	23.4

1. No spouse present.

Table B. States and Counties — Vital Statistics, Health Resources, and Crime

STATE County	Births, average 1999–2001 Total	Rate[1]	Deaths, average 1999–2001 Number Total	Infant[2]	Rate Total[1]	Infant[3]	Physicians,[4] 2000 Number	Rate[5]	Hospitals,[4] 1998 Number	Beds Number	Rate[5]	Medicare enrollees, 2003	Serious crimes known to police,[6] 2002 Total Number	Rate[7]
	32	33	34	35	36	37	38	39	40	41	42	43	44	45
WISCONSIN—Cont'd														
Dodge	969	11.3	846	5	9.9	D	97	113	3	353	424	9 979	1 718	1 972
Door	253	9.1	318	2	11.4	D	42	150	1	77	285	6 018	422	1 488
Douglas	498	11.5	459	2	10.6	D	24	55	1	42	98	7 535	2 192	4 992
Dunn	461	11.5	278	2	7.0	D	21	53	1	55	141	5 234	NA	NA
Eau Claire	1 117	12.0	692	3	7.4	D	255	274	2	519	581	13 232	3 369	3 622
Florence	43	8.5	55	0	10.9	D	4	79	0	0	0	911	122	2 364
Fond du Lac	1 148	11.8	916	7	9.4	6.4	145	149	2	220	232	16 165	2 426	2 458
Forest	110	11.0	117	1	11.7	D	2	20	0	0	0	2 092	340	3 343
Grant	522	10.5	511	3	10.3	D	43	87	3	260	527	9 347	944	1 876
Green	397	11.8	323	2	9.6	D	85	253	1	143	428	5 379	597	1 749
Green Lake	221	11.5	237	1	12.4	D	29	152	1	163	839	4 026	369	1 904
Iowa	290	12.7	201	1	8.8	D	15	66	1	82	366	3 139	332	1 437
Iron	36	5.2	82	1	12.1	D	6	87	0	0	0	1 593	185	2 658
Jackson	212	11.1	204	2	10.7	D	10	52	1	38	214	3 097	473	2 441
Jefferson	928	12.5	597	3	8.1	D	61	82	1	92	125	12 401	1 844	2 456
Juneau	270	11.1	279	3	11.4	D	14	58	1	95	399	4 979	549	2 226
Kenosha	2 147	14.3	1 207	13	8.0	5.9	204	136	2	307	213	18 992	4 275	2 817
Kewaunee	236	11.7	196	1	9.7	D	11	54	1	17	86	3 341	563	2 749
La Crosse	1 244	11.6	920	9	8.6	7.0	357	333	2	552	538	15 321	3 119	2 870
Lafayette	181	11.2	142	1	8.8	D	5	31	1	28	172	2 693	189	1 155
Langlade	220	10.6	229	1	11.1	D	24	116	1	49	239	4 286	634	3 013
Lincoln	318	10.7	324	3	10.9	D	26	88	2	125	420	5 903	737	2 451
Manitowoc	907	10.9	844	8	10.2	9.2	116	140	2	354	430	14 468	1 995	2 373
Marathon	1 513	12.0	950	10	7.5	6.4	219	174	1	270	219	17 507	2 759	2 161
Marinette	415	9.6	513	3	11.9	D	56	129	1	115	267	9 223	763	1 734
Marquette	162	10.5	170	1	11.0	D	6	38	0	0	0	3 926	259	1 613
Menominee	94	20.6	40	1	8.8	D	4	88	0	0	0	544	253	5 467
Milwaukee	14 810	15.8	8 993	145	9.6	9.8	3 113	331	14	3 537	388	134 416	59 211	6 208
Monroe	568	13.9	394	6	9.6	D	42	103	2	105	266	6 328	936	2 256
Oconto	385	10.8	353	2	9.9	D	20	56	2	49	144	5 694	816	2 257
Oneida	303	8.3	406	1	11.1	D	92	250	2	132	370	8 604	1 007	2 699
Outagamie	2 242	13.9	1 110	11	6.9	5.1	261	162	3	426	273	21 342	3 788	2 320
Ozaukee	869	10.5	592	4	7.2	D	162	197	1	82	101	12 316	1 178	1 411
Pepin	87	12.0	74	1	10.2	D	7	97	1	88	1 236	1 386	85	1 162
Pierce	393	10.7	235	2	6.4	D	6	16	1	36	101	4 758	964	2 582
Polk	482	11.6	386	5	9.3	D	43	104	3	141	364	6 858	767	1 878
Portage	779	11.6	445	3	6.6	D	82	122	1	122	188	8 693	1 777	2 607
Price	135	8.6	198	1	12.6	D	12	76	1	42	266	3 331	241	1 501
Racine	2 593	13.7	1 607	20	8.5	7.7	251	133	3	561	301	28 541	7 145	3 730
Richland	199	11.2	175	2	9.8	D	24	134	1	38	212	2 960	332	1 826
Rock	2 041	13.4	1 319	16	8.7	7.7	281	184	3	474	314	22 752	6 791	4 395
Rusk	170	11.1	183	1	11.9	D	16	104	1	142	931	3 032	427	2 743
St. Croix	897	14.1	443	6	7.0	D	45	71	3	106	180	6 720	1 355	2 207
Sauk	709	12.8	507	5	9.2	D	74	134	3	186	349	9 182	1 996	3 563
Sawyer	175	10.8	197	1	12.2	D	13	80	1	117	726	3 232	405	2 838
Shawano	471	11.6	453	3	11.2	D	19	47	1	53	137	7 178	1 103	2 674
Sheboygan	1 386	12.3	1 037	12	9.2	8.9	150	133	3	421	382	17 618	3 495	3 058
Taylor	241	12.3	181	1	9.2	D	20	102	1	155	803	3 113	281	1 408
Trempealeau	313	11.6	303	1	11.2	D	17	63	3	298	1 126	5 223	456	1 664
Vernon	380	13.5	321	2	11.4	D	22	78	2	102	373	5 252	317	1 114
Vilas	173	8.2	261	2	12.4	D	35	166	2	114	536	5 464	541	2 722
Walworth	1 115	11.9	821	7	8.7	6.3	89	95	1	88	103	13 212	2 614	2 748
Washburn	157	9.8	195	1	12.1	D	18	112	2	185	1 200	4 368	471	2 895
Washington	1 514	12.9	811	6	6.9	D	105	89	2	191	168	15 720	2 368	1 987
Waukesha	4 354	12.0	2 697	18	7.5	4.1	799	221	4	682	193	51 455	6 002	1 743
Waupaca	589	11.4	672	5	13.0	D	39	75	1	40	79	10 666	920	1 753
Waushara	225	9.7	265	1	11.5	D	11	48	1	26	120	4 562	499	2 124
Winnebago	1 858	11.9	1 240	13	7.9	7.2	320	204	2	456	304	22 481	4 281	2 692
Wood	891	11.8	685	4	9.1	D	352	466	2	708	931	14 574	1 914	2 497
WYOMING	6 166	12.5	3 997	40	8.1	6.5	762	154	26	2 309	480	68 590	17 858	3 581
Albany	367	11.4	187	2	5.8	D	56	175	1	110	377	3 084	1 295	4 005
Big Horn	139	12.2	138	1	12.1	D	7	61	1	118	1 037	2 055	128	1 106
Campbell	483	14.3	157	2	4.7	D	44	131	1	119	367	2 365	1 672	4 913
Carbon	171	11.0	139	1	8.9	D	20	128	1	50	321	2 191	579	3 666
Converse	152	12.6	89	2	7.4	D	5	41	1	34	276	1 630	320	2 629

1. Per 1,000 estimated resident population.   2. Deaths of infants under 1 year old.   3. Deaths of infants under 1 year old per 1,000 live births.   4. Data subject to copyright.   5. Per 100,000 resident population as of July 1 of the year shown.   6. Data for serious crimes have not been adjusted for underreporting; this may affect comparability between geographic areas and over time.   7. Per 100,000 population estimated by the FBI.

Table B. States and Counties — Crime, Education, Money Income, and Poverty

STATE County	Serious crimes known to police,[1] 2002 (cont'd) Rate[2] Violent	Rate[2] Property	Education — School enrollment and attainment, 2000 Enrollment[3] Total	Enrollment[3] Percent private	Attainment[4] (percent) High school graduate or less	Attainment[4] (percent) Bachelor's degree or more	Local government expenditures,[5] 2000–2001 Total current expenditures (mil dol)	Current expenditures per student (dollars)	Money income, 1999 Per capita income[6] (dollars)	Households Median income Dollars	Percent change, 1989–1999 (constant 1999 dollars)	Percent with income of $100,000 or more	Percent below poverty level, 1999 Persons	Households	Families	Families with children
	46	47	48	49	50	51	52	53	54	55	56	57	58	59	60	61
WISCONSIN—Cont'd																
Dodge	77	1 895	21 011	20.5	61.2	13.2	68.3	8 041	19 574	45 190	15.3	6.9	5.3	5.7	3.7	5.4
Door	39	1 449	5 892	11.2	50.8	21.4	36.9	8 665	21 356	38 813	10.0	8.6	6.4	6.7	4.4	6.9
Douglas	180	4 812	11 211	10.5	50.3	18.3	55.3	7 950	17 638	35 226	18.5	4.3	11.0	11.2	7.6	12.8
Dunn	NA	NA	14 115	7.3	50.2	21.1	47.9	7 882	17 520	38 753	18.0	5.7	12.9	12.3	6.3	9.0
Eau Claire	173	3 449	30 324	11.3	42.2	27.0	113.7	7 990	19 250	39 219	12.8	7.4	10.9	10.3	5.5	7.6
Florence	136	2 228	1 077	3.6	60.6	12.4	6.9	7 920	18 328	34 750	15.4	4.7	9.1	10.1	5.0	12.4
Fond du Lac	82	2 376	25 296	21.9	55.9	16.9	117.8	7 487	20 022	45 578	15.2	6.9	5.8	5.9	3.5	5.1
Forest	266	3 078	2 407	5.3	64.2	10.0	15.8	7 765	16 451	32 023	41.0	4.1	13.1	12.3	8.8	14.5
Grant	103	1 773	15 315	9.6	56.5	17.2	70.0	8 262	16 764	36 268	10.2	4.7	11.2	10.7	6.1	9.8
Green	50	1 699	8 301	7.4	56.2	16.7	48.5	8 110	20 795	43 228	13.2	7.0	5.1	5.8	3.3	4.5
Green Lake	129	1 775	4 182	15.2	60.0	14.5	27.5	7 590	19 024	39 462	14.3	5.1	7.0	7.1	3.8	6.2
Iowa	91	1 346	5 763	9.1	53.3	18.5	32.8	8 287	19 497	42 518	22.1	6.8	7.3	7.8	5.0	6.3
Iron	172	2 486	1 365	3.1	54.4	13.2	8.8	8 815	17 371	29 580	25.5	4.1	11.1	12.5	7.6	13.7
Jackson	155	2 286	4 439	6.3	62.8	11.3	25.0	7 445	17 604	37 015	28.7	5.3	9.6	9.8	5.4	7.7
Jefferson	105	2 351	18 482	20.5	53.8	17.4	102.1	8 446	21 236	46 901	13.5	8.7	5.7	5.2	3.7	6.2
Juneau	118	2 108	5 654	13.0	64.5	10.0	34.7	8 144	17 892	35 335	19.1	4.2	10.1	10.0	7.4	10.7
Kenosha	175	2 642	42 684	17.4	49.8	19.2	214.9	7 961	21 207	46 970	14.1	10.8	7.5	7.3	5.4	8.0
Kewaunee	54	2 695	4 977	16.7	63.5	11.4	26.6	7 176	18 456	43 824	21.1	5.9	5.8	6.5	4.4	5.5
La Crosse	148	2 722	33 296	14.9	42.2	25.4	131.9	8 373	19 800	39 472	9.4	7.7	10.7	10.4	5.3	8.4
Lafayette	67	1 087	4 218	6.4	61.1	13.3	28.9	8 228	16 811	37 220	13.2	4.8	9.1	9.3	6.2	8.9
Langlade	200	2 814	4 619	12.8	64.4	11.7	32.3	8 670	16 960	33 168	19.2	3.7	10.1	11.2	7.6	11.7
Lincoln	116	2 335	7 154	11.7	59.8	13.6	40.0	7 759	17 940	39 120	15.7	4.8	6.9	8.4	4.5	6.5
Manitowoc	117	2 256	20 954	22.2	58.5	15.5	87.7	7 093	20 285	43 286	17.3	6.1	6.1	5.8	3.7	5.7
Marathon	110	2 051	32 716	14.3	54.2	18.3	154.4	7 823	20 703	45 165	11.5	8.3	6.6	6.4	4.3	6.5
Marinette	57	1 677	10 876	16.6	62.2	12.9	58.5	8 070	17 492	35 256	17.2	4.6	8.3	8.6	5.6	8.4
Marquette	62	1 550	3 437	12.9	62.6	10.1	16.4	7 269	16 924	35 746	19.7	3.7	7.7	8.4	4.8	6.6
Menominee	1 491	3 976	1 645	4.7	63.8	12.9	12.6	12 761	10 625	29 440	55.2	2.4	28.8	25.0	24.8	32.7
Milwaukee	664	5 544	268 828	23.5	49.2	23.6	1 349.9	9 049	19 939	38 100	11.9	7.9	15.3	13.2	11.7	18.5
Monroe	154	2 102	10 296	15.2	60.1	13.2	51.6	7 212	17 056	37 170	11.6	4.8	12.0	10.5	8.4	12.4
Oconto	55	2 202	8 738	9.2	64.5	10.6	37.7	7 116	19 016	41 201	33.8	5.9	7.1	7.4	4.7	6.6
Oneida	126	2 573	8 435	11.3	51.4	20.0	50.1	8 646	19 746	37 619	17.1	6.5	7.4	8.2	5.3	8.0
Outagamie	92	2 228	44 269	21.2	49.6	22.5	223.4	7 336	21 943	49 613	9.3	9.9	4.7	4.9	2.9	4.2
Ozaukee	59	1 352	23 199	28.9	32.3	38.6	108.5	8 528	31 947	62 745	9.4	23.9	2.6	2.9	1.7	2.3
Pepin	82	1 080	1 844	15.2	60.2	13.3	13.7	9 026	18 288	37 609	21.7	4.9	9.1	8.8	5.8	9.4
Pierce	40	2 542	12 261	10.6	45.3	24.6	59.2	7 949	20 172	49 551	20.8	9.5	7.7	7.4	3.1	4.7
Polk	98	1 780	10 202	6.0	55.2	15.6	63.4	7 603	19 129	41 183	26.3	6.5	7.1	8.0	4.6	6.8
Portage	95	2 512	21 761	8.7	50.8	23.4	80.6	8 010	19 854	43 487	12.8	8.2	9.5	10.0	4.4	6.8
Price	25	1 477	3 685	9.2	61.1	13.0	21.1	7 809	17 837	35 249	15.8	4.9	8.9	9.2	5.7	9.2
Racine	247	3 483	51 249	21.6	49.6	20.3	238.8	8 053	21 772	48 059	9.2	10.8	8.4	7.6	5.8	9.4
Richland	209	1 617	4 510	14.1	58.7	14.1	17.7	8 876	17 042	33 998	15.3	4.4	10.1	9.6	7.2	11.3
Rock	239	4 156	39 380	13.3	55.3	16.7	220.9	8 055	20 895	45 517	10.6	9.1	7.3	7.2	5.1	7.9
Rusk	334	2 409	3 751	13.5	64.3	11.2	24.6	8 920	15 563	31 344	18.9	3.2	11.8	12.3	7.9	12.3
St. Croix	41	2 167	17 324	13.2	41.7	26.3	83.0	7 620	23 937	54 930	11.4	15.0	4.0	4.3	2.4	3.4
Sauk	91	3 472	13 531	13.0	54.3	17.6	92.1	7 728	19 695	41 941	19.1	7.0	7.2	7.4	4.8	7.3
Sawyer	84	2 754	3 740	12.0	55.2	16.5	20.3	8 467	17 634	32 287	32.8	5.6	12.7	13.0	9.9	14.2
Shawano	82	2 591	9 992	12.6	64.3	12.6	47.5	7 547	17 991	38 069	18.8	5.2	7.9	8.4	5.8	9.0
Sheboygan	116	2 942	28 868	21.5	55.5	17.9	155.8	7 904	21 509	46 237	8.9	7.8	5.2	5.2	3.7	5.4
Taylor	90	1 317	5 003	9.9	66.1	11.0	26.6	7 465	17 570	38 502	17.9	5.2	9.8	9.6	6.2	8.3
Trempealeau	51	1 613	6 266	8.4	59.9	13.3	46.2	7 961	17 681	37 889	18.2	4.5	8.3	8.9	4.9	6.7
Vernon	84	1 029	6 831	16.1	59.6	14.0	37.4	8 284	15 859	33 178	14.6	4.1	14.2	12.2	9.0	14.4
Vilas	151	2 571	4 346	8.0	54.3	17.6	32.5	10 242	18 361	33 759	23.5	5.2	8.0	7.9	5.8	9.9
Walworth	108	2 640	28 372	11.7	49.3	21.8	120.2	8 094	21 229	46 274	13.5	9.9	8.4	7.9	4.6	7.5
Washburn	123	2 772	3 591	7.9	55.9	15.2	24.7	8 247	17 341	33 716	25.7	4.8	9.9	10.8	6.6	11.3
Washington	57	1 930	30 427	22.7	46.4	21.9	149.8	7 732	24 319	57 033	10.5	14.8	3.6	3.7	2.6	3.9
Waukesha	64	1 679	97 499	24.7	35.7	34.1	498.9	8 416	29 164	62 839	4.9	21.5	2.7	2.9	1.7	2.5
Waupaca	65	1 688	12 254	13.6	61.0	14.8	76.4	7 340	18 664	40 910	16.7	6.1	6.8	7.1	4.7	7.0
Waushara	89	2 035	4 997	8.8	64.3	11.7	23.0	7 001	18 144	37 000	25.8	4.8	9.1	8.7	5.3	8.5
Winnebago	130	2 562	43 417	13.7	51.2	22.8	178.5	7 475	21 706	44 445	10.2	8.0	6.7	6.7	3.8	6.2
Wood	39	2 458	19 208	15.7	56.3	16.9	110.1	7 958	20 203	41 595	4.1	7.4	6.5	7.2	4.4	6.9
WYOMING	274	3 307	136 139	7.1	43.1	21.9	704.5	7 852	19 134	37 892	4.1	6.7	11.4	11.2	8.0	12.4
Albany	585	3 421	14 837	9.1	28.4	44.1	29.4	7 700	16 706	28 790	3.4	5.4	21.0	22.2	10.8	16.6
Big Horn	199	907	3 028	4.3	50.9	15.9	21.3	8 995	15 086	32 682	13.4	3.8	14.1	12.6	10.2	16.5
Campbell	264	4 648	9 726	5.3	47.0	15.7	55.9	7 495	20 063	49 536	-0.5	8.6	7.6	7.7	5.6	6.7
Carbon	475	3 191	3 674	4.1	51.5	17.2	26.4	9 642	18 375	36 060	-1.0	5.9	12.9	13.1	9.8	14.1
Converse	230	2 399	3 154	5.0	49.0	14.7	19.8	8 139	18 744	39 603	6.4	6.1	11.6	12.0	9.2	13.9

1. Data for serious crimes have not been adjusted for underreporting; this may affect comparability between geographic areas and over time.   2. Per 100,000 population estimated by the FBI.   3. All persons 3 years old and over enrolled in nursery school through college.   4. Persons 25 years old and over.   5. Elementary and secondary education expenditures.   6. Based on population enumerated as of April 1, 2000.

Table B. States and Counties — **Personal Income**

STATE County	Total (mil dol)	Percent change, 2001–2002	Per capita[1] Dollars	Per capita[1] Rank	Wages and salaries[2] (mil dol)	Proprietor's income (mil dol)	Dividends, interest, and rent (mil dol)	Transfer payments Total (mil dol)	Government payments to individuals Total (mil dol)	Social Security (mil dol)	Medical payments (mil dol)	Income maintenance (mil dol)	Unemployment insurance (mil dol)
	62	63	64	65	66	67	68	69	70	71	72	73	74
WISCONSIN—Cont'd													
Dodge	2 231	1.2	25 684	960	1 300	166	383	322	300	149	110	13	19
Door	885	4.2	31 292	263	394	96	269	143	136	71	49	5	8
Douglas	1 035	3.4	23 639	1 518	612	49	157	230	219	75	90	18	7
Dunn	932	4.2	22 859	1 761	560	45	159	147	137	55	54	10	7
Eau Claire	2 568	4.3	27 301	648	1 931	185	496	380	356	147	147	24	16
Florence	121	4.7	23 648	1 513	31	4	23	25	24	11	9	1	0
Fond du Lac	2 881	2.9	29 487	393	1 848	244	484	418	394	170	166	18	19
Forest	218	4.5	21 975	2 021	98	26	42	55	52	22	20	4	3
Grant	1 189	3.3	24 060	1 382	567	95	252	225	212	92	91	10	9
Green	956	2.3	28 065	539	483	67	202	136	128	60	51	6	7
Green Lake	520	2.0	26 952	708	236	43	122	94	89	44	34	4	5
Iowa	683	9.2	29 532	389	494	49	111	78	72	33	28	4	5
Iron	159	4.6	23 407	1 592	67	19	34	41	39	18	16	2	2
Jackson	499	5.1	25 835	923	314	41	91	83	78	34	31	5	5
Jefferson	2 214	1.6	28 805	468	1 245	211	370	317	298	133	131	10	15
Juneau	569	4.3	22 950	1 738	281	53	102	128	122	53	49	7	7
Kenosha	4 432	3.3	28 775	473	2 171	270	606	623	585	243	243	46	25
Kewaunee	523	1.1	25 499	1 000	246	21	92	79	74	36	28	3	6
La Crosse	3 052	3.9	28 250	516	2 447	233	531	451	424	169	179	25	17
Lafayette	370	2.0	22 724	1 812	118	30	80	62	58	28	23	3	3
Langlade	492	4.3	23 686	1 505	243	54	92	110	104	46	42	6	5
Lincoln	737	3.7	24 588	1 240	411	51	127	143	135	62	54	6	8
Manitowoc	2 233	1.5	27 097	681	1 354	124	380	372	351	166	131	14	27
Marathon	3 692	3.8	29 103	431	2 660	295	611	479	447	205	169	29	29
Marinette	1 061	5.0	24 466	1 275	699	70	176	227	217	98	88	11	11
Marquette	332	5.1	22 552	1 863	123	17	59	82	79	40	28	4	4
Menominee	85	4.6	18 394	2 845	65	3	16	26	25	7	10	4	3
Milwaukee	28 470	2.4	30 456	307	24 097	2 099	4 652	5 332	5 096	1 550	2 344	822	231
Monroe	964	4.8	23 193	1 664	632	61	178	168	157	61	61	11	9
Oconto	908	2.8	24 836	1 169	284	53	143	149	139	69	48	7	9
Oneida	1 042	4.3	28 213	519	592	99	236	212	203	96	78	8	11
Outagamie	4 955	2.9	29 850	361	4 008	317	815	547	505	241	178	26	41
Ozaukee	3 980	2.0	47 418	23	1 676	226	973	298	277	157	91	6	13
Pepin	179	4.5	24 495	1 265	74	10	33	34	32	14	14	1	1
Pierce	1 035	2.7	27 676	591	335	53	171	116	107	48	42	5	5
Polk	1 036	3.1	24 210	1 341	483	66	173	179	169	76	68	9	7
Portage	1 795	1.9	26 674	755	1 208	100	305	259	242	99	95	13	16
Price	378	4.6	24 483	1 268	219	23	76	85	81	35	34	4	3
Racine	5 785	2.2	30 331	317	3 365	258	998	817	769	338	301	58	53
Richland	409	1.8	22 603	1 851	185	24	87	85	80	34	36	5	3
Rock	4 138	3.2	26 865	725	2 828	149	640	668	629	273	244	49	43
Rusk	320	2.0	20 859	2 330	188	22	60	79	75	31	29	5	3
St. Croix	2 104	2.7	30 756	289	946	97	301	198	181	83	71	7	10
Sauk	1 581	3.7	28 298	512	1 197	104	277	232	218	101	87	11	12
Sawyer	403	6.3	24 288	1 314	213	31	93	92	87	36	36	6	4
Shawano	978	2.6	23 878	1 447	404	83	160	178	167	80	64	9	7
Sheboygan	3 465	3.1	30 612	298	2 444	301	619	451	423	206	149	20	36
Taylor	443	4.7	22 573	1 857	306	28	70	81	76	33	32	4	5
Trempealeau	689	4.6	25 338	1 033	428	45	105	132	125	51	58	6	5
Vernon	592	4.0	20 878	2 327	232	51	108	124	117	52	48	7	5
Vilas	558	4.9	25 623	974	246	32	166	129	124	67	41	5	5
Walworth	2 603	2.2	27 364	635	1 404	142	491	359	335	160	125	15	18
Washburn	375	3.9	22 851	1 763	176	15	80	104	100	42	38	5	4
Washington	4 128	1.9	34 149	156	1 898	168	759	404	373	194	132	12	25
Waukesha	15 221	2.0	41 114	54	10 729	756	2 890	1 291	1 197	649	412	34	65
Waupaca	1 377	2.8	26 297	832	726	64	224	274	261	108	115	10	12
Waushara	519	3.1	22 182	1 963	165	30	99	111	105	54	37	5	5
Winnebago	4 681	3.1	29 537	387	3 991	230	857	606	566	269	214	28	33
Wood	2 226	4.4	29 533	388	1 919	74	390	363	344	151	140	19	22
WYOMING	15 474	3.8	31 021	X	9 195	1 656	3 820	1 990	1 863	777	669	126	50
Albany	839	5.3	26 379	815	522	41	214	111	103	35	37	5	2
Big Horn	257	0.5	22 847	1 764	164	19	52	48	45	22	14	3	1
Campbell	1 093	4.4	30 253	329	1 026	63	157	89	80	30	30	4	3
Carbon	391	1.5	25 432	1 017	228	31	103	63	59	24	20	4	2
Converse	348	3.3	28 136	527	183	37	69	44	41	19	14	3	1

1. Based on the resident population estimated as of July 1 of the year shown.   2. Includes other labor income.

STATE County	Earnings, 2002								Social Security beneficiaries, December 2003		Supplemental Security Income recipients, December 2003	Housing units, 2003	
	Total (mil dol)	Farm	Goods-related[1]		Service-related and health									
			Total	Manu-facturing	Infor-mation and profes-sional and technical services	Retail trade	Finance, insur-ance, and real estate	Health services	Govern-ment	Number	Rate[2]		Total	Percent change, 2000–2003
	75	76	77	78	79	80	81	82	83	84	85	86	87	88
WISCONSIN—Cont'd														
Dodge	1 465	2.0	45.6	35.4	4.0	5.6	4.0	9.2	13.9	14 915	171	572	34 797	3.3
Door	490	1.9	D	19.5	5.1	10.3	7.3	9.1	14.1	7 060	249	215	20 687	5.6
Douglas	661	0.0	D	8.3	4.9	8.8	2.9	D	19.3	7 975	181	1 154	20 819	2.3
Dunn	605	2.8	23.4	17.5	4.2	7.4	2.8	D	25.6	6 185	150	590	16 255	6.4
Eau Claire	2 116	0.5	16.4	10.7	7.7	8.3	7.1	16.2	16.3	15 115	160	1 782	39 648	5.8
Florence	35	-2.0	27.6	21.7	D	D	D	D	32.9	1 175	231	87	4 291	1.2
Fond du Lac	2 093	1.1	43.6	35.2	4.7	6.2	4.9	9.8	11.5	17 135	175	1 119	40 501	3.1
Forest	124	0.4	D	10.5	2.7	5.3	2.9	D	43.5	2 465	248	202	8 531	2.5
Grant	662	3.1	23.0	17.0	D	8.6	5.5	D	27.0	10 225	207	788	20 212	1.4
Green	550	1.5	29.9	22.8	6.9	16.2	3.7	D	13.4	6 205	181	298	14 474	4.3
Green Lake	279	2.9	32.9	20.0	3.3	8.5	5.8	13.2	15.0	4 505	235	208	9 975	1.5
Iowa	544	1.1	D	7.0	1.8	55.0	2.2	D	10.1	3 745	161	212	10 166	6.1
Iron	85	-0.2	D	14.8	D	9.6	4.8	13.3	17.7	1 950	290	124	5 799	1.6
Jackson	355	6.3	D	8.7	1.6	5.5	3.4	6.1	33.5	3 805	195	351	8 302	3.4
Jefferson	1 456	1.4	D	35.3	4.5	8.8	5.4	9.1	11.6	13 235	171	742	31 472	4.6
Juneau	334	2.9	38.1	32.8	2.0	7.7	3.4	D	19.2	5 795	232	460	13 016	5.2
Kenosha	2 441	-0.1	D	29.8	3.8	7.0	4.3	10.5	16.1	23 755	152	2 364	62 895	4.8
Kewaunee	267	5.3	37.8	28.4	D	6.2	3.9	3.8	17.4	3 750	183	170	8 587	4.5
La Crosse	2 680	0.3	24.1	18.1	5.5	6.9	6.8	17.7	14.0	17 415	160	1 946	45 063	3.6
Lafayette	148	9.8	21.0	15.9	D	5.2	6.0	3.2	25.8	3 165	194	179	6 780	1.6
Langlade	296	4.4	D	20.3	D	12.4	3.4	D	15.5	5 005	241	380	11 524	3.0
Lincoln	462	0.8	D	35.8	2.0	7.1	7.8	D	16.6	6 515	217	363	15 230	3.7
Manitowoc	1 478	2.0	44.2	37.3	3.8	5.9	3.0	9.9	12.3	16 685	203	1 017	35 705	3.0
Marathon	2 956	1.4	34.1	28.1	5.9	8.5	9.9	8.7	10.6	20 980	165	1 904	52 989	5.2
Marinette	769	1.4	D	41.0	2.7	7.0	3.1	D	12.2	10 215	236	751	26 969	2.7
Marquette	140	1.8	44.8	37.1	2.2	6.4	4.7	4.9	19.2	4 210	283	218	8 964	3.5
Menominee	68	0.0	D	0.3	0.1	D	D	0.3	91.6	790	171	172	2 194	4.6
Milwaukee	26 196	0.0	20.1	16.9	11.0	5.3	10.8	13.6	13.1	151 125	162	32 109	401 490	0.3
Monroe	693	3.2	D	17.5	D	6.5	3.7	6.0	32.8	7 235	173	658	17 297	3.7
Oconto	338	2.7	D	28.3	3.7	8.2	3.4	D	19.5	7 565	205	445	21 079	6.4
Oneida	691	0.5	23.4	11.5	5.1	13.3	5.6	17.0	16.7	9 820	264	548	27 637	3.8
Outagamie	4 325	0.7	D	22.9	7.5	8.3	9.4	9.2	10.1	23 815	142	1 635	67 061	7.1
Ozaukee	1 902	0.2	D	30.6	7.2	6.1	13.6	8.9	9.2	14 095	166	293	33 673	5.1
Pepin	84	6.5	D	7.8	3.7	10.2	3.2	8.8	21.6	1 555	211	111	3 164	4.2
Pierce	388	2.5	D	9.9	7.2	5.8	5.8	7.9	32.7	4 925	130	259	14 453	7.1
Polk	550	2.1	38.0	28.8	4.6	7.9	4.6	10.7	17.2	8 235	190	459	22 284	5.5
Portage	1 308	2.2	D	19.1	3.9	8.3	15.7	9.3	16.5	10 325	153	737	28 005	5.3
Price	242	1.2	D	43.9	4.7	6.5	2.8	D	15.8	3 825	248	276	10 005	4.5
Racine	3 623	0.3	D	36.2	5.8	6.4	3.6	11.4	12.8	32 535	169	3 644	76 785	2.8
Richland	209	2.1	D	31.9	2.5	10.9	3.9	D	18.0	3 830	211	338	8 370	2.5
Rock	2 977	0.1	39.5	33.7	3.9	8.2	3.5	11.4	12.8	26 990	174	2 874	64 460	3.7
Rusk	210	3.1	D	35.0	3.2	8.3	2.6	D	20.9	3 550	233	339	7 969	4.7
St. Croix	1 043	1.0	35.0	25.8	6.5	9.3	5.3	8.8	12.9	8 530	120	387	28 253	16.4
Sauk	1 302	0.8	D	22.3	4.0	9.6	4.9	9.2	12.8	10 710	190	627	26 192	7.8
Sawyer	243	0.5	16.3	7.7	4.0	12.0	6.8	D	27.4	4 200	251	338	14 373	4.7
Shawano	487	6.9	D	19.8	4.3	8.3	5.4	D	20.0	8 550	208	517	18 951	3.5
Sheboygan	2 745	0.7	51.7	46.3	4.7	5.4	5.3	9.1	9.8	20 020	177	1 304	47 508	3.4
Taylor	334	1.9	D	33.5	D	6.1	3.8	D	11.2	3 675	188	238	8 824	2.7
Trempealeau	473	3.0	D	45.4	2.8	5.4	2.6	5.3	15.6	5 695	209	452	11 852	3.2
Vernon	283	3.7	16.1	11.2	3.9	8.9	10.8	D	21.6	5 970	210	507	12 779	2.9
Vilas	277	0.9	D	6.2	4.1	11.5	4.4	D	28.1	6 960	316	205	22 984	2.6
Walworth	1 546	0.1	D	26.8	5.1	7.4	4.7	6.5	17.8	15 670	162	731	46 066	5.2
Washburn	192	2.2	23.5	18.5	3.1	10.9	5.2	D	27.2	4 285	260	368	11 432	5.7
Washington	2 066	0.3	42.1	33.9	4.0	8.2	6.6	7.2	11.1	18 630	152	593	48 482	5.8
Waukesha	11 485	0.0	33.7	24.4	10.7	5.8	9.5	8.1	7.0	58 830	157	1 771	147 603	5.2
Waupaca	790	1.7	D	32.5	5.6	7.0	5.0	9.6	17.3	11 200	213	625	23 515	4.5
Waushara	195	9.2	D	13.4	3.4	10.3	5.8	D	21.0	5 705	242	360	14 343	4.9
Winnebago	4 221	0.1	D	42.3	5.1	4.6	4.6	9.5	11.9	26 385	166	1 818	67 745	4.7
Wood	1 993	1.2	26.6	21.9	3.7	6.9	2.2	31.3	10.8	15 350	204	1 166	32 933	3.9
WYOMING	10 851	0.9	D	D	D	7.4	5.8	7.0	23.8	78 745	157	5 665	229 949	2.7
Albany	563	0.2	10.3	4.1	D	7.2	D	D	45.2	3 380	106	232	15 723	3.3
Big Horn	184	2.7	32.7	3.9	4.7	5.6	2.9	D	25.7	2 335	209	158	5 152	0.9
Campbell	1 089	0.1	55.1	3.1	3.7	4.9	2.4	3.3	12.0	3 015	83	190	13 813	4.0
Carbon	259	1.3	22.8	11.1	3.6	7.7	4.1	4.8	31.0	2 460	161	136	8 395	1.1
Converse	220	0.9	36.3	2.0	D	4.8	D	D	20.4	2 005	163	95	5 751	1.4

1. Covers mining, construction, and manufacturing.   2. Per 1,000 resident population estimated as of July 1 of the year shown.

Table B. States and Counties — Housing, Labor Force, and Employment

STATE County	Housing units, 2000								Civilian labor force, 2003				Civilian employment,[6] 2000		
	Occupied units							Sub-standard units[4] (percent)		Percent change, 2002–2003	Unemployment			Percent	
	Owner-occupied					Renter-occupied								Management, professional and related occupations	Production, transportation, and material moving occupations
	Total	Percent	Median value[1]	Median owner cost as a percent of income		Median rent[3]	Median rent as a percent of income		Total		Total	Rate[5]	Total		
				With a mortgage	Without a mortgage[2]										
	89	90	91	92	93	94	95	96	97	98	99	100	101	102	103
WISCONSIN—Cont'd															
Dodge	31 417	73.5	105 800	21.5	12.0	528	20.8	1.8	48 166	3.2	2 906	6.0	43 197	25.3	28.2
Door	11 828	79.3	120 800	22.2	10.9	481	24.6	0.9	16 570	1.1	1 367	8.2	13 901	27.5	18.0
Douglas	17 808	71.5	69 900	19.3	10.4	411	23.5	1.9	23 567	1.5	1 380	5.9	20 616	26.7	16.2
Dunn	14 337	69.0	92 900	20.4	11.0	461	23.6	3.0	23 807	4.7	1 136	4.8	20 791	28.0	21.4
Eau Claire	35 822	65.0	96 300	19.8	11.0	486	24.2	2.3	55 327	2.8	2 510	4.5	49 524	31.4	15.6
Florence	2 133	85.6	82 200	19.9	12.3	385	19.6	3.0	1 896	5.5	165	8.7	2 353	24.8	22.5
Fond du Lac	36 931	73.0	101 000	19.9	10.8	500	22.1	1.6	57 216	1.2	3 110	5.4	51 374	26.3	25.3
Forest	4 043	78.9	77 400	18.9	10.7	325	20.7	3.1	5 135	3.1	377	7.3	4 044	20.5	22.5
Grant	18 465	72.4	78 000	19.2	9.9	395	22.8	1.9	25 651	3.9	1 405	5.5	25 088	29.9	19.9
Green	13 212	73.7	97 700	22.3	11.5	464	21.7	1.3	18 277	0.3	1 101	6.0	18 217	28.3	22.0
Green Lake	7 703	77.2	90 100	21.4	11.7	437	22.0	2.1	10 517	1.1	745	7.1	9 645	24.1	24.9
Iowa	8 764	75.8	91 800	21.4	12.2	502	21.5	1.6	14 509	2.8	628	4.3	12 618	30.9	17.4
Iron	3 083	80.7	58 900	20.9	13.6	308	22.1	1.5	3 406	1.7	289	8.5	2 871	23.6	19.6
Jackson	7 070	75.0	76 800	19.5	10.9	397	19.6	3.1	12 144	3.6	575	4.7	8 881	24.6	20.1
Jefferson	28 205	71.7	123 800	22.3	12.1	564	22.2	2.1	43 027	1.5	2 119	4.9	39 832	26.1	26.4
Juneau	9 696	76.9	71 200	20.2	10.8	433	22.6	2.6	10 724	0.4	1 026	9.6	11 333	22.2	26.5
Kenosha	56 057	69.1	120 900	21.4	12.5	589	24.3	3.1	85 207	3.1	5 007	5.9	73 236	28.8	19.9
Kewaunee	7 623	81.9	92 100	19.9	10.9	428	19.1	1.7	10 870	1.5	730	6.7	10 703	26.4	26.1
La Crosse	41 599	65.1	96 900	20.6	11.0	470	23.4	2.1	63 500	1.6	2 657	4.2	57 073	30.8	17.0
Lafayette	6 211	77.4	74 600	19.7	11.8	404	19.7	1.7	7 336	1.7	493	6.7	8 515	29.8	22.4
Langlade	8 452	78.7	68 600	20.0	12.0	405	24.0	2.7	9 871	0.8	886	9.0	9 703	22.4	23.9
Lincoln	11 721	78.3	86 500	19.7	11.2	433	22.8	2.1	14 972	0.7	1 059	7.1	14 530	23.5	27.1
Manitowoc	32 721	76.0	90 900	19.0	10.2	433	19.7	1.9	44 334	0.3	3 448	7.8	42 953	24.3	29.7
Marathon	47 702	75.7	95 800	19.6	9.9	484	21.6	2.7	77 392	2.2	3 583	4.6	66 550	29.7	21.8
Marinette	17 585	79.5	69 800	19.7	10.2	400	20.9	2.1	23 398	4.3	1 700	7.3	20 336	24.5	25.3
Marquette	5 986	82.3	87 000	21.7	12.4	456	21.6	2.1	7 078	1.4	658	9.3	6 621	22.1	26.0
Menominee	1 345	74.5	72 700	19.8	10.3	245	22.7	12.6	2 605	5.7	278	10.7	1 407	24.5	14.2
Milwaukee	377 729	52.6	103 200	21.1	12.6	555	24.8	4.8	487 668	0.9	34 802	7.1	436 878	32.3	18.4
Monroe	15 399	73.7	77 500	20.3	10.1	455	22.0	4.0	21 806	5.0	1 173	5.4	19 804	27.2	23.3
Oconto	13 979	82.9	89 900	20.2	10.8	429	20.6	2.2	16 361	0.3	1 577	9.6	17 680	23.9	27.4
Oneida	15 333	79.7	106 200	20.7	12.2	460	23.9	2.1	21 774	0.0	1 406	6.5	17 199	29.8	15.1
Outagamie	60 530	72.4	106 000	20.3	10.5	534	21.5	2.0	107 364	1.0	5 602	5.2	85 596	30.5	21.2
Ozaukee	30 857	76.3	177 300	21.4	11.3	642	21.2	1.1	48 874	0.9	2 115	4.3	44 203	42.8	14.1
Pepin	2 759	79.6	79 200	20.6	11.8	368	19.8	2.7	3 201	0.2	193	6.0	3 582	27.7	24.1
Pierce	13 015	73.1	123 100	21.4	10.7	542	21.2	2.9	21 466	1.9	1 112	5.2	21 095	30.1	19.6
Polk	16 254	80.1	100 200	20.8	10.9	440	23.9	2.6	23 816	1.7	1 841	7.7	20 553	26.4	26.1
Portage	25 040	70.9	98 300	19.5	9.9	477	23.8	2.4	39 454	2.6	2 009	5.1	35 677	30.0	19.1
Price	6 564	80.8	70 100	20.3	12.5	404	21.5	2.6	7 185	3.4	454	6.3	7 436	25.9	27.2
Racine	70 819	70.6	111 000	20.7	11.5	548	24.0	3.1	94 552	1.8	7 681	8.1	91 021	30.7	21.3
Richland	7 118	74.5	75 200	21.1	11.8	427	22.9	2.5	8 778	3.7	437	5.0	8 885	26.3	26.6
Rock	58 617	71.2	98 200	19.9	10.9	543	23.1	2.4	79 113	1.2	5 393	6.8	76 336	25.4	26.8
Rusk	6 095	78.6	63 200	18.7	11.1	371	22.6	3.1	7 026	-0.3	527	7.5	6 997	26.0	28.7
St. Croix	23 410	76.4	139 500	20.6	10.4	587	23.0	1.7	38 825	2.2	2 709	7.0	34 905	33.6	18.4
Sauk	21 644	73.3	107 500	21.8	11.3	508	22.3	2.2	37 552	3.2	1 671	4.4	29 108	28.0	18.9
Sawyer	6 640	76.9	94 300	20.0	12.1	386	21.2	4.0	10 413	-1.7	661	6.3	7 199	26.6	13.9
Shawano	15 815	78.2	84 000	19.8	10.5	438	21.4	2.3	21 155	2.6	1 214	5.7	20 037	26.4	23.7
Sheboygan	43 545	71.4	106 800	20.6	11.4	482	19.4	2.3	64 672	1.4	3 199	4.9	59 454	25.9	29.8
Taylor	7 529	80.4	75 600	19.2	11.5	405	19.7	3.7	11 216	5.2	716	6.4	9 836	24.4	30.1
Trempealeau	10 747	74.3	77 000	18.9	11.5	380	20.8	2.3	14 969	0.3	938	6.3	14 028	27.5	27.4
Vernon	10 825	79.1	73 400	20.7	12.1	367	22.5	5.0	14 683	3.9	799	5.4	13 113	29.9	20.9
Vilas	9 066	82.0	120 200	21.8	11.8	434	22.0	2.0	11 755	1.3	830	7.1	9 268	25.2	10.4
Walworth	34 522	69.1	128 400	22.8	11.8	588	24.1	3.1	56 505	2.3	2 464	4.4	49 128	28.6	21.3
Washburn	6 604	80.9	85 700	21.8	12.1	413	24.8	2.7	8 437	4.2	606	7.2	7 145	24.7	20.6
Washington	43 842	76.0	155 000	21.9	10.2	620	21.2	1.5	70 150	1.1	3 678	5.2	64 687	32.2	21.0
Waukesha	135 229	76.5	170 400	21.4	11.3	726	22.8	1.6	217 452	0.7	9 813	4.5	195 290	40.4	13.2
Waupaca	19 863	76.9	89 300	19.9	11.5	450	21.8	2.0	27 475	1.9	1 633	5.9	25 370	25.4	26.7
Waushara	9 336	83.4	85 100	21.9	10.9	448	22.3	2.6	12 111	4.3	813	6.7	10 530	23.5	25.0
Winnebago	61 157	68.0	97 700	20.4	10.7	500	22.0	2.1	101 205	1.1	5 053	5.0	82 666	29.4	22.4
Wood	30 135	74.3	81 400	18.1	9.9	442	22.1	1.8	41 623	2.3	2 553	6.1	37 345	26.8	22.4
WYOMING	193 608	70.0	96 600	19.7	9.9	437	22.5	3.2	278 367	3.1	12 204	4.4	241 055	30.0	12.8
Albany	13 269	51.3	118 600	19.9	9.9	464	32.6	3.0	19 704	3.9	382	1.9	17 168	40.4	8.5
Big Horn	4 312	74.4	71 800	18.7	9.9	380	20.5	4.0	5 851	2.0	267	4.6	4 800	30.1	14.0
Campbell	12 207	73.6	102 900	18.1	9.9	463	18.4	3.6	22 820	0.3	932	4.1	17 975	23.9	16.8
Carbon	6 129	70.9	76 500	17.0	9.9	377	19.4	2.9	8 121	1.3	451	5.6	7 335	23.4	13.6
Converse	4 694	74.1	84 900	17.3	9.9	349	19.4	1.8	6 582	5.5	317	4.8	5 951	23.2	17.1

1. Specified owner-occupied units. 2. Median monthly owner costs is often in the minimum category—9.9 percent or less, which is indicated as 9.9 percent. 3. Specified renter-occupied units. 4. Overcrowded or lacking complete plumbing facilities. 5. Percent of civilian labor force. 6. Persons 16 years old and over.

STATE County	Private nonfarm establishments, employment and payroll, 2001									Agriculture, 2002			
		Employment						Annual payroll		Farms			
											Percent with—		
	Number of establishments	Total	Health care and social assistance	Manufacturing	Retail trade	Finance and insurance	Professional, scientific, and technical services	Total (mil dol)	Average per employee (dollars)	Number	Less than 50 acres	500 acres and over	Farm operators whose principal occupation is farming (percent)
	104	105	106	107	108	109	110	111	112	113	114	115	116
WISCONSIN—Cont'd													
Dodge	1 836	29 021	3 561	12 310	3 228	576	499	825	28 419	1 968	29.4	8.3	66.3
Door	1 312	11 440	1 237	2 523	1 893	319	318	258	22 543	877	35.0	5.6	54.0
Douglas	1 105	14 082	1 938	1 429	2 306	332	324	316	22 453	391	15.9	8.4	46.5
Dunn	1 009	12 854	1 926	1 996	1 924	415	456	315	24 491	1 683	21.7	9.8	56.1
Eau Claire	2 707	46 924	7 835	6 222	8 038	2 606	1 635	1 241	26 442	1 174	26.6	5.1	56.0
Florence	106	661	D	212	94	D	8	12	17 828	121	21.5	4.1	49.6
Fond du Lac	2 461	44 586	5 273	11 589	6 220	1 630	2 198	1 269	28 461	1 634	27.2	8.8	67.0
Forest	306	2 366	288	372	325	79	85	50	21 117	164	23.8	11.0	40.9
Grant	1 252	13 929	1 956	3 028	2 301	815	400	297	21 330	2 490	20.2	10.1	63.9
Green	924	12 519	1 988	3 128	3 079	371	278	315	25 179	1 490	30.5	8.4	63.2
Green Lake	615	6 840	1 071	1 905	1 240	192	136	166	24 333	670	23.0	9.6	64.5
Iowa	629	10 117	859	973	5 343	191	179	270	26 736	1 686	23.1	9.9	51.7
Iron	223	2 072	315	334	368	D	28	39	19 038	62	12.9	11.3	51.6
Jackson	414	4 938	557	855	850	194	126	136	27 570	914	19.7	12.6	55.3
Jefferson	1 944	32 493	3 760	11 862	3 690	631	527	854	26 282	1 421	37.1	6.4	55.0
Juneau	670	8 170	888	2 719	1 021	173	134	193	23 665	805	26.8	8.9	53.7
Kenosha	3 147	48 734	6 930	11 013	7 178	844	1 007	1 379	28 289	466	51.9	8.6	53.9
Kewaunee	492	5 781	669	2 401	629	177	122	154	26 638	915	27.2	7.0	66.2
La Crosse	2 967	57 587	11 237	9 424	9 234	2 264	1 940	1 528	26 540	868	24.0	9.2	52.3
Lafayette	340	2 981	205	645	494	160	57	67	22 504	1 205	24.1	13.3	65.6
Langlade	598	6 527	878	1 651	1 204	214	82	153	23 462	542	22.1	11.4	62.4
Lincoln	768	9 145	1 032	3 209	1 580	227	150	226	24 736	593	27.0	5.1	60.7
Manitowoc	1 928	33 636	4 124	13 129	4 255	780	711	938	27 880	1 469	35.1	6.7	60.8
Marathon	3 401	61 840	6 919	17 695	8 263	4 844	1 721	1 844	29 812	2 898	25.8	5.9	62.9
Marinette	1 093	16 812	2 527	6 413	2 117	403	201	439	26 111	729	25.8	8.5	58.0
Marquette	340	3 285	284	1 321	450	79	29	82	24 920	624	25.8	10.6	52.9
Menominee	93	1 606	D	D	180	D	0	32	19 686	4	75.0	0.0	0.0
Milwaukee	21 210	475 478	78 313	72 605	46 670	40 043	24 323	16 792	35 316	78	62.8	1.3	57.7
Monroe	863	14 325	2 215	4 266	1 909	504	217	346	24 169	1 938	22.5	6.6	59.1
Oconto	857	8 643	949	2 903	1 129	227	185	207	23 956	1 132	22.3	6.7	59.2
Oneida	1 581	16 315	3 416	2 084	3 715	385	437	429	26 301	183	24.6	14.8	51.9
Outagamie	4 704	96 910	8 495	22 095	13 186	7 032	3 274	3 093	31 911	1 430	36.7	8.1	61.7
Ozaukee	2 866	37 848	3 756	12 221	4 799	1 702	1 745	1 253	33 119	533	41.8	4.3	56.7
Pepin	199	1 793	258	D	344	78	35	43	23 950	501	23.0	9.0	60.3
Pierce	828	6 706	531	1 118	1 264	307	269	159	23 714	1 510	30.6	6.2	53.8
Polk	1 080	11 832	1 998	3 868	1 630	351	302	287	24 297	1 659	28.7	7.7	49.9
Portage	1 618	26 869	2 581	5 166	3 840	4 057	990	759	28 265	1 197	27.6	9.2	56.1
Price	471	5 731	922	2 563	695	184	75	144	25 064	477	15.9	9.2	55.3
Racine	4 155	71 225	9 860	18 477	9 913	1 719	2 316	2 361	33 155	631	53.2	8.9	57.2
Richland	371	4 400	548	1 450	1 037	135	71	108	24 474	1 358	19.5	9.9	53.8
Rock	3 346	58 409	7 199	15 812	8 454	1 605	1 286	1 794	30 715	1 529	45.4	10.2	56.3
Rusk	325	4 544	635	1 890	657	92	D	107	23 570	715	13.8	9.4	60.6
St. Croix	1 723	21 651	2 790	5 777	3 654	508	756	587	27 089	1 864	35.7	6.4	50.5
Sauk	1 678	25 706	3 040	6 667	4 526	917	748	692	26 927	1 673	22.6	9.4	56.2
Sawyer	667	5 162	589	819	829	176	125	114	22 107	230	15.7	10.0	58.7
Shawano	920	10 686	1 528	2 089	1 752	266	226	245	22 900	1 465	23.6	6.7	68.8
Sheboygan	2 582	58 212	5 635	22 964	6 184	1 780	1 379	1 784	30 652	1 116	40.9	8.3	61.7
Taylor	462	7 486	970	3 092	934	271	91	195	26 027	1 056	17.2	8.6	64.8
Trempealeau	666	9 813	1 099	4 770	1 124	313	157	268	27 339	1 744	17.6	8.2	56.1
Vernon	637	6 448	1 540	1 152	1 201	327	144	137	21 269	2 230	22.9	5.5	60.6
Vilas	798	4 418	374	333	750	131	73	95	21 519	71	52.1	7.0	54.9
Walworth	2 592	35 437	3 430	10 066	4 378	725	1 027	930	26 249	988	41.1	11.2	56.8
Washburn	569	4 544	773	936	885	150	122	97	21 365	471	16.1	9.1	53.7
Washington	3 121	47 419	4 787	15 401	6 386	1 844	1 090	1 401	29 538	844	39.7	6.2	65.4
Waukesha	12 526	220 919	20 113	47 985	25 345	11 571	11 618	8 040	36 394	762	58.3	5.5	50.4
Waupaca	1 356	17 404	2 432	5 852	2 605	589	255	447	25 696	1 398	28.5	7.2	58.7
Waushara	525	4 650	670	877	825	104	334	89	19 247	717	28.7	10.9	58.7
Winnebago	3 719	80 820	9 972	26 401	8 721	2 756	2 045	2 708	33 505	963	32.6	8.1	60.5
Wood	1 892	38 702	8 660	8 923	5 771	1 122	588	1 218	31 458	1 108	26.1	8.5	65.7
WYOMING	18 453	178 299	25 615	9 282	29 408	6 918	6 577	4 918	27 581	9 422	21.4	44.5	61.1
Albany	1 048	10 038	1 685	562	1 959	396	784	210	20 947	320	9.4	61.9	61.6
Big Horn	290	2 574	320	319	317	90	D	71	27 690	501	25.5	27.9	60.7
Campbell	1 246	15 886	1 271	269	1 888	293	430	600	37 745	532	16.2	61.8	60.3
Carbon	572	4 513	602	D	762	130	96	112	24 873	290	17.6	56.6	65.9
Converse	384	2 780	374	36	432	91	D	76	27 372	339	13.9	58.4	64.9

STATE County	Acreage (1,000)	Percent change, 1997–2002	Average size of farm	Total irrigated (1,000)	Total cropland (1,000)	Average per farm	Average per acre	Value of machinery and equipment average per farm (dollars)	Total (mil dol)	Average per farm (dollars)	Crops	Live-stock and poultry products	$10,000 or more	$100,000 or more	Total ($1,000)	Percent of farms
	117	118	119	120	121	122	123	124	125	126	127	128	129	130	131	132

WISCONSIN—Cont'd

STATE County	117	118	119	120	121	122	123	124	125	126	127	128	129	130	131	132
Dodge	404	3.1	205	0	341	483 293	2 460	111 569	179	90 888	30.0	70.0	59.2	26.4	8 640	54.9
Door	135	10.7	154	1	99	380 435	2 132	67 519	40	45 702	37.9	62.1	37.9	12.3	1 885	44.7
Douglas	85	19.7	217	0	39	288 771	1 251	26 576	5	12 009	33.7	66.2	18.9	2.8	74	4.3
Dunn	399	8.1	237	26	255	433 524	1 838	66 769	104	61 544	32.9	67.1	40.1	15.6	6 237	56.3
Eau Claire	204	6.8	174	3	133	305 577	1 783	46 570	50	42 566	35.4	64.6	39.3	11.6	2 948	51.6
Florence	21	10.5	177	D	11	235 958	1 265	43 537	1	11 900	31.3	68.7	23.1	0.8	58	20.7
Fond du Lac	344	5.8	211	1	292	514 396	2 351	97 653	166	101 700	25.0	75.0	57.2	27.7	7 894	62.9
Forest	34	30.8	205	D	14	290 839	1 420	30 287	4	21 503	20.8	79.3	28.7	6.1	46	16.5
Grant	606	1.0	243	0	375	481 634	1 925	81 950	187	74 958	20.8	79.2	57.5	24.7	11 189	60.4
Green	307	0.7	206	5	248	493 188	2 271	85 736	117	78 668	23.1	76.9	54.5	25.8	7 430	58.2
Green Lake	148	10.4	221	3	116	447 838	1 981	65 190	46	68 294	43.5	56.5	52.7	19.6	2 627	61.0
Iowa	367	1.0	218	7	217	490 693	2 243	62 660	116	69 051	25.3	74.7	42.9	19.2	7 304	66.7
Iron	13	30.0	206	D	6	222 960	1 088	33 524	D	D	D	D	30.6	4.8	44	11.3
Jackson	258	5.7	282	5	133	435 336	1 603	65 511	70	76 329	45.7	54.3	45.4	17.6	2 855	56.5
Jefferson	248	2.5	174	10	194	555 490	3 087	90 242	139	97 621	46.2	53.8	45.2	15.3	3 951	55.1
Juneau	180	6.5	224	9	109	421 416	1 870	72 155	51	63 279	52.7	47.3	36.9	13.2	2 165	51.8
Kenosha	89	4.7	190	0	78	865 884	4 513	88 700	34	73 043	66.4	33.6	42.9	17.0	1 407	37.1
Kewaunee	174	8.1	190	0	143	485 851	2 523	100 913	105	114 551	23.3	76.7	50.2	24.0	4 060	59.6
La Crosse	174	2.4	201	1	95	425 490	1 937	59 139	42	47 987	23.3	76.7	41.1	15.9	2 240	48.6
Lafayette	343	1.5	284	0	264	643 185	2 113	110 598	131	109 057	29.1	70.9	61.1	33.2	7 676	59.3
Langlade	141	13.7	260	15	88	423 591	1 717	90 514	56	103 971	66.5	33.5	45.4	18.6	1 006	27.5
Lincoln	98	16.7	166	0	51	277 180	1 566	52 590	24	40 091	40.0	60.0	36.4	11.3	770	21.9
Manitowoc	257	4.9	175	0	210	490 353	2 808	89 166	147	100 271	14.0	86.0	46.0	22.9	6 141	51.3
Marathon	531	2.9	183	6	341	327 014	1 846	72 025	205	70 890	17.1	82.9	50.1	19.0	7 501	29.9
Marinette	149	12.9	204	2	91	344 361	1 705	73 174	41	56 036	23.0	77.0	36.9	13.7	1 742	37.3
Marquette	146	16.8	233	5	93	481 505	2 139	65 603	38	60 188	47.2	52.8	36.1	11.1	1 495	44.4
Menominee	0	NA	89	0	0	63 250	715	12 500	D	D	D	D	0.0	0.0	D	D
Milwaukee	6	0.0	72	0	4	449 510	6 418	39 603	9	115 306	96.6	3.4	53.8	25.6	62	21.8
Monroe	352	6.7	182	4	186	345 102	1 910	54 494	103	52 927	27.3	72.7	45.2	13.4	4 214	44.2
Oconto	219	7.4	193	1	154	398 963	2 011	56 822	74	65 360	20.7	79.3	41.8	17.8	3 331	48.7
Oneida	51	30.8	279	3	20	570 840	2 068	46 625	13	69 410	81.4	18.6	26.2	13.7	44	6.6
Outagamie	263	4.4	184	0	221	555 885	3 166	89 987	146	102 431	21.7	78.3	51.6	24.9	6 194	52.8
Ozaukee	75	7.1	142	0	63	579 814	4 043	62 885	38	71 901	37.8	62.2	44.8	21.2	1 602	51.6
Pepin	111	6.7	222	1	69	417 311	1 847	61 754	35	69 431	20.8	79.2	55.1	19.2	1 559	63.1
Pierce	267	-0.4	177	0	182	439 725	2 320	60 998	72	47 900	33.1	66.9	41.3	13.5	4 610	52.7
Polk	293	9.3	177	1	186	381 997	2 150	46 858	72	43 696	26.8	73.2	31.2	10.8	3 536	49.3
Portage	292	11.0	244	92	211	735 832	3 010	97 225	139	116 081	71.3	28.7	42.1	16.0	3 187	34.5
Price	104	11.8	218	D	47	332 385	1 418	40 972	15	31 315	29.2	70.8	35.0	7.8	542	19.5
Racine	124	0.8	197	5	109	800 951	4 275	74 494	73	115 949	50.9	49.1	43.6	15.7	1 726	35.2
Richland	258	8.4	190	2	133	411 654	2 182	51 167	52	38 529	18.3	81.7	36.2	9.6	3 085	57.4
Rock	344	-2.0	225	16	302	705 051	3 452	77 699	118	77 242	53.8	46.2	43.4	17.2	6 849	54.2
Rusk	173	8.8	242	0	86	494 420	1 917	70 225	30	42 325	10.0	90.0	42.2	13.3	1 449	33.4
St. Croix	310	-0.6	166	4	233	520 418	3 229	54 852	98	52 502	29.2	70.8	34.2	11.6	5 677	54.1
Sauk	353	6.0	211	12	223	551 470	2 712	76 711	116	69 375	21.5	78.5	46.4	18.4	5 368	57.5
Sawyer	54	12.5	235	0	29	460 891	1 986	51 303	13	54 368	47.4	52.6	37.0	13.5	287	17.4
Shawano	271	0.4	185	0	188	484 166	2 512	71 699	130	88 816	10.1	89.9	54.2	22.6	5 198	50.7
Sheboygan	195	7.1	175	0	167	498 165	2 953	77 259	104	93 154	20.6	79.4	50.3	23.4	3 956	43.9
Taylor	257	14.7	244	0	133	318 219	1 340	57 930	56	52 948	11.0	89.0	47.7	17.6	2 702	33.5
Trempealeau	368	7.9	211	6	220	383 248	1 794	60 664	120	68 660	18.0	82.0	42.2	15.0	5 681	64.2
Vernon	382	11.0	171	0	219	320 270	1 768	49 612	90	40 453	19.4	80.6	45.0	10.7	4 217	41.9
Vilas	10	25.0	137	1	5	447 826	3 156	93 615	5	71 009	96.9	3.1	22.5	11.3	D	D
Walworth	220	0.0	222	2	186	854 302	3 909	97 364	88	88 563	43.0	57.0	47.5	20.1	4 318	48.9
Washburn	105	7.1	224	2	47	355 917	1 741	51 740	17	36 363	32.7	67.3	32.5	8.3	548	31.0
Washington	130	2.4	154	1	105	698 726	4 051	85 299	73	86 342	38.2	61.8	52.1	20.6	2 509	40.2
Waukesha	98	-7.5	129	1	81	615 239	4 735	63 282	36	47 087	65.2	34.8	35.0	11.9	1 772	28.9
Waupaca	247	8.8	177	8	172	386 288	2 151	62 161	86	61 675	20.9	79.1	44.0	15.4	4 314	47.6
Waushara	193	10.3	269	49	137	725 229	2 589	93 896	86	119 776	77.8	22.2	40.2	17.3	1 872	41.4
Winnebago	170	1.8	177	0	138	418 923	2 519	73 577	58	60 541	33.4	66.6	41.3	14.6	2 920	53.0
Wood	228	4.1	206	6	140	390 246	1 825	73 246	80	72 528	40.1	59.9	52.0	20.0	2 427	37.5
WYOMING	34 403	0.9	3 651	1 542	2 990	1 080 945	290	74 757	864	91 688	15.9	84.1	53.2	19.2	37 913	33.6
Albany	2 384	24.0	7 451	139	100	1 607 037	228	66 210	28	88 643	6.8	93.2	55.0	23.1	612	22.2
Big Horn	412	-7.0	822	99	131	535 864	718	87 758	37	74 295	41.9	58.1	56.9	18.6	1 489	29.7
Campbell	2 986	1.4	5 613	8	196	1 138 227	177	72 806	33	62 251	1.3	98.7	52.4	16.7	2 937	33.1
Carbon	2 330	2.1	8 033	125	143	1 732 070	214	100 367	43	148 766	2.4	97.6	60.3	29.7	2 200	33.4
Converse	2 518	0.1	7 427	39	71	1 210 588	154	75 742	31	92 890	5.5	94.5	57.5	24.5	2 742	36.6

STATE County	Value of residential construction authorized by building permits, 2003		Wholesale trade, 1997				Retail trade,[1] 1997				Real estate and rental and leasing, 1997			
	New construction ($1,000)	Number of housing units	Number of establishments	Number of employees	Sales (mil dol)	Annual payroll (mil dol)	Number of establishments	Number of employees	Sales (mil dol)	Annual payroll (mil dol)	Number of establishments	Number of employees	Receipts (mil dol)	Annual payroll (mil dol)
	133	134	135	136	137	138	139	140	141	142	143	144	145	146
WISCONSIN—Cont'd														
Dodge	62 056	446	86	1 087	528.9	33.7	277	3 220	544.2	49.6	39	161	9.8	1.7
Door	51 955	406	34	159	38.9	3.3	281	1 581	258.9	24.8	55	107	14.5	1.8
Douglas	24 171	252	59	D	D	D	161	2 075	334.1	31.1	40	146	10.0	1.8
Dunn	32 966	316	43	433	98.2	9.5	156	2 060	324.0	30.0	28	50	5.1	0.5
Eau Claire	87 241	610	135	1 463	613.5	42.2	459	7 405	1 036.0	100.7	100	456	45.5	7.1
Florence	0	0	5	D	D	D	12	78	15.1	0.8	5	6	0.5	0.1
Fond du Lac	69 880	484	116	1 204	528.2	36.0	413	5 744	891.2	86.6	73	297	27.9	4.5
Forest	7 519	120	11	76	13.5	1.9	42	345	50.9	4.9	9	30	2.3	0.2
Grant	15 018	124	66	613	174.5	11.2	243	2 310	357.6	32.3	50	126	9.7	1.1
Green	45 254	313	66	588	208.8	14.1	181	3 025	572.9	66.3	18	41	7.0	0.4
Green Lake	16 125	83	19	149	32.6	3.8	113	1 297	161.4	15.7	15	42	3.0	0.4
Iowa	25 396	245	39	331	109.9	10.7	105	4 409	1 211.4	107.7	9	30	2.9	0.2
Iron	11 626	96	8	48	11.9	1.1	38	337	49.4	4.5	11	50	3.2	0.6
Jackson	13 698	130	10	74	8.7	1.1	83	919	124.7	11.6	12	24	3.9	0.6
Jefferson	70 150	493	92	1 483	466.5	42.2	253	3 519	568.2	53.1	54	177	16.5	3.0
Juneau	22 905	218	22	200	77.5	4.5	102	1 056	170.5	15.1	15	31	1.9	0.2
Kenosha	192 069	1 446	135	2 515	1 385.3	91.5	546	6 442	1 072.4	95.7	112	412	43.8	6.6
Kewaunee	18 546	130	20	139	35.5	3.4	72	655	113.6	10.3	8	11	1.0	0.1
La Crosse	84 358	584	154	3 217	1 921.6	102.5	509	9 005	1 452.6	135.6	120	774	59.2	13.3
Lafayette	10 945	84	23	170	62.2	4.0	62	526	94.8	8.8	4	4	0.3	0.0
Langlade	16 735	172	39	348	217.8	11.0	114	1 270	255.7	20.5	10	38	2.0	0.4
Lincoln	27 659	227	25	D	D	D	142	1 504	220.1	20.6	26	82	3.9	0.6
Manitowoc	38 047	299	67	611	257.1	22.0	295	3 856	561.0	55.1	50	183	14.1	2.2
Marathon	163 006	1 395	221	3 395	1 002.0	102.5	565	9 236	1 421.6	142.6	86	439	39.9	7.1
Marinette	30 820	268	33	485	93.2	14.8	187	2 008	285.9	27.4	26	45	5.3	0.6
Marquette	15 014	130	10	D	D	D	47	444	56.6	5.6	10	32	1.5	0.3
Menominee	2 613	19	2	D	D	D	13	113	15.2	1.2	1	D	D	D
Milwaukee	275 807	2 138	1 393	22 559	13 007.5	845.3	3 224	52 471	8 065.2	839.2	875	6 745	827.5	145.6
Monroe	18 450	199	46	465	241.6	12.2	139	1 618	261.8	22.8	25	85	5.6	1.1
Oconto	49 176	440	28	121	45.1	3.8	118	1 017	178.6	14.2	22	37	2.3	0.4
Oneida	58 514	447	45	441	119.9	12.8	294	3 030	471.5	45.3	63	212	24.9	4.0
Outagamie	187 833	1 278	291	4 066	1 694.0	147.5	712	11 218	1 936.3	182.2	124	702	75.6	15.0
Ozaukee	129 187	596	204	1 314	627.1	49.6	352	4 453	940.1	75.3	78	322	36.7	7.9
Pepin	4 879	42	11	90	27.4	2.1	38	434	88.7	8.6	3	6	0.6	0.1
Pierce	58 626	377	29	D	D	D	112	1 047	151.6	13.6	19	185	27.7	6.0
Polk	60 527	506	38	432	112.5	11.0	183	1 552	221.6	19.7	26	73	7.5	0.6
Portage	56 919	417	93	1 307	380.9	39.8	262	3 916	603.2	56.8	53	191	18.8	2.9
Price	18 090	193	19	211	41.5	3.3	97	726	106.9	9.9	4	12	1.5	0.2
Racine	180 204	1 188	234	4 560	3 816.9	142.4	664	9 693	1 564.1	142.0	132	746	57.7	12.1
Richland	9 353	75	16	122	32.2	1.6	76	821	128.5	11.4	11	25	1.6	0.2
Rock	111 146	988	152	2 823	1 706.4	95.8	584	8 484	1 599.7	148.4	105	364	52.9	5.6
Rusk	5 287	59	9	35	4.8	0.6	62	486	78.7	6.7	8	23	1.6	0.3
St. Croix	216 817	1 525	80	484	210.3	14.9	224	3 053	590.3	52.2	59	333	21.1	5.1
Sauk	76 421	666	68	1 090	426.4	33.6	295	4 083	582.6	62.2	45	184	22.6	3.4
Sawyer	34 371	333	8	79	23.8	3.4	100	778	133.6	12.0	24	53	5.3	0.6
Shawano	32 603	301	40	450	191.8	12.3	153	1 747	267.5	26.2	20	67	4.4	0.8
Sheboygan	89 104	599	119	2 041	1 185.0	65.4	398	5 831	911.0	88.0	85	400	38.2	6.2
Taylor	5 897	59	19	467	80.8	9.1	88	896	141.8	11.4	11	54	4.3	1.0
Trempealeau	16 848	128	39	215	125.6	5.2	126	1 017	169.4	13.5	18	49	7.3	0.8
Vernon	10 005	96	37	217	75.6	4.5	108	1 139	161.1	16.9	17	32	1.7	0.2
Vilas	44 201	336	20	69	17.0	1.5	150	764	122.8	12.8	24	D	D	D
Walworth	157 864	1 088	128	1 554	883.1	46.8	371	3 880	627.2	59.2	94	299	33.0	5.2
Washburn	29 957	277	16	90	21.9	2.1	96	975	173.6	15.4	23	70	7.0	0.9
Washington	201 664	1 226	181	2 658	1 107.9	97.0	390	5 184	1 201.5	86.0	76	276	35.0	4.1
Waukesha	471 050	2 507	1 272	16 570	11 523.8	672.1	1 385	24 345	4 094.2	392.4	413	2 432	352.9	65.0
Waupaca	75 484	499	58	406	116.3	9.5	242	2 473	416.3	36.8	34	98	7.2	1.3
Waushara	26 411	226	21	156	54.5	3.6	91	817	148.3	12.9	17	31	3.8	0.5
Winnebago	175 419	1 460	194	3 387	1 088.8	111.9	611	8 712	1 489.6	141.4	148	711	65.2	11.5
Wood	52 680	548	85	1 421	636.9	44.1	355	5 177	950.5	83.0	60	248	19.8	3.3
WYOMING	389 272	2 814	800	5 761	2 547.1	161.9	2 939	26 934	4 530.5	426.7	717	2 463	220.8	39.5
Albany	27 051	271	24	132	84.9	2.7	168	1 663	339.7	27.5	47	129	9.5	1.5
Big Horn	745	6	15	64	14.9	1.2	59	340	50.7	5.0	10	D	D	D
Campbell	22 671	159	78	658	235.4	22.9	179	1 733	280.3	28.0	37	142	11.4	1.8
Carbon	4 072	33	18	70	25.5	1.3	103	847	141.2	11.7	22	46	3.5	0.5
Converse	3 261	54	15	128	42.0	2.2	59	430	64.2	5.6	11	19	1.7	0.1

1. Establishments with payroll.

Table B. States and Counties — Professional Services, Manufacturing, and Accommodation and Foodservices

STATE County	Professional, scientific, and technical services,[1] 1997				Manufacturing, 1997				Accommodation and foodservices, 1997			
	Number of establishments	Number of employees	Receipts (mil dol)	Annual payroll (mil dol)	Number of establishments	Number of employees	Receipts (mil dol)	Annual payroll (mil dol)	Number of establishments	Number of employees	Sales (mil dol)	Annual payroll (mil dol)
	147	148	149	150	151	152	153	154	155	156	157	158
WISCONSIN—Cont'd												
Dodge	64	417	33.6	10.9	164	12 667	3 159.9	413.8	165	1 637	41.6	10.7
Door	64	251	14.7	5.0	63	2 222	267.5	59.7	243	1 796	96.4	25.1
Douglas	52	317	21.5	8.2	56	1 543	500.2	45.4	178	1 818	50.9	13.1
Dunn	43	289	17.5	7.9	60	2 910	875.4	92.0	107	1 383	33.4	9.4
Eau Claire	165	1 485	112.2	48.5	107	4 182	651.3	110.9	247	4 932	115.9	34.6
Florence	4	9	0.3	0.1	NA	NA	NA	NA	16	D	D	D
Fond du Lac	137	630	45.9	18.0	158	11 150	2 115.7	393.2	227	3 584	92.9	25.6
Forest	9	66	3.8	2.0	NA	NA	NA	NA	35	D	D	D
Grant	50	298	18.9	7.8	57	2 996	718.1	68.5	139	1 431	34.7	8.5
Green	43	180	14.2	4.4	77	3 667	840.2	93.5	92	1 182	29.1	8.3
Green Lake	24	89	5.4	1.4	61	2 383	262.0	55.8	62	707	20.0	5.7
Iowa	31	106	5.5	2.2	34	815	156.7	18.4	52	D	D	D
Iron	13	25	1.8	0.6	12	534	64.2	10.5	53	440	11.3	2.7
Jackson	25	103	4.3	2.2	20	810	134.2	17.8	52	685	17.1	4.5
Jefferson	90	598	33.0	13.6	165	12 201	2 431.5	371.8	187	2 098	52.8	13.9
Juneau	26	118	5.7	2.8	47	3 503	522.7	103.0	86	979	34.2	10.1
Kenosha	176	687	47.7	20.4	204	9 526	2 031.0	396.2	340	4 546	133.3	37.1
Kewaunee	23	73	4.3	1.4	45	2 359	314.0	67.1	53	512	11.6	2.8
La Crosse	191	1 531	117.1	52.5	161	10 171	1 382.6	313.7	300	5 533	141.9	41.4
Lafayette	15	23	1.6	0.4	21	661	134.4	14.5	36	256	5.5	1.5
Langlade	15	79	3.8	2.1	39	1 493	184.0	35.9	75	677	18.8	5.2
Lincoln	31	81	5.1	1.6	63	3 637	532.4	101.2	98	894	21.3	6.3
Manitowoc	86	538	41.8	11.9	180	13 474	2 134.1	407.2	179	2 512	59.4	16.4
Marathon	181	1 264	127.4	46.6	232	16 839	3 181.9	502.6	276	3 779	105.2	29.7
Marinette	42	132	9.1	4.0	82	6 766	1 139.1	217.9	140	1 386	36.2	9.9
Marquette	12	27	1.9	0.4	24	996	135.8	27.3	59	D	D	D
Menominee	NA	NA	NA	NA	6	705	51.0	16.6	9	D	D	D
Milwaukee	2 027	20 568	2 101.0	837.7	1 463	86 933	16 535.5	3 213.2	1 838	31 293	1 005.6	280.5
Monroe	36	143	8.7	3.4	58	3 397	745.0	79.9	110	1 186	35.8	9.3
Oconto	33	129	7.0	2.9	61	2 445	297.7	56.6	107	953	26.2	6.3
Oneida	89	363	25.7	10.3	68	2 526	395.3	78.3	209	1 903	61.6	16.9
Outagamie	275	2 371	199.9	86.7	303	21 410	5 315.4	750.7	361	6 755	192.1	53.5
Ozaukee	321	1 443	156.2	55.8	242	13 420	2 763.1	485.8	182	2 900	75.0	22.0
Pepin	6	29	1.4	0.4	NA	NA	NA	NA	26	D	D	D
Pierce	47	158	10.0	4.3	40	942	216.7	24.7	102	994	24.3	6.1
Polk	55	198	11.2	3.8	95	3 912	628.1	90.7	118	904	26.4	7.0
Portage	80	521	33.3	14.6	83	5 534	1 265.8	178.3	202	3 337	86.2	24.6
Price	23	80	4.6	1.8	46	2 957	449.6	91.7	42	D	D	D
Racine	296	1 821	134.3	55.6	379	18 869	5 229.5	664.1	360	5 324	154.7	42.2
Richland	19	67	2.9	1.1	26	1 851	373.3	52.7	32	D	D	D
Rock	182	1 002	65.1	23.5	234	19 547	10 105.6	785.3	343	5 295	151.2	41.3
Rusk	12	30	1.2	0.4	30	1 722	203.1	41.0	42	D	D	D
St. Croix	124	754	93.7	36.0	150	5 867	827.0	174.3	142	1 962	52.9	15.3
Sauk	76	549	37.0	16.8	114	6 570	1 121.2	180.8	241	3 276	123.6	32.9
Sawyer	24	76	4.2	1.6	39	859	137.3	22.4	109	613	24.3	6.1
Shawano	27	144	5.5	3.1	67	1 985	330.3	51.0	109	1 147	32.9	8.6
Sheboygan	150	1 235	92.2	40.5	239	20 047	4 252.7	628.3	237	3 714	105.9	29.1
Taylor	17	59	2.9	1.4	43	2 987	592.7	83.8	39	D	D	D
Trempealeau	29	177	7.7	3.9	62	4 678	799.9	121.8	85	713	17.1	4.9
Vernon	24	103	3.6	1.3	37	970	168.1	20.7	66	D	D	D
Vilas	20	54	3.2	1.1	NA	NA	NA	NA	188	1 451	69.9	17.3
Walworth	158	649	57.3	20.0	218	10 377	1 496.2	311.7	276	5 518	168.1	53.1
Washburn	25	126	7.7	3.2	35	793	94.7	17.1	80	521	17.6	4.3
Washington	162	1 254	102.0	26.3	321	15 660	2 360.2	499.2	217	3 737	93.7	25.7
Waukesha	1 142	9 380	1 031.1	377.8	1 148	49 130	9 434.6	1 760.3	635	11 945	372.6	104.4
Waupaca	51	165	8.7	3.1	105	5 995	1 235.3	176.0	139	1 583	41.8	11.1
Waushara	18	51	2.5	0.9	32	746	79.2	14.9	70	D	D	D
Winnebago	202	1 630	142.9	46.0	316	27 191	6 026.6	976.5	341	5 832	153.7	43.4
Wood	77	518	33.0	12.2	117	9 421	2 535.6	363.3	191	2 468	65.3	17.3
WYOMING	1 264	5 274	388.8	146.9	503	8 448	2 955.1	256.4	1 751	24 950	808.9	219.0
Albany	108	549	40.6	17.1	33	531	89.1	13.5	104	1 922	45.1	12.8
Big Horn	10	33	2.4	1.0	NA	NA	NA	NA	32	215	4.8	1.5
Campbell	80	336	22.3	8.2	NA	NA	NA	NA	77	1 346	41.9	11.1
Carbon	26	73	6.6	1.4	NA	NA	NA	NA	85	781	25.8	6.8
Converse	21	68	4.1	1.4	NA	NA	NA	NA	45	474	12.7	3.3

1. Firms subject to federal tax.

Table B. States and Counties — **Health Care and Social Assistance, Other Services, and Federal Funds**

STATE County	Health care and social assistance,[1] 1997				Other services,[1] 1997				Federal funds and grants, 2002–2003 Expenditures (mil dol)			
										Direct payments for individuals[2]		
	Number of establishments	Number of employees	Receipts (mil dol)	Annual payroll (mil dol)	Number of establishments	Number of employees	Receipts (mil dol)	Annual payroll (mil dol)	Total	Social Security and government retirement	Medicare	Food stamps and Supplemental Security Income
	159	160	161	162	163	164	165	166	167	168	169	170
WISCONSIN—Cont'd												
Dodge	137	1 252	70.0	34.5	113	402	22.2	6.0	268.1	132.1	51.3	3.4
Door	56	512	23.8	11.2	55	207	12.7	2.8	164.2	82.7	30.9	1.6
Douglas	53	718	33.5	16.0	68	397	22.5	6.0	261.9	115.4	40.9	8.1
Dunn	39	1 003	31.5	16.3	59	268	13.2	3.5	163.7	67.9	20.6	4.8
Eau Claire	180	3 052	196.1	111.8	205	1 242	64.2	19.3	414.3	177.0	66.2	12.2
Florence	4	92	3.3	1.8	3	D	D	D	24.4	13.0	4.5	0.5
Fond du Lac	157	1 748	181.2	54.2	162	945	44.4	13.7	423.8	213.1	76.9	6.3
Forest	10	326	7.5	3.3	10	21	1.4	0.4	68.5	28.3	8.9	1.1
Grant	78	969	35.0	14.4	103	331	18.7	4.2	256.2	113.5	44.6	4.3
Green	52	767	55.7	25.8	73	271	19.0	5.3	155.1	71.0	27.8	1.9
Green Lake	46	334	15.5	7.3	32	104	6.9	1.6	104.1	50.7	19.9	1.3
Iowa	39	303	18.7	7.8	27	81	5.7	1.2	94.0	37.7	13.5	1.3
Iron	10	251	8.2	3.9	10	36	1.2	0.3	43.4	21.0	8.2	0.5
Jackson	18	221	12.3	5.1	25	66	3.4	0.7	100.8	43.8	13.6	2.1
Jefferson	135	1 397	70.7	32.8	129	553	28.3	8.3	330.8	165.0	64.0	3.6
Juneau	31	300	13.9	5.8	40	155	9.4	2.5	158.7	72.1	23.2	2.5
Kenosha	263	2 517	136.9	65.9	222	1 262	68.1	19.3	607.0	286.4	119.1	18.6
Kewaunee	34	251	7.4	3.3	28	76	4.8	1.0	89.0	44.2	16.7	0.7
La Crosse	139	1 013	57.5	26.8	193	1 271	65.1	20.7	533.0	211.4	68.8	13.9
Lafayette	17	79	5.4	1.4	25	68	5.2	0.9	88.2	31.4	13.6	0.9
Langlade	26	374	17.9	8.2	41	150	7.5	1.9	117.1	55.8	21.6	2.1
Lincoln	40	453	22.2	11.8	43	190	10.3	3.1	151.9	78.3	29.0	2.2
Manitowoc	129	1 362	78.1	41.3	129	496	27.9	7.9	366.4	190.2	73.4	6.1
Marathon	200	2 672	188.8	104.9	222	1 201	79.2	20.9	537.6	231.4	85.2	13.5
Marinette	68	1 006	50.0	26.1	53	202	11.8	3.3	251.1	123.5	41.5	4.6
Marquette	18	216	8.8	4.5	21	64	3.9	1.0	92.8	51.7	17.2	1.3
Menominee	1	D	D	D	3	D	D	D	55.3	7.7	2.6	1.8
Milwaukee	2 074	27 274	1 753.0	942.9	1 412	9 778	580.6	187.3	6 003.5	1 839.3	1 033.8	289.7
Monroe	38	360	15.7	7.6	65	310	14.4	4.6	377.3	122.0	26.3	3.9
Oconto	40	559	19.8	9.7	50	86	6.4	1.1	152.9	76.4	25.9	2.7
Oneida	80	1 272	67.5	30.2	89	336	24.0	6.0	220.5	116.5	39.3	3.6
Outagamie	287	3 049	217.2	111.8	303	2 270	130.9	38.9	615.3	301.7	83.9	9.4
Ozaukee	209	1 958	112.6	53.2	161	877	41.9	13.8	329.8	180.9	56.2	1.7
Pepin	9	117	4.8	2.6	8	29	1.7	0.4	38.6	17.5	7.4	0.5
Pierce	48	646	22.1	11.5	46	168	9.8	2.7	143.0	65.6	21.3	1.6
Polk	58	652	33.8	15.9	63	226	12.3	3.2	183.2	91.5	32.9	2.9
Portage	93	1 220	68.3	39.5	101	554	44.5	10.8	253.0	117.7	38.1	5.5
Price	21	328	10.8	5.2	22	59	3.6	0.8	90.9	44.7	16.2	1.8
Racine	265	3 771	263.8	132.8	291	2 195	125.4	40.3	822.9	400.4	147.3	26.6
Richland	20	156	10.4	5.6	19	58	4.5	0.9	88.6	37.0	14.4	2.1
Rock	223	3 402	196.2	97.5	241	1 052	63.8	16.8	745.5	312.1	117.4	21.4
Rusk	21	248	7.3	3.3	21	44	3.3	0.7	89.0	38.4	13.1	2.2
St. Croix	80	787	44.6	21.7	90	324	21.3	5.6	193.8	99.2	30.1	2.1
Sauk	98	1 358	67.3	33.9	97	345	23.1	5.8	248.6	119.5	45.5	3.9
Sawyer	26	199	8.7	4.3	33	112	6.4	1.7	144.1	46.0	15.8	2.6
Shawano	44	902	28.5	12.7	56	203	13.3	2.9	198.4	93.3	32.5	2.8
Sheboygan	176	2 412	134.3	74.8	172	967	56.5	14.6	452.7	234.0	80.8	8.2
Taylor	23	276	11.4	6.3	31	97	7.1	1.5	86.4	38.4	15.5	1.5
Trempealeau	32	207	7.6	3.6	50	168	10.6	2.4	157.1	64.6	23.7	2.6
Vernon	38	259	12.0	5.8	46	72	4.5	0.9	151.7	65.4	20.9	2.9
Vilas	20	99	4.9	2.0	34	99	6.0	1.4	144.8	73.0	25.0	1.5
Walworth	168	1 504	71.9	33.9	137	496	26.8	7.9	344.6	182.0	65.6	4.4
Washburn	22	264	12.0	6.1	31	95	5.9	1.3	121.9	59.2	15.6	2.1
Washington	168	1 700	82.6	37.6	195	1 374	85.8	24.1	391.3	221.0	69.6	3.6
Waukesha	800	9 241	551.7	274.0	648	5 262	423.2	126.2	1 238.5	756.7	235.3	9.8
Waupaca	80	1 086	53.0	22.2	94	277	18.1	4.6	279.4	144.2	48.6	3.6
Waushara	19	339	10.3	4.7	35	92	6.6	1.5	119.3	60.8	20.5	1.8
Winnebago	318	3 623	264.4	132.3	260	1 778	97.3	28.9	1 239.0	299.0	123.4	12.4
Wood	121	1 308	69.7	33.1	129	651	54.0	11.4	383.5	192.7	69.8	8.1
WYOMING	1 006	7 875	493.6	210.3	980	4 866	422.8	94.8	4 226.5	1 125.5	344.9	50.5
Albany	72	601	34.9	16.1	61	358	16.7	5.3	183.2	51.3	19.7	2.8
Big Horn	7	31	2.2	0.9	18	48	2.7	0.5	92.8	30.6	11.7	1.1
Campbell	54	272	21.2	8.8	84	545	48.0	15.1	120.0	38.0	10.9	1.8
Carbon	32	255	11.3	4.9	27	71	4.8	1.2	247.9	35.3	13.0	1.2
Converse	16	96	4.4	1.4	18	47	3.6	0.7	63.7	25.3	6.8	1.3

1. Firms subject to federal tax.   2. State totals may include programs not allocated by county.

Items 159—170

	Federal funds and grants, 2002–2003 (cont'd)							Local government finances, 2002				
	Expenditures (mil dol) (cont'd)							General revenue				
	Procurement contract awards			Grants[1]							Taxes	
												Per capita[2] (dollars)
STATE County	Salaries and wages	Defense	Other	Medicaid and other health-related	Nutrition and family welfare	Education	Other	Total (mil dol)	Intergovern-mental (mil dol)	Total (mil dol)	Total	Property
	171	172	173	174	175	176	177	178	179	180	181	182
WISCONSIN—Cont'd												
Dodge	11.0	0.8	4.7	25.0	4.9	3.5	14.1	225.2	100.2	76.1	876	809
Door	18.6	1.0	4.6	14.4	2.2	1.3	2.1	102.0	32.7	53.7	1 911	1 772
Douglas	9.2	1.1	2.9	42.2	12.9	4.3	20.5	197.6	101.6	63.2	1 445	1 335
Dunn	5.6	0.1	2.9	26.0	4.8	3.8	9.2	134.7	70.2	37.6	925	850
Eau Claire	25.2	2.5	6.2	65.9	12.0	6.2	22.5	327.9	167.4	112.9	1 198	1 155
Florence	1.0	0.0	0.1	3.3	0.8	0.2	0.8	17.9	9.9	6.3	1 256	1 236
Fond du Lac	15.2	1.8	5.6	43.9	10.3	4.6	23.4	338.8	152.3	113.1	1 157	1 128
Forest	5.1	0.0	1.9	15.2	3.2	1.7	2.6	35.4	19.2	13.0	1 303	1 259
Grant	10.3	0.2	3.8	36.7	4.8	4.1	5.1	178.0	100.4	43.8	888	877
Green	5.9	0.0	1.4	14.4	2.9	2.1	4.4	114.0	57.2	35.7	1 048	1 017
Green Lake	3.9	4.1	2.0	12.0	1.9	0.9	2.4	67.7	31.2	27.9	1 461	1 431
Iowa	5.7	0.6	1.6	12.0	3.4	1.1	3.4	73.5	35.1	26.4	1 140	1 066
Iron	1.2	0.0	0.3	8.0	1.1	0.4	2.3	27.7	14.9	9.1	1 329	1 232
Jackson	4.1	0.2	1.4	21.2	4.7	1.5	2.4	72.7	39.2	16.8	867	803
Jefferson	13.2	3.8	6.6	38.4	5.3	3.8	16.5	250.4	110.7	89.4	1 189	1 096
Juneau	20.4	6.5	1.2	21.2	3.6	1.6	1.7	84.3	48.5	23.7	953	883
Kenosha	19.7	18.7	13.5	68.7	22.1	7.8	18.8	587.4	282.2	219.6	1 422	1 331
Kewaunee	3.7	0.1	1.1	8.5	1.5	1.0	1.1	66.1	35.7	18.6	913	898
La Crosse	30.1	63.6	20.1	59.3	15.0	8.4	21.8	423.2	196.0	134.8	1 246	1 136
Lafayette	3.3	0.0	0.7	11.1	1.7	1.1	9.1	70.7	36.2	16.6	1 021	1 009
Langlade	3.0	1.0	0.7	22.3	4.0	1.7	2.5	69.8	38.5	22.6	1 091	1 010
Lincoln	5.2	3.2	1.1	21.8	4.2	1.6	3.1	103.8	51.2	33.1	1 109	1 038
Manitowoc	12.9	0.2	5.3	44.3	7.6	2.9	6.4	242.9	124.4	70.8	858	832
Marathon	35.5	0.2	27.0	68.8	12.6	6.9	32.8	469.8	221.3	153.3	1 210	1 110
Marinette	10.8	0.9	14.9	36.2	5.7	2.2	5.3	140.4	74.3	44.4	1 020	989
Marquette	3.3	0.0	3.2	8.0	1.7	0.8	2.2	41.8	19.9	17.5	1 189	1 116
Menominee	0.6		0.6	12.5	5.4	7.9	13.5	24.5	20.1	2.9	616	610
Milwaukee	595.2	115.8	230.6	1 031.3	296.1	99.7	402.3	4 051.2	2 119.4	1 218.1	1 300	1 193
Monroe	77.7	65.7	21.2	32.5	5.0	2.3	11.0	132.3	75.5	33.4	803	723
Oconto	5.8	0.0	2.0	21.9	4.1	1.8	3.2	99.4	53.7	32.5	887	827
Oneida	13.7	0.1	2.3	23.3	7.9	2.0	9.5	144.0	46.2	80.6	2 185	2 054
Outagamie	25.7	35.7	16.2	68.1	11.9	6.9	36.5	629.5	294.2	215.6	1 298	1 262
Ozaukee	10.8	36.5	4.5	11.7	2.2	2.7	16.4	251.3	78.0	128.6	1 532	1 416
Pepin	1.5	0.0	0.5	6.4	1.0	0.4	0.0	29.3	18.0	8.4	1 146	1 081
Pierce	6.9	0.4	4.8	19.5	3.0	3.0	3.6	125.6	66.9	41.8	1 116	1 051
Polk	8.0	2.3	2.6	25.4	5.4	2.1	3.0	147.8	77.3	45.5	1 066	995
Portage	14.3	0.1	3.0	31.9	8.7	5.5	11.1	206.1	109.6	66.2	984	895
Price	5.9	0.0	1.0	16.0	2.3	1.0	0.8	52.4	30.0	16.5	1 072	997
Racine	27.3	17.5	8.7	110.2	32.4	12.2	29.2	602.1	322.9	190.9	999	970
Richland	3.2	0.0	0.7	17.9	2.6	0.9	2.9	60.2	28.5	14.6	808	744
Rock	21.5	78.6	7.8	99.3	26.7	12.8	29.1	555.1	317.3	165.9	1 076	1 052
Rusk	3.5	0.0	1.1	18.3	5.3	1.2	1.8	73.7	38.2	13.7	896	831
St. Croix	10.5	0.3	5.8	17.0	3.4	1.8	14.2	201.4	93.8	72.0	1 057	923
Sauk	9.0	8.3	5.2	30.1	5.2	2.7	7.5	195.3	92.0	73.7	1 326	1 103
Sawyer	4.9	30.9	0.8	21.2	4.8	3.2	10.3	51.5	21.6	24.4	1 475	1 358
Shawano	6.7	0.2	1.8	36.7	4.7	2.9	2.7	119.7	64.2	33.5	819	754
Sheboygan	15.0	4.1	25.0	44.1	10.2	5.0	15.0	408.4	192.2	144.1	1 281	1 241
Taylor	4.5	0.0	0.9	11.5	2.0	1.2	4.2	65.0	39.5	17.2	875	815
Trempealeau	6.5	2.6	1.2	28.9	7.0	1.5	8.4	120.4	63.5	30.7	1 127	1 073
Vernon	6.5	1.1	1.5	31.2	3.6	2.0	7.3	93.1	53.4	22.8	805	754
Vilas	4.3	0.0	1.2	18.4	3.6	5.2	12.1	67.3	20.1	39.5	1 828	1 681
Walworth	12.5	1.0	3.7	31.6	5.9	5.6	15.7	327.5	118.0	147.7	1 523	1 397
Washburn	7.0	0.0	1.9	17.7	2.7	1.8	8.2	59.3	26.6	25.8	1 566	1 493
Washington	20.8	2.0	3.6	28.4	6.4	3.9	25.2	361.9	141.9	156.7	1 297	1 194
Waukesha	59.0	26.5	19.1	67.3	14.5	12.4	23.9	1 171.9	367.7	610.7	1 648	1 596
Waupaca	9.3	11.6	3.1	30.4	5.0	2.7	9.6	174.9	94.0	55.4	1 059	990
Waushara	3.7	0.0	1.0	18.2	2.7	1.6	4.5	62.1	30.4	24.2	1 040	980
Winnebago	34.5	613.8	20.8	62.7	16.3	8.2	32.0	459.5	227.5	159.7	1 008	976
Wood	12.9	0.9	6.2	54.8	9.1	5.2	13.4	279.7	141.3	88.8	1 182	1 151
WYOMING	510.2	71.8	274.2	279.0	119.8	118.8	1 098.6	X	X	X	X	X
Albany	14.3	1.3	5.1	24.5	4.7	7.9	39.0	134.0	41.3	22.4	705	384
Big Horn	5.2	0.0	7.7	9.3	1.8	2.4	16.3	56.0	27.6	12.0	1 068	911
Campbell	5.9	0.7	14.9	3.9	3.1	1.1	37.3	241.1	43.3	114.4	3 168	2 445
Carbon	10.0	5.1	131.5	10.8	3.4	1.0	36.1	80.2	25.3	34.5	2 251	1 846
Converse	3.3	0.0	0.5	4.4	1.9	0.8	18.7	53.9	18.0	20.5	1 646	1 397

1. State totals may include programs not allocated by county.   2. Based on the resident population estimated as of July 1 of the year shown.

Table B. States and Counties — Local Government Finances, Government Employment, and Elections

	Local government finances, 2002 (cont'd)									Government employment, 2002			Presidential election, 2004		
	Direct general expenditure							Debt outstanding					Percent of vote cast —		
			Percent of total for —												
STATE County	Total (mil dol)	Per capita[1] (dollars)	Education	Health and hospitals	Police protection	Public welfare	Highways	Total (mil dol)	Per capita[1] (dollars)	Federal civilian	Federal military	State and local	Democratic	Republican	All other
	183	184	185	186	187	188	189	190	191	192	193	194	195	196	197
WISCONSIN—Cont'd															
Dodge	246.4	2 838	36.4	4.0	5.6	14.9	12.6	174.7	2 012	195	236	4 675	37.7	61.4	0.9
Door	108.0	3 842	40.6	6.2	4.3	3.2	13.6	69.3	2 465	84	141	1 627	47.9	51.0	1.1
Douglas	219.6	5 021	50.9	4.9	4.3	5.2	6.8	165.7	3 790	106	119	3 058	65.7	33.6	0.8
Dunn	133.8	3 288	39.9	1.6	4.2	16.9	13.6	107.4	2 638	98	110	4 053	52.0	47.0	1.0
Eau Claire	335.9	3 565	53.1	6.4	4.9	5.0	9.3	218.4	2 318	382	255	7 742	54.3	44.5	1.2
Florence	18.1	3 596	42.4	8.4	6.5	0.5	18.0	13.7	2 713	23	14	295	36.5	62.7	0.8
Fond du Lac	371.1	3 794	50.9	9.8	5.1	5.6	7.0	308.3	3 152	243	267	5 644	36.3	62.8	0.9
Forest	34.6	3 454	49.1	2.3	4.5	5.0	15.0	19.4	1 938	116	27	1 479	48.7	50.6	0.7
Grant	177.5	3 600	53.7	5.8	3.7	9.3	10.2	99.2	2 010	174	133	4 839	51.1	48.1	0.7
Green	122.1	3 582	46.0	3.6	5.0	11.5	14.7	87.9	2 580	93	92	1 900	52.5	46.6	0.9
Green Lake	67.3	3 532	45.3	5.3	6.3	4.6	11.0	51.3	2 691	64	52	1 137	35.5	63.7	0.8
Iowa	72.2	3 121	49.5	0.9	4.5	9.6	15.0	58.7	2 538	94	63	1 358	56.8	42.7	0.5
Iron	30.1	4 403	33.4	7.3	4.4	0.4	18.6	16.3	2 384	20	18	376	50.5	48.6	0.9
Jackson	69.6	3 589	40.5	10.1	3.8	14.2	12.7	32.5	1 676	56	52	3 610	54.0	45.2	0.8
Jefferson	258.3	3 436	43.7	7.8	5.4	7.7	10.9	178.5	2 375	199	203	4 068	42.6	56.5	0.9
Juneau	102.4	4 122	42.6	1.3	4.7	7.7	11.2	116.5	4 693	254	68	1 441	46.4	52.4	1.2
Kenosha	608.6	3 941	52.7	4.3	5.5	6.5	4.9	552.7	3 579	279	446	8 718	52.5	46.6	0.9
Kewaunee	74.1	3 628	45.6	10.1	3.4	1.9	20.7	42.0	2 055	72	55	1 079	46.0	52.9	1.1
La Crosse	407.3	3 766	48.6	2.6	4.8	8.2	6.4	301.7	2 790	473	310	8 904	53.4	45.6	1.0
Lafayette	73.8	4 545	45.0	9.7	2.7	11.6	14.0	48.8	3 004	66	44	1 040	52.6	46.8	0.6
Langlade	73.4	3 543	48.1	3.7	4.2	6.0	14.8	45.9	2 215	49	56	1 192	42.9	56.3	0.7
Lincoln	118.4	3 962	41.7	4.8	4.1	9.3	13.0	71.1	2 380	80	81	1 905	47.7	51.2	1.1
Manitowoc	277.8	3 369	40.4	3.1	4.9	10.0	12.3	221.9	2 691	189	242	4 232	46.8	52.2	1.0
Marathon	495.8	3 912	49.1	12.6	3.7	3.8	8.9	299.7	2 365	533	344	6 982	45.4	53.5	1.1
Marinette	155.4	3 572	41.1	11.8	6.2	5.7	11.7	118.8	2 731	125	169	2 197	45.8	53.3	0.8
Marquette	44.1	2 999	41.0	7.1	6.0	6.3	20.4	22.5	1 531	57	40	759	44.7	54.4	0.8
Menominee	22.8	4 881	58.0	5.1	3.9	14.6	8.1	9.8	2 086	(3)0	(3)13	(3)1 981	82.6	16.8	0.6
Milwaukee	4 239.4	4 524	40.6	7.0	8.0	6.3	4.6	2 740.3	2 924	9 602	2 972	56 128	61.8	37.4	0.8
Monroe	140.3	3 373	44.1	2.8	4.1	12.1	13.6	121.1	2 910	2 253	248	2 192	46.2	52.9	1.0
Oconto	115.6	3 157	47.3	6.6	3.7	4.7	15.5	102.0	2 783	115	99	1 708	43.2	55.9	1.0
Oneida	144.8	3 928	55.6	1.9	5.1	4.6	9.6	91.9	2 493	255	101	2 382	47.5	51.5	1.0
Outagamie	659.9	3 972	53.4	3.9	4.8	4.9	9.3	604.5	3 638	366	449	9 602	44.8	54.2	0.9
Ozaukee	274.1	3 266	50.7	4.4	5.9	6.6	8.5	223.2	2 660	164	227	3 761	33.4	65.9	0.7
Pepin	31.2	4 278	46.5	6.5	3.8	6.5	19.2	14.4	1 973	31	20	514	53.8	45.6	0.6
Pierce	137.9	3 684	52.6	6.2	4.0	1.7	15.7	113.2	3 025	110	101	3 331	51.2	47.8	1.1
Polk	165.5	3 877	46.0	5.6	4.5	6.3	13.5	142.6	3 340	145	116	2 425	48.0	51.1	0.9
Portage	205.0	3 045	44.0	11.3	4.8	5.9	13.4	108.6	1 614	219	187	5 248	56.2	42.5	1.3
Price	51.8	3 365	43.2	2.1	4.8	10.8	16.4	27.8	1 804	119	42	927	49.7	49.3	1.1
Racine	615.7	3 224	45.9	5.0	8.1	6.8	7.0	438.2	2 294	396	519	9 341	47.5	51.7	0.8
Richland	58.5	3 247	34.5	9.9	4.2	17.4	13.2	37.6	2 088	61	49	1 107	47.8	51.4	0.7
Rock	577.4	3 747	48.7	6.5	5.9	8.9	5.6	344.2	2 233	336	418	8 595	58.0	41.2	0.8
Rusk	78.6	5 137	34.6	16.0	3.1	11.0	13.2	40.4	2 638	58	41	1 260	48.3	50.3	1.4
St. Croix	219.3	3 219	49.3	7.7	4.1	4.9	14.0	198.8	2 919	158	184	3 408	44.9	54.3	0.8
Sauk	209.7	3 770	40.9	8.6	5.5	4.6	12.5	160.9	2 893	151	152	4 423	51.7	47.4	0.9
Sawyer	56.4	3 403	40.0	5.9	3.9	6.6	23.0	25.9	1 561	86	45	1 951	46.7	52.4	0.8
Shawano	121.3	2 964	42.4	4.3	5.0	7.2	15.1	85.6	2 092	(3)123	(3)111	(3)2 798	41.3	57.9	0.8
Sheboygan	415.8	3 696	48.5	5.7	6.0	10.5	8.0	298.5	2 654	231	315	5 953	44.1	55.1	0.8
Taylor	68.0	3 459	43.3	2.0	4.6	7.4	11.9	47.3	2 408	90	53	933	40.1	58.6	1.3
Trempealeau	124.6	4 577	44.9	3.9	2.9	16.0	10.8	87.8	3 225	127	74	1 970	57.4	41.8	0.7
Vernon	91.7	3 237	45.8	1.2	3.2	14.6	15.3	62.0	2 186	115	77	1 799	53.5	45.7	0.9
Vilas	64.8	2 996	45.9	3.4	5.7	4.7	12.4	56.8	2 624	84	59	2 207	40.9	58.3	0.8
Walworth	338.1	3 486	40.6	5.2	7.3	8.8	8.7	367.8	3 792	207	262	6 454	39.6	59.4	1.0
Washburn	61.4	3 730	42.9	1.8	3.5	9.9	21.0	26.6	1 614	120	44	1 219	49.2	49.8	1.0
Washington	400.2	3 310	45.6	5.0	5.3	6.2	8.0	380.3	3 145	265	329	5 115	29.3	70.0	0.7
Waukesha	1 206.0	3 255	55.2	2.8	6.3	3.1	6.6	1 106.9	2 987	885	1 002	16 601	32.0	67.3	0.7
Waupaca	206.1	3 940	48.1	2.3	3.9	8.2	12.1	202.9	3 879	142	142	3 601	40.0	59.1	0.8
Waushara	66.7	2 864	42.3	2.4	4.4	13.6	12.8	40.5	1 736	61	63	1 087	42.3	56.9	0.8
Winnebago	484.5	3 059	42.8	6.2	5.7	8.6	8.3	438.9	2 771	555	439	11 390	46.3	52.6	1.1
Wood	279.2	3 713	52.3	7.3	4.8	6.5	8.8	144.0	1 915	202	203	4 981	47.3	51.4	1.2
WYOMING	X	X	X	X	X	X	X	X	X	7 317	5 850	52 820	29.1	69.0	1.9
Albany	112.9	3 558	29.8	39.1	4.9	0.2	2.8	45.3	1 427	261	165	6 828	43.0	54.3	2.7
Big Horn	53.8	4 799	50.4	20.0	3.9	0.5	4.6	24.7	2 199	109	55	1 328	18.2	80.2	1.7
Campbell	199.3	5 520	33.5	28.5	4.1	0.1	7.4	49.9	1 382	89	176	3 242	16.3	82.2	1.4
Carbon	74.4	4 850	39.6	20.4	5.7	0.1	5.4	10.5	685	221	75	1 942	30.6	67.4	2.1
Converse	52.3	4 207	43.2	21.0	4.6	0.2	7.2	25.3	2 032	72	60	1 195	20.7	77.7	1.6

1. Based on the resident population estimated as of July 1 of the year shown.   3. Menominee County included with Shawano County.

STATE/ County code	CBSA code[1]	County Type[2]	STATE County	Land area,[3] (sq km) 2000	Population and population characteristics, 2003													
								Race alone or in combination, not Hispanic or Latino (percent)					Age (percent)					
					Total persons	Rank	Per square kilometer	White	Black	Am. Indian, Alaska Native	Asian and Pacific Islander	Percent Hispanic or Latino[4]	Under 5 years	5 to 17 years	18 to 24 years	25 to 34 years	35 to 44 years	45 to 54 years
				1	2	3	4	5	6	7	8	9	10	11	12	13	14	15
			WYOMING—Cont'd															
56 011	...	9	Crook	7 404	5 928	2 777	0.8	97.9	0.2	1.1	0.5	1.0	4.4	18.4	10.1	7.6	14.9	16.9
56 013	40180	7	Fremont	23 782	35 914	1 241	1.5	75.5	0.3	20.4	0.5	4.6	6.6	18.9	10.3	10.1	14.1	15.6
56 015	...	7	Goshen	5 764	12 219	2 284	2.1	89.6	0.2	1.0	0.4	9.1	5.6	17.0	10.7	9.2	13.2	15.2
56 017	...	7	Hot Springs	5 190	4 665	2 860	0.9	95.4	0.4	2.1	0.4	2.3	5.2	14.6	7.7	7.8	13.5	16.7
56 019	...	7	Johnson	10 791	7 543	2 632	0.7	97.0	0.1	1.4	0.2	2.1	4.5	16.9	9.1	9.4	12.5	16.7
56 021	16940	3	Laramie	6 957	84 083	636	12.1	83.7	3.4	1.4	1.8	11.6	6.8	18.1	10.2	13.6	15.1	14.3
56 023	...	7	Lincoln	10 539	15 208	2 085	1.4	96.5	0.2	1.0	0.6	2.4	6.3	20.9	11.0	8.9	14.2	15.2
56 025	16220	3	Natrona	13 830	68 211	736	4.9	92.7	1.2	1.6	0.8	4.9	6.6	18.1	11.0	11.7	14.2	15.5
56 027	...	9	Niobrara	6 801	2 237	3 037	0.3	97.7	0.5	0.6	0.1	1.6	4.0	16.5	8.1	7.4	15.2	17.7
56 029	...	7	Park	17 981	26 284	1 527	1.5	95.4	0.1	0.9	0.6	3.6	5.0	16.8	11.0	9.2	13.7	16.7
56 031	...	7	Platte	5 400	8 628	2 557	1.6	93.8	0.1	0.8	0.3	5.5	4.9	17.4	9.2	9.0	13.8	16.9
56 033	43260	7	Sheridan	6 535	27 111	1 501	4.1	95.4	0.4	2.0	0.7	2.5	5.3	16.8	10.0	9.9	13.4	17.3
56 035	...	9	Sublette	12 646	6 368	2 739	0.5	96.7	0.4	0.9	0.3	2.2	4.9	18.0	8.5	10.0	14.8	18.3
56 037	40540	5	Sweetwater	27 001	37 018	1 209	1.4	87.5	1.0	1.4	1.2	10.0	6.9	19.3	11.8	11.2	15.5	17.4
56 039	27220	7	Teton	10 380	18 625	1 877	1.8	89.6	0.2	0.8	1.2	8.9	5.1	13.8	7.4	20.9	16.8	18.0
56 041	21740	7	Uinta	5 391	19 700	1 821	3.7	92.7	0.3	1.6	0.6	5.8	7.7	22.7	11.6	11.0	15.5	16.4
56 043	...	7	Washakie	5 802	7 883	2 606	1.4	86.2	0.2	1.2	0.8	12.3	5.7	19.3	8.6	8.3	14.5	16.5
56 045	...	7	Weston	6 210	6 659	2 718	1.1	96.1	0.2	2.1	0.2	2.2	4.9	15.9	10.7	9.1	14.7	17.0

1. CBSA = Core Based Statistical Area. See Appendix A for explanation. See Appendix B for list of metropolitan areas with component counties. 2. County type code from the Economic Research Service of USDA Rural-Urban Continuum Codes. See Appendix A for definition. 3. Dry land or land partially or temporarily covered by water. 4. Hispanic or Latino persons may be of any race.

Table B. States and Counties — **Population and Households**

STATE County	Population, 2003 (cont'd) Age (percent) (cont'd)				Population — change and components of change, 1990–2003							Households, 2000				
					Total persons		Percent change		Components of change, 2000–2003						Percent	
	55 to 64 years	65 to 74 years	75 years and over	Percent female	1990	2000	1990–2000	2000–2003	Births	Deaths	Net migration	Number	Percent change, 1990–2000	Persons per house-hold	Female family house-holder[1]	One person
	16	17	18	19	20	21	22	23	24	25	26	27	28	29	30	31
WYOMING—Cont'd																
Crook	12.1	8.5	6.5	49.4	5 294	5 887	11.2	0.7	144	172	68	2 308	22.0	2.51	5.4	24.9
Fremont	10.8	7.7	6.0	50.5	33 662	35 804	6.4	0.3	1 556	1 241	-176	13 545	12.9	2.58	10.9	25.5
Goshen	11.6	8.7	9.4	50.0	12 373	12 538	1.3	-2.5	454	427	-342	5 061	5.7	2.38	7.7	27.6
Hot Springs	14.0	10.8	10.6	51.8	4 809	4 882	1.5	-4.4	162	223	-152	2 108	8.5	2.25	7.4	31.7
Johnson	12.4	9.0	8.4	50.9	6 145	7 075	15.1	6.6	196	252	522	2 959	23.4	2.36	7.1	28.5
Laramie	9.4	6.2	5.4	49.8	73 142	81 607	11.6	3.0	3 727	2 257	1 063	31 927	13.7	2.45	9.9	27.2
Lincoln	10.2	6.6	5.6	49.4	12 625	14 573	15.4	4.4	586	397	446	5 266	27.3	2.75	5.1	21.0
Natrona	9.5	6.8	5.8	50.4	61 226	66 533	8.7	2.5	3 011	1 951	676	26 819	12.5	2.42	10.6	27.5
Niobrara	12.9	10.8	8.8	50.5	2 499	2 407	-3.7	-7.1	61	75	-155	1 011	-2.0	2.28	6.0	29.5
Park	11.7	7.6	7.3	51.2	23 178	25 786	11.3	1.9	845	687	371	10 312	17.8	2.42	7.1	26.2
Platte	12.3	8.7	8.4	50.6	8 145	8 807	8.1	-2.0	265	281	-150	3 625	14.0	2.40	6.8	27.3
Sheridan	11.5	7.6	7.7	51.0	23 562	26 560	12.7	2.1	932	1 012	658	11 167	18.5	2.31	8.2	30.9
Sublette	11.7	7.2	4.6	48.9	4 843	5 920	22.2	7.6	188	126	380	2 371	29.3	2.47	5.3	23.6
Sweetwater	9.4	4.5	3.9	49.4	38 823	37 613	-3.1	-1.6	1 696	830	-1 493	14 105	3.6	2.62	9.2	23.6
Teton	9.9	4.7	2.5	46.4	11 173	18 251	63.3	2.0	626	256	26	7 688	68.3	2.36	5.7	27.3
Uinta	8.1	4.0	3.2	49.3	18 705	19 742	5.5	-0.2	990	367	-675	6 823	15.9	2.84	9.9	20.9
Washakie	11.5	8.7	7.9	50.3	8 388	8 289	-1.2	-4.9	317	266	-467	3 278	3.9	2.47	7.3	26.5
Weston	11.6	8.0	7.9	49.0	6 518	6 644	1.9	0.2	216	207	5	2 624	8.5	2.42	7.3	25.0

1. No spouse present.

Items 16—31

STATE County	Births, average 1999–2001		Deaths, average 1999–2001				Physicians,[4] 2000		Hospitals,[4] 1998			Medicare enrollees, 2003	Serious crimes known to police,[6] 2002	
			Number		Rate					Beds			Total	
	Total	Rate[1]	Total	Infant[2]	Total[1]	Infant[3]	Number	Rate[5]	Number	Number	Rate[5]		Number	Rate[7]
	32	33	34	35	36	37	38	39	40	41	42	43	44	45
WYOMING—Cont'd														
Crook	53	9.0	48	0	8.2	D	2	34	1	48	823	932	92	1 662
Fremont	476	13.3	351	3	9.8	D	64	179	2	177	491	5 809	1 108	3 064
Goshen	138	11.1	130	1	10.4	D	10	80	1	36	279	2 436	276	2 180
Hot Springs	47	9.7	69	0	14.1	D	6	123	1	49	1 037	1 101	117	2 373
Johnson	61	8.6	72	0	10.2	D	8	113	1	83	1 216	1 464	244	3 414
Laramie	1 130	13.8	661	7	8.1	6.2	178	218	2	266	337	11 498	3 266	3 963
Lincoln	183	12.6	108	2	7.4	D	6	41	2	33	238	2 034	213	1 499
Natrona	882	13.2	582	4	8.7	D	115	173	1	282	445	9 929	3 360	5 000
Niobrara	24	10.0	29	1	12.2	D	3	125	1	52	1 922	487	NA	NA
Park	258	10.0	230	1	8.9	D	52	202	2	356	1 381	4 517	661	2 538
Platte	87	9.8	97	1	11.0	D	6	68	1	86	997	1 732	257	2 889
Sheridan	275	10.4	287	2	10.8	D	50	188	1	64	254	4 604	621	2 315
Sublette	58	9.8	45	0	7.7	D	6	101	0	0	0	832	184	3 077
Sweetwater	524	14.0	246	5	6.6	D	41	109	1	99	249	3 832	1 587	4 178
Teton	192	10.6	72	1	4.0	D	47	258	1	104	734	1 475	570	3 092
Uinta	301	15.2	112	3	5.7	D	22	111	1	42	205	1 788	825	4 138
Washakie	101	12.2	84	1	10.1	D	11	133	1	30	346	1 474	84	1 003
Weston	65	9.8	63	1	9.6	D	3	45	1	71	1 097	1 215	167	2 864

1. Per 1,000 estimated resident population.   2. Deaths of infants under 1 year old.   3. Deaths of infants under 1 year old per 1,000 live births.   4. Data subject to copyright.   5. Per 100,000 resident population as of July 1 of the year shown.   6. Data for serious crimes have not been adjusted for underreporting; this may affect comparability between geographic areas and over time.   7. Per 100,000 population estimated by the FBI.

STATE County	Serious crimes known to police,[1] 2002 (cont'd) Rate[2]		Education School enrollment and attainment, 2000				Local government expenditures,[5] 2000–2001		Money income, 1999	Households			Percent below poverty level, 1999			
			Enrollment[3]		Attainment[4] (percent)					Median income						
	Violent	Property	Total	Percent private	High school graduate or less	Bachelor's degree or more	Total current expenditures (mil dol)	Current expenditures per student (dollars)	Per capita income[6] (dollars)	Dollars	Percent change, 1989–1999 (constant 1999 dollars)	Percent with income of $100,000 or more	Persons	Households	Families	Families with children
	46	47	48	49	50	51	52	53	54	55	56	57	58	59	60	61
WYOMING—Cont'd																
Crook	398	1 265	1 512	1.7	52.3	17.5	10.7	9 223	17 379	35 601	13.0	6.2	9.1	11.7	7.8	11.5
Fremont	227	2 837	9 531	5.4	48.4	19.7	64.4	9 492	16 519	32 503	8.7	5.0	17.6	15.3	13.3	20.4
Goshen	300	1 879	3 108	9.4	48.7	18.6	16.7	8 115	15 965	32 228	10.3	3.6	13.9	14.7	9.7	15.9
Hot Springs	223	2 150	1 043	5.0	51.9	17.9	6.6	8 474	16 858	29 888	-9.2	4.2	10.6	11.8	8.6	13.6
Johnson	168	3 247	1 652	4.2	40.8	22.2	10.6	7 946	19 030	34 012	14.3	5.8	10.1	11.5	7.2	10.1
Laramie	222	3 741	21 266	10.1	37.4	23.4	99.3	6 965	19 634	39 607	6.9	6.5	9.1	9.1	6.5	10.2
Lincoln	267	1 232	4 113	4.9	46.9	17.2	24.5	7 504	17 533	40 794	6.6	5.3	9.0	8.1	6.4	9.9
Natrona	274	4 726	18 067	5.9	42.3	20.0	87.6	7 271	18 913	36 619	-1.2	6.3	11.8	11.3	8.7	14.5
Niobrara	NA	NA	522	4.6	51.6	15.3	4.1	9 648	15 757	29 701	5.5	4.0	13.4	13.8	10.7	10.9
Park	250	2 289	6 815	7.4	42.8	23.7	30.1	7 001	18 020	35 829	2.8	5.3	12.7	11.7	8.4	14.5
Platte	349	2 541	2 147	7.0	53.6	15.2	13.6	8 431	17 530	33 866	15.5	5.3	11.7	11.1	8.5	13.0
Sheridan	82	2 233	6 752	11.9	40.4	22.4	33.6	7 851	19 407	34 538	3.8	6.9	10.7	10.7	8.6	14.6
Sublette	268	2 810	1 392	8.4	46.4	21.6	11.8	9 752	20 056	39 044	8.3	7.2	9.7	10.1	7.4	10.1
Sweetwater	271	3 906	11 129	4.9	47.3	17.0	60.7	7 989	19 575	46 537	-4.3	8.3	7.8	7.3	5.4	8.4
Teton	429	2 664	3 101	13.7	24.2	45.8	17.4	7 670	38 260	54 614	28.7	18.8	6.0	4.9	2.8	4.2
Uinta	90	4 047	5 873	5.3	50.8	15.0	37.4	7 894	16 994	44 544	-0.3	5.1	9.9	9.5	7.8	10.3
Washakie	191	812	2 112	4.7	48.2	18.7	12.4	7 768	17 780	34 943	3.3	7.3	14.1	13.1	10.0	18.9
Weston	172	2 693	1 585	2.4	55.0	14.5	10.2	8 589	17 366	32 348	-8.2	5.5	9.9	11.0	6.3	9.8

1. Data for serious crimes have not been adjusted for underreporting; this may affect comparability between geographic areas and over time. 2. Per 100,000 population estimated by the FBI. 3. All persons 3 years old and over enrolled in nursery school through college. 4. Persons 25 years old and over. 5. Elementary and secondary education expenditures. 6. Based on population enumerated as of April 1, 2000.

Table B. States and Counties — **Personal Income**

STATE County	Personal income, 2002												
			Per capita[1]						Transfer payments				
										Government payments to individuals			
	Total (mil dol)	Percent change, 2001–2002	Dollars	Rank	Wages and salaries[2] (mil dol)	Proprietor's income (mil dol)	Dividends, interest, and rent (mil dol)	Total (mil dol)	Total (mil dol)	Social Security (mil dol)	Medical payments (mil dol)	Income maintenance (mil dol)	Unemployment insurance (mil dol)
	62	63	64	65	66	67	68	69	70	71	72	73	74
WYOMING—Cont'd													
Crook..........................	178	5.6	30 284	322	69	21	39	22	20	11	6	1	0
Fremont.....................	899	3.7	24 962	1 144	477	80	200	187	178	66	79	15	6
Goshen.......................	302	1.0	24 538	1 254	120	47	70	60	57	26	21	4	1
Hot Springs	128	2.5	27 094	683	59	11	29	33	32	13	16	1	1
Johnson.....................	205	5.3	27 750	581	87	24	67	31	30	16	8	1	1
Laramie	2 570	6.0	30 949	272	1 711	188	553	340	320	121	112	23	6
Lincoln.......................	372	2.6	24 948	1 149	190	33	94	51	47	24	16	2	2
Natrona.....................	2 294	3.4	34 018	164	1 244	427	500	292	275	118	99	24	8
Niobrara....................	64	0.8	28 205	520	26	7	18	12	11	5	4	1	0
Park...........................	786	3.8	30 279	324	401	96	235	113	106	52	35	6	3
Platte........................	237	2.5	27 055	690	129	29	57	42	40	19	14	2	1
Sheridan....................	878	4.8	32 563	202	411	82	288	118	111	49	37	6	3
Sublette.....................	194	7.9	31 331	258	98	23	59	20	19	10	6	1	0
Sweetwater	1 131	1.5	30 400	311	896	78	216	128	119	47	39	8	4
Teton.........................	1 326	2.2	71 457	2	615	202	626	47	42	19	13	1	3
Uinta.........................	548	5.4	27 725	585	333	53	70	68	63	21	26	5	2
Washakie	227	-0.2	28 579	483	122	19	66	38	36	17	14	2	1
Weston......................	208	4.7	31 388	255	86	45	37	30	28	14	9	2	0

1. Based on the resident population estimated as of July 1 of the year shown.   2. Includes other labor income.

STATE County	Earnings, 2002									Social Security beneficiaries, December 2003			Housing units, 2003	
	Total (mil dol)	Farm	Goods-related[1]		Service-related and health							Supplemental Security Income recipients, December 2003		
			Total	Manu-facturing	Infor-mation and profes-sional and technical services	Retail trade	Finance, insur-ance, and real estate	Health services	Govern-ment	Number	Rate[2]		Total	Percent change, 2000–2003
	75	76	77	78	79	80	81	82	83	84	85	86	87	88
WYOMING—Cont'd														
Crook........................	89	4.9	33.3	8.4	3.2	6.3	D	D	25.6	1 150	194	35	3 045	3.7
Fremont.....................	558	1.0	20.4	2.5	5.9	9.5	4.4	D	31.4	6 910	192	753	15 929	2.5
Goshen.....................	167	16.3	D	5.1	3.9	9.4	5.6	D	23.1	2 730	223	182	5 931	0.9
Hot Springs	70	0.0	D	3.2	5.5	9.8	4.0	D	25.0	1 300	279	80	2 557	0.8
Johnson....................	111	-0.7	20.2	2.4	5.1	6.8	8.6	4.3	28.1	1 705	226	39	3 617	3.3
Laramie	1 898	0.8	11.5	4.4	D	8.1	5.9	6.7	40.2	12 605	150	1 098	35 243	3.0
Lincoln.....................	223	0.6	34.0	4.0	5.6	6.6	4.8	D	23.4	2 430	160	84	7 384	8.1
Natrona	1 671	0.0	30.9	5.8	6.7	7.6	6.9	11.4	13.5	11 425	167	1 143	30 332	1.5
Niobrara	33	9.4	D	D	D	8.3	4.4	3.6	33.1	575	257	18	1 331	-0.5
Park.........................	497	2.1	22.6	4.4	5.6	8.7	6.2	8.2	25.8	5 335	203	269	12 293	3.6
Platte.......................	158	4.9	D	2.1	4.6	8.5	4.3	D	18.2	1 910	221	98	4 592	1.4
Sheridan...................	493	0.6	14.5	2.7	8.0	9.2	8.0	10.7	27.1	5 085	188	322	12 841	2.1
Sublette....................	120	2.0	D	D	8.3	7.6	4.5	D	22.5	1 005	158	20	3 751	5.6
Sweetwater	973	0.0	D	10.6	3.0	5.9	4.6	3.4	15.6	4 375	118	323	16 084	1.0
Teton	817	-0.1	D	1.0	12.6	8.4	14.4	6.1	11.0	1 720	92	44	10 971	6.9
Uinta	386	-0.4	38.6	4.7	6.9	7.5	3.1	D	19.1	2 105	107	215	8 239	2.8
Washakie	141	1.8	27.2	13.4	6.0	5.7	4.8	D	22.6	1 685	214	68	3 692	1.0
Weston.....................	130	3.0	41.5	6.2	4.6	5.2	3.8	3.5	19.4	1 360	204	56	3 283	1.6

1. Covers mining, construction, and manufacturing.   2. Per 1,000 resident population estimated as of July 1 of the year shown.

Table B. States and Counties — Housing, Labor Force, and Employment

STATE County	Housing units, 2000 Occupied units Total	Percent	Owner-occupied Median value[1]	Median owner cost as a percent of income With a mortgage	Without a mortgage[2]	Renter-occupied Median rent[3]	Median rent as a percent of income	Substandard units[4] (percent)	Civilian labor force, 2003 Total	Percent change, 2002–2003	Unemployment Total	Rate[5]	Civilian employment,[6] 2000 Total	Percent Management, professional and related occupations	Production, transportation, and material moving occupations
	89	90	91	92	93	94	95	96	97	98	99	100	101	102	103
WYOMING—Cont'd															
Crook	2 308	80.1	85 400	16.9	9.9	393	16.8	1.7	3 032	3.7	131	4.3	2 839	29.9	15.1
Fremont	13 545	72.8	89 300	19.5	9.9	381	21.8	6.1	18 662	0.8	1 208	6.5	16 052	33.9	11.2
Goshen	5 061	70.7	77 000	20.4	11.6	368	22.2	2.2	6 220	0.7	233	3.7	5 696	31.4	15.3
Hot Springs	2 108	68.6	80 400	21.0	11.7	366	20.0	2.8	2 251	-4.2	76	3.4	2 427	34.3	9.3
Johnson	2 959	73.7	115 500	21.6	9.9	445	21.0	0.8	4 121	3.7	133	3.2	3 242	37.5	9.7
Laramie	31 927	69.1	106 400	21.0	9.9	473	24.1	2.3	44 132	4.0	1 818	4.1	36 949	32.2	13.4
Lincoln	5 266	81.4	95 300	21.3	9.9	464	18.8	4.0	7 642	14.4	440	5.8	6 506	26.8	14.8
Natrona	26 819	69.9	84 600	19.1	9.9	409	21.8	2.6	36 657	4.0	1 766	4.8	33 213	28.5	12.0
Niobrara	1 011	72.9	60 300	19.0	11.1	309	18.6	3.1	1 195	0.9	43	3.6	1 153	34.4	11.5
Park	10 312	71.3	107 300	21.2	9.9	435	22.0	2.5	16 071	4.5	693	4.3	12 333	30.3	12.3
Platte	3 625	75.8	84 100	17.4	9.9	362	18.3	2.6	4 391	-0.3	214	4.9	4 334	30.3	13.2
Sheridan	11 167	68.9	102 100	21.7	10.0	439	23.7	2.6	14 820	3.8	631	4.3	13 266	32.3	10.2
Sublette	2 371	73.5	112 000	22.1	9.9	523	22.5	3.2	3 809	9.0	106	2.8	3 033	28.6	12.4
Sweetwater	14 105	75.1	104 200	19.0	9.9	428	19.2	3.9	20 667	4.6	897	4.3	18 845	23.3	16.1
Teton	7 688	54.8	365 400	25.1	9.9	707	20.9	6.2	12 486	1.2	492	3.9	11 687	34.1	4.9
Uinta	6 823	75.2	89 400	19.2	9.9	433	18.0	3.8	11 293	-0.3	660	5.8	9 380	25.4	16.5
Washakie	3 278	73.1	83 600	18.9	9.9	393	20.3	1.9	4 647	2.8	188	4.0	3 869	29.7	11.1
Weston	2 624	78.0	66 700	17.8	9.9	364	21.8	2.1	3 194	-2.6	125	3.9	3 002	24.3	19.8

1. Specified owner-occupied units.   2. Median monthly owner costs is often in the minimum category—9.9 percent or less, which is indicated as 9.9 percent.   3. Specified renter-occupied units.   4. Overcrowded or lacking complete plumbing facilities.   5. Percent of civilian labor force.   6. Persons 16 years old and over.

	Private nonfarm establishments, employment and payroll, 2001									Agriculture, 2002			
	Employment							Annual payroll		Farms			
												Percent with—	
STATE County	Number of establish- ments	Total	Health care and social assistance	Manufac- turing	Retail trade	Finance and insurance	Professional, scientific, and technical services	Total (mil dol)	Average per employee (dollars)	Number	Less than 50 acres	500 acres and over	Farm operators whose principal occu- pation is farming (percent)
	104	105	106	107	108	109	110	111	112	113	114	115	116
WYOMING—Cont'd													
Crook	195	1 295	159	228	188	D	18	34	26 097	440	6.1	69.1	70.2
Fremont	1 298	10 394	2 023	495	1 959	372	359	230	22 133	1 019	29.3	25.8	56.8
Goshen	373	2 835	749	132	500	126	72	55	19 266	665	9.9	48.1	69.9
Hot Springs	205	1 510	411	30	208	36	30	30	19 929	147	27.9	41.5	66.7
Johnson	341	1 714	273	63	284	108	81	36	20 728	272	11.8	68.8	67.6
Laramie	2 350	27 505	5 046	1 644	5 636	1 878	1 154	683	24 841	755	18.9	46.9	57.0
Lincoln	511	3 947	291	495	667	92	84	124	31 515	495	30.9	24.2	60.6
Natrona	2 644	27 774	3 929	1 536	4 278	1 299	1 066	788	28 357	380	21.8	42.6	57.9
Niobrara	94	461	95	D	D	21	16	8	16 516	243	2.1	86.8	86.8
Park	1 162	9 002	1 350	588	1 844	345	312	205	22 818	711	40.5	21.5	54.6
Platte	285	2 132	346	133	358	93	55	53	24 972	462	13.6	49.1	68.2
Sheridan	1 110	8 959	2 011	340	1 627	380	424	211	23 526	561	26.4	40.6	55.8
Sublette	337	1 440	145	85	223	53	77	38	26 385	270	29.6	45.6	63.7
Sweetwater	1 107	14 006	1 088	912	2 346	354	262	491	35 032	170	24.7	32.4	50.6
Teton	1 675	15 045	1 092	275	1 924	405	812	403	26 760	110	33.6	23.6	41.8
Uinta	558	6 374	1 374	285	1 260	129	128	178	27 881	335	29.9	35.8	50.1
Washakie	370	3 214	727	363	405	121	121	72	22 556	184	25.5	47.3	54.3
Weston	221	1 483	254	D	240	64	16	35	23 848	221	7.7	75.1	64.7

STATE County	Acreage (1,000)	Percent change, 1997–2002	Average size of farm	Total irrigated (1,000)	Total cropland (1,000)	Average per farm	Average per acre	Value of machinery and equipment average per farm (dollars)	Total (mil dol)	Average per farm (dollars)	Crops	Live-stock and poultry products	$10,000 or more	$100,000 or more	Total ($1,000)	Percent of farms
	117	118	119	120	121	122	123	124	125	126	127	128	129	130	131	132
WYOMING—Cont'd																
Crook......................	1 523	-9.9	3 462	4	183	1 337 293	360	73 420	37	84 440	1.2	98.8	59.3	22.5	2 332	48.4
Fremont...................	2 504	-4.4	2 457	149	192	750 320	311	61 780	60	58 738	25.0	75.0	47.1	12.7	1 915	20.3
Goshen...................	1 258	-0.6	1 892	93	286	826 043	413	97 353	120	179 709	16.0	84.0	67.4	25.6	3 862	57.0
Hot Springs	877	-7.1	5 963	20	50	960 628	162	59 046	8	55 366	12.7	87.3	46.9	12.2	355	18.4
Johnson.................	2 155	1.1	7 924	39	51	2 141 370	270	88 916	26	97 275	2.3	97.7	66.5	32.4	1 844	33.1
Laramie..................	1 755	1.6	2 324	59	405	749 237	305	93 871	66	86 784	26.9	73.1	43.7	13.4	4 584	55.9
Lincoln...................	365	-10.5	737	76	118	738 290	906	62 394	24	48 872	15.3	84.7	49.1	12.7	1 202	27.7
Natrona	2 871	2.3	7 555	33	75	1 401 928	187	59 552	29	75 051	10.1	89.9	48.2	17.1	2 050	28.7
Niobrara	1 600	-0.5	6 583	38	89	1 772 218	262	82 593	35	143 527	10.0	90.0	79.0	31.3	1 438	42.8
Park.......................	810	-19.9	1 140	188	126	739 113	676	70 253	53	74 334	47.1	52.9	44.2	17.4	928	22.2
Platte.....................	1 344	4.6	2 910	75	212	951 813	335	78 476	80	172 957	9.3	90.7	55.6	19.0	2 369	47.6
Sheridan................	1 638	1.9	2 920	55	125	1 328 667	456	62 668	42	74 349	9.2	90.8	47.8	13.0	1 035	23.0
Sublette.................	586	-1.0	2 169	132	162	1 730 391	733	68 421	27	100 512	11.4	88.6	56.3	27.4	621	19.6
Sweetwater	1 480	4.2	8 707	21	36	850 926	98	45 110	7	41 755	9.7	90.3	37.1	12.9	725	23.5
Teton.....................	57	9.6	519	25	24	1 615 441	3 057	65 738	7	67 338	16.8	83.2	36.4	15.5	75	10.9
Uinta.....................	918	-2.3	2 740	83	96	1 050 378	373	57 736	19	58 025	4.3	95.7	49.3	15.5	795	20.9
Washakie................	427	-5.1	2 318	41	47	904 903	389	107 560	25	137 343	42.5	57.5	62.0	35.9	1 119	51.1
Weston...................	1 606	13.0	7 265	2	71	1 577 631	217	68 142	26	115 417	2.1	97.9	66.5	25.8	683	37.1

Table B. States and Counties — Residential Construction, Wholesale Trade, Retail Trade, and Real Estate

STATE County	Value of residential construction authorized by building permits, 2003		Wholesale trade, 1997				Retail trade,[1] 1997				Real estate and rental and leasing, 1997			
	New construction ($1,000)	Number of housing units	Number of establish-ments	Number of employees	Sales (mil dol)	Annual payroll (mil dol)	Number of establish-ments	Number of employees	Sales (mil dol)	Annual payroll (mil dol)	Number of establish-ments	Number of employees	Receipts (mil dol)	Annual payroll (mil dol)
	133	134	135	136	137	138	139	140	141	142	143	144	145	146
WYOMING—Cont'd														
Crook	3 275	31	2	D	D	D	27	180	25.7	2.4	1	D	D	D
Fremont	5 728	65	43	260	85.2	3.9	204	1 735	296.8	27.8	55	217	15.8	3.4
Goshen	1 037	6	21	240	210.9	4.1	65	509	69.3	7.7	14	33	2.1	0.3
Hot Springs	195	1	3	D	D	D	32	229	20.4	2.2	5	D	D	D
Johnson	1 771	25	12	53	6.9	0.9	56	287	38.5	3.9	11	27	2.4	0.5
Laramie	93 779	779	81	665	267.5	18.6	358	4 851	855.5	77.8	88	321	27.7	5.2
Lincoln	28 529	180	10	23	9.8	0.5	80	623	86.4	7.3	12	29	1.2	0.2
Natrona	31 358	174	206	1 853	984.1	59.2	399	3 985	645.6	65.2	106	414	39.2	8.4
Niobrara	70	1	3	D	D	D	14	84	11.9	1.0	NA	NA	NA	NA
Park	27 961	210	44	178	51.8	4.1	219	1 528	271.3	24.5	35	123	10.8	2.0
Platte	1 349	14	8	D	D	D	46	374	68.5	4.8	13	24	1.3	0.2
Sheridan	19 070	287	40	246	146.1	6.4	179	1 561	240.8	23.9	76	177	12.5	1.9
Sublette	13 726	95	7	26	10.8	0.6	33	189	26.4	2.7	10	21	2.3	0.4
Sweetwater	11 183	63	82	469	188.5	15.0	212	2 399	402.8	38.6	51	181	15.2	3.0
Teton	85 266	292	35	201	49.3	5.7	242	1 619	300.9	33.7	67	322	46.4	6.0
Uinta	6 119	56	32	226	73.2	7.3	96	1 027	174.5	15.0	29	163	12.7	3.3
Washakie	905	10	15	156	31.8	2.4	70	474	80.7	7.2	12	37	3.2	0.5
Weston	150	2	6	26	4.2	0.9	39	267	38.4	3.3	5	9	0.9	0.1

1. Establishments with payroll.

Items 133—146

Table B. States and Counties — Professional Services, Manufacturing, and Accommodation and Foodservices

STATE County	Professional, scientific, and technical services,[1] 1997				Manufacturing, 1997				Accommodation and foodservices, 1997			
	Number of establish-ments	Number of employees	Receipts (mil dol)	Annual payroll (mil dol)	Number of establish-ments	Number of employees	Receipts (mil dol)	Annual payroll (mil dol)	Number of establish-ments	Number of employees	Sales (mil dol)	Annual payroll (mil dol)
	147	148	149	150	151	152	153	154	155	156	157	158
WYOMING—Cont'd												
Crook	7	14	0.9	0.3	NA	NA	NA	NA	27	120	4.6	1.1
Fremont	78	283	16.7	6.7	41	D	D	D	152	1 397	39.9	11.4
Goshen	18	39	2.9	0.7	NA	NA	NA	NA	35	369	9.0	2.3
Hot Springs	9	28	1.3	0.5	NA	NA	NA	NA	31	234	7.2	1.8
Johnson	21	48	3.1	1.2	NA	NA	NA	NA	35	305	9.7	3.1
Laramie	199	843	64.5	24.7	48	1 349	606.3	45.2	183	3 930	106.3	31.1
Lincoln	24	84	4.2	1.7	20	579	200.8	17.4	53	369	11.5	2.7
Natrona	205	1 213	81.0	30.7	91	1 440	328.3	40.7	172	2 924	79.0	21.8
Niobrara	7	8	0.5	0.1	NA	NA	NA	NA	18	107	3.6	0.8
Park	64	218	12.2	4.3	41	524	66.1	13.9	130	1 283	90.0	21.7
Platte	19	37	3.5	1.0	NA	NA	NA	NA	40	352	9.1	2.4
Sheridan	73	304	24.1	7.4	NA	NA	NA	NA	88	1 199	36.8	10.5
Sublette	17	52	4.5	1.4	NA	NA	NA	NA	46	178	7.6	1.8
Sweetwater	58	236	17.0	7.6	29	696	458.2	36.1	109	1 838	61.3	17.5
Teton	165	577	61.8	23.6	NA	NA	NA	NA	180	4 303	166.3	43.8
Uinta	27	142	10.7	4.3	NA	NA	NA	NA	50	829	24.2	6.5
Washakie	21	70	3.0	1.2	NA	NA	NA	NA	35	320	8.4	2.1
Weston	7	19	0.9	0.3	NA	NA	NA	NA	24	155	4.1	1.1

1. Firms subject to federal tax.

STATE County	Health care and social assistance,[1] 1997				Other services,[1] 1997				Federal funds and grants, 2002–2003			
									Expenditures (mil dol)			
										Direct payments for individuals[2]		
	Number of establish-ments	Number of employees	Receipts (mil dol)	Annual payroll (mil dol)	Number of establish-ments	Number of employees	Receipts (mil dol)	Annual payroll (mil dol)	Total	Social Security and government retirement	Medicare	Food stamps and Supplemental Security Income
	159	160	161	162	163	164	165	166	167	168	169	170
WYOMING—Cont'd												
Crook	6	D	D	D	7	D	D	D	43.1	14.9	4.2	0.3
Fremont	87	1 144	73.7	28.2	64	219	17.7	4.4	246.4	84.0	33.4	6.6
Goshen	17	60	3.9	1.2	30	71	4.1	0.8	80.8	34.6	11.4	0.9
Hot Springs	11	114	5.2	2.1	14	55	1.9	0.5	49.1	16.5	6.3	0.3
Johnson	12	27	2.5	1.0	12	50	2.5	0.8	55.3	21.6	5.2	0.4
Laramie	153	1 576	105.7	51.0	127	1 122	165.2	24.3	994.4	245.7	57.2	9.6
Lincoln	16	53	2.8	0.6	21	43	3.4	0.7	92.6	32.6	8.7	0.7
Natrona	168	1 524	93.3	40.8	154	808	57.2	15.2	351.1	144.4	51.1	9.8
Niobrara	2	D	D	D	3	D	D	D	18.6	7.2	2.6	1.0
Park	63	293	20.3	9.3	60	248	23.9	5.7	206.0	67.9	20.0	2.5
Platte	15	84	4.3	1.9	19	50	3.3	0.6	66.4	26.8	8.9	0.8
Sheridan	69	537	28.9	11.8	45	214	10.5	2.9	172.5	78.8	20.2	2.9
Sublette	15	52	2.6	1.2	12	18	1.2	0.2	26.0	13.6	3.0	0.3
Sweetwater	61	457	27.5	11.5	76	359	24.0	6.6	173.0	63.5	21.4	2.3
Teton	76	288	28.1	9.1	53	242	14.4	4.6	71.7	23.7	6.5	0.4
Uinta	30	147	9.8	4.3	39	142	8.6	2.1	56.0	29.7	7.1	2.6
Washakie	15	170	6.3	2.0	28	105	6.3	1.8	59.8	21.2	9.5	0.5
Weston	9	70	3.6	1.7	8	30	1.3	0.4	61.9	18.0	6.2	0.6

1. Firms subject to federal tax.   2. State totals may include programs not allocated by county.

STATE County	Federal funds and grants, 2002–2003 (cont'd)							Local government finances, 2002				
	Expenditures (mil dol) (cont'd)							General revenue				
	Procurement contract awards		Grants[1]							Taxes		
								Total (mil dol)	Intergovernmental (mil dol)	Total (mil dol)	Per capita[2] (dollars)	
	Salaries and wages	Defense	Other	Medicaid and other health-related	Nutrition and family welfare	Education	Other				Total	Property
	171	172	173	174	175	176	177	178	179	180	181	182
WYOMING—Cont'd												
Crook	3.2	-0.9	1.0	2.9	0.4	0.3	14.8	28.8	16.2	6.7	1 135	1 007
Fremont	22.5	0.6	7.0	28.1	10.6	18.5	27.9	157.7	106.6	31.9	884	817
Goshen	6.0	0.0	0.8	14.4	2.6	0.9	1.3	44.3	29.1	8.9	727	466
Hot Springs	1.1	0.0	0.2	5.3	3.1	0.3	15.9	26.4	7.5	8.5	1 797	1 392
Johnson	5.6	0.0	1.3	2.9	0.6	1.2	15.5	33.8	13.4	8.0	1 080	814
Laramie	262.2	42.6	24.1	76.9	36.2	50.2	176.3	331.0	144.0	68.5	826	424
Lincoln	7.0	0.0	2.6	3.6	1.4	0.7	33.9	68.5	28.0	24.5	1 647	1 401
Natrona	45.6	0.8	16.1	28.6	12.7	5.0	32.0	231.9	132.2	56.6	841	568
Niobrara	1.4	0.0	0.2	1.5	0.3	0.3	3.2	10.2	5.7	3.1	1 342	1 025
Park	34.3	0.0	34.5	12.2	2.6	1.7	25.4	138.8	50.6	28.2	1 091	1 000
Platte	6.3	0.3	0.9	5.0	4.7	0.6	7.4	40.1	22.0	10.2	1 172	938
Sheridan	28.4	0.3	4.4	19.5	3.6	1.5	11.0	132.2	57.9	21.8	811	419
Sublette	4.9	0.1	1.4	0.7	0.4	0.4	1.1	52.7	12.3	35.6	5 706	5 637
Sweetwater	14.2	1.2	4.9	10.2	5.8	1.3	45.0	229.2	60.7	99.5	2 676	2 228
Teton	15.2	1.4	12.2	2.6	1.0	0.5	7.8	127.1	22.8	44.7	2 404	1 409
Uinta	3.8	0.1	0.6	2.3	3.2	1.2	5.0	103.2	34.1	50.7	2 559	2 084
Washakie	7.4	0.0	1.5	5.8	2.9	0.7	9.3	25.0	15.3	6.3	788	726
Weston	2.4	18.2	0.7	3.6	0.7	0.4	10.4	48.2	30.0	6.4	960	752

1. State totals may include programs not allocated by county.   2. Based on the resident population estimated as of July 1 of the year shown.

STATE County	Local government finances, 2002 (cont'd)							Debt outstanding		Government employment, 2002			Presidential election, 2004		
	Direct general expenditure												Percent of vote cast —		
			Percent of total for —												
	Total (mil dol)	Per capita[1] (dollars)	Educa-tion	Health and hospitals	Police protec-tion	Public welfare	High-ways	Total (mil dol)	Per capita[1] (dollars)	Federal civilian	Federal military	State and local	Demo-cratic	Republi-can	All other
	183	184	185	186	187	188	189	190	191	192	193	194	195	196	197
WYOMING—Cont'd															
Crook	26.9	4 535	46.6	18.3	3.6	0.0	5.9	2.2	370	85	29	577	14.7	83.6	1.6
Fremont	149.1	4 128	69.6	0.9	4.1	1.0	3.1	28.4	787	453	176	4 449	31.3	66.9	1.8
Goshen	43.1	3 521	65.5	1.0	3.7	0.1	2.4	11.6	951	98	60	1 107	27.0	70.9	2.1
Hot Springs	24.3	5 167	33.9	32.7	3.3	0.4	3.8	5.6	1 199	15	23	539	25.1	73.0	1.9
Johnson	32.5	4 404	39.9	31.4	4.5	0.2	3.7	11.9	1 610	111	36	746	18.2	79.9	1.9
Laramie	318.3	3 840	44.0	25.3	3.5	0.6	6.4	119.8	1 446	2 395	3 804	9 668	33.1	65.2	1.7
Lincoln	65.4	4 394	41.7	12.7	3.5	0.2	8.0	94.0	6 310	122	72	1 366	17.2	81.3	1.5
Natrona	238.1	3 536	52.2	1.4	5.6	1.2	7.0	68.4	1 016	650	328	4 633	30.9	67.3	1.8
Niobrara	8.9	3 879	57.0	2.7	5.2	0.3	6.3	18.5	8 046	25	11	300	17.5	81.0	1.4
Park	125.3	4 840	43.0	25.1	3.5	0.1	3.9	51.1	1 974	868	127	2 428	21.2	76.8	2.0
Platte	41.2	4 719	50.4	0.9	3.1	0.3	3.6	78.4	8 982	98	42	726	29.1	69.0	2.0
Sheridan	121.2	4 505	46.5	22.6	3.7	0.0	5.9	25.9	962	572	131	2 393	29.0	69.2	1.8
Sublette	35.8	5 745	44.1	5.7	5.1	0.4	7.3	22.2	3 558	112	36	592	20.0	78.0	2.0
Sweetwater	213.8	5 749	43.2	19.5	4.4	0.3	5.5	195.2	5 248	247	182	3 736	32.1	65.7	2.2
Teton	125.6	6 756	19.3	33.6	5.4	0.0	6.1	45.1	2 428	413	90	1 636	52.7	45.2	2.1
Uinta	85.8	4 333	50.4	1.0	5.6	0.2	5.6	140.3	7 086	85	96	2 034	22.5	75.4	2.2
Washakie	24.9	3 101	57.8	1.7	5.7	0.7	5.5	9.7	1 203	147	39	705	20.8	77.8	1.5
Weston	46.1	6 891	60.1	24.6	2.3	0.4	3.2	6.0	898	69	37	650	17.1	80.9	2.0

1. Based on the resident population estimated as of July 1 of the year shown.

TABLE C Highlights and Rankings

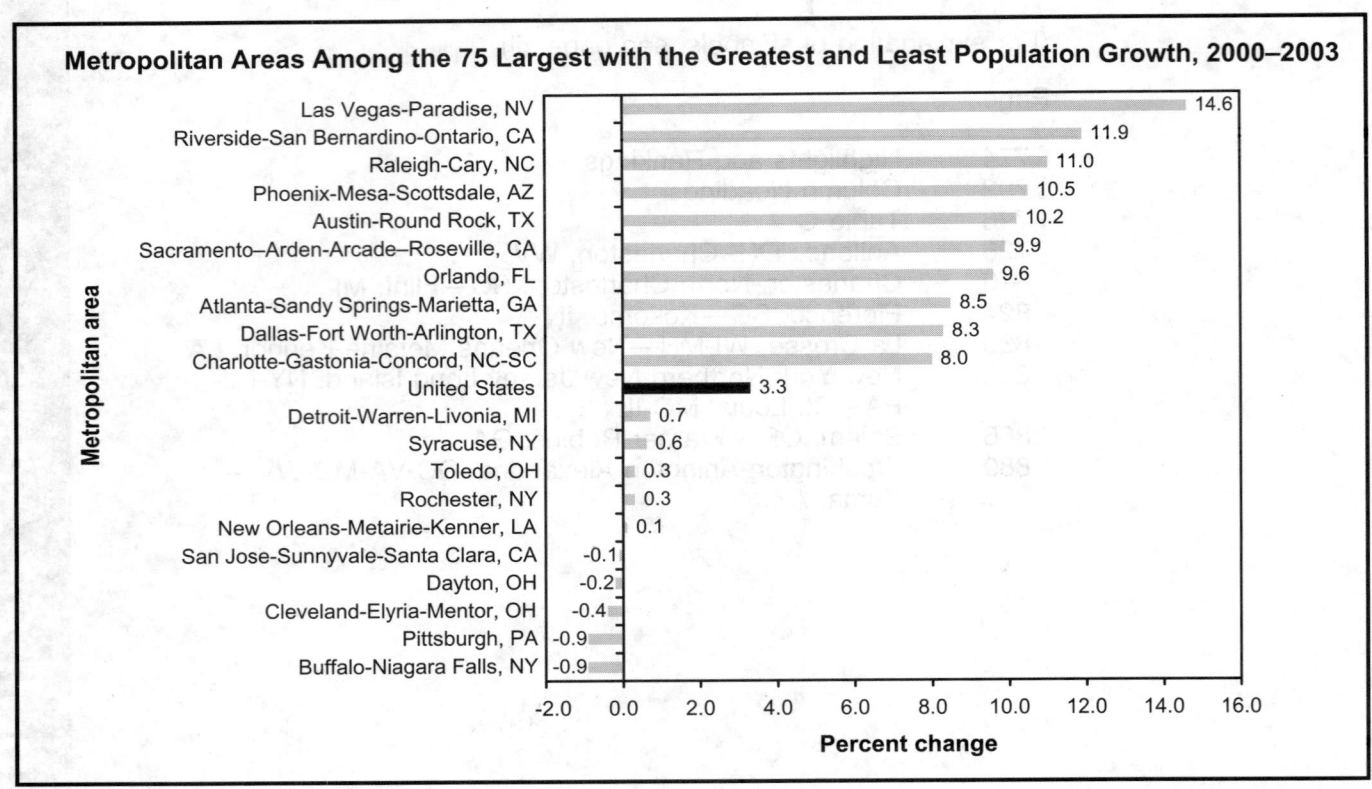

Metropolitan Areas Among the 75 Largest with the Greatest and Least Population Growth, 2000–2003

Metropolitan area	Percent change
Las Vegas-Paradise, NV	14.6
Riverside-San Bernardino-Ontario, CA	11.9
Raleigh-Cary, NC	11.0
Phoenix-Mesa-Scottsdale, AZ	10.5
Austin-Round Rock, TX	10.2
Sacramento–Arden-Arcade–Roseville, CA	9.9
Orlando, FL	9.6
Atlanta-Sandy Springs-Marietta, GA	8.5
Dallas-Fort Worth-Arlington, TX	8.3
Charlotte-Gastonia-Concord, NC-SC	8.0
United States	3.3
Detroit-Warren-Livonia, MI	0.7
Syracuse, NY	0.6
Toledo, OH	0.3
Rochester, NY	0.3
New Orleans-Metairie-Kenner, LA	0.1
San Jose-Sunnyvale-Santa Clara, CA	-0.1
Dayton, OH	-0.2
Cleveland-Elyria-Mentor, OH	-0.4
Pittsburgh, PA	-0.9
Buffalo-Niagara Falls, NY	-0.9

Four out of five Americans live in metropolitan areas, but these metropolitan areas include only one-third of all counties and a mere 25 percent of our land area. After nearly a decade of research and development, the Office of Management and Budget (OMB) recently announced new rules for defining metropolitan areas, and issued a completely new list based on the 2000 census. This new scheme defines a variety of areas called ''Core Based Statistical Areas'' (CBSAs). Along with the new definition of metropolitan areas, OMB defined a new type of area—micropolitan—that defines the many American communities with population clusters that are too small to meet the 50,000 minimum that defines a metropolitan area. Appendix C lists these new micropolitan areas as of June 2003, but, because of size constraints, *County and City Extra* continues to include only metropolitan area data in Table C.

With 18.6 million people, the New York metropolitan area is the largest, followed by Los Angeles with 12.8 million. Chicago holds third place with 9.3 million people. Another nine metropolitan areas have between 4 million and 6 million residents (Philadelphia, Dallas, Miami, Washington, Houston, Atlanta, Detroit, Boston, and San Francisco), while 38 metropolitan areas have between 1 million and 4 million people. More than half of the people in the United States live in these 50 metropolitan areas with more than 1 million residents.

The metropolitan division is another new type of statistical area definition. The 11 metropolitan areas with populations over 4 million all have a single core of 2.5 million population or more. The component counties generally are large enough to qualify as metropolitan in their own right, if they were not part of these larger areas. These large secondary population and employment centers are called metropolitan divisions. The largest metropolitan areas—New York, Los Angeles, and Chicago—also constitute the largest metropolitan divisions, with 11.4 million people in the New York-Wayne-White Plains, NY-NJ metropolitan division and nearly 9.9 million in the Los Angeles-Long Beach-Glendale, CA metropolitan division. Differences in county sizes and settlement patterns determine how many metropolitan divisions can exist within any metropolitan area. Los Angeles has only two divisions, while the much smaller Boston metropolitan area has four. Los Angeles' two divisions each consist of a single county, while New York's four divisions contain a total of 23 counties in three states.

Eleven metropolitan areas topped 10 percent growth rates: Greeley, CO and St. George, UT topped the list with more than 15 percent growth. Among the largest metropolitan areas, five had growth exceeding 10 percent, led by Las Vegas, NV with 14.6 percent. Five of the large metropolitan areas lost population since 2000. With the exception of San Jose, CA, they were all in the Great Lakes region (Pittsburgh, PA; Buffalo, NY; Cleveland, OH; and Dayton, OH).

Among metropolitan areas, New York and Los Angeles share the top spots for density as well as population. With 1,070 persons per square kilometer, the New York metropolitan area is only slightly more densely populated than the Los Angeles metropolitan area at 1021. At the other extreme, four of the largest metropolitan areas have fewer than 50 persons per square kilometer. All of these areas are located in western states (Salt Lake City, UT; Tucson, AZ; Bakersfield, CA; and Albuquerque, NM).

Three metropolitan areas had labor force growth of 6.4 percent (Blacksburg-Christiansburg-Radford, VA; McAllen-Edinburg-Pharr, TX; and St. George, UT). Among the largest metropolitan areas, Baton Rouge, LA and Riverside-San Bernardino-Ontario, CA had the highest growth rates, both with 3 percent. Nine metropolitan areas lost 3 percent or more or their labor force. San Jose-Sunnyvale-Santa Clara, CA experienced the largest proportional loss at 4.9 percent. Only one metropolitan area (Yuma, AZ) had an unemployment rate of more than 20 percent. Seventeen metropolitan areas, nine of them in California, had unemployment rates of 10 percent or more. Columbia, MO was the metropolitan area with the lowest unemployment rate—2.4 percent.

75 Largest Metropolitan Areas by 2003 Population
Selected Rankings

Population, 2003			Total land area, 2000			
Population rank	Metropolitan area	Population [col 2]	Population rank	Land area rank	Metropolitan area	Land area (square kilometers) [col 1]
1	New York-Northern New Jersey-Long Island, NY-NJ-PA	18 640 775	13	1	Riverside-San Bernardino-Ontario, CA	70 603
2	Los Angeles-Long Beach-Santa Ana, CA	12 829 272	14	2	Phoenix-Mesa-Scottsdale, AZ	37 743
3	Chicago-Naperville-Joliet, IL-IN-WI	9 333 511	50	3	Salt Lake City, UT	24 706
4	Philadelphia-Camden-Wilmington, PA-NJ-DE-MD	5 772 947	64	4	Albuquerque, NM	24 055
5	Dallas-Fort Worth-Arlington, TX	5 589 670	53	5	Tucson, AZ	23 792
6	Miami-Fort Lauderdale-Miami Beach, FL	5 288 796	5	6	Dallas-Fort Worth-Arlington, TX	23 283
7	Washington-Arlington-Alexandria, DC-VA-MD-WV	5 091 404	8	7	Houston-Baytown-Sugar Land, TX	23 124
8	Houston-Baytown-Sugar Land, TX	5 075 733	18	8	St. Louis, MO-IL	22 400
9	Atlanta-Sandy Springs-Marietta, GA	4 610 032	9	9	Atlanta-Sandy Springs-Marietta, GA	21 695
10	Detroit-Warren-Livonia, MI	4 483 853	22	10	Denver-Aurora, CO	21 676
11	Boston-Cambridge-Quincy, MA-NH	4 439 973	67	11	Bakersfield, CA	21 085
12	San Francisco-Oakland-Fremont, CA	4 157 377	35	12	Las Vegas-Paradise, NV	20 488
13	Riverside-San Bernardino-Ontario, CA	3 642 328	27	13	Kansas City, MO-KS	20 351
14	Phoenix-Mesa-Scottsdale, AZ	3 593 408	28	14	San Antonio, TX	19 012
15	Seattle-Tacoma-Bellevue, WA	3 141 777	3	15	Chicago-Naperville-Joliet, IL-IN-WI	18 679
16	Minneapolis-St. Paul-Bloomington, MN	3 083 637	1	16	New York-Northern New Jersey-Long Island, NY-NJ-PA	17 421
17	San Diego-Carlsbad-San Marcos, CA	2 930 886	25	17	Portland-Vancouver-Beaverton, OR-WA	17 311
18	St. Louis, MO-IL	2 735 927	55	18	Tulsa, OK	16 268
19	Baltimore-Towson, MD	2 616 229	16	19	Minneapolis-St. Paul-Bloomington, MN	15 704
20	Tampa-St. Petersburg-Clearwater, FL	2 531 908	56	20	Fresno, CA	15 443
21	Pittsburgh, PA	2 410 330	15	21	Seattle-Tacoma-Bellevue, WA	15 265
22	Denver-Aurora, CO	2 301 116	46	22	Richmond, VA	14 795
23	Cleveland-Elyria-Mentor, OH	2 139 512	39	23	Nashville-Davidson—Murfreesboro, TN	14 728
24	Cincinnati-Middletown, OH-KY-IN	2 047 333	7	24	Washington-Arlington-Alexandria, DC-VA-MD-WV	14 571
25	Portland-Vancouver-Beaverton, OR-WA	2 040 258	47	25	Oklahoma City, OK	14 291
26	Sacramento—Arden-Arcade—Roseville, CA	1 974 810	48	26	Birmingham-Hoover, AL	13 721
27	Kansas City, MO-KS	1 904 909	21	27	Pittsburgh, PA	13 674
28	San Antonio, TX	1 820 719	6	28	Miami-Fort Lauderdale-Miami Beach, FL	13 275
29	Orlando, FL	1 802 986	26	29	Sacramento—Arden-Arcade—Roseville, CA	13 193
30	San Jose-Sunnyvale-Santa Clara, CA	1 734 721	2	30	Los Angeles-Long Beach-Santa Ana, CA	12 563
31	Columbus, OH	1 674 589	4	31	Philadelphia-Camden-Wilmington, PA-NJ-DE-MD	11 991
32	Virginia Beach-Norfolk-Newport News, VA-NC	1 637 251	41	32	Memphis, TN-MS-AR	11 842
33	Providence-New Bedford-Fall River, RI-MA	1 623 174	24	33	Cincinnati-Middletown, OH-KY-IN	11 392
34	Indianapolis, IN	1 595 377	60	34	Omaha-Council Bluffs, NE-IA	11 300
35	Las Vegas-Paradise, NV	1 576 541	38	35	Austin-Round Rock, TX	10 940
36	Milwaukee-Waukesha-West Allis, WI	1 514 313	17	36	San Diego-Carlsbad-San Marcos, CA	10 878
37	Charlotte-Gastonia-Concord, NC-SC	1 437 427	43	37	Louisville, KY-IN	10 710
38	Austin-Round Rock, TX	1 377 633	66	38	Baton Rouge, LA	10 438
39	Nashville-Davidson—Murfreesboro, TN	1 371 302	31	39	Columbus, OH	10 318
40	New Orleans-Metairie-Kenner, LA	1 317 541	10	40	Detroit-Warren-Livonia, MI	10 137
41	Memphis, TN-MS-AR	1 239 337	34	41	Indianapolis, IN	10 007
42	Jacksonville, FL	1 202 900	71	42	Columbia, SC	9 586
43	Louisville, KY-IN	1 190 154	11	43	Boston-Cambridge-Quincy, MA-NH	9 084
44	Hartford-West Hartford-East Hartford, CT	1 177 935	29	44	Orlando, FL	9 041
45	Buffalo-Niagara Falls, NY	1 159 443	42	45	Jacksonville, FL	8 342
46	Richmond, VA	1 138 234	40	46	New Orleans-Metairie-Kenner, LA	8 167
47	Oklahoma City, OK	1 132 652	37	47	Charlotte-Gastonia-Concord, NC-SC	8 026
48	Birmingham-Hoover, AL	1 072 646	49	48	Rochester, NY	7 593
49	Rochester, NY	1 041 198	65	49	Grand Rapids-Wyoming, MI	7 324
50	Salt Lake City, UT	1 005 232	59	50	Albany-Schenectady-Troy, NY	7 298
51	Honolulu, HI	902 709	30	51	San Jose-Sunnyvale-Santa Clara, CA	6 941
52	Bridgeport-Stamford-Norwalk, CT	899 152	32	52	Virginia Beach-Norfolk-Newport News, VA-NC	6 805
53	Tucson, AZ	892 798	19	53	Baltimore-Towson, MD	6 756
54	Raleigh-Cary, NC	884 489	20	54	Tampa-St. Petersburg-Clearwater, FL	6 615
55	Tulsa, OK	879 846	12	55	San Francisco-Oakland-Fremont, CA	6 405
56	Fresno, CA	850 325	74	56	Syracuse, NY	6 189
57	Dayton, OH	846 091	54	57	Raleigh-Cary, NC	5 480
58	New Haven-Milford, CT	841 873	23	58	Cleveland-Elyria-Mentor, OH	5 191
59	Albany-Schenectady-Troy, NY	840 644	72	59	Greensboro-High Point, NC	5 188
60	Omaha-Council Bluffs, NE-IA	793 172	70	60	Springfield, MA	4 790
61	Oxnard-Thousand Oaks-Ventura, CA	791 130	61	61	Oxnard-Thousand Oaks-Ventura, CA	4 779
62	Worcester, MA	776 610	57	62	Dayton, OH	4 425
63	Allentown-Bethlehem-Easton, PA-NJ	768 036	73	63	Toledo, OH	4 195
64	Albuquerque, NM	764 869	75	64	Poughkeepsie-Newburgh-Middletown, NY	4 190
65	Grand Rapids-Wyoming, MI	762 035	33	65	Providence-New Bedford-Fall River, RI-MA	4 146
66	Baton Rouge, LA	722 646	45	66	Buffalo-Niagara Falls, NY	4 058
67	Bakersfield, CA	713 087	44	67	Hartford-West Hartford-East Hartford, CT	3 923
68	El Paso, TX	705 436	62	68	Worcester, MA	3 919
69	Akron, OH	701 644	36	69	Milwaukee-Waukesha-West Allis, WI	3 782
70	Springfield, MA	688 495	63	70	Allentown-Bethlehem-Easton, PA-NJ	3 780
71	Columbia, SC	671 407	68	71	El Paso, TX	2 624
72	Greensboro-High Point, NC	661 530	69	72	Akron, OH	2 344
73	Toledo, OH	660 874	52	73	Bridgeport-Stamford-Norwalk, CT	1 621
74	Syracuse, NY	654 194	58	74	New Haven-Milford, CT	1 569
75	Poughkeepsie-Newburgh-Middletown, NY	654 038	51	75	Honolulu, HI	1 553

75 Largest Metropolitan Areas by 2003 Population
Selected Rankings

Population density, 2003				Percent population change, 2000–2003			
Population rank	Density rank	Metropolitan area	Density (per square kilometer) [col 4]	Population rank	Percent change rank	Metropolitan area	Percent change [col 23]
1	1	New York-Northern New Jersey-Long Island, NY-NJ-PA	1 070.0	35	1	Las Vegas-Paradise, NV	14.6
2	2	Los Angeles-Long Beach-Santa Ana, CA	1 021.2	13	2	Riverside-San Bernardino-Ontario, CA	11.9
12	3	San Francisco-Oakland-Fremont, CA	649.1	54	3	Raleigh-Cary, NC	11.0
51	4	Honolulu, HI	581.3	14	4	Phoenix-Mesa-Scottsdale, AZ	10.5
52	5	Bridgeport-Stamford-Norwalk, CT	554.7	38	5	Austin-Round Rock, TX	10.2
58	6	New Haven-Milford, CT	536.6	26	6	Sacramento—Arden-Arcade—Roseville, CA	9.9
3	7	Chicago-Naperville-Joliet, IL-IN-WI	499.7	29	7	Orlando, FL	9.6
11	8	Boston-Cambridge-Quincy, MA-NH	488.8	9	8	Atlanta-Sandy Springs-Marietta, GA	8.5
4	9	Philadelphia-Camden-Wilmington, PA-NJ-DE-MD	481.4	5	9	Dallas-Fort Worth-Arlington, TX	8.3
10	10	Detroit-Warren-Livonia, MI	442.3	37	10	Charlotte-Gastonia-Concord, NC-SC	8.0
23	11	Cleveland-Elyria-Mentor, OH	412.2	67	11	Bakersfield, CA	7.8
36	12	Milwaukee-Waukesha-West Allis, WI	400.4	8	12	Houston-Baytown-Sugar Land, TX	7.6
6	13	Miami-Fort Lauderdale-Miami Beach, FL	398.4	42	13	Jacksonville, FL	7.1
33	14	Providence-New Bedford-Fall River, RI-MA	391.5	56	14	Fresno, CA	6.4
19	15	Baltimore-Towson, MD	387.2	28	14	San Antonio, TX	6.4
20	16	Tampa-St. Petersburg-Clearwater, FL	382.8	7	16	Washington-Arlington-Alexandria, DC-VA-MD-WV	6.1
7	17	Washington-Arlington-Alexandria, DC-VA-MD-WV	349.4	25	17	Portland-Vancouver-Beaverton, OR-WA	5.8
44	18	Hartford-West Hartford-East Hartford, CT	300.3	53	17	Tucson, AZ	5.8
69	19	Akron, OH	299.3	20	19	Tampa-St. Petersburg-Clearwater, FL	5.7
45	20	Buffalo-Niagara Falls, NY	285.7	22	20	Denver-Aurora, CO	5.6
17	21	San Diego-Carlsbad-San Marcos, CA	269.4	6	20	Miami-Fort Lauderdale-Miami Beach, FL	5.6
68	22	El Paso, TX	268.8	75	22	Poughkeepsie-Newburgh-Middletown, NY	5.2
30	23	San Jose-Sunnyvale-Santa Clara, CA	249.9	61	23	Oxnard-Thousand Oaks-Ventura, CA	5.0
32	24	Virginia Beach-Norfolk-Newport News, VA-NC	240.6	64	24	Albuquerque, NM	4.8
5	25	Dallas-Fort Worth-Arlington, TX	240.1	34	25	Indianapolis, IN	4.6
8	26	Houston-Baytown-Sugar Land, TX	219.5	39	26	Nashville-Davidson—Murfreesboro, TN	4.5
9	27	Atlanta-Sandy Springs-Marietta, GA	212.5	17	27	San Diego-Carlsbad-San Marcos, CA	4.2
15	28	Seattle-Tacoma-Bellevue, WA	205.8	16	28	Minneapolis-St. Paul-Bloomington, MN	3.9
63	29	Allentown-Bethlehem-Easton, PA-NJ	203.2	32	28	Virginia Beach-Norfolk-Newport News, VA-NC	3.9
29	30	Orlando, FL	199.4	31	30	Columbus, OH	3.8
62	31	Worcester, MA	198.2	68	30	El Paso, TX	3.8
16	32	Minneapolis-St. Paul-Bloomington, MN	196.4	46	30	Richmond, VA	3.8
57	33	Dayton, OH	191.2	50	30	Salt Lake City, UT	3.8
24	34	Cincinnati-Middletown, OH-KY-IN	179.7	63	34	Allentown-Bethlehem-Easton, PA-NJ	3.7
37	35	Charlotte-Gastonia-Concord, NC-SC	179.1	71	34	Columbia, SC	3.7
21	36	Pittsburgh, PA	176.3	27	34	Kansas City, MO-KS	3.7
61	37	Oxnard-Thousand Oaks-Ventura, CA	165.5	2	34	Los Angeles-Long Beach-Santa Ana, CA	3.7
31	38	Columbus, OH	162.3	62	38	Worcester, MA	3.6
54	39	Raleigh-Cary, NC	161.4	47	39	Oklahoma City, OK	3.4
40	40	New Orleans-Metairie-Kenner, LA	161.3	60	39	Omaha-Council Bluffs, NE-IA	3.4
34	41	Indianapolis, IN	159.4	15	41	Seattle-Tacoma-Bellevue, WA	3.2
73	42	Toledo, OH	157.5	51	42	Honolulu, HI	3.0
75	43	Poughkeepsie-Newburgh-Middletown, NY	156.1	65	43	Grand Rapids-Wyoming, MI	2.9
26	44	Sacramento—Arden-Arcade—Roseville, CA	149.7	72	44	Greensboro-High Point, NC	2.8
42	45	Jacksonville, FL	144.2	41	44	Memphis, TN-MS-AR	2.8
70	46	Springfield, MA	143.7	3	46	Chicago-Naperville-Joliet, IL-IN-WI	2.6
49	47	Rochester, NY	137.1	44	46	Hartford-West Hartford-East Hartford, CT	2.6
72	48	Greensboro-High Point, NC	127.5	19	48	Baltimore-Towson, MD	2.5
38	49	Austin-Round Rock, TX	125.9	33	48	Providence-New Bedford-Fall River, RI-MA	2.5
18	50	St. Louis, MO-IL	122.1	66	50	Baton Rouge, LA	2.4
25	51	Portland-Vancouver-Beaverton, OR-WA	117.9	43	50	Louisville, KY-IN	2.4
59	52	Albany-Schenectady-Troy, NY	115.2	55	50	Tulsa, OK	2.4
43	53	Louisville, KY-IN	111.1	58	53	New Haven-Milford, CT	2.2
22	54	Denver-Aurora, CO	106.2	48	54	Birmingham-Hoover, AL	2.0
74	55	Syracuse, NY	105.7	52	55	Bridgeport-Stamford-Norwalk, CT	1.9
41	56	Memphis, TN-MS-AR	104.7	24	55	Cincinnati-Middletown, OH-KY-IN	1.9
65	57	Grand Rapids-Wyoming, MI	104.0	59	57	Albany-Schenectady-Troy, NY	1.8
28	58	San Antonio, TX	95.8	1	58	New York-Northern New Jersey-Long Island, NY-NJ-PA	1.7
14	59	Phoenix-Mesa-Scottsdale, AZ	95.2	4	59	Philadelphia-Camden-Wilmington, PA-NJ-DE-MD	1.5
27	60	Kansas City, MO-KS	93.6	18	60	St. Louis, MO-IL	1.4
39	61	Nashville-Davidson—Murfreesboro, TN	93.1	70	61	Springfield, MA	1.2
47	62	Oklahoma City, OK	79.3	11	62	Boston-Cambridge-Quincy, MA-NH	1.1
48	63	Birmingham-Hoover, AL	78.2	69	63	Akron, OH	1.0
35	64	Las Vegas-Paradise, NV	76.9	36	64	Milwaukee-Waukesha-West Allis, WI	0.9
46	64	Richmond, VA	76.9	12	65	San Francisco-Oakland-Fremont, CA	0.8
60	66	Omaha-Council Bluffs, NE-IA	70.2	10	66	Detroit-Warren-Livonia, MI	0.7
71	67	Columbia, SC	70.0	74	67	Syracuse, NY	0.6
66	68	Baton Rouge, LA	69.2	49	68	Rochester, NY	0.3
56	69	Fresno, CA	55.1	73	68	Toledo, OH	0.3
55	70	Tulsa, OK	54.1	40	70	New Orleans-Metairie-Kenner, LA	0.1
13	71	Riverside-San Bernardino-Ontario, CA	51.6	30	71	San Jose-Sunnyvale-Santa Clara, CA	-0.1
50	72	Salt Lake City, UT	40.7	57	72	Dayton, OH	-0.2
53	73	Tucson, AZ	37.5	23	73	Cleveland-Elyria-Mentor, OH	-0.4
67	74	Bakersfield, CA	33.8	45	74	Buffalo-Niagara Falls, NY	-0.9
64	75	Albuquerque, NM	31.8	21	74	Pittsburgh, PA	-0.9

75 Largest Metropolitan Areas by 2003 Population
Selected Rankings

Population rank	White rank	Percent White, not Hispanic or Latino, 2003 — Metropolitan area	Percent White [col 5]	Population rank	Black rank	Percent Black, not Hispanic or Latino, 2003 — Metropolitan area	Percent Black [col 6]
21	1	Pittsburgh, PA	89.8	41	1	Memphis, TN-MS-AR	45.1
74	2	Syracuse, NY	87.4	40	2	New Orleans-Metairie-Kenner, LA	38.0
59	3	Albany-Schenectady-Troy, NY	87.1	66	3	Baton Rouge, LA	34.5
63	4	Allentown-Bethlehem-Easton, PA-NJ	86.9	71	4	Columbia, SC	34.4
69	5	Akron, OH	86.1	32	5	Virginia Beach-Norfolk-Newport News, VA-NC	32.4
62	5	Worcester, MA	86.1	46	6	Richmond, VA	31.0
24	7	Cincinnati-Middletown, OH-KY-IN	85.5	9	7	Atlanta-Sandy Springs-Marietta, GA	29.3
33	8	Providence-New Bedford-Fall River, RI-MA	85.3	48	8	Birmingham-Hoover, AL	28.2
16	9	Minneapolis-St. Paul-Bloomington, MN	84.8	19	9	Baltimore-Towson, MD	27.7
60	10	Omaha-Council Bluffs, NE-IA	84.1	7	10	Washington-Arlington-Alexandria, DC-VA-MD-WV	26.6
65	11	Grand Rapids-Wyoming, MI	83.3	72	11	Greensboro-High Point, NC	24.0
43	11	Louisville, KY-IN	83.3	10	12	Detroit-Warren-Livonia, MI	23.4
57	13	Dayton, OH	82.4	37	13	Charlotte-Gastonia-Concord, NC-SC	23.3
25	14	Portland-Vancouver-Beaverton, OR-WA	82.2	42	14	Jacksonville, FL	22.8
45	15	Buffalo-Niagara Falls, NY	82.1	4	15	Philadelphia-Camden-Wilmington, PA-NJ-DE-MD	20.4
73	16	Toledo, OH	81.9	54	16	Raleigh-Cary, NC	20.3
31	17	Columbus, OH	81.2	6	17	Miami-Fort Lauderdale-Miami Beach, FL	20.1
49	17	Rochester, NY	81.2	23	18	Cleveland-Elyria-Mentor, OH	19.9
50	19	Salt Lake City, UT	81.1	3	19	Chicago-Naperville-Joliet, IL-IN-WI	18.5
11	20	Boston-Cambridge-Quincy, MA-NH	80.9	18	19	St. Louis, MO-IL	18.5
34	21	Indianapolis, IN	80.5	1	21	New York-Northern New Jersey-Long Island, NY-NJ-PA	17.9
70	22	Springfield, MA	79.8	8	22	Houston-Baytown-Sugar Land, TX	16.7
27	23	Kansas City, MO-KS	79.1	36	22	Milwaukee-Waukesha-West Allis, WI	16.7
39	24	Nashville-Davidson–Murfreesboro, TN	78.9	39	24	Nashville-Davidson–Murfreesboro, TN	15.4
18	25	St. Louis, MO-IL	78.3	57	25	Dayton, OH	15.2
44	26	Hartford-West Hartford-East Hartford, CT	77.4	29	25	Orlando, FL	15.2
15	27	Seattle-Tacoma-Bellevue, WA	77.2	34	27	Indianapolis, IN	14.8
55	28	Tulsa, OK	77.0	31	28	Columbus, OH	14.3
75	29	Poughkeepsie-Newburgh-Middletown, NY	76.4	5	29	Dallas-Fort Worth-Arlington, TX	14.1
23	30	Cleveland-Elyria-Mentor, OH	75.2	43	30	Louisville, KY-IN	13.7
47	31	Oklahoma City, OK	75.0	27	31	Kansas City, MO-KS	13.1
20	32	Tampa-St. Petersburg-Clearwater, FL	74.6	73	32	Toledo, OH	12.7
58	33	New Haven-Milford, CT	74.2	45	33	Buffalo-Niagara Falls, NY	12.6
36	34	Milwaukee-Waukesha-West Allis, WI	73.9	58	34	New Haven-Milford, CT	12.1
52	35	Bridgeport-Stamford-Norwalk, CT	73.0	24	35	Cincinnati-Middletown, OH-KY-IN	12.0
10	36	Detroit-Warren-Livonia, MI	70.7	69	36	Akron, OH	11.8
4	37	Philadelphia-Camden-Wilmington, PA-NJ-DE-MD	70.6	49	37	Rochester, NY	11.6
42	38	Jacksonville, FL	70.5	47	38	Oklahoma City, OK	11.5
22	39	Denver-Aurora, CO	70.2	20	39	Tampa-St. Petersburg-Clearwater, FL	11.1
54	40	Raleigh-Cary, NC	69.5	52	40	Bridgeport-Stamford-Norwalk, CT	10.5
48	41	Birmingham-Hoover, AL	68.6	44	41	Hartford-West Hartford-East Hartford, CT	10.2
72	42	Greensboro-High Point, NC	68.5	75	42	Poughkeepsie-Newburgh-Middletown, NY	9.8
37	43	Charlotte-Gastonia-Concord, NC-SC	67.7	12	42	San Francisco-Oakland-Fremont, CA	9.8
19	44	Baltimore-Towson, MD	67.2	55	44	Tulsa, OK	9.6
26	45	Sacramento–Arden-Arcade–Roseville, CA	64.7	35	45	Las Vegas-Paradise, NV	9.3
46	46	Richmond, VA	64.2	21	46	Pittsburgh, PA	8.4
14	47	Phoenix-Mesa-Scottsdale, AZ	63.8	60	47	Omaha-Council Bluffs, NE-IA	8.3
29	48	Orlando, FL	62.7	65	48	Grand Rapids-Wyoming, MI	8.2
66	49	Baton Rouge, LA	62.1	13	48	Riverside-San Bernardino-Ontario, CA	8.2
32	50	Virginia Beach-Norfolk-Newport News, VA-NC	61.8	26	50	Sacramento–Arden-Arcade–Roseville, CA	8.1
71	51	Columbia, SC	61.6	74	51	Syracuse, NY	7.9
35	52	Las Vegas-Paradise, NV	60.3	38	52	Austin-Round Rock, TX	7.8
53	53	Tucson, AZ	60.1	2	52	Los Angeles-Long Beach-Santa Ana, CA	7.8
38	54	Austin-Round Rock, TX	59.9	59	54	Albany-Schenectady-Troy, NY	7.4
9	55	Atlanta-Sandy Springs-Marietta, GA	59.4	11	55	Boston-Cambridge-Quincy, MA-NH	6.8
3	56	Chicago-Naperville-Joliet, IL-IN-WI	58.9	16	56	Minneapolis-St. Paul-Bloomington, MN	6.6
5	57	Dallas-Fort Worth-Arlington, TX	57.1	15	57	Seattle-Tacoma-Bellevue, WA	6.3
61	58	Oxnard-Thousand Oaks-Ventura, CA	56.5	70	57	Springfield, MA	6.3
7	59	Washington-Arlington-Alexandria, DC-VA-MD-WV	55.8	67	59	Bakersfield, CA	6.1
17	60	San Diego-Carlsbad-San Marcos, CA	55.5	17	59	San Diego-Carlsbad-San Marcos, CA	6.1
40	61	New Orleans-Metairie-Kenner, LA	54.8	28	61	San Antonio, TX	6.0
1	62	New York-Northern New Jersey-Long Island, NY-NJ-PA	52.8	22	62	Denver-Aurora, CO	5.9
41	63	Memphis, TN-MS-AR	50.7	56	63	Fresno, CA	5.5
12	64	San Francisco-Oakland-Fremont, CA	50.0	33	64	Providence-New Bedford-Fall River, RI-MA	4.7
67	65	Bakersfield, CA	48.4	14	65	Phoenix-Mesa-Scottsdale, AZ	4.0
64	66	Albuquerque, NM	47.8	51	66	Honolulu, HI	3.9
8	67	Houston-Baytown-Sugar Land, TX	46.9	25	67	Portland-Vancouver-Beaverton, OR-WA	3.4
13	68	Riverside-San Bernardino-Ontario, CA	46.1	63	68	Allentown-Bethlehem-Easton, PA-NJ	3.3
30	69	San Jose-Sunnyvale-Santa Clara, CA	43.8	62	68	Worcester, MA	3.3
6	70	Miami-Fort Lauderdale-Miami Beach, FL	41.3	53	70	Tucson, AZ	3.2
28	71	San Antonio, TX	40.3	30	71	San Jose-Sunnyvale-Santa Clara, CA	2.8
56	72	Fresno, CA	39.5	64	72	Albuquerque, NM	2.7
2	73	Los Angeles-Long Beach-Santa Ana, CA	35.8	68	73	El Paso, TX	2.3
51	74	Honolulu, HI	31.2	61	74	Oxnard-Thousand Oaks-Ventura, CA	2.1
68	75	El Paso, TX	15.4	50	75	Salt Lake City, UT	1.4

75 Largest Metropolitan Areas by 2003 Population
Selected Rankings

Percent American Indian, Alaska Native (alone or in combination), 2003				Percent Asian and Pacific Islander (alone or in combination), 2003			
Population rank	American Indian, Alaska Native rank	Metropolitan area	Percent American Indian, Alaska Native [col 7]	Population rank	Asian and Pacific Islander rank	Metropolitan area	Percent Asian and Pacific Islander [col 8]
55	1	Tulsa, OK	10.8	51	1	Honolulu, HI	77.7
64	2	Albuquerque, NM	5.8	30	2	San Jose-Sunnyvale-Santa Clara, CA	29.5
47	2	Oklahoma City, OK	5.8	12	3	San Francisco-Oakland-Fremont, CA	23.2
53	4	Tucson, AZ	3.3	2	4	Los Angeles-Long Beach-Santa Ana, CA	14.1
14	5	Phoenix-Mesa-Scottsdale, AZ	2.3	26	5	Sacramento-Arden-Arcade-Roseville, CA	12.2
15	6	Seattle-Tacoma-Bellevue, WA	2.0	15	6	Seattle-Tacoma-Bellevue, WA	11.9
26	7	Sacramento-Arden-Arcade-Roseville, CA	1.8	17	7	San Diego-Carlsbad-San Marcos, CA	11.2
25	8	Portland-Vancouver-Beaverton, OR-WA	1.6	56	8	Fresno, CA	9.2
67	9	Bakersfield, CA	1.5	1	9	New York-Northern New Jersey-Long Island, NY-NJ-PA	9.1
56	10	Fresno, CA	1.3	7	10	Washington-Arlington-Alexandria, DC-VA-MD-WV	8.6
51	10	Honolulu, HI	1.3	35	11	Las Vegas-Paradise, NV	7.2
35	12	Las Vegas-Paradise, NV	1.2	61	12	Oxnard-Thousand Oaks-Ventura, CA	6.9
16	12	Minneapolis-St. Paul-Bloomington, MN	1.2	25	13	Portland-Vancouver-Beaverton, OR-WA	6.7
13	12	Riverside-San Bernardino-Ontario, CA	1.2	11	14	Boston-Cambridge-Quincy, MA-NH	5.9
74	12	Syracuse, NY	1.2	8	15	Houston-Baytown-Sugar Land, TX	5.8
22	16	Denver-Aurora, CO	1.1	13	16	Riverside-San Bernardino-Ontario, CA	5.5
50	16	Salt Lake City, UT	1.1	16	17	Minneapolis-St. Paul-Bloomington, MN	5.4
17	16	San Diego-Carlsbad-San Marcos, CA	1.1	3	18	Chicago-Naperville-Joliet, IL-IN-WI	5.3
65	19	Grand Rapids-Wyoming, MI	1.0	5	19	Dallas-Fort Worth-Arlington, TX	4.8
27	19	Kansas City, MO-KS	1.0	50	20	Salt Lake City, UT	4.7
12	19	San Francisco-Oakland-Fremont, CA	1.0	38	21	Austin-Round Rock, TX	4.5
32	19	Virginia Beach-Norfolk-Newport News, VA-NC	1.0	52	22	Bridgeport-Stamford-Norwalk, CT	4.2
45	23	Buffalo-Niagara Falls, NY	0.9	4	22	Philadelphia-Camden-Wilmington, PA-NJ-DE-MD	4.2
60	23	Omaha-Council Bluffs, NE-IA	0.9	9	24	Atlanta-Sandy Springs-Marietta, GA	4.1
61	23	Oxnard-Thousand Oaks-Ventura, CA	0.9	67	24	Bakersfield, CA	4.1
31	26	Columbus, OH	0.8	22	24	Denver-Aurora, CO	4.1
5	26	Dallas-Fort Worth-Arlington, TX	0.8	29	27	Orlando, FL	3.8
10	26	Detroit-Warren-Livonia, MI	0.8	54	27	Raleigh-Cary, NC	3.8
42	26	Jacksonville, FL	0.8	32	29	Virginia Beach-Norfolk-Newport News, VA-NC	3.7
36	26	Milwaukee-Waukesha-West Allis, WI	0.8	62	29	Worcester, MA	3.7
33	26	Providence-New Bedford-Fall River, RI-MA	0.8	19	31	Baltimore-Towson, MD	3.6
38	32	Austin-Round Rock, TX	0.7	47	32	Oklahoma City, OK	3.5
37	32	Charlotte-Gastonia-Concord, NC-SC	0.7	31	33	Columbus, OH	3.4
57	32	Dayton, OH	0.7	10	34	Detroit-Warren-Livonia, MI	3.3
72	32	Greensboro-High Point, NC	0.7	42	35	Jacksonville, FL	3.2
39	32	Nashville-Davidson-Murfreesboro, TN	0.7	58	35	New Haven-Milford, CT	3.2
40	32	New Orleans-Metairie-Kenner, LA	0.7	44	37	Hartford-West Hartford-East Hartford, CT	3.1
54	32	Raleigh-Cary, NC	0.7	14	38	Phoenix-Mesa-Scottsdale, AZ	3.0
46	32	Richmond, VA	0.7	59	39	Albany-Schenectady-Troy, NY	2.9
30	32	San Jose-Sunnyvale-Santa Clara, CA	0.7	36	39	Milwaukee-Waukesha-West Allis, WI	2.9
20	32	Tampa-St. Petersburg-Clearwater, FL	0.7	75	39	Poughkeepsie-Newburgh-Middletown, NY	2.9
7	32	Washington-Arlington-Alexandria, DC-VA-MD-WV	0.7	53	39	Tucson, AZ	2.9
69	43	Akron, OH	0.6	40	43	New Orleans-Metairie-Kenner, LA	2.8
59	43	Albany-Schenectady-Troy, NY	0.6	37	44	Charlotte-Gastonia-Concord, NC-SC	2.7
9	43	Atlanta-Sandy Springs-Marietta, GA	0.6	33	44	Providence-New Bedford-Fall River, RI-MA	2.7
19	43	Baltimore-Towson, MD	0.6	20	44	Tampa-St. Petersburg-Clearwater, FL	2.7
48	43	Birmingham-Hoover, AL	0.6	72	47	Greensboro-High Point, NC	2.5
71	43	Columbia, SC	0.6	27	47	Kansas City, MO-KS	2.5
34	43	Indianapolis, IN	0.6	49	47	Rochester, NY	2.5
2	43	Los Angeles-Long Beach-Santa Ana, CA	0.6	6	50	Miami-Fort Lauderdale-Miami Beach, FL	2.4
43	43	Louisville, KY-IN	0.6	46	50	Richmond, VA	2.4
58	43	New Haven-Milford, CT	0.6	64	52	Albuquerque, NM	2.3
29	43	Orlando, FL	0.6	39	52	Nashville-Davidson-Murfreesboro, TN	2.3
75	43	Poughkeepsie-Newburgh-Middletown, NY	0.6	60	52	Omaha-Council Bluffs, NE-IA	2.3
49	43	Rochester, NY	0.6	74	52	Syracuse, NY	2.3
28	43	San Antonio, TX	0.6	63	56	Allentown-Bethlehem-Easton, PA-NJ	2.2
70	43	Springfield, MA	0.6	70	56	Springfield, MA	2.2
18	43	St. Louis, MO-IL	0.6	18	58	St. Louis, MO-IL	2.1
73	43	Toledo, OH	0.6	23	59	Cleveland-Elyria-Mentor, OH	2.0
66	60	Baton Rouge, LA	0.5	57	59	Dayton, OH	2.0
11	60	Boston-Cambridge-Quincy, MA-NH	0.5	65	59	Grand Rapids-Wyoming, MI	2.0
24	60	Cincinnati-Middletown, OH-KY-IN	0.5	34	59	Indianapolis, IN	2.0
23	60	Cleveland-Elyria-Mentor, OH	0.5	69	63	Akron, OH	1.9
44	60	Hartford-West Hartford-East Hartford, CT	0.5	45	63	Buffalo-Niagara Falls, NY	1.9
8	60	Houston-Baytown-Sugar Land, TX	0.5	24	63	Cincinnati-Middletown, OH-KY-IN	1.9
41	60	Memphis, TN-MS-AR	0.5	41	63	Memphis, TN-MS-AR	1.9
1	60	New York-Northern New Jersey-Long Island, NY-NJ-PA	0.5	71	67	Columbia, SC	1.8
4	60	Philadelphia-Camden-Wilmington, PA-NJ-DE-MD	0.5	28	67	San Antonio, TX	1.8
62	60	Worcester, MA	0.5	55	67	Tulsa, OK	1.8
3	70	Chicago-Naperville-Joliet, IL-IN-WI	0.4	66	70	Baton Rouge, LA	1.7
68	70	El Paso, TX	0.4	43	71	Louisville, KY-IN	1.5
21	70	Pittsburgh, PA	0.4	21	71	Pittsburgh, PA	1.5
63	73	Allentown-Bethlehem-Easton, PA-NJ	0.3	73	71	Toledo, OH	1.5
52	73	Bridgeport-Stamford-Norwalk, CT	0.3	48	74	Birmingham-Hoover, AL	1.1
6	73	Miami-Fort Lauderdale-Miami Beach, FL	0.3	68	74	El Paso, TX	1.1

75 Largest Metropolitan Areas by 2003 Population
Selected Rankings

	Percent Hispanic or Latino,[1] 2003				Percent under 18 years old, 2002		
Population rank	Hispanic or Latino rank	Metropolitan area	Percent Hispanic or Latino [col 9]	Population rank	Under 18 years old rank	Metropolitan area	Percent under 18 years old [cols 10 and 11]
68	1	El Paso, TX	81.3	68	1	El Paso, TX	32.0
28	2	San Antonio, TX	52.1	67	2	Bakersfield, CA	30.4
56	3	Fresno, CA	46.0	56	2	Fresno, CA	30.4
2	4	Los Angeles-Long Beach-Santa Ana, CA	43.0	50	4	Salt Lake City, UT	30.3
64	5	Albuquerque, NM	42.9	13	5	Riverside-San Bernardino-Ontario, CA	29.7
67	6	Bakersfield, CA	41.5	8	6	Houston-Baytown-Sugar Land, TX	28.9
13	7	Riverside-San Bernardino-Ontario, CA	40.9	5	7	Dallas-Fort Worth-Arlington, TX	28.3
6	8	Miami-Fort Lauderdale-Miami Beach, FL	36.8	28	8	San Antonio, TX	28.1
61	9	Oxnard-Thousand Oaks-Ventura, CA	35.3	14	9	Phoenix-Mesa-Scottsdale, AZ	27.7
53	10	Tucson, AZ	31.9	41	10	Memphis, TN-MS-AR	27.6
8	11	Houston-Baytown-Sugar Land, TX	31.1	65	11	Grand Rapids-Wyoming, MI	27.3
17	12	San Diego-Carlsbad-San Marcos, CA	28.7	61	12	Oxnard-Thousand Oaks-Ventura, CA	27.2
38	13	Austin-Round Rock, TX	28.3	34	13	Indianapolis, IN	27.1
14	14	Phoenix-Mesa-Scottsdale, AZ	28.1	2	13	Los Angeles-Long Beach-Santa Ana, CA	27.1
30	15	San Jose-Sunnyvale-Santa Clara, CA	25.4	9	15	Atlanta-Sandy Springs-Marietta, GA	26.7
35	16	Las Vegas-Paradise, NV	24.4	3	16	Chicago-Naperville-Joliet, IL-IN-WI	26.5
5	17	Dallas-Fort Worth-Arlington, TX	24.3	60	16	Omaha-Council Bluffs, NE-IA	26.5
1	18	New York-Northern New Jersey-Long Island, NY-NJ-PA	20.9	35	18	Las Vegas-Paradise, NV	26.2
22	19	Denver-Aurora, CO	20.3	42	19	Jacksonville, FL	26.1
29	20	Orlando, FL	19.0	32	19	Virginia Beach-Norfolk-Newport News, VA-NC	26.1
12	21	San Francisco-Oakland-Fremont, CA	18.9	37	21	Charlotte-Gastonia-Concord, NC-SC	26.0
3	22	Chicago-Naperville-Joliet, IL-IN-WI	17.9	10	21	Detroit-Warren-Livonia, MI	26.0
26	23	Sacramento–Arden-Arcade–Roseville, CA	16.9	54	21	Raleigh-Cary, NC	26.0
50	24	Salt Lake City, UT	13.0	55	21	Tulsa, OK	26.0
52	25	Bridgeport-Stamford-Norwalk, CT	12.9	38	25	Austin-Round Rock, TX	25.9
70	26	Springfield, MA	12.1	66	25	Baton Rouge, LA	25.9
20	27	Tampa-St. Petersburg-Clearwater, FL	12.0	27	25	Kansas City, MO-KS	25.9
75	28	Poughkeepsie-Newburgh-Middletown, NY	11.5	26	25	Sacramento–Arden-Arcade–Roseville, CA	25.9
58	29	New Haven-Milford, CT	11.1	22	29	Denver-Aurora, CO	25.8
7	30	Washington-Arlington-Alexandria, DC-VA-MD-WV	10.1	36	29	Milwaukee-Waukesha-West Allis, WI	25.8
44	31	Hartford-West Hartford-East Hartford, CT	9.8	40	29	New Orleans-Metairie-Kenner, LA	25.8
25	32	Portland-Vancouver-Beaverton, OR-WA	8.7	64	32	Albuquerque, NM	25.7
63	33	Allentown-Bethlehem-Easton, PA-NJ	8.1	24	32	Cincinnati-Middletown, OH-KY-IN	25.7
33	34	Providence-New Bedford-Fall River, RI-MA	7.8	16	32	Minneapolis-St. Paul-Bloomington, MN	25.7
9	35	Atlanta-Sandy Springs-Marietta, GA	7.7	17	35	San Diego-Carlsbad-San Marcos, CA	25.6
47	36	Oklahoma City, OK	7.4	52	36	Bridgeport-Stamford-Norwalk, CT	25.3
62	37	Worcester, MA	7.3	31	36	Columbus, OH	25.3
11	38	Boston-Cambridge-Quincy, MA-NH	7.0	75	36	Poughkeepsie-Newburgh-Middletown, NY	25.3
54	38	Raleigh-Cary, NC	7.0	18	39	St. Louis, MO-IL	25.2
65	40	Grand Rapids-Wyoming, MI	6.9	7	40	Washington-Arlington-Alexandria, DC-VA-MD-WV	25.1
36	40	Milwaukee-Waukesha-West Allis, WI	6.9	29	41	Orlando, FL	25.0
51	42	Honolulu, HI	6.8	47	42	Oklahoma City, OK	24.9
37	43	Charlotte-Gastonia-Concord, NC-SC	6.5	25	42	Portland-Vancouver-Beaverton, OR-WA	24.9
15	44	Seattle-Tacoma-Bellevue, WA	6.2	30	42	San Jose-Sunnyvale-Santa Clara, CA	24.9
60	45	Omaha-Council Bluffs, NE-IA	5.7	53	42	Tucson, AZ	24.9
27	46	Kansas City, MO-KS	5.7	19	46	Baltimore-Towson, MD	24.8
4	47	Philadelphia-Camden-Wilmington, PA-NJ-DE-MD	5.4	73	46	Toledo, OH	24.8
55	48	Tulsa, OK	5.3	23	48	Cleveland-Elyria-Mentor, OH	24.7
72	49	Greensboro-High Point, NC	5.2	71	48	Columbia, SC	24.7
49	49	Rochester, NY	5.2	43	48	Louisville, KY-IN	24.7
40	51	New Orleans-Metairie-Kenner, LA	4.7	62	48	Worcester, MA	24.7
73	52	Toledo, OH	4.6	4	52	Philadelphia-Camden-Wilmington, PA-NJ-DE-MD	24.6
42	53	Jacksonville, FL	4.1	46	52	Richmond, VA	24.6
16	54	Minneapolis-St. Paul-Bloomington, MN	3.8	48	54	Birmingham-Hoover, AL	24.5
39	54	Nashville-Davidson–Murfreesboro, TN	3.8	72	55	Greensboro-High Point, NC	24.4
23	56	Cleveland-Elyria-Mentor, OH	3.5	39	56	Nashville-Davidson–Murfreesboro, TN	24.3
45	57	Buffalo-Niagara Falls, NY	3.4	1	57	New York-Northern New Jersey-Long Island, NY-NJ-PA	24.2
34	58	Indianapolis, IN	3.3	69	58	Akron, OH	24.0
59	59	Albany-Schenectady-Troy, NY	3.1	57	58	Dayton, OH	24.0
10	59	Detroit-Warren-Livonia, MI	3.1	74	58	Syracuse, NY	24.0
32	59	Virginia Beach-Norfolk-Newport News, VA-NC	3.1	49	61	Rochester, NY	23.9
71	62	Columbia, SC	2.6	6	62	Miami-Fort Lauderdale-Miami Beach, FL	23.8
41	62	Memphis, TN-MS-AR	2.6	58	62	New Haven-Milford, CT	23.8
46	62	Richmond, VA	2.6	15	64	Seattle-Tacoma-Bellevue, WA	23.7
74	62	Syracuse, NY	2.6	44	65	Hartford-West Hartford-East Hartford, CT	23.3
19	66	Baltimore-Towson, MD	2.1	11	66	Boston-Cambridge-Quincy, MA-NH	23.2
48	66	Birmingham-Hoover, AL	2.1	51	67	Honolulu, HI	23.0
31	66	Columbus, OH	2.1	33	67	Providence-New Bedford-Fall River, RI-MA	23.0
43	69	Louisville, KY-IN	2.0	70	67	Springfield, MA	23.0
66	70	Baton Rouge, LA	1.9	63	70	Allentown-Bethlehem-Easton, PA-NJ	22.9
18	71	St. Louis, MO-IL	1.7	45	71	Buffalo-Niagara Falls, NY	22.8
24	72	Cincinnati-Middletown, OH-KY-IN	1.2	12	72	San Francisco-Oakland-Fremont, CA	22.5
57	72	Dayton, OH	1.2	20	72	Tampa-St. Petersburg-Clearwater, FL	22.5
69	74	Akron, OH	0.9	59	74	Albany-Schenectady-Troy, NY	22.2
21	75	Pittsburgh, PA	0.7	21	75	Pittsburgh, PA	21.5

1. Hispanic or Latino persons may be of any race.

75 Largest Metropolitan Areas by 2003 Population
Selected Rankings

Percent 65 years old and over, 2000				Percent female-headed family households, 2000			
Population rank	65 years old and over rank	Metropolitan area	Percent 65 years old and over [cols 17 and 18]	Population rank	Female households rank	Metropolitan area	Percent female households [col 30]
20	1	Tampa-St. Petersburg-Clearwater, FL	18.0	41	1	Memphis, TN-MS-AR	19.0
21	2	Pittsburgh, PA	17.4	40	2	New Orleans-Metairie-Kenner, LA	18.2
6	3	Miami-Fort Lauderdale-Miami Beach, FL	15.8	68	3	El Paso, TX	18.0
45	4	Buffalo-Niagara Falls, NY	15.7	66	4	Baton Rouge, LA	15.9
63	5	Allentown-Bethlehem-Easton, PA-NJ	15.1	56	5	Fresno, CA	15.2
23	6	Cleveland-Elyria-Mentor, OH	14.4	1	6	New York-Northern New Jersey-Long Island, NY-NJ-PA	15.1
58	7	New Haven-Milford, CT	14.0	19	7	Baltimore-Towson, MD	14.9
33	7	Providence-New Bedford-Fall River, RI-MA	14.0	32	7	Virginia Beach-Norfolk-Newport News, VA-NC	14.9
53	9	Tucson, AZ	13.9	71	9	Columbia, SC	14.6
59	10	Albany-Schenectady-Troy, NY	13.7	67	10	Bakersfield, CA	14.5
44	10	Hartford-West Hartford-East Hartford, CT	13.7	10	10	Detroit-Warren-Livonia, MI	14.5
70	10	Springfield, MA	13.7	28	10	San Antonio, TX	14.5
57	13	Dayton, OH	13.5	48	13	Birmingham-Hoover, AL	14.4
51	13	Honolulu, HI	13.5	4	14	Philadelphia-Camden-Wilmington, PA-NJ-DE-MD	14.2
69	15	Akron, OH	13.3	46	14	Richmond, VA	14.2
4	16	Philadelphia-Camden-Wilmington, PA-NJ-DE-MD	13.1	42	16	Jacksonville, FL	14.0
74	16	Syracuse, NY	13.1	70	16	Springfield, MA	14.0
52	18	Bridgeport-Stamford-Norwalk, CT	13.0	23	18	Cleveland-Elyria-Mentor, OH	13.9
49	19	Rochester, NY	12.9	2	19	Los Angeles-Long Beach-Santa Ana, CA	13.7
18	20	St. Louis, MO-IL	12.8	6	19	Miami-Fort Lauderdale-Miami Beach, FL	13.7
73	21	Toledo, OH	12.7	9	21	Atlanta-Sandy Springs-Marietta, GA	13.6
48	22	Birmingham-Hoover, AL	12.6	58	21	New Haven-Milford, CT	13.6
1	22	New York-Northern New Jersey-Long Island, NY-NJ-PA	12.6	45	23	Buffalo-Niagara Falls, NY	13.5
11	24	Boston-Cambridge-Quincy, MA-NH	12.5	13	24	Riverside-San Bernardino-Ontario, CA	13.4
62	24	Worcester, MA	12.5	3	25	Chicago-Naperville-Joliet, IL-IN-WI	13.3
36	26	Milwaukee-Waukesha-West Allis, WI	12.4	18	25	St. Louis, MO-IL	13.3
72	27	Greensboro-High Point, NC	12.3	43	27	Louisville, KY-IN	13.2
43	28	Louisville, KY-IN	12.1	8	28	Houston-Baytown-Sugar Land, TX	13.0
55	29	Tulsa, OK	12.0	36	29	Milwaukee-Waukesha-West Allis, WI	12.9
19	30	Baltimore-Towson, MD	11.9	33	29	Providence-New Bedford-Fall River, RI-MA	12.9
29	30	Orlando, FL	11.9	64	31	Albuquerque, NM	12.8
10	32	Detroit-Warren-Livonia, MI	11.8	73	31	Toledo, OH	12.8
12	32	San Francisco-Oakland-Fremont, CA	11.8	26	33	Sacramento–Arden-Arcade–Roseville, CA	12.7
24	34	Cincinnati-Middletown, OH-KY-IN	11.6	72	34	Greensboro-High Point, NC	12.6
40	35	New Orleans-Metairie-Kenner, LA	11.4	49	35	Rochester, NY	12.5
46	36	Richmond, VA	11.3	7	35	Washington-Arlington-Alexandria, DC-VA-MD-WV	12.5
64	37	Albuquerque, NM	11.2	37	37	Charlotte-Gastonia-Concord, NC-SC	12.4
27	37	Kansas City, MO-KS	11.2	57	37	Dayton, OH	12.4
47	37	Oklahoma City, OK	11.2	29	37	Orlando, FL	12.4
14	37	Phoenix-Mesa-Scottsdale, AZ	11.2	44	40	Hartford-West Hartford-East Hartford, CT	12.3
26	41	Sacramento–Arden-Arcade–Roseville, CA	10.9	51	40	Honolulu, HI	12.3
17	41	San Diego-Carlsbad-San Marcos, CA	10.9	74	42	Syracuse, NY	12.2
42	43	Jacksonville, FL	10.8	69	43	Akron, OH	12.1
3	44	Chicago-Naperville-Joliet, IL-IN-WI	10.7	24	43	Cincinnati-Middletown, OH-KY-IN	12.1
60	44	Omaha-Council Bluffs, NE-IA	10.7	39	43	Nashville-Davidson–Murfreesboro, TN	12.1
75	44	Poughkeepsie-Newburgh-Middletown, NY	10.7	47	43	Oklahoma City, OK	12.1
71	47	Columbia, SC	10.5	5	47	Dallas-Fort Worth-Arlington, TX	12.0
65	47	Grand Rapids-Wyoming, MI	10.5	34	47	Indianapolis, IN	12.0
28	47	San Antonio, TX	10.5	35	49	Las Vegas-Paradise, NV	11.8
34	50	Indianapolis, IN	10.4	53	49	Tucson, AZ	11.8
35	51	Las Vegas-Paradise, NV	10.3	31	51	Columbus, OH	11.7
61	51	Oxnard-Thousand Oaks-Ventura, CA	10.3	27	52	Kansas City, MO-KS	11.6
32	51	Virginia Beach-Norfolk-Newport News, VA-NC	10.3	17	52	San Diego-Carlsbad-San Marcos, CA	11.6
39	54	Nashville-Davidson–Murfreesboro, TN	10.1	52	54	Bridgeport-Stamford-Norwalk, CT	11.5
25	54	Portland-Vancouver-Beaverton, OR-WA	10.1	55	54	Tulsa, OK	11.5
15	56	Seattle-Tacoma-Bellevue, WA	10.0	11	56	Boston-Cambridge-Quincy, MA-NH	11.4
31	57	Columbus, OH	9.9	62	56	Worcester, MA	11.4
68	57	El Paso, TX	9.9	59	58	Albany-Schenectady-Troy, NY	11.3
41	57	Memphis, TN-MS-AR	9.9	21	58	Pittsburgh, PA	11.3
30	57	San Jose-Sunnyvale-Santa Clara, CA	9.9	60	60	Omaha-Council Bluffs, NE-IA	11.2
2	61	Los Angeles-Long Beach-Santa Ana, CA	9.8	20	60	Tampa-St. Petersburg-Clearwater, FL	11.2
13	61	Riverside-San Bernardino-Ontario, CA	9.8	65	62	Grand Rapids-Wyoming, MI	11.0
66	63	Baton Rouge, LA	9.6	12	62	San Francisco-Oakland-Fremont, CA	11.0
56	63	Fresno, CA	9.6	61	64	Oxnard-Thousand Oaks-Ventura, CA	10.9
16	65	Minneapolis-St. Paul-Bloomington, MN	9.5	75	64	Poughkeepsie-Newburgh-Middletown, NY	10.9
37	66	Charlotte-Gastonia-Concord, NC-SC	9.4	14	66	Phoenix-Mesa-Scottsdale, AZ	10.8
67	67	Bakersfield, CA	9.0	38	67	Austin-Round Rock, TX	10.2
7	67	Washington-Arlington-Alexandria, DC-VA-MD-WV	9.0	50	67	Salt Lake City, UT	10.2
22	69	Denver-Aurora, CO	8.8	54	69	Raleigh-Cary, NC	10.1
50	70	Salt Lake City, UT	7.9	63	70	Allentown-Bethlehem-Easton, PA-NJ	10.0
54	71	Raleigh-Cary, NC	7.7	30	70	San Jose-Sunnyvale-Santa Clara, CA	10.0
5	72	Dallas-Fort Worth-Arlington, TX	7.6	25	72	Portland-Vancouver-Beaverton, OR-WA	9.9
8	72	Houston-Baytown-Sugar Land, TX	7.6	15	73	Seattle-Tacoma-Bellevue, WA	9.8
9	74	Atlanta-Sandy Springs-Marietta, GA	7.5	16	74	Minneapolis-St. Paul-Bloomington, MN	9.7
38	75	Austin-Round Rock, TX	7.0	22	75	Denver-Aurora, CO	9.6

75 Largest Metropolitan Areas by 2003 Population
Selected Rankings

Birth rate, average 1999–2001

Population rank	Birth rate rank	Metropolitan area	Birth rate (per 1,000 population) [col 33]
68	1	El Paso, TX	20.7
50	2	Salt Lake City, UT	20.0
5	3	Dallas-Fort Worth-Arlington, TX	17.7
56	3	Fresno, CA	17.7
67	5	Bakersfield, CA	17.4
8	5	Houston-Baytown-Sugar Land, TX	17.4
14	7	Phoenix-Mesa-Scottsdale, AZ	17.2
38	8	Austin-Round Rock, TX	16.9
9	9	Atlanta-Sandy Springs-Marietta, GA	16.6
28	10	San Antonio, TX	16.4
2	11	Los Angeles-Long Beach-Santa Ana, CA	16.3
13	11	Riverside-San Bernardino-Ontario, CA	16.3
41	13	Memphis, TN-MS-AR	16.2
30	14	San Jose-Sunnyvale-Santa Clara, CA	16.1
22	15	Denver-Aurora, CO	16.0
35	16	Las Vegas-Paradise, NV	15.9
54	16	Raleigh-Cary, NC	15.9
37	18	Charlotte-Gastonia-Concord, NC-SC	15.8
3	19	Chicago-Naperville-Joliet, IL-IN-WI	15.7
65	19	Grand Rapids-Wyoming, MI	15.7
34	19	Indianapolis, IN	15.7
60	22	Omaha-Council Bluffs, NE-IA	15.5
17	22	San Diego-Carlsbad-San Marcos, CA	15.5
31	24	Columbus, OH	15.2
61	24	Oxnard-Thousand Oaks-Ventura, CA	15.2
66	26	Baton Rouge, LA	15.1
55	26	Tulsa, OK	15.1
27	28	Kansas City, MO-KS	15.0
7	28	Washington-Arlington-Alexandria, DC-VA-MD-WV	15.0
64	30	Albuquerque, NM	14.8
47	30	Oklahoma City, OK	14.8
24	32	Cincinnati-Middletown, OH-KY-IN	14.7
16	32	Minneapolis-St. Paul-Bloomington, MN	14.7
39	32	Nashville-Davidson–Murfreesboro, TN	14.7
32	32	Virginia Beach-Norfolk-Newport News, VA-NC	14.7
40	36	New Orleans-Metairie-Kenner, LA	14.6
42	37	Jacksonville, FL	14.5
25	37	Portland-Vancouver-Beaverton, OR-WA	14.5
53	39	Tucson, AZ	14.4
36	40	Milwaukee-Waukesha-West Allis, WI	14.3
1	40	New York-Northern New Jersey-Long Island, NY-NJ-PA	14.3
48	42	Birmingham-Hoover, AL	14.2
51	43	Honolulu, HI	14.1
29	43	Orlando, FL	14.1
52	45	Bridgeport-Stamford-Norwalk, CT	14.0
10	45	Detroit-Warren-Livonia, MI	14.0
72	47	Greensboro-High Point, NC	13.9
26	47	Sacramento–Arden-Arcade–Roseville, CA	13.9
43	49	Louisville, KY-IN	13.7
71	50	Columbia, SC	13.6
12	51	San Francisco-Oakland-Fremont, CA	13.5
73	51	Toledo, OH	13.5
19	53	Baltimore-Towson, MD	13.4
6	53	Miami-Fort Lauderdale-Miami Beach, FL	13.4
46	53	Richmond, VA	13.4
18	53	St. Louis, MO-IL	13.4
15	57	Seattle-Tacoma-Bellevue, WA	13.3
62	57	Worcester, MA	13.3
11	59	Boston-Cambridge-Quincy, MA-NH	13.2
57	59	Dayton, OH	13.2
4	59	Philadelphia-Camden-Wilmington, PA-NJ-DE-MD	13.2
75	59	Poughkeepsie-Newburgh-Middletown, NY	13.2
23	63	Cleveland-Elyria-Mentor, OH	13.1
69	64	Akron, OH	12.6
74	64	Syracuse, NY	12.6
44	66	Hartford-West Hartford-East Hartford, CT	12.5
58	67	New Haven-Milford, CT	12.4
49	68	Rochester, NY	12.3
33	69	Providence-New Bedford-Fall River, RI-MA	12.1
20	70	Tampa-St. Petersburg-Clearwater, FL	12.0
45	71	Buffalo-Niagara Falls, NY	11.7
63	72	Allentown-Bethlehem-Easton, PA-NJ	11.6
59	73	Albany-Schenectady-Troy, NY	11.5
70	73	Springfield, MA	11.5
21	75	Pittsburgh, PA	10.7

Infant death rate, average 1999–2001

Population rank	Infant death rank	Metropolitan area	Infant death rate (per 1,000 live births) [col 37]
41	1	Memphis, TN-MS-AR	12.2
48	2	Birmingham-Hoover, AL	11.2
32	3	Virginia Beach-Norfolk-Newport News, VA-NC	9.5
42	4	Jacksonville, FL	9.4
47	5	Oklahoma City, OK	9.0
46	5	Richmond, VA	9.0
74	5	Syracuse, NY	9.0
66	8	Baton Rouge, LA	8.8
72	9	Greensboro-High Point, NC	8.7
24	10	Cincinnati-Middletown, OH-KY-IN	8.6
19	11	Baltimore-Towson, MD	8.4
37	11	Charlotte-Gastonia-Concord, NC-SC	8.4
3	11	Chicago-Naperville-Joliet, IL-IN-WI	8.4
71	11	Columbia, SC	8.4
10	15	Detroit-Warren-Livonia, MI	8.3
23	16	Cleveland-Elyria-Mentor, OH	8.1
31	17	Columbus, OH	8.0
34	17	Indianapolis, IN	8.0
36	17	Milwaukee-Waukesha-West Allis, WI	8.0
18	17	St. Louis, MO-IL	8.0
4	21	Philadelphia-Camden-Wilmington, PA-NJ-DE-MD	7.9
65	22	Grand Rapids-Wyoming, MI	7.8
40	22	New Orleans-Metairie-Kenner, LA	7.8
20	22	Tampa-St. Petersburg-Clearwater, FL	7.8
25	25	Buffalo-Niagara Falls, NY	7.6
73	26	Toledo, OH	7.5
55	26	Tulsa, OK	7.5
69	28	Akron, OH	7.4
51	28	Honolulu, HI	7.4
21	30	Pittsburgh, PA	7.3
9	31	Atlanta-Sandy Springs-Marietta, GA	7.1
44	31	Hartford-West Hartford-East Hartford, CT	7.1
67	33	Bakersfield, CA	7.0
57	34	Dayton, OH	6.9
39	34	Nashville-Davidson–Murfreesboro, TN	6.9
60	34	Omaha-Council Bluffs, NE-IA	6.9
14	34	Phoenix-Mesa-Scottsdale, AZ	6.9
27	38	Kansas City, MO-KS	6.8
13	38	Riverside-San Bernardino-Ontario, CA	6.8
7	38	Washington-Arlington-Alexandria, DC-VA-MD-WV	6.8
63	41	Allentown-Bethlehem-Easton, PA-NJ	6.6
58	41	New Haven-Milford, CT	6.6
29	41	Orlando, FL	6.6
54	41	Raleigh-Cary, NC	6.6
49	45	Rochester, NY	6.5
59	46	Albany-Schenectady-Troy, NY	6.4
64	46	Albuquerque, NM	6.4
35	46	Las Vegas-Paradise, NV	6.4
43	49	Louisville, KY-IN	6.3
53	49	Tucson, AZ	6.3
56	51	Fresno, CA	6.2
33	51	Providence-New Bedford-Fall River, RI-MA	6.2
5	53	Dallas-Fort Worth-Arlington, TX	6.1
6	53	Miami-Fort Lauderdale-Miami Beach, FL	6.1
22	55	Denver-Aurora, CO	5.9
1	55	New York-Northern New Jersey-Long Island, NY-NJ-PA	5.9
28	55	San Antonio, TX	5.9
26	58	Sacramento–Arden-Arcade–Roseville, CA	5.8
75	59	Poughkeepsie-Newburgh-Middletown, NY	5.7
17	60	San Diego-Carlsbad-San Marcos, CA	5.6
8	61	Houston-Baytown-Sugar Land, TX	5.5
16	61	Minneapolis-St. Paul-Bloomington, MN	5.5
62	61	Worcester, MA	5.5
15	64	Seattle-Tacoma-Bellevue, WA	5.3
2	65	Los Angeles-Long Beach-Santa Ana, CA	5.1
50	65	Salt Lake City, UT	5.1
52	67	Bridgeport-Stamford-Norwalk, CT	4.9
70	67	Springfield, MA	4.9
68	69	El Paso, TX	4.8
61	69	Oxnard-Thousand Oaks-Ventura, CA	4.8
25	69	Portland-Vancouver-Beaverton, OR-WA	4.8
38	72	Austin-Round Rock, TX	4.7
12	72	San Francisco-Oakland-Fremont, CA	4.7
11	74	Boston-Cambridge-Quincy, MA-NH	4.6
30	75	San Jose-Sunnyvale-Santa Clara, CA	4.4

75 Largest Metropolitan Areas by 2003 Population
Selected Rankings

Percent college graduates (bachelor's degree or more), 2000				Median household income, 1999			
Population rank	Percent college graduates rank	Metropolitan area	Percent college graduates [col 51]	Population rank	Median income rank	Metropolitan area	Median income (dollars) [col 55]
7	1	Washington-Arlington-Alexandria, DC-VA-MD-WV	42.5	52	1	Bridgeport-Stamford-Norwalk, CT	103 255
52	2	Bridgeport-Stamford-Norwalk, CT	39.9	30	2	San Jose-Sunnyvale-Santa Clara, CA	95 440
30	3	San Jose-Sunnyvale-Santa Clara, CA	39.8	12	3	San Francisco-Oakland-Fremont, CA	83 353
12	4	San Francisco-Oakland-Fremont, CA	38.8	7	4	Washington-Arlington-Alexandria, DC-VA-MD-WV	80 642
54	5	Raleigh-Cary, NC	37.6	61	5	Oxnard-Thousand Oaks-Ventura, CA	75 130
11	6	Boston-Cambridge-Quincy, MA-NH	37.0	11	6	Boston-Cambridge-Quincy, MA-NH	72 196
38	7	Austin-Round Rock, TX	36.7	1	7	New York-Northern New Jersey-Long Island, NY-NJ-PA	71 103
22	8	Denver-Aurora, CO	34.2	16	8	Minneapolis-St. Paul-Bloomington, MN	67 670
16	9	Minneapolis-St. Paul-Bloomington, MN	33.3	3	9	Chicago-Naperville-Joliet, IL-IN-WI	67 437
15	10	Seattle-Tacoma-Bellevue, WA	32.7	9	10	Atlanta-Sandy Springs-Marietta, GA	66 876
9	11	Atlanta-Sandy Springs-Marietta, GA	31.4	44	11	Hartford-West Hartford-East Hartford, CT	66 591
44	12	Hartford-West Hartford-East Hartford, CT	30.5	22	12	Denver-Aurora, CO	66 356
1	13	New York-Northern New Jersey-Long Island, NY-NJ-PA	30.3	15	13	Seattle-Tacoma-Bellevue, WA	65 948
17	14	San Diego-Carlsbad-San Marcos, CA	29.5	2	14	Los Angeles-Long Beach-Santa Ana, CA	65 428
19	15	Baltimore-Towson, MD	29.2	51	15	Honolulu, HI	65 375
59	16	Albany-Schenectady-Troy, NY	29.1	54	16	Raleigh-Cary, NC	64 636
3	17	Chicago-Naperville-Joliet, IL-IN-WI	29.0	75	17	Poughkeepsie-Newburgh-Middletown, NY	64 170
25	18	Portland-Vancouver-Beaverton, OR-WA	28.8	38	18	Austin-Round Rock, TX	64 094
5	19	Dallas-Fort Worth-Arlington, TX	28.5	5	19	Dallas-Fort Worth-Arlington, TX	64 077
31	20	Columbus, OH	28.3	10	20	Detroit-Warren-Livonia, MI	63 833
64	21	Albuquerque, NM	28.1	17	21	San Diego-Carlsbad-San Marcos, CA	63 204
37	22	Charlotte-Gastonia-Concord, NC-SC	28.0	19	22	Baltimore-Towson, MD	63 044
27	22	Kansas City, MO-KS	28.0	4	23	Philadelphia-Camden-Wilmington, PA-NJ-DE-MD	62 826
51	24	Honolulu, HI	27.9	58	24	New Haven-Milford, CT	62 220
4	25	Philadelphia-Camden-Wilmington, PA-NJ-DE-MD	27.7	37	25	Charlotte-Gastonia-Concord, NC-SC	61 810
49	25	Rochester, NY	27.7	50	26	Salt Lake City, UT	61 348
58	27	New Haven-Milford, CT	27.6	8	27	Houston-Baytown-Sugar Land, TX	60 946
46	27	Richmond, VA	27.6	62	28	Worcester, MA	59 728
50	27	Salt Lake City, UT	27.6	25	29	Portland-Vancouver-Beaverton, OR-WA	59 409
60	30	Omaha-Council Bluffs, NE-IA	27.1	26	30	Sacramento—Arden-Arcade—Roseville, CA	59 265
36	31	Milwaukee-Waukesha-West Allis, WI	27.0	14	31	Phoenix-Mesa-Scottsdale, AZ	58 886
61	32	Oxnard-Thousand Oaks-Ventura, CA	26.9	34	32	Indianapolis, IN	58 877
62	32	Worcester, MA	26.9	46	33	Richmond, VA	58 775
53	34	Tucson, AZ	26.7	36	34	Milwaukee-Waukesha-West Allis, WI	58 399
71	35	Columbia, SC	26.6	27	35	Kansas City, MO-KS	58 313
34	36	Indianapolis, IN	26.5	24	36	Cincinnati-Middletown, OH-KY-IN	58 274
26	36	Sacramento—Arden-Arcade—Roseville, CA	26.5	6	37	Miami-Fort Lauderdale-Miami Beach, FL	57 936
8	38	Houston-Baytown-Sugar Land, TX	26.4	35	38	Las Vegas-Paradise, NV	57 569
2	39	Los Angeles-Long Beach-Santa Ana, CA	26.3	31	39	Columbus, OH	57 187
39	40	Nashville-Davidson—Murfreesboro, TN	25.6	18	40	St. Louis, MO-IL	57 004
70	41	Springfield, MA	25.2	39	41	Nashville-Davidson—Murfreesboro, TN	56 868
74	41	Syracuse, NY	25.2	60	42	Omaha-Council Bluffs, NE-IA	56 352
14	43	Phoenix-Mesa-Scottsdale, AZ	25.1	23	43	Cleveland-Elyria-Mentor, OH	56 155
75	44	Poughkeepsie-Newburgh-Middletown, NY	24.9	65	44	Grand Rapids-Wyoming, MI	56 004
24	45	Cincinnati-Middletown, OH-KY-IN	24.8	49	45	Rochester, NY	55 979
29	45	Orlando, FL	24.8	63	46	Allentown-Bethlehem-Easton, PA-NJ	55 827
18	45	St. Louis, MO-IL	24.8	59	47	Albany-Schenectady-Troy, NY	55 614
69	48	Akron, OH	24.3	69	48	Akron, OH	55 460
47	49	Oklahoma City, OK	24.2	42	49	Jacksonville, FL	55 295
6	50	Miami-Fort Lauderdale-Miami Beach, FL	24.1	29	50	Orlando, FL	55 090
23	51	Cleveland-Elyria-Mentor, OH	23.9	13	51	Riverside-San Bernardino-Ontario, CA	54 501
33	52	Providence-New Bedford-Fall River, RI-MA	23.7	33	52	Providence-New Bedford-Fall River, RI-MA	54 424
32	52	Virginia Beach-Norfolk-Newport News, VA-NC	23.7	57	53	Dayton, OH	53 700
72	54	Greensboro-High Point, NC	23.4	32	54	Virginia Beach-Norfolk-Newport News, VA-NC	53 200
21	54	Pittsburgh, PA	23.4	72	55	Greensboro-High Point, NC	53 101
45	56	Buffalo-Niagara Falls, NY	23.2	41	56	Memphis, TN-MS-AR	53 044
10	56	Detroit-Warren-Livonia, MI	23.2	43	57	Louisville, KY-IN	52 981
66	58	Baton Rouge, LA	22.8	71	58	Columbia, SC	52 346
57	58	Dayton, OH	22.8	48	59	Birmingham-Hoover, AL	52 052
40	58	New Orleans-Metairie-Kenner, LA	22.8	73	60	Toledo, OH	51 640
48	61	Birmingham-Hoover, AL	22.7	74	61	Syracuse, NY	51 468
65	61	Grand Rapids-Wyoming, MI	22.7	28	62	San Antonio, TX	51 426
42	63	Jacksonville, FL	22.6	70	63	Springfield, MA	51 313
55	64	Tulsa, OK	22.5	20	64	Tampa-St. Petersburg-Clearwater, FL	50 956
28	65	San Antonio, TX	22.1	64	65	Albuquerque, NM	50 767
41	66	Memphis, TN-MS-AR	22.0	21	66	Pittsburgh, PA	49 929
63	67	Allentown-Bethlehem-Easton, PA-NJ	21.7	55	67	Tulsa, OK	49 599
20	67	Tampa-St. Petersburg-Clearwater, FL	21.7	45	68	Buffalo-Niagara Falls, NY	49 535
43	69	Louisville, KY-IN	21.2	53	69	Tucson, AZ	49 415
73	69	Toledo, OH	21.2	66	70	Baton Rouge, LA	49 207
56	71	Fresno, CA	17.5	40	71	New Orleans-Metairie-Kenner, LA	49 148
35	72	Las Vegas-Paradise, NV	17.3	47	72	Oklahoma City, OK	48 311
68	73	El Paso, TX	16.6	56	73	Fresno, CA	47 858
13	74	Riverside-San Bernardino-Ontario, CA	16.3	67	74	Bakersfield, CA	47 107
67	75	Bakersfield, CA	13.5	68	75	El Paso, TX	42 515

75 Largest Metropolitan Areas by 2003 Population
Selected Rankings

Percent of persons below the poverty level, 1999				Percent of families with children below the poverty level, 1999			
Population rank	Poverty rate rank	Metropolitan area	Poverty rate [col 58]	Population rank	Poverty rate rank for families with children	Metropolitan area	Poverty rate for families with children [col 61]
68	1	El Paso, TX	23.8	68	1	El Paso, TX	26.6
56	2	Fresno, CA	22.9	56	2	Fresno, CA	24.8
67	3	Bakersfield, CA	20.8	67	3	Bakersfield, CA	22.9
40	4	New Orleans-Metairie-Kenner, LA	18.3	40	4	New Orleans-Metairie-Kenner, LA	21.5
66	5	Baton Rouge, LA	17.1	66	5	Baton Rouge, LA	18.0
2	6	Los Angeles-Long Beach-Santa Ana, CA	16.2	2	6	Los Angeles-Long Beach-Santa Ana, CA	17.7
41	7	Memphis, TN-MS-AR	15.6	41	6	Memphis, TN-MS-AR	17.7
28	8	San Antonio, TX	15.1	28	8	San Antonio, TX	17.1
13	9	Riverside-San Bernardino-Ontario, CA	15.0	53	9	Tucson, AZ	16.4
53	10	Tucson, AZ	14.7	13	10	Riverside-San Bernardino-Ontario, CA	16.0
6	11	Miami-Fort Lauderdale-Miami Beach, FL	14.0	1	11	New York-Northern New Jersey-Long Island, NY-NJ-PA	15.7
64	12	Albuquerque, NM	13.9	70	11	Springfield, MA	15.7
8	13	Houston-Baytown-Sugar Land, TX	13.7	64	13	Albuquerque, NM	15.5
48	14	Birmingham-Hoover, AL	13.6	6	13	Miami-Fort Lauderdale-Miami Beach, FL	15.5
1	14	New York-Northern New Jersey-Long Island, NY-NJ-PA	13.6	48	15	Birmingham-Hoover, AL	15.2
47	16	Oklahoma City, OK	13.5	47	16	Oklahoma City, OK	15.0
70	17	Springfield, MA	13.1	45	17	Buffalo-Niagara Falls, NY	14.9
26	18	Sacramento—Arden-Arcade—Roseville, CA	12.7	8	18	Houston-Baytown-Sugar Land, TX	14.6
71	19	Columbia, SC	12.4	73	19	Toledo, OH	13.9
17	19	San Diego-Carlsbad-San Marcos, CA	12.4	55	20	Tulsa, OK	13.4
74	21	Syracuse, NY	12.3	33	21	Providence-New Bedford-Fall River, RI-MA	13.3
73	22	Toledo, OH	12.1	17	21	San Diego-Carlsbad-San Marcos, CA	13.3
14	23	Phoenix-Mesa-Scottsdale, AZ	12.0	74	23	Syracuse, NY	13.2
45	24	Buffalo-Niagara Falls, NY	11.9	71	24	Columbia, SC	13.1
55	25	Tulsa, OK	11.8	26	24	Sacramento—Arden-Arcade—Roseville, CA	13.1
33	26	Providence-New Bedford-Fall River, RI-MA	11.3	23	26	Cleveland-Elyria-Mentor, OH	13.0
20	27	Tampa-St. Petersburg-Clearwater, FL	11.2	43	26	Louisville, KY-IN	13.0
38	28	Austin-Round Rock, TX	11.1	14	28	Phoenix-Mesa-Scottsdale, AZ	12.7
43	29	Louisville, KY-IN	10.9	21	28	Pittsburgh, PA	12.7
23	30	Cleveland-Elyria-Mentor, OH	10.8	20	28	Tampa-St. Petersburg-Clearwater, FL	12.7
5	30	Dallas-Fort Worth-Arlington, TX	10.8	32	31	Virginia Beach-Norfolk-Newport News, VA-NC	12.5
35	30	Las Vegas-Paradise, NV	10.8	36	32	Milwaukee-Waukesha-West Allis, WI	12.4
4	30	Philadelphia-Camden-Wilmington, PA-NJ-DE-MD	10.8	42	33	Jacksonville, FL	12.0
21	30	Pittsburgh, PA	10.8	49	33	Rochester, NY	12.0
42	35	Jacksonville, FL	10.7	10	35	Detroit-Warren-Livonia, MI	11.8
29	35	Orlando, FL	10.7	72	35	Greensboro-High Point, NC	11.8
10	37	Detroit-Warren-Livonia, MI	10.6	35	35	Las Vegas-Paradise, NV	11.8
72	37	Greensboro-High Point, NC	10.6	29	38	Orlando, FL	11.7
36	37	Milwaukee-Waukesha-West Allis, WI	10.6	69	39	Akron, OH	11.6
32	37	Virginia Beach-Norfolk-Newport News, VA-NC	10.6	4	39	Philadelphia-Camden-Wilmington, PA-NJ-DE-MD	11.6
3	41	Chicago-Naperville-Joliet, IL-IN-WI	10.5	3	41	Chicago-Naperville-Joliet, IL-IN-WI	11.4
49	41	Rochester, NY	10.5	57	41	Dayton, OH	11.4
39	43	Nashville-Davidson—Murfreesboro, TN	10.3	5	43	Dallas-Fort Worth-Arlington, TX	11.3
57	44	Dayton, OH	10.0	18	43	St. Louis, MO-IL	11.3
18	44	St. Louis, MO-IL	10.0	39	45	Nashville-Davidson—Murfreesboro, TN	11.1
31	46	Columbus, OH	9.9	58	46	New Haven-Milford, CT	11.0
51	46	Honolulu, HI	9.9	24	47	Cincinnati-Middletown, OH-KY-IN	10.5
69	48	Akron, OH	9.8	31	48	Columbus, OH	10.4
19	48	Baltimore-Towson, MD	9.8	19	49	Baltimore-Towson, MD	10.3
9	50	Atlanta-Sandy Springs-Marietta, GA	9.5	51	49	Honolulu, HI	10.3
24	50	Cincinnati-Middletown, OH-KY-IN	9.5	46	49	Richmond, VA	10.3
58	50	New Haven-Milford, CT	9.5	59	52	Albany-Schenectady-Troy, NY	10.2
25	50	Portland-Vancouver-Beaverton, OR-WA	9.5	62	53	Worcester, MA	9.9
37	54	Charlotte-Gastonia-Concord, NC-SC	9.4	37	54	Charlotte-Gastonia-Concord, NC-SC	9.8
46	54	Richmond, VA	9.4	9	55	Atlanta-Sandy Springs-Marietta, GA	9.7
59	56	Albany-Schenectady-Troy, NY	9.3	25	55	Portland-Vancouver-Beaverton, OR-WA	9.7
61	57	Oxnard-Thousand Oaks-Ventura, CA	9.2	75	57	Poughkeepsie-Newburgh-Middletown, NY	9.6
75	57	Poughkeepsie-Newburgh-Middletown, NY	9.2	38	58	Austin-Round Rock, TX	9.4
62	57	Worcester, MA	9.2	63	59	Allentown-Bethlehem-Easton, PA-NJ	9.3
12	60	San Francisco-Oakland-Fremont, CA	9.1	27	59	Kansas City, MO-KS	9.3
54	61	Raleigh-Cary, NC	8.9	65	61	Grand Rapids-Wyoming, MI	9.2
65	62	Grand Rapids-Wyoming, MI	8.8	44	62	Hartford-West Hartford-East Hartford, CT	9.1
11	63	Boston-Cambridge-Quincy, MA-NH	8.5	61	62	Oxnard-Thousand Oaks-Ventura, CA	9.1
34	63	Indianapolis, IN	8.5	34	64	Indianapolis, IN	9.0
27	63	Kansas City, MO-KS	8.5	60	65	Omaha-Council Bluffs, NE-IA	8.9
15	63	Seattle-Tacoma-Bellevue, WA	8.5	12	65	San Francisco-Oakland-Fremont, CA	8.9
60	67	Omaha-Council Bluffs, NE-IA	8.4	11	67	Boston-Cambridge-Quincy, MA-NH	8.7
63	68	Allentown-Bethlehem-Easton, PA-NJ	8.3	15	68	Seattle-Tacoma-Bellevue, WA	8.5
44	68	Hartford-West Hartford-East Hartford, CT	8.3	54	69	Raleigh-Cary, NC	8.4
22	70	Denver-Aurora, CO	8.0	22	70	Denver-Aurora, CO	8.1
50	71	Salt Lake City, UT	7.9	50	71	Salt Lake City, UT	7.8
30	72	San Jose-Sunnyvale-Santa Clara, CA	7.6	52	72	Bridgeport-Stamford-Norwalk, CT	7.2
7	73	Washington-Arlington-Alexandria, DC-VA-MD-WV	7.4	7	73	Washington-Arlington-Alexandria, DC-VA-MD-WV	7.1
52	74	Bridgeport-Stamford-Norwalk, CT	6.9	30	74	San Jose-Sunnyvale-Santa Clara, CA	6.8
16	75	Minneapolis-St. Paul-Bloomington, MN	6.7	16	75	Minneapolis-St. Paul-Bloomington, MN	6.5

75 Largest Metropolitan Areas by 2003 Population
Selected Rankings

Mean value of owner-occupied housing units, 2000				Mean gross rent of renter-occupied housing units, 2000			
Population rank	Mean value rank	Metropolitan area	Mean value (dollars) [col 91]	Population rank	Mean rent rank	Metropolitan area	Mean rent (dollars) [col 94]
30	1	San Jose-Sunnyvale-Santa Clara, CA	524 976	30	1	San Jose-Sunnyvale-Santa Clara, CA	1 217
12	2	San Francisco-Oakland-Fremont, CA	420 973	12	2	San Francisco-Oakland-Fremont, CA	1 021
52	3	Bridgeport-Stamford-Norwalk, CT	397 155	61	3	Oxnard-Thousand Oaks-Ventura, CA	943
51	4	Honolulu, HI	348 564	52	4	Bridgeport-Stamford-Norwalk, CT	932
2	5	Los Angeles-Long Beach-Santa Ana, CA	298 376	7	5	Washington-Arlington-Alexandria, DC-VA-MD-WV	869
61	6	Oxnard-Thousand Oaks-Ventura, CA	297 826	51	6	Honolulu, HI	865
17	7	San Diego-Carlsbad-San Marcos, CA	284 952	17	7	San Diego-Carlsbad-San Marcos, CA	832
11	8	Boston-Cambridge-Quincy, MA-NH	266 305	2	8	Los Angeles-Long Beach-Santa Ana, CA	812
1	9	New York-Northern New Jersey-Long Island, NY-NJ-PA	261 485	11	9	Boston-Cambridge-Quincy, MA-NH	810
15	10	Seattle-Tacoma-Bellevue, WA	252 388	1	10	New York-Northern New Jersey-Long Island, NY-NJ-PA	806
7	11	Washington-Arlington-Alexandria, DC-VA-MD-WV	228 565	15	11	Seattle-Tacoma-Bellevue, WA	782
22	12	Denver-Aurora, CP	214 359	38	12	Austin-Round Rock, TX	767
25	13	Portland-Vancouver-Beaverton, OR-WA	203 484	9	13	Atlanta-Sandy Springs-Marietta, GA	749
3	14	Chicago-Naperville-Joliet, IL-IN-WI	199 800	22	14	Denver-Aurora, CP	747
50	15	Salt Lake City, UT	194 483	35	15	Las Vegas-Paradise, NV	743
26	16	Sacramento-Arden-Arcade-Roseville, CA	192 281	6	16	Miami-Fort Lauderdale-Miami Beach, FL	740
54	17	Raleigh-Cary, NC	181 226	75	17	Poughkeepsie-Newburgh-Middletown, NY	725
58	18	New Haven-Milford, CT	181 216	29	18	Orlando, FL	720
44	19	Hartford-West Hartford-East Hartford, CT	176 237	25	19	Portland-Vancouver-Beaverton, OR-WA	715
62	20	Worcester, MA	173 081	54	20	Raleigh-Cary, NC	714
9	21	Atlanta-Sandy Springs-Marietta, GA	171 035	26	21	Sacramento-Arden-Arcade-Roseville, CA	708
6	22	Miami-Fort Lauderdale-Miami Beach, FL	170 312	14	22	Phoenix-Mesa-Scottsdale, AZ	707
16	23	Minneapolis-St. Paul-Bloomington, MN	168 496	3	23	Chicago-Naperville-Joliet, IL-IN-WI	703
75	24	Poughkeepsie-Newburgh-Middletown, NY	168 348	5	24	Dallas-Fort Worth-Arlington, TX	695
35	25	Las Vegas-Paradise, NV	166 434	13	25	Riverside-San Bernardino-Ontario, CA	692
33	26	Providence-New Bedford-Fall River, RI-MA	165 860	4	26	Philadelphia-Camden-Wilmington, PA-NJ-DE-MD	691
10	27	Detroit-Warren-Livonia, MI	164 929	58	27	New Haven-Milford, CT	680
38	28	Austin-Round Rock, TX	164 223	50	28	Salt Lake City, UT	678
14	29	Phoenix-Mesa-Scottsdale, AZ	164 191	44	29	Hartford-West Hartford-East Hartford, CT	670
19	30	Baltimore-Towson, MD	163 594	16	30	Minneapolis-St. Paul-Bloomington, MN	666
13	31	Riverside-San Bernardino-Ontario, CA	163 483	37	31	Charlotte-Gastonia-Concord, NC-SC	660
37	32	Charlotte-Gastonia-Concord, NC-SC	161 062	19	32	Baltimore-Towson, MD	655
36	33	Milwaukee-Waukesha-West Allis, WI	156 918	20	33	Tampa-St. Petersburg-Clearwater, FL	646
39	34	Nashville-Davidson-Murfreesboro, TN	154 004	8	34	Houston-Baytown-Sugar Land, TX	640
4	35	Philadelphia-Camden-Wilmington, PA-NJ-DE-MD	148 160	42	35	Jacksonville, FL	638
64	36	Albuquerque, NM	147 396	32	36	Virginia Beach-Norfolk-Newport News, VA-NC	635
23	37	Cleveland-Elyria-Mentor, OH	145 872	46	37	Richmond, VA	626
53	38	Tucson, AZ	145 417	49	38	Rochester, NY	620
31	39	Columbus, OH	144 049	10	39	Detroit-Warren-Livonia, MI	618
24	40	Cincinnati-Middletown, OH-KY-IN	143 831	39	40	Nashville-Davidson-Murfreesboro, TN	616
70	41	Springfield, MA	139 232	64	41	Albuquerque, NM	613
34	42	Indianapolis, IN	138 703	36	42	Milwaukee-Waukesha-West Allis, WI	608
46	43	Richmond, VA	138 023	31	43	Columbus, OH	607
29	44	Orlando, FL	137 919	53	44	Tucson, AZ	606
32	45	Virginia Beach-Norfolk-Newport News, VA-NC	136 678	63	45	Allentown-Bethlehem-Easton, PA-NJ	605
63	46	Allentown-Bethlehem-Easton, PA-NJ	135 716	59	46	Albany-Schenectady-Troy, NY	603
5	47	Dallas-Fort Worth-Arlington, TX	135 597	27	46	Kansas City, MO-KS	603
69	48	Akron, OH	135 174	34	48	Indianapolis, IN	598
65	49	Grand Rapids-Wyoming, MI	133 109	28	49	San Antonio, TX	590
72	50	Greensboro-High Point, NC	132 289	62	49	Worcester, MA	590
42	51	Jacksonville, FL	132 102	72	51	Greensboro-High Point, NC	575
40	52	New Orleans-Metairie-Kenner, LA	130 783	23	52	Cleveland-Elyria-Mentor, OH	573
56	53	Fresno, CA	129 555	60	52	Omaha-Council Bluffs, NE-IA	573
18	54	St. Louis, MO-IL	128 742	41	54	Memphis, TN-MS-AR	570
48	55	Birmingham-Hoover, AL	128 636	56	55	Fresno, CA	569
43	56	Louisville, KY-IN	127 286	71	56	Columbia, SC	568
71	57	Columbia, SC	127 039	65	57	Grand Rapids-Wyoming, MI	566
27	58	Kansas City, MO-KS	125 941	69	58	Akron, OH	564
59	59	Albany-Schenectady-Troy, NY	124 956	67	59	Bakersfield, CA	558
8	60	Houston-Baytown-Sugar Land, TX	123 782	33	60	Providence-New Bedford-Fall River, RI-MA	557
20	61	Tampa-St. Petersburg-Clearwater, FL	122 966	57	61	Dayton, OH	555
41	62	Memphis, TN-MS-AR	122 549	70	61	Springfield, MA	555
57	63	Dayton, OH	120 633	18	63	St. Louis, MO-IL	554
60	64	Omaha-Council Bluffs, NE-IA	120 031	24	64	Cincinnati-Middletown, OH-KY-IN	552
73	65	Toledo, OH	120 000	74	65	Syracuse, NY	548
66	66	Baton Rouge, LA	118 706	40	66	New Orleans-Metairie-Kenner, LA	543
49	67	Rochester, NY	114 058	55	67	Tulsa, OK	533
67	68	Bakersfield, CA	111 850	45	68	Buffalo-Niagara Falls, NY	526
21	69	Pittsburgh, PA	105 450	66	69	Baton Rouge, LA	523
55	70	Tulsa, OK	103 945	48	70	Birmingham-Hoover, AL	520
45	71	Buffalo-Niagara Falls, NY	103 880	47	70	Oklahoma City, OK	520
28	72	San Antonio, TX	99 306	73	72	Toledo, OH	514
74	73	Syracuse, NY	98 147	43	73	Louisville, KY-IN	512
47	74	Oklahoma City, OK	95 975	21	74	Pittsburgh, PA	510
68	75	El Paso, TX	83 652	68	75	El Paso, TX	499

75 Largest Metropolitan Areas by 2003 Population
Selected Rankings

Unemployment rate, 2003				Percent of votes for George W. Bush, 2004			
Population rank	Unemployment rate rank	Metropolitan area	Unemployment rate [col 100]	Population rank	Vote for Bush rank	Metropolitan area	Percent of votes for Bush [col 196]
56	1	Fresno, CA	14.2	67	1	Bakersfield, CA	66.9
67	2	Bakersfield, CA	12.3	47	2	Oklahoma City, OK	66.7
68	3	El Paso, TX	9.7	55	3	Tulsa, OK	64.3
25	4	Portland-Vancouver-Beaverton, OR-WA	8.5	48	4	Birmingham-Hoover, AL	63.3
30	5	San Jose-Sunnyvale-Santa Clara, CA	8.3	42	5	Jacksonville, FL	63.0
65	6	Grand Rapids-Wyoming, MI	7.8	60	6	Omaha-Council Bluffs, NE-IA	61.9
73	7	Toledo, OH	7.3	5	7	Dallas-Fort Worth-Arlington, TX	61.6
10	8	Detroit-Warren-Livonia, MI	7.2	24	7	Cincinnati-Middletown, OH-KY-IN	61.6
15	8	Seattle-Tacoma-Bellevue, WA	7.2	34	9	Indianapolis, IN	61.0
8	10	Houston-Baytown-Sugar Land, TX	7.0	9	10	Atlanta-Sandy Springs-Marietta, GA	60.4
5	11	Dallas-Fort Worth-Arlington, TX	6.9	50	11	Salt Lake City, UT	60.0
3	12	Chicago-Naperville-Joliet, IL-IN-WI	6.8	28	12	San Antonio, TX	59.4
62	13	Worcester, MA	6.7	65	13	Grand Rapids-Wyoming, MI	59.2
37	14	Charlotte-Gastonia-Concord, NC-SC	6.6	8	14	Houston-Baytown-Sugar Land, TX	58.5
23	14	Cleveland-Elyria-Mentor, OH	6.6	56	15	Fresno, CA	57.9
72	14	Greensboro-High Point, NC	6.6	66	16	Baton Rouge, LA	57.6
55	14	Tulsa, OK	6.6	14	17	Phoenix-Mesa-Scottsdale, AZ	56.9
66	18	Baton Rouge, LA	6.5	13	18	Riverside-San Bernardino-Ontario, CA	56.8
1	18	New York-Northern New Jersey-Long Island, NY-NJ-PA	6.5	37	19	Charlotte-Gastonia-Concord, NC-SC	56.0
45	20	Buffalo-Niagara Falls, NY	6.4	39	19	Nashville-Davidson-Murfreesboro, TN	56.0
41	20	Memphis, TN-MS-AR	6.4	72	21	Greensboro-High Point, NC	55.4
6	22	Miami-Fort Lauderdale-Miami Beach, FL	6.3	46	22	Richmond, VA	55.3
22	23	Denver-Aurora, CO	6.2	43	23	Louisville, KY-IN	54.5
2	23	Los Angeles-Long Beach-Santa Ana, CA	6.2	71	24	Columbia, SC	54.4
36	25	Milwaukee-Waukesha-West Allis, WI	6.1	57	25	Dayton, OH	54.1
57	26	Dayton, OH	6.0	29	26	Orlando, FL	53.6
27	26	Kansas City, MO-KS	6.0	75	27	Poughkeepsie-Newburgh-Middletown, NY	53.5
58	26	New Haven-Milford, CT	6.0	54	28	Raleigh-Cary, NC	53.4
12	26	San Francisco-Oakland-Fremont, CA	6.0	32	29	Virginia Beach-Norfolk-Newport News, VA-NC	53.1
18	26	St. Louis, MO-IL	6.0	31	30	Columbus, OH	52.5
4	31	Philadelphia-Camden-Wilmington, PA-NJ-DE-MD	5.9	17	31	San Diego-Carlsbad-San Marcos, CA	52.2
13	31	Riverside-San Bernardino-Ontario, CA	5.9	26	32	Sacramento-Arden-Arcade-Roseville, CA	52.0
50	31	Salt Lake City, UT	5.9	20	33	Tampa-St. Petersburg-Clearwater, FL	51.9
63	34	Allentown-Bethlehem-Easton, PA-NJ	5.8	27	34	Kansas City, MO-KS	51.6
44	34	Hartford-West Hartford-East Hartford, CT	5.8	49	35	Rochester, NY	51.1
33	34	Providence-New Bedford-Fall River, RI-MA	5.8	61	36	Oxnard-Thousand Oaks-Ventura, CA	50.7
49	34	Rochester, NY	5.8	63	37	Allentown-Bethlehem-Easton, PA-NJ	50.6
70	34	Springfield, MA	5.8	35	38	Las Vegas-Paradise, NV	50.5
74	34	Syracuse, NY	5.8	36	39	Milwaukee-Waukesha-West Allis, WI	50.3
69	40	Akron, OH	5.7	40	40	New Orleans-Metairie-Kenner, LA	50.0
38	40	Austin-Round Rock, TX	5.7	38	41	Austin-Round Rock, TX	49.6
40	40	New Orleans-Metairie-Kenner, LA	5.7	64	42	Albuquerque, NM	48.9
21	43	Pittsburgh, PA	5.6	22	43	Denver-Aurora, CO	48.5
64	44	Albuquerque, NM	5.5	51	44	Honolulu, HI	48.3
11	44	Boston-Cambridge-Quincy, MA-NH	5.5	21	45	Pittsburgh, PA	47.6
43	44	Louisville, KY-IN	5.5	52	46	Bridgeport-Stamford-Norwalk, CT	47.3
28	44	San Antonio, TX	5.5	53	47	Tucson, AZ	47.0
26	48	Sacramento-Arden-Arcade-Roseville, CA	5.4	41	48	Memphis, TN-MS-AR	46.9
35	49	Las Vegas-Paradise, NV	5.3	19	49	Baltimore-Towson, MD	46.6
61	49	Oxnard-Thousand Oaks-Ventura, CA	5.3	74	50	Syracuse, NY	46.3
42	51	Jacksonville, FL	5.2	18	51	St. Louis, MO-IL	45.9
19	52	Baltimore-Towson, MD	5.1	16	52	Minneapolis-St. Paul-Bloomington, MN	45.8
24	53	Cincinnati-Middletown, OH-KY-IN	5.0	59	52	Albany-Schenectady-Troy, NY	45.8
47	53	Oklahoma City, OK	5.0	73	54	Toledo, OH	44.7
14	53	Phoenix-Mesa-Scottsdale, AZ	5.0	58	55	New Haven-Milford, CT	43.9
9	56	Atlanta-Sandy Springs-Marietta, GA	4.9	69	56	Akron, OH	43.8
31	56	Columbus, OH	4.9	68	57	El Paso, TX	43.3
29	56	Orlando, FL	4.9	45	58	Buffalo-Niagara Falls, NY	42.8
52	59	Bridgeport-Stamford-Norwalk, CT	4.8	62	59	Worcester, MA	42.6
71	59	Columbia, SC	4.8	10	60	Detroit-Warren-Livonia, MI	42.5
16	59	Minneapolis-St. Paul-Bloomington, MN	4.8	25	61	Portland-Vancouver-Beaverton, OR-WA	41.7
54	59	Raleigh-Cary, NC	4.8	2	62	Los Angeles-Long Beach-Santa Ana, CA	41.2
48	63	Birmingham-Hoover, AL	4.6	44	63	Hartford-West Hartford-East Hartford, CT	40.4
34	63	Indianapolis, IN	4.6	6	64	Miami-Fort Lauderdale-Miami Beach, FL	40.0
39	63	Nashville-Davidson-Murfreesboro, TN	4.6	23	65	Cleveland-Elyria-Mentor, OH	39.7
60	66	Omaha-Council Bluffs, NE-IA	4.4	1	66	New York-Northern New Jersey-Long Island, NY-NJ-PA	39.2
20	66	Tampa-St. Petersburg-Clearwater, FL	4.4	15	66	Seattle-Tacoma-Bellevue, WA	39.2
32	66	Virginia Beach-Norfolk-Newport News, VA-NC	4.4	3	68	Chicago-Naperville-Joliet, IL-IN-WI	39.0
75	69	Poughkeepsie-Newburgh-Middletown, NY	4.3	4	69	Philadelphia-Camden-Wilmington, PA-NJ-DE-MD	38.6
46	69	Richmond, VA	4.3	7	70	Washington-Arlington-Alexandria, DC-VA-MD-WV	38.0
17	69	San Diego-Carlsbad-San Marcos, CA	4.3	11	71	Boston-Cambridge-Quincy, MA-NH	37.8
53	69	Tucson, AZ	4.3	33	72	Providence-New Bedford-Fall River, RI-MA	37.7
51	73	Honolulu, HI	3.9	30	73	San Jose-Sunnyvale-Santa Clara, CA	35.0
59	74	Albany-Schenectady-Troy, NY	3.8	70	74	Springfield, MA	34.8
7	75	Washington-Arlington-Alexandria, DC-VA-MD-WV	3.5	12	75	San Francisco-Oakland-Fremont, CA	26.8

75 Largest Metropolitan Areas by 2003 Population
Selected Rankings

Manufacturing employment as a percent of total nonfarm employment, 2001				Employment in professional, scientific, and technical services as a percent of total nonfarm employment, 2001			
Population rank	Manufacturing rank	Metropolitan area	Percent employed in manufacturing [col 107/col 105]	Population rank	Services rank	Metropolitan area	Percent employed in services [col 110/col 105]
72	1	Greensboro-High Point, NC	23.9	7	1	Washington-Arlington-Alexandria, DC-VA-MD-WV	17.0
65	2	Grand Rapids-Wyoming, MI	23.2	30	2	San Jose-Sunnyvale-Santa Clara, CA	14.0
30	3	San Jose-Sunnyvale-Santa Clara, CA	19.4	12	3	San Francisco-Oakland-Fremont, CA	10.3
57	4	Dayton, OH	19.2	2	4	Los Angeles-Long Beach-Santa Ana, CA	10.2
49	5	Rochester, NY	19.2	11	5	Boston-Cambridge-Quincy, MA-NH	9.7
36	6	Milwaukee-Waukesha-West Allis, WI	19.0	17	6	San Diego-Carlsbad-San Marcos, CA	9.3
33	7	Providence-New Bedford-Fall River, RI-MA	18.5	19	7	Baltimore-Towson, MD	8.7
73	8	Toledo, OH	18.5	1	8	New York-Northern New Jersey-Long Island, NY-NJ-PA	8.6
70	9	Springfield, MA	17.6	54	9	Raleigh-Cary, NC	8.5
62	10	Worcester, MA	17.5	38	10	Austin-Round Rock, TX	8.4
23	11	Cleveland-Elyria-Mentor, OH	17.3	52	11	Bridgeport-Stamford-Norwalk, CT	8.3
63	12	Allentown-Bethlehem-Easton, PA-NJ	17.1	22	12	Denver-Aurora, CO	8.0
69	13	Akron, OH	16.9	4	13	Philadelphia-Camden-Wilmington, PA-NJ-DE-MD	7.9
45	14	Buffalo-Niagara Falls, NY	16.1	9	14	Atlanta-Sandy Springs-Marietta, GA	7.8
43	15	Louisville, KY-IN	15.9	3	15	Chicago-Naperville-Joliet, IL-IN-WI	7.5
10	16	Detroit-Warren-Livonia, MI	15.8	59	16	Albany-Schenectady-Troy, NY	7.5
68	17	El Paso, TX	15.5	32	17	Virginia Beach-Norfolk-Newport News, VA-NC	7.3
58	18	New Haven-Milford, CT	15.4	20	18	Tampa-St. Petersburg-Clearwater, FL	7.3
2	19	Los Angeles-Long Beach-Santa Ana, CA	15.2	8	19	Houston-Baytown-Sugar Land, TX	7.2
75	20	Poughkeepsie-Newburgh-Middletown, NY	15.1	15	20	Seattle-Tacoma-Bellevue, WA	7.1
24	21	Cincinnati-Middletown, OH-KY-IN	14.7	10	21	Detroit-Warren-Livonia, MI	6.9
44	22	Hartford-West Hartford-East Hartford, CT	14.5	27	22	Kansas City, MO-KS	6.8
3	23	Chicago-Naperville-Joliet, IL-IN-WI	14.5	50	23	Salt Lake City, UT	6.8
15	24	Seattle-Tacoma-Bellevue, WA	14.3	64	24	Albuquerque, NM	6.7
61	25	Oxnard-Thousand Oaks-Ventura, CA	14.3	14	25	Phoenix-Mesa-Scottsdale, AZ	6.6
74	26	Syracuse, NY	14.2	5	26	Dallas-Fort Worth-Arlington, TX	6.6
13	27	Riverside-San Bernardino-Ontario, CA	14.1	21	27	Pittsburgh, PA	6.5
55	28	Tulsa, OK	14.0	71	28	Columbia, SC	6.4
25	29	Portland-Vancouver-Beaverton, OR-WA	13.9	61	29	Oxnard-Thousand Oaks-Ventura, CA	6.4
16	30	Minneapolis-St. Paul-Bloomington, MN	13.6	6	30	Miami-Fort Lauderdale-Miami Beach, FL	6.3
37	31	Charlotte-Gastonia-Concord, NC-SC	13.1	16	31	Minneapolis-St. Paul-Bloomington, MN	6.3
52	32	Bridgeport-Stamford-Norwalk, CT	12.7	31	32	Columbus, OH	6.1
39	33	Nashville-Davidson–Murfreesboro, TN	12.6	26	33	Sacramento–Arden-Arcade–Roseville, CA	6.1
34	34	Indianapolis, IN	12.5	66	34	Baton Rouge, LA	6.0
38	35	Austin-Round Rock, TX	12.2	18	35	St. Louis, MO-IL	5.9
5	36	Dallas-Fort Worth-Arlington, TX	12.2	25	36	Portland-Vancouver-Beaverton, OR-WA	5.9
71	37	Columbia, SC	12.0	23	37	Cleveland-Elyria-Mentor, OH	5.9
18	38	St. Louis, MO-IL	12.0	60	38	Omaha-Council Bluffs, NE-IA	5.9
56	39	Fresno, CA	11.8	44	39	Hartford-West Hartford-East Hartford, CT	5.8
21	40	Pittsburgh, PA	11.3	29	40	Orlando, FL	5.8
53	41	Tucson, AZ	11.1	57	41	Dayton, OH	5.7
31	42	Columbus, OH	11.1	37	42	Charlotte-Gastonia-Concord, NC-SC	5.7
17	43	San Diego-Carlsbad-San Marcos, CA	11.1	40	43	New Orleans-Metairie-Kenner, LA	5.7
11	44	Boston-Cambridge-Quincy, MA-NH	11.0	28	44	San Antonio, TX	5.6
50	45	Salt Lake City, UT	11.0	24	45	Cincinnati-Middletown, OH-KY-IN	5.6
47	46	Oklahoma City, OK	10.9	67	46	Bakersfield, CA	5.5
46	47	Richmond, VA	10.9	48	47	Birmingham-Hoover, AL	5.4
48	48	Birmingham-Hoover, AL	10.9	53	48	Tucson, AZ	5.4
32	49	Virginia Beach-Norfolk-Newport News, VA-NC	10.7	49	49	Rochester, NY	5.2
14	50	Phoenix-Mesa-Scottsdale, AZ	10.3	51	50	Honolulu, HI	5.2
4	51	Philadelphia-Camden-Wilmington, PA-NJ-DE-MD	10.2	47	51	Oklahoma City, OK	5.1
8	52	Houston-Baytown-Sugar Land, TX	10.1	34	52	Indianapolis, IN	5.1
27	53	Kansas City, MO-KS	10.0	74	53	Syracuse, NY	5.0
60	54	Omaha-Council Bluffs, NE-IA	9.3	46	54	Richmond, VA	5.0
66	55	Baton Rouge, LA	9.2	55	55	Tulsa, OK	5.0
41	56	Memphis, TN-MS-AR	9.1	36	56	Milwaukee-Waukesha-West Allis, WI	5.0
9	57	Atlanta-Sandy Springs-Marietta, GA	8.6	58	57	New Haven-Milford, CT	4.9
64	58	Albuquerque, NM	8.5	73	58	Toledo, OH	4.7
54	59	Raleigh-Cary, NC	8.3	45	59	Buffalo-Niagara Falls, NY	4.7
67	60	Bakersfield, CA	8.3	42	60	Jacksonville, FL	4.7
19	61	Baltimore-Towson, MD	8.2	39	61	Nashville-Davidson–Murfreesboro, TN	4.7
12	62	San Francisco-Oakland-Fremont, CA	8.2	35	62	Las Vegas-Paradise, NV	4.6
59	63	Albany-Schenectady-Troy, NY	8.2	65	63	Grand Rapids-Wyoming, MI	4.5
28	64	San Antonio, TX	7.8	75	64	Poughkeepsie-Newburgh-Middletown, NY	4.5
20	65	Tampa-St. Petersburg-Clearwater, FL	7.5	69	65	Akron, OH	4.3
1	66	New York-Northern New Jersey-Long Island, NY-NJ-PA	7.5	62	66	Worcester, MA	4.3
40	67	New Orleans-Metairie-Kenner, LA	7.3	33	67	Providence-New Bedford-Fall River, RI-MA	4.2
26	68	Sacramento–Arden-Arcade–Roseville, CA	6.8	56	68	Fresno, CA	4.2
42	69	Jacksonville, FL	6.8	43	69	Louisville, KY-IN	4.1
22	70	Denver-Aurora, CO	6.6	41	70	Memphis, TN-MS-AR	3.8
6	71	Miami-Fort Lauderdale-Miami Beach, FL	6.2	72	71	Greensboro-High Point, NC	3.7
29	72	Orlando, FL	5.8	68	72	El Paso, TX	3.6
7	73	Washington-Arlington-Alexandria, DC-VA-MD-WV	3.7	70	73	Springfield, MA	3.5
51	74	Honolulu, HI	3.6	63	74	Allentown-Bethlehem-Easton, PA-NJ	3.2
35	75	Las Vegas-Paradise, NV	2.9	13	75	Riverside-San Bernardino-Ontario, CA	2.9

75 Largest Metropolitan Areas by 2003 Population
Selected Rankings

Per capita local government taxes, 2002				Violent crime rate, 2002 (violent crimes known to police)			
Population rank	Local taxes rank	Metropolitan area	Local per capita taxes (dollars) [col 181]	Population rank	Crime rate rank	Metropolitan area	Crime rate (per 100,000 population) [col 46]
1	1	New York-Northern New Jersey-Long Island, NY-NJ-PA	2 526	41	1	Memphis, TN-MS-AR	1 053
7	2	Washington-Arlington-Alexandria, DC-VA-MD-WV	2 291	19	2	Baltimore-Towson, MD	990
52	3	Bridgeport-Stamford-Norwalk, CT	2 213	64	3	Albuquerque, NM	930
30	4	San Jose-Sunnyvale-Santa Clara, CA	2 045	39	4	Nashville-Davidson-Murfreesboro, TN	897
75	5	Poughkeepsie-Newburgh-Middletown, NY	1 886	20	5	Tampa-St. Petersburg-Clearwater, FL	888
23	6	Cleveland-Elyria-Mentor, OH	1 864	71	6	Columbia, SC	884
38	7	Austin-Round Rock, TX	1 810	6	7	Miami-Fort Lauderdale-Miami Beach, FL	848
12	8	San Francisco-Oakland-Fremont, CA	1 767	42	8	Jacksonville, FL	847
3	9	Chicago-Naperville-Joliet, IL-IN-WI	1 762	70	9	Springfield, MA	840
59	10	Albany-Schenectady-Troy, NY	1 726	37	10	Charlotte-Gastonia-Concord, NC-SC	830
5	11	Dallas-Fort Worth-Arlington, TX	1 701	29	11	Orlando, FL	817
22	12	Denver-Aurora, CO	1 700	8	12	Houston-Baytown-Sugar Land, TX	768
31	13	Columbus, OH	1 673	2	13	Los Angeles-Long Beach-Santa Ana, CA	759
44	14	Hartford-West Hartford-East Hartford, CT	1 669	35	14	Las Vegas-Paradise, NV	726
8	15	Houston-Baytown-Sugar Land, TX	1 639	66	15	Baton Rouge, LA	724
49	16	Rochester, NY	1 615	10	16	Detroit-Warren-Livonia, MI	700
58	17	New Haven-Milford, CT	1 587	40	17	New Orleans-Metairie-Kenner, LA	664
4	18	Philadelphia-Camden-Wilmington, PA-NJ-DE-MD	1 567	34	18	Indianapolis, IN	663
19	19	Baltimore-Towson, MD	1 552	55	19	Tulsa, OK	647
73	20	Toledo, OH	1 523	28	20	San Antonio, TX	643
11	21	Boston-Cambridge-Quincy, MA-NH	1 514	53	21	Tucson, AZ	631
45	22	Buffalo-Niagara Falls, NY	1 485	5	22	Dallas-Fort Worth-Arlington, TX	619
69	23	Akron, OH	1 478	56	23	Fresno, CA	616
27	24	Kansas City, MO-KS	1 435	73	24	Toledo, OH	615
74	25	Syracuse, NY	1 432	68	25	El Paso, TX	606
57	26	Dayton, OH	1 430	4	26	Philadelphia-Camden-Wilmington, PA-NJ-DE-MD	595
6	27	Miami-Fort Lauderdale-Miami Beach, FL	1 403	27	27	Kansas City, MO-KS	579
9	28	Atlanta-Sandy Springs-Marietta, GA	1 398	13	28	Riverside-San Bernardino-Ontario, CA	578
36	28	Milwaukee-Waukesha-West Allis, WI	1 398	14	29	Phoenix-Mesa-Scottsdale, AZ	575
15	30	Seattle-Tacoma-Bellevue, WA	1 393	47	30	Oklahoma City, OK	543
24	31	Cincinnati-Middletown, OH-KY-IN	1 375	48	31	Birmingham-Hoover, AL	542
63	32	Allentown-Bethlehem-Easton, PA-NJ	1 369	26	32	Sacramento-Arden-Arcade-Roseville, CA	536
60	33	Omaha-Council Bluffs, NE-IA	1 346	12	33	San Francisco-Oakland-Fremont, CA	528
34	34	Indianapolis, IN	1 294	7	34	Washington-Arlington-Alexandria, DC-VA-MD-WV	518
32	35	Virginia Beach-Norfolk-Newport News, VA-NC	1 270	1	35	New York-Northern New Jersey-Long Island, NY-NJ-PA	516
40	36	New Orleans-Metairie-Kenner, LA	1 262	31	36	Columbus, OH	512
21	37	Pittsburgh, PA	1 259	9	37	Atlanta-Sandy Springs-Marietta, GA	511
62	38	Worcester, MA	1 255	60	38	Omaha-Council Bluffs, NE-IA	503
25	39	Portland-Vancouver-Beaverton, OR-WA	1 251	67	39	Bakersfield, CA	491
33	40	Providence-New Bedford-Fall River, RI-MA	1 250	17	40	San Diego-Carlsbad-San Marcos, CA	481
2	41	Los Angeles-Long Beach-Santa Ana, CA	1 234	65	41	Grand Rapids-Wyoming, MI	479
18	42	St. Louis, MO-IL	1 232	45	42	Buffalo-Niagara Falls, NY	460
41	43	Memphis, TN-MS-AR	1 211	32	42	Virginia Beach-Norfolk-Newport News, VA-NC	460
16	44	Minneapolis-St. Paul-Bloomington, MN	1 208	72	44	Greensboro-High Point, NC	458
29	45	Orlando, FL	1 207	62	45	Worcester, MA	453
46	46	Richmond, VA	1 192	36	46	Milwaukee-Waukesha-West Allis, WI	445
37	47	Charlotte-Gastonia-Concord, NC-SC	1 184	23	47	Cleveland-Elyria-Mentor, OH	442
66	48	Baton Rouge, LA	1 181	11	48	Boston-Cambridge-Quincy, MA-NH	438
14	49	Phoenix-Mesa-Scottsdale, AZ	1 166	24	49	Cincinnati-Middletown, OH-KY-IN	435
35	50	Las Vegas-Paradise, NV	1 163	46	50	Richmond, VA	423
61	51	Oxnard-Thousand Oaks-Ventura, CA	1 155	15	51	Seattle-Tacoma-Bellevue, WA	403
28	52	San Antonio, TX	1 142	22	52	Denver-Aurora, CO	385
17	53	San Diego-Carlsbad-San Marcos, CA	1 134	57	53	Dayton, OH	383
20	54	Tampa-St. Petersburg-Clearwater, FL	1 101	58	53	New Haven-Milford, CT	383
50	55	Salt Lake City, UT	1 088	54	55	Raleigh-Cary, NC	378
53	56	Tucson, AZ	1 069	21	56	Pittsburgh, PA	377
26	57	Sacramento-Arden-Arcade-Roseville, CA	1 066	59	57	Albany-Schenectady-Troy, NY	372
10	58	Detroit-Warren-Livonia, MI	1 063	38	58	Austin-Round Rock, TX	371
42	59	Jacksonville, FL	1 045	25	59	Portland-Vancouver-Beaverton, OR-WA	370
70	60	Springfield, MA	1 039	33	60	Providence-New Bedford-Fall River, RI-MA	362
48	61	Birmingham-Hoover, AL	1 035	30	61	San Jose-Sunnyvale-Santa Clara, CA	356
54	62	Raleigh-Cary, NC	993	74	62	Syracuse, NY	343
39	63	Nashville-Davidson-Murfreesboro, TN	978	50	63	Salt Lake City, UT	339
55	64	Tulsa, OK	956	16	64	Minneapolis-St. Paul-Bloomington, MN	330
71	65	Columbia, SC	953	44	65	Hartford-West Hartford-East Hartford, CT	320
43	66	Louisville, KY-IN	933	52	66	Bridgeport-Stamford-Norwalk, CT	312
68	67	El Paso, TX	917	75	67	Poughkeepsie-Newburgh-Middletown, NY	306
72	68	Greensboro-High Point, NC	886	69	68	Akron, OH	296
47	69	Oklahoma City, OK	865	51	69	Honolulu, HI	289
13	70	Riverside-San Bernardino-Ontario, CA	842	63	70	Allentown-Bethlehem-Easton, PA-NJ	272
67	71	Bakersfield, CA	835	61	71	Oxnard-Thousand Oaks-Ventura, CA	259
56	72	Fresno, CA	761	49	72	Rochester, NY	258
64	73	Albuquerque, NM	748	3	73	Chicago-Naperville-Joliet, IL-IN-WI	NA
65	74	Grand Rapids-Wyoming, MI	739	43	73	Louisville, KY-IN	NA
51	75	Honolulu, HI	596	18	73	St. Louis, MO-IL	NA

All Metropolitan Areas
Selected Rankings

Defense contracts, 2003				Non-defense contracts, 2003			
Population rank	Defense contracts rank	Metropolitan area	Defense contracts (millions of dollars) [col 172]	Population rank	Non-defense contracts rank	Metropolitan area	Non-defense contracts (millions of dollars) [col 173]
7	1	Washington-Arlington-Alexandria, DC-VA-MD-WV	18 628	7	1	Washington-Arlington-Alexandria, DC-VA-MD-WV	25 706
5	2	Dallas-Fort Worth-Arlington, TX	12 663	8	2	Houston-Baytown-Sugar Land, TX	4 599
2	3	Los Angeles-Long Beach-Santa Ana, CA	12 568	2	3	Los Angeles-Long Beach-Santa Ana, CA	4 330
18	4	St. Louis, MO-IL	5 833	12	4	San Francisco-Oakland-Fremont, CA	3 338
11	5	Boston-Cambridge-Quincy, MA-NH	5 673	1	5	New York-Northern New Jersey-Long Island, NY-NJ-PA	3 144
17	6	San Diego-Carlsbad-San Marcos, CA	4 698	76	6	Knoxville, TN	2 787
14	7	Phoenix-Mesa-Scottsdale, AZ	4 278	3	7	Chicago-Naperville-Joliet, IL-IN-WI	2 624
4	8	Philadelphia-Camden-Wilmington, PA-NJ-DE-MD	4 046	64	8	Albuquerque, NM	2 407
133	9	Huntsville, AL	4 041	194	9	Kennewick-Richland-Pasco, WA	2 397
32	10	Virginia Beach-Norfolk-Newport News,	3 921	22	10	Denver-Aurora, CO	1 845
1	11	New York-Northern New Jersey-Long Island, NY-NJ-PA	3 861	11	11	Boston-Cambridge-Quincy, MA-NH	1 749
44	12	Hartford-West Hartford-East Hartford	3 807	19	12	Baltimore-Towson, MD	1 700
30	13	San Jose-Sunnyvale-Santa Clara, CA	3 803	5	13	Dallas-Fort Worth-Arlington, TX	1 651
19	14	Baltimore-Towson, MD	2 992	89	14	Augusta-Richmond County, GA-SC	1 649
53	15	Tucson, AZ	2 782	9	15	Atlanta-Sandy Springs-Marietta, GA	1 446
8	16	Houston-Baytown-Sugar Land, TX	2 658	27	16	Kansas City, MO-KS	1 438
43	17	Louisville, KY-IN	2 382	4	17	Philadelphia-Camden-Wilmington, PA-NJ-DE-MD	1 369
164	18	Norwich-New London, CT	2 350	28	18	San Antonio, TX	1 090
15	19	Seattle-Tacoma-Bellevue, WA	2 281	93	19	Palm Bay-Melbourne-Titusville, FL	1 016
29	20	Orlando, FL	2 079	324	20	Idaho Falls, ID	983
28	21	San Antonio, TX	1 953	35	21	Las Vegas-Paradise, NV	943
9	22	Atlanta-Sandy Springs-Marietta, GA	1 841	30	22	San Jose-Sunnyvale-Santa Clara, CA	937
10	23	Detroit-Warren-Livonia, MI	1 720	21	23	Pittsburgh, PA	915
51	24	Honolulu, HI	1 625	32	24	Virginia Beach-Norfolk-Newport News,	854
3	25	Chicago-Naperville-Joliet, IL-IN-WI	1 595	18	25	St. Louis, MO-IL	848
52	26	Bridgeport-Stamford-Norwalk, CT	1 574	40	26	New Orleans-Metairie-Kenner, LA	840
84	27	Colorado Springs, CO	1 518	10	27	Detroit-Warren-Livonia, MI	808
16	28	Minneapolis-St. Paul-Bloomington, MN	1 465	24	28	Cincinnati-Middletown, OH-KY-IN	693
24	29	Cincinnati-Middletown, OH-KY-IN	1 422	47	29	Oklahoma City, OK	690
241	30	Pascagoula, MS	1 359	133	30	Huntsville, AL	674
93	31	Palm Bay-Melbourne-Titusville, FL	1 316	17	31	San Diego-Carlsbad-San Marcos, CA	638
20	32	Tampa-St. Petersburg-Clearwater, FL	1 312	181	32	Lynchburg, VA	637
40	33	New Orleans-Metairie-Kenner, LA	1 217	208	33	Johnson City, TN	633
57	34	Dayton, OH	1 194	16	34	Minneapolis-St. Paul-Bloomington, MN	631
41	35	Memphis, TN-MS-AR	1 154	14	35	Phoenix-Mesa-Scottsdale, AZ	605
100	36	Ogden-Clearfield, UT	1 146	15	36	Seattle-Tacoma-Bellevue, WA	601
21	37	Pittsburgh, PA	1 095	38	37	Austin-Round Rock, TX	565
34	38	Indianapolis, IN	1 014	6	38	Miami-Fort Lauderdale-Miami Beach, FL	562
12	39	San Francisco-Oakland-Fremont, CA	1 013	37	39	Charlotte-Gastonia-Concord, NC-SC	558
94	40	Portland-South Portland-Biddeford, M	0 998	98	40	Chattanooga, TN-GA	533
217	41	Fort Walton Beach-Crestview-Destin,	0 931	39	41	Nashville-Davidson—Murfreesboro, TN	488
42	42	Jacksonville, FL	0 925	41	42	Memphis, TN-MS-AR	483
33	43	Providence-New Bedford-Fall River, RI	0 867	23	43	Cleveland-Elyria-Mentor, OH	481
38	44	Austin-Round Rock, TX	0 809	25	44	Portland-Vancouver-Beaverton, OR-WA	437
26	45	Sacramento—Arden-Arcade—Roseville, CA	0 774	59	45	Albany-Schenectady-Troy, NY	392
47	46	Oklahoma City, OK	0 745	57	46	Dayton, OH	389
22	47	Denver-Aurora, CO	0 712	179	47	Amarillo, TX	385
31	48	Columbus, OH	0 690	26	48	Sacramento—Arden-Arcade—Roseville, CA	376
82	49	Wichita, KS	689	104	49	Durham, NC	356
13	50	Riverside-San Bernardino-Ontario, CA	683	20	50	Tampa-St. Petersburg-Clearwater, FL	343
85	51	Charleston-North Charleston, SC	663	160	51	Boulder, CO	332
140	52	Anchorage, AK	645	29	52	Orlando, FL	323
68	53	El Paso, TX	643	31	53	Columbus, OH	284
27	54	Kansas City, MO-KS	631	34	54	Indianapolis, IN	282
146	55	South Bend-Mishawaka, IN-MI	620	45	55	Buffalo-Niagara Falls, NY	274
115	56	Santa Barbara-Santa Maria-Goleta, CA	616	13	56	Riverside-San Bernardino-Ontario, CA	262
235	57	Oshkosh-Neenah, WI	614	36	57	Milwaukee-Waukesha-West Allis, WI	258
50	58	Salt Lake City, UT	610	46	58	Richmond, VA	253
61	59	Oxnard-Thousand Oaks-Ventura, CA	608	140	59	Anchorage, AK	237
138	60	Killeen-Temple-Fort Hood, TX	590	84	60	Colorado Springs, CO	218
170	61	Binghamton, NY	557	48	61	Birmingham-Hoover, AL	217
139	62	Fayetteville, NC	555	42	62	Jacksonville, FL	208
6	63	Miami-Fort Lauderdale-Miami Beach, FL	522	44	63	Hartford-West Hartford-East Hartford	202
59	64	Albany-Schenectady-Troy, NY	472	172	64	Gulfport-Biloxi, MS	201
64	65	Albuquerque, NM	470	33	65	Providence-New Bedford-Fall River, RI	198
175	66	Bremerton-Silverdale, WA	457	50	66	Salt Lake City, UT	181
118	67	York-Hanover, PA	456	231	67	Joplin, MO	180
46	68	Richmond, VA	450	51	68	Honolulu, HI	179
69	69	Akron, OH	449	52	69	Bridgeport-Stamford-Norwalk, CT	173
174	70	Cedar Rapids, IA	439	74	70	Syracuse, NY	171
148	71	Savannah, GA	391	90	71	Boise City-Nampa, ID	164
117	72	Fort Wayne, IN	387	83	72	Greenville, SC	151
197	73	Burlington-South Burlington, VT	383	60	73	Omaha-Council Bluffs, NE-IA	150
119	74	Manchester-Nashua, NH	380	58	74	New Haven-Milford, CT	149
111	75	Vallejo-Fairfield, CA	372	85	75	Charleston-North Charleston, SC	142

75 Metropolitan Areas with Highest Agricultural Sales
Selected Rankings

	Value of agricultural products sold, 2002			Number of farms, 2002		
Value of sales rank	Metropolitan area	Value of sales (millions of dollars) [col 125]	Value of sales rank	Number of farms rank	Metropolitan area	Number of farms [col 113]
1	Fresno, CA	2 759	54	1	Dallas-Fort Worth-Arlington, TX	23 143
2	Visalia-Porterville, CA	2 339	38	2	Kansas City, MO-KS	14 737
3	Salinas, CA	2 190	75	3	San Antonio, TX	13 073
4	Bakersfield, CA	2 059	23	4	Minneapolis-St. Paul-Bloomington, MN	12 437
5	Riverside-San Bernardino-Ontario, CA	1 626	25	5	St. Louis, MO-IL	12 303
6	Merced, CA	1 409	16	6	Portland-Vancouver-Beaverton, OR-WA	12 188
7	Miami-Fort Lauderdale-Miami Beach, FL	1 387	70	7	Oklahoma City, OK	10 422
8	Modesto, CA	1 229	29	8	Atlanta-Sandy Springs-Marietta, GA	9 370
9	Stockton, CA	1 222	17	9	Fayetteville-Springdale-Rogers, AR-MO	7 559
10	Phoenix-Mesa-Scottsdale, AZ	1 165	41	10	Columbus, OH	7 406
11	Greeley, CO	1 128	14	11	Chicago-Naperville-Joliet, IL-IN-WI	7 120
12	El Centro, CA	1 043	19	12	Philadelphia-Camden-Wilmington, PA-NJ-DE-MD	7 042
13	Oxnard-Thousand Oaks-Ventura, CA	1 019	1	13	Fresno, CA	6 281
14	Chicago-Naperville-Joliet, IL-IN-WI	996	37	14	Madison, WI	6 099
15	San Diego-Carlsbad-San Marcos, CA	951	43	15	Indianapolis, IN	6 034
16	Portland-Vancouver-Beaverton, OR-WA	935	28	16	Omaha-Council Bluffs, NE-IA	5 857
17	Fayetteville-Springdale-Rogers, AR-MO	903	49	17	Fort Smith, AR-OK	5 746
18	Yakima, WA	844	2	18	Visalia-Porterville, CA	5 738
19	Philadelphia-Camden-Wilmington, PA-NJ-DE-MD	813	21	19	Lancaster, PA	5 293
20	Yuma, AZ	802	15	20	San Diego-Carlsbad-San Marcos, CA	5 255
21	Lancaster, PA	798	30	21	Sacramento-Arden-Arcade-Roseville, CA	5 127
22	Hanford-Corcoran, CA	793	35	22	Boise City-Nampa, ID	5 115
23	Minneapolis-St. Paul-Bloomington, MN	769	38	23	Tampa-St. Petersburg-Clearwater, FL	4 919
24	Kennewick-Richland-Pasco, WA	751	51	24	Des Moines, IA	4 915
25	St. Louis, MO-IL	733	31	25	Lexington-Fayette, KY	4 838
26	Santa Barbara-Santa Maria-Goleta, CA	717	65	26	Seattle-Tacoma-Bellevue, WA	4 596
27	Madera, CA	710	5	27	Riverside-San Bernardino-Ontario, CA	4 572
28	Omaha-Council Bluffs, NE-IA	688	66	28	Wichita, KS	4 568
29	Atlanta-Sandy Springs-Marietta, GA	623	36	29	Salem, OR	4 527
30	Sacramento-Arden-Arcade-Roseville, CA	608	56	30	Grand Rapids-Wyoming, MI	4 323
31	Lexington-Fayette, KY	572	8	31	Modesto, CA	4 267
31	Santa Rosa-Petaluma, CA	572	73	32	Jackson, MS	4 144
33	Charlotte-Gastonia-Concord, NC-SC	566	44	33	St. Cloud, MN	4 117
34	Los Angeles-Long Beach-Santa Ana, CA	560	33	34	Charlotte-Gastonia-Concord, NC-SC	4 029
35	Boise City-Nampa, ID	552	9	35	Stockton, CA	4 026
36	Salem, OR	520	7	36	Miami-Fort Lauderdale-Miami Beach, FL	3 848
37	Madison, WI	509	48	37	Rochester, NY	3 736
38	Kansas City, MO-KS	506	18	38	Yakima, WA	3 730
38	Tampa-St. Petersburg-Clearwater, FL	506	55	39	Cedar Rapids, IA	3 655
40	Orlando, FL	505	40	40	Orlando, FL	3 594
41	Columbus, OH	473	49	41	Peoria, IL	3 518
42	Harrisonburg, VA	447	31	42	Santa Rosa-Petaluma, CA	3 447
43	Indianapolis, IN	440	46	43	Davenport-Moline-Rock Island, IA-IL	3 439
44	St. Cloud, MN	432	53	44	Sioux Falls, SD	3 302
45	Napa, CA	429	67	45	Green Bay, WI	3 164
46	Davenport-Moline-Rock Island, IA-IL	412	11	46	Greeley, CO	3 121
47	San Jose-Sunnyvale-Santa Clara, CA	406	71	47	Rochester, MN	3 091
48	Rochester, NY	398	6	48	Merced, CA	2 964
49	Fort Smith, AR-OK	397	10	49	Phoenix-Mesa-Scottsdale, AZ	2 797
49	Peoria, IL	397	60	50	Sioux City, IA-NE-SD	2 626
51	Des Moines, IA	396	58	51	Waterloo-Cedar Falls, IA	2 619
51	San Luis Obispo-Paso Robles, CA	396	64	52	Grand Forks, ND-MN	2 381
53	Sioux Falls, SD	380	51	53	San Luis Obispo-Paso Robles, CA	2 322
54	Dallas-Fort Worth-Arlington, TX	375	13	54	Oxnard-Thousand Oaks-Ventura, CA	2 318
55	Cedar Rapids, IA	373	68	55	Champaign-Urbana, IL	2 257
56	Grand Rapids-Wyoming, MI	371	24	56	Kennewick-Richland-Pasco, WA	2 256
57	Yuba City, CA	366	57	57	Yuba City, CA	2 254
58	Waterloo-Cedar Falls, IA	363	4	58	Bakersfield, CA	2 147
59	Santa Cruz-Watsonville, CA	362	74	59	Wenatchee, WA	2 140
60	Sioux City, IA-NE-SD	354	42	60	Harrisonburg, VA	2 043
61	Amarillo, TX	351	34	61	Los Angeles-Long Beach-Santa Ana, CA	1 891
61	San Francisco-Oakland-Fremont, CA	351	63	62	Fargo, ND-MN	1 838
63	Fargo, ND-MN	344	27	63	Madera, CA	1 780
64	Grand Forks, ND-MN	342	47	64	San Jose-Sunnyvale-Santa Clara, CA	1 703
65	Seattle-Tacoma-Bellevue, WA	341	61	65	Amarillo, TX	1 685
66	Wichita, KS	330	61	66	San Francisco-Oakland-Fremont, CA	1 584
67	Green Bay, WI	329	45	67	Napa, CA	1 456
68	Champaign-Urbana, IL	322	26	68	Santa Barbara-Santa Maria-Goleta, CA	1 444
69	Goldsboro, NC	318	3	69	Salinas, CA	1 216
70	Oklahoma City, OK	317	22	70	Hanford-Corcoran, CA	1154
71	Rochester, MN	309	72	71	Salisbury, MD	813
72	Salisbury, MD	302	59	72	Santa Cruz-Watsonville, CA	754
73	Jackson, MS	297	69	73	Goldsboro, NC	722
74	Wenatchee, WA	294	12	74	El Centro, CA	537
75	San Antonio, TX	293	20	75	Yuma, AZ	531

75 Metropolitan Areas with Highest Agricultural Sales
Selected Rankings

	Land in farms, 2000					Average value of agricultural land and buildings per acre, 2002		
Value of sales rank	Land in farms rank	Metropolitan area	Land in farms (1,000 acres) [col 117]	Farm land as a percent of total land area [col 117/ col 1]	Value of sales rank	Value per acre rank	Metropolitan area	Value per acre (dollars) [col 123]
54	1	Dallas-Fort Worth-Arlington, TX	3 735	16.0	45	1	Napa, CA	19 350
38	2	Kansas City, MO-KS	3 681	18.1	34	2	Los Angeles-Long Beach-Santa Ana, CA	13 693
75	3	San Antonio, TX	3 644	19.2	65	3	Seattle-Tacoma-Bellevue, WA	12 566
25	4	St. Louis, MO-IL	3 056	13.6	31	4	Santa Rosa-Petaluma, CA	11 058
4	5	Bakersfield, CA	2 731	13.0	59	5	Santa Cruz-Watsonville, CA	9 335
70	6	Oklahoma City, OK	2 586	18.1	13	6	Oxnard-Thousand Oaks-Ventura, CA	8 839
28	7	Omaha-Council Bluffs, NE-IA	2 436	21.6	19	7	Philadelphia-Camden-Wilmington, PA-NJ-DE-MD	8 063
14	8	Chicago-Naperville-Joliet, IL-IN-WI	2 333	12.5	16	8	Portland-Vancouver-Beaverton, OR-WA	7 991
66	9	Wichita, KS	2 319	21.6	21	9	Lancaster, PA	7 955
61	10	Amarillo, TX	1 992	21.0	15	10	San Diego-Carlsbad-San Marcos, CA	7 635
23	11	Minneapolis-St. Paul-Bloomington, MN	1 986	12.6	9	11	Stockton, CA	6 673
1	12	Fresno, CA	1 929	12.5	8	12	Modesto, CA	6 068
64	13	Grand Forks, ND-MN	1 867	21.2	36	13	Salem, OR	5 054
11	14	Greeley, CO	1 812	17.5	38	14	Tampa-St. Petersburg-Clearwater, FL	4 949
10	15	Phoenix-Mesa-Scottsdale, AZ	1 789	4.7	7	15	Miami-Fort Lauderdale-Miami Beach, FL	4 858
63	16	Fargo, ND-MN	1 727	23.7	20	16	Yuma, AZ	4 544
18	17	Yakima, WA	1 679	15.1	61	17	San Francisco-Oakland-Fremont, CA	4 516
41	18	Columbus, OH	1 634	15.8	29	18	Atlanta-Sandy Springs-Marietta, GA	4 287
51	19	Des Moines, IA	1 464	19.6	33	19	Charlotte-Gastonia-Concord, NC-SC	4 079
53	20	Sioux Falls, SD	1 424	21.3	42	20	Harrisonburg, VA	4 043
2	21	Visalia-Porterville, CA	1 393	11.1	2	21	Visalia-Porterville, CA	3 949
43	22	Indianapolis, IN	1 381	13.8	30	22	Sacramento-Arden-Arcade-Roseville, CA	3 940
35	23	Boise City-Nampa, ID	1 338	4.4	6	23	Merced, CA	3 826
51	24	San Luis Obispo-Paso Robles, CA	1 318	15.4	57	24	Yuba City, CA	3 824
24	25	Kennewick-Richland-Pasco, WA	1 273	16.7	26	25	Santa Barbara-Santa Maria-Goleta, CA	3 684
49	26	Peoria, IL	1 269	19.8	22	26	Hanford-Corcoran, CA	3 643
3	27	Salinas, CA	1 261	14.7	14	27	Chicago-Naperville-Joliet, IL-IN-WI	3 641
37	28	Madison, WI	1 231	17.4	1	28	Fresno, CA	3 612
17	29	Fayetteville-Springdale-Rogers, AR-MO	1 191	14.5	5	29	Riverside-San Bernardino-Ontario, CA	3 559
46	30	Davenport-Moline-Rock Island, IA-IL	1 172	19.9	3	30	Salinas, CA	3 248
60	31	Sioux City, IA-NE-SD	1 147	21.4	31	31	Lexington-Fayette, KY	3 229
68	32	Champaign-Urbana, IL	1 121	22.5	43	32	Indianapolis, IN	3 224
30	33	Sacramento-Arden-Arcade-Roseville, CA	1 113	8.4	23	33	Minneapolis-St. Paul-Bloomington, MN	3 221
5	34	Riverside-San Bernardino-Ontario, CA	1 086	1.5	41	34	Columbus, OH	3 162
49	35	Fort Smith, AR-OK	1 082	10.4	69	34	Goldsboro, NC	3 162
55	36	Cedar Rapids, IA	1 061	20.4	27	36	Madera, CA	3 120
29	37	Atlanta-Sandy Springs-Marietta, GA	1 027	4.7	72	37	Salisbury, MD	3 063
40	38	Orlando, FL	1008	11.1	56	38	Grand Rapids-Wyoming, MI	3 008
6	39	Merced, CA	1006	20.1	12	39	El Centro, CA	2 976
74	40	Wenatchee, WA	991	8.1	68	40	Champaign-Urbana, IL	2 839
47	41	San Jose-Sunnyvale-Santa Clara, CA	899	13.0	49	41	Peoria, IL	2 816
44	42	St. Cloud, MN	877	19.3	37	42	Madison, WI	2 750
73	43	Jackson, MS	863	8.9	51	43	San Luis Obispo-Paso Robles, CA	2 676
58	44	Waterloo-Cedar Falls, IA	854	21.9	58	44	Waterloo-Cedar Falls, IA	2 647
71	45	Rochester, MN	813	19.4	40	45	Orlando, FL	2 605
9	45	Stockton, CA	813	22.4	46	46	Davenport-Moline-Rock Island, IA-IL	2 531
48	47	Rochester, NY	809	10.7	67	47	Green Bay, WI	2 473
31	48	Lexington-Fayette, KY	790	20.6	25	48	St. Louis, MO-IL	2 452
8	48	Modesto, CA	790	20.4	55	49	Cedar Rapids, IA	2 390
26	50	Santa Barbara-Santa Maria-Goleta, CA	757	10.7	17	50	Fayetteville-Springdale-Rogers, AR-MO	2 361
56	51	Grand Rapids-Wyoming, MI	721	9.8	47	51	San Jose-Sunnyvale-Santa Clara, CA	2 238
16	52	Portland-Vancouver-Beaverton, OR-WA	715	4.1	71	52	Rochester, MN	2 139
27	53	Madera, CA	682	12.3	28	53	Omaha-Council Bluffs, NE-IA	2 113
7	54	Miami-Fort Lauderdale-Miami Beach, FL	650	4.9	54	54	Dallas-Fort Worth-Arlington, TX	2 067
22	55	Hanford-Corcoran, CA	646	17.9	35	55	Boise City-Nampa, ID	1 973
31	56	Santa Rosa-Petaluma, CA	627	15.4	51	56	Des Moines, IA	1 937
57	57	Yuba City, CA	606	19.0	10	57	Phoenix-Mesa-Scottsdale, AZ	1 860
67	58	Green Bay, WI	590	12.2	4	58	Bakersfield, CA	1 816
33	59	Charlotte-Gastonia-Concord, NC-SC	551	6.9	48	59	Rochester, NY	1 754
38	60	Tampa-St. Petersburg-Clearwater, FL	521	7.9	38	60	Kansas City, MO-KS	1 699
12	61	El Centro, CA	514	4.8	44	61	St. Cloud, MN	1 678
36	62	Salem, OR	510	10.2	60	62	Sioux City, IA-NE-SD	1 634
21	63	Lancaster, PA	412	16.8	24	63	Kennewick-Richland-Pasco, WA	1 569
15	64	San Diego-Carlsbad-San Marcos, CA	408	3.8	73	64	Jackson, MS	1 568
13	65	Oxnard-Thousand Oaks-Ventura, CA	332	6.9	75	65	San Antonio, TX	1 527
42	66	Harrisonburg, VA	249	11.1	49	66	Fort Smith, AR-OK	1 473
45	67	Napa, CA	238	12.2	74	67	Wenatchee, WA	1 456
20	68	Yuma, AZ	231	1.6	11	68	Greeley, CO	1 379
34	69	Los Angeles-Long Beach-Santa Ana, CA	179	1.4	53	69	Sioux Falls, SD	1 320
69	70	Goldsboro, NC	171	11.9	18	70	Yakima, WA	1 271
65	71	Seattle-Tacoma-Bellevue, WA	168	1.1	70	71	Oklahoma City, OK	1 059
72	72	Salisbury, MD	145	7.9	63	72	Fargo, ND-MN	943
59	73	Santa Cruz-Watsonville, CA	67	5.8	66	73	Wichita, KS	935
19		Philadelphia-Camden-Wilmington, PA-NJ-DE-MD	NA	NA	64	74	Grand Forks, ND-MN	814
61		San Francisco-Oakland-Fremont, CA	NA	NA	61	75	Amarillo, TX	436

COLUMN HEADINGS FOR METROPOLITAN AREAS

Table C. Metropolitan Areas — **Land Area and Population**

CBSA/ DIV code[1]	Area Name	Land area,[2] 2000 (sq km)	Population and population characteristics, 2003													
						Race alone or in combination, not Hispanic or Latino (percent)					Age (percent)					
			Total persons	Rank	Per square kilometer	White	Black	Am. Indian, Alaska Native	Asian and Pacific Islander	Percent Hispanic or Latino[3]	Under 5 years	5 to 17 years	18 to 24 years	25 to 34 years	35 to 44 years	45 to 54 years
		1	2	3	4	5	6	7	8	9	10	11	12	13	14	15

1. CBSA = Core Based Statistical Area. DIV = Metropolitan Division. See Appendix A for explanation. See Appendix B for list of metropolitan areas identified by type.   2. Dry land or land partially or temporarily covered by water.   3. Hispanic or Latino persons may be of any race.

Table C. Metropolitan Areas — **Population and Households**

Area Name	Population, 2003 (cont'd)				Population — change and components of change, 1990–2003							Households, 2000				
	Age (percent) (cont'd)				Total persons		Percent change		Components of change, 2000–2003						Percent	
	55 to 64 years	65 to 74 years	75 years and over	Percent female	1900	2000	1990– 2000	2000– 2003	Births	Deaths	Net migration	Number	Percent change, 1990– 2000	Persons per house-hold	Female family house-holder[1]	One person
	16	17	18	19	20	21	22	23	24	25	26	27	28	29	30	31

1. No spouse present.

Table C. Metropolitan Areas — **Vital Statistics, Health Resources, and Crime**

Area Name	Births, average 1999–2001		Deaths, average 1999–2001				Physicians,[4] 1998		Hospitals,[4] 1998			Medicare enrollees, 2003	Serious crimes known to police,[6] 2002	
			Number		Rate					Beds			Total	
	Total	Rate[1]	Total	Infant[2]	Total[1]	Infant[3]	Number	Rate[5]	Number	Number	Rate[6]		Number	Rate[7]
	32	33	34	35	36	37	38	39	40	41	42	43	44	45

1. Per 1,000 estimated resident population.   2. Deaths of infants under 1 year old.   3. Deaths of infants under 1 year old per 1,000 live births.   4. Data subject to copyright.   5. Per 100,000 resident population as of July 1 of the year shown.   6. Data for serious crimes have not been adjusted for underreporting; this may affect comparability between geographic areas and over time.   7. Per 100,000 population estimated by the FBI.

Table C. Metropolitan Areas — **Crime, Education, Money Income, and Poverty**

Area Name	Serious crimes known to police,[1] 2002 (cont'd)		Education							Money income, 1999				Percent below poverty level, 1999		
	Rate[2]		School enrollment and attainment, 2000				Local government expenditures,[5] 2000–2001									
			Enrollment[3]		Attainment[4] (percent)											
	Violent	Property	Total	Percent private	High school grad-uate or more	Bach-elor's degree or more	Total current expendi-tures (mil dol)	Current expendi-tures per student (dollars)	Per capita income[6] (dollars)	Mean house-hold income	Mean family income	Percent of house-holds with income of $100,000 or more	Persons	House-holds	Families	Families with children
	46	47	48	49	50	51	52	53	54	55	56	57	58	59	60	61

1. Data for serious crimes have not been adjusted for underreporting; this may affect comparability between geographic areas and over time.   2. Per 100,000 population estimated by the FBI.   3. All persons 3 years old and over enrolled in nursery school through college.   4. Persons 25 years old and over.   5. Elementary and secondary education expenditures.   6. Based on population enumerated as of April 1, 2000.

COLUMN HEADINGS FOR METROPOLITAN AREAS

Table C. Metropolitan Areas — **Personal Income**

Area Name	Personal income, 2002												
			Per capita[1]						Transfer payments				
										Government payments to individuals			
	Total (mil dol)	Percent change, 2001–2002	Dollars	Rank	Wages and salaries[2] (mil dol)	Proprietor's income (mil dol)	Dividends, interest, and rent (mil dol)	Total (mil dol)	Total (mil dol)	Social Security (mil dol)	Medical payments (mil dol)	Income mainte-nance (mil dol)	Unemploy-ment insurance (mil dol)
	62	63	64	65	66	67	68	69	70	71	72	73	74

1. Based on the resident population estimated as of July 1 of the year shown.   2. Includes other labor income.

Table C. Metropolitan Areas — **Earnings, Social Security, and Housing**

Area Name	Earnings, 2002									Social Security beneficiaries, December 2003			Housing units, 2003	
				Percent by selected industries										
			Goods related[1]		Service-related and health									
	Total (mil dol)	Farm	Total	Manu-facturing	Infor-mation, profes-sional and technical services	Retail trade	Finance and insur-ance, and real estate	Health services	Govern-ment	Number	Rate[2]	Supple-mental Security Income recipients, December 2003	Total	Percent change, 2000–2003
	75	76	77	78	79	80	81	82	83	84	85	86	87	88

1. Covers mining, construction, and manufacturing.   2. Per 1,000 resident population estimated as of July 1 of the year shown.

Table C. Metropolitan Areas — **Housing, Labor Force, and Employment**

Area Name	Housing units, 2000									Civilian labor force, 2003				Civilian employment,[5] 2000		
		Occupied units										Unemployment			Percent	
			Owner-occupied			Renter-occupied										
				Owner cost is 35 percent or more of income												
	Total	Percent	Mean value[1]	With a mort-gage	Without a mort-gage	Mean rent[2]	Rent is 35 percent or more of income	Sub-stand-ard units[3] (percent)	Total	Percent change, 2002–2003	Total	Rate[4]	Total	Management, professional, and related occupations	Production, transpor-tation, and material moving occupations
	89	90	91	92	93	94	95	96	97	98	99	100	101	102	103

1. Specified owner-occupied units.   2. Specified renter-occupied units.   3. Overcrowded or lacking complete plumbing facilities.   4. Percent of civilian labor force.   5. Persons 16 years old and over.

Table C. Metropolitan Areas — **Nonfarm Employment and Agriculture**

Area Name	Private nonfarm establishments, employment and payroll, 2001									Agriculture, 2002			
		Employment						Annual payroll		Farms			
											Percent with—		
	Number of establish-ments	Total	Health care and social assistance	Manufac-turing	Retail trade	Finance and insurance	Professional, scientific, and technical services	Total (mil dol)	Average per employee (dollars)	Number	Less than 50 acres	500 acres and over	Farm operators whose principal occu-pation is farming (percent)
	104	105	106	107	108	109	110	111	112	113	114	115	116

COLUMN HEADINGS FOR METROPOLITAN AREAS

Table C. Metropolitan Areas — Agriculture

Area Name	Agriculture, 2002 (cont'd)															
	Land in farms					Value of land and buildings (dollars)			Value of products sold				Percent of farms with sales of —		Government payments	
			Acres					Value of machinery and equipment average per farm (dollars)			Percent from —					
	Acreage (1,000)	Percent change, 1997–2002	Average size of farm	Total irrigated (1,000)	Total cropland (1,000)	Average per farm	Average per acre		Total (mil dol)	Average per farm (dollars)	Crops	Live-stock and poultry products	$10,000 or more	$100,000 or more	Total ($1,000)	Percent of farms
	117	118	119	120	121	122	123	124	125	126	127	128	129	130	131	132

Table C. Metropolitan Areas — Residential Construction, Wholesale Trade, Retail Trade, and Real Estate

Area Name	Value of residential construction authorized by building permits, 2003		Wholesale trade, 1997				Retail trade,[1] 1997				Real estate and rental and leasing, 1997			
	New construction ($1,000)	Number of housing units	Number of establish-ments	Number of employees	Sales (mil dol)	Annual payroll (mil dol)	Number of establish-ments	Number of employees	Sales (mil dol)	Annual payroll (mil dol)	Number of establish-ments	Number of employees	Receipts (mil dol)	Annual payroll (mil dol)
	133	134	135	136	137	138	139	140	141	142	143	144	145	146

1. Establishments with payroll.

Table C. Metropolitan Areas — Professional Services, Manufacturing, and Accommodation and Foodservices

Area Name	Professional, scientific, and technical services,[1] 1997				Manufacturing, 1997				Accommodation and foodservices, 1997			
	Number of establish-ments	Number of employees	Sales (mil dol)	Annual payroll (mil dol)	Number of establish-ments	Number of employees	Sales (mil dol)	Annual payroll (mil dol)	Number of establish-ments	Number of employees	Sales (mil dol)	Annual payroll (mil dol)
	147	148	149	150	151	152	153	154	155	156	157	158

1. Firms subject to federal tax.

Table C. Metropolitan Areas — Health Care and Social Assistance, Other Services, and Federal Funds

Area Name	Health care and social assistance,[1] 1997				Other services,[1] 1997				Federal funds and grants, 2002–2003			
									Expenditures (mil dol)			
										Direct payments for individuals		
	Number of establish-ments	Number of employees	Receipts (mil dol)	Annual payroll (mil dol)	Number of establish-ments	Number of employees	Receipts (mil dol)	Annual payroll (mil dol)	Total	Social Security and government retirement	Medicare	Food stamps and Supplemental Security Income
	159	160	161	162	163	164	165	166	167	168	169	170

1. Firms subject to federal tax.

Table C. Metropolitan Areas — **Federal Funds and Local Government Finances**

Area Name	Federal funds and grants, 2002–2003 (cont'd)							Local government finances, 2002				
	Expenditures (mil dol) (cont'd)							General revenue				
	Procurement contract awards			Grants							Taxes	
												Per capita[1] (dollars)	
	Salaries and wages	Defense	Other	Medicaid and other health-related	Nutrition and family welfare	Education	Other	Total (mil dol)	Intergovern-mental (mil dol)	Total (mil dol)	Total	Property
	171	172	173	174	175	176	177	178	179	180	181	182

1. Based on the resident population estimated as of July 1 of the year shown.

Table C. Metropolitan Areas — **Local Government Finances, Government Employment, and Elections**

Area Name	Local government finances, 2002 (cont'd)									Government employment, 2002			Presidential election, 2004		
	Direct general expenditure							Debt outstanding					Percent of vote cast —		
			Percent of total for —												
	Total (mil dol)	Per capita[1] (dollars)	Educa-tion	Health and hospitals	Police protec-tion	Public welfare	High-ways	Total (mil dol)	Per capita[1] (dollars)	Federal civilian	Federal military	State and local	Demo-cratic	Republi-can	All other
	183	184	185	186	187	188	189	190	191	192	193	194	195	196	197

1. Based on the resident population estimated as of July 1 of the year shown.

Table C. Metropolitan Areas — Land Area and Population

CBSA/ DIV code[1]	Area Name	Land area[2] 2000 (sq km)	Population and population characteristics, 2003													
						Race alone or in combination, not Hispanic or Latino (percent)					Age (percent)					
			Total persons	Rank	Per square kilometer	White	Black	Am. Indian, Alaska Native	Asian and Pacific Islander	Percent Hispanic or Latino[3]	Under 5 years	5 to 17 years	18 to 24 years	25 to 34 years	35 to 44 years	45 to 54 years
		1	2	3	4	5	6	7	8	9	10	11	12	13	14	15
10180	Abilene, TX	7 109	158 488	236	22.3	73.4	6.8	0.9	1.5	18.7	7.4	18.6	12.8	12.7	14.2	12.3
10420	Akron, OH	2 344	701 644	69	299.3	86.1	11.8	0.6	1.9	0.9	6.2	17.8	9.8	12.8	15.5	14.9
10500	Albany, GA	5 009	161 104	233	32.2	48.7	49.2	0.5	0.8	1.2	7.6	20.1	11.4	13.0	14.1	13.6
10580	Albany-Schenectady-Troy, NY	7 298	840 644	59	115.2	87.1	7.4	0.6	2.9	3.1	5.5	16.7	10.3	12.7	15.7	14.9
10740	Albuquerque, NM	24 055	764 869	64	31.8	48.7	2.7	5.8	2.3	42.9	7.0	18.7	10.1	13.2	15.2	14.3
10780	Alexandria, LA	5 096	146 281	257	28.7	68.4	28.7	1.2	1.0	1.6	7.3	18.9	10.5	12.1	14.6	13.6
10900	Allentown-Bethlehem-Easton, PA-NJ	3 780	768 036	63	203.2	86.9	3.3	0.3	2.2	8.1	5.6	17.3	9.2	11.6	15.9	14.6
11020	Altoona, PA	1 362	127 175	284	93.4	97.9	1.4	0.3	0.6	0.5	5.5	16.2	9.8	11.3	14.5	15.1
11100	Amarillo, TX	9 480	233 231	179	24.6	71.2	5.9	1.1	1.9	21.0	7.6	19.4	10.9	13.6	14.4	13.2
11180	Ames, IA	1 484	83 021	351	55.9	90.1	2.1	0.4	6.7	1.6	5.2	12.4	24.2	15.6	11.3	11.3
11260	Anchorage, AK	68 321	339 288	140	5.0	76.1	6.0	10.0	7.3	5.7	7.4	21.3	10.6	13.4	16.8	15.7
11300	Anderson, IN	1 171	131 121	276	112.0	89.7	8.4	0.7	0.5	1.7	6.4	17.7	9.1	12.7	14.6	14.2
11340	Anderson, SC	1 860	171 510	224	92.2	80.9	17.3	0.5	0.7	1.3	6.5	17.8	8.8	12.9	14.8	14.1
11460	Ann Arbor, MI	1 839	338 562	141	184.1	76.9	13.2	0.9	8.4	2.8	6.0	15.6	14.8	16.8	15.0	13.6
11500	Anniston-Oxford, AL	1 576	112 012	309	71.1	77.7	19.6	0.8	0.9	1.8	6.5	16.8	10.4	12.5	14.2	14.5
11540	Appleton, WI	2 486	210 794	192	84.8	93.6	0.8	1.6	2.7	2.0	6.6	19.7	9.8	13.1	17.2	13.9
11700	Asheville, NC	5 266	381 789	124	72.5	90.1	5.3	0.8	0.9	3.8	5.7	15.9	8.3	12.5	14.3	14.3
12020	Athens-Clarke County, GA	2 671	172 232	223	64.5	72.3	20.0	0.5	2.5	5.6	6.1	15.2	18.2	17.0	12.7	11.4
12060	Atlanta-Sandy Springs-Marietta, GA	21 695	4 610 032	9	212.5	59.4	29.3	0.6	4.1	7.7	7.8	18.9	9.3	16.7	17.1	13.4
12100	Atlantic City, NJ	1 453	263 410	165	181.3	64.2	17.1	0.6	6.1	13.3	6.5	18.6	8.7	12.4	16.6	14.3
12220	Auburn-Opelika, AL	1 577	119 561	296	75.8	73.3	23.4	0.5	2.2	1.5	5.7	16.6	18.8	16.1	13.0	11.2
12260	Augusta-Richmond County, GA-SC	8 492	511 487	89	60.2	60.8	35.5	0.7	2.0	2.2	7.2	19.5	10.4	13.0	15.1	14.1
12420	Austin-Round Rock, TX	10 940	1 377 633	38	125.9	59.9	7.8	0.7	4.5	28.3	8.0	17.9	11.4	18.2	16.0	12.7
12540	Bakersfield, CA	21 085	713 087	67	33.8	48.4	6.1	1.5	4.1	41.5	8.1	22.3	11.5	13.7	14.7	11.8
12580	Baltimore-Towson, MD	6 756	2 616 229	19	387.2	67.2	27.7	0.6	3.6	2.1	6.5	18.3	9.3	13.1	16.6	14.6
12620	Bangor, ME	8 795	146 982	256	16.7	97.1	0.7	1.3	1.1	0.6	5.1	16.1	11.6	11.9	15.8	15.4
12700	Barnstable Town, MA	1 024	229 545	182	224.2	95.1	2.4	0.9	1.0	1.5	4.4	14.7	7.0	9.9	14.6	14.7
12940	Baton Rouge, LA	10 438	722 646	66	69.2	62.1	34.5	0.5	1.7	1.9	7.2	18.7	12.4	13.9	14.9	13.7
12980	Battle Creek, MI	1 836	138 854	265	75.6	83.9	11.8	1.4	1.5	3.3	6.5	18.7	9.9	12.3	14.7	14.5
13020	Bay City, MI	1 151	109 452	318	95.1	93.7	1.8	1.0	0.6	4.0	5.9	17.6	9.1	11.4	15.3	15.4
13140	Beaumont-Port Arthur, TX	5 579	382 629	123	68.6	63.5	25.4	0.7	2.4	8.8	6.8	19.1	10.3	12.5	14.8	14.0
13380	Bellingham, WA	5 490	176 571	218	32.2	87.7	1.1	3.5	4.3	5.5	5.6	16.9	13.5	13.5	13.7	14.4
13460	Bend, OR	7 817	129 492	277	16.6	93.9	0.5	1.5	1.5	4.2	5.8	17.5	9.1	12.9	14.4	15.2
13740	Billings, MT	12 129	142 961	260	11.8	92.2	0.8	3.8	1.1	3.7	6.2	17.8	9.7	12.0	15.0	15.2
13780	Binghamton, NY	3 174	251 106	170	79.1	91.7	3.7	0.6	3.0	2.2	5.3	16.7	11.2	11.1	15.2	14.4
13820	Birmingham-Hoover, AL	13 721	1 072 646	48	78.2	68.6	28.2	0.6	1.1	2.1	6.7	17.8	9.2	13.8	15.2	14.5
13900	Bismarck, ND	9 219	96 828	341	10.5	95.6	0.5	3.5	0.6	0.7	5.8	17.4	11.8	12.1	15.1	15.1
13980	Blacksburg-Christiansburg-Radford, VA	2 785	152 606	243	54.8	91.7	4.6	0.5	2.8	1.3	4.8	12.6	21.7	14.5	11.9	11.9
14020	Bloomington, IN	3 422	178 974	216	52.3	93.4	2.4	0.7	3.3	1.5	5.3	14.7	19.0	14.6	13.0	12.2
14060	Bloomington-Normal, IL	3 065	156 879	237	51.2	87.4	7.2	0.4	3.1	3.2	6.3	16.5	16.8	14.8	14.2	12.5
14260	Boise City-Nampa, ID	30 529	510 876	90	16.7	87.1	0.9	1.3	2.4	9.9	7.8	19.8	10.3	14.8	14.8	13.1
14460	Boston-Cambridge-Quincy, MA-NH	9 084	4 439 972	11	488.8	80.9	6.8	0.5	5.9	7.0	6.4	16.8	9.0	14.7	17.0	14.4
14484	Boston-Quincy, MA Div	2 899	1 822 557	X	628.7	74.9	12.0	0.5	6.0	7.7	6.4	16.5	9.5	15.8	16.6	13.8
15764	Cambridge-Newton-Framingham, MA Div	2 133	1 471 724	X	690.0	83.7	4.0	0.4	8.2	4.8	6.2	16.2	8.6	15.2	17.3	14.5
21604	Essex County, MA Div	1 297	737 848	X	568.9	81.6	2.8	0.4	3.1	13.2	6.8	18.1	8.3	12.3	16.8	14.8
40484	Rockingham County-Strafford County, NH Div	2 755	407 844	X	148.0	96.5	0.9	0.5	1.7	1.2	5.8	18.5	9.1	11.8	18.3	15.7
14500	Boulder, CO	1 898	278 231	160	146.6	83.2	1.1	0.8	4.4	11.8	6.2	16.1	12.0	17.2	16.4	15.3
14540	Bowling Green, KY	2 196	107 647	322	49.0	87.5	8.4	0.6	1.7	2.9	6.3	16.3	14.0	14.3	14.2	13.2
14740	Bremerton-Silverdale, WA	1 026	240 719	175	234.6	85.7	3.6	2.9	7.4	4.6	6.2	19.0	10.6	12.3	15.6	15.4
14860	Bridgeport-Stamford-Norwalk, CT	1 621	899 152	52	554.7	73.0	10.5	0.3	4.2	12.9	6.7	18.6	7.5	11.9	17.2	14.6
15180	Brownsville-Harlingen, TX	2 346	363 092	130	154.8	13.5	0.3	0.1	0.5	85.7	10.7	23.5	10.9	13.3	12.2	10.5
15260	Brunswick, GA	3 368	96 295	342	28.6	73.3	23.5	0.6	0.7	2.7	6.6	18.7	9.3	12.2	14.7	14.1
15380	Buffalo-Niagara Falls, NY	4 058	1 159 443	45	285.7	82.1	12.6	0.9	1.9	3.4	5.6	17.2	9.4	11.9	15.4	14.7
15500	Burlington, NC	1 114	136 773	268	122.8	71.1	18.9	0.8	1.4	8.8	6.8	17.6	10.1	13.8	14.9	13.1
15540	Burlington-South Burlington, VT	3 260	203 503	197	62.4	95.8	1.2	1.2	2.2	1.0	5.4	17.5	11.5	13.3	17.0	15.2
15940	Canton-Massillon, OH	2 514	407 118	112	161.9	91.5	7.5	0.7	0.8	0.9	6.1	18.0	9.1	11.5	14.8	15.1
15980	Cape Coral-Fort Myers, FL	2 081	492 210	97	236.5	79.3	7.5	0.5	1.2	12.2	5.7	14.9	7.3	10.3	12.6	12.0
16180	Carson City, NV	371	55 311	361	149.1	79.3	1.7	2.8	1.9	15.6	6.7	16.9	8.6	12.3	14.8	14.3
16220	Casper, WY	13 830	68 211	359	4.9	92.7	1.2	1.6	0.8	4.9	6.6	18.1	11.0	11.7	14.2	15.5
16300	Cedar Rapids, IA	5 203	242 744	174	46.7	94.5	3.1	0.6	1.7	1.4	6.7	17.7	10.1	13.3	15.6	14.1
16580	Champaign-Urbana, IL	4 980	217 320	188	43.6	80.4	10.3	0.6	7.2	3.2	6.0	15.1	18.7	14.9	12.8	12.0
16620	Charleston, WV	6 559	306 836	147	46.8	93.6	5.3	0.7	1.0	0.5	5.9	16.1	8.4	12.4	14.7	16.3

1. CBSA = Core Based Statistical Area. DIV = Metropolitan Division. See Appendix A for explanation. See Appendix B for list of metropolitan areas identified by type.   2. Dry land or land partially or temporarily covered by water.   3. Hispanic or Latino persons may be of any race.

Table C. Metropolitan Areas — **Population and Households**

Area Name	Population, 2003 (cont'd) Age (percent) (cont'd) 55 to 64 years	65 to 74 years	75 years and over	Percent female	Population — change and components of change, 1990–2003 Total persons 1900	2000	Percent change 1990–2000	2000–2003	Components of change, 2000–2003 Births	Deaths	Net migration	Households, 2000 Number	Percent change, 1990–2000	Persons per house-hold	Percent Female family house-holder[1]	One person
	16	17	18	19	20	21	22	23	24	25	26	27	28	29	30	31
Abilene, TX	8.5	7.0	6.2	50.1	148 004	160 245	8.3	-1.1	7 651	4 910	-4 509	58 475	8.2	2.54	11.1	25.3
Akron, OH	9.4	6.7	6.6	51.6	657 575	694 960	5.7	1.0	28 290	20 996	-1 066	274 237	10.0	2.47	12.1	27.0
Albany, GA	8.8	5.9	5.1	52.4	146 583	157 833	7.7	2.1	7 959	4 384	-1 973	57 403	11.9	2.65	20.6	24.0
Albany-Schenectady-Troy, NY.	9.7	6.6	7.1	51.3	809 642	825 875	2.0	1.8	30 203	25 059	10 296	330 246	6.4	2.41	11.3	29.4
Albuquerque, NM	9.2	5.9	5.3	50.9	599 416	729 649	21.7	4.8	34 734	17 708	18 462	281 052	24.8	2.55	12.8	26.6
Alexandria, LA	9.7	7.0	6.0	51.8	149 082	145 035	-2.7	0.9	7 244	5 024	-853	54 193	3.8	2.57	16.3	25.6
Allentown-Bethlehem-Easton, PA-NJ	9.7	7.2	7.9	51.4	686 718	740 395	7.8	3.7	27 423	23 735	24 049	285 808	10.0	2.51	10.0	25.7
Altoona, PA	10.5	8.3	9.1	52.0	130 542	129 144	-1.1	-1.5	4 576	5 425	-1 021	51 518	2.4	2.43	11.2	27.8
Amarillo, TX	8.4	6.2	5.6	50.4	196 111	226 522	15.5	3.0	11 555	6 275	1 651	85 272	13.6	2.55	11.9	26.3
Ames, IA	6.6	4.7	5.1	48.6	74 252	79 981	7.7	3.8	2 957	1 443	1 548	29 383	13.3	2.39	5.9	26.7
Anchorage, AK	7.9	3.6	2.2	49.1	266 021	319 605	20.1	6.2	16 184	4 912	8 521	115 378	20.1	2.70	11.1	22.8
Anderson, IN	10.6	7.6	7.4	50.7	130 669	133 358	2.1	-1.7	5 418	4 817	-2 789	53 052	6.5	2.41	11.8	27.2
Anderson, SC	10.9	7.3	6.2	51.6	145 177	165 740	14.2	3.5	7 106	5 846	4 526	65 649	18.3	2.48	12.8	24.3
Ann Arbor, MI	8.0	4.3	3.9	50.2	282 937	322 895	14.1	4.9	13 323	6 034	8 923	125 327	19.9	2.41	9.3	29.5
Anniston-Oxford, AL	10.3	8.0	6.2	52.0	116 032	112 249	-3.3	-0.2	4 999	4 557	-627	45 307	5.4	2.42	13.4	26.9
Appleton, WI	8.2	5.4	5.4	50.1	174 801	201 602	15.3	4.5	9 013	4 386	4 563	75 440	21.1	2.62	7.4	23.4
Asheville, NC	11.1	8.7	8.6	51.7	308 005	369 171	19.9	3.4	14 005	13 780	12 480	154 290	23.2	2.32	9.9	27.7
Athens-Clarke County, GA	7.6	4.7	4.2	50.9	136 025	166 079	22.1	3.7	7 044	3 706	2 837	63 406	25.2	2.48	12.2	25.9
Atlanta-Sandy Springs-Marietta, GA	7.9	4.2	3.3	50.4	3 068 975	4 247 981	38.4	8.5	239 546	90 127	208 403	1 554 154	36.2	2.68	13.6	23.3
Atlantic City, NJ	9.2	6.8	6.5	51.5	224 327	252 552	12.6	4.3	11 477	8 525	8 134	95 024	11.6	2.59	14.8	27.0
Auburn-Opelika, AL	7.2	4.6	3.5	50.8	87 146	115 092	32.1	3.9	4 267	2 651	2 947	45 702	38.1	2.42	11.8	27.8
Augusta-Richmond County, GA-SC	9.1	6.1	5.0	51.5	435 799	499 684	14.7	2.4	24 524	15 187	2 679	184 801	18.4	2.61	16.7	24.3
Austin-Round Rock, TX	6.7	3.8	3.2	49.0	846 227	1 249 763	47.7	10.2	72 422	20 236	73 390	471 855	44.7	2.57	10.2	26.6
Bakersfield, CA	7.3	4.8	4.2	48.5	544 981	661 645	21.4	7.8	38 024	15 725	29 311	208 652	15.0	3.03	14.5	20.3
Baltimore-Towson, MD	9.5	6.1	5.8	51.8	2 382 172	2 552 994	7.2	2.5	111 920	78 245	24 192	974 071	10.7	2.55	14.9	26.4
Bangor, ME	10.0	7.1	6.0	51.2	146 601	144 919	-1.1	1.4	4 897	4 400	1 686	58 096	7.5	2.38	9.9	29.5
Barnstable Town, MA	11.6	11.0	11.7	52.6	186 605	222 230	19.1	3.3	6 517	9 116	9 808	94 822	22.2	2.28	9.4	29.5
Baton Rouge, LA	8.5	5.2	4.4	50.9	623 850	705 973	13.2	2.4	35 073	18 342	-324	256 637	17.9	2.64	15.9	24.2
Battle Creek, MI	9.7	7.0	6.7	51.3	135 982	137 985	1.5	0.6	6 028	4 914	-107	54 100	4.4	2.47	13.0	27.8
Bay City, MI	10.5	7.1	7.7	51.3	111 723	110 157	-1.4	-0.6	4 222	3 584	-1 261	43 930	4.1	2.47	10.9	27.2
Beaumont-Port Arthur, TX	9.1	6.9	6.3	50.1	361 218	385 090	6.6	-0.6	16 897	12 519	-6 735	142 327	6.0	2.59	14.5	25.2
Bellingham, WA	8.8	5.8	5.8	50.7	127 780	166 814	30.5	5.8	6 390	4 019	7 490	64 446	32.8	2.51	8.8	25.6
Bend, OR	10.1	6.8	5.9	50.3	74 976	115 367	53.9	12.2	4 719	3 178	12 334	45 595	56.1	2.50	8.5	22.0
Billings, MT	9.7	6.8	6.8	51.1	121 499	138 904	14.3	2.9	5 824	4 063	2 437	56 149	17.1	2.42	9.9	28.0
Binghamton, NY	10.1	7.7	8.1	51.4	264 497	252 320	-4.6	-0.5	8 768	8 262	-1 512	100 474	-0.2	2.42	10.6	29.3
Birmingham-Hoover, AL	9.5	6.6	6.0	51.8	956 668	1 052 238	10.0	2.0	48 363	35 251	8 293	412 376	13.5	2.50	14.4	26.4
Bismarck, ND	8.9	6.6	6.4	50.7	83 831	94 719	13.0	2.2	3 663	2 444	962	37 559	19.8	2.44	8.7	27.5
Blacksburg-Christiansburg-Radford, VA	9.0	5.9	5.3	49.1	140 715	151 272	7.5	0.8	4 869	4 073	579	58 443	14.0	2.36	8.7	26.7
Bloomington, IN	8.1	5.6	5.2	50.8	156 669	175 506	12.0	2.0	6 119	4 317	1 771	68 552	18.9	2.34	8.2	29.9
Bloomington-Normal, IL	7.3	4.8	4.7	51.6	129 180	150 433	16.5	4.3	6 527	3 319	3 356	56 746	21.3	2.45	8.8	27.6
Boise City-Nampa, ID	8.0	4.8	4.8	49.8	319 596	464 840	45.4	9.9	25 692	10 189	30 201	170 291	45.1	2.67	9.4	22.5
Boston-Cambridge-Quincy, MA-NH	9.4	6.2	6.3	51.5	4 133 895	4 391 344	6.2	1.1	190 492	119 507	-23 035	1 679 659	9.1	2.53	11.4	27.7
Boston-Quincy, MA Div	9.2	6.1	6.3	51.7	1 715 269	1 812 937	5.7	0.5	80 625	50 744	-20 483	695 910	8.5	2.51	12.8	29.5
Cambridge-Newton-Framingham, MA Div	9.5	6.3	6.4	51.3	1 398 468	1 465 396	4.8	0.4	60 821	38 426	-17 147	561 220	8.0	2.52	9.9	27.1
Essex County, MA Div	9.5	6.5	7.1	51.9	670 080	723 419	8.0	2.0	33 668	21 370	2 712	275 419	9.6	2.57	12.4	27.1
Rockingham County-Strafford County, NH Div	9.5	5.6	4.8	50.8	350 078	389 592	11.3	4.7	15 378	8 967	11 883	147 110	16.0	2.59	8.7	22.8
Boulder, CO	8.1	4.1	3.7	49.2	225 339	291 288	29.3	3.1	11 731	4 394	1 102	114 680	29.7	2.53	7.6	26.5
Bowling Green, KY	9.2	5.9	4.9	50.8	88 077	104 166	18.3	3.3	4 388	2 911	2 108	40 013	22.5	2.46	11.0	25.6
Bremerton-Silverdale, WA	9.6	5.4	5.2	49.1	189 731	231 969	22.3	3.8	9 571	5 973	5 319	86 416	24.8	2.60	9.5	22.6
Bridgeport-Stamford-Norwalk, CT	10.1	6.4	6.6	51.5	827 645	882 567	6.6	1.9	39 207	23 029	910	324 232	6.3	2.67	11.5	24.0
Brownsville-Harlingen, TX	6.9	5.8	5.0	52.1	260 120	335 227	28.9	8.3	27 210	5 759	6 846	97 267	32.7	3.40	17.4	15.4
Brunswick, GA	10.6	7.2	6.3	51.6	82 207	93 044	13.2	3.5	4 098	3 060	2 245	36 846	19.1	2.48	14.0	25.9
Buffalo-Niagara Falls, NY	9.8	7.6	8.1	52.0	1 189 340	1 170 111	-1.6	-0.9	43 143	40 522	-12 534	468 719	1.5	2.42	13.5	30.2
Burlington, NC	9.3	7.1	6.7	51.8	108 213	130 800	20.9	4.6	6 184	4 321	4 177	51 584	20.9	2.46	12.7	26.0
Burlington-South Burlington, VT	9.1	5.3	4.7	50.9	177 059	198 889	12.3	2.3	7 128	4 448	2 124	75 978	17.3	2.51	8.9	24.8
Canton-Massillon, OH	10.3	7.4	7.6	51.8	394 106	406 934	3.3	0.0	16 151	13 621	-2 014	159 442	6.8	2.49	11.2	25.9
Cape Coral-Fort Myers, FL	11.8	12.1	11.3	50.9	335 113	440 888	31.6	11.6	17 295	17 306	49 740	188 599	34.6	2.31	8.7	25.8
Carson City, NV	10.6	7.6	7.3	48.7	40 443	52 457	29.7	5.4	2 369	2 118	2 668	20 171	26.9	2.44	11.0	27.8
Casper, WY	9.5	6.8	5.8	50.4	61 226	66 533	8.7	2.5	3 011	1 951	676	26 819	12.5	2.42	10.6	27.5
Cedar Rapids, IA	9.2	6.3	6.5	50.5	210 640	237 230	12.6	2.3	10 649	6 039	1 120	94 059	16.2	2.45	8.7	26.9
Champaign-Urbana, IL	7.5	5.3	5.3	49.8	202 848	210 275	3.7	3.3	8 595	5 138	3 807	82 711	9.6	2.36	8.9	30.6
Charleston, WV	10.9	8.0	7.2	51.7	307 689	309 635	0.6	-0.9	11 963	11 786	-2 858	129 229	6.5	2.37	11.4	27.9

1. No spouse present.

Table C. Metropolitan Areas — Vital Statistics, Health Resources, and Crime

Area Name	Births, average 1999–2001		Deaths, average 1999–2001				Physicians,[4] 1998		Hospitals,[4] 1998			Medicare enrollees, 2003	Serious crimes known to police,[6] 2002	
			Number		Rate					Beds			Total	
	Total	Rate[1]	Total	Infant[2]	Total[1]	Infant[3]	Number	Rate[5]	Number	Number	Rate[5]		Number	Rate[7]
	32	33	34	35	36	37	38	39	40	41	42	43	44	45
Abilene, TX	2 381	14.9	1 559	37	9.8	5.2	265	261	5	579	860	23 997	6 079	3 632
Akron, OH	8 753	12.6	6 422	194	9.2	7.4	1 484	342	7	2 221	548	104 034	24 705	4 244
Albany, GA	2 431	15.4	1 355	67	8.6	9.2	232	327	3	651	853	20 735	7 399	4 483
Albany-Schenectady-Troy, NY.	9 531	11.5	7 705	184	9.3	6.4	2 240	1 072	10	2 854	1 611	131 617	25 807	3 095
Albuquerque, NM	10 792	14.8	5 307	207	7.3	6.4	2 089	500	8	1 619	308	97 991	43 831	6 355
Alexandria, LA	2 226	15.3	1 538	73	10.6	10.9	290	253	3	746	588	23 615	8 614	6 061
Allentown-Bethlehem-Easton, PA-NJ	8 586	11.6	7 256	171	9.8	6.6	1 591	692	11	2 547	1 484	129 191	18 629	2 839
Altoona, PA	1 472	11.4	1 610	23	12.5	5.2	271	210	4	593	454	25 027	3 067	2 978
Amarillo, TX	3 534	15.6	1 979	100	8.7	9.4	487	437	5	1 026	950	29 830	14 653	6 193
Ames, IA	916	11.5	456	14	5.7	5.1	144	180	2	338	449	9 020	2 853	3 554
Anchorage, AK	4 984	15.5	1 365	86	4.3	5.8	674	329	3	639	300	NA	NA	NA
Anderson, IN	1 709	12.8	1 443	46	10.8	9.0	171	128	3	659	502	22 828	NA	NA
Anderson, SC	2 219	13.4	1 723	59	10.4	8.9	256	154	1	445	277	28 369	9 096	5 361
Ann Arbor, MI.........................	4 085	12.6	1 844	98	5.7	8.0	2 127	659	5	1 637	540	32 544	12 099	3 705
Anniston-Oxford, AL...............	1 555	13.8	1 328	44	11.8	9.4	175	156	3	366	313	21 741	6 614	5 840
Appleton, WI	2 780	13.7	1 364	40	6.7	4.8	283	216	4	473	395	25 164	4 473	2 187
Asheville, NC	4 357	11.8	4 163	114	11.3	8.7	885	690	5	1 136	988	76 397	11 564	3 048
Athens-Clarke County, GA ...	2 125	12.8	1 146	60	6.9	9.4	279	361	2	486	536	18 697	8 473	5 298
Atlanta-Sandy Springs-Marietta, GA	70 881	16.6	26 621	1 516	6.2	7.1	7 920	2 660	48	9 655	5 681	404 586	199 434	4 522
Atlantic City, NJ	3 436	13.6	2 527	92	10.0	8.9	493	195	4	1 043	438	39 508	12 711	4 930
Auburn-Opelika, AL.................	1 407	12.2	759	41	6.6	9.7	138	120	1	289	288	11 506	6 584	5 670
Augusta-Richmond County, GA-SC	7 415	14.8	4 447	219	8.9	9.8	1 388	956	8	1 931	1 416	67 240	23 076	4 448
Austin-Round Rock, TX	21 344	16.9	6 334	302	5.0	4.7	2 121	482	13	1 892	557	108 630	62 161	4 762
Bakersfield, CA	11 601	17.4	4 740	245	7.1	7.0	869	131	11	1 649	261	78 689	29 148	4 249
Baltimore-Towson, MD	34 300	13.4	23 879	860	9.3	8.4	8 785	1 744	23	8 330	1 615	344 409	134 910	5 128
Bangor, ME	1 543	10.6	1 356	32	9.3	6.9	353	244	4	633	445	25 114	4 112	2 805
Barnstable Town, MA	2 019	9.1	2 738	33	12.3	5.4	453	204	2	385	185	57 608	6 117	2 761
Baton Rouge, LA	10 660	15.1	5 528	282	7.8	8.8	1 195	820	12	1 978	1 717	80 643	42 775	6 269
Battle Creek, MI	1 873	13.6	1 461	57	10.6	10.1	211	153	4	527	374	22 972	8 601	6 164
Bay City, MI............................	1 308	11.9	1 086	21	9.9	5.4	143	130	1	341	310	18 613	3 487	3 130
Beaumont-Port Arthur, TX ...	5 194	13.5	3 907	131	10.2	8.4	593	305	9	1 782	934	58 169	21 449	5 333
Bellingham, WA	2 011	12.0	1 206	24	7.2	4.0	298	179	1	228	145	23 740	8 879	5 169
Bend, OR	1 411	12.2	904	31	7.8	7.3	208	180	2	223	211	18 952	5 444	4 585
Billings, MT	1 785	12.8	1 205	35	8.7	6.5	354	390	3	566	899	21 715	6 137	4 383
Binghamton, NY	2 831	11.2	2 580	60	10.2	7.1	497	282	3	802	408	46 273	6 871	2 697
Birmingham-Hoover, AL........	14 947	14.2	10 720	503	10.2	11.2	2 835	757	19	5 372	2 232	163 760	42 539	4 464
Bismarck, ND	1 142	12.0	749	27	7.9	7.9	269	417	3	549	913	14 558	2 420	2 588
Blacksburg-Christiansburg-Radford, VA	1 566	10.3	1 238	25	8.2	5.3	216	723	4	379	1 679	21 274	2 575	1 855
Bloomington, IN	1 876	10.7	1 269	49	7.2	8.7	256	263	2	341	457	22 005	NA	NA
Bloomington-Normal, IL	1 997	13.3	1 003	37	6.7	6.2	242	161	2	322	226	17 106	NA	NA
Boise City-Nampa, ID	7 799	16.7	3 081	135	6.6	5.8	754	337	6	894	606	56 800	19 397	4 026
Boston-Cambridge-Quincy, MA-NH	57 865	13.2	36 162	805	8.2	4.6	16 225	2 281	60	14 307	2 146	618 468	120 457	2 869
Boston-Quincy, MA Div	24 461	13.5	15 281	365	8.4	5.0	9 801	1 485	25	7 579	1 223	250 643	64 696	3 654
Cambridge-Newton-Framingham, MA Div	19 075	13.0	11 691	240	8.0	4.2	4 526	309	21	4 066	286	205 867	29 820	2 095
Essex County, MA Div	9 668	13.3	6 509	141	9.0	4.9	1 314	182	9	2 044	292	111 346	19 966	2 805
Rockingham County-Strafford County, NH Div	4 662	11.9	2 680	59	6.9	4.2	584	305	5	618	345	50 612	NA	NA
Boulder, CO	3 813	13.0	1 415	59	4.8	5.2	625	215	3	360	135	30 658	7 432	2 643
Bowling Green, KY	1 362	13.1	864	30	8.3	7.3	179	216	2	623	713	14 869	NA	NA
Bremerton-Silverdale, WA ...	2 986	12.9	1 756	55	7.6	6.1	435	188	1	252	108	29 277	9 147	3 830
Bridgeport-Stamford-Norwalk, CT	12 387	14.0	7 024	182	8.0	4.9	2 512	285	8	1 965	234	124 839	22 943	2 611
Brownsville-Harlingen, TX.....	8 246	24.4	1 855	103	5.5	4.2	385	115	5	951	291	38 107	22 627	6 462
Brunswick, GA	1 228	13.2	914	38	9.8	10.3	165	286	1	337	501	15 187	6 800	6 989
Buffalo-Niagara Falls, NY ...	13 634	11.7	12 410	310	10.6	7.6	3 153	431	17	5 074	886	207 164	40 062	3 391
Burlington, NC	1 859	14.2	1 308	65	10.0	11.7	172	131	1	220	184	22 534	6 477	4 862
Burlington-South Burlington, VT..	2 537	12.7	1 342	48	6.7	6.3	723	669	3	652	567	23 971	6 427	3 191
Canton-Massillon, OH..........	5 146	12.6	4 137	114	10.2	7.4	752	256	5	1 710	458	71 055	12 562	3 757
Cape Coral-Fort Myers, FL...	5 100	11.5	5 156	102	11.6	6.7	846	192	6	1 707	434	106 110	21 515	4 667
Carson City, NV	739	14.0	581	11	11.0	5.0	116	221	1	116	235	10 596	2 074	3 635
Casper, WY	882	13.2	582	11	8.7	4.2	115	173	1	282	445	9 929	3 360	5 000
Cedar Rapids, IA	3 274	13.8	1 857	51	7.8	5.2	374	281	4	1 031	1 123	35 138	8 884	3 836
Champaign-Urbana, IL..........	2 660	12.6	1 501	71	7.1	8.9	417	376	4	629	839	25 466	NA	NA
Charleston, WV	3 754	12.1	3 637	82	11.8	7.3	717	558	7	1 384	911	58 627	10 183	3 463

1. Per 1,000 estimated resident population. 2. Deaths of infants under 1 year old. 3. Deaths of infants under 1 year old per 1,000 live births. 4. Data subject to copyright. 5. Per 100,000 resident population as of July 1 of the year shown. 6. Data for serious crimes have not been adjusted for underreporting; this may affect comparability between geographic areas and over time. 7. Per 100,000 population estimated by the FBI.

Table C. Metropolitan Areas — Crime, Education, Money Income, and Poverty

Area Name	Serious crimes known to police,[1] 2002 (cont'd) Rate[2] Violent	Property	Education — School enrollment and attainment, 2000 — Enrollment[3] Total	Percent private	Attainment[4] (percent) High school graduate or more	Bachelor's degree or more	Local government expenditures,[5] 2000–2001 Total current expenditures (mil dol)	Current expenditures per student (dollars)	Money income, 1999 Per capita income[6] (dollars)	Mean household income	Mean family income	Percent of households with income of $100,000 or more	Percent below poverty level, 1999 Persons	House-holds	Families	Families with children
	46	47	48	49	50	51	52	53	54	55	56	57	58	59	60	61
Abilene, TX	305	3 327	46 419	21.7	78.7	19.6	203.2	6 877	16 561	43 803	50 174	5.9	14.6	14.4	10.6	15.5
Akron, OH	296	3 948	188 524	14.5	85.7	24.3	834.0	7 548	22 314	55 460	64 986	11.0	9.8	9.9	7.2	11.6
Albany, GA	391	4 092	46 259	10.6	73.2	15.7	198.3	6 873	16 863	45 528	51 777	7.6	21.5	20.0	16.9	24.0
Albany-Schenectady-Troy, NY.	372	2 723	223 907	21.5	86.1	29.1	1 273.6	10 032	22 622	55 614	65 721	11.7	9.3	9.4	6.4	10.2
Albuquerque, NM	930	5 425	205 679	13.8	83.7	28.1	691.3	5 780	19 889	50 767	57 802	9.6	13.9	12.8	10.5	15.5
Alexandria, LA	931	5 130	38 040	12.8	74.4	15.7	159.8	5 905	15 872	41 819	48 306	6.2	20.7	19.7	16.4	22.7
Allentown-Bethlehem-Easton, PA-NJ	272	2 568	187 117	23.6	81.3	21.7	960.2	8 452	21 863	55 827	64 922	11.9	8.3	8.1	5.9	9.3
Altoona, PA	293	2 685	29 585	14.1	83.8	13.9	139.7	7 053	16 743	40 786	47 741	4.6	12.6	12.8	9.1	14.8
Amarillo, TX	664	5 529	64 360	9.2	80.1	20.8	257.7	6 306	18 269	47 825	55 714	7.4	13.5	13.5	10.2	15.0
Ames, IA	221	3 334	35 450	4.7	93.5	44.5	73.2	6 703	19 949	51 942	65 765	9.5	14.1	14.5	5.5	7.2
Anchorage, AK	NA	NA	92 633	11.8	89.9	27.0	474.6	7 590	24 511	66 462	73 912	17.9	8.0	7.0	5.6	8.2
Anderson, IN	NA	NA	31 151	16.5	80.1	14.4	154.0	7 660	20 090	49 458	56 849	7.6	9.3	9.3	7.0	11.3
Anderson, SC	720	4 641	39 271	13.7	73.4	15.9	174.8	6 315	18 365	45 973	53 481	6.9	12.0	13.0	9.1	13.1
Ann Arbor, MI	333	3 372	117 309	10.6	91.5	48.1	413.0	8 660	27 173	68 537	85 858	19.8	11.1	10.8	5.1	7.4
Anniston-Oxford, AL.............	689	5 152	27 855	9.5	73.9	15.2	104.4	5 744	17 367	42 443	49 263	5.9	16.1	16.9	12.4	19.5
Appleton, WI	88	2 099	55 442	20.5	88.0	22.2	253.4	7 290	21 938	58 168	66 536	9.9	4.5	4.7	2.8	4.1
Asheville, NC	273	2 775	80 802	14.2	80.9	23.1	341.1	6 658	20 062	46 976	54 432	7.2	11.2	11.4	7.7	13.0
Athens-Clarke County, GA ...	323	4 975	61 125	9.7	79.4	32.4	166.2	7 055	18 211	46 677	59 035	9.0	20.8	21.1	11.4	16.1
Atlanta-Sandy Springs-Marietta, GA	511	4 011	1 145 157	17.3	83.5	31.4	5 292.8	7 144	24 785	66 876	74 688	17.2	9.5	8.8	7.0	9.7
Atlantic City, NJ	530	4 400	66 098	14.9	78.2	18.7	457.8	10 537	21 034	54 678	62 454	10.6	10.5	10.1	7.6	10.9
Auburn-Opelika, AL.............	583	5 087	45 855	8.7	81.4	27.9	107.8	6 012	17 158	42 461	56 407	7.2	21.8	25.2	11.1	14.1
Augusta-Richmond County, GA-SC	353	4 094	139 240	12.0	78.3	20.4	564.2	6 085	18 494	48 918	55 434	8.6	15.4	15.0	12.3	17.5
Austin-Round Rock, TX	371	4 391	365 233	11.5	84.8	36.7	1 456.0	6 758	24 516	64 094	75 188	15.8	11.1	10.3	6.7	9.4
Bakersfield, CA	491	3 758	205 960	8.2	68.5	13.5	1 037.7	7 012	15 760	47 107	51 273	8.3	20.8	17.7	16.8	22.9
Baltimore-Towson, MD	990	4 138	704 168	21.5	81.9	29.2	3 226.2	8 056	24 398	63 044	72 667	15.9	9.8	9.7	7.1	10.3
Bangor, ME	73	2 732	40 435	12.0	85.7	20.3	191.4	7 780	17 801	43 568	51 282	5.8	13.7	14.4	9.7	14.6
Barnstable Town, MA	418	2 344	47 762	14.8	91.8	33.6	286.9	9 102	25 318	58 468	67 795	12.4	6.9	7.0	4.6	8.1
Baton Rouge, LA	724	5 545	214 434	19.7	79.4	22.8	681.9	6 338	18 232	49 207	56 913	9.3	17.1	16.8	13.1	18.0
Battle Creek, MI	985	5 178	36 415	13.9	83.2	16.0	199.4	8 201	19 230	48 031	55 460	7.7	11.3	10.9	8.1	12.5
Bay City, MI	259	2 871	27 880	16.3	82.4	14.2	142.8	8 216	19 698	48 695	57 046	8.7	9.7	10.1	6.7	10.9
Beaumont-Port Arthur, TX	577	4 756	102 415	9.5	78.7	14.7	484.8	6 743	17 616	46 701	53 560	8.0	15.7	15.7	13.0	18.7
Bellingham, WA	238	4 931	51 210	11.3	87.5	27.2	167.0	6 416	20 025	51 119	60 699	8.9	14.2	13.6	7.8	11.9
Bend, OR	161	4 424	27 802	12.1	88.4	25.0	143.5	7 186	21 767	54 498	62 046	10.3	9.3	8.9	6.3	9.3
Billings, MT	238	4 145	36 095	11.4	88.4	26.2	143.9	6 122	19 159	46 877	55 263	7.0	11.1	11.2	8.4	13.6
Binghamton, NY	195	2 502	69 391	10.3	84.0	22.0	403.1	9 541	19 067	46 991	55 813	7.8	11.9	11.9	8.2	13.1
Birmingham-Hoover, AL........	542	3 922	268 529	15.6	78.8	22.7	1 046.7	6 147	20 642	52 052	60 400	10.2	13.6	13.8	10.6	15.2
Bismarck, ND	89	2 499	24 947	18.2	85.8	25.5	87.9	5 669	19 572	48 510	57 800	7.1	8.3	9.6	5.7	8.9
Blacksburg-Christiansburg-Radford, VA	136	1 719	56 410	4.9	79.4	25.7	126.0	6 902	17 370	43 634	55 419	6.1	19.9	19.5	8.9	13.3
Bloomington, IN	NA	NA	64 780	7.2	84.5	29.0	160.7	7 211	18 008	44 824	56 726	7.3	16.0	16.2	7.3	10.8
Bloomington-Normal, IL	NA	NA	52 781	12.9	90.7	36.2	164.6	7 125	22 227	57 773	71 227	13.5	9.7	10.1	4.1	6.3
Boise City-Nampa, ID	316	3 710	125 572	12.7	85.9	25.5	475.5	5 561	19 940	53 521	60 250	9.7	9.4	8.9	6.8	9.9
Boston-Cambridge-Quincy, MA-NH	438	2 430	1 202 285	29.0	86.7	37.0	6 093.1	9 508	28 016	72 196	85 318	20.7	8.5	9.0	5.9	8.7
Boston-Quincy, MA Div	675	2 979	508 467	31.8	85.5	35.2	2 477.6	9 779	26 779	68 583	81 217	18.9	10.6	11.1	7.4	10.9
Cambridge-Newton-Framingham, MA Div	221	1 873	391 638	32.1	88.5	43.6	2 107.8	10 131	31 199	80 294	95 531	24.9	6.5	7.0	4.3	6.3
Essex County, MA Div	398	2 407	194 443	21.4	84.6	31.3	1 046.1	8 941	26 358	68 548	80 980	19.0	8.9	9.5	6.6	10.1
Rockingham County-Strafford County, NH Div	NA	NA	107 737	18.5	89.4	30.2	461.5	7 393	24 877	65 206	74 178	16.2	5.8	6.0	3.6	5.5
Boulder, CO	217	2 426	83 834	14.2	92.8	53.2	301.2	6 391	29 049	72 453	88 415	21.5	9.9	9.5	4.8	6.9
Bowling Green, KY	NA	NA	30 587	6.8	78.0	22.3	94.4	5 730	18 359	46 917	53 839	7.4	15.8	16.5	11.2	16.7
Bremerton-Silverdale, WA	387	3 443	62 794	12.9	90.8	25.3	264.1	6 347	22 317	57 892	64 895	11.6	8.8	8.2	6.3	9.4
Bridgeport-Stamford-Norwalk, CT	312	2 299	233 796	24.1	84.4	39.9	1 435.8	10 318	38 350	103 255	120 888	31.0	6.9	6.9	5.0	7.2
Brownsville-Harlingen, TX	431	6 031	109 790	6.1	55.2	13.4	567.0	6 771	10 960	37 115	39 116	4.8	33.1	29.3	28.2	36.5
Brunswick, GA	601	6 388	22 909	10.3	79.5	19.7	114.6	6 681	19 582	48 894	55 230	9.0	15.6	14.7	12.2	18.7
Buffalo-Niagara Falls, NY	460	2 931	313 835	20.4	83.0	23.2	1 882.0	10 502	20 143	49 535	59 253	9.1	11.9	12.1	9.0	14.9
Burlington, NC.....................	336	4 526	32 488	20.2	76.5	19.2	124.4	5 907	19 391	48 475	56 109	7.4	11.1	11.2	7.6	10.8
Burlington-South Burlington, VT....................................	134	3 057	58 802	17.5	88.5	34.8	281.7	8 830	22 158	57 019	66 426	11.4	8.8	8.9	5.5	8.0
Canton-Massillon, OH..........	315	3 442	101 519	17.2	83.2	17.3	473.3	6 868	20 154	50 543	57 932	8.3	9.3	9.4	6.9	11.5
Cape Coral-Fort Myers, FL...	646	4 021	81 283	15.7	82.3	21.1	354.5	6 070	24 542	56 641	64 570	10.6	9.7	8.6	6.7	12.3
Carson City, NV	533	3 102	12 998	8.7	82.5	18.5	55.7	6 606	20 943	51 976	59 684	9.3	10.0	9.2	6.9	11.7
Casper, WY	274	4 726	18 067	5.9	88.3	20.0	87.6	7 271	18 913	46 518	54 120	6.3	11.8	11.3	8.7	14.5
Cedar Rapids, IA	218	3 618	62 847	17.7	89.8	24.9	337.1	8 260	22 102	54 758	64 138	9.2	6.6	6.9	4.5	7.0
Champaign-Urbana, IL..........	NA	NA	81 156	7.3	90.4	34.5	207.1	7 014	19 757	49 021	62 242	8.7	14.5	14.6	6.5	9.8
Charleston, WV	350	3 113	67 767	10.3	77.6	17.9	371.6	7 663	19 089	45 597	53 073	7.2	15.6	15.6	12.4	19.2

1. Data for serious crimes have not been adjusted for underreporting; this may affect comparability between geographic areas and over time. 2. Per 100,000 population estimated by the FBI. 3. All persons 3 years old and over enrolled in nursery school through college. 4. Persons 25 years old and over. 5. Elementary and secondary education expenditures. 6. Based on population enumerated as of April 1, 2000.

Table C. Metropolitan Areas — **Personal Income**

	Personal income, 2002												
			Per capita[1]					Transfer payments					
									Government payments to individuals				
Area Name	Total (mil dol)	Percent change, 2001–2002	Dollars	Rank	Wages and salaries[2] (mil dol)	Proprietor's income (mil dol)	Dividends, interest, and rent (mil dol)	Total (mil dol)	Total (mil dol)	Social Security (mil dol)	Medical payments (mil dol)	Income mainte-nance (mil dol)	Unemploy-ment insurance (mil dol)
	62	63	64	65	66	67	68	69	70	71	72	73	74
Abilene, TX	3 837	4.4	24 179	296	2 305	394	673	718	683	256	304	62	13
Akron, OH	21 147	2.6	30 198	96	13 599	1 210	3 421	3 337	3 138	1 222	1 276	271	114
Albany, GA	3 662	4.1	22 899	327	2 405	297	585	756	710	217	308	118	20
Albany-Schenectady-Troy, NY.	26 967	3.0	32 273	55	19 732	1 828	4 513	4 411	4 192	1 527	1 678	388	120
Albuquerque, NM	21 421	4.4	28 410	138	14 889	1 592	3 618	3 088	2 890	1 036	1 211	294	78
Alexandria, LA	3 762	4.1	25 836	221	2 060	334	605	997	960	222	581	96	12
Allentown-Bethlehem-Easton, PA-NJ	23 542	3.4	31 055	80	14 065	1 576	3 916	3 887	3 694	1 530	1 583	203	227
Altoona, PA	3 165	3.4	24 758	277	2 142	224	475	774	741	237	317	59	38
Amarillo, TX	5 828	3.6	25 160	252	3 799	632	989	883	831	328	334	79	22
Ames, IA	2 173	3.3	26 944	181	1 639	144	396	250	229	105	86	11	6
Anchorage, AK	11 874	4.8	35 538	22	8 039	1 364	1 840	1 664	1 595	281	508	150	70
Anderson, IN	3 430	1.9	25 971	213	1 835	202	483	650	617	278	253	50	19
Anderson, SC	4 252	1.3	24 927	268	2 209	355	648	777	734	337	273	63	27
Ann Arbor, MI	11 801	3.0	35 295	27	10 504	694	2 113	1 037	958	424	375	73	32
Anniston-Oxford, AL	2 618	5.0	23 455	315	1 737	141	458	578	552	215	221	59	10
Appleton, WI	6 232	2.8	29 888	104	4 423	422	1 029	671	619	300	212	31	53
Asheville, NC	10 103	2.5	26 688	190	5 808	698	2 403	1 960	1 870	827	749	149	50
Athens-Clarke County, GA	4 109	3.8	24 024	300	2 884	246	802	587	538	206	233	58	9
Atlanta-Sandy Springs-Marietta, GA	149 974	1.8	33 112	45	113 820	14 595	22 755	14 012	12 720	4 773	5 450	1 247	572
Atlantic City, NJ	8 210	4.1	31 647	70	6 147	1 112	1 186	1 428	1 365	455	642	98	108
Auburn-Opelika, AL	2 530	3.8	21 418	342	1 457	149	416	357	329	140	115	39	7
Augusta-Richmond County, GA-SC	13 016	4.1	25 664	227	8 875	629	2 214	2 355	2 219	758	968	262	58
Austin-Round Rock, TX	42 671	-1.1	31 625	71	32 385	4 836	6 291	3 452	3 149	1 227	1 204	302	183
Bakersfield, CA	15 674	6.4	22 583	334	10 220	1 685	2 129	3 018	2 853	829	1 061	541	226
Baltimore-Towson, MD	92 410	3.8	35 515	24	62 339	5 740	15 016	11 743	11 087	3 960	5 141	1 007	438
Bangor, ME	3 817	4.1	26 141	206	2 643	358	509	761	728	253	321	78	17
Barnstable Town, MA	9 021	3.5	39 466	11	3 699	914	2 436	1 423	1 369	649	532	56	81
Baton Rouge, LA	18 494	3.7	25 800	223	13 240	1 167	2 808	2 876	2 690	904	1 251	341	65
Battle Creek, MI	3 621	4.2	26 168	205	2 893	141	532	701	668	268	261	70	31
Bay City, MI	2 861	1.1	26 087	208	1 634	92	497	566	540	229	213	47	27
Beaumont-Port Arthur, TX	9 689	3.4	25 348	240	6 337	825	1 500	2 003	1 918	691	911	170	65
Bellingham, WA	4 509	3.9	25 860	219	2 682	369	966	753	706	268	245	61	56
Bend, OR	3 540	5.1	28 262	145	1 935	453	857	558	529	228	172	36	49
Billings, MT	3 986	3.6	28 210	147	2 652	361	767	568	532	235	187	41	13
Binghamton, NY	6 503	2.1	25 796	224	4 498	326	1 065	1 357	1 291	535	510	134	55
Birmingham-Hoover, AL	32 651	3.7	30 567	88	22 216	3 299	5 518	4 754	4 500	1 900	1 775	460	86
Bismarck, ND	2 658	3.4	27 587	163	1 853	195	457	397	375	151	150	23	9
Blacksburg-Christiansburg-Radford, VA	3 262	3.7	21 300	343	2 429	167	523	547	510	232	187	39	14
Bloomington, IN	4 182	3.3	23 637	311	2 630	223	819	636	592	255	237	42	25
Bloomington-Normal, IL	4 798	3.9	31 064	79	4 138	245	778	450	410	196	127	33	20
Boise City-Nampa, ID	14 397	3.0	28 904	126	9 570	1 870	2 549	1 670	1 559	624	578	117	97
Boston-Cambridge-Quincy, MA-NH	188 418	0.0	42 380	5	143 843	16 868	33 751	21 656	20 598	6 822	9 875	1 458	1 678
Boston-Quincy, MA Div	77 391	0.7	42 244	X	68 220	8 371	13 297	9 878	9 442	2 664	4 984	747	689
Cambridge-Newton-Framingham, MA Div	68 485	-1.0	46 457	X	52 501	5 674	13 394	6 498	6 147	2 336	2 663	349	577
Essex County, MA Div	28 204	0.2	38 341	X	14 886	1 631	4 904	3 855	3 679	1 231	1 702	295	337
Rockingham County-Strafford County, NH Div	14 339	1.1	35 495	X	8 236	1 193	2 156	1 426	1 329	591	525	67	76
Boulder, CO	11 281	-6.6	40 405	9	8 697	902	2 489	662	598	257	207	46	52
Bowling Green, KY	2 574	4.5	24 153	297	1 874	151	409	462	435	157	189	46	12
Bremerton-Silverdale, WA	7 570	5.7	32 053	60	4 292	397	1 425	938	878	296	321	70	75
Bridgeport-Stamford-Norwalk, CT	53 433	-1.8	59 622	1	32 177	7 355	11 146	4 256	4 042	1 557	1 883	274	213
Brownsville-Harlingen, TX	5 697	6.7	16 113	360	3 409	445	743	1 500	1 421	322	697	301	37
Brunswick, GA	2 616	4.8	27 466	167	1 419	145	672	484	457	178	204	42	10
Buffalo-Niagara Falls, NY	33 076	2.8	28 437	136	22 322	2 030	5 223	6 627	6 321	2 422	2 611	683	248
Burlington, NC	3 587	1.8	26 396	200	2 209	275	651	604	572	255	221	46	32
Burlington-South Burlington, VT	6 474	2.3	31 901	65	4 953	488	1 123	779	719	270	311	73	31
Canton-Massillon, OH	11 061	2.5	27 170	174	6 751	768	1 840	1 996	1 881	791	735	157	64
Cape Coral-Fort Myers, FL	15 009	5.0	31 555	75	6 968	1 200	5 070	2 503	2 387	1 225	918	108	30
Carson City, NV	1 774	3.1	32 664	50	1 336	110	433	241	230	98	93	13	13
Casper, WY	2 294	3.4	34 068	36	1 244	427	500	292	275	118	99	24	8
Cedar Rapids, IA	7 329	1.0	30 350	93	5 434	496	1 294	973	909	416	343	55	50
Champaign-Urbana, IL	5 862	3.1	27 438	168	4 169	300	1 262	668	613	261	211	59	31
Charleston, WV	8 654	2.9	28 264	144	6 089	754	1 319	1 861	1 790	685	666	163	47

1. Based on the resident population estimated as of July 1 of the year shown.   2. Includes other labor income.

Table C. Metropolitan Areas — Earnings, Social Security, and Housing

Area Name	Earnings, 2002									Social Security beneficiaries, December 2003		Supplemental Security Income recipients, December 2003	Housing units, 2003	
	Total (mil dol)	Farm	Percent by selected industries						Government	Number	Rate[2]		Total	Percent change, 2000–2003
			Goods related[1]		Service-related and health									
			Total	Manufacturing	Information, professional and technical services	Retail trade	Finance and insurance, and real estate	Health services						
	75	76	77	78	79	80	81	82	83	84	85	86	87	88
Abilene, TX	2 699	0.4	12.4	4.5	D	8.4	7.2	D	30.1	27 615	174	3 553	66 446	1.9
Akron, OH	14 809	0.1	D	18.8	7.8	7.8	6.2	11.0	14.9	117 390	167	12 837	299 368	2.9
Albany, GA	2 702	3.3	D	D	D	7.5	D	D	22.9	24 920	155	6 882	66 387	4.1
Albany-Schenectady-Troy, NY.	21 560	0.1	D	7.8	13.8	6.3	7.9	D	26.8	149 570	178	16 769	371 378	2.1
Albuquerque, NM	16 481	0.1	D	8.7	D	7.8	7.2	D	22.7	114 525	150	16 346	325 455	6.4
Alexandria, LA	2 394	0.5	D	10.8	D	8.0	D	16.9	26.7	26 630	182	6 918	62 100	2.5
Allentown-Bethlehem-Easton, PA-NJ	15 641	0.1	D	21.3	7.9	8.0	6.5	13.0	11.1	148 525	193	13 578	319 047	3.8
Altoona, PA	2 366	0.2	D	16.1	7.1	10.5	4.0	15.3	15.8	25 500	201	4 519	55 696	1.2
Amarillo, TX	4 431	1.0	D	0.0	D	9.2	D	D	17.1	33 575	144	3 659	94 291	2.9
Ames, IA	1 783	0.7	D	12.3	5.9	6.2	3.6	6.8	44.2	9 865	119	542	41 578	5.0
Anchorage, AK	9 403	0.1	15.5	2.1	11.4	7.5	5.7	9.2	27.1	30 395	90	5 809	132 952	4.1
Anderson, IN	2 037	0.2	D	36.4	3.8	7.3	4.2	11.4	14.6	26 740	204	2 671	57 881	1.7
Anderson, SC	2 564	0.5	D	31.6	3.6	10.1	3.8	7.1	17.9	35 690	208	3 428	77 081	5.3
Ann Arbor, MI	11 198	0.0	23.4	18.7	17.0	5.5	4.0	8.5	27.0	37 955	112	3 692	139 708	6.6
Anniston-Oxford, AL	1 878	0.5	D	19.3	6.1	8.4	3.1	8.4	29.8	25 045	224	4 658	52 609	2.5
Appleton, WI	4 845	0.9	D	24.7	D	8.0	9.1	8.8	10.1	29 830	142	1 814	84 429	7.7
Asheville, NC	6 506	1.4	25.3	17.5	6.7	9.0	5.1	D	16.0	87 520	229	8 610	185 467	5.8
Athens-Clarke County, GA	3 130	1.8	D	14.0	D	7.6	D	D	32.3	22 305	130	3 938	72 822	7.8
Atlanta-Sandy Springs-Marietta, GA	128 415	0.1	D	D	D	6.5	D	D	11.5	488 925	106	70 479	1 851 094	12.6
Atlantic City, NJ	7 259	0.4	D	3.2	7.5	8.3	4.3	9.5	16.7	45 140	171	5 193	119 297	4.6
Auburn-Opelika, AL	1 607	0.4	22.1	15.7	D	9.6	4.6	7.0	34.5	15 080	126	2 804	54 096	7.5
Augusta-Richmond County, GA-SC	9 504	0.3	D	14.0	D	7.1	4.6	D	26.8	82 715	162	14 144	213 520	4.4
Austin-Round Rock, TX	37 221	0.0	21.2	14.6	16.6	6.3	9.4	D	17.9	128 630	93	15 919	558 337	12.6
Bakersfield, CA	11 905	5.0	17.7	4.4	6.2	7.3	4.2	8.0	27.1	94 080	132	29 320	242 622	4.8
Baltimore-Towson, MD	68 079	0.1	D	8.3	13.4	6.6	10.0	10.5	21.9	391 010	149	53 211	1 072 484	2.3
Bangor, ME	3 001	0.2	D	13.6	7.2	9.8	4.2	17.2	20.1	29 005	197	4 503	68 504	2.5
Barnstable Town, MA	4 614	0.1	12.9	3.2	11.4	11.2	13.0	13.2	15.8	63 295	276	3 463	151 161	2.8
Baton Rouge, LA	14 408	0.2	D	13.9	D	6.7	D	D	19.8	98 115	136	19 523	294 653	4.3
Battle Creek, MI	3 035	0.2	D	31.8	6.3	6.6	3.2	9.9	19.2	27 245	196	4 103	59 818	1.9
Bay City, MI	1 726	0.4	25.5	20.5	12.2	10.9	4.0	12.3	16.9	22 420	205	2 374	47 217	1.7
Beaumont-Port Arthur, TX	7 163	0.0	30.8	20.5	D	7.9	4.5	D	15.4	69 150	181	10 221	159 718	1.9
Bellingham, WA	3 051	2.3	D	13.8	8.2	8.6	6.0	10.3	18.4	27 825	158	3 128	78 327	6.0
Bend, OR	2 388	-0.4	21.4	9.5	10.5	11.0	9.4	13.3	14.3	23 350	180	1 366	61 723	13.1
Billings, MT	3 013	0.4	16.6	6.5	9.4	9.6	7.1	D	13.7	24 460	171	2 111	61 794	2.9
Binghamton, NY	4 824	0.3	D	26.4	7.2	6.8	4.8	11.5	19.6	53 405	213	6 540	110 965	0.7
Birmingham-Hoover, AL	25 516	0.2	18.8	9.7	D	7.5	10.2	D	13.8	195 380	182	32 601	471 192	3.7
Bismarck, ND	2 048	0.1	D	7.8	8.0	8.7	6.0	D	21.5	16 180	167	1 259	41 710	5.4
Blacksburg-Christiansburg-Radford, VA	2 597	0.3	D	26.2	D	7.1	4.2	D	29.0	24 530	161	2 723	64 732	3.2
Bloomington, IN	2 853	0.0	D	15.8	7.0	7.5	4.7	D	29.3	26 230	147	2 271	79 327	4.7
Bloomington-Normal, IL	4 384	0.0	16.3	10.8	17.4	5.8	21.3	8.8	12.7	19 295	123	1 392	63 841	6.5
Boise City-Nampa, ID	11 440	1.6	26.6	18.0	D	7.6	D	D	14.3	67 440	132	7 032	201 989	11.5
Boston-Cambridge-Quincy, MA-NH	160 711	0.0	D	11.4	19.2	5.3	14.8	9.6	10.1	673 925	152	99 119	1 777 472	1.5
Boston-Quincy, MA Div	76 591	0.0	D	5.6	16.1	4.4	23.7	11.3	10.9	269 875	148	51 464	737 707	1.2
Cambridge-Newton-Framingham, MA Div	58 175	0.0	21.6	15.5	26.1	4.9	6.6	7.1	8.4	221 055	150	24 511	582 755	1.1
Essex County, MA Div	16 517	0.1	28.7	22.1	13.3	7.6	5.9	11.8	12.0	122 570	166	20 322	291 037	1.4
Rockingham County-Strafford County, NH Div	9 429	0.1	22.2	14.0	11.6	10.3	9.1	8.5	11.1	60 425	148	2 822	165 973	4.7
Boulder, CO	9 598	0.1	23.2	17.9	28.1	5.6	6.9	6.7	14.1	27 590	99	2 429	118 413	-1.2
Bowling Green, KY	2 026	0.0	D	D	D	8.6	5.1	D	16.9	17 595	163	3 883	46 826	5.3
Bremerton-Silverdale, WA	4 689	0.1	7.0	1.5	7.3	7.1	4.1	8.1	54.5	33 375	139	3 879	96 022	3.6
Bridgeport-Stamford-Norwalk, CT	39 533	0.0	D	12.0	16.1	5.8	25.4	7.4	6.7	137 055	152	10 451	344 906	1.6
Brownsville-Harlingen, TX	3 854	1.0	13.6	9.8	5.1	9.0	4.9	17.3	27.0	44 335	122	17 229	130 222	8.8
Brunswick, GA	1 564	0.3	D	11.5	D	8.6	D	D	26.2	18 850	196	2 560	47 516	5.9
Buffalo-Niagara Falls, NY	24 352	0.2	D	20.0	9.3	6.5	8.2	10.8	17.8	234 705	202	30 150	517 863	1.2
Burlington, NC	2 484	0.0	D	24.0	5.9	7.9	6.5	10.4	9.8	26 055	190	2 346	58 775	6.0
Burlington-South Burlington, VT	5 441	0.6	D	21.3	D	8.2	D	D	15.8	28 060	138	3 329	85 775	3.7
Canton-Massillon, OH	7 520	0.8	D	26.5	D	8.9	D	D	12.0	77 350	190	7 114	172 942	1.7
Cape Coral-Fort Myers, FL	8 169	0.5	17.9	4.8	10.0	12.4	11.7	9.4	15.4	121 810	247	6 878	276 129	12.5
Carson City, NV	1 446	0.0	D	10.8	6.9	9.3	7.0	7.6	36.4	10 440	189	626	22 310	4.8
Casper, WY	1 671	0.0	30.9	5.8	6.7	7.6	6.9	11.4	13.5	11 425	167	1 143	30 332	1.5
Cedar Rapids, IA	5 930	0.8	28.8	21.6	D	7.5	8.8	D	11.0	40 770	168	2 748	104 436	5.4
Champaign-Urbana, IL	4 469	0.2	D	10.8	D	6.3	5.5	D	34.2	27 955	129	2 706	91 649	4.0
Charleston, WV	6 844	0.0	D	D	D	6.8	6.1	D	18.2	68 595	224	11 812	143 189	1.1

1. Covers mining, construction, and manufacturing.   2. Per 1,000 resident population estimated as of July 1 of the year shown.

Table C. Metropolitan Areas — **Housing, Labor Force, and Employment**

Area Name	Housing units, 2000								Civilian labor force, 2003				Civilian employment,[5] 2000		
		Occupied units									Unemployment			Percent	
			Owner-occupied			Renter-occupied									Production, transportation, and material moving occupations
				Owner cost is 35 percent or more of income										Management, professional, and related occupations	
	Total	Percent	Mean value[1]	With a mortgage	Without a mortgage	Mean rent[2]	Rent is 35 percent or more of income	Substandard units[3] (percent)	Total	Percent change, 2002–2003	Total	Rate[4]	Total		
	89	90	91	92	93	94	95	96	97	98	99	100	101	102	103
Abilene, TX	58 475	65.1	69 503	14.7	7.5	494	29.4	5.0	78 127	3.4	3 252	4.2	67 732	31.2	11.8
Akron, OH	274 237	70.5	135 174	16.7	6.9	564	30.1	1.7	376 676	1.4	21 419	5.7	342 806	32.0	17.3
Albany, GA	57 403	61.8	93 394	19.6	9.1	470	32.2	7.1	73 032	4.8	3 728	5.1	64 499	28.2	18.3
Albany-Schenectady-Troy, NY.	330 246	64.4	124 956	16.2	8.1	603	30.8	1.9	445 510	0.1	16 967	3.8	404 347	39.1	10.8
Albuquerque, NM	281 052	67.9	147 396	21.4	6.7	613	35.1	6.4	398 173	1.7	21 960	5.5	335 307	36.7	10.0
Alexandria, LA	54 193	69.8	89 297	18.4	8.0	446	34.1	4.2	67 055	2.1	4 317	6.4	57 688	30.6	12.1
Allentown-Bethlehem-Easton, PA-NJ	285 808	71.7	135 716	18.7	9.5	605	29.5	2.0	387 356	-0.9	22 311	5.8	355 911	32.2	17.3
Altoona, PA	51 518	72.9	85 966	16.5	8.0	428	30.5	1.4	65 274	-1.7	3 322	5.1	57 756	25.6	19.5
Amarillo, TX	85 272	65.9	93 915	13.8	6.4	510	30.8	6.1	123 412	3.9	4 834	3.9	105 409	29.6	14.0
Ames, IA	29 383	58.3	132 094	10.9	5.2	591	37.8	2.1	48 532	-2.7	1 304	2.7	44 535	43.0	9.1
Anchorage, AK	115 378	63.4	169 017	18.3	4.9	782	31.3	7.8	183 233	2.9	11 685	6.4	150 718	35.7	9.7
Anderson, IN	53 052	74.2	91 980	13.9	3.9	502	28.2	1.8	65 856	1.0	3 971	6.0	60 207	25.2	22.3
Anderson, SC	65 649	76.3	107 584	16.1	5.1	472	29.5	2.3	85 620	3.1	5 911	6.9	77 732	26.2	24.2
Ann Arbor, MI	125 327	59.7	206 958	15.1	5.8	731	33.9	3.5	179 803	0.9	5 770	3.2	172 373	48.3	9.7
Anniston-Oxford, AL	45 307	72.5	86 527	15.4	6.6	429	31.0	2.4	53 527	3.6	2 914	5.4	47 856	25.5	23.2
Appleton, WI	75 440	74.0	122 855	11.0	5.5	563	19.4	1.9	134 745	0.9	6 858	5.1	107 838	30.2	22.1
Asheville, NC	154 290	73.7	144 098	20.5	5.7	557	30.7	2.6	188 095	3.0	7 629	4.1	173 287	30.4	17.5
Athens-Clarke County, GA ...	63 406	56.5	139 883	16.5	5.7	568	42.0	4.7	86 841	4.5	2 627	3.0	80 714	35.0	15.8
Atlanta-Sandy Springs-Marietta, GA	1 554 154	66.8	171 035	17.2	6.9	749	29.3	5.5	2 501 514	2.6	121 568	4.9	2 153 123	37.0	12.0
Atlantic City, NJ	95 024	66.3	143 233	25.0	16.2	668	31.9	5.8	134 273	2.8	9 321	6.9	116 051	25.6	9.1
Auburn-Opelika, AL	45 702	62.1	127 707	14.8	5.8	498	47.0	3.2	53 530	4.1	2 108	3.9	52 980	33.9	15.4
Augusta-Richmond County, GA-SC	184 801	69.7	107 640	18.0	7.3	510	30.1	4.3	226 781	4.0	11 898	5.2	212 499	32.0	17.1
Austin-Round Rock, TX	471 855	58.3	164 223	15.2	8.3	767	33.1	7.7	771 328	1.2	44 135	5.7	660 769	41.9	9.3
Bakersfield, CA	208 652	62.1	111 850	23.7	8.1	558	37.1	15.5	302 324	2.0	37 147	12.3	232 461	27.0	13.5
Baltimore-Towson, MD	974 071	66.9	163 594	18.4	7.8	655	29.3	3.0	1 344 650	-0.1	68 518	5.1	1 232 921	39.8	10.2
Bangor, ME	58 096	69.8	92 403	16.0	8.2	466	33.1	2.1	81 205	1.9	4 958	6.1	69 846	30.3	15.1
Barnstable Town, MA	94 822	77.8	232 912	23.5	9.8	721	34.2	1.4	120 232	2.5	6 206	5.2	100 780	35.1	7.5
Baton Rouge, LA	256 637	69.3	118 706	16.5	6.8	523	33.0	5.6	347 707	3.0	22 564	6.5	314 223	32.3	13.0
Battle Creek, MI	54 100	73.0	95 904	15.0	6.4	496	28.8	2.8	65 876	1.3	4 850	7.4	62 956	26.9	23.8
Bay City, MI	43 930	79.3	100 725	13.6	7.2	445	27.9	1.8	53 797	0.2	4 334	8.1	50 804	26.9	18.0
Beaumont-Port Arthur, TX	142 327	70.5	75 580	15.1	8.6	492	30.2	6.2	183 381	3.0	17 410	9.5	155 964	27.5	16.1
Bellingham, WA	64 446	63.4	187 380	23.0	5.6	670	39.5	4.4	89 793	3.4	5 477	6.1	80 773	31.5	13.5
Bend, OR	45 595	72.3	189 835	22.1	5.5	683	34.8	3.6	68 771	4.1	5 316	7.7	55 754	31.3	12.8
Billings, MT	56 149	69.6	117 792	16.4	5.8	494	30.7	2.7	76 688	2.9	2 773	3.6	70 078	31.3	11.6
Binghamton, NY	100 474	67.6	87 873	14.8	6.7	488	34.0	1.9	123 506	-2.2	7 221	5.8	116 041	34.5	15.7
Birmingham-Hoover, AL	412 376	72.0	128 636	17.8	8.3	520	29.2	3.0	531 269	2.2	24 584	4.6	475 956	33.0	13.9
Bismarck, ND	37 559	70.0	105 354	10.8	6.5	460	27.1	2.1	55 941	1.8	1 926	3.4	50 280	35.0	10.3
Blacksburg-Christiansburg-Radford, VA	58 443	61.6	111 082	13.4	4.2	516	38.8	2.0	73 566	6.4	2 994	4.1	70 330	34.3	17.3
Bloomington, IN	68 552	62.4	115 330	13.9	3.7	582	43.4	2.5	91 326	2.8	3 803	4.2	87 561	34.6	14.7
Bloomington-Normal, IL	56 746	66.4	130 870	12.0	5.1	568	28.6	1.7	93 019	-1.0	2 634	2.8	80 759	37.3	10.8
Boise City-Nampa, ID	170 291	71.8	139 776	16.8	5.0	612	31.4	5.1	260 395	-0.7	13 739	5.3	230 121	34.3	13.0
Boston-Cambridge-Quincy, MA-NH	1 679 659	60.9	266 305	18.7	11.2	810	29.8	3.7	2 426 485	-1.9	134 378	5.5	2 240 183	44.0	9.8
Boston-Quincy, MA Div	695 910	56.8	256 410	19.5	11.6	822	31.4	4.6	975 245	-1.9	53 910	5.5	903 250	42.3	9.0
Cambridge-Newton-Framingham, MA Div	561 220	61.8	305 182	17.9	10.7	880	28.1	3.0	839 603	-2.7	42 732	5.1	776 273	49.7	8.4
Essex County, MA Div	275 419	63.5	262 061	19.2	11.2	666	29.7	3.8	380 796	-2.0	25 886	6.8	349 835	39.4	12.4
Rockingham County-Strafford County, NH Div	147 110	72.3	181 571	17.9	11.1	705	27.0	1.9	230 841	0.9	11 850	5.1	210 825	37.2	13.9
Boulder, CO	106 534	64.4	298 110	19.6	4.6	899	38.2	3.8	175 460	-4.4	10 147	5.8	150 999	50.5	7.5
Bowling Green, KY	40 013	66.5	116 965	15.9	7.0	493	29.1	3.0	56 742	2.1	3 084	5.4	51 436	29.0	18.8
Bremerton-Silverdale, WA	86 416	67.4	194 886	21.7	6.7	695	31.8	3.9	102 110	1.9	6 531	6.4	98 146	34.9	10.4
Bridgeport-Stamford-Norwalk, CT	324 232	69.2	397 155	23.1	14.0	932	31.7	4.2	461 385	0.7	22 320	4.8	426 638	43.7	9.3
Brownsville-Harlingen, TX	97 267	67.7	68 775	21.7	9.8	435	33.9	22.8	144 354	3.3	15 890	11.0	108 904	27.7	15.8
Brunswick, GA	36 846	70.7	160 450	20.6	8.6	553	30.3	4.5	48 903	2.2	1 943	4.0	42 436	28.6	14.4
Buffalo-Niagara Falls, NY	468 719	66.2	103 880	17.7	9.7	526	37.0	2.2	575 762	0.0	36 641	6.4	531 984	33.6	15.4
Burlington, NC	51 584	70.1	129 424	18.4	7.4	559	27.7	4.0	73 110	1.0	5 235	7.2	64 895	28.2	23.0
Burlington-South Burlington, VT	75 978	68.6	151 915	16.0	8.7	671	32.7	2.0	123 839	0.1	4 966	4.0	107 371	40.6	12.5
Canton-Massillon, OH	159 442	72.9	116 323	15.6	5.1	494	26.3	1.5	205 450	-0.2	13 943	6.8	193 806	28.1	22.1
Cape Coral-Fort Myers, FL	188 599	76.5	155 498	22.6	6.6	691	32.1	4.0	217 125	3.6	8 749	4.0	186 417	28.1	9.3
Carson City, NV	20 171	63.1	175 030	18.7	6.4	696	31.9	6.6	24 674	-0.3	1 584	6.4	23 649	30.2	13.8
Casper, WY	26 819	69.9	99 579	13.2	3.5	445	24.1	2.6	36 657	4.0	1 766	4.8	33 213	28.5	12.0
Cedar Rapids, IA	94 059	73.7	116 992	11.2	4.0	514	23.8	2.0	138 507	-3.2	6 756	4.9	126 280	33.7	15.8
Champaign-Urbana, IL	82 711	59.0	108 370	12.3	5.1	584	39.1	2.7	115 232	0.2	4 050	3.5	108 621	40.5	12.3
Charleston, WV	129 229	74.0	101 247	13.8	6.0	441	29.1	2.0	146 159	-3.2	7 739	5.3	132 085	31.5	12.9

1. Specified owner-occupied units. 2. Specified renter-occupied units. 3. Overcrowded or lacking complete plumbing facilities. 4. Percent of civilian labor force. 5. Persons 16 years old and over.

Table C. Metropolitan Areas — Nonfarm Employment and Agriculture

Table C. Metropolitan Areas — **Nonfarm Employment and Agriculture**

Area Name	Private nonfarm establishments, employment and payroll, 2001									Agriculture, 2002			
	Number of establishments	Employment						Annual payroll		Farms			
		Total	Health care and social assistance	Manufacturing	Retail trade	Finance and insurance	Professional, scientific, and technical services	Total (mil dol)	Average per employee (dollars)	Number	Percent with—		Farm operators whose principal occupation is farming (percent)
											Less than 50 acres	500 acres and over	
	104	105	106	107	108	109	110	111	112	113	114	115	116
Abilene, TX	3 983	52 689	10 658	3 466	8 214	2 629	1 356	1 214	23 041	2 994	24.6	22.8	51.6
Akron, OH	17 604	298 645	39 721	50 480	39 169	11 434	12 894	9 361	31 345	1 339	61.2	2.6	51.2
Albany, GA	3 264	50 963	7 976	9 187	8 553	1 617	1 584	1 366	26 804	1 206	31.8	26.0	52.7
Albany-Schenectady-Troy, NY.	19 333	319 714	52 039	26 193	47 729	23 732	23 960	10 461	32 720	2 404	37.9	5.5	57.5
Albuquerque, NM	17 886	281 277	37 896	23 954	39 306	15 430	18 961	8 162	29 018	2 144	66.0	15.3	51.3
Alexandria, LA	3 293	48 563	11 801	3 752	7 422	1 798	2 131	1 221	25 143	1 192	46.4	9.7	56.5
Allentown-Bethlehem-Easton, PA-NJ	17 739	292 223	43 099	49 967	37 918	15 442	9 401	9 913	33 923	2 125	60.2	5.8	53.0
Altoona, PA	3 235	49 572	8 640	8 487	8 560	1 517	2 154	1 256	25 337	504	31.0	6.7	64.9
Amarillo, TX	5 750	87 390	13 771	11 105	12 149	4 593	5 850	2 443	27 955	1 685	22.8	38.5	53.1
Ames, IA	1 927	27 973	4 414	3 727	4 971	858	1 128	669	23 916	977	30.9	24.5	64.2
Anchorage, AK	9 440	129 019	17 941	2 029	18 352	5 237	8 731	5 451	42 250	251	48.6	10.4	61.8
Anderson, IN	2 719	42 861	5 985	9 741	6 965	1 443	892	1 192	27 811	807	45.2	19.1	59.0
Anderson, SC	3 674	58 439	7 785	18 853	8 588	1 368	1 161	1 537	26 301	1 644	49.9	3.5	45.9
Ann Arbor, MI	8 270	157 248	27 705	27 425	19 877	4 185	12 105	6 588	41 896	1 325	51.4	6.5	49.4
Anniston-Oxford, AL	2 555	39 752	5 583	9 911	6 472	982	1 189	925	23 269	673	45.8	2.4	54.1
Appleton, WI	5 477	108 315	9 137	27 317	14 591	7 345	3 437	3 395	31 344	2 163	35.7	8.3	64.5
Asheville, NC	10 476	145 194	24 981	27 399	22 183	4 009	4 535	3 843	26 468	3 485	57.4	2.1	56.4
Athens-Clarke County, GA ...	3 888	54 854	8 455	10 629	9 747	1 884	2 186	1 363	24 848	1 640	44.6	3.5	55.5
Atlanta-Sandy Springs-Marietta, GA	117 524	2 155 363	178 387	184 486	262 757	125 257	167 842	81 607	37 862	9 370	53.4	3.5	49.3
Atlantic City, NJ	6 423	119 759	13 069	4 668	14 766	2 682	5 490	3 620	30 227	456	70.8	1.8	63.4
Auburn-Opelika, AL	2 016	32 564	4 964	6 217	5 205	810	698	704	21 619	336	34.8	10.7	60.1
Augusta-Richmond County, GA-SC	10 007	182 649	31 233	42 622	25 869	4 949	7 723	5 478	29 992	2 380	40.8	9.9	47.8
Austin-Round Rock, TX	32 399	580 485	56 418	71 061	74 900	29 366	48 785	22 825	39 321	8 511	42.7	10.0	51.2
Bakersfield, CA	11 063	153 457	21 188	12 760	24 264	6 278	8 503	4 529	29 513	2 147	36.4	26.8	70.1
Baltimore-Towson, MD	62 283	1 063 684	150 695	87 554	134 217	61 574	92 726	37 379	35 141	3 746	56.4	6.4	54.9
Bangor, ME	4 156	59 142	12 560	7 793	10 329	1 828	2 600	1 624	27 459	575	35.8	9.4	47.0
Barnstable Town, MA	8 442	73 481	13 312	3 287	14 586	3 004	4 026	2 243	30 525	285	89.1	0.0	45.6
Baton Rouge, LA	16 048	278 567	33 911	25 632	38 379	13 033	16 737	8 231	29 548	2 976	47.4	11.5	44.8
Battle Creek, MI	3 029	58 793	8 539	14 325	8 011	3 263	1 140	1 859	31 619	1 147	32.8	10.1	53.1
Bay City, MI	2 563	34 861	5 988	5 030	7 013	1 040	1 044	1 052	30 177	787	38.8	13.6	61.8
Beaumont-Port Arthur, TX	7 946	127 939	19 966	20 321	19 738	3 730	5 260	3 813	29 803	1 788	58.6	10.1	51.3
Bellingham, WA	5 423	58 667	6 615	8 473	9 841	2 054	2 826	1 677	28 585	1 485	62.2	2.4	54.2
Bend, OR	4 692	44 117	5 377	4 932	8 621	1 533	2 096	1 148	26 022	1 632	78.6	2.8	48.3
Billings, MT	5 291	62 536	9 350	3 395	10 227	2 716	4 807	1 668	26 673	1 982	31.2	29.0	55.3
Binghamton, NY	5 102	94 085	13 549	22 739	13 662	3 754	3 880	2 669	28 368	1 192	23.2	7.4	55.5
Birmingham-Hoover, AL	25 527	460 343	60 567	50 077	58 982	34 500	24 850	14 988	32 558	4 261	42.9	4.2	52.4
Bismarck, ND	3 010	42 380	8 872	2 401	6 592	2 117	2 677	1 105	26 074	1 801	10.8	51.5	60.5
Blacksburg-Christiansburg-Radford, VA	3 119	48 306	4 859	15 306	8 150	1 144	2 177	1 221	25 276	1 505	35.7	7.0	49.8
Bloomington, IN	3 865	56 130	8 961	9 924	9 153	1 563	2 417	1 349	24 033	1 957	36.4	6.3	46.3
Bloomington-Normal, IL	3 506	79 778	7 776	7 046	9 252	22 295	2 169	2 855	35 787	1 442	21.3	35.0	68.7
Boise City-Nampa, ID	13 918	207 781	23 843	32 955	26 540	9 194	8 808	6 098	29 348	5 115	66.9	8.3	52.6
Boston-Cambridge-Quincy, MA-NH	125 689	2 394 026	318 776	263 608	251 268	180 371	232 470	111 890	46 737	2 715	66.9	2.0	55.9
Boston-Quincy, MA Div	52 110	1 074 258	169 228	64 083	97 212	134 717	98 264	51 870	48 284	1 010	73.0	2.3	59.0
Cambridge-Newton-Framingham, MA Div	43 079	871 013	88 550	118 115	84 016	27 402	110 239	43 567	50 019	579	68.0	0.9	55.6
Essex County, MA Div	18 634	284 473	43 563	56 055	38 534	10 977	14 962	10 542	37 058	400	71.5	3.0	52.3
Rockingham County-Strafford County, NH Div	11 866	164 282	17 435	25 355	31 506	7 275	9 005	5 911	35 981	726	55.0	1.9	54.0
Boulder, CO	11 361	172 266	13 152	25 438	22 524	4 549	23 845	7 626	44 269	736	63.6	6.8	48.9
Bowling Green, KY	2 634	43 570	6 928	8 046	7 459	1 443	1 190	1 140	26 165	2 551	40.7	4.1	54.8
Bremerton-Silverdale, WA	5 377	49 570	9 376	1 946	11 113	2 067	2 987	1 279	25 802	587	89.6	0.5	53.8
Bridgeport-Stamford-Norwalk, CT	28 673	457 272	52 229	57 990	53 304	42 016	37 964	26 468	57 882	287	76.0	0.3	51.6
Brownsville-Harlingen, TX.....	5 847	86 874	20 302	10 820	14 195	2 533	2 847	1 701	19 580	1 120	59.0	14.9	59.5
Brunswick, GA	2 776	33 707	4 159	3 797	5 682	960	866	793	23 526	368	41.6	6.0	46.2
Buffalo-Niagara Falls, NY	27 077	475 627	73 802	76 501	63 373	25 977	22 446	14 290	30 045	2 090	44.5	5.5	59.8
Burlington, NC	3 355	60 291	6 972	19 378	7 682	1 665	1 208	1 562	25 908	831	43.2	3.7	52.5
Burlington-South Burlington, VT	6 513	100 553	14 009	22 362	14 357	4 343	6 218	3 199	31 814	1 342	31.2	9.9	58.0
Canton-Massillon, OH	9 902	170 694	25 975	42 258	23 632	5 776	4 728	4 722	27 664	2 086	44.8	4.3	53.4
Cape Coral-Fort Myers, FL...	12 785	147 047	17 852	7 162	29 616	4 912	9 039	3 978	27 053	643	75.3	7.5	51.2
Carson City, NV	2 333	24 411	3 010	4 236	4 126	1 152	1 388	712	29 167	21	52.4	19.0	61.9
Casper, WY	2 644	27 774	3 929	1 536	4 278	1 299	1 066	788	28 372	380	21.8	42.6	57.9
Cedar Rapids, IA	6 405	120 719	13 001	21 966	15 632	7 509	4 525	3 884	32 174	3 655	26.6	18.4	65.9
Champaign-Urbana, IL	4 887	78 105	11 353	11 103	11 944	3 254	3 708	2 061	26 388	2 257	19.9	35.9	73.9
Charleston, WV	7 638	118 062	18 630	7 740	17 002	7 301	6 297	3 486	29 527	1 098	32.4	1.9	51.1

Table C. Metropolitan Areas — **Agriculture**

Agriculture, 2002 (cont'd)

Area Name	Land in farms		Acres			Value of land and buildings (dollars)		Value of machinery and equipment average per farm (dollars)	Value of products sold		Percent from —		Percent of farms with sales of —		Government payments	
	Acreage (1,000)	Percent change, 1997–2002	Average size of farm	Total irrigated (1,000)	Total cropland (1,000)	Average per farm	Average per acre		Total (mil dol)	Average per farm (dollars)	Crops	Livestock and poultry products	$10,000 or more	$100,000 or more	Total ($1,000)	Percent of farms
	117	118	119	120	121	122	123	124	125	126	127	128	129	130	131	132
Abilene, TX	1 567	8.8	523	7	709	326 744	592	38 306	112	37 247	25.0	75.0	24.9	5.5	8 822	36.6
Akron, OH	118	12.4	88	1	81	445 564	4 510	53 564	36	26 691	73.9	26.1	28.5	6.1	1 033	13.2
Albany, GA	673	0.4	558	103	317	849 262	1 521	104 607	132	109 245	79.1	20.9	39.0	18.5	10 921	53.0
Albany-Schenectady-Troy, NY.	371	3.6	154	3	225	364 540	2 456	65 367	112	46 461	36.9	63.1	36.2	9.9	4 986	21.9
Albuquerque, NM	D	D	D	58	145	427 772	D	30 842	80	37 203	26.8	73.2	20.1	4.9	D	D
Alexandria, LA	237	-2.5	199	9	140	289 253	1 648	57 637	70	58 753	81.1	18.9	38.8	13.6	2 633	19.2
Allentown-Bethlehem-Easton, PA-NJ	266	-2.6	125	4	209	679 709	5 461	65 612	120	56 268	63.3	36.7	31.8	10.7	3 158	18.1
Altoona, PA	86	2.4	170	0	60	512 958	3 126	79 549	63	125 698	9.4	90.6	51.8	27.4	1 987	28.0
Amarillo, TX	1 992	2.8	1 182	88	753	526 361	436	58 732	351	208 490	8.7	91.3	34.1	11.2	12 250	47.3
Ames, IA	360	5.6	368	0	330	950 209	2 342	121 033	119	121 525	77.9	22.1	68.0	29.7	5 577	64.6
Anchorage, AK	47	NA	187	1	22	429 707	2 299	63 949	28	109 610	51.6	48.4	45.4	15.1	393	7.6
Anderson, IN	244	8.9	302	1	229	834 889	2 816	95 767	75	93 311	90.1	9.9	49.4	20.4	3 535	45.2
Anderson, SC	177	6.6	108	1	87	349 436	3 314	33 010	37	22 534	40.3	59.7	17.8	2.6	789	16.2
Ann Arbor, MI	175	-2.8	132	2	140	622 942	4 739	56 441	55	41 221	68.6	31.4	35.0	9.3	2 251	22.9
Anniston-Oxford, AL	75	-2.6	111	2	33	273 823	2 598	33 520	43	63 975	18.2	81.8	23.3	6.5	362	17.5
Appleton, WI	414	4.5	191	0	351	543 192	3 015	91 944	228	105 563	20.4	79.6	53.9	26.1	9 436	51.5
Asheville, NC	292	5.4	84	6	123	411 046	4 491	30 937	105	30 203	76.9	23.1	22.5	3.4	2 995	13.2
Athens-Clarke County, GA	201	2.6	122	2	74	533 261	4 286	31 540	289	175 949	5.5	94.5	34.2	18.2	1 262	29.4
Atlanta-Sandy Springs-Marietta, GA	1 027	7.9	110	D	350	445 076	4 287	30 164	623	66 503	14.8	85.2	22.8	8.5	4 079	18.1
Atlantic City, NJ	30	-3.2	67	12	19	414 096	5 796	76 470	79	172 167	99.0	1.0	39.9	19.7	D	D
Auburn-Opelika, AL	74	-2.6	220	1	22	373 440	2 280	39 870	29	86 131	D	D	26.2	3.6	302	25.0
Augusta-Richmond County, GA-SC	520	4.0	218	24	213	428 015	1 902	57 454	164	68 787	D	D	23.6	7.6	3 606	25.5
Austin-Round Rock, TX	1 888	-0.1	222	11	713	476 463	2 121	29 160	141	16 571	37.6	62.4	21.0	2.8	4 438	10.4
Bakersfield, CA	2 731	-4.2	1 272	812	998	2 213 516	1 816	195 721	2 059	958 875	86.6	13.4	60.9	43.2	13 248	16.9
Baltimore-Towson, MD	528	-7.9	141	15	400	719 370	5 101	72 941	256	68 306	63.3	36.7	35.0	11.7	9 775	24.8
Bangor, ME	107	-8.5	186	2	48	245 401	1 266	54 487	29	50 357	34.9	65.1	30.6	9.4	1 417	16.9
Barnstable Town, MA	6	20.0	21	2	3	447 947	21 421	32 869	14	48 516	62.2	37.8	42.1	12.3	D	D
Baton Rouge, LA	705	-5.4	237	9	406	511 199	1 977	60 255	195	65 561	D	D	29.8	8.7	5 606	21.0
Battle Creek, MI	240	-1.2	209	10	190	505 642	2 314	61 196	64	56 184	56.1	43.9	41.6	10.7	3 437	39.9
Bay City, MI	186	5.7	236	4	167	543 065	2 573	102 824	59	75 442	91.9	8.1	51.5	19.8	2 073	47.8
Beaumont-Port Arthur, TX	530	-9.7	297	24	230	283 334	1 029	30 406	D	D	D	D	17.6	3.5	D	D
Bellingham, WA	148	42.3	100	32	90	579 356	5 959	112 458	288	193 845	26.4	73.6	43.8	24.7	4 029	14.8
Bend, OR	138	11.3	85	44	50	423 461	5 172	23 540	21	12 857	42.7	57.3	18.0	2.5	91	1.7
Billings, MT	2 322	2.7	1 172	155	539	752 827	590	64 982	164	82 925	22.9	77.1	44.5	12.1	5 467	33.6
Binghamton, NY	227	16.4	190	1	129	386 453	2 065	77 200	59	49 271	20.2	79.8	34.6	12.8	2 849	24.1
Birmingham-Hoover, AL	551	4.8	129	7	225	307 061	2 242	34 087	254	59 662	14.1	85.9	25.3	8.2	1 372	12.9
Bismarck, ND	2 142	0.8	1 189	10	1 053	361 965	318	77 811	114	63 490	34.8	65.2	55.6	19.7	10 118	63.1
Blacksburg-Christiansburg-Radford, VA	249	3.3	165	1	106	439 653	2 556	41 690	38	25 038	20.9	79.1	31.5	4.8	816	11.4
Bloomington, IN	330	-12.0	168	2	213	338 149	2 091	41 695	61	31 181	49.2	50.8	26.9	5.3	2 733	30.0
Bloomington-Normal, IL	688	-1.3	477	1	659	1 281 279	2 912	117 586	207	143 669	86.8	13.2	76.0	41.7	10 513	71.4
Boise City-Nampa, ID	1 338	-10.6	262	435	480	507 933	1 973	66 811	552	108 010	40.6	59.4	31.2	11.7	D	D
Boston-Cambridge-Quincy, MA-NH	D	D	D	D	75	836 901	D	D	172	63 301	85.0	15.0	35.8	10.0	D	D
Boston-Quincy, MA Div	D	D	D	D	26	890 179	D	D	55	54 108	93.8	6.2	44.3	10.4	D	D
Cambridge-Newton-Framingham, MA Div	33	6.5	57	1	16	1 031 520	20 975	43 038	66	113 843	83.7	16.3	33.2	11.1	D	D
Essex County, MA Div	28	7.7	70	1	13	1 167 953	14 560	51 248	24	61 173	82.0	18.0	35.5	13.3	D	D
Rockingham County-Strafford County, NH Div	65	4.8	90	1	21	425 171	4 809	36 256	27	36 953	72.6	27.4	26.4	6.7	D	D
Boulder, CO	108	-15.6	146	31	54	1 159 421	7 639	49 483	33	44 617	66.4	33.6	25.4	5.7	262	10.5
Bowling Green, KY	349	1.5	137	0	220	259 922	1 818	42 817	71	28 002	38.0	62.0	28.1	4.9	2 359	25.1
Bremerton-Silverdale, WA	16	-15.8	27	1	7	353 586	12 869	41 280	31	52 322	43.4	56.6	15.2	4.6	105	4.3
Bridgeport-Stamford-Norwalk, CT	13	8.3	45	0	5	1 153 047	26 164	36 613	30	105 477	72.1	27.9	38.0	11.8	D	D
Brownsville-Harlingen, TX	350	-5.1	313	105	254	543 412	1 549	60 969	75	66 640	83.5	16.5	37.5	12.6	2 685	27.7
Brunswick, GA	51	27.5	139	0	13	228 265	1 635	25 956	D	D	D	D	20.9	4.1	D	D
Buffalo-Niagara Falls, NY	310	14.4	148	6	236	273 790	1 772	73 249	152	72 856	53.9	46.1	38.3	12.4	4 580	23.1
Burlington, NC	98	-9.3	118	2	45	412 829	3 867	48 571	29	34 552	36.5	63.5	29.5	7.0	400	18.3
Burlington-South Burlington, VT	283	-4.1	211	1	144	379 990	1 873	85 895	153	113 845	12.3	87.7	48.5	26.8	7 997	25.6
Canton-Massillon, OH	269	7.6	129	1	185	416 469	3 144	58 377	92	44 261	43.9	56.1	33.7	8.8	3 125	22.1
Cape Coral-Fort Myers, FL	126	-2.3	197	24	36	726 318	3 293	62 165	113	176 370	96.2	3.8	35.3	11.4	86	2.3
Carson City, NV	4	-42.9	209	2	2	651 109	3 235	75 258	1	44 190	21.8	78.2	47.6	4.8	D	D
Casper, WY	2 871	2.3	7 555	33	75	1 401 928	187	59 552	29	75 050	10.1	89.9	48.2	17.1	2 050	28.7
Cedar Rapids, IA	1 061	-1.8	290	D	909	697 208	2 390	92 224	373	101 991	60.7	39.3	63.6	27.5	19 770	66.0
Champaign-Urbana, IL	1 121	-1.3	497	6	1 087	1 426 391	2 839	141 422	322	142 767	93.4	6.6	78.6	41.5	16 704	75.4
Charleston, WV	133	7.3	122	0	37	170 143	1 428	16 089	8	7 668	74.3	25.7	8.6	0.4	97	7.4

Table C. Metropolitan Areas — Residential Construction, Wholesale Trade, Retail Trade, and Real Estate

Area Name	Value of residential construction authorized by building permits, 2003 — New construction ($1,000)	Number of housing units	Wholesale trade, 1997 — Number of establishments	Number of employees	Sales (mil dol)	Annual payroll (mil dol)	Retail trade,[1] 1997 — Number of establishments	Number of employees	Sales (mil dol)	Annual payroll (mil dol)	Real estate and rental and leasing, 1997 — Number of establishments	Number of employees	Receipts (mil dol)	Annual payroll (mil dol)
	133	134	135	136	137	138	139	140	141	142	143	144	145	146
Abilene, TX	31 266	221	251	2 174	1 086.2	58.3	729	7 975	1 526.2	129.0	180	906	89.8	17.0
Akron, OH	467 358	3 190	1 253	16 023	9 624.2	598.1	2 637	38 291	6 633.6	639.5	580	3 403	413.2	74.7
Albany, GA	87 327	907	241	D	D	D	737	8 896	1 369.9	131.0	NA	D	D	D
Albany-Schenectady-Troy, NY.	501 156	3 222	1 040	14 078	7 298.6	492.5	3 360	45 291	7 295.4	710.6	648	4 016	572.8	89.6
Albuquerque, NM	820 405	7 936	1 120	13 441	4 891.1	402.3	2 637	38 697	7 181.1	690.6	829	4 814	531.2	89.4
Alexandria, LA	64 266	580	177	D	D	D	617	7 565	1 237.6	111.8	96	D	D	D
Allentown-Bethlehem-Easton, PA-NJ	604 364	4 376	1 035	D	D	D	2 893	36 235	6 519.9	622.3	480	2 630	327.1	55.7
Altoona, PA	39 309	362	160	2 836	1 641.3	82.3	639	8 310	1 331.2	117.7	90	419	34.8	6.9
Amarillo, TX	138 165	1 050	365	D	D	D	1 022	12 490	2 397.7	212.2	261	D	D	D
Ames, IA	102 460	744	95	772	321.2	21.7	359	4 729	631.3	65.8	68	366	24.4	5.6
Anchorage, AK	411 704	2 547	456	D	D	D	1 202	17 264	3 592.2	365.9	391	2 314	335.9	58.8
Anderson, IN	71 940	581	105	1 157	428.6	31.3	521	6 790	1 123.4	101.3	112	439	35.0	7.0
Anderson, SC	152 306	1 384	186	1 704	873.0	46.4	743	8 860	1 349.1	124.7	113	418	50.3	6.6
Ann Arbor, MI	380 475	2 527	435	4 778	3 338.4	182.3	1 204	18 464	3 371.9	329.6	315	2 147	184.5	47.9
Anniston-Oxford, AL	19 804	163	130	1 688	890.9	47.0	578	6 747	982.0	92.5	73	298	24.5	4.4
Appleton, WI	253 616	1 741	336	4 540	1 792.6	159.6	818	12 833	2 169.0	202.3	142	758	78.8	15.3
Asheville, NC	521 793	3 269	489	D	D	D	1 839	20 545	3 713.5	336.1	343	1 424	171.9	28.6
Athens-Clarke County, GA	231 112	1 956	160	D	D	D	694	9 152	1 389.7	132.8	170	D	D	D
Atlanta-Sandy Springs-Marietta, GA	7 352 248	66 377	9 342	D	D	D	15 107	225 119	41 082.6	4 037.1	4 789	D	D	D
Atlantic City, NJ	249 261	2 285	234	2 312	831.5	81.0	1 258	14 308	2 513.2	253.8	236	1 424	203.3	27.0
Auburn-Opelika, AL	117 597	1 167	86	727	308.0	18.6	425	5 437	774.4	73.7	84	464	35.0	6.9
Augusta-Richmond County, GA-SC	429 116	3 592	474	D	D	D	1 964	25 055	3 969.2	378.5	423	D	D	D
Austin-Round Rock, TX	1 607 370	15 317	1 613	20 998	10 048.4	797.7	4 157	60 049	18 878.3	1 160.8	1 532	7 554	945.7	181.0
Bakersfield, CA	798 346	5 813	612	7 930	4 313.9	256.4	1 918	22 792	4 224.4	412.1	419	2 479	220.5	43.8
Baltimore-Towson, MD	1 382 777	11 133	3 494	51 526	32 627.0	1 974.7	9 585	132 311	21 687.7	2 340.4	2 331	18 521	2 397.0	476.1
Bangor, ME	70 909	638	196	2 786	938.0	85.6	796	9 433	1 654.6	148.0	146	620	66.9	9.5
Barnstable Town, MA	284 753	1 228	259	1 361	462.8	45.5	1 592	13 675	2 518.8	256.5	286	917	138.1	21.4
Baton Rouge, LA	503 280	5 351	1 010	D	D	D	2 683	37 043	5 954.9	551.7	651	D	D	D
Battle Creek, MI	50 283	394	145	1 646	1 392.4	60.8	567	7 779	1 239.0	114.7	88	425	44.2	6.7
Bay City, MI	63 809	438	123	1 393	600.0	41.7	541	6 661	1 101.7	104.8	89	364	35.4	6.8
Beaumont-Port Arthur, TX	141 215	1 384	445	5 293	2 176.2	174.4	1 526	19 904	3 467.6	299.4	345	2 024	221.2	39.9
Bellingham, WA	320 530	2 320	308	2 451	1 042.7	76.0	840	9 758	1 673.3	165.7	220	877	91.8	12.3
Bend, OR	485 150	3 145	191	1 303	571.0	39.7	687	7 130	1 297.1	128.7	198	1 028	140.5	16.9
Billings, MT	110 194	911	402	4 970	2 658.8	144.4	762	9 003	1 608.4	148.1	209	798	87.3	12.5
Binghamton, NY	57 052	378	292	D	D	D	974	13 086	1 981.4	184.2	141	668	86.4	10.7
Birmingham-Hoover, AL	956 013	6 673	2 084	D	D	D	4 443	58 350	10 003.5	913.3	889	7 137	962.2	171.6
Bismarck, ND	133 291	953	192	1 983	813.2	52.7	467	6 058	1 010.6	100.9	113	616	52.8	7.4
Blacksburg-Christiansburg-Radford, VA	91 504	773	74	D	D	D	617	7 641	1 171.0	112.8	123	686	70.6	13.1
Bloomington, IN	131 141	1 176	147	D	D	D	708	8 608	1 323.5	120.3	189	D	D	D
Bloomington-Normal, IL	150 034	1 643	212	2 268	1 348.4	87.1	632	9 242	1 474.6	142.3	134	704	99.8	14.6
Boise City-Nampa, ID	1 050 607	7 724	NA	NA	NA	NA	1 786	21 980	4 265.0	398.6	NA	D	D	D
Boston-Cambridge-Quincy, MA-NH	2 009 245	14 041	7 773	117 010	86 431.7	5 382.5	17 516	238 184	42 928.4	4 246.8	4 308	34 615	5 025.8	1 073.1
Boston-Quincy, MA Div	797 821	5 674	3 074	44 996	38 657.6	2 013.7	7 059	96 070	17 071.3	1 720.0	1 911	20 081	2 810.6	659.8
Cambridge-Newton-Framingham, MA Div	531 944	3 388	2 914	49 166	33 893.5	2 386.3	5 701	78 812	14 462.1	1 491.7	1 412	9 998	1 669.0	305.0
Essex County, MA Div	301 808	2 058	1 071	14 836	9 270.7	671.4	2 703	34 590	6 156.2	585.5	563	2 555	319.4	58.2
Rockingham County-Strafford County, NH Div	377 672	2 921	714	8 012	4 609.9	311.1	2 053	28 712	5 238.8	449.6	422	1 981	226.8	50.1
Boulder, CO	224 973	1 428	539	5 558	3 906.0	234.9	1 275	17 269	2 915.0	309.9	486	2 189	287.9	49.2
Bowling Green, KY	117 378	1 046	157	D	D	D	547	7 284	1 127.7	104.0	102	D	D	D
Bremerton-Silverdale, WA	229 865	1 460	135	925	330.9	29.9	773	10 338	1 722.1	179.5	240	1 053	103.4	16.3
Bridgeport-Stamford-Norwalk, CT	545 214	1 964	1 768	28 573	48 325.4	1 559.1	4 008	54 012	11 563.9	1 218.0	1 098	7 639	1 748.1	288.2
Brownsville-Harlingen, TX	262 230	3 444	387	3 772	1 218.9	81.6	1 117	13 089	1 904.0	179.3	283	1 208	98.5	18.1
Brunswick, GA	116 519	838	132	D	D	D	642	5 759	847.4	80.8	132	D	D	D
Buffalo-Niagara Falls, NY	438 076	2 925	1 917	28 285	15 619.1	949.0	4 514	66 786	9 643.9	957.1	849	5 834	769.9	134.2
Burlington, NC	125 303	1 163	172	1 756	550.7	53.7	643	7 630	1 245.1	117.8	97	397	69.3	7.3
Burlington-South Burlington, VT	140 341	956	359	D	D	D	1 228	D	D	D	248	1 018	127.0	20.8
Canton-Massillon, OH	251 382	1 556	542	8 422	4 235.3	281.0	1 697	23 989	3 800.8	368.5	281	1 296	127.6	23.0
Cape Coral-Fort Myers, FL	1 994 866	15 675	586	4 593	1 450.3	135.3	1 924	25 417	4 367.0	430.5	642	3 328	461.1	72.2
Carson City, NV	34 761	203	88	557	222.4	18.7	262	3 383	678.4	66.1	102	343	51.2	7.4
Casper, WY	31 358	174	206	1 853	984.1	59.2	399	3 985	645.6	65.2	106	414	39.2	8.4
Cedar Rapids, IA	161 191	1 815	449	6 395	2 612.0	184.1	1 065	14 897	2 309.4	237.5	220	1 186	131.2	26.1
Champaign-Urbana, IL	175 918	1 373	261	4 407	3 050.3	130.5	823	11 793	1 776.3	169.3	223	1 406	182.9	27.8
Charleston, WV	47 940	461	473	D	D	D	1 371	18 119	3 030.1	269.5	334	D	D	D

1. Establishments with payroll.

Items 133—146

(Abilene, TX)—(Charleston, WV) 805

Table C. Metropolitan Areas — Professional Services, Manufacturing, and Accommodation and Foodservices

Area Name	Professional, scientific, and technical services,[1] 1997				Manufacturing, 1997				Accommodation and foodservices, 1997			
	Number of establishments	Number of employees	Sales (mil dol)	Annual payroll (mil dol)	Number of establishments	Number of employees	Sales (mil dol)	Annual payroll (mil dol)	Number of establishments	Number of employees	Sales (mil dol)	Annual payroll (mil dol)
	147	148	149	150	151	152	153	154	155	156	157	158
Abilene, TX	251	1 187	96.9	31.6	NA	NA	NA	NA	308	5 746	158.2	43.6
Akron, OH	1 499	10 377	1 052.3	401.7	1 389	55 296	9 000.9	1 923.9	1 423	24 958	736.8	208.2
Albany, GA	195	D	D	D	NA	NA	NA	NA	231	D	D	D
Albany-Schenectady-Troy, NY.	1 713	15 917	1 596.5	629.1	668	26 646	6 332.1	1 004.4	1 854	24 782	859.5	243.1
Albuquerque, NM	2 042	23 692	2 620.6	1 055.3	NA	NA	NA	NA	1 406	29 552	961.3	269.7
Alexandria, LA	252	D	D	D	NA	NA	NA	NA	227	D	D	D
Allentown-Bethlehem-Easton, PA-NJ	1 373	8 122	763.8	285.3	1 084	52 355	12 622.7	1 793.9	1 482	20 733	730.1	196.8
Altoona, PA	181	1 838	151.6	53.5	157	8 966	1 592.4	251.7	254	4 003	108.8	29.6
Amarillo, TX	NA	NA	NA	NA	NA	NA	NA	NA	494	D	D	D
Ames, IA	148	970	97.9	34.7	75	3 577	988.6	108.4	202	3 598	89.1	24.5
Anchorage, AK	985	6 190	784.4	308.3	NA	NA	NA	NA	766	12 292	617.9	176.0
Anderson, IN	187	1 152	62.2	31.9	133	12 144	2 256.8	534.3	244	4 794	139.8	38.4
Anderson, SC	199	777	55.2	16.2	240	20 589	4 180.1	611.4	283	4 919	144.6	37.1
Ann Arbor, MI	993	7 818	954.4	380.0	412	29 254	7 350.2	1 395.5	627	13 266	430.2	119.5
Anniston-Oxford, AL	149	702	45.2	13.2	149	10 841	1 504.5	257.8	185	4 262	114.4	31.3
Appleton, WI	308	2 629	218.2	96.9	367	27 488	6 334.3	941.6	436	7 687	217.0	59.9
Asheville, NC	655	3 088	217.8	95.7	NA	NA	NA	NA	848	14 544	503.5	146.9
Athens-Clarke County, GA	268	1 453	117.7	60.1	NA	NA	NA	NA	311	5 596	163.8	44.8
Atlanta-Sandy Springs-Marietta, GA	12 908	113 771	13 413.7	5 222.9	NA	NA	NA	NA	7 440	D	D	D
Atlantic City, NJ	513	3 885	380.8	157.4	160	4 927	600.3	143.0	766	55 638	5 015.2	1 328.3
Auburn-Opelika, AL	129	589	50.6	16.3	88	7 016	1 232.9	194.9	199	4 165	110.3	29.6
Augusta-Richmond County, GA-SC	699	6 614	652.5	248.1	380	42 159	10 420.5	1 582.0	790	14 876	449.5	121.3
Austin-Round Rock, TX	3 699	30 168	3 460.5	1 392.3	1 192	68 826	24 924.8	2 529.4	2 211	45 599	1 605.8	453.8
Bakersfield, CA	753	6 296	525.7	224.6	390	14 306	2 824.6	379.2	1 013	14 724	493.2	129.1
Baltimore-Towson, MD	6 666	60 715	6 654.5	2 613.7	2 177	93 594	22 684.8	3 448.6	4 492	80 323	2 923.2	808.3
Bangor, ME	271	1 388	102.7	45.9	155	8 897	1 658.6	285.9	344	4 778	151.3	45.8
Barnstable Town, MA	571	1 919	173.7	63.9	226	2 561	349.4	82.4	1 144	11 852	624.3	177.3
Baton Rouge, LA	1 641	D	D	D	NA	NA	NA	NA	1 069	D	D	D
Battle Creek, MI	168	836	68.8	29.1	222	16 973	4 514.8	613.8	307	5 010	147.5	42.5
Bay City, MI	138	834	62.8	28.6	152	7 459	1 928.6	347.0	241	3 922	106.5	29.6
Beaumont-Port Arthur, TX	600	4 830	543.4	223.7	349	21 624	18 986.7	1 059.4	591	10 840	336.9	90.6
Bellingham, WA	390	2 615	246.5	109.0	314	9 184	3 947.0	281.4	429	5 926	195.5	52.8
Bend, OR	295	1 206	105.1	37.4	202	4 884	698.6	129.5	305	4 722	194.2	55.6
Billings, MT	418	2 715	201.8	75.6	NA	NA	NA	NA	417	7 108	219.6	63.1
Binghamton, NY	369	2 751	244.5	82.8	290	25 484	4 717.2	1 027.6	560	7 689	228.4	64.8
Birmingham-Hoover, AL	2 182	18 025	1 844.5	726.9	1 273	52 385	10 023.6	1 565.1	1 660	D	D	D
Bismarck, ND	206	1 890	96.1	40.8	81	2 193	673.1	74.5	205	4 065	112.5	31.9
Blacksburg-Christiansburg-Radford, VA	222	1 538	137.7	50.2	145	16 914	3 286.9	498.6	255	4 949	138.0	36.8
Bloomington, IN	242	1 758	120.3	43.7	172	11 195	2 725.1	352.6	371	D	D	D
Bloomington-Normal, IL	234	1 382	111.6	57.9	112	8 388	3 870.3	357.7	336	7 104	200.5	58.3
Boise City-Nampa, ID	958	7 050	942.6	278.0	NA	NA	NA	NA	899	15 130	452.4	125.6
Boston-Cambridge-Quincy, MA-NH	14 882	159 687	21 201.1	8 667.4	6 396	275 401	58 075.0	11 228.7	9 815	161 309	6 809.4	1 883.6
Boston-Quincy, MA Div	6 363	71 968	10 437.4	3 965.9	2 100	74 077	13 057.1	2 795.0	4 261	77 172	3 413.5	955.5
Cambridge-Newton-Framingham, MA Div	5 744	73 319	9 250.9	4 134.1	2 437	118 002	22 587.1	5 216.5	3 045	48 816	2 055.4	558.2
Essex County, MA Div	1 735	9 589	1 058.1	377.4	1 200	57 660	13 728.1	2 362.4	1 573	22 544	872.0	238.5
Rockingham County-Strafford County, NH Div	1 040	4 811	454.7	190.0	659	25 662	8 702.7	854.8	936	12 777	468.5	131.4
Boulder, CO	1 612	15 458	3 081.9	760.2	686	26 225	5 196.3	1 052.1	708	13 824	453.1	131.0
Bowling Green, KY	150	D	D	D	NA	NA	NA	NA	203	4 554	142.1	41.9
Bremerton-Silverdale, WA	443	2 226	169.0	65.5	143	1 441	142.7	36.8	399	5 998	180.2	50.6
Bridgeport-Stamford-Norwalk, CT	3 834	31 051	4 658.6	1 932.2	1 316	57 560	12 115.5	2 495.9	1 772	24 643	1 113.3	311.3
Brownsville-Harlingen, TX	339	2 278	126.5	42.7	235	12 694	1 732.8	242.4	513	8 349	278.2	71.7
Brunswick, GA	187	D	D	D	NA	NA	NA	NA	247	7 442	262.6	87.5
Buffalo-Niagara Falls, NY	2 043	16 820	1 542.6	563.3	1 561	81 398	18 458.0	3 258.6	2 735	38 792	1 143.0	329.9
Burlington, NC	173	878	66.5	29.8	282	21 490	3 324.8	588.2	246	5 028	145.1	39.9
Burlington-South Burlington, VT	573	4 044	442.0	162.9	NA	NA	NA	NA	506	D	D	D
Canton-Massillon, OH	660	3 662	316.1	110.1	669	41 134	8 524.8	1 380.8	806	14 761	400.3	110.3
Cape Coral-Fort Myers, FL	997	6 053	458.2	197.4	357	5 363	741.8	141.1	824	17 424	699.1	175.2
Carson City, NV	233	806	86.2	30.2	186	4 157	514.5	120.8	133	2 404	93.1	27.7
Casper, WY	205	1 213	81.0	30.7	91	1 440	328.3	40.7	172	2 924	79.0	21.8
Cedar Rapids, IA	414	3 078	276.1	109.3	NA	NA	NA	NA	519	8 468	253.9	71.7
Champaign-Urbana, IL	382	2 802	270.9	94.8	NA	NA	NA	NA	509	D	D	D
Charleston, WV	626	D	D	D	NA	NA	NA	NA	527	D	D	D

1. Firms subject to federal tax.

Table C. Metropolitan Areas — Health Care and Social Assistance, Other Services, and Federal Funds

Area Name	Health care and social assistance,[1] 1997				Other services,[1] 1997				Federal funds and grants, 2002–2003 Expenditures (mil dol)			
										Direct payments for individuals		
	Number of establishments	Number of employees	Receipts (mil dol)	Annual payroll (mil dol)	Number of establishments	Number of employees	Receipts (mil dol)	Annual payroll (mil dol)	Total	Social Security and government retirement	Medicare	Food stamps and Supplemental Security Income
	159	160	161	162	163	164	165	166	167	168	169	170
Abilene, TX	339	5 695	327.4	129.7	248	1 944	113.5	35.4	1 098.1	384.2	153.1	29.0
Akron, OH	1 304	15 741	964.6	484.4	1 159	7 745	418.1	133.5	3 705.6	1 376.3	748.9	122.4
Albany, GA	NA	NA	NA	NA	NA	NA	NA	NA	1 141.8	328.8	135.3	61.6
Albany-Schenectady-Troy, NY.	1 475	16 564	1 089.2	490.6	1 142	6 723	476.1	134.7	13 953.9	2 508.1	740.8	115.7
Albuquerque, NM	1 268	17 347	1 183.0	492.0	1 001	7 070	398.5	128.5	7 472.5	1 770.9	493.0	146.0
Alexandria, LA	348	5 777	310.4	130.7	177	1 014	57.5	17.3	1 091.6	348.0	186.8	50.9
Allentown-Bethlehem-Easton, PA-NJ	1 658	15 079	1 047.9	480.0	1 241	7 469	501.6	152.1	3 722.0	1 708.0	955.7	88.3
Altoona, PA	284	2 816	200.5	83.6	251	1 319	72.7	18.9	824.8	366.8	172.3	30.5
Amarillo, TX	506	D	D	D	389	D	D	D	1 468.1	449.1	182.4	33.8
Ames, IA	91	1 545	88.0	47.2	107	617	33.9	9.3	488.6	128.4	46.8	4.7
Anchorage, AK	694	5 537	542.1	217.5	471	2 846	206.4	60.3	3 379.0	545.5	102.2	51.3
Anderson, IN	206	2 232	119.4	53.5	199	1 133	60.5	19.2	710.0	351.6	153.8	27.8
Anderson, SC	244	2 970	183.4	95.2	220	1 123	65.4	22.4	770.0	401.9	137.2	24.4
Ann Arbor, MI	703	6 534	525.1	228.3	392	2 628	158.7	53.6	1 943.9	483.8	213.2	31.3
Anniston-Oxford, AL	212	2 824	185.1	81.1	206	855	45.3	15.1	1 071.0	400.7	134.3	33.7
Appleton, WI	337	3 499	238.7	122.0	351	2 400	139.0	41.0	746.2	354.9	102.8	10.7
Asheville, NC	733	8 986	599.1	289.7	568	2 753	156.0	48.3	2 242.9	1 083.9	371.1	64.5
Athens-Clarke County, GA ...	336	2 627	217.1	105.6	209	1 342	72.9	21.7	870.5	274.3	105.5	31.4
Atlanta-Sandy Springs-Marietta, GA	7 586	89 623	6 481.2	2 781.8	6 508	43 209	3 015.8	945.3	21 495.8	6 811.4	2 559.3	652.0
Atlantic City, NJ	540	5 024	376.4	175.3	429	2 485	130.7	42.1	1 601.4	566.0	308.7	34.9
Auburn-Opelika, AL	133	1 478	104.9	51.3	125	661	35.6	10.2	461.3	189.2	62.1	21.8
Augusta-Richmond County, GA-SC	917	11 756	840.5	357.2	656	3 942	207.5	64.0	4 863.6	1 173.2	389.3	130.5
Austin-Round Rock, TX	2 199	34 516	2 278.3	925.0	1 772	11 569	726.3	232.6	9 516.7	2 186.7	565.5	131.0
Bakersfield, CA	938	9 631	755.0	278.5	694	4 192	348.6	92.2	3 856.0	1 135.0	601.2	163.6
Baltimore-Towson, MD	5 234	64 227	4 263.0	1 879.9	3 885	27 412	1 724.3	541.2	22 638.7	6 012.2	2 927.6	454.8
Bangor, ME	310	3 432	209.8	98.2	208	980	82.3	20.4	963.2	356.9	125.6	36.8
Barnstable Town, MA	482	5 989	336.5	163.8	439	1 819	124.6	36.0	1 767.5	809.4	390.2	20.2
Baton Rouge, LA	1 269	19 846	1 176.0	515.0	965	D	D	D	4 459.7	1 308.3	691.1	183.4
Battle Creek, MI	300	3 100	176.3	79.3	207	1 433	91.5	26.9	971.2	352.9	148.8	33.3
Bay City, MI	210	2 225	132.9	65.2	198	1 004	55.9	16.2	582.9	258.2	121.5	20.5
Beaumont-Port Arthur, TX	921	14 230	813.2	346.4	614	4 075	236.5	69.5	2 342.2	832.7	536.7	89.9
Bellingham, WA	406	3 627	201.2	82.1	225	1 161	81.3	22.1	878.8	354.6	99.0	24.9
Bend, OR	253	2 073	147.7	57.1	159	904	56.1	18.4	532.1	305.4	73.2	15.0
Billings, MT	344	3 062	232.3	116.5	301	1 809	115.0	34.3	781.2	318.2	108.6	17.5
Binghamton, NY	389	4 234	300.8	137.3	346	1 573	103.9	27.5	1 889.8	608.3	248.0	47.4
Birmingham-Hoover, AL........	1 810	29 729	2 271.8	989.0	1 636	12 116	827.5	242.8	6 440.5	2 498.0	1 273.7	252.7
Bismarck, ND	161	1 589	128.6	59.3	184	1 030	59.7	17.9	789.4	218.4	72.6	10.1
Blacksburg-Christiansburg-Radford, VA	248	3 447	197.7	85.2	208	1 074	52.9	16.6	789.5	303.7	119.4	18.8
Bloomington, IN	309	3 335	190.2	88.2	225	1 317	77.2	22.8	871.6	329.5	111.6	21.3
Bloomington-Normal, IL	228	2 901	190.8	91.6	226	1 433	85.6	26.8	529.3	233.8	85.2	12.0
Boise City-Nampa, ID	NA	NA	NA	NA	651	D	D	D	2 542.5	934.1	242.4	55.4
Boston-Cambridge-Quincy, MA-NH	8 668	132 283	8 212.3	3 883.3	7 648	46 037	3 289.9	1 041.1	35 269.1	8 690.9	5 383.0	609.4
Boston-Quincy, MA Div	3 550	60 195	3 797.4	1 824.1	3 125	18 994	1 303.5	390.2	15 563.4	3 606.9	2 427.8	328.5
Cambridge-Newton-Framingham, MA Div	2 991	42 136	2 707.8	1 227.3	2 661	16 875	1 307.7	428.7	12 515.4	2 764.7	1 802.9	129.9
Essex County, MA Div	1 317	19 159	1 104.7	558.8	1 181	6 614	441.3	149.5	5 356.7	1 474.6	904.4	126.9
Rockingham County-Strafford County, NH Div	810	10 793	602.4	273.1	681	3 554	237.4	72.7	1 833.6	844.7	248.0	24.0
Boulder, CO	715	6 087	405.5	170.7	482	2 945	192.2	60.9	1 864.1	443.4	154.0	18.7
Bowling Green, KY	240	4 014	268.2	107.2	136	1 033	44.9	14.3	539.2	199.1	90.0	27.4
Bremerton-Silverdale, WA	473	4 466	245.3	104.1	264	1 300	77.7	23.9	2 809.5	715.0	138.9	32.3
Bridgeport-Stamford-Norwalk, CT	2 124	25 229	1 915.4	900.3	1 497	8 289	596.6	192.2	5 777.6	1 708.5	990.7	85.7
Brownsville-Harlingen, TX.....	509	11 065	498.3	216.2	338	2 279	96.3	30.0	1 665.3	423.2	248.0	142.4
Brunswick, GA	218	2 405	156.8	63.4	145	603	38.4	11.1	681.7	253.2	111.4	22.5
Buffalo-Niagara Falls, NY	2 275	29 298	1 579.8	703.1	1 908	10 373	664.7	189.8	7 531.8	2 895.1	1 272.1	233.2
Burlington, NC	212	3 555	289.1	106.9	202	1 339	80.3	23.2	584.6	300.9	115.5	14.4
Burlington-South Burlington, VT......................................	450	D	D	D	362	D	D	D	1 538.3	350.2	118.3	24.1
Canton-Massillon, OH	756	9 782	617.2	296.8	710	4 693	273.9	85.0	1 994.1	960.4	413.9	66.1
Cape Coral-Fort Myers, FL...	825	12 968	954.5	408.4	695	3 599	224.9	68.5	2 615.3	1 516.2	674.0	47.8
Carson City, NV	172	1 274	86.7	39.8	104	634	42.2	13.5	648.5	173.1	50.8	5.5
Casper, WY	168	1 524	93.3	40.8	154	808	57.2	15.2	351.1	144.4	51.1	9.8
Cedar Rapids, IA	385	4 374	285.1	145.6	427	2 486	155.5	45.8	1 458.0	486.7	162.9	23.2
Champaign-Urbana, IL..........	238	5 403	386.9	190.2	284	1 371	73.8	23.3	1 081.0	353.5	124.3	24.6
Charleston, WV	652	7 610	595.4	238.3	439	2 821	156.0	48.6	2 644.6	962.6	353.6	94.2

1. Firms subject to federal tax.

Area Name	Federal funds and grants, 2002–2003 (cont'd)							Local government finances, 2002				
	Expenditures (mil dol) (cont'd)							General revenue				
	Procurement contract awards			Grants						Taxes		
											Per capita[1] (dollars)	
	Salaries and wages	Defense	Other	Medicaid and other health-related	Nutrition and family welfare	Education	Other	Total (mil dol)	Intergovern-mental (mil dol)	Total (mil dol)	Total	Property
	171	172	173	174	175	176	177	178	179	180	181	182
Abilene, TX	245.5	76.8	20.5	88.8	16.8	7.4	47.5	371.3	162.7	150.8	950	722
Akron, OH	193.9	448.6	51.7	353.3	98.2	54.9	168.1	2 408.7	812.7	1 035.2	1 478	983
Albany, GA	140.0	50.0	40.6	152.3	44.2	19.5	31.2	508.5	259.7	179.8	1 124	656
Albany-Schenectady-Troy, NY.	525.1	471.8	392.0	1 244.3	1 204.5	966.9	5 540.4	3 245.8	1 260.6	1 441.8	1 726	1 201
Albuquerque, NM	985.4	469.7	2 407.1	612.7	109.8	65.4	336.2	2 016.5	1 095.9	564.3	748	452
Alexandria, LA	141.6	10.8	116.6	140.3	23.9	14.5	37.7	339.1	172.2	122.4	841	374
Allentown-Bethlehem-Easton, PA-NJ	180.4	245.5	41.9	293.4	58.5	22.2	75.9	2 399.9	848.2	1 037.6	1 369	1 127
Altoona, PA	53.6	0.7	15.7	103.8	22.4	4.3	42.9	298.0	157.5	96.2	753	537
Amarillo, TX	114.1	106.1	385.3	65.3	20.9	10.8	64.1	607.7	201.4	257.6	1 112	831
Ames, IA	57.7	6.3	70.6	35.9	4.0	4.1	105.6	289.1	71.3	82.8	1 026	910
Anchorage, AK	915.8	645.0	236.9	372.5	92.2	46.4	343.4	1 086.0	533.2	385.9	1 155	1 014
Anderson, IN	19.5	0.6	8.5	93.2	15.4	3.5	26.9	320.4	143.3	113.0	856	759
Anderson, SC	29.6	2.8	15.4	86.4	9.4	18.0	34.7	332.3	163.7	126.0	739	636
Ann Arbor, MI	195.0	103.0	78.3	501.1	27.0	25.6	237.0	1 017.0	452.0	370.0	1 106	1 079
Anniston-Oxford, AL	119.2	203.6	42.4	66.2	10.2	9.3	31.4	361.9	121.2	73.9	662	219
Appleton, WI	36.0	35.8	18.1	75.9	13.8	8.1	40.9	714.4	335.7	243.1	1 166	1 134
Asheville, NC	176.9	63.4	61.9	240.1	38.3	25.7	86.4	1 036.6	451.8	302.0	798	588
Athens-Clarke County, GA	114.3	7.7	32.1	130.6	26.9	17.5	110.9	607.0	162.7	161.3	943	626
Atlanta-Sandy Springs-Marietta, GA	3 227.8	1 840.7	1 445.9	1 770.0	640.4	597.4	1 659.5	14 177.0	4 596.8	6 330.9	1 398	932
Atlantic City, NJ	250.4	35.5	86.9	168.8	35.5	10.6	78.5	1 129.0	413.9	549.7	2 119	2 078
Auburn-Opelika, AL	33.4	10.3	5.7	42.7	11.8	9.6	59.5	395.9	103.2	80.1	678	297
Augusta-Richmond County, GA-SC	701.2	137.8	1 649.0	385.9	76.3	38.0	116.8	1 265.1	543.6	429.4	847	586
Austin-Round Rock, TX	613.8	809.3	565.4	871.1	803.6	1 100.5	1 739.9	4 173.9	761.9	2 442.3	1 810	1 462
Bakersfield, CA	700.7	262.7	138.4	406.8	165.1	66.6	130.1	3 749.3	2 032.9	579.6	835	659
Baltimore-Towson, MD	3 319.4	2 991.8	1 699.8	2 755.7	653.8	304.4	1 286.7	8 190.6	2 968.5	4 037.1	1 552	882
Bangor, ME	97.1	20.2	24.3	164.7	24.3	13.1	75.0	376.2	131.2	174.7	1 197	1 136
Barnstable Town, MA	140.3	107.1	33.9	101.7	18.6	13.7	124.2	725.6	178.1	427.6	1 871	1 751
Baton Rouge, LA	193.7	90.1	40.5	483.2	280.4	296.5	810.2	1 796.6	578.5	846.3	1 181	425
Battle Creek, MI	172.0	25.9	34.3	107.1	31.3	15.1	37.4	455.1	257.8	100.2	724	603
Bay City, MI	17.4	3.9	5.0	57.2	17.9	8.6	48.7	427.7	207.7	91.4	833	816
Beaumont-Port Arthur, TX	218.4	46.8	114.2	259.7	48.6	15.9	131.5	1 064.9	301.7	523.4	1 369	1 127
Bellingham, WA	48.2	122.2	17.8	85.7	23.3	10.1	61.7	451.2	189.6	167.0	958	622
Bend, OR	43.9	7.5	15.6	31.6	9.2	6.4	19.0	391.2	160.7	152.3	1 215	1 010
Billings, MT	123.5	5.9	46.8	73.0	18.7	11.2	34.8	323.5	127.9	101.0	715	679
Binghamton, NY	63.2	556.6	21.5	176.2	35.7	20.8	93.7	983.0	470.6	361.6	1 434	997
Birmingham-Hoover, AL	605.9	34.6	216.9	811.0	103.7	73.5	470.6	2 788.4	1 042.6	1 105.3	1 035	434
Bismarck, ND	71.5	21.9	13.3	59.7	46.1	59.8	171.2	234.1	84.2	87.6	909	777
Blacksburg-Christiansburg-Radford, VA	31.5	99.2	15.7	63.3	11.9	10.6	93.1	295.9	134.7	102.6	670	455
Bloomington, IN	35.5	25.9	12.3	218.3	11.3	9.9	68.3	448.3	133.4	147.8	835	683
Bloomington-Normal, IL	53.8	1.0	13.0	31.1	9.1	6.4	47.9	410.4	126.2	208.4	1 349	1 140
Boise City-Nampa, ID	322.2	87.2	163.8	257.8	74.5	77.0	283.1	1 166.6	485.5	413.1	829	772
Boston-Cambridge-Quincy, MA-NH	2 669.8	5 673.2	1 749.0	5 532.7	807.6	580.8	3 076.9	14 823.1	6 131.0	6 732.5	1 514	1 461
Boston-Quincy, MA Div	1 335.0	825.1	431.1	3 465.9	548.3	179.7	2 053.8	7 060.3	3 401.5	2 847.4	1 554	1 482
Cambridge-Newton-Framingham, MA Div	935.4	3 180.5	1 060.8	1 424.6	125.1	314.5	692.8	4 607.7	1 470.2	2 391.0	1 622	1 575
Essex County, MA Div	240.2	1 581.2	164.6	490.1	102.7	66.6	176.1	2 119.9	875.0	952.9	1 295	1 261
Rockingham County-Strafford County, NH Div	159.2	86.4	92.5	152.1	31.5	20.0	154.1	1 035.2	384.3	541.2	1 340	1 313
Boulder, CO	224.5	168.1	331.8	108.8	15.6	16.8	363.0	915.5	210.7	519.9	1 862	1 118
Bowling Green, KY	50.0	4.0	12.3	56.2	14.2	13.0	50.3	204.0	91.9	72.6	681	354
Bremerton-Silverdale, WA	1 151.0	456.5	83.9	86.2	28.0	33.4	69.2	622.1	310.0	202.1	856	622
Bridgeport-Stamford-Norwalk, CT	253.1	1 574.4	172.9	486.4	110.5	52.4	292.1	3 022.0	713.7	1 983.6	2 213	2 174
Brownsville-Harlingen, TX	99.8	13.5	20.0	399.3	87.0	36.5	148.5	995.9	580.1	247.6	700	524
Brunswick, GA	106.2	15.6	65.0	51.4	18.4	7.5	24.5	387.9	96.5	131.1	1 376	867
Buffalo-Niagara Falls, NY	593.7	263.7	274.3	1 197.9	264.3	101.0	330.1	4 731.6	2 053.9	1 727.2	1 485	1 052
Burlington, NC	15.9	9.2	6.6	68.1	9.6	7.8	28.0	289.6	152.7	83.3	613	468
Burlington-South Burlington, VT	180.4	383.4	57.3	211.2	29.6	14.7	125.5	489.1	274.2	139.2	686	644
Canton-Massillon, OH	85.5	43.1	26.8	204.4	53.5	32.1	74.7	1 151.2	565.7	408.6	1 004	752
Cape Coral-Fort Myers, FL	126.7	10.8	29.9	86.4	35.5	20.4	46.4	2 118.3	519.6	618.3	1 300	1 123
Carson City, NV	33.0	10.2	5.7	56.9	55.0	76.9	179.2	224.1	76.9	38.2	704	456
Casper, WY	45.6	0.8	16.1	28.6	12.7	5.0	32.0	231.9	132.2	56.6	841	568
Cedar Rapids, IA	72.9	439.4	48.4	97.9	25.7	6.1	42.5	728.7	289.8	268.8	1 113	1 030
Champaign-Urbana, IL	86.4	15.7	17.3	113.5	17.7	19.1	252.6	588.5	235.5	237.3	1 111	958
Charleston, WV	187.3	60.1	63.1	300.7	128.7	120.7	336.4	702.3	288.1	246.4	805	619

1. Based on the resident population estimated as of July 1 of the year shown.

Table C. Metropolitan Areas — Local Government Finances, Government Employment, and Elections

Area Name	Local government finances, 2002 (cont'd)									Government employment, 2002			Presidential election, 2004		
	Direct general expenditure							Debt outstanding					Percent of vote cast —		
			Percent of total for —												
	Total (mil dol)	Per capita[1] (dollars)	Education	Health and hospitals	Police protection	Public welfare	Highways	Total (mil dol)	Per capita[1] (dollars)	Federal civilian	Federal military	State and local	Democratic	Republican	All other
	183	184	185	186	187	188	189	190	191	192	193	194	195	196	197
Abilene, TX	362.5	2 284	55.0	6.1	6.8	0.8	4.4	187.0	1 178	1 317	5 607	11 548	22.4	77.1	0.5
Akron, OH	2 444.9	3 491	39.5	12.5	5.3	5.1	5.5	1 561.2	2 229	3 119	1 664	45 923	55.8	43.8	0.4
Albany, GA	529.3	3 310	43.7	11.3	4.4	0.7	4.1	276.0	1 726	2 509	1 123	10 962	47.5	52.1	0.4
Albany-Schenectady-Troy, NY.	3 364.7	4 027	48.1	2.6	3.6	14.8	5.3	2 355.2	2 819	7 298	3 262	99 525	52.0	45.8	2.2
Albuquerque, NM	1 952.1	2 589	50.5	2.0	7.7	0.7	4.4	1 611.6	2 137	13 582	6 199	59 115	49.9	48.9	1.2
Alexandria, LA	357.5	2 455	55.7	0.3	7.3	0.0	3.5	256.7	1 763	2 545	637	12 757	33.7	65.1	1.3
Allentown-Bethlehem-Easton, PA-NJ	2 449.2	3 231	46.4	4.1	3.2	7.5	3.1	4 158.4	5 485	2 999	1 945	35 831	48.5	50.6	0.9
Altoona, PA	269.0	2 104	57.4	0.2	3.5	3.9	4.2	310.9	2 432	920	343	8 198	33.5	65.9	0.6
Amarillo, TX	581.8	2 512	54.7	6.7	6.5	0.0	3.4	388.6	1 678	1 991	471	16 057	19.7	80.0	0.3
Ames, IA	275.8	3 420	29.1	35.7	3.2	0.7	9.4	131.1	1 625	1 062	348	17 856	52.1	46.8	1.1
Anchorage, AK	1 271.1	3 804	48.1	2.7	11.1	0.0	16.1	1 508.5	4 515	9 468	11 503	22 618	NA	NA	NA
Anderson, IN	318.6	2 412	50.0	0.7	4.7	2.4	3.5	148.2	1 122	305	353	6 616	39.9	59.3	0.8
Anderson, SC	363.2	2 129	68.1	1.7	5.2	0.2	2.8	193.7	1 136	366	637	11 083	32.0	67.0	1.0
Ann Arbor, MI	1 073.1	3 210	53.7	5.2	4.9	1.2	2.8	1 110.5	3 321	2 620	642	65 927	63.5	35.5	1.1
Anniston-Oxford, AL.............	379.7	3 402	34.7	38.7	3.7	0.0	5.3	165.2	1 480	3 928	530	7 700	33.3	65.9	0.7
Appleton, WI	752.2	3 607	51.9	4.0	4.8	5.5	10.1	692.3	3 320	476	564	10 886	44.0	55.1	0.9
Asheville, NC	1 092.6	2 886	40.5	20.1	4.1	5.8	1.5	575.2	1 519	2 983	727	22 191	44.8	54.7	0.5
Athens-Clarke County, GA ...	591.4	3 458	32.0	37.5	3.5	0.2	3.1	299.5	1 751	1 708	821	19 743	44.8	54.2	1.0
Atlanta-Sandy Springs-Marietta, GA	13 805.8	3 048	49.7	7.1	5.4	0.9	3.5	18 492.1	4 083	46 177	14 711	246 127	39.0	60.4	0.6
Atlantic City, NJ	1 146.3	4 419	50.9	0.9	7.6	1.8	2.6	965.0	3 720	2 744	596	18 374	52.6	46.6	0.8
Auburn-Opelika, AL..............	378.4	3 204	35.8	36.5	3.6	0.0	4.0	428.7	3 630	336	584	12 797	36.4	62.7	0.9
Augusta-Richmond County, GA-SC	1 290.1	2 544	52.4	5.0	4.8	0.3	3.1	1 735.3	3 422	7 074	11 654	35 862	40.4	59.0	0.6
Austin-Round Rock, TX	4 307.5	3 192	48.5	5.3	5.2	0.7	2.9	10 913.3	8 088	10 297	2 773	133 944	49.1	49.6	1.3
Bakersfield, CA	3 450.7	4 972	42.8	8.8	3.4	9.4	1.7	1 562.6	2 251	10 102	5 185	44 510	32.2	66.9	0.9
Baltimore-Towson, MD	7 788.2	2 993	52.2	1.9	7.1	0.7	4.3	6 134.9	2 358	70 264	24 155	171 249	52.2	46.6	1.2
Bangor, ME	374.1	2 562	47.3	5.5	3.7	0.1	3.9	206.3	1 413	1 360	587	12 998	49.4	48.9	1.7
Barnstable Town, MA	714.2	3 124	42.5	1.2	5.8	0.6	3.8	635.1	2 779	1 490	1 142	12 327	54.2	43.9	1.9
Baton Rouge, LA	1 743.3	2 432	46.6	5.1	5.5	0.4	4.9	2 019.5	2 817	2 708	3 182	70 780	41.5	57.6	0.9
Battle Creek, MI	466.0	3 368	55.5	5.1	4.6	3.0	5.3	311.7	2 252	3 351	299	7 897	47.7	51.2	1.1
Bay City, MI	406.3	3 705	49.6	17.0	3.7	3.4	5.6	135.6	1 236	289	215	6 437	54.4	44.6	1.0
Beaumont-Port Arthur, TX	1 054.2	2 758	48.5	4.0	5.8	0.5	3.8	1 934.1	5 060	3 108	879	23 332	44.4	55.2	0.4
Bellingham, WA	454.5	2 607	44.5	2.4	4.8	0.0	5.7	374.7	2 149	908	562	12 733	53.5	44.7	1.9
Bend, OR	410.0	3 273	49.8	4.6	6.4	0.7	6.2	341.6	2 728	837	345	6 176	42.3	56.7	1.0
Billings, MT	317.5	2 247	48.1	5.0	8.7	0.0	3.9	90.1	637	1 871	709	7 190	36.3	61.8	1.9
Binghamton, NY...................	1 048.6	4 159	50.5	2.3	2.7	12.9	4.6	631.4	2 504	977	369	21 775	47.9	49.9	2.2
Birmingham-Hoover, AL........	3 352.9	3 139	37.5	5.4	5.7	0.8	3.7	4 887.9	4 576	8 806	5 100	66 369	36.1	63.3	0.6
Bismarck, ND	217.6	2 259	46.7	1.5	5.3	3.2	11.5	151.9	1 576	1 113	653	9 618	30.5	67.9	1.6
Blacksburg-Christiansburg-Radford, VA	318.7	2 081	50.0	4.3	6.0	4.4	2.8	227.6	1 486	492	449	18 254	42.2	56.8	1.0
Bloomington, IN	445.4	2 518	38.6	5.3	2.8	3.3	4.8	278.9	1 576	533	494	21 530	47.9	51.2	0.9
Bloomington-Normal, IL	476.9	3 087	46.0	1.2	4.6	1.3	5.4	298.1	1 930	956	291	13 222	41.8	57.7	0.5
Boise City-Nampa, ID	1 200.9	2 411	49.3	2.6	6.9	0.6	6.7	674.7	1 355	5 467	1 853	32 094	33.5	65.5	1.0
Boston-Cambridge-Quincy, MA-NH	14 216.3	3 198	48.9	5.1	6.1	1.5	2.9	13 390.0	3 012	40 799	13 702	259 288	61.3	37.8	0.9
Boston-Quincy, MA Div	6 283.7	3 430	45.1	3.7	7.2	2.0	2.8	8 005.8	4 370	21 412	5 377	127 783	63.2	36.0	0.8
Cambridge-Newton-Framingham, MA Div	4 760.9	3 230	50.3	9.2	5.1	0.3	3.0	2 965.5	2 012	13 692	5 210	71 159	64.2	34.7	1.0
Essex County, MA Div	2 162.0	2 939	54.2	2.5	5.1	0.5	2.8	1 967.1	2 674	4 120	1 767	36 504	58.5	40.7	0.8
Rockingham County-Strafford County, NH Div	1 009.7	2 499	54.6	0.5	5.9	5.9	3.5	451.6	1 118	1 575	1 348	23 842	49.8	49.6	0.6
Boulder, CO	1 016.2	3 640	36.9	1.1	5.2	1.9	7.2	1 045.3	3 744	2 575	516	24 994	67.7	31.1	1.2
Bowling Green, KY	192.3	1 804	48.9	5.4	4.2	0.6	4.3	589.4	5 531	975	105	8 641	35.8	63.5	0.7
Bremerton-Silverdale, WA	593.5	2 513	50.3	4.2	3.9	0.7	4.5	475.9	2 015	14 399	13 915	12 739	51.5	46.9	1.6
Bridgeport-Stamford-Norwalk, CT	3 018.2	3 368	53.0	2.4	6.2	0.5	3.6	2 549.4	2 845	3 944	1 687	42 825	51.3	47.3	1.4
Brownsville-Harlingen, TX.....	1 051.5	2 974	64.8	1.3	4.2	0.4	2.4	1 007.2	2 849	2 209	772	23 787	49.2	50.4	0.4
Brunswick, GA	358.8	3 767	34.5	33.9	8.0	0.2	1.9	121.3	1 274	1 389	258	7 247	32.9	66.6	0.4
Buffalo-Niagara Falls, NY	4 970.4	4 273	45.2	6.6	4.2	13.1	4.5	3 414.5	2 936	10 423	2 056	78 825	54.8	42.8	2.4
Burlington, NC	295.9	2 177	48.9	9.6	6.3	6.3	1.8	133.0	979	254	235	6 106	38.1	61.6	0.3
Burlington-South Burlington, VT	464.7	2 290	61.5	0.2	4.0	0.0	6.0	377.3	1 859	2 762	1 345	14 708	61.6	36.5	2.0
Canton-Massillon, OH..........	1 120.7	2 753	51.9	6.8	5.2	7.1	4.2	425.0	1 044	1 253	936	19 929	50.0	49.5	0.5
Cape Coral-Fort Myers, FL...	1 884.6	3 962	25.3	25.8	5.0	0.6	5.1	2 732.0	5 744	1 932	783	25 049	39.1	59.8	1.1
Carson City, NV	212.8	3 919	31.7	35.3	5.0	0.7	4.4	116.5	2 145	555	79	9 786	47.9	50.5	1.6
Casper, WY	238.1	3 536	52.2	1.4	5.6	1.2	7.0	68.4	1 016	650	328	4 633	30.9	67.3	1.8
Cedar Rapids, IA	766.4	3 174	53.6	4.4	4.3	1.1	8.3	548.1	2 270	1 282	971	13 987	53.8	45.5	0.7
Champaign-Urbana, IL.........	618.6	2 895	53.9	1.7	4.4	2.7	6.5	258.7	1 211	1 442	442	33 120	47.8	51.2	1.0
Charleston, WV	688.3	2 248	57.6	3.2	4.4	0.2	1.9	670.8	2 191	2 744	1 359	24 622	47.3	52.1	0.6

1. Based on the resident population estimated as of July 1 of the year shown.

Table C. Metropolitan Areas — **Land Area and Population**

CBSA/ DIV code[1]	Area Name	Land area,[2] 2000 (sq km)	Population and population characteristics, 2003			Race alone or in combination, not Hispanic or Latino (percent)				Percent Hispanic or Latino[3]	Age (percent)					
			Total persons	Rank	Per square kilometer	White	Black	Am. Indian, Alaska Native	Asian and Pacific Islander		Under 5 years	5 to 17 years	18 to 24 years	25 to 34 years	35 to 44 years	45 to 54 years
		1	2	3	4	5	6	7	8	9	10	11	12	13	14	15
16700	Charleston-North Charleston, SC	6 711	571 631	85	85.2	64.0	31.9	0.8	2.1	2.4	6.9	18.3	11.1	14.1	15.3	13.5
16740	Charlotte-Gastonia-Concord, NC-SC...........	8 026	1 437 427	37	179.1	67.7	23.3	0.7	2.7	6.5	7.5	18.5	9.0	16.0	16.4	13.3
16820	Charlottesville, VA	4 272	181 631	213	42.5	81.1	14.0	0.5	3.1	2.5	5.8	16.1	13.3	13.6	14.7	13.8
16860	Chattanooga, TN-GA ..	5 413	485 927	98	89.8	83.0	14.3	0.7	1.4	1.6	6.2	17.0	9.7	13.4	14.8	14.7
16940	Cheyenne, WY	6 957	84 083	350	12.1	83.7	3.4	1.4	1.8	11.6	6.8	18.1	10.2	13.6	15.1	14.3
16980	Chicago-Naperville-Joliet, IL-IN-WI	18 679	9 333 511	3	499.7	58.9	18.5	0.4	5.3	17.9	7.4	19.1	9.5	14.9	15.8	13.6
16974	Chicago-Naperville-Joliet, IL Div	11 952	7 806 793	X	653.2	56.2	19.7	0.4	5.7	18.9	7.4	18.9	9.4	15.3	15.7	13.4
23844	Gary, IN Div	4 861	685 490	X	141.0	70.4	18.5	0.5	1.2	10.3	6.8	19.3	9.8	12.1	14.8	14.7
29404	Lake County-Kenosha County, IL-WI Div	1 866	841 228	X	450.8	73.9	7.1	0.5	4.9	15.0	7.5	20.5	10.2	12.9	16.8	14.0
17020	Chico, CA	4 246	211 010	191	49.7	81.8	1.9	3.1	4.8	11.3	5.4	17.1	13.2	12.7	12.4	13.5
17140	Cincinnati-Middletown, OH-KY-IN	11 392	2 047 333	24	179.7	85.5	12.0	0.5	1.9	1.2	6.9	18.8	9.9	13.4	15.9	14.2
17300	Clarksville, TN-KY	5 600	236 700	178	42.3	73.7	20.9	1.2	2.8	3.9	8.9	19.6	11.1	16.7	15.0	11.2
17420	Cleveland, TN	1 978	106 435	325	53.8	93.5	3.7	0.9	0.8	2.1	6.3	16.5	10.6	13.8	15.0	13.7
17460	Cleveland-Elyria-Mentor, OH	5 191	2 139 512	23	412.2	75.2	19.9	0.5	2.0	3.5	6.3	18.4	8.5	12.4	15.6	14.8
17660	Coeur d'Alene, ID	3 225	117 481	300	36.4	95.3	0.4	2.0	1.1	2.6	6.5	19.1	9.8	11.7	14.2	14.5
17780	College Station-Bryan, TX ..	5 454	192 603	204	35.3	65.7	12.2	0.6	3.7	18.7	6.8	15.6	23.0	15.6	11.1	9.5
17820	Colorado Springs, CO ..	6 950	572 264	84	82.3	78.2	7.5	1.6	4.1	11.6	7.7	19.7	10.4	14.1	16.5	14.1
17860	Columbia, MO	2 981	151 129	244	50.7	86.0	9.4	0.9	3.6	1.8	6.2	16.2	16.7	15.7	13.9	12.7
17900	Columbia, SC	9 586	671 407	71	70.0	61.6	34.4	0.6	1.8	2.6	6.7	18.0	11.0	14.1	15.4	14.3
17980	Columbus, GA-AL.........	5 017	287 082	154	57.2	54.8	40.3	0.8	2.1	3.5	7.4	19.0	12.5	13.9	14.5	12.9
18020	Columbus, IN	1 054	72 341	357	68.6	93.2	2.0	0.4	2.4	2.7	7.1	19.5	7.7	12.9	15.1	14.4
18140	Columbus, OH	10 318	1 674 589	31	162.3	81.2	14.3	0.8	3.4	2.1	7.2	18.1	10.1	15.6	16.0	13.7
18580	Corpus Christi, TX	4 608	406 830	114	88.3	40.3	3.3	0.6	1.4	55.1	8.0	20.3	10.4	12.6	14.4	13.5
18700	Corvallis, OR	1 752	79 335	355	45.3	87.9	1.1	1.3	6.6	5.1	5.0	14.7	17.6	14.4	12.6	14.7
19060	Cumberland, MD-WV.........	1 951	100 815	338	51.7	94.1	4.9	0.3	0.5	0.7	5.1	15.5	11.3	12.1	14.1	13.9
19100	Dallas-Fort Worth-Arlington, TX	23 283	5 589 670	5	240.1	57.1	14.1	0.8	4.8	24.3	8.4	19.9	9.9	16.2	16.3	12.8
19124	Dallas-Plano-Irving, TX Div	14 475	3 739 509	X	258.3	53.8	15.3	0.8	5.2	26.1	8.6	19.8	9.8	16.8	16.5	12.6
23104	Fort Worth-Arlington, TX Div	8 808	1 850 161	X	210.1	63.9	11.7	0.9	4.0	20.8	8.1	20.1	10.0	15.0	16.1	13.1
19140	Dalton, GA	1 643	127 279	282	77.5	76.4	2.8	0.5	1.0	20.0	8.8	19.6	9.8	15.1	15.0	12.4
19180	Danville, IL	2 329	82 804	353	35.6	85.0	11.3	0.5	0.7	3.3	6.6	17.7	9.2	12.2	14.1	14.0
19260	Danville, VA	2 626	108 628	320	41.4	65.2	33.0	0.3	0.4	1.5	6.0	16.6	8.9	10.9	14.8	15.2
19340	Davenport-Moline-Rock Island, IA-IL	5 876	374 973	127	63.8	86.4	6.6	0.6	1.6	6.1	6.5	17.6	9.8	12.5	14.6	14.8
19380	Dayton, OH	4 425	846 091	57	191.2	82.4	15.2	0.7	2.0	1.2	6.4	17.6	10.6	12.5	14.8	14.5
19460	Decatur, AL	3 304	147 204	255	44.6	82.6	12.1	2.8	0.5	3.4	6.4	18.2	8.9	12.7	15.9	14.3
19500	Decatur, IL	1 504	111 175	310	73.9	83.6	15.3	0.5	1.0	1.1	6.4	17.6	10.1	11.2	13.9	15.3
19660	Deltona-Daytona Beach-Ormond Beach, FL	2 857	468 663	101	164.0	81.0	9.9	0.7	1.4	7.9	5.1	15.3	9.0	10.5	13.5	13.3
19740	Denver-Aurora, CO	21 676	2 301 116	22	106.2	70.2	5.9	1.1	4.1	20.3	7.6	18.2	9.0	16.4	16.6	14.4
19780	Des Moines, IA	7 458	502 761	95	67.4	88.6	4.4	0.6	3.1	4.5	7.2	17.9	9.6	14.5	15.8	14.0
19820	Detroit-Warren-Livonia, MI...	10 137	4 483 853	10	442.3	70.7	23.4	0.8	3.3	3.1	6.7	19.3	8.4	13.6	16.2	14.7
19804	Detroit-Livonia-Dearborn, MI Div	1 591	2 028 778	X	1 275.2	51.0	42.8	0.9	2.6	4.2	7.2	20.6	8.6	14.0	15.4	14.0
47644	Warren-Farmington Hills-Troy, MI Div	8 546	2 455 075	X	287.3	86.9	7.4	0.8	4.0	2.3	6.2	18.2	8.2	13.4	16.8	15.2
20020	Dothan, AL	4 451	133 336	272	30.0	74.2	23.5	0.8	0.6	1.5	6.6	17.9	9.0	12.2	14.5	14.1
20100	Dover, DE	1 527	134 390	270	88.0	73.6	21.2	1.2	2.4	3.5	7.2	19.4	10.7	12.7	15.4	12.7
20220	Dubuque, IA	1 575	90 049	348	57.2	96.7	1.4	0.4	1.1	1.2	6.2	17.7	11.1	11.3	14.6	14.3
20260	Duluth, MN-WI	21 742	275 936	162	12.7	95.2	1.2	3.2	0.9	0.8	5.1	16.0	12.2	11.0	14.4	15.7
20500	Durham, NC	4 573	447 066	104	97.8	59.5	28.9	0.7	4.0	8.0	6.8	16.1	11.7	17.2	15.0	13.5
20740	Eau Claire, WI	4 268	150 959	245	35.4	96.0	0.7	0.8	2.6	0.8	5.9	17.3	13.3	12.5	14.4	13.9
20940	El Centro, CA...........	10 813	149 232	251	13.8	19.1	3.5	1.2	1.8	74.7	8.1	22.0	11.7	13.6	14.9	11.7
21060	Elizabethtown, KY...........	2 308	109 489	317	47.4	83.2	12.2	1.0	2.9	2.9	7.0	19.2	11.0	13.1	16.4	13.7
21140	Elkhart-Goshen, IN	1 201	188 779	207	157.2	82.9	5.7	0.7	1.3	10.7	8.3	21.0	9.5	13.6	14.5	13.0
21300	Elmira, NY	1 057	90 413	347	85.5	90.3	6.9	0.5	1.2	2.2	5.8	17.0	10.1	12.0	15.2	14.7
21340	El Paso, TX...........	2 624	705 436	68	268.8	15.4	2.3	0.4	1.1	81.3	9.4	22.6	10.8	13.5	14.0	11.7
21500	Erie, PA	2 077	279 966	158	134.8	90.7	6.8	0.4	0.9	2.2	6.0	17.9	11.6	11.9	14.4	14.5
21660	Eugene-Springfield, OR.......	11 795	330 527	143	28.0	90.4	1.4	2.4	3.6	5.1	5.5	16.1	11.5	13.4	13.6	15.3
21780	Evansville, IN-KY	5 934	345 680	137	58.3	92.4	6.1	0.4	0.9	1.1	6.4	17.8	10.2	12.0	15.1	14.5
21820	Fairbanks, AK	19 078	85 978	349	4.5	78.9	7.6	10.1	3.7	4.7	8.4	21.0	12.2	15.5	15.6	14.3
22020	Fargo, ND-MN	7 279	179 121	215	24.6	94.6	1.4	1.5	1.8	1.8	6.0	16.6	15.0	15.0	14.2	13.4
22140	Farmington, NM	14 281	122 272	291	8.6	45.0	0.7	39.8	0.6	15.4	8.1	22.7	12.0	12.0	14.3	12.9
22180	Fayetteville, NC	2 704	341 596	139	126.3	52.4	38.1	3.3	3.4	5.6	8.9	20.4	12.4	16.1	15.3	11.6
22220	Fayetteville-Springdale-Rogers, AR-MO	8 215	378 014	126	46.0	85.6	1.7	2.4	2.2	9.8	7.4	18.7	11.2	14.5	14.1	12.0
22380	Flagstaff, AZ	48 219	121 301	293	2.5	56.2	1.2	31.6	1.3	11.1	7.8	20.6	13.3	14.3	13.8	13.7
22420	Flint, MI	1 657	442 250	105	266.9	75.9	21.1	1.4	1.2	2.4	6.9	19.8	9.4	13.0	15.2	14.3

1. CBSA = Core Based Statistical Area. DIV = Metropolitan Division. See Appendix A for explanation. See Appendix B for list of metropolitan areas identified by type.   2. Dry land or land partially or temporarily covered by water.   3. Hispanic or Latino persons may be of any race.

Table C. Metropolitan Areas — Population and Households

Area Name	Age (percent) (cont'd)				Population — change and components of change, 1990–2003							Households, 2000				
					Total persons		Percent change		Components of change, 2000–2003						Percent		
	55 to 64 years	65 to 74 years	75 years and over	Percent female	1900	2000	1990–2000	2000–2003	Births	Deaths	Net migration	Number	Percent change, 1990–2000	Persons per household	Female family householder[1]	One person
	16	17	18	19	20	21	22	23	24	25	26	27	28	29	30	31
Charleston-North Charleston, SC..............	9.1	5.8	4.7	50.9	506 877	549 033	8.3	4.1	25 830	14 563	11 727	207 957	17.0	2.55	15.3	24.8
Charlotte-Gastonia-Concord, NC-SC	8.4	5.1	4.3	50.8	1 024 096	1 330 448	29.9	8.0	70 688	33 341	69 257	510 516	31.6	2.55	12.4	24.7
Charlottesville, VA..............	9.2	6.6	5.6	52.3	144 151	174 021	20.7	4.4	6 884	4 426	5 078	67 575	26.3	2.43	10.4	27.2
Chattanooga, TN-GA	10.4	7.3	6.2	51.8	433 039	476 531	10.0	2.0	20 082	15 827	5 439	189 607	13.9	2.46	12.8	26.0
Cheyenne, WY	9.4	6.2	5.4	49.8	73 142	81 607	11.6	3.0	3 727	2 257	1 063	31 927	13.7	2.45	9.9	27.2
Chicago-Naperville-Joliet, IL-IN-WI	8.6	5.5	5.2	51.0	8 181 939	9 098 316	11.2	2.6	465 935	232 906	-2 814	3 280 055	11.3	2.72	13.3	26.2
Chicago-Naperville-Joliet, IL Div	8.6	5.5	5.2	51.0	6 894 440	7 628 412	10.6	2.3	394 431	195 659	-26 373	2 755 393	10.3	2.72	13.6	26.9
Gary, IN Div....................	9.5	6.5	6.0	51.5	642 900	675 971	5.1	1.4	30 269	20 793	577	252 308	10.0	2.64	14.5	24.6
Lake County-Kenosha County, IL-WI Div..............	8.3	4.8	4.2	49.8	644 599	793 933	23.2	5.9	41 235	16 454	22 982	272 354	23.2	2.82	9.7	20.9
Chico, CA.......................	9.1	6.9	8.2	50.9	182 120	203 171	11.6	3.9	7 357	7 260	7 722	79 566	11.0	2.48	11.2	27.2
Cincinnati-Middletown, OH-KY-IN	8.9	6.1	5.5	51.3	1 844 888	2 009 632	8.9	1.9	94 591	57 401	137	779 226	13.2	2.52	12.1	27.2
Clarksville, TN-KY	7.2	5.3	4.1	49.6	189 279	232 000	22.6	2.0	13 795	5 646	-3 525	83 332	30.7	2.66	12.1	21.3
Cleveland, TN	10.8	7.2	5.3	50.9	87 355	104 015	19.1	2.3	4 488	3 173	1 193	40 729	24.6	2.49	10.6	23.4
Cleveland-Elyria-Mentor, OH	9.7	7.0	7.4	52.0	2 102 207	2 148 143	2.2	-0.4	91 053	70 209	-28 804	853 165	5.5	2.47	13.9	29.4
Coeur d'Alene, ID	9.7	6.5	5.9	50.5	69 795	108 685	55.7	8.1	4 866	2 929	6 871	41 308	53.3	2.60	9.2	21.9
College Station-Bryan, TX	6.3	4.4	4.0	49.8	150 998	184 885	22.4	4.2	8 629	3 467	2 679	67 744	23.9	2.53	10.6	25.6
Colorado Springs, CO	8.1	4.8	3.7	49.8	409 482	537 484	31.3	6.5	28 575	10 397	16 613	200 402	32.1	2.60	10.1	23.7
Columbia, MO	7.2	4.6	4.5	51.5	122 010	145 666	19.4	3.8	6 031	3 088	2 660	56 930	25.1	2.39	10.4	28.6
Columbia, SC	9.1	5.7	4.8	51.6	548 935	647 158	17.9	3.7	29 386	17 970	13 351	245 347	24.7	2.51	14.6	25.9
Columbus, GA-AL	8.3	6.1	5.1	50.1	266 452	281 768	5.7	1.9	14 203	8 705	-336	103 982	9.9	2.57	18.3	25.7
Columbus, IN	10.4	6.8	5.6	50.8	63 657	71 435	12.2	1.3	3 270	2 095	-234	27 936	15.5	2.52	9.7	24.0
Columbus, OH	8.4	5.3	4.6	50.8	1 405 178	1 612 694	14.8	3.8	80 908	40 890	21 637	636 602	19.2	2.46	11.7	27.7
Corpus Christi, TX	8.8	6.3	5.3	51.0	367 786	403 280	9.7	0.9	21 567	10 023	-7 911	141 590	12.9	2.79	14.5	22.2
Corvallis, OR	8.2	5.0	5.4	50.0	70 811	78 153	10.4	1.5	2 547	1 485	177	30 145	15.4	2.43	7.2	26.1
Cumberland, MD-WV	11.0	8.4	8.8	50.4	101 643	102 008	0.4	-1.2	3 378	3 923	-548	40 106	1.2	2.38	10.1	28.7
Dallas-Fort Worth-Arlington, TX	7.6	4.2	3.4	49.9	3 989 294	5 161 544	29.4	8.3	308 539	102 240	216 176	1 881 056	26.4	2.70	12.0	24.7
Dallas-Plano-Irving, TX Div	7.4	4.0	3.2	49.8	2 622 562	3 451 226	31.6	8.4	211 065	64 806	135 987	1 255 247	28.0	2.71	12.1	25.2
Fort Worth-Arlington, TX Div ..	7.9	4.7	3.7	50.2	1 366 732	1 710 318	25.1	8.2	97 474	37 434	80 189	625 809	23.4	2.69	11.7	23.9
Dalton, GA	8.9	5.6	4.0	49.9	98 609	120 031	21.7	6.0	7 576	3 047	2 681	42 671	17.8	2.79	10.9	20.0
Danville, IL	10.3	8.0	8.1	50.8	88 257	83 919	-4.9	-1.3	3 688	3 070	-1 711	33 406	-2.0	2.42	12.2	28.9
Danville, VA	11.4	8.5	8.2	52.5	108 728	110 156	1.3	-1.4	4 305	4 498	-1 226	45 291	7.0	2.39	15.3	28.2
Davenport-Moline-Rock Island, IA-IL....................	10.1	6.9	7.1	51.1	368 145	376 019	2.1	-0.3	16 065	11 382	-5 616	149 726	4.8	2.45	10.8	27.8
Dayton, OH	10.0	7.1	6.4	51.6	843 837	848 153	0.5	-0.2	36 324	26 687	-11 305	338 979	4.8	2.43	12.4	27.9
Decatur, AL	10.6	7.0	5.5	50.9	131 556	145 867	10.9	0.9	6 166	4 508	-211	57 140	16.1	2.52	11.2	24.3
Decatur, IL	10.4	7.8	7.9	52.3	117 206	114 706	-2.1	-3.1	4 692	3 726	-4 550	46 561	1.2	2.39	12.2	28.8
Deltona-Daytona Beach-Ormond Beach, FL	11.0	10.5	10.7	51.2	370 737	443 343	19.6	5.7	15 038	18 977	28 639	184 723	20.4	2.32	10.9	27.9
Denver-Aurora, CO	8.2	4.7	4.1	49.8	1 650 489	2 157 756	30.7	5.6	117 687	44 961	47 384	844 017	27.9	2.56	9.6	27.8
Des Moines, IA	8.8	5.6	5.6	51.1	416 346	481 394	15.6	4.4	24 014	12 216	9 910	189 371	16.7	2.48	9.8	26.9
Detroit-Warren-Livonia, MI	9.2	5.9	5.9	51.3	4 248 699	4 452 557	4.8	0.7	199 242	129 744	-37 535	1 696 943	7.9	2.59	14.5	27.1
Detroit-Livonia-Dearborn, MI Div	8.6	5.9	6.0	52.0	2 111 687	2 061 162	-2.4	-1.6	100 123	66 808	-65 834	768 440	-1.5	2.64	20.6	28.3
Warren-Farmington Hills-Troy, MI Div	9.7	6.0	5.8	50.7	2 137 012	2 391 395	11.9	2.7	99 119	62 936	28 299	928 503	17.2	2.55	9.5	26.0
Dothan, AL	10.5	7.7	6.9	52.2	120 352	130 861	8.7	1.9	5 760	4 684	1 524	52 836	15.3	2.45	13.6	26.2
Dover, DE	9.0	6.6	5.1	51.7	110 993	126 697	14.1	6.1	6 196	3 576	5 134	47 224	19.1	2.61	13.8	23.0
Dubuque, IA	9.3	7.2	7.5	51.2	86 403	89 143	3.2	1.0	3 783	2 831	29	33 690	9.4	2.51	8.7	26.7
Duluth, MN-WI	9.8	7.2	8.3	50.6	269 249	275 486	2.3	0.2	9 083	9 551	1 117	112 491	6.0	2.34	9.4	30.5
Durham, NC	8.2	5.1	5.0	51.5	344 665	426 493	23.7	5.5	20 429	10 630	13 605	168 704	24.9	2.41	12.7	28.4
Eau Claire, WI	8.7	6.2	6.7	51.0	137 543	148 337	7.8	1.8	5 728	4 076	1 105	57 178	13.5	2.49	8.4	26.2
El Centro, CA...................	6.9	5.6	4.5	48.0	109 303	142 361	30.2	4.8	8 443	2 613	1 072	39 384	19.9	3.33	17.1	17.1
Elizabethtown, KY	8.6	6.0	4.6	49.9	100 919	107 547	6.6	1.8	5 064	2 680	-325	39 772	17.5	2.60	11.7	22.9
Elkhart-Goshen, IN	8.5	5.5	5.3	50.1	156 198	182 791	17.0	3.3	10 127	4 675	620	66 154	16.6	2.72	10.5	22.6
Elmira, NY	9.8	7.4	8.1	50.6	95 195	91 070	-4.3	-0.7	3 500	3 081	-1 027	35 049	-0.6	2.44	12.4	27.9
El Paso, TX	7.3	5.6	4.3	52.0	591 610	679 622	14.9	3.8	46 068	11 831	-8 448	210 022	17.7	3.18	18.0	17.8
Erie, PA	9.2	6.7	7.5	51.1	275 575	280 843	1.9	-0.3	10 892	8 756	-2 852	106 507	4.9	2.51	12.1	27.6
Eugene-Springfield, OR	9.8	6.4	6.9	50.8	282 912	322 959	14.2	2.3	11 549	9 446	5 818	130 453	17.7	2.42	10.0	26.6
Evansville, IN-KY	9.7	6.9	7.0	51.7	324 858	342 815	5.5	0.8	14 131	11 568	647	136 768	8.3	2.43	10.7	27.2
Fairbanks, AK	7.2	3.0	1.8	47.9	77 720	82 840	6.6	3.8	4 843	1 196	-420	29 777	11.6	2.68	9.3	23.6
Fargo, ND-MN	7.4	5.1	5.4	50.3	153 296	174 367	13.7	2.7	6 928	3 630	1 621	69 985	21.1	2.38	8.0	29.9
Farmington, NM	7.9	5.2	3.8	50.4	91 605	113 801	24.2	7.4	6 376	2 679	4 738	37 711	31.2	2.99	14.7	19.3
Fayetteville, NC	7.0	5.0	3.1	49.4	297 569	336 609	13.1	1.5	20 019	7 463	-7 743	118 731	20.0	2.67	15.8	22.1
Fayetteville-Springdale-Rogers, AR-MO	8.6	6.1	5.3	50.1	239 495	347 045	44.9	8.9	17 769	9 309	22 205	131 939	43.9	2.57	8.8	23.4
Flagstaff, AZ	7.7	4.5	2.7	50.1	96 591	116 320	20.4	4.3	6 182	1 869	776	40 448	35.2	2.80	12.2	22.1
Flint, MI	9.3	6.5	5.3	51.9	430 459	436 141	1.3	1.4	20 460	12 979	-836	169 825	5.3	2.54	16.3	26.6

1. No spouse present.

Area Name	Births, average 1999–2001		Deaths, average 1999–2001				Physicians,[4] 1998		Hospitals,[4] 1998			Medicare enrollees, 2003	Serious crimes known to police,[6] 2002 Total	
			Number		Rate					Beds				
	Total	Rate[1]	Total	Infant[2]	Total[1]	Infant[3]	Number	Rate[5]	Number	Number	Rate[5]		Number	Rate[7]
	32	33	34	35	36	37	38	39	40	41	42	43	44	45
Charleston-North Charleston, SC..........	7 910	14.4	4 313	229	7.8	9.7	1 520	552	8	1 871	682	70 506	32 917	5 875
Charlotte-Gastonia-Concord, NC-SC..........	21 155	15.8	9 960	530	7.4	8.4	2 359	735	11	3 257	1 692	164 334	80 161	5 899
Charlottesville, VA..........	2 144	12.3	1 357	46	7.8	7.2	971	1 862	2	734	1 920	25 054	4 690	2 616
Chattanooga, TN-GA	6 150	12.9	4 853	163	10.2	8.8	1 035	643	12	1 966	1 506	76 843	26 651	5 450
Cheyenne, WY..........	1 130	13.8	661	21	8.1	6.2	178	218	2	266	337	11 498	3 266	3 963
Chicago-Naperville-Joliet, IL-IN-WI..........	142 991	15.7	71 586	3 608	7.9	8.4	21 031	1 832	103	28 027	3 014	1 089 802	NA	NA
Chicago-Naperville-Joliet, IL Div..........	120 774	15.8	60 313	3 172	7.9	8.8	18 558	1 103	84	23 522	1 591	908 105	NA	NA
Gary, IN Div..........	9 435	13.9	6 306	236	9.3	8.3	1 112	413	10	2 725	967	97 775	26 253	4 113
Lake County-Kenosha County, IL-WI Div..........	12 781	16.0	4 967	200	6.2	5.2	1 361	316	9	1 780	456	83 922	NA	NA
Chico, CA..........	2 256	11.1	2 175	31	10.7	4.6	383	189	5	661	340	37 160	7 041	3 343
Cincinnati-Middletown, OH-KY-IN..........	29 551	14.7	17 514	761	8.7	8.6	4 306	1 438	25	6 164	2 117	277 165	71 969	4 392
Clarksville, TN-KY..........	4 280	18.5	1 727	86	7.5	6.7	270	324	3	432	780	26 365	9 056	5 020
Cleveland, TN..........	1 395	13.4	985	26	9.5	6.2	137	212	3	306	588	16 705	3 990	3 765
Cleveland-Elyria-Mentor, OH	28 062	13.1	21 456	686	10.0	8.1	6 592	945	34	9 027	1 305	337 978	56 462	3 120
Coeur d'Alene, ID..........	1 502	13.8	845	34	7.8	7.5	156	144	1	187	184	17 754	4 366	3 876
College Station-Bryan, TX	2 648	14.3	1 086	41	5.9	5.2	263	222	3	289	403	17 793	9 147	4 737
Colorado Springs, CO..........	8 552	15.8	3 049	207	5.6	8.1	976	249	4	1 008	206	57 709	24 409	4 348
Columbia, MO..........	1 884	12.9	942	39	6.5	6.9	780	621	3	931	721	16 866	5 415	3 667
Columbia, SC..........	8 802	13.6	5 376	223	8.3	8.4	1 392	642	7	1 793	1 143	82 855	37 296	5 633
Columbus, GA-AL..........	4 445	15.8	2 633	197	9.3	14.8	476	586	4	991	715	38 635	14 395	4 925
Columbus, IN..........	1 069	15.0	634	27	8.9	8.4	157	220	1	237	341	10 575	2 482	3 444
Columbus, OH..........	24 529	15.2	12 427	592	7.7	8.0	3 412	845	19	4 746	1 663	192 187	94 286	6 208
Corpus Christi, TX..........	6 669	16.5	3 318	142	8.2	7.1	809	392	9	1 617	585	53 587	26 959	6 400
Corvallis, OR..........	800	10.2	448	10	5.7	4.2	179	229	1	124	159	8 656	2 860	3 555
Cumberland, MD-WV..........	1 073	10.5	1 220	25	12.0	7.8	194	311	3	525	884	20 271	2 855	2 760
Dallas-Fort Worth-Arlington, TX..........	91 785	17.7	31 683	1 667	6.1	6.1	8 712	1 099	60	11 228	1 643	486 884	315 381	5 854
Dallas-Plano-Irving, TX Div..........	62 752	18.0	20 063	1 058	5.8	5.6	6 262	792	41	7 531	1 090	312 979	213 146	5 919
Fort Worth-Arlington, TX Div..........	29 033	16.9	11 620	609	6.8	7.0	2 450	307	19	3 697	553	173 905	102 235	5 723
Dalton, GA..........	2 304	19.1	943	44	7.8	6.4	146	189	2	324	473	15 855	5 904	4 763
Danville, IL..........	1 167	13.9	956	44	11.4	12.6	141	168	2	233	277	15 773	NA	NA
Danville, VA..........	1 325	12.0	1 366	39	12.4	9.8	166	338	1	336	661	21 660	2 801	2 468
Davenport-Moline-Rock Island, IA-IL..........	5 013	13.3	3 545	114	9.4	7.6	612	469	9	1 521	1 436	59 014	NA	NA
Dayton, OH..........	11 173	13.2	8 031	231	9.5	6.9	1 995	653	11	3 454	965	132 487	37 704	4 725
Decatur, AL..........	1 972	13.5	1 380	46	9.5	7.8	158	165	4	497	560	22 730	5 177	3 587
Decatur, IL..........	1 474	12.9	1 169	43	10.2	9.7	198	173	2	581	511	20 177	NA	NA
Deltona-Daytona Beach-Ormond Beach, FL..........	4 524	10.2	5 744	91	12.9	6.7	703	159	8	1 493	353	104 449	22 177	4 830
Denver-Aurora, CO..........	34 643	16.0	13 200	617	6.1	5.9	5 520	1 294	16	4 311	928	223 773	101 827	4 771
Des Moines, IA..........	7 452	15.4	3 703	151	7.7	6.8	1 125	548	9	1 981	1 057	63 709	21 864	4 608
Detroit-Warren-Livonia, MI....	62 246	14.0	39 600	1 550	8.9	8.3	10 519	1 048	52	13 904	1 435	613 075	189 570	4 235
Detroit-Livonia-Dearborn, MI Div..........	30 886	15.0	20 360	959	9.9	10.3	4 658	226	27	8 232	389	287 693	124 239	6 022
Warren-Farmington Hills-Troy, MI Div..........	31 360	13.1	19 240	591	8.0	6.3	5 861	822	25	5 672	1 046	325 382	65 331	2 707
Dothan, AL..........	1 810	13.8	1 392	43	10.7	7.9	284	383	3	808	1 422	20 822	4 438	3 565
Dover, DE..........	1 910	15.0	1 076	50	8.5	8.7	184	145	1	190	153	18 154	5 133	3 932
Dubuque, IA..........	1 184	13.3	873	20	9.8	5.6	179	201	3	670	763	15 114	2 420	2 705
Duluth, MN-WI..........	2 877	10.4	2 985	57	10.8	6.6	501	370	11	1 663	1 626	49 355	11 398	4 058
Durham, NC..........	6 112	14.3	3 277	140	7.6	7.6	2 798	1 778	5	1 978	1 560	51 580	25 175	5 711
Eau Claire, WI..........	1 795	12.1	1 229	19	8.3	3.5	315	383	5	877	1 237	22 502	4 513	3 029
El Centro, CA..........	2 599	18.2	875	40	6.1	5.1	111	78	3	221	153	18 825	5 243	3 552
Elizabethtown, KY..........	1 627	15.1	811	52	7.5	10.7	182	245	1	296	324	14 640	NA	NA
Elkhart-Goshen, IN..........	3 187	17.4	1 425	72	7.8	7.5	228	125	2	476	276	23 188	7 821	4 224
Elmira, NY..........	1 093	12.0	967	18	10.6	5.5	216	237	2	495	538	16 716	3 035	3 301
El Paso, TX..........	14 154	20.7	3 976	202	5.8	4.8	1 047	154	6	1 829	260	79 128	30 012	4 228
Erie, PA..........	3 460	12.3	2 735	84	9.7	8.1	616	219	6	1 167	422	45 799	7 084	2 544
Eugene-Springfield, OR.......	3 681	11.4	2 829	72	8.8	6.5	636	197	4	620	197	51 244	16 667	5 014
Evansville, IN-KY..........	4 401	12.8	3 541	99	10.3	7.5	697	700	7	1 529	1 680	56 300	NA	NA
Fairbanks, AK..........	1 482	17.8	343	30	4.1	6.7	161	194	1	224	266	5 233	NA	NA
Fargo, ND-MN..........	2 296	13.2	1 168	53	6.7	7.7	446	386	3	667	571	21 247	5 672	3 262
Farmington, NM..........	1 927	16.9	738	33	6.5	5.7	152	134	1	126	119	12 891	4 103	3 535
Fayetteville, NC..........	6 148	18.3	2 211	195	6.6	10.6	554	212	2	515	181	34 778	21 264	6 112
Fayetteville-Springdale-Rogers, AR-MO..........	5 373	15.4	2 759	95	7.9	5.9	479	330	6	735	539	50 698	10 371	2 964
Flagstaff, AZ..........	1 862	16.0	524	26	4.5	4.7	208	179	2	141	123	14 208	7 480	6 047
Flint, MI..........	6 409	14.7	3 910	219	9.0	11.4	853	196	5	1 779	408	65 570	21 597	4 901

1. Per 1,000 estimated resident population.   2. Deaths of infants under 1 year old.   3. Deaths of infants under 1 year old per 1,000 live births.   4. Data subject to copyright.   5. Per 100,000 resident population as of July 1 of the year shown.   6. Data for serious crimes have not been adjusted for underreporting; this may affect comparability between geographic areas and over time.   7. Per 100,000 population estimated by the FBI.

Table C. Metropolitan Areas — Crime, Education, Money Income, and Poverty

Area Name	Serious crimes known to police,[1] 2002 (cont'd) Rate[2] Violent	Property	Education School enrollment and attainment, 2000 Enrollment[3] Total	Percent private	Attainment[4] (percent) High school graduate or more	Bachelor's degree or more	Local government expenditures,[5] 2000–2001 Total current expenditures (mil dol)	Current expenditures per student (dollars)	Money income, 1999 Per capita income[6] (dollars)	Mean household income	Mean family income	Percent of households with income of $100,000 or more	Percent below poverty level, 1999 Persons	Households	Families	Families with children
	46	47	48	49	50	51	52	53	54	55	56	57	58	59	60	61
Charleston-North Charleston, SC	854	5 020	155 163	17.4	81.3	25.0	562.5	6 205	19 772	51 315	58 721	9.5	14.0	13.7	10.7	15.5
Charlotte-Gastonia-Concord, NC-SC	830	5 070	343 006	17.2	81.3	28.0	1 425.4	6 577	23 995	61 810	70 535	13.9	9.4	8.9	6.8	9.8
Charlottesville, VA	332	2 283	53 968	12.4	82.6	38.3	191.9	7 863	23 425	58 549	69 900	12.5	11.6	11.3	6.0	8.8
Chattanooga, TN-GA	705	4 744	116 455	18.2	76.7	19.4	430.8	6 266	19 861	49 292	57 158	8.2	12.0	12.5	9.1	13.9
Cheyenne, WY	222	3 741	21 266	10.1	89.1	23.4	99.3	6 965	19 634	47 878	54 586	6.5	9.1	9.1	6.5	10.2
Chicago-Naperville-Joliet, IL-IN-WI	NA	NA	2 555 204	21.5	81.1	29.0	11 883.8	7 955	24 614	67 437	77 135	17.5	10.5	9.7	7.9	11.4
Chicago-Naperville-Joliet, IL Div	NA	NA	2 145 070	22.2	80.5	29.4	9 694.6	7 914	24 412	66 796	76 329	17.4	10.9	10.0	8.2	11.9
Gary, IN Div	433	3 681	182 415	16.3	82.4	17.3	891.6	7 710	20 509	54 321	61 973	10.0	10.5	10.4	8.1	12.6
Lake County-Kenosha County, IL-WI Div	NA	NA	227 719	18.7	86.0	34.9	1 297.7	8 469	30 050	86 059	97 876	25.3	6.1	5.7	4.3	6.1
Chico, CA	257	3 086	66 431	6.9	82.3	21.8	260.5	7 564	17 517	44 069	52 760	6.7	19.8	17.6	12.2	19.8
Cincinnati-Middletown, OH-KY-IN	435	3 958	545 020	21.8	82.4	24.8	2 251.1	7 135	22 873	58 274	68 332	12.6	9.5	9.8	6.9	10.5
Clarksville, TN-KY	477	4 543	61 884	9.9	80.8	16.2	201.9	5 467	16 383	43 785	48 132	5.4	11.7	12.3	9.4	12.7
Cleveland, TN	461	3 303	25 260	19.4	71.5	14.5	85.3	5 388	17 786	44 956	50 825	6.0	12.3	13.6	9.1	13.7
Cleveland-Elyria-Mentor, OH	442	2 679	561 473	22.8	83.0	23.9	2 760.1	8 487	22 584	56 155	66 111	11.5	10.8	10.6	8.2	13.0
Coeur d'Alene, ID	287	3 589	28 610	13.1	87.3	19.1	94.0	5 145	18 430	47 280	52 770	6.6	10.5	10.2	7.7	11.7
College Station-Bryan, TX	433	4 304	81 284	6.0	78.7	31.5	183.1	6 645	16 118	42 782	55 658	7.7	25.4	26.0	14.3	19.0
Colorado Springs, CO	416	3 932	151 657	16.1	91.4	31.8	596.7	6 086	22 059	57 989	65 460	12.2	7.9	7.8	5.6	8.5
Columbia, MO	341	3 325	52 802	12.0	88.6	39.9	146.7	6 506	19 518	48 884	61 344	8.8	14.3	14.9	7.5	11.0
Columbia, SC	884	4 749	179 090	12.5	82.1	26.6	791.8	7 226	20 262	52 346	60 685	9.6	12.4	12.1	9.1	13.1
Columbus, GA-AL	347	4 578	75 705	10.8	76.6	18.3	320.0	6 634	17 470	45 632	51 877	7.2	15.8	15.7	12.9	18.3
Columbus, IN	137	3 307	17 865	15.6	83.8	22.0	86.2	7 423	21 536	53 928	61 831	9.9	7.3	7.9	5.9	8.7
Columbus, OH	512	5 696	448 985	17.1	85.7	28.3	2 004.1	7 739	22 856	57 187	67 326	12.1	9.9	9.9	7.0	10.4
Corpus Christi, TX	597	5 803	116 162	8.1	73.9	17.7	524.4	6 528	16 853	47 241	52 114	7.6	18.3	16.9	14.7	20.4
Corvallis, OR	163	3 393	30 859	7.3	93.1	47.4	70.5	7 057	21 868	55 309	69 035	12.5	14.6	14.6	6.8	9.9
Cumberland, MD-WV	285	2 475	24 378	7.5	80.0	13.4	115.3	7 674	16 409	39 021	46 815	4.0	14.8	15.2	10.2	17.1
Dallas-Fort Worth-Arlington, TX	619	5 235	1 414 087	14.9	79.9	28.5	6 013.3	6 263	23 645	64 077	72 128	15.7	10.8	9.6	8.1	11.3
Dallas-Plano-Irving, TX Div	684	5 235	944 492	14.9	79.5	30.4	4 048.6	6 332	24 467	66 526	74 770	17.0	11.0	9.6	8.3	11.5
Fort Worth-Arlington, TX Div	487	5 236	469 595	15.1	80.8	24.8	1 964.7	6 127	21 987	59 161	66 970	13.2	10.3	9.5	7.8	10.9
Dalton, GA	371	4 392	27 812	6.8	62.4	11.1	161.2	6 739	17 820	49 679	55 277	7.5	11.8	12.0	8.8	12.0
Danville, IL	NA	NA	19 917	9.2	78.7	12.5	104.9	7 356	16 787	41 435	48 220	4.3	13.3	12.9	9.7	15.2
Danville, VA	338	2 129	24 999	12.0	67.8	11.3	108.2	6 402	17 061	40 903	47 753	4.5	15.3	15.9	11.6	19.1
Davenport-Moline-Rock Island, IA-IL	NA	NA	99 440	17.0	84.5	19.9	455.3	7 190	20 382	50 475	58 986	8.2	10.1	9.8	7.5	12.1
Dayton, OH	383	4 343	231 447	20.2	84.0	22.8	989.5	7 464	21 799	53 700	62 573	10.2	10.0	10.2	7.1	11.4
Decatur, AL	201	3 386	34 460	10.2	73.8	15.8	165.2	6 482	18 577	47 154	54 053	7.9	13.0	14.1	10.5	14.5
Decatur, IL	NA	NA	29 235	19.9	83.2	16.9	125.4	6 925	20 067	48 808	57 092	7.8	12.9	12.1	9.3	15.9
Deltona-Daytona Beach-Ormond Beach, FL	660	4 170	101 190	21.6	82.0	17.6	357.4	5 810	19 664	46 393	53 183	7.1	11.6	11.0	7.9	14.0
Denver-Aurora, CO	385	4 386	572 659	16.1	86.6	34.2	2 414.1	6 731	26 213	66 356	77 268	16.6	8.0	7.3	5.5	8.1
Des Moines, IA	272	4 337	124 259	18.4	88.5	27.9	559.5	6 643	23 116	57 784	67 832	11.4	7.5	7.3	5.0	7.7
Detroit-Warren-Livonia, MI	700	3 535	1 226 177	14.8	82.3	23.2	6 349.3	8 572	24 547	63 833	73 925	16.5	10.6	9.9	7.8	11.8
Detroit-Livonia-Dearborn, MI Div	1 176	4 846	587 853	14.3	77.0	17.2	3 024.1	8 684	20 058	53 154	60 937	11.5	16.4	14.9	12.7	18.5
Warren-Farmington Hills-Troy, MI Div	293	2 414	638 324	15.3	86.7	28.1	3 325.3	8 473	28 416	72 666	84 352	20.7	5.6	5.7	3.9	5.8
Dothan, AL	291	3 274	31 441	13.3	73.1	15.9	127.6	5 853	17 561	43 082	50 414	6.7	16.4	17.2	13.0	19.8
Dover, DE	670	3 262	35 984	13.2	79.4	18.6	200.6	8 022	18 662	49 349	55 227	8.1	10.7	10.2	8.1	12.3
Dubuque, IA	224	2 482	24 497	39.1	85.2	21.3	80.7	6 386	19 600	50 560	60 266	7.2	7.8	7.9	4.9	7.4
Duluth, MN-WI	234	3 825	74 779	10.6	86.7	20.5	335.1	7 697	18 666	44 805	54 008	5.7	11.4	11.8	7.1	11.4
Durham, NC	594	5 117	126 889	19.5	82.8	38.8	451.5	7 465	23 283	57 583	68 889	13.2	13.0	13.1	8.5	12.5
Eau Claire, WI	136	2 893	44 353	12.9	87.1	22.1	184.0	7 927	18 875	48 082	57 132	6.7	9.9	9.6	5.4	8.2
El Centro, CA	461	3 092	47 441	5.4	59.0	10.3	248.7	7 487	13 239	43 494	46 179	7.2	22.6	20.1	19.4	24.6
Elizabethtown, KY	NA	NA	28 891	10.2	80.8	14.8	104.3	5 839	17 285	45 509	51 000	5.6	10.7	10.8	8.8	12.2
Elkhart-Goshen, IN	275	3 949	44 933	14.6	75.7	15.5	225.3	6 878	20 250	54 983	61 104	9.0	7.8	7.3	5.8	8.8
Elmira, NY	335	2 966	22 739	20.1	82.1	18.6	133.0	9 873	18 264	45 469	53 168	6.6	13.0	12.9	9.1	15.5
El Paso, TX	606	3 622	226 320	8.1	65.8	16.6	986.0	6 302	13 421	42 515	45 118	6.3	23.8	21.6	20.5	26.6
Erie, PA	272	2 272	77 763	25.8	84.6	20.9	327.7	7 713	17 932	46 005	53 757	6.4	12.0	11.7	8.2	13.5
Eugene-Springfield, OR	246	4 768	90 503	9.4	87.5	25.5	367.3	7 632	19 681	48 062	56 525	7.9	14.4	14.1	9.0	14.8
Evansville, IN-KY	NA	NA	87 550	18.8	82.3	17.4	361.2	7 059	20 027	49 498	58 681	7.7	10.0	10.3	7.3	11.7
Fairbanks, AK	NA	NA	26 307	10.4	91.8	27.0	140.5	8 513	21 553	58 561	65 116	14.1	7.8	7.9	5.5	7.6
Fargo, ND-MN	146	3 116	54 942	11.9	89.7	29.4	179.8	6 424	19 910	48 679	60 805	7.7	11.0	11.5	6.2	9.2
Farmington, NM	656	2 880	36 608	6.4	76.8	13.5	144.3	5 980	14 282	42 629	46 445	5.5	21.5	19.9	18.0	23.1
Fayetteville, NC	619	5 493	97 548	12.3	83.8	18.3	351.4	6 136	17 002	45 762	50 400	6.1	13.3	13.1	10.8	14.6
Fayetteville-Springdale-Rogers, AR-MO	264	2 700	91 542	10.4	78.8	20.9	318.6	5 514	17 877	46 383	52 853	7.3	13.1	12.9	9.1	13.7
Flagstaff, AZ	575	5 472	42 187	6.7	83.8	29.9	125.4	6 231	17 139	48 723	54 981	8.5	18.2	16.1	13.1	18.8
Flint, MI	627	4 273	120 255	11.2	83.1	16.2	633.0	7 905	20 883	53 066	60 150	10.7	13.1	12.2	10.2	16.2

1. Data for serious crimes have not been adjusted for underreporting; this may affect comparability between geographic areas and over time. 2. Per 100,000 population estimated by the FBI. 3. All persons 3 years old and over enrolled in nursery school through college. 4. Persons 25 years old and over. 5. Elementary and secondary education expenditures. 6. Based on population enumerated as of April 1, 2000.

Table C. Metropolitan Areas — **Personal Income**

	Personal income, 2002												
			Per capita[1]					Transfer payments					
									Government payments to individuals				
Area Name	Total (mil dol)	Percent change, 2001–2002	Dollars	Rank	Wages and salaries[2] (mil dol)	Proprietor's income (mil dol)	Dividends, interest, and rent (mil dol)	Total (mil dol)	Total (mil dol)	Social Security (mil dol)	Medical payments (mil dol)	Income maintenance (mil dol)	Unemployment insurance (mil dol)
	62	63	64	65	66	67	68	69	70	71	72	73	74
Charleston-North Charleston, SC..................	15 176	5.1	26 972	180	10 453	1 132	2 615	2 256	2 118	751	924	236	55
Charlotte-Gastonia-Concord, NC-SC..................	46 512	3.4	32 980	47	37 074	4 384	7 074	5 160	4 826	1 923	1 909	520	265
Charlottesville, VA..............	5 755	3.2	32 164	57	3 726	542	1 428	644	601	280	231	45	18
Chattanooga, TN-GA	13 333	2.6	27 624	159	9 130	1 184	1 973	2 342	2 226	889	959	206	53
Cheyenne, WY	2 570	6.0	31 003	81	1 711	188	553	340	320	121	112	23	6
Chicago-Naperville-Joliet, IL-IN-WI	329 814	1.2	35 517	23	234 560	29 600	58 750	37 584	35 189	12 952	14 944	3 756	2 302
Chicago-Naperville-Joliet, IL Div........................	275 389	1.1	35 423	X	201 743	26 152	48 434	31 946	29 929	10 658	12 925	3 301	2 008
Gary, IN Div..................	18 740	0.7	27 454	X	10 802	960	2 799	3 060	2 889	1 227	1 139	296	120
Lake County-Kenosha County, IL-WI Div..............	35 686	2.1	43 032	X	22 015	2 488	7 517	2 579	2 371	1 067	880	159	174
Chico, CA.........................	4 999	4.5	23 895	303	2 555	480	1 022	1 150	1 100	396	422	153	41
Cincinnati-Middletown, OH-KY-IN............................	64 769	2.8	31 738	67	45 667	4 149	11 325	8 675	8 110	3 190	3 291	718	280
Clarksville, TN-KY	5 802	5.1	24 701	281	4 114	335	807	870	821	283	321	87	28
Cleveland, TN	2 655	2.6	25 090	258	1 483	408	341	488	464	190	202	39	13
Cleveland-Elyria-Mentor, OH	69 060	1.0	32 153	58	48 859	5 675	12 454	10 996	10 388	3 905	4 419	941	396
Coeur d'Alene, ID	2 761	4.6	24 229	294	1 472	264	521	476	450	200	158	29	26
College Station-Bryan, TX	3 976	3.5	21 035	345	2 790	275	685	538	495	191	195	60	7
Colorado Springs, CO..........	16 895	2.2	29 881	105	12 146	1 187	2 923	1 797	1 674	613	629	151	85
Columbia, MO	4 131	3.6	27 633	158	3 014	294	709	551	516	189	234	46	8
Columbia, SC	18 385	3.0	27 679	156	13 370	1 246	2 832	2 656	2 493	934	1 016	255	60
Columbus, GA-AL	7 410	3.5	26 171	204	5 387	418	1 304	1 276	1 201	405	473	157	36
Columbus, IN	2 172	2.2	30 320	94	1 818	155	424	283	266	130	105	19	5
Columbus, OH	53 061	3.2	31 967	64	40 965	4 237	7 552	6 495	6 026	2 123	2 452	627	234
Corpus Christi, TX	10 163	4.0	25 087	259	6 666	960	1 581	1 825	1 735	557	814	226	50
Corvallis, OR	2 399	2.8	30 515	90	1 662	166	578	248	230	109	57	17	8
Cumberland, MD-WV	2 264	4.5	22 352	337	1 321	106	360	655	630	208	291	39	20
Dallas-Fort Worth-Arlington, TX.......................................	185 167	1.6	33 765	39	138 259	26 694	23 450	16 130	14 902	5 636	5 969	1 427	1 105
Dallas-Plano-Irving, TX Div................................	130 174	1.4	35 443	X	102 098	20 548	16 709	10 552	9 729	3 620	3 905	950	812
Fort Worth-Arlington, TX Div................................	54 993	2.3	30 362	X	36 161	6 147	6 741	5 578	5 173	2 017	2 064	477	293
Dalton, GA	3 083	3.7	24 550	286	2 751	193	492	485	449	177	201	42	14
Danville, IL	1 870	1.5	22 492	336	1 168	75	350	423	401	173	136	45	21
Danville, VA	2 470	3.3	22 590	333	1 477	97	411	561	535	234	182	53	47
Davenport-Moline-Rock Island, IA-IL.....................	10 644	2.2	28 373	141	7 381	613	2 080	1 609	1 511	683	550	143	66
Dayton, OH	25 190	2.0	29 750	107	18 694	1 354	4 540	3 893	3 655	1 445	1 456	325	113
Decatur, AL	3 642	0.2	24 880	270	2 139	261	558	628	593	258	245	52	17
Decatur, IL	3 157	-0.4	28 184	149	2 275	191	615	574	545	231	185	55	37
Deltona-Daytona Beach-Ormond Beach, FL	11 380	4.7	24 770	276	5 112	527	3 048	2 476	2 363	1 147	946	127	42
Denver-Aurora, CO.............	86 526	0.7	37 940	16	61 996	11 214	14 137	7 044	6 523	2 538	2 618	588	381
Des Moines, IA	16 434	4.1	33 050	46	12 793	1 276	2 575	1 890	1 758	748	732	124	74
Detroit-Warren-Livonia, MI ...	152 800	0.7	34 076	35	112 730	12 159	23 451	20 641	19 576	7 700	8 287	2 027	1 058
Detroit-Livonia-Dearborn, MI Div............................	56 477	-0.1	27 610	X	46 126	4 093	7 527	11 018	10 533	3 475	4 761	1 500	504
Warren-Farmington Hills-Troy, MI Div......	96 323	1.2	39 499	X	66 604	8 066	15 924	9 623	9 044	4 225	3 526	527	554
Dothan, AL	3 358	3.6	25 516	233	2 030	245	591	633	602	247	236	69	11
Dover, DE	3 286	6.4	25 071	261	2 357	172	475	562	528	211	204	46	27
Dubuque, IA	2 442	3.4	27 319	171	1 809	178	535	393	369	168	151	23	13
Duluth, MN-WI	7 437	4.0	26 917	183	4 911	449	1 333	1 502	1 430	527	611	113	58
Durham, NC	13 903	2.6	31 231	77	13 440	887	2 669	1 657	1 552	605	649	155	71
Eau Claire, WI	4 010	3.5	26 681	191	2 704	297	750	638	600	247	253	38	31
El Centro, CA	2 973	8.7	20 328	351	1 810	379	318	692	658	168	252	139	60
Elizabethtown, KY	2 766	2.3	25 354	239	2 120	137	416	454	428	140	182	40	18
Elkhart-Goshen, IN	5 145	4.6	27 592	162	4 843	372	847	661	614	278	227	58	31
Elmira, NY	2 230	1.2	24 610	282	1 484	107	354	537	513	191	219	54	21
El Paso, TX	13 992	5.1	20 058	352	9 254	1 924	1 743	2 708	2 554	674	1 100	492	20
Erie, PA	7 095	2.1	25 306	245	4 842	461	1 161	1 441	1 369	527	547	132	95
Eugene-Springfield, OR.......	8 647	2.5	26 470	199	5 311	625	1 894	1 525	1 450	587	492	130	99
Evansville, IN-KY	10 021	3.1	29 129	121	7 104	709	1 839	1 571	1 485	652	602	116	45
Fairbanks, AK	2 561	5.6	30 111	98	2 018	161	407	415	399	64	137	35	19
Fargo, ND-MN....................	5 114	4.5	28 882	128	3 783	446	895	623	580	229	217	43	14
Farmington, NM	2 458	3.9	20 421	350	1 728	221	316	447	415	139	173	52	13
Fayetteville, NC	8 626	6.7	25 418	237	7 044	345	1 125	1 332	1 263	370	479	187	42
Fayetteville-Springdale-Rogers, AR-MO	9 097	5.3	24 717	280	6 815	666	1 532	1 252	1 154	550	402	97	30
Flagstaff, AZ	2 943	5.4	24 465	287	1 847	210	654	450	423	115	185	53	13
Flint, MI	11 446	1.6	25 930	215	7 611	509	1 632	2 337	2 233	822	883	297	150

1. Based on the resident population estimated as of July 1 of the year shown.   2. Includes other labor income.

Table C. Metropolitan Areas — **Earnings, Social Security, and Housing**

Area Name	Earnings, 2002									Social Security beneficiaries, December 2003		Housing units, 2003	
	Total (mil dol)	Farm	Percent by selected industries									Supplemental Security Income recipients, December 2003		
			Goods related[1]		Service-related and health					Number	Rate[2]		Total	Percent change, 2000–2003
			Total	Manufacturing	Information, profes-sional and technical services	Retail trade	Finance and insur-ance, and real estate	Health services	Govern-ment					
	75	76	77	78	79	80	81	82	83	84	85	86	87	88
Charleston-North Charleston, SC	11 585	0.2	D	10.4	9.3	8.3	7.6	8.6	26.4	85 015	149	12 538	249 288	7.0
Charlotte-Gastonia-Concord, NC-SC	41 458	0.4	21.3	14.0	D	6.4	13.7	6.0	10.2	194 700	135	21 483	615 427	12.6
Charlottesville, VA	4 268	0.4	D	0.1	D	6.9	6.8	D	32.5	28 210	155	2 627	78 924	6.8
Chattanooga, TN-GA	10 314	0.2	D	16.8	D	9.5	11.1	D	16.2	90 790	187	11 757	213 620	4.0
Cheyenne, WY	1 898	0.8	11.5	4.4	D	8.1	5.9	6.7	40.2	12 605	150	1 098	35 243	3.0
Chicago-Naperville-Joliet, IL-IN-WI	264 160	0.0	19.9	13.1	D	5.6	12.6	D	11.7	1 224 775	131	191 653	3 579 139	3.4
Chicago-Naperville-Joliet, IL Div	227 895	0.0	D	11.8	D	5.3	13.3	7.7	11.4	1 009 620	129	171 508	2 998 007	3.1
Gary, IN Div	11 762	0.2	D	22.6	D	7.8	4.7	D	13.7	116 500	170	12 685	279 632	3.7
Lake County-Kenosha County, IL-WI Div	24 503	0.0	D	21.3	10.0	8.1	9.6	6.6	14.2	98 655	117	7 460	301 500	5.5
Chico, CA	3 036	1.7	12.0	5.1	7.9	11.0	8.0	15.6	21.9	42 415	201	9 985	88 961	4.0
Cincinnati-Middletown, OH-KY-IN	49 816	-0.1	D	0.0	D	6.6	D	D	12.3	317 280	155	39 500	866 228	4.0
Clarksville, TN-KY	4 450	0.3	19.9	16.0	D	6.5	3.0	D	48.5	32 585	138	5 455	97 770	6.2
Cleveland, TN	1 891	0.6	D	30.5	3.9	7.2	8.1	D	11.7	20 625	194	2 841	46 109	4.3
Cleveland-Elyria-Mentor, OH	54 534	0.2	D	18.5	12.0	6.2	9.9	10.7	13.7	372 305	174	48 384	925 390	1.5
Coeur d'Alene, ID	1 736	0.1	20.2	8.9	8.7	11.4	6.3	10.4	19.4	21 605	184	1 815	50 643	8.7
College Station-Bryan, TX	3 065	0.2	16.1	7.4	D	7.8	5.8	D	37.7	20 400	106	2 996	80 515	7.2
Colorado Springs, CO	13 333	-0.1	D	D	16.3	7.1	7.2	7.1	27.6	67 230	117	5 756	233 766	9.9
Columbia, MO	3 308	0.0	D	7.4	D	7.8	D	D	36.8	19 695	130	2 237	65 627	7.5
Columbia, SC	14 616	0.2	17.6	11.3	D	7.6	9.9	D	25.5	100 165	149	13 631	284 767	5.8
Columbus, GA-AL	5 805	0.2	D	D	D	6.2	D	D	32.7	45 170	157	8 866	120 469	4.1
Columbus, IN	1 973	-0.1	D	43.1	4.9	5.2	7.1	7.2	11.3	12 875	178	1 185	30 523	2.2
Columbus, OH	45 202	0.0	17.9	12.2	12.2	8.3	11.4	D	16.2	218 605	131	30 145	728 515	7.1
Corpus Christi, TX	7 625	0.4	22.9	10.3	D	7.8	5.6	11.9	23.0	62 800	154	12 363	165 641	3.0
Corvallis, OR	1 828	1.7	D	26.3	9.5	4.7	3.0	10.7	27.0	10 600	134	627	33 576	5.0
Cumberland, MD-WV	1 427	0.0	D	16.4	D	8.7	3.8	D	24.5	21 605	214	2 533	45 068	0.0
Dallas-Fort Worth-Arlington, TX	164 953	0.1	D	D	D	7.2	D	D	9.6	568 685	102	71 405	2 150 449	7.6
Dallas-Plano-Irving, TX Div	122 646	0.0	D	D	D	6.9	D	7.2	9.0	363 445	97	48 442	1 437 847	7.9
Fort Worth-Arlington, TX Div	42 308	0.1	24.8	16.1	D	8.3	9.8	D	11.6	205 240	111	22 963	712 602	7.1
Dalton, GA	2 944	0.5	D	42.1	D	6.3	3.1	7.0	9.4	19 135	150	2 641	48 145	6.9
Danville, IL	1 243	0.1	D	21.9	5.1	6.9	5.7	10.0	23.4	17 745	214	2 538	36 512	0.4
Danville, VA	1 574	0.9	D	33.6	3.2	8.8	3.3	12.1	15.5	26 070	240	3 971	51 846	1.4
Davenport-Moline-Rock Island, IA-IL	7 994	0.5	D	16.7	D	7.6	D	D	16.7	68 015	181	6 348	160 888	1.5
Dayton, OH	20 048	0.0	D	20.5	D	6.2	5.6	11.0	20.4	147 245	174	16 807	371 448	1.9
Decatur, AL	2 401	1.6	D	36.0	3.8	7.4	4.3	D	14.5	27 910	190	4 372	64 207	2.9
Decatur, IL	2 466	0.0	36.6	29.2	4.7	7.5	4.3	10.8	10.1	22 655	204	3 125	50 908	1.3
Deltona-Daytona Beach-Ormond Beach, FL	5 639	1.3	D	7.4	8.2	10.9	7.5	15.3	16.5	119 140	254	9 411	224 192	5.8
Denver-Aurora, CO	73 210	0.0	D	0.0	D	5.9	12.4	D	12.3	255 640	111	25 314	973 834	8.6
Des Moines, IA	14 070	0.4	14.2	7.2	D	7.7	21.1	D	13.3	73 210	146	6 450	212 013	6.3
Detroit-Warren-Livonia, MI	124 889	0.0	D	21.6	15.6	5.8	7.5	8.6	10.1	712 945	159	104 191	1 851 044	3.0
Detroit-Livonia-Dearborn, MI Div	50 219	0.0	25.0	20.7	12.1	5.2	5.2	9.4	13.2	332 540	164	75 834	831 285	0.6
Warren-Farmington Hills-Troy, MI Div	74 670	0.0	D	22.1	17.9	6.2	9.1	8.1	8.0	380 405	155	28 357	1 019 759	5.0
Dothan, AL	2 275	4.2	D	13.7	D	10.0	5.6	D	16.6	28 320	212	5 573	61 809	3.5
Dover, DE	2 528	0.9	D	D	D	7.8	4.4	9.2	39.8	22 725	169	2 789	53 968	6.9
Dubuque, IA	1 987	1.2	D	23.7	8.7	9.0	5.6	14.5	8.1	17 160	191	1 357	36 884	3.9
Duluth, MN-WI	5 361	0.0	D	8.1	5.9	7.6	6.4	D	21.8	55 110	200	6 268	131 790	1.5
Durham, NC	14 327	0.3	D	27.2	D	4.7	5.2	11.1	17.9	61 645	138	7 456	195 537	7.7
Eau Claire, WI	3 002	0.8	23.8	17.4	6.5	8.5	5.9	14.3	16.2	25 955	172	2 687	64 025	6.2
El Centro, CA	2 189	13.4	8.5	4.4	3.0	8.4	3.4	4.0	35.7	21 950	147	9 342	46 775	6.6
Elizabethtown, KY	2 257	-0.1	D	16.7	D	7.0	3.6	D	45.7	16 985	155	3 286	45 804	5.2
Elkhart-Goshen, IN	5 215	0.1	D	53.7	3.3	4.9	3.4	6.6	6.3	27 005	143	2 265	73 973	6.0
Elmira, NY	1 591	0.3	D	20.5	5.4	9.1	4.6	14.5	21.6	19 395	215	2 887	38 135	1.0
El Paso, TX	11 178	0.1	17.4	12.2	5.9	8.2	9.9	10.2	27.6	88 945	126	23 611	235 592	5.0
Erie, PA	5 303	0.4	31.8	26.4	6.2	8.3	7.4	14.4	13.9	52 525	188	8 610	116 272	1.7
Eugene-Springfield, OR	5 936	0.4	21.9	14.8	9.4	8.9	5.6	12.6	19.3	59 135	179	5 611	143 484	3.3
Evansville, IN-KY	7 813	0.6	D	26.6	6.4	6.5	5.5	D	9.2	65 510	190	7 123	152 859	3.4
Fairbanks, AK	2 178	0.1	D	1.4	D	6.3	3.1	7.5	46.9	6 795	79	862	33 606	0.9
Fargo, ND-MN	4 229	1.8	D	8.7	9.8	8.8	9.7	D	15.0	23 670	132	2 078	78 445	6.7
Farmington, NM	1 949	3.9	27.9	3.3	3.5	8.0	3.0	8.3	22.0	15 865	130	3 540	44 462	2.9
Fayetteville, NC	7 389	0.1	D	8.4	D	6.1	2.9	D	58.3	43 625	128	8 662	137 861	5.3
Fayetteville-Springdale-Rogers, AR-MO	7 480	2.0	D	17.4	D	6.0	4.6	D	12.0	61 165	162	5 581	156 398	8.3
Flagstaff, AZ	2 057	-0.2	13.2	6.8	4.8	9.4	4.5	13.4	33.8	13 425	111	3 112	55 961	4.7
Flint, MI	8 120	0.0	33.8	28.2	9.3	7.3	4.8	11.6	14.6	77 725	176	13 190	192 176	4.7

1. Covers mining, construction, and manufacturing.   2. Per 1,000 resident population estimated as of July 1 of the year shown.

Table C. Metropolitan Areas — **Housing, Labor Force, and Employment**

Area Name	Housing units, 2000								Civilian labor force, 2003				Civilian employment,[5] 2000		
	Occupied units										Unemployment			Percent	
		Owner-occupied				Renter-occupied									
				Owner cost is 35 percent or more of income											
	Total	Percent	Mean value[1]	With a mortgage	Without a mortgage	Mean rent[2]	Rent is 35 percent or more of income	Sub-stand-ard units[3] (percent)	Total	Percent change, 2002–2003	Total	Rate[4]	Total	Management, professional, and related occupations	Production, transpor-tation, and material moving occupations
	89	90	91	92	93	94	95	96	97	98	99	100	101	102	103
Charleston-North Charleston, SC	207 957	66.5	160 960	19.2	9.0	629	32.6	3.8	290 810	3.7	13 362	4.6	247 879	32.5	13.1
Charlotte-Gastonia-Concord, NC-SC	510 516	67.6	161 062	17.0	7.3	660	27.1	4.3	775 924	2.8	50 887	6.6	681 445	34.2	15.5
Charlottesville, VA	67 575	64.3	168 388	16.1	4.7	687	35.8	3.1	85 296	0.5	2 618	3.1	85 198	44.0	8.4
Chattanooga, TN-GA	189 607	70.0	114 898	16.8	6.4	516	28.9	2.7	243 459	-0.4	9 491	3.9	228 127	29.7	20.0
Cheyenne, WY	31 927	69.1	120 934	15.6	4.5	511	26.8	2.3	44 132	4.0	1 818	4.1	36 949	32.2	13.4
Chicago-Naperville-Joliet, IL-IN-WI	3 280 055	65.2	199 800	19.8	8.9	703	29.9	6.6	4 647 489	-0.6	313 782	6.8	4 260 357	35.6	14.8
Chicago-Naperville-Joliet, IL Div	2 755 393	63.6	202 395	20.3	8.8	710	30.0	7.1	3 892 668	-0.8	269 341	6.9	3 568 661	36.0	14.6
Gary, IN Div	252 308	71.2	122 077	15.8	8.1	561	29.4	3.9	326 968	0.7	18 770	5.7	308 064	27.0	19.1
Lake County-Kenosha County, IL-WI Div	272 354	76.0	247 618	19.5	10.7	743	28.4	4.5	427 853	0.2	25 671	6.0	383 632	38.7	13.2
Chico, CA	79 566	60.7	146 827	24.1	8.1	602	43.6	6.5	91 782	1.9	7 173	7.8	82 403	31.7	11.6
Cincinnati-Middletown, OH-KY-IN	779 226	67.3	143 831	14.4	6.4	552	28.4	2.2	1 098 216	2.0	54 771	5.0	982 727	33.8	15.3
Clarksville, TN-KY	83 332	63.1	95 862	17.9	6.8	524	25.1	3.9	101 839	0.6	5 696	5.6	89 297	26.3	20.7
Cleveland, TN	40 729	70.5	109 280	19.2	6.8	453	27.8	2.7	49 271	-0.9	2 806	5.7	49 407	24.2	27.6
Cleveland-Elyria-Mentor, OH	853 165	68.1	145 872	18.9	8.1	573	30.7	2.0	1 080 117	1.2	71 421	6.6	1 011 701	33.5	16.1
Coeur d'Alene, ID	41 308	74.5	151 509	24.6	4.5	610	34.1	3.7	59 593	0.3	4 260	7.1	50 162	27.8	13.5
College Station-Bryan, TX	67 744	51.1	105 812	14.2	10.3	600	49.4	7.7	97 592	3.6	2 757	2.8	85 438	37.2	10.8
Colorado Springs, CO	200 402	65.3	176 805	19.0	4.8	709	30.4	3.9	296 688	1.4	18 720	6.3	255 893	37.1	10.6
Columbia, MO	56 930	58.7	126 774	12.0	4.0	546	35.3	2.2	93 643	-0.5	2 229	2.4	77 927	40.9	9.9
Columbia, SC	245 347	70.2	127 039	16.6	7.1	568	29.4	3.5	337 669	1.8	16 123	4.8	310 847	35.1	13.4
Columbus, GA-AL	103 982	59.8	103 825	19.1	7.6	494	29.0	4.8	133 950	3.6	7 202	5.4	112 695	29.2	17.9
Columbus, IN	27 936	74.2	127 629	13.3	3.7	569	26.5	2.0	37 961	-0.4	1 558	4.1	35 744	31.6	24.8
Columbus, OH	636 602	63.0	144 049	15.5	6.9	607	27.9	2.3	931 909	0.9	45 994	4.9	828 252	35.9	13.5
Corpus Christi, TX	141 590	63.3	85 600	19.3	10.3	561	31.1	10.0	193 527	3.1	12 948	6.7	164 508	29.4	12.1
Corvallis, OR	30 145	57.3	189 834	17.0	3.6	646	42.6	3.5	41 672	1.1	1 739	4.2	38 356	46.9	9.7
Cumberland, MD-WV	40 106	72.2	80 950	16.2	6.9	396	30.8	1.5	43 854	-1.1	2 952	6.7	41 819	25.7	19.0
Dallas-Fort Worth-Arlington, TX	1 881 056	60.2	135 597	15.3	9.4	695	26.1	9.5	2 980 658	0.9	205 337	6.9	2 550 873	36.1	12.4
Dallas-Plano-Irving, TX Div	1 255 247	58.5	145 958	15.7	9.5	715	26.1	10.3	2 008 129	0.6	143 551	7.1	1 711 770	37.3	11.7
Fort Worth-Arlington, TX Div	625 809	63.6	116 147	14.5	9.1	648	26.0	7.8	972 529	1.4	61 786	6.4	839 103	33.5	13.9
Dalton, GA	42 671	69.5	117 320	14.0	5.4	495	21.0	8.4	70 072	2.8	2 459	3.5	57 395	20.3	35.6
Danville, IL	33 406	71.8	66 305	13.0	7.0	437	27.8	2.5	37 418	0.0	3 130	8.4	35 735	24.3	23.1
Danville, VA	45 291	70.1	89 160	16.6	6.3	420	30.6	3.2	57 897	0.2	5 298	9.2	49 261	21.5	28.7
Davenport-Moline-Rock Island, IA-IL	149 726	71.7	100 706	13.0	5.2	481	26.7	2.2	196 122	-0.9	10 592	5.4	183 951	29.3	18.2
Dayton, OH	338 979	67.0	120 633	16.3	6.4	555	28.9	1.8	427 667	0.3	25 771	6.0	405 176	33.4	17.8
Decatur, AL	57 140	75.5	103 650	15.0	6.2	440	26.2	3.4	71 299	0.1	4 943	6.9	65 388	25.1	25.5
Decatur, IL	46 561	71.7	82 878	12.6	6.6	456	28.4	1.8	55 790	-2.1	4 134	7.4	52 584	28.4	19.6
Deltona-Daytona Beach-Ormond Beach, FL	184 723	75.3	108 856	23.1	6.6	623	35.6	3.3	198 240	2.5	10 061	5.1	189 035	28.8	11.8
Denver-Aurora, CO	852 163	66.9	214 359	18.9	5.4	747	30.2	5.4	1 286 726	2.1	80 318	6.2	1 155 407	38.6	10.0
Des Moines, IA	189 371	70.8	120 708	13.5	6.2	577	25.4	3.2	285 497	-1.5	11 108	3.9	257 358	35.5	11.8
Detroit-Warren-Livonia, MI	1 696 943	72.6	164 929	16.4	8.0	618	29.5	4.0	2 248 863	0.5	161 897	7.2	2 056 343	33.7	16.7
Detroit-Livonia-Dearborn, MI Div	768 440	66.6	125 213	18.1	9.2	551	32.0	5.6	922 787	1.2	83 066	9.0	851 110	28.1	19.6
Warren-Farmington Hills-Troy, MI Div	928 503	77.6	194 335	15.3	6.7	699	26.4	2.6	1 326 076	0.1	78 831	5.9	1 205 233	37.7	14.7
Dothan, AL	52 836	73.1	93 862	16.5	6.6	406	27.3	3.2	62 787	3.5	2 987	4.8	57 944	27.6	18.8
Dover, DE	47 224	70.0	126 746	18.5	5.3	578	30.0	2.9	76 366	1.8	3 229	4.2	57 895	28.5	15.3
Dubuque, IA	33 690	73.5	111 178	10.2	4.3	452	24.7	1.8	50 076	-0.9	1 996	4.0	45 728	29.7	19.7
Duluth, MN-WI	112 491	74.9	89 265	13.6	5.8	434	30.6	2.7	149 689	0.2	8 639	5.8	129 056	29.5	14.0
Durham, NC	168 704	59.5	164 466	18.2	7.6	673	33.6	5.3	242 630	2.3	11 617	4.8	218 757	44.1	10.8
Eau Claire, WI	57 178	68.9	109 346	13.0	5.4	497	26.5	2.3	87 421	2.7	4 569	5.2	77 106	29.7	18.1
El Centro, CA	39 384	58.3	116 580	25.6	9.1	529	37.6	23.0	57 322	3.5	11 146	19.4	44 092	24.7	11.7
Elizabethtown, KY	39 772	68.7	100 311	14.4	4.2	471	23.6	3.2	47 667	4.9	2 926	6.1	45 795	26.0	21.5
Elkhart-Goshen, IN	66 154	72.2	116 662	11.7	5.3	547	21.9	4.1	98 759	2.4	4 612	4.7	93 074	23.8	32.7
Elmira, NY	35 049	68.9	78 693	14.9	10.6	503	34.4	1.5	42 900	-1.7	2 829	6.6	39 220	32.0	15.9
El Paso, TX	210 022	63.6	83 652	19.8	7.9	499	33.5	14.9	298 163	2.7	28 806	9.7	240 723	29.1	16.8
Erie, PA	106 507	69.2	102 286	16.3	7.2	475	29.9	2.0	140 261	-3.1	9 678	6.9	129 325	29.2	20.5
Eugene-Springfield, OR	130 453	62.3	163 308	21.3	6.3	628	39.7	3.9	171 406	1.2	13 438	7.8	155 460	31.9	15.5
Evansville, IN-KY	136 768	71.8	101 041	12.5	5.2	467	27.6	1.9	193 443	1.9	8 244	4.3	168 281	27.3	20.3
Fairbanks, AK	29 777	54.0	139 132	17.6	4.8	705	29.3	12.6	44 837	2.2	3 108	6.9	35 258	35.8	9.6
Fargo, ND-MN	69 985	59.0	107 401	11.2	5.1	480	27.7	2.3	108 826	1.5	3 013	2.8	96 328	33.0	12.5
Farmington, NM	37 711	75.3	105 281	17.4	6.9	479	28.5	16.4	52 687	0.9	4 313	8.2	44 541	25.2	14.5
Fayetteville, NC	118 731	60.9	104 817	22.0	9.9	583	28.6	4.9	143 040	2.0	8 483	5.9	123 452	28.3	17.5
Fayetteville-Springdale-Rogers, AR-MO	131 939	66.6	115 262	15.0	5.4	532	28.6	5.9	185 446	1.0	5 882	3.2	165 338	29.9	19.5
Flagstaff, AZ	40 448	61.4	167 925	20.2	5.2	641	33.4	14.9	66 940	0.0	4 298	6.4	55 510	34.8	10.0
Flint, MI	169 825	73.2	109 844	15.2	6.6	522	33.3	3.3	186 236	-0.5	18 113	9.7	192 969	27.0	21.4

1. Specified owner-occupied units. 2. Specified renter-occupied units. 3. Overcrowded or lacking complete plumbing facilities. 4. Percent of civilian labor force. 5. Persons 16 years old and over.

Table C. Metropolitan Areas — **Nonfarm Employment and Agriculture**

Area Name	Private nonfarm establishments, employment and payroll, 2001									Agriculture, 2002			
	Number of establishments	Employment						Annual payroll		Farms			Farm operators whose principal occupation is farming (percent)
		Total	Health care and social assistance	Manufacturing	Retail trade	Finance and insurance	Professional, scientific, and technical services	Total (mil dol)	Average per employee (dollars)	Number	Percent with—		
											Less than 50 acres	500 acres and over	
	104	105	106	107	108	109	110	111	112	113	114	115	116
Charleston-North Charleston, SC	14 198	225 395	36 105	20 668	32 714	6 831	12 304	6 089	27 015	1 180	57.5	5.4	45.0
Charlotte-Gastonia-Concord, NC-SC	38 994	753 670	64 086	98 626	79 462	80 658	42 944	27 099	35 956	4 029	46.6	4.8	52.7
Charlottesville, VA	5 147	70 773	12 234	6 004	10 156	5 034	4 241	2 108	29 785	1 917	31.0	7.7	48.1
Chattanooga, TN-GA	11 309	211 566	24 994	45 747	26 090	13 915	9 800	5 888	27 831	2 397	45.3	4.1	47.9
Cheyenne, WY	2 350	27 505	5 046	1 644	5 636	1 878	1 154	683	24 832	755	18.9	46.9	57.0
Chicago-Naperville-Joliet, IL-IN-WI	227 505	4 203 543	460 967	608 456	440 510	268 114	315 921	170 488	40 558	7 120	40.9	21.4	62.9
Chicago-Naperville-Joliet, IL Div	191 653	3 603 404	392 961	496 986	358 102	241 436	284 864	147 709	40 992	4 244	36.7	22.8	67.0
Gary, IN Div	14 317	239 391	33 289	47 280	34 350	6 729	7 935	7 278	30 402	2 073	42.1	23.9	59.3
Lake County-Kenosha County, IL-WI Div	21 535	360 748	34 717	64 190	48 058	19 949	23 122	15 501	42 969	803	59.4	7.6	50.7
Chico, CA	4 652	55 931	11 186	4 763	9 478	2 360	2 693	1 308	23 386	2 128	58.9	7.4	62.8
Cincinnati-Middletown, OH-KY-IN	47 147	940 081	116 605	138 228	116 525	50 598	52 678	31 986	34 025	11 263	42.7	4.1	50.2
Clarksville, TN-KY	3 948	62 229	9 529	15 115	10 600	1 778	2 448	1 440	23 140	3 149	32.1	9.3	54.2
Cleveland, TN	2 122	40 702	5 931	12 300	4 758	1 506	810	1 070	26 289	1 195	48.6	3.6	55.1
Cleveland-Elyria-Mentor, OH	56 805	1 048 641	147 424	181 022	118 920	64 570	61 530	35 522	33 874	3 630	59.1	4.2	53.6
Coeur d'Alene, ID	3 642	36 660	5 295	4 399	6 266	997	1 938	874	23 841	828	58.0	7.7	48.4
College Station-Bryan, TX	3 710	52 190	7 290	5 409	9 021	2 161	2 662	1 251	23 970	4 455	30.2	12.3	53.1
Colorado Springs, CO	14 493	221 557	24 112	22 567	30 047	11 344	17 367	7 170	32 362	1 293	36.5	22.6	54.3
Columbia, MO	3 999	64 891	14 019	6 101	9 189	5 366	2 469	1 603	24 703	2 194	27.9	11.5	51.6
Columbia, SC	16 157	278 410	34 796	33 442	37 437	21 718	17 903	7 682	27 592	3 086	44.1	7.1	46.0
Columbus, GA-AL	5 654	103 358	11 684	18 194	13 817	7 671	3 699	2 776	26 858	836	33.0	13.8	48.9
Columbus, IN	1 914	37 892	3 964	13 199	4 373	1 157	877	1 300	34 308	608	42.3	15.1	56.7
Columbus, OH	39 095	798 795	89 120	88 553	106 504	68 562	48 668	27 281	34 153	7 406	47.3	12.1	56.0
Corpus Christi, TX	9 353	128 990	23 772	9 904	18 983	4 317	5 686	3 525	27 328	1 286	38.3	28.1	59.9
Corvallis, OR	1 936	28 257	3 767	7 681	3 132	556	1 618	949	33 585	912	71.2	5.5	49.9
Cumberland, MD-WV	2 285	30 552	6 411	5 410	5 311	1 005	803	748	24 483	743	30.4	6.7	50.9
Dallas-Fort Worth-Arlington, TX	128 167	2 591 666	220 312	315 862	294 059	156 139	170 423	100 813	38 899	23 143	54.4	5.9	46.9
Dallas-Plano-Irving, TX Div	89 710	1 902 767	150 884	220 166	198 076	122 502	137 989	78 383	41 194	13 426	52.7	6.2	48.2
Fort Worth-Arlington, TX Div	38 457	688 899	69 428	95 696	95 983	33 637	32 434	22 430	32 559	9 717	56.6	5.6	45.2
Dalton, GA	3 005	64 703	3 832	29 911	8 156	1 046	965	1 789	27 649	724	45.0	3.3	48.1
Danville, IL	1 700	28 457	4 539	6 537	3 989	1 368	492	759	26 672	909	26.7	35.4	69.6
Danville, VA	2 430	38 632	5 498	13 229	5 673	1 300	731	950	24 591	1 304	22.1	9.7	57.4
Davenport-Moline-Rock Island, IA-IL	9 543	166 736	19 941	27 076	23 005	6 978	4 781	5 043	30 245	3 439	26.7	23.0	69.9
Dayton, OH	18 871	378 948	51 369	72 899	49 840	12 852	21 687	12 107	31 949	3 787	53.3	9.2	55.4
Decatur, AL	3 146	51 078	5 533	15 682	7 087	2 047	1 144	1 379	26 998	2 905	45.7	3.7	49.6
Decatur, IL	2 685	53 746	6 856	9 487	6 821	1 619	1 028	1 702	31 667	646	28.3	36.1	73.4
Deltona-Daytona Beach-Ormond Beach, FL	10 827	132 851	19 539	10 311	25 040	4 662	5 371	3 051	22 966	1 114	80.8	3.2	48.6
Denver-Aurora, CO	67 792	1 090 399	102 358	71 956	129 913	72 734	87 397	43 356	39 762	3 951	42.3	19.3	53.8
Des Moines, IA	13 834	268 744	32 891	21 293	35 056	41 585	11 743	8 668	32 254	4 915	31.7	17.3	57.0
Detroit-Warren-Livonia, MI	105 817	1 958 403	227 719	309 057	237 836	88 555	134 669	78 525	40 096	4 798	56.3	5.4	52.4
Detroit-Livonia-Dearborn, MI Div	35 887	750 087	96 439	118 155	82 608	32 981	35 448	29 780	39 702	319	74.0	2.5	43.9
Warren-Farmington Hills-Troy, MI Div	69 930	1 208 316	131 280	190 902	155 228	55 574	99 221	48 745	40 341	4 479	55.0	5.6	53.0
Dothan, AL	3 626	53 611	9 084	10 019	8 810	1 388	1 335	1 379	25 722	2 044	29.1	13.5	54.5
Dover, DE	3 007	46 469	6 423	6 728	9 244	2 716	2 016	1 213	26 103	721	44.5	11.7	68.0
Dubuque, IA	2 645	48 677	6 525	10 458	6 749	2 289	1 018	1 247	25 618	1 481	19.9	8.5	71.2
Duluth, MN-WI	7 372	104 203	21 408	9 044	16 781	3 713	3 901	2 786	26 736	1 976	20.7	6.7	51.1
Durham, NC	10 553	232 256	33 875	42 133	23 820	7 877	21 800	9 096	39 164	2 367	45.7	4.4	59.9
Eau Claire, WI	3 934	64 205	10 526	11 679	10 884	2 996	1 950	1 670	26 010	2 795	22.0	7.4	63.3
El Centro, CA	2 270	25 103	3 401	1 588	6 484	921	662	593	23 623	537	22.0	43.9	81.2
Elizabethtown, KY	2 188	34 999	7 346	7 553	6 120	1 010	1 306	836	23 886	2 620	41.6	5.2	53.5
Elkhart-Goshen, IN	5 031	109 759	8 461	55 051	10 745	1 747	1 780	3 219	29 328	1 516	52.8	5.9	55.5
Elmira, NY	1 871	35 224	6 467	7 563	5 908	1 111	991	928	26 346	427	26.9	6.8	48.2
El Paso, TX	12 214	199 453	28 399	30 930	28 710	7 069	7 120	4 585	22 988	600	74.2	7.7	53.5
Erie, PA	6 994	122 308	17 695	35 139	16 472	4 617	3 304	3 348	27 374	1 283	37.7	3.9	55.5
Eugene-Springfield, OR	9 561	117 509	16 453	20 005	19 102	4 106	6 117	3 220	27 402	2 577	71.8	3.6	49.9
Evansville, IN-KY	8 799	159 474	22 153	34 657	21 138	5 553	5 074	4 633	29 052	2 780	36.1	18.4	56.4
Fairbanks, AK	2 230	23 024	4 657	459	4 519	667	1 035	789	34 269	187	24.1	24.1	66.3
Fargo, ND-MN	5 374	89 461	12 997	7 978	13 037	6 381	3 421	2 401	26 839	1 838	17.2	44.5	69.3
Farmington, NM	2 558	36 218	4 649	1 347	5 929	873	944	1 074	29 654	808	71.2	5.3	50.0
Fayetteville, NC	5 522	90 951	14 383	14 637	16 188	2 643	3 084	2 211	24 310	679	47.1	11.8	58.2
Fayetteville-Springdale-Rogers, AR-MO	8 624	148 387	13 408	33 297	18 423	3 678	4 810	4 404	29 679	7 559	36.1	6.0	54.9
Flagstaff, AZ	3 461	38 466	5 141	2 482	6 992	781	1 081	876	22 773	213	49.8	22.5	56.8
Flint, MI	9 087	145 300	22 241	24 689	25 376	5 543	5 585	4 789	32 959	1 051	59.1	6.6	56.8

Table C. Metropolitan Areas — **Agriculture**

	Agriculture, 2002 (cont'd)															
	Land in farms				Value of land and buildings (dollars)			Value of products sold					Percent of farms with sales of —		Government payments	
		Acres					Value of machinery and equipment average per farm (dollars)				Percent from —					
Area Name	Acreage (1,000)	Percent change, 1997–2002	Average size of farm	Total irrigated (1,000)	Total cropland (1,000)	Average per farm	Average per acre		Total (mil dol)	Average per farm (dollars)	Crops	Live-stock and poultry products	$10,000 or more	$100,000 or more	Total ($1,000)	Percent of farms
	117	118	119	120	121	122	123	124	125	126	127	128	129	130	131	132
Charleston-North Charleston, SC	162	0.6	137	2	61	449 969	3 125	45 529	57	48 046	76.7	23.3	18.6	5.1	722	14.1
Charlotte-Gastonia-Concord, NC-SC	551	9.5	137	4	301	522 967	4 079	54 009	566	140 405	D	D	30.5	15.1	4 678	22.5
Charlottesville, VA	355	5.0	185	2	148	632 823	3 474	39 430	37	19 136	36.4	63.6	26.6	3.0	817	14.2
Chattanooga, TN-GA	279	4.5	117	0	129	336 981	2 622	36 040	100	41 705	6.8	93.2	22.4	5.9	823	11.6
Cheyenne, WY	1 755	1.6	2 324	59	405	749 237	305	93 871	66	86 784	26.9	73.1	43.7	13.4	4 584	55.9
Chicago-Naperville-Joliet, IL-IN-WI	2 333	-4.7	328	D	2 173	1 201 971	3 641	110 585	996	139 948	70.7	29.3	59.3	27.6	37 101	47.9
Chicago-Naperville-Joliet, IL Div	1 470	-4.5	346	D	1 382	1 392 906	4 016	115 512	606	142 727	77.8	22.2	64.3	29.5	23 686	50.5
Gary, IN Div	735	-5.0	355	39	679	979 343	2 733	109 899	328	158 419	56.9	43.1	55.4	27.9	11 562	50.1
Lake County-Kenosha County, IL-WI Div	128	-5.9	159	1	111	767 578	4 556	86 312	62	77 580	75.4	24.6	42.7	16.2	1 853	28.3
Chico, CA	382	-5.4	179	223	257	760 934	4 401	62 857	252	118 407	96.0	4.0	53.1	22.4	9 411	12.5
Cincinnati-Middletown, OH-KY-IN	1 421	6.1	126	5	909	370 203	3 025	40 721	237	21 081	70.8	29.2	25.9	4.5	9 646	20.0
Clarksville, TN-KY	687	6.0	218	3	440	379 426	1 860	50 175	130	41 249	69.8	30.2	36.2	8.8	6 852	32.9
Cleveland, TN	126	3.3	106	0	64	368 911	3 887	49 187	81	67 545	7.7	92.3	27.4	13.6	737	13.7
Cleveland-Elyria-Mentor, OH	375	18.3	103	5	281	451 226	4 715	58 021	252	69 452	84.0	16.0	35.1	8.7	D	D
Coeur d'Alene, ID	154	17.6	186	13	68	487 329	2 265	30 418	14	17 077	85.2	14.8	15.2	3.3	685	12.4
College Station-Bryan, TX	1 213	19.9	272	51	419	399 528	1 337	35 739	158	35 475	19.5	80.5	30.9	4.7	3 072	4.4
Colorado Springs, CO	886	-6.7	685	11	120	597 343	914	55 291	34	25 925	42.8	57.2	26.8	4.5	739	17.4
Columbia, MO	540	9.8	246	8	340	471 044	1 938	35 843	65	29 662	60.5	39.5	36.5	6.0	4 573	40.3
Columbia, SC	494	2.3	160	17	216	362 071	2 191	56 546	279	90 350	D	D	22.2	8.3	3 081	18.6
Columbus, GA-AL	244	17.9	292	4	68	496 093	1 639	35 094	D	D	D	D	22.7	4.5	1 068	23.0
Columbus, IN	161	-3.6	264	9	143	765 489	2 958	86 508	42	69 689	83.0	17.0	50.2	17.1	2 365	49.5
Columbus, OH	1 634	4.1	221	3	1 380	689 887	3 162	76 269	473	63 817	62.6	37.4	39.4	12.7	25 513	38.2
Corpus Christi, TX	919	6.5	715	10	614	692 493	928	92 232	D	D	D	D	37.9	20.2	D	D
Corvallis, OR	130	-0.8	143	21	93	507 363	3 854	62 936	85	92 747	87.7	12.3	25.7	8.7	285	5.6
Cumberland, MD-WV	120	-1.6	162	D	44	286 425	1 677	23 107	16	21 978	11.7	88.3	17.0	3.1	155	12.5
Dallas-Fort Worth-Arlington, TX	3 735	6.0	161	12	1 816	344 819	2 067	28 133	375	16 204	41.1	58.9	16.7	2.4	10 148	8.3
Dallas-Plano-Irving, TX Div	2 220	4.9	165	6	1 211	333 157	1 966	30 611	221	16 492	47.5	52.5	16.7	2.6	7 252	8.6
Fort Worth-Arlington, TX Div	1 515	7.6	156	5	605	360 933	2 215	24 709	154	15 806	31.8	68.2	16.7	2.1	2 896	7.7
Dalton, GA	85	14.9	118	1	35	415 790	2 739	50 991	101	139 823	2.5	97.5	27.2	13.7	452	13.7
Danville, IL	450	-7.2	495	D	429	1 268 611	2 467	135 076	125	137 201	93.6	6.4	68.2	38.6	7 525	64.0
Danville, VA	289	NA	221	6	125	377 897	1 582	51 993	55	41 866	56.2	43.8	32.4	8.5	NA	NA
Davenport-Moline-Rock Island, IA-IL	1 172	0.9	341	16	1 042	861 615	2 531	106 594	412	119 780	68.3	31.7	65.2	30.7	22 806	66.0
Dayton, OH	653	-3.1	172	3	571	519 637	3 087	63 735	181	47 918	74.1	25.9	37.3	10.9	10 004	36.8
Decatur, AL	383	5.2	132	3	212	271 846	2 142	34 105	169	58 153	12.8	87.2	22.7	8.1	5 408	30.1
Decatur, IL	321	-0.6	496	0	303	1 504 821	3 057	131 746	91	140 646	93.5	6.5	69.0	39.8	4 688	62.1
Deltona-Daytona Beach-Ormond Beach, FL	94	-16.1	84	9	19	329 264	4 357	20 565	106	95 419	92.6	7.4	33.9	11.2	23	1.0
Denver-Aurora, CO	D	D	D	D	D	D	D	55 179	184	46 649	71.7	27.5	25.0	5.8	D	D
Des Moines, IA	1 464	-0.4	298	D	1 163	596 612	1 937	77 484	396	80 598	61.5	38.5	49.6	16.8	21 440	61.1
Detroit-Warren-Livonia, MI	598	0.8	125	9	478	557 647	4 650	66 600	233	48 581	81.3	18.7	31.7	8.7	6 602	18.6
Detroit-Livonia-Dearborn, MI Div	21	-46.2	67	1	18	443 608	6 829	53 727	28	86 392	97.8	2.2	36.1	11.9	134	10.3
Warren-Farmington Hills-Troy, MI Div	577	4.2	129	8	460	565 769	4 569	67 517	206	45 888	79.1	20.9	31.4	8.5	6 468	19.2
Dothan, AL	567	1.6	277	22	317	377 230	1 373	60 236	169	82 503	33.3	66.7	40.2	13.8	11 893	54.6
Dover, DE	185	-5.1	257	29	160	905 260	3 498	127 089	129	178 467	42.3	57.7	53.0	28.7	2 930	32.7
Dubuque, IA	316	-6.0	213	0	242	478 042	2 134	88 728	152	102 612	22.7	77.3	67.5	30.2	7 915	65.7
Duluth, MN-WI	374	12.3	189	1	187	220 309	1 244	24 119	24	12 120	42.9	57.1	21.0	2.3	463	5.0
Durham, NC	311	-5.2	131	5	132	465 947	3 614	46 886	169	71 302	22.1	77.9	33.5	12.3	1 595	20.4
Eau Claire, WI	578	2.5	207	6	372	323 780	1 617	63 711	156	55 918	23.9	76.1	46.8	17.3	8 049	48.1
El Centro, CA	514	4.9	957	477	488	2 931 721	2 976	270 910	1 043	1 942 791	62.2	37.8	82.9	69.1	3 301	32.4
Elizabethtown, KY	374	10.3	143	0	243	288 262	1 910	40 424	57	21 739	50.9	49.1	29.6	4.5	2 690	25.2
Elkhart-Goshen, IN	201	9.8	133	23	176	493 262	3 803	63 874	136	89 718	30.6	69.4	58.0	24.7	3 441	23.7
Elmira, NY	69	16.9	162	0	37	221 352	1 380	75 945	12	28 253	32.6	67.4	23.9	7.3	644	19.7
El Paso, TX	114	-53.3	190	37	51	399 653	2 187	66 508	68	113 140	42.8	57.2	29.5	11.2	421	6.8
Erie, PA	166	-1.2	129	2	106	299 506	2 320	72 463	64	50 187	65.2	34.8	42.6	12.6	1 488	19.6
Eugene-Springfield, OR	235	4.9	91	22	132	363 136	4 572	38 602	88	34 080	66.7	33.3	21.6	5.0	674	3.5
Evansville, IN-KY	931	0.0	335	D	806	698 437	2 087	101 815	272	97 690	61.0	39.0	46.9	21.2	14 049	51.6
Fairbanks, AK	110	NA	588	1	69	385 526	655	72 156	5	28 262	82.3	17.7	37.4	8.6	1 267	24.6
Fargo, ND-MN	1 727	4.7	940	16	1 616	886 324	943	173 106	344	187 095	89.6	10.4	63.5	42.0	16 946	72.6
Farmington, NM	1 757	D	2 174	67	99	705 781	324	92 036	37	45 829	72.9	27.1	15.1	2.1	D	D
Fayetteville, NC	154	-9.4	226	5	98	561 897	2 596	77 834	102	150 389	24.4	75.6	34.6	15.8	1 435	25.6
Fayetteville-Springdale-Rogers, AR-MO	1 191	4.0	158	D	532	371 685	2 361	41 254	903	119 430	1.3	98.7	36.9	16.2	1 596	6.7
Flagstaff, AZ	D	D	D	2	D	4 708 165	D	45 145	11	52 183	7.0	93.0	29.1	9.9	198	7.5
Flint, MI	143	21.2	136	1	116	512 373	3 853	55 786	29	28 004	73.6	26.4	25.5	7.3	1 601	20.7

Table C. Metropolitan Areas — **Residential Construction, Wholesale Trade, Retail Trade, and Real Estate**

Area Name	Value of residential construction authorized by building permits, 2003		Wholesale trade, 1997				Retail trade,[1] 1997				Real estate and rental and leasing, 1997			
	New construction ($1,000)	Number of housing units	Number of establishments	Number of employees	Sales (mil dol)	Annual payroll (mil dol)	Number of establishments	Number of employees	Sales (mil dol)	Annual payroll (mil dol)	Number of establishments	Number of employees	Receipts (mil dol)	Annual payroll (mil dol)
	133	134	135	136	137	138	139	140	141	142	143	144	145	146
Charleston-North Charleston, SC	900 357	7 394	606	6 644	4 402.0	209.1	2 424	29 095	4 538.1	441.1	590	3 352	366.3	62.6
Charlotte-Gastonia-Concord, NC-SC	2 376 406	18 833	3 589	47 880	40 833.7	1 893.6	5 300	72 857	13 339.7	1 257.5	1 409	11 084	1 619.9	325.2
Charlottesville, VA	267 988	2 008	167	D	D	D	795	9 290	1 534.2	149.9	210	D	D	D
Chattanooga, TN-GA	388 055	3 266	824	D	D	D	2 090	26 157	4 250.8	408.9	426	2 328	257.0	62.4
Cheyenne, WY	93 779	779	81	665	267.5	18.6	358	4 851	855.5	77.8	88	321	27.7	5.2
Chicago-Naperville-Joliet, IL-IN-WI	7 795 740	49 954	17 296	270 079	237 503.6	11 624.5	30 141	438 594	80 515.9	7 957.8	8 973	63 046	11 821.3	1 930.7
Chicago-Naperville-Joliet, IL Div	6 228 741	39 695	14 962	238 068	211 855.1	10 282.1	24 830	360 280	65 111.2	6 548.6	7 673	56 352	10 705.6	1 771.2
Gary, IN Div	617 542	4 407	788	9 347	5 184.1	318.5	2 374	33 870	5 770.0	527.6	562	2 719	346.5	57.2
Lake County-Kenosha County, IL-WI Div	949 457	5 852	1 546	22 664	20 464.4	1 023.9	2 937	44 444	9 634.7	881.6	738	3 975	769.2	102.3
Chico, CA	208 372	1 769	179	1 792	637.9	56.9	777	9 004	1 502.6	154.0	212	1 012	80.5	13.4
Cincinnati-Middletown, OH-KY-IN	1 711 376	13 181	NA	NA	NA	NA	7 377	111 692	18 230.9	1 742.9	1 898	D	D	D
Clarksville, TN-KY	161 021	2 133	NA	NA	NA	NA	911	10 315	1 736.0	159.3	192	706	82.2	10.6
Cleveland, TN	66 813	725	102	D	D	D	445	4 469	792.7	70.5	78	312	31.4	5.4
Cleveland-Elyria-Mentor, OH	1 278 449	7 040	4 451	63 745	35 605.2	2 502.0	8 445	118 837	19 784.9	1 960.1	2 067	18 457	2 178.7	389.4
Coeur d'Alene, ID	247 100	1 837	121	1 171	402.9	35.7	545	5 590	1 022.7	100.5	143	379	47.7	6.1
College Station-Bryan, TX	178 200	1 884	167	1 840	643.8	46.9	690	8 835	1 469.6	133.2	195	1 145	82.8	17.6
Colorado Springs, CO	704 299	5 449	513	6 570	1 437.4	215.6	1 973	28 322	5 092.7	512.2	777	3 246	380.6	65.3
Columbia, MO	229 918	2 101	151	1 780	733.1	53.0	643	9 079	1 494.5	137.4	176	651	75.5	11.1
Columbia, SC	679 605	6 439	894	12 518	5 401.2	414.0	2 756	36 239	5 766.1	549.9	575	D	D	D
Columbus, GA-AL	226 443	1 991	245	D	D	D	1 101	13 981	2 246.1	216.0	274	D	D	D
Columbus, IN	43 725	283	114	910	714.3	29.8	397	4 658	680.6	66.1	68	268	37.2	5.8
Columbus, OH	2 307 281	16 423	2 386	D	D	D	5 878	97 091	17 315.4	1 688.6	1 634	11 701	1 226.3	262.5
Corpus Christi, TX	185 031	1 997	551	5 354	1 933.8	162.5	1 576	19 777	3 257.0	307.3	462	2 743	352.6	65.9
Corvallis, OR	65 414	439	63	681	112.6	15.9	294	3 175	473.9	53.2	111	379	38.9	5.5
Cumberland, MD-WV	27 718	217	89	D	D	D	488	5 701	806.2	76.1	68	232	26.3	3.7
Dallas-Fort Worth-Arlington, TX	7 108 546	52 813	10 098	D	D	D	17 038	245 533	49 943.9	4 719.1	5 862	D	D	D
Dallas-Plano-Irving, TX Div	5 106 336	35 649	7 499	D	D	D	11 307	165 431	33 847.7	3 250.0	4 322	D	D	D
Fort Worth-Arlington, TX Div	2 002 210	17 164	2 599	35 056	22 793.0	1 260.1	5 731	80 102	16 096.2	1 469.1	1 540	8 712	1 186.4	203.5
Dalton, GA	85 231	859	373	4 574	4 012.9	133.4	616	6 651	1 235.0	117.3	102	410	64.0	8.6
Danville, IL	7 032	70	102	2 221	1 257.5	68.5	351	4 505	639.2	64.4	63	265	17.6	4.2
Danville, VA	37 468	328	101	D	D	D	547	5 957	886.0	84.8	82	333	29.2	5.3
Davenport-Moline-Rock Island, IA-IL	163 734	1 279	730	9 943	6 032.9	323.0	1 644	23 159	3 719.3	375.2	336	2 169	231.1	48.4
Dayton, OH	544 259	4 109	1 140	16 647	12 501.3	631.4	3 190	51 210	7 989.1	766.0	736	4 137	484.2	88.8
Decatur, AL	47 685	429	199	D	D	D	683	7 147	1 253.1	105.1	104	465	41.3	8.3
Decatur, IL	63 005	526	158	1 815	3 249.3	57.4	506	6 967	1 129.6	110.4	98	515	39.9	8.5
Deltona-Daytona Beach-Ormond Beach, FL	915 622	6 416	488	4 314	1 629.7	105.4	1 865	23 251	3 887.6	360.5	546	2 856	277.6	49.8
Denver-Aurora, CO	2 801 809	17 359	4 589	D	D	D	7 983	112 268	21 245.6	2 183.2	3 306	22 899	3 265.2	592.0
Des Moines, IA	779 461	5 502	1 037	D	D	D	2 041	31 689	5 060.2	515.4	510	3 557	595.3	86.0
Detroit-Warren-Livonia, MI	2 800 831	19 900	7 368	101 743	114 887.6	4 605.2	16 504	234 369	44 777.1	4 272.2	3 924	27 693	4 046.3	698.5
Detroit-Livonia-Dearborn, MI Div	686 927	5 638	2 357	40 193	37 963.4	1 614.4	6 690	85 476	15 852.1	1 483.7	1 256	9 014	1 478.6	225.7
Warren-Farmington Hills-Troy, MI Div	2 113 904	14 262	5 011	61 550	76 924.2	2 990.8	9 814	148 893	28 925.0	2 788.5	2 668	18 679	2 567.7	472.8
Dothan, AL	46 159	455	249	D	D	D	861	9 138	1 481.3	143.0	117	D	D	D
Dover, DE	230 804	2 167	110	D	D	D	594	7 864	1 325.4	128.3	128	506	49.4	8.0
Dubuque, IA	75 481	541	157	1 845	926.5	50.8	525	6 583	935.5	100.2	89	341	32.8	4.9
Duluth, MN-WI	160 285	1 349	364	D	D	D	1 377	15 824	2 452.7	236.8	227	1 126	101.0	17.3
Durham, NC	749 161	5 103	415	5 567	2 962.6	189.6	1 734	21 878	3 346.1	352.2	405	1 852	228.7	41.4
Eau Claire, WI	146 719	1 162	184	2 117	850.9	63.9	664	9 880	1 517.3	140.6	126	543	50.7	7.9
El Centro, CA	138 271	1 201	189	1 951	673.7	41.0	521	5 991	989.4	98.8	86	408	33.2	6.5
Elizabethtown, KY	103 464	957	75	615	138.1	13.3	463	5 725	939.5	87.2	89	251	24.0	3.7
Elkhart-Goshen, IN	145 593	1 175	382	5 031	2 246.1	160.0	751	10 866	1 973.6	179.6	171	884	78.1	13.9
Elmira, NY	18 528	145	107	1 667	447.2	49.2	412	5 963	875.9	82.9	66	345	47.9	7.4
El Paso, TX	307 811	5 271	1 000	11 129	6 089.3	309.6	2 134	28 986	4 698.9	430.5	550	2 458	285.3	48.1
Erie, PA	77 850	769	334	4 069	1 277.8	131.9	1 225	16 323	2 562.1	239.0	180	834	75.5	13.8
Eugene-Springfield, OR	254 145	1 534	535	6 144	2 498.6	179.6	1 462	18 145	3 322.6	328.3	463	2 042	226.5	35.0
Evansville, IN-KY	214 595	1 904	542	D	D	D	1 612	21 528	3 400.9	328.9	324	D	D	D
Fairbanks, AK	39 408	257	75	737	266.0	27.7	359	4 431	927.9	99.5	91	687	79.1	17.3
Fargo, ND-MN	220 943	2 266	433	6 710	3 166.1	200.4	765	12 525	2 127.2	199.1	201	1 194	121.6	18.7
Farmington, NM	44 360	367	158	1 278	381.9	35.7	494	5 896	990.8	96.7	87	495	35.1	15.3
Fayetteville, NC	272 007	2 267	212	2 556	875.6	69.3	1 135	15 415	2 630.8	245.2	283	1 206	138.9	23.7
Fayetteville-Springdale-Rogers, AR-MO	575 975	6 287	463	D	D	D	1 430	16 532	2 590.8	245.2	336	1 242	143.6	20.0
Flagstaff, AZ	147 566	1 189	112	D	D	D	653	7 217	1 081.2	112.1	175	662	75.3	13.0
Flint, MI	310 073	2 240	422	5 884	1 899.4	217.2	1 809	25 369	4 521.3	409.3	350	1 613	193.6	28.7

1. Establishments with payroll.

Table C. Metropolitan Areas — **Professional Services, Manufacturing, and Accommodation and Foodservices**

Area Name	Professional, scientific, and technical services,[1] 1997				Manufacturing, 1997				Accommodation and foodservices, 1997			
	Number of establish-ments	Number of employees	Sales (mil dol)	Annual payroll (mil dol)	Number of establish-ments	Number of employees	Sales (mil dol)	Annual payroll (mil dol)	Number of establish-ments	Number of employees	Sales (mil dol)	Annual payroll (mil dol)
	147	148	149	150	151	152	153	154	155	156	157	158
Charleston-North Charleston, SC.................	1 110	8 539	784.0	314.6	415	20 595	6 588.9	687.5	1 097	24 251	836.2	232.8
Charlotte-Gastonia-Concord, NC-SC.................	3 132	31 509	3 209.0	1 238.8	2 146	115 038	27 829.9	3 525.7	2 450	50 080	1 714.6	465.1
Charlottesville, VA.................	440	2 643	211.6	86.7	NA	NA	NA	NA	359	7 524	269.4	80.9
Chattanooga, TN-GA	782	D	D	D	718	44 986	7 694.5	1 284.2	898	D	D	D
Cheyenne, WY	199	843	64.5	24.7	48	1 349	606.3	45.2	183	3 930	106.3	31.1
Chicago-Naperville-Joliet, IL-IN-WI	25 617	244 101	31 468.9	12 081.2	14 026	656 705	143 834.3	24 591.2	16 496	D	D	D
Chicago-Naperville-Joliet, IL Div	22 233	222 270	29 172.4	11 165.3	12 222	532 229	109 009.7	19 092.4	13 636	244 814	10 234.0	2 758.8
Gary, IN Div..................	1 004	6 759	572.5	198.4	631	52 415	19 107.4	2 442.4	1 275	D	D	D
Lake County-Kenosha County, IL-WI Div........	2 380	15 072	1 724.0	717.5	1 173	72 061	15 717.2	3 056.4	1 585	24 636	909.1	247.4
Chico, CA..........................	308	1 513	130.7	45.0	232	4 944	771.6	128.4	380	5 920	156.2	43.3
Cincinnati-Middletown, OH-KY-IN	4 064	40 060	4 150.2	1 572.7	NA	NA	NA	NA	3 842	D	D	D
Clarksville, TN-KY................	211	D	D	D	NA	NA	NA	NA	368	7 228	197.1	58.0
Cleveland, TN	122	D	D	D	164	14 035	3 003.8	382.1	156	2 693	86.6	23.0
Cleveland-Elyria-Mentor, OH	5 276	46 861	4 894.9	1 984.4	4 457	189 878	42 393.7	7 241.1	4 377	78 476	2 495.6	668.6
Coeur d'Alene, ID	245	1 121	81.8	32.8	195	4 472	592.1	116.9	298	4 086	137.7	37.9
College Station-Bryan, TX	299	2 149	203.9	75.5	NA	NA	NA	NA	318	6 113	182.8	51.9
Colorado Springs, CO	1 434	10 670	1 215.6	472.2	NA	NA	NA	NA	1 066	23 328	866.7	242.9
Columbia, MO	280	1 607	113.6	39.5	NA	NA	NA	NA	324	6 135	183.0	49.2
Columbia, SC.......................	1 360	9 841	1 083.2	378.1	574	34 051	8 414.0	1 086.4	1 159	D	D	D
Columbus, GA-AL	327	D	D	D	NA	NA	NA	NA	478	D	D	D
Columbus, IN	152	777	58.5	24.7	145	13 311	3 096.7	412.1	135	3 114	102.4	28.4
Columbus, OH	3 610	35 282	3 852.7	1 406.1	1 644	87 503	25 986.5	3 171.1	3 170	63 217	2 085.0	602.8
Corpus Christi, TX	768	5 111	453.1	170.9	NA	NA	NA	NA	911	14 706	475.3	126.7
Corvallis, OR	210	1 367	116.7	50.1	106	8 547	1 391.9	494.5	205	2 807	85.9	24.0
Cumberland, MD-WV...........	114	581	28.6	14.6	83	5 307	922.2	179.6	213	2 920	88.7	23.2
Dallas-Fort Worth-Arlington, TX....................................	13 340	123 634	14 609.9	5 999.4	NA	NA	NA	NA	8 222	D	D	D
Dallas-Plano-Irving, TX Div	10 122	102 942	12 596.9	5 230.1	NA	NA	NA	NA	5 612	D	D	D
Fort Worth-Arlington, TX Div	3 218	20 692	2 013.0	769.3	2 334	105 790	20 094.1	3 845.8	2 610	53 811	1 946.6	533.9
Dalton, GA	163	996	68.3	31.1	479	32 694	7 368.4	809.3	182	3 058	112.0	30.5
Danville, IL	94	331	27.9	8.6	104	7 055	1 696.1	228.9	185	2 570	68.5	20.0
Danville, VA	102	759	31.4	12.8	106	D	D	D	170	2 767	85.4	24.4
Davenport-Moline-Rock Island, IA-IL	619	4 337	355.0	134.7	NA	NA	NA	NA	898	15 354	434.1	124.5
Dayton, OH	1 711	18 587	1 904.6	692.9	1 394	78 373	19 782.5	3 067.6	1 622	32 071	988.3	279.2
Decatur, AL	193	984	74.4	28.9	243	D	D	D	218	4 276	114.6	32.6
Decatur, IL	156	1 101	90.0	36.1	134	11 616	6 114.2	479.4	233	4 105	123.6	35.7
Deltona-Daytona Beach-Ormond Beach, FL	844	4 048	346.4	120.7	392	10 216	1 212.6	263.2	1 051	19 758	635.6	167.0
Denver-Aurora, CO	8 172	63 734	7 537.2	2 986.6	NA	NA	NA	NA	4 241	86 195	3 094.7	878.7
Des Moines, IA	1 057	10 960	866.0	352.9	NA	NA	NA	NA	1 061	18 785	576.4	167.8
Detroit-Warren-Livonia, MI	9 901	105 568	11 313.5	4 818.6	7 569	348 575	111 823.3	15 544.9	7 710	140 982	4 794.7	1 319.9
Detroit-Livonia-Dearborn, MI Div..............................	2 512	29 950	3 133.0	1 233.0	2 390	133 703	54 375.0	6 514.3	3 313	58 336	2 023.7	542.5
Warren-Farmington Hills-Troy, MI Div	7 389	75 618	8 180.5	3 585.6	5 179	214 872	57 448.3	9 030.6	4 397	82 646	2 771.0	777.4
Dothan, AL	204	1 264	78.2	28.5	169	12 766	2 011.3	299.9	241	D	D	D
Dover, DE	155	1 091	69.4	30.3	82	7 985	1 965.5	209.8	234	3 796	118.4	31.9
Dubuque, IA	117	802	56.4	23.5	133	10 687	3 074.9	386.9	233	3 838	94.7	27.4
Duluth, MN-WI	403	2 636	176.5	77.9	314	9 120	1 804.6	291.0	843	11 236	364.1	92.8
Durham, NC	1 060	9 963	1 289.2	440.6	374	44 945	13 465.0	1 354.9	847	D	D	D
Eau Claire, WI	219	1 715	129.2	55.6	219	10 624	1 641.1	314.6	379	6 254	150.2	43.1
El Centro, CA.......................	113	519	46.2	15.8	61	1 481	241.6	40.6	238	2 723	89.3	23.0
Elizabethtown, KY.................	125	539	36.3	13.8	80	7 803	1 659.2	226.9	151	D	D	D
Elkhart-Goshen, IN	246	1 465	111.6	36.0	894	56 087	8 999.9	1 610.8	354	6 202	189.4	51.7
Elmira, NY	104	827	56.5	18.3	94	9 098	1 357.3	278.1	213	2 965	86.2	24.4
El Paso, TX	927	5 777	398.1	161.7	652	36 723	7 966.5	773.9	1 094	19 292	703.3	194.0
Erie, PA	379	2 330	177.7	62.4	570	32 813	5 779.3	1 142.3	614	9 599	265.2	73.3
Eugene-Springfield, OR	797	4 682	374.3	138.8	624	19 262	3 881.8	589.8	809	12 022	387.8	110.5
Evansville, IN-KY	626	4 600	320.6	124.1	494	D	D	D	687	D	D	D
Fairbanks, AK	167	784	70.5	28.1	NA	NA	NA	NA	184	2 488	112.1	29.4
Fargo, ND-MN.....................	328	2 625	189.0	75.5	221	7 982	1 741.6	209.2	401	8 799	235.7	66.6
Farmington, NM	166	919	50.9	19.9	71	1 147	257.8	30.3	173	3 478	100.0	27.3
Fayetteville, NC	342	2 114	144.0	48.2	132	15 433	3 181.7	457.4	514	10 843	323.8	92.5
Fayetteville-Springdale-Rogers, AR-MO	609	2 929	281.8	91.5	440	32 805	5 521.2	768.9	645	10 063	291.6	80.4
Flagstaff, AZ........................	181	777	58.8	21.6	95	D	D	D	477	9 409	407.7	105.8
Flint, MI	660	4 149	274.3	125.2	355	34 414	11 240.3	1 744.6	794	13 618	403.9	111.2

1. Firms subject to federal tax.

Area Name	Health care and social assistance,[1] 1997				Other services,[1] 1997				Federal funds and grants, 2002–2003 Expenditures (mil dol)			
									Total	Direct payments for individuals		
	Number of establishments	Number of employees	Receipts (mil dol)	Annual payroll (mil dol)	Number of establishments	Number of employees	Receipts (mil dol)	Annual payroll (mil dol)		Social Security and government retirement	Medicare	Food stamps and Supplemental Security Income
	159	160	161	162	163	164	165	166	167	168	169	170
Charleston-North Charleston, SC	1 050	12 478	812.1	329.6	863	5 636	321.0	102.9	4 368.1	1 437.2	397.3	124.0
Charlotte-Gastonia-Concord, NC-SC	2 003	28 834	2 066.1	929.4	2 215	14 923	961.8	300.1	5 579.9	2 381.8	869.6	191.2
Charlottesville, VA	320	3 859	232.5	96.4	271	1 548	85.9	29.4	1 106.4	395.8	139.1	18.0
Chattanooga, TN-GA	924	13 083	957.3	426.0	701	4 513	268.7	81.2	3 473.7	1 178.5	542.6	112.1
Cheyenne, WY	153	1 576	105.7	51.0	127	1 122	165.2	24.3	994.4	245.7	57.2	9.6
Chicago-Naperville-Joliet, IL-IN-WI	16 260	179 799	12 997.6	5 688.0	13 520	93 235	6 691.5	2 054.4	46 091.1	15 219.1	8 672.2	1 890.7
Chicago-Naperville-Joliet, IL Div	13 472	151 952	11 095.9	4 810.5	11 293	78 544	5 690.5	1 742.8	38 760.4	12 402.3	7 452.9	1 676.0
Gary, IN Div	1 315	13 167	868.5	396.9	1 030	7 567	464.0	151.4	3 448.3	1 489.3	725.7	153.5
Lake County-Kenosha County, IL-WI Div	1 473	14 680	1 033.2	480.6	1 197	7 124	537.0	160.2	3 882.3	1 327.4	493.6	61.2
Chico, CA	553	5 261	299.4	114.3	261	1 454	147.1	25.3	1 190.7	502.8	256.5	55.0
Cincinnati-Middletown, OH-KY-IN	3 407	D	D	D	3 029	20 649	1 307.6	412.3	11 587.1	3 890.3	1 756.9	341.3
Clarksville, TN-KY	274	3 683	199.5	84.9	275	1 203	66.9	17.9	2 494.5	566.1	142.1	48.4
Cleveland, TN	219	10 426	448.4	203.2	111	1 341	71.7	26.6	493.8	232.1	104.7	22.2
Cleveland-Elyria-Mentor, OH	4 338	51 455	3 203.1	1 524.5	3 733	26 240	1 884.4	525.0	12 708.0	4 653.9	2 649.8	467.6
Coeur d'Alene, ID	267	2 561	137.1	55.6	176	836	47.5	12.9	607.8	283.4	71.2	14.1
College Station-Bryan, TX	287	3 248	227.5	91.4	233	1 371	72.7	20.2	2 029.2	269.1	96.4	25.3
Colorado Springs, CO	1 160	10 647	715.9	313.3	782	4 628	270.4	90.8	5 294.3	1 426.2	285.2	56.5
Columbia, MO	344	4 322	329.8	133.4	240	1 293	68.5	20.8	769.9	253.6	109.9	22.8
Columbia, SC	1 065	14 024	978.3	448.4	983	6 365	369.8	111.3	4 843.8	1 591.5	419.1	122.0
Columbus, GA-AL	398	D	D	D	401	D	D	D	2 562.4	778.8	226.5	83.5
Columbus, IN	142	1 633	106.6	57.3	101	703	39.4	13.8	369.7	151.1	58.1	8.7
Columbus, OH	2 895	37 992	2 377.8	1 178.0	2 162	15 881	955.3	306.2	10 399.2	2 973.5	1 134.8	267.8
Corpus Christi, TX	959	16 426	869.2	387.9	632	3 974	233.0	71.1	2 722.5	842.7	390.5	107.2
Corvallis, OR	148	1 994	140.5	52.6	88	461	26.3	7.9	393.4	135.8	38.7	8.2
Cumberland, MD-WV	207	1 896	126.8	58.0	173	918	46.3	13.7	713.2	291.3	172.1	19.9
Dallas-Fort Worth-Arlington, TX	10 191	131 811	9 902.5	4 062.3	7 371	D	D	D	32 528.1	7 596.3	3 283.3	628.7
Dallas-Plano-Irving, TX Div	7 057	92 671	7 368.5	2 955.5	4 930	D	D	D	16 046.8	4 737.4	2 153.5	432.5
Fort Worth-Arlington, TX Div	3 134	39 140	2 534.0	1 106.8	2 441	16 072	1 038.5	320.1	16 481.3	2 858.9	1 129.9	196.2
Dalton, GA	146	1 690	131.3	58.3	137	731	51.3	16.0	436.0	208.2	88.7	17.8
Danville, IL	103	1 343	83.4	38.6	133	627	33.3	9.9	529.3	230.6	91.1	22.6
Danville, VA	172	1 931	120.4	55.8	204	1 028	50.2	14.2	611.4	271.6	107.7	22.3
Davenport-Moline-Rock Island, IA-IL	679	6 730	450.9	208.1	656	4 163	253.1	74.7	2 115.3	918.6	325.2	64.5
Dayton, OH	1 569	20 455	1 277.4	613.0	1 342	12 299	626.5	226.2	6 883.7	2 077.2	799.9	139.6
Decatur, AL	262	3 263	197.6	92.1	197	1 417	74.4	23.5	742.6	338.4	134.3	29.2
Decatur, IL	204	2 546	155.6	70.3	189	1 456	86.0	28.7	599.4	278.9	114.2	28.0
Deltona-Daytona Beach-Ormond Beach, FL	906	10 079	596.8	253.3	707	3 094	163.6	47.8	2 878.2	1 465.3	679.7	69.4
Denver-Aurora, CO	4 358	D	D	D	3 551	D	D	D	12 713.9	3 619.3	1 395.4	224.9
Des Moines, IA	910	10 726	705.5	346.4	809	5 023	319.1	95.8	2 986.2	1 006.8	354.0	57.9
Detroit-Warren-Livonia, MI	8 953	91 064	5 907.7	2 852.5	6 641	48 135	3 314.1	1 045.9	24 589.7	8 864.3	5 343.1	987.9
Detroit-Livonia-Dearborn, MI Div	3 115	35 576	2 186.2	1 040.1	2 621	20 451	1 407.6	440.8	13 268.4	4 137.1	2 913.7	767.0
Warren-Farmington Hills-Troy, MI Div	5 838	55 488	3 721.5	1 812.4	4 020	27 684	1 906.5	605.1	11 321.3	4 727.2	2 429.4	220.9
Dothan, AL	259	4 859	387.3	176.6	228	1 162	65.3	19.4	879.3	358.7	133.9	36.3
Dover, DE	192	2 157	137.6	59.6	215	1 016	56.0	16.8	1 158.7	359.0	86.2	22.0
Dubuque, IA	124	2 376	185.8	89.3	172	889	51.2	14.9	438.3	199.4	82.4	8.9
Duluth, MN-WI	468	6 344	290.1	149.0	438	2 314	154.9	44.0	1 785.9	731.7	265.7	49.2
Durham, NC	689	9 208	503.1	237.0	586	3 309	184.5	62.7	3 391.3	762.6	301.8	59.1
Eau Claire, WI	257	4 182	242.1	133.3	279	1 525	84.3	24.3	701.9	298.5	111.7	17.7
El Centro, CA	172	1 665	103.7	40.8	107	506	34.5	9.4	765.9	210.3	123.2	41.9
Elizabethtown, KY	200	2 405	158.3	72.9	147	859	45.9	14.8	1 013.4	332.6	75.0	23.2
Elkhart-Goshen, IN	233	3 281	187.7	78.0	345	2 427	164.1	47.3	594.4	318.4	109.1	21.1
Elmira, NY	162	1 675	123.1	60.7	108	553	36.1	9.8	539.2	228.8	92.2	19.3
El Paso, TX	984	16 524	1 165.3	455.8	824	5 779	265.7	87.6	4 317.6	1 203.5	469.7	216.6
Erie, PA	560	5 498	423.4	190.6	476	2 174	135.0	39.6	1 512.9	625.8	299.4	64.5
Eugene-Springfield, OR	751	7 176	492.8	217.7	473	3 210	194.0	57.1	1 741.0	758.5	247.0	75.8
Evansville, IN-KY	651	10 487	633.1	291.4	552	4 087	246.8	76.8	1 888.2	785.8	350.0	63.6
Fairbanks, AK	146	1 007	96.4	45.9	129	658	52.2	14.6	1 142.2	126.7	27.4	9.7
Fargo, ND-MN	300	6 435	499.1	203.1	337	2 358	133.4	41.0	901.8	311.0	97.2	19.0
Farmington, NM	169	1 379	85.8	39.6	176	1 076	66.4	18.7	575.5	193.4	60.4	26.1
Fayetteville, NC	430	6 437	377.3	164.5	419	2 682	148.6	45.8	4 296.1	903.0	158.6	81.0
Fayetteville-Springdale-Rogers, AR-MO	522	5 418	323.0	156.0	451	2 677	149.9	46.3	1 396.0	731.6	220.2	42.0
Flagstaff, AZ	240	1 627	107.5	45.8	183	899	54.7	14.2	799.3	225.7	62.6	29.0
Flint, MI	1 037	9 466	610.5	310.7	627	4 165	255.2	74.4	2 292.2	940.7	510.5	128.4

1. Firms subject to federal tax.

Table C. Metropolitan Areas — Federal Funds and Local Government Finances

Area Name	Federal funds and grants, 2002–2003 (cont'd) — Expenditures (mil dol) (cont'd)							Local government finances, 2002 — General revenue				
	Procurement contract awards			Grants						Taxes		
	Salaries and wages	Defense	Other	Medicaid and other health-related	Nutrition and family welfare	Education	Other	Total (mil dol)	Intergovern-mental (mil dol)	Total (mil dol)	Per capita[1] (dollars) Total	Property
	171	172	173	174	175	176	177	178	179	180	181	182
Charleston-North Charleston, SC	847.0	662.9	142.3	437.1	58.2	44.9	169.4	1 467.8	560.0	579.8	1 030	797
Charlotte-Gastonia-Concord, NC-SC	433.2	74.1	557.9	491.5	126.6	88.7	265.6	5 327.6	1 621.7	1 670.2	1 184	930
Charlottesville, VA	93.6	30.3	38.6	231.0	12.3	14.3	121.9	424.5	169.5	199.8	1 117	741
Chattanooga, TN-GA	526.9	15.6	532.6	330.0	63.6	40.5	84.3	1 611.8	409.6	445.0	922	626
Cheyenne, WY	262.2	42.6	24.1	76.9	36.2	50.2	176.3	331.0	144.0	68.5	826	424
Chicago-Naperville-Joliet, IL-IN-WI	4 749.6	1 594.7	2 624.0	5 421.0	1 206.5	395.8	3 004.8	34 269.7	11 123.2	16 366.8	1 762	1 438
Chicago-Naperville-Joliet, IL Div	3 562.4	1 249.5	2 480.1	4 785.2	1 043.6	346.0	2 672.6	28 843.1	9 377.8	13 950.5	1 794	1 426
Gary, IN Div	139.1	48.4	38.9	457.5	111.3	21.0	211.5	2 424.8	824.9	852.1	1 248	1 178
Lake County-Kenosha County, IL-WI Div	1 048.1	296.8	104.9	178.3	51.6	28.8	120.8	3 001.9	920.4	1 564.3	1 886	1 762
Chico, CA	31.2	0.4	27.2	151.0	44.5	18.8	47.1	787.5	493.5	150.3	718	521
Cincinnati-Middletown, OH-KY-IN	1 036.2	1 421.5	692.5	1 336.5	257.7	114.3	570.1	6 659.4	2 373.5	2 805.5	1 375	939
Clarksville, TN-KY	1 141.3	303.1	48.4	113.9	22.8	16.8	52.6	417.5	191.6	152.5	649	381
Cleveland, TN	19.6	0.0	6.8	67.4	9.7	7.2	13.5	235.2	77.8	55.5	524	372
Cleveland-Elyria-Mentor, OH	1 232.2	315.0	481.4	1 643.9	362.8	162.0	554.6	9 143.3	3 278.9	4 004.5	1 864	1 181
Coeur d'Alene, ID	36.2	17.4	50.6	50.5	7.3	2.6	66.9	479.5	116.1	89.3	784	737
College Station-Bryan, TX	68.0	20.2	26.3	161.4	16.4	12.0	1 289.7	419.0	114.6	217.3	1 150	914
Colorado Springs, CO	1 422.2	1 517.8	217.6	129.8	51.3	44.9	103.9	1 719.8	549.4	579.3	1 025	612
Columbia, MO	113.7	12.5	16.0	103.0	12.1	20.3	76.3	361.9	123.2	149.9	1 003	606
Columbia, SC	829.4	249.8	117.1	470.7	188.7	228.6	532.2	1 777.7	656.7	632.9	953	867
Columbus, GA-AL	902.8	204.4	18.1	191.9	49.3	25.5	42.7	692.1	348.4	235.5	832	541
Columbus, IN	21.5	32.0	4.0	39.0	9.0	1.1	37.9	298.9	67.7	75.7	1 057	877
Columbus, OH	900.8	689.7	284.1	1 230.4	867.8	531.8	1 346.0	6 179.1	2 227.6	2 776.9	1 673	1 053
Corpus Christi, TX	426.8	277.0	33.2	323.9	70.3	25.2	166.1	1 155.3	407.4	503.9	1 244	1 010
Corvallis, OR	42.2	4.4	10.3	41.5	6.0	6.2	83.4	202.6	95.2	68.5	872	782
Cumberland, MD-WV	42.9	19.7	14.5	85.3	15.8	8.3	31.3	260.8	137.9	75.9	750	507
Dallas-Fort Worth-Arlington, TX	2 993.7	12 662.9	1 650.7	1 722.0	311.6	169.7	1 245.5	16 714.4	3 477.1	9 329.0	1 701	1 346
Dallas-Plano-Irving, TX Div	1 950.0	2 691.6	1 385.1	1 234.4	226.7	113.1	965.3	11 568.9	2 122.1	6 626.2	1 804	1 422
Fort Worth-Arlington, TX Div	1 043.7	9 971.3	265.6	487.6	84.9	56.6	280.3	5 145.5	1 355.0	2 702.8	1 492	1 192
Dalton, GA	16.5	4.2	9.5	49.3	8.9	9.1	18.8	405.8	163.0	136.8	1 089	631
Danville, IL	64.3	1.8	8.2	45.1	13.9	4.0	32.5	228.2	119.0	64.3	774	681
Danville, VA	17.9	22.8	12.3	93.8	15.7	11.6	24.6	244.5	131.8	67.6	618	393
Davenport-Moline-Rock Island, IA-IL	283.5	131.2	35.5	141.2	49.0	19.4	82.2	1 138.3	466.4	420.9	1 122	951
Dayton, OH	1 270.3	1 194.3	389.2	512.7	127.2	69.5	206.1	3 063.9	1 163.6	1 211.1	1 430	914
Decatur, AL	106.4	-9.7	6.5	82.4	16.0	10.7	15.6	426.5	151.2	82.5	564	321
Decatur, IL	26.3	0.3	21.5	62.5	14.2	5.1	27.4	327.5	134.9	106.3	949	833
Deltona-Daytona Beach-Ormond Beach, FL	93.8	111.5	30.4	133.1	32.6	28.7	195.3	1 475.6	402.7	469.9	1 023	830
Denver-Aurora, CO	2 066.1	712.4	1 845.0	1 069.7	387.2	265.7	935.7	8 798.5	2 166.6	3 877.2	1 700	952
Des Moines, IA	364.9	54.7	75.7	300.7	158.9	118.1	408.7	1 662.1	580.6	666.0	1 339	1 169
Detroit-Warren-Livonia, MI	1 797.7	1 719.8	807.6	2 687.4	801.3	317.9	1 082.9	16 770.8	8 803.1	4 768.1	1 063	920
Detroit-Livonia-Dearborn, MI Div	1 042.7	55.4	568.2	2 044.8	630.4	198.9	794.7	9 102.1	5 083.5	2 250.0	1 100	833
Warren-Farmington Hills-Troy, MI Div	755.1	1 664.4	239.4	642.5	171.0	119.0	288.2	7 668.6	3 719.7	2 518.1	1 033	992
Dothan, AL	27.8	43.2	15.3	97.3	16.0	11.4	26.6	491.4	164.7	78.1	593	207
Dover, DE	250.0	125.4	8.3	83.0	13.0	66.9	124.8	313.3	209.7	51.1	390	357
Dubuque, IA	18.9	4.1	3.8	48.4	10.0	2.0	39.8	234.8	96.8	85.9	961	793
Duluth, MN-WI	164.5	16.8	34.9	272.8	69.4	25.8	122.4	1 197.9	585.7	262.0	948	861
Durham, NC	329.2	85.0	355.9	1 041.4	45.8	62.1	298.5	1 220.3	513.4	492.0	1 105	899
Eau Claire, WI	37.1	12.7	9.2	103.1	19.8	10.4	44.0	495.9	262.6	161.8	1 076	1 020
El Centro, CA	82.3	19.3	21.4	115.0	40.9	28.0	64.1	844.1	474.3	103.9	710	521
Elizabethtown, KY	479.1	7.1	8.1	43.2	10.0	6.1	20.6	275.7	95.1	49.8	456	273
Elkhart-Goshen, IN	18.3	11.7	7.0	59.7	9.7	3.9	26.7	466.6	185.0	204.3	1 095	928
Elmira, NY	25.9	4.4	6.1	94.9	17.8	6.0	38.1	333.9	168.0	109.7	1 210	797
El Paso, TX	744.3	643.3	125.2	473.6	110.7	63.9	143.0	2 086.8	1 013.5	639.8	917	721
Erie, PA	93.4	29.4	22.5	161.9	47.4	12.9	122.3	763.7	375.9	250.4	893	716
Eugene-Springfield, OR	112.0	16.7	47.7	254.2	53.2	41.9	97.7	1 081.6	520.8	301.5	923	793
Evansville, IN-KY	83.3	183.3	11.4	209.6	36.9	10.5	110.0	853.3	303.2	347.4	1 010	846
Fairbanks, AK	402.7	283.0	34.3	104.7	23.9	25.0	94.3	241.4	135.7	81.5	959	865
Fargo, ND-MN	144.6	11.3	23.2	79.2	19.5	7.7	131.0	535.0	208.3	179.8	1 015	866
Farmington, NM	79.3	1.2	15.5	99.2	15.7	37.5	27.7	414.1	228.8	85.4	710	390
Fayetteville, NC	2 166.7	555.4	45.2	183.9	57.1	34.5	59.3	1 096.5	427.0	223.4	658	506
Fayetteville-Springdale-Rogers, AR-MO	103.7	22.2	29.7	104.1	19.9	19.8	77.5	722.8	373.5	191.1	519	180
Flagstaff, AZ	141.2	4.7	33.3	140.1	26.7	46.4	64.7	381.0	180.2	132.6	1 102	703
Flint, MI	92.6	0.4	27.2	283.2	106.8	41.4	96.3	1 332.5	824.1	232.4	526	510

1. Based on the resident population estimated as of July 1 of the year shown.

Table C. Metropolitan Areas — Local Government Finances, Government Employment, and Elections

Area Name	Local government finances, 2002 (cont'd)									Government employment, 2002			Presidential election, 2004		
	Direct general expenditure							Debt outstanding					Percent of vote cast —		
			Percent of total for —												
	Total (mil dol)	Per capita[1] (dollars)	Education	Health and hospitals	Police protection	Public welfare	Highways	Total (mil dol)	Per capita[1] (dollars)	Federal civilian	Federal military	State and local	Democratic	Republican	All other
	183	184	185	186	187	188	189	190	191	192	193	194	195	196	197
Charleston-North Charleston, SC	1 514.5	2 692	51.7	2.0	6.1	0.3	2.3	1 987.6	3 532	7 798	12 603	45 293	42.7	55.7	1.6
Charlotte-Gastonia-Concord, NC-SC	5 312.5	3 767	34.7	25.1	4.7	5.1	2.4	5 611.1	3 979	6 274	2 896	89 033	43.6	56.0	0.4
Charlottesville, VA	431.3	2 410	55.0	2.1	4.9	5.9	1.3	317.6	1 775	1 442	720	27 705	51.6	47.6	0.8
Chattanooga, TN-GA	1 517.8	3 145	31.7	29.8	5.2	1.6	3.1	1 340.7	2 778	6 698	1 495	29 405	38.6	60.7	0.7
Cheyenne, WY	318.3	3 840	44.0	25.3	3.5	0.6	6.4	119.8	1 446	2 395	3 804	9 668	33.1	65.2	1.7
Chicago-Naperville-Joliet, IL-IN-WI	35 681.8	3 842	42.4	4.2	6.8	1.3	5.3	42 511.5	4 578	61 691	39 873	506 197	60.4	39.0	0.6
Chicago-Naperville-Joliet, IL Div	30 215.2	3 887	41.3	4.1	7.2	0.9	5.6	38 103.8	4 901	53 589	14 737	427 125	61.4	38.0	0.6
Gary, IN Div	2 413.5	3 536	40.7	7.2	4.4	5.4	3.0	1 614.7	2 366	2 190	1 824	37 644	44.9	54.0	1.1
Lake County-Kenosha County, IL-WI Div	3 053.0	3 682	55.0	2.2	5.2	2.0	4.1	2 793.0	3 368	5 912	23 312	41 428	50.7	48.5	0.8
Chico, CA	797.8	3 814	46.6	6.2	3.7	13.6	2.9	229.5	1 097	534	298	15 051	44.4	54.0	1.6
Cincinnati-Middletown, OH-KY-IN	6 709.0	3 288	39.9	6.4	6.0	5.1	4.0	8 256.4	4 046	17 827	4 302	114 345	37.9	61.6	0.5
Clarksville, TN-KY	453.3	1 930	50.5	1.9	5.4	1.0	4.9	598.4	2 548	5 305	25 834	12 380	39.1	60.3	0.6
Cleveland, TN	239.1	2 260	43.5	28.1	4.6	0.0	3.8	173.8	1 643	337	345	5 527	28.7	70.6	0.7
Cleveland-Elyria-Mentor, OH	9 080.1	4 228	39.4	10.4	5.6	5.8	3.6	8 853.0	4 122	18 054	5 589	126 523	59.8	39.7	0.5
Coeur d'Alene, ID	399.0	3 501	37.8	32.2	3.5	0.5	4.6	105.2	924	660	410	7 815	32.3	66.4	1.3
College Station-Bryan, TX	427.4	2 261	44.0	3.3	5.9	0.6	8.0	414.0	2 190	1 078	464	30 189	31.6	67.7	0.8
Colorado Springs, CO	1 779.0	3 146	40.2	17.6	6.0	2.1	6.7	2 024.5	3 581	10 038	29 313	31 302	31.9	66.9	1.2
Columbia, MO	371.4	2 485	51.7	2.6	4.7	1.3	7.2	351.5	2 351	1 956	485	28 841	49.1	50.3	0.6
Columbia, SC	1 828.1	2 752	52.6	15.8	4.5	0.0	0.6	1 436.5	2 163	8 474	13 138	67 998	44.6	54.4	1.0
Columbus, GA-AL	723.8	2 556	53.1	5.6	6.4	0.1	3.2	503.8	1 779	5 330	20 851	16 646	47.9	51.7	0.4
Columbus, IN	303.3	4 234	32.8	39.5	2.1	2.0	2.6	152.4	2 128	247	191	5 162	32.3	67.0	0.7
Columbus, OH	6 308.5	3 801	40.4	7.9	5.6	5.6	4.4	6 215.8	3 745	13 361	4 478	142 674	47.0	52.5	0.5
Corpus Christi, TX	1 124.1	2 775	56.2	6.4	5.5	0.4	3.2	1 113.5	2 749	5 754	6 418	26 008	40.7	58.9	0.4
Corvallis, OR	229.2	2 916	36.1	7.0	7.1	1.6	4.8	125.3	1 594	685	282	11 432	58.2	40.6	1.1
Cumberland, MD-WV	256.7	2 534	56.4	0.6	3.0	3.7	5.6	144.5	1 426	656	290	7 168	33.9	65.2	0.9
Dallas-Fort Worth-Arlington, TX	17 378.8	3 169	49.2	8.1	5.4	0.2	3.6	26 540.0	4 839	43 872	13 308	288 333	37.9	61.6	0.5
Dallas-Plano-Irving, TX Div	12 205.7	3 323	48.1	7.8	5.1	0.2	3.4	17 561.4	4 781	29 793	8 621	197 943	39.5	60.0	0.5
Fort Worth-Arlington, TX Div	5 173.1	2 856	51.6	8.8	6.1	0.2	4.0	8 978.6	4 957	14 079	4 687	90 390	34.9	64.6	0.5
Dalton, GA	404.0	3 217	49.4	14.0	3.1	0.3	4.9	429.7	3 422	292	299	6 731	26.5	73.0	0.5
Danville, IL	237.7	2 859	57.8	1.5	5.5	2.7	5.8	72.5	872	1 485	153	4 785	43.7	55.6	0.7
Danville, VA	246.1	2 251	46.7	4.1	5.6	5.7	3.4	261.8	2 394	266	287	6 242	40.3	58.1	1.6
Davenport-Moline-Rock Island, IA-IL	1 168.0	3 113	51.6	4.7	4.6	1.5	6.5	721.1	1 922	6 315	1 177	21 117	52.6	46.7	0.6
Dayton, OH	2 928.8	3 459	41.3	3.7	7.0	7.6	5.1	2 181.4	2 576	17 134	7 718	48 272	45.5	54.1	0.4
Decatur, AL	441.8	3 018	41.3	23.3	3.7	0.4	4.0	581.8	3 975	383	643	8 609	33.3	65.9	0.8
Decatur, IL	302.2	2 698	44.9	2.6	6.0	1.0	6.3	175.3	1 565	356	215	6 298	45.1	54.4	0.5
Deltona-Daytona Beach-Ormond Beach, FL	1 512.4	3 292	34.9	21.8	6.5	0.7	4.5	1 254.8	2 731	1 321	722	20 183	50.5	48.9	0.7
Denver-Aurora, CO	9 370.7	4 109	33.2	5.4	6.1	3.1	12.4	13 910.1	6 099	28 787	6 479	141 030	50.3	48.5	1.2
Des Moines, IA	1 723.5	3 466	46.7	9.4	4.4	1.2	5.4	1 488.9	2 994	5 485	2 322	33 027	49.9	49.4	0.7
Detroit-Warren-Livonia, MI	18 270.7	4 075	44.9	6.8	5.6	1.5	5.2	17 031.7	3 798	28 708	8 700	214 334	56.6	42.5	0.9
Detroit-Livonia-Dearborn, MI Div	10 348.5	5 059	38.0	7.3	5.7	2.0	4.6	10 316.2	5 043	16 294	3 978	109 689	69.3	29.9	0.8
Warren-Farmington Hills-Troy, MI Div	7 922.3	3 249	53.9	6.1	5.5	0.8	6.0	6 715.5	2 754	12 414	4 722	104 645	47.9	51.2	1.0
Dothan, AL	533.4	4 053	28.5	40.0	3.6	1.0	4.5	417.6	3 173	473	579	9 500	25.3	74.2	0.5
Dover, DE	315.7	2 409	75.8	0.8	4.3	0.0	1.2	160.7	1 226	1 683	4 775	14 117	42.6	56.4	0.9
Dubuque, IA	235.6	2 636	39.3	5.5	5.5	4.0	9.4	66.9	749	276	382	3 684	56.4	42.8	0.7
Duluth, MN-WI	1 178.2	4 264	35.1	7.3	4.2	10.0	9.0	952.9	3 449	2 167	1 039	24 547	65.0	33.9	1.1
Durham, NC	1 211.8	2 722	43.7	7.0	6.1	7.5	1.7	1 031.8	2 318	5 107	909	46 470	63.5	36.1	0.4
Eau Claire, WI	523.0	3 480	50.8	6.5	5.8	4.1	11.0	339.0	2 256	598	408	11 082	52.2	46.7	1.1
El Centro, CA	859.0	5 874	42.7	17.1	3.3	8.0	3.2	508.6	3 478	1 845	479	13 906	53.9	44.9	1.2
Elizabethtown, KY	279.3	2 560	36.2	40.6	2.4	0.2	2.6	228.7	2 096	4 448	9 967	6 825	31.4	67.8	0.8
Elkhart-Goshen, IN	481.9	2 584	53.9	0.9	5.2	4.1	3.5	396.6	2 127	295	499	7 485	29.3	70.1	0.6
Elmira, NY	367.7	4 058	46.7	2.3	3.0	18.5	7.0	230.6	2 544	434	138	6 818	43.3	54.2	2.5
El Paso, TX	2 124.7	3 046	57.0	12.0	5.1	0.1	1.1	1 755.4	2 516	8 445	12 179	48 528	56.2	43.3	0.5
Erie, PA	782.7	2 792	44.3	0.7	2.6	18.1	3.0	1 188.5	4 239	1 416	811	15 403	53.8	45.7	0.5
Eugene-Springfield, OR	1 105.1	3 383	46.6	4.5	5.8	3.5	6.2	844.0	2 584	1 879	957	23 798	58.3	40.8	1.0
Evansville, IN-KY	854.8	2 485	43.0	1.1	5.5	2.5	3.8	1 087.0	3 160	1 384	831	16 339	39.1	60.3	0.6
Fairbanks, AK	238.9	2 809	56.9	0.4	5.5	0.0	2.8	143.4	1 686	3 198	8 270	7 567	NA	NA	NA
Fargo, ND-MN	567.0	3 202	37.4	1.2	3.9	4.9	7.4	684.4	3 865	2 198	1 060	12 943	41.3	57.2	1.5
Farmington, NM	431.8	3 587	56.0	0.2	3.8	1.3	4.6	1 050.0	8 723	1 571	326	9 707	32.9	65.7	1.4
Fayetteville, NC	1 107.1	3 262	39.5	32.6	4.8	5.5	1.2	674.7	1 988	9 954	47 877	23 074	48.3	51.4	0.3
Fayetteville-Springdale-Rogers, AR-MO	677.0	1 839	56.1	3.1	6.8	0.1	5.7	528.2	1 435	1 793	1 620	20 457	36.2	62.6	1.2
Flagstaff, AZ	376.9	3 133	42.4	2.9	6.5	2.0	7.5	428.8	3 564	3 322	226	12 620	55.8	43.4	0.7
Flint, MI	1 364.2	3 090	58.8	8.6	2.8	1.0	3.5	603.3	1 367	1 454	761	24 332	60.0	39.2	0.7

1. Based on the resident population estimated as of July 1 of the year shown.

Table C. Metropolitan Areas — Land Area and Population

CBSA/ DIV code[1]	Area Name	Land area,[2] 2000 (sq km)	Total persons	Rank	Per square kilometer	White	Black	Am. Indian, Alaska Native	Asian and Pacific Islander	Percent Hispanic or Latino[3]	Under 5 years	5 to 17 years	18 to 24 years	25 to 34 years	35 to 44 years	45 to 54 years
			1	2	3	4	5	6	7	8	9	10	11	12	13	14	15
22500	Florence, SC	3 525	196 291	201	55.7	57.1	41.2	0.4	0.8	1.1	6.9	18.5	9.8	12.8	14.5	14.7
22520	Florence-Muscle Shoals, AL	3 274	141 499	264	43.2	85.8	12.6	0.7	0.4	1.1	5.8	16.7	9.7	12.3	14.5	14.4
22540	Fond du Lac, WI	1 872	97 833	340	52.3	95.3	1.2	0.7	1.0	2.5	5.6	17.9	10.6	11.7	15.7	14.7
22660	Fort Collins-Loveland, CO	6 737	266 610	163	39.6	88.0	1.1	1.1	2.4	8.9	6.1	16.9	12.7	15.4	14.9	14.6
22900	Fort Smith, AR-OK	10 362	279 777	159	27.0	83.3	4.1	8.5	2.3	5.3	7.2	19.0	9.7	12.7	14.5	13.4
23020	Fort Walton Beach-Crestview-Destin, FL	2 423	178 104	217	73.5	82.9	9.9	1.3	4.3	4.3	7.0	18.3	9.6	13.0	16.2	13.5
23060	Fort Wayne, IN	3 529	399 716	117	113.3	84.3	10.4	0.7	1.8	4.2	7.6	20.3	9.4	13.2	14.8	14.1
23420	Fresno, CA	15 443	850 325	56	55.1	39.5	5.5	1.3	9.2	46.0	8.1	22.3	11.8	13.8	13.8	11.7
23460	Gadsden, AL	1 385	103 035	332	74.4	82.6	14.9	0.7	0.5	2.0	6.2	17.1	9.1	12.6	13.8	14.4
23540	Gainesville, FL	3 168	239 211	176	75.5	70.8	20.2	0.7	4.1	5.7	5.5	14.5	19.2	15.9	12.3	12.4
23580	Gainesville, GA	1 020	156 101	238	153.0	69.1	6.8	0.5	1.6	22.6	8.7	18.9	10.7	16.4	14.8	11.7
24020	Glens Falls, NY	4 415	126 587	286	28.7	95.6	1.9	0.5	0.6	1.9	4.9	17.0	9.4	12.0	15.7	14.9
24140	Goldsboro, NC	1 431	113 104	306	79.0	59.6	33.9	0.7	1.4	5.5	7.6	19.0	9.7	13.5	15.5	13.5
24220	Grand Forks, ND-MN	8 827	95 641	343	10.8	92.9	1.5	2.6	1.6	2.8	5.6	16.8	15.9	13.5	13.8	13.2
24300	Grand Junction, CO	8 619	124 676	287	14.5	88.0	0.6	1.3	0.9	10.3	6.1	17.7	10.6	11.8	13.7	14.5
24340	Grand Rapids-Wyoming, MI	7 324	762 035	65	104.0	83.3	8.2	1.0	2.0	6.9	7.4	19.9	10.5	13.9	15.6	13.6
24500	Great Falls, MT	6 988	79 561	354	11.4	90.3	1.9	5.9	1.7	2.6	6.4	18.1	10.0	11.7	15.1	14.1
24540	Greeley, CO	10 335	211 272	190	20.4	68.3	0.7	0.9	1.4	29.7	7.8	19.9	13.2	14.7	14.1	12.3
24580	Green Bay, WI	4 841	291 247	152	60.2	91.2	1.5	2.4	2.2	3.7	6.5	18.5	10.3	13.2	16.6	14.2
24660	Greensboro-High Point, NC.	5 188	661 530	72	127.5	68.5	24.0	0.7	2.5	5.2	6.8	17.6	9.4	14.4	15.4	13.9
24780	Greenville, NC	2 375	158 680	234	66.8	59.3	35.3	0.5	1.2	4.5	7.0	17.0	14.6	15.8	13.7	12.7
24860	Greenville, SC	5 185	578 485	83	111.6	77.1	17.6	0.5	1.6	4.0	6.5	17.4	10.6	14.0	15.2	13.7
25060	Gulfport-Biloxi, MS	3 893	248 965	172	64.0	75.2	20.0	1.0	3.1	2.3	7.2	18.4	10.5	13.7	15.3	13.5
25180	Hagerstown-Martinsburg, MD-WV	2 612	237 582	177	91.0	91.2	7.0	0.5	1.0	1.4	6.1	17.5	9.1	13.4	15.9	14.0
25260	Hanford-Corcoran, CA	3 603	138 564	266	38.5	42.3	8.4	1.3	3.9	45.4	7.7	20.1	12.5	17.1	16.5	10.9
25420	Harrisburg-Carlisle, PA	4 219	517 468	88	122.7	85.6	10.0	0.4	2.4	2.7	5.7	17.0	9.4	12.3	15.5	15.4
25500	Harrisonburg, VA	2 249	110 535	312	49.1	88.9	3.5	0.3	1.9	6.4	5.8	15.1	19.8	12.0	13.1	12.2
25540	Hartford-West Hartford-East Hartford, CT	3 923	1 177 935	44	300.3	77.4	10.2	0.5	3.1	9.8	5.8	17.5	9.2	12.1	16.4	14.8
25620	Hattiesburg, MS	4 171	128 631	278	30.8	71.3	26.6	0.5	1.0	1.3	7.1	18.1	13.9	14.6	13.7	12.1
25860	Hickory-Lenoir-Morganton, NC	4 243	350 140	135	82.5	85.4	7.0	0.4	2.8	5.0	6.4	17.8	8.7	14.0	15.3	14.0
25980	Hinesville-Fort Stewart, GA .	2 382	69 705	358	29.3	53.3	38.7	1.1	3.4	6.4	12.3	23.1	13.4	18.2	15.3	9.4
26100	Holland-Grand Haven, MI	1 465	249 391	171	170.2	88.8	1.4	0.6	2.7	7.4	7.1	20.0	12.5	12.7	15.2	13.1
26180	Honolulu, HI	1 553	902 709	51	581.3	31.2	3.9	1.3	77.7	6.8	6.8	16.2	10.0	14.0	15.0	13.8
26300	Hot Springs, AR	1 754	91 188	346	52.0	88.0	8.5	1.3	0.8	2.7	5.8	15.7	8.2	10.9	13.2	13.4
26380	Houma-Bayou Cane-Thibodaux, LA	6 059	197 388	200	32.6	77.8	16.0	4.7	1.0	1.7	7.1	19.6	11.4	12.7	15.7	13.2
26420	Houston-Baytown-Sugar Land, TX	23 124	5 075 733	8	219.5	46.9	16.7	0.5	5.8	31.1	8.3	20.6	10.0	15.2	15.8	13.5
26580	Huntington-Ashland, WV-KY-OH	4 528	286 517	156	63.3	96.2	2.8	0.6	0.6	0.7	5.7	15.9	10.1	12.8	14.0	14.6
26620	Huntsville, AL	3 556	357 907	133	100.6	73.8	21.8	1.5	2.5	2.2	6.4	18.3	9.8	13.2	16.7	13.8
26820	Idaho Falls, ID	7 675	107 201	324	14.0	89.7	0.6	1.0	1.2	8.5	8.3	22.7	11.1	11.4	13.7	13.1
26900	Indianapolis, IN	10 007	1 595 377	34	159.4	80.5	14.8	0.6	2.0	3.3	7.6	19.5	8.9	14.5	16.3	13.6
26980	Iowa City, IA	3 064	136 862	267	44.7	89.6	3.2	0.5	5.2	2.6	5.8	14.3	17.1	17.1	13.8	12.8
27060	Ithaca, NY	1 233	101 411	336	82.2	83.0	4.3	0.8	10.1	3.6	4.1	13.0	24.2	14.4	12.1	12.2
27100	Jackson, MI	1 830	162 321	230	88.7	88.8	8.6	1.0	0.8	2.4	6.1	18.6	9.3	12.9	16.0	14.6
27140	Jackson, MS	9 650	510 060	92	52.9	52.0	46.3	0.4	1.0	1.1	7.4	19.2	10.9	13.9	15.0	13.7
27180	Jackson, TN	2 190	109 715	316	50.1	67.4	30.2	0.5	0.9	1.8	6.8	17.9	11.9	13.3	14.7	13.7
27260	Jacksonville, FL	8 342	1 202 900	42	144.2	70.5	22.8	0.8	3.2	4.1	7.1	19.0	9.5	13.4	15.8	14.0
27340	Jacksonville, NC	1 986	147 524	254	74.3	73.9	19.4	1.4	3.7	4.8	10.8	17.5	22.0	15.6	13.0	9.1
27500	Janesville, WI	1 866	154 794	240	83.0	89.7	5.2	0.6	1.3	4.5	6.6	19.1	9.5	12.5	15.7	14.2
27620	Jefferson City, MO	5 836	142 778	262	24.5	90.3	7.5	0.9	0.9	1.3	6.2	17.7	10.8	14.1	16.3	14.2
27740	Johnson City, TN	2 210	186 181	208	84.2	94.9	3.1	0.6	0.7	1.5	5.4	14.9	10.0	14.0	14.6	14.2
27780	Johnstown, PA	1 782	149 453	249	83.9	95.6	3.3	0.2	0.5	1.0	4.9	15.1	9.8	11.0	14.1	15.5
27860	Jonesboro, AR	3 804	110 041	314	28.9	88.2	9.0	0.7	0.7	2.2	7.0	17.6	11.6	14.2	13.7	13.0
27900	Joplin, MO	3 279	162 145	231	49.4	92.7	1.7	2.8	1.0	3.7	7.3	18.3	10.5	12.7	14.0	13.2
28020	Kalamazoo-Portage, MI	3 037	320 320	145	105.5	85.0	9.6	1.2	2.1	4.1	6.5	17.9	12.7	13.2	14.2	14.1
28100	Kankakee-Bradley, IL	1 753	105 625	329	60.3	77.7	15.9	0.5	1.0	5.9	7.1	19.2	10.7	12.6	14.3	13.6
28140	Kansas City, MO-KS	20 351	1 904 909	27	93.6	79.1	13.1	1.0	2.5	5.7	7.2	18.7	9.2	14.0	16.0	14.1
28420	Kennewick-Richland-Pasco, WA	7 629	209 786	194	27.5	72.7	1.7	1.1	2.6	23.1	7.8	21.1	11.0	12.7	14.2	13.5
28660	Killeen-Temple-Fort Hood, TX	7 313	343 329	138	46.9	61.2	19.4	1.3	3.8	17.1	9.8	20.1	12.3	16.4	14.6	10.6
28700	Kingsport-Bristol-Bristol, TN-VA	5 211	299 703	149	57.5	96.8	2.1	0.5	0.5	0.8	5.4	15.6	8.3	12.5	14.8	14.9
28740	Kingston, NY	2 918	181 111	214	62.1	85.6	6.3	0.8	1.7	7.0	5.0	16.7	10.0	12.1	16.5	15.5
28940	Knoxville, TN	4 810	636 863	76	132.4	90.8	6.7	0.7	1.5	1.4	5.9	16.1	10.0	13.6	15.2	14.5
29020	Kokomo, IN	1 433	101 302	337	70.7	91.2	6.4	0.7	1.2	1.7	6.9	18.9	8.4	12.3	14.8	14.5

1. CBSA = Core Based Statistical Area. DIV = Metropolitan Division. See Appendix A for explanation. See Appendix B for list of metropolitan areas identified by type. 2. Dry land or land partially or temporarily covered by water. 3. Hispanic or Latino persons may be of any race.

Table C. Metropolitan Areas — **Population and Households**

Area Name	Population, 2003 (cont'd) Age (percent) (cont'd)				Population — change and components of change, 1990–2003							Households, 2000				
					Total persons		Percent change		Components of change, 2000–2003						Percent	
	55 to 64 years	65 to 74 years	75 years and over	Percent female	1900	2000	1990–2000	2000–2003	Births	Deaths	Net migration	Number	Percent change, 1990–2000	Persons per house-hold	Female family house-holder[1]	One person
	16	17	18	19	20	21	22	23	24	25	26	27	28	29	30	31
Florence, SC	10.2	6.5	5.6	52.8	176 195	193 155	9.6	1.6	9 230	6 723	842	72 940	17.2	2.58	18.3	24.7
Florence-Muscle Shoals, AL..	11.0	8.2	7.3	52.1	131 327	142 950	8.9	-1.0	5 214	4 983	-1 524	58 549	14.8	2.40	11.3	26.3
Fond du Lac, WI	9.3	6.7	7.6	51.0	90 083	97 296	8.0	0.6	3 498	3 062	219	36 931	13.1	2.52	7.8	25.4
Fort Collins-Loveland, CO	8.2	5.0	4.5	49.9	186 136	251 494	35.1	6.0	10 620	5 053	9 569	97 164	37.9	2.52	7.9	23.4
Fort Smith, AR-OK	10.1	6.9	6.0	50.6	234 078	273 170	16.7	2.4	13 403	9 025	2 430	104 506	18.2	2.56	11.1	24.4
Fort Walton Beach-Crestview-Destin, FL.........	9.1	7.8	4.6	49.5	143 777	170 498	18.6	4.5	7 754	4 518	4 432	66 269	24.3	2.49	10.2	23.5
Fort Wayne, IN	8.6	5.7	5.8	50.8	354 435	390 156	10.1	2.5	19 641	10 284	557	150 858	13.6	2.54	11.2	26.7
Fresno, CA	7.2	4.9	4.7	49.8	667 479	799 407	19.8	6.4	46 000	17 895	23 410	252 940	14.5	3.09	15.2	20.6
Gadsden, AL	10.7	8.1	7.8	52.0	99 840	103 459	3.6	-0.4	4 228	4 326	-248	41 615	7.6	2.44	13.1	26.3
Gainesville, FL	7.7	5.2	4.7	50.9	191 263	232 392	21.5	2.9	8 740	5 707	4 090	92 530	24.1	2.36	12.2	28.7
Gainesville, GA	8.1	5.1	3.9	49.0	95 434	139 277	45.9	12.1	9 323	3 358	10 806	47 381	36.5	2.89	10.8	19.2
Glens Falls, NY	10.6	7.6	7.0	50.0	118 539	124 345	4.9	1.8	4 082	3 915	2 159	48 184	12.5	2.48	10.4	25.8
Goldsboro, NC	9.2	6.9	5.0	50.6	104 666	113 329	8.3	-0.2	5 748	3 449	-2 510	42 612	15.5	2.55	15.4	24.5
Grand Forks, ND-MN	7.9	5.7	6.5	49.6	103 272	97 478	-5.6	-1.9	3 572	2 595	-2 861	37 505	0.5	2.44	8.7	28.5
Grand Junction, CO	9.2	7.5	7.4	51.1	93 145	116 255	24.8	6.6	4 846	3 829	6 749	45 823	26.4	2.47	9.8	25.1
Grand Rapids-Wyoming, MI .	8.1	5.3	5.2	50.2	645 918	740 482	14.6	2.9	36 794	17 743	2 944	272 130	17.4	2.65	11.0	24.6
Great Falls, MT	10.0	7.4	7.0	50.6	77 691	80 357	3.4	-1.0	3 337	2 682	-1 431	32 547	8.0	2.41	9.9	28.8
Greeley, CO	7.4	4.3	3.7	49.7	131 821	180 936	37.3	16.8	10 243	3 831	23 269	63 247	33.2	2.86	8.7	21.0
Green Bay, WI	8.6	5.7	5.7	50.1	243 698	282 599	16.0	3.1	12 313	7 150	3 881	108 897	20.6	2.52	8.5	25.9
Greensboro-High Point, NC..	9.6	6.5	5.8	51.6	540 041	643 430	19.1	2.8	29 338	18 302	7 730	256 315	20.8	2.45	12.6	26.5
Greenville, NC	7.6	5.3	4.5	52.0	123 864	152 772	23.3	3.9	7 431	3 909	2 608	59 235	29.1	2.45	14.7	27.6
Greenville, SC	9.8	6.2	5.6	50.9	472 155	559 940	18.6	3.3	24 223	16 463	11 261	217 152	22.7	2.48	12.1	25.9
Gulfport-Biloxi, MS	9.4	6.8	5.1	50.3	207 875	246 190	18.4	1.1	11 863	7 680	-1 368	93 182	24.1	2.55	14.3	25.4
Hagerstown-Martinsburg, MD-WV	9.6	6.8	6.0	49.5	192 774	222 771	15.6	6.6	9 077	6 918	12 484	85 440	18.9	2.48	10.5	25.3
Hanford-Corcoran, CA	6.3	3.9	3.3	42.7	101 469	129 461	27.6	7.0	7 008	2 301	4 472	34 418	18.3	3.18	14.3	17.0
Harrisburg-Carlisle, PA	9.9	7.2	7.1	51.4	474 242	509 074	7.3	1.6	19 222	15 826	5 438	202 380	10.2	2.41	10.5	28.0
Harrisonburg, VA	8.3	6.1	6.0	51.3	88 189	108 193	22.7	2.2	4 256	2 702	784	38 488	23.9	2.58	8.3	23.6
Hartford-West Hartford-East Hartford, CT	9.9	6.5	7.2	51.5	1 123 678	1 148 618	2.2	2.6	44 654	33 371	18 981	445 870	5.2	2.48	12.3	27.3
Hattiesburg, MS	8.2	5.7	4.9	52.2	109 603	123 812	13.0	3.9	6 082	3 686	2 522	45 999	15.5	2.56	15.1	25.3
Hickory-Lenoir-Morganton, NC	10.6	7.2	5.8	50.4	292 405	341 851	16.9	2.4	14 644	10 562	4 073	133 966	19.2	2.50	10.8	24.2
Hinesville-Fort Stewart, GA ..	5.1	2.8	1.9	47.5	58 947	71 914	22.0	-3.1	5 453	1 035	-6 836	22 957	32.5	2.92	14.8	17.1
Holland-Grand Haven, MI	8.0	5.0	5.1	50.8	187 768	238 314	26.9	4.6	11 508	4 731	4 522	81 662	30.3	2.81	7.5	19.6
Honolulu, HI	9.7	6.7	6.8	49.9	836 231	876 156	4.8	3.0	43 246	20 749	4 569	286 450	8.0	2.95	12.3	21.6
Hot Springs, AR	11.5	10.7	10.0	51.4	73 397	88 068	20.0	3.5	3 350	4 240	3 939	37 813	22.6	2.28	10.1	28.8
Houma-Bayou Cane-Thibodaux, LA	9.1	6.0	4.6	51.0	182 842	194 477	6.4	1.5	9 398	5 126	-1 214	68 054	12.2	2.81	13.3	19.4
Houston-Baytown-Sugar Land, TX	7.8	4.4	3.2	50.0	3 767 218	4 715 407	25.2	7.6	274 215	93 534	179 349	1 656 799	22.5	2.80	13.0	23.4
Huntington-Ashland, WV-KY-OH	11.1	8.3	7.1	51.6	288 189	288 649	0.2	-0.7	10 897	10 964	-1 833	117 697	6.1	2.40	11.4	26.9
Huntsville, AL	9.5	6.6	4.6	50.7	293 047	342 376	16.8	4.5	14 615	9 063	10 134	134 643	21.4	2.47	11.6	26.5
Idaho Falls, ID	8.4	5.2	4.7	50.0	88 750	101 677	14.6	5.4	5 877	2 492	2 252	34 654	18.8	2.90	8.9	20.4
Indianapolis, IN	8.4	5.4	5.0	51.0	1 294 217	1 525 104	17.8	4.6	78 336	41 290	32 278	594 874	20.1	2.51	12.0	26.9
Iowa City, IA	7.1	4.4	4.6	50.5	115 731	131 676	13.8	3.9	5 405	2 418	2 374	52 136	19.8	2.36	6.8	29.7
Ithaca, NY	7.5	4.6	4.7	50.3	94 097	96 501	2.6	5.1	2 753	1 979	4 219	36 420	9.2	2.32	8.2	32.5
Jackson, MI	9.4	6.3	6.3	48.9	149 756	158 422	5.8	2.5	6 524	4 684	2 170	58 168	8.4	2.55	12.0	24.6
Jackson, MS	8.4	5.6	5.0	52.1	446 941	497 197	11.2	2.6	25 626	14 273	1 702	180 556	14.4	2.65	18.6	25.0
Jackson, TN	9.0	6.1	6.1	51.8	90 801	107 377	18.3	2.2	4 958	3 288	766	41 212	20.6	2.50	15.3	25.7
Jacksonville, FL	9.1	5.9	4.9	51.2	925 213	1 122 750	21.4	7.1	53 942	32 532	58 202	432 627	23.9	2.54	14.0	24.7
Jacksonville, NC	5.5	4.5	2.5	43.7	149 838	150 355	0.3	-1.9	10 298	2 596	-10 794	48 122	18.4	2.72	11.6	18.6
Janesville, WI	9.4	6.5	6.2	50.6	139 510	152 307	9.2	1.6	6 537	4 380	505	58 617	12.2	2.54	10.9	25.1
Jefferson City, MO	8.9	5.9	5.6	48.5	120 704	140 052	16.0	1.9	5 656	4 096	1 274	51 637	19.1	2.50	9.7	26.3
Johnson City, TN	11.0	7.6	7.0	51.0	160 390	181 607	13.2	2.5	6 436	6 586	4 813	75 197	20.1	2.34	10.6	27.4
Johnstown, PA	10.4	8.9	10.6	51.3	163 062	152 598	-6.4	-2.1	4 816	6 427	-1 404	60 531	-2.4	2.38	10.4	29.8
Jonesboro, AR	9.7	6.4	5.8	51.4	93 620	107 762	15.1	2.1	4 998	3 594	987	42 327	18.7	2.47	11.9	25.1
Joplin, MO	9.6	6.8	6.7	51.2	134 910	157 322	16.6	3.1	7 838	5 416	2 547	61 552	16.1	2.50	10.4	25.7
Kalamazoo-Portage, MI	8.8	5.8	5.7	51.2	293 471	314 866	7.3	1.7	13 528	8 550	748	121 461	11.3	2.48	11.0	26.8
Kankakee-Bradley, IL	9.1	6.6	6.3	51.3	96 255	103 833	7.9	1.7	5 078	3 809	660	38 182	10.3	2.61	13.1	24.9
Kansas City, MO-KS	9.0	5.7	5.5	51.0	1 636 527	1 836 038	12.2	3.7	90 973	50 389	28 366	717 761	14.1	2.51	11.6	27.1
Kennewick-Richland-Pasco, WA	8.4	4.9	4.4	49.3	150 033	191 822	27.9	9.4	10 617	4 061	11 360	67 706	24.4	2.81	10.4	22.0
Killeen-Temple-Fort Hood, TX	6.6	4.6	3.9	49.6	268 820	330 714	23.0	3.8	21 718	6 578	-2 376	112 011	25.9	2.72	11.9	21.3
Kingsport-Bristol-Bristol, TN-VA	12.2	8.6	7.4	51.7	275 678	298 484	8.3	0.4	10 561	11 053	1 911	124 021	14.8	2.41	9.6	26.4
Kingston, NY	10.5	6.8	6.4	50.3	165 380	177 749	7.5	1.9	5 778	5 340	3 043	67 499	11.0	2.47	10.9	27.9
Knoxville, TN	10.3	7.1	6.4	51.5	534 910	616 079	15.2	3.4	24 427	19 930	16 538	253 005	19.5	2.37	10.7	27.8
Kokomo, IN	11.0	7.2	6.5	51.5	96 946	101 541	4.7	-0.2	4 491	3 511	-1 135	41 269	9.9	2.43	10.9	27.4

1. No spouse present.

Table C. Metropolitan Areas — **Vital Statistics, Health Resources, and Crime**

Area Name	Births, average 1999–2001		Deaths, average 1999–2001				Physicians,[4] 1998		Hospitals,[4] 1998			Medicare enrollees, 2003	Serious crimes known to police,[6] 2002	
			Number		Rate					Beds			Total	
	Total	Rate[1]	Total	Infant[2]	Total[1]	Infant[3]	Number	Rate[5]	Number	Number	Rate[5]		Number	Rate[7]
	32	33	34	35	36	37	38	39	40	41	42	43	44	45
Florence, SC	2 836	14.7	2 033	113	10.5	13.3	349	319	6	915	838	29 981	12 698	6 422
Florence-Muscle Shoals, AL.	1 677	11.8	1 503	36	10.5	7.2	227	318	4	907	1 273	26 830	4 189	2 929
Fond du Lac, WI	1 148	11.8	316	22	9.4	6.4	145	149	2	220	232	16 165	2 426	2 458
Fort Collins-Loveland, CO	3 222	12.7	1 485	47	5.9	4.9	433	172	3	375	162	28 548	9 906	3 759
Fort Smith, AR-OK..........	4 075	14.9	2 778	95	10.2	7.8	418	514	6	952	1 330	45 185	11 304	4 084
Fort Walton Beach-Crestview-Destin, FL........	2 343	13.7	1 325	51	7.8	7.3	298	175	3	433	256	26 727	5 449	3 056
Fort Wayne, IN....................	5 985	15.3	3 155	117	8.1	6.5	766	503	6	1 286	1 196	52 445	14 759	4 054
Fresno, CA....................	14 193	17.7	5 492	262	6.8	6.2	1 341	168	14	2 118	280	94 572	49 847	6 015
Gadsden, AL..................	1 329	12.8	1 294	37	12.5	9.3	185	179	2	538	517	19 773	5 421	5 194
Gainesville, FL...............	2 654	11.4	1 680	74	7.2	9.3	1 211	613	3	1 057	532	29 482	13 360	5 498
Gainesville, GA..............	2 744	19.5	1 007	61	7.2	7.4	213	153	2	447	375	17 273	5 230	3 594
Glens Falls, NY..............	1 281	10.3	1 202	28	9.7	7.3	218	347	2	553	905	21 873	2 999	2 389
Goldsboro, NC...............	1 750	15.4	1 072	56	9.5	10.7	152	134	1	267	238	17 762	5 777	4 932
Grand Forks, ND-MN......	1 185	12.2	801	20	8.2	5.6	209	351	4	665	1 432	12 833	3 738	3 940
Grand Junction, CO........	1 464	12.6	1 135	34	9.7	7.7	286	246	3	422	374	21 588	3 955	3 451
Grand Rapids-Wyoming, MI .	11 614	15.7	5 404	272	7.3	7.8	1 428	428	7	1 646	709	92 647	27 903	3 744
Great Falls, MT..............	1 053	13.1	764	29	9.5	9.2	198	246	2	402	509	13 233	5 043	6 226
Greeley, CO..................	3 065	16.7	1 136	59	6.2	6.4	260	144	1	326	204	19 380	8 193	4 716
Green Bay, WI...............	3 802	13.4	2 138	73	7.6	6.4	423	283	6	698	523	37 330	8 026	2 800
Greensboro-High Point, NC..	8 986	13.9	5 590	235	8.7	8.7	1 043	377	6	1 632	798	96 334	33 530	5 072
Greenville, NC...............	2 211	14.5	1 191	74	7.8	11.2	514	398	1	571	451	19 612	9 219	5 838
Greenville, SC...............	7 601	13.6	4 938	143	8.8	6.3	950	357	7	1 526	620	84 136	24 954	4 353
Gulfport-Biloxi, MS.........	3 713	15.1	2 363	106	9.6	9.5	509	430	6	822	828	37 267	13 731	6 236
Hagerstown-Martinsburg, MD-WV...........	2 812	12.6	2 078	54	9.3	6.4	375	422	3	573	868	35 310	6 314	2 803
Hanford-Corcoran, CA	2 155	16.7	706	38	5.5	5.9	119	92	3	175	147	11 430	3 900	2 906
Harrisburg-Carlisle, PA	5 923	11.6	4 870	99	9.6	5.6	1 508	678	7	1 987	849	82 134	11 968	2 504
Harrisonburg, VA............	1 324	12.2	822	21	7.6	5.3	141	324	1	264	790	13 750	1 813	1 626
Hartford-West Hartford-East Hartford, CT...........	14 351	12.5	10 364	304	9.0	7.1	3 360	682	12	2 690	498	180 643	34 707	3 494
Hattiesburg, MS.............	1 862	15.0	1 156	50	9.3	8.9	271	532	4	777	1 661	17 846	NA	NA
Hickory-Lenoir-Morganton, NC...........	4 625	13.5	3 172	113	9.3	8.1	498	491	6	812	869	53 658	11 711	3 333
Hinesville-Fort Stewart, GA ..	1 653	23.0	319	52	4.4	10.5	54	88	1	49	83	4 121	2 748	3 711
Holland-Grand Haven, MI	3 652	15.3	1 444	76	6.0	6.9	205	86	3	336	150	29 533	5 435	2 255
Honolulu, HI..................	12 421	15.4	5 896	277	6.7	7.4	2 518	287	10	2 316	265	126 752	57 271	6 360
Hot Springs, AR.............	1 034	11.7	1 245	24	14.1	7.7	205	233	2	441	525	23 127	3 995	4 475
Houma-Bayou Cane-Thibodaux, LA...........	2 899	14.9	1 520	108	7.8	12.4	300	304	5	647	660	26 492	8 705	4 523
Houston-Baytown-Sugar Land, TX...........	82 561	17.4	28 620	1 372	6.0	5.5	9 952	1 111	58	12 797	1 579	432 380	258 150	5 307
Huntington-Ashland, WV-KY-OH...........	3 400	11.8	3 373	85	11.7	8.3	624	906	5	1 460	2 155	55 613	NA	NA
Huntsville, AL................	4 613	13.4	2 680	102	7.8	7.4	545	257	4	960	471	46 661	14 637	4 243
Idaho Falls, ID...............	1 777	17.4	702	37	6.9	6.9	152	192	1	270	335	12 830	3 231	3 066
Indianapolis, IN.............	24 042	15.7	12 488	575	8.2	8.0	3 928	1 260	22	4 997	1 831	190 606	62 034	4 788
Iowa City, IA.................	1 671	12.7	730	23	5.5	4.6	1 062	1 023	3	1 085	1 371	14 032	4 186	3 168
Ithaca, NY...................	872	9.0	614	22	6.3	8.4	183	190	1	204	212	11 004	3 005	3 085
Jackson, MI..................	2 048	12.9	1 428	64	9.0	10.4	220	139	2	507	325	24 460	5 750	3 754
Jackson, MS.................	7 629	15.3	4 343	280	8.7	12.2	1 300	815	12	2 560	1 827	66 653	NA	NA
Jackson, TN.................	1 529	14.2	1 016	50	9.4	10.9	291	333	2	710	826	15 792	6 055	5 534
Jacksonville, FL.............	16 371	14.5	9 693	461	8.6	9.4	2 395	735	13	3 270	1 288	151 482	62 291	5 873
Jacksonville, NC............	3 213	21.5	773	77	5.2	8.0	175	116	1	133	93	13 248	3 560	2 304
Janesville, WI...............	2 041	13.4	1 319	47	8.7	7.7	281	184	3	474	314	22 752	6 791	4 395
Jefferson City, MO..........	1 761	12.6	1 261	40	9.0	7.6	227	429	4	326	514	19 503	3 320	2 338
Johnson City, TN............	2 060	11.4	1 960	54	10.8	8.7	510	590	5	739	1 045	32 949	7 630	4 123
Johnstown, PA...............	1 531	10.0	1 971	37	12.9	8.1	342	224	4	872	559	32 844	2 423	1 957
Jonesboro, AR...............	1 537	14.3	1 054	43	9.8	9.3	228	307	2	425	548	16 753	5 151	4 715
Joplin, MO...................	2 399	15.2	1 654	57	10.5	7.9	301	429	5	759	818	26 397	7 394	4 636
Kalamazoo-Portage, MI	4 205	13.3	2 575	99	8.2	7.8	803	377	4	1 041	652	43 818	15 455	4 919
Kankakee-Bradley, IL........	1 536	14.8	1 109	43	10.7	9.3	172	166	2	482	472	16 616	NA	NA
Kansas City, MO-KS...........	27 686	15.0	15 313	565	8.3	6.8	4 109	1 663	35	6 411	3 154	245 834	87 657	5 254
Kennewick-Richland-Pasco, WA...........	3 254	16.9	1 228	62	6.4	6.4	300	282	4	430	514	22 589	7 382	3 737
Killeen-Temple-Fort Hood, TX...........	6 471	19.6	2 033	144	6.2	7.4	738	411	6	825	524	32 656	14 520	4 217
Kingsport-Bristol-Bristol, TN-VA...........	3 328	11.2	3 318	90	11.1	9.0	581	195	5	990	342	60 055	10 374	3 399
Kingston, NY.................	1 780	10.0	1 604	27	9.0	5.1	300	169	3	413	248	27 798	4 069	2 338
Knoxville, TN................	7 536	12.2	6 002	116	9.7	5.1	1 581	813	9	2 435	1 223	101 631	27 546	4 388
Kokomo, IN..................	1 397	13.8	1 034	27	10.2	6.4	162	283	3	416	1 053	16 315	3 948	4 320

1. Per 1,000 estimated resident population. 2. Deaths of infants under 1 year old. 3. Deaths of infants under 1 year old per 1,000 live births. 4. Data subject to copyright. 5. Per 100,000 resident population as of July 1 of the year shown. 6. Data for serious crimes have not been adjusted for underreporting; this may affect comparability between geographic areas and over time. 7. Per 100,000 population estimated by the FBI.

Area Name	Serious crimes known to police,[1] 2002 (cont'd) Rate[2]		Education School enrollment and attainment, 2000 Enrollment[3]		Attainment[4] (percent)		Local government expenditures,[5] 2000–2001		Money income, 1999				Percent below poverty level, 1999			
	Violent	Property	Total	Percent private	High school graduate or more	Bachelor's degree or more	Total current expenditures (mil dol)	Current expenditures per student (dollars)	Per capita income[6] (dollars)	Mean household income	Mean family income	Percent of households with income of $100,000 or more	Persons	Households	Families	Families with children
	46	47	48	49	50	51	52	53	54	55	56	57	58	59	60	61
Florence, SC	924	5 498	51 534	13.4	71.8	16.9	218.2	6 457	17 320	45 108	51 499	6.8	17.8	17.8	14.5	20.0
Florence-Muscle Shoals, AL	196	2 732	34 615	10.3	75.2	16.8	137.4	6 343	18 205	43 946	51 338	6.6	14.2	15.5	10.8	16.2
Fond du Lac, WI	82	2 376	25 296	21.9	84.2	16.9	117.8	7 487	20 022	51 682	59 762	6.9	5.8	5.9	3.5	5.1
Fort Collins-Loveland, CO	272	3 488	80 102	10.7	92.3	39.5	252.8	6 292	23 689	60 516	71 091	13.9	9.2	9.1	4.3	6.1
Fort Smith, AR-OK	460	3 624	66 582	7.8	73.2	13.2	295.6	5 830	15 970	41 079	46 486	5.2	15.7	15.6	12.2	17.9
Fort Walton Beach-Crestview-Destin, FL	345	2 711	44 445	10.8	88.0	24.2	171.3	5 644	20 918	52 400	58 200	9.1	8.8	8.5	6.6	10.8
Fort Wayne, IN	277	3 777	106 191	22.9	85.8	21.3	460.2	7 424	21 294	54 359	63 662	9.8	8.6	8.2	6.2	9.6
Fresno, CA	616	5 398	263 942	7.0	67.5	17.5	1 300.6	7 181	15 495	47 858	52 247	8.6	22.9	18.2	17.6	24.8
Gadsden, AL	771	4 423	23 661	11.1	74.1	13.4	90.8	5 742	16 783	41 044	48 040	5.6	15.7	16.2	12.3	18.9
Gainesville, FL	813	4 685	93 758	8.1	87.0	36.7	196.2	6 055	18 187	44 501	57 882	8.5	22.2	22.8	12.1	16.8
Gainesville, GA	320	3 274	33 309	10.4	70.5	18.7	156.2	6 427	19 690	56 988	62 780	11.0	12.4	11.0	8.5	11.9
Glens Falls, NY	267	2 122	30 527	9.3	82.0	18.9	217.2	9 777	19 368	48 783	55 346	7.4	9.6	9.3	7.0	11.1
Goldsboro, NC	442	4 489	29 896	13.3	77.2	15.0	118.7	6 090	17 010	43 941	49 471	5.4	13.8	13.8	10.2	15.2
Grand Forks, ND-MN	150	3 790	32 683	5.8	86.6	24.2	106.9	6 527	17 679	44 693	54 355	5.7	11.9	12.5	7.8	11.8
Grand Junction, CO	199	3 252	29 470	10.7	85.0	22.0	116.3	5 698	18 715	46 576	54 216	7.1	10.2	10.2	7.0	11.0
Grand Rapids-Wyoming, MI	479	3 264	208 882	19.0	84.3	22.7	1 022.5	7 996	20 905	56 004	64 221	10.5	8.8	8.4	6.3	9.2
Great Falls, MT	389	5 837	20 212	14.0	87.1	21.5	82.1	5 982	17 566	42 308	48 510	5.4	13.5	13.4	10.4	17.1
Greeley, CO	336	4 380	55 843	8.6	79.6	21.6	190.5	6 264	18 958	53 541	60 091	9.5	12.5	11.7	8.0	11.9
Green Bay, WI	171	2 629	74 891	18.7	85.4	20.1	363.7	7 684	21 197	54 107	62 778	9.0	6.8	7.0	4.6	6.9
Greensboro-High Point, NC	458	4 614	163 561	14.2	78.2	23.4	644.8	6 409	21 416	53 101	62 062	10.2	10.6	10.7	7.8	11.8
Greenville, NC	635	5 203	50 387	8.5	78.0	23.9	145.4	6 250	17 897	44 872	54 907	7.0	20.3	20.8	13.8	19.3
Greenville, SC	718	3 636	148 623	19.4	76.9	23.1	517.8	6 028	20 377	51 695	60 373	9.8	11.6	11.7	8.4	12.2
Gulfport-Biloxi, MS	379	5 857	62 348	14.5	79.5	17.9	219.8	5 520	17 791	45 595	51 646	6.3	14.7	14.4	11.7	16.9
Hagerstown-Martinsburg, MD-WV	317	2 485	50 076	11.9	77.6	14.5	249.7	7 063	19 222	47 688	54 186	6.8	10.3	10.4	7.6	11.5
Hanford-Corcoran, CA	304	2 602	37 449	9.6	68.8	10.4	177.5	7 000	15 848	48 709	49 728	7.5	19.5	15.8	15.8	22.2
Harrisburg-Carlisle, PA	282	2 222	124 019	18.8	84.2	24.3	637.4	7 832	22 447	55 040	64 337	10.4	8.2	8.1	5.8	9.4
Harrisonburg, VA	152	1 475	35 610	13.3	73.6	21.4	100.5	6 957	17 338	47 391	56 115	6.9	15.5	14.6	6.9	10.6
Hartford-West Hartford-East Hartford, CT	320	3 174	309 449	15.6	84.0	30.5	1 818.9	9 764	26 277	66 591	78 367	17.9	8.3	8.2	5.9	9.1
Hattiesburg, MS	NA	NA	39 205	11.3	79.8	22.6	114.2	5 346	16 096	42 314	49 622	6.4	19.4	19.4	14.9	20.3
Hickory-Lenoir-Morganton, NC	224	3 109	77 271	9.7	70.3	13.6	338.9	5 992	18 723	47 140	53 605	6.4	9.8	10.1	7.1	10.9
Hinesville-Fort Stewart, GA	305	3 406	19 965	8.1	84.9	13.2	78.6	5 848	13 673	39 298	40 889	4.0	15.6	15.4	14.1	18.1
Holland-Grand Haven, MI	170	2 085	73 944	22.2	86.6	26.0	365.8	7 518	21 676	62 159	69 839	12.8	5.5	5.3	3.1	4.4
Honolulu, HI	289	6 072	234 038	23.3	84.8	27.9	1 216.6	6 599	21 998	65 375	72 281	18.2	9.9	9.7	7.0	10.3
Hot Springs, AR	488	3 986	18 185	10.1	78.3	18.0	75.0	5 864	18 631	42 947	50 180	6.1	14.6	14.0	10.5	19.6
Houma-Bayou Cane-Thibodaux, LA	512	4 011	53 565	16.0	66.7	12.3	203.8	5 834	15 939	44 823	49 497	6.1	17.9	17.2	14.5	19.7
Houston-Baytown-Sugar Land, TX	768	4 539	1 354 503	12.1	76.3	26.4	6 035.7	6 381	21 657	60 946	68 038	15.0	13.7	12.3	10.9	14.6
Huntington-Ashland, WV-KY-OH	NA	NA	69 942	7.7	76.6	14.9	311.5	6 924	16 628	40 137	47 082	5.1	17.9	18.3	13.7	21.4
Huntsville, AL	363	3 880	94 606	16.3	83.3	30.9	344.1	6 227	22 073	55 343	63 893	12.3	10.9	11.3	8.4	12.6
Idaho Falls, ID	215	2 851	31 008	7.1	87.2	24.2	124.9	5 227	17 481	50 885	56 761	8.3	10.2	10.0	7.5	11.3
Indianapolis, IN	663	4 125	390 690	19.7	84.3	26.5	1 834.5	7 358	23 302	58 877	68 519	12.9	8.5	8.3	6.2	9.0
Iowa City, IA	425	2 743	49 987	8.7	91.6	42.0	107.1	6 379	21 593	53 335	69 723	10.7	13.8	14.3	5.2	7.7
Ithaca, NY	135	2 949	42 942	52.3	91.4	47.5	141.2	10 659	19 659	50 577	66 014	10.8	17.6	17.1	6.8	10.6
Jackson, MI	505	3 249	41 089	15.4	84.2	16.3	213.1	8 263	20 171	53 012	59 722	8.9	9.0	8.7	6.5	10.5
Jackson, MS	NA	NA	144 456	19.1	79.9	26.2	430.7	5 184	18 690	50 539	57 645	9.2	17.0	15.9	13.6	18.9
Jackson, TN	820	4 714	29 345	28.6	77.2	20.1	96.0	5 961	18 863	48 416	55 799	8.0	14.0	14.4	10.9	15.5
Jacksonville, FL	847	5 026	301 544	17.8	83.4	22.6	1 070.6	5 670	21 632	55 295	63 117	10.9	10.7	10.5	8.1	12.0
Jacksonville, NC	162	2 141	37 631	8.8	84.3	14.8	124.2	5 875	14 853	40 734	43 570	4.1	12.9	12.2	10.8	14.8
Janesville, WI	239	4 156	39 380	13.3	83.9	16.7	220.9	8 055	20 895	53 448	61 084	9.1	7.3	7.2	5.1	7.9
Jefferson City, MO	333	2 005	35 729	23.4	81.7	21.2	118.7	5 893	18 889	49 551	57 179	6.6	8.7	8.9	6.0	8.8
Johnson City, TN	437	3 686	42 544	8.1	73.7	18.5	146.5	5 740	17 370	41 053	48 236	5.4	14.8	16.0	10.9	16.7
Johnstown, PA	263	1 694	34 592	18.5	80.0	13.7	177.4	9 100	16 058	39 387	46 797	4.1	12.5	13.2	9.4	15.7
Jonesboro, AR	347	4 368	28 676	7.3	73.5	17.3	102.0	5 555	16 139	40 580	47 449	5.4	16.8	17.5	13.0	18.7
Joplin, MO	537	4 099	38 568	12.1	79.6	16.4	148.8	5 522	16 653	41 926	48 119	4.9	13.5	13.4	9.7	14.8
Kalamazoo-Portage, MI	506	4 412	98 385	12.1	86.3	26.9	417.7	8 160	20 804	52 914	62 961	10.3	11.8	11.3	6.9	10.8
Kankakee-Bradley, IL	NA	NA	28 166	18.3	79.8	15.0	132.9	7 117	19 055	50 488	57 293	7.9	11.4	10.5	8.7	13.3
Kansas City, MO-KS	579	4 675	485 870	17.3	86.6	28.0	2 133.6	6 772	23 102	58 313	67 886	12.2	8.5	8.5	6.2	9.3
Kennewick-Richland-Pasco, WA	256	3 482	54 796	9.1	80.1	23.3	263.6	6 640	19 798	55 664	61 441	10.8	12.6	10.8	9.6	14.3
Killeen-Temple-Fort Hood, TX	406	3 812	89 697	11.1	83.5	18.0	403.9	6 304	16 580	46 107	50 624	6.2	11.7	11.3	9.4	13.2
Kingsport-Bristol-Bristol, TN-VA	382	3 017	62 706	11.4	73.1	15.5	290.6	6 544	18 061	42 805	49 581	5.5	13.6	14.9	10.5	16.1
Kingston, NY	300	2 028	46 246	12.5	81.7	25.0	319.0	11 076	20 846	52 982	61 120	10.8	11.4	10.5	7.2	11.2
Knoxville, TN	566	3 822	154 421	12.8	80.2	24.6	531.6	5 893	20 823	49 999	59 264	9.3	12.2	13.1	8.5	13.2
Kokomo, IN	385	3 935	24 268	12.5	83.4	17.1	130.8	7 692	22 029	53 693	62 034	10.3	8.8	8.6	5.9	9.9

1. Data for serious crimes have not been adjusted for underreporting; this may affect comparability between geographic areas and over time. 2. Per 100,000 population estimated by the FBI. 3. All persons 3 years old and over enrolled in nursery school through college. 4. Persons 25 years old and over. 5. Elementary and secondary education expenditures. 6. Based on population enumerated as of April 1, 2000.

Table C. Metropolitan Areas — **Personal Income**

Area Name	Personal income, 2002												
	Total (mil dol)	Per capita[1]			Wages and salaries[2] (mil dol)	Proprietor's income (mil dol)	Dividends, interest, and rent (mil dol)	Transfer payments	Government payments to individuals				
		Percent change, 2001–2002	Dollars	Rank				Total (mil dol)	Total (mil dol)	Social Security (mil dol)	Medical payments (mil dol)	Income maintenance (mil dol)	Unemployment insurance (mil dol)
	62	63	64	65	66	67	68	69	70	71	72	73	74
Florence, SC	4 863	2.6	24 917	269	3 388	303	694	1 023	974	311	434	134	35
Florence-Muscle Shoals, AL	3 226	0.4	22 724	331	1 764	202	614	709	676	310	245	55	25
Fond du Lac, WI	2 881	2.9	29 455	112	1 848	244	484	418	394	170	166	18	19
Fort Collins-Loveland, CO	8 296	2.4	31 352	76	5 317	742	1 569	750	690	313	249	47	36
Fort Smith, AR-OK	6 399	2.3	22 989	324	3 889	780	966	1 298	1 227	473	502	126	34
Fort Walton Beach-Crestview-Destin, FL	5 254	7.9	29 902	103	3 904	270	1 184	739	700	264	279	47	9
Fort Wayne, IN	11 486	1.9	28 958	124	8 697	785	2 076	1 513	1 414	636	554	117	50
Fresno, CA	19 544	6.2	23 416	316	12 315	2 151	2 777	4 074	3 875	937	1 578	745	360
Gadsden, AL	2 365	3.2	22 938	325	1 249	145	357	561	537	229	221	51	9
Gainesville, FL	5 934	3.7	25 041	263	4 422	271	1 148	958	900	305	415	89	11
Gainesville, GA	3 795	3.4	24 929	267	2 540	323	704	524	481	201	210	41	10
Glens Falls, NY	3 149	3.6	25 172	250	1 844	190	577	637	604	244	250	56	23
Goldsboro, NC	2 641	2.9	23 381	319	1 757	79	428	530	505	176	217	65	13
Grand Forks, ND-MN	2 475	4.7	25 772	225	1 782	164	432	384	362	135	146	27	12
Grand Junction, CO	3 167	5.2	26 083	209	1 891	239	662	550	523	223	200	44	15
Grand Rapids-Wyoming, MI	21 688	2.0	28 618	133	16 717	1 999	3 246	2 830	2 650	1 117	940	286	199
Great Falls, MT	2 113	3.9	26 616	194	1 316	179	445	362	343	142	125	27	7
Greeley, CO	5 000	2.3	24 389	289	2 897	637	709	616	569	212	240	56	29
Green Bay, WI	8 641	3.8	29 875	106	6 637	526	1 582	1 026	953	435	345	57	68
Greensboro-High Point, NC	18 708	1.8	28 435	137	14 257	1 315	3 283	2 806	2 651	1 109	1 037	258	132
Greenville, NC	3 790	2.4	24 193	295	2 529	175	636	652	615	204	273	98	22
Greenville, SC	15 573	1.5	27 086	177	11 587	978	2 633	2 358	2 215	963	884	189	68
Gulfport-Biloxi, MS	6 213	4.2	24 863	271	4 596	415	1 058	1 173	1 111	388	511	108	16
Hagerstown-Martinsburg, MD-WV	6 028	4.3	26 121	207	3 634	296	912	1 007	951	391	354	69	34
Hanford-Corcoran, CA	2 505	7.1	18 550	357	1 685	182	317	492	461	118	189	80	44
Harrisburg-Carlisle, PA	16 366	4.1	31 806	66	14 118	1 072	2 765	2 301	2 170	890	885	134	100
Harrisonburg, VA	2 562	1.1	23 385	318	2 010	179	470	340	313	163	105	23	6
Hartford-West Hartford-East Hartford, CT	44 403	1.7	38 013	14	34 011	3 910	6 991	5 796	5 518	2 145	2 501	405	288
Hattiesburg, MS	2 893	5.0	22 810	330	1 816	256	483	591	558	198	245	64	9
Hickory-Lenoir-Morganton, NC	8 887	0.8	25 447	236	5 924	. 714	1 532	1 550	1 467	617	576	129	96
Hinesville-Fort Stewart, GA	1 290	4.9	17 791	358	1 383	36	173	200	184	44	84	29	6
Holland-Grand Haven, MI	6 769	1.5	27 526	164	4 942	326	1 161	755	696	351	222	42	53
Honolulu, HI	28 301	5.1	31 585	72	20 522	1 893	4 924	3 277	3 104	1 317	1 067	401	139
Hot Springs, AR	2 292	3.5	25 450	234	1 128	139	646	546	522	232	211	35	12
Houma-Bayou Cane-Thibodaux, LA	4 773	3.8	24 246	292	3 111	334	709	867	816	308	376	96	13
Houston-Baytown-Sugar Land, TX	173 757	1.9	34 846	30	118 649	34 346	20 982	15 522	14 404	5 064	6 456	1 568	687
Huntington-Ashland, WV-KY-OH	6 630	3.4	23 167	322	4 197	289	1 029	1 697	1 625	581	610	182	36
Huntsville, AL	10 223	3.8	28 900	127	9 120	526	1 769	1 215	1 132	485	413	108	28
Idaho Falls, ID	2 605	4.4	24 819	274	1 630	280	429	376	353	149	143	26	15
Indianapolis, IN	51 841	2.1	32 922	48	38 769	4 512	8 547	5 888	5 496	2 294	2 168	494	221
Iowa City, IA	4 087	3.5	30 183	97	3 107	316	748	399	363	166	140	23	13
Ithaca, NY	2 521	4.1	25 412	238	2 057	134	531	358	332	133	122	38	10
Jackson, MI	4 030	2.6	25 035	264	2 539	167	650	731	693	295	264	68	38
Jackson, MS	13 550	3.1	26 805	185	9 267	1 208	2 165	2 250	2 119	752	926	274	34
Jackson, TN	2 766	3.1	25 309	244	2 218	251	370	515	491	175	212	56	17
Jacksonville, FL	35 338	4.0	30 008	100	25 145	2 135	6 489	4 648	4 365	1 658	1 780	433	111
Jacksonville, NC	3 808	5.9	25 557	232	3 066	114	479	453	427	130	170	54	13
Janesville, WI	4 138	3.2	26 854	184	2 828	149	640	668	629	273	244	49	43
Jefferson City, MO	3 708	2.0	26 082	210	2 743	259	654	557	524	221	225	36	14
Johnson City, TN	4 205	3.4	22 915	326	2 577	293	630	961	920	349	395	78	28
Johnstown, PA	3 590	2.6	23 861	305	1 967	230	587	1 017	979	351	447	65	45
Jonesboro, AR	2 399	2.7	21 914	340	1 551	169	387	497	468	174	195	50	17
Joplin, MO	3 747	2.6	23 389	317	2 545	304	603	767	729	282	325	67	18
Kalamazoo-Portage, MI	8 673	2.7	27 213	173	6 164	418	1 415	1 338	1 262	535	493	135	53
Kankakee-Bradley, IL	2 716	2.5	25 951	214	1 598	119	456	513	486	187	200	47	28
Kansas City, MO-KS	61 255	2.5	32 422	51	45 028	5 113	9 805	7 570	7 094	2 865	3 020	523	293
Kennewick-Richland-Pasco, WA	5 469	6.4	26 926	182	4 038	297	790	872	817	272	322	82	69
Killeen-Temple-Fort Hood, TX	8 231	5.2	24 351	291	6 167	397	1 118	1 082	1 016	326	391	104	31
Kingsport-Bristol-Bristol, TN-VA	7 317	2.7	24 437	288	4 637	512	1 228	1 566	1 498	670	589	127	36
Kingston, NY	4 864	3.3	27 024	179	2 201	287	845	919	872	335	392	82	27
Knoxville, TN	17 922	4.5	28 449	135	12 658	1 841	2 807	2 866	2 726	1 164	1 126	241	57
Kokomo, IN	2 892	2.4	28 529	134	2 649	121	430	464	439	207	174	35	11

1. Based on the resident population estimated as of July 1 of the year shown. 2. Includes other labor income.

Table C. Metropolitan Areas — Earnings, Social Security, and Housing

Area Name	Earnings, 2002									Social Security beneficiaries, December 2003		Housing units, 2003	
	Total (mil dol)	Farm	Percent by selected industries										
			Goods related[1]		Service-related and health				Govern-ment	Number	Rate[2]	Supplemental Security Income recipients, December 2003	
			Total	Manu-facturing	Infor-mation, profes-sional and technical services	Retail trade	Finance and insur-ance, and real estate	Health services					Total	Percent change, 2000–2003
	75	76	77	78	79	80	81	82	83	84	85	86	87	88
Florence, SC	3 692	-0.1	D	25.4	5.5	8.2	8.3	D	17.4	35 205	179	8 393	82 905	2.6
Florence-Muscle Shoals, AL	1 966	0.5	D	17.0	D	10.5	4.8	9.1	27.3	32 430	229	4 674	66 834	2.2
Fond du Lac, WI	2 093	1.1	43.6	35.2	4.7	6.2	4.9	9.8	11.5	17 135	175	1 119	40 501	3.1
Fort Collins-Loveland, CO	6 059	0.4	31.8	20.2	9.7	7.6	6.6	8.6	19.2	32 770	123	1 851	116 467	10.5
Fort Smith, AR-OK	4 669	1.7	D	23.3	D	7.2	4.1	D	13.3	55 370	198	9 126	118 629	2.8
Fort Walton Beach-Crestview-Destin, FL	4 174	0.0	D	3.5	10.3	7.3	7.1	6.1	44.4	29 935	168	2 475	83 243	5.9
Fort Wayne, IN	9 482	0.1	D	23.2	D	6.3	8.9	D	9.7	61 675	154	5 307	169 813	4.6
Fresno, CA	14 466	3.4	15.6	8.6	6.8	7.9	6.4	11.9	21.8	105 300	124	38 896	281 327	3.9
Gadsden, AL	1 393	1.2	D	19.1	4.6	8.8	5.1	18.5	14.7	24 265	236	4 422	47 038	2.3
Gainesville, FL	4 694	0.6	D	4.3	8.4	7.2	6.3	D	37.6	32 865	137	5 495	107 235	6.2
Gainesville, GA	2 863	0.9	34.4	27.0	4.6	7.3	7.9	12.3	12.3	21 105	135	2 276	57 011	11.7
Glens Falls, NY	2 034	1.0	D	16.8	D	9.5	5.1	13.3	21.0	25 525	202	3 020	63 155	2.4
Goldsboro, NC	1 836	0.6	D	14.7	2.9	7.8	3.9	10.7	35.1	20 995	186	4 359	48 951	3.5
Grand Forks, ND-MN	1 945	3.1	D	6.9	4.9	8.7	3.8	D	32.7	14 305	150	1 192	41 895	1.2
Grand Junction, CO	2 130	0.3	19.8	6.7	7.0	10.5	7.6	14.9	17.6	24 020	193	2 088	53 167	9.8
Grand Rapids-Wyoming, MI	18 715	0.3	32.9	26.4	D	7.1	7.4	9.8	9.6	110 445	145	13 880	305 429	4.2
Great Falls, MT	1 494	0.4	D	2.9	7.6	9.3	7.5	16.6	30.8	15 055	189	1 514	35 469	0.7
Greeley, CO	3 534	7.4	29.4	15.5	4.9	7.4	8.2	8.2	13.4	23 325	110	2 402	79 672	20.4
Green Bay, WI	7 163	0.7	D	21.6	D	6.9	8.1	D	11.8	44 345	152	3 771	125 512	6.2
Greensboro-High Point, NC	15 572	0.8	D	21.7	8.7	7.5	8.5	D	11.2	112 785	170	12 407	292 069	6.2
Greenville, NC	2 704	0.4	D	15.7	5.3	7.9	4.8	10.7	32.5	23 695	149	5 634	71 853	9.2
Greenville, SC	12 565	0.2	D	21.1	D	8.4	7.2	D	13.6	99 755	172	10 953	251 882	5.4
Gulfport-Biloxi, MS	5 011	-0.1	11.1	6.1	6.4	6.8	3.7	D	35.3	44 125	177	7 744	113 079	6.6
Hagerstown-Martinsburg, MD-WV	3 930	0.2	D	15.1	7.3	9.3	9.0	D	20.2	41 080	173	4 105	99 784	6.2
Hanford-Corcoran, CA	1 867	5.8	D	9.0	2.4	6.0	2.8	7.3	47.1	13 965	101	4 264	38 340	4.9
Harrisburg-Carlisle, PA	15 190	0.2	D	9.3	D	6.7	10.4	10.5	22.1	89 170	172	7 833	223 421	2.9
Harrisonburg, VA	2 189	1.4	D	28.1	6.1	9.1	4.3	9.4	15.2	17 225	156	1 336	42 808	4.4
Hartford-West Hartford-East Hartford, CT	37 921	0.2	D	15.1	10.9	6.1	19.6	10.5	14.3	202 445	172	19 073	481 421	2.0
Hattiesburg, MS	2 072	0.8	D	11.1	D	9.9	5.4	15.2	25.7	21 830	170	4 411	51 957	3.0
Hickory-Lenoir-Morganton, NC	6 638	1.3	D	37.2	D	7.3	3.5	D	12.8	65 490	187	5 944	152 226	5.1
Hinesville-Fort Stewart, GA	1 419	0.1	D	D	D	D	D	D	79.7	5 605	80	1 142	27 404	4.6
Holland-Grand Haven, MI	5 268	1.5	48.9	42.0	4.5	6.2	4.5	5.1	11.9	34 135	137	1 924	93 282	7.4
Honolulu, HI	22 415	0.3	7.9	2.1	9.9	6.7	6.4	9.0	34.2	136 730	151	15 918	322 845	2.2
Hot Springs, AR	1 267	0.8	19.4	11.3	5.1	10.7	5.7	21.0	15.0	24 615	270	2 631	45 670	1.6
Houma-Bayou Cane-Thibodaux, LA	3 445	0.4	30.4	11.2	4.5	7.1	7.3	8.0	13.4	33 775	171	6 829	77 554	3.4
Houston-Baytown-Sugar Land, TX	152 995	0.1	D	13.2	D	5.6	8.7	D	9.8	510 670	101	85 914	1 931 181	7.3
Huntington-Ashland, WV-KY-OH	4 486	0.0	19.5	12.9	6.1	8.5	5.2	D	18.5	61 455	214	14 447	130 689	0.6
Huntsville, AL	9 646	0.2	D	22.2	18.9	6.1	3.3	D	27.0	54 080	151	7 614	152 642	3.7
Idaho Falls, ID	1 910	3.6	13.7	5.4	D	9.2	4.1	D	14.4	15 760	147	1 649	39 180	6.6
Indianapolis, IN	43 281	0.1	D	17.1	D	6.7	11.1	D	12.4	225 295	141	21 387	693 774	7.6
Iowa City, IA	3 423	0.8	D	8.8	8.5	6.6	4.6	D	41.8	16 260	119	1 267	58 478	7.5
Ithaca, NY	2 191	0.5	13.0	10.1	8.1	5.4	3.7	D	12.5	12 790	126	1 571	39 917	3.3
Jackson, MI	2 705	0.0	27.4	21.4	4.0	9.4	5.1	11.6	17.8	28 775	177	3 587	65 532	4.2
Jackson, MS	10 474	0.6	D	7.8	11.8	7.7	9.0	D	21.1	81 165	159	17 775	205 390	4.5
Jackson, TN	2 470	-0.1	D	23.7	D	9.6	4.3	D	18.6	18 925	172	3 199	46 702	5.2
Jacksonville, FL	27 280	0.2	D	6.7	D	7.7	13.3	9.7	18.4	177 840	148	23 423	511 624	7.7
Jacksonville, NC	3 181	0.1	4.6	1.2	2.3	4.7	1.9	3.1	75.2	16 075	109	2 385	59 356	6.5
Janesville, WI	2 977	0.1	39.5	33.7	3.9	8.2	3.5	11.4	12.8	26 990	174	2 874	64 460	3.7
Jefferson City, MO	3 002	0.4	D	9.5	D	8.0	5.6	D	36.0	23 750	166	1 900	59 512	4.9
Johnson City, TN	2 870	0.4	24.6	19.0	D	8.9	6.0	D	20.2	39 165	210	5 439	84 189	2.8
Johnstown, PA	2 197	0.5	14.3	9.0	9.1	9.7	7.0	18.0	19.5	36 215	242	4 715	66 182	0.6
Jonesboro, AR	1 721	-0.1	D	19.8	5.4	8.7	6.4	17.0	16.9	20 370	185	4 157	47 770	3.4
Joplin, MO	2 848	0.8	D	25.0	4.1	9.1	4.0	14.8	11.0	31 265	193	3 746	69 813	3.5
Kalamazoo-Portage, MI	6 581	0.7	D	27.0	6.1	7.7	6.8	10.6	15.5	52 270	163	6 655	138 389	3.9
Kankakee-Bradley, IL	1 717	1.5	27.8	21.2	D	9.2	5.3	15.6	15.7	18 995	180	2 573	41 752	2.8
Kansas City, MO-KS	50 141	0.0	17.0	9.9	D	D	D	D	14.6	282 605	148	25 248	809 721	5.5
Kennewick-Richland-Pasco, WA	4 335	4.6	12.7	6.7	20.1	6.7	3.5	7.7	17.9	26 855	128	3 081	77 110	7.0
Killeen-Temple-Fort Hood, TX	6 564	0.1	10.3	5.9	D	6.5	3.6	8.3	54.8	38 885	113	5 340	130 359	6.7
Kingsport-Bristol-Bristol, TN-VA	5 149	0.1	D	30.5	D	8.7	4.2	12.2	11.5	72 605	242	10 253	140 259	2.9
Kingston, NY	2 489	0.6	15.8	10.4	7.2	11.3	5.8	13.7	26.0	33 120	183	4 266	79 456	2.3
Knoxville, TN	14 499	0.1	D	14.5	D	10.1	6.4	11.4	15.1	119 125	187	15 508	288 323	4.4
Kokomo, IN	2 771	0.5	D	58.9	3.5	5.8	2.9	D	10.3	19 760	195	1 803	45 673	2.7

1. Covers mining, construction, and manufacturing.   2. Per 1,000 resident population estimated as of July 1 of the year shown.

Table C. Metropolitan Areas — Housing, Labor Force, and Employment

Area Name	Housing units, 2000 Occupied units Total	Percent	Owner-occupied Mean value[1]	Owner cost is 35 percent or more of income With a mortgage	Without a mortgage	Renter-occupied Mean rent[2]	Rent is 35 percent or more of income	Sub-standard units[3] (percent)	Civilian labor force, 2003 Total	Percent change, 2002–2003	Unemployment Total	Rate[4]	Civilian employment,[5] 2000 Total	Percent Management, professional, and related occupations	Production, transportation, and material moving occupations
	89	90	91	92	93	94	95	96	97	98	99	100	101	102	103
Florence, SC	72 940	74.4	103 034	18.0	8.5	447	31.1	4.2	93 518	1.9	8 140	8.7	84 398	28.3	20.5
Florence-Muscle Shoals, AL	58 549	74.2	99 881	17.7	7.3	431	32.5	1.9	63 335	-1.2	5 015	7.9	62 016	25.4	22.1
Fond du Lac, WI	36 931	73.0	117 671	11.9	7.7	513	23.4	1.6	57 216	1.2	3 110	5.4	51 374	26.3	25.3
Fort Collins-Loveland, CO	97 164	67.7	201 557	17.7	4.7	726	35.0	2.6	155 314	1.2	8 840	5.7	136 903	39.6	11.5
Fort Smith, AR-OK	104 506	70.4	81 199	15.5	6.5	426	26.8	5.1	126 765	-0.8	7 152	5.6	118 959	24.9	25.8
Fort Walton Beach-Crestview-Destin, FL	66 269	66.4	132 178	17.1	4.7	634	27.0	3.2	91 434	2.6	2 477	2.7	71 992	32.0	9.2
Fort Wayne, IN	150 858	72.6	108 136	11.5	3.6	530	26.0	2.4	211 480	-0.5	11 609	5.5	197 724	30.7	20.6
Fresno, CA	252 940	56.5	129 555	24.4	8.4	569	37.9	17.6	399 098	1.2	56 815	14.2	301 306	29.5	13.3
Gadsden, AL	41 615	74.4	85 218	18.7	7.3	392	28.5	2.1	47 192	0.1	2 863	6.1	43 426	25.3	23.2
Gainesville, FL	92 530	56.6	120 186	18.5	7.0	599	45.1	3.9	119 242	0.8	2 927	2.5	111 049	43.0	7.1
Gainesville, GA	47 381	71.1	156 861	17.7	7.2	631	27.2	8.8	80 368	3.9	2 832	3.5	66 587	26.3	24.0
Glens Falls, NY	48 184	72.0	111 252	19.5	9.2	544	32.2	2.0	62 228	2.6	3 056	4.9	57 428	28.8	16.6
Goldsboro, NC	42 612	65.3	105 809	17.4	7.9	462	25.4	4.1	51 492	-1.0	3 026	5.9	47 140	28.1	18.8
Grand Forks, ND-MN	37 505	60.2	96 954	13.0	6.0	474	29.6	2.8	54 556	1.0	2 108	3.9	47 732	31.6	12.2
Grand Junction, CO	45 823	72.7	141 565	20.3	4.2	575	35.5	3.3	66 793	3.8	3 806	5.7	55 046	29.3	12.9
Grand Rapids-Wyoming, MI	272 130	73.2	133 109	13.2	5.7	566	26.6	3.5	410 824	0.7	31 870	7.8	364 330	29.7	21.7
Great Falls, MT	32 547	64.9	106 331	19.5	4.5	438	29.4	3.5	36 527	0.8	1 674	4.6	34 792	30.5	10.4
Greeley, CO	63 247	68.7	162 079	21.3	7.7	589	34.2	7.1	101 880	3.3	6 830	6.7	87 626	29.5	15.9
Green Bay, WI	108 897	68.8	128 669	12.2	6.8	533	23.2	2.8	173 496	2.8	9 618	5.5	148 913	29.5	20.3
Greensboro-High Point, NC	256 315	67.0	132 289	17.3	6.2	575	27.7	3.8	354 381	0.5	23 228	6.6	326 667	30.3	20.5
Greenville, NC	59 235	60.0	116 913	17.1	12.3	497	36.5	5.0	82 615	0.3	5 456	6.6	72 458	32.5	15.6
Greenville, SC	217 152	70.3	129 070	16.1	5.9	549	29.4	3.0	283 380	2.3	15 818	5.6	272 996	30.9	19.5
Gulfport-Biloxi, MS	93 182	66.7	110 211	19.0	9.3	538	30.2	5.0	112 133	2.2	5 053	4.5	105 272	27.4	12.1
Hagerstown-Martinsburg, MD-WV	85 440	69.8	121 382	16.9	6.2	493	24.6	1.9	115 590	-0.1	5 307	4.6	104 330	26.0	19.7
Hanford-Corcoran, CA	34 418	55.9	110 416	21.6	7.4	577	32.9	16.0	49 138	3.7	7 162	14.6	39 511	25.9	13.7
Harrisburg-Carlisle, PA	202 380	69.7	125 310	15.8	6.5	568	25.3	2.0	293 960	-1.5	11 128	3.8	251 256	33.8	15.0
Harrisonburg, VA	38 488	64.7	128 592	15.5	5.1	526	29.6	3.8	60 916	1.0	1 511	2.5	53 484	28.2	21.3
Hartford-West Hartford-East Hartford, CT	445 870	66.3	176 237	16.6	10.1	670	29.3	3.0	596 605	0.3	34 494	5.8	565 554	39.6	12.1
Hattiesburg, MS	45 999	67.5	94 838	20.9	9.2	472	34.1	4.6	59 065	3.5	2 548	4.3	54 735	30.4	15.0
Hickory-Lenoir-Morganton, NC	133 966	74.3	115 939	16.6	5.7	500	22.5	3.7	177 228	-1.5	15 526	8.8	176 415	22.2	34.3
Hinesville-Fort Stewart, GA	22 957	53.1	87 202	21.2	12.0	533	24.8	6.5	24 552	2.6	1 202	4.9	21 198	23.4	16.1
Holland-Grand Haven, MI	81 662	80.8	157 260	12.0	3.8	613	23.9	3.0	139 957	-0.3	8 625	6.2	123 168	31.8	21.7
Honolulu, HI	286 450	54.5	348 586	29.0	4.0	865	33.9	16.4	436 442	1.7	16 901	3.9	383 148	33.8	8.8
Hot Springs, AR	37 813	71.2	113 499	19.2	4.9	512	32.3	2.8	37 697	-0.1	2 432	6.5	36 530	27.7	14.8
Houma-Bayou Cane-Thibodaux, LA	68 054	76.7	95 011	16.4	7.2	450	28.2	6.5	99 388	3.1	3 851	3.9	78 613	25.2	18.9
Houston-Baytown-Sugar Land, TX	1 656 799	60.9	123 782	15.7	9.0	640	27.0	11.8	2 584 531	2.4	180 728	7.0	2 140 728	35.1	12.6
Huntington-Ashland, WV-KY-OH	117 697	72.3	84 674	18.0	5.8	424	34.6	1.9	123 244	1.0	7 329	5.9	115 087	27.6	15.6
Huntsville, AL	134 643	71.2	124 754	12.8	4.9	509	26.9	2.5	184 176	4.9	8 289	4.5	164 625	40.4	14.8
Idaho Falls, ID	34 654	76.4	109 519	13.6	4.5	523	31.2	5.3	60 385	3.0	2 054	3.4	46 598	35.0	12.1
Indianapolis, IN	594 874	67.6	138 703	14.3	5.8	598	27.6	2.7	868 643	1.3	39 846	4.6	774 031	34.1	15.1
Iowa City, IA	52 136	59.6	143 778	12.6	4.4	598	41.2	2.4	84 670	-3.8	2 836	3.3	75 021	41.6	10.2
Ithaca, NY	36 420	53.8	124 098	16.0	8.7	673	43.8	2.6	55 119	1.6	1 687	3.1	48 192	50.2	7.5
Jackson, MI	58 168	76.5	114 931	12.8	4.8	513	29.7	2.4	79 492	1.5	6 331	8.0	71 695	27.5	21.7
Jackson, MS	180 556	69.9	105 315	17.9	8.8	534	30.9	6.4	262 226	3.0	11 636	4.4	223 384	34.1	13.2
Jackson, TN	41 212	68.4	100 887	14.4	7.2	508	31.2	3.0	59 214	-2.5	3 411	5.8	50 652	29.8	20.1
Jacksonville, FL	432 627	67.5	132 102	17.7	6.1	638	28.1	4.4	602 268	0.4	31 198	5.2	529 169	31.9	11.9
Jacksonville, NC	48 122	58.1	104 044	19.0	6.6	534	23.2	4.4	51 531	1.1	2 953	5.7	49 020	26.1	11.4
Janesville, WI	58 617	71.2	110 704	13.0	5.6	542	24.7	2.4	79 113	1.2	5 393	6.8	76 336	25.4	26.8
Jefferson City, MO	51 637	72.8	105 806	10.7	3.6	441	21.1	2.1	82 076	2.1	2 855	3.5	69 206	31.6	14.5
Johnson City, TN	75 197	71.1	107 563	18.4	5.9	450	29.9	2.1	88 847	-1.8	4 968	5.6	84 524	28.2	19.0
Johnstown, PA	60 531	74.7	74 403	17.9	7.8	373	27.0	1.2	64 914	-1.7	4 402	6.8	61 115	27.9	17.2
Jonesboro, AR	42 327	64.6	89 303	16.1	7.6	446	33.4	2.9	54 406	-1.2	3 316	6.1	50 744	26.4	22.8
Joplin, MO	61 552	70.1	83 176	13.4	5.8	444	26.2	3.2	84 466	0.3	4 450	5.3	73 961	25.9	23.8
Kalamazoo-Portage, MI	121 461	68.9	126 503	13.0	5.4	548	32.4	2.8	166 361	1.5	9 811	5.9	156 365	32.6	17.5
Kankakee-Bradley, IL	38 182	69.4	116 145	18.1	7.6	553	31.3	3.7	52 354	-0.3	4 027	7.7	48 227	26.1	20.7
Kansas City, MO-KS	717 761	68.2	125 941	13.7	6.4	603	25.7	3.1	1 052 918	2.2	63 539	6.0	919 353	35.4	12.8
Kennewick-Richland-Pasco, WA	67 706	68.1	131 811	14.8	4.2	586	28.7	9.1	104 534	3.8	8 122	7.8	85 746	34.9	12.9
Killeen-Temple-Fort Hood, TX	112 011	56.6	88 492	16.2	6.6	570	24.8	6.9	133 696	2.3	7 343	5.5	118 987	30.1	13.7
Kingsport-Bristol-Bristol, TN-VA	124 021	76.1	101 212	17.0	6.0	426	24.3	2.0	143 171	0.3	8 724	6.1	131 054	26.5	22.6
Kingston, NY	67 499	70.2	128 255	20.9	12.4	638	37.3	2.7	86 454	0.6	3 693	4.3	83 748	35.4	12.1
Knoxville, TN	253 005	70.2	124 299	17.4	6.0	502	31.1	1.9	338 114	-0.2	11 969	3.5	294 630	33.6	14.4
Kokomo, IN	41 269	73.0	105 114	12.1	4.6	521	26.9	1.7	50 698	0.6	3 287	6.5	47 717	25.9	26.8

1. Specified owner-occupied units. 2. Specified renter-occupied units. 3. Overcrowded or lacking complete plumbing facilities. 4. Percent of civilian labor force. 5. Persons 16 years old and over.

Table C. Metropolitan Areas — Nonfarm Employment and Agriculture

Area Name	Number of establishments	Total	Health care and social assistance	Manufacturing	Retail trade	Finance and insurance	Professional, scientific, and technical services	Total (mil dol)	Average per employee (dollars)	Number	Less than 50 acres	500 acres and over	Farm operators whose principal occupation is farming (percent)
	104	105	106	107	108	109	110	111	112	113	114	115	116
Florence, SC	4 522	78 012	12 150	17 621	12 017	5 136	1 907	2 119	27 162	973	35.7	15.6	55.4
Florence-Muscle Shoals, AL	3 359	49 578	7 062	10 848	8 177	1 484	1 163	1 077	21 723	2 069	42.1	5.9	47.6
Fond du Lac, WI	2 461	44 586	5 273	11 589	6 220	1 630	2 198	1 269	28 462	1 634	27.2	8.8	67.0
Fort Collins-Loveland, CO	8 160	96 202	10 443	12 980	15 956	3 070	6 329	2 878	29 916	1 564	61.5	9.8	48.3
Fort Smith, AR-OK	5 832	105 601	15 172	29 633	14 172	2 987	4 658	2 639	24 990	5 746	32.8	7.8	53.4
Fort Walton Beach-Crestview-Destin, FL	4 771	60 333	7 770	2 896	11 891	2 351	4 613	1 421	23 553	465	49.7	3.4	46.5
Fort Wayne, IN	10 307	194 215	24 702	40 914	24 834	10 617	7 591	5 932	30 543	3 021	41.4	12.7	57.7
Fresno, CA	15 337	218 995	33 357	25 833	32 648	10 618	9 190	6 206	28 339	6 281	58.1	11.5	69.5
Gadsden, AL	2 133	32 845	5 386	6 397	4 821	957	552	770	23 443	974	52.1	2.3	50.0
Gainesville, FL	5 363	85 948	17 498	4 597	14 140	4 380	5 570	2 128	24 759	1 901	61.4	5.8	49.8
Gainesville, GA	3 403	56 748	5 893	19 007	7 021	2 303	1 288	1 617	28 494	834	61.0	1.4	54.9
Glens Falls, NY	3 447	43 045	6 469	8 467	7 329	1 728	1 330	1 286	29 876	959	26.9	12.9	60.6
Goldsboro, NC	2 317	38 610	7 354	9 144	5 892	1 146	731	911	23 595	722	42.5	13.3	66.5
Grand Forks, ND-MN	2 566	36 902	7 620	3 480	7 427	1 138	1 060	871	23 603	2 381	11.8	40.4	65.1
Grand Junction, CO	4 073	44 063	7 127	3 790	7 602	1 437	2 019	1 164	26 417	1 599	66.4	7.6	51.2
Grand Rapids-Wyoming, MI	18 260	364 943	39 730	84 574	46 627	17 106	16 570	12 253	33 575	4 323	43.3	7.5	52.7
Great Falls, MT	2 519	27 540	5 594	937	5 281	2 064	1 007	607	22 041	1 037	26.8	37.0	56.8
Greeley, CO	4 281	58 214	5 899	9 809	8 227	3 939	2 010	1 784	30 646	3 121	31.5	21.3	57.8
Green Bay, WI	7 697	145 892	16 848	31 928	18 411	10 376	5 089	4 504	30 872	3 164	31.4	6.7	62.5
Greensboro-High Point, NC	18 149	335 279	31 556	80 085	40 673	18 844	12 466	10 076	30 053	3 549	46.0	3.8	56.7
Greenville, NC	3 437	56 376	11 329	9 453	8 438	1 844	2 106	1 382	24 514	719	29.9	25.0	72.5
Greenville, SC	14 525	289 228	24 223	56 546	31 300	10 229	12 497	8 823	30 505	2 462	51.1	4.0	42.8
Gulfport-Biloxi, MS	5 433	89 933	13 517	5 075	13 516	2 871	3 851	2 195	24 407	1 046	50.1	3.1	45.6
Hagerstown-Martinsburg, MD-WV	5 070	81 313	13 654	13 645	13 550	7 368	2 032	2 236	27 499	1 629	43.6	4.2	55.3
Hanford-Corcoran, CA	1 550	19 929	2 832	3 283	3 644	651	358	485	24 336	1 154	48.7	18.7	67.2
Harrisburg-Carlisle, PA	12 913	261 367	33 527	25 469	33 285	20 741	13 136	8 128	31 098	2 720	37.8	4.3	58.6
Harrisonburg, VA	2 738	48 260	5 625	14 080	6 950	1 161	1 454	1 275	26 419	2 043	40.7	3.9	62.9
Hartford-West Hartford-East Hartford, CT	29 781	567 921	80 871	82 612	64 035	74 678	33 013	23 509	41 395	1 448	66.6	2.1	50.1
Hattiesburg, MS	2 992	43 221	8 501	5 952	7 748	1 791	1 769	1 028	23 785	1 336	42.1	3.1	45.2
Hickory-Lenoir-Morganton, NC	8 142	165 808	15 823	77 056	17 516	3 004	2 411	4 242	25 584	2 226	53.8	2.7	54.7
Hinesville-Fort Stewart, GA	753	9 956	1 655	1 009	2 196	510	285	207	20 791	144	27.1	17.4	39.6
Holland-Grand Haven, MI	5 995	105 640	9 837	40 168	12 908	2 372	3 441	3 286	31 106	1 291	54.3	5.0	56.8
Honolulu, HI	20 801	320 461	38 942	11 549	43 687	15 971	16 596	9 624	30 032	794	91.4	2.4	69.9
Hot Springs, AR	2 616	30 794	6 349	3 908	5 970	846	827	685	22 245	386	42.0	3.6	51.3
Houma-Bayou Cane-Thibodaux, LA	4 570	67 037	8 353	6 983	11 259	1 768	2 456	1 951	29 103	561	40.5	13.9	51.7
Houston-Baytown-Sugar Land, TX	108 781	2 006 031	191 654	201 870	234 401	90 046	144 087	80 659	40 208	15 175	51.2	8.4	48.3
Huntington-Ashland, WV-KY-OH	6 249	93 687	19 466	12 463	15 473	4 509	3 390	2 505	26 738	2 301	31.0	2.6	50.7
Huntsville, AL	8 293	147 076	16 439	30 261	19 789	3 608	20 446	4 798	32 623	2 352	45.5	6.6	53.4
Idaho Falls, ID	3 024	41 341	5 167	3 159	6 689	1 184	9 259	1 234	29 849	1 747	53.7	17.2	52.0
Indianapolis, IN	40 200	783 894	98 336	98 352	98 154	49 195	39 718	27 600	35 209	6 034	52.2	12.7	52.8
Iowa City, IA	3 321	58 059	13 705	6 129	9 385	1 694	1 961	1 529	26 335	2 461	26.7	15.8	67.5
Ithaca, NY	2 143	43 074	3 672	4 045	4 801	991	2 122	1 128	26 187	563	38.9	8.9	55.1
Jackson, MI	3 398	53 738	7 815	11 774	8 516	1 506	1 294	1 608	29 923	1 265	46.2	6.0	48.4
Jackson, MS	12 083	210 150	33 304	20 196	30 033	11 995	8 696	5 734	27 285	4 144	33.7	7.6	47.7
Jackson, TN	2 834	55 724	8 419	13 084	7 819	1 371	1 261	1 484	26 631	1 252	34.3	7.7	47.3
Jacksonville, FL	29 257	501 262	57 451	34 044	64 827	54 415	23 420	14 907	29 739	1 445	66.9	5.2	50.4
Jacksonville, NC	2 562	29 978	4 142	1 564	6 841	945	928	559	18 647	404	44.3	5.7	59.4
Janesville, WI	3 346	58 409	7 199	15 812	8 454	1 605	1 286	1 794	30 714	1 529	45.4	10.2	56.3
Jefferson City, MO	3 471	53 276	8 192	6 589	7 391	2 330	1 364	1 348	25 302	4 950	20.6	9.9	54.0
Johnson City, TN	3 717	63 823	10 716	12 496	9 149	3 400	1 491	1 537	24 082	2 652	63.0	1.9	52.9
Johnstown, PA	3 520	49 418	10 115	6 010	7 866	3 371	2 672	1 160	23 473	634	34.4	5.8	48.9
Jonesboro, AR	2 676	38 977	6 169	9 928	6 388	1 122	832	918	23 552	1 178	23.1	40.2	70.5
Joplin, MO	4 084	71 194	11 171	15 974	9 852	1 608	1 308	1 746	24 525	3 142	34.1	6.9	56.9
Kalamazoo-Portage, MI	7 433	129 474	17 791	23 590	17 821	4 871	5 871	4 287	33 111	1 968	48.8	6.6	55.0
Kankakee-Bradley, IL	2 275	37 535	5 922	6 877	5 669	1 816	682	1 066	28 400	722	22.6	32.3	72.2
Kansas City, MO-KS	49 547	904 200	101 995	90 157	111 732	59 347	61 832	31 157	34 458	14 737	32.2	11.7	53.8
Kennewick-Richland-Pasco, WA	4 451	63 639	7 672	7 096	10 198	1 522	6 740	2 061	32 386	2 256	57.9	16.7	61.5
Killeen-Temple-Fort Hood, TX	5 213	86 465	20 053	8 533	13 234	3 937	4 270	2 121	24 530	4 162	33.9	15.1	51.1
Kingsport-Bristol-Bristol, TN-VA	6 366	109 720	14 579	30 187	15 751	2 952	2 665	3 117	28 409	6 778	49.6	2.1	51.9
Kingston, NY	4 363	46 676	8 387	6 227	8 686	2 288	2 333	1 177	25 216	532	44.7	6.6	64.1
Knoxville, TN	15 915	279 771	38 155	39 784	40 445	11 875	21 484	8 408	30 053	4 847	55.1	1.5	47.1
Kokomo, IN	2 293	45 642	5 594	17 064	6 694	1 161	650	1 803	39 503	896	34.8	22.0	65.5

Table C. Metropolitan Areas — **Agriculture**

	Agriculture, 2002 (cont'd)															
	Land in farms					Value of land and buildings (dollars)		Value of machinery and equipment average per farm (dollars)	Value of products sold				Percent of farms with sales of —		Government payments	
			Acres								Percent from —					
Area Name	Acreage (1,000)	Percent change, 1997–2002	Average size of farm	Total irrigated (1,000)	Total cropland (1,000)	Average per farm	Average per acre		Total (mil dol)	Average per farm (dollars)	Crops	Live-stock and poultry products	$10,000 or more	$100,000 or more	Total ($1,000)	Percent of farms
	117	118	119	120	121	122	123	124	125	126	127	128	129	130	131	132
Florence, SC	333	1.8	342	3	201	450 654	1 292	105 066	75	76 705	65.2	34.8	36.4	14.6	3 452	36.1
Florence-Muscle Shoals, AL	340	0.0	164	3	186	248 768	1 641	37 602	63	30 320	35.9	64.1	21.7	4.9	3 943	28.6
Fond du Lac, WI	344	5.8	211	1	292	514 396	2 351	97 653	166	101 700	25.0	75.0	57.2	27.7	7 894	62.9
Fort Collins-Loveland, CO	522	-3.7	334	59	140	778 424	2 311	62 865	101	64 639	32.6	67.4	24.6	5.9	766	12.1
Fort Smith, AR-OK	1 082	-3.9	188	17	508	260 325	1 473	36 395	397	69 129	8.6	91.4	32.6	10.3	1 339	9.4
Fort Walton Beach-Crestview-Destin, FL	55	7.8	119	0	20	292 073	2 539	70 199	7	14 065	54.7	45.3	16.1	2.6	418	21.9
Fort Wayne, IN	683	7.2	226	D	618	620 518	2 810	78 443	183	60 650	69.9	30.1	49.1	15.5	10 792	50.3
Fresno, CA	1 929	2.6	307	1 099	1 230	1 101 948	3 612	99 231	2 759	439 328	77.9	22.1	71.9	32.7	18 898	8.5
Gadsden, AL	90	-5.3	93	0	45	252 802	2 856	31 743	48	49 003	5.5	94.5	21.5	8.4	587	15.0
Gainesville, FL	304	10.1	160	17	107	462 167	2 981	28 895	103	54 299	42.4	57.6	27.2	6.2	1 030	8.3
Gainesville, GA	62	21.6	74	0	21	336 075	5 384	37 639	170	204 137	0.8	99.2	34.5	21.6	491	20.9
Glens Falls, NY	213	4.4	222	1	132	298 501	1 410	89 868	84	88 098	16.7	83.3	49.2	21.0	D	D
Goldsboro, NC	171	-25.3	237	7	127	722 503	3 162	124 792	318	440 064	13.7	86.3	61.2	38.5	2 524	33.8
Grand Forks, ND-MN	1 867	2.2	784	25	1 685	635 430	814	163 847	342	143 649	91.3	8.7	49.7	29.3	26 288	79.7
Grand Junction, CO	385	-7.7	241	66	120	553 679	1 426	48 705	59	37 038	49.9	50.1	30.1	6.7	879	11.1
Grand Rapids-Wyoming, MI	721	1.5	167	21	547	525 136	3 008	70 229	371	85 925	50.9	49.1	33.1	11.9	13 078	33.7
Great Falls, MT	1 389	-3.6	1 339	42	507	603 928	425	58 769	51	49 160	36.8	63.2	42.9	13.1	6 100	43.7
Greeley, CO	1 812	-5.3	581	326	878	759 282	1 379	112 747	1 128	361 376	18.2	81.8	47.6	17.3	13 111	37.6
Green Bay, WI	590	5.2	186	1	467	462 465	2 473	78 424	329	103 843	17.2	82.8	47.9	22.4	11 948	51.3
Greensboro-High Point, NC	404	2.5	114	8	180	406 663	3 773	52 482	222	62 548	30.3	69.7	31.3	13.0	1 816	17.4
Greenville, NC	284	-4.4	394	10	213	1 020 660	2 598	125 199	279	388 061	31.1	68.9	63.7	41.7	5 608	40.8
Greenville, SC	276	13.1	112	3	120	407 296	3 010	35 723	40	16 441	54.8	45.2	14.4	2.1	748	11.6
Gulfport-Biloxi, MS	120	25.0	115	0	37	290 278	2 424	21 727	13	12 260	44.3	55.7	19.6	2.2	197	7.1
Hagerstown-Martinsburg, MD-WV	225	-0.9	138	D	142	471 573	3 455	48 342	79	48 668	30.3	69.8	32.7	13.5	2 679	19.3
Hanford-Corcoran, CA	646	-1.7	559	407	500	2 012 543	3 643	167 431	793	687 228	49.8	50.2	65.8	42.5	10 038	25.1
Harrisburg-Carlisle, PA	367	6.4	135	2	282	504 204	3 986	57 769	206	75 710	17.7	82.3	42.7	20.3	5 294	28.2
Harrisonburg, VA	249	NA	122	4	148	498 534	4 043	56 927	447	218 631	3.0	97.0	55.8	38.1	4 811	17.5
Hartford-West Hartford-East Hartford, CT	105	-2.8	72	7	57	734 942	10 425	54 660	199	137 531	78.9	21.1	34.6	11.6	D	D
Hattiesburg, MS	155	2.0	116	1	50	272 232	2 234	32 149	54	40 184	8.1	91.9	22.3	8.7	605	13.5
Hickory-Lenoir-Morganton, NC	204	2.5	92	4	103	356 506	4 177	41 429	135	60 680	27.7	72.3	29.3	13.8	1 014	14.1
Hinesville-Fort Stewart, GA	40	0.0	275	1	9	464 359	1 805	30 831	8	57 382	20.9	79.1	24.3	8.3	77	19.4
Holland-Grand Haven, MI	165	-3.5	128	14	138	574 104	4 352	85 231	278	214 952	59.4	40.6	49.6	22.3	3 435	23.3
Honolulu, HI	71	-11.3	89	14	29	738 577	8 358	37 543	179	225 845	83.1	16.9	58.2	17.1	60	1.8
Hot Springs, AR	46	7.0	120	0	18	258 863	2 260	23 075	10	24 938	22.9	77.1	15.0	3.4	D	D
Houma-Bayou Cane-Thibodaux, LA	204	8.5	364	D	90	547 138	1 562	93 116	42	75 011	75.7	24.3	37.1	12.1	157	13.2
Houston-Baytown-Sugar Land, TX	2 977	4.6	196	87	1 232	390 225	1 938	30 855	278	18 295	56.2	43.8	21.0	3.2	16 943	6.2
Huntington-Ashland, WV-KY-OH	280	14.8	122	0	93	156 106	1 366	21 260	15	6 427	57.3	42.7	12.3	0.6	349	12.4
Huntsville, AL	424	-8.6	180	13	283	395 951	2 188	48 722	90	38 232	63.0	37.0	24.7	7.2	5 908	30.6
Idaho Falls, ID	783	0.1	448	344	554	597 141	1 480	91 767	278	159 038	68.0	32.0	36.3	16.0	8 992	31.1
Indianapolis, IN	1 381	-2.5	229	D	1 228	746 219	3 224	76 146	440	73 002	D	D	41.0	15.4	21 350	33.9
Iowa City, IA	635	4.8	258	0	542	582 008	2 321	92 274	279	113 549	42.0	58.0	61.0	26.6	14 798	67.1
Ithaca, NY	101	6.3	179	0	67	304 567	1 686	252 933	42	74 437	21.1	78.9	36.4	13.0	1 492	24.5
Jackson, MI	193	6.6	153	5	145	453 511	2 902	48 062	43	34 068	49.2	50.8	31.1	6.5	2 994	28.4
Jackson, MS	863	21.5	208	2	309	360 521	1 568	42 551	297	71 724	10.9	89.1	22.1	8.2	6 897	22.8
Jackson, TN	241	10.0	192	3	163	416 810	2 240	53 605	32	25 511	78.2	21.8	20.8	4.8	2 428	45.3
Jacksonville, FL	D	D	D	26	53	510 232	D	36 375	172	119 105	46.1	53.9	21.3	10.4	D	D
Jacksonville, NC	64	1.6	158	2	44	427 198	2 949	78 796	90	222 911	19.4	80.6	47.0	24.8	586	21.3
Janesville, WI	344	-2.0	225	16	302	705 051	3 452	77 699	118	77 242	53.8	46.2	43.4	17.2	6 849	54.2
Jefferson City, MO	1 116	7.6	226	8	611	383 469	1 613	44 312	213	42 986	20.7	79.3	40.6	7.1	6 214	36.8
Johnson City, TN	180	8.4	68	1	111	288 692	3 959	51 786	50	18 783	D	D	20.5	2.7	546	8.3
Johnstown, PA	88	0.0	139	0	58	421 590	2 687	48 999	18	28 773	43.1	56.9	25.9	6.2	819	26.5
Jonesboro, AR	732	-4.3	621	530	675	965 158	1 652	155 456	181	153 397	97.3	2.7	62.6	37.4	29 584	48.4
Joplin, MO	557	5.7	177	9	318	278 293	1 622	33 360	204	64 918	14.2	85.8	34.7	7.6	2 809	27.7
Kalamazoo-Portage, MI	324	0.0	165	53	252	532 833	3 139	77 718	251	127 695	77.1	22.9	41.3	15.0	4 107	25.2
Kankakee-Bradley, IL	347	-1.4	481	14	334	1 342 239	2 812	137 679	120	166 150	92.0	8.0	74.4	37.5	4 886	66.1
Kansas City, MO-KS	3 681	4.9	250	25	2 448	427 148	1 699	54 859	506	34 308	53.1	46.9	34.9	6.6	30 042	39.0
Kennewick-Richland-Pasco, WA	1 273	8.2	564	429	946	857 738	1 569	152 140	751	332 914	88.4	11.6	48.6	29.2	14 769	26.1
Killeen-Temple-Fort Hood, TX	1 357	-8.8	326	4	479	396 986	1 186	31 463	89	21 359	26.9	73.1	26.2	3.0	2 412	17.1
Kingsport-Bristol-Bristol, TN-VA	624	68.2	92	2	292	231 149	2 457	34 510	108	15 905	30.6	69.4	20.8	2.4	1 257	7.5
Kingston, NY	83	20.3	157	4	39	534 962	3 539	81 821	34	64 692	83.5	16.5	39.5	10.7	777	12.8
Knoxville, TN	377	8.6	78	1	220	351 847	4 477	39 472	102	21 096	D	D	15.6	2.0	1 004	8.2
Kokomo, IN	308	0.7	344	D	290	993 923	3 163	108 718	113	125 570	73.6	26.4	65.8	27.5	5 060	55.0

Area Name	Value of residential construction authorized by building permits, 2003		Wholesale trade, 1997				Retail trade,[1] 1997				Real estate and rental and leasing, 1997			
	New construction ($1,000)	Number of housing units	Number of establishments	Number of employees	Sales (mil dol)	Annual payroll (mil dol)	Number of establishments	Number of employees	Sales (mil dol)	Annual payroll (mil dol)	Number of establishments	Number of employees	Receipts (mil dol)	Annual payroll (mil dol)
	133	134	135	136	137	138	139	140	141	142	143	144	145	146
Florence, SC	24 765	251	287	3 705	1 745.6	100.7	1 069	11 650	1 890.7	174.7	143	480	48.1	8.5
Florence-Muscle Shoals, AL	30 974	442	209	3 132	773.2	75.8	735	8 461	1 308.3	119.9	121	434	41.9	7.5
Fond du Lac, WI	69 880	484	116	1 204	528.2	36.0	413	5 744	891.2	86.6	73	297	27.9	4.5
Fort Collins-Loveland, CO	431 406	3 003	311	2 630	805.6	75.9	1 201	13 810	2 440.5	234.2	360	1 497	190.0	27.8
Fort Smith, AR-OK	91 104	914	353	D	D	D	1 214	13 746	2 166.4	193.8	220	904	97.8	15.2
Fort Walton Beach-Crestview-Destin, FL	298 170	1 749	139	959	248.3	23.9	931	11 322	1 754.9	165.7	280	1 582	140.3	29.0
Fort Wayne, IN	402 454	2 631	753	12 836	7 209.5	401.8	1 544	24 687	3 919.6	390.0	386	2 151	279.8	46.0
Fresno, CA	834 578	5 753	971	13 004	5 845.2	415.5	2 492	30 231	5 574.6	548.9	593	3 496	376.5	67.3
Gadsden, AL	29 584	335	135	D	D	D	452	4 935	737.8	65.9	68	273	23.9	4.4
Gainesville, FL	182 452	1 763	235	D	D	D	957	12 932	1 964.4	189.0	285	1 645	156.2	28.6
Gainesville, GA	221 199	1 830	238	3 407	1 777.8	100.6	548	6 357	1 240.8	114.6	105	398	44.3	9.0
Glens Falls, NY	93 495	778	137	D	D	D	675	6 929	1 115.8	109.8	87	341	45.3	6.1
Goldsboro, NC	63 909	690	151	2 217	891.1	59.4	523	6 169	1 033.0	88.1	81	263	21.0	4.5
Grand Forks, ND-MN	65 209	674	187	1 926	758.6	51.3	503	6 973	1 146.4	101.1	85	590	37.2	7.9
Grand Junction, CO	195 007	1 589	198	1 461	531.1	42.8	600	6 409	1 152.7	115.0	133	658	62.6	11.6
Grand Rapids-Wyoming, MI	596 197	4 284	1 433	29 351	16 168.7	1 072.5	2 714	43 480	7 329.5	736.9	633	4 273	510.8	92.2
Great Falls, MT	26 348	201	141	1 231	1 114.8	32.6	427	5 049	803.0	81.8	100	395	30.4	4.6
Greeley, CO	602 260	3 963	247	2 829	1 334.6	84.9	505	6 195	1 155.5	109.2	154	576	65.4	9.5
Green Bay, WI	374 458	3 111	509	6 740	2 928.7	219.3	1 140	16 648	2 861.3	264.2	227	1 096	119.6	19.2
Greensboro-High Point, NC	617 980	4 816	1 580	23 599	14 207.7	937.4	2 937	38 612	6 644.1	663.3	646	4 139	480.9	88.9
Greenville, NC	154 335	1 736	194	2 275	1 281.6	69.1	681	8 258	1 432.5	129.0	125	503	51.9	8.0
Greenville, SC	467 509	4 469	1 056	D	D	D	2 424	30 755	5 447.8	462.7	501	2 496	317.6	53.5
Gulfport-Biloxi, MS	252 643	1 962	242	2 409	736.7	60.8	1 070	12 561	1 891.7	179.9	249	991	86.2	14.7
Hagerstown-Martinsburg, MD-WV	352 146	2 832	215	D	D	D	986	11 805	1 826.9	175.7	177	731	63.0	10.9
Hanford-Corcoran, CA	102 676	1 017	60	623	411.6	15.8	316	3 690	629.3	60.0	66	235	20.8	3.3
Harrisburg-Carlisle, PA	346 733	2 831	618	D	D	D	2 221	32 181	5 497.6	531.8	380	235	20.8	3.3
Harrisonburg, VA	86 206	728	119	2 111	1 288.9	56.1	550	6 236	1 047.0	99.4	82	715	96.3	17.8
Hartford-West Hartford-East Hartford, CT	515 802	4 137	1 676	28 388	17 900.5	1 205.6	4 853	64 199	10 937.9	1 168.5	1 102	7 492	1 142.5	205.4
Hattiesburg, MS	13 612	133	145	D	D	D	633	8 012	1 165.2	108.6	123	484	42.2	6.9
Hickory-Lenoir-Morganton, NC	235 992	1 619	487	7 360	3 606.0	227.2	1 524	17 319	2 935.2	264.7	236	883	103.3	16.9
Hinesville-Fort Stewart, GA	40 194	336	15	D	D	D	174	1 799	262.1	22.6	40	D	D	D
Holland-Grand Haven, MI	340 051	2 451	326	3 471	2 213.3	110.2	828	12 375	1 920.7	193.1	168	774	93.6	15.9
Honolulu, HI	589 007	3 473	1 463	15 423	6 079.9	487.0	3 269	44 960	8 264.7	823.6	1 221	7 746	1 219.9	208.4
Hot Springs, AR	14 102	129	110	898	966.5	25.5	498	5 023	875.8	74.8	106	285	33.9	5.7
Houma-Bayou Cane-Thibodaux, LA	98 120	1 053	300	3 189	1 119.0	88.3	805	10 106	1 634.1	143.7	218	2 077	303.7	63.4
Houston-Baytown-Sugar Land, TX	5 939 092	56 571	8 865	D	D	D	15 329	217 241	40 118.1	3 698.6	4 954	38 233	4 697.3	935.0
Huntington-Ashland, WV-KY-OH	16 176	179	349	D	D	D	1 326	16 323	2 410.6	232.2	236	D	D	D
Huntsville, AL	135 477	2 397	520	D	D	D	1 479	19 814	3 015.3	291.4	366	1 735	178.2	31.7
Idaho Falls, ID	109 010	1 183	211	2 995	909.2	71.2	528	6 053	993.3	95.8	76	376	19.9	3.7
Indianapolis, IN	2 276 191	15 784	2 968	D	D	D	5 910	90 357	16 045.8	1 526.2	1 642	11 692	1 440.0	262.3
Iowa City, IA	223 050	1 555	129	D	D	D	595	7 960	1 146.5	120.9	136	594	68.0	10.4
Ithaca, NY	41 486	336	71	432	239.6	13.8	373	4 367	616.3	65.7	81	450	42.1	8.2
Jackson, MI	99 930	831	196	2 339	1 047.2	83.7	564	8 108	1 289.4	126.9	96	465	41.9	7.3
Jackson, MS	395 286	3 569	805	11 649	5 488.2	368.8	2 029	29 198	4 497.5	445.5	477	2 287	258.0	39.2
Jackson, TN	69 435	761	171	2 248	790.8	61.8	647	8 650	1 296.3	122.7	95	443	44.0	7.7
Jacksonville, FL	2 277 701	15 821	1 724	D	D	D	4 475	59 674	10 425.0	984.3	1 202	7 596	1 092.9	182.3
Jacksonville, NC	113 629	1 048	69	D	D	D	564	6 542	1 090.1	96.7	129	497	53.0	7.5
Janesville, WI	111 146	988	152	2 823	1 706.4	95.8	584	8 484	1 599.7	148.4	105	364	52.9	5.6
Jefferson City, MO	62 909	496	169	D	D	D	579	6 827	1 173.1	102.6	107	D	D	D
Johnson City, TN	115 395	944	199	D	D	D	746	8 817	1 447.3	131.2	148	616	56.2	9.8
Johnstown, PA	29 753	237	144	2 115	580.7	57.5	693	8 555	1 244.8	111.5	77	347	32.4	5.1
Jonesboro, AR	61 111	690	164	1 815	688.7	43.3	591	6 349	972.4	90.8	100	401	45.8	6.7
Joplin, MO	54 825	599	250	2 575	1 092.1	64.3	790	9 302	1 444.3	133.6	151	585	50.3	9.3
Kalamazoo-Portage, MI	303 138	2 462	398	6 683	2 030.6	244.9	1 245	18 115	2 892.0	274.4	285	2 201	192.5	42.9
Kankakee-Bradley, IL	97 360	671	126	1 628	809.3	47.2	388	5 594	907.0	88.5	85	348	34.9	5.9
Kansas City, MO-KS	2 012 048	14 935	3 719	D	D	D	6 986	100 459	18 416.2	1 751.6	1 956	D	D	D
Kennewick-Richland-Pasco, WA	340 314	2 249	199	2 161	856.0	55.7	770	9 296	1 696.2	161.5	193	1 126	125.4	23.5
Killeen-Temple-Fort Hood, TX	272 637	2 675	183	D	D	D	1 038	12 752	2 096.6	193.2	296	1 260	102.7	17.8
Kingsport-Bristol-Bristol, TN-VA	105 631	1 250	349	D	D	D	1 391	15 838	2 594.1	238.2	221	918	100.8	16.0
Kingston, NY	122 196	805	183	2 163	522.0	59.5	771	8 107	1 278.3	132.1	135	418	54.6	7.9
Knoxville, TN	475 809	3 899	1 148	D	D	D	2 835	39 468	7 219.6	662.3	648	3 663	422.1	80.8
Kokomo, IN	61 469	403	130	D	D	D	461	6 556	1 077.7	96.4	95	329	39.7	5.6

1. Establishments with payroll.

Table C. Metropolitan Areas — Professional Services, Manufacturing, and Accommodation and Foodservices

Area Name	Professional, scientific, and technical services,[1] 1997				Manufacturing, 1997				Accommodation and foodservices, 1997			
	Number of establishments	Number of employees	Sales (mil dol)	Annual payroll (mil dol)	Number of establishments	Number of employees	Sales (mil dol)	Annual payroll (mil dol)	Number of establishments	Number of employees	Sales (mil dol)	Annual payroll (mil dol)
	147	148	149	150	151	152	153	154	155	156	157	158
Florence, SC	239	1 494	105.9	39.2	202	17 013	4 168.8	514.1	336	5 821	178.5	48.8
Florence-Muscle Shoals, AL.	225	963	67.7	22.5	233	13 126	2 376.7	375.7	249	4 324	113.5	31.8
Fond du Lac, WI	137	630	45.9	18.0	158	11 150	2 115.7	393.2	227	3 584	92.9	25.6
Fort Collins-Loveland, CO	711	3 815	336.3	134.2	384	15 840	3 890.7	645.0	647	10 779	343.6	95.0
Fort Smith, AR-OK	368	2 526	149.8	56.4	NA	NA	NA	NA	478	7 357	219.5	58.5
Fort Walton Beach-Crestview-Destin, FL	417	3 181	264.0	113.5	133	3 448	296.5	81.5	401	8 450	261.7	73.0
Fort Wayne, IN	714	5 727	478.8	167.3	691	44 527	10 581.2	1 585.5	723	14 940	452.6	133.2
Fresno, CA	1 184	11 156	584.1	234.3	696	27 552	5 667.6	704.3	1 256	19 886	631.9	169.6
Gadsden, AL	122	621	36.6	13.7	136	8 775	1 577.0	277.0	169	3 223	85.0	23.6
Gainesville, FL	580	3 826	294.6	127.1	NA	NA	NA	NA	447	D	D	D
Gainesville, GA	217	972	91.6	32.0	226	16 519	4 293.7	443.1	202	4 192	148.5	41.6
Glens Falls, NY	210	1 239	136.3	42.7	183	7 866	1 462.7	266.7	507	4 662	199.3	56.4
Goldsboro, NC	129	596	43.4	16.0	101	9 495	1 417.5	231.1	158	2 953	84.4	23.1
Grand Forks, ND-MN	138	925	61.0	28.6	92	3 087	551.8	75.3	260	5 253	118.8	33.8
Grand Junction, CO	275	1 283	91.3	39.2	167	3 605	484.2	99.2	247	4 555	124.7	36.3
Grand Rapids-Wyoming, MI .	1 441	12 355	1 149.9	471.4	1 402	89 200	16 628.2	3 481.7	1 185	23 415	691.4	201.4
Great Falls, MT	176	994	69.3	28.6	80	925	228.5	23.9	267	3 592	109.7	29.4
Greeley, CO	221	964	72.2	27.9	208	10 773	4 338.5	345.4	271	4 047	106.8	29.4
Green Bay, WI	429	3 550	282.1	123.0	502	30 629	7 069.1	1 139.4	693	11 648	321.2	91.0
Greensboro-High Point, NC .	1 361	8 948	821.5	292.1	1 397	86 070	17 373.5	2 378.0	1 198	24 337	773.6	222.9
Greenville, NC	229	1 326	89.5	35.8	NA	NA	NA	NA	247	5 459	156.4	42.6
Greenville, SC	1 183	11 751	3 406.3	558.6	878	63 609	12 257.9	1 909.2	1 079	22 209	635.8	177.7
Gulfport-Biloxi, MS	403	2 728	211.4	80.9	NA	NA	NA	NA	467	D	D	D
Hagerstown-Martinsburg, MD-WV	254	1 484	120.2	41.2	NA	NA	NA	NA	379	6 457	207.0	57.6
Hanford-Corcoran, CA	74	358	26.8	8.6	65	2 796	748.7	90.6	156	2 037	65.1	16.2
Harrisburg-Carlisle, PA	993	9 358	892.1	354.9	475	29 520	6 980.9	986.3	1 087	18 546	644.4	176.3
Harrisonburg, VA	141	832	64.4	25.0	112	12 959	4 838.3	372.3	188	4 024	124.4	33.4
Hartford-West Hartford-East Hartford, CT	2 720	23 268	2 760.9	1 086.4	2 053	89 601	15 058.3	3 772.4	2 341	35 958	1 268.8	371.0
Hattiesburg, MS	207	1 008	76.0	26.4	113	D	D	D	217	D	D	D
Hickory-Lenoir-Morganton, NC	415	1 921	135.5	50.3	1 012	78 514	9 907.8	1 925.5	573	10 632	299.2	84.0
Hinesville-Fort Stewart, GA ..	32	D	D	D	NA	NA	NA	NA	71	1 248	36.9	9.3
Holland-Grand Haven, MI	344	2 565	192.0	91.9	591	38 244	7 688.1	1 310.8	328	6 073	173.2	50.4
Honolulu, HI	1 917	13 729	1 400.6	546.8	685	11 161	2 692.2	300.9	2 125	53 916	3 036.8	852.8
Hot Springs, AR	167	673	46.3	17.4	108	3 827	795.5	100.0	222	4 005	120.2	36.8
Houma-Bayou Cane-Thibodaux, LA	329	2 597	216.7	78.3	185	6 454	963.7	202.2	302	4 687	154.5	42.0
Houston-Baytown-Sugar Land, TX	11 698	116 394	17 056.2	5 983.1	NA	NA	NA	NA	7 044	140 579	5 350.3	1 425.5
Huntington-Ashland, WV-KY-OH	368	2 232	152.3	62.8	244	14 500	5 562.0	539.0	517	9 415	274.4	74.7
Huntsville, AL	835	13 490	1 629.7	619.6	404	35 060	8 312.7	1 388.1	584	12 811	391.8	107.4
Idaho Falls, ID	226	7 366	750.5	339.2	132	3 214	362.3	67.7	198	D	D	D
Indianapolis, IN	3 465	29 817	3 036.1	1 132.7	NA	NA	NA	NA	2 908	62 759	2 084.6	595.6
Iowa City, IA	197	1 218	87.7	31.0	121	5 080	2 706.6	162.3	313	6 002	155.1	43.9
Ithaca, NY	188	1 411	135.8	49.5	94	3 613	667.1	123.6	312	3 477	113.2	31.7
Jackson, MI	200	1 354	90.8	45.5	351	12 248	2 271.8	422.0	267	4 467	137.0	37.7
Jackson, MS	949	7 318	731.0	276.0	439	23 634	4 737.3	597.1	740	D	D	D
Jackson, TN	148	1 009	79.1	37.1	162	13 282	3 549.4	401.2	202	4 416	144.3	39.2
Jacksonville, FL	2 514	19 425	1 728.5	756.6	NA	NA	NA	NA	2 065	42 825	1 448.5	387.8
Jacksonville, NC	137	725	34.9	11.9	37	1 829	346.4	37.7	249	4 420	127.9	34.5
Janesville, WI	182	1 002	65.1	23.5	234	19 547	10 105.6	785.3	343	5 295	151.2	41.3
Jefferson City, MO	216	1 041	83.1	32.4	136	D	D	D	224	D	D	D
Johnson City, TN	244	1 491	84.0	28.4	221	13 848	1 776.8	344.6	256	6 041	169.6	48.7
Johnstown, PA	184	1 619	98.6	42.3	153	7 403	1 349.5	186.3	314	4 143	111.4	30.6
Jonesboro, AR	167	715	55.5	19.8	149	8 781	1 624.7	227.4	309	5 764	159.5	46.0
Joplin, MO	182	1 092	60.7	25.3	261	16 219	2 847.5	399.6	309	5 764	159.5	46.0
Kalamazoo-Portage, MI	558	3 805	343.2	148.1	526	26 886	5 116.4	973.0	598	10 994	312.2	93.3
Kankakee-Bradley, IL	132	507	32.7	12.7	116	6 937	2 253.2	263.8	229	3 563	100.4	27.4
Kansas City, MO-KS	4 472	44 707	4 780.8	1 911.6	NA	NA	NA	NA	3 357	D	D	D
Kennewick-Richland-Pasco, WA	318	7 537	938.9	369.0	168	6 764	2 046.0	208.6	343	5 328	170.7	46.1
Killeen-Temple-Fort Hood, TX	245	2 231	185.3	57.4	NA	NA	NA	NA	464	D	D	D
Kingsport-Bristol-Bristol, TN-VA	419	D	D	D	NA	NA	NA	NA	465	D	D	D
Kingston, NY	321	2 013	183.7	69.3	215	6 449	785.0	183.7	468	5 662	215.7	63.1
Knoxville, TN	1 289	16 756	1 724.9	690.7	791	40 617	8 336.4	1 246.8	1 131	23 785	749.1	212.1
Kokomo, IN	122	503	35.4	11.7	102	20 972	4 931.5	1 108.4	207	4 232	124.3	34.2

1. Firms subject to federal tax.

Table C. Metropolitan Areas — Health Care and Social Assistance, Other Services, and Federal Funds

Area Name	Health care and social assistance,[1] 1997				Other services,[1] 1997				Federal funds and grants, 2002–2003 Expenditures (mil dol)			
										Direct payments for individuals		
	Number of establishments	Number of employees	Receipts (mil dol)	Annual payroll (mil dol)	Number of establishments	Number of employees	Receipts (mil dol)	Annual payroll (mil dol)	Total	Social Security and government retirement	Medicare	Food stamps and Supplemental Security Income
	159	160	161	162	163	164	165	166	167	168	169	170
Florence, SC	351	6 566	466.7	220.5	271	1 619	95.8	27.4	1 120.2	418.4	178.8	71.1
Florence-Muscle Shoals, AL	295	3 607	256.2	110.4	234	1 367	71.5	21.1	940.5	430.8	157.5	27.8
Fond du Lac, WI	157	1 748	181.2	54.2	162	945	44.4	13.7	423.8	213.1	76.9	6.3
Fort Collins-Loveland, CO	530	4 957	296.2	133.5	384	2 151	127.6	39.0	1 088.2	417.0	141.8	15.8
Fort Smith, AR-OK	472	7 710	461.4	207.5	343	1 966	124.1	31.6	1 482.5	662.9	266.1	66.3
Fort Walton Beach-Crestview-Destin, FL	356	5 134	412.2	142.7	313	1 531	86.3	25.5	2 939.9	770.1	134.5	16.9
Fort Wayne, IN	638	10 090	668.0	305.6	683	5 029	306.3	97.2	1 978.8	742.9	280.4	54.8
Fresno, CA	1 614	15 504	1 103.7	463.9	947	6 026	458.9	120.0	4 074.2	1 210.2	529.5	237.6
Gadsden, AL	199	4 291	312.8	127.9	132	570	34.8	9.5	627.0	297.7	145.6	30.8
Gainesville, FL	509	6 520	436.6	201.6	321	D	D	D	1 419.8	450.8	186.9	39.1
Gainesville, GA	245	2 626	230.0	95.8	184	860	56.2	15.3	565.8	247.7	93.8	17.6
Glens Falls, NY	191	1 985	130.0	64.3	169	668	51.3	14.7	636.3	300.3	107.1	17.2
Goldsboro, NC	181	2 357	114.4	56.0	151	998	58.5	18.5	903.9	288.5	96.3	28.8
Grand Forks, ND-MN	133	1 967	81.4	51.1	168	968	49.3	14.4	796.2	171.4	70.5	10.1
Grand Junction, CO	264	2 504	150.7	69.9	188	1 018	73.9	19.1	641.2	309.6	97.3	17.3
Grand Rapids-Wyoming, MI	1 257	14 256	919.6	459.0	1 189	8 102	563.3	166.1	2 935.8	1 284.6	492.1	109.6
Great Falls, MT	205	1 729	104.2	40.5	153	690	43.3	11.4	768.2	234.1	72.4	13.2
Greeley, CO	209	2 279	138.2	56.5	215	1 130	67.8	17.9	651.9	262.5	105.0	18.6
Green Bay, WI	454	6 277	386.9	203.1	469	2 812	154.6	48.5	1 141.8	519.9	166.6	25.1
Greensboro-High Point, NC	1 101	14 661	994.6	468.3	1 082	6 661	444.6	124.8	3 184.2	1 332.6	500.2	96.0
Greenville, NC	220	3 605	226.7	120.2	168	912	52.4	14.6	723.9	267.7	109.6	40.7
Greenville, SC	860	10 297	720.0	359.4	846	5 195	328.7	96.6	2 791.5	1 189.0	407.4	90.5
Gulfport-Biloxi, MS	438	6 215	458.9	174.7	341	1 884	100.7	32.2	2 462.4	722.3	254.6	59.1
Hagerstown-Martinsburg, MD-WV	350	4 122	272.2	119.0	313	1 961	106.4	32.7	1 326.1	571.8	189.8	29.1
Hanford-Corcoran, CA	142	1 544	99.7	40.9	88	331	25.4	5.8	776.8	182.7	76.3	25.0
Harrisburg-Carlisle, PA	1 015	11 271	748.8	353.7	848	4 961	313.7	97.8	5 971.9	1 721.9	498.1	55.5
Harrisonburg, VA	167	1 913	111.4	52.2	179	917	61.2	17.1	398.7	227.1	67.2	9.1
Hartford-West Hartford-East Hartford, CT	2 490	34 766	2 323.9	1 117.7	2 136	12 552	871.9	269.8	10 751.0	2 522.7	1 293.4	159.8
Hattiesburg, MS	189	3 348	228.7	121.6	138	898	55.9	15.6	663.5	266.5	112.2	33.4
Hickory-Lenoir-Morganton, NC	498	7 610	491.1	220.8	459	2 462	147.7	44.9	1 505.3	718.8	257.6	43.9
Hinesville-Fort Stewart, GA	48	602	25.7	9.3	62	D	D	D	339.7	127.5	23.5	13.0
Holland-Grand Haven, MI	332	4 128	213.1	105.4	346	2 032	141.6	40.5	801.3	409.4	118.4	9.7
Honolulu, HI	1 730	13 474	1 231.7	563.1	1 097	8 402	560.8	170.7	9 056.3	2 219.8	645.0	179.5
Hot Springs, AR	202	3 342	226.8	93.7	133	670	31.1	10.0	628.3	341.4	139.7	20.4
Houma-Bayou Cane-Thibodaux, LA	319	3 564	230.6	110.6	267	2 468	212.0	59.0	978.7	359.2	199.5	59.5
Houston-Baytown-Sugar Land, TX	8 632	112 883	7 932.7	3 278.4	6 650	54 471	3 721.9	1 139.9	24 184.0	6 376.1	3 194.9	832.8
Huntington-Ashland, WV-KY-OH	531	6 775	465.8	228.5	409	2 510	129.8	40.8	1 981.8	820.5	325.7	112.1
Huntsville, AL	658	7 547	539.1	225.7	530	2 873	152.8	50.8	7 123.9	957.0	226.3	60.4
Idaho Falls, ID	260	3 278	233.8	93.4	152	735	51.7	13.4	1 421.0	195.1	60.3	14.5
Indianapolis, IN	2 843	39 172	2 557.0	1 179.0	2 335	17 358	1 045.5	326.7	9 500.1	3 075.2	1 243.8	230.3
Iowa City, IA	220	2 393	114.1	49.2	188	887	54.6	14.5	746.2	198.8	64.1	9.2
Ithaca, NY	157	1 307	85.1	35.3	108	555	32.4	8.8	607.2	152.8	49.6	10.5
Jackson, MI	299	2 649	180.0	85.7	238	1 294	77.2	22.2	722.6	342.1	148.3	29.2
Jackson, MS	830	13 030	925.9	396.0	658	4 403	289.6	83.2	3 792.0	1 087.2	410.7	145.6
Jackson, TN	214	3 917	299.8	152.7	182	1 106	60.3	19.0	577.7	218.8	105.9	28.4
Jacksonville, FL	2 155	30 059	2 192.9	996.3	1 878	11 060	718.8	217.9	8 596.7	2 877.2	1 036.7	182.8
Jacksonville, NC	188	2 489	127.1	57.5	195	914	45.5	13.4	2 079.2	366.3	55.7	22.2
Janesville, WI	223	3 402	196.2	97.5	241	1 052	63.8	16.8	745.5	312.1	117.4	21.4
Jefferson City, MO	223	2 718	155.9	81.4	194	972	49.8	14.7	1 792.9	439.8	128.9	17.2
Johnson City, TN	329	4 898	332.4	147.5	249	1 508	73.1	25.6	1 720.2	490.3	183.8	46.3
Johnstown, PA	351	2 749	180.8	92.5	220	1 097	69.8	19.0	1 203.8	454.5	264.2	35.1
Jonesboro, AR	234	3 672	254.5	119.9	143	672	43.2	10.8	623.1	223.9	92.6	30.5
Joplin, MO	298	3 468	204.8	86.7	299	1 411	79.5	21.4	951.7	356.4	153.4	32.5
Kalamazoo-Portage, MI	561	6 434	441.8	221.0	507	3 144	195.0	61.3	1 435.2	608.6	248.4	53.2
Kankakee-Bradley, IL	168	1 730	107.6	53.0	162	954	59.8	18.3	522.8	224.7	122.7	23.2
Kansas City, MO-KS	3 471	D	D	D	3 131	19 587	1 233.9	376.1	11 732.3	3 868.0	1 743.8	263.6
Kennewick-Richland-Pasco, WA	416	3 510	223.5	89.8	245	1 351	83.8	24.9	3 225.0	356.1	111.6	28.1
Killeen-Temple-Fort Hood, TX	345	6 831	447.5	156.6	394	2 046	98.5	30.9	3 881.6	822.2	179.2	42.4
Kingsport-Bristol-Bristol, TN-VA	530	7 615	514.7	241.3	414	2 315	126.3	38.1	1 775.8	836.3	312.7	74.3
Kingston, NY	343	3 292	191.7	75.6	243	938	55.6	15.1	863.2	379.8	155.8	25.7
Knoxville, TN	1 272	14 508	1 207.2	569.6	961	6 022	321.4	102.3	6 523.6	1 558.8	598.0	138.4
Kokomo, IN	189	2 163	127.5	57.5	152	1 090	51.2	16.4	485.1	242.8	104.1	17.2

1. Firms subject to federal tax.

Items 159—170

Area Name	Federal funds and grants, 2002–2003 (cont'd) Expenditures (mil dol) (cont'd) Procurement contract awards			Grants				Local government finances, 2002 General revenue		Taxes		
	Salaries and wages	Defense	Other	Medicaid and other health-related	Nutrition and family welfare	Education	Other	Total (mil dol)	Intergovernmental (mil dol)	Total (mil dol)	Per capita[1] (dollars) Total	Property
	171	172	173	174	175	176	177	178	179	180	181	182
Florence, SC	52.3	2.9	13.2	241.9	30.2	24.3	46.8	400.2	202.1	138.1	707	552
Florence-Muscle Shoals, AL.	115.8	1.9	29.8	80.2	10.8	11.6	49.5	544.8	168.6	106.1	748	436
Fond du Lac, WI	15.2	1.8	5.6	43.9	10.3	4.6	23.4	338.8	152.3	113.1	1 157	1 128
Fort Collins-Loveland, CO	141.5	27.6	91.6	103.7	18.1	12.2	99.5	838.3	220.7	397.0	1 500	953
Fort Smith, AR-OK	117.8	27.5	13.0	184.5	25.5	28.1	71.1	563.1	327.7	137.3	493	204
Fort Walton Beach-Crestview-Destin, FL	915.2	930.7	25.6	48.8	17.4	16.2	48.7	428.4	190.3	142.4	810	675
Fort Wayne, IN	156.4	387.2	74.4	156.2	35.0	8.6	43.7	961.2	340.4	438.8	1 106	970
Fresno, CA	539.5	119.8	131.9	579.8	256.4	97.4	205.7	3 668.6	2 338.5	634.8	761	549
Gadsden, AL	19.4	0.5	10.4	76.4	9.9	9.8	15.8	201.2	98.2	69.5	674	200
Gainesville, FL	185.2	10.7	39.6	244.1	37.8	23.8	154.1	605.9	255.0	195.0	823	712
Gainesville, GA	28.7	27.7	28.8	49.0	27.9	6.8	31.3	652.1	168.3	182.4	1 198	673
Glens Falls, NY	27.7	8.1	6.5	98.5	17.5	9.6	31.8	527.3	215.4	220.2	1 760	1 331
Goldsboro, NC	202.7	76.1	11.4	109.6	24.9	11.4	26.0	285.6	184.2	57.3	508	361
Grand Forks, ND-MN	151.9	129.0	18.1	69.9	20.2	15.3	60.8	362.4	177.3	91.1	948	780
Grand Junction, CO	66.9	17.1	21.3	54.0	11.7	6.8	29.4	324.0	129.3	132.4	1 091	610
Grand Rapids-Wyoming, MI	211.6	129.5	74.6	298.1	73.8	43.2	158.9	2 393.9	1 303.0	560.0	739	654
Great Falls, MT	215.1	72.6	10.8	78.0	12.6	6.3	34.7	167.8	72.0	54.5	686	671
Greeley, CO	42.1	3.9	15.1	82.0	23.2	15.0	41.0	551.1	195.4	226.8	1 106	840
Green Bay, WI	78.5	15.3	61.6	126.7	29.9	17.1	55.1	1 106.2	464.7	340.7	1 178	1 149
Greensboro-High Point, NC.	275.0	197.2	124.2	295.4	63.3	53.2	186.4	1 680.2	764.7	582.6	886	711
Greenville, NC	27.1	16.4	6.9	140.6	24.6	16.9	25.9	403.6	232.3	96.6	617	453
Greenville, SC	132.1	264.2	151.0	253.7	41.5	16.7	37.4	1 899.3	483.8	481.9	838	711
Gulfport-Biloxi, MS	761.5	186.8	200.7	102.6	27.9	15.0	91.6	922.0	318.4	225.3	902	770
Hagerstown-Martinsburg, MD-WV	209.5	71.0	53.2	97.7	20.7	8.2	56.9	517.6	216.6	195.4	847	582
Hanford-Corcoran, CA	284.3	1.9	25.0	73.8	34.3	19.1	17.5	443.4	293.6	67.5	500	366
Harrisburg-Carlisle, PA	553.4	311.5	72.4	482.7	629.5	369.3	1 152.5	1 568.7	495.7	642.7	1 249	868
Harrisonburg, VA	21.8	3.1	10.8	26.6	4.0	5.2	10.4	223.7	89.2	88.9	811	519
Hartford-West Hartford-East Hartford, CT	451.3	3 806.6	201.5	925.1	297.8	206.4	798.6	3 323.4	1 070.7	1 949.0	1 669	1 646
Hattiesburg, MS	43.2	17.1	8.0	74.1	16.0	8.6	53.6	539.7	120.5	85.7	676	609
Hickory-Lenoir-Morganton, NC	58.2	149.2	22.9	137.7	27.3	30.4	36.7	1 023.1	423.4	227.3	651	507
Hinesville-Fort Stewart, GA	65.7	53.8	1.9	22.3	9.3	11.7	6.5	173.1	90.3	49.7	686	392
Holland-Grand Haven, MI	32.6	56.8	67.8	37.7	10.4	11.3	30.9	628.1	341.6	174.1	708	690
Honolulu, HI	2 737.5	1 624.6	179.2	520.9	176.9	179.9	537.8	1 021.2	176.7	534.4	596	427
Hot Springs, AR	34.3	5.7	9.2	44.8	7.1	8.6	11.3	181.6	98.0	46.0	511	168
Houma-Bayou Cane-Thibodaux, LA	27.3	87.3	20.2	104.5	22.2	17.6	37.8	728.4	256.0	184.3	936	331
Houston-Baytown-Sugar Land, TX	1 893.2	2 658.1	4 598.9	2 338.9	421.0	229.8	1 266.8	15 545.6	3 945.0	8 171.1	1 639	1 346
Huntington-Ashland, WV-KY-OH	158.5	13.5	38.7	298.6	53.2	27.6	104.1	645.5	344.6	171.6	600	447
Huntsville, AL	788.7	4 040.6	673.5	128.6	19.0	25.1	147.4	1 918.1	337.1	243.8	689	273
Idaho Falls, ID	53.4	14.9	983.1	43.0	10.3	2.1	26.6	242.6	137.5	62.4	595	574
Indianapolis, IN	975.9	1 014.2	281.9	876.5	363.7	241.4	854.7	5 312.2	1 810.2	2 037.9	1 294	1 109
Iowa City, IA	83.2	3.0	76.9	224.6	6.4	8.3	40.7	321.1	115.5	131.6	972	890
Ithaca, NY	22.4	6.4	8.8	105.9	12.4	12.5	198.1	348.4	136.2	151.3	1 525	1 085
Jackson, MI	28.2	14.6	10.5	77.6	27.2	10.4	21.7	465.9	306.5	75.2	467	411
Jackson, MS	335.1	219.6	138.9	450.2	206.0	198.9	508.2	1 133.4	537.6	370.8	734	684
Jackson, TN	36.6	0.5	7.6	111.3	10.6	9.6	24.7	612.9	87.8	115.7	1 059	532
Jacksonville, FL	1 863.1	925.3	208.1	519.0	147.2	86.6	663.3	3 184.3	1 104.4	1 230.5	1 045	785
Jacksonville, NC	1 269.5	257.1	8.5	48.0	12.8	9.7	17.1	370.2	164.1	72.8	488	341
Janesville, WI	21.5	78.6	7.8	99.3	26.7	12.8	29.1	555.1	317.3	165.9	1 076	1 052
Jefferson City, MO	51.6	3.6	9.0	178.0	233.4	211.3	494.8	230.9	86.8	104.5	735	499
Johnson City, TN	107.6	13.1	633.1	153.8	15.1	14.8	41.9	328.6	132.8	114.3	623	392
Johnstown, PA	96.1	110.5	23.1	109.9	21.4	7.2	63.3	415.8	210.2	105.7	702	545
Jonesboro, AR	31.0	1.0	7.6	88.3	17.4	10.4	49.0	243.4	131.6	53.7	491	226
Joplin, MO	35.1	10.4	179.5	108.4	19.0	13.5	25.6	323.2	132.9	124.3	776	462
Kalamazoo-Portage, MI	86.1	40.1	31.6	194.9	51.6	29.5	57.5	961.0	483.2	240.8	756	736
Kankakee-Bradley, IL	30.5	2.1	4.3	55.7	16.2	6.1	23.9	284.4	141.0	98.1	937	882
Kansas City, MO-KS	1 829.4	631.3	1 438.4	919.7	184.3	104.7	577.7	6 186.0	1 919.4	2 711.6	1 435	899
Kennewick-Richland-Pasco, WA	87.6	32.2	2 397.4	68.2	29.4	14.1	59.3	894.1	312.2	174.6	860	531
Killeen-Temple-Fort Hood, TX	1 908.8	589.7	34.0	105.6	23.5	61.9	76.6	865.2	426.8	249.4	738	563
Kingsport-Bristol-Bristol, TN-VA	79.2	63.6	26.8	268.7	35.5	21.1	33.1	561.1	238.7	216.4	723	482
Kingston, NY	34.6	15.8	13.2	173.9	21.4	11.7	23.0	735.6	259.1	370.5	2 058	1 591
Knoxville, TN	389.0	157.9	2 787.2	444.2	59.8	49.7	252.3	1 491.9	443.1	651.2	1 034	647
Kokomo, IN	21.5	0.2	6.0	53.2	11.0	2.0	15.0	355.3	99.2	133.3	1 315	1 157

1. Based on the resident population estimated as of July 1 of the year shown.

Table C. Metropolitan Areas — Local Government Finances, Government Employment, and Elections

Area Name	Direct general expenditure — Total (mil dol)	Per capita[1] (dollars)	Percent of total for — Education	Health and hospitals	Police protection	Public welfare	Highways	Debt outstanding — Total (mil dol)	Per capita[1] (dollars)	Government employment, 2002 — Federal civilian	Federal military	State and local	Presidential election, 2004 Percent of vote cast — Democratic	Republican	All other
	183	184	185	186	187	188	189	190	191	192	193	194	195	196	197
Florence, SC	412.5	2 114	62.3	1.6	5.3	0.4	2.1	369.4	1 893	787	727	15 422	44.3	54.8	0.8
Florence-Muscle Shoals, AL	537.3	3 785	27.3	46.0	2.9	0.1	3.6	411.0	2 895	1 696	628	10 508	41.4	57.9	0.7
Fond du Lac, WI	371.1	3 794	50.9	9.8	5.1	5.6	7.0	308.3	3 152	243	267	5 644	36.3	62.8	0.9
Fort Collins-Loveland, CO	757.5	2 863	41.7	1.4	5.8	4.4	5.6	1 077.2	4 071	2 365	425	23 082	46.6	51.9	1.6
Fort Smith, AR-OK	560.8	2 015	60.2	1.9	5.0	0.1	7.2	406.2	1 459	1 521	1 340	13 938	37.4	61.9	0.7
Fort Walton Beach-Crestview-Destin, FL	436.0	2 481	53.7	1.8	6.1	0.3	4.8	150.4	856	6 309	16 779	7 511	21.6	77.6	0.8
Fort Wayne, IN	998.2	2 517	51.1	0.6	3.9	3.9	4.6	663.4	1 672	2 329	1 062	18 981	34.5	64.9	0.6
Fresno, CA	3 604.4	4 319	48.6	6.1	5.2	10.6	3.0	2 388.8	2 862	9 631	1 205	55 815	41.3	57.9	0.8
Gadsden, AL	202.9	1 968	50.0	2.3	9.0	0.1	5.3	105.9	1 027	329	455	4 997	35.9	63.3	0.8
Gainesville, FL	626.6	2 644	46.9	1.2	8.6	0.2	3.6	838.6	3 539	3 146	430	40 948	54.5	44.5	0.9
Gainesville, GA	668.4	4 391	31.7	37.6	2.7	0.5	2.5	434.4	2 854	485	364	8 263	42.4	55.1	2.5
Glens Falls, NY	555.9	4 443	51.7	3.0	2.2	12.2	6.4	276.3	2 209	417	182	9 751	42.4	55.1	2.5
Goldsboro, NC	281.2	2 489	52.9	5.7	3.8	6.8	1.5	95.0	841	1 260	4 624	8 535	37.4	62.4	0.2
Grand Forks, ND-MN	354.2	3 688	33.5	1.2	3.9	5.3	6.7	367.9	3 830	1 395	3 369	10 776	42.0	56.4	1.6
Grand Junction, CO	326.3	2 688	40.5	1.7	7.5	6.2	10.2	240.1	1 977	1 149	183	7 115	31.6	67.1	1.3
Grand Rapids-Wyoming, MI	2 582.8	3 408	48.0	6.5	4.6	1.5	4.5	3 027.3	3 995	3 294	1 345	33 985	39.8	59.2	1.0
Great Falls, MT	164.5	2 071	53.5	2.1	8.1	1.1	6.4	59.6	750	1 496	3 997	3 874	40.9	56.9	2.2
Greeley, CO	563.2	2 747	49.2	2.2	5.1	1.3	7.8	612.1	2 986	578	312	12 235	35.9	62.7	1.3
Green Bay, WI	1 206.2	4 170	45.2	5.2	4.3	3.6	8.6	1 024.9	3 544	1 161	833	18 448	44.5	54.6	0.9
Greensboro-High Point, NC	1 775.0	2 698	48.1	6.1	6.1	6.6	2.1	1 081.3	1 643	4 289	1 213	36 755	44.3	55.4	0.4
Greenville, NC	434.7	2 775	45.2	6.0	5.3	6.7	2.3	232.2	1 482	429	288	19 580	45.8	54.0	0.2
Greenville, SC	1 881.2	3 272	35.6	36.8	3.7	0.2	1.6	1 950.1	3 392	2 028	2 194	37 393	32.1	66.8	1.1
Gulfport-Biloxi, MS	939.6	3 760	34.4	24.9	6.1	0.4	5.9	499.1	1 997	7 734	13 037	15 256	34.2	64.9	0.9
Hagerstown-Martinsburg, MD-WV	491.1	2 128	63.9	3.2	4.1	0.5	2.9	379.7	1 645	3 498	766	11 769	35.2	63.9	0.9
Hanford-Corcoran, CA	449.9	3 332	49.2	6.1	4.1	9.2	2.8	173.7	1 286	952	6 469	10 644	34.0	65.2	0.8
Harrisburg-Carlisle, PA	1 755.4	3 412	52.1	3.5	2.7	5.6	3.2	3 005.2	5 840	8 585	2 387	56 055	39.9	59.6	0.5
Harrisonburg, VA	227.7	2 078	51.5	3.1	4.4	4.4	3.2	382.3	3 490	367	293	8 726	29.4	70.1	0.6
Hartford-West Hartford-East Hartford, CT	3 204.0	2 743	53.8	0.8	6.5	1.3	4.3	1 425.0	1 220	6 979	2 235	89 102	57.9	40.4	1.7
Hattiesburg, MS	510.2	4 023	23.9	47.6	2.6	0.1	4.2	835.9	6 591	780	901	14 127	29.1	70.2	0.7
Hickory-Lenoir-Morganton, NC	928.9	2 660	45.9	20.1	4.0	8.2	1.3	335.8	961	822	603	22 171	33.2	66.5	0.3
Hinesville-Fort Stewart, GA	167.5	2 310	59.1	10.3	4.7	1.5	3.8	53.0	730	2 825	15 635	3 842	48.3	51.3	0.4
Holland-Grand Haven, MI	642.3	2 612	53.7	7.0	2.6	0.8	8.9	849.9	3 456	470	489	13 760	27.6	71.6	0.8
Honolulu, HI	1 197.5	1 336	0.0	1.6	14.0	0.0	9.1	2 297.0	2 564	27 715	51 297	64 964	51.1	48.3	0.6
Hot Springs, AR	178.6	1 983	51.6	0.3	7.3	0.0	5.7	145.8	1 619	593	406	3 914	44.9	54.1	0.9
Houma-Bayou Cane-Thibodaux, LA	687.2	3 491	35.2	35.9	3.7	0.5	3.3	313.2	1 591	431	879	13 657	34.4	64.4	1.2
Houston-Baytown-Sugar Land, TX	16 838.8	3 377	48.3	7.2	5.0	0.2	3.8	29 832.2	5 983	26 419	10 965	298 162	41.0	58.5	0.5
Huntington-Ashland, WV-KY-OH	652.6	2 280	56.0	8.1	3.5	2.5	2.4	417.6	1 459	2 775	825	16 235	44.8	54.5	0.7
Huntsville, AL	1 211.2	3 424	32.7	33.7	3.6	0.1	2.9	1 571.6	4 443	14 937	3 061	25 379	38.7	60.5	0.9
Idaho Falls, ID	246.3	2 346	57.8	3.7	5.5	0.7	4.2	96.5	920	827	377	5 684	19.8	79.1	1.1
Indianapolis, IN	5 479.2	3 480	38.4	14.5	3.9	1.6	4.2	6 409.7	4 071	13 970	5 078	98 272	38.3	61.0	0.7
Iowa City, IA	330.4	2 440	38.5	8.6	4.5	0.6	10.5	430.0	3 176	1 580	560	28 650	60.7	38.1	1.1
Ithaca, NY	371.9	3 494	50.0	4.0	2.9	7.9	7.0	250.7	2 527	308	159	6 065	63.5	33.5	3.0
Jackson, MI	500.8	3 111	50.0	14.1	2.7	2.1	4.6	312.3	1 940	434	278	10 032	43.4	55.6	1.0
Jackson, MS	1 156.5	2 288	54.5	3.4	6.7	0.7	5.7	1 214.0	2 402	5 239	2 854	50 674	42.0	57.2	0.8
Jackson, TN	591.7	5 414	19.4	58.7	2.5	0.0	2.4	372.0	3 404	569	358	11 336	42.3	57.3	0.4
Jacksonville, FL	3 408.1	2 894	42.5	1.9	6.5	1.0	2.9	8 207.7	6 970	17 231	26 137	51 429	36.3	63.0	0.7
Jacksonville, NC	380.3	2 552	40.5	30.6	3.7	5.5	0.6	105.9	711	5 357	39 788	7 098	30.1	69.6	0.3
Janesville, WI	577.4	3 747	48.7	6.5	5.9	8.9	5.6	344.2	2 233	336	418	8 595	58.0	41.2	0.8
Jefferson City, MO	240.6	1 693	57.3	1.8	5.0	0.0	7.3	172.8	1 216	830	442	26 853	32.3	67.2	0.5
Johnson City, TN	332.2	1 811	48.2	7.8	6.1	0.1	6.4	424.7	2 314	1 994	611	12 782	31.7	67.7	0.6
Johnstown, PA	429.7	2 856	43.7	6.2	3.2	10.4	4.1	608.9	4 047	1 241	573	8 602	48.7	50.8	0.5
Jonesboro, AR	227.4	2 077	50.8	0.3	4.7	0.2	8.8	428.4	3 913	504	490	7 374	47.2	51.6	1.1
Joplin, MO	329.1	2 054	59.0	7.1	4.7	0.3	8.9	101.8	636	488	480	8 645	28.4	71.1	0.5
Kalamazoo-Portage, MI	982.5	3 083	50.8	11.0	5.8	1.2	5.3	1 170.7	3 673	1 329	555	21 665	50.4	48.6	1.0
Kankakee-Bradley, IL	301.3	2 878	54.3	1.0	5.9	0.2	7.0	143.9	1 375	329	193	6 097	44.4	54.9	0.7
Kansas City, MO-KS	6 146.9	3 254	46.2	8.0	6.2	0.8	5.3	7 234.2	3 829	27 058	9 611	120 175	47.7	51.6	0.8
Kennewick-Richland-Pasco, WA	642.6	3 164	47.7	11.6	3.9	0.0	4.6	6 984.6	34 388	1 323	619	13 734	32.6	66.1	1.4
Killeen-Temple-Fort Hood, TX	842.4	2 492	64.3	4.6	4.2	0.3	2.3	928.7	2 747	7 777	43 775	22 299	32.4	67.1	0.5
Kingsport-Bristol-Bristol, TN-VA	607.0	2 027	55.7	1.3	5.5	2.0	4.1	441.2	1 473	1 281	920	14 301	32.3	66.8	0.9
Kingston, NY	776.1	4 312	50.6	3.2	3.0	15.3	5.2	358.1	1 989	461	268	13 975	54.1	43.3	2.6
Knoxville, TN	1 442.1	2 289	41.8	10.6	5.8	1.3	3.5	1 820.4	2 890	5 199	2 198	46 778	35.8	63.3	0.9
Kokomo, IN	362.0	3 571	37.1	21.3	4.5	2.1	3.1	206.8	2 040	342	271	7 179	33.9	65.3	0.8

1. Based on the resident population estimated as of July 1 of the year shown.

Table C. Metropolitan Areas — Land Area and Population

CBSA/DIV code[1]	Area Name	Land area,[2] 2000 (sq km)	Population and population characteristics, 2003												
			Total persons	Rank	Per square kilometer	Race alone or in combination, not Hispanic or Latino (percent)				Percent Hispanic or Latino[3]	Age (percent)					
						White	Black	Am. Indian, Alaska Native	Asian and Pacific Islander		Under 5 years	5 to 17 years	18 to 24 years	25 to 34 years	35 to 44 years	45 to 54 years
		1	2	3	4	5	6	7	8	9	10	11	12	13	14	15
29100	La Crosse, WI-MN	2 619	128 592	279	49.1	94.8	1.2	0.6	3.4	0.9	5.6	17.2	13.7	12.5	14.3	14.0
29140	Lafayette, IN	3 310	184 536	209	55.8	87.9	2.4	0.6	4.9	5.2	6.0	15.7	19.9	14.9	12.4	11.4
29180	Lafayette, LA	2 615	244 150	173	93.4	70.8	26.2	0.5	1.4	1.7	7.3	19.2	11.5	14.0	15.5	13.8
29340	Lake Charles, LA	6 175	193 597	203	31.4	73.8	23.9	0.6	0.9	1.5	7.2	18.9	11.1	12.6	14.9	13.8
29460	Lakeland, FL	4 855	510 458	91	105.1	72.9	14.6	0.7	1.4	11.4	6.8	18.0	9.1	11.6	13.3	12.2
29540	Lancaster, PA	2 458	482 775	99	196.4	89.6	3.2	0.3	1.8	6.0	6.7	19.1	9.8	11.7	14.9	13.8
29620	Lansing-East Lansing, MI	4 421	455 836	103	103.1	83.1	9.3	1.1	3.5	4.9	6.1	17.6	13.7	13.7	14.3	14.2
29700	Laredo, TX	8 694	213 615	189	24.6	4.3	0.1	0.1	0.4	95.1	12.5	24.8	11.1	14.9	12.7	9.6
29740	Las Cruces, NM	9 861	182 165	212	18.5	31.9	1.6	1.1	1.2	64.9	7.9	20.6	13.2	13.0	13.1	11.8
29820	Las Vegas-Paradise, NV	20 488	1 576 541	35	76.9	60.3	9.3	1.2	7.2	24.4	7.6	18.6	8.8	15.7	15.0	12.2
29940	Lawrence, KS	1 183	102 983	333	87.1	86.3	4.9	3.3	4.3	3.5	5.7	14.1	21.5	17.2	12.3	11.6
30020	Lawton, OK	2 770	113 890	304	41.1	64.3	21.8	6.9	4.1	7.3	8.1	19.4	13.7	15.0	14.6	11.3
30140	Lebanon, PA	937	122 652	290	130.9	92.6	1.4	0.3	1.0	5.2	5.6	17.0	9.1	11.5	15.0	14.4
30300	Lewiston, ID-WA	3 845	58 324	360	15.2	93.3	0.4	4.7	0.9	1.9	6.0	16.9	9.8	11.4	13.7	14.3
30340	Lewiston-Auburn, ME	1 218	106 115	326	87.1	97.0	1.3	0.8	1.0	1.1	5.7	17.0	9.9	12.0	16.3	14.4
30460	Lexington-Fayette, KY	3 830	422 247	109	110.2	83.7	11.1	0.5	2.4	3.4	6.7	16.2	11.2	16.1	15.6	13.9
30620	Lima, OH	1 047	108 241	321	103.4	85.4	13.1	0.6	0.9	1.5	7.0	18.3	10.8	11.7	14.5	14.3
30700	Lincoln, NE	3 662	277 666	161	75.8	89.9	3.4	1.0	3.7	3.5	7.0	16.3	14.0	15.3	14.1	13.4
30780	Little Rock-North Little Rock, AR	10 594	628 293	80	59.3	74.0	22.7	0.9	1.5	2.1	7.0	18.3	9.8	14.3	15.2	13.9
30860	Logan, UT-ID	4 739	107 538	323	22.7	89.7	0.6	0.8	2.4	7.3	10.6	20.9	17.1	17.0	10.3	9.0
30980	Longview, TX	4 624	198 155	199	42.9	72.1	18.0	0.9	0.7	9.2	7.1	18.8	10.4	12.2	14.4	13.5
31020	Longview, WA	2 949	95 146	344	32.3	91.4	0.9	2.8	1.8	5.2	6.2	19.0	9.7	11.9	14.4	14.7
31100	Los Angeles-Long Beach-Santa Ana, CA	12 563	12 829 272	2	1 021.2	35.8	7.8	0.6	14.1	43.0	7.4	19.7	9.8	15.8	15.9	12.7
31084	Los Angeles-Long Beach-Glendale, CA Div	10 518	9 871 506	X	938.5	31.3	9.7	0.6	13.5	46.3	7.5	19.8	10.0	16.0	15.7	12.6
42044	Santa Ana-Anaheim-Irvine, CA Div	2 045	2 957 766	X	1 446.3	50.9	1.8	0.7	16.3	32.1	7.4	19.1	9.3	15.3	16.4	13.1
31140	Louisville, KY-IN	10 710	1 190 154	43	111.1	83.3	13.7	0.6	1.5	2.0	6.7	18.0	9.0	13.5	15.9	14.7
31180	Lubbock, TX	4 660	257 188	167	55.2	61.5	7.6	0.6	1.4	29.6	7.6	18.1	14.2	14.5	13.0	12.0
31340	Lynchburg, VA	5 502	231 036	181	42.0	79.7	18.7	0.6	0.9	1.0	5.7	17.1	10.7	11.8	14.6	14.5
31420	Macon, GA	4 467	226 022	185	50.6	55.5	42.2	0.5	1.1	1.3	7.3	19.2	10.0	13.2	15.0	13.9
31460	Madera, CA	5 532	133 463	271	24.1	46.4	3.7	1.9	1.9	47.2	7.6	20.6	11.4	13.5	13.9	12.2
31540	Madison, WI	7 092	526 742	87	74.3	88.9	4.3	0.7	4.2	3.4	6.1	16.3	12.1	15.4	15.9	14.5
31700	Manchester-Nashua, NH	2 270	394 663	119	173.9	92.1	1.8	0.6	2.9	3.6	6.3	19.1	8.2	12.9	18.2	15.1
31900	Mansfield, OH	1 287	128 267	281	99.7	88.7	10.1	0.7	0.8	0.9	6.2	17.8	9.1	12.2	15.0	14.8
32580	McAllen-Edinburg-Pharr, TX	4 066	635 540	77	156.3	9.7	0.3	0.1	0.7	89.2	11.3	24.4	11.5	14.3	12.0	9.5
32780	Medford, OR	7 214	190 077	206	26.3	90.0	0.7	2.1	1.9	7.4	5.6	17.6	9.6	11.3	13.1	15.2
32820	Memphis, TN-MS-AR	11 842	1 239 337	41	104.7	50.7	45.1	0.5	1.9	2.6	7.6	20.0	9.8	14.3	15.4	14.0
32900	Merced, CA	4 995	231 574	180	46.4	39.8	4.0	1.1	7.3	49.5	8.4	24.1	12.0	13.5	13.6	10.9
33100	Miami-Fort Lauderdale-Miami Beach, FL	13 275	5 288 796	6	398.4	41.3	20.1	0.3	2.4	36.8	6.5	17.3	8.2	12.9	15.8	13.1
22744	Fort Lauderdale-Pompano Beach-Deerfield Beach, FL Div	3 122	1 731 347	X	554.6	53.1	24.1	0.4	3.4	20.2	6.6	17.7	7.8	13.1	16.6	13.6
33124	Miami-Miami Beach-Kendall, FL Div	5 040	2 341 167	X	464.5	18.8	19.5	0.2	1.7	60.5	6.8	17.8	9.0	13.8	15.9	12.9
48424	West Palm Beach-Boca Raton-Boynton Beach, FL Div	5 113	1 216 282	X	237.9	67.6	15.7	0.4	2.3	14.9	5.8	15.9	7.5	10.9	14.4	12.6
33140	Michigan City-La Porte, IN	1 549	109 878	315	70.9	85.8	10.6	0.8	0.6	3.5	6.4	18.0	9.3	12.9	15.5	14.9
33260	Midland, TX	2 332	118 624	297	50.9	60.4	6.7	0.6	1.1	31.8	7.6	21.5	10.4	11.5	14.6	14.3
33340	Milwaukee-Waukesha-West Allis, WI	3 782	1 514 313	36	400.4	73.9	16.7	0.8	2.9	6.9	6.9	18.9	9.4	13.1	15.8	14.5
33460	Minneapolis-St. Paul-Bloomington, MN	15 704	3 083 637	16	196.4	84.8	6.6	1.2	5.4	3.8	7.0	18.7	9.4	14.8	17.2	14.3
33540	Missoula, MT	6 729	98 616	339	14.7	94.3	0.6	3.4	1.7	1.7	5.6	15.9	13.3	14.9	14.2	15.2
33660	Mobile, AL	3 194	399 747	116	125.2	62.0	34.6	1.1	2.0	1.2	7.3	19.6	10.1	13.0	14.6	13.7
33700	Modesto, CA	3 869	492 233	96	127.2	55.7	3.1	1.5	5.9	36.0	7.6	22.0	11.1	13.8	14.5	12.1
33740	Monroe, LA	3 854	170 864	226	44.3	64.3	33.4	0.5	0.8	1.5	7.4	19.5	11.4	13.5	13.6	13.0
33780	Monroe, MI	1 427	150 673	246	105.6	95.0	2.3	0.8	0.8	2.2	5.8	19.5	9.8	12.0	16.1	15.2
33860	Montgomery, AL	7 057	352 536	134	50.0	56.2	41.6	0.6	1.3	1.3	7.2	18.7	10.9	13.9	15.2	13.5
34060	Morgantown, WV	2 614	114 075	303	43.6	94.0	3.0	0.5	2.7	0.9	4.9	13.8	16.9	14.9	13.2	13.4
34100	Morristown, TN	1 852	127 215	283	68.7	92.0	3.0	0.5	0.6	4.4	6.1	16.3	9.7	13.7	14.8	13.5
34580	Mount Vernon-Anacortes, WA	4 494	109 234	319	24.3	83.4	0.7	2.4	2.4	12.5	6.1	18.4	10.5	11.6	13.9	14.3
34620	Muncie, IN	1 019	117 488	299	115.3	91.2	7.1	0.6	1.1	1.1	5.9	16.2	15.5	12.8	12.8	12.7
34740	Muskegon-Norton Shores, MI	1 319	173 090	221	131.2	80.9	14.8	1.5	0.7	3.8	6.7	19.7	9.8	12.4	15.2	14.2
34820	Myrtle Beach-Conway-North Myrtle Beach, SC	2 936	210 757	193	71.8	79.7	16.2	0.8	1.2	3.1	6.1	15.3	9.0	13.8	14.5	13.4
34900	Napa, CA	1 952	131 607	274	67.4	66.8	1.8	1.2	5.4	26.6	5.9	17.3	9.7	12.6	14.5	14.6
34940	Naples-Marco Island, FL	5 246	286 634	155	54.6	70.2	5.8	0.3	0.9	23.3	6.1	14.7	7.7	10.7	12.6	11.2
34980	Nashville-Davidson—Murfreesboro, TN	14 728	1 371 302	39	93.1	78.9	15.4	0.7	2.3	3.8	7.0	18.0	10.0	15.2	16.3	14.1
35300	New Haven-Milford, CT	1 569	841 873	58	536.6	74.2	12.1	0.6	3.2	11.1	6.0	17.8	9.2	12.8	16.0	14.2
35380	New Orleans-Metairie-Kenner, LA	8 167	1 317 541	40	161.3	54.8	38.0	0.7	2.8	4.7	7.1	18.7	10.1	13.3	15.3	14.5

1. CBSA = Core Based Statistical Area. DIV = Metropolitan Division. See Appendix A for explanation. See Appendix B for list of metropolitan areas identified by type.   2. Dry land or land partially or temporarily covered by water.   3. Hispanic or Latino persons may be of any race.

Table C. Metropolitan Areas — **Population and Households**

Area Name	Population, 2003 (cont'd) Age (percent) (cont'd) 55 to 64 years	65 to 74 years	75 years and over	Percent female	Total persons 1900	2000	Percent change 1990–2000	2000–2003	Components of change, 2000–2003 Births	Deaths	Net migration	Households, 2000 Number	Percent change, 1990–2000	Persons per household	Percent Female family householder[1]	One person
	16	17	18	19	20	21	22	23	24	25	26	27	28	29	30	31
La Crosse, WI-MN	8.5	6.3	6.7	51.3	116 401	126 838	9.0	1.4	4 680	3 661	915	49 232	13.2	2.46	8.2	27.9
Lafayette, IN	7.4	4.8	5.0	48.7	158 848	178 541	12.4	3.4	7 108	4 144	3 203	66 502	18.3	2.45	8.1	27.2
Lafayette, LA	8.0	5.5	4.3	51.2	208 859	239 086	14.5	2.1	11 970	5 795	-904	89 536	19.3	2.61	14.4	24.5
Lake Charles, LA	9.1	6.7	5.3	51.1	177 394	193 568	9.1	0.0	9 289	5 890	-3 296	72 205	13.7	2.62	14.4	23.8
Lakeland, FL	10.2	9.3	8.4	50.8	405 382	483 924	19.4	5.5	22 432	17 252	21 204	187 233	20.0	2.52	12.0	24.1
Lancaster, PA	9.2	6.8	7.2	51.1	422 822	470 658	11.3	2.6	21 472	13 791	5 098	172 560	14.3	2.64	8.6	23.1
Lansing-East Lansing, MI	8.8	5.2	4.9	51.3	432 684	447 728	3.5	1.8	18 314	10 100	-74	172 413	9.9	2.48	11.1	27.4
Laredo, TX	5.9	4.1	3.3	51.8	133 239	193 117	44.9	10.6	19 319	2 817	4 219	50 740	47.3	3.75	18.3	12.4
Las Cruces, NM	7.9	6.2	4.7	50.8	135 510	174 682	28.9	4.3	9 701	3 449	1 308	59 556	32.2	2.85	14.7	21.3
Las Vegas-Paradise, NV	9.2	6.2	4.1	49.1	741 368	1 375 765	85.6	14.6	74 427	36 304	159 627	512 253	78.5	2.65	11.8	24.5
Lawrence, KS	6.4	4.0	4.0	50.2	81 798	99 962	22.2	3.0	3 856	1 805	1 092	38 486	27.7	2.37	8.5	28.5
Lawton, OK	7.3	5.7	4.3	48.3	111 486	114 996	3.1	-1.0	6 149	2 765	-4 569	39 808	6.0	2.63	14.1	23.4
Lebanon, PA	10.2	8.0	8.4	51.2	113 744	120 327	5.8	1.9	4 453	4 047	2 042	46 551	9.0	2.49	9.2	25.2
Lewiston, ID-WA	10.3	7.9	8.8	51.3	51 359	57 961	12.9	0.6	2 224	1 920	106	23 650	14.7	2.41	9.2	25.2
Lewiston-Auburn, ME	9.7	6.9	7.2	51.3	105 259	103 793	-1.4	2.2	3 914	3 427	1 886	42 028	5.0	2.38	10.8	28.3
Lexington-Fayette, KY	8.7	5.4	4.8	50.9	348 428	408 326	17.2	3.4	18 659	10 657	6 080	163 854	22.2	2.39	11.5	28.2
Lima, OH	9.4	6.9	7.1	50.0	109 755	108 473	-1.2	-0.2	4 991	3 698	-1 466	40 646	3.1	2.52	12.4	26.3
Lincoln, NE	7.8	5.2	5.3	50.0	229 091	266 787	16.5	4.1	12 619	6 059	4 564	105 200	19.3	2.41	8.9	28.8
Little Rock-North Little Rock, AR	9.3	6.1	5.3	51.4	534 943	610 518	14.1	2.9	29 188	17 775	6 505	241 094	18.4	2.47	13.1	26.4
Logan, UT-ID	5.3	3.7	3.9	50.5	79 415	102 720	29.3	4.7	7 729	1 651	-1 252	31 019	30.1	3.24	7.0	14.7
Longview, TX	9.5	7.3	6.5	50.7	180 053	194 042	7.8	2.1	9 350	6 973	1 913	73 341	8.3	2.56	12.5	24.9
Longview, WA	10.4	6.7	6.6	50.5	82 119	92 948	13.2	2.4	3 971	2 906	1 257	35 850	13.3	2.55	10.7	24.3
Los Angeles-Long Beach-Santa Ana, CA	8.0	5.1	4.7	50.4	11 273 720	12 365 627	9.7	3.7	644 086	248 249	68 477	4 069 061	6.6	2.99	13.7	23.8
Los Angeles-Long Beach-Glendale, CA Div	7.8	5.1	4.7	50.5	8 863 052	9 519 338	7.4	3.7	498 085	193 782	48 018	3 133 774	4.8	2.98	14.7	24.6
Santa Ana-Anaheim-Irvine, CA Div	8.5	5.2	4.8	50.2	2 410 668	2 846 289	18.1	3.9	146 001	54 467	20 459	935 287	13.1	3.00	10.7	21.1
Louisville, KY-IN	9.5	6.4	5.7	51.3	1 056 156	1 161 975	10.0	2.4	51 830	36 099	12 555	462 241	14.3	2.46	13.2	27.0
Lubbock, TX	7.7	5.9	5.2	51.0	229 940	249 700	8.6	3.0	12 826	6 295	974	95 020	13.1	2.53	12.5	27.0
Lynchburg, VA	10.8	7.8	6.9	51.9	206 226	228 616	10.9	1.1	8 524	7 628	1 753	89 736	16.2	2.43	12.0	26.8
Macon, GA	9.1	6.2	5.7	53.1	206 786	222 368	7.5	1.6	11 001	7 509	224	84 338	11.2	2.56	18.6	25.7
Madera, CA	7.9	5.8	4.9	51.5	88 090	123 109	39.8	8.4	6 987	3 030	6 439	36 155	27.4	3.18	12.2	25.8
Madison, WI	8.2	4.9	4.9	50.3	432 323	501 774	16.1	5.0	20 723	11 112	15 641	202 687	21.3	2.39	7.9	28.8
Manchester-Nashua, NH	9.2	5.3	5.1	50.5	335 838	380 841	13.4	3.6	16 126	9 010	6 957	144 455	16.0	2.58	9.5	24.3
Mansfield, OH	10.4	7.7	6.9	49.7	126 137	128 852	2.2	-0.5	5 231	3 978	-1 782	49 534	4.1	2.47	11.4	26.5
McAllen-Edinburg-Pharr, TX	6.0	4.9	4.3	51.4	383 545	569 463	48.5	11.6	49 286	8 565	25 815	156 824	51.6	3.60	15.7	13.1
Medford, OR	10.6	7.5	8.2	51.4	146 387	181 269	23.8	4.9	6 727	6 322	8 454	71 532	25.0	2.48	10.5	25.1
Memphis, TN-MS-AR	8.4	5.3	4.6	51.8	1 067 263	1 205 204	12.9	2.8	64 735	35 000	4 549	448 473	16.5	2.63	19.0	25.3
Merced, CA	6.9	4.8	4.0	49.7	178 403	210 554	18.0	10.0	12 731	4 513	12 722	63 815	15.3	3.25	14.1	17.7
Miami-Fort Lauderdale-Miami Beach, FL	9.4	7.6	8.2	51.5	4 056 228	5 007 564	23.5	5.6	228 689	155 606	206 729	1 905 394	20.1	2.58	13.7	26.9
Fort Lauderdale-Pompano Beach-Deerfield Beach, FL Div	9.0	6.5	8.2	51.5	1 255 531	1 623 018	29.3	6.7	74 147	52 831	87 403	654 445	23.8	2.45	12.5	29.6
Miami-Miami Beach-Kendall, FL Div	9.7	7.2	6.2	51.6	1 937 194	2 253 362	16.3	3.9	108 905	59 296	36 807	776 774	12.2	2.84	17.2	23.3
West Palm Beach-Boca Raton-Boynton Beach, FL Div	9.6	9.7	12.2	51.4	863 503	1 131 184	31.0	7.5	45 637	43 479	82 519	474 175	29.7	2.34	9.7	29.2
Michigan City-La Porte, IN	9.7	6.8	6.7	48.6	107 066	110 106	2.8	-0.2	4 533	3 446	-1 229	41 050	6.7	2.52	11.7	25.2
Midland, TX	7.9	6.4	5.4	51.6	106 611	116 009	8.8	2.3	5 863	2 881	-321	42 745	9.8	2.68	11.4	24.2
Milwaukee-Waukesha-West Allis, WI	8.9	6.1	6.3	51.4	1 432 149	1 500 741	4.8	0.9	69 944	43 028	-12 760	587 657	9.3	2.50	12.9	28.7
Minneapolis-St. Paul-Bloomington, MN	8.4	4.8	4.7	50.5	2 538 776	2 968 806	16.9	3.9	142 247	61 536	32 668	1 136 615	18.4	2.56	9.7	26.7
Missoula, MT	9.0	5.0	5.0	50.0	78 687	95 802	21.8	2.9	3 614	2 186	1 476	38 439	24.9	2.40	9.2	28.0
Mobile, AL	9.4	6.4	5.7	52.1	378 643	399 843	5.6	0.0	19 685	13 007	-6 638	150 179	9.7	2.61	17.7	24.8
Modesto, CA	7.5	5.1	4.8	50.5	370 522	446 997	20.6	10.1	24 333	11 511	31 924	145 146	15.8	3.03	13.7	19.4
Monroe, LA	8.7	6.6	5.6	52.4	162 987	170 053	4.3	0.5	8 654	5 418	-2 328	64 073	10.4	2.57	17.3	25.6
Monroe, MI	9.6	6.0	5.2	50.4	133 600	145 945	9.2	3.2	5 460	4 025	3 397	53 772	15.6	2.69	10.1	21.7
Montgomery, AL	8.8	6.2	5.3	51.6	305 175	346 528	13.6	1.7	17 310	10 103	-1 255	129 717	18.4	2.54	17.0	26.4
Morgantown, WV	8.8	6.0	5.6	49.6	104 546	111 200	6.4	2.6	3 656	3 172	2 460	44 990	13.3	2.34	8.5	29.4
Morristown, TN	11.5	7.8	5.5	50.5	100 591	123 081	22.4	3.4	5 151	4 173	3 199	48 636	27.5	2.48	10.3	23.5
Mount Vernon-Anacortes, WA	9.6	6.8	7.3	50.5	79 545	102 979	29.5	6.1	4 456	3 164	4 985	38 852	27.1	2.60	9.7	23.3
Muncie, IN	9.8	7.0	6.6	52.0	119 659	118 769	-0.7	-1.1	4 429	3 793	-1 849	47 131	4.3	2.37	10.9	28.2
Muskegon-Norton Shores, MI	8.9	6.3	6.4	50.3	158 983	170 200	7.1	1.7	7 737	5 286	643	63 330	9.6	2.59	13.9	25.2
Myrtle Beach-Conway-North Myrtle Beach, SC	11.1	9.1	5.9	50.8	144 053	196 629	36.5	7.2	8 364	6 326	11 866	81 800	46.7	2.37	11.5	25.8
Napa, CA	10.1	6.6	7.9	49.9	110 765	124 279	12.2	5.9	5 008	4 185	6 492	45 402	9.9	2.62	9.9	25.8
Naples-Marco Island, FL	11.8	12.6	10.5	49.5	152 099	251 377	65.3	14.0	11 086	7 839	31 384	102 973	66.9	2.39	7.2	24.5
Nashville-Davidson—Murfreesboro, TN	8.9	5.5	4.6	50.8	1 048 216	1 311 789	25.1	4.5	63 530	35 127	30 484	510 222	27.7	2.50	12.1	26.1
New Haven-Milford, CT	9.5	6.3	7.7	51.8	804 219	824 008	2.5	2.2	33 007	25 383	11 168	319 040	4.7	2.50	13.6	28.2
New Orleans-Metairie-Kenner, LA	9.2	6.0	5.4	52.0	1 264 383	1 316 510	4.1	0.1	63 434	39 920	-22 746	498 587	7.6	2.59	18.2	27.2

1. No spouse present.

Area Name	Births, average 1999–2001 Total	Rate[1]	Deaths, average 1999–2001 Number Total	Number Infant[2]	Rate Total[1]	Rate Infant[3]	Physicians,[4] 1998 Number	Rate[5]	Hospitals,[4] 1998 Number	Beds Number	Beds Rate[5]	Medicare enrollees, 2003	Serious crimes known to police,[6] 2002 Total Number	Rate[7]
	32	33	34	35	36	37	38	39	40	41	42	43	44	45
La Crosse, WI-MN	1 456	11.5	1 113	31	8.8	7.1	367	384	3	641	1 000	18 833	3 448	2 677
Lafayette, IN	2 284	12.8	1 311	57	7.3	8.3	300	264	2	477	343	20 029	5 465	3 566
Lafayette, LA	3 631	15.2	1 780	103	7.4	9.5	471	272	6	1 036	574	28 439	11 054	4 808
Lake Charles, LA	2 914	15.1	1 790	88	9.3	10.1	307	196	7	889	776	27 580	11 040	5 788
Lakeland, FL	6 783	14.0	5 275	160	10.9	7.9	714	148	5	1 430	316	93 608	25 818	5 133
Lancaster, PA	6 763	14.3	4 235	143	9.0	7.0	756	161	5	1 118	245	73 091	12 033	2 833
Lansing-East Lansing, MI	5 735	12.8	3 125	98	7.0	5.7	1 003	439	7	1 632	683	55 388	16 224	3 608
Laredo, TX	5 721	29.3	926	96	4.7	5.6	167	86	2	377	200	18 329	13 468	6 677
Las Cruces, NM	3 001	17.1	1 077	49	6.1	5.4	240	137	1	221	131	22 166	NA	NA
Las Vegas-Paradise, NV	22 082	15.9	10 505	424	7.6	6.4	1 969	143	8	2 249	194	182 306	72 126	4 820
Lawrence, KS	1 195	11.9	529	16	5.3	4.5	135	135	1	167	179	9 567	4 651	4 606
Lawton, OK	1 914	16.7	842	37	7.3	6.4	186	162	2	339	299	13 205	5 919	5 084
Lebanon, PA	1 417	11.8	1 256	26	10.4	6.1	208	173	2	216	184	21 824	2 850	2 468
Lewiston, ID-WA	696	12.0	616	18	10.6	8.6	115	358	2	161	519	11 311	2 234	3 802
Lewiston-Auburn, ME	1 213	11.7	1 047	21	10.1	5.8	247	238	2	440	434	18 740	3 547	3 366
Lexington-Fayette, KY	5 639	13.8	3 215	120	7.9	7.1	1 424	948	9	2 228	2 026	51 148	NA	NA
Lima, OH	1 579	14.6	1 113	41	10.3	8.7	203	187	3	581	542	16 855	4 956	4 703
Lincoln, NE	3 882	14.5	1 826	72	6.8	6.2	497	250	4	751	599	32 950	16 224	6 018
Little Rock-North Little Rock, AR	8 849	14.5	5 305	241	8.7	9.1	1 755	699	10	2 805	1 036	84 220	39 882	6 444
Logan, UT-ID	2 398	23.4	504	33	4.9	4.6	117	151	2	204	745	9 075	2 199	2 064
Longview, TX	2 835	14.6	2 155	77	11.1	9.1	246	274	4	556	615	33 182	10 581	5 251
Longview, WA	1 267	13.6	909	28	9.7	7.4	159	171	1	209	228	15 448	5 984	6 253
Los Angeles-Long Beach-Santa Ana, CA	202 122	16.3	76 504	3 096	6.2	5.1	29 248	464	151	37 253	583	1 338 861	476 868	3 720
Los Angeles-Long Beach-Glendale, CA Div	155 765	16.3	59 775	2 451	6.3	5.2	22 877	240	114	30 364	330	1 029 780	394 591	3 998
Santa Ana-Anaheim-Irvine, CA Div	46 357	16.2	16 729	645	5.9	4.6	6 371	224	37	6 889	253	309 081	82 277	2 788
Louisville, KY-IN	15 982	13.7	11 018	302	9.5	6.3	2 603	1 231	18	4 672	2 249	173 845	NA	NA
Lubbock, TX	3 932	15.7	2 039	88	8.1	7.5	747	321	7	1 586	1 161	31 878	16 028	6 145
Lynchburg, VA	2 646	11.6	2 298	51	10.1	6.4	301	774	3	695	3 436	42 556	5 453	2 315
Macon, GA	3 338	15.0	2 291	128	10.3	12.8	520	448	5	1 004	822	33 606	15 047	6 471
Madera, CA	2 085	16.8	898	35	7.2	5.6	107	87	2	124	108	19 091	5 037	3 947
Madison, WI	6 344	12.6	3 327	123	6.6	6.5	1 705	571	7	1 541	1 075	60 530	15 671	3 584
Manchester-Nashua, NH	4 983	13.0	2 708	70	7.1	4.7	732	192	5	938	258	48 117	NA	NA
Mansfield, OH	1 644	12.8	1 276	36	9.9	7.3	185	144	3	411	323	21 933	6 728	5 190
McAllen-Edinburg-Pharr, TX	14 846	25.8	2 799	189	4.9	4.2	513	90	5	1 036	198	58 418	34 075	5 742
Medford, OR	2 089	11.5	1 867	31	10.3	4.9	400	221	3	471	272	33 915	8 344	4 472
Memphis, TN-MS-AR	19 489	16.2	10 673	711	8.8	12.2	2 477	631	19	5 422	1 624	146 180	86 028	7 349
Merced, CA	3 827	18.0	1 371	64	6.5	5.6	215	102	4	402	203	21 018	11 141	5 104
Miami-Fort Lauderdale-Miami Beach, FL	67 290	13.4	48 343	1 229	9.6	6.1	12 626	743	59	17 489	1 089	812 930	317 101	6 056
Fort Lauderdale-Pompano Beach-Deerfield Beach, FL Div	21 837	13.4	16 201	424	9.9	6.5	3 487	215	20	5 538	368	244 892	73 096	4 307
Miami-Miami Beach-Kendall, FL Div	32 072	14.2	18 920	539	8.4	5.6	6 355	282	25	8 657	402	321 353	168 968	7 171
West Palm Beach-Boca Raton-Boynton Beach, FL Div	13 380	11.8	13 222	266	11.6	6.6	2 784	246	14	3 294	319	246 685	75 037	6 343
Michigan City-La Porte, IN	1 404	12.7	1 051	32	9.5	7.6	160	145	3	468	428	16 605	5 027	4 568
Midland, TX	1 831	15.7	888	40	7.6	7.3	179	154	2	318	266	14 662	4 730	3 904
Milwaukee-Waukesha-West Allis, WI	21 548	14.3	13 093	517	8.7	8.0	4 179	838	21	4 492	850	213 907	68 759	4 582
Minneapolis-St. Paul-Bloomington, MN	43 906	14.7	18 897	729	6.3	5.5	6 318	1 436	32	6 454	2 202	330 821	121 048	4 026
Missoula, MT	1 110	11.6	654	13	6.8	3.9	257	268	2	336	378	11 664	NA	NA
Mobile, AL	6 156	15.4	3 919	193	9.8	10.4	925	231	6	1 762	441	59 320	24 377	6 400
Modesto, CA	7 322	16.2	3 453	157	7.7	7.1	648	145	7	1 478	347	58 154	27 932	6 027
Monroe, LA	2 584	15.2	1 649	88	9.7	11.4	325	250	7	1 072	962	23 965	NA	NA
Monroe, MI	1 824	12.5	1 165	29	8.0	5.3	114	78	1	173	121	19 848	4 409	2 987
Montgomery, AL	5 289	15.3	3 092	125	8.9	7.9	579	391	7	1 346	778	49 636	22 163	6 961
Morgantown, WV	1 133	10.2	989	23	8.9	6.8	501	676	3	620	920	15 026	2 743	2 502
Morristown, TN	1 612	13.1	1 230	27	10.0	5.6	112	223	3	369	712	22 588	4 769	3 803
Mount Vernon-Anacortes, WA	1 382	13.4	942	26	9.1	6.3	211	205	3	307	309	17 462	6 727	6 344
Muncie, IN	1 411	11.9	1 153	44	9.7	10.4	267	225	1	428	366	18 631	4 320	3 591
Muskegon-Norton Shores, MI	2 386	14.0	1 608	76	9.4	10.6	296	174	3	618	371	27 920	10 117	5 878
Myrtle Beach-Conway-North Myrtle Beach, SC	2 502	12.7	1 876	64	9.5	8.5	272	138	3	480	275	33 827	16 397	8 165
Napa, CA	1 518	12.1	1 267	11	10.1	2.4	376	303	3	1 429	1 198	22 036	3 574	2 774
Naples-Marco Island, FL	3 146	12.4	2 356	53	9.3	5.6	557	222	2	500	251	54 158	9 738	3 704
Nashville-Davidson—Murfreesboro, TN	19 378	14.7	10 573	403	8.0	6.9	3 309	1 483	26	4 840	3 706	162 946	71 712	5 365
New Haven-Milford, CT	10 262	12.4	7 760	204	9.4	6.6	3 280	398	8	2 268	286	131 800	31 184	3 952
New Orleans-Metairie-Kenner, LA	19 184	14.6	12 163	447	9.2	7.8	4 154	1 251	29	6 043	2 208	179 082	68 124	5 166

1. Per 1,000 estimated resident population.   2. Deaths of infants under 1 year old.   3. Deaths of infants under 1 year old per 1,000 live births.   4. Data subject to copyright.   5. Per 100,000 resident population as of July 1 of the year shown.   6. Data for serious crimes have not been adjusted for underreporting; this may affect comparability between geographic areas and over time.   7. Per 100,000 population estimated by the FBI.

Table C. Metropolitan Areas — Crime, Education, Money Income, and Poverty

Area Name	Serious crimes known to police,[1] 2002 (cont'd) Rate[2] Violent	Property	Education — School enrollment and attainment, 2000 — Enrollment Total[3]	Percent private	Attainment[4] (percent) High school graduate or more	Bachelor's degree or more	Local government expenditures,[5] 2000–2001 Total current expenditures (mil dol)	Current expenditures per student (dollars)	Money income, 1999 Per capita income[6] (dollars)	Mean household income	Mean family income	Percent of households with income of $100,000 or more	Percent below poverty level, 1999 Persons	Households	Families	Families with children
	46	47	48	49	50	51	52	53	54	55	56	57	58	59	60	61
La Crosse, WI-MN	138	2 539	38 579	14.8	89.0	24.6	156.5	8 066	19 649	49 460	59 764	7.5	10.0	10.0	5.1	7.9
Lafayette, IN	214	3 352	67 855	8.2	87.1	29.2	165.2	6 875	19 268	49 799	61 137	9.0	13.8	13.8	6.7	9.8
Lafayette, LA	605	4 202	69 554	19.2	76.4	22.0	209.5	5 578	18 202	47 839	55 559	8.4	16.9	17.1	13.2	17.6
Lake Charles, LA	645	5 142	52 863	13.5	76.6	16.4	195.6	5 717	17 588	46 516	52 715	7.4	15.3	15.7	12.6	17.3
Lakeland, FL	566	4 567	114 180	15.4	74.8	14.9	467.5	5 882	18 302	46 511	52 304	6.6	12.9	11.9	9.4	15.5
Lancaster, PA	216	2 617	115 931	23.7	77.4	20.5	536.9	7 861	20 398	54 889	62 233	9.7	7.8	7.0	5.3	8.0
Lansing-East Lansing, MI	460	3 148	149 664	10.0	88.6	28.4	622.9	8 455	21 653	55 361	66 045	11.2	11.0	11.1	6.4	10.0
Laredo, TX	588	6 089	67 101	6.8	53.0	13.9	309.0	6 084	10 759	40 467	41 829	6.2	31.2	28.1	26.7	32.8
Las Cruces, NM	NA	NA	60 034	6.1	70.0	22.3	219.2	5 952	13 999	40 277	44 920	5.3	25.4	22.3	20.2	28.9
Las Vegas-Paradise, NV	726	4 094	329 929	9.3	79.5	17.3	1 279.9	5 525	21 785	57 569	63 702	11.5	10.8	9.5	7.9	11.8
Lawrence, KS	361	4 244	42 645	9.3	92.4	42.7	85.5	6 563	19 952	50 570	67 609	9.0	15.9	17.1	6.2	8.9
Lawton, OK	637	4 446	32 582	7.0	85.2	19.1	126.2	5 663	15 728	41 621	46 651	5.2	15.6	15.4	13.2	18.6
Lebanon, PA	288	2 179	26 552	19.6	78.6	15.4	121.3	6 786	19 773	49 854	57 585	7.7	7.5	7.4	5.4	8.9
Lewiston, ID-WA	177	3 625	14 657	8.5	85.6	18.6	64.9	6 919	18 262	44 327	51 802	5.9	13.3	12.8	9.7	16.3
Lewiston-Auburn, ME	130	3 236	25 970	19.7	79.8	14.4	130.8	7 890	18 734	45 209	53 036	5.4	11.1	12.1	7.5	12.3
Lexington-Fayette, KY	NA	NA	114 238	17.3	83.2	29.8	376.0	6 448	22 008	53 751	64 628	11.0	11.9	12.2	8.2	12.4
Lima, OH	480	4 223	28 722	19.3	82.5	13.4	126.7	6 816	17 511	45 618	52 652	6.7	12.1	12.5	9.6	14.9
Lincoln, NE	488	5 530	81 929	18.0	90.3	32.0	271.6	7 034	21 086	52 338	63 410	9.3	9.4	9.6	5.4	8.6
Little Rock-North Little Rock, AR	623	5 821	162 119	16.6	83.0	24.2	604.6	6 240	20 122	50 271	58 281	8.8	12.1	11.8	9.0	13.8
Logan, UT-ID	97	1 967	41 160	4.2	90.1	29.6	99.1	4 521	14 940	48 919	54 006	7.3	12.8	12.4	7.7	9.1
Longview, TX	515	4 735	49 902	10.5	77.3	16.2	246.8	6 591	17 635	45 919	52 555	6.8	14.9	14.8	11.8	17.5
Longview, WA	373	5 880	23 679	9.6	83.2	13.3	113.6	6 416	18 583	47 326	53 649	7.3	14.0	12.7	10.3	16.5
Los Angeles-Long Beach-Santa Ana, CA	759	2 961	3 778 747	15.5	72.2	26.3	15 043.9	6 917	21 867	65 428	71 133	17.0	16.2	13.4	12.7	17.7
Los Angeles-Long Beach-Glendale, CA Div	902	3 096	2 931 076	15.7	69.9	24.9	11 870.8	7 063	20 683	61 811	67 022	15.1	17.9	15.1	14.4	19.9
Santa Ana-Anaheim-Irvine, CA Div	278	2 510	847 671	14.8	79.5	30.8	3 173.1	6 421	25 826	77 543	84 272	23.5	10.3	7.7	7.0	10.1
Louisville, KY-IN	NA	NA	290 252	20.9	80.9	21.2	1 194.1	6 811	21 350	52 981	61 581	10.1	10.9	11.1	8.4	13.0
Lubbock, TX	1 023	5 123	82 911	9.0	77.9	24.0	293.0	6 685	17 242	44 581	54 137	7.0	18.1	18.3	12.3	18.2
Lynchburg, VA	231	2 084	57 649	24.8	75.9	18.7	220.2	6 188	18 839	47 068	53 912	7.1	11.4	11.8	8.5	13.1
Macon, GA	361	6 110	60 971	18.8	76.1	18.7	236.8	6 372	18 703	48 781	56 702	8.6	17.1	17.0	13.6	20.0
Madera, CA	586	3 360	35 998	7.3	65.4	12.0	171.1	6 907	14 682	48 050	51 112	8.2	21.4	16.5	15.9	23.1
Madison, WI	236	3 348	150 852	11.0	91.3	36.9	671.6	8 681	24 321	59 235	72 587	12.2	8.9	8.8	3.9	5.9
Manchester-Nashua, NH	NA	NA	103 468	23.9	87.0	30.1	430.8	6 518	25 198	65 582	75 122	16.6	6.3	6.4	4.3	6.3
Mansfield, OH	174	5 017	31 084	13.4	80.2	12.6	172.8	7 939	18 582	47 025	53 478	6.9	10.6	10.3	8.2	13.7
McAllen-Edinburg-Pharr, TX	487	5 255	188 181	3.8	50.5	12.9	1 003.7	6 952	9 899	35 591	36 896	4.7	35.9	31.9	31.3	39.1
Medford, OR	264	4 209	44 630	10.6	85.0	22.3	210.3	7 204	19 498	48 729	55 919	8.0	12.5	11.9	8.9	14.7
Memphis, TN-MS-AR	1 053	6 295	340 891	16.0	79.0	22.0	1 232.8	5 670	19 992	53 044	60 609	10.5	15.6	14.8	12.6	17.7
Merced, CA	645	4 458	70 396	6.8	63.8	11.0	359.3	6 963	14 257	46 185	49 349	6.9	21.7	17.8	16.9	22.8
Miami-Fort Lauderdale-Miami Beach, FL	848	5 208	1 309 212	20.0	76.2	24.1	4 849.4	6 268	22 339	57 936	65 784	12.8	14.0	13.3	10.8	15.5
Fort Lauderdale-Pompano Beach-Deerfield Beach, FL Div	545	3 762	410 814	20.7	82.0	24.5	1 470.0	5 853	23 170	56 805	66 119	12.8	11.5	10.8	8.7	12.6
Miami-Miami Beach-Kendall, FL Div	1 116	6 054	643 727	19.4	67.9	21.7	2 415.3	6 552	18 497	52 753	57 886	10.8	18.0	18.1	14.5	19.3
West Palm Beach-Boca Raton-Boynton Beach, FL Div	747	5 597	254 671	20.4	83.6	27.7	964.2	6 266	28 801	67 994	79 591	16.2	9.9	9.0	6.9	11.5
Michigan City-La Porte, IN	245	4 322	27 395	14.3	80.6	14.0	126.6	7 089	18 913	49 448	56 357	7.1	8.7	8.7	6.3	9.7
Midland, TX	495	3 408	34 805	13.3	79.2	24.8	151.9	6 590	20 369	54 539	62 263	11.9	12.9	12.1	10.3	14.6
Milwaukee-Waukesha-West Allis, WI	445	4 137	419 953	24.1	84.5	27.0	2 107.2	8 759	23 158	58 399	68 974	12.4	10.6	9.6	7.7	12.4
Minneapolis-St. Paul-Bloomington, MN	330	3 696	830 788	17.7	90.6	33.3	3 948.4	7 779	26 219	67 670	79 376	16.9	6.7	6.3	4.2	6.5
Missoula, MT	NA	NA	30 019	8.5	91.0	32.8	88.9	6 391	17 808	43 812	53 644	6.2	14.8	15.5	8.8	13.4
Mobile, AL	597	5 803	110 152	21.3	76.7	18.6	351.1	5 404	17 178	45 263	51 411	6.7	18.5	18.3	15.6	22.8
Modesto, CA	538	5 489	136 838	9.2	70.4	14.1	658.4	6 767	16 913	51 437	55 910	9.1	16.0	13.6	12.3	17.3
Monroe, LA	NA	NA	49 399	10.8	77.6	21.2	173.6	5 496	16 780	43 871	51 647	7.1	20.4	19.4	15.6	22.8
Monroe, MI	274	2 714	39 786	3.3	83.1	14.3	195.6	7 909	22 458	60 326	67 695	13.7	7.0	7.3	4.8	6.7
Montgomery, AL	576	6 385	97 327	18.9	78.9	24.2	315.4	5 591	18 659	48 744	55 620	9.0	15.8	15.0	12.1	17.9
Morgantown, WV	240	2 262	36 648	6.0	80.8	26.0	108.3	7 169	16 180	39 097	50 030	6.0	21.6	22.5	12.4	18.2
Morristown, TN	380	3 423	26 822	11.7	68.4	12.2	102.9	5 191	16 875	41 984	48 111	5.3	14.8	15.7	11.0	15.8
Mount Vernon-Anacortes, WA	186	6 158	26 225	8.9	84.0	20.8	131.8	6 975	21 256	55 622	62 390	9.5	11.1	9.5	7.9	11.6
Muncie, IN	293	3 297	37 225	5.9	81.6	20.4	133.1	7 891	19 233	47 415	56 168	7.3	15.1	15.4	9.0	13.7
Muskegon-Norton Shores, MI	629	5 249	46 749	9.7	83.1	13.9	261.8	8 001	17 967	46 749	53 590	6.6	11.4	11.1	8.8	13.8
Myrtle Beach-Conway-North Myrtle Beach, SC	973	7 193	42 752	10.8	81.1	18.7	204.1	6 829	19 944	47 313	53 488	7.1	12.0	11.2	8.4	14.4
Napa, CA	268	2 506	33 203	18.3	80.4	26.4	138.4	7 154	26 395	70 985	80 378	18.6	8.3	6.9	5.6	8.8
Naples-Marco Island, FL	538	3 166	46 873	13.8	81.8	27.9	228.8	6 690	31 195	75 125	84 576	18.1	10.3	7.8	6.6	13.1
Nashville-Davidson—Murfreesboro, TN	897	4 468	334 926	20.5	80.3	25.6	1 159.7	5 864	22 438	56 868	66 119	11.5	10.3	10.4	7.6	11.1
New Haven-Milford, CT	383	3 568	225 396	23.5	83.0	27.6	1 252.1	9 757	24 439	62 220	73 421	15.8	9.5	9.7	7.0	11.0
New Orleans-Metairie-Kenner, LA	664	4 503	379 440	29.6	77.7	22.8	1 170.4	6 136	18 906	49 148	56 796	9.3	18.3	17.4	14.8	21.5

1. Data for serious crimes have not been adjusted for underreporting; this may affect comparability between geographic areas and over time.   2. Per 100,000 population estimated by the FBI.   3. All persons 3 years old and over enrolled in nursery school through college.   4. Persons 25 years old and over.   5. Elementary and secondary education expenditures.   6. Based on population enumerated as of April 1, 2000.

Table C. Metropolitan Areas — **Personal Income**

Area Name	Personal income, 2002												
	Total (mil dol)	Percent change, 2001-2002	Per capita[1] Dollars	Rank	Wages and salaries[2] (mil dol)	Proprietor's income (mil dol)	Dividends, interest, and rent (mil dol)	Transfer payments Total (mil dol)	Government payments to individuals Total (mil dol)	Social Security (mil dol)	Medical payments (mil dol)	Income mainte-nance (mil dol)	Unemploy-ment insurance (mil dol)
	62	63	64	65	66	67	68	69	70	71	72	73	74
La Crosse, WI-MN	3 612	3.8	28 220	146	2 604	266	648	536	503	204	214	29	20
Lafayette, IN	4 549	1.3	25 072	260	3 458	313	868	555	510	245	174	38	18
Lafayette, LA	6 636	2.4	27 359	170	5 121	547	1 098	1 004	941	306	454	111	19
Lake Charles, LA	4 701	2.6	24 359	290	3 345	299	760	897	848	315	387	85	19
Lakeland, FL	12 891	4.7	25 848	220	7 193	906	2 498	2 389	2 267	1 045	838	221	44
Lancaster, PA	14 001	2.9	29 256	117	9 083	1 174	2 607	1 952	1 830	862	707	119	72
Lansing-East Lansing, MI	12 614	2.8	27 807	154	10 051	625	1 871	1 717	1 610	678	625	159	73
Laredo, TX	3 437	6.9	16 555	359	2 359	352	346	720	674	140	329	149	14
Las Cruces, NM	3 674	7.3	20 564	347	2 023	310	606	753	706	209	315	109	14
Las Vegas-Paradise, NV	44 572	5.0	29 282	116	31 915	3 219	8 188	5 305	4 979	2 104	1 896	401	312
Lawrence, KS	2 658	2.8	25 978	212	1 674	139	461	294	266	113	104	18	11
Lawton, OK	2 686	3.9	23 683	309	2 006	134	384	439	416	135	142	50	4
Lebanon, PA	3 380	2.6	27 888	152	1 621	227	557	577	546	248	222	26	25
Lewiston, ID-WA	1 515	3.0	26 321	201	931	122	291	315	302	127	118	23	12
Lewiston-Auburn, ME	2 809	5.5	26 802	186	1 779	154	348	580	556	190	265	59	14
Lexington-Fayette, KY	12 967	3.1	31 142	78	10 066	1 286	2 301	1 547	1 441	575	523	135	43
Lima, OH	2 728	2.0	25 231	248	2 185	190	491	497	466	198	173	42	17
Lincoln, NE	8 222	4.0	29 988	101	6 083	676	1 495	960	895	373	348	71	20
Little Rock-North Little Rock, AR	17 831	3.1	28 628	131	12 989	1 408	2 855	2 745	2 579	953	1 067	236	91
Logan, UT-ID	2 099	3.5	19 916	354	1 370	125	361	273	249	103	81	23	8
Longview, TX	5 062	2.6	25 657	228	2 908	581	933	982	938	368	414	82	28
Longview, WA	2 373	1.5	25 107	256	1 534	172	401	530	504	188	179	52	52
Los Angeles-Long Beach-Santa Ana, CA	413 165	2.7	32 418	52	288 864	54 397	68 810	53 336	50 294	13 516	23 469	8 357	1 964
Los Angeles-Long Beach-Glendale, CA Div	300 898	2.6	30 683	X	215 001	39 950	50 124	43 511	41 170	10 091	19 907	7 325	1 554
Santa Ana-Anaheim-Irvine, CA Div	112 267	2.8	38 205	X	73 863	14 448	18 687	9 825	9 124	3 426	3 561	1 033	410
Louisville, KY-IN	36 195	2.1	30 600	86	24 826	2 830	6 566	5 216	4 914	1 988	2 009	436	211
Lubbock, TX	6 365	4.2	25 016	265	4 150	635	1 017	1 103	1 046	350	513	108	13
Lynchburg, VA	5 850	1.3	25 450	234	3 641	342	1 075	1 058	1 002	446	375	77	35
Macon, GA	6 214	4.4	27 612	161	3 894	455	1 063	1 135	1 071	350	501	130	27
Madera, CA	2 527	6.2	19 399	356	1 292	281	404	571	540	171	203	90	45
Madison, WI	18 001	4.7	34 644	32	13 915	1 277	3 383	1 758	1 627	703	646	110	80
Manchester-Nashua, NH	13 914	0.6	35 458	25	9 764	987	1 929	1 418	1 324	570	567	83	40
Mansfield, OH	3 222	3.3	25 171	251	2 380	135	473	619	583	246	228	49	23
McAllen-Edinburg-Pharr, TX	9 056	7.3	14 738	361	5 171	1 009	1 084	2 404	2 266	460	1 076	558	63
Medford, OR	4 942	4.3	26 509	197	2 714	532	1 168	911	869	383	284	72	60
Memphis, TN-MS-AR	37 496	3.3	30 471	91	27 362	4 492	4 614	5 162	4 880	1 634	2 066	794	143
Merced, CA	4 640	4.8	20 586	346	2 278	592	634	1 067	1 013	238	449	187	83
Miami-Fort Lauderdale-Miami Beach, FL	168 639	3.2	32 232	56	100 053	12 001	43 861	25 440	24 160	8 612	11 689	2 318	712
Fort Lauderdale-Pompano Beach-Deerfield Beach, FL Div	54 173	3.1	31 696	X	30 191	3 119	12 140	7 381	6 963	2 809	3 123	501	247
Miami-Miami Beach-Kendall, FL Div	62 037	3.6	26 596	X	45 908	5 036	11 171	11 646	11 075	2 832	6 048	1 526	315
West Palm Beach-Boca Raton-Boynton Beach, FL Div	52 429	2.9	44 044	X	23 954	3 846	20 551	6 413	6 121	2 970	2 517	291	150
Michigan City-La Porte, IN	2 729	1.2	24 723	279	1 728	125	495	477	450	203	173	36	21
Midland, TX	3 956	0.8	33 620	40	2 193	750	803	450	424	177	175	43	14
Milwaukee-Waukesha-West Allis, WI	51 798	2.2	34 247	34	38 400	3 249	9 274	7 324	6 944	2 550	2 980	873	334
Minneapolis-St. Paul-Bloomington, MN	115 502	2.1	37 812	17	89 285	7 721	20 162	11 439	10 639	3 883	4 678	865	668
Missoula, MT	2 626	5.2	26 768	188	1 847	302	508	349	325	127	114	30	9
Mobile, AL	9 033	1.9	22 573	335	6 591	598	1 400	1 908	1 813	681	740	241	44
Modesto, CA	11 372	4.3	23 572	313	6 508	1 045	1 627	2 140	2 025	609	829	303	160
Monroe, LA	4 224	4.9	24 831	273	2 692	412	652	841	797	251	384	101	15
Monroe, MI	4 328	2.2	28 998	122	2 140	158	607	587	552	251	212	38	29
Montgomery, AL	9 665	4.4	27 518	165	6 795	755	1 687	1 529	1 447	531	555	208	26
Morgantown, WV	2 778	4.3	24 725	278	1 965	212	455	545	519	173	215	39	9
Morristown, TN	2 873	3.8	22 886	328	1 743	258	395	647	619	237	273	57	22
Mount Vernon-Anacortes, WA	3 135	3.8	29 325	115	1 728	334	682	552	523	202	193	42	45
Muncie, IN	2 992	1.6	25 314	243	1 987	152	541	549	520	225	207	46	19
Muskegon-Norton Shores, MI	4 082	1.7	23 765	306	2 579	187	571	863	823	329	308	109	55
Myrtle Beach-Conway-North Myrtle Beach, SC	5 059	3.5	24 554	285	3 216	337	1 056	961	910	417	335	83	31
Napa, CA	4 983	2.8	38 252	12	2 894	556	1 130	579	548	216	233	34	26
Naples-Marco Island, FL	11 601	4.1	41 928	6	4 687	892	5 559	1 214	1 146	662	398	49	16
Nashville-Davidson—Murfreesboro, TN	43 317	3.1	32 013	62	30 180	6 449	5 818	5 249	4 949	1 898	2 171	451	195
New Haven-Milford, CT	29 532	2.0	35 340	26	18 761	2 168	4 501	4 527	4 328	1 545	2 084	333	210
New Orleans-Metairie-Kenner, LA	38 085	3.6	28 956	125	24 677	4 412	5 936	6 572	6 233	1 983	3 019	828	105

1. Based on the resident population estimated as of July 1 of the year shown.   2. Includes other labor income.

Table C. Metropolitan Areas — Earnings, Social Security, and Housing

Area Name	Earnings, 2002									Social Security beneficiaries, December 2003		Supplemental Security Income recipients, December 2003	Housing units, 2003	
			Percent by selected industries											
			Goods related[1]		Service-related and health									
	Total (mil dol)	Farm	Total	Manu-facturing	Infor-mation, profes-sional and technical services	Retail trade	Finance and insur-ance, and real estate	Health services	Govern-ment	Number	Rate[2]		Total	Percent change, 2000–2003
	75	76	77	78	79	80	81	82	83	84	85	86	87	88
La Crosse, WI-MN	2 870	0.3	D	17.8	5.9	7.0	D	D	14.4	21 235	165	2 141	53 406	3.4
Lafayette, IN	3 771	0.5	D	27.0	4.2	6.7	D	D	24.6	24 000	130	1 690	75 720	6.9
Lafayette, LA	5 668	0.2	30.5	6.1	9.6	8.1	7.8	D	10.8	34 685	142	6 780	102 825	4.5
Lake Charles, LA	3 644	-0.1	34.7	20.7	D	D	D	D	14.2	32 805	169	5 158	84 796	4.3
Lakeland, FL	8 099	1.2	20.6	12.7	7.3	9.6	6.8	10.9	15.1	112 470	220	13 978	240 055	6.0
Lancaster, PA	10 257	0.7	36.2	25.6	8.2	8.9	6.1	10.0	8.8	83 225	172	7 288	186 695	3.7
Lansing-East Lansing, MI	10 676	0.2	22.1	16.3	D	6.8	8.9	9.1	27.6	65 310	143	7 892	189 520	4.2
Laredo, TX	2 711	-0.2	9.4	1.4	5.3	10.3	7.5	10.2	26.4	21 105	99	8 740	61 127	10.7
Las Cruces, NM	2 332	5.9	D	4.9	8.3	7.5	3.7	12.2	35.6	25 490	140	5 753	69 241	6.2
Las Vegas-Paradise, NV	35 134	0.0	14.8	3.1	4.8	7.8	9.1	6.7	13.4	218 970	139	23 009	648 682	15.9
Lawrence, KS	1 812	0.0	D	9.0	15.0	6.8	5.0	7.4	30.7	10 925	106	922	43 026	6.9
Lawton, OK	2 140	0.3	D	9.6	4.3	6.1	3.6	5.8	56.5	15 795	139	2 547	45 787	0.8
Lebanon, PA	1 848	0.7	D	24.5	D	9.2	D	14.2	17.9	24 980	204	1 724	51 164	3.7
Lewiston, ID-WA	1 053	0.5	D	15.2	5.2	9.6	6.8	15.1	18.4	13 140	225	1 499	25 726	1.6
Lewiston-Auburn, ME	1 933	0.7	21.7	15.1	9.8	10.4	D	16.2	12.1	21 455	202	3 436	46 971	2.2
Lexington-Fayette, KY	11 352	2.8	27.3	20.8	D	7.0	5.3	D	16.4	60 450	143	9 986	185 640	5.9
Lima, OH	2 375	-0.5	35.4	29.5	3.9	8.0	3.8	16.2	14.2	19 635	181	2 466	44 601	0.8
Lincoln, NE	6 759	0.3	19.8	13.4	10.1	6.2	8.2	D	21.2	36 970	133	3 505	115 785	4.6
Little Rock-North Little Rock, AR	14 397	0.2	14.9	8.7	D	6.9	D	D	22.2	103 955	165	14 842	273 964	4.6
Logan, UT-ID	1 495	3.3	D	20.5	7.1	7.5	3.1	6.7	25.0	10 695	99	559	35 217	7.0
Longview, TX	3 489	0.9	29.0	12.8	D	10.3	5.5	D	11.7	37 110	187	5 172	82 612	1.8
Longview, WA	1 706	0.5	D	25.5	3.6	8.0	3.8	11.5	14.5	18 790	197	2 555	39 996	3.6
Los Angeles-Long Beach-Santa Ana, CA	343 261	0.2	17.4	12.3	18.7	6.6	11.1	7.7	12.4	1 356 400	106	450 147	4 316 003	1.8
Los Angeles-Long Beach-Glendale, CA Div	254 950	0.1	16.1	11.8	20.1	6.3	9.9	8.0	13.4	1 030 955	104	388 235	3 311 721	1.2
Santa Ana-Anaheim-Irvine, CA Div	88 311	0.3	20.9	13.5	14.5	7.2	14.4	6.8	9.4	325 445	110	61 912	1 004 282	3.6
Louisville, KY-IN	27 656	0.0	D	0.0	8.6	6.7	D	D	12.2	202 485	170	28 226	515 028	4.6
Lubbock, TX	4 786	0.9	D	5.8	D	10.2	D	15.3	22.2	36 760	143	5 180	108 687	4.7
Lynchburg, VA	3 983	0.2	D	28.3	D	8.7	6.8	D	13.1	47 340	205	5 110	101 722	3.7
Macon, GA	4 349	0.4	D	D	D	7.3	D	D	14.3	39 755	176	8 344	97 403	3.6
Madera, CA	1 573	7.4	D	9.2	D	8.2	3.6	14.1	22.0	19 155	144	4 441	42 779	5.9
Madison, WI	15 193	0.4	D	11.6	11.0	8.4	10.6	D	24.1	68 705	130	6 422	226 883	6.7
Manchester-Nashua, NH	10 751	0.0	26.7	20.3	13.1	9.1	10.9	9.9	9.6	56 680	144	4 056	156 036	4.1
Mansfield, OH	2 514	0.2	38.9	34.5	5.5	8.0	3.8	11.3	16.6	24 675	192	2 755	54 332	2.4
McAllen-Edinburg-Pharr, TX	6 180	1.0	12.0	4.9	5.2	11.1	5.1	18.3	26.7	68 910	108	29 368	214 555	11.4
Medford, OR	3 246	0.3	18.8	9.2	6.7	13.0	6.1	14.0	16.2	39 415	207	3 100	80 476	6.3
Memphis, TN-MS-AR	31 854	0.0	D	15.7	10.3	D	7.5	9.3	D	14.1	176 480	142	41 160	508 985	5.9
Merced, CA	2 870	11.5	19.2	13.6	3.2	8.6	3.3	8.8	20.8	28 230	122	10 061	72 669	6.3
Miami-Fort Lauderdale-Miami Beach, FL	112 054	0.4	11.6	5.2	14.0	8.1	11.4	9.7	14.1	878 380	166	170 194	2 252 686	4.8
Fort Lauderdale-Pompano Beach-Deerfield Beach, FL Div	33 309	0.1	12.9	5.6	12.7	9.7	12.4	9.3	14.3	273 865	158	31 065	773 642	4.4
Miami-Miami Beach-Kendall, FL Div	50 944	0.3	9.7	4.9	14.9	7.3	10.6	9.3	16.1	332 530	142	123 324	891 553	4.6
West Palm Beach-Boca Raton-Boynton Beach, FL Div	27 800	0.9	13.3	5.4	14.1	7.7	11.9	11.1	10.4	271 985	224	15 805	587 491	5.6
Michigan City-La Porte, IN	1 853	0.2	32.3	24.6	4.1	7.5	3.8	12.5	16.4	19 650	179	1 673	46 699	2.4
Midland, TX	2 944	-0.1	44.4	3.4	8.0	6.2	6.5	6.3	11.7	17 410	147	2 102	48 854	1.7
Milwaukee-Waukesha-West Allis, WI	41 648	0.0	D	20.4	10.4	5.7	10.3	11.6	11.2	242 680	160	34 766	631 248	2.1
Minneapolis-St. Paul-Bloomington, MN	97 007	0.1	20.4	14.2	13.2	6.0	11.9	D	12.0	376 260	122	40 183	1 238 608	5.9
Missoula, MT	2 150	-0.1	D	6.2	10.2	10.0	6.4	15.6	18.7	13 345	135	1 637	43 515	5.3
Mobile, AL	7 189	0.4	21.4	12.7	9.8	8.2	6.2	11.0	17.3	72 950	182	13 910	171 249	3.7
Modesto, CA	7 553	3.4	21.8	13.4	5.6	10.5	5.1	11.6	17.1	66 870	136	19 593	160 358	6.3
Monroe, LA	3 104	0.8	D	D	12.2	8.4	7.4	D	16.3	27 695	162	5 937	72 778	2.5
Monroe, MI	2 298	0.6	42.4	32.3	D	7.6	3.5	6.5	12.9	24 210	161	1 966	60 164	6.5
Montgomery, AL	7 550	0.4	D	9.9	D	6.5	8.1	D	29.3	59 580	169	13 687	149 395	3.3
Morgantown, WV	2 177	-0.1	18.6	9.5	6.7	6.2	3.5	D	35.2	17 860	157	2 754	50 597	0.9
Morristown, TN	2 002	0.0	D	38.3	D	8.4	D	D	11.3	26 755	210	4 132	56 165	4.5
Mount Vernon-Anacortes, WA	2 061	4.4	23.2	13.5	8.0	10.4	7.2	8.8	19.2	20 175	185	1 801	44 880	5.2
Muncie, IN	2 139	0.3	D	22.1	5.2	7.7	5.6	17.9	19.4	22 030	188	2 653	51 938	1.8
Muskegon-Norton Shores, MI	2 765	0.3	D	27.2	6.2	10.9	4.4	12.8	16.0	33 510	194	5 267	71 302	4.0
Myrtle Beach-Conway-North Myrtle Beach, SC	3 553	-0.7	15.7	5.4	8.2	13.0	12.5	8.1	13.9	45 520	216	4 399	134 761	10.4
Napa, CA	3 450	4.4	D	19.1	7.7	6.8	7.7	9.8	13.6	22 055	168	2 068	50 889	4.8
Naples-Marco Island, FL	5 579	2.1	17.6	2.3	9.6	9.9	12.6	10.8	9.6	62 080	217	2 131	167 244	15.7
Nashville-Davidson—Murfreesboro, TN	36 629	0.0	18.9	13.1	D	7.5	D	D	10.8	194 260	142	22 818	579 791	6.7
New Haven-Milford, CT	20 929	0.1	21.0	14.9	13.5	7.6	7.3	13.4	13.2	146 070	174	15 256	344 790	1.2
New Orleans-Metairie-Kenner, LA	29 088	0.0	D	7.8	D	D	7.2	D	17.0	210 865	160	48 910	557 378	1.6

1. Covers mining, construction, and manufacturing.   2. Per 1,000 resident population estimated as of July 1 of the year shown.

Table C. Metropolitan Areas — **Housing, Labor Force, and Employment**

Area Name	Housing units, 2000								Civilian labor force, 2003				Civilian employment,[5] 2000		
	Occupied units										Unemployment			Percent	
			Owner-occupied			Renter-occupied									
				Owner cost is 35 percent or more of income											
	Total	Percent	Mean value[1]	With a mortgage	Without a mortgage	Mean rent[2]	Rent is 35 percent or more of income	Substandard units[3] (percent)	Total	Percent change, 2002–2003	Total	Rate[4]	Total	Management, professional, and related occupations	Production, transportation, and material moving occupations
	89	90	91	92	93	94	95	96	97	98	99	100	101	102	103
La Crosse, WI-MN	49 232	67.6	112 078	12.8	6.2	493	26.0	1.9	75 048	1.3	3 234	4.3	67 178	31.2	17.0
Lafayette, IN	66 502	59.7	123 924	12.8	4.2	582	36.8	3.6	94 012	-1.4	4 005	4.3	89 689	34.6	18.4
Lafayette, LA	89 536	69.1	116 753	16.6	6.9	490	29.7	5.5	122 726	1.8	5 756	4.7	107 714	32.1	13.2
Lake Charles, LA	72 205	72.2	97 501	14.1	6.5	478	30.7	5.2	91 417	0.9	6 022	6.6	83 592	26.7	15.2
Lakeland, FL	187 233	73.4	99 883	18.3	5.9	536	28.4	5.2	218 348	0.3	13 208	6.0	206 460	26.2	16.1
Lancaster, PA	172 560	70.9	135 567	15.5	6.4	607	26.4	2.7	255 433	-1.9	10 090	4.0	235 686	28.1	22.0
Lansing-East Lansing, MI	172 413	67.2	123 282	13.1	5.4	583	32.8	2.7	249 773	1.0	12 300	4.9	229 037	34.6	14.3
Laredo, TX	50 740	65.7	86 801	26.2	10.6	474	33.5	27.8	84 173	4.7	6 177	7.3	62 558	26.7	14.6
Las Cruces, NM	59 556	67.5	110 607	18.5	6.5	476	37.8	11.4	78 324	4.0	5 866	7.5	67 685	32.3	11.6
Las Vegas-Paradise, NV	512 253	59.1	166 434	23.3	6.0	743	32.5	9.5	813 832	1.7	43 057	5.3	637 339	24.4	9.5
Lawrence, KS	38 486	51.9	140 902	13.8	2.8	602	39.5	2.7	58 116	0.9	2 705	4.7	55 212	40.4	10.1
Lawton, OK	39 808	60.3	82 946	16.6	7.2	480	30.0	4.7	42 878	1.4	1 553	3.6	40 436	29.5	14.3
Lebanon, PA	46 551	72.7	113 390	16.3	6.5	491	22.4	2.1	67 620	-1.4	2 553	3.8	59 767	25.4	23.2
Lewiston, ID-WA	23 650	68.2	122 385	17.4	5.9	502	32.2	2.7	36 697	-0.9	1 607	4.4	27 067	27.7	16.9
Lewiston-Auburn, ME	42 028	63.4	100 434	16.3	7.7	452	25.2	2.0	61 734	1.7	2 994	4.8	51 522	26.0	19.0
Lexington-Fayette, KY	163 854	59.9	132 682	13.0	4.4	545	30.5	2.4	217 710	1.4	8 870	4.1	212 710	36.6	14.2
Lima, OH	40 646	72.1	93 856	14.2	5.6	463	28.9	1.7	52 574	1.9	3 703	7.0	47 919	25.0	25.6
Lincoln, NE	105 200	61.1	124 506	12.3	3.5	557	29.0	3.0	163 770	1.4	6 523	4.0	148 223	35.7	13.6
Little Rock-North Little Rock, AR	241 094	66.6	109 352	13.7	6.9	548	30.1	3.6	319 562	-1.2	16 645	5.2	291 948	33.2	13.8
Logan, UT-ID	31 019	66.4	143 803	17.8	5.0	532	28.2	6.8	54 466	4.0	1 991	3.7	49 392	31.9	19.2
Longview, TX	73 341	71.0	82 798	15.3	7.9	485	28.2	5.8	100 151	2.3	6 481	6.5	82 624	26.8	18.7
Longview, WA	35 850	67.6	146 795	18.8	4.5	543	33.9	4.7	40 499	-0.6	4 152	10.3	39 888	23.6	21.1
Los Angeles-Long Beach-Santa Ana, CA	4 069 061	51.0	298 376	30.3	7.7	812	36.0	21.8	6 364 437	0.4	396 831	6.2	5 292 253	35.2	14.7
Los Angeles-Long Beach-Glendale, CA Div	3 133 774	47.9	286 633	31.8	8.2	773	36.5	23.5	4 788 827	0.0	337 116	7.0	3 953 415	34.3	15.5
Santa Ana-Anaheim-Irvine, CA Div	935 287	61.4	329 206	26.6	6.0	990	34.0	16.0	1 575 610	1.9	59 715	3.8	1 338 838	38.1	12.5
Louisville, KY-IN	462 241	69.5	127 286	14.9	5.4	512	27.1	2.5	620 126	0.6	34 072	5.5	566 388	30.4	18.5
Lubbock, TX	95 028	59.5	83 711	15.6	8.5	537	37.8	6.6	133 573	2.0	4 877	3.7	117 360	33.1	10.9
Lynchburg, VA	89 736	74.3	116 206	16.0	4.1	473	26.4	2.3	110 052	-1.4	5 746	5.2	108 184	28.4	19.7
Macon, GA	84 338	65.9	106 164	17.5	7.1	478	31.5	4.1	106 800	4.8	4 650	4.4	95 263	30.3	15.5
Madera, CA	36 155	66.2	135 421	27.3	8.4	575	36.3	15.8	57 114	1.3	7 213	12.6	42 166	24.7	15.2
Madison, WI	202 687	60.1	163 569	14.9	7.3	663	30.3	2.9	330 246	2.5	10 609	3.2	286 006	41.6	11.4
Manchester-Nashua, NH	144 455	64.9	159 258	15.3	11.1	711	26.0	2.4	224 213	2.4	10 745	4.8	202 366	37.8	14.8
Mansfield, OH	49 534	71.6	99 305	15.7	5.0	457	26.0	1.9	61 365	1.1	4 790	7.8	58 219	23.9	26.0
McAllen-Edinburg-Pharr, TX	156 824	73.1	66 759	24.1	9.7	428	32.8	25.5	232 358	6.4	31 580	13.6	180 121	26.3	14.4
Medford, OR	71 532	66.5	169 383	23.2	5.5	650	37.3	4.9	97 407	3.4	7 150	7.3	80 714	30.6	14.4
Memphis, TN-MS-AR	448 473	66.0	122 549	19.5	9.2	570	31.5	5.4	612 452	0.0	39 084	6.4	546 714	31.1	15.8
Merced, CA	63 815	58.7	129 318	25.3	8.3	549	34.2	20.5	89 745	2.5	13 281	14.8	75 321	25.6	17.4
Miami-Fort Lauderdale-Miami Beach, FL	1 905 394	66.0	170 312	27.9	11.8	740	38.3	12.5	2 565 585	-0.1	160 708	6.3	2 164 907	32.2	10.2
Fort Lauderdale-Pompano Beach-Deerfield Beach, FL Div	654 445	69.5	162 733	25.9	12.1	798	36.8	7.7	877 270	0.9	48 646	5.5	758 939	33.3	9.3
Miami-Miami Beach-Kendall, FL Div	776 774	57.8	162 594	32.3	14.0	680	40.1	20.6	1 103 718	-1.2	79 512	7.2	921 208	30.2	11.9
West Palm Beach-Boca Raton-Boynton Beach, FL Div	474 175	74.7	190 261	24.0	9.0	806	35.6	5.8	584 597	0.5	32 550	5.6	484 760	34.4	8.4
Michigan City-La Porte, IN	41 050	75.2	111 628	13.9	6.1	516	27.4	2.6	54 146	-1.6	3 725	6.9	51 097	24.5	23.4
Midland, TX	42 745	69.5	91 209	15.3	8.7	529	27.1	6.5	64 381	3.9	2 886	4.5	51 628	34.9	10.4
Milwaukee-Waukesha-West Allis, WI	587 657	61.1	156 918	15.3	8.2	608	29.0	3.6	824 144	0.9	50 408	6.1	741 058	35.1	17.0
Minneapolis-St. Paul-Bloomington, MN	1 136 615	72.4	168 496	13.3	5.2	666	28.6	3.7	1 833 761	0.3	87 528	4.8	1 619 473	38.9	12.9
Missoula, MT	38 439	61.9	156 573	21.5	7.3	564	41.1	3.4	56 671	4.1	2 189	3.9	50 436	32.3	10.9
Mobile, AL	150 179	68.9	102 275	18.9	8.8	484	33.9	4.9	197 415	3.0	13 809	7.0	164 654	29.0	16.2
Modesto, CA	145 146	61.9	145 969	24.4	7.6	631	36.5	14.2	216 655	1.3	24 952	11.5	174 328	26.5	17.5
Monroe, LA	64 073	66.5	96 984	17.2	6.3	454	34.1	5.4	86 195	1.6	5 250	6.1	73 333	30.0	13.8
Monroe, MI	53 772	80.9	145 678	13.2	5.8	559	29.0	2.2	75 335	1.1	5 477	7.3	70 344	24.8	24.1
Montgomery, AL	129 717	69.9	114 135	16.5	7.6	539	31.4	4.3	170 948	3.3	9 032	5.3	147 819	33.5	13.9
Morgantown, WV	44 990	66.7	106 056	16.3	5.7	475	46.6	2.2	53 955	-0.6	2 200	4.1	49 576	34.8	12.4
Morristown, TN	48 636	76.3	102 658	19.2	5.7	416	25.7	3.3	64 904	-2.5	4 077	6.3	57 031	21.8	29.7
Mount Vernon-Anacortes, WA	38 852	69.7	189 005	24.3	6.1	702	34.1	6.4	54 054	2.4	4 178	7.7	45 729	28.5	15.5
Muncie, IN	47 131	67.2	86 505	13.9	5.4	487	36.1	1.5	60 050	-0.5	3 470	5.8	55 773	30.1	17.6
Muskegon-Norton Shores, MI	63 330	77.7	101 350	14.3	6.4	459	31.7	3.0	82 442	0.3	8 745	10.6	76 788	24.3	25.8
Myrtle Beach-Conway-North Myrtle Beach, SC	81 800	73.0	144 456	20.2	5.9	599	30.5	3.3	110 408	6.3	5 671	5.1	97 577	26.2	10.1
Napa, CA	45 402	65.1	327 177	25.3	6.5	875	31.2	9.3	70 642	1.7	3 234	4.6	58 501	34.6	11.4
Naples-Marco Island, FL	102 973	75.6	259 155	26.3	8.1	820	29.9	7.0	121 111	4.1	5 484	4.5	105 436	28.4	8.1
Nashville-Davidson-Murfreesboro, TN	510 222	66.8	154 004	17.2	6.1	616	29.1	3.4	723 032	-0.8	33 244	4.6	667 968	33.8	15.3
New Haven-Milford, CT	319 040	63.1	181 216	20.1	12.8	680	32.7	3.2	436 099	0.4	26 351	6.0	396 326	37.0	13.6
New Orleans-Metairie-Kenner, LA	498 587	61.5	130 783	20.2	8.2	543	34.2	6.2	595 948	1.9	33 966	5.7	570 997	33.0	11.3

1. Specified owner-occupied units. 2. Specified renter-occupied units. 3. Overcrowded or lacking complete plumbing facilities. 4. Percent of civilian labor force. 5. Persons 16 years old and over.

Table C. Metropolitan Areas — **Nonfarm Employment and Agriculture**

	Private nonfarm establishments, employment and payroll, 2001								Agriculture, 2002			
	Employment						Annual payroll		Farms			
										Percent with—		
Area Name	Number of establishments	Total	Health care and social assistance	Manufacturing	Retail trade	Finance and insurance	Professional, scientific, and technical services	Total (mil dol)	Average per employee (dollars)	Number	Less than 50 acres	500 acres and over	Farm operators whose principal occupation is farming (percent)
	104	105	106	107	108	109	110	111	112	113	114	115	116
La Crosse, WI-MN	3 355	61 123	11 956	9 949	9 760	2 462	2 039	1 605	26 259	1 899	21.3	10.2	57.4
Lafayette, IN	3 830	69 077	8 493	19 946	11 028	3 622	2 336	2 031	29 402	1 628	35.6	25.5	61.3
Lafayette, LA	7 398	113 136	16 494	8 458	15 739	3 275	7 455	3 267	28 877	1 043	65.4	8.5	54.4
Lake Charles, LA	4 363	71 455	9 923	10 424	10 484	1 821	3 249	2 025	28 340	1 279	43.2	16.5	46.5
Lakeland, FL	9 606	155 412	18 491	16 461	23 562	11 712	5 822	4 269	27 469	3 114	65.1	6.0	52.1
Lancaster, PA	11 524	214 803	27 559	50 760	32 915	7 202	7 634	6 340	29 515	5 293	44.5	1.2	74.3
Lansing-East Lansing, MI	10 270	167 961	21 640	22 784	27 415	10 855	8 376	5 248	31 245	3 418	44.6	9.2	52.0
Laredo, TX	4 150	53 255	8 398	1 282	10 055	2 471	1 410	1 110	20 843	568	7.9	49.1	52.1
Las Cruces, NM	3 226	37 764	6 956	2 516	6 599	1 319	2 682	816	21 608	1 691	81.1	5.6	45.4
Las Vegas-Paradise, NV	30 365	650 239	46 806	18 985	76 824	24 093	30 059	19 522	30 023	253	79.8	3.2	42.7
Lawrence, KS	2 599	36 544	4 767	4 024	6 266	837	1 568	828	22 658	874	35.8	11.3	51.5
Lawton, OK	2 169	27 466	5 162	3 437	4 777	1 162	1 318	645	23 484	1 188	23.7	16.8	53.1
Lebanon, PA	2 597	38 962	6 654	9 981	6 526	878	949	1 031	26 462	1 104	46.4	1.5	63.0
Lewiston, ID-WA	1 590	20 079	3 596	3 273	3 508	1 181	429	543	27 043	621	37.8	38.2	57.8
Lewiston-Auburn, ME	2 799	45 920	7 581	7 675	6 492	2 763	2 337	1 203	26 198	334	40.7	7.5	55.4
Lexington-Fayette, KY	11 059	205 731	29 051	37 598	28 719	7 409	12 255	6 314	30 691	4 838	42.6	7.8	59.0
Lima, OH	2 861	50 220	9 059	10 106	7 660	1 268	1 074	1 383	27 539	968	36.9	11.3	54.8
Lincoln, NE	7 550	133 304	19 566	17 257	17 763	10 738	8 320	3 668	27 516	2 469	33.3	21.6	57.8
Little Rock-North Little Rock, AR	16 229	286 105	44 158	30 469	37 071	14 827	13 441	8 250	28 836	3 732	37.0	10.8	53.2
Logan, UT-ID	2 742	34 345	3 739	10 232	5 317	810	1 488	756	22 012	1 986	47.9	12.6	45.8
Longview, TX	5 098	72 742	9 761	12 937	10 898	2 334	2 603	1 947	26 766	3 071	37.3	6.8	48.8
Longview, WA	2 274	32 336	4 587	7 962	4 631	822	779	1 041	32 193	532	66.0	1.7	53.4
Los Angeles-Long Beach-Santa Ana, CA	307 878	5 298 837	501 038	807 646	521 067	273 015	540 456	198 266	37 417	1 891	85.5	3.3	53.3
Los Angeles-Long Beach-Glendale, CA Div	227 941	3 889 686	389 885	590 921	376 071	182 983	432 820	143 585	36 914	1 543	86.8	3.5	54.4
Santa Ana-Anaheim-Irvine, CA Div	79 937	1 409 151	111 153	216 725	144 996	90 032	107 636	54 681	38 804	348	79.3	2.3	48.0
Louisville, KY-IN	29 486	546 755	68 703	86 888	69 385	31 612	22 681	17 165	31 394	10 700	42.1	4.4	53.3
Lubbock, TX	6 636	97 481	17 251	6 760	16 086	4 641	3 320	2 298	23 574	1 515	25.6	35.6	64.5
Lynchburg, VA	5 780	94 251	10 995	24 061	12 853	4 697	4 308	2 711	28 764	2 802	24.4	7.0	52.2
Macon, GA	5 349	87 003	14 684	10 031	13 279	6 741	3 133	2 467	28 355	896	34.5	10.8	49.4
Madera, CA	1 871	24 012	2 807	5 091	3 178	409	600	520	21 656	1 780	45.2	13.3	72.8
Madison, WI	14 631	256 911	33 767	33 182	39 387	20 511	16 384	8 131	31 649	6 099	32.8	9.2	55.9
Manchester-Nashua, NH	10 781	182 450	21 751	37 319	27 708	7 608	9 954	6 783	37 177	481	59.9	1.7	48.0
Mansfield, OH	3 010	50 976	6 630	14 003	7 925	1 277	1 036	1 388	27 228	1 086	37.0	4.9	57.9
McAllen-Edinburg-Pharr, TX	8 382	120 612	23 271	10 373	23 568	4 380	4 735	2 462	20 413	2 104	59.8	12.1	53.0
Medford, OR	5 442	62 806	9 306	7 033	11 089	1 809	1 817	1 653	26 319	1 953	70.3	3.6	53.0
Memphis, TN-MS-AR	26 059	566 067	62 083	51 271	67 322	23 025	21 351	18 037	31 864	4 544	39.9	13.1	50.3
Merced, CA	2 997	39 990	5 679	8 497	6 945	1 025	806	974	24 356	2 964	50.0	11.9	71.1
Miami-Fort Lauderdale-Miami Beach, FL	156 131	1 955 176	241 185	121 228	285 526	111 145	122 657	63 690	32 575	3 848	87.9	3.2	51.9
Fort Lauderdale-Pompano Beach-Deerfield Beach, FL Div	51 036	640 214	77 111	36 497	99 787	37 780	39 520	20 140	31 458	494	90.3	2.6	51.0
Miami-Miami Beach-Kendall, FL Div	67 703	845 720	102 250	56 439	116 258	47 607	54 137	27 251	32 222	2 244	89.6	1.5	51.3
West Palm Beach-Boca Raton-Boynton Beach, FL Div	37 392	469 242	61 824	28 292	69 481	25 758	29 000	16 299	34 735	1 110	83.3	6.9	53.6
Michigan City-La Porte, IN	2 625	39 545	4 989	9 587	6 450	773	1 030	1 086	27 462	817	41.2	17.6	57.0
Midland, TX	4 038	48 396	5 384	2 199	6 318	1 734	2 240	1 508	31 160	477	48.6	16.6	36.9
Milwaukee-Waukesha-West Allis, WI	39 723	781 664	106 969	148 212	83 200	55 160	38 776	27 486	35 163	2 217	47.4	5.3	57.9
Minneapolis-St. Paul-Bloomington, MN	85 864	1 642 398	184 835	223 635	196 174	113 263	102 767	64 714	39 402	12 437	44.1	6.7	52.5
Missoula, MT	3 674	42 622	6 724	2 892	7 785	1 607	2 248	1 071	25 128	641	55.5	11.4	44.6
Mobile, AL	9 227	152 459	21 491	18 956	21 088	4 979	7 919	4 254	27 903	740	56.8	6.8	53.5
Modesto, CA	8 298	125 928	18 205	22 640	20 488	3 670	3 896	3 515	27 913	4 267	66.4	6.1	64.9
Monroe, LA	4 365	66 928	10 712	8 103	9 636	6 420	3 869	1 723	25 744	997	41.3	7.3	51.0
Monroe, MI	2 502	39 441	4 133	9 349	6 830	947	914	1 368	34 685	1 183	51.2	10.1	55.9
Montgomery, AL	8 010	132 053	16 567	16 516	20 027	8 561	6 999	3 542	26 823	2 129	32.8	14.2	53.9
Morgantown, WV	2 575	36 984	10 115	3 223	5 569	842	1 360	945	25 552	1 395	24.7	3.9	51.8
Morristown, TN	2 295	44 481	4 361	18 813	5 501	824	447	1 136	25 539	3 263	50.9	1.3	51.4
Mount Vernon-Anacortes, WA	3 278	35 392	5 149	5 295	7 092	926	1 188	998	28 198	872	59.7	4.9	60.9
Muncie, IN	2 649	48 787	7 993	8 718	6 956	1 615	2 012	1 324	27 138	687	48.5	13.5	60.0
Muskegon-Norton Shores, MI	3 583	56 495	8 196	15 757	8 389	1 286	1 746	1 700	30 091	545	55.2	5.1	53.0
Myrtle Beach-Conway-North Myrtle Beach, SC	7 211	86 594	7 425	6 233	16 570	3 292	2 927	1 902	21 965	988	40.9	8.9	54.0
Napa, CA	3 848	52 052	9 319	10 622	6 427	1 526	1 850	1 771	34 024	1 456	70.5	7.2	54.9
Naples-Marco Island, FL	8 705	98 832	12 643	2 852	18 469	4 478	5 034	2 875	29 090	273	56.8	21.6	54.2
Nashville-Davidson—Murfreesboro, TN	34 260	648 093	79 976	81 499	80 428	37 384	30 260	21 269	32 818	16 730	43.7	5.3	49.4
New Haven-Milford, CT	20 549	335 101	58 639	51 556	42 975	15 051	16 547	12 445	37 138	486	71.4	1.2	51.9
New Orleans-Metairie-Kenner, LA	31 543	535 752	76 571	39 304	70 214	23 358	30 295	15 866	29 614	975	66.9	5.2	50.1

Table C. Metropolitan Areas — **Agriculture**

	Agriculture, 2002 (cont'd)															
	Land in farms					Value of land and buildings (dollars)		Value of machinery and equipment average per farm (dollars)	Value of products sold				Percent of farms with sales of —		Government payments	
			Acres								Percent from —					
Area Name	Acreage (1,000)	Percent change, 1997–2002	Average size of farm	Total irrigated (1,000)	Total cropland (1,000)	Average per farm	Average per acre		Total (mil dol)	Average per farm (dollars)	Crops	Live-stock and poultry products	$10,000 or more	$100,000 or more	Total ($1,000)	Percent of farms
	117	118	119	120	121	122	123	124	125	126	127	128	129	130	131	132
La Crosse, WI-MN	428	-8.5	225	1	247	380 780	1 562	61 905	108	56 983	26.7	73.3	47.2	16.4	6 891	56.0
Lafayette, IN	670	-6.6	412	D	623	1 088 234	2 688	128 382	243	149 205	74.0	26.0	62.1	32.7	10 137	53.3
Lafayette, LA	156	-6.0	149	13	126	335 030	2 385	66 380	49	46 586	90.8	9.2	22.2	7.0	1 151	8.6
Lake Charles, LA	552	-0.7	432	30	203	666 856	1 431	38 275	22	17 235	D	D	24.4	4.0	3 830	12.7
Lakeland, FL	627	1.0	201	116	190	588 641	2 899	36 440	285	91 454	87.5	12.5	55.2	16.4	200	1.0
Lancaster, PA	412	5.1	78	6	333	610 359	7 955	68 923	798	150 831	11.1	88.9	68.3	39.6	6 846	11.4
Lansing-East Lansing, MI	679	2.0	199	7	569	529 924	2 673	72 630	203	59 403	57.3	42.7	38.3	11.7	10 540	36.1
Laredo, TX	2 043	-6.1	3 596	7	90	1 622 339	446	32 621	24	41 618	5.4	94.6	25.0	5.1	343	7.9
Las Cruces, NM	581	0.0	343	83	95	593 335	1 565	65 938	252	148 934	48.9	51.1	27.5	9.5	2 420	7.5
Las Vegas-Paradise, NV	69	-2.8	272	D	10	962 798	3 567	54 791	17	67 206	39.0	61.0	19.4	6.3	34	5.1
Lawrence, KS	201	-8.2	230	2	129	411 999	2 010	49 084	24	27 446	53.3	46.7	29.9	6.4	1 360	39.7
Lawton, OK	425	-2.3	358	0	178	280 816	768	46 020	33	27 687	25.2	74.8	36.9	6.5	2 198	32.1
Lebanon, PA	125	12.6	113	2	103	592 004	5 349	74 969	191	173 101	9.0	91.0	57.3	37.6	2 921	20.1
Lewiston, ID-WA	624	-3.1	1 005	3	292	781 650	699	138 809	49	79 691	83.1	16.9	39.1	19.0	5 210	38.5
Lewiston-Auburn, ME	56	0.0	167	1	22	443 764	2 421	72 201	97	289 368	7.4	92.6	38.9	15.0	606	13.8
Lexington-Fayette, KY	790	-5.6	163	5	488	546 223	3 229	55 061	572	118 267	12.2	87.8	45.5	12.2	2 629	17.6
Lima, OH	188	-1.1	194	0	168	576 950	3 031	72 666	41	42 628	73.3	26.7	48.8	12.3	2 859	56.9
Lincoln, NE	813	9.6	329	146	671	639 612	1 884	85 912	188	76 160	57.6	42.4	48.2	17.5	11 378	61.6
Little Rock-North Little Rock, AR	865	-0.3	232	D	570	391 771	1 663	52 462	181	48 435	54.3	45.7	26.9	8.8	12 580	13.6
Logan, UT-ID	490	-4.5	247	130	278	406 681	1 480	70 992	146	73 531	15.3	84.7	37.8	14.2	5 599	33.6
Longview, TX	516	4.5	168	2	218	225 676	1 405	29 772	83	26 891	20.2	79.8	22.7	3.1	D	D
Longview, WA	40	29.0	74	3	14	410 960	5 118	37 772	31	57 444	35.5	64.5	17.1	7.7	66	1.5
Los Angeles-Long Beach-Santa Ana, CA	179	-5.3	95	36	66	723 311	13 693	55 559	560	296 091	98.2	1.8	34.4	16.1	108	2.2
Los Angeles-Long Beach-Glendale, CA Div	111	-15.3	72	26	51	432 687	15 544	46 652	281	182 309	96.9	3.1	31.7	13.8	78	2.0
Santa Ana-Anaheim-Irvine, CA Div	68	17.2	195	10	15	2 011 911	10 661	95 053	279	800 592	99.6	0.4	46.6	26.4	30	3.2
Louisville, KY-IN	1 440	0.6	135	5	913	378 190	2 680	44 178	288	26 960	48.2	51.8	32.0	5.3	9 786	24.3
Lubbock, TX	1 047	-5.2	691	298	761	420 715	650	99 152	183	120 912	55.5	44.5	47.3	21.5	16 015	60.4
Lynchburg, VA	523	NA	187	3	229	421 490	2 318	37 788	48	17 135	21.8	78.2	26.1	2.9	1 729	22.9
Macon, GA	205	18.5	229	7	58	439 598	2 013	45 408	81	89 882	21.4	78.6	27.9	8.7	1 106	21.3
Madera, CA	682	6.2	383	317	362	1 209 723	3 120	92 867	710	399 120	71.1	28.9	66.8	36.5	3 160	7.1
Madison, WI	1 231	2.2	202	13	897	554 807	2 750	75 271	509	83 484	31.7	68.3	45.6	19.0	25 311	57.0
Manchester-Nashua, NH	40	5.3	83	0	14	477 112	5 619	33 501	15	30 701	76.0	24.0	26.4	6.2	470	7.9
Mansfield, OH	159	1.9	146	0	120	403 516	2 734	50 742	46	42 683	42.6	57.4	42.2	13.8	2 057	34.4
McAllen-Edinburg-Pharr, TX	593	-6.8	282	170	405	483 683	2 015	48 731	202	96 042	90.3	9.7	44.2	12.0	6 509	18.2
Medford, OR	252	2.4	129	50	68	428 469	2 824	43 963	54	27 748	69.8	30.2	18.5	2.9	278	5.9
Memphis, TN-MS-AR	1 556	0.0	342	227	1 147	608 461	1 752	72 889	271	59 532	84.6	15.4	25.1	9.8	25 816	28.5
Merced, CA	1 006	14.1	339	519	593	1 363 034	3 826	114 594	1 409	475 457	42.4	57.6	70.2	36.0	11 479	15.3
Miami-Fort Lauderdale-Miami Beach, FL	650	-9.8	169	467	555	844 179	4 858	46 451	1 387	360 575	98.8	1.2	50.3	18.2	598	1.3
Fort Lauderdale-Pompano Beach-Deerfield Beach, FL Div	24	-22.6	48	5	7	450 331	20 423	30 471	50	100 455	89.9	10.1	43.9	10.3	163	1.6
Miami-Miami Beach-Kendall, FL Div	90	5.9	400	44	67	545 496	9 726	42 997	578	257 576	99.2	0.8	55.5	18.0	136	1.2
West Palm Beach-Boca Raton-Boynton Beach, FL Div	536	-11.4	483	418	481	1 623 283	3 348	60 546	760	684 565	99.1	0.9	42.6	22.0	299	1.4
Michigan City-La Porte, IN	243	-2.0	298	32	222	787 647	2 653	100 522	79	97 140	70.2	29.8	48.3	21.1	4 367	48.7
Midland, TX	362	-58.1	758	7	73	281 759	384	22 642	7	15 516	54.0	46.0	15.9	3.4	1 308	28.5
Milwaukee-Waukesha-West Allis, WI	309	0.0	139	2	253	632 675	4 309	70 735	156	70 397	47.7	52.3	44.6	18.0	5 945	38.4
Minneapolis-St. Paul-Bloomington, MN	1 986	D	160	102	1 533	512 034	3 221	61 001	769	61 805	60.1	39.9	38.1	12.6	25 980	37.6
Missoula, MT	258	-1.5	403	19	44	608 634	1 438	37 745	8	13 044	33.3	66.7	20.0	2.5	142	10.0
Mobile, AL	101	-16.5	136	2	52	454 768	3 361	43 995	75	101 446	87.1	12.9	38.6	11.1	1 366	13.0
Modesto, CA	790	7.8	185	401	408	1 062 751	6 068	77 381	1 229	287 932	46.2	53.8	59.2	24.6	8 589	7.8
Monroe, LA	167	9.9	168	9	84	356 122	1 843	51 572	141	140 966	7.7	92.3	38.9	21.4	1 838	18.3
Monroe, MI	217	3.3	184	6	200	578 759	3 152	79 298	92	77 974	93.4	6.6	45.4	12.5	4 129	34.1
Montgomery, AL	632	-1.7	297	6	239	533 943	1 688	47 091	108	50 718	28.1	71.9	30.6	6.7	4 743	23.1
Morgantown, WV	203	-3.3	145	0	77	215 900	1 403	26 693	13	9 097	16.9	83.1	18.9	1.1	270	7.0
Morristown, TN	269	8.9	82	D	157	255 433	3 165	37 447	60	18 287	37.1	62.9	20.2	2.4	717	11.2
Mount Vernon-Anacortes, WA	114	22.6	131	18	76	613 134	5 113	99 671	217	249 294	70.1	29.9	43.5	21.1	1 835	14.7
Muncie, IN	190	9.8	276	D	177	684 845	2 540	101 639	50	73 048	86.9	13.1	47.6	15.7	2 239	45.6
Muskegon-Norton Shores, MI	74	1.4	136	7	49	356 820	3 008	63 674	46	84 956	63.8	36.2	33.0	12.3	1 134	18.5
Myrtle Beach-Conway-North Myrtle Beach, SC	188	2.2	191	1	101	439 723	2 171	75 665	54	55 112	70.8	29.2	31.5	11.9	1 777	27.8
Napa, CA	238	12.3	163	53	76	2 734 325	19 350	72 725	429	294 650	99.1	0.9	67.6	30.1	225	2.1
Naples-Marco Island, FL	181	-34.7	662	55	91	1 652 022	2 660	123 655	268	980 352	98.6	1.4	56.4	29.3	D	D
Nashville-Davidson—Murfreesboro, TN	1 939	5.0	116	4	1 041	348 341	3 084	37 947	251	15 027	54.4	45.6	21.1	2.7	4 500	11.7
New Haven-Milford, CT	26	4.0	53	1	14	929 815	13 630	69 982	57	117 650	91.9	8.1	34.4	12.8	292	4.9
New Orleans-Metairie-Kenner, LA	D	D	D	1	46	486 150	3 447	31 064	32	33 137	D	D	26.8	5.2	D	D

Table C. Metropolitan Areas — Residential Construction, Wholesale Trade, Retail Trade, and Real Estate

Area Name	Value of residential construction authorized by building permits, 2003		Wholesale trade, 1997				Retail trade,[1] 1997				Real estate and rental and leasing, 1997			
	New construction ($1,000)	Number of housing units	Number of establishments	Number of employees	Sales (mil dol)	Annual payroll (mil dol)	Number of establishments	Number of employees	Sales (mil dol)	Annual payroll (mil dol)	Number of establishments	Number of employees	Receipts (mil dol)	Annual payroll (mil dol)
	133	134	135	136	137	138	139	140	141	142	143	144	145	146
La Crosse, WI-MN	99 220	680	185	3 753	1 991.6	112.6	579	9 505	1 528.9	141.6	125	785	61.0	13.4
Lafayette, IN	168 237	1 519	177	D	D	D	684	10 675	1 640.7	153.6	171	D	D	D
Lafayette, LA	190 568	1 574	520	6 592	2 737.0	231.7	1 111	15 722	2 657.8	248.8	374	3 177	418.2	90.4
Lake Charles, LA	118 794	1 458	263	3 251	2 149.5	95.5	809	10 640	1 635.3	149.5	214	1 175	107.5	20.8
Lakeland, FL	566 697	6 823	639	8 329	4 176.2	212.7	1 816	22 751	3 844.3	360.9	214	1 175	107.5	20.8
Lakeland, FL	566 697	6 823	639	8 329	4 176.2	212.7	1 816	22 751	3 844.3	360.9	214	1 175	107.5	20.8
Lancaster, PA	336 665	2 690	663	11 020	10 936.6	341.6	2 012	29 237	4 671.7	480.8	281	1 906	247.2	41.9
Lansing-East Lansing, MI	376 458	3 156	507	7 289	4 509.5	261.8	1 756	26 727	4 317.5	424.4	410	3 493	281.7	63.8
Laredo, TX	136 485	1 671	339	2 453	1 105.4	51.1	730	9 051	1 524.6	138.8	155	574	64.3	10.0
Las Cruces, NM	223 160	1 767	122	978	283.6	25.0	511	6 266	1 059.1	98.1	175	530	44.8	7.4
Las Vegas-Paradise, NV	3 888 554	36 732	1 298	15 824	6 366.0	526.9	3 803	58 477	12 321.5	1 201.7	1 521	12 437	1 672.5	291.4
Lawrence, KS	115 372	1 060	88	777	248.8	21.0	453	5 664	758.5	80.3	122	434	46.4	6.6
Lawton, OK	18 666	162	84	766	200.6	16.4	436	5 216	691.8	67.8	133	523	48.7	8.1
Lebanon, PA	87 551	744	118	D	D	D	490	6 480	1 209.1	106.8	59	270	29.2	4.0
Lewiston, ID-WA	23 254	155	81	D	D	D	297	3 546	624.4	62.4	59	258	18.7	3.9
Lewiston-Auburn, ME	66 287	508	126	1 244	277.8	35.7	533	6 362	1 247.1	96.4	109	418	46.9	7.2
Lexington-Fayette, KY	494 375	3 975	635	D	D	D	1 795	27 264	4 358.8	409.0	462	2 336	341.7	44.9
Lima, OH	44 094	284	190	D	D	D	542	7 908	1 291.4	116.0	107	454	37.7	6.8
Lincoln, NE	310 620	2 498	329	D	D	D	1 059	16 298	2 351.1	238.8	277	1 525	151.9	25.7
Little Rock-North Little Rock, AR	581 458	4 098	1 090	D	D	D	2 665	35 407	6 295.6	549.5	626	D	D	D
Logan, UT-ID	125 196	988	104	818	176.5	15.3	394	5 625	737.8	75.5	72	452	25.1	6.8
Longview, TX	43 800	332	400	4 129	2 105.0	128.2	979	11 025	1 882.8	173.8	164	742	81.3	17.9
Longview, WA	60 241	436	81	D	D	D	414	4 744	811.5	82.1	98	396	49.8	7.2
Los Angeles-Long Beach-Santa Ana, CA	4 645 279	30 151	28 503	362 330	271 648.3	13 450.0	36 661	470 231	95 707.0	9 341.0	14 469	106 060	18 323.4	3 195.4
Los Angeles-Long Beach-Glendale, CA Div	3 049 103	20 903	21 474	259 217	177 244.9	9 450.4	27 577	343 656	69 534.2	6 769.0	10 932	76 904	13 608.6	2 256.3
Santa Ana-Anaheim-Irvine, CA Div	1 596 176	9 248	7 029	103 113	94 403.4	3 999.6	9 084	126 575	26 172.8	2 572.0	3 537	29 156	4 714.8	939.1
Louisville, KY-IN	1 116 095	8 632	1 991	D	D	D	4 601	66 863	10 352.3	1 046.4	1 146	D	D	D
Lubbock, TX	278 963	2 956	517	6 799	3 933.2	186.1	1 117	14 764	2 714.8	241.2	299	1 911	134.2	30.8
Lynchburg, VA	205 087	1 421	233	D	D	D	992	12 575	2 052.4	196.9	195	633	59.3	11.6
Macon, GA	205 903	1 871	305	D	D	D	1 051	13 837	2 113.7	207.3	NA	D	D	D
Madera, CA	164 821	1 227	87	623	265.8	18.8	313	3 173	527.3	53.0	60	217	22.3	3.8
Madison, WI	838 524	6 117	778	11 114	4 812.5	371.9	2 178	36 993	6 479.7	652.6	561	3 604	381.4	72.3
Manchester-Nashua, NH	299 055	2 051	721	8 588	4 792.9	366.4	1 692	25 208	4 927.0	455.6	436	2 269	233.8	53.1
Mansfield, OH	63 167	490	157	1 902	633.2	53.8	590	8 848	1 297.7	127.7	98	407	43.3	6.3
McAllen-Edinburg-Pharr, TX	445 581	8 060	600	6 395	1 981.7	124.6	1 582	20 862	3 337.6	313.1	346	1 347	116.3	18.5
Medford, OR	275 725	2 138	284	2 678	1 022.7	69.8	835	9 564	2 075.3	172.2	248	1 003	95.9	15.2
Memphis, TN-MS-AR	1 200 452	9 605	2 090	D	D	D	4 544	67 990	10 860.6	1 045.5	988	7 593	913.0	177.5
Merced, CA	369 472	2 742	117	1 333	699.9	36.4	551	6 122	1 102.1	108.0	121	461	46.0	5.7
Miami-Fort Lauderdale-Miami Beach, FL	5 297 831	39 595	15 481	126 528	81 271.1	4 357.6	21 585	261 145	50 431.6	4 761.8	7 357	43 596	6 374.3	1 065.7
Fort Lauderdale-Pompano Beach-Deerfield Beach, FL Div	1 118 886	8 218	4 359	38 614	26 122.2	1 414.7	6 804	89 290	17 979.8	1 639.9	2 263	14 394	2 196.6	351.6
Miami-Miami Beach-Kendall, FL Div	1 697 336	15 533	8 935	70 050	43 604.4	2 235.9	9 814	110 292	20 720.6	1 995.8	3 378	19 793	2 853.9	465.8
West Palm Beach-Boca Raton-Boynton Beach, FL Div	2 481 609	15 844	2 187	17 864	11 544.5	707.0	4 967	61 563	11 731.2	1 126.1	1 716	9 409	1 323.8	248.3
Michigan City-La Porte, IN	50 610	417	135	1 525	658.5	44.6	552	6 312	1 041.7	95.7	95	313	31.0	4.9
Midland, TX	30 268	260	297	2 708	1 938.6	93.9	549	6 649	1 226.3	108.5	185	899	90.0	17.8
Milwaukee-Waukesha-West Allis, WI	1 077 708	6 467	3 050	43 101	26 266.3	1 664.0	5 351	86 453	14 301.0	1 392.9	1 442	9 775	1 252.1	222.6
Minneapolis-St. Paul-Bloomington, MN	4 466 757	27 623	6 464	D	D	D	10 519	173 134	31 195.7	2 969.7	3 518	24 708	3 360.4	614.7
Missoula, MT	61 773	947	183	1 991	775.9	50.0	540	6 800	1 069.0	105.7	138	593	46.2	8.2
Mobile, AL	162 509	1 684	699	8 647	3 332.9	252.1	1 681	22 860	3 404.5	338.1	380	2 170	228.7	43.3
Modesto, CA	604 567	4 119	417	5 118	2 264.4	159.1	1 368	17 706	3 282.2	319.2	340	2 033	244.5	42.4
Monroe, LA	65 113	543	259	2 987	1 266.2	83.7	826	10 227	1 575.8	141.8	185	827	81.5	13.0
Monroe, MI	153 782	1 160	96	1 213	731.5	46.2	448	5 489	1 035.0	91.1	74	278	30.0	4.4
Montgomery, AL	185 322	1 772	476	5 932	3 121.7	167.9	1 533	20 193	3 181.6	297.3	355	D	D	D
Morgantown, WV	9 213	90	107	887	536.3	24.4	460	5 578	824.2	82.1	128	503	45.3	7.0
Morristown, TN	68 595	598	121	1 491	552.6	42.3	502	5 395	952.6	80.3	74	248	32.4	3.9
Mount Vernon-Anacortes, WA	124 682	904	122	1 018	344.4	30.2	614	6 096	1 070.7	107.0	114	406	48.3	7.3
Muncie, IN	130 660	563	119	1 501	653.4	45.8	548	7 340	1 118.7	105.4	119	433	46.9	8.4
Muskegon-Norton Shores, MI	105 853	969	162	1 852	891.4	57.6	591	8 672	1 365.4	132.3	112	469	55.5	7.2
Myrtle Beach-Conway-North Myrtle Beach, SC	624 543	5 130	230	1 824	481.5	49.5	1 522	14 457	2 505.2	230.7	360	3 026	259.6	59.7
Napa, CA	183 470	607	153	1 296	533.0	46.4	525	5 292	952.6	102.8	153	1 068	84.2	15.7
Naples-Marco Island, FL	977 445	5 820	350	2 076	813.8	63.0	1 343	15 366	2 627.1	274.1	509	2 874	305.2	66.0
Nashville-Davidson—Murfreesboro, TN	1 826 560	13 549	2 264	D	D	D	5 549	75 112	13 076.2	1 284.4	1 445	D	D	D
New Haven-Milford, CT	244 015	1 826	1 316	15 458	8 028.3	633.3	3 335	41 942	7 725.2	775.9	761	4 030	477.5	89.0
New Orleans-Metairie-Kenner, LA	970 784	6 129	2 167	D	D	D	5 186	68 807	10 960.6	1 066.1	1 310	10 670	1 239.4	231.7

1. Establishments with payroll.

Table C. Metropolitan Areas — Professional Services, Manufacturing, and Accommodation and Foodservices

Area Name	Professional, scientific, and technical services,[1] 1997				Manufacturing, 1997				Accommodation and foodservices, 1997			
	Number of establishments	Number of employees	Sales (mil dol)	Annual payroll (mil dol)	Number of establishments	Number of employees	Sales (mil dol)	Annual payroll (mil dol)	Number of establishments	Number of employees	Sales (mil dol)	Annual payroll (mil dol)
	147	148	149	150	151	152	153	154	155	156	157	158
La Crosse, WI-MN	211	1 584	121.8	53.2	NA	NA	NA	NA	333	5 793	148.8	42.7
Lafayette, IN	242	1 342	109.9	38.2	162	19 448	8 078.6	755.1	357	D	D	D
Lafayette, LA	828	5 884	547.8	211.5	259	8 920	2 128.3	219.8	434	D	D	D
Lake Charles, LA	359	2 550	190.1	72.2	NA	NA	NA	NA	305	8 073	308.4	75.8
Lakeland, FL	712	4 006	347.6	135.4	480	20 627	5 999.9	633.5	711	13 383	419.3	113.2
Lancaster, PA	639	5 130	439.8	165.6	918	52 908	10 585.4	1 752.0	877	15 724	506.4	145.6
Lansing-East Lansing, MI	897	6 161	598.0	253.6	428	D	D	D	836	17 358	489.7	139.4
Laredo, TX	210	1 029	69.6	23.1	87	1 402	258.6	28.1	253	4 350	144.7	37.4
Las Cruces, NM	222	1 334	107.3	45.7	111	2 290	395.5	46.9	253	4 278	121.7	32.6
Las Vegas-Paradise, NV	2 405	20 281	2 105.8	832.7	814	D	D	D	2 164	185 322	12 412.3	3 771.0
Lawrence, KS	192	1 280	84.5	33.1	76	4 240	728.8	120.0	240	4 627	120.7	34.2
Lawton, OK	127	1 062	63.0	30.5	51	3 325	900.8	119.8	203	3 660	96.9	28.9
Lebanon, PA	113	608	42.2	17.9	199	9 376	1 710.3	254.3	209	2 687	76.0	22.3
Lewiston, ID-WA	99	455	31.4	12.1	NA	NA	NA	NA	143	1 955	59.1	17.4
Lewiston-Auburn, ME	151	1 672	191.6	54.3	183	8 233	1 218.6	226.6	180	2 438	77.4	23.3
Lexington-Fayette, KY	963	9 290	1 135.5	312.2	482	D	D	D	831	19 166	630.8	180.7
Lima, OH	171	951	59.8	21.9	132	9 529	6 631.7	407.8	231	4 260	127.5	33.1
Lincoln, NE	504	7 209	691.7	212.3	285	16 361	3 966.8	532.4	582	11 819	331.1	95.0
Little Rock-North Little Rock, AR	1 453	10 982	995.4	430.4	NA	NA	NA	NA	1 068	D	D	D
Logan, UT-ID	161	921	51.8	20.4	NA	NA	NA	NA	126	2 162	53.8	14.1
Longview, TX	337	1 838	161.6	51.6	287	14 913	3 660.0	490.2	347	5 464	173.0	48.7
Longview, WA	116	677	43.7	18.9	125	8 309	2 496.5	364.4	214	3 208	97.1	28.7
Los Angeles-Long Beach-Santa Ana, CA	31 032	421 925	41 407.6	16 308.0	23 682	838 238	145 840.5	27 954.9	21 115	372 455	15 316.0	4 124.5
Los Angeles-Long Beach-Glendale, CA Div	22 194	346 290	31 678.8	12 767.4	17 915	622 302	106 706.4	20 311.3	15 718	267 157	11 074.3	2 991.3
Santa Ana-Anaheim-Irvine, CA Div	8 838	75 635	9 728.8	3 540.6	5 767	215 936	39 134.1	7 643.6	5 397	105 298	4 241.7	1 133.2
Louisville, KY-IN	2 395	17 835	1 666.8	567.8	NA	NA	NA	NA	2 018	D	D	D
Lubbock, TX	487	2 522	199.0	67.8	NA	NA	NA	NA	527	11 188	333.2	87.9
Lynchburg, VA	361	3 456	328.2	130.6	316	24 294	5 504.2	798.8	342	D	D	D
Macon, GA	398	D	D	D	NA	NA	NA	NA	387	D	D	D
Madera, CA	81	364	42.3	10.7	94	3 913	952.3	120.8	162	2 136	73.0	18.7
Madison, WI	1 233	11 101	969.1	420.6	706	32 694	6 259.6	1 041.9	1 235	D	D	D
Manchester-Nashua, NH	1 210	7 164	741.2	330.5	737	36 656	6 260.7	1 397.9	702	12 020	412.7	120.6
Mansfield, OH	168	933	73.3	23.5	220	15 212	2 444.7	567.1	272	4 613	140.1	38.6
McAllen-Edinburg-Pharr, TX	482	2 682	193.4	62.7	261	10 284	1 428.2	178.3	626	10 871	352.1	90.1
Medford, OR	341	1 917	99.5	35.4	301	7 428	1 424.0	201.7	474	6 253	205.3	60.3
Memphis, TN-MS-AR	1 911	16 249	1 565.2	585.0	NA	NA	NA	NA	1 759	52 472	2 354.6	639.9
Merced, CA	138	668	41.0	15.8	123	8 381	2 431.5	198.2	269	3 265	108.4	27.2
Miami-Fort Lauderdale-Miami Beach, FL	17 657	92 064	9 932.7	3 945.2	6 049	129 787	20 656.7	3 917.3	9 128	177 871	7 333.8	1 934.9
Fort Lauderdale-Pompano Beach-Deerfield Beach, FL Div	5 625	27 496	2 940.7	1 103.7	1 967	37 134	5 788.3	1 115.4	3 206	61 243	2 474.5	615.5
Miami-Miami Beach-Kendall, FL Div	7 821	42 781	4 640.0	1 856.0	3 031	66 391	8 523.9	1 663.8	3 835	75 597	3 199.5	878.5
West Palm Beach-Boca Raton-Boynton Beach, FL Div	4 211	21 787	2 352.0	985.5	1 051	26 262	6 344.5	1 138.1	2 087	41 031	1 659.8	440.9
Michigan City-La Porte, IN	145	707	40.1	13.9	189	10 835	2 007.9	351.2	234	3 394	106.1	29.0
Midland, TX	350	2 088	245.0	75.6	135	2 435	326.1	76.5	231	3 814	123.9	34.2
Milwaukee-Waukesha-West Allis, WI	3 652	32 645	3 390.3	1 297.6	3 174	165 143	31 093.4	5 958.5	2 872	49 875	1 546.9	432.6
Minneapolis-St. Paul-Bloomington, MN	9 814	81 621	9 422.4	3 672.7	5 348	234 192	44 599.9	8 760.7	5 131	111 217	3 757.3	1 111.5
Missoula, MT	276	1 617	109.7	45.2	136	2 690	562.3	89.4	329	4 782	145.6	40.4
Mobile, AL	769	5 949	518.6	205.9	445	22 130	5 494.8	835.3	649	12 767	370.1	102.2
Modesto, CA	478	2 974	232.5	81.3	435	25 056	6 886.6	823.1	676	9 877	312.7	80.4
Monroe, LA	370	2 071	147.0	51.1	NA	NA	NA	NA	284	D	D	D
Monroe, MI	120	501	36.3	14.1	138	9 278	2 560.1	425.6	219	3 339	98.0	26.2
Montgomery, AL	653	4 818	449.5	202.7	313	D	D	D	538	D	D	D
Morgantown, WV	176	1 014	76.3	24.9	86	2 719	667.0	91.9	237	4 039	102.2	30.1
Morristown, TN	104	D	D	D	220	18 787	2 654.1	459.9	161	D	D	D
Mount Vernon-Anacortes, WA	209	732	55.7	20.6	185	5 026	2 917.7	148.9	277	3 614	118.1	31.5
Muncie, IN	153	1 691	87.8	37.3	176	9 972	1 764.5	402.6	228	4 981	126.7	35.6
Muskegon-Norton Shores, MI	229	1 087	91.2	40.4	335	16 398	2 903.3	562.1	321	5 256	153.8	42.2
Myrtle Beach-Conway-North Myrtle Beach, SC	400	1 766	135.5	53.8	160	6 687	927.8	173.4	1 044	20 246	881.7	228.5
Napa, CA	268	1 752	301.7	132.2	277	8 466	2 139.7	320.7	347	6 250	287.1	80.3
Naples-Marco Island, FL	743	3 074	414.1	196.5	205	2 305	259.0	62.4	518	11 599	536.7	140.9
Nashville-Davidson—Murfreesboro, TN	2 729	D	D	D	NA	NA	NA	NA	2 329	D	D	D
New Haven-Milford, CT	1 885	11 285	1 191.0	466.6	1 592	59 380	12 073.9	2 285.0	1 644	21 581	804.7	221.4
New Orleans-Metairie-Kenner, LA	3 392	24 902	2 476.3	966.9	996	40 880	22 513.7	1 523.7	2 639	60 687	2 363.0	650.9

1. Firms subject to federal tax.

848 (La Crosse, WI-MN)—(New Orleans-Metairie-Kenner, LA) Items 147—158

Table C. Metropolitan Areas — Health Care and Social Assistance, Other Services, and Federal Funds

Area Name	Health care and social assistance,[1] 1997				Other services,[1] 1997				Federal funds and grants, 2002–2003 Expenditures (mil dol)			
										Direct payments for individuals		
	Number of establishments	Number of employees	Receipts (mil dol)	Annual payroll (mil dol)	Number of establishments	Number of employees	Receipts (mil dol)	Annual payroll (mil dol)	Total	Social Security and government retirement	Medicare	Food stamps and Supplemental Security Income
	159	160	161	162	163	164	165	166	167	168	169	170
La Crosse, WI-MN	156	1 187	65.0	30.1	226	1 348	71.6	22.0	629.7	255.4	83.4	15.2
Lafayette, IN......................	215	3 215	230.7	108.8	257	1 712	108.5	32.4	743.1	288.8	103.4	16.3
Lafayette, LA......................	650	8 144	609.3	239.0	389	2 534	167.6	51.0	1 030.2	376.1	193.5	53.9
Lake Charles, LA	409	4 779	321.2	132.5	270	1 944	124.9	36.3	1 075.7	386.0	208.6	44.1
Lakeland, FL	643	9 886	657.7	279.4	611	3 224	199.6	60.6	2 549.2	1 325.8	538.7	100.5
Lancaster, PA	710	8 212	523.8	252.0	808	4 429	276.4	81.6	1 972.5	994.7	368.8	46.6
Lansing-East Lansing, MI	882	7 532	497.6	237.9	612	3 933	212.9	68.2	4 230.9	1 215.7	343.4	69.3
Laredo, TX	227	4 330	207.1	94.8	190	951	48.0	13.3	896.2	192.2	116.6	70.2
Las Cruces, NM	272	3 149	177.9	75.3	169	1 025	43.9	13.2	1 241.1	347.6	95.4	56.5
Las Vegas-Paradise, NV	2 053	29 105	2 567.0	988.7	1 324	11 045	707.8	221.1	7 170.4	3 078.6	937.9	192.6
Lawrence, KS	175	1 648	88.7	41.8	132	782	42.5	13.5	398.2	143.7	45.8	7.4
Lawton, OK	208	2 349	141.5	52.8	146	778	36.3	10.9	1 286.5	350.2	68.6	26.6
Lebanon, PA	194	1 655	107.1	49.7	192	785	52.1	13.6	746.9	318.8	113.0	9.6
Lewiston, ID-WA	152	1 913	100.8	40.7	108	602	32.1	9.2	373.5	162.5	59.0	12.1
Lewiston-Auburn, ME...........	221	2 542	149.6	68.4	191	714	46.2	12.9	597.3	248.1	104.0	29.1
Lexington-Fayette, KY	809	12 693	894.6	389.9	658	4 217	225.9	71.5	2 271.1	764.4	261.6	78.7
Lima, OH...........................	201	2 625	161.8	86.0	182	1 071	61.2	17.0	711.3	379.1	101.4	25.2
Lincoln, NE........................	570	6 642	387.1	190.0	455	2 629	143.2	44.1	1 705.6	544.4	144.6	29.3
Little Rock-North Little Rock, AR	1 300	15 848	1 124.4	525.4	930	D	D	D	4 694.0	1 540.9	506.5	120.3
Logan, UT-ID	177	1 379	85.6	30.2	135	661	37.5	9.8	407.1	138.1	40.0	6.2
Longview, TX	414	6 321	348.8	148.3	300	1 924	124.0	34.6	992.1	470.9	220.8	36.8
Longview, WA	168	1 933	110.4	48.6	138	706	43.7	13.4	487.3	229.6	80.8	22.8
Los Angeles-Long Beach-Santa Ana, CA	27 264	262 812	21 281.0	8 333.6	17 383	114 788	8 188.3	2 334.3	68 977.7	16 038.1	12 357.2	2 707.8
Los Angeles-Long Beach-Glendale, CA Div	20 278	196 543	15 709.6	6 162.8	13 134	86 614	6 086.4	1 734.3	56 540.1	11 907.8	9 921.3	2 356.7
Santa Ana-Anaheim-Irvine, CA Div.................	6 986	66 269	5 571.4	2 170.8	4 249	28 174	2 101.9	600.0	12 437.5	4 130.4	2 435.9	351.0
Louisville, KY-IN.................	2 238	34 669	2 229.7	988.4	1 887	12 566	777.2	243.6	8 223.1	2 554.7	1 122.9	145.5
Lubbock, TX.......................	628	D	D	D	412	3 064	179.6	53.3	1 283.8	460.2	286.0	47.5
Lynchburg, VA....................	323	4 244	227.7	109.4	366	1 800	101.1	30.8	1 766.2	637.5	174.1	30.7
Macon, GA.........................	518	9 138	686.4	272.3	353	1 901	118.3	36.0	1 420.3	532.8	255.0	72.0
Madera, CA........................	155	1 238	69.8	26.0	95	386	27.8	7.0	522.3	218.2	103.8	21.9
Madison, WI.......................	913	11 048	797.3	345.8	777	4 813	284.8	95.6	3 794.9	1 006.2	293.4	40.8
Manchester-Nashua, NH	742	9 268	587.4	284.8	640	4 143	286.7	93.3	2 137.2	760.3	248.0	33.4
Mansfield, OH	256	2 797	156.8	72.6	199	1 512	81.1	31.0	635.3	288.1	120.9	22.5
McAllen-Edinburg-Pharr, TX .	833	15 858	1 167.0	431.0	479	2 465	114.3	30.6	2 608.3	588.1	370.1	243.2
Medford, OR	384	3 810	244.3	110.5	222	1 192	80.6	21.6	1 013.2	505.8	142.3	37.7
Memphis, TN-MS-AR............	2 013	25 989	2 169.1	912.3	1 658	12 239	776.3	243.5	8 480.1	2 261.5	1 006.3	417.2
Merced, CA........................	323	2 668	167.8	64.2	171	813	49.2	14.3	964.5	343.3	147.7	65.2
Miami-Fort Lauderdale-Miami Beach, FL...............	13 663	152 049	11 643.2	4 738.0	9 260	53 301	3 514.8	968.8	29 054.8	9 980.7	8 525.4	1 201.1
Fort Lauderdale-Pompano Beach-Deerfield Beach, FL Div................................	4 226	51 708	3 879.0	1 603.0	3 246	19 188	1 397.3	373.4	8 104.9	3 341.6	2 761.4	225.9
Miami-Miami Beach-Kendall, FL Div..............	6 157	60 718	4 782.5	1 877.5	3 901	22 435	1 391.0	385.8	14 036.7	3 253.7	3 662.8	854.9
West Palm Beach-Boca Raton-Boynton Beach, FL Div................................	3 280	39 623	2 981.7	1 257.5	2 113	11 678	726.5	209.6	6 913.2	3 385.4	2 101.1	120.4
Michigan City-La Porte, IN....	181	1 995	137.2	64.5	189	929	49.9	17.3	494.0	237.9	110.2	18.1
Midland, TX........................	245	2 971	251.9	102.6	228	1 509	112.2	29.3	427.6	205.1	93.8	18.1
Milwaukee-Waukesha-West Allis, WI	3 251	40 173	2 499.9	1 307.7	2 416	17 291	1 131.5	351.4	7 963.1	2 997.9	1 394.8	304.7
Minneapolis-St. Paul-Bloomington, MN	5 073	70 207	4 109.1	2 082.1	4 471	41 363	2 493.7	875.7	14 802.0	4 836.0	1 890.4	347.9
Missoula, MT......................	285	2 305	151.7	70.7	184	956	61.9	17.0	540.5	188.6	56.6	14.0
Mobile, AL	561	10 565	742.2	347.1	648	4 775	305.4	91.0	2 320.3	939.0	453.7	137.3
Modesto, CA	805	9 346	656.1	253.2	538	3 154	210.7	58.7	2 046.9	764.8	389.7	105.8
Monroe, LA	375	5 817	352.2	159.0	238	1 386	77.2	22.9	897.7	314.7	204.9	54.9
Monroe, MI	171	1 480	90.2	41.9	141	892	60.7	22.4	574.9	291.7	131.4	15.8
Montgomery, AL..................	657	D	D	D	505	3 238	169.3	51.9	3 741.8	1 076.2	307.5	107.9
Morgantown, WV	171	3 036	199.8	97.5	178	1 293	80.2	23.6	783.9	231.6	93.2	23.1
Morristown, TN...................	181	2 686	140.3	53.8	127	578	34.6	10.5	666.5	306.3	125.9	32.7
Mount Vernon-Anacortes, WA	219	2 291	142.9	67.5	151	880	60.6	18.6	539.0	270.3	95.4	17.3
Muncie, IN.........................	223	3 304	200.9	94.2	186	1 530	98.7	24.4	596.1	259.5	108.0	26.7
Muskegon-Norton Shores, MI	272	2 682	157.8	82.2	234	1 299	67.2	21.8	877.4	381.0	154.5	42.7
Myrtle Beach-Conway-North Myrtle Beach, SC..............	326	4 036	295.9	117.8	336	1 477	91.5	25.5	1 023.4	525.3	147.6	38.1
Napa, CA...........................	357	3 272	229.2	90.5	165	916	60.2	17.1	702.1	310.5	182.2	9.8
Naples-Marco Island, FL.......	492	5 124	404.9	175.0	431	2 035	109.6	34.8	1 224.6	761.3	273.8	17.1
Nashville-Davidson—Murfreesboro, TN.............	2 551	45 978	3 248.6	1 400.0	1 929	13 432	898.7	272.1	7 838.1	2 599.6	1 121.7	226.1
New Haven-Milford, CT	1 855	26 597	1 750.3	800.2	1 634	9 237	633.4	191.6	5 199.6	1 786.8	1 076.5	131.0
New Orleans-Metairie-Kenner, LA	2 887	46 774	3 001.0	1 241.9	1 922	13 945	894.1	270.6	9 928.6	2 581.0	1 706.6	481.7

1. Firms subject to federal tax.

Area Name	Federal funds and grants, 2002–2003 (cont'd)							Local government finances, 2002				
	Expenditures (mil dol) (cont'd)							General revenue				
	Procurement contract awards			Grants							Taxes	
											Per capita[1] (dollars)	
	Salaries and wages	Defense	Other	Medicaid and other health-related	Nutrition and family welfare	Education	Other	Total (mil dol)	Intergovernmental (mil dol)	Total (mil dol)	Total	Property
	171	172	173	174	175	176	177	178	179	180	181	182
La Crosse, WI-MN	33.9	63.9	20.9	70.6	16.6	9.4	33.7	480.8	231.9	146.8	1 147	1 053
Lafayette, IN	40.8	23.2	11.5	83.1	10.3	7.0	124.1	419.7	143.1	188.3	1 038	891
Lafayette, LA	68.8	17.7	40.2	151.5	25.8	23.0	49.7	492.4	181.1	217.7	897	314
Lake Charles, LA	41.4	122.7	55.6	100.0	19.3	13.9	58.6	634.6	178.2	288.8	1 496	594
Lakeland, FL	86.0	18.3	21.3	176.3	66.8	35.3	149.2	1 170.9	487.4	363.3	729	593
Lancaster, PA	97.2	82.8	50.9	146.5	36.7	15.1	92.5	1 089.3	348.2	504.6	1 054	831
Lansing-East Lansing, MI	186.2	116.3	40.3	408.2	512.4	356.8	889.5	1 512.5	812.2	375.6	828	731
Laredo, TX	74.0	10.6	29.5	219.0	98.5	23.4	40.2	693.7	352.4	196.7	948	714
Las Cruces, NM	146.6	219.1	78.6	139.6	29.9	15.6	77.7	459.5	284.2	110.7	620	305
Las Vegas-Paradise, NV	861.3	187.1	942.8	450.5	112.1	73.8	258.4	5 571.3	1 975.7	1 770.4	1 163	726
Lawrence, KS	31.1	10.9	4.0	56.3	7.1	35.3	38.8	308.3	70.1	106.8	1 044	743
Lawton, OK	583.2	121.1	10.5	48.3	20.1	16.8	25.2	321.8	123.2	61.2	539	266
Lebanon, PA	115.8	27.6	21.6	37.4	6.2	2.3	84.4	294.8	95.7	112.4	927	705
Lewiston, ID-WA	14.6	7.3	8.9	55.9	12.4	6.0	22.6	149.1	68.5	48.9	850	775
Lewiston-Auburn, ME	22.7	1.6	4.4	117.2	17.3	6.3	38.2	276.0	110.3	134.3	1 282	1 255
Lexington-Fayette, KY	229.6	225.4	95.7	246.8	42.4	35.1	176.4	881.4	241.8	447.5	1 075	449
Lima, OH	33.4	36.8	6.8	61.1	16.1	8.5	26.5	334.0	164.7	111.3	1 029	695
Lincoln, NE	176.3	47.8	34.8	182.5	103.0	93.3	288.3	809.3	259.0	358.9	1 309	995
Little Rock-North Little Rock, AR	684.4	259.2	130.4	382.7	167.8	168.4	654.5	1 461.3	736.5	359.4	577	270
Logan, UT-ID	23.3	40.6	34.5	35.9	12.3	9.5	31.6	219.8	111.4	54.5	517	332
Longview, TX	33.5	1.4	7.2	145.0	27.8	7.6	26.7	515.5	179.3	237.7	1 205	966
Longview, WA	15.2	1.6	13.4	57.7	20.2	17.6	23.0	303.7	134.8	86.8	918	636
Los Angeles-Long Beach-Santa Ana, CA	4 184.4	12 568.4	4 330.4	8 820.4	3 059.5	959.5	3 141.6	57 621.7	30 174.8	15 721.1	1 234	748
Los Angeles-Long Beach-Glendale, CA Div	3 404.4	10 431.2	3 695.6	7 884.8	2 746.4	796.6	2 730.4	47 021.0	25 648.4	11 982.8	1 222	713
Santa Ana-Anaheim-Irvine, CA Div	779.9	2 137.1	634.8	935.5	313.1	162.9	411.2	10 600.7	4 526.5	3 738.3	1 272	863
Louisville, KY-IN	553.1	2 381.7	134.8	630.4	139.8	83.1	372.8	3 011.1	959.1	1 103.2	933	581
Lubbock, TX	86.0	16.4	12.9	135.2	25.5	12.9	119.0	772.6	274.4	236.6	930	707
Lynchburg, VA	52.7	22.7	637.3	97.6	18.9	13.4	59.4	535.0	254.6	187.5	816	569
Macon, GA	105.3	19.8	57.8	192.1	40.3	25.8	83.5	1 026.6	250.7	263.2	1 169	728
Madera, CA	15.5	0.4	6.3	85.4	26.9	10.3	15.9	406.6	257.5	81.0	622	473
Madison, WI	301.7	31.5	131.9	582.3	251.4	247.3	817.3	1 911.6	784.0	796.5	1 533	1 405
Manchester-Nashua, NH	279.7	380.3	46.4	198.9	30.1	18.2	116.9	1 031.6	419.4	467.3	1 191	1 154
Mansfield, OH	62.0	2.5	7.8	68.3	16.2	9.6	26.8	426.9	208.6	146.5	1 144	776
McAllen-Edinburg-Pharr, TX	127.9	219.6	26.2	538.9	123.2	69.7	190.2	1 786.3	1 109.4	426.0	693	546
Medford, OR	94.6	0.9	35.8	95.3	24.5	13.8	50.4	506.9	268.2	166.2	892	731
Memphis, TN-MS-AR	985.6	1 153.6	482.9	1 262.4	227.6	84.3	451.7	3 624.3	1 287.3	1 489.8	1 211	823
Merced, CA	46.3	5.5	17.2	147.8	70.0	28.1	44.4	990.7	632.7	139.5	619	477
Miami-Fort Lauderdale-Miami Beach, FL	2 057.5	522.4	561.5	3 911.8	571.7	278.1	1 013.3	20 629.5	5 902.7	7 340.4	1 403	1 106
Fort Lauderdale-Pompano Beach-Deerfield Beach, FL Div	495.5	233.2	154.2	352.9	114.7	79.0	241.6	6 696.1	1 713.2	2 278.7	1 333	1 060
Miami-Miami Beach-Kendall, FL Div	1 205.6	174.8	281.6	3 318.4	369.9	151.2	486.9	9 594.8	3 185.1	2 965.2	1 271	950
West Palm Beach-Boca Raton-Boynton Beach, FL Div	356.3	114.4	125.7	240.5	87.1	47.9	284.7	4 338.5	1 004.3	2 096.5	1 761	1 477
Michigan City-La Porte, IN	15.2	4.7	4.3	50.2	12.1	2.8	26.5	338.0	125.1	134.8	1 221	1 132
Midland, TX	37.8	1.5	6.4	27.5	5.8	7.5	15.0	449.9	130.5	161.3	1 371	1 084
Milwaukee-Waukesha-West Allis, WI	685.8	180.9	257.8	1 138.7	319.2	118.7	467.8	5 836.4	2 706.9	2 114.1	1 398	1 304
Minneapolis-St. Paul-Bloomington, MN	1 426.7	1 464.7	630.9	1 753.3	543.3	344.9	1 256.7	12 385.2	5 450.6	3 690.8	1 208	1 126
Missoula, MT	85.5	3.8	51.5	66.4	13.0	9.7	35.1	192.6	77.4	79.4	810	788
Mobile, AL	178.9	77.2	48.8	227.9	57.0	37.3	108.4	984.6	434.0	373.3	933	316
Modesto, CA	75.9	15.0	94.6	307.5	125.7	36.8	79.6	2 047.7	1 179.3	405.9	841	554
Monroe, LA	39.0	5.3	9.1	148.7	20.5	14.2	61.1	467.4	202.8	207.3	1 219	423
Monroe, MI	16.0	2.2	5.5	40.7	18.0	8.1	37.5	438.2	204.5	119.6	801	773
Montgomery, AL	574.9	324.8	116.5	303.2	201.6	206.2	466.8	691.7	346.8	219.9	626	164
Morgantown, WV	117.6	9.4	134.5	75.3	9.4	7.9	61.7	183.9	85.2	62.2	554	445
Morristown, TN	21.8	1.2	3.9	116.1	18.1	10.7	13.6	191.6	88.3	70.8	564	323
Mount Vernon-Anacortes, WA	21.6	8.2	15.5	46.3	17.8	14.7	21.1	486.8	171.9	114.6	1 072	729
Muncie, IN	23.5	1.8	7.5	91.0	15.5	6.7	35.7	283.9	129.8	110.7	937	845
Muskegon-Norton Shores, MI	28.2	60.1	20.7	109.3	36.4	15.7	21.0	619.9	331.1	112.8	656	590
Myrtle Beach-Conway-North Myrtle Beach, SC	31.6	5.1	7.6	99.0	17.2	11.3	117.4	655.9	175.2	271.3	1 317	957
Napa, CA	17.2	10.6	4.2	58.7	19.0	8.9	72.9	548.9	230.7	208.3	1 599	1 198
Naples-Marco Island, FL	40.4	7.1	27.1	37.5	28.4	8.6	16.7	779.6	148.9	427.6	1 545	1 373
Nashville-Davidson—Murfreesboro, TN	712.6	90.9	488.2	1 076.8	304.5	304.2	776.1	3 238.1	1 016.4	1 322.9	978	736
New Haven-Milford, CT	351.7	113.4	148.5	924.8	135.0	71.3	388.7	2 724.1	1 145.3	1 326.0	1 587	1 559
New Orleans-Metairie-Kenner, LA	1 030.7	1 217.2	839.9	1 071.7	195.9	119.4	437.4	4 183.7	1 326.4	1 659.7	1 262	510

1. Based on the resident population estimated as of July 1 of the year shown.

Area Name	Local government finances, 2002 (cont'd)									Government employment, 2002			Presidential election, 2004		
	Direct general expenditure							Debt outstanding					Percent of vote cast —		
					Percent of total for —										
	Total (mil dol)	Per capita¹ (dollars)	Educa-tion	Health and hospitals	Police protec-tion	Public welfare	High-ways	Total (mil dol)	Per capita¹ (dollars)	Federal civilian	Federal military	State and local	Demo-cratic	Republi-can	All other
	183	184	185	186	187	188	189	190	191	192	193	194	195	196	197
La Crosse, WI-MN	482.9	3 773	50.3	2.5	4.5	7.7	7.3	349.6	2 731	555	378	9 956	52.5	46.4	1.1
Lafayette, IN	401.6	2 213	47.5	0.6	5.0	2.7	5.3	224.5	1 238	655	530	21 787	38.0	61.0	1.0
Lafayette, LA	524.5	2 163	47.5	2.3	7.0	0.1	6.5	755.4	3 114	1 063	1 058	13 299	39.5	58.9	1.6
Lake Charles, LA	617.6	3 200	41.8	8.7	6.0	0.3	6.0	787.8	4 082	639	851	13 645	40.6	58.4	1.0
Lakeland, FL	1 180.7	2 368	48.9	1.7	8.5	0.8	3.9	1 703.8	3 416	2 763	762	24 830	40.8	58.6	0.6
Lancaster, PA	1 180.7	2 467	48.5	3.8	4.0	4.8	3.3	1 962.3	4 100	1 470	1 284	18 780	33.5	65.9	0.6
Lansing-East Lansing, MI	1 581.8	3 487	50.4	6.4	3.9	5.2	4.2	1 784.3	3 933	2 745	1 208	56 887	52.0	47.0	1.0
Laredo, TX	733.4	3 533	60.3	1.7	5.3	1.2	5.6	827.9	3 988	2 082	387	14 979	57.0	42.7	0.3
Las Cruces, NM	437.1	2 447	62.4	0.5	5.4	1.3	4.0	268.6	1 503	3 394	538	16 323	50.7	48.2	1.0
Las Vegas-Paradise, NV	5 563.2	3 655	34.8	8.4	7.2	1.3	8.4	9 579.5	6 293	9 540	9 933	66 505	47.9	50.5	1.6
Lawrence, KS	294.3	2 876	32.9	29.8	4.6	0.1	4.0	258.6	2 528	554	332	15 516	56.7	41.4	1.8
Lawton, OK	311.8	2 749	48.9	29.3	3.9	0.0	3.0	119.5	1 054	3 203	14 034	8 386	36.2	63.8	0.0
Lebanon, PA	276.8	2 284	48.1	9.7	2.9	9.7	3.3	349.9	2 887	1 976	339	5 101	32.5	66.7	0.8
Lewiston, ID-WA	146.4	2 544	47.2	4.1	6.1	0.4	9.5	68.4	1 188	243	198	4 891	37.0	61.7	1.3
Lewiston-Auburn, ME	249.1	2 377	50.8	0.1	3.9	0.3	6.4	178.3	1 701	342	415	5 326	54.3	43.8	1.9
Lexington-Fayette, KY	922.6	2 216	38.9	2.5	6.4	1.7	4.0	1 656.5	3 978	4 416	455	37 696	42.4	56.8	0.9
Lima, OH	338.5	3 131	53.0	3.4	5.0	5.5	5.7	113.9	1 053	442	254	7 251	33.2	66.4	0.4
Lincoln, NE	818.5	2 985	52.8	2.3	3.7	1.8	6.6	911.8	3 326	2 742	1 005	29 392	41.3	57.3	1.4
Little Rock-North Little Rock, AR	1 411.5	2 266	48.4	5.9	6.9	0.0	4.7	1 295.4	2 080	9 162	7 681	53 759	47.6	51.4	1.0
Logan, UT-ID	208.6	1 979	54.6	6.8	4.5	0.3	4.6	161.8	1 536	392	424	9 894	15.2	82.7	2.1
Longview, TX	500.4	2 536	57.7	7.7	5.5	0.1	4.2	444.9	2 255	482	368	11 055	28.5	71.3	0.2
Longview, WA	324.8	3 437	42.3	3.3	4.6	0.0	4.0	335.6	3 550	250	282	5 451	52.9	45.7	1.4
Los Angeles-Long Beach-Santa Ana, CA	53 254.2	4 178	38.9	8.1	6.8	9.9	3.6	55 040.7	4 319	64 327	21 771	707 453	57.6	41.2	1.2
Los Angeles-Long Beach-Glendale, CA Div	43 227.9	4 408	37.5	9.1	6.7	10.6	3.5	42 997.4	4 385	52 776	16 711	560 846	62.9	35.9	1.2
Santa Ana-Anaheim-Irvine, CA Div	10 026.3	3 412	45.3	3.7	7.4	6.8	4.3	12 043.2	4 098	11 551	5 060	146 607	39.3	59.6	1.1
Louisville, KY-IN	3 072.1	2 597	39.6	9.0	5.0	1.3	2.8	6 076.0	5 137	9 084	1 732	66 032	44.8	54.5	0.7
Lubbock, TX	763.6	3 001	40.9	27.0	4.9	0.1	2.2	485.3	1 907	1 251	526	22 827	24.2	75.3	0.4
Lynchburg, VA	519.4	2 259	50.8	5.4	4.8	4.5	2.9	542.3	2 359	835	617	13 418	34.7	64.4	0.9
Macon, GA	1 026.8	4 563	29.7	41.5	3.3	0.3	2.7	737.2	3 276	1 676	682	13 394	46.1	53.4	0.5
Madera, CA	419.7	3 222	50.5	6.2	3.9	9.8	4.8	100.3	770	340	179	7 791	34.7	64.2	1.1
Madison, WI	1 943.0	3 739	47.1	2.1	5.3	9.8	6.2	1 680.4	3 234	4 648	1 483	72 570	64.1	35.0	0.9
Manchester-Nashua, NH	1 067.0	2 719	51.4	0.6	5.3	4.4	4.5	822.8	2 097	3 944	1 095	16 769	48.2	51.2	0.6
Mansfield, OH	406.3	3 174	48.9	7.1	4.7	6.8	6.0	176.8	1 381	655	295	9 056	39.7	59.8	0.5
McAllen-Edinburg-Pharr, TX	1 904.3	3 099	68.3	2.5	3.6	2.0	2.2	1 396.9	2 273	2 599	1 148	40 942	54.9	44.8	0.3
Medford, OR	517.0	2 773	46.1	6.4	5.5	0.0	5.9	303.4	1 628	1 671	522	9 351	43.5	55.5	0.9
Memphis, TN-MS-AR	3 868.5	3 144	39.6	10.4	7.2	0.2	2.5	4 690.7	3 812	16 121	6 199	75 994	52.5	46.9	0.6
Merced, CA	967.1	4 290	51.3	4.4	3.3	11.9	2.4	342.2	1 518	788	311	13 124	42.3	56.6	1.1
Miami-Fort Lauderdale-Miami Beach, FL	20 272.2	3 875	33.5	13.5	8.0	1.2	1.8	22 300.7	4 262	29 758	11 029	274 570	59.3	40.0	0.8
Fort Lauderdale-Pompano Beach-Deerfield Beach, FL Div	6 697.0	3 918	32.1	21.9	8.6	0.7	2.2	6 304.7	3 689	7 191	2 956	86 715	64.3	34.5	1.2
Miami-Miami Beach-Kendall, FL Div	9 325.1	3 998	33.6	12.0	7.2	1.3	1.1	11 299.6	4 844	18 422	6 180	132 095	53.6	45.9	0.5
West Palm Beach-Boca Raton-Boynton Beach, FL Div	4 250.2	3 570	35.4	3.5	8.6	1.8	3.0	4 696.4	3 945	4 145	1 893	55 760	60.4	39.0	0.6
Michigan City-La Porte, IN	303.9	2 753	45.7	1.3	4.3	4.5	4.2	168.5	1 526	225	313	7 606	60.8	38.5	0.7
Midland, TX	447.1	3 799	38.4	31.7	4.9	0.0	1.7	243.9	2 073	553	218	7 886	17.9	81.7	0.4
Milwaukee-Waukesha-West Allis, WI	6 119.7	4 046	44.2	5.9	7.4	5.6	5.4	4 450.7	2 943	10 916	4 530	81 605	49.0	50.3	0.7
Minneapolis-St. Paul-Bloomington, MN	12 490.6	4 089	40.0	6.1	4.5	6.6	6.1	16 423.2	5 376	20 419	11 161	204 805	53.0	45.8	1.1
Missoula, MT	192.9	1 967	53.2	2.7	9.0	0.3	3.7	119.6	1 219	1 475	482	8 112	51.4	45.7	2.8
Mobile, AL	1 041.5	2 603	42.1	4.4	6.2	0.8	6.3	1 005.3	2 512	2 420	2 597	25 724	40.6	58.7	0.7
Modesto, CA	1 932.9	4 007	48.7	9.8	4.8	9.9	3.1	2 408.4	4 992	1 175	665	25 595	40.8	58.3	0.9
Monroe, LA	499.6	2 937	47.7	4.4	4.4	0.2	5.7	351.0	2 063	592	733	13 667	33.4	65.5	1.1
Monroe, MI	424.3	2 843	53.7	6.5	3.4	1.0	6.5	559.2	3 747	259	258	6 305	48.7	50.5	0.8
Montgomery, AL	711.6	2 026	50.9	3.7	6.9	0.1	5.9	432.6	1 232	6 755	6 392	31 348	42.0	57.6	0.4
Morgantown, WV	179.3	1 595	63.0	0.5	3.9	0.1	1.8	207.1	1 843	1 525	479	16 063	43.9	55.2	0.9
Morristown, TN	194.1	1 546	60.5	1.5	5.6	0.1	5.4	139.7	1 113	359	408	6 000	32.9	66.5	0.7
Mount Vernon-Anacortes, WA	454.2	4 249	33.7	29.1	4.0	0.0	6.2	335.5	3 138	414	319	9 358	48.5	49.9	1.6
Muncie, IN	276.4	2 339	51.4	0.9	5.4	4.7	3.6	98.3	832	392	321	10 375	42.7	56.5	0.8
Muskegon-Norton Shores, MI	618.9	3 603	53.7	6.7	3.4	11.4	4.2	463.2	2 696	396	310	9 238	55.2	43.9	0.9
Myrtle Beach-Conway-North Myrtle Beach, SC	694.1	3 369	41.1	11.7	5.1	0.3	5.9	575.6	2 794	461	767	10 980	36.3	62.0	1.7
Napa, CA	547.2	4 201	42.0	5.2	5.9	5.6	4.7	163.3	1 254	429	179	9 198	59.7	39.0	1.3
Naples-Marco Island, FL	808.8	2 923	45.1	1.0	10.2	0.6	8.9	757.3	2 737	657	420	11 002	34.1	65.0	0.9
Nashville-Davidson—Murfreesboro, TN	3 510.4	2 594	41.3	7.2	5.9	0.9	3.3	5 769.8	4 264	11 046	5 069	75 674	43.3	56.0	0.7
New Haven-Milford, CT	2 648.9	3 170	52.5	1.6	5.7	1.7	3.2	2 085.5	2 496	6 464	1 729	43 378	54.2	43.9	1.9
New Orleans-Metairie-Kenner, LA	4 040.4	3 072	33.8	18.1	6.1	0.7	5.0	4 830.0	3 672	15 541	10 069	88 337	49.1	50.0	0.9

1. Based on the resident population estimated as of July 1 of the year shown.

Table C. Metropolitan Areas — Land Area and Population

CBSA/ DIV code[1]	Area Name	Land area,[2] 2000 (sq km)	Total persons	Rank	Per square kilometer	White	Black	Am. Indian, Alaska Native	Asian and Pacific Islander	Percent Hispanic or Latino[3]	Under 5 years	5 to 17 years	18 to 24 years	25 to 34 years	35 to 44 years	45 to 54 years
		1	2	3	4	5	6	7	8	9	10	11	12	13	14	15
35620	New York-Northern New Jersey-Long Island, NY-NJ-PA	17 421	18 640 775	1	1 070.0	52.8	17.9	0.5	9.1	20.9	6.7	17.5	8.6	14.5	16.4	13.8
20764	Edison, NJ Div	4 461	2 270 950	X	509.1	74.0	7.4	0.4	9.2	10.0	6.5	17.9	8.1	12.6	16.7	14.1
35004	Nassau-Suffolk, NY Div	3 106	2 807 500	X	903.9	74.0	9.4	0.4	5.0	12.1	6.2	17.9	8.4	12.0	16.8	14.7
35084	Newark-Union, NJ-PA Div	5 690	2 140 397	X	376.2	59.4	22.0	0.4	4.8	14.4	6.9	18.7	8.2	12.8	17.0	14.5
35644	New York-Wayne-White Plains, NY-NJ Div	4 164	11 421 928	X	2 743.0	42.1	21.3	0.5	10.9	26.4	6.9	17.1	8.9	15.8	16.1	13.4
35660	Niles-Benton Harbor, MI	1 479	162 766	229	110.1	79.0	16.4	0.9	1.7	3.4	6.4	18.6	9.5	11.4	14.7	14.6
35980	Norwich-New London, CT	1 725	263 992	164	153.0	85.4	6.4	1.7	3.2	5.5	5.8	17.6	9.4	12.4	17.1	14.5
36100	Ocala, FL	4 089	280 288	157	68.5	80.1	11.9	0.8	1.0	7.0	5.4	16.0	8.0	9.7	12.7	11.8
36140	Ocean City, NJ	661	101 845	334	154.1	91.0	4.9	0.4	0.8	3.6	5.0	16.5	7.8	9.8	14.5	14.5
36220	Odessa, TX	2 334	122 692	289	52.6	48.9	4.5	0.7	0.7	45.7	8.6	21.4	11.2	12.6	14.0	13.0
36260	Ogden-Clearfield, UT	3 858	468 942	100	121.6	87.0	1.6	0.9	2.5	9.3	9.5	22.7	12.8	14.1	13.0	11.2
36420	Oklahoma City, OK	14 291	1 132 652	47	79.3	75.0	11.5	5.8	3.5	7.4	7.1	17.8	11.2	14.1	14.7	13.7
36500	Olympia, WA	1 883	221 950	186	117.9	85.9	3.2	2.6	6.9	4.8	5.8	17.7	10.4	13.0	15.0	15.6
36540	Omaha-Council Bluffs, NE-IA	11 300	793 172	60	70.2	84.1	8.3	0.9	2.3	5.8	7.5	19.0	10.1	14.2	15.4	13.7
36740	Orlando, FL	9 041	1 802 986	29	199.4	62.7	15.2	0.6	3.8	19.0	6.8	18.2	9.5	14.3	15.7	13.0
36780	Oshkosh-Neenah, WI	1 136	158 500	235	139.5	94.2	1.3	0.8	2.3	2.1	5.8	17.1	11.5	13.3	16.3	14.2
36980	Owensboro, KY	2 346	110 845	311	47.2	94.5	4.4	0.4	0.6	1.0	7.1	18.2	9.6	12.0	14.8	14.2
37100	Oxnard-Thousand Oaks-Ventura, CA	4 779	791 130	61	165.5	56.5	2.1	0.9	6.9	35.3	7.0	20.2	9.8	13.1	16.0	14.0
37340	Palm Bay-Melbourne-Titusville, FL	2 637	505 711	93	191.8	83.9	9.1	0.8	2.3	5.2	5.1	16.5	8.2	9.7	15.2	13.6
37460	Panama City-Lynn Haven, FL	1 978	155 193	239	78.5	84.2	11.4	1.4	2.5	2.1	6.4	17.6	9.0	12.3	15.7	14.0
37620	Parkersburg-Marietta, WV-OH	3 538	163 155	228	46.1	97.7	1.3	0.6	0.7	0.5	5.6	16.7	9.1	11.5	15.0	15.3
37700	Pascagoula, MS	3 122	154 335	241	49.4	75.6	20.4	0.7	2.1	2.1	7.2	19.6	10.1	13.0	15.4	13.6
37860	Pensacola-Ferry Pass-Brent, FL	4 349	428 978	108	98.6	77.1	17.9	1.7	3.1	2.1	6.5	17.9	11.4	12.5	15.0	13.5
37900	Peoria, IL	6 399	365 995	129	57.2	88.0	9.3	0.6	1.5	1.8	6.5	17.7	9.8	12.5	14.2	14.6
37980	Philadelphia-Camden-Wilmington, PA-NJ-DE-MD	11 991	5 772 947	4	481.4	70.6	20.4	0.5	4.2	5.4	6.3	18.3	9.3	12.9	16.0	14.2
15804	Camden, NJ Div	3 501	1 225 252	X	350.0	74.2	16.1	0.5	3.7	6.8	6.3	18.9	9.0	12.6	16.7	14.4
37964	Philadelphia, PA Div	5 609	3 875 021	X	690.9	68.8	22.2	0.5	4.7	4.9	6.3	18.1	9.3	12.9	15.7	14.2
48864	Wilmington, DE-MD-NJ Div	2 881	672 674	X	233.5	74.4	18.1	0.5	3.0	5.1	6.5	18.2	10.0	13.5	16.2	14.1
38060	Phoenix-Mesa-Scottsdale, AZ	37 743	3 593 408	14	95.2	63.8	4.0	2.3	3.0	28.1	8.2	19.5	9.8	15.3	14.4	11.7
38220	Pine Bluff, AR	5 294	106 001	327	20.0	51.7	46.5	0.6	0.7	1.1	6.9	18.0	11.5	12.8	14.8	13.8
38300	Pittsburgh, PA	13 674	2 410 330	21	176.3	89.8	8.4	0.4	1.5	0.7	5.3	16.2	8.6	11.5	15.3	15.4
38340	Pittsfield, MA	2 412	133 310	273	55.3	94.5	2.6	0.5	1.4	2.0	4.7	16.2	9.8	10.4	14.8	15.4
38540	Pocatello, ID	6 523	83 003	352	12.7	88.6	0.8	3.5	1.8	6.8	8.5	19.5	12.5	14.0	12.8	13.5
38860	Portland-South Portland-Biddeford, ME	5 388	505 408	94	93.8	96.5	1.2	0.6	1.7	1.0	5.4	17.2	8.6	12.0	16.9	15.8
38900	Portland-Vancouver-Beaverton, OR-WA	17 311	2 040 258	25	117.9	82.2	3.4	1.6	6.7	8.7	6.8	18.1	9.2	15.4	15.7	14.9
38940	Port St. Lucie-Fort Pierce, FL	2 922	348 569	136	119.3	77.4	12.2	0.6	1.2	9.4	5.2	15.9	7.7	9.3	13.2	12.4
39100	Poughkeepsie-Newburgh-Middletown, NY	4 190	654 038	75	156.1	76.4	9.8	0.6	2.9	11.5	6.2	19.1	10.5	12.2	16.7	14.2
39140	Prescott, AZ	21 039	184 433	210	8.8	87.0	0.5	2.2	0.9	10.5	5.1	15.8	8.5	9.2	11.8	13.9
39300	Providence-New Bedford-Fall River, RI-MA	4 146	1 623 174	33	391.5	85.3	4.7	0.8	2.7	7.8	5.8	17.2	10.2	12.9	16.0	14.1
39340	Provo-Orem, UT	13 961	406 851	113	29.1	89.7	0.5	0.9	2.7	7.5	12.0	22.5	16.3	17.6	10.0	8.0
39380	Pueblo, CO	6 187	148 751	252	24.0	57.5	2.0	1.1	0.9	39.3	6.7	18.5	10.4	13.0	13.9	13.4
39460	Punta Gorda, FL	1 796	153 392	242	85.4	90.3	4.8	0.4	1.2	3.8	3.8	12.2	6.0	7.4	10.6	11.5
39540	Racine, WI	863	192 284	205	222.8	79.6	11.2	0.7	1.1	8.6	6.8	19.2	9.5	11.8	16.3	14.6
39580	Raleigh-Cary, NC	5 480	884 489	54	161.4	69.5	20.3	0.7	3.8	7.0	7.6	18.4	9.5	16.9	17.2	13.2
39660	Rapid City, SD	16 179	116 596	301	7.2	89.0	1.7	7.6	1.7	2.5	7.4	18.6	11.1	12.8	14.8	14.2
39740	Reading, PA	2 224	385 307	121	173.2	84.6	4.0	0.3	1.3	10.6	6.0	17.9	9.8	11.9	15.6	14.1
39820	Redding, CA	9 804	175 650	219	17.9	88.3	1.3	4.2	2.7	6.6	5.4	18.3	10.2	10.6	13.7	14.6
39900	Reno-Sparks, NV	17 108	374 364	128	21.9	73.6	2.1	2.3	5.5	18.4	6.9	18.1	9.5	14.1	15.2	14.3
40060	Richmond, VA	14 795	1 138 234	46	76.9	64.2	31.0	0.7	2.4	2.6	6.4	18.2	9.6	13.4	16.2	14.8
40140	Riverside-San Bernardino-Ontario, CA	70 603	3 642 328	13	51.6	46.1	8.2	1.2	5.5	40.9	7.5	22.2	11.0	13.5	14.7	11.6
40220	Roanoke, VA	4 852	290 497	153	59.9	84.9	12.8	0.5	1.3	1.4	5.8	16.6	8.6	11.9	15.1	15.5
40340	Rochester, MN	4 189	172 459	222	41.2	90.9	2.7	0.5	4.4	2.4	6.8	18.8	9.2	13.5	16.6	13.8
40380	Rochester, NY	7 593	1 041 198	49	137.1	81.2	11.6	0.6	2.5	5.2	5.8	18.1	10.2	12.3	15.9	14.7
40420	Rockford, IL	2 059	330 790	142	160.7	79.0	10.1	0.6	2.1	9.5	6.9	19.2	9.3	13.3	15.2	13.9
40580	Rocky Mount, NC	2 707	144 627	258	53.4	51.8	44.1	0.6	0.6	3.5	7.0	19.3	8.9	12.5	15.2	14.9
40660	Rome, GA	1 329	93 368	345	70.3	79.1	13.4	0.5	1.2	6.5	7.1	17.7	11.2	13.5	14.2	12.8
40900	Sacramento—Arden-Arcade—Roseville, CA.	13 193	1 974 810	26	149.7	64.7	8.1	1.8	12.2	16.9	6.6	19.3	10.3	13.8	15.2	13.6
40980	Saginaw-Saginaw Township North, MI	2 095	209 327	195	99.9	72.8	19.7	0.8	1.1	6.9	6.5	19.2	9.8	12.0	14.4	14.7
41060	St. Cloud, MN	4 539	174 074	220	38.4	95.4	1.5	0.6	1.9	1.5	6.3	17.6	15.1	13.6	14.7	12.6
41100	St. George, UT	6 285	104 132	331	16.6	91.6	0.5	1.9	1.6	5.7	8.8	20.8	13.1	12.5	9.9	8.7
41140	St. Joseph, MO-KS	4 303	122 934	288	28.6	92.5	5.0	0.9	0.6	2.0	6.0	17.2	10.8	12.9	15.7	13.8
41180	St. Louis, MO-IL	22 400	2 735 927	18	122.1	78.3	18.5	0.6	2.1	1.7	6.5	18.7	9.5	12.8	15.8	14.3

1. CBSA = Core Based Statistical Area. DIV = Metropolitan Division. See Appendix A for explanation. See Appendix B for list of metropolitan areas identified by type. 2. Dry land or land partially or temporarily covered by water. 3. Hispanic or Latino persons may be of any race.

Table C. Metropolitan Areas — **Population and Households**

Area Name	Age (percent) (cont'd)				Total persons		Percent change		Components of change, 2000–2003			Households, 2000			Percent	
	55 to 64 years	65 to 74 years	75 years and over	Percent female	1900	2000	1990–2000	2000–2003	Births	Deaths	Net migration	Number	Percent change, 1990–2000	Persons per house-hold	Female family house-holder[1]	One person
	16	17	18	19	20	21	22	23	24	25	26	27	28	29	30	31
New York-Northern New Jersey-Long Island, NY-NJ-PA	9.5	6.4	6.2	51.9	16 863 671	18 323 002	8.7	1.7	858 023	479 797	-60 282	6 676 963	8.1	2.69	15.1	27.0
Edison, NJ Div	9.4	6.9	7.2	51.3	1 898 329	2 173 869	14.5	4.5	94 922	65 708	69 489	799 437	15.4	2.67	9.8	24.0
Nassau-Suffolk, NY Div	10.2	6.9	6.4	51.3	2 609 212	2 753 913	5.5	1.9	116 643	74 565	14 219	916 686	7.1	2.95	10.9	18.6
Newark-Union, NJ-PA Div	9.8	6.1	5.8	51.6	1 959 933	2 098 843	7.1	2.0	97 108	57 093	3 774	751 513	7.3	2.73	14.1	23.7
New York-Wayne-White Plains, NY-NJ Div	9.3	6.3	5.9	52.2	10 396 197	11 296 377	8.7	1.1	549 350	282 431	-147 764	4 209 327	7.2	2.63	17.3	29.9
Niles-Benton Harbor, MI	10.2	7.2	7.2	51.4	161 378	162 453	0.7	0.2	7 022	5 285	-1 342	63 569	4.2	2.49	13.2	27.1
Norwich-New London, CT	9.7	6.4	6.5	50.5	254 957	259 088	1.6	1.9	9 822	7 209	2 585	99 835	7.1	2.48	11.0	26.4
Ocala, FL	11.2	12.5	11.1	51.7	194 835	258 916	32.9	8.3	9 627	11 591	22 792	106 755	36.6	2.36	10.7	25.0
Ocean City, NJ	11.7	10.0	10.2	51.9	95 089	102 326	7.6	-0.5	3 318	4 308	620	42 148	11.3	2.36	10.9	30.2
Odessa, TX	8.1	6.2	4.8	51.3	118 934	121 123	1.8	1.3	7 061	3 038	-2 416	43 846	3.6	2.72	13.7	24.0
Ogden-Clearfield, UT	6.8	4.6	4.0	49.7	351 799	442 656	25.8	5.9	29 327	8 481	5 913	138 945	28.2	3.14	9.8	16.6
Oklahoma City, OK	9.0	6.0	5.2	50.8	971 042	1 095 421	12.8	3.4	53 588	32 249	16 373	429 743	15.4	2.47	12.1	27.4
Olympia, WA	9.7	5.6	5.6	51.0	161 238	207 355	28.6	7.0	8 192	5 351	11 735	81 625	31.3	2.50	10.3	25.1
Omaha-Council Bluffs, NE-IA	8.4	5.6	5.1	50.7	685 797	767 041	11.8	3.4	39 902	19 864	6 510	294 502	14.5	2.55	11.2	26.7
Orlando, FL	8.6	6.5	5.4	50.6	1 224 844	1 644 561	34.3	9.6	78 067	43 820	120 376	625 248	34.4	2.58	12.4	23.5
Oshkosh-Neenah, WI	8.9	6.2	6.3	50.1	140 320	156 763	11.7	1.1	5 940	4 100	80	61 157	14.9	2.43	8.3	24.9
Owensboro, KY	10.1	7.1	6.5	51.5	104 681	109 875	5.0	0.9	5 211	3 620	-534	43 232	9.4	2.48	11.2	26.5
Oxnard-Thousand Oaks-Ventura, CA	8.8	5.3	5.0	50.0	669 016	753 197	12.6	5.0	36 775	15 319	17 453	243 234	11.9	3.04	10.9	18.9
Palm Bay-Melbourne-Titusville, FL	11.0	10.5	9.1	50.9	398 978	476 230	19.4	6.2	15 668	17 425	30 726	198 195	22.8	2.35	10.2	26.9
Panama City-Lynn Haven, FL	10.1	8.0	5.6	50.5	126 994	148 217	16.7	4.7	6 223	4 695	5 498	59 597	21.8	2.43	12.0	26.0
Parkersburg-Marietta, WV-OH	11.3	8.1	7.4	51.4	161 907	164 624	1.7	-0.9	5 934	5 939	-1 340	66 583	6.5	2.42	10.1	26.1
Pascagoula, MS	10.0	6.3	4.3	50.1	131 916	150 564	14.1	2.5	7 290	4 390	984	54 418	17.7	2.72	14.0	20.6
Pensacola-Ferry Pass-Brent, FL	9.5	7.3	5.5	50.3	344 406	412 153	19.7	4.1	17 686	12 396	11 527	154 842	20.5	2.50	13.8	24.7
Peoria, IL	9.9	7.2	7.5	51.4	358 552	366 899	2.3	-0.2	15 679	11 736	-4 631	143 607	5.0	2.47	10.5	26.9
Philadelphia-Camden-Wilmington, PA-NJ-DE-MD	9.4	6.5	6.6	51.8	5 435 550	5 687 147	4.6	1.5	242 935	177 934	24 152	2 134 404	7.3	2.58	14.2	26.9
Camden, NJ Div	9.3	6.2	5.9	51.2	1 127 972	1 186 999	5.2	3.2	49 205	33 927	23 441	430 832	9.3	2.69	13.0	23.5
Philadelphia, PA Div	9.4	6.7	7.0	52.1	3 728 991	3 849 647	3.2	0.7	165 063	125 591	-11 798	1 459 119	5.5	2.55	14.8	28.3
Wilmington, DE-MD-NJ Div	9.3	6.0	5.5	51.2	578 587	650 501	12.4	3.4	28 667	18 416	12 509	244 453	14.9	2.58	13.1	24.8
Phoenix-Mesa-Scottsdale, AZ	8.1	5.9	5.3	49.6	2 238 498	3 251 876	45.3	10.5	189 687	81 449	231 611	1 194 250	41.0	2.67	10.8	24.4
Pine Bluff, AR	9.5	6.5	6.3	49.5	106 958	107 341	0.4	-1.2	4 897	3 548	-2 654	38 093	3.9	2.59	17.6	25.5
Pittsburgh, PA	10.3	8.2	9.2	52.1	2 468 289	2 431 087	-1.5	-0.9	82 346	94 156	-7 113	995 505	2.0	2.37	11.3	29.9
Pittsfield, MA	10.9	8.3	9.5	52.0	139 352	134 953	-3.2	-1.2	3 956	5 157	-329	56 006	3.1	2.30	11.0	31.6
Pocatello, ID	8.1	5.3	5.1	50.6	73 112	83 103	13.7	-0.1	4 750	2 005	-2 875	29 752	15.4	2.71	9.9	22.6
Portland-South Portland-Biddeford, ME	9.9	6.6	6.6	51.3	441 257	487 568	10.5	3.7	17 425	14 067	14 677	196 669	16.4	2.42	9.5	26.9
Portland-Vancouver-Beaverton, OR-WA	8.8	4.9	5.2	50.2	1 523 741	1 927 881	26.5	5.8	89 812	48 332	71 912	745 531	25.8	2.54	9.9	26.3
Port St. Lucie-Fort Pierce, FL	10.8	11.7	11.8	50.9	251 071	319 426	27.2	9.1	11 329	12 931	30 026	132 221	30.7	2.37	9.5	25.8
Poughkeepsie-Newburgh-Middletown, NY	9.1	5.6	5.1	49.9	567 033	621 517	9.6	3.2	26 240	15 555	21 881	214 324	12.2	2.75	10.9	22.9
Prescott, AZ	12.7	11.4	9.8	50.8	107 714	167 517	55.5	10.1	5 687	6 480	17 293	70 171	56.7	2.33	8.1	26.7
Providence-New Bedford-Fall River, RI-MA	9.3	6.5	7.5	51.8	1 509 789	1 582 997	4.8	2.5	61 596	48 951	28 790	613 835	8.5	2.49	12.9	27.9
Provo-Orem, UT	4.9	3.4	3.0	50.5	269 407	376 774	39.9	8.0	33 306	5 485	-113	102 393	42.3	3.59	8.0	11.3
Pueblo, CO	8.9	7.4	7.3	51.0	123 051	141 472	15.0	5.1	6 434	4 651	5 434	54 579	16.0	2.52	13.3	26.6
Punta Gorda, FL	13.7	17.0	16.5	52.3	110 975	141 627	27.6	8.3	3 345	6 933	14 885	63 864	31.9	2.18	7.2	26.0
Racine, WI	9.3	6.1	6.0	50.5	175 034	188 831	7.9	1.8	8 441	5 264	467	70 819	11.1	2.59	12.3	24.5
Raleigh-Cary, NC	7.7	4.3	3.4	50.2	544 031	797 071	46.5	11.0	43 137	15 601	59 215	306 478	45.4	2.53	10.1	25.2
Rapid City, SD	8.4	6.3	5.4	50.2	103 221	112 818	9.3	3.3	5 725	2 769	966	43 446	15.4	2.52	11.0	24.8
Reading, PA	9.5	7.1	7.4	50.9	336 523	373 638	11.0	3.1	15 068	11 887	8 647	141 570	10.9	2.55	9.9	24.6
Redding, CA	10.7	7.4	7.3	51.2	147 036	163 256	11.0	7.6	6 179	5 720	11 773	63 426	13.3	2.52	11.9	24.7
Reno-Sparks, NV	9.6	5.9	4.6	49.2	257 193	342 885	33.3	9.2	16 412	8 951	23 911	133 546	29.3	2.53	10.3	27.0
Richmond, VA	9.3	5.9	5.4	51.6	949 244	1 096 957	15.6	3.8	48 645	31 418	24 265	425 100	17.5	2.49	14.2	26.0
Riverside-San Bernardino-Ontario, CA	7.1	5.1	4.7	50.0	2 588 793	3 254 821	25.7	11.9	176 412	78 312	284 594	1 034 812	19.4	3.07	13.4	19.5
Roanoke, VA	10.9	7.9	7.6	52.0	268 513	288 309	7.4	0.8	11 027	10 236	1 580	119 366	12.6	2.35	11.5	28.2
Rochester, MN	8.9	5.6	5.8	50.6	141 945	163 618	15.3	5.4	7 803	3 492	4 688	62 504	18.2	2.56	7.7	25.1
Rochester, NY	9.7	6.2	6.7	51.4	1 002 410	1 037 831	3.5	0.3	40 158	28 841	-7 470	397 303	6.1	2.51	12.5	27.2
Rockford, IL	9.3	6.2	6.1	50.8	283 719	320 204	12.9	3.3	14 850	9 131	5 040	122 577	13.8	2.57	11.4	24.6
Rocky Mount, NC	9.7	6.7	5.8	52.5	133 369	143 026	7.2	1.1	6 940	4 883	-289	54 036	9.5	2.59	17.1	24.6
Rome, GA	9.4	7.1	6.5	51.5	81 251	90 565	11.5	3.1	4 401	3 160	1 631	34 028	11.5	2.55	13.0	24.5
Sacramento--Arden-Arcade--Roseville, CA	8.3	5.6	5.3	50.8	1 506 792	1 796 857	19.3	9.9	83 612	44 626	137 370	665 298	19.6	2.65	12.7	25.0
Saginaw-Saginaw Township North, MI	9.9	6.8	6.8	51.8	211 946	210 039	-0.9	-0.3	9 008	6 848	-2 753	80 430	2.8	2.54	15.4	26.0
St. Cloud, MN	7.4	5.5	5.4	49.9	149 509	167 392	12.0	4.0	7 360	3 552	3 010	60 669	19.6	2.63	7.8	24.1
St. George, UT	7.1	8.2	8.0	50.6	48 560	90 354	86.1	15.2	5 904	2 274	10 037	29 939	96.2	2.97	8.0	17.5
St. Joseph, MO-KS	9.0	6.9	7.7	49.0	115 816	122 336	5.6	-0.7	4 736	4 312	-1 219	46 531	5.6	2.46	10.8	27.8
St. Louis, MO-IL	9.2	6.5	6.3	51.7	2 580 720	2 698 687	4.6	1.4	117 711	83 895	4 121	1 048 279	7.5	2.52	13.3	27.3

1. No spouse present.

Table C. Metropolitan Areas — Vital Statistics, Health Resources, and Crime

Area Name	Births, average 1999–2001		Deaths, average 1999–2001				Physicians,[4] 1998		Hospitals,[4] 1998			Medicare enrollees, 2003	Serious crimes known to police,[6] 2002	
			Number		Rate					Beds			Total	
	Total	Rate[1]	Total	Infant[2]	Total[1]	Infant[3]	Number	Rate[5]	Number	Number	Rate[5]		Number	Rate[7]
	32	33	34	35	36	37	38	39	40	41	42	43	44	45
New York-Northern New Jersey-Long Island, NY-NJ-PA	262 201	14.3	148 416	4 637	8.1	5.9	59 125	6 305	177	70 142	7 945	2 527 769	515 974	2 787
Edison, NJ Div	29 536	13.5	20 201	444	9.3	5.0	5 050	928	17	5 571	999	342 666	51 581	2 324
Nassau-Suffolk, NY Div	36 844	13.4	22 519	572	8.2	5.2	8 926	654	28	10 161	764	427 077	58 936	2 135
Newark-Union, NJ-PA Div	29 968	14.3	17 672	619	8.4	6.9	5 819	1 217	27	9 674	1 899	278 439	72 629	3 402
New York-Wayne-White Plains, NY-NJ Div	165 853	14.7	88 025	3 002	7.8	6.0	39 330	3 506	105	44 736	4 283	1 479 587	332 828	2 919
Niles-Benton Harbor, MI	2 182	13.4	1 639	66	10.1	10.1	268	165	4	733	457	29 034	6 883	4 190
Norwich-New London, CT	2 671	10.3	1 998	60	7.7	7.5	539	208	2	428	174	39 390	NA	NA
Ocala, FL	2 874	11.1	3 410	67	13.1	7.8	368	142	2	534	221	72 671	10 784	3 983
Ocean City, NJ	1 034	10.1	1 346	29	13.2	9.3	153	150	1	239	244	22 252	4 707	4 506
Odessa, TX	2 196	18.0	979	46	8.0	7.0	189	156	2	401	319	15 937	7 498	5 927
Ogden-Clearfield, UT	8 887	20.0	2 466	130	5.6	4.9	527	303	4	832	423	44 492	17 078	3 720
Oklahoma City, OK	16 197	14.8	9 657	436	8.8	9.0	2 289	674	20	3 879	1 410	140 357	70 687	6 373
Olympia, WA	2 541	12.2	1 580	34	7.6	4.5	446	215	2	437	216	29 554	8 901	4 169
Omaha-Council Bluffs, NE-IA	11 953	15.5	5 907	247	7.7	6.9	1 888	803	14	3 447	2 016	98 110	42 897	5 747
Orlando, FL	23 269	14.1	13 034	462	7.9	6.6	2 770	592	19	4 593	1 150	248 436	98 196	5 710
Oshkosh-Neenah, WI	1 858	11.9	1 240	40	7.9	7.2	320	204	2	456	304	22 481	4 281	2 692
Owensboro, KY	1 589	14.5	1 095	30	10.0	6.3	151	222	3	552	841	18 725	3 184	3 435
Oxnard-Thousand Oaks-Ventura, CA	11 515	15.2	4 712	165	6.2	4.8	1 299	172	8	1 451	198	91 182	17 694	2 266
Palm Bay-Melbourne-Titusville, FL	4 847	10.1	5 189	73	10.9	5.0	819	172	5	1 190	255	103 480	23 277	4 674
Panama City-Lynn Haven, FL	1 960	13.2	1 413	50	9.5	8.5	239	161	2	478	325	25 461	9 673	6 241
Parkersburg-Marietta, WV-OH	1 861	11.3	1 845	35	11.2	6.3	276	397	4	758	979	30 095	3 577	2 280
Pascagoula, MS	2 219	14.7	1 335	51	8.8	7.7	215	217	3	499	611	20 469	6 172	4 567
Pensacola-Ferry Pass-Brent, FL	5 441	13.2	3 734	165	9.0	10.1	784	314	6	1 792	753	64 956	18 235	4 231
Peoria, IL	4 840	13.2	3 597	119	9.8	8.2	736	543	6	1 262	808	59 809	NA	NA
Philadelphia-Camden-Wilmington, PA-NJ-DE-MD	75 353	13.2	54 632	1 775	9.6	7.9	17 730	2 708	81	20 111	3 312	841 688	196 425	3 470
Camden, NJ Div	15 487	13.0	10 474	342	8.8	7.4	2 745	638	12	3 328	765	167 371	37 062	3 058
Philadelphia, PA Div	50 956	13.2	38 646	1 186	10.0	7.8	13 568	1 575	61	14 951	1 677	585 929	132 772	3 513
Wilmington, DE-MD-NJ Div	8 911	13.7	5 512	247	8.5	9.2	1 417	495	8	1 832	870	88 388	26 591	3 971
Phoenix-Mesa-Scottsdale, AZ	56 444	17.2	24 234	1 163	7.4	6.9	6 144	256	29	6 561	439	416 913	232 943	6 854
Pine Bluff, AR	1 516	14.1	1 105	39	10.3	8.6	146	201	1	484	593	16 073	6 203	5 701
Pittsburgh, PA	26 044	10.7	28 735	572	11.8	7.3	6 928	1 152	38	10 823	2 280	460 650	58 077	2 729
Pittsfield, MA	1 237	9.2	1 592	9	11.8	2.4	327	242	4	595	447	26 737	2 845	2 156
Pocatello, ID	1 488	17.9	623	28	7.5	6.3	139	268	3	289	824	10 306	2 555	2 966
Portland-South Portland-Biddeford, ME	5 401	11.1	4 261	84	8.7	5.2	1 251	639	10	1 501	790	78 328	13 730	2 774
Portland-Vancouver-Beaverton, OR-WA	28 020	14.5	14 335	402	7.4	4.8	4 609	1 092	18	3 623	844	234 359	100 140	5 046
Port St. Lucie-Fort Pierce, FL	3 429	10.7	3 875	68	12.1	6.6	580	381	4	792	536	79 114	14 622	4 377
Poughkeepsie-Newburgh-Middletown, NY	8 236	13.2	4 759	142	7.6	5.7	1 171	380	9	1 740	579	85 648	14 538	2 338
Prescott, AZ	1 709	10.2	1 927	35	11.5	6.8	247	147	2	186	125	39 042	7 515	4 218
Providence-New Bedford-Fall River, RI-MA	19 172	12.1	15 012	358	9.5	6.2	3 563	1 169	15	4 046	1 241	261 178	55 454	3 455
Provo-Orem, UT	10 157	26.8	1 601	145	4.2	4.8	402	157	5	630	446	29 215	13 639	3 523
Pueblo, CO	1 962	13.8	1 399	35	9.9	5.9	325	230	2	563	417	25 964	7 410	4 999
Punta Gorda, FL	1 010	7.1	2 139	16	15.0	5.3	292	206	3	652	483	41 473	4 839	3 267
Racine, WI	2 593	13.7	1 607	60	8.5	7.7	251	133	3	561	301	28 541	7 145	3 730
Raleigh-Cary, NC	12 731	15.9	4 643	252	5.8	6.6	1 330	317	9	1 489	496	85 016	35 114	4 296
Rapid City, SD	1 725	15.3	838	46	7.4	8.9	276	416	2	442	894	16 486	4 839	4 254
Reading, PA	4 623	12.4	3 633	101	9.7	7.3	637	170	3	874	246	61 325	10 891	3 212
Redding, CA	1 875	11.4	1 712	34	10.4	6.0	379	232	5	656	399	33 800	5 669	3 349
Reno-Sparks, NV	4 958	14.4	2 619	95	7.6	6.4	735	217	4	1 009	322	45 320	17 557	4 708
Richmond, VA	14 694	13.4	9 551	397	8.7	9.0	2 715	2 498	14	3 804	3 042	149 328	47 090	4 202
Riverside-San Bernardino-Ontario, CA	53 403	16.3	23 590	1 085	7.2	6.8	4 783	292	35	6 713	430	399 208	142 954	4 236
Roanoke, VA	3 386	11.7	3 108	87	10.8	8.6	730	1 459	4	1 116	2 234	50 139	7 684	2 587
Rochester, MN	2 352	14.3	1 096	44	6.7	6.2	1 536	1 338	5	1 455	1 686	21 630	4 100	2 505
Rochester, NY	12 720	12.3	8 838	247	8.5	6.5	2 871	799	14	3 657	1 705	158 696	36 768	3 521
Rockford, IL	4 577	14.3	2 797	109	8.7	7.9	652	301	5	1 026	668	46 764	NA	NA
Rocky Mount, NC	2 089	14.6	1 487	69	10.4	11.0	190	245	3	412	543	23 523	8 153	5 547
Rome, GA	1 303	14.4	973	28	10.7	7.2	239	264	2	505	593	15 212	3 756	3 966
Sacramento—Arden-Arcade—Roseville, CA	25 258	13.9	13 316	443	7.3	5.8	3 891	740	17	3 841	641	245 669	88 380	4 744
Saginaw-Saginaw Township North, MI	2 835	13.5	2 001	77	9.5	9.1	442	210	3	848	404	34 090	10 242	4 822
St. Cloud, MN	2 289	13.6	1 095	41	6.5	6.0	305	243	5	655	511	22 627	5 360	3 138
St. George, UT	1 809	19.9	678	25	7.4	4.6	115	127	1	103	125	16 219	2 386	2 546
St. Joseph, MO-KS	1 510	12.4	1 329	35	10.9	7.7	173	283	2	482	1 656	19 916	5 544	4 481
St. Louis, MO-IL	36 221	13.4	25 697	870	9.5	8.0	6 602	1 892	48	10 738	3 958	400 667	NA	NA

1. Per 1,000 estimated resident population.   2. Deaths of infants under 1 year old.   3. Deaths of infants under 1 year old per 1,000 live births.   4. Data subject to copyright.   5. Per 100,000 resident population as of July 1 of the year shown.   6. Data for serious crimes have not been adjusted for underreporting; this may affect comparability between geographic areas and over time.   7. Per 100,000 population estimated by the FBI.

Table C. Metropolitan Areas — Crime, Education, Money Income, and Poverty

Area Name	Serious crimes known to police,[1] 2002 (cont'd) Rate[2] Violent	Property	School enrollment and attainment, 2000 — Enrollment[3] Total	Percent private	High school grad-uate or more	Bach-elor's degree or more	Local government expenditures,[5] 2000–2001 Total current expendi-tures (mil dol)	Current expendi-tures per student (dollars)	Money income, 1999 Per capita income[6] (dollars)	Mean house-hold income	Mean family income	Percent of house-holds with income of $100,000 or more	Percent below poverty level, 1999 Persons	House-holds	Families	Families with children
	46	47	48	49	50	51	52	53	54	55	56	57	58	59	60	61
New York-Northern New Jersey-Long Island, NY-NJ-PA	516	2 271	4 951 884	25.2	78.7	30.3	31 278.4	11 749	26 232	71 103	80 778	20.2	13.6	13.0	10.9	15.7
Edison, NJ Div	197	2 127	561 948	21.3	85.7	32.0	3 509.7	10 509	28 588	76 995	88 308	23.6	6.2	5.9	4.2	6.2
Nassau-Suffolk, NY Div	208	1 927	745 166	21.6	86.4	31.3	5 950.0	13 047	29 278	86 983	96 064	28.8	5.6	5.5	3.7	5.3
Newark-Union, NJ-PA Div	503	2 899	564 425	22.1	82.2	32.2	3 901.4	11 864	28 849	79 681	91 824	24.5	9.4	9.3	7.2	10.4
New York-Wayne-White Plains, NY-NJ Div	655	2 264	3 080 345	27.4	74.8	29.4	17 917.3	11 610	24 550	64 993	72 960	16.9	17.8	16.7	15.0	21.2
Niles-Benton Harbor, MI	541	3 649	42 978	20.4	81.9	19.6	229.5	8 196	19 952	50 165	57 716	8.7	12.7	11.6	9.3	14.4
Norwich-New London, CT	NA	NA	67 054	16.9	86.0	26.2	392.1	9 785	24 678	62 459	71 403	14.5	6.4	6.7	4.5	7.3
Ocala, FL	785	3 198	54 173	14.4	78.2	13.7	224.2	5 813	17 848	42 571	48 417	5.5	13.1	12.2	9.2	16.6
Ocean City, NJ	327	4 178	23 063	16.7	81.9	22.0	176.9	11 488	24 172	57 755	66 582	12.3	8.6	8.3	6.4	10.1
Odessa, TX	526	5 400	36 067	5.9	68.0	12.0	164.4	6 126	15 031	41 077	46 332	5.2	18.7	18.4	16.1	21.8
Ogden-Clearfield, UT	211	3 508	142 213	7.4	88.9	24.6	473.1	4 621	18 917	59 500	65 178	11.8	6.9	7.0	5.3	7.5
Oklahoma City, OK	543	5 830	307 909	12.7	83.5	24.2	1 055.5	5 683	19 291	48 311	56 625	8.0	13.5	13.1	9.9	15.0
Olympia, WA	293	3 876	56 997	12.6	89.5	29.8	249.4	6 604	22 415	56 343	64 757	10.8	8.8	8.8	5.8	9.4
Omaha-Council Bluffs, NE-IA	503	5 244	218 320	20.3	87.8	27.1	866.0	6 635	21 892	56 352	65 999	10.9	8.4	8.1	5.8	8.9
Orlando, FL	817	4 893	432 945	16.9	82.8	24.8	1 548.0	5 621	21 232	55 090	61 877	10.9	10.7	9.8	7.7	11.7
Oshkosh-Neenah, WI	130	2 562	43 417	13.7	86.3	22.8	178.5	7 475	21 706	54 034	63 493	8.0	6.7	6.7	3.8	6.2
Owensboro, KY	231	3 204	27 174	19.2	79.5	15.6	112.7	6 371	18 334	45 943	53 352	5.8	12.8	13.2	10.0	15.2
Oxnard-Thousand Oaks-Ventura, CA	259	2 007	224 449	14.5	80.1	26.9	886.4	6 340	24 600	75 130	81 413	22.8	9.2	7.2	6.4	9.1
Palm Bay-Melbourne-Titusville, FL	821	3 853	112 005	18.0	86.3	23.6	393.2	5 570	21 484	51 028	58 849	9.3	9.5	9.1	6.8	11.2
Panama City-Lynn Haven, FL	748	5 492	36 970	10.0	81.0	17.7	154.3	5 992	18 700	45 929	52 952	6.6	13.0	12.7	9.8	15.9
Parkersburg-Marietta, WV-OH	151	2 129	38 352	12.2	82.2	14.7	197.5	7 253	17 878	43 595	49 708	6.0	13.1	12.9	10.1	16.9
Pascagoula, MS	317	4 249	39 553	7.9	79.6	15.5	148.1	4 992	17 332	46 889	52 059	7.0	13.2	13.5	10.8	15.8
Pensacola-Ferry Pass-Brent, FL	599	3 632	109 544	16.6	83.0	21.5	389.7	5 762	19 054	48 230	54 730	7.7	13.8	13.3	10.8	16.9
Peoria, IL	NA	NA	96 122	19.3	84.7	20.8	423.2	7 125	21 238	53 125	61 640	9.5	9.8	9.2	6.9	11.5
Philadelphia-Camden-Wilmington, PA-NJ-DE-MD	595	2 875	1 572 300	28.4	82.4	27.7	7 589.1	9 061	23 972	62 826	73 318	16.0	10.8	10.7	7.9	11.6
Camden, NJ Div	360	2 698	326 354	18.4	83.6	25.2	2 174.6	10 657	23 852	64 875	73 680	16.8	7.5	7.4	5.5	8.1
Philadelphia, PA Div	672	2 841	1 067 074	32.3	81.7	28.8	4 547.5	8 456	23 931	62 019	73 359	15.7	12.3	12.1	9.0	13.3
Wilmington, DE-MD-NJ Div	585	3 386	178 872	23.7	84.3	26.3	867.0	9 060	24 432	64 028	72 421	16.0	8.4	7.9	5.7	8.6
Phoenix-Mesa-Scottsdale, AZ	575	6 279	876 279	11.6	81.9	25.1	2 911.8	5 202	21 907	58 886	66 068	12.9	12.0	9.9	8.2	12.7
Pine Bluff, AR	753	4 948	27 984	6.8	73.3	14.1	104.0	5 608	15 016	40 824	46 530	5.2	20.0	19.1	15.5	23.5
Pittsburgh, PA	377	2 352	587 732	19.8	84.9	23.4	2 897.5	8 337	20 779	49 929	59 655	9.1	10.8	11.3	7.8	12.7
Pittsfield, MA	359	1 797	34 081	18.8	85.1	26.0	205.6	9 940	21 807	51 859	62 683	9.7	9.5	10.2	6.5	11.6
Pocatello, ID	305	2 661	27 810	7.3	86.4	24.0	88.7	5 617	16 863	46 352	53 646	7.0	14.1	14.2	9.9	14.6
Portland-South Portland-Biddeford, ME	124	2 650	124 290	16.5	88.6	29.2	637.1	8 061	22 648	55 542	65 220	10.3	8.0	8.3	5.6	8.9
Portland-Vancouver-Beaverton, OR-WA	370	4 676	495 479	16.8	87.2	28.8	2 273.7	7 286	23 293	59 409	68 596	13.1	9.5	8.7	6.4	9.7
Port St. Lucie-Fort Pierce, FL	618	3 760	67 807	14.9	80.8	19.7	283.7	6 187	23 072	54 908	62 891	10.3	11.6	9.8	8.0	14.3
Poughkeepsie-Newburgh-Middletown, NY	306	2 031	180 039	21.7	82.8	24.9	1 109.7	10 140	22 653	64 170	72 686	16.6	9.2	8.4	6.4	9.6
Prescott, AZ	422	3 796	37 187	13.2	84.7	21.1	124.5	5 137	19 727	46 398	52 951	7.4	11.9	11.0	7.9	14.5
Providence-New Bedford-Fall River, RI-MA	362	3 093	428 475	22.3	76.3	23.7	2 209.8	8 875	21 448	54 424	64 348	11.3	11.3	12.0	8.5	13.3
Provo-Orem, UT	104	3 419	151 416	29.2	90.7	31.0	372.0	4 447	15 496	56 073	60 212	10.9	12.0	10.7	6.8	7.9
Pueblo, CO	515	4 484	37 564	8.4	81.3	18.3	144.1	5 797	17 163	43 720	50 681	5.8	14.9	14.5	11.2	17.5
Punta Gorda, FL	331	2 936	22 784	12.4	82.1	17.6	102.5	5 968	21 806	47 734	54 910	7.3	8.2	8.1	5.3	10.9
Racine, WI	247	3 483	51 249	21.6	82.9	20.3	238.8	8 053	21 772	57 304	65 189	10.8	8.4	7.6	5.8	9.4
Raleigh-Cary, NC	378	3 918	218 197	16.7	86.3	37.6	833.9	6 394	25 187	64 636	74 768	16.9	8.9	8.5	5.9	8.4
Rapid City, SD	309	3 945	30 782	11.6	87.8	23.3	114.3	5 685	18 668	47 446	54 395	6.7	11.1	10.6	8.5	13.6
Reading, PA	421	2 791	94 301	17.3	78.0	18.5	493.0	7 656	21 232	54 872	63 207	10.2	9.4	8.8	6.3	10.3
Redding, CA	487	2 862	45 010	11.8	83.3	16.6	222.7	7 316	17 738	45 204	51 664	7.2	15.4	13.9	11.3	18.1
Reno-Sparks, NV	556	4 151	90 635	9.6	84.0	23.7	328.1	5 785	24 271	61 398	70 505	12.8	9.9	9.1	6.6	10.3
Richmond, VA	423	3 780	288 134	15.0	81.4	27.6	1 262.6	6 838	23 195	58 775	67 828	12.8	9.4	9.4	6.9	10.3
Riverside-San Bernardino-Ontario, CA	578	3 659	1 021 008	11.0	74.6	16.3	4 582.1	6 547	17 726	54 501	58 815	11.5	15.0	12.8	11.7	16.0
Roanoke, VA	290	2 297	66 525	16.1	79.4	21.0	311.7	7 075	21 006	49 924	58 734	8.4	9.5	9.8	6.9	11.2
Rochester, MN	170	2 335	44 708	14.8	89.9	30.5	211.2	6 875	23 627	60 847	70 662	13.2	6.3	6.4	3.9	5.8
Rochester, NY	258	3 263	296 065	20.7	84.3	27.7	1 828.9	10 342	21 809	55 979	65 330	11.7	10.5	10.2	7.5	12.0
Rockford, IL	NA	NA	83 889	20.8	81.3	18.8	387.7	7 409	21 246	54 874	63 269	10.3	9.3	9.0	6.7	10.2
Rocky Mount, NC	448	5 099	36 855	10.8	71.8	13.9	163.2	6 076	17 142	44 596	51 050	6.7	15.8	15.9	12.5	18.2
Rome, GA	338	3 628	23 133	18.5	71.5	15.8	103.2	6 603	17 808	46 495	52 469	7.3	14.4	14.3	10.8	16.1
Sacramento—Arden-Arcade—Roseville, CA	536	4 209	545 383	11.6	84.6	26.5	2 375.2	7 091	22 302	59 265	67 245	14.0	12.7	10.7	8.7	13.1
Saginaw-Saginaw Township North, MI	971	3 851	58 489	11.9	81.6	15.9	292.1	7 956	19 438	49 950	56 870	9.3	13.9	13.1	11.0	17.4
St. Cloud, MN	175	2 963	53 219	18.6	86.0	21.0	216.7	7 311	19 170	51 898	61 206	8.1	8.4	8.9	4.3	6.0
St. George, UT	226	2 320	26 270	8.6	87.6	21.0	82.1	4 467	15 873	47 254	51 845	6.9	11.2	9.7	7.7	13.0
St. Joseph, MO-KS	203	4 278	30 974	11.3	81.4	16.4	122.1	6 109	17 387	43 977	50 302	5.4	11.5	12.3	8.2	12.5
St. Louis, MO-IL	NA	NA	745 583	23.9	83.1	24.8	3 124.4	7 243	22 473	57 004	66 514	11.9	10.0	9.8	7.5	11.3

1. Data for serious crimes have not been adjusted for underreporting; this may affect comparability between geographic areas and over time. 2. Per 100,000 population estimated by the FBI. 3. All persons 3 years old and over enrolled in nursery school through college. 4. Persons 25 years old and over. 5. Elementary and secondary education expenditures. 6. Based on population enumerated as of April 1, 2000.

Table C. Metropolitan Areas — **Personal Income**

Area Name	Personal income, 2002												
			Per capita[1]					Transfer payments					
									Government payments to individuals				
	Total (mil dol)	Percent change, 2001–2002	Dollars	Rank	Wages and salaries[2] (mil dol)	Proprietor's income (mil dol)	Dividends, interest, and rent (mil dol)	Total (mil dol)	Total (mil dol)	Social Security (mil dol)	Medical payments (mil dol)	Income maintenance (mil dol)	Unemployment insurance (mil dol)
	62	63	64	65	66	67	68	69	70	71	72	73	74
New York-Northern New Jersey-Long Island, NY-NJ-PA	755 390	0.5	40 606	7	517 834	81 833	126 593	111 997	107 228	29 215	58 013	10 685	5 074
Edison, NJ Div	90 194	1.5	40 045	X	55 650	6 313	15 227	10 687	10 136	4 281	4 262	381	717
Nassau-Suffolk, NY Div	121 159	1.0	43 216	X	60 374	8 962	22 954	14 477	13 742	5 454	6 180	922	461
Newark-Union, NJ-PA Div	92 243	1.2	43 259	X	60 633	8 489	15 637	10 260	9 737	3 417	4 497	694	703
New York-Wayne-White Plains, NY-NJ Div	451 793	0.1	39 579	X	341 177	58 070	72 776	76 573	73 613	16 063	43 073	8 688	3 193
Niles-Benton Harbor, MI	4 305	1.9	26 527	196	2 753	269	729	830	791	325	317	93	32
Norwich-New London, CT	9 203	3.7	35 034	28	6 759	535	1 570	1 201	1 140	454	502	76	58
Ocala, FL	6 437	4.4	23 617	312	2 908	347	1 588	1 559	1 492	785	548	106	18
Ocean City, NJ	3 549	5.5	34 790	31	1 479	241	738	738	713	263	328	26	68
Odessa, TX	2 732	2.8	22 336	338	1 869	220	386	531	503	179	219	64	22
Ogden-Clearfield, UT	11 587	4.0	25 147	255	7 150	546	1 799	1 254	1 151	432	390	126	53
Oklahoma City, OK	31 219	2.6	27 843	153	21 206	3 652	5 137	4 270	4 009	1 572	1 531	438	114
Olympia, WA	6 719	4.0	30 872	83	3 776	399	1 069	976	917	342	307	69	71
Omaha-Council Bluffs, NE-IA	26 012	3.0	33 159	44	18 440	2 427	4 588	3 115	2 930	1 099	1 276	245	70
Orlando, FL	48 431	4.5	27 640	157	36 460	3 402	7 900	6 932	6 503	2 626	2 704	575	173
Oshkosh-Neenah, WI	4 681	3.1	29 552	109	3 991	230	857	606	566	269	214	28	33
Owensboro, KY	2 759	0.8	25 010	266	1 801	200	476	530	501	210	203	45	22
Oxnard-Thousand Oaks-Ventura, CA	27 006	3.2	34 450	33	14 924	2 291	4 623	2 774	2 589	996	975	266	169
Palm Bay-Melbourne-Titusville, FL	13 770	3.7	27 786	155	8 298	664	3 025	2 566	2 446	1 163	936	136	52
Panama City-Lynn Haven, FL	3 889	6.4	25 602	231	2 519	215	779	743	707	263	301	63	14
Parkersburg-Marietta, WV-OH	4 054	4.0	24 813	275	2 751	253	639	899	858	339	333	80	21
Pascagoula, MS	3 497	1.4	22 848	329	2 126	156	530	668	629	258	266	54	16
Pensacola-Ferry Pass-Brent, FL	10 544	3.1	24 840	272	6 453	436	2 006	1 889	1 789	683	722	176	22
Peoria, IL	10 685	1.8	29 208	119	7 422	538	2 159	1 603	1 508	709	529	132	81
Philadelphia-Camden-Wilmington, PA-NJ-DE-MD	205 346	3.1	35 701	21	140 050	16 410	33 817	30 178	28 718	10 017	13 443	2 478	1 545
Camden, NJ Div	40 353	4.0	33 298	X	23 872	2 526	5 470	5 779	5 484	2 029	2 481	342	332
Philadelphia, PA Div	142 093	2.9	36 690	X	98 256	12 397	24 466	21 554	20 565	6 891	9 818	1 940	1 092
Wilmington, DE-MD-NJ Div	22 900	2.8	34 325	X	17 922	1 487	3 881	2 844	2 669	1 097	1 144	196	122
Phoenix-Mesa-Scottsdale, AZ	99 387	3.0	28 395	139	70 166	8 970	16 331	12 637	11 829	4 884	4 722	1 018	312
Pine Bluff, AR	2 180	2.0	20 535	348	1 469	86	310	512	484	159	180	71	18
Pittsburgh, PA	78 241	2.4	32 355	54	50 029	8 297	12 793	14 268	13 650	5 340	5 955	917	744
Pittsfield, MA	4 437	4.2	33 245	42	2 561	377	978	848	816	300	394	55	44
Pocatello, ID	1 886	3.0	22 673	332	1 196	151	281	330	312	107	103	27	16
Portland-South Portland-Biddeford, ME	15 849	3.6	31 663	69	10 690	1 053	2 981	2 213	2 099	833	925	181	41
Portland-Vancouver-Beaverton, OR-WA	64 755	1.4	32 115	59	45 398	5 834	11 547	8 200	7 725	2 717	2 769	639	832
Port St. Lucie-Fort Pierce, FL	10 663	4.7	31 581	73	4 084	457	4 103	1 990	1 908	936	748	107	39
Poughkeepsie-Newburgh-Middletown, NY	19 702	2.3	30 568	87	10 719	1 161	2 888	2 924	2 756	1 033	1 226	255	95
Prescott, AZ	3 927	5.8	21 932	339	1 669	250	1 166	857	816	475	224	47	11
Providence-New Bedford-Fall River, RI-MA	49 645	3.3	30 775	85	29 984	3 015	7 795	8 942	8 559	2 815	4 051	744	493
Provo-Orem, UT	7 850	1.9	19 804	355	5 322	687	1 051	1 007	918	337	342	85	51
Pueblo, CO	3 489	3.5	23 754	307	1 928	218	551	941	907	246	499	85	18
Punta Gorda, FL	4 036	6.3	27 146	175	1 435	216	1 439	992	955	521	356	29	7
Racine, WI	5 785	2.2	30 286	95	3 365	258	998	817	769	338	301	58	53
Raleigh-Cary, NC	28 613	1.2	33 305	41	19 760	2 038	4 468	2 675	2 473	956	980	247	168
Rapid City, SD	3 171	4.1	27 495	166	2 113	204	693	455	431	177	166	35	5
Reading, PA	11 262	2.8	29 473	111	7 112	681	1 939	1 830	1 732	732	695	117	111
Redding, CA	4 558	5.7	26 531	195	2 441	529	817	1 053	1 012	355	417	124	42
Reno-Sparks, NV	13 425	2.2	36 706	20	8 614	1 027	3 679	1 257	1 179	515	434	82	71
Richmond, VA	36 061	2.4	32 018	61	26 965	2 191	6 192	4 236	3 965	1 746	1 515	360	120
Riverside-San Bernardino-Ontario, CA	84 301	5.3	23 982	301	44 425	7 294	12 574	14 035	13 199	4 351	5 301	1 970	638
Roanoke, VA	8 467	3.5	29 247	118	6 170	556	1 610	1 304	1 234	555	407	89	44
Rochester, MN	5 741	4.4	33 887	38	4 591	382	993	640	595	247	260	38	28
Rochester, NY	31 716	1.6	30 415	92	22 039	2 130	5 399	5 589	5 315	1 921	2 266	650	244
Rockford, IL	8 861	2.2	27 077	178	6 431	396	1 527	1 327	1 242	574	424	111	100
Rocky Mount, NC	3 548	0.5	24 589	284	2 366	220	565	739	705	236	297	101	34
Rome, GA	2 346	4.5	25 333	241	1 570	129	405	476	449	177	206	40	10
Sacramento—Arden-Arcade—Roseville, CA	59 829	4.1	30 996	82	41 635	5 166	9 629	8 565	8 104	2 503	3 506	1 091	365
Saginaw-Saginaw Township North, MI	5 306	1.0	25 256	246	4 257	237	798	1 105	1 055	418	401	149	56
St. Cloud, MN	4 593	4.9	26 675	192	3 472	273	803	609	564	219	219	39	35
St. George, UT	1 994	6.2	20 052	353	1 113	161	465	382	359	181	118	28	7
St. Joseph, MO-KS	2 940	2.8	24 132	298	1 855	204	485	578	548	220	239	42	16
St. Louis, MO-IL	88 410	2.6	32 396	53	61 985	5 299	17 029	12 203	11 542	4 714	4 800	1 073	396

1. Based on the resident population estimated as of July 1 of the year shown.　　2. Includes other labor income.

Table C. Metropolitan Areas — Earnings, Social Security, and Housing

Area Name	Earnings, 2002									Social Security beneficiaries, December 2003		Supplemental Security Income recipients, December 2003	Housing units, 2003	
			Percent by selected industries											
			Goods related[1]		Service-related and health									
	Total (mil dol)	Farm	Total	Manu- facturing	Infor- mation, profes- sional and technical services	Retail trade	Finance and insur- ance, and real estate	Health services	Govern- ment	Number	Rate[2]		Total	Percent change, 2000–2003
	75	76	77	78	79	80	81	82	83	84	85	86	87	88
New York-Northern New Jersey-Long Island, NY-NJ-PA	599 667	0.0	D	D	18.3	5.2	D	9.3	12.3	2 721 495	146	562 170	7 218 576	1.8
Edison, NJ Div	61 962	0.1	D	11.2	20.1	7.5	9.7	8.7	12.8	387 370	171	23 399	908 811	3.8
Nassau-Suffolk, NY Div	69 336	0.1	D	7.9	13.9	8.0	11.8	12.7	16.0	481 890	172	37 693	996 139	1.6
Newark-Union, NJ-PA Div	69 122	0.1	D	11.6	17.3	6.3	12.1	8.5	13.3	310 330	145	40 328	820 836	2.0
New York-Wayne-White Plains, NY-NJ Div	399 247	0.0	D	D	19.0	4.2	D	8.9	11.4	1 541 905	135	460 750	4 492 790	1.4
Niles-Benton Harbor, MI	3 021	0.3	37.9	33.2	5.0	7.0	4.2	9.2	11.8	32 180	198	4 957	74 788	1.8
Norwich-New London, CT	7 295	0.6	D	18.6	9.7	6.5	3.1	9.2	31.9	44 330	168	3 162	112 883	2.0
Ocala, FL	3 255	1.7	20.0	11.7	6.4	12.5	6.8	12.4	18.0	84 365	301	6 637	133 766	9.1
Ocean City, NJ	1 720	0.3	D	1.9	6.1	11.7	9.2	9.5	26.1	25 265	248	1 498	94 624	3.9
Odessa, TX	2 089	-0.3	28.1	10.3	D	10.8	6.1	8.5	17.3	18 630	152	3 388	50 923	2.9
Ogden-Clearfield, UT	7 696	0.1	D	14.6	D	7.8	4.7	7.7	33.0	48 980	104	3 888	158 926	8.3
Oklahoma City, OK	24 859	0.1	D	13.4	D	7.3	7.2	D	24.3	166 030	147	19 580	489 392	3.7
Olympia, WA	4 176	0.8	10.0	4.0	6.5	9.0	5.4	10.8	42.2	35 160	158	3 628	91 349	5.4
Omaha-Council Bluffs, NE-IA	20 867	0.2	15.1	7.5	D	7.2	10.3	D	15.1	111 240	140	10 561	327 550	5.1
Orlando, FL	39 862	0.5	13.7	6.5	13.6	7.8	9.8	9.3	11.3	284 245	158	37 402	758 716	11.0
Oshkosh-Neenah, WI	4 221	0.1	D	42.3	5.1	4.6	4.6	9.5	11.9	26 385	166	1 818	67 745	4.7
Owensboro, KY	2 000	3.1	D	24.9	D	7.8	5.0	D	16.8	22 325	201	3 618	49 233	6.1
Oxnard-Thousand Oaks-Ventura, CA	17 215	3.3	22.7	16.6	11.1	7.4	10.9	7.2	16.5	101 275	128	14 939	262 015	4.1
Palm Bay-Melbourne-Titusville, FL	8 962	0.1	D	16.7	11.4	8.0	4.4	11.4	17.1	120 435	238	8 589	237 766	7.1
Panama City-Lynn Haven, FL	2 734	0.1	D	5.5	7.2	9.2	5.9	13.1	29.3	29 710	191	3 862	82 260	4.9
Parkersburg-Marietta, WV-OH	3 004	0.2	D	D	D	8.9	D	D	16.1	34 495	211	5 312	74 699	0.9
Pascagoula, MS	2 281	0.1	D	33.7	D	6.5	D	6.6	23.9	27 585	179	3 327	62 456	5.5
Pensacola-Ferry Pass-Brent, FL	6 889	0.3	12.4	5.3	8.8	7.8	4.8	12.5	33.4	78 295	183	10 503	182 112	4.8
Peoria, IL	7 960	0.5	D	25.0	D	6.0	D	D	11.5	68 235	186	6 772	156 844	2.3
Philadelphia-Camden-Wilmington, PA-NJ-DE-MD	156 461	0.2	D	12.1	D	6.5	11.8	11.3	12.5	949 280	164	146 789	2 330 747	2.1
Camden, NJ Div	26 398	0.2	18.9	12.4	11.0	8.5	9.1	11.3	17.5	194 090	158	20 245	470 658	3.2
Philadelphia, PA Div	110 653	0.2	D	12.2	17.4	6.1	12.1	11.7	11.4	650 470	168	116 436	1 591 570	1.7
Wilmington, DE-MD-NJ Div	19 409	0.3	D	11.0	D	5.8	14.3	9.1	11.7	104 720	156	10 108	268 519	3.2
Phoenix-Mesa-Scottsdale, AZ	79 136	0.6	20.5	11.2	D	8.3	12.0	8.4	12.6	498 170	139	48 485	1 478 815	11.1
Pine Bluff, AR	1 555	1.3	D	21.2	D	D	D	D	27.7	18 720	177	4 335	43 899	1.8
Pittsburgh, PA	58 326	0.1	D	13.9	13.1	7.0	D	12.3	11.2	517 005	214	62 748	1 096 538	1.7
Pittsfield, MA	2 938	0.1	23.7	16.8	8.0	8.8	6.9	16.7	11.4	30 225	227	3 770	66 915	0.9
Pocatello, ID	1 347	3.5	D	12.9	D	8.3	5.4	D	26.8	11 245	135	1 545	32 824	2.7
Portland-South Portland-Biddeford, ME	11 743	0.1	D	D	10.1	8.6	10.3	13.0	17.3	89 645	177	8 105	242 861	4.1
Portland-Vancouver-Beaverton, OR-WA	51 232	0.8	D	15.5	11.8	6.6	D	9.0	13.3	268 330	132	30 623	830 930	5.1
Port St. Lucie-Fort Pierce, FL	4 541	0.9	D	5.4	8.8	10.7	8.9	14.3	15.4	93 395	268	6 488	169 631	8.2
Poughkeepsie-Newburgh-Middletown, NY	11 880	0.4	22.6	16.7	8.4	8.4	5.2	12.1	22.7	100 335	153	11 094	238 111	4.0
Prescott, AZ	1 919	0.1	20.2	6.1	6.6	10.8	6.1	11.7	21.6	49 885	270	2 912	90 529	10.8
Providence-New Bedford-Fall River, RI-MA	32 999	0.1	D	16.0	D	7.9	7.9	13.0	16.7	294 285	181	47 941	666 520	1.5
Provo-Orem, UT	6 009	0.5	D	12.5	16.1	8.4	5.4	8.8	14.6	34 980	86	3 291	119 898	11.9
Pueblo, CO	2 145	-0.5	D	10.6	4.4	9.7	6.2	17.3	22.7	28 160	189	4 876	62 798	6.6
Punta Gorda, FL	1 651	0.8	D	2.5	8.0	12.1	6.8	19.4	13.7	52 115	340	1 713	85 109	6.7
Racine, WI	3 623	0.3	D	36.2	5.8	6.4	3.6	11.4	12.8	32 535	169	3 644	76 785	2.8
Raleigh-Cary, NC	21 798	0.3	D	9.9	D	7.5	8.2	6.6	17.1	101 005	114	13 160	371 090	12.6
Rapid City, SD	2 318	-0.2	15.1	7.1	6.4	9.0	6.8	D	26.3	19 425	167	1 872	49 876	5.2
Reading, PA	7 793	0.9	31.2	24.4	8.5	7.7	6.8	10.0	11.3	71 085	184	6 824	155 828	3.7
Redding, CA	2 970	0.4	D	5.1	7.5	10.8	5.5	16.1	20.2	38 770	221	8 991	72 193	4.9
Reno-Sparks, NV	9 641	0.1	D	8.1	D	7.7	D	D	14.7	53 520	143	4 660	160 126	10.0
Richmond, VA	29 156	0.2	D	D	10.9	0.0	D	D	19.4	176 625	155	21 416	475 952	5.1
Riverside-San Bernardino-Ontario, CA	51 719	0.7	21.0	10.6	6.0	9.4	7.4	9.5	21.5	463 525	127	106 429	1 267 866	6.9
Roanoke, VA	6 726	0.2	D	D	D	8.1	8.6	D	13.7	58 215	200	6 104	133 807	3.2
Rochester, MN	4 973	0.7	D	20.2	5.2	5.8	3.5	D	9.3	25 380	147	1 921	71 039	9.1
Rochester, NY	24 170	0.4	D	24.1	D	6.4	5.4	D	14.2	185 275	178	24 383	435 359	1.9
Rockford, IL	6 827	0.3	D	30.8	D	6.8	6.6	D	10.6	55 600	168	5 872	134 758	3.8
Rocky Mount, NC	2 585	1.4	D	24.3	6.0	7.8	7.7	D	16.7	27 480	190	5 987	63 852	4.6
Rome, GA	1 699	0.3	D	26.7	5.9	7.1	4.6	16.5	14.2	18 285	196	2 918	38 009	3.8
Sacramento—Arden-Arcade—Roseville, CA	46 801	0.4	16.1	7.2	11.7	7.5	9.1	8.1	28.7	267 360	135	66 130	772 656	8.1
Saginaw-Saginaw Township North, MI	4 494	0.2	D	31.6	5.8	7.5	5.7	13.3	12.6	40 415	193	7 107	87 439	2.3
St. Cloud, MN	3 746	0.9	27.4	19.3	D	9.9	6.1	D	15.4	25 110	144	2 105	68 397	7.3
St. George, UT	1 273	-0.1	D	6.0	6.4	13.1	7.7	12.6	14.8	19 550	188	779	42 129	15.5
St. Joseph, MO-KS	2 060	0.5	D	D	D	8.2	6.1	D	17.5	23 125	188	2 396	51 293	1.4
St. Louis, MO-IL	67 284	0.1	D	D	D	6.2	D	D	12.8	461 890	169	51 485	1 169 408	3.2

1. Covers mining, construction, and manufacturing.   2. Per 1,000 resident population estimated as of July 1 of the year shown.

Table C. Metropolitan Areas — Housing, Labor Force, and Employment

Area Name	Housing units, 2000								Civilian labor force, 2003				Civilian employment,[5] 2000		
	Occupied units										Unemployment			Percent	
			Owner-occupied			Renter-occupied									
				Owner cost is 35 percent or more of income											
	Total	Percent	Mean value[1]	With a mortgage	Without a mortgage	Mean rent[2]	Rent is 35 percent or more of income	Sub-standard units[3] (percent)	Total	Percent change, 2002–2003	Total	Rate[4]	Total	Management, professional, and related occupations	Production, transportation, and material moving occupations
	89	90	91	92	93	94	95	96	97	98	99	100	101	102	103
New York-Northern New Jersey-Long Island, NY-NJ-PA	6 676 963	50.7	261 485	26.1	16.0	806	33.5	10.1	9 095 043	-0.3	587 341	6.5	8 145 601	38.4	10.7
Edison, NJ Div	799 437	74.5	211 541	22.2	14.7	862	30.9	4.1	1 169 126	0.2	61 288	5.2	1 032 807	40.5	10.6
Nassau-Suffolk, NY Div	916 686	80.0	266 806	27.6	17.5	998	35.7	3.8	1 485 799	0.7	62 348	4.2	1 314 250	38.2	9.3
Newark-Union, NJ-PA Div	751 513	62.1	261 983	22.5	15.6	752	30.7	5.9	1 104 979	0.8	65 561	5.9	981 370	39.4	11.9
New York-Wayne-White Plains, NY-NJ Div	4 209 327	37.8	286 972	29.0	15.8	795	33.8	13.3	5 335 139	-0.9	398 144	7.5	4 817 174	37.9	10.9
Niles-Benton Harbor, MI	63 569	72.2	120 727	15.6	6.6	491	30.4	3.4	80 294	1.6	5 873	7.3	76 557	29.3	21.3
Norwich-New London, CT	99 835	66.7	173 185	17.0	8.4	651	24.9	2.2	146 905	2.2	7 069	4.8	125 194	35.6	10.8
Ocala, FL	106 755	79.8	99 169	20.9	5.2	559	32.2	3.5	105 823	2.1	4 731	4.5	98 248	26.4	14.5
Ocean City, NJ	42 148	74.3	184 082	26.6	16.2	671	35.1	2.0	46 070	2.7	4 575	9.9	44 503	31.5	8.0
Odessa, TX	43 846	68.6	58 446	15.2	8.2	443	28.1	9.0	63 234	3.8	4 482	7.1	50 029	23.8	16.4
Ogden-Clearfield, UT	138 945	76.5	166 098	17.7	3.3	604	27.8	4.6	238 361	1.9	14 140	5.9	206 126	32.4	14.0
Oklahoma City, OK	429 743	65.2	95 975	14.9	6.0	520	30.0	4.4	577 906	0.0	28 977	5.0	517 986	32.1	13.1
Olympia, WA	81 625	66.6	169 788	18.4	6.9	682	32.0	4.0	110 328	5.1	6 327	5.7	100 487	37.4	10.0
Omaha-Council Bluffs, NE-IA	294 502	66.8	120 031	12.8	6.0	573	25.2	3.1	441 647	0.5	19 587	4.4	393 280	34.6	12.6
Orlando, FL	625 248	66.3	137 919	20.5	6.6	720	33.0	6.0	974 118	1.4	47 792	4.9	801 512	32.6	10.2
Oshkosh-Neenah, WI	61 157	68.0	121 099	12.1	6.6	521	22.2	2.1	101 205	1.1	5 053	5.0	82 666	29.4	22.4
Owensboro, KY	43 232	72.1	93 610	12.1	5.2	421	26.3	2.5	56 418	0.8	3 698	6.6	51 121	27.0	21.4
Oxnard-Thousand Oaks-Ventura, CA	243 234	67.6	297 826	26.9	6.5	943	32.8	12.7	430 313	1.4	22 655	5.3	348 338	36.5	11.5
Palm Bay-Melbourne-Titusville, FL	198 195	74.6	119 262	19.2	5.0	636	32.3	2.8	224 783	0.6	11 069	4.9	207 366	34.9	10.8
Panama City-Lynn Haven, FL	59 597	68.6	118 233	18.0	5.3	560	30.4	3.6	71 864	2.4	3 887	5.4	64 883	28.5	10.8
Parkersburg-Marietta, WV-OH	66 583	75.1	91 457	13.8	4.8	425	30.9	1.7	82 080	-0.6	5 341	6.5	72 176	27.8	19.4
Pascagoula, MS	54 418	76.0	96 085	15.3	8.9	527	28.6	5.0	77 390	2.6	4 681	6.0	63 887	27.2	16.4
Pensacola-Ferry Pass-Brent, FL	154 842	71.0	115 431	19.3	6.3	571	33.6	3.5	180 900	1.4	7 348	4.1	170 127	30.7	11.7
Peoria, IL	143 607	72.7	104 325	12.7	5.4	496	26.6	1.8	189 940	-0.8	10 551	5.6	175 149	32.4	16.1
Philadelphia-Camden-Wilmington, PA-NJ-DE-MD	2 134 404	70.0	148 160	19.8	12.2	691	32.4	3.5	3 600 361	-0.9	211 555	5.9	2 645 623	37.7	11.5
Camden, NJ Div	430 832	74.7	140 713	20.3	14.5	703	31.3	3.3	632 197	1.1	34 256	5.4	566 027	36.2	12.2
Philadelphia, PA Div	1 459 119	68.4	149 734	20.4	12.4	688	33.3	3.6	2 629 431	-1.4	159 998	6.1	1 757 963	38.4	11.1
Wilmington, DE-MD-NJ Div	244 453	71.0	153 214	16.2	6.7	689	28.6	2.9	338 733	-0.8	17 301	5.1	321 633	36.6	12.4
Phoenix-Mesa-Scottsdale, AZ	1 194 250	68.0	164 191	18.9	6.0	707	32.1	8.8	1 806 556	0.9	90 245	5.0	1 488 583	33.4	11.1
Pine Bluff, AR	38 093	68.6	68 915	16.3	10.2	462	33.9	5.3	45 172	-1.2	4 038	8.9	41 478	26.7	22.3
Pittsburgh, PA	995 505	71.5	105 450	18.4	8.6	510	30.3	1.4	1 216 114	-2.2	68 016	5.6	1 104 971	33.6	13.7
Pittsfield, MA	56 006	66.9	143 853	17.9	8.4	522	29.3	1.2	68 651	-0.2	3 493	5.1	65 253	35.1	11.9
Pocatello, ID	29 752	71.0	104 271	14.4	6.0	457	32.1	4.6	43 811	-0.6	2 406	5.5	38 966	31.9	13.8
Portland-South Portland-Biddeford, ME	196 669	69.4	156 707	17.7	9.7	611	29.6	1.6	267 973	1.6	10 227	3.8	251 373	35.4	13.4
Portland-Vancouver-Beaverton, OR-WA	745 531	62.9	203 484	21.3	7.0	715	31.6	5.3	1 099 740	0.0	93 083	8.5	971 454	35.2	14.3
Port St. Lucie-Fort Pierce, FL	132 221	78.8	147 065	23.7	7.1	654	34.5	4.1	145 745	3.0	9 612	6.6	128 896	28.3	10.7
Poughkeepsie-Newburgh-Middletown, NY	214 324	67.9	168 348	20.5	11.0	725	33.6	3.7	300 357	1.4	12 962	4.3	282 537	35.6	11.2
Prescott, AZ	70 171	73.4	170 962	26.4	4.4	647	38.5	4.7	81 771	2.7	2 689	3.3	68 098	28.3	11.6
Providence-New Bedford-Fall River, RI-MA	613 835	60.6	165 860	18.5	11.1	557	29.2	3.0	852 185	2.4	49 608	5.8	759 640	32.8	16.1
Provo-Orem, UT	102 393	67.1	186 262	21.1	4.6	632	30.8	8.2	185 764	1.5	8 707	4.7	169 528	36.2	11.6
Pueblo, CO	54 579	70.4	111 798	21.7	6.3	517	36.9	4.5	63 232	2.2	4 599	7.3	59 715	28.2	13.3
Punta Gorda, FL	63 864	83.7	124 010	26.6	7.1	667	31.6	1.9	52 708	-3.2	2 297	4.4	50 690	27.2	9.3
Racine, WI	70 819	70.6	128 537	13.9	6.6	559	28.6	3.1	94 552	1.8	7 681	8.1	91 021	30.7	21.3
Raleigh-Cary, NC	306 478	67.7	181 226	15.3	7.1	714	29.2	3.6	490 043	2.1	23 371	4.8	425 793	43.6	9.8
Rapid City, SD	43 446	66.6	109 206	13.9	5.0	505	28.2	3.3	65 412	1.9	2 182	3.3	55 556	30.9	12.6
Reading, PA	141 570	74.0	117 313	17.1	8.6	565	28.0	2.8	184 361	-3.7	11 479	6.2	180 881	29.3	21.3
Redding, CA	63 426	66.1	140 465	27.4	6.9	598	38.7	5.3	81 927	2.4	6 389	7.8	65 828	30.4	12.3
Reno-Sparks, NV	133 546	59.5	208 095	22.8	6.1	721	31.1	8.8	201 789	0.2	8 848	4.4	173 505	29.5	12.1
Richmond, VA	425 100	68.8	138 023	15.7	6.2	626	29.3	2.9	587 526	-0.2	25 341	4.3	540 913	35.8	12.5
Riverside-San Bernardino-Ontario, CA	1 034 812	66.6	163 483	26.2	7.8	692	37.2	14.0	1 688 311	3.0	99 621	5.9	1 264 128	28.0	15.7
Roanoke, VA	119 366	70.7	125 904	16.8	4.5	503	25.5	2.0	155 899	-1.4	5 922	3.8	141 911	30.5	16.1
Rochester, MN	62 504	77.7	131 742	9.8	3.6	573	28.1	2.7	106 572	0.4	4 627	4.3	87 676	41.5	12.1
Rochester, NY	397 303	67.9	114 058	16.5	9.8	620	36.5	2.1	545 692	-0.3	31 651	5.8	497 240	37.6	15.1
Rockford, IL	122 577	71.1	109 635	15.4	6.6	543	25.9	3.3	169 163	-0.8	14 579	8.6	155 101	29.1	22.5
Rocky Mount, NC	54 036	66.3	105 837	19.5	10.1	490	31.0	5.8	70 398	-0.8	6 320	9.0	62 329	25.6	23.2
Rome, GA	34 028	66.8	103 133	18.2	6.9	490	27.4	4.6	48 176	4.3	2 090	4.3	40 403	27.1	22.7
Sacramento-Arden-Arcade-Roseville, CA	665 298	61.3	192 281	23.1	6.3	708	34.7	8.2	972 689	2.2	52 549	5.4	815 041	37.3	9.8
Saginaw-Saginaw Township North, MI	80 430	73.8	97 255	13.7	6.5	528	34.6	3.4	100 157	1.5	9 393	9.4	91 113	27.3	18.0
St. Cloud, MN	60 669	72.3	113 132	11.7	5.2	482	24.1	2.4	106 414	-0.1	5 290	5.0	91 416	29.3	19.3
St. George, UT	29 939	74.0	164 691	27.6	3.9	629	32.8	6.9	47 927	6.4	2 110	4.4	35 646	26.9	13.2
St. Joseph, MO-KS	46 531	70.1	86 025	13.2	4.8	455	27.5	2.0	61 038	-0.7	3 658	6.0	55 078	28.0	18.2
St. Louis, MO-IL	1 048 279	71.7	128 742	14.0	5.8	554	28.9	2.7	1 444 122	1.9	86 057	6.0	1 294 013	34.1	14.0

1. Specified owner-occupied units.   2. Specified renter-occupied units.   3. Overcrowded or lacking complete plumbing facilities.   4. Percent of civilian labor force.   5. Persons 16 years old and over.

Table C. Metropolitan Areas — Nonfarm Employment and Agriculture

Area Name	Private nonfarm establishments, employment and payroll, 2001									Agriculture, 2002			
		Employment						Annual payroll		Farms			
											Percent with—		Farm operators whose principal occupation is farming (percent)
	Number of establishments	Total	Health care and social assistance	Manufacturing	Retail trade	Finance and insurance	Professional, scientific, and technical services	Total (mil dol)	Average per employee (dollars)	Number	Less than 50 acres	500 acres and over	
	104	105	106	107	108	109	110	111	112	113	114	115	116
New York-Northern New Jersey-Long Island, NY-NJ-PA	516 366	7 693 970	1 127 886	574 736	794 477	664 242	664 909	391 063	50 827	5 970	D	D	D
Edison, NJ Div	60 168	914 528	105 680	87 201	119 527	50 878	96 586	39 321	42 996	1 826	78.3	3.2	52.8
Nassau-Suffolk, NY Div	91 431	1 100 827	167 457	101 075	157 531	69 373	81 212	41 433	37 638	716	77.4	1.4	61.3
Newark-Union, NJ-PA Div	60 239	962 004	116 980	106 377	97 782	51 432	78 729	45 481	47 277	3 034	69.5	2.1	47.1
New York-Wayne-White Plains, NY-NJ Div	304 528	4 716 611	737 769	280 083	419 637	492 559	408 382	264 828	56 148	394	D	D	D
Niles-Benton Harbor, MI	3 956	59 622	7 936	15 058	7 663	1 360	1 554	1 813	30 408	1 093	53.4	7.6	62.4
Norwich-New London, CT	5 739	105 598	14 293	18 266	13 418	2 113	5 861	3 681	34 859	677	56.0	2.4	50.7
Ocala, FL	5 521	71 560	11 453	8 888	14 739	2 374	2 462	1 748	24 427	2 930	75.4	3.1	61.0
Ocean City, NJ	4 012	26 099	3 716	915	5 452	917	1 239	736	28 200	197	77.2	1.0	64.0
Odessa, TX	2 983	40 725	6 006	3 827	6 449	989	1 110	1 115	27 379	287	65.9	16.4	46.7
Ogden-Clearfield, UT	9 230	131 178	17 040	23 267	23 117	5 063	7 350	3 360	25 614	1 849	74.6	4.0	45.0
Oklahoma City, OK	29 877	438 014	61 755	47 899	59 183	21 847	22 239	11 910	27 191	10 422	33.0	12.2	52.3
Olympia, WA	5 068	53 827	9 665	3 166	9 654	2 533	3 303	1 517	28 183	1 155	76.0	2.1	50.6
Omaha-Council Bluffs, NE-IA	20 454	374 547	48 449	34 656	49 614	31 798	21 970	11 953	31 913	5 857	27.0	28.5	67.2
Orlando, FL	45 521	818 126	75 971	47 046	106 193	38 115	47 082	24 281	29 679	3 594	74.7	4.8	47.7
Oshkosh-Neenah, WI	3 719	80 820	9 972	26 401	8 721	2 756	2 045	2 708	33 507	963	32.6	8.1	60.5
Owensboro, KY	2 680	44 259	6 773	9 419	6 581	1 737	1 362	1 197	27 045	1 893	37.4	11.1	57.6
Oxnard-Thousand Oaks-Ventura, CA	17 510	249 865	23 633	35 728	34 892	17 372	15 873	8 550	34 218	2 318	73.6	4.4	57.3
Palm Bay-Melbourne-Titusville, FL	11 484	164 500	23 839	18 049	26 086	4 589	14 872	5 003	30 413	555	73.5	7.6	53.3
Panama City-Lynn Haven, FL	4 179	52 887	7 902	3 165	9 851	2 836	2 320	1 235	23 352	116	73.3	2.6	59.5
Parkersburg-Marietta, WV-OH	4 040	62 264	9 478	14 040	9 792	2 308	1 623	1 674	26 886	2 074	25.5	3.2	50.5
Pascagoula, MS	2 639	43 568	5 173	14 074	6 253	995	2 476	1 279	29 356	1 105	59.7	2.2	45.6
Pensacola-Ferry Pass-Brent, FL	8 582	126 927	20 967	7 464	19 428	4 377	6 234	3 243	25 550	1 179	62.0	6.0	53.4
Peoria, IL	8 759	158 989	24 074	22 913	19 715	6 689	6 359	5 204	32 732	3 518	25.7	24.0	66.3
Philadelphia-Camden-Wilmington, PA-NJ-DE-MD	143 378	2 550 674	362 175	259 260	305 709	221 397	201 932	99 647	39 067	7 042	64.2	4.4	55.1
Camden, NJ Div	28 681	432 974	60 567	51 440	64 367	28 192	28 662	14 812	34 210	1 814	70.5	4.8	55.1
Philadelphia, PA Div	95 317	1 786 340	264 156	175 271	204 886	151 833	156 052	70 958	39 723	3 649	64.4	2.7	55.4
Wilmington, DE-MD-NJ Div	19 380	331 360	37 452	32 549	36 456	41 372	17 218	13 877	41 879	1 579	56.7	7.8	54.4
Phoenix-Mesa-Scottsdale, AZ	75 135	1 402 848	126 219	144 713	175 333	97 687	92 935	46 119	32 875	2 797	70.5	13.1	59.4
Pine Bluff, AR	1 871	28 983	4 917	8 109	4 765	895	673	724	24 980	913	25.7	23.2	68.6
Pittsburgh, PA	60 671	1 055 049	162 816	119 198	133 032	57 399	68 778	34 894	33 073	7 859	37.8	2.9	48.1
Pittsfield, MA	4 414	57 538	10 120	7 781	8 787	2 514	2 027	1 717	29 841	401	43.9	10.2	58.1
Pocatello, ID	2 017	27 250	3 813	4 050	4 915	1 488	1 577	648	23 780	1 364	49.0	23.7	48.5
Portland-South Portland-Biddeford, ME	16 404	218 107	33 539	26 142	32 539	14 968	12 408	6 842	31 370	1 439	55.8	2.9	45.5
Portland-Vancouver-Beaverton, OR-WA	56 943	878 379	91 910	122 394	109 480	43 505	51 745	31 786	36 187	12 188	78.2	2.0	48.1
Port St. Lucie-Fort Pierce, FL	8 214	89 472	14 149	5 195	17 867	3 221	4 702	2 318	25 908	895	58.9	15.3	56.3
Poughkeepsie-Newburgh-Middletown, NY	15 082	194 292	32 889	29 433	32 634	7 042	8 820	6 205	31 936	1 373	42.8	7.8	63.0
Prescott, AZ	5 127	46 530	6 472	3 750	8 126	1 239	1 677	1 063	22 845	575	66.1	15.0	52.3
Providence-New Bedford-Fall River, RI-MA	41 902	597 959	100 715	110 696	88 776	30 258	25 132	18 589	31 087	1 482	62.8	1.2	51.6
Provo-Orem, UT	7 792	143 146	13 294	16 519	18 930	3 072	11 618	3 609	25 212	2 282	69.3	8.2	45.0
Pueblo, CO	3 194	44 636	9 894	4 026	7 048	1 738	1 604	1 120	25 092	801	38.2	27.3	56.7
Punta Gorda, FL	3 149	29 956	7 007	611	7 214	1 166	1 424	711	23 735	284	60.9	13.4	45.1
Racine, WI	4 155	71 225	9 860	18 477	9 913	1 719	2 316	2 361	33 148	631	53.2	8.9	57.2
Raleigh-Cary, NC	24 129	392 240	40 571	32 748	51 001	19 244	33 407	13 158	33 546	2 564	46.8	6.9	61.2
Rapid City, SD	3 826	47 408	8 452	4 843	7 545	2 796	1 616	1 160	24 468	1 591	15.2	51.1	69.8
Reading, PA	8 210	151 116	17 147	39 293	20 413	8 360	7 470	4 701	31 109	1 791	48.4	4.5	63.5
Redding, CA	4 510	47 871	9 847	3 576	8 341	1 313	2 220	1 274	26 613	1 126	64.1	10.6	52.4
Reno-Sparks, NV	11 237	174 611	17 501	11 787	21 910	6 331	8 515	5 342	30 594	338	64.8	13.9	41.4
Richmond, VA	28 884	508 499	58 385	55 373	63 909	54 666	25 516	16 885	33 206	4 261	35.4	9.9	54.5
Riverside-San Bernardino-Ontario, CA	54 585	877 495	104 435	123 999	131 495	25 589	25 056	24 427	27 837	4 572	80.1	4.3	53.2
Roanoke, VA	8 198	143 818	19 149	19 962	22 196	12 337	5 096	3 889	27 041	2 192	31.6	6.2	53.1
Rochester, MN	4 162	89 722	30 639	16 532	11 941	2 081	2 116	3 067	34 183	3 091	31.4	14.4	61.5
Rochester, NY	23 103	438 702	63 130	84 369	57 704	15 123	22 950	14 885	33 930	3 736	40.7	10.7	60.5
Rockford, IL	7 755	144 720	18 359	40 646	18 181	5 989	5 046	4 535	31 336	1 171	40.2	16.7	64.2
Rocky Mount, NC	3 228	57 880	7 350	14 707	7 458	2 607	1 340	1 590	27 471	759	37.4	20.8	67.6
Rome, GA	2 026	36 749	6 806	7 953	4 842	1 105	961	925	25 171	663	41.2	4.7	45.6
Sacramento—Arden-Arcade—Roseville, CA	41 105	645 016	76 048	44 035	88 431	47 988	39 058	21 777	33 762	5 127	69.3	8.1	58.4
Saginaw-Saginaw Township North, MI	4 905	91 399	15 479	19 306	14 202	2 859	3 172	2 982	32 626	1 359	38.8	12.1	58.9
St. Cloud, MN	4 795	83 069	11 828	16 750	14 120	2 622	2 008	2 243	27 002	4 117	24.5	8.2	65.5
St. George, UT	2 633	28 038	3 845	2 398	5 870	776	918	615	21 935	481	53.2	14.3	46.6
St. Joseph, MO-KS	2 923	42 332	6 648	7 051	6 327	2 370	918	1 085	25 631	2 997	23.5	16.2	57.0
St. Louis, MO-IL	68 047	1 238 792	158 989	148 068	152 115	70 484	73 489	42 523	34 326	12 303	31.3	13.5	56.9

Table C. Metropolitan Areas — Agriculture

Area Name	Land in farms Acreage (1,000)	Land in farms Percent change, 1997–2002	Acres Average size of farm	Acres Total irrigated (1,000)	Acres Total cropland (1,000)	Value of land and buildings (dollars) Average per farm	Value of land and buildings (dollars) Average per acre	Value of machinery and equipment average per farm (dollars)	Value of products sold Total (mil dol)	Value of products sold Average per farm (dollars)	Percent from — Crops	Percent from — Livestock and poultry products	Percent of farms with sales of — $10,000 or more	Percent of farms with sales of — $100,000 or more	Government payments Total ($1,000)	Government payments Percent of farms
	117	118	119	120	121	122	123	124	125	126	127	128	129	130	131	132
New York-Northern New Jersey-Long Island, NY-NJ-PA	D	D	D	D	D	D	D	D	D	D	D	D	29.5	9.7	D	D
Edison, NJ Div	117	-19.3	64	10	77	821 105	15 594	60 510	130	71 219	85.5	14.5	31.4	9.6	D	D
Nassau-Suffolk, NY Div	35	0.0	49	16	27	889 364	18 522	196 758	209	292 504	D	D	58.9	27.9	D	D
Newark-Union, NJ-PA Div	212	D	70	3	129	766 427	11 098	36 250	108	35 658	85.4	14.6	19.9	4.9	D	D
New York-Wayne-White Plains, NY-NJ Div	D	D	D	D	D	D	D	D	D	D	D	D	40.6	14.2	D	D
Niles-Benton Harbor, MI	174	0.0	159	19	143	604 737	3 898	89 999	97	88 487	87.4	12.6	48.9	15.6	3 016	30.2
Norwich-New London, CT	59	-13.2	87	1	27	558 698	6 889	44 033	123	181 516	58.9	41.1	25.7	9.2	647	7.1
Ocala, FL	271	1.9	92	6	87	443 694	4 992	27 589	88	29 874	20.9	79.1	19.6	4.3	362	1.1
Ocean City, NJ	10	0.0	51	2	5	341 959	7 049	31 825	11	57 112	95.6	4.4	24.9	8.1	D	D
Odessa, TX	504	9.1	1 755	1	4	261 924	141	18 504	2	6 526	14.9	85.1	13.9	1.4	236	5.9
Ogden-Clearfield, UT	D	D	D	63	85	455 385	D	44 009	64	34 871	52.7	47.3	24.4	6.7	1 031	10.0
Oklahoma City, OK	2 586	4.4	248	19	1 242	256 583	1 059	37 736	317	30 378	23.8	76.2	32.7	5.6	9 352	22.7
Olympia, WA	74	32.1	64	7	30	400 151	8 458	37 299	115	99 286	43.0	57.0	20.6	6.1	243	2.8
Omaha-Council Bluffs, NE-IA	2 436	4.5	416	172	2 133	891 612	2 113	107 949	688	117 505	62.0	38.0	62.1	27.5	33 320	62.1
Orlando, FL	1 008	0.0	280	56	179	726 108	2 605	37 882	505	140 489	92.6	7.4	42.2	14.2	334	1.2
Oshkosh-Neenah, WI	170	1.8	177	0	138	418 923	2 519	73 577	58	60 541	33.4	66.6	41.3	14.6	2 920	53.0
Owensboro, KY	452	0.4	239	2	358	455 369	1 835	63 608	137	72 360	52.5	47.5	40.3	13.9	4 804	37.0
Oxnard-Thousand Oaks-Ventura, CA	332	-4.0	143	102	124	1 441 670	8 839	66 436	1 019	439 544	98.7	1.3	61.0	31.4	1 217	4.5
Palm Bay-Melbourne-Titusville, FL	188	-32.1	338	25	23	783 045	2 385	42 237	42	75 962	83.7	16.3	39.8	9.4	52	1.1
Panama City-Lynn Haven, FL	11	57.1	94	0	3	243 482	2 626	20 307	2	18 595	87.2	12.7	15.5	3.4	D	D
Parkersburg-Marietta, WV-OH	282	4.1	136	D	113	218 111	1 586	43 670	26	12 743	42.7	57.2	18.0	2.6	D	D
Pascagoula, MS	106	43.2	96	1	42	270 112	3 356	23 601	19	17 594	67.3	32.7	18.6	2.5	409	8.3
Pensacola-Ferry Pass-Brent, FL	148	3.5	126	8	91	365 033	2 533	33 964	37	31 105	80.5	19.5	23.5	6.3	4 896	23.5
Peoria, IL	1 269	-2.6	361	D	1 147	1 036 861	2 816	107 973	397	112 952	81.9	18.1	66.3	30.3	17 645	63.0
Philadelphia-Camden-Wilmington, PA-NJ-DE-MD	D	D	D	D	523	813 476	D	62 517	813	115 414	77.3	22.7	35.3	15.6	D	D
Camden, NJ Div	172	0.6	95	27	112	751 498	7 854	57 904	163	89 802	91.1	8.9	32.7	14.2	D	D
Philadelphia, PA Div	D	D	D	D	218	817 885	D	54 612	481	131 916	77.0	23.0	36.8	17.4	D	D
Wilmington, DE-MD-NJ Div	245	-3.9	155	23	194	874 489	5 282	86 084	168	106 700	64.8	35.2	34.7	13.1	D	D
Phoenix-Mesa-Scottsdale, AZ	1 789	-11.1	640	454	541	1 189 151	1 860	109 447	1 165	416 497	48.8	51.2	35.4	21.1	19 873	12.2
Pine Bluff, AR	511	1.0	559	290	425	709 665	1 257	125 386	223	244 042	45.4	54.6	52.8	31.9	16 124	29.8
Pittsburgh, PA	908	19.3	116	3	554	317 974	2 668	45 285	186	23 664	54.9	45.1	23.0	4.7	4 634	15.9
Pittsfield, MA	69	9.5	171	0	26	783 518	5 639	58 867	22	54 177	44.7	55.3	36.9	11.7	330	6.2
Pocatello, ID	782	6.7	574	169	569	484 281	870	86 887	144	105 383	72.0	28.0	26.0	10.1	12 388	36.9
Portland-South Portland-Biddeford, ME	132	4.8	92	2	50	394 113	3 742	45 266	41	28 224	D	D	25.8	7.0	645	7.7
Portland-Vancouver-Beaverton, OR-WA	715	6.1	59	93	439	459 348	7 991	45 849	935	76 685	83.6	16.4	26.2	7.4	2 809	4.9
Port St. Lucie-Fort Pierce, FL	428	4.1	478	158	217	1 384 486	2 933	55 697	256	285 544	82.9	17.1	52.4	21.7	793	2.2
Poughkeepsie-Newburgh-Middletown, NY	220	8.9	160	6	130	714 215	5 334	110 026	98	71 331	63.3	36.7	45.3	14.1	2 436	16.1
Prescott, AZ	720	-6.7	1 253	10	29	737 949	621	37 030	37	64 960	D	D	25.6	7.3	272	4.5
Providence-New Bedford-Fall River, RI-MA	97	5.4	66	6	39	709 616	10 532	49 086	85	57 292	81.8	18.2	39.3	11.9	D	D
Provo-Orem, UT	613	-5.8	269	107	206	558 754	1 808	41 848	129	56 624	37.1	62.9	25.7	7.4	2 777	15.1
Pueblo, CO	774	-6.0	967	25	118	626 878	491	64 567	42	52 000	26.6	73.4	37.5	8.4	1 610	23.6
Punta Gorda, FL	192	-33.8	674	25	42	1 171 466	1 726	50 286	48	170 077	88.3	11.7	38.0	14.1	D	D
Racine, WI	124	0.8	197	5	109	800 951	4 275	74 494	73	115 949	50.9	49.1	43.6	15.7	1 726	35.2
Raleigh-Cary, NC	415	-10.0	162	15	234	624 880	3 996	60 047	242	94 416	55.8	44.2	36.9	15.0	3 446	26.6
Rapid City, SD	3 439	10.3	2 161	18	870	659 746	297	73 255	110	68 832	15.4	84.6	55.9	19.5	5 307	38.2
Reading, PA	216	-2.7	120	2	173	661 305	5 527	63 509	287	160 233	41.8	58.2	50.1	24.5	3 805	22.8
Redding, CA	334	5.4	296	46	71	519 775	1 733	22 962	22	19 496	38.0	62.0	27.0	4.4	268	7.3
Reno-Sparks, NV	802	D	2 373	D	50	1 728 520	599	111 529	D	D	55.7	44.3	22.2	8.0	222	5.9
Richmond, VA	949	NA	223	D	485	584 193	2 501	48 124	238	55 937	D	D	29.3	9.1	9 240	28.1
Riverside-San Bernardino-Ontario, CA	1 086	-24.2	237	239	330	974 177	3 559	66 163	1 626	355 669	48.4	51.6	45.1	19.0	3 508	3.6
Roanoke, VA	349	NA	159	2	156	384 721	2 399	40 839	54	24 600	19.7	80.3	28.6	5.5	2 255	20.3
Rochester, MN	813	1.1	263	D	663	560 844	2 139	96 252	309	99 870	49.3	50.7	54.5	23.3	13 522	56.2
Rochester, NY	809	1.5	217	12	622	378 850	1 754	106 560	398	106 489	61.7	38.3	43.8	17.7	13 615	32.4
Rockford, IL	338	0.3	289	3	310	916 736	3 159	88 066	110	93 954	75.4	24.6	54.9	23.7	5 789	54.7
Rocky Mount, NC	324	-6.6	427	20	210	999 359	2 286	114 210	206	271 831	46.3	53.7	52.6	34.1	4 816	42.2
Rome, GA	91	9.6	138	1	31	358 778	2 650	28 802	29	43 163	7.9	92.1	17.5	4.2	317	14.2
Sacramento—Arden-Arcade—Roseville, CA	1 113	2.4	217	466	597	874 807	3 940	61 289	608	118 510	83.5	16.5	32.4	13.0	11 894	9.4
Saginaw-Saginaw Township North, MI	325	9.1	239	3	287	469 112	2 068	82 227	91	67 132	88.2	11.8	48.9	14.6	4 927	50.3
St. Cloud, MN	877	6.7	213	52	674	367 440	1 678	74 895	432	104 925	20.6	79.4	56.0	23.7	14 454	50.0
St. George, UT	217	33.1	451	15	41	781 922	1 659	39 157	7	15 085	41.6	58.4	27.7	3.5	330	11.9
St. Joseph, MO-KS	854	0.9	285	0	636	467 373	1 508	76 118	118	39 526	66.4	33.6	45.6	10.2	11 965	60.1
St. Louis, MO-IL	3 056	3.2	248	D	2 354	626 060	2 452	69 129	733	59 580	63.1	36.9	43.3	13.6	34 273	46.3

Table C. Metropolitan Areas — Residential Construction, Wholesale Trade, Retail Trade, and Real Estate

Area Name	Value of residential construction authorized by building permits, 2003		Wholesale trade, 1997				Retail trade,[1] 1997				Real estate and rental and leasing, 1997			
	New construction ($1,000)	Number of housing units	Number of establishments	Number of employees	Sales (mil dol)	Annual payroll (mil dol)	Number of establishments	Number of employees	Sales (mil dol)	Annual payroll (mil dol)	Number of establishments	Number of employees	Receipts (mil dol)	Annual payroll (mil dol)
	133	134	135	136	137	138	139	140	141	142	143	144	145	146
New York-Northern New Jersey-Long Island, NY-NJ-PA	5 848 532	49 812	43 361	D	D	D	72 804	749 750	143 307.4	14 796.3	28 668	151 922	31 159.1	4 907.6
Edison, NJ Div	1 244 786	10 331	4 164	60 666	49 777.0	2 703.5	8 756	113 042	21 798.6	2 086.7	1 872	9 793	1 628.1	280.5
Nassau-Suffolk, NY Div	940 523	4 182	7 524	78 508	45 747.2	3 214.0	13 144	149 961	29 993.3	2 968.6	3 438	15 766	2 904.1	453.6
Newark-Union, NJ-PA Div	888 617	7 277	4 509	D	D	D	8 369	92 758	18 417.9	1 866.6	2 306	13 184	2 596.2	378.6
New York-Wayne-White Plains, NY-NJ Div	2 774 606	28 022	27 164	313 668	294 921.1	14 355.2	42 535	393 989	73 097.6	7 874.4	21 052	113 179	24 030.7	3 794.9
Niles-Benton Harbor, MI	114 986	608	193	1 887	938.3	60.0	674	8 078	1 302.5	125.6	164	627	186.3	10.5
Norwich-New London, CT	173 106	1 222	201	2 279	801.6	81.9	1 182	13 923	2 405.0	240.3	188	723	82.4	13.8
Ocala, FL	779 354	6 475	309	3 219	999.6	80.0	1 014	13 159	2 221.4	202.1	244	786	88.4	13.8
Ocean City, NJ	233 617	1 693	74	907	201.0	21.6	784	4 990	961.1	102.7	208	589	126.5	18.9
Odessa, TX	25 924	173	355	3 518	1 047.6	117.9	538	6 060	1 139.9	104.4	136	853	87.8	18.1
Ogden-Clearfield, UT	621 518	4 422	435	D	D	D	1 249	20 486	3 587.9	329.8	351	D	D	D
Oklahoma City, OK	1 043 624	8 082	1 884	D	D	D	4 434	55 949	10 121.4	900.5	1 264	6 622	725.7	127.7
Olympia, WA	326 704	2 014	201	1 805	580.3	57.5	730	9 008	1 616.8	166.3	218	884	89.7	13.5
Omaha-Council Bluffs, NE-IA	763 665	6 370	1 336	D	D	D	2 951	48 311	7 968.5	789.0	765	D	D	D
Orlando, FL	3 647 261	28 233	3 149	36 667	29 509.1	1 200.9	6 795	93 025	16 865.0	1 538.7	2 200	19 964	2 647.1	473.6
Oshkosh-Neenah, WI	175 419	1 460	194	3 387	1 088.8	111.9	611	8 712	1 489.6	141.4	148	711	65.2	11.5
Owensboro, KY	47 476	603	153	D	D	D	522	6 388	923.9	90.2	85	D	D	D
Oxnard-Thousand Oaks-Ventura, CA	729 831	3 567	1 088	13 811	10 402.7	522.6	2 348	30 831	6 476.6	608.7	672	3 254	409.0	73.4
Palm Bay-Melbourne-Titusville, FL	999 716	6 169	577	4 389	1 362.4	136.2	1 856	23 867	3 900.5	370.3	525	2 443	220.0	45.3
Panama City-Lynn Haven, FL	425 631	3 676	173	1 406	422.1	34.2	832	9 558	1 496.8	148.1	229	1 018	76.8	15.6
Parkersburg-Marietta, WV-OH	24 662	229	195	D	D	D	783	9 441	1 543.6	141.0	132	568	61.5	10.9
Pascagoula, MS	94 560	897	82	D	D	D	582	6 825	1 041.0	90.3	105	377	29.9	5.7
Pensacola-Ferry Pass-Brent, FL	519 377	4 801	470	5 065	1 719.1	135.4	1 620	20 217	3 435.8	305.6	389	1 625	159.4	27.8
Peoria, IL	230 224	1 757	522	D	D	D	1 447	20 158	3 448.1	320.3	300	D	D	D
Philadelphia-Camden-Wilmington, PA-NJ-DE-MD	2 325 386	21 080	9 467	D	D	D	21 817	293 703	53 672.8	5 383.1	4 814	36 419	9 659.0	980.8
Camden, NJ Div	540 115	5 598	2 072	30 319	28 369.0	1 165.9	4 611	63 464	11 464.9	1 138.9	850	6 694	1 303.1	192.8
Philadelphia, PA Div	1 439 808	11 677	6 660	88 835	68 225.8	3 826.7	14 617	193 656	35 826.2	3 621.4	3 085	25 653	3 490.8	691.3
Wilmington, DE-MD-NJ Div	345 463	3 805	735	D	D	D	2 589	36 583	6 381.7	622.8	879	4 072	4 865.1	96.7
Phoenix-Mesa-Scottsdale, AZ	7 871 171	54 860	4 840	62 284	39 724.9	2 284.0	9 618	149 267	30 011.8	2 856.3	3 502	22 551	3 079.9	558.2
Pine Bluff, AR	11 103	214	90	D	D	D	440	5 107	766.4	75.5	64	D	D	D
Pittsburgh, PA	968 596	6 513	3 859	51 417	39 287.3	1 845.1	9 974	135 502	21 949.5	2 041.4	1 940	12 460	1 983.8	295.1
Pittsfield, MA	79 197	417	136	D	D	D	832	8 513	1 280.7	137.7	122	410	43.9	7.5
Pocatello, ID	43 217	412	115	1 078	355.5	28.4	366	4 368	741.6	68.2	65	D	D	D
Portland-South Portland-Biddeford, ME	533 389	3 505	794	10 474	4 190.6	339.8	2 595	29 218	5 274.5	488.7	613	3 481	363.6	76.2
Portland-Vancouver-Beaverton, OR-WA	2 331 717	16 003	4 129	D	D	D	6 905	98 157	19 292.2	1 929.1	2 578	15 973	1 967.0	364.1
Port St. Lucie-Fort Pierce, FL	1 159 355	9 690	372	2 957	1 005.3	77.5	1 322	16 069	2 841.2	272.6	389	1 638	204.5	39.8
Poughkeepsie-Newburgh-Middletown, NY	444 589	2 909	722	D	D	D	2 535	30 637	5 307.2	516.1	534	2 577	322.0	51.1
Prescott, AZ	406 155	2 984	150	1 134	480.6	29.1	757	7 325	1 203.1	120.8	226	737	88.2	15.6
Providence-New Bedford-Fall River, RI-MA	569 467	4 035	2 299	30 851	19 188.9	1 106.3	6 534	78 147	12 664.4	1 263.3	1 297	6 213	767.0	137.3
Provo-Orem, UT	686 281	4 341	328	6 324	2 774.3	191.1	1 007	16 135	2 526.7	248.1	241	D	D	D
Pueblo, CO	123 160	1 282	113	1 101	390.3	27.5	600	7 040	1 180.7	121.7	131	486	58.8	8.2
Punta Gorda, FL	373 507	2 522	103	446	117.2	11.2	515	6 840	1 063.3	100.4	167	601	60.7	10.1
Racine, WI	180 204	1 188	234	4 560	3 816.9	142.4	664	9 693	1 564.1	142.0	132	746	57.7	12.1
Raleigh-Cary, NC	1 626 738	12 660	1 400	20 583	14 262.0	866.1	3 332	44 392	8 426.0	750.8	876	5 058	888.2	134.3
Rapid City, SD	108 638	858	195	2 161	770.5	60.2	662	7 500	1 247.9	122.0	142	607	56.8	9.8
Reading, PA	263 911	1 991	439	7 051	3 121.7	253.0	1 468	19 302	3 330.7	326.2	215	1 324	191.3	28.1
Redding, CA	187 920	1 358	217	1 786	566.6	51.9	713	8 113	1 354.5	140.3	199	878	80.3	14.6
Reno-Sparks, NV	744 658	5 033	641	D	D	D	1 352	19 500	3 758.6	390.9	615	D	D	D
Richmond, VA	1 166 982	9 177	1 763	D	D	D	4 466	61 801	9 641.0	965.9	1 039	D	D	D
Riverside-San Bernardino-Ontario, CA	6 843 021	42 252	2 947	37 405	20 969.7	1 222.4	8 402	115 373	21 951.8	2 129.4	2 324	12 267	1 452.1	252.9
Roanoke, VA	195 269	1 627	550	7 028	2 627.7	221.9	1 437	20 601	3 149.6	319.5	279	2 425	166.4	41.9
Rochester, MN	316 432	2 016	172	1 696	810.5	51.9	758	10 584	1 626.8	156.1	142	705	92.8	10.8
Rochester, NY	476 089	3 422	1 437	17 973	10 358.7	719.8	3 746	58 701	8 811.0	851.1	773	6 542	738.9	137.0
Rockford, IL	225 231	2 625	553	D	D	D	1 181	18 200	2 953.2	289.7	251	1 255	171.3	25.7
Rocky Mount, NC	68 365	762	172	2 806	1 493.1	87.8	720	7 516	1 249.7	114.5	123	758	95.8	15.1
Rome, GA	61 712	502	112	1 163	523.3	35.8	442	4 991	808.1	75.0	56	313	26.8	5.2
Sacramento—Arden-Arcade—Roseville, CA	4 076 375	22 832	1 960	30 491	15 598.3	1 051.5	5 466	74 401	14 122.4	1 446.4	1 851	12 578	1 359.6	266.0
Saginaw-Saginaw Township North, MI	94 363	699	269	3 643	1 614.3	120.1	1 101	14 917	2 477.0	228.2	155	820	80.1	14.0
St. Cloud, MN	247 300	2 015	238	4 771	1 604.3	145.5	763	11 222	1 851.1	170.0	150	733	64.2	11.5
St. George, UT	330 082	2 729	85	641	238.5	18.0	406	4 829	879.4	77.3	102	332	31.8	4.6
St. Joseph, MO-KS	36 276	304	185	D	D	D	501	5 908	972.8	87.6	101	D	D	D
St. Louis, MO-IL	2 031 624	14 754	4 919	D	D	D	10 209	144 561	24 658.0	2 545.8	2 663	D	D	D

1. Establishments with payroll.

Table C. Metropolitan Areas — Professional Services, Manufacturing, and Accommodation and Foodservices

Area Name	Professional, scientific, and technical services,[1] 1997				Manufacturing, 1997				Accommodation and foodservices, 1997			
	Number of establishments	Number of employees	Sales (mil dol)	Annual payroll (mil dol)	Number of establishments	Number of employees	Sales (mil dol)	Annual payroll (mil dol)	Number of establishments	Number of employees	Sales (mil dol)	Annual payroll (mil dol)
	147	148	149	150	151	152	153	154	155	156	157	158
New York-Northern New Jersey-Long Island, NY-NJ-PA	54 491	509 164	70 884.8	27 347.9	NA	NA	NA	NA	34 043	421 554	21 563.1	6 001.7
Edison, NJ Div	7 209	74 499	7 980.3	3 457.3	2 249	86 266	22 094.5	3 411.1	4 259	54 733	2 228.4	606.4
Nassau-Suffolk, NY Div	9 464	55 636	5 982.3	2 199.0	4 188	113 034	19 126.5	3 984.3	5 676	64 915	2 811.1	767.6
Newark-Union, NJ-PA Div	7 113	64 615	8 592.9	3 365.1	NA	NA	NA	NA	4 046	50 353	2 290.5	632.0
New York-Wayne-White Plains, NY-NJ Div	30 705	314 414	48 329.3	18 326.5	15 665	360 042	55 761.1	10 853.1	20 062	251 553	14 233.1	3 995.7
Niles-Benton Harbor, MI	255	1 338	124.6	48.9	397	16 996	2 394.2	539.1	383	5 328	163.5	44.0
Norwich-New London, CT	463	3 944	338.9	162.2	237	19 888	2 962.8	1 035.1	590	8 652	333.0	95.7
Ocala, FL	361	1 882	132.9	52.8	215	9 620	1 287.8	238.0	363	6 558	200.9	54.1
Ocean City, NJ	211	795	69.1	26.7	82	813	110.4	19.1	961	4 642	368.1	95.0
Odessa, TX	192	1 005	69.1	26.5	203	3 526	1 286.2	115.6	234	3 806	119.9	32.9
Ogden-Clearfield, UT	606	4 478	278.8	118.0	NA	NA	NA	NA	596	11 649	308.6	86.8
Oklahoma City, OK	2 964	16 559	1 462.4	567.2	NA	NA	NA	NA	2 135	D	D	D
Olympia, WA	401	2 571	198.1	86.2	156	3 218	761.0	100.7	406	6 076	193.0	56.6
Omaha-Council Bluffs, NE-IA	1 571	D	D	D	NA	NA	NA	NA	1 567	D	D	D
Orlando, FL	4 465	34 147	3 378.8	1 344.4	1 564	47 086	8 327.2	1 627.8	3 013	103 403	5 399.4	1 274.6
Oshkosh-Neenah, WI	202	1 630	142.9	46.0	316	27 191	6 026.6	976.5	341	5 832	153.7	43.4
Owensboro, KY	161	892	58.1	23.6	NA	NA	NA	NA	168	D	D	D
Oxnard-Thousand Oaks-Ventura, CA	1 597	10 829	1 229.3	464.9	1 008	33 562	6 163.4	1 136.3	1 200	21 879	775.3	209.4
Palm Bay-Melbourne-Titusville, FL	1 073	11 192	1 195.6	455.0	494	20 832	3 450.7	753.9	860	16 207	495.3	136.3
Panama City-Lynn Haven, FL	268	1 730	138.9	56.1	136	3 492	719.0	108.7	483	9 268	336.3	84.8
Parkersburg-Marietta, WV-OH	222	D	D	D	NA	NA	NA	NA	335	5 930	180.3	51.9
Pascagoula, MS	180	1 676	138.7	63.3	NA	NA	NA	NA	216	D	D	D
Pensacola-Ferry Pass-Brent, FL	669	4 446	340.0	143.7	295	9 421	2 641.8	336.2	612	13 071	404.7	106.9
Peoria, IL	572	5 630	452.6	202.6	NA	NA	NA	NA	859	D	D	D
Philadelphia-Camden-Wilmington, PA-NJ-DE-MD	14 570	158 340	19 344.2	7 856.2	7 119	277 284	76 020.9	10 584.1	10 354	153 363	5 865.6	1 602.8
Camden, NJ Div	2 916	24 524	2 491.7	1 023.7	1 431	50 834	14 446.3	1 886.7	1 978	29 330	1 033.4	283.1
Philadelphia, PA Div	10 091	122 555	15 488.7	6 310.5	5 127	196 886	51 005.1	7 388.9	7 207	102 939	4 055.8	1 099.7
Wilmington, DE-MD-NJ Div	1 563	11 261	1 363.8	522.0	561	29 564	10 569.5	1 308.5	1 169	21 094	776.4	220.0
Phoenix-Mesa-Scottsdale, AZ	7 228	58 051	5 136.8	2 141.5	3 438	148 277	35 312.7	5 199.8	5 134	116 068	4 335.7	1 207.2
Pine Bluff, AR	93	D	D	D	NA	NA	NA	NA	140	D	D	D
Pittsburgh, PA	5 002	54 933	6 069.3	2 305.6	3 092	124 410	24 582.5	4 450.3	5 010	84 882	2 620.3	736.6
Pittsfield, MA	247	1 420	129.3	50.6	207	9 176	1 423.0	344.7	485	7 060	247.3	75.6
Pocatello, ID	114	951	48.0	22.7	70	4 371	930.4	140.5	204	2 868	77.6	21.1
Portland-South Portland-Biddeford, ME	1 315	7 916	735.0	303.9	669	D	D	D	1 579	18 489	749.6	207.1
Portland-Vancouver-Beaverton, OR-WA	5 350	38 593	3 763.0	1 566.3	NA	NA	NA	NA	4 050	69 820	2 500.7	711.0
Port St. Lucie-Fort Pierce, FL	666	3 040	233.4	94.1	296	5 504	1 097.9	161.8	503	8 635	315.4	83.0
Poughkeepsie-Newburgh-Middletown, NY	1 196	5 792	553.3	210.3	556	D	D	D	1 245	13 006	508.6	131.4
Prescott, AZ	304	1 043	71.1	25.4	189	3 511	445.8	91.3	444	5 614	180.4	48.6
Providence-New Bedford-Fall River, RI-MA	3 142	18 967	1 742.8	654.0	3 450	124 962	18 133.4	3 942.8	3 729	51 142	1 778.2	493.2
Provo-Orem, UT	592	D	D	D	NA	NA	NA	NA	414	8 562	234.8	66.3
Pueblo, CO	192	981	49.7	19.3	107	4 688	1 021.3	147.0	321	4 969	142.4	38.1
Punta Gorda, FL	194	1 083	73.3	37.3	74	587	77.7	13.8	218	3 935	123.5	31.9
Racine, WI	296	1 821	134.3	55.6	379	18 869	5 229.5	664.1	360	5 324	154.7	42.2
Raleigh-Cary, NC	2 534	18 795	2 043.1	815.4	808	32 636	12 486.9	1 044.1	1 417	D	D	D
Rapid City, SD	228	1 176	95.9	31.7	NA	NA	NA	NA	380	5 642	179.4	48.4
Reading, PA	546	5 520	476.6	215.2	587	41 614	7 729.4	1 510.7	706	10 091	330.4	90.9
Redding, CA	304	1 636	127.0	51.6	177	3 526	635.0	118.7	402	5 070	161.7	41.7
Reno-Sparks, NV	1 198	6 438	661.0	260.2	NA	NA	NA	NA	788	34 566	1 818.2	583.8
Richmond, VA	2 463	D	D	D	NA	NA	NA	NA	1 809	D	D	D
Riverside-San Bernardino-Ontario, CA	3 124	17 060	1 648.7	537.1	3 412	109 582	19 354.7	3 159.5	4 482	79 231	2 899.1	782.9
Roanoke, VA	586	D	D	D	NA	NA	NA	NA	590	D	D	D
Rochester, MN	253	2 266	172.2	86.7	145	13 733	3 852.5	570.9	349	D	D	D
Rochester, NY	1 996	17 058	1 800.5	674.3	1 409	102 161	25 205.5	4 100.7	2 045	29 900	972.0	277.7
Rockford, IL	601	D	D	D	842	45 586	8 908.4	1 767.5	609	10 249	324.9	88.8
Rocky Mount, NC	155	989	77.8	27.2	154	17 599	3 328.4	501.8	220	4 228	133.7	36.4
Rome, GA	131	650	61.6	19.7	120	9 583	1 892.4	280.0	151	2 572	87.8	22.9
Sacramento—Arden-Arcade—Roseville, CA	3 750	27 466	2 973.5	1 121.9	1 489	47 690	14 550.8	1 688.8	3 443	56 414	1 878.5	505.6
Saginaw-Saginaw Township North, MI	320	2 908	195.1	86.5	239	20 681	5 172.2	1 148.6	408	9 236	270.5	78.9
St. Cloud, MN	249	1 504	113.7	47.3	272	15 406	2 516.8	440.5	362	6 520	177.2	47.5
St. George, UT	131	605	38.8	15.4	92	1 949	243.4	48.4	195	3 580	113.2	31.6
St. Joseph, MO-KS	161	849	66.9	22.6	NA	NA	NA	NA	247	3 823	111.3	31.0
St. Louis, MO-IL	5 990	59 855	6 706.2	2 422.5	NA	NA	NA	NA	5 226	D	D	D

1. Firms subject to federal tax.

Table C. Metropolitan Areas — Health Care and Social Assistance, Other Services, and Federal Funds

Area Name	Health care and social assistance,[1] 1997				Other services,[1] 1997				Federal funds and grants, 2002–2003 Expenditures (mil dol)		Direct payments for individuals	
	Number of establishments	Number of employees	Receipts (mil dol)	Annual payroll (mil dol)	Number of establishments	Number of employees	Receipts (mil dol)	Annual payroll (mil dol)	Total	Social Security and government retirement	Medicare	Food stamps and Supplemental Security Income
	159	160	161	162	163	164	165	166	167	168	169	170
New York-Northern New Jersey-Long Island, NY-NJ-PA	38 909	366 723	29 029.4	12 097.6	31 898	156 084	10 825.3	3 208.8	112 902.7	33 662.8	22 272.5	4 298.8
Edison, NJ Div	4 814	46 906	3 757.4	1 547.4	3 703	17 994	1 255.0	370.6	12 349.9	5 001.4	2 437.0	146.3
Nassau-Suffolk, NY Div	7 528	78 746	6 113.9	2 534.1	6 187	29 595	2 050.4	608.4	16 001.4	6 291.1	3 313.2	221.3
Newark-Union, NJ-PA Div	5 004	44 054	3 384.3	1 492.0	3 981	21 610	1 565.2	486.3	11 184.6	3 947.9	2 210.7	314.3
New York-Wayne-White Plains, NY-NJ Div	21 563	197 017	15 773.8	6 524.1	18 027	86 885	5 954.7	1 743.5	73 366.8	18 422.4	14 311.6	3 616.9
Niles-Benton Harbor, MI	281	2 395	154.1	71.3	262	1 452	77.6	25.1	876.4	389.3	172.5	41.6
Norwich-New London, CT	490	7 493	521.3	227.8	391	2 113	137.6	37.8	3 993.7	637.7	263.7	25.1
Ocala, FL	466	6 512	466.6	185.9	369	1 680	93.9	29.4	1 647.3	987.0	364.1	48.0
Ocean City, NJ	208	1 289	94.5	43.3	168	803	42.6	14.7	688.0	322.1	180.7	9.0
Odessa, TX	227	3 674	163.7	68.9	233	1 777	194.4	40.8	500.9	212.4	116.0	30.0
Ogden-Clearfield, UT	692	D	D	D	508	D	D	D	3 912.2	997.3	192.9	41.3
Oklahoma City, OK	2 545	32 892	2 044.4	902.6	1 608	11 492	651.0	197.4	8 762.5	2 656.0	887.2	206.9
Olympia, WA	459	4 551	322.8	137.0	264	1 356	79.0	24.2	2 283.3	688.1	139.8	32.5
Omaha-Council Bluffs, NE-IA	1 275	16 240	1 021.6	495.1	1 312	8 563	516.3	160.8	4 535.7	1 638.5	568.2	100.1
Orlando, FL	3 136	38 208	2 746.1	1 240.2	2 626	16 893	1 040.1	314.7	9 792.0	3 859.5	1 585.2	268.2
Oshkosh-Neenah, WI	318	3 623	264.4	132.3	260	1 778	97.3	28.9	1 239.0	299.0	123.4	12.4
Owensboro, KY	221	2 785	192.2	79.6	165	880	54.9	15.5	555.0	252.8	106.9	28.0
Oxnard-Thousand Oaks-Ventura, CA	1 591	13 110	1 086.6	413.1	875	5 577	442.5	126.7	4 065.6	1 343.8	636.3	72.3
Palm Bay-Melbourne-Titusville, FL	1 017	10 631	783.2	358.0	728	3 778	206.4	63.8	5 545.5	1 856.5	608.2	64.6
Panama City-Lynn Haven, FL	317	4 398	315.8	131.2	246	1 569	85.5	27.6	1 324.0	523.6	158.1	27.6
Parkersburg-Marietta, WV-OH	308	D	D	D	287	D	D	D	1 058.9	422.8	179.5	41.6
Pascagoula, MS	249	1 929	132.9	56.5	189	823	45.0	12.6	2 146.5	373.6	131.6	30.8
Pensacola-Ferry Pass-Brent, FL	662	11 163	748.8	344.1	557	3 672	210.4	73.6	3 501.6	1 423.1	375.1	83.9
Peoria, IL	568	6 953	478.1	244.0	577	3 719	258.2	81.8	1 916.7	811.7	355.3	62.8
Philadelphia-Camden-Wilmington, PA-NJ-DE-MD	11 744	131 099	9 224.8	4 266.3	9 129	54 031	3 659.6	1 125.0	38 985.6	12 481.4	7 456.1	1 211.0
Camden, NJ Div	2 276	24 502	1 733.6	813.2	1 926	11 255	739.2	227.7	7 746.7	2 659.5	1 239.1	156.2
Philadelphia, PA Div	8 247	93 426	6 529.4	3 004.3	6 226	36 945	2 557.5	775.3	27 814.7	8 477.1	5 622.6	967.8
Wilmington, DE-MD-NJ Div	1 221	13 171	961.8	448.8	977	5 831	362.9	122.0	3 424.1	1 344.7	594.4	87.0
Phoenix-Mesa-Scottsdale, AZ	5 980	65 092	4 618.6	2 016.1	4 168	30 680	2 040.5	606.3	20 089.6	6 528.9	2 589.1	519.7
Pine Bluff, AR	203	D	D	D	126	814	47.9	14.9	951.4	245.4	101.1	42.6
Pittsburgh, PA	5 558	60 722	4 163.4	1 836.0	4 400	25 308	1 672.9	469.8	18 584.8	6 713.2	4 194.1	477.6
Pittsfield, MA	268	4 334	254.6	113.7	231	1 074	62.7	18.7	1 087.9	342.7	213.0	21.7
Pocatello, ID	164	1 450	81.5	39.8	123	628	36.8	10.5	403.2	166.0	46.3	15.2
Portland-South Portland-Biddeford, ME	1 169	12 377	762.5	378.2	770	4 449	289.6	88.3	3 818.9	1 177.5	386.1	70.7
Portland-Vancouver-Beaverton, OR-WA	3 893	40 387	2 664.5	1 163.0	2 822	18 155	1 283.4	388.4	9 441.4	3 565.3	1 324.1	316.3
Port St. Lucie-Fort Pierce, FL	677	10 392	756.4	294.8	517	2 226	138.1	38.8	2 078.3	1 198.9	543.0	47.8
Poughkeepsie-Newburgh-Middletown, NY	1 234	10 599	714.6	304.7	996	4 390	314.5	84.0	3 387.8	1 262.3	520.5	74.1
Prescott, AZ	377	3 014	167.5	66.8	231	1 004	59.1	16.1	980.9	608.0	146.6	22.6
Providence-New Bedford-Fall River, RI-MA	2 918	38 183	2 170.9	998.0	2 827	12 942	842.2	247.3	10 817.7	3 503.9	1 861.7	301.5
Provo-Orem, UT	604	7 516	425.6	180.3	347	2 283	106.5	29.7	1 063.9	442.5	144.0	28.2
Pueblo, CO	299	3 459	203.9	98.4	194	912	47.5	13.9	930.9	400.6	149.8	41.0
Punta Gorda, FL	305	4 286	306.9	134.7	189	674	37.4	10.2	970.8	611.9	290.4	12.4
Racine, WI	265	3 771	263.8	132.8	291	2 195	125.4	40.3	822.9	400.4	147.3	26.6
Raleigh-Cary, NC	1 372	19 521	1 247.9	567.2	1 180	7 681	600.8	163.6	4 895.3	1 452.4	452.6	96.3
Rapid City, SD	245	2 449	169.8	67.4	225	1 114	61.0	18.5	897.4	300.5	70.2	17.4
Reading, PA	601	6 387	412.6	200.5	559	3 102	183.2	56.4	1 670.8	832.0	373.4	49.2
Redding, CA	487	5 441	387.9	156.8	241	1 289	86.4	22.8	1 061.2	483.3	201.7	48.3
Reno-Sparks, NV	780	D	D	D	NA	NA	NA	NA	1 743.0	718.3	225.7	38.2
Richmond, VA	1 946	D	D	D	1 832	12 594	809.4	253.2	7 547.5	2 643.4	894.3	168.3
Riverside-San Bernardino-Ontario, CA	4 621	51 493	3 956.7	1 505.8	3 219	21 301	1 425.5	406.0	14 663.2	5 710.4	2 948.5	606.6
Roanoke, VA	507	D	D	D	634	D	D	D	1 781.6	765.8	258.4	39.6
Rochester, MN	211	2 623	121.7	58.2	248	1 626	90.2	26.4	827.7	281.4	108.6	15.3
Rochester, NY	1 681	17 432	1 130.7	473.5	1 412	7 221	482.3	139.3	5 836.5	2 183.7	984.7	177.6
Rockford, IL	467	6 223	480.2	232.3	532	3 899	243.5	78.4	1 355.7	635.4	232.8	52.0
Rocky Mount, NC	205	4 459	280.0	115.3	211	1 247	74.6	20.8	831.3	314.9	131.8	42.3
Rome, GA	165	4 018	345.6	131.4	95	721	41.6	14.1	440.4	205.1	92.4	22.0
Sacramento—Arden-Arcade—Roseville, CA	3 549	33 932	2 659.3	1 118.6	2 237	15 481	1 116.3	336.3	17 706.0	4 658.4	1 500.6	406.5
Saginaw-Saginaw Township North, MI	410	3 465	248.1	121.5	336	2 127	126.7	39.1	1 153.2	484.0	217.6	63.8
St. Cloud, MN	267	3 669	258.3	130.5	281	1 667	102.7	27.6	716.8	307.2	91.7	15.6
St. George, UT	193	1 722	114.0	41.2	98	433	32.9	8.4	406.5	245.8	55.7	7.4
St. Joseph, MO-KS	209	2 709	153.8	69.8	198	911	55.6	15.5	664.9	284.6	131.5	25.0
St. Louis, MO-IL	5 349	63 577	3 991.6	1 825.4	4 591	27 848	1 766.7	560.7	21 989.5	6 100.1	2 904.4	550.6

1. Firms subject to federal tax.

Table C. Metropolitan Areas — **Federal Funds and Local Government Finances**

	Federal funds and grants, 2002–2003 (cont'd)							Local government finances, 2002				
	Expenditures (mil dol) (cont'd)							General revenue				
	Procurement contract awards			Grants							Taxes	
											Per capita[1] (dollars)	
Area Name	Salaries and wages	Defense	Other	Medicaid and other health-related	Nutrition and family welfare	Education	Other	Total (mil dol)	Intergovernmental (mil dol)	Total (mil dol)	Total	Property
	171	172	173	174	175	176	177	178	179	180	181	182
New York-Northern New Jersey-Long Island, NY-NJ-PA	8 016.8	3 860.9	3 144.2	22 804.3	3 760.8	1 292.7	7 615.9	99 272.8	35 276.1	46 997.8	2 526	1 662
Edison, NJ Div	1 022.2	1 178.0	462.7	844.9	124.4	57.4	965.3	7 665.2	2 254.6	4 342.4	1 928	1 899
Nassau-Suffolk, NY Div	1 362.7	1 137.7	740.1	1 778.6	234.0	154.0	637.3	14 152.4	3 966.7	8 583.0	3 061	2 407
Newark-Union, NJ-PA Div	972.1	428.0	295.2	1 414.1	308.7	92.7	1 014.4	7 991.0	2 607.7	4 311.6	2 022	1 981
New York-Wayne-White Plains, NY-NJ Div	4 659.9	1 117.2	1 646.2	18 766.7	3 093.7	988.6	4 998.9	69 464.2	26 447.1	29 760.8	2 607	1 373
Niles-Benton Harbor, MI	25.5	2.1	13.7	137.2	29.5	14.1	36.4	472.4	270.6	114.2	704	684
Norwich-New London, CT	411.3	2 349.7	43.9	129.5	27.0	24.5	67.1	796.9	295.1	396.9	1 511	1 488
Ocala, FL	40.9	8.3	18.8	94.1	35.3	15.2	21.6	601.0	256.6	174.7	641	543
Ocean City, NJ	61.6	16.6	14.0	37.3	7.3	4.9	31.2	518.3	149.7	278.8	2 733	2 655
Odessa, TX	11.7	0.2	2.9	49.0	17.6	8.9	43.8	487.3	161.7	136.1	1 113	884
Ogden-Clearfield, UT	1 058.0	1 145.7	115.0	179.0	51.5	12.2	91.4	1 079.3	485.2	349.7	759	523
Oklahoma City, OK	1 827.6	744.5	690.4	541.9	272.0	230.2	583.9	2 726.2	951.9	970.4	865	426
Olympia, WA	67.6	10.7	12.5	197.4	253.1	236.1	612.2	622.7	284.7	218.0	1 002	701
Omaha-Council Bluffs, NE-IA	771.5	240.6	150.2	505.8	105.8	70.5	260.3	2 292.4	765.1	1 055.7	1 346	994
Orlando, FL	617.3	2 078.5	322.7	406.5	136.6	96.8	313.3	5 932.6	1 730.8	2 114.8	1 207	894
Oshkosh-Neenah, WI	34.5	613.8	20.8	62.7	16.3	8.2	32.0	459.5	227.5	159.7	1 008	976
Owensboro, KY	22.1	3.0	5.2	50.6	21.8	6.5	45.9	319.7	97.2	71.4	647	386
Oxnard-Thousand Oaks-Ventura, CA	687.9	608.4	110.8	255.1	95.7	48.1	182.2	3 092.5	1 427.8	905.2	1 155	875
Palm Bay-Melbourne-Titusville, FL	432.8	1 315.8	1 016.1	88.6	37.1	24.3	79.0	1 320.3	486.6	408.5	824	650
Panama City-Lynn Haven, FL	337.5	160.8	32.8	62.3	21.1	15.0	-26.3	581.6	172.5	145.7	959	630
Parkersburg-Marietta, WV-OH	130.0	12.7	58.1	106.6	22.5	14.4	53.1	367.7	183.9	120.7	739	599
Pascagoula, MS	142.9	1 359.3	6.2	36.8	16.0	8.7	33.5	479.2	145.0	126.2	824	752
Pensacola-Ferry Pass-Brent, FL	807.9	280.5	51.0	211.2	68.5	32.8	110.6	1 072.8	433.0	309.0	728	526
Peoria, IL	177.9	117.6	41.6	117.8	37.5	13.9	132.2	989.4	427.8	358.7	981	848
Philadelphia-Camden-Wilmington, PA-NJ-DE-MD	3 851.4	4 046.4	1 369.4	4 947.9	916.9	266.3	1 858.7	21 523.5	8 563.5	9 013.3	1 567	1 116
Camden, NJ Div	827.3	1 415.6	309.2	545.0	137.6	55.7	323.4	4 879.5	1 923.3	2 062.1	1 702	1 679
Philadelphia, PA Div	2 726.7	2 584.9	976.3	4 036.6	681.1	183.0	1 190.7	14 944.9	5 903.0	6 376.4	1 646	1 017
Wilmington, DE-MD-NJ Div	297.4	46.0	83.9	366.3	98.3	27.6	344.5	1 699.1	737.3	574.9	862	671
Phoenix-Mesa-Scottsdale, AZ	1 495.7	4 277.8	605.0	1 862.6	525.6	429.7	857.4	10 909.1	4 490.8	4 082.2	1 166	748
Pine Bluff, AR	75.6	134.8	11.6	127.5	20.5	12.3	142.8	200.4	124.6	43.1	406	189
Pittsburgh, PA	1 236.4	1 095.0	915.4	2 227.3	360.7	87.3	1 057.8	8 260.9	3 457.8	3 045.4	1 259	940
Pittsfield, MA	66.8	103.1	141.4	107.8	22.6	13.0	48.5	377.7	177.4	160.5	1 203	1 160
Pocatello, ID	32.4	1.5	11.9	52.9	6.8	3.8	27.6	273.5	96.2	62.5	752	725
Portland-South Portland-Biddeford, ME	542.3	998.4	44.3	330.3	51.6	20.8	149.6	1 382.7	366.4	810.8	1 620	1 581
Portland-Vancouver-Beaverton, OR-WA	1 160.2	285.5	436.6	1 291.9	235.0	128.7	561.7	6 995.2	2 815.5	2 522.2	1 251	956
Port St. Lucie-Fort Pierce, FL	54.5	25.6	32.7	68.4	30.8	20.9	35.8	998.6	287.9	432.8	1 282	1 153
Poughkeepsie-Newburgh-Middletown, NY	385.4	353.4	48.8	466.8	63.5	41.1	136.1	2 523.8	941.6	1 215.3	1 886	1 436
Prescott, AZ	64.5	3.2	25.4	62.4	10.8	12.2	18.8	488.0	202.0	207.2	1 157	744
Providence-New Bedford-Fall River, RI-MA	917.4	867.2	197.8	1 680.0	319.9	195.5	825.0	4 145.7	1 703.0	2 016.1	1 250	1 217
Provo-Orem, UT	70.6	42.8	34.7	131.1	35.5	13.1	61.5	898.4	426.2	284.0	716	472
Pueblo, CO	60.8	15.4	10.3	141.0	41.8	15.0	33.6	379.0	170.7	150.6	1 026	624
Punta Gorda, FL	18.1	0.1	4.9	9.4	9.2	4.5	7.0	373.9	76.3	176.8	1 189	823
Racine, WI	27.3	17.5	8.7	110.2	32.4	12.2	29.2	602.1	322.9	190.9	999	970
Raleigh-Cary, NC	334.8	61.3	131.7	520.7	423.0	348.4	977.7	2 359.5	909.0	853.0	993	763
Rapid City, SD	230.2	62.0	24.9	48.3	14.9	14.9	90.4	274.3	93.3	132.0	1 145	805
Reading, PA	77.8	31.2	28.5	137.9	29.2	11.6	64.3	1 128.6	412.3	493.7	1 292	1 024
Redding, CA	73.4	1.4	25.9	114.9	49.6	17.9	34.1	741.2	438.1	144.5	841	639
Reno-Sparks, NV	195.1	72.3	100.6	167.8	33.1	24.6	134.4	1 389.6	559.6	483.2	1 321	841
Richmond, VA	1 068.3	449.7	252.9	618.9	342.4	305.7	665.0	3 329.9	1 335.2	1 342.1	1 192	857
Riverside-San Bernardino-Ontario, CA	1 447.6	683.4	261.6	1 268.6	606.1	266.9	670.2	14 860.6	8 420.1	2 961.4	842	600
Roanoke, VA	190.6	158.6	104.9	123.4	31.7	17.3	50.7	797.9	347.4	326.4	1 127	725
Rochester, MN	64.8	9.0	40.8	213.8	13.3	9.1	40.9	591.0	277.8	141.0	832	737
Rochester, NY	293.1	348.0	115.2	900.9	179.7	109.1	314.5	4 343.7	1 943.2	1 684.6	1 615	1 218
Rockford, IL	72.2	101.8	21.1	111.0	25.5	15.4	56.5	931.0	370.7	395.6	1 209	1 151
Rocky Mount, NC	38.2	6.8	10.2	146.7	31.4	13.3	48.8	594.8	290.1	97.8	678	535
Rome, GA	16.6	1.5	3.1	56.0	11.9	6.4	14.8	423.0	134.3	90.6	978	581
Sacramento—Arden-Arcade—Roseville, CA	868.0	774.2	375.7	1 625.7	2 790.1	1 684.9	2 765.0	8 729.0	4 408.9	2 057.2	1 066	701
Saginaw-Saginaw Township North, MI	86.4	6.0	30.6	146.5	54.0	19.2	29.8	617.3	369.5	118.5	564	468
St. Cloud, MN	84.6	1.7	23.6	76.7	17.5	12.2	32.2	558.2	287.7	143.1	831	772
St. George, UT	51.0	1.3	4.7	15.6	5.7	3.7	8.8	226.9	88.9	83.6	840	536
St. Joseph, MO-KS	38.6	1.9	13.5	86.0	14.3	7.9	33.1	272.6	115.8	104.2	855	509
St. Louis, MO-IL	1 933.8	5 833.1	847.7	2 136.4	342.9	162.0	873.4	7 772.3	2 862.8	3 362.4	1 232	820

1. Based on the resident population estimated as of July 1 of the year shown.

Table C. Metropolitan Areas — Local Government Finances, Government Employment, and Elections

	Local government finances, 2002 (cont'd)									Government employment, 2002			Presidential election, 2004		
	Direct general expenditure							Debt outstanding					Percent of vote cast —		
			Percent of total for —												
Area Name	Total (mil dol)	Per capita[1] (dollars)	Education	Health and hospitals	Police protection	Public welfare	Highways	Total (mil dol)	Per capita[1] (dollars)	Federal civilian	Federal military	State and local	Democratic	Republican	All other
	183	184	185	186	187	188	189	190	191	192	193	194	195	196	197
New York-Northern New Jersey-Long Island, NY-NJ-PA	100 671.1	5 412	36.1	7.7	6.8	11.0	2.4	103 826.2	5 581	131 014	31 218	1 116 293	59.5	39.2	1.2
Edison, NJ Div	7 683.7	3 411	55.9	1.2	5.9	2.7	3.3	6 800.4	3 019	16 128	5 697	121 285	46.9	52.2	0.9
Nassau-Suffolk, NY Div	14 686.9	5 239	51.1	4.3	7.5	6.7	2.7	11 144.5	3 975	19 518	4 948	165 476	50.6	47.7	1.7
Newark-Union, NJ-PA Div	7 773.6	3 646	48.6	2.6	7.7	3.6	3.0	5 501.0	2 580	16 978	3 380	138 509	53.9	45.2	0.9
New York-Wayne-White Plains, NY-NJ Div	70 526.9	6 179	29.5	9.6	6.6	13.6	2.2	80 380.4	7 042	78 390	17 193	691 023	67.5	31.3	1.2
Niles-Benton Harbor, MI	478.0	2 946	53.4	6.6	4.0	1.1	6.7	224.8	1 385	419	305	8 228	44.0	55.0	1.0
Norwich-New London, CT	765.8	2 915	58.0	0.8	6.1	0.8	4.2	573.3	2 183	2 694	9 268	37 176	55.8	42.2	2.0
Ocala, FL	560.3	2 056	51.6	0.8	7.5	0.4	5.4	482.0	1 769	716	415	14 678	41.0	58.2	0.8
Ocean City, NJ	515.8	5 056	40.9	2.2	5.9	3.7	6.2	515.3	5 052	390	1 431	8 312	42.2	56.7	1.1
Odessa, TX	478.2	3 910	41.3	33.8	3.9	0.0	1.6	261.0	2 134	200	229	9 055	23.7	75.9	0.4
Ogden-Clearfield, UT	1 062.2	2 305	53.8	1.6	5.9	1.5	3.6	579.9	1 259	19 577	6 885	24 233	22.1	75.8	2.1
Oklahoma City, OK	2 825.3	2 520	44.7	8.3	7.1	0.1	6.2	2 259.0	2 015	26 365	12 226	83 135	33.3	66.7	0.0
Olympia, WA	591.1	2 716	50.9	4.8	4.2	0.0	6.5	432.7	1 988	986	694	34 373	55.5	42.6	1.9
Omaha-Council Bluffs, NE-IA	2 373.5	3 026	48.1	2.9	5.3	0.5	6.1	2 591.7	3 304	8 420	10 873	46 992	37.0	61.9	1.1
Orlando, FL	5 881.9	3 357	40.4	2.9	6.6	0.9	6.0	10 770.5	6 147	10 086	3 262	90 280	45.7	53.6	0.6
Oshkosh-Neenah, WI	484.5	3 059	42.8	6.2	5.7	8.6	8.3	438.9	2 771	555	439	11 390	46.3	52.6	1.1
Owensboro, KY	312.3	2 831	35.1	5.8	3.1	0.5	2.7	1 728.9	15 672	361	105	8 869	38.7	60.5	0.8
Oxnard-Thousand Oaks-Ventura, CA	2 995.6	3 821	43.8	7.7	5.8	5.1	3.7	1 705.7	2 176	7 613	7 659	36 272	48.1	50.7	1.1
Palm Bay-Melbourne-Titusville, FL	1 298.3	2 620	40.8	9.6	5.9	0.5	4.3	1 287.0	2 597	5 505	3 171	21 641	41.6	57.7	0.8
Panama City-Lynn Haven, FL	580.7	3 823	37.9	24.1	5.8	0.5	4.3	461.8	3 040	3 018	4 644	7 466	28.1	71.2	0.7
Parkersburg-Marietta, WV-OH	361.1	2 210	61.0	4.8	3.7	5.9	4.7	397.2	2 431	2 194	555	8 231	38.1	61.3	0.6
Pascagoula, MS	470.0	3 071	34.6	29.0	4.0	0.1	4.9	543.6	3 551	832	2 981	10 062	29.2	70.1	0.7
Pensacola-Ferry Pass-Brent, FL	1 086.0	2 558	49.1	1.9	7.1	0.4	5.1	1 740.7	4 101	6 736	16 669	21 751	29.9	69.1	0.9
Peoria, IL	997.2	2 726	50.1	1.4	4.6	1.4	6.6	473.6	1 295	2 813	729	18 932	44.4	55.0	0.6
Philadelphia-Camden-Wilmington, PA-NJ-DE-MD	21 175.2	3 681	42.6	6.8	5.6	4.5	3.4	31 008.5	5 391	59 775	22 703	288 938	60.8	38.6	0.6
Camden, NJ Div	4 573.1	3 774	56.5	1.9	5.5	2.7	5.0	5 170.4	4 266	9 804	6 915	72 529	56.5	42.7	0.9
Philadelphia, PA Div	14 834.4	3 830	36.7	9.0	5.5	5.5	2.3	24 133.3	6 232	45 278	12 381	176 801	62.7	36.9	0.4
Wilmington, DE-MD-NJ Div	1 767.7	2 650	55.8	0.9	6.4	1.0	8.0	1 704.8	2 555	4 693	3 407	39 608	56.6	42.5	0.9
Phoenix-Mesa-Scottsdale, AZ	10 804.2	3 087	38.8	3.4	6.8	5.4	3.9	16 974.5	4 850	20 019	12 709	185 907	42.5	56.9	0.6
Pine Bluff, AR	194.4	1 831	55.7	0.2	7.8	0.0	6.0	119.2	1 123	1 667	521	8 388	61.0	37.2	1.8
Pittsburgh, PA	8 344.6	3 451	42.4	6.5	3.6	6.3	3.6	15 853.4	6 556	18 940	7 225	111 578	51.8	47.6	0.7
Pittsfield, MA	399.3	2 992	58.5	0.4	3.4	0.1	5.9	295.9	2 217	429	309	7 695	73.3	25.8	0.8
Pocatello, ID	267.4	3 215	38.3	27.3	5.3	0.6	4.3	98.1	1 179	536	309	8 977	36.4	62.5	1.0
Portland-South Portland-Biddeford, ME	1 299.9	2 597	51.6	0.4	4.4	2.0	5.0	949.3	1 896	7 917	5 690	28 264	55.1	43.1	1.7
Portland-Vancouver-Beaverton, OR-WA	7 054.1	3 498	42.5	3.3	5.1	2.5	5.1	8 755.7	4 342	17 285	6 383	110 146	57.3	41.7	0.9
Port St. Lucie-Fort Pierce, FL	935.8	2 772	42.8	0.6	8.2	1.5	3.7	1 518.7	4 498	869	593	14 633	47.5	51.6	0.9
Poughkeepsie-Newburgh-Middletown, NY	2 645.3	4 104	53.5	3.5	3.5	10.8	4.2	1 718.3	2 666	6 576	6 721	42 970	44.8	53.5	1.7
Prescott, AZ	474.3	2 649	36.4	1.5	6.2	8.2	12.9	376.6	2 103	1 181	327	9 236	37.7	61.6	0.7
Providence-New Bedford-Fall River, RI-MA	4 208.6	2 609	55.7	0.4	6.5	0.4	2.8	2 534.9	1 571	11 102	9 718	84 869	61.0	37.7	1.3
Provo-Orem, UT	859.2	2 168	56.2	2.2	6.0	0.2	4.1	1 051.5	2 653	1 103	1 587	22 119	11.0	86.1	2.9
Pueblo, CO	360.7	2 456	44.9	1.7	5.5	6.3	5.6	425.3	2 896	676	223	10 946	52.5	46.5	1.0
Punta Gorda, FL	351.7	2 261	37.1	1.4	7.5	0.8	12.7	271.3	1 825	254	227	4 944	42.9	55.7	1.4
Racine, WI	615.7	3 224	45.9	5.0	8.1	6.8	7.0	438.2	2 294	396	519	9 341	47.5	51.7	0.8
Raleigh-Cary, NC	2 457.2	2 860	46.4	6.8	4.7	4.5	3.1	7 915.3	9 213	4 844	2 235	76 299	46.2	53.4	0.4
Rapid City, SD	275.3	2 387	50.8	1.1	5.4	0.4	9.5	131.1	1 137	2 491	4 068	6 753	30.4	67.9	1.8
Reading, PA	1 161.3	3 039	51.7	4.3	3.6	5.4	2.7	1 879.8	4 920	1 081	1 047	19 736	46.5	52.9	0.6
Redding, CA	693.0	4 034	41.3	8.2	4.5	11.0	3.8	441.3	2 569	1 244	238	12 962	31.2	67.5	1.2
Reno-Sparks, NV	1 346.3	3 681	30.2	0.9	8.2	2.5	13.6	2 026.2	5 540	3 185	538	21 809	47.9	50.5	1.6
Richmond, VA	3 366.9	2 989	45.3	7.3	5.6	4.7	2.5	3 154.7	2 801	15 193	9 570	98 197	44.2	55.3	0.5
Riverside-San Bernardino-Ontario, CA	14 352.2	4 083	43.7	9.7	6.8	9.2	3.1	11 666.5	3 319	16 386	20 780	195 878	42.2	56.8	1.0
Roanoke, VA	809.1	2 795	42.0	2.9	5.1	5.4	2.3	819.3	2 830	3 643	790	16 288	39.0	60.3	0.8
Rochester, MN	609.1	3 595	40.1	1.5	3.8	9.5	8.8	1 532.4	9 045	993	585	9 199	46.1	52.7	1.2
Rochester, NY	4 682.6	4 491	50.5	3.1	3.4	13.0	4.6	3 100.9	2 974	4 538	1 548	72 319	47.0	51.1	1.9
Rockford, IL	983.4	3 005	51.9	1.3	5.6	2.6	5.7	691.4	2 113	1 161	605	15 381	48.3	51.0	0.6
Rocky Mount, NC	573.1	3 972	38.1	26.3	3.4	5.8	1.2	72.9	505	550	251	10 547	51.0	48.8	0.2
Rome, GA	388.5	4 195	34.5	40.8	2.7	0.1	2.0	198.0	2 139	160	246	6 115	31.7	67.7	0.6
Sacramento-Arden-Arcade—Roseville, CA	8 260.6	4 280	39.5	4.2	6.0	11.1	5.3	10 912.9	5 654	12 458	3 536	223 574	47.0	52.0	1.0
Saginaw-Saginaw Township North, MI	630.6	3 001	50.1	11.1	4.7	0.9	5.2	427.0	2 033	1 283	382	11 146	53.4	45.9	0.8
St. Cloud, MN	563.5	3 273	46.4	3.0	4.0	6.4	11.4	865.7	5 028	1 484	597	10 971	43.7	54.8	1.5
St. George, UT	210.3	2 115	52.4	0.4	5.0	0.0	6.9	331.7	3 335	479	394	4 557	16.4	81.6	2.0
St. Joseph, MO-KS	286.8	2 354	58.7	1.7	3.8	0.1	7.0	276.1	2 266	640	368	9 305	43.4	55.8	0.8
St. Louis, MO-IL	7 765.6	2 846	52.3	2.5	6.5	0.5	5.5	6 246.8	2 289	30 051	14 301	142 011	53.6	45.9	0.5

1. Based on the resident population estimated as of July 1 of the year shown.

Table C. Metropolitan Areas — Land Area and Population

| CBSA/ DIV code[1] | Area Name | Land area,[2] 2000 (sq km) | Population and population characteristics, 2003 | | | | Race alone or in combination, not Hispanic or Latino (percent) | | | | | Age (percent) | | | | | |
| | | | Total persons | Rank | Per square kilometer | White | Black | Am. Indian, Alaska Native | Asian and Pacific Islander | Percent Hispanic or Latino[3] | Under 5 years | 5 to 17 years | 18 to 24 years | 25 to 34 years | 35 to 44 years | 45 to 54 years |
		1	2	3	4	5	6	7	8	9	10	11	12	13	14	15
41420	Salem, OR	4 985	362 990	131	72.8	77.9	1.1	2.2	2.8	17.8	7.1	19.1	10.9	13.7	13.6	13.3
41500	Salinas, CA	8 604	414 449	110	48.2	40.0	3.8	0.9	7.5	49.7	8.0	20.0	11.3	15.3	14.9	12.4
41540	Salisbury, MD	1 824	112 822	308	61.9	69.6	27.1	0.5	1.7	2.0	6.0	16.5	13.4	12.1	14.9	13.8
41620	Salt Lake City, UT	24 706	1 005 232	50	40.7	81.1	1.4	1.1	4.7	13.0	9.3	21.0	11.9	16.2	13.7	12.0
41660	San Angelo, TX	6 665	105 270	330	15.8	62.4	3.6	0.8	1.1	32.9	7.3	18.5	12.7	12.2	13.7	12.7
41700	San Antonio, TX	19 012	1 820 719	28	95.8	40.3	6.0	0.6	1.8	52.1	7.8	20.3	10.6	14.0	14.7	12.7
41740	San Diego-Carlsbad-San Marcos, CA	10 878	2 930 886	17	269.4	55.5	6.1	1.1	11.2	28.7	7.2	18.4	10.8	15.4	15.7	13.0
41780	Sandusky, OH	660	78 709	356	119.3	88.6	9.4	0.6	0.6	2.2	5.8	17.8	8.5	10.6	14.9	15.5
41860	San Francisco-Oakland-Fremont, CA	6 405	4 157 377	12	649.1	50.0	9.8	1.0	23.2	18.9	6.4	16.1	7.9	15.9	17.1	15.1
36084	Oakland-Fremont-Hayward, CA Div	3 775	2 462 166	X	652.2	48.2	12.8	1.1	21.0	20.2	6.9	18.2	8.8	14.6	16.7	14.8
41884	San Francisco-San Mateo-Redwood City, CA Div	2 630	1 695 211	X	644.6	52.6	5.4	0.7	26.5	17.1	5.7	13.1	6.6	17.7	17.8	15.6
41940	San Jose-Sunnyvale-Santa Clara, CA	6 941	1 734 721	30	249.9	43.8	2.8	0.7	29.5	25.4	7.5	17.4	8.3	16.4	17.6	13.9
42020	San Luis Obispo-Paso Robles, CA	8 558	253 118	168	29.6	77.3	2.2	1.5	3.6	17.3	4.7	15.5	13.1	12.2	14.4	15.2
42060	Santa Barbara-Santa Maria-Goleta, CA	7 089	403 134	115	56.9	57.1	2.3	1.1	5.1	36.1	6.6	17.8	12.8	13.7	14.4	12.8
42100	Santa Cruz-Watsonville, CA	1 153	251 584	169	218.2	67.2	1.2	1.3	4.7	27.7	6.3	16.6	11.7	13.9	15.7	16.7
42140	Santa Fe, NM	4 945	136 423	269	27.6	46.3	0.8	3.0	1.3	49.5	5.7	17.0	9.1	12.1	15.3	17.1
42220	Santa Rosa-Petaluma, CA	4 082	466 725	102	114.3	74.3	1.9	1.7	4.8	19.8	5.9	17.6	9.8	12.3	15.4	16.4
42260	Sarasota-Bradenton-Venice, FL	3 399	633 597	78	186.4	84.5	6.5	0.5	1.3	7.9	5.0	14.0	6.7	9.5	12.5	12.6
42340	Savannah, GA	3 521	304 325	148	86.4	61.8	34.6	0.6	2.1	2.0	7.3	18.6	10.8	14.2	14.8	13.2
42540	Scranton—Wilkes-Barre, PA	4 524	552 139	86	122.0	96.1	1.8	0.2	0.8	1.5	4.9	15.7	9.3	11.3	14.7	14.6
42660	Seattle-Tacoma-Bellevue, WA	15 265	3 141 777	15	205.8	77.2	6.3	2.0	11.9	6.2	6.3	17.4	9.3	15.3	17.1	15.0
42644	Seattle-Bellevue-Everett, WA Div	10 917	2 400 820	X	219.9	76.7	5.6	1.8	12.9	6.1	6.1	16.7	8.9	15.7	17.4	15.4
45104	Tacoma, WA Div	4 348	740 957	X	170.4	78.8	8.6	2.6	8.4	6.3	6.8	19.4	10.8	13.9	16.0	13.8
43100	Sheboygan, WI	1 330	113 376	305	85.2	90.5	1.2	0.6	4.4	3.9	5.7	18.3	9.6	12.2	16.3	14.8
43300	Sherman-Denison, TX	2 418	115 153	302	47.6	84.6	6.0	2.4	0.8	8.0	6.9	18.2	10.3	11.8	14.1	13.4
43340	Shreveport-Bossier City, LA	6 730	378 331	125	56.2	57.7	39.0	0.8	1.3	2.1	7.3	19.0	10.4	13.0	14.2	13.7
43580	Sioux City, IA-NE-SD	5 369	142 857	261	26.6	83.2	2.2	2.0	3.1	10.9	7.4	19.3	10.3	13.1	14.4	13.8
43620	Sioux Falls, SD	6 680	198 377	198	29.7	93.5	2.1	2.1	1.5	2.0	7.3	18.7	10.5	14.1	15.6	13.5
43780	South Bend-Mishawaka, IN-MI	2 460	317 733	146	129.2	82.9	11.4	1.0	1.9	4.7	6.9	18.8	11.2	12.3	14.3	14.0
43900	Spartanburg, SC	2 100	261 281	166	124.4	73.4	21.5	0.5	2.0	3.4	6.4	18.0	9.4	13.6	15.1	14.2
44060	Spokane, WA	4 568	431 027	107	94.4	91.7	2.3	2.3	3.0	3.1	6.3	18.1	11.2	13.1	14.8	14.6
44100	Springfield, IL	3 063	204 468	196	66.8	87.6	10.2	0.6	1.5	1.3	6.4	17.8	8.7	12.8	15.7	15.3
44140	Springfield, MA	4 790	688 495	70	143.7	79.8	6.3	0.6	2.2	12.1	5.6	17.4	12.0	12.0	15.0	14.5
44180	Springfield, MO	7 797	384 654	122	49.3	95.0	2.0	1.4	1.2	1.7	6.3	17.0	11.9	13.7	14.3	13.2
44220	Springfield, OH	1 036	143 351	259	138.4	88.9	9.6	0.9	0.8	1.3	6.6	17.9	9.9	11.5	14.0	14.6
44300	State College, PA	2 868	141 636	263	49.4	91.3	2.8	0.3	4.9	1.5	4.2	12.6	23.3	14.5	12.4	11.3
44700	Stockton, CA	3 624	632 760	79	174.6	45.7	7.8	1.4	14.6	33.4	7.7	21.8	11.3	13.5	14.4	12.0
44940	Sumter, SC	1 723	105 958	328	61.5	48.1	49.2	0.6	1.5	1.6	8.0	20.0	10.6	12.5	15.1	13.0
45060	Syracuse, NY	6 189	654 194	74	105.7	87.4	7.9	1.2	2.3	2.6	6.0	18.0	10.9	11.9	15.6	14.4
45220	Tallahassee, FL	6 183	327 879	144	53.0	61.4	33.1	0.6	1.9	3.9	6.2	15.8	15.4	15.3	13.9	13.7
45300	Tampa-St. Petersburg-Clearwater, FL	6 615	2 531 908	20	382.8	74.6	11.1	0.7	2.7	12.0	6.0	16.5	8.0	12.1	14.8	13.5
45460	Terre Haute, IN	3 794	169 745	227	44.7	93.5	4.7	0.7	1.2	0.9	6.1	17.2	12.2	12.7	14.0	13.9
45500	Texarkana, TX-Texarkana, AR	3 916	131 591	275	33.6	71.5	24.1	1.2	0.6	3.6	6.8	18.2	10.1	13.4	14.5	13.5
45780	Toledo, OH	4 195	660 874	73	157.5	81.9	12.7	0.6	1.5	4.6	6.5	18.3	11.0	13.1	14.5	14.4
45820	Topeka, KS	8 398	226 268	184	26.9	84.4	7.7	2.1	1.2	6.5	6.7	18.2	9.5	11.9	14.9	15.0
45940	Trenton-Ewing, NJ	585	361 981	132	618.8	62.7	20.2	0.4	6.8	10.9	6.3	17.6	10.7	13.2	16.0	14.3
46060	Tucson, AZ	23 792	892 798	53	37.5	60.1	3.2	3.3	2.9	31.9	6.9	18.0	10.4	13.4	13.8	13.1
46140	Tulsa, OK	16 268	879 846	55	54.1	77.0	9.6	10.8	1.8	5.3	7.2	18.8	9.8	13.3	14.9	14.1
46220	Tuscaloosa, AL	6 770	194 645	202	28.8	62.3	35.5	0.5	1.0	1.3	6.6	17.1	13.9	14.2	13.5	13.6
46340	Tyler, TX	2 405	184 015	211	76.5	67.4	18.8	0.8	0.9	13.0	7.3	19.0	10.7	12.6	13.5	13.0
46540	Utica-Rome, NY	6 796	298 077	150	43.9	90.5	5.1	0.5	1.5	3.3	5.2	17.0	10.0	11.7	15.2	14.4
46660	Valdosta, GA	4 115	122 181	292	29.7	63.1	32.7	0.8	1.4	3.0	7.2	18.7	13.1	15.3	14.7	11.9
46700	Vallejo-Fairfield, CA	2 148	412 336	111	192.0	50.3	16.3	1.5	16.6	19.9	7.0	20.4	10.1	13.5	16.1	14.3
46940	Vero Beach, FL	1 303	120 463	294	92.5	82.9	8.6	0.4	1.0	7.6	4.9	14.4	7.5	9.0	12.1	12.2
47020	Victoria, TX	5 824	112 965	307	19.4	52.4	5.4	0.4	1.3	40.9	7.8	20.5	9.9	11.8	14.4	13.5
47220	Vineland-Millville-Bridgeton, NJ	1 267	149 306	250	117.8	57.5	20.3	1.2	1.2	21.0	6.8	18.5	9.2	14.4	15.7	13.3
47260	Virginia Beach-Norfolk-Newport News, VA-NC	6 805	1 637 251	32	240.6	61.8	32.4	1.0	3.7	3.1	7.1	19.0	11.3	13.7	16.1	13.1
47300	Visalia-Porterville, CA	12 494	390 791	120	31.3	40.6	1.7	1.3	3.6	53.8	8.9	23.5	11.9	13.1	13.3	11.3
47380	Waco, TX	2 698	219 807	187	81.5	63.9	15.2	0.7	1.4	19.8	7.5	18.9	14.3	12.5	13.0	12.0
47580	Warner Robins, GA	976	120 434	295	123.4	70.0	25.3	0.8	2.5	2.9	7.1	20.3	10.5	13.1	16.5	13.2

1. CBSA = Core Based Statistical Area. DIV = Metropolitan Division. See Appendix A for explanation. See Appendix B for list of metropolitan areas identified by type.   2. Dry land or land partially or temporarily covered by water.   3. Hispanic or Latino persons may be of any race.

Table C. Metropolitan Areas — **Population and Households**

Area Name	Population, 2003 (cont'd) Age (percent) (cont'd)				Population — change and components of change, 1990–2003							Households, 2000				
					Total persons		Percent change		Components of change, 2000–2003						Percent	
	55 to 64 years	65 to 74 years	75 years and over	Percent female	1900	2000	1990–2000	2000–2003	Births	Deaths	Net migration	Number	Percent change, 1990–2000	Persons per house-hold	Female family house-holder[1]	One person
	16	17	18	19	20	21	22	23	24	25	26	27	28	29	30	31
Salem, OR	8.7	5.9	6.6	49.8	278 024	347 214	24.9	4.5	16 920	9 949	9 122	124 699	22.7	2.68	10.7	23.7
Salinas, CA	7.7	5.1	4.7	48.2	355 660	401 762	13.0	3.2	22 995	7 909	-2 469	121 236	7.3	3.14	11.6	21.2
Salisbury, MD	9.3	6.7	6.1	51.0	97 779	109 391	11.9	3.1	4 572	3 478	2 430	40 579	13.5	2.50	14.3	25.8
Salt Lake City, UT	6.9	4.1	3.8	49.4	768 075	968 858	26.1	3.8	63 324	18 193	-9 344	318 150	25.0	3.00	10.2	20.6
San Angelo, TX	8.8	7.0	6.8	51.6	100 087	105 781	5.7	-0.5	5 048	3 124	-2 436	40 197	11.6	2.53	11.8	27.1
San Antonio, TX	8.1	5.6	4.9	51.0	1 407 745	1 711 703	21.6	6.4	91 502	38 348	56 448	601 265	23.4	2.78	14.5	23.1
San Diego-Carlsbad-San Marcos, CA	7.9	5.4	5.5	49.6	2 498 016	2 813 833	12.6	4.2	141 510	64 583	43 141	994 677	12.1	2.73	11.6	24.2
Sandusky, OH	11.3	8.0	7.9	51.3	76 781	79 551	3.6	-1.1	3 008	2 648	-1 165	31 727	9.7	2.45	11.2	27.0
San Francisco-Oakland-Fremont, CA	9.6	5.9	5.9	50.5	3 711 756	4 123 740	11.1	0.8	181 732	97 201	-53 133	1 551 948	9.1	2.61	11.0	28.0
Oakland-Fremont-Hayward, CA Div	9.2	5.3	5.2	50.9	2 108 078	2 392 557	13.5	2.9	113 384	54 127	10 330	867 495	11.2	2.71	12.4	24.8
San Francisco-San Mateo-Redwood City, CA Div	10.3	6.7	6.8	49.9	1 603 678	1 731 183	8.0	-2.1	68 348	43 074	-63 463	684 453	6.5	2.47	9.3	32.1
San Jose-Sunnyvale-Santa Clara, CA	8.9	5.3	4.6	49.2	1 534 274	1 735 819	13.1	-0.1	88 787	29 501	-63 703	581 748	9.4	2.93	10.0	21.2
San Luis Obispo-Paso Robles, CA	9.3	6.9	7.3	48.6	217 162	246 681	13.6	2.6	7 879	6 571	5 240	92 739	15.5	2.49	9.1	26.0
Santa Barbara-Santa Maria-Goleta, CA	8.4	6.2	6.6	49.9	369 608	399 347	8.0	0.9	18 192	9 494	-5 003	136 622	5.3	2.80	10.0	24.3
Santa Cruz-Watsonville, CA	9.2	4.8	5.2	50.0	229 734	255 602	11.3	-1.6	11 161	5 501	-9 866	91 139	9.1	2.71	10.2	25.1
Santa Fe, NM	11.3	6.2	4.8	51.0	98 928	129 292	30.7	5.5	4 953	2 498	4 753	52 482	38.7	2.42	11.7	29.4
Santa Rosa-Petaluma, CA	10.0	5.8	6.7	50.6	388 222	458 614	18.1	1.8	18 313	12 653	2 748	172 403	15.7	2.60	10.4	25.7
Sarasota-Bradenton-Venice, FL	11.8	12.5	14.2	51.9	489 483	589 959	20.5	7.4	19 325	26 348	49 177	262 397	21.2	2.20	8.4	29.6
Savannah, GA	8.8	6.0	5.4	51.5	257 899	293 000	13.6	3.9	14 948	8 943	5 352	111 105	17.0	2.56	15.9	25.2
Scranton—Wilkes-Barre, PA	10.7	8.6	10.3	52.0	575 322	560 625	-2.6	-1.5	17 526	25 137	-348	227 667	2.1	2.37	11.5	31.0
Seattle-Tacoma-Bellevue, WA	8.9	5.0	5.0	50.1	2 559 136	3 043 878	18.9	3.2	129 987	67 907	36 774	1 196 568	19.4	2.49	9.8	27.7
Seattle-Bellevue-Everett, WA Div	9.1	4.9	5.1	50.1	1 972 933	2 343 058	18.8	2.5	97 614	50 434	11 448	935 768	18.8	2.45	9.2	28.6
Tacoma, WA Div	8.5	5.3	4.7	50.2	586 203	700 820	19.6	5.7	32 373	17 473	25 326	260 800	21.5	2.60	11.8	24.3
Sheboygan, WI	9.2	6.6	7.3	49.7	103 877	112 646	8.4	0.6	3 941	3 370	271	43 545	12.8	2.50	7.3	26.1
Sherman-Denison, TX	9.9	7.4	7.2	51.3	95 019	110 595	16.4	4.1	5 232	4 066	3 445	42 849	16.3	2.51	11.4	25.5
Shreveport-Bossier City, LA	9.1	6.7	6.1	52.1	360 009	375 965	4.4	0.6	18 787	12 191	-4 038	144 293	8.4	2.54	18.2	27.1
Sioux City, IA-NE-SD	8.6	6.1	6.7	50.7	131 350	143 053	8.9	-0.1	7 187	4 112	-3 307	53 586	9.1	2.61	10.7	25.9
Sioux Falls, SD	7.7	5.5	5.8	50.2	153 500	187 093	21.9	6.0	9 419	4 728	6 654	72 492	23.7	2.50	8.8	26.7
South Bend-Mishawaka, IN-MI	8.8	6.4	7.0	51.4	296 529	316 663	6.8	0.3	14 187	9 571	-3 382	120 419	8.9	2.51	12.0	27.1
Spartanburg, SC	10.2	6.6	5.8	51.3	226 793	253 791	11.9	3.0	10 800	8 634	5 524	97 735	15.7	2.52	13.8	24.8
Spokane, WA	8.9	5.9	6.4	50.8	361 333	417 939	15.7	3.1	17 573	12 002	7 987	163 611	15.5	2.46	11.0	28.1
Springfield, IL	9.7	6.6	6.8	52.1	189 550	201 437	6.3	1.5	8 768	6 400	-160	83 595	9.5	2.37	11.5	30.5
Springfield, MA	9.2	6.3	7.4	52.2	672 964	680 014	1.0	1.2	24 975	20 804	4 877	260 745	5.3	2.48	14.0	28.5
Springfield, MO	9.1	6.6	6.4	51.1	298 818	368 374	23.3	4.4	15 714	11 563	12 325	145 304	26.7	2.43	9.4	26.4
Springfield, OH	10.8	7.4	7.4	51.8	147 538	144 742	-1.9	-1.0	6 113	5 371	-2 055	56 648	2.6	2.49	12.8	26.0
State College, PA	7.5	5.4	4.8	48.8	124 812	135 758	8.8	4.3	3 887	2 935	5 000	49 323	15.6	2.45	6.1	26.6
Stockton, CA	7.5	4.9	4.9	49.9	480 628	563 598	17.3	12.3	31 670	14 415	50 843	181 629	14.8	3.00	14.0	20.7
Sumter, SC	8.6	6.4	5.2	51.8	101 276	104 646	3.3	1.3	5 736	3 074	-1 294	37 728	15.3	2.68	18.3	23.2
Syracuse, NY	9.4	6.5	6.6	51.7	659 924	650 154	-1.5	0.6	25 826	18 428	-2 837	252 043	3.3	2.49	12.2	28.0
Tallahassee, FL	8.4	5.1	4.2	51.6	259 107	320 304	23.6	2.4	13 512	7 527	1 713	125 533	28.9	2.41	14.2	28.2
Tampa-St. Petersburg-Clearwater, FL	10.2	8.7	9.3	51.6	2 067 959	2 395 997	15.9	5.7	95 394	95 307	134 281	1 009 316	16.1	2.33	11.2	29.7
Terre Haute, IN	9.3	6.7	7.5	50.2	166 578	170 943	2.6	-0.7	6 708	6 523	-1 279	65 795	4.1	2.43	10.8	28.1
Texarkana, TX-Texarkana, AR	9.6	6.7	6.7	50.2	120 132	129 749	8.0	1.4	5 654	4 267	569	48 695	8.5	2.50	15.3	25.9
Toledo, OH	9.1	6.3	6.4	51.5	654 157	659 188	0.8	0.3	28 767	20 901	-5 754	259 973	5.7	2.47	12.8	28.5
Topeka, KS	9.9	7.0	6.9	51.1	210 257	224 551	6.8	0.8	9 881	7 613	-373	89 600	9.1	2.44	10.7	28.0
Trenton-Ewing, NJ	9.2	6.0	6.2	51.1	325 759	350 761	7.7	3.2	15 164	9 590	6 030	125 807	7.6	2.62	13.8	25.6
Tucson, AZ	9.1	7.2	6.7	51.1	666 957	843 746	26.5	5.8	39 894	24 828	34 396	332 350	27.0	2.47	11.8	28.5
Tulsa, OK	9.6	6.4	5.6	51.0	761 019	859 532	12.9	2.4	42 553	26 346	4 371	337 215	13.4	2.50	11.5	26.9
Tuscaloosa, AL	8.4	6.2	5.3	51.6	176 151	192 034	9.0	0.8	8 753	5 996	-1 091	74 863	16.5	2.44	15.4	28.3
Tyler, TX	9.2	7.3	6.5	51.9	151 309	174 706	15.5	5.3	8 786	5 629	6 267	65 692	15.7	2.59	12.3	24.7
Utica-Rome, NY	10.1	7.4	8.8	50.5	316 645	299 896	-5.3	-0.6	10 174	11 123	-676	116 230	-1.1	2.44	11.6	29.1
Valdosta, GA	7.8	5.4	4.5	50.3	99 244	119 560	20.5	2.2	5 790	3 224	123	42 666	23.7	2.63	15.9	24.0
Vallejo-Fairfield, CA	8.3	5.2	4.5	49.7	339 469	394 542	16.2	4.5	18 983	8 290	7 447	130 403	15.0	2.90	13.8	19.6
Vero Beach, FL	11.1	13.0	14.7	51.4	90 208	112 947	25.2	6.7	3 692	5 216	8 821	49 137	29.1	2.25	8.9	28.2
Victoria, TX	9.2	6.9	5.8	51.0	99 394	111 663	12.3	1.2	5 798	2 801	-1 639	40 157	14.0	2.74	12.1	22.2
Vineland-Millville-Bridgeton, NJ	9.0	6.3	6.4	48.8	138 053	146 438	6.1	2.0	6 933	5 059	1 123	49 143	4.3	2.73	17.3	23.6
Virginia Beach-Norfolk-Newport News, VA-NC	8.3	5.5	4.8	50.6	1 450 855	1 576 370	8.7	3.9	76 493	39 421	23 930	580 278	13.0	2.60	14.9	23.4
Visalia-Porterville, CA	7.2	4.9	4.5	49.8	311 932	368 021	18.0	6.2	23 563	8 695	8 130	110 385	12.8	3.28	14.5	17.1
Waco, TX	8.0	6.2	6.3	51.4	189 123	213 517	12.9	2.9	10 680	6 189	2 014	78 859	12.3	2.59	13.6	26.0
Warner Robins, GA	8.3	5.6	3.7	50.8	89 208	110 765	24.2	8.7	5 540	2 788	6 834	40 911	26.1	2.65	14.0	22.1

1. No spouse present.

Table C. Metropolitan Areas — Vital Statistics, Health Resources, and Crime

Area Name	Births, average 1999–2001		Deaths, average 1999–2001				Physicians,[4] 1998		Hospitals,[4] 1998			Medicare enrollees, 2003	Serious crimes known to police,[6] 2002	
			Number		Rate					Beds			Total	
	Total	Rate[1]	Total	Infant[2]	Total[1]	Infant[3]	Number	Rate[5]	Number	Number	Rate[5]		Number	Rate[7]
	32	33	34	35	36	37	38	39	40	41	42	43	44	45
Salem, OR	5 261	15.1	2 949	87	8.5	5.5	563	279	4	517	257	51 191	22 607	6 344
Salinas, CA	6 732	16.7	2 412	110	6.0	5.4	673	168	4	675	185	43 750	14 426	3 463
Salisbury, MD	1 398	12.8	1 057	45	9.6	10.7	244	363	2	439	665	16 500	5 163	4 580
Salt Lake City, UT	19 448	20.0	5 366	300	5.5	5.1	2 330	457	10	1 962	340	88 603	60 469	6 028
San Angelo, TX	1 589	15.1	1 022	43	9.7	9.0	213	205	3	478	465	16 387	6 177	5 591
San Antonio, TX	28 159	16.4	12 621	499	7.3	5.9	4 136	754	21	4 369	755	216 513	115 504	6 460
San Diego-Carlsbad-San Marcos, CA	43 809	15.5	19 685	739	7.0	5.6	7 062	251	25	6 828	246	350 167	105 363	3 612
Sandusky, OH	937	11.8	822	22	10.3	7.8	157	197	2	444	567	13 908	3 296	4 138
San Francisco-Oakland-Fremont, CA	55 943	13.5	29 811	786	7.2	4.7	13 065	1 704	49	12 437	1 519	526 857	190 501	4 456
Oakland-Fremont-Hayward, CA Div	34 563	14.4	16 579	531	6.9	5.1	5 736	479	27	5 829	495	280 877	121 462	4 897
San Francisco-San Mateo-Redwood City, CA Div	21 380	12.3	13 233	255	7.6	4.0	7 329	1 225	22	6 608	1 024	245 980	69 039	3 847
San Jose-Sunnyvale-Santa Clara, CA	27 983	16.1	9 183	371	5.3	4.4	4 605	325	16	4 589	480	177 959	47 681	2 650
San Luis Obispo-Paso Robles, CA	2 411	9.8	2 013	33	8.1	4.6	581	236	6	636	271	40 110	7 603	2 973
Santa Barbara-Santa Maria-Goleta, CA	5 599	14.0	2 938	85	7.4	5.1	998	250	8	1 314	337	56 246	10 041	2 425
Santa Cruz-Watsonville, CA	3 658	14.3	1 682	46	6.6	4.2	531	208	2	395	163	28 062	10 136	3 825
Santa Fe, NM	1 612	12.4	798	32	6.2	6.6	329	254	1	208	169	16 964	6 339	4 965
Santa Rosa-Petaluma, CA	5 594	12.2	3 827	80	8.3	4.8	1 066	232	8	889	205	64 105	16 031	3 372
Sarasota-Bradenton-Venice, FL	5 874	9.9	8 153	120	13.8	6.8	1 411	466	6	2 175	796	161 625	31 396	5 089
Savannah, GA	4 518	15.4	2 650	110	9.0	8.1	647	389	4	1 256	780	40 120	18 099	6 004
Scranton—Wilkes-Barre, PA	5 479	9.8	7 670	102	13.7	6.2	1 240	547	12	2 543	1 190	115 273	11 629	2 569
Seattle-Tacoma-Bellevue, WA	40 736	13.3	20 801	645	6.8	5.3	8 187	673	31	5 834	513	354 128	170 288	5 460
Seattle-Bellevue-Everett, WA Div	30 685	13.1	15 560	448	6.6	4.9	6 795	474	24	4 776	357	267 541	125 984	5 255
Tacoma, WA Div	10 051	14.3	5 241	197	7.4	6.5	1 392	199	7	1 058	156	86 587	44 304	6 142
Sheboygan, WI	1 386	12.3	1 037	37	9.2	8.9	150	133	3	421	382	17 618	3 495	3 058
Sherman-Denison, TX	1 538	13.9	1 282	37	11.6	8.0	190	172	3	540	525	19 015	4 889	4 232
Shreveport-Bossier City, LA	5 636	15.0	3 710	209	9.9	12.4	1 007	499	10	1 860	1 033	55 367	24 357	6 459
Sioux City, IA-NE-SD	2 264	15.8	1 257	49	8.8	7.2	246	360	2	681	670	21 436	6 779	4 743
Sioux Falls, SD	2 879	15.4	1 443	58	7.7	6.7	519	465	1	926	1 603	25 453	4 667	2 680
South Bend-Mishawaka, IN-MI	4 461	14.1	2 935	106	9.3	7.9	556	231	5	893	439	47 718	16 614	5 306
Spartanburg, SC	3 350	13.2	2 551	70	10.0	7.0	418	165	3	681	275	41 603	13 903	5 351
Spokane, WA	5 535	13.2	3 641	82	8.7	4.9	993	238	4	1 274	312	61 613	24 322	5 766
Springfield, IL	2 685	13.3	1 929	58	9.6	7.2	645	356	3	1 336	698	31 300	NA	NA
Springfield, MA	7 816	11.5	6 562	114	9.7	4.9	1 559	612	10	2 101	730	108 877	31 622	4 712
Springfield, MO	4 977	13.5	3 480	95	9.4	6.4	710	449	6	1 731	1 021	60 220	17 407	4 661
Springfield, OH	1 934	13.4	1 666	46	11.5	7.9	202	140	2	464	319	24 374	7 784	5 357
State College, PA	1 242	9.1	852	17	6.3	4.6	244	180	2	232	175	16 231	2 831	2 076
Stockton, CA	9 425	16.5	4 359	178	7.6	6.3	762	135	8	1 140	207	71 307	37 878	6 483
Sumter, SC	1 675	16.0	921	48	8.8	9.6	127	121	1	230	215	14 509	6 521	6 087
Syracuse, NY	8 181	12.6	5 712	222	8.8	9.0	1 777	556	8	2 279	1 054	102 118	21 958	3 389
Tallahassee, FL	4 100	12.8	2 295	146	7.2	11.9	527	390	2	812	374	35 472	18 743	5 596
Tampa-St. Petersburg-Clearwater, FL	28 964	12.0	28 761	677	10.2	7.8	5 427	769	33	8 131	1 303	469 339	147 810	5 899
Terre Haute, IN	2 133	12.5	2 001	55	11.7	8.6	258	374	5	714	1 335	28 423	NA	NA
Texarkana, TX-Texarkana, AR	1 752	13.5	1 344	38	10.3	7.2	210	258	4	711	851	20 191	6 508	4 847
Toledo, OH	8 881	13.5	6 344	201	9.6	7.5	1 650	578	11	2 901	984	96 759	36 678	6 387
Topeka, KS	3 045	13.6	2 315	90	10.3	9.9	501	440	4	777	1 175	36 974	13 878	6 238
Trenton-Ewing, NJ	4 595	13.1	3 027	105	8.6	7.6	1 046	298	5	1 674	505	52 272	13 186	3 682
Tucson, AZ	12 184	14.4	7 383	232	8.7	6.3	2 266	269	9	2 078	263	134 558	67 628	7 537
Tulsa, OK	12 987	15.1	7 835	294	9.1	7.5	1 671	615	18	2 876	2 509	121 391	43 532	5 002
Tuscaloosa, AL	2 705	14.1	1 792	104	9.3	12.8	331	304	4	782	1 331	28 204	9 740	5 328
Tyler, TX	2 639	15.1	1 722	61	9.8	7.7	492	282	3	558	331	28 959	9 062	5 021
Utica-Rome, NY	3 225	10.8	3 353	75	11.2	7.8	535	284	6	1 279	916	56 305	8 089	2 763
Valdosta, GA	1 772	14.9	991	64	8.3	12.0	170	258	4	424	1 150	14 623	5 257	4 227
Vallejo-Fairfield, CA	5 739	14.5	2 489	84	6.3	4.9	703	178	4	522	138	42 954	17 953	4 389
Vero Beach, FL	1 091	9.6	1 514	24	13.4	7.3	249	220	2	480	484	32 651	4 732	4 006
Victoria, TX	1 772	15.8	915	25	8.2	4.7	202	349	4	663	1 075	16 135	5 370	4 604
Vineland-Millville-Bridgeton, NJ	2 038	13.9	1 529	81	10.4	13.2	240	164	3	631	450	22 649	7 547	5 048
Virginia Beach-Norfolk-Newport News, VA-NC	23 182	14.7	11 967	661	7.6	9.5	3 294	2 988	17	3 960	3 383	192 331	71 923	4 428
Visalia-Porterville, CA	7 116	19.3	2 634	131	7.1	6.1	431	117	7	854	240	42 622	18 592	4 873
Waco, TX	3 227	15.1	1 989	77	9.3	8.0	359	168	3	638	314	31 068	14 889	6 676
Warner Robins, GA	1 562	14.1	775	46	7.0	9.8	127	115	2	236	223	13 146	5 250	4 533

1. Per 1,000 estimated resident population.   2. Deaths of infants under 1 year old.   3. Deaths of infants under 1 year old per 1,000 live births.   4. Data subject to copyright.   5. Per 100,000 resident population as of July 1 of the year shown.   6. Data for serious crimes have not been adjusted for underreporting; this may affect comparability between geographic areas and over time.   7. Per 100,000 population estimated by the FBI.

Table C. Metropolitan Areas — Crime, Education, Money Income, and Poverty

Area Name	Serious crimes known to police,[1] 2002 (cont'd) Rate[2]		Education						Money income, 1999				Percent below poverty level, 1999			
			School enrollment and attainment, 2000				Local government expenditures,[5] 2000–2001									
			Enrollment[3]		Attainment[4] (percent)											
	Violent	Property	Total	Percent private	High school graduate or more	Bachelor's degree or more	Total current expenditures (mil dol)	Current expenditures per student (dollars)	Per capita income[6] (dollars)	Mean household income	Mean family income	Percent of households with income of $100,000 or more	Persons	Households	Families	Families with children
	46	47	48	49	50	51	52	53	54	55	56	57	58	59	60	61
Salem, OR	241	6 103	91 093	14.4	80.4	20.8	432.8	7 364	18 565	50 208	56 624	7.9	13.1	11.3	9.0	14.4
Salinas, CA	469	2 995	117 126	10.7	68.4	22.5	506.6	6 985	20 165	63 944	68 162	15.2	13.5	10.3	9.7	14.0
Salisbury, MD	804	3 776	31 590	11.5	78.1	19.5	135.0	7 848	18 446	47 805	56 137	7.8	14.3	13.8	10.0	15.1
Salt Lake City, UT	339	5 688	296 488	11.2	87.0	27.6	875.8	4 568	20 444	61 348	68 189	13.3	7.9	7.6	5.6	7.8
San Angelo, TX	377	5 214	30 194	5.8	76.3	19.5	130.8	6 708	17 378	44 277	51 585	5.9	15.1	14.8	11.1	16.4
San Antonio, TX	643	5 818	493 250	13.5	77.1	22.1	2 163.7	6 599	18 443	51 426	57 305	9.8	15.1	13.7	11.9	17.1
San Diego-Carlsbad-San Marcos, CA	481	3 131	827 975	13.4	82.6	29.5	3 487.5	7 141	22 926	63 204	70 321	15.7	12.4	10.3	8.9	13.3
Sandusky, OH	222	3 915	19 104	14.2	84.0	16.6	130.0	9 100	21 530	53 326	62 350	9.1	8.3	8.3	6.0	9.7
San Francisco-Oakland-Fremont, CA	528	3 927	1 112 300	19.9	84.2	38.8	4 063.8	7 259	31 771	83 353	95 230	26.2	9.1	8.1	6.1	8.9
Oakland-Fremont-Hayward, CA Div	562	4 335	687 395	16.8	84.2	35.0	2 620.4	6 929	28 241	77 011	87 542	24.0	9.7	8.5	6.7	9.7
San Francisco-San Mateo-Redwood City, CA Div	483	3 364	424 905	24.8	84.2	43.6	1 443.4	7 945	36 651	91 393	107 054	29.0	8.4	7.6	5.2	7.6
San Jose-Sunnyvale-Santa Clara, CA	356	2 294	492 343	19.6	83.2	39.8	1 915.3	7 214	32 432	95 440	103 849	34.2	7.6	6.1	5.0	6.8
San Luis Obispo-Paso Robles, CA	273	2 700	77 496	8.9	85.6	26.7	248.6	6 727	21 864	55 550	65 049	12.0	12.8	11.8	6.8	9.9
Santa Barbara-Santa Maria-Goleta, CA	322	2 104	127 198	13.4	79.2	29.4	454.4	6 883	23 059	65 782	74 651	16.0	14.3	11.6	8.5	13.0
Santa Cruz-Watsonville, CA	415	3 410	76 840	13.1	83.2	34.2	302.9	7 493	26 396	72 455	81 395	21.9	11.9	9.5	6.7	9.8
Santa Fe, NM	530	4 434	33 486	20.6	84.5	36.9	83.8	5 459	23 594	57 571	65 049	13.0	12.0	11.5	9.4	13.4
Santa Rosa-Petaluma, CA	309	3 063	125 553	13.6	84.9	28.5	538.1	7 302	25 724	67 258	76 638	18.1	8.1	7.0	4.7	6.9
Sarasota-Bradenton-Venice, FL	625	4 464	107 822	16.6	84.7	24.6	461.2	6 397	25 669	56 753	66 382	11.2	8.8	8.0	6.0	11.5
Savannah, GA	619	5 385	82 370	19.4	79.9	23.2	313.5	6 383	20 752	53 979	62 904	10.4	14.5	14.3	11.0	16.6
Scranton—Wilkes-Barre, PA	272	2 296	132 799	27.5	81.5	17.5	591.8	8 226	18 372	44 362	53 900	6.5	10.8	11.7	7.7	12.3
Seattle-Tacoma-Bellevue, WA	403	5 057	799 046	16.1	89.3	32.7	3 189.8	6 572	26 332	65 948	76 064	16.1	8.5	8.0	5.7	8.5
Seattle-Bellevue-Everett, WA Div	357	4 898	607 726	16.6	90.0	36.1	2 352.7	6 582	27 942	69 007	80 579	17.6	8.0	7.5	5.2	7.6
Tacoma, WA Div	555	5 587	191 320	14.3	86.9	20.6	837.2	6 545	20 948	54 972	61 571	10.4	10.5	9.6	7.5	11.3
Sheboygan, WI	116	2 942	28 868	21.5	84.4	17.9	155.8	7 904	21 509	54 105	62 181	7.8	5.2	5.2	3.7	5.4
Sherman-Denison, TX	275	3 957	27 885	12.0	80.2	17.2	126.0	6 357	18 862	48 129	55 167	7.5	11.3	12.1	8.4	13.2
Shreveport-Bossier City, LA	805	5 653	103 063	10.5	79.2	19.2	426.7	6 186	17 625	45 182	51 977	7.4	19.5	18.3	15.6	23.1
Sioux City, IA-NE-SD	429	4 314	38 087	16.5	80.9	18.5	175.6	6 852	18 736	49 363	57 323	7.2	10.0	9.6	7.2	10.8
Sioux Falls, SD	250	2 430	49 192	18.6	88.1	25.1	176.8	5 657	20 624	52 380	62 033	8.5	7.1	7.3	4.8	7.2
South Bend-Mishawaka, IN-MI	386	4 920	89 547	29.4	82.1	21.7	376.1	7 978	19 711	50 848	59 267	8.7	10.3	9.7	7.4	12.1
Spartanburg, SC	848	4 504	61 998	13.8	73.1	18.2	295.0	6 900	18 738	47 774	55 201	7.5	12.3	12.8	9.2	13.4
Spokane, WA	418	5 348	117 842	15.5	89.1	25.0	493.6	6 799	19 233	48 118	56 818	7.9	12.3	12.2	8.3	12.9
Springfield, IL	NA	NA	51 573	17.3	88.1	28.1	209.5	6 616	23 074	55 041	65 055	10.4	9.3	8.4	6.5	10.4
Springfield, MA	840	3 872	201 287	18.7	82.4	25.2	1 042.5	9 593	20 140	51 313	60 211	9.5	13.1	12.8	9.6	15.7
Springfield, MO	453	4 208	101 077	16.6	83.0	21.3	321.3	5 524	18 098	44 869	52 559	6.4	12.4	12.5	8.2	12.7
Springfield, OH	409	4 948	36 734	15.9	81.2	14.9	183.7	7 390	19 501	49 016	56 009	7.9	10.7	10.1	7.9	12.9
State College, PA	120	1 956	56 564	7.1	88.2	36.3	132.2	9 155	18 020	47 820	62 292	8.5	18.8	17.7	6.1	8.7
Stockton, CA	937	5 546	176 188	12.5	71.2	14.5	809.3	6 687	17 365	52 852	58 108	10.6	17.7	14.5	13.5	19.0
Sumter, SC	1 030	5 058	30 345	15.0	74.3	15.8	119.8	6 283	15 657	42 505	47 944	5.3	16.2	16.3	13.1	18.2
Syracuse, NY	343	3 046	188 890	20.3	84.5	25.2	1 118.1	9 640	20 254	51 468	60 591	9.9	12.3	12.3	8.5	13.2
Tallahassee, FL	804	4 791	114 737	10.3	84.7	34.1	293.6	6 362	19 705	48 931	60 937	9.2	17.9	18.3	10.7	15.0
Tampa-St. Petersburg-Clearwater, FL	888	5 011	549 586	18.3	81.5	21.7	2 072.0	6 019	21 784	50 956	59 425	9.4	11.2	10.4	7.8	12.7
Terre Haute, IN	NA	NA	46 597	11.2	81.2	17.4	191.2	6 935	17 343	43 455	51 666	5.8	12.3	12.9	9.0	13.7
Texarkana, TX-Texarkana, AR	545	4 301	32 069	7.6	76.4	15.0	141.5	6 173	17 072	43 892	50 954	6.2	18.2	17.4	14.3	22.0
Toledo, OH	615	5 771	193 153	16.8	84.1	21.2	818.8	7 885	20 652	51 640	61 071	9.5	12.1	12.1	8.7	13.9
Topeka, KS	572	5 666	57 298	14.4	88.0	23.6	245.5	6 486	20 312	50 019	58 508	7.6	9.1	9.3	6.2	9.7
Trenton-Ewing, NJ	531	3 151	99 649	26.5	81.8	34.0	698.3	12 454	27 914	76 166	89 633	23.0	8.6	8.6	5.9	8.9
Tucson, AZ	631	6 906	236 404	10.8	83.4	26.7	721.5	5 491	19 785	49 415	57 686	9.0	14.7	13.3	10.5	16.4
Tulsa, OK	647	4 355	231 319	16.2	83.2	22.5	856.0	5 581	19 720	49 599	57 788	8.6	11.8	11.7	9.0	13.4
Tuscaloosa, AL	527	4 801	59 553	10.4	76.8	21.9	184.0	6 080	18 155	45 329	54 667	7.2	18.9	20.4	13.3	19.0
Tyler, TX	506	4 514	46 077	11.9	80.2	22.5	179.8	5 836	19 072	49 992	57 729	9.1	13.8	13.2	10.2	15.0
Utica-Rome, NY	305	2 458	76 818	13.8	79.1	17.7	474.0	9 538	18 006	44 900	52 365	6.2	12.9	12.8	9.6	16.0
Valdosta, GA	432	3 795	37 175	8.4	75.0	17.4	137.7	6 564	16 099	42 072	48 601	5.9	19.4	19.3	15.0	20.8
Vallejo-Fairfield, CA	545	3 844	116 471	12.9	83.8	21.4	480.2	6 572	21 731	64 228	69 772	16.5	8.3	7.4	6.1	8.5
Vero Beach, FL	396	3 610	22 308	17.2	81.6	23.1	92.3	6 161	27 227	62 018	73 662	12.4	9.3	8.5	6.3	11.8
Victoria, TX	571	4 033	31 262	11.4	74.6	15.2	151.9	7 216	18 069	49 332	55 472	8.1	13.8	13.3	11.0	15.8
Vineland-Millville-Bridgeton, NJ	692	4 357	37 622	13.0	68.5	11.7	303.7	11 923	17 376	48 956	54 477	8.2	15.0	13.7	11.3	16.7
Virginia Beach-Norfolk-Newport News, VA-NC	460	3 968	443 075	15.4	84.6	23.7	1 876.8	6 802	20 313	53 200	59 546	9.7	10.6	10.4	8.4	12.5
Visalia-Porterville, CA	658	4 214	118 065	6.6	61.7	11.5	612.1	7 146	14 006	45 974	48 595	7.6	23.9	19.0	18.8	26.6
Waco, TX	581	6 095	68 392	24.0	76.6	19.1	263.8	6 726	17 174	45 523	53 569	7.5	17.6	17.6	12.4	17.6
Warner Robins, GA	265	4 268	32 495	10.5	84.3	19.8	141.5	6 571	19 515	51 364	56 934	8.5	10.2	9.8	8.4	12.3

1. Data for serious crimes have not been adjusted for underreporting; this may affect comparability between geographic areas and over time.　2. Per 100,000 population estimated by the FBI.　3. All persons 3 years old and over enrolled in nursery school through college.　4. Persons 25 years old and over.　5. Elementary and secondary education expenditures.　6. Based on population enumerated as of April 1, 2000.

Table C. Metropolitan Areas — **Personal Income**

Area Name	Personal income, 2002 Total (mil dol)	Percent change, 2001–2002	Per capita[1] Dollars	Rank	Wages and salaries[2] (mil dol)	Proprietor's income (mil dol)	Dividends, interest, and rent (mil dol)	Transfer payments Total (mil dol)	Government payments to individuals Total (mil dol)	Social Security (mil dol)	Medical payments (mil dol)	Income maintenance (mil dol)	Unemployment insurance (mil dol)
	62	63	64	65	66	67	68	69	70	71	72	73	74
Salem, OR	9 032	3.4	25 242	247	5 472	713	1 722	1 614	1 532	573	587	143	102
Salinas, CA	13 091	3.1	31 666	68	7 363	1 993	2 878	1 556	1 458	464	547	181	141
Salisbury, MD	2 712	2.8	24 242	293	1 816	129	472	523	495	182	226	44	15
Salt Lake City, UT	28 540	2.2	28 620	132	23 556	2 825	4 627	2 797	2 572	1 031	865	272	160
San Angelo, TX	2 684	2.3	25 617	230	1 681	176	549	464	442	171	190	43	7
San Antonio, TX	48 884	3.3	27 361	169	31 649	6 367	7 415	6 884	6 492	2 118	2 841	753	172
San Diego-Carlsbad-San Marcos, CA	101 293	4.3	34 849	29	68 484	10 924	18 898	11 439	10 772	3 620	4 549	1 257	398
Sandusky, OH	2 378	1.6	30 023	99	1 567	200	428	385	363	156	138	24	13
San Francisco-Oakland-Fremont, CA	195 396	-2.4	46 751	2	133 063	21 779	38 901	17 407	16 410	5 493	6 863	1 913	981
Oakland-Fremont-Hayward, CA Div	99 478	-0.7	40 362	X	61 050	8 565	16 882	10 135	9 547	3 016	4 166	1 129	565
San Francisco-San Mateo-Redwood City, CA Div	95 918	-4.1	55 934	X	72 013	13 214	22 019	7 272	6 863	2 477	2 698	785	415
San Jose-Sunnyvale-Santa Clara, CA	79 596	-7.0	45 759	3	72 491	7 468	15 023	6 158	5 743	1 884	2 238	635	540
San Luis Obispo-Paso Robles, CA	7 599	4.1	29 987	102	3 838	927	2 051	1 010	949	441	313	88	32
Santa Barbara-Santa Maria-Goleta, CA	13 701	3.2	33 990	37	7 981	1 530	3 973	1 546	1 451	611	499	164	56
Santa Cruz-Watsonville, CA	9 707	-1.4	38 245	13	4 519	1 033	2 030	943	883	303	329	98	79
Santa Fe, NM	4 417	6.5	32 834	49	2 332	518	1 177	476	440	190	168	38	9
Santa Rosa-Petaluma, CA	17 391	1.1	37 130	19	9 003	1 770	3 922	1 863	1 751	720	667	141	95
Sarasota-Bradenton-Venice, FL	23 264	4.1	37 514	18	10 239	1 694	8 441	3 569	3 417	1 799	1 288	140	42
Savannah, GA	8 449	4.0	28 183	150	5 598	416	1 651	1 354	1 269	455	559	129	29
Scranton—Wilkes-Barre, PA	15 279	2.5	27 622	160	9 315	1 187	2 641	3 434	3 292	1 256	1 443	195	176
Seattle-Tacoma-Bellevue, WA	118 739	1.4	37 986	15	90 450	10 746	19 808	12 814	11 974	4 144	4 070	969	1 269
Seattle-Bellevue-Everett, WA Div	97 372	0.9	40 681	X	78 697	9 497	16 678	9 609	8 961	3 163	2 996	675	992
Tacoma, WA Div	21 368	3.6	29 180	X	11 754	1 249	3 130	3 205	3 012	981	1 075	295	277
Sheboygan, WI	3 465	3.1	30 805	84	2 444	301	619	451	423	206	149	20	36
Sherman-Denison, TX	2 644	1.3	23 222	320	1 612	154	440	538	513	202	219	34	17
Shreveport-Bossier City, LA	9 789	3.2	25 905	217	6 415	820	1 704	1 872	1 776	582	826	225	39
Sioux City, IA-NE-SD	3 869	1.4	27 093	176	2 715	359	694	598	561	228	242	45	16
Sioux Falls, SD	6 223	4.1	31 970	63	4 413	799	1 073	651	610	284	244	36	8
South Bend-Mishawaka, IN-MI	8 947	2.8	28 100	151	5 460	949	1 572	1 333	1 254	567	487	119	39
Spartanburg, SC	6 523	3.1	25 154	254	5 076	313	938	1 144	1 079	468	400	99	53
Spokane, WA	11 382	2.8	26 624	193	7 874	791	2 048	2 128	2 013	674	761	192	158
Springfield, IL	6 416	2.4	31 575	74	4 805	443	1 229	855	802	356	292	82	35
Springfield, MA	20 066	3.3	29 326	114	12 079	1 094	3 078	4 159	3 996	1 151	2 083	369	237
Springfield, MO	9 705	4.0	25 625	229	6 120	1 186	1 716	1 650	1 560	628	653	130	34
Springfield, OH	3 762	0.0	26 231	203	2 013	161	575	771	730	262	322	68	28
State College, PA	3 560	4.9	25 700	226	2 749	273	628	495	460	189	154	26	22
Stockton, CA	14 788	3.6	24 073	299	8 507	1 152	2 195	2 960	2 813	743	1 306	435	166
Sumter, SC	2 270	4.3	21 578	341	1 631	338	482	457		149	182	70	16
Syracuse, NY	18 423	3.9	28 191	148	13 322	1 143	2 711	3 372	3 200	1 205	1 333	365	128
Tallahassee, FL	8 547	3.1	26 068	211	6 510	446	1 410	1 134	1 053	384	410	136	18
Tampa-St. Petersburg-Clearwater, FL	73 986	3.4	29 710	108	49 287	3 655	15 541	12 623	12 015	5 183	5 033	849	254
Terre Haute, IN	3 934	2.5	23 174	321	2 519	208	741	822	779	316	330	67	25
Texarkana, TX-Texarkana, AR	3 128	4.0	23 873	304	1 861	279	576	604	573	198	264	67	10
Toledo, OH	18 891	2.4	28 644	130	13 821	1 164	3 090	3 239	3 052	1 092	1 289	302	117
Topeka, KS	6 401	2.7	28 349	143	4 463	369	1 095	1 056	994	397	390	67	32
Trenton-Ewing, NJ	14 582	2.2	40 566	8	11 962	1 014	2 653	1 877	1 789	630	851	125	99
Tucson, AZ	22 213	4.6	25 207	249	13 654	1 233	4 963	3 946	3 744	1 470	1 597	322	61
Tulsa, OK	26 827	1.9	30 558	89	16 553	4 668	4 419	3 561	3 356	1 427	1 307	279	108
Tuscaloosa, AL	4 871	3.5	25 158	253	3 284	352	781	911	865	318	368	105	15
Tyler, TX	5 114	4.0	28 351	142	3 275	708	997	819	779	320	327	65	19
Utica-Rome, NY	7 348	2.8	24 599	283	4 636	394	1 184	1 721	1 643	609	717	176	56
Valdosta, GA	2 790	7.5	23 030	323	1 834	169	482	541	508	154	239	62	14
Vallejo-Fairfield, CA	11 912	2.7	28 978	123	5 890	539	1 605	1 475	1 379	448	519	166	96
Vero Beach, FL	4 699	3.3	39 820	10	1 591	206	2 366	734	705	369	268	27	13
Victoria, TX	2 908	1.2	25 825	222	1 902	245	564	495	470	179	211	47	14
Vineland-Millville-Bridgeton, NJ	3 823	5.9	25 872	218	2 497	286	482	925	889	259	444	74	79
Virginia Beach-Norfolk-Newport News, VA-NC	45 773	4.4	28 379	140	34 932	2 277	7 034	5 630	5 267	2 060	1 961	549	187
Visalia-Porterville, CA	8 076	4.3	21 154	344	4 513	979	1 099	1 881	1 790	429	741	345	186
Waco, TX	5 212	4.1	23 940	302	3 553	457	825	893	844	328	310	92	18
Warner Robins, GA	3 027	7.0	25 923	216	2 510	128	476	399	367	118	170	41	12

1. Based on the resident population estimated as of July 1 of the year shown.   2. Includes other labor income.

Table C. Metropolitan Areas — Earnings, Social Security, and Housing

Area Name	Earnings, 2002									Social Security beneficiaries, December 2003		Housing units, 2003		
	Total (mil dol)	Farm	Goods related[1]		Service-related and health							Supplemental Security Income recipients, December 2003		Percent change, 2000–2003
			Total	Manu-facturing	Infor-mation, profes-sional and technical services	Retail trade	Finance and insur-ance, and real estate	Health services	Govern-ment	Number	Rate[2]		Total	
	75	76	77	78	79	80	81	82	83	84	85	86	87	88
Salem, OR	6 185	3.6	15.8	9.2	5.3	7.3	5.4	12.8	30.4	58 965	162	6 067	138 232	4.2
Salinas, CA	9 356	11.1	10.8	5.1	7.0	7.5	6.3	6.6	21.8	49 470	119	8 957	135 569	2.9
Salisbury, MD	1 945	0.7	D	10.8	D	8.3	4.9	D	21.2	19 225	170	2 361	46 387	4.3
Salt Lake City, UT	26 381	0.0	17.7	10.1	D	7.5	10.6	D	15.6	103 625	103	9 656	361 286	5.5
San Angelo, TX	1 858	0.2	D	10.1	D	D	D	14.8	27.5	18 635	177	2 399	45 568	1.6
San Antonio, TX	38 016	0.3	D	6.5	D	7.9	11.1	D	22.9	252 195	139	44 470	687 437	6.0
San Diego-Carlsbad-San Marcos, CA	79 407	0.5	16.7	9.9	17.3	6.7	9.8	7.0	22.8	375 965	128	79 578	1 085 515	4.4
Sandusky, OH	1 766	0.2	37.0	32.1	3.4	6.4	3.7	9.5	13.9	15 095	192	1 245	36 403	1.4
San Francisco-Oakland-Fremont, CA	154 842	0.1	D	8.2	22.0	6.5	13.9	7.3	12.6	532 340	128	132 690	1 645 363	2.4
Oakland-Fremont-Hayward, CA Div	69 616	0.1	20.6	12.4	16.3	7.1	8.3	9.4	14.7	296 135	120	70 890	920 279	2.9
San Francisco-San Mateo-Redwood City, CA Div	85 227	0.1	D	4.7	26.6	6.0	18.4	5.6	11.0	236 205	139	61 800	725 084	1.8
San Jose-Sunnyvale-Santa Clara, CA	79 959	0.3	D	29.3	23.4	4.9	5.9	5.3	7.6	180 255	104	43 335	614 059	3.1
San Luis Obispo-Paso Robles, CA	4 765	2.8	17.1	6.6	9.2	9.9	7.2	10.0	21.1	44 985	178	5 345	107 819	5.4
Santa Barbara-Santa Maria-Goleta, CA	9 511	4.1	16.3	9.4	13.1	8.0	8.2	8.7	19.8	61 505	153	9 640	146 867	2.8
Santa Cruz-Watsonville, CA	5 552	3.7	D	9.6	13.5	9.7	8.0	9.5	16.1	31 135	124	5 475	100 173	1.3
Santa Fe, NM	2 850	0.2	11.5	2.6	11.8	10.7	10.1	9.6	26.0	19 815	145	2 019	59 766	3.6
Santa Rosa-Petaluma, CA	10 773	1.7	26.2	15.8	11.1	8.5	8.9	10.3	13.5	71 245	153	9 315	189 818	3.6
Sarasota-Bradenton-Venice, FL	11 933	1.1	D	8.4	11.9	9.6	8.1	13.1	9.6	175 580	277	7 364	345 910	7.9
Savannah, GA	6 014	0.0	D	14.7	7.3	7.7	5.4	D	19.7	46 775	154	7 475	130 179	6.2
Scranton—Wilkes-Barre, PA	10 502	0.2	23.4	17.8	8.3	8.5	7.0	14.4	14.2	131 200	238	14 603	255 306	1.0
Seattle-Tacoma-Bellevue, WA	101 196	0.1	20.6	14.1	20.3	6.4	8.5	7.6	14.4	395 905	126	51 949	1 319 766	5.1
Seattle-Bellevue-Everett, WA Div	88 193	0.1	21.2	15.0	22.5	6.3	8.6	6.9	12.0	294 645	123	36 903	1 026 567	4.9
Tacoma, WA Div	13 003	0.2	16.2	8.4	5.5	7.8	7.5	12.6	30.6	101 260	137	15 046	293 199	5.8
Sheboygan, WI	2 745	0.7	51.7	46.3	4.7	5.4	5.3	9.1	9.8	20 020	177	1 304	47 508	3.4
Sherman-Denison, TX	1 766	0.2	32.2	24.3	4.7	9.9	8.2	16.0	12.5	21 415	186	2 176	49 360	2.2
Shreveport-Bossier City, LA	7 235	0.1	20.6	10.8	D	7.1	4.9	D	23.8	63 285	167	13 393	163 782	2.5
Sioux City, IA-NE-SD	3 073	2.2	D	D	D	6.7	D	D	12.2	23 640	165	2 312	57 655	1.3
Sioux Falls, SD	5 212	2.1	D	10.2	6.6	8.2	16.8	D	9.4	29 455	148	2 238	82 560	9.2
South Bend-Mishawaka, IN-MI	6 409	0.2	D	23.5	8.1	7.2	5.9	D	10.7	54 790	172	4 982	135 052	3.2
Spartanburg, SC	5 389	0.2	39.2	32.9	4.9	7.7	4.3	7.2	13.9	49 690	190	6 129	112 636	5.3
Spokane, WA	8 664	0.2	16.6	10.1	8.2	9.6	8.6	14.6	20.3	69 715	162	10 083	180 977	3.4
Springfield, IL	5 248	0.3	D	3.4	9.2	6.0	9.9	D	32.8	36 675	179	4 846	93 138	2.6
Springfield, MA	13 174	0.2	D	14.3	7.4	7.7	8.2	14.2	19.6	122 525	178	26 389	279 526	1.1
Springfield, MO	7 306	0.1	21.3	15.1	7.4	10.7	7.3	D	13.2	69 425	180	7 826	166 670	6.5
Springfield, OH	2 174	0.3	30.3	25.3	3.9	10.2	4.0	14.0	16.0	27 120	189	3 606	61 840	1.3
State College, PA	3 022	0.2	16.1	10.5	9.4	6.5	4.4	7.8	42.4	18 695	132	1 655	55 667	4.7
Stockton, CA	9 659	2.6	19.7	10.0	5.8	9.4	6.3	9.8	19.9	81 180	128	26 331	205 364	8.6
Sumter, SC	1 715	0.3	D	21.3	3.0	6.5	3.5	8.5	36.4	17 620	166	4 106	42 968	2.9
Syracuse, NY	14 464	0.3	D	16.3	10.6	6.6	7.5	D	17.0	118 345	181	15 937	282 614	1.6
Tallahassee, FL	6 956	1.0	D	2.5	D	6.3	5.6	D	40.0	42 010	128	8 003	145 227	6.2
Tampa-St. Petersburg-Clearwater, FL	52 942	0.5	D	7.4	13.0	8.2	10.4	11.0	13.0	537 040	212	56 020	1 204 611	5.3
Terre Haute, IN	2 727	0.1	D	21.7	D	11.1	4.3	D	19.4	32 670	192	3 750	73 885	1.9
Texarkana, TX-Texarkana, AR	2 140	1.3	18.8	13.0	D	10.1	5.5	16.1	23.1	23 290	177	4 356	55 763	2.9
Toledo, OH	14 985	0.2	D	23.5	D	7.3	5.7	D	15.5	107 770	163	15 723	292 872	2.6
Topeka, KS	4 832	-0.2	D	9.3	D	8.1	9.5	D	23.4	40 910	181	4 232	99 297	3.0
Trenton-Ewing, NJ	12 977	0.0	D	4.4	18.9	4.9	12.3	8.3	24.0	56 975	157	7 958	136 986	2.8
Tucson, AZ	14 887	0.1	D	13.3	10.0	8.0	5.8	11.6	24.6	152 730	171	15 877	391 234	6.7
Tulsa, OK	21 221	0.0	30.2	21.0	11.7	7.4	6.4	D	9.6	143 490	163	14 730	378 457	3.3
Tuscaloosa, AL	3 636	0.8	33.9	21.2	5.0	7.2	D	D	24.6	35 000	180	8 173	88 550	5.0
Tyler, TX	3 984	1.0	21.1	13.2	9.6	12.1	9.4	17.9	12.5	32 965	179	4 103	74 211	3.5
Utica-Rome, NY	5 030	0.6	17.4	13.2	7.4	7.8	7.3	13.8	25.4	64 430	216	9 247	135 616	0.6
Valdosta, GA	2 003	1.8	D	0.0	D	9.7	D	D	34.3	17 915	147	3 857	50 702	5.3
Vallejo-Fairfield, CA	6 429	0.5	20.0	9.3	4.7	9.6	4.7	11.4	29.2	49 420	120	10 204	141 837	5.4
Vero Beach, FL	1 798	1.6	D	6.2	9.2	11.4	8.6	16.5	13.1	36 335	302	1 373	63 594	9.8
Victoria, TX	2 148	-0.2	D	D	D	9.5	D	D	14.4	19 075	169	2 692	47 637	2.2
Vineland-Millville-Bridgeton, NJ	2 783	1.8	25.0	19.4	5.0	9.2	4.3	11.7	25.8	25 955	174	4 663	53 692	1.6
Virginia Beach-Norfolk-Newport News, VA-NC	37 209	0.1	12.6	8.2	D	5.8	D	7.0	38.3	224 235	137	29 730	648 255	4.1
Visalia-Porterville, CA	5 492	10.6	15.4	8.9	3.8	8.1	5.0	7.0	22.9	51 120	131	17 079	124 970	4.5
Waco, TX	4 010	0.5	24.7	18.0	5.9	7.7	10.1	10.5	17.3	35 450	161	5 278	87 375	3.0
Warner Robins, GA	2 638	0.1	9.1	6.6	6.7	5.8	2.5	4.8	61.1	15 195	126	2 426	49 774	11.8

1. Covers mining, construction, and manufacturing.   2. Per 1,000 resident population estimated as of July 1 of the year shown.

Table C. Metropolitan Areas — Housing, Labor Force, and Employment

Area Name	Total	Percent	Mean value[1]	With a mortgage	Without a mortgage	Mean rent[2]	Rent is 35 percent or more of income	Sub-standard units[3] (percent)	Total	Percent change, 2002-2003	Total	Rate[4]	Total	Management, professional, and related occupations	Production, transportation, and material moving occupations
	89	90	91	92	93	94	95	96	97	98	99	100	101	102	103
Salem, OR	124 699	63.9	154 551	21.7	5.7	625	32.8	7.6	183 064	1.9	14 155	7.7	155 929	30.0	15.2
Salinas, CA	121 236	54.7	347 704	30.5	7.6	849	32.5	20.8	198 582	0.6	20 701	10.4	163 987	29.2	11.1
Salisbury, MD	40 579	67.1	111 531	17.5	8.9	549	34.2	2.7	59 463	-2.2	3 199	5.4	51 579	29.7	14.5
Salt Lake City, UT	318 150	69.6	194 483	20.2	4.9	678	29.2	6.2	543 428	1.1	31 820	5.9	479 758	32.7	13.0
San Angelo, TX	40 197	64.4	77 194	15.7	7.6	492	30.4	5.7	52 399	1.7	2 019	3.9	46 267	27.9	13.3
San Antonio, TX	601 265	64.5	99 306	16.4	7.9	590	28.9	9.5	888 450	2.3	48 728	5.5	737 324	32.5	11.2
San Diego-Carlsbad-San Marcos, CA	994 677	55.4	284 952	27.6	6.6	832	35.6	12.2	1 482 241	1.7	63 137	4.3	1 241 258	37.7	9.9
Sandusky, OH	31 727	72.0	130 482	15.8	7.2	533	25.8	1.5	44 123	1.4	2 629	6.0	37 750	26.9	23.5
San Francisco-Oakland-Fremont, CA	1 551 948	55.4	420 973	26.7	7.6	1 021	31.7	11.3	2 171 415	-1.6	130 921	6.0	2 062 508	44.0	9.2
Oakland-Fremont-Hayward, CA Div	867 495	60.5	347 050	25.4	7.4	925	33.0	10.7	1 268 008	-0.7	79 663	6.3	1 144 190	41.8	10.5
San Francisco-San Mateo-Redwood City, CA Div	684 453	49.0	547 206	29.2	7.8	1 116	30.4	12.1	903 407	-2.9	51 258	5.7	918 318	46.7	7.5
San Jose-Sunnyvale-Santa Clara, CA	581 748	60.1	524 976	25.1	6.1	1 217	30.3	14.6	924 066	-4.9	76 255	8.3	867 575	48.0	11.3
San Luis Obispo-Paso Robles, CA	92 739	61.5	267 605	29.1	6.5	775	42.0	5.9	121 184	0.4	4 112	3.4	109 669	34.3	9.8
Santa Barbara-Santa Maria-Goleta, CA	136 622	56.1	383 707	30.8	6.5	920	40.3	13.2	209 136	2.4	8 433	4.0	180 716	35.4	9.6
Santa Cruz-Watsonville, CA	91 139	60.0	426 041	30.9	7.8	997	38.6	11.6	139 017	-1.5	11 718	8.4	129 380	40.3	8.9
Santa Fe, NM	52 482	68.6	255 529	25.9	8.2	725	36.5	5.7	71 175	3.5	2 664	3.7	64 930	41.7	6.4
Santa Rosa-Petaluma, CA	172 403	64.1	319 124	28.0	5.7	897	34.0	7.2	257 544	-1.9	12 578	4.9	229 227	35.0	11.4
Sarasota-Bradenton-Venice, FL	262 397	76.8	165 729	23.5	6.7	740	33.8	3.1	305 869	2.4	10 649	3.5	247 212	30.5	10.9
Savannah, GA	111 105	64.3	136 552	19.2	9.1	603	34.2	4.6	149 022	4.4	5 879	3.9	130 209	31.2	13.9
Scranton—Wilkes-Barre, PA	227 667	69.7	104 338	19.6	10.8	449	27.7	1.1	276 592	-1.5	16 224	5.9	252 570	28.4	18.5
Seattle-Tacoma-Bellevue, WA	1 196 568	62.1	252 388	22.5	7.3	782	30.7	5.2	1 720 973	0.1	124 211	7.2	1 545 414	38.8	11.8
Seattle-Bellevue-Everett, WA Div	935 768	61.7	274 388	22.3	7.4	811	30.2	5.2	1 365 279	-0.5	96 495	7.1	1 231 256	41.0	10.9
Tacoma, WA Div	260 800	63.5	175 746	23.3	6.9	666	32.5	5.2	355 694	2.4	27 716	7.8	314 158	30.1	15.1
Sheboygan, WI	43 545	71.4	123 742	11.7	6.2	496	18.2	2.3	64 672	1.4	3 199	4.9	59 454	25.9	29.8
Sherman-Denison, TX	42 849	70.5	84 065	15.5	9.1	550	26.3	4.4	52 208	2.4	3 839	7.4	50 801	29.6	17.5
Shreveport-Bossier City, LA	144 293	66.1	94 615	16.0	8.1	488	30.3	5.5	176 205	1.6	12 999	7.4	157 230	28.8	14.9
Sioux City, IA-NE-SD	53 586	69.3	92 062	12.3	5.9	515	25.1	4.8	72 932	-3.5	3 670	5.0	71 816	28.1	20.4
Sioux Falls, SD	72 492	67.5	116 236	11.3	4.5	531	23.5	2.3	119 088	1.7	3 505	2.9	103 410	31.3	14.7
South Bend-Mishawaka, IN-MI	120 419	73.3	105 483	14.3	5.1	543	28.6	2.9	162 983	0.3	7 806	4.8	152 351	30.5	19.9
Spartanburg, SC	97 735	72.0	112 795	16.7	5.8	500	27.4	3.6	132 272	2.9	9 548	7.2	119 910	26.6	24.5
Spokane, WA	163 611	65.5	131 738	20.6	5.9	562	34.8	3.6	217 808	1.4	14 828	6.8	191 295	33.0	12.7
Springfield, IL	83 595	70.5	111 198	12.3	5.5	522	25.9	1.8	104 879	-2.5	5 506	5.2	104 012	39.0	8.4
Springfield, MA	260 745	63.1	139 232	17.3	10.3	555	31.8	3.4	345 469	-0.8	20 064	5.8	326 465	34.5	15.5
Springfield, MO	145 304	67.7	107 903	16.5	4.6	489	30.6	2.6	197 852	1.3	8 236	4.2	181 023	29.0	16.7
Springfield, OH	56 648	71.5	103 939	15.4	6.0	511	28.7	1.7	69 490	-0.2	5 065	7.3	67 204	27.0	22.8
State College, PA	49 323	60.2	133 541	16.3	5.2	621	43.7	4.1	68 746	-2.5	2 331	3.4	64 663	41.6	11.1
Stockton, CA	181 629	60.4	164 517	24.9	7.4	653	37.1	14.4	278 922	2.4	28 154	10.1	219 000	27.1	16.8
Sumter, SC	37 728	69.5	92 696	15.1	8.8	497	26.9	4.2	46 235	4.0	3 641	7.9	41 372	24.9	23.1
Syracuse, NY	252 043	67.0	98 147	16.4	9.9	548	35.0	2.1	333 100	0.2	19 280	5.8	302 516	34.7	14.5
Tallahassee, FL	125 533	62.4	126 167	17.6	8.0	607	42.8	4.4	175 172	0.5	6 084	3.5	156 988	41.3	7.0
Tampa-St. Petersburg-Clearwater, FL	1 009 316	70.8	122 966	20.7	7.4	646	32.0	4.3	1 331 291	0.6	58 133	4.4	1 079 627	32.8	11.2
Terre Haute, IN	65 795	71.9	82 550	12.5	6.4	440	29.6	2.1	81 962	2.0	4 666	5.7	76 313	27.0	19.2
Texarkana, TX-Texarkana, AR	48 695	70.0	78 620	15.4	7.5	462	32.0	4.3	57 416	0.5	3 129	5.4	52 805	27.2	17.6
Toledo, OH	259 973	68.1	120 000	15.6	7.0	514	30.6	2.0	345 808	0.3	25 184	7.3	315 539	29.9	20.0
Topeka, KS	89 600	70.9	91 386	11.8	5.9	529	28.9	2.8	121 796	1.3	6 064	5.0	111 464	32.9	13.4
Trenton-Ewing, NJ	125 807	67.0	196 431	19.5	16.1	765	29.2	4.4	191 314	2.2	9 158	4.8	166 647	43.2	9.7
Tucson, AZ	332 350	64.3	145 417	19.9	5.9	606	35.6	7.5	426 018	-0.1	18 398	4.3	370 768	35.0	9.4
Tulsa, OK	337 215	67.4	103 945	14.7	6.6	533	27.7	4.1	448 749	-1.1	29 646	6.6	408 255	31.7	14.2
Tuscaloosa, AL	74 863	65.6	123 224	17.2	8.0	497	38.0	4.0	95 057	2.1	4 230	4.4	83 348	30.7	17.8
Tyler, TX	65 692	69.7	103 167	16.3	8.3	551	31.7	6.3	97 127	2.8	4 800	4.9	77 518	30.3	16.1
Utica-Rome, NY	116 230	68.1	84 587	16.7	10.1	477	33.4	1.8	145 102	-0.2	7 724	5.3	131 963	31.0	15.8
Valdosta, GA	42 666	64.5	98 969	18.6	9.4	501	34.0	5.1	60 695	5.4	1 820	3.0	50 793	25.9	17.2
Vallejo-Fairfield, CA	130 403	65.2	202 766	23.8	7.6	830	32.6	9.1	212 559	1.8	12 654	6.0	172 355	30.9	13.0
Vero Beach, FL	49 137	77.6	177 983	22.6	6.1	683	34.4	3.1	52 931	5.8	3 981	7.5	45 494	28.0	9.4
Victoria, TX	40 157	69.2	81 856	12.8	6.6	511	25.7	7.5	56 464	0.1	3 212	5.7	49 659	28.0	15.9
Vineland-Millville-Bridgeton, NJ	49 143	67.9	102 201	21.6	12.8	591	36.1	5.8	66 369	2.3	5 739	8.6	59 129	24.8	20.9
Virginia Beach-Norfolk-Newport News, VA-NC	580 278	63.0	136 678	20.4	7.3	635	30.8	3.8	796 763	2.1	35 221	4.4	685 479	33.5	11.9
Visalia-Porterville, CA	110 385	61.5	119 908	24.8	7.4	545	34.6	19.8	174 584	0.6	27 107	15.5	134 094	25.3	14.2
Waco, TX	78 859	60.2	82 577	15.9	6.5	522	34.4	6.6	105 310	2.3	5 398	5.1	94 076	30.0	15.5
Warner Robins, GA	40 911	68.5	103 469	14.2	6.2	574	26.7	3.7	58 123	4.9	1 783	3.1	48 653	31.7	12.6

1. Specified owner-occupied units.   2. Specified renter-occupied units.   3. Overcrowded or lacking complete plumbing facilities.   4. Percent of civilian labor force.   5. Persons 16 years old and over.

Table C. Metropolitan Areas — Nonfarm Employment and Agriculture

Area Name	Private nonfarm establishments, employment and payroll, 2001									Agriculture, 2002			
	Number of establishments	Employment						Annual payroll		Farms			Farm operators whose principal occupation is farming (percent)
		Total	Health care and social assistance	Manufacturing	Retail trade	Finance and insurance	Professional, scientific, and technical services	Total (mil dol)	Average per employee (dollars)	Number	Percent with—		
											Less than 50 acres	500 acres and over	
	104	105	106	107	108	109	110	111	112	113	114	115	116
Salem, OR	8 642	107 747	17 310	12 904	16 859	6 263	3 436	2 852	26 469	4 527	69.8	4.6	52.8
Salinas, CA	8 719	106 740	12 690	6 863	17 717	3 618	5 638	3 393	31 788	1 216	42.5	21.8	69.0
Salisbury, MD	2 910	40 604	7 485	5 689	6 672	1 215	1 225	1 036	25 515	813	50.8	9.8	65.8
Salt Lake City, UT	28 210	504 735	47 439	55 453	62 027	33 250	34 091	15 807	31 317	1 649	64.8	10.9	44.6
San Angelo, TX	2 567	35 873	6 140	3 866	5 532	1 661	1 276	870	24 252	1 175	40.6	31.4	53.8
San Antonio, TX	35 890	654 777	90 131	51 110	82 821	42 894	36 695	19 563	29 877	13 073	36.6	12.1	51.3
San Diego-Carlsbad-San Marcos, CA	69 059	1 081 762	114 863	119 555	144 791	47 431	100 820	39 694	36 694	5 255	89.1	1.9	50.4
Sandusky, OH	2 026	31 521	3 734	8 816	4 788	699	713	1 022	32 423	392	41.6	16.3	55.9
San Francisco-Oakland-Fremont, CA	120 030	2 048 499	203 976	167 915	212 924	143 145	211 345	102 517	50 045	1 584	58.0	14.1	55.3
Oakland-Fremont-Hayward, CA Div	58 753	1 000 061	111 230	115 047	110 720	51 365	77 652	44 162	44 159	1 016	61.4	11.7	53.4
San Francisco-San Mateo-Redwood City, CA Div	61 277	1 048 438	92 746	52 868	102 204	91 780	133 693	58 355	55 659	568	51.9	18.5	58.6
San Jose-Sunnyvale-Santa Clara, CA	46 290	1 054 261	72 709	204 213	90 201	22 290	147 609	68 594	65 064	1 703	66.5	13.1	56.6
San Luis Obispo-Paso Robles, CA	7 136	79 094	13 042	6 972	13 213	2 678	3 949	2 163	27 347	2 322	54.2	16.0	60.2
Santa Barbara-Santa Maria-Goleta, CA	11 005	140 797	16 352	16 416	20 911	5 514	9 035	4 606	32 714	1 444	60.9	14.2	61.6
Santa Cruz-Watsonville, CA	7 001	81 466	10 424	8 247	13 207	2 065	5 641	2 605	31 977	754	74.1	2.1	64.9
Santa Fe, NM	4 730	44 482	5 826	1 342	9 068	1 838	2 459	1 205	27 090	460	65.2	13.3	51.7
Santa Rosa-Petaluma, CA	13 526	172 665	23 284	29 381	25 972	8 941	8 327	6 005	34 778	3 447	70.7	5.9	55.6
Sarasota-Bradenton-Venice, FL	17 204	226 340	31 892	17 954	35 760	8 163	12 424	6 166	27 242	1 223	57.7	12.8	52.5
Savannah, GA	7 559	119 481	16 671	15 055	18 343	4 167	4 173	3 382	28 306	329	41.6	12.2	50.2
Scranton—Wilkes-Barre, PA	13 612	231 817	37 879	37 681	33 367	10 571	7 222	5 967	25 740	1 195	33.1	3.5	53.8
Seattle-Tacoma-Bellevue, WA	90 476	1 470 610	159 468	210 456	179 078	69 782	103 831	63 242	43 004	4 596	83.2	0.8	52.7
Seattle-Bellevue-Everett, WA Div	74 903	1 262 626	124 864	189 163	146 401	61 009	96 309	56 949	45 104	3 122	84.5	0.8	52.7
Tacoma, WA Div	15 573	207 984	34 604	21 293	32 677	8 773	7 522	6 293	30 257	1 474	80.7	0.7	52.8
Sheboygan, WI	2 582	58 212	5 635	22 964	6 184	1 780	1 379	1 784	30 647	1 116	40.9	8.3	61.7
Sherman-Denison, TX	2 560	39 252	7 590	9 235	6 142	2 413	968	1 062	27 056	2 597	46.9	6.6	49.4
Shreveport-Bossier City, LA	8 599	145 730	24 675	15 634	19 869	4 535	4 858	3 815	26 179	1 639	39.9	12.7	49.9
Sioux City, IA-NE-SD	3 894	72 618	9 122	19 401	10 167	2 648	1 567	2 011	27 693	2 626	20.4	28.3	66.9
Sioux Falls, SD	6 287	108 449	18 763	13 046	14 743	13 953	3 170	2 945	27 156	3 302	25.0	30.2	67.2
South Bend-Mishawaka, IN-MI	7 265	130 073	16 115	23 388	18 767	5 126	5 180	3 812	29 307	1 663	47.0	10.8	54.7
Spartanburg, SC	6 266	119 590	13 745	32 668	14 083	2 657	3 349	3 525	29 476	1 412	55.7	2.3	45.5
Spokane, WA	11 632	169 945	28 568	19 722	24 914	9 646	8 240	5 036	29 633	2 225	52.2	12.1	50.2
Springfield, IL	5 523	84 768	18 150	4 058	12 398	5 852	3 969	2 388	28 171	1 299	31.4	28.7	61.8
Springfield, MA	17 449	252 623	44 714	44 512	35 367	13 135	8 934	7 577	29 993	1 586	46.5	2.9	51.6
Springfield, MO	10 425	163 294	27 007	22 270	24 144	7 763	6 720	3 980	24 373	8 389	34.3	6.7	55.1
Springfield, OH	2 694	49 568	7 688	11 540	7 245	1 662	966	1 317	26 570	756	52.1	12.8	56.9
State College, PA	3 163	46 374	5 667	8 176	8 038	1 835	3 227	1 158	24 971	1 213	37.6	4.2	48.2
Stockton, CA	10 350	163 533	21 693	24 237	23 203	6 901	4 277	4 742	28 997	4 026	62.6	8.2	67.4
Sumter, SC	1 875	35 830	3 774	12 719	4 759	1 024	712	867	24 198	537	42.8	12.5	46.0
Syracuse, NY	15 129	270 338	37 078	38 495	36 953	13 318	13 652	8 518	31 509	2 141	31.7	9.2	62.3
Tallahassee, FL	7 711	106 725	18 742	4 287	17 892	4 833	9 270	2 888	27 060	1 168	55.9	7.1	46.1
Tampa-St. Petersburg-Clearwater, FL	61 924	1 042 912	124 209	78 541	137 228	72 532	75 750	32 602	31 261	4 919	77.5	3.6	53.0
Terre Haute, IN	3 836	61 587	9 972	11 070	12 168	1 834	1 391	1 570	25 492	1 689	37.9	19.0	55.1
Texarkana, TX-Texarkana, AR	2 823	42 004	7 692	6 317	7 060	1 354	849	1 049	24 974	1 853	32.5	10.0	56.4
Toledo, OH	15 990	297 173	48 926	54 966	39 679	9 058	14 091	9 256	31 147	2 771	42.1	15.3	58.5
Topeka, KS	5 680	89 113	18 854	7 517	12 461	5 974	4 227	2 471	27 729	4 599	24.1	17.9	54.0
Trenton-Ewing, NJ	10 088	182 869	23 280	10 463	19 822	17 276	17 804	8 063	44 092	304	72.4	4.6	46.4
Tucson, AZ	18 828	293 987	41 187	32 749	43 012	8 963	15 860	8 327	28 324	517	72.7	11.6	54.7
Tulsa, OK	23 127	380 655	44 818	53 326	45 345	18 636	18 891	12 232	32 134	9 518	36.8	10.5	49.2
Tuscaloosa, AL	4 285	73 021	11 707	13 959	10 550	1 722	2 334	1 993	27 294	1 329	27.8	15.8	57.6
Tyler, TX	4 919	75 564	14 203	11 052	11 459	2 773	3 464	2 236	29 591	2 264	47.8	4.5	47.9
Utica-Rome, NY	6 081	100 123	19 450	18 105	14 841	8 595	3 008	2 613	26 098	1 777	22.5	9.4	65.1
Valdosta, GA	2 750	39 535	6 446	5 792	7 155	1 106	1 441	897	22 689	1 120	35.5	13.9	46.2
Vallejo-Fairfield, CA	6 584	100 819	15 835	10 116	17 904	3 734	3 760	3 109	30 837	915	60.3	12.3	61.0
Vero Beach, FL	3 437	39 804	6 790	3 036	8 163	1 712	1 721	992	24 922	480	64.4	12.3	55.0
Victoria, TX	2 719	38 563	6 177	6 657	5 855	1 431	1 156	1 123	29 121	2 598	27.8	18.6	54.5
Vineland-Millville-Bridgeton, NJ	2 997	44 657	6 954	10 778	7 013	1 308	1 351	1 347	30 163	616	62.8	5.4	61.9
Virginia Beach-Norfolk-Newport News, VA-NC	34 304	575 072	68 290	61 405	85 915	25 331	41 815	15 960	27 753	1 402	52.2	13.8	58.0
Visalia-Porterville, CA	5 937	79 078	11 634	12 291	13 174	3 282	2 114	2 000	25 291	5 738	61.2	8.4	66.5
Waco, TX	4 780	85 175	13 644	14 270	10 571	4 081	2 352	2 128	24 984	2 571	46.7	8.8	49.3
Warner Robins, GA	1 996	27 694	3 789	2 595	5 746	929	3 462	640	23 110	360	48.6	10.3	44.7

Table C. Metropolitan Areas — **Agriculture**

Area Name	Land in farms					Value of land and buildings (dollars)		Value of machinery and equipment average per farm (dollars)	Value of products sold				Percent of farms with sales of —		Government payments	
			Acres								Percent from —					
	Acreage (1,000)	Percent change, 1997–2002	Average size of farm	Total irrigated (1,000)	Total cropland (1,000)	Average per farm	Average per acre		Total (mil dol)	Average per farm (dollars)	Crops	Live-stock and poultry products	$10,000 or more	$100,000 or more	Total ($1,000)	Percent of farms
	117	118	119	120	121	122	123	124	125	126	127	128	129	130	131	132
Salem, OR	510	6.7	113	113	376	521 850	5 054	78 327	520	114 922	82.9	17.1	33.0	13.2	1 513	7.7
Salinas, CA	1 261	-18.3	1 037	253	368	3 222 212	3 248	260 030	2 190	1 801 086	98.7	1.3	61.6	43.2	1 131	7.8
Salisbury, MD	145	0.0	178	9	102	536 305	3 063	78 307	302	371 305	11.6	88.4	62.6	47.6	2 519	37.9
Salt Lake City, UT	873	-12.3	529	61	138	669 536	1 212	39 345	57	34 588	30.7	69.3	24.1	7.1	1 088	9.5
San Angelo, TX	1 381	-14.2	1 175	28	223	539 845	475	58 984	101	85 711	18.8	81.2	31.2	9.4	4 877	27.8
San Antonio, TX	3 644	2.0	279	116	1 114	434 151	1 527	28 391	293	22 397	43.4	56.6	20.4	2.5	9 763	13.6
San Diego-Carlsbad-San Marcos, CA	408	-14.1	78	68	108	740 112	7 635	32 597	951	180 925	92.8	7.2	44.9	13.7	324	0.8
Sandusky, OH	95	5.6	242	0	83	819 142	3 118	82 603	33	83 181	90.0	10.0	55.1	18.6	1 090	45.4
San Francisco-Oakland-Fremont, CA	D	D	D	46	D	1 403 095	D	53 594	351	221 487	D	D	42.2	15.9	D	D
Oakland-Fremont-Hayward, CA Div	344	-15.3	339	39	69	1 207 944	4 715	45 063	133	131 342	85.7	14.3	36.5	11.0	D	D
San Francisco-San Mateo-Redwood City, CA Div	D	D	D	7	D	1 752 167	D	68 853	217	382 734	D	D	52.3	24.6	D	D
San Jose-Sunnyvale-Santa Clara, CA	899	8.3	528	58	108	1 302 147	2 238	52 220	406	238 633	85.5	14.5	39.8	16.6	405	4.9
San Luis Obispo-Paso Robles, CA	1 318	1.2	568	74	266	1 523 567	2 676	64 723	396	170 712	92.4	7.6	46.5	16.7	2 951	11.5
Santa Barbara-Santa Maria-Goleta, CA	757	-7.3	524	108	155	1 893 146	3 684	118 593	717	496 715	95.9	4.1	54.4	29.2	538	3.3
Santa Cruz-Watsonville, CA	67	-5.6	89	24	28	1 179 533	9 335	81 260	362	479 975	97.5	2.5	59.5	31.6	233	3.6
Santa Fe, NM	684	4.9	1 486	19	38	764 738	485	27 412	12	25 615	74.1	25.9	13.5	3.5	387	6.7
Santa Rosa-Petaluma, CA	627	9.8	182	76	163	1 710 715	11 058	60 466	572	165 857	75.6	24.4	49.9	19.1	1 897	4.8
Sarasota-Bradenton-Venice, FL	423	6.5	345	60	151	1 012 479	3 100	42 126	286	234 081	90.9	9.1	41.9	13.7	D	D
Savannah, GA	79	-9.2	241	D	25	450 604	1 765	37 858	7	21 474	79.0	21.0	25.2	4.0	286	26.4
Scranton—Wilkes-Barre, PA	168	13.5	141	1	97	440 565	3 009	56 073	48	40 454	61.5	38.5	32.1	10.8	971	20.1
Seattle-Tacoma-Bellevue, WA	168	9.8	36	16	89	441 620	12 566	32 510	341	74 232	48.5	51.5	23.8	7.7	2 085	3.9
Seattle-Bellevue-Everett, WA Div	110	7.8	35	9	61	449 443	14 075	31 464	247	79 117	52.9	47.1	25.6	8.5	1 873	4.6
Tacoma, WA Div	57	11.8	39	6	28	425 050	9 655	34 726	94	63 887	37.1	62.9	19.8	6.0	212	2.4
Sheboygan, WI	195	7.1	175	0	167	498 165	2 953	77 259	104	93 154	20.6	79.4	50.3	23.4	3 956	43.9
Sherman-Denison, TX	441	5.8	170	2	232	342 282	1 921	28 228	42	16 121	47.8	52.2	20.3	2.8	1 315	11.1
Shreveport-Bossier City, LA	415	-5.9	254	7	191	358 157	1 441	42 476	51	31 309	39.6	60.4	25.0	7.0	4 392	19.0
Sioux City, IA-NE-SD	1 147	1.0	437	70	974	717 528	1 634	100 387	354	134 899	53.7	46.3	61.4	27.6	18 382	66.2
Sioux Falls, SD	1 424	2.4	431	D	1 230	585 537	1 320	104 991	380	115 071	55.2	44.8	68.2	30.1	15 172	58.9
South Bend-Mishawaka, IN-MI	354	6.9	213	45	297	488 922	2 576	80 127	115	68 949	66.1	33.9	40.3	14.0	5 571	42.3
Spartanburg, SC	126	17.8	90	2	59	346 877	4 029	35 260	25	17 894	64.5	35.5	16.8	2.5	388	9.7
Spokane, WA	643	9.0	289	12	422	566 929	2 114	56 915	94	42 181	82.3	17.7	28.3	9.8	4 279	23.0
Springfield, IL	623	-2.2	480	3	576	1 273 826	2 728	127 907	188	144 486	88.4	11.6	57.0	32.9	8 595	64.3
Springfield, MA	163	-1.2	103	4	65	538 854	5 363	52 188	102	64 098	70.3	29.7	34.8	13.0	1 487	9.5
Springfield, MO	1 412	4.9	168	1	782	328 164	1 993	32 822	224	26 757	8.7	91.3	35.7	5.5	5 017	20.7
Springfield, OH	165	-4.1	219	2	143	724 496	3 539	78 700	71	93 796	78.3	21.7	38.4	13.5	2 866	39.0
State College, PA	165	21.3	136	1	104	447 167	3 400	47 969	53	44 011	27.8	72.2	38.0	13.8	1 654	18.3
Stockton, CA	813	0.5	202	520	575	1 203 010	6 673	91 721	1 222	303 640	74.3	25.7	63.0	30.6	7 118	8.3
Sumter, SC	136	-2.2	253	6	85	511 947	1 958	62 688	55	102 693	27.7	72.3	25.1	10.4	1 378	39.3
Syracuse, NY	428	-1.8	200	3	279	326 253	1 589	100 032	175	81 875	28.4	71.6	43.2	19.8	7 587	27.2
Tallahassee, FL	286	8.7	245	11	60	521 160	2 087	36 316	121	103 402	86.7	13.3	22.4	4.0	989	18.2
Tampa-St. Petersburg-Clearwater, FL	521	12.3	106	56	D	478 342	4 949	38 627	506	102 927	75.9	24.1	31.2	8.7	886	1.7
Terre Haute, IN	563	-1.1	333	D	480	663 380	2 092	83 347	128	75 559	85.1	14.9	46.5	18.5	8 225	47.6
Texarkana, TX-Texarkana, AR	466	7.1	251	12	223	348 541	1 429	38 480	75	40 412	20.5	79.5	28.7	7.1	2 489	9.9
Toledo, OH	695	1.2	251	6	644	668 600	2 703	97 434	217	78 183	76.6	23.4	53.4	17.4	10 716	54.1
Topeka, KS	1 665	0.7	362	25	840	343 336	913	55 794	152	33 104	40.2	59.8	40.2	7.8	9 271	47.2
Trenton-Ewing, NJ	25	-10.7	82	1	20	1 884 550	18 855	45 689	12	40 286	89.0	11.0	31.3	9.9	140	9.5
Tucson, AZ	D	D	D	35	47	1 567 404	D	56 938	69	133 228	81.8	18.2	31.7	11.4	1 630	7.0
Tulsa, OK	2 843	0.8	299	11	845	270 529	883	27 873	204	21 423	28.2	71.8	25.2	3.5	4 275	15.6
Tuscaloosa, AL	392	2.9	295	2	112	418 804	1 356	57 832	85	63 649	9.7	90.3	28.5	9.4	1 840	28.3
Tyler, TX	287	14.3	127	2	129	213 780	1 566	27 419	64	28 051	75.0	25.0	20.4	2.4	106	1.3
Utica-Rome, NY	380	6.1	214	1	243	238 565	1 177	71 909	128	72 142	22.9	77.1	49.6	21.9	5 965	31.2
Valdosta, GA	358	11.2	319	36	151	505 931	1 633	63 253	113	100 993	84.7	15.3	35.2	11.3	4 526	40.2
Vallejo-Fairfield, CA	351	-3.0	384	125	195	1 564 886	3 834	81 554	191	208 567	83.1	16.9	47.2	19.6	2 457	15.2
Vero Beach, FL	191	13.7	399	95	103	1 146 115	2 969	41 314	117	243 569	94.3	5.7	59.8	21.9	78	2.7
Victoria, TX	1 268	14.8	488	10	374	425 978	896	39 960	65	24 977	38.3	61.7	31.7	5.1	4 334	14.5
Vineland-Millville-Bridgeton, NJ	71	7.6	115	19	54	585 323	4 714	88 585	123	199 143	97.8	2.2	45.3	23.7	254	7.6
Virginia Beach-Norfolk-Newport News, VA-NC	D	D	D	5	291	752 651	D	90 642	161	114 729	D	D	44.3	16.8	6 834	30.0
Visalia-Porterville, CA	1 393	6.3	243	652	770	948 550	3 949	90 642	2 339	407 560	51.1	48.9	68.9	33.7	12 816	9.2
Waco, TX	538	9.1	209	3	298	273 080	1 248	30 959	61	23 746	35.6	64.4	20.4	3.9	1 846	10.5
Warner Robins, GA	75	-13.8	210	5	39	469 980	2 197	73 606	24	65 567	34.0	66.0	27.2	9.7	930	23.1

Area Name	Value of residential construction authorized by building permits, 2003		Wholesale trade, 1997				Retail trade,[1] 1997				Real estate and rental and leasing, 1997			
	New construction ($1,000)	Number of housing units	Number of establishments	Number of employees	Sales (mil dol)	Annual payroll (mil dol)	Number of establishments	Number of employees	Sales (mil dol)	Annual payroll (mil dol)	Number of establishments	Number of employees	Receipts (mil dol)	Annual payroll (mil dol)
	133	134	135	136	137	138	139	140	141	142	143	144	145	146
Salem, OR	291 284	1 979	367	3 672	1 271.3	100.6	1 224	16 229	2 904.9	290.6	434	1 893	209.0	38.2
Salinas, CA	351 583	1 355	473	7 530	4 747.4	267.9	1 558	16 413	3 035.9	327.9	386	1 837	236.4	38.9
Salisbury, MD	122 185	1 298	149	D	D	D	537	6 596	1 062.1	106.1	101	610	54.5	11.4
Salt Lake City, UT	1 072 044	8 145	2 069	29 788	15 492.6	1 025.4	3 546	56 926	10 630.1	985.7	1 220	8 213	939.5	170.6
San Angelo, TX	30 985	265	162	D	D	D	475	5 423	892.2	84.4	135	D	D	D
San Antonio, TX	1 655 531	13 375	2 120	27 460	13 669.4	872.5	5 477	74 948	13 647.5	1 275.7	1 566	9 552	1 186.3	215.1
San Diego-Carlsbad-San Marcos, CA	2 999 360	18 031	4 159	53 589	26 543.9	2 273.7	9 109	119 022	22 215.3	2 241.1	3 742	23 069	3 250.0	573.9
Sandusky, OH	41 265	334	94	1 123	397.0	31.0	382	4 784	732.0	71.4	77	292	27.2	5.1
San Francisco-Oakland-Fremont, CA	3 068 970	14 828	8 548	105 888	92 055.3	4 712.3	14 485	185 082	36 687.8	3 868.6	5 888	42 903	7 392.1	1 273.0
Oakland-Fremont-Hayward, CA Div	2 393 842	11 352	4 391	62 404	62 758.8	2 673.8	7 068	96 839	19 781.7	1 980.6	2 721	16 493	2 618.2	438.3
San Francisco-San Mateo-Redwood City, CA Div	675 128	3 476	4 157	43 484	29 296.5	2 038.5	7 417	88 243	16 906.1	1 888.0	3 167	26 410	4 773.9	834.7
San Jose-Sunnyvale-Santa Clara, CA	1 069 948	7 103	3 511	67 294	68 306.5	3 913.4	5 395	81 652	16 950.4	1 727.6	2 002	12 680	2 470.9	374.2
San Luis Obispo-Paso Robles, CA	414 092	2 260	244	1 904	561.5	46.8	1 132	10 917	1 780.7	182.4	319	1 243	149.7	20.9
Santa Barbara-Santa Maria-Goleta, CA	292 550	1 461	469	4 282	1 636.0	137.5	1 653	19 187	3 183.5	354.0	558	2 733	708.8	71.0
Santa Cruz-Watsonville, CA	188 571	1 066	342	4 472	1 541.8	140.3	986	11 794	1 970.2	215.5	314	1 649	166.5	27.1
Santa Fe, NM	70 719	561	167	1 260	340.2	39.3	846	7 868	1 422.9	149.4	200	D	D	D
Santa Rosa-Petaluma, CA	394 616	2 252	619	7 430	3 069.7	259.4	1 808	22 190	4 146.2	443.7	576	2 394	329.3	48.5
Sarasota-Bradenton-Venice, FL	1 576 292	9 025	797	5 470	2 123.5	162.7	2 607	32 476	5 747.6	538.2	836	3 322	449.0	68.3
Savannah, GA	353 197	2 526	374	D	D	D	1 413	17 355	2 718.0	267.1	312	D	D	D
Scranton—Wilkes-Barre, PA	202 765	1 530	697	D	D	D	2 571	33 353	5 037.0	476.4	364	2 019	187.5	39.7
Seattle-Tacoma-Bellevue, WA	3 308 653	20 601	6 473	79 828	58 406.6	3 200.9	11 347	154 800	30 171.0	3 099.6	4 496	28 355	3 981.0	706.7
Seattle-Bellevue-Everett, WA Div	2 604 940	15 449	5 692	70 504	53 787.7	2 873.9	9 058	125 844	24 702.8	2 549.5	3 789	23 948	3 585.2	625.5
Tacoma, WA Div	703 713	5 152	781	9 324	4 618.9	327.0	2 289	28 956	5 468.2	550.1	707	4 407	395.8	81.2
Sheboygan, WI	89 104	599	119	2 041	1 185.0	65.4	398	5 831	911.0	88.0	85	400	38.2	6.2
Sherman-Denison, TX	31 528	337	132	958	406.1	25.1	474	6 213	1 092.0	98.5	104	351	32.0	5.8
Shreveport-Bossier City, LA	264 344	2 243	589	D	D	D	1 499	19 531	3 288.6	304.0	368	1 641	158.7	29.9
Sioux City, IA-NE-SD	54 917	437	274	D	D	D	664	D	D	D	135	D	D	D
Sioux Falls, SD	248 385	2 520	422	5 846	2 478.5	174.1	915	D	D	D	199	D	D	D
South Bend-Mishawaka, IN-MI	210 957	1 366	526	7 431	3 641.5	241.8	1 212	17 807	2 941.9	263.6	243	1 341	134.9	26.3
Spartanburg, SC	178 007	2 081	484	6 234	3 965.3	214.8	1 117	13 785	2 311.6	213.5	198	898	90.4	17.9
Spokane, WA	304 404	2 550	788	11 268	4 878.5	360.9	1 730	22 246	4 122.6	433.9	503	2 674	289.1	47.4
Springfield, IL	126 808	1 075	274	3 621	1 588.1	122.4	877	12 374	2 050.2	191.6	215	885	87.5	14.7
Springfield, MA	254 072	1 663	769	D	D	D	2 761	34 531	5 295.3	538.4	546	2 453	312.7	50.5
Springfield, MO	405 614	3 455	700	10 242	5 405.8	282.9	1 761	21 335	3 913.9	348.0	426	1 965	166.2	34.8
Springfield, OH	33 033	273	124	1 704	1 035.2	49.6	528	7 439	1 102.9	107.9	82	317	32.4	5.0
State College, PA	113 521	1 022	100	D	D	D	617	7 861	1 153.9	108.7	111	704	83.1	14.0
Stockton, CA	1 273 912	7 041	560	9 751	7 651.7	319.3	1 594	19 957	3 679.6	364.7	436	2 602	257.7	52.3
Sumter, SC	55 151	653	84	671	208.6	18.1	425	4 841	782.0	72.8	74	277	26.6	4.3
Syracuse, NY	215 233	1 703	1 128	14 865	11 459.6	550.5	2 630	37 747	5 582.7	556.1	511	4 418	409.5	97.3
Tallahassee, FL	359 395	3 526	306	D	D	D	1 303	17 550	2 533.3	255.2	331	1 927	209.4	34.4
Tampa-St. Petersburg-Clearwater, FL	3 757 592	29 281	4 304	53 358	35 721.1	1 808.6	9 142	128 351	24 184.1	2 199.6	2 759	15 239	1 805.0	323.2
Terre Haute, IN	41 491	359	199	D	D	D	743	12 135	2 730.5	192.5	116	D	D	D
Texarkana, TX-Texarkana, AR	45 460	651	183	D	D	D	612	6 734	1 194.8	104.0	112	585	65.1	9.3
Toledo, OH	394 336	3 205	1 030	14 098	8 250.2	481.8	2 646	38 812	6 436.9	612.7	592	3 662	404.1	76.4
Topeka, KS	191 930	1 378	240	2 484	1 034.1	69.0	973	12 050	1 831.0	184.9	223	D	D	D
Trenton-Ewing, NJ	93 357	1 188	472	8 480	4 403.0	291.5	1 442	18 217	3 183.1	326.1	289	1 685	256.7	43.1
Tucson, AZ	1 263 700	7 910	929	9 257	2 759.8	266.0	2 785	39 285	6 853.8	693.4	978	6 631	676.6	130.5
Tulsa, OK	563 969	4 354	1 676	D	D	D	3 236	42 895	7 570.2	687.9	938	4 889	543.0	99.8
Tuscaloosa, AL	135 066	1 194	200	D	D	D	869	11 406	1 627.3	157.8	172	1 108	86.3	14.2
Tyler, TX	97 151	657	297	3 103	1 237.7	93.9	805	9 773	1 868.6	170.2	189	895	93.2	20.7
Utica-Rome, NY	63 000	481	278	D	D	D	1 225	14 847	2 159.5	210.2	208	748	88.9	12.6
Valdosta, GA	102 019	1 050	148	D	D	D	622	D	D	D	94	D	D	D
Vallejo-Fairfield, CA	447 292	2 642	262	3 909	2 170.1	145.7	1 116	15 046	2 789.4	281.0	321	1 344	164.9	24.5
Vero Beach, FL	419 919	2 430	147	D	D	D	667	7 793	1 143.9	121.5	170	714	76.5	12.9
Victoria, TX	23 381	244	174	1 812	476.8	49.9	495	5 877	997.2	91.7	109	D	D	D
Vineland-Millville-Bridgeton, NJ	39 439	374	189	2 230	989.4	69.4	578	7 157	1 226.5	130.1	115	486	52.0	9.4
Virginia Beach-Norfolk-Newport News, VA-NC	1 294 756	10 353	1 588	D	D	D	6 027	83 091	12 714.0	1 260.5	NA	NA	NA	NA
Visalia-Porterville, CA	297 258	2 270	343	5 120	2 527.7	135.1	1 107	12 742	2 135.7	211.8	206	809	97.7	12.6
Waco, TX	100 476	891	315	3 755	1 716.3	102.1	862	10 227	1 797.8	162.7	212	1 086	131.4	21.4
Warner Robins, GA	149 639	1 648	54	454	236.5	14.7	403	5 818	941.2	86.6	88	347	43.4	5.1

1. Establishments with payroll.

Table C. Metropolitan Areas — **Professional Services, Manufacturing, and Accommodation and Foodservices**

Area Name	Professional, scientific, and technical services,[1] 1997				Manufacturing, 1997				Accommodation and foodservices, 1997			
	Number of establishments	Number of employees	Sales (mil dol)	Annual payroll (mil dol)	Number of establishments	Number of employees	Sales (mil dol)	Annual payroll (mil dol)	Number of establishments	Number of employees	Sales (mil dol)	Annual payroll (mil dol)
	147	148	149	150	151	152	153	154	155	156	157	158
Salem, OR	582	2 908	224.5	88.3	465	15 009	2 590.2	417.8	606	9 869	312.3	85.9
Salinas, CA	694	2 998	293.1	109.2	302	7 070	1 329.4	223.7	905	16 869	835.3	226.0
Salisbury, MD	187	1 048	80.5	31.0	NA	NA	NA	NA	187	3 299	97.3	28.0
Salt Lake City, UT	2 520	22 772	2 393.6	923.1	1 508	56 022	10 441.2	1 784.6	1 744	39 436	1 321.6	371.3
San Angelo, TX	155	D	D	D	NA	NA	NA	NA	197	D	D	D
San Antonio, TX	3 184	23 151	2 139.8	835.9	NA	NA	NA	NA	3 059	D	D	D
San Diego-Carlsbad-San Marcos, CA	7 144	59 761	7 072.3	2 725.7	3 407	118 868	22 233.6	4 223.5	5 426	105 069	4 237.9	1 157.4
Sandusky, OH	107	470	38.4	17.2	117	9 176	2 251.5	409.2	248	4 622	167.9	46.6
San Francisco-Oakland-Fremont, CA	15 194	137 404	19 496.4	7 693.2	5 837	177 255	45 307.8	7 144.0	9 721	160 020	7 550.1	2 117.5
Oakland-Fremont-Hayward, CA Div	6 345	49 557	6 362.8	2 518.4	3 230	113 175	33 982.6	4 692.0	4 288	61 734	2 475.3	656.2
San Francisco-San Mateo-Redwood City, CA Div	8 849	87 847	13 133.6	5 174.8	2 607	64 080	11 325.2	2 452.0	5 433	98 286	5 074.8	1 461.3
San Jose-Sunnyvale-Santa Clara, CA	6 389	71 763	10 454.4	4 429.3	3 539	252 107	72 893.6	13 158.2	3 575	61 292	2 620.7	685.6
San Luis Obispo-Paso Robles, CA	529	2 292	212.2	76.7	323	6 322	1 156.3	182.3	674	10 534	382.5	101.7
Santa Barbara-Santa Maria-Goleta, CA	981	6 344	711.2	270.6	502	14 985	2 770.4	584.2	952	17 195	633.1	177.1
Santa Cruz-Watsonville, CA	678	3 073	384.1	132.1	387	10 011	2 135.0	315.2	591	8 223	305.5	80.8
Santa Fe, NM	464	1 964	205.9	85.1	162	1 436	124.8	31.7	361	7 498	304.8	89.1
Santa Rosa-Petaluma, CA	1 171	5 682	565.8	239.1	793	24 209	5 119.8	968.8	1 005	13 993	490.2	132.2
Sarasota-Bradenton-Venice, FL	1 515	7 664	663.0	263.1	663	18 965	2 988.3	571.3	1 077	20 531	723.3	196.6
Savannah, GA	528	2 908	224.6	88.3	NA	NA	NA	NA	641	D	D	D
Scranton—Wilkes-Barre, PA	856	6 356	489.8	190.2	749	D	D	D	1 270	17 923	531.0	144.1
Seattle-Tacoma-Bellevue, WA	8 699	71 272	7 817.2	3 136.6	4 510	214 481	50 659.4	9 305.9	6 782	111 577	4 323.2	1 219.6
Seattle-Bellevue-Everett, WA Div	7 725	66 307	7 372.9	2 962.6	3 830	192 198	46 383.5	8 600.7	5 564	92 769	3 719.6	1 050.3
Tacoma, WA Div	974	4 965	444.3	174.0	680	22 283	4 275.9	705.2	1 218	18 808	603.6	169.3
Sheboygan, WI	150	1 235	92.2	40.5	239	20 047	4 252.7	628.3	237	3 714	105.9	29.1
Sherman-Denison, TX	162	715	52.6	19.6	140	10 223	3 557.3	365.4	200	3 312	104.8	30.7
Shreveport-Bossier City, LA	672	3 832	309.7	114.0	308	15 741	5 385.4	555.0	596	D	D	D
Sioux City, IA-NE-SD	239	1 127	85.0	27.8	NA	NA	NA	NA	333	4 980	147.5	40.0
Sioux Falls, SD	397	2 474	188.5	75.0	NA	NA	NA	NA	459	8 642	236.1	67.0
South Bend-Mishawaka, IN-MI	572	4 196	381.7	159.1	544	23 819	4 720.5	794.8	613	11 328	325.2	92.1
Spartanburg, SC	330	2 445	215.8	95.7	481	35 102	7 534.6	1 108.6	465	9 520	244.2	68.7
Spokane, WA	886	5 738	444.5	186.9	572	20 892	3 994.6	681.4	904	14 456	453.2	128.5
Springfield, IL	489	3 323	280.3	118.8	NA	NA	NA	NA	521	D	D	D
Springfield, MA	1 113	6 878	520.9	216.9	1 101	44 810	7 757.8	1 578.5	1 413	20 023	627.9	176.8
Springfield, MO	680	4 377	380.4	127.3	561	D	D	D	762	13 833	401.0	114.2
Springfield, OH	146	738	43.5	16.7	230	13 231	4 071.5	520.0	248	4 662	132.8	36.6
State College, PA	211	2 332	167.5	85.9	159	8 546	1 409.3	255.4	287	5 241	154.8	41.2
Stockton, CA	575	3 531	277.7	111.2	553	24 646	5 879.1	749.6	826	11 413	376.9	96.5
Sumter, SC	116	471	29.1	8.9	84	12 655	2 050.4	303.0	133	2 311	70.0	19.1
Syracuse, NY	1 254	11 265	1 008.1	395.4	687	40 897	9 331.8	1 570.5	1 495	21 085	656.7	194.4
Tallahassee, FL	912	7 106	716.8	297.3	NA	NA	NA	NA	536	10 619	320.7	82.9
Tampa-St. Petersburg-Clearwater, FL	6 398	62 828	6 186.2	2 318.5	2 580	77 098	12 701.1	2 246.2	4 138	81 729	2 952.0	780.5
Terre Haute, IN	217	1 160	79.8	24.6	199	D	D	D	381	D	D	D
Texarkana, TX-Texarkana, AR	162	733	66.0	20.2	100	6 330	1 471.1	227.7	221	3 819	128.7	31.6
Toledo, OH	1 203	11 220	1 111.9	389.2	1 010	58 467	16 980.9	2 294.8	1 550	25 936	826.8	221.6
Topeka, KS	449	3 361	239.2	96.6	NA	NA	NA	NA	467	7 374	215.8	57.9
Trenton-Ewing, NJ	1 223	10 930	1 407.3	586.2	352	13 537	2 413.6	579.7	703	9 870	394.0	109.9
Tucson, AZ	1 811	12 214	1 124.2	430.9	764	26 746	4 455.2	1 064.7	1 524	32 305	1 041.9	292.2
Tulsa, OK	2 229	14 876	1 517.6	553.9	NA	NA	NA	NA	1 680	28 016	899.5	240.0
Tuscaloosa, AL	273	1 774	135.8	52.0	NA	NA	NA	NA	334	D	D	D
Tyler, TX	392	2 464	284.0	93.0	213	10 969	2 299.1	381.1	294	5 834	175.1	47.8
Utica-Rome, NY	402	2 504	185.9	65.7	351	20 050	3 147.7	582.9	681	7 156	220.7	61.4
Valdosta, GA	151	D	D	D	NA	NA	NA	NA	NA	NA	NA	NA
Vallejo-Fairfield, CA	391	2 149	179.3	66.2	277	9 175	3 496.4	331.0	568	8 747	291.1	73.8
Vero Beach, FL	281	1 296	103.1	43.3	116	1 825	219.8	55.4	204	3 527	112.4	31.6
Victoria, TX	178	998	77.0	30.6	NA	NA	NA	NA	221	3 349	97.4	26.6
Vineland-Millville-Bridgeton, NJ	200	1 061	88.9	34.1	210	12 985	1 896.1	398.3	218	2 554	78.8	21.1
Virginia Beach-Norfolk-Newport News, VA-NC	2 588	27 184	2 098.3	888.5	NA	NA	NA	NA	2 937	D	D	D
Visalia-Porterville, CA	335	1 788	265.6	45.0	282	11 439	3 167.3	314.5	510	7 020	232.3	56.8
Waco, TX	292	2 039	133.0	57.4	261	16 474	3 855.6	481.7	400	6 900	220.7	59.8
Warner Robins, GA	135	1 504	111.5	44.5	66	D	D	D	183	3 753	102.5	28.4

1. Firms subject to federal tax.

Area Name	Health care and social assistance,[1] 1997				Other services,[1] 1997				Federal funds and grants, 2002–2003			
									Expenditures (mil dol)			
										Direct payments for individuals		
	Number of establishments	Number of employees	Receipts (mil dol)	Annual payroll (mil dol)	Number of establishments	Number of employees	Receipts (mil dol)	Annual payroll (mil dol)	Total	Social Security and government retirement	Medicare	Food stamps and Supplemental Security Income
	159	160	161	162	163	164	165	166	167	168	169	170
Salem, OR	721	6 475	379.6	166.5	431	2 232	131.2	41.0	2 331.3	824.2	246.8	68.6
Salinas, CA	708	5 613	430.5	177.7	445	2 416	172.1	48.0	2 106.6	730.1	316.2	46.3
Salisbury, MD	219	2 771	172.9	92.5	162	1 053	66.9	18.9	570.1	231.9	99.2	17.3
Salt Lake City, UT	1 835	23 517	1 601.1	660.5	1 337	9 857	635.9	188.9	5 112.4	1 461.5	457.3	90.1
San Angelo, TX	NA	NA	NA	NA	NA	NA	NA	NA	678.4	253.5	89.7	18.1
San Antonio, TX	3 315	56 579	3 264.3	1 341.9	2 511	16 941	933.6	300.1	14 255.2	4 499.8	1 435.2	368.3
San Diego-Carlsbad-San Marcos, CA	5 508	53 541	4 232.7	1 656.5	3 811	24 273	1 648.1	466.0	24 045.1	5 770.4	2 670.5	438.6
Sandusky, OH	168	1 369	87.3	45.4	123	647	29.0	9.2	420.5	192.4	89.4	10.9
San Francisco-Oakland-Fremont, CA	9 856	86 991	7 014.9	2 891.3	6 516	40 319	3 138.7	918.1	25 998.6	6 987.5	4 139.6	737.7
Oakland-Fremont-Hayward, CA Div	5 158	51 394	4 144.8	1 697.8	3 365	21 627	1 712.7	503.7	14 289.7	3 921.2	2 257.1	417.2
San Francisco-San Mateo-Redwood City, CA Div	4 698	35 597	2 870.1	1 193.5	3 151	18 692	1 426.0	414.4	11 708.9	3 066.3	1 882.5	320.4
San Jose-Sunnyvale-Santa Clara, CA	3 806	38 672	3 052.3	1 248.6	2 517	17 039	1 370.7	403.6	11 408.1	2 292.7	1 193.3	265.9
San Luis Obispo-Paso Robles, CA	599	5 083	375.3	161.3	294	1 446	96.2	25.9	1 113.7	544.3	240.3	24.9
Santa Barbara-Santa Maria-Goleta, CA	934	6 609	516.9	199.8	536	3 054	192.1	57.4	2 724.0	799.8	355.2	49.1
Santa Cruz-Watsonville, CA	631	4 739	309.8	121.7	330	1 614	112.1	31.3	992.7	370.0	219.6	29.6
Santa Fe, NM	298	2 831	164.1	74.0	170	854	54.5	15.8	1 173.4	316.7	69.7	13.0
Santa Rosa-Petaluma, CA	1 241	11 357	766.6	319.5	676	3 604	252.0	74.0	2 039.1	916.1	460.5	48.1
Sarasota-Bradenton-Venice, FL	1 504	21 183	1 513.0	613.2	939	4 701	259.7	81.9	3 999.2	2 300.4	1 114.1	55.7
Savannah, GA	493	6 733	487.2	243.2	439	2 921	184.1	61.1	2 861.0	677.4	291.9	73.4
Scranton—Wilkes-Barre, PA	1 318	13 748	868.2	384.1	891	4 508	255.0	70.0	4 013.3	1 623.1	945.5	96.1
Seattle-Tacoma-Bellevue, WA	6 866	66 709	4 402.9	1 924.6	4 979	30 918	2 290.2	682.4	18 729.8	5 891.5	2 038.8	459.8
Seattle-Bellevue-Everett, WA Div	5 427	52 672	3 537.2	1 540.6	4 071	25 488	1 935.5	567.9	13 677.2	4 130.0	1 600.1	323.0
Tacoma, WA Div	1 439	14 037	865.7	384.0	908	5 430	354.7	114.5	5 052.6	1 761.5	438.7	136.8
Sheboygan, WI	176	2 412	134.3	74.8	172	967	56.5	14.6	452.7	234.0	80.8	8.2
Sherman-Denison, TX	278	4 362	225.0	104.6	123	649	32.9	9.6	561.4	294.3	126.7	15.5
Shreveport-Bossier City, LA	676	10 842	724.8	320.1	555	3 489	222.7	64.8	2 506.1	851.2	402.8	121.2
Sioux City, IA-NE-SD	268	2 670	212.0	99.9	247	1 687	103.4	31.5	852.0	285.0	126.1	17.5
Sioux Falls, SD	329	4 930	373.1	205.0	338	2 047	115.7	34.6	994.2	369.6	115.8	17.1
South Bend-Mishawaka, IN-MI	542	6 232	469.0	217.4	512	4 067	268.1	84.3	2 163.8	647.7	280.9	52.9
Spartanburg, SC	377	4 899	364.5	167.8	377	2 038	153.4	41.2	1 115.6	579.9	192.6	47.1
Spokane, WA	991	11 137	681.4	306.8	699	4 355	258.4	78.5	2 554.2	1 014.6	368.1	83.9
Springfield, IL	370	7 740	482.4	206.5	362	2 352	146.2	47.4	3 216.4	748.6	201.6	37.2
Springfield, MA	1 138	17 170	1 010.3	468.4	1 053	5 381	363.9	109.2	4 076.4	1 414.2	766.3	167.8
Springfield, MO	578	8 869	578.9	272.7	675	4 036	219.2	64.1	1 822.7	850.7	302.6	63.2
Springfield, OH	240	2 758	159.6	78.1	202	1 384	72.8	21.4	837.3	377.7	158.7	31.9
State College, PA	212	2 520	169.1	72.4	159	958	52.2	14.5	961.1	228.5	89.5	10.9
Stockton, CA	949	9 252	664.0	273.5	690	3 838	265.3	74.2	2 675.1	986.9	462.6	158.2
Sumter, SC	128	1 347	81.0	40.6	123	827	47.5	14.1	877.5	267.8	72.2	37.3
Syracuse, NY	1 100	11 339	826.5	386.8	976	6 385	463.2	131.1	3 749.7	1 438.5	555.6	116.4
Tallahassee, FL	487	6 883	480.1	218.1	452	2 798	157.1	50.1	4 111.4	801.2	203.2	63.7
Tampa-St. Petersburg-Clearwater, FL	5 794	80 476	5 822.4	2 384.4	3 972	23 499	1 466.1	441.2	16 181.1	6 936.9	3 888.9	413.2
Terre Haute, IN	327	4 270	280.3	91.6	249	1 626	78.3	23.4	1 052.2	404.5	203.2	32.3
Texarkana, TX-Texarkana, AR	267	4 304	255.0	119.1	179	1 170	69.3	20.0	971.0	348.0	161.1	35.7
Toledo, OH	1 197	17 069	1 048.6	528.4	1 097	7 078	437.9	131.2	3 328.6	1 282.6	734.8	148.0
Topeka, KS	382	6 526	332.4	170.7	369	2 118	142.7	44.9	1 974.4	700.8	190.6	33.7
Trenton-Ewing, NJ	792	6 837	576.4	260.0	538	2 985	210.3	62.1	3 730.2	967.5	448.5	51.0
Tucson, AZ	1 614	19 280	1 283.3	563.9	1 171	7 575	437.9	138.1	8 108.7	2 213.3	782.8	163.2
Tulsa, OK	1 833	25 449	1 579.5	700.8	1 255	7 769	536.6	156.2	4 102.6	1 801.6	766.1	149.9
Tuscaloosa, AL	288	3 870	234.8	121.1	268	1 554	84.9	26.3	1 189.1	408.8	191.8	61.6
Tyler, TX	430	5 047	396.8	186.2	288	2 032	116.3	35.4	921.7	413.6	181.0	29.1
Utica-Rome, NY	484	4 753	312.3	143.5	414	2 245	174.7	44.2	1 982.4	784.3	325.1	61.8
Valdosta, GA	NA	NA	NA	NA	NA	NA	NA	NA	838.6	241.6	100.2	34.3
Vallejo-Fairfield, CA	628	6 046	480.3	199.2	446	3 104	210.4	70.1	2 442.4	907.0	228.3	59.2
Vero Beach, FL	287	3 388	263.7	96.4	206	944	45.4	13.7	832.3	464.7	240.3	10.4
Victoria, TX	260	3 781	246.6	100.4	186	1 087	67.9	19.5	532.1	223.1	104.7	20.7
Vineland-Millville-Bridgeton, NJ	238	2 191	161.8	74.8	243	1 156	65.2	20.6	874.8	303.4	187.8	31.8
Virginia Beach-Norfolk-Newport News, VA-NC	2 605	30 548	1 790.4	879.0	2 467	D	D	D	18 213.7	4 526.1	1 098.7	269.9
Visalia-Porterville, CA	588	5 102	334.0	127.8	308	1 544	115.2	28.7	1 634.1	521.9	277.6	91.9
Waco, TX	353	4 861	265.9	126.4	329	2 065	114.1	34.4	1 236.2	499.9	150.6	44.3
Warner Robins, GA	181	1 927	125.5	52.7	162	744	38.3	11.3	1 769.9	376.4	69.1	20.4

1. Firms subject to federal tax.

Table C. Metropolitan Areas — Federal Funds and Local Government Finances

Area Name	Federal funds and grants, 2002–2003 (cont'd) Expenditures (mil dol) (cont'd)							Local government finances, 2002 General revenue				
	Procurement contract awards			Grants							Taxes	
												Per capita[1] (dollars)	
	Salaries and wages	Defense	Other	Medicaid and other health-related	Nutrition and family welfare	Education	Other	Total (mil dol)	Intergovernmental (mil dol)	Total (mil dol)	Total	Property
	171	172	173	174	175	176	177	178	179	180	181	182
Salem, OR	99.0	3.3	26.2	278.1	180.0	167.7	404.1	1 095.9	600.3	285.3	797	704
Salinas, CA	489.3	102.0	46.4	168.0	74.3	38.6	74.6	2 112.1	858.5	478.1	1 156	795
Salisbury, MD	31.2	18.6	10.2	79.5	18.4	10.0	35.2	280.9	118.4	110.1	984	600
Salt Lake City, UT	713.7	609.5	181.3	619.2	195.6	121.9	575.2	2 736.3	979.1	1 085.4	1 088	728
San Angelo, TX	155.7	31.3	4.5	62.2	9.3	4.5	29.9	225.4	90.0	98.4	939	702
San Antonio, TX	2 602.1	1 952.8	1 089.8	1 267.0	231.3	120.0	481.6	5 239.8	1 960.0	2 040.2	1 142	946
San Diego-Carlsbad-San Marcos, CA	5 842.9	4 697.8	637.6	2 043.2	564.0	246.0	937.9	11 595.6	5 406.4	3 296.2	1 134	822
Sandusky, OH	15.1	30.3	10.9	27.1	9.8	5.1	24.8	287.5	98.8	118.8	1 500	1 128
San Francisco-Oakland-Fremont, CA	2 670.2	1 012.8	3 338.4	4 112.1	651.9	287.3	1 739.3	22 084.3	8 427.9	7 385.4	1 767	1 134
Oakland-Fremont-Hayward, CA Div	1 196.0	528.1	2 452.4	1 870.7	443.8	185.7	875.9	12 189.8	4 878.3	3 676.8	1 492	980
San Francisco-San Mateo-Redwood City, CA Div	1 474.1	484.7	885.9	2 241.4	208.2	101.6	863.5	9 894.5	3 549.6	3 708.6	2 163	1 355
San Jose-Sunnyvale-Santa Clara, CA	731.8	3 802.9	937.1	1 052.4	224.6	113.9	719.3	8 950.2	3 211.1	3 556.6	2 045	1 449
San Luis Obispo-Paso Robles, CA	45.3	14.6	15.0	100.6	41.0	12.8	49.6	966.5	379.7	369.1	1 457	1 134
Santa Barbara-Santa Maria-Goleta, CA	314.6	615.9	82.2	187.6	55.4	35.7	191.6	1 883.2	763.0	507.8	1 260	934
Santa Cruz-Watsonville, CA	35.4	14.0	14.3	148.3	34.6	19.4	88.5	1 096.8	493.0	328.5	1 294	927
Santa Fe, NM	71.0	14.2	130.2	148.8	103.4	118.3	174.4	355.1	162.6	129.0	959	524
Santa Rosa-Petaluma, CA	140.5	22.3	43.0	208.6	58.4	26.7	90.7	1 933.3	822.8	574.3	1 226	933
Sarasota-Bradenton-Venice, FL	125.6	29.9	32.3	107.1	40.7	27.8	138.6	2 176.1	427.4	742.6	1 197	955
Savannah, GA	961.8	391.1	25.4	192.9	56.2	25.3	115.5	946.4	320.3	418.1	1 395	884
Scranton—Wilkes-Barre, PA	251.9	186.3	88.9	378.6	70.0	17.1	171.5	1 321.4	484.1	566.2	1 024	741
Seattle-Tacoma-Bellevue, WA	3 047.1	2 280.5	600.6	2 506.1	376.4	169.7	1 146.6	12 004.5	4 190.0	4 355.4	1 393	825
Seattle-Bellevue-Everett, WA Div	1 684.2	1 868.3	526.6	2 055.2	260.7	117.7	944.2	9 844.7	3 222.4	3 631.4	1 517	864
Tacoma, WA Div	1 363.0	412.2	73.9	450.9	115.7	52.0	202.3	2 159.8	967.6	724.0	989	699
Sheboygan, WI	15.0	4.1	25.0	44.1	10.2	5.0	15.0	408.4	192.2	144.1	1 281	1 241
Sherman-Denison, TX	18.3	2.6	5.7	64.6	8.1	3.3	11.9	278.2	110.1	114.4	1 005	802
Shreveport-Bossier City, LA	471.7	69.8	50.8	302.3	52.4	31.9	117.6	1 035.0	400.9	485.4	1 285	594
Sioux City, IA-NE-SD	71.8	112.2	22.7	89.8	20.9	12.0	45.2	433.5	184.9	169.3	1 186	933
Sioux Falls, SD	133.0	15.0	57.0	76.8	10.9	3.9	93.7	460.0	125.9	258.7	1 329	1 057
South Bend-Mishawaka, IN-MI	81.0	619.6	118.5	180.8	31.8	12.2	102.4	921.0	347.6	337.4	1 060	993
Spartanburg, SC	34.9	1.2	10.3	153.8	21.5	15.8	37.2	703.2	239.3	242.1	934	831
Spokane, WA	375.0	73.2	67.2	305.5	73.1	36.3	106.1	1 212.2	598.5	361.8	846	577
Springfield, IL	134.2	5.4	22.9	307.8	779.6	414.9	529.1	556.7	218.1	224.6	1 105	1 005
Springfield, MA	400.4	92.6	98.3	526.2	148.1	69.2	314.3	2 007.1	1 067.4	710.6	1 039	1 016
Springfield, MO	165.4	4.8	41.7	218.7	35.0	24.0	67.9	783.2	281.9	313.5	828	447
Springfield, OH	58.1	16.8	6.1	108.6	22.8	10.8	31.8	414.5	208.8	144.9	1 010	692
State College, PA	35.6	160.7	14.1	88.0	12.2	10.0	253.0	280.2	82.7	125.5	906	641
Stockton, CA	177.1	44.9	49.9	429.5	161.4	48.4	91.3	2 641.7	1 495.5	511.3	832	572
Sumter, SC	240.0	40.2	14.4	117.0	21.1	13.7	34.2	214.6	127.0	67.2	639	496
Syracuse, NY	288.5	244.6	171.4	500.8	99.4	54.9	211.5	2 600.0	1 234.9	935.6	1 432	1 032
Tallahassee, FL	135.5	45.4	39.3	589.1	517.4	604.6	964.9	974.4	414.1	283.9	866	601
Tampa-St. Petersburg-Clearwater, FL	1 406.1	1 311.6	343.0	861.4	261.7	166.3	437.4	7 344.5	2 514.5	2 740.9	1 101	866
Terre Haute, IN	110.9	41.8	29.2	140.4	18.3	7.0	32.7	394.8	157.4	151.6	893	864
Texarkana, TX-Texarkana, AR	114.2	79.2	9.3	115.8	18.9	7.5	68.2	308.2	155.1	91.1	696	477
Toledo, OH	196.6	32.0	99.0	423.2	100.7	54.4	162.2	2 362.8	900.1	1 004.6	1 523	964
Topeka, KS	201.9	28.8	32.1	177.8	130.1	123.3	319.2	697.2	265.9	263.7	1 168	917
Trenton-Ewing, NJ	183.0	107.7	115.3	472.8	306.2	294.9	737.3	1 637.7	606.7	796.6	2 216	2 190
Tucson, AZ	731.5	2 781.6	136.8	753.1	116.6	92.0	250.8	2 528.7	1 190.0	942.2	1 069	786
Tulsa, OK	318.7	125.9	95.3	356.6	116.4	73.7	237.4	2 142.7	767.9	839.6	956	547
Tuscaloosa, AL	78.5	43.7	51.3	141.9	26.6	21.8	126.8	702.6	255.5	128.8	665	245
Tyler, TX	54.6	46.0	12.7	114.8	14.9	8.7	29.3	405.1	159.9	175.8	969	743
Utica-Rome, NY	151.4	76.4	22.0	327.0	43.8	26.4	114.0	1 149.7	589.0	390.9	1 309	898
Valdosta, GA	183.1	93.0	4.8	88.8	24.6	10.9	24.6	467.5	150.9	115.5	953	483
Vallejo-Fairfield, CA	500.1	371.7	35.2	150.8	52.8	28.5	96.3	1 734.9	876.8	409.0	995	644
Vero Beach, FL	25.6	33.5	6.1	22.4	10.2	5.2	10.5	335.0	68.4	175.5	1 487	1 204
Victoria, TX	21.9	16.2	4.5	72.2	14.6	7.1	27.2	444.6	95.4	181.2	1 610	1 368
Vineland-Millville-Bridgeton, NJ	47.9	41.8	10.0	142.5	33.3	13.0	51.2	601.2	393.4	134.6	911	893
Virginia Beach-Norfolk-Newport News, VA-NC	6 108.7	3 921.2	854.0	536.8	171.6	142.9	392.0	5 256.4	2 103.3	2 047.7	1 270	855
Visalia-Porterville, CA	69.4	12.0	31.8	326.2	124.7	44.4	62.1	2 104.0	1 228.0	222.4	583	408
Waco, TX	119.5	76.5	15.6	157.8	22.5	11.8	61.3	739.1	240.8	217.0	997	732
Warner Robins, GA	884.5	277.8	53.4	36.5	16.8	7.2	16.3	385.5	129.5	108.3	927	511

1. Based on the resident population estimated as of July 1 of the year shown.

Table C. Metropolitan Areas — Local Government Finances, Government Employment, and Elections

Area Name	Direct general expenditure Total (mil dol)	Per capita[1] (dollars)	Education	Health and hospitals	Police protection	Public welfare	Highways	Debt outstanding Total (mil dol)	Per capita[1] (dollars)	Federal civilian	Federal military	State and local	Democratic	Republican	All other
	183	184	185	186	187	188	189	190	191	192	193	194	195	196	197
Salem, OR	1 166.3	3 259	54.0	7.2	5.0	0.0	4.0	764.9	2 138	1 511	986	36 493	44.5	54.6	0.9
Salinas, CA	2 022.0	4 891	36.9	22.1	4.3	5.7	3.6	704.5	1 704	4 724	5 785	25 661	60.0	38.9	1.1
Salisbury, MD	286.4	2 560	54.6	1.3	4.7	2.9	5.1	159.5	1 426	402	305	8 988	41.1	58.0	0.9
Salt Lake City, UT	2 681.3	2 689	43.3	2.6	6.0	0.0	4.9	5 360.0	5 375	10 392	4 553	80 674	37.2	60.0	2.8
San Angelo, TX	214.5	2 047	53.6	3.4	6.3	0.0	4.1	211.5	2 019	1 322	3 432	7 672	23.9	75.6	0.4
San Antonio, TX	5 506.8	3 082	54.3	9.2	4.6	2.5	2.5	9 557.9	5 350	27 694	40 803	112 978	40.1	59.4	0.6
San Diego-Carlsbad-San Marcos, CA	11 583.5	3 985	43.1	8.0	5.5	6.3	2.6	8 707.3	2 996	39 014	116 506	185 393	46.9	52.2	1.0
Sandusky, OH	291.7	3 683	46.3	2.1	5.4	8.3	3.9	135.3	1 708	195	182	5 659	53.3	46.5	0.2
San Francisco-Oakland-Fremont, CA	21 775.9	5 210	28.1	13.3	5.8	7.6	4.0	25 265.1	6 045	38 388	7 771	268 967	72.1	26.8	1.2
Oakland-Fremont-Hayward, CA Div	12 027.2	4 880	32.1	12.8	5.3	7.5	3.9	14 069.9	5 709	16 265	4 620	150 541	68.9	29.9	1.1
San Francisco-San Mateo-Redwood City, CA Div	9 748.7	5 685	23.1	14.0	6.4	7.7	4.2	11 195.2	6 528	22 123	3 151	118 426	76.3	22.5	1.2
San Jose-Sunnyvale-Santa Clara, CA	8 884.8	5 108	36.6	8.5	4.5	6.6	5.7	7 733.5	4 446	10 582	2 899	88 960	63.8	35.0	1.2
San Luis Obispo-Paso Robles, CA	937.7	3 700	41.2	7.9	5.0	8.4	5.6	295.7	1 167	634	379	20 722	46.1	52.5	1.4
Santa Barbara-Santa Maria-Goleta, CA	1 833.5	4 549	38.8	15.6	4.6	5.5	4.2	833.6	2 068	3 760	3 872	30 539	54.9	43.9	1.3
Santa Cruz-Watsonville, CA	1 118.5	4 407	39.5	7.0	4.8	7.8	3.4	558.9	2 202	562	349	18 439	73.2	24.9	1.8
Santa Fe, NM	346.1	2 572	42.4	0.6	8.3	2.4	6.9	435.6	3 238	1 260	368	15 885	71.0	28.0	1.0
Santa Rosa-Petaluma, CA	1 961.9	4 189	38.0	7.8	5.4	5.7	4.3	1 544.1	3 297	1 773	1 275	27 362	67.3	31.2	1.6
Sarasota-Bradenton-Venice, FL	2 115.6	3 412	33.7	17.7	6.4	1.1	4.2	1 748.9	2 820	1 974	975	22 993	44.1	54.8	1.0
Savannah, GA	950.2	3 170	40.2	7.6	6.2	0.4	4.3	887.5	2 960	2 613	5 361	18 032	44.3	55.3	0.4
Scranton-Wilkes-Barre, PA	1 365.5	2 469	48.5	0.6	3.4	3.7	4.2	1 724.1	3 117	4 596	1 538	27 130	52.5	46.3	1.2
Seattle-Tacoma-Bellevue, WA	11 572.6	3 702	34.3	8.9	4.7	0.3	5.2	16 711.3	5 346	32 853	39 784	215 138	59.6	39.2	1.3
Seattle-Bellevue-Everett, WA Div	9 399.1	3 927	31.2	10.0	4.8	0.2	5.3	14 436.2	6 031	23 386	14 205	172 151	62.0	36.8	1.3
Tacoma, WA Div	2 173.5	2 968	47.7	4.3	4.1	0.3	4.8	2 275.1	3 107	9 467	25 579	42 987	50.6	48.2	1.2
Sheboygan, WI	415.8	3 696	48.5	5.7	6.0	10.5	8.0	298.5	2 654	231	315	5 953	44.1	55.1	0.8
Sherman-Denison, TX	279.5	2 455	57.3	3.9	4.5	0.7	3.8	297.7	2 615	344	213	5 551	30.2	69.4	0.4
Shreveport-Bossier City, LA	1 003.5	2 656	49.7	1.2	6.1	0.1	4.0	1 051.8	2 783	4 435	7 678	26 245	42.9	56.5	0.6
Sioux City, IA-NE-SD	438.6	3 071	53.3	2.5	5.1	1.1	7.6	265.2	1 857	1 007	583	8 012	46.6	52.7	0.7
Sioux Falls, SD	454.6	2 335	51.8	1.1	5.3	0.8	10.0	377.7	1 940	2 235	1 122	8 685	39.7	58.8	1.4
South Bend-Mishawaka, IN-MI	960.4	3 016	47.2	1.1	4.0	3.6	2.9	800.9	2 515	1 250	867	15 210	47.4	52.0	0.7
Spartanburg, SC	690.7	2 663	53.6	0.8	4.3	0.2	1.9	2 168.9	8 364	498	968	16 757	34.7	64.1	1.2
Spokane, WA	1 134.0	2 653	52.4	2.9	5.0	0.0	4.2	804.5	1 882	4 417	4 901	28 423	43.7	54.8	1.6
Springfield, IL	589.5	2 901	46.0	1.2	6.8	0.7	7.7	605.8	2 981	2 127	393	29 264	40.0	59.2	0.8
Springfield, MA	2 014.4	2 944	55.3	0.5	5.2	0.7	3.5	2 358.6	3 447	6 208	1 772	51 245	64.2	34.8	1.0
Springfield, MO	878.1	2 319	48.6	4.9	5.3	1.4	5.6	722.6	1 908	2 490	1 164	21 359	34.8	64.6	0.6
Springfield, OH	401.8	2 802	50.9	5.6	6.0	8.4	4.5	160.0	1 116	624	338	7 464	48.6	51.0	0.5
State College, PA	305.9	2 208	44.2	4.2	2.8	6.3	3.5	312.4	2 255	437	461	37 562	47.8	51.6	0.6
Stockton, CA	2 467.8	4 017	44.7	9.5	5.3	10.2	4.3	1 511.0	2 460	4 017	871	34 430	45.8	53.4	0.8
Sumter, SC	196.6	1 869	68.1	1.1	6.4	0.6	1.8	117.4	1 116	1 091	5 988	6 048	50.5	48.9	0.6
Syracuse, NY	2 834.2	4 337	48.6	2.8	3.2	12.3	5.3	1 904.3	2 914	4 800	1 288	49 794	51.6	46.3	2.1
Tallahassee, FL	941.2	2 871	44.5	0.8	7.1	1.0	6.4	2 197.3	6 702	1 926	652	61 478	61.3	38.1	0.6
Tampa-St. Petersburg-Clearwater, FL	7 099.7	2 851	41.9	1.4	7.1	2.3	3.9	9 553.0	3 836	18 408	10 765	117 787	47.2	51.9	1.0
Terre Haute, IN	405.3	2 388	50.4	5.9	2.5	1.8	4.3	382.5	2 253	1 394	482	11 762	43.3	56.0	0.8
Texarkana, TX-Texarkana, AR	317.2	2 421	56.8	2.1	8.6	0.3	5.5	237.4	1 812	3 228	370	7 650	37.2	62.5	0.3
Toledo, OH	2 305.5	3 496	41.5	5.3	5.7	6.1	4.3	1 863.8	2 826	2 549	1 662	48 992	55.0	44.7	0.3
Topeka, KS	663.6	2 939	53.9	2.4	5.7	0.5	4.1	1 061.7	4 702	2 940	847	24 149	41.9	56.6	1.4
Trenton-Ewing, NJ	1 554.6	4 325	53.8	1.1	5.5	4.3	1.6	1 564.9	4 353	2 894	551	48 450	61.0	38.1	0.9
Tucson, AZ	2 435.1	2 763	38.6	6.8	8.1	3.0	6.7	2 753.4	3 124	8 861	7 989	65 221	52.4	47.0	0.6
Tulsa, OK	2 199.2	2 505	49.6	3.0	6.3	1.4	3.6	2 418.2	2 755	4 842	3 313	43 936	35.7	64.3	0.0
Tuscaloosa, AL	758.8	3 919	33.4	40.1	3.4	0.1	5.3	445.1	2 299	1 457	874	20 796	42.2	57.1	0.6
Tyler, TX	396.4	2 185	60.3	6.6	5.5	1.4	2.7	305.6	1 684	965	340	11 269	27.1	72.5	0.4
Utica-Rome, NY	1 271.9	4 258	53.4	2.2	2.6	11.2	6.5	945.5	3 165	2 142	530	25 068	41.9	55.6	2.5
Valdosta, GA	470.5	3 884	35.3	38.9	4.1	0.4	4.3	70.6	583	984	4 259	10 293	39.3	60.3	0.4
Vallejo-Fairfield, CA	1 732.4	4 214	35.5	4.9	6.7	7.4	4.5	1 450.9	3 530	4 257	8 157	23 296	57.8	41.2	0.9
Vero Beach, FL	303.2	2 569	39.5	2.8	9.1	0.6	5.8	325.3	2 757	393	178	4 678	39.0	60.1	0.8
Victoria, TX	453.7	4 029	42.9	28.5	4.8	0.2	3.6	336.9	2 992	286	257	8 350	30.8	68.7	0.4
Vineland-Millville-Bridgeton, NJ	574.1	3 885	61.4	1.9	3.9	6.5	2.1	275.0	1 861	737	211	13 443	52.3	45.9	1.8
Virginia Beach-Norfolk-Newport News, VA-NC	5 390.5	3 342	46.0	6.5	4.7	4.2	2.5	5 492.0	3 405	44 714	114 992	104 382	46.4	53.1	0.5
Visalia-Porterville, CA	2 052.3	5 376	41.3	20.9	2.8	9.0	2.2	638.3	1 672	1 356	525	28 444	32.8	66.3	0.8
Waco, TX	768.0	3 528	44.5	3.7	4.4	0.2	2.2	3 092.5	14 205	2 886	441	13 566	33.8	65.8	0.3
Warner Robins, GA	393.5	3 370	40.8	29.0	3.9	0.0	2.2	133.7	1 145	12 657	5 716	7 277	33.3	66.1	0.5

1. Based on the resident population estimated as of July 1 of the year shown.

Table C. Metropolitan Areas — **Land Area and Population**

CBSA/ DIV code[1]	Area Name	Land area,[2] 2000 (sq km)	Population and population characteristics, 2003													
						Race alone or in combination, not Hispanic or Latino (percent)					Age (percent)					
			Total persons	Rank	Per square kilometer	White	Black	Am. Indian, Alaska Native	Asian and Pacific Islander	Percent Hispanic or Latino[3]	Under 5 years	5 to 17 years	18 to 24 years	25 to 34 years	35 to 44 years	45 to 54 years
		1	2	3	4	5	6	7	8	9	10	11	12	13	14	15
47900	Washington-Arlington-Alexandria, DC-VA-MD-WV	14 571	5 091 404	7	349.4	55.8	26.6	0.7	8.6	10.1	7.1	18.0	8.8	15.1	17.1	14.6
13644	Bethesda-Frederick-Gaithersburg, MD Div ...	3 000	1 132 543	X	377.5	65.5	13.5	0.6	11.7	10.6	7.0	18.4	7.7	13.2	17.2	15.3
47894	Washington-Arlington-Alexandria, DC-VA-MD-WV Div...	11 571	3 958 861	X	342.1	53.1	30.3	0.7	7.8	10.0	7.2	17.8	9.1	15.7	17.1	14.4
47940	Waterloo-Cedar Falls, IA	3 905	162 127	232	41.5	90.6	6.9	0.4	1.4	1.7	5.7	16.3	13.5	11.8	12.9	14.4
48140	Wausau, WI	4 001	127 168	285	31.8	93.3	0.5	0.6	5.4	0.9	5.9	19.3	9.5	11.9	16.1	14.7
48260	Weirton-Steubenville, WV-OH	1 506	128 569	280	85.4	94.8	4.3	0.4	0.5	0.6	5.1	15.3	9.0	10.9	14.0	16.2
48300	Wenatchee, WA.................	12 281	101 726	335	8.3	77.8	0.3	1.4	1.0	20.4	6.8	19.8	10.0	11.1	14.4	14.5
48540	Wheeling, WV-OH	2 462	150 361	247	61.1	95.9	3.4	0.4	0.6	0.5	5.1	15.8	9.4	11.2	14.3	16.0
48620	Wichita, KS	10 744	582 781	82	54.2	80.0	8.4	1.9	3.7	8.1	7.5	19.8	9.9	13.3	15.1	13.9
48660	Wichita Falls, TX............	6 825	149 653	248	21.9	77.0	8.9	1.5	2.2	12.1	7.0	18.2	13.7	12.3	14.7	12.7
48700	Williamsport, PA	3 198	118 438	298	37.0	94.5	4.6	0.4	0.6	0.6	5.3	16.7	10.8	11.2	14.9	14.9
48900	Wilmington, NC	4 984	293 207	151	58.8	79.8	16.6	0.8	0.8	2.8	5.9	15.6	9.8	13.9	14.2	13.7
49020	Winchester, VA-WV	2 760	110 246	313	39.9	91.3	4.7	0.5	1.0	3.5	6.0	18.1	9.6	13.0	16.0	13.9
49180	Winston-Salem, NC	3 787	437 550	106	115.5	71.7	20.1	0.5	1.2	7.3	6.9	17.6	8.9	14.0	15.5	14.1
49340	Worcester, MA.................	3 919	776 610	62	198.2	86.1	3.3	0.5	3.7	7.3	6.4	18.3	9.2	13.0	16.9	14.3
49420	Yakima, WA..................	11 127	226 727	183	20.4	55.7	1.1	4.8	1.3	38.3	8.7	22.1	10.8	12.8	13.5	12.4
49620	York-Hanover, PA...............	2 343	394 919	118	168.6	92.0	4.2	0.4	1.2	3.2	5.8	17.7	8.7	12.0	16.3	15.1
49660	Youngstown-Warren-Boardman, OH-PA.......	4 412	593 340	81	134.5	86.9	11.1	0.5	0.7	1.7	5.7	17.3	9.1	11.2	14.3	15.2
49700	Yuba City, CA	3 194	148 135	253	46.4	63.6	2.8	3.1	11.1	22.3	7.4	20.9	10.9	12.8	14.2	12.3
49740	Yuma, AZ....................	14 281	171 134	225	12.0	41.8	1.7	1.5	1.2	54.4	8.8	21.4	10.3	11.2	12.5	9.9

1. CBSA = Core Based Statistical Area. DIV = Metropolitan Division. See Appendix A for explanation. See Appendix B for list of metropolitan areas identified by type. 2. Dry land or land partially or temporarily covered by water. 3. Hispanic or Latino persons may be of any race.

Table C. Metropolitan Areas — **Population and Households**

Area Name	55 to 64 years	65 to 74 years	75 years and over	Percent female	1900	2000	1990–2000	2000–2003	Births	Deaths	Net migration	Number	Percent change, 1990–2000	Persons per house-hold	Female family house-holder[1]	One person
	16	17	18	19	20	21	22	23	24	25	26	27	28	29	30	31
Washington-Arlington-Alexandria, DC-VA-MD-WV	9.3	4.9	4.1	51.2	4 122 259	4 796 183	16.3	6.1	242 818	98 813	147 246	1 800 263	17.7	2.61	12.5	26.5
Bethesda-Frederick-Gaithersburg, MD Div	9.6	5.5	5.4	51.7	913 083	1 068 618	17.0	6.0	52 164	22 524	34 770	394 625	17.9	2.67	10.3	23.7
Washington-Arlington-Alexandria, DC-VA-MD-WV Div	9.2	4.7	3.7	51.1	3 209 176	3 727 565	16.2	6.2	190 654	76 289	112 476	1 405 638	17.7	2.59	13.1	27.3
Waterloo-Cedar Falls, IA	9.5	6.9	7.9	51.9	158 640	163 706	3.2	-1.0	6 315	4 984	-2 913	63 527	5.7	2.45	9.8	26.6
Wausau, WI	9.3	6.2	6.8	50.1	115 400	125 834	9.0	1.1	4 848	3 187	-196	47 702	14.8	2.60	7.4	23.6
Weirton-Steubenville, WV-OH	11.2	9.5	9.2	52.1	142 523	132 008	-7.4	-2.6	4 283	5 855	-1 785	54 491	-1.3	2.36	11.1	27.9
Wenatchee, WA	9.3	6.7	6.8	50.3	78 455	99 219	26.5	2.5	4 508	2 518	575	36 747	21.1	2.66	9.0	23.5
Wheeling, WV-OH	10.7	8.6	9.4	51.6	159 301	153 172	-3.8	-1.8	4 981	6 118	-1 584	62 249	-1.0	2.35	11.1	29.6
Wichita, KS	8.2	5.9	5.9	50.4	511 111	571 166	11.7	2.0	29 063	15 612	-1 508	220 440	12.3	2.55	10.3	27.3
Wichita Falls, TX	8.5	7.0	6.0	49.0	140 375	151 524	7.9	-1.2	6 779	4 589	-4 093	56 109	7.8	2.50	11.2	26.6
Williamsport, PA	10.1	7.9	8.2	50.9	118 710	120 044	1.1	-1.3	4 153	3 988	-1 702	47 003	4.6	2.44	10.3	26.9
Wilmington, NC	11.2	8.2	5.9	51.1	200 124	274 532	37.2	6.8	11 102	8 467	15 786	114 675	44.6	2.34	11.1	26.4
Winchester, VA-WV	9.8	6.7	5.5	50.2	84 168	102 997	22.4	7.0	4 199	2 886	5 879	40 053	26.2	2.52	9.7	24.1
Winston-Salem, NC	9.7	6.8	5.9	51.7	361 426	421 961	16.7	3.7	19 727	12 661	8 933	169 685	17.5	2.42	12.4	27.3
Worcester, MA	8.8	5.8	6.7	51.1	709 711	750 963	5.8	3.6	32 950	22 353	16 650	283 927	9.1	2.56	11.4	26.2
Yakima, WA	8.2	5.4	5.7	50.1	188 823	222 581	17.9	1.9	13 450	5 421	-3 936	73 993	12.1	2.96	12.5	21.5
York-Hanover, PA	10.1	6.9	6.5	50.8	339 574	381 751	12.4	3.4	14 791	10 811	9 338	148 219	15.2	2.52	9.0	23.3
Youngstown-Warren-Boardman, OH-PA	10.4	8.2	8.9	51.7	613 604	602 964	-1.7	-1.6	22 497	22 926	-8 843	238 319	2.4	2.46	12.9	27.9
Yuba City, CA	8.6	6.1	5.1	50.0	122 643	139 149	13.5	6.5	7 216	3 971	5 823	47 568	10.9	2.87	12.4	21.4
Yuma, AZ	8.5	9.5	7.0	49.8	106 895	160 026	49.7	6.9	9 973	3 290	4 599	53 848	50.5	2.86	11.2	18.5

1. No spouse present.

Area Name	Births, average 1999–2001		Deaths, average 1999–2001				Physicians,[4] 1998		Hospitals,[4] 1998			Medicare enrollees, 2003	Serious crimes known to police,[6] 2002	
			Number		Rate					Beds			Total	
	Total	Rate[1]	Total	Infant[2]	Total[1]	Infant[3]	Number	Rate[5]	Number	Number	Rate[5]		Number	Rate[7]
	32	33	34	35	36	37	38	39	40	41	42	43	44	45
Washington-Arlington-Alexandria, DC-VA-MD-WV	72 516	15.0	29 642	1 474	6.2	6.8	10 855	4 657	38	10 793	11 421	480 361	202 398	4 135
Bethesda-Frederick-Gaithersburg, MD Div	15 716	14.6	6 509	233	6.1	4.9	5 080	692	6	1 741	311	123 970	35 094	3 187
Washington-Arlington-Alexandria, DC-VA-MD-WV Div..	56 800	15.2	23 133	1 241	6.2	7.3	5 775	3 965	32	9 052	11 110	356 391	167 304	4 410
Waterloo-Cedar Falls, IA	1 944	11.9	1 510	35	9.2	6.0	304	342	6	771	1 541	26 717	6 334	3 855
Wausau, WI	1 513	12.0	950	29	7.5	6.4	219	174	1	270	219	17 507	2 759	2 161
Weirton-Steubenville, WV-OH	1 357	10.3	1 759	30	13.3	7.4	158	355	3	643	1 294	27 888	2 407	2 053
Wenatchee, WA	1 422	14.3	788	15	8.0	3.5	214	345	3	246	410	15 331	4 550	4 454
Wheeling, WV-OH................	1 568	10.3	1 957	39	12.8	8.3	361	734	6	1 198	2 343	30 302	NA	NA
Wichita, KS	9 129	15.9	4 763	207	8.3	7.6	1 152	625	11	2 343	1 852	78 040	29 177	5 169
Wichita Falls, TX.................	2 081	13.8	1 461	64	9.7	10.3	281	230	4	455	631	22 014	9 560	6 040
Williamsport, PA.................	1 327	11.1	1 249	31	10.4	7.8	248	207	4	612	522	21 787	2 789	2 485
Wilmington, NC	3 357	12.2	2 481	69	9.0	6.9	476	369	5	777	721	49 311	16 587	5 902
Winchester, VA-WV	1 325	12.8	866	25	8.4	6.3	217	897	2	412	1 858	15 766	3 105	2 945
Winston-Salem, NC	6 037	14.3	3 835	186	9.1	10.3	1 173	549	6	1 837	1 074	66 298	22 722	5 253
Worcester, MA	10 006	13.3	6 766	166	9.0	5.5	2 028	270	12	2 248	307	112 188	19 590	2 688
Yakima, WA	4 226	19.0	1 734	83	7.8	6.5	370	166	4	481	221	28 709	14 319	6 248
York-Hanover, PA	4 548	11.9	3 313	61	8.7	4.5	641	168	3	768	206	58 951	7 312	2 396
Youngstown-Warren-Boardman, OH-PA	7 028	11.7	7 055	185	11.7	8.8	1 212	600	10	2 582	1 319	113 408	NA	NA
Yuba City, CA...................	2 209	15.8	1 215	36	8.7	5.4	226	323	2	260	384	20 038	6 357	4 407
Yuma, AZ........................	2 969	18.5	985	59	6.2	6.6	156	97	1	275	208	20 451	5 671	3 685

1. Per 1,000 estimated resident population.   2. Deaths of infants under 1 year old.   3. Deaths of infants under 1 year old per 1,000 live births.   4. Data subject to copyright.   5. Per 100,000 resident population as of July 1 of the year shown.   6. Data for serious crimes have not been adjusted for underreporting; this may affect comparability between geographic areas and over time.   7. Per 100,000 population estimated by the FBI.

Area Name	Serious crimes known to police,[1] 2002 (cont'd) Rate[2]		Education						Money income, 1999				Percent below poverty level, 1999			
			School enrollment and attainment, 2000				Local government expenditures,[5] 2000–2001									
			Enrollment[3]		Attainment[4] (percent)											
	Violent	Property	Total	Percent private	High school graduate or more	Bachelor's degree or more	Total current expenditures (mil dol)	Current expenditures per student (dollars)	Per capita income[6] (dollars)	Mean household income	Mean family income	Percent of households with income of $100,000 or more	Persons	Households	Families	Families with children
	46	47	48	49	50	51	52	53	54	55	56	57	58	59	60	61
Washington-Arlington-Alexandria, DC-VA-MD-WV	518	3 617	1 338 102	22.2	87.0	42.5	6 582.3	8 639	30 650	80 642	91 694	25.6	7.4	6.7	5.1	7.1
Bethesda-Frederick-Gaithersburg, MD Div	272	2 915	294 103	23.4	89.8	50.2	1 538.8	8 996	33 806	90 619	103 186	30.0	5.3	4.8	3.6	4.9
Washington-Arlington-Alexandria, DC-VA-MD-WV Div	589	3 821	1 043 999	21.8	86.1	40.2	5 043.5	8 536	29 745	77 840	88 214	24.3	8.0	7.3	5.5	7.8
Waterloo-Cedar Falls, IA	290	3 565	50 587	14.2	86.6	22.3	174.9	6 934	18 949	47 861	57 179	6.9	11.3	11.2	6.8	10.8
Wausau, WI	110	2 051	32 716	14.3	83.8	18.3	154.4	7 823	20 703	54 081	61 718	8.3	6.6	6.4	4.3	6.5
Weirton-Steubenville, WV-OH................	245	1 808	30 097	18.8	81.6	12.1	143.3	7 268	16 911	40 556	46 671	4.5	13.5	13.8	10.4	17.5
Wenatchee, WA	189	4 265	27 022	9.6	78.9	20.0	128.2	6 479	18 575	49 916	57 040	8.3	13.1	11.6	9.6	14.9
Wheeling, WV-OH................	NA	NA	36 033	17.0	81.2	14.6	158.5	7 482	16 748	40 266	47 585	4.6	15.4	15.8	11.8	19.1
Wichita, KS	481	4 688	162 193	16.7	85.4	24.3	625.4	6 195	20 584	52 506	61 240	8.8	9.1	9.1	6.7	10.1
Wichita Falls, TX	691	5 350	40 750	9.0	80.0	19.2	175.2	6 606	17 058	43 890	50 865	5.8	12.7	12.9	9.9	14.3
Williamsport, PA.................	184	2 301	29 073	15.5	80.6	15.1	150.3	7 870	17 224	43 006	50 325	5.7	11.5	11.9	7.9	13.0
Wilmington, NC	493	5 409	66 089	11.4	82.6	24.2	262.6	6 778	21 469	50 662	59 062	9.2	13.0	13.1	8.9	14.4
Winchester, VA-WV	213	2 731	24 752	13.3	76.4	18.3	126.4	7 230	19 726	50 222	56 817	7.8	9.9	10.0	6.6	9.7
Winston-Salem, NC	511	4 742	104 176	19.0	79.8	24.0	428.6	6 572	21 984	53 897	62 755	10.3	10.5	10.7	7.6	11.5
Worcester, MA	453	2 235	205 456	21.3	83.5	26.9	1 121.4	8 610	22 983	59 728	69 968	14.8	9.2	9.6	6.8	9.9
Yakima, WA	271	5 977	63 808	8.8	68.7	15.3	315.3	6 595	15 606	45 692	49 997	7.0	19.7	16.4	14.8	21.9
York-Hanover, PA	186	2 210	90 912	17.9	80.7	18.4	378.3	6 717	21 086	53 506	60 720	8.8	6.7	6.7	4.6	7.1
Youngstown-Warren-Boardman, OH-PA...........	NA	NA	147 352	15.8	82.6	16.3	738.9	7 760	18 721	46 578	54 186	6.8	11.5	11.5	8.8	14.8
Yuba City, CA	476	3 931	41 727	7.2	72.5	13.2	211.4	7 133	15 998	45 960	50 917	7.2	17.8	15.6	13.9	20.1
Yuma, AZ	632	3 053	43 353	4.7	65.8	11.8	159.5	5 226	14 802	42 912	45 285	6.0	19.2	15.8	15.5	24.4

1. Data for serious crimes have not been adjusted for underreporting; this may affect comparability between geographic areas and over time. 2. Per 100,000 population estimated by the FBI. 3. All persons 3 years old and over enrolled in nursery school through college. 4. Persons 25 years old and over. 5. Elementary and secondary education expenditures. 6. Based on population enumerated as of April 1, 2000.

Table C. Metropolitan Areas — **Personal Income**

Area Name	Personal income, 2002 Total (mil dol)	Percent change, 2001–2002	Per capita[1] Dollars	Rank	Wages and salaries[2] (mil dol)	Proprietor's income (mil dol)	Dividends, interest, and rent (mil dol)	Transfer payments Total (mil dol)	Government payments to individuals Total (mil dol)	Social Security (mil dol)	Medical payments (mil dol)	Income maintenance (mil dol)	Unemployment insurance (mil dol)
	62	63	64	65	66	67	68	69	70	71	72	73	74
Washington-Arlington-Alexandria, DC-VA-MD-WV	214 441	3.0	42 664	4	176 833	16 683	35 119	15 071	13 867	4 901	6 138	1 321	487
Bethesda-Frederick-Gaithersburg, MD Div	54 247	3.8	48 466	X	31 918	4 404	10 957	3 367	3 085	1 320	1 294	199	76
Washington-Arlington-Alexandria, DC-VA-MD-WV Div	160 194	2.8	41 002	X	144 915	12 279	24 162	11 703	10 782	3 580	4 843	1 122	411
Waterloo-Cedar Falls, IA	4 354	3.6	26 697	189	3 074	315	782	768	725	312	300	54	25
Wausau, WI	3 692	3.8	29 133	120	2 660	295	611	479	447	205	169	29	29
Weirton-Steubenville, WV-OH..................	3 072	3.0	23 692	308	1 848	144	524	808	774	324	315	61	12
Wenatchee, WA	2 644	4.8	26 319	202	1 550	260	521	495	468	172	180	40	43
Wheeling, WV-OH................	3 776	2.6	25 094	257	2 195	204	784	916	878	351	356	71	20
Wichita, KS	17 158	2.0	29 513	110	12 019	1 690	2 798	2 409	2 250	931	906	184	111
Wichita Falls, TX	3 982	4.2	26 484	198	2 516	406	748	631	599	235	249	52	15
Williamsport, PA..................	2 980	1.6	25 042	262	1 881	274	503	619	588	238	225	46	49
Wilmington, NC	7 689	2.8	26 790	187	4 353	692	1 693	1 419	1 351	565	541	125	55
Winchester, VA-WV	2 955	4.1	27 302	172	1 981	250	508	385	359	174	123	28	11
Winston-Salem, NC	12 775	2.2	29 437	113	8 806	824	2 596	1 837	1 735	752	688	157	70
Worcester, MA	25 580	0.8	33 207	43	14 986	1 600	3 427	3 807	3 624	1 243	1 658	272	328
Yakima, WA	5 324	4.0	23 681	310	3 165	489	895	1 202	1 141	311	500	148	112
York-Hanover, PA	11 222	3.0	28 833	129	6 938	543	1 859	1 605	1 506	707	556	97	86
Youngstown-Warren-Boardman, OH-PA	15 107	2.4	25 333	241	9 323	807	2 563	3 423	3 257	1 309	1 378	274	112
Yuba City, CA	3 416	5.1	23 572	313	1 819	330	497	799	765	201	324	116	51
Yuma, AZ	3 431	15.6	20 495	349	2 000	591	440	644	606	202	222	81	54

1. Based on the resident population estimated as of July 1 of the year shown.   2. Includes other labor income.

Table C. Metropolitan Areas — Earnings, Social Security, and Housing

	Earnings, 2002									Social Security beneficiaries, December 2003			Housing units, 2003	
Area Name		Percent by selected industries												
			Goods related[1]		Service-related and health									
	Total (mil dol)	Farm	Total	Manufacturing	Information, professional and technical services	Retail trade	Finance and insurance, and real estate	Health services	Government	Number	Rate[2]	Supplemental Security Income recipients, December 2003	Total	Percent change, 2000–2003
	75	76	77	78	79	80	81	82	83	84	85	86	87	88
Washington-Arlington-Alexandria, DC-VA-MD-WV	193 516	0.0	D	2.1	D	4.5	D	D	27.6	511 194	100	65 637	1 997 918	5.7
Bethesda-Frederick-Gaithersburg, MD Div	36 322	0.1	12.1	5.3	23.4	5.8	10.1	8.0	21.0	127 995	113	12 208	428 900	5.2
Washington-Arlington-Alexandria, DC-VA-MD-WV Div	157 194	0.0	D	1.4	D	4.2	D	D	29.1	383 199	97	53 429	1 569 018	5.8
Waterloo-Cedar Falls, IA	3 389	2.0	D	26.6	5.6	7.6	7.1	D	15.6	30 670	189	3 110	68 025	2.4
Wausau, WI	2 956	1.4	34.1	28.1	5.9	8.5	9.9	8.7	10.6	20 980	165	1 904	52 989	5.2
Weirton-Steubenville, WV-OH	1 992	0.1	D	32.6	D	6.5	3.0	D	12.5	31 215	243	3 644	59 333	0.3
Wenatchee, WA	1 810	7.6	D	5.9	4.8	9.8	4.0	14.8	21.2	17 670	174	1 588	44 570	2.8
Wheeling, WV-OH	2 400	-0.1	D	13.1	D	8.8	5.2	D	17.0	34 875	232	4 290	68 697	-0.7
Wichita, KS	13 708	0.1	39.3	32.5	D	6.4	5.2	10.9	12.7	89 560	154	8 818	247 127	3.6
Wichita Falls, TX	2 921	0.7	D	14.0	D	7.5	D	11.2	34.5	25 080	168	3 112	63 076	1.5
Williamsport, PA	2 155	0.3	34.0	29.1	5.7	8.6	4.8	12.8	16.8	24 690	208	3 232	53 380	1.7
Wilmington, NC	5 046	0.4	D	11.1	D	9.5	8.8	D	19.4	59 720	204	6 740	166 056	9.4
Winchester, VA-WV	2 231	0.3	D	26.4	D	9.1	4.5	D	11.6	18 840	171	1 899	47 749	5.9
Winston-Salem, NC	9 630	0.2	D	19.8	D	7.3	9.3	D	9.5	76 180	174	7 734	193 479	5.7
Worcester, MA	16 585	0.1	23.8	17.5	10.8	7.2	7.8	12.6	14.4	126 480	163	18 745	305 895	2.6
Yakima, WA	3 654	12.2	15.7	11.4	4.6	7.9	4.0	13.2	19.3	33 365	147	5 469	80 694	1.9
York-Hanover, PA	7 481	0.1	37.7	29.5	5.8	8.0	4.4	10.6	11.4	69 645	176	6 037	163 981	4.6
Youngstown-Warren-Boardman, OH-PA	10 129	0.2	32.7	27.2	5.0	9.3	5.4	14.1	13.8	128 170	216	15 587	260 132	1.3
Yuba City, CA	2 149	3.7	14.0	6.4	4.7	9.0	4.3	11.3	32.9	22 900	155	7 043	52 930	3.9
Yuma, AZ	2 591	19.4	D	3.2	3.5	7.1	2.3	8.0	28.2	24 295	142	2 950	79 336	7.0

1. Covers mining, construction, and manufacturing.   2. Per 1,000 resident population estimated as of July 1 of the year shown.

Table C. Metropolitan Areas — Housing, Labor Force, and Employment

	Housing units, 2000								Civilian labor force, 2003				Civilian employment,[5] 2000		
	Occupied units										Unemployment			Percent	
		Owner-occupied				Renter-occupied									
				Owner cost is 35 percent or more of income											Production, transportation, and material moving occupations
Area Name	Total	Percent	Mean value[1]	With a mortgage	Without a mortgage	Mean rent[2]	Rent is 35 percent or more of income	Substandard units[3] (percent)	Total	Percent change, 2002–2003	Total	Rate[4]	Total	Management, professional, and related occupations	
	89	90	91	92	93	94	95	96	97	98	99	100	101	102	103
Washington-Arlington-Alexandria, DC-VA-MD-WV	1 800 263	63.7	228 565	17.1	6.1	869	26.2	6.1	2 783 869	0.9	97 985	3.5	2 488 601	49.1	6.4
Bethesda-Frederick-Gaithersburg, MD Div	394 625	70.0	260 336	16.8	6.0	956	27.3	5.0	615 690	0.6	16 733	2.7	561 680	53.7	5.4
Washington-Arlington-Alexandria, DC-VA-MD-WV Div	1 405 638	62.0	218 463	17.2	6.2	849	25.9	6.5	2 168 179	1.0	81 252	3.7	1 926 921	47.7	6.6
Waterloo-Cedar Falls, IA	63 527	71.0	91 487	10.7	4.5	487	32.3	2.5	89 490	-2.3	4 053	4.5	82 272	30.7	17.9
Wausau, WI	47 702	75.7	110 908	12.6	5.9	502	20.6	2.7	77 392	2.2	3 583	4.6	66 550	29.7	21.8
Weirton-Steubenville, WV-OH	54 491	75.4	77 550	16.4	5.5	403	29.5	1.4	55 438	0.1	3 670	6.6	54 762	22.5	21.3
Wenatchee, WA	36 747	66.6	169 432	23.2	6.6	552	32.9	8.9	53 450	1.5	4 693	8.8	42 665	29.7	12.3
Wheeling, WV-OH...................	62 249	73.6	78 871	16.0	5.2	377	27.8	1.5	72 845	-1.2	3 781	5.2	63 546	27.1	16.7
Wichita, KS	220 440	68.1	97 355	12.4	5.7	537	25.9	3.9	301 012	0.5	21 569	7.2	275 271	32.0	16.4
Wichita Falls, TX...................	56 109	65.0	74 191	14.4	8.5	525	28.4	3.7	70 874	0.8	3 441	4.9	64 042	29.0	15.8
Williamsport, PA...................	47 003	69.5	97 759	17.8	8.3	465	31.2	1.4	56 982	-2.0	3 601	6.3	54 817	24.4	22.6
Wilmington, NC	114 675	71.9	171 931	23.1	8.1	629	37.9	2.6	147 865	2.6	8 499	5.7	131 489	30.3	12.7
Winchester, VA-WV	40 053	71.8	127 678	15.2	3.9	580	26.3	3.0	58 965	1.3	2 166	3.7	51 663	28.3	20.2
Winston-Salem, NC	169 685	70.0	134 710	16.0	6.5	537	26.6	3.5	221 412	0.9	12 311	5.6	207 704	32.7	18.5
Worcester, MA	283 927	64.1	173 081	16.3	10.1	590	27.1	2.7	388 557	-0.7	25 906	6.7	366 942	37.6	14.7
Yakima, WA	73 993	64.4	131 944	20.6	6.8	558	34.4	14.7	112 155	2.2	11 849	10.6	88 074	27.4	16.5
York-Hanover, PA...................	148 219	76.1	124 730	16.7	6.3	552	24.7	1.6	197 758	-2.3	9 841	5.0	195 962	28.4	22.7
Youngstown-Warren-Boardman, OH-PA	238 319	74.0	94 337	16.1	6.9	465	29.5	1.9	282 738	0.5	20 244	7.2	263 062	26.1	22.6
Yuba City, CA	47 568	58.2	126 793	24.2	7.0	535	33.5	11.7	59 612	1.2	8 241	13.8	51 203	26.3	15.9
Yuma, AZ	53 848	72.2	102 451	22.1	5.2	539	31.1	15.4	74 376	1.7	17 501	23.5	49 213	26.7	12.2

1. Specified owner-occupied units.   2. Specified renter-occupied units.   3. Overcrowded or lacking complete plumbing facilities.   4. Percent of civilian labor force.   5. Persons 16 years old and over.

Table C. Metropolitan Areas — Nonfarm Employment and Agriculture

Area Name	Private nonfarm establishments, employment and payroll, 2001									Agriculture, 2002			
	Number of establish-ments	Employment						Annual payroll		Farms			Farm operators whose principal occu-pation is farming (percent)
		Total	Health care and social assistance	Manufac-turing	Retail trade	Finance and insurance	Professional, scientific, and technical services	Total (mil dol)	Average per employee (dollars)	Number	Percent with—		
											Less than 50 acres	500 acres and over	
	104	105	106	107	108	109	110	111	112	113	114	115	116
Washington-Arlington-Alexandria, DC-VA-MD-WV	107 056	1 820 986	159 632	68 156	234 947	90 700	308 817	78 244	42 968	8 316	52.3	5.1	51.2
Bethesda-Frederick-Gaithersburg, MD Div	31 042	482 989	51 629	21 382	61 336	30 409	72 603	20 177	41 775	1 850	49.1	5.8	54.3
Washington-Arlington-Alexandria, DC-VA-MD-WV Div	76 014	1 337 997	108 003	46 774	173 611	60 291	236 214	58 067	43 398	6 466	53.2	4.9	50.3
Waterloo-Cedar Falls, IA	4 084	70 814	10 933	15 437	10 547	3 906	1 921	1 894	26 746	2 619	28.1	20.3	67.2
Wausau, WI	3 401	61 840	6 919	17 695	8 263	4 844	1 721	1 844	29 819	2 898	25.8	5.9	62.9
Weirton-Steubenville, WV-OH....................................	2 644	43 648	7 004	13 432	5 500	1 242	703	1 184	27 126	644	32.1	4.8	52.6
Wenatchee, WA	2 808	28 689	4 795	2 442	5 238	972	827	769	26 805	2 140	60.6	12.5	69.6
Wheeling, WV-OH................	3 722	54 093	12 227	3 870	9 042	2 403	1 707	1 294	23 922	1 625	23.6	3.9	49.6
Wichita, KS	14 527	262 659	35 363	69 877	31 398	9 595	8 080	8 469	32 243	4 568	25.9	26.4	58.8
Wichita Falls, TX.................	3 565	48 557	10 120	7 494	7 934	1 941	1 175	1 181	24 322	1 993	22.9	28.9	59.7
Williamsport, PA..................	2 825	47 378	7 968	12 858	7 295	1 724	1 329	1 209	25 518	1 323	30.7	3.3	52.5
Wilmington, NC	8 441	102 561	14 342	12 207	17 649	3 489	5 478	2 724	26 560	644	48.6	7.9	58.4
Winchester, VA-WV	2 798	46 405	6 564	11 315	7 351	1 322	1 649	1 309	28 208	1 355	34.7	7.6	50.9
Winston-Salem, NC	10 455	200 996	27 108	31 598	23 510	17 248	9 283	6 307	31 379	3 466	49.0	2.9	56.8
Worcester, MA	18 129	299 548	52 786	52 317	36 430	16 991	12 813	10 392	34 692	1 094	51.4	2.4	52.5
Yakima, WA	4 698	60 204	10 574	9 182	9 948	1 621	1 655	1 571	26 095	3 730	66.5	5.7	62.7
York-Hanover, PA	8 234	156 588	18 502	42 979	22 368	4 129	4 454	4 761	30 405	2 546	61.5	3.9	48.5
Youngstown-Warren-Boardman, OH-PA	13 934	220 139	36 736	47 606	33 490	6 937	6 259	6 143	27 905	2 907	36.2	3.4	54.1
Yuba City, CA	2 519	26 548	4 750	3 060	5 238	885	738	713	26 857	2 254	47.1	11.6	63.1
Yuma, AZ............................	2 539	32 820	4 881	2 317	7 076	970	863	715	21 785	531	56.9	18.3	63.7

Table C. Metropolitan Areas — **Agriculture**

Area Name	Agriculture, 2002 (cont'd)															
	Land in farms					Value of land and buildings (dollars)		Value of machinery and equipment average per farm (dollars)	Value of products sold				Percent of farms with sales of —		Government payments	
			Acres								Percent from —					
	Acreage (1,000)	Percent change, 1997–2002	Average size of farm	Total irrigated (1,000)	Total cropland (1,000)	Average per farm	Average per acre		Total (mil dol)	Average per farm (dollars)	Crops	Live-stock and poultry products	$10,000 or more	$100,000 or more	Total ($1,000)	Percent of farms
	117	118	119	120	121	122	123	124	125	126	127	128	129	130	131	132
Washington-Arlington-Alexandria, DC-VA-MD-WV	D	D	D	11	682	D	D	D	D	D	41.9	58.1	27.3	6.4	9 458	14.9
Bethesda-Frederick-Gaithersburg, MD Div	271	-7.5	146	3	201	766 871	5 506	72 533	138	74 804	41.1	58.9	35.1	13.6	5 246	24.1
Washington-Arlington-Alexandria, DC-VA-MD-WV Div	D	D	D	8	481	D	D	D	D	D	42.5	57.5	25.1	4.4	4 212	12.2
Waterloo-Cedar Falls, IA	854	0.9	326	D	789	867 995	2 647	124 326	363	138 523	62.0	38.0	69.6	32.4	14 657	68.9
Wausau, WI	531	2.9	183	6	341	327 014	1 846	72 025	205	70 890	17.1	82.9	50.1	19.0	7 501	29.9
Weirton-Steubenville, WV-OH	88	-4.3	137	0	44	199 859	1 803	43 303	8	12 561	40.8	59.2	21.6	3.1	D	D
Wenatchee, WA	991	-3.8	463	59	602	610 536	1 456	66 651	294	137 268	96.2	3.8	67.8	32.2	12 405	30.5
Wheeling, WV-OH	255	3.2	157	0	114	216 216	1 360	37 503	19	11 978	29.6	70.4	17.8	3.4	634	12.1
Wichita, KS	2 319	1.4	508	78	1 612	479 589	935	82 677	330	72 243	50.0	50.0	49.9	16.4	14 186	47.2
Wichita Falls, TX	1 492	-3.9	749	7	432	441 946	601	43 435	113	56 689	12.0	88.0	40.6	10.9	4 811	32.4
Williamsport, PA	177	30.1	134	2	104	315 040	2 318	48 714	49	37 187	32.9	67.1	29.2	10.8	1 370	22.2
Wilmington, NC	D	D	D	7	65	550 219	D	63 576	140	217 179	30.5	69.5	39.6	19.3	854	17.4
Winchester, VA-WV	251	NA	185	1	106	483 842	2 544	39 089	41	30 468	42.1	57.9	26.4	5.2	838	10.5
Winston-Salem, NC	352	5.4	102	4	183	386 261	3 533	48 615	116	33 494	40.5	59.5	25.8	7.4	1 212	15.2
Worcester, MA	104	1.0	95	1	42	661 544	7 378	46 309	69	62 682	50.8	49.2	32.5	10.1	1 098	8.4
Yakima, WA	1 679	-0.2	450	269	361	577 843	1 271	84 172	844	226 239	60.2	39.8	55.0	23.0	10 501	19.7
York-Hanover, PA	285	9.2	112	2	223	542 750	4 805	51 153	148	57 985	38.1	61.9	30.9	10.9	3 070	17.6
Youngstown-Warren-Boardman, OH-PA	367	4.0	126	1	252	325 055	2 612	50 472	102	35 021	41.3	58.7	37.3	9.2	3 862	23.8
Yuba City, CA	606	8.8	269	342	395	922 493	3 824	98 498	366	162 273	91.5	8.5	62.0	30.3	13 356	17.5
Yuma, AZ	231	-2.9	435	197	213	1 998 970	4 544	201 464	802	1 511 051	D	D	59.3	39.2	3 419	11.9

Area Name	Value of residential construction authorized by building permits, 2003		Wholesale trade, 1997				Retail trade,[1] 1997				Real estate and rental and leasing, 1997			
	New construction ($1,000)	Number of housing units	Number of establishments	Number of employees	Sales (mil dol)	Annual payroll (mil dol)	Number of establishments	Number of employees	Sales (mil dol)	Annual payroll (mil dol)	Number of establishments	Number of employees	Receipts (mil dol)	Annual payroll (mil dol)
	133	134	135	136	137	138	139	140	141	142	143	144	145	146
Washington-Arlington-Alexandria, DC-VA-MD-WV	4 342 128	35 847	4 514	D	D	D	16 599	237 815	42 847.2	4 507.3	5 213	D	D	D
Bethesda-Frederick-Gaithersburg, MD Div	665 746	6 265	1 183	17 535	9 643.6	872.9	3 741	56 955	10 753.7	1 144.6	1 308	12 237	1 409.4	323.3
Washington-Arlington-Alexandria, DC-VA-MD-WV Div	3 676 382	29 582	3 331	D	D	D	12 858	180 860	32 093.5	3 362.7	3 905	D	D	D
Waterloo-Cedar Falls, IA	100 509	690	231	3 214	1 276.4	91.2	762	10 800	1 550.9	158.3	147	612	73.1	13.0
Wausau, WI	163 006	1 395	221	3 395	1 002.0	102.5	565	9 236	1 421.6	142.6	86	439	39.9	7.1
Weirton-Steubenville, WV-OH	16 828	156	100	D	D	D	556	6 335	828.7	81.8	86	310	24.9	5.0
Wenatchee, WA	92 346	663	146	1 948	864.3	58.7	506	5 139	882.6	90.7	139	625	48.8	10.7
Wheeling, WV-OH	6 569	55	189	D	D	D	744	9 588	1 328.9	129.8	121	D	D	D
Wichita, KS	379 476	3 648	933	10 763	6 335.7	358.9	2 247	29 439	4 916.0	480.9	622	2 857	354.5	56.7
Wichita Falls, TX	51 693	534	236	2 099	493.4	48.3	659	7 646	1 275.4	113.4	154	D	D	D
Williamsport, PA	36 215	289	137	2 195	481.9	51.4	605	7 600	1 149.3	108.4	78	299	32.2	4.7
Wilmington, NC	882 768	6 455	414	4 221	1 393.0	112.0	1 433	15 748	3 056.9	262.5	366	2 183	192.3	39.1
Winchester, VA-WV	150 320	1 137	135	1 882	614.6	50.8	553	6 681	1 103.8	110.7	95	385	39.8	8.6
Winston-Salem, NC	387 922	3 406	561	D	D	D	1 858	23 415	4 200.8	384.6	387	1 943	286.5	40.0
Worcester, MA	528 334	3 629	1 026	12 865	12 038.3	493.9	2 796	35 415	6 231.7	606.7	537	3 019	391.6	70.5
Yakima, WA	82 139	606	291	4 871	1 853.8	141.9	854	10 174	1 741.6	174.9	212	1 018	99.9	17.0
York-Hanover, PA	367 185	3 148	450	9 498	3 428.1	275.9	1 447	20 356	3 250.6	315.4	236	1 138	128.3	21.5
Youngstown-Warren-Boardman, OH-PA	183 422	1 431	762	10 118	4 000.7	299.6	2 718	36 889	5 776.1	541.2	432	2 448	255.9	46.2
Yuba City, CA	235 045	1 597	130	D	D	D	446	5 129	851.3	86.7	118	592	51.9	7.4
Yuma, AZ	217 343	1 915	132	2 376	512.9	41.3	455	5 984	1 035.7	94.5	113	485	48.4	7.0

1. Establishments with payroll.

Area Name	Professional, scientific, and technical services,[1] 1997				Manufacturing, 1997				Accommodation and foodservices, 1997			
	Number of establish-ments	Number of employees	Sales (mil dol)	Annual payroll (mil dol)	Number of establish-ments	Number of employees	Sales (mil dol)	Annual payroll (mil dol)	Number of establish-ments	Number of employees	Sales (mil dol)	Annual payroll (mil dol)
	147	148	149	150	151	152	153	154	155	156	157	158
Washington-Arlington-Alexandria, DC-VA-MD-WV	19 264	282 573	37 496.0	14 895.4	NA	NA	NA	NA	8 455	D	D	D
Bethesda-Frederick-Gaithersburg, MD Div	4 763	53 007	6 293.7	2 549.5	689	22 985	4 621.0	949.0	1 711	31 276	1 255.3	352.5
Washington-Arlington-Alexandria, DC-VA-MD-WV Div	14 501	229 566	31 202.3	12 345.9	NA	NA	NA	NA	6 744	D	D	D
Waterloo-Cedar Falls, IA	243	1 662	110.4	47.8	NA	NA	NA	NA	363	D	D	D
Wausau, WI	181	1 264	127.4	46.6	232	16 839	3 181.9	502.6	276	3 779	105.2	29.7
Weirton-Steubenville, WV-OH	153	627	42.2	13.0	104	11 530	3 206.2	458.6	308	D	D	D
Wenatchee, WA	141	676	50.3	20.9	NA	NA	NA	NA	286	3 679	120.4	33.4
Wheeling, WV-OH	220	1 350	114.3	34.1	NA	NA	NA	NA	361	5 078	147.5	41.0
Wichita, KS	1 087	6 775	561.9	226.5	746	67 496	12 412.6	2 761.5	1 166	20 614	659.4	188.0
Wichita Falls, TX	225	1 099	89.2	33.2	NA	NA	NA	NA	293	5 317	162.1	47.7
Williamsport, PA	137	1 014	68.8	27.1	208	12 982	2 460.4	370.2	283	3 571	106.1	28.5
Wilmington, NC	622	3 469	277.1	111.6	299	11 841	3 847.3	450.0	658	11 176	364.0	97.9
Winchester, VA-WV	162	968	49.1	22.2	NA	NA	NA	NA	203	3 341	114.8	34.5
Winston-Salem, NC	865	5 823	552.7	210.7	520	34 265	11 038.2	1 116.5	782	D	D	D
Worcester, MA	1 432	7 909	824.4	329.8	1 336	61 344	11 303.4	2 340.9	1 522	21 242	715.1	195.6
Yakima, WA	223	1 298	119.4	43.2	239	10 163	2 090.5	264.6	411	5 371	178.6	47.8
York-Hanover, PA	502	3 457	268.4	105.2	661	45 754	8 156.9	1 557.5	635	10 721	318.7	91.1
Youngstown-Warren-Boardman, OH-PA	834	5 222	368.4	156.7	885	57 559	15 786.4	2 347.5	1 255	19 929	572.6	157.6
Yuba City, CA	143	572	37.3	14.3	114	2 792	602.2	76.1	187	2 383	75.9	21.9
Yuma, AZ	148	666	48.1	17.3	66	3 041	389.5	54.6	245	4 158	130.0	31.3

1. Firms subject to federal tax.

Table C. Metropolitan Areas — Health Care and Social Assistance, Other Services, and Federal Funds

Area Name	Health care and social assistance,[1] 1997				Other services,[1] 1997				Federal funds and grants, 2002–2003 Expenditures (mil dol)			
										Direct payments for individuals		
	Number of establishments	Number of employees	Receipts (mil dol)	Annual payroll (mil dol)	Number of establishments	Number of employees	Receipts (mil dol)	Annual payroll (mil dol)	Total	Social Security and government retirement	Medicare	Food stamps and Supplemental Security Income
	159	160	161	162	163	164	165	166	167	168	169	170
Washington-Arlington-Alexandria, DC-VA-MD-WV	NA	NA	NA	NA	7 241	49 350	3 481.9	1 085.3	98 384.7	12 353.2	3 099.4	537.7
Bethesda-Frederick-Gaithersburg, MD Div	2 753	23 219	1 907.5	797.7	1 678	10 692	752.5	250.7	15 215.4	2 519.5	755.4	77.9
Washington-Arlington-Alexandria, DC-VA-MD-WV Div	NA	NA	NA	NA	5 563	38 658	2 729.4	834.6	83 169.3	9 833.7	2 344.0	459.7
Waterloo-Cedar Falls, IA	284	2 687	190.3	92.6	298	1 721	95.1	29.0	805.1	360.3	154.2	25.8
Wausau, WI	200	2 672	188.8	104.9	222	1 201	79.2	20.9	537.6	231.4	85.2	13.5
Weirton-Steubenville, WV-OH	256	3 315	154.4	69.3	197	1 166	54.4	16.8	870.1	392.7	214.8	33.8
Wenatchee, WA	167	2 351	186.4	73.5	154	518	38.6	10.2	513.7	218.2	77.1	12.6
Wheeling, WV-OH	357	4 025	207.0	88.9	228	1 451	75.0	24.4	974.1	424.7	203.9	37.7
Wichita, KS	953	17 904	1 276.4	528.5	946	5 741	359.3	109.5	3 488.4	1 193.0	491.8	82.8
Wichita Falls, TX	284	D	D	D	238	1 571	89.4	29.3	1 295.7	408.4	141.7	26.1
Williamsport, PA	218	2 050	134.4	58.6	176	887	57.5	15.2	652.4	286.8	131.4	22.7
Wilmington, NC	531	7 255	461.9	191.5	440	2 275	141.9	41.4	1 648.6	781.7	229.7	57.1
Winchester, VA-WV	192	2 111	154.5	82.4	171	816	49.7	15.4	441.6	251.4	69.8	12.4
Winston-Salem, NC	634	9 346	686.8	283.7	616	3 999	214.6	73.5	2 038.7	932.1	339.4	62.9
Worcester, MA	1 244	20 902	1 425.3	599.7	1 182	6 312	444.3	122.9	3 926.5	1 467.5	931.8	117.7
Yakima, WA	391	4 594	298.6	129.8	277	1 408	87.6	26.8	1 171.5	410.3	159.5	54.4
York-Hanover, PA	586	6 842	469.4	214.2	585	3 058	202.4	58.0	2 074.9	852.0	296.5	38.9
Youngstown-Warren-Boardman, OH-PA	1 408	15 755	894.1	411.6	928	5 533	306.0	89.6	3 532.9	1 586.4	838.3	143.0
Yuba City, CA	252	2 702	248.1	79.0	148	821	53.9	14.3	966.2	316.8	134.5	39.3
Yuma, AZ	224	2 428	154.1	60.1	158	855	46.5	13.6	1 021.7	321.5	126.7	36.2

1. Firms subject to federal tax.

Area Name	Federal funds and grants, 2002–2003 (cont'd)							Local government finances, 2002				
	Expenditures (mil dol) (cont'd)							General revenue				
	Procurement contract awards			Grants							Taxes	
											Per capita[1] (dollars)	
	Salaries and wages	Defense	Other	Medicaid and other health-related	Nutrition and family welfare	Education	Other	Total (mil dol)	Intergovern-mental (mil dol)	Total (mil dol)	Total	Property
	171	172	173	174	175	176	177	178	179	180	181	182
Washington-Arlington-Alexandria, DC-VA-MD-WV	27 520.0	18 628.0	25 706.4	3 044.3	523.6	549.7	4 478.4	22 487.7	7 195.0	11 515.2	2 291	1 244
Bethesda-Frederick-Gaithersburg, MD Div	3 809.1	1 553.3	4 925.7	910.5	47.1	36.3	531.6	4 484.9	899.0	2 807.7	2 508	1 414
Washington-Arlington-Alexandria, DC-VA-MD-WV Div	23 710.9	17 074.6	20 780.7	2 133.9	476.6	513.3	3 946.9	18 002.8	6 296.0	8 707.6	2 229	1 195
Waterloo-Cedar Falls, IA	40.9	1.3	8.6	98.5	25.8	12.8	40.0	490.3	188.3	177.0	1 085	875
Wausau, WI	35.5	0.2	27.0	68.8	12.6	6.9	32.8	469.8	221.3	153.3	1 210	1 110
Weirton-Steubenville, WV-OH	24.1	2.0	7.3	87.4	21.0	9.4	66.4	293.1	145.7	103.1	795	646
Wenatchee, WA	43.8	11.1	20.9	53.6	15.1	6.9	25.5	342.6	155.7	94.9	945	685
Wheeling, WV-OH	49.7	9.5	12.9	96.9	27.3	17.4	77.0	359.6	173.9	112.6	748	540
Wichita, KS	431.9	688.5	63.4	265.1	77.6	24.0	106.1	1 574.4	693.0	533.2	917	693
Wichita Falls, TX	355.4	144.1	52.0	76.7	15.7	8.9	48.3	355.1	121.7	153.0	1 018	771
Williamsport, PA	38.7	32.1	12.2	65.3	17.0	4.0	29.0	307.2	138.0	108.0	907	633
Wilmington, NC	79.7	106.5	56.3	182.3	30.5	18.6	80.4	1 278.2	348.1	341.4	1 189	939
Winchester, VA-WV	29.1	1.3	14.3	39.4	5.6	6.4	5.9	272.0	97.2	115.4	1 066	751
Winston-Salem, NC	89.9	29.3	46.9	347.7	42.9	29.6	83.5	1 012.0	487.6	367.9	848	669
Worcester, MA	219.1	106.7	22.9	626.8	101.6	67.0	225.1	2 425.0	1 185.9	967.1	1 255	1 188
Yakima, WA	72.1	23.0	17.1	207.2	87.5	34.5	61.2	653.3	400.4	149.8	666	445
York-Hanover, PA	141.7	456.3	38.1	130.3	22.9	7.7	70.2	994.2	306.8	416.4	1 070	823
Youngstown-Warren-Boardman, OH-PA	141.6	19.3	32.3	393.3	112.5	45.8	175.1	1 697.9	834.3	574.2	963	713
Yuba City, CA	195.6	0.7	22.2	115.3	41.5	19.9	27.6	599.8	384.8	97.6	673	510
Yuma, AZ	258.5	66.6	16.1	86.7	30.5	19.9	41.7	441.6	243.5	124.8	746	407

1. Based on the resident population estimated as of July 1 of the year shown.

Table C. Metropolitan Areas — **Local Government Finances, Government Employment, and Elections**

Area Name	Local government finances, 2002 (cont'd)									Government employment, 2002			Presidential election, 2004		
	Direct general expenditure							Debt outstanding					Percent of vote cast —		
			Percent of total for —												
	Total (mil dol)	Per capita[1] (dollars)	Education	Health and hospitals	Police protection	Public welfare	Highways	Total (mil dol)	Per capita[1] (dollars)	Federal civilian	Federal military	State and local	Democratic	Republican	All other
	183	184	185	186	187	188	189	190	191	192	193	194	195	196	197
Washington-Arlington-Alexandria, DC-VA-MD-WV	21 242.7	4 226	40.7	4.6	5.4	9.3	2.2	20 079.9	3 995	347 084	76 025	273 280	61.2	38.0	0.8
Bethesda-Frederick-Gaithersburg, MD Div	3 893.8	3 479	52.4	2.3	5.3	3.1	3.5	3 827.4	3 419	45 879	8 068	51 914	60.3	38.6	1.0
Washington-Arlington-Alexandria, DC-VA-MD-WV Div	17 348.9	4 441	38.1	5.1	5.4	10.7	1.9	16 252.6	4 160	301 205	67 957	221 366	61.5	37.8	0.7
Waterloo-Cedar Falls, IA	474.9	2 912	46.0	6.5	4.2	4.6	9.3	296.3	1 817	660	669	13 122	52.2	47.2	0.6
Wausau, WI	495.8	3 912	49.1	12.6	3.7	3.8	8.9	299.7	2 365	533	344	6 982	45.4	53.5	1.1
Weirton-Steubenville, WV-OH	295.9	2 282	51.1	5.6	4.0	6.5	5.1	212.4	1 638	363	399	6 134	51.1	48.3	0.6
Wenatchee, WA	317.5	3 161	49.1	9.8	3.9	0.0	6.2	1 326.5	13 204	925	309	7 233	34.9	63.9	1.2
Wheeling, WV-OH	352.7	2 344	52.1	0.7	4.5	6.6	5.1	445.5	2 961	726	508	9 605	47.3	52.1	0.6
Wichita, KS	1 546.3	2 660	48.1	2.8	5.2	0.2	9.0	2 351.9	4 045	5 045	4 597	33 877	35.1	63.6	1.4
Wichita Falls, TX	356.6	2 371	51.2	4.4	5.5	0.7	3.9	488.7	3 250	2 610	10 619	10 635	27.1	72.4	0.5
Williamsport, PA	323.5	2 719	55.1	0.0	2.3	4.8	3.8	457.1	3 841	593	320	8 201	31.8	67.4	0.8
Wilmington, NC	1 349.5	4 702	29.3	34.9	5.3	4.2	0.9	859.4	2 994	1 324	752	21 633	42.2	57.5	0.3
Winchester, VA-WV	262.2	2 423	58.4	0.9	4.1	2.5	3.5	270.3	2 497	470	318	5 999	33.4	65.9	0.8
Winston-Salem, NC	1 073.9	2 475	45.2	6.2	5.9	6.6	2.6	722.5	1 665	1 357	756	21 639	40.1	59.6	0.3
Worcester, MA	2 314.6	3 005	56.5	0.7	4.3	0.1	3.5	2 689.5	3 491	2 933	1 937	46 687	56.5	42.6	0.9
Yakima, WA	645.9	2 873	56.9	1.8	4.4	1.2	5.2	331.0	1 472	1 343	755	14 772	38.9	59.9	1.2
York-Hanover, PA	1 052.0	2 703	46.5	6.8	3.5	4.1	2.8	1 465.8	3 766	3 643	1 500	13 695	35.4	63.8	0.7
Youngstown-Warren-Boardman, OH-PA	1 664.0	2 790	50.8	6.0	4.9	5.7	4.5	966.6	1 621	2 207	1 441	31 608	59.7	39.7	0.6
Yuba City, CA	568.3	3 921	48.0	5.9	3.6	11.6	3.6	151.0	1 042	1 452	3 616	9 571	31.8	67.1	1.1
Yuma, AZ	439.5	2 625	50.0	2.0	5.4	0.6	5.7	315.9	1 887	2 643	4 305	9 432	40.6	58.9	0.6

1. Based on the resident population estimated as of July 1 of the year shown.

Cities of 25,000 or More

(For explanation of symbols, see page xii)

TABLE D Highlights and Rankings

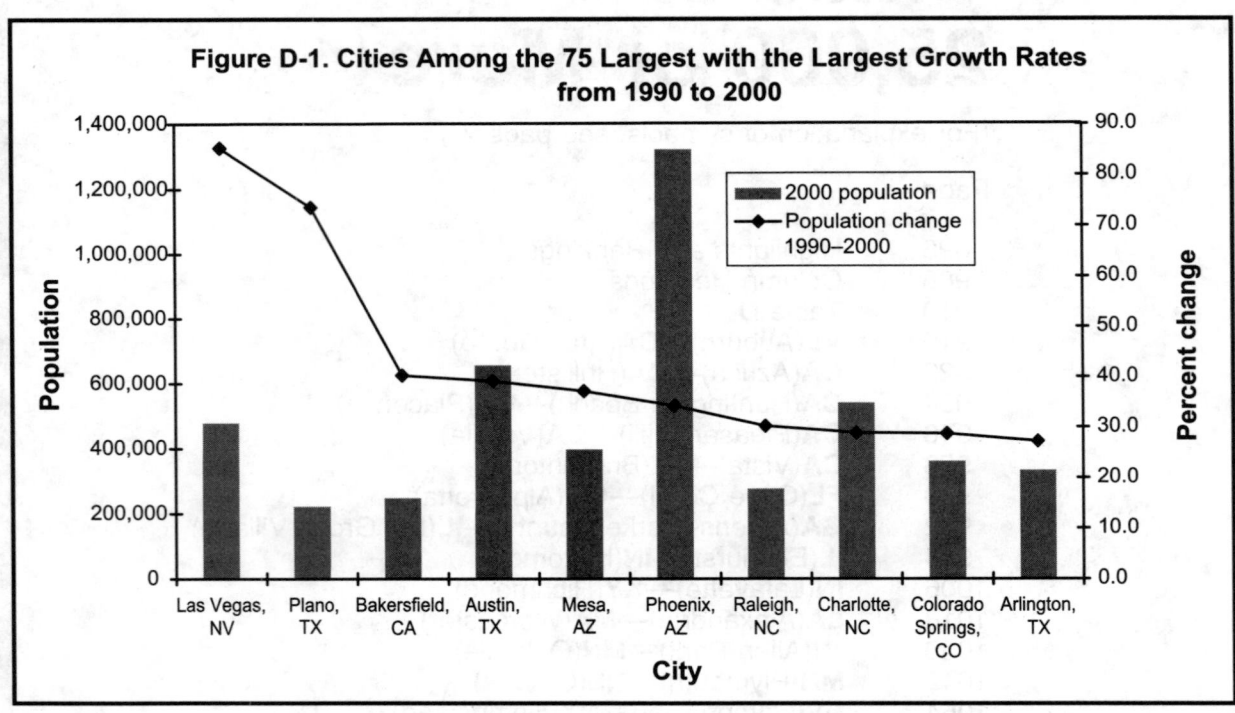

Figure D-1. Cities Among the 75 Largest with the Largest Growth Rates from 1990 to 2000

Legend: 2000 population; Population change 1990–2000

Cities (x-axis): Las Vegas, NV; Plano, TX; Bakersfield, CA; Austin, TX; Mesa, AZ; Phoenix, AZ; Raleigh, NC; Charlotte, NC; Colorado Springs, CO; Arlington, TX

There are 1,237 cities with populations of 25,000 or more based on the April 1, 2000 census counts. In 2003, nine cities had populations over 1 million people, topped by New York City with 8 million, Los Angeles with 3.8 million, and Chicago with 2.9 million. California has four cities among the nation's 20 largest: Los Angeles, San Diego, San Jose, and San Francisco; and Texas has five: Houston, San Antonio, Dallas, Austin, and Forth Worth. In 2003, San Antonio grew larger than Dallas, and became the 8th largest city in the United States. San Antonio ranked 14th among the largest cities in population growth from 2000 to 2003.

Among the largest cities, 25 had growth exceeding 15 percent from 1990 to 2000. Most of these cities are located in just six states: Nevada, Texas, California, Arizona, North Carolina, and Colorado. The growth in cities located in western states continued from 2000 to 2003. The 13 cities with the highest growth rates, each exceeding 5.5 percent, are located in the same six states.

Since the 2000 census, seven of the 20 largest cities lost population. St. Louis lost 4.6 percent, and Detroit and Cincinnati lost 4.1 percent, with Cleveland and Baltimore both losing 3.5 percent or more. Among the 68 cities with populations exceeding 250,000, 20 lost population from 2000 to 2003.

Juneau, AK, is the nation's largest city in terms of land area, with over 7,000 square kilometers, an area 5.8 times the size of Los Angeles. Seventeen cities in the United States have land area larger than New York City (which has a land area of about 785 square kilometers). Cities with very large land areas tend to be in the West, but some cities with boundaries coextensive with their respective counties (such as the Nashville-Davidson consolidated city in Tennessee or Indianapolis, IN) also have particularly large land areas. The median land area for all places of 25,000 or more was about 54 square kilometers.

The labor force of Broomfield, CO grew by more than 16 percent from 2002 to 2003. Three other cities had labor forces that increased by more than 7 percent during the year—Kingsville city, TX; Kannapolis city, NC; and Twin Falls city, ID. Fourteen cities lost 5 percent or more of their labor force. With the exception of Marion, IN, these cities are located in California, almost all of them in the San Jose area. Among the 75 largest cities, Riverside has the fifth highest labor force growth, and San Francisco and San Jose, CA rank 74th and 75th respectively.

Fourteen cities had unemployment rates over 15 percent, many of them agricultural centers in California. Among large cities, three of the 10 highest unemployment rates were in California: Fresno (12.8 percent), Stockton (11.9 percent), and Oakland (10.6 percent). Newark and Jersey City, NJ were also in the top 10, at 12.3 percent and 9.9 percent respectively.

75 Largest Cities by 2003 Population
Selected Rankings

Population, 2003			Total land area, 2000				Population density, 2003			
Population rank	City	Population [col 2]	Population rank	Land area rank	City	Land area (square kilometers) [col 1]	Population rank	Density rank	City	Density (per square kilometer) [col 4]
1	New York City, NY	8 085 742	67	1	Anchorage city, AK	4 395.8	1	1	New York City, NY	10 292.4
2	Los Angeles city, CA	3 819 951	13	2	Jacksonville city, FL	1 962.4	14	2	San Francisco city, CA	6 217.4
3	Chicago city, IL	2 869 121	29	3	Oklahoma City, OK	1 572.1	73	3	Jersey City, NJ	6 194.2
4	Houston city, TX	2 009 690	4	4	Houston city, TX	1 500.7	3	4	Chicago city, IL	4 877.0
5	Philadelphia city, PA	1 479 339	24	5	Nashville-Davidson consolidated city, TN	1 300.9	51	5	Santa Ana city, CA	4 872.1
6	Phoenix city, AZ	1 388 416	6	6	Phoenix city, AZ	1 229.9	23	6	Boston city, MA	4 638.1
7	San Diego city, CA	1 266 753	2	7	Los Angeles city, CA	1 214.9	64	7	Newark city, NJ	4 511.5
8	San Antonio city, TX	1 214 725	8	8	San Antonio city, TX	1 055.6	5	8	Philadelphia city, PA	4 227.9
9	Dallas city, TX	1 208 318	12	9	Indianapolis consolidated city, IN	949.2	46	9	Miami city, FL	4 078.1
10	Detroit city, MI	911 402	9	10	Dallas city, TX	887.2	32	10	Long Beach city, CA	3 640.6
11	San Jose city, CA	898 349	7	11	San Diego city, CA	840.0	26	11	Washington city, DC	3 543.3
12	Indianapolis consolidated city, IN	793 430	38	12	Kansas City, MO	812.1	2	12	Los Angeles city, CA	3 144.3
13	Jacksonville city, FL	773 781	1	13	New York City, NY	785.6	18	13	Baltimore city, MD	3 003.7
14	San Francisco city, CA	751 682	20	14	Fort Worth city, TX	757.7	43	14	Oakland city, CA	2 746.9
15	Columbus city, OH	728 432	68	15	Lexington-Fayette, KY	736.9	60	15	Buffalo city, NY	2 709.3
16	Austin city, TX	672 011	17	16	Memphis city, TN	723.4	47	16	Minneapolis city, MN	2 624.4
17	Memphis city, TN	645 978	16	17	Austin city, TX	651.4	52	17	Anaheim city, CA	2 621.1
18	Baltimore city, MD	628 670	22	18	El Paso city, TX	645.1	25	18	Seattle city, WA	2 620.2
19	Milwaukee city, WI	586 941	39	19	Virginia Beach city, VA	643.1	10	19	Detroit city, MI	2 535.9
20	Fort Worth city, TX	585 122	21	20	Charlotte city, NC	627.5	19	20	Milwaukee city, WI	2 359.1
21	Charlotte city, NC	584 658	3	21	Chicago city, IL	588.3	35	21	Cleveland city, OH	2 296.3
22	El Paso city, TX	584 113	15	22	Columbus city, OH	544.6	54	22	Pittsburgh city, PA	2 259.3
23	Boston city, MA	581 616	31	23	Tucson city, AZ	504.2	53	23	St. Louis city, MO	2 071.2
24	Nashville-Davidson consolidated city, TN	569 842	48	24	Colorado Springs city, CO	481.1	62	24	St. Paul city, MN	2 051.2
25	Seattle city, WA	569 101	44	25	Tulsa city, OK	473.1	11	25	San Jose city, CA	1 983.5
26	Washington city, DC	563 384	33	26	Albuquerque city, NM	467.9	65	26	Stockton city, CA	1 915.8
27	Denver city, CO	557 478	34	27	New Orleans city, LA	467.6	37	27	Sacramento city, CA	1 770.0
28	Portland city, OR	538 544	11	28	San Jose city, CA	452.9	30	28	Las Vegas city, NV	1 761.6
29	Oklahoma City, OK	523 303	63	29	Corpus Christi city, TX	400.5	72	29	Norfolk city, VA	1 736.5
30	Las Vegas city, NV	517 017	27	30	Denver city, CO	397.2	45	30	Honolulu CDP, HI	1 712.4
31	Tucson city, AZ	507 658	74	31	Birmingham city, AL	388.3	36	31	Fresno city, CA	1 670.2
32	Long Beach city, CA	475 460	59	32	Aurora city, CO	369.1	70	32	St. Petersburg city, FL	1 603.7
33	Albuquerque city, NM	471 856	10	33	Detroit city, MI	359.4	56	33	Cincinnati city, OH	1 571.9
34	New Orleans city, LA	469 032	50	34	Wichita city, KS	351.6	28	34	Portland city, OR	1 548.0
35	Cleveland city, OH	461 324	5	35	Philadelphia city, PA	349.9	69	35	Louisville city, KY	1 546.1
36	Fresno city, CA	451 455	28	36	Portland city, OR	347.9	7	36	San Diego city, CA	1 508.0
37	Sacramento city, CA	445 335	41	37	Atlanta city, GA	341.2	58	37	Toledo city, OH	1 479.8
38	Kansas City, MO	442 768	40	38	Mesa city, AZ	323.7	49	38	Arlington city, TX	1 430.3
39	Virginia Beach city, VA	439 467	42	39	Omaha city, NE	299.7	27	39	Denver city, CO	1 403.5
40	Mesa city, AZ	432 376	57	40	Raleigh city, NC	296.8	61	40	Riverside city, CA	1 391.6
41	Atlanta city, GA	423 019	30	41	Las Vegas city, NV	293.5	9	41	Dallas city, TX	1 361.9
42	Omaha city, NE	404 267	66	42	Bakersfield city, CA	292.9	42	42	Omaha city, NE	1 348.9
43	Oakland city, CA	398 844	55	43	Tampa city, FL	290.2	4	43	Houston city, TX	1 339.2
44	Tulsa city, OK	387 807	36	44	Fresno city, CA	270.3	15	44	Columbus city, OH	1 337.6
45	Honolulu CDP, HI	380 149	37	45	Sacramento city, CA	251.6	40	45	Mesa city, AZ	1 335.7
46	Miami city, FL	376 815	19	46	Milwaukee city, WI	248.8	71	46	Plano city, TX	1 305.2
47	Minneapolis city, MN	373 188	49	47	Arlington city, TX	248.2	41	47	Atlanta city, GA	1 239.8
48	Colorado Springs city, CO	370 448	45	48	Honolulu CDP, HI	222.0	75	48	Lincoln city, NE	1 218.8
49	Arlington city, TX	355 007	25	49	Seattle city, WA	217.2	8	49	San Antonio city, TX	1 150.7
50	Wichita city, KS	354 617	18	50	Baltimore city, MD	209.3	6	50	Phoenix city, AZ	1 128.9
51	Santa Ana city, CA	342 510	58	51	Toledo city, OH	208.8	55	51	Tampa city, FL	1 094.6
52	Anaheim city, CA	332 361	61	52	Riverside city, CA	202.3	57	52	Raleigh city, NC	1 067.4
53	St. Louis city, MO	332 223	56	53	Cincinnati city, OH	201.9	16	53	Austin city, TX	1 031.6
54	Pittsburgh city, PA	325 337	35	54	Cleveland city, OH	200.9	50	54	Wichita city, KS	1 008.6
55	Tampa city, FL	317 647	75	55	Lincoln city, NE	193.3	33	55	Albuquerque city, NM	1 008.5
56	Cincinnati city, OH	317 361	71	56	Plano city, TX	185.4	31	56	Tucson city, AZ	1 006.9
57	Raleigh city, NC	316 802	69	57	Louisville city, KY	160.9	34	57	New Orleans city, LA	1 003.1
58	Toledo city, OH	308 973	53	58	St. Louis city, MO	160.4	21	58	Charlotte city, NC	931.7
59	Aurora city, CO	290 418	26	59	Washington city, DC	159.0	66	59	Bakersfield city, CA	925.3
60	Buffalo city, NY	285 018	70	60	St. Petersburg city, FL	154.4	22	60	El Paso city, TX	905.5
61	Riverside city, CA	281 514	43	61	Oakland city, CA	145.2	17	61	Memphis city, TN	893.0
62	St. Paul city, MN	280 404	54	62	Pittsburgh city, PA	144.0	12	62	Indianapolis consolidated city, IN	835.9
63	Corpus Christi city, TX	279 208	47	63	Minneapolis city, MN	142.2	44	63	Tulsa city, OK	819.7
64	Newark city, NJ	277 911	65	64	Stockton city, CA	141.7	59	64	Aurora city, CO	786.8
65	Stockton city, CA	271 466	72	65	Norfolk city, VA	139.2	20	65	Fort Worth city, TX	772.2
66	Bakersfield city, CA	271 035	62	66	St. Paul city, MN	136.7	48	66	Colorado Springs city, CO	770.0
67	Anchorage city, AK	270 951	32	67	Long Beach city, CA	130.6	63	67	Corpus Christi city, TX	697.1
68	Lexington-Fayette, KY	266 798	52	68	Anaheim city, CA	126.8	39	68	Virginia Beach city, VA	683.4
69	Louisville city, KY	248 762	23	69	Boston city, MA	125.4	74	69	Birmingham city, AL	609.4
70	St. Petersburg city, FL	247 610	14	70	San Francisco city, CA	120.9	38	70	Kansas City, MO	545.2
71	Plano city, TX	241 991	60	71	Buffalo city, NY	105.2	24	71	Nashville-Davidson consolidated city, TN	438.0
72	Norfolk city, VA	241 727	46	72	Miami city, FL	92.4	13	72	Jacksonville city, FL	394.3
73	Jersey City, NJ	239 097	51	73	Santa Ana city, CA	70.3	68	73	Lexington-Fayette, KY	362.1
74	Birmingham city, AL	236 620	64	74	Newark city, NJ	61.6	29	74	Oklahoma City, OK	332.9
75	Lincoln city, NE	235 594	73	75	Jersey City, NJ	38.6	67	75	Anchorage city, AK	61.6

75 Largest Cities by 2003 Population
Selected Rankings

Population rank	Percent change rank	City	Percent change [col 8]	Population rank	White, not Hispanic or Latino rank	City	Percent White, not Hispanic or Latino [col 15]	Population rank	Black rank	City	Percent Black [col 10]
		Percent population change, 2000–2003				**Percent White, not Hispanic or Latino, 2000**				**Percent Black, 2000**	
57	1	Raleigh city, NC	14.7	75	1	Lincoln city, NE	87.8	10	1	Detroit city, MI	82.8
65	2	Stockton city, CA	11.4	68	2	Lexington-Fayette, KY	79.1	74	2	Birmingham city, AL	74.0
61	3	Riverside city, CA	10.3	28	3	Portland city, OR	75.5	34	3	New Orleans city, LA	67.9
66	4	Bakersfield city, CA	9.7	42	4	Omaha city, NE	75.4	18	4	Baltimore city, MD	65.2
20	5	Fort Worth city, TX	9.4	48	5	Colorado Springs city, CO	75.3	41	5	Atlanta city, GA	62.1
37	5	Sacramento city, CA	9.4	40	6	Mesa city, AZ	73.2	17	6	Memphis city, TN	61.9
40	7	Mesa city, AZ	9.1	71	7	Plano city, TX	72.8	26	7	Washington city, DC	61.3
71	8	Plano city, TX	9.0	50	8	Wichita city, KS	71.7	64	8	Newark city, NJ	55.0
21	9	Charlotte city, NC	8.1	67	9	Anchorage city, AK	69.9	35	9	Cleveland city, OH	52.1
30	9	Las Vegas city, NV	8.1	39	10	Virginia Beach city, VA	69.5	53	9	St. Louis city, MO	52.1
49	11	Arlington city, TX	6.6	70	11	St. Petersburg city, FL	68.6	72	11	Norfolk city, VA	45.3
8	12	San Antonio city, TX	6.1	25	12	Seattle city, WA	67.9	5	12	Philadelphia city, PA	44.3
36	13	Fresno city, CA	5.6	58	13	Toledo city, OH	67.8	56	13	Cincinnati city, OH	44.0
33	14	Albuquerque city, NM	5.2	12	14	Indianapolis consolidated city, IN	67.7	60	14	Buffalo city, NY	38.6
13	14	Jacksonville city, FL	5.2	44	15	Tulsa city, OK	67.1	19	14	Milwaukee city, WI	38.6
59	16	Aurora city, CO	5.1	15	16	Columbus city, OH	66.9	43	16	Oakland city, CA	37.6
6	16	Phoenix city, AZ	5.1	54	16	Pittsburgh city, PA	66.9	3	17	Chicago city, IL	37.4
55	18	Tampa city, FL	4.7	24	18	Nashville-Davidson consolidated city, TN	65.1	69	18	Louisville city, KY	33.9
75	19	Lincoln city, NE	4.4	29	19	Oklahoma City, OK	64.7	21	19	Charlotte city, NC	33.4
31	20	Tucson city, AZ	4.3	62	20	St. Paul city, MN	64.0	38	20	Kansas City, MO	32.3
67	21	Anchorage city, AK	4.1	47	21	Minneapolis city, MN	62.5	73	21	Jersey City, NJ	30.0
46	22	Miami city, FL	4.0	13	22	Jacksonville city, FL	62.2	13	22	Jacksonville city, FL	29.7
42	23	Omaha city, NE	3.7	69	23	Louisville city, KY	61.9	57	23	Raleigh city, NC	28.6
22	24	El Paso city, TX	3.6	57	24	Raleigh city, NC	60.3	1	24	New York City, NY	28.4
7	25	San Diego city, CA	3.5	49	25	Arlington city, TX	59.6	54	25	Pittsburgh city, PA	28.1
2	26	Los Angeles city, CA	3.4	59	26	Aurora city, CO	59.2	23	26	Boston city, MA	27.7
29	26	Oklahoma City, OK	3.4	30	27	Las Vegas city, NV	58.0	55	27	Tampa city, FL	27.2
39	28	Virginia Beach city, VA	3.3	38	28	Kansas City, MO	57.6	24	28	Nashville-Davidson consolidated city, TN	26.6
72	29	Norfolk city, VA	3.1	6	29	Phoenix city, AZ	55.8	9	29	Dallas city, TX	26.5
32	30	Long Beach city, CA	3.0	21	30	Charlotte city, NC	55.1	12	30	Indianapolis consolidated city, IN	26.1
50	30	Wichita city, KS	3.0	31	31	Tucson city, AZ	54.2	15	31	Columbus city, OH	26.0
4	32	Houston city, TX	2.9	16	32	Austin city, TX	52.9	4	32	Houston city, TX	25.9
48	33	Colorado Springs city, CO	2.6	56	33	Cincinnati city, OH	52.5	58	33	Toledo city, OH	24.8
16	34	Austin city, TX	2.4	27	34	Denver city, CO	51.9	46	34	Miami city, FL	24.2
15	34	Columbus city, OH	2.4	60	35	Buffalo city, NY	51.8	70	35	St. Petersburg city, FL	23.2
68	34	Lexington-Fayette, KY	2.4	66	36	Bakersfield city, CA	51.1	20	36	Fort Worth city, TX	20.8
45	37	Honolulu CDP, HI	2.3	55	37	Tampa city, FL	51.0	47	37	Minneapolis city, MN	20.5
28	38	Portland city, OR	1.8	33	38	Albuquerque city, NM	49.9	39	38	Virginia Beach city, VA	20.0
9	39	Dallas city, TX	1.7	23	39	Boston city, MA	49.5	37	39	Sacramento city, CA	17.3
41	40	Atlanta city, GA	1.6	7	40	San Diego city, CA	49.4	44	40	Tulsa city, OK	16.5
64	40	Newark city, NJ	1.6	72	41	Norfolk city, VA	47.0	29	41	Oklahoma City, OK	16.4
52	42	Anaheim city, CA	1.3	20	42	Fort Worth city, TX	45.8	32	42	Long Beach city, CA	16.0
51	42	Santa Ana city, CA	1.3	61	43	Riverside city, CA	45.6	59	43	Aurora city, CO	15.0
1	44	New York City, NY	1.0	19	44	Milwaukee city, WI	45.4	49	44	Arlington city, TX	14.5
25	44	Seattle city, WA	1.0	14	45	San Francisco city, CA	43.6	42	45	Omaha city, NE	14.2
63	46	Corpus Christi city, TX	0.6	53	46	St. Louis city, MO	42.9	68	46	Lexington-Fayette, KY	14.1
27	47	Denver city, CO	0.5	5	47	Philadelphia city, PA	42.5	62	47	St. Paul city, MN	13.4
11	48	San Jose city, CA	0.4	37	48	Sacramento city, CA	40.5	65	48	Stockton city, CA	12.5
38	49	Kansas City, MO	0.3	35	49	Cleveland city, OH	38.8	50	49	Wichita city, KS	12.4
12	50	Indianapolis consolidated city, IN	0.2	63	50	Corpus Christi city, TX	38.5	27	50	Denver city, CO	12.1
24	51	Nashville-Davidson consolidated city, TN	0.0	36	51	Fresno city, CA	37.3	2	51	Los Angeles city, CA	12.0
43	52	Oakland city, CA	-0.2	11	52	San Jose city, CA	36.0	30	52	Las Vegas city, NV	11.3
70	53	St. Petersburg city, FL	-0.3	52	53	Anaheim city, CA	35.9	16	53	Austin city, TX	10.7
73	54	Jersey City, NJ	-0.4	1	54	New York City, NY	35.0	66	54	Bakersfield city, CA	10.0
17	55	Memphis city, TN	-0.6	9	55	Dallas city, TX	34.6	25	55	Seattle city, WA	9.9
3	56	Chicago city, IL	-0.9	17	56	Memphis city, TN	33.3	36	56	Fresno city, CA	9.2
23	57	Boston city, MA	-1.3	32	57	Long Beach city, CA	33.1	7	57	San Diego city, CA	8.9
44	57	Tulsa city, OK	-1.3	65	58	Stockton city, CA	32.2	14	58	San Francisco city, CA	8.6
58	59	Toledo city, OH	-1.5	8	59	San Antonio city, TX	31.8	61	59	Riverside city, CA	8.4
26	59	Washington city, DC	-1.5	41	60	Atlanta city, GA	31.3	28	60	Portland city, OR	7.9
19	61	Milwaukee city, WI	-1.7	3	60	Chicago city, IL	31.3	48	61	Colorado Springs city, CO	7.8
62	62	St. Paul city, MN	-2.3	18	62	Baltimore city, MD	31.0	8	62	San Antonio city, TX	7.4
47	63	Minneapolis city, MN	-2.5	4	63	Houston city, TX	30.8	67	63	Anchorage city, AK	7.2
5	63	Philadelphia city, PA	-2.5	2	64	Los Angeles city, CA	29.7	6	64	Phoenix city, AZ	5.8
74	65	Birmingham city, AL	-2.6	26	65	Washington city, DC	27.8	71	65	Plano city, TX	5.4
60	65	Buffalo city, NY	-2.6	34	66	New Orleans city, LA	26.6	63	66	Corpus Christi city, TX	5.1
54	67	Pittsburgh city, PA	-2.8	73	67	Jersey City, NJ	23.6	31	66	Tucson city, AZ	5.1
69	68	Louisville city, KY	-2.9	74	68	Birmingham city, AL	23.5	11	68	San Jose city, CA	4.1
34	69	New Orleans city, LA	-3.2	43	68	Oakland city, CA	23.5	33	69	Albuquerque city, NM	3.8
14	69	San Francisco city, CA	-3.2	45	70	Honolulu CDP, HI	18.7	75	69	Lincoln city, NE	3.8
18	71	Baltimore city, MD	-3.5	22	71	El Paso city, TX	18.3	22	71	El Paso city, TX	3.5
35	72	Cleveland city, OH	-3.6	64	72	Newark city, NJ	14.2	52	72	Anaheim city, CA	3.2
56	73	Cincinnati city, OH	-4.2	51	73	Santa Ana city, CA	12.4	40	73	Mesa city, AZ	3.1
10	73	Detroit city, MI	-4.2	46	74	Miami city, FL	11.8	45	74	Honolulu CDP, HI	2.4
53	75	St. Louis city, MO	-4.6	10	75	Detroit city, MI	10.5	51	75	Santa Ana city, CA	2.1

75 Largest Cities by 2003 Population
Selected Rankings

	Percent American Indian, Alaska Native, 2000				Percent Asian and Pacific Islander, 2000				Percent Hispanic or Latino,[1] 2000		
Population rank	American Indian, Alaska Native rank	City	Percent American Indian, Alaska Native [col 11]	Population rank	Asian and Pacific Islander rank	City	Percent Asian and Pacific Islander [col 12]	Population rank	Hispanic or Latino rank	City	Percent Hispanic or Latino [col 14]
67	1	Anchorage city, AK	10.4	45	1	Honolulu CDP, HI	83.3	22	1	El Paso city, TX	76.6
44	2	Tulsa city, OK	7.7	14	2	San Francisco city, CA	33.4	51	2	Santa Ana city, CA	76.1
29	3	Oklahoma City, OK	5.7	11	3	San Jose city, CA	29.6	46	3	Miami city, FL	65.8
33	4	Albuquerque city, NM	4.9	65	4	Stockton city, CA	23.9	8	4	San Antonio city, TX	58.7
47	5	Minneapolis city, MN	3.3	37	5	Sacramento city, CA	20.6	63	5	Corpus Christi city, TX	54.3
31	6	Tucson city, AZ	3.2	73	6	Jersey City, NJ	17.9	52	6	Anaheim city, CA	46.8
37	7	Sacramento city, CA	2.8	43	7	Oakland city, CA	17.4	2	7	Los Angeles city, CA	46.5
6	8	Phoenix city, AZ	2.7	7	8	San Diego city, CA	16.4	33	8	Albuquerque city, NM	39.9
36	9	Fresno city, CA	2.6	25	9	Seattle city, WA	15.9	36	8	Fresno city, CA	39.9
66	10	Bakersfield city, CA	2.5	32	10	Long Beach city, CA	15.4	61	10	Riverside city, CA	38.1
40	11	Mesa city, AZ	2.3	52	11	Anaheim city, CA	13.9	4	11	Houston city, TX	37.4
28	11	Portland city, OR	2.3	62	11	St. Paul city, MN	13.9	32	12	Long Beach city, CA	35.8
65	11	Stockton city, CA	2.3	36	13	Fresno city, CA	13.0	31	13	Tucson city, AZ	35.7
50	11	Wichita city, KS	2.3	2	14	Los Angeles city, CA	11.4	9	14	Dallas city, TX	35.6
27	15	Denver city, CO	2.2	1	15	New York City, NY	11.1	6	15	Phoenix city, AZ	34.1
61	16	Riverside city, CA	2.1	71	15	Plano city, TX	11.1	66	16	Bakersfield city, CA	32.5
25	16	Seattle city, WA	2.1	51	17	Santa Ana city, CA	9.9	65	16	Stockton city, CA	32.5
62	16	St. Paul city, MN	2.1	67	18	Anchorage city, AK	8.5	27	18	Denver city, CO	31.7
48	19	Colorado Springs city, CO	1.9	23	19	Boston city, MA	8.4	16	19	Austin city, TX	30.5
59	20	Aurora city, CO	1.8	28	20	Portland city, OR	8.2	11	20	San Jose city, CA	30.2
32	21	Long Beach city, CA	1.7	61	21	Riverside city, CA	7.4	20	21	Fort Worth city, TX	29.8
43	21	Oakland city, CA	1.7	47	22	Minneapolis city, MN	7.2	64	22	Newark city, NJ	29.5
51	21	Santa Ana city, CA	1.7	30	23	Las Vegas city, NV	6.9	73	23	Jersey City, NJ	28.3
52	24	Anaheim city, CA	1.5	49	24	Arlington city, TX	6.8	1	24	New York City, NY	27.0
30	24	Las Vegas city, NV	1.5	39	25	Virginia Beach city, VA	6.3	3	25	Chicago city, IL	26.0
19	24	Milwaukee city, WI	1.5	4	26	Houston city, TX	5.9	7	26	San Diego city, CA	25.4
11	24	San Jose city, CA	1.5	59	27	Aurora city, CO	5.7	30	27	Las Vegas city, NV	23.6
60	28	Buffalo city, NY	1.4	16	28	Austin city, TX	5.6	43	28	Oakland city, CA	21.9
45	28	Honolulu CDP, HI	1.4	66	28	Bakersfield city, CA	5.6	37	29	Sacramento city, CA	21.6
2	28	Los Angeles city, CA	1.4	3	30	Chicago city, IL	5.1	59	30	Aurora city, CO	19.8
8	31	San Antonio city, TX	1.3	5	30	Philadelphia city, PA	5.1	40	31	Mesa city, AZ	19.7
7	31	San Diego city, CA	1.3	50	32	Wichita city, KS	4.7	55	32	Tampa city, FL	19.3
49	33	Arlington city, TX	1.2	48	33	Colorado Springs city, CO	4.3	49	33	Arlington city, TX	18.3
22	33	El Paso city, TX	1.2	29	34	Oklahoma City, OK	4.2	23	34	Boston city, MA	14.4
38	33	Kansas City, MO	1.2	15	35	Columbus city, OH	4.0	14	35	San Francisco city, CA	14.1
75	33	Lincoln city, NE	1.2	21	36	Charlotte city, NC	3.9	48	36	Colorado Springs city, CO	12.0
42	33	Omaha city, NE	1.2	72	36	Norfolk city, VA	3.9	19	36	Milwaukee city, WI	12.0
14	33	San Francisco city, CA	1.2	57	36	Raleigh city, NC	3.9	29	38	Oklahoma City, OK	10.1
16	39	Austin city, TX	1.1	27	39	Denver city, CO	3.6	71	38	Plano city, TX	10.1
63	39	Corpus Christi city, TX	1.1	13	39	Jacksonville city, FL	3.6	50	40	Wichita city, KS	9.6
20	39	Fort Worth city, TX	1.1	75	39	Lincoln city, NE	3.6	5	41	Philadelphia city, PA	8.5
1	39	New York City, NY	1.1	19	42	Milwaukee city, WI	3.5	62	42	St. Paul city, MN	7.9
72	39	Norfolk city, VA	1.1	31	42	Tucson city, AZ	3.5	26	42	Washington city, DC	7.9
15	44	Columbus city, OH	1.0	70	44	St. Petersburg city, FL	3.3	47	44	Minneapolis city, MN	7.6
9	44	Dallas city, TX	1.0	9	45	Dallas city, TX	3.2	60	45	Buffalo city, NY	7.5
73	44	Jersey City, NJ	1.0	20	45	Fort Worth city, TX	3.2	42	45	Omaha city, NE	7.5
39	44	Virginia Beach city, VA	1.0	54	45	Pittsburgh city, PA	3.2	21	47	Charlotte city, NC	7.4
23	48	Boston city, MA	0.9	26	45	Washington city, DC	3.2	35	48	Cleveland city, OH	7.3
35	48	Cleveland city, OH	0.9	33	49	Albuquerque city, NM	3.1	44	49	Tulsa city, OK	7.2
10	48	Detroit city, MI	0.9	68	50	Lexington-Fayette, KY	2.9	57	50	Raleigh city, NC	7.0
70	48	St. Petersburg city, FL	0.9	24	50	Nashville-Davidson consolidated city, TN	2.9	38	51	Kansas City, MO	6.9
55	48	Tampa city, FL	0.9	55	50	Tampa city, FL	2.9	28	52	Portland city, OR	6.8
58	48	Toledo city, OH	0.9	6	53	Phoenix city, AZ	2.8	67	53	Anchorage city, AK	5.7
18	54	Baltimore city, MD	0.8	34	54	New Orleans city, LA	2.6	58	54	Toledo city, OH	5.5
56	54	Cincinnati city, OH	0.8	38	55	Kansas City, MO	2.5	25	55	Seattle city, WA	5.3
4	54	Houston city, TX	0.8	40	56	Mesa city, AZ	2.4	10	56	Detroit city, MI	5.0
13	54	Jacksonville city, FL	0.8	53	56	St. Louis city, MO	2.4	24	57	Nashville-Davidson consolidated city, TN	4.6
64	54	Newark city, NJ	0.8	41	58	Atlanta city, GA	2.3	41	58	Atlanta city, GA	4.5
71	54	Plano city, TX	0.8	8	58	San Antonio city, TX	2.3	45	59	Honolulu CDP, HI	4.4
57	54	Raleigh city, NC	0.8	44	58	Tulsa city, OK	2.3	13	60	Jacksonville city, FL	4.2
53	54	St. Louis city, MO	0.8	42	61	Omaha city, NE	2.2	70	60	St. Petersburg city, FL	4.2
26	54	Washington city, DC	0.8	18	62	Baltimore city, MD	1.9	39	60	Virginia Beach city, VA	4.2
21	63	Charlotte city, NC	0.7	56	62	Cincinnati city, OH	1.9	12	63	Indianapolis consolidated city, IN	3.9
3	63	Chicago city, IL	0.7	63	62	Corpus Christi city, TX	1.9	72	64	Norfolk city, VA	3.8
12	63	Indianapolis consolidated city, IN	0.7	60	65	Buffalo city, NY	1.8	75	65	Lincoln city, NE	3.6
69	63	Louisville city, KY	0.7	12	65	Indianapolis consolidated city, IN	1.8	68	66	Lexington-Fayette, KY	3.3
24	63	Nashville-Davidson consolidated city, TN	0.7	69	65	Louisville city, KY	1.8	34	67	New Orleans city, LA	3.1
5	63	Philadelphia city, PA	0.7	17	65	Memphis city, TN	1.8	17	68	Memphis city, TN	3.0
54	63	Pittsburgh city, PA	0.7	64	65	Newark city, NJ	1.8	15	69	Columbus city, OH	2.5
68	70	Lexington-Fayette, KY	0.6	35	70	Cleveland city, OH	1.7	53	70	St. Louis city, MO	2.0
41	71	Atlanta city, GA	0.5	22	70	El Paso city, TX	1.7	69	71	Louisville city, KY	1.9
74	71	Birmingham city, AL	0.5	10	72	Detroit city, MI	1.4	18	72	Baltimore city, MD	1.7
17	71	Memphis city, TN	0.5	58	72	Toledo city, OH	1.4	74	73	Birmingham city, AL	1.6
46	71	Miami city, FL	0.5	74	74	Birmingham city, AL	1.1	56	74	Cincinnati city, OH	1.3
34	71	New Orleans city, LA	0.5	46	74	Miami city, FL	1.1	54	74	Pittsburgh city, PA	1.3

1. Hispanic or Latino persons may be of any race.

899

75 Largest Cities by 2003 Population
Selected Rankings

Percent under 18 years old, 2000				Percent 65 years old and over, 2000				Median household income, 1999			
Population rank	Under 18 years old rank	City	Percent under 18 years old [col 16 and 17]	Population rank	65 years old and over rank	City	Percent 65 years old and over [col 23 and 24]	Population rank	Median income rank	City	Median income (dollars) [col 44]
51	1	Santa Ana city, CA	34.2	45	1	Honolulu CDP, HI	17.8	71	1	Plano city, TX	78 722
36	2	Fresno city, CA	32.9	70	2	St. Petersburg city, FL	17.4	11	2	San Jose city, CA	70 243
66	3	Bakersfield city, CA	32.7	46	3	Miami city, FL	17.0	67	3	Anchorage city, AK	55 546
65	4	Stockton city, CA	32.4	54	4	Pittsburgh city, PA	16.4	14	4	San Francisco city, CA	55 221
10	5	Detroit city, MI	31.1	69	5	Louisville city, KY	14.7	39	5	Virginia Beach city, VA	48 705
22	5	El Paso city, TX	31.1	5	6	Philadelphia city, PA	14.1	49	6	Arlington city, TX	47 622
52	7	Anaheim city, CA	30.2	53	7	St. Louis city, MO	13.7	52	7	Anaheim city, CA	47 122
61	8	Riverside city, CA	30.1	14	8	San Francisco city, CA	13.6	21	8	Charlotte city, NC	46 975
67	9	Anchorage city, AK	29.2	60*	9	Buffalo city, NY	13.5	57	9	Raleigh city, NC	46 612
32	9	Long Beach city, CA	29.2	74	10	Birmingham city, AL	13.4	59	10	Aurora city, CO	46 507
6	11	Phoenix city, AZ	29.0	40	11	Mesa city, AZ	13.3	25	11	Seattle city, WA	45 736
19	12	Milwaukee city, WI	28.7	18	12	Baltimore city, MD	13.2	7	12	San Diego city, CA	45 733
71	12	Plano city, TX	28.7	58	13	Toledo city, OH	13.1	45	13	Honolulu CDP, HI	45 112
8	14	San Antonio city, TX	28.6	44	14	Tulsa city, OK	13.1	48	14	Colorado Springs city, CO	45 081
35	15	Cleveland city, OH	28.5	35	15	Cleveland city, OH	12.5	30	15	Las Vegas city, NV	44 069
49	16	Arlington city, TX	28.3	55	16	Tampa city, FL	12.5	51	16	Santa Ana city, CA	43 412
20	16	Fort Worth city, TX	28.3	56	17	Cincinnati city, OH	12.3	40	17	Mesa city, AZ	42 817
63	18	Corpus Christi city, TX	28.2	26	18	Washington city, DC	12.2	16	18	Austin city, TX	42 689
64	19	Newark city, NJ	28.0	25	19	Seattle city, WA	12.0	61	19	Riverside city, CA	41 646
17	20	Memphis city, TN	27.9	33	20	Albuquerque city, NM	11.9	6	20	Phoenix city, AZ	41 207
59	21	Aurora city, CO	27.6	31	20	Tucson city, AZ	11.9	75	21	Lincoln city, NE	40 605
39	22	Virginia Beach city, VA	27.5	50	20	Wichita city, KS	11.9	13	22	Jacksonville city, FL	40 316
4	23	Houston city, TX	27.4	38	23	Kansas City, MO	11.8	12	23	Indianapolis consolidated city, IN	40 154
40	24	Mesa city, AZ	27.3	42	23	Omaha city, NE	11.8	28	24	Portland city, OR	40 146
37	24	Sacramento city, CA	27.3	34	25	New Orleans city, LA	11.7	26	25	Washington city, DC	40 127
62	26	St. Paul city, MN	27.1	1	25	New York City, NY	11.7	43	26	Oakland city, CA	40 055
50	26	Wichita city, KS	27.1	30	27	Las Vegas city, NV	11.6	42	27	Omaha city, NE	40 006
13	28	Jacksonville city, FL	26.7	29	28	Oklahoma City, OK	11.5	66	28	Bakersfield city, CA	39 982
34	28	New Orleans city, LA	26.7	28	28	Portland city, OR	11.5	50	29	Wichita city, KS	39 939
48	30	Colorado Springs city, CO	26.5	37	30	Sacramento city, CA	11.4	68	30	Lexington-Fayette, KY	39 813
9	30	Dallas city, TX	26.5	27	31	Denver city, CO	11.2	24	31	Nashville-Davidson consolidated city, TN	39 797
2	30	Los Angeles city, CA	26.5	24	31	Nashville-Davidson consolidated city, TN	11.2	23	32	Boston city, MA	39 629
11	33	San Jose city, CA	26.4	63	33	Corpus Christi city, TX	11.1	27	33	Denver city, CO	39 500
60	34	Buffalo city, NY	26.3	12	34	Indianapolis consolidated city, IN	11.0	62	34	St. Paul city, MN	38 774
3	35	Chicago city, IL	26.2	17	35	Memphis city, TN	10.9	3	35	Chicago city, IL	38 625
58	35	Toledo city, OH	26.2	19	35	Milwaukee city, WI	10.9	1	36	New York City, NY	38 293
30	37	Las Vegas city, NV	25.9	72	35	Norfolk city, VA	10.9	33	37	Albuquerque city, NM	38 272
53	38	St. Louis city, MO	25.7	22	38	El Paso city, TX	10.6	47	38	Minneapolis city, MN	37 974
12	39	Indianapolis consolidated city, IN	25.6	10	39	Detroit city, MI	10.5	15	39	Columbus city, OH	37 897
42	39	Omaha city, NE	25.6	43	39	Oakland city, CA	10.5	73	40	Jersey City, NJ	37 862
29	41	Oklahoma City, OK	25.5	7	39	San Diego city, CA	10.5	9	41	Dallas city, TX	37 628
38	42	Kansas City, MO	25.4	23	42	Boston city, MA	10.4	32	42	Long Beach city, CA	37 270
5	43	Philadelphia city, PA	25.3	75	42	Lincoln city, NE	10.4	38	43	Kansas City, MO	37 198
74	44	Birmingham city, AL	25.0	8	42	San Antonio city, TX	10.4	20	44	Fort Worth city, TX	37 074
43	44	Oakland city, CA	25.0	3	45	Chicago city, IL	10.3	37	45	Sacramento city, CA	37 049
18	46	Baltimore city, MD	24.8	13	45	Jacksonville city, FL	10.3	2	46	Los Angeles city, CA	36 687
44	46	Tulsa city, OK	24.8	62	45	St. Paul city, MN	10.3	4	47	Houston city, TX	36 616
21	48	Charlotte city, NC	24.7	65	48	Stockton city, CA	10.2	63	48	Corpus Christi city, TX	36 414
73	48	Jersey City, NJ	24.7	68	49	Lexington-Fayette, KY	10.0	8	49	San Antonio city, TX	36 214
55	48	Tampa city, FL	24.7	41	50	Atlanta city, GA	9.7	65	50	Stockton city, CA	35 453
33	51	Albuquerque city, NM	24.6	73	50	Jersey City, NJ	9.7	44	51	Tulsa city, OK	35 316
56	52	Cincinnati city, OH	24.5	2	50	Los Angeles city, CA	9.7	29	52	Oklahoma City, OK	34 947
31	52	Tucson city, AZ	24.5	48	53	Colorado Springs city, CO	9.6	41	53	Atlanta city, GA	34 770
1	54	New York City, NY	24.3	20	53	Fort Worth city, TX	9.6	70	54	St. Petersburg city, FL	34 597
15	55	Columbus city, OH	24.2	36	55	Fresno city, CA	9.3	55	55	Tampa city, FL	34 415
72	56	Norfolk city, VA	24.1	64	55	Newark city, NJ	9.3	58	56	Toledo city, OH	32 546
7	57	San Diego city, CA	24.0	32	57	Long Beach city, CA	9.1	17	57	Memphis city, TN	32 285
69	58	Louisville city, KY	23.6	47	57	Minneapolis city, MN	9.1	36	58	Fresno city, CA	32 236
75	59	Lincoln city, NE	23.0	61	59	Riverside city, CA	9.0	19	59	Milwaukee city, WI	32 216
16	60	Austin city, TX	22.5	21	60	Charlotte city, NC	8.8	22	60	El Paso city, TX	32 124
41	61	Atlanta city, GA	22.3	15	60	Columbus city, OH	8.8	72	61	Norfolk city, VA	31 815
24	62	Nashville-Davidson consolidated city, TN	22.2	66	62	Bakersfield city, CA	8.7	31	62	Tucson city, AZ	30 981
47	63	Minneapolis city, MN	22.0	9	63	Dallas city, TX	8.6	5	63	Philadelphia city, PA	30 746
27	64	Denver city, CO	21.9	39	64	Virginia Beach city, VA	8.5	18	64	Baltimore city, MD	30 078
46	65	Miami city, FL	21.8	4	65	Houston city, TX	8.4	10	65	Detroit city, MI	29 526
70	66	St. Petersburg city, FL	21.5	57	65	Raleigh city, NC	8.4	56	66	Cincinnati city, OH	29 493
68	67	Lexington-Fayette, KY	21.3	11	67	San Jose city, CA	8.3	69	67	Louisville city, KY	28 843
28	68	Portland city, OR	21.1	52	68	Anaheim city, CA	8.2	54	68	Pittsburgh city, PA	28 588
57	69	Raleigh city, NC	20.8	6	69	Phoenix city, AZ	8.1	53	69	St. Louis city, MO	27 156
26	70	Washington city, DC	20.1	59	70	Aurora city, CO	7.4	34	70	New Orleans city, LA	27 133
54	71	Pittsburgh city, PA	19.9	16	71	Austin city, TX	6.7	64	71	Newark city, NJ	26 913
23	72	Boston city, MA	19.7	49	72	Arlington city, TX	6.1	74	72	Birmingham city, AL	26 735
45	73	Honolulu CDP, HI	19.2	67	73	Anchorage city, AK	5.5	35	73	Cleveland city, OH	25 928
25	74	Seattle city, WA	15.6	51	73	Santa Ana city, CA	5.5	60	74	Buffalo city, NY	24 536
14	75	San Francisco city, CA	14.6	71	75	Plano city, TX	5.0	46	75	Miami city, FL	23 483

75 Largest Cities by 2003 Population
Selected Rankings

Percent of persons below the poverty level, 1999				Percent high school graduates or less, 2000				Percent college graduates (bachelor's degree or more), 2000			
Population rank	Poverty rate rank	City	Poverty rate [col 47]	Population rank	Percent high school graduates or less rank	City	Percent high school graduates or less [col 41]	Population rank	Percent college graduates rank	City	Percent college graduates [col 42]
46	1	Miami city, FL	28.5	51	1	Santa Ana city, CA	72.8	71	1	Plano city, TX	53.3
64	2	Newark city, NJ	28.4	64	2	Newark city, NJ	72.5	25	2	Seattle city, WA	47.2
34	3	New Orleans city, LA	27.9	46	3	Miami city, FL	67.1	14	3	San Francisco city, CA	45.0
60	4	Buffalo city, NY	26.6	35	4	Cleveland city, OH	64.2	57	4	Raleigh city, NC	44.9
35	5	Cleveland city, OH	26.3	5	5	Philadelphia city, PA	62.1	16	5	Austin city, TX	40.4
36	6	Fresno city, CA	26.2	10	6	Detroit city, MI	60.4	26	6	Washington city, DC	39.1
10	7	Detroit city, MI	26.1	18	7	Baltimore city, MD	59.8	47	7	Minneapolis city, MN	37.4
74	8	Birmingham city, AL	24.7	53	8	St. Louis city, MO	56.2	21	8	Charlotte city, NC	36.4
53	9	St. Louis city, MO	24.6	19	9	Milwaukee city, WI	55.3	23	9	Boston city, MA	35.6
41	10	Atlanta city, GA	24.4	60	10	Buffalo city, NY	54.5	68	9	Lexington-Fayette, KY	35.6
65	11	Stockton city, CA	23.9	65	11	Stockton city, CA	54.1	7	11	San Diego city, CA	35.0
18	12	Baltimore city, MD	22.9	58	12	Toledo city, OH	54.0	41	12	Atlanta city, GA	34.6
5	12	Philadelphia city, PA	22.9	22	13	El Paso city, TX	53.9	27	13	Denver city, CO	34.5
32	14	Long Beach city, CA	22.8	73	14	Jersey City, NJ	53.0	48	14	Colorado Springs city, CO	33.6
22	15	El Paso city, TX	22.2	69	15	Louisville city, KY	52.8	75	15	Lincoln city, NE	33.3
2	16	Los Angeles city, CA	22.1	74	16	Birmingham city, AL	52.2	28	16	Portland city, OR	32.6
56	17	Cincinnati city, OH	21.9	1	16	New York City, NY	52.2	62	17	St. Paul city, MN	32.0
69	18	Louisville city, KY	21.6	52	18	Anaheim city, CA	52.1	33	18	Albuquerque city, NM	31.8
19	19	Milwaukee city, WI	21.3	17	19	Memphis city, TN	51.6	11	19	San Jose city, CA	31.6
1	20	New York City, NY	21.2	54	20	Pittsburgh city, PA	51.5	45	20	Honolulu CDP, HI	31.1
17	21	Memphis city, TN	20.6	20	21	Fort Worth city, TX	51.3	43	21	Oakland city, CA	30.9
54	22	Pittsburgh city, PA	20.4	3	22	Chicago city, IL	51.2	24	22	Nashville-Davidson consolidated city, TN	30.5
26	23	Washington city, DC	20.2	72	22	Norfolk city, VA	51.2	49	23	Arlington city, TX	30.4
37	24	Sacramento city, CA	20.0	36	24	Fresno city, CA	51.1	15	24	Columbus city, OH	29.0
51	25	Santa Ana city, CA	19.8	2	25	Los Angeles city, CA	50.8	67	25	Anchorage city, AK	28.9
3	26	Chicago city, IL	19.6	30	26	Las Vegas city, NV	50.4	42	26	Omaha city, NE	28.7
23	27	Boston city, MA	19.5	4	27	Houston city, TX	50.0	44	27	Tulsa city, OK	28.3
72	28	Norfolk city, VA	19.4	9	28	Dallas city, TX	49.3	39	28	Virginia Beach city, VA	28.1
43	28	Oakland city, CA	19.4	56	29	Cincinnati city, OH	49.1	9	29	Dallas city, TX	27.7
4	30	Houston city, TX	19.2	8	29	San Antonio city, TX	49.1	73	30	Jersey City, NJ	27.5
73	31	Jersey City, NJ	18.6	63	31	Corpus Christi city, TX	48.9	1	31	New York City, NY	27.4
31	32	Tucson city, AZ	18.4	34	32	New Orleans city, LA	48.8	4	32	Houston city, TX	27.0
55	33	Tampa city, FL	18.1	55	33	Tampa city, FL	48.4	56	33	Cincinnati city, OH	26.6
66	34	Bakersfield city, CA	18.0	61	34	Riverside city, CA	48.1	54	34	Pittsburgh city, PA	26.2
58	35	Toledo city, OH	17.9	12	35	Indianapolis consolidated city, IN	48.0	34	35	New Orleans city, LA	25.8
9	36	Dallas city, TX	17.8	66	36	Bakersfield city, CA	47.5	38	36	Kansas City, MO	25.7
63	37	Corpus Christi city, TX	17.6	13	37	Jacksonville city, FL	47.3	3	37	Chicago city, IL	25.5
8	38	San Antonio city, TX	17.3	32	38	Long Beach city, CA	46.2	12	37	Indianapolis consolidated city, IN	25.5
47	39	Minneapolis city, MN	16.9	6	38	Phoenix city, AZ	46.2	2	37	Los Angeles city, CA	25.5
29	40	Oklahoma City, OK	16.0	70	40	St. Petersburg city, FL	46.1	55	40	Tampa city, FL	25.4
20	41	Fort Worth city, TX	15.9	41	41	Atlanta city, GA	45.4	50	41	Wichita city, KS	25.3
6	42	Phoenix city, AZ	15.8	38	41	Kansas City, MO	45.4	59	42	Aurora city, CO	24.6
61	42	Riverside city, CA	15.8	23	43	Boston city, MA	45.1	29	43	Oklahoma City, OK	24.0
62	44	St. Paul city, MN	15.6	29	44	Oklahoma City, OK	44.9	32	44	Long Beach city, CA	23.9
15	45	Columbus city, OH	14.8	50	45	Wichita city, KS	44.8	37	44	Sacramento city, CA	23.9
7	46	San Diego city, CA	14.6	37	46	Sacramento city, CA	44.2	31	46	Tucson city, AZ	22.9
16	47	Austin city, TX	14.4	43	47	Oakland city, CA	43.7	70	47	St. Petersburg city, FL	22.8
27	48	Denver city, CO	14.3	31	48	Tucson city, AZ	43.6	6	48	Phoenix city, AZ	22.7
38	48	Kansas City, MO	14.3	15	49	Columbus city, OH	43.5	20	49	Fort Worth city, TX	22.3
52	50	Anaheim city, CA	14.1	24	50	Nashville-Davidson consolidated city, TN	43.1	40	50	Mesa city, AZ	21.6
44	50	Tulsa city, OK	14.1	26	51	Washington city, DC	42.8	8	50	San Antonio city, TX	21.6
33	52	Albuquerque city, NM	13.5	45	52	Honolulu CDP, HI	42.6	69	52	Louisville city, KY	21.3
70	53	St. Petersburg city, FL	13.3	62	53	St. Paul city, MN	41.9	13	53	Jacksonville city, FL	21.1
28	54	Portland city, OR	13.1	27	54	Denver city, CO	41.1	17	54	Memphis city, TN	20.9
24	55	Nashville-Davidson consolidated city, TN	13.0	42	54	Omaha city, NE	41.1	52	55	Anaheim city, CA	19.6
68	56	Lexington-Fayette, KY	12.9	40	56	Mesa city, AZ	41.0	63	55	Corpus Christi city, TX	19.6
13	57	Jacksonville city, FL	12.2	44	57	Tulsa city, OK	40.9	72	55	Norfolk city, VA	19.6
30	58	Las Vegas city, NV	11.9	59	58	Aurora city, CO	39.8	66	58	Bakersfield city, CA	19.3
45	59	Honolulu CDP, HI	11.8	11	58	San Jose city, CA	39.8	18	59	Baltimore city, MD	19.1
12	59	Indianapolis consolidated city, IN	11.8	33	60	Albuquerque city, NM	38.2	61	59	Riverside city, CA	19.1
25	59	Seattle city, WA	11.8	68	61	Lexington-Fayette, KY	36.6	53	59	St. Louis city, MO	19.1
57	62	Raleigh city, NC	11.5	28	61	Portland city, OR	36.6	36	62	Fresno city, CA	19.0
42	63	Omaha city, NE	11.3	49	63	Arlington city, TX	36.0	74	63	Birmingham city, AL	18.5
14	63	San Francisco city, CA	11.3	47	64	Minneapolis city, MN	35.8	60	64	Buffalo city, NY	18.3
50	65	Wichita city, KS	11.2	39	65	Virginia Beach city, VA	35.5	22	64	El Paso city, TX	18.3
21	66	Charlotte city, NC	10.6	21	66	Charlotte city, NC	35.0	19	64	Milwaukee city, WI	18.3
75	67	Lincoln city, NE	10.1	75	67	Lincoln city, NE	34.3	30	67	Las Vegas city, NV	18.2
49	68	Arlington city, TX	9.9	7	68	San Diego city, CA	34.2	5	68	Philadelphia city, PA	17.9
59	69	Aurora city, CO	8.9	67	69	Anchorage city, AK	33.9	58	69	Toledo city, OH	16.8
40	69	Mesa city, AZ	8.9	16	70	Austin city, TX	33.6	46	70	Miami city, FL	16.2
11	71	San Jose city, CA	8.8	14	71	San Francisco city, CA	32.7	65	71	Stockton city, CA	15.4
48	72	Colorado Springs city, CO	8.7	48	72	Colorado Springs city, CO	31.2	35	72	Cleveland city, OH	11.4
67	73	Anchorage city, AK	7.3	57	73	Raleigh city, NC	27.7	10	73	Detroit city, MI	11.0
39	74	Virginia Beach city, VA	6.5	25	74	Seattle city, WA	25.8	51	74	Santa Ana city, CA	9.2
71	75	Plano city, TX	4.3	71	75	Plano city, TX	18.3	64	75	Newark city, NJ	9.0

Percent female-headed family households, 2000				Percent of households composed of one person, 2000				Percent change in housing units, 1990–2000			
Population rank	Female-headed family households rank	City	Percent female households [col 29]	Population rank	One person household rank	City	Percent one person households [col 30]	Population rank	Percent change rank	City	Percent change [col 51]
10	1	Detroit city, MI	31.6	26	1	Washington city, DC	43.8	71	1	Plano city, TX	81.7
64	2	Newark city, NJ	29.3	56	2	Cincinnati city, OH	42.8	30	2	Las Vegas city, NV	73.9
18	3	Baltimore city, MD	25.0	25	3	Seattle city, WA	40.8	21	3	Charlotte city, NC	35.2
35	4	Cleveland city, OH	24.8	47	4	Minneapolis city, MN	40.3	66	4	Bakersfield city, CA	33.4
74	5	Birmingham city, AL	24.6	53	5	St. Louis city, MO	40.3	57	5	Raleigh city, NC	30.3
34	6	New Orleans city, LA	24.5	54	6	Pittsburgh city, PA	39.4	16	6	Austin city, TX	27.5
17	7	Memphis city, TN	23.8	27	7	Denver city, CO	39.3	40	7	Mesa city, AZ	25.1
60	8	Buffalo city, NY	22.3	14	8	San Francisco city, CA	38.6	75	8	Lincoln city, NE	20.4
5	8	Philadelphia city, PA	22.3	41	9	Atlanta city, GA	38.5	28	9	Portland city, OR	19.6
53	10	St. Louis city, MO	21.3	69	10	Louisville city, KY	37.9	48	10	Colorado Springs city, CO	19.5
19	11	Milwaukee city, WI	21.1	60	11	Buffalo city, NY	37.7	33	11	Albuquerque city, NM	18.9
41	12	Atlanta city, GA	20.7	23	12	Boston city, MA	37.1	68	11	Lexington-Fayette, KY	18.9
73	13	Jersey City, NJ	20.2	62	13	St. Paul city, MN	35.9	8	13	San Antonio city, TX	18.5
69	14	Louisville city, KY	19.2	70	14	St. Petersburg city, FL	35.6	15	14	Columbus city, OH	17.7
1	15	New York City, NY	19.1	35	15	Cleveland city, OH	35.2	6	15	Phoenix city, AZ	17.5
3	16	Chicago city, IL	18.9	18	16	Baltimore city, MD	34.9	49	16	Arlington city, TX	15.8
26	16	Washington city, DC	18.9	28	17	Portland city, OR	34.6	42	17	Omaha city, NE	15.4
72	18	Norfolk city, VA	18.8	74	18	Birmingham city, AL	34.4	36	18	Fresno city, CA	15.2
46	19	Miami city, FL	18.7	15	19	Columbus city, OH	34.1	22	19	El Paso city, TX	14.8
56	20	Cincinnati city, OH	18.6	38	19	Kansas City, MO	34.1	31	20	Tucson city, AZ	14.3
22	21	El Paso city, TX	18.5	44	21	Tulsa city, OK	33.9	65	21	Stockton city, CA	13.1
43	22	Oakland city, CA	17.7	5	22	Philadelphia city, PA	33.8	50	22	Wichita city, KS	12.6
36	23	Fresno city, CA	17.6	55	23	Tampa city, FL	33.7	24	23	Nashville-Davidson consolidated city, TN	10.4
65	24	Stockton city, CA	17.3	19	24	Milwaukee city, WI	33.5	39	23	Virginia Beach city, VA	10.4
58	25	Toledo city, OH	17.2	24	25	Nashville-Davidson consolidated city, TN	33.4	12	25	Indianapolis consolidated city, IN	10.0
54	26	Pittsburgh city, PA	16.5	34	26	New Orleans city, LA	33.2	59	26	Aurora city, CO	9.4
23	27	Boston city, MA	16.4	57	27	Raleigh city, NC	33.1	17	27	Memphis city, TN	9.2
8	27	San Antonio city, TX	16.4	9	28	Dallas city, TX	32.9	45	28	Honolulu CDP, HI	8.8
32	29	Long Beach city, CA	16.1	16	29	Austin city, TX	32.8	7	28	San Diego city, CA	8.8
55	29	Tampa city, FL	16.1	58	29	Toledo city, OH	32.8	11	30	San Jose city, CA	8.7
13	31	Jacksonville city, FL	16.0	3	31	Chicago city, IL	32.6	25	31	Seattle city, WA	8.6
38	31	Kansas City, MO	16.0	43	32	Oakland city, CA	32.5	20	32	Fort Worth city, TX	8.5
66	33	Bakersfield city, CA	15.5	31	33	Tucson city, AZ	32.3	13	32	Jacksonville city, FL	8.5
63	34	Corpus Christi city, TX	15.4	12	34	Indianapolis consolidated city, IN	32.0	4	34	Houston city, TX	7.7
37	34	Sacramento city, CA	15.4	37	34	Sacramento city, CA	32.0	63	35	Corpus Christi city, TX	7.6
4	36	Houston city, TX	15.3	1	36	New York City, NY	31.9	29	36	Oklahoma City, OK	7.4
12	37	Indianapolis consolidated city, IN	15.0	42	36	Omaha city, NE	31.9	61	37	Riverside city, CA	7.1
9	38	Dallas city, TX	14.9	68	38	Lexington-Fayette, KY	31.7	52	38	Anaheim city, CA	7.0
61	39	Riverside city, CA	14.8	50	39	Wichita city, KS	31.2	1	38	New York City, NY	7.0
20	40	Fort Worth city, TX	14.7	29	40	Oklahoma City, OK	30.7	37	40	Sacramento city, CA	6.9
15	41	Columbus city, OH	14.5	33	41	Albuquerque city, NM	30.5	67	41	Anchorage city, AK	6.6
2	41	Los Angeles city, CA	14.5	17	41	Memphis city, TN	30.5	14	42	San Francisco city, CA	5.5
24	43	Nashville-Davidson consolidated city, TN	14.3	75	43	Lincoln city, NE	30.4	27	43	Denver city, CO	4.9
62	44	St. Paul city, MN	13.9	46	43	Miami city, FL	30.4	55	44	Tampa city, FL	4.7
70	45	St. Petersburg city, FL	13.8	72	45	Norfolk city, VA	30.2	9	45	Dallas city, TX	4.0
31	45	Tucson city, AZ	13.8	10	46	Detroit city, MI	29.7	73	46	Jersey City, NJ	3.2
21	47	Charlotte city, NC	13.7	45	46	Honolulu CDP, HI	29.7	2	47	Los Angeles city, CA	2.9
51	48	Santa Ana city, CA	13.5	4	48	Houston city, TX	29.6	46	48	Miami city, FL	2.7
29	49	Oklahoma City, OK	13.2	32	48	Long Beach city, CA	29.6	41	49	Atlanta city, GA	2.3
52	50	Anaheim city, CA	13.1	21	50	Charlotte city, NC	29.5	3	50	Chicago city, IL	1.8
59	50	Aurora city, CO	13.1	73	51	Jersey City, NJ	29.2	43	50	Oakland city, CA	1.8
42	52	Omaha city, NE	13.0	20	52	Fort Worth city, TX	28.6	44	50	Tulsa city, OK	1.8
33	53	Albuquerque city, NM	12.9	2	53	Los Angeles city, CA	28.5	32	53	Long Beach city, CA	0.7
6	53	Phoenix city, AZ	12.9	7	54	San Diego city, CA	28.0	23	54	Boston city, MA	0.4
44	53	Tulsa city, OK	12.9	59	55	Aurora city, CO	27.4	38	55	Kansas City, MO	0.3
39	56	Virginia Beach city, VA	12.4	48	56	Colorado Springs city, CO	27.0	51	56	Santa Ana city, CA	-0.5
47	57	Minneapolis city, MN	12.3	64	57	Newark city, NJ	26.6	70	57	St. Petersburg city, FL	-0.7
30	58	Las Vegas city, NV	12.2	13	58	Jacksonville city, FL	26.2	18	58	Baltimore city, MD	-1.1
45	59	Honolulu CDP, HI	12.1	6	59	Phoenix city, AZ	25.4	26	59	Washington city, DC	-1.3
49	60	Arlington city, TX	11.8	8	60	San Antonio city, TX	25.1	62	60	St. Paul city, MN	-1.6
11	61	San Jose city, CA	11.7	30	61	Las Vegas city, NV	25.0	58	60	Toledo city, OH	-1.6
50	62	Wichita city, KS	11.6	49	62	Arlington city, TX	24.7	56	62	Cincinnati city, OH	-1.8
67	63	Anchorage city, AK	11.5	40	63	Mesa city, AZ	24.2	5	63	Philadelphia city, PA	-1.9
68	63	Lexington-Fayette, KY	11.5	67	64	Anchorage city, AK	23.4	19	64	Milwaukee city, WI	-2.0
57	65	Raleigh city, NC	11.4	36	65	Fresno city, CA	23.3	69	65	Louisville city, KY	-2.2
7	65	San Diego city, CA	11.4	63	66	Corpus Christi city, TX	23.2	64	66	Newark city, NJ	-2.3
16	67	Austin city, TX	10.8	65	67	Stockton city, CA	22.9	47	67	Minneapolis city, MN	-2.4
27	67	Denver city, CO	10.8	66	68	Bakersfield city, CA	21.5	35	68	Cleveland city, OH	-3.8
28	67	Portland city, OR	10.8	61	68	Riverside city, CA	21.5	54	69	Pittsburgh city, PA	-4.0
48	70	Colorado Springs city, CO	10.6	39	70	Virginia Beach city, VA	20.4	60	70	Buffalo city, NY	-4.2
40	70	Mesa city, AZ	10.6	71	71	Plano city, TX	20.2	72	71	Norfolk city, VA	-4.4
75	72	Lincoln city, NE	9.5	22	72	El Paso city, TX	19.2	34	72	New Orleans city, LA	-4.6
14	73	San Francisco city, CA	8.9	11	73	San Jose city, CA	18.4	74	73	Birmingham city, AL	-4.9
25	74	Seattle city, WA	8.1	52	74	Anaheim city, CA	18.1	10	74	Detroit city, MI	-8.5
71	75	Plano city, TX	7.5	51	75	Santa Ana city, CA	12.7	53	75	St. Louis city, MO	-9.5

75 Largest Cities by 2003 Population
Selected Rankings

Unemployment rate, 2003				Percent change in civilian labor force, 2002–2003				Per capita local government taxes, 2002			
Population rank	Unemployment rate rank	City	Unemployment rate [col 64]	Population rank	Percent change rank	City	Percent change [col 62]	Population rank	Local taxes rank	City	Local per capita taxes (dollars) [col 121]
10	1	Detroit city, MI	14.6	62	1	St. Paul city, MN	4.4	26	1	Washington city, DC	5 654
36	2	Fresno city, CA	12.8	59	2	Aurora city, CO	3.6	1	2	New York City, NY	2 750
35	3	Cleveland city, OH	12.7	27	3	Denver city, CO	3.2	14	3	San Francisco city, CA	2 223
64	4	Newark city, NJ	12.3	63	4	Corpus Christi city, TX	3.1	23	4	Boston city, MA	1 781
65	5	Stockton city, CA	11.9	61	5	Riverside city, CA	2.9	45	5	Honolulu CDP, HI	1 413
43	6	Oakland city, CA	10.6	22	6	El Paso city, TX	2.7	5	6	Philadelphia city, PA	1 369
46	7	Miami city, FL	10.4	4	7	Houston city, TX	2.5	39	7	Virginia Beach city, VA	1 343
60	8	Buffalo city, NY	10.2	74	8	Birmingham city, AL	2.4	27	8	Denver city, CO	1 307
53	9	St. Louis city, MO	10.1	21	8	Charlotte city, NC	2.4	53	9	St. Louis city, MO	1 264
73	10	Jersey City, NJ	9.9	10	8	Detroit city, MI	2.4	18	10	Baltimore city, MD	1 262
19	11	Milwaukee city, WI	9.7	8	8	San Antonio city, TX	2.4	25	11	Seattle city, WA	1 207
11	12	San Jose city, CA	9.6	53	8	St. Louis city, MO	2.4	72	12	Norfolk city, VA	1 206
28	13	Portland city, OR	9.5	65	8	Stockton city, CA	2.4	67	13	Anchorage city, AK	1 196
22	14	El Paso city, TX	9.3	38	14	Kansas City, MO	2.3	24	13	Nashville-Davidson consolidated city, TN	1 196
66	15	Bakersfield city, CA	9.1	72	15	Norfolk city, VA	2.2	74	15	Birmingham city, AL	1 089
9	15	Dallas city, TX	9.1	37	16	Sacramento city, CA	2.1	56	16	Cincinnati city, OH	1 086
58	15	Toledo city, OH	9.1	39	16	Virginia Beach city, VA	2.1	38	17	Kansas City, MO	1 053
18	18	Baltimore city, MD	8.6	41	18	Atlanta city, GA	2.0	10	18	Detroit city, MI	985
20	19	Fort Worth city, TX	8.5	57	18	Raleigh city, NC	2.0	43	19	Oakland city, CA	920
1	20	New York City, NY	8.4	67	20	Anchorage city, AK	1.9	35	20	Cleveland city, OH	908
4	21	Houston city, TX	8.3	34	20	New Orleans city, LA	1.9	34	21	New Orleans city, LA	851
3	22	Chicago city, IL	8.2	52	22	Anaheim city, CA	1.8	54	22	Pittsburgh city, PA	841
2	23	Los Angeles city, CA	8.0	66	22	Bakersfield city, CA	1.8	69	23	Louisville city, KY	804
41	24	Atlanta city, GA	7.9	33	24	Albuquerque city, NM	1.7	12	24	Indianapolis consolidated city, IN	792
25	24	Seattle city, WA	7.9	45	24	Honolulu CDP, HI	1.7	13	25	Jacksonville city, FL	774
50	24	Wichita city, KS	7.9	30	24	Las Vegas city, NV	1.7	68	26	Lexington-Fayette, KY	748
17	27	Memphis city, TN	7.7	7	24	San Diego city, CA	1.7	11	27	San Jose city, CA	741
5	28	Philadelphia city, PA	7.6	56	28	Cincinnati city, OH	1.6	47	28	Minneapolis city, MN	726
27	29	Denver city, CO	7.4	51	28	Santa Ana city, CA	1.6	15	29	Columbus city, OH	712
38	29	Kansas City, MO	7.4	48	30	Colorado Springs city, CO	1.4	3	30	Chicago city, IL	708
56	31	Cincinnati city, OH	7.3	20	30	Fort Worth city, TX	1.4	29	31	Oklahoma City, OK	675
74	32	Birmingham city, AL	7.2	68	30	Lexington-Fayette, KY	1.4	59	32	Aurora city, CO	670
26	33	Washington city, DC	7.0	75	30	Lincoln city, NE	1.4	9	33	Dallas city, TX	659
44	34	Tulsa city, OK	6.9	49	34	Arlington city, TX	1.3	71	34	Plano city, TX	653
37	35	Sacramento city, CA	6.8	36	35	Fresno city, CA	1.2	44	35	Tulsa city, OK	638
14	35	San Francisco city, CA	6.8	69	35	Louisville city, KY	1.2	2	36	Los Angeles city, CA	637
51	35	Santa Ana city, CA	6.8	16	37	Austin city, TX	1.1	55	37	Tampa city, FL	630
59	38	Aurora city, CO	6.6	35	37	Cleveland city, OH	1.1	41	38	Atlanta city, GA	626
63	38	Corpus Christi city, TX	6.6	12	39	Indianapolis consolidated city, IN	1.0	46	39	Miami city, FL	618
34	38	New Orleans city, LA	6.6	40	39	Mesa city, AZ	1.0	20	40	Fort Worth city, TX	611
32	41	Long Beach city, CA	6.5	64	41	Newark city, NJ	0.9	16	41	Austin city, TX	606
69	41	Louisville city, KY	6.5	6	41	Phoenix city, AZ	0.9	4	42	Houston city, TX	603
72	41	Norfolk city, VA	6.5	15	43	Columbus city, OH	0.8	28	43	Portland city, OR	599
48	44	Colorado Springs city, CO	6.4	19	43	Milwaukee city, WI	0.8	37	43	Sacramento city, CA	599
21	45	Charlotte city, NC	6.3	42	43	Omaha city, NE	0.8	64	45	Newark city, NJ	591
16	46	Austin city, TX	6.2	55	46	Tampa city, FL	0.6	7	45	San Diego city, CA	591
8	46	San Antonio city, TX	6.2	9	47	Dallas city, TX	0.5	42	47	Omaha city, NE	587
23	48	Boston city, MA	6.0	71	47	Plano city, TX	0.5	58	48	Toledo city, OH	584
61	48	Riverside city, CA	6.0	70	47	St. Petersburg city, FL	0.5	17	49	Memphis city, TN	562
13	50	Jacksonville city, FL	5.8	50	47	Wichita city, KS	0.5	6	50	Phoenix city, AZ	547
67	51	Anchorage city, AK	5.7	13	51	Jacksonville city, FL	0.4	52	51	Anaheim city, CA	545
49	51	Arlington city, TX	5.7	29	51	Oklahoma City, OK	0.4	21	52	Charlotte city, NC	539
15	51	Columbus city, OH	5.7	58	51	Toledo city, OH	0.4	60	53	Buffalo city, NY	507
29	54	Oklahoma City, OK	5.6	18	54	Baltimore city, MD	0.3	73	54	Jersey City, NJ	503
57	54	Raleigh city, NC	5.6	60	55	Buffalo city, NY	0.2	33	55	Albuquerque city, NM	493
12	56	Indianapolis consolidated city, IN	5.5	47	55	Minneapolis city, MN	0.2	32	55	Long Beach city, CA	493
47	56	Minneapolis city, MN	5.5	32	57	Long Beach city, CA	0.0	31	57	Tucson city, AZ	486
54	56	Pittsburgh city, PA	5.5	2	57	Los Angeles city, CA	0.0	49	58	Arlington city, TX	457
62	56	St. Paul city, MN	5.5	28	59	Portland city, OR	-0.1	70	59	St. Petersburg city, FL	451
6	60	Phoenix city, AZ	5.4	31	59	Tucson city, AZ	-0.1	48	60	Colorado Springs city, CO	449
71	61	Plano city, TX	5.3	26	61	Washington city, DC	-0.3	62	60	St. Paul city, MN	449
33	62	Albuquerque city, NM	5.2	17	62	Memphis city, TN	-0.4	51	62	Santa Ana city, CA	400
30	62	Las Vegas city, NV	5.2	25	62	Seattle city, WA	-0.4	63	63	Corpus Christi city, TX	399
42	62	Omaha city, NE	5.2	24	64	Nashville-Davidson consolidated city, TN	-0.9	57	64	Raleigh city, NC	398
70	65	St. Petersburg city, FL	5.1	43	64	Oakland city, CA	-0.9	75	65	Lincoln city, NE	388
55	65	Tampa city, FL	5.1	3	66	Chicago city, IL	-1.1	65	66	Stockton city, CA	387
31	67	Tucson city, AZ	4.8	1	67	New York City, NY	-1.2	8	67	San Antonio city, TX	372
24	68	Nashville-Davidson consolidated city, TN	4.5	5	68	Philadelphia city, PA	-1.4	61	68	Riverside city, CA	367
52	69	Anaheim city, CA	4.4	44	68	Tulsa city, OK	-1.4	22	69	El Paso city, TX	361
7	70	San Diego city, CA	4.3	46	70	Miami city, FL	-1.5	19	70	Milwaukee city, WI	352
75	71	Lincoln city, NE	4.2	23	71	Boston city, MA	-2.3	30	71	Las Vegas city, NV	331
40	71	Mesa city, AZ	4.2	54	71	Pittsburgh city, PA	-2.3	36	72	Fresno city, CA	323
45	73	Honolulu CDP, HI	3.9	73	73	Jersey City, NJ	-2.7	66	73	Bakersfield city, CA	322
68	74	Lexington-Fayette, KY	3.8	14	74	San Francisco city, CA	-3.2	50	74	Wichita city, KS	316
39	75	Virginia Beach city, VA	3.7	11	75	San Jose city, CA	-5.2	40	75	Mesa city, AZ	284

Violent crime rate, 2002 (violent crimes known to police)

Population rank	Violent crime rate rank	City	Violent crime rate (per 100,000 population) [col 37]
41	1	Atlanta city, GA	2 289
53	2	St. Louis city, MO	2 124
10	3	Detroit city, MI	2 073
18	4	Baltimore city, MD	2 055
55	5	Tampa city, FL	1 982
46	6	Miami city, FL	1 907
70	7	St. Petersburg city, FL	1 704
26	8	Washington city, DC	1 633
17	9	Memphis city, TN	1 572
24	10	Nashville-Davidson consolidated city, TN	1 549
3	11	Chicago city, IL	1 498
65	12	Stockton city, CA	1 461
9	13	Dallas city, TX	1 371
43	14	Oakland city, CA	1 367
38	15	Kansas City, MO	1 352
2	16	Los Angeles city, CA	1 350
35	17	Cleveland city, OH	1 322
5	18	Philadelphia city, PA	1 316
74	19	Birmingham city, AL	1 301
56	20	Cincinnati city, OH	1 275
60	21	Buffalo city, NY	1 272
4	22	Houston city, TX	1 223
73	23	Jersey City, NJ	1 186
21	24	Charlotte city, NC	1 172
23	25	Boston city, MA	1 166
64	26	Newark city, NJ	1 143
54	27	Pittsburgh city, PA	1 108
44	28	Tulsa city, OK	1 086
33	29	Albuquerque city, NM	1 069
47	30	Minneapolis city, MN	1 056
58	31	Toledo city, OH	1009
19	32	Milwaukee city, WI	955
34	33	New Orleans city, LA	937
12	34	Indianapolis consolidated city, IN	935
13	35	Jacksonville city, FL	916
31	36	Tucson city, AZ	910
15	37	Columbus city, OH	908
36	38	Fresno city, CA	853
37	39	Sacramento city, CA	841
28	40	Portland city, OR	828
29	41	Oklahoma City, OK	822
8	42	San Antonio city, TX	817
62	43	St. Paul city, MN	805
1	44	New York City, NY	790
69	45	Louisville city, KY	785
30	46	Las Vegas city, NV	779
61	47	Riverside city, CA	766
20	48	Fort Worth city, TX	760
32	49	Long Beach city, CA	758
14	50	San Francisco city, CA	752
6	51	Phoenix city, AZ	728
42	52	Omaha city, NE	718
63	53	Corpus Christi city, TX	712
25	54	Seattle city, WA	705
57	55	Raleigh city, NC	689
40	56	Mesa city, AZ	685
50	57	Wichita city, KS	681
22	58	El Paso city, TX	661
67	59	Anchorage city, AK	644
49	60	Arlington city, TX	633
59	61	Aurora city, CO	631
7	62	San Diego city, CA	567
75	63	Lincoln city, NE	559
72	63	Norfolk city, VA	559
51	65	Santa Ana city, CA	551
68	66	Lexington-Fayette, KY	542
27	67	Denver city, CO	534
48	68	Colorado Springs city, CO	508
16	69	Austin city, TX	467
11	70	San Jose city, CA	446
66	71	Bakersfield city, CA	418
52	72	Anaheim city, CA	408
45	73	Honolulu CDP, HI	289
71	74	Plano city, TX	288
39	75	Virginia Beach city, VA	219

Percent of city expenditures for police protection, 2002

Population rank	Police expenditures rank	City	Percent of city expenditures [col 132]
51	1	Santa Ana city, CA	26.9
65	2	Stockton city, CA	25.7
40	3	Mesa city, AZ	25.6
61	4	Riverside city, CA	25.5
19	5	Milwaukee city, WI	23.0
66	6	Bakersfield city, CA	22.9
46	7	Miami city, FL	22.6
20	8	Fort Worth city, TX	21.4
36	8	Fresno city, CA	21.4
73	10	Jersey City, NJ	21.3
59	11	Aurora city, CO	21.1
58	12	Toledo city, OH	20.9
3	13	Chicago city, IL	20.0
49	14	Arlington city, TX	19.2
55	15	Tampa city, FL	19.1
21	16	Charlotte city, NC	19.0
35	16	Cleveland city, OH	19.0
15	18	Columbus city, OH	18.8
22	18	El Paso city, TX	18.8
31	20	Tucson city, AZ	18.6
63	21	Corpus Christi city, TX	18.1
64	22	Newark city, NJ	17.8
2	23	Los Angeles city, CA	17.3
4	24	Houston city, TX	16.9
70	25	St. Petersburg city, FL	16.8
57	26	Raleigh city, NC	16.5
8	26	San Antonio city, TX	16.5
52	28	Anaheim city, CA	16.4
38	29	Kansas City, MO	16.0
30	30	Las Vegas city, NV	15.9
32	30	Long Beach city, CA	15.9
33	32	Albuquerque city, NM	15.8
37	32	Sacramento city, CA	15.8
74	34	Birmingham city, AL	15.3
42	34	Omaha city, NE	15.3
44	34	Tulsa city, OK	15.3
69	37	Louisville city, KY	15.2
6	37	Phoenix city, AZ	15.2
53	39	St. Louis city, MO	15.1
7	40	San Diego city, CA	14.9
54	41	Pittsburgh city, PA	14.8
47	42	Minneapolis city, MN	14.6
29	42	Oklahoma City, OK	14.6
71	44	Plano city, TX	14.4
28	45	Portland city, OR	14.4
45	46	Honolulu CDP, HI	14.2
56	47	Cincinnati city, OH	13.4
67	48	Anchorage city, AK	13.2
62	49	St. Paul city, MN	13.0
50	50	Wichita city, KS	12.9
34	51	New Orleans city, LA	12.3
11	51	San Jose city, CA	12.3
41	53	Atlanta city, GA	12.2
25	54	Seattle city, WA	12.1
16	55	Austin city, TX	12.0
68	55	Lexington-Fayette, KY	12.0
18	57	Baltimore city, MD	11.8
75	57	Lincoln city, NE	11.8
9	59	Dallas city, TX	11.6
43	60	Oakland city, CA	10.9
23	61	Boston city, MA	10.4
5	62	Philadelphia city, PA	10.3
17	63	Memphis city, TN	10.2
13	64	Jacksonville city, FL	10.1
48	65	Colorado Springs city, CO	9.0
27	66	Denver city, CO	7.9
12	66	Indianapolis consolidated city, IN	7.9
14	68	San Francisco city, CA	7.8
10	69	Detroit city, MI	7.7
24	70	Nashville-Davidson consolidated city, TN	7.1
1	71	New York City, NY	6.9
60	72	Buffalo city, NY	6.6
26	73	Washington city, DC	6.0
72	74	Norfolk city, VA	5.1
39	75	Virginia Beach city, VA	4.8

City government per capita debt outstanding, 2002

Population rank	Debt rank	City	Debt per capita (dollars) [col 138]
14	1	San Francisco city, CA	10 685
41	2	Atlanta city, GA	9 838
26	3	Washington city, DC	9 117
13	4	Jacksonville city, FL	8 961
27	5	Denver city, CO	8 913
1	6	New York City, NY	7 908
43	7	Oakland city, CA	6 852
16	8	Austin city, TX	6 536
24	9	Nashville-Davidson consolidated city, TN	6 160
45	10	Honolulu CDP, HI	6 074
35	11	Cleveland city, OH	5 474
10	12	Detroit city, MI	5 454
25	13	Seattle city, WA	5 451
55	14	Tampa city, FL	5 400
67	15	Anchorage city, AK	5 097
72	16	Norfolk city, VA	5 026
53	17	St. Louis city, MO	4 891
52	18	Anaheim city, CA	4 838
47	19	Minneapolis city, MN	4 666
3	20	Chicago city, IL	4 554
74	21	Birmingham city, AL	4 223
9	22	Dallas city, TX	4 216
4	23	Houston city, TX	4 082
8	24	San Antonio city, TX	4 030
32	25	Long Beach city, CA	3 981
12	26	Indianapolis consolidated city, IN	3 810
21	27	Charlotte city, NC	3 778
44	28	Tulsa city, OK	3 696
28	29	Portland city, OR	3 692
5	30	Philadelphia city, PA	3 456
54	31	Pittsburgh city, PA	3 446
11	32	San Jose city, CA	3 281
6	33	Phoenix city, AZ	3 198
2	34	Los Angeles city, CA	3 191
34	35	New Orleans city, LA	3 094
48	36	Colorado Springs city, CO	3 069
37	37	Sacramento city, CA	2 893
23	38	Boston city, MA	2 880
62	39	St. Paul city, MN	2 874
61	40	Riverside city, CA	2 788
69	41	Louisville city, KY	2 558
18	42	Baltimore city, MD	2 456
70	43	St. Petersburg city, FL	2 331
15	44	Columbus city, OH	2 310
60	45	Buffalo city, NY	2 288
63	46	Corpus Christi city, TX	2 225
39	47	Virginia Beach city, VA	2 215
31	48	Tucson city, AZ	2 200
68	49	Lexington-Fayette, KY	2 190
7	50	San Diego city, CA	2 024
38	51	Kansas City, MO	1 979
20	52	Fort Worth city, TX	1 974
33	53	Albuquerque city, NM	1 924
73	53	Jersey City, NJ	1 924
36	55	Fresno city, CA	1 890
50	56	Wichita city, KS	1 889
40	57	Mesa city, AZ	1 819
29	58	Oklahoma City, OK	1 806
65	59	Stockton city, CA	1 710
75	60	Lincoln city, NE	1 706
17	61	Memphis city, TN	1 677
56	62	Cincinnati city, OH	1 495
51	63	Santa Ana city, CA	1 489
59	64	Aurora city, CO	1 406
22	65	El Paso city, TX	1 398
71	66	Plano city, TX	1 331
64	67	Newark city, NJ	1 295
46	68	Miami city, FL	1 291
19	69	Milwaukee city, WI	1 250
49	70	Arlington city, TX	1 182
42	71	Omaha city, NE	1 174
58	72	Toledo city, OH	1 064
57	73	Raleigh city, NC	864
66	74	Bakersfield city, CA	846
30	75	Las Vegas city, NV	688

All Cities
Selected Rankings

Defense procurement contracts, 2002–2003

Population rank	Defense contract rank	City	Defense contracts (millions of dollars) [col 108]
20	1	Fort Worth city, TX	9 711
53	2	St. Louis city, MO	4 907
32	3	Long Beach city, CA	4 173
7	4	San Diego city, CA	4 054
128	5	Huntsville city, AL	3 898
174	6	Sunnyvale city, CA	3 363
31	7	Tucson city, AZ	2 695
69	8	Louisville city, KY	2 199
94	9	Orlando city, FL	1 906
72	10	Norfolk city, VA	1 841
5	11	Philadelphia city, PA	1 783
26	12	Washington city, DC	1 753
25	13	Seattle city, WA	1 624
6	14	Phoenix city, AZ	1 549
8	15	San Antonio city, TX	1 503
1 260	16	Pascagoula city, MS	1 358
288	17	Lynn city, MA	1 332
40	18	Mesa city, AZ	1 317
173	19	Alexandria city, VA	1 298
56	20	Cincinnati city, OH	1 183
179	21	Sterling Heights city, MI	1 110
480	22	Marietta city, GA	1 089
4	23	Houston city, TX	1 008
175	24	Palmdale city, CA	998
12	25	Indianapolis consolidated city, IN	996
34	26	New Orleans city, LA	995
166	27	Grand Prairie city, TX	963
1 196	28	Clearfield city, UT	878
380	29	Melbourne city, FL	876
48	30	Colorado Springs city, CO	798
239	31	Cambridge city, MA	772
441	32	Redondo Beach city, CA	754
134	33	Tempe city, AZ	727
47	34	Minneapolis city, MN	694
18	35	Baltimore city, MD	693
273	36	Carson city, CA	649
50	37	Wichita city, KS	634
466	38	Oshkosh city, WI	601
132	39	Dayton city, OH	588
52	40	Anaheim city, CA	502
22	41	El Paso city, TX	494
3	42	Chicago city, IL	473
70	42	St. Petersburg city, FL	473
901	44	Annapolis city, MD	464
118	45	Salt Lake City, UT	456
189	46	Cedar Rapids city, IA	438
361	47	Round Rock city, TX	434
39	48	Virginia Beach city, VA	429
86	49	Akron city, OH	419
877	50	Manassas city, VA	418
37	51	Sacramento city, CA	417
667	52	Mishawaka city, IN	408
13	53	Jacksonville city, FL	396
806	54	York city, PA	395
486	55	Schenectady city, NY	393
154	56	Pasadena city, TX	391
45	57	Honolulu CDP, HI	375
346	58	McKinney city, TX	373
67	59	Anchorage city, AK	371
83	60	Scottsdale city, AZ	370
2	61	Los Angeles city, CA	368
833	62	Burlington city, VT	365
15	63	Columbus city, OH	363
567	64	Rockville city, MD	360
168	65	Warren city, MI	357
9	66	Dallas city, TX	356
16	67	Austin city, TX	355
80	68	Fort Wayne city, IN	354
1 127	69	Deer Park city, TX	345
124	70	Irvine city, CA	339
542	71	Taunton city, MA	332
691	72	Middletown city, CT	327
14	72	San Francisco city, CA	327
248	74	Portsmouth city, VA	326
33	75	Albuquerque city, NM	325

Non-defense procurement contracts, 2002–2003

Population rank	Non-defense contract rank	City	Non-defense contracts (millions of dollars) [col 109]
26	1	Washington city, DC	9 623
4	2	Houston city, TX	4 213
765	3	Richland city, WA	2 386
33	4	Albuquerque city, NM	2 338
1 183	5	Oak Ridge city, TN	2 300
567	6	Rockville city, MD	2 194
237	7	Berkeley city, CA	1 986
163	8	Pasadena city, CA	1 667
1 239	9	Aiken city, SC	1 592
1	10	New York City, NY	1 210
8	11	San Antonio city, TX	1 008
41	12	Atlanta city, GA	985
616	13	Idaho Falls city, ID	979
18	14	Baltimore city, MD	903
30	15	Las Vegas city, NV	829
249	16	Richardson city, TX	801
38	17	Kansas City, MO	696
448	18	Lynchburg city, VA	617
34	19	New Orleans city, LA	577
14	20	San Francisco city, CA	536
56	21	Cincinnati city, OH	512
3	22	Chicago city, IL	509
173	23	Alexandria city, VA	491
21	24	Charlotte city, NC	482
137	25	Chattanooga city, TN	476
7	26	San Diego city, CA	462
551	27	Frederick city, MD	449
534	28	Johnson City, TN	426
2	29	Los Angeles city, CA	395
27	30	Denver city, CO	390
120	31	Amarillo city, TX	375
929	32	Leavenworth city, KS	373
17	33	Memphis city, TN	369
5	34	Philadelphia city, PA	335
123	35	Knoxville city, TN	323
35	36	Cleveland city, OH	298
257	37	Dearborn city, MI	285
108	38	Huntington Beach city, CA	282
486	39	Schenectady city, NY	278
24	40	Nashville-Davidsn consol. city, TN	277
536	41	Gaithersburg city, MD	276
1 273	42	Paducah city, KY	273
361	43	Round Rock city, TX	267
25	44	Seattle city, WA	266
53	45	St. Louis city, MO	264
150	46	Hampton city, VA	262
28	47	Portland city, OR	244
54	48	Pittsburgh city, PA	232
128	48	Huntsville city, AL	232
275	50	Boulder city, CO	226
47	51	Minneapolis city, MN	194
15	52	Columbus city, OH	188
37	53	Sacramento city, CA	185
60	54	Buffalo city, NY	184
239	55	Cambridge city, MA	183
23	56	Boston city, MA	180
937	57	Beverly Hills city, CA	177
12	58	Indianapolis consolidated city, IN	175
851	59	Marlborough city, MA	171
67	59	Anchorage city, AK	171
704	59	Joplin city, MO	171
29	62	Oklahoma City, OK	170
9	63	Dallas city, TX	160
16	64	Austin city, TX	158
74	65	Birmingham city, AL	152
46	66	Miami city, FL	142
19	67	Milwaukee city, WI	134
94	68	Orlando city, FL	133
20	69	Fort Worth city, TX	132
10	70	Detroit city, MI	126
6	71	Phoenix city, AZ	121
1 286	72	Carlsbad city, NM	120
555	73	Greenville city, SC	119
96	74	Durham city, NC	118
116	74	Newport News city, VA	118

Federal grants, 2002–2003

Population rank	Grants rank	City	Grants (millions of dollars) [col 110]
1	1	New York City, NY	23 905
37	2	Sacramento city, CA	6 536
26	3	Washington city, DC	4 310
16	4	Austin city, TX	3 516
23	5	Boston city, MA	3 499
272	6	Albany city, NY	2 692
3	7	Chicago city, IL	2 349
139	8	Tallahassee city, FL	2 341
15	9	Columbus city, OH	2 281
41	10	Atlanta city, GA	2 238
18	11	Baltimore city, MD	2 152
669	12	Harrisburg city, PA	2 129
2	13	Los Angeles city, CA	2 047
206	14	Springfield city, IL	1 857
57	15	Raleigh city, NC	1 548
196	16	Lansing city, MI	1 547
81	17	Madison city, WI	1 531
5	18	Philadelphia city, PA	1 531
7	19	San Diego city, CA	1 519
24	20	Nashville-Davidson consolidated city, TN	1 367
25	21	Seattle city, WA	1 326
314	22	Trenton city, NJ	1 308
386	23	College Station city, TX	1 279
4	24	Houston city, TX	1 270
27	25	Denver city, CO	1 243
106	26	Richmond city, VA	1 205
12	27	Indianapolis consolidated city, IN	1 152
740	28	Olympia city, WA	1 099
6	29	Phoenix city, AZ	1 060
14	30	San Francisco city, CA	1 044
62	31	St. Paul city, MN	1 006
79	32	Baton Rouge city, LA	981
54	33	Pittsburgh city, PA	976
865	34	Jefferson City, MO	962
1 181	35	Frankfort city, KY	833
93	36	Montgomery city, AL	812
29	37	Oklahoma City, OK	805
119	38	Jackson city, MS	788
45	39	Honolulu CDP, HI	768
239	40	Cambridge city, MA	766
198	41	Columbia city, SC	758
118	42	Salt Lake City, UT	735
10	43	Detroit city, MI	619
115	43	Little Rock city, AR	619
96	45	Durham city, NC	615
157	46	Salem city, OR	612
184	47	Hartford city, CT	609
47	48	Minneapolis city, MN	606
35	49	Cleveland city, OH	599
205	50	Ann Arbor city, MI	596
8	51	San Antonio city, TX	581
34	52	New Orleans city, LA	548
190	53	Topeka city, KS	540
183	54	New Haven city, CT	523
103	55	Des Moines city, IA	517
1 043	55	Juneau city, AK	517
121	57	Providence city, RI	508
74	58	Birmingham city, AL	490
617	59	Charleston city, WV	488
9	60	Dallas city, TX	485
75	61	Lincoln city, NE	465
567	62	Rockville city, MD	451
56	63	Cincinnati city, OH	446
64	64	Newark city, NJ	441
53	65	St. Louis city, MO	424
440	66	Santa Fe city, NM	421
28	67	Portland city, OR	408
84	68	Rochester city, NY	408
237	69	Berkeley city, CA	405
648	70	Chapel Hill town, NC	401
19	71	Milwaukee city, WI	387
275	72	Boulder city, CO	380
33	73	Albuquerque city, NM	374
46	74	Miami city, FL	368
31	75	Tucson city, AZ	366

COLUMN HEADINGS FOR CITIES

Table D. Cities — **Land Area and Population**

STATE Place code	City	Land area,[1] 2000 (sq km)	Population, 2003			Population characteristics, 2000							
						Percent							
							Race (alone or in combination)					Hispanic or Latino[2]	Non-Hispanic White
			Total persons	Rank	Per square kilometer	White	Black	Am. Indian, Alaska Native	Asian and Pacific Islander	Other race			
		1	2	3	4	5	6	7	8	9		10	11

1. Dry land or land partially or temporarily covered by water.   2. Hispanic or Latino persons may be of any race.

Table D. Cities — **Population and Households**

City	Population characteristics, 2000 (cont'd)										Population			
	Age of population (percent)										Census counts		Percent change	
	Under 5 years	5 to 17 years	18 to 24 years	25 to 34 years	35 to 44 years	45 to 54 years	55 to 64 years	65 to 74 years	75 years and over	Percent female	1990	2000	1990–2000	2000–2003
	12	13	14	15	16	17	18	19	20	21	22	23	24	25

********table 37********

Table D. Cities — **Group Quarters, Crime, and Education**

City	Households, 2000					Persons in group quarters, 2000				Serious crimes known to police,[2] 2002				Education, 2000			
		Percent					Institutional			Total	Rate[2]			School enrollment[4]		Attainment[5] (percent)	
	Number	Percent change, 1990–2000	Persons per household	Female family householder[1]	One-person	Total	Total	Persons in nursing homes	Non-institutional	Number	Rate[3]	Violent	Property	Public	Private	High school graduate or less	Bachelor's degree or more
	26	27	28	29	30	31	32	33	34	35	36	37	38	39	40	41	42

1. No spouse present.   2. Data for serious crimes have not been adjusted for underreporting. This may affect comparability between geographic areas and over time.   3. Per 100,000 population estimated by the FBI.   4. All persons 3 years old and over enrolled in nursery school through college.   5. Persons 25 years old and over.

Table D. Cities — **Income, Poverty, and Housing**

City	Money income, 1999							Housing units, 2000				
		Households			Percent below poverty					Vacant units		
		Median income			Persons		Families					
	Per capita income[1] (dollars)	Dollars	Percent change, 1989–1999 (constant 1999 dollars)	Percent with income of $100,000 or more	Total	Percent change in rate, 1989–1999	Total	Total	Percent change, 1990–2000	Vacant units for sale or rent[2]	For seasonal use (percent)	Home owner vacancy rate	Renter vacancy rate
	43	44	45	46	47	48	49	50	51	52	53	54	55

1. Based on population enumerated as of April 1, 2000.   2. Includes units rented or sold but not occupied.

906

COLUMN HEADINGS FOR CITIES

Table D. Cities — Housing, Labor Force, Employment, and Disability

City	Housing units, 2000 (cont'd)					Civilian labor force, 2003				Civilian employment,[2] 2000			Disability, 2000
		Occupied units						Unemployment			Percent		
	Total	Percent owner occupied	Percent renter occupied	Average size owner occupied	Average size renter occupied	Total	Percent change, 2002–2003	Total	Rate[1]	Total	Management, professional, and related occupations	Production, transportation, and material moving occupations	Employment disabled persons[3] (percent)
	56	57	58	59	60	61	62	63	64	65	66	67	68

1. Percent of civilian labor force.   2. Persons 16 years old and over.   3. Persons 16 to 64 years old.

Table D. Cities — Construction, Wholesale Trade, and Retail Trade

City	Value of residential construction authorized by building permits, 2003			Wholesale trade, 1997				Retail trade,[1] 1997			
	New construction ($1,000)	Number of housing units	Percent single family	Number of establishments	Number of employees	Sales (mil dol)	Annual payroll (mil dol)	Number of establishments	Number of employees	Sales (mil dol)	Annual payroll (mil dol)
	69	70	71	72	73	74	75	76	77	78	79

1. Establishments with payroll.

Table D. Cities — Real Estate, Professional Services, and Manufacturing

City	Real estate and rental and leasing, 1997				Professional, scientific, and technical services,[1] 1997				Manufacturing, 1997			
	Number of establishments	Number of employees	Receipts (mil dol)	Annual payroll (mil dol)	Number of establishments	Number of employees	Receipts (mil dol)	Annual payroll (mil dol)	Number of establishments	Number of employees	Receipts (mil dol)	Annual payroll (mil dol)
	80	81	82	83	84	85	86	87	88	89	90	91

1. Firms subject to federal tax.

Table D. Cities — Accommodation and Foodservices, Entertainment, and Health Care

City	Accommodation and foodservices, 1997				Arts, entertainment, and recreation,[1] 1997				Health care and social assistance,[1] 1997			
	Number of establishments	Number of employees	Sales (mil dol)	Annual payroll (mil dol)	Number of establishments	Number of employees	Receipts (mil dol)	Annual payroll (mil dol)	Number of establishments	Number of employees	Receipts (mil dol)	Annual payroll (mil dol)
	92	93	94	95	96	97	98	99	100	101	102	103

1. Firms subject to federal tax.

COLUMN HEADINGS FOR CITIES

Table D. Cities — **Other Services and Federal Funds**

City	Other services,[1] 1997				Selected federal funds, 2002–2003 (mil dol)								
					Procurement contracts		Grants						
	Number of establish-ments	Number of employees	Receipts (mil dol)	Annual payroll (mil dol)	Defense	Other	Total[2]	Medicaid and other health related	Nutrition and family welfare	Energy and envi-ronment	Education	Housing and community develop-ment	Direct payments for individuals for educational assistance
	104	105	106	107	108	109	110	111	112	113	114	115	116

1. Firms subject to federal tax.   2. Includes program categories not shown separately. State totals include additional categories not allocated by city.

Table D. Cities — **City Government Finances**

City	City government finances, 2002									
	General revenue							General expenditure		
		Intergovernmental		Taxes					Per capita[1] (dollars)	
					Per capita[1] (dollars)					
	Total (mil dol)	Total (mil dol)	Percent from state government	Total (mil dol)	Total	Property	Sales and gross receipts	Total (mil dol)	Total	Capital outlays
	117	118	119	120	121	122	123	124	125	126

1. Based on population estimated as of July 1 of the year shown.

Table D. Cities — **City Government Finances (cont'd)**

City	City government finances, 2002 (cont'd)									
	General expenditure									
	Percent of total for—									
	Public welfare	Highways	Parking facilities	Education	Health and hospitals	Police protection	Sewerage and sanitation	Parks and recreation	Housing and community development	Interest on debt
	127	128	129	130	131	132	133	134	135	136

Table D. Cities — **City Government Finances, City Government Employment, and Climate**

City	City government finances, 2002 (cont'd)			City government employment, 2002	Climate[2]							
	Debt outstanding				Average daily temperature (degrees Fahrenheit)							
					Mean		Limits					
	Total (mil dol)	Per capita[1] (dollars)	Percent utility		January	July	January[3]	July[4]	Annual precipitation (inches)	Heating degree days	Cooling degree days
	137	138	139	140	141	142	143	144	145	146	147

1. Based on the population estimated as of July 1 of the year shown.   2. Represents normal values based on the 30-year period, 1961–1990.   3. Average daily minimum.   4. Average daily maximum.

Table D. Cities — Land Area and Population

STATE Place code	City	Land area,[1] 2000 (sq km)	Population, 2003 Total persons	Population, 2003 Rank	Population, 2003 Per square kilometer	Race (alone or in combination) White	Black	Am. Indian, Alaska Native	Asian and Pacific Islander	Other race	Hispanic or Latino[2]	Non-Hispanic White
		1	2	3	4	5	6	7	8	9	10	11
00 00000	UNITED STATES............	9 161 924.0	290 809 777	X	31.7	77.1	12.9	1.5	4.5	6.6	12.5	69.1
01 00000	ALABAMA	131 426.4	4 500 752	X	34.2	72.0	26.3	1.0	1.0	0.9	1.7	70.3
01 03076	Auburn......	101.3	46 923	682	463.2	79.0	17.1	0.6	3.8	0.8	1.5	77.2
01 05980	Bessemer.......	105.4	29 108	1 091	276.2	29.4	70.0	0.6	0.4	0.5	1.1	28.5
01 07000	Birmingham.........	388.3	236 620	74	609.4	24.6	74.0	0.5	1.1	0.9	1.6	23.5
01 20104	Decatur......	138.3	54 239	584	392.2	76.6	20.0	1.1	1.1	2.6	5.6	72.6
01 21184	Dothan......	224.3	60 036	496	267.7	68.1	30.5	0.6	1.1	0.7	1.3	66.7
01 26896	Florence......	64.6	35 852	896	555.0	79.3	19.5	0.6	0.9	0.8	1.3	77.7
01 28696	Gadsden.......	93.2	37 619	851	403.6	63.6	34.5	0.7	0.9	1.5	2.7	61.6
01 35800	Homewood......	21.5	24 399	1 229	1 134.8	80.7	15.6	0.5	3.0	1.4	2.8	78.1
01 35896	Hoover......	111.7	65 070	443	582.5	88.5	7.0	0.4	3.4	1.9	3.8	85.5
01 37000	Huntsville......	450.8	164 237	127	364.3	65.9	30.9	1.3	2.8	1.0	2.0	63.4
01 45784	Madison......	60.0	34 080	947	568.0	81.8	13.4	1.4	4.3	1.1	2.3	78.6
01 50000	Mobile......	305.4	193 464	110	633.5	51.1	46.7	0.6	1.8	0.8	1.4	49.8
01 51000	Montgomery......	402.4	200 123	93	497.3	48.4	50.1	0.5	1.5	0.6	1.2	47.1
01 59472	Phenix City......	63.7	28 444	1 113	446.5	53.5	45.3	0.5	0.9	0.8	1.5	52.3
01 62496	Prichard......	65.8	27 983	1 133	425.3	14.6	85.1	0.7	0.4	0.2	0.6	14.1
01 77256	Tuscaloosa.........	145.7	79 294	345	544.2	54.8	43.1	0.4	1.9	0.9	1.4	53.5
02 00000	ALASKA	1 481 346.9	648 818	X	0.4	74.0	4.3	19.0	6.1	2.4	4.1	67.6
02 03000	Anchorage......	4 395.8	270 951	67	61.6	77.2	7.2	10.4	8.5	3.3	5.7	69.9
02 24230	Fairbanks......	82.5	30 970	1 035	375.4	72.3	12.9	13.3	5.0	3.6	6.1	64.2
02 36400	Juneau	7 036.1	31 187	1 024	4.4	80.5	1.4	16.6	7.4	1.8	3.4	73.3
04 00000	ARIZONA	294 312.2	5 580 811	X	19.0	77.9	3.6	5.7	2.6	13.2	25.3	63.8
04 02830	Apache Junction	88.7	34 027	951	383.6	94.5	0.8	1.8	1.1	3.9	8.8	87.9
04 04720	Avondale......	106.9	54 710	573	511.8	66.6	5.9	2.0	2.9	26.7	46.2	44.5
04 08220	Bullhead City......	117.1	36 255	885	309.6	88.1	1.2	2.1	1.6	9.8	20.2	75.4
04 10530	Casa Grande......	124.8	29 700	1 077	238.0	67.8	4.9	6.0	1.6	23.4	39.1	50.4
04 12000	Chandler......	149.9	211 299	87	1 409.6	79.7	4.1	1.8	5.4	12.3	21.0	68.6
04 23620	Flagstaff......	164.7	55 893	550	339.4	80.4	2.2	11.3	1.9	7.3	16.1	69.5
04 27400	Gilbert......	111.3	145 250	151	1 305.0	88.2	3.0	1.1	4.7	6.0	11.9	79.9
04 27820	Glendale......	144.2	232 838	76	1 614.7	78.5	5.5	2.1	3.8	13.8	24.8	64.7
04 39370	Lake Havasu City...............	111.5	49 124	645	440.6	95.7	0.4	1.3	1.1	3.0	7.9	89.5
04 46000	Mesa......	323.7	432 376	40	1 335.7	84.1	3.1	2.3	2.4	11.1	19.7	73.2
04 51600	Oro Valley town	82.4	34 355	940	416.9	94.5	1.4	0.7	2.6	2.4	7.5	88.2
04 54050	Peoria......	358.0	127 580	175	356.4	87.1	3.3	1.2	2.9	8.2	15.4	77.9
04 55000	Phoenix......	1 229.9	1 388 416	6	1 128.9	73.8	5.8	2.7	2.8	18.4	34.1	55.8
04 57380	Prescott......	96.0	37 576	853	391.4	94.4	0.7	2.0	1.4	3.3	8.2	88.2
04 65000	Scottsdale......	477.1	217 989	83	456.9	93.6	1.5	1.0	2.7	2.9	7.0	88.0
04 66820	Sierra Vista......	397.5	39 841	806	100.2	77.3	12.5	1.9	6.3	7.5	15.8	65.4
04 71510	Surprise city......	180.0	50 585	627	281.0	87.8	3.0	0.8	1.5	8.9	23.3	71.8
04 73000	Tempe......	103.8	158 880	133	1 530.6	80.2	4.4	2.7	6.1	10.2	17.9	69.7
04 77000	Tucson......	504.2	507 658	31	1 006.9	73.3	5.1	3.2	3.5	19.0	35.7	54.2
04 85540	Yuma......	276.2	81 605	327	295.5	71.7	3.8	2.2	2.4	23.9	45.7	47.5
05 00000	ARKANSAS......	134 855.9	2 725 714	X	20.2	81.2	16.0	1.4	1.1	1.8	3.2	78.6
05 15190	Conway	90.8	47 840	671	526.9	85.1	12.5	0.7	1.6	1.3	2.3	83.0
05 23290	Fayetteville......	112.5	62 078	471	551.8	88.6	5.8	2.3	3.5	2.5	4.9	84.0
05 24550	Fort Smith	130.4	81 562	330	625.5	79.6	9.4	3.2	5.2	5.8	8.8	74.0
05 33400	Hot Springs	85.2	36 770	874	431.6	80.5	17.5	1.5	1.1	1.3	3.8	76.5
05 34750	Jacksonville......	68.3	30 393	1 052	445.0	71.0	25.9	1.1	3.0	1.7	3.4	67.2
05 35710	Jonesboro......	206.3	57 435	526	278.4	86.4	11.6	0.8	1.2	1.3	2.3	84.2
05 41000	Little Rock	301.0	184 053	114	611.5	56.1	41.0	0.7	2.0	1.6	2.7	54.0
05 50450	North Little Rock	116.1	59 687	501	514.1	63.5	34.6	1.0	0.9	1.4	2.4	61.5
05 55310	Pine Bluff	118.1	53 905	589	456.4	32.8	66.3	0.5	1.0	0.3	0.8	32.0
05 60410	Rogers......	86.8	42 795	750	493.0	87.4	0.7	1.7	1.8	10.3	19.3	76.9
05 66080	Springdale......	81.1	52 471	603	647.0	83.4	1.1	1.8	4.0	12.2	19.7	74.1
05 68810	Texarkana......	82.5	28 900	1 096	350.3	67.2	31.5	1.2	0.6	1.0	1.8	65.0
05 74540	West Memphis	68.6	28 014	1 132	408.4	42.6	56.3	0.5	0.7	0.6	1.0	41.8
06 00000	CALIFORNIA......	403 932.8	35 484 453	X	87.8	63.4	7.4	1.9	13.0	19.4	32.4	46.7
06 00562	Alameda......	28.0	71 805	393	2 564.5	61.9	7.5	1.6	30.1	5.5	9.3	52.5
06 00884	Alhambra......	19.7	87 754	300	4 454.5	33.0	2.1	1.2	49.1	18.8	35.5	13.8
06 02000	Anaheim......	126.8	332 361	52	2 621.1	59.0	3.2	1.5	13.9	27.6	46.8	35.9
06 02252	Antioch......	69.8	101 124	241	1 448.8	71.2	11.1	2.3	10.5	12.5	22.1	55.9
06 02364	Apple Valley......	189.9	60 076	495	316.4	80.3	8.8	2.3	3.4	9.9	18.6	67.7
06 02462	Arcadia......	28.4	55 443	555	1 952.2	47.9	1.5	0.7	47.7	5.9	10.6	40.1
06 03064	Atascadero......	69.2	27 015	1 169	390.4	91.9	2.8	2.2	2.3	4.4	10.5	82.7

1. Dry land or land partially or temporarily covered by water. 2. Hispanic or Latino persons may be of any race.

Table D. Cities — **Population and Households**

City	Population characteristics, 2000 (cont'd) Age of population (percent)									Percent female	Population Census counts		Population Percent change	
	Under 5 years	5 to 17 years	18 to 24 years	25 to 34 years	35 to 44 years	45 to 54 years	55 to 64 years	65 to 74 years	75 years and over		1990	2000	1990–2000	2000–2003
	12	13	14	15	16	17	18	19	20	21	22	23	24	25
UNITED STATES..............	6.8	18.9	9.7	14.2	16.0	13.4	8.6	6.5	5.9	50.9	248 790 925	281 421 906	13.1	3.3
ALABAMA	6.7	18.6	9.9	13.6	15.4	13.5	9.3	7.1	5.9	51.7	4 040 389	4 447 100	10.1	1.2
Auburn..................................	4.1	11.2	44.6	12.7	9.2	7.4	4.3	3.2	3.2	50.1	33 830	42 987	27.1	9.2
Bessemer............................	7.7	19.1	9.6	12.3	13.7	12.6	8.5	8.2	8.2	54.7	33 581	29 672	-11.6	-1.9
Birmingham.........................	6.8	18.2	11.1	14.9	15.1	12.9	7.5	6.7	6.7	53.9	265 347	242 820	-8.5	-2.6
Decatur...............................	6.8	18.6	8.8	13.7	15.9	13.8	9.3	7.0	6.1	52.0	49 917	53 929	8.0	0.6
Dothan................................	6.9	18.6	8.4	12.9	15.3	14.0	9.4	7.6	6.9	53.1	54 131	57 737	6.6	4.0
Florence..............................	5.8	15.7	13.7	12.4	13.2	12.5	9.2	8.7	8.8	54.3	36 426	36 264	-0.4	-1.1
Gadsden..............................	6.6	16.5	9.5	12.7	12.6	12.8	9.2	9.7	10.4	54.0	42 523	38 978	-8.3	-3.5
Homewood...........................	6.3	14.0	17.8	19.6	14.3	11.5	5.8	4.5	6.1	53.8	23 644	25 043	5.9	-2.6
Hoover.................................	6.6	18.2	7.9	15.3	17.4	15.3	8.4	5.8	5.1	51.3	39 988	62 742	56.9	3.7
Huntsville............................	6.2	17.0	10.7	13.5	15.9	13.3	10.1	7.7	5.7	51.9	159 880	158 216	-1.0	3.8
Madison...............................	7.8	22.5	6.8	13.9	21.9	14.5	7.1	3.4	2.1	50.6	14 792	29 329	98.3	16.2
Mobile.................................	7.3	19.2	10.8	13.6	14.4	12.7	8.3	6.9	6.8	53.2	199 973	198 915	1.4	-2.7
Montgomery	7.1	18.9	12.1	14.7	15.0	12.6	7.7	6.1	5.7	53.1	190 350	201 568	5.9	-0.7
Phenix City	7.1	19.2	9.6	14.0	14.7	12.4	8.8	8.0	6.3	53.7	25 311	28 265	11.7	0.6
Prichard..............................	7.8	23.6	11.4	10.3	14.3	12.7	8.3	6.0	5.5	54.3	34 320	28 633	-16.6	-2.3
Tuscaloosa	5.7	14.1	24.5	13.5	11.9	11.5	6.9	6.3	5.5	52.4	77 866	77 906	0.2	1.8
ALASKA	7.6	22.8	9.1	14.3	18.2	15.1	7.1	3.6	2.1	48.3	550 043	626 932	14.0	3.5
Anchorage	7.7	21.5	9.6	15.4	18.5	14.9	7.0	3.4	2.1	49.4	226 338	260 283	15.0	4.1
Fairbanks	9.6	19.8	14.7	18.5	14.4	10.8	5.6	3.6	3.0	48.7	30 843	30 224	-2.0	2.5
Juneau	6.5	20.9	8.1	14.0	18.8	18.0	7.7	3.5	2.6	49.6	26 751	30 711	14.8	1.5
ARIZONA	7.5	19.2	10.0	14.5	15.0	12.2	8.6	7.1	5.9	50.1	3 665 339	5 130 632	40.0	8.8
Apache Junction	6.3	14.2	6.9	11.6	12.1	11.0	12.6	14.4	10.9	51.1	18 092	31 814	75.8	7.0
Avondale	9.8	24.5	9.7	16.8	16.2	11.5	6.2	3.2	2.1	49.4	17 595	35 883	103.9	52.5
Bullhead City	6.4	16.1	7.3	11.3	13.2	13.0	13.6	11.5	7.7	50.3	21 951	33 769	53.8	7.4
Casa Grande	8.7	22.2	9.3	13.1	13.3	11.0	8.6	8.2	5.6	50.7	19 076	25 224	32.2	17.7
Chandler..............................	9.1	20.7	8.6	19.0	19.0	11.8	6.0	3.4	2.4	50.1	89 862	176 581	96.5	19.7
Flagstaff..............................	6.7	17.6	21.7	16.4	14.1	12.2	6.1	3.1	2.2	50.4	45 857	52 894	15.3	5.7
Gilbert.................................	10.3	23.9	7.4	18.4	19.4	11.7	5.2	2.4	1.4	50.3	29 149	109 697	276.3	32.4
Glendale..............................	8.5	21.6	10.8	15.5	16.4	12.7	7.1	4.0	3.4	50.1	147 070	218 812	48.0	6.4
Lake Havasu City.................	4.7	14.8	5.7	8.8	12.8	12.7	15.0	15.2	10.3	50.8	24 363	41 938	72.1	17.1
Mesa...................................	8.2	19.1	11.2	15.5	14.2	11.1	7.3	6.7	6.6	50.5	289 199	396 375	37.1	9.1
Oro Valley town	5.0	16.5	4.5	8.3	15.3	14.8	12.9	14.3	8.4	51.5	8 627	29 700	244.3	15.7
Peoria..................................	7.4	21.0	6.7	13.9	16.8	11.9	8.0	6.9	7.5	52.0	51 080	108 364	113.8	17.7
Phoenix	8.7	20.3	10.9	17.2	16.0	11.9	6.9	4.4	3.7	49.1	988 015	1 321 045	34.2	5.1
Prescott	3.7	12.1	11.2	8.1	10.8	13.9	13.4	13.8	13.0	50.8	26 592	33 938	27.6	10.7
Scottsdale	5.2	14.2	6.6	14.3	16.1	15.1	11.9	9.2	7.5	51.8	130 099	202 705	55.8	7.5
Sierra Vista	7.7	18.1	13.0	15.4	13.8	11.0	8.9	7.1	5.0	49.8	32 983	37 775	14.5	5.5
Surprise city	7.3	12.6	7.0	13.6	8.8	8.9	16.4	17.1	8.4	50.9	7 122	30 848	333.1	64.0
Tempe	5.7	14.1	21.3	19.4	13.8	11.8	6.7	3.9	3.3	48.3	141 993	158 625	11.7	0.2
Tucson	7.2	17.3	13.8	15.7	14.9	11.8	7.3	6.0	5.9	51.0	415 444	486 699	18.3	4.3
Yuma	8.7	20.9	11.9	13.5	13.6	10.1	7.4	7.4	6.5	50.2	56 966	77 515	36.1	5.3
ARKANSAS.........................	6.8	18.7	9.8	13.2	14.9	13.1	9.6	7.4	6.6	51.2	2 350 624	2 673 400	13.7	2.0
Conway	6.9	16.4	22.4	15.7	13.5	10.3	5.8	4.3	4.7	52.5	26 481	43 167	63.0	10.8
Fayetteville..........................	6.5	13.4	25.7	17.3	12.6	10.5	5.3	4.1	4.6	49.3	42 247	58 047	37.4	6.9
Fort Smith	7.6	17.8	9.8	14.3	15.0	13.1	8.7	6.7	7.0	51.5	72 798	80 268	10.3	1.6
Hot Springs	5.9	14.3	8.2	11.4	13.9	12.9	10.1	10.7	12.6	53.1	33 095	35 750	10.1	2.9
Jacksonville.........................	9.5	19.5	12.8	17.7	15.6	10.6	7.1	4.7	2.7	49.9	29 101	29 916	2.8	1.6
Jonesboro............................	6.7	16.2	16.6	14.5	13.6	12.5	8.1	6.2	5.6	52.1	46 535	55 515	19.3	3.5
Little Rock	7.1	17.6	10.0	16.1	15.6	14.1	7.9	5.7	5.9	52.9	175 727	183 133	4.2	0.5
North Little Rock	7.1	18.3	9.0	13.4	14.9	13.8	8.7	7.3	7.3	53.3	61 829	60 433	-2.3	-1.2
Pine Bluff............................	7.4	20.1	12.2	12.7	14.2	12.0	7.7	6.6	7.1	52.7	57 140	55 085	-3.6	-2.1
Rogers................................	8.9	20.6	9.0	15.9	15.6	11.1	7.2	5.7	6.1	51.2	24 692	38 829	57.3	10.2
Springdale...........................	9.3	19.7	10.7	16.3	15.1	11.1	7.6	5.2	5.0	50.4	29 945	45 798	52.9	14.6
Texarkana	7.6	18.3	10.1	14.2	14.3	12.8	8.7	6.9	7.1	52.1	22 631	26 448	16.9	9.3
West Memphis	8.5	23.0	9.8	13.7	14.5	11.9	8.1	5.4	5.0	53.6	28 259	27 666	-2.1	1.3
CALIFORNIA......................	7.3	20.0	9.9	15.4	16.2	12.8	7.7	5.6	5.0	50.2	29 785 857	33 871 648	13.8	4.8
Alameda..............................	5.6	15.9	7.0	15.3	18.2	15.8	8.8	6.5	6.8	52.0	73 979	72 259	-2.3	-0.6
Alhambra.............................	6.2	16.1	9.7	18.0	16.0	12.9	7.9	6.4	6.8	52.9	82 087	85 804	4.5	2.3
Anaheim..............................	9.2	21.0	10.5	17.8	15.7	11.0	6.7	4.4	3.8	50.0	266 406	328 014	23.1	1.3
Antioch................................	8.6	23.6	8.2	14.0	18.4	13.0	6.7	4.1	3.3	51.0	62 195	90 532	45.6	11.7
Apple Valley	7.1	24.4	7.8	10.0	15.1	12.7	9.0	7.9	5.9	51.6	46 079	54 239	17.7	10.8
Arcadia...............................	4.6	18.7	7.5	10.8	16.4	16.3	10.3	7.5	8.0	53.0	48 284	53 054	9.9	4.5
Atascadero	5.4	20.3	8.3	10.9	17.8	17.1	8.7	6.1	5.4	48.5	23 138	26 411	14.1	2.3

Table D. Cities — Group Quarters, Crime, and Education

City	Households, 2000					Persons in group quarters, 2000				Serious crimes known to police[2] 2002				Education, 2000			
	Number	Percent change, 1990–2000	Persons per household	Female family householder[1]	One-person	Total	Institutional Total	Persons in nursing homes	Non-institutional	Total Number	Rate[3]	Violent	Property	School enrollment[4] Public	Private	Attainment[5] (percent) High school graduate or less	Bachelor's degree or more
	26	27	28	29	30	31	32	33	34	35	36	37	38	39	40	41	42
UNITED STATES	105 480 101	14.7	2.59	12.2	25.8	7 778 633	4 059 039	1 720 500	3 719 594	11 877 218	4 119	495	3 624	64 083 103	12 549 824	48.2	24.4
ALABAMA	1 737 080	15.3	2.49	14.2	26.1	114 720	65 363	26 697	49 357	200 331	4 465	444	4 021	994 978	160 526	55.1	19.0
Auburn	18 421	37.0	2.12	7.7	36.8	3 855	177	104	3 678	2 282	5 262	383	4 879	24 050	1 551	21.6	56.0
Bessemer	11 537	-8.3	2.52	29.2	29.0	629	594	305	35	NA	NA	NA	NA	6 384	1 155	64.4	9.2
Birmingham	98 782	-6.3	2.37	24.6	34.4	8 852	3 902	1 895	4 950	21 265	8 681	1 301	7 380	57 241	8 985	52.2	18.5
Decatur	21 824	14.1	2.43	13.4	28.9	923	621	299	302	3 810	7 003	399	6 604	11 702	1 595	46.8	23.7
Dothan	23 685	14.5	2.39	15.4	28.4	1 127	1 030	556	97	3 072	5 274	364	4 910	11 540	2 640	48.5	22.9
Florence	15 820	6.1	2.20	14.0	33.8	1 477	736	474	741	1 869	5 109	473	4 636	9 252	1 244	49.3	25.0
Gadsden	16 456	-6.0	2.28	18.1	33.9	1 430	878	454	552	3 934	10 004	1 821	8 184	7 523	900	58.4	14.4
Homewood	10 688	4.9	2.16	11.4	36.2	1 937	134	0	1 803	1 560	6 175	408	5 767	5 503	3 061	20.8	54.2
Hoover	25 191	56.8	2.47	7.2	25.9	491	454	440	37	1 916	3 027	327	2 700	12 876	3 379	20.7	52.6
Huntsville	66 742	5.8	2.29	13.7	32.3	5 575	1 666	736	3 909	10 167	6 370	602	5 768	36 398	8 068	34.7	36.1
Madison	11 143	86.7	2.61	9.6	23.9	254	208	179	46	930	3 143	189	2 954	7 294	1 738	18.3	52.0
Mobile	78 480	4.0	2.46	19.9	30.2	2 727	1 512	1 512	3 453	17 949	6 997	536	6 460	43 887	13 104	46.8	24.9
Montgomery	78 384	12.0	2.44	19.1	30.1	10 187	2 870	1 134	7 317	17 617	8 663	725	7 938	47 759	12 029	43.0	29.4
Phenix City	11 517	18.2	2.40	22.1	30.4	674	609	314	65	1 156	4 054	438	3 616	6 656	744	62.4	12.6
Prichard	9 841	-11.5	2.84	36.0	23.4	733	423	180	310	2 925	10 126	1 679	8 447	7 970	977	70.5	6.7
Tuscaloosa	31 381	6.5	2.22	15.7	35.2	8 102	1 934	704	6 168	5 774	7 346	597	6 750	26 770	3 005	44.8	30.9
ALASKA	221 600	17.3	2.74	10.8	23.5	19 349	4 824	803	14 525	27 745	4 310	563	3 746	166 991	18 769	39.5	24.7
Anchorage	94 822	14.7	2.67	11.5	23.4	7 014	1 915	291	5 099	13 670	5 114	644	4 471	65 258	9 367	33.9	28.9
Fairbanks	11 075	1.7	2.56	12.6	27.4	1 899	327	81	1 572	1 606	5 174	915	4 259	7 614	801	40.2	19.4
Juneau	11 543	16.6	2.60	10.5	24.4	678	229	39	449	816	2 587	263	2 324	7 975	802	28.8	36.0
ARIZONA	1 901 327	38.9	2.64	11.1	24.8	109 850	63 768	13 607	46 082	348 467	6 386	553	5 833	1 253 669	148 171	43.3	23.5
Apache Junction	13 775	78.8	2.29	8.5	27.2	223	0	0	223	1 908	5 639	319	5 320	5 089	622	58.2	9.0
Avondale	10 640	116.4	3.36	12.7	12.9	146	146	121	0	NA	NA	NA	NA	10 192	826	52.0	16.2
Bullhead City	13 909	57.6	2.42	11.1	25.3	117	79	77	38	1 722	4 795	490	4 305	6 415	334	62.4	8.6
Casa Grande	8 920	37.3	2.80	15.1	21.7	274	123	123	151	2 173	8 100	962	7 139	6 547	584	54.0	17.8
Chandler	62 377	98.1	2.82	10.5	19.3	782	478	392	304	11 204	5 966	276	5 690	45 850	5 961	30.7	32.5
Flagstaff	19 306	33.9	2.59	11.6	23.2	2 853	177	73	2 676	5 597	9 950	951	8 999	20 549	1 562	27.2	39.4
Gilbert	35 405	277.4	3.10	8.3	12.7	66	54	54	12	5 284	4 529	158	4 372	32 021	4 664	23.4	36.1
Glendale	75 700	41.0	2.85	12.8	21.3	2 857	1 014	987	1 843	15 475	6 650	581	6 069	57 372	8 364	43.2	21.0
Lake Havasu City	17 911	80.6	2.32	7.7	22.8	321	236	233	85	1 819	4 078	184	3 895	7 697	665	48.8	13.1
Mesa	146 643	36.0	2.68	10.6	24.2	3 949	2 189	1 705	1 760	33 335	7 908	685	7 223	99 540	10 749	41.0	21.6
Oro Valley town	12 249	330.4	2.41	4.9	19.4	159	27	27	132	523	1 656	66	1 589	5 879	965	21.2	43.5
Peoria	39 184	114.7	2.73	9.1	20.5	1 514	873	855	641	5 877	5 100	245	4 855	26 695	3 252	39.7	21.7
Phoenix	465 834	25.9	2.79	12.9	25.4	22 468	12 948	1 674	9 520	109 916	7 824	728	7 096	319 144	43 575	46.2	22.7
Prescott	15 098	31.5	2.11	7.9	32.1	2 044	862	733	1 182	2 034	5 635	391	5 245	6 314	2 094	33.2	30.6
Scottsdale	90 669	57.5	2.22	7.5	30.8	1 677	479	409	1 198	10 134	4 701	224	4 477	37 109	8 259	22.9	44.1
Sierra Vista	14 196	21.6	2.48	10.4	25.1	2 575	259	259	2 316	1 660	4 132	306	3 826	9 460	1 147	31.3	25.7
Surprise city	12 484	453.9	2.46	5.4	17.9	124	66	54	58	NA	NA	NA	NA	4 746	610	43.9	20.5
Tempe	63 602	14.5	2.41	9.7	28.5	5 242	406	394	4 836	17 819	10 563	735	9 828	49 538	5 224	27.8	39.6
Tucson	192 891	18.6	2.42	13.8	32.3	19 182	7 942	1 202	11 240	50 171	9 693	910	8 783	130 573	14 519	43.6	22.9
Yuma	26 649	38.2	2.79	13.1	21.7	3 144	1 065	581	2 079	5 387	3 735	663	3 072	20 728	1 266	51.9	16.2
ARKANSAS	1 042 696	17.0	2.49	12.1	25.6	73 908	45 152	21 379	28 756	112 672	4 158	424	3 733	602 713	72 396	58.8	16.7
Conway	16 039	70.0	2.44	11.2	26.1	4 037	533	382	3 504	2 463	5 629	206	5 423	12 646	2 972	37.1	36.0
Fayetteville	23 798	40.9	2.21	9.6	34.0	5 350	1 420	823	3 930	3 027	5 144	377	4 767	19 492	1 881	33.7	41.2
Fort Smith	32 398	9.3	2.42	12.3	30.7	1 990	1 632	618	358	7 498	9 215	877	8 337	16 067	2 615	52.8	18.6
Hot Springs	16 096	11.1	2.12	12.4	38.4	1 586	1 086	704	500	3 694	10 193	1 043	9 150	6 355	760	57.5	16.6
Jacksonville	10 890	10.5	2.64	14.6	22.0	1 204	41	40	1 163	1 731	5 708	462	5 246	7 246	829	47.5	15.4
Jonesboro	22 219	23.6	2.38	12.2	27.5	2 575	712	480	1 863	3 252	5 779	464	5 315	15 156	1 425	48.4	26.6
Little Rock	77 352	6.6	2.30	16.1	33.8	4 915	2 774	1 026	2 141	20 680	11 139	1 299	9 841	38 256	11 211	36.2	35.5
North Little Rock	25 542	2.2	2.35	17.6	32.0	520	403	403	117	5 840	9 533	849	8 684	13 102	2 444	50.1	22.0
Pine Bluff	19 956	-4.4	2.57	23.8	29.2	3 821	2 644	745	1 177	5 286	9 466	1 343	8 123	14 974	1 051	58.8	17.6
Rogers	14 005	44.3	2.74	10.1	22.2	476	420	409	56	1 538	3 907	201	3 707	8 650	1 186	52.6	21.1
Springdale	16 149	41.3	2.80	10.5	22.0	574	509	286	65	2 197	4 732	681	4 052	9 996	1 171	57.1	17.7
Texarkana	10 384	19.4	2.45	18.7	28.3	1 057	902	287	155	1 916	7 146	683	6 464	5 760	788	58.7	14.7
West Memphis	10 051	1.7	2.70	25.1	24.8	514	462	211	52	1 880	6 704	966	5 737	7 650	541	64.3	11.5
CALIFORNIA	11 502 870	10.8	2.87	12.6	23.5	819 754	413 656	120 724	406 098	1 384 872	3 944	593	3 350	8 703 390	1 426 600	43.3	26.6
Alameda	30 226	3.9	2.35	11.4	32.2	1 077	469	331	608	2 928	3 908	399	3 509	14 741	4 102	28.1	42.2
Alhambra	29 111	3.1	2.88	16.4	22.5	1 923	971	931	952	2 594	2 916	256	2 660	21 426	4 390	46.6	27.5
Anaheim	96 969	10.7	3.34	13.1	18.1	3 796	1 290	1 215	2 506	12 198	3 587	408	3 179	84 865	12 506	52.1	19.6
Antioch	29 338	37.1	3.07	13.5	15.9	416	262	252	154	3 418	3 642	729	2 913	25 504	3 574	43.0	18.2
Apple Valley	18 557	19.0	2.90	14.2	18.0	363	176	136	187	2 241	3 985	441	3 544	15 496	1 624	45.4	16.4
Arcadia	19 149	4.3	2.74	11.9	22.3	581	419	419	162	1 622	2 949	273	2 676	12 720	3 275	27.1	44.4
Atascadero	9 531	-12.3	2.62	11.4	22.0	1 466	1 282	65	184	922	3 367	325	3 042	6 926	912	37.4	20.3

1. No spouse present.   2. Data for serious crimes have not been adjusted for underreporting. This may affect comparability between geographic areas and over time.   3. Per 100,000 population estimated by the FBI.   4. All persons 3 years old and over enrolled in nursery school through college.   5. Persons 25 years old and over.

City	Money income, 1999							Housing units, 2000					
	Households				Percent below poverty					Vacant units			
	Median income				Persons		Families						
	Per capita income[1] (dollars)	Dollars	Percent change, 1989–1999 (constant 1999 dollars)	Percent with income of $100,000 or more	Total	Percent change in rate, 1989–1999	Total	Total	Percent change, 1990–2000	Vacant units for sale or rent[2]	For seasonal use (percent)	Home owner vacancy rate	Renter vacancy rate
	43	44	45	46	47	48	49	50	51	52	53	54	55
UNITED STATES..............	21 587	41 994	4.0	12.3	12.4	-5.3	9.2	115 904 641	13.3	10 424 540	3.1	1.7	6.8
ALABAMA	18 189	34 135	7.7	7.6	16.1	-12.0	12.5	1 963 711	17.6	226 631	2.4	2.0	11.8
Auburn................................	16 431	17 206	-1.0	7.9	38.1	-4.5	14.0	20 043	36.6	1 622	0.5	3.0	8.8
Bessemer............................	12 232	23 066	5.1	2.8	27.2	-8.4	24.2	12 790	-7.2	1 253	0.1	1.9	7.0
Birmingham.........................	15 663	26 735	3.7	4.5	24.7	-0.4	20.9	111 927	-4.9	13 145	0.3	2.7	11.6
Decatur...............................	20 431	37 192	-7.7	9.4	14.9	17.3	11.9	23 950	16.0	2 126	0.3	2.3	12.9
Dothan................................	20 539	35 000	1.0	10.0	15.6	-8.2	12.7	25 920	16.8	2 235	0.5	2.3	10.5
Florence	19 464	28 330	-1.7	7.9	20.4	10.3	14.4	17 707	11.3	1 887	0.6	3.0	12.6
Gadsden.............................	15 610	24 823	-3.7	5.0	22.9	12.3	18.1	18 797	-1.8	2 341	0.3	3.5	10.8
Homewood	25 491	45 431	10.8	14.8	7.6	13.4	4.4	11 494	7.1	806	0.3	1.6	9.5
Hoover................................	33 361	61 982	3.1	27.0	3.4	13.3	2.1	27 150	59.3	1 959	0.7	1.9	12.1
Huntsville............................	24 015	41 074	-5.3	13.0	12.8	10.3	9.8	73 670	8.6	6 928	0.7	2.7	12.8
Madison..............................	27 821	63 849	10.7	22.7	5.8	38.1	4.4	12 121	83.2	978	0.7	3.2	13.4
Mobile................................	18 072	31 445	4.3	7.7	21.2	-5.4	17.9	86 187	4.1	7 707	0.5	1.7	9.1
Montgomery	19 385	35 627	0.8	9.6	17.7	-2.2	13.9	86 787	13.2	8 403	0.3	2.5	9.9
Phenix City	14 619	26 720	-2.9	3.4	21.3	-4.1	18.8	13 250	22.5	1 733	0.2	3.6	15.9
Prichard..............................	10 626	19 544	25.7	2.8	35.5	-19.5	31.8	11 336	-13.0	1 495	0.2	1.7	12.6
Tuscaloosa	19 129	27 731	5.5	8.2	23.6	-11.6	14.2	34 857	11.7	3 476	0.4	2.1	11.3
ALASKA	22 660	51 571	-7.3	16.1	9.4	4.4	6.7	260 978	12.2	39 378	8.2	1.9	7.8
Anchorage	25 287	55 546	-5.9	18.8	7.3	2.8	5.1	100 368	6.6	5 546	1.1	1.4	5.3
Fairbanks	19 814	40 577	-5.7	9.9	10.5	1.0	7.4	12 357	-1.4	1 282	1.0	2.4	10.0
Juneau	26 719	62 034	-3.7	19.7	6.0	7.1	3.7	12 282	15.5	739	1.5	0.9	5.7
ARIZONA	20 275	40 558	9.6	10.8	13.9	-11.5	9.9	2 189 189	31.9	287 862	6.5	2.1	9.2
Apache Junction	16 806	33 170	25.4	2.7	11.6	-30.5	7.3	22 771	78.5	8 996	29.8	5.3	26.7
Avondale............................	16 919	49 153	50.6	11.1	13.8	-51.1	10.3	11 419	104.7	779	0.5	2.7	12.2
Bullhead City......................	16 250	30 221	-9.4	4.0	15.1	18.0	11.3	18 430	37.0	4 521	13.3	4.4	9.2
Casa Grande......................	15 917	36 212	4.0	7.0	16.0	-8.0	12.4	11 041	49.1	2 121	7.8	2.7	18.4
Chandler............................	23 904	58 416	14.0	16.6	6.6	-32.0	4.6	66 592	90.4	4 215	1.6	1.5	10.2
Flagstaff	18 637	37 146	-2.6	9.9	17.4	1.2	10.6	21 396	31.2	2 090	4.6	2.1	5.3
Gilbert................................	24 795	68 032	23.3	21.5	3.2	-48.4	2.5	37 007	247.3	1 602	0.7	2.1	5.2
Glendale............................	19 124	45 015	5.8	11.3	11.9	3.5	8.8	79 667	30.1	3 967	0.4	1.4	6.7
Lake Havasu City................	20 403	36 499	-5.8	7.3	9.5	17.3	6.6	23 018	79.2	5 107	17.3	2.3	7.8
Mesa.................................	19 601	42 817	5.3	9.6	8.9	-6.3	6.2	175 701	25.1	29 058	10.3	2.4	10.7
Oro Valley town	31 134	61 037	NA	20.6	3.1	NA	2.4	13 946	290.0	1 697	6.3	2.2	14.5
Peoria................................	22 726	52 199	13.6	12.1	5.3	-32.9	3.3	42 573	94.0	3 389	3.0	2.3	10.0
Phoenix..............................	19 833	41 207	4.7	11.5	15.8	11.3	11.5	495 832	17.5	29 998	0.9	1.4	7.9
Prescott	22 565	35 446	17.2	9.7	13.1	-1.5	7.4	17 144	28.0	2 046	6.0	2.7	6.1
Scottsdale	39 158	57 484	9.6	26.0	5.8	-1.7	3.4	104 974	52.1	14 305	7.6	2.3	10.6
Sierra Vista	18 436	38 427	-3.3	6.6	10.5	-1.9	8.0	15 685	21.3	1 489	1.1	2.0	10.7
Surprise city	21 451	44 156	NA	7.5	8.7	NA	5.6	16 260	209.4	3 776	13.3	3.2	31.6
Tempe................................	22 406	42 361	-1.1	12.6	14.3	5.1	7.5	67 068	9.1	3 466	0.8	1.0	6.1
Tucson...............................	16 322	30 981	6.0	5.0	18.4	-8.9	13.7	209 609	14.3	16 718	1.7	1.6	8.1
Yuma	16 730	35 374	-1.6	7.6	14.7	-8.1	12.1	34 475	51.9	7 826	11.7	1.6	12.3
ARKANSAS.....................	16 904	32 182	13.3	6.0	15.8	-17.3	12.0	1 173 043	17.2	130 347	2.5	2.5	9.6
Conway	18 509	37 063	23.8	9.5	16.3	-3.6	9.3	17 289	70.5	1 250	0.3	3.2	8.3
Fayetteville.........................	18 311	31 345	10.0	7.9	19.9	0.5	11.4	25 467	35.2	1 669	0.5	2.7	6.1
Fort Smith	18 994	32 157	0.4	8.1	15.8	14.5	12.1	35 341	6.9	2 943	0.4	2.5	8.1
Hot Springs	17 961	26 040	23.4	5.8	19.2	-22.9	13.7	18 813	7.2	2 717	2.9	3.2	11.9
Jacksonville........................	16 369	35 460	5.5	4.2	14.2	22.4	11.9	11 890	9.2	1 000	0.5	2.3	8.9
Jonesboro	17 884	32 196	2.8	7.3	17.4	5.5	12.9	24 263	24.2	2 044	0.4	2.5	10.4
Little Rock	23 209	37 572	4.0	11.6	14.3	-2.1	11.1	84 793	4.7	7 441	0.5	1.7	9.7
North Little Rock	19 662	35 578	10.5	7.8	16.1	-6.4	12.4	27 567	1.1	2 025	0.3	2.2	8.4
Pine Bluff...........................	14 637	27 247	5.9	5.0	25.5	-7.9	20.6	22 484	-3.0	2 528	0.3	2.0	9.2
Rogers...............................	19 761	40 474	15.0	10.9	12.8	47.1	9.4	14 836	44.2	831	0.4	2.6	5.9
Springdale	16 855	36 729	7.7	6.8	12.5	33.0	8.8	16 962	41.3	813	0.3	2.3	4.4
Texarkana	17 130	31 343	22.7	6.1	21.7	-13.9	17.2	11 721	18.9	1 337	0.4	2.8	15.1
West Memphis	13 679	27 399	-7.5	5.3	28.3	23.6	23.7	11 022	4.9	971	0.3	1.7	10.2
CALIFORNIA....................	22 711	47 493	-1.3	17.3	14.2	13.6	10.6	12 214 549	9.2	711 679	1.9	1.4	3.7
Alameda.............................	30 982	56 285	9.9	22.6	8.2	20.6	6.0	31 644	3.7	1 418	0.5	0.5	2.4
Alhambra............................	17 350	39 213	-7.0	9.4	14.3	-3.4	11.5	30 069	1.6	958	0.3	1.3	2.1
Anaheim.............................	18 266	47 122	-11.5	14.5	14.1	33.0	10.4	99 719	7.0	2 750	0.2	0.9	3.2
Antioch	22 152	60 359	9.7	19.1	8.5	-6.6	6.5	30 116	31.1	778	0.1	0.9	3.4
Apple Valley	17 830	40 421	-11.6	9.7	17.3	61.7	13.3	20 163	20.9	1 606	0.7	3.4	7.8
Arcadia	28 400	56 100	-11.8	23.9	7.9	51.9	6.7	19 970	2.5	821	0.6	1.8	2.4
Atascadero	20 029	48 725	3.2	11.0	9.0	15.4	6.9	9 848	11.0	317	0.7	0.9	2.7

1. Based on population enumerated as of April 1, 2000.   2. Includes units rented or sold but not occupied.

Table D. Cities — Housing, Labor Force, Employment, and Disability

City	Housing units, 2000 (cont'd) Occupied units — Total	Percent owner occupied	Percent renter occupied	Average size owner occupied	Average size renter occupied	Civilian labor force, 2003 — Total	Percent change, 2002–2003	Unemployment — Total	Rate[1]	Civilian employment,[2] 2000 — Total	Percent Management, professional, and related occupations	Production, transportation, and material moving occupations	Disability, 2000 Employment disabled persons[3] (percent)
	56	57	58	59	60	61	62	63	64	65	66	67	68
UNITED STATES............	105 480 101	66.2	33.8	2.69	2.40	146 178 717	0.9	8 750 000	6.0	129 721 512	33.6	14.6	11.9
ALABAMA	1 737 080	72.5	27.5	2.57	2.30	2 147 321	2.5	124 662	5.8	1 920 189	29.5	19.0	13.7
Auburn............................	18 421	40.9	59.1	2.45	1.90	19 175	4.1	773	4.0	19 077	45.5	7.1	6.2
Bessemer.........................	11 537	59.2	40.8	2.53	2.49	14 134	2.5	1 170	8.3	10 193	22.0	19.7	17.0
Birmingham.....................	98 782	53.7	46.3	2.49	2.23	129 580	2.4	9 316	7.2	98 574	28.0	15.4	17.7
Decatur...........................	21 824	63.8	36.2	2.52	2.26	27 376	0.2	2 055	7.5	24 331	30.5	21.3	12.6
Dothan............................	23 685	62.9	37.1	2.47	2.26	30 612	3.3	1 384	4.5	25 707	33.4	14.4	11.7
Florence..........................	15 820	58.5	41.5	2.33	2.02	16 316	-3.6	1 751	10.7	15 217	31.8	16.4	12.8
Gadsden..........................	16 456	63.6	36.4	2.29	2.27	16 011	-0.5	1 227	7.7	14 200	25.4	24.6	15.3
Homewood.......................	10 688	54.6	45.4	2.34	1.95	13 397	2.2	325	2.4	13 908	52.8	4.9	6.7
Hoover............................	25 191	66.0	34.0	2.68	2.07	26 663	2.1	487	1.8	33 718	52.8	4.1	5.9
Huntsville........................	66 742	61.6	38.4	2.42	2.07	103 122	4.9	4 606	4.5	75 646	44.3	11.9	9.5
Madison...........................	11 143	70.3	29.7	2.81	2.13	10 660	4.9	252	2.4	16 030	56.8	8.7	6.2
Mobile.............................	78 480	59.3	40.7	2.55	2.32	98 564	3.0	7 928	8.0	81 223	34.0	13.3	14.4
Montgomery.....................	78 384	61.9	38.1	2.51	2.33	100 564	3.4	5 498	5.5	86 741	37.0	11.4	13.5
Phenix City......................	11 517	52.7	47.3	2.47	2.31	13 675	3.8	1 081	7.9	11 323	28.1	20.8	15.0
Prichard..........................	9 841	58.4	41.6	2.81	2.87	10 597	3.9	976	9.2	8 767	16.2	23.8	19.3
Tuscaloosa......................	31 381	47.7	52.3	2.43	2.04	39 303	2.0	1 905	4.8	34 279	36.3	13.8	9.6
ALASKA	221 600	62.5	37.5	2.89	2.49	331 675	2.5	26 561	8.0	281 532	34.4	10.8	8.3
Anchorage.......................	94 822	60.1	39.9	2.81	2.46	147 868	1.9	8 470	5.7	125 737	36.8	9.6	8.2
Fairbanks........................	11 075	34.9	65.1	2.62	2.53	16 496	2.3	1 303	7.9	11 197	30.4	9.7	9.1
Juneau............................	11 543	63.7	36.3	2.78	2.29	16 984	1.8	1 053	6.2	16 537	42.3	7.0	7.0
ARIZONA	1 901 327	68.0	32.0	2.69	2.53	2 690 294	0.9	150 935	5.6	2 233 004	32.7	10.9	12.2
Apache Junction	13 775	82.1	17.9	2.27	2.38	12 249	1.3	594	4.8	12 613	18.9	15.7	16.5
Avondale.........................	10 640	77.6	22.4	3.35	3.39	16 078	0.3	1 504	9.4	15 670	28.7	15.8	13.1
Bullhead City...................	13 909	60.3	39.7	2.31	2.58	20 048	3.4	1 083	5.4	14 321	16.6	7.6	18.9
Casa Grande....................	8 920	64.0	36.0	2.80	2.79	15 323	1.2	859	5.6	10 196	28.1	16.2	15.9
Chandler..........................	62 377	73.6	26.4	2.86	2.70	109 002	1.1	4 056	3.7	92 646	40.8	10.4	9.4
Flagstaff.........................	19 306	48.2	51.8	2.74	2.46	35 998	-0.2	1 819	5.1	29 223	37.9	8.2	9.0
Gilbert............................	35 405	84.9	15.1	3.16	2.72	64 499	1.1	2 248	3.5	56 609	43.6	8.2	7.6
Glendale..........................	75 700	64.8	35.2	2.97	2.63	126 635	0.9	6 268	4.9	103 474	31.4	11.9	12.9
Lake Havasu City..............	17 911	77.6	22.4	2.29	2.45	21 026	3.8	543	2.6	16 536	22.9	13.4	11.9
Mesa...............................	146 643	66.4	33.6	2.74	2.54	231 337	1.0	9 718	4.2	185 711	30.9	12.3	11.0
Oro Valley town	12 249	84.2	15.8	2.47	2.12	15 129	0.1	438	2.9	12 495	52.1	5.7	7.3
Peoria.............................	39 184	84.3	15.7	2.78	2.45	54 769	1.1	2 091	3.8	49 793	33.9	10.4	11.3
Phoenix...........................	465 834	60.7	39.3	2.89	2.63	831 658	0.9	45 216	5.4	611 019	30.9	12.0	13.2
Prescott..........................	15 098	65.2	34.8	2.14	2.07	20 589	2.6	758	3.7	13 427	37.4	9.3	11.0
Scottsdale.......................	90 669	69.6	30.4	2.32	1.97	119 185	1.1	4 261	3.6	104 436	46.9	4.5	8.3
Sierra Vista.....................	14 196	52.2	47.8	2.43	2.53	16 243	1.2	652	4.0	13 739	34.0	6.9	10.7
Surprise city....................	12 484	88.3	11.7	2.37	3.14	12 244	0.5	977	8.0	10 443	27.9	10.4	13.9
Tempe.............................	63 602	51.0	49.0	2.59	2.22	136 599	1.0	5 781	4.2	90 791	39.7	9.4	10.0
Tucson............................	192 891	53.4	46.6	2.48	2.24	265 189	-0.1	12 653	4.8	216 006	32.0	9.6	12.6
Yuma..............................	26 649	63.5	36.5	2.80	2.78	39 642	1.8	6 479	16.3	28 024	30.2	10.0	12.3
ARKANSAS....................	1 042 696	69.4	30.6	2.54	2.40	1 264 519	-1.3	78 132	6.2	1 173 399	27.7	21.0	13.8
Conway............................	16 039	55.1	44.9	2.66	2.17	20 867	-1.1	1 217	5.8	21 639	36.4	12.6	9.3
Fayetteville.....................	23 798	42.2	57.8	2.45	2.04	33 347	1.0	1 105	3.3	29 222	40.4	11.0	10.0
Fort Smith.......................	32 398	56.3	43.7	2.52	2.29	41 761	-1.8	2 120	5.1	36 634	28.7	25.4	15.0
Hot Springs.....................	16 096	57.3	42.7	2.18	2.05	16 146	0.2	1 284	8.0	14 448	27.9	14.5	17.1
Jacksonville.....................	10 890	47.3	52.7	2.58	2.69	12 626	-1.1	1 004	8.0	11 951	25.4	17.0	14.9
Jonesboro........................	22 219	57.7	42.3	2.49	2.24	31 102	-0.9	1 622	5.2	27 622	31.8	17.9	13.7
Little Rock.......................	77 352	57.4	42.6	2.46	2.10	100 580	-1.3	5 175	5.1	88 680	41.6	9.8	11.6
North Little Rock	25 542	57.5	42.5	2.39	2.29	31 980	-1.3	1 701	5.3	28 388	31.5	13.9	13.2
Pine Bluff........................	19 956	58.8	41.2	2.56	2.58	23 893	-1.3	2 534	10.6	20 119	26.0	23.4	15.8
Rogers.............................	14 005	63.2	36.8	2.77	2.69	21 667	0.8	575	2.7	18 265	29.9	22.5	13.3
Springdale.......................	16 149	60.4	39.6	2.77	2.85	23 514	0.9	661	2.8	21 417	25.5	22.4	9.9
Texarkana........................	10 384	60.9	39.1	2.46	2.42	9 885	-2.5	427	4.3	11 142	28.6	18.4	13.1
West Memphis	10 051	56.0	44.0	2.73	2.66	13 638	0.5	957	7.0	10 697	23.7	20.4	16.3
CALIFORNIA...................	11 502 870	56.9	43.1	2.93	2.79	17 460 005	0.5	1 177 322	6.7	14 718 928	36.0	12.7	12.8
Alameda..........................	30 226	47.9	52.1	2.50	2.22	41 091	-0.8	2 022	4.9	37 291	48.2	8.1	10.3
Alhambra.........................	29 111	39.2	60.8	3.04	2.78	43 496	-0.1	2 512	5.8	37 421	36.8	13.1	12.5
Anaheim..........................	96 969	50.0	50.0	3.24	3.45	174 159	1.8	7 660	4.4	142 825	27.5	18.8	14.7
Antioch...........................	29 338	71.0	29.0	3.14	2.90	38 477	-0.3	2 830	7.4	41 598	29.1	11.3	10.1
Apple Valley....................	18 557	70.0	30.0	2.83	3.08	26 883	3.0	1 650	6.1	19 758	31.1	14.0	12.4
Arcadia...........................	19 149	62.3	37.7	2.91	2.47	25 846	-0.2	896	3.5	23 412	50.5	5.2	8.1
Atascadero.......................	9 531	65.6	34.4	2.71	2.44	14 257	0.4	371	2.6	12 284	32.7	10.1	11.3

1. Percent of civilian labor force.   2. Persons 16 years old and over.   3. Persons 16 to 64 years old.

City	Value of residential construction authorized by building permits, 2003			Wholesale trade, 1997				Retail trade,[1] 1997			
	New construction ($1,000)	Number of housing units	Percent single family	Number of establish-ments	Number of employees	Sales (mil dol)	Annual payroll (mil dol)	Number of establish-ments	Number of employees	Sales (mil dol)	Annual payroll (mil dol)
	69	70	71	72	73	74	75	76	77	78	79
UNITED STATES..............	249 693 105	1 889 214	77.3	453 471	5 794 312	4 058 480.1	214 915.5	1 118 446	13 991 004	2 460 963.0	237 201.0
ALABAMA	2 463 568	22 256	79.4	6 315	79 229	40 986.3	2 394.7	20 163	231 665	36 623.3	3 381.7
Auburn..............................	104 810	1 085	53.9	26	D	D	D	198	2 851	385.1	37.2
Bessemer..........................	7 871	77	100.0	70	1 423	922.7	47.8	209	2 773	519.0	45.1
Birmingham	42 049	390	39.0	736	14 656	6 744.4	494.1	1 150	16 618	3 085.5	294.7
Decatur.............................	25 851	205	100.0	138	1 785	868.5	51.9	410	4 920	921.9	74.2
Dothan..............................	37 901	373	100.0	180	1 918	643.2	49.1	547	7 148	1 199.2	116.0
Florence............................	18 653	271	41.0	72	1 842	349.0	43.6	353	5 049	710.0	68.7
Gadsden...........................	4 178	90	33.3	70	1 031	283.2	28.3	290	3 148	503.5	45.2
Homewood........................	7 467	31	100.0	154	1 998	1 083.3	68.3	254	4 276	565.0	61.6
Hoover..............................	190 151	831	92.8	126	1 240	1 767.6	57.1	203	4 812	874.2	82.0
Huntsville.........................	68 470	1 495	35.1	361	3 968	2 828.5	143.7	945	14 647	2 268.6	219.3
Madison	43 190	669	80.6	56	563	332.0	20.9	77	1 211	146.3	15.8
Mobile..............................	35 687	238	98.3	491	6 314	2 669.0	195.4	1 140	17 003	2 573.2	261.2
Montgomery	104 654	1 067	71.4	365	4 733	2 701.0	141.0	1 091	15 619	2 425.3	232.3
Phenix City	27 417	331	85.5	17	453	91.2	11.6	127	1 470	181.1	18.6
Prichard...........................	1 047	11	100.0	27	476	147.7	15.5	77	566	71.1	8.8
Tuscaloosa........................	95 882	884	69.5	117	1 153	516.6	37.2	577	8 496	1 250.9	122.3
ALASKA	560 200	3 531	49.3	784	6 860	2 989.8	256.8	2 866	32 502	6 251.4	670.5
Anchorage........................	391 600	2 387	37.1	434	4 748	1 989.1	181.4	1 001	15 115	3 114.9	319.3
Fairbanks	1 102	12	100.0	51	590	178.3	21.8	248	3 356	727.0	77.2
Juneau	18 208	117	72.6	33	196	96.3	8.2	173	1 807	312.7	37.2
ARIZONA	10 518 958	74 996	87.8	6 689	80 155	45 763.9	2 748.9	16 283	232 050	43 960.9	4 223.9
Apache Junction	17 627	212	89.6	12	D	D	D	80	980	143.5	14.7
Avondale..........................	204 863	1 461	83.6	7	D	D	D	38	582	141.8	10.1
Bullhead City.....................	52 780	514	99.6	NA	NA	NA	NA	NA	NA	NA	NA
Casa Grande......................	110 892	1 035	75.7	35	326	93.5	8.5	182	2 103	336.6	31.6
Chandler...........................	791 507	4 658	81.7	162	1 952	1 254.0	59.2	283	5 528	1 190.7	127.1
Flagstaff	78 720	755	55.1	80	739	505.0	18.2	367	5 011	784.6	79.0
Gilbert..............................	605 273	3 862	100.0	74	301	119.1	9.4	110	1 870	362.7	39.2
Glendale...........................	122 005	1 078	67.0	160	2 130	848.8	57.3	598	11 308	2 311.9	203.3
Lake Havasu City................	162 883	1 737	78.4	42	189	44.0	4.4	228	2 290	377.6	37.9
Mesa................................	455 756	2 931	84.4	347	2 797	1 280.8	109.0	1 405	23 747	4 348.7	420.2
Oro Valley town	118 590	496	100.0	NA	NA	NA	NA	NA	NA	NA	NA
Peoria..............................	217 258	1 892	81.6	25	113	37.6	3.3	149	2 558	454.5	46.6
Phoenix............................	1 711 776	11 946	76.1	2 447	37 073	21 861.7	1 383.9	3 807	58 531	11 407.6	1 123.2
Prescott............................	133 050	683	90.0	47	302	113.6	7.8	251	2 822	513.7	52.5
Scottsdale	241 489	1 809	64.5	634	3 997	2 749.3	164.0	1 232	16 189	3 614.6	342.4
Sierra Vista	28 365	402	100.0	15	D	D	D	145	2 321	371.4	37.1
Surprise city	668 258	5 291	93.6	NA	NA	NA	NA	NA	NA	NA	NA
Tempe	79 418	857	9.0	659	10 322	9 609.2	370.2	728	13 575	3 491.9	295.3
Tucson	308 417	2 737	88.6	615	6 532	1 801.0	190.1	2 079	30 607	5 370.2	547.7
Yuma	97 954	685	100.0	65	635	207.9	19.8	300	4 376	697.9	66.2
ARKANSAS.......................	1 541 009	14 839	67.9	3 619	41 385	27 515.4	1 136.6	12 600	132 335	21 643.7	1 904.4
Conway	93 507	739	87.8	54	D	D	D	248	3 111	526.2	47.8
Fayetteville.......................	149 138	1 869	33.3	88	1 202	6 024.6	43.7	401	5 711	790.0	79.9
Fort Smith	31 164	292	54.1	219	1 942	660.3	52.1	599	8 197	1 282.6	121.4
Hot Springs	14 102	129	100.0	NA	NA	NA	NA	NA	NA	NA	NA
Jacksonville......................	18 345	163	97.5	17	D	D	D	109	1 394	239.8	22.5
Jonesboro	54 736	609	77.5	111	1 342	458.1	30.6	410	5 146	770.3	73.8
Little Rock	188 520	1 027	70.6	555	10 270	4 550.3	332.1	1 101	15 944	2 590.5	236.9
North Little Rock.................	15 439	128	56.3	219	3 255	4 712.8	91.6	466	7 671	1 328.5	121.9
Pine Bluff	3 263	139	41.0	69	D	D	D	349	4 359	653.5	66.0
Rogers..............................	99 092	711	73.8	44	495	712.8	14.8	204	2 669	418.5	39.1
Springdale........................	145 843	2 065	37.4	163	1 775	673.2	51.4	278	3 463	615.0	58.8
Texarkana	16 111	297	44.1	46	739	200.8	18.1	147	1 413	243.3	20.2
West Memphis	7 234	163	86.5	41	477	281.9	14.5	151	2 170	402.2	27.0
CALIFORNIA.....................	31 778 214	191 948	72.9	57 842	755 513	551 230.6	29 900.2	106 357	1 354 797	263 118.3	26 362.7
Alameda...........................	18 902	67	88.1	68	538	353.4	24.5	204	2 329	408.5	48.5
Alhambra	3 283	20	50.0	427	1 972	747.1	46.3	249	3 672	983.2	76.0
Anaheim	60 267	373	68.4	962	12 779	15 533.1	457.4	963	13 119	2 773.7	278.2
Antioch	57 822	255	99.2	32	273	85.6	9.1	197	2 898	500.1	51.4
Apple Valley	79 923	644	99.5	21	109	14.8	2.0	68	960	146.6	14.6
Arcadia.............................	64 733	255	78.8	309	1 131	569.8	30.2	283	4 000	509.7	59.8
Atascadero	31 459	180	90.0	14	95	36.0	2.8	129	1 374	226.0	21.3

1. Establishments with payroll.

Table D. Cities — **Real Estate, Professional Services, and Manufacturing**

City	Real estate and rental and leasing, 1997				Professional, scientific, and technical services,[1] 1997				Manufacturing, 1997			
	Number of establish-ments	Number of employees	Receipts (mil dol)	Annual payroll (mil dol)	Number of establish-ments	Number of employees	Receipts (mil dol)	Annual payroll (mil dol)	Number of establish-ments	Number of employees	Receipts (mil dol)	Annual payroll (mil dol)
	80	81	82	83	84	85	86	87	88	89	90	91
UNITED STATES.............	288 274	1 702 540	241 268.5	41 597.5	615 305	5 212 745	579 542.1	225 376.0	363 753	16 888 016	3 842 061.4	572 101.1
ALABAMA	3 664	20 629	2 130.3	396.7	7 076	54 413	5 295.6	2 051.4	5 444	352 618	67 970.1	10 187.8
Auburn..............................	53	357	27.0	5.4	63	340	32.1	11.7	28	1 708	270.3	34.8
Bessemer...........................	26	96	9.2	1.7	53	180	10.9	3.9	45	2 164	367.9	70.0
Birmingham.......................	275	3 000	442.9	81.9	815	9 020	991.8	390.3	382	19 057	3 179.5	621.0
Decatur.............................	81	404	35.2	7.3	139	822	63.8	25.5	124	8 495	3 219.0	291.1
Dothan..............................	84	313	32.8	5.8	160	1 147	69.1	26.4	102	8 269	1 311.0	212.8
Florence............................	63	261	25.4	5.3	136	718	49.3	16.9	83	6 049	743.8	140.9
Gadsden............................	43	162	18.7	3.3	103	468	32.1	12.6	67	6 067	1 241.0	217.5
Homewood.........................	57	502	73.3	12.1	179	1 568	113.9	44.9	40	1 472	403.1	43.6
Hoover..............................	44	282	28.3	5.2	168	858	96.1	32.8	NA	NA	NA	NA
Huntsville..........................	278	1 339	138.7	24.6	666	12 461	1 532.3	571.7	240	25 793	6 694.3	1 014.6
Madison............................	28	206	22.9	4.2	53	191	24.3	8.9	28	D	D	D
Mobile..............................	291	1 685	175.6	31.9	674	5 495	496.7	196.6	213	11 631	1 907.4	445.0
Montgomery.......................	287	2 140	175.4	39.3	540	4 295	407.0	189.2	190	10 312	1 798.7	269.0
Phenix City........................	33	109	11.5	1.4	38	D	D	D	34	2 566	864.2	91.6
Prichard............................	8	26	2.7	0.4	2	D	D	D	22	1 038	340.1	40.2
Tuscaloosa	129	985	66.6	12.5	210	1 556	107.6	44.2	89	6 020	1 058.9	179.1
ALASKA	716	4 014	543.2	98.3	1 437	7 892	945.9	370.8	488	10 770	3 305.0	331.2
Anchorage.........................	356	2 145	322.2	56.8	907	5 939	767.2	301.3	187	2 022	322.3	62.9
Fairbanks	64	408	38.9	9.2	118	592	52.5	21.9	NA	NA	NA	NA
Juneau	49	249	38.3	4.0	96	415	44.9	18.5	NA	NA	NA	NA
ARIZONA	5 450	32 529	4 110.1	747.4	10 163	75 789	6 669.4	2 724.7	4 917	193 616	43 030.3	6 753.6
Apache Junction	36	94	10.5	1.0	12	28	1.7	0.8	NA	NA	NA	NA
Avondale...........................	14	33	4.4	0.8	14	46	4.1	1.5	NA	NA	NA	NA
Bullhead City.....................	NA	NA	NA	NA	NA	NA	NA	NA	NA	NA	NA	NA
Casa Grande......................	34	120	12.3	2.1	22	342	9.5	4.7	27	1 626	307.1	52.1
Chandler...........................	101	449	66.2	9.1	208	746	69.3	25.0	135	9 668	4 744.3	352.0
Flagstaff	116	439	53.3	9.4	143	702	53.7	19.9	62	1 798	505.2	67.7
Gilbert..............................	54	205	23.0	3.8	111	494	64.8	23.1	78	2 228	311.5	57.4
Glendale...........................	150	897	101.4	15.5	167	768	36.9	14.5	156	6 398	1 075.9	244.0
Lake Havasu City................	54	126	15.9	2.2	55	171	12.8	3.6	82	1 845	274.7	37.4
Mesa................................	367	1 576	194.3	28.1	628	4 950	282.8	128.5	258	13 921	3 367.1	530.7
Oro Valley town	NA	NA	NA	NA	NA	NA	NA	NA	NA	NA	NA	NA
Peoria..............................	48	349	31.1	5.5	46	430	9.1	3.5	34	558	54.3	13.8
Phoenix............................	1 485	13 109	1 768.6	331.3	3 664	36 761	3 328.5	1 470.5	1 706	69 401	14 649.6	2 532.4
Prescott............................	101	272	35.4	5.2	144	547	41.0	13.9	65	1 509	178.0	36.7
Scottsdale	570	2 480	430.0	81.2	1 222	6 295	713.2	252.4	257	8 254	1 128.2	192.1
Sierra Vista	48	236	18.6	3.4	72	1 196	103.1	43.1	NA	NA	NA	NA
Surprise city	NA	NA	NA	NA	NA	NA	NA	NA	NA	NA	NA	NA
Tempe..............................	293	2 069	274.4	50.3	671	5 531	454.7	160.2	498	24 105	5 414.8	865.2
Tucson	647	4 879	485.7	98.2	1 331	9 883	886.9	349.6	520	20 152	3 483.6	841.2
Yuma	78	323	24.7	4.2	125	597	44.2	16.1	36	2 481	348.1	44.5
ARKANSAS........................	2 269	9 761	1 001.6	163.2	4 125	23 094	1 825.8	719.6	3 316	230 153	45 186.0	5 778.4
Conway............................	57	133	17.8	2.0	70	482	40.7	11.6	67	7 242	1 205.9	183.1
Fayetteville........................	116	507	61.8	7.9	217	1 023	80.5	26.7	68	5 962	948.9	144.2
Fort Smith	120	557	63.9	10.2	209	1 197	91.6	27.3	206	20 817	3 949.8	521.5
Hot Springs	NA	NA	NA	NA	NA	NA	NA	NA	66	2 756	610.0	68.2
Jacksonville.......................	35	D	D	D	29	99	5.5	2.2	32	1 995	309.5	53.7
Jonesboro	79	D	D	D	137	652	51.9	18.9	97	6 234	1 126.9	170.7
Little Rock	323	2 685	290.6	50.2	979	8 734	827.9	372.9	251	12 570	2 457.9	365.9
North Little Rock	68	356	28.8	6.1	125	898	64.0	24.7	91	4 073	1 095.8	110.4
Pine Bluff..........................	52	334	22.8	5.6	79	387	27.2	7.6	75	D	D	D
Rogers..............................	56	245	27.2	3.8	104	485	38.9	14.6	71	7 083	1 047.8	181.4
Springdale.........................	57	175	27.9	3.4	97	560	37.4	16.3	106	D	D	D
Texarkana	24	75	4.9	0.8	36	D	D	D	20	2 230	491.5	98.7
West Memphis	24	111	12.3	2.2	43	292	13.2	4.4	33	D	D	D
CALIFORNIA......................	37 244	243 288	38 288.4	6 570.5	78 635	805 856	89 555.7	35 258.6	49 418	1 809 667	379 612.4	65 762.8
Alameda............................	81	313	49.5	6.5	209	1 576	221.4	89.0	56	2 298	1 009.1	127.3
Alhambra...........................	95	343	43.4	7.7	170	1 000	55.7	18.6	125	3 248	308.5	81.8
Anaheim............................	335	3 019	358.3	88.3	556	4 422	451.5	165.3	896	38 330	6 019.8	1 358.7
Antioch.............................	42	270	35.8	4.2	68	254	15.2	5.4	38	577	117.7	20.2
Apple Valley	35	140	14.9	3.3	26	69	5.4	2.4	NA	NA	NA	NA
Arcadia.............................	112	492	63.9	10.4	141	804	83.6	29.5	72	971	201.2	29.0
Atascadero	26	82	9.3	0.9	38	119	9.1	2.7	NA	NA	NA	NA

1. Firms subject to federal tax.

Table D. Cities — Accommodation and Foodservices, Entertainment, and Health Care

City	Accommodation and foodservices, 1997				Arts, entertainment, and recreation,[1] 1997				Health care and social assistance,[1] 1997			
	Number of establishments	Number of employees	Sales (mil dol)	Annual payroll (mil dol)	Number of establishments	Number of employees	Receipts (mil dol)	Annual payroll (mil dol)	Number of establishments	Number of employees	Receipts (mil dol)	Annual payroll (mil dol)
	92	93	94	95	96	97	98	99	100	101	102	103
UNITED STATES..............	545 060	9 451 056	350 389.1	97 003.9	79 637	1 207 943	85 129.3	26 115.0	531 069	6 231 768	418 602.2	182 256.3
ALABAMA	6 955	134 719	3 881.8	1 059.6	791	9 381	435.7	105.0	7 121	104 492	7 116.7	3 104.8
Auburn.............................	125	3 013	76.3	20.2	12	0	0.0	0.0	48	316	20.2	8.7
Bessemer.........................	52	1 459	33.3	9.3	5	55	1.6	0.5	71	851	46.3	25.1
Birmingham......................	524	10 504	346.8	99.6	41	1 092	58.2	13.1	675	10 682	985.1	442.3
Decatur............................	137	3 117	86.5	25.3	20	134	4.8	1.1	196	2 088	146.4	67.7
Dothan.............................	176	3 527	111.0	28.3	21	233	8.2	2.6	209	4 502	370.9	170.3
Florence..........................	109	2 242	59.6	17.4	15	0	0.0	0.0	176	2 120	153.1	64.4
Gadsden..........................	102	1 953	56.7	15.7	10	103	4.0	1.4	156	3 611	285.8	114.8
Homewood.......................	107	2 467	99.1	25.9	12	51	1.8	0.5	158	5 628	498.8	184.9
Hoover.............................	90	1 916	60.3	17.2	12	112	3.4	0.9	99	1 628	82.5	36.2
Huntsville........................	400	8 853	282.1	76.6	50	884	22.4	6.6	502	5 883	457.4	193.9
Madison...........................	56	1 432	39.1	11.3	6	58	0.9	0.3	39	548	28.3	11.3
Mobile.............................	482	10 102	301.6	84.8	51	849	37.8	7.2	490	9 662	697.9	328.5
Montgomery.....................	411	9 983	277.3	76.5	35	526	19.4	4.8	534	8 898	637.4	262.1
Phenix City......................	60	882	30.4	7.9	3	0	0.0	0.0	36	691	33.7	11.0
Prichard...........................	26	D	D	D	NA	NA	NA	NA	13	320	13.6	6.1
Tuscaloosa.......................	252	6 355	171.6	47.4	20	204	4.9	1.7	203	1 920	157.6	84.6
ALASKA	1 763	20 587	1 065.5	301.5	320	3 055	168.3	34.9	1 143	8 156	758.1	309.4
Anchorage........................	640	11 364	574.0	165.8	101	1 455	81.2	16.2	599	5 053	508.6	203.8
Fairbanks.........................	121	1 989	86.7	23.4	26	312	17.4	2.3	99	768	79.0	39.9
Juneau.............................	94	1 117	57.7	16.1	21	232	14.4	3.0	81	437	40.1	16.6
ARIZONA	9 089	184 323	6 633.0	1 823.2	1 071	24 416	2 033.3	475.1	9 155	97 091	6 687.9	2 893.3
Apache Junction	48	809	20.6	5.5	4	53	2.1	0.8	24	600	30.0	14.3
Avondale	18	179	6.4	1.6	4	0	0.0	0.0	14	223	10.4	4.6
Bullhead City....................	NA	NA	NA	NA	NA	NA	NA	NA	NA	NA	NA	NA
Casa Grande....................	68	1 240	40.8	9.4	5	36	2.6	0.3	73	584	42.9	18.1
Chandler..........................	207	3 846	130.2	35.9	25	0	0.0	0.0	235	2 420	148.7	69.4
Flagstaff..........................	268	5 144	179.7	47.0	24	687	19.7	6.2	205	1 485	98.8	42.9
Gilbert.............................	44	783	24.3	6.3	14	286	14.6	3.5	78	1 255	71.6	31.4
Glendale..........................	293	6 042	187.0	51.1	21	492	24.4	5.5	373	4 208	288.3	124.4
Lake Havasu City...............	117	1 911	54.7	15.8	14	130	8.2	2.1	96	797	51.9	22.3
Mesa...............................	577	12 355	411.4	108.9	59	975	45.4	11.4	799	9 068	585.8	248.8
Oro Valley town	NA	NA	NA	NA	NA	NA	NA	NA	NA	NA	NA	NA
Peoria.............................	74	1 128	35.4	10.0	8	102	6.0	1.5	106	1 791	112.5	50.6
Phoenix...........................	2 223	50 269	2 008.7	555.1	255	6 004	462.3	158.4	2 677	30 034	2 243.6	994.8
Prescott...........................	140	2 037	64.1	17.3	12	117	9.0	2.0	175	1 480	86.6	32.9
Scottsdale........................	563	18 396	723.5	211.8	113	3 408	276.0	58.8	773	7 095	525.0	226.4
Sierra Vista......................	77	1 455	38.4	10.1	6	78	1.8	0.5	77	946	59.6	22.7
Surprise city	NA	NA	NA	NA	NA	NA	NA	NA	NA	NA	NA	NA
Tempe.............................	514	10 694	345.4	95.9	60	1 069	126.1	57.1	369	3 613	262.3	104.7
Tucson............................	1 151	23 782	704.4	199.1	116	2 174	109.3	25.6	1 196	14 955	1 045.8	457.0
Yuma..............................	174	3 274	97.4	24.5	20	0	0.0	0.0	195	2 274	140.2	55.0
ARKANSAS......................	4 663	73 397	2 179.7	589.9	594	5 343	228.7	56.8	4 571	59 960	3 655.1	1 609.7
Conway	91	2 125	61.0	16.8	13	0	0.0	0.0	122	1 231	72.1	33.2
Fayetteville.......................	222	3 881	110.7	31.4	23	227	8.0	2.1	167	1 690	121.0	60.1
Fort Smith	239	4 463	133.1	36.6	19	0	0.0	0.0	263	4 345	326.9	147.4
Hot Springs	NA	NA	NA	NA	NA	NA	NA	NA	NA	NA	NA	NA
Jacksonville......................	52	893	27.3	6.9	6	68	1.5	0.7	44	614	28.3	14.5
Jonesboro	118	D	D	D	29	181	8.2	2.2	198	3 087	237.9	112.4
Little Rock........................	490	10 389	329.0	95.8	55	640	28.6	8.3	704	9 469	777.5	361.7
North Little Rock	186	4 378	126.0	34.4	19	192	10.1	3.6	188	1 610	117.4	52.3
Pine Bluff.........................	118	D	D	D	12	0	0.0	0.0	181	1 671	108.4	47.5
Rogers.............................	78	1 369	37.8	10.2	8	168	7.0	2.6	95	1 159	63.6	33.6
Springdale........................	124	2 099	66.2	17.9	14	90	3.2	0.7	105	1 120	67.0	29.6
Texarkana	71	1 290	44.2	11.3	5	0	0.0	0.0	32	0	0.0	0.0
West Memphis	65	1 307	45.6	11.7	9	0	0.0	0.0	55	660	38.1	15.0
CALIFORNIA......................	62 532	1 052 715	42 261.1	11 437.2	12 015	182 004	15 913.8	6 296.6	69 857	664 539	51 968.0	20 619.3
Alameda...........................	165	1 908	66.9	17.9	24	583	95.8	53.9	159	1 631	84.6	36.0
Alhambra..........................	172	2 627	91.0	24.2	15	103	4.8	1.4	197	2 031	133.4	49.7
Anaheim...........................	689	18 054	818.6	222.9	50	0	0.0	0.0	730	8 305	726.8	264.4
Antioch............................	109	1 501	54.1	13.5	19	191	6.7	1.7	136	1 297	102.8	40.3
Apple Valley	41	612	17.2	4.2	1	0	0.0	0.0	142	750	123.3	49.6
Arcadia............................	134	2 232	84.4	21.0	45	2 114	105.6	35.4	244	1 806	140.2	62.3
Atascadero	46	616	18.5	4.9	5	81	1.9	0.5	71	315	20.1	6.5

1. Firms subject to federal tax.

Items 92—103

City	Other services,[1] 1997				Selected federal funds, 2002–2003 (mil dol)								
					Procurement contracts		Grants						
	Number of establishments	Number of employees	Receipts (mil dol)	Annual payroll (mil dol)	Defense	Other	Total[2]	Medicaid and other health related	Nutrition and family welfare	Energy and environment	Education	Housing and community development	Direct payments for individuals for educational assistance
	104	105	106	107	108	109	110	111	112	113	114	115	116
UNITED STATES..............	420 950	2 493 574	163 033.3	48 452.6	200 182.8	125 964.9	435 095.3	208 825.0	61 370.6	5 638.4	36 926.8	31 457.3	14 937.6
ALABAMA	6 329	37 061	2 241.7	659.3	5 510.4	1 557.0	6 649.1	3 251.9	769.6	86.5	596.5	362.7	270.9
Auburn.........................	53	326	16.0	4.9	10.0	2.1	55.4	0.0	5.6	1.7	3.2	3.0	10.0
Bessemer......................	65	406	28.7	8.4	1.2	0.2	6.5	0.1	0.0	0.0	0.3	5.5	1.7
Birmingham..................	456	4 311	265.4	85.5	20.1	152.4	490.4	325.9	17.5	24.9	10.6	64.3	27.5
Decatur........................	115	1 054	51.5	18.1	-12.3	0.9	16.4	0.0	6.9	0.5	0.9	7.6	0.0
Dothan.........................	160	921	50.2	14.9	17.9	2.9	12.6	0.0	4.6	0.0	1.6	5.2	5.4
Florence	101	673	29.7	10.1	0.2	1.0	10.9	0.0	1.1	0.0	0.0	9.0	5.8
Gadsden.......................	79	379	22.4	6.0	0.3	7.2	15.7	3.2	2.1	0.0	2.8	5.5	5.9
Homewood	90	766	55.4	17.3	0.0	1.0	0.2	0.0	0.0	0.0	0.0	0.0	0.0
Hoover.........................	71	512	23.7	8.5	0.0	0.0	0.7	0.0	0.0	0.0	0.0	0.3	0.0
Huntsville	358	2 234	120.9	41.1	3 897.6	231.9	81.4	6.2	3.1	1.4	5.2	13.2	8.3
Madison	31	170	7.9	2.7	12.2	2.1	1.4	0.0	0.0	0.0	0.1	0.8	0.0
Mobile..........................	429	3 308	215.2	63.1	72.2	28.8	101.2	34.9	0.0	4.6	10.6	39.0	24.6
Montgomery	371	2 688	138.6	43.7	91.8	95.8	811.9	104.4	161.8	40.9	183.4	68.4	28.2
Phenix City	63	328	18.2	5.6	1.0	0.0	5.7	0.0	1.3	0.0	0.6	3.7	3.4
Prichard.......................	35	183	7.9	2.4	0.1	0.1	15.7	0.0	8.5	0.0	0.0	7.0	0.0
Tuscaloosa	182	1 234	64.9	20.7	41.4	44.5	60.9	10.0	5.7	5.1	8.4	12.6	25.3
ALASKA	852	4 364	331.0	93.4	1 236.7	443.4	3 022.3	1 103.1	241.7	107.0	307.4	127.3	12.6
Anchorage	393	2 576	185.8	54.8	371.2	170.7	349.1	184.1	34.6	6.3	22.6	41.4	7.4
Fairbanks	83	459	33.5	9.9	23.9	27.2	142.4	49.9	5.4	4.3	20.3	12.8	3.7
Juneau	56	240	15.8	4.5	1.4	6.6	517.3	24.7	31.0	71.3	96.8	7.3	0.8
ARIZONA	6 494	43 669	2 794.0	829.6	7 564.1	992.9	7 235.1	3 688.3	1 041.7	69.9	776.7	367.0	335.1
Apache Junction	33	120	5.2	1.5	0.0	0.0	0.1	0.0	0.0	0.0	0.0	0.1	0.0
Avondale	19	83	6.0	1.3	0.2	0.0	2.0	0.0	0.0	0.0	0.7	0.6	3.3
Bullhead City	NA	NA	NA	NA	0.0	0.9	1.7	0.0	0.0	0.0	0.0	0.4	0.0
Casa Grande	35	284	12.1	4.4	0.0	0.8	4.1	1.2	0.0	0.0	1.1	1.3	0.0
Chandler.......................	157	1 010	54.0	18.5	108.2	26.2	8.5	0.0	0.0	0.0	0.3	6.9	2.0
Flagstaff	132	726	44.1	11.7	3.5	7.3	50.2	6.0	8.8	3.6	10.9	2.2	15.4
Gilbert	68	321	20.4	8.4	42.8	19.7	1.0	0.0	0.0	0.0	0.2	0.4	16.4
Glendale.......................	271	1 442	93.0	25.3	3.8	20.4	15.4	0.0	0.0	0.0	1.2	13.7	12.3
Lake Havasu City...........	72	473	32.5	9.4	0.1	0.8	0.8	0.0	0.0	0.0	0.1	0.6	0.1
Mesa............................	548	3 686	220.9	71.2	1 317.4	62.5	35.9	0.7	0.5	0.0	1.4	19.0	12.3
Oro Valley town	NA	NA	NA	NA	0.0	0.2	0.6	0.0	0.0	0.0	0.0	0.0	0.0
Peoria	77	454	24.8	7.6	2.8	1.6	2.4	0.0	0.0	0.0	0.2	2.0	0.0
Phoenix	1 836	15 938	1 141.9	321.2	1 548.9	120.6	1 060.0	130.8	234.7	40.2	219.4	109.1	135.2
Prescott	104	548	27.5	8.2	2.7	19.2	4.5	1.5	0.0	0.1	1.6	0.6	4.0
Scottsdale	410	2 733	159.9	52.2	369.5	114.8	22.0	5.0	1.3	2.3	1.3	10.5	10.1
Sierra Vista	40	207	8.6	2.7	1.6	1.9	4.0	0.0	0.0	0.0	1.1	2.0	0.1
Surprise city	NA	NA	NA	NA	0.0	0.0	4.8	3.9	0.0	0.0	0.2	0.2	0.0
Tempe..........................	324	2 511	184.1	57.9	726.5	14.8	99.8	26.1	0.0	1.8	17.4	7.5	40.5
Tucson	852	5 858	340.0	107.1	2 694.9	85.8	365.8	143.1	18.0	8.0	25.1	59.4	58.1
Yuma	114	649	32.8	9.8	54.0	10.4	26.0	0.4	7.9	0.1	3.0	7.8	6.1
ARKANSAS....................	3 553	18 809	1 113.9	310.5	577.7	286.4	4 540.9	2 171.5	507.2	25.5	373.7	217.2	165.1
Conway.........................	69	484	25.5	7.5	1.0	0.3	73.5	0.8	5.2	0.0	1.0	1.9	10.9
Fayetteville	107	774	33.5	11.1	1.0	10.2	54.1	4.0	3.4	1.2	4.7	5.4	11.3
Fort Smith	171	1 225	68.8	19.8	9.0	2.1	14.0	0.0	0.1	0.0	0.4	10.6	6.8
Hot Springs	NA	NA	NA	NA	0.5	4.5	8.6	0.0	1.2	0.0	0.0	6.7	0.0
Jacksonville	42	162	8.1	2.4	5.0	0.0	6.2	0.0	0.0	0.0	0.0	5.5	0.2
Jonesboro	103	561	34.7	9.1	0.1	2.1	19.1	0.0	7.7	0.0	1.6	8.1	18.3
Little Rock	428	2 983	183.5	52.5	91.6	82.7	618.9	119.0	116.3	23.7	128.6	57.1	21.0
North Little Rock	149	960	60.0	18.1	15.4	11.4	13.4	0.9	0.0	0.0	0.0	11.7	9.2
Pine Bluff	101	728	39.1	12.3	14.5	3.7	32.9	4.5	2.7	0.0	4.7	11.5	11.8
Rogers	65	370	18.6	5.7	1.7	1.0	7.7	0.0	2.8	0.0	0.4	1.3	0.0
Springdale	97	573	32.1	10.1	19.2	0.8	3.3	0.0	0.0	0.0	0.7	2.4	0.5
Texarkana	37	290	13.6	4.4	1.7	0.0	11.1	0.0	2.2	0.0	0.0	7.3	0.0
West Memphis	52	391	23.0	6.6	0.2	0.2	9.3	3.0	0.0	0.0	1.6	4.2	2.2
CALIFORNIA...................	44 642	282 762	20 521.5	5 852.2	26 078.5	10 971.0	51 328.8	23 533.6	10 635.1	536.5	4 555.6	4 037.7	1 612.2
Alameda........................	93	479	33.1	9.4	10.3	44.9	20.0	0.8	1.2	0.6	0.1	15.4	3.1
Alhambra......................	100	497	37.5	11.1	0.0	0.4	8.3	5.3	0.0	0.0	0.0	3.0	0.5
Anaheim	473	3 487	305.4	77.4	502.0	10.0	42.4	0.0	0.0	1.3	1.8	38.3	5.0
Antioch	79	452	32.4	9.7	3.3	0.5	4.4	0.0	0.0	0.0	0.6	3.7	1.9
Apple Valley	21	123	6.9	1.5	0.2	2.1	0.9	0.0	0.0	0.1	0.2	0.6	0.0
Arcadia	92	303	18.7	4.8	6.6	2.7	45.2	40.3	0.0	1.9	0.0	1.8	0.0
Atascadero	41	180	12.7	2.9	0.0	0.0	0.3	0.0	0.0	0.0	0.0	0.1	0.0

1. Firms subject to federal tax.   2. Includes program categories not shown separately. State totals include additional categories not allocated by city.

City	City government finances, 2002								
	General revenue						General expenditure		
	Intergovernmental			Taxes				Per capita[1] (dollars)	
					Per capita[1] (dollars)				
	Total (mil dol)	Total (mil dol)	Percent from state government	Total (mil dol)	Total	Property	Sales and gross receipts	Total (mil dol)	Total	Capital outlays
	117	118	119	120	121	122	123	124	125	126
UNITED STATES..............	X	X	X	X	X	X	X	X	X	X
ALABAMA	X	X	X	X	X	X	X	X	X	X
Auburn........................	44.7	1.8	77.1	31.2	688	164	306	39.6	871	112
Bessemer....................	37.2	5.0	50.0	25.4	864	154	502	37.5	1 276	118
Birmingham	383.8	38.7	48.4	260.7	1 089	176	434	466.1	1 947	200
Decatur.......................	185.4	12.0	61.1	26.9	498	45	362	183.4	3 400	446
Dothan........................	56.1	2.3	71.8	39.6	672	46	593	85.6	1 450	325
Florence	NA	NA	NA	NA	NA	NA	NA	NA	NA	NA
Gadsden......................	51.7	5.0	48.8	34.8	917	74	437	47.9	1 262	87
Homewood	36.0	1.5	20.1	31.5	1 269	219	907	34.2	1 381	294
Hoover........................	72.0	3.6	55.3	60.2	936	98	693	69.5	1 081	278
Huntsville....................	220.5	31.9	74.8	128.1	788	104	562	206.6	1 271	239
Madison	22.4	1.3	48.1	15.3	473	94	321	23.7	734	157
Mobile........................	274.8	14.6	86.3	170.4	875	55	684	273.9	1 405	306
Montgomery	155.0	16.2	45.7	113.8	565	87	345	154.7	768	64
Phenix City	NA	NA	NA	NA	NA	NA	NA	NA	NA	NA
Prichard......................	NA	NA	NA	NA	NA	NA	NA	NA	NA	NA
Tuscaloosa	85.2	16.5	20.9	48.3	610	95	346	77.5	980	221
ALASKA	X	X	X	X	X	X	X	X	X	X
Anchorage...................	858.5	396.4	92.7	321.8	1 196	1 070	92	1 042.4	3 875	1 377
Fairbanks	21.9	6.4	61.5	11.8	384	244	121	33.2	1 079	418
Juneau	166.5	36.0	88.6	64.1	2 086	869	995	151.8	4 937	509
ARIZONA	X	X	X	X	X	X	X	X	X	X
Apache Junction	23.1	11.4	100.0	9.9	291	5	235	26.1	768	285
Avondale.....................	43.5	7.9	87.5	24.1	495	45	265	31.2	639	73
Bullhead City................	36.8	12.9	100.0	9.0	255	1	222	33.1	935	221
Casa Grande................	33.7	9.8	96.4	15.2	530	91	382	31.8	1 107	176
Chandler.....................	237.4	91.7	61.6	88.9	440	76	295	222.4	1 101	320
Flagstaff.....................	92.5	34.7	64.3	33.0	598	155	407	89.6	1 624	433
Gilbert........................	130.6	29.0	95.6	70.5	522	94	226	120.8	895	441
Glendale......................	222.1	67.8	82.6	86.9	377	100	236	236.7	1 026	208
Lake Havasu City..........	49.8	17.7	95.7	24.4	525	141	328	46.4	999	311
Mesa.........................	385.5	145.4	73.7	121.4	284	0	243	480.4	1 126	308
Oro Valley town	26.2	11.8	82.5	9.3	276	36	198	25.9	770	250
Peoria........................	139.6	32.4	85.9	54.8	444	111	285	135.9	1 103	202
Phoenix	2 125.1	749.2	55.0	750.6	547	138	373	1 981.8	1 445	259
Prescott......................	65.5	15.6	85.9	26.3	725	132	557	56.3	1 551	608
Scottsdale	354.6	63.7	85.8	189.3	877	212	584	320.3	1 485	357
Sierra Vista	31.8	13.5	97.6	10.4	267	0	250	38.4	984	286
Surprise city	72.8	6.1	100.0	34.0	762	58	518	89.6	2 006	1 057
Tempe	241.2	60.0	68.4	120.0	752	160	576	223.4	1 401	250
Tucson	598.0	241.3	60.1	244.6	486	86	366	543.2	1 080	125
Yuma	76.9	25.3	94.0	36.3	451	95	329	77.6	965	248
ARKANSAS...................	X	X	X	X	X	X	X	X	X	X
Conway	45.2	5.9	54.1	15.3	334	29	296	38.6	840	109
Fayetteville	72.5	15.6	36.3	34.4	567	25	529	60.7	999	240
Fort Smith...................	99.8	26.4	48.8	43.8	537	102	418	86.9	1 066	214
Hot Springs	56.8	12.3	61.4	25.0	688	2	668	52.2	1 436	348
Jacksonville.................	114.9	8.1	31.1	10.9	359	0	355	93.6	3 082	153
Jonesboro	64.2	15.3	35.1	15.1	266	52	196	57.6	1 012	233
Little Rock	239.6	67.1	48.5	71.9	391	131	228	240.5	1 307	151
North Little Rock	64.2	19.7	22.8	22.1	368	82	268	71.3	1 188	256
Pine Bluff....................	42.2	14.1	39.5	14.7	272	55	200	42.1	778	60
Rogers........................	36.4	7.3	37.8	14.1	340	47	274	29.1	700	102
Springdale	38.6	11.8	42.8	14.6	286	52	219	39.2	769	220
Texarkana	25.8	7.1	43.3	9.2	326	86	235	25.1	886	201
West Memphis	23.9	6.0	49.3	9.7	344	20	290	22.2	793	21
CALIFORNIA..................	X	X	X	X	X	X	X	X	X	X
Alameda	99.1	13.6	79.7	49.8	683	336	269	113.1	1 551	394
Alhambra	78.9	16.5	68.8	33.5	382	132	217	75.7	863	278
Anaheim	437.0	93.9	40.4	181.4	545	150	368	430.1	1 293	219
Antioch	60.5	10.5	88.4	27.1	271	110	122	54.0	541	113
Apple Valley	26.7	5.5	85.1	9.8	168	49	77	27.1	467	111
Arcadia	45.6	6.4	72.5	27.4	500	180	279	42.7	777	204
Atascadero	19.0	3.6	99.9	9.7	361	134	177	14.9	555	165

1. Based on population estimated as of July 1 of the year shown.

City	City government finances, 2002 (cont'd)									
	General expenditure									
	Percent of total for—									
	Public welfare	Highways	Parking facilities	Education	Health and hospitals	Police protection	Sewerage and sanitation	Parks and recreation	Housing and community development	Interest on debt
	127	128	129	130	131	132	133	134	135	136
UNITED STATES..............	X	X	X	X	X	X	X	X	X	X
ALABAMA	X	X	X	X	X	X	X	X	X	X
Auburn...............	0.4	12.3	0.0	10.6	1.9	11.3	17.2	8.0	0.9	12.1
Bessemer...............	2.6	4.5	0.0	2.6	0.0	19.7	6.8	2.3	4.8	3.9
Birmingham...............	0.0	2.7	1.9	2.4	0.7	15.3	8.7	6.1	7.2	8.0
Decatur...............	0.0	4.0	0.0	0.0	55.7	4.6	9.4	8.0	1.3	7.4
Dothan...............	0.2	7.0	0.0	16.0	0.8	12.1	18.6	8.2	0.0	4.2
Florence...............	NA	NA	NA	NA	NA	NA	NA	NA	NA	NA
Gadsden...............	0.0	7.1	0.0	1.4	0.4	17.9	11.9	8.7	3.8	6.1
Homewood...............	0.0	2.0	0.0	8.7	0.4	19.5	10.0	5.5	0.0	0.9
Hoover...............	0.0	6.7	0.0	0.0	0.5	17.9	8.8	11.4	0.6	6.9
Huntsville...............	0.2	3.8	1.1	0.0	1.6	13.2	13.0	11.1	5.2	13.6
Madison...............	0.0	28.6	0.0	0.0	0.0	15.1	6.3	7.6	0.0	9.7
Mobile...............	0.0	9.1	0.0	0.0	0.2	13.7	13.7	7.7	0.0	12.2
Montgomery...............	0.2	11.8	0.4	5.3	1.4	18.5	9.5	14.6	2.1	2.0
Phenix City...............	NA	NA	NA	NA	NA	NA	NA	NA	NA	NA
Prichard...............	NA	NA	NA	NA	NA	NA	NA	NA	NA	NA
Tuscaloosa...............	0.0	11.1	1.6	0.0	0.3	18.2	16.3	4.8	1.3	1.0
ALASKA	X	X	X	X	X	X	X	X	X	X
Anchorage...............	0.0	18.7	0.3	45.1	3.1	13.2	2.7	5.3	0.0	3.1
Fairbanks...............	0.0	11.9	0.0	0.0	0.2	37.1	0.0	0.0	0.0	1.2
Juneau...............	0.0	5.6	0.1	34.6	26.7	5.2	3.1	6.0	1.5	1.1
ARIZONA	X	X	X	X	X	X	X	X	X	X
Apache Junction	0.0	22.9	0.0	0.0	0.0	18.0	0.0	6.5	0.0	1.3
Avondale...............	2.5	13.4	0.0	0.0	0.0	14.9	17.2	7.0	0.0	6.7
Bullhead City...............	0.0	7.7	0.0	0.0	0.0	27.1	13.1	4.8	0.0	9.0
Casa Grande...............	0.0	12.3	0.0	0.0	0.6	22.7	14.9	15.3	3.8	3.0
Chandler...............	0.0	12.6	0.0	0.0	0.0	18.3	21.6	7.7	6.1	3.4
Flagstaff...............	0.0	17.3	0.0	0.0	0.0	10.9	14.7	6.2	1.8	5.1
Gilbert...............	0.0	10.6	0.0	0.0	0.0	12.8	18.2	12.4	0.3	5.2
Glendale...............	0.1	10.7	0.0	0.0	0.0	14.9	15.6	6.4	5.3	4.5
Lake Havasu City...............	0.0	10.5	0.0	0.0	0.3	15.0	20.8	8.2	0.1	2.3
Mesa...............	0.3	11.1	0.0	0.0	0.0	25.6	18.1	9.2	6.4	5.2
Oro Valley town...............	0.0	19.4	0.0	0.0	0.0	28.9	0.2	9.2	0.0	3.6
Peoria...............	0.0	9.4	0.0	0.4	0.0	11.3	12.0	12.0	1.3	5.2
Phoenix...............	0.0	4.4	0.1	0.9	0.0	15.2	15.2	9.6	4.9	8.9
Prescott...............	0.0	31.0	0.0	0.0	0.3	10.5	20.5	8.4	3.0	4.7
Scottsdale...............	0.0	6.1	0.0	0.0	0.0	15.4	10.5	9.5	1.8	9.1
Sierra Vista...............	0.0	17.0	0.0	0.0	0.0	13.6	20.0	14.3	0.0	5.3
Surprise city...............	0.0	7.8	0.0	0.0	0.0	7.8	6.2	53.1	0.0	4.4
Tempe...............	0.0	7.4	0.0	0.0	0.0	20.8	6.9	13.0	8.0	2.8
Tucson...............	0.0	9.2	0.0	0.0	0.0	18.6	4.8	10.0	8.5	6.0
Yuma...............	0.0	18.5	0.0	0.0	0.5	18.0	15.0	13.6	2.9	4.8
ARKANSAS......................	X	X	X	X	X	X	X	X	X	X
Conway	0.8	6.8	0.0	0.0	0.0	15.3	22.1	1.4	0.0	16.1
Fayetteville...............	0.0	10.8	1.1	0.0	0.8	11.9	22.5	5.3	1.5	4.2
Fort Smith...............	0.0	19.6	0.2	0.0	0.0	13.1	26.7	5.6	1.4	2.4
Hot Springs...............	0.0	8.9	1.4	0.0	0.7	15.4	20.5	15.2	5.4	3.3
Jacksonville...............	0.0	2.5	0.0	0.0	78.7	4.0	4.9	1.8	0.3	1.3
Jonesboro...............	0.0	16.4	0.1	0.0	0.7	8.8	12.5	5.9	0.9	34.9
Little Rock...............	0.0	8.2	0.3	0.0	3.4	17.0	13.4	5.8	1.6	8.8
North Little Rock	0.1	4.3	0.0	0.0	0.5	21.4	21.4	6.5	3.6	4.3
Pine Bluff...............	0.0	8.5	0.0	0.0	0.6	23.2	21.5	9.5	4.9	4.6
Rogers...............	0.0	8.9	0.0	0.0	0.0	18.9	15.2	11.7	0.2	9.1
Springdale...............	0.0	6.9	0.0	0.0	0.6	16.7	22.2	5.0	2.4	1.0
Texarkana...............	0.6	21.1	0.0	0.0	0.5	22.4	14.2	1.2	1.9	12.8
West Memphis	0.2	9.8	0.0	0.0	0.8	22.1	14.8	4.9	4.4	13.4
CALIFORNIA......................	X	X	X	X	X	X	X	X	X	X
Alameda...............	0.0	7.3	0.1	0.0	2.4	17.3	6.2	7.6	8.8	1.8
Alhambra...............	0.0	17.7	1.1	0.0	2.5	18.8	9.3	8.1	18.7	6.9
Anaheim...............	0.0	7.9	0.0	0.0	0.2	16.4	8.8	10.8	18.0	16.6
Antioch...............	0.0	17.7	0.0	0.0	1.2	29.4	4.6	9.2	13.3	13.6
Apple Valley...............	0.0	32.3	0.0	0.0	1.4	18.5	23.3	9.1	2.6	1.9
Arcadia...............	0.0	12.3	0.0	0.0	0.3	33.6	1.4	4.1	4.8	3.2
Atascadero...............	0.0	15.6	0.0	0.0	0.0	25.5	9.9	10.9	1.3	1.6

City	City government finances, 2002 (cont'd) Debt outstanding — Total (mil dol)	Per capita[1] (dollars)	Percent utility	City government employment, 2002	Climate[2] — Average daily temperature (degrees Fahrenheit) — Mean — January	July	Limits — January[3]	July[4]	Annual precipitation (inches)	Heating degree days	Cooling degree days
	137	138	139	140	141	142	143	144	145	146	147
UNITED STATES..............	X	X	X	X	X	X	X	X	X	X	X
ALABAMA	X	X	X	X	X	X	X	X	X	X	X
Auburn.............................	121.7	2 682	16.5	489	43.1	79.2	32.7	89.3	56.47	2 612	1 865
Bessemer.........................	49.2	1 675	55.0	446	41.7	79.7	30.5	91.4	59.11	2 893	1 777
Birmingham	1 011.0	4 223	26.6	4 629	41.5	79.8	31.3	89.9	54.58	2 918	1 797
Decatur............................	270.9	5 022	11.2	1 778	38.8	79.0	29.2	89.0	57.18	3 323	1 651
Dothan.............................	80.2	1 359	9.3	1 020	48.2	80.0	37.2	91.0	55.61	1 903	2 204
Florence	NA	NA	NA	853	38.7	79.7	29.0	90.3	53.85	3 325	1 736
Gadsden..........................	52.9	1 392	14.0	650	39.1	78.9	28.7	89.5	55.31	3 317	1 610
Homewood	7.0	282	0.0	352	NA	NA	NA	NA	NA	NA	NA
Hoover.............................	97.7	1 520	0.0	590	41.5	79.8	31.3	89.9	54.58	2 918	1 797
Huntsville........................	504.7	3 105	12.1	2 564	38.8	79.0	29.2	89.0	57.18	3 323	1 651
Madison	90.0	2 783	49.1	286	NA	NA	NA	NA	NA	NA	NA
Mobile	661.5	3 395	5.0	2 953	49.9	82.3	40.0	91.3	63.96	1 702	2 627
Montgomery	145.5	723	48.4	2 901	46.1	81.3	35.8	91.1	53.43	2 224	2 212
Phenix City......................	NA	NA	NA	328	45.7	81.9	35.2	91.8	51.00	2 261	2 284
Prichard...........................	NA	NA	NA	307	49.9	82.3	40.0	91.3	63.96	1 702	2 627
Tuscaloosa	126.2	1 594	73.6	1 064	42.8	81.1	32.4	91.1	54.90	2 661	2 070
ALASKA	X	X	X	X	X	X	X	X	X	X	X
Anchorage	1 370.9	5 097	27.8	9 255	14.9	58.4	8.4	65.2	15.91	10 570	0
Fairbanks	7.2	234	0.0	184	10.1	62.5	18.5	72.3	10.87	13 940	84
Juneau	47.5	1 545	5.7	1 905	24.2	56.0	19.0	63.9	54.31	8 897	0
ARIZONA	X	X	X	X	X	X	X	X	X	X	X
Apache Junction	15.2	448	50.8	228	NA	NA	NA	NA	NA	NA	NA
Avondale..........................	40.9	840	5.0	278	NA	NA	NA	NA	NA	NA	NA
Bullhead City	57.4	1 620	0.0	325	NA	NA	NA	NA	NA	NA	NA
Casa Grande....................	17.5	609	0.0	296	NA	NA	NA	NA	NA	NA	NA
Chandler	290.0	1 436	49.4	1 464	51.9	90.2	38.1	104.8	9.04	1 490	3 476
Flagstaff	103.7	1 879	23.8	731	28.7	66.3	15.2	81.9	22.80	7 131	145
Gilbert..............................	181.1	1 341	0.0	692	51.9	90.2	38.1	104.8	9.04	1 490	3 476
Glendale..........................	225.0	976	24.8	1 726	53.6	93.5	41.2	105.9	7.66	1 350	4 162
Lake Havasu City..............	23.9	515	15.1	502	NA	NA	NA	NA	NA	NA	NA
Mesa...............................	776.2	1 819	44.5	3 801	52.9	91.2	39.5	105.5	8.50	1 366	3 635
Oro Valley town	51.0	1 515	68.1	251	NA	NA	NA	NA	NA	NA	NA
Peoria..............................	206.5	1 676	45.9	906	53.6	93.5	41.2	105.9	7.66	1 350	4 162
Phoenix	4 387.4	3 198	4.1	13 421	53.6	93.5	41.2	105.9	7.66	1 350	4 162
Prescott...........................	46.8	1 290	9.2	477	36.2	73.1	21.9	88.1	19.63	4 995	631
Scottsdale	625.2	2 898	16.6	2 030	53.6	93.5	41.2	105.9	7.66	1 350	4 162
Sierra Vista	39.3	1 008	0.0	373	45.1	78.5	26.8	93.5	18.63	2 928	1 441
Surprise city	63.3	1 418	0.0	141	NA	NA	NA	NA	NA	NA	NA
Tempe	236.6	1 484	33.2	1 926	52.6	90.6	37.8	106.7	8.88	1 464	3 530
Tucson	1 107.2	2 200	30.3	6 018	51.3	86.6	38.6	99.4	12.00	1 678	2 954
Yuma	69.9	870	16.3	876	56.5	93.7	44.2	106.6	3.17	927	4 305
ARKANSAS......................	X	X	X	X	X	X	X	X	X	X	X
Conway	124.1	2 702	34.4	384	39.0	81.4	27.9	93.1	49.36	3 147	1 917
Fayetteville	57.8	951	35.6	615	34.0	78.7	22.9	89.3	44.04	4 141	1 401
Fort Smith	166.7	2 045	26.5	825	36.9	81.5	25.5	93.0	40.90	3 478	1 894
Hot Springs	75.3	2 071	17.8	494	39.3	81.7	28.5	93.3	56.52	3 181	1 958
Jacksonville.....................	22.2	730	5.1	711	38.5	81.4	29.4	91.5	49.25	3 228	1 916
Jonesboro........................	340.9	5 992	16.0	568	36.6	81.7	27.9	92.3	47.19	3 504	1 940
Little Rock	335.3	1 822	0.0	2 607	39.1	81.9	29.1	92.4	50.86	3 155	2 005
North Little Rock	172.2	2 869	75.0	916	38.5	81.4	29.4	91.5	49.25	3 228	1 916
Pine Bluff........................	26.5	490	0.0	413	40.0	81.8	29.6	92.4	52.36	3 016	2 050
Rogers.............................	39.8	959	8.1	360	NA	NA	NA	NA	NA	NA	NA
Springdale	20.1	394	74.8	476	34.0	78.7	22.9	89.3	44.04	4 141	1 401
Texarkana	65.1	2 302	33.5	202	NA	NA	NA	NA	NA	NA	NA
West Memphis	56.4	2 014	25.0	375	37.0	81.1	27.4	90.9	50.77	3 438	1 871
CALIFORNIA....................	X	X	X	X	X	X	X	X	X	X	X
Alameda..........................	114.2	1 567	34.2	847	49.9	62.1	43.3	70.0	24.30	2 902	115
Alhambra	91.6	1 045	0.8	461	55.7	75.2	41.7	89.2	17.90	1 433	1 427
Anaheim..........................	1 609.2	4 838	28.1	2 794	57.4	72.6	45.6	82.6	12.27	1 238	1 175
Antioch............................	153.6	1 538	8.5	351	44.5	73.8	35.9	90.8	12.80	2 837	1 066
Apple Valley	9.0	156	0.0	75	44.2	79.3	30.0	97.4	5.51	3 127	1 525
Arcadia............................	39.4	718	0.0	337	55.7	75.2	41.7	89.2	17.90	1 433	1 427
Atascadero	3.2	121	0.0	129	NA	NA	NA	NA	NA	NA	NA

1. Based on the population estimated as of July 1 of the year shown. 2. Represents normal values based on the 30-year period, 1961–1990. 3. Average daily minimum. 4. Average daily maximum.

Table D. Cities — Land Area and Population

STATE Place code	City	Land area,[1] 2000 (sq km)	Population, 2003			Population characteristics, 2000 Percent						
			Total persons	Rank	Per square kilometer	Race (alone or in combination)					Hispanic or Latino[2]	Non-Hispanic White
						White	Black	Am. Indian, Alaska Native	Asian and Pacific Islander	Other race		
		1	2	3	4	5	6	7	8	9	10	11
	CALIFORNIA—Cont'd											
06 03386	Azusa	23.1	46 962	680	2 033.0	57.2	4.4	2.1	7.7	34.7	63.8	24.2
06 03526	Bakersfield	292.9	271 035	66	925.3	65.5	10.0	2.5	5.6	21.1	32.5	51.1
06 03666	Baldwin Park	17.3	78 747	350	4 551.8	43.9	1.9	2.0	12.6	44.2	78.7	7.3
06 04870	Bell	6.4	37 694	849	5 889.7	52.9	1.5	1.6	1.5	47.4	90.9	5.8
06 04982	Bellflower	15.7	74 863	374	4 768.3	50.1	14.1	1.7	11.9	27.6	43.2	30.7
06 04996	Bell Gardens	6.4	45 491	712	7 108.0	52.3	1.1	2.0	1.0	48.2	93.4	4.7
06 05108	Belmont	11.7	24 499	1 228	2 093.9	78.8	2.0	0.8	18.7	4.3	8.3	70.4
06 05290	Benicia	33.4	26 941	1 177	806.6	83.5	5.8	2.0	10.4	4.2	9.0	73.9
06 06000	Berkeley	27.1	102 049	236	3 765.6	63.7	15.3	1.6	19.1	6.5	9.7	55.2
06 06308	Beverly Hills	14.7	34 941	925	2 376.9	89.3	2.1	0.4	8.8	4.1	4.6	82.0
06 08100	Brea	27.3	37 889	843	1 387.9	80.7	1.6	1.2	10.7	9.9	20.3	66.5
06 08786	Buena Park	27.4	78 934	349	2 880.8	57.4	4.5	1.8	23.6	18.5	33.5	38.2
06 08954	Burbank	44.9	103 359	231	2 302.0	77.7	2.6	1.2	10.8	14.0	24.9	59.4
06 09066	Burlingame	11.2	27 387	1 149	2 445.3	80.3	1.4	0.7	16.2	5.5	10.6	71.3
06 09710	Calexico	16.1	32 517	989	2 019.7	49.5	0.6	0.9	2.4	50.2	95.3	2.4
06 10046	Camarillo	49.0	60 445	490	1 233.6	83.8	1.9	1.2	9.2	7.7	15.5	72.8
06 10345	Campbell	14.5	37 149	867	2 562.0	77.0	3.0	1.4	16.6	6.9	13.3	66.0
06 11194	Carlsbad	97.0	87 372	303	900.7	89.2	1.3	1.1	5.9	5.7	11.7	80.5
06 11530	Carson	48.8	93 747	272	1 921.0	29.0	26.6	1.3	28.0	20.6	34.9	12.0
06 12048	Cathedral City	49.7	48 528	656	976.4	68.9	3.3	1.6	4.7	25.9	50.0	42.0
06 12524	Ceres	18.0	37 828	846	2 101.6	69.0	3.3	2.8	7.0	23.7	37.9	50.2
06 12552	Cerritos	22.3	52 800	600	2 367.7	29.5	7.2	0.8	61.4	5.1	10.4	21.4
06 13014	Chico	71.9	67 509	422	938.9	86.1	2.8	2.6	5.6	7.5	12.3	77.2
06 13210	Chino	54.5	71 928	391	1 319.8	59.8	8.3	1.7	6.4	28.9	47.4	37.6
06 13392	Chula Vista	126.6	199 060	95	1 572.4	59.9	5.4	1.4	14.1	25.4	49.6	31.7
06 13756	Claremont	34.0	34 964	924	1 028.4	77.1	5.8	1.3	13.6	6.7	15.4	65.0
06 14218	Clovis	44.3	78 558	351	1 773.3	79.8	2.4	2.8	8.0	11.8	20.3	67.5
06 14890	Colton	39.1	50 602	626	1 294.2	46.7	12.0	2.0	6.8	37.9	60.7	20.8
06 15044	Compton	26.2	95 835	262	3 657.8	19.4	41.2	1.2	1.7	40.3	56.8	1.0
06 16000	Concord	78.1	124 977	181	1 600.2	75.8	3.8	1.8	12.6	12.5	21.8	60.9
06 16350	Corona	91.0	142 454	159	1 565.4	66.5	7.2	1.6	9.6	20.7	35.7	47.0
06 16532	Costa Mesa	40.5	109 563	213	2 705.3	73.2	1.8	1.4	8.9	19.1	31.8	56.8
06 16742	Covina	18.0	48 160	664	2 675.6	66.2	5.6	1.7	11.7	20.0	40.3	42.3
06 17568	Culver City	13.2	39 788	810	3 014.2	63.8	13.6	1.8	14.5	12.8	23.7	48.1
06 17610	Cupertino	28.3	50 479	628	1 783.7	52.8	1.0	0.6	46.6	2.2	4.0	47.8
06 17750	Cypress	17.1	47 215	676	2 761.1	69.3	3.4	1.4	23.5	7.1	15.7	57.1
06 17918	Daly City	19.6	100 819	243	5 143.8	30.2	5.4	1.0	55.2	14.8	22.3	17.7
06 17946	Dana Point	17.2	35 745	898	2 078.2	89.8	1.2	1.2	3.8	7.0	15.5	78.8
06 17988	Danville	46.9	42 547	753	907.2	88.6	1.1	0.6	10.7	1.8	4.7	83.0
06 18100	Davis	27.1	64 348	448	2 374.5	74.2	3.1	1.5	20.4	6.0	9.6	65.9
06 18394	Delano	26.2	42 801	749	1 633.6	29.2	5.8	1.4	17.8	50.4	68.5	9.2
06 19192	Diamond Bar	38.2	58 160	521	1 522.5	44.1	5.3	0.9	45.3	8.9	18.5	31.0
06 19766	Downey	32.2	110 360	212	3 427.3	57.6	4.2	1.4	9.0	32.8	57.9	28.7
06 20018	Dublin	32.6	35 581	904	1 091.4	72.7	10.5	1.4	12.8	6.7	13.5	62.3
06 20956	East Palo Alto	6.6	31 915	1 005	4 835.6	30.0	24.2	1.6	11.8	37.5	58.8	6.5
06 21712	El Cajon	37.7	95 159	267	2 524.1	79.3	6.5	2.0	4.9	13.7	22.5	64.5
06 21782	El Centro	24.8	37 985	840	1 531.7	50.0	3.5	1.5	4.2	44.6	74.6	18.1
06 22230	El Monte	24.7	121 740	190	4 928.7	39.2	1.0	1.9	19.4	42.8	72.4	7.4
06 22678	Encinitas	49.5	60 340	491	1 219.0	89.3	0.9	1.0	4.5	7.4	14.8	79.0
06 22804	Escondido	94.0	136 093	166	1 447.8	72.0	2.9	2.3	5.9	22.0	38.7	51.9
06 23042	Eureka	24.5	25 808	1 209	1 053.4	86.9	2.2	7.3	5.0	3.8	7.8	78.6
06 23182	Fairfield	97.5	102 762	232	1 054.0	61.9	17.1	2.1	15.8	11.4	18.8	49.0
06 24638	Folsom	56.3	62 628	463	1 112.4	80.9	6.4	1.3	9.1	6.1	9.5	74.2
06 24680	Fontana	93.5	151 903	141	1 624.6	49.3	12.9	2.0	5.8	35.6	57.7	23.9
06 25338	Foster City	9.7	28 866	1 100	2 975.9	62.8	2.5	0.6	36.0	2.6	5.3	55.9
06 25380	Fountain Valley	23.1	55 747	554	2 413.3	67.8	1.5	1.2	28.5	5.6	10.7	58.5
06 26000	Fremont	198.6	204 525	91	1 029.8	52.4	3.8	1.3	40.8	8.0	13.5	41.4
06 27000	Fresno	270.3	451 455	36	1 670.2	54.0	9.2	2.6	13.0	26.6	39.9	37.3
06 28000	Fullerton	57.5	131 249	170	2 282.6	65.2	2.7	1.4	17.9	17.2	30.2	48.7
06 28168	Gardena	15.1	59 941	497	3 969.6	27.5	27.2	1.3	30.1	19.5	31.8	12.2
06 29000	Garden Grove	46.7	167 029	126	3 576.6	50.3	1.8	1.4	33.2	17.7	32.5	32.5
06 29504	Gilroy	41.1	43 817	732	1 066.1	63.6	2.3	2.4	6.3	31.2	53.8	38.0
06 30000	Glendale	79.4	200 499	92	2 525.2	73.1	1.6	0.7	17.9	17.0	19.7	54.2
06 30014	Glendora	49.6	50 853	619	1 025.3	83.9	1.8	1.2	7.9	9.5	21.7	67.9
06 31960	Hanford	33.9	45 368	713	1 338.3	69.2	5.6	2.3	4.3	24.6	38.7	49.9
06 32548	Hawthorne	15.7	86 173	308	5 488.7	33.0	34.4	1.4	8.9	27.8	44.3	13.0
06 33000	Hayward	114.8	141 336	161	1 231.1	48.2	12.3	1.9	25.2	20.6	34.2	29.2
06 33182	Hemet	66.4	65 044	444	979.6	83.6	3.2	2.1	2.4	12.4	23.1	70.3
06 33434	Hesperia	174.4	69 179	409	396.7	78.5	4.7	2.5	2.2	17.1	29.4	62.4
06 33588	Highland	35.3	48 516	657	1 374.4	60.5	13.3	2.4	7.9	21.5	36.6	41.7
06 34120	Hollister	17.0	36 555	881	2 150.3	63.8	1.8	2.2	4.7	33.4	55.1	38.5

1. Dry land or land partially or temporarily covered by water. 2. Hispanic or Latino persons may be of any race.

Table D. Cities — **Population and Households**

	Population characteristics, 2000 (cont'd)										Population			
	Age of population (percent)										Census counts		Percent change	
City	Under 5 years	5 to 17 years	18 to 24 years	25 to 34 years	35 to 44 years	45 to 54 years	55 to 64 years	65 to 74 years	75 years and over	Percent female	1990	2000	1990–2000	2000–2003
	12	13	14	15	16	17	18	19	20	21	22	23	24	25
CALIFORNIA—Cont'd														
Azusa	9.3	21.6	15.5	17.2	14.2	9.5	5.8	3.9	3.0	50.6	41 203	44 712	8.5	5.0
Bakersfield	8.8	23.9	10.1	14.4	15.5	12.0	6.6	4.5	4.2	51.4	176 264	247 057	40.2	9.7
Baldwin Park	9.7	25.3	11.9	16.4	14.2	10.6	5.9	3.6	2.5	50.0	69 330	75 837	9.4	3.8
Bell	10.8	24.5	12.9	19.0	13.3	9.3	4.8	3.0	2.4	49.5	34 365	36 664	6.7	2.8
Bellflower	9.5	22.3	10.3	16.8	15.2	11.0	6.4	4.3	4.1	51.3	61 815	72 878	17.9	2.7
Bell Gardens	11.4	28.0	12.9	18.2	13.3	8.1	4.1	2.4	1.6	49.4	42 315	44 054	4.1	3.3
Belmont	6.0	13.3	6.5	16.8	19.1	15.0	10.1	7.0	6.2	50.8	24 165	25 123	4.0	-2.5
Benicia	5.6	21.5	6.5	10.2	18.1	19.2	9.6	5.2	4.1	51.4	24 437	26 865	9.9	0.3
Berkeley	4.0	10.1	21.6	17.9	13.9	13.9	8.4	4.9	5.3	50.9	102 724	102 743	0.0	-0.7
Beverly Hills	3.7	16.2	6.3	14.1	15.2	15.8	10.9	8.1	9.5	54.5	31 971	33 784	5.7	3.4
Brea	6.1	19.6	8.5	13.7	16.7	14.9	9.3	6.4	4.9	51.2	32 873	35 410	7.7	7.0
Buena Park	8.1	21.4	9.7	15.8	16.6	11.9	7.3	5.5	3.8	50.4	68 784	78 282	13.8	0.8
Burbank	5.7	16.5	7.7	17.3	18.1	13.3	8.5	6.0	6.8	51.5	93 649	100 316	7.1	3.0
Burlingame	5.6	13.6	5.5	18.1	18.7	14.4	8.7	6.5	8.8	52.2	26 666	28 158	5.6	-2.7
Calexico	7.8	27.1	9.9	12.5	14.7	11.0	6.6	6.4	4.0	53.4	18 633	27 109	45.5	19.9
Camarillo	6.6	18.7	6.5	11.9	16.6	13.7	9.0	7.2	9.8	51.6	52 297	57 077	9.1	5.9
Campbell	6.5	15.0	7.6	20.4	19.9	13.5	7.4	5.0	4.7	50.4	36 088	38 138	5.7	-2.6
Carlsbad	6.4	16.9	6.2	13.4	18.5	16.0	8.6	7.1	6.9	51.1	63 292	78 247	23.6	11.7
Carson	6.9	21.5	9.9	13.5	15.0	12.7	9.8	6.6	4.1	51.7	83 995	89 730	6.8	4.5
Cathedral City	8.8	22.3	8.8	15.0	15.6	10.1	7.1	6.7	5.5	49.3	30 085	42 647	41.8	13.8
Ceres	8.6	25.7	10.1	13.7	16.3	11.2	6.3	4.7	3.4	50.8	26 413	34 609	31.0	9.3
Cerritos	4.7	19.8	8.8	10.9	14.9	17.9	13.4	6.1	3.6	51.3	53 244	51 488	-3.3	2.5
Chico	6.0	15.1	27.0	15.1	11.7	10.2	5.0	3.9	6.0	50.9	39 970	59 954	50.0	12.6
Chino	7.2	21.3	12.3	16.3	17.9	13.1	6.1	3.3	2.5	44.6	59 682	67 168	12.5	7.1
Chula Vista	7.8	20.9	9.4	15.2	16.4	11.8	7.4	6.0	5.0	51.5	135 160	173 556	28.4	14.7
Claremont	4.3	16.3	18.6	9.8	13.0	14.2	9.1	7.1	7.5	53.0	32 610	33 998	4.3	2.8
Clovis	7.6	23.1	9.2	13.2	17.2	13.5	6.9	4.7	4.6	52.0	50 323	68 468	36.1	14.7
Colton	10.0	24.9	11.9	16.7	14.9	10.0	5.2	3.7	2.7	50.7	40 213	47 662	18.3	6.2
Compton	10.4	28.1	11.5	15.0	13.7	8.8	5.6	4.2	2.7	51.0	90 454	93 493	3.4	2.5
Concord	7.1	18.2	9.0	15.5	17.3	13.9	8.3	5.7	5.0	50.6	111 308	121 780	9.4	2.6
Corona	9.8	23.6	8.9	17.3	17.8	11.1	5.7	3.2	2.6	50.5	75 943	124 966	64.6	14.0
Costa Mesa	7.1	16.1	11.2	21.5	17.5	11.5	6.5	4.6	3.9	48.8	96 357	108 724	12.8	0.8
Covina	7.4	20.7	9.5	14.7	16.4	12.6	7.8	6.0	4.9	52.1	43 332	46 837	8.1	2.8
Culver City	5.5	15.4	6.6	15.1	18.2	15.8	9.5	7.0	6.9	53.3	38 793	38 816	0.1	2.5
Cupertino	6.1	20.6	5.2	12.1	21.0	15.4	8.7	5.8	5.2	50.1	39 967	50 546	26.5	-0.1
Cypress	6.0	21.0	7.9	12.4	17.8	14.3	10.1	6.6	4.0	51.3	42 655	46 229	8.4	2.1
Daly City	6.0	16.4	10.5	16.4	15.8	13.7	9.0	6.9	5.2	50.8	92 088	103 621	12.5	-2.7
Dana Point	5.6	15.0	7.1	14.2	17.1	17.2	10.8	7.4	5.7	50.0	31 896	35 110	10.1	1.8
Danville	7.1	21.5	4.2	8.2	19.4	18.6	10.7	5.3	5.0	51.5	31 306	41 715	33.2	2.0
Davis	4.6	14.0	30.9	14.9	12.2	11.3	5.4	3.3	3.4	52.3	46 322	60 308	30.2	6.7
Delano	9.1	23.4	12.4	17.2	15.5	9.3	5.6	4.1	3.4	43.5	22 762	38 824	70.6	10.2
Diamond Bar	5.7	21.3	8.8	11.9	17.7	17.6	9.5	4.7	2.8	51.0	53 672	56 287	4.9	3.3
Downey	8.0	21.2	9.8	16.5	14.7	11.5	7.3	5.3	5.7	51.4	91 444	107 323	17.4	2.8
Dublin	5.9	15.1	9.3	21.4	22.8	14.2	6.7	3.1	1.5	47.3	23 229	29 973	29.0	18.7
East Palo Alto	10.0	25.0	13.4	18.6	13.9	8.8	5.1	3.2	1.9	48.5	23 451	29 506	25.8	8.2
El Cajon	8.2	19.7	11.2	15.5	15.8	11.3	7.0	5.6	5.8	51.2	88 918	94 869	6.7	0.3
El Centro	8.4	25.3	9.7	13.8	15.1	11.7	6.7	5.5	3.9	50.9	31 405	37 835	20.5	0.4
El Monte	10.0	24.1	12.1	17.4	14.1	9.7	5.7	4.0	3.0	49.5	106 162	115 965	9.2	5.0
Encinitas	5.9	17.2	7.2	14.7	18.6	18.1	7.8	4.9	5.5	50.2	55 406	58 014	4.7	4.0
Escondido	8.8	20.9	10.4	15.9	15.5	11.0	6.5	4.9	6.1	50.4	108 648	133 559	22.9	1.9
Eureka	5.7	16.6	11.6	13.8	15.0	15.2	8.3	6.5	7.2	50.5	27 025	26 128	-3.3	-1.2
Fairfield	8.5	21.3	11.1	14.9	16.4	12.0	6.8	5.0	3.9	50.2	78 650	96 178	22.3	6.8
Folsom	6.9	17.3	6.6	17.2	21.8	14.6	6.8	4.4	4.4	44.8	29 802	51 884	74.1	20.7
Fontana	10.3	27.5	10.3	16.3	16.0	10.1	4.6	2.7	2.0	50.4	87 535	128 929	47.3	17.8
Foster City	5.9	15.3	5.9	16.8	18.5	16.2	11.4	6.1	4.0	50.8	28 176	28 803	2.2	0.2
Fountain Valley	6.0	17.5	7.9	13.4	16.7	14.8	12.4	6.6	4.7	51.1	53 691	54 978	2.4	1.4
Fremont	7.4	18.3	7.7	17.3	19.5	13.7	7.7	4.9	3.5	49.7	173 339	203 413	17.3	0.5
Fresno	9.1	23.8	11.8	14.8	14.1	11.0	6.2	4.7	4.6	50.9	354 091	427 652	20.8	5.6
Fullerton	7.0	18.2	11.5	16.6	15.7	12.0	7.7	5.9	5.5	50.6	114 144	126 003	10.4	4.2
Gardena	7.5	18.3	8.7	16.5	15.8	12.0	8.8	7.0	5.4	51.3	51 481	57 746	12.2	3.8
Garden Grove	7.9	20.5	9.2	16.9	16.6	11.6	7.7	5.5	4.0	49.9	142 965	165 196	15.5	1.1
Gilroy	9.4	23.1	10.0	16.4	16.3	11.9	6.1	3.7	3.1	50.2	31 487	41 464	31.7	5.7
Glendale	5.7	16.7	8.4	14.9	17.3	14.1	9.0	7.2	6.7	52.3	180 038	194 973	8.3	2.8
Glendora	6.3	21.3	7.6	12.0	17.1	14.1	9.1	6.7	5.9	51.7	47 832	49 415	3.3	2.9
Hanford	8.7	22.9	9.8	14.7	14.9	11.6	7.1	5.2	5.1	51.0	30 463	41 686	36.8	8.8
Hawthorne	10.1	21.6	11.3	19.5	15.3	10.3	5.8	3.5	2.7	51.9	71 349	84 112	17.9	2.5
Hayward	7.9	18.9	10.9	17.5	15.8	11.9	6.9	5.2	4.9	50.4	114 705	140 030	22.1	0.9
Hemet	6.5	16.0	7.2	10.2	10.4	8.6	8.0	12.8	20.2	54.2	43 366	58 812	35.6	10.6
Hesperia	7.9	24.9	9.3	11.6	15.7	12.2	7.4	6.1	4.9	50.7	50 418	62 582	24.1	10.5
Highland	9.5	26.1	9.0	14.1	15.9	12.2	6.7	4.0	2.5	51.2	34 439	44 605	29.5	8.8
Hollister	10.0	24.6	9.5	16.4	17.4	10.7	5.1	3.6	2.7	49.5	19 318	34 413	78.1	6.2

	Households, 2000					Persons in group quarters, 2000				Serious crimes known to police,[2] 2002				Education, 2000			
				Percent			Institutional			Total		Rate[2]		School enrollment[4]		Attainment[5] (percent)	
City	Number	Percent change, 1990–2000	Persons per house-hold	Female family house-holder[1]	One-person	Total	Total	Persons in nursing homes	Non-institutional	Number	Rate[3]	Violent	Property	Public	Private	High school grad-uate or less	Bach-elor's degree or more
	26	27	28	29	30	31	32	33	34	35	36	37	38	39	40	41	42
CALIFORNIA—Cont'd																	
Azusa	12 549	-0.8	3.41	17.1	18.7	1 949	69	45	1 880	1 475	3 182	395	2 787	11 901	3 764	59.2	14.2
Bakersfield	83 441	33.6	2.92	15.5	21.5	3 813	2 018	1 125	1 795	11 846	4 625	418	4 207	73 221	7 934	47.5	19.3
Baldwin Park	16 961	2.1	4.44	17.5	8.1	606	278	260	328	1 908	2 427	382	2 045	23 911	1 890	73.6	9.0
Bell	8 918	-1.1	4.05	18.3	11.0	538	97	97	441	874	2 299	645	1 655	11 440	792	82.7	4.0
Bellflower	23 367	2.0	3.09	19.0	21.1	623	253	253	370	2 954	3 910	605	3 305	20 310	3 422	55.8	12.9
Bell Gardens	9 466	2.4	4.61	19.6	7.2	456	301	123	155	1 243	2 722	698	2 023	15 662	579	84.1	4.0
Belmont	10 418	3.1	2.35	7.1	27.2	627	103	103	524	553	2 123	346	1 778	3 960	1 890	19.7	51.7
Benicia	10 328	12.2	2.60	11.9	23.6	54	27	27	27	552	1 982	165	1 817	7 279	1 215	25.9	37.3
Berkeley	44 955	3.5	2.16	9.5	38.1	5 822	246	185	5 576	10 271	9 643	684	8 958	32 932	6 421	16.4	64.3
Beverly Hills	15 035	3.2	2.24	8.1	38.2	39	1	0	38	1 333	3 806	380	3 426	6 192	2 385	22.2	54.5
Brea	13 067	6.9	2.70	10.5	23.0	128	22	0	106	1 532	4 173	196	3 977	8 952	1 746	30.2	33.5
Buena Park	23 332	5.1	3.32	14.8	14.4	934	325	306	609	2 371	2 921	291	2 631	21 272	3 229	48.7	19.7
Burbank	41 608	5.9	2.39	11.5	33.6	826	476	462	350	3 216	3 092	262	2 830	20 944	5 301	38.2	29.0
Burlingame	12 511	1.5	2.21	7.7	35.6	486	428	428	58	1 010	3 460	277	3 182	4 887	1 572	22.1	47.9
Calexico	6 814	44.1	3.96	22.0	10.4	103	0	0	103	1 110	3 949	249	3 700	9 988	532	69.0	9.1
Camarillo	21 438	18.4	2.62	8.2	24.1	939	393	211	546	1 091	1 844	206	1 638	12 918	2 801	30.1	32.9
Campbell	15 920	4.0	2.38	10.1	30.4	290	106	106	184	1 176	2 974	200	2 774	7 863	1 833	27.1	39.7
Carlsbad	31 521	26.1	2.46	8.6	24.8	787	535	535	252	2 273	2 802	259	2 543	16 537	3 515	21.1	45.7
Carson	24 648	3.5	3.59	17.2	14.2	1 210	242	236	968	3 446	3 704	801	2 903	24 559	4 000	50.8	18.1
Cathedral City	14 027	28.5	3.03	11.9	23.2	145	0	0	145	1 932	4 370	495	3 874	11 144	701	54.8	14.7
Ceres	10 435	21.6	3.31	15.7	14.1	99	57	52	42	2 470	6 884	527	6 357	10 262	779	63.3	8.3
Cerritos	15 390	2.4	3.34	10.9	8.9	93	30	30	63	2 430	4 552	365	4 187	14 433	2 735	25.5	43.7
Chico	23 476	51.4	2.42	11.3	29.3	3 063	497	486	2 566	2 665	4 288	434	3 853	25 310	1 290	29.7	33.6
Chino	17 304	10.7	3.43	12.9	14.1	7 816	7 634	0	182	2 464	3 538	465	3 073	18 431	2 598	55.3	13.0
Chula Vista	57 705	20.7	2.99	14.9	19.5	1 079	647	165	432	7 463	4 148	495	3 652	49 034	6 509	43.8	22.2
Claremont	11 281	7.7	2.56	10.4	24.9	5 104	465	384	4 639	1 075	3 050	247	2 803	6 800	6 673	22.0	52.4
Clovis	24 347	33.3	2.79	13.2	22.3	480	253	224	227	3 242	4 567	165	4 402	20 519	2 028	38.2	23.1
Colton	14 520	7.8	3.26	19.5	19.4	264	123	123	141	2 286	4 626	435	4 191	14 891	1 671	56.2	12.2
Compton	22 327	0.0	4.16	27.7	13.2	650	93	73	557	4 530	4 674	1 867	2 806	30 562	2 609	73.1	5.9
Concord	44 020	5.0	2.74	12.3	23.2	1 354	706	706	648	5 661	4 484	339	4 145	28 052	4 814	38.4	25.9
Corona	37 839	58.2	3.29	11.2	14.4	632	431	337	201	4 430	3 419	269	3 150	35 476	5 412	40.8	22.0
Costa Mesa	39 206	4.6	2.69	10.3	28.1	3 270	1 268	260	2 002	3 826	3 394	240	3 155	25 138	5 614	38.0	29.1
Covina	15 971	2.8	2.89	16.3	20.8	602	279	247	323	2 267	4 669	408	4 261	12 679	2 084	44.7	18.8
Culver City	16 611	2.8	2.31	12.8	34.5	524	241	170	283	1 448	3 598	328	3 270	7 764	1 979	28.1	41.2
Cupertino	18 204	18.5	2.75	7.8	19.6	448	377	377	71	1 218	2 324	149	2 175	12 734	2 554	13.6	65.4
Cypress	15 654	9.6	2.93	13.3	17.6	321	5	5	316	1 090	2 274	165	2 109	12 899	2 229	32.1	31.2
Daly City	30 775	6.1	3.34	14.2	18.1	790	532	524	258	2 199	2 047	281	1 766	23 152	6 603	38.7	29.1
Dana Point	14 456	13.8	2.41	8.8	26.0	242	95	95	147	687	1 887	179	1 709	6 648	1 630	24.5	41.0
Danville	14 816	33.9	2.78	7.1	15.5	464	94	94	370	647	1 496	35	1 461	9 801	2 237	14.6	59.4
Davis	22 948	28.0	2.50	8.2	25.0	2 970	254	254	2 716	1 864	2 981	205	2 777	28 484	2 088	11.5	68.6
Delano	8 409	34.8	4.02	18.4	10.8	5 057	4 982	177	75	2 412	5 993	206	5 786	10 852	747	78.0	5.5
Diamond Bar	17 651	4.4	3.18	11.1	12.5	118	51	48	67	909	1 558	187	1 371	16 448	2 977	26.2	42.3
Downey	33 989	3.0	3.11	15.8	19.1	1 765	1 423	412	342	3 651	3 281	393	2 889	29 672	4 715	52.6	17.3
Dublin	9 325	37.1	2.65	9.1	21.3	5 292	5 262	0	30	722	2 323	138	2 185	5 687	1 308	34.3	32.9
East Palo Alto	6 976	0.3	4.20	19.8	18.2	189	41	41	148	1 200	3 923	876	3 047	8 757	1 035	69.8	10.6
El Cajon	34 199	4.0	2.70	16.0	24.1	2 483	1 429	1 388	1 054	4 776	4 856	552	4 304	25 001	2 799	50.1	14.5
El Centro	11 439	18.7	3.23	18.7	18.8	887	749	112	138	1 590	4 054	818	3 235	12 883	648	56.1	14.0
El Monte	27 034	3.5	4.24	18.5	10.9	1 270	623	572	647	3 592	2 988	622	2 366	35 175	2 588	75.7	7.1
Encinitas	22 830	9.9	2.52	8.8	25.7	559	415	393	144	1 597	2 655	294	2 361	12 767	2 682	21.1	50.0
Escondido	43 817	11.6	3.01	11.7	22.4	1 765	696	696	1 069	5 495	3 968	439	3 529	33 465	4 594	48.6	20.1
Eureka	10 957	-1.6	2.26	14.0	35.3	1 355	487	110	868	2 323	8 576	845	7 730	6 491	327	45.1	16.9
Fairfield	30 870	21.4	2.98	14.2	17.0	4 229	1 886	986	2 343	5 353	5 369	580	4 789	25 718	3 434	39.5	20.4
Folsom	17 190	96.4	2.61	8.0	21.8	6 944	3 228	87	3 716	1 685	3 133	244	2 889	11 609	2 302	30.2	37.6
Fontana	34 014	28.9	3.78	15.5	10.9	499	218	189	281	4 312	3 226	683	2 543	41 767	3 535	59.6	10.3
Foster City	11 613	3.6	2.47	7.1	23.6	87	67	67	20	502	1 681	121	1 561	5 658	1 260	14.9	59.8
Fountain Valley	18 162	4.3	3.00	10.5	16.0	512	169	167	343	1 604	2 814	163	2 651	13 116	2 823	29.7	34.4
Fremont	68 237	13.4	2.96	9.2	16.5	1 759	755	484	1 004	5 704	2 705	185	2 520	46 240	10 915	28.5	43.2
Fresno	140 079	15.0	2.99	17.6	23.3	8 187	4 527	1 691	3 660	33 909	7 648	853	6 796	135 827	10 118	51.1	19.0
Fullerton	43 609	6.7	2.83	11.0	23.5	2 770	884	846	1 886	4 774	3 655	276	3 378	33 356	5 930	37.0	31.3
Gardena	20 324	12.1	2.80	18.1	25.5	804	556	509	248	2 492	4 162	1 042	3 120	14 227	2 404	51.8	16.6
Garden Grove	45 791	2.8	3.56	13.0	15.2	2 234	788	701	1 446	5 430	3 171	462	2 708	45 468	5 809	54.8	15.0
Gilroy	11 869	24.8	3.46	14.2	14.3	430	219	143	211	1 754	4 080	730	3 350	11 190	1 598	50.0	19.1
Glendale	71 805	4.7	2.68	11.8	25.7	2 864	1 715	1 689	1 149	4 535	2 244	245	1 999	44 955	11 123	40.2	32.1
Glendora	16 819	3.0	2.88	12.1	19.1	1 007	786	671	221	1 253	2 446	164	2 282	12 759	2 881	34.6	25.7
Hanford	13 931	28.3	2.93	15.4	20.6	848	718	358	130	1 698	3 929	338	3 591	11 896	1 186	51.9	14.4
Hawthorne	28 536	5.2	2.93	23.2	24.5	500	308	308	192	3 067	3 517	764	2 753	23 821	3 122	56.9	12.7
Hayward	44 804	11.7	3.08	14.5	20.9	2 138	755	751	1 383	5 508	3 794	413	3 381	34 184	5 475	50.7	19.9
Hemet	25 252	45.2	2.26	11.2	34.4	1 679	919	871	760	2 794	4 582	405	4 177	11 099	1 141	57.4	10.8
Hesperia	19 966	20.6	3.12	13.8	16.5	331	196	104	135	2 079	3 204	288	2 916	18 316	1 674	58.1	8.0
Highland	13 478	19.1	3.29	19.0	15.4	240	8	8	232	1 775	3 838	387	3 451	14 244	1 720	51.6	16.1
Hollister	9 716	64.8	3.52	12.2	12.7	171	159	62	12	1 114	3 122	350	2 772	9 925	1 172	51.6	15.0

1. No spouse present.   2. Data for serious crimes have not been adjusted for underreporting. This may affect comparability between geographic areas and over time.   3. Per 100,000 population estimated by the FBI.   4. All persons 3 years old and over enrolled in nursery school through college.   5. Persons 25 years old and over.

Table D. Cities — Income, Poverty, and Housing

City	Per capita income[1] (dollars)	Median income — Dollars	Median income — Percent change, 1989–1999 (constant 1999 dollars)	Percent with income of $100,000 or more	Percent below poverty — Persons — Total	Percent below poverty — Persons — Percent change in rate, 1989–1999	Percent below poverty — Families — Total	Housing units, 2000 — Total	Percent change, 1990–2000	Vacant units for sale or rent[2]	For seasonal use (percent)	Home owner vacancy rate	Renter vacancy rate
	43	44	45	46	47	48	49	50	51	52	53	54	55
CALIFORNIA—Cont'd													
Azusa	13 412	39 191	-8.5	8.0	18.8	31.5	15.1	13 013	-1.7	464	0.2	1.1	4.0
Bakersfield	17 678	39 982	-7.5	10.0	18.0	20.0	14.6	88 262	33.4	4 821	0.3	2.0	6.2
Baldwin Park	11 562	41 629	-5.2	7.9	18.2	15.9	15.4	17 430	1.5	469	0.1	1.2	1.9
Bell	9 905	29 946	-1.0	3.8	24.1	-7.7	21.2	9 215	-2.0	297	0.5	1.7	1.9
Bellflower	15 982	39 362	-10.4	8.1	15.8	64.6	12.8	24 247	0.5	880	0.2	1.8	3.0
Bell Gardens	8 415	30 597	-4.4	3.8	27.3	4.6	25.3	9 788	2.5	322	0.1	2.7	1.7
Belmont	42 812	80 905	18.4	38.7	4.0	-14.9	1.7	10 577	2.5	159	0.2	0.3	1.0
Benicia	31 226	67 617	1.3	28.1	4.3	-20.4	3.1	10 547	10.0	219	0.4	0.5	2.4
Berkeley	30 477	44 485	11.3	20.8	20.0	14.3	8.3	46 875	2.5	1 920	0.6	0.7	2.8
Beverly Hills	65 507	70 945	-2.8	37.9	9.1	37.9	7.9	15 856	0.8	821	0.9	1.6	3.3
Brea	26 307	59 759	-13.2	21.9	5.3	51.4	3.4	13 327	5.4	260	0.3	0.5	2.1
Buena Park	18 031	50 336	-9.6	13.1	11.3	41.3	8.0	23 826	2.7	494	0.1	0.8	2.2
Burbank	25 713	47 467	-1.8	15.1	10.5	26.5	8.1	42 847	4.0	1 239	0.4	0.9	2.1
Burlingame	43 565	68 526	20.0	32.1	5.7	21.3	3.7	12 869	-0.3	358	0.6	0.4	2.2
Calexico	9 981	28 929	15.5	6.3	25.7	-20.4	22.6	6 983	44.5	169	0.3	1.0	1.1
Camarillo	28 635	62 457	-3.6	24.5	5.3	20.5	3.6	21 946	17.2	508	0.3	0.9	1.9
Campbell	34 441	67 214	17.7	28.0	4.8	-17.2	3.2	16 286	2.7	366	0.6	0.4	1.5
Carlsbad	34 863	65 145	6.0	28.4	5.9	-13.2	3.4	33 798	24.1	2 277	2.6	2.2	4.1
Carson	17 107	52 284	-11.3	13.7	9.3	34.8	7.2	25 337	3.7	689	0.1	1.1	2.6
Cathedral City	16 215	38 887	-6.4	9.3	13.6	0.0	10.2	17 893	17.5	3 866	10.5	4.1	5.2
Ceres	14 420	40 736	-1.8	6.8	12.9	-16.8	10.1	10 773	18.7	338	0.1	1.0	3.8
Cerritos	25 249	73 030	-8.0	29.9	5.0	25.0	4.0	15 607	1.6	217	0.2	0.4	1.7
Chico	16 970	29 359	15.0	6.7	26.6	-16.9	12.7	24 386	49.7	910	0.3	1.8	2.6
Chino	17 574	55 401	-1.7	16.4	8.3	12.2	6.3	17 898	10.9	594	0.1	0.9	5.2
Chula Vista	18 556	44 861	4.3	11.8	10.6	8.2	8.6	59 495	19.4	1 790	0.4	1.0	3.1
Claremont	28 843	65 910	-8.3	27.5	8.0	50.9	6.0	11 559	6.7	278	0.4	0.7	2.2
Clovis	18 690	42 283	-0.7	10.3	10.6	2.9	7.6	25 250	33.7	903	0.2	1.5	4.0
Colton	13 460	35 777	-7.7	6.2	19.6	25.6	18.2	15 680	6.2	1 160	0.3	3.4	7.0
Compton	10 389	31 819	-5.2	5.7	28.0	1.8	25.5	23 795	2.4	1 468	0.1	3.7	5.1
Concord	24 727	55 597	-0.7	18.1	7.6	13.4	5.2	45 083	3.1	1 063	0.3	0.5	2.3
Corona	21 001	59 615	1.9	17.6	8.3	0.0	6.0	39 271	48.0	1 432	0.2	1.9	3.8
Costa Mesa	23 342	50 732	-6.3	16.0	12.6	37.0	8.2	40 406	2.0	1 200	0.3	0.8	2.8
Covina	20 231	48 474	-7.3	13.6	11.6	52.6	8.9	16 364	1.6	393	0.1	0.8	2.5
Culver City	29 025	51 792	-10.3	18.7	8.6	28.4	5.5	17 130	1.1	519	0.2	1.2	2.1
Cupertino	44 749	100 411	15.7	50.3	4.8	50.0	3.7	18 682	16.4	478	0.4	0.6	1.8
Cypress	25 798	64 377	-6.0	24.5	6.0	33.3	4.6	16 028	8.9	374	0.6	0.6	2.9
Daly City	21 900	62 310	11.7	22.3	7.1	-1.4	4.2	31 311	3.8	536	0.3	0.3	1.7
Dana Point	37 938	63 043	-13.9	28.5	6.7	-6.9	3.4	15 682	6.9	1 226	4.6	1.2	4.2
Danville	50 773	114 064	14.0	59.3	2.2	4.8	1.3	15 130	32.0	314	0.3	0.6	5.5
Davis	22 937	42 454	8.8	18.9	24.5	-3.9	5.4	23 617	29.2	669	0.4	0.8	2.7
Delano	11 068	28 143	-0.5	5.1	28.2	19.0	25.7	8 830	36.2	421	0.3	1.1	5.6
Diamond Bar	25 472	68 871	-15.5	28.0	6.0	71.4	5.0	17 959	1.7	308	0.2	0.7	1.9
Downey	18 197	45 667	-8.1	12.5	11.1	37.0	9.3	34 759	1.3	770	0.2	1.0	1.5
Dublin	29 451	77 283	7.1	32.5	2.9	-31.0	1.9	9 872	41.2	547	0.4	0.7	8.1
East Palo Alto	13 774	45 006	14.7	12.9	16.2	-7.4	13.5	7 091	-3.5	115	0.2	0.3	1.0
El Cajon	16 698	35 566	-5.8	7.3	16.7	29.5	13.5	35 190	2.1	991	0.3	0.6	2.7
El Centro	13 874	33 161	-1.9	7.5	22.8	-2.1	20.6	12 263	20.5	824	2.4	1.2	4.9
El Monte	10 316	32 439	-13.9	6.3	26.1	16.0	22.5	27 758	2.2	724	0.2	1.2	1.4
Encinitas	34 336	63 954	3.3	28.7	7.3	-12.0	3.8	23 843	7.8	1 013	1.9	0.9	2.6
Escondido	18 241	42 567	-3.7	11.9	13.4	19.6	9.3	45 050	7.2	1 233	0.2	1.0	2.7
Eureka	16 174	25 849	-11.8	4.4	23.7	26.7	15.8	11 637	-1.2	680	0.5	2.0	4.7
Fairfield	20 617	51 151	3.2	14.7	9.3	25.7	7.1	31 792	20.6	922	0.2	0.7	3.9
Folsom	30 210	73 175	16.6	30.4	7.3	40.4	2.6	17 968	90.8	772	0.4	1.6	7.1
Fontana	14 208	45 782	-4.2	8.8	14.7	28.9	12.2	35 908	22.2	1 894	0.1	3.1	4.2
Foster City	45 754	95 279	17.3	47.2	2.9	0.0	1.7	12 009	2.2	396	1.1	0.3	2.6
Fountain Valley	26 521	69 734	-7.7	28.6	4.3	22.9	3.0	18 473	2.5	311	0.3	0.5	2.3
Fremont	31 411	76 579	11.3	33.5	5.4	25.6	3.6	69 452	11.3	1 215	0.3	0.6	1.7
Fresno	15 010	32 236	-3.7	7.6	26.2	9.2	20.5	149 025	15.2	8 946	0.2	1.9	6.4
Fullerton	23 370	50 269	-10.7	17.4	11.4	16.3	8.0	44 771	4.2	1 162	0.2	0.8	2.8
Gardena	17 263	38 988	-12.2	8.8	15.7	60.2	12.3	21 041	10.5	717	0.2	1.2	3.3
Garden Grove	16 209	47 754	-10.9	12.5	13.9	33.7	10.5	46 703	1.6	912	0.2	0.7	2.0
Gilroy	22 071	62 135	12.9	23.0	10.4	-19.4	7.3	12 152	24.4	283	0.1	0.6	1.6
Glendale	22 227	41 805	-9.5	14.8	15.5	7.6	13.6	73 713	2.2	1 908	0.3	0.9	1.9
Glendora	25 993	60 013	-3.1	21.0	5.9	18.0	3.9	17 145	1.6	326	0.2	0.6	2.1
Hanford	17 504	37 582	5.0	8.7	17.3	10.2	14.2	14 721	26.8	790	0.4	2.1	6.0
Hawthorne	15 022	31 887	-23.4	6.2	20.3	46.0	18.4	29 629	1.4	1 093	0.2	1.4	3.3
Hayward	19 695	51 177	5.6	14.3	10.0	3.1	7.2	45 922	8.8	1 118	0.2	0.6	2.6
Hemet	16 226	26 839	-2.0	3.3	16.3	16.4	12.4	29 401	49.3	4 149	2.6	3.1	19.2
Hesperia	15 487	40 201	-2.8	6.6	14.1	12.8	11.1	21 348	23.0	1 382	0.4	2.7	7.3
Highland	16 039	41 230	-2.8	10.9	21.5	36.1	17.5	14 858	18.3	1 380	0.2	3.7	12.6
Hollister	18 857	56 104	27.1	17.6	9.5	-18.8	6.9	9 924	59.5	208	0.2	0.6	2.3

1. Based on population enumerated as of April 1, 2000.   2. Includes units rented or sold but not occupied.

Table D. Cities — Housing, Labor Force, Employment, and Disability

City	Housing units, 2000 (cont'd) Occupied units					Civilian labor force, 2003		Unemployment		Civilian employment,[2] 2000	Percent		Disability, 2000
	Total	Percent owner occupied	Percent renter occupied	Average size owner occupied	Average size renter occupied	Total	Percent change, 2002–2003	Total	Rate[1]	Total	Management, professional, and related occupations	Production, transportation, and material moving occupations	Employment disabled persons[3] (percent)
	56	57	58	59	60	61	62	63	64	65	66	67	68

CALIFORNIA—Cont'd

City	56	57	58	59	60	61	62	63	64	65	66	67	68
Azusa	12 549	50.5	49.5	3.34	3.48	22 464	0.0	1 780	7.9	17 851	23.6	20.3	17.3
Bakersfield	83 441	60.5	39.5	3.01	2.77	105 444	1.8	9 571	9.1	102 001	32.0	11.6	13.6
Baldwin Park	16 961	61.0	39.0	4.43	4.45	32 916	0.0	2 658	8.1	26 153	15.0	29.5	19.4
Bell	8 918	30.9	69.1	4.36	3.91	15 517	0.2	1 837	11.8	12 406	12.5	35.7	16.9
Bellflower	23 367	40.3	59.7	3.20	3.02	34 065	-0.1	1 918	5.6	29 322	24.4	18.2	13.3
Bell Gardens	9 466	23.8	76.2	4.67	4.59	18 381	0.2	2 355	12.8	13 048	8.9	38.5	23.3
Belmont	10 418	60.2	39.8	2.59	1.99	15 464	-2.6	636	4.1	14 238	54.4	5.9	7.5
Benicia	10 328	70.7	29.3	2.73	2.27	17 849	1.7	708	4.0	14 139	45.7	8.3	10.6
Berkeley	44 955	42.7	57.3	2.40	1.98	65 717	-0.8	4 138	6.3	55 832	61.4	5.0	7.8
Beverly Hills	15 035	43.4	56.6	2.73	1.87	18 470	-0.2	669	3.6	15 916	60.0	2.8	10.6
Brea	13 067	64.2	35.8	2.88	2.37	22 852	2.0	595	2.6	18 207	44.2	9.1	9.0
Buena Park	23 332	57.1	42.9	3.28	3.36	43 353	1.8	1 952	4.5	34 538	29.0	17.0	12.5
Burbank	41 608	43.5	56.5	2.61	2.22	55 830	-0.1	2 729	4.9	49 399	41.1	9.8	11.0
Burlingame	12 511	47.9	52.1	2.58	1.87	15 549	-2.6	526	3.4	15 385	52.4	4.8	8.6
Calexico	6 814	55.2	44.8	4.19	3.68	9 110	3.7	2 396	26.3	8 483	19.0	11.2	12.7
Camarillo	21 438	73.5	26.5	2.63	2.59	31 535	1.4	1 313	4.2	26 484	42.7	8.4	8.7
Campbell	15 920	48.2	51.8	2.55	2.22	23 635	-5.1	1 422	6.0	21 759	50.3	8.0	9.4
Carlsbad	31 521	67.4	32.6	2.52	2.33	42 337	1.7	1 447	3.4	38 763	49.2	5.3	8.6
Carson	24 648	77.9	22.1	3.57	3.68	46 698	0.0	3 209	6.9	37 300	26.8	20.0	15.5
Cathedral City	14 027	65.2	34.8	2.95	3.18	23 188	2.9	1 251	5.4	17 300	22.0	8.7	19.6
Ceres	10 435	66.2	33.8	3.29	3.34	15 152	1.3	1 754	11.6	13 098	19.1	22.7	16.1
Cerritos	15 390	83.5	16.5	3.30	3.56	30 767	-0.2	1 081	3.5	24 366	48.1	7.7	9.1
Chico	23 476	40.4	59.6	2.52	2.35	23 705	1.9	1 790	7.6	27 463	35.3	9.0	8.0
Chino	17 304	68.7	31.3	3.51	3.26	36 453	3.0	1 513	4.2	26 981	28.5	18.4	11.8
Chula Vista	57 705	57.4	42.6	3.09	2.85	77 676	1.7	3 497	4.5	71 195	33.0	10.4	12.8
Claremont	11 281	66.7	33.3	2.74	2.20	18 369	-0.1	739	4.0	16 046	57.4	5.2	7.9
Clovis	24 347	60.4	39.6	2.95	2.56	34 340	1.2	3 039	8.8	31 486	35.2	10.0	11.3
Colton	14 520	52.0	48.0	3.53	2.97	25 872	3.0	1 920	7.4	18 927	22.2	22.0	14.0
Compton	22 327	56.3	43.7	4.16	4.15	37 374	0.3	5 131	13.7	27 119	15.0	32.4	18.2
Concord	44 020	62.6	37.4	2.69	2.81	76 510	-0.4	3 928	5.1	59 655	34.0	9.3	12.3
Corona	37 839	67.5	32.5	3.39	3.06	61 944	2.9	3 090	5.0	57 276	32.8	15.4	11.6
Costa Mesa	39 206	40.5	59.5	2.66	2.71	71 397	1.9	2 344	3.3	56 681	35.9	9.3	11.2
Covina	15 971	58.4	41.6	3.02	2.72	24 746	-0.1	1 265	5.1	21 459	30.5	13.9	12.8
Culver City	16 611	54.4	45.6	2.34	2.26	24 239	-0.1	955	3.9	20 285	49.8	6.0	10.9
Cupertino	18 204	63.6	36.4	2.83	2.62	25 119	-5.0	1 223	4.9	23 959	71.0	4.3	7.1
Cypress	15 654	69.4	30.6	2.96	2.87	28 716	1.9	1 018	3.5	22 650	42.2	9.7	8.5
Daly City	30 775	59.8	40.2	3.48	3.13	51 931	-2.6	3 397	6.5	50 885	29.4	11.6	15.6
Dana Point	14 456	62.0	38.0	2.38	2.46	22 057	2.0	663	3.0	18 900	42.5	6.2	10.2
Danville	14 816	89.1	10.9	2.83	2.38	21 305	-0.6	573	2.7	20 907	58.1	3.6	6.3
Davis	22 948	44.6	55.4	2.64	2.39	36 319	3.3	1 441	4.0	31 571	60.5	4.7	4.2
Delano	8 409	59.4	40.6	4.16	3.80	13 301	2.9	3 863	29.0	9 319	15.7	18.6	19.2
Diamond Bar	17 651	82.6	17.4	3.21	3.05	32 283	-0.2	1 094	3.4	26 788	47.4	7.5	9.3
Downey	33 989	51.8	48.2	3.26	2.94	50 061	-0.1	2 599	5.2	44 108	28.7	16.7	14.5
Dublin	9 325	64.9	35.1	2.80	2.37	12 525	-0.8	498	4.0	14 476	46.7	6.8	8.4
East Palo Alto	6 976	43.5	56.5	4.69	3.83	11 457	-2.5	1 447	12.6	11 349	18.2	14.5	18.5
El Cajon	34 199	40.5	59.5	2.67	2.72	51 920	1.7	2 688	5.2	40 337	25.4	11.5	14.2
El Centro	11 439	50.2	49.8	3.34	3.12	17 433	3.5	3 274	18.8	13 043	28.5	10.4	13.8
El Monte	27 034	41.0	59.0	4.03	4.39	49 984	0.1	4 495	9.0	40 582	15.4	33.8	17.8
Encinitas	22 830	64.2	35.8	2.61	2.35	40 360	1.7	1 163	2.9	31 399	50.7	4.7	9.7
Escondido	43 817	53.2	46.8	2.93	3.10	67 264	1.7	2 961	4.4	57 426	27.9	14.3	12.6
Eureka	10 957	46.5	53.5	2.29	2.23	13 193	-0.1	865	6.6	10 694	24.3	12.7	17.2
Fairfield	30 870	59.7	40.3	2.99	2.97	46 649	1.9	3 040	6.5	39 186	29.3	13.9	13.8
Folsom	17 196	76.3	23.7	2.75	2.18	15 428	2.0	573	3.7	23 465	51.9	5.3	8.4
Fontana	34 014	68.1	31.9	3.87	3.58	54 242	3.0	3 023	5.6	47 452	20.8	24.2	15.8
Foster City	11 613	61.5	38.5	2.64	2.21	18 310	-2.6	751	4.1	16 051	61.9	3.6	7.8
Fountain Valley	18 162	74.7	25.3	3.07	2.79	36 670	1.9	1 143	3.1	27 621	43.6	8.9	8.7
Fremont	68 237	64.5	35.5	3.08	2.73	111 116	-0.8	5 245	4.7	102 187	49.8	11.3	8.7
Fresno	140 079	50.6	49.4	2.94	3.05	203 087	1.2	25 991	12.8	159 776	30.4	12.9	14.7
Fullerton	43 609	53.9	46.1	2.87	2.77	75 806	1.9	2 779	3.7	59 332	37.0	13.7	11.3
Gardena	20 324	47.3	52.7	2.85	2.76	28 735	-0.1	1 616	5.6	23 899	27.9	18.8	13.9
Garden Grove	45 791	59.6	40.4	3.49	3.67	88 406	1.8	4 349	4.9	69 356	25.0	22.1	16.5
Gilroy	11 869	61.2	38.8	3.27	3.75	17 271	-5.3	2 298	13.3	19 259	28.6	15.0	12.7
Glendale	71 805	38.4	61.6	2.72	2.65	98 811	0.0	6 562	6.6	85 113	40.5	10.3	15.1
Glendora	16 819	73.6	26.4	2.97	2.62	26 707	-0.1	1 095	4.1	23 711	39.9	9.9	10.0
Hanford	13 931	59.0	41.0	2.96	2.89	18 069	3.7	2 314	12.8	15 891	30.0	13.0	11.5
Hawthorne	28 536	25.9	74.1	3.36	2.78	41 927	0.0	2 772	6.6	32 803	23.3	16.7	16.8
Hayward	44 804	53.2	46.8	3.13	3.02	65 529	-0.8	4 510	6.9	63 270	26.7	18.7	17.1
Hemet	25 252	64.6	35.4	2.15	2.46	16 861	2.9	1 437	8.5	16 958	22.7	16.2	16.8
Hesperia	19 966	72.3	27.7	3.08	3.23	27 639	3.0	1 939	7.0	22 533	20.9	20.7	14.2
Highland	13 478	66.6	33.4	3.22	3.44	21 514	3.0	1 460	6.8	17 058	28.9	14.7	13.5
Hollister	9 716	67.0	33.0	3.51	3.55	15 007	3.0	1 818	12.1	15 122	29.3	14.2	13.8

1. Percent of civilian labor force.   2. Persons 16 years old and over.   3. Persons 16 to 64 years old.

City	New construction ($1,000)	Number of housing units	Percent single family	Number of establish-ments	Number of employees	Sales (mil dol)	Annual payroll (mil dol)	Number of establish-ments	Number of employees	Sales (mil dol)	Annual payroll (mil dol)
	Value of residential construction authorized by building permits, 2003			Wholesale trade, 1997				Retail trade,[1] 1997			
	69	70	71	72	73	74	75	76	77	78	79
CALIFORNIA—Cont'd											
Azusa	44 645	164	100.0	56	939	412.9	26.6	89	1 226	307.0	26.7
Bakersfield	568 122	3 795	96.5	291	3 891	2 747.6	144.2	918	12 207	2 382.2	230.0
Baldwin Park	10 658	74	100.0	152	1 323	744.9	40.7	125	1 041	204.5	21.2
Bell	2 944	27	100.0	71	1 287	591.7	39.2	62	483	102.1	10.3
Bellflower	6 953	61	67.2	44	316	62.6	6.9	169	2 116	439.4	41.0
Bell Gardens	686	7	100.0	35	319	147.1	7.9	80	584	104.0	9.5
Belmont	2 394	10	100.0	46	779	428.9	58.0	64	810	228.1	23.4
Benicia	19 655	131	56.5	78	1 542	747.9	68.0	76	825	137.1	16.0
Berkeley	25 541	286	11.9	136	1 389	438.2	61.0	536	6 313	1 238.7	131.9
Beverly Hills	30 750	37	91.9	186	1 256	928.6	60.1	414	5 910	1 377.4	170.8
Brea	44 378	248	95.6	235	2 926	2 548.1	121.4	296	5 094	765.5	75.6
Buena Park	4 490	29	27.6	157	2 150	1 322.6	74.7	235	3 793	966.6	88.5
Burbank	42 249	305	20.3	261	3 956	5 069.4	162.2	381	5 981	1 306.1	110.6
Burlingame	9 157	23	100.0	244	1 597	2 062.5	70.2	192	2 282	546.3	59.3
Calexico	54 165	525	78.7	62	352	167.8	6.5	182	2 091	291.3	28.2
Camarillo	59 097	282	84.4	128	1 892	632.8	82.1	249	3 110	607.9	58.9
Campbell	17 364	62	100.0	NA	NA	NA	NA	NA	NA	NA	NA
Carlsbad	194 108	1 265	40.8	266	4 290	2 140.3	174.8	355	4 855	1 120.5	106.7
Carson	8 968	79	87.3	338	7 029	5 176.5	273.5	216	4 505	949.5	100.0
Cathedral City	117 825	803	48.1	35	250	52.5	7.9	169	2 421	574.0	52.6
Ceres	50 626	375	93.6	20	D	D	D	81	1 350	222.7	20.9
Cerritos	5 039	13	100.0	276	5 313	3 940.4	201.6	279	7 822	1 934.3	159.8
Chico	110 325	946	66.0	109	1 300	469.1	44.3	420	5 812	987.8	97.7
Chino	47 111	160	100.0	217	2 830	1 296.1	107.0	184	2 963	554.2	55.6
Chula Vista	616 716	3 143	68.0	265	1 717	681.3	46.0	546	7 502	1 276.6	125.7
Claremont	15 785	58	65.5	29	210	91.1	7.9	97	1 251	321.6	26.7
Clovis	298 375	1 433	96.2	44	219	89.1	5.6	262	4 319	853.0	78.4
Colton	6 881	42	100.0	60	846	279.4	27.3	103	1 682	327.6	33.1
Compton	4 110	48	91.7	135	3 114	1 325.1	108.7	148	1 811	375.2	33.5
Concord	71 893	333	55.0	203	1 677	1 264.6	68.7	481	7 295	1 654.9	164.3
Corona	123 979	726	50.4	220	2 958	2 396.6	102.7	270	4 513	1 066.4	96.0
Costa Mesa	14 113	85	100.0	373	5 888	7 388.3	289.9	693	12 297	2 343.3	251.8
Covina	131	2	0.0	97	652	333.2	20.4	177	2 632	537.9	52.3
Culver City	1 717	8	100.0	201	3 449	1 638.7	160.4	341	4 970	884.9	97.6
Cupertino	14 703	36	100.0	92	1 464	1 935.2	117.9	248	3 355	509.2	55.0
Cypress	28 876	127	100.0	99	3 799	7 999.8	230.9	100	1 254	310.6	25.7
Daly City	10 823	39	94.9	47	550	209.7	21.4	240	3 214	524.9	52.3
Dana Point	31 303	77	61.0	46	143	136.8	5.1	114	1 295	306.3	27.6
Danville	3 624	22	100.0	75	286	328.4	13.2	139	1 599	352.8	31.1
Davis	32 849	240	25.8	27	93	29.5	4.1	139	1 885	324.6	37.4
Delano	24 228	240	95.0	16	160	67.1	5.3	99	1 016	161.9	16.1
Diamond Bar	10 361	14	100.0	174	1 100	1 241.9	31.3	102	1 031	204.3	17.4
Downey	12 534	86	25.6	98	1 112	635.1	43.5	295	4 694	1 061.1	103.6
Dublin	207 532	766	27.9	81	546	270.6	20.4	154	2 499	614.1	57.2
East Palo Alto	16 607	79	59.5	7	D	D	D	20	79	16.2	1.2
El Cajon	18 653	129	100.0	116	1 262	369.2	34.0	497	6 539	1 211.8	123.6
El Centro	31 625	219	95.4	47	334	137.5	8.6	172	2 393	417.7	43.0
El Monte	21 565	205	51.2	314	3 461	2 389.6	129.8	245	3 320	1 335.3	96.6
Encinitas	54 509	240	77.9	81	461	234.6	17.0	224	2 525	493.4	50.6
Escondido	116 213	498	99.2	171	1 172	377.2	38.9	600	9 390	1 765.6	186.0
Eureka	3 782	41	36.6	56	587	166.3	17.3	271	3 173	539.7	53.9
Fairfield	120 788	1 067	56.3	60	1 016	913.8	37.1	336	5 090	940.9	93.0
Folsom	188 925	783	93.7	23	D	D	D	162	2 134	444.9	41.6
Fontana	274 253	1 340	100.0	69	2 432	1 925.2	64.6	209	4 001	773.6	75.1
Foster City	0	0	0.0	97	1 595	862.6	98.2	60	1 171	246.9	23.9
Fountain Valley	22 329	118	54.2	157	1 429	1 951.1	63.4	218	3 242	632.2	57.4
Fremont	27 302	87	100.0	656	10 975	15 406.2	477.3	440	6 544	1 705.1	152.1
Fresno	297 275	2 296	67.4	655	8 209	3 934.0	269.4	1 546	19 850	3 589.5	362.8
Fullerton	147 929	750	93.1	225	3 596	2 331.2	134.9	292	4 361	938.6	88.0
Gardena	1 556	11	81.8	198	1 708	606.8	51.2	175	2 196	439.3	44.1
Garden Grove	17 488	108	81.5	240	3 031	1 469.9	101.4	413	5 618	1 247.9	116.3
Gilroy	75 266	247	100.0	43	D	D	D	273	3 118	664.8	60.1
Glendale	16 983	137	10.9	315	2 813	1 057.6	101.1	725	9 426	1 844.2	188.1
Glendora	15 049	39	100.0	50	546	322.9	22.8	133	1 758	341.5	34.7
Hanford	47 922	503	88.9	27	218	114.5	4.7	184	2 512	414.6	41.2
Hawthorne	5 515	33	78.8	55	821	218.9	28.2	187	2 581	528.4	49.1
Hayward	101 081	496	100.0	598	9 655	5 283.1	364.3	438	6 541	1 460.6	147.6
Hemet	143 682	798	100.0	19	87	49.1	3.3	221	3 349	561.7	60.0
Hesperia	161 181	1 088	95.0	38	187	98.2	4.9	129	1 161	200.2	21.4
Highland	105 995	366	100.0	6	148	25.1	3.0	50	578	109.1	9.2
Hollister	207	2	100.0	27	687	161.6	19.4	93	1 400	233.1	25.5

1. Establishments with payroll.

Table D. Cities — Real Estate, Professional Services, and Manufacturing

City	Real estate and rental and leasing, 1997				Professional, scientific, and technical services,[1] 1997				Manufacturing, 1997			
	Number of establishments	Number of employees	Receipts (mil dol)	Annual payroll (mil dol)	Number of establishments	Number of employees	Receipts (mil dol)	Annual payroll (mil dol)	Number of establishments	Number of employees	Receipts (mil dol)	Annual payroll (mil dol)
	80	81	82	83	84	85	86	87	88	89	90	91
CALIFORNIA—Cont'd												
Azusa	28	107	14.7	2.4	14	36	2.9	1.4	126	5 017	905.9	197.7
Bakersfield	229	1 333	117.2	23.2	519	2 793	249.5	89.5	160	4 560	416.0	107.9
Baldwin Park	26	94	12.5	1.9	14	122	9.6	3.0	141	2 854	232.1	68.5
Bell	12	90	15.8	2.9	10	192	7.6	3.9	29	940	177.3	28.8
Bellflower	84	340	40.8	5.9	47	227	15.4	5.8	NA	NA	NA	NA
Bell Gardens	10	26	2.0	0.2	4	D	D	D	70	1 672	163.3	42.2
Belmont	35	320	28.0	4.9	81	408	49.8	19.6	NA	NA	NA	NA
Benicia	40	172	28.5	4.6	79	758	74.4	26.2	85	2 063	1 650.0	88.1
Berkeley	162	681	108.8	15.4	464	2 554	332.6	130.2	199	5 247	996.6	212.8
Beverly Hills	424	2 214	423.9	77.5	908	4 940	909.9	319.0	64	501	45.1	10.9
Brea	53	351	43.8	9.1	151	1 724	162.6	47.0	187	8 461	1 145.1	316.5
Buena Park	49	398	55.6	12.5	67	887	97.0	43.3	126	7 108	1 358.5	227.8
Burbank	173	1 853	709.6	81.5	368	126 307	4 972.4	2 707.5	298	9 355	1 131.2	306.9
Burlingame	147	966	183.2	24.0	255	1 802	247.6	108.0	83	2 286	408.5	90.9
Calexico	19	84	5.1	1.2	20	79	5.2	2.3	NA	NA	NA	NA
Camarillo	58	316	41.1	9.3	176	1 468	176.2	68.1	173	8 487	1 513.5	296.9
Campbell	NA	NA	NA	NA	NA	NA	NA	NA	156	3 307	613.5	133.6
Carlsbad	139	1 054	134.8	29.7	351	3 377	423.7	136.3	205	12 384	2 418.9	458.0
Carson	70	2 884	544.1	103.7	77	775	94.1	32.4	321	13 958	5 207.9	477.5
Cathedral City	36	223	25.6	3.9	30	100	10.5	2.6	NA	NA	NA	NA
Ceres	24	99	8.3	1.4	11	51	2.9	1.2	32	835	131.1	24.0
Cerritos	55	282	41.6	6.7	111	1 627	342.0	111.6	117	5 463	801.1	169.4
Chico	101	531	48.9	8.0	171	1 026	99.3	34.4	107	2 455	403.7	63.1
Chino	40	209	38.3	4.4	80	585	60.6	17.2	259	9 897	1 294.7	245.8
Chula Vista	161	750	93.6	11.9	156	706	57.8	19.4	158	5 626	1 029.2	210.9
Claremont	28	149	14.2	3.4	114	726	75.5	22.7	29	1 309	177.6	58.0
Clovis	46	256	29.4	3.9	72	355	23.4	8.6	55	2 320	259.4	56.0
Colton	28	144	14.8	3.3	31	438	43.6	13.9	54	1 668	278.2	45.4
Compton	23	166	25.7	3.6	23	D	D	D	179	8 188	1 108.1	215.3
Concord	119	620	123.2	18.4	256	2 044	246.9	102.2	145	2 554	353.3	97.6
Corona	86	861	69.3	18.4	133	733	81.3	25.2	291	10 424	1 817.4	313.2
Costa Mesa	216	1 751	312.8	58.2	552	6 031	908.1	338.7	310	11 091	1 757.6	429.6
Covina	74	358	41.5	7.6	142	783	50.4	18.5	119	3 226	359.5	114.5
Culver City	100	1 040	91.6	26.0	249	2 290	243.0	82.3	119	2 789	253.7	76.1
Cupertino	78	373	67.1	11.7	296	2 091	343.7	141.2	49	2 626	295.1	112.9
Cypress	45	152	27.5	3.8	75	924	104.5	42.4	40	1 341	200.4	41.8
Daly City	49	208	43.1	3.9	69	215	19.9	7.2	NA	NA	NA	NA
Dana Point	36	158	25.3	3.3	85	276	31.1	10.2	NA	NA	NA	NA
Danville	83	597	70.6	12.9	182	862	104.9	48.0	NA	NA	NA	NA
Davis	71	487	42.3	8.5	110	588	95.0	24.7	NA	NA	NA	NA
Delano	13	38	3.7	0.5	10	172	7.3	5.2	NA	NA	NA	NA
Diamond Bar	54	395	41.2	14.2	135	1 020	133.8	47.2	NA	NA	NA	NA
Downey	111	533	62.7	10.9	123	458	38.1	14.0	102	7 464	1 419.0	372.8
Dublin	31	204	31.6	2.9	100	666	98.3	27.4	26	606	75.1	23.4
East Palo Alto	16	40	6.1	0.6	4	D	D	D	13	767	196.5	42.5
El Cajon	145	656	62.8	12.5	150	1 481	62.4	27.7	187	6 102	654.3	194.1
El Centro	31	128	10.6	1.4	56	334	34.3	11.2	NA	NA	NA	NA
El Monte	46	267	39.5	5.5	81	293	38.3	10.4	238	8 068	882.2	211.8
Encinitas	90	296	51.3	6.8	213	711	85.6	34.7	NA	NA	NA	NA
Escondido	163	964	157.4	20.8	260	1 173	109.1	39.0	190	4 330	563.8	114.5
Eureka	48	231	14.7	3.8	107	565	39.8	14.7	44	686	128.5	20.6
Fairfield	84	395	41.4	6.6	111	520	41.9	15.6	53	2 955	1 036.1	121.7
Folsom	34	105	14.2	2.4	78	329	39.7	16.2	23	648	79.2	26.2
Fontana	47	271	42.4	6.2	20	66	3.8	1.2	111	4 811	1 128.7	153.9
Foster City	46	719	115.4	36.6	148	1 858	349.2	142.4	26	1 866	563.4	115.8
Fountain Valley	55	327	45.8	9.6	164	1 350	191.5	55.5	111	2 645	1 302.2	84.6
Fremont	195	1 168	186.4	26.5	497	4 632	512.0	226.0	464	34 623	10 765.3	1 593.4
Fresno	398	2 598	273.1	51.1	913	10 110	505.0	205.4	412	15 225	3 099.8	395.1
Fullerton	122	700	82.1	15.5	260	2 543	427.3	120.0	228	10 916	2 217.1	375.8
Gardena	49	211	41.2	5.3	54	227	20.1	6.9	339	7 739	849.2	208.3
Garden Grove	103	555	85.0	13.1	184	1 228	95.2	29.2	354	9 710	2 255.3	269.5
Gilroy	42	136	21.6	2.8	46	221	18.1	8.4	61	2 538	426.9	76.7
Glendale	226	1 421	299.0	43.4	585	4 637	469.8	186.6	329	7 280	784.7	217.7
Glendora	58	207	22.9	3.5	77	329	44.8	12.8	53	1 321	194.4	49.3
Hanford	38	161	12.4	2.2	55	274	21.3	7.0	27	1 672	376.3	62.6
Hawthorne	56	151	16.9	1.9	33	241	19.1	10.3	114	5 719	1 006.6	234.6
Hayward	163	1 217	217.4	32.9	215	1 525	164.7	64.6	385	11 817	2 287.2	430.1
Hemet	61	328	31.4	5.0	72	270	19.8	7.0	25	972	106.5	19.9
Hesperia	30	88	8.4	1.2	35	115	10.2	2.1	66	1 212	157.6	26.3
Highland	18	61	5.7	0.8	11	33	1.7	0.5	NA	NA	NA	NA
Hollister	22	67	12.0	1.1	41	133	12.1	4.7	49	1 346	231.1	39.7

1. Firms subject to federal tax.

928 CA(Azusa)—CA(Hollister)   Items 80—91

Table D. Cities — Accommodation and Foodservices, Entertainment, and Health Care

City	Accommodation and foodservices, 1997				Arts, entertainment, and recreation,[1] 1997				Health care and social assistance,[1] 1997			
	Number of establishments	Number of employees	Sales (mil dol)	Annual payroll (mil dol)	Number of establishments	Number of employees	Receipts (mil dol)	Annual payroll (mil dol)	Number of establishments	Number of employees	Receipts (mil dol)	Annual payroll (mil dol)
	92	93	94	95	96	97	98	99	100	101	102	103
CALIFORNIA—Cont'd												
Azusa	63	894	31.4	7.8	4	106	4.3	1.2	34	445	12.5	5.2
Bakersfield	472	7 956	272.6	72.8	50	1 027	35.6	10.6	639	7 112	600.4	217.4
Baldwin Park	60	839	32.6	7.6	3	0	0.0	0.0	56	1 505	85.0	42.7
Bell	50	684	25.5	5.5	NA	NA	NA	NA	23	210	12.9	4.9
Bellflower	88	1 057	38.9	8.8	9	79	6.0	1.4	115	2 474	255.0	86.3
Bell Gardens	37	382	15.7	3.3	5	0	0.0	0.0	20	371	15.4	7.0
Belmont	60	619	28.3	7.2	5	49	1.7	0.5	48	361	24.1	9.4
Benicia	54	D	D	D	9	22	1.8	0.2	49	286	17.3	5.8
Berkeley	367	4 711	198.6	56.9	38	447	25.4	6.6	420	2 272	203.9	78.6
Beverly Hills	188	6 230	297.9	92.7	573	2 856	975.1	551.7	769	3 162	443.4	165.8
Brea	103	2 393	85.0	21.9	6	0	0.0	0.0	100	1 059	88.8	30.6
Buena Park	119	2 750	102.0	27.9	14	3 603	157.3	61.4	80	818	53.1	19.5
Burbank	236	4 756	201.0	53.0	167	1 831	296.0	190.2	326	2 921	258.4	103.2
Burlingame	123	4 988	287.4	83.8	18	246	17.0	3.0	151	1 441	92.2	40.3
Calexico	54	625	21.7	5.7	1	0	0.0	0.0	19	108	5.7	1.6
Camarillo	112	1 846	69.7	17.6	16	194	12.6	3.1	144	826	65.1	24.9
Campbell	NA	NA	NA	NA	NA	NA	NA	NA	NA	NA	NA	NA
Carlsbad	165	4 176	186.3	50.3	14	204	15.9	4.0	119	767	51.9	20.3
Carson	118	1 606	63.6	15.7	7	60	4.0	0.7	116	1 009	63.5	21.6
Cathedral City	86	957	32.4	8.3	7	570	46.8	12.3	38	355	26.9	8.2
Ceres	43	566	20.4	4.8	3	0	0.0	0.0	36	311	13.7	4.7
Cerritos	99	1 972	72.9	21.6	8	202	9.3	2.0	114	1 128	64.9	25.7
Chico	210	3 754	94.1	26.0	23	479	13.3	4.2	300	3 478	208.1	80.1
Chino	89	1 816	56.9	14.9	9	275	11.2	3.4	102	1 441	110.9	39.4
Chula Vista	280	4 370	157.2	39.9	26	408	27.1	6.6	319	2 169	190.0	68.2
Claremont	70	1 235	40.0	11.5	10	278	12.4	4.4	92	701	40.7	15.8
Clovis	133	D	D	D	11	0	0.0	0.0	124	1 026	55.5	22.0
Colton	75	1 021	33.5	8.6	7	10	11.2	1.1	56	838	52.5	21.8
Compton	63	687	23.4	5.5	6	0	0.0	0.0	50	370	24.8	8.3
Concord	217	3 607	141.2	38.0	15	426	12.5	4.3	327	3 277	213.1	87.4
Corona	136	2 311	77.8	19.7	18	230	14.5	3.3	168	1 720	103.8	40.6
Costa Mesa	315	6 638	282.7	75.4	37	686	35.1	11.7	210	1 730	132.4	46.2
Covina	106	1 603	63.3	16.0	8	131	5.5	1.8	181	2 400	163.1	72.9
Culver City	153	2 491	118.9	33.5	80	174	67.2	37.7	176	3 249	265.2	89.8
Cupertino	138	2 657	109.4	30.5	6	114	5.5	1.4	138	1 158	80.8	27.7
Cypress	89	1 400	48.5	12.4	16	882	66.3	25.6	72	912	59.7	26.1
Daly City	115	2 049	82.4	21.4	14	394	12.5	3.9	195	1 623	133.2	53.8
Dana Point	72	2 515	140.5	34.8	14	120	17.3	2.8	62	338	25.9	10.5
Danville	99	D	D	D	11	801	20.2	6.9	97	636	45.0	17.9
Davis	118	1 930	57.1	14.3	12	171	5.8	1.8	132	989	72.5	34.8
Delano	43	D	D	D	1	0	0.0	0.0	46	366	21.7	8.4
Diamond Bar	69	1 021	35.2	9.1	7	148	7.3	1.6	122	893	74.7	20.5
Downey	183	2 964	116.6	30.0	10	169	6.6	2.0	239	3 288	228.7	93.4
Dublin	55	1 285	46.1	11.3	6	74	3.3	1.0	42	713	90.7	30.3
East Palo Alto	13	182	9.0	2.0	NA	NA	NA	NA	4	3	0.3	0.0
El Cajon	211	2 819	103.4	25.4	15	270	11.0	2.8	210	2 970	199.4	80.7
El Centro	96	1 294	43.0	10.9	3	58	1.1	0.4	96	1 065	74.4	28.7
El Monte	128	1 317	53.2	11.7	5	33	1.4	0.5	112	1 448	77.5	30.6
Encinitas	148	2 207	73.4	20.7	23	163	9.9	2.9	228	1 666	152.1	54.3
Escondido	233	3 505	123.8	32.9	20	413	17.9	4.7	272	3 026	185.9	79.8
Eureka	146	1 951	64.7	17.1	11	121	3.0	0.8	124	1 164	89.8	32.4
Fairfield	133	2 346	79.5	20.2	14	284	11.0	3.5	179	1 563	122.5	48.8
Folsom	103	D	D	D	8	136	4.6	1.5	81	1 137	71.0	30.0
Fontana	119	1 530	55.8	13.5	3	0	0.0	0.0	71	2 494	233.5	85.1
Foster City	62	1 206	51.2	13.4	10	165	8.7	2.8	53	356	21.4	9.1
Fountain Valley	128	1 974	74.1	18.0	11	611	19.1	5.7	259	3 313	312.7	124.0
Fremont	290	4 612	176.8	44.2	27	782	25.4	7.8	431	4 438	368.1	140.0
Fresno	799	13 915	433.4	119.8	63	1 118	50.3	13.3	1 189	12 047	919.3	385.7
Fullerton	199	3 792	137.0	37.0	17	434	23.8	7.5	268	2 615	229.5	100.3
Gardena	162	1 734	68.0	16.8	5	0	0.0	0.0	152	2 163	131.7	53.2
Garden Grove	278	3 868	138.1	36.5	15	0	0.0	0.0	353	3 847	274.8	94.8
Gilroy	83	1 147	48.3	10.4	4	75	1.6	0.5	99	1 235	77.9	34.4
Glendale	304	4 915	191.2	51.4	70	583	54.6	18.9	618	5 699	422.9	160.7
Glendora	78	1 149	39.2	10.4	5	58	2.1	0.6	147	1 710	101.6	43.4
Hanford	91	1 256	40.7	10.3	6	83	2.4	0.5	94	1 310	84.7	34.7
Hawthorne	98	1 272	57.8	12.4	4	16	0.8	0.1	123	1 295	89.7	35.8
Hayward	236	2 959	112.9	27.9	16	204	9.0	2.5	197	3 352	285.4	128.4
Hemet	106	1 332	44.5	11.2	8	141	5.0	1.5	177	1 973	143.3	55.1
Hesperia	68	873	26.7	7.1	4	39	1.5	0.6	63	308	25.7	6.8
Highland	35	D	D	D	1	0	0.0	0.0	30	577	37.5	16.8
Hollister	50	653	22.3	5.8	2	0	0.0	0.0	54	339	18.2	6.9

1. Firms subject to federal tax.

Table D. Cities — Other Services and Federal Funds

City	Other services,[1] 1997				Selected federal funds, 2002–2003 (mil dol)								
					Procurement contracts		Grants						
	Number of establishments	Number of employees	Receipts (mil dol)	Annual payroll (mil dol)	Defense	Other	Total[2]	Medicaid and other health related	Nutrition and family welfare	Energy and environment	Education	Housing and community development	Direct payments for individuals for educational assistance
	104	105	106	107	108	109	110	111	112	113	114	115	116
CALIFORNIA—Cont'd													
Azusa	53	279	19.1	5.0	75.9	60.4	4.8	0.2	0.0	0.0	0.3	4.4	3.4
Bakersfield	346	2 300	168.0	45.7	5.5	6.5	60.9	0.6	21.3	2.5	6.5	17.2	25.1
Baldwin Park	59	234	15.7	4.7	1.3	0.6	13.2	0.0	0.0	0.0	1.9	11.2	0.3
Bell	34	138	13.2	3.8	9.2	5.7	0.5	0.0	0.0	0.2	0.0	0.2	1.2
Bellflower	117	599	42.6	11.9	1.5	0.2	3.4	0.0	0.0	0.0	1.3	2.0	0.1
Bell Gardens	33	240	14.8	4.7	0.0	0.9	0.9	0.0	0.0	0.0	0.0	0.8	0.0
Belmont	47	239	16.2	4.3	0.2	0.8	1.1	0.0	0.0	0.0	0.3	0.6	1.1
Benicia	52	705	55.0	21.4	166.5	17.4	1.7	0.0	0.0	0.0	0.0	1.8	0.0
Berkeley	203	1 353	84.4	27.3	60.9	1 985.7	405.2	164.0	3.5	10.1	31.8	34.6	31.0
Beverly Hills	221	1 546	86.6	28.0	2.3	176.8	1.8	0.0	0.0	0.0	0.7	0.9	0.1
Brea	91	941	71.6	26.7	24.5	4.8	0.5	0.0	0.0	0.4	0.0	0.0	-0.1
Buena Park	66	384	19.5	5.7	3.2	0.4	3.1	0.0	0.0	0.0	0.3	2.7	0.0
Burbank	218	1 805	146.6	42.0	37.9	1.2	20.5	0.0	0.0	0.0	1.1	11.9	2.2
Burlingame	106	587	47.5	14.4	22.1	9.6	5.9	3.1	0.1	0.0	0.0	0.0	0.0
Calexico	14	37	3.3	0.9	0.0	0.3	2.8	0.0	0.0	0.0	0.0	2.3	0.0
Camarillo	82	719	59.1	18.7	102.9	15.3	5.5	0.0	0.4	0.0	0.8	3.3	8.7
Campbell	NA	NA	NA	NA	0.3	0.0	7.3	0.1	0.0	0.0	1.1	6.0	0.0
Carlsbad	86	650	38.7	11.0	34.1	8.8	16.2	2.3	0.0	0.2	0.8	3.9	0.2
Carson	97	1 177	90.1	29.8	649.1	3.3	12.9	2.0	0.3	0.0	3.2	4.9	14.0
Cathedral City	84	506	35.8	10.4	0.1	0.1	2.3	0.0	0.0	0.0	0.6	0.1	0.0
Ceres	33	139	9.8	1.9	0.4	0.1	2.2	0.0	0.0	0.0	0.5	1.7	0.0
Cerritos	63	585	35.2	12.8	2.3	0.7	3.9	0.0	0.0	0.0	0.0	0.0	0.6
Chico	136	1 016	112.6	17.6	0.3	15.4	13.8	0.3	0.8	0.0	3.3	5.3	17.0
Chino	97	1 159	70.5	23.4	0.6	0.8	1.3	0.0	0.0	0.0	0.0	1.2	0.0
Chula Vista	184	1 118	67.0	20.5	52.3	7.6	13.5	0.0	0.4	0.5	1.4	7.4	10.1
Claremont	31	164	6.3	2.2	1.1	0.0	13.6	2.4	0.0	0.1	1.7	4.0	4.7
Clovis	102	568	36.6	9.9	0.1	9.8	2.5	0.4	0.0	0.0	0.1	0.0	5.5
Colton	42	514	23.4	7.8	3.3	5.7	5.1	0.0	0.0	0.0	0.5	2.6	3.6
Compton	60	425	23.1	6.6	16.6	3.4	32.9	0.0	0.0	0.0	2.6	29.3	5.3
Concord	209	1 382	113.9	35.3	10.8	4.0	20.8	1.0	0.0	0.7	0.9	8.9	0.2
Corona	135	1 080	108.0	31.0	21.9	2.1	2.1	0.0	0.0	0.0	0.0	2.0	0.0
Costa Mesa	292	1 610	117.7	34.6	115.3	1.4	6.9	0.0	0.0	0.0	2.3	4.4	10.4
Covina	116	571	40.2	11.4	3.4	1.2	27.8	0.0	0.0	0.0	0.5	2.0	0.0
Culver City	132	1 053	77.3	25.7	6.6	12.6	8.3	1.3	0.0	0.3	1.6	3.8	4.2
Cupertino	53	277	21.9	4.6	1.0	0.8	2.0	0.0	0.0	0.0	0.6	1.4	5.7
Cypress	82	608	49.0	13.6	5.9	8.7	0.4	0.0	0.0	0.0	0.0	0.4	7.0
Daly City	89	428	30.9	8.9	14.7	1.4	8.7	0.0	0.0	0.0	0.0	8.4	0.6
Dana Point	33	130	7.8	2.3	0.0	0.1	1.6	0.0	0.0	0.0	1.5	0.1	0.0
Danville	44	192	11.9	3.7	0.3	0.1	0.2	0.0	0.0	0.0	0.0	0.1	0.0
Davis	48	252	16.9	5.0	3.3	24.0	222.5	132.2	0.0	10.6	5.4	9.3	24.7
Delano	20	48	3.9	0.9	0.0	1.6	1.7	0.0	0.0	0.0	0.0	1.8	0.0
Diamond Bar	48	204	16.5	4.9	9.7	2.3	0.0	0.0	0.0	0.0	0.0	0.0	0.0
Downey	140	1 475	80.0	25.3	6.1	0.2	235.9	0.6	222.1	0.4	10.1	2.3	0.0
Dublin	64	451	44.3	15.4	9.8	4.6	0.3	0.1	0.0	0.4	0.0	0.2	0.0
East Palo Alto	6	11	1.4	0.2	0.0	0.0	7.2	3.4	0.0	0.0	0.0	3.3	0.0
El Cajon	170	1 160	84.5	21.6	5.9	4.2	19.6	0.2	0.0	0.1	2.8	11.5	10.6
El Centro	43	265	13.8	4.6	14.1	13.8	17.8	0.6	0.0	0.0	6.7	2.5	0.0
El Monte	132	738	46.4	12.8	11.5	1.7	9.4	0.0	0.0	0.0	1.0	8.2	1.7
Encinitas	92	790	42.4	13.3	1.1	0.5	4.1	0.4	0.0	1.7	0.2	1.0	0.0
Escondido	242	1 222	84.7	24.6	15.5	2.1	13.5	5.1	0.0	0.0	0.6	6.1	0.0
Eureka	88	504	33.2	9.6	0.2	3.6	10.8	0.3	1.4	0.2	1.2	5.5	5.7
Fairfield	118	659	40.1	13.6	8.5	1.5	19.7	0.0	0.0	0.0	5.8	9.8	0.0
Folsom	46	244	14.3	3.2	5.2	3.5	1.9	0.0	0.0	0.0	0.1	1.0	0.0
Fontana	103	578	37.2	12.6	0.7	0.2	6.3	0.0	0.0	0.0	0.5	5.6	0.0
Foster City	24	141	8.7	4.3	2.3	7.8	0.0	0.0	0.0	0.0	0.0	0.0	0.0
Fountain Valley	102	851	52.5	19.0	5.8	0.2	4.3	0.4	0.0	0.1	0.4	1.2	1.3
Fremont	293	1 742	129.7	38.1	8.9	2.9	17.6	2.3	9.9	0.0	0.2	4.9	10.5
Fresno	626	4 602	358.9	94.9	6.1	62.5	139.7	10.3	28.1	2.3	15.5	60.8	55.7
Fullerton	172	798	68.5	19.0	114.1	66.0	10.0	1.1	0.0	0.1	3.2	3.8	31.1
Gardena	136	820	56.0	17.8	36.2	3.4	13.2	0.0	0.0	0.0	0.2	2.9	3.2
Garden Grove	228	1 373	94.7	23.8	27.0	5.9	21.7	0.1	0.1	0.0	1.0	19.5	2.9
Gilroy	63	733	42.7	12.8	0.4	0.2	5.4	0.0	0.0	0.0	0.8	4.5	1.9
Glendale	304	2 164	135.2	49.8	13.9	16.4	28.0	1.1	0.0	0.8	3.6	21.6	14.7
Glendora	81	660	34.7	10.2	1.2	0.2	3.7	0.0	0.0	0.0	0.1	1.3	6.3
Hanford	50	207	13.8	3.3	0.0	23.1	10.9	0.0	5.8	0.0	2.2	2.3	0.0
Hawthorne	112	442	36.6	8.7	13.7	4.1	11.5	0.8	0.0	0.0	2.1	8.2	0.2
Hayward	243	2 490	211.8	56.0	10.3	2.1	23.4	3.8	0.0	0.3	8.6	7.8	17.2
Hemet	70	399	22.2	6.1	0.1	1.0	5.0	0.0	0.0	0.0	1.7	3.2	0.2
Hesperia	93	466	28.7	7.1	-0.1	0.0	1.0	0.0	0.0	0.0	0.0	0.8	0.0
Highland	23	88	4.7	1.7	0.2	0.0	0.1	0.0	0.0	0.0	0.0	0.0	0.0
Hollister	40	171	16.1	2.7	17.0	0.5	2.2	0.0	0.0	0.0	0.1	2.0	0.0

1. Firms subject to federal tax. 2. Includes program categories not shown separately. State totals include additional categories not allocated by city.

Table D. Cities — **City Government Finances**

	City government finances, 2002									
City	General revenue							General expenditure		
		Intergovernmental		Taxes					Per capita[1] (dollars)	
					Per capita[1] (dollars)					
	Total (mil dol)	Total (mil dol)	Percent from state government	Total (mil dol)	Total	Property	Sales and gross receipts	Total (mil dol)	Total	Capital outlays
	117	118	119	120	121	122	123	124	125	126

CALIFORNIA—Cont'd

City	117	118	119	120	121	122	123	124	125	126
Azusa	48.4	8.5	75.8	22.9	495	149	259	40.9	882	124
Bakersfield	201.5	31.8	84.1	84.0	322	88	209	172.9	662	106
Baldwin Park	30.9	11.9	55.4	12.7	163	56	95	28.7	368	24
Bell	24.5	4.6	88.0	10.3	276	119	138	22.7	608	188
Bellflower	26.4	7.6	87.7	15.4	206	33	159	26.2	352	111
Bell Gardens	25.1	6.0	80.0	14.0	310	59	54	27.7	611	210
Belmont	29.3	3.1	89.1	19.3	776	501	218	28.9	1 165	157
Benicia	33.2	3.2	93.2	20.3	746	357	346	28.9	1 064	216
Berkeley	231.5	46.8	73.6	93.5	902	356	354	231.3	2 231	214
Beverly Hills	142.2	4.7	94.8	86.8	2 490	591	990	145.4	4 173	739
Brea	71.8	4.9	95.8	45.6	1 231	714	478	56.6	1 530	136
Buena Park	62.1	9.2	70.2	36.0	456	155	282	51.0	645	159
Burbank	177.5	29.1	58.7	88.7	862	407	414	167.2	1 625	341
Burlingame	43.3	3.6	100.0	26.3	947	237	651	54.2	1 950	604
Calexico	29.6	7.0	98.5	10.9	353	133	154	24.9	810	158
Camarillo	53.7	7.9	82.9	23.6	397	133	222	34.4	579	157
Campbell	39.4	4.4	100.0	22.7	607	261	312	52.9	1 413	613
Carlsbad	140.9	15.8	72.7	68.3	789	287	427	94.5	1 090	234
Carson	97.5	23.8	100.0	56.8	611	264	297	90.0	969	352
Cathedral City	42.0	4.6	96.8	30.5	659	391	228	40.7	878	153
Ceres	20.6	3.9	96.5	10.9	297	77	166	22.5	614	219
Cerritos	96.9	4.9	99.5	52.6	1 000	456	515	142.3	2 705	1 343
Chico	64.0	8.5	91.1	38.3	581	195	320	51.2	777	170
Chino	71.8	8.6	100.0	26.7	382	170	180	69.6	995	103
Chula Vista	230.5	34.6	94.4	91.2	470	104	222	202.1	1 042	195
Claremont	27.4	3.4	88.0	12.8	369	106	234	26.8	769	168
Clovis	75.4	12.9	88.4	25.2	338	96	193	69.1	928	224
Colton	42.3	5.4	97.0	17.3	348	158	161	41.0	822	111
Compton	98.0	16.7	72.5	48.2	505	266	217	90.6	948	169
Concord	104.7	14.7	91.8	61.6	492	188	244	109.8	877	221
Corona	158.3	16.9	86.1	68.8	498	187	219	149.1	1 078	164
Costa Mesa	80.9	10.6	100.0	54.4	494	145	327	83.8	761	38
Covina	39.2	6.6	90.6	23.9	498	191	287	43.5	906	295
Culver City	118.1	11.3	57.5	64.8	1 632	635	799	101.6	2 559	578
Cupertino	47.3	5.3	78.4	25.2	504	72	384	36.4	728	103
Cypress	35.9	4.6	93.7	23.6	499	180	288	26.4	558	53
Daly City	86.1	18.2	62.3	32.5	319	126	151	84.5	829	165
Dana Point	24.8	4.3	93.5	16.9	472	99	343	17.2	481	125
Danville	29.0	4.5	87.1	13.4	315	143	120	24.2	568	157
Davis	80.7	16.8	77.4	39.0	608	200	206	66.5	1 036	213
Delano	26.9	11.2	91.2	6.9	163	66	66	20.9	497	193
Diamond Bar	17.7	5.2	94.6	9.1	156	40	98	17.4	301	110
Downey	71.5	15.4	82.4	35.9	327	96	212	63.9	582	79
Dublin	61.6	3.8	98.0	46.6	1 356	262	437	42.3	1 231	359
East Palo Alto	20.9	6.1	57.1	8.6	270	160	90	17.8	562	89
El Cajon	73.2	14.5	74.6	38.2	400	121	261	73.2	766	94
El Centro	89.6	5.4	74.9	14.5	385	111	252	99.7	2 645	655
El Monte	62.6	13.6	97.3	40.5	338	96	218	68.9	574	111
Encinitas	54.2	5.9	100.0	28.9	483	268	208	54.5	912	353
Escondido	133.8	18.9	98.3	54.0	398	142	229	118.2	870	215
Eureka	30.8	4.7	78.2	16.0	619	161	434	32.1	1 242	404
Fairfield	129.8	30.0	42.5	69.4	681	269	254	95.2	934	209
Folsom	96.3	11.9	69.7	53.6	875	250	282	77.5	1 264	160
Fontana	156.0	16.9	75.3	81.7	569	263	183	127.6	889	119
Foster City	49.6	3.1	99.6	32.8	1 123	797	216	41.2	1 412	228
Fountain Valley	50.7	8.1	83.3	29.7	534	247	256	46.5	837	287
Fremont	173.0	23.8	94.8	111.3	538	281	190	186.6	902	291
Fresno	399.5	92.7	71.8	143.8	323	106	175	433.1	973	265
Fullerton	102.1	16.0	79.3	56.1	435	180	166	90.9	706	168
Gardena	47.6	13.0	85.8	28.7	482	60	287	30.4	510	6
Garden Grove	107.7	42.1	45.8	51.1	305	142	139	96.2	574	86
Gilroy	46.0	4.6	100.0	22.6	523	90	374	39.3	912	159
Glendale	233.0	51.5	58.9	91.1	457	163	275	151.1	758	48
Glendora	30.4	4.7	98.9	15.5	306	136	149	26.2	519	106
Hanford	30.2	6.2	72.6	11.4	258	72	145	32.4	731	246
Hawthorne	100.2	52.9	80.8	29.5	344	79	197	103.0	1 199	70
Hayward	140.7	28.5	88.9	70.9	497	161	271	114.5	802	143
Hemet	42.2	6.3	97.0	21.7	342	146	153	48.1	759	161
Hesperia	27.2	6.2	88.4	17.4	260	92	132	24.2	360	32
Highland	22.5	5.8	80.7	8.6	182	80	51	16.0	339	110
Hollister	31.5	4.7	99.8	14.6	402	222	108	28.1	772	105

1. Based on population estimated as of July 1 of the year shown.

Table D. Cities — **City Government Finances (cont'd)**

City	City government finances, 2002 (cont'd)									
	General expenditure									
	Percent of total for—									
	Public welfare	Highways	Parking facilities	Education	Health and hospitals	Police protection	Sewerage and sanitation	Parks and recreation	Housing and community development	Interest on debt
	127	128	129	130	131	132	133	134	135	136
CALIFORNIA—Cont'd										
Azusa	0.0	8.4	0.0	0.0	0.9	25.0	7.0	7.0	13.8	10.3
Bakersfield	0.0	9.1	0.4	0.0	0.0	22.9	22.6	7.2	1.5	6.8
Baldwin Park	0.0	15.8	0.0	0.0	0.1	33.6	0.6	4.8	24.4	6.5
Bell	0.0	9.7	0.0	0.0	0.0	27.2	6.7	8.4	24.7	7.4
Bellflower	0.0	19.0	0.0	0.0	0.4	30.0	0.0	15.2	17.4	2.0
Bell Gardens	0.0	4.7	0.0	0.0	0.0	29.6	1.5	12.4	28.4	3.0
Belmont	0.0	7.7	0.0	0.0	0.0	23.4	17.2	10.3	6.0	5.2
Benicia	0.0	9.2	0.0	0.0	0.0	17.0	15.5	13.3	1.8	5.8
Berkeley	0.0	5.3	1.9	0.0	10.5	14.5	14.5	4.4	5.3	6.1
Beverly Hills	0.0	10.4	6.5	0.0	2.3	19.7	8.2	13.0	0.9	7.8
Brea	0.0	8.6	0.0	0.0	2.9	25.2	3.8	5.8	10.6	19.0
Buena Park	0.0	13.6	0.0	0.0	0.0	28.4	4.6	6.7	10.2	6.7
Burbank	0.0	12.0	0.3	0.0	6.5	17.3	16.4	4.6	7.3	4.9
Burlingame	0.0	31.4	1.5	0.0	0.0	12.7	9.1	10.4	0.0	2.5
Calexico	0.0	12.6	0.0	0.0	1.9	16.4	17.7	2.9	19.7	7.2
Camarillo	0.0	31.5	0.0	0.0	0.4	17.9	24.4	0.0	1.9	3.7
Campbell	0.0	15.0	0.0	0.0	0.0	17.4	0.5	7.6	34.9	2.4
Carlsbad	0.0	16.3	0.0	0.0	0.0	16.4	4.5	9.3	5.9	5.3
Carson	0.0	30.8	0.0	0.0	0.1	15.9	0.0	8.8	22.4	3.1
Cathedral City	0.0	7.5	0.0	0.0	1.6	16.7	0.0	9.5	33.0	11.8
Ceres	0.0	11.8	0.0	0.0	0.0	29.3	12.0	5.0	22.2	3.3
Cerritos	0.0	10.0	0.0	0.0	0.1	6.0	3.0	3.5	27.8	10.2
Chico	0.0	9.6	0.5	0.0	0.2	21.1	5.3	5.3	13.2	6.5
Chino	0.0	22.5	0.0	0.0	5.0	23.8	20.0	1.0	12.4	6.5
Chula Vista	0.0	16.2	0.2	0.0	0.7	19.4	9.4	4.7	6.1	18.0
Claremont	0.0	13.4	0.0	0.0	1.3	23.7	19.6	16.7	9.0	2.3
Clovis	0.0	19.2	0.0	0.0	0.4	19.4	19.8	3.8	5.0	13.6
Colton	0.0	4.0	0.0	0.0	0.3	19.8	10.0	2.3	16.7	14.7
Compton	0.0	13.0	0.0	0.0	1.5	14.7	8.5	2.3	12.9	6.2
Concord	0.0	17.5	0.0	0.0	0.0	24.5	10.5	12.6	16.2	4.6
Corona	0.0	6.8	0.1	0.0	0.8	16.0	17.3	6.0	4.4	23.6
Costa Mesa	0.0	11.1	0.0	0.0	0.0	36.9	1.0	5.1	1.2	3.9
Covina	0.0	6.1	0.1	0.0	0.4	20.2	6.7	5.8	8.8	5.8
Culver City	0.0	5.4	0.1	0.0	2.7	20.2	10.4	5.4	22.1	10.3
Cupertino	0.0	23.0	0.0	0.0	0.9	16.6	4.7	24.1	0.1	7.1
Cypress	0.0	17.6	0.0	0.0	0.0	36.4	0.8	14.8	7.5	6.0
Daly City	0.0	16.4	0.0	0.0	0.0	19.0	18.0	11.0	8.2	0.0
Dana Point	0.0	27.1	0.0	0.0	1.2	31.3	0.0	13.2	0.0	0.0
Danville	0.0	19.6	0.2	0.0	1.7	19.6	0.0	14.3	18.1	1.6
Davis	0.0	10.4	0.0	0.0	0.2	13.0	16.4	15.6	11.5	6.2
Delano	0.0	4.9	0.0	0.0	1.5	19.3	35.2	3.8	8.2	4.5
Diamond Bar	0.0	36.7	0.0	0.0	0.4	24.7	1.0	19.0	0.0	0.0
Downey	0.0	18.9	0.0	0.0	3.2	30.0	1.2	7.3	3.9	3.6
Dublin	0.0	18.8	0.0	0.0	0.9	18.2	2.4	8.3	1.0	0.3
East Palo Alto	0.0	7.7	0.0	0.0	0.4	32.1	8.2	4.0	17.8	14.9
El Cajon	0.0	13.0	0.0	0.0	5.5	27.7	15.8	6.4	6.8	4.0
El Centro	0.0	6.7	0.0	0.0	66.2	5.6	6.0	1.5	3.1	3.0
El Monte	0.0	11.6	0.1	0.0	0.1	31.4	0.0	6.6	12.2	3.7
Encinitas	0.0	25.5	0.0	0.0	1.3	14.0	5.7	21.0	4.3	1.9
Escondido	0.0	11.7	0.0	0.0	0.2	21.5	26.2	3.2	5.8	8.3
Eureka	0.0	10.6	0.0	0.0	0.0	18.6	15.4	5.1	17.1	7.5
Fairfield	0.0	23.8	0.0	0.0	0.2	17.1	0.2	11.2	12.9	10.2
Folsom	0.0	7.9	0.0	0.0	0.1	14.0	11.7	13.0	2.2	11.1
Fontana	0.0	10.9	0.0	0.0	0.4	15.4	14.3	3.5	9.4	25.2
Foster City	0.0	3.6	0.0	0.0	0.0	16.0	7.5	12.7	28.4	11.8
Fountain Valley	0.0	24.9	0.0	0.0	3.4	21.6	5.9	7.4	16.8	5.1
Fremont	0.0	12.5	0.0	0.0	3.1	23.3	0.8	8.0	12.4	8.4
Fresno	0.0	9.9	0.8	0.0	1.5	21.4	19.6	15.7	4.6	7.5
Fullerton	0.0	13.6	0.0	0.0	1.5	29.3	8.8	6.8	8.9	2.3
Gardena	0.0	7.7	0.0	0.0	7.9	39.0	2.7	6.7	0.0	7.6
Garden Grove	0.0	10.3	0.0	0.0	4.1	29.7	0.0	2.9	30.5	4.1
Gilroy	0.0	16.0	0.0	0.0	0.0	34.0	12.1	12.0	0.0	4.9
Glendale	0.0	10.0	2.4	0.0	0.4	22.3	10.4	5.1	14.0	5.2
Glendora	0.0	20.3	0.0	0.0	0.8	29.0	11.9	12.3	7.4	4.0
Hanford	0.0	14.3	0.0	0.0	0.3	13.9	22.2	17.1	7.1	3.6
Hawthorne	0.0	6.5	0.0	0.0	0.0	27.3	10.4	2.8	12.2	3.5
Hayward	0.0	15.5	0.4	0.0	1.0	29.1	9.4	3.1	4.2	3.4
Hemet	0.0	13.6	0.1	0.0	0.4	23.7	15.5	0.8	14.6	3.3
Hesperia	0.0	19.8	0.0	0.0	4.2	24.5	0.0	0.0	6.6	8.3
Highland	0.0	29.2	0.0	0.0	4.4	23.9	0.0	0.8	6.1	7.7
Hollister	0.0	24.8	0.0	0.0	0.8	13.8	14.0	2.9	7.2	6.4

Table D. Cities — City Government Finances, City Government Employment, and Climate

City	Total (mil dol) 137	Per capita¹ (dollars) 138	Percent utility 139	City government employment, 2002 140	Mean January 141	Mean July 142	Limits January³ 143	Limits July⁴ 144	Annual precipitation (inches) 145	Heating degree days 146	Cooling degree days 147
CALIFORNIA—Cont'd											
Azusa	76.1	1 642	0.0	319	55.8	75.0	43.6	89.0	19.37	1 453	1 394
Bakersfield	220.9	846	2.2	1 275	47.8	84.1	38.6	98.5	5.72	2 182	2 365
Baldwin Park	48.0	617	0.0	349	55.7	75.2	41.7	89.2	17.90	1 433	1 427
Bell	31.3	837	0.0	115	58.3	74.3	48.9	84.0	14.77	1 154	1 537
Bellflower	16.7	224	0.0	147	55.9	73.1	44.9	82.7	11.80	1 430	1 201
Bell Gardens	18.9	418	27.3	175	58.3	74.3	48.9	84.0	14.77	1 154	1 537
Belmont	36.2	1 458	0.0	136	NA	NA	NA	NA	NA	NA	NA
Benicia	28.0	1 031	5.3	233	NA	NA	NA	NA	NA	NA	NA
Berkeley	213.5	2 060	0.0	1 468	49.9	62.1	43.3	70.0	24.30	2 902	115
Beverly Hills	236.2	6 777	7.2	866	57.2	70.4	46.5	79.2	13.06	1 391	986
Brea	237.9	6 424	8.1	450	57.4	72.6	45.6	82.6	12.27	1 238	1 175
Buena Park	47.6	603	2.1	345	57.4	72.6	45.6	82.6	12.27	1 238	1 175
Burbank	265.6	2 580	41.1	1 369	54.5	75.6	41.3	90.2	15.87	1 609	1 424
Burlingame	36.4	1 312	0.0	328	48.7	62.7	41.8	71.6	19.70	3 016	145
Calexico	29.8	968	0.0	201	NA	NA	NA	NA	NA	NA	NA
Camarillo	36.7	617	0.0	137	55.3	66.1	44.2	74.4	14.38	1 992	416
Campbell	20.4	546	0.0	219	49.4	69.5	40.6	82.4	14.42	2 387	594
Carlsbad	89.1	1 029	2.6	762	54.5	67.6	44.1	73.5	10.93	2 010	555
Carson	93.5	1 006	0.0	516	56.1	69.7	45.3	78.8	13.57	1 568	794
Cathedral City	77.3	1 670	0.0	202	56.4	92.0	42.5	108.7	5.31	985	4 014
Ceres	11.9	324	0.0	159	45.6	77.1	37.4	94.2	12.10	2 605	1 401
Cerritos	212.1	4 031	0.0	445	55.9	73.1	44.9	82.7	11.80	1 430	1 201
Chico	66.5	1 009	0.0	434	44.0	77.4	34.5	94.2	26.32	2 953	1 360
Chino	99.8	1 427	4.8	368	54.3	74.6	40.7	90.4	16.62	1 713	1 273
Chula Vista	627.0	3 234	0.0	1 286	55.3	68.2	45.3	73.1	9.34	1 798	638
Claremont	10.1	289	0.0	213	54.3	74.6	40.7	90.4	16.62	1 713	1 273
Clovis	161.7	2 170	1.8	442	45.7	81.9	37.4	98.6	10.60	2 556	1 967
Colton	151.3	3 035	18.9	398	53.6	79.4	40.3	97.0	15.42	1 719	1 804
Compton	120.9	1 266	0.0	505	56.1	69.7	45.3	78.8	13.57	1 568	794
Concord	140.3	1 120	0.0	592	44.5	73.8	35.9	90.8	12.80	2 837	1 066
Corona	415.3	3 002	8.4	828	53.9	75.4	40.5	92.1	11.83	1 747	1 339
Costa Mesa	52.7	479	0.0	664	55.2	67.1	46.8	71.8	10.85	1 866	500
Covina	56.2	1 170	4.8	214	54.3	74.6	40.7	90.4	16.62	1 713	1 273
Culver City	201.7	5 082	0.0	819	57.2	70.4	46.5	79.2	13.06	1 391	986
Cupertino	42.6	852	0.0	173	49.4	69.5	40.6	82.4	14.42	2 387	594
Cypress	39.5	836	0.0	215	57.4	72.6	45.6	82.6	12.27	1 238	1 175
Daly City	0.0	0	0.0	613	48.7	62.7	41.8	71.6	19.70	3 016	145
Dana Point	0.0	0	0.0	32	53.7	67.2	41.5	75.8	12.19	2 157	493
Danville	10.3	241	0.0	95	46.1	71.6	35.5	89.8	14.21	2 909	780
Davis	66.4	1 034	0.0	447	44.5	74.1	36.3	92.7	18.13	2 911	1 041
Delano	15.0	356	0.0	252	NA	NA	NA	NA	NA	NA	NA
Diamond Bar	0.0	0	0.0	51	54.3	74.6	40.7	90.4	16.62	1 713	1 273
Downey	34.8	317	1.6	506	58.3	74.3	48.9	84.0	14.77	1 154	1 537
Dublin	1.7	49	0.0	94	NA	NA	NA	NA	NA	NA	NA
East Palo Alto	45.8	1 446	0.0	77	NA	NA	NA	NA	NA	NA	NA
El Cajon	49.6	519	0.0	553	56.6	72.5	44.6	83.4	12.80	1 400	1 110
El Centro	49.9	1 325	2.7	905	54.6	91.3	39.3	107.5	2.71	1 156	3 741
El Monte	82.9	691	22.8	425	55.7	75.2	41.7	89.2	17.90	1 433	1 427
Encinitas	47.6	797	49.8	212	54.5	67.6	44.1	73.5	10.93	2 010	555
Escondido	155.1	1 141	0.0	963	55.2	70.5	43.1	81.3	13.04	1 802	868
Eureka	41.7	1 613	0.0	349	48.0	57.0	41.5	61.8	37.53	4 496	0
Fairfield	217.5	2 133	30.4	609	45.5	72.0	36.2	88.5	21.38	2 767	898
Folsom	147.7	2 412	12.6	534	45.6	77.2	37.7	94.2	23.91	2 683	1 422
Fontana	644.7	4 489	0.0	462	56.0	78.6	44.5	94.8	15.63	1 478	1 922
Foster City	76.3	2 613	0.0	247	48.7	68.7	38.9	83.4	19.74	2 563	486
Fountain Valley	36.8	662	0.0	275	57.4	72.6	45.6	82.6	12.27	1 238	1 175
Fremont	334.2	1 615	0.0	1 074	49.0	66.7	41.1	76.1	13.73	2 578	410
Fresno	841.5	1 890	5.9	3 466	45.7	81.9	37.4	98.6	10.60	2 556	1 967
Fullerton	44.7	347	4.4	726	57.4	72.6	45.6	82.6	12.27	1 238	1 175
Gardena	36.2	608	0.0	401	56.1	69.7	45.3	78.8	13.57	1 568	794
Garden Grove	102.1	610	17.1	728	57.4	72.6	45.6	82.6	12.27	1 238	1 175
Gilroy	41.2	954	0.0	289	47.4	70.9	35.6	88.3	19.77	2 668	719
Glendale	163.9	822	22.6	1 841	54.5	75.6	41.3	90.2	15.87	1 609	1 424
Glendora	16.2	320	0.0	258	54.3	74.6	40.7	90.4	16.62	1 713	1 273
Hanford	37.1	837	2.1	239	43.9	78.8	34.3	95.9	7.95	2 816	1 551
Hawthorne	61.9	720	0.0	413	56.8	69.1	47.8	75.3	12.01	1 458	727
Hayward	90.2	632	5.6	903	49.0	66.7	41.1	76.1	13.73	2 578	410
Hemet	35.9	567	13.0	307	50.2	77.6	39.3	96.2	17.33	2 432	1 451
Hesperia	59.8	892	0.0	88	44.2	79.3	30.0	97.4	5.51	3 127	1 525
Highland	26.9	572	0.0	35	53.6	79.4	40.3	97.0	15.42	1 719	1 804
Hollister	28.6	785	0.0	180	NA	NA	NA	NA	NA	NA	NA

1. Based on the population estimated as of July 1 of the year shown. 2. Represents normal values based on the 30-year period, 1961–1990. 3. Average daily minimum. 4. Average daily maximum.

STATE Place code	City	Land area,[1] 2000 (sq km)	Population, 2003 Total persons	Rank	Per square kilometer	White	Black	Am. Indian, Alaska Native	Asian and Pacific Islander	Other race	Hispanic or Latino[2]	Non-Hispanic White
		1	2	3	4	5	6	7	8	9	10	11
	CALIFORNIA—Cont'd											
06 36000	Huntington Beach	68.4	194 248	108	2 839.9	82.7	1.1	1.5	11.5	7.4	14.7	71.9
06 36056	Huntington Park	7.8	63 139	461	8 094.7	45.9	1.0	1.3	1.1	55.6	95.6	2.7
06 36294	Imperial Beach	11.1	27 151	1 160	2 446.0	67.5	6.4	2.1	10.5	20.5	40.1	43.5
06 36448	Indio	69.1	58 241	520	842.9	52.1	3.1	1.5	2.2	45.2	75.4	19.5
06 36546	Inglewood	23.7	115 208	202	4 861.1	21.9	48.7	1.4	2.1	30.4	46.0	4.1
06 36770	Irvine	119.6	170 561	123	1 426.1	65.2	1.8	0.6	32.7	4.7	7.4	57.0
06 39248	Laguna Niguel	38.0	64 326	449	1 692.8	86.8	1.6	0.8	9.5	5.2	10.4	77.4
06 39290	La Habra	19.0	59 703	500	3 142.3	67.1	2.0	1.6	7.4	26.9	49.0	41.4
06 39486	Lake Elsinore	87.6	34 914	928	398.6	69.8	6.2	2.5	3.7	23.3	38.0	51.4
06 39496	Lake Forest	32.4	76 738	366	2 368.5	79.8	2.3	1.2	11.8	9.4	18.6	66.7
06 39892	Lakewood	24.4	81 300	331	3 332.0	66.8	8.1	1.6	16.7	12.4	22.8	52.4
06 40004	La Mesa	24.0	54 571	577	2 273.8	84.4	5.8	1.5	6.1	6.8	13.5	73.7
06 40032	La Mirada	20.3	48 887	651	2 408.2	67.9	2.3	1.4	16.5	16.0	33.5	47.1
06 40130	Lancaster	243.5	125 896	179	517.0	67.0	17.5	2.3	5.4	13.4	24.1	52.4
06 40340	La Puente	9.0	42 143	762	4 682.6	43.4	2.4	1.9	8.3	49.4	83.1	6.7
06 40830	La Verne	21.5	33 005	978	1 535.1	80.9	3.7	1.3	8.8	9.8	23.1	63.6
06 40886	Lawndale..............................	5.1	32 490	991	6 370.6	47.5	13.6	1.8	12.3	31.7	52.1	21.9
06 41992	Livermore	62.0	77 744	358	1 253.9	85.9	2.1	1.6	8.2	7.1	14.4	74.4
06 42202	Lodi	31.7	61 027	479	1 925.1	78.4	0.9	1.8	7.1	17.0	27.1	63.5
06 42524	Lompoc	30.1	41 167	782	1 367.7	70.3	8.4	3.0	6.0	18.1	37.3	47.9
06 43000	Long Beach..........................	130.6	475 460	32	3 640.6	48.9	16.0	1.7	15.4	23.6	35.8	33.1
06 43280	Los Altos	16.4	27 173	1 157	1 656.9	82.9	0.6	0.5	17.5	1.5	3.0	78.2
06 44000	Los Angeles	1 214.9	3 819 951	2	3 144.3	51.2	12.0	1.4	11.4	29.4	46.5	29.7
06 44028	Los Banos	20.8	30 538	1 047	1 468.2	63.7	5.1	2.5	4.4	30.8	50.4	39.8
06 44112	Los Gatos............................	27.7	27 976	1 135	1 010.0	89.7	1.1	0.8	9.5	2.5	5.2	83.3
06 44574	Lynwood...............................	12.6	71 619	395	5 684.0	37.3	14.0	1.7	1.5	50.0	82.3	2.9
06 45022	Madera	31.8	47 952	667	1 507.9	52.9	4.4	3.9	2.3	42.3	67.8	25.1
06 45400	Manhattan Beach	10.2	36 007	891	3 530.1	91.6	0.9	0.6	7.9	1.9	5.2	85.4
06 45484	Manteca	41.2	59 500	502	1 444.2	79.6	3.5	2.8	6.0	14.8	25.1	64.1
06 45778	Marina	22.7	18 919	1 230	833.4	49.4	16.3	2.2	23.8	17.1	23.2	37.8
06 46114	Martinez	31.7	36 595	880	1 154.4	85.2	4.0	2.0	9.0	4.9	10.2	75.5
06 46492	Maywood..............................	3.0	28 751	1 105	9 583.7	47.2	0.5	1.4	0.7	54.8	96.3	2.6
06 46870	Menlo Park	26.2	29 811	1 072	1 137.8	74.9	7.6	1.0	10.1	9.9	15.6	66.4
06 46898	Merced	51.4	69 512	405	1 352.4	56.3	7.3	2.5	13.2	26.2	41.4	37.8
06 47766	Milpitas	35.1	63 081	462	1 797.2	34.4	4.4	1.3	55.5	9.7	16.6	23.8
06 48256	Mission Viejo	48.3	95 831	263	1 984.1	86.4	1.6	0.9	9.6	5.3	12.1	76.0
06 48354	Modesto	92.7	206 872	89	2 231.6	74.2	4.8	2.6	8.9	15.8	25.6	59.6
06 48648	Monrovia	35.6	37 996	839	1 067.3	66.9	9.5	1.8	8.6	18.2	35.2	46.6
06 48788	Montclair..............................	13.2	34 776	933	2 634.5	48.7	6.9	1.7	9.6	38.1	60.0	23.6
06 48816	Montebello...........................	21.4	63 747	454	2 978.8	51.5	1.1	1.8	12.7	38.5	74.6	11.1
06 48872	Monterey	21.9	29 960	1 064	1 368.0	84.8	3.2	1.5	9.9	5.4	10.9	75.0
06 48914	Monterey Park	19.8	62 213	470	3 142.1	23.7	0.7	1.0	63.9	14.3	28.9	7.3
06 49138	Moorpark	49.3	35 168	920	713.3	77.8	1.9	1.2	7.2	15.9	27.8	62.4
06 49270	Moreno Valley	132.7	157 063	134	1 183.6	51.4	21.6	1.9	8.3	23.1	38.4	32.2
06 49278	Morgan Hill	30.2	34 128	945	1 130.1	76.7	2.2	2.1	8.6	16.1	27.5	61.3
06 49670	Mountain View	31.2	69 366	406	2 223.3	67.2	3.1	0.9	23.1	10.1	18.3	55.2
06 50076	Murrieta	73.5	66 729	430	907.9	85.4	4.1	1.6	6.1	7.5	17.5	71.8
06 50258	Napa....................................	45.8	75 560	370	1 649.8	83.8	0.8	2.0	2.9	14.6	26.8	68.2
06 50398	National City.........................	19.1	58 292	519	3 051.9	39.1	6.6	1.6	21.7	36.9	59.1	14.1
06 50916	Newark	36.2	43 042	745	1 189.0	57.8	4.7	1.6	26.4	17.2	28.6	40.3
06 51182	Newport Beach	38.3	78 043	356	2 037.7	93.8	0.7	0.6	5.1	1.7	4.7	89.0
06 52526	Norwalk	25.1	107 155	220	4 269.1	48.6	5.1	1.8	13.1	36.2	62.9	18.9
06 52582	Novato	71.8	48 383	660	673.9	86.2	2.7	1.3	7.1	6.9	13.1	76.3
06 53000	Oakland	145.2	398 844	43	2 746.9	34.7	37.6	1.7	17.4	14.1	21.9	23.5
06 53322	Oceanside	105.1	167 082	125	1 589.7	70.6	7.4	1.7	9.3	16.7	30.2	53.6
06 53896	Ontario	128.9	167 402	124	1 298.7	52.2	8.3	1.8	5.4	37.9	59.9	26.6
06 53980	Orange	60.6	132 197	169	2 181.5	73.7	2.0	1.4	10.9	15.9	32.2	54.6
06 54652	Oxnard	65.6	180 872	116	2 757.2	45.9	4.4	2.0	9.3	43.4	66.2	20.6
06 54806	Pacifica	32.7	37 291	863	1 140.4	75.0	4.2	1.6	20.1	6.3	14.6	61.3
06 55156	Palmdale..............................	271.8	127 759	174	470.0	59.1	15.8	1.9	5.3	23.5	37.7	41.0
06 55184	Palm Desert	63.1	45 624	708	723.0	88.9	1.6	0.9	3.3	7.8	17.1	77.6
06 55254	Palm Springs	244.1	45 228	714	185.3	81.0	4.4	1.6	4.7	11.5	23.7	66.5
06 55282	Palo Alto	61.3	57 233	530	933.7	78.6	2.5	0.7	19.4	2.3	4.6	72.8
06 55520	Paradise	47.3	26 796	1 179	566.5	96.2	0.4	2.3	1.9	2.0	4.3	91.2
06 55618	Paramount	12.3	56 660	537	4 606.5	38.5	14.3	1.7	5.0	45.5	72.3	9.0
06 56000	Pasadena	59.8	141 114	162	2 359.8	57.7	15.6	1.5	11.6	19.3	33.4	39.1
06 56700	Perris	81.3	41 208	780	506.9	45.8	17.3	2.5	4.3	36.2	56.2	22.8
06 56784	Petaluma	35.7	55 175	561	1 545.5	87.8	1.7	1.5	5.7	7.7	14.6	77.0
06 56924	Pico Rivera	21.5	65 317	440	3 038.0	54.3	0.9	1.9	3.3	45.1	88.3	7.7
06 57456	Pittsburg	40.4	61 004	481	1 510.0	48.9	20.7	1.9	16.5	19.8	32.2	31.2
06 57526	Placentia	17.1	48 210	662	2 819.3	70.8	2.1	1.5	12.6	16.8	31.1	53.7

1. Dry land or land partially or temporarily covered by water. 2. Hispanic or Latino persons may be of any race.

Table D. Cities — **Population and Households**

City	Under 5 years	5 to 17 years	18 to 24 years	25 to 34 years	35 to 44 years	45 to 54 years	55 to 64 years	65 to 74 years	75 years and over	Percent female	1990	2000	1990–2000	2000–2003
	12	13	14	15	16	17	18	19	20	21	22	23	24	25
CALIFORNIA—Cont'd														
Huntington Beach	6.2	16.1	8.4	17.4	17.5	14.2	9.8	5.9	4.5	49.9	181 519	189 594	4.4	2.5
Huntington Park	10.4	25.4	13.0	18.7	13.6	9.0	4.8	3.1	2.0	49.9	56 129	61 348	9.3	2.9
Imperial Beach	8.4	21.1	13.9	17.0	15.3	11.0	5.8	4.4	3.1	50.1	26 512	26 992	1.8	0.6
Indio	10.4	24.9	11.1	15.7	13.7	8.9	6.3	5.2	3.9	49.7	36 850	49 116	33.3	18.6
Inglewood	9.1	23.3	10.2	16.4	15.5	11.5	6.9	4.1	3.0	52.5	109 602	112 580	2.7	2.3
Irvine	5.6	17.9	14.4	15.0	17.3	14.9	7.7	3.9	3.3	51.6	110 330	143 072	29.7	19.2
Laguna Niguel	7.0	19.6	6.0	12.7	20.2	16.8	8.8	5.1	3.8	51.3	44 723	61 891	38.4	3.9
La Habra	8.4	20.7	10.3	16.4	15.3	11.2	7.0	5.4	5.4	50.7	51 263	58 974	15.0	1.2
Lake Elsinore	9.8	26.2	9.3	14.7	17.4	10.5	5.4	3.9	2.8	50.1	19 733	28 928	46.6	20.7
Lake Forest	7.1	19.9	8.0	15.0	18.3	15.1	8.1	4.0	4.6	50.8	56 065	58 707	4.7	30.7
Lakewood	7.1	20.5	8.1	13.9	17.2	13.6	7.8	6.1	5.8	51.6	73 553	79 345	7.9	2.5
La Mesa	5.7	14.1	9.9	16.5	16.4	12.8	7.5	7.1	10.0	52.8	52 911	54 749	3.5	-0.3
La Mirada	6.3	19.9	10.7	12.4	16.1	12.1	8.7	7.7	6.1	51.7	40 452	46 783	15.7	4.5
Lancaster	8.0	24.3	9.5	13.8	17.5	11.6	6.6	4.6	4.0	49.2	97 300	118 718	22.0	6.0
La Puente	9.0	24.8	11.6	16.7	14.3	9.7	6.2	4.7	2.9	50.0	36 955	41 063	11.1	2.6
La Verne	5.8	19.4	9.7	11.2	16.2	15.1	9.4	6.6	6.6	51.9	30 843	31 638	2.6	4.3
Lawndale	9.3	22.6	10.2	19.5	16.4	10.6	5.9	3.5	2.1	49.4	27 331	31 711	16.0	2.5
Livermore	7.7	20.4	7.1	14.8	20.3	14.0	8.1	4.3	3.2	50.0	56 741	73 345	29.3	6.0
Lodi	7.9	20.3	9.6	13.3	14.8	12.1	7.7	6.5	7.8	51.2	51 874	56 999	9.9	7.1
Lompoc	8.0	22.0	8.9	15.6	17.7	11.4	7.1	5.3	4.0	46.9	37 649	41 103	9.2	0.2
Long Beach	8.4	20.8	10.9	17.2	15.7	11.6	6.4	4.4	4.7	50.9	429 321	461 522	7.5	3.0
Los Altos	5.9	17.8	3.5	7.2	17.3	16.9	12.2	9.0	10.3	51.8	26 599	27 693	4.1	-1.9
Los Angeles	7.7	18.8	11.1	18.2	15.8	11.6	7.0	5.1	4.6	50.2	3 485 557	3 694 820	6.0	3.4
Los Banos	9.4	25.8	8.9	13.7	16.1	10.6	6.2	5.0	4.3	50.2	14 519	25 869	78.2	18.0
Los Gatos	5.0	16.2	4.3	12.9	18.5	16.1	11.7	7.4	7.9	52.5	27 357	28 592	4.5	-2.2
Lynwood	10.6	27.4	13.1	17.3	13.9	9.0	4.5	2.4	1.8	48.9	61 945	69 845	12.8	2.5
Madera	10.7	24.7	12.5	15.7	12.6	9.4	5.5	4.7	4.2	49.3	29 283	43 207	47.5	11.0
Manhattan Beach	6.5	15.8	4.1	17.7	19.8	16.1	9.6	5.9	4.5	49.6	32 063	33 852	5.6	6.4
Manteca	7.5	24.1	8.8	13.1	17.4	12.8	7.0	4.9	4.4	51.0	40 773	49 258	20.8	20.8
Marina	5.7	15.6	14.0	19.7	18.7	11.6	6.8	5.2	2.7	42.8	26 512	25 101	-5.3	-24.6
Martinez	5.6	17.1	7.3	13.4	19.2	17.5	9.8	5.4	4.8	50.4	31 800	35 866	12.8	2.0
Maywood	11.4	25.6	13.2	19.4	13.2	8.5	4.5	2.5	1.7	49.0	27 893	28 083	0.7	2.4
Menlo Park	6.6	15.3	6.2	17.4	17.4	13.3	8.0	6.7	9.2	51.5	28 403	30 785	8.4	-3.2
Merced	9.2	25.5	11.4	13.8	13.6	10.8	6.3	4.9	4.6	51.1	56 155	63 893	13.8	8.8
Milpitas	7.2	17.5	9.5	19.0	19.0	13.3	7.5	4.6	2.4	47.4	50 690	62 698	23.7	0.6
Mission Viejo	6.9	20.2	6.6	11.7	18.8	15.5	9.4	5.5	5.4	51.1	79 464	93 102	27.9	2.9
Modesto	7.6	22.5	9.6	13.5	15.5	12.8	7.6	5.6	5.5	51.5	164 746	188 856	14.6	9.5
Monrovia	8.0	19.3	8.0	16.9	17.1	12.7	7.5	5.0	5.4	52.0	35 733	36 929	3.3	2.9
Montclair	8.9	24.3	10.7	15.7	14.7	11.0	6.5	4.4	3.9	50.1	28 434	33 049	16.2	5.2
Montebello	8.1	20.5	10.4	16.6	13.8	10.6	7.6	6.7	5.7	52.0	59 564	62 150	4.3	2.6
Monterey	5.0	11.6	13.1	18.1	15.6	13.6	8.1	6.7	8.2	50.8	31 954	29 674	-7.1	1.0
Monterey Park	5.6	15.7	8.4	15.0	15.2	13.0	9.3	9.6	8.3	52.0	60 738	60 051	-1.1	3.6
Moorpark	8.1	26.1	8.6	12.4	19.9	14.8	5.6	2.7	1.8	50.1	25 494	31 415	23.2	11.9
Moreno Valley	8.8	28.0	10.5	12.9	16.6	12.1	5.6	3.4	2.0	51.1	118 779	142 381	19.9	10.3
Morgan Hill	8.1	22.4	7.6	13.5	18.2	14.8	7.9	3.9	3.6	50.4	23 928	33 556	40.2	1.7
Mountain View	6.0	11.9	8.3	24.6	18.8	12.6	7.2	5.3	5.2	48.3	67 365	70 708	5.0	-1.9
Murrieta	7.5	26.2	6.4	10.9	19.9	11.0	6.6	7.1	4.3	51.0	18 557	44 282	138.6	50.7
Napa	6.8	19.0	8.5	14.1	15.5	13.9	8.5	6.2	7.6	50.9	61 865	72 585	17.3	4.1
National City	8.1	22.0	14.0	15.0	14.0	10.0	5.9	6.0	5.1	49.4	54 249	54 260	0.0	7.4
Newark	7.2	20.0	9.5	16.5	17.8	12.8	8.3	4.9	3.0	49.6	37 861	42 471	12.2	1.3
Newport Beach	4.0	11.7	6.5	17.0	16.0	15.2	12.0	8.8	8.8	50.5	66 643	70 032	5.1	11.4
Norwalk	8.6	23.5	10.7	15.7	14.8	10.9	6.7	5.1	3.9	50.5	94 279	103 298	9.6	3.7
Novato	5.9	17.2	6.4	12.6	17.4	16.9	10.7	6.6	6.4	51.6	47 585	47 630	0.1	1.6
Oakland	7.1	17.9	9.7	18.1	15.8	13.5	7.4	5.2	5.3	51.7	372 242	399 484	7.3	-0.2
Oceanside	7.6	20.0	10.2	14.8	16.2	11.1	6.5	6.7	6.9	50.5	128 090	161 029	25.7	3.8
Ontario	9.7	24.7	11.2	16.9	15.4	10.6	5.5	3.3	2.6	49.9	133 179	158 007	18.6	5.9
Orange	7.4	19.3	9.9	16.5	16.8	12.6	7.9	5.4	4.3	49.8	110 658	128 821	16.4	2.6
Oxnard	8.9	22.8	11.8	16.2	14.7	10.8	6.5	4.7	3.4	48.9	142 560	170 358	19.5	6.2
Pacifica	5.7	17.5	7.7	14.4	18.4	17.3	9.3	5.8	4.0	50.7	37 670	38 390	1.9	-2.9
Palmdale	9.3	28.7	8.5	12.7	18.4	11.3	5.4	3.4	2.2	50.9	73 314	116 670	66.0	9.5
Palm Desert	4.5	12.8	6.2	10.1	12.5	12.8	13.4	14.6	12.9	51.9	23 252	41 155	77.0	10.9
Palm Springs	4.7	12.3	6.1	10.4	13.8	13.8	12.6	12.9	13.4	48.1	40 144	42 807	6.6	5.7
Palo Alto	5.1	16.1	4.9	14.5	17.9	16.0	9.9	7.1	8.5	51.1	55 900	58 598	4.8	-2.3
Paradise	4.3	16.1	5.9	7.8	13.3	14.6	10.8	11.3	15.9	53.4	25 401	26 408	4.0	1.5
Paramount	11.0	25.9	12.0	18.1	13.8	8.9	5.1	2.9	2.2	50.9	47 669	55 266	15.9	2.5
Pasadena	6.9	16.2	9.3	18.5	16.4	12.5	8.0	5.8	6.3	51.1	131 586	133 936	1.8	5.4
Perris	10.8	28.8	9.9	15.7	15.1	8.7	4.8	3.4	2.8	51.0	21 500	36 189	68.3	13.9
Petaluma	6.6	19.6	7.2	12.9	18.6	15.7	8.4	5.2	5.9	51.1	43 166	54 548	26.4	1.1
Pico Rivera	8.2	22.7	10.5	15.5	14.2	10.6	7.2	6.3	4.7	50.9	59 177	63 428	7.2	3.0
Pittsburg	8.3	22.5	10.4	14.9	16.3	12.5	6.8	4.5	3.7	50.9	47 607	56 769	19.2	7.5
Placentia	7.4	19.6	9.5	16.2	15.8	13.2	9.2	5.4	3.7	50.4	41 259	46 488	12.7	3.7

Table D. Cities — Group Quarters, Crime, and Education

City	Households, 2000 Number	Percent change, 1990–2000	Persons per house-hold	Percent Female family householder[1]	Percent One-person	Persons in group quarters, 2000 Total	Institutional Total	Persons in nursing homes	Non-institutional	Serious crimes Total Number	Rate[3]	Violent	Property	School enrollment[4] Public	Private	Attainment High school graduate or less	Bachelor's degree or more
	26	27	28	29	30	31	32	33	34	35	36	37	38	39	40	41	42
CALIFORNIA—Cont'd																	
Huntington Beach	73 657	6.9	2.56	9.6	24.3	792	496	434	296	4 385	2 231	172	2 058	43 133	9 123	26.7	36.0
Huntington Park	14 860	6.9	4.12	20.3	10.9	181	16	0	165	2 963	4 659	752	3 907	19 516	1 032	82.7	4.7
Imperial Beach	9 272	2.1	2.84	18.1	21.4	666	0	0	666	836	2 987	579	2 409	7 542	697	50.1	11.7
Indio	13 871	29.1	3.48	16.7	16.0	856	551	197	305	2 332	4 580	974	3 606	14 519	723	67.5	8.6
Inglewood	36 805	1.9	3.02	24.9	25.3	1 370	745	409	625	4 107	3 519	793	2 726	31 988	5 584	56.4	13.3
Irvine	51 199	27.2	2.66	9.8	22.8	7 112	103	103	7 009	3 624	2 443	109	2 335	47 413	6 722	15.1	58.4
Laguna Niguel	23 217	35.2	2.65	8.8	20.6	303	41	41	262	1 085	1 691	108	1 583	13 898	3 809	17.4	47.8
La Habra	18 947	4.6	3.08	13.5	21.0	595	252	252	343	1 824	2 983	257	2 726	15 754	2 333	49.9	18.2
Lake Elsinore	8 817	45.4	3.27	13.8	16.2	73	0	0	73	1 406	4 688	790	3 898	8 841	770	56.2	12.5
Lake Forest	20 008	-7.9	2.89	10.3	19.4	838	558	558	280	1 400	1 777	161	1 616	14 352	2 797	28.4	33.9
Lakewood	26 853	2.9	2.95	13.4	18.4	194	112	112	82	3 112	3 783	411	3 372	20 406	4 349	39.3	20.7
La Mesa	24 186	4.2	2.22	11.6	34.2	1 046	820	781	226	2 357	4 153	365	3 788	12 745	2 222	31.4	27.6
La Mirada	14 580	14.5	3.10	10.4	17.3	1 639	222	222	1 417	1 040	2 144	322	1 823	11 387	4 190	40.1	25.2
Lancaster	38 224	16.2	2.92	17.0	22.1	7 015	6 402	749	613	5 123	4 162	1 107	3 056	33 622	5 479	47.7	15.8
La Puente	9 461	4.9	4.34	17.9	10.1	32	0	0	32	932	2 189	538	1 651	12 683	929	72.8	7.8
La Verne	11 070	3.1	2.79	11.5	19.6	708	159	156	549	770	2 347	296	2 052	7 606	2 594	30.8	31.6
Lawndale	9 555	3.6	3.31	19.0	18.8	86	0	0	86	975	2 966	794	2 172	9 237	1 247	62.7	12.5
Livermore	26 123	26.5	2.80	9.3	18.8	201	128	128	73	2 209	2 905	195	2 710	18 439	3 048	30.4	31.6
Lodi	20 692	8.9	2.71	12.2	25.4	1 024	683	628	341	3 293	5 573	487	5 085	13 225	2 013	52.6	15.6
Lompoc	13 059	4.4	2.88	14.8	23.5	3 439	3 245	106	194	1 380	3 238	401	2 837	11 660	720	50.7	13.8
Long Beach	163 088	2.6	2.77	16.1	29.6	10 181	3 378	2 371	6 803	19 303	4 034	758	3 276	133 079	15 666	46.2	23.9
Los Altos	10 462	6.4	2.61	5.4	18.7	419	297	297	122	265	923	73	850	5 016	1 996	10.3	71.3
Los Angeles	1 275 412	4.8	2.83	14.5	28.5	82 597	30 446	12 853	52 151	190 992	4 986	1 350	3 636	907 807	191 820	50.8	25.5
Los Banos	7 721	61.8	3.33	12.4	15.8	175	149	149	26	776	2 893	436	2 457	7 759	443	58.3	9.9
Los Gatos	11 988	6.3	2.33	7.2	29.7	702	553	553	149	605	2 041	148	1 893	5 086	1 810	13.8	58.9
Lynwood	14 395	1.7	4.70	20.6	7.7	2 200	1 622	391	578	2 570	3 549	1 229	2 320	23 140	1 603	80.5	4.5
Madera	11 978	30.8	3.57	17.5	16.8	438	201	201	237	2 605	5 815	1 060	4 755	12 934	730	70.2	9.3
Manhattan Beach	14 474	3.4	2.34	5.8	29.3	14	0	0	14	1 113	3 171	237	2 935	6 273	1 719	11.3	67.6
Manteca	16 368	21.8	2.98	13.0	18.6	477	288	288	189	2 570	5 033	351	4 682	13 636	1 414	53.9	11.0
Marina	6 745	-14.7	2.79	15.1	21.4	6 307	4 087	0	2 220	499	1 918	300	1 618	6 311	832	53.6	14.3
Martinez	14 300	14.3	2.41	11.0	27.4	1 350	1 217	219	133	1 321	3 553	148	3 405	7 323	1 935	29.2	32.1
Maywood	6 469	-0.4	4.33	16.9	8.4	94	90	90	4	584	2 006	453	1 553	8 873	395	86.8	2.3
Menlo Park	12 387	4.8	2.41	8.5	32.1	952	625	312	327	742	2 325	222	2 102	4 952	2 251	20.8	61.7
Merced	20 435	11.8	3.06	18.2	22.6	1 370	810	222	560	5 080	7 669	752	6 917	20 512	1 726	54.0	13.6
Milpitas	17 132	21.5	3.47	10.9	11.5	3 174	3 116	24	58	2 229	3 429	306	3 123	14 324	3 310	34.1	36.5
Mission Viejo	32 449	28.9	2.84	8.1	17.3	1 065	32	32	1 033	1 670	1 730	120	1 610	22 972	4 959	22.1	41.2
Modesto	64 959	12.1	2.86	14.7	22.5	3 208	1 853	1 261	1 355	12 981	6 630	517	6 113	51 947	5 451	49.8	16.5
Monrovia	13 502	2.0	2.71	15.4	26.0	293	93	85	200	1 079	2 818	366	2 453	8 706	2 010	41.6	25.1
Montclair	8 800	3.1	3.69	16.3	15.0	612	181	181	431	2 139	6 243	698	5 545	9 652	960	62.7	9.6
Montebello	18 844	1.2	3.28	20.1	17.1	309	277	256	32	2 419	3 754	480	3 275	17 035	2 652	61.8	14.3
Monterey	12 600	-0.7	2.13	8.4	37.0	2 842	300	290	2 542	1 369	4 450	429	4 021	5 400	1 917	24.2	46.2
Monterey Park	19 564	0.3	3.06	15.8	17.3	277	85	85	192	1 739	2 793	288	2 506	13 948	2 765	48.8	25.1
Moorpark	8 994	18.0	3.49	9.7	9.9	12	5	0	7	260	798	55	743	9 626	1 308	31.7	34.2
Moreno Valley	39 225	12.2	3.61	17.1	11.0	697	6	0	691	6 902	4 676	842	3 834	47 482	4 830	50.2	14.0
Morgan Hill	10 846	38.9	3.05	11.1	15.1	505	306	155	199	1 035	2 975	218	2 757	8 321	1 779	30.8	33.5
Mountain View	31 242	4.2	2.25	7.3	35.6	504	307	278	197	2 112	2 881	447	2 434	11 392	4 191	22.8	55.3
Murrieta	14 320	421.1	3.08	8.1	14.5	186	63	63	123	NA	NA	NA	NA	12 898	2 262	34.2	23.0
Napa	26 978	12.8	2.64	11.1	26.8	1 459	689	467	770	2 326	3 091	343	2 748	17 020	2 871	41.9	23.3
National City	15 018	1.7	3.39	21.1	16.7	3 343	215	215	3 128	2 736	4 864	978	3 886	15 915	941	66.6	9.0
Newark	12 992	8.1	3.26	11.6	14.1	89	0	0	89	2 015	4 576	336	4 240	10 702	1 868	44.0	24.2
Newport Beach	33 071	7.2	2.09	6.1	35.3	940	427	418	513	2 554	3 518	138	3 380	10 610	4 520	12.9	58.5
Norwalk	26 887	2.1	3.79	16.6	12.7	1 349	961	588	388	3 576	3 339	697	2 643	30 260	3 660	63.5	10.6
Novato	18 524	1.6	2.52	10.3	25.2	982	618	521	364	1 260	2 552	148	2 404	10 320	2 305	27.4	37.0
Oakland	150 790	4.3	2.60	17.7	32.5	7 175	2 894	1 475	4 281	29 875	7 213	1 367	5 847	94 346	20 111	43.7	30.9
Oceanside	56 488	20.9	2.83	11.0	22.7	1 280	181	156	1 099	6 964	4 171	668	3 503	40 254	4 916	41.4	22.2
Ontario	43 525	8.1	3.60	15.5	15.1	1 141	428	412	713	8 296	5 064	640	4 425	46 323	4 387	61.1	10.5
Orange	40 930	11.3	3.02	11.6	19.5	5 332	3 297	268	2 035	3 872	2 899	207	2 692	29 869	7 525	39.2	28.0
Oxnard	43 576	10.9	3.85	14.1	14.6	2 597	503	475	2 094	5 373	3 042	480	2 562	48 043	4 219	60.0	13.7
Pacifica	13 994	4.9	2.73	11.0	21.2	181	142	133	39	818	2 055	226	1 829	8 094	2 620	29.9	33.8
Palmdale	34 285	56.2	3.40	16.2	13.9	94	3	3	91	5 374	4 443	955	3 488	38 199	3 985	50.9	13.3
Palm Desert	19 184	81.1	2.13	7.7	32.4	227	152	152	75	2 193	5 140	354	4 786	6 806	1 346	30.7	31.4
Palm Springs	20 516	10.2	2.05	8.5	41.6	696	279	279	417	3 908	8 806	895	7 911	6 751	975	40.1	26.6
Palo Alto	25 216	4.2	2.30	7.0	32.6	668	433	343	235	1 778	2 927	176	2 751	11 044	3 976	9.4	71.0
Paradise	11 591	4.9	2.22	10.3	32.0	620	317	287	303	1 005	3 671	248	3 422	5 080	958	41.1	19.4
Paramount	13 972	7.5	3.93	21.7	14.6	320	300	143	20	2 290	3 997	752	3 245	17 468	1 645	70.7	7.0
Pasadena	51 844	3.3	2.52	12.1	33.7	3 518	1 333	1 236	2 185	4 881	3 515	473	3 042	27 119	11 508	33.9	41.3
Perris	9 652	43.5	3.73	18.8	12.2	232	111	105	121	1 749	4 662	632	4 030	11 755	916	65.1	6.6
Petaluma	19 932	24.1	2.70	10.6	22.6	740	321	321	419	1 607	2 842	138	2 704	12 992	2 324	33.4	30.1
Pico Rivera	16 468	2.9	3.83	17.8	12.8	350	335	335	15	1 655	2 517	620	1 896	18 182	1 766	70.9	7.1
Pittsburg	17 741	13.4	3.17	17.2	18.0	506	179	163	327	2 922	4 965	355	4 610	15 720	2 510	50.2	14.7
Placentia	15 037	12.5	3.07	11.2	16.0	303	89	89	214	952	1 975	309	1 666	12 019	2 301	36.3	31.3

1. No spouse present. 2. Data for serious crimes have not been adjusted for underreporting. This may affect comparability between geographic areas and over time. 3. Per 100,000 population estimated by the FBI. 4. All persons 3 years old and over enrolled in nursery school through college. 5. Persons 25 years old and over.

Table D. Cities — Income, Poverty, and Housing

City	Money income, 1999							Housing units, 2000					
	Households				Percent below poverty						Vacant units		
	Median income				Persons		Families						
	Per capita income[1] (dollars)	Dollars	Percent change, 1989–1999 (constant 1999 dollars)	Percent with income of $100,000 or more	Total	Percent change in rate, 1989–1999	Total	Total	Percent change, 1990–2000	Vacant units for sale or rent[2]	For seasonal use (percent)	Home owner vacancy rate	Renter vacancy rate
	43	44	45	46	47	48	49	50	51	52	53	54	55
CALIFORNIA—Cont'd													
Huntington Beach	31 964	64 824	-4.7	26.4	6.6	26.9	4.3	75 662	4.0	2 005	0.7	0.9	2.0
Huntington Park	9 340	28 941	-8.7	4.0	25.2	3.7	23.3	15 335	5.6	475	0.1	2.3	1.9
Imperial Beach	16 003	35 882	0.9	5.9	18.8	6.2	14.1	9 739	2.2	467	1.8	0.8	3.0
Indio	13 525	34 624	-0.8	6.7	21.5	1.4	16.8	16 909	29.8	3 038	12.8	2.4	4.9
Inglewood	14 776	34 269	-14.6	6.8	22.5	36.4	19.4	38 648	-0.2	1 843	0.1	1.5	3.5
Irvine	32 196	72 057	-4.8	32.3	9.1	42.2	5.0	53 711	27.2	2 512	0.7	1.1	3.5
Laguna Niguel	39 167	80 733	-2.3	38.9	4.1	32.3	2.8	23 885	26.4	668	0.8	0.8	3.3
La Habra	18 923	47 652	-11.3	13.1	12.9	61.3	9.1	19 441	4.1	494	0.2	1.3	2.1
Lake Elsinore	15 413	41 884	1.2	10.2	17.0	42.9	14.7	9 505	36.2	688	0.9	3.3	7.0
Lake Forest	28 583	67 967	NA	27.2	5.3	NA	3.2	20 486	NA	478	0.1	0.8	4.1
Lakewood	22 095	58 214	-3.1	16.6	7.4	51.0	5.6	27 310	1.9	457	0.1	0.6	1.9
La Mesa	22 372	41 693	-0.4	8.4	9.4	2.2	5.2	24 943	3.3	757	0.3	0.7	2.8
La Mirada	22 404	61 632	-2.7	19.6	5.6	43.6	3.7	14 811	10.9	231	0.2	0.7	1.7
Lancaster	16 935	41 127	-20.3	9.7	16.4	65.7	13.8	41 745	15.3	3 521	0.3	3.4	8.8
La Puente	11 336	41 222	-7.8	7.8	18.9	35.0	16.3	9 660	4.0	199	0.1	1.2	1.3
La Verne	26 689	61 326	-2.0	22.8	4.7	6.8	2.5	11 286	1.6	216	0.2	0.6	2.6
Lawndale	13 702	39 012	-16.0	6.1	17.3	32.1	14.3	9 869	0.9	314	0.3	1.3	2.5
Livermore	31 062	75 322	14.1	30.4	5.3	1.9	3.8	26 610	23.8	487	0.2	0.4	2.0
Lodi	18 719	39 570	-4.2	10.2	16.7	32.5	12.3	21 378	8.7	686	0.2	1.2	2.9
Lompoc	15 509	37 587	-11.8	6.3	15.4	2.0	12.6	13 621	2.7	562	0.2	0.8	4.0
Long Beach	19 040	37 270	-13.1	12.0	22.8	35.7	19.3	171 632	0.7	8 544	0.4	2.2	4.2
Los Altos	66 776	126 740	18.5	61.0	2.4	100.0	1.1	10 727	6.1	265	0.3	0.3	6.2
Los Angeles	20 671	36 687	-11.7	13.6	22.1	16.9	18.3	1 337 706	2.9	62 294	0.4	1.8	3.5
Los Banos	15 582	43 690	31.9	7.9	12.1	-37.6	9.8	8 049	58.8	328	0.6	1.3	3.1
Los Gatos	56 094	94 319	21.4	47.8	4.3	-6.5	3.1	12 367	4.6	379	0.9	0.5	2.3
Lynwood	9 542	35 888	2.9	4.9	23.5	7.8	21.0	14 987	3.2	592	0.2	2.4	2.7
Madera	11 674	31 033	7.9	5.8	32.5	20.8	25.6	12 521	31.4	543	0.2	1.5	3.8
Manhattan Beach	61 136	100 750	10.7	50.5	3.2	-15.8	2.0	15 034	2.3	560	1.1	1.0	3.0
Manteca	18 241	46 677	-1.0	10.1	9.7	-2.0	7.2	16 937	21.1	569	0.2	1.1	3.1
Marina	18 860	43 000	10.2	10.1	13.1	35.1	10.7	8 537	3.3	1 792	0.3	6.4	2.9
Martinez	29 701	63 010	2.0	24.0	5.2	-11.9	3.2	14 597	12.5	297	0.1	0.5	2.0
Maywood	8 926	30 480	-11.3	3.2	24.5	15.0	23.1	6 701	0.3	232	0.1	1.8	1.6
Menlo Park	53 341	84 609	24.8	43.2	6.9	6.2	4.2	12 714	3.8	327	0.8	0.3	1.5
Merced	13 115	30 429	-8.4	5.3	27.9	11.2	22.4	21 532	13.5	1 097	0.2	1.6	5.1
Milpitas	27 823	84 429	12.8	38.8	5.0	2.0	3.3	17 364	20.0	232	0.1	0.4	2.1
Mission Viejo	33 302	78 248	-4.6	34.9	3.8	90.0	2.3	32 985	25.0	536	0.3	0.6	2.3
Modesto	17 797	40 394	-5.2	9.6	15.7	20.8	12.2	67 179	10.4	2 220	0.2	1.2	3.3
Monrovia	21 686	45 375	-5.4	14.7	13.1	5.6	9.7	13 957	0.1	455	0.2	1.0	2.5
Montclair	13 556	40 797	-8.2	8.1	17.4	4.2	14.2	9 066	1.7	266	0.1	1.2	3.6
Montebello	15 125	38 805	-8.1	9.2	17.0	21.4	14.2	19 416	1.2	572	0.2	1.0	2.7
Monterey	27 133	49 109	5.3	15.2	7.8	18.2	4.4	13 382	-0.9	782	2.7	1.0	2.3
Monterey Park	17 661	40 724	-7.0	12.3	15.6	-4.9	12.4	20 209	-0.4	645	0.3	1.9	1.9
Moorpark	25 383	76 642	-5.5	30.4	7.0	62.8	4.3	9 094	14.9	100	0.1	0.5	1.2
Moreno Valley	14 983	47 387	-16.4	9.9	14.2	69.0	11.6	41 431	9.2	2 206	0.2	2.8	5.9
Morgan Hill	33 047	81 958	14.1	39.3	4.7	4.4	3.3	11 091	36.0	245	0.3	0.6	2.6
Mountain View	39 693	69 362	21.7	31.5	6.8	9.7	3.6	32 432	3.0	1 190	0.9	0.6	1.6
Murrieta	23 290	60 911	NA	19.9	4.3	NA	3.0	14 921	NA	601	0.7	1.7	5.1
Napa	23 642	49 154	3.1	15.7	8.9	15.6	6.1	27 776	11.5	798	0.6	0.8	1.9
National City	11 582	29 826	0.3	3.7	22.0	3.3	19.8	15 422	1.2	404	0.1	0.5	2.3
Newark	23 641	69 350	2.3	26.3	5.5	10.0	4.2	13 150	7.0	158	0.2	0.4	1.2
Newport Beach	63 015	83 455	2.9	42.5	4.4	-22.8	2.1	37 288	7.0	4 217	5.3	1.8	8.0
Norwalk	14 022	46 047	-10.1	8.8	11.9	28.0	9.5	27 554	1.1	667	0.1	1.4	2.0
Novato	32 402	63 453	2.9	27.0	5.6	33.3	3.1	18 994	1.1	470	0.3	0.9	2.5
Oakland	21 936	40 055	10.0	14.5	19.4	3.2	16.2	157 508	1.8	6 718	0.3	1.0	2.7
Oceanside	20 329	46 301	3.0	12.1	11.6	14.9	8.2	59 581	16.6	3 093	2.4	1.0	3.2
Ontario	14 244	42 452	-11.7	8.4	15.5	14.0	12.2	45 182	6.2	1 657	0.2	1.6	3.3
Orange	24 294	58 994	-5.7	21.9	10.0	25.0	6.8	41 904	10.2	974	0.2	1.1	2.0
Oxnard	15 288	48 603	-2.7	12.7	15.1	20.8	11.4	45 166	9.5	1 590	1.6	1.0	1.8
Pacifica	30 183	71 737	12.3	28.4	2.9	-35.6	1.2	14 245	3.7	251	0.3	0.2	1.9
Palmdale	16 384	46 941	-16.8	11.2	15.8	77.5	12.9	37 096	52.0	2 811	0.3	3.1	9.6
Palm Desert	33 463	48 316	-3.6	19.2	9.2	29.6	5.9	28 021	53.6	8 837	23.0	2.3	8.3
Palm Springs	25 957	35 973	-2.8	12.7	15.1	19.8	11.2	30 823	1.0	10 307	23.5	3.2	11.0
Palo Alto	56 257	90 377	21.6	45.6	4.8	4.3	3.2	26 048	3.4	832	0.8	0.6	2.0
Paradise	19 267	31 863	3.3	5.7	12.4	11.7	9.7	12 374	6.4	783	0.8	2.5	6.2
Paramount	11 487	36 749	-5.7	5.2	21.9	24.4	19.1	14 591	6.3	619	0.2	3.4	3.1
Pasadena	28 186	46 012	-2.4	19.6	15.9	6.7	11.6	54 132	2.1	2 288	0.6	1.4	2.9
Perris	11 425	35 522	-7.6	5.1	20.4	29.9	18.1	10 553	36.0	901	1.0	4.0	7.2
Petaluma	27 087	61 679	12.2	23.1	6.0	42.9	3.3	20 304	22.7	372	0.3	0.5	1.7
Pico Rivera	13 011	41 564	-10.0	8.2	12.6	8.6	11.6	16 807	3.0	339	0.0	0.9	2.3
Pittsburg	18 241	50 557	-2.3	12.5	11.5	6.5	8.7	18 300	9.5	559	0.2	0.9	3.8
Placentia	23 843	62 803	-8.2	22.9	8.7	13.0	5.7	15 326	11.6	289	0.2	0.6	2.3

1. Based on population enumerated as of April 1, 2000. 2. Includes units rented or sold but not occupied.

Table D. Cities — Housing, Labor Force, Employment, and Disability

City	Housing units, 2000 (cont'd) Occupied units					Civilian labor force, 2003		Unemployment		Civilian employment,[2] 2000	Percent		Disability, 2000
	Total	Percent owner occupied	Percent renter occupied	Average size owner occupied	Average size renter occupied	Total	Percent change, 2002–2003	Total	Rate[1]	Total	Management, professional, and related occupations	Production, transportation, and material moving occupations	Employment disabled persons[3] (percent)
	56	57	58	59	60	61	62	63	64	65	66	67	68
CALIFORNIA—Cont'd													
Huntington Beach	73 657	60.6	39.4	2.58	2.54	130 910	2.0	3 737	2.9	102 866	44.0	7.8	9.0
Huntington Park	14 860	27.4	72.6	4.65	3.92	27 331	0.2	3 346	12.2	20 307	11.8	38.3	16.4
Imperial Beach	9 272	30.0	70.0	2.79	2.86	13 434	1.6	975	7.3	10 459	22.8	12.6	15.1
Indio	13 871	56.2	43.8	3.45	3.51	25 950	2.9	2 216	8.5	17 801	17.2	10.5	16.7
Inglewood	36 805	36.3	63.7	3.24	2.90	58 633	0.1	5 622	9.6	42 375	24.6	16.3	17.0
Irvine	51 199	60.0	40.0	2.78	2.46	74 356	2.0	1 960	2.6	73 707	57.7	4.3	6.9
Laguna Niguel	23 217	75.0	25.0	2.68	2.56	30 808	2.0	690	2.2	31 814	50.3	5.1	7.2
La Habra	18 947	56.6	43.4	3.04	3.13	32 895	1.8	1 431	4.4	26 044	28.6	15.8	14.4
Lake Elsinore	8 817	64.6	35.4	3.29	3.25	12 495	2.9	842	6.7	11 352	21.9	17.6	12.0
Lake Forest	20 008	72.0	28.0	2.93	2.79	42 208	2.0	1 184	2.8	31 282	41.3	7.7	8.5
Lakewood	26 853	72.0	28.0	2.94	2.97	41 238	-0.1	1 710	4.1	37 351	34.0	13.0	10.8
La Mesa	24 186	47.2	52.8	2.35	2.10	34 716	1.7	1 214	3.5	27 212	37.0	8.2	8.8
La Mirada	14 580	82.0	18.0	3.15	2.85	22 777	-0.1	995	4.4	21 162	36.1	12.3	10.4
Lancaster	38 224	61.4	38.6	3.01	2.78	48 567	0.0	3 253	6.7	43 178	32.3	12.5	13.4
La Puente	9 461	60.9	39.1	4.50	4.09	18 293	0.1	1 614	8.8	15 032	15.4	32.8	15.6
La Verne	11 070	77.5	22.5	2.84	2.63	17 104	-0.2	644	3.8	15 607	43.3	9.3	10.8
Lawndale	9 555	33.2	66.8	3.41	3.26	15 884	0.0	1 144	7.2	13 198	20.6	17.2	16.3
Livermore	26 123	72.2	27.8	2.86	2.65	36 092	-0.8	1 701	4.7	38 525	41.8	9.4	9.2
Lodi	20 692	54.6	45.4	2.65	2.77	32 687	2.4	2 442	7.5	24 177	27.6	17.0	15.6
Lompoc	13 059	51.6	48.4	2.83	2.94	18 762	2.4	1 046	5.6	15 265	26.1	12.6	14.7
Long Beach	163 088	41.0	59.0	2.81	2.74	223 373	0.0	14 630	6.5	189 487	34.3	14.8	14.0
Los Altos	10 462	85.6	14.4	2.67	2.21	14 696	-5.0	746	5.1	12 711	74.7	2.9	4.7
Los Angeles	1 275 412	38.6	61.4	2.99	2.73	1 922 525	0.0	153 520	8.0	1 532 074	34.2	15.2	15.2
Los Banos	7 721	67.9	32.1	3.29	3.40	7 640	2.5	1 087	14.2	9 290	27.0	15.8	14.8
Los Gatos	11 988	65.3	34.7	2.54	1.92	17 205	-5.0	887	5.2	15 148	64.4	3.4	6.3
Lynwood	14 395	47.1	52.9	5.09	4.35	26 513	0.2	3 164	11.9	20 998	12.5	35.1	16.7
Madera	11 978	52.7	47.3	3.38	3.78	18 576	1.3	3 353	18.1	14 187	19.9	18.3	16.4
Manhattan Beach	14 474	65.1	34.9	2.60	1.85	22 105	-0.2	499	2.3	19 225	64.3	2.1	7.5
Manteca	16 368	63.0	37.0	3.06	2.85	24 952	2.4	2 017	8.1	20 561	24.8	17.8	13.7
Marina	6 745	45.8	54.2	2.77	2.80	11 893	0.7	812	6.8	9 446	26.3	9.3	12.7
Martinez	14 300	68.8	31.2	2.53	2.16	21 962	-0.5	992	4.5	19 169	41.3	7.0	8.7
Maywood	6 469	29.4	70.6	4.74	4.15	13 541	0.2	1 584	11.7	9 339	10.2	42.8	19.7
Menlo Park	12 387	57.0	43.0	2.67	2.07	15 007	-2.6	586	3.9	15 429	62.8	5.3	7.8
Merced	20 435	46.5	53.5	2.93	3.18	27 259	2.5	3 998	14.7	22 267	27.4	15.5	14.4
Milpitas	17 132	69.8	30.2	3.49	3.44	29 023	-5.2	2 461	8.5	30 302	45.5	16.4	13.5
Mission Viejo	32 449	81.4	18.6	2.87	2.71	47 265	2.0	1 081	2.3	46 858	46.7	6.5	7.7
Modesto	64 959	58.7	41.3	2.89	2.81	98 576	1.3	10 140	10.3	76 567	28.4	16.1	14.3
Monrovia	13 502	47.9	52.1	2.75	2.68	20 303	-0.1	1 204	5.9	16 851	37.3	10.7	12.6
Montclair	8 800	60.6	39.4	3.59	3.84	19 288	3.0	1 103	5.7	12 502	19.3	23.6	16.6
Montebello	18 844	47.5	52.5	3.28	3.28	29 800	0.0	1 918	6.4	22 867	25.8	19.6	15.7
Monterey	12 600	38.5	61.5	2.29	2.03	17 727	0.7	672	3.8	13 933	46.3	5.3	9.7
Monterey Park	19 564	54.0	46.0	2.97	3.16	30 378	-0.1	1 785	5.9	24 270	34.3	14.0	12.9
Moorpark	8 994	82.1	17.9	3.43	3.78	16 919	1.4	671	4.0	15 091	40.7	9.8	9.0
Moreno Valley	39 225	71.1	28.9	3.63	3.56	86 939	2.9	5 641	6.5	56 429	25.2	17.6	13.2
Morgan Hill	10 846	72.5	27.5	2.98	3.21	13 406	-5.1	871	6.5	16 295	44.5	7.9	8.8
Mountain View	31 242	41.5	58.5	2.30	2.21	45 097	-5.1	2 582	5.7	41 126	62.5	5.8	9.3
Murrieta	14 320	79.7	20.3	3.18	2.70	13 875	2.9	625	4.5	18 850	34.6	10.6	7.6
Napa	26 978	60.6	39.4	2.59	2.71	40 114	1.7	2 131	5.3	34 378	32.7	12.2	11.4
National City	15 018	35.0	65.0	3.63	3.26	23 972	1.7	1 872	7.8	17 764	15.4	19.4	17.1
Newark	12 992	70.6	29.4	3.22	3.37	24 024	-0.8	1 431	6.0	20 452	32.2	17.6	12.5
Newport Beach	33 071	55.7	44.3	2.30	1.83	47 723	2.0	1 127	2.4	38 316	57.6	3.2	6.9
Norwalk	26 887	65.8	34.2	3.85	3.67	47 897	0.0	3 041	6.3	39 231	21.1	23.2	17.1
Novato	18 524	67.6	32.4	2.50	2.56	25 836	-2.7	904	3.5	24 873	43.4	6.4	11.5
Oakland	150 790	41.4	58.6	2.76	2.49	199 843	-0.9	21 135	10.6	174 743	39.2	12.3	14.8
Oceanside	56 488	62.1	37.9	2.82	2.85	71 308	1.7	3 683	5.2	68 063	31.5	13.7	13.7
Ontario	43 525	57.6	42.4	3.64	3.55	89 160	3.0	4 925	5.5	62 417	20.7	24.0	16.0
Orange	40 930	62.6	37.4	2.91	3.20	73 631	1.9	2 656	3.6	61 620	37.0	11.3	12.2
Oxnard	43 576	57.3	42.7	3.79	3.94	87 626	1.3	6 618	7.6	70 395	21.6	19.6	16.3
Pacifica	13 994	68.6	31.4	2.88	2.41	22 257	-2.6	903	4.1	21 302	39.1	9.3	9.6
Palmdale	34 285	71.0	29.0	3.43	3.33	35 067	0.0	2 319	6.6	43 474	28.2	15.9	12.2
Palm Desert	19 184	66.9	33.1	2.12	2.16	18 962	2.9	676	3.6	17 384	37.3	4.8	12.9
Palm Springs	20 516	60.8	39.2	2.03	2.09	30 753	2.9	1 435	4.7	17 841	31.5	6.1	18.4
Palo Alto	25 216	57.2	42.8	2.55	1.96	34 298	-5.0	1 460	4.3	31 369	76.0	2.4	6.3
Paradise	11 591	70.9	29.1	2.23	2.21	10 783	1.9	660	6.1	9 763	30.4	12.3	13.8
Paramount	13 972	42.9	57.1	3.91	3.95	22 948	0.1	2 171	9.5	18 858	18.0	29.3	17.7
Pasadena	51 844	45.8	54.2	2.64	2.41	73 994	-0.1	4 456	6.0	63 104	48.0	7.8	13.6
Perris	9 652	68.1	31.9	3.79	3.58	13 442	2.9	1 174	8.7	11 934	17.7	25.1	16.0
Petaluma	19 932	70.1	29.9	2.75	2.59	29 934	-2.0	1 190	4.0	28 162	36.5	10.4	9.3
Pico Rivera	16 468	70.4	29.6	3.90	3.67	28 857	0.0	2 328	8.1	23 489	19.4	27.5	17.5
Pittsburg	17 741	62.8	37.2	3.24	3.05	28 516	-0.2	2 224	7.8	24 671	24.0	13.7	15.8
Placentia	15 037	69.0	31.0	2.92	3.40	27 913	1.9	946	3.4	23 497	39.3	12.0	7.8

1. Percent of civilian labor force.   2. Persons 16 years old and over.   3. Persons 16 to 64 years old.

Table D. Cities — Construction, Wholesale Trade, and Retail Trade

City	Value of residential construction authorized by building permits, 2003			Wholesale trade, 1997				Retail trade,[1] 1997			
	New construction ($1,000)	Number of housing units	Percent single family	Number of establishments	Number of employees	Sales (mil dol)	Annual payroll (mil dol)	Number of establishments	Number of employees	Sales (mil dol)	Annual payroll (mil dol)
	69	70	71	72	73	74	75	76	77	78	79
CALIFORNIA—Cont'd											
Huntington Beach	50 974	305	40.7	477	4 819	2 484.3	171.6	601	8 063	1 700.6	160.6
Huntington Park	403	3	33.3	58	1 167	374.8	35.9	173	1 658	296.2	30.9
Imperial Beach	3 962	23	100.0	6	34	6.6	0.5	43	254	34.1	3.5
Indio	232 508	1 716	100.0	33	D	D	D	136	1 752	327.0	32.3
Inglewood	2 657	20	40.0	102	1 455	509.8	48.9	231	2 567	527.9	47.2
Irvine	307 540	2 804	37.9	894	17 641	29 723.1	881.0	400	6 137	1 368.5	137.1
Laguna Niguel	27 833	110	100.0	102	337	462.7	14.3	146	2 911	526.8	50.2
La Habra	6 070	34	76.5	67	479	175.2	14.8	158	2 378	392.2	43.6
Lake Elsinore	102 448	612	90.7	12	53	14.6	1.6	162	1 826	269.4	26.5
Lake Forest	0	0	0.0	NA	NA	NA	NA	NA	NA	NA	NA
Lakewood	1 606	18	5.6	43	315	58.6	7.4	250	4 211	637.0	66.1
La Mesa	9 551	65	53.8	36	222	70.3	7.5	281	4 491	872.1	84.6
La Mirada	4 923	113	4.4	114	2 755	2 521.4	118.2	95	1 394	287.7	29.0
Lancaster	152 481	972	100.0	61	652	198.1	17.2	326	3 906	715.8	75.5
La Puente	452	7	14.3	18	D	D	D	100	1 125	228.2	19.9
La Verne	12 340	70	78.6	45	340	220.7	11.3	84	1 229	212.8	21.1
Lawndale	611	5	100.0	22	D	D	D	96	1 108	303.9	21.8
Livermore	124 529	431	75.2	129	1 708	1 133.7	74.4	188	2 931	593.7	55.4
Lodi	54 509	275	100.0	58	1 050	415.4	30.3	218	2 970	529.7	53.8
Lompoc	473	2	100.0	17	D	D	D	111	1 439	245.7	23.9
Long Beach	21 894	271	24.7	402	5 257	8 218.0	200.8	998	11 047	1 939.9	197.4
Los Altos	23 670	36	100.0	51	D	D	D	115	920	163.6	20.0
Los Angeles	812 450	7 361	19.5	8 327	87 405	49 609.3	3 065.1	10 639	118 117	22 932.8	2 342.9
Los Banos	74 308	509	100.0	15	D	D	D	75	939	143.9	17.3
Los Gatos	13 661	43	86.0	65	440	272.6	24.2	199	2 216	484.9	53.6
Lynwood	2 263	19	78.9	44	747	259.6	23.3	83	925	179.9	17.1
Madera	57 833	506	83.2	33	D	D	D	141	1 918	302.5	31.5
Manhattan Beach	58 455	168	92.9	54	442	403.3	27.1	159	2 794	612.3	51.1
Manteca	140 483	759	98.2	23	D	D	D	147	1 996	359.3	36.2
Marina	1 910	10	100.0	9	59	18.7	1.9	41	475	59.9	6.7
Martinez	2 832	12	66.7	41	446	654.3	20.1	78	1 224	281.7	27.9
Maywood	92	1	100.0	16	164	54.3	4.7	47	572	86.7	8.9
Menlo Park	12 587	18	100.0	68	1 674	779.9	107.2	139	1 930	558.1	49.8
Merced	145 481	1 288	78.7	37	576	416.7	18.7	265	3 722	674.7	65.8
Milpitas	1 306	1	100.0	224	4 470	3 747.0	206.3	318	4 934	804.5	89.2
Mission Viejo	0	0	0.0	142	783	465.7	38.5	256	3 702	775.0	67.7
Modesto	146 605	924	93.5	164	2 111	870.5	66.9	704	10 008	1 765.7	177.1
Monrovia	6 457	40	95.0	109	1 020	282.7	32.9	141	2 617	553.2	48.3
Montclair	714	3	100.0	57	499	129.2	14.1	290	5 363	709.9	84.8
Montebello	351	3	100.0	123	1 929	1 474.6	77.0	242	3 468	630.0	62.2
Monterey	2 733	20	15.0	56	1 324	1 460.5	49.7	264	2 785	381.0	44.5
Monterey Park	22 540	111	62.2	268	1 656	864.8	44.3	169	1 683	275.2	26.2
Moorpark	32 649	249	20.5	56	773	242.3	31.4	33	452	77.9	9.5
Moreno Valley	417 648	2 435	81.6	25	80	47.0	2.5	277	3 997	691.2	74.9
Morgan Hill	79 548	311	76.8	48	1 593	625.5	66.5	94	1 453	278.8	28.4
Mountain View	14 539	92	97.8	180	5 479	2 612.0	283.5	296	4 458	977.6	98.8
Murrieta	365 606	2 413	63.4	NA	NA	NA	NA	NA	NA	NA	NA
Napa	35 093	165	77.6	84	568	202.5	17.0	319	3 712	648.8	69.6
National City	4 023	21	100.0	119	1 302	814.1	39.9	324	5 030	1 052.3	105.7
Newark	357	2	0.0	83	1 410	683.9	56.6	218	3 470	626.8	60.2
Newport Beach	71 111	173	80.9	289	7 136	2 642.8	140.7	440	5 947	1 140.2	125.1
Norwalk	253	2	100.0	84	815	610.1	28.7	172	2 810	630.1	57.4
Novato	108 998	486	94.0	111	981	423.1	34.9	192	2 619	543.8	59.5
Oakland	179 313	1 085	28.0	526	7 662	3 553.2	285.6	1 030	10 190	2 146.5	213.1
Oceanside	185 859	1 036	55.9	125	1 694	925.6	42.1	388	4 916	781.2	82.4
Ontario	24 021	189	46.0	371	7 262	5 425.5	251.6	461	7 653	1 769.1	152.1
Orange	29 838	153	94.8	403	5 751	4 685.5	228.2	484	5 519	1 227.3	123.8
Oxnard	230 553	1 036	87.4	175	2 818	922.9	110.6	487	6 821	1 398.7	135.8
Pacifica	2 580	11	63.6	7	14	7.3	0.6	70	721	127.3	12.1
Palmdale	176 387	957	100.0	36	268	71.7	8.4	208	2 852	543.0	53.3
Palm Desert	77 059	338	70.1	68	403	125.6	11.0	364	4 024	669.7	71.7
Palm Springs	128 015	611	99.3	40	D	D	D	225	2 759	438.1	49.1
Palo Alto	27 688	110	52.7	104	1 382	1 019.1	126.5	307	6 097	1 337.7	139.9
Paradise	14 459	93	100.0	8	D	D	D	84	859	120.9	13.3
Paramount	1 640	13	100.0	200	2 752	888.6	83.4	115	1 515	230.2	24.5
Pasadena	109 742	1 040	10.9	200	2 492	2 219.5	108.6	567	8 330	1 553.1	160.9
Perris	188 773	1 269	100.0	13	106	29.6	2.7	66	2 544	471.0	39.6
Petaluma	47 997	259	59.8	113	1 948	579.8	60.5	276	3 307	618.6	65.7
Pico Rivera	3 121	17	100.0	86	1 532	620.1	51.9	108	1 554	303.9	33.8
Pittsburg	108 903	778	62.0	31	378	147.4	14.6	111	2 158	369.0	38.6
Placentia	56 656	532	14.1	129	1 264	477.6	45.6	110	1 525	334.6	38.1

1. Establishments with payroll.

Items 69—79

CA(Huntington Beach)—CA(Placentia) 939

City	Real estate and rental and leasing, 1997				Professional, scientific, and technical services,[1] 1997				Manufacturing, 1997			
	Number of establish-ments	Number of employees	Receipts (mil dol)	Annual payroll (mil dol)	Number of establish-ments	Number of employees	Receipts (mil dol)	Annual payroll (mil dol)	Number of establish-ments	Number of employees	Receipts (mil dol)	Annual payroll (mil dol)
	80	81	82	83	84	85	86	87	88	89	90	91
CALIFORNIA—Cont'd												
Huntington Beach	228	1 188	262.2	38.0	460	2 632	258.9	100.8	417	14 927	2 377.3	594.8
Huntington Park	12	77	6.4	0.7	18	92	8.0	2.6	163	5 042	575.4	133.5
Imperial Beach	25	D	D	D	7	17	1.1	0.3	NA	NA	NA	NA
Indio	32	177	22.9	3.7	34	85	10.6	2.5	NA	NA	NA	NA
Inglewood	71	636	124.8	15.1	51	576	161.8	40.1	74	2 554	384.3	79.7
Irvine	320	4 308	678.7	157.1	1 419	18 430	2 874.4	1 057.0	479	34 067	8 500.6	1 319.0
Laguna Niguel	61	315	51.6	9.4	170	575	68.6	29.0	NA	NA	NA	NA
La Habra	40	163	19.3	2.7	58	233	22.9	8.8	87	1 371	155.0	39.4
Lake Elsinore	21	76	8.7	1.2	17	40	3.0	1.1	53	778	61.0	17.7
Lake Forest	NA	NA	NA	NA	NA	NA	NA	NA	NA	NA	NA	NA
Lakewood	40	224	40.7	4.1	57	702	44.4	15.0	NA	NA	NA	NA
La Mesa	116	648	65.6	12.2	163	536	46.3	14.9	NA	NA	NA	NA
La Mirada	24	177	25.9	6.4	52	256	56.6	10.2	74	4 323	757.0	132.1
Lancaster	76	420	54.6	8.6	87	438	42.2	16.5	50	845	79.0	15.3
La Puente	18	122	9.0	1.6	10	66	8.0	2.8	NA	NA	NA	NA
La Verne	17	171	15.6	3.5	42	339	36.2	10.2	43	1 062	188.6	35.0
Lawndale	27	237	23.4	3.6	25	184	11.4	4.8	NA	NA	NA	NA
Livermore	57	306	46.9	8.9	120	1 591	200.7	84.7	112	2 897	499.5	89.7
Lodi	68	763	51.9	15.2	86	440	24.1	11.1	99	3 149	475.3	88.6
Lompoc	33	144	13.2	2.4	26	108	8.1	3.3	NA	NA	NA	NA
Long Beach	404	2 934	372.0	62.8	740	8 083	788.2	308.4	332	27 548	8 786.9	1 400.3
Los Altos	78	199	57.1	6.8	213	903	137.2	53.6	NA	NA	NA	NA
Los Angeles	4 998	39 094	7 382.2	1 219.5	10 755	122 686	14 539.9	5 668.2	7 222	186 758	27 378.2	5 302.8
Los Banos	16	46	7.7	0.5	20	98	6.1	2.7	14	D	D	D
Los Gatos	102	402	61.2	12.1	261	1 307	217.4	94.0	61	1 055	136.4	50.2
Lynwood	13	78	8.2	1.2	11	48	7.8	1.9	62	2 516	289.0	56.6
Madera	19	89	8.9	1.4	34	204	16.7	6.3	38	1 260	190.9	33.9
Manhattan Beach	89	356	46.5	11.3	178	681	97.7	34.4	NA	NA	NA	NA
Manteca	45	213	19.8	3.8	28	96	8.5	2.8	28	1 779	208.2	38.4
Marina	22	D	D	D	12	28	1.6	0.6	NA	NA	NA	NA
Martinez	33	187	27.6	4.7	90	311	25.5	10.1	33	D	D	D
Maywood	5	D	D	D	3	D	D	D	31	514	32.7	9.1
Menlo Park	91	796	120.8	32.6	254	3 754	642.2	268.7	78	6 371	1 478.0	369.8
Merced	67	320	30.5	4.5	83	471	29.9	11.4	42	2 326	457.3	64.3
Milpitas	45	236	71.9	9.4	140	1 123	188.7	60.4	202	27 550	7 129.6	1 364.6
Mission Viejo	85	862	131.0	29.2	178	883	98.7	40.3	46	1 466	272.3	70.3
Modesto	171	1 003	136.2	22.0	328	2 342	181.0	64.2	137	7 462	2 124.8	265.5
Monrovia	26	98	9.6	2.0	92	736	79.1	31.7	130	5 150	725.6	199.4
Montclair	20	144	11.4	2.9	27	152	8.3	2.7	72	854	95.0	19.9
Montebello	60	294	49.3	7.5	57	205	15.5	3.9	112	4 850	642.2	133.7
Monterey	100	581	60.4	10.6	222	1 044	114.8	44.9	61	1 317	159.6	44.1
Monterey Park	81	350	82.8	7.5	113	334	28.8	8.7	79	1 841	170.4	43.9
Moorpark	13	43	7.4	1.3	41	554	82.7	20.5	52	2 578	370.1	79.4
Moreno Valley	49	207	18.3	3.1	43	196	10.3	2.5	19	1 095	143.7	20.8
Morgan Hill	41	115	27.0	2.9	77	482	41.2	17.4	68	2 304	365.3	91.8
Mountain View	121	771	102.8	16.4	446	7 957	1 238.2	497.9	235	20 837	9 372.0	1 298.7
Murrieta	NA	NA	NA	NA	NA	NA	NA	NA	NA	NA	NA	NA
Napa	85	712	53.4	10.5	160	1 248	244.0	109.3	104	2 694	591.2	84.7
National City	46	197	30.1	3.7	50	554	16.8	8.9	100	1 744	342.7	45.1
Newark	34	224	64.4	5.1	67	872	78.2	28.5	84	2 989	597.5	124.1
Newport Beach	521	5 612	1 233.7	229.0	1 031	7 343	1 120.3	413.7	109	5 136	1 481.8	255.6
Norwalk	44	206	25.7	4.1	51	435	13.5	5.6	75	1 234	159.9	28.9
Novato	79	434	64.0	10.1	177	1 446	151.4	62.1	82	1 669	263.1	65.2
Oakland	476	2 712	406.9	66.7	1 110	8 673	1 130.3	466.2	574	13 913	2 048.1	426.2
Oceanside	94	445	59.7	7.8	169	865	62.3	22.8	157	3 749	416.5	97.5
Ontario	115	1 008	201.5	25.1	119	1 048	121.9	47.2	420	16 296	3 257.5	483.4
Orange	164	947	140.4	24.4	497	6 459	611.3	217.4	338	10 463	1 452.6	309.4
Oxnard	100	464	57.2	9.5	175	1 069	102.5	35.4	172	6 935	1 440.7	220.8
Pacifica	21	58	12.0	1.1	45	97	11.3	4.4	NA	NA	NA	NA
Palmdale	58	193	24.7	3.4	47	227	18.5	6.3	44	D	D	D
Palm Desert	89	425	51.1	10.7	200	746	79.7	23.1	57	702	82.2	18.9
Palm Springs	113	518	91.4	12.3	130	596	54.3	20.6	37	734	107.6	22.5
Palo Alto	155	1 336	258.1	44.1	731	9 034	1 724.7	720.1	114	7 983	2 232.0	362.6
Paradise	37	D	D	D	28	74	4.5	1.1	NA	NA	NA	NA
Paramount	42	232	28.6	4.6	28	417	26.8	10.3	268	6 401	1 081.7	199.4
Pasadena	239	2 059	244.6	40.8	872	10 199	1 292.9	484.8	151	2 877	389.0	87.4
Perris	17	58	4.8	0.8	10	43	2.1	0.8	40	2 616	421.7	59.7
Petaluma	71	399	41.9	6.9	145	1 158	119.2	51.6	119	4 998	1 403.7	249.8
Pico Rivera	24	240	45.9	6.7	16	179	15.3	4.9	81	3 122	518.5	89.0
Pittsburg	22	170	35.4	3.6	26	150	12.4	3.5	46	2 362	1 503.1	118.3
Placentia	36	411	23.4	6.6	60	372	41.2	15.5	134	3 438	447.2	85.9

1. Firms subject to federal tax.

City	Accommodation and foodservices, 1997				Arts, entertainment, and recreation,[1] 1997				Health care and social assistance,[1] 1997			
	Number of establishments	Number of employees	Sales (mil dol)	Annual payroll (mil dol)	Number of establishments	Number of employees	Receipts (mil dol)	Annual payroll (mil dol)	Number of establishments	Number of employees	Receipts (mil dol)	Annual payroll (mil dol)
	92	93	94	95	96	97	98	99	100	101	102	103
CALIFORNIA—Cont'd												
Huntington Beach	378	6 467	237.9	64.3	35	843	54.4	14.6	460	3 937	274.7	106.3
Huntington Park	74	D	D	D	4	124	4.2	1.2	116	1 260	96.2	36.3
Imperial Beach	47	430	13.9	3.7	2	0	0.0	0.0	14	339	16.2	6.2
Indio	74	1 050	42.0	9.5	10	0	0.0	0.0	80	1 011	82.3	30.9
Inglewood	127	1 694	74.1	15.9	33	2 581	393.7	118.8	274	4 043	314.1	131.0
Irvine	300	8 073	338.2	91.4	45	954	68.6	16.3	364	3 296	292.5	119.6
Laguna Niguel	109	D	D	D	11	177	8.6	3.3	129	563	42.6	17.2
La Habra	98	1 526	49.8	12.9	2	0	0.0	0.0	75	1 900	160.9	66.0
Lake Elsinore	53	759	23.1	6.3	6	176	3.3	2.1	35	206	13.0	4.5
Lake Forest	NA	NA	NA	NA	NA	NA	NA	NA	NA	NA	NA	NA
Lakewood	147	2 837	91.7	23.5	13	282	9.3	2.7	130	1 546	123.2	52.8
La Mesa	152	3 516	120.9	35.2	10	170	4.7	1.6	296	3 397	229.7	90.4
La Mirada	72	1 084	44.3	11.0	7	103	7.3	1.3	76	951	61.3	24.9
Lancaster	148	2 716	92.4	23.0	13	182	8.4	2.4	266	3 606	307.0	106.5
La Puente	57	521	20.7	4.6	1	0	0.0	0.0	38	206	16.8	4.6
La Verne	43	744	25.2	6.3	1	0	0.0	0.0	35	239	17.1	6.8
Lawndale	46	594	22.9	5.8	3	0	0.0	0.0	59	365	28.2	8.3
Livermore	119	1 755	64.8	15.6	11	205	8.6	2.0	119	1 159	60.9	31.7
Lodi	124	1 561	51.1	12.8	9	169	9.2	2.6	145	1 433	100.6	36.7
Lompoc	77	1 109	37.7	8.9	4	39	0.9	0.2	59	337	26.1	10.5
Long Beach	678	11 571	445.8	120.7	53	867	56.4	12.3	898	9 999	899.4	383.9
Los Altos	60	1 250	47.5	13.3	7	120	3.5	1.3	112	766	68.9	26.1
Los Angeles	6 215	103 676	4 523.1	1 249.1	4 229	23 403	4 530.8	2 178.7	7 491	74 565	6 051.2	2 351.7
Los Banos	41	452	16.9	4.1	3	0	0.0	0.0	41	225	12.8	3.9
Los Gatos	120	2 282	79.4	23.4	17	309	11.8	4.7	269	3 611	227.4	110.8
Lynwood	56	478	21.0	4.4	1	0	0.0	0.0	100	818	71.9	27.6
Madera	64	D	D	D	6	59	1.4	0.4	93	936	52.3	19.0
Manhattan Beach	126	2 782	121.9	33.6	23	303	18.6	7.2	129	587	55.4	24.7
Manteca	80	D	D	D	11	188	8.3	2.0	84	1 024	69.9	28.3
Marina	29	341	13.9	3.1	4	63	1.2	0.5	15	149	7.2	2.7
Martinez	77	802	27.9	7.4	4	12	0.7	0.1	39	1 214	98.8	45.2
Maywood	27	278	12.3	2.6	3	5	0.5	0.0	21	219	13.1	5.0
Menlo Park	83	1 352	67.5	17.7	15	89	8.3	2.3	114	1 284	109.5	47.2
Merced	129	1 755	55.2	13.7	13	159	3.4	0.9	204	1 929	127.8	48.7
Milpitas	192	3 839	147.6	37.2	16	329	14.9	3.1	123	1 065	99.2	35.9
Mission Viejo	130	2 184	73.5	18.4	19	316	12.8	3.6	268	2 229	207.1	82.7
Modesto	334	5 931	182.2	48.3	39	693	23.0	6.1	513	6 951	524.4	204.4
Monrovia	73	1 502	56.7	15.8	7	110	4.5	1.8	49	633	47.2	16.5
Montclair	73	D	D	D	5	124	5.3	1.0	70	1 526	98.6	40.4
Montebello	118	1 579	55.9	13.4	5	0	0.0	0.0	155	1 300	103.0	39.0
Monterey	205	4 733	236.7	62.8	25	261	24.0	10.3	230	2 053	168.4	71.8
Monterey Park	128	2 039	84.0	22.8	6	0	0.0	0.0	203	2 641	201.9	83.2
Moorpark	26	D	D	D	7	0	0.0	0.0	18	115	7.1	2.5
Moreno Valley	129	2 149	66.6	18.0	17	246	10.4	3.1	156	1 298	75.0	25.6
Morgan Hill	80	1 038	39.3	8.8	9	111	3.0	1.0	55	490	32.1	10.7
Mountain View	221	3 463	173.7	41.4	15	308	13.0	3.8	236	1 871	175.4	75.8
Murrieta	NA	NA	NA	NA	NA	NA	NA	NA	NA	NA	NA	NA
Napa	189	2 720	111.3	30.5	14	329	10.2	3.1	259	2 345	151.2	61.4
National City	148	1 844	63.7	16.5	6	119	7.2	1.3	112	1 088	66.4	27.2
Newark	103	1 684	74.6	17.6	4	60	1.4	0.3	38	208	14.9	4.6
Newport Beach	339	8 404	371.7	106.7	61	1 348	77.4	20.8	582	3 923	411.0	175.9
Norwalk	118	1 651	64.4	14.8	6	148	6.6	1.3	97	982	58.1	20.6
Novato	109	1 341	50.4	13.2	13	220	15.7	5.2	130	998	79.9	34.0
Oakland	738	9 390	436.3	121.3	62	1 218	183.1	103.0	886	8 669	854.1	338.6
Oceanside	239	3 893	126.1	33.9	14	482	18.2	6.6	215	1 448	131.3	44.8
Ontario	210	4 760	217.0	58.8	12	379	13.6	4.0	114	1 780	196.1	58.1
Orange	246	4 307	171.0	45.5	36	533	19.1	5.6	481	5 069	496.9	201.6
Oxnard	220	4 487	166.6	47.0	34	352	16.9	4.7	309	2 564	194.2	78.7
Pacifica	62	575	24.9	6.0	4	67	1.6	0.6	34	249	12.8	5.0
Palmdale	111	2 286	74.6	19.2	8	181	6.0	1.8	110	926	58.4	21.4
Palm Desert	149	5 164	214.5	63.9	29	720	35.7	11.7	121	855	53.8	20.4
Palm Springs	220	4 974	197.4	57.4	19	929	42.6	13.6	210	2 790	279.7	98.9
Palo Alto	248	5 211	240.7	72.5	16	230	16.2	9.2	285	1 900	188.4	70.1
Paradise	52	658	16.3	4.3	4	83	2.3	0.7	96	745	37.6	13.2
Paramount	55	559	21.7	4.9	2	0	0.0	0.0	76	1 199	86.2	30.9
Pasadena	364	8 048	313.4	92.9	68	853	56.2	19.7	562	6 453	547.7	216.5
Perris	41	583	17.9	4.8	1	0	0.0	0.0	30	285	13.2	4.7
Petaluma	138	2 010	64.1	17.3	15	264	11.3	3.7	151	1 375	77.0	33.4
Pico Rivera	71	1 004	37.3	9.0	3	0	0.0	0.0	80	887	49.0	22.6
Pittsburg	66	864	30.3	8.2	4	21	0.6	0.1	57	500	27.9	10.6
Placentia	77	1 250	47.3	11.1	5	0	0.0	0.0	67	584	47.0	18.7

1. Firms subject to federal tax.

Table D. Cities — Other Services and Federal Funds

City	Other services,[1] 1997				Selected federal funds, 2002–2003 (mil dol)								
					Procurement contracts		Grants						Direct payments for individuals for educational assistance
	Number of establishments	Number of employees	Receipts (mil dol)	Annual payroll (mil dol)	Defense	Other	Total[2]	Medicaid and other health related	Nutrition and family welfare	Energy and environment	Education	Housing and community development	
	104	105	106	107	108	109	110	111	112	113	114	115	116
CALIFORNIA—Cont'd													
Huntington Beach	344	1 807	138.1	37.3	82.2	281.8	6.5	0.0	0.0	0.9	0.9	3.9	6.6
Huntington Park	63	299	20.8	5.8	0.0	1.1	3.4	0.0	0.0	0.0	0.0	3.3	0.0
Imperial Beach	21	116	3.9	1.0	6.8	0.2	2.8	0.0	0.0	0.0	0.4	0.7	0.0
Indio	54	288	17.3	5.6	0.1	0.0	7.5	0.0	0.4	0.1	0.0	6.6	0.0
Inglewood	139	1 037	62.0	17.6	26.1	4.0	29.3	1.8	0.0	0.0	0.0	21.3	1.7
Irvine	232	2 270	143.4	49.5	338.5	31.8	184.2	122.0	0.1	10.7	5.8	5.0	24.5
Laguna Niguel	58	411	26.0	7.9	0.1	2.4	13.7	0.0	0.0	12.6	0.0	1.1	0.0
La Habra	107	597	37.1	9.8	0.0	0.2	2.6	0.0	0.0	0.1	0.0	2.5	0.0
Lake Elsinore	31	129	7.9	1.9	3.1	0.0	0.4	0.0	0.0	0.0	0.0	0.4	0.0
Lake Forest	NA	NA	NA	NA	12.5	0.2	0.7	0.0	0.0	0.0	0.0	0.6	7.7
Lakewood	73	740	40.5	16.1	0.8	0.0	2.5	0.0	0.0	0.0	0.0	2.4	0.0
La Mesa	99	661	29.0	9.6	0.4	0.6	5.4	0.0	2.1	0.0	0.1	3.1	4.1
La Mirada	36	256	13.3	4.3	15.4	1.1	0.4	0.0	0.0	0.0	0.0	0.4	2.4
Lancaster	117	676	51.1	11.9	21.2	0.9	9.4	0.0	0.0	0.0	0.8	8.3	7.3
La Puente	34	100	7.0	1.3	4.0	0.0	7.2	0.0	0.0	0.0	0.4	6.8	1.3
La Verne	28	130	5.8	1.5	6.7	0.4	0.9	0.0	0.0	0.0	0.0	0.6	4.4
Lawndale	85	398	26.0	6.5	0.0	0.2	2.4	0.0	0.0	0.0	1.2	1.2	0.0
Livermore	93	734	82.4	26.9	9.9	2.2	19.7	9.1	0.0	0.0	0.1	6.7	1.1
Lodi	107	458	32.0	8.0	9.9	9.9	0.9	0.0	0.0	0.0	0.0	0.3	0.0
Lompoc	46	239	13.8	3.7	1.1	4.9	4.6	0.4	0.0	0.0	2.8	1.4	0.0
Long Beach	482	3 892	286.5	96.3	4 173.2	42.7	128.8	5.1	10.2	0.3	17.8	81.4	59.7
Los Altos	54	219	13.4	4.3	0.6	1.8	1.8	1.5	0.0	0.0	0.1	0.1	1.5
Los Angeles	5 358	33 761	2 397.4	631.4	368.0	394.8	2 047.1	725.2	34.8	37.3	74.6	879.0	236.0
Los Banos	23	102	6.2	2.2	0.0	0.6	7.7	0.0	0.0	0.5	0.0	0.5	0.0
Los Gatos	82	341	21.9	6.0	0.3	1.8	1.2	0.3	0.0	0.0	0.0	0.7	0.0
Lynwood	34	185	9.9	2.3	0.5	0.2	5.9	0.0	0.0	0.0	0.0	4.8	0.4
Madera	48	229	15.9	4.2	0.1	0.3	11.0	3.8	3.1	0.2	0.0	3.2	0.1
Manhattan Beach	67	388	21.7	5.8	0.2	0.1	0.0	0.0	0.0	0.0	0.0	0.0	0.1
Manteca	58	657	54.4	14.9	0.0	0.5	0.8	0.0	0.0	0.0	0.0	0.7	0.0
Marina	17	57	4.0	0.8	0.1	0.0	4.7	0.0	0.0	0.1	0.0	0.2	0.0
Martinez	42	152	13.3	3.6	94.8	12.0	36.3	4.3	18.9	0.1	0.8	8.9	1.3
Maywood	24	94	6.2	1.8	0.7	0.0	0.4	0.0	0.0	0.0	0.0	0.4	0.0
Menlo Park	53	359	27.2	9.0	58.6	46.0	36.3	25.5	0.0	2.1	1.2	1.9	0.0
Merced	71	460	25.7	8.2	0.0	0.2	30.4	6.0	7.8	0.2	3.4	5.9	7.6
Milpitas	96	721	74.8	18.4	2.5	4.3	4.9	0.0	0.0	0.0	0.0	4.8	1.1
Mission Viejo	122	655	70.7	16.5	0.3	2.5	1.9	0.0	0.0	0.0	0.5	1.0	2.5
Modesto	245	1 474	95.5	28.5	5.9	58.9	55.8	0.0	34.6	0.0	2.3	14.9	12.0
Monrovia	71	356	22.7	6.5	11.7	2.5	3.4	0.1	0.0	0.0	0.0	2.5	0.8
Montclair	67	599	43.1	14.1	0.1	0.0	0.9	0.0	0.0	0.0	0.0	0.8	0.0
Montebello	106	813	53.4	15.9	22.3	0.5	2.5	0.0	0.0	0.0	0.2	2.1	0.7
Monterey	80	540	30.9	9.2	46.3	25.8	18.5	0.3	0.2	0.8	2.9	8.5	2.0
Monterey Park	80	368	22.3	6.2	0.0	0.4	8.2	0.4	0.0	0.0	0.6	3.8	10.6
Moorpark	26	125	9.5	2.4	2.5	0.0	0.5	0.0	0.0	0.0	0.5	0.0	0.3
Moreno Valley	94	380	21.2	6.1	6.6	0.9	8.3	0.0	0.0	0.0	3.5	4.0	0.3
Morgan Hill	47	265	16.5	4.6	11.4	0.7	1.5	0.0	0.0	0.1	0.5	0.6	0.0
Mountain View	151	883	74.8	23.1	7.0	23.2	19.9	7.1	0.0	3.0	0.6	6.8	0.0
Murrieta	NA	NA	NA	NA	3.4	0.0	0.1	0.0	0.0	0.0	0.0	0.0	0.0
Napa	118	639	44.4	12.3	10.6	0.3	20.1	0.0	5.5	0.1	3.1	10.0	2.1
National City	123	838	54.9	17.0	19.4	0.8	31.7	0.1	10.3	0.2	0.5	20.3	0.3
Newark	60	360	29.6	8.1	3.1	1.2	1.4	0.0	0.0	0.3	0.0	0.9	0.5
Newport Beach	159	1 117	70.3	22.1	27.6	11.2	2.7	1.6	0.0	0.9	0.0	1.3	0.5
Norwalk	74	337	21.9	6.0	1.8	1.2	10.0	0.2	0.0	0.2	1.3	7.9	13.7
Novato	91	646	45.7	14.7	1.9	7.4	13.2	9.7	0.2	0.3	0.4	0.9	0.0
Oakland	597	3 524	268.3	78.3	66.8	35.1	307.4	76.6	18.3	9.6	8.7	145.1	15.4
Oceanside	149	1 022	66.0	18.4	6.4	4.4	18.3	0.0	0.1	0.2	5.9	9.4	1.8
Ontario	194	2 069	145.3	47.8	48.7	3.0	9.6	0.0	0.0	0.0	0.9	5.3	0.5
Orange	260	1 821	124.6	36.1	250.3	6.2	72.7	1.1	0.0	0.0	0.5	66.7	6.2
Oxnard	183	1 011	71.2	17.9	27.3	11.9	33.4	0.0	10.9	0.0	2.2	17.7	0.5
Pacifica	34	119	8.0	2.3	0.1	0.0	5.0	0.3	0.0	0.0	0.0	4.7	0.0
Palmdale	73	366	22.3	5.5	998.2	4.8	7.1	0.0	0.0	0.0	0.0	6.5	0.0
Palm Desert	95	704	36.5	11.3	0.2	0.4	2.5	0.5	0.0	0.0	0.9	0.6	4.4
Palm Springs	90	563	33.9	9.8	0.0	1.0	7.3	0.7	0.0	0.1	0.0	2.7	0.3
Palo Alto	107	964	101.1	29.4	83.7	97.6	339.8	300.3	0.0	7.3	1.5	10.9	0.4
Paradise	35	106	8.0	1.9	0.0	0.0	1.0	0.0	0.0	0.0	0.2	0.7	0.0
Paramount	68	677	53.7	16.0	2.0	0.7	2.9	0.0	0.0	0.4	0.2	2.2	0.3
Pasadena	300	1 843	133.9	33.9	71.6	1 666.5	236.8	43.6	13.6	18.0	3.8	41.6	18.7
Perris	18	61	7.0	2.1	0.7	5.0	0.8	0.9	0.4	0.0	0.4	0.4	0.0
Petaluma	97	543	44.6	12.3	3.1	5.0	4.5	0.9	0.4	0.0	0.6	2.2	0.0
Pico Rivera	59	708	32.7	10.1	1.2	0.0	6.0	0.0	0.0	0.0	0.4	5.5	0.0
Pittsburg	46	289	15.2	6.8	0.0	0.0	21.4	0.2	0.0	0.0	3.9	16.6	0.0
Placentia	60	298	24.5	7.3	4.2	2.2	21.1	0.0	0.0	0.0	0.5	0.9	0.0

1. Firms subject to federal tax. 2. Includes program categories not shown separately. State totals include additional categories not allocated by city.

City	City government finances, 2002									
	General revenue							General expenditure		
		Intergovernmental		Taxes					Per capita[1] (dollars)	
					Per capita[1] (dollars)					
	Total (mil dol)	Total (mil dol)	Percent from state government	Total (mil dol)	Total	Property	Sales and gross receipts	Total (mil dol)	Total	Capital outlays
	117	118	119	120	121	122	123	124	125	126
CALIFORNIA—Cont'd										
Huntington Beach	179.6	30.5	78.2	93.3	481	168	261	205.3	1 059	264
Huntington Park	41.0	8.4	89.3	18.9	300	117	159	39.8	631	48
Imperial Beach	17.4	6.1	56.1	5.1	188	79	92	17.5	641	8
Indio	60.2	5.4	83.3	21.2	392	138	214	36.5	673	56
Inglewood	128.6	48.2	59.4	49.1	427	81	270	123.3	1 072	143
Irvine	142.3	20.9	71.3	81.7	504	93	343	203.4	1 254	351
Laguna Niguel	31.2	7.0	81.3	19.6	311	124	164	25.9	411	147
La Habra	48.5	15.0	90.9	22.5	376	150	207	44.2	737	94
Lake Elsinore	28.6	4.2	89.6	18.4	578	296	196	34.1	1 069	277
Lake Forest	34.3	8.4	91.9	21.9	284	86	184	25.1	326	99
Lakewood	43.2	9.5	93.0	23.4	289	88	186	38.1	469	58
La Mesa	39.7	7.4	90.0	21.2	385	95	274	38.7	704	139
La Mirada	37.7	4.2	92.8	23.1	476	257	195	38.2	789	107
Lancaster	98.3	19.3	92.0	58.2	467	243	184	99.5	799	216
La Puente	11.1	4.6	87.8	5.3	126	16	97	8.6	205	25
La Verne	28.7	4.1	92.1	15.6	476	252	176	25.6	784	76
Lawndale	15.2	5.1	66.7	6.8	209	20	164	14.9	461	149
Livermore	124.0	19.7	95.0	37.9	495	203	263	125.1	1 632	579
Lodi	63.5	15.9	97.0	28.7	474	91	356	36.2	597	20
Lompoc	30.8	5.5	90.8	12.1	293	70	205	29.6	715	117
Long Beach	882.8	185.7	50.8	232.9	493	165	278	936.2	1 982	515
Los Altos	24.6	2.8	97.9	13.1	479	223	197	22.5	824	174
Los Angeles	6 018.7	1 011.4	47.7	2 420.5	637	224	259	6 503.1	1 712	386
Los Banos	17.9	3.4	76.9	7.2	243	83	107	21.6	731	220
Los Gatos	29.1	3.1	97.1	19.6	696	304	310	30.7	1 089	372
Lynwood	35.9	9.0	100.0	15.1	211	98	104	39.4	552	70
Madera	34.0	7.6	61.3	14.1	306	104	165	36.9	797	269
Manhattan Beach	45.9	5.2	89.0	24.8	699	256	305	38.2	1 076	97
Manteca	58.4	8.5	63.4	22.6	396	178	134	46.4	815	250
Marina	15.0	3.8	76.8	5.9	279	102	164	10.4	490	47
Martinez	26.7	11.0	89.5	10.8	295	119	146	19.3	525	128
Maywood	9.9	2.9	100.0	4.8	167	64	88	7.8	271	15
Menlo Park	47.0	5.1	99.3	30.0	989	524	378	59.3	1 958	830
Merced	52.9	7.4	100.0	21.0	308	112	168	54.5	798	211
Milpitas	107.6	9.1	99.2	67.4	1 058	660	361	123.6	1 940	675
Mission Viejo	60.7	11.9	85.0	40.0	416	172	210	68.0	707	275
Modesto	177.7	34.8	77.4	93.7	460	52	267	151.1	743	148
Monrovia	36.4	5.5	88.7	21.7	573	276	262	30.9	816	47
Montclair	32.5	4.5	94.9	20.6	598	204	359	29.9	870	62
Montebello	64.9	15.6	73.3	35.0	550	251	269	58.1	913	225
Monterey	70.1	6.0	100.0	35.0	1 181	297	782	61.6	2 078	539
Monterey Park	47.0	9.4	85.7	25.1	406	207	171	45.8	741	102
Moorpark	24.5	3.1	88.1	12.4	359	133	109	15.4	446	132
Moreno Valley	78.6	15.5	90.8	45.5	302	113	172	75.7	502	101
Morgan Hill	49.8	3.5	99.9	31.0	917	590	210	47.9	1 418	765
Mountain View	139.7	9.3	88.1	74.5	1 064	565	394	109.4	1 562	276
Murrieta	68.8	35.4	13.1	26.8	496	124	137	53.0	980	644
Napa	63.0	14.9	69.6	34.3	457	161	215	58.2	775	199
National City	58.1	15.7	48.7	27.6	497	164	314	57.8	1 041	185
Newark	40.5	4.8	94.6	26.3	606	164	387	37.7	869	88
Newport Beach	131.2	10.0	93.0	69.8	894	412	393	135.4	1 734	249
Norwalk	60.1	18.2	67.1	29.4	277	77	187	62.0	585	190
Novato	38.1	5.1	96.8	19.0	395	159	181	36.9	767	133
Oakland	920.3	137.1	46.6	370.5	920	367	266	1 115.4	2 769	1 049
Oceanside	182.0	39.4	96.7	50.8	306	132	125	172.3	1 039	178
Ontario	202.5	26.7	69.5	104.2	631	252	311	175.3	1 062	193
Orange	103.6	16.7	89.6	62.4	474	197	243	99.8	758	116
Oxnard	174.8	26.5	69.8	75.6	425	155	196	172.4	968	204
Pacifica	33.1	9.0	98.1	11.0	291	148	116	38.6	1 022	342
Palmdale	79.7	18.7	100.0	47.5	382	200	144	86.1	692	142
Palm Desert	115.3	4.6	95.7	77.0	1 737	1 083	554	107.7	2 430	678
Palm Springs	110.7	29.7	20.0	47.3	1 062	372	638	102.2	2 296	463
Palo Alto	202.0	9.9	75.9	52.1	905	228	564	166.2	2 888	489
Paradise	10.5	4.3	74.1	5.3	197	107	72	10.3	385	48
Paramount	35.4	10.4	75.7	19.5	345	147	174	33.4	592	171
Pasadena	293.3	47.3	69.1	122.0	873	278	513	200.4	1 435	41
Perris	24.9	4.8	97.0	14.2	370	126	168	20.4	532	22
Petaluma	64.9	11.4	83.0	32.3	584	272	234	63.7	1 153	290
Pico Rivera	37.0	13.7	71.7	16.5	255	80	149	37.8	583	130
Pittsburg	72.0	7.1	85.4	38.2	631	426	182	56.5	933	168
Placentia	32.5	6.4	88.5	18.0	377	126	190	36.5	763	179

1. Based on population estimated as of July 1 of the year shown.

City	Public welfare	Highways	Parking facilities	Education	Health and hospitals	Police protection	Sewerage and sanitation	Parks and recreation	Housing and community development	Interest on debt
	127	128	129	130	131	132	133	134	135	136
CALIFORNIA—Cont'd										
Huntington Beach	0.0	16.9	0.6	0.0	3.0	21.6	5.5	14.1	6.7	4.2
Huntington Park	0.0	6.1	1.2	0.0	0.3	29.0	2.5	4.8	9.6	29.1
Imperial Beach	0.0	21.5	0.0	0.0	0.6	20.9	27.2	2.9	0.6	0.4
Indio	0.0	10.2	0.0	0.0	3.8	20.9	0.0	3.3	5.6	14.3
Inglewood	0.0	6.5	0.2	0.0	1.8	26.1	8.8	6.0	12.9	3.6
Irvine	0.0	17.0	0.0	0.0	0.6	17.9	0.0	10.1	1.4	20.9
Laguna Niguel	0.0	15.6	0.0	0.0	0.9	21.4	0.0	44.6	0.3	0.0
La Habra	0.0	16.8	0.0	0.0	3.8	26.6	6.4	7.7	4.2	5.7
Lake Elsinore	0.0	19.5	0.0	0.0	0.2	11.8	0.0	10.5	17.2	23.0
Lake Forest	0.0	37.4	0.0	0.0	0.1	27.0	0.0	15.3	7.9	0.2
Lakewood	0.0	15.5	0.0	0.0	0.8	16.2	10.0	18.7	15.0	4.5
La Mesa	0.0	17.7	0.2	0.0	0.3	22.2	18.5	10.9	2.8	1.9
La Mirada	0.0	14.3	0.0	0.0	0.3	16.4	0.0	13.0	12.6	12.7
Lancaster	0.0	23.6	0.0	0.0	0.2	13.1	0.0	11.0	27.9	14.3
La Puente	0.0	15.6	0.0	0.0	0.9	44.6	0.0	10.5	0.1	1.2
La Verne	0.0	12.1	0.0	0.0	3.6	26.6	1.9	9.3	15.8	7.6
Lawndale	0.0	9.0	0.0	0.0	0.5	24.7	0.1	10.8	29.8	4.9
Livermore	0.0	13.4	0.1	0.0	1.0	16.0	10.5	1.5	9.2	4.4
Lodi	0.0	12.7	0.0	0.0	0.5	24.1	13.4	11.5	1.3	3.9
Lompoc	0.0	14.5	0.0	0.0	0.6	19.3	37.8	6.4	1.1	0.2
Long Beach	0.0	9.6	0.1	0.0	4.0	15.9	7.9	2.9	9.6	8.7
Los Altos	0.0	10.7	0.0	0.0	0.0	21.2	16.6	22.0	0.0	0.1
Los Angeles	0.0	8.6	0.1	0.0	0.6	17.3	8.8	5.1	2.7	7.1
Los Banos	0.0	15.6	0.0	0.0	0.3	18.4	17.4	11.6	9.8	0.7
Los Gatos	0.0	25.6	0.0	0.0	0.0	31.3	2.1	6.5	8.8	0.8
Lynwood	0.0	16.0	0.0	0.0	0.2	15.8	8.2	9.6	12.3	4.4
Madera	0.0	15.1	0.1	0.0	2.0	19.5	19.0	6.2	13.6	3.2
Manhattan Beach	0.0	13.7	2.5	0.0	4.8	33.0	10.7	12.1	0.0	0.0
Manteca	0.0	18.2	0.0	0.0	0.5	15.6	32.0	10.2	4.8	3.0
Marina	0.0	12.2	0.0	0.0	0.0	38.2	0.0	3.4	9.2	3.1
Martinez	0.0	26.2	2.0	0.0	0.0	37.4	0.0	14.1	0.7	1.1
Maywood	0.0	10.9	0.0	0.0	0.7	52.8	0.0	16.7	6.1	5.0
Menlo Park	0.0	10.0	0.0	0.0	0.3	14.5	2.4	16.6	37.1	6.9
Merced	0.0	8.7	0.5	0.0	0.4	20.8	25.1	11.4	8.1	2.5
Milpitas	0.0	12.1	0.0	0.0	3.4	12.7	10.8	3.8	21.3	7.4
Mission Viejo	0.0	25.9	0.0	0.0	1.2	11.7	0.0	14.2	3.4	3.7
Modesto	0.0	16.3	0.4	0.0	0.5	25.6	14.8	11.6	2.4	4.7
Monrovia	0.0	10.5	0.0	0.0	2.5	30.3	3.5	9.1	6.9	11.1
Montclair	0.0	10.1	0.0	0.0	2.5	26.7	11.6	6.2	12.9	8.1
Montebello	0.0	2.5	0.0	0.0	0.0	22.5	4.1	10.3	18.8	8.5
Monterey	0.0	8.5	5.2	0.0	0.0	13.6	2.0	15.7	1.3	2.5
Monterey Park	0.0	10.8	0.0	0.0	1.0	23.7	9.4	6.7	10.0	6.1
Moorpark	0.0	22.5	0.0	0.0	1.2	18.9	1.1	14.6	15.6	3.6
Moreno Valley	0.0	16.9	0.0	0.0	2.1	26.2	0.0	11.0	13.3	4.1
Morgan Hill	0.0	10.7	0.0	0.0	0.1	12.3	10.5	2.7	46.8	4.0
Mountain View	0.0	10.8	0.0	0.0	0.0	14.9	16.8	14.4	0.9	3.7
Murrieta	0.0	26.0	0.0	0.0	0.1	27.0	0.0	7.3	0.1	2.1
Napa	0.0	26.5	0.7	0.0	1.6	23.2	5.6	10.3	6.1	0.8
National City	0.0	7.0	0.0	0.0	0.2	23.8	12.7	4.2	27.3	5.1
Newark	0.0	12.3	0.0	0.0	11.9	25.8	0.5	14.3	4.8	11.2
Newport Beach	0.0	12.0	0.0	0.0	1.2	17.1	5.4	19.9	0.5	17.6
Norwalk	0.0	23.5	1.0	0.0	0.0	16.3	0.0	8.6	17.5	7.9
Novato	0.0	19.6	0.0	0.0	0.0	23.8	0.0	9.3	5.3	20.3
Oakland	0.0	5.9	0.5	0.0	1.5	10.9	1.3	3.7	4.4	10.4
Oceanside	0.0	7.1	0.0	0.0	0.0	17.1	19.6	2.6	12.7	9.7
Ontario	0.0	8.7	0.0	0.0	2.9	24.1	13.5	5.4	12.0	8.9
Orange	0.0	12.2	0.0	0.0	4.1	25.0	7.8	6.6	9.3	5.3
Oxnard	0.0	9.8	0.0	0.0	0.0	19.9	25.6	9.0	5.6	5.4
Pacifica	0.0	14.8	0.0	0.0	0.0	15.6	14.6	8.0	1.9	3.2
Palmdale	0.0	9.6	0.0	0.0	0.9	14.8	0.0	3.9	20.3	15.3
Palm Desert	0.0	16.9	0.0	0.0	0.1	8.9	0.0	8.9	37.9	13.1
Palm Springs	0.0	4.0	0.2	0.0	0.6	15.3	6.2	7.8	5.3	8.9
Palo Alto	0.0	13.9	0.0	0.0	0.3	11.4	29.3	10.4	0.2	1.4
Paradise	0.0	13.9	0.0	0.0	1.6	32.4	2.7	0.0	0.0	0.2
Paramount	0.0	23.0	0.0	0.0	0.8	23.4	0.0	13.9	15.5	10.8
Pasadena	0.0	6.2	3.3	0.0	6.5	19.7	4.7	6.2	9.2	7.8
Perris	0.0	16.8	0.0	0.0	0.9	27.7	7.3	4.3	4.9	21.3
Petaluma	0.0	15.4	0.0	0.0	4.0	16.5	20.6	8.1	13.8	3.7
Pico Rivera	0.0	10.8	0.0	0.0	4.0	15.9	0.0	21.4	7.2	8.0
Pittsburg	0.0	21.8	0.0	0.0	1.8	23.7	1.1	6.7	17.7	19.7
Placentia	0.0	20.3	0.0	0.0	0.0	25.9	5.1	10.5	11.0	4.8

Table D. Cities — City Government Finances, City Government Employment, and Climate

City	City government finances, 2002 (cont'd) Debt outstanding Total (mil dol)	Per capita[1] (dollars)	Percent utility	City government employment, 2002	Climate[2] Average daily temperature (degrees Fahrenheit) Mean January	July	Limits January[3]	July[4]	Annual precipitation (inches)	Heating degree days	Cooling degree days
	137	138	139	140	141	142	143	144	145	146	147
CALIFORNIA—Cont'd											
Huntington Beach	182.2	940	14.8	1 390	55.2	67.1	46.8	71.8	10.85	1 866	500
Huntington Park	158.0	2 509	0.0	208	58.3	74.3	48.9	84.0	14.77	1 154	1 537
Imperial Beach	2.1	76	0.0	74	55.3	68.2	45.3	73.1	9.34	1 798	638
Indio	74.5	1 373	0.0	177	56.4	92.0	42.5	108.7	5.31	985	4 014
Inglewood	136.2	1 184	2.5	821	56.8	69.1	47.8	75.3	12.01	1 458	727
Irvine	818.8	5 050	0.0	835	54.5	71.6	41.4	83.7	11.81	1 784	973
Laguna Niguel	0.0	0	0.0	62	53.7	67.2	41.5	75.8	12.19	2 157	493
La Habra	54.9	914	0.0	389	57.4	72.6	45.6	82.6	12.27	1 238	1 175
Lake Elsinore	183.7	5 766	0.0	51	NA	NA	NA	NA	NA	NA	NA
Lake Forest	1.4	18	0.0	26	NA	NA	NA	NA	NA	NA	NA
Lakewood	34.2	422	14.0	245	55.9	73.1	44.9	82.7	11.80	1 430	1 201
La Mesa	11.8	215	0.0	279	56.6	72.5	44.6	83.4	12.80	1 400	1 110
La Mirada	81.1	1 672	0.0	167	57.4	72.6	45.6	82.6	12.27	1 238	1 175
Lancaster	328.0	2 633	0.0	286	45.1	80.7	31.9	97.1	6.92	2 948	1 720
La Puente	2.2	52	0.0	44	55.7	75.2	41.7	89.2	17.90	1 433	1 427
La Verne	24.4	744	0.0	221	54.3	74.6	40.7	90.4	16.62	1 713	1 273
Lawndale	10.9	335	0.0	77	56.1	69.7	45.3	78.8	13.57	1 568	794
Livermore	134.9	1 760	0.0	449	46.1	71.6	35.5	89.8	14.21	2 909	780
Lodi	90.2	1 487	60.0	384	45.1	73.9	36.4	91.4	17.11	2 809	1 020
Lompoc	9.8	236	75.2	393	52.9	62.9	40.1	72.9	13.95	2 651	265
Long Beach	1 880.5	3 981	2.7	5 986	55.9	73.1	44.9	82.7	11.80	1 430	1 201
Los Altos	0.2	8	0.0	144	47.5	66.4	37.7	78.4	14.96	2 911	297
Los Angeles	12 121.1	3 191	34.3	50 012	58.3	74.3	48.9	84.0	14.77	1 154	1 537
Los Banos	10.2	346	0.6	139	NA	NA	NA	NA	NA	NA	NA
Los Gatos	3.9	136	0.0	181	49.4	69.5	40.6	82.4	14.42	2 387	594
Lynwood	36.6	513	25.9	217	58.3	74.3	48.9	84.0	14.77	1 154	1 537
Madera	23.2	503	0.0	241	44.7	79.7	35.5	97.8	11.15	2 741	1 632
Manhattan Beach	4.3	120	100.0	307	56.8	69.1	47.8	75.3	12.01	1 458	727
Manteca	21.5	377	0.0	301	45.0	77.7	37.0	94.4	13.95	2 707	1 470
Marina	6.4	304	0.0	84	51.7	60.0	43.3	68.1	18.72	3 125	55
Martinez	14.9	405	76.5	231	49.9	63.2	42.0	71.0	22.20	2 574	199
Maywood	10.1	353	0.0	88	58.3	74.3	48.9	84.0	14.77	1 154	1 537
Menlo Park	89.5	2 957	0.0	294	47.5	66.4	37.7	78.4	14.96	2 911	297
Merced	36.1	529	0.0	415	45.1	78.6	35.7	96.9	12.01	2 692	1 500
Milpitas	189.0	2 966	0.0	561	49.4	69.5	40.6	82.4	14.42	2 387	594
Mission Viejo	63.5	660	0.0	144	54.5	71.6	41.4	83.7	11.81	1 784	973
Modesto	191.3	940	12.1	1 258	45.6	77.1	37.4	94.2	12.10	2 605	1 401
Monrovia	66.9	1 767	0.0	277	55.8	75.0	43.6	89.0	19.37	1 453	1 394
Montclair	39.4	1 147	0.0	167	54.3	74.6	40.7	90.4	16.62	1 713	1 273
Montebello	110.0	1 730	0.0	576	58.3	74.3	48.9	84.0	14.77	1 154	1 537
Monterey	32.8	1 107	0.0	484	51.7	60.0	43.3	68.1	18.72	3 125	55
Monterey Park	43.1	697	0.0	404	55.7	75.2	41.7	89.2	17.90	1 433	1 427
Moorpark	20.5	592	0.0	58	54.6	67.8	41.2	80.8	17.39	2 039	569
Moreno Valley	67.4	447	0.0	378	53.6	76.9	41.2	93.7	10.00	1 796	1 500
Morgan Hill	48.3	1 429	8.4	158	NA	NA	NA	NA	NA	NA	NA
Mountain View	78.1	1 116	0.0	668	47.5	66.4	37.7	78.4	14.96	2 911	297
Murrieta	19.2	355	0.0	146	NA	NA	NA	NA	NA	NA	NA
Napa	20.6	274	47.5	436	47.1	67.9	37.2	82.1	25.12	2 844	456
National City	48.8	879	0.0	355	57.4	71.0	48.9	76.2	9.90	1 256	984
Newark	61.6	1 421	0.0	318	49.0	66.7	41.1	76.1	13.73	2 578	410
Newport Beach	353.7	4 529	3.1	955	55.2	67.1	46.8	71.8	10.85	1 866	500
Norwalk	83.8	790	0.0	330	55.9	73.1	44.9	82.7	11.80	1 430	1 201
Novato	118.8	2 469	0.0	243	46.4	67.0	36.8	82.5	24.60	3 050	335
Oakland	2 759.7	6 852	0.0	5 265	49.9	62.1	43.3	70.0	24.30	2 902	115
Oceanside	305.0	1 838	9.1	1 045	54.5	67.6	44.1	73.5	10.93	2 010	555
Ontario	296.6	1 797	0.0	1 171	54.3	74.6	40.7	90.4	16.62	1 713	1 273
Orange	147.7	1 123	1.3	739	57.4	72.6	45.6	82.6	12.27	1 238	1 175
Oxnard	150.7	847	0.0	1 296	55.3	66.1	44.2	74.4	14.38	1 992	416
Pacifica	23.6	625	0.0	257	48.7	62.7	41.8	71.6	19.70	3 016	145
Palmdale	215.9	1 736	0.0	357	45.1	80.7	31.9	97.1	6.92	2 948	1 720
Palm Desert	252.0	5 685	0.0	133	NA	NA	NA	NA	NA	NA	NA
Palm Springs	167.0	3 750	0.0	504	56.4	92.0	42.5	108.7	5.31	985	4 014
Palo Alto	63.2	1 098	0.0	1 174	47.5	66.4	37.7	78.4	14.96	2 911	297
Paradise	0.0	0	0.0	144	45.4	77.2	36.9	90.8	52.71	3 214	1 342
Paramount	99.1	1 754	0.3	131	55.9	73.1	44.9	82.7	11.80	1 430	1 201
Pasadena	450.1	3 221	19.7	1 789	55.8	75.0	43.6	89.0	19.37	1 453	1 394
Perris	90.4	2 361	0.0	49	NA	NA	NA	NA	NA	NA	NA
Petaluma	66.1	1 196	14.9	359	46.4	67.0	36.8	82.5	24.60	3 050	335
Pico Rivera	64.4	993	34.9	329	58.3	74.3	48.9	84.0	14.77	1 154	1 537
Pittsburg	252.1	4 165	5.7	321	44.5	73.8	35.9	90.8	12.80	2 837	1 066
Placentia	36.6	765	0.0	180	57.4	72.6	45.6	82.6	12.27	1 238	1 175

1. Based on the population estimated as of July 1 of the year shown.   2. Represents normal values based on the 30-year period, 1961–1990.   3. Average daily minimum.   4. Average daily maximum.

Table D. Cities — Land Area and Population

STATE Place code	City	Land area,[1] 2000 (sq km)	Population, 2003			Population characteristics, 2000						
						Percent						
									Race (alone or in combination)			
			Total persons	Rank	Per square kilometer	White	Black	Am. Indian, Alaska Native	Asian and Pacific Islander	Other race	Hispanic or Latino[2]	Non-Hispanic White
		1	2	3	4	5	6	7	8	9	10	11
	CALIFORNIA—Cont'd											
06 57764	Pleasant Hill	18.4	33 859	956	1 840.2	85.4	2.1	1.3	11.9	3.8	8.4	76.6
06 57792	Pleasanton	56.1	65 982	437	1 176.1	83.6	1.7	0.9	14.0	3.7	7.9	75.8
06 58072	Pomona	59.2	154 147	137	2 603.8	45.6	10.4	2.0	8.6	38.6	64.5	17.0
06 58240	Porterville	36.3	42 484	757	1 170.4	58.6	1.7	2.9	5.9	35.9	49.4	42.0
06 58520	Poway	101.6	49 201	644	484.3	86.5	2.1	1.2	9.7	4.8	10.4	77.2
06 59451	Rancho Cucamonga	97.0	151 640	144	1 563.3	71.0	8.9	1.6	7.9	16.3	27.8	54.8
06 59514	Rancho Palos Verdes	35.4	42 265	758	1 193.9	70.1	2.4	0.6	28.1	2.4	5.7	63.1
06 59920	Redding	151.4	87 579	302	578.5	91.7	1.5	3.8	4.0	2.5	5.4	85.7
06 59962	Redlands	91.9	67 859	418	738.4	77.4	5.1	1.8	6.8	13.5	24.1	63.3
06 60018	Redondo Beach	16.3	66 337	435	4 069.8	82.7	3.1	1.2	11.8	6.2	13.5	70.8
06 60102	Redwood City	50.4	73 472	382	1 457.8	72.6	3.0	1.2	11.6	16.1	31.2	53.9
06 60466	Rialto	56.6	98 091	253	1 733.1	43.3	23.7	2.1	4.0	32.4	51.2	21.5
06 60620	Richmond	77.6	102 327	234	1 318.6	35.0	37.8	1.6	14.6	16.7	26.5	21.2
06 62000	Riverside	202.3	281 514	61	1 391.6	63.6	8.4	2.1	7.4	23.9	38.1	45.6
06 62364	Rocklin	41.9	46 937	681	1 120.2	91.7	1.3	1.8	6.3	3.0	7.9	83.4
06 62546	Rohnert Park	16.7	41 871	768	2 507.2	84.9	2.9	2.1	8.3	7.6	13.6	74.0
06 62896	Rosemead	13.3	55 262	559	4 155.0	29.0	0.9	1.4	50.3	22.0	41.3	8.0
06 62938	Roseville	78.9	98 359	252	1 246.6	89.2	1.7	1.6	6.0	5.2	11.5	79.8
06 64000	Sacramento	251.6	445 335	37	1 770.0	52.6	17.3	2.8	20.6	13.7	21.6	40.5
06 64224	Salinas	49.2	147 840	148	3 004.9	49.4	3.9	2.0	8.3	41.9	64.1	24.2
06 65000	San Bernardino	152.3	195 357	105	1 282.7	49.4	17.8	2.5	5.7	30.4	47.5	28.9
06 65028	San Bruno	14.1	39 602	813	2 808.7	63.1	2.6	1.2	26.2	14.8	24.1	46.9
06 65042	San Buenaventura (Ventura)	54.6	104 140	227	1 907.3	82.7	2.0	2.5	4.5	13.0	24.3	68.1
06 65070	San Carlos	15.3	27 004	1 170	1 765.0	88.1	1.0	0.7	10.3	4.0	7.7	80.2
06 65084	San Clemente	45.6	57 768	525	1 266.8	90.4	1.1	1.3	4.0	6.2	15.9	78.4
06 66000	San Diego	840.0	1 266 753	7	1 508.0	63.9	8.9	1.3	16.4	14.7	25.4	49.4
06 66070	San Dimas	40.2	36 000	892	895.5	78.5	3.8	1.5	11.2	9.7	23.3	61.1
06 67000	San Francisco	120.9	751 682	14	6 217.4	53.0	8.6	1.2	33.4	8.5	14.1	43.6
06 67042	San Gabriel	10.7	40 987	784	3 830.6	35.9	1.3	1.3	50.8	14.2	30.7	17.4
06 68000	San Jose	452.9	898 349	11	1 983.5	51.5	4.1	1.5	29.6	18.7	30.2	36.0
06 68028	San Juan Capistrano	36.8	34 796	931	945.5	81.7	1.1	1.7	3.0	16.2	33.1	62.3
06 68084	San Leandro	34.0	80 139	340	2 357.0	55.9	11.0	1.7	26.5	11.3	20.1	42.3
06 68154	San Luis Obispo	27.6	44 202	728	1 601.5	87.2	1.9	1.5	6.9	6.3	11.7	78.7
06 68196	San Marcos	61.5	64 242	451	1 044.6	71.3	2.8	1.5	6.4	22.8	36.9	53.9
06 68252	San Mateo	31.6	91 157	284	2 884.7	70.2	3.1	1.1	19.6	11.4	20.5	56.5
06 68294	San Pablo	6.7	31 041	1 030	4 633.0	36.3	19.9	2.0	19.5	29.6	44.6	16.2
06 68364	San Rafael	43.0	55 805	552	1 297.8	79.6	3.0	1.3	7.3	13.7	23.3	65.9
06 68378	San Ramon	30.0	45 907	704	1 530.2	79.9	2.3	0.9	17.6	3.2	7.2	72.3
06 69000	Santa Ana	70.3	342 510	51	4 872.1	46.6	2.1	1.7	9.9	44.3	76.1	12.4
06 69070	Santa Barbara	49.1	88 251	296	1 797.4	77.5	2.2	1.9	3.9	18.6	35.0	58.3
06 69084	Santa Clara	47.6	102 095	235	2 144.9	59.6	2.8	1.1	32.3	9.4	16.0	48.3
06 69088	Santa Clarita	123.9	162 742	129	1 313.5	83.0	2.6	1.3	7.0	10.3	20.5	69.3
06 69112	Santa Cruz	32.5	54 262	583	1 669.6	82.7	2.5	2.1	7.0	10.8	17.4	72.0
06 69196	Santa Maria	50.1	81 944	325	1 635.6	62.5	2.3	3.1	6.2	31.4	59.7	32.0
06 70000	Santa Monica	21.4	87 162	306	4 073.0	81.9	4.5	1.1	9.0	7.9	13.4	71.9
06 70042	Santa Paula	11.9	28 879	1 099	2 426.8	59.4	0.7	2.1	1.5	41.0	71.2	26.4
06 70098	Santa Rosa	103.9	153 386	139	1 476.3	81.4	2.9	2.6	5.6	12.3	19.2	70.9
06 70224	Santee	41.6	52 942	599	1 272.6	90.3	2.0	1.7	4.9	5.4	11.4	80.8
06 70280	Saratoga	31.4	29 309	1 086	933.4	69.4	0.5	0.4	31.0	1.2	3.1	65.1
06 70742	Seaside	22.9	33 897	955	1 480.2	54.5	14.8	2.2	15.7	21.0	34.5	36.4
06 72016	Simi Valley	101.5	117 115	198	1 153.8	84.7	1.7	1.6	8.0	8.1	16.8	72.7
06 73080	South Gate	19.1	98 966	251	5 181.5	45.8	1.2	1.3	1.3	55.2	92.0	6.0
06 73262	South San Francisco	23.4	59 415	506	2 539.1	49.6	3.5	1.4	34.1	18.9	31.8	30.5
06 73962	Stanton	8.1	37 853	844	4 673.2	53.6	2.7	1.7	18.2	29.2	48.9	30.2
06 75000	Stockton	141.7	271 466	65	1 915.8	47.7	12.5	2.3	23.9	20.8	32.5	32.2
06 75630	Suisun City	10.4	26 968	1 173	2 593.1	50.6	21.7	2.1	23.7	11.3	17.8	38.6
06 77000	Sunnyvale	56.8	128 549	173	2 263.2	56.7	2.7	1.1	34.9	9.1	15.5	46.5
06 78120	Temecula	68.0	76 836	365	1 129.9	82.6	4.3	1.7	7.0	9.1	19.0	69.3
06 78148	Temple City	10.4	36 325	883	3 492.8	51.5	1.1	0.9	40.6	9.5	20.5	37.7
06 78582	Thousand Oaks	142.1	124 192	185	874.0	87.7	1.4	1.0	7.3	5.6	13.1	77.7
06 80000	Torrance	53.2	142 621	157	2 680.8	63.1	2.7	1.1	31.9	6.3	12.8	52.4
06 80238	Tracy	54.4	72 456	387	1 331.9	70.9	6.4	2.0	11.4	16.4	27.7	54.0
06 80644	Tulare	43.0	47 421	674	1 102.8	61.6	5.8	2.4	3.0	33.3	45.6	43.8
06 80812	Turlock	34.5	63 467	458	1 839.6	77.0	1.8	1.8	6.3	18.6	29.4	60.4
06 80854	Tustin	29.5	68 478	415	2 321.3	62.5	3.5	1.3	17.0	20.5	34.2	44.8
06 81204	Union City	49.9	69 309	407	1 389.0	34.9	7.6	1.3	48.8	14.7	24.0	20.4
06 81344	Upland	39.2	72 040	389	1 837.8	71.1	8.4	1.6	8.8	15.0	27.5	54.8
06 81554	Vacaville	70.1	94 129	269	1 342.8	76.8	11.2	2.1	7.3	8.7	17.9	63.2
06 81666	Vallejo	78.2	119 708	193	1 530.8	40.4	25.8	1.8	29.2	10.1	15.9	30.4
06 82590	Victorville	188.5	74 987	372	397.8	66.0	13.4	2.4	5.2	19.3	33.5	47.5
06 82954	Visalia	74.0	100 612	244	1 359.6	73.1	2.3	2.4	6.3	20.3	35.6	54.9

1. Dry land or land partially or temporarily covered by water.   2. Hispanic or Latino persons may be of any race.

City	Population characteristics, 2000 (cont'd)										Population			
	Age of population (percent)										Census counts		Percent change	
	Under 5 years	5 to 17 years	18 to 24 years	25 to 34 years	35 to 44 years	45 to 54 years	55 to 64 years	65 to 74 years	75 years and over	Percent female	1990	2000	1990–2000	2000–2003
	12	13	14	15	16	17	18	19	20	21	22	23	24	25
CALIFORNIA—Cont'd														
Pleasant Hill	6.1	15.3	7.2	14.4	18.0	16.8	9.0	6.2	7.0	51.5	31 583	32 837	4.0	3.1
Pleasanton	6.8	21.4	5.5	12.5	20.8	16.5	8.9	4.3	3.3	50.9	50 570	63 654	25.9	3.7
Pomona	9.4	25.2	13.0	15.9	14.6	10.2	5.3	3.5	2.9	49.4	131 700	149 473	13.5	3.1
Porterville	9.5	24.8	10.8	14.0	14.0	11.2	6.3	4.4	5.0	50.9	29 521	39 615	34.2	7.2
Poway	6.0	24.7	7.1	9.5	18.6	17.0	8.5	4.5	4.1	50.8	43 396	48 044	10.7	2.4
Rancho Cucamonga	7.0	22.9	9.9	14.6	18.6	14.4	6.6	3.5	2.6	50.0	101 409	127 743	26.0	18.7
Rancho Palos Verdes	4.9	18.1	4.7	7.0	16.0	16.5	14.2	11.1	7.6	51.6	41 667	41 145	-1.3	2.7
Redding	6.6	19.5	9.7	11.8	14.6	13.4	8.9	7.5	8.0	52.1	66 176	80 865	21.7	8.3
Redlands	6.2	20.0	10.7	13.0	14.9	14.2	8.4	5.9	6.7	52.8	62 667	63 591	1.5	6.7
Redondo Beach	5.7	13.1	6.1	20.9	22.1	15.5	8.0	4.7	3.7	49.6	60 167	63 261	5.1	4.9
Redwood City	7.5	15.7	8.4	18.9	18.5	13.2	7.6	4.7	5.5	49.7	66 072	75 402	14.1	-2.6
Rialto	9.5	28.2	10.4	13.8	15.3	10.8	5.6	3.9	2.6	51.1	72 395	91 873	26.9	6.8
Richmond	7.7	20.0	9.9	15.9	15.5	13.3	7.9	5.2	4.7	51.4	86 019	99 216	15.3	3.1
Riverside	8.0	22.1	12.9	14.6	15.3	11.6	6.4	4.6	4.4	50.7	226 546	255 166	12.6	10.3
Rocklin	7.9	22.1	7.0	13.9	19.8	13.8	7.0	4.9	3.7	51.1	18 806	36 330	93.2	29.2
Rohnert Park	6.3	19.0	14.8	15.1	16.9	13.4	6.4	3.9	4.2	51.5	36 326	42 236	16.3	-0.9
Rosemead	7.5	20.0	10.5	16.3	15.3	12.0	7.7	6.1	4.6	50.9	51 638	53 505	3.6	3.3
Roseville	7.3	19.5	7.0	13.8	17.0	12.7	8.3	7.5	6.9	52.1	44 685	79 921	78.9	23.1
Sacramento	7.1	20.2	10.4	15.6	15.1	12.8	7.4	5.7	5.7	51.4	369 365	407 018	10.2	9.4
Salinas	9.3	22.8	11.8	17.9	15.7	10.2	5.3	3.8	3.3	46.8	108 777	151 060	38.9	-2.1
San Bernardino	9.8	25.4	11.0	14.7	14.9	10.1	5.9	4.3	3.9	50.8	170 036	185 401	9.0	5.4
San Bruno	6.1	16.9	8.2	16.4	18.0	14.6	8.5	6.1	5.2	50.6	38 961	40 165	3.1	-1.4
San Buenaventura (Ventura)	6.6	18.5	7.8	14.1	17.4	14.6	8.3	6.3	6.5	50.8	92 557	100 916	9.0	3.2
San Carlos	7.0	15.1	4.3	13.5	19.6	16.4	9.8	6.5	7.8	51.9	26 382	27 718	5.1	-2.6
San Clemente	6.5	17.6	7.2	13.7	17.9	15.4	8.6	6.9	6.2	49.4	41 100	49 936	21.5	15.7
San Diego	6.7	17.3	12.4	17.7	16.2	12.1	7.0	5.4	5.1	49.6	1 110 623	1 223 400	10.2	3.5
San Dimas	5.9	19.7	8.9	12.0	16.1	15.8	9.8	5.8	6.1	52.0	32 398	34 980	8.0	2.9
San Francisco	4.1	10.5	9.1	23.2	17.2	13.9	8.4	6.9	6.7	49.2	723 959	776 733	7.3	-3.2
San Gabriel	6.7	16.8	8.6	16.7	16.6	12.8	8.3	6.3	7.1	52.0	37 120	39 804	7.2	3.0
San Jose	7.6	18.8	9.9	18.0	17.4	12.4	7.6	4.7	3.6	49.2	782 224	894 943	14.4	0.4
San Juan Capistrano	7.2	20.9	7.8	12.0	15.4	14.6	9.1	6.2	6.9	50.8	26 183	33 826	29.2	2.7
San Leandro	6.3	15.9	7.8	15.2	16.8	13.7	8.3	7.4	8.6	51.8	68 223	79 452	16.5	0.9
San Luis Obispo	3.4	10.8	33.6	12.4	11.2	10.7	5.8	5.0	7.1	48.6	41 958	44 174	5.3	0.1
San Marcos	8.8	20.3	9.4	16.4	15.9	10.9	6.4	5.4	6.4	50.4	38 974	54 977	41.1	16.9
San Mateo	6.1	14.3	7.2	17.7	17.4	13.7	8.5	6.7	8.4	51.1	85 619	92 482	8.0	-1.4
San Pablo	9.1	22.6	10.9	17.0	14.8	10.7	6.2	4.1	4.5	50.9	25 158	30 215	20.1	2.7
San Rafael	5.8	13.7	8.1	16.6	16.7	15.4	9.4	6.5	7.9	50.5	48 410	56 063	15.8	-0.5
San Ramon	7.4	18.9	5.8	14.7	21.0	17.4	8.8	3.4	2.7	50.7	35 303	44 722	26.7	2.6
Santa Ana	10.3	23.9	12.8	19.5	14.5	8.7	4.8	3.1	2.4	48.2	293 827	337 977	15.0	1.3
Santa Barbara	5.6	14.1	13.8	17.1	15.2	13.1	7.3	5.8	7.9	50.8	85 571	92 325	7.9	-4.4
Santa Clara	6.5	13.4	11.3	21.9	17.2	11.7	7.4	5.6	5.1	49.1	93 613	102 361	9.3	-0.3
Santa Clarita	7.8	22.5	8.1	14.2	19.4	13.9	6.9	3.8	3.3	50.5	120 050	151 088	25.9	7.7
Santa Cruz	4.9	12.5	20.5	17.1	15.5	14.7	6.3	4.0	4.5	50.2	49 711	54 593	9.8	-0.6
Santa Maria	9.0	22.6	11.6	15.7	13.9	9.7	6.2	5.6	5.7	49.2	61 552	77 423	25.8	5.8
Santa Monica	4.1	10.5	6.1	20.3	19.8	15.7	9.1	6.4	7.9	51.8	86 905	84 084	-3.2	3.7
Santa Paula	8.8	22.6	10.9	15.6	14.1	10.4	6.8	5.3	5.3	49.1	25 062	28 598	14.1	1.0
Santa Rosa	6.5	17.8	9.5	14.3	15.7	14.4	7.9	5.9	8.0	51.2	113 261	147 595	30.3	3.9
Santee	6.7	21.5	8.4	13.7	19.1	14.3	7.3	4.7	4.2	51.8	52 902	52 975	0.1	-0.1
Saratoga	5.4	20.7	4.0	5.8	18.0	17.5	12.4	9.1	7.1	50.9	28 061	29 843	6.4	-1.8
Seaside	9.7	20.6	11.1	19.4	15.1	10.1	5.7	5.2	3.3	49.1	38 826	31 696	-18.4	6.9
Simi Valley	7.3	21.1	7.9	14.1	18.7	14.7	8.4	4.5	3.1	50.5	100 218	111 351	11.1	5.2
South Gate	10.1	25.5	12.5	17.5	14.0	9.6	5.2	2.9	2.5	50.4	86 284	96 375	11.7	2.7
South San Francisco	6.5	17.8	9.2	15.4	16.6	13.3	8.6	7.0	5.6	50.4	54 312	60 552	11.5	-1.9
Stanton	9.3	21.1	10.5	18.4	14.9	9.7	6.5	4.9	4.7	49.4	30 491	37 403	22.7	1.2
Stockton	8.6	23.8	11.0	13.6	13.8	11.8	7.1	5.2	5.0	51.3	210 943	243 771	15.6	11.4
Suisun City	7.7	24.9	8.9	13.5	19.1	13.9	6.4	3.4	2.3	50.5	22 704	26 118	15.0	3.3
Sunnyvale	7.0	13.4	7.7	23.2	18.1	11.9	8.0	5.7	4.9	48.6	117 324	131 760	12.3	-2.4
Temecula	8.9	25.8	7.8	13.5	19.7	11.6	5.5	4.4	2.7	50.6	27 177	57 716	113.0	33.1
Temple City	5.7	18.3	8.1	12.5	16.4	15.5	9.6	6.6	7.3	52.4	31 153	33 377	7.1	8.8
Thousand Oaks	6.7	19.3	7.1	12.3	17.6	15.8	10.1	5.8	5.3	50.9	104 381	117 005	12.1	6.1
Torrance	5.7	17.3	6.8	13.4	18.9	14.6	9.2	7.5	6.5	51.4	133 107	137 946	3.6	3.4
Tracy	9.4	25.0	7.5	15.5	19.6	11.3	5.4	3.3	3.1	50.0	33 558	56 929	69.6	27.3
Tulare	9.6	25.0	10.5	14.2	14.5	10.4	6.4	4.9	4.4	51.4	33 249	43 994	32.3	7.8
Turlock	8.1	21.8	11.4	14.4	14.4	11.4	6.7	5.6	6.2	51.9	42 224	55 810	32.2	13.7
Tustin	8.6	18.2	9.3	20.4	17.7	11.5	7.1	4.1	3.1	51.0	50 689	67 504	33.2	1.4
Union City	7.3	20.5	9.8	16.0	16.8	13.8	7.8	4.6	3.5	50.3	53 762	66 869	24.4	3.6
Upland	7.0	20.3	9.6	13.8	15.4	14.3	8.8	5.9	4.9	51.9	63 374	68 393	7.9	5.3
Vacaville	6.6	20.3	9.0	16.3	19.2	13.4	6.9	4.5	3.7	45.8	71 476	88 625	24.0	6.2
Vallejo	7.2	20.4	9.0	13.6	16.0	14.6	8.0	5.6	5.6	51.6	109 199	116 760	6.9	2.5
Victorville	8.6	25.6	8.6	13.2	15.5	10.6	6.8	6.2	5.0	51.6	50 103	64 029	27.8	17.1
Visalia	8.1	23.2	9.6	13.7	14.8	12.4	7.3	5.3	5.5	51.8	75 659	91 565	21.0	9.9

City	Households, 2000					Persons in group quarters, 2000				Serious crimes known to police,[2] 2002				Education, 2000			
				Percent			Institutional			Total		Rate[2]		School enrollment[4]		Attainment[5] (percent)	
	Number	Percent change, 1990–2000	Persons per household	Female family householder[1]	One-person	Total	Total	Persons in nursing homes	Non-institutional	Number	Rate[3]	Violent	Property	Public	Private	High school graduate or less	Bachelor's degree or more
	26	27	28	29	30	31	32	33	34	35	36	37	38	39	40	41	42
CALIFORNIA—Cont'd																	
Pleasant Hill	13 753	5.8	2.35	9.1	29.1	460	305	305	155	2 102	6 174	446	5 728	6 935	1 741	24.4	42.5
Pleasanton	23 311	26.1	2.72	7.8	19.3	235	161	161	74	1 795	2 720	123	2 597	15 983	2 636	20.5	47.3
Pomona	37 855	3.9	3.82	16.3	15.4	5 041	1 906	788	3 135	6 132	3 957	870	3 087	48 108	4 599	63.7	12.8
Porterville	11 884	24.0	3.20	17.7	19.1	1 632	1 123	276	509	1 817	4 424	426	3 998	12 501	665	61.4	11.0
Poway	15 467	11.4	3.08	10.5	12.6	426	354	354	72	971	1 949	195	1 755	14 379	2 276	25.1	39.3
Rancho Cucamonga	40 863	21.5	3.04	12.8	16.8	3 626	1 858	0	1 768	3 966	2 995	211	2 784	37 378	5 497	35.6	23.3
Rancho Palos Verdes	15 256	2.1	2.66	6.8	16.8	509	166	166	343	572	1 341	169	1 172	8 852	1 908	16.1	58.0
Redding	32 103	23.0	2.44	13.0	27.6	2 377	1 216	478	1 161	3 389	4 042	508	3 534	19 785	3 232	40.2	19.4
Redlands	23 593	7.3	2.61	13.0	26.0	1 966	541	535	1 425	2 997	4 546	648	3 898	15 370	5 015	31.6	35.2
Redondo Beach	28 566	6.9	2.21	9.0	33.1	187	96	5	91	1 884	2 873	303	2 569	11 249	3 155	21.4	48.0
Redwood City	28 060	10.1	2.62	9.9	27.1	1 927	1 481	269	446	2 482	3 175	436	2 739	14 140	4 413	34.6	35.7
Rialto	24 659	12.6	3.69	18.6	13.4	804	265	248	539	3 847	4 039	934	3 105	30 409	2 523	61.2	8.7
Richmond	34 625	5.7	2.82	20.1	26.2	1 628	953	165	675	7 838	7 620	1 165	6 455	25 464	4 047	46.5	22.4
Riverside	82 005	8.7	3.02	14.8	21.5	7 798	2 881	1 180	4 917	15 161	5 731	766	4 965	76 384	10 293	48.1	19.1
Rocklin	13 258	87.7	2.74	9.4	18.7	20	6	6	14	1 059	2 812	125	2 687	10 327	1 384	22.3	36.1
Rohnert Park	15 503	15.6	2.65	11.9	24.0	1 101	0	0	1 101	1 828	4 175	281	3 894	12 497	1 539	35.5	24.7
Rosemead	13 913	1.5	3.80	17.4	12.6	612	387	280	225	1 518	2 737	519	2 217	15 411	1 641	65.7	12.9
Roseville	30 783	85.4	2.57	10.1	23.1	928	713	646	215	3 821	4 612	259	4 352	19 932	2 462	30.0	31.4
Sacramento	154 581	7.0	2.57	15.4	32.0	9 002	4 831	1 917	4 171	30 780	7 294	841	6 454	111 172	13 379	44.2	23.9
Salinas	38 298	14.8	3.66	14.8	17.1	10 805	8 756	361	2 049	6 834	4 364	727	3 637	42 588	3 519	63.2	12.3
San Bernardino	56 330	3.4	3.19	21.1	21.1	5 849	3 765	664	2 084	13 755	7 156	1 292	5 864	57 338	5 239	60.6	11.6
San Bruno	14 677	0.3	2.72	11.2	25.5	221	122	122	99	1 221	2 932	231	2 702	8 823	2 362	37.6	26.2
San Buenaventura (Ventura)	38 524	8.8	2.56	11.7	26.5	2 370	1 376	426	994	3 648	3 487	273	3 213	23 700	4 744	33.9	29.2
San Carlos	11 455	3.7	2.40	7.2	25.7	183	145	145	38	578	2 011	104	1 907	4 746	1 839	20.8	49.8
San Clemente	19 395	16.1	2.56	7.8	23.4	292	62	62	230	877	1 694	129	1 565	10 619	2 507	26.4	36.1
San Diego	450 691	11.0	2.61	11.4	28.0	45 818	6 637	3 285	39 181	50 124	3 952	567	3 385	317 233	54 154	34.2	35.0
San Dimas	12 163	11.1	2.78	11.6	21.0	1 209	372	215	837	886	2 443	279	2 165	8 132	2 622	30.6	28.4
San Francisco	329 700	7.9	2.30	8.9	38.6	19 757	4 200	1 685	15 557	42 671	5 299	752	4 547	134 631	48 332	32.7	45.0
San Gabriel	12 587	3.0	3.10	15.2	18.2	755	681	510	74	1 054	2 554	451	2 103	9 657	2 028	49.1	24.6
San Jose	276 598	10.5	3.20	11.7	18.4	10 864	3 846	2 106	7 018	24 139	2 602	446	2 156	224 127	38 221	39.8	31.6
San Juan Capistrano	10 930	21.2	3.06	8.5	19.7	426	305	181	121	596	1 700	188	1 511	8 099	1 882	37.5	30.7
San Leandro	30 642	5.2	2.57	12.7	28.5	827	517	471	310	4 606	5 592	606	4 986	16 320	3 801	45.3	23.3
San Luis Obispo	18 639	10.0	2.27	7.2	32.7	1 862	362	362	1 500	2 093	4 570	349	4 221	19 855	954	24.1	40.9
San Marcos	18 111	33.0	3.03	9.6	20.3	148	15	15	133	1 472	2 583	339	2 244	15 006	1 418	46.6	20.0
San Mateo	37 338	5.2	2.44	9.1	31.6	1 316	609	477	707	2 846	2 968	357	2 612	17 091	4 378	32.2	38.6
San Pablo	9 051	4.0	3.29	19.7	22.5	465	367	367	98	2 052	6 551	919	5 631	8 938	927	63.7	10.4
San Rafael	22 371	10.2	2.42	9.0	32.1	2 020	1 083	765	937	1 883	3 240	243	2 997	9 457	2 860	29.5	43.6
San Ramon	16 944	31.9	2.63	7.0	21.1	85	47	5	38	1 127	2 431	84	2 347	10 260	2 265	15.3	52.7
Santa Ana	73 002	1.9	4.55	13.5	12.7	5 624	3 482	752	2 142	12 038	3 436	551	2 885	100 160	6 447	72.8	9.2
Santa Barbara	35 605	3.7	2.47	9.5	32.9	4 517	477	477	4 040	3 072	3 209	541	2 668	21 650	5 790	33.8	39.6
Santa Clara	38 526	5.4	2.58	9.5	25.9	2 787	459	427	2 328	3 228	3 042	293	2 749	18 575	8 830	30.2	42.4
Santa Clarita	50 787	32.0	2.95	9.8	18.7	1 393	370	370	1 023	3 195	2 040	195	1 845	40 570	7 772	32.6	29.1
Santa Cruz	20 442	12.8	2.44	9.6	29.3	4 634	373	29	4 261	3 569	6 306	813	5 493	17 229	1 860	25.4	44.4
Santa Maria	22 146	11.2	3.40	13.3	20.0	2 162	1 438	380	724	2 110	2 629	350	2 279	20 672	1 597	61.7	11.0
Santa Monica	44 497	-0.8	1.83	7.5	51.2	2 516	941	790	1 575	4 701	5 393	756	4 637	13 424	4 454	21.0	54.8
Santa Paula	8 136	6.2	3.49	13.4	17.2	243	129	129	114	893	3 012	327	2 685	7 491	746	64.9	8.6
Santa Rosa	56 036	22.6	2.57	11.0	27.8	3 806	1 558	649	2 248	6 531	4 268	408	3 860	34 970	5 082	36.4	27.6
Santee	18 470	3.9	2.81	13.0	18.2	1 043	899	211	144	1 380	2 513	251	2 261	14 549	1 804	38.9	17.0
Saratoga	10 450	4.0	2.83	4.9	14.3	251	215	208	36	348	1 125	74	1 050	6 162	2 298	11.2	68.2
Seaside	9 833	-7.6	3.21	13.9	18.1	103	28	28	75	935	2 845	456	2 389	8 533	1 147	53.3	17.5
Simi Valley	36 421	13.8	3.04	10.7	14.7	800	163	133	637	1 756	1 521	120	1 402	27 849	5 496	36.7	24.9
South Gate	23 213	3.5	4.15	18.4	10.4	141	61	61	80	3 423	3 426	517	2 908	31 508	2 319	80.6	4.9
South San Francisco	19 677	6.3	3.05	13.2	19.9	443	148	148	295	1 541	2 455	182	2 273	13 056	3 951	44.2	25.2
Stanton	10 767	4.5	3.43	14.8	21.5	518	278	278	240	888	2 290	346	1 944	10 118	1 015	60.9	11.9
Stockton	78 556	14.2	3.04	17.3	22.9	5 316	1 739	1 643	3 577	21 114	8 354	1 461	6 893	70 536	10 519	54.1	15.4
Suisun City	7 987	19.3	3.26	13.1	14.3	94	61	61	33	908	3 353	233	3 121	7 812	1 146	40.0	17.3
Sunnyvale	52 539	8.8	2.49	8.2	27.1	875	499	484	376	2 569	1 881	141	1 740	23 398	6 857	24.0	50.8
Temecula	18 293	100.4	3.15	10.0	12.6	22	0	0	22	2 151	3 595	361	3 234	16 607	2 917	31.8	25.0
Temple City	11 338	2.6	2.90	14.3	19.7	511	413	409	98	528	1 526	197	1 329	8 064	1 759	37.0	28.5
Thousand Oaks	41 793	14.6	2.75	8.7	19.6	1 951	270	253	1 681	2 030	1 673	130	1 543	26 901	6 840	24.1	42.2
Torrance	54 542	3.7	2.51	10.3	27.5	1 249	686	609	563	4 541	3 175	338	2 837	31 405	6 676	29.6	36.4
Tracy	17 620	57.2	3.21	10.7	14.4	345	153	153	192	2 537	4 298	234	4 065	16 571	2 179	43.8	18.0
Tulare	13 543	24.7	3.22	17.1	16.7	447	214	175	233	3 022	6 626	1 066	5 560	13 126	968	64.9	8.2
Turlock	18 408	25.3	2.92	13.1	21.2	2 080	504	504	1 576	3 769	6 514	486	6 028	15 880	1 728	54.1	19.1
Tustin	23 831	30.0	2.82	12.3	24.1	418	35	18	383	2 197	3 139	310	2 829	16 817	2 601	35.7	33.4
Union City	18 642	18.7	3.57	12.2	11.3	342	215	215	127	2 566	3 701	358	3 344	17 572	2 972	40.6	29.5
Upland	24 551	6.4	2.76	14.3	21.1	585	316	308	269	2 795	3 942	450	3 492	17 155	3 940	38.0	26.7
Vacaville	28 105	24.2	2.83	12.4	19.2	9 218	9 149	261	69	2 482	2 701	294	2 407	21 964	2 863	41.8	19.4
Vallejo	39 601	5.9	2.90	16.5	22.7	1 745	819	644	926	7 117	5 879	894	4 986	28 748	5 205	42.7	21.1
Victorville	20 893	46.7	3.03	16.1	19.4	670	406	266	264	3 634	5 474	453	5 021	19 940	1 353	52.9	10.6
Visalia	30 883	18.3	2.91	14.1	20.7	1 622	893	681	729	6 309	6 646	908	5 738	25 636	3 143	46.2	18.9

1. No spouse present. 2. Data for serious crimes have not been adjusted for underreporting. This may affect comparability between geographic areas and over time. 3. Per 100,000 population estimated by the FBI. 4. All persons 3 years old and over enrolled in nursery school through college. 5. Persons 25 years old and over.

Table D. Cities — Income, Poverty, and Housing

City	Money income, 1999							Housing units, 2000					
	Households				Percent below poverty					Vacant units			
	Median income				Persons		Families						
	Per capita income[1] (dollars)	Dollars	Percent change, 1989–1999 (constant 1999 dollars)	Percent with income of $100,000 or more	Total	Percent change in rate, 1989–1999	Total	Total	Percent change, 1990–2000	Vacant units for sale or rent[2]	For seasonal use (percent)	Home owner vacancy rate	Renter vacancy rate
	43	44	45	46	47	48	49	50	51	52	53	54	55
CALIFORNIA—Cont'd													
Pleasant Hill	33 076	67 489	7.1	27.1	5.0	38.9	2.7	14 034	2.8	281	0.5	0.5	1.4
Pleasanton	41 623	90 859	13.7	44.3	2.6	8.3	1.6	23 968	23.8	657	0.7	0.5	3.2
Pomona	13 336	40 021	-7.3	10.1	21.6	17.4	17.1	39 598	2.9	1 743	0.2	2.2	3.2
Porterville	12 745	32 046	7.6	4.9	25.7	-4.1	20.3	12 691	26.0	807	0.4	2.0	7.2
Poway	29 788	71 708	0.2	32.0	4.3	7.5	3.1	15 714	9.2	247	0.2	0.3	2.1
Rancho Cucamonga	23 702	60 931	-1.8	20.9	7.1	29.1	4.9	42 134	15.9	1 271	0.1	1.2	4.1
Rancho Palos Verdes	46 250	95 503	-10.9	47.5	2.9	-9.4	2.0	15 709	1.6	453	0.7	0.8	3.7
Redding	18 207	34 194	-1.5	7.5	15.6	9.1	11.3	33 802	24.1	1 699	0.5	1.9	4.6
Redlands	24 237	48 155	-3.3	17.0	10.5	16.7	7.7	24 790	6.9	1 197	0.4	2.2	5.0
Redondo Beach	38 305	69 173	-0.8	29.6	5.9	5.4	4.0	29 543	4.7	977	0.6	1.2	2.6
Redwood City	34 042	66 748	15.6	29.9	6.0	-27.7	3.9	28 921	7.7	861	0.8	0.4	2.3
Rialto	13 375	41 254	-15.3	8.4	17.4	43.8	13.8	26 045	9.3	1 386	0.1	2.9	5.6
Richmond	19 788	44 210	2.3	12.0	16.2	0.6	13.4	36 044	4.4	1 419	0.3	1.2	3.1
Riverside	17 882	41 646	-10.9	11.7	15.8	32.8	11.7	85 974	7.1	3 969	0.3	1.9	4.8
Rocklin	26 910	64 737	19.2	24.4	4.5	-19.6	3.1	14 421	90.8	1 163	0.3	1.7	17.1
Rohnert Park	23 035	51 942	7.1	14.2	8.0	-5.9	3.2	15 808	13.6	305	0.4	0.5	2.2
Rosemead	12 146	36 181	-9.5	7.3	22.8	14.0	19.4	14 345	1.5	432	0.2	1.0	2.2
Roseville	27 021	57 367	6.8	18.3	4.9	-27.9	3.4	31 925	79.5	1 142	0.4	1.3	4.5
Sacramento	18 721	37 049	-2.2	9.4	20.0	16.3	15.3	163 957	6.9	9 376	0.4	2.0	5.4
Salinas	14 495	43 720	4.1	9.8	16.7	7.1	12.8	39 659	14.7	1 361	0.2	1.0	3.8
San Bernardino	12 925	31 140	-9.2	5.4	27.6	21.1	23.5	63 535	8.0	7 205	0.2	6.1	9.7
San Bruno	26 360	62 081	10.0	22.2	4.4	-8.3	3.1	14 980	-1.3	303	0.5	0.4	1.7
San Buenaventura (Ventura)	25 065	52 298	-3.4	17.2	9.0	36.4	6.4	39 803	6.6	1 279	0.9	0.8	2.8
San Carlos	46 628	88 460	20.5	42.8	2.7	0.0	1.4	11 691	3.1	236	0.3	0.3	2.0
San Clemente	34 169	63 507	1.9	28.7	7.6	8.6	4.6	20 653	10.3	1 258	3.7	0.9	2.5
San Diego	23 609	45 733	1.0	15.6	14.6	9.0	10.6	469 689	8.8	18 998	1.1	0.8	3.2
San Dimas	28 321	62 885	-6.9	24.9	6.3	16.7	3.6	12 503	8.9	340	0.4	1.0	2.6
San Francisco	34 556	55 221	23.0	24.7	11.3	-11.0	7.8	346 527	5.5	16 827	1.1	0.8	2.5
San Gabriel	16 807	41 791	-4.5	11.7	15.9	4.6	12.5	12 909	1.4	322	0.3	0.9	1.8
San Jose	26 697	70 243	13.1	30.8	8.8	-5.4	6.0	281 841	8.7	5 243	0.3	0.4	1.8
San Juan Capistrano	29 926	62 392	0.4	25.8	10.7	72.6	6.6	11 320	17.8	390	0.6	1.0	6.1
San Leandro	23 895	51 081	6.6	14.9	6.4	28.0	4.5	31 334	3.8	692	0.3	0.6	2.2
San Luis Obispo	20 386	31 926	-8.5	10.5	26.6	-2.9	7.1	19 306	8.0	667	0.6	1.1	2.3
San Marcos	18 657	45 908	6.9	12.5	12.0	10.1	7.8	18 862	30.3	751	0.3	1.4	3.3
San Mateo	36 176	64 757	12.4	28.5	6.1	-1.6	3.6	38 249	3.6	911	0.6	0.5	1.6
San Pablo	14 303	37 184	8.6	7.1	18.1	-4.7	15.5	9 340	-0.8	289	0.4	0.9	2.1
San Rafael	35 762	60 994	8.3	27.9	10.2	25.9	5.6	22 948	8.6	577	0.5	0.9	1.7
San Ramon	42 336	95 856	12.2	47.6	2.0	17.6	1.4	17 552	29.7	608	0.7	0.4	3.5
Santa Ana	12 152	43 412	-8.1	10.1	19.8	9.4	16.1	74 588	-0.5	1 586	0.1	0.8	1.9
Santa Barbara	26 466	47 498	5.0	17.7	13.4	5.5	7.7	37 076	2.3	1 471	1.4	0.7	2.3
Santa Clara	31 755	69 466	15.6	29.3	7.8	25.8	4.5	39 630	4.6	1 104	0.6	0.4	1.8
Santa Clarita	26 841	66 717	-6.3	25.8	6.4	73.0	4.7	52 442	27.5	1 655	0.2	1.2	4.8
Santa Cruz	25 758	50 605	18.2	19.4	16.5	5.1	6.6	21 504	11.1	1 062	2.4	0.7	1.4
Santa Maria	13 780	36 541	-7.8	6.8	19.7	17.3	15.5	22 847	8.1	701	0.2	0.9	3.1
Santa Monica	42 874	50 714	4.9	23.6	10.4	10.6	5.4	47 863	0.2	3 366	1.6	1.4	4.3
Santa Paula	15 736	41 651	-1.9	10.8	14.7	20.5	12.2	8 341	3.5	205	0.2	0.5	2.2
Santa Rosa	24 495	50 931	7.6	15.8	8.5	2.4	5.1	57 578	20.6	1 542	0.5	0.7	2.1
Santee	21 311	53 624	2.1	12.7	5.4	0.0	3.8	18 833	3.1	363	0.2	0.5	2.2
Saratoga	65 400	139 895	20.1	67.1	2.8	100.0	1.8	10 649	3.2	199	0.3	0.3	3.4
Seaside	15 183	41 393	7.5	7.8	12.1	-0.8	9.3	11 005	-2.1	1 172	0.2	2.9	1.5
Simi Valley	26 586	70 370	-2.9	26.4	5.8	61.1	3.9	37 272	12.6	851	0.1	0.9	3.8
South Gate	10 602	35 695	-2.6	5.3	19.2	10.3	17.4	24 269	5.8	1 056	1.5	2.1	1.7
South San Francisco	23 562	61 764	7.1	21.3	5.2	-11.9	3.5	20 138	5.5	461	0.3	0.7	1.3
Stanton	14 197	39 127	-12.7	6.6	18.0	32.4	13.4	11 011	2.4	244	0.2	0.9	2.0
Stockton	15 405	35 453	-1.8	8.2	23.9	11.7	18.9	82 042	13.1	3 486	0.2	1.4	4.3
Suisun City	20 386	60 848	10.8	14.4	6.5	-30.9	4.6	8 146	15.9	159	0.1	0.8	3.1
Sunnyvale	36 524	74 409	19.4	33.7	5.4	14.9	3.7	53 753	5.8	1 214	0.6	0.5	1.3
Temecula	21 557	59 516	0.1	17.0	6.7	36.7	5.6	19 099	79.2	806	0.4	1.4	7.2
Temple City	20 267	48 722	-6.5	13.2	9.3	66.1	7.2	11 674	1.1	336	0.4	0.9	1.9
Thousand Oaks	34 314	76 815	0.6	35.1	5.0	19.0	3.2	42 958	13.8	1 165	0.5	0.9	2.9
Torrance	28 144	56 489	-10.9	21.0	6.4	25.5	4.5	55 967	1.9	1 425	0.3	1.0	2.4
Tracy	21 397	62 794	16.1	18.5	7.0	-5.4	5.2	18 087	48.6	467	0.2	1.1	2.8
Tulare	13 655	33 637	1.4	6.0	20.7	-3.3	16.9	14 253	26.0	710	0.3	1.3	5.4
Turlock	16 844	39 050	6.5	8.2	16.2	22.7	12.4	19 095	24.0	687	0.3	1.7	2.8
Tustin	25 932	55 985	8.4	21.3	8.5	25.0	5.8	25 501	32.1	1 670	0.4	0.9	2.5
Union City	22 890	71 926	13.9	28.4	6.5	0.0	4.8	18 877	16.1	235	0.1	0.5	1.3
Upland	23 343	48 734	-13.6	17.3	12.0	53.8	9.1	25 467	4.0	916	0.2	1.6	3.9
Vacaville	21 557	57 667	5.5	17.3	6.1	0.0	4.3	28 696	21.3	591	0.2	0.7	2.8
Vallejo	20 415	50 030	1.7	14.2	10.1	18.8	7.7	41 219	3.3	1 618	0.3	1.2	4.5
Victorville	14 454	36 187	-6.1	5.3	18.7	26.4	15.3	22 498	44.0	1 605	0.5	2.8	7.9
Visalia	18 422	41 349	4.5	11.5	16.8	-4.5	12.9	32 654	20.3	1 771	0.3	2.2	6.4

1. Based on population enumerated as of April 1, 2000.   2. Includes units rented or sold but not occupied.

City	Housing units, 2000 (cont'd) Occupied units					Civilian labor force, 2003				Civilian employment,[2] 2000			Disability, 2000
								Unemployment			Percent		
	Total	Percent owner occupied	Percent renter occupied	Average size owner occupied	Average size renter occupied	Total	Percent change, 2002–2003	Total	Rate[1]	Total	Management, professional, and related occupations	Production, transportation, and material moving occupations	Employment disabled persons[3] (percent)
	56	57	58	59	60	61	62	63	64	65	66	67	68
CALIFORNIA—Cont'd													
Pleasant Hill	13 753	63.5	36.5	2.53	2.05	22 606	-0.5	807	3.6	17 788	48.9	5.2	7.8
Pleasanton	23 311	73.4	26.6	2.87	2.30	34 130	-0.8	1 178	3.5	33 608	52.2	5.8	6.6
Pomona	37 855	57.3	42.7	3.86	3.76	64 451	0.0	5 603	8.7	53 512	22.2	24.3	17.1
Porterville	11 884	56.4	43.6	3.19	3.20	15 964	0.6	2 939	18.4	14 152	26.5	13.6	15.0
Poway	15 467	77.7	22.3	3.12	2.95	28 239	1.7	769	2.7	22 994	44.4	7.3	7.5
Rancho Cucamonga	40 863	70.2	29.8	3.20	2.66	73 388	3.0	2 676	3.6	61 950	35.6	12.0	10.0
Rancho Palos Verdes	15 256	81.6	18.4	2.67	2.65	23 151	-0.2	517	2.2	18 399	62.9	4.8	7.1
Redding	32 103	56.7	43.3	2.47	2.41	38 907	2.4	3 032	7.8	33 747	31.9	10.5	12.3
Redlands	23 593	60.4	39.6	2.71	2.46	40 381	3.0	1 483	3.7	29 942	45.8	8.8	9.5
Redondo Beach	28 566	49.5	50.5	2.37	2.05	43 790	-0.2	1 425	3.3	38 106	53.1	4.9	8.2
Redwood City	28 060	53.0	47.0	2.61	2.63	38 137	-2.6	1 761	4.6	40 100	42.3	9.1	10.3
Rialto	24 659	68.4	31.6	3.74	3.59	44 519	3.0	2 746	6.2	32 460	20.2	23.6	14.1
Richmond	34 625	53.3	46.7	2.87	2.76	52 150	-0.1	5 445	10.4	42 769	32.9	13.3	14.2
Riverside	82 005	56.6	43.4	3.18	2.81	173 840	2.9	10 436	6.0	106 805	30.9	15.2	11.8
Rocklin	13 258	72.7	27.3	2.88	2.35	16 492	2.1	735	4.5	18 486	43.8	7.1	8.1
Rohnert Park	15 503	58.4	41.6	2.83	2.40	25 791	-1.9	1 412	5.5	22 617	30.7	11.3	10.3
Rosemead	13 913	48.8	51.2	3.67	3.92	24 382	0.0	1 959	8.0	20 250	22.3	24.8	18.3
Roseville	30 783	69.5	30.5	2.67	2.34	37 268	2.2	1 860	5.0	37 256	41.8	8.3	9.6
Sacramento	154 581	50.1	49.9	2.65	2.50	219 730	2.1	15 002	6.8	169 787	36.2	11.0	14.6
Salinas	38 298	50.1	49.9	3.65	3.67	65 663	0.6	8 929	13.6	54 902	21.4	14.4	18.9
San Bernardino	56 330	52.4	47.6	3.25	3.12	92 855	3.1	7 747	8.3	62 289	23.3	18.2	15.3
San Bruno	14 677	63.0	37.0	2.76	2.66	22 234	-2.6	1 108	5.0	21 364	32.2	10.2	11.3
San Buenaventura (Ventura)	38 524	58.7	41.3	2.62	2.46	60 341	1.4	2 490	4.1	49 791	39.2	10.0	10.8
San Carlos	11 455	72.7	27.3	2.55	2.02	15 484	-2.6	456	2.9	15 128	56.1	4.5	7.4
San Clemente	19 395	62.4	37.6	2.59	2.51	26 727	2.0	782	2.9	24 654	40.9	7.8	8.1
San Diego	450 691	49.5	50.5	2.71	2.52	679 817	1.7	29 484	4.3	557 382	41.8	9.0	11.1
San Dimas	12 163	73.7	26.3	2.87	2.51	19 057	-0.2	622	3.3	17 042	42.2	8.9	10.5
San Francisco	329 700	35.0	65.0	2.73	2.06	403 095	-3.2	27 476	6.8	427 823	48.3	7.5	12.1
San Gabriel	12 587	47.6	52.4	3.15	3.06	19 406	-0.1	1 141	5.9	16 837	34.0	14.4	12.9
San Jose	276 598	61.8	38.2	3.22	3.16	459 293	-5.2	44 003	9.6	436 890	40.8	14.3	13.7
San Juan Capistrano	10 930	78.9	21.1	2.91	3.60	16 071	2.0	463	2.9	14 815	35.2	9.2	10.5
San Leandro	30 642	60.6	39.4	2.70	2.36	39 645	-0.8	2 369	6.0	37 829	32.8	15.1	14.1
San Luis Obispo	18 639	41.9	58.1	2.35	2.22	26 288	0.4	970	3.7	22 057	39.0	6.3	6.7
San Marcos	18 111	66.0	34.0	2.83	3.40	22 932	1.7	937	4.1	24 503	29.0	15.5	10.2
San Mateo	37 338	53.9	46.1	2.53	2.34	50 527	-2.6	2 594	5.1	48 275	43.2	7.9	12.5
San Pablo	9 051	49.1	50.9	3.40	3.18	13 688	0.0	1 534	11.2	10 818	20.2	16.2	19.2
San Rafael	22 371	53.8	46.2	2.31	2.53	27 840	-2.8	1 511	5.4	29 076	45.1	5.9	14.5
San Ramon	16 944	71.3	28.7	2.84	2.12	26 147	-0.6	806	3.1	25 761	54.8	4.0	6.0
Santa Ana	73 002	49.3	50.7	4.54	4.57	177 171	1.6	12 005	6.8	127 530	16.5	26.7	18.9
Santa Barbara	35 605	42.0	58.0	2.51	2.43	53 920	2.5	1 839	3.4	47 759	40.9	8.0	11.6
Santa Clara	38 526	46.1	53.9	2.69	2.49	60 231	-5.1	4 664	7.7	55 528	51.3	10.6	9.4
Santa Clarita	50 787	74.7	25.3	3.00	2.78	66 967	-0.2	2 243	3.3	75 361	40.9	8.9	7.8
Santa Cruz	20 442	46.6	53.4	2.51	2.39	30 876	-1.5	2 281	7.4	29 644	45.1	6.7	8.1
Santa Maria	22 146	55.9	44.1	3.18	3.68	31 747	2.4	1 851	5.8	30 656	17.8	14.8	18.0
Santa Monica	44 497	29.8	70.2	2.24	1.66	55 913	-0.1	2 567	4.6	47 059	60.3	3.7	9.3
Santa Paula	8 136	57.7	42.3	3.29	3.75	14 788	1.3	1 250	8.5	11 213	18.2	17.0	15.9
Santa Rosa	56 036	58.5	41.5	2.56	2.57	73 671	-1.9	3 496	4.7	72 513	34.1	12.4	12.7
Santee	18 470	71.0	29.0	2.80	2.84	33 593	1.7	1 209	3.6	26 300	31.4	9.6	8.5
Saratoga	10 450	90.0	10.0	2.88	2.37	15 481	-5.0	781	5.0	13 344	72.5	2.9	5.0
Seaside	9 833	44.0	56.0	2.99	3.39	17 238	0.6	1 527	8.9	12 822	20.4	10.0	12.9
Simi Valley	36 421	77.6	22.4	3.09	2.85	71 319	1.4	3 251	4.6	57 001	38.2	10.1	10.7
South Gate	23 213	46.9	53.1	4.42	3.90	40 858	0.1	4 230	10.4	32 200	15.0	33.1	16.9
South San Francisco	19 677	62.5	37.5	3.02	3.11	29 883	-2.6	1 896	6.3	29 796	30.1	13.3	11.3
Stanton	10 767	48.9	51.1	3.18	3.66	19 090	1.6	1 281	6.7	14 695	19.6	24.8	17.5
Stockton	78 556	51.6	48.4	2.99	3.08	115 177	2.4	13 675	11.9	89 165	26.5	17.0	14.9
Suisun City	7 987	73.6	26.4	3.34	3.03	13 856	1.9	990	7.1	11 943	26.0	14.5	13.6
Sunnyvale	52 539	47.6	52.4	2.60	2.39	75 938	-5.1	5 332	7.0	72 756	59.5	7.6	9.0
Temecula	18 293	73.4	26.6	3.27	2.84	21 488	2.9	813	3.8	25 179	35.5	12.0	8.2
Temple City	11 338	63.1	36.9	2.96	2.79	16 888	-0.1	742	4.4	15 102	37.9	9.9	10.5
Thousand Oaks	41 793	75.3	24.7	2.80	2.61	72 622	1.4	3 179	4.4	59 051	48.6	6.4	9.9
Torrance	54 542	56.0	44.0	2.68	2.29	80 322	-0.2	3 037	3.8	67 573	45.7	7.9	9.6
Tracy	17 620	72.2	27.8	3.28	3.02	22 194	2.4	1 870	8.4	25 492	30.7	15.7	12.5
Tulare	13 543	60.5	39.5	3.16	3.30	18 182	0.6	2 433	13.4	15 882	20.7	18.2	13.7
Turlock	18 408	55.8	44.2	2.98	2.85	25 182	1.3	2 550	10.1	22 284	30.2	17.6	12.3
Tustin	23 831	49.6	50.4	2.70	2.70	33 273	1.9	1 284	3.9	34 906	40.5	11.1	11.6
Union City	18 642	71.3	28.7	3.59	3.52	32 142	-0.8	1 625	5.1	31 280	35.7	18.8	14.9
Upland	24 551	58.9	41.1	2.83	2.66	46 821	3.0	1 823	3.9	32 077	36.0	12.2	11.8
Vacaville	28 105	66.7	33.3	2.90	2.68	43 012	1.7	2 076	4.8	37 609	31.1	13.1	10.5
Vallejo	39 601	63.2	36.8	2.99	2.76	67 075	1.9	4 419	6.6	51 420	29.3	13.5	14.4
Victorville	20 893	65.1	34.9	3.05	3.00	22 332	3.0	1 766	7.9	22 385	25.6	16.2	12.0
Visalia	30 883	62.7	37.3	2.88	2.97	43 788	0.6	4 439	10.1	38 401	34.1	11.9	11.4

1. Percent of civilian labor force. 2. Persons 16 years old and over. 3. Persons 16 to 64 years old.

City	Value of residential construction authorized by building permits, 2003			Wholesale trade, 1997				Retail trade,[1] 1997			
	New construction ($1,000)	Number of housing units	Percent single family	Number of establishments	Number of employees	Sales (mil dol)	Annual payroll (mil dol)	Number of establishments	Number of employees	Sales (mil dol)	Annual payroll (mil dol)
	69	70	71	72	73	74	75	76	77	78	79
CALIFORNIA—Cont'd											
Pleasant Hill	7 424	24	12.5	35	338	153.9	15.3	159	2 383	382.2	36.2
Pleasanton	87 153	253	100.0	253	5 868	13 804.0	331.2	349	5 665	1 068.2	107.5
Pomona	29 384	267	34.8	229	2 982	1 184.8	87.3	269	3 216	599.5	63.6
Porterville	28 014	322	69.9	23	398	150.5	6.3	165	2 097	340.6	35.1
Poway	40 205	166	49.4	60	530	263.4	20.3	139	2 036	442.8	38.9
Rancho Cucamonga	332 391	1 860	63.1	219	2 594	1 529.4	86.3	233	3 947	708.9	70.5
Rancho Palos Verdes	16 770	29	100.0	46	101	110.7	5.6	49	595	109.7	10.8
Redding	92 478	602	78.6	152	1 311	436.3	40.5	501	6 513	1 128.3	115.6
Redlands	81 736	396	85.1	37	496	161.2	16.3	208	3 313	560.8	60.4
Redondo Beach	49 225	191	100.0	77	552	366.7	23.2	287	3 968	538.5	62.8
Redwood City	1 958	22	100.0	128	1 376	1 099.4	72.6	256	4 199	1 097.2	104.5
Rialto	27 294	125	96.8	50	553	924.3	21.3	115	1 708	313.9	29.0
Richmond	64 033	425	47.3	105	1 396	690.9	47.6	224	2 510	453.7	45.6
Riverside	232 487	2 018	34.1	267	3 395	1 723.0	104.9	800	11 452	2 279.3	219.7
Rocklin	132 228	467	100.0	68	968	567.2	34.4	84	1 365	217.1	24.2
Rohnert Park	19 286	209	1.0	35	D	D	D	108	2 203	390.8	40.7
Rosemead	16 619	65	100.0	100	D	D	D	134	1 155	190.1	18.1
Roseville	426 793	1 941	75.6	77	1 520	668.4	66.1	279	5 514	1 545.9	134.7
Sacramento	683 067	6 016	59.9	594	10 553	5 538.2	369.9	1 296	18 093	3 039.6	329.7
Salinas	97 326	544	47.2	200	3 802	2 308.0	145.6	496	7 173	1 332.5	146.3
San Bernardino	36 092	317	58.4	150	2 728	1 050.2	88.0	640	9 571	1 903.9	181.0
San Bruno	6 968	27	100.0	35	244	452.9	10.8	138	2 833	656.6	57.9
San Buenaventura (Ventura)	21 663	221	9.5	201	2 816	639.9	98.2	483	6 334	1 249.8	128.2
San Carlos	2 306	5	100.0	129	1 504	671.4	57.1	142	1 503	315.9	36.4
San Clemente	180 375	673	98.8	144	1 293	748.4	48.7	173	1 587	286.7	27.5
San Diego	742 826	6 561	29.4	2 178	33 766	18 478.4	1 634.8	4 128	54 308	10 018.2	1 020.3
San Dimas	5 502	15	100.0	102	970	1 271.8	34.0	101	1 295	210.7	22.3
San Francisco	118 445	1 430	4.4	1 900	17 677	12 219.1	779.8	3 841	39 693	6 795.0	830.6
San Gabriel	17 341	75	84.0	156	599	195.5	12.8	173	1 475	306.7	26.7
San Jose	488 402	4 336	26.2	1 423	25 578	27 076.8	1 398.6	2 169	34 278	6 905.0	700.5
San Juan Capistrano	10 034	26	100.0	66	391	212.3	14.1	122	1 427	326.9	32.4
San Leandro	14 584	60	96.7	324	4 402	2 533.3	176.1	351	5 952	1 116.7	113.9
San Luis Obispo	38 206	298	51.7	69	554	161.6	14.4	319	3 845	606.1	62.8
San Marcos	328 724	1 709	72.0	155	1 843	495.5	63.8	229	2 275	525.1	48.7
San Mateo	27 493	156	37.8	156	2 138	1 840.2	179.4	400	6 247	1 082.8	120.7
San Pablo	24 672	148	98.0	13	41	11.5	0.8	139	1 552	315.2	31.7
San Rafael	10 295	38	94.7	221	1 775	754.6	66.1	411	4 637	1 075.2	115.7
San Ramon	3 300	39	0.0	162	2 759	7 459.8	175.5	143	1 962	380.0	38.7
Santa Ana	46 367	184	76.1	571	8 899	4 113.4	357.2	876	11 543	2 302.6	232.1
Santa Barbara	25 549	95	54.7	157	1 145	379.8	35.2	655	7 589	1 220.4	143.3
Santa Clara	147 294	1 113	21.8	593	13 779	20 791.0	892.0	414	6 703	1 758.7	187.6
Santa Clarita	163 473	598	99.5	75	576	392.6	37.4	297	3 720	736.6	66.9
Santa Cruz	28 168	285	22.1	92	888	170.1	23.7	282	3 626	578.9	62.3
Santa Maria	144 303	934	71.9	117	1 350	451.7	43.7	353	4 928	810.5	89.5
Santa Monica	45 308	272	18.4	234	2 608	3 792.3	124.3	726	8 018	2 200.3	190.0
Santa Paula	3 393	15	100.0	32	765	265.1	19.4	72	515	124.4	7.4
Santa Rosa	92 718	756	64.7	182	2 088	716.2	71.3	758	10 653	2 118.8	220.5
Santee	19 379	191	30.4	63	418	106.6	11.2	125	2 234	401.5	40.1
Saratoga	58 856	213	39.4	48	D	D	D	64	569	102.7	12.1
Seaside	83 596	210	100.0	15	123	23.6	2.9	83	1 204	353.3	32.5
Simi Valley	145 528	893	43.6	146	2 050	843.9	76.9	279	3 806	852.4	69.0
South Gate	8 244	115	8.7	86	1 417	1 327.5	41.1	154	1 738	361.1	32.0
South San Francisco	57 172	244	51.6	472	7 370	4 778.9	302.0	187	2 558	585.9	56.6
Stanton	5 825	35	71.4	39	732	127.9	18.7	96	1 136	238.9	21.6
Stockton	528 957	3 208	97.5	262	4 027	2 949.0	125.9	742	9 842	1 771.4	178.2
Suisun City	33 590	127	100.0	11	D	D	D	37	360	65.7	7.0
Sunnyvale	41 573	270	25.2	386	8 677	7 425.4	574.6	373	6 319	1 659.8	150.3
Temecula	199 861	1 532	83.3	77	973	579.6	37.4	211	2 817	687.7	63.0
Temple City	15 543	252	15.9	75	311	90.7	5.9	89	1 033	142.4	14.9
Thousand Oaks	141 714	569	62.7	202	1 997	6 480.3	96.3	504	7 185	1 706.4	153.1
Torrance	30 589	146	91.8	618	7 802	14 366.0	405.3	794	12 773	3 023.3	265.0
Tracy	236 935	1 494	99.9	30	299	219.5	9.7	196	2 464	401.0	38.4
Tulare	31 389	304	93.4	40	478	135.9	12.4	154	2 095	315.5	35.4
Turlock	126 492	976	89.8	53	409	166.4	12.5	166	1 898	352.6	34.6
Tustin	4 908	24	20.8	232	3 233	2 236.2	139.6	235	4 916	1 691.7	138.3
Union City	34 190	134	68.7	179	4 640	2 722.5	186.2	88	2 227	510.9	49.6
Upland	38 335	233	100.0	108	579	191.3	16.0	224	2 684	528.4	54.3
Vacaville	129 916	536	89.9	35	392	110.2	9.9	302	3 830	701.5	67.0
Vallejo	43 346	236	100.0	32	387	220.4	12.8	279	4 187	791.0	83.2
Victorville	369 421	2 279	92.3	29	227	63.6	8.3	304	4 766	839.9	81.0
Visalia	175 506	1 080	92.0	137	1 344	1 050.8	44.4	436	6 124	1 042.9	100.7

1. Establishments with payroll.

City	Real estate and rental and leasing, 1997				Professional, scientific, and technical services,[1] 1997				Manufacturing, 1997			
	Number of establish-ments	Number of employees	Receipts (mil dol)	Annual payroll (mil dol)	Number of establish-ments	Number of employees	Receipts (mil dol)	Annual payroll (mil dol)	Number of establish-ments	Number of employees	Receipts (mil dol)	Annual payroll (mil dol)
	80	81	82	83	84	85	86	87	88	89	90	91
CALIFORNIA—Cont'd												
Pleasant Hill	49	204	26.6	4.8	116	1 058	104.8	65.0	NA	NA	NA	NA
Pleasanton	101	442	92.0	17.7	328	3 797	614.7	185.4	100	1 759	328.4	77.1
Pomona	81	424	50.7	9.4	92	555	41.7	16.3	253	9 792	1 551.4	301.9
Porterville	32	105	16.7	1.3	38	113	9.0	2.2	35	1 045	161.4	28.1
Poway	54	225	25.3	4.1	97	366	51.4	15.6	52	1 397	227.6	41.2
Rancho Cucamonga	80	460	47.5	9.6	200	955	100.1	33.7	243	9 913	2 009.1	311.7
Rancho Palos Verdes	46	127	28.8	3.0	86	228	25.4	10.8	NA	NA	NA	NA
Redding	146	664	59.8	11.1	261	1 519	115.4	48.6	110	1 351	166.2	38.0
Redlands	67	247	32.5	3.9	122	656	56.6	22.4	54	1 803	196.1	41.3
Redondo Beach	91	295	51.7	5.8	197	4 408	740.9	278.7	40	D	D	D
Redwood City	88	1 279	114.1	31.6	301	3 687	552.7	232.1	98	4 606	930.1	238.6
Rialto	41	176	22.1	3.3	28	164	9.5	3.6	66	1 935	299.0	50.2
Richmond	54	242	46.7	6.7	115	923	89.0	43.9	137	4 640	2 979.0	207.8
Riverside	250	1 276	145.0	28.3	466	3 195	333.6	101.4	289	10 901	1 687.2	322.4
Rocklin	21	105	14.7	1.9	40	149	17.7	5.7	32	798	216.0	26.7
Rohnert Park	42	239	51.8	6.4	53	429	27.5	32.6	48	781	136.2	27.6
Rosemead	28	126	11.3	2.7	48	343	21.2	3.7	82	1 759	149.6	38.1
Roseville	79	922	82.3	21.6	188	1 357	132.6	55.8	57	D	D	D
Sacramento	415	3 058	367.3	80.1	1 456	11 899	1 355.5	544.8	423	15 763	3 582.7	579.1
Salinas	104	546	71.7	11.7	201	1 078	89.1	35.0	97	2 752	641.6	96.0
San Bernardino	152	556	68.7	11.7	264	1 877	176.7	66.1	150	4 140	589.5	106.1
San Bruno	29	138	49.6	4.4	69	394	41.9	20.0	NA	NA	NA	NA
San Buenaventura (Ventura)	175	790	94.5	19.4	389	2 574	234.3	91.6	157	3 126	374.7	90.9
San Carlos	52	246	32.1	6.9	132	805	66.7	27.8	148	3 712	561.6	144.4
San Clemente	65	236	35.6	4.7	157	767	107.0	31.3	91	1 452	189.3	49.3
San Diego	1 954	14 038	2 109.3	386.8	4 584	46 351	5 780.7	2 278.2	1 444	65 599	14 315.4	2 562.7
San Dimas	29	172	27.3	4.0	82	1 542	237.8	62.5	99	2 382	321.7	73.1
San Francisco	1 627	14 492	2 721.2	472.9	4 984	58 942	9 016.6	3 517.4	1 247	25 037	3 978.9	642.4
San Gabriel	65	223	29.0	4.5	69	211	15.6	4.0	54	628	36.5	11.0
San Jose	794	6 088	1 140.3	179.0	2 393	24 773	3 370.6	1 426.5	1 225	86 726	26 808.1	4 263.5
San Juan Capistrano	49	212	31.1	8.0	107	527	72.7	28.8	44	1 108	176.6	40.7
San Leandro	120	1 838	242.1	50.5	152	1 720	149.5	65.3	257	9 002	2 260.6	310.7
San Luis Obispo	106	501	53.5	7.8	236	1 214	120.9	46.8	78	1 521	195.0	43.9
San Marcos	40	232	25.6	4.4	69	320	25.1	9.5	227	5 981	872.1	172.1
San Mateo	161	1 892	252.5	54.5	462	2 997	396.6	179.4	77	531	67.5	18.4
San Pablo	26	132	22.8	2.7	15	101	11.6	4.6	NA	NA	NA	NA
San Rafael	152	1 458	203.0	41.9	433	1 893	231.2	94.6	149	1 809	223.2	58.3
San Ramon	68	548	146.3	24.8	282	3 271	558.6	203.7	NA	NA	NA	NA
Santa Ana	254	2 951	451.6	89.3	834	7 761	763.3	311.5	961	30 246	4 052.4	878.1
Santa Barbara	257	1 397	551.8	45.4	520	2 950	363.6	133.4	155	2 204	262.6	68.7
Santa Clara	146	973	307.9	30.1	583	10 210	1 378.6	588.8	711	46 029	12 884.0	2 398.9
Santa Clarita	111	506	74.4	10.9	140	777	79.4	23.1	66	1 136	164.3	39.5
Santa Cruz	80	327	41.9	5.5	239	985	109.7	39.1	122	2 969	866.8	101.2
Santa Maria	69	383	32.6	6.3	119	848	49.4	21.1	86	2 608	452.4	63.7
Santa Monica	334	1 932	338.8	70.0	995	7 478	1 124.9	444.8	147	4 065	560.6	141.0
Santa Paula	15	171	10.9	2.0	28	162	15.0	5.0	NA	NA	NA	NA
Santa Rosa	235	959	133.4	20.5	539	2 613	251.4	95.4	203	9 598	1 784.1	418.2
Santee	45	173	22.6	3.1	39	201	13.1	3.8	127	2 356	216.9	61.1
Saratoga	55	264	49.4	8.7	152	572	67.1	27.8	NA	NA	NA	NA
Seaside	12	58	7.4	1.0	14	40	2.9	1.1	NA	NA	NA	NA
Simi Valley	68	341	36.1	6.9	164	1 228	168.2	55.0	157	4 709	1 208.3	170.5
South Gate	27	129	83.2	4.4	21	394	78.9	14.1	200	7 603	1 330.9	214.9
South San Francisco	72	1 328	346.3	44.3	109	2 634	396.7	127.5	193	10 151	2 011.2	485.9
Stanton	25	101	18.2	2.0	13	98	6.5	2.9	64	1 251	117.2	31.4
Stockton	208	1 223	125.6	25.2	336	2 326	197.4	76.7	191	8 783	1 809.8	256.7
Suisun City	7	43	5.5	0.8	10	30	2.6	0.5	NA	NA	NA	NA
Sunnyvale	122	780	131.0	20.6	521	9 031	1 180.3	550.0	438	43 471	11 208.6	2 683.0
Temecula	51	287	29.9	4.8	116	1 009	93.7	26.4	107	4 321	1 113.4	145.6
Temple City	14	58	6.4	0.7	33	98	6.2	1.8	NA	NA	NA	NA
Thousand Oaks	145	731	114.8	16.5	464	2 279	274.0	105.6	137	4 172	602.0	158.9
Torrance	303	1 890	293.5	41.4	684	4 953	655.1	245.7	328	16 065	4 364.1	719.9
Tracy	34	115	15.8	1.9	58	299	19.9	7.4	48	2 527	651.2	77.5
Tulare	24	73	10.0	1.0	41	187	13.6	5.8	35	1 797	1 331.8	61.0
Turlock	33	128	21.5	2.3	45	229	19.5	6.3	69	3 636	857.2	93.0
Tustin	126	652	109.6	17.7	387	2 569	314.1	113.9	141	6 771	1 446.3	282.5
Union City	24	84	15.5	2.1	48	257	24.4	7.8	93	3 696	677.5	128.1
Upland	89	513	44.9	9.3	134	753	43.2	16.4	95	1 510	224.1	40.1
Vacaville	80	312	43.2	6.2	72	285	21.6	8.2	58	2 382	355.8	71.1
Vallejo	68	317	29.8	4.6	88	458	31.0	13.0	40	682	198.2	23.0
Victorville	44	221	24.2	5.1	66	355	26.1	9.4	29	773	216.3	27.8
Visalia	97	406	52.8	7.9	202	1 171	229.2	31.9	87	3 873	821.2	106.7

1. Firms subject to federal tax.

City	Accommodation and foodservices, 1997				Arts, entertainment, and recreation,[1] 1997				Health care and social assistance,[1] 1997			
	Number of establish-ments	Number of employees	Sales (mil dol)	Annual payroll (mil dol)	Number of establish-ments	Number of employees	Receipts (mil dol)	Annual payroll (mil dol)	Number of establish-ments	Number of employees	Receipts (mil dol)	Annual payroll (mil dol)
	92	93	94	95	96	97	98	99	100	101	102	103
CALIFORNIA—Cont'd												
Pleasant Hill	72	1 268	49.1	12.2	10	137	6.4	1.9	98	727	51.0	19.9
Pleasanton	187	3 699	152.5	40.7	31	531	39.4	15.3	198	1 903	234.6	64.3
Pomona	165	2 603	94.5	23.8	11	365	47.5	12.0	214	2 315	150.9	60.3
Porterville	79	1 143	35.4	8.0	5	0	0.0	0.0	95	1 040	61.9	20.0
Poway	80	1 086	39.5	10.2	13	282	12.8	2.6	140	923	74.5	30.1
Rancho Cucamonga	153	D	D	D	14	298	15.0	4.3	148	1 524	88.7	31.3
Rancho Palos Verdes	34	694	26.2	6.4	4	74	5.3	1.1	71	275	24.1	11.4
Redding	254	3 849	120.5	31.6	22	261	8.5	2.6	413	4 908	355.9	143.8
Redlands	119	1 865	59.1	16.1	11	279	8.7	2.6	172	2 695	158.5	74.1
Redondo Beach	161	3 122	126.1	34.8	19	247	11.0	3.8	132	995	85.0	36.7
Redwood City	173	3 138	130.4	35.2	24	618	28.9	9.0	220	2 232	209.9	96.5
Rialto	64	1 152	32.5	8.0	4	0	0.0	0.0	78	792	33.1	12.3
Richmond	83	947	29.8	7.4	11	90	9.9	3.0	118	1 345	94.2	42.8
Riverside	397	6 281	208.3	56.7	34	573	23.8	6.5	540	7 486	622.4	244.5
Rocklin	51	1 053	29.7	8.2	7	180	4.3	1.7	45	202	15.0	4.7
Rohnert Park	74	1 792	60.0	16.4	10	169	6.3	2.3	54	336	18.7	7.4
Rosemead	103	1 159	43.0	10.1	4	0	0.0	0.0	76	742	44.1	17.6
Roseville	167	3 185	102.0	27.2	15	205	5.9	1.3	241	2 603	239.9	88.4
Sacramento	877	14 847	528.8	142.9	81	1 285	96.4	18.8	993	10 610	883.1	385.6
Salinas	226	3 118	105.3	27.2	17	247	17.8	2.8	281	2 272	192.3	78.2
San Bernardino	322	5 345	177.5	47.7	22	406	17.6	4.8	376	3 826	309.9	126.5
San Bruno	59	971	38.1	10.2	7	0	0.0	0.0	65	910	103.8	41.3
San Buenaventura (Ventura)	251	4 544	166.4	47.0	38	474	20.7	5.1	342	2 578	228.6	85.4
San Carlos	83	755	32.0	9.1	4	53	1.2	0.6	73	411	30.9	11.1
San Clemente	117	1 269	56.8	14.3	13	299	11.9	3.2	124	1 032	70.7	28.9
San Diego	2 776	61 170	2 607.4	706.7	267	6 439	479.5	188.9	2 642	28 497	2 464.6	977.0
San Dimas	59	1 156	39.5	10.0	15	331	26.4	6.9	78	899	52.2	23.2
San Francisco	3 258	60 113	3 281.1	955.7	332	6 402	632.3	240.8	2 260	14 360	1 209.7	478.5
San Gabriel	134	1 535	57.2	15.2	8	44	1.8	0.4	140	1 066	66.2	24.3
San Jose	1 478	23 699	981.3	249.5	106	2 907	209.4	82.8	1 701	18 436	1 371.8	567.1
San Juan Capistrano	58	932	33.3	9.1	14	294	12.9	5.2	71	464	55.4	19.1
San Leandro	170	2 256	79.3	22.0	11	134	5.2	1.5	198	3 891	242.4	106.2
San Luis Obispo	173	3 535	114.4	30.9	15	121	4.7	1.8	239	2 987	219.4	107.1
San Marcos	92	1 555	48.5	14.0	15	251	11.1	3.1	66	558	28.3	11.4
San Mateo	235	3 428	148.7	44.0	39	730	39.1	17.9	343	2 321	179.4	73.0
San Pablo	60	788	29.4	7.0	5	0	0.0	0.0	75	863	60.7	26.7
San Rafael	198	2 429	93.4	23.8	31	303	23.8	6.0	214	2 269	159.7	72.8
San Ramon	99	D	D	D	12	898	23.1	8.0	153	1 198	109.6	42.4
Santa Ana	454	6 519	264.5	67.0	28	542	53.0	16.1	677	5 708	426.3	168.0
Santa Barbara	385	7 545	294.4	84.9	43	395	28.3	10.3	416	3 277	286.2	109.5
Santa Clara	309	6 513	316.3	82.6	24	2 699	100.5	28.6	149	2 998	274.6	129.7
Santa Clarita	151	2 432	80.8	22.6	40	369	23.1	8.5	205	1 678	122.1	49.2
Santa Cruz	216	3 339	124.5	33.9	27	966	35.6	13.1	143	1 195	80.9	28.1
Santa Maria	146	2 593	79.1	22.8	10	114	4.7	1.0	219	1 706	118.7	45.8
Santa Monica	375	9 894	461.9	127.1	403	1 697	329.4	170.9	742	5 019	552.4	218.0
Santa Paula	38	396	12.8	3.1	1	0	0.0	0.0	33	353	12.0	4.4
Santa Rosa	339	5 122	175.4	47.2	39	688	36.5	11.7	609	6 325	479.8	208.0
Santee	70	D	D	D	12	207	9.0	2.9	62	401	21.9	9.3
Saratoga	42	548	28.6	7.2	6	95	3.8	1.7	61	410	26.9	10.3
Seaside	54	953	35.8	9.6	3	8	0.4	0.1	14	68	4.1	1.1
Simi Valley	157	2 789	92.7	23.8	21	555	18.5	5.7	196	1 283	120.4	46.6
South Gate	98	966	36.6	8.1	5	18	1.2	0.1	89	694	46.1	16.9
South San Francisco	152	3 819	221.9	64.4	13	153	11.0	2.7	105	1 635	163.0	71.8
Stanton	75	785	29.9	7.2	7	0	0.0	0.0	25	107	6.2	1.9
Stockton	398	5 902	197.7	51.5	42	660	22.4	7.2	558	5 597	432.7	184.4
Suisun City	26	D	D	D	4	38	0.5	0.2	27	160	6.3	2.5
Sunnyvale	293	4 987	226.5	59.8	20	227	12.7	3.3	235	2 474	249.6	80.0
Temecula	107	2 274	75.3	20.9	13	231	9.2	2.9	102	818	59.0	18.1
Temple City	46	D	D	D	4	10	0.7	0.2	45	712	27.2	11.1
Thousand Oaks	234	5 150	179.9	47.7	45	272	23.3	10.5	388	4 125	369.8	135.0
Torrance	400	7 747	296.4	79.5	37	923	53.4	20.3	795	6 134	520.6	221.2
Tracy	88	1 368	43.8	10.8	10	107	4.9	1.1	70	682	35.4	13.4
Tulare	73	786	27.3	6.4	6	0	0.0	0.0	82	638	45.3	14.4
Turlock	87	1 146	35.9	9.2	13	83	2.2	0.6	121	1 067	70.4	25.4
Tustin	143	2 877	97.9	26.9	17	721	34.1	9.0	237	2 551	172.9	68.3
Union City	69	648	25.1	5.9	1	0	0.0	0.0	64	550	50.2	15.0
Upland	114	D	D	D	14	229	11.4	2.5	244	1 644	132.0	57.0
Vacaville	121	2 260	77.0	20.5	8	188	4.5	1.6	119	1 115	90.6	31.2
Vallejo	172	2 225	73.3	18.7	15	484	42.4	6.9	215	2 725	232.6	107.0
Victorville	143	2 588	83.8	22.8	8	215	6.6	2.3	120	1 606	121.4	37.6
Visalia	204	3 751	123.5	31.7	15	0	0.0	0.0	283	2 532	183.7	77.2

1. Firms subject to federal tax.

City	Other services,[1] 1997				Selected federal funds, 2002–2003 (mil dol)								
					Procurement contracts		Grants						
	Number of establishments	Number of employees	Receipts (mil dol)	Annual payroll (mil dol)	Defense	Other	Total[2]	Medicaid and other health related	Nutrition and family welfare	Energy and environment	Education	Housing and community development	Direct payments for individuals for educational assistance
	104	105	106	107	108	109	110	111	112	113	114	115	116
CALIFORNIA—Cont'd													
Pleasant Hill	50	290	12.4	4.1	1.1	1.2	2.2	0.0	0.6	0.0	0.0	1.5	0.1
Pleasanton	107	722	63.5	18.8	21.5	5.1	2.5	0.6	0.0	0.6	0.2	0.7	0.0
Pomona	141	813	62.7	16.3	66.2	5.5	24.2	3.5	0.0	4.0	3.3	12.0	22.3
Porterville	36	149	11.1	2.2	0.7	1.6	9.5	4.4	0.0	0.2	1.0	3.0	-0.1
Poway	65	276	21.4	5.3	9.4	2.7	6.5	2.4	0.0	0.0	3.1	0.6	0.2
Rancho Cucamonga	131	1 016	63.7	19.7	9.9	4.3	2.2	0.0	0.0	0.0	0.4	1.6	7.3
Rancho Palos Verdes	24	181	15.4	4.8	5.1	0.4	2.9	0.0	0.0	2.3	0.6	0.0	0.0
Redding	171	1 064	69.7	18.6	0.2	6.9	29.3	3.4	8.6	0.5	4.5	6.9	6.8
Redlands	89	451	27.8	6.6	19.3	9.9	10.4	0.0	0.0	0.0	1.4	2.0	3.7
Redondo Beach	108	913	83.6	26.1	754.1	89.2	13.3	3.3	0.0	0.0	0.0	6.3	0.0
Redwood City	135	804	64.8	19.2	13.5	3.6	19.7	3.6	0.0	0.2	1.6	10.4	1.2
Rialto	58	456	53.0	11.2	1.6	0.0	5.4	0.0	0.1	0.0	0.0	5.0	0.0
Richmond	108	547	48.4	13.4	9.6	5.0	40.4	0.3	0.9	0.0	0.7	37.0	0.0
Riverside	327	2 316	154.0	41.8	5.9	9.6	184.1	13.2	49.8	4.2	10.9	68.2	40.1
Rocklin	36	177	9.7	2.1	0.6	0.1	2.3	0.0	0.0	0.0	0.0	2.3	6.3
Rohnert Park	43	243	15.5	4.8	2.7	1.5	8.6	0.0	3.2	0.0	3.3	0.3	5.1
Rosemead	72	265	15.7	3.6	0.4	0.7	2.5	0.0	0.0	0.3	0.0	2.1	0.9
Roseville	107	1 310	132.2	44.7	1.9	6.1	4.8	0.0	0.0	0.0	0.0	3.1	0.0
Sacramento	572	4 272	335.0	95.0	416.9	184.7	6 536.1	551.8	2 439.9	252.0	1 530.1	232.1	99.2
Salinas	155	943	74.0	21.3	2.5	4.8	27.2	5.3	6.5	0.0	4.8	5.5	5.3
San Bernardino	211	1 459	96.9	26.2	31.0	29.9	122.7	9.7	35.3	1.6	12.9	46.1	38.1
San Bruno	72	438	36.9	10.2	2.6	0.8	0.8	0.0	0.0	0.0	0.8	0.0	3.6
San Buenaventura (Ventura)	162	1 407	132.3	38.8	0.0	0.0	0.0	0.0	0.0	0.0	0.0	0.0	0.0
San Carlos	82	542	47.9	14.8	8.6	1.2	1.9	1.4	0.2	0.0	0.0	0.0	0.0
San Clemente	61	335	19.4	5.6	7.9	0.6	0.7	0.0	0.0	0.3	0.0	0.4	0.0
San Diego	1 827	12 658	867.9	239.3	4 054.4	462.4	1 519.3	813.7	129.9	31.3	55.0	192.1	88.1
San Dimas	62	566	46.6	16.3	2.8	1.3	1.9	0.0	0.0	0.5	0.8	0.6	0.5
San Francisco	1 477	8 794	634.9	179.0	326.5	535.9	1 044.2	627.0	15.0	3.8	31.4	235.0	99.6
San Gabriel	78	433	32.4	9.9	1.3	0.1	0.9	0.2	0.0	0.0	0.4	0.3	0.0
San Jose	1 146	7 214	546.3	156.7	158.2	65.4	184.2	13.3	13.9	1.0	23.1	85.4	38.0
San Juan Capistrano	43	215	16.3	4.6	2.7	1.7	0.1	0.0	0.0	0.0	0.0	0.0	0.0
San Leandro	155	1 057	99.8	29.6	27.7	37.2	5.5	0.7	0.0	0.0	0.4	3.2	0.0
San Luis Obispo	92	601	33.5	9.3	10.2	0.6	37.5	0.4	20.9	0.0	1.8	10.0	15.6
San Marcos	97	507	39.9	11.6	6.6	1.7	12.7	8.2	0.1	0.0	3.8	0.0	10.1
San Mateo	195	964	67.9	19.8	6.5	4.0	24.4	4.4	0.0	0.5	1.0	15.2	2.0
San Pablo	39	197	12.9	3.3	0.1	0.5	8.1	0.9	0.0	0.2	3.1	2.9	3.4
San Rafael	230	1 178	108.8	32.4	0.4	2.2	13.7	2.2	2.5	1.0	0.9	5.1	1.3
San Ramon	91	805	61.5	18.4	6.3	0.8	0.7	0.0	0.0	0.6	0.0	0.1	0.0
Santa Ana	432	3 105	267.0	79.4	89.5	25.6	118.2	7.2	49.3	0.5	7.6	36.6	10.3
Santa Barbara	205	1 130	70.6	20.7	98.8	21.3	153.4	18.4	0.1	8.5	4.5	29.8	24.7
Santa Clara	229	2 002	206.8	65.9	98.8	12.3	35.7	2.5	0.5	0.7	2.6	26.3	4.3
Santa Clarita	146	786	54.5	14.7	11.7	0.4	3.0	0.0	0.0	0.5	0.5	1.3	5.7
Santa Cruz	99	522	37.4	10.7	3.3	3.0	78.4	19.9	4.0	3.3	2.0	22.1	10.8
Santa Maria	121	750	45.5	12.5	75.6	2.6	6.5	0.0	0.0	0.0	1.0	2.5	3.7
Santa Monica	300	1 982	135.0	37.9	110.9	4.4	72.2	42.3	0.1	0.2	6.5	16.3	9.4
Santa Paula	28	94	7.5	1.4	0.7	0.0	7.1	0.0	0.0	0.0	0.5	4.1	0.0
Santa Rosa	274	1 594	106.0	32.8	7.1	6.8	37.1	3.2	5.7	0.5	3.0	16.0	5.5
Santee	101	517	36.3	10.3	1.4	0.5	3.7	0.0	0.0	0.0	0.4	3.3	0.0
Saratoga	30	215	10.8	4.0	0.5	0.0	3.2	0.0	0.0	1.4	0.0	1.6	2.5
Seaside	48	235	20.6	5.4	0.7	0.0	8.5	0.0	0.0	0.0	3.5	3.4	4.2
Simi Valley	130	659	49.5	13.6	28.5	37.4	1.6	0.0	0.0	0.3	0.2	1.1	0.2
South Gate	84	275	22.8	5.0	0.7	0.3	11.4	0.0	0.0	0.0	0.0	11.3	1.9
South San Francisco	137	1 472	106.9	33.6	13.3	0.5	17.2	4.3	6.3	0.0	0.0	2.9	0.0
Stanton	67	231	21.6	4.9	0.3	0.0	0.0	0.0	0.0	0.0	0.0	0.0	0.1
Stockton	318	1 733	111.6	34.0	31.4	14.7	65.8	6.1	21.3	1.0	4.8	27.6	25.0
Suisun City	18	114	6.7	2.0	0.2	0.2	6.6	0.4	0.0	0.0	0.2	5.9	3.4
Sunnyvale	192	1 459	111.7	34.0	3 362.9	32.2	17.7	7.3	0.0	0.7	0.0	7.3	0.3
Temecula	81	506	35.7	9.6	3.4	1.8	1.2	0.0	0.1	0.5	0.2	0.1	0.2
Temple City	39	202	9.7	3.7	0.0	0.0	0.2	0.0	0.0	0.0	0.2	0.0	0.0
Thousand Oaks	154	970	75.8	23.4	38.3	2.2	11.2	0.0	0.0	1.2	1.1	2.5	1.2
Torrance	270	1 467	111.8	31.7	315.6	27.5	51.4	29.0	0.0	11.6	1.5	8.6	8.1
Tracy	48	293	14.7	3.9	3.7	2.2	3.3	0.0	0.0	0.0	0.1	2.7	0.0
Tulare	53	232	17.4	4.3	0.2	4.3	7.5	0.5	0.0	0.0	0.2	6.6	0.1
Turlock	75	478	27.7	6.9	0.4	12.9	5.4	0.0	0.0	0.0	1.5	1.6	7.9
Tustin	95	771	61.9	17.0	12.4	19.6	3.6	0.8	0.0	0.0	0.0	2.2	0.0
Union City	47	496	63.2	13.2	7.0	7.6	15.2	12.8	0.0	0.0	0.0	1.5	0.0
Upland	80	410	28.0	7.5	0.2	5.2	8.0	0.0	0.0	0.0	1.7	5.6	0.0
Vacaville	84	423	29.2	7.6	0.6	0.8	7.4	0.4	0.0	0.0	0.0	5.2	0.0
Vallejo	134	906	54.7	17.6	18.9	1.7	19.3	0.0	0.0	1.9	0.8	16.3	0.5
Victorville	82	497	29.4	8.4	1.2	13.4	8.0	0.0	0.0	0.0	0.3	3.4	9.3
Visalia	140	877	67.1	17.3	4.1	2.5	36.4	0.0	16.7	0.0	3.3	5.2	18.5

1. Firms subject to federal tax.   2. Includes program categories not shown separately. State totals include additional categories not allocated by city.

Table D. Cities — City Government Finances

City	General revenue — Total (mil dol)	Intergovernmental — Total (mil dol)	Intergovernmental — Percent from state government	Taxes — Total (mil dol)	Taxes — Per capita (dollars) Total	Taxes — Per capita Property	Taxes — Per capita Sales and gross receipts	General expenditure — Total (mil dol)	General expenditure — Per capita (dollars) Total	General expenditure — Per capita Capital outlays
	117	118	119	120	121	122	123	124	125	126
CALIFORNIA—Cont'd										
Pleasant Hill	25.4	2.8	98.9	15.8	471	133	266	24.3	725	244
Pleasanton	121.9	20.6	43.8	57.3	867	438	339	111.4	1 684	302
Pomona	112.2	17.4	82.1	68.0	443	178	238	113.7	740	100
Porterville	29.5	5.0	98.0	12.2	295	66	198	34.0	822	235
Poway	84.4	6.0	85.6	41.7	850	587	217	89.2	1 817	376
Rancho Cucamonga	151.3	14.6	84.7	88.9	619	371	157	104.3	726	122
Rancho Palos Verdes	21.9	4.2	93.4	14.6	347	101	212	22.9	543	204
Redding	116.8	20.8	41.9	37.9	442	161	252	115.5	1 348	530
Redlands	71.0	8.9	86.4	36.1	541	167	156	67.8	1 016	245
Redondo Beach	79.5	10.5	89.5	39.8	605	211	329	78.1	1 187	278
Redwood City	102.8	10.7	86.4	58.6	787	357	345	107.0	1 437	440
Rialto	62.1	11.2	82.0	26.2	271	139	110	52.3	541	71
Richmond	143.6	24.6	64.9	77.1	752	320	368	130.1	1 268	184
Riverside	267.5	48.8	88.4	100.7	367	101	233	232.5	848	171
Rocklin	42.0	5.6	99.8	25.1	580	147	150	34.4	794	85
Rohnert Park	49.7	4.9	97.1	18.9	447	221	198	57.4	1 355	312
Rosemead	25.8	10.6	67.8	11.8	214	91	103	30.3	552	212
Roseville	218.0	42.0	24.1	87.9	958	163	503	221.2	2 410	1 246
Sacramento	785.0	192.4	51.5	260.9	599	206	300	666.9	1 532	316
Salinas	96.1	23.4	74.0	51.8	348	83	222	87.9	591	110
San Bernardino	196.9	35.7	54.1	89.6	468	133	291	165.9	866	72
San Bruno	38.8	6.2	72.7	16.2	412	112	218	48.1	1 221	138
San Buenaventura (Ventura)	107.9	24.4	90.0	50.6	488	132	289	96.0	926	213
San Carlos	35.2	3.5	98.2	19.8	729	361	282	36.0	1 324	411
San Clemente	72.2	8.3	92.6	40.2	718	184	128	54.6	975	308
San Diego	1 903.3	432.9	32.2	744.7	591	208	310	1 774.2	1 409	353
San Dimas	23.7	4.2	85.4	13.2	369	152	186	20.5	571	148
San Francisco	4 843.5	1 726.2	77.9	1 698.8	2 223	978	722	4 793.1	6 273	1 028
San Gabriel	18.9	4.2	100.0	11.7	287	111	150	17.7	435	86
San Jose	1 463.5	257.5	40.4	666.8	741	307	285	1 519.3	1 687	498
San Juan Capistrano	30.3	3.5	99.6	19.4	559	301	211	26.5	764	122
San Leandro	93.7	11.4	86.6	58.7	728	181	445	94.4	1 171	102
San Luis Obispo	59.9	13.7	79.3	26.8	606	118	453	56.1	1 267	446
San Marcos	94.8	7.6	88.6	47.6	765	393	235	81.8	1 317	485
San Mateo	110.0	11.9	90.7	64.4	701	314	254	136.0	1 480	583
San Pablo	23.8	3.3	98.1	15.3	492	237	133	21.1	682	233
San Rafael	61.0	5.8	100.0	36.0	640	208	364	68.7	1 221	317
San Ramon	49.7	5.5	99.0	28.4	614	241	282	49.8	1 077	320
Santa Ana	276.2	62.3	80.6	137.2	400	150	217	283.2	825	183
Santa Barbara	163.7	24.9	86.2	66.3	742	238	460	138.6	1 551	302
Santa Clara	273.0	15.5	81.8	103.6	1 017	443	530	193.4	1 899	396
Santa Clarita	107.9	26.8	66.2	61.5	383	43	206	82.0	511	194
Santa Cruz	107.1	14.0	82.2	41.5	770	271	391	98.4	1 827	428
Santa Maria	80.3	11.3	74.7	32.5	407	61	270	58.5	731	136
Santa Monica	303.2	36.3	45.4	165.2	1 903	536	1 013	231.3	2 664	569
Santa Paula	16.0	5.3	66.8	5.6	195	110	70	13.4	464	59
Santa Rosa	196.3	27.2	67.1	69.7	454	106	295	241.2	1 572	681
Santee	30.6	6.5	90.5	16.8	316	160	140	29.7	557	70
Saratoga	17.1	3.6	95.9	8.4	283	136	78	22.8	772	248
Seaside	22.3	3.0	99.2	16.0	496	163	316	19.0	587	114
Simi Valley	91.5	15.8	74.3	43.5	373	149	177	83.9	720	142
South Gate	44.9	13.0	79.3	21.0	213	83	101	79.8	808	371
South San Francisco	97.3	14.2	100.0	50.0	833	450	311	79.6	1 328	370
Stanton	18.9	4.0	86.9	10.6	280	118	150	16.4	432	93
Stockton	253.3	53.9	71.0	101.8	387	79	253	239.4	911	108
Suisun City	21.2	2.7	99.2	12.8	476	346	112	25.6	951	350
Sunnyvale	196.5	24.8	94.7	75.1	579	197	334	181.1	1 396	204
Temecula	68.0	10.8	63.8	47.5	643	222	331	64.6	876	215
Temple City	12.3	3.5	89.4	5.6	157	52	76	9.3	262	9
Thousand Oaks	129.0	11.8	90.3	68.3	557	165	278	127.6	1 040	340
Torrance	195.2	42.6	59.9	109.9	776	160	544	160.8	1 135	115
Tracy	121.3	17.7	71.4	27.4	403	183	195	87.3	1 283	354
Tulare	37.6	7.4	84.1	15.7	341	91	203	39.3	854	99
Turlock	49.5	8.8	69.5	19.8	321	80	200	38.3	621	184
Tustin	47.0	10.6	85.0	29.2	425	159	250	50.6	738	171
Union City	51.1	8.3	90.9	34.3	490	255	193	56.3	806	204
Upland	56.1	7.8	99.9	21.7	305	141	127	47.4	668	114
Vacaville	120.8	21.8	65.2	53.8	575	293	158	135.0	1 442	610
Vallejo	229.4	49.9	93.6	54.0	451	132	267	191.6	1 600	287
Victorville	69.1	9.7	64.9	35.4	500	123	336	52.8	745	156
Visalia	96.9	16.2	78.2	33.5	346	102	187	80.8	834	225

1. Based on population estimated as of July 1 of the year shown.

Table D. Cities — City Government Finances (cont'd)

City	City government finances, 2002 (cont'd)									
	General expenditure									
	Percent of total for—									
	Public welfare	Highways	Parking facilities	Education	Health and hospitals	Police protection	Sewerage and sanitation	Parks and recreation	Housing and community development	Interest on debt
	127	128	129	130	131	132	133	134	135	136
CALIFORNIA—Cont'd										
Pleasant Hill	0.0	27.2	0.0	0.0	0.3	27.1	0.3	0.0	14.5	12.2
Pleasanton	0.0	11.7	0.0	0.0	0.5	13.7	9.8	14.5	1.7	12.0
Pomona	0.0	16.3	0.0	0.0	0.3	25.3	6.0	2.8	19.4	7.1
Porterville	0.0	24.7	0.1	0.0	0.4	13.9	20.4	9.5	1.3	9.5
Poway	0.0	4.0	0.0	0.0	2.0	12.2	9.2	5.6	30.9	21.4
Rancho Cucamonga	0.0	17.9	0.0	0.0	0.6	11.9	0.4	4.2	16.9	11.9
Rancho Palos Verdes	0.0	34.3	0.0	0.0	0.4	12.1	1.0	23.8	10.2	1.4
Redding	0.0	4.4	0.0	0.0	0.3	14.3	24.6	4.7	18.2	5.3
Redlands	0.0	16.2	0.0	0.0	3.0	21.5	23.8	5.8	2.0	6.8
Redondo Beach	0.0	9.5	0.0	0.0	5.1	21.6	1.3	8.9	8.5	4.6
Redwood City	0.0	30.3	0.4	0.0	0.4	18.6	8.1	7.0	4.4	2.6
Rialto	0.0	12.5	0.0	0.0	0.0	28.7	10.8	3.9	4.7	14.0
Richmond	0.0	4.9	0.0	0.0	0.0	24.5	7.4	11.8	9.2	10.0
Riverside	0.0	14.6	0.0	0.0	0.7	25.5	8.9	9.6	6.7	11.6
Rocklin	0.0	9.8	0.0	0.0	0.5	15.4	0.0	17.9	10.8	9.1
Rohnert Park	0.0	4.8	0.0	0.0	1.3	13.3	32.2	8.7	20.1	4.7
Rosemead	0.0	8.7	0.0	0.0	0.5	22.1	0.0	11.5	39.7	6.3
Roseville	0.0	23.0	0.0	0.0	0.2	6.4	30.4	8.8	4.3	7.7
Sacramento	0.0	8.3	2.3	0.0	2.0	15.8	8.2	8.5	18.6	7.5
Salinas	0.0	13.5	0.0	0.0	3.1	27.2	5.8	9.5	3.9	7.4
San Bernardino	0.0	3.5	0.1	0.0	1.8	25.9	19.6	4.1	10.7	8.9
San Bruno	0.0	8.3	0.0	0.0	0.0	17.7	19.1	8.2	10.9	0.0
San Buenaventura (Ventura)	0.0	18.6	0.3	0.0	0.9	22.5	10.5	11.4	2.4	2.5
San Carlos	0.0	12.5	0.0	0.0	0.1	14.9	8.6	12.8	18.6	3.6
San Clemente	0.0	33.8	0.2	0.0	0.7	13.2	7.7	14.5	1.2	5.1
San Diego	0.0	3.2	0.5	0.0	0.2	14.9	20.6	8.6	9.5	7.2
San Dimas	0.0	26.1	0.1	0.0	0.4	19.8	0.1	15.6	14.6	5.6
San Francisco	11.0	3.5	0.6	1.9	20.1	7.8	2.5	4.9	1.3	8.1
San Gabriel	0.0	10.5	0.0	0.0	0.0	35.6	0.0	7.3	1.3	0.3
San Jose	0.0	6.9	0.4	0.0	1.5	12.3	13.8	9.8	20.6	7.2
San Juan Capistrano	0.0	15.9	0.8	0.0	0.1	16.6	7.8	13.3	17.3	11.2
San Leandro	0.0	8.3	0.3	0.0	1.4	20.8	8.7	5.3	9.9	3.7
San Luis Obispo	0.0	16.5	12.5	0.0	0.0	15.1	11.0	9.4	6.7	2.7
San Marcos	0.0	15.4	0.0	0.0	1.1	10.5	0.0	4.2	23.4	16.3
San Mateo	0.0	9.6	0.8	0.0	0.7	15.1	10.8	12.1	18.1	4.7
San Pablo	0.0	12.2	0.0	0.0	0.0	33.6	0.0	5.8	25.9	14.2
San Rafael	0.0	11.9	1.6	0.0	4.8	20.4	0.0	11.1	17.0	3.8
San Ramon	0.0	29.4	0.0	0.0	0.2	12.9	0.4	18.9	15.0	7.0
Santa Ana	0.0	11.6	0.5	0.0	0.5	26.9	3.9	8.7	12.6	11.9
Santa Barbara	0.0	10.8	2.8	0.0	0.4	16.5	5.9	9.4	8.4	1.5
Santa Clara	0.0	8.6	0.9	0.0	0.2	14.6	12.5	6.9	12.7	5.6
Santa Clarita	0.0	28.6	0.0	0.0	0.0	13.7	4.4	20.0	1.2	3.1
Santa Cruz	0.0	8.6	2.8	0.0	2.4	15.2	27.7	10.5	6.9	2.5
Santa Maria	0.0	20.2	0.0	0.0	0.0	20.8	23.3	6.4	1.5	3.5
Santa Monica	0.0	5.8	0.1	0.0	0.0	22.8	8.0	13.2	10.8	4.7
Santa Paula	0.0	10.7	0.0	0.0	0.9	27.5	14.5	4.7	4.8	2.2
Santa Rosa	0.0	7.8	1.4	0.0	0.5	14.0	42.8	8.3	5.6	4.1
Santee	0.0	10.6	0.0	0.0	3.8	26.7	0.7	5.2	17.7	2.2
Saratoga	0.0	14.4	0.7	0.0	3.8	14.5	0.0	12.5	0.8	2.6
Seaside	0.0	5.8	0.0	0.0	0.0	32.2	0.0	16.3	12.6	4.0
Simi Valley	0.0	15.7	0.0	0.0	0.8	22.0	13.4	0.3	7.9	19.4
South Gate	0.0	7.1	0.0	0.0	0.0	19.7	4.3	4.4	19.9	6.1
South San Francisco	0.0	25.0	0.3	0.0	4.2	15.4	10.0	8.8	7.9	3.4
Stanton	0.0	22.9	0.0	0.0	0.0	30.2	1.3	2.2	9.5	8.1
Stockton	0.0	10.9	0.0	0.0	0.5	25.7	12.7	7.5	2.7	10.8
Suisun City	0.0	12.7	0.0	0.0	0.0	13.7	0.9	4.3	43.9	18.1
Sunnyvale	0.0	8.0	5.8	0.0	1.0	14.2	32.2	9.8	3.9	4.0
Temecula	0.0	7.8	0.0	0.0	0.1	13.3	0.0	22.7	24.4	4.0
Temple City	0.0	14.2	1.3	0.0	1.5	30.5	0.2	13.5	1.4	2.3
Thousand Oaks	0.0	20.1	0.0	0.0	0.1	11.9	16.8	7.6	7.4	4.2
Torrance	0.0	13.4	0.0	0.0	0.0	26.1	5.0	7.2	3.7	5.4
Tracy	0.0	20.5	0.0	0.0	0.1	9.3	16.8	10.2	4.1	10.3
Tulare	0.0	9.5	0.2	0.0	2.2	15.5	26.0	5.9	6.7	12.2
Turlock	0.0	17.9	0.0	0.0	0.6	24.3	13.1	10.4	5.8	3.8
Tustin	0.0	23.6	0.0	0.0	0.2	28.4	0.0	6.3	5.4	10.7
Union City	0.0	8.8	0.1	0.0	2.3	24.7	0.0	8.1	24.9	9.1
Upland	0.0	13.3	0.0	0.0	0.5	19.5	23.9	6.1	4.7	14.4
Vacaville	0.0	8.2	0.0	0.0	2.9	12.7	29.8	8.8	17.2	6.2
Vallejo	0.0	7.4	0.0	0.0	0.1	15.3	6.9	26.5	15.7	5.9
Victorville	0.0	9.4	0.0	0.0	1.2	19.4	21.1	10.5	4.0	4.5
Visalia	0.0	11.8	0.0	0.0	0.0	17.6	27.7	8.6	5.1	5.3

Table D. Cities — **City Government Finances, City Government Employment, and Climate**

City	City government finances, 2002 (cont'd) Debt outstanding			City government employment, 2002	Climate[2] Average daily temperature (degrees Fahrenheit)						
					Mean		Limits				
	Total (mil dol)	Per capita[1] (dollars)	Percent utility		January	July	January[3]	July[4]	Annual precipitation (inches)	Heating degree days	Cooling degree days
	137	138	139	140	141	142	143	144	145	146	147
CALIFORNIA—Cont'd											
Pleasant Hill	49.1	1 463	0.0	138	44.5	73.8	35.9	90.8	12.80	2 837	1 066
Pleasanton	212.7	3 215	0.0	559	46.1	71.6	35.5	89.8	14.21	2 909	780
Pomona	237.4	1 546	26.3	743	54.3	74.6	40.7	90.4	16.62	1 713	1 273
Porterville	61.8	1 496	12.3	290	46.4	81.8	36.4	98.3	11.03	2 374	1 998
Poway	348.6	7 098	1.3	248	56.6	72.5	44.6	83.4	12.80	1 400	1 110
Rancho Cucamonga	338.2	2 353	0.0	430	56.0	78.6	44.5	94.8	15.63	1 478	1 922
Rancho Palos Verdes	5.5	129	0.0	56	56.1	69.7	45.3	78.8	13.57	1 568	794
Redding	246.2	2 875	51.8	833	45.5	81.5	35.7	98.3	33.30	2 855	1 797
Redlands	97.0	1 453	21.9	508	52.8	78.4	39.6	95.8	12.80	1 875	1 673
Redondo Beach	66.2	1 007	0.0	597	56.8	69.1	47.8	75.3	12.01	1 458	727
Redwood City	63.0	846	0.0	642	48.7	68.7	38.9	83.4	19.74	2 563	486
Rialto	114.8	1 188	5.5	366	53.6	79.4	40.3	97.0	15.42	1 719	1 804
Richmond	215.7	2 104	0.0	988	49.9	63.2	42.0	71.0	22.20	2 574	199
Riverside	764.4	2 788	41.3	2 055	53.9	77.9	40.5	94.4	9.58	1 678	1 651
Rocklin	83.0	1 919	0.0	287	NA	NA	NA	NA	NA	NA	NA
Rohnert Park	45.3	1 071	0.0	206	47.4	67.6	37.0	83.8	30.30	2 883	489
Rosemead	34.3	623	0.0	89	55.7	75.2	41.7	89.2	17.90	1 433	1 427
Roseville	406.1	4 426	14.0	921	45.6	77.2	37.7	94.2	23.91	2 683	1 422
Sacramento	1 259.3	2 893	0.0	4 268	45.2	75.7	37.7	93.2	17.52	2 749	1 237
Salinas	101.7	684	0.0	712	50.5	62.5	40.0	71.1	12.44	2 964	181
San Bernardino	427.9	2 233	1.1	1 477	53.6	79.4	40.3	97.0	15.42	1 719	1 804
San Bruno	0.3	6	0.0	267	48.7	62.7	41.8	71.6	19.70	3 016	145
San Buenaventura (Ventura)	68.8	664	19.7	703	55.3	66.1	44.2	74.4	14.38	1 992	416
San Carlos	21.7	800	0.0	137	48.7	68.7	38.9	83.4	19.74	2 563	486
San Clemente	45.5	812	0.0	185	53.7	67.2	41.5	75.8	12.19	2 157	493
San Diego	2 549.6	2 024	0.0	11 324	57.4	71.0	48.9	76.2	9.90	1 256	984
San Dimas	18.3	511	0.0	88	54.3	74.6	40.7	90.4	16.62	1 713	1 273
San Francisco	8 163.8	10 685	4.3	28 931	51.1	59.1	45.8	64.6	19.71	3 005	65
San Gabriel	1.0	23	0.0	369	55.7	75.2	41.7	89.2	17.90	1 433	1 427
San Jose	2 954.6	3 281	0.0	7 195	49.4	69.5	40.6	82.4	14.42	2 387	594
San Juan Capistrano	62.4	1 802	13.7	95	53.7	67.2	41.5	75.8	12.19	2 157	493
San Leandro	65.1	807	0.0	453	49.9	62.1	43.3	70.0	24.30	2 902	115
San Luis Obispo	36.7	830	31.8	446	52.5	65.2	41.5	78.1	23.46	2 498	335
San Marcos	278.4	4 480	0.0	228	55.2	70.5	43.1	81.3	13.04	1 802	868
San Mateo	133.9	1 456	0.0	712	48.7	68.7	38.9	83.4	19.74	2 563	486
San Pablo	58.6	1 892	0.0	56	49.9	63.2	42.0	71.0	22.20	2 574	199
San Rafael	56.9	1 011	0.0	457	48.8	67.7	40.6	81.6	35.74	2 581	449
San Ramon	56.6	1 224	0.0	107	46.1	71.6	35.5	89.8	14.21	2 909	780
Santa Ana	511.2	1 489	3.7	1 976	57.4	72.6	45.6	82.6	12.27	1 238	1 175
Santa Barbara	115.4	1 291	19.6	1 302	52.0	65.4	40.3	73.9	16.25	2 438	289
Santa Clara	339.9	3 337	46.4	1 123	49.4	69.5	40.6	82.4	14.42	2 387	594
Santa Clarita	45.4	283	0.0	395	54.5	75.6	41.3	90.2	15.87	1 609	1 424
Santa Cruz	55.1	1 024	1.9	1 053	49.9	63.5	38.8	75.7	28.99	2 969	148
Santa Maria	54.9	686	0.0	438	51.1	63.1	38.3	73.3	12.36	2 984	169
Santa Monica	174.3	2 008	0.0	1 866	57.2	65.5	49.6	69.3	13.21	1 819	446
Santa Paula	4.6	159	0.0	137	54.6	67.8	41.2	80.8	17.39	2 039	569
Santa Rosa	440.7	2 871	0.0	1 292	47.4	67.6	37.0	83.8	30.30	2 883	489
Santee	13.2	248	0.0	135	56.6	72.5	44.6	83.4	12.80	1 400	1 110
Saratoga	15.0	509	0.0	67	49.4	69.5	40.6	82.4	14.42	2 387	594
Seaside	11.6	358	0.0	156	51.7	60.0	43.3	68.1	18.72	3 125	55
Simi Valley	200.7	1 721	0.0	617	54.6	67.8	41.2	80.8	17.39	2 039	569
South Gate	123.1	1 246	34.2	408	58.3	74.3	48.9	84.0	14.77	1 154	1 537
South San Francisco	50.5	843	0.0	506	48.7	62.7	41.8	71.6	19.70	3 016	145
Stanton	22.0	581	0.0	30	57.4	72.6	45.6	82.6	12.27	1 238	1 175
Stockton	449.4	1 710	3.2	2 118	45.0	77.7	37.0	94.4	13.95	2 707	1 470
Suisun City	79.7	2 954	0.0	103	NA	NA	NA	NA	NA	NA	NA
Sunnyvale	131.2	1 012	0.0	931	49.4	69.5	40.6	82.4	14.42	2 387	594
Temecula	74.5	1 009	0.0	163	53.9	75.4	40.5	92.1	11.83	1 747	1 339
Temple City	4.0	112	0.0	53	55.7	75.2	41.7	89.2	17.90	1 433	1 427
Thousand Oaks	120.1	979	0.0	548	55.3	66.1	44.2	74.4	14.38	1 992	416
Torrance	138.2	976	4.8	1 619	56.1	69.7	45.3	78.8	13.57	1 568	794
Tracy	163.3	2 400	1.1	434	45.2	76.2	36.7	92.1	11.85	2 659	1 321
Tulare	87.0	1 893	0.0	446	45.4	80.4	37.0	96.0	10.15	2 511	1 762
Turlock	32.8	532	0.0	355	45.6	77.1	37.4	94.2	12.10	2 605	1 401
Tustin	96.9	1 411	8.4	308	54.5	71.6	41.4	83.7	11.81	1 784	973
Union City	91.4	1 307	0.0	320	49.0	66.7	41.1	76.1	13.73	2 578	410
Upland	97.1	1 368	0.0	422	54.3	74.6	40.7	90.4	16.62	1 713	1 273
Vacaville	201.3	2 152	0.0	663	45.2	75.2	36.1	94.1	23.84	2 764	1 154
Vallejo	332.5	2 775	24.6	606	49.9	63.2	42.0	71.0	22.20	2 574	199
Victorville	57.0	805	0.0	372	44.2	79.3	30.0	97.4	5.51	3 127	1 525
Visalia	78.3	808	0.0	583	45.4	80.4	37.0	96.0	10.15	2 511	1 762

1. Based on the population estimated as of July 1 of the year shown.   2. Represents normal values based on the 30-year period, 1961–1990.   3. Average daily minimum.   4. Average daily maximum.

Table D. Cities — Land Area and Population

STATE Place code	City	Land area,[1] 2000 (sq km)	Population, 2003 Total persons	Rank	Per square kilometer	White	Black	Am. Indian, Alaska Native	Asian and Pacific Islander	Other race	Hispanic or Latino[2]	Non-Hispanic White
		1	2	3	4	5	6	7	8	9	10	11
	CALIFORNIA—Cont'd											
06 82996	Vista	48.4	91 813	279	1 897.0	68.3	5.1	1.9	6.1	23.8	38.9	49.9
06 83332	Walnut	23.3	31 089	1 028	1 334.3	30.8	4.6	0.6	58.2	9.7	19.3	18.2
06 83346	Walnut Creek	51.6	65 151	441	1 262.6	86.8	1.5	0.9	11.0	3.2	6.0	80.6
06 83668	Watsonville	16.4	46 159	701	2 814.6	47.3	1.1	2.6	4.6	49.9	75.1	19.4
06 84200	West Covina	41.7	108 251	217	2 595.9	47.5	7.1	1.4	24.8	24.4	45.7	23.0
06 84410	West Hollywood	4.9	36 731	877	7 496.1	89.4	3.7	0.9	5.0	4.6	8.8	81.4
06 84550	Westminster	26.2	89 493	288	3 415.8	49.0	1.4	1.4	40.2	12.1	21.7	36.2
06 84816	West Sacramento	54.2	37 897	842	699.2	70.2	3.3	3.3	10.9	19.7	30.0	54.6
06 85292	Whittier	37.9	85 368	311	2 252.5	67.6	1.6	2.1	4.6	29.5	55.9	37.6
06 86328	Woodland	26.7	50 988	617	1 909.7	71.0	1.7	2.6	5.5	24.4	38.8	53.0
06 86832	Yorba Linda	50.2	62 358	467	1 242.2	84.2	1.5	1.0	12.8	3.9	10.3	74.8
06 86972	Yuba City	24.3	48 998	647	2 016.4	70.7	3.4	3.2	11.2	16.6	24.6	59.0
06 87042	Yucaipa	71.9	46 171	700	642.2	88.3	1.2	2.2	2.1	9.8	18.3	76.7
08 00000	COLORADO	268 627.2	4 550 688	X	16.9	85.2	4.4	1.9	3.0	8.5	17.1	74.5
08 03455	Arvada	84.6	101 972	237	1 205.3	93.1	1.0	1.4	3.0	4.1	9.8	85.5
08 04000	Aurora	369.1	290 418	59	786.8	72.3	15.0	1.8	5.7	9.9	19.8	59.2
08 07850	Boulder	63.1	93 051	274	1 474.7	90.5	1.6	1.0	5.1	4.4	8.2	84.2
08 09280	Broomfield	70.2	42 169	761	600.7	90.8	1.2	1.3	5.1	4.2	9.1	83.7
08 16000	Colorado Springs	481.1	370 448	48	770.0	83.9	7.8	1.9	4.3	6.3	12.0	75.3
08 20000	Denver	397.2	557 478	27	1 403.5	68.3	12.1	2.2	3.6	17.7	31.7	51.9
08 24785	Englewood	17.0	32 762	988	1 927.2	90.0	1.9	2.3	2.5	6.0	13.0	81.0
08 27425	Fort Collins	120.5	125 740	180	1 043.5	92.0	1.4	1.3	3.5	4.6	8.8	85.4
08 31660	Grand Junction	79.8	44 382	725	556.2	93.6	0.9	1.8	1.3	4.6	10.9	85.9
08 32155	Greeley	77.5	83 414	321	1 076.3	82.9	1.2	1.5	2.0	15.4	29.5	66.8
08 43000	Lakewood	107.7	142 474	158	1 322.9	89.5	1.9	2.0	3.5	5.9	14.5	78.9
08 45255	Littleton	35.0	40 599	788	1 160.0	93.6	1.5	1.4	2.3	3.3	8.4	86.8
08 45970	Longmont	56.4	79 556	344	1 410.6	86.7	0.8	1.6	2.3	10.9	19.1	76.8
08 46465	Loveland	63.6	56 436	540	887.4	94.7	0.6	1.4	1.3	4.1	8.6	88.6
08 54330	Northglenn	19.2	32 943	979	1 715.8	85.7	2.0	2.0	4.0	9.6	20.3	72.9
08 62000	Pueblo	116.7	103 648	229	888.2	79.4	2.9	2.7	1.2	17.6	44.1	51.1
08 77290	Thornton	69.6	96 584	259	1 387.7	85.5	1.9	2.0	3.4	10.5	21.3	72.4
08 83835	Westminster	81.6	103 391	230	1 267.0	86.6	1.6	1.5	6.5	6.7	15.2	75.9
08 84440	Wheat Ridge	23.5	31 782	1 009	1 352.4	91.5	1.2	1.9	2.0	6.1	13.5	82.1
09 00000	CONNECTICUT	12 548.0	3 483 372	X	277.6	83.3	10.0	0.7	2.9	5.5	9.4	77.5
09 08000	Bridgeport	41.4	139 664	163	3 373.5	48.5	33.2	1.0	4.1	19.0	31.9	30.9
09 08420	Bristol	68.7	60 722	487	883.9	93.0	3.4	0.7	1.8	2.8	5.3	89.3
09 18430	Danbury	109.1	77 353	361	709.0	79.2	7.6	0.7	6.2	10.3	15.8	68.1
09 37000	Hartford	44.8	124 387	183	2 776.5	30.8	40.6	1.2	2.6	30.6	40.5	17.8
09 46450	Meriden	61.5	58 962	512	958.7	82.7	7.7	0.8	1.7	10.2	21.1	69.9
09 47290	Middletown	105.9	46 918	683	443.0	82.2	13.7	0.8	3.3	3.0	5.3	77.5
09 47500	Milford	58.4	53 869	590	922.4	94.6	2.2	0.4	2.7	1.3	3.3	91.3
09 49880	Naugatuck Borough	42.4	31 700	1 013	747.6	93.4	3.5	0.7	1.9	2.4	4.5	88.9
09 50370	New Britain	34.5	71 572	396	2 074.6	72.5	12.3	0.8	2.7	15.7	26.8	58.8
09 52000	New Haven	48.8	124 512	182	2 551.5	45.9	39.3	1.2	4.7	13.0	21.4	35.6
09 52280	New London	14.3	26 201	1 196	1 832.2	67.6	21.8	2.3	3.2	11.5	19.7	56.1
09 55990	Norwalk	59.1	84 170	317	1 424.2	76.1	16.3	0.6	3.8	6.3	15.6	64.3
09 56200	Norwich	73.4	36 227	886	493.6	85.8	9.0	2.4	2.7	4.3	6.1	80.4
09 68100	Shelton	79.2	39 121	825	494.0	95.6	1.3	0.5	2.2	1.7	3.5	92.1
09 73000	Stamford	97.8	120 107	192	1 228.1	71.9	16.5	0.5	5.6	8.7	16.8	61.2
09 76500	Torrington	103.1	35 756	897	346.8	94.3	2.7	0.6	2.2	1.8	3.3	91.5
09 80000	Waterbury	74.0	108 130	218	1 461.2	69.7	18.0	1.0	2.1	13.2	21.8	58.2
09 82800	West Haven	28.1	53 004	598	1 886.3	76.2	17.4	0.7	3.4	5.2	9.1	69.7
10 00000	DELAWARE	5 059.7	817 491	X	161.6	75.9	20.1	0.8	2.5	2.6	4.8	72.5
10 21200	Dover	58.0	32 808	985	565.7	56.7	38.8	1.2	4.0	2.4	4.1	53.3
10 50670	Newark	23.1	29 821	1 071	1 291.0	88.7	6.5	0.5	4.8	1.3	2.5	85.7
10 77580	Wilmington	28.1	72 051	388	2 564.1	36.6	57.8	0.8	0.9	6.0	9.8	32.1
11 00000	DISTRICT OF COLUMBIA	159.0	563 384	X	3 543.3	32.2	61.3	0.8	3.2	5.0	7.9	27.8
11 50000	Washington	159.0	563 384	26	3 543.3	32.2	61.3	0.8	3.2	5.0	7.9	27.8
12 00000	FLORIDA	139 669.8	17 019 068	X	121.9	79.7	15.5	0.7	2.3	4.4	16.8	65.4
12 00950	Altamonte Springs	23.0	40 942	785	1 780.1	81.6	10.7	0.8	3.8	6.3	15.9	69.5
12 01700	Apopka	62.3	30 703	1 042	492.8	76.0	16.5	0.7	2.4	7.2	18.1	63.0
12 07300	Boca Raton	70.4	78 449	352	1 114.3	92.1	4.3	0.4	2.6	2.6	8.5	84.2
12 07875	Boynton Beach	41.1	64 384	447	1 566.5	71.4	24.6	0.4	2.1	4.2	9.2	64.4
12 07950	Bradenton	31.4	52 498	602	1 671.9	79.4	15.8	0.6	1.1	4.8	11.3	71.6

1. Dry land or land partially or temporarily covered by water.   2. Hispanic or Latino persons may be of any race.

958 **CA(Vista)—FL(Bradenton)**

City	Population characteristics, 2000 (cont'd)										Population			
	Age of population (percent)										Census counts		Percent change	
	Under 5 years	5 to 17 years	18 to 24 years	25 to 34 years	35 to 44 years	45 to 54 years	55 to 64 years	65 to 74 years	75 years and over	Percent female	1990	2000	1990–2000	2000–2003
	12	13	14	15	16	17	18	19	20	21	22	23	24	25
CALIFORNIA—Cont'd														
Vista	8.6	21.1	11.4	16.5	16.2	10.7	5.5	4.8	5.2	50.0	71 861	89 857	25.0	2.2
Walnut	4.9	22.9	9.8	9.8	17.4	19.5	8.9	4.3	2.6	50.8	29 105	30 004	3.1	3.6
Walnut Creek	4.4	13.2	5.2	12.2	14.8	14.5	10.3	9.8	15.5	53.8	60 569	64 296	6.2	1.3
Watsonville	9.3	24.7	11.8	16.4	14.1	9.7	5.4	4.2	4.4	49.8	31 099	44 265	42.3	4.3
West Covina	7.6	20.9	10.0	14.9	15.6	12.7	7.9	5.8	4.5	51.4	96 226	105 080	9.2	3.0
West Hollywood	1.6	4.0	6.3	26.4	22.2	13.8	8.5	8.0	9.0	44.8	36 118	35 716	-1.1	2.8
Westminster	7.3	18.7	8.8	16.8	15.8	12.4	9.2	6.6	4.5	50.0	78 293	88 207	12.7	1.5
West Sacramento	7.7	22.1	9.1	12.5	15.2	12.2	8.5	7.0	5.6	50.6	28 898	31 615	9.4	19.9
Whittier	7.8	20.5	10.0	15.1	15.5	11.7	6.9	5.8	6.7	51.4	77 671	83 680	7.7	2.0
Woodland	8.1	21.7	9.6	14.6	15.7	12.7	7.2	4.9	5.6	51.0	40 230	49 151	22.2	3.7
Yorba Linda	6.0	23.3	7.3	9.6	18.9	18.1	9.2	4.5	3.2	50.9	52 422	58 918	12.4	5.8
Yuba City	8.1	20.9	10.7	14.9	14.5	11.4	7.3	6.0	6.2	51.1	27 385	36 758	34.2	33.3
Yucaipa	6.5	22.0	7.6	11.0	16.2	13.0	8.2	7.0	8.4	51.7	32 819	41 207	25.6	12.0
COLORADO	6.9	18.7	10.0	15.4	17.1	14.3	7.9	5.3	4.4	49.6	3 294 473	4 301 261	30.6	5.8
Arvada	6.4	19.8	7.8	12.4	18.0	15.5	9.4	6.2	4.5	51.0	89 261	102 153	14.4	-0.2
Aurora	8.1	19.5	10.1	17.7	17.0	13.3	6.9	4.1	3.3	50.5	222 103	276 393	24.4	5.1
Boulder	4.1	10.7	25.9	19.5	13.6	12.4	6.0	3.7	4.1	48.4	85 127	94 673	11.2	-1.7
Broomfield	7.8	21.5	7.7	16.2	20.1	13.9	6.2	4.1	2.5	49.8	24 638	38 272	55.3	10.2
Colorado Springs	7.5	19.0	10.3	15.4	17.4	13.5	7.4	5.1	4.5	50.5	280 430	360 890	28.7	2.6
Denver	6.8	15.1	10.7	20.5	15.6	12.8	7.2	5.5	5.7	49.5	467 610	554 636	18.6	0.5
Englewood	5.8	14.5	9.6	18.2	17.7	12.9	7.1	5.6	8.6	50.5	29 396	31 727	7.9	3.3
Fort Collins	5.9	15.6	22.1	16.9	14.6	11.7	5.4	3.8	4.0	49.8	87 491	118 652	35.6	6.0
Grand Junction	5.6	15.6	11.9	11.9	14.4	13.9	8.8	8.3	9.6	51.3	32 893	41 986	27.6	5.7
Greeley	7.5	18.2	19.0	14.3	13.0	11.4	6.5	4.9	5.2	51.0	60 454	76 930	27.3	8.4
Lakewood	6.1	16.2	9.6	15.7	16.8	14.2	9.4	6.5	5.6	50.6	126 475	144 126	14.0	-1.1
Littleton	5.7	17.6	8.2	13.0	17.1	15.1	9.1	7.2	7.0	51.4	33 711	40 340	19.7	0.6
Longmont	7.8	20.1	8.5	15.1	18.0	13.8	7.4	4.6	4.6	50.5	51 976	71 093	36.8	11.9
Loveland	7.0	19.9	7.8	13.6	17.0	14.0	8.1	6.3	6.2	51.0	37 357	50 608	35.5	11.5
Northglenn	7.3	19.4	9.9	16.1	16.8	11.4	8.8	6.7	3.5	50.0	27 195	31 575	16.1	4.3
Pueblo	6.7	18.4	10.3	12.5	14.1	13.0	8.4	8.2	8.4	51.6	98 640	102 121	3.5	1.5
Thornton	8.8	21.2	9.6	18.0	18.0	13.0	5.8	3.2	2.4	50.3	55 031	82 384	49.7	17.2
Westminster	7.3	19.6	9.6	17.6	18.4	14.3	6.8	3.8	2.7	50.0	74 619	100 940	35.3	2.4
Wheat Ridge	6.1	15.1	7.6	13.3	16.0	14.0	9.0	7.8	11.2	52.7	29 419	32 913	11.9	-3.4
CONNECTICUT	6.6	18.2	8.0	13.3	17.1	14.1	9.1	6.8	7.0	51.6	3 287 116	3 405 565	3.6	2.3
Bridgeport	8.2	20.3	11.2	15.9	14.7	11.1	7.3	5.5	5.9	52.3	141 686	139 529	-1.5	0.1
Bristol	6.3	16.9	7.2	15.1	17.4	13.5	8.8	7.3	7.6	51.6	60 640	60 062	-1.0	1.1
Danbury	6.5	15.1	10.2	17.8	17.6	13.4	8.3	5.6	5.4	51.0	65 585	74 848	14.1	3.3
Hartford	8.3	21.8	12.6	15.5	14.3	11.0	7.1	4.9	4.6	52.2	139 739	121 578	-13.0	2.3
Meriden	7.1	18.6	8.1	14.1	16.1	13.5	8.3	6.6	7.5	51.6	59 479	58 244	-2.1	1.2
Middletown	6.5	15.2	8.3	17.6	17.5	13.0	8.5	6.2	7.2	51.7	42 762	43 167	0.9	8.7
Milford	6.0	16.3	5.9	14.0	17.7	15.2	10.0	7.4	7.5	51.6	48 139	52 305	4.7	3.0
Naugatuck Borough	6.9	19.9	7.3	14.9	18.2	13.1	7.9	5.4	6.3	51.4	30 625	30 989	1.2	2.3
New Britain	6.6	17.5	12.5	14.9	14.0	11.5	7.1	6.9	8.8	52.1	75 491	71 538	-5.2	0.0
New Haven	7.1	18.4	16.4	17.8	13.4	10.2	6.6	4.8	5.4	52.1	130 474	123 626	-5.2	0.7
New London	6.7	16.2	17.6	15.0	14.6	11.2	6.7	5.6	6.5	51.1	28 540	25 671	-10.1	2.1
Norwalk	6.9	15.2	7.0	17.7	17.9	13.3	9.3	6.9	5.9	51.2	78 331	82 951	5.9	1.5
Norwich	6.4	17.7	8.9	14.0	16.2	13.4	8.1	7.3	8.1	52.5	37 391	36 117	-3.4	0.3
Shelton	6.2	17.4	5.8	12.2	17.8	15.2	10.5	7.3	7.5	51.6	35 418	38 101	7.6	2.7
Stamford	6.9	15.2	7.4	17.8	17.3	12.9	8.7	7.1	6.8	51.6	108 056	117 083	8.4	2.6
Torrington	6.0	17.1	6.4	13.4	17.6	13.5	8.6	7.5	10.1	51.6	33 687	35 202	4.5	1.6
Waterbury	7.6	18.9	8.9	14.8	15.1	11.7	8.0	6.7	8.2	52.7	108 961	107 271	-1.6	0.8
West Haven	6.2	16.9	9.7	14.9	16.3	13.4	8.4	6.9	7.3	52.3	54 021	52 360	-3.1	1.2
DELAWARE	6.6	18.3	9.6	13.9	16.3	13.3	9.1	7.2	5.8	51.4	666 168	783 600	17.6	4.3
Dover	6.7	16.9	15.7	13.7	14.2	11.5	8.0	6.7	6.7	52.9	27 630	32 135	16.3	2.1
Newark	3.0	9.5	43.6	11.2	8.7	9.0	5.9	4.6	4.5	54.0	26 463	28 547	7.9	4.5
Wilmington	6.8	19.0	9.8	16.4	15.6	12.2	7.6	6.1	6.5	52.3	71 529	72 664	1.6	-0.8
DISTRICT OF COLUMBIA	5.7	14.4	12.7	17.8	15.3	13.2	8.7	6.3	5.9	52.9	606 900	572 059	-5.7	-1.5
Washington	5.7	14.4	12.7	17.8	15.3	13.2	8.7	6.3	5.9	52.9	606 900	572 059	-5.7	-1.5
FLORIDA	5.9	16.9	8.3	13.0	15.5	12.9	9.8	9.1	8.5	51.2	12 938 071	15 982 378	23.5	6.5
Altamonte Springs	5.9	14.5	10.8	20.8	16.3	12.8	8.2	5.3	5.4	51.9	35 167	41 200	17.2	-0.6
Apopka	8.5	19.7	8.6	16.2	17.4	11.9	7.6	5.7	4.4	51.6	13 611	26 642	95.7	15.2
Boca Raton	4.7	14.2	8.1	10.6	15.8	15.2	11.5	9.8	10.0	51.3	61 486	74 764	21.6	4.9
Boynton Beach	5.7	14.1	6.4	13.3	14.8	11.0	8.7	11.0	14.8	53.2	46 284	60 389	30.5	6.6
Bradenton	6.1	15.4	7.7	12.2	13.1	11.5	8.4	10.4	15.0	52.6	43 769	49 504	13.1	6.0

Table D. Cities — Group Quarters, Crime, and Education

City	Households, 2000					Persons in group quarters, 2000				Serious crimes known to police,[2] 2002				Education, 2000			
				Percent			Institutional			Total		Rate[2]		School enrollment[4]		Attainment[5] (percent)	
	Number	Percent change, 1990–2000	Persons per household	Female family householder[1]	One-person	Total	Total	Persons in nursing homes	Non-institutional	Number	Rate[3]	Violent	Property	Public	Private	High school graduate or less	Bachelor's degree or more
	26	27	28	29	30	31	32	33	34	35	36	37	38	39	40	41	42
CALIFORNIA—Cont'd																	
Vista	28 877	13.8	3.03	12.7	20.5	2 266	1 262	378	1 004	3 184	3 418	425	2 993	23 458	2 767	46.3	19.6
Walnut	8 260	5.3	3.63	9.9	5.8	40	24	24	16	396	1 273	170	1 103	9 350	1 745	25.5	41.9
Walnut Creek	30 301	6.9	2.09	6.7	38.0	964	513	513	451	2 779	4 169	203	3 967	10 842	3 005	17.6	54.0
Watsonville	11 381	20.6	3.84	16.4	17.6	553	223	212	330	2 259	4 923	702	4 221	12 731	933	71.0	8.7
West Covina	31 411	4.4	3.32	15.8	14.8	808	195	167	613	4 238	3 890	332	3 558	28 036	5 756	44.4	21.9
West Hollywood	23 120	2.4	1.53	4.4	60.5	230	0	0	230	2 078	5 612	1 118	4 494	3 546	1 251	25.4	46.8
Westminster	26 406	5.3	3.32	12.4	16.9	552	203	203	349	3 114	3 405	379	3 026	23 363	2 987	50.2	18.1
West Sacramento	11 404	3.2	2.75	15.4	27.1	206	112	112	94	2 052	6 261	1 315	4 946	8 962	619	60.2	9.8
Whittier	28 271	2.3	2.88	14.3	22.4	2 348	1 159	374	1 189	2 578	2 972	354	2 618	20 818	5 338	44.6	21.9
Woodland	16 751	18.0	2.89	12.9	21.0	790	451	413	339	1 512	2 967	410	2 557	12 824	1 594	51.9	18.0
Yorba Linda	19 252	14.8	3.05	8.3	12.4	135	6	0	129	1 005	1 645	70	1 575	15 807	3 893	21.5	41.5
Yuba City	13 290	25.6	2.70	14.3	26.5	916	701	449	215	2 296	6 025	472	5 552	9 507	829	52.5	14.4
Yucaipa	15 193	14.1	2.67	11.6	25.3	572	430	329	142	899	2 104	129	1 976	10 920	1 540	46.6	14.3
COLORADO	1 658 238	29.3	2.53	9.6	26.3	102 955	52 741	18 495	50 214	195 936	4 348	352	3 995	1 003 508	162 496	36.3	32.7
Arvada	39 019	19.2	2.60	9.7	23.1	751	143	120	608	4 148	3 876	163	3 713	23 088	4 546	35.0	29.0
Aurora	105 625	18.5	2.60	13.1	27.4	2 089	1 411	812	678	18 019	6 222	631	5 591	64 567	9 245	39.8	24.6
Boulder	39 596	14.2	2.20	6.5	33.7	7 479	1 144	621	6 335	3 743	3 774	233	3 541	32 230	3 918	14.1	66.9
Broomfield	13 842	58.8	2.76	8.2	19.3	7	0	0	7	NA	NA	NA	NA	9 760	1 760	27.9	37.9
Colorado Springs	141 516	27.7	2.50	10.6	27.0	7 153	3 665	1 827	3 488	20 445	5 407	508	4 899	80 673	17 782	31.2	33.6
Denver	239 235	13.4	2.27	10.8	39.3	12 719	6 216	2 621	6 503	32 025	5 511	534	4 977	105 149	25 336	41.1	34.5
Englewood	14 392	8.6	2.15	10.8	37.9	728	622	576	106	2 228	6 703	168	6 534	5 693	1 238	45.7	23.0
Fort Collins	45 882	36.2	2.45	7.9	26.0	6 055	903	538	5 152	5 371	4 320	351	3 970	41 214	3 712	22.4	48.4
Grand Junction	17 865	39.5	2.23	9.4	33.2	2 180	823	224	1 357	2 647	6 017	350	5 667	9 207	1 275	41.8	26.2
Greeley	27 647	22.1	2.63	10.8	25.6	4 221	1 177	658	3 044	5 275	6 545	391	6 154	24 214	2 152	43.4	26.4
Lakewood	60 531	17.2	2.32	10.8	30.7	3 800	2 721	1 357	1 079	8 939	5 920	288	5 632	28 800	6 227	35.3	32.8
Littleton	17 313	24.5	2.29	9.2	33.3	611	541	332	70	1 551	3 670	151	3 518	8 446	1 660	29.0	40.1
Longmont	26 667	36.3	2.64	10.1	23.7	615	420	414	195	874	1 173	94	1 079	16 196	2 715	37.4	31.3
Loveland	19 741	40.5	2.55	9.8	23.4	361	295	278	66	2 169	4 091	224	3 866	11 555	2 074	37.5	27.5
Northglenn	11 610	18.1	2.71	11.8	23.0	163	163	163	0	1 964	5 937	514	5 423	7 103	878	45.9	19.4
Pueblo	40 307	5.2	2.44	15.1	30.0	3 894	2 942	1 115	952	6 145	5 743	678	5 066	24 713	2 112	52.5	16.8
Thornton	28 882	51.6	2.83	11.5	18.7	550	490	430	60	5 502	6 374	514	5 860	20 327	2 734	45.5	19.9
Westminster	38 343	37.8	2.62	9.6	23.7	487	380	290	107	NA	NA	NA	NA	23 919	4 092	36.1	31.3
Wheat Ridge	14 559	10.8	2.20	11.4	35.4	844	505	477	339	2 047	5 936	502	5 434	6 099	1 048	44.5	25.1
CONNECTICUT	1 301 670	5.8	2.53	12.1	26.4	107 939	55 256	32 223	52 683	103 719	2 997	311	2 686	731 418	179 451	44.5	31.4
Bridgeport	50 307	-3.9	2.70	24.0	29.0	3 596	1 919	942	1 677	8 551	6 031	1 196	4 836	32 459	8 507	66.3	12.2
Bristol	24 886	3.9	2.38	11.5	28.9	771	588	588	183	1 883	3 085	416	2 669	11 674	2 334	57.1	16.2
Danbury	27 183	12.8	2.64	10.5	26.2	3 128	2 010	684	1 118	2 198	2 890	201	2 689	14 611	3 300	51.7	27.1
Hartford	44 986	-12.6	2.58	29.6	33.2	5 355	2 290	920	3 065	10 870	8 799	1 252	7 547	33 754	4 212	69.6	12.4
Meriden	22 951	-1.2	2.49	15.2	28.9	1 141	875	815	266	2 622	4 430	225	4 206	12 698	2 245	57.4	16.4
Middletown	18 554	10.3	2.23	11.6	35.0	1 874	1 427	557	447	1 108	2 526	119	2 407	7 675	2 695	46.2	30.4
Milford	20 900	10.9	2.48	9.7	26.6	537	420	420	117	2 027	3 814	145	3 669	9 682	2 592	42.4	29.3
Naugatuck Borough	11 829	4.4	2.60	12.8	24.9	220	194	194	26	603	1 915	114	1 801	7 209	1 385	52.6	19.0
New Britain	28 558	-5.3	2.40	17.7	33.1	3 071	897	897	2 174	3 481	4 789	440	4 348	17 643	2 790	63.9	16.6
New Haven	47 094	-3.9	2.40	22.9	36.1	10 599	2 662	1 117	7 937	9 458	7 529	1 373	6 156	27 972	15 403	54.6	27.1
New London	10 181	-5.0	2.26	17.8	37.8	2 706	247	247	2 459	1 196	4 585	567	4 018	5 628	2 535	54.8	19.6
Norwalk	32 711	7.0	2.51	12.2	28.2	865	527	527	338	2 974	3 528	401	3 127	15 108	4 231	42.3	34.2
Norwich	15 091	0.5	2.34	15.0	32.0	749	388	379	361	1 257	3 425	411	3 014	7 638	1 276	55.0	18.9
Shelton	14 190	13.9	2.65	8.5	21.8	561	541	351	20	439	1 134	52	1 082	7 195	2 221	41.9	29.9
Stamford	45 399	8.2	2.54	11.5	28.7	1 753	891	818	862	2 398	2 016	235	1 780	21 290	5 809	42.3	39.6
Torrington	14 743	6.2	2.33	10.3	32.1	834	653	653	181	1 117	3 123	417	2 706	7 059	903	59.0	15.7
Waterbury	42 622	-1.3	2.46	19.1	31.4	2 214	1 562	1 362	652	6 524	5 985	535	5 450	22 692	5 185	62.6	13.9
West Haven	21 090	-0.9	2.42	15.6	31.0	1 259	449	345	810	1 989	3 738	222	3 517	10 751	3 144	55.7	19.1
DELAWARE	298 736	20.7	2.54	13.1	25.0	24 583	11 510	4 852	13 073	31 803	3 939	599	3 340	164 193	45 786	48.8	25.0
Dover	12 340	24.6	2.35	16.7	31.4	3 118	842	699	2 276	1 947	5 880	580	5 301	8 372	1 844	40.6	28.8
Newark	8 989	20.4	2.43	7.2	27.2	6 727	141	141	6 586	1 415	4 811	666	4 144	12 713	2 549	24.7	51.3
Wilmington	28 617	0.2	2.39	23.8	37.1	4 228	2 785	553	1 443	5 068	6 769	1 521	5 248	16 055	3 275	55.7	21.4
DISTRICT OF COLUMBIA	248 338	-0.5	2.16	18.9	43.8	35 562	7 964	3 759	27 598	45 799	8 022	1 633	6 389	105 998	51 477	42.8	39.1
Washington	248 338	-0.5	2.16	18.9	43.8	35 562	7 964	3 759	27 598	45 799	8 022	1 633	6 389	105 998	51 477	42.8	39.1
FLORIDA	6 337 929	23.4	2.46	12.0	26.6	388 945	248 350	88 828	140 595	905 957	5 421	770	4 650	3 257 226	676 053	48.9	22.3
Altamonte Springs	18 821	22.0	2.17	12.0	36.1	428	419	405	9	2 084	4 837	441	4 396	7 501	2 235	31.5	31.2
Apopka	9 562	87.1	2.76	14.4	18.6	217	135	135	82	2 061	7 398	962	6 436	5 531	1 233	43.5	22.0
Boca Raton	31 848	21.1	2.26	7.1	29.5	2 806	548	536	2 258	2 890	3 696	262	3 434	11 549	7 172	27.1	44.2
Boynton Beach	26 210	29.2	2.26	10.9	33.0	1 091	912	897	179	5 277	8 356	944	7 413	10 386	1 957	49.2	20.7
Bradenton	21 379	13.3	2.24	12.1	34.1	1 586	1 415	990	171	3 758	7 259	885	6 375	9 284	1 226	51.6	20.5

1. No spouse present. 2. Data for serious crimes have not been adjusted for underreporting. This may affect comparability between geographic areas and over time. 3. Per 100,000 population estimated by the FBI. 4. All persons 3 years old and over enrolled in nursery school through college. 5. Persons 25 years old and over.

Table D. Cities — **Income, Poverty, and Housing**

City	Money income, 1999 — Per capita income[1] (dollars)	Households — Median income — Dollars	Households — Median income — Percent change, 1989–1999 (constant 1999 dollars)	Percent with income of $100,000 or more	Percent below poverty — Persons — Total	Percent below poverty — Persons — Percent change in rate, 1989–1999	Percent below poverty — Families — Total	Housing units, 2000 — Total	Percent change, 1990–2000	Vacant units — Vacant units for sale or rent[2]	Vacant units — For seasonal use (percent)	Vacant units — Home owner vacancy rate	Vacant units — Renter vacancy rate
	43	44	45	46	47	48	49	50	51	52	53	54	55
CALIFORNIA—Cont'd													
Vista	18 027	42 594	-2.6	10.3	14.2	21.4	10.0	29 814	8.7	937	0.2	1.0	3.3
Walnut	25 196	81 015	-6.3	34.7	6.5	58.5	5.8	8 395	3.8	135	0.3	0.7	2.2
Walnut Creek	39 875	63 238	3.4	27.0	3.7	-2.6	1.7	31 425	4.9	1 124	0.6	1.1	2.8
Watsonville	13 205	37 617	0.1	7.9	19.1	24.8	15.4	11 695	18.0	314	0.3	0.6	2.9
West Covina	19 342	53 002	-7.1	15.2	9.0	16.9	6.8	32 058	3.0	647	0.1	0.7	2.2
West Hollywood	38 302	38 914	-1.2	13.6	11.5	0.9	7.3	24 110	1.2	990	0.8	1.7	2.4
Westminster	18 218	49 450	-11.0	15.4	13.5	18.4	10.7	26 940	4.2	534	0.1	0.7	2.3
West Sacramento	15 245	31 718	1.4	5.4	22.3	20.5	17.2	12 133	4.1	729	0.3	1.3	6.6
Whittier	21 409	49 256	-3.6	16.2	10.5	34.6	7.8	28 977	0.8	706	0.2	0.9	2.1
Woodland	18 042	44 449	4.5	9.2	11.9	24.0	9.2	17 120	15.5	369	0.2	0.7	2.1
Yorba Linda	36 173	89 593	-1.8	43.4	3.0	57.9	2.5	19 567	12.8	315	0.2	0.6	1.9
Yuba City	15 928	32 858	4.1	6.3	18.1	-2.7	14.5	13 912	25.7	622	0.3	1.4	4.7
Yucaipa	18 949	39 144	7.2	11.2	11.2	47.4	8.8	16 112	12.9	919	0.4	2.0	6.6
COLORADO	24 049	47 203	16.6	14.2	9.3	-20.5	6.2	1 808 037	22.4	149 799	4.0	1.4	5.5
Arvada	24 679	55 541	6.0	16.1	5.2	-17.5	3.5	39 733	15.0	714	0.1	0.6	2.5
Aurora	21 095	46 507	4.2	9.7	8.9	20.3	6.8	109 260	9.4	3 635	0.2	1.1	3.5
Boulder	27 262	44 748	13.3	17.9	17.4	-8.4	6.4	40 726	12.3	1 130	0.6	0.6	2.2
Broomfield	26 488	63 903	21.7	20.7	4.2	-17.6	2.1	14 322	57.4	480	0.4	1.0	6.3
Colorado Springs	22 496	45 081	16.0	11.6	8.7	-20.2	6.1	148 690	19.5	7 174	0.5	1.2	6.2
Denver	24 101	39 500	17.1	11.5	14.3	-16.4	10.6	251 435	4.9	12 200	0.6	1.7	4.5
Englewood	20 904	38 943	14.0	6.3	8.2	-24.8	4.9	14 916	0.1	524	0.1	0.7	4.3
Fort Collins	22 133	44 459	23.4	12.4	14.0	-17.6	5.5	47 755	35.1	1 873	0.4	1.4	4.1
Grand Junction	19 692	33 152	29.6	7.8	11.9	-44.9	7.5	18 784	37.1	919	0.4	1.7	5.9
Greeley	17 775	36 414	15.5	7.9	16.9	-13.3	10.1	28 972	20.8	1 325	0.2	1.9	4.8
Lakewood	25 575	48 109	5.1	12.5	7.1	-6.6	4.8	62 422	12.1	1 891	0.3	0.7	3.6
Littleton	28 681	50 583	10.7	18.6	6.0	-17.8	3.9	18 084	22.4	771	0.3	0.7	7.2
Longmont	23 409	51 174	17.1	14.5	7.8	0.0	5.9	27 394	33.8	727	0.3	1.1	2.6
Loveland	21 889	47 119	14.8	10.6	5.7	-27.8	4.0	20 299	38.0	558	0.3	1.0	2.8
Northglenn	20 253	48 276	3.5	7.9	5.4	1.9	3.8	12 051	15.4	441	0.2	0.7	6.8
Pueblo	16 026	29 650	7.6	4.8	17.8	-17.6	13.9	43 121	5.5	2 814	0.2	1.7	8.5
Thornton	21 471	54 445	18.7	11.7	5.2	-36.6	4.0	29 573	41.0	691	0.1	0.9	4.7
Westminster	25 482	56 323	14.2	15.7	4.7	-28.8	3.1	39 318	31.6	975	0.3	0.5	4.3
Wheat Ridge	22 636	38 983	2.4	8.5	8.9	6.0	5.9	14 931	5.7	372	0.3	0.6	2.4
CONNECTICUT	28 766	53 935	-3.8	20.2	7.9	16.2	5.6	1 385 975	4.9	84 305	1.7	1.1	5.6
Bridgeport	16 306	34 658	-10.1	7.3	18.4	7.6	16.2	54 367	-5.0	4 060	0.2	1.9	5.6
Bristol	23 362	47 422	-7.7	10.8	6.6	50.0	4.8	26 125	4.5	1 239	0.3	1.1	5.2
Danbury	24 500	53 664	-8.9	17.7	8.0	37.9	5.9	28 519	9.9	1 336	1.3	1.1	3.4
Hartford	13 428	24 820	-16.6	4.0	30.6	11.3	28.2	50 644	-9.7	5 658	0.3	2.0	9.2
Meriden	20 597	43 237	-11.1	9.8	11.0	50.7	8.5	24 631	-0.8	1 680	0.2	1.7	7.3
Middletown	25 720	47 162	-6.8	15.6	7.5	7.1	4.3	19 697	8.8	1 143	0.5	1.5	5.8
Milford	28 882	61 183	3.2	19.5	3.7	0.0	2.4	21 962	9.0	1 062	1.6	0.7	6.1
Naugatuck Borough	22 757	51 247	-4.4	11.4	6.4	52.4	4.9	12 341	3.4	512	0.2	0.9	5.0
New Britain	18 404	34 185	-15.5	6.2	16.4	28.1	13.3	31 164	-3.6	2 606	0.2	1.7	6.1
New Haven	16 393	29 604	-14.6	6.9	24.4	14.6	20.5	52 941	-2.1	5 847	0.3	3.7	7.1
New London	18 437	33 809	-4.5	5.8	15.8	4.6	13.4	11 560	-3.4	1 379	1.1	2.5	9.8
Norwalk	31 781	59 839	-7.5	24.7	7.2	38.5	5.0	33 753	4.7	1 042	0.6	0.6	2.9
Norwich	20 742	39 181	-0.7	8.3	11.5	-3.4	8.3	16 600	0.8	1 509	1.3	2.3	7.0
Shelton	29 893	67 292	0.2	26.2	3.2	28.0	2.5	14 707	13.3	517	0.7	0.9	5.8
Stamford	34 987	60 556	-9.5	27.8	7.9	25.4	5.4	47 317	6.9	1 918	1.0	0.6	3.0
Torrington	21 406	41 841	-11.6	8.7	7.4	42.3	4.5	16 147	6.5	1 404	2.7	1.9	7.0
Waterbury	17 701	34 285	-16.4	7.1	16.0	32.2	12.7	46 827	-0.8	4 205	0.3	2.2	7.6
West Haven	21 121	42 393	-11.7	9.9	8.8	44.3	6.6	22 336	-1.5	1 246	0.3	1.5	6.6
DELAWARE	23 305	47 381	1.1	14.0	9.2	5.7	6.5	343 072	18.3	44 336	7.6	1.5	8.2
Dover	19 445	38 669	-8.1	8.9	13.8	10.4	11.5	13 195	25.8	855	0.4	2.0	6.7
Newark	20 376	48 758	-5.9	18.5	20.1	15.5	4.1	9 294	18.2	305	0.2	1.1	4.0
Wilmington	20 236	35 116	-1.0	9.7	21.3	17.7	16.8	32 138	2.9	3 521	0.2	2.6	8.4
DISTRICT OF COLUMBIA	28 659	40 127	-2.8	16.4	20.2	19.5	16.7	274 845	-1.3	26 507	0.8	2.9	5.9
Washington	28 659	40 127	-2.8	16.4	20.2	19.5	16.7	274 845	-1.3	26 507	0.8	2.9	5.9
FLORIDA	21 557	38 819	5.1	10.4	12.5	-1.6	9.0	7 302 947	19.7	965 018	6.6	2.2	9.3
Altamonte Springs	23 216	41 578	-1.9	8.2	7.4	-3.9	5.6	19 992	16.6	1 171	1.0	1.5	5.7
Apopka	19 189	43 651	6.0	10.2	9.5	-17.4	7.1	10 091	76.7	529	1.3	1.8	4.5
Boca Raton	45 628	60 248	6.0	30.7	6.7	21.8	4.1	37 547	13.6	5 699	11.2	1.4	7.0
Boynton Beach	22 573	39 845	2.9	8.2	10.2	6.3	7.4	30 643	20.0	4 433	9.6	2.1	7.8
Bradenton	20 133	34 902	-0.1	6.0	13.6	6.3	9.7	24 887	12.5	3 508	7.5	2.1	9.4

1. Based on population enumerated as of April 1, 2000.   2. Includes units rented or sold but not occupied.

City	Housing units, 2000 (cont'd)					Civilian labor force, 2003				Civilian employment,[2] 2000			Disability, 2000
		Occupied units						Unemployment			Percent		
	Total	Percent owner occupied	Percent renter occupied	Average size owner occupied	Average size renter occupied	Total	Percent change, 2002–2003	Total	Rate[1]	Total	Management, professional, and related occupations	Production, transportation, and material moving occupations	Employment disabled persons[3] (percent)
	56	57	58	59	60	61	62	63	64	65	66	67	68
CALIFORNIA—Cont'd													
Vista	28 877	54.2	45.8	2.89	3.20	41 761	1.7	2 029	4.9	38 226	27.9	14.8	14.4
Walnut	8 260	88.9	11.1	3.62	3.73	16 444	-0.1	672	4.1	14 009	48.0	8.4	9.4
Walnut Creek	30 301	68.3	31.7	2.16	1.94	38 781	-0.5	1 412	3.6	30 386	55.5	3.6	7.2
Watsonville	11 381	48.1	51.9	3.55	4.11	17 133	-1.1	2 958	17.3	17 285	16.8	18.6	15.8
West Covina	31 411	66.5	33.5	3.38	3.19	53 056	-0.1	2 514	4.7	44 969	31.7	14.6	12.7
West Hollywood	23 120	21.6	78.4	1.55	1.53	25 034	0.0	1 684	6.7	22 084	54.1	4.3	12.3
Westminster	26 406	60.2	39.8	3.21	3.48	48 935	1.8	2 217	4.5	38 093	29.7	19.8	15.6
West Sacramento	11 404	54.5	45.5	2.60	2.94	17 364	3.4	1 188	6.8	11 893	20.8	16.2	15.7
Whittier	28 271	57.8	42.2	2.94	2.80	41 209	-0.1	1 906	4.6	36 470	33.7	14.7	12.9
Woodland	16 751	58.5	41.5	2.93	2.82	28 100	3.3	1 619	5.8	21 682	27.2	16.2	13.5
Yorba Linda	19 252	84.7	15.3	3.11	2.71	34 880	2.0	745	2.1	30 133	49.9	6.0	5.9
Yuba City	13 290	47.4	52.6	2.76	2.64	16 086	0.7	2 519	15.7	14 174	26.7	15.3	14.5
Yucaipa	15 193	74.2	25.8	2.64	2.79	18 495	3.0	726	3.9	17 264	29.5	13.5	13.2
COLORADO	1 658 238	67.3	32.7	2.64	2.30	2 477 874	1.7	149 692	6.0	2 205 194	37.4	10.5	9.9
Arvada	39 019	75.7	24.3	2.70	2.30	63 510	-3.4	4 101	6.5	54 614	35.8	10.8	8.4
Aurora	105 625	63.9	36.1	2.65	2.50	168 276	3.6	11 162	6.6	143 506	30.7	12.0	11.8
Boulder	39 596	49.5	50.5	2.30	2.11	72 699	-4.4	4 445	6.1	54 894	53.6	5.2	5.5
Broomfield	13 842	76.8	23.2	2.90	2.32	23 683	16.7	1 451	6.1	20 612	44.2	10.9	7.5
Colorado Springs	141 516	60.8	39.2	2.65	2.27	210 049	1.4	13 468	6.4	176 527	38.2	10.3	9.0
Denver	239 235	52.5	47.5	2.41	2.10	302 697	3.2	22 261	7.4	284 340	37.9	10.4	13.7
Englewood	14 392	52.2	47.8	2.32	1.98	21 638	3.3	1 513	7.0	17 354	30.1	11.8	14.2
Fort Collins	45 882	57.0	43.0	2.61	2.24	74 904	1.2	4 550	6.1	65 670	42.9	9.7	5.5
Grand Junction	17 865	62.6	37.4	2.35	2.03	20 061	4.0	1 394	6.9	19 892	32.4	11.5	11.4
Greeley	27 647	58.4	41.6	2.76	2.45	47 283	3.3	3 184	6.7	36 350	30.7	14.8	11.5
Lakewood	60 531	60.9	39.1	2.41	2.17	92 051	-3.7	5 513	6.0	79 034	38.9	9.2	10.1
Littleton	17 313	62.1	37.9	2.49	1.97	24 825	3.2	1 612	6.5	21 772	41.3	7.8	9.1
Longmont	26 667	65.6	34.4	2.72	2.50	40 605	-4.4	2 938	7.2	37 355	37.5	12.7	9.2
Loveland	19 741	69.4	30.6	2.62	2.37	29 457	1.1	1 600	5.4	26 164	33.0	14.6	8.8
Northglenn	11 610	67.4	32.6	2.88	2.34	22 630	6.6	1 323	5.8	16 584	28.8	15.3	8.8
Pueblo	40 307	65.6	34.4	2.49	2.34	49 895	2.2	3 770	7.6	41 160	26.6	13.0	13.9
Thornton	28 882	77.7	22.3	2.91	2.57	44 186	6.6	2 651	6.0	44 181	28.6	15.2	10.9
Westminster	38 343	69.7	30.3	2.75	2.31	59 393	2.0	2 905	4.9	57 705	37.5	11.4	8.4
Wheat Ridge	14 559	54.6	45.4	2.29	2.10	19 401	-3.7	1 217	6.3	16 513	31.6	11.9	12.3
CONNECTICUT	1 301 670	66.8	33.2	2.67	2.25	1 803 108	0.6	99 147	5.5	1 664 440	39.1	12.0	11.0
Bridgeport	50 307	43.2	56.8	2.74	2.67	63 754	2.2	6 370	10.0	56 916	21.8	19.2	17.3
Bristol	24 886	61.9	38.1	2.60	2.03	31 947	0.1	2 065	6.5	31 219	28.6	18.8	15.3
Danbury	27 183	58.3	41.7	2.67	2.59	40 335	1.1	1 782	4.4	40 070	32.5	14.2	12.0
Hartford	44 986	24.6	75.4	2.76	2.52	51 792	1.8	5 971	11.5	42 402	21.6	16.9	18.4
Meriden	22 951	59.9	40.1	2.59	2.34	31 445	0.6	2 208	7.0	28 103	28.9	16.9	12.5
Middletown	18 554	51.3	48.7	2.49	1.95	23 768	0.6	1 439	6.1	22 559	43.3	10.7	10.1
Milford	20 900	77.3	22.7	2.61	2.02	28 122	0.7	1 516	5.4	28 158	39.5	11.9	10.7
Naugatuck Borough	11 829	66.5	33.5	2.79	2.22	17 074	1.3	1 226	7.2	15 591	30.3	19.0	12.2
New Britain	28 558	42.7	57.3	2.50	2.32	34 436	0.7	2 993	8.7	31 794	25.5	21.8	15.8
New Haven	47 094	29.6	70.4	2.60	2.32	58 493	0.7	4 418	7.6	49 358	37.3	14.2	13.8
New London	10 181	37.9	62.1	2.39	2.17	13 805	2.5	913	6.6	11 469	27.5	11.5	15.9
Norwalk	32 711	62.0	38.0	2.61	2.35	48 841	0.4	2 165	4.4	44 731	40.8	9.1	11.8
Norwich	15 091	52.5	47.5	2.51	2.16	20 369	3.0	1 309	6.4	17 577	27.6	10.8	16.1
Shelton	14 190	81.8	18.2	2.76	2.15	20 652	1.0	1 202	5.8	20 372	41.0	10.9	7.9
Stamford	45 399	56.7	43.3	2.65	2.39	66 538	0.1	2 765	4.2	60 947	42.0	8.4	14.8
Torrington	14 743	64.6	35.4	2.50	2.02	19 252	1.1	1 256	6.5	17 530	25.4	19.8	12.7
Waterbury	42 622	47.6	52.4	2.58	2.36	53 591	0.9	4 907	9.2	45 484	25.1	21.4	16.4
West Haven	21 090	55.2	44.8	2.62	2.18	28 940	0.0	1 744	6.0	26 725	27.5	15.5	13.0
DELAWARE	298 736	72.3	27.7	2.61	2.37	417 256	-0.6	18 290	4.4	376 811	35.3	12.5	11.2
Dover	12 340	52.3	47.7	2.50	2.19	18 883	1.8	792	4.2	14 174	35.4	10.3	11.0
Newark	8 989	54.5	45.5	2.53	2.31	14 343	-2.1	395	2.8	14 362	44.7	6.9	5.4
Wilmington	28 617	50.1	49.9	2.45	2.33	33 936	-2.6	1 771	5.2	30 412	33.0	12.1	14.5
DISTRICT OF COLUMBIA	248 338	40.8	59.2	2.31	2.06	302 286	-0.3	21 096	7.0	263 108	51.1	5.2	13.5
Washington	248 338	40.8	59.2	2.31	2.06	302 286	-0.3	21 096	7.0	263 108	51.1	5.2	13.5
FLORIDA	6 337 929	70.1	29.9	2.49	2.39	8 164 237	0.9	420 433	5.1	6 995 047	31.5	10.8	14.2
Altamonte Springs	18 821	41.8	58.2	2.38	2.02	31 404	1.4	1 507	4.8	24 292	38.9	7.6	12.5
Apopka	9 562	75.8	24.2	2.75	2.81	10 795	1.3	516	4.8	13 176	33.8	11.3	14.8
Boca Raton	31 848	75.6	24.4	2.33	2.04	44 898	0.6	1 601	3.6	35 076	45.6	4.8	10.1
Boynton Beach	26 210	72.8	27.2	2.27	2.24	29 600	0.5	1 685	5.7	26 671	29.6	8.3	15.4
Bradenton	21 379	61.7	38.3	2.25	2.22	28 867	2.3	1 235	4.3	20 924	28.0	13.7	17.4

1. Percent of civilian labor force.   2. Persons 16 years old and over.   3. Persons 16 to 64 years old.

Table D. Cities — **Construction, Wholesale Trade, and Retail Trade**

City	Value of residential construction authorized by building permits, 2003			Wholesale trade, 1997				Retail trade,[1] 1997			
	New construction ($1,000)	Number of housing units	Percent single family	Number of establish-ments	Number of employees	Sales (mil dol)	Annual payroll (mil dol)	Number of establish-ments	Number of employees	Sales (mil dol)	Annual payroll (mil dol)
	69	70	71	72	73	74	75	76	77	78	79
CALIFORNIA—Cont'd											
Vista	50 035	395	20.5	110	1 592	426.5	48.7	233	3 212	665.6	61.5
Walnut	11 649	117	7.7	247	1 212	1 278.7	33.7	60	553	91.4	9.9
Walnut Creek	15 839	76	68.4	121	1 177	2 402.7	64.5	339	5 859	1 240.9	132.8
Watsonville	91 035	508	71.7	57	1 641	750.6	57.2	142	1 551	302.1	31.5
West Covina	22 782	153	43.8	59	199	114.2	6.0	297	5 218	972.8	88.3
West Hollywood	16 320	113	38.9	135	862	457.9	34.3	324	2 794	571.2	69.2
Westminster	20 945	170	28.8	86	585	202.6	15.4	444	5 042	1 051.9	93.0
West Sacramento	130 687	902	67.4	154	4 361	3 109.2	145.5	101	1 098	215.7	23.0
Whittier	1 375	3	100.0	90	696	660.3	29.0	247	3 181	618.1	64.6
Woodland	50 075	450	61.6	74	2 953	1 561.0	92.8	165	2 372	406.5	43.6
Yorba Linda	121 520	360	72.2	157	4 351	1 700.6	65.0	116	1 726	371.3	34.1
Yuba City	140 541	900	83.3	48	390	181.5	14.1	231	3 273	528.8	54.7
Yucaipa	72 520	518	100.0	23	208	72.1	4.7	79	646	108.6	10.7
COLORADO	6 258 256	39 569	85.5	7 383	88 364	60 310.4	3 282.0	18 299	225 647	40 536.0	4 163.3
Arvada	71 159	385	83.9	122	1 075	282.1	30.2	294	4 106	660.1	70.2
Aurora	325 762	2 150	61.4	289	4 800	4 326.8	189.1	842	13 348	2 335.9	230.7
Boulder	23 409	163	53.4	251	2 548	1 598.3	100.1	699	9 587	1 544.9	169.8
Broomfield	103 841	637	63.6	64	527	202.6	22.4	90	1 384	290.4	27.9
Colorado Springs	NA	NA	NA	417	5 911	1 205.2	200.8	1 644	25 565	4 669.3	466.5
Denver	339 366	3 036	69.9	1 681	26 604	16 177.1	972.8	2 410	30 080	5 600.9	628.0
Englewood	492	3	100.0	220	3 278	4 291.7	137.6	275	3 427	941.1	82.5
Fort Collins	204 373	1 384	69.4	110	D	D	D	603	8 644	1 437.0	141.5
Grand Junction	NA	NA	NA	141	1 123	390.4	32.7	467	5 179	965.9	94.4
Greeley	116 646	853	93.0	107	1 098	442.2	33.9	297	4 511	764.8	75.3
Lakewood	76 880	387	71.6	221	1 326	957.5	53.3	654	9 359	1 801.6	179.4
Littleton	16 284	94	64.9	114	1 093	875.4	43.9	360	7 383	1 599.0	145.1
Longmont	124 577	857	90.0	79	1 519	1 751.6	81.3	300	4 269	776.4	76.8
Loveland	118 208	1 004	77.9	62	611	186.4	18.0	264	3 101	613.5	52.3
Northglenn	1 427	16	100.0	26	145	59.7	4.1	106	1 276	268.0	27.2
Pueblo	NA	NA	NA	90	890	360.3	24.0	532	6 586	1 117.2	114.5
Thornton	269 270	1 850	77.6	47	438	557.6	18.8	158	4 013	729.2	80.0
Westminster	110 269	586	82.6	94	688	272.5	26.9	372	6 483	1 093.4	104.6
Wheat Ridge	7 426	58	63.8	66	648	268.3	18.1	198	2 747	589.2	57.6
CONNECTICUT	1 664 859	10 435	78.4	5 283	77 716	75 821.6	3 595.3	14 574	186 935	34 938.9	3 634.3
Bridgeport	5 791	86	86.0	131	1 665	601.2	63.7	342	3 755	665.8	81.6
Bristol	18 194	140	100.0	58	839	251.9	32.1	215	2 741	556.1	50.7
Danbury	21 301	206	96.6	125	2 150	904.0	69.9	497	8 262	1 715.5	166.6
Hartford	23 077	335	26.0	171	4 575	3 038.6	214.5	419	3 644	764.8	87.0
Meriden	7 897	97	97.9	67	745	220.4	25.1	256	3 678	570.1	59.6
Middletown	7 284	203	43.8	51	672	220.3	22.8	148	2 020	377.6	40.0
Milford	27 675	284	25.4	153	1 925	776.7	80.7	342	5 645	1 133.3	106.0
Naugatuck Borough	8 476	66	100.0	22	372	152.2	13.0	77	1 139	186.9	18.6
New Britain	2 476	34	82.4	41	575	279.0	24.0	203	2 068	435.7	42.8
New Haven	6 862	77	61.0	130	1 399	737.6	50.9	390	3 377	506.2	64.4
New London	2 773	52	100.0	22	223	63.8	8.3	146	1 799	428.6	43.8
Norwalk	22 996	130	43.1	210	4 143	3 682.2	338.1	411	7 133	1 792.5	180.7
Norwich	15 829	247	49.4	29	480	175.8	15.2	181	2 749	468.5	47.8
Shelton	13 992	85	100.0	47	1 111	921.7	54.0	94	1 626	381.2	30.7
Stamford	37 906	96	93.8	354	5 992	22 164.2	430.8	545	6 973	1 798.1	186.7
Torrington	11 289	111	100.0	52	603	209.8	23.9	201	2 531	454.5	43.5
Waterbury	3 707	138	35.5	113	1 462	494.9	51.7	481	5 527	982.0	96.4
West Haven	1 576	26	100.0	57	1 000	490.0	41.5	140	1 479	277.2	28.4
DELAWARE	790 664	7 760	87.0	906	13 509	12 585.5	619.5	3 736	47 116	8 237.0	798.7
Dover	31 944	518	25.9	40	D	D	D	310	5 026	802.9	77.2
Newark	1 600	23	39.1	52	D	D	D	204	3 796	760.8	70.1
Wilmington	5 026	134	50.7	106	1 736	1 158.1	70.1	354	3 674	708.5	71.7
DISTRICT OF COLUMBIA	95 696	1 427	10.7	348	5 008	3 918.6	223.0	2 075	19 608	2 788.8	351.5
Washington	95 696	1 427	10.7	348	5 008	3 918.6	223.0	2 075	19 608	2 788.8	351.5
FLORIDA	28 351 596	213 567	73.4	31 214	296 139	187 079.9	9 678.2	66 643	841 814	151 191.2	14 169.5
Altamonte Springs	7 323	103	4.9	152	1 137	897.2	51.0	407	6 342	896.6	94.8
Apopka	59 492	598	99.0	47	481	132.3	13.5	105	1 664	261.1	23.2
Boca Raton	57 441	89	100.0	525	6 440	4 325.7	322.1	744	9 092	1 438.2	163.8
Boynton Beach	31 368	333	94.3	92	498	171.1	14.4	219	2 757	405.0	42.2
Bradenton	6 980	49	91.8	37	219	98.3	6.5	241	3 294	519.6	50.1

1. Establishments with payroll.

Table D. Cities — Real Estate, Professional Services, and Manufacturing

City	Real estate and rental and leasing, 1997				Professional, scientific, and technical services,[1] 1997				Manufacturing, 1997			
	Number of establishments	Number of employees	Receipts (mil dol)	Annual payroll (mil dol)	Number of establishments	Number of employees	Receipts (mil dol)	Annual payroll (mil dol)	Number of establishments	Number of employees	Receipts (mil dol)	Annual payroll (mil dol)
	80	81	82	83	84	85	86	87	88	89	90	91
CALIFORNIA—Cont'd												
Vista	105	590	63.3	9.0	143	668	59.5	19.1	153	5 607	743.9	148.9
Walnut	18	106	15.1	3.2	54	347	20.8	6.7	48	665	146.7	23.0
Walnut Creek	230	1 342	233.6	42.0	718	5 790	750.6	313.9	45	1 417	355.1	63.5
Watsonville	48	234	19.2	3.4	57	333	32.9	12.1	81	3 482	555.6	87.0
West Covina	48	141	21.0	2.8	109	660	42.7	16.2	NA	NA	NA	NA
West Hollywood	97	752	139.3	21.0	205	2 868	288.9	123.8	NA	NA	NA	NA
Westminster	73	352	41.4	6.3	95	257	16.5	4.6	128	1 984	168.5	43.7
West Sacramento	51	435	90.5	14.8	42	571	79.8	23.4	68	2 487	712.9	91.5
Whittier	83	317	33.2	6.4	144	649	55.2	21.6	76	2 733	298.3	69.4
Woodland	50	291	30.2	4.5	58	299	24.1	9.5	65	2 309	484.6	77.6
Yorba Linda	54	208	63.8	5.1	115	596	63.0	23.3	72	1 523	205.8	70.6
Yuba City	69	449	36.1	5.7	90	386	24.7	9.6	35	759	234.1	27.2
Yucaipa	35	120	15.9	1.6	28	64	4.0	1.2	NA	NA	NA	NA
COLORADO	6 663	38 224	4 853.5	883.8	14 315	103 008	12 887.7	4 625.1	5 480	173 069	40 012.8	6 176.8
Arvada	110	558	47.0	9.5	210	1 123	179.2	40.5	106	3 022	432.0	100.6
Aurora	301	1 921	222.7	48.1	451	3 226	379.3	128.9	139	2 360	342.4	75.3
Boulder	281	1 425	201.4	35.5	948	D	D	D	282	9 940	1 758.8	415.7
Broomfield	44	123	12.9	1.9	94	429	29.9	12.9	92	7 101	1 389.9	284.5
Colorado Springs	661	2 826	333.1	58.4	1 227	10 126	1 161.5	451.6	418	17 439	4 204.3	565.9
Denver	1 201	11 339	1 771.9	287.0	3 147	29 056	3 640.3	1 455.0	976	26 320	4 867.8	816.2
Englewood	70	1 044	147.1	28.4	195	898	103.7	38.7	200	4 684	617.2	145.2
Fort Collins	194	928	111.6	17.3	410	2 650	243.3	102.6	124	8 117	2 334.6	351.8
Grand Junction	93	497	46.3	7.9	210	1 174	80.7	36.3	113	3 212	446.0	91.0
Greeley	107	447	50.6	7.5	154	715	53.6	21.1	71	5 073	1 926.5	120.0
Lakewood	257	1 330	129.3	28.8	615	4 788	461.3	193.8	125	1 720	359.0	72.1
Littleton	89	462	39.6	7.4	269	1 054	91.8	37.3	67	1 860	279.0	60.0
Longmont	78	348	41.1	5.9	188	915	74.6	32.4	152	4 688	556.7	136.6
Loveland	76	303	40.9	4.9	123	543	38.5	13.0	66	5 214	1 260.8	225.2
Northglenn	40	232	22.7	4.4	42	232	21.3	7.4	42	616	102.8	17.4
Pueblo	107	450	51.0	7.6	176	939	46.5	17.9	70	2 818	578.4	96.2
Thornton	34	325	20.8	6.2	42	264	11.4	3.8	26	1 587	279.3	44.5
Westminster	88	441	60.1	7.2	187	968	67.6	28.5	70	2 450	659.3	95.7
Wheat Ridge	49	226	40.5	4.1	144	993	93.9	37.8	58	1 413	295.2	53.1
CONNECTICUT	3 372	20 635	3 522.8	609.3	9 393	71 058	9 115.8	3 700.1	5 844	252 330	46 938.2	10 452.1
Bridgeport	94	342	57.0	8.3	184	1 528	172.6	79.3	249	10 340	1 424.4	375.0
Bristol	33	131	22.7	2.9	73	292	20.7	8.2	158	4 542	580.5	159.0
Danbury	76	1 739	535.3	66.1	231	1 744	199.7	81.6	130	6 556	1 302.0	281.0
Hartford	191	1 708	282.2	62.7	405	6 197	891.3	322.3	112	2 183	254.5	60.6
Meriden	66	307	36.0	6.4	74	721	60.4	20.2	103	4 353	751.2	162.9
Middletown	52	249	42.7	5.1	88	686	76.4	32.5	58	5 256	1 662.2	222.0
Milford	43	193	31.8	4.5	158	1 081	126.0	49.3	206	6 100	1 104.5	258.8
Naugatuck Borough	16	78	8.0	1.0	32	83	8.5	2.6	63	2 957	737.5	109.8
New Britain	37	223	26.0	5.6	71	376	39.4	15.0	141	5 329	845.0	193.2
New Haven	140	847	113.3	19.1	418	2 855	339.9	137.1	106	4 177	750.6	147.2
New London	23	147	14.7	3.6	100	886	72.4	34.1	NA	NA	NA	NA
Norwalk	94	443	144.3	18.2	378	3 173	420.7	174.2	170	6 713	1 420.5	297.7
Norwich	30	128	12.2	2.0	75	407	34.1	16.8	48	1 403	254.5	44.8
Shelton	22	473	80.5	18.1	108	934	103.6	42.7	77	4 923	728.6	211.8
Stamford	216	1 816	358.0	74.5	720	10 898	1 713.6	787.5	183	6 126	2 515.3	229.6
Torrington	26	127	10.3	2.1	51	176	18.5	4.3	83	3 770	443.8	118.7
Waterbury	100	436	58.5	10.6	152	848	78.7	28.4	219	6 433	1 085.3	220.9
West Haven	43	100	13.1	1.9	53	463	25.3	8.8	62	5 258	1 623.1	276.5
DELAWARE	1 101	5 243	5 006.5	118.3	1 717	12 382	1 430.4	553.4	675	41 084	13 397.3	1 474.3
Dover	71	294	30.6	4.7	89	820	52.3	23.9	29	3 902	1 338.5	111.5
Newark	60	335	73.9	6.5	96	509	57.5	23.1	52	D	D	D
Wilmington	269	1 015	2 425.1	24.8	450	4 322	690.2	266.2	102	D	D	D
DISTRICT OF COLUMBIA	934	7 725	1 354.2	275.4	3 760	61 123	10 365.2	3 935.5	200	2 858	320.2	101.1
Washington	934	7 725	1 354.2	275.4	3 760	61 123	10 365.2	3 935.5	200	2 858	320.2	101.1
FLORIDA	20 388	118 086	15 360.4	2 652.2	42 403	276 263	27 231.1	10 803.5	15 992	433 149	77 477.5	13 185.1
Altamonte Springs	102	533	85.6	15.2	252	1 411	119.6	45.9	NA	NA	NA	NA
Apopka	20	64	8.8	1.1	43	213	12.1	3.8	28	808	123.7	35.5
Boca Raton	344	2 096	378.2	69.8	1 029	4 922	612.4	237.1	175	4 828	639.0	211.2
Boynton Beach	76	276	41.3	6.6	152	996	56.2	24.5	65	D	D	D
Bradenton	76	261	39.0	4.9	196	814	74.5	30.1	34	D	D	D

1. Firms subject to federal tax.

City	Accommodation and foodservices, 1997				Arts, entertainment, and recreation,[1] 1997				Health care and social assistance,[1] 1997			
	Number of establishments	Number of employees	Sales (mil dol)	Annual payroll (mil dol)	Number of establishments	Number of employees	Receipts (mil dol)	Annual payroll (mil dol)	Number of establishments	Number of employees	Receipts (mil dol)	Annual payroll (mil dol)
	92	93	94	95	96	97	98	99	100	101	102	103
CALIFORNIA—Cont'd												
Vista	127	1 380	48.3	11.7	9	306	18.8	5.5	167	2 233	174.0	61.7
Walnut	30	D	D	D	5	18	1.7	0.2	48	549	19.6	6.9
Walnut Creek	197	3 719	156.6	42.1	25	469	16.2	5.1	353	4 391	369.2	178.9
Watsonville	81	908	32.9	8.0	4	167	4.7	1.5	101	774	45.7	16.6
West Covina	146	2 285	82.1	23.7	6	187	8.0	1.8	272	2 713	223.7	86.1
West Hollywood	184	4 676	205.4	61.6	254	1 001	264.0	140.7	191	934	139.4	53.3
Westminster	206	2 288	81.2	20.2	11	0	0.0	0.0	225	1 651	121.9	46.4
West Sacramento	66	910	30.5	7.9	1	0	0.0	0.0	40	408	17.5	8.2
Whittier	140	2 443	77.7	20.0	16	258	11.0	5.0	266	2 671	250.9	87.3
Woodland	83	1 157	38.1	9.8	10	0	0.0	0.0	76	913	41.4	13.5
Yorba Linda	68	1 573	49.7	13.4	6	199	18.6	4.4	108	705	52.1	19.4
Yuba City	79	1 269	39.4	11.4	10	149	4.6	1.4	169	1 778	198.3	56.5
Yucaipa	40	627	19.1	5.0	2	0	0.0	0.0	48	529	32.5	9.3
COLORADO	10 064	195 126	6 705.5	1 937.4	1 494	30 541	1 909.6	625.0	8 611	85 370	5 790.8	2 538.1
Arvada	150	D	D	D	18	234	7.0	2.4	168	1 255	74.0	27.7
Aurora	424	8 844	278.3	76.8	56	901	40.9	10.5	516	8 108	602.1	236.7
Boulder	363	8 078	272.8	79.0	53	692	34.7	13.5	391	2 990	225.1	93.2
Broomfield	49	D	D	D	10	104	4.0	1.2	45	303	17.6	7.7
Colorado Springs	829	19 464	703.1	199.8	122	1 522	66.1	18.6	1 048	10 148	690.0	302.8
Denver	1 564	33 749	1 335.2	386.0	150	1 772	291.8	146.8	1 478	15 938	1 197.2	562.3
Englewood	96	D	D	D	12	274	10.0	2.3	192	1 846	200.2	99.9
Fort Collins	311	6 749	190.8	54.6	26	529	14.3	4.1	344	3 354	206.7	95.1
Grand Junction	180	3 697	102.8	30.0	18	208	7.2	2.8	229	2 229	138.0	65.0
Greeley	153	2 654	70.5	19.3	25	260	6.1	2.0	157	1 785	118.2	47.6
Lakewood	317	6 234	202.4	60.1	44	957	50.7	12.2	350	3 861	227.8	96.5
Littleton	139	D	D	D	14	183	8.7	2.2	170	1 896	125.3	50.2
Longmont	140	2 460	82.6	22.9	22	278	12.6	2.5	151	1 845	103.3	44.4
Loveland	103	1 728	53.9	13.6	9	73	3.1	0.6	128	1 187	73.6	32.3
Northglenn	49	1 128	39.2	10.9	5	97	3.0	0.8	33	482	27.1	11.5
Pueblo	280	4 547	131.6	35.3	26	0	0.0	0.0	282	3 349	199.9	96.5
Thornton	109	2 616	85.2	23.5	12	194	7.6	1.9	105	1 324	87.0	37.6
Westminster	170	3 812	118.0	33.9	13	263	8.4	2.8	153	1 486	93.5	42.6
Wheat Ridge	99	1 707	54.2	15.5	15	96	4.2	1.1	186	1 818	147.9	72.5
CONNECTICUT	6 903	96 556	3 746.6	1 062.8	1 046	27 236	2 526.8	589.2	7 515	100 363	6 849.7	3 199.3
Bridgeport	163	D	D	D	20	166	19.6	3.4	252	4 422	332.3	144.2
Bristol	98	D	D	D	13	178	18.7	3.7	116	1 460	93.5	45.4
Danbury	181	2 803	111.4	30.0	27	224	11.4	3.2	192	3 359	232.0	129.4
Hartford	313	4 733	172.8	50.4	16	227	58.9	33.2	324	3 772	466.7	249.5
Meriden	106	1 232	49.6	12.3	6	0	0.0	0.0	113	1 567	107.8	47.3
Middletown	103	1 094	44.5	12.0	8	21	2.4	0.3	123	1 694	134.3	61.2
Milford	168	2 647	99.0	25.6	21	441	25.0	9.4	139	2 380	125.7	57.8
Naugatuck Borough	42	D	D	D	2	0	0.0	0.0	36	520	30.3	11.5
New Britain	95	D	D	D	7	68	5.2	1.2	118	2 004	154.0	84.7
New Haven	262	3 327	137.8	37.8	15	282	81.6	5.9	331	3 999	391.2	171.7
New London	95	1 392	48.1	14.0	8	0	0.0	0.0	103	1 953	195.7	71.5
Norwalk	202	1 944	93.2	25.7	41	314	40.4	7.7	234	2 389	203.9	99.9
Norwich	78	1 379	47.9	13.4	10	123	6.4	1.9	139	1 971	129.2	68.1
Shelton	74	862	40.9	10.2	4	21	1.1	0.3	61	1 036	70.8	35.5
Stamford	281	3 980	198.4	55.0	56	752	116.1	25.0	340	2 938	265.5	115.6
Torrington	72	866	30.9	8.6	8	68	7.9	0.7	94	1 601	86.9	37.0
Waterbury	198	2 472	83.9	23.4	22	190	19.0	2.5	248	4 374	316.6	153.6
West Haven	97	1 238	42.6	12.1	8	37	9.1	0.6	60	967	49.3	24.6
DELAWARE	1 605	26 969	1 009.0	280.8	216	4 074	240.1	62.0	1 465	15 980	1 131.6	526.4
Dover	134	2 689	82.3	22.2	10	0	0.0	0.0	128	1 428	94.3	42.6
Newark	123	2 829	111.2	26.6	9	138	5.5	1.4	126	1 456	167.5	73.8
Wilmington	219	3 798	155.9	50.5	21	754	24.2	7.8	249	2 106	190.5	90.0
DISTRICT OF COLUMBIA	1 700	42 650	2 263.5	701.4	171	1 564	161.9	56.1	1 464	13 692	1 054.8	476.7
Washington	1 700	42 650	2 263.5	701.4	171	1 564	161.9	56.1	1 464	13 692	1 054.8	476.7
FLORIDA	28 999	608 834	24 165.3	6 239.5	4 763	103 980	7 871.5	1 972.9	35 568	447 117	32 559.1	13 610.7
Altamonte Springs	156	4 756	167.2	47.5	17	164	9.1	2.1	192	2 032	166.3	70.2
Apopka	52	1 097	28.2	7.1	7	86	3.5	0.9	32	205	13.9	4.8
Boca Raton	297	5 635	279.0	61.5	76	1 502	73.6	23.1	547	5 483	470.9	194.5
Boynton Beach	101	2 001	63.0	18.1	15	26	6.6	0.9	190	2 277	165.9	70.6
Bradenton	104	1 652	55.2	13.2	13	37	4.4	1.4	226	6 301	470.7	176.5

1. Firms subject to federal tax.

Table D. Cities — Other Services and Federal Funds

City	Other services,[1] 1997				Selected federal funds, 2002–2003 (mil dol)								
					Procurement contracts		Grants						
	Number of establishments	Number of employees	Receipts (mil dol)	Annual payroll (mil dol)	Defense	Other	Total[2]	Medicaid and other health related	Nutrition and family welfare	Energy and environment	Education	Housing and community development	Direct payments for individuals for educational assistance
	104	105	106	107	108	109	110	111	112	113	114	115	116
CALIFORNIA—Cont'd													
Vista	101	594	38.4	11.8	15.1	3.0	2.4	0.8	0.1	0.0	0.2	0.9	0.6
Walnut	50	423	27.9	10.8	4.2	0.1	1.4	0.0	0.0	0.0	0.9	0.0	9.8
Walnut Creek	177	1 051	71.7	21.3	76.2	64.1	2.4	0.2	0.0	0.0	0.0	1.0	0.0
Watsonville	53	188	12.4	3.1	9.9	3.4	5.5	1.6	0.0	0.1	1.5	1.7	0.0
West Covina	59	244	13.8	3.6	2.4	0.9	10.4	0.7	6.5	0.0	0.2	2.7	1.9
West Hollywood	146	883	47.8	14.7	0.6	0.0	3.0	0.0	0.0	0.0	0.0	1.8	0.0
Westminster	154	770	51.3	13.3	0.1	0.1	3.0	0.0	0.0	1.0	0.1	1.7	0.9
West Sacramento	62	372	36.2	9.5	7.0	6.7	3.7	0.0	1.2	1.1	0.0	0.6	0.0
Whittier	143	751	62.2	16.7	3.1	0.4	6.9	0.0	0.0	0.4	2.6	2.8	10.4
Woodland	79	379	26.9	7.5	3.1	3.1	6.1	0.0	0.0	0.2	0.2	5.0	0.0
Yorba Linda	76	516	29.4	8.9	18.0	3.6	0.0	0.0	0.0	0.0	0.0	0.0	0.0
Yuba City	78	527	31.9	9.2	0.0	10.3	6.7	1.8	0.0	0.0	1.1	3.2	0.0
Yucaipa	41	174	11.5	3.0	0.4	0.0	0.0	0.0	0.0	0.0	0.0	0.0	0.0
COLORADO	6 793	39 363	2 571.1	770.0	2 471.0	2 670.7	6 014.4	2 033.6	707.9	108.4	450.0	429.6	208.0
Arvada	158	768	53.8	15.1	1.7	44.3	8.8	0.0	0.0	0.0	0.0	8.7	0.0
Aurora	375	2 132	132.3	40.2	21.2	47.4	26.3	0.0	0.0	0.0	2.9	16.8	3.4
Boulder	235	1 652	114.9	36.3	116.4	226.4	380.4	48.8	2.1	17.9	6.7	8.3	15.3
Broomfield	54	446	23.7	8.0	18.9	5.7	1.6	0.7	0.0	0.6	0.0	0.0	0.0
Colorado Springs	659	4 163	241.0	82.0	797.7	92.6	64.7	6.0	9.2	0.0	8.0	21.6	17.0
Denver	1 101	8 212	604.5	172.8	111.9	389.9	1 243.1	375.3	214.9	59.9	166.1	165.5	91.7
Englewood	164	894	67.2	20.4	126.0	75.5	26.1	0.1	1.1	0.1	2.4	3.2	0.0
Fort Collins	184	1 160	70.3	21.7	24.6	52.8	146.0	56.1	2.6	7.7	4.5	13.0	13.5
Grand Junction	147	886	67.5	17.3	17.1	10.4	19.8	0.8	0.1	0.0	0.3	15.1	6.6
Greeley	123	734	40.2	11.6	2.4	4.7	36.0	3.4	5.1	0.0	5.3	18.2	8.5
Lakewood	299	1 550	85.8	27.9	4.5	80.9	20.3	2.2	1.0	4.1	0.0	11.6	0.4
Littleton	112	793	57.5	18.5	144.1	69.0	13.3	1.0	0.0	0.1	0.3	8.3	2.9
Longmont	120	583	33.1	10.5	38.6	35.5	15.2	1.6	1.1	0.1	0.0	3.3	0.0
Loveland	78	473	23.0	7.3	2.7	11.9	5.6	0.2	0.9	0.0	0.0	0.6	0.0
Northglenn	45	345	17.5	5.1	0.4	0.0	0.7	0.0	0.0	0.0	0.0	0.6	0.0
Pueblo	166	846	43.3	12.9	4.0	5.8	36.2	4.3	0.4	0.1	5.9	23.3	15.6
Thornton	67	743	49.5	14.5	42.8	2.2	3.1	0.0	0.0	0.0	0.0	3.0	0.0
Westminster	105	493	28.1	9.9	2.8	8.1	5.2	0.5	0.0	0.3	1.0	3.2	7.2
Wheat Ridge	105	600	45.3	13.6	4.3	3.6	4.3	0.0	0.0	2.8	0.0	1.1	0.0
CONNECTICUT	6 121	34 089	2 370.2	727.8	7 894.8	589.5	5 376.1	2 623.0	695.9	81.0	388.7	573.0	99.9
Bridgeport	161	932	71.9	22.1	61.0	7.2	68.8	5.2	8.8	0.2	3.7	48.5	6.7
Bristol	92	434	23.8	6.5	1.5	0.0	8.3	0.0	0.0	0.0	0.0	7.9	0.0
Danbury	152	853	59.2	17.8	38.4	25.0	28.8	0.2	0.1	11.2	1.6	14.8	2.4
Hartford	212	1 129	76.3	21.4	26.8	16.4	608.9	100.8	139.3	34.6	123.9	140.6	5.6
Meriden	96	447	29.9	10.2	8.1	37.3	13.0	3.7	0.0	-0.7	0.0	9.0	0.2
Middletown	87	462	54.6	14.7	327.3	0.2	57.3	9.9	0.0	0.6	0.5	10.2	3.3
Milford	130	789	50.9	17.4	7.7	1.1	4.4	0.4	0.0	0.0	0.3	3.5	0.0
Naugatuck Borough	52	261	18.3	5.9	1.3	0.0	3.1	0.0	0.0	0.0	0.1	2.8	0.0
New Britain	100	530	40.7	11.5	1.8	6.3	23.8	1.0	2.3	2.4	1.5	16.2	6.8
New Haven	254	1 748	119.4	35.9	11.3	21.1	523.2	358.7	6.9	13.2	17.4	85.4	15.5
New London	66	409	23.3	8.1	8.8	14.0	20.3	0.3	0.1	0.0	2.6	16.4	2.0
Norwalk	179	880	73.9	23.5	34.6	2.3	20.0	0.0	1.4	0.6	1.2	16.3	3.7
Norwich	74	422	23.9	7.1	0.0	0.0	10.2	0.0	0.0	0.0	0.1	9.5	1.6
Shelton	47	237	14.5	4.7	41.9	66.9	1.6	0.0	0.0	0.0	0.0	1.6	0.0
Stamford	219	1 133	83.5	25.5	52.0	9.7	33.2	0.0	2.6	0.0	1.2	27.0	0.2
Torrington	76	303	17.5	4.8	2.2	5.6	6.0	0.4	0.0	0.0	0.0	5.5	0.0
Waterbury	188	1 001	62.9	19.4	3.8	0.8	46.0	3.0	3.9	0.0	2.2	33.9	3.5
West Haven	111	643	46.4	15.9	1.1	12.9	8.3	0.0	1.2	0.0	0.1	6.4	3.0
DELAWARE	1 198	7 006	420.5	140.7	164.3	80.5	1 180.8	475.5	144.8	28.3	114.6	84.3	112.8
Dover	103	678	36.1	11.4	9.3	1.7	105.1	1.6	1.0	11.5	50.4	18.0	7.9
Newark	69	473	27.4	11.6	8.6	3.4	113.5	26.1	5.6	5.7	3.0	7.1	6.0
Wilmington	166	1 236	72.4	27.0	10.3	19.9	96.1	10.5	17.4	1.7	7.4	33.4	93.2
DISTRICT OF COLUMBIA	978	6 218	404.8	111.1	1 753.1	9 622.8	4 310.2	1 415.5	291.2	114.3	316.2	767.0	55.1
Washington	978	6 218	404.8	111.1	1 753.1	9 622.8	4 310.2	1 415.5	291.2	114.3	316.2	767.0	55.1
FLORIDA	26 121	146 360	9 123.6	2 665.7	7 998.7	2 900.3	17 463.1	8 388.3	2 576.4	157.6	1 704.1	1 201.7	707.9
Altamonte Springs	110	778	48.9	15.3	0.9	1.2	0.4	0.0	0.0	0.0	0.0	0.0	0.1
Apopka	50	303	17.1	5.3	64.9	1.2	2.5	0.2	0.0	0.0	0.0	2.2	0.0
Boca Raton	310	1 823	129.2	37.3	5.6	6.2	16.3	6.0	0.0	0.3	0.5	2.4	1.2
Boynton Beach	114	469	27.1	7.1	0.3	0.3	2.3	0.0	0.0	0.0	0.0	1.5	0.0
Bradenton	99	531	29.3	8.6	2.5	0.6	15.6	0.0	4.6	0.0	3.1	5.6	9.2

1. Firms subject to federal tax.   2. Includes program categories not shown separately. State totals include additional categories not allocated by city.

City	General revenue Total (mil dol)	Intergovernmental Total (mil dol)	Intergovernmental Percent from state government	Taxes Total (mil dol)	Taxes Per capita[1] (dollars) Total	Taxes Per capita[1] (dollars) Property	Taxes Per capita[1] (dollars) Sales and gross receipts	General expenditure Total (mil dol)	General expenditure Per capita[1] (dollars) Total	General expenditure Per capita[1] (dollars) Capital outlays
	117	118	119	120	121	122	123	124	125	126
CALIFORNIA—Cont'd										
Vista	71.9	10.0	87.4	33.1	361	165	134	70.9	774	218
Walnut	31.9	3.2	95.2	21.3	691	588	61	31.3	1 016	156
Walnut Creek	59.0	6.2	95.8	34.3	524	137	352	65.7	1 006	303
Watsonville	48.8	4.7	97.7	22.3	479	199	220	49.0	1 051	233
West Covina	73.4	13.1	81.8	42.1	391	181	191	61.5	571	41
West Hollywood	55.9	4.6	89.0	28.2	768	217	477	53.5	1 458	333
Westminster	58.6	12.2	80.5	37.3	417	150	236	49.1	549	95
West Sacramento	58.3	7.6	74.4	31.8	871	473	359	95.1	2 603	1 142
Whittier	60.6	13.9	99.9	26.7	313	76	217	57.5	673	71
Woodland	45.8	10.7	91.3	23.4	460	156	240	54.3	1 068	429
Yorba Linda	69.9	14.3	33.0	34.2	560	350	111	63.1	1 034	288
Yuba City	39.6	6.8	82.2	17.2	365	135	186	33.2	704	178
Yucaipa	21.9	7.8	96.8	9.3	213	68	67	14.7	334	95
COLORADO	X	X	X	X	X	X	X	X	X	X
Arvada	102.0	18.3	51.3	42.1	412	33	361	85.7	838	187
Aurora	306.2	23.1	60.9	191.7	670	88	557	287.2	1 004	197
Boulder	182.3	18.9	100.0	119.7	1 271	214	980	179.7	1 909	110
Broomfield	95.6	3.3	75.1	81.1	1 985	251	997	60.9	1 491	409
Colorado Springs	673.1	50.5	34.4	166.8	449	49	399	721.4	1 944	484
Denver	1 912.3	232.8	95.8	732.6	1 307	282	828	1 899.8	3 390	355
Englewood	55.0	4.0	82.4	31.4	954	87	843	51.6	1 565	260
Fort Collins	198.6	26.4	80.0	91.8	736	109	612	180.3	1 446	475
Grand Junction	64.6	9.8	40.4	36.0	834	87	744	73.6	1 704	348
Greeley	70.7	9.0	55.9	41.6	506	71	418	77.0	937	248
Lakewood	107.7	16.7	64.1	61.6	429	45	366	112.1	780	163
Littleton	56.9	10.5	26.2	30.8	762	125	602	52.0	1 287	21
Longmont	103.2	5.5	54.7	53.4	678	124	555	131.1	1 666	821
Loveland	78.4	7.3	100.0	32.4	586	86	468	70.6	1 278	487
Northglenn	38.8	2.2	85.7	21.1	628	202	399	19.5	579	36
Pueblo	89.6	13.7	35.5	53.0	512	76	434	74.0	716	111
Thornton	95.5	7.5	45.3	65.3	698	116	534	84.4	901	304
Westminster	158.4	10.2	41.0	70.1	676	38	615	263.8	2 546	1 586
Wheat Ridge	22.7	3.2	100.0	14.5	449	96	329	26.4	817	109
CONNECTICUT	X	X	X	X	X	X	X	X	X	X
Bridgeport	499.4	276.2	96.0	178.5	1 274	1 266	0	504.8	3 603	119
Bristol	147.1	59.5	98.7	74.6	1 232	1 211	0	149.3	2 467	253
Danbury	178.0	41.7	95.1	112.9	1 468	1 419	0	165.4	2 151	91
Hartford	339.8	134.7	65.7	175.3	1 407	1 375	0	301.9	2 424	121
Meriden	164.0	71.8	98.1	79.4	1 354	1 353	0	159.4	2 716	37
Middletown	120.8	40.1	100.0	67.3	1 523	1 511	0	121.7	2 756	379
Milford	138.2	21.9	100.0	105.0	1 964	1 932	0	130.8	2 445	41
Naugatuck Borough	76.6	34.7	98.5	38.1	1 212	1 194	0	76.6	2 438	7
New Britain	233.9	135.0	97.0	79.1	1 105	1 094	0	200.6	2 801	30
New Haven	606.9	399.6	96.6	140.8	1 134	1 084	0	713.8	5 748	1 657
New London	91.6	50.8	89.4	30.5	1 170	1 152	0	87.3	3 350	142
Norwalk	240.2	54.3	97.0	175.0	2 081	2 040	0	237.5	2 823	244
Norwich	104.9	45.4	100.0	43.9	1 221	1 208	0	99.3	2 759	72
Shelton	89.4	13.7	93.6	66.1	1 701	1 669	0	87.6	2 254	269
Stamford	381.4	58.9	98.4	272.7	2 275	2 230	0	366.4	3 058	141
Torrington	NA	NA	NA	NA	NA	NA	NA	NA	NA	NA
Waterbury	370.6	188.1	96.7	154.8	1 434	1 434	0	310.9	2 882	299
West Haven	128.8	54.9	97.4	64.8	1 228	1 221	0	125.0	2 370	60
DELAWARE	X	X	X	X	X	X	X	X	X	X
Dover	22.4	2.9	73.7	9.3	285	190	0	24.6	754	79
Newark	16.7	2.2	91.0	5.7	190	147	0	21.7	727	71
Wilmington	135.8	14.1	72.3	81.7	1 127	360	28	146.3	2 018	98
DISTRICT OF COLUMBIA	X	X	X	X	X	X	X	X	X	X
Washington	6 237.8	2 189.7	0.0	3 227.9	5 654	1 407	1 727	6 378.5	11 173	2 053
FLORIDA	X	X	X	X	X	X	X	X	X	X
Altamonte Springs	46.3	5.7	71.9	20.6	502	256	210	38.9	949	127
Apopka	28.3	6.4	88.8	10.0	338	121	195	25.2	848	105
Boca Raton	144.9	22.3	35.1	68.6	886	471	356	119.0	1 537	237
Boynton Beach	72.4	9.3	70.8	34.4	540	317	165	63.9	1 003	123
Bradenton	40.5	3.3	22.7	20.7	402	152	231	36.3	707	47

1. Based on population estimated as of July 1 of the year shown.

City	City government finances, 2002 (cont'd)									
	General expenditure									
	Percent of total for—									
	Public welfare	Highways	Parking facilities	Education	Health and hospitals	Police protection	Sewerage and sanitation	Parks and recreation	Housing and community development	Interest on debt
	127	128	129	130	131	132	133	134	135	136
CALIFORNIA—Cont'd										
Vista	0.0	10.6	0.0	0.0	4.2	15.8	17.3	9.9	16.4	5.1
Walnut	0.0	13.4	0.0	0.0	0.6	9.2	0.0	7.4	56.2	7.8
Walnut Creek	0.0	13.8	6.2	0.0	0.0	19.8	0.0	24.3	2.1	0.8
Watsonville	0.0	13.7	0.0	0.0	1.4	16.8	17.0	8.4	9.4	2.0
West Covina	0.0	8.3	0.0	0.0	1.9	33.1	0.0	6.5	12.4	9.1
West Hollywood	0.0	11.8	7.7	0.0	0.0	21.9	2.8	4.1	16.8	3.6
Westminster	0.0	13.2	0.0	0.0	1.8	39.9	0.0	6.9	14.4	4.0
West Sacramento	0.0	26.6	0.0	0.0	0.2	10.6	8.1	2.7	5.3	19.5
Whittier	0.0	10.6	0.3	0.0	0.0	36.4	14.0	12.9	5.3	2.8
Woodland	0.0	23.9	0.5	0.0	0.0	19.3	5.8	7.3	2.8	5.2
Yorba Linda	0.0	31.5	0.0	0.0	0.3	10.4	5.5	10.4	22.9	4.2
Yuba City	0.0	16.4	0.0	0.0	0.4	18.6	17.9	6.5	9.8	4.1
Yucaipa	0.0	23.1	0.0	0.0	3.8	23.8	0.0	12.1	2.8	7.7
COLORADO	X	X	X	X	X	X	X	X	X	X
Arvada	0.9	24.2	0.0	0.0	0.0	18.4	10.0	24.6	5.0	3.9
Aurora	0.0	16.2	0.0	0.0	0.0	21.1	8.4	14.4	2.0	3.7
Boulder	0.0	14.2	1.8	0.0	0.0	9.2	3.4	11.4	10.9	3.4
Broomfield	4.0	7.3	0.0	0.0	0.0	27.3	11.7	11.9	4.1	17.5
Colorado Springs	0.0	11.9	0.5	0.0	40.1	9.0	8.0	5.0	1.5	2.0
Denver	6.6	4.3	0.4	0.0	2.8	7.9	2.5	8.2	1.9	13.8
Englewood	0.0	10.7	0.0	0.0	0.0	14.0	16.4	20.1	4.5	3.5
Fort Collins	0.3	12.4	0.4	0.0	0.0	11.3	6.2	14.3	4.3	3.7
Grand Junction	0.0	26.8	0.2	0.0	0.0	16.6	16.9	11.7	2.3	0.4
Greeley	0.0	11.3	0.1	0.0	0.2	17.3	4.4	17.2	1.7	3.3
Lakewood	0.0	11.8	1.2	0.0	0.7	22.9	2.2	18.7	4.3	6.8
Littleton	0.6	20.0	0.0	0.0	3.0	15.5	11.8	5.7	0.0	1.5
Longmont	0.0	12.5	0.0	0.0	0.1	9.9	16.4	37.1	0.5	2.1
Loveland	4.9	7.9	0.0	0.0	0.0	13.8	12.9	12.1	0.5	0.2
Northglenn	0.0	9.9	0.0	0.0	0.0	29.7	13.3	17.6	4.5	0.1
Pueblo	0.0	11.8	0.2	0.0	1.2	19.1	5.1	10.7	3.6	3.3
Thornton	0.0	17.6	0.0	0.0	0.0	8.2	9.3	21.3	2.3	9.9
Westminster	0.0	2.9	0.0	0.0	0.0	34.3	1.4	16.4	0.9	8.0
Wheat Ridge	0.0	20.1	0.0	0.0	0.0	23.2	0.0	18.1	4.9	2.6
CONNECTICUT	X	X	X	X	X	X	X	X	X	X
Bridgeport	0.9	1.5	0.0	49.2	2.4	7.1	4.9	1.0	2.7	7.2
Bristol	2.4	5.5	0.0	54.9	1.8	7.4	9.1	1.7	0.6	1.6
Danbury	0.2	3.3	0.4	55.9	1.9	7.9	2.5	2.7	0.3	2.0
Hartford	4.3	5.9	0.6	0.0	3.0	12.3	8.2	2.6	14.4	1.2
Meriden	0.2	1.7	0.1	54.5	1.9	5.8	3.3	1.4	0.8	2.1
Middletown	0.0	2.6	0.1	47.1	0.8	11.5	3.6	1.9	0.0	2.5
Milford	0.0	1.7	0.0	56.4	1.4	5.9	6.4	0.6	0.5	2.8
Naugatuck Borough	0.0	1.7	0.0	61.5	1.9	4.9	1.3	1.7	0.0	2.1
New Britain	0.9	2.2	0.0	57.3	0.9	5.9	7.8	4.9	1.7	6.4
New Haven	5.0	2.5	2.1	42.9	0.8	4.3	2.1	1.7	0.7	2.0
New London	0.0	1.4	0.7	51.7	2.3	9.8	6.9	2.7	2.8	2.3
Norwalk	0.3	8.2	0.0	52.9	1.6	6.3	0.1	1.4	0.6	2.6
Norwich	1.9	1.0	0.3	57.2	0.0	8.7	6.5	3.9	1.5	2.4
Shelton	1.6	2.6	0.0	57.8	1.8	4.8	4.2	1.2	0.5	1.6
Stamford	0.1	2.7	0.2	50.0	5.8	11.7	6.5	3.8	0.6	3.2
Torrington	NA	NA	NA	NA	NA	NA	NA	NA	NA	NA
Waterbury	0.1	1.8	0.3	59.0	1.4	8.2	6.0	3.4	1.8	2.8
West Haven	0.6	2.8	0.0	59.2	1.0	10.3	6.0	1.4	0.7	2.6
DELAWARE	X	X	X	X	X	X	X	X	X	X
Dover	0.0	7.9	0.0	0.0	0.0	38.1	25.4	2.7	1.2	2.0
Newark	0.0	9.5	2.5	0.0	0.0	24.5	25.4	8.1	0.9	1.1
Wilmington	0.0	14.2	2.1	0.0	0.0	24.2	11.4	7.0	5.9	9.2
DISTRICT OF COLUMBIA	X	X	X	X	X	X	X	X	X	X
Washington	22.9	1.1	0.1	18.4	8.7	6.0	4.0	4.8	1.4	3.7
FLORIDA	X	X	X	X	X	X	X	X	X	X
Altamonte Springs	0.0	7.5	0.0	0.0	0.0	20.1	16.4	9.2	0.0	0.0
Apopka	0.0	8.1	0.0	0.0	0.0	19.8	21.3	4.8	0.0	2.6
Boca Raton	0.0	5.7	0.0	0.0	0.0	17.6	9.9	23.9	3.6	8.3
Boynton Beach	0.3	1.6	0.0	0.0	0.0	19.2	25.5	13.5	0.7	6.2
Bradenton	4.4	5.5	0.4	0.0	0.0	21.0	31.5	5.7	3.6	0.0

City	City government finances, 2002 (cont'd) Debt outstanding Total (mil dol)	Per capita[1] (dollars)	Percent utility	City government employment, 2002	Climate[2] Average daily temperature (degrees Fahrenheit) Mean January	Mean July	Limits January[3]	July[4]	Annual precipitation (inches)	Heating degree days	Cooling degree days
	137	138	139	140	141	142	143	144	145	146	147
CALIFORNIA—Cont'd											
Vista	107.1	1 170	0.0	337	55.2	70.5	43.1	81.3	13.04	1 802	868
Walnut	39.0	1 268	0.0	46	54.3	74.6	40.7	90.4	16.62	1 713	1 273
Walnut Creek	13.3	203	0.0	439	44.5	73.8	35.9	90.8	12.80	2 837	1 066
Watsonville	32.9	705	22.2	384	49.4	61.8	38.3	71.3	21.73	3 213	107
West Covina	107.6	999	0.0	479	55.7	75.2	41.7	89.2	17.90	1 433	1 427
West Hollywood	31.1	847	0.0	152	58.3	74.3	48.9	84.0	14.77	1 154	1 537
Westminster	50.5	565	8.5	356	57.4	72.6	45.6	82.6	12.27	1 238	1 175
West Sacramento	264.7	7 242	0.0	319	45.2	75.7	37.7	93.2	17.52	2 749	1 237
Whittier	55.7	652	11.9	473	55.7	75.2	41.7	89.2	17.90	1 433	1 427
Woodland	46.4	912	0.0	363	44.5	76.9	35.9	96.3	19.43	2 777	1 387
Yorba Linda	85.7	1 403	0.0	80	57.4	72.6	45.6	82.6	12.27	1 238	1 175
Yuba City	26.2	554	18.7	253	45.6	78.8	37.2	96.0	21.04	2 524	1 607
Yucaipa	24.6	561	0.0	49	52.8	78.4	39.6	95.8	12.80	1 875	1 673
COLORADO	X	X	X	X	X	X	X	X	X	X	X
Arvada	115.3	1 128	28.7	726	30.2	71.9	17.1	85.7	15.86	6 158	554
Aurora	402.1	1 406	24.7	2 496	29.7	73.5	16.1	88.2	15.40	6 020	679
Boulder	210.5	2 235	20.5	1 475	32.6	73.0	19.9	87.5	18.58	5 554	649
Broomfield	283.2	6 937	19.5	572	NA	NA	NA	NA	NA	NA	NA
Colorado Springs	1 139.3	3 069	72.4	7 109	28.8	70.8	16.1	84.4	16.24	6 415	419
Denver	4 994.9	8 913	4.2	13 005	29.7	73.5	16.1	88.2	15.40	6 020	679
Englewood	57.2	1 736	23.2	530	29.7	73.5	16.1	88.2	15.40	6 020	679
Fort Collins	198.3	1 591	32.3	1 771	27.7	71.5	14.1	85.5	15.07	6 368	479
Grand Junction	10.4	240	1.3	650	25.0	78.8	14.5	93.6	8.64	5 548	1 183
Greeley	83.0	1 010	47.7	808	26.1	73.5	12.3	89.1	13.97	6 306	645
Lakewood	121.9	848	0.0	1 001	30.2	71.9	17.1	85.7	15.86	6 158	554
Littleton	12.1	301	0.0	405	30.2	71.9	17.1	85.7	15.86	6 158	554
Longmont	78.9	1 003	5.4	858	26.6	72.4	11.7	88.7	13.60	6 443	562
Loveland	1.8	32	0.0	687	27.7	71.5	14.1	85.5	15.07	6 368	479
Northglenn	34.2	1 016	95.5	295	29.7	73.5	16.1	88.2	15.40	6 020	679
Pueblo	129.9	1 256	42.6	868	29.8	77.1	14.2	93.0	11.19	5 413	973
Thornton	218.7	2 336	35.2	663	29.7	73.5	16.1	88.2	15.40	6 020	679
Westminster	307.0	2 964	16.6	877	30.2	71.9	17.1	85.7	15.86	6 158	554
Wheat Ridge	10.7	330	0.0	294	30.2	71.9	17.1	85.7	15.86	6 158	554
CONNECTICUT	X	X	X	X	X	X	X	X	X	X	X
Bridgeport	829.3	5 919	0.0	5 075	28.9	73.7	21.9	81.7	41.66	5 537	724
Bristol	45.3	748	22.6	1 683	24.6	73.7	15.8	85.0	44.14	6 151	677
Danbury	110.3	1 435	18.0	1 982	23.8	71.3	13.2	83.6	44.50	6 492	486
Hartford	54.7	439	0.0	2 399	24.6	73.7	15.8	85.0	44.14	6 151	677
Meriden	164.3	2 800	5.5	1 882	27.1	72.8	19.2	83.3	49.72	5 945	633
Middletown	61.4	1 391	0.0	1 447	27.1	72.8	19.2	83.3	49.72	5 945	633
Milford	63.0	1 179	0.0	1 769	NA	NA	NA	NA	NA	NA	NA
Naugatuck Borough	17.5	556	0.0	965	27.1	72.8	19.2	83.3	49.72	5 945	633
New Britain	229.5	3 205	0.0	2 173	24.6	73.7	15.8	85.0	44.14	6 151	677
New Haven	447.4	3 603	0.0	5 676	28.9	73.7	21.9	81.7	41.66	5 537	724
New London	32.3	1 241	13.3	987	27.7	71.4	18.5	80.7	48.16	5 951	472
Norwalk	139.4	1 657	0.0	2 439	27.5	72.9	17.9	83.5	46.80	5 865	613
Norwich	53.2	1 478	0.0	1 045	27.6	72.2	17.5	82.7	50.01	5 869	551
Shelton	28.7	740	0.0	933	28.9	73.7	21.9	81.7	41.66	5 537	724
Stamford	308.7	2 576	0.0	3 615	27.4	72.6	17.6	84.4	49.43	5 778	613
Torrington	NA	NA	NA	986	23.6	70.7	13.5	82.0	49.28	6 636	418
Waterbury	237.3	2 200	1.3	3 680	27.1	72.8	19.2	83.3	49.72	5 945	633
West Haven	69.7	1 322	0.0	1 324	28.9	73.7	21.9	81.7	41.66	5 537	724
DELAWARE	X	X	X	X	X	X	X	X	X	X	X
Dover	39.1	1 201	78.8	357	33.8	77.2	25.0	87.7	44.14	4 337	1 199
Newark	5.8	194	0.0	260	31.3	76.0	22.3	87.2	42.61	4 825	1 033
Wilmington	269.1	3 712	12.1	1 452	30.6	76.4	22.4	85.6	40.84	4 937	1 046
DISTRICT OF COLUMBIA	X	X	X	X	X	X	X	X	X	X	X
Washington	5 204.7	9 117	0.0	35 040	34.6	80.0	26.8	88.5	38.63	4 047	1 549
FLORIDA	X	X	X	X	X	X	X	X	X	X	X
Altamonte Springs	0.0	0	0.0	452	59.7	82.3	48.6	91.5	48.11	686	3 381
Apopka	21.0	708	47.8	340	NA	NA	NA	NA	NA	NA	NA
Boca Raton	224.5	2 900	30.6	1 349	66.2	82.5	56.8	91.2	59.15	262	4 038
Boynton Beach	66.9	1 051	0.0	830	65.1	82.2	55.7	89.9	60.75	323	3 891
Bradenton	22.9	447	100.0	552	60.2	81.4	49.0	90.8	53.71	678	3 186

1. Based on the population estimated as of July 1 of the year shown.   2. Represents normal values based on the 30-year period, 1961–1990.   3. Average daily minimum.   4. Average daily maximum.

Table D. Cities — Land Area and Population

STATE Place code	City	Land area,[1] 2000 (sq km)	Population, 2003			Population characteristics, 2000 — Percent						
								Race (alone or in combination)				
			Total persons	Rank	Per square kilometer	White	Black	Am. Indian, Alaska Native	Asian and Pacific Islander	Other race	Hispanic or Latino[2]	Non-Hispanic White
		1	2	3	4	5	6	7	8	9	10	11
	FLORIDA—Cont'd											
12 10275	Cape Coral	272.4	118 737	194	435.9	94.4	2.4	0.6	1.3	2.9	8.3	87.5
12 12875	Clearwater	65.5	108 272	216	1 653.0	85.4	10.4	0.7	2.0	3.3	9.0	78.1
12 13275	Coconut Creek	29.9	48 198	663	1 612.0	87.9	6.8	0.3	3.1	4.2	11.7	77.8
12 14125	Cooper City	16.4	28 853	1 101	1 759.3	90.6	3.6	0.4	4.8	2.8	15.6	75.7
12 14250	Coral Gables	34.0	42 539	755	1 251.1	93.2	3.6	0.3	2.1	2.4	46.6	47.7
12 14400	Coral Springs	61.9	127 005	177	2 051.8	83.3	10.2	0.4	4.2	4.6	15.5	69.9
12 16475	Davie	86.6	80 364	336	928.0	88.9	5.2	0.6	3.5	4.3	18.8	72.2
12 16525	Daytona Beach	152.0	64 581	445	424.9	63.6	33.5	0.8	2.3	1.7	3.5	60.3
12 16725	Deerfield Beach	34.8	65 694	438	1 887.8	78.9	17.2	0.4	1.8	4.6	8.7	71.2
12 17100	Delray Beach	39.8	63 321	459	1 591.0	67.5	29.7	0.4	1.9	4.6	7.0	61.8
12 18575	Dunedin	26.9	36 715	878	1 364.9	95.9	2.2	0.6	1.4	1.1	3.3	92.4
12 24000	Fort Lauderdale	82.2	162 917	128	1 982.0	65.6	31.5	0.5	1.6	4.7	9.5	57.5
12 24125	Fort Myers	82.4	51 028	613	619.3	57.8	35.2	0.7	1.5	7.9	14.5	49.2
12 24300	Fort Pierce	38.2	37 841	845	990.6	50.9	42.8	0.7	1.2	7.6	15.0	41.4
12 25175	Gainesville	124.8	109 146	214	874.6	70.1	24.0	0.7	5.3	2.2	6.4	64.1
12 27322	Greenacres City	12.1	31 111	1 027	2 571.2	85.0	7.3	0.6	2.4	7.3	21.2	69.2
12 28452	Hallandale Beach	10.9	35 369	913	3 244.9	79.1	17.0	0.5	1.6	4.8	18.8	62.6
12 30000	Hialeah	49.8	226 401	78	4 546.2	91.2	2.9	0.3	0.7	8.6	90.3	8.1
12 32000	Hollywood	70.8	143 408	155	2 025.5	80.7	13.2	0.6	2.7	6.3	22.5	61.6
12 32275	Homestead	37.0	34 182	942	923.8	64.1	25.0	0.8	1.4	14.2	51.8	22.9
12 35000	Jacksonville	1 962.4	773 781	13	394.3	66.0	29.7	0.8	3.6	2.1	4.2	62.2
12 35875	Jupiter town	51.8	45 100	715	870.7	95.8	1.4	0.4	1.7	1.9	7.3	89.4
12 36550	Key West	15.4	25 031	1 224	1 625.4	86.7	10.0	0.8	1.8	3.0	16.5	71.4
12 36950	Kissimmee	43.2	54 598	576	1 263.8	70.8	11.3	1.0	4.3	17.5	41.7	43.7
12 38250	Lakeland	118.7	87 860	299	740.2	74.8	22.1	0.7	1.8	2.5	6.4	69.5
12 39075	Lake Worth	14.6	35 612	903	2 439.2	67.4	21.3	1.4	1.4	13.4	29.7	48.1
12 39425	Largo	40.6	71 166	398	1 752.9	94.0	3.1	0.7	2.1	1.6	4.2	89.9
12 39525	Lauderdale Lakes	9.3	31 571	1 015	3 394.7	25.1	72.0	0.4	1.8	6.0	5.5	21.2
12 39550	Lauderhill	18.9	59 096	510	3 126.8	35.0	61.9	0.4	2.4	4.5	6.9	29.5
12 43125	Margate	22.8	54 954	567	2 410.3	81.0	13.1	0.6	3.7	5.4	15.3	67.8
12 43975	Melbourne	78.2	74 545	375	953.3	86.4	10.1	0.9	3.2	1.9	5.5	80.7
12 45000	Miami	92.4	376 815	46	4 078.1	69.5	24.2	0.5	1.1	9.5	65.8	11.8
12 45025	Miami Beach	18.2	89 312	290	4 907.3	89.8	4.8	0.5	2.0	6.6	53.4	40.9
12 45975	Miramar	76.4	96 646	257	1 265.0	46.2	46.2	0.4	4.2	8.3	29.4	21.6
12 49425	North Lauderdale	10.0	33 534	962	3 353.4	52.7	38.3	0.6	4.2	9.9	21.1	36.7
12 49450	North Miami	21.9	59 310	508	2 708.2	36.7	58.1	0.7	3.0	6.6	23.2	18.1
12 49475	North Miami Beach	12.8	40 345	793	3 152.0	49.3	41.8	0.6	5.2	8.6	30.0	24.8
12 50575	Oakland Park	16.3	31 462	1 019	1 930.2	68.4	25.1	0.6	2.8	7.9	17.9	53.9
12 50750	Ocala	100.1	47 921	669	478.7	74.2	22.7	0.9	1.5	2.5	5.7	69.6
12 53000	Orlando	242.2	199 336	94	823.0	63.4	28.3	0.7	3.6	7.7	17.5	50.8
12 53150	Ormond Beach	66.7	37 617	852	564.0	95.2	2.9	0.5	1.7	0.7	2.2	92.5
12 53575	Oviedo	39.2	27 940	1 139	712.8	85.3	9.5	0.7	3.3	3.6	12.2	75.0
12 54000	Palm Bay	164.8	85 076	313	516.2	83.6	12.2	0.8	2.5	3.7	8.6	76.2
12 54075	Palm Beach Gardens	144.2	41 834	769	290.1	94.6	2.6	0.3	2.5	1.1	5.6	89.1
12 54700	Panama City	53.1	37 085	870	698.4	75.2	22.0	1.4	2.3	1.1	2.9	72.3
12 55775	Pembroke Pines	85.6	148 927	147	1 739.8	78.0	14.6	0.4	4.9	5.9	28.2	52.7
12 55925	Pensacola	58.8	54 897	568	933.6	66.1	31.2	1.1	2.3	0.9	2.1	63.7
12 56975	Pinellas Park	38.2	46 449	692	1 215.9	91.1	2.5	1.1	4.8	2.9	6.3	85.3
12 57425	Plantation	56.3	84 929	314	1 508.5	80.0	15.1	0.4	3.8	3.8	13.1	68.0
12 57550	Plant City	58.6	31 117	1 026	531.0	73.0	16.6	0.7	1.3	10.2	17.4	64.3
12 58050	Pompano Beach	53.2	88 064	297	1 655.3	69.3	27.7	0.5	1.4	4.9	9.9	60.8
12 58575	Port Orange	64.0	50 930	618	795.8	96.4	1.7	0.6	1.5	0.8	2.5	93.7
12 58715	Port St. Lucie	195.6	105 507	223	539.4	89.2	7.7	0.6	1.7	2.6	7.5	82.8
12 60975	Riviera Beach	21.6	31 733	1 012	1 469.1	28.5	69.4	0.5	1.4	2.5	4.5	25.4
12 63000	St. Petersburg	154.4	247 610	70	1 603.7	73.0	23.2	0.9	3.3	2.0	4.2	68.6
12 63650	Sanford	49.5	43 556	737	879.9	61.5	33.1	1.0	1.5	5.2	10.4	54.6
12 64175	Sarasota	38.6	53 259	596	1 379.8	78.4	16.8	0.9	1.4	4.5	11.9	69.8
12 69700	Sunrise	47.1	89 136	291	1 892.5	71.5	21.9	0.4	4.1	5.6	17.1	57.0
12 70600	Tallahassee	247.9	153 938	138	621.0	61.7	34.9	0.7	3.0	1.6	4.2	57.8
12 70675	Tamarac	29.5	57 967	524	1 965.0	84.0	11.6	0.4	2.1	4.9	14.9	71.4
12 71000	Tampa	290.2	317 647	55	1 094.6	66.3	27.2	0.9	2.9	5.8	19.3	51.0
12 71900	Titusville	55.1	41 752	771	757.7	85.0	13.2	0.9	1.4	1.1	3.5	81.3
12 76582	Weston city	61.5	62 243	469	1 012.1	89.7	4.2	0.2	3.8	4.5	30.2	61.8
12 76600	West Palm Beach	142.8	88 932	293	622.8	59.7	34.0	0.8	2.1	6.9	18.2	46.0
12 78275	Winter Haven	45.8	27 137	1 162	592.5	72.5	24.5	0.5	1.4	3.3	4.9	69.1
12 78325	Winter Springs	37.2	31 808	1 007	855.1	90.5	5.2	0.6	2.4	3.5	10.5	81.6
13 00000	**GEORGIA**	149 976.2	8 684 715	X	57.9	66.1	29.2	0.6	2.5	2.9	5.3	62.6
13 01052	Albany	143.8	76 202	368	529.9	33.7	65.2	0.5	0.9	0.6	1.2	32.7
13 01696	Alpharetta	55.3	35 139	922	635.4	84.9	6.8	0.5	6.3	3.1	5.5	80.7

1. Dry land or land partially or temporarily covered by water.   2. Hispanic or Latino persons may be of any race.

City	Under 5 years	5 to 17 years	18 to 24 years	25 to 34 years	35 to 44 years	45 to 54 years	55 to 64 years	65 to 74 years	75 years and over	Percent female	Census counts 1990	Census counts 2000	Percent change 1990–2000	Percent change 2000–2003
	12	13	14	15	16	17	18	19	20	21	22	23	24	25
FLORIDA—Cont'd														
Cape Coral	5.5	17.1	5.8	11.2	15.6	13.9	11.4	10.5	9.1	51.5	74 991	102 286	36.4	16.1
Clearwater	5.2	14.0	8.0	12.8	14.8	13.7	10.1	9.7	11.8	52.1	98 669	108 787	10.3	-0.5
Coconut Creek	6.2	11.8	5.6	16.0	15.3	10.5	8.1	9.5	17.0	53.5	27 269	43 566	59.8	10.6
Cooper City	6.1	25.3	6.3	9.4	20.8	18.1	7.5	4.1	2.6	51.5	21 335	27 939	31.0	3.3
Coral Gables	4.9	12.5	13.9	13.7	15.3	13.9	10.0	7.5	8.3	53.3	40 091	42 249	5.4	0.7
Coral Springs	6.9	23.8	7.9	13.2	19.1	16.4	6.7	3.1	2.9	51.3	78 864	117 549	49.1	8.0
Davie	6.7	19.7	8.2	14.5	18.9	14.5	8.2	5.4	4.0	51.3	47 143	75 720	60.6	6.1
Daytona Beach	5.0	12.6	16.6	13.1	12.5	11.5	9.0	9.4	10.4	50.1	61 991	64 112	3.4	0.7
Deerfield Beach	4.8	10.8	6.5	14.2	14.2	11.0	9.2	10.8	18.5	53.4	46 997	64 583	37.4	1.7
Delray Beach	5.0	13.2	6.3	12.4	14.7	12.6	9.8	10.8	15.1	52.3	47 184	60 020	27.2	5.5
Dunedin	3.8	11.8	5.4	10.3	14.2	13.6	11.0	12.9	17.0	54.2	34 427	35 691	3.7	2.9
Fort Lauderdale	5.3	14.1	7.7	15.1	17.7	14.9	9.9	7.8	7.5	47.6	149 238	152 397	2.1	6.9
Fort Myers	8.1	18.2	11.4	15.8	14.5	10.8	6.8	6.2	8.1	50.6	44 947	48 208	7.3	5.8
Fort Pierce	7.6	19.6	9.8	12.5	13.5	11.0	8.5	8.7	8.8	50.7	36 830	37 516	1.9	0.9
Gainesville	4.6	13.2	29.4	15.0	11.6	10.5	5.9	4.8	5.0	51.1	91 482	95 447	12.2	14.4
Greenacres City	6.1	14.8	7.6	14.7	13.8	10.7	8.7	11.9	11.7	53.2	18 683	27 569	47.6	12.8
Hallandale Beach	4.0	9.2	5.3	11.0	11.9	11.1	11.7	14.7	21.1	53.9	30 997	34 282	10.6	NA
Hialeah	5.8	17.2	8.2	14.2	15.1	12.0	10.9	9.5	7.1	51.9	188 008	226 419	20.4	0.0
Hollywood	5.9	15.4	7.0	14.4	16.9	13.7	9.4	8.0	9.4	51.5	121 720	139 357	14.5	2.9
Homestead	10.6	22.5	12.8	17.3	13.8	9.3	5.7	4.2	3.7	48.3	26 694	31 909	19.5	7.1
Jacksonville	7.3	19.4	9.7	15.5	16.8	13.1	7.8	5.5	4.8	51.6	635 042	735 617	9.3	5.2
Jupiter town	5.2	15.5	5.1	11.4	17.5	14.8	11.6	11.1	7.8	50.7	26 753	39 328	57.9	14.7
Key West	4.7	11.3	8.4	18.0	19.2	16.9	9.6	6.3	5.5	45.0	24 832	25 478	2.6	-1.8
Kissimmee	7.8	19.2	12.0	18.7	16.2	11.5	6.9	4.5	3.1	50.5	30 337	47 814	57.6	14.2
Lakeland	6.2	15.2	10.3	12.5	12.2	11.2	9.4	10.6	12.4	53.5	70 576	78 452	11.2	12.0
Lake Worth	7.1	15.8	10.6	16.2	16.5	12.0	7.6	6.3	7.9	47.9	28 564	35 133	23.0	1.4
Largo	4.2	11.4	6.1	11.4	13.7	11.9	11.1	13.4	16.7	53.5	65 910	69 371	5.3	2.6
Lauderdale Lakes	7.6	20.1	8.7	12.7	14.2	10.8	8.1	7.1	10.7	55.2	27 341	31 705	16.0	-0.4
Lauderhill	7.5	19.1	8.7	14.8	15.5	11.5	6.8	6.2	9.9	54.2	49 015	57 585	17.5	2.6
Margate	6.0	14.9	6.5	13.6	15.6	12.2	9.5	7.9	13.8	52.8	42 985	53 909	25.4	1.9
Melbourne	5.4	15.3	9.3	12.6	15.8	12.4	9.6	9.7	10.0	51.5	60 034	71 382	18.9	4.4
Miami	5.9	15.9	8.8	15.0	15.4	12.2	9.9	8.9	8.1	50.3	358 648	362 470	1.1	4.0
Miami Beach	3.9	9.5	7.8	20.9	17.3	12.4	8.9	8.8	10.5	48.8	92 639	87 933	-5.1	1.6
Miramar	8.7	22.3	8.6	16.4	19.0	12.1	6.6	3.8	2.5	52.4	40 663	72 739	78.9	32.9
North Lauderdale	8.0	21.8	10.7	17.5	17.7	11.7	5.6	3.2	3.7	51.6	26 473	32 264	21.9	3.9
North Miami	8.1	20.0	11.3	15.8	16.0	12.5	7.1	4.8	4.4	51.9	50 001	59 880	19.8	-1.0
North Miami Beach	7.1	20.2	9.4	14.2	16.8	13.3	7.7	5.5	5.8	52.2	35 361	40 786	15.3	-1.1
Oakland Park	6.7	14.1	9.0	18.6	20.2	13.7	7.6	5.4	4.7	47.8	26 326	30 966	17.6	1.6
Ocala	5.9	17.3	9.3	12.1	14.1	11.7	9.2	9.0	11.4	52.7	42 045	45 943	9.3	4.3
Orlando	6.6	15.4	10.7	21.1	16.2	11.6	7.0	5.7	5.7	51.6	164 674	185 951	12.9	7.2
Ormond Beach	4.2	15.0	4.5	8.5	13.9	14.8	11.7	13.3	14.2	53.3	29 721	36 301	22.1	3.6
Oviedo	8.4	23.6	7.1	15.1	21.5	12.8	5.8	3.6	2.2	50.5	11 114	26 316	136.8	6.2
Palm Bay	6.1	20.4	7.6	12.1	17.5	12.6	8.9	8.7	6.0	51.2	62 543	79 413	27.0	7.1
Palm Beach Gardens	4.5	14.2	5.1	10.6	15.6	15.4	13.4	11.4	9.7	52.6	24 139	35 058	45.2	19.3
Panama City	6.1	16.9	9.6	13.8	16.0	13.0	8.7	7.8	8.1	51.4	34 396	36 417	5.9	1.8
Pembroke Pines	7.1	18.5	6.4	14.9	18.6	12.2	7.1	7.0	8.2	53.4	65 566	137 427	109.6	8.4
Pensacola	5.7	17.2	8.9	12.1	14.8	14.5	9.6	8.9	8.3	53.0	59 198	56 255	-5.0	-2.4
Pinellas Park	5.5	15.8	6.7	13.3	15.9	12.3	9.8	9.5	11.0	52.3	43 571	45 658	4.8	1.7
Plantation	6.0	17.1	7.1	14.7	17.3	15.2	9.5	6.2	6.9	52.5	66 814	82 934	24.1	2.4
Plant City	8.3	21.1	8.9	14.2	14.9	12.0	8.2	6.6	5.7	51.8	22 754	29 915	31.5	4.0
Pompano Beach	5.3	12.5	7.4	13.5	15.6	12.5	10.0	9.9	13.5	50.7	72 411	78 191	8.0	12.6
Port Orange	4.5	15.3	5.9	10.3	14.6	14.2	11.5	12.4	11.2	52.4	35 399	45 823	29.4	11.1
Port St. Lucie	5.8	18.5	5.9	11.4	16.7	13.0	9.8	10.5	8.3	51.4	55 761	88 769	59.2	18.9
Riviera Beach	7.1	22.1	8.0	12.0	13.8	11.8	10.3	8.3	6.7	52.3	27 646	29 884	8.1	6.2
St. Petersburg	5.7	15.8	7.7	13.8	16.5	13.9	9.2	8.1	9.3	52.3	240 318	248 232	3.3	-0.3
Sanford	7.5	19.3	10.7	16.6	15.9	12.2	7.2	5.5	5.0	50.3	32 387	38 291	18.2	13.7
Sarasota	5.3	13.1	9.2	13.4	14.6	12.8	9.6	9.6	12.4	51.4	50 897	52 715	3.6	1.0
Sunrise	6.4	18.5	7.3	14.7	16.9	11.9	6.5	6.5	11.2	53.2	65 683	85 779	30.6	3.9
Tallahassee	5.2	12.2	29.7	15.9	11.9	10.9	5.9	4.1	4.1	52.8	124 773	150 624	20.7	2.2
Tamarac	4.4	9.0	5.3	12.1	11.3	10.1	10.0	14.4	23.4	55.3	44 822	55 588	24.0	4.3
Tampa	6.8	17.9	10.0	15.8	16.5	12.7	7.9	6.4	6.1	51.2	280 015	303 447	8.4	4.7
Titusville	5.7	17.3	6.9	10.9	15.3	12.4	10.8	11.2	9.6	52.4	39 394	40 670	3.2	2.7
Weston city	9.0	23.4	5.0	14.5	21.7	13.3	6.4	4.2	2.5	51.5	9 829	49 286	401.4	26.3
West Palm Beach	6.1	15.3	9.8	16.0	15.5	12.6	8.8	7.6	8.4	50.7	67 764	82 103	21.2	8.3
Winter Haven	5.7	15.2	6.8	11.0	12.5	11.5	9.8	11.8	15.6	54.0	24 725	26 487	7.1	2.5
Winter Springs	6.0	21.0	7.3	11.5	17.9	16.4	9.0	6.3	4.5	51.5	22 151	31 666	43.0	0.4
GEORGIA	7.3	19.2	10.2	15.9	16.5	13.2	8.1	5.3	4.3	50.8	6 478 149	8 186 453	26.4	6.1
Albany	7.8	20.0	13.0	14.2	13.5	12.0	7.6	6.3	5.6	54.0	78 804	76 939	-2.4	-1.0
Alpharetta	8.5	18.6	7.2	19.2	21.3	13.1	6.3	3.4	2.4	50.4	13 002	34 854	168.1	0.8

Table D. Cities — **Group Quarters, Crime, and Education**

City	Households, 2000					Persons in group quarters, 2000				Serious crimes known to police,[2] 2002				Education, 2000			
				Percent			Institutional			Total		Rate[2]		School enrollment[4]		Attainment[5] (percent)	
	Number	Percent change, 1990–2000	Persons per household	Female family householder[1]	One-person	Total	Total	Persons in nursing homes	Non-institutional	Number	Rate[3]	Violent	Property	Public	Private	High school graduate or less	Bachelor's degree or more
	26	27	28	29	30	31	32	33	34	35	36	37	38	39	40	41	42
FLORIDA—Cont'd																	
Cape Coral	40 768	37.0	2.49	9.3	19.7	591	550	550	41	4 086	3 820	364	3 456	18 641	3 486	50.1	17.5
Clearwater	48 449	9.8	2.17	11.3	35.5	3 863	1 457	1 437	2 406	6 544	5 752	987	4 765	18 082	4 350	44.4	23.9
Coconut Creek	20 093	48.0	2.16	7.7	32.5	197	113	113	84	1 236	2 713	283	2 430	6 305	1 800	41.3	27.1
Cooper City	9 123	30.8	3.06	11.9	10.8	1	0	0	1	816	2 793	178	2 615	8 044	1 780	30.5	38.2
Coral Gables	16 793	8.6	2.31	9.1	31.5	3 510	97	51	3 413	2 863	6 480	416	6 064	4 457	8 613	19.3	58.3
Coral Springs	39 522	46.3	2.96	13.3	15.2	567	305	305	262	3 918	3 187	238	2 950	30 226	7 250	33.9	33.9
Davie	28 682	60.2	2.64	12.6	22.3	97	33	33	64	3 699	4 672	400	4 271	16 703	5 461	44.9	25.8
Daytona Beach	28 605	3.8	2.06	14.5	39.4	5 097	1 492	1 315	3 605	7 181	10 711	1 395	9 316	11 114	6 990	49.5	18.8
Deerfield Beach	31 392	35.8	2.02	9.6	40.3	1 168	659	305	509	1 928	2 855	425	2 430	9 044	2 443	50.5	21.2
Delray Beach	26 787	25.2	2.22	10.2	35.3	530	304	216	226	4 665	7 433	942	6 491	9 923	2 518	42.6	29.3
Dunedin	17 258	8.6	2.01	8.8	37.9	943	209	209	734	1 087	2 912	268	2 644	4 919	1 330	42.2	22.4
Fort Lauderdale	68 468	3.1	2.14	11.5	40.3	5 559	3 979	617	1 580	11 681	7 330	883	6 447	24 853	7 891	45.3	27.9
Fort Myers	19 107	5.3	2.40	18.4	33.8	2 307	2 205	784	102	5 118	10 152	2 130	8 022	10 149	1 633	58.3	18.3
Fort Pierce	14 407	1.7	2.56	19.3	31.1	705	8	0	697	4 329	11 034	2 098	8 937	8 905	884	65.1	12.7
Gainesville	37 279	16.8	2.25	13.3	32.6	11 507	1 989	386	9 518	6 016	6 027	766	5 261	42 016	2 574	29.6	42.8
Greenacres City	12 059	46.4	2.29	12.5	29.7	0	0	0	0	NA	NA	NA	NA	4 798	660	54.1	17.4
Hallandale Beach	18 051	5.3	1.88	9.1	45.2	368	133	133	235	NA	NA	NA	NA	4 332	1 188	57.7	19.8
Hialeah	70 704	19.1	3.15	17.4	14.7	3 652	2 304	1 603	1 348	12 217	5 160	634	4 526	49 256	7 555	73.0	10.4
Hollywood	59 673	12.8	2.31	13.4	34.4	1 751	858	812	893	9 171	6 293	702	5 591	24 940	7 410	49.8	21.9
Homestead	10 095	8.4	3.10	22.4	20.9	575	432	400	143	3 793	11 367	2 176	9 191	8 347	779	70.7	9.8
Jacksonville	284 499	10.6	2.53	16.0	26.2	15 317	6 579	3 401	8 738	51 021	6 633	916	5 717	163 990	37 489	47.3	21.1
Jupiter town	16 945	58.8	2.32	8.4	25.8	91	70	70	21	1 717	4 175	353	3 822	6 427	1 916	32.9	34.7
Key West	11 016	5.7	2.23	8.2	31.4	893	518	95	375	2 199	8 254	679	7 574	3 868	674	40.2	27.3
Kissimmee	17 121	51.3	2.77	15.8	20.9	461	321	192	140	3 471	6 942	942	6 000	10 955	1 590	52.9	16.3
Lakeland	33 509	13.0	2.23	13.7	32.9	3 710	1 247	1 090	2 463	5 360	6 533	811	5 723	13 767	4 740	51.0	20.9
Lake Worth	13 828	10.1	2.49	11.5	33.6	761	645	645	116	3 424	9 320	1 331	7 989	7 063	1 093	57.6	16.4
Largo	34 041	6.6	1.99	9.0	38.5	1 786	922	696	864	3 050	4 204	358	3 846	9 388	1 875	52.1	16.4
Lauderdale Lakes	12 099	1.1	2.59	22.2	30.1	350	337	337	13	1 002	3 022	679	2 344	7 935	1 368	66.2	12.5
Lauderhill	22 810	7.9	2.49	20.1	31.0	842	210	112	632	2 949	4 897	850	4 047	13 618	2 341	53.9	16.2
Margate	22 714	20.0	2.36	10.2	30.8	345	247	247	98	1 768	3 136	344	2 792	9 677	1 834	53.5	17.0
Melbourne	30 788	22.8	2.22	11.5	32.9	3 064	1 451	694	1 613	5 329	7 139	1 439	5 700	12 773	4 663	44.1	21.3
Miami	134 198	3.0	2.61	18.7	30.4	11 611	8 333	1 517	3 278	33 952	8 957	1 907	7 050	78 681	12 185	67.1	16.2
Miami Beach	46 194	-6.3	1.87	8.5	48.7	1 336	796	671	540	10 390	11 299	1 171	10 128	12 603	4 991	41.7	33.5
Miramar	23 058	60.2	3.15	19.1	14.3	28	0	0	28	3 437	4 519	596	3 923	19 874	4 558	45.6	20.7
North Lauderdale	10 799	19.0	2.99	19.3	19.6	0	0	0	0	758	2 247	495	1 752	8 740	1 435	55.8	13.5
North Miami	20 541	2.1	2.85	20.1	26.9	1 255	547	498	708	5 605	8 951	1 410	7 541	17 986	3 654	58.8	15.8
North Miami Beach	13 987	0.1	2.89	19.5	23.9	426	386	382	40	2 793	6 548	764	5 784	10 971	1 585	59.1	14.2
Oakland Park	13 502	11.6	2.26	13.3	35.1	440	13	13	427	1 598	4 935	735	4 200	5 896	1 229	49.8	21.2
Ocala	18 646	7.2	2.29	15.9	31.8	3 260	2 537	1 070	723	4 159	8 657	1 397	7 260	9 155	1 801	50.2	19.4
Orlando	80 883	23.1	2.25	15.4	35.0	4 041	2 489	1 031	1 552	21 133	10 868	1 861	9 007	36 847	7 508	42.3	28.2
Ormond Beach	15 629	23.0	2.27	8.8	27.1	766	571	475	195	1 223	3 222	274	2 948	5 950	1 481	37.4	29.1
Oviedo	8 556	125.5	3.07	9.9	10.5	78	41	41	37	748	2 718	385	2 333	7 976	1 364	26.2	41.3
Palm Bay	30 336	30.0	2.60	12.2	21.8	390	263	236	127	4 129	4 972	834	4 138	18 656	3 047	48.0	16.7
Palm Beach Gardens	15 599	63.2	2.23	8.9	27.7	325	142	142	183	1 872	5 106	346	4 760	5 110	2 130	26.4	43.8
Panama City	14 819	5.5	2.30	15.4	32.2	2 351	2 091	503	260	3 107	8 159	853	7 305	8 014	1 016	50.5	18.9
Pembroke Pines	51 989	94.6	2.62	11.1	24.1	1 288	1 261	105	27	4 751	3 306	263	3 043	29 966	7 892	38.5	28.7
Pensacola	24 524	2.3	2.27	16.7	32.9	496	342	305	154	3 121	5 305	782	4 523	12 086	2 454	37.6	32.4
Pinellas Park	19 444	6.9	2.31	11.6	30.2	802	484	312	318	3 134	6 564	584	5 980	7 578	1 866	58.3	11.9
Plantation	33 244	25.5	2.48	11.2	25.8	475	417	417	58	4 435	5 114	300	4 814	15 274	6 586	33.0	36.7
Plant City	10 849	29.2	2.73	14.8	22.9	337	269	269	68	2 432	7 774	857	6 917	7 221	867	56.4	16.6
Pompano Beach	35 197	9.5	2.13	10.9	38.6	3 239	2 647	453	592	4 178	5 110	959	4 151	11 985	2 935	51.4	21.6
Port Orange	19 574	30.8	2.32	9.6	25.7	504	414	399	90	1 128	2 354	61	2 294	8 112	1 782	49.9	17.0
Port St. Lucie	33 909	64.0	2.60	10.0	18.2	574	331	319	243	2 922	3 148	291	2 857	18 368	2 763	51.1	15.0
Riviera Beach	11 387	10.2	2.60	23.5	27.6	313	137	116	176	4 437	14 198	1 734	12 464	7 830	1 044	56.6	17.7
St. Petersburg	109 663	3.7	2.20	13.8	35.6	6 502	3 297	2 840	3 205	20 914	8 057	1 704	6 353	46 408	12 252	46.1	22.8
Sanford	14 237	17.5	2.57	19.2	27.0	1 696	1 302	50	394	3 283	8 199	677	7 522	8 828	1 253	55.3	14.0
Sarasota	23 427	2.7	2.12	12.3	38.3	3 122	1 870	1 083	1 252	4 699	8 524	1 146	7 378	9 153	1 628	47.4	25.7
Sunrise	33 308	26.6	2.54	13.8	27.2	1 066	771	685	295	4 290	4 783	491	4 292	18 525	4 289	49.1	20.0
Tallahassee	63 217	25.3	2.17	13.2	34.7	13 157	3 720	930	9 437	11 880	7 542	1 027	6 516	61 151	5 567	26.8	45.0
Tamarac	27 423	19.7	2.00	9.4	36.3	609	310	310	299	1 129	1 942	258	1 684	7 003	1 293	53.8	17.3
Tampa	124 758	8.7	2.36	16.1	33.7	8 918	3 000	763	5 918	35 380	11 150	1 982	9 168	66 360	15 901	48.4	25.4
Titusville	17 200	6.1	2.32	12.6	29.9	825	638	536	187	2 146	5 046	856	4 190	8 329	1 181	46.0	19.2
Weston city	16 576	NA	2.97	9.0	13.8	0	0	0	0	NA	NA	NA	NA	11 313	4 722	18.9	50.9
West Palm Beach	34 769	20.8	2.26	13.6	37.6	3 635	970	734	2 665	10 603	12 350	1 386	10 964	15 270	4 024	46.9	26.9
Winter Haven	11 833	8.2	2.17	12.8	36.0	762	442	436	320	2 504	9 040	744	8 297	4 307	809	56.5	16.7
Winter Springs	11 774	47.0	2.69	11.1	18.8	36	0	0	36	623	1 881	248	1 634	7 665	1 419	30.9	36.3
GEORGIA	3 006 369	27.0	2.65	14.5	23.6	233 822	126 023	34 812	107 799	385 830	4 507	459	4 048	1 892 158	319 500	50.1	24.3
Albany	28 620	2.5	2.54	25.2	28.8	4 237	1 614	490	2 623	5 430	6 749	639	6 110	20 962	2 579	54.7	18.2
Alpharetta	13 911	164.2	2.50	7.3	27.7	80	2	0	78	1 565	4 294	332	3 962	6 677	2 224	17.1	57.1

1. No spouse present.   2. Data for serious crimes have not been adjusted for underreporting. This may affect comparability between geographic areas and over time.   3. Per 100,000 population estimated by the FBI.   4. All persons 3 years old and over enrolled in nursery school through college.   5. Persons 25 years old and over.

Table D. Cities — Income, Poverty, and Housing

City	Money income, 1999							Housing units, 2000					
	Households				Percent below poverty					Vacant units			
	Median income				Persons		Families						
	Per capita income[1] (dollars)	Dollars	Percent change, 1989–1999 (constant 1999 dollars)	Percent with income of $100,000 or more	Total	Percent change in rate, 1989–1999	Total	Total	Percent change, 1990–2000	Vacant units for sale or rent[2]	For seasonal use (percent)	Home owner vacancy rate	Renter vacancy rate
	43	44	45	46	47	48	49	50	51	52	53	54	55
FLORIDA—Cont'd													
Cape Coral	21 021	43 410	3.6	8.2	7.0	18.6	5.3	45 653	32.4	4 885	6.2	1.8	7.9
Clearwater	22 786	36 494	2.6	9.4	12.3	15.0	8.4	56 802	5.5	8 353	7.6	2.4	9.3
Coconut Creek	25 590	43 980	-1.4	10.5	7.1	73.2	5.1	22 182	40.6	2 089	4.1	2.4	10.0
Cooper City	27 474	75 166	12.5	28.1	3.2	-13.5	2.9	9 289	26.4	166	0.5	0.7	2.9
Coral Gables	46 163	66 839	4.7	35.5	6.9	6.2	4.3	17 849	7.8	1 056	1.7	1.5	4.2
Coral Springs	25 282	58 459	0.2	22.7	8.0	53.8	6.3	41 337	38.8	1 815	0.7	1.6	5.1
Davie	23 271	47 014	-5.0	15.8	9.8	25.6	6.9	31 284	57.3	2 602	3.3	2.6	5.3
Daytona Beach	17 530	25 439	1.6	5.3	23.6	4.9	16.9	33 345	3.7	4 740	6.4	2.6	8.4
Deerfield Beach	23 296	34 041	-6.0	8.7	12.5	26.3	9.2	37 343	29.7	5 951	10.2	1.8	5.5
Delray Beach	29 350	43 371	3.6	15.1	11.8	4.4	8.2	31 702	15.2	4 915	11.0	1.5	7.8
Dunedin	23 460	34 813	0.0	8.1	8.2	15.5	4.8	19 952	8.4	2 694	6.2	2.3	13.8
Fort Lauderdale	27 798	37 887	3.5	14.3	17.7	3.5	13.8	80 862	-0.5	12 394	8.5	2.5	7.7
Fort Myers	17 312	28 514	-4.0	6.6	21.8	5.3	18.1	21 836	2.1	2 729	3.7	3.7	10.0
Fort Pierce	14 345	25 121	-1.1	4.6	30.9	5.8	25.4	17 170	-0.5	2 763	6.1	3.1	13.0
Gainesville	16 779	28 164	-0.5	7.7	26.7	1.5	15.3	40 105	15.9	2 826	0.4	2.0	6.8
Greenacres City	19 298	36 941	-6.0	5.3	7.2	1.4	5.0	14 153	26.5	2 094	8.4	2.3	10.5
Hallandale Beach	22 464	28 266	0.9	6.6	16.8	5.0	13.1	25 022	0.9	6 971	19.7	2.6	9.0
Hialeah	12 402	29 492	-6.4	4.1	18.6	2.2	16.0	72 142	16.0	1 438	0.2	1.0	1.7
Hollywood	22 097	36 714	-0.1	10.1	13.2	20.0	9.9	68 426	8.1	8 753	7.2	2.2	7.1
Homestead	11 357	26 775	-3.2	4.0	31.8	6.4	29.1	11 162	3.6	1 067	1.3	3.7	8.0
Jacksonville	20 337	40 316	5.2	9.3	12.2	-4.7	9.4	308 826	8.5	24 327	0.3	1.8	9.0
Jupiter town	35 088	54 945	7.0	22.9	4.8	-17.2	3.0	20 943	43.4	3 998	14.4	1.4	11.1
Key West	26 316	43 021	13.9	12.2	10.2	-1.9	5.8	13 306	8.9	2 290	8.3	2.3	9.3
Kissimmee	15 071	33 949	-8.4	3.7	15.4	30.5	12.3	19 642	44.4	2 521	5.6	2.6	9.2
Lakeland	19 760	33 119	0.8	6.8	15.0	7.1	10.7	38 980	11.6	5 471	5.5	3.5	9.4
Lake Worth	15 517	30 034	3.2	4.5	20.0	17.0	15.8	15 861	1.5	2 033	5.5	2.6	7.9
Largo	20 848	32 217	-1.3	4.4	9.1	23.0	6.0	40 261	4.0	6 220	8.6	3.0	10.2
Lauderdale Lakes	14 039	26 932	-3.3	3.0	22.5	58.5	19.9	14 325	2.9	2 226	9.7	2.9	6.8
Lauderhill	17 243	32 515	-9.4	6.0	17.8	72.8	15.5	25 751	-2.0	2 941	5.3	3.1	5.8
Margate	20 308	38 722	1.2	7.1	8.4	9.1	5.5	24 740	14.3	2 026	3.9	2.3	6.2
Melbourne	19 175	34 571	-0.6	6.3	11.5	-10.2	8.6	33 678	20.0	2 890	2.5	2.3	8.5
Miami	15 128	23 483	3.3	6.8	28.5	-8.7	23.5	148 388	2.7	14 190	2.0	2.9	6.6
Miami Beach	27 853	27 322	32.8	11.7	21.8	-13.5	17.0	59 723	-4.3	13 529	12.8	7.6	8.8
Miramar	18 462	50 289	4.6	11.7	8.2	-2.4	7.0	25 905	69.9	2 847	0.4	9.7	6.6
North Lauderdale	15 557	40 050	-17.9	5.1	13.7	104.5	11.5	11 444	16.8	645	0.9	3.1	5.8
North Miami	14 581	29 778	-11.0	6.5	23.9	54.2	20.7	22 281	0.8	1 740	1.6	2.2	5.8
North Miami Beach	14 699	31 377	-6.4	5.6	20.5	58.9	18.4	15 350	-3.0	1 363	3.9	2.6	4.7
Oakland Park	18 873	35 493	-4.7	5.7	16.5	58.7	13.3	14 509	4.6	1 007	2.8	2.0	4.6
Ocala	18 021	30 888	5.6	6.6	18.1	-9.0	13.2	20 501	5.3	1 855	1.6	2.3	8.0
Orlando	21 216	35 732	1.8	7.7	15.9	0.6	13.3	88 486	20.5	7 603	1.3	1.8	8.3
Ormond Beach	26 364	43 364	-1.3	13.5	6.1	-9.0	4.2	17 258	21.6	1 629	4.7	1.7	10.4
Oviedo	23 831	64 119	18.7	19.2	4.6	-41.0	3.3	8 977	113.1	421	0.3	1.4	11.9
Palm Bay	16 992	36 508	-10.3	4.5	9.5	9.2	7.1	32 902	25.2	2 566	2.0	2.6	9.0
Palm Beach Gardens	42 975	59 776	-0.4	26.1	5.6	24.4	3.5	18 317	50.5	2 718	10.0	1.6	10.0
Panama City	17 830	31 572	7.4	5.8	17.2	-12.2	12.1	16 548	3.9	1 729	0.9	2.5	11.2
Pembroke Pines	23 843	52 629	7.5	15.7	5.4	5.9	3.9	55 296	87.2	3 307	2.1	2.1	5.8
Pensacola	21 438	34 779	3.3	9.0	16.1	-14.8	12.7	26 995	2.4	2 471	0.7	2.2	10.0
Pinellas Park	18 701	35 048	-0.1	4.1	9.3	0.0	6.5	21 843	6.1	2 399	4.5	2.6	8.9
Plantation	28 250	53 746	-4.4	20.5	6.4	82.9	4.3	34 999	19.0	1 755	1.7	1.3	5.2
Plant City	18 815	37 584	10.7	8.9	14.7	-17.4	11.3	11 797	26.2	948	0.9	2.4	7.8
Pompano Beach	23 938	36 073	-9.5	10.9	17.0	6.3	13.1	44 496	4.2	9 299	15.8	1.9	7.1
Port Orange	20 628	38 783	9.0	6.0	7.6	-7.3	5.0	21 102	24.0	1 528	3.5	1.7	5.6
Port St. Lucie	18 059	40 509	-7.4	5.6	7.9	46.3	5.7	36 785	51.7	2 876	3.6	2.0	8.1
Riviera Beach	19 847	32 111	-3.8	9.9	23.0	1.8	19.0	14 220	1.0	2 833	13.8	1.9	8.6
St. Petersburg	21 107	34 597	9.2	7.6	13.3	-2.2	9.2	124 618	-0.7	14 955	3.9	2.4	9.1
Sanford	15 219	31 163	-7.3	4.8	17.8	9.2	13.2	15 623	12.9	1 386	0.9	2.7	6.6
Sarasota	23 197	34 077	1.9	9.1	16.7	25.6	12.4	26 898	-0.3	3 471	6.6	2.2	7.8
Sunrise	18 713	40 998	-3.3	7.3	9.7	49.2	7.3	35 661	21.7	2 353	1.9	2.4	5.8
Tallahassee	18 981	30 571	-3.0	8.0	24.7	10.8	12.6	68 417	23.9	5 200	0.6	2.1	7.7
Tamarac	22 243	34 290	-4.4	6.0	8.9	53.4	6.1	29 750	13.8	2 327	3.3	2.7	4.8
Tampa	21 953	34 415	12.5	10.5	18.1	-6.7	14.0	135 776	4.7	11 018	0.6	2.1	7.8
Titusville	18 901	35 607	-6.8	7.2	12.4	17.0	9.3	19 178	5.5	1 978	3.4	2.3	10.6
Weston city	35 490	80 920	NA	37.6	5.0	NA	3.9	18 943	NA	2 367	4.7	2.8	5.3
West Palm Beach	23 188	36 774	3.3	11.5	18.9	16.7	14.5	40 461	15.7	5 692	5.0	2.9	10.3
Winter Haven	20 383	31 884	0.2	5.4	15.0	11.1	10.5	13 912	9.1	2 079	5.5	3.8	11.8
Winter Springs	26 166	53 247	-2.3	21.0	4.2	27.3	3.3	12 306	41.4	532	0.7	1.2	9.0
GEORGIA	21 154	42 433	8.8	12.3	13.0	-11.6	9.9	3 281 737	24.4	275 368	1.5	1.9	8.2
Albany	15 485	28 639	-2.6	6.7	27.1	-1.5	21.5	32 062	4.8	3 442	0.4	2.7	10.7
Alpharetta	39 432	71 207	19.5	33.6	5.2	40.5	2.9	14 670	149.2	759	0.7	1.7	5.6

1. Based on population enumerated as of April 1, 2000.   2. Includes units rented or sold but not occupied.

Table D. Cities — Housing, Labor Force, Employment, and Disability

City	Housing units, 2000 (cont'd) Occupied units					Civilian labor force, 2003				Civilian employment,[2] 2000			Disability, 2000
	Total	Percent owner occupied	Percent renter occupied	Average size owner occupied	Average size renter occupied	Total	Percent change, 2002–2003	Unemployment Total	Rate[1]	Total	Percent Management, professional, and related occupations	Production, transportation, and material moving occupations	Employment disabled persons[3] (percent)
	56	57	58	59	60	61	62	63	64	65	66	67	68
FLORIDA—Cont'd													
Cape Coral	40 768	80.0	20.0	2.48	2.54	49 540	3.6	1 954	3.9	47 623	28.6	9.5	13.6
Clearwater	48 449	62.1	37.9	2.19	2.12	59 217	0.5	2 781	4.7	51 663	34.1	10.5	15.0
Coconut Creek	20 093	75.5	24.5	2.17	2.13	17 061	0.9	1 102	6.5	20 283	37.6	6.7	8.6
Cooper City	9 123	92.2	7.8	3.07	3.00	16 105	1.1	485	3.0	14 536	45.3	5.7	5.9
Coral Gables	16 793	65.8	34.2	2.56	1.83	24 538	-1.0	927	3.8	20 753	59.9	2.9	7.6
Coral Springs	39 522	65.0	35.0	3.08	2.73	59 952	1.0	2 397	4.0	59 432	39.5	7.0	10.9
Davie	28 682	76.5	23.5	2.74	2.29	37 651	1.0	1 822	4.8	38 361	34.1	8.8	10.3
Daytona Beach	28 605	47.3	52.7	2.15	1.98	34 666	2.4	2 332	6.7	27 504	26.1	12.6	14.3
Deerfield Beach	31 392	70.2	29.8	1.98	2.12	28 589	1.0	1 420	5.0	28 174	30.7	9.4	16.3
Delray Beach	26 787	69.7	30.3	2.19	2.30	30 249	0.4	2 348	7.8	25 672	33.6	9.0	17.0
Dunedin	17 258	71.4	28.6	2.09	1.81	18 929	0.6	720	3.8	16 008	35.2	7.3	15.9
Fort Lauderdale	68 468	55.4	44.6	2.18	2.10	107 942	0.8	7 472	6.9	72 444	33.4	9.8	16.0
Fort Myers	19 107	39.7	60.3	2.50	2.34	31 510	3.6	1 779	5.6	20 470	25.6	9.8	17.3
Fort Pierce	14 407	53.2	46.8	2.40	2.73	20 842	2.4	2 627	12.6	14 299	19.9	15.5	23.4
Gainesville	37 279	47.7	52.3	2.39	2.12	51 684	0.6	1 469	2.8	44 249	45.9	5.5	7.8
Greenacres City	12 059	70.9	29.1	2.17	2.56	14 081	0.5	729	5.2	11 774	24.9	11.2	17.7
Hallandale Beach	18 051	66.6	33.4	1.80	2.03	14 957	0.8	1 132	7.6	13 329	27.7	11.0	14.9
Hialeah	70 704	50.7	49.3	3.35	2.95	110 232	-1.3	8 294	7.5	82 251	16.5	24.0	17.5
Hollywood	59 673	62.2	37.8	2.43	2.10	83 194	0.9	5 228	6.3	65 326	31.3	10.0	14.1
Homestead	10 095	36.0	64.0	2.74	3.31	13 721	-1.2	936	6.8	12 530	17.2	9.8	18.6
Jacksonville	284 499	63.2	36.8	2.64	2.34	390 804	0.4	22 510	5.8	343 319	31.2	12.4	14.1
Jupiter town	16 945	81.3	18.7	2.31	2.33	19 393	0.6	756	3.9	19 152	40.5	6.7	11.6
Key West	11 016	45.6	54.4	2.24	2.23	15 577	1.0	350	2.2	13 777	29.8	6.0	12.9
Kissimmee	17 121	44.9	55.1	2.88	2.67	32 974	1.5	1 966	6.0	23 431	20.7	10.3	18.2
Lakeland	33 509	60.3	39.7	2.24	2.22	38 108	0.3	2 110	5.5	33 000	30.8	15.7	15.3
Lake Worth	13 828	52.4	47.6	2.41	2.57	19 814	0.5	1 207	6.1	16 291	21.8	10.4	15.4
Largo	34 041	67.4	32.6	2.01	1.93	37 450	0.6	1 432	3.8	30 558	29.2	12.4	16.8
Lauderdale Lakes	12 099	62.2	37.8	2.41	2.89	16 366	0.8	1 270	7.8	12 221	20.0	13.8	18.8
Lauderhill	22 810	59.4	40.6	2.40	2.62	33 820	0.9	1 947	5.8	24 892	26.2	10.8	20.5
Margate	22 714	80.1	19.9	2.37	2.33	27 925	0.9	1 532	5.5	24 664	27.5	9.9	14.7
Melbourne	30 788	62.1	37.9	2.34	2.02	34 130	0.6	1 927	5.6	32 512	31.4	11.0	14.0
Miami	134 198	34.9	65.1	2.79	2.52	191 929	-1.5	19 932	10.4	129 981	23.8	13.8	19.3
Miami Beach	46 194	36.6	63.4	2.00	1.80	46 945	-1.3	3 939	8.4	40 744	40.3	6.8	15.7
Miramar	23 058	80.1	19.9	3.23	2.83	31 059	1.0	1 547	5.0	33 734	31.3	9.9	12.5
North Lauderdale	10 799	63.7	36.3	3.03	2.92	21 385	0.9	1 116	5.2	15 506	23.6	11.7	18.9
North Miami	20 541	50.5	49.5	3.10	2.61	30 345	-1.3	2 351	7.7	23 559	24.3	13.8	20.3
North Miami Beach	13 987	61.8	38.2	2.98	2.74	19 783	-1.1	1 171	5.9	16 048	22.0	13.0	15.4
Oakland Park	13 502	50.7	49.3	2.23	2.29	22 183	1.0	1 059	4.8	16 838	26.4	13.2	16.5
Ocala	18 646	57.2	42.8	2.34	2.22	24 441	2.1	1 159	4.7	18 831	31.8	12.0	14.4
Orlando	80 883	40.8	59.2	2.38	2.16	128 580	1.3	6 760	5.3	96 783	33.3	9.8	15.1
Ormond Beach	15 629	81.7	18.3	2.32	2.06	16 041	2.5	571	3.6	15 669	40.3	6.8	9.9
Oviedo	8 556	85.6	14.4	3.09	2.92	8 466	1.4	330	3.9	14 077	43.8	6.5	7.5
Palm Bay	30 336	75.3	24.7	2.63	2.54	36 646	0.6	1 871	5.1	35 906	29.4	12.1	13.5
Palm Beach Gardens	15 599	79.5	20.5	2.26	2.08	18 036	0.7	503	2.8	16 884	46.9	5.7	8.7
Panama City	14 819	57.8	42.2	2.35	2.23	19 288	2.3	1 252	6.5	14 702	32.2	10.4	13.8
Pembroke Pines	51 989	80.2	19.8	2.65	2.48	46 333	1.1	1 692	3.7	65 239	40.7	7.2	8.1
Pensacola	24 524	63.3	36.7	2.34	2.16	28 009	1.4	1 285	4.6	24 419	38.3	8.7	11.6
Pinellas Park	19 444	75.1	24.9	2.29	2.36	26 189	0.6	1 071	4.1	21 264	23.2	18.1	18.2
Plantation	33 244	71.7	28.3	2.58	2.23	52 254	1.0	2 119	4.1	43 748	43.0	6.2	9.8
Plant City	10 849	65.7	34.3	2.73	2.71	15 324	0.6	623	4.1	12 830	25.5	18.5	15.0
Pompano Beach	35 197	62.8	37.2	2.07	2.23	47 155	0.8	3 096	6.6	33 103	28.6	11.0	18.2
Port Orange	19 574	82.1	17.9	2.33	2.24	20 205	2.5	778	3.9	20 814	30.1	9.5	12.3
Port St. Lucie	33 909	83.3	16.7	2.55	2.83	35 780	2.9	2 063	5.8	39 493	26.6	10.7	15.3
Riviera Beach	11 387	59.2	40.8	2.47	2.78	18 654	0.3	1 822	9.8	11 664	24.5	14.7	19.8
St. Petersburg	109 663	63.5	36.5	2.32	2.00	144 274	0.5	7 371	5.1	117 892	34.0	12.7	16.8
Sanford	14 237	55.4	44.6	2.63	2.49	22 296	1.3	1 390	6.2	16 923	25.0	15.0	16.0
Sarasota	23 427	58.4	41.6	2.08	2.17	34 661	2.4	1 411	4.1	23 298	29.0	9.8	16.4
Sunrise	33 308	73.8	26.2	2.58	2.43	43 463	1.0	2 195	5.1	40 074	31.7	9.5	12.8
Tallahassee	63 217	43.8	56.2	2.35	2.04	87 826	0.1	3 491	4.0	75 613	46.0	5.2	6.3
Tamarac	27 423	79.9	20.1	1.94	2.27	24 009	0.9	1 448	6.0	22 619	28.4	9.0	18.7
Tampa	124 758	55.0	45.0	2.49	2.20	198 493	0.6	10 153	5.1	136 492	34.0	10.9	15.1
Titusville	17 200	68.0	32.0	2.33	2.28	22 328	0.6	1 086	4.9	17 071	33.6	13.0	11.3
Weston city	16 576	81.8	18.2	3.02	2.78	NA	NA	NA	NA	22 702	51.7	4.6	6.6
West Palm Beach	34 769	52.0	48.0	2.31	2.20	51 319	0.4	3 606	7.0	37 813	32.1	10.0	18.3
Winter Haven	11 833	59.1	40.9	2.26	2.05	12 689	0.3	702	5.5	10 029	26.2	14.1	18.0
Winter Springs	11 774	80.3	19.7	2.72	2.55	17 177	1.4	730	4.2	16 191	43.4	6.9	9.5
GEORGIA	3 006 369	67.5	32.5	2.71	2.51	4 414 014	3.1	207 191	4.7	3 839 756	32.7	15.7	12.6
Albany	28 620	47.4	52.6	2.54	2.54	34 660	3.9	2 126	6.1	28 934	30.5	16.4	14.9
Alpharetta	13 911	60.3	39.7	2.81	2.02	9 934	2.7	218	2.2	19 059	54.6	4.0	6.5

1. Percent of civilian labor force.   2. Persons 16 years old and over.   3. Persons 16 to 64 years old.

City	Value of residential construction authorized by building permits, 2003			Wholesale trade, 1997				Retail trade,[1] 1997			
	New construction ($1,000)	Number of housing units	Percent single family	Number of establishments	Number of employees	Sales (mil dol)	Annual payroll (mil dol)	Number of establishments	Number of employees	Sales (mil dol)	Annual payroll (mil dol)
	69	70	71	72	73	74	75	76	77	78	79
FLORIDA—Cont'd											
Cape Coral	470 177	5 063	85.2	94	D	D	D	300	3 747	515.3	52.9
Clearwater	32 569	436	20.0	301	2 173	1 020.3	65.6	775	11 505	2 535.5	222.9
Coconut Creek	12 363	255	1.2	41	85	61.1	3.9	55	1 016	420.4	27.5
Cooper City	32 968	183	100.0	49	158	116.5	5.3	72	1 079	136.9	13.6
Coral Gables	23 854	61	100.0	268	1 981	4 723.1	117.7	315	3 652	795.2	75.6
Coral Springs	14 683	378	4.5	259	2 588	915.1	88.7	417	6 395	950.0	92.3
Davie	92 878	909	58.0	267	2 285	1 406.1	56.1	303	3 690	684.8	71.6
Daytona Beach	21 598	193	44.0	90	1 028	393.2	27.6	546	7 481	1 466.9	126.7
Deerfield Beach	15 861	133	39.1	211	3 391	6 510.8	153.8	278	4 340	885.8	81.8
Delray Beach	72 253	568	67.6	120	569	231.5	19.2	344	4 265	1 467.3	102.4
Dunedin	12 209	67	100.0	41	217	81.8	8.4	129	1 346	175.4	20.0
Fort Lauderdale	140 518	713	58.5	761	8 279	6 347.6	336.0	1 203	13 080	3 192.2	287.9
Fort Myers	141 172	1 417	32.9	207	2 258	557.6	65.2	614	8 593	1 695.1	160.2
Fort Pierce	27 984	376	8.5	59	899	260.3	19.1	257	2 844	431.0	39.9
Gainesville	36 846	586	21.0	138	1 296	620.9	40.8	498	6 521	1 098.3	104.8
Greenacres City	64 340	520	84.2	NA	NA	NA	NA	NA	NA	NA	NA
Hallandale Beach	76 720	620	2.4	90	524	121.7	12.1	134	1 932	263.0	29.1
Hialeah	13 026	152	5.3	576	4 040	1 114.6	99.0	945	10 430	1 530.9	151.2
Hollywood	150 037	476	17.9	361	2 408	1 191.1	80.0	556	6 758	1 234.9	121.6
Homestead	196 142	1 565	78.5	35	D	D	D	122	1 636	303.0	27.8
Jacksonville	917 997	8 152	70.7	1 394	21 860	16 590.0	760.3	3 134	44 276	8 034.1	761.4
Jupiter town	193 206	945	67.1	67	397	284.3	18.4	196	1 904	327.8	35.0
Key West	5 706	47	100.0	32	D	D	D	332	3 117	421.1	48.3
Kissimmee	90 896	667	75.1	43	D	D	D	309	3 517	531.7	52.3
Lakeland	36 745	281	91.5	164	2 468	2 191.2	66.1	621	9 559	1 559.9	148.6
Lake Worth	4 522	43	86.0	69	D	D	D	183	1 519	274.6	26.4
Largo	15 300	135	45.9	179	1 593	526.0	46.4	382	4 358	626.5	66.1
Lauderdale Lakes	0	0	0.0	19	D	D	D	78	713	142.1	13.2
Lauderhill	7 210	106	1.9	51	193	63.6	4.9	159	1 884	534.1	33.3
Margate	1 138	23	4.3	97	381	195.8	10.3	198	3 187	848.1	68.2
Melbourne	53 191	320	100.0	142	1 124	388.1	38.5	446	6 394	1 137.5	111.6
Miami	290 031	2 601	5.1	1 810	12 885	7 178.4	388.8	2 533	21 675	3 681.5	362.5
Miami Beach	34 610	206	13.6	136	470	255.9	12.5	466	3 680	504.2	62.1
Miramar	244 893	1 676	79.5	84	1 479	712.8	57.9	115	2 063	341.1	29.3
North Lauderdale	13 638	292	0.0	13	27	8.8	0.6	48	950	121.2	11.7
North Miami	3 238	42	88.1	108	574	183.1	16.2	235	3 402	705.8	83.2
North Miami Beach	2 350	7	71.4	96	379	180.7	11.3	217	2 775	541.4	47.8
Oakland Park	1 930	14	64.3	223	1 500	489.7	49.2	275	2 719	517.4	53.6
Ocala	48 440	702	30.1	198	2 243	680.8	54.6	602	8 560	1 470.4	136.7
Orlando	400 058	3 449	45.6	676	9 637	4 389.2	315.3	1 406	18 296	3 786.5	334.3
Ormond Beach	70 972	304	100.0	58	622	207.6	17.9	170	2 231	257.1	30.2
Oviedo	98 627	383	99.5	35	129	85.7	3.8	72	1 082	153.4	14.4
Palm Bay	234 803	1 496	100.0	46	264	117.5	11.0	150	2 174	307.1	28.1
Palm Beach Gardens	253 157	1 431	57.2	80	271	239.9	13.9	307	5 612	836.9	91.0
Panama City	246 565	2 341	7.3	88	686	246.5	18.1	415	5 461	916.9	88.6
Pembroke Pines	27 686	255	34.5	135	417	233.3	13.9	375	7 362	1 650.7	125.8
Pensacola	20 119	141	82.3	151	1 992	552.8	53.9	470	6 415	991.4	93.9
Pinellas Park	35 457	509	21.2	115	1 234	391.7	33.0	241	5 235	1 530.8	104.9
Plantation	52 824	184	100.0	229	878	629.3	35.0	441	6 511	1 137.4	109.9
Plant City	6 261	71	91.5	69	1 383	568.8	42.2	159	2 594	451.7	40.7
Pompano Beach	14 253	208	33.2	503	5 616	2 386.7	177.8	587	6 828	1 571.8	140.1
Port Orange	141 412	1 056	71.3	38	207	62.0	5.6	109	1 572	207.5	21.8
Port St. Lucie	635 875	6 403	94.5	NA	NA	NA	NA	NA	NA	NA	NA
Riviera Beach	35 303	432	99.1	101	1 627	1 088.9	55.3	114	847	157.3	17.9
St. Petersburg	58 157	907	46.3	293	3 147	2 221.3	112.5	933	12 942	2 228.7	208.2
Sanford	72 014	1 024	51.2	84	1 046	249.6	28.1	303	3 960	628.4	57.7
Sarasota	77 603	159	49.1	123	890	329.3	23.9	512	5 601	931.6	93.9
Sunrise	26 803	359	78.6	246	2 713	1 728.5	123.1	448	7 971	1 355.2	133.7
Tallahassee	200 564	2 297	51.7	204	2 181	602.2	62.6	864	13 270	1 721.2	188.5
Tamarac	47 881	618	14.6	95	706	433.5	24.9	208	2 516	350.8	38.4
Tampa	297 517	2 740	61.3	1 048	18 497	15 906.4	630.9	1 792	25 054	4 756.7	428.9
Titusville	40 819	323	96.6	29	186	42.3	4.0	182	2 602	386.5	37.1
Weston city	20 414	236	38.1	NA	NA	NA	NA	NA	NA	NA	NA
West Palm Beach	489 739	3 480	44.4	188	1 897	1 356.4	68.4	615	9 261	1 968.5	188.4
Winter Haven	25 434	388	38.1	69	1 098	359.7	24.1	269	3 253	552.5	54.5
Winter Springs	43 466	186	100.0	38	118	32.1	2.7	32	196	24.4	2.5
GEORGIA	10 837 216	96 704	83.4	13 978	191 078	163 647.5	7 519.7	33 073	420 676	72 212.5	6 943.6
Albany	30 319	427	31.1	171	2 151	971.2	63.8	548	7 595	1 134.8	112.6
Alpharetta	36 506	267	100.0	185	5 776	9 870.4	307.6	317	6 233	945.6	105.9

1. Establishments with payroll.

City	Real estate and rental and leasing, 1997				Professional, scientific, and technical services,[1] 1997				Manufacturing, 1997			
	Number of establish-ments	Number of employees	Receipts (mil dol)	Annual payroll (mil dol)	Number of establish-ments	Number of employees	Receipts (mil dol)	Annual payroll (mil dol)	Number of establish-ments	Number of employees	Receipts (mil dol)	Annual payroll (mil dol)
	80	81	82	83	84	85	86	87	88	89	90	91
FLORIDA—Cont'd												
Cape Coral	97	287	51.9	5.7	164	1 469	68.7	36.9	77	549	46.5	12.9
Clearwater	201	961	93.6	20.2	634	4 100	397.1	169.3	182	3 191	342.9	84.8
Coconut Creek	25	85	15.7	2.1	57	128	15.3	4.6	NA	NA	NA	NA
Cooper City	28	78	13.7	1.7	69	213	12.5	5.0	NA	NA	NA	NA
Coral Gables	260	1 266	176.7	35.4	1 109	5 707	606.4	248.3	82	1 186	139.8	34.5
Coral Springs	136	452	86.7	12.5	421	1 587	127.9	45.8	111	1 447	156.1	39.0
Davie	113	401	57.9	10.2	214	669	68.7	22.8	63	1 931	200.4	44.4
Daytona Beach	151	975	106.9	18.2	280	1 761	152.3	53.4	63	1 931	200.4	44.4
Deerfield Beach	84	495	67.3	12.4	218	1 350	142.0	67.7	100	2 511	333.9	78.4
Delray Beach	85	356	41.4	8.0	180	1 773	197.9	89.0	67	613	84.4	18.2
Dunedin	28	107	17.9	2.5	122	2 328	257.0	75.7	NA	NA	NA	NA
Fort Lauderdale	495	4 013	799.5	117.2	1 656	8 971	1 086.8	448.4	352	7 546	1 001.7	247.2
Fort Myers	151	983	148.9	21.6	322	2 093	179.2	80.7	95	1 743	296.7	47.9
Fort Pierce	53	236	23.7	4.1	95	848	47.2	21.0	NA	NA	NA	NA
Gainesville	171	876	97.7	17.1	371	2 547	199.1	84.0	85	1 688	414.3	57.7
Greenacres City	NA	NA	NA	NA	NA	NA	NA	NA	NA	NA	NA	NA
Hallandale Beach	50	109	21.0	2.1	66	243	20.8	8.4	55	733	78.3	18.7
Hialeah	252	884	199.3	21.1	237	1 710	81.2	31.9	690	18 397	1 822.3	425.4
Hollywood	219	1 351	160.8	29.7	607	3 377	307.9	136.6	169	3 498	769.6	92.6
Homestead	25	95	7.4	2.1	38	144	11.1	4.3	NA	NA	NA	NA
Jacksonville	886	6 374	918.5	158.4	1 959	17 491	1 552.9	690.0	754	28 237	7 231.0	944.1
Jupiter town	76	368	42.0	8.7	193	751	83.3	29.0	NA	NA	NA	NA
Key West	111	476	49.5	7.8	106	334	28.0	10.0	NA	NA	NA	NA
Kissimmee	130	2 347	207.3	47.6	93	382	28.6	9.6	32	526	79.5	15.1
Lakeland	139	689	81.7	13.0	256	1 911	172.6	66.6	81	4 007	652.3	127.5
Lake Worth	44	218	20.4	4.8	92	382	29.0	12.7	46	523	40.3	10.8
Largo	108	648	76.9	11.8	178	819	90.9	27.9	138	2 544	229.8	60.6
Lauderdale Lakes	22	928	123.5	23.3	17	60	5.9	1.9	NA	NA	NA	NA
Lauderhill	54	412	30.4	6.2	103	394	25.4	9.1	NA	NA	NA	NA
Margate	53	338	40.4	5.8	100	300	32.1	8.4	NA	NA	NA	NA
Melbourne	115	642	63.4	11.4	297	2 072	209.7	87.0	91	4 435	1 282.6	160.6
Miami	729	4 625	719.5	119.7	2 447	16 969	2 231.5	955.7	575	7 490	1 021.7	188.8
Miami Beach	313	1 909	189.7	33.1	298	1 048	107.2	36.4	NA	NA	NA	NA
Miramar	33	131	18.4	2.8	59	368	37.7	13.6	36	729	124.9	25.1
North Lauderdale	9	30	2.6	0.5	25	249	27.5	12.4	NA	NA	NA	NA
North Miami	95	535	57.7	10.7	123	716	36.8	14.5	63	529	44.6	10.3
North Miami Beach	69	242	33.5	4.8	185	722	72.7	34.4	48	647	100.9	16.0
Oakland Park	72	286	38.8	5.7	156	1 520	145.8	49.0	166	1 855	193.8	48.8
Ocala	145	487	57.5	8.5	252	1 557	112.0	47.1	138	7 680	1 023.1	185.3
Orlando	457	6 995	991.3	194.8	1 348	14 678	1 505.2	630.4	281	12 168	2 390.5	522.5
Ormond Beach	79	412	43.9	8.1	119	573	47.5	15.2	47	1 039	100.1	26.4
Oviedo	23	66	9.7	1.0	50	166	13.4	7.4	NA	NA	NA	NA
Palm Bay	47	335	25.2	6.3	76	306	27.3	11.5	61	8 325	1 171.6	358.6
Palm Beach Gardens	86	361	67.9	11.3	225	1 039	116.0	48.0	NA	NA	NA	NA
Panama City	86	363	32.4	6.0	155	840	63.1	25.0	63	2 255	514.8	74.8
Pembroke Pines	95	422	77.8	9.4	226	785	65.6	23.6	54	632	80.0	15.7
Pensacola	115	511	52.2	9.5	372	3 047	234.9	106.7	75	1 865	475.7	62.9
Pinellas Park	37	157	18.6	3.0	85	622	40.3	17.7	190	7 653	1 136.3	209.6
Plantation	145	788	94.2	15.4	489	2 583	280.2	77.4	53	D	D	D
Plant City	37	127	12.0	2.1	52	193	11.9	5.5	54	3 990	935.0	101.3
Pompano Beach	190	953	141.1	24.3	278	1 367	142.4	41.3	284	6 711	783.8	187.8
Port Orange	38	223	16.6	3.2	43	267	23.2	8.8	NA	NA	NA	NA
Port St. Lucie	NA	NA	NA	NA	NA	NA	NA	NA	NA	NA	NA	NA
Riviera Beach	42	136	24.3	3.1	58	240	31.1	13.2	73	1 439	213.2	42.1
St. Petersburg	287	1 531	177.4	31.2	842	10 581	792.7	373.1	203	7 389	1 237.3	227.1
Sanford	32	276	24.1	4.6	63	342	24.8	12.6	61	2 270	253.6	50.2
Sarasota	184	864	124.4	20.4	483	2 969	329.2	137.7	89	1 529	136.6	35.5
Sunrise	74	706	78.1	13.3	187	643	94.5	22.1	71	2 405	201.3	50.6
Tallahassee	241	1 659	179.5	30.0	704	6 304	654.0	277.3	102	D	D	D
Tamarac	62	452	43.7	10.1	175	724	74.5	28.6	NA	NA	NA	NA
Tampa	526	4 489	599.8	110.6	1 780	26 172	3 145.2	1 112.8	463	13 213	2 442.1	364.2
Titusville	36	127	10.3	1.4	79	286	25.2	11.4	46	614	49.9	12.3
Weston city	NA	NA	NA	NA	NA	NA	NA	NA	NA	NA	NA	NA
West Palm Beach	203	1 508	142.6	39.8	758	6 079	644.2	305.8	154	7 014	2 269.2	402.8
Winter Haven	67	431	42.6	9.3	115	510	41.1	17.6	42	818	188.3	24.1
Winter Springs	22	56	6.0	1.0	59	164	20.9	5.2	NA	NA	NA	NA
GEORGIA	7 794	47 669	6 912.9	1 308.8	17 810	138 198	15 266.4	5 908.8	9 083	533 830	124 526.8	15 534.1
Albany	122	618	79.3	12.1	164	1 286	94.6	36.6	76	D	D	D
Alpharetta	60	335	76.5	14.2	259	2 413	384.5	124.5	44	2 279	589.2	88.9

1. Firms subject to federal tax.

City	Accommodation and foodservices, 1997				Arts, entertainment, and recreation,[1] 1997				Health care and social assistance,[1] 1997			
	Number of establish-ments	Number of employees	Sales (mil dol)	Annual payroll (mil dol)	Number of establish-ments	Number of employees	Receipts (mil dol)	Annual payroll (mil dol)	Number of establish-ments	Number of employees	Receipts (mil dol)	Annual payroll (mil dol)
	92	93	94	95	96	97	98	99	100	101	102	103
FLORIDA—Cont'd												
Cape Coral	122	1 787	60.0	16.5	23	228	12.0	2.6	168	1 330	98.3	41.2
Clearwater	401	7 830	339.3	84.1	40	512	28.3	7.6	522	6 373	426.7	186.0
Coconut Creek	19	116	5.3	1.3	7	21	1.1	0.2	39	351	15.8	7.0
Cooper City	31	611	16.1	4.7	8	42	4.0	0.6	65	498	28.2	13.0
Coral Gables	172	3 701	153.3	47.3	27	347	25.6	4.9	462	3 479	311.4	121.0
Coral Springs	179	3 218	109.9	27.5	46	731	33.5	10.0	362	2 500	189.9	76.6
Davie	138	D	D	D	33	439	99.7	49.5	110	880	48.7	20.9
Daytona Beach	321	7 016	247.2	62.6	29	1 007	101.0	17.9	221	3 362	202.2	92.9
Deerfield Beach	140	2 438	105.0	25.5	23	325	120.4	13.0	117	1 398	97.8	32.7
Delray Beach	138	2 233	84.2	21.8	23	247	9.6	4.3	200	1 880	125.5	55.7
Dunedin	77	916	32.0	7.9	9	121	4.7	1.3	130	1 232	81.0	41.1
Fort Lauderdale	698	19 971	941.5	221.9	117	1 481	116.7	52.2	699	8 023	570.5	267.4
Fort Myers	213	4 338	145.1	38.1	19	483	14.0	4.4	292	7 275	566.7	252.3
Fort Pierce	113	1 751	53.8	14.3	9	71	5.4	1.6	140	2 991	216.0	88.0
Gainesville	273	4 610	140.2	36.2	35	523	18.8	4.7	281	2 442	157.1	77.9
Greenacres City	NA	NA	NA	NA	NA	NA	NA	NA	NA	NA	NA	NA
Hallandale Beach	67	1 610	46.0	13.3	17	0	0.0	0.0	107	767	59.2	23.1
Hialeah	268	3 248	129.7	31.2	31	282	30.1	5.8	680	9 124	698.4	233.9
Hollywood	320	4 871	163.4	44.6	72	1 419	103.5	18.3	450	6 097	514.4	211.2
Homestead	67	990	32.8	8.2	6	0	0.0	0.0	68	460	29.4	11.2
Jacksonville	1 420	28 354	917.2	244.2	173	2 808	187.6	94.3	1 579	23 107	1 729.8	810.5
Jupiter town	96	2 152	73.5	21.3	28	420	42.1	16.0	143	873	69.8	31.8
Key West	286	5 476	307.5	74.5	29	293	36.4	14.8	60	534	38.7	18.1
Kissimmee	205	6 281	480.2	80.2	34	1 065	52.9	16.0	182	2 772	195.0	80.6
Lakeland	222	5 146	160.4	42.8	24	321	12.2	3.5	265	4 898	329.3	133.3
Lake Worth	78	852	32.9	9.2	9	282	10.7	4.4	93	1 055	54.3	22.2
Largo	176	2 854	89.8	21.8	16	114	5.0	1.3	249	5 499	401.1	156.2
Lauderdale Lakes	27	326	11.6	3.0	2	0	0.0	0.0	81	2 560	219.5	83.6
Lauderhill	63	D	D	D	11	139	4.1	2.1	111	1 580	76.4	32.8
Margate	97	D	D	D	19	194	9.2	2.6	143	1 952	136.6	53.2
Melbourne	182	3 407	96.8	28.1	22	360	15.7	3.6	263	3 690	309.3	141.3
Miami	912	16 953	764.8	202.7	123	2 733	470.2	146.5	1 319	12 101	980.0	375.5
Miami Beach	466	12 714	551.0	160.3	56	409	51.0	10.8	330	3 313	292.4	123.4
Miramar	44	425	15.6	3.4	7	25	1.0	0.4	65	956	102.1	36.3
North Lauderdale	36	431	14.0	3.3	2	0	0.0	0.0	19	123	5.2	2.0
North Miami	107	1 952	66.6	16.7	23	117	8.1	1.8	115	2 044	132.1	63.0
North Miami Beach	74	911	32.8	8.4	16	344	28.1	6.9	194	3 116	237.7	113.8
Oakland Park	115	1 729	70.7	17.5	13	155	24.9	3.6	138	2 503	200.5	76.2
Ocala	203	4 763	141.2	39.0	16	204	7.7	1.8	346	5 464	416.1	167.4
Orlando	581	18 872	753.5	214.0	122	0	0.0	0.0	676	7 391	683.5	321.8
Ormond Beach	113	2 485	70.5	19.8	23	277	9.0	2.8	180	2 294	144.4	62.9
Oviedo	25	D	D	D	7	158	8.1	1.8	41	352	19.6	8.9
Palm Bay	80	1 152	35.5	9.4	13	119	5.2	1.2	121	1 032	70.3	31.2
Palm Beach Gardens	96	2 340	93.6	25.8	20	268	19.5	4.2	239	2 888	255.2	94.4
Panama City	175	3 471	129.5	33.3	24	271	10.4	2.6	200	3 295	257.7	104.1
Pembroke Pines	190	4 009	134.3	34.4	37	392	19.8	5.0	298	1 916	139.4	55.0
Pensacola	183	4 156	130.5	35.3	31	392	25.4	4.5	315	3 553	287.5	145.0
Pinellas Park	92	1 565	60.4	14.1	15	135	7.5	2.0	83	1 293	64.0	33.9
Plantation	164	3 601	136.1	35.5	33	320	17.9	4.6	505	7 694	649.6	267.0
Plant City	58	1 070	30.7	8.3	9	274	6.1	2.1	86	847	50.1	22.4
Pompano Beach	229	3 035	124.9	34.1	35	513	38.2	7.4	195	2 304	140.5	60.9
Port Orange	66	1 403	40.7	11.4	7	30	1.3	0.4	77	568	34.0	11.8
Port St. Lucie	NA	NA	NA	NA	NA	NA	NA	NA	NA	NA	NA	NA
Riviera Beach	41	741	33.1	8.2	11	58	5.3	1.5	29	145	6.7	2.4
St. Petersburg	432	7 827	268.8	76.2	50	825	20.2	11.6	783	9 333	656.0	289.4
Sanford	81	1 594	51.4	13.8	13	145	5.5	2.0	72	1 964	140.0	55.9
Sarasota	241	4 628	183.5	49.5	39	757	42.2	9.1	380	3 285	288.3	136.3
Sunrise	163	3 065	115.9	27.8	21	443	19.5	3.4	193	2 942	196.5	74.7
Tallahassee	401	8 819	268.9	69.8	42	385	13.5	3.7	393	5 607	405.0	189.0
Tamarac	102	D	D	D	12	141	8.2	2.0	207	3 294	225.5	86.0
Tampa	842	20 303	782.8	212.3	114	5 723	471.6	167.7	1 014	14 076	1 178.9	467.3
Titusville	80	2 005	52.8	15.8	14	151	7.5	1.9	119	1 302	85.5	39.5
Weston city	NA	NA	NA	NA	NA	NA	NA	NA	NA	NA	NA	NA
West Palm Beach	294	5 797	223.0	60.1	45	630	44.5	13.0	421	5 793	389.8	187.5
Winter Haven	116	2 223	63.0	15.8	7	17	0.6	0.1	149	2 460	182.0	85.8
Winter Springs	12	167	4.6	1.2	8	43	2.3	0.7	20	104	5.4	2.1
GEORGIA	13 829	274 322	9 689.9	2 695.1	1 653	23 437	1 533.7	408.9	13 960	173 768	12 065.1	5 158.0
Albany	188	3 688	116.6	31.2	11	156	7.4	1.6	245	3 266	238.2	109.6
Alpharetta	126	2 355	95.8	26.1	19	275	16.3	5.5	115	672	72.1	25.2

1. Firms subject to federal tax.

Table D. Cities — Other Services and Federal Funds

City	Other services,[1] 1997 Number of establish-ments	Number of employees	Receipts (mil dol)	Annual payroll (mil dol)	Procurement contracts Defense	Procurement contracts Other	Grants Total[2]	Medicaid and other health related	Nutrition and family welfare	Energy and environment	Education	Housing and community develop-ment	Direct payments for individuals for educational assistance
	104	105	106	107	108	109	110	111	112	113	114	115	116
FLORIDA—Cont'd													
Cape Coral	137	550	40.5	11.5	0.4	0.1	0.9	0.0	0.0	0.0	0.0	0.5	0.2
Clearwater	259	1 915	159.2	47.9	163.8	22.6	26.2	0.8	0.5	10.6	1.6	9.4	2.3
Coconut Creek	29	131	7.0	2.3	0.2	0.0	0.0	0.0	0.0	0.0	0.0	0.0	0.0
Cooper City	28	104	5.5	1.3	3.8	0.0	0.0	0.0	0.0	0.0	0.0	0.0	0.0
Coral Gables	122	752	35.7	12.4	1.2	3.0	127.0	110.8	0.8	1.5	0.0	0.0	0.0
Coral Springs	192	747	34.8	9.7	3.1	26.2	4.5	0.0	0.0	0.0	0.0	4.6	0.0
Davie	205	962	84.9	24.5	1.7	0.9	1.5	0.0	0.0	0.0	0.0	0.6	0.0
Daytona Beach	138	788	36.6	12.6	9.9	1.3	34.6	1.9	0.5	0.0	8.0	10.3	24.7
Deerfield Beach	128	918	39.1	14.2	43.3	2.2	2.3	0.0	0.0	0.0	0.0	2.1	0.2
Delray Beach	157	860	57.9	16.8	1.5	1.5	6.1	0.0	0.0	0.0	0.0	5.6	0.2
Dunedin	62	297	14.7	4.3	0.3	0.2	0.3	0.0	0.0	0.0	0.0	0.3	0.2
Fort Lauderdale	524	3 508	392.4	73.3	31.0	23.5	89.1	26.3	14.1	0.4	6.0	26.5	75.2
Fort Myers	200	1 504	89.5	29.6	1.5	5.3	43.4	11.2	5.2	0.0	2.5	12.7	11.5
Fort Pierce	90	497	26.9	8.6	3.8	7.5	20.0	1.3	0.0	0.1	4.0	5.1	5.7
Gainesville	209	1 096	69.1	20.5	7.9	26.6	268.8	111.1	8.3	6.6	10.3	28.3	37.3
Greenacres City	NA	NA	NA	NA	0.0	0.0	0.2	0.0	0.0	0.0	0.0	0.0	0.0
Hallandale Beach	90	470	28.6	9.3	0.0	0.2	0.9	0.0	0.0	0.0	0.0	0.7	0.0
Hialeah	465	1 893	113.4	29.5	5.0	13.9	35.2	0.0	0.0	0.0	0.0	0.3	13.2
Hollywood	288	2 096	143.6	42.5	4.2	1.0	11.0	0.1	0.0	0.1	0.0	34.0	0.8
Homestead	43	183	10.9	2.9	1.0	11.5	16.3	0.0	0.0	0.0	0.0	8.4	0.0
Jacksonville	1 448	9 054	604.7	184.3	395.7	109.3	201.2	16.4	16.4	0.7	9.6	15.7	0.0
Jupiter town	91	419	24.2	7.4	1.9	2.2	0.4	0.0	0.0	0.7	9.6	139.2	36.1
Key West	68	280	16.2	4.3	112.1	4.2	12.4	0.7	1.4	0.3	0.0	0.0	0.0
Kissimmee	97	552	29.4	9.7	1.6	0.1	8.5	1.8	0.0	0.0	1.8	3.4	0.5
Lakeland	161	941	44.6	14.7	1.6	1.4	13.0	0.0	0.0	0.0	0.0	12.5	4.9
Lake Worth	93	343	22.3	5.6	3.8	1.4	3.0	1.0	0.0	0.0	2.0	0.0	14.4
Largo	176	771	47.4	14.9	60.1	18.9	17.4	0.4	0.0	2.3	4.2	1.2	0.0
Lauderdale Lakes	29	77	3.8	0.9	0.0	0.0	7.8	0.0	0.0	0.0	0.0	7.8	0.0
Lauderhill	89	462	21.2	6.1	0.1	0.2	1.8	0.0	0.0	0.0	0.0	1.6	0.0
Margate	130	541	34.4	9.6	0.2	0.0	0.5	0.0	0.0	0.0	0.0	0.5	0.0
Melbourne	135	809	40.8	13.5	876.4	114.0	16.7	1.4	0.0	0.0	0.2	5.8	2.3
Miami	836	5 045	337.2	85.8	135.9	141.6	368.0	73.4	47.2	13.2	26.3	132.7	169.3
Miami Beach	163	1 023	41.7	13.6	0.3	0.4	48.4	15.0	0.0	0.0	0.0	33.0	0.4
Miramar	53	228	18.3	5.7	2.8	0.6	1.0	0.2	0.0	0.0	0.0	0.6	0.0
North Lauderdale	34	232	20.9	5.6	0.0	0.0	0.1	0.0	0.0	0.0	0.0	0.0	0.0
North Miami	116	418	20.3	5.6	1.3	0.8	3.3	0.0	0.0	0.5	0.0	0.0	0.0
North Miami Beach	105	514	27.0	8.4	0.2	0.5	2.9	0.0	0.0	0.5	0.0	2.5	0.0
Oakland Park	205	766	55.9	13.7	120.1	9.7	0.2	0.0	0.0	0.0	0.0	0.0	0.0
Ocala	223	1 171	65.7	21.0	6.6	9.8	29.6	0.0	7.2	0.0	2.2	17.3	7.6
Orlando	440	4 650	289.2	89.0	1 906.2	133.1	177.2	17.4	15.7	5.2	8.8	34.5	45.9
Ormond Beach	58	305	14.0	4.0	1.3	0.5	2.6	0.0	0.0	0.0	0.0	1.9	0.0
Oviedo	37	166	7.6	2.2	1.9	0.3	0.0	0.0	0.0	0.0	0.0	0.0	0.0
Palm Bay	81	286	17.5	5.1	40.0	2.2	1.9	0.0	0.0	0.0	0.0	0.0	0.0
Palm Beach Gardens	77	453	20.9	7.7	0.9	9.5	0.8	0.0	0.0	0.0	0.0	1.1	0.2
Panama City	112	798	38.6	11.9	49.2	10.4	22.2	0.1	3.7	0.0	3.5	13.0	5.9
Pembroke Pines	159	1 096	54.0	17.8	0.2	1.4	1.2	0.0	0.0	0.0	0.0	1.1	0.0
Pensacola	115	952	52.3	15.0	143.0	15.1	42.6	0.1	5.5	0.3	4.2	24.4	16.4
Pinellas Park	135	840	50.6	14.8	3.1	0.9	13.7	4.2	0.0	0.0	6.8	1.9	0.2
Plantation	154	1 178	71.7	21.8	0.9	5.7	0.4	0.0	0.0	0.0	0.0	0.3	0.0
Plant City	44	241	15.3	4.2	7.4	0.4	2.2	0.0	0.0	0.0	0.0	1.2	0.0
Pompano Beach	270	2 338	163.6	52.6	9.6	1.8	9.9	0.9	0.0	0.0	0.0	9.2	4.1
Port Orange	55	215	9.1	2.8	0.0	0.1	0.6	0.0	0.0	0.0	0.0	0.4	0.0
Port St. Lucie	NA	NA	NA	NA	0.1	0.0	0.6	0.0	0.0	0.0	0.0	0.1	0.0
Riviera Beach	51	220	19.5	4.9	8.5	0.7	7.8	0.1	0.0	0.0	0.0	7.4	0.0
St. Petersburg	412	2 116	125.0	40.0	472.6	10.2	74.4	6.6	13.2	0.4	2.0	29.2	0.0
Sanford	86	319	20.6	5.9	16.8	0.6	13.8	3.6	0.0	0.0	1.8	6.9	8.6
Sarasota	179	1 186	61.0	22.2	17.1	3.4	23.3	0.7	3.0	1.9	1.1	6.4	1.6
Sunrise	127	558	33.7	10.0	3.3	2.9	2.3	0.0	0.0	0.0	0.0	1.6	0.0
Tallahassee	322	2 179	121.6	40.2	43.7	25.4	2 340.7	415.6	471.3	104.9	579.4	78.1	54.9
Tamarac	99	469	24.7	6.9	0.0	0.4	0.6	0.0	0.0	0.0	0.0	0.0	0.0
Tampa	785	5 358	358.9	109.7	226.9	75.0	232.2	85.1	23.9	2.4	21.3	58.7	44.4
Titusville	81	388	23.4	7.3	5.3	2.0	12.4	0.0	0.0	0.1	0.0	4.0	0.0
Weston city	NA	NA	NA	NA	0.0	0.0	0.1	0.0	0.0	0.0	0.0	0.0	0.0
West Palm Beach	220	1 476	97.8	31.1	55.1	32.7	73.5	17.3	13.0	0.3	5.1	19.7	9.0
Winter Haven	83	408	24.6	7.5	0.3	0.2	11.2	0.0	5.2	0.0	1.2	4.6	2.0
Winter Springs	19	47	4.1	1.1	0.7	0.0	0.5	0.0	0.0	0.0	0.0	0.0	0.0
GEORGIA	11 482	69 422	4 580.7	1 407.5	3 323.8	1 918.7	10 561.2	5 050.9	1 594.2	120.3	1 031.2	740.3	359.6
Albany	159	1 110	66.0	21.3	38.2	31.7	27.7	3.8	5.3	0.0	5.1	11.1	16.2
Alpharetta	82	850	37.0	9.1	86.9	3.5	1.3	0.4	0.0	0.0	0.0	0.7	0.0

1. Firms subject to federal tax.   2. Includes program categories not shown separately. State totals include additional categories not allocated by city.

Table D. Cities — **City Government Finances**

City	General revenue Total (mil dol)	Intergovernmental Total (mil dol)	Intergovernmental Percent from state government	Taxes Total (mil dol)	Taxes Per capita¹ (dollars) Total	Taxes Per capita¹ (dollars) Property	Taxes Sales and gross receipts	General expenditure Total (mil dol)	General expenditure Per capita¹ (dollars) Total	General expenditure Capital outlays
	117	118	119	120	121	122	123	124	125	126
FLORIDA—Cont'd										
Cape Coral	132.5	13.6	91.3	41.0	363	252	83	80.3	711	106
Clearwater	162.3	27.2	72.2	64.7	597	256	301	181.7	1 678	504
Coconut Creek	30.8	5.0	85.9	17.2	359	174	148	27.7	581	26
Cooper City	20.1	3.6	100.0	11.0	380	213	138	23.0	796	0
Coral Gables	90.2	7.3	65.0	54.5	1 279	722	298	96.3	2 259	307
Coral Springs	84.4	14.5	87.4	47.3	377	176	165	81.4	648	95
Davie	57.0	7.8	100.0	36.9	462	245	174	59.3	742	133
Daytona Beach	75.3	11.7	89.0	32.0	496	228	238	78.3	1 212	168
Deerfield Beach	60.6	7.6	83.3	26.2	400	291	87	62.2	947	48
Delray Beach	77.4	11.0	80.2	40.1	643	434	166	86.8	1 394	143
Dunedin	29.1	5.7	16.8	11.1	302	133	151	26.7	727	33
Fort Lauderdale	237.6	29.5	51.0	120.5	762	443	267	231.3	1 462	149
Fort Myers	90.9	16.2	45.7	30.2	604	286	260	94.3	1 888	314
Fort Pierce	NA	NA	NA	NA	NA	NA	NA	NA	NA	NA
Gainesville	109.5	28.7	74.5	27.9	293	131	142	112.5	1 182	206
Greenacres City	13.4	2.7	97.6	8.9	291	130	128	12.3	403	3
Hallandale Beach	NA	NA	NA	NA	NA	NA	NA	NA	NA	NA
Hialeah	177.7	32.1	45.7	89.0	390	175	193	180.9	793	124
Hollywood	160.7	26.1	68.9	65.4	457	257	178	162.9	1 137	175
Homestead	NA	NA	NA	NA	NA	NA	NA	NA	NA	NA
Jacksonville	1 252.3	173.2	70.3	589.8	774	468	288	1 478.6	1 939	555
Jupiter town	34.6	8.6	92.2	17.5	404	164	151	26.3	606	69
Key West	64.6	14.5	100.0	13.4	529	413	0	55.9	2 212	122
Kissimmee	56.1	20.3	33.0	13.5	276	124	135	45.3	925	38
Lakeland	123.3	26.8	30.6	28.6	332	123	184	103.8	1 205	69
Lake Worth	45.6	11.8	92.4	13.6	383	234	130	42.7	1 200	114
Largo	68.2	12.1	60.1	27.0	382	106	258	70.8	1 002	171
Lauderdale Lakes	20.1	3.7	66.1	8.7	274	97	159	21.1	666	99
Lauderhill	26.6	7.2	75.9	12.5	212	122	64	29.3	499	92
Margate	37.9	6.5	92.3	22.0	402	204	181	34.9	637	16
Melbourne	78.8	11.4	66.4	28.2	382	144	213	75.5	1 023	241
Miami	462.0	87.1	36.5	231.6	618	376	204	442.1	1 180	100
Miami Beach	278.1	30.2	75.6	129.3	1 444	766	305	253.9	2 834	314
Miramar	65.1	7.4	89.5	36.9	408	196	107	70.3	778	200
North Lauderdale	20.1	3.6	89.1	9.5	285	104	124	20.0	601	29
North Miami	45.2	7.9	60.2	16.8	281	182	84	44.0	733	64
North Miami Beach	44.5	5.8	96.7	16.4	403	197	170	44.4	1 088	152
Oakland Park	NA	NA	NA	NA	NA	NA	NA	NA	NA	NA
Ocala	69.1	8.1	37.9	24.6	523	246	243	72.3	1 540	247
Orlando	405.4	94.7	39.5	142.4	735	356	284	404.0	2 085	384
Ormond Beach	NA	NA	NA	NA	NA	NA	NA	NA	NA	NA
Oviedo	20.5	2.9	76.6	10.3	373	190	158	26.3	952	73
Palm Bay	49.0	9.3	85.7	28.4	342	171	151	49.4	595	118
Palm Beach Gardens	NA	NA	NA	NA	NA	NA	NA	NA	NA	NA
Panama City	35.0	4.7	82.6	19.4	528	140	194	34.1	928	199
Pembroke Pines	116.2	14.7	84.7	45.4	309	139	109	120.7	823	149
Pensacola	83.0	19.2	49.5	34.4	622	202	395	93.3	1 689	331
Pinellas Park	54.6	4.8	81.7	23.6	510	200	282	42.5	917	145
Plantation	64.8	9.4	97.3	36.4	430	203	184	64.9	766	126
Plant City	34.4	6.2	68.6	14.3	462	416	0	29.2	942	123
Pompano Beach	100.0	9.0	52.4	54.5	626	299	270	86.7	995	81
Port Orange	42.1	2.5	100.0	16.4	333	124	191	35.5	720	102
Port St. Lucie	61.9	12.8	47.2	20.7	210	95	86	66.2	672	189
Riviera Beach	37.6	5.7	95.3	22.4	736	470	229	37.7	1 237	122
St. Petersburg	339.5	58.3	54.5	112.1	451	241	184	338.7	1 363	345
Sanford	NA	NA	NA	NA	NA	NA	NA	NA	NA	NA
Sarasota	89.9	6.6	90.6	42.2	791	223	524	69.0	1 294	0
Sunrise	109.7	10.9	93.7	29.0	328	224	46	115.9	1 310	396
Tallahassee	210.0	32.6	79.2	58.8	379	112	237	225.4	1 453	275
Tamarac	44.9	6.3	83.6	18.1	314	206	78	27.8	483	33
Tampa	507.2	61.4	62.4	198.6	630	283	302	531.9	1 688	358
Titusville	31.9	5.6	74.9	15.4	375	178	177	31.6	769	69
Weston city	29.6	4.9	77.3	14.6	237	80	115	30.0	487	150
West Palm Beach	158.6	19.8	44.6	68.6	792	474	235	133.2	1 539	141
Winter Haven	33.2	3.3	69.5	14.9	563	212	329	36.0	1 361	298
Winter Springs	18.3	3.1	91.8	8.8	280	116	140	15.8	504	63
GEORGIA	X	X	X	X	X	X	X	X	X	X
Albany	97.9	41.4	38.4	23.5	308	188	91	92.7	1 215	223
Alpharetta	42.8	4.2	6.4	28.3	793	500	229	50.3	1 407	381

1. Based on population estimated as of July 1 of the year shown.

City	Public welfare	Highways	Parking facilities	Education	Health and hospitals	Police protection	Sewerage and sanitation	Parks and recreation	Housing and community development	Interest on debt
	127	128	129	130	131	132	133	134	135	136
FLORIDA—Cont'd										
Cape Coral	0.0	8.4	0.0	0.0	0.0	18.1	6.3	12.9	0.3	13.2
Clearwater	0.0	2.9	1.5	0.0	0.0	16.5	20.3	8.8	0.3	0.7
Coconut Creek	0.0	15.2	0.0	0.0	0.0	29.3	11.4	12.5	2.4	3.7
Cooper City	0.0	6.6	18.6	0.0	0.0	26.4	9.3	9.7	0.0	0.4
Coral Gables	0.0	5.0	2.7	0.0	0.0	26.4	14.8	7.9	0.4	2.2
Coral Springs	0.0	5.5	0.0	0.0	0.0	29.2	3.9	14.6	0.0	5.6
Davie	0.0	5.7	0.0	0.0	0.0	34.1	0.0	23.3	0.0	3.6
Daytona Beach	0.0	9.5	0.0	0.0	0.0	26.2	22.3	7.8	7.7	1.3
Deerfield Beach	3.2	2.8	0.1	0.0	0.0	15.4	23.6	7.0	1.2	1.3
Delray Beach	0.2	7.9	0.1	0.0	0.0	22.1	3.0	14.2	1.8	7.4
Dunedin	0.0	2.3	0.0	0.0	0.0	11.1	31.5	16.8	0.0	0.6
Fort Lauderdale	0.0	3.6	2.3	0.0	0.0	28.6	8.8	13.9	5.7	3.1
Fort Myers	0.0	9.4	0.0	0.0	0.0	15.3	19.8	15.9	12.1	6.6
Fort Pierce	NA	NA	NA	NA	NA	NA	NA	NA	NA	NA
Gainesville	0.1	8.0	0.0	0.0	0.0	19.6	22.7	6.9	3.3	5.9
Greenacres City	0.0	9.0	0.0	0.0	0.0	38.8	5.4	8.6	0.0	0.7
Hallandale Beach	NA	NA	NA	NA	NA	NA	NA	NA	NA	NA
Hialeah	0.3	10.1	0.0	0.0	0.0	16.9	20.3	6.6	5.4	1.6
Hollywood	0.0	6.4	1.4	0.0	0.0	30.7	21.5	6.1	2.5	0.2
Homestead	NA	NA	NA	NA	NA	NA	NA	NA	NA	NA
Jacksonville	2.3	3.3	0.2	0.0	3.1	10.1	22.4	4.4	1.2	11.7
Jupiter town	0.0	1.9	0.0	0.0	0.0	34.4	7.6	13.0	0.0	3.8
Key West	0.0	3.8	0.6	0.0	0.0	10.9	29.1	4.6	0.0	5.9
Kissimmee	0.0	12.8	0.0	0.0	0.0	24.5	4.9	13.8	8.7	2.5
Lakeland	0.0	11.7	0.4	0.0	0.0	20.2	14.2	12.9	2.2	7.3
Lake Worth	0.0	6.9	0.1	0.0	0.0	20.4	22.6	10.8	3.8	1.3
Largo	0.0	2.1	0.0	0.0	0.0	14.7	34.2	9.4	3.8	2.9
Lauderdale Lakes	1.8	4.1	0.0	0.0	0.0	24.2	2.3	13.5	5.3	5.0
Lauderhill	0.0	3.5	0.0	0.0	0.0	28.5	13.4	9.7	0.0	2.4
Margate	0.0	10.7	0.0	0.0	0.0	37.2	2.2	8.2	1.8	0.8
Melbourne	0.0	6.7	0.0	0.0	0.0	20.6	22.6	10.5	3.0	1.6
Miami	0.0	2.2	1.7	0.0	0.0	22.6	7.6	6.1	9.8	7.4
Miami Beach	0.2	2.0	5.6	0.0	0.5	20.0	14.4	17.3	4.6	9.4
Miramar	0.0	3.6	0.0	0.0	0.0	19.0	14.8	5.6	0.0	2.9
North Lauderdale	0.0	4.3	0.0	0.0	0.0	31.0	5.6	12.1	0.0	4.1
North Miami	2.1	5.8	0.0	0.0	0.0	25.0	26.1	13.8	1.5	5.6
North Miami Beach	0.0	7.8	0.0	0.0	0.0	23.5	23.6	8.2	0.0	2.6
Oakland Park	NA	NA	NA	NA	NA	NA	NA	NA	NA	NA
Ocala	0.0	10.0	0.1	0.0	0.0	19.2	32.7	6.6	0.8	2.7
Orlando	0.8	11.6	1.8	0.0	0.0	17.1	20.1	7.9	3.5	5.7
Ormond Beach	NA	NA	NA	NA	NA	NA	NA	NA	NA	NA
Oviedo	0.0	5.1	0.0	0.0	0.0	58.7	1.5	8.0	0.1	3.4
Palm Bay	0.0	21.9	0.0	0.0	0.0	22.3	12.5	3.5	4.6	2.1
Palm Beach Gardens	NA	NA	NA	NA	NA	NA	NA	NA	NA	NA
Panama City	0.0	17.3	0.0	0.0	0.6	19.2	9.6	10.7	2.1	4.6
Pembroke Pines	0.0	4.1	0.0	0.0	0.0	17.5	7.8	12.2	4.5	3.9
Pensacola	0.2	6.5	0.0	0.0	0.0	17.6	5.8	11.0	12.1	9.8
Pinellas Park	0.0	14.6	0.0	0.0	3.0	18.8	21.4	6.3	0.0	2.8
Plantation	0.0	8.9	0.0	0.0	0.0	35.2	6.3	11.2	1.5	2.4
Plant City	0.0	6.4	0.0	0.0	0.0	18.0	30.8	24.9	1.8	2.0
Pompano Beach	0.0	4.8	0.0	0.0	10.8	26.5	18.8	10.5	1.5	3.0
Port Orange	0.0	6.8	0.0	0.0	0.0	17.1	21.3	13.4	0.0	5.1
Port St. Lucie	0.0	15.4	0.0	0.0	1.4	15.4	28.1	11.2	2.6	9.8
Riviera Beach	0.0	8.0	0.0	0.0	0.0	26.0	8.4	12.4	2.4	0.8
St. Petersburg	0.7	2.6	0.7	0.0	1.6	16.8	28.6	12.6	1.4	7.0
Sanford	NA	NA	NA	NA	NA	NA	NA	NA	NA	NA
Sarasota	0.0	5.0	0.6	0.0	0.0	27.1	24.5	17.0	2.6	2.9
Sunrise	0.0	3.8	0.0	0.0	0.0	13.7	24.5	6.9	23.1	6.1
Tallahassee	3.1	13.4	0.2	0.0	0.1	15.1	23.0	7.3	1.4	7.0
Tamarac	0.8	8.8	0.0	0.0	0.0	27.0	16.3	3.5	2.4	2.9
Tampa	2.9	7.2	4.0	0.0	0.0	19.1	23.5	9.5	1.9	16.1
Titusville	0.3	3.4	0.0	0.0	0.0	23.8	12.6	3.6	3.7	3.5
Weston city	0.0	11.7	0.0	0.0	0.0	12.4	11.9	23.2	10.3	1.7
West Palm Beach	0.0	8.8	1.6	0.0	2.0	26.6	5.1	6.3	7.7	5.4
Winter Haven	0.0	4.9	0.0	0.0	0.0	22.5	43.0	8.4	0.9	1.7
Winter Springs	0.0	15.9	0.0	0.0	0.0	23.1	8.3	9.5	0.0	4.7
GEORGIA	X	X	X	X	X	X	X	X	X	X
Albany	0.0	7.0	0.0	0.0	0.0	13.0	18.1	9.4	4.2	0.9
Alpharetta	0.0	14.4	0.0	0.0	0.0	11.6	6.6	16.3	0.0	5.8

City	City government finances, 2002 (cont'd) Debt outstanding Total (mil dol)	Per capita[1] (dollars)	Percent utility	City government employment, 2002	Climate[2] Average daily temperature (degrees Fahrenheit) Mean January	July	Limits January[3]	July[4]	Annual precipitation (inches)	Heating degree days	Cooling degree days
	137	138	139	140	141	142	143	144	145	146	147
FLORIDA—Cont'd											
Cape Coral	126.0	1 116	22.8	1 203	63.8	82.8	53.2	91.1	53.37	418	3 855
Clearwater	155.4	1 434	62.7	1 734	59.9	82.1	50.0	90.2	43.92	726	3 396
Coconut Creek	18.3	384	0.0	306	66.2	82.5	56.8	91.2	59.15	262	4 038
Cooper City	7.7	268	84.5	219	NA	NA	NA	NA	NA	NA	NA
Coral Gables	62.9	1 476	0.0	862	67.2	82.6	59.2	89.0	55.91	200	4 198
Coral Springs	119.0	947	21.3	816	66.2	82.5	56.8	91.2	59.15	262	4 038
Davie	76.7	961	41.9	595	67.2	82.6	57.9	90.1	60.64	205	4 124
Daytona Beach	61.5	952	72.3	1 183	57.5	81.2	46.9	89.8	47.89	909	2 919
Deerfield Beach	30.1	459	22.0	547	66.2	82.5	56.8	91.2	59.15	262	4 038
Delray Beach	91.7	1 473	0.0	733	66.2	82.5	56.8	91.2	59.15	262	4 038
Dunedin	34.3	934	59.4	377	59.9	82.1	50.0	90.2	43.92	726	3 396
Fort Lauderdale	112.4	711	8.8	2 778	67.2	82.6	57.9	90.1	60.64	205	4 124
Fort Myers	217.1	4 346	46.4	977	63.8	82.8	53.2	91.1	53.37	418	3 855
Fort Pierce	NA	NA	NA	638	62.5	81.4	51.6	90.4	50.06	490	3 441
Gainesville	406.5	4 271	74.8	2 004	53.7	80.7	42.5	90.7	51.81	1 316	2 570
Greenacres City	2.9	95	0.0	182	NA	NA	NA	NA	NA	NA	NA
Hallandale Beach	NA	NA	NA	694	67.2	82.6	57.9	90.1	60.64	205	4 124
Hialeah	84.1	369	3.4	1 595	66.3	82.4	56.8	89.8	63.01	273	4 012
Hollywood	110.6	772	97.2	1 603	67.2	82.6	57.9	90.1	60.64	205	4 124
Homestead	NA	NA	NA	380	65.3	81.1	54.5	90.1	58.74	277	3 603
Jacksonville	6 832.7	8 961	50.1	10 205	NA	NA	NA	NA	NA	NA	NA
Jupiter town	57.3	1 320	51.9	348	NA	NA	NA	NA	NA	NA	NA
Key West	64.4	2 548	0.0	448	NA	NA	NA	NA	NA	NA	NA
Kissimmee	363.8	7 435	93.7	954	61.0	81.7	48.7	91.4	46.11	603	3 324
Lakeland	746.4	8 662	78.1	2 126	61.1	82.5	50.4	92.2	47.54	588	3 546
Lake Worth	34.6	974	60.6	543	65.1	82.2	55.7	89.9	60.75	323	3 891
Largo	31.7	449	0.0	826	59.9	82.1	50.0	90.2	43.92	726	3 396
Lauderdale Lakes	19.7	622	0.0	163	67.2	82.6	57.9	90.1	60.64	205	4 124
Lauderhill	29.0	494	48.3	421	67.2	82.6	57.9	90.1	60.64	205	4 124
Margate	38.9	710	86.8	469	66.2	82.5	56.8	91.2	59.15	262	4 038
Melbourne	102.6	1 390	82.6	871	60.9	81.1	50.7	90.0	45.49	644	3 193
Miami	483.7	1 291	0.0	3 860	67.2	82.6	59.2	89.0	55.91	200	4 198
Miami Beach	444.9	4 967	0.0	1 771	68.1	82.6	62.3	86.9	45.35	139	4 157
Miramar	87.1	964	52.8	770	66.3	82.4	56.8	89.8	63.01	273	4 012
North Lauderdale	10.3	309	0.0	158	66.2	82.5	56.8	91.2	59.15	262	4 038
North Miami	35.8	597	14.9	538	66.3	82.4	56.8	89.8	63.01	273	4 012
North Miami Beach	42.7	1 046	16.0	506	68.1	82.6	62.3	86.9	45.35	139	4 157
Oakland Park	NA	NA	NA	324	67.2	82.6	57.9	90.1	60.64	205	4 124
Ocala	133.5	2 844	76.5	1 177	57.5	81.5	45.1	92.2	51.59	930	3 046
Orlando	366.3	1 891	0.0	3 428	59.7	82.3	48.6	91.5	48.11	686	3 381
Ormond Beach	NA	NA	NA	360	57.5	81.2	46.9	89.8	47.89	909	2 919
Oviedo	21.3	772	26.1	229	NA	NA	NA	NA	NA	NA	NA
Palm Bay	120.1	1 447	83.1	766	60.9	81.1	50.7	90.0	45.49	644	3 193
Palm Beach Gardens	NA	NA	NA	397	NA	NA	NA	NA	NA	NA	NA
Panama City	43.3	1 179	45.2	522	50.7	80.8	39.1	90.0	65.06	1 681	2 409
Pembroke Pines	100.8	687	0.0	1 082	66.3	82.4	56.8	89.8	63.01	273	4 012
Pensacola	155.7	2 819	10.1	997	50.6	82.1	41.4	89.9	62.25	1 617	2 636
Pinellas Park	27.4	590	31.7	552	60.7	83.1	52.9	89.8	48.62	603	3 626
Plantation	55.1	650	57.7	809	67.2	82.6	57.9	90.1	60.64	205	4 124
Plant City	29.7	958	61.8	382	NA	NA	NA	NA	NA	NA	NA
Pompano Beach	87.0	998	55.2	657	66.2	82.5	56.8	91.2	59.15	262	4 038
Port Orange	127.6	2 587	62.0	356	57.5	81.2	46.9	89.8	47.89	909	2 919
Port St. Lucie	325.7	3 305	57.9	749	62.5	81.4	51.6	90.4	50.06	490	3 441
Riviera Beach	15.1	496	60.9	420	65.1	82.2	55.7	89.9	60.75	323	3 891
St. Petersburg	579.4	2 331	13.4	3 300	60.7	83.1	52.9	89.8	48.62	603	3 626
Sanford	NA	NA	NA	435	58.2	81.5	46.8	91.6	48.81	831	3 004
Sarasota	111.9	2 099	49.6	924	60.2	81.4	49.0	90.8	53.71	678	3 186
Sunrise	330.1	3 731	65.6	919	67.2	82.6	57.9	90.1	60.64	205	4 124
Tallahassee	533.7	3 440	58.7	2 992	50.5	81.3	38.1	91.3	65.71	1 705	2 518
Tamarac	29.9	521	51.0	366	66.2	82.5	56.8	91.2	59.15	262	4 038
Tampa	1 701.6	5 400	7.7	4 325	59.9	82.1	50.0	90.2	43.92	726	3 396
Titusville	71.3	1 733	76.9	480	58.6	81.3	47.3	91.4	54.07	803	3 057
Weston city	11.8	192	14.5	3	NA	NA	NA	NA	NA	NA	NA
West Palm Beach	211.6	2 445	45.7	1 349	65.1	82.2	55.7	89.9	60.75	323	3 891
Winter Haven	56.4	2 133	79.0	520	NA	NA	NA	NA	NA	NA	NA
Winter Springs	43.0	1 375	61.9	265	NA	NA	NA	NA	NA	NA	NA
GEORGIA	X	X	X	X	X	X	X	X	X	X	X
Albany	91.3	1 196	80.2	1 244	46.5	80.8	33.8	91.9	51.48	2 205	2 206
Alpharetta	54.8	1 534	3.6	307	NA	NA	NA	NA	NA	NA	NA

1. Based on the population estimated as of July 1 of the year shown.   2. Represents normal values based on the 30-year period, 1961–1990.   3. Average daily minimum.   4. Average daily maximum.

STATE Place code	City	Land area,[1] 2000 (sq km)	Population, 2003			Population characteristics, 2000 Percent						
								Race (alone or in combination)				
			Total persons	Rank	Per square kilometer	White	Black	Am. Indian, Alaska Native	Asian and Pacific Islander	Other race	Hispanic or Latino[2]	Non-Hispanic White
		1	2	3	4	5	6	7	8	9	10	11
	GEORGIA—Cont'd											
13 03436	Athens-Clarke County..........	312.8	103 691	228	331.5	66.1	27.8	0.5	3.7	3.5	6.3	62.0
13 04000	Atlanta..........	341.2	423 019	41	1 239.8	34.0	62.1	0.5	2.3	2.5	4.5	31.3
13 04200	Augusta-Richmond County ...	839.3	198 149	98	236.1	46.8	50.7	0.7	2.2	1.5	2.8	44.4
13 19000	Columbus..........	560.1	185 702	113	331.6	51.8	44.6	0.8	2.3	2.5	4.5	48.7
13 21380	Dalton city..........	51.3	30 341	1 054	591.4	68.6	8.2	0.7	2.2	23.2	40.2	49.7
13 25720	East Point..........	35.6	37 220	865	1 045.5	16.9	79.0	0.6	1.1	4.0	7.6	13.0
13 31908	Gainesville..........	70.1	29 806	1 073	425.2	66.5	16.1	0.6	3.1	15.4	33.2	47.8
13 38964	Hinesville..........	42.0	29 396	1 083	699.9	44.2	48.2	1.1	4.2	6.7	9.1	38.8
13 44340	La Grange..........	75.0	26 576	1 187	354.3	50.0	47.9	0.5	1.2	1.5	2.4	48.4
13 49000	Macon	144.5	95 267	265	659.3	35.9	62.9	0.4	0.9	0.7	1.2	35.0
13 49756	Marietta..........	56.7	61 282	474	1 080.8	58.4	30.5	0.8	3.6	9.5	16.9	48.6
13 59724	Peachtree City..........	60.3	33 010	977	547.4	88.9	6.5	0.6	4.3	1.3	3.7	85.1
13 66668	Rome..........	76.1	35 303	914	463.9	64.5	28.2	0.7	1.9	6.4	10.3	59.2
13 67284	Roswell..........	98.5	78 229	354	794.2	82.9	9.1	0.6	4.4	5.0	10.6	75.5
13 69000	Savannah..........	193.6	127 573	176	659.0	39.8	57.8	0.6	2.1	1.3	2.2	37.9
13 71492	Smyrna..........	36.0	45 610	709	1 266.9	61.3	28.1	0.9	4.6	7.8	13.8	53.5
13 78800	Valdosta..........	77.5	45 059	716	581.4	48.6	49.0	0.6	1.8	1.3	2.2	46.7
13 80508	Warner Robins..........	59.0	54 264	582	919.7	64.1	32.8	0.8	2.7	1.7	3.8	60.5
15 00000	**HAWAII**	16 634.5	1 257 608	X	75.6	39.3	2.8	2.1	81.3	3.9	7.2	22.9
15 14650	Hilo CDP..........	140.6	NA	1 231	NA	38.7	1.2	2.6	96.0	4.3	8.8	15.9
15 17000	Honolulu CDP..........	222.0	380 149	45	1 712.4	30.1	2.4	1.4	83.3	2.4	4.4	18.7
15 23150	Kailua CDP..........	17.2	NA	1 231	NA	64.3	1.6	2.4	63.8	3.0	6.1	42.3
15 28250	Kaneohe CDP..........	17.0	NA	1 231	NA	41.3	1.5	2.1	91.7	2.9	7.2	19.3
15 51050	Mililani CDP..........	10.1	NA	1 231	NA	38.3	4.3	1.9	84.5	3.9	7.8	19.2
15 62600	Pearl City CDP..........	12.9	NA	1 231	NA	30.1	3.6	1.6	86.8	3.9	7.3	16.0
15 77750	Waimalu CDP..........	15.3	NA	1 231	NA	29.7	3.5	1.6	86.4	3.6	6.0	16.1
15 79700	Waipahu CDP..........	6.7	NA	1 231	NA	13.7	1.7	1.4	100.5	3.5	6.1	4.1
16 00000	**IDAHO**	214 314.3	1 366 332	X	6.4	92.8	0.6	2.1	1.5	5.0	7.9	88.0
16 08830	Boise City..........	165.2	190 117	112	1 150.8	94.4	1.1	1.4	3.0	2.6	4.5	89.9
16 12250	Caldwell..........	29.4	31 041	1 030	1 055.8	77.6	0.8	1.8	1.7	21.1	28.1	68.3
16 16750	Coeur d'Alene	34.0	37 262	864	1 095.9	97.6	0.4	1.8	1.2	1.0	2.7	94.1
16 39700	Idaho Falls	44.2	51 507	609	1 165.3	93.6	0.9	1.3	1.5	4.4	7.2	89.4
16 46540	Lewiston	42.7	30 937	1 036	724.5	96.7	0.4	2.6	1.3	0.8	1.9	94.1
16 52120	Meridian city	30.5	41 127	783	1 348.4	96.3	0.7	1.0	2.3	1.9	3.7	92.4
16 56260	Nampa..........	51.4	64 269	450	1 250.4	86.1	0.7	1.7	1.8	12.7	17.9	78.2
16 64090	Pocatello	73.1	51 009	615	697.8	94.2	1.0	2.1	2.1	2.9	4.9	90.4
16 82810	Twin Falls	31.1	36 742	876	1 181.4	94.0	0.4	1.4	1.6	5.0	8.9	87.6
17 00000	**ILLINOIS**	143 960.8	12 653 544	X	87.9	75.1	15.6	0.6	3.9	6.8	12.3	67.8
17 00243	Addison..........	24.4	36 767	875	1 506.8	77.5	2.7	0.6	8.6	13.1	28.4	60.0
17 01114	Alton..........	40.5	29 841	1 069	736.8	73.8	25.7	0.7	0.7	1.0	1.5	71.6
17 02154	Arlington Heights..........	42.5	75 784	369	1 783.2	91.6	1.1	0.2	6.6	1.7	4.5	87.6
17 03012	Aurora..........	99.8	162 184	130	1 625.1	70.5	11.9	0.7	3.6	16.2	32.6	52.1
17 04013	Bartlett..........	38.4	37 558	854	978.1	88.4	2.3	0.4	8.5	2.0	5.5	83.6
17 04845	Belleville..........	48.8	41 209	779	844.4	82.8	16.1	0.6	1.2	0.7	1.6	80.5
17 05573	Berwyn..........	10.1	52 534	601	5 201.4	76.8	1.6	0.9	3.2	21.3	38.0	56.4
17 06613	Bloomington	58.3	68 507	414	1 175.1	86.5	9.5	0.5	3.5	1.9	3.3	83.3
17 07133	Bolingbrook	53.1	66 151	436	1 245.8	66.7	21.6	0.7	7.3	6.7	13.1	57.9
17 09447	Buffalo Grove	23.8	43 237	740	1 816.7	89.7	0.9	0.1	9.1	1.4	3.3	86.5
17 09642	Burbank..........	10.8	28 049	1 130	2 597.1	93.8	0.4	0.5	2.2	6.4	11.1	84.3
17 10487	Calumet City	18.8	38 688	831	2 057.9	40.3	53.9	0.7	0.8	6.7	10.9	34.4
17 11332	Carol Stream	23.0	40 114	795	1 744.1	80.2	4.7	0.5	12.0	4.8	10.0	73.0
17 11358	Carpentersville..........	19.3	34 815	929	1 803.9	72.0	4.7	1.0	2.6	23.4	40.6	51.9
17 12385	Champaign..........	44.0	71 958	390	1 635.4	74.9	16.5	0.6	7.6	2.6	4.0	71.3
17 14000	Chicago..........	588.3	2 869 121	3	4 877.0	44.3	37.4	0.7	5.1	15.6	26.0	31.3
17 14026	Chicago Heights..........	24.8	32 297	997	1 302.3	47.2	38.9	0.8	0.7	15.1	23.8	36.8
17 14351	Cicero..........	15.1	83 029	323	5 498.6	51.9	1.3	1.3	1.3	48.2	77.4	19.6
17 17887	Crystal Lake	42.1	40 021	798	950.6	95.0	0.7	0.4	2.5	2.6	7.0	89.6
17 18563	Danville..........	44.0	33 106	973	752.4	71.8	25.5	0.6	1.5	2.7	4.6	68.3
17 18823	Decatur..........	107.6	79 285	346	736.8	79.1	20.6	0.5	0.9	0.7	1.2	77.0
17 19161	De Kalb	32.7	41 348	777	1 264.5	81.2	9.7	0.6	5.3	5.3	7.7	75.6
17 19642	Des Plaines	37.4	56 450	539	1 509.4	86.1	1.2	0.6	8.3	5.8	14.0	76.0
17 20292	Dolton..........	11.8	25 176	1 223	2 133.6	15.0	83.1	0.5	0.8	1.8	3.1	13.2
17 20591	Downers Grove..........	36.9	49 222	643	1 333.9	91.1	2.1	0.3	6.2	1.4	3.6	87.8
17 22255	East St. Louis..........	36.4	30 573	1 045	839.9	1.5	98.2	0.5	0.2	0.3	0.7	1.2
17 23074	Elgin..........	64.8	97 117	255	1 498.7	73.0	7.5	0.8	4.5	17.2	34.3	53.8
17 23256	Elk Grove Village	28.6	34 666	936	1 212.1	87.1	1.6	0.3	9.5	2.8	6.2	82.4

1. Dry land or land partially or temporarily covered by water.   2. Hispanic or Latino persons may be of any race.

Table D. Cities — Population and Households

City	Under 5 years	5 to 17 years	18 to 24 years	25 to 34 years	35 to 44 years	45 to 54 years	55 to 64 years	65 to 74 years	75 years and over	Percent female	1990	2000	1990–2000	2000–2003
	12	13	14	15	16	17	18	19	20	21	22	23	24	25
GEORGIA—Cont'd														
Athens-Clarke County..........	5.2	12.6	31.3	16.4	11.0	9.5	5.9	4.1	3.9	51.2	86 522	101 489	15.9	2.2
Atlanta.............................	6.4	15.9	13.3	19.7	15.5	12.0	7.4	5.0	4.7	50.4	393 929	416 474	5.7	1.6
Augusta-Richmond County ...	7.1	19.7	12.0	14.8	15.0	12.6	7.9	6.0	4.8	51.8	189 719	199 775	5.3	-0.8
Columbus...........................	7.3	19.5	11.9	14.6	15.2	12.2	7.5	6.5	5.2	51.4	178 685	186 291	3.9	-0.3
Dalton city.........................	8.9	18.4	12.0	17.0	13.3	11.4	7.5	5.6	5.9	49.0	22 218	27 912	25.6	8.7
East Point..........................	8.7	20.6	11.9	16.1	15.2	12.8	6.7	4.1	3.9	52.8	34 595	39 595	14.5	-6.0
Gainesville.........................	8.3	16.7	15.1	18.3	12.3	10.3	6.6	5.7	6.8	50.5	17 885	25 578	43.0	16.5
Hinesville..........................	10.6	23.6	13.8	19.1	16.9	8.9	4.1	2.0	1.1	50.7	21 596	30 392	40.7	-3.3
La Grange..........................	7.7	20.7	11.0	13.8	13.1	11.7	7.5	6.8	7.7	53.9	25 574	25 998	1.7	2.2
Macon	7.8	19.2	11.3	13.6	13.8	12.3	7.8	7.1	7.2	55.6	107 365	97 255	-9.4	-2.0
Marietta............................	7.9	14.5	14.1	24.1	15.4	10.2	5.5	3.7	4.6	49.7	44 129	58 748	33.1	4.3
Peachtree City	6.1	25.5	5.8	8.8	19.7	18.0	8.2	4.2	3.8	51.2	19 027	31 580	66.0	4.5
Rome................................	6.7	17.5	12.1	14.2	13.5	11.8	8.3	7.6	8.3	52.6	30 425	34 980	15.3	0.9
Roswell.............................	6.9	17.5	8.2	17.0	18.1	16.3	8.4	4.0	3.5	50.0	47 986	79 334	65.3	-1.4
Savannah...........................	7.0	18.6	13.2	14.8	13.7	11.6	7.9	6.5	6.8	52.8	137 812	131 510	-4.6	-3.0
Smyrna.............................	6.9	12.6	10.8	26.7	17.1	11.3	6.2	4.4	3.9	51.2	32 453	40 999	26.3	11.2
Valdosta............................	7.7	18.4	18.4	14.6	12.6	11.0	6.8	5.4	5.0	53.7	40 038	43 724	9.2	3.1
Warner Robins	7.2	20.3	9.6	15.5	16.4	12.1	8.1	6.4	4.4	51.5	43 861	48 804	11.3	11.2
HAWAII	6.5	18.0	9.5	14.1	15.8	14.1	8.8	7.0	6.2	49.8	1 108 229	1 211 537	9.3	3.8
Hilo CDP	5.6	19.0	10.3	10.7	13.7	14.3	9.6	8.5	8.2	51.1	37 808	40 759	7.8	NA
Honolulu CDP	5.1	14.1	8.9	14.5	15.4	14.4	9.7	8.7	9.1	50.9	377 059	371 657	-1.4	2.3
Kailua CDP	5.7	18.4	7.2	12.0	16.6	16.5	9.7	7.6	6.1	50.5	36 818	36 513	-0.8	NA
Kaneohe CDP	5.8	18.8	8.2	12.6	16.5	14.1	9.3	8.3	6.5	51.0	35 448	34 970	-1.3	NA
Mililani CDP	5.8	21.4	9.2	11.9	16.5	18.6	9.5	4.6	2.5	50.1	29 359	28 608	-2.6	NA
Pearl City CDP...................	5.1	13.7	13.7	14.7	12.4	11.1	12.0	10.5	6.6	46.5	30 993	30 976	0.1	NA
Waimalu CDP	5.4	16.0	9.5	14.8	16.6	17.2	10.2	6.3	3.8	49.4	29 967	29 371	-2.0	NA
Waipahu CDP	6.9	19.6	9.5	13.4	13.3	11.6	9.8	8.6	7.2	50.6	31 435	33 108	5.3	NA
IDAHO	7.5	21.0	10.7	13.1	14.9	13.2	8.3	5.9	5.4	49.9	1 006 734	1 293 953	28.5	5.6
Boise City..........................	7.1	18.3	11.7	16.3	16.1	13.6	7.0	4.8	5.3	50.5	126 685	185 787	46.7	2.3
Caldwell............................	9.6	21.3	13.1	14.6	12.7	10.6	7.0	5.1	5.9	51.1	18 586	25 967	41.1	19.5
Coeur d'Alene	6.9	18.1	11.7	13.7	14.3	13.0	7.6	6.6	8.2	51.6	24 561	34 514	40.5	8.0
Idaho Falls	8.2	22.1	10.1	12.9	14.6	13.0	7.9	5.8	5.4	50.5	43 973	50 730	15.4	1.5
Lewiston	5.9	17.3	10.7	12.3	14.5	13.4	8.9	8.0	9.1	51.2	28 082	30 904	10.0	0.1
Meridian city......................	11.4	22.3	6.9	19.8	17.3	10.4	5.4	3.6	2.9	50.9	9 596	34 919	263.9	17.8
Nampa..............................	10.5	20.4	12.5	17.6	12.7	9.2	5.9	5.0	6.2	51.0	28 365	51 867	82.9	23.9
Pocatello	8.3	18.3	16.7	14.7	12.6	12.0	6.9	5.2	5.2	50.8	46 117	51 466	11.6	-0.9
Twin Falls	7.8	18.6	12.1	12.8	13.4	12.1	8.1	6.7	8.3	52.0	27 634	34 469	24.7	6.6
ILLINOIS	7.1	19.1	9.8	14.6	16.0	13.1	8.4	6.2	5.9	51.0	11 430 602	12 419 293	8.6	1.9
Addison	7.6	18.6	11.3	16.6	15.4	12.8	9.3	5.3	3.1	49.2	32 053	35 914	12.0	2.4
Alton	7.2	18.5	9.1	14.5	14.5	12.0	8.0	7.3	8.7	53.1	33 060	30 496	-7.8	-2.1
Arlington Heights.................	6.0	17.1	6.0	13.2	16.6	14.7	10.3	7.9	8.2	51.9	75 463	76 031	0.8	-0.3
Aurora	10.6	21.2	10.2	19.4	16.5	10.6	5.4	3.1	3.1	49.6	99 672	142 990	43.5	13.4
Bartlett.............................	10.7	21.1	5.4	16.4	21.4	13.4	6.1	3.3	2.3	50.6	19 395	36 706	89.3	2.3
Belleville	6.2	17.3	9.0	14.1	16.2	12.5	7.6	7.8	9.4	52.9	42 806	41 410	-3.3	-0.5
Berwyn	7.9	18.3	9.6	16.1	15.6	11.7	7.3	6.0	7.4	51.3	45 426	54 016	18.9	-2.7
Bloomington	7.4	17.6	12.5	16.8	16.5	12.8	6.5	5.0	5.0	51.5	51 889	64 808	24.9	5.7
Bolingbrook	9.5	22.7	8.4	16.8	18.4	13.5	6.4	2.4	1.9	50.1	40 843	56 321	37.9	17.5
Buffalo Grove	6.6	22.3	5.3	11.7	20.5	16.8	7.8	5.2	3.9	51.6	36 417	42 909	17.8	0.8
Burbank	5.9	19.3	9.9	12.2	15.9	13.2	9.6	7.7	6.3	51.2	27 600	27 902	1.1	0.5
Calumet City	7.7	21.0	8.6	14.7	16.0	11.6	7.6	6.3	6.4	53.5	37 840	39 071	3.3	-1.0
Carol Stream	8.2	22.7	9.1	16.5	20.2	12.6	5.0	2.6	3.1	50.7	31 759	40 438	27.3	-0.8
Carpentersville	10.5	22.6	10.9	19.7	15.7	10.0	5.3	3.6	1.7	48.4	23 049	30 586	32.7	13.8
Champaign.........................	5.0	12.8	31.7	15.1	11.6	10.0	5.4	4.5	3.9	49.3	63 502	67 518	6.3	6.6
Chicago	7.5	18.7	11.2	18.4	15.0	11.4	7.5	5.5	4.8	51.5	2 783 726	2 896 016	4.0	-0.9
Chicago Heights.................	9.2	22.5	10.2	14.2	13.7	11.0	7.4	6.4	5.5	51.3	32 966	32 776	-0.6	-1.5
Cicero...............................	10.9	23.7	12.7	18.2	13.7	8.8	4.8	3.4	3.7	48.6	67 436	85 616	27.0	-3.0
Crystal Lake	8.1	23.5	6.7	13.4	19.7	13.0	6.6	4.5	4.5	50.6	24 692	38 000	53.9	5.3
Danville.............................	7.1	17.8	9.5	13.6	14.1	12.7	8.6	7.9	8.7	50.2	33 828	33 904	0.2	-2.4
Decatur.............................	6.7	17.3	11.1	12.1	13.9	13.5	9.0	8.2	8.2	53.2	83 900	81 860	-2.4	-3.1
De Kalb	5.4	11.6	39.2	14.0	9.7	7.6	4.4	3.8	4.3	50.5	35 076	39 018	11.2	6.0
Des Plaines........................	5.9	16.5	7.5	12.9	16.3	14.0	9.8	8.3	8.9	51.6	53 414	58 720	9.9	-3.9
Dolton...............................	7.5	24.5	8.3	12.3	17.5	13.5	7.1	4.8	4.4	53.6	23 956	25 614	6.9	-1.7
Downers Grove	6.2	18.5	6.6	12.1	17.2	16.0	9.0	6.5	7.9	52.0	47 464	48 724	4.0	1.0
East St. Louis	8.6	24.2	9.7	11.9	12.7	11.8	8.5	7.1	5.4	55.1	40 944	31 542	-23.0	-3.1
Elgin	9.2	19.8	10.7	17.5	16.1	11.8	6.4	4.2	4.4	50.0	77 014	94 487	22.7	2.8
Elk Grove Village	6.0	18.9	7.4	13.1	18.7	15.1	9.1	7.0	4.8	51.3	33 429	34 727	3.9	-0.2

Table D. Cities — Group Quarters, Crime, and Education

City	Households, 2000					Persons in group quarters, 2000				Serious crimes known to police,[2] 2002				Education, 2000			
				Percent			Institutional			Total		Rate[2]		School enrollment[4]		Attainment[5] (percent)	
	Number	Percent change, 1990–2000	Persons per household	Female family householder[1]	One-person	Total	Total	Persons in nursing homes	Non-institutional	Number	Rate[3]	Violent	Property	Public	Private	High school graduate or less	Bachelor's degree or more
	26	27	28	29	30	31	32	33	34	35	36	37	38	39	40	41	42
GEORGIA—Cont'd																	
Athens-Clarke County	39 706	NA	2.35	13.3	29.7	8 180	1 179	567	7 001	6 656	6 339	418	5 921	40 725	3 647	40.6	39.8
Atlanta	168 147	8.0	2.30	20.7	38.5	28 947	8 938	1 225	20 009	49 451	11 355	2 289	9 066	87 475	25 659	45.4	34.6
Augusta-Richmond County	73 920	7.6	2.55	20.8	27.7	10 911	3 193	498	7 718	12 569	6 017	387	5 630	50 041	6 566	51.7	18.7
Columbus	69 819	6.0	2.54	19.6	26.7	9 107	3 249	1 053	5 858	12 382	6 374	428	5 946	45 411	5 539	49.3	20.3
Dalton city	9 689	10.9	2.81	11.5	27.6	685	508	365	177	2 111	7 233	654	6 578	5 794	479	63.0	18.3
East Point	14 553	8.8	2.69	28.9	27.4	438	149	132	289	2 852	6 888	833	6 055	9 659	1 795	56.6	17.6
Gainesville	8 537	23.0	2.79	15.2	29.5	1 760	1 189	190	571	2 162	8 083	819	7 265	4 654	921	56.7	24.2
Hinesville	10 528	40.3	2.89	16.7	17.4	12	0	0	12	1 812	5 702	485	5 217	8 548	738	41.9	17.3
La Grange	10 022	2.6	2.50	23.5	30.1	895	429	139	466	2 372	8 725	511	8 214	6 453	1 172	59.4	21.0
Macon	38 444	-6.6	2.44	25.7	31.7	3 595	1 668	911	1 927	10 515	10 340	628	9 711	23 025	4 821	60.3	17.2
Marietta	23 895	20.3	2.39	13.8	32.8	1 561	483	459	1 078	3 170	5 160	479	4 682	11 568	2 939	39.1	34.1
Peachtree City	10 876	75.1	2.89	8.4	16.0	152	152	152	0	272	824	42	781	8 539	1 474	21.7	46.2
Rome	13 320	10.9	2.47	17.0	30.9	2 114	1 422	495	692	2 129	5 820	634	5 186	7 418	1 591	60.7	18.9
Roswell	30 207	66.1	2.61	8.6	23.1	628	53	0	575	2 033	2 451	272	2 178	15 823	4 383	20.5	52.6
Savannah	51 375	-1.1	2.45	21.7	31.4	5 497	2 120	642	3 377	11 595	8 432	865	7 567	31 801	7 409	52.2	20.2
Smyrna	18 372	23.8	2.21	11.4	37.5	466	66	21	400	2 191	5 111	399	4 712	7 049	1 743	34.2	40.3
Valdosta	16 692	18.0	2.50	19.5	28.4	1 952	475	355	1 477	3 028	6 623	573	6 050	14 279	1 426	50.3	24.9
Warner Robins	19 550	16.9	2.48	16.6	28.1	409	292	292	117	3 384	6 631	419	6 212	12 558	1 209	49.0	16.7
HAWAII	403 240	13.2	2.92	12.4	21.9	35 782	7 690	2 949	28 092	75 238	6 044	262	5 782	255 215	65 627	43.9	26.2
Hilo CDP	14 577	9.4	2.70	15.2	24.1	1 391	479	465	912	NA	NA	NA	NA	11 301	1 002	45.5	24.3
Honolulu CDP	140 337	4.3	2.57	12.1	29.7	11 286	3 039	1 638	8 247	57 271	6 360	289	6 072	67 640	23 875	42.6	31.1
Kailua CDP	12 229	3.3	2.98	12.2	16.6	69	5	0	64	NA	NA	NA	NA	6 597	3 651	31.9	39.4
Kaneohe CDP	10 976	3.4	3.14	13.7	15.4	499	276	136	223	NA	NA	NA	NA	7 250	2 502	41.0	29.5
Mililani CDP	9 010	2.7	3.17	10.2	10.6	4	0	0	4	NA	NA	NA	NA	7 006	1 677	29.5	31.8
Pearl City CDP	8 921	0.5	3.17	12.3	14.9	2 727	117	110	2 610	NA	NA	NA	NA	5 600	1 300	46.7	20.1
Waimalu CDP	10 524	1.5	2.78	11.1	21.0	90	1	0	89	NA	NA	NA	NA	5 740	1 793	34.5	32.4
Waipahu CDP	7 566	0.0	4.23	18.1	11.1	1 134	27	25	1 107	NA	NA	NA	NA	7 674	1 197	64.6	11.1
IDAHO	469 645	30.2	2.69	8.7	22.4	31 496	17 717	5 735	13 779	42 547	3 173	255	2 918	323 683	44 896	43.8	21.7
Boise City	74 438	46.4	2.44	10.0	28.0	4 013	2 569	1 109	1 444	8 841	4 591	354	4 237	44 287	6 066	30.1	33.6
Caldwell	8 963	33.7	2.79	13.9	23.3	931	514	178	417	2 169	8 059	498	7 561	5 796	1 069	61.2	11.7
Coeur d'Alene	13 985	35.7	2.39	11.5	28.2	1 062	867	526	195	2 245	6 276	481	5 795	7 981	996	43.3	19.5
Idaho Falls	18 793	17.3	2.65	10.2	25.3	946	672	93	274	2 224	4 230	285	3 944	13 181	1 036	38.0	28.2
Lewiston	12 795	11.1	2.36	9.3	27.9	662	405	368	257	1 293	4 037	150	3 887	7 236	797	45.5	19.6
Meridian city	11 829	227.5	2.93	8.8	14.5	263	153	153	110	NA	NA	NA	NA	8 597	1 243	34.4	27.1
Nampa	18 090	77.1	2.77	11.4	22.6	1 844	688	496	1 156	3 016	5 610	519	5 091	11 652	2 448	52.0	16.0
Pocatello	19 334	12.5	2.58	10.5	25.0	1 663	280	265	1 383	1 711	3 208	276	2 932	16 444	1 365	34.9	27.9
Twin Falls	13 274	26.8	2.51	11.0	26.8	1 167	575	339	592	2 298	6 432	523	5 909	8 159	901	48.5	16.5
ILLINOIS	4 591 779	9.3	2.63	12.3	26.8	321 781	174 727	91 887	147 054	506 086	4 016	621	3 396	2 787 463	663 141	46.3	26.1
Addison	11 649	8.6	3.07	10.2	16.9	201	0	0	201	NA	NA	NA	NA	7 550	1 639	55.8	19.5
Alton	12 518	-3.5	2.36	17.4	33.3	942	633	429	309	NA	NA	NA	NA	6 750	1 448	52.0	16.1
Arlington Heights	30 763	6.8	2.44	6.3	29.0	919	793	790	126	NA	NA	NA	NA	13 541	4 614	26.6	46.5
Aurora	46 489	37.9	3.04	12.0	20.6	1 889	1 015	824	874	6 034	4 159	497	3 662	32 885	7 864	46.3	29.9
Bartlett	12 179	91.3	3.00	7.0	14.2	113	49	0	64	NA	NA	NA	NA	9 012	1 814	29.9	38.3
Belleville	17 603	-0.8	2.27	13.5	35.1	1 476	1 304	928	172	NA	NA	NA	NA	8 783	2 096	46.5	17.6
Berwyn	19 702	2.1	2.73	12.8	29.4	181	140	140	41	NA	NA	NA	NA	11 088	2 895	54.5	17.2
Bloomington	26 642	24.0	2.34	9.7	32.8	2 447	555	330	1 892	NA	NA	NA	NA	14 590	4 146	35.1	39.7
Bolingbrook	17 416	40.6	3.22	10.9	14.2	279	270	270	9	NA	NA	NA	NA	14 656	2 518	36.1	29.2
Buffalo Grove	15 708	17.8	2.72	6.6	22.1	236	234	234	2	NA	NA	NA	NA	10 721	2 014	18.7	55.9
Burbank	9 317	1.6	2.98	12.1	18.9	117	71	56	46	NA	NA	NA	NA	5 866	1 439	64.8	9.3
Calumet City	15 139	-1.9	2.58	22.4	29.8	22	0	0	22	NA	NA	NA	NA	9 701	1 963	50.9	13.9
Carol Stream	13 872	22.4	2.91	9.6	21.1	85	83	83	2	NA	NA	NA	NA	10 554	1 852	35.1	32.0
Carpentersville	8 872	28.5	3.45	11.5	13.9	4	0	0	4	NA	NA	NA	NA	8 093	674	61.5	12.2
Champaign	27 071	12.0	2.23	9.0	36.6	7 239	307	253	6 932	NA	NA	NA	NA	30 053	2 235	28.3	44.3
Chicago	1 061 928	3.6	2.67	18.9	32.6	59 547	27 323	13 839	32 224	191 199	6 507	1 498	5 009	614 543	203 891	51.2	25.5
Chicago Heights	10 703	-2.1	3.00	22.3	22.9	644	236	236	408	NA	NA	NA	NA	8 674	1 568	58.7	12.3
Cicero	23 115	-0.3	3.70	13.7	17.5	198	190	190	8	NA	NA	NA	NA	21 806	3 236	77.4	6.1
Crystal Lake	13 070	51.1	2.89	8.4	20.2	276	221	221	55	NA	NA	NA	NA	10 259	1 760	31.2	36.2
Danville	13 327	-3.4	2.35	15.1	33.9	2 522	2 361	376	161	NA	NA	NA	NA	7 033	949	58.7	15.7
Decatur	34 086	0.2	2.30	14.1	32.7	3 448	1 590	903	1 858	NA	NA	NA	NA	15 773	4 899	55.4	17.0
De Kalb	13 081	23.9	2.42	9.4	29.6	7 374	380	380	6 994	NA	NA	NA	NA	19 583	1 143	33.6	18.0
Des Plaines	22 362	11.9	2.58	9.0	28.5	1 000	858	858	142	NA	NA	NA	NA	11 350	2 469	46.5	24.7
Dolton	8 512	2.1	2.98	26.1	20.8	231	231	231	0	NA	NA	NA	NA	7 292	1 365	43.8	15.4
Downers Grove	18 979	7.5	2.53	7.2	27.4	768	381	381	387	NA	NA	NA	NA	9 641	3 439	27.3	46.4
East St. Louis	11 178	-14.4	2.80	40.6	27.8	272	182	119	90	NA	NA	NA	NA	9 422	516	62.5	9.1
Elgin	31 543	17.4	2.94	11.3	23.3	1 908	1 145	613	763	NA	NA	NA	NA	21 090	4 262	51.2	20.5
Elk Grove Village	13 278	10.6	2.60	8.6	25.6	221	149	149	72	NA	NA	NA	NA	7 580	1 590	37.3	31.6

1. No spouse present. 2. Data for serious crimes have not been adjusted for underreporting. This may affect comparability between geographic areas and over time. 3. Per 100,000 population estimated by the FBI. 4. All persons 3 years old and over enrolled in nursery school through college. 5. Persons 25 years old and over.

City	Per capita income[1] (dollars)	Median income Dollars	Percent change, 1989–1999 (constant 1999 dollars)	Percent with income of $100,000 or more	Persons Total	Percent change in rate, 1989–1999	Families Total	Total	Percent change, 1990–2000	Vacant units for sale or rent[2]	For seasonal use (percent)	Home owner vacancy rate	Renter vacancy rate
	43	44	45	46	47	48	49	50	51	52	53	54	55
GEORGIA—Cont'd													
Athens-Clarke County	17 123	28 403	48.0	8.2	28.3	-28.0	14.8	42 126	127.7	2 420	0.4	1.6	4.9
Atlanta	25 772	34 770	16.2	15.1	24.4	-10.6	21.3	186 925	2.3	18 778	0.6	4.1	7.2
Augusta-Richmond County	17 088	33 086	-2.5	6.4	19.6	NA	16.2	82 312	6.5	8 392	0.3	2.6	10.7
Columbus	18 262	34 798	7.7	8.0	15.7	-15.6	12.8	76 182	7.4	6 363	0.3	1.7	10.5
Dalton city	20 575	34 312	4.2	11.7	16.0	8.1	11.9	10 229	7.1	540	0.2	1.5	5.3
East Point	15 175	31 874	-11.4	5.3	20.7	22.5	17.2	15 637	-0.2	1 084	0.2	1.7	5.2
Gainesville	19 128	36 605	6.1	12.0	21.8	16.6	16.1	9 076	18.6	539	0.3	2.0	5.7
Hinesville	14 300	35 013	6.0	4.3	14.8	-15.4	13.8	11 742	46.1	1 214	0.3	4.9	10.0
La Grange	16 640	29 719	1.2	8.4	21.4	0.5	18.2	11 000	0.5	978	0.4	2.1	8.4
Macon	16 082	27 405	-3.0	5.7	25.5	4.5	21.6	44 341	-2.5	5 897	0.2	2.9	14.2
Marietta	23 409	40 645	10.5	11.6	15.7	10.6	11.5	25 227	8.9	1 332	0.2	1.5	5.2
Peachtree City	31 667	76 458	6.3	34.0	2.3	4.5	1.7	11 313	73.0	437	0.6	1.2	7.9
Rome	17 327	30 930	9.2	7.9	20.3	8.6	15.3	14 508	10.8	1 188	0.3	2.2	9.1
Roswell	36 012	71 726	2.3	34.0	5.0	51.5	2.8	31 300	54.1	1 093	0.3	1.0	5.3
Savannah	16 921	29 038	-2.2	5.8	21.8	-3.5	17.7	57 437	-2.3	6 062	0.3	1.7	9.1
Smyrna	27 637	47 572	4.6	14.2	8.9	34.8	6.7	19 633	16.7	1 261	0.4	3.3	4.5
Valdosta	16 472	29 046	-1.1	7.9	24.7	3.8	18.8	18 907	21.1	2 215	0.3	3.1	13.2
Warner Robins	18 121	38 401	-3.8	4.8	13.2	11.9	11.0	21 688	19.9	2 138	0.2	2.8	12.1
HAWAII	21 525	49 820	-4.5	16.6	10.7	28.9	7.6	460 542	18.1	57 302	5.6	1.6	8.2
Hilo CDP	18 220	39 139	-2.9	9.9	17.1	17.9	11.1	16 026	13.4	1 449	1.3	1.2	10.9
Honolulu CDP	24 191	45 112	-9.7	17.0	11.8	40.5	7.9	158 663	8.8	18 326	3.3	1.7	10.2
Kailua CDP	29 299	72 784	-2.0	31.8	5.4	58.8	3.3	12 780	4.5	551	1.3	0.8	4.1
Kaneohe CDP	23 476	66 006	-1.3	24.2	6.1	24.5	4.4	11 472	5.7	496	0.4	0.8	5.5
Mililani CDP	24 427	73 067	-1.7	26.1	3.2	88.2	2.5	9 280	4.3	270	0.2	1.0	4.9
Pearl City CDP	21 683	62 036	-9.0	21.5	6.2	77.1	4.0	9 181	2.0	260	0.2	0.6	3.2
Waimalu CDP	25 913	61 210	-12.4	22.4	5.9	90.3	4.1	10 999	3.6	475	0.3	1.1	6.0
Waipahu CDP	14 484	49 444	-4.1	17.5	13.8	3.0	10.6	8 033	3.8	467	0.0	1.0	8.0
IDAHO	17 841	37 572	10.7	7.3	11.8	-11.3	8.3	527 824	27.7	58 179	5.2	2.2	7.6
Boise City	22 696	42 432	8.5	10.9	8.4	-10.6	5.9	77 850	46.1	3 412	0.5	1.5	5.2
Caldwell	13 657	30 848	10.2	3.8	16.0	0.0	12.6	9 603	34.7	640	0.2	2.5	7.9
Coeur d'Alene	17 454	33 001	10.3	4.3	12.8	-9.2	9.3	14 929	36.3	944	0.6	2.4	7.6
Idaho Falls	18 857	40 512	0.9	8.4	10.9	3.8	7.8	19 771	17.4	978	0.4	1.5	5.9
Lewiston	19 091	36 606	6.0	6.0	12.0	6.2	8.4	13 394	11.1	599	0.4	1.2	5.4
Meridian city	20 150	53 276	NA	11.0	5.6	NA	4.6	12 293	228.2	464	0.2	2.7	2.9
Nampa	14 491	34 758	31.3	3.3	12.4	-33.0	8.7	19 379	80.1	1 289	0.3	3.4	7.5
Pocatello	17 425	34 326	2.4	7.0	15.4	0.7	10.7	20 627	9.9	1 293	0.4	2.3	7.8
Twin Falls	16 439	32 641	4.7	4.7	14.1	-2.1	9.8	14 162	28.6	888	0.4	2.0	8.1
ILLINOIS	23 104	46 590	7.5	14.4	10.7	-10.1	7.8	4 885 615	8.4	293 836	0.6	1.5	6.2
Addison	21 201	54 090	-2.7	17.3	9.6	104.3	7.2	11 805	7.1	156	0.2	0.4	1.4
Alton	16 817	31 213	1.2	4.4	18.7	-6.0	14.7	13 894	-2.2	1 376	0.2	2.3	10.1
Arlington Heights	33 544	67 807	-1.7	28.6	2.5	4.2	1.6	31 725	4.3	962	0.3	1.2	4.6
Aurora	22 131	54 861	16.5	17.5	8.5	-19.0	6.2	48 797	37.0	2 308	0.2	1.6	6.1
Bartlett	29 652	79 718	15.2	33.0	1.9	-26.9	1.2	12 356	85.6	177	0.1	0.6	4.7
Belleville	18 990	35 979	0.4	5.5	11.7	30.0	9.3	19 142	0.3	1 539	0.1	2.1	8.9
Berwyn	19 113	43 833	4.1	9.1	7.9	38.6	6.2	20 691	3.2	989	0.2	1.3	4.4
Bloomington	24 751	46 496	17.9	15.1	7.8	-22.0	4.3	28 431	25.6	1 789	0.2	2.1	8.1
Bolingbrook	23 468	67 852	9.4	22.8	4.1	28.1	2.9	17 884	38.8	468	0.1	1.2	4.4
Buffalo Grove	36 696	80 525	7.0	37.2	2.3	53.3	1.3	16 166	16.6	458	1.7	0.4	2.9
Burbank	18 923	49 388	-1.8	10.7	5.1	18.6	4.5	9 518	2.4	201	0.1	0.8	2.2
Calumet City	18 123	38 902	-3.9	5.8	12.2	24.5	9.8	15 947	-3.9	808	0.1	2.1	6.3
Carol Stream	25 152	64 893	7.0	22.2	3.4	-2.9	2.4	14 200	17.4	328	0.1	0.9	3.5
Carpentersville	17 424	54 526	11.5	11.7	8.5	-19.8	6.7	9 113	27.1	241	0.1	0.9	3.1
Champaign	18 664	32 795	6.3	8.2	22.1	-2.6	8.1	28 556	9.8	1 485	0.2	1.4	5.1
Chicago	20 175	38 625	9.3	11.6	19.6	-9.3	16.6	1 152 868	1.8	90 940	0.4	1.7	5.7
Chicago Heights	14 963	36 958	-0.2	7.3	17.5	-12.9	13.7	11 444	-1.5	741	0.1	2.6	6.5
Cicero	12 489	38 044	4.2	5.2	15.5	11.5	13.2	24 640	-0.8	1 525	0.3	2.0	3.4
Crystal Lake	26 146	66 872	7.7	22.7	3.5	66.7	2.6	13 459	50.0	389	0.3	1.1	4.3
Danville	16 476	30 431	1.5	5.3	18.1	-6.2	13.4	14 886	-2.9	1 559	0.2	3.1	11.8
Decatur	19 009	33 111	-3.2	6.7	16.5	3.8	12.1	37 239	-0.6	3 153	0.3	1.9	11.7
De Kalb	16 261	35 153	3.1	7.4	21.3	-12.7	9.0	13 619	24.8	538	0.3	1.6	3.6
Des Plaines	24 146	53 638	-5.3	14.3	4.6	109.1	3.0	22 851	11.4	489	0.2	0.6	3.5
Dolton	18 102	48 020	-2.7	8.6	8.4	71.4	6.7	8 944	4.1	432	0.1	2.7	4.9
Downers Grove	31 580	65 539	1.1	26.6	2.3	-8.0	1.3	19 477	7.2	498	0.3	0.9	3.5
East St. Louis	11 169	21 324	25.7	3.2	35.1	-20.0	31.8	12 899	-17.4	1 721	0.1	1.9	7.7
Elgin	21 112	52 605	10.1	13.6	8.1	3.8	6.4	32 665	16.9	1 122	0.2	1.1	4.9
Elk Grove Village	28 515	62 132	-5.4	20.5	2.0	-25.9	1.5	13 513	8.8	235	0.2	0.3	4.3

1. Based on population enumerated as of April 1, 2000.   2. Includes units rented or sold but not occupied.

Table D. Cities — Housing, Labor Force, Employment, and Disability

City	Housing units, 2000 (cont'd) — Occupied units					Civilian labor force, 2003				Civilian employment,[2] 2000			Disability, 2000
	Total	Percent owner occupied	Percent renter occupied	Average size owner occupied	Average size renter occupied	Total	Percent change, 2002–2003	Unemployment Total	Rate[1]	Total	Percent Management, professional, and related occupations	Production, transportation, and material moving occupations	Employment disabled persons[3] (percent)
	56	57	58	59	60	61	62	63	64	65	66	67	68
GEORGIA—Cont'd													
Athens-Clarke County	39 706	42.0	58.0	2.45	2.27	51 327	4.3	1 569	3.1	49 159	36.9	14.5	8.4
Atlanta	168 147	43.7	56.3	2.37	2.25	240 663	2.0	18 897	7.9	182 936	40.6	11.2	13.4
Augusta-Richmond County	73 920	58.0	42.0	2.62	2.46	84 447	3.9	4 570	5.4	78 906	30.5	16.0	15.6
Columbus	69 819	56.4	43.6	2.57	2.49	89 672	3.7	4 424	4.9	75 677	30.7	16.5	14.3
Dalton city	9 689	47.9	52.1	2.71	2.90	15 162	4.4	667	4.4	12 354	23.3	38.6	19.2
East Point	14 553	45.4	54.6	2.63	2.74	22 605	2.1	1 643	7.3	17 300	23.2	18.1	19.0
Gainesville	8 537	43.7	56.3	2.67	2.88	14 416	3.9	599	4.2	11 019	27.9	27.5	16.8
Hinesville	10 528	49.6	50.4	3.02	2.75	9 983	2.6	520	5.2	9 848	25.8	14.6	9.2
La Grange	10 022	46.8	53.2	2.49	2.52	13 916	2.4	1 084	7.8	11 341	27.6	26.3	16.9
Macon	38 444	50.1	49.9	2.46	2.41	50 738	4.5	2 710	5.3	37 214	27.9	15.5	15.5
Marietta	23 895	37.6	62.4	2.36	2.41	37 198	2.3	2 040	5.5	32 172	33.5	9.3	12.7
Peachtree City	10 876	81.2	18.8	2.95	2.65	14 085	3.0	578	4.1	15 571	46.4	12.3	6.5
Rome	13 320	53.0	47.0	2.50	2.43	16 493	4.1	940	5.7	14 451	27.4	25.1	16.5
Roswell	30 207	67.0	33.0	2.68	2.46	36 166	2.7	800	2.2	44 613	48.5	5.2	7.8
Savannah	51 375	50.3	49.7	2.52	2.38	69 510	4.3	3 370	4.8	53 594	28.6	14.0	16.2
Smyrna	18 372	50.1	49.9	2.18	2.23	29 999	2.5	1 205	4.0	23 499	42.7	9.1	12.1
Valdosta	16 692	47.7	52.3	2.56	2.45	24 528	5.5	912	3.7	19 071	29.2	15.6	12.9
Warner Robins	19 550	57.5	42.5	2.49	2.45	28 225	4.9	934	3.3	20 827	28.5	12.8	12.7
HAWAII	403 240	56.5	43.5	3.07	2.71	618 310	1.9	26 512	4.3	537 909	32.2	8.9	11.4
Hilo CDP	14 577	60.9	39.1	2.78	2.58	NA	NA	NA	NA	16 766	33.6	8.9	9.9
Honolulu CDP	140 337	46.9	53.1	2.75	2.40	436 442	1.7	16 901	3.9	169 982	35.7	7.8	11.8
Kailua CDP	12 229	69.7	30.3	3.09	2.72	NA	NA	NA	NA	18 152	43.5	6.5	6.3
Kaneohe CDP	10 976	68.1	31.9	3.19	3.03	NA	NA	NA	NA	16 511	37.6	7.6	8.8
Mililani CDP	9 010	75.9	24.1	3.16	3.21	NA	NA	NA	NA	14 662	37.7	7.4	6.6
Pearl City CDP	8 921	68.7	31.3	3.24	3.00	NA	NA	NA	NA	12 703	27.0	9.2	9.2
Waimalu CDP	10 524	62.1	37.9	2.94	2.53	NA	NA	NA	NA	15 490	36.6	7.2	8.2
Waipahu CDP	7 566	53.4	46.6	4.63	3.76	NA	NA	NA	NA	13 120	14.7	14.5	18.4
IDAHO	469 645	72.4	27.6	2.75	2.52	692 543	1.0	37 440	5.4	599 453	31.4	14.2	9.4
Boise City	74 438	64.0	36.0	2.58	2.19	112 117	-0.7	5 178	4.6	99 605	38.8	9.9	8.2
Caldwell	8 963	65.3	34.7	2.83	2.72	14 841	-0.5	1 137	7.7	11 403	23.8	22.0	11.9
Coeur d'Alene	13 985	61.8	38.2	2.48	2.25	21 051	0.5	1 153	5.5	16 154	27.8	12.2	10.8
Idaho Falls	18 793	68.3	31.7	2.80	2.32	30 834	3.0	1 075	3.5	23 528	37.9	9.9	8.5
Lewiston	12 795	66.8	33.2	2.48	2.12	20 603	-1.5	633	3.1	15 064	26.9	17.4	10.4
Meridian city	11 829	84.3	15.7	2.98	2.67	7 897	-0.7	327	4.1	17 554	37.2	9.5	9.0
Nampa	18 090	69.5	30.5	2.80	2.69	21 542	-0.5	1 558	7.2	23 425	26.2	18.7	9.7
Pocatello	19 334	66.2	33.8	2.72	2.30	29 071	-0.7	1 485	5.1	25 244	33.8	12.2	7.5
Twin Falls	13 274	62.5	37.5	2.57	2.41	19 129	7.1	810	4.2	15 780	26.7	15.8	12.5
ILLINOIS	4 591 779	67.3	32.7	2.76	2.37	6 330 059	-0.6	422 263	6.7	5 833 185	34.2	15.7	10.8
Addison	11 649	68.4	31.6	3.09	3.01	20 716	-0.7	1 479	7.1	17 568	26.9	21.7	12.8
Alton	12 518	65.4	34.6	2.42	2.24	13 330	0.9	1 274	9.6	13 044	25.5	18.4	13.7
Arlington Heights	30 763	76.7	23.3	2.60	1.91	42 588	-1.0	2 069	4.9	39 845	50.5	7.3	7.5
Aurora	46 489	70.1	29.9	3.17	2.71	80 200	0.0	6 546	8.2	68 525	33.3	20.5	13.8
Bartlett	12 179	93.1	6.9	3.03	2.72	20 644	-0.5	1 177	5.7	19 514	43.2	9.8	7.5
Belleville	17 603	60.2	39.8	2.44	2.00	20 597	0.6	2 295	11.1	19 775	28.7	14.0	12.3
Berwyn	19 702	61.5	38.5	3.05	2.23	26 521	-0.7	1 855	7.0	24 780	26.2	20.1	12.6
Bloomington	26 642	63.1	36.9	2.59	1.92	41 717	-1.0	1 298	3.1	35 871	40.7	10.4	7.6
Bolingbrook	17 416	85.2	14.8	3.30	2.75	34 189	-0.4	2 321	6.8	29 297	36.8	13.7	8.1
Buffalo Grove	15 708	87.1	12.9	2.80	2.13	24 784	-1.2	1 137	4.6	22 941	54.9	5.6	5.7
Burbank	9 317	83.0	17.0	3.09	2.46	14 101	-1.0	891	6.3	13 321	16.8	25.4	10.7
Calumet City	15 139	63.3	36.7	2.74	2.31	19 012	-1.0	1 727	9.1	16 981	24.6	19.7	12.6
Carol Stream	13 872	70.5	29.5	3.15	2.34	22 836	-1.0	1 269	5.6	21 546	37.7	13.1	6.1
Carpentersville	8 872	79.9	20.1	3.46	3.40	17 357	-0.2	1 632	9.4	13 538	19.7	24.7	13.0
Champaign	27 071	47.4	52.6	2.43	2.05	38 822	0.1	1 248	3.2	35 034	45.1	8.7	5.2
Chicago	1 061 928	43.8	56.2	2.90	2.49	1 299 278	-1.1	106 429	8.2	1 220 040	33.5	16.2	15.1
Chicago Heights	10 703	62.8	37.2	2.97	2.97	14 304	-0.4	1 511	10.6	12 420	24.0	21.9	12.1
Cicero	23 115	55.2	44.8	3.94	3.40	37 701	-0.7	3 367	8.9	30 543	11.2	35.5	18.1
Crystal Lake	13 070	79.3	20.7	3.04	2.30	21 310	-0.4	1 502	7.0	18 759	40.7	11.9	5.3
Danville	13 327	62.5	37.5	2.42	2.25	14 805	-0.2	1 619	10.9	12 862	27.1	21.8	12.8
Decatur	34 086	66.4	33.6	2.35	2.20	38 783	-2.2	3 492	9.0	35 794	27.4	20.1	12.7
De Kalb	13 081	41.9	58.1	2.67	2.24	20 995	-0.4	1 029	4.9	19 482	37.0	11.7	6.9
Des Plaines	22 362	79.3	20.7	2.70	2.13	33 449	-0.7	2 677	8.0	28 638	32.2	14.7	11.4
Dolton	8 512	81.6	18.4	3.10	2.47	13 081	-0.5	1 348	10.3	11 564	27.3	18.6	11.8
Downers Grove	18 979	79.2	20.8	2.70	1.86	26 594	-0.9	1 410	5.3	25 280	49.0	7.7	6.3
East St. Louis	11 178	52.9	47.1	2.78	2.82	9 576	-0.2	1 331	13.9	9 302	21.9	18.4	20.3
Elgin	31 543	70.2	29.8	3.01	2.77	51 726	-0.2	4 825	9.3	46 221	28.0	22.6	13.3
Elk Grove Village	13 278	76.7	23.3	2.74	2.12	20 280	-0.9	1 147	5.7	19 451	36.7	11.8	9.0

1. Percent of civilian labor force.   2. Persons 16 years old and over.   3. Persons 16 to 64 years old.

City	Value of residential construction authorized by building permits, 2003			Wholesale trade, 1997				Retail trade,[1] 1997			
	New construction ($1,000)	Number of housing units	Percent single family	Number of establish-ments	Number of employees	Sales (mil dol)	Annual payroll (mil dol)	Number of establish-ments	Number of employees	Sales (mil dol)	Annual payroll (mil dol)
	69	70	71	72	73	74	75	76	77	78	79
GEORGIA—Cont'd											
Athens-Clarke County	116 521	1 340	61.0	NA	NA	NA	NA	NA	NA	NA	NA
Atlanta	488 410	6 893	14.2	1 164	15 406	17 285.9	636.9	2 044	26 738	4 229.8	491.1
Augusta-Richmond County	89 287	873	74.3	NA	NA	NA	NA	NA	NA	NA	NA
Columbus	109 656	1 226	57.4	208	2 884	1 316.5	91.3	845	11 718	1 950.9	186.6
Dalton city	20 284	316	23.1	248	D	D	D	372	5 098	919.6	89.2
East Point	2 189	19	100.0	39	673	396.0	17.0	91	1 160	155.4	16.8
Gainesville	24 915	421	34.9	116	1 512	1 035.2	44.0	331	4 250	773.2	74.6
Hinesville	32 927	249	71.1	7	41	6.5	0.8	133	1 635	239.4	20.7
La Grange	13 855	145	96.6	42	397	189.3	12.9	202	2 809	445.6	43.5
Macon	25 915	346	43.1	210	2 776	984.0	81.8	765	10 586	1 630.2	159.5
Marietta	28 531	143	100.0	342	4 471	2 719.7	190.6	409	7 391	1 948.2	167.1
Peachtree City	60 784	300	100.0	70	680	378.1	24.3	80	1 354	174.9	19.1
Rome	NA	NA	NA	76	795	309.9	25.5	343	4 389	707.0	65.8
Roswell	77 120	482	95.2	309	2 912	6 033.5	151.9	321	4 720	1 298.8	118.4
Savannah	25 096	213	70.4	220	2 737	1 487.2	90.9	962	12 394	1 894.3	188.8
Smyrna	88 981	531	100.0	117	1 906	3 411.0	82.4	226	4 820	927.2	81.0
Valdosta	34 281	349	91.7	109	1 027	408.0	27.5	379	4 892	758.2	72.7
Warner Robins	66 199	916	81.0	31	310	184.1	10.5	238	3 790	607.1	58.0
HAWAII	1 316 090	7 284	85.3	1 872	18 532	7 147.5	576.0	5 088	64 218	11 317.8	1 161.8
Hilo CDP	NA	NA	NA	87	811	314.2	22.0	261	3 696	552.2	63.0
Honolulu CDP	589 007	3 473	83.8	1 114	11 332	4 537.5	354.2	2 258	27 812	5 483.5	534.7
Kailua CDP	NA	NA	NA	26	81	58.4	3.9	104	1 758	227.9	27.5
Kaneohe CDP	NA	NA	NA	22	84	23.1	1.9	137	2 171	371.8	37.7
Mililani CDP	NA	NA	NA	14	115	37.5	6.3	50	1 181	176.8	19.5
Pearl City CDP	NA	NA	NA	37	517	176.1	14.8	50	1 062	239.7	18.8
Waimalu CDP	NA	NA	NA	18	86	10.0	1.5	84	1 259	251.7	27.0
Waipahu CDP	NA	NA	NA	60	1 246	364.7	41.3	119	1 908	378.3	39.6
IDAHO	1 942 662	15 091	83.5	1 980	22 828	10 127.8	628.0	5 848	63 732	11 649.6	1 079.7
Boise City	142 032	1 221	60.4	367	5 235	4 637.4	200.1	939	12 880	2 505.9	230.0
Caldwell	66 086	684	95.0	35	263	76.0	5.8	120	1 270	287.0	26.7
Coeur d'Alene	48 527	452	82.3	53	398	247.0	13.3	292	3 576	692.1	66.3
Idaho Falls	22 248	239	89.1	125	1 529	572.0	38.9	398	4 758	790.0	76.9
Lewiston	12 750	78	76.9	55	557	183.1	14.7	220	2 749	453.6	47.2
Meridian city	211 134	1 627	88.1	NA	NA	NA	NA	NA	NA	NA	NA
Nampa	154 438	1 501	82.1	70	890	377.1	23.8	216	2 664	563.2	49.0
Pocatello	17 846	167	92.2	89	883	270.6	24.2	239	2 809	538.4	48.8
Twin Falls	48 167	609	65.8	109	1 190	330.7	26.9	299	4 013	726.7	65.6
ILLINOIS	9 105 577	62 211	72.9	21 956	325 847	275 978.4	13 325.5	44 568	610 790	108 002.2	10 596.0
Addison	11 175	105	33.3	257	4 566	2 649.9	182.1	123	2 754	801.0	63.9
Alton	1 981	43	11.6	27	327	79.2	11.6	207	2 404	392.6	36.8
Arlington Heights	30 480	88	88.6	326	3 664	4 427.1	192.3	326	4 970	1 302.5	92.7
Aurora	148 628	1 559	53.6	140	2 212	5 262.0	93.8	463	7 942	1 171.5	121.0
Bartlett	28 360	157	84.7	43	115	70.8	4.7	39	486	77.2	7.8
Belleville	15 390	130	100.0	42	D	D	D	231	3 073	543.4	55.4
Berwyn	248	2	100.0	29	141	98.1	4.7	147	1 578	272.8	27.8
Bloomington	79 163	861	51.2	109	1 137	566.5	50.5	364	5 300	905.1	85.6
Bolingbrook	143 494	1 108	100.0	54	1 076	1 102.0	34.9	102	2 786	456.9	43.9
Buffalo Grove	2 461	17	100.0	190	2 251	2 784.6	111.8	123	1 705	357.6	40.9
Burbank	9 877	78	100.0	10	84	9.1	1.4	91	1 794	290.2	26.0
Calumet City	2 261	32	75.0	20	D	D	D	194	4 775	715.1	72.1
Carol Stream	13 728	98	100.0	103	3 552	4 950.8	157.4	80	1 349	299.7	26.6
Carpentersville	90 000	360	100.0	12	D	D	D	38	401	57.4	6.1
Champaign	54 127	405	46.2	76	1 414	689.0	38.3	379	6 227	825.3	82.6
Chicago	723 721	8 138	12.6	3 312	50 029	31 971.1	1 970.1	7 885	86 703	13 882.1	1 553.2
Chicago Heights	1 977	19	100.0	51	890	371.9	25.6	93	1 165	308.7	26.4
Cicero	0	0	0.0	45	669	403.7	29.5	133	1 869	347.4	32.3
Crystal Lake	30 483	202	100.0	95	854	439.4	33.9	203	3 291	618.9	55.4
Danville	3 870	27	100.0	60	1 802	1 004.0	55.1	214	3 212	434.2	44.2
Decatur	32 950	325	82.5	129	1 609	3 119.0	50.6	372	5 334	882.6	87.8
De Kalb	24 800	225	73.8	20	D	D	D	130	2 153	297.9	32.1
Des Plaines	32 142	241	19.9	224	5 611	4 724.2	258.4	197	2 592	562.6	51.8
Dolton	399	5	100.0	8	91	21.3	3.3	60	851	116.8	12.6
Downers Grove	46 936	156	100.0	171	3 009	3 195.4	143.0	267	5 969	1 591.6	135.1
East St. Louis	1 282	16	100.0	23	D	D	D	73	617	71.2	8.6
Elgin	25 427	233	76.8	169	2 985	2 158.1	129.4	226	3 887	862.8	82.4
Elk Grove Village	1 590	7	100.0	621	10 899	8 110.0	479.7	152	3 039	550.1	68.2

1. Establishments with payroll.

Table D. Cities — Real Estate, Professional Services, and Manufacturing

City	Real estate and rental and leasing, 1997				Professional, scientific, and technical services,[1] 1997				Manufacturing, 1997			
	Number of establish-ments	Number of employees	Receipts (mil dol)	Annual payroll (mil dol)	Number of establish-ments	Number of employees	Receipts (mil dol)	Annual payroll (mil dol)	Number of establish-ments	Number of employees	Receipts (mil dol)	Annual payroll (mil dol)
	80	81	82	83	84	85	86	87	88	89	90	91
GEORGIA—Cont'd												
Athens-Clarke County	NA	NA	NA	NA	NA	NA	NA	NA	90	9 388	1 368.5	234.9
Atlanta	832	8 689	1 485.7	318.5	2 573	38 245	5 305.7	1 969.6	499	21 497	5 822.0	688.7
Augusta-Richmond County	NA	NA	NA	NA	NA	NA	NA	NA	NA	NA	NA	NA
Columbus	224	1 197	142.7	27.3	264	1 607	146.2	43.6	158	D	D	D
Dalton city	67	301	56.7	7.1	110	736	59.2	27.3	260	21 534	4 970.4	540.2
East Point	35	542	32.6	8.9	31	159	12.2	4.8	41	1 199	286.7	40.6
Gainesville	53	221	29.3	5.8	143	781	76.2	26.4	95	7 365	1 543.3	178.2
Hinesville	35	D	D	D	27	D	D	D	NA	NA	NA	NA
La Grange	34	135	14.1	2.5	50	221	15.8	6.9	70	8 540	1 634.0	257.6
Macon	157	986	137.1	24.3	308	1 792	163.4	51.7	154	10 650	5 388.6	419.5
Marietta	149	1 091	132.6	23.7	419	3 087	267.4	99.7	158	4 886	924.1	169.1
Peachtree City	31	84	13.0	1.9	82	274	30.4	11.4	37	5 277	1 304.1	161.8
Rome	40	266	20.6	4.5	108	579	53.9	17.4	88	5 342	1 070.6	154.1
Roswell	132	716	126.5	21.2	500	2 323	268.8	103.2	58	759	164.3	24.7
Savannah	194	974	115.7	23.0	367	2 239	188.1	75.7	131	4 579	1 279.7	139.3
Smyrna	92	527	158.0	18.5	173	1 327	153.2	75.6	50	1 032	136.8	36.6
Valdosta	73	438	31.4	6.9	117	674	41.6	16.9	70	4 816	1 272.4	118.9
Warner Robins	61	254	36.6	3.9	89	969	89.0	35.3	34	D	D	D
HAWAII	1 753	12 446	1 824.1	311.9	2 480	15 743	1 574.0	606.5	921	15 109	3 192.5	405.0
Hilo CDP	78	378	37.1	6.5	124	573	35.6	13.8	58	716	80.2	17.5
Honolulu CDP	973	6 707	968.4	179.3	1 650	12 014	1 282.5	503.2	491	7 639	904.9	187.7
Kailua CDP	30	114	15.6	2.7	67	202	20.4	7.8	NA	NA	NA	NA
Kaneohe CDP	30	114	10.2	2.4	25	97	7.6	2.6	NA	NA	NA	NA
Mililani CDP	12	36	3.4	0.6	14	87	11.1	5.7	NA	NA	NA	NA
Pearl City CDP	15	49	6.2	1.1	12	91	6.4	2.6	NA	NA	NA	NA
Waimalu CDP	22	151	10.2	3.3	22	380	12.3	6.1	NA	NA	NA	NA
Waipahu CDP	25	113	14.7	3.1	15	49	3.7	1.4	NA	NA	NA	NA
IDAHO	1 236	4 870	450.3	73.9	2 364	19 669	2 046.1	756.2	1 647	66 184	16 952.9	2 099.8
Boise City	294	1 536	167.7	28.2	675	5 927	868.9	252.1	210	16 823	5 780.6	753.4
Caldwell	18	100	6.2	1.2	40	124	10.0	3.4	64	1 956	239.1	41.1
Coeur d'Alene	83	252	32.6	4.3	155	790	59.2	24.6	61	1 169	193.6	32.5
Idaho Falls	65	365	18.9	3.5	187	7 210	740.5	334.8	79	2 107	217.8	44.9
Lewiston	39	178	11.5	2.5	65	D	D	D	44	D	D	D
Meridian city	NA	NA	NA	NA	NA	NA	NA	NA	NA	NA	NA	NA
Nampa	48	103	12.8	1.5	54	306	19.9	7.6	71	5 798	3 008.7	179.9
Pocatello	59	221	21.4	3.1	97	885	44.5	21.2	52	2 315	385.7	70.4
Twin Falls	58	218	24.6	3.5	119	493	35.2	12.4	64	2 400	512.1	51.8
ILLINOIS	11 411	73 819	12 830.0	2 101.4	30 378	274 714	33 855.1	13 105.4	17 953	887 350	200 020.0	31 837.9
Addison	34	239	39.6	8.4	99	1 146	77.9	21.4	388	10 598	1 461.1	346.9
Alton	33	121	14.3	2.1	63	350	25.8	11.0	31	1 716	358.4	66.1
Arlington Heights	104	913	139.9	27.2	430	4 523	446.5	146.0	120	10 976	3 052.9	645.6
Aurora	90	486	51.8	10.0	204	1 937	115.4	53.1	148	8 759	2 743.1	387.4
Bartlett	11	56	7.3	1.5	66	93	11.9	4.1	22	1 426	304.7	58.4
Belleville	58	247	22.8	4.1	177	1 119	101.2	43.2	60	2 239	307.7	65.7
Berwyn	25	106	9.1	1.5	59	128	10.3	3.3	22	585	79.5	23.6
Bloomington	78	323	43.1	5.5	173	1 005	89.4	38.2	59	D	D	D
Bolingbrook	29	158	15.2	2.2	78	291	24.9	10.2	21	2 453	807.9	153.8
Buffalo Grove	45	324	36.0	9.0	219	1 244	154.1	67.5	54	3 889	652.1	138.3
Burbank	12	68	5.5	1.0	17	85	4.3	1.1	NA	NA	NA	NA
Calumet City	22	108	9.8	1.3	34	119	7.1	2.0	19	757	155.3	23.4
Carol Stream	20	105	14.5	2.4	62	319	26.4	12.0	91	5 123	973.3	190.8
Carpentersville	13	96	13.5	2.3	17	46	3.6	1.5	40	2 066	294.4	73.7
Champaign	108	859	106.3	18.2	183	1 654	202.0	67.0	67	2 846	393.2	74.8
Chicago	2 971	25 827	5 226.4	899.1	8 115	118 842	17 205.3	6 757.5	3 195	130 372	26 745.9	4 178.4
Chicago Heights	21	132	11.5	2.4	42	327	27.5	12.4	71	4 061	982.5	149.0
Cicero	22	115	10.8	1.5	30	305	16.3	6.2	123	5 613	973.2	190.7
Crystal Lake	52	249	30.6	4.5	143	510	43.3	18.8	99	5 437	756.3	186.8
Danville	48	D	D	D	77	287	25.8	7.7	60	4 864	1 363.4	160.5
Decatur	88	498	38.7	8.3	144	1 026	81.1	33.4	98	D	D	D
De Kalb	36	200	26.4	3.1	49	149	12.5	3.5	47	2 648	535.3	71.2
Des Plaines	85	1 293	691.3	40.4	281	5 785	649.1	213.5	164	12 021	1 849.6	411.0
Dolton	12	75	10.8	1.7	9	38	3.0	1.5	23	1 196	263.3	38.2
Downers Grove	67	397	73.5	10.5	272	1 843	182.2	69.8	104	5 174	692.7	203.0
East St. Louis	20	69	6.2	1.3	8	D	D	D	22	564	134.7	20.9
Elgin	78	433	68.5	10.9	185	1 437	164.1	53.8	175	9 955	1 779.0	345.8
Elk Grove Village	55	467	86.9	14.7	146	2 803	339.3	115.5	550	23 239	3 916.5	864.4

1. Firms subject to federal tax.

Table D. Cities — Accommodation and Foodservices, Entertainment, and Health Care

City	Accommodation and foodservices, 1997				Arts, entertainment, and recreation,[1] 1997				Health care and social assistance,[1] 1997			
	Number of establishments	Number of employees	Sales (mil dol)	Annual payroll (mil dol)	Number of establishments	Number of employees	Receipts (mil dol)	Annual payroll (mil dol)	Number of establishments	Number of employees	Receipts (mil dol)	Annual payroll (mil dol)
	92	93	94	95	96	97	98	99	100	101	102	103
GEORGIA—Cont'd												
Athens-Clarke County	NA	NA	NA	NA	NA	NA	NA	NA	NA	NA	NA	NA
Atlanta	1 361	37 792	1 604.8	478.7	157	3 937	379.9	88.0	1 134	12 059	1 040.0	480.2
Augusta-Richmond County	NA	NA	NA	NA	NA	NA	NA	NA	NA	NA	NA	NA
Columbus	365	D	D	D	37	D	D	D	343	5 225	439.9	171.6
Dalton city	118	2 350	84.6	23.3	7	41	2.0	0.6	106	1 275	102.0	47.6
East Point	48	1 084	45.3	12.6	4	51	1.2	0.4	87	981	62.3	28.0
Gainesville	127	2 449	83.4	23.7	17	155	5.8	1.9	191	2 352	215.0	89.3
Hinesville	54	1 052	31.3	7.7	3	0	0.0	0.0	40	402	20.5	7.3
La Grange	59	1 026	31.3	7.9	3	60	1.0	0.4	62	970	65.0	32.3
Macon	273	5 786	175.0	47.3	25	275	8.2	2.2	430	7 536	627.8	247.8
Marietta	235	4 203	163.2	45.4	25	454	24.5	6.5	284	3 777	303.5	137.1
Peachtree City	50	1 442	61.3	16.6	10	42	1.5	0.6	49	398	25.6	11.2
Rome	118	2 246	78.9	20.2	10	56	4.7	0.8	147	3 735	330.8	125.1
Roswell	151	3 072	115.8	33.6	24	259	12.1	3.7	204	2 257	217.3	78.6
Savannah	413	9 619	334.6	90.1	42	475	21.0	5.8	370	5 400	405.8	216.0
Smyrna	142	3 028	109.5	30.7	13	241	13.1	2.4	121	1 458	104.3	38.3
Valdosta	138	2 787	83.0	23.6	15	120	5.1	1.1	165	2 399	148.0	65.9
Warner Robins	120	2 510	69.5	18.6	8	102	2.5	1.0	128	1 370	98.0	41.5
HAWAII	3 081	88 083	5 007.9	1 507.5	386	6 925	409.6	116.6	2 360	18 221	1 646.3	730.8
Hilo CDP	116	1 881	64.7	18.5	11	129	4.2	1.0	180	1 643	155.4	53.9
Honolulu CDP	1 503	42 549	2 604.0	733.4	159	2 592	143.5	43.2	1 194	9 866	925.5	427.4
Kailua CDP	83	D	D	D	9	248	11.8	3.4	108	526	44.1	20.8
Kaneohe CDP	60	1 009	36.9	9.5	6	72	4.1	1.4	63	587	37.6	16.3
Mililani CDP	27	D	D	D	3	149	6.8	2.2	25	169	15.6	7.2
Pearl City CDP	42	734	27.9	7.2	5	37	2.2	0.6	29	296	26.4	9.1
Waimalu CDP	43	884	39.8	10.2	9	208	11.2	3.0	66	463	49.1	25.3
Waipahu CDP	77	1 287	48.7	12.6	1	0	0.0	0.0	53	239	22.7	10.2
IDAHO	2 978	42 067	1 232.5	345.7	457	4 425	174.1	45.2	2 551	26 365	1 548.3	680.1
Boise City	511	10 138	316.3	89.0	56	825	28.2	8.2	587	5 728	433.0	204.9
Caldwell	59	749	21.2	5.6	6	73	1.4	0.5	58	982	69.7	26.9
Coeur d'Alene	173	2 943	101.0	27.7	22	266	13.2	4.1	183	1 886	111.0	44.0
Idaho Falls	170	3 335	88.6	25.4	19	203	3.8	1.2	225	3 094	226.9	90.4
Lewiston	97	1 415	42.0	12.3	11	0	0.0	0.0	109	0	0.0	0.0
Meridian city	NA	NA	NA	NA	NA	NA	NA	NA	NA	NA	NA	NA
Nampa	96	1 701	46.1	12.3	9	97	4.1	0.8	98	1 580	86.4	45.5
Pocatello	133	2 031	56.4	15.4	18	206	4.4	1.5	145	1 280	72.5	35.8
Twin Falls	125	2 160	58.3	17.1	19	96	4.0	0.9	127	2 028	108.7	49.4
ILLINOIS	23 984	397 300	14 826.8	4 018.7	3 097	46 972	3 640.3	1 040.6	21 122	248 667	16 870.2	7 441.8
Addison	53	990	39.2	8.7	9	57	2.8	0.8	40	233	16.1	7.0
Alton	99	1 821	57.1	15.0	11	0	0.0	0.0	111	1 344	93.1	47.7
Arlington Heights	147	2 953	124.2	32.5	23	398	35.7	9.1	269	3 153	246.5	121.9
Aurora	192	3 122	110.3	29.1	20	0	0.0	0.0	191	3 113	253.8	111.8
Bartlett	30	D	D	D	6	0	0.0	0.0	36	293	16.8	6.3
Belleville	132	2 260	61.8	17.0	13	220	7.1	2.0	198	2 228	147.3	75.6
Berwyn	101	D	D	D	6	65	5.1	1.7	107	763	67.2	30.6
Bloomington	192	4 221	124.7	37.1	19	226	8.3	1.8	145	1 814	129.6	64.1
Bolingbrook	57	988	34.4	8.7	7	54	1.9	0.5	54	673	30.0	12.1
Buffalo Grove	74	D	D	D	15	76	5.6	1.1	108	1 102	91.4	39.7
Burbank	69	D	D	D	3	0	0.0	0.0	25	469	27.8	11.6
Calumet City	106	1 674	51.4	12.8	5	98	6.0	1.1	57	917	42.6	14.9
Carol Stream	50	864	29.5	7.8	9	201	5.1	2.1	62	513	43.7	21.7
Carpentersville	27	679	23.0	6.7	3	34	1.0	0.3	11	48	3.8	1.3
Champaign	252	5 728	152.1	42.5	22	280	6.9	2.5	121	2 269	161.7	67.1
Chicago	5 148	92 348	4 481.9	1 194.1	563	7 547	864.0	361.1	4 019	43 898	3 217.3	1 284.8
Chicago Heights	54	762	23.5	6.2	2	0	0.0	0.0	46	1 130	95.3	40.8
Cicero	89	914	37.8	9.3	24	575	79.9	10.9	33	1 063	51.6	18.6
Crystal Lake	73	1 589	52.8	14.4	15	200	8.4	1.7	128	1 554	76.2	37.7
Danville	116	1 893	53.3	15.5	8	80	2.8	0.7	82	1 285	78.7	36.8
Decatur	196	D	D	D	16	213	5.6	2.0	185	2 354	147.7	67.0
De Kalb	94	1 719	45.4	11.1	5	0	0.0	0.0	34	385	26.5	13.2
Des Plaines	144	2 408	104.6	26.8	11	87	3.5	1.1	182	2 088	175.4	69.1
Dolton	36	530	14.8	3.9	6	40	1.2	0.3	24	597	23.5	11.2
Downers Grove	117	3 415	126.4	35.1	15	192	5.9	1.8	180	2 091	192.7	81.9
East St. Louis	37	476	18.6	4.1	2	0	0.0	0.0	41	419	26.1	7.5
Elgin	129	2 019	76.4	20.2	17	0	0.0	0.0	178	1 864	135.5	71.5
Elk Grove Village	85	1 442	63.6	16.6	8	65	5.8	1.2	105	1 228	120.3	57.9

1. Firms subject to federal tax.

Table D. Cities — Other Services and Federal Funds

City	Other services,[1] 1997				Selected federal funds, 2002–2003 (mil dol)								
					Procurement contracts		Grants						
	Number of establishments	Number of employees	Receipts (mil dol)	Annual payroll (mil dol)	Defense	Other	Total[2]	Medicaid and other health related	Nutrition and family welfare	Energy and environment	Education	Housing and community development	Direct payments for individuals for educational assistance
	104	105	106	107	108	109	110	111	112	113	114	115	116
GEORGIA—Cont'd													
Athens-Clarke County	NA	NA	NA	NA	2.6	1.0	65.6	47.0	8.3	0.0	0.0	1.3	0.0
Atlanta	903	7 202	498.6	149.4	290.8	984.9	2 238.4	498.4	304.4	95.5	391.7	305.8	96.6
Augusta-Richmond County	NA	NA	NA	NA	10.1	32.5	86.6	39.9	10.9	0.6	4.8	24.7	14.6
Columbus	305	2 004	104.7	35.8	6.5	1.4	32.1	1.4	5.3	0.9	2.9	20.1	9.8
Dalton city	88	453	32.3	9.4	2.6	2.5	5.5	0.5	0.0	0.2	0.5	3.8	3.4
East Point	51	443	41.0	14.6	0.2	0.2	3.1	0.0	0.0	0.0	0.0	2.4	0.0
Gainesville	101	624	37.8	11.0	27.5	22.8	24.7	0.1	19.2	0.0	0.1	4.0	3.7
Hinesville	40	174	10.1	2.6	53.0	0.4	10.8	0.0	0.0	0.0	7.3	3.1	0.0
La Grange	61	320	19.7	6.3	2.9	0.5	13.1	0.5	7.4	0.0	0.0	4.1	2.3
Macon	247	1 385	82.9	26.7	15.4	41.2	54.6	4.5	4.5	0.0	7.9	23.6	20.8
Marietta	213	1 640	108.2	37.9	1 088.8	21.6	20.4	1.2	0.0	0.0	0.2	14.0	5.3
Peachtree City	35	297	12.5	4.4	2.4	0.9	0.5	0.0	0.0	0.0	0.0	0.5	0.0
Rome	73	642	35.9	12.4	0.8	0.2	5.9	0.0	0.0	0.1	0.6	4.5	7.1
Roswell	172	1 241	137.7	29.0	22.0	3.5	2.9	0.0	0.0	2.6	0.0	0.0	0.1
Savannah	270	1 877	110.5	37.2	184.3	9.3	55.9	6.3	6.5	0.8	6.3	25.2	22.8
Smyrna	75	491	34.4	10.4	4.0	10.2	4.4	0.1	0.0	0.0	0.0	3.9	0.0
Valdosta	107	572	30.1	8.6	44.4	1.2	13.9	0.6	6.1	0.0	1.4	4.2	9.4
Warner Robins	107	563	27.3	8.3	116.8	9.6	8.1	0.0	6.8	0.0	0.0	1.1	1.4
HAWAII	1 476	10 375	683.2	206.4	1 750.2	228.2	1 911.0	657.0	278.7	33.7	236.3	158.9	36.3
Hilo CDP	76	476	28.6	8.9	NA	NA	NA	NA	NA	NA	NA	NA	NA
Honolulu CDP	748	5 786	395.5	117.0	374.6	115.9	767.9	106.9	73.1	30.6	160.9	90.6	22.4
Kailua CDP	36	229	13.3	4.7	NA	NA	NA	NA	NA	NA	NA	NA	NA
Kaneohe CDP	55	729	37.0	12.2	NA	NA	NA	NA	NA	NA	NA	NA	NA
Mililani CDP	18	91	3.6	1.2	NA	NA	NA	NA	NA	NA	NA	NA	NA
Pearl City CDP	27	197	15.6	4.6	NA	NA	NA	NA	NA	NA	NA	NA	NA
Waimalu CDP	28	220	13.5	4.3	NA	NA	NA	NA	NA	NA	NA	NA	NA
Waipahu CDP	55	291	22.9	7.4	NA	NA	NA	NA	NA	NA	NA	NA	NA
IDAHO	1 858	9 461	550.6	151.7	207.2	1 324.2	1 858.2	743.3	215.2	64.6	175.6	77.3	84.0
Boise City	319	2 584	132.7	39.8	6.1	64.2	309.8	32.9	46.1	52.3	67.6	9.4	16.7
Caldwell	41	214	13.4	3.8	0.3	1.6	9.1	0.0	5.4	0.0	0.9	0.8	0.9
Coeur d'Alene	89	529	28.2	7.7	9.0	40.9	8.5	0.5	2.2	0.1	0.4	3.1	4.9
Idaho Falls	112	591	38.1	10.4	14.9	979.0	11.3	0.4	1.6	3.9	0.0	2.1	1.1
Lewiston	82	527	27.7	8.0	0.0	4.0	11.3	0.0	3.1	0.0	1.8	4.0	4.0
Meridian city	NA	NA	NA	NA	4.9	7.3	5.7	0.0	0.0	0.0	0.0	0.3	0.0
Nampa	87	412	20.6	5.9	52.2	51.4	6.4	4.1	0.0	0.0	0.0	1.1	1.4
Pocatello	89	475	29.3	8.3	1.4	7.1	18.8	2.4	1.3	1.5	1.7	4.6	18.0
Twin Falls	83	542	26.3	7.9	0.6	3.1	9.5	1.6	4.3	0.3	0.3	1.2	6.9
ILLINOIS	18 806	118 317	8 296.8	2 503.0	2 513.7	3 215.1	15 720.0	7 013.3	2 603.5	228.0	1 461.9	1 627.0	592.2
Addison	110	855	74.8	22.4	6.7	0.7	3.6	0.0	0.0	0.0	0.0	3.6	0.0
Alton	70	393	25.8	7.5	3.4	0.4	12.9	0.1	6.2	0.0	0.1	4.5	0.0
Arlington Heights	149	1 055	56.5	19.9	5.9	1.1	7.5	0.0	0.2	0.2	0.7	5.6	0.0
Aurora	154	949	58.8	19.5	11.6	1.6	27.1	12.0	0.0	0.0	0.8	14.1	1.6
Bartlett	32	153	8.5	3.1	0.1	0.1	0.0	0.0	0.0	0.0	0.0	0.0	0.0
Belleville	119	652	38.1	13.2	115.1	0.8	18.9	0.0	0.0	0.0	0.6	10.9	7.6
Berwyn	66	333	25.0	6.2	0.0	0.1	2.0	0.0	0.0	0.0	0.3	1.7	0.0
Bloomington	136	965	60.2	19.1	1.0	4.2	18.8	2.2	3.0	0.0	0.0	5.7	1.3
Bolingbrook	56	351	25.7	6.8	2.0	0.2	3.7	0.0	0.0	0.0	0.0	3.7	0.0
Buffalo Grove	59	547	40.8	12.4	30.1	29.4	0.0	0.0	0.0	0.0	0.0	0.0	0.0
Burbank	31	124	9.5	2.7	0.0	0.0	0.0	0.0	0.0	0.0	0.0	0.0	0.0
Calumet City	45	224	14.1	4.0	0.0	0.1	3.1	0.0	0.0	0.0	0.0	3.1	0.0
Carol Stream	47	471	35.6	10.2	4.7	1.7	6.2	0.0	0.0	0.0	0.0	6.1	0.0
Carpentersville	16	53	3.4	1.1	5.1	0.0	14.6	0.0	0.0	0.0	0.0	14.6	0.0
Champaign	127	741	38.0	13.0	7.0	2.9	246.1	58.9	1.1	20.4	1.1	6.8	6.6
Chicago	3 333	23 886	1 820.5	502.9	473.4	509.0	2 349.2	586.6	153.3	11.0	100.0	919.4	277.7
Chicago Heights	52	349	17.4	5.4	0.4	3.9	4.9	0.0	0.1	0.0	0.7	4.0	2.5
Cicero	72	465	34.4	11.4	1.3	0.0	2.8	0.0	0.0	0.0	0.0	2.5	0.0
Crystal Lake	96	622	36.9	11.7	5.3	0.0	1.8	0.1	0.0	0.0	0.0	1.7	1.2
Danville	77	487	23.3	7.8	1.6	4.1	13.4	0.0	4.0	0.0	0.6	8.3	2.8
Decatur	144	1 278	73.6	25.6	0.3	17.2	28.7	2.2	2.3	0.0	0.9	16.7	5.1
De Kalb	58	282	13.0	3.8	0.0	0.0	24.8	2.3	0.1	0.2	7.2	11.8	15.0
Des Plaines	145	1 042	88.7	27.7	1.2	8.2	12.9	0.2	0.0	10.8	1.1	0.7	2.2
Dolton	26	190	13.4	4.4	0.0	0.0	2.7	2.1	0.0	0.0	0.0	0.5	0.0
Downers Grove	117	1 153	104.3	37.9	33.2	4.1	6.3	1.8	0.0	0.3	0.0	4.2	0.9
East St. Louis	28	177	10.0	2.8	1.2	9.1	26.5	10.5	0.2	0.0	0.6	14.3	0.1
Elgin	126	1 292	78.5	28.4	16.0	1.1	16.7	1.1	0.0	0.0	3.2	12.1	4.1
Elk Grove Village	97	918	77.7	28.0	24.3	1.1	6.3	5.9	0.0	0.0	0.0	0.0	0.0

1. Firms subject to federal tax.   2. Includes program categories not shown separately. State totals include additional categories not allocated by city.

City	General revenue Total (mil dol)	Intergovernmental Total (mil dol)	Intergovernmental Percent from state government	Taxes Total (mil dol)	Taxes Per capita[1] (dollars) Total	Taxes Per capita[1] (dollars) Property	Taxes Per capita[1] (dollars) Sales and gross receipts	General expenditure Total (mil dol)	General expenditure Per capita[1] (dollars) Total	General expenditure Per capita[1] (dollars) Capital outlays
	117	118	119	120	121	122	123	124	125	126
GEORGIA—Cont'd										
Athens-Clarke County..........	139.1	49.9	24.0	46.5	447	285	133	137.1	1 320	340
Atlanta..............................	1 245.5	152.3	7.0	266.1	626	260	243	1 088.9	2 563	564
Augusta-Richmond County ...	234.5	86.6	15.8	70.9	358	184	152	212.6	1 074	209
Columbus............................	238.6	95.2	31.2	79.5	428	285	76	231.8	1 247	214
Dalton city..........................	67.2	3.9	30.9	11.4	383	247	99	80.5	2 692	1 450
East Point...........................	32.8	10.3	1.5	10.0	263	143	103	45.2	1 193	250
Gainesville..........................	49.2	9.7	29.3	13.1	467	213	190	58.6	2 093	917
Hinesville............................	16.1	3.4	10.3	6.9	226	129	84	15.8	517	70
La Grange	29.3	4.3	1.8	3.8	143	0	114	32.5	1 229	275
Macon................................	87.1	32.0	1.8	34.4	358	155	168	88.8	926	38
Marietta	66.1	11.7	46.6	24.4	393	135	169	85.2	1 374	207
Peachtree City	18.3	6.0	3.3	9.5	294	146	126	19.5	603	159
Rome.................................	49.7	16.7	12.5	14.8	419	209	141	47.1	1 338	161
Roswell..............................	61.7	14.6	4.9	28.1	356	218	107	66.2	838	196
Savannah............................	198.5	47.1	18.5	67.2	527	288	183	196.8	1 541	193
Smyrna...............................	32.8	0.9	34.0	19.9	436	285	109	35.7	781	87
Valdosta	47.0	20.8	15.2	14.0	312	163	120	44.4	994	303
Warner Robins	34.8	5.2	35.3	16.0	304	169	108	33.3	634	48
HAWAII	X	X	X	X	X	X	X	X	X	X
Hilo CDP	NA	NA	NA	NA	NA	NA	NA	NA	NA	NA
Honolulu CDP	1 000.2	171.7	35.1	534.4	1 413	1 011	369	1 181.4	3 124	832
Kailua CDP	NA	NA	NA	NA	NA	NA	NA	NA	NA	NA
Kaneohe CDP	NA	NA	NA	NA	NA	NA	NA	NA	NA	NA
Mililani CDP	NA	NA	NA	NA	NA	NA	NA	NA	NA	NA
Pearl City CDP	NA	NA	NA	NA	NA	NA	NA	NA	NA	NA
Waimalu CDP	NA	NA	NA	NA	NA	NA	NA	NA	NA	NA
Waipahu CDP	NA	NA	NA	NA	NA	NA	NA	NA	NA	NA
IDAHO............................	X	X	X	X	X	X	X	X	X	X
Boise City...........................	174.9	21.2	46.6	74.7	393	324	27	191.0	1 006	276
Caldwell..............................	22.0	5.3	44.1	7.4	250	205	0	23.9	812	324
Coeur d'Alene	27.3	4.4	86.6	11.2	309	234	46	27.8	767	170
Idaho Falls	53.8	14.5	40.9	17.1	334	316	8	52.1	1 021	256
Lewiston.............................	NA	NA	NA	NA	NA	NA	NA	NA	NA	NA
Meridian city.......................	17.7	2.6	58.9	6.9	177	122	14	15.8	405	106
Nampa...............................	55.8	6.8	89.8	23.9	396	346	13	47.2	783	171
Pocatello	43.4	10.5	63.6	17.4	339	309	21	41.6	811	154
Twin Falls...........................	NA	NA	NA	NA	NA	NA	NA	NA	NA	NA
ILLINOIS	X	X	X	X	X	X	X	X	X	X
Addison..............................	31.8	9.3	97.9	9.9	272	128	98	34.0	935	111
Alton..................................	33.3	17.7	100.0	7.3	242	109	119	36.4	1 205	303
Arlington Heights.................	75.4	22.8	93.8	40.3	527	413	92	68.3	894	159
Aurora................................	157.8	54.9	94.5	73.9	471	250	177	158.7	1 011	189
Bartlett	21.6	5.6	96.4	8.9	237	164	32	28.1	753	165
Belleville.............................	35.8	13.4	99.3	13.0	315	197	95	35.9	868	131
Berwyn...............................	48.6	9.7	92.2	25.5	479	312	86	81.1	1 522	666
Bloomington	73.2	26.6	95.5	31.8	472	214	241	72.3	1 073	180
Bolingbrook	56.7	19.1	100.0	23.4	373	148	174	86.0	1 369	636
Buffalo Grove......................	38.7	11.8	100.0	16.7	386	241	111	38.1	881	76
Burbank..............................	18.0	5.9	100.0	10.3	365	218	67	20.8	741	114
Calumet City	32.5	10.9	98.7	18.2	468	291	157	37.6	968	93
Carol Stream	22.1	10.1	99.6	6.1	152	12	114	18.8	466	55
Carpentersville....................	19.7	5.6	91.5	8.9	259	126	95	23.2	677	205
Champaign..........................	63.7	22.7	95.1	28.4	410	175	214	62.9	906	125
Chicago..............................	4 886.9	1 297.9	68.4	2 042.3	708	222	437	5 529.2	1 916	425
Chicago Heights..................	29.8	8.3	68.2	15.8	484	330	70	32.6	1 000	118
Cicero................................	74.1	19.9	99.6	41.9	497	307	119	75.9	901	235
Crystal Lake	32.5	14.5	100.0	9.5	240	189	34	24.8	626	0
Danville..............................	29.4	13.7	91.9	9.1	274	105	152	28.4	850	44
Decatur..............................	78.0	26.3	84.5	20.6	258	104	141	58.4	731	77
De Kalb	27.8	11.1	84.6	12.8	319	156	155	25.5	637	32
Des Plaines	58.9	16.0	95.5	32.0	546	312	171	60.3	1 027	221
Dolton................................	17.0	4.8	100.0	7.3	289	168	71	19.4	762	37
Downers Grove....................	41.9	18.9	94.1	13.8	283	138	130	45.2	925	55
East St. Louis......................	39.9	25.7	78.2	11.5	372	260	99	32.1	1 037	143
Elgin..................................	112.4	48.8	96.7	33.7	349	266	64	113.0	1 170	348
Elk Grove Village	44.9	16.4	95.3	21.4	611	328	229	36.2	1 034	24

1. Based on population estimated as of July 1 of the year shown.

City	City government finances, 2002 (cont'd)									
	General expenditure									
	Percent of total for—									
	Public welfare	Highways	Parking facilities	Education	Health and hospitals	Police protection	Sewerage and sanitation	Parks and recreation	Housing and community development	Interest on debt
	127	128	129	130	131	132	133	134	135	136
GEORGIA—Cont'd										
Athens-Clarke County	0.5	8.5	0.5	0.0	6.3	11.9	12.0	8.1	1.9	0.5
Atlanta	0.0	5.0	0.0	0.0	0.0	12.2	23.3	4.5	0.7	11.2
Augusta-Richmond County	0.5	7.5	0.0	0.0	8.1	13.7	13.5	7.4	4.9	5.1
Columbus	0.2	6.4	0.0	0.0	8.4	16.1	7.5	9.9	2.4	4.9
Dalton city	0.5	11.2	0.0	0.3	0.0	6.4	41.9	5.1	0.1	1.5
East Point	0.0	4.8	0.0	0.0	0.0	19.4	14.8	4.2	0.3	3.7
Gainesville	4.1	4.2	0.0	0.0	0.0	10.5	52.1	5.8	1.4	0.9
Hinesville	0.0	12.6	0.0	0.0	0.0	25.1	30.0	2.1	2.1	0.0
La Grange	0.1	6.8	0.0	0.0	0.5	17.3	31.3	6.6	3.9	2.2
Macon	0.0	3.4	0.1	0.0	0.3	17.0	5.4	5.4	5.0	2.4
Marietta	7.8	6.8	0.0	0.0	0.0	13.6	11.8	1.2	3.5	5.3
Peachtree City	0.0	20.6	0.0	0.0	0.8	23.1	0.0	16.7	0.0	1.9
Rome	0.0	5.6	0.0	17.0	0.2	12.0	21.7	2.1	4.4	2.9
Roswell	0.0	15.6	0.0	0.0	0.1	15.6	11.1	21.1	1.5	5.6
Savannah	0.7	4.6	0.0	0.0	0.0	14.3	33.0	8.8	5.4	3.3
Smyrna	0.0	9.5	0.0	0.0	0.0	18.9	20.8	9.4	3.7	3.6
Valdosta	0.0	11.4	0.0	0.0	0.0	17.8	21.0	10.4	2.3	0.0
Warner Robins	0.4	9.0	0.0	0.0	0.0	20.5	23.2	3.7	10.3	0.3
HAWAII	X	X	X	X	X	X	X	X	X	X
Hilo CDP	NA	NA	NA	NA	NA	NA	NA	NA	NA	NA
Honolulu CDP	0.0	9.3	0.0	0.0	1.6	14.2	21.6	14.0	2.5	7.6
Kailua CDP	NA	NA	NA	NA	NA	NA	NA	NA	NA	NA
Kaneohe CDP	NA	NA	NA	NA	NA	NA	NA	NA	NA	NA
Mililani CDP	NA	NA	NA	NA	NA	NA	NA	NA	NA	NA
Pearl City CDP	NA	NA	NA	NA	NA	NA	NA	NA	NA	NA
Waimalu CDP	NA	NA	NA	NA	NA	NA	NA	NA	NA	NA
Waipahu CDP	NA	NA	NA	NA	NA	NA	NA	NA	NA	NA
IDAHO	X	X	X	X	X	X	X	X	X	X
Boise City	0.0	1.0	0.5	0.0	0.3	12.6	24.0	5.9	1.7	4.7
Caldwell	0.0	9.7	0.0	0.0	0.0	27.7	28.0	5.4	1.6	2.6
Coeur d'Alene	0.0	15.0	0.3	0.0	0.0	18.9	18.2	5.9	0.0	3.2
Idaho Falls	0.0	7.1	0.0	0.0	3.4	14.8	23.4	12.6	0.0	0.3
Lewiston	NA	NA	NA	NA	NA	NA	NA	NA	NA	NA
Meridian city	0.0	0.7	0.0	0.0	0.5	26.0	30.5	7.7	0.0	0.0
Nampa	0.0	9.9	0.0	0.0	0.0	15.8	21.2	24.3	2.3	2.9
Pocatello	0.0	8.5	0.0	0.0	1.1	16.6	26.1	8.4	1.0	2.0
Twin Falls	NA	NA	NA	NA	NA	NA	NA	NA	NA	NA
ILLINOIS	X	X	X	X	X	X	X	X	X	X
Addison	0.0	17.0	0.0	0.0	0.0	24.1	12.4	0.0	3.8	16.7
Alton	0.0	6.8	0.0	0.0	0.0	32.2	11.3	6.1	4.5	7.2
Arlington Heights	0.0	13.8	1.0	0.0	2.4	19.8	2.8	0.1	2.4	6.3
Aurora	0.7	10.9	0.6	0.0	0.9	23.5	5.1	3.6	0.7	11.2
Bartlett	0.0	15.6	0.3	0.0	0.0	21.5	8.1	12.9	3.3	6.3
Belleville	0.0	14.8	0.5	0.0	4.9	15.8	11.0	3.2	0.0	7.0
Berwyn	1.4	46.8	0.0	0.0	0.0	14.5	4.8	1.4	0.6	6.7
Bloomington	0.0	15.1	1.3	0.0	0.0	15.7	9.3	15.9	2.4	2.3
Bolingbrook	0.0	14.2	0.0	0.0	0.0	12.4	12.9	1.7	0.0	4.1
Buffalo Grove	0.0	7.9	0.0	0.0	0.0	22.5	10.1	5.9	0.0	3.6
Burbank	0.0	8.3	0.0	0.0	0.0	22.6	0.0	0.0	0.0	4.0
Calumet City	0.0	15.6	0.0	0.0	0.5	20.2	4.8	0.0	0.0	8.6
Carol Stream	0.0	24.9	0.0	0.0	0.0	42.1	8.6	0.0	0.0	1.7
Carpentersville	0.0	6.1	0.0	0.0	0.0	26.5	27.6	0.1	1.3	1.7
Champaign	0.3	9.5	3.0	0.0	0.0	15.6	3.9	0.0	2.6	1.6
Chicago	2.6	12.4	0.0	0.0	3.4	20.0	8.1	1.3	3.7	10.7
Chicago Heights	0.0	13.7	0.0	0.0	0.0	21.8	9.3	2.4	0.0	10.9
Cicero	0.3	9.2	0.0	0.0	1.3	17.0	4.5	0.0	5.7	5.9
Crystal Lake	0.0	17.4	0.0	0.0	0.0	23.2	6.8	0.0	0.0	11.7
Danville	0.0	10.8	0.7	0.0	0.0	24.6	8.3	6.6	5.0	4.9
Decatur	0.0	15.6	1.3	0.0	0.0	22.6	3.5	2.0	4.9	4.8
De Kalb	0.0	22.3	0.0	0.0	0.0	22.5	4.4	2.2	1.6	6.1
Des Plaines	1.0	7.4	0.6	0.0	0.0	19.9	8.6	0.2	0.8	5.7
Dolton	0.0	15.7	0.0	0.0	0.0	21.4	4.6	7.3	11.4	4.7
Downers Grove	0.0	20.8	0.9	0.0	0.0	22.5	1.5	0.0	1.5	8.9
East St. Louis	0.0	10.9	0.0	0.0	0.0	20.5	1.9	0.0	18.2	0.7
Elgin	0.4	8.7	0.0	0.0	0.0	18.0	4.5	16.1	2.6	4.0
Elk Grove Village	0.0	21.4	0.0	0.0	0.8	25.8	4.7	0.0	0.6	2.3

City	City government finances, 2002 (cont'd) Debt outstanding			City government employment, 2002	Climate[2] Average daily temperature (degrees Fahrenheit) Mean		Limits				
	Total (mil dol)	Per capita[1] (dollars)	Percent utility		January	July	January[3]	July[4]	Annual precipitation (inches)	Heating degree days	Cooling degree days
	137	138	139	140	141	142	143	144	145	146	147
GEORGIA—Cont'd											
Athens-Clarke County..........	52.8	508	86.0	1 524	41.8	79.6	32.0	89.6	49.74	2 893	1 709
Atlanta..............................	4 179.7	9 838	48.8	8 270	41.0	78.8	31.5	88.0	50.77	2 991	1 667
Augusta-Richmond County ...	330.2	1 669	55.4	2 533	NA	NA	NA	NA	NA	NA	NA
Columbus..........................	275.2	1 480	46.1	3 211	NA	NA	NA	NA	NA	NA	NA
Dalton city.......................	299.4	10 015	70.0	550	NA	NA	NA	NA	NA	NA	NA
East Point.........................	90.8	2 398	50.1	589	41.0	78.8	31.5	88.0	50.77	2 991	1 667
Gainesville........................	118.1	4 222	93.9	594	NA	NA	NA	NA	NA	NA	NA
Hinesville.........................	9.6	313	99.7	152	NA	NA	NA	NA	NA	NA	NA
La Grange	49.9	1 889	72.0	378	43.4	79.0	31.9	90.1	54.52	2 667	1 696
Macon	34.2	357	0.0	1 430	45.4	81.2	34.2	91.9	44.63	2 334	2 125
Marietta	110.1	1 776	0.0	758	41.0	78.8	31.5	88.0	50.77	2 991	1 667
Peachtree City	6.2	192	0.0	230	NA	NA	NA	NA	NA	NA	NA
Rome...............................	66.6	1 889	65.7	628	38.4	76.9	27.0	87.3	55.33	3 467	1 337
Roswell............................	66.5	841	0.2	704	41.0	78.8	31.5	88.0	50.77	2 991	1 667
Savannah..........................	200.8	1 572	41.6	2 188	48.9	81.8	38.1	91.1	49.22	1 847	2 365
Smyrna	29.3	641	19.5	395	41.0	78.8	31.5	88.0	50.77	2 991	1 667
Valdosta	6.8	153	100.0	549	49.0	80.7	36.7	92.1	52.24	1 844	2 350
Warner Robins	28.2	537	96.4	493	45.4	81.2	34.2	91.9	44.63	2 334	2 125
HAWAII	X	X	X	X	X	X	X	X	X	X	X
Hilo CDP...........................	NA	NA	NA	NA	71.7	75.8	63.6	83.0	129.19	0	3 284
Honolulu CDP.....................	2 297.0	6 074	5.3	9 231	71.4	78.9	62.4	87.7	21.53	0	3 845
Kailua CDP........................	NA	NA	NA	NA	71.3	77.0	65.5	82.2	79.91	0	3 482
Kaneohe CDP.....................	NA	NA	NA	NA	71.3	77.0	65.5	82.2	79.91	0	3 482
Mililani CDP......................	NA	NA	NA	NA	71.4	78.9	62.4	87.7	21.53	0	3 845
Pearl City CDP	NA	NA	NA	NA	71.4	78.9	62.4	87.7	21.53	0	3 845
Waimalu CDP.....................	NA	NA	NA	NA	71.4	78.9	62.4	87.7	21.53	0	3 845
Waipahu CDP	NA	NA	NA	NA	71.4	78.9	62.4	87.7	21.53	0	3 845
IDAHO..................	X	X	X	X	X	X	X	X	X	X	X
Boise City.........................	198.5	1 045	0.0	1 429	29.0	74.0	21.6	90.2	12.11	5 861	754
Caldwell...........................	19.3	656	0.0	188	NA	NA	NA	NA	NA	NA	NA
Coeur d'Alene	19.1	526	10.1	281	NA	NA	NA	NA	NA	NA	NA
Idaho Falls	40.9	800	79.8	612	18.2	68.6	10.0	86.0	10.88	8 063	305
Lewiston...........................	NA	NA	NA	324	33.6	74.1	27.6	89.0	12.43	5 270	814
Meridian city.....................	4.0	102	0.0	168	NA	NA	NA	NA	NA	NA	NA
Nampa..............................	17.8	295	0.0	419	29.0	74.0	21.6	90.2	12.11	5 861	754
Pocatello	9.1	178	0.0	517	23.3	70.6	14.4	88.1	12.14	7 180	421
Twin Falls.........................	NA	NA	NA	266	26.9	68.8	18.6	85.0	10.40	6 769	329
ILLINOIS	X	X	X	X	X	X	X	X	X	X	X
Addison	79.4	2 182	0.0	245	21.0	73.2	12.9	83.7	35.82	6 536	752
Alton................................	32.7	1 085	0.0	293	27.0	78.5	17.9	88.4	38.43	5 214	1 346
Arlington Heights................	65.2	854	2.4	621	21.0	73.2	12.9	83.7	35.82	6 536	752
Aurora.............................	311.3	1 983	4.8	1 070	19.7	73.1	10.7	84.2	36.88	6 699	702
Bartlett............................	26.5	709	3.4	149	NA	NA	NA	NA	NA	NA	NA
Belleville	36.4	881	0.0	324	29.9	77.4	20.3	89.4	38.37	4 774	1 271
Berwyn	87.8	1 647	0.0	398	21.0	73.2	12.9	83.7	35.82	6 536	752
Bloomington	29.5	437	0.0	584	23.9	75.9	15.4	86.7	37.10	5 759	1 117
Bolingbrook.......................	103.1	1 642	7.0	351	19.7	73.1	10.7	84.2	36.88	6 699	702
Buffalo Grove	26.6	615	6.4	267	21.0	73.2	12.9	83.7	35.82	6 536	752
Burbank............................	11.5	409	0.0	221	22.4	75.1	14.9	84.4	37.38	6 176	940
Calumet City	53.5	1 378	0.0	405	23.7	74.1	15.2	85.5	36.82	6 043	857
Carol Stream	4.5	111	0.0	199	21.0	73.2	12.9	83.7	35.82	6 536	752
Carpentersville	12.9	376	0.0	175	NA	NA	NA	NA	NA	NA	NA
Champaign.........................	24.7	356	0.0	289	23.8	75.0	16.0	85.3	39.71	5 854	985
Chicago............................	13 145.1	4 554	7.8	40 921	22.4	75.1	14.9	84.4	37.38	6 176	940
Chicago Heights..................	64.9	1 991	0.0	392	20.6	73.7	12.2	83.8	37.12	6 541	780
Cicero..............................	68.2	809	0.0	553	22.4	75.1	14.9	84.4	37.38	6 176	940
Crystal Lake	40.6	1 025	7.0	279	NA	NA	NA	NA	NA	NA	NA
Danville............................	20.7	620	0.0	309	25.1	75.2	16.1	86.8	40.18	5 610	1 005
Decatur............................	72.2	904	37.3	590	25.2	76.2	16.0	87.9	40.16	5 522	1 120
De Kalb	31.2	778	19.2	259	17.7	73.0	8.9	83.8	36.35	7 034	682
Des Plaines	103.4	1 760	5.1	477	21.0	73.2	12.9	83.7	35.82	6 536	752
Dolton..............................	15.0	591	0.0	165	NA	NA	NA	NA	NA	NA	NA
Downers Grove...................	65.1	1 332	0.0	415	21.0	73.2	12.9	83.7	35.82	6 536	752
East St. Louis.....................	3.5	112	0.0	249	28.4	78.4	18.9	89.6	37.86	5 001	1 329
Elgin................................	141.7	1 468	49.7	659	18.3	71.9	9.3	82.7	35.19	7 084	603
Elk Grove Village	15.5	444	0.0	343	21.0	73.2	12.9	83.7	35.82	6 536	752

1. Based on the population estimated as of July 1 of the year shown.   2. Represents normal values based on the 30-year period, 1961–1990.   3. Average daily minimum.   4. Average daily maximum.

Table D. Cities — Land Area and Population

STATE Place code	City	Land area,[1] 2000 (sq km)	Population, 2003 Total persons	Rank	Per square kilometer	Population characteristics, 2000 Percent — Race (alone or in combination) White	Black	Am. Indian, Alaska Native	Asian and Pacific Islander	Other race	Hispanic or Latino[2]	Non-Hispanic White
		1	2	3	4	5	6	7	8	9	10	11
	ILLINOIS—Cont'd											
17 23620	Elmhurst	26.6	44 054	730	1 656.2	94.2	1.0	0.3	4.2	1.3	4.0	90.5
17 23724	Elmwood Park	4.9	24 876	1 226	5 076.7	93.8	0.7	0.4	2.5	5.1	11.0	84.6
17 24582	Evanston	20.1	74 360	376	3 699.5	67.4	24.1	0.6	7.2	4.0	6.1	62.6
17 27884	Freeport	29.6	25 867	1 204	873.9	83.8	15.2	0.5	1.4	1.5	2.1	80.9
17 28326	Galesburg	43.8	32 809	984	749.1	85.9	11.3	0.6	1.3	2.9	5.0	82.1
17 29730	Glendale Heights	14.0	32 848	982	2 346.3	66.1	5.4	0.6	21.2	9.8	18.4	54.8
17 29756	Glen Ellyn	17.1	27 210	1 155	1 591.2	90.9	2.4	0.3	5.5	2.7	4.7	87.0
17 29938	Glenview	34.8	44 818	719	1 287.9	86.8	1.7	0.3	10.9	1.8	4.1	83.1
17 30926	Granite City	43.2	31 294	1 022	724.4	96.1	2.2	1.0	0.8	1.3	2.9	93.1
17 32018	Gurnee	34.7	30 396	1 051	876.0	83.9	5.6	0.6	9.1	3.0	6.0	78.7
17 32746	Hanover Park	17.6	37 643	850	2 138.8	70.7	6.6	0.7	13.0	12.2	26.7	53.5
17 33383	Harvey	16.0	29 367	1 085	1 835.4	11.1	80.8	0.7	0.7	8.7	12.8	6.3
17 34722	Highland Park	32.0	30 897	1 037	965.5	92.2	2.1	0.3	2.8	3.9	8.9	86.4
17 35411	Hoffman Estates	51.0	50 108	633	982.5	76.1	4.8	0.5	16.2	4.7	10.5	68.3
17 38570	Joliet	98.6	123 570	186	1 253.2	71.1	18.8	0.7	1.6	10.1	18.4	61.0
17 38934	Kankakee	31.8	26 995	1 171	848.9	52.5	42.1	0.8	0.6	6.1	9.3	47.8
17 42028	Lansing	17.5	27 976	1 135	1 598.6	86.7	11.0	0.5	0.9	2.1	5.7	82.0
17 44407	Lombard	25.1	42 971	748	1 712.0	88.3	3.0	0.5	7.8	2.1	4.8	84.1
17 47774	Maywood	7.0	26 398	1 193	3 771.1	10.8	83.8	0.6	0.4	6.3	10.5	5.5
17 49867	Moline	40.4	43 064	744	1 065.9	90.1	3.7	0.6	1.6	5.9	11.9	82.3
17 51089	Mount Prospect	26.4	55 784	553	2 113.0	82.2	2.1	0.5	11.9	5.3	11.8	73.8
17 51349	Mundelein	22.3	32 251	998	1 446.2	80.5	1.9	0.6	7.3	11.8	24.2	66.5
17 51622	Naperville	91.6	137 894	164	1 505.4	86.2	3.3	0.3	10.4	1.1	3.2	82.9
17 53000	Niles	15.2	29 945	1 066	1 970.1	84.7	0.6	0.4	13.6	2.6	5.0	80.3
17 53234	Normal	35.3	48 649	652	1 378.2	88.8	8.4	0.4	2.6	1.3	2.6	86.2
17 53481	Northbrook	33.5	34 061	950	1 016.7	90.1	0.7	0.1	9.5	0.7	1.8	87.8
17 53559	North Chicago	20.3	36 601	879	1 803.0	50.7	37.7	1.7	5.1	9.1	18.2	39.1
17 54638	Oak Forest	14.6	28 229	1 122	1 933.5	91.7	3.8	0.5	3.1	2.5	5.9	86.6
17 54820	Oak Lawn	22.3	55 136	562	2 472.5	95.1	1.3	0.4	2.1	2.9	5.3	89.9
17 54885	Oak Park	12.2	50 824	620	4 165.9	71.1	23.9	0.7	5.1	2.4	4.5	66.2
17 56640	Orland Park	49.6	54 011	587	1 088.9	94.6	0.8	0.2	3.9	1.7	3.7	91.0
17 57225	Palatine	33.6	66 848	428	1 989.5	84.7	2.5	0.4	8.3	6.0	14.1	74.9
17 57875	Park Ridge	18.2	37 460	859	2 058.2	96.1	0.3	0.2	3.1	1.1	2.9	93.5
17 58447	Pekin	34.1	33 190	970	973.3	96.5	2.7	0.7	0.5	0.3	1.3	94.8
17 59000	Peoria	115.0	112 907	206	981.8	71.1	26.2	0.6	2.7	1.7	2.5	68.3
17 62367	Quincy	37.9	39 922	801	1 053.4	94.1	5.4	0.5	0.7	0.6	0.9	92.5
17 65000	Rockford	145.1	151 725	142	1 045.7	74.9	18.4	0.8	2.7	5.8	10.2	68.4
17 65078	Rock Island	41.2	38 857	828	943.1	79.1	18.5	0.7	1.1	3.0	5.9	74.3
17 66040	Round Lake Beach	12.9	28 093	1 128	2 177.8	77.0	3.6	1.2	2.7	18.5	31.3	62.1
17 66703	St. Charles	36.2	32 010	1 002	884.3	94.6	1.9	0.4	2.1	2.0	5.5	90.4
17 68003	Schaumburg	49.2	74 342	377	1 511.0	80.2	3.7	0.4	15.0	2.5	5.3	75.5
17 70122	Skokie	26.0	63 633	457	2 447.4	71.6	5.0	0.4	22.7	3.6	5.7	65.6
17 72000	Springfield	139.9	113 586	205	811.9	82.3	16.2	0.6	1.8	0.7	1.2	80.3
17 73157	Streamwood	18.9	37 477	858	1 982.9	79.7	4.3	0.7	9.6	8.5	16.8	69.0
17 75484	Tinley Park	38.7	53 792	592	1 390.0	94.3	2.1	0.3	2.7	1.8	4.1	90.5
17 77005	Urbana	27.2	38 725	829	1 423.7	69.0	15.2	0.6	15.4	2.4	3.5	65.4
17 79293	Waukegan	59.6	91 452	283	1 534.4	53.0	20.3	1.0	4.2	25.2	44.8	30.9
17 81048	Wheaton	29.1	55 016	564	1 890.6	91.0	3.1	0.3	5.5	1.5	3.7	87.5
17 81087	Wheeling	21.8	35 495	908	1 628.2	78.5	2.7	0.5	9.9	10.6	20.7	66.4
17 82075	Wilmette	13.9	27 266	1 153	1 961.6	90.7	0.7	0.2	9.0	0.6	2.1	88.0
17 83245	Woodridge	21.6	33 695	959	1 560.0	77.0	8.7	0.5	12.0	4.1	9.2	70.1
18 00000	INDIANA	92 894.8	6 195 643	X	66.7	88.6	8.8	0.6	1.3	2.0	3.5	85.8
18 01468	Anderson	103.7	58 394	518	563.1	83.3	15.7	0.8	0.8	1.1	2.1	80.9
18 05860	Bloomington	51.1	70 642	401	1 382.4	88.8	4.9	0.8	6.2	1.6	2.5	85.7
18 10342	Carmel	46.1	43 083	743	934.6	93.4	1.7	0.4	4.8	0.6	1.7	91.3
18 14734	Columbus	67.2	39 058	826	581.2	92.4	3.2	0.4	3.6	1.7	2.8	90.0
18 19486	East Chicago	31.0	31 366	1 021	1 011.8	38.5	36.8	0.8	0.4	26.1	51.6	12.1
18 20728	Elkhart	55.3	51 682	608	934.6	74.1	16.0	1.1	1.6	10.3	14.8	66.8
18 22000	Evansville	105.4	117 881	196	1 118.4	87.5	11.7	0.6	1.0	0.7	1.1	85.6
18 23278	Fishers town	56.2	47 790	673	850.4	93.2	3.2	0.3	3.7	0.7	2.0	90.9
18 25000	Fort Wayne	204.5	219 495	80	1 073.3	77.4	18.5	0.9	2.0	3.6	5.8	73.1
18 27000	Gary	130.1	99 961	245	768.3	13.0	85.3	0.7	0.4	2.7	4.9	10.1
18 28386	Goshen	34.2	29 787	1 074	871.0	84.9	2.1	0.6	1.4	13.1	19.3	76.7
18 29898	Greenwood	37.0	39 545	816	1 068.8	97.2	0.6	0.4	1.7	0.8	1.9	95.4
18 31000	Hammond	59.3	80 547	334	1 358.3	74.8	15.3	1.0	0.8	11.0	21.0	62.4
18 34114	Hobart	67.9	26 972	1 172	397.2	95.1	1.6	0.6	0.8	3.4	8.1	89.0
18 36000	Indianapolis	949.2	793 430	12	835.9	70.7	26.1	0.7	1.8	2.4	3.9	67.7
18 38358	Jeffersonville	35.2	28 025	1 131	796.2	84.3	14.9	0.8	1.2	0.9	1.8	81.5
18 40392	Kokomo	41.9	46 154	702	1 101.5	86.8	11.3	0.9	1.4	1.5	2.6	83.8

1. Dry land or land partially or temporarily covered by water.   2. Hispanic or Latino persons may be of any race.

City	Under 5 years	5 to 17 years	18 to 24 years	25 to 34 years	35 to 44 years	45 to 54 years	55 to 64 years	65 to 74 years	75 years and over	Percent female	1990	2000	1990–2000	2000–2003
	12	13	14	15	16	17	18	19	20	21	22	23	24	25
ILLINOIS—Cont'd														
Elmhurst	7.0	18.6	7.0	11.3	17.2	14.0	9.0	7.1	8.9	51.9	42 029	42 762	1.7	3.0
Elmwood Park	5.7	16.2	8.2	13.9	16.6	13.4	9.4	8.1	8.5	52.4	23 206	25 405	9.5	-2.1
Evanston	5.8	14.4	16.4	17.3	14.7	12.8	7.9	5.1	5.7	52.9	73 233	74 239	1.4	0.2
Freeport	6.6	17.8	8.5	12.8	15.0	12.4	8.8	8.1	10.0	53.4	25 840	26 443	2.3	-2.2
Galesburg	5.7	15.4	11.8	12.9	14.1	13.2	8.7	8.4	9.7	49.9	33 530	33 706	0.5	-2.7
Glendale Heights	8.0	18.9	11.5	20.1	16.7	13.0	6.9	3.1	1.9	49.0	27 915	31 765	13.8	3.4
Glen Ellyn	7.8	20.5	6.2	12.1	17.9	15.3	8.7	6.2	5.1	51.2	24 919	26 999	8.3	0.8
Glenview	6.5	19.1	5.2	9.5	15.8	16.5	11.4	8.6	7.4	52.0	38 436	41 847	8.9	7.1
Granite City	6.0	18.7	8.3	12.9	16.2	12.7	8.8	8.5	7.8	52.0	32 766	31 301	-4.5	0.0
Gurnee	9.6	20.7	5.5	15.8	21.3	13.4	6.5	4.1	3.1	51.5	13 715	28 834	110.2	5.4
Hanover Park	8.8	22.7	10.9	17.3	17.8	12.3	6.2	2.6	1.5	48.5	32 918	38 278	16.3	-1.7
Harvey	9.6	25.5	10.8	13.5	13.1	10.9	7.9	5.0	3.6	52.0	29 771	30 000	0.8	-2.1
Highland Park	7.4	19.6	4.6	9.6	15.9	16.4	11.4	8.5	6.5	51.0	30 575	31 365	2.6	-1.5
Hoffman Estates	7.2	20.9	8.7	15.4	18.5	15.3	7.3	3.9	2.8	50.2	46 363	49 495	6.8	1.2
Joliet	9.3	20.2	10.1	17.6	15.5	10.1	6.2	5.1	6.0	50.5	77 217	106 221	37.6	16.3
Kankakee	8.3	21.1	9.7	14.3	14.4	11.6	7.1	5.9	7.4	52.1	27 541	27 491	-0.2	-1.8
Lansing	6.4	17.9	7.8	12.8	16.3	13.7	9.4	8.0	7.7	52.6	28 131	28 332	0.7	-1.3
Lombard	6.1	16.8	7.9	16.1	17.3	13.0	8.2	6.4	8.1	51.5	39 408	42 322	7.4	1.5
Maywood	8.0	23.7	10.4	13.6	14.1	11.8	8.7	6.0	3.6	53.2	27 139	26 987	-0.6	-2.2
Moline	6.5	17.6	9.2	12.8	15.0	14.2	9.4	7.7	7.7	52.2	43 080	43 768	1.6	-1.6
Mount Prospect	6.6	16.4	8.2	15.3	16.0	12.9	9.9	8.5	6.3	50.3	53 168	56 265	5.8	-0.9
Mundelein	9.2	22.2	8.3	16.2	19.7	12.7	5.4	3.7	2.5	48.9	21 224	30 935	45.8	4.3
Naperville	8.4	23.4	6.4	13.1	20.6	15.4	6.5	3.1	3.1	51.1	85 806	128 358	49.6	7.4
Niles	3.8	12.9	6.9	10.5	13.5	13.4	11.3	12.4	15.4	53.3	28 375	30 068	6.0	-0.4
Normal	4.9	12.6	38.1	12.3	10.8	8.7	5.0	3.9	3.7	53.0	40 023	45 386	13.4	7.2
Northbrook	5.7	19.8	4.4	6.7	15.1	17.0	12.6	9.9	8.7	51.7	32 565	33 435	2.6	1.9
North Chicago	8.0	16.1	34.7	17.0	10.5	5.7	3.5	2.5	2.0	39.0	34 978	35 918	2.7	1.9
Oak Forest	6.7	19.3	9.1	13.8	17.2	15.1	9.6	5.2	4.0	50.2	26 202	28 051	7.1	0.6
Oak Lawn	5.4	16.6	7.2	11.2	15.0	13.0	9.4	10.5	11.3	53.1	56 182	55 245	-1.7	-0.2
Oak Park	6.9	17.3	6.7	17.3	17.9	16.5	7.9	4.5	5.1	53.5	53 648	52 524	-2.1	-3.2
Orland Park	5.4	19.0	7.1	9.2	15.5	16.3	11.0	8.9	7.5	52.2	35 720	51 077	43.0	5.7
Palatine	7.3	17.5	8.5	18.0	17.8	13.7	8.3	5.0	3.8	50.2	41 554	65 479	57.6	2.1
Park Ridge	5.8	18.7	5.5	8.3	16.2	15.1	10.7	9.6	10.1	52.6	37 075	37 775	1.9	-0.8
Pekin	6.5	16.7	9.3	14.4	15.9	12.9	8.5	8.1	7.6	50.9	32 254	33 857	5.0	-2.0
Peoria	7.4	18.3	12.0	13.8	13.4	12.7	8.1	6.8	7.4	52.7	113 508	112 936	-0.5	0.0
Quincy	5.9	17.4	10.0	12.1	13.8	12.3	8.7	8.5	11.4	53.1	39 682	40 366	1.7	-1.1
Rockford	7.7	18.9	9.2	14.9	14.8	12.5	7.9	6.7	7.4	51.8	142 815	150 115	5.9	1.1
Rock Island	6.4	16.5	13.1	12.0	13.7	13.3	8.6	7.6	8.7	52.8	40 630	39 684	-2.3	-2.1
Round Lake Beach	11.3	23.7	9.4	18.9	17.5	9.9	4.7	2.5	2.1	49.6	16 406	25 859	57.6	8.6
St. Charles	6.3	21.5	7.4	12.3	17.4	16.7	8.3	5.0	5.2	50.2	22 636	27 896	23.3	14.7
Schaumburg	6.0	15.9	8.3	19.2	17.1	14.9	9.1	4.7	4.8	51.3	68 586	75 386	9.9	-1.4
Skokie	5.2	17.8	7.0	10.2	14.7	15.5	10.0	9.2	10.3	52.6	59 432	63 348	6.6	0.4
Springfield	6.6	17.4	8.8	14.3	15.5	14.4	8.6	7.0	7.4	53.0	105 412	111 454	5.7	1.9
Streamwood	8.7	19.4	8.2	18.7	18.6	12.8	7.5	3.8	2.3	49.9	31 197	36 407	16.7	2.9
Tinley Park	6.6	20.0	8.1	12.9	18.2	15.5	8.0	5.7	5.0	51.6	37 115	48 401	30.4	11.1
Urbana	4.4	10.5	36.2	16.3	10.1	8.4	4.8	4.2	5.2	47.3	36 383	36 395	0.0	6.4
Waukegan	9.6	20.6	12.1	18.4	15.0	10.6	5.8	4.2	3.7	49.2	69 481	87 901	26.5	4.0
Wheaton	6.3	19.8	10.5	12.2	16.5	15.4	8.0	5.4	5.8	51.3	51 441	55 416	7.7	-0.7
Wheeling	6.6	16.8	9.4	18.0	17.1	13.9	7.8	5.3	4.9	50.8	29 911	34 496	15.3	2.9
Wilmette	7.1	22.6	3.6	5.5	16.2	17.2	10.6	8.6	8.6	52.1	26 694	27 651	3.6	-1.4
Woodridge	7.6	19.7	9.2	17.2	18.8	14.7	7.5	3.3	2.0	50.3	26 359	30 934	17.4	8.9
INDIANA	7.0	18.9	10.1	13.7	15.8	13.4	8.7	6.5	5.9	51.0	5 544 156	6 080 485	9.7	1.9
Anderson	6.9	16.3	11.2	14.0	13.6	12.2	9.1	8.0	8.6	52.6	59 518	59 734	0.4	-2.2
Bloomington	4.1	8.6	42.3	15.4	9.2	7.9	4.7	3.8	4.0	51.4	62 735	69 291	11.7	1.9
Carmel	7.9	22.4	4.8	11.0	18.9	16.4	8.9	5.1	4.6	51.4	25 380	37 733	48.7	14.2
Columbus	7.4	18.3	8.0	14.2	15.3	13.8	9.3	6.9	6.8	51.9	33 948	39 059	15.1	0.0
East Chicago	9.1	21.4	11.1	13.4	13.4	10.8	7.5	7.4	5.9	52.2	33 892	32 414	-4.4	-3.2
Elkhart	9.4	19.0	11.1	17.1	14.6	11.0	6.9	5.2	5.5	50.8	44 661	51 874	16.2	-0.4
Evansville	6.4	16.3	11.5	13.7	14.9	12.5	8.4	7.7	8.5	53.0	126 272	121 582	-3.7	-3.0
Fishers town	11.9	20.3	5.4	23.4	21.4	10.2	4.0	2.2	1.2	51.1	7 189	37 835	426.3	26.3
Fort Wayne	7.8	19.2	10.7	15.2	14.9	12.4	7.3	6.0	6.4	51.6	195 680	205 727	7.2	6.7
Gary	8.4	21.5	10.1	11.5	13.5	13.1	9.0	7.5	5.3	54.2	116 646	102 746	-11.9	-2.7
Goshen	7.9	18.0	12.9	16.3	13.7	10.5	7.0	5.6	8.0	49.8	23 794	29 383	23.5	1.4
Greenwood	7.7	17.6	9.6	16.5	15.6	12.6	8.1	5.8	6.5	52.1	26 507	36 037	36.0	9.7
Hammond	8.1	19.2	9.8	14.4	15.7	12.2	7.6	6.5	6.5	51.2	84 236	83 048	-1.4	-3.0
Hobart	6.1	17.5	8.6	13.6	16.1	13.8	9.2	7.6	7.5	51.5	24 440	25 363	3.8	6.3
Indianapolis	7.3	18.3	10.1	16.5	16.3	12.7	7.6	5.8	5.2	51.6	731 726	791 926	6.7	0.2
Jeffersonville	6.7	16.9	8.7	15.1	16.2	14.6	9.2	6.9	5.7	52.0	24 016	27 362	13.9	2.4
Kokomo	7.8	17.1	9.4	14.7	14.3	13.1	9.2	7.2	7.2	52.7	44 996	46 113	2.5	0.1

Table D. Cities — Group Quarters, Crime, and Education

City	Households, 2000					Persons in group quarters, 2000				Serious crimes known to police,[2] 2002				Education, 2000			
				Percent			Institutional			Total		Rate[2]		School enrollment[4]		Attainment[5] (percent)	
	Number	Percent change, 1990–2000	Persons per household	Female family householder[1]	One-person	Total	Total	Persons in nursing homes	Non-institutional	Number	Rate[3]	Violent	Property	Public	Private	High school graduate or less	Bachelor's degree or more
	26	27	28	29	30	31	32	33	34	35	36	37	38	39	40	41	42
ILLINOIS—Cont'd																	
Elmhurst	15 627	3.3	2.63	7.4	24.6	1 591	851	821	740	NA	NA	NA	NA	8 191	3 720	28.9	45.1
Elmwood Park	9 858	4.1	2.55	12.4	29.2	243	239	239	4	NA	NA	NA	NA	4 312	1 969	52.1	19.5
Evanston	29 651	6.1	2.27	10.9	36.3	6 964	559	559	6 405	NA	NA	NA	NA	12 149	15 041	19.0	62.4
Freeport	11 222	3.5	2.29	12.6	33.7	730	548	460	182	NA	NA	NA	NA	5 465	1 217	52.9	17.1
Galesburg	13 237	-0.3	2.24	12.4	34.6	4 079	2 561	646	1 518	NA	NA	NA	NA	6 142	1 966	55.0	14.9
Glendale Heights	10 791	12.3	2.94	9.9	22.8	16	6	0	10	NA	NA	NA	NA	7 247	1 460	43.4	26.7
Glen Ellyn	10 207	8.4	2.63	6.8	25.2	109	22	22	87	NA	NA	NA	NA	5 794	1 893	18.2	58.8
Glenview	15 464	15.9	2.67	6.9	20.7	532	316	310	216	NA	NA	NA	NA	8 530	2 995	20.0	55.9
Granite City	12 773	-1.8	2.43	13.7	29.4	294	209	209	85	NA	NA	NA	NA	7 158	799	61.5	9.8
Gurnee	10 629	98.3	2.71	7.8	22.7	30	0	0	30	NA	NA	NA	NA	6 916	1 853	24.4	47.8
Hanover Park	11 105	10.5	3.44	11.8	13.5	66	26	0	40	NA	NA	NA	NA	9 727	1 366	49.9	20.2
Harvey	8 990	-0.7	3.30	31.8	20.7	362	154	88	208	NA	NA	NA	NA	9 574	795	58.8	8.2
Highland Park	11 521	4.5	2.71	5.8	19.5	196	0	0	196	NA	NA	NA	NA	6 672	1 713	18.5	61.6
Hoffman Estates	17 034	7.0	2.89	9.6	19.9	263	263	259	0	NA	NA	NA	NA	12 714	2 515	33.9	35.9
Joliet	36 182	35.1	2.81	13.3	24.7	4 494	3 566	1 548	928	4 764	4 420	555	3 866	22 622	5 625	51.5	18.6
Kankakee	10 020	-3.6	2.60	21.2	31.5	1 447	1 252	302	195	NA	NA	NA	NA	6 622	1 147	61.7	13.2
Lansing	11 416	4.9	2.48	11.4	27.9	0	0	0	0	NA	NA	NA	NA	5 029	1 863	49.8	18.2
Lombard	16 487	9.6	2.49	7.9	28.7	1 341	688	688	653	NA	NA	NA	NA	7 559	3 416	34.2	36.0
Maywood	7 937	-1.2	3.38	30.2	19.1	189	0	0	189	NA	NA	NA	NA	7 403	1 268	57.6	10.3
Moline	18 492	1.2	2.35	10.4	31.9	350	290	222	60	NA	NA	NA	NA	9 342	1 337	47.5	20.8
Mount Prospect	21 585	6.4	2.60	7.2	25.1	66	5	0	61	NA	NA	NA	NA	10 530	2 806	38.1	35.4
Mundelein	9 858	38.5	3.12	9.0	17.0	177	0	0	177	NA	NA	NA	NA	7 413	1 673	38.3	39.9
Naperville	43 751	50.3	2.89	5.9	18.8	1 986	943	812	1 043	2 424	1 861	58	1 803	33 553	8 395	15.3	60.6
Niles	12 002	11.4	2.39	8.5	30.6	1 350	1 163	1 163	187	NA	NA	NA	NA	4 752	1 546	47.8	24.8
Normal	15 157	27.8	2.43	9.3	26.6	8 584	428	360	8 156	NA	NA	NA	NA	21 695	1 623	28.6	42.4
Northbrook	12 203	7.1	2.68	5.3	18.9	751	515	515	236	NA	NA	NA	NA	6 955	1 973	16.4	62.2
North Chicago	7 661	7.3	3.09	18.9	21.8	12 282	1 691	0	10 591	NA	NA	NA	NA	7 526	1 273	51.2	14.8
Oak Forest	9 785	10.4	2.81	9.7	20.7	534	485	0	49	NA	NA	NA	NA	5 563	1 953	44.1	22.5
Oak Lawn	22 220	3.5	2.46	10.1	30.9	490	471	471	19	NA	NA	NA	NA	8 709	4 158	50.8	20.9
Oak Park	23 079	2.1	2.26	11.6	37.0	379	225	225	154	NA	NA	NA	NA	10 696	4 191	16.0	62.1
Orland Park	18 675	54.4	2.71	7.9	20.6	437	411	411	26	NA	NA	NA	NA	10 570	3 297	38.9	31.7
Palatine	25 518	68.3	2.56	8.3	27.5	217	144	144	73	NA	NA	NA	NA	13 129	3 051	30.2	41.4
Park Ridge	14 219	5.6	2.61	8.0	24.1	667	494	493	173	NA	NA	NA	NA	6 799	2 983	26.2	46.2
Pekin	13 380	2.3	2.37	11.4	29.5	2 209	2 001	299	208	NA	NA	NA	NA	7 031	832	56.5	13.4
Peoria	45 199	0.5	2.38	15.5	33.2	5 428	1 795	1 261	3 633	9 117	7 957	721	7 236	22 632	10 105	42.9	28.0
Quincy	16 546	2.9	2.30	11.6	33.7	2 364	1 618	1 428	746	NA	NA	NA	NA	7 283	3 075	52.6	19.3
Rockford	59 158	7.9	2.46	14.8	30.7	4 326	2 945	1 875	1 381	13 615	8 939	768	8 172	29 727	8 488	53.4	19.8
Rock Island	16 148	-0.6	2.31	14.2	34.5	2 435	632	444	1 803	NA	NA	NA	NA	7 981	3 356	49.8	18.7
Round Lake Beach	7 349	49.9	3.50	10.5	14.0	140	140	140	0	NA	NA	NA	NA	6 560	1 006	54.3	16.1
St. Charles	10 351	27.3	2.62	8.0	23.5	810	677	171	133	NA	NA	NA	NA	6 730	1 171	30.3	42.9
Schaumburg	31 799	15.3	2.36	8.1	32.3	436	430	430	6	NA	NA	NA	NA	15 072	3 350	31.3	38.9
Skokie	23 223	2.3	2.68	9.9	23.6	1 139	722	655	417	NA	NA	NA	NA	12 865	4 509	33.4	42.6
Springfield	48 621	8.0	2.24	12.9	36.1	2 556	1 515	1 035	1 041	9 539	8 436	1 102	7 334	21 739	6 153	41.6	30.9
Streamwood	12 095	21.8	2.99	9.2	17.3	225	211	189	14	NA	NA	NA	NA	8 436	1 617	43.4	26.5
Tinley Park	17 478	37.9	2.73	8.6	23.1	717	644	101	73	NA	NA	NA	NA	11 080	2 277	41.4	24.8
Urbana	14 327	8.5	2.14	8.7	36.6	5 735	618	400	5 117	NA	NA	NA	NA	18 610	731	24.7	53.3
Waukegan	27 787	13.2	3.09	14.6	24.2	2 090	1 011	353	1 079	NA	NA	NA	NA	21 110	3 300	60.8	16.3
Wheaton	19 377	9.0	2.64	7.3	24.5	4 200	1 710	932	2 490	NA	NA	NA	NA	11 860	5 924	19.5	57.3
Wheeling	13 280	6.5	2.57	9.0	30.1	370	366	366	4	NA	NA	NA	NA	7 236	1 402	41.8	32.1
Wilmette	10 039	3.3	2.73	6.4	21.1	223	126	126	97	NA	NA	NA	NA	6 074	2 309	11.0	72.6
Woodridge	11 382	18.3	2.71	10.5	23.5	86	0	0	86	NA	NA	NA	NA	7 067	1 751	29.9	39.0
INDIANA	2 336 306	13.1	2.53	11.1	25.9	178 154	90 885	48 745	87 269	230 966	3 750	357	3 393	1 337 569	265 985	55.1	19.4
Anderson	25 274	4.0	2.28	15.1	33.1	2 179	856	599	1 323	NA	NA	NA	NA	10 838	3 260	61.5	13.1
Bloomington	26 468	26.1	2.09	7.8	39.1	14 005	873	327	13 132	2 744	3 910	155	3 754	36 478	1 954	25.1	54.8
Carmel	13 597	49.2	2.74	6.6	18.9	521	454	454	67	718	1 879	55	1 824	8 500	2 639	17.0	58.4
Columbus	15 985	24.4	2.39	11.0	29.1	814	781	552	33	2 251	5 690	197	5 492	7 860	1 571	46.7	27.6
East Chicago	11 707	-3.4	2.75	26.7	28.6	192	106	106	86	2 489	7 581	1 955	5 625	8 214	1 141	73.4	7.1
Elkhart	20 072	14.6	2.55	15.3	30.3	658	292	283	366	4 288	8 161	407	7 753	10 642	1 461	63.3	13.4
Evansville	52 273	-1.3	2.24	13.7	35.1	4 720	2 463	1 567	2 257	6 154	4 997	538	4 459	23 286	6 486	55.8	16.7
Fishers town	14 044	423.6	2.69	6.6	20.7	1	0	0	1	682	1 780	170	1 610	8 296	2 395	13.3	60.1
Fort Wayne	83 333	19.7	2.41	14.6	32.6	5 036	2 865	1 988	2 171	12 152	5 831	406	5 426	43 088	13 417	49.6	19.4
Gary	38 244	-6.6	2.66	30.9	28.9	849	535	481	314	5 812	5 584	727	4 857	26 892	3 241	62.4	10.1
Goshen	10 675	18.2	2.61	10.1	27.5	1 524	856	369	668	1 430	4 805	622	4 183	5 413	1 431	62.5	18.5
Greenwood	14 931	40.9	2.37	9.9	29.9	577	439	376	138	2 012	5 512	562	4 950	6 531	1 676	46.0	23.7
Hammond	32 026	-0.4	2.58	16.9	29.7	394	116	116	278	5 397	6 416	741	5 675	18 106	3 428	63.6	11.3
Hobart	9 855	22.1	2.55	10.4	24.1	248	211	211	37	1 399	5 445	452	4 994	5 347	751	56.1	14.2
Indianapolis	324 342	9.5	2.39	15.0	32.0	17 915	11 375	5 425	6 540	48 503	6 032	935	5 097	155 592	45 102	48.0	25.5
Jeffersonville	11 643	33.1	2.30	14.8	32.1	628	461	198	167	1 479	5 336	285	5 051	5 543	873	56.2	14.9
Kokomo	20 273	8.6	2.24	14.1	35.2	694	556	422	138	3 146	6 735	589	6 147	8 810	1 368	58.5	15.8

1. No spouse present. 2. Data for serious crimes have not been adjusted for underreporting. This may affect comparability between geographic areas and over time. 3. Per 100,000 population estimated by the FBI. 4. All persons 3 years old and over enrolled in nursery school through college. 5. Persons 25 years old and over.

Table D. Cities — **Income, Poverty, and Housing**

City	Money income, 1999						Housing units, 2000					
	Households			Percent below poverty					Vacant units			
	Median income			Persons		Families						
	Per capita income[1] (dollars)	Dollars	Percent change, 1989–1999 (constant 1999 dollars)	Percent with income of $100,000 or more	Total	Percent change in rate, 1989–1999	Total	Total	Percent change, 1990–2000	Vacant units for sale or rent[2]	For seasonal use (percent)	Home owner vacancy rate	Renter vacancy rate
	43	44	45	46	47	48	49	50	51	52	53	54	55
ILLINOIS—Cont'd												
Elmhurst	32 015	69 794	4.7	29.1	2.5	78.6	1.9	16 147	4.3	520	0.8	1.0	4.8
Elmwood Park	22 526	47 315	2.3	11.3	5.2	-1.9	3.6	10 150	3.8	292	0.2	0.9	2.8
Evanston	33 645	56 335	2.0	26.0	11.1	13.3	5.1	30 817	5.7	1 166	0.4	1.2	3.2
Freeport	18 680	35 399	6.4	4.8	13.1	4.8	9.9	12 471	6.4	1 249	0.3	2.0	14.6
Galesburg	17 214	31 987	6.0	4.9	14.7	-17.9	10.7	14 133	-1.3	896	0.2	1.8	7.5
Glendale Heights	21 911	56 285	-2.2	13.4	6.1	125.9	4.7	11 105	8.8	314	0.1	0.5	5.0
Glen Ellyn	39 783	74 846	7.3	36.7	2.8	27.3	1.3	10 515	7.9	308	0.4	0.8	3.2
Glenview	43 384	80 730	1.8	40.4	2.0	17.6	1.4	15 853	15.2	389	0.5	0.7	3.2
Granite City	17 691	35 615	3.6	4.5	11.3	-14.4	8.8	14 022	1.0	1 249	0.1	1.7	13.6
Gurnee	31 517	75 742	14.9	31.5	3.0	3.4	2.0	10 929	96.2	300	0.4	0.5	5.9
Hanover Park	19 960	61 358	3.2	15.6	6.1	117.9	4.7	11 343	9.0	238	0.0	0.5	5.1
Harvey	12 336	31 958	2.5	4.6	21.7	-15.2	20.3	10 158	-1.2	1 168	0.1	3.3	8.9
Highland Park	55 331	100 967	4.5	50.6	3.8	35.7	2.3	11 934	4.4	413	0.8	1.1	3.2
Hoffman Estates	26 669	65 937	-0.8	24.8	4.4	120.0	3.4	17 387	4.7	353	0.1	0.6	4.3
Joliet	19 390	47 761	14.8	10.8	10.8	-16.9	7.7	38 176	31.4	1 994	0.1	1.6	6.7
Kankakee	15 479	30 469	11.6	5.0	21.4	-8.9	18.1	10 965	-3.6	945	0.2	3.6	8.4
Lansing	22 547	47 554	-3.4	9.4	5.4	100.0	3.5	11 748	5.0	332	0.1	1.3	4.9
Lombard	27 667	60 015	1.0	18.9	3.8	46.2	2.0	17 019	7.4	532	0.4	0.7	6.0
Maywood	14 915	41 942	1.4	8.9	13.4	-11.8	11.1	8 475	-0.8	538	0.1	2.3	6.9
Moline	21 557	39 363	6.5	8.4	9.5	-7.8	7.1	19 487	1.3	995	0.4	1.1	6.4
Mount Prospect	26 464	57 165	-8.5	19.3	4.6	39.4	3.1	21 952	4.8	367	0.1	0.5	2.5
Mundelein	26 280	69 651	12.8	25.9	4.6	-6.1	3.0	10 167	37.4	309	0.2	1.2	6.3
Naperville	35 551	88 771	8.4	42.8	2.2	46.7	1.6	45 651	47.7	1 900	0.5	1.3	8.7
Niles	23 543	48 627	-6.5	12.7	5.4	45.9	3.2	12 256	10.9	254	0.3	0.4	1.1
Normal	17 775	40 379	-4.2	10.4	19.3	-11.1	5.6	15 683	27.5	526	0.2	1.0	4.0
Northbrook	50 765	95 665	-2.9	48.2	2.3	27.8	1.2	12 492	7.0	289	0.5	0.7	2.5
North Chicago	14 564	38 180	11.4	6.6	15.1	1.3	12.0	8 377	5.7	716	0.3	2.0	5.2
Oak Forest	23 487	60 073	3.1	16.0	3.6	20.0	2.7	10 022	10.6	237	0.1	1.3	3.1
Oak Lawn	23 877	47 585	-8.4	13.2	5.4	58.8	3.9	22 846	4.6	626	0.2	1.4	4.0
Oak Park	36 340	59 183	8.9	25.7	5.6	21.7	3.6	23 723	0.6	644	0.2	0.8	2.7
Orland Park	30 467	67 574	-2.8	27.1	3.1	29.2	2.1	19 045	52.6	370	0.3	0.9	3.4
Palatine	30 661	63 321	-3.2	24.0	4.8	92.0	3.5	26 223	65.4	705	0.3	0.6	4.5
Park Ridge	36 046	73 154	3.1	31.4	2.4	84.6	1.7	14 646	6.0	427	0.3	1.2	4.3
Pekin	19 616	37 972	12.2	6.8	9.4	-32.4	6.8	14 038	1.9	658	0.2	1.3	5.4
Peoria	20 512	36 397	3.9	9.8	18.8	-0.5	14.1	49 125	1.8	3 926	0.2	1.9	10.3
Quincy	17 479	30 956	8.0	4.4	12.2	-18.7	9.2	18 043	2.9	1 497	0.3	1.8	9.9
Rockford	19 781	37 667	-0.9	8.7	14.0	4.5	10.5	63 570	9.3	4 412	0.2	1.7	8.4
Rock Island	19 202	34 729	7.1	6.4	14.5	-24.9	10.9	17 542	-2.0	1 394	0.2	1.8	9.8
Round Lake Beach	18 113	59 359	20.7	12.4	5.1	-25.0	3.2	7 608	50.9	259	0.3	1.6	3.2
St. Charles	33 969	69 424	10.8	29.8	3.4	36.0	2.1	11 072	30.2	721	1.0	2.3	10.5
Schaumburg	30 587	60 941	-3.6	20.0	3.0	11.1	2.0	33 093	12.2	1 294	0.4	0.5	6.8
Skokie	27 136	57 375	1.0	21.1	5.4	38.5	4.2	23 702	2.3	479	0.3	0.8	1.9
Springfield	23 324	39 388	4.7	10.0	11.7	-7.1	8.4	53 733	10.7	5 112	0.3	2.4	11.0
Streamwood	23 961	65 076	-0.7	18.0	3.0	15.4	2.3	12 371	19.8	276	0.1	1.3	3.2
Tinley Park	25 207	61 648	6.2	18.0	2.5	0.0	1.1	18 037	36.4	559	0.1	1.6	3.4
Urbana	15 969	27 819	-4.6	6.7	27.3	25.2	13.3	15 311	9.3	984	0.3	1.5	7.3
Waukegan	17 368	42 335	0.6	9.7	13.9	46.3	10.7	29 243	13.3	1 456	0.2	1.5	6.0
Wheaton	34 147	73 385	4.6	33.6	3.6	-29.4	2.4	19 881	6.7	504	0.2	0.7	3.8
Wheeling	24 989	55 491	3.6	14.6	5.3	65.6	2.7	13 697	5.4	417	0.4	0.5	4.9
Wilmette	55 611	106 773	11.5	54.0	2.3	9.5	1.3	10 319	2.7	280	0.7	0.7	2.7
Woodridge	27 851	61 944	3.4	22.3	3.8	31.0	2.9	11 708	14.8	326	0.2	0.8	4.6
INDIANA	20 397	41 567	7.4	9.2	9.5	-11.2	6.7	2 532 319	12.7	196 013	1.3	1.8	8.8
Anderson	19 142	32 577	4.4	5.5	13.4	-25.6	10.8	27 643	4.9	2 369	0.4	2.3	9.2
Bloomington	16 481	25 377	2.7	8.2	29.6	-6.0	10.3	28 400	28.9	1 932	0.6	2.7	6.3
Carmel	38 906	81 583	11.4	38.5	2.5	56.3	1.6	14 107	46.3	510	0.3	1.5	7.0
Columbus	22 055	41 723	7.6	10.2	8.1	-25.7	6.5	17 162	27.5	1 177	0.4	2.2	8.6
East Chicago	13 517	26 538	1.9	4.6	24.4	-4.7	22.5	13 261	-1.7	1 554	0.2	2.2	8.8
Elkhart	17 890	34 863	2.6	5.8	13.6	8.8	11.1	21 688	13.3	1 616	0.4	2.4	8.2
Evansville	18 388	31 963	3.7	4.9	13.7	-6.2	10.1	57 065	-1.9	4 792	0.4	2.2	8.1
Fishers town	31 891	75 638	NA	27.5	1.8	NA	1.1	15 241	NA	1 197	0.4	2.3	18.8
Fort Wayne	18 517	36 518	3.2	6.1	12.5	8.7	9.6	90 915	17.8	7 582	0.3	1.9	10.7
Gary	14 383	27 195	4.4	5.3	25.8	-12.2	22.2	43 630	-7.3	5 386	0.2	2.5	8.3
Goshen	18 899	39 383	1.3	6.3	9.3	22.4	6.0	11 264	18.3	589	0.5	2.0	5.4
Greenwood	23 003	46 176	4.2	10.6	7.0	14.8	4.6	16 042	40.7	1 111	0.5	2.3	10.7
Hammond	16 254	35 528	-1.6	4.4	14.3	5.9	12.0	34 139	0.6	2 113	0.2	1.6	6.4
Hobart	21 508	47 759	2.7	8.5	4.8	-5.9	2.9	10 299	24.1	444	0.3	1.8	5.8
Indianapolis	21 789	40 154	2.8	9.8	11.8	-5.6	9.0	356 980	10.0	32 638	0.3	2.0	11.0
Jeffersonville	19 656	37 234	15.6	6.8	10.1	-32.2	6.9	12 402	32.3	759	0.4	1.6	7.7
Kokomo	20 083	36 258	2.7	6.2	13.0	-20.7	9.6	22 292	9.6	2 019	0.7	2.3	10.3

1. Based on population enumerated as of April 1, 2000.   2. Includes units rented or sold but not occupied.

City	Housing units, 2000 (cont'd)					Civilian labor force, 2003				Civilian employment,[2] 2000			Disability, 2000
	Occupied units							Unemployment			Percent		
	Total	Percent owner occupied	Percent renter occupied	Average size owner occupied	Average size renter occupied	Total	Percent change, 2002–2003	Total	Rate[1]	Total	Management, professional, and related occupations	Production, transportation, and material moving occupations	Employment disabled persons[3] (percent)
	56	57	58	59	60	61	62	63	64	65	66	67	68
ILLINOIS—Cont'd													
Elmhurst	15 627	83.3	16.7	2.78	1.92	23 278	-0.8	1 122	4.8	21 719	47.4	7.5	5.4
Elmwood Park	9 858	65.6	34.4	2.79	2.09	12 902	-0.7	763	5.9	12 730	27.2	16.4	9.6
Evanston	29 651	52.7	47.3	2.50	2.01	40 707	-1.4	2 089	5.1	38 220	60.7	5.1	6.8
Freeport	11 222	68.2	31.8	2.42	2.02	12 782	-1.2	1 290	10.1	12 001	28.1	23.2	10.8
Galesburg	13 237	64.3	35.7	2.35	2.03	16 400	-1.2	1 319	8.0	14 665	26.7	22.0	10.2
Glendale Heights	10 791	70.1	29.9	3.22	2.28	19 720	-0.4	1 365	6.9	17 275	30.7	19.3	13.4
Glen Ellyn	10 207	77.4	22.6	2.78	2.14	14 835	-0.7	911	6.1	13 540	53.3	6.2	6.5
Glenview	15 464	88.0	12.0	2.70	2.45	22 297	-0.9	1 016	4.6	20 508	53.6	6.1	7.8
Granite City	12 773	70.5	29.5	2.51	2.23	14 976	0.4	1 354	9.0	14 022	21.8	24.0	13.5
Gurnee	10 629	78.4	21.6	2.92	1.96	17 357	-0.8	833	4.8	15 113	50.4	7.6	6.7
Hanover Park	11 105	82.3	17.7	3.38	3.72	21 740	-0.2	1 666	7.7	19 669	26.4	19.9	11.9
Harvey	8 990	56.4	43.6	3.38	3.19	12 072	-1.0	1 429	11.8	10 205	20.0	22.0	16.6
Highland Park	11 521	82.1	17.9	2.72	2.66	15 716	-1.0	548	3.5	15 679	55.6	3.5	7.4
Hoffman Estates	17 034	76.5	23.5	3.06	2.33	28 895	-0.9	1 596	5.5	26 728	41.2	11.9	9.1
Joliet	36 182	70.4	29.6	2.93	2.52	52 529	0.1	4 871	9.3	46 915	27.6	18.3	12.0
Kankakee	10 020	53.4	46.6	2.68	2.50	12 201	0.0	1 550	12.7	10 834	22.5	25.4	15.8
Lansing	11 416	75.3	24.7	2.61	2.09	14 885	-0.1	1 023	6.9	13 712	29.8	15.0	7.4
Lombard	16 487	74.9	25.1	2.64	2.02	24 436	-0.7	1 516	6.2	22 315	39.9	9.2	7.3
Maywood	7 937	62.8	37.2	3.65	2.91	12 702	-0.6	1 478	11.6	10 926	20.7	23.3	14.6
Moline	18 492	67.3	32.7	2.47	2.09	22 160	-0.2	1 265	5.7	21 526	29.3	18.4	8.9
Mount Prospect	21 585	71.5	28.5	2.67	2.43	32 386	-0.9	1 593	4.9	29 617	39.4	12.9	9.5
Mundelein	9 858	79.7	20.3	3.10	3.18	18 208	-0.2	1 253	6.9	15 509	41.3	12.8	11.2
Naperville	43 751	79.7	20.3	3.11	2.02	71 366	-0.9	3 799	5.3	64 686	56.0	4.7	4.7
Niles	12 002	76.5	23.5	2.50	2.03	15 288	-0.8	778	5.1	13 732	31.3	14.9	10.3
Normal	15 157	55.2	44.8	2.57	2.25	28 366	-1.1	648	2.3	23 803	35.5	7.6	5.0
Northbrook	12 203	91.7	8.3	2.74	1.97	17 409	-1.0	711	4.1	15 937	57.7	3.3	5.3
North Chicago	7 661	36.3	63.7	3.14	3.06	8 530	-0.6	1 032	12.1	8 938	25.2	20.1	13.5
Oak Forest	9 785	81.7	18.3	3.00	2.00	15 675	-0.6	937	6.0	14 683	32.2	12.8	9.0
Oak Lawn	22 220	82.9	17.1	2.56	1.99	27 688	-0.7	1 661	6.0	25 044	31.9	14.1	10.0
Oak Park	23 079	56.3	43.7	2.67	1.73	29 951	-0.9	1 494	5.0	29 983	60.5	5.1	5.1
Orland Park	18 675	91.1	8.9	2.76	2.20	27 508	-0.6	1 449	5.3	24 816	40.5	9.9	5.5
Palatine	25 518	69.3	30.7	2.65	2.34	39 273	-0.8	2 307	5.9	36 911	43.8	10.0	10.1
Park Ridge	14 219	87.6	12.4	2.71	1.88	19 482	-0.9	791	4.1	18 376	50.3	6.7	6.7
Pekin	13 380	67.2	32.8	2.50	2.08	16 708	-0.9	1 183	7.1	15 538	24.7	20.0	10.7
Peoria	45 199	59.7	40.3	2.49	2.21	55 969	-0.8	3 628	6.5	49 878	38.3	11.8	9.8
Quincy	16 546	66.4	33.6	2.43	2.03	21 511	0.6	1 270	5.9	19 071	27.2	18.4	10.6
Rockford	59 158	61.1	38.9	2.59	2.26	75 761	-0.3	8 426	11.1	67 868	29.1	22.6	13.8
Rock Island	16 148	65.1	34.9	2.41	2.12	18 457	-0.4	1 109	6.0	18 255	27.3	17.8	9.8
Round Lake Beach	7 349	84.6	15.4	3.54	3.27	14 224	0.1	1 201	8.4	12 437	23.3	19.3	10.7
St. Charles	10 351	74.0	26.0	2.81	2.06	17 260	-1.1	1 244	7.2	15 050	42.8	8.9	7.9
Schaumburg	31 799	69.4	30.6	2.52	1.99	46 419	-1.0	2 538	5.5	43 988	44.3	9.6	7.0
Skokie	23 223	75.2	24.8	2.77	2.41	32 988	-1.1	1 562	4.7	30 076	46.3	9.7	10.6
Springfield	48 621	62.8	37.2	2.38	2.01	58 544	-2.4	3 856	6.6	56 704	40.3	7.7	9.9
Streamwood	12 095	89.6	10.4	3.00	2.96	22 350	-0.2	1 631	7.3	19 801	33.1	14.1	9.8
Tinley Park	17 478	84.9	15.1	2.86	1.99	27 827	-0.7	1 441	5.2	25 055	36.2	11.3	6.3
Urbana	14 327	37.0	63.0	2.35	2.02	20 944	-0.1	728	3.5	18 028	52.9	6.7	4.9
Waukegan	27 787	56.5	43.5	3.35	2.74	45 439	-0.4	3 706	8.2	38 501	22.6	25.0	14.3
Wheaton	19 377	74.1	25.9	2.84	2.08	29 697	-1.0	1 340	4.5	28 048	53.8	5.2	4.9
Wheeling	13 280	66.6	33.4	2.78	2.15	21 808	-1.0	1 231	5.6	19 329	35.2	14.8	12.0
Wilmette	10 039	86.8	13.2	2.83	2.11	13 476	-1.0	442	3.3	12 541	66.8	2.1	4.5
Woodridge	11 382	67.2	32.8	2.94	2.24	20 201	-1.0	1 004	5.0	17 005	43.2	10.0	7.4
INDIANA	2 336 306	71.4	28.6	2.64	2.24	3 187 734	0.6	163 367	5.1	2 965 174	28.7	21.4	11.3
Anderson	25 274	63.8	36.2	2.31	2.21	29 954	1.0	2 277	7.6	26 228	22.8	21.6	13.4
Bloomington	26 468	35.3	64.7	2.30	1.97	34 589	4.5	1 289	3.7	34 523	43.9	6.4	4.2
Carmel	13 597	79.1	20.9	2.92	2.03	27 008	1.0	630	2.3	19 004	56.2	4.3	5.1
Columbus	15 985	64.9	35.1	2.50	2.20	18 675	-0.4	838	4.5	18 937	35.1	22.9	10.7
East Chicago	11 707	44.6	55.4	2.95	2.59	13 445	-0.1	1 370	10.2	10 421	17.3	28.0	16.7
Elkhart	20 072	53.5	46.5	2.64	2.45	27 279	2.3	1 703	6.2	24 899	20.0	39.3	16.6
Evansville	52 273	60.0	40.0	2.38	2.02	72 172	0.5	3 415	4.7	58 253	25.0	19.9	13.3
Fishers town	14 044	77.5	22.5	2.90	1.98	19 837	1.0	211	1.1	21 999	55.5	3.8	2.8
Fort Wayne	83 333	61.6	38.4	2.57	2.14	102 134	-0.5	6 918	6.8	100 677	28.7	20.4	11.7
Gary	38 244	55.8	44.2	2.66	2.68	47 316	-0.4	5 685	12.0	35 903	20.6	21.3	17.1
Goshen	10 675	63.6	36.4	2.65	2.55	14 984	2.4	644	4.3	14 638	24.8	35.1	11.0
Greenwood	14 931	62.5	37.5	2.64	1.93	21 362	1.0	565	2.6	19 370	35.6	12.3	9.1
Hammond	32 026	63.2	36.8	2.70	2.37	40 099	0.4	2 518	6.3	34 598	20.5	22.4	12.7
Hobart	9 855	80.2	19.8	2.63	2.21	11 352	0.9	383	3.4	12 287	25.3	18.5	8.5
Indianapolis	324 342	58.7	41.3	2.53	2.18	442 681	1.0	24 180	5.5	397 032	32.9	15.2	12.7
Jeffersonville	11 643	62.2	37.8	2.41	2.11	13 088	-0.8	605	4.6	13 852	26.9	19.6	11.5
Kokomo	20 273	61.1	38.9	2.31	2.12	22 741	1.0	1 871	8.2	21 063	23.7	28.0	12.6

1. Percent of civilian labor force.   2. Persons 16 years old and over.   3. Persons 16 to 64 years old.

Table D. Cities — Construction, Wholesale Trade, and Retail Trade

City	Value of residential construction authorized by building permits, 2003			Wholesale trade, 1997				Retail trade,[1] 1997			
	New construction ($1,000)	Number of housing units	Percent single family	Number of establish-ments	Number of employees	Sales (mil dol)	Annual payroll (mil dol)	Number of establish-ments	Number of employees	Sales (mil dol)	Annual payroll (mil dol)
	69	70	71	72	73	74	75	76	77	78	79
ILLINOIS—Cont'd											
Elmhurst	64 629	234	100.0	197	6 605	2 264.9	341.4	188	2 898	850.4	74.0
Elmwood Park	7 337	55	20.0	17	33	25.2	1.1	52	567	86.0	9.2
Evanston	38 618	542	2.4	95	992	403.3	30.0	292	4 370	746.0	87.1
Freeport	3 040	24	50.0	25	230	80.1	5.6	135	2 155	346.3	34.9
Galesburg	947	6	100.0	42	527	210.5	14.5	198	3 304	409.3	45.9
Glendale Heights	600	3	100.0	79	2 417	1 337.5	96.7	63	1 390	332.8	29.7
Glen Ellyn	29 026	74	100.0	72	220	364.7	15.2	113	1 498	257.7	29.2
Glenview	71 951	218	100.0	146	1 753	866.8	77.3	166	1 909	515.6	45.4
Granite City	4 498	39	92.3	36	578	859.5	19.2	110	1 456	250.2	22.7
Gurnee	8 145	48	95.8	66	1 036	477.9	43.6	227	4 329	640.4	60.8
Hanover Park	4 470	42	100.0	26	558	333.7	26.0	76	1 094	157.6	18.5
Harvey	2 076	26	76.9	30	659	277.7	26.5	66	777	141.1	15.8
Highland Park	29 576	115	56.5	106	410	1 106.1	22.0	180	2 419	570.5	52.4
Hoffman Estates	28 045	186	100.0	107	1 094	1 790.1	67.9	104	1 657	332.8	36.7
Joliet	206 861	1 687	100.0	90	952	216.2	28.9	405	7 042	1 281.5	119.9
Kankakee	1 253	11	100.0	40	403	205.9	13.6	115	1 289	212.3	24.5
Lansing	3 217	23	100.0	43	589	310.3	23.1	158	3 073	472.9	48.1
Lombard	11 809	59	100.0	180	3 003	3 228.9	137.2	282	5 138	858.2	91.3
Maywood	904	7	100.0	10	68	21.3	1.7	45	332	90.3	7.0
Moline	6 741	38	89.5	73	1 072	766.8	43.6	325	5 164	805.5	81.6
Mount Prospect	9 137	87	19.5	136	2 164	3 162.7	109.9	232	4 285	573.1	66.2
Mundelein	15 466	135	100.0	82	755	269.5	31.3	135	1 762	292.0	32.3
Naperville	166 346	668	91.9	310	3 398	12 942.4	192.8	396	7 212	1 506.7	143.3
Niles	9 368	80	10.0	95	2 178	661.9	72.5	234	5 190	1 147.9	91.2
Normal	44 009	608	71.7	35	D	D	D	152	2 843	398.2	39.8
Northbrook	68 490	290	41.4	375	4 107	3 172.5	190.8	269	4 258	723.0	86.2
North Chicago	2 695	41	82.9	22	777	269.7	37.9	37	343	69.2	11.3
Oak Forest	8 868	79	36.7	31	323	173.7	12.4	58	549	155.3	14.3
Oak Lawn	9 056	69	82.6	39	139	71.2	3.9	239	4 298	1 039.9	92.0
Oak Park	1 965	13	100.0	57	242	146.1	9.4	181	1 624	240.0	26.7
Orland Park	136 924	586	68.8	73	476	150.1	16.4	374	7 389	1 244.9	117.8
Palatine	40 632	232	49.1	167	799	689.3	36.4	217	2 943	554.5	54.6
Park Ridge	36 600	107	81.3	108	457	605.4	18.1	117	1 432	305.0	29.0
Pekin	15 748	105	70.5	28	D	D	D	152	2 429	463.8	41.5
Peoria	51 070	501	58.1	231	3 831	5 321.3	138.6	566	9 434	1 501.0	149.3
Quincy	17 740	135	76.3	82	1 175	403.4	34.0	275	4 308	607.1	62.0
Rockford	25 510	384	58.9	320	4 838	1 812.5	167.6	679	11 718	1 875.3	185.9
Rock Island	2 719	20	100.0	80	1 728	543.6	53.9	128	1 365	201.1	20.0
Round Lake Beach	2 843	29	100.0	6	D	D	D	62	1 422	224.9	21.3
St. Charles	35 021	193	89.6	120	1 554	1 329.1	64.4	239	3 595	577.3	59.4
Schaumburg	5 280	22	100.0	431	9 640	12 007.5	536.1	523	12 331	2 262.6	227.5
Skokie	27 223	164	23.2	234	3 921	6 222.6	230.0	413	7 088	981.6	118.7
Springfield	71 347	643	53.0	162	2 370	963.3	80.0	618	9 812	1 634.3	154.7
Streamwood	16 204	75	100.0	32	184	93.9	7.3	64	891	163.7	12.4
Tinley Park	122 980	813	67.8	41	350	172.7	12.9	130	2 456	494.0	44.1
Urbana	20 266	326	47.9	32	D	D	D	109	1 836	287.3	30.4
Waukegan	13 620	91	93.4	73	2 423	1 016.1	94.6	288	4 373	735.2	78.2
Wheaton	23 304	68	100.0	115	369	408.2	15.1	217	2 919	513.3	51.7
Wheeling	7 540	78	100.0	203	3 111	1 473.3	134.3	101	1 707	366.7	31.7
Wilmette	29 558	71	100.0	47	134	214.6	6.8	133	1 571	241.0	27.0
Woodridge	36 775	153	100.0	33	1 109	536.7	41.0	64	1 308	203.3	19.3
INDIANA	5 392 722	39 421	80.9	8 896	112 705	66 350.1	3 737.8	24 954	337 867	57 241.6	5 273.8
Anderson	15 702	174	54.0	60	885	247.7	23.1	346	5 079	833.0	77.0
Bloomington	NA	NA	NA	72	868	284.5	26.7	443	6 424	1 010.6	91.4
Carmel	233 065	1 009	88.6	175	1 670	2 788.6	90.4	184	3 663	720.9	69.9
Columbus	NA	NA	NA	81	698	588.1	22.4	286	3 941	566.8	55.6
East Chicago	113	2	100.0	60	1 115	953.8	39.0	60	610	83.6	10.6
Elkhart	6 578	79	54.4	168	2 457	1 147.6	80.3	330	5 168	920.2	82.5
Evansville	16 540	181	91.2	296	4 051	1 480.3	123.3	870	13 655	2 092.6	211.3
Fishers town	213 841	1 385	100.0	NA	NA	NA	NA	NA	NA	NA	NA
Fort Wayne	51 463	501	62.3	531	8 532	4 041.7	281.3	1 058	17 653	2 859.6	283.0
Gary	19 775	205	35.6	65	1 480	534.5	52.1	218	2 361	359.8	30.8
Goshen	24 437	252	68.7	29	D	D	D	171	2 885	494.2	47.7
Greenwood	60 462	688	46.2	61	501	552.5	19.7	258	4 847	728.5	70.1
Hammond	2 649	20	100.0	95	1 366	961.1	44.5	251	3 388	556.3	52.0
Hobart	31 896	314	68.8	23	223	150.2	10.1	136	2 254	397.6	36.3
Indianapolis	598 353	4 607	73.3	1 863	D	D	D	3 405	56 872	10 305.6	990.4
Jeffersonville	21 095	178	98.9	59	831	430.2	23.0	108	1 608	264.4	24.7
Kokomo	24 950	194	77.8	73	601	553.3	22.3	346	5 564	878.7	81.5

1. Establishments with payroll.

Table D. Cities — **Real Estate, Professional Services, and Manufacturing**

City	Real estate and rental and leasing, 1997				Professional, scientific, and technical services,[1] 1997				Manufacturing, 1997			
	Number of establishments	Number of employees	Receipts (mil dol)	Annual payroll (mil dol)	Number of establishments	Number of employees	Receipts (mil dol)	Annual payroll (mil dol)	Number of establishments	Number of employees	Receipts (mil dol)	Annual payroll (mil dol)
	80	81	82	83	84	85	86	87	88	89	90	91
ILLINOIS—Cont'd												
Elmhurst	68	472	73.1	15.8	229	1 044	107.7	47.0	85	2 882	421.0	103.1
Elmwood Park	12	32	4.7	0.5	27	106	4.9	2.2	NA	NA	NA	NA
Evanston	128	603	101.5	15.1	357	2 085	227.6	80.7	67	2 310	321.7	74.4
Freeport	23	97	9.0	1.5	49	223	16.3	6.5	40	7 645	1 058.2	280.7
Galesburg	35	148	11.0	1.8	47	257	19.3	7.0	48	D	D	D
Glendale Heights	8	82	16.1	1.4	41	176	23.8	6.6	48	2 304	327.2	87.7
Glen Ellyn	44	184	26.2	4.2	172	1 037	90.5	37.8	NA	NA	NA	NA
Glenview	54	178	29.7	4.4	214	523	82.3	23.8	68	1 481	222.9	54.2
Granite City	31	186	14.6	3.5	45	278	33.1	15.8	28	5 632	1 857.1	234.5
Gurnee	23	284	58.5	6.9	101	610	73.3	23.9	63	2 769	517.6	96.5
Hanover Park	15	71	13.3	1.1	30	79	6.3	2.9	NA	NA	NA	NA
Harvey	10	38	3.4	0.7	9	57	7.2	2.8	48	2 361	699.2	110.4
Highland Park	58	125	27.0	4.0	226	576	83.5	26.3	44	D	D	D
Hoffman Estates	35	158	24.1	3.1	160	1 676	268.0	89.1	23	971	191.2	45.6
Joliet	74	304	34.9	5.4	172	1 047	93.5	40.7	104	7 268	3 814.8	323.6
Kankakee	27	163	16.3	2.8	67	305	20.8	8.2	32	2 502	673.5	96.0
Lansing	42	163	17.5	3.0	56	220	35.3	8.8	34	870	171.4	29.7
Lombard	63	703	75.2	24.6	212	1 630	192.4	85.6	102	1 718	246.3	62.2
Maywood	9	41	5.5	1.1	8	52	4.2	1.6	28	603	74.0	19.1
Moline	61	370	52.8	9.1	91	576	43.1	18.6	61	2 150	500.4	89.7
Mount Prospect	46	224	31.0	5.2	181	849	95.0	29.3	46	3 457	553.4	134.8
Mundelein	16	435	19.9	4.8	79	438	64.7	23.0	92	3 691	553.3	124.5
Naperville	139	606	105.6	16.2	588	3 513	404.3	173.6	84	2 334	348.9	80.4
Niles	32	254	31.5	5.8	97	745	50.2	23.1	102	6 376	1 023.3	242.4
Normal	40	336	48.9	7.9	30	172	5.8	2.3	19	D	D	D
Northbrook	126	659	144.6	25.6	569	7 553	695.5	379.1	123	4 672	840.3	161.1
North Chicago	12	D	D	D	19	135	14.7	6.2	28	1 606	356.6	51.7
Oak Forest	21	86	6.9	2.2	46	188	13.6	5.1	22	519	85.7	16.1
Oak Lawn	60	271	29.5	4.5	110	271	23.9	8.2	31	527	57.1	17.5
Oak Park	59	383	40.5	7.3	226	915	88.4	34.4	43	679	82.8	22.3
Orland Park	64	253	57.9	6.5	167	632	58.3	19.9	55	2 195	477.7	92.4
Palatine	75	439	67.8	9.7	225	1 039	113.0	43.5	76	2 830	453.6	91.9
Park Ridge	54	318	59.0	9.3	229	1 517	150.3	64.9	NA	NA	NA	NA
Pekin	23	134	12.7	3.0	55	223	12.8	5.2	28	D	D	D
Peoria	154	753	92.9	16.8	299	4 031	337.5	154.2	113	5 666	1 381.6	197.3
Quincy	50	209	17.0	2.7	96	442	36.7	11.6	57	2 995	774.0	96.6
Rockford	150	806	104.7	18.1	440	4 666	258.8	107.6	477	26 100	4 467.4	998.8
Rock Island	41	185	17.1	3.1	101	1 022	69.1	30.6	58	1 927	238.5	47.7
Round Lake Beach	8	27	5.2	0.6	12	37	1.4	0.4	NA	NA	NA	NA
St. Charles	40	230	27.2	3.6	146	1 676	120.9	70.1	118	7 053	1 360.7	238.7
Schaumburg	132	1 130	299.0	39.4	457	4 468	592.6	238.8	190	8 709	1 448.1	404.8
Skokie	116	756	351.9	46.4	351	2 378	326.6	114.3	212	9 083	1 815.5	310.1
Springfield	145	624	69.8	11.3	398	3 008	255.1	108.9	84	2 850	462.9	82.2
Streamwood	13	107	3.5	1.0	38	62	5.0	2.0	45	918	148.4	36.8
Tinley Park	23	129	9.7	2.0	83	287	22.7	7.4	33	1 140	197.1	40.2
Urbana	36	138	48.3	4.1	61	534	27.1	11.4	33	D	D	D
Waukegan	61	335	47.8	8.0	143	1 293	116.9	59.9	95	6 037	986.8	213.6
Wheaton	59	253	40.1	6.7	381	1 859	191.9	82.1	34	508	63.1	19.0
Wheeling	36	307	41.6	13.2	144	1 022	124.4	45.4	186	10 194	2 306.9	415.8
Wilmette	56	242	31.7	6.4	146	258	36.6	15.6	NA	NA	NA	NA
Woodridge	30	160	20.6	3.1	49	208	22.9	11.6	16	741	192.6	30.5
INDIANA	5 427	28 948	3 269.1	572.6	9 795	69 393	5 974.2	2 207.5	9 303	625 692	142 270.7	22 121.4
Anderson	68	307	23.2	5.0	126	889	49.2	26.2	59	8 999	1 769.1	456.0
Bloomington	140	822	75.7	14.2	167	1 285	91.2	31.3	61	5 013	1 751.3	159.4
Carmel	74	519	82.6	13.8	235	2 517	251.2	105.1	53	1 304	177.8	44.2
Columbus	50	228	30.5	4.8	123	694	50.7	22.3	96	11 647	2 273.1	366.2
East Chicago	14	128	21.2	4.0	17	135	14.0	5.5	51	16 068	4 894.2	812.3
Elkhart	89	371	42.5	7.0	136	898	67.3	20.7	349	17 947	3 023.5	554.5
Evansville	198	1 327	148.7	23.5	359	3 237	231.8	89.9	213	15 029	3 446.0	528.1
Fishers town	NA	NA	NA	NA	NA	NA	NA	NA	NA	NA	NA	NA
Fort Wayne	238	1 582	193.2	35.5	505	4 954	412.1	144.6	390	22 830	4 258.9	846.3
Gary	62	272	32.2	4.5	46	403	54.8	12.6	62	10 066	3 377.4	511.3
Goshen	36	190	15.6	3.1	49	195	15.2	4.2	105	7 397	1 070.8	200.8
Greenwood	46	208	26.9	3.8	96	506	31.2	12.3	45	1 013	289.6	36.1
Hammond	62	553	77.2	17.6	101	1 364	79.7	30.2	76	4 195	1 468.0	171.4
Hobart	25	113	14.5	2.3	28	128	7.3	2.3	NA	NA	NA	NA
Indianapolis	1 048	D	D	D	2 174	22 189	2 356.5	875.1	1 094	D	D	D
Jeffersonville	46	206	34.0	2.7	86	316	26.5	7.9	75	3 671	584.0	105.3
Kokomo	73	281	35.3	5.2	87	393	30.1	10.1	66	D	D	D

1. Firms subject to federal tax.

Table D. Cities — Accommodation and Foodservices, Entertainment, and Health Care

City	Accommodation and foodservices, 1997				Arts, entertainment, and recreation,[1] 1997				Health care and social assistance,[1] 1997			
	Number of establishments	Number of employees	Sales (mil dol)	Annual payroll (mil dol)	Number of establishments	Number of employees	Receipts (mil dol)	Annual payroll (mil dol)	Number of establishments	Number of employees	Receipts (mil dol)	Annual payroll (mil dol)
	92	93	94	95	96	97	98	99	100	101	102	103
ILLINOIS—Cont'd												
Elmhurst	83	D	D	D	8	123	4.8	1.8	144	2 235	208.5	91.9
Elmwood Park	34	492	21.0	5.4	NA	NA	NA	NA	39	395	23.4	9.5
Evanston	177	2 491	110.1	30.1	29	157	8.4	3.0	237	2 145	220.7	114.5
Freeport	78	1 108	31.4	7.5	3	7	0.5	0.1	58	574	32.9	17.2
Galesburg	104	D	D	D	12	77	3.1	0.5	63	1 119	68.1	25.5
Glendale Heights	43	D	D	D	7	189	9.5	1.7	25	1 178	52.7	25.9
Glen Ellyn	52	847	40.9	7.9	9	54	2.1	0.8	65	480	30.6	11.5
Glenview	104	1 842	76.3	21.7	31	206	15.9	7.2	123	1 032	74.8	37.5
Granite City	72	937	28.6	7.5	7	62	3.1	1.1	80	898	61.2	23.6
Gurnee	91	2 322	92.7	23.6	9	0	0.0	0.0	82	696	59.1	27.6
Hanover Park	47	626	23.3	6.0	2	0	0.0	0.0	35	429	25.0	12.4
Harvey	38	504	13.7	3.6	1	0	0.0	0.0	53	819	61.8	34.9
Highland Park	71	968	41.6	10.9	15	188	6.0	2.4	158	1 238	97.1	52.1
Hoffman Estates	83	1 653	72.1	18.4	15	194	10.0	2.8	169	3 590	305.3	121.8
Joliet	191	3 300	107.9	28.1	16	0	0.0	0.0	232	2 607	225.9	108.3
Kankakee	69	900	26.5	7.2	8	102	5.9	1.2	86	777	58.3	28.7
Lansing	75	1 331	46.3	12.5	9	68	3.9	1.0	39	259	14.2	6.1
Lombard	95	2 231	87.6	24.3	16	380	49.8	5.0	104	1 475	91.6	38.9
Maywood	33	363	19.3	4.7	1	0	0.0	0.0	23	121	9.0	3.6
Moline	163	3 304	90.5	25.7	16	103	6.6	1.2	137	1 515	113.0	54.2
Mount Prospect	101	D	D	D	6	92	5.7	1.4	82	1 053	62.3	24.8
Mundelein	61	D	D	D	9	72	6.1	1.3	37	291	14.7	6.0
Naperville	233	4 972	184.8	53.0	33	650	22.0	6.9	309	3 625	247.7	100.3
Niles	102	1 774	59.9	16.4	9	98	3.1	0.8	90	1 405	78.5	31.7
Normal	93	2 250	60.2	16.8	2	0	0.0	0.0	52	701	44.0	21.4
Northbrook	112	1 602	75.1	21.1	25	551	20.2	9.7	168	1 935	133.6	71.2
North Chicago	56	934	31.3	8.9	1	0	0.0	0.0	10	71	5.1	2.8
Oak Forest	36	532	16.1	4.5	4	18	1.2	0.3	49	397	34.8	16.5
Oak Lawn	96	2 205	74.4	20.2	6	77	5.4	1.3	214	2 249	207.2	109.4
Oak Park	81	1 458	49.3	14.6	19	88	4.6	1.3	219	1 964	144.5	64.3
Orland Park	127	2 676	98.7	26.2	16	515	18.1	5.6	170	1 408	91.9	39.3
Palatine	115	1 887	69.5	17.6	26	209	11.5	2.9	103	842	58.5	28.5
Park Ridge	61	755	25.9	6.3	9	88	5.3	2.4	179	1 523	189.6	84.4
Pekin	75	1 319	34.6	10.0	7	59	1.5	0.5	67	803	45.2	21.4
Peoria	344	6 592	203.4	59.1	33	690	28.7	9.6	311	4 072	349.3	186.0
Quincy	117	2 098	62.9	17.5	16	173	3.7	1.1	106	1 490	93.2	49.4
Rockford	347	6 984	223.7	61.1	45	429	16.7	4.2	349	4 885	397.9	196.2
Rock Island	92	1 178	33.6	8.3	12	530	24.6	8.1	77	816	46.1	19.7
Round Lake Beach	28	353	13.2	3.2	1	0	0.0	0.0	15	183	9.9	4.5
St. Charles	104	3 175	98.1	33.5	12	60	5.6	0.8	64	428	31.7	14.7
Schaumburg	210	5 836	239.2	62.7	15	326	16.9	3.4	171	2 134	177.9	67.5
Skokie	138	2 572	101.0	27.8	34	266	11.3	2.6	252	3 679	218.6	91.4
Springfield	373	6 820	209.9	62.0	45	553	39.7	7.8	307	7 266	466.0	199.5
Streamwood	38	612	24.2	6.3	5	93	2.9	1.0	35	399	24.7	8.3
Tinley Park	62	1 037	34.9	9.4	14	208	29.9	4.2	75	529	31.8	13.0
Urbana	104	2 038	62.9	18.4	6	0	0.0	0.0	32	0	0.0	0.0
Waukegan	152	2 101	79.5	19.7	18	312	9.5	3.1	124	1 448	93.4	46.1
Wheaton	84	2 007	62.2	16.6	9	194	8.0	2.7	137	1 520	133.1	50.5
Wheeling	57	D	D	D	7	29	1.9	0.5	38	342	23.7	8.5
Wilmette	45	D	D	D	18	21	2.6	0.9	95	467	43.0	20.8
Woodridge	25	466	15.3	4.5	8	249	9.8	3.0	56	404	26.3	11.3
INDIANA	11 705	215 710	6 646.3	1 865.3	1 500	24 903	1 918.3	516.1	10 236	132 416	8 132.3	3 675.3
Anderson	160	4 055	116.4	32.8	21	0	0.0	0.0	158	1 520	91.5	41.3
Bloomington	275	6 020	165.8	45.1	17	56	7.9	0.7	200	2 054	148.2	69.9
Carmel	79	1 636	57.7	16.3	21	246	11.9	3.5	131	1 520	123.2	53.3
Columbus	110	2 721	88.6	24.6	10	59	2.7	0.5	133	1 519	102.0	54.9
East Chicago	57	494	16.0	3.6	3	0	0.0	0.0	28	253	11.6	5.2
Elkhart	184	3 093	94.5	26.9	14	140	4.3	1.5	114	1 500	106.4	41.7
Evansville	396	D	D	D	43	1 804	140.5	31.4	368	7 358	475.3	227.9
Fishers town	NA	NA	NA	NA	NA	NA	NA	NA	NA	NA	NA	NA
Fort Wayne	506	11 413	350.9	103.0	58	674	28.1	8.8	434	7 242	424.5	191.2
Gary	120	1 465	43.7	11.4	9	0	0.0	0.0	127	1 160	71.5	31.8
Goshen	66	1 403	41.7	11.4	7	41	2.2	0.6	59	709	36.5	15.4
Greenwood	107	2 419	66.4	19.3	18	229	9.5	2.4	83	1 232	76.2	31.9
Hammond	164	2 024	71.3	17.3	10	0	0.0	0.0	69	558	44.4	17.7
Hobart	55	D	D	D	9	106	2.9	0.9	44	597	34.7	13.6
Indianapolis	1 751	D	D	D	230	4 451	428.7	175.8	1 752	26 194	1 802.7	829.6
Jeffersonville	66	D	D	D	8	35	2.1	0.6	98	1 475	88.9	38.9
Kokomo	160	3 637	109.6	29.9	21	279	8.6	2.6	150	1 761	110.3	50.7

1. Firms subject to federal tax.

City	Other services,[1] 1997 Number of establish-ments	Number of employees	Receipts (mil dol)	Annual payroll (mil dol)	Procurement contracts Defense	Other	Grants Total[2]	Medicaid and other health related	Nutrition and family welfare	Energy and envi-ronment	Education	Housing and community develop-ment	Direct payments for individuals for educational assistance
	104	105	106	107	108	109	110	111	112	113	114	115	116
ILLINOIS—Cont'd													
Elmhurst	103	892	64.7	21.9	8.4	0.2	0.8	0.0	0.0	0.1	0.0	0.7	2.0
Elmwood Park	27	136	5.5	1.9	0.0	0.0	0.0	0.0	0.0	0.0	0.0	0.0	0.0
Evanston	98	529	32.2	11.1	25.7	0.8	255.2	180.5	1.4	6.6	3.8	6.8	9.8
Freeport	58	295	13.5	4.0	1.0	0.0	4.2	0.0	1.1	0.4	0.6	1.9	1.9
Galesburg	64	330	20.4	5.7	0.0	0.1	5.0	0.0	0.0	0.0	1.0	3.5	4.7
Glendale Heights	24	127	11.5	3.9	0.1	0.0	3.7	1.0	0.0	0.0	0.0	2.6	0.0
Glen Ellyn	41	267	14.1	4.7	0.0	0.5	1.9	0.0	0.0	0.0	0.1	1.8	5.4
Glenview	101	752	38.0	13.6	5.6	0.4	1.5	0.0	0.0	0.0	0.1	0.6	0.0
Granite City	62	390	20.8	6.9	5.4	0.2	3.2	0.0	0.0	0.0	0.0	1.9	0.0
Gurnee	56	405	26.1	7.6	0.4	0.2	2.0	0.0	0.0	0.0	0.0	2.0	0.0
Hanover Park	36	261	14.3	6.9	0.0	0.0	0.0	0.0	0.0	0.0	0.0	0.0	0.1
Harvey	29	278	30.3	11.5	0.5	0.4	3.8	1.4	0.0	0.0	1.0	1.0	0.0
Highland Park	79	453	30.1	8.9	0.2	0.3	2.0	0.0	0.0	0.0	0.1	1.8	0.0
Hoffman Estates	45	277	14.8	4.4	0.4	0.5	0.5	0.1	0.0	0.0	0.0	0.3	2.2
Joliet	128	888	59.2	16.9	5.3	0.8	24.5	0.8	5.5	0.0	0.6	17.1	4.9
Kankakee	60	361	23.8	7.1	2.0	0.0	14.2	0.0	2.5	1.0	2.1	7.2	3.8
Lansing	78	678	38.4	13.6	0.1	0.0	0.5	0.0	0.0	0.0	0.0	0.5	0.0
Lombard	117	1 049	104.5	35.9	12.3	6.5	5.7	0.0	0.0	0.7	0.0	2.1	0.2
Maywood	19	86	5.8	1.6	0.5	0.0	27.7	16.6	0.0	0.0	4.4	6.6	0.0
Moline	105	681	51.2	13.4	4.8	3.2	12.9	0.0	0.0	0.5	1.2	7.6	5.9
Mount Prospect	84	365	24.9	6.1	0.9	0.3	7.0	0.0	0.0	0.0	0.0	6.9	0.1
Mundelein	70	586	102.5	24.3	0.9	7.8	1.5	0.0	0.0	0.0	0.4	1.1	0.0
Naperville	173	1 311	72.4	24.0	11.5	7.5	6.7	0.2	0.0	2.6	0.0	3.6	1.3
Niles	70	639	52.5	16.2	0.4	4.2	0.7	0.0	0.0	0.0	0.0	0.2	0.1
Normal	51	337	16.3	5.3	0.0	0.1	10.2	0.6	0.1	0.0	3.9	2.1	13.2
Northbrook	69	686	47.3	17.4	0.9	0.7	2.6	1.2	0.0	0.0	0.1	1.1	0.0
North Chicago	11	94	4.7	1.8	2.6	13.5	33.0	7.7	0.0	0.0	8.7	15.3	0.5
Oak Forest	43	315	31.8	7.5	0.0	0.0	0.0	0.0	0.0	0.0	0.0	0.0	0.4
Oak Lawn	111	656	39.3	12.5	0.0	1.8	1.1	0.3	0.0	0.2	0.0	0.5	0.8
Oak Park	90	585	40.4	12.6	0.2	0.3	11.9	1.7	0.0	0.0	0.0	9.2	0.0
Orland Park	104	833	44.0	14.0	0.3	0.4	0.1	0.0	0.0	0.0	0.0	0.0	0.0
Palatine	127	915	68.7	20.2	0.1	2.0	5.0	0.0	0.0	0.0	0.0	5.0	3.6
Park Ridge	73	402	21.0	7.0	0.1	1.4	0.3	0.0	0.1	0.0	0.1	0.0	0.0
Pekin	66	352	18.5	5.4	2.9	4.4	8.1	0.0	0.0	0.0	0.8	6.8	0.0
Peoria	202	1 996	146.6	48.0	5.4	8.7	91.3	1.7	6.0	11.0	1.8	54.1	10.0
Quincy	113	636	36.2	11.6	16.3	0.8	8.9	0.1	1.7	0.0	1.7	2.0	4.6
Rockford	293	2 654	165.0	54.3	82.1	5.3	51.6	6.5	3.8	0.4	7.0	28.5	6.0
Rock Island	79	618	33.8	10.0	17.4	0.8	19.5	0.0	4.6	0.1	0.3	12.9	1.5
Round Lake Beach	23	111	6.3	2.0	0.0	0.0	2.4	0.0	0.0	0.0	0.0	2.4	0.0
St. Charles	73	455	26.8	8.4	0.6	0.7	4.9	0.0	0.0	0.2	0.0	1.0	0.0
Schaumburg	188	1 498	109.8	35.5	9.2	0.5	6.4	1.3	0.0	0.0	0.1	2.6	0.0
Skokie	172	1 403	81.8	26.3	19.3	16.4	2.3	0.0	0.0	0.0	0.0	2.3	0.4
Springfield	248	1 813	112.8	37.3	4.3	6.7	1 856.5	218.2	763.5	144.8	409.3	32.4	6.5
Streamwood	47	241	16.4	4.7	0.0	0.3	0.1	0.0	0.0	0.0	0.0	0.0	0.0
Tinley Park	52	311	17.5	5.7	0.2	0.1	0.8	0.0	0.0	0.0	0.0	0.7	0.0
Urbana	48	296	14.8	4.9	1.4	1.3	54.9	0.7	3.9	0.4	13.2	5.9	16.0
Waukegan	111	493	33.7	9.7	1.6	1.9	32.1	1.8	5.4	0.0	0.4	22.5	0.3
Wheaton	95	551	30.8	10.3	0.1	0.8	20.4	1.3	0.0	0.3	0.2	16.1	1.6
Wheeling	65	545	72.3	14.7	3.4	0.5	1.0	0.3	0.0	0.0	0.0	0.7	0.1
Wilmette	53	400	27.8	9.9	0.2	0.0	1.0	0.0	0.0	0.0	0.0	0.8	0.0
Woodridge	27	148	8.5	2.3	0.0	0.4	0.5	0.1	0.0	0.0	0.0	0.5	1.4
INDIANA	9 243	60 711	3 701.4	1 127.8	2 566.7	734.8	7 313.0	3 628.8	941.8	118.9	627.4	505.3	433.3
Anderson	127	784	43.3	14.2	0.6	0.3	15.1	0.6	2.6	0.0	0.6	9.0	2.5
Bloomington	119	725	35.1	11.3	1.9	4.5	209.6	146.1	2.3	5.1	6.9	11.2	17.1
Carmel	79	552	44.6	13.2	0.2	0.4	1.6	0.3	0.0	1.3	0.0	0.0	0.0
Columbus	81	574	34.0	12.1	24.6	0.9	21.7	0.0	2.4	12.4	0.1	5.0	0.0
East Chicago	40	492	41.3	15.8	4.8	0.1	14.9	2.6	0.0	0.0	0.0	12.2	0.0
Elkhart	145	1 163	69.1	20.6	1.9	1.2	8.6	0.0	0.0	0.0	0.5	8.0	0.0
Evansville	304	2 787	161.4	51.7	167.3	-9.4	28.7	2.3	4.9	0.0	0.8	16.7	8.6
Fishers town	NA	NA	NA	NA	0.6	0.2	0.1	0.0	0.0	0.0	0.0	0.0	0.0
Fort Wayne	447	3 741	237.4	74.6	353.6	47.9	32.1	1.3	4.9	0.0	1.6	20.9	13.1
Gary	78	558	31.0	9.7	4.9	0.4	35.0	0.0	0.2	1.5	2.2	29.0	7.0
Goshen	65	524	37.7	10.0	9.8	0.0	3.1	0.0	0.0	0.0	0.1	3.0	0.9
Greenwood	85	681	39.9	14.4	0.3	0.1	2.9	0.0	0.0	0.0	0.0	2.9	0.1
Hammond	120	937	54.0	19.1	9.0	4.7	8.9	1.3	0.0	0.0	0.4	7.1	0.1
Hobart	48	427	26.5	9.6	0.0	0.0	0.5	0.0	0.0	0.0	0.4	0.1	0.2
Indianapolis	1 320	11 727	702.1	221.8	996.4	175.0	1 152.2	132.4	240.5	77.2	214.2	168.2	274.2
Jeffersonville	53	485	28.4	10.0	0.2	4.9	9.8	0.0	1.9	0.0	0.7	5.6	0.1
Kokomo	107	849	37.6	12.3	0.2	0.2	10.3	0.0	2.4	0.0	0.0	6.6	1.7

1. Firms subject to federal tax.   2. Includes program categories not shown separately. State totals include additional categories not allocated by city.

Table D. Cities — **City Government Finances**

	City government finances, 2002									
	General revenue							General expenditure		
		Intergovernmental		Taxes					Per capita[1] (dollars)	
					Per capita[1] (dollars)					
City	Total (mil dol)	Total (mil dol)	Percent from state government	Total (mil dol)	Total	Property	Sales and gross receipts	Total (mil dol)	Total	Capital outlays
	117	118	119	120	121	122	123	124	125	126
ILLINOIS—Cont'd										
Elmhurst	50.1	18.0	98.7	19.1	440	222	184	54.7	1 261	110
Elmwood Park	19.6	5.4	90.6	11.9	472	306	80	15.0	596	23
Evanston	125.3	33.3	91.2	55.2	752	380	285	155.0	2 111	861
Freeport	19.8	8.2	89.6	5.2	200	119	20	21.5	828	86
Galesburg	26.5	10.3	99.2	9.6	288	163	109	25.7	772	30
Glendale Heights	27.7	8.6	98.7	9.6	292	148	113	25.2	763	65
Glen Ellyn	32.3	6.5	93.5	9.3	342	201	109	26.2	964	138
Glenview	50.0	15.8	72.6	19.5	442	267	133	76.1	1 728	812
Granite City	NA	NA	NA	NA	NA	NA	NA	NA	NA	NA
Gurnee	28.6	16.5	88.7	7.8	260	10	198	23.0	764	73
Hanover Park	24.8	6.8	100.0	11.2	295	192	62	24.8	651	50
Harvey	22.2	6.4	79.4	13.6	458	327	73	19.4	653	0
Highland Park	43.8	12.8	93.6	22.9	750	401	265	36.0	1 180	87
Hoffman Estates	67.9	12.8	98.2	37.9	761	588	136	57.2	1 149	322
Joliet	137.4	67.7	94.9	40.1	339	116	177	147.6	1 246	307
Kankakee	33.7	12.5	71.4	10.1	370	210	111	35.2	1 295	262
Lansing	27.9	9.7	100.0	13.3	474	386	46	23.2	823	82
Lombard	41.5	16.1	94.5	13.9	321	149	141	39.2	907	274
Maywood	27.4	5.9	90.6	17.8	664	514	83	34.8	1 302	307
Moline	NA	NA	NA	NA	NA	NA	NA	NA	NA	NA
Mount Prospect	44.5	15.8	95.8	22.9	408	201	158	47.3	843	201
Mundelein	23.3	7.9	96.8	10.7	335	208	83	21.6	675	0
Naperville	130.4	38.8	94.9	54.9	406	240	147	138.2	1 021	247
Niles	38.0	16.0	96.0	18.3	608	228	360	42.6	1 416	215
Normal	35.9	12.1	94.1	15.0	318	107	193	34.9	741	153
Northbrook	36.1	11.7	99.9	16.2	479	325	48	41.5	1 222	218
North Chicago	17.3	7.2	97.6	6.6	183	67	97	18.9	524	24
Oak Forest	14.5	5.4	93.7	6.6	232	191	0	17.5	618	183
Oak Lawn	43.4	18.7	95.0	14.4	260	185	46	42.4	766	52
Oak Park	65.6	16.4	77.6	34.1	661	462	167	65.6	1 272	229
Orland Park	45.2	22.3	100.0	11.5	216	146	28	53.2	997	286
Palatine	50.9	17.4	84.7	22.9	345	255	61	58.5	881	202
Park Ridge	30.8	8.5	99.0	20.1	532	287	159	36.9	977	89
Pekin	29.6	11.1	89.8	7.4	221	127	86	35.0	1 046	110
Peoria	121.9	50.5	94.0	47.0	417	166	230	120.6	1 070	266
Quincy	34.3	16.8	90.6	9.8	246	144	83	32.1	804	103
Rockford	130.1	61.0	83.2	48.8	323	251	35	139.3	922	142
Rock Island	45.4	17.1	91.3	12.1	309	204	90	42.5	1 089	176
Round Lake Beach	11.7	6.5	96.2	4.0	144	66	33	7.8	279	0
St. Charles	41.4	13.1	98.5	13.6	438	170	193	54.4	1 756	624
Schaumburg	86.7	46.3	99.4	29.3	391	22	324	87.7	1 170	252
Skokie	61.3	20.4	97.9	35.0	554	359	142	51.3	813	9
Springfield	116.4	43.3	87.5	37.3	333	168	155	155.3	1 389	429
Streamwood	20.6	7.6	97.4	10.4	277	134	82	20.8	553	154
Tinley Park	34.4	15.5	95.0	11.9	228	194	0	23.3	446	0
Urbana	32.0	12.7	68.2	12.5	328	126	182	29.6	773	176
Waukegan	61.6	23.3	91.7	23.1	253	140	91	58.8	644	85
Wheaton	36.1	12.9	98.8	14.8	267	191	67	35.5	642	7
Wheeling	29.8	11.6	97.5	12.2	344	229	102	32.3	910	154
Wilmette	24.5	6.5	100.0	13.0	474	287	130	29.8	1 081	226
Woodridge	19.9	8.6	100.0	8.5	251	115	42	18.3	542	49
INDIANA	X	X	X	X	X	X	X	X	X	X
Anderson	62.2	14.8	69.4	29.8	507	354	8	60.0	1 019	105
Bloomington	125.9	10.1	86.1	24.4	348	238	7	135.8	1 940	640
Carmel	49.4	8.8	38.1	24.4	596	271	5	64.0	1 566	86
Columbus	37.0	13.0	49.3	11.5	296	288	4	38.0	981	19
East Chicago	92.8	18.5	71.7	41.4	1 303	701	598	77.6	2 447	76
Elkhart	66.3	20.6	61.5	25.3	489	423	3	67.4	1 302	108
Evansville	136.8	27.3	62.0	61.1	513	338	7	150.5	1 264	138
Fishers town	26.3	2.5	52.0	14.6	329	136	3	29.1	654	213
Fort Wayne	144.7	19.3	83.8	75.9	361	287	0	171.6	817	142
Gary	163.6	45.0	70.3	65.9	653	639	0	177.3	1 756	385
Goshen	23.9	6.7	53.0	7.8	262	223	0	25.9	872	51
Greenwood	46.1	7.7	28.4	8.0	206	197	3	42.5	1 092	68
Hammond	141.9	15.0	55.7	29.9	368	358	0	146.2	1 796	265
Hobart	26.0	4.1	96.5	10.4	393	364	0	30.4	1 149	45
Indianapolis	1 643.4	518.0	82.7	628.8	792	624	55	1 825.8	2 301	509
Jeffersonville	NA	NA	NA	NA	NA	NA	NA	NA	NA	NA
Kokomo	NA	NA	NA	NA	NA	NA	NA	NA	NA	NA

1. Based on population estimated as of July 1 of the year shown.

Items 117—126

IL(Elmhurst)—IN(Kokomo) 1003

City	City government finances, 2002 (cont'd)									
	General expenditure									
	Percent of total for—									
	Public welfare	Highways	Parking facilities	Education	Health and hospitals	Police protection	Sewerage and sanitation	Parks and recreation	Housing and community development	Interest on debt
	127	128	129	130	131	132	133	134	135	136
ILLINOIS—Cont'd										
Elmhurst	0.3	20.0	0.7	0.0	0.6	17.5	8.1	1.5	0.0	6.6
Elmwood Park	0.0	3.0	0.0	0.0	0.0	21.2	8.0	5.3	0.0	0.6
Evanston	4.9	7.8	7.1	0.0	1.9	10.1	30.6	7.9	4.1	5.9
Freeport	0.5	11.1	0.0	0.0	0.2	17.2	17.6	0.8	1.6	4.9
Galesburg	0.0	13.3	0.0	0.0	0.0	18.0	4.6	10.8	0.0	10.1
Glendale Heights	0.0	16.9	0.0	0.0	0.0	22.8	11.7	14.9	0.0	3.1
Glen Ellyn	0.0	25.1	0.6	0.0	0.0	16.3	16.1	12.2	0.0	3.6
Glenview	0.0	8.8	0.3	0.0	0.0	10.5	2.0	0.0	0.0	4.5
Granite City	NA	NA	NA	NA	NA	NA	NA	NA	NA	NA
Gurnee	0.0	12.6	0.0	0.0	0.0	29.6	4.8	0.0	0.0	2.3
Hanover Park	0.0	17.8	1.1	0.0	0.0	25.2	4.9	0.0	0.0	13.3
Harvey	0.0	13.9	1.4	0.0	0.0	23.4	9.6	0.0	0.0	6.0
Highland Park	0.0	14.5	2.2	0.0	0.0	18.7	1.2	9.1	0.0	4.3
Hoffman Estates	0.0	7.4	0.0	0.0	1.0	17.9	2.8	0.5	0.0	14.6
Joliet	0.0	24.5	0.6	0.0	0.0	17.1	8.2	15.0	0.8	1.3
Kankakee	0.0	17.0	0.0	0.0	0.0	16.3	21.4	0.1	3.1	7.2
Lansing	0.0	5.0	0.0	0.0	0.0	30.1	7.0	0.1	0.0	12.8
Lombard	0.0	27.3	0.0	0.0	0.0	16.5	9.1	0.0	0.0	2.0
Maywood	0.0	7.0	0.0	0.0	0.0	17.1	2.9	2.8	0.0	5.2
Moline	NA	NA	NA	NA	NA	NA	NA	NA	NA	NA
Mount Prospect	2.7	19.9	0.8	0.0	0.0	20.3	9.3	0.6	0.5	2.7
Mundelein	0.0	17.8	0.1	0.0	0.0	25.2	10.6	0.0	0.0	3.9
Naperville	0.1	26.9	1.5	0.0	0.0	18.3	7.9	3.4	0.3	5.4
Niles	0.0	10.3	0.0	0.0	0.0	18.0	4.9	3.6	0.0	5.7
Normal	0.0	12.9	0.0	0.0	0.0	17.8	5.3	13.1	0.2	3.8
Northbrook	0.0	26.5	0.0	0.0	0.0	19.7	2.0	0.0	0.9	3.0
North Chicago	0.0	8.9	0.0	0.0	0.0	28.2	7.6	0.0	3.4	2.5
Oak Forest	0.0	24.6	1.6	0.0	0.0	24.7	4.5	0.0	0.0	3.2
Oak Lawn	0.0	10.6	0.1	0.0	1.2	21.9	8.2	0.6	1.0	3.7
Oak Park	0.0	9.3	5.0	0.0	1.3	18.9	4.0	0.0	16.9	3.8
Orland Park	0.0	5.7	0.0	0.0	0.0	22.6	9.5	12.2	1.0	3.3
Palatine	0.0	11.0	3.7	0.0	0.9	19.1	9.6	0.0	0.3	6.9
Park Ridge	0.0	15.4	0.8	0.0	0.5	18.1	10.5	0.4	0.7	1.4
Pekin	0.0	11.2	0.0	0.0	0.0	16.0	12.4	0.0	0.7	10.7
Peoria	0.0	12.3	2.1	0.0	0.0	15.1	1.5	1.8	14.4	5.5
Quincy	0.8	14.5	0.0	0.0	0.0	18.5	11.7	0.2	1.8	9.2
Rockford	8.7	16.4	0.8	0.0	0.1	22.4	5.7	0.0	5.5	4.3
Rock Island	0.0	8.7	0.5	0.0	0.0	19.1	11.8	13.5	2.5	4.2
Round Lake Beach	0.0	23.8	0.2	0.0	0.0	44.4	0.0	0.0	0.0	11.9
St. Charles	0.0	26.7	0.0	0.0	1.2	12.9	4.3	0.0	0.0	3.2
Schaumburg	0.0	9.7	5.2	0.0	2.6	26.7	7.0	3.6	1.4	2.3
Skokie	0.7	8.4	0.0	0.0	1.8	20.3	6.3	2.8	0.4	7.1
Springfield	0.0	15.0	0.4	0.0	1.9	15.8	4.0	2.4	4.8	2.3
Streamwood	0.0	23.3	0.0	0.0	0.0	28.6	0.0	1.5	0.7	2.4
Tinley Park	0.0	16.5	1.4	0.0	0.0	38.1	3.5	0.0	0.0	3.3
Urbana	0.5	28.9	3.2	0.0	0.0	15.7	2.7	0.0	9.9	6.3
Waukegan	0.0	10.3	0.7	0.0	0.0	31.8	6.8	2.4	6.7	4.9
Wheaton	0.3	18.5	1.1	0.0	0.0	26.0	4.4	1.0	3.5	3.0
Wheeling	0.0	22.2	0.2	0.0	0.0	25.8	5.6	0.0	0.1	1.8
Wilmette	0.0	32.5	1.1	0.0	0.6	19.8	10.7	0.0	0.0	2.7
Woodridge	0.0	12.0	0.0	0.0	0.0	34.1	2.0	0.2	0.0	6.9
INDIANA	X	X	X	X	X	X	X	X	X	X
Anderson	0.0	6.6	0.4	0.0	1.0	15.6	19.8	5.8	4.3	2.9
Bloomington	0.4	6.0	1.0	0.0	2.5	5.9	61.4	5.2	0.8	1.7
Carmel	0.0	3.9	0.0	0.0	0.7	10.8	18.2	0.2	0.0	3.6
Columbus	0.0	6.4	0.2	0.0	3.2	12.4	12.9	15.6	0.9	1.8
East Chicago	0.0	4.1	0.0	0.0	7.5	16.0	25.1	0.3	5.2	2.0
Elkhart	0.1	5.6	2.1	0.0	0.5	15.0	18.2	6.2	1.2	1.3
Evansville	0.9	3.7	0.2	0.0	1.8	15.8	13.2	6.6	2.6	3.8
Fishers town	0.0	8.2	0.0	0.0	0.0	16.0	22.0	3.5	0.0	2.9
Fort Wayne	0.0	9.7	0.8	0.0	1.0	18.9	14.1	8.5	2.1	3.3
Gary	0.0	5.6	0.0	0.0	3.2	11.5	14.1	16.0	4.0	3.8
Goshen	0.0	4.7	0.0	0.0	1.4	12.8	18.4	4.2	1.7	3.1
Greenwood	0.1	4.9	0.0	0.0	0.0	10.3	4.1	2.7	1.5	2.1
Hammond	0.0	4.1	0.0	0.0	0.6	10.6	8.6	12.0	4.6	3.4
Hobart	0.0	5.6	0.3	0.0	0.0	11.1	12.7	1.7	0.0	0.6
Indianapolis	3.5	5.3	0.1	0.0	22.0	7.9	9.6	5.8	9.7	10.1
Jeffersonville	NA	NA	NA	NA	NA	NA	NA	NA	NA	NA
Kokomo	NA	NA	NA	NA	NA	NA	NA	NA	NA	NA

City	City government finances, 2002 (cont'd) Debt outstanding Total (mil dol)	Per capita[1] (dollars)	Percent utility	City government employment, 2002	Climate[2] Average daily temperature (degrees Fahrenheit) Mean January	July	Limits January[3]	July[4]	Annual precipitation (inches)	Heating degree days	Cooling degree days
	137	138	139	140	141	142	143	144	145	146	147
ILLINOIS—Cont'd											
Elmhurst..................	79.9	1 840	8.3	365	21.0	73.2	12.9	83.7	35.82	6 536	752
Elmwood Park................	6.2	247	78.6	167	NA	NA	NA	NA	NA	NA	NA
Evanston..................	234.9	3 199	3.6	820	21.0	73.2	12.9	83.7	35.82	6 536	752
Freeport..................	17.7	682	0.0	197	17.1	72.9	7.8	84.2	33.08	7 169	645
Galesburg.................	41.4	1 244	0.0	306	21.1	75.1	12.5	85.3	36.55	6 314	925
Glendale Heights	22.5	683	0.0	235	21.0	73.2	12.9	83.7	35.82	6 536	752
Glen Ellyn.................	18.5	679	0.0	180	NA	NA	NA	NA	NA	NA	NA
Glenview..................	104.3	2 369	7.2	391	21.0	73.2	12.9	83.7	35.82	6 536	752
Granite City...............	NA	NA	NA	221	28.4	78.4	18.9	89.6	37.86	5 001	1 329
Gurnee...................	8.6	284	19.1	203	NA	NA	NA	NA	NA	NA	NA
Hanover Park...............	48.5	1 275	0.0	205	21.0	73.2	12.9	83.7	35.82	6 536	752
Harvey...................	19.1	644	0.0	288	20.6	73.7	12.2	83.8	37.12	6 541	780
Highland Park	27.5	901	31.3	343	21.0	73.2	12.9	83.7	35.82	6 536	752
Hoffman Estates	235.3	4 725	0.0	383	18.3	71.9	9.3	82.7	35.19	7 084	603
Joliet....................	49.2	415	30.5	848	20.7	73.8	11.8	84.6	36.26	6 463	776
Kankakee..................	51.6	1 899	0.0	289	21.1	74.6	12.3	85.2	35.31	6 322	921
Lansing...................	44.7	1 589	0.0	172	23.7	74.1	15.2	85.5	36.82	6 043	857
Lombard..................	9.2	213	0.0	312	21.0	73.2	12.9	83.7	35.82	6 536	752
Maywood..................	73.8	2 763	1.8	247	21.0	73.2	12.9	83.7	35.82	6 536	752
Moline...................	NA	NA	NA	423	19.9	75.2	11.3	85.9	39.08	6 474	911
Mount Prospect..............	23.9	426	1.6	315	21.0	73.2	12.9	83.7	35.82	6 536	752
Mundelein.................	19.6	614	3.3	174	NA	NA	NA	NA	NA	NA	NA
Naperville................	154.6	1 142	21.9	1 179	19.7	73.1	10.7	84.2	36.88	6 699	702
Niles	45.2	1 504	24.0	315	21.0	73.2	12.9	83.7	35.82	6 536	752
Normal...................	15.3	324	0.0	337	23.9	75.9	15.4	86.7	37.10	5 759	1 117
Northbrook................	38.7	1 139	38.5	323	21.0	73.2	12.9	83.7	35.82	6 536	752
North Chicago..............	10.2	281	0.0	193	19.3	71.2	10.8	81.1	34.20	7 136	542
Oak Forest................	11.8	414	0.0	135	20.6	73.7	12.2	83.8	37.12	6 541	780
Oak Lawn.................	41.4	747	40.4	424	22.4	75.1	14.9	84.4	37.38	6 176	940
Oak Park.................	55.3	1 071	33.3	514	22.4	75.1	14.9	84.4	37.38	6 176	940
Orland Park...............	34.1	640	0.0	498	20.6	73.7	12.2	83.8	37.12	6 541	780
Palatine..................	91.9	1 383	0.0	380	21.0	73.2	12.9	83.7	35.82	6 536	752
Park Ridge	11.1	293	0.0	283	21.0	73.2	12.9	83.7	35.82	6 536	752
Pekin....................	52.8	1 578	0.0	268	21.6	75.5	13.2	85.7	36.25	6 148	982
Peoria...................	158.6	1 407	0.0	992	21.6	75.5	13.2	85.7	36.25	6 148	982
Quincy...................	41.2	1 032	0.0	429	23.9	76.7	15.6	86.8	39.66	5 763	1 106
Rockford.................	110.1	729	25.4	1 250	18.2	73.2	9.8	83.8	36.28	6 969	702
Rock Island...............	39.0	1 000	40.8	466	19.9	75.2	11.3	85.9	39.08	6 474	911
Round Lake Beach	21.3	762	0.0	98	NA	NA	NA	NA	NA	NA	NA
St. Charles...............	32.9	1 064	11.4	280	NA	NA	NA	NA	NA	NA	NA
Schaumburg................	86.1	1 149	0.0	775	21.0	73.2	12.9	83.7	35.82	6 536	752
Skokie...................	85.4	1 354	4.0	585	21.0	73.2	12.9	83.7	35.82	6 536	752
Springfield................	290.5	2 597	65.2	1 784	24.2	76.5	15.9	86.9	35.25	5 688	1 141
Streamwood...............	7.8	208	25.1	201	18.3	71.9	9.3	82.7	35.19	7 084	603
Tinley Park...............	27.8	533	12.5	249	20.6	73.7	12.2	83.8	37.12	6 541	780
Urbana...................	25.2	659	0.0	291	23.8	75.0	16.0	85.3	39.71	5 854	985
Waukegan.................	105.8	1 159	3.4	614	19.3	71.2	10.8	81.1	34.20	7 136	542
Wheaton..................	27.4	496	0.0	352	21.1	73.9	12.3	86.0	36.68	6 354	818
Wheeling.................	14.6	412	0.0	230	21.0	73.2	12.9	83.7	35.82	6 536	752
Wilmette	31.3	1 137	50.3	202	21.0	73.2	12.9	83.7	35.82	6 536	752
Woodridge................	21.2	629	22.3	173	19.7	73.1	10.7	84.2	36.88	6 699	702
INDIANA................	X	X	X	X	X	X	X	X	X	X	X
Anderson.................	47.8	813	14.6	949	24.8	73.5	17.4	83.7	38.47	5 916	812
Bloomington	58.1	831	18.9	662	27.3	75.8	18.1	85.9	43.14	5 309	1 068
Carmel..................	43.7	1 068	10.3	400	25.5	75.4	17.2	85.5	39.94	5 615	1 014
Columbus................	20.3	522	40.4	474	22.0	72.1	13.6	83.6	37.50	6 576	644
East Chicago..............	23.7	747	0.0	853	23.7	74.1	15.2	85.5	36.82	6 043	857
Elkhart..................	23.6	456	35.9	626	23.3	72.9	16.1	82.9	39.14	6 331	728
Evansville................	111.7	938	11.0	1 268	30.1	78.4	21.2	89.1	43.14	4 708	1 376
Fishers town..............	18.8	424	0.0	239	NA	NA	NA	NA	NA	NA	NA
Fort Wayne	95.9	457	13.5	1 908	22.9	74.0	15.3	84.6	34.75	6 273	824
Gary....................	129.3	1 280	0.0	1 690	23.7	74.1	15.2	85.5	36.82	6 043	857
Goshen..................	17.1	576	29.8	242	NA	NA	NA	NA	NA	NA	NA
Greenwood...............	23.0	591	0.0	292	25.5	75.4	17.2	85.5	39.94	5 615	1 014
Hammond................	14.1	173	0.0	1 090	23.7	74.1	15.2	85.5	36.82	6 043	857
Hobart..................	3.7	139	0.0	265	NA	NA	NA	NA	NA	NA	NA
Indianapolis..............	3 024.2	3 810	18.8	12 645	NA	NA	NA	NA	NA	NA	NA
Jeffersonville..............	NA	NA	NA	222	NA	NA	NA	NA	NA	NA	NA
Kokomo..................	NA	NA	NA	542	22.1	73.1	13.6	84.4	39.89	6 429	770

1. Based on the population estimated as of July 1 of the year shown.   2. Represents normal values based on the 30-year period, 1961–1990.   3. Average daily minimum.   4. Average daily maximum.

STATE Place code	City	Land area,[1] 2000 (sq km)	Total persons	Rank	Per square kilometer	White	Black	Am. Indian, Alaska Native	Asian and Pacific Islander	Other race	Hispanic or Latino[2]	Non-Hispanic White
			Population, 2003			Population characteristics, 2000 — Percent — Race (alone or in combination)						
		1	2	3	4	5	6	7	8	9	10	11
	INDIANA—Cont'd											
18 40788	Lafayette	52.0	61 229	476	1 177.5	90.4	3.6	0.9	1.5	5.2	9.1	84.9
18 42426	Lawrence	52.0	40 795	786	784.5	80.2	16.4	0.7	2.3	2.3	4.7	76.0
18 46908	Marion	34.4	30 609	1 043	889.8	81.6	16.8	1.1	1.0	2.0	3.6	77.8
18 48528	Merrillville	86.2	30 990	1 034	359.5	71.6	23.6	0.8	1.9	4.6	9.7	64.5
18 48798	Michigan City	50.8	32 335	996	636.5	71.4	27.7	0.9	0.8	1.7	3.1	67.8
18 49932	Mishawaka	40.7	48 396	659	1 189.1	93.3	4.3	1.0	1.8	1.6	2.8	90.2
18 51876	Muncie	62.6	66 521	433	1 062.6	87.1	11.7	0.7	1.3	0.9	1.4	85.0
18 52326	New Albany	37.9	36 973	872	975.5	91.5	7.9	0.8	0.8	0.9	1.4	89.4
18 54180	Noblesville city, IN	46.4	33 046	976	712.2	97.2	1.4	0.5	1.2	0.8	1.4	95.7
18 61092	Portage	65.9	34 915	927	529.8	94.2	1.8	0.8	1.0	4.1	9.9	86.7
18 64260	Richmond	60.1	38 201	837	635.6	88.8	10.2	0.8	1.1	1.4	2.0	85.9
18 71000	South Bend	100.2	105 540	222	1 053.3	68.4	26.1	1.0	1.8	5.8	8.5	63.3
18 75428	Terre Haute	80.9	58 096	523	718.1	88.0	10.7	0.9	1.6	0.9	1.6	85.3
18 78326	Valparaiso	28.2	28 365	1 116	1 005.9	95.7	1.9	0.7	2.0	1.4	3.3	92.1
18 82862	West Lafayette	14.3	29 835	1 070	2 086.4	84.6	2.7	0.4	12.4	1.7	3.2	81.5
19 00000	IOWA	144 701.0	2 944 062	X	20.3	94.9	2.5	0.6	1.6	1.6	2.8	92.6
19 01855	Ames	55.9	53 284	595	953.2	88.4	3.0	0.4	8.4	1.1	2.0	86.3
19 02305	Ankeny	43.4	31 144	1 025	717.6	97.7	1.0	0.3	1.3	0.6	1.1	96.4
19 06355	Bettendorf	55.0	31 456	1 020	571.9	96.0	1.9	0.6	1.8	0.9	2.5	93.5
19 09550	Burlington	36.4	25 966	1 202	713.4	92.9	5.9	0.7	1.0	1.2	2.1	90.6
19 11755	Cedar Falls	73.3	36 429	882	497.0	96.1	2.0	0.4	2.0	0.7	1.1	94.6
19 12000	Cedar Rapids	163.5	122 542	188	749.5	93.5	4.6	0.7	2.2	0.9	1.7	90.9
19 14430	Clinton	92.1	27 437	1 146	297.9	95.1	3.8	0.8	0.9	0.8	1.7	92.9
19 16860	Council Bluffs	96.8	58 656	516	606.0	95.9	1.4	0.9	0.9	2.2	4.5	92.5
19 19000	Davenport	162.6	97 512	254	599.7	85.8	10.4	1.0	2.4	3.0	5.4	81.3
19 21000	Des Moines	196.3	196 093	103	998.9	84.1	8.9	0.8	4.1	4.4	6.6	79.6
19 22395	Dubuque	68.6	57 204	531	833.9	97.0	1.5	0.5	1.1	0.9	1.6	95.4
19 28515	Fort Dodge	37.7	25 917	1 203	687.5	93.7	4.4	0.6	1.1	1.6	2.9	91.1
19 38595	Iowa City	62.6	63 807	453	1 019.3	88.8	4.4	0.6	6.3	1.7	2.9	85.8
19 49485	Marion	31.1	28 756	1 104	924.6	97.8	0.9	0.4	1.2	0.6	1.1	96.4
19 49755	Marshalltown	46.7	25 860	1 207	553.7	88.4	1.8	0.7	1.4	9.6	12.6	83.6
19 50160	Mason City	66.8	28 274	1 120	423.3	96.7	1.7	0.5	1.1	1.6	3.4	93.4
19 73335	Sioux City	141.9	83 876	318	591.1	87.2	3.1	2.8	3.3	6.0	10.9	80.6
19 79950	Urbandale	53.6	31 868	1 006	594.6	96.0	1.9	0.3	2.1	0.8	1.6	94.3
19 82425	Waterloo	157.3	67 054	427	426.3	83.4	14.7	0.6	1.2	2.2	2.6	80.6
19 83910	West Des Moines	69.4	51 699	607	744.9	93.8	2.2	0.4	3.2	1.7	3.0	91.1
20 00000	KANSAS	211 899.6	2 723 507	X	12.9	87.9	6.3	1.8	2.2	4.0	7.0	83.1
20 18250	Dodge City	32.7	25 568	1 213	781.9	73.7	2.4	1.2	2.8	22.6	42.9	51.5
20 21275	Emporia	25.6	26 666	1 185	1 041.6	80.9	3.6	1.2	3.0	13.9	21.5	71.1
20 25325	Garden City	22.1	27 216	1 154	1 231.5	71.1	1.9	1.6	4.1	24.1	43.9	49.8
20 33625	Hutchinson	54.7	40 783	787	745.6	90.6	5.0	1.4	0.9	4.4	7.7	85.4
20 36000	Kansas City	321.8	145 757	150	452.9	58.1	31.3	1.7	2.2	9.9	16.8	48.9
20 38900	Lawrence	72.8	82 120	324	1 128.0	86.4	6.2	4.0	4.7	2.0	3.6	82.1
20 39000	Leavenworth	60.9	35 211	917	578.2	79.1	17.6	1.6	2.5	2.4	5.1	74.1
20 39075	Leawood	39.1	28 888	1 098	738.8	95.9	1.6	0.3	2.5	0.4	1.3	94.2
20 39350	Lenexa	88.8	41 995	767	472.9	90.9	3.7	0.9	4.2	2.1	4.0	87.5
20 44250	Manhattan	38.9	44 733	721	1 149.9	89.0	5.6	1.0	4.8	1.8	3.5	85.4
20 52575	Olathe	140.3	105 274	225	750.3	90.2	4.3	0.9	3.3	3.2	5.4	86.2
20 53775	Overland Park	147.0	160 368	132	1 090.9	91.9	2.9	0.7	4.4	1.7	3.8	88.4
20 62700	Salina	58.9	45 833	705	778.1	89.8	4.5	1.3	2.4	4.4	6.7	85.4
20 64500	Shawnee	108.1	54 093	585	500.4	92.0	3.5	0.8	3.2	2.5	4.4	88.2
20 71000	Topeka	145.1	122 008	189	840.9	81.2	13.2	2.5	1.6	5.1	8.9	75.1
20 79000	Wichita	351.6	354 617	50	1 008.6	77.8	12.4	2.3	4.7	6.1	9.6	71.7
21 00000	KENTUCKY	102 895.5	4 117 827	X	40.0	91.0	7.7	0.6	1.0	0.8	1.5	89.3
21 08902	Bowling Green	91.7	50 663	624	552.5	82.6	13.3	0.6	2.6	3.0	4.1	79.1
21 17848	Covington	34.0	42 687	752	1 255.5	88.5	11.0	0.7	0.6	0.9	1.4	86.3
21 28900	Frankfort	38.2	27 408	1 148	717.5	83.2	15.7	0.5	1.4	1.0	1.5	81.1
21 35866	Henderson	38.8	27 468	1 144	707.9	88.2	11.0	0.5	0.5	0.8	1.3	86.7
21 37918	Hopkinsville	62.2	28 678	1 107	461.4	67.2	31.6	0.6	1.2	0.9	1.7	65.3
21 40222	Jeffersontown	25.8	26 331	1 194	1 020.6	88.0	9.2	0.6	2.1	1.7	2.5	85.5
21 46027	Lexington-Fayette	736.9	266 798	68	362.1	82.4	14.1	0.6	2.9	1.7	3.3	79.1
21 48000	Louisville	160.9	248 762	69	1 546.1	64.2	33.9	0.7	1.8	1.2	1.9	61.9
21 58620	Owensboro	45.1	54 312	581	1 204.3	91.8	7.6	0.5	0.8	0.7	1.0	90.1
21 58836	Paducah	50.5	25 565	1 214	506.2	74.2	25.0	0.8	1.0	0.7	1.4	72.1
21 65226	Richmond	49.5	29 080	1 092	587.5	89.7	9.1	0.8	1.4	0.7	1.2	87.5

1. Dry land or land partially or temporarily covered by water.   2. Hispanic or Latino persons may be of any race.

Table D. Cities — **Population and Households**

City	Population characteristics, 2000 (cont'd)										Population			
	Age of population (percent)										Census counts		Percent change	
	Under 5 years	5 to 17 years	18 to 24 years	25 to 34 years	35 to 44 years	45 to 54 years	55 to 64 years	65 to 74 years	75 years and over	Percent female	1990	2000	1990–2000	2000–2003
	12	13	14	15	16	17	18	19	20	21	22	23	24	25
INDIANA—Cont'd														
Lafayette	7.0	16.2	14.2	17.4	13.9	11.8	7.4	5.9	6.1	50.6	45 933	56 397	26.4	8.6
Lawrence	9.1	20.9	7.7	17.3	18.9	11.8	6.2	4.5	3.7	51.2	26 849	38 915	44.9	4.8
Marion	6.5	16.7	12.5	12.5	13.5	12.1	9.2	8.3	8.7	53.0	32 607	31 320	-3.9	-2.3
Merrillville	6.6	18.0	8.7	13.7	15.7	13.7	8.5	6.9	8.2	52.3	27 257	30 560	12.1	1.4
Michigan City	7.6	17.4	9.6	15.1	15.6	12.6	8.0	6.9	7.2	49.6	33 822	32 900	-2.7	-1.7
Mishawaka	7.1	16.9	11.8	16.3	14.4	12.0	7.4	6.5	7.5	52.7	42 635	46 557	9.2	3.9
Muncie	5.8	13.9	24.6	12.9	11.2	10.3	8.0	6.6	6.6	52.7	71 170	67 430	-5.3	-1.3
New Albany	6.9	17.2	9.6	14.0	15.2	13.2	8.6	7.6	7.8	53.1	36 322	37 603	3.5	-1.7
Noblesville city, IN	9.3	20.2	7.3	17.0	17.5	13.0	7.2	4.4	4.1	50.9	17 655	28 590	61.9	15.6
Portage	7.2	18.9	9.4	13.8	16.1	14.2	8.6	6.0	5.8	51.5	29 062	33 496	15.3	4.2
Richmond	6.8	16.6	11.0	13.7	13.7	12.5	9.1	8.1	8.3	53.0	38 705	39 124	1.1	-2.4
South Bend	8.3	19.0	10.4	15.5	13.8	11.5	6.7	6.8	8.0	52.3	105 511	107 789	2.2	-2.1
Terre Haute	6.2	15.2	18.7	13.4	13.2	11.2	7.2	6.5	8.3	50.7	57 475	59 614	3.7	-2.5
Valparaiso	5.9	15.3	17.4	14.5	13.6	13.0	7.2	5.8	7.3	52.1	24 414	27 428	12.3	3.4
West Lafayette	2.5	7.9	54.6	10.2	6.7	6.5	3.9	3.1	4.6	42.8	26 144	28 778	10.1	3.7
IOWA	6.4	18.6	10.2	12.4	15.2	13.4	8.8	7.2	7.7	50.9	2 776 831	2 926 324	5.4	0.6
Ames	4.4	10.2	40.0	14.2	9.6	8.7	5.2	3.9	3.8	47.8	47 198	50 731	7.5	5.0
Ankeny	8.4	18.8	11.4	16.9	16.5	13.0	7.1	4.2	3.7	51.5	18 482	27 117	46.7	14.9
Bettendorf	6.2	20.1	6.7	11.4	16.6	16.9	9.7	6.5	5.9	51.5	28 139	31 275	11.1	0.6
Burlington	6.6	17.9	8.9	12.4	14.3	13.7	9.0	7.9	9.3	52.4	27 208	26 839	-1.4	-3.3
Cedar Falls	4.4	13.6	30.6	9.5	11.0	12.0	7.0	5.4	6.5	53.1	34 298	36 145	5.4	0.8
Cedar Rapids	7.1	17.3	10.8	15.2	15.5	13.0	8.0	6.4	6.7	51.3	108 772	120 758	11.0	1.5
Clinton	6.6	18.0	9.1	11.6	15.1	13.1	9.4	8.0	9.1	52.3	29 201	27 772	-4.9	-1.2
Council Bluffs	7.2	18.8	10.3	14.2	15.4	12.5	8.2	7.2	6.1	51.6	54 315	58 268	7.3	0.7
Davenport	7.4	18.8	10.7	15.1	14.9	13.0	7.9	6.0	6.2	51.4	95 333	98 359	3.2	-0.9
Des Moines	7.5	17.3	10.6	16.3	15.5	12.6	7.8	6.0	6.4	51.6	193 189	198 682	2.8	-1.3
Dubuque	6.2	17.4	11.8	11.9	14.6	13.1	8.5	7.7	8.9	52.6	57 538	57 686	0.3	-0.8
Fort Dodge	6.8	17.5	10.7	11.3	13.9	12.8	8.5	8.2	10.4	52.5	26 057	25 136	-2.9	3.1
Iowa City	4.6	11.6	32.8	16.4	11.7	10.6	5.2	3.5	3.5	51.0	59 735	62 220	4.2	2.6
Marion	7.4	19.0	8.2	15.3	16.6	13.5	8.6	5.9	5.5	51.4	20 422	26 294	28.8	9.4
Marshalltown	6.7	17.8	8.9	12.3	13.7	13.7	9.2	8.1	9.5	50.5	25 178	26 009	3.3	-0.6
Mason City	6.2	17.3	10.2	11.9	14.8	13.2	8.5	8.4	9.4	52.6	29 040	29 172	0.5	-3.1
Sioux City	7.9	19.2	11.0	14.2	14.3	12.6	7.6	6.6	6.7	51.2	80 505	85 013	5.6	-1.3
Urbandale	6.7	19.6	7.0	13.4	17.9	15.6	9.0	6.1	4.6	51.7	23 775	29 072	22.3	9.6
Waterloo	7.0	17.6	10.6	13.6	13.8	13.6	8.4	7.3	8.0	52.0	66 467	68 747	3.4	-2.5
West Des Moines	7.7	16.9	9.7	19.2	16.3	13.0	7.3	5.3	4.5	52.1	31 702	46 403	46.4	11.4
KANSAS	7.0	19.5	10.3	13.0	15.6	13.2	8.2	6.5	6.7	50.6	2 477 588	2 688 418	8.5	1.3
Dodge City	9.9	21.3	12.3	16.3	13.7	10.3	6.2	4.6	5.3	48.4	21 129	25 176	19.2	1.6
Emporia	7.3	18.0	19.4	13.9	13.3	10.8	6.2	4.8	6.2	51.1	25 512	26 760	4.9	-0.4
Garden City	10.2	22.5	11.6	16.2	14.9	10.5	6.1	4.1	4.1	49.4	24 097	28 451	18.1	-4.3
Hutchinson	6.6	16.6	11.0	12.8	15.1	12.7	8.5	7.8	9.1	49.6	39 308	40 787	3.8	0.0
Kansas City	8.1	20.4	10.6	14.5	14.9	12.1	7.7	6.1	5.5	51.1	151 521	146 866	-3.1	-0.8
Lawrence	5.4	13.1	30.7	16.2	12.2	10.2	4.9	3.6	3.6	50.3	65 608	80 098	22.1	2.5
Leavenworth	8.2	19.5	8.8	15.6	19.2	12.1	6.9	4.9	4.8	47.1	38 495	35 420	-8.0	-0.6
Leawood	6.3	23.8	4.2	5.9	17.4	19.6	10.1	7.0	5.6	51.0	19 693	27 656	40.4	4.5
Lenexa	6.4	19.3	9.5	14.7	17.3	16.5	7.7	3.5	5.1	51.1	34 110	40 238	18.0	4.4
Manhattan	4.6	11.2	39.2	14.0	10.0	8.6	4.6	3.6	4.2	48.5	43 081	44 831	4.1	-0.2
Olathe	9.4	21.5	9.2	18.0	18.7	12.8	5.4	2.8	2.4	50.1	63 402	92 962	46.6	13.2
Overland Park	7.1	19.0	7.0	14.6	17.9	14.9	8.0	5.8	5.6	51.6	111 790	149 080	33.4	7.6
Salina	7.1	18.8	10.0	13.6	15.1	12.8	8.3	7.1	7.1	51.1	42 299	45 679	8.0	0.3
Shawnee	7.7	19.1	7.8	15.8	18.4	14.6	8.1	5.0	3.5	50.8	37 962	47 996	26.4	12.7
Topeka	7.0	17.2	9.9	14.0	14.8	13.5	8.4	7.4	7.7	52.0	119 883	122 377	2.1	-0.3
Wichita	8.0	19.1	10.1	15.0	15.7	12.8	7.4	6.0	5.9	50.7	304 017	344 284	13.2	3.0
KENTUCKY	6.6	18.0	9.9	14.1	15.9	13.8	9.2	6.8	5.7	51.1	3 686 892	4 041 769	9.6	1.9
Bowling Green	6.0	14.2	23.5	14.5	12.4	10.4	7.1	5.9	6.0	51.6	41 688	49 296	18.2	2.8
Covington	7.8	18.0	10.0	17.3	16.0	11.9	7.1	5.9	6.0	51.1	43 646	43 370	-0.6	-1.6
Frankfort	6.2	15.4	11.7	15.3	15.0	13.6	8.8	7.0	6.9	52.3	26 535	27 741	4.5	-1.2
Henderson	6.7	16.9	9.2	14.1	15.3	13.7	8.8	7.8	7.4	52.8	25 945	27 373	5.5	0.3
Hopkinsville	7.4	19.0	9.7	13.7	14.6	12.1	8.7	7.6	7.3	53.2	29 809	30 089	0.9	-4.7
Jeffersontown	7.2	17.5	7.7	16.2	17.2	14.6	8.7	6.0	4.8	51.9	23 223	26 633	14.7	-1.1
Lexington-Fayette	6.2	15.1	14.6	17.1	16.1	13.2	7.6	5.3	4.7	50.9	225 366	260 512	15.6	2.4
Louisville	6.6	17.0	10.4	14.7	15.7	13.2	7.8	7.3	7.4	52.7	269 555	256 231	-4.9	-2.9
Owensboro	6.8	17.4	9.8	12.7	14.7	13.1	9.2	8.2	8.1	53.3	53 577	54 067	0.9	0.5
Paducah	6.5	16.0	8.5	12.3	13.9	13.2	9.2	8.8	11.4	54.5	27 256	26 307	-3.5	-2.8
Richmond	6.0	11.6	31.7	16.6	10.9	8.3	5.5	4.6	4.9	52.5	21 183	27 152	28.2	7.1

Table D. Cities — Group Quarters, Crime, and Education

City	Households, 2000					Persons in group quarters, 2000				Serious crimes known to police,[2] 2002				Education, 2000			
				Percent			Institutional			Total		Rate[2]		School enrollment[4]		Attainment[5] (percent)	
	Number	Percent change, 1990–2000	Persons per household	Female family householder[1]	One-person	Total	Total	Persons in nursing homes	Non-institutional	Number	Rate[3]	Violent	Property	Public	Private	High school graduate or less	Bachelor's degree or more
	26	27	28	29	30	31	32	33	34	35	36	37	38	39	40	41	42
INDIANA—Cont'd																	
Lafayette	24 060	33.1	2.31	10.2	33.2	709	524	505	185	3 346	5 857	399	5 458	13 180	1 726	51.2	23.7
Lawrence	14 853	40.0	2.60	13.0	24.8	286	263	263	23	1 101	2 793	416	2 377	8 724	2 023	43.2	26.8
Marion	12 462	-1.8	2.30	14.7	33.8	2 631	1 119	623	1 512	2 166	6 827	864	5 964	5 541	2 210	65.9	13.4
Merrillville	11 678	16.7	2.57	12.6	26.1	555	432	396	123	1 077	3 479	110	3 370	7 247	943	50.0	20.2
Michigan City	12 550	0.1	2.41	18.1	30.9	2 661	2 585	385	76	2 386	7 160	387	6 773	7 026	1 246	63.5	12.1
Mishawaka	20 248	12.5	2.23	13.0	35.8	1 305	354	215	951	4 119	8 734	316	8 418	8 999	2 747	55.6	18.1
Muncie	27 322	0.5	2.24	13.0	34.1	6 201	1 036	574	5 165	3 214	4 706	416	4 290	23 096	1 164	58.7	19.0
New Albany	15 959	8.6	2.31	16.1	30.8	680	615	509	65	3 109	8 162	593	7 569	7 384	1 442	57.0	15.9
Noblesville city, IN	10 576	59.0	2.64	9.2	21.3	645	628	235	17	671	2 317	142	2 175	6 552	1 044	32.7	40.9
Portage	12 746	21.2	2.60	12.2	23.9	406	358	358	48	1 559	4 595	253	4 341	7 389	898	63.8	10.1
Richmond	16 287	4.5	2.29	13.9	33.0	1 832	859	418	973	2 220	5 602	495	5 107	7 775	1 620	62.1	13.8
South Bend	42 908	1.5	2.45	17.0	32.5	2 817	1 662	1 072	1 155	8 203	7 513	751	6 762	21 971	6 646	53.6	20.3
Terre Haute	22 870	6.4	2.28	14.0	34.9	7 401	2 873	674	4 528	NA	NA	NA	NA	16 614	2 579	55.8	19.7
Valparaiso	10 867	21.0	2.27	9.7	33.4	2 708	743	498	1 965	881	3 171	284	2 887	5 034	3 476	38.2	34.5
West Lafayette	10 462	14.3	2.26	4.4	32.7	5 138	215	215	4 923	610	2 093	79	2 014	18 753	1 038	14.0	69.7
IOWA	1 149 276	8.0	2.46	8.6	27.2	104 169	50 256	33 428	53 913	101 265	3 448	286	3 163	669 809	122 248	50.0	21.2
Ames	18 085	15.8	2.30	5.3	28.5	9 122	186	137	8 936	2 075	4 076	263	3 812	26 256	1 019	17.0	58.6
Ankeny	10 339	53.0	2.57	7.3	21.8	558	235	235	323	649	2 385	77	2 308	6 808	1 130	27.3	39.1
Bettendorf	12 474	17.0	2.48	8.1	26.0	294	180	178	114	965	3 075	360	2 715	7 182	1 479	30.3	38.8
Burlington	11 102	1.1	2.36	12.0	31.0	633	475	339	158	1 310	4 864	568	4 296	5 260	988	53.4	16.1
Cedar Falls	12 833	9.8	2.45	7.5	25.5	4 694	524	524	4 170	1 143	3 151	303	2 848	15 324	976	32.5	39.2
Cedar Rapids	49 820	14.1	2.36	10.0	30.2	3 369	1 407	985	1 962	7 336	6 053	354	5 699	25 135	6 390	39.2	28.4
Clinton	11 427	-2.1	2.36	11.7	30.2	787	326	107	461	NA	NA	NA	NA	5 873	1 119	56.2	14.9
Council Bluffs	22 889	8.3	2.49	14.3	27.9	1 329	858	432	471	6 884	11 773	893	10 880	12 816	1 534	57.6	13.9
Davenport	39 124	5.2	2.44	13.4	29.5	2 877	1 471	875	1 406	9 601	9 726	1 564	8 162	21 108	6 723	48.2	21.5
Des Moines	80 504	2.6	2.39	12.6	31.9	6 537	2 670	1 586	3 867	13 829	6 936	392	6 543	38 472	10 647	50.5	21.8
Dubuque	22 560	5.2	2.37	10.0	31.0	4 167	1 047	867	3 120	2 095	3 619	276	3 342	9 075	6 474	53.4	23.3
Fort Dodge	10 470	-0.3	2.29	11.4	30.8	1 165	815	599	350	1 912	7 580	761	6 819	5 284	997	50.6	19.4
Iowa City	25 202	14.8	2.23	6.7	33.8	6 110	462	115	5 648	2 221	3 557	572	2 985	28 444	1 778	20.6	55.9
Marion	10 458	34.6	2.47	8.4	26.0	430	230	230	200	361	1 368	68	1 300	5 841	1 019	35.8	29.1
Marshalltown	10 175	2.0	2.44	10.8	29.7	1 224	1 146	1 024	78	1 631	6 249	854	5 394	5 577	583	56.6	18.0
Mason City	12 368	2.8	2.27	10.3	33.5	1 125	616	476	509	1 757	6 002	133	5 868	5 978	1 118	47.0	20.0
Sioux City	32 054	5.1	2.57	12.2	27.7	2 674	1 172	777	1 502	5 759	6 750	636	6 114	17 933	4 609	54.2	19.0
Urbandale	11 484	27.4	2.51	7.1	24.2	304	252	252	52	1 047	3 589	230	3 359	6 179	1 678	25.2	43.7
Waterloo	28 169	4.2	2.39	13.3	30.0	1 551	819	413	732	4 236	6 140	468	5 672	14 991	2 935	52.8	19.4
West Des Moines	19 826	52.8	2.33	7.7	30.5	299	220	214	79	1 810	3 887	103	3 784	9 029	2 950	21.9	48.5
KANSAS	1 037 891	9.9	2.51	9.3	27.0	81 950	45 396	25 248	36 554	110 997	4 087	377	3 710	654 604	102 356	43.8	25.8
Dodge City	8 395	10.3	2.94	10.3	23.5	493	274	202	219	1 574	6 189	491	5 697	6 406	546	53.4	17.3
Emporia	10 253	5.1	2.47	9.4	31.1	1 465	318	196	1 147	1 622	6 000	366	5 634	8 846	291	49.7	23.8
Garden City	9 338	15.7	2.99	10.8	22.1	572	237	151	335	2 051	7 136	647	6 489	7 788	535	57.4	14.5
Hutchinson	16 335	4.3	2.31	10.3	31.7	2 974	2 711	571	263	773	1 876	114	1 762	8 573	1 003	47.9	17.2
Kansas City	55 500	-2.9	2.62	18.2	29.2	1 348	872	540	476	NA	NA	NA	NA	34 366	5 198	61.0	11.7
Lawrence	31 388	28.0	2.30	8.7	30.6	7 957	437	343	7 520	3 961	4 895	402	4 494	33 713	2 830	25.6	47.7
Leavenworth	12 035	4.9	2.60	11.6	27.1	4 103	3 462	157	641	1 515	4 234	598	3 636	8 203	1 776	44.6	27.0
Leawood	9 841	42.9	2.81	5.1	15.2	45	42	38	3	574	2 054	193	1 861	5 866	2 750	9.6	68.0
Lenexa	15 574	22.5	2.54	7.6	24.3	670	668	668	2	NA	NA	NA	NA	8 923	2 440	19.3	49.8
Manhattan	16 949	15.4	2.30	6.6	30.5	5 794	369	294	5 425	NA	NA	NA	NA	22 421	1 007	23.3	48.2
Olathe	32 314	50.7	2.83	9.0	18.4	1 595	742	625	853	3 299	3 513	340	3 173	23 413	5 156	27.9	39.9
Overland Park	59 703	32.9	2.47	7.4	27.4	1 588	1 433	1 139	155	3 436	2 281	167	2 115	30 607	8 386	19.0	52.1
Salina	18 523	7.1	2.39	10.5	30.1	1 367	685	429	682	2 987	6 473	332	6 141	9 928	1 970	48.3	20.3
Shawnee	18 522	27.2	2.58	8.2	22.7	248	198	198	50	1 536	3 168	179	2 988	10 165	2 905	28.2	39.5
Topeka	52 190	4.5	2.27	13.1	35.0	4 078	3 336	1 604	742	11 294	9 136	800	8 336	24 453	5 266	47.3	25.3
Wichita	139 087	12.9	2.44	11.6	31.2	4 877	3 196	1 514	1 681	24 104	6 930	681	6 250	78 315	17 019	44.8	25.3
KENTUCKY	1 590 647	15.3	2.47	11.8	26.0	114 804	62 057	29 266	52 747	118 799	2 903	279	2 624	859 020	148 432	59.4	17.1
Bowling Green	19 277	20.7	2.27	13.1	33.5	5 489	1 101	573	4 388	3 498	7 007	721	6 286	15 863	952	48.9	26.9
Covington	18 257	5.4	2.31	16.5	36.5	1 120	842	451	278	NA	NA	NA	NA	8 517	1 782	63.5	13.3
Frankfort	12 314	11.6	2.14	14.1	37.6	1 331	594	98	737	NA	NA	NA	NA	5 912	734	50.7	24.9
Henderson	11 693	10.9	2.27	14.1	32.1	808	677	359	131	NA	NA	NA	NA	5 284	763	60.8	14.0
Hopkinsville	12 174	6.8	2.39	18.2	29.7	999	894	451	105	2 008	6 590	391	6 200	6 591	1 076	56.1	16.0
Jeffersontown	10 653	19.7	2.46	10.7	26.4	402	400	400	2	NA	NA	NA	NA	4 933	1 977	33.6	32.6
Lexington-Fayette	108 288	21.0	2.29	11.5	31.7	12 723	4 722	1 423	8 001	12 521	4 746	542	4 205	64 583	11 747	36.6	35.6
Louisville	111 414	-1.5	2.22	19.2	37.9	8 527	3 664	2 065	4 863	15 439	5 950	785	5 165	54 253	12 990	52.8	21.3
Owensboro	22 659	4.6	2.29	13.9	33.3	2 223	1 103	750	1 120	2 582	4 716	258	4 458	10 237	2 585	56.1	17.8
Paducah	11 825	-1.1	2.12	16.2	39.3	1 212	1 132	641	80	1 962	7 365	642	6 723	5 217	773	54.5	18.6
Richmond	10 795	49.7	2.14	12.8	34.7	4 074	372	183	3 702	1 630	5 928	375	5 554	10 342	525	48.4	25.7

1. No spouse present. 2. Data for serious crimes have not been adjusted for underreporting. This may affect comparability between geographic areas and over time. 3. Per 100,000 population estimated by the FBI. 4. All persons 3 years old and over enrolled in nursery school through college. 5. Persons 25 years old and over.

City	Money income, 1999							Housing units, 2000					
	Households				Percent below poverty					Vacant units			
	Median income				Persons		Families						
	Per capita income[1] (dollars)	Dollars	Percent change, 1989–1999 (constant 1999 dollars)	Percent with income of $100,000 or more	Total	Percent change in rate, 1989–1999	Total	Total	Percent change, 1990–2000	Vacant units for sale or rent[2]	For seasonal use (percent)	Home owner vacancy rate	Renter vacancy rate
	43	44	45	46	47	48	49	50	51	52	53	54	55
INDIANA—Cont'd													
Lafayette	19 217	35 859	-1.2	5.8	12.1	36.0	8.0	25 602	32.9	1 542	0.3	1.6	6.8
Lawrence	22 543	47 838	20.1	12.5	6.7	-9.5	4.8	16 292	40.2	1 439	0.3	3.4	15.3
Marion	16 378	30 440	3.0	5.8	16.9	-10.6	12.6	13 820	-1.3	1 358	0.2	2.4	10.6
Merrillville	22 293	49 545	1.8	8.6	4.3	19.4	2.6	12 303	19.2	625	0.3	1.9	8.3
Michigan City	16 995	33 732	8.6	4.2	13.3	-18.9	10.4	14 221	1.6	1 671	3.4	2.7	8.2
Mishawaka	18 434	33 986	4.1	4.2	9.9	8.8	7.3	21 572	13.4	1 324	0.4	1.6	6.7
Muncie	15 814	26 613	2.4	3.8	23.1	-2.9	14.3	30 205	1.3	2 883	0.3	2.2	9.3
New Albany	18 365	34 923	8.6	4.8	13.7	-11.6	11.4	17 098	9.7	1 139	0.3	1.7	7.4
Noblesville city, IN	28 813	61 455	24.8	21.4	5.4	-28.0	4.3	11 294	58.4	718	0.6	1.7	11.1
Portage	20 146	47 500	6.8	7.4	7.5	-5.1	5.8	13 375	23.1	629	0.4	1.3	8.0
Richmond	17 096	30 210	9.2	4.5	15.7	-23.4	12.1	17 647	4.2	1 360	0.4	2.0	9.4
South Bend	17 121	32 439	0.1	5.1	16.7	16.0	13.6	46 349	1.3	3 441	0.5	2.0	7.6
Terre Haute	15 728	28 018	9.1	4.6	19.2	-5.9	14.8	25 636	6.5	2 766	0.3	3.2	11.9
Valparaiso	22 509	45 799	7.9	10.5	9.1	5.8	4.8	11 559	24.4	692	0.5	1.5	7.4
West Lafayette	18 337	24 869	-15.0	11.9	38.3	12.0	9.5	10 819	14.3	357	0.2	1.4	2.5
IOWA	19 674	39 469	12.0	7.3	9.1	-20.9	6.0	1 232 511	7.8	83 235	1.3	1.7	6.8
Ames	18 881	36 042	8.9	9.6	20.4	-15.4	7.6	18 757	16.8	672	0.3	1.2	3.3
Ankeny	25 143	55 162	12.2	14.1	4.0	-28.6	2.5	10 882	55.8	543	0.2	3.4	5.5
Bettendorf	28 053	54 217	0.4	17.1	4.8	2.1	3.3	13 044	17.9	570	0.5	1.5	7.3
Burlington	19 450	33 770	0.1	4.9	12.6	-8.0	10.0	11 985	1.8	883	0.4	2.0	9.1
Cedar Falls	19 140	40 226	6.9	9.8	16.7	-0.6	5.6	13 271	10.0	438	0.2	0.8	3.4
Cedar Rapids	22 589	43 704	3.4	8.9	7.5	-25.0	4.9	52 240	14.9	2 420	0.3	1.5	5.8
Clinton	17 320	34 159	7.9	3.7	12.5	-1.6	10.0	12 412	-1.4	985	0.4	1.8	11.2
Council Bluffs	18 143	36 221	7.8	5.3	10.3	-15.6	8.2	24 340	9.4	1 451	0.3	1.4	9.3
Davenport	18 828	37 242	5.7	6.4	14.1	-9.6	10.5	41 350	2.5	2 226	0.3	1.6	7.3
Des Moines	19 467	38 408	7.1	6.3	11.4	-11.6	7.9	85 067	2.1	4 563	0.2	1.4	6.8
Dubuque	19 616	36 785	1.3	6.5	9.5	-12.8	5.5	23 819	6.4	1 259	0.3	0.8	8.0
Fort Dodge	18 018	33 361	9.0	4.9	11.6	-9.4	7.7	11 168	-0.4	698	0.4	1.5	8.2
Iowa City	20 269	34 977	6.0	10.4	21.7	-7.3	6.7	26 083	16.1	881	0.2	2.4	2.2
Marion	23 158	48 591	8.2	11.3	5.2	-20.0	3.9	10 968	37.1	510	0.3	2.6	5.7
Marshalltown	19 113	35 688	-2.8	5.5	12.5	31.6	8.8	10 857	2.1	682	0.6	1.7	7.8
Mason City	18 899	33 852	4.3	5.9	10.0	4.2	7.2	13 029	2.8	661	0.3	1.5	5.4
Sioux City	18 666	37 429	11.2	7.0	11.2	-18.8	7.9	33 816	5.1	1 762	0.2	1.4	7.8
Urbandale	29 021	59 744	4.2	17.9	3.7	37.0	2.5	11 869	27.7	385	0.3	1.2	5.1
Waterloo	18 558	34 092	7.6	5.8	13.7	-18.9	10.0	29 499	1.6	1 330	0.2	0.9	5.9
West Des Moines	31 405	54 139	-1.8	18.7	4.5	36.4	2.8	20 815	52.3	989	0.7	1.6	5.9
KANSAS	20 506	40 624	10.8	9.3	9.9	-13.9	6.7	1 131 200	8.3	93 309	0.9	2.0	8.8
Dodge City	15 538	37 156	11.6	6.1	13.9	10.3	11.1	8 976	8.7	581	0.3	1.5	8.3
Emporia	15 157	30 809	1.4	3.8	17.9	7.2	12.4	11 019	2.7	766	0.3	1.5	7.5
Garden City	15 200	37 752	0.4	4.7	14.3	53.8	9.9	9 907	15.4	569	0.2	1.5	7.3
Hutchinson	17 964	32 645	3.1	4.8	12.7	5.8	9.8	17 693	3.1	1 358	0.3	1.7	10.1
Kansas City	15 737	33 011	5.4	4.7	17.1	-4.5	13.0	61 446	-4.7	5 946	0.3	1.9	8.4
Lawrence	19 378	34 669	12.7	8.5	18.9	-21.6	7.3	32 761	26.5	1 373	0.1	1.9	3.6
Leavenworth	18 785	40 681	0.4	5.9	9.1	-4.2	6.8	12 936	2.9	901	0.2	2.0	6.3
Leawood	49 139	102 496	1.7	51.7	1.3	0.0	0.5	10 129	40.5	288	0.7	0.7	7.4
Lenexa	30 212	61 990	-1.7	23.2	3.4	-20.9	1.8	16 378	21.4	804	0.4	0.7	8.4
Manhattan	16 566	30 463	5.3	7.9	24.2	-1.6	8.7	17 690	13.7	741	0.3	1.3	3.4
Olathe	24 498	61 111	14.5	17.2	4.1	0.0	2.4	33 343	48.2	1 029	0.1	1.6	3.3
Overland Park	32 069	62 116	4.5	24.6	3.2	14.3	2.1	62 586	30.3	2 883	0.6	1.0	8.1
Salina	18 593	36 066	7.0	5.6	9.6	-21.3	6.7	19 599	6.5	1 076	0.3	1.6	7.3
Shawnee	28 142	59 626	13.2	19.7	3.3	-19.5	2.2	19 086	25.4	564	0.2	1.0	4.9
Topeka	19 555	35 928	-0.1	6.5	12.4	0.8	8.5	56 435	3.2	4 245	0.2	1.6	7.2
Wichita	20 647	39 939	6.1	8.3	11.2	-10.4	8.4	152 119	12.6	13 032	0.3	2.0	12.0
KENTUCKY	18 093	33 672	11.2	7.2	15.8	-16.8	12.7	1 750 927	16.2	160 280	1.7	1.8	8.7
Bowling Green	17 621	29 047	7.9	7.2	21.8	-8.8	15.7	21 290	21.7	2 013	0.4	2.6	10.1
Covington	16 841	30 735	8.9	4.2	18.4	-7.1	15.5	20 448	7.0	2 191	0.3	3.1	9.7
Frankfort	20 512	34 980	1.4	6.4	13.9	6.9	9.5	13 422	13.0	1 108	0.5	1.5	9.9
Henderson	17 925	30 427	2.5	5.2	16.5	-2.9	13.2	12 652	11.4	959	0.5	1.9	7.2
Hopkinsville	15 796	30 419	6.0	4.6	16.8	-22.9	13.6	13 260	8.4	1 086	0.2	2.7	7.9
Jeffersontown	23 977	51 999	-0.7	12.7	4.3	26.5	3.7	11 220	19.8	567	1.0	0.9	8.6
Lexington-Fayette	23 109	39 813	5.6	11.5	12.9	-8.5	8.2	116 167	18.9	7 879	0.8	1.1	8.4
Louisville	18 193	28 843	6.6	6.0	21.6	-4.4	17.9	121 275	-2.2	9 861	0.3	1.8	7.5
Owensboro	17 968	31 867	8.0	5.0	15.9	-15.9	12.2	24 302	5.3	1 643	0.4	1.9	7.7
Paducah	18 417	26 137	13.1	6.5	22.4	-5.9	18.0	13 221	0.5	1 396	0.5	3.3	10.4
Richmond	15 815	25 533	21.9	4.1	25.0	-21.1	16.6	11 857	50.7	1 062	0.3	3.5	8.8

1. Based on population enumerated as of April 1, 2000.   2. Includes units rented or sold but not occupied.

Table D. Cities — **Housing, Labor Force, Employment, and Disability**

City	Housing units, 2000 (cont'd)					Civilian labor force, 2003				Civilian employment,[2] 2000			Disability, 2000
	Occupied units							Unemployment			Percent		
	Total	Percent owner occupied	Percent renter occupied	Average size owner occupied	Average size renter occupied	Total	Percent change, 2002–2003	Total	Rate[1]	Total	Management, professional, and related occupations	Production, transportation, and material moving occupations	Employment disabled persons[3] (percent)
	56	57	58	59	60	61	62	63	64	65	66	67	68
INDIANA—Cont'd													
Lafayette	24 060	52.9	47.1	2.45	2.16	27 369	-1.8	1 079	3.9	29 770	29.8	21.2	9.6
Lawrence	14 853	75.8	24.2	2.68	2.37	16 176	1.0	792	4.9	20 549	36.0	12.8	10.3
Marion	12 462	62.1	37.9	2.42	2.11	13 409	-6.0	1 518	11.3	12 820	23.0	29.5	10.3
Merrillville	11 678	70.6	29.4	2.79	2.03	14 455	0.9	416	2.9	15 292	28.3	19.7	13.7
Michigan City	12 550	61.1	38.9	2.49	2.28	16 802	-1.7	1 582	9.4	14 254	21.3	22.2	9.5
Mishawaka	20 248	56.8	43.2	2.47	1.92	25 006	0.1	1 130	4.5	24 223	27.1	20.1	12.2
Muncie	27 322	55.8	44.2	2.27	2.20	34 545	-0.4	2 537	7.3	30 591	27.7	17.1	10.7
New Albany	15 959	59.3	40.7	2.40	2.18	20 795	-0.7	926	4.5	18 084	25.5	20.8	12.4
Noblesville city, IN	10 576	74.1	25.9	2.79	2.21	18 332	1.1	532	2.9	14 912	43.9	10.3	7.8
Portage	12 746	72.5	27.5	2.70	2.33	16 809	1.1	1 054	6.3	16 094	20.7	23.2	10.3
Richmond	16 287	58.7	41.3	2.33	2.23	18 983	0.5	1 383	7.3	17 716	23.8	25.7	12.2
South Bend	42 908	63.1	36.9	2.50	2.35	56 632	0.0	3 680	6.5	47 107	28.2	22.0	12.4
Terre Haute	22 870	59.5	40.5	2.38	2.14	26 540	2.2	1 780	6.7	25 556	28.5	15.2	11.7
Valparaiso	10 867	55.1	44.9	2.56	1.92	14 899	1.2	570	3.8	13 870	38.3	11.7	7.6
West Lafayette	10 462	32.2	67.8	2.57	2.11	14 506	-1.7	753	5.2	13 725	52.7	6.0	4.5
IOWA	1 149 276	72.3	27.7	2.57	2.15	1 612 328	-3.0	72 223	4.5	1 489 816	31.3	18.1	9.3
Ames	18 085	46.1	53.9	2.52	2.11	31 279	-2.7	932	3.0	28 883	47.3	6.7	3.7
Ankeny	10 339	71.8	28.2	2.79	2.00	13 912	-1.6	291	2.1	15 822	40.9	9.3	6.5
Bettendorf	12 474	77.3	22.7	2.64	1.95	17 228	-1.9	539	3.1	16 098	42.2	11.5	7.4
Burlington	11 102	70.2	29.8	2.49	2.06	14 099	-2.6	1 094	7.8	12 841	24.3	24.7	10.3
Cedar Falls	12 833	64.3	35.7	2.55	2.27	21 197	-1.7	853	4.0	20 282	37.3	10.2	6.4
Cedar Rapids	49 820	69.0	31.0	2.50	2.03	74 949	-2.8	3 776	5.0	64 645	34.6	15.3	8.4
Clinton	11 427	69.3	30.7	2.48	2.10	15 066	-4.3	1 020	6.8	12 653	22.2	26.9	12.7
Council Bluffs	22 889	65.0	35.0	2.60	2.28	33 102	-0.4	2 030	6.1	28 879	23.5	18.1	13.3
Davenport	39 124	65.2	34.8	2.58	2.18	53 186	-1.8	2 785	5.2	47 737	28.7	17.7	11.0
Des Moines	80 504	64.7	35.3	2.53	2.12	128 612	-1.2	6 460	5.0	100 956	29.1	14.0	12.3
Dubuque	22 560	67.5	32.5	2.58	1.95	33 089	-0.9	1 468	4.4	28 902	29.6	19.5	8.8
Fort Dodge	10 470	66.4	33.6	2.44	1.99	12 982	-2.3	611	4.7	11 875	28.3	19.5	9.7
Iowa City	25 202	46.5	53.5	2.46	2.02	44 680	-3.9	1 544	3.5	36 515	43.6	7.8	5.6
Marion	10 458	78.3	21.7	2.65	1.82	14 381	-3.0	459	3.2	15 060	35.2	12.4	8.0
Marshalltown	10 175	70.1	29.9	2.53	2.20	13 512	-1.3	769	5.7	12 134	26.9	24.1	11.7
Mason City	12 368	67.4	32.6	2.44	1.92	16 222	-1.4	555	3.4	14 461	27.8	19.7	8.5
Sioux City	32 054	66.2	33.8	2.71	2.29	43 749	-4.2	2 446	5.6	42 039	27.1	20.5	12.1
Urbandale	11 484	77.6	22.4	2.67	1.94	17 357	-1.6	389	2.2	16 627	45.8	7.3	5.7
Waterloo	28 169	67.1	32.9	2.47	2.20	36 074	-1.6	2 074	5.7	32 079	27.6	21.5	12.0
West Des Moines	19 826	62.1	37.9	2.58	1.90	23 092	-1.5	664	2.9	27 332	50.0	5.5	7.1
KANSAS	1 037 891	69.2	30.8	2.63	2.25	1 434 070	1.7	77 299	5.4	1 316 283	33.9	15.0	10.2
Dodge City	8 395	60.7	39.3	3.01	2.84	12 569	3.9	403	3.2	11 710	22.8	27.5	13.3
Emporia	10 253	53.6	46.4	2.71	2.18	14 764	3.2	726	4.9	13 183	24.1	24.6	10.1
Garden City	9 338	61.6	38.4	3.16	2.71	13 040	0.1	482	3.7	13 030	24.0	26.9	12.1
Hutchinson	16 335	64.7	35.3	2.43	2.11	20 039	0.0	1 039	5.2	18 234	27.3	18.7	13.4
Kansas City	55 500	62.0	38.0	2.69	2.52	73 380	3.2	9 047	12.3	62 940	21.5	21.4	16.1
Lawrence	31 388	45.9	54.1	2.57	2.07	46 774	0.9	2 371	5.1	44 705	41.9	9.1	7.0
Leavenworth	12 035	50.8	49.2	2.47	2.74	14 150	2.1	1 140	8.1	13 044	30.4	10.5	15.1
Leawood	9 841	92.8	7.2	2.87	2.01	13 013	2.0	399	3.1	13 304	62.0	2.3	4.9
Lenexa	15 574	62.7	37.3	2.85	2.01	28 136	2.0	1 195	4.2	23 257	48.2	6.5	4.8
Manhattan	16 949	42.9	57.1	2.54	2.12	21 421	3.0	679	3.2	23 726	39.9	6.3	4.1
Olathe	32 314	71.5	28.5	3.02	2.36	49 508	2.1	2 520	5.1	51 774	43.0	8.8	8.9
Overland Park	59 703	68.3	31.7	2.72	1.94	90 895	2.0	3 651	4.0	80 823	50.9	5.3	6.8
Salina	18 523	66.1	33.9	2.51	2.16	26 257	1.1	1 078	4.1	23 377	27.3	19.0	9.9
Shawnee	18 522	74.4	25.6	2.78	1.98	31 319	2.1	1 629	5.2	27 235	43.4	9.6	7.0
Topeka	52 190	60.7	39.3	2.40	2.07	65 866	0.2	3 764	5.7	59 101	33.0	13.2	13.1
Wichita	139 087	61.6	38.4	2.61	2.17	182 442	0.5	14 488	7.9	165 868	31.6	16.0	12.0
KENTUCKY	1 590 647	70.8	29.2	2.55	2.27	1 956 384	1.2	120 475	6.2	1 798 264	28.7	19.7	13.9
Bowling Green	19 277	47.0	53.0	2.34	2.21	25 695	1.2	191	0.7	24 173	29.1	17.6	11.9
Covington	18 257	49.3	50.7	2.53	2.11	19 987	2.0	1 109	5.5	19 715	23.6	18.7	15.3
Frankfort	12 314	52.0	48.0	2.27	2.01	14 546	1.0	641	4.4	13 048	35.6	13.7	12.9
Henderson	11 693	57.3	42.7	2.39	2.11	14 421	0.7	959	6.7	12 543	24.3	24.8	13.5
Hopkinsville	12 174	57.9	42.1	2.39	2.39	14 973	4.4	1 110	7.4	12 217	26.6	22.1	13.5
Jeffersontown	10 653	69.8	30.2	2.60	2.15	16 177	0.1	563	3.5	14 264	40.1	11.7	17.2
Lexington-Fayette	108 288	55.3	44.7	2.47	2.07	141 070	1.4	5 394	3.8	139 174	40.4	11.2	7.2
Louisville	111 414	52.5	47.5	2.33	2.10	120 872	1.2	7 899	6.5	113 532	30.7	16.5	10.3
Owensboro	22 659	60.2	39.8	2.38	2.14	28 365	1.2	2 026	7.1	24 523	29.4	19.3	14.6
Paducah	11 825	52.9	47.1	2.22	2.01	10 753	-0.1	212	2.0	10 286	31.1	14.4	15.0
Richmond	10 795	35.2	64.8	2.31	2.05	12 874	1.5	989	7.7	13 421	27.5	13.7	14.7

1. Percent of civilian labor force.   2. Persons 16 years old and over.   3. Persons 16 to 64 years old.

City	Value of residential construction authorized by building permits, 2003			Wholesale trade, 1997				Retail trade,[1] 1997			
	New construction ($1,000)	Number of housing units	Percent single family	Number of establishments	Number of employees	Sales (mil dol)	Annual payroll (mil dol)	Number of establishments	Number of employees	Sales (mil dol)	Annual payroll (mil dol)
	69	70	71	72	73	74	75	76	77	78	79
INDIANA—Cont'd											
Lafayette	33 803	483	39.8	83	1 027	218.2	26.3	410	6 608	1 060.4	100.8
Lawrence	54 114	366	92.9	34	346	110.7	11.0	116	1 418	241.4	25.6
Marion	NA	NA	NA	43	431	118.8	13.4	233	3 131	524.9	46.2
Merrillville	20 355	237	26.6	63	681	284.0	24.3	308	5 485	965.6	87.5
Michigan City	8 212	99	78.8	55	726	248.0	22.7	299	3 759	562.4	57.1
Mishawaka	20 404	173	69.9	87	1 278	667.0	41.4	393	8 081	1 479.9	116.8
Muncie	82 710	305	10.5	80	1 151	444.0	37.6	406	5 648	863.3	83.7
New Albany	14 013	130	93.8	69	D	D	D	174	1 886	265.7	30.0
Noblesville city, IN	211 984	1 336	67.4	103	1 178	771.7	42.0	115	1 766	320.0	28.4
Portage	26 162	228	99.1	27	612	364.5	18.3	80	1 185	197.2	17.5
Richmond	6 589	59	88.1	68	1 362	1 148.3	45.7	249	3 582	585.7	54.6
South Bend	NA	NA	NA	250	4 759	2 191.4	155.5	440	6 597	939.1	98.6
Terre Haute	9 967	136	61.8	114	1 390	592.3	36.6	411	7 586	1 963.8	129.8
Valparaiso	19 942	131	52.7	44	403	254.6	13.0	177	3 403	534.3	53.0
West Lafayette	14 122	148	35.1	9	D	D	D	79	1 660	188.4	17.2
IOWA	2 062 916	16 082	73.6	5 399	63 596	35 453.7	1 820.1	14 695	175 694	26 723.8	2 633.4
Ames	74 698	597	43.7	50	380	129.6	10.8	246	3 922	510.8	54.6
Ankeny	119 767	1 040	98.8	58	1 094	411.4	34.3	93	1 677	284.0	25.2
Bettendorf	26 084	133	91.0	78	665	516.4	26.3	124	1 821	252.2	28.9
Burlington	2 578	20	80.0	33	330	152.2	7.9	132	2 108	259.3	31.0
Cedar Falls	42 165	227	68.7	38	723	420.6	22.3	180	2 611	429.5	41.4
Cedar Rapids	50 019	695	54.5	285	4 914	1 986.5	139.7	640	10 952	1 638.6	172.0
Clinton	5 304	39	100.0	36	277	77.4	6.0	153	1 883	321.5	34.3
Council Bluffs	36 040	384	47.9	68	1 155	836.3	36.0	287	4 400	717.2	67.5
Davenport	59 972	588	48.6	252	3 458	2 372.4	111.8	545	8 810	1 416.2	147.5
Des Moines	76 125	658	62.5	408	6 500	2 459.9	221.1	897	13 577	2 103.9	231.6
Dubuque	16 612	182	42.9	97	1 164	656.2	32.3	382	5 537	734.3	80.4
Fort Dodge	3 771	28	67.9	53	D	D	D	216	2 932	374.4	40.5
Iowa City	107 774	741	42.9	38	D	D	D	333	5 448	775.2	79.8
Marion	46 952	626	40.6	35	292	106.2	8.5	112	1 210	200.3	22.3
Marshalltown	12 697	90	71.1	39	D	D	D	155	2 296	295.0	31.8
Mason City	11 200	83	59.0	55	657	344.1	19.1	218	3 451	519.7	47.4
Sioux City	9 352	106	69.8	188	D	D	D	469	7 174	1 049.7	108.3
Urbandale	160 497	835	75.1	101	1 574	1 391.1	64.8	127	2 441	484.8	46.8
Waterloo	16 638	188	42.6	102	1 750	389.1	49.3	347	6 030	807.8	88.5
West Des Moines	73 492	439	49.0	118	1 665	3 625.2	68.3	274	5 081	608.2	68.4
KANSAS	1 895 406	15 049	76.4	5 085	59 954	42 209.9	1 946.8	12 271	140 412	22 571.9	2 191.1
Dodge City	5 360	73	78.1	43	506	286.0	14.5	146	1 832	323.6	28.6
Emporia	4 618	83	28.9	35	535	182.9	13.3	163	1 870	274.3	26.6
Garden City	3 785	32	100.0	33	D	D	D	155	2 284	335.9	33.7
Hutchinson	10 488	69	100.0	60	955	345.4	28.8	238	2 966	510.3	50.7
Kansas City	23 388	197	100.0	293	6 566	3 864.7	216.5	404	4 622	851.0	83.3
Lawrence	84 467	800	38.5	77	644	207.0	18.7	413	5 420	731.5	77.8
Leavenworth	11 563	82	100.0	13	D	D	D	128	1 638	272.0	24.3
Leawood	87 449	297	97.6	87	606	981.5	24.9	95	1 895	201.3	25.6
Lenexa	82 603	352	100.0	383	6 605	3 410.9	248.5	226	3 574	634.4	70.7
Manhattan	47 081	553	30.4	41	517	141.7	12.7	294	3 570	484.4	47.8
Olathe	173 132	1 366	89.2	181	3 333	1 536.1	130.5	319	4 695	1 106.9	97.8
Overland Park	233 701	1 429	60.3	513	5 130	12 533.4	244.3	745	13 018	2 208.7	222.6
Salina	14 861	107	100.0	81	989	421.4	28.4	302	4 285	663.4	62.7
Shawnee	128 526	994	54.8	75	593	376.5	18.7	165	2 439	459.1	44.2
Topeka	54 583	467	78.6	177	1 900	706.5	56.7	706	10 166	1 559.8	160.2
Wichita	162 717	1 702	85.4	682	8 221	4 005.0	274.3	1 580	22 657	3 834.5	381.9
KENTUCKY	2 346 693	20 404	85.4	5 051	69 309	37 242.9	2 071.2	17 369	212 189	33 332.7	3 128.1
Bowling Green	51 470	548	47.3	128	1 795	1 276.6	50.3	458	6 764	1 048.2	96.3
Covington	12 023	251	74.5	35	312	159.3	11.2	173	1 869	310.1	32.4
Frankfort	6 696	95	41.1	26	D	D	D	179	2 893	382.0	34.9
Henderson	8 457	92	76.1	59	D	D	D	192	2 203	415.4	36.1
Hopkinsville	12 041	107	58.9	66	D	D	D	241	2 498	406.0	39.6
Jeffersontown	6 675	65	53.8	221	3 629	1 512.5	128.7	172	4 097	767.6	73.1
Lexington-Fayette	285 972	2 309	95.5	NA	NA	NA	NA	NA	NA	NA	NA
Louisville	5 993	83	56.6	677	14 614	8 597.4	488.2	1 166	15 744	2 069.0	240.0
Owensboro	43 987	561	87.3	105	1 272	564.7	33.6	393	4 356	656.1	63.4
Paducah	6 255	44	100.0	112	D	D	D	432	5 688	914.3	81.8
Richmond	28 213	365	65.2	29	572	249.1	21.3	195	2 838	429.3	37.4

1. Establishments with payroll.

Table D. Cities — Real Estate, Professional Services, and Manufacturing

City	Real estate and rental and leasing, 1997				Professional, scientific, and technical services,[1] 1997				Manufacturing, 1997			
	Number of establishments	Number of employees	Receipts (mil dol)	Annual payroll (mil dol)	Number of establishments	Number of employees	Receipts (mil dol)	Annual payroll (mil dol)	Number of establishments	Number of employees	Receipts (mil dol)	Annual payroll (mil dol)
	80	81	82	83	84	85	86	87	88	89	90	91
INDIANA—Cont'd												
Lafayette	87	411	45.4	7.0	134	972	79.1	27.8	71	D	D	D
Lawrence	33	149	12.6	2.7	39	146	14.8	4.3	30	626	61.9	19.6
Marion	39	154	11.4	2.2	53	320	14.5	4.9	56	8 037	1 537.0	356.6
Merrillville	60	302	26.7	4.6	177	1 609	167.0	56.3	35	641	82.1	17.7
Michigan City	35	148	13.4	2.2	64	406	21.3	7.4	69	4 621	946.9	153.3
Mishawaka	56	248	29.7	4.6	113	1 067	99.9	40.6	128	5 253	636.5	162.9
Muncie	90	341	37.4	6.6	111	1 480	65.3	27.6	109	7 185	1 305.6	302.4
New Albany	43	214	17.2	3.4	114	877	69.8	25.3	100	6 779	1 168.7	188.2
Noblesville city, IN	28	115	26.3	2.3	78	428	52.3	17.3	38	1 419	292.7	45.5
Portage	26	148	22.3	3.0	43	228	22.7	10.1	22	2 172	1 124.5	112.6
Richmond	48	187	20.7	3.4	54	343	24.4	11.3	95	8 093	1 500.2	250.1
South Bend	104	853	80.4	18.0	292	2 564	235.7	99.2	200	10 066	1 850.1	361.8
Terre Haute	68	404	30.9	7.2	133	836	55.2	16.9	92	5 998	1 398.4	200.3
Valparaiso	48	257	31.2	4.2	90	527	42.5	15.6	54	2 134	552.2	82.4
West Lafayette	45	D	D	D	38	137	16.5	5.4	20	D	D	D
IOWA	2 518	12 619	1 457.5	249.0	4 670	31 115	2 435.6	887.9	3 749	235 880	62 413.7	7 573.3
Ames	48	304	20.7	5.0	104	808	88.3	31.2	44	2 344	824.1	75.3
Ankeny	24	94	10.6	1.5	49	251	17.6	7.6	14	2 225	879.6	111.2
Bettendorf	42	182	27.4	3.7	65	356	33.3	12.3	28	1 127	130.9	34.3
Burlington	37	394	46.6	9.7	49	219	15.8	5.0	37	4 089	891.2	142.0
Cedar Falls	35	96	13.1	1.7	61	627	35.3	16.8	50	1 911	261.7	61.5
Cedar Rapids	154	996	110.4	22.1	296	2 391	229.8	89.3	164	21 491	6 194.2	890.3
Clinton	35	141	9.4	1.3	41	156	9.8	3.2	28	3 649	1 780.1	126.9
Council Bluffs	52	273	24.8	4.5	78	458	39.1	12.5	41	D	D	D
Davenport	107	1 184	111.3	28.4	229	1 571	138.5	44.1	121	6 380	2 984.9	248.0
Des Moines	235	1 848	263.9	43.8	450	6 867	527.9	218.0	234	11 168	2 841.7	375.8
Dubuque	80	322	30.0	4.5	98	733	51.9	22.3	86	D	D	D
Fort Dodge	45	D	D	D	61	309	21.9	8.2	44	1 976	911.3	61.3
Iowa City	89	438	50.3	7.8	125	761	62.2	21.0	48	2 945	2 339.2	102.7
Marion	23	83	10.3	2.2	32	418	24.1	13.1	39	607	74.8	21.0
Marshalltown	27	239	20.2	6.1	45	193	12.6	4.7	38	D	D	D
Mason City	38	126	13.3	1.9	53	321	23.0	9.6	37	3 308	677.9	88.8
Sioux City	105	D	D	D	169	907	71.3	23.1	94	6 018	1 853.7	160.2
Urbandale	38	219	82.2	4.6	90	968	82.9	27.2	23	861	288.2	31.9
Waterloo	84	438	47.1	8.5	122	876	64.9	27.6	93	11 413	4 848.1	487.4
West Des Moines	87	853	163.2	23.4	214	1 911	167.4	74.8	43	1 390	194.6	43.6
KANSAS	2 602	13 005	1 525.8	259.6	5 345	39 534	3 559.3	1 396.0	3 309	193 742	46 296.4	6 532.5
Dodge City	33	106	10.7	1.6	49	439	27.6	12.5	19	D	D	D
Emporia	31	D	D	D	37	D	D	D	30	D	D	D
Garden City	34	111	9.4	1.8	53	320	20.2	8.0	NA	2 365	364.0	71.2
Hutchinson	41	142	52.1	2.0	75	407	23.9	10.3	47	2 365	364.0	71.2
Kansas City	119	684	82.4	14.7	146	1 098	86.1	32.4	249	14 624	7 562.1	623.8
Lawrence	111	409	45.6	6.4	175	1 216	77.4	30.1	56	3 439	541.6	86.2
Leavenworth	25	113	13.0	1.8	51	637	73.1	19.4	NA	NA	NA	NA
Leawood	44	201	33.0	5.7	122	800	93.7	37.0	NA	NA	NA	NA
Lenexa	62	441	48.4	9.1	216	3 229	299.5	121.2	133	7 703	1 506.0	232.7
Manhattan	73	241	19.1	3.0	87	665	55.5	20.9	NA	NA	NA	NA
Olathe	75	381	46.9	8.1	182	636	62.0	22.4	117	4 902	842.3	181.4
Overland Park	281	2 692	430.0	72.1	795	11 091	1 306.2	527.1	106	1 632	226.4	50.7
Salina	64	268	32.3	4.1	80	697	51.6	20.2	68	5 496	985.3	160.7
Shawnee	49	226	29.1	4.2	95	201	19.2	7.7	42	D	D	D
Topeka	186	1 187	87.3	22.0	376	3 131	224.9	91.5	124	D	D	D
Wichita	480	2 483	317.6	50.4	865	6 100	518.0	210.6	496	52 170	8 579.6	2 158.6
KENTUCKY	3 227	16 284	1 961.6	314.3	6 189	41 991	3 820.3	1 260.1	4 218	288 405	86 636.1	9 198.1
Bowling Green	92	379	36.2	5.5	130	869	53.1	18.4	88	D	D	D
Covington	36	301	19.1	5.7	100	754	77.0	31.4	45	1 491	321.1	40.7
Frankfort	32	D	D	D	95	655	59.5	24.7	28	2 760	504.5	79.1
Henderson	39	172	15.2	3.3	62	265	17.1	5.4	62	6 189	1 557.8	192.9
Hopkinsville	57	212	23.3	3.4	71	272	21.4	6.6	48	4 406	775.0	114.5
Jeffersontown	45	751	100.4	18.7	117	1 615	182.6	47.6	107	4 447	632.0	139.8
Lexington-Fayette	NA	NA	NA	NA	NA	NA	NA	NA	283	17 403	4 313.9	654.0
Louisville	332	2 698	331.7	60.0	1 024	9 645	948.4	334.6	456	29 078	17 225.4	1 076.2
Owensboro	61	433	30.8	7.3	127	809	53.2	22.3	86	D	D	D
Paducah	63	373	56.9	10.5	120	886	62.7	20.4	40	1 634	300.9	51.9
Richmond	41	155	14.9	1.7	52	201	10.8	3.6	35	1 981	583.1	55.4

1. Firms subject to federal tax.

City	Accommodation and foodservices, 1997				Arts, entertainment, and recreation,[1] 1997				Health care and social assistance,[1] 1997			
	Number of establishments	Number of employees	Sales (mil dol)	Annual payroll (mil dol)	Number of establishments	Number of employees	Receipts (mil dol)	Annual payroll (mil dol)	Number of establishments	Number of employees	Receipts (mil dol)	Annual payroll (mil dol)
	92	93	94	95	96	97	98	99	100	101	102	103
INDIANA—Cont'd												
Lafayette	152	3 092	94.7	27.6	13	220	5.8	1.7	129	2 390	188.5	94.0
Lawrence	52	802	23.2	6.6	10	0	0.0	0.0	30	0	0.0	0.0
Marion	92	1 901	54.9	15.3	8	73	3.0	0.6	96	1 531	67.5	33.1
Merrillville	134	3 640	118.2	33.5	13	313	12.9	3.6	251	2 761	197.2	95.3
Michigan City	106	1 679	55.1	15.0	10	0	0.0	0.0	93	1 164	87.5	40.3
Mishawaka	164	3 655	104.8	29.8	17	270	7.5	2.3	102	1 129	73.3	32.3
Muncie	174	4 337	109.2	30.4	18	255	6.8	1.8	182	2 555	173.4	81.1
New Albany	87	1 408	44.5	12.8	11	69	2.1	0.8	135	1 730	103.1	43.7
Noblesville city, IN	51	1 050	29.3	8.7	12	177	6.7	2.0	60	649	40.5	18.6
Portage	56	951	28.1	8.0	8	43	1.8	0.4	46	494	24.6	10.6
Richmond	103	2 158	63.6	18.4	12	89	3.5	0.8	86	985	51.5	27.0
South Bend	257	4 868	142.8	40.8	16	178	7.1	1.7	303	4 038	344.7	165.3
Terre Haute	217	4 308	126.8	36.2	18	144	4.2	1.1	211	3 023	226.9	71.1
Valparaiso	90	1 672	49.5	14.0	8	83	3.4	0.8	139	1 369	101.5	47.7
West Lafayette	86	1 860	47.0	13.5	5	26	0.9	0.2	31	329	21.8	6.2
IOWA	6 830	99 148	2 762.8	769.5	875	14 169	919.8	220.3	4 876	56 374	3 183.2	1 540.6
Ames	168	3 173	79.0	21.7	15	289	9.0	2.7	62	1 142	76.9	41.1
Ankeny	50	1 022	29.5	8.1	11	47	2.5	0.5	41	641	21.1	9.7
Bettendorf	72	1 712	49.5	15.8	11	0	0.0	0.0	66	480	35.2	11.9
Burlington	89	D	D	D	8	96	3.4	0.7	79	643	45.2	19.6
Cedar Falls	99	2 182	47.9	15.3	6	0	0.0	0.0	62	616	33.4	16.9
Cedar Rapids	350	6 760	209.8	59.5	30	544	14.0	4.3	266	3 172	226.4	116.5
Clinton	91	1 184	32.1	9.0	11	0	0.0	0.0	69	646	39.8	15.0
Council Bluffs	146	3 338	174.2	45.1	19	0	0.0	0.0	93	1 220	71.4	40.2
Davenport	262	5 707	167.0	48.5	39	0	0.0	0.0	228	2 501	196.1	97.8
Des Moines	514	9 234	293.7	86.7	41	495	45.1	6.0	409	4 536	403.6	201.9
Dubuque	179	3 220	80.1	23.7	20	1 106	73.7	19.1	104	2 146	179.0	85.8
Fort Dodge	78	1 274	35.5	10.3	5	46	1.2	0.3	79	674	49.2	23.6
Iowa City	178	3 743	89.2	25.5	20	213	6.0	1.7	124	1 312	76.7	30.6
Marion	38	D	D	D	8	65	1.9	0.4	35	348	17.5	7.4
Marshalltown	70	981	27.3	7.9	8	0	0.0	0.0	48	532	29.0	14.2
Mason City	88	1 495	39.1	11.1	11	0	0.0	0.0	62	1 118	74.0	46.3
Sioux City	214	3 544	103.2	28.4	28	0	0.0	0.0	209	1 986	181.2	87.3
Urbandale	48	776	25.7	7.2	13	232	4.4	1.4	52	719	38.5	16.1
Waterloo	163	3 120	82.1	22.2	17	184	8.4	2.1	156	1 494	131.2	64.7
West Des Moines	118	2 641	78.4	24.8	16	275	10.3	3.6	158	2 146	121.3	63.7
KANSAS	5 677	91 173	2 685.7	757.1	652	7 618	374.5	91.0	4 793	66 613	4 116.1	1 771.8
Dodge City	64	D	D	D	6	81	1.6	0.6	57	765	64.8	24.3
Emporia	96	1 593	36.2	9.7	9	67	1.6	0.4	60	696	32.4	16.4
Garden City	61	1 261	37.6	10.6	6	0	0.0	0.0	48	576	40.4	19.0
Hutchinson	103	1 927	56.7	14.6	5	69	1.3	0.3	73	1 172	93.1	45.3
Kansas City	212	2 962	102.6	28.7	23	0	0.0	0.0	199	3 705	288.5	101.4
Lawrence	222	4 511	117.9	33.6	33	263	8.9	2.3	159	1 399	80.1	37.2
Leavenworth	63	1 104	27.6	8.3	7	39	1.0	0.3	56	429	21.7	10.5
Leawood	37	D	D	D	7	100	3.6	1.3	76	488	45.6	22.5
Lenexa	89	1 994	69.7	19.2	14	212	7.3	2.0	95	2 157	161.8	55.9
Manhattan	153	3 003	75.3	21.2	12	0	0.0	0.0	92	936	55.1	22.0
Olathe	128	2 785	79.2	23.7	15	96	4.7	1.5	154	1 897	106.9	53.2
Overland Park	340	8 788	316.7	93.8	56	1 105	45.0	13.5	447	7 629	570.2	243.5
Salina	127	2 357	66.1	20.0	11	0	0.0	0.0	123	0	0.0	0.0
Shawnee	77	D	D	D	13	110	3.7	1.1	58	661	31.9	13.5
Topeka	353	D	D	D	34	546	17.2	4.1	308	5 637	307.4	159.0
Wichita	852	15 891	528.1	151.1	78	0	0.0	0.0	701	14 506	1 103.3	450.4
KENTUCKY	6 546	129 442	4 056.1	1 140.6	906	10 580	550.2	126.3	6 805	94 720	5 936.2	2 620.3
Bowling Green	182	4 306	134.0	39.5	21	136	4.0	0.9	218	3 778	259.3	103.6
Covington	133	2 283	87.5	24.3	10	114	5.8	1.4	38	695	24.0	13.1
Frankfort	85	D	D	D	6	84	2.8	1.1	84	1 234	87.2	36.1
Henderson	75	1 392	40.8	11.8	7	0	0.0	0.0	89	680	48.3	19.2
Hopkinsville	72	1 713	42.4	14.9	10	38	1.6	0.4	91	0	0.0	0.0
Jeffersontown	79	2 869	98.7	27.4	13	176	12.8	2.4	65	1 467	128.5	37.5
Lexington-Fayette	NA	NA	NA	NA	NA	NA	NA	NA	NA	NA	NA	NA
Louisville	648	15 529	507.6	147.7	94	1 991	130.7	21.1	799	14 394	998.1	472.7
Owensboro	121	2 865	87.4	23.2	17	147	5.4	1.3	178	2 374	174.7	73.5
Paducah	167	3 808	117.5	33.3	15	142	4.9	1.7	157	1 927	167.2	85.5
Richmond	79	1 806	51.1	14.7	5	32	0.6	0.1	82	794	41.9	19.1

1. Firms subject to federal tax.

City	Other services,[1] 1997				Selected federal funds, 2002–2003 (mil dol)								
					Procurement contracts		Grants						Direct payments for individuals for educational assistance
	Number of establishments	Number of employees	Receipts (mil dol)	Annual payroll (mil dol)	Defense	Other	Total[2]	Medicaid and other health related	Nutrition and family welfare	Energy and environment	Education	Housing and community development	
	104	105	106	107	108	109	110	111	112	113	114	115	116
INDIANA—Cont'd													
Lafayette	146	1 118	78.2	22.4	7.5	1.5	22.5	0.8	3.0	3.3	0.0	13.9	0.7
Lawrence	48	256	15.0	4.6	0.1	1.8	0.0	0.0	0.0	0.0	0.0	0.0	0.0
Marion	67	335	15.5	4.8	0.0	10.3	10.8	0.0	0.0	0.0	0.0	0.0	0.0
Merrillville	91	654	43.8	15.0	0.1	1.7	10.5	0.0	2.0	0.0	0.5	6.9	4.8
Michigan City	76	465	26.2	9.7	3.9	1.0	6.4	0.0	9.5	0.0	0.4	0.3	0.4
Mishawaka	102	693	43.4	13.3	408.4	72.2	7.6	0.2	1.9	0.0	0.7	3.7	0.2
Muncie	141	1 346	87.8	21.3	1.6	2.2	17.6	0.2	0.2	0.0	0.0	7.2	1.7
New Albany	82	543	28.8	10.0	0.7	0.5	5.2	1.4	1.5	0.0	3.9	6.9	11.5
									1.6			3.2	3.9
Noblesville city, IN	45	287	18.8	5.1	0.0	0.0	3.2	0.1	0.1	0.0	0.0	3.1	0.1
Portage	52	357	21.4	7.0	0.1	0.0	0.9	0.0	0.0	0.0	0.0	0.7	0.0
Richmond	82	423	20.6	6.5	1.5	1.1	8.6	0.0	1.7	0.2	0.0	6.6	4.6
South Bend	220	2 470	172.6	55.3	205.9	32.1	43.0	1.3	5.5	2.0	0.4	29.9	8.2
Terre Haute	129	1 162	54.9	16.3	8.8	19.9	15.4	1.1	2.0	0.0	3.1	7.2	9.9
Valparaiso	90	552	30.7	8.9	1.7	4.0	6.9	0.0	0.0	0.2	0.5	4.4	2.5
West Lafayette	38	216	8.1	3.0	15.7	3.1	108.3	34.3	0.3	12.0	4.9	3.4	17.0
IOWA	5 234	24 383	1 486.5	411.3	658.2	451.0	3 877.3	1 838.7	520.4	17.3	338.6	225.0	188.2
Ames	78	472	27.8	7.7	6.3	67.7	108.1	21.8	0.8	10.8	2.4	2.6	16.1
Ankeny	40	220	21.3	4.6	0.2	0.2	2.6	0.0	0.0	0.0	1.4	0.3	9.4
Bettendorf	52	396	21.0	7.5	0.9	0.3	1.1	0.0	0.0	0.0	0.0	1.1	0.0
Burlington	44	222	12.1	3.3	0.3	0.1	6.8	0.0	3.3	0.0	0.0	3.4	0.0
Cedar Falls	50	308	18.4	6.0	0.3	0.9	12.1	0.7	0.0	1.7	5.7	2.9	9.0
Cedar Rapids	251	1 651	95.8	29.4	438.3	35.6	24.3	2.0	0.4	0.0	1.3	10.3	21.5
Clinton	59	248	14.4	3.9	0.2	0.0	5.0	0.0	0.0	0.0	1.0	1.8	0.6
Council Bluffs	100	536	31.8	9.6	0.0	0.4	17.2	1.0	0.1	0.0	1.4	9.3	3.2
Davenport	206	1 376	79.7	25.7	43.5	14.5	29.4	4.8	4.1	0.3	7.0	11.1	20.9
Des Moines	368	2 531	153.5	49.1	23.7	21.2	517.3	72.2	114.5	-6.6	104.4	75.4	7.6
Dubuque	130	773	40.3	12.7	3.7	0.3	16.2	0.1	1.6	0.2	0.4	10.0	4.7
Fort Dodge	68	374	18.9	6.0	10.9	0.6	7.8	0.0	1.6	0.0	0.8	3.5	4.7
Iowa City	104	569	32.4	9.6	2.9	72.7	228.2	190.2	1.0	3.0	4.5	10.1	10.5
Marion	47	227	14.6	4.7	0.4	0.0	1.1	0.0	0.0	0.4	0.0	0.6	0.0
Marshalltown	50	236	13.9	3.7	0.1	0.1	19.0	0.0	3.6	0.0	1.4	1.9	1.6
Mason City	72	371	16.8	5.7	0.0	0.4	10.0	0.0	2.3	2.3	0.3	3.4	2.5
Sioux City	155	1 195	59.0	18.9	1.3	0.7	35.8	3.3	3.6	0.0	5.9	11.7	8.1
Urbandale	53	431	27.7	9.3	0.0	1.4	0.1	0.0	0.0	0.0	0.0	0.0	0.0
Waterloo	132	1 121	55.1	18.5	0.6	0.3	22.5	2.2	4.6	0.3	1.9	11.3	6.0
West Des Moines	75	586	26.7	8.5	20.7	0.6	1.7	0.7	0.0	0.0	0.1	0.9	16.1
KANSAS	4 604	24 081	1 548.4	452.9	1 219.2	800.9	3 415.0	1 422.1	483.1	50.3	394.5	193.6	131.4
Dodge City	45	213	12.5	3.4	0.0	0.1	7.6	0.0	1.5	0.0	2.1	1.1	1.5
Emporia	64	289	14.5	4.2	0.2	0.0	7.2	1.0	0.0	0.0	4.1	1.8	5.1
Garden City	63	319	16.1	4.9	0.0	0.1	3.4	1.0	0.0	0.0	1.5	0.8	1.8
Hutchinson	79	403	20.0	6.3	0.1	0.1	9.3	0.0	2.3	0.0	2.0	2.5	3.0
Kansas City	215	1 325	74.0	24.2	3.5	24.1	88.3	52.2	7.3	0.2	1.8	22.6	6.4
Lawrence	119	738	38.7	13.0	10.8	0.7	99.7	33.6	0.8	4.3	33.4	5.2	10.8
Leavenworth	50	241	11.9	4.0	16.2	373.3	8.4	0.0	0.0	0.0	0.1	7.9	0.5
Leawood	30	202	10.2	3.7	0.2	0.0	0.4	0.3	0.0	0.0	0.0	0.0	0.0
Lenexa	94	925	99.5	25.2	4.1	16.0	1.4	0.0	0.2	0.1	0.0	0.3	0.0
Manhattan	83	439	18.0	5.8	9.6	8.1	57.9	9.5	1.4	5.4	7.2	1.2	15.6
Olathe	141	814	49.1	15.5	14.9	4.2	11.3	0.0	1.1	0.3	2.0	6.4	2.1
Overland Park	261	1 823	109.3	38.1	6.3	35.7	6.7	0.0	1.2	0.0	0.0	5.3	0.0
Salina	99	526	31.9	9.9	1.0	2.4	10.0	0.1	3.5	0.0	1.1	2.6	1.4
Shawnee	71	384	26.1	8.7	3.1	17.5	1.3	0.0	0.0	0.0	0.0	1.3	0.0
Topeka	277	1 782	120.3	39.3	26.1	15.7	539.7	55.5	102.6	33.3	115.8	61.1	6.9
Wichita	675	4 622	283.2	89.0	633.7	24.6	69.6	6.0	10.8	2.5	7.6	23.4	16.5
KENTUCKY	5 383	31 164	1 870.3	551.4	3 223.4	1 895.7	6 634.1	3 246.3	848.1	63.6	567.1	402.8	234.3
Bowling Green	116	976	40.7	13.6	3.9	1.4	27.5	0.8	5.8	1.1	8.4	6.6	15.5
Covington	76	391	26.0	8.3	0.5	12.9	56.6	1.7	3.1	0.0	2.1	10.0	1.0
Frankfort	55	385	20.5	8.6	0.2	0.9	832.5	83.3	178.4	40.6	182.0	67.1	4.3
Henderson	57	475	30.2	10.0	13.3	0.2	6.8	0.5	0.0	0.0	0.0	4.8	0.1
Hopkinsville	67	247	16.0	4.0	3.8	0.8	8.7	0.0	0.0	0.0	0.3	5.3	0.0
Jeffersontown	74	730	57.8	16.8	0.0	0.1	0.4	0.0	0.0	0.0	0.0	0.3	0.0
Lexington-Fayette	NA	NA	NA	NA	196.2	33.1	236.7	96.5	12.7	12.0	15.0	27.9	93.9
Louisville	580	4 014	240.6	73.6	2 198.5	53.9	242.8	69.1	16.2	1.4	23.4	73.1	36.0
Owensboro	119	747	43.7	12.8	3.0	1.0	29.2	0.5	11.6	0.0	1.2	13.4	2.5
Paducah	93	645	43.7	10.8	0.0	272.9	16.1	0.8	1.6	0.0	1.0	7.6	0.5
Richmond	42	270	10.8	3.4	24.4	0.8	33.2	1.3	4.4	0.0	1.5	4.3	14.7

1. Firms subject to federal tax.   2. Includes program categories not shown separately. State totals include additional categories not allocated by city.

City	City government finances, 2002									
	General revenue							General expenditure		
		Intergovernmental		Taxes					Per capita[1] (dollars)	
					Per capita[1] (dollars)					
	Total (mil dol)	Total (mil dol)	Percent from state government	Total (mil dol)	Total	Property	Sales and gross receipts	Total (mil dol)	Total	Capital outlays
	117	118	119	120	121	122	123	124	125	126
INDIANA—Cont'd										
Lafayette	74.9	17.0	91.6	27.3	451	354	4	60.7	1 002	23
Lawrence	20.3	3.6	78.9	8.9	220	188	8	21.3	526	84
Marion	22.5	6.0	73.0	12.1	395	266	0	23.2	756	44
Merrillville	12.5	3.2	81.7	7.2	233	207	8	17.5	566	53
Michigan City	NA	NA	NA	NA	NA	NA	NA	NA	NA	NA
Mishawaka	41.8	9.5	79.1	22.8	471	403	3	43.6	902	71
Muncie	55.2	14.8	71.0	30.0	447	378	0	54.3	809	30
New Albany	NA	NA	NA	NA	NA	NA	NA	NA	NA	NA
Noblesville city, IN	31.8	2.9	100.0	19.0	598	281	2	37.0	1 160	218
Portage	23.3	3.5	84.6	10.4	301	288	4	27.4	793	54
Richmond	NA	NA	NA	NA	NA	NA	NA	NA	NA	NA
South Bend	176.5	27.9	81.2	62.9	590	489	5	192.5	1 806	176
Terre Haute	47.4	11.4	64.8	25.8	440	428	0	47.1	804	77
Valparaiso	24.1	3.5	86.7	10.0	356	335	9	21.4	759	50
West Lafayette	35.1	4.0	78.3	10.5	363	241	3	32.4	1 112	113
IOWA	X	X	X	X	X	X	X	X	X	X
Ames	146.7	18.1	79.5	17.6	346	277	52	139.5	2 740	423
Ankeny	23.0	3.0	87.3	12.7	426	385	23	21.4	715	172
Bettendorf	34.2	5.3	80.1	21.2	672	443	214	38.5	1 219	356
Burlington	26.1	6.2	53.2	12.3	473	306	159	29.7	1 139	317
Cedar Falls	44.1	7.3	59.2	17.2	470	336	111	39.4	1 075	268
Cedar Rapids	181.7	39.3	54.1	65.4	534	460	59	195.5	1 596	517
Clinton	NA	NA	NA	NA	NA	NA	NA	NA	NA	NA
Council Bluffs	69.1	10.6	62.3	39.2	668	399	252	79.3	1 353	634
Davenport	117.0	30.0	60.3	53.2	544	435	96	120.3	1 231	299
Des Moines	288.1	69.1	63.9	101.9	514	469	35	345.4	1 744	511
Dubuque	73.7	20.1	40.8	26.4	463	297	142	80.3	1 408	502
Fort Dodge	25.2	5.0	55.7	11.3	454	368	75	25.9	1 042	305
Iowa City	78.8	22.2	57.5	24.6	386	360	12	92.2	1 445	502
Marion	19.6	4.1	63.4	10.6	384	330	39	17.7	641	135
Marshalltown	21.3	5.1	61.2	10.8	413	259	140	21.0	806	51
Mason City	27.7	6.7	52.4	13.6	479	326	133	24.2	849	148
Sioux City	112.4	35.4	32.6	47.5	565	421	131	112.8	1 341	432
Urbandale	19.9	3.6	96.4	14.2	454	373	54	19.0	609	106
Waterloo	83.3	21.4	40.6	39.1	577	414	150	73.4	1 083	259
West Des Moines	NA	NA	NA	NA	NA	NA	NA	NA	NA	NA
KANSAS	X	X	X	X	X	X	X	X	X	X
Dodge City	24.4	7.3	88.8	10.1	397	202	189	25.3	998	333
Emporia	19.7	2.6	46.0	7.6	286	168	110	27.4	1 025	324
Garden City	22.9	3.5	42.4	9.5	345	154	182	22.4	809	110
Hutchinson	35.8	7.9	43.9	15.8	387	199	181	28.8	706	30
Kansas City	283.1	32.0	49.5	117.6	800	562	233	288.2	1 961	162
Lawrence	157.4	13.7	35.5	30.0	367	175	185	153.7	1 884	76
Leavenworth	28.9	8.0	74.0	14.1	399	278	112	26.5	748	135
Leawood	34.4	7.8	19.0	19.0	672	346	266	26.7	945	55
Lenexa	54.6	7.9	21.9	33.2	804	399	375	61.5	1 491	518
Manhattan	25.9	4.0	63.1	14.7	335	208	117	30.7	700	20
Olathe	91.1	12.3	40.6	35.5	350	225	111	85.8	846	28
Overland Park	103.7	16.0	82.9	70.5	445	95	319	108.4	684	169
Salina	50.8	10.6	28.9	20.0	434	178	195	46.7	1 015	170
Shawnee	47.9	7.1	38.6	20.6	390	201	171	60.1	1 140	454
Topeka	133.9	17.8	45.8	69.8	572	244	318	121.8	997	140
Wichita	350.7	111.0	41.1	112.2	316	197	101	365.7	1 030	332
KENTUCKY	X	X	X	X	X	X	X	X	X	X
Bowling Green	57.3	5.6	32.5	30.7	611	152	8	51.7	1 029	43
Covington	57.7	13.2	44.9	30.3	706	117	45	56.4	1 313	308
Frankfort	40.3	2.6	56.8	21.1	765	96	0	42.4	1 534	313
Henderson	27.7	6.1	33.4	8.8	321	125	30	26.6	971	125
Hopkinsville	31.6	6.4	34.4	13.9	474	102	21	28.1	958	80
Jeffersontown	25.1	1.0	59.2	12.4	476	115	8	20.7	793	80
Lexington-Fayette	324.7	45.1	56.1	197.1	748	141	29	352.9	1 339	258
Louisville	402.6	101.2	56.0	202.2	804	208	5	390.0	1 551	211
Owensboro	62.1	10.1	41.5	22.9	422	123	9	66.5	1 228	116
Paducah	46.1	13.4	16.7	22.2	867	183	20	45.1	1 763	324
Richmond	25.2	3.7	76.6	13.1	466	56	26	26.0	926	38

1. Based on population estimated as of July 1 of the year shown.

City	City government finances, 2002 (cont'd)									
	General expenditure									
	Percent of total for—									
	Public welfare	Highways	Parking facilities	Education	Health and hospitals	Police protection	Sewerage and sanitation	Parks and recreation	Housing and community development	Interest on debt
	127	128	129	130	131	132	133	134	135	136
INDIANA—Cont'd										
Lafayette	0.0	8.3	0.1	0.0	0.0	13.2	38.9	5.8	0.9	0.7
Lawrence	0.0	21.1	0.1	0.0	1.3	20.6	12.9	5.0	0.0	0.1
Marion	0.0	9.8	0.1	0.0	0.0	19.2	13.3	3.9	4.2	0.8
Merrillville	0.0	12.2	0.0	0.0	4.2	20.7	0.0	1.3	13.9	2.2
Michigan City	NA	NA	NA	NA	NA	NA	NA	NA	NA	NA
Mishawaka	0.0	9.6	0.0	0.0	2.3	12.6	9.7	5.6	3.3	4.3
Muncie	0.0	6.9	0.0	0.0	0.4	22.3	26.9	2.7	5.3	0.1
New Albany	NA	NA	NA	NA	NA	NA	NA	NA	NA	NA
Noblesville city, IN	0.0	9.9	0.1	0.0	0.8	11.2	15.8	5.8	6.2	6.6
Portage	0.0	15.0	0.0	0.0	0.2	13.5	17.1	5.3	0.0	0.8
Richmond	NA	NA	NA	NA	NA	NA	NA	NA	NA	NA
South Bend	0.9	3.9	0.4	0.0	0.0	11.3	21.0	11.2	2.4	2.4
Terre Haute	0.0	7.4	0.2	0.0	0.0	12.5	14.9	7.3	8.7	3.0
Valparaiso	0.0	7.7	0.2	0.0	0.0	12.7	28.7	16.0	0.0	0.0
West Lafayette	0.0	6.5	0.0	0.0	0.0	11.5	33.5	3.9	1.7	1.2
IOWA	X	X	X	X	X	X	X	X	X	X
Ames	0.7	13.5	0.2	0.0	58.6	3.6	4.8	4.8	1.1	2.9
Ankeny	0.0	12.8	0.0	0.0	3.2	14.8	6.5	18.2	6.4	10.7
Bettendorf	0.0	24.2	0.0	0.0	3.2	12.4	7.9	18.4	1.2	7.3
Burlington	0.2	25.2	0.3	0.0	3.1	12.4	17.9	10.4	1.4	6.1
Cedar Falls	0.0	29.0	0.4	0.0	1.1	8.0	13.3	8.5	4.0	5.6
Cedar Rapids	0.0	16.6	1.5	0.0	1.7	10.1	20.2	18.5	4.8	7.7
Clinton	NA	NA	NA	NA	NA	NA	NA	NA	NA	NA
Council Bluffs	0.0	19.8	0.1	0.0	1.3	12.4	24.5	12.4	4.8	3.8
Davenport	0.0	21.7	8.4	0.0	0.5	6.1	11.5	14.0	5.7	11.7
Des Moines	0.0	6.5	1.3	0.0	0.9	10.1	13.2	5.8	4.6	6.6
Dubuque	0.3	16.1	1.0	0.0	1.3	11.4	8.9	9.1	9.1	2.7
Fort Dodge	0.3	14.7	0.3	0.0	0.9	10.3	14.4	7.2	5.3	5.1
Iowa City	0.0	15.1	2.5	0.0	0.5	7.7	24.5	3.9	8.9	9.3
Marion	0.2	21.7	0.0	0.0	0.0	17.6	17.7	5.9	4.7	2.4
Marshalltown	0.1	17.9	0.0	0.0	0.3	18.9	15.8	10.0	7.6	7.6
Mason City	0.0	16.1	0.3	0.0	0.6	16.4	13.8	8.7	8.2	4.2
Sioux City	0.0	11.2	0.8	0.0	0.2	12.0	10.0	13.7	7.5	4.9
Urbandale	0.0	15.9	0.0	0.0	2.6	18.1	7.0	12.8	1.6	6.6
Waterloo	0.3	15.2	1.2	0.0	3.5	9.5	18.6	6.4	10.6	10.6
West Des Moines	NA	NA	NA	NA	NA	NA	NA	NA	NA	NA
KANSAS	X	X	X	X	X	X	X	X	X	X
Dodge City	0.0	4.7	0.0	0.0	1.5	10.5	10.2	14.4	0.0	5.6
Emporia	0.0	9.0	0.2	0.0	3.3	13.0	31.1	15.2	0.6	2.6
Garden City	0.0	9.9	0.0	0.0	0.0	16.1	13.7	11.5	0.8	9.6
Hutchinson	0.0	7.5	0.0	0.0	0.3	14.1	20.5	5.7	0.0	5.4
Kansas City	0.0	7.2	0.0	0.0	1.2	12.4	5.2	2.2	2.7	32.3
Lawrence	0.2	3.7	0.4	0.0	56.8	6.2	8.1	4.3	0.9	3.0
Leavenworth	0.0	8.2	0.0	0.0	0.0	16.8	11.1	5.9	7.3	3.4
Leawood	0.0	25.9	0.0	0.0	0.0	20.5	0.0	8.5	0.0	9.1
Lenexa	0.0	33.4	0.0	0.0	0.6	14.1	0.0	2.2	0.0	15.5
Manhattan	0.0	5.4	0.0	0.0	0.6	22.1	10.3	8.3	2.1	11.0
Olathe	0.0	3.1	0.0	0.0	0.0	16.1	13.1	2.1	4.9	23.3
Overland Park	0.0	11.0	0.0	0.0	0.5	19.7	0.0	9.4	1.0	3.9
Salina	0.2	36.5	0.0	0.0	0.5	11.0	13.8	13.4	8.0	3.1
Shawnee	0.0	8.8	0.0	0.0	0.0	13.1	0.0	9.2	0.0	16.4
Topeka	1.9	8.1	1.1	0.0	7.2	16.6	11.8	12.7	7.5	11.7
Wichita	0.8	25.3	0.0	0.0	1.2	12.9	9.3	9.6	11.2	8.0
KENTUCKY	X	X	X	X	X	X	X	X	X	X
Bowling Green	1.6	9.8	0.0	0.0	0.0	10.9	7.9	11.2	6.3	18.8
Covington	1.1	12.8	1.0	0.0	0.0	19.1	3.6	1.3	13.4	5.6
Frankfort	4.0	3.2	0.0	0.0	5.1	8.4	12.4	5.4	1.2	7.1
Henderson	0.0	3.9	0.0	0.0	0.0	14.1	28.3	3.1	6.6	3.7
Hopkinsville	0.0	6.3	0.0	0.0	0.0	11.9	15.7	1.3	26.4	8.7
Jeffersontown	0.0	6.7	0.0	0.0	1.7	18.4	9.9	1.5	0.7	49.4
Lexington-Fayette	4.2	7.0	0.2	0.2	3.5	12.0	18.5	5.4	2.3	10.3
Louisville	1.5	7.1	1.9	0.0	0.3	15.2	4.5	8.5	7.2	4.6
Owensboro	2.0	4.3	0.0	0.0	0.0	11.4	9.4	5.0	5.4	29.8
Paducah	0.0	10.3	0.0	0.0	0.0	12.0	13.9	2.1	10.0	0.9
Richmond	0.0	2.4	0.0	0.0	0.0	8.8	8.7	5.7	12.6	28.1

City	City government finances, 2002 (cont'd) Debt outstanding — Total (mil dol)	Per capita[1] (dollars)	Percent utility	City government employment, 2002	Climate[2] — Average daily temperature (degrees Fahrenheit) — Mean — January	July	Limits — January[3]	July[4]	Annual precipitation (inches)	Heating degree days	Cooling degree days
	137	138	139	140	141	142	143	144	145	146	147
INDIANA—Cont'd											
Lafayette	18.3	302	36.3	657	22.5	73.5	13.9	84.4	36.05	6 228	806
Lawrence	0.4	9	0.0	184	25.5	75.4	17.2	85.5	39.94	5 615	1 014
Marion	8.9	290	63.6	281	23.1	73.3	14.7	84.4	37.56	6 260	760
Merrillville	13.5	438	0.0	133	23.7	74.1	15.2	85.5	36.82	6 043	857
Michigan City	NA	NA	NA	463	23.7	74.1	15.2	85.5	36.82	6 043	857
Mishawaka	64.7	1 341	44.3	561	23.3	72.9	16.1	82.9	39.14	6 331	728
Muncie	0.9	14	0.0	627	23.6	74.4	15.7	84.4	37.88	6 027	878
New Albany	NA	NA	NA	287	31.7	77.2	23.2	87.0	44.39	4 514	1 288
Noblesville city, IN	44.5	1 396	0.0	263	NA	NA	NA	NA	NA	NA	NA
Portage	3.9	113	0.0	231	23.7	74.1	15.2	85.5	36.82	6 043	857
Richmond	NA	NA	NA	596	24.9	73.1	15.9	84.5	39.95	5 963	759
South Bend	120.6	1 132	17.9	1 466	23.3	72.9	16.1	82.9	39.14	6 331	728
Terre Haute	29.9	511	0.0	629	25.3	75.6	16.2	86.6	41.19	5 581	1 025
Valparaiso	0.0	0	0.0	219	NA	NA	NA	NA	NA	NA	NA
West Lafayette	0.0	0	0.0	179	23.8	74.9	15.8	86.0	35.80	5 940	935
IOWA	X	X	X	X	X	X	X	X	X	X	X
Ames	84.9	1 667	12.5	578	18.2	74.2	8.8	85.3	32.94	6 776	816
Ankeny	51.4	1 719	3.7	169	NA	NA	NA	NA	NA	NA	NA
Bettendorf	55.9	1 773	0.0	262	19.9	75.2	11.3	85.9	39.08	6 474	911
Burlington	36.2	1 391	0.0	266	21.8	75.7	13.1	85.8	36.06	6 158	992
Cedar Falls	57.6	1 571	20.7	408	14.6	73.1	5.4	83.9	33.70	7 406	702
Cedar Rapids	275.3	2 247	0.0	1 368	17.6	74.2	9.2	84.6	33.72	6 924	788
Clinton	NA	NA	NA	228	20.3	75.1	11.3	86.1	35.21	6 324	941
Council Bluffs	84.5	1 440	3.8	510	21.1	76.9	10.9	87.9	29.86	6 300	1 072
Davenport	227.4	2 325	0.0	860	19.9	75.2	11.3	85.9	39.08	6 474	911
Des Moines	539.2	2 722	7.7	2 219	19.4	76.6	10.7	86.7	33.12	6 497	1 036
Dubuque	44.1	773	0.0	594	15.9	72.3	7.7	82.4	38.36	7 327	593
Fort Dodge	28.3	1 136	4.2	213	16.2	73.8	6.6	85.1	33.93	7 261	768
Iowa City	267.8	4 197	11.4	595	20.6	76.3	11.5	87.5	36.31	6 227	1 047
Marion	10.7	387	0.0	153	NA	NA	NA	NA	NA	NA	NA
Marshalltown	33.4	1 280	5.8	222	16.9	73.3	7.2	84.8	34.43	7 170	695
Mason City	14.9	524	7.9	293	13.2	72.5	4.2	83.6	32.74	7 837	623
Sioux City	101.0	1 200	6.6	869	17.7	75.7	7.7	86.5	25.86	6 893	907
Urbandale	22.8	732	0.0	168	NA	NA	NA	NA	NA	NA	NA
Waterloo	134.7	1 988	0.9	593	14.6	73.1	5.4	83.9	33.70	7 406	702
West Des Moines	NA	NA	NA	350	19.4	76.6	10.7	86.7	33.12	6 497	1 036
KANSAS	X	X	X	X	X	X	X	X	X	X	X
Dodge City	23.1	910	0.0	225	NA	NA	NA	NA	NA	NA	NA
Emporia	29.8	1 114	25.3	274	28.7	79.3	17.9	91.3	36.84	4 856	1 414
Garden City	45.9	1 660	35.4	290	NA	NA	NA	NA	NA	NA	NA
Hutchinson	44.4	1 089	16.8	401	28.1	80.7	16.4	93.6	29.22	5 103	1 489
Kansas City	1 373.1	9 342	0.0	2 693	25.7	78.5	16.7	88.7	37.62	5 393	1 288
Lawrence	111.4	1 365	23.9	1 629	29.2	80.3	19.2	91.3	39.28	4 734	1 565
Leavenworth	23.3	657	0.0	319	27.0	78.5	16.7	90.1	40.54	5 192	1 313
Leawood	55.6	1 967	0.0	237	NA	NA	NA	NA	NA	NA	NA
Lenexa	152.0	3 684	0.0	394	28.0	78.2	18.3	88.7	39.56	5 029	1 308
Manhattan	66.0	1 506	0.0	306	27.8	80.0	17.3	91.4	33.82	5 043	1 478
Olathe	343.3	3 385	10.5	722	28.0	78.2	18.3	88.7	39.56	5 029	1 308
Overland Park	117.8	744	0.0	730	28.0	78.2	18.3	88.7	39.56	5 029	1 308
Salina	45.9	998	46.7	534	28.1	80.9	17.6	92.6	29.82	5 101	1 534
Shawnee	190.4	3 613	0.0	260	28.0	78.2	18.3	88.7	39.56	5 029	1 308
Topeka	299.5	2 453	24.2	1 718	26.7	78.5	16.3	89.3	35.23	5 265	1 304
Wichita	670.8	1 889	13.7	3 067	29.5	81.4	19.2	92.8	29.33	4 791	1 628
KENTUCKY	X	X	X	X	X	X	X	X	X	X	X
Bowling Green	206.1	4 103	4.6	590	32.9	77.9	23.6	88.7	50.93	4 328	1 370
Covington	90.3	2 101	0.0	394	28.1	75.1	19.5	85.5	41.33	5 248	996
Frankfort	65.7	2 375	18.8	509	29.8	75.5	19.4	87.3	42.52	5 002	1 038
Henderson	29.6	1 079	58.8	476	32.2	77.8	23.4	88.6	44.80	4 323	1 393
Hopkinsville	94.0	3 212	12.4	384	32.0	77.7	22.1	89.5	50.79	4 437	1 365
Jeffersontown	160.9	6 150	0.2	112	NA	NA	NA	NA	NA	NA	NA
Lexington-Fayette	577.4	2 190	0.0	3 795	30.8	75.8	22.4	85.8	44.55	4 783	1 140
Louisville	643.1	2 558	44.1	4 439	31.7	77.2	23.2	87.0	44.39	4 514	1 288
Owensboro	416.2	7 683	41.0	707	32.2	77.9	23.1	89.3	46.65	4 334	1 415
Paducah	25.3	989	54.4	521	32.6	78.8	23.5	89.0	49.31	4 279	1 475
Richmond	103.5	3 685	0.0	230	NA	NA	NA	NA	NA	NA	NA

1. Based on the population estimated as of July 1 of the year shown.   2. Represents normal values based on the 30-year period, 1961–1990.   3. Average daily minimum.   4. Average daily maximum.

Table D. Cities — Land Area and Population

STATE Place code	City	Land area,[1] 2000 (sq km)	Population, 2003 Total persons	Rank	Per square kilometer	Population characteristics, 2000 — Percent — Race (alone or in combination) White	Black	Am. Indian, Alaska Native	Asian and Pacific Islander	Other race	Hispanic or Latino[2]	Non-Hispanic White
		1	2	3	4	5	6	7	8	9	10	11
22 00000	LOUISIANA	112 824.7	4 496 334	X	39.9	64.8	32.9	1.0	1.5	1.1	2.4	62.5
22 00975	Alexandria	68.4	45 649	707	667.4	43.2	55.3	0.6	1.5	0.5	1.0	42.0
22 05000	Baton Rouge	199.0	225 090	79	1 131.1	46.4	50.4	0.5	3.0	0.8	1.7	44.7
22 08920	Bossier City	105.8	58 111	522	549.3	73.1	23.4	1.1	2.6	1.9	4.0	69.4
22 36255	Houma	36.3	32 025	1 000	882.2	68.7	26.7	4.4	1.0	1.0	1.8	66.6
22 39475	Kenner	39.2	70 202	404	1 790.9	70.1	22.9	0.8	3.3	5.3	13.6	59.8
22 40735	Lafayette	123.3	111 667	211	905.7	69.0	28.9	0.5	1.7	1.0	1.9	67.1
22 41155	Lake Charles	104.0	70 735	400	680.1	51.1	47.5	0.7	1.3	0.8	1.4	49.5
22 51410	Monroe	74.3	52 163	605	702.1	37.2	61.4	0.3	1.3	0.4	1.0	36.4
22 54035	New Iberia	27.4	32 502	990	1 186.2	57.8	38.9	0.6	3.1	0.9	1.5	56.3
22 55000	New Orleans	467.6	469 032	34	1 003.1	28.9	67.9	0.5	2.6	1.5	3.1	26.6
22 70000	Shreveport	267.1	198 364	97	742.7	47.4	51.2	0.7	1.1	0.7	1.6	45.9
22 70805	Slidell	30.5	26 947	1 176	883.5	84.4	14.0	1.0	1.1	1.0	2.7	81.2
23 00000	MAINE	79 931.1	1 305 728	X	16.3	97.9	0.7	1.0	1.0	0.4	0.7	96.5
23 02795	Bangor	89.2	31 550	1 016	353.7	96.3	1.4	1.6	1.6	0.6	1.0	94.4
23 38740	Lewiston	88.3	35 922	894	406.8	97.3	1.6	1.0	1.2	0.7	1.3	95.0
23 60545	Portland	54.9	63 635	456	1 159.1	92.8	3.2	1.0	3.7	1.2	1.5	90.6
24 00000	MARYLAND	25 314.1	5 508 909	X	217.6	65.4	28.8	0.7	4.6	2.5	4.3	62.1
24 01600	Annapolis	17.4	36 178	888	2 079.2	63.8	32.1	0.6	2.4	2.8	6.4	59.0
24 04000	Baltimore	209.3	628 670	18	3 003.7	32.6	65.2	0.8	1.9	1.2	1.7	31.0
24 08775	Bowie	41.7	53 660	593	1 286.8	64.4	32.0	1.0	3.8	1.5	2.9	61.1
24 30325	Frederick	52.9	56 128	544	1 061.0	79.1	16.0	0.8	3.9	2.9	4.8	75.0
24 31175	Gaithersburg	26.1	57 365	529	2 197.9	61.6	15.7	0.8	15.2	11.2	19.8	49.1
24 36075	Hagerstown	27.6	36 953	873	1 338.9	87.6	11.2	0.7	1.3	1.1	1.8	85.2
24 67675	Rockville	34.8	55 213	560	1 586.6	70.2	9.9	0.9	16.3	6.2	11.7	61.9
25 00000	MASSACHUSETTS	20 305.6	6 433 422	X	316.8	86.2	6.3	0.6	4.3	5.1	6.8	81.9
25 00765	Agawam	60.2	28 528	1 109	473.9	97.4	1.1	0.4	1.2	0.7	1.8	95.5
25 02690	Attleboro	71.3	43 502	738	610.1	92.7	2.0	0.6	4.0	2.6	4.3	89.1
25 03600	Barnstable Town	155.5	48 907	650	314.5	93.8	3.5	1.1	1.2	3.0	1.7	90.8
25 05595	Beverly	43.0	40 255	794	936.2	96.9	1.4	0.4	1.6	0.7	1.8	94.8
25 07000	Boston	125.4	581 616	23	4 638.1	56.8	27.7	0.9	8.4	10.9	14.4	49.5
25 09000	Brockton	55.6	95 090	268	1 710.3	64.4	23.3	0.9	2.9	16.5	8.0	58.2
25 11000	Cambridge	16.7	101 587	238	6 083.1	71.2	13.8	0.8	13.3	5.7	7.4	64.6
25 13205	Chelsea	5.7	34 106	946	5 983.5	63.3	8.7	0.9	5.4	28.5	48.4	38.3
25 13660	Chicopee	59.2	54 992	565	928.9	91.4	2.8	0.5	1.3	5.9	8.8	86.9
25 21990	Everett	8.8	37 540	856	4 265.9	84.1	7.5	0.7	3.9	9.4	9.5	75.2
25 23000	Fall River	80.3	92 760	277	1 155.2	93.3	3.2	0.6	2.8	2.8	3.3	89.5
25 23875	Fitchburg	71.9	39 948	800	555.6	84.2	4.7	0.9	5.0	8.4	15.0	75.2
25 25100	Franklin	69.3	30 175	1 057	435.4	96.7	1.3	0.3	2.1	0.5	1.1	95.3
25 26150	Gloucester	67.2	30 730	1 040	457.3	97.9	0.9	0.4	1.0	0.9	1.5	96.2
25 29405	Haverhill	86.3	60 326	492	699.0	91.4	3.0	0.6	1.8	5.3	8.8	86.3
25 30840	Holyoke	55.1	40 015	799	726.2	68.0	4.6	0.8	1.2	28.4	41.4	54.0
25 34550	Lawrence	18.0	72 492	386	4 027.3	53.5	7.6	1.3	3.3	41.0	59.7	34.1
25 35075	Leominster	74.8	42 000	766	561.5	88.9	4.4	0.5	3.0	5.6	11.0	81.5
25 37000	Lowell	35.7	104 351	226	2 923.0	71.4	5.0	0.6	18.2	9.0	14.0	62.5
25 37490	Lynn	28.0	89 571	287	3 199.0	71.0	12.6	0.9	7.7	12.8	18.4	62.5
25 37875	Malden	13.1	55 816	551	4 260.8	74.2	9.7	0.5	14.8	4.5	4.8	69.6
25 38715	MarlBorough	54.6	37 980	841	695.6	90.3	2.6	0.6	4.3	5.0	6.1	84.9
25 39835	Medford	21.1	54 734	572	2 594.0	88.2	7.1	0.4	4.4	2.4	2.6	85.0
25 40115	Melrose	12.2	26 784	1 180	2 195.4	96.4	1.3	0.4	2.5	1.0	1.0	94.5
25 40710	Methuen	58.0	44 850	718	773.3	90.9	1.8	0.4	2.8	6.0	9.6	85.8
25 45000	New Bedford	52.1	94 112	270	1 806.4	82.9	6.8	1.4	1.2	14.0	10.2	75.2
25 45560	Newton	46.8	84 323	316	1 801.8	89.3	2.4	0.3	8.4	1.2	2.5	86.4
25 46330	Northampton	89.2	29 287	1 087	328.3	91.7	2.8	0.9	3.8	3.0	5.2	87.8
25 52490	Peabody	42.5	49 759	637	1 170.8	95.5	1.3	0.3	1.7	3.0	3.4	92.4
25 53960	Pittsfield	105.5	44 779	720	424.4	94.0	4.6	0.6	1.5	1.1	2.0	91.6
25 55745	Quincy	43.5	89 059	292	2 047.3	81.0	2.6	0.4	16.0	1.8	2.1	78.4
25 56585	Revere	15.3	47 002	678	3 072.0	86.9	3.6	0.6	6.0	6.9	9.4	79.4
25 59105	Salem	21.0	42 067	764	2 003.2	87.4	3.9	0.6	2.6	8.2	11.2	82.4
25 62535	Somerville	10.6	76 296	367	7 197.7	80.6	7.9	0.6	7.4	8.6	8.8	72.7
25 67000	Springfield	83.1	152 157	140	1 831.0	58.7	22.9	1.0	2.8	18.9	27.2	48.8
25 69170	Taunton	120.7	56 781	535	470.4	93.4	3.5	0.5	1.1	3.8	3.9	89.8
25 72600	Waltham	32.9	58 894	514	1 790.1	84.4	5.0	0.4	7.9	4.4	8.5	78.4
25 76030	Westfield	120.6	40 560	789	336.3	95.8	1.2	0.6	1.2	2.6	5.0	92.1
25 81035	Woburn	32.8	37 809	847	1 152.7	91.5	2.2	0.3	5.3	1.9	3.1	89.0
25 82000	Worcester	97.3	175 706	121	1 805.8	79.8	8.0	1.0	5.5	9.3	15.1	70.8

1. Dry land or land partially or temporarily covered by water.   2. Hispanic or Latino persons may be of any race.

City	Under 5 years	5 to 17 years	18 to 24 years	25 to 34 years	35 to 44 years	45 to 54 years	55 to 64 years	65 to 74 years	75 years and over	Percent female	Census counts 1990	Census counts 2000	Percent change 1990–2000	Percent change 2000–2003
	12	13	14	15	16	17	18	19	20	21	22	23	24	25
LOUISIANA	7.1	20.2	10.6	13.5	15.5	13.1	8.5	6.3	5.2	51.6	4 221 826	4 468 976	5.9	0.6
Alexandria	7.3	20.8	9.2	11.8	14.4	12.7	8.7	7.5	7.6	54.5	49 049	46 342	-5.5	-1.5
Baton Rouge	6.8	17.6	17.5	13.9	13.3	11.9	7.5	5.8	5.6	52.5	219 531	227 818	3.8	-1.2
Bossier City......................	8.0	20.2	11.0	14.7	15.6	11.5	7.9	6.1	4.8	51.4	52 721	56 461	7.1	2.9
Houma	7.4	20.5	9.8	13.3	16.0	12.6	8.3	6.6	5.7	51.3	30 495	32 393	6.2	-1.1
Kenner..............................	7.0	20.3	9.4	14.1	16.4	15.1	8.7	5.2	3.7	52.0	72 033	70 517	-2.1	-0.4
Lafayette	6.4	18.6	13.3	14.0	15.5	13.3	7.7	6.3	4.9	51.8	101 865	110 257	8.3	1.3
Lake Charles......................	6.9	18.6	11.5	12.5	14.4	12.9	8.5	7.7	6.9	52.4	70 580	71 757	1.7	-1.4
Monroe	7.6	22.0	15.0	12.4	12.7	11.0	6.5	6.2	6.6	54.3	54 909	53 107	-3.3	-1.8
New Iberia	8.2	21.6	9.7	12.4	14.4	12.2	8.1	6.8	6.6	53.2	31 828	32 623	2.5	-0.4
New Orleans	6.9	19.8	11.4	14.5	14.8	13.1	7.8	6.0	5.7	53.1	496 938	484 674	-2.5	-3.2
Shreveport........................	7.1	19.8	10.7	13.2	14.1	13.0	8.2	6.9	7.0	53.4	198 518	200 145	0.8	-0.9
Slidell	6.7	20.3	7.6	12.5	16.0	13.8	9.5	7.2	6.5	52.1	24 124	25 695	6.5	4.9
MAINE	5.5	18.1	8.1	12.4	16.7	15.1	9.7	7.5	6.8	51.3	1 227 928	1 274 923	3.8	2.4
Bangor..............................	5.7	15.5	12.4	14.7	15.6	13.9	8.1	6.7	7.4	52.8	33 181	31 473	-5.1	0.2
Lewiston	5.6	15.2	12.6	12.9	14.0	12.7	9.3	8.3	9.4	52.4	39 757	35 690	-10.2	0.7
Portland............................	5.1	13.6	10.7	19.3	16.8	13.3	7.3	6.3	7.6	52.1	64 157	64 249	0.1	-1.0
MARYLAND	6.7	18.9	8.5	14.1	17.3	14.3	8.9	6.1	5.2	51.7	4 780 753	5 296 486	10.8	4.0
Annapolis	6.7	15.0	9.3	17.7	15.7	14.3	9.3	6.3	5.7	52.6	33 195	35 838	8.0	0.9
Baltimore	6.4	18.4	10.9	14.3	15.6	12.8	8.4	6.9	6.3	53.4	736 014	651 154	-11.5	-3.5
Bowie................................	7.5	19.4	5.7	14.5	20.5	13.8	9.2	5.7	3.7	52.2	37 642	50 269	33.5	6.7
Frederick	7.5	17.7	9.3	17.7	17.6	12.4	6.7	5.3	6.0	52.4	40 186	52 767	31.3	6.4
Gaithersburg	8.2	16.8	9.0	18.9	18.8	13.4	6.6	3.5	4.8	51.3	39 676	52 613	32.6	9.0
Hagerstown........................	7.9	17.6	9.0	15.8	15.3	12.3	7.8	6.8	7.6	53.2	35 306	36 687	3.9	0.7
Rockville	6.3	17.1	7.0	14.2	17.9	14.8	9.7	6.8	6.3	51.2	44 830	47 388	5.7	16.5
MASSACHUSETTS	6.3	17.4	9.1	14.6	16.7	13.8	8.6	6.7	6.8	51.8	6 016 425	6 349 097	5.5	1.3
Agawam	5.5	16.5	6.5	12.6	17.0	15.4	9.7	7.4	9.3	52.5	27 323	28 144	3.0	1.4
Attleboro	7.0	18.4	6.8	15.7	18.2	12.7	8.3	6.4	6.5	51.4	38 383	42 068	9.6	3.4
Barnstable Town	5.2	16.7	5.6	10.4	16.4	14.9	10.6	10.5	9.6	52.2	40 949	47 821	16.8	2.3
Beverly	6.3	15.4	9.0	13.6	17.2	14.5	8.3	7.2	8.4	52.7	38 195	39 862	4.4	1.0
Boston..............................	5.4	14.3	16.2	21.2	14.7	10.8	7.0	5.3	5.1	51.9	574 283	589 141	2.6	-1.3
Brockton............................	7.3	20.6	9.1	14.6	15.9	12.4	8.4	5.8	5.9	52.1	92 788	94 304	1.6	0.8
Cambridge..........................	4.1	9.2	21.2	24.9	13.8	11.0	6.8	4.6	4.5	51.0	95 802	101 355	5.8	0.2
Chelsea..............................	8.1	19.2	10.6	19.0	15.6	9.8	6.5	5.4	5.8	49.8	28 710	35 080	22.2	-2.8
Chicopee............................	5.5	17.2	8.5	13.2	15.6	13.3	9.2	8.5	9.1	52.4	56 632	54 653	-3.5	0.6
Everett..............................	5.9	15.7	8.9	18.4	16.4	11.8	8.1	7.5	7.2	52.4	35 701	38 037	6.5	-1.3
Fall River	6.4	17.8	9.2	15.6	14.2	11.7	8.3	7.6	9.4	53.3	92 703	91 938	-0.8	0.9
Fitchburg	6.7	19.1	11.6	13.9	14.9	11.7	7.5	6.7	7.9	52.3	41 194	39 102	-5.1	2.2
Franklin	9.4	20.9	6.5	13.6	21.5	13.3	6.6	4.6	3.6	51.0	22 095	29 560	33.8	2.1
Gloucester........................	5.8	16.2	6.5	12.5	17.4	16.1	9.9	8.3	7.3	52.1	28 716	30 273	5.4	1.5
Haverhill	7.4	18.3	7.7	15.7	17.8	12.8	7.6	5.9	6.9	52.5	51 418	58 969	14.7	2.3
Holyoke	7.9	21.5	9.0	13.0	13.8	11.5	7.7	6.7	8.9	53.2	43 704	39 838	-8.8	0.4
Lawrence..........................	9.0	23.0	11.1	15.8	14.6	10.5	6.2	4.4	5.4	52.2	70 207	72 043	2.6	0.6
Leominster	7.1	18.4	7.2	14.9	17.5	13.1	8.2	6.8	6.9	51.9	38 145	41 303	8.3	1.7
Lowell	7.3	19.6	11.9	17.1	15.3	11.0	6.8	5.4	5.4	50.7	103 439	105 167	1.7	-0.8
Lynn	7.3	19.7	9.1	15.1	15.9	12.4	7.7	6.3	6.5	51.6	81 245	89 050	9.6	0.6
Malden	5.8	14.1	8.5	20.2	16.7	12.5	8.3	7.0	6.8	51.9	53 884	56 340	4.6	-0.9
MarlBorough......................	7.0	16.2	7.0	17.5	19.2	13.2	8.4	5.8	5.7	50.7	31 813	36 255	14.0	4.8
Medford	4.9	13.1	11.0	17.0	15.6	12.4	8.7	8.1	9.2	53.1	57 407	55 765	-2.9	-1.8
Melrose	6.7	15.3	5.4	14.5	17.5	15.2	9.1	7.6	8.7	53.0	28 150	27 134	-3.6	-1.3
Methuen	6.3	18.5	7.3	13.6	17.4	13.5	8.1	7.1	8.3	52.1	39 990	43 789	9.5	2.4
New Bedford	6.7	18.2	9.5	14.3	14.4	11.9	8.2	7.7	9.0	52.9	99 922	93 768	-6.2	0.4
Newton..............................	5.2	16.0	10.3	12.9	15.3	16.0	9.2	7.1	8.0	53.5	82 585	83 829	1.5	0.6
Northampton	4.1	12.9	15.4	14.1	15.8	16.3	7.6	5.9	7.9	56.9	29 289	28 978	-1.1	1.1
Peabody	5.8	16.4	6.2	12.4	17.1	14.5	10.2	9.1	8.4	52.1	47 264	48 129	1.8	3.4
Pittsfield	5.9	17.2	6.9	12.6	15.7	13.7	9.4	8.8	9.8	52.5	48 622	45 793	-5.8	-2.2
Quincy	5.1	12.4	8.1	19.7	16.3	13.1	9.0	8.0	8.3	52.3	84 985	88 025	3.6	1.2
Revere..............................	5.8	15.2	7.9	16.5	16.1	12.4	9.4	8.3	8.3	51.6	42 786	47 283	10.5	-0.6
Salem	5.6	14.6	10.4	17.0	16.3	13.7	8.2	6.9	7.2	53.6	38 091	40 407	6.1	4.1
Somerville..........................	4.5	10.3	15.9	27.6	15.0	10.1	6.2	5.2	5.2	51.3	76 210	77 478	1.7	-1.5
Springfield	7.6	21.3	11.4	14.0	14.4	11.6	7.2	6.1	6.4	52.8	156 983	152 082	-3.1	0.0
Taunton............................	7.1	17.8	8.0	15.9	17.3	12.7	8.4	6.3	6.6	51.9	49 832	55 976	12.3	1.4
Waltham	4.7	10.8	16.8	19.1	15.3	12.0	8.2	6.6	6.5	50.7	57 878	59 226	2.3	-0.6
Westfield	5.9	17.9	12.6	12.3	15.7	13.7	8.2	6.6	7.1	51.6	38 372	40 072	4.4	1.2
Woburn	5.8	15.3	6.9	17.3	17.6	12.9	8.8	8.6	6.8	51.1	35 943	37 258	3.7	1.5
Worcester..........................	6.5	17.1	13.3	15.5	14.8	11.4	7.2	6.3	7.8	52.0	169 759	172 648	1.7	1.8

Table D. Cities — Group Quarters, Crime, and Education

City	Households, 2000 Number	Percent change, 1990–2000	Persons per house-hold	Percent Female family house-holder[1]	One-person	Persons in group quarters, 2000 Total	Institutional Total	Persons in nursing homes	Non-institu-tional	Serious crimes known to police[2] 2002 Total Number	Rate[3]	Violent	Property	Education 2000 School enrollment[4] Public	Private	High school graduate or less	Bachelor's degree or more
	26	27	28	29	30	31	32	33	34	35	36	37	38	39	40	41	42
LOUISIANA	1 656 053	10.5	2.62	16.6	25.3	135 965	90 002	31 521	45 963	228 528	5 098	662	4 436	1 030 634	240 665	57.6	18.7
Alexandria	17 816	-1.8	2.50	23.2	30.4	1 782	1 281	761	501	5 554	11 948	2 063	9 885	11 068	1 544	57.1	19.5
Baton Rouge	88 973	6.8	2.42	19.0	31.7	12 453	3 406	1 397	9 047	18 949	8 292	1 168	7 124	64 790	12 959	43.3	31.7
Bossier City	21 197	11.4	2.58	15.8	24.7	1 695	852	569	843	4 187	7 393	927	6 466	14 633	1 419	49.0	18.2
Houma	11 634	9.2	2.72	16.7	24.1	800	681	119	119	2 125	6 540	1 188	5 352	6 535	2 131	64.6	14.3
Kenner	25 652	2.4	2.72	16.3	23.2	698	437	414	261	3 357	4 746	443	4 304	12 660	7 148	50.6	21.3
Lafayette	43 506	19.8	2.43	14.6	29.4	4 438	1 966	924	2 472	8 431	7 623	943	6 680	26 567	7 028	42.2	31.3
Lake Charles	27 974	4.3	2.44	18.7	30.0	3 570	2 208	820	1 362	4 881	6 781	966	5 816	16 839	3 279	54.1	20.2
Monroe	19 421	1.5	2.54	25.3	31.3	3 706	1 373	714	2 333	NA	NA	NA	NA	16 413	1 851	48.8	26.9
New Iberia	11 756	5.5	2.70	20.5	25.2	932	467	362	465	2 178	6 656	843	5 812	7 848	1 045	70.6	12.3
New Orleans	188 251	0.0	2.48	24.5	33.2	17 641	9 772	2 976	7 869	31 206	6 419	937	5 482	109 563	40 533	48.8	25.8
Shreveport	78 662	4.0	2.48	21.5	30.8	5 391	3 476	1 979	1 915	16 389	8 164	1 018	7 145	49 265	6 406	51.8	22.2
Slidell	9 480	13.9	2.67	14.0	20.4	347	324	305	23	2 398	9 304	799	8 505	5 599	1 305	46.6	22.0
MAINE	518 200	11.4	2.39	9.5	27.0	34 912	13 091	9 339	21 821	34 381	2 656	108	2 548	275 158	45 883	50.8	22.9
Bangor	13 713	2.4	2.12	12.8	37.6	2 360	789	468	1 571	1 630	5 101	122	4 979	6 643	1 578	44.3	26.5
Lewiston	15 290	-3.4	2.17	11.8	35.9	2 543	764	693	1 779	1 789	4 937	218	4 719	6 238	2 935	65.6	12.6
Portland	29 714	5.2	2.08	10.5	40.1	2 443	924	527	1 519	3 525	5 404	291	5 112	12 405	2 541	37.6	36.4
MARYLAND	1 980 859	13.3	2.61	14.1	25.0	134 056	69 318	26 716	64 738	259 120	4 747	770	3 978	1 174 026	301 458	42.9	31.4
Annapolis	15 303	8.8	2.30	16.3	32.9	706	212	212	494	2 330	6 309	1 140	5 169	6 163	2 562	37.9	38.7
Baltimore	257 996	-6.7	2.42	25.0	34.9	25 753	12 634	4 204	13 119	55 820	8 319	2 055	6 264	141 851	42 662	59.8	19.1
Bowie	18 188	41.1	2.74	11.0	19.7	471	327	327	144	NA	NA	NA	NA	10 283	4 196	25.6	43.0
Frederick	20 891	33.3	2.42	12.8	30.0	2 110	969	969	1 141	2 710	4 984	1 206	3 777	11 028	2 572	42.8	29.9
Gaithersburg	19 621	29.1	2.65	11.2	27.8	623	268	268	355	NA	NA	NA	NA	10 875	2 516	29.5	46.5
Hagerstown	15 849	5.2	2.26	15.9	35.4	829	412	392	417	1 764	4 666	635	4 031	7 380	626	66.1	11.8
Rockville	17 247	10.1	2.65	9.5	23.8	1 642	1 269	643	373	NA	NA	NA	NA	9 407	2 702	27.1	52.9
MASSACHUSETTS	2 443 580	8.7	2.51	11.9	28.0	221 216	88 453	55 837	132 763	198 890	3 094	484	2 610	1 276 945	449 166	42.5	33.2
Agawam	11 260	7.9	2.43	9.8	28.0	726	726	726	0	843	2 959	284	2 674	5 515	1 171	49.0	21.4
Attleboro	16 019	13.0	2.57	10.6	25.7	831	609	609	222	973	2 285	289	1 996	8 496	1 973	50.0	23.5
Barnstable Town	19 626	18.2	2.38	10.7	27.7	1 204	600	328	604	1 653	3 414	698	2 716	9 069	1 768	35.7	32.2
Beverly	15 750	6.4	2.39	9.7	29.9	2 170	774	770	1 396	853	2 114	280	1 834	6 766	3 398	37.0	36.5
Boston	239 528	4.8	2.31	16.4	37.1	35 077	8 481	3 930	26 596	35 706	5 986	1 166	4 820	101 700	83 684	45.1	35.6
Brockton	33 675	2.5	2.74	19.9	26.6	1 876	1 367	927	509	5 179	5 425	1 124	4 301	23 857	3 422	59.9	14.0
Cambridge	42 615	8.1	2.03	9.7	41.4	14 663	505	272	14 158	4 306	4 196	484	3 712	11 962	25 761	22.7	65.1
Chelsea	11 888	12.7	2.87	20.1	28.8	953	878	878	75	1 890	5 322	1 917	3 404	8 048	1 679	70.6	10.0
Chicopee	23 117	2.2	2.32	14.2	32.7	1 006	310	310	696	2 488	4 497	761	3 736	10 750	2 424	63.2	12.3
Everett	15 435	6.2	2.45	15.2	31.3	231	214	214	17	1 152	2 992	322	2 670	7 102	1 995	64.1	14.7
Fall River	38 759	3.9	2.32	16.5	34.2	1 891	1 472	1 351	419	4 869	5 231	995	4 236	18 749	3 111	69.5	10.7
Fitchburg	14 943	-2.7	2.50	14.6	30.3	1 745	567	517	1 178	1 699	4 292	740	3 552	9 679	1 422	59.8	15.4
Franklin	10 152	194.4	2.85	8.5	18.3	626	66	66	560	122	408	37	371	6 769	2 123	30.6	42.7
Gloucester	12 592	8.7	2.38	10.6	30.7	360	265	265	95	740	2 415	238	2 176	5 399	1 485	45.8	27.5
Haverhill	22 976	17.4	2.51	13.4	28.6	1 397	851	794	546	1 776	2 975	466	2 509	12 516	3 038	47.5	23.4
Holyoke	14 967	-5.6	2.57	22.1	30.9	1 381	1 188	1 180	193	3 346	8 296	1 145	7 151	9 773	1 899	59.6	16.9
Lawrence	24 463	0.8	2.90	25.7	25.5	1 044	801	551	243	3 195	4 381	724	3 657	19 166	3 511	71.4	10.0
Leominster	16 491	11.2	2.48	12.5	27.9	394	296	296	98	1 197	2 863	151	2 712	8 561	2 165	50.8	21.9
Lowell	37 887	2.3	2.67	17.4	29.0	3 841	1 120	1 120	2 721	4 258	3 999	797	3 202	25 803	4 883	60.9	18.1
Lynn	33 511	6.2	2.62	17.6	31.0	1 344	738	738	606	3 924	4 352	951	3 402	20 755	3 564	59.7	16.4
Malden	23 009	5.0	2.42	12.3	32.2	605	379	379	226	NA	NA	NA	NA	9 341	3 811	49.6	26.2
Marlborough	14 501	19.3	2.47	9.0	28.4	489	346	346	143	710	1 934	213	1 722	6 427	2 200	37.9	35.6
Medford	22 067	1.1	2.43	11.8	28.7	2 204	536	536	1 668	1 486	2 632	138	2 494	7 464	6 682	45.9	31.7
Melrose	10 982	0.4	2.44	8.7	29.7	329	291	291	38	342	1 245	87	1 158	4 688	1 540	32.8	40.1
Methuen	16 532	12.9	2.62	12.2	25.3	483	319	319	164	1 235	2 786	196	2 590	9 171	2 377	51.4	23.0
New Bedford	38 178	-1.6	2.40	18.9	31.6	1 986	1 507	1 291	479	3 299	3 475	768	2 707	20 171	2 773	70.1	10.7
Newton	31 201	5.9	2.51	8.0	25.5	5 578	621	612	4 957	890	1 049	92	957	13 374	11 260	17.6	68.0
Northampton	11 880	6.4	2.14	10.1	37.3	3 602	1 090	675	2 512	1 039	3 541	539	3 003	5 128	3 715	32.0	46.1
Peabody	18 581	5.8	2.55	10.4	25.4	720	535	524	185	1 467	3 011	209	2 801	9 086	2 616	49.6	23.1
Pittsfield	19 704	-1.1	2.26	13.1	34.0	1 267	910	621	357	1 166	2 515	375	2 140	9 330	1 375	53.5	21.1
Quincy	38 883	9.0	2.22	10.5	37.6	1 586	780	655	806	2 455	2 755	296	2 459	12 868	6 197	43.5	31.8
Revere	19 463	11.6	2.41	13.9	32.7	318	255	255	63	1 945	4 063	485	3 579	8 288	2 325	63.7	13.5
Salem	17 492	10.7	2.24	13.3	34.9	1 160	162	149	998	1 057	2 584	196	2 388	8 599	1 803	43.2	31.1
Somerville	31 555	4.1	2.38	10.3	31.0	2 515	316	280	2 199	2 569	3 275	444	2 832	9 998	10 593	43.2	40.6
Springfield	57 130	-1.1	2.57	23.8	30.2	5 533	1 648	829	3 885	14 302	9 289	2 015	7 274	36 595	10 026	59.5	15.4
Taunton	22 045	17.0	2.50	13.4	28.2	820	592	394	228	1 641	2 896	494	2 402	11 193	2 289	60.4	15.1
Waltham	23 207	12.0	2.29	8.9	34.2	5 991	749	459	5 242	1 129	1 883	158	1 724	8 197	8 375	40.0	38.4
Westfield	14 797	7.0	2.54	10.6	25.9	2 468	511	370	1 957	1 043	2 571	592	1 979	10 569	1 466	47.4	24.2
Woburn	14 997	11.2	2.47	10.9	28.7	244	100	100	144	992	2 630	241	2 389	6 180	2 030	44.3	29.5
Worcester	67 028	4.9	2.41	15.6	33.0	11 107	2 893	2 542	8 214	8 397	4 804	763	4 041	35 752	15 874	52.7	23.3

1. No spouse present. 2. Data for serious crimes have not been adjusted for underreporting. This may affect comparability between geographic areas and over time. 3. Per 100,000 population estimated by the FBI. 4. All persons 3 years old and over enrolled in nursery school through college. 5. Persons 25 years old and over.

Table D. Cities — Income, Poverty, and Housing

City	Per capita income[1] (dollars)	Money income, 1999 — Households — Median income — Dollars	Percent change, 1989–1999 (constant 1999 dollars)	Percent with income of $100,000 or more	Percent below poverty — Persons — Total	Percent change in rate, 1989–1999	Families — Total	Housing units, 2000 — Total	Percent change, 1990–2000	Vacant units for sale or rent[2]	Vacant units — For seasonal use (percent)	Home owner vacancy rate	Renter vacancy rate
	43	44	45	46	47	48	49	50	51	52	53	54	55
LOUISIANA	16 912	32 566	10.4	7.4	19.6	-16.9	15.8	1 847 181	7.6	191 128	2.1	1.6	9.3
Alexandria	16 242	26 097	4.7	7.5	27.4	-4.9	23.2	19 806	-2.7	1 990	0.3	2.0	10.7
Baton Rouge	18 512	30 368	3.2	9.3	24.0	-8.4	18.0	97 388	0.3	8 415	0.3	1.6	8.8
Bossier City	17 032	36 561	5.0	6.4	14.8	-7.5	11.4	23 026	5.6	1 829	0.5	2.1	9.8
Houma	17 720	34 471	32.3	8.2	20.8	-21.2	16.4	12 514	9.0	880	0.1	1.3	8.0
Kenner	19 615	39 946	-2.2	10.4	13.6	-4.2	11.0	27 378	0.4	1 726	0.3	0.9	10.1
Lafayette	21 031	35 996	14.3	10.8	16.3	-25.6	11.6	46 865	16.1	3 359	0.5	1.4	9.1
Lake Charles	17 922	30 774	7.9	7.8	19.6	-16.9	16.3	31 429	5.3	3 455	0.4	2.1	13.6
Monroe	15 933	25 864	18.7	7.8	32.3	-14.6	26.3	21 278	-1.5	1 857	0.3	1.8	7.6
New Iberia	13 084	26 079	4.9	4.2	29.5	2.8	24.9	12 880	3.7	1 124	0.4	1.5	7.2
New Orleans	17 258	27 133	9.3	7.8	27.9	-11.7	23.7	215 091	-4.6	26 840	1.1	2.2	7.9
Shreveport	17 759	30 526	2.9	7.4	22.8	-9.9	18.7	86 802	-0.8	8 140	0.4	1.8	10.9
Slidell	19 947	42 856	-7.5	10.7	11.8	16.8	9.5	10 133	11.5	653	0.4	1.5	11.2
MAINE	19 533	37 240	-0.5	7.1	10.9	0.9	7.8	651 901	11.0	133 701	15.6	1.7	7.0
Bangor	19 295	29 740	-10.3	7.4	16.6	10.7	11.9	14 587	1.5	874	1.0	2.0	4.2
Lewiston	17 905	29 191	-9.7	4.2	15.5	11.5	10.0	16 470	-3.8	1 180	0.4	1.3	8.8
Portland	22 698	35 650	-0.2	7.0	14.1	0.7	9.7	31 862	1.8	2 148	3.0	0.5	3.6
MARYLAND	25 614	52 868	-0.1	18.1	8.5	2.4	6.1	2 145 283	13.4	164 424	1.8	1.6	6.1
Annapolis	27 180	49 243	3.2	16.4	12.7	5.0	9.5	16 165	6.0	862	1.2	1.4	3.8
Baltimore	16 978	30 078	-6.9	6.3	22.9	4.6	18.8	300 477	-1.1	42 481	0.5	3.6	7.6
Bowie	30 703	76 778	-4.2	28.7	1.6	45.5	0.7	18 718	43.3	530	0.2	1.2	4.5
Frederick	23 053	47 700	1.8	11.5	7.4	-7.5	4.8	22 106	33.1	1 215	0.3	2.7	5.3
Gaithersburg	27 323	59 879	2.1	21.8	7.1	18.3	4.9	20 674	28.7	1 053	0.5	1.5	6.1
Hagerstown	17 153	30 796	0.3	3.8	18.1	14.6	15.1	17 089	4.4	1 240	0.2	3.4	5.7
Rockville	30 518	68 074	-2.7	29.8	7.8	34.5	5.6	17 786	9.5	539	0.2	0.8	4.5
MASSACHUSETTS	25 952	50 502	1.7	17.7	9.3	4.5	6.7	2 621 989	6.0	178 409	3.6	0.7	3.5
Agawam	22 562	49 390	NA	10.4	5.6	NA	4.3	11 659	7.3	399	0.6	0.8	4.2
Attleboro	22 660	50 807	3.2	11.5	6.2	-3.1	3.7	16 554	10.0	535	0.2	0.7	3.8
Barnstable Town	25 554	46 811	NA	13.6	8.8	NA	6.3	25 018	7.1	5 392	19.0	1.1	3.7
Beverly	28 626	53 984	1.5	18.4	5.7	-13.6	4.0	16 275	4.0	525	0.8	0.4	3.1
Boston	23 353	39 629	1.1	12.8	19.5	4.3	15.3	251 935	0.4	12 407	0.6	1.0	3.0
Brockton	17 163	39 507	-7.3	7.9	14.5	6.6	12.1	34 837	-1.5	1 162	0.1	0.5	3.3
Cambridge	31 156	47 979	7.8	19.6	12.9	20.6	8.7	44 725	6.5	2 110	1.3	0.9	2.6
Chelsea	14 628	30 161	-10.7	6.6	23.3	-3.3	20.6	12 337	6.6	449	0.2	1.1	1.6
Chicopee	18 646	35 672	-8.1	4.9	12.3	25.5	9.6	24 424	3.1	1 307	0.4	0.9	4.8
Everett	19 845	40 661	-1.7	7.9	11.8	22.9	9.2	15 908	3.2	473	0.1	0.5	2.2
Fall River	16 118	29 014	-3.8	4.2	17.1	19.6	14.0	41 857	3.7	3 098	0.2	1.4	6.7
Fitchburg	17 256	37 004	1.6	6.6	15.0	7.1	12.1	16 002	-4.0	1 059	0.2	1.4	6.5
Franklin	27 849	71 174	NA	28.2	2.8	NA	2.2	10 327	34.3	175	0.3	0.3	2.9
Gloucester	25 595	47 722	8.7	12.9	8.8	17.3	7.1	13 958	6.3	1 366	6.9	0.8	2.7
Haverhill	23 280	49 833	0.4	13.4	9.1	3.4	7.0	23 737	11.3	761	0.3	0.5	3.1
Holyoke	15 913	30 441	-0.9	5.9	26.4	2.7	22.6	16 210	-4.2	1 243	0.2	0.9	6.9
Lawrence	13 360	27 983	-6.1	5.0	24.3	-11.6	21.2	25 601	-4.9	1 138	0.2	1.0	3.0
Leominster	21 769	44 893	-7.1	11.1	9.5	31.9	7.2	16 976	9.3	485	0.2	0.5	2.6
Lowell	17 557	39 192	-0.6	8.1	16.8	-6.7	13.6	39 468	-2.1	1 581	0.2	1.2	3.1
Lynn	17 492	37 364	-2.6	8.1	16.5	3.8	13.2	34 637	0.1	1 126	0.2	0.7	2.3
Malden	22 004	45 654	-1.1	10.9	9.2	22.7	6.6	23 634	1.8	625	0.3	0.4	2.1
MarlBorough	28 723	56 879	2.5	20.4	6.8	19.3	4.7	14 903	14.4	402	0.4	0.5	2.4
Medford	24 707	52 476	0.5	16.7	6.4	-7.2	4.1	22 687	0.2	620	0.2	0.5	2.5
Melrose	30 347	62 811	6.0	23.3	3.3	-21.4	1.6	11 248	-0.4	266	0.4	0.4	1.6
Methuen	22 305	49 627	NA	13.4	7.4	NA	5.8	16 885	9.4	353	0.2	0.3	2.8
New Bedford	15 602	27 569	-9.4	4.2	20.2	20.2	17.3	41 511	-0.6	3 333	0.3	1.9	6.9
Newton	45 708	86 052	7.2	42.8	4.3	0.0	2.6	32 112	5.3	911	0.8	0.5	2.1
Northampton	24 022	41 808	0.1	11.8	9.8	-14.8	5.7	12 405	5.6	525	1.0	0.4	3.4
Peabody	24 827	54 829	2.5	17.5	5.3	15.2	3.7	18 898	3.6	317	0.3	0.3	1.7
Pittsfield	20 549	35 655	-11.5	7.7	11.4	17.5	8.9	21 366	0.4	1 662	1.2	1.5	9.0
Quincy	26 001	47 121	-2.2	13.7	7.3	7.4	5.2	40 093	6.3	1 210	0.5	0.4	2.7
Revere	19 698	37 067	-10.0	9.0	14.6	25.9	11.9	20 181	7.8	718	0.4	0.5	2.3
Salem	23 857	44 033	0.4	12.1	9.7	-17.1	6.3	18 175	5.9	683	0.4	0.9	2.5
Somerville	23 628	46 315	6.2	13.3	12.5	8.7	8.4	32 477	2.2	922	0.3	0.8	1.6
Springfield	15 232	30 417	-11.8	5.0	23.1	14.9	19.3	61 172	-0.2	4 042	0.3	1.3	6.1
Taunton	19 899	42 932	-1.1	8.0	10.0	20.5	8.0	22 908	13.0	863	0.1	0.6	4.7
Waltham	26 364	54 010	4.4	18.9	7.0	7.7	3.6	23 880	9.9	673	0.5	0.3	2.2
Westfield	20 600	45 240	0.5	9.8	11.3	41.3	6.9	15 441	6.7	644	0.5	1.0	2.8
Woburn	26 207	54 897	-4.3	16.8	6.1	19.6	4.5	15 391	9.1	394	0.5	0.4	2.2
Worcester	18 614	35 623	-8.4	8.2	17.9	17.0	14.1	70 723	2.0	3 695	0.4	0.9	4.1

1. Based on population enumerated as of April 1, 2000.   2. Includes units rented or sold but not occupied.

Table D. Cities — Housing, Labor Force, Employment, and Disability

City	Housing units, 2000 (cont'd) Occupied units					Civilian labor force, 2003				Civilian employment,[2] 2000			Disability, 2000
	Total	Percent owner occupied	Percent renter occupied	Average size owner occupied	Average size renter occupied	Total	Percent change, 2002–2003	Unemployment Total	Rate[1]	Total	Percent Management, professional, and related occupations	Production, transportation, and material moving occupations	Employment disabled persons[3] (percent)
	56	57	58	59	60	61	62	63	64	65	66	67	68
LOUISIANA	1 656 053	67.9	32.1	2.70	2.44	2 037 050	1.9	133 531	6.6	1 851 777	29.9	14.1	12.9
Alexandria	17 816	57.4	42.6	2.53	2.47	22 374	2.0	1 797	8.0	17 094	32.8	10.3	16.4
Baton Rouge	88 973	52.2	47.8	2.58	2.25	119 614	3.3	7 849	6.6	101 130	36.7	10.3	12.1
Bossier City	21 197	60.0	40.0	2.60	2.56	28 724	1.7	1 848	6.4	23 637	28.5	12.5	11.2
Houma	11 634	67.7	32.3	2.80	2.54	16 193	3.1	645	4.0	12 649	26.0	15.3	15.3
Kenner	25 652	60.8	39.2	2.87	2.49	38 082	1.9	1 938	5.1	33 496	31.4	10.8	13.5
Lafayette	43 506	58.3	41.7	2.63	2.15	57 977	2.1	2 892	5.0	51 252	39.6	9.0	10.3
Lake Charles	27 974	57.6	42.4	2.51	2.34	36 783	1.2	2 948	8.0	30 219	28.8	11.9	13.2
Monroe	19 421	49.6	50.4	2.56	2.52	25 054	1.8	2 096	8.4	20 357	32.6	9.7	14.6
New Iberia	11 756	62.6	37.4	2.70	2.69	14 697	-0.6	1 116	7.6	11 481	24.5	16.9	11.7
New Orleans	188 251	46.5	53.5	2.60	2.37	194 424	1.9	12 863	6.6	191 739	34.7	10.4	13.6
Shreveport	78 662	59.0	41.0	2.52	2.41	94 265	1.6	7 297	7.7	82 432	30.2	14.0	14.1
Slidell	9 480	76.1	23.9	2.71	2.57	15 820	1.6	594	3.8	11 329	34.3	10.1	13.2
MAINE	518 200	71.6	28.4	2.54	2.03	693 083	1.9	35 015	5.1	624 011	31.5	15.3	11.7
Bangor	13 713	47.5	52.5	2.43	1.85	18 356	1.3	623	3.4	15 591	34.8	9.0	13.4
Lewiston	15 290	47.2	52.8	2.44	1.92	21 090	1.8	1 023	4.9	16 572	25.0	18.4	14.4
Portland	29 714	42.5	57.5	2.41	1.84	36 943	2.0	1 256	3.4	35 150	39.7	9.9	11.7
MARYLAND	1 980 859	67.7	32.3	2.73	2.35	2 904 139	0.3	130 827	4.5	2 608 457	41.3	9.5	10.8
Annapolis	15 303	51.7	48.3	2.36	2.23	22 091	-0.4	1 399	6.3	19 341	42.9	6.9	10.5
Baltimore	257 996	50.3	49.7	2.57	2.27	288 454	0.3	24 810	8.6	256 036	32.4	13.4	16.6
Bowie	18 188	85.0	15.0	2.79	2.45	25 219	0.6	662	2.6	27 218	52.7	5.2	7.0
Frederick	20 891	55.6	44.4	2.59	2.22	29 373	0.9	1 085	3.7	27 647	39.2	9.8	9.6
Gaithersburg	19 621	52.6	47.4	2.86	2.42	27 853	0.5	906	3.3	28 578	48.6	6.1	8.9
Hagerstown	15 849	41.9	58.1	2.36	2.19	21 102	-0.3	1 019	4.8	17 292	21.2	19.2	12.4
Rockville	17 247	67.7	32.3	2.71	2.54	29 261	0.5	905	3.1	24 110	55.6	4.8	7.6
MASSACHUSETTS	2 443 580	61.7	38.3	2.72	2.17	3 415 518	-1.5	198 311	5.8	3 161 087	41.1	11.3	11.8
Agawam	11 260	73.6	26.4	2.63	1.90	15 494	-0.9	870	5.6	14 871	33.2	14.1	9.4
Attleboro	16 019	63.8	36.2	2.81	2.16	23 663	0.7	1 459	6.2	22 063	33.6	19.4	12.5
Barnstable Town	19 626	76.2	23.8	2.43	2.19	26 054	2.4	1 171	4.5	22 677	35.3	7.7	12.1
Beverly	15 750	60.0	40.0	2.70	1.93	21 967	-2.4	1 018	4.6	20 609	42.4	9.0	9.6
Boston	239 528	32.2	67.8	2.51	2.22	309 552	-2.3	18 710	6.0	285 859	44.3	8.3	14.2
Brockton	33 675	54.6	45.4	2.98	2.46	48 762	0.2	3 540	7.3	42 560	23.9	20.4	20.6
Cambridge	42 615	32.3	67.7	2.16	1.97	58 546	-2.7	2 106	3.6	56 241	66.8	4.3	7.2
Chelsea	11 888	28.9	71.1	2.87	2.87	15 532	-1.4	1 228	7.9	13 173	17.9	23.4	22.9
Chicopee	23 117	59.3	40.7	2.46	2.11	27 591	-0.7	1 927	7.0	25 804	22.8	23.4	14.7
Everett	15 435	41.4	58.6	2.67	2.29	19 861	-1.4	1 378	6.9	18 231	24.9	13.8	16.4
Fall River	38 759	34.9	65.1	2.66	2.14	43 790	1.7	3 932	9.0	39 674	22.4	24.3	18.7
Fitchburg	14 943	51.6	48.4	2.64	2.35	18 109	0.1	1 654	9.1	17 536	27.2	21.4	13.4
Franklin	10 152	81.2	18.8	3.06	1.92	16 373	-2.3	772	4.7	15 008	46.7	8.1	8.3
Gloucester	12 592	59.7	40.3	2.60	2.04	16 337	-2.0	1 167	7.1	15 314	36.1	13.4	9.1
Haverhill	22 976	60.2	39.8	2.69	2.23	30 983	-2.1	2 550	8.2	29 676	34.3	17.0	13.8
Holyoke	14 967	41.5	58.5	2.66	2.50	15 866	-0.6	1 338	8.4	14 848	30.4	18.3	17.6
Lawrence	24 463	32.2	67.8	3.02	2.85	29 861	-1.9	4 410	14.8	25 772	20.7	27.9	23.5
Leominster	16 491	57.9	42.1	2.71	2.16	21 997	-0.5	1 603	7.3	20 221	32.8	17.7	12.4
Lowell	37 887	43.0	57.0	2.87	2.53	54 257	-3.4	4 652	8.6	47 735	28.4	22.6	15.6
Lynn	33 511	45.6	54.4	2.81	2.46	42 251	-1.2	3 220	7.6	39 243	25.8	17.2	17.9
Malden	23 009	43.3	56.7	2.86	2.08	31 280	-1.7	1 946	6.2	29 903	35.6	10.9	15.2
Marlborough	14 501	61.0	39.0	2.68	2.13	22 468	-2.5	1 197	5.3	20 321	42.8	10.5	11.2
Medford	22 067	58.6	41.4	2.62	2.15	30 324	-2.1	1 611	5.3	29 024	42.1	8.5	11.8
Melrose	10 982	67.0	33.0	2.78	1.75	14 687	-2.5	717	4.9	14 700	48.6	7.1	9.0
Methuen	16 532	71.9	28.1	2.79	2.19	22 677	-1.9	2 057	9.1	20 810	36.0	15.4	13.6
New Bedford	38 178	43.8	56.2	2.60	2.25	41 772	-0.5	4 339	10.4	38 482	20.8	25.1	16.9
Newton	31 201	69.5	30.5	2.70	2.08	47 938	-2.7	1 631	3.4	45 018	65.3	3.3	6.8
Northampton	11 880	53.5	46.5	2.44	1.79	15 734	-1.2	580	3.7	16 291	50.2	8.1	8.2
Peabody	18 581	71.2	28.8	2.75	2.06	27 144	-2.1	1 404	5.2	24 341	36.4	11.4	12.5
Pittsfield	19 704	60.8	39.2	2.45	1.97	21 834	-0.6	1 202	5.5	21 266	32.4	11.0	12.7
Quincy	38 883	49.0	51.0	2.59	1.87	50 973	-1.8	3 040	6.0	47 911	40.1	7.9	11.4
Revere	19 463	50.0	50.0	2.64	2.19	23 955	-1.3	1 730	7.2	21 184	25.5	13.3	17.8
Salem	17 492	49.1	50.9	2.40	2.09	23 108	-1.8	1 427	6.2	21 684	37.4	11.9	11.7
Somerville	31 555	30.6	69.4	2.59	2.28	45 449	-2.4	2 168	4.8	45 967	47.9	8.5	12.9
Springfield	57 130	49.9	50.1	2.61	2.52	66 827	-0.7	5 659	8.5	60 651	27.1	17.8	18.7
Taunton	22 045	61.2	38.8	2.73	2.14	29 277	-1.7	1 904	6.5	28 391	26.3	19.8	13.4
Waltham	23 207	46.0	54.0	2.60	2.03	34 221	-2.4	1 802	5.3	33 290	45.3	8.8	9.8
Westfield	14 797	67.8	32.2	2.68	2.25	20 321	-1.2	1 064	5.2	19 843	32.5	15.4	12.0
Woburn	14 997	61.2	38.8	2.74	2.04	22 422	-2.4	1 158	5.2	20 287	38.4	10.9	11.5
Worcester	67 028	43.3	56.7	2.57	2.28	81 757	-0.6	5 873	7.2	77 475	33.2	16.3	15.9

1. Percent of civilian labor force.   2. Persons 16 years old and over.   3. Persons 16 to 64 years old.

City	Value of residential construction authorized by building permits, 2003			Wholesale trade, 1997				Retail trade,[1] 1997			
	New construction ($1,000)	Number of housing units	Percent single family	Number of establishments	Number of employees	Sales (mil dol)	Annual payroll (mil dol)	Number of establishments	Number of employees	Sales (mil dol)	Annual payroll (mil dol)
	69	70	71	72	73	74	75	76	77	78	79
LOUISIANA	2 595 720	22 220	83.2	6 390	76 350	46 972.3	2 375.2	17 863	224 412	35 807.9	3 307.9
Alexandria	24 948	202	90.1	101	1 255	427.5	32.5	362	5 064	777.6	76.3
Baton Rouge	77 416	1 222	34.0	594	7 871	2 925.2	283.0	1 408	20 737	3 382.5	328.9
Bossier City	79 351	1 025	42.1	77	1 023	1 111.3	28.2	305	4 370	761.7	67.0
Houma	NA	NA	NA	102	1 276	429.7	38.6	246	3 088	437.5	42.4
Kenner	23 215	103	88.3	170	D	D	D	350	5 765	968.9	86.5
Lafayette	NA	NA	NA	321	4 159	1 864.0	137.4	818	12 689	2 104.3	198.9
Lake Charles	41 389	475	42.3	141	2 039	533.0	56.0	483	6 705	1 019.8	96.4
Monroe	13 063	157	58.6	139	1 867	680.8	56.9	470	6 314	1 058.1	94.4
New Iberia	9 556	68	64.7	82	1 139	279.8	36.2	214	2 748	505.3	43.3
New Orleans	281 293	917	57.8	484	6 086	2 450.5	210.2	1 871	20 405	2 771.3	315.6
Shreveport	103 733	674	97.6	422	5 186	1 723.0	154.9	930	12 010	2 056.5	198.3
Slidell	9 609	102	100.0	48	D	D	D	322	4 324	666.3	59.3
MAINE	1 066 671	7 933	92.1	1 726	19 932	7 305.6	616.2	7 074	72 897	12 737.1	1 164.2
Bangor	6 070	60	66.7	92	1 600	620.5	49.2	335	5 340	999.7	87.9
Lewiston	10 763	94	94.7	60	D	D	D	202	2 548	593.1	40.1
Portland	28 498	264	61.0	233	3 538	1 477.5	113.0	422	5 380	1 292.3	97.5
MARYLAND	3 723 627	29 914	78.2	6 283	92 458	54 906.6	3 656.3	19 798	274 260	46 428.2	4 914.0
Annapolis	19 256	147	100.0	89	646	419.0	28.6	466	6 238	1 032.9	111.3
Baltimore	51 421	695	29.6	792	14 152	6 171.2	499.2	2 256	23 159	3 438.4	414.7
Bowie	NA	NA	NA	26	D	D	D	104	2 284	339.1	35.5
Frederick	30 203	489	60.5	123	2 088	634.0	68.4	464	7 724	1 308.2	132.7
Gaithersburg	39 116	479	35.9	76	D	D	D	333	6 573	1 340.1	128.7
Hagerstown	11 585	175	72.6	79	967	301.6	28.3	305	4 123	689.7	62.4
Rockville	97 683	967	43.4	131	2 656	2 937.3	150.0	305	4 250	983.6	97.4
MASSACHUSETTS	3 141 366	20 257	64.4	9 993	146 827	112 792.4	6 484.8	26 209	335 736	58 578.0	5 894.8
Agawam	15 987	71	97.2	NA	NA	NA	NA	NA	NA	NA	NA
Attleboro	13 680	123	82.9	40	394	172.1	16.7	158	2 973	476.3	38.8
Barnstable Town	32 266	130	87.7	NA	NA	NA	NA	NA	NA	NA	NA
Beverly	9 971	46	100.0	46	331	210.8	18.0	146	1 820	350.5	34.2
Boston	117 182	1 508	6.6	770	9 857	7 574.9	437.2	2 262	26 624	4 255.7	472.0
Brockton	11 401	122	62.3	84	1 666	604.2	58.1	359	5 414	932.4	106.4
Cambridge	17 299	22	100.0	145	3 696	1 457.9	183.4	538	7 290	1 113.4	124.6
Chelsea	1 425	14	7.1	116	D	D	D	98	1 260	241.4	24.6
Chicopee	4 166	43	76.7	57	D	D	D	183	2 372	382.8	34.0
Everett	1 926	17	17.6	75	1 269	925.6	59.8	85	595	123.9	11.4
Fall River	7 719	133	77.4	87	1 079	401.8	27.4	349	3 408	592.4	61.1
Fitchburg	17 977	120	96.7	45	D	D	D	170	2 011	349.8	39.2
Franklin	18 472	68	100.0	NA	NA	NA	NA	NA	NA	NA	NA
Gloucester	13 824	91	57.1	66	318	227.8	11.0	123	1 300	227.6	23.7
Haverhill	15 449	141	69.5	71	703	157.7	19.4	158	2 202	420.7	39.3
Holyoke	7 522	58	82.8	47	765	245.6	24.3	218	3 305	451.3	46.8
Lawrence	4 808	52	53.8	72	1 119	344.5	37.1	158	1 255	328.4	29.9
Leominster	17 875	109	96.3	56	602	408.7	22.4	209	3 166	494.2	45.4
Lowell	18 429	145	89.0	88	1 159	353.9	41.5	256	2 514	472.4	44.1
Lynn	13 364	116	60.3	61	856	419.5	31.4	213	2 658	429.8	43.9
Malden	3 853	55	87.3	48	845	463.8	29.8	161	1 869	364.6	31.9
MarlBorough	8 441	60	90.0	104	3 725	2 244.5	201.3	219	3 074	494.3	59.0
Medford	726	10	60.0	64	1 146	386.2	40.2	185	2 918	547.4	50.3
Melrose	1 985	17	41.2	18	238	67.3	5.8	73	818	130.2	14.2
Methuen	12 606	108	100.0	NA	NA	NA	NA	NA	NA	NA	NA
New Bedford	13 384	179	89.9	146	2 111	782.7	59.4	325	3 273	499.4	52.2
Newton	32 019	148	54.7	175	2 587	1 857.5	109.0	390	5 701	978.1	113.9
Northampton	10 232	47	100.0	22	D	D	D	206	2 525	380.0	41.5
Peabody	29 081	387	6.7	109	2 817	2 689.7	132.4	282	4 899	886.4	86.4
Pittsfield	7 869	44	100.0	51	D	D	D	243	3 362	527.9	56.0
Quincy	84 084	733	2.0	89	859	384.8	28.0	271	5 146	822.5	84.0
Revere	18 188	242	5.8	30	D	D	D	140	1 882	302.8	31.3
Salem	1 150	5	100.0	49	456	175.3	20.7	172	1 880	292.7	32.1
Somerville	4 857	26	46.2	80	1 020	352.0	35.0	208	3 307	559.0	53.0
Springfield	16 844	187	67.4	166	2 524	1 989.4	116.4	565	7 313	1 123.3	120.1
Taunton	13 462	88	86.4	73	1 364	644.5	56.2	252	3 261	417.2	44.5
Waltham	40 810	429	16.8	158	4 158	4 387.3	279.2	258	3 185	587.5	64.8
Westfield	12 171	57	100.0	51	879	765.3	23.9	152	2 191	335.8	32.2
Woburn	3 495	19	100.0	288	4 495	2 780.6	216.5	223	3 640	754.3	86.2
Worcester	60 863	690	60.9	216	2 085	803.4	70.0	722	8 854	1 530.5	157.3

1. Establishments with payroll.

City	Real estate and rental and leasing, 1997				Professional, scientific, and technical services,[1] 1997				Manufacturing, 1997			
	Number of establishments	Number of employees	Receipts (mil dol)	Annual payroll (mil dol)	Number of establishments	Number of employees	Receipts (mil dol)	Annual payroll (mil dol)	Number of establishments	Number of employees	Receipts (mil dol)	Annual payroll (mil dol)
	80	81	82	83	84	85	86	87	88	89	90	91
LOUISIANA	4 151	28 571	3 342.1	642.2	9 077	63 642	5 754.6	2 159.0	3 545	165 777	80 424.0	6 054.5
Alexandria	61	375	34.5	5.4	173	1 114	90.1	31.3	32	D	D	D
Baton Rouge	388	3 279	271.4	64.5	1 114	9 708	856.1	330.0	265	5 598	1 444.6	201.2
Bossier City	54	238	23.5	3.8	72	286	19.3	6.7	57	1 915	211.4	45.4
Houma	70	1 269	199.9	43.9	118	737	65.4	24.7	57	2 086	269.5	74.5
Kenner	71	1 404	128.2	25.5	116	599	42.9	17.0	68	1 693	161.2	45.6
Lafayette	252	1 850	238.5	51.0	703	5 264	502.4	194.3	125	3 434	538.4	89.1
Lake Charles	137	714	62.3	12.3	273	1 738	127.6	45.4	66	D	D	D
Monroe	113	628	58.0	9.7	251	1 593	115.8	40.6	58	3 061	408.0	76.1
New Iberia	62	998	175.9	36.4	100	427	29.5	10.7	51	1 427	209.0	46.8
New Orleans	481	3 538	407.4	72.3	1 420	12 469	1 401.8	551.5	261	10 453	2 305.0	362.2
Shreveport	213	1 069	110.4	20.4	531	3 033	274.8	102.6	177	D	D	D
Slidell	45	273	35.3	4.3	102	546	45.5	15.0	31	611	73.0	11.1
MAINE	1 343	5 929	601.7	114.2	2 552	13 747	1 215.6	474.8	1 812	82 288	14 097.6	2 591.1
Bangor	81	347	47.2	6.1	147	869	70.4	33.0	46	D	D	D
Lewiston	50	172	16.4	2.7	73	1 215	153.4	38.2	79	D	D	D
Portland	172	1 618	163.4	37.3	436	3 645	363.9	152.7	119	3 905	624.9	107.0
MARYLAND	5 065	39 502	4 764.7	971.3	14 115	146 814	15 940.2	6 483.8	3 996	163 992	36 505.9	5 840.5
Annapolis	80	530	74.4	14.9	370	2 142	253.7	95.2	NA	NA	NA	NA
Baltimore	597	4 807	568.2	124.9	1 395	14 695	1 645.0	666.3	688	30 216	9 822.2	1 006.2
Bowie	39	175	34.0	3.4	113	1 662	66.9	39.8	NA	NA	NA	NA
Frederick	111	617	73.2	14.9	255	3 129	224.7	105.5	79	3 097	505.1	100.3
Gaithersburg	84	D	D	D	278	6 826	1 197.7	432.5	42	1 993	318.0	89.8
Hagerstown	54	D	D	D	107	607	36.3	15.4	64	3 361	593.1	96.9
Rockville	74	1 172	183.4	32.7	673	14 867	1 598.6	673.9	68	1 438	166.2	52.9
MASSACHUSETTS	5 834	41 233	5 925.4	1 214.1	18 086	177 345	22 744.1	9 261.4	9 554	417 135	77 876.6	16 379.0
Agawam	NA	NA	NA	NA	NA	NA	NA	NA	NA	NA	NA	NA
Attleboro	33	153	23.1	4.4	50	169	17.0	5.7	143	9 714	1 412.0	333.5
Barnstable Town	NA	NA	NA	NA	NA	NA	NA	NA	NA	NA	NA	NA
Beverly	36	140	20.4	3.2	91	325	43.0	15.9	83	3 861	726.1	168.1
Boston	826	12 736	1 550.8	426.5	3 053	49 765	7 871.3	2 949.9	536	18 944	3 941.5	671.5
Brockton	53	257	35.3	5.4	138	1 181	78.6	30.8	121	3 009	378.0	92.0
Cambridge	143	1 144	206.7	36.8	738	20 339	2 751.9	1 341.2	106	3 050	585.2	98.1
Chelsea	29	98	13.3	2.4	34	342	37.6	14.6	62	2 084	341.4	66.0
Chicopee	34	165	26.5	3.5	35	131	10.7	3.9	109	4 974	990.0	184.6
Everett	13	85	7.6	1.8	29	251	16.3	7.4	77	2 216	297.0	82.1
Fall River	76	302	33.2	5.3	145	586	48.2	16.7	199	12 366	1 364.5	337.3
Fitchburg	36	161	12.1	3.1	67	259	19.1	6.9	89	3 896	653.6	145.3
Franklin	NA	NA	NA	NA	NA	NA	NA	NA	NA	NA	NA	NA
Gloucester	33	99	10.9	3.1	69	215	26.2	9.5	64	3 948	846.8	137.2
Haverhill	35	176	19.5	3.9	99	631	45.4	19.0	119	3 885	545.9	130.8
Holyoke	37	271	18.3	3.9	51	459	25.4	9.1	88	4 223	886.8	139.0
Lawrence	38	206	20.7	3.7	63	424	23.9	9.0	120	6 252	1 052.4	207.9
Leominster	46	193	23.9	4.2	68	323	31.4	11.3	135	6 003	1 256.0	196.3
Lowell	63	466	41.9	7.3	144	1 389	138.2	48.3	101	5 709	888.1	193.3
Lynn	47	254	31.0	5.5	80	233	18.9	7.0	67	6 870	2 101.8	325.2
Malden	44	264	31.6	4.5	71	715	29.5	12.7	63	1 929	309.2	63.8
Marlborough	31	174	35.6	4.6	138	2 020	338.4	125.5	90	4 959	1 592.9	258.0
Medford	23	183	35.5	4.8	85	429	52.3	20.2	52	924	98.3	24.9
Melrose	13	30	4.6	0.6	76	336	29.9	11.9	NA	NA	NA	NA
Methuen	NA	NA	NA	NA	NA	NA	NA	NA	NA	NA	NA	NA
New Bedford	64	238	25.1	4.7	165	653	49.0	19.1	151	9 839	1 259.9	273.8
Newton	140	1 506	281.6	49.2	540	4 235	451.7	209.0	87	2 999	542.6	110.2
Northampton	52	152	22.2	2.3	107	468	33.0	12.7	39	1 471	264.5	46.3
Peabody	42	263	20.8	4.9	114	836	85.6	35.3	98	4 028	690.1	164.5
Pittsfield	55	218	22.0	4.2	112	821	70.1	30.3	59	D	D	D
Quincy	72	691	158.6	18.2	222	1 972	209.5	84.6	72	753	127.3	25.9
Revere	26	152	18.3	3.3	35	102	10.1	3.7	NA	NA	NA	NA
Salem	36	157	20.7	4.3	154	511	46.3	15.4	70	1 733	190.2	54.9
Somerville	35	158	20.9	2.8	140	776	94.8	33.6	83	2 574	433.0	96.2
Springfield	119	688	101.4	18.0	321	2 198	188.1	82.4	174	7 199	1 161.1	258.9
Taunton	35	180	35.3	3.8	80	591	31.4	13.3	71	4 465	709.0	174.4
Waltham	96	779	227.7	30.8	308	5 834	737.4	329.4	161	7 431	1 217.2	351.5
Westfield	33	118	13.0	2.2	48	308	30.5	13.7	105	3 786	634.7	132.6
Woburn	57	1 245	165.4	33.7	195	2 113	243.4	99.7	195	5 778	876.7	226.8
Worcester	139	1 313	201.7	33.8	445	2 718	232.7	93.3	278	13 475	2 139.5	528.5

1. Firms subject to federal tax.

City	Accommodation and foodservices, 1997				Arts, entertainment, and recreation,[1] 1997				Health care and social assistance,[1] 1997			
	Number of establishments	Number of employees	Sales (mil dol)	Annual payroll (mil dol)	Number of establishments	Number of employees	Receipts (mil dol)	Annual payroll (mil dol)	Number of establishments	Number of employees	Receipts (mil dol)	Annual payroll (mil dol)
	92	93	94	95	96	97	98	99	100	101	102	103
LOUISIANA	7 151	147 016	5 259.9	1 408.9	1 016	22 828	1 958.1	412.9	8 580	129 773	7 967.6	3 341.5
Alexandria	138	2 717	80.7	22.2	15	79	7.9	1.1	236	4 053	243.9	101.7
Baton Rouge	594	13 431	409.5	113.6	59	2 688	273.4	46.0	769	11 992	793.7	364.8
Bossier City	150	5 379	292.7	67.9	21	0	0.0	0.0	90	1 461	81.0	32.3
Houma	86	1 262	41.8	13.2	14	130	6.9	1.6	112	1 181	102.1	53.3
Kenner	160	3 712	148.4	35.4	18	0	0.0	0.0	100	1 821	95.6	37.3
Lafayette	329	8 380	250.9	73.3	44	990	44.7	8.2	558	6 842	564.7	218.9
Lake Charles	183	6 092	239.5	59.7	25	0	0.0	0.0	299	3 622	268.0	111.3
Monroe	172	3 734	116.9	29.5	18	127	10.0	1.7	233	3 869	253.0	112.0
New Iberia	71	1 186	29.6	7.7	12	0	0.0	0.0	126	1 566	106.3	38.7
New Orleans	1 105	32 081	1 371.8	377.5	117	3 609	271.8	61.7	1 022	19 447	1 245.4	530.6
Shreveport	374	7 150	219.3	61.2	66	1 832	234.5	33.6	532	8 680	612.4	274.1
Slidell	147	2 637	83.5	20.9	16	175	8.7	1.5	159	2 196	132.6	56.4
MAINE	3 714	39 624	1 509.3	428.8	524	5 456	254.4	64.0	2 727	28 944	1 608.4	766.3
Bangor	144	2 709	88.4	27.2	20	212	39.9	1.9	181	2 230	154.4	74.5
Lewiston	77	1 032	32.2	9.7	10	148	4.4	1.4	133	1 460	97.3	45.2
Portland	275	4 084	147.4	42.4	38	353	19.1	5.0	284	3 230	245.0	125.1
MARYLAND	9 049	161 273	5 972.5	1 644.7	1 460	19 398	1 412.4	494.8	10 841	116 241	8 060.7	3 538.0
Annapolis	166	4 426	169.2	49.5	34	296	16.5	4.4	146	1 678	124.1	63.5
Baltimore	1 328	20 021	849.9	232.0	107	2 147	338.7	168.5	1 220	16 856	1 093.8	486.1
Bowie	44	1 031	33.4	9.1	18	209	17.9	6.6	111	652	43.3	18.3
Frederick	178	3 687	123.2	33.4	26	401	17.3	4.1	230	2 439	167.0	79.5
Gaithersburg	144	3 327	129.5	35.1	20	458	15.3	4.3	108	875	61.5	27.3
Hagerstown	124	2 604	78.5	22.3	13	135	7.2	1.2	143	1 748	146.0	67.0
Rockville	183	2 703	104.9	28.1	32	828	63.9	14.8	196	1 863	136.1	59.5
MASSACHUSETTS	14 800	227 476	9 269.9	2 575.6	1 781	22 598	1 578.5	518.6	11 887	182 902	11 361.4	5 310.5
Agawam	NA	NA	NA	NA	NA	NA	NA	NA	NA	NA	NA	NA
Attleboro	81	1 697	53.9	15.0	5	57	5.8	1.2	74	1 003	66.1	29.0
Barnstable Town	NA	NA	NA	NA	NA	NA	NA	NA	NA	NA	NA	NA
Beverly	79	909	33.3	8.8	13	123	7.6	2.2	108	2 108	125.3	74.5
Boston	1 907	39 831	2 049.1	576.1	165	3 463	433.2	186.3	963	19 284	1 437.5	701.5
Brockton	150	2 658	88.2	24.9	15	177	4.3	1.3	188	3 962	271.5	132.7
Cambridge	413	7 766	404.3	111.9	40	529	46.2	7.5	201	2 433	219.3	93.9
Chelsea	62	D	D	D	2	0	0.0	0.0	23	577	26.8	11.9
Chicopee	125	1 608	52.8	14.0	6	63	2.6	0.8	51	1 145	53.3	23.1
Everett	55	D	D	D	4	32	1.1	0.2	51	327	20.2	9.8
Fall River	181	2 276	78.3	20.9	11	34	1.9	0.3	202	2 493	154.3	80.8
Fitchburg	101	1 370	46.9	12.7	5	0	0.0	0.0	90	1 051	63.0	28.4
Franklin	NA	NA	NA	NA	NA	NA	NA	NA	NA	NA	NA	NA
Gloucester	101	1 031	42.4	13.0	11	74	5.1	1.6	45	432	26.1	12.3
Haverhill	123	D	D	D	15	464	15.9	4.7	76	1 858	100.4	54.5
Holyoke	81	1 153	39.7	10.0	11	58	6.4	1.7	95	1 287	86.0	40.7
Lawrence	84	D	D	D	4	0	0.0	0.0	57	0	0.0	0.0
Leominster	95	1 344	42.5	11.6	9	68	3.2	0.9	68	708	55.2	18.1
Lowell	174	D	D	D	10	154	6.1	2.2	145	2 311	146.5	69.6
Lynn	131	D	D	D	8	40	1.9	0.7	131	1 835	104.8	51.6
Malden	89	938	36.5	9.5	9	85	4.2	0.9	88	1 525	60.6	30.5
MarlBorough	115	2 024	80.0	23.4	11	158	4.6	1.3	59	881	54.8	22.5
Medford	87	1 201	42.6	11.4	3	61	2.7	0.6	93	1 051	70.9	31.3
Melrose	30	364	13.9	3.8	3	0	0.0	0.0	76	1 035	69.9	40.1
Methuen	NA	NA	NA	NA	NA	NA	NA	NA	NA	NA	NA	NA
New Bedford	209	2 019	70.7	17.4	14	87	4.3	1.0	153	3 383	163.6	80.5
Newton	163	3 699	172.1	49.1	37	347	22.4	6.8	338	4 519	247.4	118.9
Northampton	97	1 873	57.9	17.4	14	85	3.5	0.9	104	1 389	84.1	41.8
Peabody	135	2 408	97.9	27.4	7	77	3.6	1.6	90	1 792	84.5	41.2
Pittsfield	125	2 083	61.6	18.0	18	0	0.0	0.0	128	2 115	144.5	60.0
Quincy	201	2 943	115.2	30.9	20	217	11.8	3.0	203	3 576	180.9	80.6
Revere	84	D	D	D	3	0	0.0	0.0	50	710	34.3	15.1
Salem	116	1 556	51.5	14.9	16	67	5.3	1.5	122	1 187	79.8	41.1
Somerville	154	D	D	D	19	264	18.4	4.8	60	577	37.3	14.5
Springfield	278	4 770	146.3	43.3	16	191	8.5	2.9	333	5 394	358.0	168.0
Taunton	101	D	D	D	9	57	2.1	0.5	88	1 425	93.0	45.2
Waltham	172	2 852	123.3	30.9	18	225	12.7	2.7	131	1 759	177.9	60.2
Westfield	73	1 095	29.8	7.8	9	63	3.5	1.1	56	661	32.9	13.3
Woburn	77	1 528	74.5	18.0	13	109	6.8	2.9	79	2 458	140.1	55.1
Worcester	415	6 202	200.3	54.7	21	521	13.9	5.0	385	8 418	651.3	280.7

1. Firms subject to federal tax.

Table D. Cities — Other Services and Federal Funds

	Other services,[1] 1997				Selected federal funds, 2002–2003 (mil dol)								
					Procurement contracts		Grants						
City	Number of establishments	Number of employees	Receipts (mil dol)	Annual payroll (mil dol)	Defense	Other	Total[2]	Medicaid and other health related	Nutrition and family welfare	Energy and environment	Education	Housing and community development	Direct payments for individuals for educational assistance
	104	105	106	107	108	109	110	111	112	113	114	115	116
LOUISIANA	5 998	39 764	2 595.2	767.2	1 951.3	1 243.4	7 820.3	4 071.3	1 008.4	81.5	693.7	459.1	276.7
Alexandria	109	629	38.1	11.9	7.6	9.1	18.8	0.6	5.9	0.0	2.3	6.5	4.9
Baton Rouge	539	4 223	249.6	80.1	13.7	7.3	980.8	69.2	209.7	62.2	251.7	82.9	51.8
Bossier City	123	701	36.8	10.7	1.3	0.3	7.6	0.0	2.5	0.0	0.0	5.0	4.7
Houma	94	857	87.0	22.1	2.0	0.7	0.3	0.0	0.0	0.0	0.0	0.3	0.0
Kenner	157	815	49.3	14.4	1.8	0.3	5.7	0.0	0.0	0.0	0.0	5.6	1.1
Lafayette	263	1 938	116.5	37.6	11.4	28.4	40.2	2.4	9.2	1.2	6.2	13.1	16.3
Lake Charles	165	1 213	68.5	20.8	118.1	43.0	28.9	1.6	2.6	0.0	1.1	16.4	10.9
Monroe	114	828	40.2	12.5	4.8	0.8	36.9	2.9	4.5	0.0	1.3	18.3	11.1
New Iberia	79	414	28.3	8.2	1.7	1.3	11.0	1.2	0.0	0.0	0.9	6.2	0.6
New Orleans	605	4 684	257.7	77.8	994.8	576.5	547.8	219.2	23.5	9.3	28.2	103.1	74.7
Shreveport	332	2 328	153.6	45.8	7.3	33.7	88.3	18.2	10.0	0.4	4.3	41.5	12.4
Slidell	93	439	29.5	7.7	16.9	1.5	3.7	0.0	0.0	0.2	0.0	2.2	0.6
MAINE	1 923	8 820	612.3	169.6	1 175.6	136.1	2 609.8	1 428.7	292.0	46.7	181.3	177.2	72.7
Bangor	87	553	47.2	11.8	6.0	9.9	32.2	2.2	5.4	0.1	2.1	7.7	4.3
Lewiston	75	0	0.0	0.0	0.1	0.2	18.6	0.0	3.3	0.1	0.0	13.3	1.7
Portland	179	1 171	84.8	24.3	84.9	4.3	69.6	12.2	5.0	2.4	3.0	26.4	22.4
MARYLAND	7 871	55 241	3 561.3	1 129.2	7 171.2	9 044.7	8 632.1	4 437.8	963.9	129.5	583.2	615.9	180.1
Annapolis	141	1 411	66.6	23.4	464.1	60.2	75.4	0.5	6.0	9.0	9.9	26.1	0.5
Baltimore	891	6 733	426.4	131.5	693.3	902.7	2 151.8	987.9	288.3	72.6	200.9	233.4	77.5
Bowie	47	244	10.9	3.7	2.9	28.7	7.8	0.3	0.2	0.0	3.3	0.2	4.0
Frederick	157	1 030	79.2	22.1	165.1	449.4	213.8	201.8	2.0	0.0	0.1	4.8	2.4
Gaithersburg	124	884	59.9	18.6	201.4	276.1	33.4	27.6	0.7	0.1	0.5	3.9	0.2
Hagerstown	108	717	30.5	10.0	21.7	7.7	26.8	0.6	3.4	0.0	0.3	15.3	4.4
Rockville	186	1 753	166.0	54.8	359.8	2 193.7	451.4	321.8	5.5	8.3	10.3	33.1	11.5
MASSACHUSETTS	10 806	61 557	4 359.8	1 338.6	6 364.8	1 992.7	13 328.3	7 346.5	1 275.8	244.5	816.7	1 607.4	421.1
Agawam	NA	NA	NA	NA	1.0	0.0	0.2	0.0	0.0	0.0	0.0	0.0	0.0
Attleboro	55	238	15.0	4.3	1.5	9.0	4.0	0.1	0.0	0.5	0.0	3.2	0.0
Barnstable Town	NA	NA	NA	NA	0.0	0.0	0.0	0.0	0.0	0.0	0.0	0.0	0.0
Beverly	55	294	19.0	5.9	21.5	3.9	26.7	11.6	2.9	0.1	0.0	9.9	1.1
Boston	1 021	7 625	519.3	150.1	125.9	179.8	3 498.8	1 775.0	272.6	122.9	62.4	683.6	69.4
Brockton	142	754	45.8	12.1	2.1	14.7	33.8	3.2	0.9	0.6	1.7	24.2	4.2
Cambridge	148	1 024	91.0	21.6	772.2	182.9	765.9	430.7	4.4	71.5	14.3	31.4	16.2
Chelsea	31	153	15.2	4.4	0.5	0.8	19.9	0.1	2.1	0.0	0.3	10.6	0.0
Chicopee	89	476	31.6	9.7	11.6	12.5	10.0	0.0	0.0	0.0	0.0	8.5	1.4
Everett	69	403	31.1	9.3	2.6	0.3	4.8	0.0	0.0	0.0	0.0	4.6	0.0
Fall River	154	730	39.8	12.1	3.7	0.2	46.5	1.4	5.1	1.4	2.0	34.5	5.3
Fitchburg	70	331	22.4	6.8	0.5	0.2	15.3	0.9	4.6	0.2	0.8	7.3	1.6
Franklin	NA	NA	NA	NA	3.3	0.9	0.5	0.0	0.0	0.0	0.0	0.0	0.0
Gloucester	55	201	12.6	4.1	2.1	12.0	7.5	0.0	1.4	0.0	0.0	5.3	0.0
Haverhill	85	466	26.3	8.5	0.2	0.2	18.8	0.0	1.6	0.4	1.4	15.4	5.0
Holyoke	59	294	16.0	5.2	0.1	1.6	39.5	4.4	9.5	0.0	0.7	18.7	4.8
Lawrence	94	842	56.3	19.1	1.5	0.5	42.3	4.4	5.9	0.3	3.5	29.5	0.0
Leominster	71	362	21.2	6.5	0.0	0.0	8.1	0.0	0.0	0.0	0.5	6.7	0.0
Lowell	149	738	46.4	13.6	23.4	7.5	58.0	4.7	5.1	6.8	4.2	27.9	10.2
Lynn	110	527	33.1	10.4	1 332.1	0.8	52.0	1.7	2.2	0.0	0.8	46.5	0.0
Malden	106	536	38.7	9.6	3.6	5.5	215.5	0.4	1.6	0.5	193.8	17.9	0.8
Marlborough	77	696	91.1	23.3	229.2	170.8	6.4	0.0	0.0	1.3	0.0	5.3	0.0
Medford	96	698	55.3	18.8	3.0	1.2	25.4	3.0	0.0	1.1	0.2	13.2	4.3
Melrose	42	170	11.1	3.5	0.5	0.0	5.3	0.0	0.0	0.0	0.0	5.8	0.0
Methuen	NA	NA	NA	NA	0.9	1.1	0.4	0.0	0.0	0.0	0.1	0.0	0.0
New Bedford	142	890	66.6	17.8	27.5	8.9	45.6	1.5	2.6	2.5	5.3	31.1	0.2
Newton	159	1 057	73.4	21.7	4.3	18.2	60.0	13.3	0.2	0.9	6.4	12.6	9.0
Northampton	67	286	21.3	6.0	31.5	0.2	14.3	1.4	2.0	0.0	2.8	5.6	0.0
Peabody	110	543	34.8	10.7	4.2	2.7	11.1	0.1	0.0	0.0	0.0	10.8	0.0
Pittsfield	102	0	0.0	0.0	102.3	1.3	20.5	0.0	2.3	0.1	0.7	15.8	1.5
Quincy	161	934	62.8	19.6	248.1	32.4	30.8	1.4	2.9	0.0	0.2	24.6	3.3
Revere	78	285	19.5	5.2	0.1	0.3	10.5	0.0	0.0	0.0	0.0	10.1	0.0
Salem	76	330	26.3	6.7	1.5	7.2	14.7	0.7	0.0	0.0	6.0	7.9	4.0
Somerville	112	920	58.4	20.6	5.6	4.3	107.8	66.9	2.8	1.7	3.7	29.6	0.0
Springfield	223	1 636	108.0	35.0	3.2	4.3	89.9	4.7	0.1	0.9	6.9	74.4	14.1
Taunton	77	355	24.5	6.6	332.3	0.1	13.2	0.0	2.2	0.2	0.0	7.4	0.1
Waltham	137	710	70.2	19.0	48.2	11.7	61.3	34.3	3.0	3.7	0.5	14.1	5.5
Westfield	71	329	19.5	6.5	2.8	0.2	25.9	0.0	1.8	0.0	0.5	3.4	2.3
Woburn	101	765	62.5	26.3	31.2	9.9	17.3	8.1	0.0	0.0	0.0	3.6	2.5
Worcester	310	2 203	134.8	42.2	20.5	9.6	225.8	125.8	10.4	2.6	9.3	60.9	17.0

1. Firms subject to federal tax.   2. Includes program categories not shown separately. State totals include additional categories not allocated by city.

Table D. Cities — City Government Finances

City	General revenue Total (mil dol)	Intergovernmental Total (mil dol)	Intergovernmental Percent from state government	Taxes Total (mil dol)	Taxes Per capita[1] (dollars) Total	Taxes Per capita[1] (dollars) Property	Taxes Per capita[1] (dollars) Sales and gross receipts	General expenditure Total (mil dol)	General expenditure Per capita[1] (dollars) Total	General expenditure Per capita[1] (dollars) Capital outlays
	117	118	119	120	121	122	123	124	125	126
LOUISIANA	X	X	X	X	X	X	X	X	X	X
Alexandria	54.4	15.1	8.3	28.4	619	109	464	56.1	1 222	274
Baton Rouge	644.6	88.3	49.5	335.1	1 485	484	953	587.9	2 605	375
Bossier City	77.1	6.7	68.6	49.1	859	134	689	67.2	1 177	341
Houma	274.9	49.4	82.4	63.7	1 982	783	1 153	267.6	8 329	985
Kenner	67.7	36.4	5.1	18.7	266	77	61	74.0	1 049	252
Lafayette	197.0	27.9	48.1	98.3	884	326	533	219.2	1 970	615
Lake Charles	79.1	13.9	13.9	51.9	734	76	619	66.0	933	192
Monroe	102.6	26.6	25.9	57.3	1 093	166	883	112.4	2 146	796
New Iberia	22.4	2.9	15.4	15.4	475	85	352	22.3	687	101
New Orleans	946.7	242.4	66.2	403.3	851	349	445	852.8	1 800	266
Shreveport	273.0	53.0	39.7	153.0	769	242	493	260.8	1 310	308
Slidell	32.4	4.0	3.3	23.3	879	170	646	34.7	1 313	420
MAINE	X	X	X	X	X	X	X	X	X	X
Bangor	96.5	24.8	89.4	41.9	1 329	1 181	125	121.0	3 835	292
Lewiston	81.9	30.0	95.6	42.8	1 200	1 190	0	82.5	2 315	274
Portland	217.2	42.8	95.7	109.2	1 709	1 671	0	242.9	3 803	725
MARYLAND	X	X	X	X	X	X	X	X	X	X
Annapolis	46.2	12.4	36.4	21.5	594	502	34	47.0	1 298	111
Baltimore	2 418.6	1 381.2	88.4	806.2	1 262	775	99	2 159.8	3 382	478
Bowie	23.2	8.7	32.5	10.8	207	179	13	21.3	410	43
Frederick	54.2	18.5	37.3	23.6	420	391	11	62.4	1 114	355
Gaithersburg	33.2	9.8	26.9	14.4	256	184	13	33.7	598	223
Hagerstown	42.4	7.3	48.0	14.0	382	357	7	34.3	937	111
Rockville	58.4	13.2	34.4	23.8	452	388	20	57.3	1 090	227
MASSACHUSETTS	X	X	X	X	X	X	X	X	X	X
Agawam	64.1	21.5	100.0	34.3	1 208	1 201	2	69.4	2 444	161
Attleboro	95.1	43.5	98.8	40.1	929	893	16	87.7	2 033	74
Barnstable Town	119.2	23.5	94.2	76.8	1 573	1 501	45	113.5	2 322	125
Beverly	93.1	24.9	91.1	56.6	1 407	1 378	16	102.0	2 535	432
Boston	2 574.6	1 188.9	92.0	1 049.5	1 781	1 660	63	2 470.9	4 193	317
Brockton	288.1	176.2	98.7	85.0	890	829	46	288.2	3 020	188
Cambridge	728.3	229.9	72.0	207.8	2 041	1 885	81	748.4	7 351	788
Chelsea	112.5	75.3	95.2	25.8	739	700	16	113.1	3 239	200
Chicopee	128.5	67.2	96.9	49.4	900	876	15	123.6	2 254	113
Everett	92.6	37.0	98.6	50.5	1 337	1 297	18	118.8	3 146	525
Fall River	219.0	149.5	95.9	45.6	492	472	5	253.6	2 737	426
Fitchburg	104.9	64.0	96.0	29.6	744	720	10	111.8	2 813	182
Franklin	75.5	27.0	99.8	40.2	1 340	1 300	16	93.6	3 124	943
Gloucester	74.9	19.7	92.8	44.8	1 461	1 416	26	73.1	2 382	110
Haverhill	179.6	62.0	96.2	58.6	983	964	6	181.9	3 050	63
Holyoke	152.6	93.5	96.4	38.1	956	926	21	150.5	3 774	149
Lawrence	227.4	180.8	94.2	33.6	464	441	13	235.3	3 247	450
Leominster	89.1	46.4	97.0	36.7	877	856	8	85.6	2 044	176
Lowell	300.0	202.0	96.1	71.5	681	668	4	289.9	2 763	133
Lynn	260.2	160.5	97.5	72.6	811	789	13	257.5	2 874	56
Malden	128.7	63.6	89.9	48.6	865	855	0	136.8	2 436	21
MarlBorough	90.0	21.2	94.2	61.7	1 618	1 550	38	86.2	2 259	209
Medford	124.1	44.4	91.2	65.3	1 184	1 169	4	163.4	2 964	766
Melrose	58.8	18.6	99.0	34.1	1 265	1 257	0	71.8	2 663	361
Methuen	98.4	44.9	96.0	47.0	1 053	1 025	5	101.0	2 263	139
New Bedford	266.9	165.7	93.2	67.3	715	685	18	302.3	3 213	340
Newton	243.0	36.4	87.0	177.3	2 114	2 049	15	257.0	3 064	278
Northampton	68.8	23.3	87.0	30.7	1 059	1 026	13	62.9	2 169	147
Peabody	116.9	38.7	84.8	59.5	1 197	1 143	24	125.8	2 533	220
Pittsfield	125.5	62.9	88.3	49.4	1 097	1 081	10	130.8	2 906	143
Quincy	213.5	69.6	87.6	124.1	1 391	1 355	10	226.1	2 535	162
Revere	96.1	47.4	96.9	45.5	958	915	15	103.5	2 179	22
Salem	106.7	39.5	86.4	53.1	1 260	1 245	5	108.0	2 562	34
Somerville	163.7	83.0	90.7	70.9	922	895	7	189.3	2 461	184
Springfield	541.8	373.9	87.5	118.0	777	761	6	603.7	3 974	388
Taunton	119.0	60.6	96.0	47.4	837	816	7	126.6	2 234	140
Waltham	158.7	31.3	94.5	106.6	1 805	1 727	41	141.8	2 400	286
Westfield	98.6	47.7	96.0	41.4	1 027	1 012	5	99.6	2 471	202
Woburn	96.6	23.4	96.2	60.4	1 590	1 531	37	100.1	2 633	136
Worcester	494.1	291.1	92.6	158.4	905	875	4	536.1	3 064	309

1. Based on population estimated as of July 1 of the year shown.

City	City government finances, 2002 (cont'd)									
	General expenditure									
	Percent of total for—									
	Public welfare	Highways	Parking facilities	Education	Health and hospitals	Police protection	Sewerage and sanitation	Parks and recreation	Housing and community development	Interest on debt
	127	128	129	130	131	132	133	134	135	136
LOUISIANA	X	X	X	X	X	X	X	X	X	X
Alexandria	0.0	5.8	0.0	0.0	0.3	17.9	22.5	14.8	7.5	3.8
Baton Rouge	0.3	8.1	0.1	0.0	7.7	8.9	12.6	5.7	5.6	9.7
Bossier City	0.0	11.6	0.0	0.0	3.7	14.2	12.3	7.4	7.0	6.1
Houma	1.0	2.6	0.0	0.3	57.9	5.1	5.6	2.0	2.5	2.3
Kenner	0.9	18.9	0.0	0.0	0.1	23.1	11.5	10.8	5.3	3.4
Lafayette	0.1	12.9	0.2	0.0	2.1	12.0	7.9	6.5	7.0	8.2
Lake Charles	0.0	16.2	0.0	0.4	0.9	13.4	12.6	11.4	16.6	1.0
Monroe	0.0	14.1	0.0	0.0	0.0	8.6	19.9	8.1	17.4	2.2
New Iberia	0.2	8.9	0.0	0.0	0.6	18.4	27.8	5.1	9.2	3.4
New Orleans	0.4	5.7	0.9	0.0	2.4	12.3	13.6	2.0	11.7	6.8
Shreveport	0.0	5.3	0.1	0.0	0.0	13.0	12.5	4.9	11.2	7.5
Slidell	0.0	15.8	0.0	0.0	0.8	17.7	15.3	5.5	7.5	5.2
MAINE	X	X	X	X	X	X	X	X	X	X
Bangor	0.0	0.0	1.0	27.5	1.5	4.3	5.6	2.7	1.3	1.1
Lewiston	0.6	7.0	0.0	44.7	0.0	5.1	6.2	1.8	8.4	3.3
Portland	7.6	3.7	0.0	30.6	0.9	2.1	7.2	2.8	0.0	3.1
MARYLAND	X	X	X	X	X	X	X	X	X	X
Annapolis	0.0	15.4	1.5	0.0	0.0	23.3	12.1	5.4	0.9	2.8
Baltimore	0.3	5.4	0.5	46.9	3.0	11.8	5.5	2.8	2.0	3.4
Bowie	0.0	13.1	0.0	0.0	0.6	3.3	30.5	18.6	0.1	0.9
Frederick	0.0	19.6	2.3	0.0	0.0	20.0	9.0	10.8	0.8	3.3
Gaithersburg	0.0	5.8	0.0	0.0	0.8	10.5	5.0	27.8	1.6	0.0
Hagerstown	0.0	6.4	1.0	0.0	0.0	26.5	19.0	7.7	6.0	3.2
Rockville	0.0	12.5	0.3	0.0	0.4	7.6	12.1	33.1	2.5	2.8
MASSACHUSETTS	X	X	X	X	X	X	X	X	X	X
Agawam	0.1	5.3	0.0	52.2	0.6	4.7	4.4	1.1	0.0	2.3
Attleboro	0.4	2.5	0.0	61.8	0.5	5.4	5.4	1.4	0.5	4.6
Barnstable Town	0.1	3.4	0.0	53.4	0.7	7.4	3.3	2.4	0.4	4.1
Beverly	0.1	4.1	0.0	53.0	0.4	5.0	9.7	1.8	1.4	2.7
Boston	4.9	2.1	0.1	33.3	7.5	10.4	6.3	1.1	4.2	2.6
Brockton	0.2	2.6	0.1	59.2	0.2	4.8	4.6	1.4	0.0	1.0
Cambridge	0.1	0.7	0.1	17.1	55.8	3.7	2.8	1.4	0.6	1.1
Chelsea	0.2	1.8	0.0	54.4	0.3	6.4	2.0	0.1	1.3	4.4
Chicopee	0.6	3.8	0.0	61.0	0.4	5.7	5.8	1.6	1.1	0.7
Everett	0.2	2.9	0.0	53.0	0.6	5.4	3.1	1.2	0.7	2.7
Fall River	0.5	5.0	0.0	56.1	1.0	6.5	3.1	0.5	2.5	1.7
Fitchburg	0.0	2.7	0.2	53.4	0.4	5.4	5.9	0.4	2.2	2.6
Franklin	0.1	3.3	0.0	73.2	0.2	3.8	5.5	0.4	0.0	1.4
Gloucester	0.1	1.7	0.0	53.3	1.6	6.6	7.3	1.4	0.0	4.4
Haverhill	1.7	2.1	0.0	41.3	24.9	4.4	4.2	0.4	1.3	2.5
Holyoke	7.5	2.8	0.2	58.6	0.3	6.2	3.8	0.6	2.3	2.0
Lawrence	0.1	1.4	0.3	68.5	0.1	4.5	1.8	0.3	0.9	2.2
Leominster	0.2	5.2	0.1	63.0	0.3	6.0	8.1	0.9	0.6	1.3
Lowell	0.2	2.3	0.5	59.2	0.8	6.8	5.1	1.2	0.8	3.1
Lynn	2.5	2.9	0.3	58.7	0.4	6.0	4.2	0.2	1.2	2.1
Malden	1.7	2.0	1.9	47.1	0.2	5.0	2.3	0.5	5.5	4.1
MarlBorough	0.1	6.1	0.0	53.7	0.3	6.5	10.7	0.4	1.3	2.5
Medford	0.1	2.0	0.0	58.8	0.2	5.6	3.8	0.6	1.3	1.0
Melrose	0.0	2.4	0.0	54.8	0.3	5.3	2.2	2.5	0.2	0.5
Methuen	0.2	4.5	0.0	57.2	0.6	5.9	2.6	0.2	1.0	4.0
New Bedford	0.2	2.1	0.1	47.9	1.1	6.4	6.6	0.8	1.7	4.2
Newton	0.1	3.6	0.0	57.2	0.5	5.2	3.6	1.5	1.7	0.7
Northampton	0.2	3.9	0.7	44.5	1.1	5.9	6.9	1.1	3.3	4.9
Peabody	0.1	3.0	0.4	51.3	0.7	4.9	2.8	4.5	3.0	1.3
Pittsfield	0.1	2.0	0.0	51.9	0.3	3.8	5.1	0.5	1.8	3.7
Quincy	0.2	2.6	0.0	38.2	0.6	9.0	3.8	1.4	2.1	1.4
Revere	0.4	4.3	0.0	52.6	0.3	6.0	2.1	0.2	1.3	0.7
Salem	0.2	2.1	0.5	49.6	0.4	6.5	3.9	1.7	1.4	2.4
Somerville	0.1	3.0	0.0	43.2	0.6	7.3	2.5	0.4	4.5	1.5
Springfield	0.1	1.0	0.0	53.9	0.3	6.6	3.9	1.0	1.4	2.6
Taunton	4.3	3.4	0.0	54.6	0.4	7.2	3.4	0.8	1.4	2.2
Waltham	0.2	4.3	0.2	46.3	0.4	9.6	10.5	0.4	1.2	0.7
Westfield	0.1	5.4	0.0	57.6	1.4	4.9	4.1	0.3	0.8	4.0
Woburn	0.1	5.4	0.0	51.2	0.3	6.8	2.9	1.0	0.0	0.9
Worcester	0.1	2.3	0.0	53.5	0.9	5.9	3.6	1.1	1.4	5.1

Table D. Cities — City Government Finances, City Government Employment, and Climate

City	City government finances, 2002 (cont'd) Debt outstanding			City government employment, 2002	Climate[2] Average daily temperature (degrees Fahrenheit) Mean		Limits		Annual precipitation (inches)	Heating degree days	Cooling degree days
	Total (mil dol)	Per capita[1] (dollars)	Percent utility		January	July	January[3]	July[4]			
	137	138	139	140	141	142	143	144	145	146	147
LOUISIANA	X	X	X	X	X	X	X	X	X	X	X
Alexandria	82.8	1 805	58.6	889	46.8	82.4	36.4	92.5	58.50	2 003	2 477
Baton Rouge	1 069.4	4 738	0.0	6 531	49.8	82.3	39.6	91.4	60.89	1 669	2 690
Bossier City	84.6	1 479	14.8	777	45.1	82.7	34.8	93.0	46.11	2 264	2 368
Houma	157.2	4 893	21.0	2 576	52.1	81.6	42.0	90.4	62.91	1 429	2 668
Kenner	48.0	681	0.0	717	51.3	81.9	41.8	90.6	61.88	1 513	2 655
Lafayette	482.8	4 339	30.9	2 532	50.6	82.1	41.2	90.6	58.36	1 587	2 673
Lake Charles	14.1	199	0.0	822	50.4	82.2	41.1	90.8	54.84	1 616	2 650
Monroe	103.5	1 977	7.9	1 168	44.2	82.3	34.6	92.4	51.48	2 407	2 323
New Iberia	15.6	479	0.0	277	50.4	81.7	40.5	90.7	59.56	1 609	2 596
New Orleans	1 465.7	3 094	1.1	9 570	51.3	81.9	41.8	90.6	61.88	1 513	2 655
Shreveport	601.3	3 021	21.5	2 754	45.1	82.7	34.8	93.0	46.11	2 264	2 368
Slidell	37.5	1 416	6.6	337	NA	NA	NA	NA	NA	NA	NA
MAINE	X	X	X	X	X	X	X	X	X	X	X
Bangor	59.1	1 875	0.0	1 244	17.5	68.2	8.2	78.1	41.23	7 930	251
Lewiston	69.5	1 949	8.5	1 137	20.2	70.7	11.1	80.7	45.30	7 244	398
Portland	230.4	3 606	0.0	2 721	20.8	68.6	11.4	78.8	44.34	7 378	268
MARYLAND	X	X	X	X	X	X	X	X	X	X	X
Annapolis	30.2	833	14.9	496	33.6	77.6	24.6	87.6	41.81	4 382	1 271
Baltimore	1 568.6	2 456	16.0	28 083	31.8	77.0	23.4	87.2	40.76	4 707	1 137
Bowie	2.2	42	0.0	242	33.6	77.6	24.6	87.6	41.81	4 382	1 271
Frederick	79.2	1 413	16.6	526	31.4	74.7	23.1	85.3	40.25	4 810	925
Gaithersburg	0.0	0	0.0	280	30.7	74.7	21.4	85.8	41.11	5 093	889
Hagerstown	19.8	539	37.8	448	28.7	74.9	20.3	85.8	38.60	5 293	909
Rockville	28.7	546	0.0	612	30.7	74.7	21.4	85.8	41.11	5 093	889
MASSACHUSETTS	X	X	X	X	X	X	X	X	X	X	X
Agawam	30.0	1 056	0.0	766	NA	NA	NA	NA	NA	NA	NA
Attleboro	110.3	2 555	19.5	1 300	25.9	71.2	15.5	82.3	46.68	6 346	457
Barnstable Town	123.8	2 535	0.0	1 547	NA	NA	NA	NA	NA	NA	NA
Beverly	72.9	1 811	6.2	1 023	28.6	73.5	21.6	81.8	41.51	5 641	678
Boston	1 696.9	2 880	0.0	21 460	28.6	73.5	21.6	81.8	41.51	5 641	678
Brockton	82.3	863	9.0	3 136	26.9	71.2	16.9	82.2	45.50	6 225	461
Cambridge	216.6	2 128	22.7	2 830	28.6	73.5	21.6	81.8	41.51	5 641	678
Chelsea	95.6	2 737	4.3	1 345	28.6	73.5	21.6	81.8	41.51	5 641	678
Chicopee	21.8	398	1.4	2 043	26.8	74.1	17.6	85.4	43.88	5 754	751
Everett	96.5	2 554	0.0	1 100	28.6	73.5	21.6	81.8	41.51	5 641	678
Fall River	116.9	1 262	0.3	2 853	30.6	73.5	23.4	81.3	47.34	5 426	729
Fitchburg	84.9	2 136	22.1	1 169	23.4	71.3	13.4	81.5	47.02	6 698	485
Franklin	82.3	2 746	7.3	939	NA	NA	NA	NA	NA	NA	NA
Gloucester	110.3	3 596	12.3	1 040	28.6	73.5	21.6	81.8	41.51	5 641	678
Haverhill	115.6	1 939	3.9	1 787	24.7	72.5	15.2	83.8	44.43	6 413	575
Holyoke	71.8	1 802	27.7	2 342	26.8	74.1	17.6	85.4	43.88	5 754	751
Lawrence	132.3	1 826	8.3	2 846	24.7	72.5	15.4	82.6	42.80	6 322	555
Leominster	51.3	1 224	8.1	1 208	23.4	71.3	13.4	81.5	47.02	6 698	485
Lowell	191.7	1 828	7.2	3 890	24.3	73.3	14.7	84.8	42.07	6 339	610
Lynn	227.4	2 538	48.3	2 543	28.6	73.5	21.6	81.8	41.51	5 641	678
Malden	121.7	2 167	0.2	1 536	28.6	73.5	21.6	81.8	41.51	5 641	678
MarlBorough	47.1	1 235	12.6	1 045	23.4	71.3	13.4	81.5	47.02	6 698	485
Medford	100.5	1 823	2.4	1 282	28.6	73.5	21.6	81.8	41.51	5 641	678
Melrose	28.7	1 066	0.7	695	28.6	73.5	21.6	81.8	41.51	5 641	678
Methuen	82.5	1 849	1.5	1 308	NA	NA	NA	NA	NA	NA	NA
New Bedford	234.1	2 488	1.8	3 873	30.6	73.5	23.4	81.3	47.34	5 426	729
Newton	71.6	853	0.0	2 970	28.6	73.5	21.6	81.8	41.51	5 641	678
Northampton	64.7	2 232	10.0	852	23.6	71.8	12.2	84.6	42.50	6 404	522
Peabody	72.3	1 456	31.4	1 611	24.5	71.0	14.3	82.7	46.64	6 573	425
Pittsfield	80.4	1 786	4.9	1 680	21.4	68.9	11.0	81.5	43.47	7 060	293
Quincy	71.9	806	15.5	2 180	27.4	71.5	18.5	81.5	47.69	6 072	450
Revere	18.3	386	0.5	1 080	28.6	73.5	21.6	81.8	41.51	5 641	678
Salem	74.2	1 761	0.3	1 510	28.6	73.5	21.6	81.8	41.51	5 641	678
Somerville	78.6	1 021	2.2	1 985	28.6	73.5	21.6	81.8	41.51	5 641	678
Springfield	321.6	2 117	0.0	7 038	26.8	74.1	17.6	85.4	43.88	5 754	751
Taunton	97.4	1 720	13.8	1 707	25.9	71.2	15.5	82.3	46.68	6 346	457
Waltham	66.8	1 131	3.7	1 461	28.6	73.5	21.6	81.8	41.51	5 641	678
Westfield	103.2	2 559	11.0	1 493	26.8	74.1	17.6	85.4	43.88	5 754	751
Woburn	39.9	1 051	4.2	1 127	24.5	71.0	14.3	82.7	46.64	6 573	425
Worcester	589.0	3 366	12.5	5 484	22.8	69.7	15.0	79.3	47.75	6 979	333

1. Based on the population estimated as of July 1 of the year shown. 2. Represents normal values based on the 30-year period, 1961–1990. 3. Average daily minimum. 4. Average daily maximum.

Table D. Cities — **Land Area and Population**

STATE Place code	City	Land area,[1] 2000 (sq km)	Population, 2003 Total persons	Population, 2003 Rank	Population, 2003 Per square kilometer	Population characteristics, 2000 Percent — Race (alone or in combination) White	Black	Am. Indian, Alaska Native	Asian and Pacific Islander	Other race	Hispanic or Latino[2]	Non-Hispanic White
		1	2	3	4	5	6	7	8	9	10	11
26 00000	MICHIGAN	147 121.2	10 079 985	X	68.5	81.8	14.8	1.3	2.2	2.0	3.3	78.6
26 01380	Allen Park	18.2	28 762	1 103	1 580.3	96.8	0.8	0.9	1.1	1.7	4.7	92.5
26 03000	Ann Arbor	70.0	114 498	204	1 635.7	77.3	9.9	0.9	13.1	2.1	3.3	72.8
26 05920	Battle Creek	110.9	53 827	591	485.4	76.9	19.4	1.7	2.3	2.7	4.6	72.6
26 06020	Bay City	27.0	35 428	910	1 312.1	93.4	3.5	1.7	0.7	3.2	6.7	87.8
26 12060	Burton	60.8	30 890	1 038	508.1	94.0	4.1	1.8	1.1	1.3	2.3	90.9
26 21000	Dearborn	63.1	96 670	256	1 532.0	96.1	1.5	0.6	2.7	8.7	3.0	84.8
26 21020	Dearborn Heights	30.3	57 373	528	1 893.5	94.3	2.4	0.9	2.9	2.4	3.4	89.3
26 22000	Detroit	359.4	911 402	10	2 535.9	13.8	82.8	0.9	1.4	3.6	5.0	10.5
26 24120	East Lansing	29.1	47 245	675	1 623.5	82.7	8.1	0.7	9.1	1.6	2.7	79.4
26 24290	Eastpointe	13.2	33 394	964	2 529.8	93.7	5.1	1.2	1.2	0.5	1.3	91.2
26 27440	Farmington Hills	86.2	80 874	333	938.2	84.7	7.4	0.6	8.3	1.2	1.5	81.9
26 29000	Flint	87.1	120 292	191	1 381.1	43.7	55.3	2.2	0.8	1.6	3.0	40.0
26 31420	Garden City	15.2	29 547	1 080	1 943.9	97.4	1.3	0.9	1.0	0.7	2.0	94.6
26 34000	Grand Rapids	115.6	195 601	104	1 692.1	69.9	22.0	1.5	2.1	7.9	13.1	62.5
26 38640	Holland	42.9	34 666	936	808.1	80.4	3.2	1.1	4.1	14.0	22.2	70.0
26 40680	Inkster	16.2	29 478	1 081	1 819.6	27.1	69.5	1.4	3.8	1.3	1.6	24.5
26 41420	Jackson	28.7	35 152	921	1 224.8	77.0	22.0	1.7	0.9	2.4	4.0	72.2
26 42160	Kalamazoo	63.9	75 312	371	1 178.6	73.5	22.4	1.6	3.1	3.2	4.3	69.5
26 42820	Kentwood	54.5	46 487	691	853.0	83.0	10.2	1.0	6.3	2.2	3.9	79.0
26 46000	Lansing	90.8	118 379	195	1 303.7	69.0	24.4	2.0	3.4	6.1	10.0	61.4
26 47800	Lincoln Park	15.2	39 131	824	2 574.4	94.9	2.4	1.3	0.7	2.5	6.4	89.2
26 49000	Livonia	92.5	99 487	249	1 075.5	96.5	1.1	0.6	2.3	0.7	1.7	94.1
26 50560	Madison Heights	18.6	30 463	1 048	1 637.8	92.1	2.1	1.1	5.7	1.8	1.6	88.5
26 53780	Midland	86.0	42 175	760	490.4	94.5	2.1	0.7	3.1	0.8	1.9	92.2
26 56020	Mount Pleasant	20.2	25 687	1 210	1 271.6	90.7	4.3	2.2	3.3	1.4	2.5	88.0
26 56320	Muskegon	37.2	39 825	807	1 070.6	63.5	33.4	2.3	0.9	3.6	6.4	57.9
26 59440	Novi	78.9	50 786	621	643.7	88.6	2.2	0.5	9.4	0.9	1.8	86.1
26 59920	Oak Park	13.0	29 146	1 090	2 242.0	50.5	47.3	0.8	2.8	3.0	1.3	46.4
26 65440	Pontiac	51.8	67 152	426	1 296.4	41.8	49.9	1.5	2.9	7.6	12.8	34.5
26 65560	Portage	83.4	45 679	706	547.7	92.4	4.5	0.9	3.1	1.1	1.9	89.6
26 65820	Port Huron	20.9	31 747	1 010	1 519.0	89.2	9.2	1.8	0.8	2.0	4.3	84.5
26 69035	Rochester Hills	85.1	68 754	412	807.9	90.0	2.7	0.6	7.3	0.8	2.3	87.1
26 69800	Roseville	25.4	47 925	668	1 886.8	94.9	3.0	1.1	2.0	0.7	1.5	92.4
26 70040	Royal Oak	30.6	58 650	517	1 916.7	96.1	1.8	0.7	2.1	0.8	1.3	93.9
26 70520	Saginaw	45.2	59 235	509	1 310.5	49.4	44.9	1.2	0.7	7.1	11.7	42.7
26 70760	St. Clair Shores	29.9	61 896	472	2 070.1	97.9	0.8	0.9	1.1	0.4	1.2	96.0
26 74900	Southfield	67.9	77 488	360	1 141.2	41.0	55.8	0.9	3.7	1.9	1.2	38.3
26 74960	Southgate	17.8	30 064	1 062	1 689.0	94.8	2.3	0.9	2.0	1.2	4.0	90.9
26 76460	Sterling Heights	94.9	126 182	178	1 329.6	93.0	1.5	0.6	5.5	1.9	1.3	89.8
26 79000	Taylor	61.2	65 589	439	1 071.7	87.9	9.5	1.5	2.0	1.3	3.2	84.0
26 80700	Troy	86.9	81 071	332	932.9	83.9	2.3	0.5	14.1	1.2	1.5	81.3
26 84000	Warren	88.8	136 016	167	1 531.7	93.3	3.1	1.1	3.7	1.1	1.4	90.4
26 86000	Westland	53.0	85 707	310	1 617.1	89.0	7.4	1.1	3.3	1.4	2.5	85.6
26 88900	Wyandotte	13.7	27 432	1 147	2 002.3	97.8	0.8	1.3	0.6	1.1	2.9	94.3
26 88940	Wyoming	63.3	70 205	403	1 109.1	86.6	5.8	1.3	3.4	5.7	9.7	80.4
27 00000	MINNESOTA	206 189.1	5 059 375	X	24.5	90.8	4.1	1.6	3.4	1.8	2.9	88.2
27 01486	Andover	88.3	28 938	1 094	327.7	97.6	0.9	0.8	1.4	0.5	1.0	95.8
27 01900	Apple Valley	44.9	48 938	649	1 089.9	93.3	2.5	0.6	4.1	1.3	2.0	90.9
27 06382	Blaine	87.7	50 425	629	575.0	95.1	1.4	1.3	3.1	1.0	1.7	92.6
27 06616	Bloomington	91.9	83 080	322	904.0	89.5	4.1	0.7	5.8	1.7	2.7	86.9
27 07948	Brooklyn Center	20.6	28 362	1 117	1 376.8	73.8	15.9	1.5	9.8	2.5	2.8	70.4
27 07966	Brooklyn Park	67.5	67 781	419	1 004.2	73.6	15.9	1.1	10.2	2.4	2.9	70.3
27 08794	Burnsville	64.4	59 805	498	928.6	89.5	5.2	0.9	5.0	2.0	2.9	86.3
27 13114	Coon Rapids	58.7	62 310	468	1 061.5	94.8	2.7	1.1	2.2	1.0	1.5	92.4
27 13456	Cottage Grove	88.0	31 800	1 008	361.4	94.7	2.8	0.8	1.9	1.2	2.5	92.2
27 17000	Duluth	176.1	85 734	309	486.8	94.3	2.2	3.4	1.5	0.5	1.1	92.1
27 17288	Eagan	83.7	64 006	452	764.7	89.7	4.1	0.7	6.1	1.5	2.2	86.9
27 18116	Eden Prairie	83.9	59 470	504	708.8	91.9	2.8	0.4	5.5	0.9	1.6	89.7
27 18188	Edina	40.8	46 656	687	1 143.5	95.2	1.5	0.3	3.6	0.6	1.1	93.6
27 22814	Fridley	26.3	27 169	1 158	1 033.0	91.2	4.4	1.5	3.7	2.3	2.6	87.5
27 31076	Inver Grove Heights	74.2	31 281	1 023	421.6	93.5	2.8	0.9	2.6	2.3	4.2	89.8
27 35180	Lakeville	93.7	47 805	672	510.2	95.4	1.7	0.7	2.6	1.0	1.9	93.3
27 39878	Mankato	39.4	33 925	953	861.0	93.6	2.4	0.7	3.3	1.4	2.2	91.5
27 40166	Maple Grove	85.1	57 172	532	671.8	95.8	1.4	0.5	3.0	0.5	1.1	94.1
27 40382	Maplewood	44.9	35 945	893	800.6	90.3	4.4	1.0	5.1	1.2	2.2	87.6
27 43000	Minneapolis	142.2	373 188	47	2 624.4	68.0	20.5	3.3	7.2	5.8	7.6	62.5
27 43252	Minnetonka	70.3	50 690	622	721.1	95.3	1.8	0.4	2.8	0.8	1.3	93.7
27 43864	Moorhead	34.8	32 786	986	942.1	93.8	1.1	2.6	1.9	2.6	4.5	90.1
27 47680	Oakdale	28.7	27 673	1 143	964.2	93.9	3.0	0.8	3.0	1.3	2.7	90.7

1. Dry land or land partially or temporarily covered by water.   2. Hispanic or Latino persons may be of any race.

	Population characteristics, 2000 (cont'd)										Population			
	Age of population (percent)										Census counts		Percent change	
City	Under 5 years	5 to 17 years	18 to 24 years	25 to 34 years	35 to 44 years	45 to 54 years	55 to 64 years	65 to 74 years	75 years and over	Percent female	1990	2000	1990–2000	2000–2003
	12	13	14	15	16	17	18	19	20	21	22	23	24	25
MICHIGAN	6.8	19.4	9.4	13.7	16.1	13.8	8.7	6.5	5.8	51.0	9 295 287	9 938 444	6.9	1.4
Allen Park	5.3	16.8	6.5	12.0	16.3	13.7	8.5	9.2	11.7	52.4	31 092	29 376	-5.5	-2.1
Ann Arbor	5.0	11.7	26.8	18.3	13.0	11.3	6.0	4.1	3.8	50.6	109 608	114 024	4.0	0.4
Battle Creek	7.3	19.9	8.7	14.5	15.0	13.1	8.0	6.7	6.9	52.1	53 516	53 364	-0.3	0.9
Bay City	7.0	18.5	9.4	14.8	15.6	12.7	7.8	6.5	7.6	51.8	38 936	36 817	-5.4	-3.8
Burton	7.3	20.1	8.4	14.9	17.1	12.8	8.2	6.5	4.6	51.1	27 437	30 308	10.5	1.9
Dearborn	8.3	19.6	8.3	14.5	14.6	11.9	7.2	6.5	9.0	50.3	89 286	97 775	9.5	-1.1
Dearborn Heights	6.4	16.1	7.5	14.0	15.5	12.4	9.3	9.8	9.0	51.8	60 838	58 264	-4.2	-1.5
Detroit	8.0	23.1	9.7	15.2	14.4	12.2	7.1	5.6	4.9	52.9	1 027 974	951 270	-7.5	-4.2
East Lansing	2.5	6.5	58.6	10.6	5.8	6.2	3.7	2.5	3.6	51.9	50 677	46 525	-8.2	1.5
Eastpointe	6.4	18.1	7.6	15.2	17.1	12.6	6.6	7.7	8.8	51.5	35 283	34 077	-3.4	-2.0
Farmington Hills	6.0	17.1	6.7	14.5	16.8	15.3	9.3	7.0	7.4	51.6	74 614	82 111	10.0	-1.5
Flint	9.0	21.6	10.3	15.1	14.3	11.9	7.3	5.8	4.7	53.0	140 925	124 943	-11.3	-3.7
Garden City	6.2	18.9	7.6	14.7	17.9	12.9	8.2	8.5	5.0	50.6	31 846	30 047	-5.6	-1.7
Grand Rapids	8.3	18.8	13.1	17.2	14.3	10.8	6.0	5.2	6.4	51.1	189 126	197 800	4.6	-0.3
Holland	8.0	18.2	17.5	14.4	13.0	9.9	5.6	5.4	8.2	52.6	30 745	35 048	14.0	-1.1
Inkster	8.0	21.8	9.2	15.8	14.5	11.9	7.9	6.1	4.7	52.3	30 772	30 115	-2.1	-2.1
Jackson	9.1	20.6	9.8	15.8	14.6	11.4	6.8	5.6	6.4	52.3	37 425	36 316	-3.0	-3.2
Kalamazoo	6.2	14.1	27.6	15.0	11.8	9.6	5.6	4.5	5.6	51.8	80 277	77 145	-3.9	-2.4
Kentwood	7.7	18.9	10.4	17.1	16.6	12.6	6.9	5.0	4.9	51.8	37 826	45 255	19.6	2.7
Lansing	8.2	18.6	11.4	17.6	15.2	12.4	6.9	5.2	4.5	52.0	127 321	119 128	-6.4	-0.6
Lincoln Park	6.9	17.4	8.5	16.4	16.3	12.9	7.4	7.1	7.0	51.1	41 832	40 008	-4.4	-2.2
Livonia	5.6	18.2	6.3	11.3	17.4	14.9	9.4	8.9	8.0	51.5	100 850	100 545	-0.3	-1.1
Madison Heights	6.2	15.9	8.1	17.9	17.5	12.3	7.9	8.0	6.2	51.1	32 196	31 101	-3.4	-2.1
Midland	6.5	19.4	10.2	12.2	15.7	14.0	8.2	6.8	7.1	52.1	38 053	41 685	9.5	1.2
Mount Pleasant	3.4	8.1	54.1	9.8	7.0	6.5	3.7	3.1	4.3	54.8	23 299	25 946	11.4	-1.0
Muskegon	7.6	18.1	11.6	16.6	15.5	11.6	6.4	5.5	6.9	47.7	39 809	40 105	0.7	-0.7
Novi	7.4	20.2	6.7	15.2	20.4	14.7	7.2	4.3	3.8	50.8	32 998	47 386	43.6	7.2
Oak Park	6.8	21.4	8.0	14.4	15.4	14.0	7.8	5.9	6.3	53.2	30 468	29 793	-2.2	-2.2
Pontiac	8.9	21.7	10.3	17.4	14.9	11.5	6.8	4.7	3.8	51.3	71 136	66 337	-6.7	1.2
Portage	6.9	19.5	8.5	13.8	16.0	14.7	8.7	6.5	5.3	52.1	41 042	44 897	9.4	1.7
Port Huron	7.8	19.2	9.7	14.8	14.9	12.1	7.5	6.5	7.6	52.4	33 694	32 338	-4.0	-1.8
Rochester Hills	6.5	19.4	6.7	12.1	18.0	17.1	9.5	5.5	5.2	51.3	61 766	68 825	11.4	-0.1
Roseville	6.5	16.6	8.2	16.5	16.5	12.4	7.8	7.9	7.5	51.6	51 412	48 129	-6.4	-0.4
Royal Oak	5.2	12.6	7.5	21.2	17.6	13.6	7.4	6.7	8.3	51.2	65 410	60 062	-8.2	-2.4
Saginaw	8.6	23.0	9.9	14.1	14.2	12.1	6.6	5.8	5.6	53.4	69 512	61 799	-11.1	-4.1
St. Clair Shores	5.1	15.1	6.2	12.6	16.2	13.7	9.4	11.1	10.7	52.4	68 107	63 096	-7.4	-1.9
Southfield	5.6	16.0	7.9	15.8	14.8	15.4	9.3	6.8	8.4	54.1	75 727	78 296	3.4	-1.0
Southgate	5.4	16.1	8.3	14.8	15.9	14.2	9.1	8.4	7.8	51.8	30 771	30 136	-2.1	-0.2
Sterling Heights	6.2	17.9	8.5	14.3	16.1	15.0	10.3	5.8	5.9	51.0	117 810	124 471	5.7	1.4
Taylor	7.5	19.7	9.3	15.3	15.7	12.6	8.9	6.7	4.2	51.8	70 811	65 868	-7.0	-0.4
Troy	6.2	20.0	6.7	12.1	17.6	17.0	10.1	5.8	4.5	50.5	72 884	80 959	11.1	0.1
Warren	6.4	16.6	7.6	14.9	15.9	11.8	9.7	9.1	8.2	51.1	144 864	138 247	-4.6	-1.6
Westland	6.9	16.3	9.0	17.3	16.5	12.4	8.2	7.0	6.3	51.9	84 724	86 602	2.2	-1.0
Wyandotte	5.6	17.1	8.3	14.2	17.4	14.1	7.6	7.6	8.2	51.0	30 938	28 006	-9.5	-2.0
Wyoming	8.0	20.0	10.9	17.3	16.4	11.8	6.2	5.1	4.3	50.6	63 891	69 368	8.6	1.2
MINNESOTA	6.7	19.5	9.6	13.7	16.8	13.5	8.2	6.0	6.1	50.5	4 375 665	4 919 479	12.4	2.8
Andover	9.2	26.3	6.0	14.5	21.9	13.1	6.1	1.7	1.1	49.2	15 216	26 588	74.7	8.8
Apple Valley	7.2	22.5	7.2	13.9	19.2	16.3	8.2	3.3	2.2	51.1	34 598	45 527	31.6	7.5
Blaine	7.8	21.3	8.7	15.8	19.1	14.2	7.8	3.7	1.6	49.9	38 975	44 942	15.3	12.2
Bloomington	5.3	15.3	8.0	13.6	15.8	15.1	11.3	8.7	7.0	51.7	86 335	85 172	-1.3	-2.5
Brooklyn Center	6.7	18.3	9.6	14.8	15.3	11.6	8.1	8.3	7.1	51.3	28 887	29 172	1.0	-2.8
Brooklyn Park	8.1	20.7	9.7	16.8	18.2	14.0	6.9	3.7	1.9	50.3	56 381	67 388	19.5	0.6
Burnsville	7.1	19.1	10.1	16.9	17.1	13.7	8.7	4.4	2.8	50.7	51 288	60 220	17.4	-0.7
Coon Rapids	7.5	21.2	8.9	15.2	18.1	13.6	8.2	4.6	2.7	51.3	52 978	61 607	16.3	1.1
Cottage Grove	8.5	24.2	7.4	15.6	18.8	13.6	7.2	3.6	1.3	50.2	22 935	30 582	33.3	4.0
Duluth	5.4	15.9	16.2	12.1	14.1	13.4	7.9	6.5	8.6	51.7	85 493	86 918	1.7	-1.4
Eagan	8.1	21.9	7.4	16.7	21.6	14.2	6.0	2.7	1.5	50.8	47 409	63 557	34.1	0.7
Eden Prairie	7.8	22.6	6.2	14.6	21.0	16.1	6.8	3.0	1.9	50.9	39 311	54 901	39.7	8.3
Edina	5.4	17.5	4.4	8.8	14.8	15.9	10.6	10.1	12.6	54.2	46 075	47 425	2.9	-1.6
Fridley	6.7	15.9	10.2	15.4	15.6	13.4	11.0	7.7	4.2	50.6	28 335	27 449	-3.1	-1.0
Inver Grove Heights	7.2	20.1	9.2	15.4	18.5	13.9	7.8	4.7	3.1	50.5	22 477	29 751	32.4	5.1
Lakeville	10.1	26.0	5.9	15.2	22.6	12.1	5.3	1.9	0.9	49.4	24 854	43 128	73.5	10.8
Mankato	4.9	12.0	32.5	13.1	10.8	9.8	5.6	4.9	6.4	50.8	31 459	32 427	3.1	4.9
Maple Grove	7.4	23.3	6.6	13.7	21.2	17.0	6.7	2.6	1.5	50.5	38 736	50 365	30.0	13.5
Maplewood	6.5	18.2	7.7	13.0	16.9	13.8	8.7	7.4	7.7	52.2	30 954	34 947	12.9	2.9
Minneapolis	6.6	15.4	14.4	20.6	15.9	12.0	5.9	4.0	5.1	49.8	368 383	382 618	3.9	-1.2
Minnetonka	5.3	17.8	6.0	11.7	16.8	18.1	10.3	7.2	6.8	52.1	48 370	51 301	6.1	-1.2
Moorhead	5.8	16.8	23.1	10.9	13.3	10.9	6.3	5.8	6.9	53.1	32 295	32 177	-0.4	1.9
Oakdale	7.7	21.3	7.2	15.0	19.6	13.2	7.5	4.7	3.7	51.8	18 377	26 653	45.0	3.8

Table D. Cities — **Group Quarters, Crime, and Education**

City	Households, 2000: Number	Households, 2000: Percent change, 1990–2000	Households, 2000: Persons per household	Households, 2000: Percent: Female family householder[1]	Households, 2000: Percent: One-person	Persons in group quarters, 2000: Total	Persons in group quarters, 2000: Institutional: Total	Persons in group quarters, 2000: Institutional: Persons in nursing homes	Persons in group quarters, 2000: Noninstitutional	Serious crimes known to police,[2] 2002: Total: Number	Serious crimes known to police,[2] 2002: Total: Rate[3]	Serious crimes known to police,[2] 2002: Rate[2]: Violent	Serious crimes known to police,[2] 2002: Rate[2]: Property	Education, 2000: School enrollment[4]: Public	Education, 2000: School enrollment[4]: Private	Education, 2000: Attainment[5] (percent): High school graduate or less	Education, 2000: Attainment[5] (percent): Bachelor's degree or more
	26	27	28	29	30	31	32	33	34	35	36	37	38	39	40	41	42
MICHIGAN	3 785 661	10.7	2.56	12.5	26.2	249 889	126 132	50 113	123 757	389 366	3 874	540	3 334	2 397 577	382 801	47.9	21.8
Allen Park	11 974	-0.5	2.43	9.9	28.2	306	295	292	11	688	2 316	125	2 191	5 835	1 227	47.5	19.7
Ann Arbor	45 693	9.7	2.22	7.5	35.5	12 389	519	303	11 870	3 727	3 232	261	2 971	46 866	5 022	13.3	69.3
Battle Creek	21 348	-0.5	2.43	16.1	31.6	1 522	1 075	366	447	4 715	8 737	1 557	7 181	12 344	1 591	50.4	17.2
Bay City	15 208	-2.3	2.38	14.7	32.9	585	197	4	388	1 618	4 346	449	3 897	8 014	1 410	56.8	12.8
Burton	11 699	12.0	2.58	12.8	25.3	110	0	0	110	1 977	6 450	509	5 941	6 952	1 010	56.6	11.2
Dearborn	36 770	3.7	2.65	9.4	30.9	401	224	154	177	5 681	5 746	1 122	4 624	23 838	4 490	46.6	26.4
Dearborn Heights	23 276	-0.7	2.47	10.8	28.0	687	527	367	160	1 238	2 101	127	1 974	10 730	3 034	55.8	16.7
Detroit	336 428	-10.1	2.77	31.6	29.7	19 701	10 509	4 597	9 192	85 035	8 840	2 073	6 767	257 711	37 912	60.4	11.0
East Lansing	14 390	6.6	2.22	5.7	36.2	14 573	229	229	14 344	1 455	3 093	395	2 697	31 255	1 573	10.4	70.4
Eastpointe	13 595	1.1	2.50	12.3	28.8	79	0	0	79	1 350	3 917	493	3 424	6 833	1 468	59.7	11.3
Farmington Hills	33 559	14.8	2.41	6.6	29.6	1 313	547	417	766	1 798	2 165	210	1 956	17 082	4 178	26.0	47.9
Flint	48 744	-9.6	2.51	27.5	31.9	2 559	1 013	186	1 546	9 712	7 687	1 354	6 332	33 354	3 419	57.6	11.3
Garden City	11 479	2.4	2.62	11.2	24.0	18	2	0	16	814	2 679	309	2 370	6 853	954	58.0	9.0
Grand Rapids	73 217	6.1	2.57	15.8	30.8	9 694	4 415	2 592	5 279	11 292	5 645	1 089	4 556	40 826	16 572	48.1	23.8
Holland	11 971	13.2	2.67	10.8	26.8	3 096	520	516	2 576	1 314	3 707	310	3 397	7 039	4 406	49.3	26.9
Inkster	11 169	-0.3	2.67	26.8	27.9	252	77	73	175	1 472	4 833	1 373	3 461	7 863	1 095	58.7	12.1
Jackson	14 210	-3.5	2.48	19.9	32.0	1 104	599	327	505	2 821	7 459	1 177	6 283	8 401	1 413	53.6	13.1
Kalamazoo	29 413	0.0	2.30	14.7	34.8	9 539	1 285	501	8 254	6 316	8 096	1 092	7 004	27 966	3 933	39.4	32.7
Kentwood	18 477	21.2	2.43	10.8	30.9	362	180	125	182	1 671	3 651	264	3 387	10 211	2 287	37.4	31.5
Lansing	49 505	-2.2	2.39	17.0	33.2	872	502	314	370	6 601	5 479	1 072	4 407	31 530	4 137	44.4	21.2
Lincoln Park	16 204	-0.3	2.46	13.3	29.3	128	116	110	12	1 969	4 867	373	4 493	7 956	1 308	66.1	6.9
Livonia	38 089	6.1	2.59	8.0	22.9	1 891	1 181	1 019	710	2 779	2 733	209	2 524	22 371	4 710	38.6	29.7
Madison Heights	13 299	3.5	2.33	10.5	33.8	160	139	139	21	1 303	4 143	254	3 889	6 628	902	54.8	18.5
Midland	16 743	13.0	2.42	8.7	28.6	1 220	459	355	761	957	2 270	180	2 090	9 879	2 576	29.1	41.9
Mount Pleasant	8 449	26.8	2.38	8.5	29.6	5 868	627	261	5 241	900	3 430	236	3 194	16 040	617	32.8	40.3
Muskegon	14 569	-1.4	2.42	20.2	34.4	4 827	4 459	333	368	3 482	8 585	1 149	7 436	9 122	1 243	59.4	8.7
Novi	18 726	47.5	2.52	7.1	28.1	267	202	202	65	1 493	3 116	104	3 011	11 905	1 749	22.8	49.1
Oak Park	11 104	2.0	2.68	19.5	26.6	23	0	0	23	1 076	3 571	405	3 166	7 299	2 294	40.5	27.2
Pontiac	24 234	-2.2	2.68	25.2	29.4	1 441	647	283	794	4 004	5 969	1 631	4 338	17 854	1 571	63.6	10.3
Portage	18 138	17.3	2.45	9.7	27.2	415	120	120	295	2 183	4 808	264	4 544	10 947	1 730	31.2	36.8
Port Huron	12 961	-1.5	2.43	17.5	31.9	839	441	195	398	1 377	4 211	584	3 627	7 455	618	58.9	11.3
Rochester Hills	26 315	17.7	2.59	6.8	24.0	783	280	280	503	NA	NA	NA	NA	15 911	4 130	25.6	47.3
Roseville	19 976	2.2	2.40	12.7	30.8	184	153	153	31	2 500	5 137	349	4 787	9 665	1 319	62.6	7.2
Royal Oak	28 880	1.9	2.06	7.5	40.8	506	223	194	283	1 508	2 483	173	2 310	11 233	2 611	31.4	39.9
Saginaw	23 182	-11.4	2.60	27.3	29.5	1 438	746	319	692	4 847	7 756	2 418	5 338	17 578	1 428	61.7	10.4
St. Clair Shores	27 434	0.8	2.28	10.0	32.7	484	372	372	112	1 734	2 718	259	2 459	11 264	2 403	49.4	18.1
Southfield	33 987	5.8	2.27	14.3	36.2	1 223	673	610	550	4 543	5 738	1 076	4 662	16 624	4 695	32.0	36.7
Southgate	12 836	5.8	2.33	9.7	32.3	198	171	91	27	1 389	4 558	220	4 338	6 184	986	58.4	12.7
Sterling Heights	46 319	13.4	2.66	8.5	24.1	1 198	672	650	526	3 353	2 664	193	2 471	28 556	4 585	45.2	23.0
Taylor	24 776	-0.3	2.63	17.4	23.1	695	580	438	115	3 425	5 142	441	4 700	14 642	2 223	65.2	7.0
Troy	30 018	14.7	2.69	6.0	22.8	235	0	0	235	2 077	2 537	115	2 422	20 062	3 760	25.2	50.0
Warren	55 551	1.7	2.47	11.7	28.8	1 302	1 002	996	300	5 361	3 835	612	3 223	28 480	3 972	58.9	13.0
Westland	36 533	10.3	2.34	12.1	32.6	942	848	599	94	3 043	3 475	340	3 134	17 981	2 743	53.4	16.1
Wyandotte	11 816	-4.1	2.36	11.9	31.9	94	41	0	53	1 086	3 835	286	3 549	5 484	1 239	56.9	12.7
Wyoming	26 536	9.8	2.60	12.0	26.6	358	87	87	271	2 741	3 907	475	3 433	16 136	2 893	51.6	17.0
MINNESOTA	1 895 127	15.0	2.52	8.9	26.9	135 883	63 058	40 506	72 825	177 454	3 535	268	3 268	1 146 595	215 912	40.9	27.4
Andover	8 107	83.0	3.28	5.5	8.4	12	0	0	12	732	2 698	63	2 635	7 414	1 338	30.9	28.0
Apple Valley	16 344	46.6	2.77	9.0	19.3	237	192	192	45	1 378	2 966	127	2 839	12 012	1 607	24.1	41.0
Blaine	15 898	24.0	2.82	11.1	17.0	103	0	0	103	2 370	5 168	172	4 996	11 255	1 449	42.1	19.7
Bloomington	36 400	5.5	2.30	8.2	29.6	1 326	727	665	599	4 007	4 611	192	4 419	15 315	3 705	31.3	35.4
Brooklyn Center	11 430	1.8	2.52	13.4	28.2	387	183	171	204	2 037	6 843	447	6 396	6 556	780	47.9	16.7
Brooklyn Park	24 432	19.8	2.75	12.1	22.0	218	15	15	203	3 202	4 657	345	4 312	16 994	2 759	34.6	27.3
Burnsville	23 687	23.8	2.53	10.0	24.8	343	131	29	212	2 187	3 559	173	3 387	13 904	2 426	27.1	36.8
Coon Rapids	22 578	29.4	2.71	12.2	20.1	362	184	184	178	2 750	4 375	137	4 238	14 942	2 320	39.8	21.4
Cottage Grove	9 932	44.9	3.07	8.8	11.0	59	0	0	59	817	2 618	131	2 487	8 167	1 241	35.8	23.9
Duluth	35 500	2.7	2.26	11.4	34.5	6 561	2 154	1 119	4 407	5 331	6 011	422	5 589	23 106	3 789	41.1	28.2
Eagan	23 773	36.4	2.67	8.4	23.0	165	0	0	165	1 773	2 734	88	2 646	15 336	3 445	20.2	47.7
Eden Prairie	20 457	41.6	2.68	7.7	22.0	174	77	77	97	1 312	2 342	120	2 222	13 326	3 163	14.7	57.1
Edina	20 996	5.7	2.24	5.8	34.0	290	262	262	28	1 217	2 515	99	2 416	8 816	2 348	16.3	58.5
Fridley	11 328	3.8	2.40	11.6	26.8	218	53	53	165	1 629	5 816	314	5 502	5 492	799	43.6	24.4
Inver Grove Heights	11 257	44.3	2.62	10.3	21.5	263	213	162	50	1 029	3 390	165	3 225	6 881	1 203	36.5	29.6
Lakeville	13 609	73.3	3.17	7.5	10.7	39	0	0	39	949	2 157	55	2 102	12 472	1 545	26.0	35.7
Mankato	12 367	10.2	2.31	8.8	32.2	3 839	328	254	3 511	1 991	6 017	181	5 836	12 105	1 556	35.5	32.2
Maple Grove	17 532	39.9	2.87	7.5	15.8	68	0	0	68	1 238	2 409	119	2 290	13 483	1 865	23.6	41.7
Maplewood	13 758	19.7	2.48	10.5	27.0	817	337	337	480	2 561	7 182	278	6 904	6 692	1 843	41.9	25.6
Minneapolis	162 352	1.0	2.25	12.3	40.3	18 064	5 701	4 199	12 363	26 630	6 821	1 056	5 765	90 792	19 383	35.8	37.4
Minnetonka	21 393	14.5	2.37	6.8	27.3	635	345	212	290	1 269	2 424	84	2 340	9 919	2 719	19.9	51.6
Moorhead	11 660	5.4	2.43	9.8	29.2	3 836	524	382	3 312	1 262	3 844	247	3 597	9 372	3 201	37.0	29.5
Oakdale	10 243	52.9	2.59	11.1	25.2	109	0	0	109	1 257	4 622	235	4 387	6 184	1 498	37.9	24.3

1. No spouse present. 2. Data for serious crimes have not been adjusted for underreporting. This may affect comparability between geographic areas and over time. 3. Per 100,000 population estimated by the FBI. 4. All persons 3 years old and over enrolled in nursery school through college. 5. Persons 25 years old and over.

City	Per capita income[1] (dollars)	Households Median income Dollars	Percent change, 1989–1999 (constant 1999 dollars)	Percent with income of $100,000 or more	Persons Total	Percent change in rate, 1989–1999	Families Total	Housing units, 2000 Total	Percent change, 1990–2000	Vacant units Vacant units for sale or rent[2]	For seasonal use (percent)	Home owner vacancy rate	Renter vacancy rate
	43	44	45	46	47	48	49	50	51	52	53	54	55
MICHIGAN	22 168	44 667	7.2	12.7	10.5	-19.8	7.4	4 234 279	10.0	448 618	5.5	1.6	6.8
Allen Park	24 980	51 992	-3.1	12.9	3.2	-3.0	1.9	12 254	0.2	280	0.2	0.6	4.4
Ann Arbor	26 419	46 299	3.3	18.4	16.6	3.1	4.6	47 218	7.3	1 525	0.5	1.0	2.6
Battle Creek	18 424	35 491	4.4	7.1	14.4	-21.3	10.7	23 525	1.2	2 177	0.4	2.5	12.1
Bay City	16 550	30 425	5.9	5.3	14.6	-19.3	10.3	16 259	-0.7	1 051	0.4	1.7	7.4
Burton	20 548	44 050	9.4	8.6	8.7	-39.2	5.5	12 348	13.9	649	0.2	2.7	5.3
Dearborn	21 488	44 560	-5.0	13.8	16.1	49.1	12.2	38 981	5.6	2 211	1.2	1.5	6.1
Dearborn Heights	22 829	48 222	-2.4	10.9	6.1	10.9	4.4	23 913	0.1	637	0.3	0.9	3.8
Detroit	14 717	29 526	17.3	6.3	26.1	-19.4	21.7	375 096	-8.5	38 668	0.2	1.6	8.3
East Lansing	16 333	28 217	-15.0	12.1	34.8	3.0	11.0	15 321	6.4	931	0.3	1.2	6.3
Eastpointe	20 665	46 261	1.1	8.0	6.4	30.6	4.2	13 965	2.1	370	0.2	0.9	4.5
Farmington Hills	36 134	67 493	-3.4	30.8	4.1	36.7	2.4	34 858	11.8	1 299	0.8	0.5	5.1
Flint	15 733	28 015	3.3	5.5	26.4	-13.7	22.9	55 464	-5.6	6 720	0.3	2.7	13.1
Garden City	21 651	51 841	-0.3	10.2	4.5	4.7	3.3	11 719	3.0	240	0.2	0.5	3.6
Grand Rapids	17 661	37 224	3.3	6.6	15.7	-2.5	11.9	77 960	5.8	4 743	0.3	1.3	6.6
Holland	18 823	42 291	2.6	8.6	10.6	-10.2	6.7	12 533	11.5	562	0.9	1.4	3.3
Inkster	16 711	35 950	6.2	6.2	19.5	-15.9	15.2	12 013	-0.3	844	0.2	1.7	7.7
Jackson	15 230	31 294	11.8	4.0	19.6	-20.6	15.2	15 241	-2.9	1 031	0.3	1.5	7.9
Kalamazoo	16 897	31 189	0.0	6.8	24.3	-7.3	13.6	31 798	1.0	2 385	0.4	2.1	6.9
Kentwood	22 463	45 812	-0.7	10.2	6.3	26.0	5.0	19 507	19.4	1 030	0.5	1.3	7.0
Lansing	17 924	34 833	-1.8	4.7	16.9	-12.9	13.2	53 159	-1.4	3 654	0.4	2.0	7.2
Lincoln Park	20 140	42 515	3.3	6.5	7.7	-9.4	6.1	16 821	0.3	617	0.3	1.0	5.8
Livonia	27 923	63 018	-3.6	21.8	3.2	23.1	2.0	38 658	5.5	569	0.2	0.4	2.7
Madison Heights	21 429	42 326	-0.8	7.8	8.9	6.0	7.0	13 623	3.0	324	0.3	0.8	3.0
Midland	26 818	48 444	-6.9	19.6	8.8	-7.4	5.5	17 773	15.1	1 030	0.8	1.7	6.7
Mount Pleasant	13 177	24 572	-4.7	5.7	37.2	-3.9	11.4	8 878	25.6	429	0.4	1.7	4.5
Muskegon	14 283	27 929	10.9	3.2	20.5	-22.6	16.8	15 999	0.1	1 430	0.5	2.9	7.8
Novi	35 992	71 918	12.6	32.1	2.2	-33.3	1.6	19 649	44.9	923	0.5	1.2	7.0
Oak Park	21 677	48 697	0.4	12.3	9.4	-13.8	7.8	11 370	0.2	266	0.2	1.1	2.7
Pontiac	15 842	31 207	5.8	5.8	22.1	-17.2	18.0	26 336	-1.0	2 102	0.2	2.0	8.6
Portage	25 414	49 410	-5.8	15.0	4.8	14.3	3.1	18 880	17.0	742	0.4	1.4	5.2
Port Huron	17 100	31 327	8.3	5.5	16.9	-23.5	13.4	14 003	-0.2	1 042	0.7	2.0	7.9
Rochester Hills	35 070	74 912	1.4	33.8	3.4	30.8	2.3	27 263	15.8	948	0.5	1.0	6.1
Roseville	19 823	41 220	-5.1	6.0	7.9	27.4	6.1	20 519	2.5	543	0.3	0.9	3.3
Royal Oak	30 990	52 252	5.6	15.8	4.3	-6.5	2.0	29 942	2.7	1 062	0.7	0.8	4.5
Saginaw	13 816	26 485	11.1	4.2	28.5	-10.1	24.7	25 639	-8.4	2 457	0.2	2.2	7.6
St. Clair Shores	25 009	49 047	-1.1	11.3	3.7	2.8	2.6	28 208	1.0	774	0.5	0.8	4.0
Southfield	28 096	51 802	-5.0	17.1	7.4	27.6	5.8	35 698	1.8	1 711	0.3	1.1	5.8
Southgate	23 219	46 927	-4.4	9.9	4.6	0.0	2.6	13 361	6.9	525	0.5	1.2	4.8
Sterling Heights	24 958	60 494	-3.1	19.1	5.2	44.4	4.0	47 547	12.4	1 228	0.3	0.9	3.7
Taylor	19 638	42 944	-2.1	9.3	10.8	-9.2	8.9	25 905	0.7	1 129	0.2	1.5	5.8
Troy	35 936	77 538	4.2	36.2	2.7	-3.6	1.7	30 872	13.5	854	0.7	0.5	3.7
Warren	21 407	44 626	-7.7	9.6	7.4	13.8	5.2	57 249	1.9	1 698	0.3	0.8	4.4
Westland	22 615	46 308	-1.5	9.4	6.8	-4.2	4.7	38 077	10.3	1 544	0.3	1.5	5.2
Wyandotte	22 185	43 740	15.0	8.2	6.2	-36.1	4.7	12 303	-4.0	487	0.3	1.1	4.4
Wyoming	19 287	43 164	3.3	7.0	7.3	2.8	5.1	27 506	9.8	970	0.2	1.0	5.6
MINNESOTA	23 198	47 111	13.4	12.6	7.9	-22.5	5.1	2 065 946	11.8	170 819	5.1	0.9	4.1
Andover	26 317	76 241	22.0	25.6	2.0	-44.4	1.2	8 205	81.6	98	0.1	0.6	1.1
Apple Valley	29 477	69 752	3.9	25.6	2.1	-40.0	1.1	16 536	43.3	192	0.2	0.3	2.2
Blaine	22 777	59 219	9.1	12.9	3.0	-42.3	2.1	16 169	22.7	271	0.1	0.8	0.9
Bloomington	29 782	54 628	-2.6	17.7	4.0	8.1	2.3	37 104	3.6	704	0.4	0.3	3.0
Brooklyn Center	19 695	44 570	-2.9	6.8	7.4	4.2	4.7	11 598	-1.0	168	0.2	0.4	2.3
Brooklyn Park	23 199	56 572	5.2	15.2	5.1	-32.0	3.8	24 846	16.8	414	0.2	0.4	2.9
Burnsville	27 093	57 965	-1.1	17.9	5.1	21.4	3.7	24 261	19.8	574	0.4	0.4	3.4
Coon Rapids	22 915	55 550	-1.7	12.4	4.8	0.0	3.6	22 828	26.1	250	0.2	0.5	1.1
Cottage Grove	23 348	65 825	6.4	17.3	2.2	-15.4	1.8	10 024	41.1	92	0.1	0.2	4.3
Duluth	18 969	33 766	7.5	6.7	15.5	-6.6	8.6	36 994	2.7	1 494	0.5	1.0	3.4
Eagan	30 167	67 388	7.6	25.3	2.9	3.6	1.9	24 390	32.2	617	0.3	0.2	5.6
Eden Prairie	38 854	78 328	10.1	36.2	3.5	12.9	2.8	21 026	36.5	569	0.7	0.4	3.9
Edina	44 195	66 019	0.4	32.4	3.3	3.1	2.0	21 669	3.3	673	1.4	0.5	2.5
Fridley	23 022	48 372	-2.3	9.5	7.3	19.7	5.3	11 504	0.8	176	0.2	0.4	2.0
Inver Grove Heights	25 493	59 090	11.7	18.8	4.2	-41.7	3.0	11 457	40.6	200	0.2	0.6	2.2
Lakeville	26 492	72 404	20.0	26.0	2.0	-33.3	1.5	13 799	70.3	190	0.2	0.5	2.3
Mankato	17 652	33 956	12.4	5.8	19.0	-24.6	8.5	12 759	9.2	392	0.2	0.9	2.6
Maple Grove	30 544	76 111	11.9	29.4	1.4	-39.1	0.8	17 745	36.8	213	0.2	0.3	2.3
Maplewood	24 387	51 596	1.4	13.7	4.8	-22.6	3.0	14 004	15.5	246	0.4	0.4	1.9
Minneapolis	22 685	37 974	11.6	10.4	16.9	-8.6	11.9	168 606	-2.4	6 254	0.5	0.7	2.8
Minnetonka	40 410	69 979	2.8	30.2	2.6	23.8	1.5	22 228	10.5	835	1.1	0.4	5.0
Moorhead	17 150	34 781	6.7	6.4	16.3	-18.1	8.2	12 180	5.8	520	0.2	0.8	6.3
Oakdale	24 107	56 299	2.1	14.7	3.6	-37.9	2.9	10 394	49.9	151	0.2	0.5	1.8

1. Based on population enumerated as of April 1, 2000.   2. Includes units rented or sold but not occupied.

City	Housing units, 2000 (cont'd) Occupied units — Total	Percent owner occupied	Percent renter occupied	Average size owner occupied	Average size renter occupied	Civilian labor force, 2003 — Total	Percent change, 2002–2003	Unemployment — Total	Rate[1]	Civilian employment,[2] 2000 — Total	Percent Management, professional, and related occupations	Production, transportation, and material moving occupations	Disability, 2000 Employment disabled persons[3] (percent)
	56	57	58	59	60	61	62	63	64	65	66	67	68
MICHIGAN	3 785 661	73.8	26.2	2.67	2.24	5 042 094	0.8	368 121	7.3	4 637 461	31.5	18.5	10.7
Allen Park	11 974	87.9	12.1	2.51	1.82	14 367	0.1	560	3.9	13 510	33.6	16.0	7.3
Ann Arbor	45 693	45.3	54.7	2.43	2.06	70 375	0.9	1 914	2.7	61 271	61.0	4.0	5.4
Battle Creek	21 348	65.8	34.2	2.52	2.25	24 895	1.5	2 114	8.5	23 052	26.7	22.8	13.5
Bay City	15 208	69.5	30.5	2.51	2.09	17 805	0.6	1 884	10.6	16 481	24.9	18.7	11.8
Burton	11 699	80.8	19.2	2.67	2.23	11 868	-0.3	1 285	10.8	13 720	22.6	23.1	11.1
Dearborn	36 770	73.4	26.6	2.75	2.38	40 602	0.2	1 809	4.5	38 790	37.8	14.7	11.8
Dearborn Heights	23 276	85.4	14.6	2.53	2.14	29 486	0.2	1 238	4.2	25 982	28.1	17.2	11.3
Detroit	336 428	54.9	45.1	2.84	2.68	391 159	2.4	57 291	14.6	331 441	21.6	22.5	18.8
East Lansing	14 390	32.0	68.0	2.41	2.13	29 212	1.3	1 764	6.0	24 520	44.6	4.3	3.5
Eastpointe	13 595	88.0	12.0	2.56	2.09	19 669	0.1	1 135	5.8	16 544	23.0	21.2	9.0
Farmington Hills	33 559	66.9	33.1	2.72	1.77	48 112	-0.4	1 695	3.5	42 200	53.3	7.4	6.8
Flint	48 744	58.8	41.2	2.45	2.59	52 838	0.4	8 700	16.5	45 885	21.0	24.6	15.8
Garden City	11 479	86.2	13.8	2.71	2.03	16 435	0.2	691	4.2	14 614	22.6	21.6	11.5
Grand Rapids	73 217	59.7	40.3	2.69	2.39	117 962	1.2	12 807	10.9	92 392	29.2	21.7	12.7
Holland	11 971	67.1	32.9	2.73	2.55	21 563	-0.1	1 606	7.4	17 226	29.0	26.5	8.1
Inkster	11 169	58.0	42.0	2.76	2.55	13 288	1.4	1 340	10.1	11 859	21.6	24.4	15.2
Jackson	14 210	57.6	42.4	2.55	2.38	19 062	2.2	2 184	11.5	15 601	23.0	25.0	13.2
Kalamazoo	29 413	47.7	52.3	2.43	2.18	43 515	1.9	3 460	8.0	37 141	32.2	14.7	8.8
Kentwood	18 477	61.0	39.0	2.71	1.99	27 201	-0.1	1 403	5.2	24 402	35.0	19.4	9.0
Lansing	49 505	57.5	42.5	2.49	2.26	67 511	1.4	4 533	6.7	57 751	27.9	15.9	12.1
Lincoln Park	16 204	79.1	20.9	2.57	2.06	19 813	0.5	1 106	5.6	18 565	17.5	25.0	12.3
Livonia	38 089	88.8	11.2	2.68	1.86	52 799	0.0	1 687	3.2	49 783	41.1	12.0	6.7
Madison Heights	13 299	70.1	29.9	2.50	1.93	20 096	-0.1	1 340	6.7	15 673	29.5	17.1	12.2
Midland	16 743	69.7	30.3	2.63	1.92	22 130	-0.2	1 021	4.6	19 747	46.2	9.5	6.7
Mount Pleasant	8 449	34.3	65.7	2.43	2.35	14 147	-0.2	621	4.4	13 123	29.2	6.1	3.9
Muskegon	14 569	56.9	43.1	2.58	2.21	18 270	0.8	2 533	13.9	15 136	19.1	28.7	18.6
Novi	18 726	71.1	28.9	2.78	1.88	21 527	-0.4	822	3.8	25 956	53.0	8.5	4.8
Oak Park	11 104	74.8	25.2	2.74	2.52	17 306	-0.2	1 047	6.0	13 495	34.8	15.9	11.6
Pontiac	24 234	52.8	47.2	2.76	2.59	35 010	0.6	4 953	14.1	26 640	18.5	25.2	15.8
Portage	18 138	68.9	31.1	2.71	1.88	25 424	1.0	872	3.4	23 566	39.0	13.3	7.5
Port Huron	12 961	57.2	42.8	2.54	2.29	17 847	1.4	2 130	11.9	14 518	20.6	27.5	11.7
Rochester Hills	26 315	79.1	20.9	2.76	1.92	38 351	-0.3	1 531	4.0	36 044	53.3	7.8	6.7
Roseville	19 976	75.2	24.8	2.53	2.01	31 169	0.5	2 532	8.1	23 201	19.5	21.6	10.7
Royal Oak	28 880	70.1	29.9	2.24	1.65	41 725	-0.3	1 781	4.3	35 487	48.0	8.6	6.4
Saginaw	23 182	63.6	36.4	2.61	2.59	28 138	3.5	4 508	16.0	22 500	21.3	19.1	14.1
St. Clair Shores	27 434	85.8	14.2	2.36	1.81	40 696	0.2	2 483	6.1	29 878	31.4	15.6	9.8
Southfield	33 987	54.1	45.9	2.64	1.83	48 014	-0.2	2 712	5.6	39 714	43.9	12.6	12.1
Southgate	12 836	70.6	29.4	2.58	1.73	15 700	0.2	681	4.3	14 588	27.3	18.6	10.0
Sterling Heights	46 319	79.0	21.0	2.87	1.88	76 551	0.1	4 175	5.5	64 340	35.5	14.6	9.6
Taylor	24 776	70.8	29.2	2.67	2.53	33 933	0.6	2 168	6.4	29 509	17.5	25.7	12.3
Troy	30 018	77.3	22.7	2.92	1.91	46 251	-0.4	1 443	3.1	42 032	54.8	7.2	6.9
Warren	55 551	80.4	19.6	2.55	2.12	86 810	0.4	6 713	7.7	64 188	25.4	21.7	9.9
Westland	36 533	62.7	37.3	2.57	1.97	45 697	0.2	2 040	4.5	43 776	27.0	20.8	10.1
Wyandotte	11 816	73.0	27.0	2.53	1.91	14 041	0.5	813	5.8	13 701	22.9	20.1	9.4
Wyoming	26 536	67.6	32.4	2.80	2.18	44 538	0.5	3 418	7.7	36 608	23.4	26.9	11.5
MINNESOTA	1 895 127	74.6	25.4	2.69	2.03	2 923 083	0.3	145 399	5.0	2 580 046	35.8	14.9	8.6
Andover	8 107	95.7	4.3	3.32	2.34	17 020	0.1	663	3.9	14 497	36.9	13.8	5.6
Apple Valley	16 344	88.0	12.0	2.86	2.14	29 686	0.1	1 144	3.9	26 513	40.6	9.3	6.0
Blaine	15 898	90.5	9.5	2.87	2.32	30 616	0.4	1 492	4.9	25 918	30.9	19.0	10.1
Bloomington	36 400	70.6	29.4	2.48	1.88	56 060	0.0	2 488	4.4	47 821	41.0	10.4	8.6
Brooklyn Center	11 430	68.7	31.3	2.70	2.13	17 180	0.6	1 007	5.9	14 967	28.0	18.4	10.7
Brooklyn Park	24 432	73.4	26.6	2.94	2.22	44 278	0.3	2 314	5.2	38 056	34.3	16.2	8.8
Burnsville	23 687	68.1	31.9	2.71	2.14	40 103	0.1	1 706	4.3	35 703	39.4	9.4	9.3
Coon Rapids	22 578	80.4	19.6	2.81	2.30	38 991	0.3	1 932	5.0	34 659	32.9	16.2	7.3
Cottage Grove	9 932	91.4	8.6	3.09	2.92	17 878	0.4	776	4.3	16 833	32.3	14.5	6.5
Duluth	35 500	64.1	35.9	2.46	1.91	48 408	0.1	2 289	4.7	41 826	34.3	10.4	10.1
Eagan	23 773	75.0	25.0	2.85	2.11	42 950	-0.1	1 510	3.5	37 336	49.0	8.4	6.5
Eden Prairie	20 457	78.3	21.7	2.83	2.11	37 693	-0.2	1 363	3.6	30 916	53.0	6.4	5.9
Edina	20 996	76.5	23.5	2.42	1.66	26 418	-0.1	915	3.5	22 913	55.2	4.1	4.8
Fridley	11 328	67.7	32.3	2.51	2.19	18 075	0.3	953	5.3	15 546	31.5	17.7	10.1
Inver Grove Heights	11 257	77.5	22.5	2.72	2.27	19 075	0.4	838	4.4	17 174	38.0	11.9	7.6
Lakeville	13 609	91.8	8.2	3.22	2.55	27 998	0.1	832	3.0	23 312	37.9	11.4	7.7
Mankato	12 367	52.9	47.1	2.51	2.09	22 686	-0.4	932	4.1	18 652	30.1	16.4	7.0
Maple Grove	17 532	92.7	7.3	2.92	2.24	36 007	-0.1	1 298	3.6	30 045	46.6	7.6	4.7
Maplewood	13 758	75.7	24.3	2.67	1.90	21 588	4.5	923	4.3	18 354	34.5	13.4	8.7
Minneapolis	162 352	51.4	48.6	2.43	2.05	220 430	0.2	12 054	5.5	207 890	41.1	12.0	10.1
Minnetonka	21 393	75.7	24.3	2.55	1.79	32 505	-0.2	1 175	3.6	29 393	50.6	6.5	5.8
Moorhead	11 660	63.7	36.3	2.65	2.05	20 182	1.4	484	2.4	16 615	32.6	11.5	7.8
Oakdale	10 243	80.5	19.5	2.75	1.94	17 508	0.4	729	4.2	14 688	35.3	11.3	7.1

1. Percent of civilian labor force.   2. Persons 16 years old and over.   3. Persons 16 to 64 years old.

— **Construction, Wholesale Trade, and Retail Trade**

City	Value of residential construction authorized by building permits, 2003			Wholesale trade, 1997				Retail trade,[1] 1997			
	New construction ($1,000)	Number of housing units	Percent single family	Number of establishments	Number of employees	Sales (mil dol)	Annual payroll (mil dol)	Number of establishments	Number of employees	Sales (mil dol)	Annual payroll (mil dol)
	69	70	71	72	73	74	75	76	77	78	79
MICHIGAN	7 052 549	53 913	83.0	13 936	189 057	158 757.3	7 629.6	39 564	529 441	93 706.1	8 922.3
Allen Park	458	3	100.0	30	399	272.4	27.0	104	852	115.4	13.5
Ann Arbor	37 707	347	76.9	174	1 767	1 399.0	80.6	647	9 645	1 369.5	154.4
Battle Creek	15 022	108	94.4	59	976	1 139.7	37.5	266	3 825	632.7	58.2
Bay City	661	11	100.0	63	938	409.2	27.0	221	2 081	400.1	36.6
Burton	16 723	167	100.0	31	560	136.3	17.7	228	3 754	513.5	56.3
Dearborn	12 554	47	95.7	156	1 822	1 104.2	78.4	557	9 607	1 752.5	170.9
Dearborn Heights	6 596	30	100.0	30	237	101.6	8.4	187	2 455	391.6	38.8
Detroit	53 844	486	78.6	740	12 878	14 616.4	541.3	2 253	17 886	3 188.7	289.1
East Lansing	2 646	22	100.0	22	D	D	D	119	2 471	304.0	32.3
Eastpointe	523	9	100.0	NA	NA	NA	NA	NA	NA	NA	NA
Farmington Hills	19 943	102	100.0	416	5 457	7 318.4	266.7	328	4 696	1 100.4	104.2
Flint	863	8	100.0	139	1 970	728.3	62.0	531	5 157	864.6	86.3
Garden City	4 013	40	100.0	18	139	24.1	4.2	111	1 300	392.1	31.5
Grand Rapids	21 055	222	67.6	485	8 890	4 426.2	345.5	795	11 578	2 018.1	214.8
Holland	15 898	101	45.5	64	1 011	549.2	35.3	230	3 525	612.3	58.7
Inkster	1 991	19	100.0	8	79	27.0	3.0	55	470	86.7	7.9
Jackson	1 345	15	100.0	100	1 311	633.6	52.1	237	3 671	567.5	56.3
Kalamazoo	9 218	73	45.2	155	2 389	687.3	84.8	337	4 265	727.2	70.5
Kentwood	26 231	229	96.9	121	3 845	3 354.0	142.9	267	5 718	855.4	84.4
Lansing	20 448	380	17.4	190	3 186	933.4	103.9	523	8 178	1 486.6	150.2
Lincoln Park	965	12	100.0	22	187	40.0	5.2	159	2 644	352.5	35.9
Livonia	26 532	239	100.0	424	8 691	6 430.2	337.7	644	9 668	1 591.2	167.7
Madison Heights	5 592	63	100.0	141	2 960	2 722.8	152.0	193	3 744	717.8	66.4
Midland	9 131	84	81.0	54	478	240.4	19.6	256	3 673	584.7	59.4
Mount Pleasant	9 411	217	19.8	38	D	D	D	130	2 193	288.1	29.0
Muskegon	4 862	52	57.7	53	669	237.7	22.3	176	2 571	413.0	42.5
Novi	91 512	740	54.1	163	3 940	2 851.9	185.1	323	6 100	1 177.8	105.4
Oak Park	60	1	100.0	91	1 178	627.7	44.3	182	2 510	401.9	55.2
Pontiac	16 912	213	100.0	76	D	D	D	228	2 548	502.3	44.6
Portage	54 032	344	82.6	83	2 431	692.7	94.7	338	6 404	879.0	85.9
Port Huron	3 067	29	93.1	30	285	173.1	11.4	168	1 936	375.7	40.3
Rochester Hills	82 314	519	69.6	175	1 405	1 302.5	66.9	240	4 340	968.3	92.3
Roseville	5 962	110	90.9	78	973	383.6	39.0	293	5 807	966.3	91.2
Royal Oak	9 906	52	100.0	118	915	590.0	37.8	297	4 193	773.9	85.4
Saginaw	636	10	100.0	76	1 182	317.9	39.0	206	1 898	260.6	30.5
St. Clair Shores	6 447	48	100.0	86	548	605.4	23.5	234	3 306	547.8	58.4
Southfield	17 739	139	100.0	440	6 838	15 374.8	426.0	566	8 925	1 987.7	182.6
Southgate	15 673	220	34.5	17	D	D	D	171	3 836	888.7	70.3
Sterling Heights	71 517	799	100.0	155	2 409	952.0	106.0	495	9 680	1 598.9	160.0
Taylor	24 166	238	74.8	86	1 931	1 872.1	66.3	343	6 038	1 037.0	102.3
Troy	47 930	343	100.0	521	7 489	11 690.9	384.1	607	12 184	2 410.8	226.9
Warren	9 436	149	53.0	274	4 379	2 802.5	169.5	563	8 524	1 730.7	172.0
Westland	47 244	403	99.5	76	738	280.8	27.9	335	6 533	1 160.5	101.2
Wyandotte	14 324	97	72.2	31	286	59.5	9.4	107	753	122.2	13.3
Wyoming	31 295	337	66.5	223	7 193	3 330.3	272.5	308	5 510	934.6	101.4
MINNESOTA	6 269 475	42 046	77.8	9 348	131 787	99 444.5	5 024.0	20 883	282 282	48 077.7	4 525.7
Andover	30 455	209	85.6	14	47	10.3	1.2	35	430	72.0	6.3
Apple Valley	60 335	527	43.8	49	244	245.7	12.9	112	2 761	529.3	46.5
Blaine	115 044	813	99.3	59	964	316.5	33.0	199	3 100	504.4	45.5
Bloomington	18 730	123	22.0	485	8 222	10 687.5	402.2	587	12 036	2 079.0	201.3
Brooklyn Center	1 858	17	100.0	54	540	329.1	20.1	133	3 435	675.0	58.0
Brooklyn Park	70 492	474	93.7	97	1 270	580.1	52.7	154	4 656	1 220.1	93.6
Burnsville	26 270	200	32.0	225	2 563	1 605.0	88.5	372	7 850	1 272.9	123.4
Coon Rapids	57 200	332	100.0	39	456	172.3	19.7	151	3 412	573.7	49.3
Cottage Grove	52 945	283	100.0	5	15	7.1	0.5	44	1 066	151.6	13.3
Duluth	23 847	161	85.1	129	1 611	778.7	49.3	536	7 277	1 037.0	110.8
Eagan	48 576	391	47.1	163	3 496	2 059.3	144.7	140	3 251	555.1	57.4
Eden Prairie	115 237	726	69.7	319	6 208	5 447.1	303.0	188	3 597	676.4	61.9
Edina	24 154	83	38.6	300	2 906	5 783.3	145.7	377	8 123	1 182.9	132.6
Fridley	3 328	25	68.0	94	1 593	817.6	61.3	107	2 863	482.5	47.0
Inver Grove Heights	87 772	627	31.6	24	393	166.0	9.8	58	1 516	435.5	32.6
Lakeville	152 402	780	88.1	51	564	256.8	17.0	68	1 247	349.6	27.1
Mankato	72 979	730	70.1	74	1 179	415.5	32.9	266	4 823	702.4	66.1
Maple Grove	141 635	850	49.4	95	1 606	1 252.8	86.2	97	1 569	277.6	24.9
Maplewood	26 917	202	48.5	41	421	126.1	12.1	254	4 936	854.6	77.5
Minneapolis	161 116	1 235	26.8	841	14 152	13 527.1	644.3	1 333	15 860	2 344.0	287.7
Minnetonka	28 315	69	88.4	288	4 016	7 374.9	189.6	352	7 410	1 157.6	116.5
Moorhead	34 312	369	55.6	36	507	220.1	12.0	138	2 113	361.6	28.7
Oakdale	13 871	108	48.1	20	77	32.6	2.4	61	975	198.4	17.7

1. Establishments with payroll.

Table D. Cities — **Real Estate, Professional Services, and Manufacturing**

City	Real estate and rental and leasing, 1997				Professional, scientific, and technical services,[1] 1997				Manufacturing, 1997			
	Number of establish-ments	Number of employees	Receipts (mil dol)	Annual payroll (mil dol)	Number of establish-ments	Number of employees	Receipts (mil dol)	Annual payroll (mil dol)	Number of establish-ments	Number of employees	Receipts (mil dol)	Annual payroll (mil dol)
	80	81	82	83	84	85	86	87	88	89	90	91
MICHIGAN	8 302	50 941	6 492.7	1 126.2	18 614	162 971	16 231.7	6 882.9	16 045	833 429	214 900.7	34 418.9
Allen Park	26	109	14.0	1.7	50	492	52.2	19.3	20	D	D	D
Ann Arbor	147	1 414	107.4	33.2	621	6 371	809.0	320.8	131	4 330	599.8	160.0
Battle Creek	53	270	32.0	5.2	96	568	51.6	22.3	81	10 194	3 337.7	409.4
Bay City	42	175	14.7	3.3	95	621	46.5	22.6	79	4 174	794.7	198.3
Burton	28	152	14.7	3.9	29	437	24.6	8.9	41	D	D	D
Dearborn	81	1 132	375.6	44.8	215	2 747	252.8	127.1	119	13 098	5 533.8	764.4
Dearborn Heights	35	192	19.2	2.6	67	348	20.3	10.9	NA	NA	NA	NA
Detroit	380	2 279	233.2	47.2	718	12 794	1 594.4	604.3	825	47 487	19 778.5	2 312.2
East Lansing	59	367	32.6	10.0	110	687	57.9	24.9	NA	NA	NA	NA
Eastpointe	NA	NA	NA	NA	NA	NA	NA	NA	NA	NA	NA	NA
Farmington Hills	206	3 754	429.5	89.1	656	7 600	829.1	359.6	155	5 109	993.8	225.3
Flint	101	476	59.8	8.7	253	1 497	101.8	46.6	94	D	D	D
Garden City	16	49	5.8	0.7	13	28	2.7	1.6	NA	NA	NA	NA
Grand Rapids	225	1 461	162.6	30.9	661	6 066	647.4	257.7	459	30 971	5 140.1	1 309.1
Holland	54	258	32.6	5.6	76	682	55.4	26.3	117	16 130	3 246.8	615.7
Inkster	8	47	4.7	0.7	9	30	1.8	0.7	NA	NA	NA	NA
Jackson	43	160	19.4	2.5	109	966	60.6	30.8	143	4 453	826.1	149.8
Kalamazoo	110	1 317	113.6	27.7	227	1 861	169.7	76.7	153	7 499	1 450.5	253.8
Kentwood	62	504	51.8	11.0	95	1 096	80.8	35.4	99	9 998	1 550.8	332.1
Lansing	105	1 730	103.8	27.5	279	2 201	240.7	108.0	131	D	D	D
Lincoln Park	26	100	11.8	1.4	24	530	62.4	27.5	NA	NA	NA	NA
Livonia	120	799	149.1	21.5	384	6 668	553.6	224.0	350	17 012	4 243.0	826.7
Madison Heights	48	510	57.3	9.6	118	2 302	235.2	95.6	227	6 683	1 060.2	282.2
Midland	45	168	22.1	2.8	108	603	61.6	19.9	49	5 289	1 671.1	278.9
Mount Pleasant	30	520	16.4	6.3	66	384	25.1	13.0	15	D	D	D
Muskegon	26	134	13.1	1.9	90	568	52.1	23.1	108	6 918	1 231.0	236.7
Novi	53	254	34.7	6.3	126	1 436	166.9	66.6	87	2 448	378.8	104.4
Oak Park	34	374	30.3	7.1	47	368	43.3	12.5	78	1 632	208.1	63.4
Pontiac	45	299	27.5	5.6	54	510	28.4	12.4	58	8 474	4 570.2	378.7
Portage	55	354	30.1	6.9	114	953	85.2	38.4	78	5 667	902.2	239.4
Port Huron	36	131	17.7	2.7	75	397	30.2	14.2	74	5 789	1 355.6	184.8
Rochester Hills	51	223	41.0	6.1	184	2 952	190.4	81.8	140	7 936	1 264.0	285.9
Roseville	47	179	20.6	2.8	58	846	28.6	14.0	202	6 582	930.5	257.1
Royal Oak	67	212	44.2	4.6	207	1 903	300.2	75.8	98	2 397	531.4	96.3
Saginaw	33	176	10.9	2.6	116	1 023	73.2	32.0	78	7 667	2 289.5	420.8
St. Clair Shores	47	244	40.0	4.1	160	862	59.9	31.4	68	2 756	335.0	76.7
Southfield	292	3 001	356.3	89.2	938	13 035	1 584.8	696.8	115	4 564	748.8	211.7
Southgate	19	87	8.8	2.1	26	335	15.8	9.3	NA	NA	NA	NA
Sterling Heights	87	410	64.3	9.7	234	2 657	302.7	136.2	314	21 628	6 777.9	1 241.7
Taylor	56	627	128.3	21.0	63	893	45.3	17.4	90	2 662	652.4	94.2
Troy	169	1 527	191.3	41.2	843	15 151	1 644.7	822.1	396	11 872	1 678.0	470.9
Warren	108	682	105.2	15.4	193	4 180	391.2	203.1	518	23 404	8 065.3	1 157.2
Westland	54	410	51.2	7.5	69	415	41.5	16.6	79	2 533	402.6	91.5
Wyandotte	13	99	4.3	2.3	43	161	9.9	4.0	49	2 227	511.1	96.0
Wyoming	63	851	150.2	23.3	80	967	63.4	25.6	185	11 933	2 055.0	539.2
MINNESOTA	5 051	30 172	3 886.4	687.2	12 391	96 677	10 447.9	4 091.3	8 091	382 530	76 244.9	13 126.1
Andover	4	D	D	D	41	95	8.0	3.7	NA	NA	NA	NA
Apple Valley	37	152	18.3	2.7	107	266	21.5	9.6	NA	NA	NA	NA
Blaine	36	282	33.9	4.6	81	334	27.6	11.3	134	3 147	368.3	106.2
Bloomington	191	2 224	211.3	67.1	578	7 762	967.6	376.6	209	10 538	1 655.5	420.8
Brooklyn Center	33	216	21.5	4.0	70	386	31.4	13.8	44	1 723	242.3	66.6
Brooklyn Park	41	283	28.3	5.5	116	865	86.2	41.8	109	5 406	860.9	226.8
Burnsville	90	507	69.6	10.0	212	956	96.4	33.9	113	4 055	723.6	148.1
Coon Rapids	58	293	25.8	4.7	95	452	35.0	13.4	61	2 613	379.1	102.8
Cottage Grove	19	77	7.2	1.1	27	54	7.1	2.0	10	D	D	D
Duluth	109	694	54.9	11.3	197	1 446	98.3	43.4	97	2 751	534.2	88.9
Eagan	69	367	56.3	8.3	214	879	105.8	42.2	85	4 169	3 294.1	169.5
Eden Prairie	96	1 562	399.5	68.4	330	3 902	441.0	170.8	146	9 873	1 528.6	412.6
Edina	199	1 253	166.9	33.6	522	4 975	699.1	238.0	93	3 007	479.4	109.4
Fridley	27	177	31.9	3.5	84	389	37.6	17.1	159	9 797	1 673.7	382.5
Inver Grove Heights	10	66	10.5	0.7	45	170	19.8	6.3	NA	NA	NA	NA
Lakeville	31	111	10.8	2.0	59	178	10.3	4.9	63	3 186	646.4	108.8
Mankato	57	333	28.5	6.1	81	569	46.1	15.7	62	3 721	1 476.4	116.6
Maple Grove	31	130	14.6	1.6	138	356	36.0	14.9	105	5 685	1 028.2	227.8
Maplewood	52	234	25.8	3.9	81	501	47.7	23.4	32	712	110.2	21.6
Minneapolis	518	4 246	587.8	121.4	1 977	27 509	3 565.9	1 384.7	699	25 906	3 953.5	951.1
Minnetonka	98	786	188.8	24.1	363	1 994	212.8	90.0	118	7 462	1 457.8	296.9
Moorhead	33	D	D	D	44	268	21.4	9.0	26	926	205.3	29.1
Oakdale	18	80	7.3	1.4	58	234	29.1	7.0	NA	NA	NA	NA

1. Firms subject to federal tax.

Table D. Cities — **Accommodation and Foodservices, Entertainment, and Health Care**

City	Accommodation and foodservices, 1997				Arts, entertainment, and recreation,[1] 1997				Health care and social assistance,[1] 1997			
	Number of establish-ments	Number of employees	Sales (mil dol)	Annual payroll (mil dol)	Number of establish-ments	Number of employees	Receipts (mil dol)	Annual payroll (mil dol)	Number of establish-ments	Number of employees	Receipts (mil dol)	Annual payroll (mil dol)
	92	93	94	95	96	97	98	99	100	101	102	103
MICHIGAN	18 958	320 014	10 158.7	2 835.8	2 693	34 161	2 202.8	664.6	18 943	186 954	11 811.5	5 696.8
Allen Park	62	1 276	34.5	8.7	11	325	18.1	8.9	85	885	52.1	24.4
Ann Arbor	344	8 266	273.7	75.9	43	533	18.8	5.6	305	2 913	242.0	88.6
Battle Creek	162	3 033	91.4	26.9	15	187	7.6	2.0	181	1 988	113.0	53.0
Bay City	111	1 629	41.3	11.1	10	107	6.6	1.5	98	1 092	70.1	37.3
Burton	82	1 445	43.2	12.1	7	39	1.7	0.4	75	462	28.2	13.7
Dearborn	267	5 771	221.3	62.0	23	764	25.0	6.5	330	2 666	238.9	111.3
Dearborn Heights	104	1 814	57.0	14.3	9	107	3.9	1.2	95	791	46.9	20.9
Detroit	1 108	15 426	576.0	150.4	66	1 773	173.5	73.6	900	12 747	730.3	371.9
East Lansing	113	2 372	62.9	17.0	8	314	6.0	2.2	101	1 098	75.5	34.8
Eastpointe	NA	NA	NA	NA	NA	NA	NA	NA	NA	NA	NA	NA
Farmington Hills	181	3 779	131.4	38.2	34	374	24.2	6.6	313	2 982	224.2	97.7
Flint	266	3 824	112.9	29.8	10	107	3.6	1.1	292	2 900	206.0	100.9
Garden City	54	740	26.4	6.1	3	16	0.9	0.2	73	549	44.1	22.4
Grand Rapids	386	8 134	262.6	78.5	44	679	25.6	7.3	462	5 625	413.0	221.3
Holland	87	2 258	57.3	19.1	8	162	4.9	1.8	86	1 412	83.0	42.1
Inkster	28	164	8.9	2.0	2	0	0.0	0.0	20	104	3.9	1.7
Jackson	111	1 769	57.9	14.6	11	196	6.5	1.5	168	1 384	114.9	52.8
Kalamazoo	206	4 217	112.1	33.8	23	529	14.3	4.7	191	2 875	216.5	112.9
Kentwood	102	2 798	84.7	24.7	14	315	11.6	2.9	57	669	40.9	16.6
Lansing	260	5 620	159.8	47.7	25	462	41.7	6.3	254	2 316	184.3	95.5
Lincoln Park	79	D	D	D	11	119	3.4	0.8	68	965	58.8	27.1
Livonia	266	6 399	213.6	57.1	35	697	92.1	12.7	371	3 919	264.2	113.0
Madison Heights	102	2 250	77.9	19.6	15	245	14.6	3.9	82	703	56.9	24.3
Midland	93	2 330	68.0	20.5	13	181	8.6	3.2	176	1 599	105.1	52.8
Mount Pleasant	71	1 921	49.9	14.3	6	147	2.4	1.0	73	745	42.8	20.3
Muskegon	82	D	D	D	15	220	7.1	2.0	126	1 370	97.5	52.2
Novi	96	2 778	90.9	28.7	15	138	10.1	2.2	96	974	59.9	29.1
Oak Park	45	743	22.4	5.9	8	84	4.1	0.8	62	364	21.4	10.4
Pontiac	130	D	D	D	9	0	0.0	0.0	90	792	65.6	30.0
Portage	110	2 752	78.6	23.4	13	250	7.0	1.9	109	1 077	62.2	28.6
Port Huron	69	1 143	38.4	10.3	10	115	5.4	1.0	131	978	87.3	46.6
Rochester Hills	103	2 592	76.7	22.4	16	142	16.7	2.7	197	1 885	111.0	52.5
Roseville	111	2 563	83.2	22.3	12	254	10.2	2.4	96	789	59.5	27.6
Royal Oak	143	3 071	107.0	32.9	17	110	6.9	1.5	171	1 157	89.9	42.5
Saginaw	123	1 928	55.5	15.2	7	72	5.5	1.2	128	1 243	81.3	42.2
St. Clair Shores	128	D	D	D	25	218	12.6	3.2	202	1 473	119.8	58.6
Southfield	283	4 739	195.6	54.5	29	566	22.1	8.1	602	8 302	533.1	276.2
Southgate	74	D	D	D	9	31	1.2	0.3	69	795	58.0	27.3
Sterling Heights	202	4 083	126.3	36.7	21	173	14.1	4.0	210	2 114	140.7	61.6
Taylor	154	2 789	84.4	22.9	13	188	6.6	2.0	102	1 411	68.3	33.0
Troy	225	5 330	202.4	57.3	32	362	66.8	8.6	324	3 065	211.4	113.5
Warren	301	5 435	193.3	51.4	21	396	15.6	4.3	314	4 053	286.7	139.7
Westland	154	3 022	94.1	25.1	14	193	8.9	2.4	132	1 848	103.3	44.5
Wyandotte	68	901	26.8	7.2	8	79	2.9	0.7	46	317	28.4	12.7
Wyoming	131	2 557	78.1	21.9	12	191	6.7	2.1	75	1 097	57.9	23.4
MINNESOTA	9 982	179 487	5 934.2	1 688.8	1 593	27 958	1 469.7	477.9	8 033	106 839	5 864.5	2 946.0
Andover	8	193	5.0	1.2	3	0	0.0	0.0	17	86	2.6	0.9
Apple Valley	37	1 011	33.8	9.0	5	73	2.3	0.6	54	837	38.6	19.7
Blaine	52	1 568	43.9	12.7	9	133	4.4	1.1	56	576	27.0	11.5
Bloomington	246	9 049	383.3	106.7	37	1 896	87.3	26.0	153	2 105	112.1	66.5
Brooklyn Center	45	1 456	44.5	14.1	9	242	5.7	2.2	53	758	44.6	23.2
Brooklyn Park	68	D	D	D	12	261	7.6	2.2	70	1 017	41.0	18.4
Burnsville	108	3 101	92.2	27.0	20	461	7.2	3.0	121	2 359	106.4	50.8
Coon Rapids	77	1 705	53.7	15.5	17	423	12.3	2.7	110	2 280	121.4	64.0
Cottage Grove	23	357	10.1	2.7	4	72	2.6	0.9	30	338	16.7	8.3
Duluth	241	4 872	156.3	43.1	31	279	9.7	2.3	224	2 800	137.0	72.6
Eagan	102	2 541	82.7	26.6	16	426	14.2	3.8	98	855	47.9	18.4
Eden Prairie	106	2 189	85.9	24.6	23	1 837	125.7	68.0	86	1 349	113.6	36.7
Edina	89	D	D	D	26	114	10.4	2.7	327	4 058	301.4	154.4
Fridley	45	1 145	28.2	8.8	8	256	5.1	2.1	56	793	60.6	34.1
Inver Grove Heights	24	460	13.0	3.8	5	91	2.3	0.8	35	425	17.1	9.0
Lakeville	27	671	23.0	7.0	10	88	5.0	1.5	31	204	9.7	4.4
Mankato	111	2 295	62.4	17.1	15	86	3.2	0.7	102	1 840	91.5	46.8
Maple Grove	55	1 552	42.1	12.5	8	103	4.4	1.7	66	666	32.7	16.0
Maplewood	87	2 249	64.1	18.8	14	137	5.6	1.4	78	967	67.5	34.6
Minneapolis	921	20 653	828.9	246.8	139	2 506	233.4	77.4	672	9 019	622.7	318.0
Minnetonka	110	2 804	108.4	32.9	33	320	23.6	6.9	111	2 170	114.0	54.6
Moorhead	65	1 349	32.2	9.7	4	57	1.1	0.4	43	380	20.2	9.2
Oakdale	27	364	11.1	3.1	8	26	2.5	0.7	28	197	6.5	2.8

1. Firms subject to federal tax.

Table D. Cities — Other Services and Federal Funds

City	Other services,[1] 1997				Selected federal funds, 2002–2003 (mil dol)								
	Number of establishments	Number of employees	Receipts (mil dol)	Annual payroll (mil dol)	Procurement contracts		Grants						Direct payments for individuals for educational assistance
					Defense	Other	Total[2]	Medicaid and other health related	Nutrition and family welfare	Energy and environment	Education	Housing and community development	
	104	105	106	107	108	109	110	111	112	113	114	115	116
MICHIGAN	14 705	93 792	6 159.1	1 893.8	2 494.2	1 389.8	12 970.0	6 173.8	2 317.3	225.5	1 193.3	838.8	419.9
Allen Park	58	300	13.0	4.5	0.0	0.0	0.0	0.0	0.0	0.0	0.0	0.0	0.0
Ann Arbor	168	1 129	73.0	23.1	81.7	54.6	595.9	396.3	4.3	23.0	13.0	12.2	24.6
Battle Creek	94	892	52.8	16.2	23.5	29.9	20.9	3.9	6.3	0.0	3.7	4.8	4.7
Bay City	90	541	31.7	9.8	2.4	0.3	8.6	0.0	0.0	0.0	3.1	5.2	12.6
Burton	57	402	24.3	7.2	0.0	0.0	0.5	0.0	0.0	0.0	0.0	0.5	0.0
Dearborn	180	1 200	76.3	28.2	2.0	284.9	14.3	0.7	0.0	1.9	0.7	7.1	17.8
Dearborn Heights	98	619	37.1	12.2	0.0	0.0	1.2	0.0	0.0	0.0	0.0	1.2	0.0
Detroit	829	7 518	467.3	149.6	25.2	125.5	618.9	128.1	55.5	11.1	14.3	189.6	43.2
East Lansing	36	268	11.2	4.1	0.9	3.4	176.6	43.7	0.9	11.0	9.2	4.2	22.8
Eastpointe	NA	NA	NA	NA	0.0	0.0	0.0	0.0	0.0	0.0	0.0	0.0	0.0
Farmington Hills	155	1 205	69.4	24.3	4.9	1.7	2.3	0.0	0.0	0.0	0.0	2.1	0.3
Flint	199	1 384	84.1	23.4	0.2	6.7	68.0	2.9	12.1	0.0	4.7	41.2	53.2
Garden City	65	333	21.9	6.4	0.0	0.2	0.5	0.0	0.0	0.0	0.0	0.5	0.0
Grand Rapids	334	2 478	168.6	53.8	66.4	30.9	64.6	5.9	10.7	0.0	5.3	31.9	29.5
Holland	87	603	37.1	12.5	16.1	22.0	11.4	0.1	3.1	0.0	0.9	4.0	1.4
Inkster	19	93	6.2	1.7	0.1	0.1	6.5	0.0	0.7	0.0	0.4	5.2	0.0
Jackson	97	669	38.2	10.6	14.6	3.5	21.9	1.8	6.9	0.0	1.0	11.9	3.9
Kalamazoo	174	1 469	92.2	30.2	25.4	6.8	57.8	7.1	5.6	2.7	11.8	22.1	19.9
Kentwood	79	1 026	75.0	20.8	0.1	0.2	6.0	0.0	0.0	0.0	0.0	6.0	0.0
Lansing	204	1 413	77.6	24.2	113.3	6.4	1 547.0	183.7	462.0	147.0	323.4	115.9	32.4
Lincoln Park	87	523	30.1	9.5	0.0	0.0	2.8	0.0	0.0	0.0	0.0	2.8	0.0
Livonia	245	2 467	232.2	71.0	14.7	1.7	6.2	0.0	0.0	0.0	0.6	5.5	6.2
Madison Heights	85	956	62.6	20.9	5.5	0.6	3.4	0.0	0.0	0.0	0.0	3.4	0.3
Midland	83	556	37.3	9.9	0.6	0.1	5.8	1.4	0.0	1.1	0.2	3.0	4.6
Mount Pleasant	47	266	11.4	3.4	0.0	0.2	10.6	4.5	0.2	0.3	1.8	2.2	13.3
Muskegon	51	380	19.2	6.7	55.4	14.1	11.4	1.3	0.5	0.0	1.5	6.7	3.8
Novi	72	694	47.8	17.8	0.0	0.4	0.0	0.0	0.0	0.0	0.0	0.0	0.0
Oak Park	41	172	13.0	3.5	0.0	0.4	2.2	0.0	0.0	0.0	0.0	2.1	0.6
Pontiac	105	775	47.1	14.1	3.2	1.0	48.9	0.2	8.8	1.5	2.1	34.7	0.0
Portage	100	692	40.8	12.8	0.1	0.0	2.5	0.0	0.0	0.0	1.6	0.7	0.1
Port Huron	62	383	20.2	5.8	6.5	1.3	12.5	0.0	2.4	0.0	0.8	7.3	2.7
Rochester Hills	76	491	41.5	12.0	0.5	0.5	3.2	0.0	0.0	0.1	0.2	0.0	0.0
Roseville	110	559	38.9	13.1	18.4	1.3	6.5	0.0	0.0	0.0	0.0	6.5	0.0
Royal Oak	129	1 014	65.2	24.7	0.2	0.4	6.5	2.4	0.0	0.1	0.0	3.9	0.1
Saginaw	93	507	28.1	8.4	5.9	15.9	25.7	3.9	4.6	0.0	0.6	12.1	2.7
St. Clair Shores	136	778	36.6	11.5	0.0	3.6	2.1	0.0	0.0	0.0	0.2	1.8	0.1
Southfield	170	1 565	99.6	32.3	17.0	1.5	13.6	2.3	3.2	4.5	0.0	3.4	0.2
Southgate	56	546	54.1	13.6	0.0	0.0	3.1	0.0	0.0	0.0	0.1	2.0	1.9
Sterling Heights	169	1 217	82.0	29.2	1 109.9	4.1	8.5	0.0	0.0	0.0	0.0	8.2	0.0
Taylor	96	623	54.2	14.3	0.8	0.0	22.2	0.0	0.0	0.0	0.0	22.0	0.1
Troy	185	1 951	169.6	50.8	15.9	90.2	38.1	22.0	0.0	10.4	0.3	4.7	1.0
Warren	278	2 122	152.3	47.3	356.9	2.3	3.4	0.0	0.0	0.0	0.8	2.5	6.4
Westland	107	913	60.7	20.4	1.3	0.2	22.9	0.0	16.5	0.0	0.0	6.2	0.1
Wyandotte	62	422	21.0	7.1	0.0	0.1	1.7	0.0	0.0	1.3	0.0	0.3	0.0
Wyoming	165	1 161	75.3	24.5	0.1	0.1	3.4	0.0	0.0	0.0	0.0	3.3	0.0
MINNESOTA	7 614	55 723	3 394.6	1 103.6	1 541.9	864.0	6 913.5	3 363.4	1 061.8	129.5	542.5	530.1	252.7
Andover	21	93	4.1	1.5	0.0	0.0	0.0	0.0	0.0	0.0	0.0	0.0	0.0
Apple Valley	48	353	19.4	6.3	0.0	0.2	2.7	0.3	0.0	0.0	0.0	2.4	0.0
Blaine	63	429	26.3	9.3	0.0	0.0	4.9	0.0	3.5	0.0	0.0	0.7	0.0
Bloomington	177	5 563	200.1	136.3	49.7	5.5	7.8	1.5	0.0	0.0	0.0	5.6	0.0
Brooklyn Center	45	404	16.3	5.7	0.4	0.4	2.0	0.5	0.0	0.0	0.0	1.0	0.0
Brooklyn Park	84	679	39.6	12.3	0.4	0.3	2.2	0.0	0.0	0.0	0.0	2.1	0.0
Burnsville	120	1 019	55.4	19.1	23.9	1.9	5.9	0.0	0.0	0.0	0.0	5.3	0.2
Coon Rapids	70	431	26.2	7.5	0.0	0.2	6.1	0.8	0.0	0.0	0.0	5.3	0.0
Cottage Grove	22	242	7.1	2.6	0.0	0.0	0.6	0.0	0.0	0.0	0.3	0.3	0.0
Duluth	186	1 122	71.5	21.4	2.6	5.2	45.1	3.0	3.1	0.3	3.0	20.9	12.0
Eagan	95	1 634	102.7	41.9	55.4	2.6	0.2	0.0	0.0	0.0	0.0	0.2	0.0
Eden Prairie	83	1 777	155.9	61.0	24.7	51.3	5.7	0.4	0.0	0.9	0.0	4.0	0.1
Edina	104	1 356	63.3	25.6	1.1	23.0	5.7	1.6	0.0	0.0	0.0	3.4	0.0
Fridley	59	512	44.2	10.9	4.8	0.2	1.1	0.0	0.0	0.0	0.0	1.0	0.0
Inver Grove Heights	39	272	20.4	7.2	0.4	0.7	0.4	0.0	0.2	0.0	0.0	0.2	0.0
Lakeville	28	175	12.5	3.4	1.5	1.3	0.5	0.0	0.0	0.0	0.2	0.1	0.0
Mankato	82	579	30.5	9.2	0.1	0.1	9.5	0.4	2.4	0.8	1.4	3.9	9.4
Maple Grove	51	311	16.5	6.1	0.8	0.6	0.7	0.0	0.0	0.3	0.0	0.3	0.0
Maplewood	74	541	28.0	8.2	0.0	0.0	3.9	0.0	0.0	0.0	0.0	3.9	0.0
Minneapolis	672	7 965	499.0	155.1	693.9	193.5	606.4	290.6	20.8	23.5	34.0	97.8	85.5
Minnetonka	76	738	42.2	17.3	1.8	0.1	9.6	0.9	0.0	5.7	0.0	3.0	0.0
Moorhead	59	264	15.6	4.5	0.1	0.0	8.4	1.9	1.7	0.0	0.1	1.8	8.9
Oakdale	26	191	12.0	2.7	0.2	0.0	6.0	0.3	0.0	0.0	0.0	2.6	0.0

1. Firms subject to federal tax.   2. Includes program categories not shown separately. State totals include additional categories not allocated by city.

City	City government finances, 2002								
	General revenue						General expenditure		
	Intergovernmental			Taxes				Per capita[1] (dollars)	
					Per capita[1] (dollars)				
	Total (mil dol)	Total (mil dol)	Percent from state government	Total (mil dol)	Total	Property	Sales and gross receipts	Total (mil dol)	Total	Capital outlays
	117	118	119	120	121	122	123	124	125	126
MICHIGAN	X	X	X	X	X	X	X	X	X	X
Allen Park........................	28.9	7.3	98.8	15.2	523	509	0	30.3	1 040	17
Ann Arbor........................	138.0	36.3	66.4	60.7	526	502	0	146.6	1 273	106
Battle Creek	77.1	23.3	62.1	25.8	482	251	0	78.5	1 462	173
Bay City	54.7	20.4	49.9	12.3	343	331	0	50.3	1 404	348
Burton.............................	18.7	5.9	84.9	5.1	168	151	0	19.8	652	113
Dearborn.........................	136.9	22.7	80.6	67.6	691	668	0	152.7	1 561	343
Dearborn Heights..............	50.3	13.0	80.3	23.1	398	382	0	64.8	1 116	263
Detroit.............................	3 876.2	2 403.7	83.9	911.5	985	447	165	4 436.0	4 795	1 017
East Lansing	44.5	12.6	88.3	14.4	311	281	0	57.5	1 244	325
Eastpointe	27.9	6.9	93.2	11.8	350	329	0	25.8	763	10
Farmington Hills	76.1	15.8	90.3	37.7	462	440	0	87.0	1 068	144
Flint................................	NA	NA	NA	NA	NA	NA	NA	NA	NA	NA
Garden City......................	29.3	7.1	93.3	9.8	329	314	0	30.3	1 013	107
Grand Rapids....................	235.9	73.1	66.3	82.7	421	141	0	306.4	1 559	311
Holland	41.2	10.6	69.4	15.6	451	439	0	40.4	1 166	294
Inkster	20.1	7.7	88.5	8.1	270	260	0	21.1	704	35
Jackson...........................	39.6	14.7	63.2	14.1	396	191	0	46.4	1 308	418
Kalamazoo	116.1	28.3	77.5	31.7	417	401	0	109.1	1 438	229
Kentwood	30.9	7.0	97.5	14.6	315	290	0	29.4	634	101
Lansing............................	222.2	52.9	61.7	68.5	578	326	0	210.6	1 776	306
Lincoln Park	37.9	10.8	81.6	17.8	449	418	0	33.6	846	19
Livonia............................	106.5	27.2	64.8	43.4	433	415	0	114.7	1 143	154
Madison Heights	35.3	8.0	73.5	17.7	578	549	0	35.7	1 164	164
Midland...........................	62.9	11.3	74.9	29.7	706	693	0	43.0	1 022	74
Mount Pleasant.................	18.2	6.0	93.3	4.9	187	174	0	24.1	926	328
Muskegon........................	43.0	16.1	60.9	15.5	393	194	0	44.0	1 116	223
Novi	52.2	8.0	89.7	26.0	529	495	0	49.4	1 006	315
Oak Park	24.6	6.7	97.4	13.7	466	455	0	28.6	972	83
Pontiac............................	149.5	34.1	81.0	48.7	736	482	0	115.4	1 745	233
Portage............................	36.2	9.3	93.7	19.0	421	397	0	41.8	926	206
Port Huron	49.8	14.1	55.7	20.8	645	437	0	45.6	1 412	116
Rochester Hills	50.9	10.8	97.6	23.4	341	317	0	53.4	778	137
Roseville..........................	45.3	12.3	73.0	19.0	393	384	0	42.9	887	66
Royal Oak	63.3	16.9	61.4	26.9	454	355	0	70.9	1 197	339
Saginaw	72.0	23.3	77.4	22.0	366	110	2	72.3	1 202	88
St. Clair Shores.................	55.4	14.8	72.3	24.7	394	372	0	52.8	841	108
Southfield........................	98.5	21.3	72.9	55.4	711	679	0	116.0	1 490	221
Southgate........................	27.4	5.8	96.6	12.9	423	409	0	27.7	910	191
Sterling Heights.................	98.1	22.0	92.1	46.7	370	355	0	94.1	746	80
Taylor	103.6	19.7	72.2	41.3	626	593	0	117.1	1 777	519
Troy	91.5	17.9	86.3	49.2	609	590	0	127.2	1 573	693
Warren............................	129.9	30.4	88.3	66.7	484	471	0	135.3	983	148
Westland	72.5	22.6	66.2	22.6	262	251	0	74.0	857	6
Wyandotte	NA	NA	NA	NA	NA	NA	NA	NA	NA	NA
Wyoming..........................	62.8	19.9	61.2	22.2	316	294	0	62.2	884	166
MINNESOTA....................	X	X	X	X	X	X	X	X	X	X
Andover...........................	18.8	1.7	91.7	6.3	222	199	0	16.5	579	253
Apple Valley	33.5	5.7	98.2	15.2	314	280	12	33.7	695	169
Blaine.............................	48.3	6.0	90.8	12.5	257	213	5	46.2	952	496
Bloomington	116.7	18.6	61.5	53.6	638	517	75	102.4	1 218	408
Brooklyn Center	35.3	5.8	96.2	13.5	470	414	29	33.4	1 162	274
Brooklyn Park	62.7	8.7	89.0	29.2	429	402	0	57.9	850	213
Burnsville........................	70.1	8.2	73.6	24.9	415	369	6	66.0	1 100	233
Coon Rapids	62.3	16.7	97.3	16.5	265	207	39	46.8	751	190
Cottage Grove	24.1	3.2	91.7	7.8	251	212	0	21.4	689	221
Duluth.............................	175.4	60.8	75.9	35.8	414	212	195	142.9	1 653	195
Eagan.............................	55.9	4.3	95.5	19.9	311	263	7	54.1	845	326
Eden Prairie	57.3	2.8	84.6	25.1	438	388	0	35.4	618	95
Edina..............................	55.1	5.1	93.2	26.7	566	518	0	51.0	1 082	238
Fridley............................	21.2	4.0	89.9	8.3	304	276	6	20.2	737	96
Inver Grove Heights............	26.8	3.7	95.3	10.1	329	296	0	22.2	722	122
Lakeville	30.6	4.5	75.0	11.6	249	197	7	38.5	831	416
Mankato	48.3	15.5	76.9	13.6	409	274	100	51.0	1 538	506
Maple Grove	79.9	19.4	85.8	22.6	398	318	0	67.1	1 183	621
Maplewood.......................	31.1	3.1	94.7	10.1	282	244	2	36.8	1 029	225
Minneapolis......................	750.1	203.3	78.8	272.8	726	548	122	630.6	1 679	155
Minnetonka.......................	35.9	4.4	95.8	17.2	337	291	1	31.4	615	102
Moorhead	36.9	13.8	79.0	4.7	143	117	14	59.5	1 827	884
Oakdale...........................	22.9	2.7	88.7	8.7	315	287	2	20.8	756	183

1. Based on population estimated as of July 1 of the year shown.

City	City government finances, 2002 (cont'd)									
	General expenditure									
	Percent of total for—									
	Public welfare	Highways	Parking facilities	Education	Health and hospitals	Police protection	Sewerage and sanitation	Parks and recreation	Housing and community development	Interest on debt
	127	128	129	130	131	132	133	134	135	136
MICHIGAN	X	X	X	X	X	X	X	X	X	X
Allen Park	0.0	16.4	0.0	0.0	0.0	16.2	17.0	4.4	0.0	0.8
Ann Arbor	1.2	6.0	5.8	0.0	0.0	14.1	13.9	5.8	7.3	3.2
Battle Creek	0.0	8.5	0.8	0.0	0.0	16.0	20.2	5.6	4.8	7.1
Bay City	0.0	16.0	0.1	0.0	0.6	13.4	18.8	2.2	22.5	1.3
Burton	0.0	13.3	0.0	0.0	0.0	21.4	33.2	1.0	0.0	4.1
Dearborn	0.7	13.2	1.4	0.0	0.4	14.9	14.3	12.8	4.0	3.7
Dearborn Heights	0.0	5.8	0.0	0.0	0.0	15.3	25.0	2.2	2.1	1.2
Detroit	0.0	3.5	0.7	45.3	2.6	7.7	11.6	2.8	2.3	2.6
East Lansing	0.5	8.8	5.3	0.0	0.0	14.2	22.3	15.3	0.0	6.3
Eastpointe	0.0	9.8	0.0	0.0	0.0	23.7	11.7	6.7	0.0	2.3
Farmington Hills	0.0	13.0	0.0	0.0	0.0	18.3	14.8	9.6	0.6	1.8
Flint	NA	NA	NA	NA	NA	NA	NA	NA	NA	NA
Garden City	0.0	18.9	0.0	0.0	0.0	15.1	21.4	4.4	0.0	15.8
Grand Rapids	0.0	7.5	3.4	0.0	0.0	20.1	10.5	5.3	6.9	7.5
Holland	0.0	16.5	0.5	0.0	2.7	17.2	18.3	14.0	1.3	1.6
Inkster	0.0	19.7	0.0	0.0	0.0	32.7	1.1	2.8	0.9	1.1
Jackson	0.0	11.2	0.1	0.0	0.0	16.5	13.2	9.2	26.8	0.6
Kalamazoo	0.0	8.6	0.0	0.0	0.0	24.6	20.8	4.1	2.6	19.8
Kentwood	0.0	19.4	0.0	0.1	0.0	24.1	7.3	3.8	0.0	0.0
Lansing	0.8	5.3	2.6	0.0	0.0	8.4	16.1	6.0	7.4	11.3
Lincoln Park	1.3	15.4	0.0	0.0	1.3	22.9	17.0	6.7	5.0	0.4
Livonia	1.1	11.9	0.0	0.0	0.8	20.1	20.5	16.4	0.5	3.4
Madison Heights	0.0	13.1	0.0	0.0	0.0	20.6	16.1	5.6	4.1	0.3
Midland	0.0	13.7	0.2	0.0	0.0	9.3	12.8	10.9	4.5	3.6
Mount Pleasant	0.0	12.1	0.4	0.0	0.0	13.4	29.0	10.0	1.7	3.3
Muskegon	0.0	21.3	0.0	0.0	0.0	16.3	10.9	16.9	5.5	2.0
Novi	0.0	30.2	0.0	0.0	0.9	17.2	1.1	7.3	0.0	11.7
Oak Park	0.0	14.1	0.0	0.0	0.0	25.3	14.5	4.9	0.0	6.1
Pontiac	0.0	6.5	1.5	0.0	0.5	16.2	11.5	12.5	2.9	3.1
Portage	0.3	22.9	0.0	0.0	3.7	18.9	10.1	9.4	0.6	5.1
Port Huron	0.0	11.7	0.5	0.0	0.1	15.1	24.4	14.1	6.4	2.9
Rochester Hills	0.0	23.6	0.0	0.0	0.0	10.9	13.3	6.4	0.0	3.9
Roseville	0.0	10.5	0.0	0.0	1.0	21.3	13.7	2.5	3.2	2.1
Royal Oak	0.0	4.7	10.8	0.0	1.0	13.9	22.9	9.1	5.7	2.6
Saginaw	0.0	10.0	0.5	0.0	0.0	18.6	16.0	2.1	7.8	10.0
St. Clair Shores	0.0	14.6	0.0	0.0	0.6	17.8	18.9	9.0	1.4	2.3
Southfield	0.6	13.6	2.2	0.0	0.0	15.3	2.6	9.3	3.3	4.2
Southgate	0.0	9.5	0.0	0.0	0.0	16.9	14.4	22.5	0.0	0.2
Sterling Heights	0.0	14.7	0.0	0.0	0.0	22.3	14.5	5.1	0.0	2.3
Taylor	0.0	36.1	0.0	0.0	0.0	8.9	4.4	7.9	11.7	4.9
Troy	0.0	26.8	0.0	0.0	0.0	16.2	8.1	24.1	0.5	1.3
Warren	0.0	8.4	0.0	0.0	0.0	23.4	13.7	3.5	0.7	3.0
Westland	1.2	13.0	0.0	0.0	0.0	18.3	17.2	3.3	4.6	1.8
Wyandotte	NA	NA	NA	NA	NA	NA	NA	NA	NA	NA
Wyoming	0.0	16.4	0.0	0.0	0.5	20.7	12.2	5.9	7.5	4.7
MINNESOTA	X	X	X	X	X	X	X	X	X	X
Andover	0.0	20.3	0.0	0.0	0.0	6.7	7.2	9.2	23.9	11.3
Apple Valley	0.0	16.3	0.0	0.0	0.0	16.3	10.5	15.5	0.0	11.9
Blaine	0.0	2.7	0.0	0.0	0.0	10.1	13.9	5.7	8.8	6.0
Bloomington	0.0	11.7	0.0	0.0	6.2	13.1	8.9	12.3	1.3	5.6
Brooklyn Center	0.3	15.1	0.0	0.0	0.0	13.9	12.1	20.6	0.0	11.7
Brooklyn Park	0.0	8.2	0.0	0.0	0.0	16.2	8.0	17.5	2.9	6.5
Burnsville	0.0	18.8	0.0	0.0	0.0	11.6	8.2	6.4	5.9	28.5
Coon Rapids	0.0	17.3	0.0	0.0	0.7	10.5	8.1	11.4	3.5	22.0
Cottage Grove	0.0	32.7	0.0	0.0	4.1	16.2	6.5	14.8	0.0	6.2
Duluth	0.0	10.5	0.5	0.0	0.0	10.4	11.9	9.6	3.2	8.7
Eagan	0.0	3.9	0.0	0.0	0.0	13.7	15.0	8.4	2.5	10.2
Eden Prairie	1.1	16.5	0.0	0.0	0.2	16.3	14.7	12.7	1.6	17.2
Edina	0.8	7.2	0.0	0.0	0.4	8.0	8.7	14.6	21.4	13.9
Fridley	0.0	19.7	0.0	0.0	0.0	18.7	15.5	5.5	6.7	8.8
Inver Grove Heights	0.0	23.9	0.0	0.0	0.0	14.4	7.0	22.3	0.0	10.7
Lakeville	0.0	23.6	0.0	0.0	0.1	14.4	14.8	9.8	5.1	7.0
Mankato	0.0	26.3	0.8	0.0	0.0	10.5	10.8	4.3	16.8	6.7
Maple Grove	0.0	44.6	0.0	0.0	0.0	6.8	9.6	11.5	0.8	8.7
Maplewood	0.0	15.2	0.0	0.0	2.2	11.7	9.9	13.4	0.0	22.4
Minneapolis	0.0	9.4	10.2	0.0	3.5	14.6	12.8	11.2	8.4	10.2
Minnetonka	0.0	10.2	0.0	0.0	0.5	18.9	18.4	17.8	4.9	5.1
Moorhead	0.0	19.8	0.0	0.0	0.2	9.6	9.2	6.3	2.5	5.2
Oakdale	0.0	27.8	0.0	0.0	0.0	14.4	10.7	5.3	0.0	13.3

City	City government finances, 2002 (cont'd) Debt outstanding Total (mil dol)	Per capita[1] (dollars)	Percent utility	City government employment, 2002	Climate[2] Average daily temperature (degrees Fahrenheit) Mean January	July	Limits January[3]	July[4]	Annual precipitation (inches)	Heating degree days	Cooling degree days
	137	138	139	140	141	142	143	144	145	146	147
MICHIGAN	X	X	X	X	X	X	X	X	X	X	X
Allen Park	3.6	125	0.0	200	22.9	72.9	15.5	83.8	32.71	6 500	677
Ann Arbor	118.8	1 031	30.6	1 128	23.2	73.0	16.2	83.7	32.81	6 379	713
Battle Creek	123.9	2 310	13.0	695	22.5	71.7	14.9	83.2	35.70	6 677	575
Bay City	19.9	556	62.2	449	22.0	72.2	14.7	84.1	29.51	6 763	599
Burton	13.9	459	1.4	100	21.5	70.6	14.2	81.5	30.28	6 979	483
Dearborn	145.8	1 491	0.0	1 343	22.9	72.9	15.5	83.8	32.71	6 500	677
Dearborn Heights	33.0	568	0.0	378	22.9	72.9	15.5	83.8	32.71	6 500	677
Detroit	5 045.0	5 454	26.0	36 833	24.7	74.2	18.7	83.3	32.09	6 167	805
East Lansing	70.6	1 526	0.0	469	20.1	70.5	12.4	81.9	29.68	7 228	458
Eastpointe	9.2	273	0.0	215	24.7	74.2	18.7	83.3	32.09	6 167	805
Farmington Hills	39.5	485	0.0	498	22.2	72.4	14.8	83.8	30.56	6 653	647
Flint	0.0	0	0.0	3 762	21.5	70.6	14.2	81.5	30.28	6 979	483
Garden City	71.4	2 390	0.0	202	22.9	72.9	15.5	83.8	32.71	6 500	677
Grand Rapids	422.0	2 146	30.9	2 132	21.8	71.6	14.7	82.8	36.04	6 973	534
Holland	23.0	662	63.9	439	23.3	70.8	16.8	81.9	36.25	6 747	529
Inkster	6.8	228	0.0	240	22.9	72.3	15.6	83.3	32.62	6 569	626
Jackson	5.2	145	22.3	361	21.5	72.2	14.3	83.2	29.73	6 791	621
Kalamazoo	472.6	6 230	5.8	1 012	23.7	73.5	16.4	84.9	37.03	6 230	764
Kentwood	10.0	216	4.2	226	21.8	71.6	14.7	82.8	36.04	6 973	534
Lansing	552.4	4 658	30.0	2 197	20.9	70.8	13.3	82.6	30.62	7 101	490
Lincoln Park	1.9	49	46.3	239	22.9	72.9	15.5	83.8	32.71	6 500	677
Livonia	104.6	1 042	3.9	862	22.9	72.9	15.5	83.8	32.71	6 500	677
Madison Heights	5.6	182	9.8	246	24.7	74.2	18.7	83.3	32.09	6 167	805
Midland	40.2	956	15.2	427	22.0	72.2	14.7	84.1	29.51	6 763	599
Mount Pleasant	22.4	862	33.6	158	NA	NA	NA	NA	NA	NA	NA
Muskegon	22.9	581	44.3	323	23.3	70.3	17.7	80.3	32.56	6 924	431
Novi	87.7	1 786	0.0	310	21.0	71.0	13.6	81.4	29.95	7 064	515
Oak Park	29.8	1 012	11.3	237	24.7	74.2	18.7	83.3	32.09	6 167	805
Pontiac	90.3	1 365	4.7	926	22.2	72.4	14.8	83.8	30.56	6 653	647
Portage	57.9	1 282	1.0	244	23.7	73.5	16.4	84.9	37.03	6 230	764
Port Huron	40.3	1 247	24.8	408	22.4	71.7	15.4	81.5	30.34	6 898	544
Rochester Hills	51.8	755	0.0	253	22.2	72.4	14.8	83.8	30.56	6 653	647
Roseville	13.4	278	0.0	361	24.7	74.2	18.7	83.3	32.09	6 167	805
Royal Oak	65.0	1 097	0.0	459	24.7	74.2	18.7	83.3	32.09	6 167	805
Saginaw	149.4	2 487	5.3	583	22.7	73.0	15.7	84.4	30.89	6 538	675
St. Clair Shores	21.9	349	0.0	358	24.7	73.5	17.4	83.7	33.23	6 185	737
Southfield	93.9	1 206	0.0	838	22.2	72.4	14.8	83.8	30.56	6 653	647
Southgate	12.5	410	13.7	220	22.9	72.3	15.6	83.3	32.62	6 569	626
Sterling Heights	31.6	250	0.0	716	23.1	71.3	16.7	81.3	31.36	6 777	526
Taylor	92.4	1 403	0.0	677	22.9	72.3	15.6	83.3	32.62	6 569	626
Troy	64.8	801	0.0	551	22.2	72.4	14.8	83.8	30.56	6 653	647
Warren	107.3	779	0.0	1 132	24.7	74.2	18.7	83.3	32.09	6 167	805
Westland	19.4	225	0.0	449	22.9	72.3	15.6	83.3	32.62	6 569	626
Wyandotte	NA	NA	NA	138	22.9	72.9	15.5	83.8	32.71	6 500	677
Wyoming	59.3	843	21.7	486	21.8	71.6	14.7	82.8	36.04	6 973	534
MINNESOTA	X	X	X	X	X	X	X	X	X	X	X
Andover	55.6	1 949	0.0	61	NA	NA	NA	NA	NA	NA	NA
Apple Valley	52.1	1 075	2.2	201	11.3	72.4	0.9	84.5	32.42	8 048	590
Blaine	53.8	1 109	0.5	159	11.8	73.6	2.8	84.0	28.32	7 981	682
Bloomington	119.1	1 416	0.0	573	11.8	73.6	2.8	84.0	28.32	7 981	682
Brooklyn Center	64.4	2 239	0.0	197	11.8	73.6	2.8	84.0	28.32	7 981	682
Brooklyn Park	61.5	903	10.3	375	11.8	73.6	2.8	84.0	28.32	7 981	682
Burnsville	230.6	3 842	0.0	295	11.8	73.6	2.8	84.0	28.32	7 981	682
Coon Rapids	152.3	2 443	6.8	242	11.8	73.6	2.8	84.0	28.32	7 981	682
Cottage Grove	35.6	1 144	8.9	124	NA	NA	NA	NA	NA	NA	NA
Duluth	242.8	2 810	2.5	1 157	7.0	66.1	-2.2	77.1	30.00	9 818	180
Eagan	112.4	1 754	5.5	267	11.8	73.6	2.8	84.0	28.32	7 981	682
Eden Prairie	96.8	1 688	18.0	295	11.8	73.6	2.8	84.0	28.32	7 981	682
Edina	116.2	2 466	1.7	285	11.8	73.6	2.8	84.0	28.32	7 981	682
Fridley	29.3	1 070	12.0	200	11.8	73.6	2.8	84.0	28.32	7 981	682
Inver Grove Heights	44.7	1 453	15.9	159	NA	NA	NA	NA	NA	NA	NA
Lakeville	54.7	1 179	0.0	259	NA	NA	NA	NA	NA	NA	NA
Mankato	110.2	3 324	5.1	258	11.7	73.1	1.2	84.7	29.51	8 005	670
Maple Grove	118.8	2 095	6.5	282	11.8	73.6	2.8	84.0	28.32	7 981	682
Maplewood	111.3	3 116	0.0	367	11.8	73.6	2.8	84.0	28.32	7 981	682
Minneapolis	1 752.6	4 666	3.3	6 318	11.8	73.6	2.8	84.0	28.32	7 981	682
Minnetonka	30.7	600	28.3	250	11.8	73.6	2.8	84.0	28.32	7 981	682
Moorhead	113.0	3 469	30.8	328	5.9	71.1	-3.6	83.4	19.45	9 254	537
Oakdale	44.4	1 609	0.0	90	NA	NA	NA	NA	NA	NA	NA

1. Based on the population estimated as of July 1 of the year shown.   2. Represents normal values based on the 30-year period, 1961–1990.   3. Average daily minimum.   4. Average daily maximum.

STATE Place code	City	Land area,[1] 2000 (sq km)	Population, 2003 Total persons	Rank	Per square kilometer	White	Black	Am. Indian, Alaska Native	Asian and Pacific Islander	Other race	Hispanic or Latino[2]	Non-Hispanic White
		1	2	3	4	5	6	7	8	9	10	11
	MINNESOTA—Cont'd											
27 51730	Plymouth	85.2	69 164	410	811.8	92.5	3.2	0.6	4.3	0.8	1.6	90.4
27 54214	Richfield	17.9	34 079	949	1 903.9	83.2	7.9	1.3	6.1	4.3	6.3	78.8
27 54880	Rochester	102.6	92 507	278	901.6	88.7	4.3	0.6	6.4	1.9	3.0	85.8
27 55852	Roseville	34.3	33 105	974	965.2	90.9	3.5	0.7	5.6	1.1	2.0	88.5
27 56896	St. Cloud	78.1	59 458	505	761.3	92.9	2.9	1.2	3.6	0.8	1.3	91.1
27 57220	St. Louis Park	27.7	44 114	729	1 592.6	90.3	5.2	0.9	3.8	1.7	2.9	87.5
27 58000	St. Paul	136.7	280 404	62	2 051.2	69.6	13.4	2.1	13.9	5.2	7.9	64.0
27 59998	Shoreview	29.0	27 105	1 164	934.7	94.5	1.2	0.6	4.3	0.8	1.3	92.5
27 71032	Winona	47.2	26 641	1 186	564.4	95.3	1.3	0.6	3.2	0.8	1.3	93.7
27 71428	Woodbury	90.6	49 415	639	545.4	91.4	3.1	0.6	5.7	0.9	2.1	88.8
28 00000	MISSISSIPPI	121 488.5	2 881 281	X	23.7	61.9	36.6	0.7	0.9	0.7	1.4	60.7
28 06220	Biloxi	98.5	48 972	648	497.2	73.4	19.8	1.1	6.3	2.0	3.6	69.7
28 15380	Columbus	55.5	24 959	1 225	449.7	44.1	54.9	0.3	0.9	0.7	1.1	43.3
28 29180	Greenville	69.6	39 521	817	567.8	29.2	69.9	0.2	1.0	0.3	0.7	28.7
28 29700	Gulfport	147.4	71 810	392	487.2	63.5	34.1	1.0	1.9	1.3	2.6	60.9
28 31020	Hattiesburg	127.6	46 664	686	365.7	50.6	47.7	0.4	1.5	0.7	1.4	49.3
28 36000	Jackson	271.7	179 599	118	661.0	28.2	71.1	0.4	0.8	0.3	0.8	27.5
28 46640	Meridian	116.9	39 559	815	338.4	44.4	54.7	0.4	0.8	0.4	1.1	43.5
28 55360	Pascagoula	39.3	25 865	1 205	658.1	68.0	29.3	0.5	1.3	2.0	3.9	65.2
28 69280	Southaven	87.5	34 760	934	397.3	91.0	6.8	0.6	1.0	1.4	2.3	89.3
28 74840	Tupelo	132.4	35 297	915	266.6	70.1	28.7	0.3	1.0	0.7	1.4	68.7
28 76720	Vicksburg	85.2	26 005	1 201	305.2	38.1	60.8	0.4	0.7	0.6	1.0	37.4
29 00000	MISSOURI	178 413.7	5 704 484	X	32.0	86.1	11.7	1.1	1.5	1.2	2.1	83.8
29 03160	Ballwin	23.2	31 006	1 033	1 336.5	94.4	1.7	0.5	3.8	0.8	1.9	92.2
29 06652	Blue Springs	47.1	49 398	640	1 048.8	94.6	3.4	1.0	1.4	1.2	2.8	91.6
29 11242	Cape Girardeau	62.9	35 741	899	568.2	88.5	9.9	0.9	1.5	0.6	1.1	86.7
29 13600	Chesterfield	81.6	47 067	677	576.8	92.0	2.0	0.3	5.9	0.5	1.6	90.1
29 15670	Columbia	137.4	88 534	294	644.4	83.3	11.7	0.9	4.9	1.3	2.1	80.4
29 24778	Florissant	29.4	51 018	614	1 735.3	86.9	12.2	0.6	1.0	0.9	1.5	84.8
29 27190	Gladstone	20.7	27 089	1 165	1 308.6	94.7	2.4	1.1	1.8	1.7	3.6	91.1
29 31276	Hazelwood	41.1	25 848	1 208	628.9	81.7	16.8	0.7	1.7	0.9	1.6	79.3
29 35000	Independence	202.9	112 079	209	552.4	94.0	3.2	1.6	1.6	2.0	3.7	90.1
29 37000	Jefferson City	70.6	37 550	855	531.9	82.7	15.4	1.0	1.7	0.9	1.6	80.7
29 37592	Joplin	81.4	46 373	695	569.7	93.9	3.3	3.0	1.1	1.4	2.5	90.2
29 38000	Kansas City	812.1	442 768	38	545.2	62.5	32.3	1.2	2.5	4.1	6.9	57.6
29 39044	Kirkwood	23.9	27 294	1 152	1 142.0	91.6	7.5	0.4	1.1	0.4	1.1	90.0
29 41348	Lee's Summit	154.1	77 052	363	500.0	94.5	3.9	0.8	1.4	0.9	2.0	91.9
29 42032	Liberty	69.8	27 982	1 134	400.9	95.3	3.0	1.1	1.0	1.4	2.7	92.4
29 46586	Maryland Heights	55.4	25 583	1 212	461.8	86.2	5.9	0.5	7.6	0.9	2.3	83.8
29 54074	O'Fallon	58.2	63 677	455	1 094.1	96.3	2.6	0.6	1.1	0.6	1.5	94.4
29 60788	Raytown	25.7	29 747	1 075	1 157.5	85.8	12.4	1.1	1.3	1.3	2.3	83.0
29 64082	St. Charles	52.7	61 253	475	1 162.3	94.4	3.9	0.7	1.4	1.0	2.0	92.1
29 64550	St. Joseph	113.5	72 663	383	640.2	93.2	5.7	0.9	0.8	1.0	2.6	90.2
29 65000	St. Louis	160.4	332 223	53	2 071.2	45.2	52.1	0.8	2.4	1.5	2.0	42.9
29 65126	St. Peters	54.9	53 397	594	972.6	95.2	3.1	0.5	1.6	0.7	1.5	93.3
29 70000	Springfield	189.5	150 867	145	796.1	93.5	3.9	1.7	1.9	1.2	2.3	90.5
29 75220	University City	15.2	37 757	848	2 484.0	50.6	46.4	0.6	3.4	0.9	1.6	48.4
29 79820	Wildwood	171.0	34 145	944	199.7	95.5	1.8	0.4	2.7	0.5	1.4	93.8
30 00000	MONTANA	376 979.1	917 621	X	2.4	92.2	0.5	7.4	0.9	0.9	2.0	89.5
30 06550	Billings	87.3	95 220	266	1 090.7	93.7	0.9	4.5	1.0	1.9	4.2	89.9
30 08950	Bozeman	32.6	30 753	1 039	943.3	96.1	0.5	1.9	2.3	0.9	1.6	93.8
30 11390	Butte-Silver Bow	1 860.4	33 208	969	17.8	96.7	0.3	3.0	0.8	0.8	2.7	93.7
30 32800	Great Falls	50.5	56 155	543	1 112.0	92.2	1.4	6.6	1.6	0.9	2.4	88.7
30 35600	Helena	36.3	26 718	1 184	736.0	96.4	0.4	3.0	1.2	0.7	1.7	93.8
30 50200	Missoula	61.6	60 722	487	985.7	95.3	0.6	3.4	1.8	0.8	1.8	92.6
31 00000	NEBRASKA	199 098.6	1 739 291	X	8.7	90.8	4.4	1.3	1.7	3.3	5.5	87.3
31 03950	Bellevue	34.4	46 734	685	1 358.5	88.0	7.0	1.1	3.2	3.4	5.9	83.2
31 17670	Fremont	19.2	25 198	1 222	1 312.4	96.0	0.7	0.7	1.0	2.6	4.3	93.6
31 19595	Grand Island	55.6	43 771	733	787.2	88.0	0.6	0.6	1.7	10.5	15.9	81.4
31 25055	Kearney	28.4	28 211	1 125	993.3	96.2	1.0	0.7	1.3	2.1	4.1	93.1
31 28000	Lincoln	193.3	235 594	75	1 218.8	91.0	3.8	1.2	3.6	2.4	3.6	87.8
31 37000	Omaha	299.7	404 267	42	1 348.9	80.0	14.2	1.2	2.2	4.5	7.5	75.4

1. Dry land or land partially or temporarily covered by water.   2. Hispanic or Latino persons may be of any race.

City	Under 5 years	5 to 17 years	18 to 24 years	25 to 34 years	35 to 44 years	45 to 54 years	55 to 64 years	65 to 74 years	75 years and over	Percent female	Census counts 1990	Census counts 2000	Percent change 1990–2000	Percent change 2000–2003
	12	13	14	15	16	17	18	19	20	21	22	23	24	25
MINNESOTA—Cont'd														
Plymouth	7.0	20.1	7.4	13.8	19.2	16.1	8.9	4.8	2.8	50.7	50 889	65 894	29.5	5.0
Richfield	6.0	14.2	9.3	16.9	16.5	12.7	8.0	7.1	9.3	51.0	35 710	34 439	-3.6	-1.0
Rochester	7.5	18.3	9.1	16.2	17.2	12.5	7.7	5.5	6.0	51.4	70 729	85 806	21.3	7.8
Roseville	4.6	13.7	11.1	12.4	14.4	13.3	10.4	9.2	11.0	53.5	33 485	33 690	0.6	-1.7
St. Cloud	5.5	15.2	24.1	14.2	13.4	11.1	6.2	5.2	5.1	49.6	48 812	59 107	21.1	0.6
St. Louis Park	6.0	12.7	8.7	21.2	16.5	12.8	7.4	6.1	8.6	52.5	43 787	44 126	0.8	0.0
St. Paul	7.6	19.5	12.5	16.8	15.3	11.9	6.2	4.6	5.7	51.6	272 235	287 151	5.5	-2.3
Shoreview	5.5	20.6	6.9	10.3	18.2	18.8	9.9	5.9	3.8	51.5	24 587	25 924	5.4	4.6
Winona	4.5	13.5	27.5	10.5	11.7	11.0	7.0	5.8	8.4	53.0	25 435	27 069	6.4	-1.6
Woodbury	9.6	21.0	5.9	16.8	20.2	13.8	6.6	3.6	2.5	51.5	20 075	46 463	131.4	6.4
MISSISSIPPI	7.2	20.1	10.9	13.4	15.0	12.7	8.6	6.5	5.5	51.7	2 575 475	2 844 658	10.5	1.3
Biloxi	7.3	16.9	14.3	15.1	15.2	11.5	7.7	6.7	5.3	49.5	46 319	50 644	9.3	-3.3
Columbus	7.1	18.9	12.0	13.5	13.1	11.7	8.1	7.3	8.2	54.8	23 799	25 944	9.0	-3.8
Greenville	8.6	22.8	10.1	12.6	13.6	12.6	7.8	6.0	5.8	53.9	45 226	41 633	-7.9	-5.1
Gulfport	7.1	18.9	11.1	14.8	15.6	12.7	8.3	6.5	4.9	50.4	64 045	71 127	11.1	1.0
Hattiesburg	6.7	14.8	24.4	15.0	11.3	9.6	6.3	5.5	6.3	54.0	45 325	44 779	-1.2	4.2
Jackson	7.8	20.7	12.4	14.5	14.6	12.1	7.0	5.5	5.4	53.5	202 062	184 256	-8.8	-2.5
Meridian	7.6	19.6	9.9	13.3	13.3	11.8	8.0	7.8	8.7	54.3	41 036	39 968	-2.6	-1.0
Pascagoula	7.8	19.0	12.0	14.2	14.7	12.0	8.3	6.5	5.4	49.6	25 899	26 200	1.2	-1.3
Southaven	7.6	19.6	9.0	16.7	15.8	12.9	9.7	5.5	3.4	51.2	18 705	28 977	61.4	20.0
Tupelo	7.5	20.0	8.1	14.5	16.0	12.8	8.7	6.1	6.3	53.0	30 685	34 211	11.5	3.2
Vicksburg	7.9	20.4	9.3	13.3	14.6	12.0	7.6	6.9	7.9	54.7	26 886	26 407	-1.8	-1.5
MISSOURI	6.6	18.9	9.6	13.2	15.9	13.3	9.1	7.0	6.5	51.4	5 116 901	5 595 211	9.3	2.0
Ballwin	7.3	19.8	6.4	12.1	17.8	14.8	9.7	7.6	4.6	51.5	27 054	31 283	46.1	-0.9
Blue Springs	7.4	22.1	8.7	14.8	17.2	15.1	7.7	3.9	3.2	51.1	40 103	48 080	19.9	2.7
Cape Girardeau	5.4	15.2	18.4	12.7	12.9	12.2	7.7	6.9	8.6	52.8	34 475	35 349	2.5	1.1
Chesterfield	5.6	19.1	5.9	8.9	16.2	18.0	11.7	7.3	7.4	52.2	42 325	46 802	10.6	0.6
Columbia	5.8	14.0	26.7	15.9	12.8	10.5	5.8	4.1	4.5	52.1	69 133	84 531	22.3	4.7
Florissant	6.5	18.1	8.2	13.5	16.5	11.7	8.4	9.0	8.1	52.8	51 038	50 497	-1.1	1.0
Gladstone	5.4	15.6	8.6	13.1	15.1	15.3	11.1	8.8	7.0	51.9	26 243	26 365	0.5	2.7
Hazelwood	6.1	18.5	9.7	14.8	16.9	13.6	8.8	6.6	5.0	52.0	15 512	26 206	68.9	-1.4
Independence	6.6	17.3	8.7	13.2	15.7	13.4	9.6	8.1	7.4	52.2	112 301	113 288	0.9	-1.1
Jefferson City	5.8	15.0	11.0	15.6	16.4	14.2	7.8	6.7	7.3	48.7	35 517	39 636	11.6	-5.3
Joplin	7.1	16.1	13.5	13.6	13.7	12.1	8.2	7.4	8.3	52.5	41 175	45 504	11.3	1.9
Kansas City	7.2	18.2	9.7	16.4	16.1	12.8	7.9	6.2	5.6	51.7	434 829	441 545	1.5	0.3
Kirkwood	6.0	17.4	5.9	11.9	15.7	15.7	9.2	8.1	10.1	54.3	28 318	27 324	-3.5	-0.1
Lee's Summit	8.0	21.1	6.6	14.1	19.0	13.6	7.3	4.7	5.6	52.1	46 418	70 700	52.3	9.0
Liberty	6.7	20.9	10.4	13.4	16.8	13.7	7.7	5.2	5.2	52.1	20 459	26 232	28.2	6.7
Maryland Heights	5.9	15.6	9.8	20.2	17.1	12.9	9.1	5.6	3.9	50.6	25 440	25 756	1.2	-0.7
O'Fallon	10.5	22.9	6.4	18.6	20.2	9.7	5.6	3.8	2.3	50.7	17 427	46 169	164.9	37.9
Raytown	5.8	16.7	7.8	12.4	15.6	13.3	9.2	9.5	9.8	53.0	30 601	30 388	-0.7	-2.1
St. Charles	6.2	17.1	12.0	14.1	16.4	13.3	8.7	6.4	5.8	50.9	50 634	60 321	19.1	1.5
St. Joseph	6.4	17.7	11.6	13.4	15.1	12.2	8.1	7.2	8.2	51.1	71 852	73 990	3.0	-1.8
St. Louis	6.7	19.0	10.6	15.6	15.3	11.8	7.2	6.6	7.1	53.0	396 685	348 189	-12.2	-4.6
St. Peters	7.4	22.5	7.4	13.9	19.7	14.5	6.7	4.4	3.4	51.3	40 660	51 381	26.4	3.9
Springfield	5.9	14.0	17.4	14.5	13.5	11.8	7.9	7.0	7.9	51.8	140 494	151 580	7.9	-0.5
University City	6.1	15.7	11.3	16.4	14.8	13.1	9.4	6.8	6.5	54.3	40 087	37 428	-6.6	0.9
Wildwood	8.2	25.0	4.8	10.0	21.5	17.6	7.6	3.4	2.1	50.8	16 527	32 884	99.0	3.8
MONTANA	6.1	19.4	9.5	11.4	15.7	15.0	9.4	6.9	6.5	50.2	799 065	902 195	12.9	1.7
Billings	6.5	17.5	10.1	13.2	15.5	13.7	8.6	7.2	7.7	51.9	81 125	89 847	10.8	6.0
Bozeman	5.0	11.1	33.0	17.1	11.5	10.1	4.3	3.2	4.8	47.4	22 660	27 509	21.4	11.8
Butte-Silver Bow	5.8	17.9	9.6	11.2	15.4	14.2	9.8	7.7	8.3	50.6	33 252	34 606	2.0	-4.0
Great Falls	6.4	18.5	9.0	12.0	15.8	13.2	9.5	7.7	8.0	51.5	55 125	56 690	2.8	-0.9
Helena	5.8	16.6	11.1	11.4	15.2	16.7	9.3	6.4	7.5	52.4	24 609	25 780	4.8	3.6
Missoula	5.3	14.4	20.7	15.7	13.7	13.1	6.6	4.7	5.6	50.3	42 918	57 053	32.9	6.4
NEBRASKA	6.8	19.5	10.2	13.0	15.4	13.2	8.3	6.8	6.8	50.7	1 578 417	1 711 263	8.4	1.6
Bellevue	7.1	20.3	10.2	14.7	16.3	12.7	9.0	6.0	3.5	50.4	39 240	44 382	13.1	5.3
Fremont	6.3	17.9	11.0	11.9	14.8	12.3	8.4	8.4	9.1	52.4	23 680	25 174	6.3	0.1
Grand Island	7.8	19.1	9.5	13.8	14.9	12.9	7.8	6.9	7.3	50.5	39 487	42 940	8.7	1.9
Kearney	6.7	15.5	23.9	13.9	12.3	11.1	6.0	4.7	6.0	51.9	24 396	27 431	12.4	2.8
Lincoln	6.7	16.3	16.4	15.9	14.8	12.6	6.9	5.2	5.2	50.2	191 972	225 581	17.5	4.4
Omaha	7.2	18.4	11.0	15.5	15.4	12.9	7.8	6.1	5.7	51.3	344 463	390 007	13.8	3.7

Table D. Cities — **Group Quarters, Crime, and Education**

City	Households, 2000 Number	Percent change, 1990–2000	Persons per house-hold	Female family house-holder[1]	One-person	Persons in group quarters, 2000 Total	Institutional Total	Persons in nursing homes	Non-institu-tional	Serious crimes known to police[2] 2002 Total Number	Rate[3]	Violent	Property	School enrollment[4] Public	Private	High school graduate or less	Bachelor's degree or more
	26	27	28	29	30	31	32	33	34	35	36	37	38	39	40	41	42
MINNESOTA—Cont'd																	
Plymouth	24 820	35.2	2.60	7.6	21.8	1 450	935	97	515	1 926	2 865	109	2 756	14 231	3 982	19.1	51.0
Richfield	15 073	-3.1	2.25	10.5	33.7	488	241	241	247	1 363	3 879	415	3 463	5 619	1 371	38.3	27.3
Rochester	34 116	22.2	2.43	8.5	29.7	2 879	1 559	531	1 320	2 999	3 425	260	3 165	18 510	4 266	30.4	38.1
Roseville	14 598	7.6	2.20	7.2	33.6	1 642	702	649	940	1 659	4 826	140	4 686	5 334	2 756	30.3	42.3
St. Cloud	22 652	26.4	2.40	9.4	30.2	4 724	1 661	506	3 063	3 235	5 364	312	5 052	18 590	2 849	37.5	29.6
St. Louis Park	20 782	4.3	2.08	8.6	37.9	914	541	541	373	1 398	3 105	122	2 983	7 266	2 095	26.7	43.2
St. Paul	112 109	1.7	2.46	13.9	35.9	11 196	3 240	2 352	7 956	17 803	6 076	805	5 271	65 164	23 596	41.9	32.0
Shoreview	10 125	12.6	2.54	7.9	24.1	171	0	0	171	471	1 781	60	1 720	5 939	1 503	23.1	46.9
Winona	10 301	10.4	2.27	8.4	35.2	3 653	566	537	3 087	828	2 998	69	2 929	8 510	2 329	44.0	26.3
Woodbury	16 676	140.7	2.76	6.9	18.8	440	359	359	81	1 154	2 434	84	2 350	10 689	2 662	19.3	49.3
MISSISSIPPI	1 046 434	14.8	2.63	17.3	24.6	95 414	50 826	18 382	44 588	119 442	4 159	343	3 816	688 942	100 961	56.5	16.9
Biloxi	19 588	17.7	2.42	14.0	30.1	3 270	520	219	2 750	3 852	7 534	643	6 891	10 654	1 630	44.6	19.2
Columbus	10 062	10.1	2.42	21.7	31.3	1 574	903	491	671	1 732	6 613	260	6 353	6 610	1 114	54.6	22.9
Greenville	14 784	-3.5	2.77	27.7	25.8	719	575	393	144	4 455	10 600	830	9 769	10 806	1 653	59.8	17.5
Gulfport	26 943	70.6	2.51	18.2	27.7	3 424	1 512	243	1 912	5 818	8 102	454	7 648	15 674	2 713	48.9	19.1
Hattiesburg	17 295	8.7	2.29	19.4	34.4	5 136	1 409	601	3 727	3 526	7 800	529	7 271	14 918	2 152	42.9	28.9
Jackson	67 841	-5.6	2.61	25.3	28.9	7 201	2 485	1 100	4 716	17 648	9 488	969	8 519	47 620	10 740	42.4	27.1
Meridian	15 966	-1.3	2.39	23.3	33.2	1 855	1 356	408	499	1 812	4 491	416	4 074	10 157	1 014	54.0	17.6
Pascagoula	9 878	1.1	2.52	18.8	27.0	1 327	455	120	872	2 344	8 862	578	8 284	5 834	651	52.9	15.6
Southaven	11 007	80.0	2.62	12.4	21.3	125	121	121	4	2 057	7 032	202	6 830	6 312	1 192	52.6	14.3
Tupelo	13 395	14.4	2.47	16.2	28.0	1 114	905	548	209	2 230	6 457	365	6 092	8 228	1 020	41.5	26.7
Vicksburg	10 364	25.4	2.49	24.2	32.0	601	502	379	99	2 400	9 003	1 227	7 776	6 196	849	52.6	19.1
MISSOURI	2 194 594	11.9	2.48	11.6	27.3	162 058	90 430	48 708	71 628	261 077	4 602	539	4 064	1 205 378	274 195	51.4	21.6
Ballwin	11 797	50.3	2.65	8.0	20.6	1	0	0	1	352	1 110	57	1 053	5 981	2 943	23.9	46.7
Blue Springs	17 286	27.8	2.77	10.5	18.1	246	206	206	40	1 972	4 046	203	3 842	12 110	1 805	37.4	27.4
Cape Girardeau	14 380	7.0	2.24	10.9	33.6	3 070	983	938	2 087	2 179	6 080	181	5 899	9 666	1 484	46.5	29.3
Chesterfield	18 060	37.7	2.53	5.4	23.6	1 073	1 070	1 001	3	1 018	2 145	84	2 061	8 187	4 491	16.9	60.6
Columbia	33 689	30.4	2.26	10.3	33.1	8 459	595	549	7 864	3 837	4 477	478	3 999	31 746	3 688	26.7	50.5
Florissant	20 399	6.4	2.44	13.2	28.8	781	557	557	224	1 287	2 514	141	2 373	9 162	3 680	47.4	17.4
Gladstone	11 484	9.0	2.27	10.3	29.9	279	230	230	49	795	2 974	161	2 813	4 569	1 105	41.4	25.1
Hazelwood	10 954	72.4	2.38	12.7	32.1	132	3	0	129	786	2 958	361	2 597	5 438	1 486	45.9	22.5
Independence	47 390	4.6	2.37	12.3	30.1	1 140	590	383	550	8 483	7 386	568	6 818	21 653	3 719	55.5	15.2
Jefferson City	15 794	11.5	2.21	10.8	36.1	4 734	3 993	456	741	1 596	3 972	709	3 262	7 056	2 558	42.4	30.8
Joplin	19 101	9.3	2.28	12.3	32.4	1 906	676	618	1 230	3 689	7 996	447	7 550	8 876	2 312	49.6	20.7
Kansas City	183 981	3.6	2.35	16.0	34.1	9 096	4 958	2 418	4 138	44 940	10 040	1 352	8 687	93 260	23 509	45.4	25.7
Kirkwood	11 763	4.9	2.29	9.0	33.5	341	250	223	91	732	2 642	159	2 484	4 550	2 447	21.1	51.5
Lee's Summit	26 417	49.8	2.65	8.9	22.0	779	746	746	33	2 040	2 846	93	2 753	17 067	3 288	37.3	37.3
Liberty	9 511	32.6	2.62	10.9	22.4	1 280	430	233	850	671	2 523	402	2 121	6 027	1 734	37.3	32.0
Maryland Heights	11 302	6.0	2.25	9.5	33.8	344	324	263	20	1 089	4 170	119	4 052	4 729	1 459	34.8	38.7
O'Fallon	15 389	141.1	2.98	8.6	14.1	368	105	105	263	NA	NA	NA	NA	11 132	2 566	37.8	27.2
Raytown	12 855	1.2	2.32	12.6	30.3	552	518	471	34	1 161	3 768	266	3 502	6 012	1 047	46.2	19.5
St. Charles	24 210	11.7	2.38	10.2	29.6	2 641	771	452	1 870	1 842	3 012	185	2 827	10 808	3 007	43.8	26.6
St. Joseph	29 026	2.2	2.39	12.8	30.4	4 618	3 159	740	1 459	4 738	6 316	257	6 059	16 421	2 376	56.1	17.1
St. Louis	147 076	-10.8	2.30	21.3	40.3	10 632	4 667	2 943	5 965	50 429	14 286	2 124	12 161	71 341	26 990	56.2	19.1
St. Peters	18 435	21.1	2.78	9.7	20.3	146	127	127	19	1 672	3 210	299	2 910	12 294	3 547	36.2	27.2
Springfield	64 691	12.8	2.17	10.9	35.3	11 019	3 122	1 376	7 897	12 066	7 852	690	7 161	35 907	8 196	47.7	23.0
University City	16 453	-0.6	2.25	16.3	34.2	409	238	214	171	2 220	5 850	416	5 434	6 361	4 776	29.7	45.0
Wildwood	10 837	NA	3.02	4.6	12.4	148	69	52	79	NA	NA	NA	NA	8 101	2 947	16.1	57.4
MONTANA	358 667	17.1	2.45	8.9	27.4	24 762	12 068	6 470	12 694	31 948	3 513	352	3 161	217 183	24 571	44.1	24.4
Billings	37 525	13.1	2.32	10.8	31.3	2 683	1 572	971	1 111	4 846	5 351	237	5 113	20 084	2 929	40.7	28.5
Bozeman	10 877	24.3	2.26	7.3	30.4	2 901	304	262	2 597	NA	NA	NA	NA	11 457	729	21.0	49.5
Butte-Silver Bow	14 432	3.8	2.32	10.5	32.8	1 092	715	397	377	1 693	4 853	473	4 380	8 184	1 255	49.2	21.7
Great Falls	23 834	5.3	2.31	11.1	31.9	1 531	1 272	449	259	4 528	7 924	465	7 458	11 993	2 015	45.6	22.4
Helena	11 541	10.7	2.14	10.4	37.5	1 096	312	248	784	NA	NA	NA	NA	5 068	1 291	31.4	39.8
Missoula	24 141	36.6	2.23	10.0	33.6	3 286	487	108	2 799	NA	NA	NA	NA	18 013	1 455	30.4	38.0
NEBRASKA	666 184	10.6	2.49	9.1	27.6	50 818	26 011	16 195	24 807	73 606	4 257	314	3 943	398 031	82 674	44.7	23.7
Bellevue	16 937	48.2	2.61	11.3	23.2	223	101	101	122	1 679	3 744	125	3 619	10 664	2 467	36.6	25.2
Fremont	10 171	7.9	2.38	9.4	29.1	938	368	340	570	1 083	4 258	86	4 171	4 877	1 520	56.1	15.8
Grand Island	16 426	7.8	2.55	10.4	27.1	1 091	770	631	321	2 894	6 670	309	6 361	9 044	1 123	53.5	15.8
Kearney	10 549	17.6	2.37	9.7	28.7	2 411	391	279	2 020	1 357	4 896	263	4 632	8 972	849	33.1	34.9
Lincoln	90 485	20.0	2.36	9.5	30.4	11 643	3 689	959	7 954	15 005	6 583	559	6 023	57 839	11 854	34.3	33.3
Omaha	156 738	17.1	2.42	13.0	31.9	10 581	5 760	2 808	4 821	28 781	7 303	718	6 585	82 927	26 724	41.1	28.7

1. No spouse present. 2. Data for serious crimes have not been adjusted for underreporting. This may affect comparability between geographic areas and over time. 3. Per 100,000 population estimated by the FBI. 4. All persons 3 years old and over enrolled in nursery school through college. 5. Persons 25 years old and over.

City	Per capita income[1] (dollars)	Median income Dollars	Percent change, 1989–1999 (constant 1999 dollars)	Percent with income of $100,000 or more	Percent below poverty Persons Total	Percent change in rate, 1989–1999	Families Total	Housing units, 2000 Total	Percent change, 1990–2000	Vacant units for sale or rent[2]	For seasonal use (percent)	Home owner vacancy rate	Renter vacancy rate
	43	44	45	46	47	48	49	50	51	52	53	54	55
MINNESOTA—Cont'd													
Plymouth	36 309	77 008	11.7	33.8	2.6	-23.5	1.5	25 258	28.8	438	0.5	0.3	2.1
Richfield	24 709	45 519	4.6	9.5	6.3	14.5	3.9	15 357	-4.6	284	0.2	0.4	2.4
Rochester	24 811	49 090	4.6	14.2	7.8	0.0	4.7	35 346	22.0	1 230	0.5	0.7	4.0
Roseville	27 755	51 056	0.4	15.8	4.2	13.5	2.6	14 917	4.9	319	0.5	0.5	2.3
St. Cloud	19 769	37 346	15.8	8.9	13.1	-33.2	5.0	23 249	23.5	597	0.3	0.6	2.8
St. Louis Park	28 970	49 260	5.4	13.0	5.2	2.0	3.0	21 140	2.2	358	0.3	0.4	1.7
St. Paul	20 216	38 774	8.9	9.3	15.6	-6.6	11.7	115 713	-1.6	3 604	0.4	0.7	2.8
Shoreview	32 399	69 719	6.3	27.7	2.1	-25.0	1.3	10 289	10.9	164	0.4	0.5	2.3
Winona	16 783	32 845	8.7	5.0	17.3	0.6	6.5	10 666	10.2	365	0.2	0.8	4.1
Woodbury	32 606	76 109	11.0	30.2	1.7	-32.0	0.8	17 541	132.6	865	0.6	1.4	13.3
MISSISSIPPI	15 853	31 330	15.8	6.0	19.9	-21.0	16.0	1 161 953	15.0	115 519	1.9	1.6	9.2
Biloxi	17 809	34 106	28.1	5.9	14.6	-31.8	11.2	22 115	17.2	2 527	1.3	2.4	9.9
Columbus	16 848	27 393	7.1	7.4	25.7	-10.1	21.0	11 112	12.2	1 050	0.5	2.2	9.2
Greenville	13 992	25 928	6.9	5.6	29.6	-7.5	25.7	16 251	-1.5	1 467	0.1	1.9	8.6
Gulfport	17 554	32 779	15.2	5.7	17.7	-12.8	14.1	29 559	62.1	2 616	1.1	2.0	10.3
Hattiesburg	15 102	24 409	16.6	5.7	28.3	-21.2	21.5	19 258	9.0	1 963	0.5	2.4	9.9
Jackson	17 116	30 414	-2.7	7.3	23.5	3.5	19.6	75 678	-4.7	7 837	0.4	2.2	11.7
Meridian	15 255	25 085	3.7	5.2	28.6	2.9	24.6	17 890	0.8	1 924	0.3	3.3	8.8
Pascagoula	16 891	32 042	-4.6	6.3	20.7	5.1	18.1	10 931	-1.1	1 053	0.5	1.7	11.7
Southaven	20 759	46 691	-4.7	7.6	6.7	-2.9	5.3	11 462	81.6	455	0.2	1.6	5.4
Tupelo	22 024	38 401	2.6	9.7	12.7	0.8	10.2	14 551	18.0	1 156	0.4	1.4	10.9
Vicksburg	16 174	28 466	23.1	5.9	23.0	-30.7	19.3	11 654	26.0	1 290	0.4	2.0	12.3
MISSOURI	19 936	37 934	7.1	8.8	11.7	-12.0	8.6	2 442 017	11.0	247 423	2.7	2.1	9.0
Ballwin	29 520	66 458	6.0	25.8	3.2	28.0	2.0	12 062	47.9	265	0.2	0.5	5.6
Blue Springs	23 444	55 402	3.3	14.2	4.8	2.1	3.9	17 733	24.5	447	0.2	1.0	3.7
Cape Girardeau	18 918	32 452	6.7	6.8	15.2	-15.6	8.5	15 827	8.2	1 447	0.5	2.9	11.3
Chesterfield	43 288	83 802	-6.8	42.1	2.6	23.8	1.8	18 738	33.7	678	0.7	0.9	6.3
Columbia	19 507	33 729	13.8	9.4	19.2	-14.3	9.4	35 916	30.4	2 227	0.3	2.5	6.2
Florissant	20 622	44 462	-10.1	6.4	4.0	21.2	2.7	21 027	6.2	628	0.2	1.0	5.8
Gladstone	25 105	46 333	-7.6	9.9	4.7	34.3	3.1	11 919	7.6	435	0.2	1.2	5.8
Hazelwood	22 311	45 110	-4.6	8.7	6.3	40.0	4.3	11 433	69.0	479	0.4	1.5	5.5
Independence	19 384	38 012	0.2	6.0	8.6	-9.5	6.4	50 213	4.0	2 823	0.2	1.6	7.2
Jefferson City	21 268	39 628	6.9	8.0	11.5	18.6	7.3	16 987	10.0	1 193	0.8	2.2	7.4
Joplin	17 738	30 555	17.1	5.5	14.8	-12.9	10.5	21 328	10.1	2 227	0.3	3.5	10.8
Kansas City	20 753	37 198	3.6	8.3	14.3	-6.5	11.1	202 334	0.3	18 353	0.3	1.9	9.6
Kirkwood	32 012	55 122	-2.6	21.3	4.6	64.3	2.8	12 306	5.2	543	0.4	1.3	6.2
Lee's Summit	26 891	60 905	16.8	20.1	3.8	-20.8	2.8	27 311	45.6	894	0.2	1.2	5.4
Liberty	23 415	52 745	7.9	13.3	5.0	-3.8	3.8	9 973	30.5	462	0.3	1.8	6.4
Maryland Heights	24 918	48 689	-7.6	10.1	5.3	47.2	3.8	11 846	3.3	544	0.5	0.7	7.4
O'Fallon	21 774	60 179	22.6	13.2	3.3	-35.3	2.6	15 920	137.1	531	0.2	1.9	6.4
Raytown	21 634	41 949	-2.4	6.9	5.0	4.2	3.1	13 309	0.7	454	0.1	1.1	5.5
St. Charles	23 607	47 782	3.6	13.0	6.3	-3.1	4.6	25 283	8.8	1 073	0.4	0.9	6.2
St. Joseph	17 445	32 663	9.0	4.9	13.0	-22.2	9.1	31 752	1.5	2 726	0.3	2.0	7.6
St. Louis	16 108	27 156	3.9	4.6	24.6	0.0	20.8	176 354	-9.5	29 278	0.3	3.5	11.8
St. Peters	22 792	57 898	-4.9	13.2	2.7	3.8	1.5	18 776	19.0	341	0.2	0.8	3.8
Springfield	17 711	29 563	2.0	5.4	15.9	-10.7	9.9	69 650	11.5	4 959	0.4	2.5	7.1
University City	26 901	40 902	-5.3	15.3	14.7	14.8	9.5	17 485	-1.2	1 032	0.2	1.5	6.8
Wildwood	38 485	94 006	NA	45.8	2.2	NA	1.6	11 229	NA	392	0.3	0.8	11.4
MONTANA	17 151	33 024	6.9	5.6	14.6	-9.3	10.5	412 633	14.3	53 966	5.9	2.2	7.6
Billings	19 207	35 147	2.0	6.6	12.0	-4.0	9.2	39 293	9.3	1 768	0.4	1.2	5.3
Bozeman	16 104	32 156	24.9	4.8	20.2	-19.8	9.2	11 577	27.0	700	0.9	2.1	4.9
Butte-Silver Bow	17 009	30 402	6.7	4.9	14.9	1.4	10.7	16 176	4.5	1 744	1.1	3.1	12.6
Great Falls	18 059	32 436	4.5	5.5	14.5	-1.4	11.1	25 250	4.5	1 416	0.3	1.4	7.0
Helena	20 020	34 416	0.6	6.0	14.5	25.0	9.3	12 133	9.8	592	0.5	1.4	5.3
Missoula	17 166	30 366	7.5	5.8	19.7	3.7	11.7	25 225	36.4	1 084	0.5	1.0	3.6
NEBRASKA	19 613	39 250	12.3	8.1	9.7	-12.6	6.7	722 668	9.4	56 484	1.6	1.8	7.6
Bellevue	20 903	47 201	10.1	8.9	5.9	3.5	4.1	17 439	45.8	502	0.1	0.8	4.1
Fremont	18 006	36 700	10.3	5.3	8.8	-6.4	5.1	10 576	7.4	405	0.2	0.9	4.4
Grand Island	17 071	36 044	7.2	5.7	12.8	14.3	9.9	17 421	9.9	995	0.1	2.0	7.4
Kearney	17 713	34 829	11.2	5.7	13.4	-18.8	7.4	11 099	18.4	550	0.3	1.9	5.3
Lincoln	20 984	40 605	7.7	8.9	10.1	-10.6	5.8	95 199	20.4	4 714	0.3	1.3	6.2
Omaha	21 756	40 006	10.6	10.0	11.3	-10.3	7.8	165 731	15.4	8 993	0.3	1.0	7.2

1. Based on population enumerated as of April 1, 2000.   2. Includes units rented or sold but not occupied.

Table D. Cities — Housing, Labor Force, Employment, and Disability

City	Housing units, 2000 (cont'd) Occupied units					Civilian labor force, 2003				Civilian employment,[2] 2000			Disability, 2000
	Total	Percent owner occupied	Percent renter occupied	Average size owner occupied	Average size renter occupied	Total	Percent change, 2002–2003	Unemployment Total	Rate[1]	Total	Percent Management, professional, and related occupations	Percent Production, transportation, and material moving occupations	Employment disabled persons[3] (percent)
	56	57	58	59	60	61	62	63	64	65	66	67	68
MINNESOTA—Cont'd													
Plymouth	24 820	76.5	23.5	2.76	2.08	43 475	-0.1	1 609	3.7	37 324	51.4	7.0	5.5
Richfield	15 073	67.6	32.4	2.42	1.91	21 985	0.3	1 020	4.6	19 449	32.5	12.0	12.1
Rochester	34 116	71.0	29.0	2.64	1.93	59 253	1.5	2 627	4.4	45 411	46.8	9.5	8.2
Roseville	14 598	67.5	32.5	2.44	1.69	21 199	3.6	678	3.2	18 075	48.5	9.2	6.7
St. Cloud	22 652	55.9	44.1	2.66	2.07	38 505	-0.1	2 001	5.2	33 010	30.9	15.3	7.0
St. Louis Park	20 782	63.6	36.4	2.26	1.77	29 422	0.0	1 188	4.0	26 660	45.8	8.9	7.5
St. Paul	112 109	54.8	45.2	2.72	2.15	163 039	4.4	8 886	5.5	141 663	37.8	14.0	10.3
Shoreview	10 125	87.2	12.8	2.64	1.91	18 159	4.0	646	3.6	14 951	52.0	8.5	5.7
Winona	10 301	60.9	39.1	2.46	1.99	15 726	-1.1	899	5.7	14 097	28.3	19.5	7.2
Woodbury	16 676	85.2	14.8	2.87	2.13	29 911	-0.1	909	3.0	25 655	52.1	7.2	5.7
MISSISSIPPI	1 046 434	72.3	27.7	2.67	2.52	1 312 127	1.6	83 135	6.3	1 173 314	27.4	20.4	14.4
Biloxi	19 588	48.9	51.1	2.47	2.37	19 347	1.7	1 070	5.5	20 366	28.2	9.6	16.1
Columbus	10 062	54.3	45.7	2.48	2.35	10 867	-3.0	1 412	13.0	10 082	30.4	19.0	11.0
Greenville	14 784	55.8	44.2	2.72	2.83	17 048	-2.2	1 747	10.2	14 847	28.0	21.7	13.5
Gulfport	26 943	58.7	41.3	2.57	2.43	33 846	2.1	1 629	4.8	30 133	26.8	11.5	15.8
Hattiesburg	17 295	44.6	55.4	2.47	2.15	21 691	3.2	1 211	5.6	19 701	31.9	13.3	9.9
Jackson	67 841	58.0	42.0	2.68	2.51	101 272	2.9	5 674	5.6	77 632	31.4	13.7	15.3
Meridian	15 966	56.3	43.7	2.43	2.33	17 072	2.8	1 458	8.5	14 720	30.8	15.6	12.7
Pascagoula	9 878	56.8	43.2	2.55	2.48	13 492	1.8	807	6.0	10 182	28.0	16.1	13.3
Southaven	11 007	72.3	27.7	2.65	2.54	18 984	3.6	525	2.8	15 078	27.2	14.7	10.6
Tupelo	13 395	62.2	37.8	2.59	2.28	18 348	-0.1	948	5.2	16 382	34.6	20.1	13.6
Vicksburg	10 364	56.4	43.6	2.50	2.48	12 461	-0.8	948	7.6	10 783	29.1	18.6	15.3
MISSOURI	2 194 594	70.3	29.7	2.59	2.20	3 020 592	1.3	170 126	5.6	2 657 924	31.5	16.3	10.8
Ballwin	11 797	82.9	17.1	2.76	2.11	13 297	2.1	337	2.5	16 277	46.8	6.6	5.5
Blue Springs	17 286	74.2	25.8	2.92	2.34	24 257	2.1	949	3.9	26 276	36.5	11.1	8.8
Cape Girardeau	14 380	57.3	42.7	2.42	2.01	21 453	-0.1	997	4.6	17 674	33.1	13.6	9.2
Chesterfield	18 060	77.9	22.1	2.75	1.77	21 415	2.1	549	2.6	23 606	57.6	3.6	3.6
Columbia	33 689	47.3	52.7	2.50	2.04	53 506	-0.5	1 317	2.5	45 630	45.5	7.2	7.1
Florissant	20 399	76.8	23.2	2.56	2.05	30 030	2.2	1 186	3.9	24 867	29.9	14.0	8.9
Gladstone	11 484	68.6	31.4	2.43	1.92	20 290	2.2	672	3.3	14 184	31.1	12.5	8.8
Hazelwood	10 954	64.6	35.4	2.62	1.95	16 291	2.2	729	4.5	14 293	33.2	14.1	11.8
Independence	47 390	67.8	32.2	2.47	2.15	66 847	2.2	3 778	5.7	55 381	25.9	17.4	11.4
Jefferson City	15 794	58.6	41.4	2.43	1.90	22 990	2.2	795	3.5	18 981	39.6	10.1	9.5
Joplin	19 101	57.6	42.4	2.36	2.18	25 427	0.3	1 392	5.5	21 305	28.7	18.8	12.0
Kansas City	183 981	57.7	42.3	2.52	2.11	270 420	2.3	19 903	7.4	212 016	34.1	13.0	13.6
Kirkwood	11 763	77.1	22.9	2.44	1.81	15 453	2.2	544	3.5	14 210	52.6	5.6	5.4
Lee's Summit	26 417	75.6	24.4	2.86	1.99	28 138	2.1	1 036	3.7	37 310	44.6	8.6	5.6
Liberty	9 511	73.5	26.5	2.76	2.24	14 708	2.2	590	4.0	13 543	37.9	11.0	7.5
Maryland Heights	11 302	62.6	37.4	2.46	1.89	18 023	2.2	543	3.0	15 103	43.8	9.6	8.9
O'Fallon	15 389	89.5	10.5	3.04	2.42	15 484	2.2	707	4.6	23 718	35.9	12.6	6.1
Raytown	12 855	73.9	26.1	2.42	2.05	18 399	2.1	744	4.0	14 874	30.4	14.0	11.9
St. Charles	24 210	64.6	35.4	2.63	1.93	47 060	2.1	1 923	4.1	31 912	34.4	12.8	8.0
St. Joseph	29 026	64.8	35.2	2.49	2.20	37 355	-0.8	2 316	6.2	32 924	27.1	17.7	11.4
St. Louis	147 076	46.9	53.1	2.49	2.12	161 963	2.4	16 347	10.1	143 850	29.7	15.4	14.7
St. Peters	18 435	85.4	14.6	2.89	2.13	37 961	2.1	1 366	3.6	28 337	35.8	11.8	7.0
Springfield	64 691	53.7	46.3	2.27	2.06	87 278	1.6	3 728	4.3	75 199	27.7	15.5	10.7
University City	16 453	57.8	42.2	2.47	1.94	23 916	2.4	1 735	7.3	19 257	51.2	8.2	11.0
Wildwood	10 837	90.4	9.6	3.13	1.98	16 895	2.2	653	3.9	16 609	55.4	4.3	3.9
MONTANA	358 667	69.1	30.9	2.55	2.22	474 910	2.5	22 494	4.7	425 977	33.1	11.2	9.3
Billings	37 525	64.0	36.0	2.48	2.04	52 090	3.0	1 835	3.5	45 560	31.8	10.8	9.7
Bozeman	10 877	42.9	57.1	2.43	2.13	20 861	3.3	674	3.2	15 796	37.6	9.2	5.3
Butte-Silver Bow	14 432	70.4	29.6	2.46	1.99	16 680	1.5	852	5.1	15 768	32.4	11.1	9.7
Great Falls	23 834	63.0	37.0	2.48	2.03	26 891	0.8	1 278	4.8	24 909	31.2	10.3	10.7
Helena	11 541	57.3	42.7	2.35	1.86	14 923	2.9	547	3.7	13 291	44.9	7.1	8.8
Missoula	24 141	50.2	49.8	2.47	1.98	31 166	4.1	1 322	4.2	30 391	35.2	8.4	7.4
NEBRASKA	666 184	67.4	32.6	2.63	2.20	976 034	2.1	39 370	4.0	877 237	33.0	15.1	9.4
Bellevue	16 937	66.1	33.9	2.76	2.32	20 580	0.6	768	3.7	22 583	32.4	11.6	8.8
Fremont	10 171	63.4	36.6	2.51	2.16	14 306	2.3	758	5.3	12 819	22.8	21.7	11.1
Grand Island	16 426	62.7	37.3	2.71	2.28	26 032	2.2	1 166	4.5	21 260	23.9	21.2	12.7
Kearney	10 549	56.5	43.5	2.59	2.08	18 632	1.4	725	3.9	15 762	29.7	12.7	7.9
Lincoln	90 485	58.0	42.0	2.59	2.05	140 027	1.4	5 868	4.2	126 176	36.0	13.3	8.1
Omaha	156 738	59.6	40.4	2.64	2.10	219 348	0.8	11 422	5.2	199 054	34.8	12.6	10.7

1. Percent of civilian labor force.   2. Persons 16 years old and over.   3. Persons 16 to 64 years old.

City	Value of residential construction authorized by building permits, 2003			Wholesale trade, 1997				Retail trade,[1] 1997			
	New construction ($1,000)	Number of housing units	Percent single family	Number of establishments	Number of employees	Sales (mil dol)	Annual payroll (mil dol)	Number of establishments	Number of employees	Sales (mil dol)	Annual payroll (mil dol)
	69	70	71	72	73	74	75	76	77	78	79
MINNESOTA—Cont'd											
Plymouth	111 509	660	53.9	350	11 437	6 950.7	412.4	165	4 057	1 460.4	109.5
Richfield	43 970	256	7.0	37	322	110.1	11.6	148	2 746	438.7	46.2
Rochester	176 028	1 157	79.6	88	843	443.4	28.6	502	8 675	1 311.7	126.4
Roseville	24 296	203	16.3	151	2 334	1 227.2	89.6	350	8 031	1 210.6	122.9
St. Cloud	28 470	267	83.1	98	2 835	985.2	100.4	373	6 530	1 065.3	99.1
St. Louis Park	14 473	128	7.8	229	2 817	2 204.8	118.5	232	3 851	671.5	69.7
St. Paul	85 659	774	19.8	456	7 746	4 075.5	323.5	872	12 246	1 907.3	225.7
Shoreview	31 680	240	10.0	40	798	221.1	34.6	37	810	117.0	9.7
Winona	16 874	170	33.5	57	508	360.7	13.4	173	2 135	313.6	30.4
Woodbury	121 994	491	92.7	30	180	129.6	7.0	144	2 530	341.2	31.6
MISSISSIPPI	1 268 335	12 010	84.4	3 173	36 520	18 445.2	1 012.1	12 791	138 372	20 774.5	1 935.3
Biloxi	83 574	502	44.6	44	551	175.3	14.0	259	3 162	403.2	44.9
Columbus	4 183	38	100.0	76	969	287.2	26.2	318	3 644	567.8	51.2
Greenville	1 181	26	38.5	55	610	333.9	19.9	252	3 048	413.2	41.6
Gulfport	35 242	305	95.4	98	1 147	286.1	27.6	395	4 958	861.5	77.8
Hattiesburg	9 741	85	97.6	93	1 266	1 119.3	28.4	385	5 542	818.7	78.7
Jackson	21 938	393	23.7	404	6 820	2 828.5	218.4	968	15 841	2 595.6	265.7
Meridian	5 300	35	94.3	94	1 770	942.1	48.0	434	5 009	753.0	72.8
Pascagoula	1 890	13	100.0	30	271	173.1	8.6	186	2 632	499.8	41.5
Southaven	67 979	655	98.8	25	D	D	D	109	2 377	295.4	28.2
Tupelo	13 307	96	100.0	156	1 721	670.7	46.5	431	5 785	895.2	84.7
Vicksburg	3 401	25	100.0	38	325	134.4	9.8	257	2 973	402.8	39.8
MISSOURI	3 596 524	29 309	77.6	9 522	125 929	91 411.9	4 639.8	24 181	297 556	51 269.9	4 945.0
Ballwin	3 517	23	100.0	58	201	164.0	7.3	117	1 889	433.5	32.0
Blue Springs	28 012	328	44.8	61	372	195.0	12.7	171	2 833	534.3	51.2
Cape Girardeau	14 235	127	56.7	111	1 183	539.0	31.9	359	4 893	780.6	73.0
Chesterfield	NA	NA	NA	243	2 023	3 024.1	98.0	218	3 564	380.5	47.5
Columbia	173 462	1 667	55.5	106	1 466	596.4	44.5	491	7 836	1 270.8	116.7
Florissant	0	0	0.0	48	415	95.1	11.7	227	4 432	688.2	68.7
Gladstone	8 407	47	100.0	22	101	31.0	2.8	104	1 828	317.2	31.3
Hazelwood	3 646	31	100.0	47	1 539	2 653.9	65.9	78	1 036	252.1	27.5
Independence	44 150	405	98.5	106	981	410.8	30.2	507	8 120	1 278.4	128.0
Jefferson City	24 269	172	80.8	83	D	D	D	260	4 191	694.0	64.4
Joplin	20 699	220	100.0	142	1 495	651.9	38.6	438	6 287	970.6	89.8
Kansas City	331 773	2 703	70.4	898	18 053	12 630.3	702.2	1 843	27 774	5 773.0	511.0
Kirkwood	10 303	63	63.5	97	637	286.6	22.4	140	1 994	437.9	44.9
Lee's Summit	164 861	1 176	84.4	101	975	907.8	31.0	195	2 709	475.3	46.3
Liberty	29 534	231	100.0	26	D	D	D	102	1 215	197.3	19.2
Maryland Heights	2 378	21	81.0	258	4 975	2 687.7	187.6	127	3 459	717.3	80.0
O'Fallon	138 323	1 355	84.0	43	487	355.8	19.3	107	1 645	237.7	24.0
Raytown	5 035	77	24.7	53	487	342.5	22.6	137	2 804	498.7	49.2
St. Charles	24 287	180	86.7	109	1 055	354.2	31.2	300	3 815	650.0	61.3
St. Joseph	24 436	211	73.9	139	1 556	1 106.3	42.9	382	4 733	777.6	71.2
St. Louis	116 774	1 215	13.7	902	16 599	10 582.9	646.4	1 241	14 511	2 361.7	282.4
St. Peters	35 364	256	96.1	67	594	666.2	19.6	308	5 619	1 000.8	95.7
Springfield	80 920	823	47.9	488	8 326	4 908.2	249.7	1 106	16 060	2 937.4	266.7
University City	4 280	20	100.0	54	615	180.3	20.7	105	1 366	164.1	20.6
Wildwood	NA	NA	NA	NA	NA	NA	NA	NA	NA	NA	NA
MONTANA	411 698	3 767	62.1	1 577	14 381	7 709.5	372.3	5 042	48 337	7 779.1	746.5
Billings	105 712	850	76.0	314	4 128	2 295.1	121.1	642	8 103	1 432.0	133.8
Bozeman	76 444	606	56.8	73	697	230.6	20.8	307	3 387	492.7	52.2
Butte-Silver Bow	3 609	37	94.6	55	534	192.0	10.7	220	2 147	333.1	32.0
Great Falls	21 865	174	81.6	111	1 030	1 039.8	27.8	389	4 895	782.9	79.8
Helena	10 655	86	65.1	62	692	193.1	16.5	248	2 603	456.6	42.4
Missoula	61 773	947	45.2	145	1 675	515.4	42.7	463	6 166	990.0	97.1
NEBRASKA	1 250 209	10 339	83.7	3 157	41 002	38 015.4	1 170.2	8 295	102 684	16 529.3	1 554.6
Bellevue	89 395	617	79.1	12	15	3.4	0.3	124	2 335	379.2	34.6
Fremont	10 064	105	61.9	30	329	306.4	10.3	149	2 093	441.1	34.8
Grand Island	19 451	160	63.1	94	D	D	D	307	4 256	658.5	63.6
Kearney	40 165	348	73.9	44	D	D	D	198	2 903	399.2	44.0
Lincoln	280 931	2 271	82.3	270	D	D	D	952	15 326	2 197.5	225.2
Omaha	321 856	2 915	88.5	932	15 973	10 907.3	533.0	1 786	33 724	5 479.3	572.3

1. Establishments with payroll.

City	Real estate and rental and leasing, 1997				Professional, scientific, and technical services,[1] 1997				Manufacturing, 1997			
	Number of establish-ments	Number of employees	Receipts (mil dol)	Annual payroll (mil dol)	Number of establish-ments	Number of employees	Receipts (mil dol)	Annual payroll (mil dol)	Number of establish-ments	Number of employees	Receipts (mil dol)	Annual payroll (mil dol)
	80	81	82	83	84	85	86	87	88	89	90	91
MINNESOTA—Cont'd												
Plymouth	93	427	93.4	11.9	303	2 114	286.5	101.0	207	12 651	2 096.5	498.1
Richfield	36	367	34.4	5.2	60	423	19.8	7.7	NA	NA	NA	NA
Rochester	111	617	71.2	9.4	184	2 082	155.3	81.8	64	D	D	D
Roseville	81	824	133.2	19.8	217	2 022	222.0	71.0	88	5 238	604.9	196.0
St. Cloud	101	568	52.6	9.6	141	1 012	78.1	33.8	75	7 189	981.7	194.0
St. Louis Park	155	1 346	180.9	26.8	384	3 228	321.2	135.2	113	4 241	707.5	159.9
St. Paul	304	2 507	235.6	53.0	803	6 333	646.5	290.9	375	20 215	5 536.6	737.5
Shoreview	20	106	15.2	1.7	76	425	37.3	17.4	35	1 870	269.1	71.8
Winona	35	D	D	D	57	197	12.9	4.1	83	5 992	921.5	170.7
Woodbury	28	181	26.6	3.6	103	227	33.4	9.7	17	1 062	253.4	39.4
MISSISSIPPI	2 125	8 354	794.2	132.1	3 627	21 671	1 761.6	662.1	3 008	227 800	39 658.3	5 599.4
Biloxi	61	281	26.9	3.9	100	618	53.3	20.0	36	D	D	D
Columbus	53	294	25.9	5.0	77	383	27.2	10.1	57	D	D	D
Greenville	63	264	23.4	3.6	66	299	31.7	8.8	49	4 313	904.0	105.3
Gulfport	101	418	39.5	7.3	182	909	75.7	28.5	67	1 885	259.3	50.4
Hattiesburg	89	364	32.9	5.5	156	827	63.3	20.9	62	4 625	942.4	103.4
Jackson	263	1 455	147.7	23.6	619	5 424	552.0	219.2	173	9 337	1 709.3	236.9
Meridian	66	242	22.5	3.5	106	452	32.5	9.8	70	D	D	D
Pascagoula	34	156	11.7	2.9	81	648	72.4	31.1	39	D	D	D
Southaven	23	118	19.2	2.6	33	177	11.2	4.4	NA	NA	NA	NA
Tupelo	58	268	23.1	4.5	131	838	62.7	26.3	109	8 813	1 470.7	231.3
Vicksburg	41	121	13.6	1.9	67	565	33.3	17.0	32	2 813	748.9	76.3
MISSOURI	5 500	31 301	3 991.1	698.1	10 601	93 792	9 953.3	3 643.6	7 497	371 448	93 115.5	11 647.0
Ballwin	28	130	30.5	3.2	87	637	67.2	28.3	NA	NA	NA	NA
Blue Springs	43	211	26.1	3.4	94	344	21.7	9.2	41	978	127.5	28.2
Cape Girardeau	73	238	26.1	4.6	91	639	41.3	14.6	52	3 602	1 246.9	111.3
Chesterfield	120	555	73.7	13.4	252	2 513	252.1	116.2	42	1 489	207.7	47.8
Columbia	147	566	69.9	10.0	232	1 242	88.8	29.9	62	4 277	1 376.1	120.7
Florissant	33	125	24.5	3.2	61	579	24.2	10.2	NA	NA	NA	NA
Gladstone	38	300	20.2	7.1	71	305	25.8	13.0	NA	NA	NA	NA
Hazelwood	18	104	19.7	2.6	41	D	D	D	36	5 349	6 583.2	258.2
Independence	114	425	48.9	7.9	183	1 079	73.1	29.2	108	3 711	812.5	129.1
Jefferson City	65	172	20.8	3.3	157	881	73.1	29.5	39	3 603	1 046.8	114.9
Joplin	85	394	32.4	6.2	109	750	45.4	19.6	108	5 585	849.8	148.2
Kansas City	516	4 660	816.0	126.5	1 317	17 551	1 907.7	806.7	575	27 888	7 155.5	998.5
Kirkwood	39	184	26.6	5.3	111	482	48.9	20.4	41	1 272	136.5	41.1
Lee's Summit	82	307	40.7	5.5	156	691	65.3	27.1	77	2 577	456.7	72.1
Liberty	30	229	33.2	5.2	71	446	30.9	11.5	23	D	D	D
Maryland Heights	31	454	55.7	16.2	119	2 918	301.1	105.3	132	4 858	980.3	171.6
O'Fallon	21	100	8.0	1.4	37	173	12.4	5.0	54	D	D	D
Raytown	28	121	12.0	1.8	69	427	21.0	9.4	33	663	58.0	17.5
St. Charles	76	624	254.7	15.8	194	1 805	119.8	37.2	83	2 565	360.2	78.7
St. Joseph	85	D	D	D	130	D	D	D	91	D	D	D
St. Louis	401	3 520	402.9	76.7	963	13 915	1 819.8	663.7	802	33 836	8 605.5	1 243.6
St. Peters	39	197	20.0	3.7	64	607	37.2	16.5	69	3 822	1 489.7	126.4
Springfield	283	1 570	136.4	29.6	509	3 691	338.6	111.7	310	18 260	3 673.5	488.3
University City	43	395	26.8	6.9	98	452	49.3	20.2	NA	NA	NA	NA
Wildwood	NA	NA	NA	NA	NA	NA	NA	NA	NA	NA	NA	NA
MONTANA	1 186	4 265	353.4	58.1	2 082	10 735	769.4	297.7	1 160	19 611	4 866.3	560.1
Billings	170	712	77.8	11.4	367	2 502	186.2	69.9	141	D	D	D
Bozeman	74	257	24.5	3.6	181	833	69.2	27.8	75	906	101.3	20.4
Butte-Silver Bow	39	134	11.3	2.0	88	861	60.2	25.7	NA	NA	NA	NA
Great Falls	90	357	26.8	4.2	162	962	66.8	27.7	64	853	221.2	22.1
Helena	70	353	24.1	4.8	139	947	72.2	30.6	NA	NA	NA	NA
Missoula	124	536	42.7	7.1	250	1 553	103.7	43.7	94	1 103	151.0	28.1
NEBRASKA	1 587	8 240	891.1	160.8	3 076	25 720	2 273.4	838.0	1 960	106 690	27 859.2	3 040.5
Bellevue	30	146	12.9	2.1	61	1 166	128.7	48.7	10	1 070	146.1	20.9
Fremont	34	169	13.1	2.4	40	257	11.7	5.2	40	1 469	316.4	34.7
Grand Island	56	170	19.6	2.9	90	401	31.3	11.7	59	5 107	1 714.9	139.1
Kearney	40	D	D	D	58	331	20.7	7.9	21	1 518	214.8	40.9
Lincoln	254	1 460	147.6	25.0	464	D	D	D	234	D	D	D
Omaha	511	4 278	524.0	103.2	1 121	11 882	1 075.5	447.0	497	24 767	6 528.1	787.2

1. Firms subject to federal tax.

Table D. Cities — Accommodation and Foodservices, Entertainment, and Health Care

City	Accommodation and foodservices, 1997				Arts, entertainment, and recreation,[1] 1997				Health care and social assistance,[1] 1997			
	Number of establish-ments	Number of employees	Sales (mil dol)	Annual payroll (mil dol)	Number of establish-ments	Number of employees	Receipts (mil dol)	Annual payroll (mil dol)	Number of establish-ments	Number of employees	Receipts (mil dol)	Annual payroll (mil dol)
	92	93	94	95	96	97	98	99	100	101	102	103
MINNESOTA—Cont'd												
Plymouth	72	2 130	107.4	31.6	17	98	8.8	2.6	120	1 207	83.9	47.9
Richfield	52	1 414	45.4	12.6	7	69	2.9	0.6	63	686	33.7	14.2
Rochester	247	5 624	196.7	56.4	22	322	14.1	4.0	145	2 151	97.4	48.7
Roseville	103	3 362	102.3	31.1	12	152	10.3	1.7	97	1 407	66.0	33.8
St. Cloud	142	3 759	100.5	27.5	26	251	11.9	3.0	179	2 765	213.6	111.4
St. Louis Park	89	2 255	66.5	20.6	24	937	38.7	8.4	164	2 542	165.7	83.5
St. Paul	599	10 532	350.9	105.5	72	764	32.1	9.4	578	9 286	622.3	349.4
Shoreview	22	346	11.9	3.6	4	4	0.4	0.2	46	453	25.3	11.4
Winona	85	1 501	40.0	10.6	10	134	7.3	2.1	57	498	31.4	13.9
Woodbury	64	1 514	49.0	15.2	9	243	8.1	2.5	72	1 075	52.0	23.6
MISSISSIPPI	4 050	84 834	3 064.8	814.5	483	21 239	1 394.0	371.7	4 139	55 529	3 632.3	1 547.0
Biloxi	144	4 911	183.2	51.8	32	8 696	587.8	164.3	118	2 554	192.8	77.2
Columbus	95	1 995	56.4	14.3	17	0	0.0	0.0	113	986	74.7	27.6
Greenville	80	1 400	44.7	11.7	12	0	0.0	0.0	106	1 108	74.5	29.0
Gulfport	156	3 017	87.4	23.0	23	0	0.0	0.0	190	2 279	181.5	68.3
Hattiesburg	161	3 502	101.1	26.5	13	118	5.4	2.2	125	2 489	177.6	100.1
Jackson	396	9 427	293.3	85.0	22	312	21.7	4.4	506	7 381	584.0	263.4
Meridian	138	2 777	85.8	23.5	12	53	2.1	0.6	142	1 932	160.2	80.5
Pascagoula	59	1 272	36.0	9.9	4	8	0.3	0.1	103	821	65.0	29.5
Southaven	38	783	23.5	6.0	5	0	0.0	0.0	56	594	43.6	18.1
Tupelo	134	2 662	78.3	21.7	8	0	0.0	0.0	136	1 928	162.5	91.1
Vicksburg	88	3 193	156.9	37.2	11	0	0.0	0.0	59	1 856	142.8	54.6
MISSOURI	11 150	203 849	6 780.8	1 933.3	1 493	29 484	1 803.9	684.2	10 213	131 485	7 885.4	3 596.7
Ballwin	43	956	28.5	8.4	8	97	2.6	0.8	54	529	39.6	20.0
Blue Springs	83	1 868	52.0	14.9	14	178	4.1	1.7	111	1 126	64.5	24.4
Cape Girardeau	103	2 468	77.0	21.5	12	75	6.4	0.9	162	1 850	146.5	67.9
Chesterfield	78	D	D	D	23	161	9.4	2.5	197	2 562	183.9	88.4
Columbia	278	5 731	173.6	46.6	25	473	14.4	4.3	287	3 639	308.7	123.8
Florissant	131	D	D	D	11	159	4.4	1.6	160	1 701	94.4	44.6
Gladstone	52	D	D	D	4	72	2.0	0.6	79	898	51.8	23.0
Hazelwood	48	1 065	35.8	9.7	8	96	4.4	1.8	29	413	31.2	11.6
Independence	221	4 577	143.1	41.5	20	238	11.9	2.7	214	3 759	233.7	110.8
Jefferson City	118	2 619	80.6	23.6	9	100	9.2	1.6	149	1 863	122.2	69.6
Joplin	187	4 118	116.1	33.9	18	147	4.4	1.1	208	2 049	146.1	66.6
Kansas City	1 053	26 879	1 042.5	312.3	97	3 530	296.5	174.0	949	13 404	1 011.8	508.2
Kirkwood	55	1 113	30.2	9.6	10	79	2.4	0.9	109	776	70.4	31.8
Lee's Summit	89	1 798	53.6	15.6	19	202	5.8	1.8	98	872	49.9	22.3
Liberty	47	816	26.5	8.2	4	52	1.6	0.4	79	852	55.3	29.1
Maryland Heights	75	3 097	126.7	38.8	8	91	19.0	1.3	36	1 834	135.9	49.8
O'Fallon	48	D	D	D	6	72	3.1	0.9	38	385	15.5	5.9
Raytown	60	921	25.4	7.1	6	107	3.6	1.3	59	582	21.6	9.3
St. Charles	176	3 783	113.6	31.9	22	2 085	157.1	46.5	155	2 052	180.6	91.7
St. Joseph	189	3 133	94.2	26.1	17	0	0.0	0.0	173	0	0.0	0.0
St. Louis	954	18 843	686.6	195.8	68	3 603	378.4	209.4	581	9 806	612.5	263.9
St. Peters	111	2 492	65.0	19.2	21	262	7.3	2.2	121	1 339	82.0	34.9
Springfield	545	11 243	335.8	96.2	45	536	16.5	5.0	411	6 608	509.0	244.3
University City	67	D	D	D	5	0	0.0	0.0	64	676	23.1	10.5
Wildwood	NA	NA	NA	NA	NA	NA	NA	NA	NA	NA	NA	NA
MONTANA	3 278	38 533	1 198.9	325.4	639	5 638	306.5	62.2	2 034	15 673	928.6	412.6
Billings	303	6 137	186.2	53.7	75	882	57.1	9.5	310	2 685	216.0	109.3
Bozeman	137	2 339	64.0	18.1	28	325	27.3	4.2	127	1 009	58.9	25.4
Butte-Silver Bow	130	1 354	47.8	12.3	25	185	9.8	2.1	114	1 055	53.4	24.7
Great Falls	223	3 277	95.8	27.0	41	349	18.0	4.2	201	1 721	103.9	40.5
Helena	135	2 186	60.5	16.6	26	421	16.1	3.5	138	1 144	67.2	26.1
Missoula	259	4 322	129.7	36.4	48	505	34.2	7.7	251	2 112	143.4	67.2
NEBRASKA	4 070	61 048	1 726.6	488.2	517	5 957	258.6	58.1	3 057	34 763	2 027.7	970.3
Bellevue	78	1 196	35.1	10.1	9	136	6.6	1.4	42	531	21.2	10.5
Fremont	68	1 295	36.6	9.2	9	70	2.3	0.6	66	615	36.0	15.9
Grand Island	139	2 702	67.7	20.2	13	314	15.7	2.4	103	0	0.0	0.0
Kearney	100	2 225	62.8	18.0	12	118	3.6	1.0	82	745	64.0	35.1
Lincoln	518	10 856	309.7	89.2	51	1 035	36.3	9.7	531	6 264	373.5	182.5
Omaha	960	18 796	590.8	176.1	116	1 870	70.3	17.3	865	10 874	793.5	374.4

1. Firms subject to federal tax.

Table D. Cities — Other Services and Federal Funds

City	Other services,[1] 1997				Selected federal funds, 2002–2003 (mil dol)								
					Procurement contracts		Grants						Direct payments for individuals for educational assistance
	Number of establishments	Number of employees	Receipts (mil dol)	Annual payroll (mil dol)	Defense	Other	Total[2]	Medicaid and other health related	Nutrition and family welfare	Energy and environment	Education	Housing and community development	
	104	105	106	107	108	109	110	111	112	113	114	115	116
MINNESOTA—Cont'd													
Plymouth	71	566	45.6	13.9	82.6	1.1	6.4	0.0	0.0	2.9	0.0	2.0	0.0
Richfield	59	396	27.1	9.0	0.0	0.0	3.0	0.0	0.0	0.0	0.0	2.9	0.0
Rochester	145	1 221	60.3	18.0	8.1	11.1	173.7	159.8	2.0	0.0	1.0	9.7	3.9
Roseville	100	1 166	89.1	29.3	0.7	2.0	5.3	1.2	0.0	0.0	0.0	1.3	0.0
St. Cloud	121	1 006	60.7	18.8	1.2	2.4	11.1	0.1	0.0	0.0	4.2	6.1	11.8
St. Louis Park	111	775	52.2	16.5	0.1	1.5	4.1	0.0	0.0	0.0	0.0	3.6	0.0
St. Paul	420	3 054	177.5	55.7	238.5	87.7	1 005.5	101.9	207.3	84.1	185.2	150.7	42.5
Shoreview	17	180	6.5	2.6	10.4	0.7	0.3	0.0	0.0	0.0	0.0	0.3	0.0
Winona	51	260	14.1	3.7	2.3	1.8	3.6	0.3	0.0	0.0	0.6	1.3	7.0
Woodbury	28	277	15.2	6.0	0.0	0.0	0.0	0.0	0.0	0.0	0.0	0.0	0.0
MISSISSIPPI	3 491	17 449	1 057.1	299.6	2 126.4	499.3	5 318.5	2 763.2	689.0	81.3	474.2	260.6	239.1
Biloxi	66	468	21.7	6.7	4.1	18.2	31.1	8.2	0.5	0.0	2.9	9.2	0.0
Columbus	88	501	29.8	8.5	23.8	0.7	5.7	0.0	0.0	0.0	0.0	3.1	2.9
Greenville	91	438	24.5	7.1	2.6	1.8	17.6	0.0	6.2	0.0	4.8	4.8	0.4
Gulfport	137	918	48.9	16.7	75.8	29.4	34.3	0.0	9.1	0.3	2.2	6.8	0.8
Hattiesburg	75	653	40.3	11.9	13.3	2.7	56.2	5.0	5.1	2.7	2.7	9.9	21.7
Jackson	342	2 848	166.8	52.3	50.4	40.3	787.8	127.8	161.4	55.6	165.4	83.3	30.0
Meridian	115	609	30.8	9.2	28.9	4.0	10.2	2.6	0.0	0.0	0.6	3.2	6.3
Pascagoula	60	349	19.9	5.3	1 358.3	2.4	8.2	0.9	0.0	0.0	0.4	3.0	0.0
Southaven	54	245	14.2	3.7	0.0	0.3	3.8	0.0	0.0	0.0	0.0	3.8	0.0
Tupelo	97	780	47.0	20.6	0.3	2.3	16.4	0.2	5.5	2.3	0.7	3.9	4.4
Vicksburg	59	244	13.1	3.8	51.3	15.4	4.5	0.0	0.0	0.0	0.0	3.9	0.0
MISSOURI	9 427	52 060	3 203.3	963.1	6 243.8	1 747.9	8 655.1	4 617.2	1 033.0	106.6	684.0	609.3	298.8
Ballwin	42	222	13.8	5.0	5.8	17.1	0.0	0.0	0.0	0.0	0.0	0.0	0.1
Blue Springs	102	662	25.9	9.3	0.1	0.1	3.1	0.0	0.0	0.0	1.0	1.6	0.0
Cape Girardeau	82	442	26.9	8.4	0.7	44.7	13.0	2.3	0.0	1.5	2.7	0.9	7.6
Chesterfield	67	517	20.6	8.0	6.9	18.0	2.8	1.0	0.0	1.2	0.0	0.0	28.8
Columbia	183	1 155	59.4	19.0	4.5	6.4	126.5	42.7	4.1	6.9	12.8	8.9	19.0
Florissant	106	582	32.7	11.3	0.5	0.3	2.9	0.0	0.0	0.0	1.3	0.3	0.4
Gladstone	68	311	19.5	5.8	0.0	0.1	0.2	0.0	0.0	0.0	0.0	0.0	0.0
Hazelwood	34	226	14.6	4.7	10.7	3.4	0.0	0.0	0.0	0.0	0.0	0.0	0.0
Independence	215	1 180	59.9	20.3	284.6	13.4	30.8	0.0	0.0	0.0	2.0	21.5	0.3
Jefferson City	84	498	23.9	7.4	3.0	3.9	962.3	121.0	226.6	78.0	205.2	10.2	3.6
Joplin	150	929	50.2	14.7	9.9	170.7	14.2	0.8	5.6	1.8	0.6	5.3	8.1
Kansas City	793	6 083	420.5	123.3	122.5	696.1	250.6	66.1	19.5	1.3	10.3	123.2	45.6
Kirkwood	46	294	20.1	6.8	0.3	0.0	0.8	0.0	0.0	0.0	0.0	0.7	0.0
Lee's Summit	94	507	27.1	9.1	0.6	9.0	7.1	0.0	0.0	0.0	0.5	4.4	0.0
Liberty	55	256	13.8	4.3	0.0	0.1	2.5	0.0	0.0	0.0	0.0	2.5	1.1
Maryland Heights	51	485	40.4	12.7	51.9	35.9	0.0	0.0	0.0	0.0	0.0	0.0	0.0
O'Fallon	71	486	32.6	11.2	0.3	0.0	0.7	0.0	0.0	0.0	0.0	0.0	0.0
Raytown	69	525	36.8	10.2	0.0	0.0	0.9	0.0	0.2	0.0	0.0	0.7	0.0
St. Charles	141	711	40.9	12.5	228.9	2.6	11.0	1.5	4.6	0.5	0.0	3.8	3.5
St. Joseph	151	755	44.4	12.7	1.9	7.7	21.7	3.1	2.8	0.0	0.5	14.1	5.6
St. Louis	673	4 693	334.1	101.2	4 906.9	263.6	423.6	74.8	31.6	5.0	14.4	201.7	54.8
St. Peters	111	816	38.0	13.6	3.0	6.7	0.1	0.0	0.0	0.0	0.0	0.1	2.1
Springfield	438	3 184	166.0	51.8	1.6	21.5	51.1	2.6	11.7	0.7	4.2	19.5	29.1
University City	66	680	37.2	14.1	0.0	0.0	2.0	0.0	0.0	0.0	0.0	1.9	0.0
Wildwood	NA	NA	NA	NA	0.1	0.0	0.0	0.0	0.0	0.0	0.0	0.0	0.0
MONTANA	1 612	6 986	449.1	117.0	190.0	307.3	1 938.5	652.7	219.4	37.6	216.9	86.2	61.7
Billings	238	1 477	94.4	26.8	5.8	33.0	29.5	6.1	3.5	0.1	3.6	8.2	6.8
Bozeman	76	443	20.9	6.1	6.1	4.7	80.1	22.5	2.1	3.5	2.5	1.1	10.2
Butte-Silver Bow	71	282	16.6	4.3	5.8	16.0	6.9	0.4	0.0	0.8	0.3	1.7	2.8
Great Falls	127	606	36.6	9.7	9.3	5.0	28.0	4.5	2.3	0.4	1.7	8.9	3.6
Helena	67	367	20.9	5.9	1.6	8.8	303.2	32.5	48.6	22.0	57.8	25.9	9.6
Missoula	155	805	49.9	14.5	3.3	21.6	48.6	12.7	2.9	2.9	4.9	5.4	13.4
NEBRASKA	3 288	16 940	1 039.2	297.1	312.2	296.1	2 511.9	1 065.7	346.9	38.0	236.7	135.1	84.7
Bellevue	58	268	15.8	5.0	27.3	0.2	18.0	0.0	0.0	0.0	14.2	3.5	2.4
Fremont	67	285	13.7	3.9	0.9	4.3	1.5	0.0	0.7	0.0	0.0	0.6	1.6
Grand Island	107	639	36.8	10.4	6.3	14.3	17.2	0.0	0.1	0.0	0.9	4.0	4.1
Kearney	67	398	25.0	7.3	0.1	0.2	5.9	0.0	2.5	0.0	0.5	2.3	5.2
Lincoln	395	2 466	130.8	41.3	46.3	20.3	465.0	59.9	81.6	35.5	77.2	45.1	25.0
Omaha	817	6 339	367.5	119.9	23.2	98.0	158.9	60.7	8.0	0.7	12.9	39.1	26.1

1. Firms subject to federal tax.   2. Includes program categories not shown separately. State totals include additional categories not allocated by city.

Table D. Cities — **City Government Finances**

City	City government finances, 2002									
	General revenue							General expenditure		
		Intergovernmental		Taxes					Per capita¹ (dollars)	
					Per capita¹ (dollars)					
	Total (mil dol)	Total (mil dol)	Percent from state government	Total (mil dol)	Total	Property	Sales and gross receipts	Total (mil dol)	Total	Capital outlays
	117	118	119	120	121	122	123	124	125	126
MINNESOTA—Cont'd										
Plymouth	50.8	12.4	77.0	17.0	253	218	0	44.3	658	185
Richfield	46.2	20.0	67.4	13.3	384	337	7	47.2	1 360	721
Rochester	149.1	20.9	80.8	37.3	412	258	123	152.3	1 683	400
Roseville	39.7	5.9	78.9	17.7	528	468	7	33.2	993	193
St. Cloud	92.2	23.5	96.4	22.3	373	255	85	90.1	1 507	551
St. Louis Park	65.2	11.8	89.9	17.6	398	353	0	62.5	1 417	430
St. Paul	510.5	189.7	68.7	127.6	449	294	125	461.5	1 625	292
Shoreview	18.3	2.4	78.7	7.0	258	232	7	16.0	595	88
Winona	27.6	9.8	96.1	7.6	287	230	35	22.3	839	125
Woodbury	51.3	11.6	32.6	15.2	309	266	0	64.6	1 314	704
MISSISSIPPI	X	X	X	X	X	X	X	X	X	X
Biloxi	73.5	37.5	96.7	19.0	381	313	52	78.3	1 572	33
Columbus	25.0	12.8	93.6	5.3	211	152	35	22.4	888	89
Greenville	30.9	12.3	99.8	10.6	262	188	25	31.1	773	118
Gulfport	263.5	25.6	100.0	24.1	332	219	97	266.1	3 670	172
Hattiesburg	45.5	18.4	84.1	16.8	368	257	104	41.0	895	117
Jackson	179.3	61.9	66.0	64.8	358	303	41	168.3	930	154
Meridian	33.5	13.0	100.0	12.1	307	257	44	30.5	771	16
Pascagoula	21.9	7.8	80.1	6.5	250	202	42	24.3	934	140
Southaven	NA	NA	NA	NA	NA	NA	NA	NA	NA	NA
Tupelo	44.6	25.2	84.1	7.4	211	189	11	45.1	1 289	364
Vicksburg	34.4	17.1	96.9	8.8	334	296	0	34.0	1 298	285
MISSOURI	X	X	X	X	X	X	X	X	X	X
Ballwin	NA	NA	NA	NA	NA	NA	NA	NA	NA	NA
Blue Springs	31.4	4.4	50.5	13.2	267	77	182	32.8	664	155
Cape Girardeau	39.0	3.1	96.4	24.8	696	43	623	32.1	901	105
Chesterfield	31.4	15.2	18.4	12.6	268	149	98	40.0	848	473
Columbia	93.4	11.3	53.2	42.3	487	86	393	102.3	1 176	282
Florissant	22.9	15.5	18.2	3.3	66	0	47	23.3	467	89
Gladstone	NA	NA	NA	NA	NA	NA	NA	NA	NA	NA
Hazelwood	20.1	8.6	16.2	8.7	334	50	81	22.4	861	165
Independence	99.6	24.0	44.7	47.8	423	65	339	120.3	1 064	292
Jefferson City	35.0	1.7	100.0	22.1	564	92	463	36.7	939	274
Joplin	36.7	4.8	70.2	22.4	484	21	449	40.6	878	230
Kansas City	787.2	79.5	33.3	466.8	1 053	180	470	710.2	1 601	449
Kirkwood	NA	NA	NA	NA	NA	NA	NA	NA	NA	NA
Lee's Summit	88.3	8.0	30.4	49.8	665	241	400	82.3	1 098	369
Liberty	21.6	1.6	37.9	11.7	426	127	283	28.1	1 021	396
Maryland Heights	37.4	26.5	65.2	5.5	214	8	164	26.4	1 025	384
O'Fallon	42.6	1.2	100.0	23.7	398	115	250	50.9	853	40
Raytown	NA	NA	NA	NA	NA	NA	NA	NA	NA	NA
St. Charles	84.4	18.9	92.6	50.7	834	268	545	93.5	1 539	740
St. Joseph	71.2	10.6	69.2	34.3	469	124	309	68.7	939	185
St. Louis	833.7	132.4	39.9	427.7	1 264	171	587	912.1	2 696	728
St. Peters	48.2	6.1	56.1	26.2	490	106	375	57.9	1 081	348
Springfield	183.7	24.8	44.6	85.7	568	55	490	240.6	1 593	675
University City	28.4	10.1	20.6	11.2	297	128	152	25.8	681	23
Wildwood	7.8	5.3	18.4	2.0	58	0	54	6.7	198	4
MONTANA	X	X	X	X	X	X	X	X	X	X
Billings	76.1	18.8	66.7	19.0	206	158	0	78.2	850	94
Bozeman	28.2	5.8	74.5	8.0	272	246	0	26.7	905	156
Butte-Silver Bow	41.7	11.4	61.6	16.1	481	463	0	36.0	1 079	51
Great Falls	41.5	8.6	84.5	13.1	234	214	0	43.0	766	90
Helena	33.2	9.9	86.0	6.4	241	209	0	29.6	1 123	142
Missoula	34.8	5.6	79.7	15.1	254	221	0	41.7	701	62
NEBRASKA	X	X	X	X	X	X	X	X	X	X
Bellevue	39.9	5.3	80.2	18.1	391	152	140	37.5	810	369
Fremont	28.8	4.6	59.3	15.4	613	113	178	23.0	911	279
Grand Island	43.3	6.3	90.8	18.5	430	157	236	42.9	997	247
Kearney	25.6	7.6	69.7	6.9	248	44	197	17.7	633	60
Lincoln	203.4	56.3	68.9	90.1	388	128	191	192.8	830	243
Omaha	389.7	57.8	70.0	234.3	587	212	313	460.9	1 154	419

1. Based on population estimated as of July 1 of the year shown.

City	City government finances, 2002 (cont'd)									
	General expenditure									
	Percent of total for—									
	Public welfare	Highways	Parking facilities	Education	Health and hospitals	Police protection	Sewerage and sanitation	Parks and recreation	Housing and community development	Interest on debt
	127	128	129	130	131	132	133	134	135	136
MINNESOTA—Cont'd										
Plymouth	0.0	21.3	0.0	0.0	0.0	13.8	12.8	13.1	0.9	10.0
Richfield	0.0	39.1	0.0	0.0	0.1	12.1	5.0	8.0	8.0	3.0
Rochester	0.0	9.9	1.8	0.0	0.1	7.3	7.6	14.4	1.8	36.1
Roseville	0.0	17.0	0.0	0.0	0.0	12.7	12.5	14.0	1.0	18.9
St. Cloud	0.0	17.6	0.8	0.0	1.4	10.4	13.8	5.5	0.5	18.6
St. Louis Park	0.0	9.2	0.0	0.0	0.0	8.4	9.5	8.5	25.5	26.5
St. Paul	0.0	8.5	0.9	0.0	0.9	13.0	5.6	18.9	18.4	6.3
Shoreview	0.0	15.6	0.0	0.0	0.2	7.4	16.7	25.8	7.9	9.5
Winona	0.3	11.1	0.0	0.2	0.0	14.7	6.3	9.8	10.5	13.4
Woodbury	0.0	32.7	0.0	0.0	2.0	7.1	6.0	23.4	0.0	11.6
MISSISSIPPI	X	X	X	X	X	X	X	X	X	X
Biloxi	0.3	29.8	0.0	0.0	0.0	15.9	12.5	6.0	1.0	2.5
Columbus	0.0	11.3	0.0	0.0	0.0	20.2	12.9	2.3	1.9	1.7
Greenville	0.0	13.2	0.0	0.0	1.3	26.4	11.9	3.6	0.5	2.4
Gulfport	0.0	2.4	0.0	0.0	74.0	6.2	4.0	1.8	2.0	0.0
Hattiesburg	0.0	13.4	0.5	0.0	1.2	17.5	11.1	8.3	1.8	9.4
Jackson	2.0	10.4	0.0	0.0	0.4	17.2	15.7	5.9	2.4	4.3
Meridian	0.0	20.3	0.0	0.0	0.0	17.5	13.9	6.3	4.0	5.6
Pascagoula	0.3	10.4	0.0	0.0	0.0	17.5	22.0	5.5	4.0	1.8
Southaven	NA	NA	NA	NA	NA	NA	NA	NA	NA	NA
Tupelo	0.0	10.7	0.0	0.0	0.0	17.5	9.9	10.7	0.0	8.2
Vicksburg	0.1	8.3	0.0	0.0	0.1	23.7	9.0	6.2	1.1	2.8
MISSOURI	X	X	X	X	X	X	X	X	X	X
Ballwin	NA	NA	NA	NA	NA	NA	NA	NA	NA	NA
Blue Springs	0.0	13.4	0.0	0.0	0.0	23.2	21.1	17.6	2.1	7.9
Cape Girardeau	0.0	21.2	0.0	0.0	0.8	15.0	19.2	9.8	3.3	6.6
Chesterfield	0.0	26.6	0.0	0.0	0.0	15.7	4.2	4.9	0.0	8.5
Columbia	0.9	11.0	1.7	0.0	2.9	12.4	24.8	12.0	1.8	3.1
Florissant	0.9	15.6	0.0	0.0	2.0	30.1	0.0	26.1	0.4	1.9
Gladstone	NA	NA	NA	NA	NA	NA	NA	NA	NA	NA
Hazelwood	0.0	7.4	0.0	0.0	0.0	23.9	1.0	6.7	2.9	4.7
Independence	0.0	9.3	0.0	0.0	1.8	16.2	12.2	7.4	3.5	7.0
Jefferson City	0.0	5.6	1.7	0.0	0.0	16.4	19.1	8.9	0.0	4.7
Joplin	0.0	27.5	0.0	0.0	3.1	16.7	10.8	8.6	1.9	2.5
Kansas City	0.8	11.4	0.1	0.0	3.4	16.0	6.9	9.8	1.9	3.3
Kirkwood	NA	NA	NA	NA	NA	NA	NA	NA	NA	NA
Lee's Summit	0.0	20.9	0.0	0.0	0.0	13.9	14.0	15.8	1.1	3.2
Liberty	0.8	14.4	0.0	0.0	0.0	12.2	21.5	24.7	5.0	2.0
Maryland Heights	0.0	40.9	0.0	0.0	0.0	24.9	0.4	12.4	0.0	1.7
O'Fallon	0.0	10.3	0.0	0.0	0.0	10.9	7.1	5.0	0.0	34.9
Raytown	NA	NA	NA	NA	NA	NA	NA	NA	NA	NA
St. Charles	0.0	17.9	0.5	0.0	0.0	18.5	7.0	6.1	0.4	4.5
St. Joseph	0.5	18.8	0.4	0.0	2.9	11.1	10.6	8.6	4.5	18.2
St. Louis	0.0	1.9	1.4	0.0	3.6	15.1	2.0	2.9	5.4	7.0
St. Peters	0.0	21.2	0.0	0.0	0.9	13.9	16.3	11.7	0.1	3.6
Springfield	2.4	6.3	0.0	0.0	1.4	14.3	13.0	9.8	4.8	5.3
University City	0.0	10.6	0.3	0.0	0.0	30.7	9.8	5.1	0.0	5.9
Wildwood	0.0	46.7	0.0	0.0	0.0	25.8	0.0	0.1	0.0	0.0
MONTANA	X	X	X	X	X	X	X	X	X	X
Billings	0.0	7.3	2.2	0.0	0.0	24.8	15.8	6.6	4.2	3.2
Bozeman	3.4	4.8	0.4	0.0	1.5	13.5	19.1	5.5	0.0	3.3
Butte-Silver Bow	0.2	8.6	0.0	0.0	7.8	15.3	9.0	5.4	3.8	9.5
Great Falls	0.0	20.2	1.4	0.0	0.5	14.8	16.3	8.5	5.3	3.1
Helena	0.0	11.2	3.6	0.0	0.3	16.0	24.2	8.6	0.5	4.8
Missoula	0.0	5.0	0.0	0.0	4.3	17.6	10.7	6.7	3.0	5.1
NEBRASKA	X	X	X	X	X	X	X	X	X	X
Bellevue	0.0	25.8	0.0	0.0	0.0	12.7	8.8	2.5	0.1	3.4
Fremont	0.0	15.8	0.0	0.0	0.0	10.7	32.9	8.8	1.6	1.3
Grand Island	0.2	22.6	0.0	0.0	1.7	14.0	12.1	8.7	0.7	3.8
Kearney	0.0	10.6	0.0	0.0	0.0	22.1	18.7	12.8	6.4	3.9
Lincoln	0.0	20.8	1.2	0.0	7.1	11.8	5.6	6.7	4.5	2.6
Omaha	0.0	11.1	0.0	0.0	0.0	15.3	11.2	8.1	1.2	4.8

City	City government finances, 2002 (cont'd) Debt outstanding Total (mil dol)	Per capita[1] (dollars)	Percent utility	City government employment, 2002	Climate[2] Average daily temperature (degrees Fahrenheit) Mean January	July	Limits January[3]	July[4]	Annual precipitation (inches)	Heating degree days	Cooling degree days
	137	138	139	140	141	142	143	144	145	146	147
MINNESOTA—Cont'd											
Plymouth	70.3	1 045	0.4	273	11.8	73.6	2.8	84.0	28.32	7 981	682
Richfield	29.5	849	0.0	135	11.8	73.6	2.8	84.0	28.32	7 981	682
Rochester	1 227.0	13 556	3.0	852	11.5	70.9	2.6	81.8	29.66	8 250	472
Roseville	72.7	2 174	0.0	217	11.8	73.6	2.8	84.0	28.32	7 981	682
St. Cloud	360.7	6 037	17.3	461	8.1	70.1	-2.4	82.6	27.43	8 928	415
St. Louis Park	293.1	6 644	0.0	301	11.8	73.6	2.8	84.0	28.32	7 981	682
St. Paul	816.4	2 874	3.8	3 064	11.8	73.6	2.8	84.0	28.32	7 981	682
Shoreview	33.9	1 257	7.9	88	NA	NA	NA	NA	NA	NA	NA
Winona	51.3	1 932	11.9	201	14.1	73.2	4.0	85.0	32.57	7 694	662
Woodbury	120.5	2 451	1.4	175	NA	NA	NA	NA	NA	NA	NA
MISSISSIPPI	X	X	X	X	X	X	X	X	X	X	X
Biloxi	37.7	757	0.0	598	51.0	82.3	42.3	90.0	61.76	1 507	2 666
Columbus	46.7	1 850	83.9	336	NA	NA	NA	NA	NA	NA	NA
Greenville	25.1	624	53.0	506	41.2	81.9	31.0	92.5	53.38	2 778	2 153
Gulfport	0.0	0	0.0	2 630	50.7	82.3	41.2	91.3	62.72	1 551	2 645
Hattiesburg	75.4	1 646	18.8	713	46.0	81.3	34.3	91.8	60.58	2 180	2 265
Jackson	306.7	1 696	34.7	2 325	44.1	81.5	32.7	92.4	55.37	2 467	2 215
Meridian	57.8	1 462	53.8	513	45.0	81.0	33.4	92.1	56.71	2 444	2 138
Pascagoula	9.7	372	33.7	308	48.9	82.1	39.3	90.3	63.72	1 761	2 617
Southaven	NA	NA	NA	248	NA	NA	NA	NA	NA	NA	NA
Tupelo	66.5	1 900	15.2	476	39.9	80.6	30.9	90.7	55.87	3 079	1 908
Vicksburg	15.8	604	15.1	609	NA	NA	NA	NA	NA	NA	NA
MISSOURI	X	X	X	X	X	X	X	X	X	X	X
Ballwin	NA	NA	NA	176	NA	NA	NA	NA	NA	NA	NA
Blue Springs	38.7	782	1.9	279	25.7	78.5	16.7	88.7	37.62	5 393	1 288
Cape Girardeau	50.0	1 402	19.2	546	31.7	79.6	22.6	90.2	46.31	4 386	1 543
Chesterfield	49.7	1 054	0.0	190	29.3	79.8	20.8	89.3	37.51	4 758	1 534
Columbia	118.2	1 359	51.0	1 168	27.6	77.4	18.5	88.6	39.05	5 212	1 189
Florissant	6.9	138	0.0	305	29.3	79.8	20.8	89.3	37.51	4 758	1 534
Gladstone	NA	NA	NA	169	25.7	78.5	16.7	88.7	37.62	5 393	1 288
Hazelwood	17.8	685	0.0	196	NA	NA	NA	NA	NA	NA	NA
Independence	190.7	1 687	30.0	1 188	25.7	78.5	16.7	88.7	37.62	5 393	1 288
Jefferson City	62.8	1 607	0.0	392	27.4	77.4	15.3	90.1	38.43	5 302	1 175
Joplin	17.6	382	0.0	417	32.3	80.0	22.7	90.2	43.23	4 303	1 560
Kansas City	877.6	1 979	17.5	6 872	25.7	78.5	16.7	88.7	37.62	5 393	1 288
Kirkwood	NA	NA	NA	281	29.3	79.8	20.8	89.3	37.51	4 758	1 534
Lee's Summit	92.9	1 239	17.5	551	28.0	78.3	17.5	90.2	39.84	4 993	1 316
Liberty	30.9	1 121	39.7	203	NA	NA	NA	NA	NA	NA	NA
Maryland Heights	9.3	360	0.0	204	29.3	79.8	20.8	89.3	37.51	4 758	1 534
O'Fallon	310.6	5 204	5.8	236	NA	NA	NA	NA	NA	NA	NA
Raytown	NA	NA	NA	180	25.7	78.5	16.7	88.7	37.62	5 393	1 288
St. Charles	97.0	1 597	0.0	485	27.5	77.6	17.2	89.2	37.74	5 179	1 226
St. Joseph	214.4	2 931	0.0	634	24.6	78.1	14.7	88.9	35.69	5 590	1 254
St. Louis	1 654.8	4 891	2.5	7 329	28.4	78.4	18.9	89.6	37.86	5 001	1 329
St. Peters	66.6	1 243	26.1	460	27.5	77.6	17.2	89.2	37.74	5 179	1 226
Springfield	386.6	2 560	43.9	2 785	31.1	78.1	20.4	89.6	43.04	4 638	1 320
University City	19.9	526	0.0	434	29.3	79.8	20.8	89.3	37.51	4 758	1 534
Wildwood	0.0	0	0.0	14	NA	NA	NA	NA	NA	NA	NA
MONTANA	X	X	X	X	X	X	X	X	X	X	X
Billings	39.3	427	6.2	815	22.8	72.5	13.7	86.7	15.08	7 164	652
Bozeman	19.6	664	12.2	268	NA	NA	NA	NA	NA	NA	NA
Butte-Silver Bow	65.0	1 946	33.4	472	NA	NA	NA	NA	NA	NA	NA
Great Falls	32.1	573	29.1	492	21.2	68.2	11.6	83.3	15.21	7 741	388
Helena	31.6	1 200	23.3	267	NA	NA	NA	NA	NA	NA	NA
Missoula	36.0	605	0.0	350	22.7	66.8	15.4	83.4	13.46	7 792	280
NEBRASKA	X	X	X	X	X	X	X	X	X	X	X
Bellevue	19.8	429	0.0	236	21.1	76.9	10.9	87.9	29.86	6 300	1 072
Fremont	13.0	517	65.5	289	NA	NA	NA	NA	NA	NA	NA
Grand Island	87.0	2 022	70.2	435	21.9	76.7	11.1	88.5	24.90	6 421	997
Kearney	13.1	470	13.1	235	NA	NA	NA	NA	NA	NA	NA
Lincoln	396.3	1 706	80.1	2 625	21.3	78.2	10.1	90.0	28.26	6 278	1 134
Omaha	468.8	1 174	0.0	2 835	21.1	76.9	10.9	87.9	29.86	6 300	1 072

1. Based on the population estimated as of July 1 of the year shown.   2. Represents normal values based on the 30-year period, 1961–1990.   3. Average daily minimum.   4. Average daily maximum.

Table D. Cities — Land Area and Population

STATE Place code	City	Land area,[1] 2000 (sq km)	Population, 2003 Total persons	Rank	Per square kilometer	White	Black	Am. Indian, Alaska Native	Asian and Pacific Islander	Other race	Hispanic or Latino[2]	Non-Hispanic White
		1	2	3	4	5	6	7	8	9	10	11
32 00000	NEVADA	284 448.0	2 241 154	X	7.9	78.4	7.5	2.1	6.4	9.7	19.7	65.2
32 09700	Carson City	371.3	55 311	557	149.0	87.2	2.1	3.3	2.5	7.2	14.2	78.5
32 31900	Henderson	206.4	214 852	85	1 040.9	87.5	4.4	1.4	6.2	4.4	10.7	78.2
32 40000	Las Vegas	293.5	517 017	30	1 761.6	73.2	11.3	1.5	6.9	11.6	23.6	58.0
32 51800	North Las Vegas	203.3	144 502	152	710.8	59.8	20.2	1.5	5.4	18.2	37.6	37.1
32 60600	Reno	179.0	193 882	109	1 083.1	80.5	3.2	2.1	7.2	10.8	19.2	69.2
32 68400	Sparks	62.0	77 295	362	1 246.7	81.4	2.9	1.9	6.8	10.7	19.7	69.5
33 00000	NEW HAMPSHIRE	23 227.3	1 287 687	X	55.4	97.0	1.0	0.6	1.7	0.9	1.7	95.1
33 14200	Concord	166.5	41 823	770	251.2	96.7	1.4	0.8	1.9	0.7	1.5	94.6
33 18820	Dover	69.2	28 216	1 124	407.7	95.8	1.5	0.7	2.8	0.7	1.1	93.8
33 45140	Manchester	85.5	108 871	215	1 273.3	93.3	2.6	0.7	2.8	2.5	4.6	89.3
33 50260	Nashua	80.0	87 285	305	1 091.1	90.5	2.5	0.6	4.4	3.7	6.2	86.5
33 65140	Rochester	116.9	29 654	1 078	253.7	98.0	0.8	0.6	1.2	0.5	0.9	96.6
34 00000	NEW JERSEY	19 210.8	8 638 396	X	449.7	74.4	14.4	0.6	6.3	6.9	13.3	66.0
34 02080	Atlantic City	29.4	40 385	792	1 373.6	29.2	45.9	1.2	11.7	16.7	24.9	19.4
34 03580	Bayonne	14.6	60 905	482	4 171.6	82.0	6.3	0.5	5.0	10.4	17.8	69.9
34 05170	Bergenfield Borough	7.5	26 181	1 198	3 490.8	64.9	7.8	0.7	21.5	8.3	17.0	54.0
34 10000	Camden	22.8	80 089	341	3 512.7	19.0	55.3	1.2	3.3	25.4	38.8	7.1
34 13690	Clifton	29.3	79 823	343	2 724.3	80.3	3.3	0.5	7.3	13.4	19.8	67.6
34 19390	East Orange	10.2	69 212	408	6 785.5	4.5	92.8	0.9	1.0	4.9	4.7	2.7
34 21000	Elizabeth	31.7	123 215	187	3 886.9	60.2	21.6	0.8	3.0	20.5	49.5	26.8
34 21480	Englewood	12.8	26 106	1 200	2 039.5	44.8	41.5	1.0	6.1	11.5	21.8	32.0
34 22470	Fair Lawn Borough	13.4	31 585	1 014	2 357.1	92.7	1.0	0.2	5.5	2.1	5.5	87.7
34 24420	Fort Lee Borough	6.6	37 139	869	5 627.1	64.6	2.1	0.2	32.4	2.9	7.9	57.4
34 25770	Garfield	5.5	29 701	1 076	5 400.2	85.4	4.0	0.6	3.2	10.1	20.1	72.4
34 28680	Hackensack	10.7	43 493	739	4 064.8	56.3	26.5	1.1	8.2	13.3	25.9	39.9
34 32250	Hoboken	3.3	39 482	818	11 964.2	83.1	5.1	0.5	5.0	9.3	20.2	70.5
34 36000	Jersey City	38.6	239 097	73	6 194.2	37.7	30.0	1.0	17.9	19.6	28.3	23.6
34 36510	Kearny	23.7	39 853	805	1 681.6	79.5	4.6	0.6	6.2	13.5	27.3	60.3
34 40350	Linden	28.0	39 877	804	1 424.2	68.5	24.4	0.5	2.8	7.7	14.4	57.9
34 41310	Long Branch	13.5	31 523	1 018	2 335.0	71.5	20.0	0.8	2.3	9.9	20.7	56.9
34 46680	Millville	109.7	27 119	1 163	247.2	77.9	16.2	1.2	1.1	6.1	11.2	71.6
34 51000	Newark	61.6	277 911	64	4 511.5	29.4	55.0	0.8	1.8	17.6	29.5	14.2
34 51210	New Brunswick	13.5	49 803	636	3 689.1	51.7	24.5	1.2	6.1	21.0	39.0	32.9
34 55950	Paramus Borough	27.1	26 503	1 190	978.0	80.4	1.3	0.2	18.0	1.6	4.9	75.5
34 56550	Passaic	8.1	68 528	413	8 460.2	39.0	15.2	1.2	6.3	43.5	62.5	18.3
34 57000	Paterson	21.9	150 782	146	6 885.0	35.0	34.6	1.0	2.8	32.9	50.1	13.2
34 58200	Perth Amboy	12.4	48 447	658	3 907.0	50.9	11.4	1.1	2.0	40.3	69.8	18.9
34 59190	Plainfield	15.6	48 025	665	3 078.5	24.4	63.9	1.1	1.5	14.0	25.2	11.5
34 61530	Rahway	10.3	26 779	1 183	2 599.9	62.3	28.7	0.8	4.1	7.6	13.9	53.2
34 65790	Sayreville Borough	41.2	42 064	765	1 021.0	78.0	9.1	0.4	11.4	3.3	7.3	72.0
34 74000	Trenton	19.8	85 314	312	4 308.8	34.5	53.6	0.8	1.6	12.9	21.5	24.6
34 74630	Union City	3.3	66 573	432	20 173.6	64.2	5.3	1.2	2.8	33.7	82.3	13.3
34 76070	Vineland	177.9	57 057	533	320.7	69.8	14.8	1.1	1.6	16.1	30.0	54.8
34 79040	Westfield	17.4	29 951	1 065	1 721.3	91.1	4.3	0.3	4.8	1.0	2.8	87.9
34 79610	West New York	2.6	46 348	696	17 826.2	66.7	4.8	1.1	3.5	31.8	78.7	15.5
35 00000	NEW MEXICO	314 309.4	1 874 614	X	6.0	69.9	2.3	10.5	1.7	19.4	42.1	44.7
35 01780	Alamogordo	50.1	35 551	906	709.6	79.1	6.4	1.8	2.7	14.5	32.0	57.8
35 02000	Albuquerque	467.9	471 856	33	1 008.5	75.3	3.8	4.9	3.1	17.5	39.9	49.9
35 12150	Carlsbad	73.5	25 303	1 219	344.3	79.7	2.6	1.9	1.0	17.4	36.7	58.8
35 16420	Clovis	58.0	32 815	983	565.8	74.3	8.3	1.8	2.4	17.0	33.4	55.6
35 25800	Farmington	68.8	41 420	775	602.0	73.4	1.3	18.4	0.9	9.2	17.7	62.8
35 32520	Hobbs	49.0	28 311	1 119	577.8	66.9	7.4	1.8	0.6	27.2	42.2	48.9
35 39380	Las Cruces	134.9	76 990	364	570.7	72.6	2.9	2.7	1.9	24.2	51.7	42.0
35 63460	Rio Rancho	190.2	58 981	511	310.1	82.0	3.4	3.4	2.4	13.1	27.7	64.1
35 64930	Roswell	74.9	44 228	727	590.5	73.9	2.9	2.1	1.1	23.6	44.3	50.9
35 70500	Santa Fe	96.7	66 476	434	687.4	80.1	1.0	3.3	1.9	18.3	47.8	47.1
36 00000	NEW YORK	122 283.1	19 190 115	X	156.9	70.0	17.0	0.9	6.4	9.1	15.1	62.0
36 01000	Albany	55.4	93 919	271	1 695.3	65.1	29.9	1.0	4.0	3.2	5.6	61.1
36 03078	Auburn	21.7	28 121	1 127	1 295.9	89.9	8.6	0.8	0.8	1.7	2.8	87.4
36 06607	Binghamton	27.0	46 310	697	1 715.2	85.7	10.0	0.8	4.0	2.8	3.9	81.7
36 11000	Buffalo	105.2	285 018	60	2 709.3	56.2	38.6	1.4	1.8	4.7	7.5	51.8
36 24229	Elmira	18.9	30 336	1 055	1 605.1	84.4	14.9	0.9	0.8	1.9	3.1	80.8
36 27485	Freeport	11.9	43 726	734	3 674.5	46.8	34.7	1.2	2.0	21.1	33.5	31.6
36 29113	Glen Cove	17.2	26 781	1 182	1 557.0	82.9	7.0	0.6	5.0	7.8	20.0	68.2
36 33139	Hempstead	9.5	53 162	597	5 596.0	28.5	54.7	1.4	2.0	18.4	31.8	13.2

1. Dry land or land partially or temporarily covered by water. 2. Hispanic or Latino persons may be of any race.

City	Under 5 years	5 to 17 years	18 to 24 years	25 to 34 years	35 to 44 years	45 to 54 years	55 to 64 years	65 to 74 years	75 years and over	Percent female	Census counts 1990	Census counts 2000	Percent change 1990–2000	Percent change 2000–2003
	12	13	14	15	16	17	18	19	20	21	22	23	24	25
NEVADA	7.3	18.3	9.0	15.3	16.1	13.5	9.5	6.6	4.4	49.1	1 201 675	1 998 257	66.3	12.2
Carson City	6.3	17.1	7.9	12.9	16.0	14.7	10.2	7.8	7.1	48.3	40 443	52 457	29.7	5.4
Henderson	6.8	18.3	7.9	15.4	17.1	14.4	10.0	6.4	3.7	50.4	64 948	175 381	170.0	22.5
Las Vegas	7.7	18.2	8.8	16.1	15.9	12.5	9.2	7.1	4.5	49.2	258 877	478 434	85.3	8.1
North Las Vegas	10.4	23.6	9.6	18.5	15.8	10.0	6.4	3.7	2.0	49.0	47 849	115 488	141.4	25.1
Reno	7.0	16.2	11.8	15.9	15.6	13.6	8.5	6.1	5.3	48.9	134 230	180 480	34.8	7.4
Sparks	7.4	19.5	9.2	14.7	16.9	13.8	8.3	5.6	4.6	50.6	53 367	66 346	24.3	16.5
NEW HAMPSHIRE	6.1	18.9	8.4	13.0	17.9	14.9	8.9	6.3	5.6	50.8	1 109 252	1 235 786	11.4	4.2
Concord	5.8	17.3	8.3	15.2	17.8	14.3	7.7	5.8	7.9	50.5	36 006	40 687	13.0	2.8
Dover	5.7	15.2	11.2	17.2	16.7	12.6	7.7	6.5	7.3	52.0	25 042	26 884	7.4	5.0
Manchester	6.7	17.0	9.5	16.9	16.5	12.9	7.6	6.1	6.8	51.0	99 332	107 006	7.7	1.7
Nashua	6.5	18.1	8.1	15.9	17.6	13.6	8.5	6.1	5.5	50.6	79 662	86 605	8.7	0.8
Rochester	6.8	18.5	7.7	14.2	17.4	13.4	8.6	7.3	6.2	51.4	26 630	28 461	6.9	4.2
NEW JERSEY	6.7	18.1	8.0	14.1	17.1	13.8	9.0	6.8	6.4	51.5	7 747 750	8 414 350	8.9	2.7
Atlantic City	7.5	18.2	8.9	15.8	15.2	11.5	8.7	7.3	6.8	51.0	37 986	40 517	6.7	-0.3
Bayonne	5.8	16.3	8.2	14.6	16.1	13.8	8.7	8.0	8.6	52.7	61 464	61 842	0.6	-1.5
Bergenfield Borough	6.8	18.1	7.3	13.4	17.6	14.3	9.0	6.9	6.6	52.2	24 458	26 247	7.3	-0.3
Camden	9.1	25.5	12.0	15.3	14.1	9.9	6.4	4.5	3.1	51.5	87 492	79 904	-8.7	0.2
Clifton	6.0	15.6	7.7	14.4	16.3	13.8	8.7	7.9	9.7	52.3	71 984	78 672	9.3	1.5
East Orange	7.9	20.2	9.8	15.2	14.9	12.1	8.7	6.3	5.0	55.0	73 552	69 824	-5.1	-0.9
Elizabeth	7.7	18.6	10.8	17.2	16.5	11.6	7.7	5.2	4.8	50.5	110 002	120 568	9.6	2.2
Englewood	6.9	17.0	7.4	14.6	15.9	14.3	10.5	7.3	6.0	53.0	24 850	26 203	5.4	-0.4
Fair Lawn Borough	5.3	17.5	6.0	10.3	16.5	16.3	9.3	8.9	9.8	52.5	30 548	31 637	3.6	-0.2
Fort Lee Borough	5.3	12.2	5.1	15.3	17.2	13.9	10.9	10.2	10.0	53.3	31 997	35 461	10.8	4.7
Garfield	6.1	16.3	9.6	17.0	16.2	13.0	7.8	6.7	7.4	51.3	26 727	29 786	11.4	-0.3
Hackensack	5.8	12.4	8.6	20.7	17.7	13.4	8.9	6.3	6.2	50.3	37 049	42 677	15.2	1.9
Hoboken	3.2	7.3	15.3	37.9	13.9	8.1	5.4	4.6	4.5	49.1	33 397	38 577	15.5	2.3
Jersey City	6.9	17.8	10.7	19.4	15.7	11.8	7.9	5.2	4.5	51.2	228 517	240 055	5.0	-0.4
Kearny	5.7	15.7	10.7	18.5	17.2	13.1	8.2	5.6	5.2	48.4	34 874	40 513	16.2	-1.6
Linden	6.0	16.5	8.2	14.6	15.8	13.5	9.1	7.5	8.8	52.5	36 701	39 394	7.3	1.2
Long Branch	7.0	16.8	10.2	16.5	15.9	12.6	8.2	6.6	6.3	51.5	28 658	31 340	9.4	0.6
Millville	7.0	21.0	8.6	13.4	15.4	13.2	8.5	6.5	6.4	52.8	25 992	26 847	3.3	1.0
Newark	7.8	20.2	12.1	16.9	15.1	10.9	7.8	5.3	4.0	51.5	275 221	273 546	-0.6	1.6
New Brunswick	7.0	13.1	34.0	17.6	10.6	7.1	4.2	3.2	3.3	50.4	41 711	48 573	16.5	2.5
Paramus Borough	5.2	18.1	5.5	9.0	15.7	14.4	10.7	10.5	11.0	51.4	25 004	25 737	2.9	3.0
Passaic	9.6	21.2	12.5	17.5	14.2	10.5	6.4	4.2	3.9	50.1	58 041	67 861	16.9	1.0
Paterson	8.4	21.4	11.2	16.5	15.5	11.3	7.5	4.6	3.7	51.4	140 891	149 222	5.9	1.0
Perth Amboy	8.0	20.4	11.4	16.5	15.1	11.3	7.0	5.1	5.1	50.4	41 967	47 303	12.7	2.4
Plainfield	7.9	19.6	10.2	15.9	16.7	12.2	8.3	5.0	4.2	51.1	46 577	47 829	2.7	0.4
Rahway	6.3	17.6	7.8	14.7	17.3	13.5	8.3	7.2	7.3	52.3	25 325	26 500	4.6	1.1
Sayreville Borough	6.7	16.8	7.3	16.3	18.0	13.8	8.7	6.5	5.9	51.0	34 998	40 377	15.4	4.2
Trenton	7.6	20.1	10.1	16.7	15.2	11.5	7.4	5.8	5.6	50.6	88 675	85 403	-3.7	-0.1
Union City	7.4	17.9	11.0	18.0	16.3	11.4	8.0	5.9	4.1	49.9	58 012	67 088	15.6	-0.8
Vineland	6.2	19.5	8.3	13.6	15.4	13.8	9.1	6.9	7.2	52.1	54 780	56 271	2.7	1.4
Westfield	8.0	20.4	4.0	11.2	18.4	15.7	8.8	6.6	6.9	52.1	28 870	29 644	2.7	1.0
West New York	6.7	15.6	10.9	18.6	15.5	11.1	8.8	7.3	5.4	50.9	38 125	45 768	20.0	1.3
NEW MEXICO	7.2	20.8	9.8	12.9	15.5	13.5	8.7	6.5	5.2	50.8	1 515 069	1 819 046	20.1	3.1
Alamogordo	7.6	21.0	9.2	14.2	15.5	11.5	8.3	7.4	5.3	50.6	27 596	35 582	28.9	-0.1
Albuquerque	6.9	17.7	10.6	15.0	16.0	13.8	8.2	6.1	5.8	51.4	384 915	448 607	16.5	5.2
Carlsbad	7.3	19.8	8.4	11.1	13.6	13.5	9.1	8.1	9.1	51.8	24 952	25 625	2.7	-1.3
Clovis	8.3	21.7	9.4	13.1	14.9	11.5	8.0	6.7	6.3	52.0	30 954	32 667	5.5	0.5
Farmington	7.6	21.7	9.9	12.5	16.0	13.7	7.9	5.8	4.9	51.0	33 997	37 844	11.3	9.4
Hobbs	8.1	22.3	10.3	13.1	14.9	11.5	7.8	6.7	5.2	50.0	29 121	28 657	-1.6	-1.2
Las Cruces	7.0	18.1	16.0	13.4	13.4	11.1	7.8	7.1	6.0	51.5	62 360	74 267	19.1	3.7
Rio Rancho	7.5	21.7	7.0	13.7	18.4	13.1	7.0	5.7	6.0	51.5	32 512	51 765	59.2	13.9
Roswell	7.4	21.1	9.9	11.3	13.6	12.3	8.3	7.8	8.2	51.8	44 260	45 293	2.3	-2.4
Santa Fe	5.4	14.9	8.9	13.7	15.3	17.3	10.7	7.3	6.6	52.2	56 537	62 203	10.0	6.9
NEW YORK	6.5	18.2	9.3	14.5	16.2	13.5	8.9	6.7	6.2	51.8	17 990 778	18 976 457	5.5	1.1
Albany	5.6	14.3	19.3	15.9	13.4	11.3	6.9	5.9	7.4	52.5	100 031	95 658	-4.4	-1.8
Auburn	6.3	16.5	9.3	14.8	15.5	12.6	7.2	7.2	10.6	50.3	31 258	28 574	-8.6	-1.6
Binghamton	6.1	15.5	13.2	13.0	13.7	12.5	8.5	7.7	9.9	52.7	53 008	47 380	-10.6	-2.3
Buffalo	7.1	19.2	11.3	14.4	14.9	12.0	7.6	6.8	6.7	53.0	328 175	292 648	-10.8	-2.6
Elmira	7.0	18.1	13.0	14.2	15.7	11.5	6.7	6.5	7.3	49.7	33 724	30 940	-8.3	-2.0
Freeport	6.9	19.5	9.1	15.1	16.9	13.5	8.5	5.7	4.8	51.9	39 894	43 783	9.7	-0.1
Glen Cove	6.2	15.0	8.1	14.7	15.9	13.0	9.5	8.1	9.4	51.9	24 149	26 622	10.2	0.6
Hempstead	7.9	18.4	16.3	17.1	14.4	10.5	7.1	4.3	4.1	52.2	45 982	56 554	23.0	-6.0

Table D. Cities — Group Quarters, Crime, and Education

City	Households, 2000 Number	Percent change, 1990–2000	Persons per household	Percent Female family householder[1]	Percent One-person	Persons in group quarters, 2000 Total	Institutional Total	Persons in nursing homes	Non-institutional	Serious crimes known to police,[2] 2002 Total Number	Rate[3]	Violent	Property	School enrollment[4] Public	Private	Attainment[5] (percent) High school graduate or less	Bachelor's degree or more
	26	27	28	29	30	31	32	33	34	35	36	37	38	39	40	41	42
NEVADA	751 165	61.1	2.62	11.1	24.9	33 675	22 173	4 895	11 502	97 752	4 498	638	3 860	448 044	44 841	48.7	18.2
Carson City	20 171	26.9	2.44	11.0	27.8	3 223	3 102	272	121	2 074	3 635	533	3 102	11 868	1 130	45.4	18.5
Henderson	66 331	185.5	2.63	10.0	20.3	1 026	741	492	285	5 781	3 030	238	2 792	39 798	4 841	39.5	23.7
Las Vegas	176 750	77.2	2.66	12.2	25.0	8 185	5 416	1 258	2 769	56 810	4 925	779	4 146	101 429	12 302	50.4	18.2
North Las Vegas	34 018	134.2	3.36	15.2	13.6	1 338	1 223	577	115	7 367	5 865	1 030	4 835	31 420	1 801	61.3	10.2
Reno	73 904	29.0	2.38	10.6	32.6	4 496	1 633	651	2 863	11 626	5 922	756	5 166	44 006	4 143	41.3	25.0
Sparks	24 601	19.6	2.67	12.0	24.3	623	551	429	72	3 741	5 184	484	4 700	16 002	1 617	45.7	17.8
NEW HAMPSHIRE	474 606	15.4	2.53	9.1	24.4	35 539	13 784	9 316	21 755	28 306	2 220	161	2 059	264 403	68 485	42.7	28.7
Concord	16 281	14.5	2.30	11.4	32.7	3 267	2 819	684	448	1 267	3 018	102	2 916	8 471	2 054	39.5	30.7
Dover	11 573	11.9	2.26	10.3	31.0	757	646	493	111	NA	NA	NA	NA	5 454	1 340	37.0	32.4
Manchester	44 247	9.7	2.36	11.7	31.7	2 692	1 442	883	1 250	3 545	3 211	219	2 992	20 228	6 033	49.8	22.3
Nashua	34 614	11.5	2.46	10.4	28.3	1 403	639	588	764	NA	NA	NA	NA	17 074	5 626	39.9	31.5
Rochester	11 434	11.9	2.46	11.4	25.7	293	221	201	72	834	2 840	208	2 632	5 680	1 213	55.1	15.2
NEW JERSEY	3 064 645	9.7	2.68	12.6	24.5	194 821	110 169	51 493	84 652	259 789	3 024	375	2 650	1 735 248	482 584	47.3	29.8
Atlantic City	15 848	0.7	2.46	23.2	37.2	1 475	332	332	1 143	5 345	12 922	1 603	11 319	8 636	1 353	68.9	10.4
Bayonne	25 545	0.9	2.42	15.1	32.8	142	0	0	142	1 099	1 741	329	1 411	11 198	3 667	58.6	20.9
Bergenfield Borough	8 981	2.1	2.92	11.8	20.8	56	8	0	48	322	1 202	97	1 105	5 201	1 803	41.8	32.3
Camden	24 177	-9.2	3.12	37.7	22.5	4 375	3 454	420	921	6 125	7 508	1 817	5 692	24 148	2 227	77.6	5.4
Clifton	30 244	4.1	2.59	11.5	27.9	386	244	244	142	2 627	3 271	256	3 014	14 082	4 836	54.5	23.6
East Orange	26 024	-4.4	2.63	28.8	33.0	1 304	925	553	379	5 956	8 355	2 135	6 220	16 491	4 213	58.7	15.0
Elizabeth	40 482	3.5	2.91	19.1	24.6	2 916	2 313	497	603	7 149	5 808	735	5 073	26 604	6 046	70.3	12.1
Englewood	9 273	3.4	2.79	17.4	24.8	286	156	156	130	661	2 471	254	2 217	4 355	2 370	42.4	36.7
Fair Lawn Borough	11 806	2.7	2.67	9.0	21.3	168	139	139	29	567	1 755	161	1 594	5 723	2 042	33.8	44.8
Fort Lee Borough	16 544	8.6	2.14	7.4	39.0	34	0	0	34	625	1 726	47	1 679	4 974	2 131	31.1	48.2
Garfield	11 250	2.8	2.64	13.8	27.4	70	0	0	70	583	1 917	125	1 792	5 793	1 570	65.9	14.0
Hackensack	18 113	10.0	2.26	13.0	39.8	1 662	990	306	672	1 317	3 023	287	2 736	6 992	2 112	47.5	29.1
Hoboken	19 418	29.1	1.92	9.0	41.8	1 288	158	0	1 130	1 530	3 885	452	3 433	3 682	3 465	28.8	59.4
Jersey City	88 632	7.6	2.67	20.2	29.2	3 377	1 563	1 326	1 814	12 182	4 971	1 186	3 785	48 790	19 155	53.0	27.5
Kearny	13 539	8.6	2.81	13.2	21.8	2 520	2 423	160	97	1 210	2 926	239	2 686	7 849	2 473	63.9	17.4
Linden	15 052	4.8	2.60	15.3	27.9	253	246	246	7	1 879	4 672	361	4 312	7 797	1 809	62.8	14.1
Long Branch	12 594	9.1	2.47	15.9	34.1	205	70	70	135	1 046	3 269	447	2 822	6 801	1 552	55.0	20.2
Millville	10 043	4.2	2.65	17.9	25.1	258	123	123	135	1 590	5 801	657	5 144	6 565	627	64.6	12.2
Newark	91 382	-0.2	2.85	29.3	26.6	12 773	7 451	2 420	5 322	17 814	6 379	1 143	5 235	65 935	14 193	72.5	9.0
New Brunswick	13 057	2.7	3.23	18.0	24.3	6 446	109	90	6 337	2 940	5 929	722	5 207	19 440	1 225	64.4	19.2
Paramus Borough	8 082	3.9	3.00	8.0	14.4	1 507	1 244	651	263	2 209	8 407	396	8 011	5 198	1 479	39.8	38.7
Passaic	19 458	3.9	3.46	21.7	20.3	579	200	200	379	3 345	4 828	1 249	3 580	14 566	4 896	71.0	13.7
Paterson	44 710	1.7	3.25	26.8	20.4	3 821	2 139	201	1 682	6 842	4 491	765	3 727	34 950	8 083	73.9	8.2
Perth Amboy	14 562	2.5	3.20	21.0	20.6	702	379	358	323	1 697	3 514	507	3 007	11 338	1 692	73.3	9.7
Plainfield	15 137	0.1	3.10	24.5	21.1	907	550	399	357	2 413	4 942	1 057	3 885	10 862	2 545	57.8	18.5
Rahway	10 028	4.2	2.63	15.6	28.0	160	118	118	42	863	3 190	248	2 942	4 927	1 764	55.3	18.6
Sayreville Borough	14 955	17.3	2.68	11.1	22.3	246	194	194	52	835	2 026	189	1 836	7 552	2 293	51.2	24.9
Trenton	29 437	-4.3	2.75	27.1	29.7	4 401	3 301	512	1 100	6 150	7 054	1 700	5 354	18 674	4 776	69.6	9.2
Union City	22 872	11.0	2.92	19.3	23.0	355	181	181	174	2 212	3 230	453	2 777	15 108	3 012	71.0	12.5
Vineland	19 930	6.4	2.70	16.8	23.7	2 402	1 052	606	1 350	3 733	6 498	789	5 710	12 390	2 453	64.3	14.3
Westfield	10 622	3.2	2.77	7.1	19.3	267	177	177	90	334	1 104	13	1 090	6 209	2 112	19.8	62.5
West New York	16 719	16.0	2.74	16.9	27.5	28	0	0	28	1 440	3 082	392	2 690	8 838	1 669	67.8	16.4
NEW MEXICO	677 971	24.9	2.63	13.2	25.4	36 307	19 178	6 810	17 129	94 196	5 078	740	4 338	476 022	57 764	47.7	23.5
Alamogordo	13 704	30.7	2.57	11.7	25.2	426	364	182	62	1 215	3 348	287	3 062	9 557	842	46.9	14.6
Albuquerque	183 236	19.1	2.40	12.9	30.5	9 344	4 043	1 835	5 301	35 762	7 817	1 069	6 748	107 068	17 941	38.2	31.8
Carlsbad	9 957	7.4	2.51	13.1	26.6	654	517	378	137	1 727	6 609	570	6 039	6 160	752	58.3	14.5
Clovis	12 458	6.7	2.57	14.9	26.8	596	500	300	96	2 239	6 721	588	6 133	9 645	494	50.4	15.7
Farmington	13 982	16.7	2.67	12.4	22.6	509	348	221	161	2 253	5 838	1 109	4 729	10 400	786	44.4	19.7
Hobbs	10 040	-2.0	2.72	14.6	23.4	1 333	1 226	176	107	2 061	7 052	1 201	5 851	7 911	564	60.2	12.9
Las Cruces	29 184	22.6	2.46	15.1	27.9	2 399	1 147	243	1 252	3 826	5 052	416	4 636	23 611	1 745	41.9	28.0
Rio Rancho	18 995	62.9	2.70	10.3	20.8	418	257	257	161	1 443	2 734	265	2 468	13 263	1 877	37.2	24.8
Roswell	17 068	5.4	2.58	14.9	27.1	1 192	554	322	638	3 633	7 865	1 087	6 779	12 105	1 250	52.4	16.9
Santa Fe	27 569	21.0	2.20	12.1	36.4	1 474	415	415	1 059	4 929	7 770	640	7 130	11 023	3 588	32.6	40.0
NEW YORK	7 056 860	6.3	2.61	14.7	28.1	580 461	262 262	123 852	318 199	537 121	2 804	496	2 308	3 987 395	1 229 635	48.7	27.4
Albany	40 709	-3.4	2.11	16.1	41.9	9 902	2 046	1 418	7 856	6 774	7 015	1 453	5 562	24 770	7 555	43.2	32.5
Auburn	11 411	-4.4	2.27	14.7	36.3	2 620	2 200	445	420	1 147	3 976	243	3 734	5 875	784	58.8	13.6
Binghamton	21 089	-6.8	2.19	13.8	40.3	1 244	911	632	333	2 366	4 946	429	4 518	11 929	1 496	51.8	21.3
Buffalo	122 720	-10.1	2.29	22.3	37.7	11 126	5 203	2 767	5 923	19 017	6 437	1 272	5 165	69 241	15 917	51.8	17.0
Elmira	11 475	-7.7	2.37	18.4	34.5	3 732	2 514	331	1 218	1 978	6 333	519	5 814	6 172	1 974	61.4	14.6
Freeport	13 504	2.0	3.20	17.8	21.2	637	375	375	262	1 212	2 742	425	2 317	9 921	2 256	53.6	20.5
Glen Cove	9 461	11.8	2.72	12.7	24.1	876	558	558	318	275	1 023	67	956	4 648	1 689	48.5	27.9
Hempstead	15 188	4.1	3.41	27.0	20.8	4 741	1 001	1 001	3 740	1 455	2 548	687	1 862	12 530	5 929	61.5	16.0

1. No spouse present. 2. Data for serious crimes have not been adjusted for underreporting. This may affect comparability between geographic areas and over time. 3. Per 100,000 population estimated by the FBI. 4. All persons 3 years old and over enrolled in nursery school through college. 5. Persons 25 years old and over.

Table D. Cities — Income, Poverty, and Housing

City	Per capita income[1] (dollars)	Median income Dollars	Percent change, 1989–1999 (constant 1999 dollars)	Percent with income of $100,000 or more	Percent below poverty Persons Total	Persons Percent change in rate, 1989–1999	Families Total	Housing units, 2000 Total	Percent change, 1990–2000	Vacant units for sale or rent[2]	For seasonal use (percent)	Home owner vacancy rate	Renter vacancy rate
	43	44	45	46	47	48	49	50	51	52	53	54	55
NEVADA	21 989	44 581	7.0	11.3	10.5	2.9	7.5	827 457	59.5	76 292	2.0	2.6	9.7
Carson City	20 943	41 809	-1.4	9.3	10.0	25.0	6.9	21 283	28.0	1 112	0.5	1.5	6.8
Henderson	26 815	55 949	7.3	17.4	5.6	-21.1	3.9	71 149	180.1	4 818	1.2	2.2	9.4
Las Vegas	22 060	44 069	7.2	12.1	11.9	3.5	8.6	190 724	73.9	13 974	0.9	2.5	8.4
North Las Vegas	16 023	46 057	43.3	8.3	14.8	-30.8	11.8	36 600	131.1	2 582	0.2	2.1	12.0
Reno	22 520	40 530	6.3	10.4	12.6	9.6	8.3	79 453	29.4	5 549	0.5	2.2	7.9
Sparks	21 122	45 745	5.0	9.7	8.0	11.1	6.5	26 025	20.2	1 424	0.2	2.4	7.0
NEW HAMPSHIRE	23 844	49 467	1.3	13.8	6.5	1.6	4.3	547 024	8.6	72 418	10.3	1.0	3.5
Concord	21 976	42 447	-3.5	8.6	8.0	19.4	6.2	16 881	7.5	600	0.7	0.8	2.9
Dover	23 459	43 873	3.6	10.3	8.4	-10.6	4.8	11 924	5.5	351	0.6	0.7	1.8
Manchester	21 244	40 774	-4.9	7.6	10.6	17.8	7.7	45 892	3.5	1 645	0.5	0.5	3.1
Nashua	25 209	51 969	-4.5	15.9	6.8	4.6	5.0	35 387	6.0	773	0.5	0.4	1.6
Rochester	18 859	40 596	-1.9	6.2	8.4	33.3	6.3	11 836	6.9	402	0.7	0.9	2.8
NEW JERSEY	27 006	55 146	0.3	21.3	8.5	11.8	6.3	3 310 275	7.6	245 630	3.3	1.2	4.5
Atlantic City	15 402	26 969	-1.2	5.3	23.6	-5.6	19.1	20 219	-6.5	4 371	9.6	6.2	7.3
Bayonne	21 553	41 566	-3.2	11.6	10.1	14.8	8.4	26 826	1.4	1 281	0.2	0.9	3.6
Bergenfield Borough	24 706	62 172	1.2	23.2	3.5	6.1	2.6	9 147	1.2	166	0.2	0.4	1.8
Camden	9 815	23 421	0.3	2.2	35.5	-3.0	32.8	29 769	-1.2	5 592	0.1	5.1	6.1
Clifton	23 638	50 619	-5.6	16.0	6.3	34.0	4.3	31 060	3.5	816	0.2	0.7	2.4
East Orange	16 488	32 346	-10.2	7.6	19.2	8.5	15.9	28 485	-1.7	2 461	0.1	2.3	6.8
Elizabeth	15 114	35 175	-5.2	7.2	17.8	10.6	15.6	42 838	3.7	2 356	0.3	1.5	3.4
Englewood	35 275	58 379	-7.1	27.4	8.9	6.0	6.6	9 614	2.2	341	0.4	1.0	2.5
Fair Lawn Borough	32 273	72 127	8.1	29.9	3.7	27.6	2.6	12 006	2.1	200	0.2	0.4	1.9
Fort Lee Borough	37 899	58 161	-6.7	25.6	7.9	31.7	5.7	17 446	3.6	902	1.5	1.3	3.9
Garfield	19 530	42 748	0.5	9.4	7.8	5.4	6.4	11 698	2.1	448	0.3	0.8	2.9
Hackensack	26 856	49 316	-5.8	14.4	9.3	32.9	6.8	18 945	7.0	832	0.6	1.3	3.8
Hoboken	43 195	62 550	33.5	28.3	11.0	-32.9	10.0	19 915	14.3	497	0.3	0.6	1.7
Jersey City	19 410	37 862	-3.0	11.5	18.6	-1.6	16.4	93 648	3.2	5 016	0.3	1.9	3.3
Kearny	20 886	47 757	-6.1	13.3	8.6	41.0	6.1	13 872	3.3	333	0.2	0.6	2.1
Linden	21 314	46 345	-3.9	11.2	6.4	14.3	5.0	15 567	4.4	515	0.2	1.1	3.0
Long Branch	20 532	38 651	-6.3	10.7	16.7	13.6	13.9	13 983	2.6	1 389	5.0	1.3	3.6
Millville	18 632	40 378	-3.9	8.1	15.2	32.2	12.1	10 652	4.9	609	0.5	2.0	5.8
Newark	13 009	26 913	-7.5	5.3	28.4	8.0	25.5	100 141	-2.3	8 759	0.1	2.0	5.6
New Brunswick	14 308	36 080	-5.1	8.7	27.0	22.7	16.9	13 893	2.5	836	0.3	2.0	3.4
Paramus Borough	29 295	76 918	-3.0	34.5	3.3	10.0	1.4	8 209	4.0	127	0.2	0.5	2.2
Passaic	12 874	33 594	-6.2	6.7	21.2	24.7	18.4	20 194	2.9	736	0.2	2.0	1.9
Paterson	13 257	32 778	-9.5	7.0	22.2	20.0	19.2	47 169	2.2	2 459	0.1	1.7	3.8
Perth Amboy	14 989	37 608	-1.4	9.0	17.6	15.8	14.3	15 236	1.5	674	0.2	1.5	2.8
Plainfield	19 052	46 683	-9.7	15.7	15.9	30.3	12.2	16 180	0.7	1 043	0.1	2.3	5.0
Rahway	22 481	50 729	-7.4	13.3	7.1	10.9	5.4	10 381	3.9	353	0.1	1.2	3.3
Sayreville Borough	24 736	58 919	-4.8	18.0	4.7	51.6	3.4	15 235	14.1	280	0.1	0.6	1.6
Trenton	14 621	31 074	-10.1	5.9	21.1	16.6	17.6	33 843	0.8	4 406	0.1	4.0	8.4
Union City	13 997	30 642	-11.1	5.6	21.4	17.6	18.6	23 741	5.1	869	0.2	1.0	2.3
Vineland	18 797	40 076	-2.9	9.8	13.8	26.6	9.8	20 958	7.2	1 028	0.5	1.7	4.4
Westfield	47 187	98 390	9.7	49.4	2.7	50.0	1.7	10 819	2.2	197	0.4	0.3	2.7
West New York	16 719	31 980	-9.7	8.5	18.9	15.2	16.1	17 360	9.9	641	0.3	1.4	2.5
NEW MEXICO	17 261	34 133	5.5	7.6	18.4	-10.7	14.5	780 579	23.5	102 608	4.1	2.2	11.6
Alamogordo	14 662	30 928	-6.3	3.1	16.5	22.2	13.2	15 920	33.0	2 216	1.1	3.5	18.0
Albuquerque	20 884	38 272	3.4	9.7	13.5	-3.6	10.0	198 465	18.9	15 229	0.4	1.9	11.8
Carlsbad	16 496	30 658	0.9	5.0	16.5	-20.3	13.1	11 421	8.0	1 464	0.6	3.3	20.1
Clovis	15 561	28 878	1.3	5.1	21.0	-1.9	17.2	14 269	9.9	1 811	0.5	5.1	12.2
Farmington	18 167	37 663	-3.0	7.8	16.0	5.3	12.9	15 077	14.9	1 095	0.7	1.5	9.5
Hobbs	14 209	28 100	-8.3	5.3	24.2	-2.4	20.2	11 968	-2.9	1 928	0.3	4.0	21.1
Las Cruces	15 704	30 375	-4.4	4.7	23.3	3.1	17.2	31 682	23.4	2 498	0.7	2.3	9.3
Rio Rancho	20 322	47 169	11.4	7.4	5.1	10.9	3.7	20 209	64.0	1 214	0.5	2.3	12.2
Roswell	14 589	27 252	-7.3	4.4	22.6	4.6	18.7	19 327	5.9	2 259	0.6	3.3	14.2
Santa Fe	25 454	40 392	0.1	11.7	12.3	0.0	9.5	30 533	23.7	2 964	5.2	1.7	5.5
NEW YORK	23 389	43 393	-2.0	15.3	14.6	12.3	11.5	7 679 307	6.3	622 447	3.1	1.6	4.6
Albany	18 281	30 041	-11.1	6.8	21.7	18.6	16.0	45 288	-2.0	4 579	0.2	3.3	7.0
Auburn	17 083	30 281	1.2	4.6	16.5	19.6	12.5	12 637	-0.4	1 226	0.2	2.7	11.4
Binghamton	17 067	25 665	-8.6	4.9	23.7	18.5	16.5	23 971	-2.7	2 882	0.3	3.9	11.2
Buffalo	14 991	24 536	-1.2	4.1	26.6	3.9	23.0	145 574	-4.2	22 854	0.2	4.2	11.1
Elmira	14 495	27 292	9.5	3.8	23.1	4.1	17.9	12 895	-3.1	1 420	0.3	3.2	10.9
Freeport	21 288	55 948	-5.2	19.5	10.6	43.2	8.0	13 819	1.2	315	0.3	1.1	1.1
Glen Cove	26 627	55 503	-3.9	21.9	9.1	42.2	6.2	9 734	10.6	273	0.7	0.9	1.3
Hempstead	15 735	45 234	-8.3	13.8	17.7	42.7	14.4	15 579	3.1	391	0.1	1.1	1.7

1. Based on population enumerated as of April 1, 2000.   2. Includes units rented or sold but not occupied.

City	Total	Percent owner occupied	Percent renter occupied	Average size owner occupied	Average size renter occupied	Total	Percent change, 2002–2003	Total	Rate[1]	Total	Management, professional, and related occupations	Production, transportation, and material moving occupations	Employment disabled persons[3] (percent)
	56	57	58	59	60	61	62	63	64	65	66	67	68
NEVADA	751 165	60.9	39.1	2.71	2.47	1 141 351	1.1	59 439	5.2	933 280	25.7	10.4	14.5
Carson City	20 171	63.1	36.9	2.46	2.41	24 674	-0.3	1 584	6.4	23 649	30.2	13.8	11.8
Henderson	66 331	70.5	29.5	2.71	2.43	70 364	1.8	3 033	4.3	89 198	30.9	8.5	10.5
Las Vegas	176 750	59.1	40.9	2.76	2.52	287 500	1.7	15 031	5.2	214 301	25.5	9.0	16.4
North Las Vegas	34 018	70.1	29.9	3.27	3.56	44 632	1.4	4 053	9.1	45 740	17.9	12.3	17.0
Reno	73 904	47.5	52.5	2.53	2.25	106 245	0.2	5 060	4.8	90 372	29.2	11.0	13.4
Sparks	24 601	59.7	40.3	2.76	2.54	42 473	0.2	1 702	4.0	34 039	24.2	15.2	15.1
NEW HAMPSHIRE	474 606	69.7	30.3	2.70	2.14	718 885	1.8	30 734	4.3	650 871	35.8	14.8	10.1
Concord	16 281	51.4	48.6	2.62	1.96	24 387	2.8	710	2.9	20 337	39.4	10.4	10.5
Dover	11 573	51.2	48.8	2.54	1.96	16 310	2.0	564	3.5	15 261	39.3	12.2	8.4
Manchester	44 247	46.0	54.0	2.61	2.14	62 761	3.8	2 840	4.5	55 825	29.8	18.0	13.0
Nashua	34 614	56.9	43.1	2.66	2.20	49 802	1.6	2 884	5.8	45 738	39.6	15.4	11.5
Rochester	11 434	66.8	33.2	2.56	2.26	15 468	0.8	664	4.3	14 668	25.0	21.9	12.1
NEW JERSEY	3 064 645	65.6	34.4	2.81	2.43	4 375 020	0.5	256 983	5.9	3 950 029	38.0	12.0	11.6
Atlantic City	15 848	28.9	71.1	2.66	2.38	20 948	3.1	2 506	12.0	15 408	13.7	10.4	22.9
Bayonne	25 545	40.0	60.0	2.61	2.28	30 453	-2.6	1 638	5.4	27 565	32.0	14.0	15.4
Bergenfield Borough	8 981	71.1	28.9	3.09	2.49	13 735	-0.1	769	5.6	13 241	38.1	11.3	12.1
Camden	24 177	46.1	53.9	3.16	3.09	33 881	1.6	5 717	16.9	22 973	16.8	25.7	20.0
Clifton	30 244	60.9	39.1	2.75	2.33	37 618	0.2	1 916	5.1	37 317	32.3	16.6	11.6
East Orange	26 024	26.6	73.4	3.27	2.40	37 095	0.9	3 609	9.7	27 399	24.6	15.1	17.7
Elizabeth	40 482	29.7	70.3	3.25	2.76	58 828	0.8	6 012	10.2	47 671	18.2	28.4	19.2
Englewood	9 273	59.4	40.6	2.91	2.63	13 684	-0.1	808	5.9	12 495	38.6	12.4	13.3
Fair Lawn Borough	11 806	80.0	20.0	2.80	2.11	15 772	-0.1	660	4.2	15 727	48.1	7.8	10.3
Fort Lee Borough	16 544	56.2	43.8	2.13	2.15	17 106	-0.1	906	5.3	17 205	51.6	5.9	10.2
Garfield	11 250	40.2	59.8	2.80	2.54	14 255	-0.1	1 002	7.0	14 412	20.5	20.7	21.7
Hackensack	18 113	32.4	67.6	2.49	2.15	22 027	-0.1	1 414	6.4	21 953	35.6	13.6	15.3
Hoboken	19 418	22.6	77.4	1.96	1.91	19 962	-2.6	1 117	5.6	25 661	61.0	4.6	8.2
Jersey City	88 632	28.2	71.8	2.98	2.55	113 929	-2.7	11 253	9.9	103 448	33.0	15.5	17.0
Kearny	13 539	48.0	52.0	3.00	2.63	18 755	-2.6	1 060	5.7	17 741	26.8	17.0	14.8
Linden	15 052	58.7	41.3	2.75	2.39	19 881	0.9	1 371	6.9	18 772	23.0	20.5	12.0
Long Branch	12 594	42.4	57.6	2.61	2.37	17 360	1.9	1 517	8.7	14 263	28.6	12.1	14.9
Millville	10 043	63.9	36.1	2.71	2.54	13 112	2.3	982	7.5	11 791	24.8	19.8	12.5
Newark	91 382	23.8	76.2	3.22	2.74	118 996	0.9	14 588	12.3	90 819	18.9	21.2	21.1
New Brunswick	13 057	26.3	73.7	3.01	3.30	24 761	-1.6	2 339	9.4	23 832	24.9	21.2	12.3
Paramus Borough	8 082	90.7	9.3	3.00	2.94	12 874	-0.1	526	4.1	11 793	44.1	7.2	6.9
Passaic	19 458	27.0	73.0	3.63	3.40	28 457	0.4	3 351	11.8	25 638	18.0	33.5	18.9
Paterson	44 710	31.5	68.5	3.59	3.10	67 331	0.4	7 997	11.9	52 545	16.7	27.4	24.6
Perth Amboy	14 562	40.5	59.5	3.24	3.17	24 299	-1.6	2 820	11.6	18 698	17.5	31.3	18.4
Plainfield	15 137	50.1	49.9	3.16	3.04	27 001	0.8	2 407	8.9	22 997	24.0	22.5	15.1
Rahway	10 028	62.7	37.3	2.84	2.26	14 552	0.9	805	5.5	12 605	30.6	15.3	11.6
Sayreville Borough	14 955	67.7	32.3	2.84	2.35	21 959	-1.5	948	4.3	19 923	35.5	12.0	10.1
Trenton	29 437	45.5	54.5	2.83	2.69	45 804	1.9	4 634	10.1	32 470	21.5	16.3	18.3
Union City	22 872	18.2	81.8	2.98	2.90	30 020	-2.7	2 976	9.9	25 874	17.1	31.2	21.2
Vineland	19 930	66.2	33.8	2.74	2.63	26 952	2.3	2 265	8.4	24 633	26.3	19.6	17.4
Westfield	10 622	81.7	18.3	2.94	1.99	16 364	0.9	506	3.1	14 575	60.5	4.5	6.3
West New York	16 719	19.9	80.1	2.70	2.74	19 967	-2.7	1 560	7.8	18 358	19.8	26.5	22.3
NEW MEXICO	677 971	70.0	30.0	2.72	2.41	896 867	2.5	57 200	6.4	763 116	34.0	10.7	12.3
Alamogordo	13 704	60.7	39.3	2.61	2.49	12 430	2.7	744	6.0	12 440	28.6	12.4	11.6
Albuquerque	183 236	60.4	39.6	2.55	2.16	257 656	1.7	13 318	5.2	216 913	38.5	8.7	11.6
Carlsbad	9 957	71.5	28.5	2.56	2.38	12 162	1.4	933	7.7	10 065	25.2	12.5	13.5
Clovis	12 458	62.3	37.7	2.58	2.57	16 137	2.6	654	4.1	12 708	27.9	13.2	11.2
Farmington	13 982	68.4	31.6	2.74	2.51	23 180	0.3	1 164	5.0	16 928	30.2	12.1	9.5
Hobbs	10 040	67.9	32.1	2.76	2.64	13 491	1.4	687	5.1	10 002	25.5	13.8	14.3
Las Cruces	29 184	58.1	41.9	2.60	2.28	39 570	4.0	2 810	7.1	31 866	36.9	7.7	10.0
Rio Rancho	18 995	81.5	18.5	2.75	2.51	25 927	1.4	1 271	4.9	24 582	34.5	9.9	9.9
Roswell	17 068	68.4	31.6	2.64	2.47	19 749	3.1	1 775	9.0	16 582	27.3	15.7	13.8
Santa Fe	27 569	58.2	41.8	2.31	2.05	41 745	3.4	1 406	3.4	32 461	43.0	5.5	11.0
NEW YORK	7 056 860	53.0	47.0	2.78	2.41	9 315 319	-0.3	588 959	6.3	8 382 988	36.7	11.7	13.2
Albany	40 709	37.6	62.4	2.31	1.98	54 881	0.3	2 720	5.0	43 663	40.9	7.4	11.6
Auburn	11 411	51.9	48.1	2.48	2.05	13 751	0.7	1 050	7.6	12 096	26.1	18.7	15.0
Binghamton	21 089	43.0	57.0	2.33	2.08	23 365	-2.4	1 956	8.4	20 001	31.2	15.1	13.3
Buffalo	122 720	43.5	56.5	2.47	2.16	144 543	0.2	14 705	10.2	114 062	29.2	17.2	15.4
Elmira	11 475	48.3	51.7	2.49	2.26	13 577	-1.9	1 350	9.9	11 583	27.3	16.2	13.8
Freeport	13 504	65.2	34.8	3.23	3.14	23 613	0.5	1 074	4.5	20 567	27.4	15.7	15.7
Glen Cove	9 461	58.5	41.5	2.75	2.67	13 480	0.5	598	4.4	12 099	34.4	8.9	10.2
Hempstead	15 188	43.2	56.8	3.70	3.19	28 610	0.5	1 853	6.5	24 612	21.9	14.9	16.1

1. Percent of civilian labor force.　2. Persons 16 years old and over.　3. Persons 16 to 64 years old.

City	Value of residential construction authorized by building permits, 2003 — New construction ($1,000)	Number of housing units	Percent single family	Wholesale trade, 1997 — Number of establishments	Number of employees	Sales (mil dol)	Annual payroll (mil dol)	Retail trade,[1] 1997 — Number of establishments	Number of employees	Sales (mil dol)	Annual payroll (mil dol)
	69	70	71	72	73	74	75	76	77	78	79
NEVADA	4 879 197	43 366	76.3	2 253	27 251	12 806.9	918.5	6 222	89 452	18 220.8	1 798.2
Carson City	34 761	203	97.0	88	557	222.4	18.7	262	3 383	678.4	66.1
Henderson	747 903	4 869	87.6	85	729	301.2	21.7	321	5 824	1 252.6	113.6
Las Vegas	1 060 389	9 183	74.7	500	6 266	2 208.8	209.2	1 516	24 600	5 811.5	535.7
North Las Vegas	567 399	5 096	90.2	91	1 903	735.5	67.5	138	2 277	433.9	39.7
Reno	313 354	2 301	79.7	286	3 487	3 043.4	118.6	928	14 619	2 865.8	294.2
Sparks	214 258	1 632	81.9	290	5 391	2 376.7	188.2	256	3 559	640.2	71.2
NEW HAMPSHIRE	1 207 854	8 641	76.2	2 033	22 631	11 371.1	875.0	6 645	84 170	15 890.1	1 428.2
Concord	25 148	245	51.0	63	848	268.7	28.8	331	4 578	943.6	75.7
Dover	23 559	277	52.0	44	329	114.9	9.2	119	1 603	270.1	27.6
Manchester	35 115	361	47.4	226	3 185	1 368.2	115.0	561	7 594	1 547.6	140.5
Nashua	12 816	177	63.8	160	2 028	1 527.4	102.3	492	9 611	1 848.8	161.2
Rochester	18 666	245	40.0	26	829	88.8	20.1	143	2 154	371.2	35.4
NEW JERSEY	3 781 901	32 984	67.2	17 812	266 944	227 366.7	11 886.1	34 837	420 724	79 914.9	7 926.0
Atlantic City	6 908	62	95.2	24	203	63.5	7.0	255	1 832	296.5	31.8
Bayonne	23 931	231	22.1	57	1 127	1 081.0	45.7	224	1 588	232.1	31.8
Bergenfield Borough	542	2	100.0	39	D	D	D	117	904	241.6	21.4
Camden	8 668	112	100.0	92	1 184	480.5	40.8	158	1 212	241.7	24.1
Clifton	10 110	85	97.6	215	2 474	2 579.4	104.8	286	4 075	767.8	79.0
East Orange	5 754	84	9.5	17	D	D	D	131	939	149.1	17.0
Elizabeth	33 572	550	0.9	158	3 181	2 119.1	120.3	396	3 947	723.8	65.1
Englewood	11 856	71	47.9	159	1 658	1 162.2	89.0	169	1 593	528.9	41.2
Fair Lawn Borough	987	5	100.0	83	715	1 264.7	31.1	116	1 199	241.7	24.1
Fort Lee Borough	7 303	38	44.7	250	1 942	4 352.2	119.2	158	1 588	300.7	28.9
Garfield	1 263	15	6.7	61	D	D	D	81	817	137.5	17.4
Hackensack	1 947	19	63.2	279	2 902	2 434.3	131.5	284	3 895	719.8	82.1
Hoboken	52 905	555	20.7	83	575	742.6	25.7	152	974	130.0	12.7
Jersey City	86 784	924	0.2	278	5 701	2 510.8	202.7	809	8 787	1 536.0	144.6
Kearny	1 334	14	21.4	98	1 231	539.9	56.3	131	1 550	237.3	28.5
Linden	5 106	75	6.7	131	1 475	1 861.5	56.8	195	2 303	502.4	50.3
Long Branch	8 020	94	100.0	41	394	523.2	14.7	73	785	147.5	15.1
Millville	6 477	85	100.0	25	D	D	D	100	1 621	257.7	26.4
Newark	130 148	1 652	9.4	426	5 393	2 319.3	192.0	832	5 920	912.8	101.5
New Brunswick	6 650	86	34.9	63	908	249.1	28.8	136	1 208	149.7	18.5
Paramus Borough	8 532	28	92.9	167	2 785	2 943.1	157.9	623	13 648	2 438.3	249.3
Passaic	2 917	47	46.8	95	919	296.4	29.4	218	1 961	440.1	38.5
Paterson	1 470	37	100.0	211	2 804	1 105.6	104.4	382	2 513	409.3	48.1
Perth Amboy	20 038	180	53.3	62	871	514.8	32.8	152	1 302	215.5	21.8
Plainfield	468	6	100.0	35	381	97.9	11.3	122	813	136.3	16.0
Rahway	14 797	331	3.3	56	912	444.9	38.1	86	609	166.1	13.3
Sayreville Borough	25 965	264	99.2	48	335	117.6	12.0	104	1 673	243.0	24.8
Trenton	0	0	0.0	81	987	317.6	32.9	240	2 039	353.9	41.1
Union City	5 901	105	0.0	88	509	166.2	15.8	319	1 504	265.0	25.5
Vineland	21 791	179	95.5	123	1 184	542.7	38.8	308	3 680	643.8	69.6
Westfield	9 752	53	96.2	53	280	327.2	20.4	170	1 338	234.3	25.8
West New York	7 253	146	0.0	64	413	160.7	14.8	217	1 028	150.4	17.0
NEW MEXICO	1 703 302	13 759	86.2	2 182	21 344	7 397.6	601.1	7 421	86 300	14 984.5	1 455.5
Alamogordo	26 585	161	100.0	17	94	25.2	2.0	164	1 996	287.6	28.5
Albuquerque	607 016	6 181	82.3	919	10 636	3 630.1	330.3	2 004	30 720	5 914.6	568.7
Carlsbad	4 578	55	100.0	33	202	53.9	6.0	151	1 599	250.8	28.4
Clovis	18 207	161	62.7	33	268	95.3	5.9	221	2 352	330.5	33.3
Farmington	23 179	231	73.2	115	1 002	276.8	28.5	359	4 854	806.9	79.0
Hobbs	5 744	38	76.3	85	708	253.8	20.6	175	1 914	336.1	34.8
Las Cruces	133 519	1 258	63.3	79	656	194.2	17.8	407	5 655	955.6	89.1
Rio Rancho	97 364	1 038	98.4	NA	NA	NA	NA	NA	NA	NA	NA
Roswell	3 856	33	100.0	61	514	196.9	12.0	243	2 542	384.3	37.7
Santa Fe	70 719	561	100.0	146	1 207	319.7	37.7	782	7 504	1 368.3	143.1
NEW YORK	6 193 971	49 708	48.7	37 499	414 249	319 697.6	17 185.8	75 241	805 208	139 303.9	14 329.8
Albany	6 526	112	2.7	164	2 401	1 438.6	90.4	492	6 830	1 074.2	113.2
Auburn	689	5	100.0	44	424	131.5	12.1	183	2 671	412.1	41.4
Binghamton	1 734	12	100.0	80	1 018	305.7	26.6	202	3 239	452.3	45.2
Buffalo	6 021	58	87.9	468	7 225	3 273.0	235.5	916	10 187	1 243.9	154.3
Elmira	772	6	100.0	46	552	136.6	15.1	119	1 685	234.8	23.8
Freeport	1 958	16	100.0	120	969	350.6	30.6	162	1 964	431.1	39.9
Glen Cove	1 905	6	33.3	50	519	186.6	23.8	114	1 167	251.5	24.3
Hempstead	1 685	15	100.0	58	547	191.9	21.0	208	1 584	570.3	43.1

1. Establishments with payroll.

City	Real estate and rental and leasing, 1997				Professional, scientific, and technical services,[1] 1997				Manufacturing, 1997			
	Number of establish-ments	Number of employees	Receipts (mil dol)	Annual payroll (mil dol)	Number of establish-ments	Number of employees	Receipts (mil dol)	Annual payroll (mil dol)	Number of establish-ments	Number of employees	Receipts (mil dol)	Annual payroll (mil dol)
	80	81	82	83	84	85	86	87	88	89	90	91
NEVADA	2 460	16 890	2 276.5	381.5	4 171	28 963	2 974.4	1 171.1	1 615	37 849	6 361.8	1 178.0
Carson City	102	343	51.2	7.4	233	806	86.2	30.2	186	4 157	514.5	120.8
Henderson	111	1 335	161.1	31.9	166	691	72.1	28.8	60	3 131	939.0	96.8
Las Vegas	608	4 009	498.6	83.6	1 344	13 489	1 308.4	563.5	274	3 884	493.8	114.1
North Las Vegas	49	451	79.8	16.6	35	580	73.6	19.4	74	6 086	1 076.3	191.6
Reno	419	2 266	342.9	47.6	860	4 999	486.1	197.6	192	4 477	684.6	136.2
Sparks	86	495	63.0	11.8	111	881	86.2	33.8	182	4 477	684.6	136.2
NEW HAMPSHIRE	1 399	6 639	719.4	151.1	3 341	18 268	1 626.6	713.1	2 328	98 934	19 813.1	3 361.4
Concord	62	D	D	D	216	1 340	132.0	60.7	56	3 016	372.7	89.6
Dover	36	114	15.6	1.9	71	415	20.8	9.5	58	3 300	525.2	111.4
Manchester	143	821	86.2	19.2	339	3 297	314.8	144.4	191	8 952	1 394.5	289.7
Nashua	119	541	62.9	14.0	333	1 454	168.5	70.9	179	11 164	1 990.4	521.2
Rochester	26	79	10.8	1.5	35	354	29.4	12.6	38	2 694	1 218.0	74.8
NEW JERSEY	8 292	47 558	8 881.9	1 376.5	25 849	220 238	25 943.8	10 441.0	11 812	409 788	97 060.8	15 430.2
Atlantic City	63	773	112.1	13.2	82	758	74.4	37.7	NA	NA	NA	NA
Bayonne	40	208	25.3	4.9	66	278	13.7	4.8	52	1 747	556.1	60.6
Bergenfield Borough	23	82	11.0	1.6	39	103	11.9	4.5	NA	NA	NA	NA
Camden	32	285	18.9	5.2	42	308	30.7	13.0	81	2 757	557.8	117.6
Clifton	94	346	46.7	10.1	271	2 605	232.0	83.8	211	9 631	1 780.5	374.9
East Orange	78	346	52.8	7.5	66	1 368	187.4	60.2	NA	NA	NA	NA
Elizabeth	129	505	58.1	9.2	115	401	40.0	14.1	129	5 983	1 143.6	191.0
Englewood	67	198	47.0	5.9	126	690	116.8	40.1	83	2 143	425.6	78.8
Fair Lawn Borough	30	99	14.6	2.5	210	1 075	175.6	56.9	62	3 146	589.3	116.4
Fort Lee Borough	139	462	112.2	12.6	260	1 658	230.9	70.9	NA	NA	NA	NA
Garfield	15	36	10.0	1.1	37	122	11.8	3.3	105	3 293	521.4	90.8
Hackensack	155	2 624	487.4	77.0	512	3 354	367.9	142.3	140	2 551	391.7	85.2
Hoboken	61	306	41.8	7.3	146	871	126.0	53.6	69	1 655	311.0	47.5
Jersey City	212	1 082	188.2	25.3	353	3 553	522.8	184.9	190	5 770	1 039.2	179.8
Kearny	32	320	62.1	13.1	58	199	17.9	5.4	69	2 068	361.9	62.7
Linden	44	279	36.8	6.5	53	318	20.9	9.5	164	8 202	6 332.5	364.1
Long Branch	31	72	14.7	1.5	36	109	8.7	3.3	24	505	58.5	15.2
Millville	10	27	3.4	0.5	38	112	8.5	2.7	52	4 684	609.5	154.4
Newark	193	3 108	502.7	75.5	281	4 559	722.5	245.1	439	14 960	3 353.1	491.9
New Brunswick	37	185	36.0	3.8	127	634	74.6	29.6	78	2 689	689.9	114.0
Paramus Borough	60	575	139.4	18.1	211	2 181	273.1	115.2	32	1 541	238.2	70.8
Passaic	50	215	34.8	5.4	49	344	26.7	11.1	144	4 687	433.2	108.6
Paterson	77	419	45.6	9.9	75	477	34.7	11.7	340	8 436	1 748.4	277.2
Perth Amboy	20	109	15.6	2.6	35	146	11.7	3.9	53	2 408	865.6	85.9
Plainfield	31	123	18.4	2.8	40	247	21.5	8.7	42	1 128	154.9	30.9
Rahway	21	117	15.8	2.5	35	270	22.0	13.9	68	3 316	1 153.8	167.4
Sayreville Borough	23	98	17.7	1.9	71	217	19.7	10.8	24	2 272	860.7	101.2
Trenton	56	447	56.2	8.8	109	730	83.2	40.4	89	2 790	370.8	104.7
Union City	47	135	17.5	1.9	78	207	18.8	5.3	133	1 563	102.3	29.4
Vineland	79	362	41.9	7.1	112	718	64.1	24.5	105	6 223	913.0	186.9
Westfield	39	137	53.7	7.6	191	1 086	119.2	47.5	NA	NA	NA	NA
West New York	45	185	34.6	4.2	63	168	18.9	6.7	172	1 970	142.2	34.3
NEW MEXICO	1 887	8 844	893.9	165.2	3 702	31 535	3 243.4	1 307.3	1 593	39 664	17 906.1	1 135.8
Alamogordo	34	140	9.9	1.8	45	187	8.3	3.2	18	562	92.1	10.1
Albuquerque	677	4 251	480.0	80.6	1 746	D	D	D	592	D	D	D
Carlsbad	36	132	9.0	2.5	36	168	15.9	6.6	NA	NA	NA	NA
Clovis	51	D	D	D	60	210	11.6	4.4	NA	NA	NA	NA
Farmington	62	403	29.4	14.0	125	768	42.8	17.2	47	695	74.1	16.9
Hobbs	38	279	34.3	8.2	51	283	17.1	7.3	NA	NA	NA	NA
Las Cruces	138	448	40.6	6.4	184	970	66.1	27.1	65	1 433	253.4	28.6
Rio Rancho	NA	NA	NA	NA	NA	NA	NA	NA	30	D	D	D
Roswell	72	D	D	D	84	456	37.3	13.6	40	D	D	D
Santa Fe	174	798	99.9	18.1	408	1 864	194.8	81.9	136	1 155	95.2	23.7
NEW YORK	27 214	145 326	27 770.1	4 447.8	45 619	416 892	57 475.0	21 773.1	23 908	785 891	146 720.2	26 515.8
Albany	124	1 000	142.7	22.4	377	3 579	433.5	151.9	86	1 933	420.5	62.6
Auburn	35	130	16.3	2.4	61	458	32.0	14.0	64	3 087	556.3	92.6
Binghamton	46	283	21.1	3.3	138	909	76.2	26.3	79	5 994	1 266.4	199.6
Buffalo	217	1 635	279.0	48.1	592	5 811	608.6	217.4	466	20 307	4 527.2	748.4
Elmira	24	D	D	D	58	411	37.8	11.0	30	2 531	334.5	70.3
Freeport	39	189	27.2	4.7	98	345	33.5	13.2	122	3 330	392.4	92.7
Glen Cove	30	87	14.6	2.6	80	276	36.9	11.2	32	2 597	448.4	82.3
Hempstead	40	203	40.8	5.4	88	633	56.1	18.5	38	674	84.1	20.3

1. Firms subject to federal tax.

City	Accommodation and foodservices, 1997				Arts, entertainment, and recreation,[1] 1997				Health care and social assistance,[1] 1997			
	Number of establishments	Number of employees	Sales (mil dol)	Annual payroll (mil dol)	Number of establishments	Number of employees	Receipts (mil dol)	Annual payroll (mil dol)	Number of establishments	Number of employees	Receipts (mil dol)	Annual payroll (mil dol)
	92	93	94	95	96	97	98	99	100	101	102	103
NEVADA	3 632	241 672	15 322.7	4 665.3	811	23 960	1 667.5	465.8	3 226	39 476	3 406.5	1 358.9
Carson City	133	2 404	93.1	27.7	39	1 001	51.0	13.7	172	1 274	86.7	39.8
Henderson	167	3 736	206.8	55.0	48	2 654	150.3	43.6	186	1 694	125.9	49.9
Las Vegas	872	43 124	2 283.7	836.1	193	4 384	374.3	84.0	1 021	17 184	1 624.8	605.1
North Las Vegas	53	2 276	127.6	37.4	10	1 636	62.1	25.8	47	1 937	110.6	36.8
Reno	565	26 468	1 406.6	462.7	80	2 854	139.7	44.3	589	5 514	509.3	234.4
Sparks	117	5 118	253.5	71.8	28	1 173	65.6	19.7	115	1 657	117.1	43.5
NEW HAMPSHIRE	3 029	43 942	1 543.5	449.8	460	6 545	365.0	99.6	2 373	28 889	1 734.1	836.3
Concord.............	119	2 266	73.5	21.6	17	0	0.0	0.0	136	2 141	156.5	84.4
Dover.............	61	D	D	D	4	14	1.1	0.1	102	1 425	73.1	34.7
Manchester	230	4 115	140.2	38.4	24	342	13.6	4.0	231	2 887	195.4	99.0
Nashua	182	3 677	131.1	39.3	19	252	19.0	6.9	197	2 922	197.4	93.0
Rochester.............	61	761	24.6	6.7	8	92	3.7	1.1	62	643	34.9	18.6
NEW JERSEY	16 974	251 872	13 407.4	3 608.2	2 393	27 187	1 981.2	602.2	18 905	172 723	13 702.4	5 900.2
Atlantic City	205	48 506	4 717.1	1 246.0	16	100	11.2	2.7	57	624	34.1	17.3
Bayonne	114	D	D	D	9	66	3.1	1.1	130	791	70.7	30.5
Bergenfield Borough	49	D	D	D	10	97	4.0	1.3	31	162	17.0	6.1
Camden.............	84	583	25.2	5.8	2	0	0.0	0.0	74	1 020	74.7	39.6
Clifton.............	142	D	D	D	19	123	7.9	1.8	271	2 248	355.8	98.4
East Orange.............	59	955	37.2	9.4	2	0	0.0	0.0	113	1 707	85.6	36.1
Elizabeth	227	2 132	117.9	30.0	7	30	9.5	5.4	174	1 037	80.6	34.7
Englewood	46	496	25.9	7.0	17	75	6.5	2.1	187	1 492	161.5	77.7
Fair Lawn Borough	59	566	22.5	6.1	11	68	3.4	0.8	171	1 203	124.0	54.6
Fort Lee Borough	96	1 062	53.6	15.0	14	70	16.2	4.1	162	1 724	96.8	44.6
Garfield.............	48	305	12.2	3.1	4	13	0.5	0.2	22	80	5.8	1.5
Hackensack	108	D	D	D	12	149	16.9	3.3	250	2 583	233.5	113.0
Hoboken.............	132	1 150	46.9	12.6	13	78	3.6	1.0	80	389	42.3	14.4
Jersey City	345	2 789	121.3	32.5	27	227	17.4	6.6	329	2 776	214.8	89.8
Kearny.............	74	D	D	D	2	0	0.0	0.0	62	266	19.6	8.4
Linden.............	103	987	39.2	11.1	3	0	0.0	0.0	54	543	38.4	15.0
Long Branch.............	77	941	39.2	12.5	7	41	2.8	0.8	88	650	61.3	29.2
Millville.............	44	408	14.3	3.8	2	0	0.0	0.0	41	452	32.1	13.0
Newark.............	454	5 346	335.0	88.5	5	59	2.2	0.6	310	2 971	198.3	91.9
New Brunswick	131	1 614	67.3	19.5	2	0	0.0	0.0	94	1 271	241.9	64.0
Paramus Borough	128	2 306	98.4	25.4	17	304	9.7	2.7	137	1 230	102.1	40.2
Passaic.............	68	418	19.3	4.4	4	9	1.4	0.2	82	718	55.5	24.5
Paterson.............	154	861	39.9	10.3	5	12	1.4	0.3	157	800	78.2	36.4
Perth Amboy	71	448	18.9	3.8	2	0	0.0	0.0	66	794	52.8	21.8
Plainfield.............	46	D	D	D	1	0	0.0	0.0	69	668	53.3	23.2
Rahway.............	66	572	24.5	6.3	4	0	0.0	0.0	41	281	28.7	16.5
Sayreville Borough	45	414	15.5	3.8	3	0	0.0	0.0	49	481	30.0	12.2
Trenton.............	187	1 131	51.8	13.3	3	0	0.0	0.0	100	1 298	83.0	40.6
Union City	143	D	D	D	7	22	2.8	0.6	136	1 186	59.7	24.7
Vineland.............	100	1 531	44.8	12.3	8	56	2.2	0.5	130	1 081	81.3	37.9
Westfield.............	64	D	D	D	5	13	1.4	0.3	151	1 423	106.3	50.4
West New York	66	502	17.5	4.2	6	15	3.8	1.2	75	493	31.3	11.6
NEW MEXICO	3 825	67 134	2 144.9	599.1	440	8 679	520.4	115.4	2 923	32 824	2 057.3	864.3
Alamogordo.............	73	1 068	29.3	7.7	10	80	1.4	0.5	61	491	27.0	11.6
Albuquerque.............	1 082	24 747	813.2	228.8	121	2 980	150.1	39.2	1 073	15 510	1 085.5	450.0
Carlsbad.............	62	1 059	34.3	9.3	6	18	0.4	0.1	64	969	64.9	24.1
Clovis.............	79	1 605	45.7	13.0	10	0	0.0	0.0	94	0	0.0	0.0
Farmington.............	121	2 783	79.8	21.7	10	108	2.3	0.7	143	1 122	75.4	34.5
Hobbs.............	78	1 152	33.5	8.9	9	0	0.0	0.0	68	966	64.5	20.3
Las Cruces.............	208	3 396	103.2	27.2	17	134	7.0	1.9	246	2 587	157.4	65.5
Rio Rancho	NA	NA	NA	NA	NA	NA	NA	NA	NA	NA	NA	NA
Roswell.............	106	1 859	51.5	13.7	5	46	1.4	0.3	112	772	44.8	21.3
Santa Fe	329	7 045	288.9	84.5	67	878	136.9	16.3	286	2 785	161.9	73.3
NEW YORK	38 045	473 327	21 671.1	6 101.1	7 311	77 057	7 029.0	2 284.6	36 054	358 075	26 008.3	10 970.9
Albany.............	365	4 395	152.2	41.1	23	600	11.9	5.0	239	3 154	263.9	134.2
Auburn.............	94	1 266	34.3	10.0	16	98	4.9	1.4	119	879	56.2	23.9
Binghamton.............	157	2 278	64.8	18.9	14	254	9.3	1.6	145	1 672	100.6	47.0
Buffalo.............	678	8 280	252.3	70.5	55	1 170	68.7	40.9	436	7 567	431.0	218.8
Elmira.............	80	D	D	D	4	28	2.2	0.6	92	813	70.5	36.2
Freeport.............	71	586	27.2	8.1	17	46	5.1	1.1	85	804	66.2	23.3
Glen Cove	50	D	D	D	12	96	4.1	1.0	98	980	72.0	28.8
Hempstead.............	53	709	30.8	8.1	9	0	0.0	0.0	109	3 294	167.8	75.5

1. Firms subject to federal tax.

Table D. Cities — Other Services and Federal Funds

City	Other services,[1] 1997				Selected federal funds, 2002–2003 (mil dol)								
					Procurement contracts		Grants						Direct payments for individuals for educational assistance
	Number of establishments	Number of employees	Receipts (mil dol)	Annual payroll (mil dol)	Defense	Other	Total[2]	Medicaid and other health related	Nutrition and family welfare	Energy and environment	Education	Housing and community development	
	104	105	106	107	108	109	110	111	112	113	114	115	116
NEVADA	2 175	16 185	1 061.7	328.0	386.7	1 085.6	1 955.0	765.3	264.5	74.4	207.3	151.6	49.9
Carson City	104	634	42.2	13.5	10.2	3.8	336.1	35.9	52.5	28.4	73.6	12.4	1.8
Henderson	108	975	55.9	18.7	1.5	30.9	3.8	0.0	0.0	0.0	0.5	3.2	0.0
Las Vegas	594	5 323	328.7	105.8	42.0	829.4	167.3	21.6	13.5	27.5	19.5	39.7	14.3
North Las Vegas	56	843	55.7	19.5	0.4	4.9	30.1	0.0	0.0	0.0	0.2	25.7	22.6
Reno	326	2 230	137.3	45.9	15.0	73.4	163.9	27.8	12.2	9.4	9.0	27.8	9.4
Sparks	140	874	68.1	19.3	48.8	2.2	4.3	0.2	0.1	1.4	0.4	1.4	0.0
NEW HAMPSHIRE	2 159	11 379	794.5	236.6	531.1	207.2	1 865.3	801.4	176.9	45.0	133.4	148.9	55.6
Concord	103	589	50.4	12.9	1.1	5.9	333.1	31.1	47.9	37.5	55.8	34.2	14.3
Dover	40	226	16.0	4.8	0.1	1.2	5.2	0.0	0.0	0.0	0.2	4.5	2.6
Manchester	222	1 642	116.4	39.2	12.3	3.9	47.4	1.3	3.9	0.0	0.6	17.7	8.9
Nashua	153	1 197	90.9	28.8	317.5	4.5	25.3	0.9	0.0	0.0	0.3	15.7	2.9
Rochester	47	231	16.3	4.4	1.8	6.1	2.2	0.0	0.0	0.0	0.0	2.1	0.4
NEW JERSEY	15 077	78 644	5 434.8	1 665.1	3 873.1	1 587.9	11 480.9	5 007.2	1 408.0	125.3	892.8	1 254.9	287.3
Atlantic City	68	725	27.7	9.2	0.4	1.6	50.9	0.0	8.0	0.0	0.2	39.5	0.0
Bayonne	100	315	26.2	10.1	17.5	3.6	17.3	0.0	1.3	0.4	0.3	10.4	0.0
Bergenfield Borough	69	258	16.3	5.0	0.2	0.0	1.0	0.0	0.0	0.0	0.0	1.0	0.0
Camden	64	673	36.8	11.0	74.4	11.8	77.6	7.4	11.1	0.2	0.5	53.0	0.1
Clifton	160	661	57.4	18.7	113.8	3.1	11.0	0.0	0.0	0.0	0.3	9.7	0.3
East Orange	61	388	57.1	12.8	0.1	8.5	44.8	0.8	4.1	0.0	0.0	38.6	0.0
Elizabeth	175	1 114	84.3	25.8	13.2	20.7	26.0	2.9	0.0	0.0	0.0	22.3	2.1
Englewood	83	397	23.5	7.7	2.5	18.8	11.4	0.8	0.0	0.2	0.8	9.4	0.1
Fair Lawn Borough	77	840	55.6	23.3	1.4	0.0	0.1	0.0	0.0	0.1	0.0	0.0	0.1
Fort Lee Borough	94	469	26.3	8.2	0.3	1.0	16.3	0.1	0.0	0.0	0.0	16.1	0.0
Garfield	62	200	17.9	4.3	0.6	0.0	0.0	0.0	0.0	0.0	0.0	0.0	0.0
Hackensack	157	1 230	84.2	27.6	11.5	0.6	29.3	1.5	3.5	0.6	0.7	20.7	1.0
Hoboken	75	238	15.3	4.2	8.8	0.9	34.0	1.0	1.7	0.0	2.1	17.3	2.0
Jersey City	303	2 357	114.2	32.8	4.2	6.6	135.8	9.9	12.5	0.2	4.7	94.4	26.5
Kearny	80	245	15.3	4.1	0.1	0.0	0.5	0.0	0.0	0.0	0.0	0.3	0.0
Linden	113	699	60.2	19.5	0.9	0.7	7.2	0.0	0.0	0.0	0.5	5.4	0.0
Long Branch	63	287	16.3	5.0	1.3	0.2	8.4	0.1	0.0	0.0	0.0	8.2	0.0
Millville	40	270	14.2	4.8	1.3	0.0	10.0	0.0	0.0	0.0	2.3	7.6	0.0
Newark	400	2 826	185.4	60.6	50.6	36.9	441.2	95.2	32.4	5.1	8.2	200.9	17.8
New Brunswick	66	433	20.5	6.7	11.7	7.4	126.1	27.8	2.9	9.7	3.2	14.0	36.8
Paramus Borough	68	893	60.0	21.7	0.2	0.5	5.8	0.0	0.0	0.0	0.0	0.1	8.3
Passaic	73	395	24.9	8.4	5.1	0.1	19.3	0.0	0.9	0.0	0.0	16.4	0.0
Paterson	193	1 182	83.5	28.1	5.6	2.4	66.8	10.5	6.9	0.2	2.2	43.8	7.2
Perth Amboy	75	399	29.3	9.3	-0.2	2.4	4.0	0.7	0.0	0.0	0.1	3.2	0.5
Plainfield	48	192	13.8	4.5	0.0	0.0	13.4	2.8	0.0	0.0	0.9	9.6	0.5
Rahway	62	251	22.8	7.2	4.4	0.0	10.7	0.0	0.0	0.0	0.0	3.8	0.0
Sayreville Borough	52	260	13.4	3.9	0.3	1.6	5.1	0.0	0.0	0.0	0.0	4.8	0.0
Trenton	102	552	40.6	11.0	44.9	9.7	1 308.2	200.3	262.4	81.2	282.0	109.0	14.0
Union City	106	341	20.5	5.5	1.5	0.0	11.0	0.0	0.0	0.0	0.4	10.5	0.0
Vineland	140	647	34.2	11.8	33.1	3.3	18.4	0.0	0.0	0.5	1.5	10.4	4.3
Westfield	80	426	24.4	8.4	0.0	0.1	1.3	0.0	0.0	0.0	0.0	1.2	0.0
West New York	71	227	12.1	3.0	0.4	0.0	12.8	1.3	3.7	0.0	0.0	7.8	0.4
NEW MEXICO	2 318	13 448	759.1	227.2	955.4	4 863.6	4 322.3	1 887.2	502.3	117.6	519.7	149.3	116.7
Alamogordo	46	215	10.3	2.7	19.8	0.6	4.3	0.0	0.0	0.9	2.7	0.3	0.3
Albuquerque	788	6 073	339.0	111.0	325.2	2 338.1	373.9	93.4	19.5	26.3	24.6	67.6	48.7
Carlsbad	54	241	19.2	4.1	1.8	119.9	12.4	0.0	5.2	3.6	0.0	2.4	0.1
Clovis	67	302	15.5	4.2	1.7	0.7	7.4	0.0	0.0	0.0	1.4	4.9	3.6
Farmington	122	900	54.6	15.6	0.1	6.5	11.1	0.5	0.2	0.0	4.4	2.5	5.0
Hobbs	68	432	34.4	9.7	0.0	0.2	8.6	0.0	2.4	0.0	1.1	5.1	4.0
Las Cruces	132	688	33.4	9.5	68.4	73.6	59.0	14.4	5.2	6.6	2.9	8.9	24.1
Rio Rancho	NA	NA	NA	NA	0.2	0.4	1.6	0.0	0.0	0.4	1.3	0.3	0.0
Roswell	67	309	17.4	4.6	2.0	5.7	11.5	0.0	0.0	0.4	3.0	5.0	0.3
Santa Fe	159	825	52.0	15.1	13.2	16.0	421.3	61.4	94.0	63.0	113.3	10.9	5.1
NEW YORK	30 104	146 365	10 014.6	2 858.7	4 252.8	3 505.4	47 574.7	26 018.6	5 892.8	273.3	2 772.6	3 612.2	1 308.8
Albany	147	1 060	98.5	27.8	22.0	40.9	2 692.3	347.6	89.5	65.7	914.5	170.3	159.5
Auburn	55	313	24.5	5.6	1.0	1.8	13.0	0.0	1.1	2.1	0.5	5.5	3.9
Binghamton	89	452	27.2	8.4	91.1	3.6	34.3	5.0	4.5	0.4	2.2	14.1	9.3
Buffalo	440	2 527	155.8	47.1	110.1	183.9	319.8	120.2	25.1	1.5	10.0	92.8	43.0
Elmira	37	195	16.3	4.1	3.2	0.3	16.8	0.0	1.3	0.3	0.0	11.4	2.5
Freeport	95	343	29.3	7.7	2.5	0.6	4.2	0.0	0.0	0.0	1.0	3.0	0.0
Glen Cove	78	255	20.6	5.4	2.7	0.0	8.8	0.0	0.6	0.2	0.0	8.0	0.0
Hempstead	91	1 284	72.7	26.9	0.6	0.2	59.5	0.5	7.9	0.0	0.5	36.7	9.4

1. Firms subject to federal tax. 2. Includes program categories not shown separately. State totals include additional categories not allocated by city.

Table D. Cities — **City Government Finances**

City	City government finances, 2002									
	General revenue							General expenditure		
		Intergovernmental		Taxes					Per capita[1] (dollars)	
					Per capita[1] (dollars)					
	Total (mil dol)	Total (mil dol)	Percent from state government	Total (mil dol)	Total	Property	Sales and gross receipts	Total (mil dol)	Total	Capital outlays
	117	118	119	120	121	122	123	124	125	126
NEVADA	X	X	X	X	X	X	X	X	X	X
Carson City	160.0	28.7	91.9	26.0	479	232	209	143.8	2 648	135
Henderson	230.8	70.2	88.2	71.1	345	190	110	247.3	1 200	328
Las Vegas	573.6	211.8	82.3	168.4	331	163	93	556.0	1 093	282
North Las Vegas	160.5	57.5	52.7	47.9	353	221	66	164.5	1 211	262
Reno	247.4	72.3	61.9	83.0	436	252	95	274.7	1 444	595
Sparks	77.6	22.7	91.4	29.2	396	236	37	88.4	1 198	220
NEW HAMPSHIRE	X	X	X	X	X	X	X	X	X	X
Concord	46.1	4.3	69.1	27.4	663	626	0	44.9	1 085	160
Dover	72.4	28.5	75.0	36.2	1 302	1 281	0	72.6	2 612	402
Manchester	283.4	132.6	72.6	83.6	771	671	0	314.7	2 904	211
Nashua	236.8	89.0	91.3	121.6	1 386	1 373	0	242.7	2 767	663
Rochester	68.8	29.7	92.8	34.9	1 189	1 043	0	66.7	2 273	258
NEW JERSEY	X	X	X	X	X	X	X	X	X	X
Atlantic City	158.4	33.7	55.6	105.9	2 636	2 550	0	164.8	4 101	678
Bayonne	192.3	62.7	88.9	102.3	1 661	1 642	0	184.9	3 001	184
Bergenfield Borough	NA	NA	NA	NA	NA	NA	NA	NA	NA	NA
Camden	NA	NA	NA	NA	NA	NA	NA	NA	NA	NA
Clifton	NA	NA	NA	NA	NA	NA	NA	NA	NA	NA
East Orange	284.0	190.3	97.4	69.0	989	989	0	278.9	3 999	238
Elizabeth	162.2	55.8	83.0	69.3	562	529	18	139.2	1 129	32
Englewood	NA	NA	NA	NA	NA	NA	NA	NA	NA	NA
Fair Lawn Borough	NA	NA	NA	NA	NA	NA	NA	NA	NA	NA
Fort Lee Borough	NA	NA	NA	NA	NA	NA	NA	NA	NA	NA
Garfield	66.7	26.8	90.0	26.0	874	861	0	61.5	2 067	55
Hackensack	54.4	7.5	81.5	41.3	950	933	0	58.0	1 333	29
Hoboken	78.7	33.6	48.7	20.8	525	476	12	73.1	1 851	4
Jersey City	442.7	179.4	65.6	120.8	503	458	3	396.5	1 651	95
Kearny	67.2	32.2	100.0	30.2	749	744	0	49.7	1 234	121
Linden	NA	NA	NA	NA	NA	NA	NA	NA	NA	NA
Long Branch	49.7	20.1	58.1	21.1	668	640	3	42.9	1 358	158
Millville	24.0	9.2	83.0	8.4	314	302	0	22.2	826	31
Newark	678.1	347.6	47.7	163.8	591	420	54	636.6	2 298	214
New Brunswick	190.3	112.1	86.7	45.0	912	878	1	196.9	3 987	469
Paramus Borough	NA	NA	NA	NA	NA	NA	NA	NA	NA	NA
Passaic	79.6	35.6	52.1	37.5	548	533	1	77.0	1 125	63
Paterson	174.9	75.2	65.7	72.7	482	482	0	185.3	1 229	67
Perth Amboy	61.4	30.9	66.8	20.9	433	426	0	57.3	1 190	180
Plainfield	NA	NA	NA	NA	NA	NA	NA	NA	NA	NA
Rahway	34.6	9.9	58.4	19.3	717	695	2	39.9	1 482	232
Sayreville Borough	40.0	18.7	67.0	16.4	392	375	2	34.4	823	61
Trenton	390.8	311.5	99.9	51.8	605	582	2	410.1	4 788	368
Union City	203.1	156.4	95.4	37.4	559	545	1	203.8	3 046	153
Vineland	52.5	18.5	79.7	18.3	325	305	2	50.8	902	93
Westfield	NA	NA	NA	NA	NA	NA	NA	NA	NA	NA
West New York	120.5	79.4	96.8	33.1	707	692	0	127.8	2 725	140
NEW MEXICO	X	X	X	X	X	X	X	X	X	X
Alamogordo	27.8	9.1	90.9	10.8	309	68	228	25.2	719	76
Albuquerque	705.8	242.4	69.9	228.7	493	170	300	628.1	1 354	350
Carlsbad	26.0	8.7	91.7	9.0	358	52	301	23.5	934	67
Clovis	26.4	10.8	69.1	9.9	305	31	271	26.1	803	135
Farmington	114.1	25.5	94.7	20.0	494	23	460	113.5	2 799	252
Hobbs	33.9	13.9	93.1	12.1	426	38	385	36.4	1 278	240
Las Cruces	95.0	14.3	74.8	52.9	705	87	604	83.4	1 111	178
Rio Rancho	46.2	8.5	92.6	17.6	312	90	214	36.5	644	125
Roswell	NA	NA	NA	NA	NA	NA	NA	NA	NA	NA
Santa Fe	131.2	44.2	89.1	50.1	770	21	726	119.7	1 837	327
NEW YORK	X	X	X	X	X	X	X	X	X	X
Albany	131.8	52.6	43.2	41.8	446	383	34	141.9	1 513	220
Auburn	34.3	12.9	38.8	9.0	318	274	31	35.0	1 243	123
Binghamton	55.2	25.7	26.3	18.8	402	374	19	65.4	1 398	211
Buffalo	1 007.6	757.2	79.9	145.9	507	435	53	1 031.8	3 587	220
Elmira	26.8	13.4	41.4	8.2	271	240	24	32.0	1 052	186
Freeport	38.9	3.3	71.7	23.5	535	502	10	45.9	1 045	168
Glen Cove	35.0	11.9	61.8	17.1	635	542	23	39.5	1 468	272
Hempstead	50.5	13.7	87.7	29.9	559	527	16	55.5	1 037	79

1. Based on population estimated as of July 1 of the year shown.

City	City government finances, 2002 (cont'd)									
	General expenditure									
	Percent of total for—									
	Public welfare	Highways	Parking facilities	Education	Health and hospitals	Police protection	Sewerage and sanitation	Parks and recreation	Housing and community development	Interest on debt
	127	128	129	130	131	132	133	134	135	136
NEVADA	X	X	X	X	X	X	X	X	X	X
Carson City	1.1	6.6	0.0	0.0	52.2	7.4	2.8	5.1	0.7	1.8
Henderson	0.0	3.9	0.0	0.0	0.0	14.7	5.3	23.4	2.7	9.6
Las Vegas	0.1	11.1	0.6	0.0	0.4	15.9	5.8	11.9	2.1	3.6
North Las Vegas	0.0	7.5	0.1	0.0	0.3	17.8	5.4	9.6	6.2	2.7
Reno...............................	0.0	40.2	0.2	0.0	0.3	18.3	6.9	3.5	1.7	4.1
Sparks	0.2	11.6	0.3	0.0	0.1	15.1	11.9	7.9	1.6	3.6
NEW HAMPSHIRE	X	X	X	X	X	X	X	X	X	X
Concord...........................	2.5	10.0	1.8	0.0	0.9	12.6	12.1	5.8	0.0	3.6
Dover...............................	1.2	2.5	0.3	44.9	0.0	6.3	5.1	3.1	0.5	4.8
Manchester	0.7	5.4	0.5	37.0	1.1	5.7	2.6	2.6	10.8	6.9
Nashua	0.6	2.6	0.1	56.2	0.8	5.4	5.2	1.1	0.4	3.1
Rochester	1.4	2.6	0.0	54.6	0.3	5.6	6.0	0.8	0.5	6.2
NEW JERSEY	X	X	X	X	X	X	X	X	X	X
Atlantic City	2.3	2.7	0.0	0.0	4.0	24.2	1.7	2.9	14.9	3.0
Bayonne	3.5	0.7	0.4	49.8	0.8	9.5	5.4	1.4	6.3	1.4
Bergenfield Borough	NA	NA	NA	NA	NA	NA	NA	NA	NA	NA
Camden...........................	NA	NA	NA	NA	NA	NA	NA	NA	NA	NA
Clifton.............................	NA	NA	NA	NA	NA	NA	NA	NA	NA	NA
East Orange.....................	0.3	0.6	0.1	66.0	1.0	7.3	4.2	0.9	1.5	0.8
Elizabeth	0.0	3.7	1.7	0.0	2.9	23.3	13.2	5.2	7.3	4.2
Englewood	NA	NA	NA	NA	NA	NA	NA	NA	NA	NA
Fair Lawn Borough	NA	NA	NA	NA	NA	NA	NA	NA	NA	NA
Fort Lee Borough	NA	NA	NA	NA	NA	NA	NA	NA	NA	NA
Garfield............................	1.4	3.2	4.0	55.9	0.5	9.7	6.6	1.2	2.8	1.4
Hackensack......................	0.3	12.3	1.0	0.0	0.9	18.9	11.8	1.7	3.5	1.9
Hoboken...........................	0.0	1.1	5.7	0.0	0.9	17.6	5.8	3.1	20.7	5.2
Jersey City	0.2	1.8	0.4	0.0	1.0	21.3	14.9	1.8	16.1	5.0
Kearny	0.0	6.9	0.0	0.0	1.4	25.2	13.7	2.4	0.0	4.0
Linden.............................	NA	NA	NA	NA	NA	NA	NA	NA	NA	NA
Long Branch	0.0	8.8	1.5	0.0	1.1	16.3	11.8	1.9	25.4	1.6
Millville............................	0.0	3.5	0.0	0.0	1.2	21.9	22.0	3.3	10.4	0.6
Newark............................	1.0	1.6	0.0	0.0	4.7	17.8	9.1	1.6	28.0	2.6
New Brunswick	0.0	0.5	2.3	58.0	0.3	6.2	3.0	0.8	9.7	6.0
Paramus Borough	NA	NA	NA	NA	NA	NA	NA	NA	NA	NA
Passaic............................	0.0	2.8	0.0	1.6	2.1	18.6	10.9	1.2	24.9	1.3
Paterson..........................	1.3	4.2	1.8	0.0	4.7	19.0	15.2	2.3	13.3	2.4
Perth Amboy	0.5	10.1	0.7	0.0	0.8	19.2	10.7	2.7	9.2	4.2
Plainfield..........................	NA	NA	NA	NA	NA	NA	NA	NA	NA	NA
Rahway	0.4	6.0	0.0	0.0	1.7	20.1	7.5	3.7	9.3	2.2
Sayreville Borough.............	0.0	8.0	0.0	0.0	0.8	23.9	13.9	3.0	13.5	3.8
Trenton	0.1	0.8	1.6	56.6	1.6	7.2	4.7	0.9	3.5	1.1
Union City	0.1	0.5	0.7	65.5	0.5	7.2	2.8	0.5	6.5	1.0
Vineland	0.0	6.1	0.0	0.0	7.7	17.8	14.0	1.2	7.0	4.1
Westfield..........................	NA	NA	NA	NA	NA	NA	NA	NA	NA	NA
West New York	0.0	3.2	0.6	63.0	0.2	7.8	4.3	1.9	0.7	1.1
NEW MEXICO	X	X	X	X	X	X	X	X	X	X
Alamogordo......................	0.0	10.4	0.0	0.0	0.0	20.7	10.9	13.5	3.2	3.1
Albuquerque.....................	0.9	8.8	5.0	0.0	1.6	15.8	10.5	10.9	3.1	4.8
Carlsbad..........................	1.1	17.0	0.0	0.0	0.6	20.2	19.0	12.6	0.8	0.5
Clovis..............................	0.0	8.6	0.0	0.0	0.0	18.7	15.5	6.4	10.4	5.2
Farmington	0.0	9.3	0.0	0.0	0.1	6.2	5.5	5.9	0.0	49.6
Hobbs.............................	0.0	6.9	0.0	0.0	1.4	19.8	12.1	16.8	0.0	2.7
Las Cruces	0.0	14.8	0.0	0.0	0.0	17.0	14.8	6.5	2.0	6.4
Rio Rancho	0.0	12.9	0.0	0.0	0.1	34.1	18.7	11.0	1.7	1.8
Roswell............................	NA	NA	NA	NA	NA	NA	NA	NA	NA	NA
Santa Fe	3.9	12.1	2.3	0.0	0.0	12.8	13.1	11.4	4.3	8.1
NEW YORK	X	X	X	X	X	X	X	X	X	X
Albany.............................	0.0	9.8	0.0	0.0	0.1	22.8	7.7	5.5	0.0	12.6
Auburn.............................	0.0	10.5	0.7	0.0	0.0	13.3	16.4	4.3	5.5	13.1
Binghamton	1.9	5.4	0.8	0.0	0.0	13.1	19.0	3.5	5.1	9.3
Buffalo.............................	0.0	4.7	0.3	56.1	0.2	6.6	4.6	1.3	6.2	2.3
Elmira..............................	0.0	14.2	0.9	0.0	0.2	17.3	4.2	4.5	5.4	3.0
Freeport...........................	0.0	11.3	0.1	0.0	0.0	24.0	8.2	6.9	2.0	3.9
Glen Cove	7.2	5.9	0.0	0.0	0.5	19.2	11.6	5.1	12.4	6.3
Hempstead........................	0.0	8.4	0.4	0.0	0.0	26.3	4.0	3.7	14.6	3.0

City	City government finances, 2002 (cont'd)			City government employment, 2002	Climate[2]						
	Debt outstanding				Average daily temperature (degrees Fahrenheit)						
					Mean		Limits				
	Total (mil dol)	Per capita[1] (dollars)	Percent utility		January	July	January[3]	July[4]	Annual precipitation (inches)	Heating degree days	Cooling degree days
	137	138	139	140	141	142	143	144	145	146	147
NEVADA	X	X	X	X	X	X	X	X	X	X	X
Carson City	73.3	1 349	24.5	1 453	33.6	69.9	20.7	89.5	10.87	5 691	401
Henderson	510.0	2 474	26.9	1 684	45.5	91.1	33.6	105.9	4.13	2 407	3 201
Las Vegas	350.0	688	0.0	2 581	45.5	91.1	33.6	105.9	4.13	2 407	3 201
North Las Vegas	95.3	701	0.9	1 235	45.5	91.1	33.6	105.9	4.13	2 407	3 201
Reno	393.2	2 067	0.0	1 535	32.9	71.6	20.7	91.9	7.53	5 674	508
Sparks	68.2	925	0.0	629	32.9	71.6	20.7	91.9	7.53	5 674	508
NEW HAMPSHIRE	X	X	X	X	X	X	X	X	X	X	X
Concord	70.2	1 695	18.7	448	18.6	69.5	7.4	82.4	36.37	7 554	328
Dover	62.8	2 262	24.0	995	22.2	69.8	11.0	82.9	42.18	7 002	347
Manchester	447.8	4 131	4.7	3 265	18.6	69.5	7.4	82.4	36.37	7 554	328
Nashua	161.4	1 840	0.0	2 674	21.4	70.2	10.0	82.4	43.00	7 110	382
Rochester	82.6	2 816	0.0	813	21.5	70.2	10.4	83.2	46.85	7 052	397
NEW JERSEY	X	X	X	X	X	X	X	X	X	X	X
Atlantic City	143.1	3 562	19.2	1 746	30.9	74.7	21.4	84.5	40.29	5 169	826
Bayonne	81.7	1 326	0.0	2 301	29.5	74.9	23.3	82.2	43.50	5 362	874
Bergenfield Borough	NA	NA	NA	185	NA	NA	NA	NA	NA	NA	NA
Camden	NA	NA	NA	1 513	31.8	76.6	23.7	86.6	45.56	4 725	1 085
Clifton	NA	NA	NA	654	28.3	74.9	19.4	85.9	49.79	5 486	838
East Orange	48.6	697	36.8	2 862	30.6	77.8	23.4	87.0	43.97	4 888	1 201
Elizabeth	108.6	881	0.0	1 439	30.6	77.8	23.4	87.0	43.97	4 888	1 201
Englewood	NA	NA	NA	735	NA	NA	NA	NA	NA	NA	NA
Fair Lawn Borough	NA	NA	NA	252	28.3	74.9	19.4	85.9	49.79	5 486	838
Fort Lee Borough	NA	NA	NA	335	29.5	74.9	23.3	82.2	43.50	5 362	874
Garfield	19.5	656	18.8	183	28.3	74.9	19.4	85.9	49.79	5 486	838
Hackensack	47.2	1 085	0.0	438	28.3	74.9	19.4	85.9	49.79	5 486	838
Hoboken	73.7	1 865	0.0	678	29.5	74.9	23.3	82.2	43.50	5 362	874
Jersey City	462.0	1 924	11.3	3 424	29.5	74.9	23.3	82.2	43.50	5 362	874
Kearny	40.4	1 002	2.2	368	30.6	77.8	23.4	87.0	43.97	4 888	1 201
Linden	NA	NA	NA	649	30.6	77.8	23.4	87.0	43.97	4 888	1 201
Long Branch	19.5	618	0.0	403	30.6	73.7	22.3	82.3	47.13	5 253	746
Millville	8.2	303	6.7	276	31.1	75.9	22.5	85.3	42.28	4 946	983
Newark	358.8	1 295	9.7	5 754	30.6	77.8	23.4	87.0	43.97	4 888	1 201
New Brunswick	250.3	5 067	3.2	3 874	29.0	74.6	20.6	84.9	47.02	5 340	804
Paramus Borough	NA	NA	NA	359	28.3	74.9	19.4	85.9	49.79	5 486	838
Passaic	21.5	314	0.0	704	28.3	74.9	19.4	85.9	49.79	5 486	838
Paterson	76.6	508	10.7	1 816	28.3	74.9	19.4	85.9	49.79	5 486	838
Perth Amboy	51.1	1 061	7.3	490	29.0	74.6	20.6	84.9	47.02	5 340	804
Plainfield	NA	NA	NA	596	29.4	75.0	21.5	86.4	49.00	5 227	891
Rahway	38.6	1 436	20.4	364	30.6	77.8	23.4	87.0	43.97	4 888	1 201
Sayreville Borough	31.0	742	15.3	245	29.0	74.6	20.6	84.9	47.02	5 340	804
Trenton	177.7	2 075	30.9	4 344	29.6	75.4	20.5	87.3	45.43	5 172	937
Union City	51.6	771	0.0	2 263	29.5	74.9	23.3	82.2	43.50	5 362	874
Vineland	129.8	2 305	39.8	738	31.1	75.9	22.5	85.3	42.28	4 946	983
Westfield	NA	NA	NA	265	29.7	74.8	20.3	86.6	48.75	5 239	841
West New York	24.1	515	0.0	1 362	29.5	74.9	23.3	82.2	43.50	5 362	874
NEW MEXICO	X	X	X	X	X	X	X	X	X	X	X
Alamogordo	23.1	658	41.9	338	42.6	80.4	28.3	94.9	12.74	2 908	1 764
Albuquerque	892.7	1 924	25.5	6 466	34.2	78.5	21.7	92.5	8.88	4 425	1 244
Carlsbad	25.0	990	77.5	335	NA	NA	NA	NA	NA	NA	NA
Clovis	16.2	499	0.0	346	36.5	76.9	22.3	90.5	17.51	4 068	1 156
Farmington	851.9	21 002	6.3	711	28.6	75.0	15.7	92.3	8.26	5 495	803
Hobbs	22.2	780	25.2	492	42.5	79.8	28.0	92.8	16.78	2 851	1 790
Las Cruces	114.3	1 524	17.6	1 447	41.8	80.4	26.4	94.2	9.40	3 155	1 618
Rio Rancho	21.5	380	31.3	484	34.2	78.5	21.7	92.5	8.88	4 425	1 244
Roswell	NA	NA	NA	568	39.5	80.7	24.7	94.6	12.58	3 267	1 776
Santa Fe	250.6	3 848	27.2	1 308	30.4	69.0	13.7	84.9	16.37	6 138	324
NEW YORK	X	X	X	X	X	X	X	X	X	X	X
Albany	299.2	3 191	0.0	1 472	20.6	71.8	11.0	84.0	36.17	6 894	507
Auburn	83.3	2 957	0.2	353	23.1	71.5	15.1	81.7	36.57	6 782	501
Binghamton	66.8	1 430	37.4	648	21.1	69.2	14.3	78.6	36.99	7 273	337
Buffalo	658.3	2 288	16.8	11 731	23.6	71.1	17.0	80.2	38.58	6 747	477
Elmira	38.2	1 257	50.3	328	22.8	69.7	13.4	82.7	33.32	6 982	373
Freeport	62.7	1 426	26.3	425	31.2	75.5	24.9	82.8	41.59	5 027	921
Glen Cove	44.6	1 659	2.2	251	NA	NA	NA	NA	NA	NA	NA
Hempstead	41.9	784	3.6	439	31.0	74.4	25.0	82.6	44.68	5 316	853

1. Based on the population estimated as of July 1 of the year shown. 2. Represents normal values based on the 30-year period, 1961–1990. 3. Average daily minimum. 4. Average daily maximum.

Table D. Cities — Land Area and Population

STATE Place code	City	Land area,[1] 2000 (sq km)	Population, 2003 Total persons	Rank	Per square kilometer	Population characteristics, 2000 — Percent — Race (alone or in combination) White	Black	Am. Indian, Alaska Native	Asian and Pacific Islander	Other race	Hispanic or Latino[2]	Non-Hispanic White
		1	2	3	4	5	6	7	8	9	10	11
	NEW YORK—Cont'd											
36 38077	Ithaca	14.1	30 343	1 053	2 152.0	76.4	7.8	1.0	15.6	2.8	5.3	71.3
36 38264	Jamestown	23.3	30 726	1 041	1 318.7	93.5	4.5	1.2	0.7	2.4	4.9	89.0
36 42554	Lindenhurst	9.7	28 469	1 111	2 934.9	95.8	1.1	0.4	1.8	2.8	6.5	89.8
36 43335	Long Beach	5.5	35 415	912	6 439.1	85.9	6.8	0.5	3.0	6.2	12.8	77.1
36 47042	Middletown	13.3	25 863	1 206	1 944.6	72.1	17.4	1.5	2.3	11.4	25.1	56.8
36 49121	Mount Vernon	11.3	68 404	416	6 053.5	30.9	62.2	0.9	3.0	7.8	10.4	24.4
36 50034	Newburgh	9.9	28 412	1 114	2 869.9	45.9	35.5	1.5	1.3	21.1	36.3	28.2
36 50617	New Rochelle	26.8	72 582	384	2 708.3	70.2	20.3	0.6	3.9	8.4	20.1	55.8
36 51000	New York	785.6	8 085 742	1	10 292.4	47.5	28.4	1.1	11.1	17.0	27.0	35.0
36 51055	Niagara Falls	36.4	53 989	588	1 483.2	77.9	19.8	2.4	1.0	1.1	2.0	75.3
36 53682	North Tonawanda	26.2	32 359	995	1 235.1	98.5	0.5	0.6	0.7	0.4	1.1	97.1
36 59223	Port Chester	6.1	27 955	1 138	4 582.8	67.0	7.6	0.7	2.5	29.3	46.2	42.8
36 59641	Poughkeepsie	13.3	30 174	1 058	2 268.7	55.3	38.5	1.2	2.0	7.2	10.6	49.2
36 63000	Rochester	92.8	215 093	84	2 317.8	50.9	40.7	1.3	2.9	8.4	12.8	44.3
36 63418	Rome	194.1	34 512	938	177.8	89.7	8.5	0.6	1.3	2.1	4.7	85.5
36 65255	Saratoga Springs	73.6	27 332	1 151	371.4	94.8	3.8	0.7	1.3	0.9	1.9	92.6
36 65508	Schenectady	28.1	61 016	480	2 171.4	79.6	16.8	1.0	2.8	3.6	5.9	74.5
36 70420	Spring Valley	5.4	25 509	1 216	4 723.9	40.3	48.3	0.8	6.9	10.2	15.4	30.9
36 73000	Syracuse	65.0	144 001	154	2 215.4	67.1	27.5	2.2	3.9	3.2	5.3	62.4
36 75484	Troy	27.0	48 649	652	1 801.8	82.2	12.6	0.7	4.0	3.1	4.3	78.7
36 76540	Utica	42.3	59 485	503	1 406.3	82.0	14.0	0.7	2.7	3.7	5.8	76.5
36 76705	Valley Stream	8.9	36 214	887	4 069.0	80.4	8.3	0.4	7.9	5.8	12.3	71.4
36 78608	Watertown	23.2	26 782	1 181	1 154.4	91.2	6.1	1.2	1.9	2.3	3.6	87.8
36 81677	White Plains	25.4	55 900	549	2 200.8	67.5	17.1	0.8	5.5	13.2	23.5	54.2
36 84000	Yonkers	46.8	197 388	100	4 217.7	63.2	18.1	0.9	5.7	16.8	25.9	50.7
37 00000	**NORTH CAROLINA**	126 160.6	8 407 248	X	66.6	73.1	22.1	1.6	1.8	2.8	4.7	70.2
37 02140	Asheville	106.0	69 045	411	651.4	79.3	18.2	0.8	1.3	2.1	3.8	76.0
37 09060	Burlington	55.1	46 271	698	839.8	67.3	25.6	0.7	2.1	5.8	10.1	62.0
37 10740	Cary	109.0	99 824	246	915.8	83.7	6.6	0.6	8.9	2.2	4.3	79.7
37 11800	Chapel Hill	51.2	49 301	641	962.9	79.4	12.1	0.9	8.0	1.6	3.2	76.1
37 12000	Charlotte	627.5	584 658	21	931.7	59.4	33.4	0.7	3.9	4.4	7.4	55.1
37 14100	Concord	133.6	58 943	513	441.2	79.8	15.5	0.6	1.5	3.9	7.8	75.0
37 19000	Durham	245.1	198 376	96	809.4	46.8	44.6	0.8	4.2	5.6	8.6	42.4
37 22920	Fayetteville	152.2	124 372	184	817.2	50.7	43.8	1.8	3.4	3.4	5.7	46.6
37 25580	Gastonia	119.3	67 781	419	568.2	71.0	26.1	0.5	1.5	2.1	5.5	67.3
37 26880	Goldsboro	64.2	38 484	834	599.4	44.2	53.2	0.8	2.0	1.6	2.7	41.9
37 28000	Greensboro	271.2	229 110	77	844.8	56.6	38.2	0.9	3.3	2.8	4.4	53.6
37 28080	Greenville	66.2	67 190	425	1 015.0	62.4	34.7	0.6	2.3	1.5	2.1	60.6
37 31060	Hickory	72.7	39 476	819	543.0	78.3	14.6	0.5	4.5	3.8	7.7	73.2
37 31400	High Point	127.0	91 543	281	720.8	61.6	32.3	0.8	4.0	3.0	4.9	58.5
37 34200	Jacksonville	115.2	67 386	423	584.9	66.6	25.5	1.6	3.7	6.6	10.0	60.8
37 35200	Kannapolis	77.3	38 178	838	493.9	78.7	16.9	0.6	1.2	3.8	6.3	75.2
37 43920	Monroe	63.6	28 222	1 123	443.7	61.4	28.2	0.7	0.9	10.4	21.4	49.6
37 55000	Raleigh	296.8	316 802	57	1 067.4	64.7	28.6	0.8	3.9	4.0	7.0	60.3
37 57500	Rocky Mount	92.1	55 984	547	607.9	41.7	56.5	0.6	1.0	1.3	1.8	40.3
37 58860	Salisbury	46.0	26 548	1 188	577.1	58.4	38.2	0.7	1.8	2.4	4.3	55.4
37 74440	Wilmington	106.2	91 137	285	858.2	71.5	26.3	0.7	1.2	1.5	2.6	69.4
37 74540	Wilson	60.3	45 921	703	761.5	47.4	47.9	0.5	0.9	4.4	7.3	43.9
37 75000	Winston-Salem	281.9	190 299	111	675.1	56.7	37.9	0.6	1.5	4.9	8.6	52.4
38 00000	**NORTH DAKOTA**	178 646.8	633 837	X	3.5	93.4	0.8	5.5	0.9	0.6	1.2	91.7
38 07200	Bismarck	69.6	56 344	542	809.5	95.6	0.4	3.9	0.7	0.3	0.7	94.3
38 25700	Fargo	98.3	91 484	282	930.7	95.4	1.4	1.7	2.1	0.9	1.3	93.4
38 32060	Grand Forks	49.8	48 618	654	976.3	94.6	1.2	3.5	1.4	0.8	1.9	92.3
38 53380	Minot	37.7	35 424	911	939.6	94.6	1.8	3.5	1.0	0.7	1.5	92.4
39 00000	**OHIO**	106 055.8	11 435 798	X	107.8	86.1	12.1	0.7	1.5	1.1	1.9	84.0
39 01000	Akron	160.8	212 215	86	1 319.7	68.9	29.7	0.9	1.9	0.8	1.2	66.7
39 03828	Barberton	23.3	27 462	1 145	1 178.6	93.7	5.9	0.8	0.5	0.4	0.6	92.0
39 04720	Beavercreek	68.4	39 196	821	573.0	94.5	1.6	0.5	4.1	0.5	1.1	92.6
39 07972	Bowling Green	26.3	29 382	1 084	1 117.2	93.1	3.2	0.6	2.3	2.3	3.5	90.6
39 09680	Brunswick	32.5	34 788	932	1 070.4	97.8	0.9	0.4	1.1	0.6	1.4	96.2
39 12000	Canton	53.2	79 255	348	1 489.8	77.1	22.9	1.5	0.6	1.2	1.2	73.8
39 15000	Cincinnati	201.9	317 361	56	1 571.9	54.2	44.0	0.8	1.9	1.0	1.3	52.5
39 16000	Cleveland	200.9	461 324	35	2 296.3	43.2	52.1	0.9	1.7	4.6	7.3	38.8
39 16014	Cleveland Heights	21.0	49 016	646	2 334.1	54.2	43.3	0.8	3.1	1.2	1.6	51.7
39 18000	Columbus	544.6	728 432	15	1 337.6	69.8	26.0	1.0	4.0	2.0	2.5	66.9
39 19778	Cuyahoga Falls	66.2	50 375	630	761.0	96.6	2.1	0.5	1.2	0.4	0.6	95.4
39 21000	Dayton	144.5	161 696	131	1 119.0	54.8	44.3	1.0	1.0	1.0	1.6	52.6

1. Dry land or land partially or temporarily covered by water.   2. Hispanic or Latino persons may be of any race.

Table D. Cities — Population and Households

City	Under 5 years	5 to 17 years	18 to 24 years	25 to 34 years	35 to 44 years	45 to 54 years	55 to 64 years	65 to 74 years	75 years and over	Percent female	Census counts 1990	Census counts 2000	Percent change 1990–2000	Percent change 2000–2003
	12	13	14	15	16	17	18	19	20	21	22	23	24	25
NEW YORK—Cont'd														
Ithaca	2.5	6.8	53.8	12.6	7.4	7.1	3.5	2.8	3.5	49.4	29 541	29 287	-0.9	3.6
Jamestown	7.6	18.3	9.1	13.5	14.7	12.9	8.0	7.5	8.5	52.3	34 681	31 730	-8.5	-3.2
Lindenhurst	6.9	19.8	7.1	14.5	19.5	13.5	7.6	6.3	4.7	51.4	26 879	27 819	3.5	2.3
Long Beach	4.9	13.7	6.6	16.5	17.9	14.9	8.9	7.6	9.1	51.9	33 510	35 462	5.8	-0.1
Middletown	7.9	19.9	9.4	15.3	15.6	12.4	7.5	5.4	6.6	51.7	24 160	25 388	5.1	1.9
Mount Vernon	7.1	18.3	8.3	14.9	16.2	13.1	9.3	6.5	6.4	54.9	67 153	68 381	1.8	0.0
Newburgh	9.8	23.4	12.7	15.1	13.7	9.4	6.7	4.5	4.6	52.6	26 454	28 259	6.8	0.5
New Rochelle	6.8	17.3	8.7	14.0	15.5	13.1	9.2	7.6	7.9	52.5	67 265	72 182	7.3	0.6
New York	6.8	17.5	10.0	17.1	15.8	12.6	8.5	6.2	5.5	52.6	7 322 564	8 008 278	9.4	1.0
Niagara Falls	6.4	18.3	8.6	12.4	15.3	12.5	7.9	8.7	9.9	53.2	61 840	55 593	-10.1	-2.9
North Tonawanda	5.7	18.1	8.6	12.3	16.7	14.8	8.3	8.2	7.5	51.4	34 989	33 262	-4.9	-2.7
Port Chester	7.0	15.5	10.8	18.5	16.7	11.5	7.1	6.3	6.6	49.4	24 728	27 867	12.7	0.3
Poughkeepsie	7.6	18.3	12.2	15.0	14.2	11.4	7.7	6.6	7.0	52.2	28 844	29 871	3.6	1.0
Rochester	7.8	20.3	11.6	17.1	15.0	11.4	6.7	4.5	5.5	52.2	230 356	219 773	-4.6	-2.1
Rome	5.9	16.3	8.5	14.3	15.6	13.2	9.2	7.8	9.4	48.8	44 350	34 950	-21.2	-1.3
Saratoga Springs	5.3	14.0	15.5	13.2	14.3	14.6	8.8	6.1	8.2	52.5	25 001	26 186	4.7	4.4
Schenectady	7.0	17.3	11.6	14.4	15.3	11.7	7.4	6.6	8.6	52.2	65 566	61 821	-5.7	-1.3
Spring Valley	9.6	22.5	10.7	16.4	15.3	11.5	7.3	3.8	2.9	50.3	21 802	25 464	16.8	0.2
Syracuse	6.9	18.0	16.8	14.5	13.4	11.0	6.5	5.8	7.1	52.9	163 860	147 306	-10.1	-2.2
Troy	6.4	15.7	17.6	14.9	13.6	10.9	7.2	6.5	7.2	50.5	54 269	49 170	-9.4	-1.1
Utica	6.7	17.4	10.0	13.2	13.7	11.8	8.4	8.1	10.7	53.0	68 637	60 651	-11.6	-1.9
Valley Stream	5.8	17.7	7.7	12.6	16.6	14.7	8.7	8.2	8.1	52.3	33 946	36 368	7.1	-0.4
Watertown	7.8	18.2	10.4	15.1	14.5	11.4	7.1	6.8	8.7	52.5	29 429	26 705	-9.3	0.3
White Plains	6.2	15.0	7.5	16.0	16.5	13.9	9.7	7.6	7.5	52.7	48 718	53 077	8.9	5.3
Yonkers	7.0	17.3	8.8	15.4	15.2	12.3	8.9	7.7	7.3	53.0	188 082	196 086	4.3	0.7
NORTH CAROLINA	6.7	17.7	10.0	15.1	16.0	13.5	9.0	6.6	5.4	51.0	6 632 448	8 049 313	21.4	4.4
Asheville	5.4	14.2	10.3	14.3	14.4	14.0	9.1	8.6	9.7	53.2	63 379	68 889	8.7	0.2
Burlington	6.5	17.2	8.9	14.6	14.4	12.6	8.8	8.5	8.5	53.0	39 498	44 917	13.7	3.0
Cary	8.1	21.0	6.6	16.9	21.6	14.1	6.3	3.1	2.3	50.2	44 394	94 536	112.9	5.6
Chapel Hill	3.6	11.5	37.1	14.2	10.2	9.9	5.5	3.9	4.2	54.9	38 711	48 715	25.8	1.2
Charlotte	7.1	17.6	10.4	19.1	17.1	12.9	7.1	4.7	4.1	51.0	419 558	540 828	28.9	8.1
Concord	7.9	18.3	8.9	17.1	16.4	12.3	7.9	5.6	5.5	51.1	29 591	55 977	89.2	5.3
Durham	7.2	15.8	14.1	20.1	15.5	11.8	6.3	4.6	4.7	51.9	138 894	187 035	34.7	6.1
Fayetteville	7.5	17.9	12.7	16.4	14.8	11.7	8.0	6.5	4.5	52.1	75 850	121 015	59.5	2.8
Gastonia	7.0	17.9	8.8	15.4	15.1	13.4	8.6	7.3	6.5	52.7	54 725	66 277	21.1	2.3
Goldsboro	7.1	17.9	11.4	14.6	15.2	12.0	8.0	7.3	6.4	50.8	40 736	39 043	-4.1	-1.4
Greensboro	6.3	15.9	14.1	16.7	14.9	12.5	7.6	6.1	5.8	52.8	185 125	223 891	21.8	2.3
Greenville	5.6	13.3	28.7	16.6	11.6	9.9	5.6	4.6	4.2	53.7	46 274	60 476	30.6	11.1
Hickory	6.9	16.3	11.2	16.1	14.6	12.8	8.5	7.0	6.6	51.9	28 474	37 222	30.7	6.1
High Point	7.5	18.5	9.3	15.6	16.2	13.0	8.0	6.1	5.7	52.2	69 428	85 839	23.6	6.6
Jacksonville	9.6	14.6	36.3	15.8	10.1	5.6	3.1	2.8	2.0	39.0	78 031	66 715	-14.5	1.0
Kannapolis	7.0	17.1	9.0	15.1	15.4	12.0	8.8	7.6	8.0	51.6	31 592	36 910	16.8	3.4
Monroe	8.8	18.1	11.6	18.2	14.4	10.6	7.4	5.7	5.2	49.4	18 623	26 228	40.8	7.6
Raleigh	6.3	14.5	15.9	20.7	15.9	11.9	6.4	4.4	4.0	50.5	218 859	276 093	30.2	14.7
Rocky Mount	7.0	20.7	8.9	13.1	15.4	13.8	8.1	6.7	6.3	54.0	53 078	55 893	13.1	0.2
Salisbury	6.4	15.4	13.1	12.4	12.7	11.9	8.2	8.3	11.6	52.6	23 626	26 462	12.0	0.3
Wilmington	5.3	13.1	17.2	15.5	13.0	12.1	8.5	7.7	7.6	53.3	55 530	75 838	36.6	20.2
Wilson	7.4	18.6	9.8	14.0	14.9	13.4	8.4	7.1	6.3	53.2	38 400	44 405	15.6	3.4
Winston-Salem	6.7	16.6	11.7	15.6	14.8	12.7	8.2	7.0	6.7	53.0	162 292	185 776	23.1	2.4
NORTH DAKOTA	6.1	18.9	11.4	12.0	15.3	13.3	8.3	7.1	7.6	50.1	638 800	642 200	0.5	-1.3
Bismarck	6.0	17.5	11.1	13.2	15.9	14.1	8.3	7.0	6.8	51.6	49 272	55 532	12.7	1.5
Fargo	6.4	14.8	19.2	16.7	14.4	12.2	6.3	5.0	5.1	50.0	74 084	90 599	22.3	1.0
Grand Forks	5.9	15.5	22.9	14.2	13.5	11.9	6.4	4.7	5.1	49.5	49 417	49 321	-0.2	-1.4
Minot	6.6	16.6	13.3	13.4	14.0	12.7	7.9	7.2	8.1	51.8	34 544	36 567	5.9	-3.1
OHIO	6.6	18.8	9.3	14.8	15.9	13.8	8.9	7.0	6.3	51.4	10 847 115	11 353 140	4.7	0.7
Akron	7.2	18.1	10.5	15.3	15.0	12.7	7.6	6.7	6.8	52.2	223 019	217 074	-2.7	-2.2
Barberton	7.7	17.1	8.4	13.7	14.6	12.8	8.4	8.5	8.8	53.3	27 623	27 899	1.0	-1.6
Beavercreek	5.2	20.1	6.3	9.5	17.5	17.8	11.5	7.0	5.2	50.6	33 626	37 984	13.0	3.2
Bowling Green	3.7	9.4	46.6	11.0	8.5	8.4	4.8	3.7	4.0	53.2	28 303	29 636	4.7	-0.9
Brunswick	7.3	20.5	8.1	14.9	17.8	14.4	8.8	4.9	3.4	50.9	28 218	33 388	18.3	4.2
Canton	7.8	18.8	9.8	14.4	14.8	12.5	7.6	6.8	7.5	53.3	84 161	80 806	-4.0	-1.9
Cincinnati	7.2	17.3	12.9	16.9	14.7	11.7	7.0	6.0	6.3	52.8	364 114	331 285	-9.0	-4.2
Cleveland	8.1	20.4	9.5	15.0	15.4	11.5	7.5	6.6	5.9	52.6	505 616	478 403	-5.4	-3.6
Cleveland Heights	6.2	17.7	9.2	16.7	15.0	15.0	8.6	6.2	5.5	53.3	54 052	49 958	-7.6	-1.9
Columbus	7.5	16.7	14.0	19.6	15.5	11.4	6.5	4.7	4.1	51.4	632 945	711 470	12.4	2.4
Cuyahoga Falls	6.5	15.9	7.9	15.9	16.1	13.2	8.4	8.1	8.0	52.5	48 950	49 374	0.9	2.0
Dayton	7.1	18.0	14.2	14.1	14.9	12.1	7.6	6.4	5.6	51.8	182 011	166 179	-8.7	-2.7

Table D. Cities — Group Quarters, Crime, and Education

City	Households, 2000 Number	Percent change, 1990–2000	Persons per household	Percent Female family householder[1]	Percent One-person	Persons in group quarters, 2000 Total	Institutional Total	Persons in nursing homes	Non-institutional	Serious crimes known to police,[2] 2002 Total Number	Rate[3]	Violent	Property	Education, 2000 School enrollment[4] Public	Private	Attainment[5] (percent) High school graduate or less	Bachelor's degree or more
	26	27	28	29	30	31	32	33	34	35	36	37	38	39	40	41	42
NEW YORK—Cont'd																	
Ithaca	10 287	7.0	2.13	7.8	43.3	7 417	180	171	7 237	1 311	4 434	156	4 278	4 870	14 211	27.0	57.9
Jamestown	13 558	-5.0	2.29	14.5	35.0	735	341	300	394	1 258	3 927	506	3 422	7 129	651	55.1	14.8
Lindenhurst	9 061	5.4	3.06	11.8	17.0	125	0	0	125	NA	NA	NA	NA	6 494	1 156	56.2	16.4
Long Beach	14 923	9.8	2.26	10.8	36.7	1 714	900	814	814	632	1 765	304	1 461	5 598	2 116	36.7	37.0
Middletown	9 466	7.7	2.62	16.7	30.0	581	199	191	382	865	3 375	312	3 063	5 690	992	55.0	17.0
Mount Vernon	25 729	2.2	2.63	23.0	30.0	748	539	517	209	2 183	3 162	633	2 529	13 783	4 807	52.1	24.2
Newburgh	9 144	1.5	2.97	25.4	27.1	1 105	193	20	912	1 889	6 621	2 058	4 564	8 077	957	69.5	11.2
New Rochelle	26 189	3.4	2.68	12.5	28.0	2 116	1 108	1 108	1 008	1 854	2 544	360	2 185	12 652	6 660	43.2	38.3
New York	3 021 588	7.2	2.59	19.1	31.9	182 430	75 870	42 480	106 560	250 630	3 100	790	2 310	1 609 315	607 930	52.2	27.4
Niagara Falls	24 099	-7.2	2.27	18.3	35.9	806	505	505	301	3 847	6 855	996	5 859	11 726	2 217	61.2	12.5
North Tonawanda	13 671	0.3	2.43	11.1	29.5	99	79	79	20	639	1 903	149	1 754	6 940	1 402	51.3	19.5
Port Chester	9 531	4.7	2.89	13.6	26.7	275	218	208	57	883	3 139	377	2 762	4 804	1 649	60.4	20.6
Poughkeepsie	12 014	1.2	2.40	19.7	35.4	985	559	180	426	1 306	4 331	942	3 389	6 678	1 914	55.1	19.5
Rochester	88 999	-4.9	2.36	23.3	37.1	9 422	3 991	2 556	5 431	16 911	7 622	805	6 817	51 452	15 890	55.6	20.1
Rome	13 653	-13.3	2.30	13.9	33.2	3 498	3 152	490	346	770	2 182	179	2 004	6 372	1 126	58.6	15.7
Saratoga Springs	10 784	11.3	2.21	9.6	35.0	2 300	442	379	1 858	542	2 050	140	1 910	4 285	3 035	34.4	38.9
Schenectady	26 265	-5.3	2.23	16.7	38.6	3 265	1 128	706	2 137	3 197	5 123	790	4 333	12 348	4 316	54.7	19.0
Spring Valley	7 566	0.7	3.33	21.4	20.6	296	86	77	210	206	801	210	591	5 409	3 128	54.9	19.9
Syracuse	59 482	-8.4	2.29	19.3	38.2	10 989	2 267	1 623	8 722	9 791	6 584	1 021	5 562	31 331	19 114	52.9	23.2
Troy	19 996	-3.7	2.26	16.3	36.6	3 988	846	606	3 142	2 496	5 028	633	4 396	9 453	6 318	54.5	19.4
Utica	25 100	-11.5	2.28	16.9	37.4	3 404	1 714	1 151	1 690	3 168	5 174	596	4 578	12 438	3 089	57.6	15.2
Valley Stream	12 484	5.3	2.91	11.5	20.2	55	0	0	55	NA	NA	NA	NA	8 023	1 872	48.3	24.9
Watertown	11 036	-3.4	2.32	14.2	34.5	1 097	741	601	356	791	2 934	271	2 663	5 909	899	51.9	17.3
White Plains	20 921	7.7	2.47	11.3	33.4	1 414	651	644	763	2 033	3 794	370	3 425	9 326	3 537	37.8	41.1
Yonkers	74 351	3.1	2.61	17.2	29.2	2 320	869	801	1 451	4 676	2 362	451	1 911	35 372	16 339	52.6	24.8
NORTH CAROLINA	3 132 013	24.4	2.49	12.5	25.4	253 881	106 659	50 892	147 222	392 826	4 721	470	4 251	1 762 124	281 101	50.3	22.5
Asheville	30 690	13.6	2.14	13.0	36.8	3 211	1 363	743	1 848	4 861	6 827	668	6 158	13 826	1 811	41.4	30.4
Burlington	18 280	9.9	2.40	14.9	30.3	1 111	749	714	362	3 722	8 017	631	7 386	9 104	1 398	54.5	21.7
Cary	34 906	106.4	2.69	6.3	21.0	569	497	497	72	2 253	2 306	115	2 191	23 046	4 893	15.6	60.7
Chapel Hill	17 808	29.2	2.22	7.5	31.2	9 247	345	290	8 902	2 505	4 975	469	4 506	23 973	1 744	11.8	73.7
Charlotte	215 449	35.5	2.45	13.7	29.5	12 228	5 081	2 428	7 147	48 597	7 513	1 172	6 340	115 669	27 752	35.0	36.4
Concord	20 962	94.0	2.61	11.5	23.6	1 346	756	617	590	2 894	5 002	299	4 703	12 006	2 132	47.4	22.8
Durham	74 981	33.9	2.37	15.9	31.9	9 373	2 341	1 605	7 032	14 461	7 480	936	6 544	38 130	16 355	35.0	41.8
Fayetteville	48 414	63.3	2.42	17.1	28.2	3 962	1 481	1 052	2 481	10 594	8 469	914	7 556	29 042	5 485	40.5	24.2
Gastonia	25 945	23.6	2.50	16.3	26.5	1 479	1 176	921	303	5 652	8 250	1 131	7 119	13 716	2 222	53.5	20.2
Goldsboro	14 630	9.0	2.40	20.4	30.5	3 901	2 704	480	1 197	3 219	7 976	783	7 193	8 642	1 442	52.6	17.2
Greensboro	92 394	23.8	2.30	14.6	32.6	11 307	1 902	1 848	9 405	15 128	6 537	708	5 829	54 924	9 587	38.1	33.9
Greenville	25 204	48.1	2.18	13.8	35.4	5 590	413	381	5 177	5 225	8 359	891	7 467	23 850	1 626	33.3	38.4
Hickory	15 372	30.3	2.35	12.3	32.2	1 164	400	400	764	3 143	8 169	590	7 579	7 401	1 666	45.7	28.0
High Point	33 519	21.8	2.49	16.3	27.2	2 303	949	608	1 354	6 413	7 228	789	6 439	18 417	4 483	48.6	25.5
Jacksonville	17 175	57.3	2.83	12.3	16.6	18 053	383	197	17 670	955	1 385	189	1 196	14 166	1 516	42.6	17.8
Kannapolis	14 804	23.2	2.46	13.5	26.5	502	486	390	16	1 136	2 978	412	2 566	7 419	810	62.8	12.0
Monroe	9 029	52.1	2.83	15.9	23.3	673	507	380	166	1 733	6 392	572	5 821	5 063	913	59.5	15.6
Raleigh	112 608	31.2	2.30	11.4	33.1	17 316	4 935	1 116	12 381	17 833	6 249	689	5 560	66 649	14 765	27.7	44.9
Rocky Mount	21 435	13.6	2.55	20.9	27.4	1 164	420	420	744	5 710	9 883	782	9 101	13 860	1 989	56.4	20.1
Salisbury	10 276	12.2	2.29	17.4	34.3	2 979	1 290	1 096	1 689	1 763	6 446	731	5 714	5 315	1 732	51.2	24.1
Wilmington	34 359	46.9	2.10	14.0	36.6	3 589	725	376	2 864	8 811	11 240	1 273	9 967	19 343	2 282	40.1	31.0
Wilson	17 296	19.6	2.47	19.3	29.4	1 645	992	792	653	3 147	6 856	765	6 092	9 556	1 937	57.8	19.2
Winston-Salem	76 247	27.3	2.32	16.6	33.4	9 114	3 145	1 988	5 969	14 669	7 639	841	6 799	37 373	11 405	45.0	30.3
NORTH DAKOTA	257 152	6.8	2.41	7.8	29.3	23 631	9 688	7 254	13 943	15 258	2 406	78	2 328	163 677	15 990	44.0	22.0
Bismarck	23 185	20.0	2.32	9.3	31.0	1 728	1 334	597	394	1 698	3 097	82	3 015	11 482	2 706	35.7	29.4
Fargo	39 268	30.2	2.20	7.8	34.6	4 015	817	648	3 198	3 291	3 679	146	3 532	25 587	2 397	30.5	34.4
Grand Forks	19 677	6.2	2.31	10.0	31.4	3 817	566	461	3 251	2 452	5 035	125	4 910	17 635	790	34.5	30.3
Minot	15 520	11.1	2.27	10.0	32.5	1 310	518	387	792	1 064	2 947	105	2 842	8 910	745	41.6	24.1
OHIO	4 445 773	8.8	2.49	12.1	27.3	299 121	172 368	93 157	126 753	469 104	4 107	351	3 756	2 475 221	539 239	53.1	21.1
Akron	90 116	0.2	2.35	17.7	33.1	4 908	2 259	1 027	2 649	13 313	6 096	552	5 544	51 459	7 799	55.5	18.0
Barberton	11 523	4.0	2.39	15.4	30.1	394	319	238	75	1 420	5 060	242	4 817	5 605	662	66.9	10.6
Beavercreek	14 071	20.3	2.66	5.8	17.5	555	453	453	102	1 544	4 041	120	3 920	8 126	2 590	30.0	42.9
Bowling Green	10 266	20.7	2.21	7.5	34.3	6 951	356	268	6 595	1 102	3 696	148	3 549	16 183	677	31.5	44.2
Brunswick	11 883	31.6	2.79	9.3	17.7	255	185	185	70	NA	NA	NA	NA	7 456	1 683	51.6	19.4
Canton	32 489	-2.9	2.39	19.1	33.0	3 042	1 555	1 124	1 487	6 280	7 725	875	6 851	17 422	3 518	65.6	11.8
Cincinnati	148 095	-4.0	2.15	18.6	42.8	13 436	6 502	3 325	6 934	28 351	8 507	1 275	7 232	72 320	21 159	49.1	26.6
Cleveland	190 638	-4.6	2.44	24.8	35.2	13 434	6 962	3 670	6 472	33 209	6 900	1 322	5 578	106 866	26 803	64.2	11.4
Cleveland Heights	20 913	-0.5	2.38	14.1	32.6	261	157	155	104	768	1 528	50	1 478	9 393	5 880	24.0	50.0
Columbus	301 534	17.3	2.30	14.5	34.1	17 659	5 412	3 797	12 247	66 261	9 258	908	8 350	176 556	32 155	43.5	29.0
Cuyahoga Falls	21 655	6.2	2.26	10.1	32.6	399	316	304	83	1 919	3 863	145	3 719	9 348	2 129	42.3	25.6
Dayton	67 409	-7.2	2.30	20.6	36.8	10 829	3 336	959	7 493	15 990	9 565	1 218	8 347	34 748	15 380	56.8	14.4

1. No spouse present. 2. Data for serious crimes have not been adjusted for underreporting. This may affect comparability between geographic areas and over time. 3. Per 100,000 population estimated by the FBI. 4. All persons 3 years old and over enrolled in nursery school through college. 5. Persons 25 years old and over.

Table D. Cities — Income, Poverty, and Housing

City	Money income, 1999							Housing units, 2000					
	Households				Percent below poverty					Vacant units			
	Median income				Persons		Families						
	Per capita income[1] (dollars)	Dollars	Percent change, 1989–1999 (constant 1999 dollars)	Percent with income of $100,000 or more	Total	Percent change in rate, 1989–1999	Total	Total	Percent change, 1990–2000	Vacant units for sale or rent[2]	For seasonal use (percent)	Home owner vacancy rate	Renter vacancy rate
	43	44	45	46	47	48	49	50	51	52	53	54	55
NEW YORK—Cont'd													
Ithaca	13 408	21 441	-10.0	5.8	40.2	2.0	13.5	10 736	6.6	449	0.4	2.1	2.7
Jamestown	15 316	25 837	-6.6	3.7	19.5	4.3	15.8	15 027	-2.8	1 469	0.2	2.6	9.8
Lindenhurst	22 150	61 667	-1.5	20.2	6.4	82.9	4.9	9 277	4.9	216	0.3	0.7	2.6
Long Beach	31 069	56 289	1.0	22.4	9.4	13.3	6.3	16 128	5.0	1 205	4.2	1.0	3.2
Middletown	18 947	39 570	-2.5	9.8	17.5	26.8	13.5	10 124	6.8	658	0.2	2.0	4.2
Mount Vernon	20 827	41 128	-12.2	13.8	14.2	20.3	11.8	27 048	3.1	1 319	0.2	2.0	4.0
Newburgh	13 360	30 332	1.6	5.0	25.8	-1.5	23.0	10 476	4.8	1 332	0.3	2.0	7.6
New Rochelle	31 956	55 513	-5.0	26.4	10.5	38.2	7.9	26 995	2.3	806	0.6	6.8	2.3
New York	22 402	38 293	-4.4	13.7	21.2	9.8	18.5	3 200 912	7.0	179 324	0.9	1.7	3.2
Niagara Falls	15 721	26 800	-3.4	4.0	19.5	4.8	15.6	27 837	-2.8	3 738	0.2	2.7	16.0
North Tonawanda	19 264	39 154	-1.5	6.6	7.2	18.0	5.4	14 425	3.0	754	0.3	1.3	7.8
Port Chester	21 131	45 381	-4.1	15.8	13.0	60.5	10.1	9 772	2.7	241	0.2	1.4	1.4
Poughkeepsie	16 759	29 389	-20.8	7.8	22.7	54.4	18.4	13 153	0.3	1 139	0.5	3.3	5.8
Rochester	15 588	27 123	-11.4	4.7	25.9	10.2	23.4	99 789	-1.3	10 790	0.2	3.8	5.8
Rome	18 604	33 643	3.3	5.8	15.0	24.0	12.0	16 272	-2.3	2 619	0.2	3.3	9.0
Saratoga Springs	26 250	45 130	8.6	13.0	8.8	-1.1	5.5	11 584	7.7	800	2.9	1.2	14.6
Schenectady	17 076	29 378	-10.1	4.2	20.8	39.6	16.8	30 272	0.1	4 007	0.3	4.6	9.3
Spring Valley	14 861	41 311	-8.9	9.2	18.7	79.8	15.2	7 812	-3.7	246	0.2	2.2	2.3
Syracuse	15 168	25 000	-12.4	5.0	27.3	20.3	21.7	68 192	-4.6	8 710	0.3	4.8	11.8
Troy	16 796	29 844	-4.9	4.8	19.1	11.0	14.3	23 093	1.0	3 097	0.5	4.2	9.2
Utica	15 248	24 916	-7.0	3.9	24.5	12.9	19.8	29 186	-6.2	4 086	0.3	3.6	12.9
Valley Stream	25 636	63 243	-0.5	23.0	3.5	9.4	2.4	12 688	4.3	204	0.2	0.6	1.8
Watertown	16 354	28 429	-7.1	4.4	19.3	22.2	14.4	12 450	0.4	1 414	0.3	4.5	11.5
White Plains	33 825	58 545	-1.0	26.5	9.8	27.3	6.5	21 576	4.2	655	0.8	0.8	2.1
Yonkers	22 793	44 663	-8.6	15.6	15.5	40.9	13.0	77 589	2.7	3 238	0.4	1.3	3.5
NORTH CAROLINA	20 307	39 184	9.4	9.4	12.3	-5.4	9.0	3 523 944	25.0	391 931	3.8	2.0	8.8
Asheville	20 024	32 772	9.5	6.9	15.5	-2.5	10.3	33 567	13.0	2 877	1.3	2.6	8.1
Burlington	19 640	35 301	-0.9	7.8	13.7	38.4	9.7	19 567	10.6	1 287	0.3	2.1	7.7
Cary	32 974	75 122	20.9	32.8	3.4	6.3	2.1	36 863	104.7	1 957	0.6	1.9	8.2
Chapel Hill	24 133	39 140	-4.5	20.2	21.6	34.2	6.4	18 976	27.8	1 168	0.7	1.4	6.5
Charlotte	26 823	46 975	9.7	15.9	10.6	-1.9	7.8	230 434	35.2	14 985	0.3	2.2	8.4
Concord	21 523	46 094	34.7	12.9	8.2	-32.2	5.8	22 485	93.6	1 523	0.3	2.4	7.3
Durham	22 526	41 160	12.4	11.7	15.0	0.7	11.3	80 797	33.3	5 816	0.6	2.6	6.7
Fayetteville	19 141	36 287	10.9	7.6	14.8	-21.3	11.7	53 565	68.9	5 151	0.3	2.8	10.4
Gastonia	19 592	36 924	6.1	9.8	15.0	5.6	11.8	27 857	25.5	1 912	0.2	2.1	7.4
Goldsboro	16 614	29 456	9.9	5.1	19.2	-9.4	15.4	16 372	14.1	1 742	0.2	2.5	6.8
Greensboro	22 986	39 661	1.1	11.2	12.3	6.0	8.6	99 305	23.5	6 911	0.4	2.0	7.2
Greenville	18 476	28 648	-5.9	8.1	26.1	-1.9	15.6	28 145	55.9	2 941	0.4	3.0	5.6
Hickory	23 263	37 236	1.8	11.5	11.3	0.0	8.4	16 571	30.5	1 199	0.4	2.1	8.0
High Point	21 303	40 137	19.3	10.6	13.2	3.9	10.5	35 952	22.3	2 433	0.5	2.2	7.0
Jacksonville	14 237	32 544	-5.7	4.4	14.1	18.5	12.5	18 312	55.1	1 137	0.2	2.9	5.2
Kannapolis	17 539	35 532	18.2	5.5	10.5	-11.0	7.7	15 941	25.4	1 137	0.2	1.8	7.9
Monroe	17 970	40 457	30.1	8.3	17.2	3.0	11.7	9 621	51.6	592	0.3	3.3	4.3
Raleigh	25 113	46 612	6.9	14.6	11.5	-2.5	7.1	120 699	30.3	8 091	0.4	2.1	8.3
Rocky Mount	17 804	32 661	1.1	8.0	20.1	11.0	15.8	24 167	19.8	2 732	0.3	2.2	6.3
Salisbury	18 864	32 923	1.8	7.2	16.0	2.6	12.2	11 288	14.0	1 012	0.5	3.1	7.0
Wilmington	21 503	31 099	12.3	8.5	19.6	-11.3	13.3	38 678	46.1	4 319	1.3	3.6	11.0
Wilson	17 813	31 169	6.0	7.9	21.6	-8.1	16.5	18 660	21.3	1 364	0.3	2.4	4.8
Winston-Salem	22 468	37 006	4.0	10.7	15.2	0.0	11.3	82 593	25.8	6 346	0.3	2.2	9.7
NORTH DAKOTA	17 769	34 604	11.0	5.7	11.9	-17.4	8.3	289 677	4.8	32 525	2.9	2.7	8.2
Bismarck	20 789	39 422	4.0	7.3	8.4	-13.4	5.7	24 217	20.9	1 032	0.4	1.1	5.5
Fargo	21 101	35 510	4.4	8.1	11.8	-13.9	6.6	41 200	29.9	1 932	0.5	1.6	5.1
Grand Forks	18 395	34 194	0.0	5.9	14.6	0.7	9.3	20 838	6.4	1 161	0.4	2.4	6.7
Minot	18 011	32 218	1.1	5.4	12.8	-10.5	8.8	16 475	9.5	955	0.6	1.7	6.2
OHIO	21 003	40 956	6.2	9.8	10.6	-15.2	7.8	4 783 051	9.4	337 278	1.0	1.6	8.3
Akron	17 596	31 835	6.4	5.1	17.5	-14.6	14.0	97 315	1.0	7 199	0.3	1.8	8.8
Barberton	17 764	32 178	10.4	4.6	13.3	-21.3	11.5	12 163	3.7	640	0.2	1.5	5.4
Beavercreek	30 298	68 801	4.2	24.6	2.4	-31.4	1.5	14 769	21.6	698	0.5	1.3	13.6
Bowling Green	15 032	30 599	4.6	6.4	25.3	-6.3	8.0	10 667	19.0	401	0.3	1.1	3.8
Brunswick	21 937	56 288	2.3	10.9	4.6	9.5	3.2	12 251	29.7	368	0.1	0.9	7.0
Canton	15 544	28 730	8.0	4.1	19.2	-12.3	15.4	35 502	-2.8	3 013	0.1	2.2	10.2
Cincinnati	19 962	29 493	4.5	7.4	21.9	-9.9	18.2	166 012	-1.8	17 917	0.4	2.2	9.9
Cleveland	14 291	25 928	8.3	3.4	26.3	-8.4	22.9	215 856	-3.8	25 218	0.4	2.1	10.8
Cleveland Heights	25 804	46 731	-3.5	15.3	10.6	24.7	7.4	21 798	-0.3	885	0.2	1.2	5.0
Columbus	20 450	37 897	5.8	7.4	14.8	-14.0	10.8	327 175	17.7	25 641	0.3	2.0	8.3
Cuyahoga Falls	22 550	42 263	1.8	7.1	6.1	-7.6	4.5	22 727	6.9	1 072	0.3	1.2	6.7
Dayton	15 547	27 423	3.2	4.0	23.0	-13.2	18.2	77 321	-3.8	9 912	0.2	3.0	12.7

1. Based on population enumerated as of April 1, 2000.   2. Includes units rented or sold but not occupied.

Table D. Cities — Housing, Labor Force, Employment, and Disability

City	Housing units, 2000 (cont'd) Occupied units Total	Percent owner occupied	Percent renter occupied	Average size owner occupied	Average size renter occupied	Civilian labor force, 2003 Total	Percent change, 2002–2003	Unemployment Total	Rate[1]	Civilian employment,[2] 2000 Total	Percent Management, professional, and related occupations	Production, transportation, and material moving occupations	Disability, 2000 Employment disabled persons[3] (percent)
	56	57	58	59	60	61	62	63	64	65	66	67	68
NEW YORK—Cont'd													
Ithaca	10 287	26.0	74.0	2.30	2.07	15 732	1.5	548	3.5	13 587	53.8	3.9	4.4
Jamestown	13 558	51.3	48.7	2.46	2.10	15 696	-0.9	1 105	7.0	13 946	26.7	23.3	12.9
Lindenhurst	9 061	80.6	19.4	3.21	2.43	16 020	0.7	792	4.9	13 442	27.2	14.3	10.7
Long Beach	14 923	53.4	46.6	2.45	2.05	18 758	0.5	989	5.3	17 978	42.3	6.8	16.2
Middletown	9 466	45.7	54.3	2.68	2.57	13 853	2.1	759	5.5	10 852	26.6	14.3	16.3
Mount Vernon	25 729	36.5	63.5	2.93	2.45	34 892	0.1	2 168	6.2	30 980	34.2	8.8	18.2
Newburgh	9 144	30.7	69.3	2.88	3.01	13 498	2.5	1 330	9.9	10 547	18.0	27.2	20.4
New Rochelle	26 189	50.3	49.7	2.87	2.48	36 881	0.2	1 586	4.3	33 757	42.3	7.0	12.1
New York	3 021 588	30.2	69.8	2.81	2.50	3 682 973	-1.2	308 075	8.4	3 277 825	36.8	10.9	16.4
Niagara Falls	24 099	57.6	42.4	2.40	2.10	28 287	0.1	3 310	11.7	22 258	24.3	18.7	14.2
North Tonawanda	13 671	68.7	31.3	2.65	1.93	18 508	-0.2	1 136	6.1	16 589	29.8	19.8	9.0
Port Chester	9 531	43.2	56.8	2.76	3.00	14 030	0.2	686	4.9	13 452	25.6	11.4	20.8
Poughkeepsie	12 014	36.8	63.2	2.46	2.37	14 078	0.5	890	6.3	12 483	30.3	11.6	16.1
Rochester	88 999	40.2	59.8	2.54	2.24	117 566	-0.3	11 576	9.8	91 927	31.0	17.7	15.5
Rome	13 653	57.1	42.9	2.45	2.11	17 143	-0.3	925	5.4	13 990	30.6	15.2	14.6
Saratoga Springs	10 784	55.8	44.2	2.49	1.87	14 496	0.0	610	4.2	13 582	43.2	7.3	8.0
Schenectady	26 265	44.7	55.3	2.37	2.12	32 206	0.5	1 834	5.7	27 077	29.7	12.5	15.2
Spring Valley	7 566	31.4	68.6	3.41	3.29	12 855	1.5	733	5.7	11 152	25.2	13.7	17.5
Syracuse	59 482	40.3	59.7	2.48	2.16	76 144	0.0	6 116	8.0	60 729	32.6	14.5	12.9
Troy	19 996	40.1	59.9	2.45	2.13	26 801	-0.2	1 674	6.2	21 899	32.4	13.8	14.4
Utica	25 100	48.8	51.2	2.41	2.15	30 408	-0.3	2 222	7.3	24 342	27.1	17.7	15.9
Valley Stream	12 484	80.3	19.7	3.06	2.27	18 206	0.5	806	4.4	17 554	33.5	8.1	11.9
Watertown	11 036	43.0	57.0	2.51	2.18	12 389	0.7	997	8.0	9 972	29.7	12.9	13.2
White Plains	20 921	52.2	47.8	2.53	2.41	27 915	0.2	1 169	4.2	26 397	45.9	6.4	13.0
Yonkers	74 351	43.2	56.8	2.68	2.55	95 244	0.2	5 165	5.4	84 182	34.1	10.1	16.4
NORTH CAROLINA	3 132 013	69.4	30.6	2.54	2.37	4 229 772	1.5	272 826	6.5	3 824 741	31.2	18.7	13.3
Asheville	30 690	56.8	43.2	2.24	2.01	37 212	3.0	1 911	5.1	32 757	34.5	13.2	11.7
Burlington	18 280	59.4	40.6	2.39	2.40	26 290	1.0	2 004	7.6	21 559	29.2	23.5	14.9
Cary	34 906	72.8	27.2	2.86	2.23	43 046	2.3	1 460	3.4	51 657	59.9	4.7	5.6
Chapel Hill	17 808	42.9	57.1	2.49	2.01	25 285	2.5	922	3.6	24 455	56.9	3.3	3.6
Charlotte	215 449	57.5	42.5	2.56	2.30	323 785	2.4	20 423	6.3	285 601	38.1	11.8	11.7
Concord	20 962	67.6	32.4	2.65	2.52	20 753	5.7	1 845	8.9	28 167	32.6	15.9	10.7
Durham	74 981	48.9	51.1	2.44	2.30	95 981	2.0	5 651	5.9	94 705	46.5	8.9	11.0
Fayetteville	48 414	53.3	46.7	2.50	2.32	40 556	2.1	2 280	5.6	46 173	33.3	14.5	14.9
Gastonia	25 945	56.7	43.3	2.54	2.44	30 658	1.5	2 537	8.3	30 154	28.5	24.1	16.2
Goldsboro	14 630	42.5	57.5	2.37	2.42	15 426	-1.1	1 177	7.6	12 829	31.0	17.7	18.0
Greensboro	92 394	53.0	47.0	2.42	2.17	124 728	0.7	8 045	6.5	114 542	35.9	13.9	11.7
Greenville	25 204	39.3	60.7	2.39	2.04	31 177	0.1	2 553	8.2	30 412	38.5	10.3	8.7
Hickory	15 372	55.0	45.0	2.39	2.30	18 499	-2.3	2 220	12.0	19 211	31.9	23.1	12.4
High Point	33 519	59.0	41.0	2.53	2.44	44 553	0.6	3 344	7.5	42 250	30.3	21.5	15.5
Jacksonville	17 175	39.2	60.8	2.67	2.94	14 131	1.1	777	5.5	15 660	30.6	9.1	9.9
Kannapolis	14 804	66.7	33.3	2.43	2.52	20 978	7.2	2 712	12.9	17 598	21.1	24.6	17.8
Monroe	9 029	56.1	43.9	2.66	3.04	13 637	2.3	1 342	9.8	12 334	25.8	22.1	16.7
Raleigh	112 069	51.6	48.4	2.43	2.15	194 789	2.0	10 851	5.6	154 114	45.1	7.7	8.6
Rocky Mount	21 435	55.0	45.0	2.56	2.54	25 788	-1.0	2 640	10.2	23 229	30.3	20.6	14.0
Salisbury	10 276	53.5	46.5	2.29	2.28	13 408	6.4	1 428	10.7	10 650	31.4	24.7	18.3
Wilmington	34 359	48.6	51.4	2.20	2.01	39 275	1.9	2 532	6.4	36 629	32.9	11.5	12.5
Wilson	17 296	51.0	49.0	2.50	2.44	20 744	1.0	2 391	11.5	19 254	28.4	22.4	19.3
Winston-Salem	76 247	55.8	44.2	2.34	2.28	83 223	0.7	5 790	7.0	86 940	35.4	16.4	12.2
NORTH DAKOTA	257 152	66.6	33.4	2.60	2.02	346 471	0.8	13 746	4.0	316 632	33.3	12.4	9.3
Bismarck	23 185	63.4	36.6	2.59	1.86	34 839	1.7	1 051	3.0	30 002	36.2	9.6	9.8
Fargo	39 268	47.1	52.9	2.61	1.84	56 731	1.5	1 549	2.7	52 744	34.1	11.5	8.7
Grand Forks	19 677	50.7	49.3	2.68	1.94	28 897	1.0	951	3.3	26 715	32.0	10.9	8.2
Minot	15 520	62.4	37.6	2.51	1.87	19 153	0.4	752	3.9	17 436	33.0	9.7	10.1
OHIO	4 445 773	69.1	30.9	2.62	2.19	5 915 176	1.2	363 385	6.1	5 402 175	31.0	19.0	10.3
Akron	90 116	59.4	40.6	2.45	2.21	118 370	1.4	9 405	7.9	99 310	26.0	19.6	12.9
Barberton	11 523	65.1	34.9	2.44	2.29	13 827	1.4	1 056	7.6	12 486	20.1	24.1	13.4
Beavercreek	14 071	84.5	15.5	2.74	2.22	19 575	0.1	623	3.2	19 126	51.2	9.0	3.7
Bowling Green	10 266	42.2	57.8	2.45	2.03	17 395	-0.1	1 098	6.3	15 549	36.0	14.2	5.4
Brunswick	11 883	80.6	19.4	2.92	2.23	20 848	1.4	1 230	6.0	17 522	31.0	17.0	8.6
Canton	32 489	59.7	40.3	2.51	2.22	39 291	0.5	4 125	10.5	34 475	21.5	24.1	12.4
Cincinnati	148 095	39.0	61.0	2.43	1.97	174 973	1.6	12 747	7.3	150 574	35.8	13.5	12.5
Cleveland	190 638	48.5	51.5	2.56	2.32	208 756	1.1	26 501	12.7	180 459	22.5	22.3	15.9
Cleveland Heights	20 913	62.1	37.9	2.63	1.95	28 579	1.1	1 232	4.3	26 602	53.5	8.6	8.5
Columbus	301 534	49.1	50.9	2.48	2.13	417 203	0.8	23 661	5.7	374 892	35.5	12.7	10.7
Cuyahoga Falls	21 655	65.7	34.3	2.46	1.89	29 551	1.3	1 178	4.0	25 524	34.5	13.9	9.4
Dayton	67 409	52.8	47.2	2.36	2.24	78 050	0.9	8 415	10.8	69 126	25.7	20.0	13.6

1. Percent of civilian labor force. 2. Persons 16 years old and over. 3. Persons 16 to 64 years old.

City	Value of residential construction authorized by building permits, 2003			Wholesale trade, 1997				Retail trade,[1] 1997			
	New construction ($1,000)	Number of housing units	Percent single family	Number of establishments	Number of employees	Sales (mil dol)	Annual payroll (mil dol)	Number of establishments	Number of employees	Sales (mil dol)	Annual payroll (mil dol)
	69	70	71	72	73	74	75	76	77	78	79
NEW YORK—Cont'd											
Ithaca	4 250	64	3.1	42	268	166.9	9.2	273	3 581	491.0	52.8
Jamestown	50	1	100.0	65	583	172.1	15.3	149	2 638	425.1	39.0
Lindenhurst	761	7	100.0	65	389	310.4	12.2	102	991	170.4	20.4
Long Beach	2 958	29	37.9	26	23	29.3	1.1	93	549	88.4	10.0
Middletown	3 922	52	100.0	41	400	111.0	10.5	304	4 504	751.2	67.5
Mount Vernon	2 955	35	25.7	123	1 708	673.5	65.0	240	1 739	303.5	38.0
Newburgh	340	3	100.0	57	683	199.7	21.5	121	1 277	197.7	21.8
New Rochelle	14 458	132	9.1	147	1 221	614.1	55.8	256	2 581	609.4	51.0
New York	NA	NA	NA	18 482	185 407	182 107.1	8 614.3	28 456	232 494	41 912.2	4 731.1
Niagara Falls	559	6	100.0	60	708	204.4	16.8	255	3 437	438.9	45.0
North Tonawanda	1 812	14	100.0	38	D	D	D	103	1 159	134.6	15.3
Port Chester	1 905	9	33.3	60	960	306.8	33.8	130	1 704	237.7	26.7
Poughkeepsie	3 867	52	3.8	50	D	D	D	172	1 475	195.6	23.7
Rochester	11 778	163	11.0	441	7 329	5 193.4	308.2	756	8 251	1 140.8	131.9
Rome	1 398	12	100.0	24	146	31.4	3.5	164	2 177	321.6	29.9
Saratoga Springs	33 907	174	62.6	28	294	188.3	8.8	183	2 348	375.0	35.9
Schenectady	271	4	100.0	57	1 060	425.5	41.3	235	2 169	338.4	35.5
Spring Valley	0	0	0.0	49	D	D	D	111	1 102	294.1	23.7
Syracuse	836	10	100.0	262	3 569	1 529.4	124.9	708	8 860	1 346.8	147.4
Troy	2 958	36	100.0	55	482	201.7	13.5	168	2 258	330.2	34.3
Utica	715	9	66.7	94	1 341	448.8	37.7	218	2 461	346.5	36.0
Valley Stream	150	1	100.0	119	779	592.1	35.9	251	2 873	586.8	51.2
Watertown	1 988	22	100.0	52	554	168.3	15.4	273	3 743	519.4	52.6
White Plains	70 951	320	3.8	139	1 781	3 222.7	127.4	497	6 946	1 176.7	133.4
Yonkers	15 722	139	17.3	228	2 460	1 037.6	84.2	620	8 171	1 533.4	144.8
NORTH CAROLINA	10 267 977	79 226	84.4	12 284	157 774	98 080.1	5 574.1	35 563	416 287	72 356.8	6 697.4
Asheville	75 967	399	57.6	211	2 134	777.0	64.8	794	10 637	1 762.0	170.8
Burlington	23 511	290	95.9	89	1 080	332.4	35.6	419	5 403	829.4	82.3
Cary	114 020	604	93.5	132	1 260	1 728.9	57.9	410	7 311	1 218.3	108.2
Chapel Hill	87 935	465	99.6	33	123	254.9	5.2	223	3 347	480.6	58.4
Charlotte	NA	NA	NA	2 150	32 325	30 244.7	1 319.9	2 306	35 463	6 830.3	662.5
Concord	NA	NA	NA	74	1 000	691.7	28.7	228	3 734	667.0	61.3
Durham	344 284	2 800	65.5	182	2 736	1 652.9	80.4	909	12 206	1 833.1	195.7
Fayetteville	65 343	581	62.3	140	1 653	549.5	45.8	755	12 055	2 089.9	193.4
Gastonia	52 890	448	79.7	127	1 197	726.9	41.8	442	6 895	1 128.1	103.3
Goldsboro	10 817	95	100.0	101	1 799	738.2	47.8	371	4 996	812.4	70.5
Greensboro	177 764	1 656	80.0	783	14 701	9 531.0	629.7	1 294	19 942	3 390.0	350.0
Greenville	72 238	1 155	37.5	122	1 196	527.2	30.2	474	6 729	1 144.5	105.3
Hickory	11 637	131	52.7	194	4 048	1 990.6	127.8	493	7 484	1 291.3	122.2
High Point	109 885	966	77.0	315	2 996	1 885.3	102.7	501	6 575	1 173.9	117.6
Jacksonville	31 772	250	100.0	28	156	36.4	3.7	321	4 561	758.4	69.2
Kannapolis	NA	NA	NA	16	D	D	D	189	2 223	350.9	33.3
Monroe	19 239	141	100.0	77	1 112	367.7	37.5	240	3 094	585.6	53.4
Raleigh	583 870	5 634	67.2	778	11 873	8 296.7	553.2	1 618	22 689	4 568.5	414.5
Rocky Mount	20 526	304	87.5	99	1 744	896.0	58.6	392	4 833	825.3	76.4
Salisbury	NA	NA	NA	65	729	235.7	19.6	252	3 412	574.2	55.2
Wilmington	NA	NA	NA	209	2 748	994.0	74.1	743	9 566	1 952.2	163.6
Wilson	29 794	317	74.8	93	1 075	422.1	29.1	319	3 975	663.1	60.4
Winston-Salem	125 507	1 378	76.8	331	4 649	2 543.7	149.8	1 101	15 734	2 769.2	260.4
NORTH DAKOTA	397 521	3 721	63.0	1 604	16 992	8 618.4	454.4	3 569	40 685	6 702.1	616.1
Bismarck	61 484	478	55.0	134	1 472	591.2	42.0	356	5 081	808.4	82.0
Fargo	84 488	981	46.4	246	4 603	2 168.8	148.5	486	9 166	1 588.9	153.0
Grand Forks	43 239	487	38.4	97	D	D	D	312	5 345	889.2	77.5
Minot	10 748	120	56.7	62	D	D	D	292	4 534	711.7	69.8
OHIO	7 502 920	53 041	80.5	17 322	254 226	158 310.2	9 192.2	44 521	630 098	102 938.8	9 924.5
Akron	39 696	598	49.2	334	4 956	2 808.5	175.7	908	11 912	1 731.7	192.5
Barberton	8 694	67	100.0	42	401	122.2	15.0	93	873	123.8	12.6
Beavercreek	NA	NA	NA	41	289	287.2	12.0	230	4 947	707.4	64.8
Bowling Green	NA	NA	NA	23	164	63.3	4.4	124	1 895	262.5	23.7
Brunswick	19 424	124	100.0	44	464	155.8	13.3	102	1 285	307.8	24.9
Canton	15 351	184	78.3	141	2 493	1 072.0	75.1	391	5 050	775.7	78.8
Cincinnati	52 652	641	23.9	705	15 388	10 660.8	671.6	1 334	18 093	3 017.0	308.7
Cleveland	40 029	450	82.7	921	16 936	7 155.4	622.5	1 607	15 454	2 378.3	276.7
Cleveland Heights	671	5	100.0	27	58	52.7	1.7	154	1 594	278.7	28.8
Columbus	585 281	6 538	48.8	1 092	24 483	13 539.2	1 002.5	2 717	51 028	8 595.5	897.7
Cuyahoga Falls	16 843	117	84.6	79	530	157.2	16.8	207	3 683	760.3	64.7
Dayton	29 435	277	100.0	287	5 256	3 296.5	209.5	529	6 801	1 045.2	113.7

1. Establishments with payroll.

Table D. Cities — Real Estate, Professional Services, and Manufacturing

City	Real estate and rental and leasing, 1997				Professional, scientific, and technical services,[1] 1997				Manufacturing, 1997			
	Number of establish- ments	Number of employees	Receipts (mil dol)	Annual payroll (mil dol)	Number of establish- ments	Number of employees	Receipts (mil dol)	Annual payroll (mil dol)	Number of establish- ments	Number of employees	Receipts (mil dol)	Annual payroll (mil dol)
	80	81	82	83	84	85	86	87	88	89	90	91
NEW YORK—Cont'd												
Ithaca	50	357	29.9	6.3	137	1 215	111.1	42.5	61	2 775	515.3	97.0
Jamestown	34	148	18.4	3.0	75	394	27.9	10.8	83	5 056	666.9	150.2
Lindenhurst	12	43	5.5	0.7	42	168	13.5	4.9	68	802	82.0	20.5
Long Beach	42	99	19.0	2.4	50	122	16.8	5.8	NA	NA	NA	NA
Middletown	38	146	23.7	2.2	80	272	19.0	8.2	46	1 581	256.6	44.3
Mount Vernon	109	504	85.5	16.1	80	313	34.5	10.1	147	4 405	602.1	142.3
Newburgh	34	142	19.3	2.8	57	578	86.7	26.2	48	1 467	116.9	28.5
New Rochelle	146	552	80.6	11.1	175	1 416	61.5	22.9	61	1 167	138.9	36.8
New York	16 530	90 795	19 526.3	3 086.7	19 790	249 961	40 075.3	15 355.4	10 569	207 975	27 735.8	5 504.1
Niagara Falls	37	226	23.4	4.4	79	320	32.0	8.2	69	3 942	1 234.0	183.7
North Tonawanda	8	46	4.2	0.4	37	150	9.2	3.9	61	2 131	522.2	72.6
Port Chester	38	221	47.0	7.9	61	407	49.7	14.5	42	1 054	137.1	30.8
Poughkeepsie	49	490	28.6	6.5	121	858	91.1	36.9	38	D	D	D
Rochester	203	1 511	188.9	34.8	718	6 970	706.4	277.6	533	51 405	12 269.7	2 218.8
Rome	36	162	14.6	2.7	55	467	51.0	16.2	49	2 278	547.5	72.9
Saratoga Springs	35	128	13.1	2.0	97	508	26.9	8.8	28	1 782	374.0	59.5
Schenectady	27	118	11.7	2.1	130	1 112	136.9	44.9	66	3 401	1 302.9	154.9
Spring Valley	23	66	13.5	1.1	35	151	27.6	4.5	NA	NA	NA	NA
Syracuse	167	2 595	172.7	59.6	486	5 193	484.7	185.4	163	10 193	1 958.1	409.5
Troy	39	166	20.3	3.7	102	946	70.3	29.9	41	1 727	196.9	53.2
Utica	54	193	26.0	3.4	157	1 046	75.2	27.0	102	4 095	509.2	118.7
Valley Stream	56	191	37.6	5.0	139	781	73.2	32.6	NA	NA	NA	NA
Watertown	44	222	27.2	3.5	65	452	27.1	13.0	41	1 855	279.9	56.0
White Plains	179	641	167.5	21.0	579	3 165	450.5	169.2	NA	NA	NA	NA
Yonkers	336	1 106	227.8	29.4	217	948	96.3	30.3	131	4 074	742.6	132.6
NORTH CAROLINA	7 346	39 349	5 026.0	900.6	14 351	101 610	9 760.9	3 693.5	11 306	773 548	161 900.5	21 297.9
Asheville	149	829	107.1	17.9	353	2 115	152.3	70.5	142	6 168	1 405.3	164.7
Burlington	58	292	60.6	5.7	91	475	36.6	16.3	110	8 811	1 435.6	208.6
Cary	99	397	74.4	12.8	385	2 538	309.3	135.9	65	2 767	384.7	89.3
Chapel Hill	83	D	D	D	228	1 541	128.5	55.1	NA	NA	NA	NA
Charlotte	859	8 677	1 285.6	272.3	1 958	23 207	2 648.9	1 044.1	787	31 811	6 504.0	1 058.5
Concord	51	297	38.7	6.4	80	510	36.8	16.7	78	6 253	6 968.6	225.4
Durham	213	1 162	146.0	27.8	470	4 648	689.2	204.0	123	D	D	D
Fayetteville	197	867	90.5	16.9	272	1 849	122.9	42.9	78	9 100	2 170.0	295.1
Gastonia	67	308	27.1	5.1	139	648	52.1	20.6	211	12 666	2 385.8	360.0
Goldsboro	69	242	18.1	4.3	101	519	38.7	14.2	64	4 644	579.8	116.1
Greensboro	361	2 807	324.3	63.6	763	5 741	542.0	192.7	411	21 305	5 903.6	711.5
Greenville	100	431	44.7	6.9	177	1 131	75.6	30.9	60	4 006	1 827.2	143.5
Hickory	100	489	65.5	10.5	172	939	73.6	26.6	253	17 501	2 235.8	441.1
High Point	90	500	51.6	9.6	206	1 579	127.6	51.5	288	17 182	2 247.9	465.0
Jacksonville	75	365	41.2	5.8	92	590	26.6	9.1	NA	NA	NA	NA
Kannapolis	29	156	15.3	3.3	46	229	12.3	5.6	21	D	D	D
Monroe	40	138	16.9	2.7	80	587	51.1	16.1	105	9 686	1 829.3	269.5
Raleigh	494	3 291	624.6	95.0	1 465	12 856	1 424.1	566.8	328	7 954	2 147.1	241.5
Rocky Mount	75	395	48.5	7.2	89	610	52.6	19.1	65	7 886	1 475.0	220.3
Salisbury	50	197	19.2	3.8	81	340	35.8	11.5	100	5 790	984.3	166.7
Wilmington	159	755	85.8	14.6	347	2 508	198.9	81.7	139	5 257	1 241.1	202.0
Wilson	52	181	17.5	2.7	79	D	D	D	70	7 534	2 821.1	238.5
Winston-Salem	280	1 527	252.2	34.5	575	4 515	465.8	179.4	241	17 789	4 449.7	583.0
NORTH DAKOTA	657	3 325	287.0	46.3	1 077	7 076	418.0	175.7	704	21 956	5 115.9	604.8
Bismarck	90	D	D	D	174	D	D	D	48	D	D	D
Fargo	144	1 017	107.3	16.6	246	2 129	147.9	58.0	133	5 206	1 057.5	131.2
Grand Forks	63	494	31.8	6.7	102	710	48.4	23.2	43	1 536	231.9	33.7
Minot	55	D	D	D	80	797	37.0	17.1	41	D	D	D
OHIO	9 692	62 628	7 243.7	1 334.6	21 182	182 805	18 294.7	6 948.0	17 974	984 201	241 902.9	35 950.5
Akron	163	1 276	112.6	27.8	480	4 837	564.6	203.3	370	12 822	2 020.4	451.8
Barberton	10	60	4.1	1.1	27	112	7.3	2.5	77	4 140	535.5	122.5
Beavercreek	31	138	26.4	3.1	141	2 040	231.2	92.4	31	826	167.7	31.4
Bowling Green	33	156	13.4	2.1	48	331	34.0	8.8	41	3 107	429.8	96.6
Brunswick	15	71	10.6	1.5	41	228	18.2	5.9	29	658	93.6	21.0
Canton	82	375	32.5	6.7	198	1 160	105.8	42.3	182	13 120	3 233.5	461.9
Cincinnati	512	3 571	431.5	99.0	1 282	18 517	2 137.0	830.5	604	28 917	6 540.2	1 021.8
Cleveland	346	3 159	328.8	76.0	1 284	19 671	2 502.5	987.2	1 270	44 400	8 675.8	1 662.2
Cleveland Heights	56	267	26.9	3.5	109	235	19.9	7.1	NA	NA	NA	NA
Columbus	788	7 701	770.2	179.2	1 825	20 837	2 377.4	875.1	685	32 243	8 409.3	1 173.3
Cuyahoga Falls	49	305	25.3	5.3	109	964	44.7	20.5	88	3 220	531.9	111.4
Dayton	155	1 017	115.7	25.7	407	4 535	550.6	181.8	350	20 112	3 579.4	811.2

1. Firms subject to federal tax.

Table D. Cities — **Accommodation and Foodservices, Entertainment, and Health Care**

City	Accommodation and foodservices, 1997				Arts, entertainment, and recreation,[1] 1997				Health care and social assistance,[1] 1997			
	Number of establishments	Number of employees	Sales (mil dol)	Annual payroll (mil dol)	Number of establishments	Number of employees	Receipts (mil dol)	Annual payroll (mil dol)	Number of establishments	Number of employees	Receipts (mil dol)	Annual payroll (mil dol)
	92	93	94	95	96	97	98	99	100	101	102	103
NEW YORK—Cont'd												
Ithaca	213	2 718	81.3	23.3	20	210	6.6	2.0	95	681	52.1	21.5
Jamestown	96	897	26.1	6.9	8	56	2.8	0.7	114	1 335	61.6	29.7
Lindenhurst	65	684	24.8	6.2	9	0	0.0	0.0	44	259	21.6	8.9
Long Beach	43	269	12.5	3.2	11	104	5.3	1.8	104	1 180	85.0	32.1
Middletown	104	1 465	47.9	13.0	14	94	4.4	1.0	102	1 207	83.3	37.0
Mount Vernon	63	376	15.8	3.9	13	43	4.9	1.9	109	951	53.8	22.3
Newburgh	62	D	D	D	3	0	0.0	0.0	80	822	52.9	24.8
New Rochelle	123	D	D	D	34	580	32.2	8.5	202	1 459	125.3	51.5
New York	13 726	182 381	11 000.4	3 119.7	3 332	32 475	4 458.9	1 527.7	13 210	125 076	9 746.8	3 988.2
Niagara Falls	221	3 253	104.6	28.4	9	108	3.5	0.9	101	1 341	49.7	21.4
North Tonawanda	60	477	12.4	3.3	11	100	3.5	0.8	54	214	13.4	5.3
Port Chester	74	637	31.7	8.2	5	73	4.8	1.1	40	376	29.2	12.1
Poughkeepsie	91	894	39.8	9.7	13	149	6.0	1.8	126	1 365	102.7	45.7
Rochester	516	6 498	222.5	63.9	53	703	40.8	10.2	396	6 278	415.2	186.7
Rome	85	957	28.2	7.9	13	48	1.9	0.5	87	1 003	57.0	27.7
Saratoga Springs	121	2 107	87.7	26.4	14	0	0.0	0.0	85	882	64.1	25.9
Schenectady	182	1 453	51.5	14.3	13	0	0.0	0.0	171	2 027	127.2	60.1
Spring Valley	37	454	16.1	4.2	5	37	1.1	0.3	33	449	17.7	7.0
Syracuse	414	5 253	167.9	50.7	28	290	18.9	3.6	356	4 374	375.4	196.5
Troy	127	1 590	46.1	13.6	14	50	2.9	0.4	152	1 924	110.4	49.4
Utica	149	1 625	50.4	14.1	10	79	2.9	0.6	172	1 534	119.3	50.0
Valley Stream	89	1 133	41.7	10.4	12	33	6.7	2.7	113	749	67.4	26.9
Watertown	122	1 642	57.2	15.1	13	97	3.9	1.0	100	888	67.8	37.6
White Plains	180	2 103	113.8	29.2	28	231	22.2	7.6	327	3 565	283.3	139.9
Yonkers	249	2 103	102.2	25.2	32	536	49.1	10.5	375	3 612	261.6	107.8
NORTH CAROLINA	14 579	262 848	8 625.0	2 393.2	2 090	23 481	1 632.6	470.5	12 582	173 770	10 708.8	4 859.6
Asheville	356	7 242	268.0	81.4	38	788	51.3	15.6	366	4 785	376.6	192.9
Burlington	151	3 553	103.7	28.3	11	114	3.8	1.1	143	3 022	261.9	94.6
Cary	187	3 765	132.8	37.5	25	472	22.1	7.0	206	2 223	138.9	62.2
Chapel Hill	211	3 566	130.1	38.0	20	165	5.1	1.4	157	1 694	95.5	48.5
Charlotte	1 277	27 598	1 008.7	279.1	154	1 896	341.5	123.0	1 001	15 218	1 208.9	543.4
Concord	89	1 915	66.4	18.0	19	248	34.7	6.8	104	1 710	118.0	61.0
Durham	386	7 800	295.9	81.9	31	363	17.3	4.8	341	5 018	276.0	137.4
Fayetteville	354	8 134	246.8	67.2	35	601	18.7	6.1	336	5 054	328.7	142.6
Gastonia	166	3 346	107.0	29.1	16	179	5.0	1.4	189	2 807	189.2	91.8
Goldsboro	125	2 553	73.0	19.9	11	111	3.4	1.0	144	1 798	98.1	48.2
Greensboro	653	15 531	489.3	142.7	76	727	29.0	9.0	567	8 420	596.2	293.4
Greenville	198	4 854	138.7	38.1	29	410	12.2	4.2	167	2 805	194.9	105.4
Hickory	195	4 498	127.5	37.4	18	194	9.0	2.1	169	3 752	296.4	125.9
High Point	184	3 023	97.1	27.9	23	347	47.7	4.5	180	1 913	170.1	75.5
Jacksonville	137	2 729	76.7	20.4	16	123	4.0	1.1	138	2 078	109.3	49.0
Kannapolis	58	909	31.0	8.4	10	155	7.5	2.6	37	422	19.4	7.2
Monroe	95	1 909	57.7	14.0	9	65	1.7	0.5	80	944	62.1	30.6
Raleigh	780	16 886	606.2	171.3	95	899	39.9	10.6	731	10 956	833.0	387.7
Rocky Mount	118	2 549	81.2	22.1	15	100	3.8	1.3	132	2 849	192.4	77.9
Salisbury	103	2 104	61.9	17.1	12	79	3.0	0.7	131	1 667	94.9	44.4
Wilmington	289	6 562	203.5	56.9	38	467	16.4	5.0	329	5 047	344.8	146.6
Wilson	115	2 463	76.2	20.5	11	89	2.9	0.8	110	1 740	93.3	46.0
Winston-Salem	479	10 328	327.7	94.0	45	451	18.0	5.6	446	6 048	555.7	225.7
NORTH DAKOTA	1 827	26 330	684.9	189.0	248	3 154	164.3	32.6	1 013	13 181	904.1	386.4
Bismarck	149	3 444	95.7	27.6	15	0	0.0	0.0	131	1 437	121.0	55.4
Fargo	242	6 616	178.7	51.5	29	452	18.8	4.0	205	5 753	466.9	187.7
Grand Forks	152	3 941	88.4	26.1	19	166	4.8	1.0	75	1 414	62.9	43.4
Minot	131	2 678	68.0	19.8	26	170	6.1	1.6	97	1 010	88.6	27.8
OHIO	22 631	401 206	12 411.0	3 444.2	2 902	37 210	2 308.6	706.6	20 399	261 520	15 440.1	7 477.0
Akron	489	7 364	223.9	62.6	48	777	47.8	10.9	415	5 418	410.5	229.6
Barberton	57	692	22.5	5.8	4	42	1.1	0.3	63	755	48.6	20.7
Beavercreek	69	D	D	D	9	177	9.0	2.7	72	948	64.1	31.7
Bowling Green	87	1 808	39.7	11.0	5	66	1.7	0.5	45	533	26.3	12.7
Brunswick	48	824	21.4	6.0	5	77	1.6	0.6	45	660	27.5	13.2
Canton	208	3 620	100.1	27.0	16	155	8.2	2.0	185	2 703	196.6	107.3
Cincinnati	829	16 006	564.1	158.1	84	1 340	181.4	100.3	862	12 504	869.7	469.4
Cleveland	1 099	17 757	674.4	176.9	84	2 738	354.1	143.9	531	9 272	590.9	300.6
Cleveland Heights	83	D	D	D	13	88	2.8	0.8	112	736	48.6	20.5
Columbus	1 508	32 807	1 160.0	334.7	133	2 316	93.4	23.3	1 325	18 567	1 299.0	675.2
Cuyahoga Falls	123	2 695	79.8	23.5	7	68	2.8	0.7	155	1 311	77.7	39.9
Dayton	327	5 098	180.7	48.0	27	329	14.4	3.8	319	4 624	307.4	167.5

1. Firms subject to federal tax.

Table D. Cities — Other Services and Federal Funds

City	Other services,[1] 1997				Selected federal funds, 2002–2003 (mil dol)								
					Procurement contracts		Grants						
	Number of establishments	Number of employees	Receipts (mil dol)	Annual payroll (mil dol)	Defense	Other	Total[2]	Medicaid and other health related	Nutrition and family welfare	Energy and environment	Education	Housing and community development	Direct payments for individuals for educational assistance
	104	105	106	107	108	109	110	111	112	113	114	115	116
NEW YORK—Cont'd													
Ithaca	62	382	20.6	5.7	5.2	4.7	265.4	63.8	2.8	7.6	6.3	4.4	18.8
Jamestown	55	256	18.8	4.5	48.7	0.5	8.6	0.0	0.0	0.0	0.4	6.0	5.1
Lindenhurst	92	345	28.6	7.7	6.5	0.2	0.2	0.0	0.0	0.2	0.0	6.0	5.1
Long Beach	51	203	9.4	2.7	0.3	0.2	10.0	0.0	0.0	0.0	0.3	9.6	0.2
Middletown	91	519	28.3	8.7	2.4	3.2	4.5	0.6	1.5	0.0	0.2	9.6	0.2
Mount Vernon	133	674	48.7	15.7	1.5	0.1	37.0	9.1	0.0	0.0	0.0	27.6	2.7
Newburgh	49	194	14.3	4.1	4.2	0.8	16.6	1.1	2.1	0.0	0.2	8.9	0.2
New Rochelle	141	508	38.0	9.9	0.2	0.3	28.5	0.1	0.0	0.0	1.3	26.2	19.5
New York	11 623	56 487	3 779.9	1 088.6	323.1	1 210.4	23 905.3	16 454.6	2 703.6	-0.6	825.2	2 193.7	511.3
Niagara Falls	81	329	19.7	5.1	5.8	2.3	17.7	0.0	0.1	0.0	2.9	13.4	0.1
North Tonawanda	57	186	12.5	3.4	5.7	0.1	6.2	0.0	3.3	0.0	0.0	2.6	0.0
Port Chester	81	310	26.5	6.9	2.8	0.0	6.7	0.0	0.0	0.0	0.6	5.8	0.1
Poughkeepsie	70	273	21.4	4.8	1.2	2.0	33.8	1.5	0.4	0.0	1.2	21.9	8.4
Rochester	387	2 530	184.8	55.0	215.1	37.8	407.7	181.0	15.6	55.9	30.8	67.5	43.7
Rome	50	237	13.7	3.7	46.6	4.5	10.1	0.0	3.7	0.0	0.0	6.2	0.0
Saratoga Springs	46	224	12.5	3.2	2.9	0.8	2.8	0.2	0.0	0.0	0.0	2.2	2.0
Schenectady	113	798	54.6	15.1	393.0	278.1	49.8	3.4	4.1	7.7	3.3	26.4	5.6
Spring Valley	45	115	9.7	2.4	0.8	0.3	15.9	0.9	1.7	0.0	0.0	13.3	0.0
Syracuse	260	1 995	129.8	42.1	144.8	40.1	135.3	35.1	9.4	4.1	7.2	48.5	27.6
Troy	75	367	25.3	6.8	7.0	0.7	128.4	5.0	5.3	69.7	2.4	16.1	15.3
Utica	98	713	33.5	10.7	17.3	0.8	23.6	1.5	0.0	0.0	2.6	17.3	22.6
Valley Stream	119	998	37.6	13.0	0.0	0.5	0.9	0.0	0.0	0.0	0.9	0.5	0.5
Watertown	59	323	21.3	6.2	4.3	1.1	13.7	7.6	2.0	0.0	1.1	8.5	4.0
White Plains	115	735	48.8	15.1	3.9	4.0	41.8	7.6	0.0	0.0	0.6	22.3	3.6
Yonkers	278	961	64.7	18.6	24.6	0.6	52.3	0.5	0.4	0.0	4.3	45.8	0.2
NORTH CAROLINA	11 483	64 802	4 060.6	1 204.0	1 988.2	1 806.2	11 613.2	6 238.1	1 545.5	110.1	986.9	605.2	401.8
Asheville	214	1 324	78.2	25.6	13.7	32.3	35.5	4.9	7.1	0.3	1.1	15.8	5.5
Burlington	109	744	38.7	12.5	8.2	2.7	11.2	0.3	0.0	0.0	1.1	9.7	0.0
Cary	151	1 114	76.4	22.9	4.6	11.3	6.9	3.3	0.0	0.4	0.0	0.2	0.0
Chapel Hill	65	429	20.2	7.0	2.4	36.0	400.6	313.6	6.4	5.4	19.7	1.5	8.6
Charlotte	1 045	8 575	557.9	177.1	45.8	481.8	117.7	23.3	6.6	1.0	17.3	40.7	32.4
Concord	96	489	26.4	8.4	0.0	0.2	6.4	0.5	1.0	0.2	1.3	2.2	2.2
Durham	294	2 088	111.5	39.6	59.8	118.3	615.3	516.8	3.4	12.0	17.6	13.6	19.3
Fayetteville	239	1 835	98.5	31.9	46.7	13.2	41.9	0.5	5.9	0.0	12.6	19.2	19.6
Gastonia	131	926	50.3	14.6	1.4	0.2	9.0	0.0	3.6	0.0	0.0	4.7	0.0
Goldsboro	108	844	49.6	16.0	0.5	2.3	13.6	0.0	5.0	0.0	0.8	6.4	3.4
Greensboro	476	3 853	270.4	77.9	160.4	29.4	81.7	6.7	7.9	0.4	17.5	19.2	26.5
Greenville	114	742	39.2	11.6	16.4	2.5	21.1	8.9	0.0	0.2	3.6	4.7	13.9
Hickory	138	919	51.1	17.6	0.5	0.7	8.1	0.0	0.0	0.0	0.8	2.6	4.7
High Point	154	813	42.7	13.7	4.0	32.3	16.2	0.0	0.0	0.0	0.8	14.5	3.7
Jacksonville	107	596	27.5	9.1	15.6	4.5	12.8	0.0	1.5	0.0	2.4	7.2	4.1
Kannapolis	65	295	19.6	5.8	0.0	0.0	7.3	0.2	1.2	0.0	0.0	5.9	0.0
Monroe	78	528	26.8	8.0	10.1	0.9	8.2	0.0	3.8	2.0	0.0	2.3	0.0
Raleigh	575	4 540	371.6	97.6	53.1	70.2	1 547.5	180.7	373.7	78.6	310.2	65.4	41.3
Rocky Mount	114	830	49.8	14.3	6.3	0.1	15.1	0.0	4.2	0.0	0.6	8.3	4.0
Salisbury	77	395	21.9	7.3	0.2	12.7	13.4	0.0	6.6	0.0	1.8	4.8	9.6
Wilmington	224	1 496	90.8	28.3	15.2	45.8	73.6	34.5	1.9	0.2	3.8	20.0	12.0
Wilson	75	614	28.2	9.6	2.7	0.5	8.4	2.3	0.0	0.0	0.8	4.1	4.9
Winston-Salem	352	2 623	135.0	47.3	18.3	26.1	174.1	131.0	3.7	0.0	0.5	21.7	17.4
NORTH DAKOTA	1 281	6 294	364.3	101.3	262.1	135.4	1 537.1	417.2	161.4	28.1	157.9	65.2	48.7
Bismarck	132	808	44.1	13.6	1.7	4.2	233.1	22.2	35.1	15.1	57.8	16.3	12.2
Fargo	206	1 813	98.9	31.0	7.0	10.7	56.9	8.6	2.9	0.2	2.4	7.3	6.2
Grand Forks	94	673	33.7	10.8	27.9	7.4	58.7	13.3	1.7	10.0	10.7	8.5	9.7
Minot	87	510	22.6	7.1	10.2	7.6	22.8	0.7	3.9	0.0	11.5	3.3	4.1
OHIO	17 314	116 165	7 087.5	2 165.7	4 271.2	2 276.4	15 687.5	7 841.1	2 614.5	222.9	1 268.8	1 253.3	510.1
Akron	368	2 522	138.9	45.3	419.0	4.9	86.2	7.6	10.2	0.2	3.1	39.7	23.7
Barberton	51	322	17.4	5.7	1.6	0.0	2.5	1.0	0.0	0.5	0.1	1.0	0.2
Beavercreek	63	351	21.4	6.2	59.3	4.9	0.9	0.0	0.0	0.0	0.0	0.0	0.0
Bowling Green	40	281	14.4	4.7	0.6	0.0	12.6	3.9	0.0	0.0	2.7	0.3	0.0
Brunswick	49	283	17.0	4.9	0.7	0.2	1.0	0.0	0.0	0.0	2.7	2.9	12.6
Canton	153	1 009	66.1	21.5	7.2	3.0	45.6	2.0	5.8	1.8	2.8	0.8	0.0
Cincinnati	609	4 476	297.6	92.4	1 183.4	511.6	445.5	203.9	29.1	7.9	10.4	26.4	10.7
Cleveland	749	5 448	377.6	103.4	175.2	297.9	598.6	318.7	32.9	16.1	15.8	170.3	42.2
Cleveland Heights	65	457	28.9	8.8	0.1	0.1	7.8	0.0	0.0	0.0	0.0	144.1	66.4
Columbus	998	8 317	509.7	163.0	362.6	187.9	2 281.3	399.2	696.3	163.9	429.7	7.6	0.0
Cuyahoga Falls	92	532	28.7	9.3	3.1	1.7	3.8	0.0	0.0	0.2	0.0	225.8	67.4
Dayton	279	2 613	171.8	56.8	587.8	89.7	136.1	18.4	18.5	3.1	12.2	3.4	1.9
												60.8	36.4

1. Firms subject to federal tax. 2. Includes program categories not shown separately. State totals include additional categories not allocated by city.

City	City government finances, 2002									
	General revenue							General expenditure		
	Intergovernmental			Taxes					Per capita[1] (dollars)	
					Per capita[1] (dollars)					
	Total (mil dol)	Total (mil dol)	Percent from state government	Total (mil dol)	Total	Property	Sales and gross receipts	Total (mil dol)	Total	Capital outlays
	117	118	119	120	121	122	123	124	125	126
NEW YORK—Cont'd										
Ithaca	36.2	7.4	33.4	17.4	582	286	270	41.8	1 393	273
Jamestown	52.0	23.7	60.6	10.6	343	320	13	57.8	1 863	58
Lindenhurst	8.8	2.1	62.6	4.3	154	121	17	9.0	319	80
Long Beach	53.2	11.7	38.9	26.3	739	641	42	51.7	1 454	225
Middletown	24.2	7.8	34.2	9.8	380	335	23	26.3	1 020	123
Mount Vernon	75.1	18.5	39.7	45.7	665	451	173	71.8	1 047	79
Newburgh	33.6	11.1	40.1	11.3	399	347	37	33.6	1 185	110
New Rochelle	98.0	23.7	47.0	58.4	806	449	315	96.3	1 328	166
New York	52 718.0	22 536.3	85.1	22 235.2	2 750	1 100	568	54 501.7	6 742	864
Niagara Falls	90.6	35.5	34.8	34.3	631	457	162	83.1	1 528	118
North Tonawanda	29.6	11.1	34.8	12.6	387	333	42	30.6	939	100
Port Chester	27.8	4.3	37.9	12.6	452	413	17	33.0	1 180	328
Poughkeepsie	41.6	21.0	23.4	13.3	443	396	23	45.2	1 502	210
Rochester	860.6	582.0	76.8	180.9	833	758	58	882.1	4 062	414
Rome	39.2	11.5	78.4	20.6	594	362	222	39.8	1 147	167
Saratoga Springs	30.1	11.5	25.7	11.1	411	304	46	29.0	1 072	85
Schenectady	61.2	24.9	33.0	21.2	345	302	27	71.3	1 161	124
Spring Valley	22.6	8.2	13.3	12.6	491	468	13	25.0	976	102
Syracuse	450.5	356.1	76.7	26.5	183	139	23	515.5	3 551	310
Troy	52.9	26.2	47.0	16.7	342	305	24	51.2	1 049	146
Utica	65.5	26.2	71.8	27.7	462	239	210	69.7	1 163	218
Valley Stream	23.2	2.0	73.2	18.0	494	453	16	23.2	636	88
Watertown	29.2	15.7	26.9	8.8	344	310	23	33.3	1 301	120
White Plains	112.3	11.0	43.2	70.5	1 272	538	664	110.2	1 989	213
Yonkers	674.1	374.7	95.5	247.4	1 255	854	277	690.2	3 499	227
NORTH CAROLINA	X	X	X	X	X	X	X	X	X	X
Asheville	84.3	25.9	30.5	34.2	494	418	16	84.5	1 222	98
Burlington	42.2	11.7	39.3	15.4	335	306	2	45.5	989	129
Cary	116.7	20.6	30.6	49.9	509	458	13	105.2	1 073	339
Chapel Hill	55.6	26.8	24.2	23.2	450	396	19	42.0	813	78
Charlotte	957.8	237.6	24.3	312.8	539	402	68	746.6	1 286	372
Concord	68.5	17.4	26.1	26.9	459	442	5	65.6	1 121	69
Durham	207.2	48.9	31.3	89.1	455	382	9	184.4	941	93
Fayetteville	117.3	31.2	30.8	37.0	298	267	9	110.1	886	78
Gastonia	68.1	22.7	41.5	20.9	308	274	14	71.9	1 060	149
Goldsboro	45.7	24.1	72.6	9.8	254	227	8	43.7	1 136	225
Greensboro	269.6	63.7	33.5	110.3	483	427	23	265.0	1 161	89
Greenville	76.3	28.1	17.8	20.8	318	262	21	85.0	1 298	204
Hickory	54.7	14.8	32.0	24.2	615	545	29	55.8	1 419	314
High Point	110.6	24.4	40.7	44.3	489	418	18	98.8	1 090	124
Jacksonville	35.0	13.4	31.4	11.6	174	154	3	35.3	527	68
Kannapolis	25.6	7.4	38.4	11.2	294	284	4	24.5	645	135
Monroe	35.4	6.3	35.2	10.9	395	371	3	30.0	1 090	218
Raleigh	282.9	74.6	33.9	122.3	398	333	15	303.1	987	181
Rocky Mount	87.8	45.1	78.0	15.0	268	237	9	81.1	1 447	94
Salisbury	35.9	7.4	44.1	11.7	442	420	1	30.1	1 136	47
Wilmington	105.3	22.3	35.8	45.6	503	469	7	85.3	941	113
Wilson	49.1	14.1	46.0	13.9	305	273	5	44.5	977	40
Winston-Salem	210.9	55.2	37.8	75.6	400	352	12	226.4	1 198	246
NORTH DAKOTA	X	X	X	X	X	X	X	X	X	X
Bismarck	67.6	14.2	33.0	21.9	389	197	174	54.4	967	256
Fargo	102.0	17.4	70.9	31.3	343	175	147	118.8	1 302	603
Grand Forks	88.4	27.3	50.7	23.2	477	166	285	107.2	2 209	1 012
Minot	30.4	4.4	88.5	16.6	467	194	261	33.1	929	416
OHIO	X	X	X	X	X	X	X	X	X	X
Akron	322.9	67.1	70.3	164.0	765	137	8	336.0	1 568	346
Barberton	28.4	7.1	80.0	11.6	418	47	0	29.8	1 078	263
Beavercreek	16.5	4.7	100.0	7.9	208	192	11	19.2	506	76
Bowling Green	33.5	4.6	100.0	16.0	542	66	38	31.4	1 066	239
Brunswick	19.1	3.7	67.8	10.2	289	46	5	20.6	586	95
Canton	91.4	21.3	27.3	45.2	566	36	0	86.0	1 078	44
Cincinnati	792.8	270.1	36.2	351.7	1 086	183	29	706.4	2 181	569
Cleveland	954.4	229.4	67.9	424.8	908	166	61	912.4	1 950	335
Cleveland Heights	54.3	8.5	33.0	33.0	664	199	8	51.0	1 025	210
Columbus	1 063.9	205.5	65.8	516.0	712	50	22	1 081.3	1 491	269
Cuyahoga Falls	54.7	7.7	39.8	26.2	531	175	13	53.8	1 093	211
Dayton	307.2	48.5	46.5	128.7	791	107	0	312.9	1 924	274

1. Based on population estimated as of July 1 of the year shown.

Table D. Cities — City Government Finances (cont'd)

City	Public welfare	Highways	Parking facilities	Education	Health and hospitals	Police protection	Sewerage and sanitation	Parks and recreation	Housing and community development	Interest on debt
	127	128	129	130	131	132	133	134	135	136
NEW YORK—Cont'd										
Ithaca	0.0	15.8	0.8	0.0	0.0	14.7	13.3	9.3	4.7	1.9
Jamestown	0.0	4.1	0.1	44.4	0.0	8.3	8.1	2.8	0.0	7.4
Lindenhurst	0.0	30.8	0.1	0.0	0.0	0.0	8.1	7.9	0.0	1.2
Long Beach	0.0	11.5	0.0	0.1	0.0	22.1	14.4	10.8	0.7	2.8
Middletown	0.0	6.4	0.0	0.0	0.0	20.2	15.8	4.1	3.2	7.7
Mount Vernon	9.9	2.5	0.0	0.0	0.1	19.2	6.2	3.5	5.1	3.4
Newburgh	0.0	5.4	0.2	0.0	0.0	23.9	12.3	7.2	1.6	8.8
New Rochelle	7.6	5.1	1.7	0.0	0.3	21.6	4.9	2.7	7.4	7.5
New York	16.1	1.6	0.0	26.4	10.5	6.9	4.5	1.3	5.8	4.5
Niagara Falls	4.0	9.1	0.7	0.0	0.1	15.0	14.5	11.8	4.1	3.4
North Tonawanda	0.0	13.2	0.0	0.0	0.1	14.4	17.4	6.9	1.4	3.1
Port Chester	0.0	25.1	0.0	0.0	0.2	16.6	5.8	3.9	8.2	5.4
Poughkeepsie	4.8	9.5	1.1	0.0	0.1	19.7	10.7	2.3	3.7	6.5
Rochester	0.0	2.0	0.3	57.9	0.1	6.5	2.2	1.9	2.0	1.8
Rome	0.0	10.1	0.7	0.0	0.3	13.5	8.2	2.9	4.1	5.4
Saratoga Springs	0.0	13.0	0.3	0.0	0.2	16.4	8.9	10.0	0.7	1.9
Schenectady	0.0	8.3	0.9	0.0	0.0	17.7	15.4	2.8	4.0	10.7
Spring Valley	23.4	5.2	0.2	0.1	0.0	24.4	0.3	3.3	6.1	2.0
Syracuse	0.0	4.4	0.0	56.4	0.0	6.3	1.7	1.7	1.4	6.1
Troy	0.0	9.1	0.8	0.0	0.4	18.5	8.3	3.6	6.0	8.4
Utica	4.8	13.3	0.9	0.0	0.0	15.3	3.2	5.1	3.4	10.4
Valley Stream	0.0	18.1	0.6	0.0	0.4	0.9	17.8	12.4	0.0	4.4
Watertown	0.0	10.4	0.2	0.0	0.0	14.7	10.1	3.2	1.3	6.2
White Plains	3.7	7.6	7.0	0.0	0.0	19.4	6.4	5.7	1.5	1.8
Yonkers	0.0	0.9	0.4	56.4	0.0	9.0	2.9	1.1	0.0	3.9
NORTH CAROLINA	X	X	X	X	X	X	X	X	X	X
Asheville	0.0	9.9	1.8	0.0	0.1	15.2	22.7	12.4	4.6	3.0
Burlington	0.0	7.2	0.0	0.0	2.9	23.2	24.0	11.5	1.6	4.7
Cary	0.0	18.6	0.0	0.0	0.0	9.1	15.9	16.4	0.6	2.9
Chapel Hill	0.0	7.0	3.0	0.0	0.0	21.0	7.8	6.9	7.6	2.2
Charlotte	0.0	12.9	0.1	0.0	0.5	19.0	10.3	1.6	5.3	8.1
Concord	0.0	4.4	0.0	0.0	0.0	13.3	22.2	7.3	1.1	7.7
Durham	0.0	7.7	0.7	0.0	0.0	18.7	22.1	7.4	3.3	4.6
Fayetteville	0.0	10.6	0.2	0.0	0.0	21.8	20.2	5.7	2.7	7.9
Gastonia	0.0	5.7	0.0	0.0	0.0	16.9	21.5	7.1	3.2	7.8
Goldsboro	0.0	6.7	0.0	0.0	0.3	13.3	14.2	6.4	0.4	3.1
Greensboro	0.0	7.8	0.4	0.0	0.0	18.9	17.1	13.3	4.1	3.5
Greenville	0.0	9.7	0.0	0.0	0.0	13.6	16.8	6.5	19.0	4.4
Hickory	0.0	8.2	0.0	0.0	0.1	12.1	19.4	11.9	1.8	3.2
High Point	0.0	8.4	0.8	0.0	0.0	14.5	13.2	6.5	2.3	4.6
Jacksonville	0.0	5.6	0.0	0.0	0.0	20.8	25.9	11.4	1.7	4.7
Kannapolis	0.0	10.8	0.0	0.0	0.0	20.3	21.2	4.0	1.8	2.3
Monroe	0.0	5.4	0.0	0.0	0.0	17.9	19.3	13.7	2.6	3.7
Raleigh	0.4	13.9	1.6	0.0	0.0	16.5	15.1	13.9	2.4	4.4
Rocky Mount	0.0	5.7	0.0	0.0	0.0	10.7	16.9	6.6	3.5	1.3
Salisbury	0.0	9.5	0.0	0.0	0.1	18.7	22.0	8.9	2.7	4.5
Wilmington	0.0	6.2	2.4	0.0	0.0	18.7	19.8	11.6	2.6	2.6
Wilson	0.0	6.1	0.2	0.0	0.0	17.0	25.2	8.6	12.7	2.2
Winston-Salem	0.0	9.0	3.5	0.0	0.0	16.8	19.1	10.4	6.9	4.5
NORTH DAKOTA	X	X	X	X	X	X	X	X	X	X
Bismarck	0.0	25.1	1.0	0.0	1.6	12.7	10.2	4.1	2.1	8.3
Fargo	0.3	4.6	1.2	0.0	3.3	6.6	7.1	12.1	1.5	8.2
Grand Forks	0.0	3.8	0.3	0.0	1.6	5.7	18.3	9.0	5.5	9.8
Minot	0.8	8.2	0.3	0.0	0.0	12.5	9.0	3.2	0.0	2.6
OHIO	X	X	X	X	X	X	X	X	X	X
Akron	0.0	12.5	4.3	0.0	7.5	13.9	11.0	4.0	1.2	5.4
Barberton	0.0	10.6	0.0	0.0	5.4	15.7	13.6	17.4	5.1	1.1
Beavercreek	0.0	24.7	0.0	0.0	1.1	29.6	0.0	15.5	0.4	5.6
Bowling Green	0.0	9.2	0.7	0.0	0.6	24.0	16.7	3.3	4.2	3.1
Brunswick	0.0	11.8	0.0	0.0	0.2	15.3	8.4	12.0	1.6	2.1
Canton	0.0	6.9	0.1	0.0	4.9	18.7	11.7	3.0	10.9	2.4
Cincinnati	0.0	3.6	0.8	0.0	5.1	13.4	17.3	5.5	3.9	1.8
Cleveland	0.3	5.1	0.3	0.0	3.7	19.0	5.4	6.7	13.4	5.3
Cleveland Heights	0.5	11.4	1.8	0.0	0.8	15.5	9.0	7.3	6.7	2.9
Columbus	0.0	8.7	0.1	0.0	5.5	18.8	16.8	7.6	1.5	8.9
Cuyahoga Falls	0.5	16.5	0.0	0.0	0.5	14.4	11.1	11.2	0.6	2.2
Dayton	0.0	11.0	0.0	0.0	0.0	16.5	9.5	3.8	4.1	5.4

Table D. Cities — City Government Finances, City Government Employment, and Climate

City	City government finances, 2002 (cont'd) — Debt outstanding — Total (mil dol)	Per capita[1] (dollars)	Percent utility	City government employment, 2002	Climate[2] — Average daily temperature (degrees Fahrenheit) — Mean — January	July	Limits — January[3]	July[4]	Annual precipitation (inches)	Heating degree days	Cooling degree days
	137	138	139	140	141	142	143	144	145	146	147
NEW YORK—Cont'd											
Ithaca	23.1	769	19.5	463	21.5	68.6	12.9	79.8	35.40	7 207	288
Jamestown	52.9	1 703	71.4	865	24.3	70.5	17.8	78.7	45.82	6 591	461
Lindenhurst	2.7	95	0.0	88	31.2	75.5	24.9	82.8	41.59	5 027	921
Long Beach	40.6	1 140	35.2	497	31.2	75.5	24.9	82.8	41.59	5 027	921
Middletown	35.3	1 371	17.3	326	NA	NA	NA	NA	NA	NA	NA
Mount Vernon	26.8	390	0.0	748	28.7	74.1	19.7	85.7	46.01	5 470	779
Newburgh	33.6	1 185	18.4	244	27.4	75.2	19.3	86.5	47.51	5 550	896
New Rochelle	126.6	1 747	0.0	625	28.7	74.1	19.7	85.7	46.01	5 470	779
New York	63 934.1	7 908	25.2	426 560	31.5	76.8	25.3	85.2	47.25	4 805	1 096
Niagara Falls	109.5	2 015	61.5	804	23.6	71.1	17.0	80.2	38.58	6 747	477
North Tonawanda	16.0	492	3.2	338	23.6	71.1	17.0	80.2	38.58	6 747	477
Port Chester	32.5	1 162	0.0	172	NA	NA	NA	NA	NA	NA	NA
Poughkeepsie	55.3	1 839	5.2	406	23.8	72.2	14.2	83.8	40.72	6 391	566
Rochester	345.4	1 590	8.6	10 722	23.6	70.2	16.3	80.7	31.96	6 734	425
Rome	44.4	1 280	6.0	435	20.1	70.2	12.7	80.3	45.09	7 305	423
Saratoga Springs	8.7	321	0.0	298	20.1	71.1	9.3	84.1	40.88	6 998	452
Schenectady	86.2	1 404	12.9	715	21.8	71.7	13.2	82.6	36.46	6 881	537
Spring Valley	12.2	477	0.0	147	NA	NA	NA	NA	NA	NA	NA
Syracuse	475.7	3 277	2.7	6 485	22.4	70.4	14.2	81.7	38.93	6 834	438
Troy	116.2	2 380	3.7	641	21.3	73.0	11.6	83.8	36.18	6 758	599
Utica	92.8	1 548	0.2	805	20.1	70.2	12.7	80.3	45.09	7 305	423
Valley Stream	20.1	552	0.0	279	31.2	75.5	24.9	82.8	41.59	5 027	921
Watertown	41.7	1 630	39.2	371	17.9	68.6	8.3	79.6	32.04	7 753	299
White Plains	62.3	1 125	8.6	1 007	27.2	73.3	20.2	82.1	48.92	5 832	691
Yonkers	454.4	2 304	3.1	5 664	28.7	74.1	19.7	85.7	46.01	5 470	779
NORTH CAROLINA	X	X	X	X	X	X	X	X	X	X	X
Asheville	95.1	1 374	64.0	1 020	35.7	72.8	24.8	83.0	47.59	4 308	787
Burlington	40.2	873	10.5	623	37.5	78.2	27.0	88.9	44.96	3 680	1 408
Cary	127.3	1 298	62.1	1 038	38.9	78.1	28.8	88.0	41.43	3 457	1 417
Chapel Hill	25.9	501	0.0	634	37.2	76.8	25.7	88.7	46.02	3 802	1 233
Charlotte	2 193.2	3 778	19.5	5 538	39.3	79.3	29.6	88.9	43.09	3 341	1 582
Concord	130.2	2 225	39.0	826	38.5	78.8	27.2	90.0	45.70	3 497	1 541
Durham	347.0	1 771	16.7	2 008	37.1	77.1	25.1	88.8	48.10	3 867	1 278
Fayetteville	247.0	1 987	44.6	1 732	40.3	79.4	29.1	89.7	46.72	3 169	1 623
Gastonia	116.5	1 718	22.1	1 016	39.8	78.2	29.1	88.9	46.63	3 338	1 464
Goldsboro	37.0	962	29.9	470	41.0	79.8	30.5	89.9	49.27	3 040	1 689
Greensboro	337.4	1 479	17.6	2 761	36.7	76.9	26.6	86.9	42.62	3 865	1 253
Greenville	116.3	1 776	49.6	1 118	40.6	78.8	29.6	89.5	49.00	3 129	1 561
Hickory	44.6	1 134	20.8	663	37.7	76.8	27.8	86.6	49.38	3 728	1 258
High Point	125.6	1 386	19.3	1 413	38.9	77.9	29.0	88.3	44.52	3 420	1 400
Jacksonville	34.2	511	0.0	418	44.9	79.5	35.0	86.8	54.75	2 506	1 815
Kannapolis	47.1	1 238	57.1	214	38.5	78.8	27.2	90.0	45.70	3 497	1 541
Monroe	35.3	1 281	51.0	428	NA	NA	NA	NA	NA	NA	NA
Raleigh	265.2	864	3.1	3 204	38.8	78.6	28.9	88.3	44.97	3 397	1 493
Rocky Mount	26.2	468	39.5	782	39.9	78.4	29.4	88.9	45.69	3 321	1 447
Salisbury	58.4	2 207	62.9	443	NA	NA	NA	NA	NA	NA	NA
Wilmington	124.3	1 372	53.3	1 110	44.9	80.1	34.4	88.5	54.27	2 470	1 926
Wilson	41.6	913	62.8	668	39.4	78.5	28.4	89.4	46.96	3 371	1 519
Winston-Salem	363.7	1 925	28.8	2 310	38.9	77.9	29.0	88.3	44.52	3 420	1 400
NORTH DAKOTA	X	X	X	X	X	X	X	X	X	X	X
Bismarck	72.6	1 291	0.0	534	9.2	70.4	-1.7	84.4	15.47	8 968	488
Fargo	221.9	2 433	21.3	695	5.9	71.1	-3.6	83.4	19.45	9 254	537
Grand Forks	211.9	4 366	8.8	502	4.3	69.1	-5.3	81.6	18.34	9 733	453
Minot	26.0	729	31.5	326	9.0	69.9	0.4	82.0	18.57	9 193	492
OHIO	X	X	X	X	X	X	X	X	X	X	X
Akron	361.3	1 686	16.1	2 590	24.8	71.9	16.9	82.3	36.82	6 160	625
Barberton	16.4	591	16.0	257	24.8	71.9	16.9	82.3	36.82	6 160	625
Beavercreek	16.2	426	0.0	132	26.0	74.2	17.9	84.9	36.64	5 708	886
Bowling Green	28.4	963	0.0	286	22.7	73.0	14.4	84.6	32.77	6 482	694
Brunswick	9.8	279	0.0	179	24.8	71.9	17.6	82.4	36.63	6 201	621
Canton	45.7	573	30.8	1 115	24.8	71.9	16.9	82.3	36.82	6 160	625
Cincinnati	484.2	1 495	36.1	6 846	29.8	76.4	21.2	86.6	40.70	4 928	1 135
Cleveland	2 561.2	5 474	37.8	9 155	24.8	71.9	17.6	82.4	36.63	6 201	621
Cleveland Heights	31.7	637	3.2	558	24.8	71.9	17.6	82.4	36.63	6 201	621
Columbus	1 675.0	2 310	20.7	8 710	26.4	73.2	18.5	83.7	38.09	5 708	797
Cuyahoga Falls	36.1	732	38.7	855	24.8	71.9	16.9	82.3	36.82	6 160	625
Dayton	304.3	1 871	10.6	3 003	26.0	74.2	17.9	84.9	36.64	5 708	886

1. Based on the population estimated as of July 1 of the year shown. 2. Represents normal values based on the 30-year period, 1961–1990. 3. Average daily minimum. 4. Average daily maximum.

Table D. Cities — Land Area and Population

STATE Place code	City	Land area,[1] 2000 (sq km)	Population, 2003 Total persons	Rank	Per square kilometer	White	Black	Am. Indian, Alaska Native	Asian and Pacific Islander	Other race	Hispanic or Latino[2]	Non-Hispanic White
		1	2	3	4	5	6	7	8	9	10	11
	OHIO—Cont'd											
39 21434	Delaware	38.8	28 358	1 118	730.9	94.3	4.6	0.9	1.2	0.8	1.2	92.2
39 22694	Dublin	54.7	33 606	960	614.4	90.5	2.0	0.3	8.0	0.3	1.0	88.9
39 23380	East Cleveland	8.0	26 255	1 195	3 281.9	5.2	94.6	0.9	0.5	0.5	0.8	4.5
39 25256	Elyria	51.5	56 096	546	1 089.2	83.7	15.6	1.1	1.0	1.4	2.8	80.0
39 25704	Euclid	27.7	51 260	611	1 850.5	67.6	31.6	0.6	1.3	0.7	1.1	65.8
39 25914	Fairborn	33.8	32 474	992	960.8	89.2	7.1	1.0	4.1	0.9	1.7	86.3
39 25970	Fairfield	54.4	42 544	754	782.1	90.9	6.6	0.4	2.6	0.8	1.5	89.0
39 27048	Findlay	44.5	39 797	808	894.3	94.8	1.8	0.5	2.1	2.1	3.9	91.8
39 29106	Gahanna	32.1	33 224	968	1 035.0	87.7	8.8	0.6	3.8	0.7	1.3	85.7
39 29428	Garfield Heights	18.7	29 881	1 067	1 597.9	81.5	17.2	0.5	1.1	0.6	1.3	80.0
39 32592	Grove City	36.1	29 165	1 089	807.9	97.2	1.9	0.6	0.9	0.5	1.2	95.4
39 33012	Hamilton	56.0	60 763	486	1 085.1	90.1	8.0	0.8	0.7	1.7	2.6	88.0
39 36610	Huber Heights	54.5	38 240	835	701.7	86.8	10.9	0.8	2.9	1.0	1.7	83.9
39 39872	Kent	22.5	28 082	1 129	1 248.1	87.9	10.2	0.7	2.6	0.9	1.3	85.3
39 40040	Kettering	48.4	56 494	538	1 167.2	96.3	2.0	0.5	1.9	0.6	1.1	94.5
39 41664	Lakewood	14.4	54 378	579	3 776.3	95.6	2.5	0.7	1.9	2.1	2.2	91.7
39 41720	Lancaster	46.8	35 914	895	767.4	98.3	1.0	0.8	0.7	0.3	0.8	96.8
39 43554	Lima	33.1	40 549	790	1 225.0	71.5	28.2	0.9	0.7	1.3	2.0	68.4
39 44856	Lorain	62.2	67 955	417	1 092.5	73.2	17.8	1.2	0.6	11.5	21.0	61.1
39 47138	Mansfield	77.5	50 688	623	654.0	78.5	20.9	1.0	0.9	0.8	1.2	76.1
39 47306	Maple Heights	13.4	25 490	1 217	1 902.2	52.8	45.4	0.6	2.1	0.9	1.2	51.2
39 47754	Marion	29.4	37 300	862	1 268.7	91.4	7.6	0.6	0.7	0.9	1.3	89.6
39 48244	Massillon	43.4	31 542	1 017	726.8	89.6	10.4	0.8	0.4	0.5	1.0	87.5
39 48790	Medina	28.8	26 487	1 191	919.7	96.0	3.5	0.6	1.0	0.4	1.0	93.9
39 49056	Mentor	69.3	50 004	634	721.6	97.9	0.8	0.2	1.4	0.3	0.7	96.8
39 49840	Middletown	66.5	51 941	606	781.1	88.2	11.4	0.7	0.6	0.6	0.9	86.5
39 54040	Newark	50.6	46 601	689	921.0	95.6	3.9	0.8	0.9	0.5	0.8	93.6
39 56882	North Olmsted	30.1	33 481	963	1 112.3	95.6	1.2	0.4	3.2	1.4	1.7	92.8
39 57008	North Royalton	55.1	29 598	1 079	537.2	96.9	0.8	0.2	2.4	0.5	1.0	95.5
39 61000	Parma	51.7	83 861	319	1 622.1	96.7	1.3	0.3	2.0	0.9	1.5	94.7
39 66390	Reynoldsburg	27.4	32 878	981	1 199.9	86.6	11.2	0.7	2.3	1.1	1.8	84.0
39 70380	Sandusky	26.0	27 030	1 167	1 039.6	77.0	23.1	0.8	0.6	1.6	3.1	73.0
39 71682	Shaker Heights	16.3	28 459	1 112	1 746.0	61.7	35.4	0.7	3.9	1.0	1.2	59.3
39 74118	Springfield	58.2	64 483	446	1 108.0	79.9	19.6	1.1	1.0	0.8	1.2	77.5
39 74944	Stow	44.3	34 290	941	774.0	96.1	1.8	0.4	2.3	0.5	0.9	94.6
39 75098	Strongsville	63.8	44 560	724	698.4	95.1	1.5	0.2	3.6	0.6	1.3	93.3
39 77000	Toledo	208.8	308 973	58	1 479.8	72.4	24.8	0.9	1.4	3.2	5.5	67.8
39 77504	Trotwood city	79.1	27 070	1 166	342.2	40.1	59.8	1.0	0.5	0.8	0.8	38.3
39 79002	Upper Arlington	25.3	32 406	994	1 280.9	95.4	0.8	0.3	3.9	0.4	1.0	93.9
39 80892	Warren	41.7	46 608	688	1 117.7	73.6	26.5	0.7	0.7	0.6	1.0	71.4
39 83342	Westerville	32.1	34 922	926	1 087.9	94.6	3.7	0.4	1.9	0.6	1.1	92.9
39 83622	Westlake	41.2	32 024	1 001	777.3	94.4	1.1	0.2	4.7	1.1	1.3	92.1
39 88000	Youngstown	87.8	79 271	347	902.9	52.6	45.5	1.1	0.6	3.0	5.2	48.9
39 88084	Zanesville	29.1	25 277	1 220	868.6	88.0	12.7	1.3	0.4	0.6	0.8	85.0
40 00000	OKLAHOMA	177 846.9	3 511 532	X	19.7	80.3	8.3	11.4	1.8	3.0	5.2	74.1
40 04450	Bartlesville	54.7	34 708	935	634.5	87.4	3.8	11.8	1.4	1.5	3.0	80.6
40 09050	Broken Arrow	116.5	83 607	320	717.7	88.8	4.2	6.6	2.4	1.8	3.6	83.5
40 23200	Edmond	220.5	71 643	394	324.9	89.2	4.5	4.0	4.0	1.4	2.8	85.1
40 23950	Enid	191.6	46 436	693	242.4	89.7	4.5	3.7	2.1	2.9	4.7	85.3
40 41850	Lawton	194.6	91 730	280	471.4	65.2	25.0	5.5	4.5	5.2	9.4	57.8
40 48350	Midwest City	63.7	54 662	574	858.1	73.0	20.9	5.9	2.7	2.1	4.1	67.6
40 49200	Moore	56.3	44 987	717	799.1	89.2	3.6	7.5	2.4	2.4	5.1	82.1
40 50050	Muskogee	96.7	38 635	832	399.5	66.3	19.3	17.8	1.2	1.9	3.3	60.0
40 52500	Norman	458.4	99 197	250	216.4	86.0	5.0	7.0	4.2	1.9	3.9	80.3
40 55000	Oklahoma City	1 572.1	523 303	29	332.9	71.7	16.4	5.7	4.2	6.2	10.1	64.7
40 59850	Ponca City	46.9	25 596	1 211	545.8	87.7	3.3	9.2	1.1	2.5	4.4	82.5
40 66800	Shawnee	109.5	29 446	1 082	268.9	80.9	4.8	16.3	1.4	1.2	2.7	75.8
40 70300	Stillwater	72.1	41 320	778	573.1	85.5	4.8	5.8	5.8	1.5	2.5	81.3
40 75000	Tulsa	473.1	387 807	44	819.7	73.9	16.5	7.7	2.3	4.2	7.2	67.1
41 00000	OREGON	248 630.5	3 559 596	X	14.3	89.3	2.1	2.5	4.2	5.2	8.0	83.5
41 01000	Albany	41.1	43 091	742	1 048.4	94.0	0.8	2.4	2.2	3.4	6.1	89.0
41 05350	Beaverton	42.3	80 520	335	1 903.5	81.5	2.4	1.4	12.0	6.7	11.1	73.6
41 05800	Bend	82.9	59 779	499	721.1	96.0	0.5	1.7	1.8	2.2	4.6	91.6
41 15800	Corvallis	35.2	50 126	631	1 424.0	88.6	1.6	1.6	8.1	3.3	5.7	83.3
41 23850	Eugene	104.9	142 185	160	1 355.4	91.5	2.0	2.3	5.1	3.1	5.0	86.0
41 31250	Gresham	57.4	95 816	264	1 669.3	86.1	2.6	2.0	5.0	8.5	11.9	78.9
41 34100	Hillsboro	55.9	77 709	359	1 390.1	80.4	1.7	1.6	8.2	11.7	18.9	70.3
41 38500	Keizer	18.7	34 154	943	1 826.4	88.6	1.2	2.5	2.6	8.7	12.3	81.7

1. Dry land or land partially or temporarily covered by water.   2. Hispanic or Latino persons may be of any race.

Table D. Cities — **Population and Households**

City	Population characteristics, 2000 (cont'd) Age of population (percent)									Percent female	Population Census counts		Percent change	
	Under 5 years	5 to 17 years	18 to 24 years	25 to 34 years	35 to 44 years	45 to 54 years	55 to 64 years	65 to 74 years	75 years and over		1990	2000	1990–2000	2000–2003
	12	13	14	15	16	17	18	19	20	21	22	23	24	25
OHIO—Cont'd														
Delaware	7.9	16.7	14.5	16.2	14.8	11.7	7.2	5.6	5.3	52.2	19 966	25 243	26.4	12.3
Dublin	8.2	23.9	4.8	12.2	21.2	17.6	6.7	3.1	2.3	50.5	16 366	31 392	91.8	7.1
East Cleveland	7.4	22.3	9.0	12.5	14.1	12.2	9.2	7.8	5.5	55.7	33 096	27 217	-17.8	-3.5
Elyria	7.9	18.7	8.9	14.8	15.5	12.9	8.4	6.6	6.4	52.0	56 746	55 953	-1.4	0.3
Euclid	6.3	16.0	6.8	14.5	16.2	12.7	8.3	8.3	10.8	54.3	54 875	52 717	-3.9	-2.8
Fairborn	6.0	15.1	18.4	15.3	13.9	11.7	8.0	6.9	4.7	51.4	31 300	32 052	2.4	1.3
Fairfield	6.3	18.0	9.5	15.9	16.4	14.6	8.6	6.1	4.6	51.3	39 709	42 097	6.0	1.1
Findlay	7.0	16.8	11.9	14.1	14.6	12.8	8.6	6.7	7.4	52.3	35 703	38 967	9.1	2.1
Gahanna	6.8	22.1	6.5	12.0	19.7	16.1	8.2	4.9	3.8	51.5	23 898	32 636	36.6	1.8
Garfield Heights	6.3	17.7	7.3	13.5	15.8	12.7	8.0	8.3	10.3	53.3	31 739	30 734	-3.2	-2.8
Grove City	7.7	20.5	7.4	14.4	17.2	13.5	8.2	6.3	4.8	51.4	19 661	27 075	37.7	7.7
Hamilton	7.5	18.3	9.8	14.6	15.3	12.5	7.7	7.5	6.8	51.9	61 438	60 690	-1.2	0.1
Huber Heights	7.3	20.1	8.6	15.1	16.0	14.3	9.3	6.0	3.3	51.3	38 696	38 212	-1.3	0.1
Kent	5.0	11.4	40.0	13.0	10.0	8.8	4.2	3.7	3.9	54.2	28 835	27 906	-3.2	0.6
Kettering	5.8	16.7	7.5	14.2	15.2	13.1	9.2	9.3	9.0	52.5	60 569	57 502	-5.1	-1.8
Lakewood	5.9	15.1	9.5	20.7	16.5	13.0	7.0	5.7	6.5	51.9	59 718	56 646	-5.1	-4.0
Lancaster	7.7	16.9	9.3	14.7	14.3	12.2	9.0	8.0	8.0	52.7	34 507	35 335	2.4	1.6
Lima	8.1	19.0	11.5	14.1	14.6	11.8	7.6	6.6	6.7	49.8	45 553	40 081	-12.0	1.2
Lorain	8.0	20.4	9.0	13.5	14.7	12.5	8.0	7.2	6.7	52.6	71 245	68 652	-3.6	-1.0
Mansfield	7.2	16.7	9.3	14.8	14.9	12.9	8.7	7.7	7.7	50.4	50 627	49 346	-2.5	2.7
Maple Heights	6.3	19.4	6.7	13.5	17.4	12.6	7.5	7.9	8.6	53.3	27 089	26 156	-3.4	-2.5
Marion	7.0	18.2	9.3	15.1	15.7	13.2	8.2	6.9	6.4	49.4	34 075	35 318	3.6	5.6
Massillon	6.6	18.7	7.9	13.1	15.0	13.1	9.4	8.2	7.9	51.9	30 969	31 325	1.1	0.7
Medina	9.2	20.7	7.2	16.1	17.7	12.6	6.3	4.7	5.6	52.1	19 231	25 139	30.7	5.4
Mentor	6.0	19.9	6.5	11.1	17.8	16.5	9.9	6.6	5.6	51.5	47 491	50 278	5.9	-0.5
Middletown	7.2	17.8	9.3	14.0	15.3	13.0	8.6	7.8	7.1	52.2	46 758	51 605	12.1	0.7
Newark	7.5	17.8	9.4	13.8	15.3	12.7	8.4	7.2	7.7	52.7	44 396	46 279	4.2	0.7
North Olmsted	5.5	18.2	7.3	11.5	16.1	15.6	10.9	8.2	6.8	51.7	34 204	34 113	-0.3	-1.9
North Royalton	5.4	18.9	7.7	12.2	18.5	16.7	8.7	6.4	5.6	51.2	23 197	28 648	23.5	3.3
Parma	5.8	16.5	7.0	13.8	15.9	12.6	8.9	9.0	10.6	52.3	87 876	85 655	-2.5	-2.1
Reynoldsburg	7.1	19.5	8.0	14.8	17.1	14.9	8.5	6.0	4.2	52.4	25 748	32 069	24.5	2.5
Sandusky	7.2	18.6	9.2	13.1	15.4	12.9	8.4	7.5	7.6	52.8	29 764	27 844	-6.5	-2.9
Shaker Heights	6.2	20.0	5.3	11.7	15.7	15.7	9.8	7.9	7.7	54.5	30 955	29 405	-5.0	-3.2
Springfield	7.5	18.0	11.5	13.5	13.5	12.5	8.2	7.1	8.1	52.8	70 487	65 358	-7.3	-1.3
Stow	6.6	19.4	7.4	13.5	17.7	15.3	8.2	6.1	5.9	51.6	27 998	32 139	14.8	6.7
Strongsville	6.2	20.0	6.2	10.5	18.0	17.3	10.3	6.4	4.9	51.2	35 308	43 858	24.2	1.6
Toledo	7.3	18.9	11.0	15.2	14.6	12.2	7.6	6.6	6.5	52.1	332 943	313 619	-5.8	-1.5
Trotwood city	6.2	20.1	7.5	11.8	14.8	14.0	9.8	7.7	8.2	54.4	8 816	27 420	211.0	-1.3
Upper Arlington	5.5	19.4	4.4	9.6	15.5	16.9	10.2	9.0	9.6	52.8	34 128	33 686	-1.3	-3.8
Warren	7.9	18.4	8.6	13.3	13.9	12.2	8.9	8.3	8.5	53.5	50 793	46 832	-7.8	-0.5
Westerville	6.1	20.8	9.1	10.1	17.0	17.8	8.8	5.4	5.0	52.6	30 269	35 318	16.7	-1.1
Westlake	5.1	17.7	5.6	11.1	15.7	16.7	9.9	7.6	10.7	52.8	27 018	31 719	17.4	1.0
Youngstown	7.1	18.7	10.1	12.5	13.9	12.4	8.0	8.6	8.8	52.1	95 732	82 026	-14.3	-3.4
Zanesville	8.1	18.6	9.5	14.0	13.7	12.1	8.4	7.4	8.1	54.0	26 778	25 586	-4.5	-1.2
OKLAHOMA	6.8	19.0	10.3	13.1	15.2	13.1	9.2	7.0	6.2	50.9	3 145 576	3 450 654	9.7	1.8
Bartlesville	6.2	18.8	8.1	10.8	13.9	13.9	9.8	9.1	9.4	52.6	34 256	34 748	1.4	-0.1
Broken Arrow	8.0	22.9	7.7	14.1	18.2	14.6	7.0	4.3	3.2	51.2	58 082	74 859	29.0	11.7
Edmond	7.0	20.5	11.3	12.8	16.8	14.8	8.0	4.7	4.1	51.6	52 310	68 315	30.6	4.9
Enid	6.9	17.8	9.6	12.6	15.0	12.6	8.9	7.9	8.5	51.8	45 309	47 045	3.8	-1.3
Lawton	8.4	19.5	15.3	16.6	14.8	9.9	6.4	5.2	4.1	47.9	80 561	92 757	15.1	-1.1
Midwest City	7.3	19.1	10.7	13.8	14.9	12.9	7.9	7.1	6.1	52.2	52 267	54 088	3.5	1.1
Moore	7.7	21.8	9.3	15.5	17.0	13.1	8.4	4.6	2.6	51.6	40 318	41 138	2.0	9.4
Muskogee	7.5	18.2	9.7	12.1	13.7	12.7	8.7	7.9	9.5	53.0	37 708	38 310	1.6	0.8
Norman	5.9	15.3	21.4	15.0	14.1	12.3	7.0	4.8	4.2	49.8	80 071	95 694	19.5	3.7
Oklahoma City	7.3	18.2	10.7	15.1	15.7	13.2	8.3	6.1	5.4	51.1	444 724	506 132	13.8	3.4
Ponca City	7.2	19.1	8.5	11.2	14.4	13.4	8.7	8.4	9.2	52.4	26 359	25 919	-1.7	-1.2
Shawnee	7.4	16.9	15.2	12.5	13.0	11.3	8.3	7.5	7.8	51.9	26 017	28 692	10.3	2.6
Stillwater	4.7	10.5	38.2	14.4	10.0	8.2	5.3	3.7	4.9	49.3	36 676	39 065	6.5	5.8
Tulsa	7.2	17.6	10.9	14.9	15.0	13.3	8.2	6.6	6.2	51.7	367 302	393 049	7.0	-1.3
OREGON	6.5	18.2	9.6	13.8	15.4	14.8	8.9	6.4	6.4	50.4	2 842 337	3 421 399	20.4	4.0
Albany	7.6	18.8	9.6	14.5	14.9	13.7	8.2	5.6	7.1	51.4	33 523	40 852	21.9	5.5
Beaverton	7.2	17.7	10.6	18.4	16.7	13.6	6.8	4.0	5.0	50.6	53 307	76 129	42.8	5.8
Bend	6.9	17.6	10.2	15.5	15.6	14.3	7.5	6.0	6.4	50.7	23 740	52 029	119.2	14.9
Corvallis	4.9	12.8	28.4	14.8	12.1	11.3	5.5	4.4	5.6	50.2	44 757	49 322	10.2	1.6
Eugene	5.3	15.0	17.3	14.9	13.5	14.6	7.2	5.3	6.8	51.0	112 733	137 893	22.3	3.1
Gresham	8.0	19.6	11.1	14.7	15.6	13.7	7.5	4.7	5.1	50.6	68 285	90 205	32.2	6.2
Hillsboro	9.3	19.0	11.4	21.2	15.8	11.3	5.7	3.1	3.1	48.6	37 598	70 186	86.7	10.7
Keizer	8.1	19.7	8.2	15.0	15.1	13.5	8.4	6.0	6.2	51.5	21 884	32 203	47.2	6.1

Items 12—25

Table D. Cities — **Group Quarters, Crime, and Education**

City	Households, 2000 Number (26)	Percent change, 1990-2000 (27)	Persons per household (28)	Percent Female family householder[1] (29)	Percent One-person (30)	Persons in group quarters, 2000 Total (31)	Institutional Total (32)	Persons in nursing homes (33)	Non-institutional (34)	Serious crimes Total Number (35)	Rate[3] (36)	Rate Violent (37)	Rate Property (38)	School enrollment[4] Public (39)	School enrollment[4] Private (40)	Attainment High school graduate or less (41)	Bachelor's degree or more (42)
OHIO—Cont'd																	
Delaware	9 520	33.4	2.45	11.1	26.9	1 924	360	351	1 564	1 052	4 143	343	3 800	4 807	2 354	45.9	26.8
Dublin	11 209	103.0	2.80	5.0	18.5	50	50	50	0	760	2 407	60	2 346	7 839	2 168	13.7	64.7
East Cleveland	11 210	-16.1	2.39	30.3	38.0	449	339	290	110	100	365	351	15	7 255	862	64.1	8.5
Elyria	22 409	4.6	2.46	15.1	28.5	934	864	407	70	NA	NA	NA	NA	11 308	2 307	56.0	13.1
Euclid	24 353	-2.2	2.14	15.2	39.7	626	507	445	119	2 178	4 107	281	3 826	9 317	3 292	51.0	19.6
Fairborn	13 615	7.4	2.28	12.4	31.0	1 031	87	87	944	1 672	5 185	270	4 916	9 091	969	47.8	21.8
Fairfield	16 960	10.9	2.44	9.7	26.6	654	411	411	243	1 931	4 560	390	4 170	8 391	2 061	42.1	27.3
Findlay	15 905	12.7	2.36	9.9	30.2	1 505	636	559	869	NA	NA	NA	NA	7 518	2 897	49.3	24.3
Gahanna	11 990	26.8	2.70	9.2	20.9	221	211	208	10	1 040	3 168	110	3 058	7 250	2 231	30.7	40.4
Garfield Heights	12 452	-0.2	2.43	15.3	30.0	421	268	245	153	480	1 552	188	1 365	5 658	1 699	61.9	12.0
Grove City	10 265	39.1	2.61	10.3	22.4	281	180	180	101	851	3 124	147	2 978	5 874	1 514	49.1	22.0
Hamilton	24 188	0.8	2.45	15.3	29.3	1 340	1 014	459	326	5 513	9 030	932	8 098	11 745	2 262	65.6	12.2
Huber Heights	14 392	6.5	2.64	12.0	20.5	199	91	91	108	1 889	4 914	208	4 706	8 540	1 812	44.7	18.9
Kent	9 772	10.9	2.27	13.3	32.4	5 725	92	91	5 633	1 000	3 562	289	3 274	13 999	630	36.9	37.0
Kettering	25 657	-1.7	2.22	9.5	33.4	435	341	341	94	2 164	3 741	157	3 584	11 035	3 225	35.8	31.0
Lakewood	26 693	-1.1	2.09	9.7	43.6	772	411	406	361	1 376	2 415	142	2 272	10 237	2 918	36.3	35.9
Lancaster	14 852	6.2	2.35	12.9	30.3	450	415	317	35	1 335	3 756	236	3 519	6 684	1 163	60.5	13.3
Lima	15 410	-5.5	2.42	19.7	32.1	2 741	2 177	327	564	3 286	8 150	1 114	7 036	9 207	1 384	65.7	9.5
Lorain	26 434	0.9	2.57	19.2	27.4	723	529	499	194	2 901	4 200	392	3 808	15 673	2 831	63.7	9.9
Mansfield	20 182	0.1	2.28	15.2	34.8	3 346	2 871	339	475	4 006	8 070	351	7 719	9 645	1 508	62.2	13.4
Maple Heights	10 489	-0.6	2.47	17.0	29.9	224	189	189	35	50	190	4	186	5 646	1 502	58.1	12.9
Marion	13 551	2.8	2.44	14.1	29.3	2 204	2 112	201	92	1 911	5 379	208	5 170	7 628	796	68.8	8.8
Massillon	12 677	4.7	2.40	13.8	29.6	853	697	284	156	NA	NA	NA	NA	6 214	1 198	64.5	12.4
Medina	9 467	33.3	2.60	10.6	25.1	521	494	266	27	NA	NA	NA	NA	5 765	1 135	39.9	32.5
Mentor	18 797	12.4	2.65	8.9	20.5	476	324	320	152	1 578	3 120	89	3 031	10 890	2 457	40.8	27.4
Middletown	21 469	16.9	2.38	14.6	29.6	578	488	426	90	3 753	7 229	324	6 906	10 049	1 531	61.3	13.1
Newark	19 312	8.5	2.35	13.4	31.5	926	808	611	118	2 609	5 604	215	5 389	9 202	1 694	59.8	14.7
North Olmsted	13 517	6.8	2.50	8.6	26.5	316	272	272	44	71	207	32	175	6 379	2 139	40.9	27.1
North Royalton	11 250	28.3	2.51	7.4	26.7	363	236	236	127	30	104	35	69	5 599	2 161	42.6	29.4
Parma	35 126	1.3	2.40	10.2	29.2	1 224	1 145	979	79	1 512	1 755	107	1 648	14 481	5 175	53.7	17.8
Reynoldsburg	12 849	28.7	2.49	12.3	25.8	103	91	86	12	1 216	3 769	158	3 611	6 860	1 742	42.0	27.1
Sandusky	11 851	-1.7	2.31	16.4	34.9	473	322	322	151	2 081	7 429	436	6 994	5 590	1 067	63.9	11.2
Shaker Heights	12 220	-3.4	2.39	12.9	30.2	198	133	93	65	790	2 671	162	2 508	6 014	2 403	16.4	61.7
Springfield	26 254	-3.6	2.38	16.6	32.2	2 820	1 304	996	1 516	7 226	10 990	893	10 097	13 031	3 697	61.6	12.7
Stow	12 317	22.1	2.57	8.4	23.7	540	463	463	77	773	2 391	87	2 304	7 260	1 740	35.7	36.2
Strongsville	16 209	32.0	2.69	6.4	19.9	329	258	258	71	282	639	41	598	8 880	3 092	33.3	37.0
Toledo	128 925	-1.5	2.38	17.2	32.8	6 895	2 636	2 031	4 259	26 717	8 468	1 009	7 459	71 886	17 683	54.0	16.8
Trotwood city	11 110	208.3	2.40	21.5	29.8	724	619	582	105	NA	NA	NA	NA	6 495	991	54.6	15.0
Upper Arlington	13 985	0.2	2.39	6.9	28.2	314	314	227	0	NA	NA	NA	NA	7 432	1 794	12.5	67.5
Warren	19 288	-5.1	2.37	19.4	32.9	1 161	1 039	702	122	NA	NA	NA	NA	9 866	1 429	66.4	10.9
Westerville	12 663	24.4	2.67	8.3	20.9	1 558	575	575	983	1 153	3 245	99	3 147	7 992	3 272	26.9	44.6
Westlake	12 826	25.0	2.37	5.8	32.0	1 266	1 091	960	175	169	530	22	508	5 142	2 755	29.6	45.3
Youngstown	32 177	-13.1	2.39	22.9	30.4	4 994	3 498	723	1 496	5 915	7 168	1 162	6 006	18 540	3 808	68.4	9.7
Zanesville	10 572	-2.3	2.36	18.0	33.4	663	519	342	144	2 358	9 161	571	8 590	5 607	551	66.4	11.4
OKLAHOMA	1 342 293	11.3	2.49	11.4	26.7	112 375	66 746	28 021	45 629	165 715	4 743	503	4 240	832 166	98 699	50.9	20.3
Bartlesville	14 565	3.9	2.35	9.7	29.5	552	285	234	267	1 592	4 525	364	4 161	7 562	1 112	41.3	30.7
Broken Arrow	26 159	35.8	2.84	9.7	15.7	517	476	430	41	2 281	3 009	219	2 790	19 348	4 336	32.5	30.9
Edmond	25 256	34.7	2.63	9.1	20.6	1 869	460	386	1 409	1 761	2 546	106	2 440	19 484	3 259	22.6	47.8
Enid	18 955	4.1	2.39	11.2	29.1	1 725	1 221	937	504	2 985	6 267	527	5 740	10 067	1 275	52.9	20.0
Lawton	31 778	7.5	2.61	15.3	24.6	9 784	3 082	788	6 702	5 515	5 872	709	5 163	24 637	1 855	45.1	19.3
Midwest City	22 161	8.7	2.42	16.5	28.6	478	436	407	42	2 318	4 233	318	3 915	13 304	1 644	45.7	17.0
Moore	14 848	9.4	2.75	13.3	18.2	263	190	190	73	1 729	4 151	324	3 827	10 824	1 403	45.0	16.8
Muskogee	15 523	2.9	2.39	15.4	31.8	1 274	922	615	352	2 318	5 976	732	5 244	8 734	465	54.6	17.5
Norman	38 834	21.7	2.31	9.5	30.3	6 071	1 123	786	4 948	3 769	3 890	231	3 659	33 934	2 590	29.7	39.8
Oklahoma City	204 434	14.4	2.41	13.2	30.7	13 133	8 455	2 790	4 678	49 929	9 743	822	8 921	112 632	20 469	44.9	24.0
Ponca City	10 636	-0.9	2.38	11.1	30.0	587	392	320	195	1 542	5 876	774	5 103	5 565	665	49.0	21.5
Shawnee	11 311	9.4	2.38	14.4	30.4	1 753	379	307	1 374	1 724	5 935	685	5 250	6 508	1 887	54.2	18.5
Stillwater	15 604	10.1	2.13	7.7	34.6	5 902	288	200	5 614	1 432	3 621	245	3 375	20 143	530	25.0	48.0
Tulsa	165 743	6.6	2.31	12.9	33.9	10 433	4 722	2 476	5 711	30 119	7 568	1 086	6 482	78 865	23 937	40.9	28.3
OREGON	1 333 723	20.9	2.51	9.8	26.1	77 491	37 901	14 677	39 590	171 443	4 868	292	4 576	753 762	122 730	41.1	25.1
Albany	16 108	36.7	2.49	11.7	26.1	687	492	155	195	2 783	6 619	174	6 445	9 332	1 270	43.5	18.4
Beaverton	30 821	39.5	2.44	9.7	29.7	917	287	233	630	3 350	4 275	237	4 038	16 195	3 073	27.9	39.1
Bend	21 062	147.0	2.42	9.7	26.1	1 011	497	238	514	3 344	6 245	271	5 974	11 198	1 728	33.7	29.4
Corvallis	19 630	17.2	2.26	7.2	31.5	4 887	322	253	4 565	1 972	3 885	144	3 741	21 083	1 071	19.1	53.1
Eugene	58 110	25.6	2.27	9.1	31.7	6 086	1 672	726	4 414	9 308	6 558	330	6 228	41 194	4 193	27.8	37.3
Gresham	33 327	29.7	2.67	12.0	24.3	1 128	714	605	414	6 154	6 628	519	6 109	19 801	3 177	45.2	18.4
Hillsboro	25 079	95.2	2.76	9.0	23.4	950	796	192	154	3 759	5 203	253	4 950	15 501	2 712	37.5	29.5
Keizer	12 110	45.3	2.64	11.2	22.4	280	233	233	47	1 426	4 302	151	4 151	7 613	783	42.3	20.4

1. No spouse present.   2. Data for serious crimes have not been adjusted for underreporting. This may affect comparability between geographic areas and over time.   3. Per 100,000 population estimated by the FBI.   4. All persons 3 years old and over enrolled in nursery school through college.   5. Persons 25 years old and over.

Table D. Cities — Income, Poverty, and Housing

City	Money income, 1999							Housing units, 2000					
	Households				Percent below poverty					Vacant units			
	Median income				Persons		Families						
	Per capita income[1] (dollars)	Dollars	Percent change, 1989–1999 (constant 1999 dollars)	Percent with income of $100,000 or more	Total	Percent change in rate, 1989–1999	Total	Total	Percent change, 1990–2000	Vacant units for sale or rent[2]	For seasonal use (percent)	Home owner vacancy rate	Renter vacancy rate
	43	44	45	46	47	48	49	50	51	52	53	54	55
OHIO—Cont'd													
Delaware	20 633	46 030	18.2	8.9	7.3	-25.5	4.8	10 208	33.3	688	0.3	1.7	9.2
Dublin	41 122	91 162	-5.8	45.1	2.7	170.0	2.1	12 038	103.4	829	1.7	1.3	12.8
East Cleveland	12 602	20 542	-6.6	2.6	32.0	15.1	28.0	13 491	-11.1	2 281	0.1	3.6	15.4
Elyria	19 344	38 156	5.5	6.7	11.7	-14.6	9.5	23 841	5.8	1 432	0.3	1.5	8.8
Euclid	19 664	35 151	-2.8	4.5	9.7	24.4	7.1	26 123	-1.7	1 770	0.1	1.4	9.8
Fairborn	18 662	36 889	-0.4	5.6	14.1	-8.4	8.9	14 419	8.5	804	0.4	1.7	6.6
Fairfield	24 556	50 316	-2.8	12.0	4.2	10.5	2.5	17 789	9.3	829	0.4	0.9	7.6
Findlay	21 328	40 883	-0.1	9.4	9.1	7.1	5.9	17 152	14.3	1 247	0.5	2.0	8.5
Gahanna	29 040	66 031	17.0	25.1	3.7	-26.0	2.2	12 390	24.9	400	0.5	0.6	5.9
Garfield Heights	18 988	39 278	1.9	4.4	8.5	44.1	6.0	12 998	0.0	546	0.1	1.3	7.6
Grove City	22 305	52 064	12.8	13.0	4.6	-20.7	3.3	10 712	39.6	447	0.3	1.9	5.5
Hamilton	17 493	35 365	15.0	4.8	13.4	-20.2	10.6	25 913	2.2	1 725	0.3	1.5	7.1
Huber Heights	20 951	49 073	-3.7	9.0	5.9	37.2	4.2	14 938	4.4	546	0.2	1.3	5.8
Kent	15 015	29 582	2.6	7.0	25.2	-8.4	15.4	10 435	12.5	663	0.2	1.8	6.4
Kettering	27 009	45 051	-2.8	11.1	4.6	9.5	3.2	26 936	-0.6	1 279	0.5	1.3	6.9
Lakewood	23 945	40 527	4.8	9.2	8.9	4.7	6.1	28 416	-0.4	1 723	0.5	0.9	6.4
Lancaster	17 648	33 321	10.6	4.6	10.6	-24.8	8.7	15 891	7.7	1 039	0.8	1.6	7.1
Lima	13 882	27 067	-4.3	3.1	22.7	5.1	19.2	17 631	-5.5	2 221	0.4	2.5	12.9
Lorain	16 340	33 917	4.6	5.5	17.1	-13.6	14.2	28 231	2.5	1 797	0.2	1.6	7.2
Mansfield	17 726	30 176	-0.6	5.2	16.3	-8.4	13.2	22 267	1.6	2 085	0.4	2.1	10.6
Maple Heights	18 676	40 414	1.7	4.5	5.9	47.5	4.7	10 935	1.3	446	0.1	1.8	5.7
Marion	16 247	33 124	9.9	3.9	13.8	-17.9	10.9	14 713	3.3	1 162	0.2	2.3	8.0
Massillon	17 633	32 734	2.3	5.1	10.7	-25.7	8.3	13 567	5.9	890	0.2	1.8	7.2
Medina	21 709	50 226	13.4	12.5	5.7	-32.1	5.1	9 924	34.9	457	0.2	1.4	6.4
Mentor	24 592	57 230	1.2	16.0	2.7	-6.9	1.8	19 301	12.4	504	0.4	0.9	5.6
Middletown	19 773	36 215	4.8	6.5	12.6	-18.2	9.2	23 144	19.4	1 675	0.2	2.2	8.5
Newark	17 819	34 791	12.3	5.5	13.0	-16.7	10.1	20 625	8.7	1 313	0.3	2.1	6.8
North Olmsted	24 329	52 542	-1.4	13.7	4.1	32.3	2.8	14 059	7.5	542	0.4	1.1	7.9
North Royalton	26 610	57 398	4.3	18.1	2.3	-8.0	1.2	11 754	29.0	504	0.4	1.5	7.0
Parma	21 293	43 920	-1.8	7.3	4.9	19.5	3.3	36 414	2.3	1 288	0.2	0.8	7.2
Reynoldsburg	23 388	51 108	2.3	11.2	5.5	25.0	4.4	13 434	26.9	585	0.3	1.2	7.1
Sandusky	18 111	31 133	2.8	4.0	15.3	-0.6	12.2	13 323	-0.7	1 472	3.5	2.0	9.6
Shaker Heights	41 354	63 983	-6.9	30.3	6.9	97.1	5.3	12 982	-2.9	762	0.4	1.1	8.2
Springfield	16 660	32 193	11.9	5.4	16.9	-19.1	13.5	29 309	-0.9	3 055	0.4	2.6	10.7
Stow	25 509	57 525	8.0	16.2	4.0	29.0	2.9	12 852	22.8	535	0.4	1.4	6.4
Strongsville	29 722	68 660	0.4	26.0	2.2	-4.3	1.3	16 863	28.7	654	0.5	0.9	10.1
Toledo	17 388	32 546	-2.4	5.2	17.9	-6.3	14.2	139 871	-1.6	10 946	0.3	1.5	8.8
Trotwood city	18 329	34 931	NA	6.6	15.3	NA	13.6	12 020	220.6	910	0.2	2.1	9.6
Upper Arlington	42 025	72 116	1.0	32.8	2.4	71.4	1.7	14 432	0.4	447	0.7	0.9	4.1
Warren	16 808	30 147	-0.9	4.3	19.4	-3.0	16.2	21 279	-2.3	1 991	0.2	2.5	11.5
Westerville	29 401	69 135	6.7	29.6	3.5	25.0	2.5	13 143	24.9	480	0.3	1.0	8.4
Westlake	37 142	64 963	1.5	26.6	2.5	19.0	1.3	13 648	23.9	822	0.7	1.9	8.9
Youngstown	13 293	24 201	5.6	2.7	24.8	-14.5	20.4	37 159	-8.9	4 982	0.2	2.3	11.5
Zanesville	15 192	26 642	12.3	3.0	22.4	-13.5	19.3	11 662	-0.9	1 090	0.2	3.4	7.6
OKLAHOMA	17 646	33 400	5.4	6.6	14.7	-12.0	11.2	1 514 400	7.7	172 107	2.1	2.5	10.6
Bartlesville	21 195	35 827	-12.2	10.9	12.7	14.4	9.4	16 091	1.2	1 526	0.6	1.9	7.9
Broken Arrow	21 555	53 507	5.9	13.0	4.5	-30.8	3.4	27 085	32.6	926	0.1	1.3	6.9
Edmond	26 517	54 556	7.9	19.0	7.2	-1.4	4.4	26 380	28.1	1 124	0.2	1.4	6.3
Enid	17 471	32 227	5.5	5.3	14.8	3.5	11.1	21 255	-2.0	2 300	0.4	2.9	11.2
Lawton	15 397	32 521	0.0	4.7	16.3	2.5	14.2	36 433	5.2	4 655	0.2	4.9	13.5
Midwest City	17 220	35 027	-3.6	4.2	13.9	24.1	11.2	23 853	4.4	1 692	0.3	2.1	9.1
Moore	17 689	43 409	-2.0	5.5	7.6	-5.0	6.3	15 801	6.6	953	0.8	1.7	9.3
Muskogee	15 351	26 418	0.8	4.6	19.2	-14.7	14.6	17 517	-0.9	1 994	0.4	2.6	10.2
Norman	20 630	36 713	8.6	9.9	15.0	0.0	7.8	41 547	16.5	2 713	0.4	1.7	8.0
Oklahoma City	19 098	34 947	1.0	7.8	16.0	0.6	12.4	228 149	7.4	23 715	0.5	2.2	12.3
Ponca City	17 732	31 406	-11.5	6.6	16.0	49.5	12.7	11 871	-3.4	1 235	0.8	2.3	11.0
Shawnee	15 676	27 659	8.3	5.1	17.8	-16.0	13.8	12 651	7.4	1 340	1.1	2.4	9.1
Stillwater	15 789	25 432	2.3	6.6	27.3	3.4	12.6	16 827	6.7	1 223	0.4	2.2	5.8
Tulsa	21 534	35 316	2.2	9.7	14.1	-6.0	10.9	179 405	1.8	13 662	0.5	1.6	8.7
OREGON	20 940	40 916	11.8	10.0	11.6	-6.5	7.9	1 452 709	21.7	118 986	2.5	2.3	7.3
Albany	18 570	39 409	19.8	6.6	11.6	-21.1	9.3	17 374	41.0	1 266	0.3	2.6	9.8
Beaverton	25 419	47 863	4.9	15.2	7.8	21.9	5.0	32 500	34.9	1 679	0.3	2.0	6.0
Bend	21 624	40 857	17.9	9.5	10.5	-20.5	6.9	22 507	150.0	1 445	1.5	2.6	5.5
Corvallis	19 317	35 236	13.0	9.8	20.6	-1.9	9.7	20 909	20.8	1 279	0.3	2.2	7.1
Eugene	21 315	35 850	5.2	9.6	17.1	0.6	8.7	61 444	28.0	3 334	0.4	1.7	6.6
Gresham	19 588	43 442	1.6	8.8	12.5	50.6	8.4	35 309	30.9	1 982	0.3	2.4	6.9
Hillsboro	21 680	51 737	16.2	12.9	9.2	10.8	6.0	27 211	103.9	2 132	0.6	4.0	8.2
Keizer	20 119	45 052	7.9	9.1	9.3	31.0	6.2	12 774	49.0	664	0.2	2.8	6.7

1. Based on population enumerated as of April 1, 2000.   2. Includes units rented or sold but not occupied.

Table D. Cities — Housing, Labor Force, Employment, and Disability

	Housing units, 2000 (cont'd) — Occupied units					Civilian labor force, 2003		Unemployment		Civilian employment,[2] 2000	Percent		Disability, 2000
City	Total	Percent owner occupied	Percent renter occupied	Average size owner occupied	Average size renter occupied	Total	Percent change, 2002–2003	Total	Rate[1]	Total	Management, professional, and related occupations	Production, transportation, and material moving occupations	Employment disabled persons[3] (percent)
	56	57	58	59	60	61	62	63	64	65	66	67	68
OHIO—Cont'd													
Delaware	9 520	60.3	39.7	2.63	2.17	20 688	0.8	933	4.5	12 737	37.3	14.7	7.6
Dublin	11 209	76.8	23.2	3.04	1.99	19 584	0.4	254	1.3	15 956	59.8	3.3	4.3
East Cleveland	11 210	35.5	64.5	2.75	2.19	14 627	1.2	2 139	14.6	9 384	20.4	19.0	16.1
Elyria	22 409	64.6	35.4	2.57	2.25	31 038	1.3	2 437	7.9	27 001	24.0	24.3	12.9
Euclid	24 353	59.5	40.5	2.34	1.84	27 157	1.1	1 439	5.3	24 961	30.6	16.5	12.8
Fairborn	13 615	51.7	48.3	2.39	2.15	16 626	0.5	1 105	6.6	15 502	30.8	13.8	9.7
Fairfield	16 960	65.4	34.6	2.63	2.09	32 174	2.7	988	3.1	23 011	39.4	12.4	9.2
Findlay	15 905	64.8	35.2	2.47	2.14	24 045	-0.5	1 195	5.0	20 167	30.1	24.0	7.9
Gahanna	11 990	77.7	22.3	2.86	2.16	17 791	0.6	643	3.6	17 420	46.5	8.1	7.0
Garfield Heights	12 452	79.9	20.1	2.51	2.15	15 275	1.1	809	5.3	14 336	23.9	18.3	11.8
Grove City	10 265	72.5	27.5	2.73	2.29	13 099	0.6	407	3.1	14 068	34.0	11.6	8.2
Hamilton	24 188	60.7	39.3	2.52	2.35	38 420	2.7	2 577	6.7	27 031	22.6	21.8	12.6
Huber Heights	14 392	72.0	28.0	2.64	2.64	20 194	0.3	1 001	5.0	19 015	30.1	19.9	10.3
Kent	9 772	37.8	62.2	2.58	2.08	17 467	1.7	1 105	6.3	15 586	32.1	13.1	7.7
Kettering	25 657	66.6	33.4	2.39	1.90	31 660	0.1	1 012	3.2	29 337	39.5	13.0	8.4
Lakewood	26 693	45.2	54.8	2.53	1.74	33 149	1.1	1 449	4.4	32 020	41.0	10.4	7.7
Lancaster	14 852	59.4	40.6	2.41	2.26	22 015	0.9	1 482	6.7	16 783	23.8	18.5	12.2
Lima	15 410	56.8	43.2	2.44	2.40	19 651	2.2	2 178	11.1	15 893	18.4	29.9	15.4
Lorain	26 434	61.2	38.8	2.61	2.51	33 796	1.4	3 556	10.5	29 021	20.4	27.0	12.8
Mansfield	20 182	57.6	42.4	2.36	2.17	22 901	1.4	2 248	9.8	20 811	23.2	25.8	12.9
Maple Heights	10 489	83.8	16.2	2.55	2.09	13 481	1.1	635	4.7	12 304	25.2	21.9	10.0
Marion	13 551	63.5	36.5	2.52	2.32	16 758	-0.4	1 273	7.6	15 299	19.2	28.9	14.8
Massillon	12 677	69.0	31.0	2.50	2.20	14 867	0.1	1 243	8.4	14 614	22.2	27.1	12.3
Medina	9 467	66.3	33.7	2.86	2.09	12 994	1.5	819	6.3	12 480	36.2	14.3	9.5
Mentor	18 797	87.5	12.5	2.69	2.33	28 376	1.3	1 524	5.4	27 399	36.1	16.9	7.7
Middletown	21 469	60.1	39.9	2.47	2.24	30 226	2.7	1 998	6.6	23 710	24.3	24.2	13.6
Newark	19 312	58.2	41.8	2.47	2.18	25 864	2.1	2 048	7.9	21 636	23.7	20.9	12.0
North Olmsted	13 517	79.7	20.3	2.62	2.01	18 275	1.1	575	3.1	17 935	37.7	11.8	7.1
North Royalton	11 250	74.9	25.1	2.75	1.80	12 725	1.1	435	3.4	15 783	37.1	12.7	8.5
Parma	35 126	77.5	22.5	2.52	2.00	43 744	1.1	1 412	3.2	41 447	30.0	15.3	8.9
Reynoldsburg	12 849	65.1	34.9	2.63	2.23	18 413	0.6	548	3.0	17 319	36.0	11.8	7.7
Sandusky	11 851	56.5	43.5	2.42	2.17	16 842	1.7	1 442	8.6	13 001	19.0	27.1	12.4
Shaker Heights	12 220	64.9	35.1	2.66	1.89	16 384	1.1	578	3.5	14 813	63.3	5.5	10.9
Springfield	26 254	57.2	42.8	2.42	2.33	31 224	-0.2	2 865	9.2	27 890	24.4	24.1	14.1
Stow	12 317	72.1	27.9	2.79	1.99	17 254	1.2	475	2.8	16 928	42.3	12.5	7.6
Strongsville	16 209	82.7	17.3	2.85	1.92	19 434	1.1	625	3.2	23 309	42.2	10.4	6.3
Toledo	128 925	59.8	40.2	2.50	2.19	162 924	0.4	14 862	9.1	140 270	25.7	21.3	13.3
Trotwood city	11 110	62.6	37.4	2.46	2.30	14 338	0.6	1 075	7.5	11 530	24.6	25.1	16.3
Upper Arlington	13 985	81.3	18.7	2.51	1.85	20 944	0.5	375	1.8	16 723	64.1	2.9	4.4
Warren	19 288	58.4	41.6	2.39	2.33	22 333	2.0	2 570	11.5	18 198	21.1	28.1	14.0
Westerville	12 663	79.2	20.8	2.82	2.09	22 070	0.5	528	2.4	18 778	47.6	7.0	4.6
Westlake	12 826	74.8	25.2	2.61	1.67	14 030	1.1	380	2.7	15 727	52.9	5.8	5.8
Youngstown	32 177	64.0	36.0	2.40	2.38	34 686	1.7	4 685	13.5	28 659	18.7	24.2	14.7
Zanesville	10 572	54.6	45.4	2.42	2.28	13 154	0.9	1 425	10.8	10 542	22.8	25.7	14.1
OKLAHOMA	1 342 293	68.4	31.6	2.55	2.36	1 696 060	0.1	96 034	5.7	1 545 296	30.3	15.4	12.5
Bartlesville	14 565	70.4	29.6	2.39	2.24	14 296	5.5	863	6.0	14 889	37.6	12.8	14.0
Broken Arrow	26 159	78.7	21.3	2.90	2.62	35 526	-2.0	1 501	4.2	38 764	38.0	9.9	8.2
Edmond	25 256	72.8	27.2	2.78	2.23	32 553	-0.1	998	3.1	35 062	45.7	6.1	7.8
Enid	18 955	67.2	32.8	2.40	2.37	20 857	0.8	827	4.0	20 680	26.5	14.6	12.9
Lawton	31 778	54.7	45.3	2.58	2.65	33 283	1.4	1 228	3.7	30 818	28.6	13.6	10.8
Midwest City	22 161	61.2	38.8	2.43	2.40	29 092	0.4	1 611	5.5	24 015	28.0	14.2	13.1
Moore	14 848	75.8	24.2	2.75	2.76	27 203	-0.2	873	3.2	20 212	28.2	14.7	11.1
Muskogee	15 523	61.9	38.1	2.45	2.27	17 388	-3.1	1 142	6.6	14 826	27.0	18.3	15.0
Norman	38 834	55.2	44.8	2.53	2.04	54 577	0.0	2 318	4.2	49 568	41.4	7.6	7.3
Oklahoma City	204 434	59.4	40.6	2.51	2.27	263 618	0.4	14 840	5.6	235 565	31.3	13.6	13.6
Ponca City	10 636	68.1	31.9	2.41	2.33	12 198	-4.2	901	7.4	10 900	32.0	15.9	12.3
Shawnee	11 311	59.9	40.1	2.40	2.36	13 037	1.0	855	6.6	12 328	28.5	15.5	12.4
Stillwater	15 604	41.8	58.2	2.38	1.94	22 467	-0.1	597	2.7	20 967	41.3	9.5	5.4
Tulsa	165 743	55.6	44.4	2.41	2.18	223 113	-1.4	15 299	6.9	190 954	34.5	12.0	12.3
OREGON	1 333 723	64.3	35.7	2.59	2.36	1 858 879	1.0	152 151	8.2	1 627 769	33.1	14.7	10.6
Albany	16 108	59.5	40.5	2.57	2.38	20 113	0.9	1 772	8.8	19 312	28.5	18.7	9.9
Beaverton	30 821	47.7	52.3	2.67	2.23	49 521	0.0	3 338	6.7	40 922	43.3	10.3	8.4
Bend	21 062	62.9	37.1	2.48	2.32	20 201	4.1	1 354	6.7	26 565	33.9	11.4	8.4
Corvallis	19 630	44.9	55.1	2.50	2.07	25 722	1.2	1 138	4.4	23 841	48.5	8.3	7.7
Eugene	58 110	51.8	48.2	2.47	2.05	71 626	1.1	5 060	7.1	69 094	39.3	11.9	6.9
Gresham	33 327	54.9	45.1	2.78	2.54	43 920	-0.2	2 988	6.8	44 024	26.1	15.9	10.8
Hillsboro	25 079	52.3	47.7	2.92	2.58	30 702	0.0	2 231	7.3	36 427	37.6	13.9	9.9
Keizer	12 110	64.7	35.3	2.67	2.57	15 904	1.9	1 118	7.0	15 425	32.2	12.7	10.2

1. Percent of civilian labor force.   2. Persons 16 years old and over.   3. Persons 16 to 64 years old.

Table D. Cities — Construction, Wholesale Trade, and Retail Trade

City	Value of residential construction authorized by building permits, 2003			Wholesale trade, 1997				Retail trade,[1] 1997			
	New construction ($1,000)	Number of housing units	Percent single family	Number of establishments	Number of employees	Sales (mil dol)	Annual payroll (mil dol)	Number of establishments	Number of employees	Sales (mil dol)	Annual payroll (mil dol)
	69	70	71	72	73	74	75	76	77	78	79
OHIO—Cont'd											
Delaware	66 241	533	91.2	29	171	63.0	5.2	110	1 600	278.5	22.6
Dublin	123 497	493	95.1	123	1 514	1 568.1	72.0	150	2 181	611.5	48.7
East Cleveland	0	0	0.0	12	D	D	D	69	515	54.3	6.7
Elyria	21 781	224	100.0	65	647	183.1	19.0	272	4 415	705.6	66.1
Euclid	3 251	9	100.0	72	2 532	1 342.3	174.3	169	2 418	314.7	32.5
Fairborn	15 901	179	72.6	15	253	138.1	8.3	101	1 326	224.4	19.0
Fairfield	16 573	123	100.0	93	1 683	1 279.8	60.5	182	3 254	710.6	60.6
Findlay	24 353	142	84.5	61	607	336.0	17.8	259	3 665	569.3	52.3
Gahanna	13 270	85	100.0	49	421	278.9	19.3	89	1 296	189.2	17.6
Garfield Heights	1 668	14	100.0	51	1 487	810.2	71.4	78	1 287	179.9	18.6
Grove City	75 050	742	62.5	34	712	349.1	22.3	77	1 173	161.3	15.2
Hamilton	21 839	374	33.2	75	1 404	890.5	51.2	233	2 755	375.3	40.3
Huber Heights	NA	NA	NA	21	295	160.1	13.1	129	2 150	276.6	26.1
Kent	9 083	51	64.7	28	189	61.0	6.1	74	1 215	338.1	26.3
Kettering	4 936	30	100.0	73	924	595.4	43.1	228	4 821	756.0	71.2
Lakewood	0	0	0.0	62	617	255.7	22.8	155	1 767	300.6	30.9
Lancaster	23 549	156	100.0	40	364	97.7	12.2	270	3 868	540.0	57.9
Lima	1 918	32	31.3	89	1 197	436.2	32.8	188	2 143	361.9	33.5
Lorain	17 493	148	100.0	40	877	199.0	23.6	175	2 148	314.9	29.5
Mansfield	10 115	105	61.0	96	1 344	445.3	36.2	273	3 186	486.6	53.1
Maple Heights	1 518	14	100.0	27	709	250.5	20.3	135	1 750	197.9	23.0
Marion	2 183	42	57.1	32	287	84.7	8.8	156	1 750	197.9	37.4
Massillon	20 513	204	84.8	33	1 158	833.3	45.5	128	1 831	296.6	28.1
Medina	18 073	104	100.0	59	655	307.3	22.6	112	2 217	243.1	24.7
Mentor	21 195	104	80.8	138	1 828	477.5	56.8	401	7 492	1 316.3	120.6
Middletown	9 173	114	56.1	40	876	302.2	29.0	193	2 232	327.0	33.5
Newark	193 697	1 257	82.8	43	447	178.5	14.8	192	2 038	323.3	32.9
North Olmsted	6 785	69	42.0	57	D	D	D	324	5 444	935.6	76.9
North Royalton	31 842	227	83.3	70	459	220.9	17.0	74	754	137.7	12.2
Parma	4 969	37	100.0	73	981	290.8	34.1	366	5 440	794.1	80.8
Reynoldsburg	30 063	219	100.0	33	432	147.9	8.9	101	1 214	151.7	16.6
Sandusky	3 748	27	70.4	47	498	147.8	15.1	224	3 016	419.7	43.4
Shaker Heights	3 632	13	100.0	34	245	337.0	8.8	89	1 187	203.9	19.6
Springfield	4 609	49	51.0	69	1 126	657.6	30.5	328	4 983	724.2	70.6
Stow	34 319	223	98.2	46	727	451.2	23.7	99	1 971	266.4	29.2
Strongsville	28 409	160	100.0	85	1 516	632.2	62.8	226	4 434	511.3	57.4
Toledo	32 943	490	63.3	487	7 731	3 692.8	259.5	1 281	18 732	2 513.1	280.4
Trotwood city	3 158	32	100.0	NA	NA	NA	NA	NA	NA	NA	NA
Upper Arlington	4 987	9	100.0	48	366	242.9	12.3	124	1 511	156.7	21.3
Warren	763	9	55.6	62	728	265.2	19.2	281	4 639	761.2	82.1
Westerville	7 027	50	76.0	74	963	831.9	35.1	136	1 989	283.7	28.1
Westlake	30 932	87	97.7	174	2 482	2 050.2	123.6	148	2 532	401.0	41.4
Youngstown	3 572	42	95.2	153	2 251	702.1	69.5	347	3 442	487.4	56.3
Zanesville	1 607	10	100.0	41	813	337.3	22.0	266	3 226	506.9	46.6
OKLAHOMA	1 861 185	14 968	85.0	5 191	59 641	32 132.3	1 756.1	14 352	161 613	27 065.6	2 406.9
Bartlesville	15 899	90	100.0	28	112	24.1	2.4	183	2 431	409.8	36.6
Broken Arrow	86 813	672	99.7	113	1 218	420.4	42.5	217	2 956	616.0	48.5
Edmond	164 405	886	76.3	96	399	156.0	11.9	274	3 549	522.6	50.4
Enid	16 070	174	32.2	96	D	D	D	282	3 333	488.6	46.9
Lawton	15 579	129	96.1	80	751	173.1	15.9	392	5 005	664.4	65.5
Midwest City	41 881	481	38.0	28	D	D	D	220	4 401	742.7	60.8
Moore	82 039	744	100.0	40	350	93.5	6.7	114	1 592	237.5	22.3
Muskogee	13 306	117	75.2	65	830	231.7	21.2	281	3 221	505.6	48.0
Norman	99 324	854	72.5	79	987	397.6	27.0	399	5 268	968.0	82.5
Oklahoma City	461 469	3 733	91.1	1 307	19 128	14 323.2	572.8	2 145	28 167	5 337.0	490.8
Ponca City	5 863	30	100.0	32	226	145.7	6.3	158	1 963	280.5	27.0
Shawnee	8 309	73	100.0	25	D	D	D	221	2 535	358.3	33.9
Stillwater	27 814	188	86.2	30	399	135.1	8.8	193	2 639	370.6	34.2
Tulsa	79 429	581	79.3	1 237	16 094	8 372.1	577.7	1 905	28 474	5 100.5	484.1
OREGON	3 770 948	25 015	71.5	5 943	74 790	53 679.1	2 578.7	14 467	178 349	33 396.8	3 308.8
Albany	52 285	398	95.5	55	731	214.6	21.7	198	2 773	461.9	45.4
Beaverton	48 079	307	83.7	271	3 919	5 353.3	189.0	399	6 830	1 584.6	146.0
Bend	219 285	1 825	63.3	108	868	374.3	27.1	391	4 511	848.6	85.6
Corvallis	48 687	348	56.0	29	387	45.4	7.4	236	2 792	413.7	46.7
Eugene	118 224	611	91.5	356	3 977	1 687.8	125.2	826	11 203	2 036.4	209.4
Gresham	110 700	869	46.1	64	722	507.8	23.5	277	4 397	905.4	79.6
Hillsboro	203 126	1 578	46.0	83	1 007	325.5	41.7	225	3 704	884.3	78.6
Keizer	20 679	124	77.4	19	D	D	D	69	512	97.7	10.8

1. Establishments with payroll.

Table D. Cities — **Real Estate, Professional Services, and Manufacturing**

City	Real estate and rental and leasing, 1997				Professional, scientific, and technical services,[1] 1997				Manufacturing, 1997			
	Number of establishments	Number of employees	Receipts (mil dol)	Annual payroll (mil dol)	Number of establishments	Number of employees	Receipts (mil dol)	Annual payroll (mil dol)	Number of establishments	Number of employees	Receipts (mil dol)	Annual payroll (mil dol)
	80	81	82	83	84	85	86	87	88	89	90	91
OHIO—Cont'd												
Delaware	35	103	14.4	2.4	50	225	15.7	6.5	38	2 370	832.1	99.7
Dublin	72	514	84.2	20.4	185	2 204	422.6	115.7	24	1 142	157.6	36.8
East Cleveland	21	116	11.9	1.8	4	10	0.7	0.1	NA	NA	NA	NA
Elyria	46	233	26.7	3.7	97	506	43.8	18.5	132	7 704	1 610.8	260.2
Euclid	49	358	29.4	6.5	60	378	31.3	15.3	108	8 223	1 627.6	326.0
Fairborn	27	121	14.3	1.9	65	1 932	200.6	84.2	14	779	139.5	27.0
Fairfield	45	387	38.1	8.2	69	461	33.8	13.7	84	3 096	492.8	95.9
Findlay	55	D	D	D	91	445	31.8	12.7	66	7 559	1 397.3	271.5
Gahanna	22	81	14.0	1.6	70	568	53.0	23.9	28	517	74.4	16.1
Garfield Heights	13	46	6.5	0.6	42	435	42.6	19.4	48	1 502	189.3	48.1
Grove City	21	81	9.3	1.2	40	137	10.5	3.5	20	1 165	221.1	42.1
Hamilton	55	303	23.7	5.6	102	756	38.9	17.8	86	3 717	692.2	136.9
Huber Heights	24	212	27.0	6.4	26	246	14.7	7.0	34	D	D	D
Kent	28	154	14.8	1.9	41	145	8.8	2.6	72	2 412	343.0	70.2
Kettering	66	348	38.3	6.1	142	1 360	132.7	53.2	51	5 025	831.9	269.9
Lakewood	47	282	31.4	5.3	110	526	36.0	16.6	41	1 128	182.1	44.1
Lancaster	47	200	18.5	3.0	79	337	22.9	8.8	78	4 282	625.1	134.0
Lima	48	201	15.3	3.1	98	556	38.5	14.2	48	3 856	1 743.7	209.3
Lorain	55	212	16.2	3.3	66	782	39.2	20.8	64	7 745	6 669.5	340.4
Mansfield	53	214	25.8	3.7	111	673	42.7	17.4	126	7 844	1 256.5	265.4
Maple Heights	18	79	5.4	1.2	12	47	3.1	1.2	31	576	77.9	19.0
Marion	38	150	12.9	3.1	56	313	17.7	6.7	48	2 723	784.9	92.6
Massillon	14	54	4.1	0.8	42	253	15.0	6.6	64	4 737	975.6	144.7
Medina	27	105	13.4	1.7	90	380	29.0	11.3	87	3 813	759.5	123.9
Mentor	48	308	29.9	5.4	140	659	62.8	23.7	244	8 617	1 450.4	274.8
Middletown	59	245	27.5	4.4	73	557	92.8	20.6	71	7 187	3 662.9	353.0
Newark	45	199	16.9	3.5	88	821	40.5	16.6	49	4 017	770.2	133.4
North Olmsted	27	127	19.9	3.4	70	466	33.4	15.7	NA	NA	NA	NA
North Royalton	15	65	5.4	1.0	50	148	21.6	5.1	84	1 111	135.2	37.4
Parma	55	438	47.3	7.9	102	1 001	42.6	14.8	58	5 002	972.8	278.8
Reynoldsburg	48	221	26.6	3.6	80	497	42.9	21.3	15	591	213.0	16.0
Sandusky	37	165	13.7	2.7	62	336	26.9	13.6	66	5 206	799.0	223.4
Shaker Heights	29	162	19.0	2.7	97	489	56.5	18.8	NA	NA	NA	NA
Springfield	49	223	21.2	3.8	91	532	27.4	11.2	115	D	D	D
Stow	27	144	16.3	2.1	64	229	14.5	4.9	72	2 527	342.5	89.4
Strongsville	39	199	18.7	3.3	117	447	35.4	16.2	76	3 286	650.9	122.7
Toledo	255	1 729	192.4	37.6	584	5 500	569.5	183.3	462	25 446	9 282.3	1 101.0
Trotwood city	NA	NA	NA	NA	NA	NA	NA	NA	NA	NA	NA	NA
Upper Arlington	48	D	D	D	128	552	46.9	18.3	NA	NA	NA	NA
Warren	57	267	28.4	5.0	127	715	50.3	21.1	69	12 471	3 247.4	629.7
Westerville	44	293	29.7	5.3	148	864	68.2	30.3	37	1 206	191.5	49.8
Westlake	55	592	76.8	15.4	162	1 047	85.6	37.5	55	1 662	308.7	54.8
Youngstown	60	436	32.3	6.4	126	906	80.2	35.5	148	4 658	954.0	166.5
Zanesville	46	172	20.1	3.5	54	344	27.1	10.0	53	4 194	599.0	112.2
OKLAHOMA	3 344	15 354	1 576.0	284.5	7 009	40 633	3 543.0	1 323.7	4 087	164 060	37 453.2	4 963.2
Bartlesville	41	D	D	D	68	762	73.5	23.0	31	930	139.7	40.2
Broken Arrow	52	189	21.3	3.4	141	484	42.5	12.9	129	4 191	614.9	136.8
Edmond	91	789	106.8	12.4	219	687	68.6	19.9	39	929	91.0	23.2
Enid	65	277	23.8	4.6	89	D	D	D	54	D	D	D
Lawton	123	500	47.1	7.9	119	1 008	60.2	29.1	45	D	D	D
Midwest City	60	257	25.6	3.7	68	625	47.2	20.2	18	D	D	D
Moore	25	84	6.2	1.1	35	190	11.0	3.5	NA	NA	NA	NA
Muskogee	50	208	16.0	3.1	63	326	23.0	7.2	61	3 476	760.7	117.4
Norman	132	514	40.7	7.8	288	1 239	106.8	37.2	83	2 442	679.6	71.6
Oklahoma City	705	4 136	464.1	87.2	1 848	12 251	1 100.3	449.3	759	38 354	9 658.1	1 251.1
Ponca City	30	78	9.4	1.2	57	776	33.7	14.0	45	D	D	D
Shawnee	47	165	17.4	2.3	61	269	20.3	6.1	41	2 799	545.5	96.3
Stillwater	55	236	12.1	2.7	85	550	40.1	15.9	28	2 195	814.6	68.4
Tulsa	684	3 904	451.4	84.0	1 688	12 883	1 355.7	504.0	872	29 436	5 526.1	986.6
OREGON	4 556	23 058	2 704.0	470.9	8 117	52 514	4 734.6	1 925.0	5 768	213 111	47 666.0	7 095.3
Albany	47	218	21.4	3.4	82	431	30.1	13.6	68	3 538	630.7	124.2
Beaverton	169	1 115	124.7	16.4	280	1 804	195.5	75.6	135	9 717	2 310.1	383.4
Bend	105	457	49.8	8.2	192	846	72.9	25.1	119	3 422	496.3	87.4
Corvallis	87	322	33.1	4.4	149	1 051	80.9	39.8	51	6 510	895.8	420.5
Eugene	276	1 408	165.7	24.9	605	3 899	333.5	123.5	340	9 524	1 330.3	277.1
Gresham	102	461	53.3	8.1	106	262	19.1	6.6	82	5 338	795.6	183.2
Hillsboro	60	203	28.6	3.6	143	1 165	143.7	69.9	173	8 734	1 977.3	339.4
Keizer	44	137	20.7	2.4	36	62	5.2	1.6	NA	NA	NA	NA

1. Firms subject to federal tax.

City	Accommodation and foodservices, 1997				Arts, entertainment, and recreation,[1] 1997				Health care and social assistance,[1] 1997			
	Number of establishments	Number of employees	Sales (mil dol)	Annual payroll (mil dol)	Number of establishments	Number of employees	Receipts (mil dol)	Annual payroll (mil dol)	Number of establishments	Number of employees	Receipts (mil dol)	Annual payroll (mil dol)
	92	93	94	95	96	97	98	99	100	101	102	103
OHIO—Cont'd												
Delaware	67	1 258	34.5	9.9	5	31	1.2	0.4	68	726	42.1	18.1
Dublin	93	1 966	67.9	18.8	20	374	28.0	8.4	96	1 894	151.7	67.7
East Cleveland	29	454	14.1	3.8	1	0	0.0	0.0	21	288	16.0	7.1
Elyria	124	2 278	68.6	17.6	9	120	4.3	1.2	124	1 188	91.7	49.0
Euclid	83	D	D	D	9	90	2.1	0.6	95	1 712	97.0	56.3
Fairborn	79	1 656	50.5	14.6	5	39	0.7	0.2	33	276	15.8	5.5
Fairfield	81	1 727	48.5	13.6	15	195	6.2	1.7	110	1 602	96.2	44.0
Findlay	143	2 766	74.7	22.3	8	56	2.2	0.6	105	1 183	77.0	39.2
Gahanna	64	1 272	38.2	11.5	6	133	6.5	2.7	72	562	32.4	14.4
Garfield Heights	54	D	D	D	NA	NA	NA	NA	61	416	37.7	15.7
Grove City	75	1 521	52.5	14.9	6	503	22.8	5.1	56	625	38.7	18.8
Hamilton	130	2 184	62.1	17.0	10	93	2.4	0.6	115	1 128	70.0	37.5
Huber Heights	79	1 524	45.2	12.5	6	61	1.5	0.5	64	671	35.6	15.1
Kent	84	1 328	33.3	9.9	2	0	0.0	0.0	40	385	22.2	8.7
Kettering	115	D	D	D	16	213	7.1	2.5	177	2 267	149.1	76.6
Lakewood	112	1 356	41.3	10.7	8	43	1.9	0.5	138	1 479	100.2	58.4
Lancaster	100	2 249	66.3	18.4	12	84	9.8	1.7	141	1 458	84.7	41.5
Lima	93	1 427	43.7	11.7	4	29	0.7	0.2	142	1 633	122.7	67.6
Lorain	99	D	D	D	15	168	8.2	1.9	139	1 775	115.6	65.1
Mansfield	143	2 289	74.0	20.3	15	260	4.7	1.5	176	1 887	111.4	53.7
Maple Heights	47	575	19.3	5.0	7	51	2.5	0.5	57	504	31.6	12.1
Marion	67	1 395	41.6	10.8	8	66	2.2	0.4	106	1 678	96.8	48.6
Massillon	79	1 107	31.0	7.5	4	45	0.7	0.2	49	742	39.0	17.2
Medina	54	1 394	40.4	11.9	3	0	0.0	0.0	92	926	54.4	26.0
Mentor	127	3 338	86.5	24.9	19	166	9.1	2.3	106	1 248	65.1	27.3
Middletown	97	2 370	69.5	20.0	11	130	5.6	2.3	109	1 157	82.7	43.1
Newark	102	1 335	40.6	11.1	10	139	3.9	1.2	118	2 582	114.3	60.0
North Olmsted	117	2 617	72.3	20.6	9	86	1.9	0.6	77	760	42.5	19.1
North Royalton	45	558	15.5	4.3	1	0	0.0	0.0	41	773	29.0	13.4
Parma	189	2 778	76.2	20.4	16	355	4.5	1.3	209	2 058	161.8	69.5
Reynoldsburg	75	1 043	33.6	9.0	6	71	2.5	1.2	67	396	23.7	10.8
Sandusky	123	2 853	104.9	28.8	18	0	0.0	0.0	119	877	62.2	31.9
Shaker Heights	38	779	22.6	6.1	4	11	0.6	0.2	68	1 248	42.2	22.9
Springfield	169	3 258	95.0	26.3	8	80	3.2	0.9	190	2 001	130.6	64.6
Stow	44	886	23.6	6.2	11	114	4.2	1.3	59	747	47.7	20.0
Strongsville	95	2 151	51.4	13.4	8	91	3.2	0.8	72	468	29.0	12.3
Toledo	737	13 187	424.0	112.3	80	1 230	66.2	16.3	596	8 240	543.8	267.6
Trotwood city	NA	NA	NA	NA	NA	NA	NA	NA	NA	NA	NA	NA
Upper Arlington	53	1 016	29.6	9.2	6	10	0.3	0.1	78	714	39.9	17.8
Warren	137	2 415	67.9	18.4	13	110	5.3	1.7	211	1 996	122.0	53.0
Westerville	62	D	D	D	10	559	13.8	4.2	140	1 904	121.1	56.2
Westlake	70	1 936	61.5	16.9	14	155	4.3	1.3	161	2 122	111.7	49.3
Youngstown	177	2 467	79.3	19.9	12	161	4.1	1.0	216	2 964	190.2	91.1
Zanesville	105	2 097	61.4	16.9	5	73	1.6	0.4	116	1 203	96.1	45.4
OKLAHOMA	6 534	105 934	3 151.3	856.8	746	8 904	531.4	110.3	6 991	91 803	5 061.4	2 244.0
Bartlesville	83	1 443	47.1	13.1	10	0	0.0	0.0	99	819	59.4	29.8
Broken Arrow	101	1 789	49.3	14.0	18	403	15.3	5.1	123	1 822	73.7	35.3
Edmond	124	2 603	76.9	22.2	25	263	13.0	4.5	186	2 148	120.0	53.7
Enid	117	1 889	51.6	14.6	14	0	0.0	0.0	143	0	0.0	0.0
Lawton	179	3 391	89.1	25.0	19	0	0.0	0.0	196	2 295	139.0	51.9
Midwest City	98	1 973	56.3	16.0	16	134	2.7	0.8	127	2 273	161.3	62.4
Moore	68	1 107	31.7	8.7	8	85	2.2	0.5	53	617	23.4	10.7
Muskogee	109	1 959	54.9	14.2	10	0	0.0	0.0	150	2 195	97.7	44.1
Norman	225	4 779	139.9	38.6	34	348	22.9	3.8	236	2 426	148.1	66.7
Oklahoma City	1 071	21 553	684.2	188.8	109	2 521	104.8	31.3	1 474	18 208	1 308.1	586.6
Ponca City	62	1 054	29.5	7.8	11	0	0.0	0.0	84	593	35.1	14.9
Shawnee	111	2 439	70.0	19.2	6	0	0.0	0.0	84	1 273	62.3	27.0
Stillwater	114	2 398	56.0	15.6	11	87	1.7	0.5	88	1 012	51.0	23.6
Tulsa	1 035	19 183	643.9	172.6	106	1 305	92.5	19.0	1 240	17 228	1 244.7	553.7
OREGON	8 363	124 425	4 385.7	1 236.6	968	16 098	875.8	260.6	7 328	68 285	4 431.4	1 899.6
Albany	98	1 633	50.9	14.6	13	169	6.1	1.3	92	887	53.7	25.1
Beaverton	200	3 738	146.2	41.7	29	575	34.9	8.7	184	1 521	103.3	36.6
Bend	161	2 136	79.1	22.2	29	1 313	34.2	10.1	167	1 593	116.5	45.3
Corvallis	177	2 545	78.8	22.0	14	213	7.1	2.5	129	1 925	137.8	51.3
Eugene	452	7 351	234.5	68.1	48	641	20.7	6.5	489	4 929	373.8	162.3
Gresham	166	3 321	105.0	30.3	20	300	10.9	3.6	176	1 477	92.0	37.9
Hillsboro	130	2 613	82.3	23.1	12	151	3.8	1.3	146	1 197	79.4	33.7
Keizer	28	930	21.8	6.4	11	133	6.9	1.6	41	397	17.6	7.4

1. Firms subject to federal tax.

Table D. Cities — Other Services and Federal Funds

City	Other services,[1] 1997				Selected federal funds, 2002–2003 (mil dol)								
					Procurement contracts		Grants						Direct payments for individuals for educational assistance
	Number of establishments	Number of employees	Receipts (mil dol)	Annual payroll (mil dol)	Defense	Other	Total[2]	Medicaid and other health related	Nutrition and family welfare	Energy and environment	Education	Housing and community development	
	104	105	106	107	108	109	110	111	112	113	114	115	116
OHIO—Cont'd													
Delaware	31	130	7.1	2.2	0.1	1.3	6.3	0.2	0.0	0.0	1.3	4.4	1.6
Dublin	49	581	33.8	11.7	150.8	0.5	0.7	0.0	0.0	0.3	0.0	0.1	0.0
East Cleveland	22	96	3.7	1.1	0.0	0.0	11.0	0.0	0.1	0.0	0.0	11.2	0.0
Elyria	75	479	28.8	8.0	9.2	0.8	8.9	0.0	0.0	0.0	0.2	7.7	7.0
Euclid	98	566	34.8	10.3	1.5	0.1	3.1	0.0	0.0	0.0	0.0	3.2	0.0
Fairborn	60	524	24.7	11.7	36.5	13.4	6.0	0.0	0.0	0.0	1.5	4.2	0.4
Fairfield	102	616	42.5	13.1	57.7	1.4	5.4	0.0	4.2	0.0	0.0	1.1	0.2
Findlay	74	566	30.3	10.0	0.0	0.2	5.2	0.0	2.5	0.0	0.6	1.8	3.8
Gahanna	43	576	34.6	10.1	0.4	0.4	2.3	0.0	0.0	0.0	0.0	2.2	0.0
Garfield Heights	48	266	15.0	4.8	3.3	0.1	0.3	0.0	0.0	0.0	0.0	0.1	0.0
Grove City	43	307	17.3	5.4	0.1	0.4	0.7	0.0	0.0	0.0	0.0	0.6	0.0
Hamilton	83	421	27.3	6.9	0.2	0.2	13.7	0.0	0.0	0.0	1.0	11.5	0.4
Huber Heights	51	286	14.5	4.4	4.3	0.1	0.0	0.0	0.0	0.0	0.0	0.0	0.0
Kent	35	201	9.5	3.1	3.3	0.1	27.9	2.5	0.0	0.6	8.7	6.5	30.9
Kettering	88	707	31.9	11.6	1.8	0.3	3.1	0.0	0.0	0.0	0.0	3.1	0.0
Lakewood	72	431	26.5	8.5	0.0	0.6	6.4	0.4	0.0	0.0	0.0	5.9	0.3
Lancaster	73	437	23.8	8.0	0.0	0.1	9.6	0.3	1.6	0.7	0.2	6.4	0.0
Lima	75	489	21.9	6.4	33.4	0.4	12.3	0.0	0.0	0.0	0.3	11.2	5.9
Lorain	85	689	37.6	12.4	2.8	2.0	18.3	0.2	6.4	0.0	0.1	9.4	1.4
Mansfield	112	955	47.1	20.2	2.5	0.6	7.2	0.8	0.4	0.0	0.3	5.3	3.5
Maple Heights	49	270	22.8	5.2	0.1	0.0	0.1	0.0	0.0	0.0	0.0	0.0	0.0
Marion	62	298	15.3	4.8	0.9	3.0	12.1	0.1	5.8	0.0	0.0	5.4	1.9
Massillon	61	318	15.3	4.7	0.1	0.0	4.4	2.0	0.0	0.0	0.0	2.2	0.0
Medina	56	381	22.4	7.7	0.8	0.4	2.3	0.0	0.0	0.0	0.1	1.9	0.0
Mentor	138	1 002	67.1	21.7	8.4	3.4	1.2	0.0	0.7	0.0	0.0	0.4	0.1
Middletown	91	578	28.8	9.5	9.0	0.0	5.2	0.7	0.0	0.0	0.0	4.3	0.0
Newark	80	518	29.1	9.5	103.9	0.4	14.0	0.7	2.9	0.0	0.0	9.9	3.0
North Olmsted	99	634	29.1	10.8	0.7	1.5	0.0	0.0	0.0	0.0	0.0	0.3	0.0
North Royalton	64	353	23.9	6.5	2.1	0.0	0.3	0.0	0.0	0.0	0.0	0.3	0.0
Parma	160	1 313	67.3	22.2	0.0	0.1	2.3	0.0	0.0	0.0	2.0	2.3	0.0
Reynoldsburg	63	283	17.5	5.0	0.4	0.5	4.4	0.0	0.0	0.0	0.3	0.0	0.0
Sandusky	73	384	16.0	5.2	28.8	8.5	18.4	0.0	1.9	0.0	0.0	2.9	0.1
Shaker Heights	40	294	14.1	4.9	0.0	0.0	2.1	0.2	0.6	0.0	0.0	1.1	0.0
Springfield	125	1 053	50.4	14.8	16.0	0.6	25.2	0.7	0.0	4.1	0.8	16.5	5.9
Stow	48	350	13.5	5.1	2.4	0.1	1.1	0.0	0.0	0.0	0.0	1.0	0.0
Strongsville	64	524	44.6	13.6	0.4	0.8	3.5	0.0	0.0	0.0	0.0	3.1	0.0
Toledo	571	3 880	247.0	74.5	26.0	67.5	120.3	24.7	12.5	0.4	3.9	55.5	20.1
Trotwood city	NA	NA	NA	NA	0.0	0.0	2.3	0.0	0.0	0.0	0.0	2.1	0.0
Upper Arlington	36	237	11.0	3.6	0.0	0.0	0.0	0.0	0.0	0.0	0.0	0.0	0.0
Warren	104	481	30.0	7.5	1.8	0.6	17.7	0.0	5.0	0.0	0.3	11.7	1.6
Westerville	50	321	17.5	5.9	2.7	2.0	5.8	0.1	0.0	0.8	2.3	2.0	1.9
Westlake	58	485	31.1	10.3	3.5	4.1	0.3	0.3	0.0	0.0	0.0	0.0	0.0
Youngstown	144	1 145	70.6	24.4	2.7	2.7	26.1	1.4	6.8	0.2	2.0	13.5	13.1
Zanesville	79	750	40.7	13.8	2.6	0.2	6.3	0.0	1.8	0.0	0.4	3.8	3.3
OKLAHOMA	4 572	26 308	1 599.4	458.5	1 470.5	1 017.3	5 135.6	2 259.8	784.4	69.7	570.0	347.0	207.9
Bartlesville	61	335	19.7	6.6	0.1	1.1	8.4	0.1	0.0	0.2	0.2	6.1	1.1
Broken Arrow	111	698	37.7	12.9	1.4	1.1	1.5	0.0	0.0	0.0	0.3	0.9	0.2
Edmond	102	598	30.0	9.6	8.7	2.8	7.6	0.1	0.0	0.0	1.8	3.5	9.3
Enid	91	446	23.2	6.5	0.7	0.7	6.5	0.0	0.1	0.0	0.3	5.2	0.4
Lawton	135	709	33.5	9.8	7.4	5.6	25.6	1.3	4.3	2.1	7.3	9.2	6.8
Midwest City	69	393	19.3	5.4	288.9	2.2	4.9	0.1	0.0	0.0	0.0	4.5	0.3
Moore	45	255	15.6	4.7	0.0	3.5	2.8	0.0	0.0	0.0	0.8	1.9	1.1
Muskogee	61	362	21.0	6.4	0.5	24.1	10.1	0.1	2.7	0.0	1.9	3.0	2.7
Norman	112	679	32.3	9.7	1.3	28.5	49.3	7.0	5.8	2.5	3.6	4.4	16.4
Oklahoma City	892	7 677	445.6	135.6	161.4	170.4	805.2	162.1	158.0	35.6	152.0	89.2	30.2
Ponca City	49	226	13.8	3.9	103.2	0.0	6.4	2.7	0.4	0.1	0.8	2.1	0.2
Shawnee	49	214	11.8	3.4	2.9	0.3	15.7	4.3	2.7	0.4	2.3	4.6	3.7
Stillwater	67	372	16.1	4.8	27.4	2.3	77.9	5.1	0.3	1.1	21.3	2.8	15.5
Tulsa	794	5 621	399.7	115.3	112.2	43.7	117.5	11.2	10.3	4.5	7.7	57.7	29.0
OREGON	4 794	28 185	1 897.5	561.9	474.4	723.8	5 103.2	2 364.0	694.4	78.0	444.6	303.4	169.8
Albany	64	397	22.3	7.8	0.2	8.6	3.2	0.0	0.0	0.5	0.0	1.5	5.9
Beaverton	140	924	62.5	17.8	30.4	3.3	5.3	0.6	0.0	0.3	0.5	2.7	0.0
Bend	96	694	41.9	14.4	7.4	3.0	8.0	0.0	0.5	2.0	0.4	1.8	3.8
Corvallis	66	371	18.7	5.9	3.9	6.6	103.1	17.3	0.9	8.3	3.1	2.8	14.8
Eugene	260	2 135	130.9	38.7	6.8	14.1	126.9	62.9	1.3	3.0	23.1	15.0	28.0
Gresham	117	732	45.5	14.8	1.5	0.2	8.2	0.0	4.8	0.0	0.6	2.1	5.4
Hillsboro	103	493	36.9	11.5	7.0	0.9	6.0	0.0	2.3	0.1	0.2	2.0	0.0
Keizer	35	117	7.2	1.9	0.0	0.0	0.1	0.0	0.0	0.0	0.0	0.1	0.0

1. Firms subject to federal tax.   2. Includes program categories not shown separately. State totals include additional categories not allocated by city.

City	City government finances, 2002									
	General revenue							General expenditure		
		Intergovernmental		Taxes					Per capita[1] (dollars)	
					Per capita[1] (dollars)					
	Total (mil dol)	Total (mil dol)	Percent from state government	Total (mil dol)	Total	Property	Sales and gross receipts	Total (mil dol)	Total	Capital outlays
	117	118	119	120	121	122	123	124	125	126
OHIO—Cont'd										
Delaware	26.0	3.7	88.6	11.8	445	56	0	21.4	807	241
Dublin	72.3	3.7	79.5	55.5	1 692	85	44	76.2	2 321	988
East Cleveland	NA	NA	NA	NA	NA	NA	NA	NA	NA	NA
Elyria	48.1	4.5	83.3	25.1	446	62	5	63.1	1 121	310
Euclid	53.0	5.8	69.2	27.1	521	97	15	56.0	1 080	46
Fairborn	25.9	5.0	78.9	9.0	278	86	0	24.3	748	77
Fairfield	42.8	6.1	82.1	23.4	556	82	8	48.8	1 158	441
Findlay	40.0	4.5	100.0	17.9	455	73	0	46.6	1 182	452
Gahanna	29.9	6.2	67.0	14.5	433	35	6	22.4	668	190
Garfield Heights	26.0	5.3	97.0	16.7	552	248	0	25.6	847	33
Grove City	26.0	3.3	52.4	16.9	582	78	5	27.0	933	397
Hamilton	69.9	12.1	77.8	25.5	424	71	0	86.1	1 432	516
Huber Heights	25.1	3.9	95.5	14.6	384	91	0	26.8	705	101
Kent	24.4	4.0	84.7	12.2	438	82	5	25.3	913	228
Kettering	54.4	10.0	91.5	32.0	565	137	0	52.3	922	177
Lakewood	54.9	11.7	100.0	30.7	555	237	0	51.8	937	82
Lancaster	35.7	6.9	87.0	13.8	383	40	0	38.6	1 070	201
Lima	39.8	8.8	67.8	16.0	391	28	2	43.7	1 071	6
Lorain	53.0	19.3	100.0	22.6	334	52	0	59.0	872	211
Mansfield	49.3	12.4	60.4	25.8	509	66	4	51.6	1 017	171
Maple Heights	22.0	5.8	80.7	12.6	490	191	0	24.3	942	178
Marion	28.4	5.6	93.3	13.6	368	35	4	34.6	931	214
Massillon	31.0	5.9	82.0	14.2	450	55	0	23.7	751	3
Medina	19.0	2.9	68.0	10.5	401	140	0	24.4	934	301
Mentor	51.1	9.1	93.1	33.4	666	96	7	57.4	1 144	42
Middletown	56.5	13.9	92.9	23.5	458	93	0	75.3	1 471	402
Newark	34.0	8.9	90.9	16.1	347	57	0	37.4	806	87
North Olmsted	39.1	5.1	100.0	21.8	644	291	8	46.1	1 364	304
North Royalton	21.5	2.9	100.0	12.4	406	123	4	19.2	626	56
Parma	60.4	15.1	45.2	34.0	402	102	4	59.2	701	80
Reynoldsburg	20.5	3.3	98.3	10.9	332	20	15	24.2	739	204
Sandusky	27.9	3.6	100.0	14.2	517	81	136	27.1	991	92
Shaker Heights	45.2	5.1	61.8	28.9	1 002	221	2	43.7	1 515	198
Springfield	61.9	15.0	54.5	31.4	490	41	25	52.6	820	95
Stow	26.6	6.7	100.0	17.6	520	177	0	26.3	776	218
Strongsville	46.4	4.7	100.0	28.1	632	179	0	46.9	1 053	126
Toledo	347.1	57.7	69.3	180.4	584	50	18	342.7	1 109	183
Trotwood city	14.2	3.7	81.0	7.6	280	85	6	15.2	560	36
Upper Arlington	37.7	4.0	15.7	26.1	792	232	0	31.3	951	163
Warren	58.5	8.4	46.0	18.5	391	32	8	47.7	1 009	57
Westerville	47.9	7.8	100.0	25.7	725	223	11	56.8	1 598	587
Westlake	49.4	8.5	97.3	28.8	895	383	7	47.2	1 468	502
Youngstown	89.6	18.0	61.9	35.6	444	26	11	79.0	987	85
Zanesville	26.7	6.2	100.0	13.5	531	42	0	24.6	966	41
OKLAHOMA	X	X	X	X	X	X	X	X	X	X
Bartlesville	31.1	1.9	24.1	17.3	498	69	417	30.6	879	216
Broken Arrow	53.0	1.1	82.7	32.5	391	71	297	48.3	582	144
Edmond	55.9	1.9	53.0	31.6	448	0	405	59.5	843	166
Enid	39.0	3.4	61.4	21.8	469	2	452	26.7	574	98
Lawton	61.6	5.7	20.4	29.2	320	15	297	46.4	508	36
Midwest City	42.4	2.7	6.2	20.6	379	5	359	41.0	751	43
Moore	27.3	1.1	49.6	14.4	329	25	282	26.6	609	50
Muskogee	NA	NA	NA	NA	NA	NA	NA	NA	NA	NA
Norman	226.1	6.0	71.4	45.3	463	11	435	233.2	2 384	257
Oklahoma City	711.0	72.3	46.3	350.2	675	79	580	750.6	1 446	538
Ponca City	20.3	1.2	13.7	7.9	307	8	286	23.9	928	116
Shawnee	NA	NA	NA	NA	NA	NA	NA	NA	NA	NA
Stillwater	34.6	2.4	100.0	19.6	482	44	426	36.5	899	241
Tulsa	615.5	70.3	15.9	250.2	638	73	523	590.1	1 506	373
OREGON	X	X	X	X	X	X	X	X	X	X
Albany	39.5	5.4	84.5	22.1	525	340	93	45.1	1 070	197
Beaverton	50.4	11.7	58.4	23.0	288	195	60	46.7	585	131
Bend	46.9	7.1	49.2	27.6	485	218	98	52.5	921	376
Corvallis	54.6	8.1	43.5	21.8	438	327	90	80.3	1 613	115
Eugene	190.8	36.4	25.8	81.9	583	473	26	205.4	1 463	328
Gresham	75.4	9.8	64.1	37.9	400	218	81	78.9	833	78
Hillsboro	71.3	4.0	98.3	40.3	531	380	84	63.8	840	113
Keizer	NA	NA	NA	NA	NA	NA	NA	NA	NA	NA

1. Based on population estimated as of July 1 of the year shown.

Table D. Cities — **City Government Finances (cont'd)**

City	Public welfare	Highways	Parking facilities	Education	Health and hospitals	Police protection	Sewerage and sanitation	Parks and recreation	Housing and community development	Interest on debt
	127	128	129	130	131	132	133	134	135	136
OHIO—Cont'd										
Delaware	0.0	10.4	0.2	0.0	0.0	15.5	16.9	5.9	2.3	1.5
Dublin	0.0	24.4	0.0	0.0	0.2	8.8	5.3	22.6	0.0	8.8
East Cleveland	NA	NA	NA	NA	NA	NA	NA	NA	NA	NA
Elyria	0.0	6.7	0.0	0.0	3.3	17.2	25.0	3.6	2.2	2.0
Euclid	0.0	5.9	0.0	0.0	0.9	18.3	25.0	6.6	3.0	6.4
Fairborn	0.0	6.4	0.0	0.0	0.3	20.2	18.2	1.4	3.7	1.4
Fairfield	0.0	22.5	0.0	0.0	0.8	13.2	16.9	8.3	0.0	3.3
Findlay	0.0	7.8	0.2	0.0	1.5	12.6	37.7	2.9	0.0	3.9
Gahanna	0.0	19.6	0.0	0.0	0.2	21.5	8.6	7.2	10.4	1.8
Garfield Heights	0.0	6.8	0.0	0.0	0.4	21.3	8.6	4.0	0.7	4.3
Grove City	0.0	13.8	0.0	0.0	0.7	21.9	4.6	9.6	3.7	5.4
Hamilton	0.0	6.1	0.7	0.0	2.6	14.6	14.6	3.0	4.6	3.8
Huber Heights	0.0	13.5	0.0	0.0	0.0	22.2	10.5	1.0	0.4	5.9
Kent	0.0	5.5	0.0	0.0	1.7	19.2	17.0	3.8	2.4	4.3
Kettering	0.0	25.3	0.0	0.0	0.0	17.3	0.0	18.1	3.4	1.0
Lakewood	0.0	4.9	0.5	0.0	6.2	12.5	15.5	5.4	6.1	8.1
Lancaster	0.0	10.8	0.0	0.0	2.9	15.6	23.6	4.8	2.1	1.0
Lima	0.0	8.1	0.0	0.0	0.0	19.2	21.4	2.5	9.3	1.2
Lorain	0.0	5.6	0.0	0.0	2.6	14.4	23.9	6.7	14.1	2.6
Mansfield	0.2	20.2	0.0	0.0	0.2	18.5	11.5	1.9	3.3	0.4
Maple Heights	0.0	6.9	0.0	0.0	0.3	23.3	8.0	4.6	0.4	1.9
Marion	0.0	8.4	0.2	0.0	3.0	15.6	23.7	3.4	1.2	2.0
Massillon	0.0	8.5	0.0	0.0	2.4	15.6	18.4	5.4	0.8	5.8
Medina	0.0	2.7	0.0	0.0	0.5	15.8	9.3	11.3	2.3	1.5
Mentor	0.0	27.6	0.0	0.0	0.0	15.3	1.1	13.8	0.5	4.6
Middletown	0.0	11.7	0.2	0.0	2.3	12.8	13.0	4.2	7.8	2.5
Newark	2.3	13.3	0.1	0.0	2.1	17.9	12.0	6.6	4.0	0.5
North Olmsted	0.6	13.0	0.0	0.0	0.4	13.2	17.6	12.0	0.0	9.1
North Royalton	0.0	9.1	0.0	0.0	1.5	25.4	22.4	2.9	3.4	1.1
Parma	0.0	9.0	0.0	0.0	1.8	19.0	1.7	6.7	8.1	7.3
Reynoldsburg	0.0	3.6	0.0	0.0	0.6	23.9	17.0	4.7	0.0	4.8
Sandusky	0.0	5.8	0.0	0.0	0.1	17.1	22.2	2.7	2.8	4.2
Shaker Heights	0.0	7.2	0.0	0.0	0.8	19.7	8.4	8.7	8.6	0.1
Springfield	0.0	8.6	0.0	0.0	1.3	22.8	11.5	3.8	0.7	2.9
Stow	0.0	25.1	0.0	0.0	1.8	12.5	0.0	5.8	4.3	1.5
Strongsville	0.0	15.1	0.0	0.0	3.0	18.5	13.4	9.0	3.3	3.6
Toledo	0.0	8.0	0.0	0.0	4.7	20.9	16.6	1.6	3.9	5.5
Trotwood city	0.0	11.1	0.0	0.0	0.0	33.5	12.9	3.6	0.6	0.6
Upper Arlington	0.0	7.3	2.4	0.0	0.5	16.0	8.0	8.0	0.3	2.9
Warren	0.0	9.2	0.2	0.0	1.5	12.5	16.1	1.2	6.4	4.6
Westerville	0.0	10.9	0.0	0.0	0.0	11.6	11.4	27.6	0.0	2.9
Westlake	0.0	5.4	0.0	0.0	1.0	14.0	11.3	6.1	0.0	8.4
Youngstown	0.0	9.8	0.0	0.0	2.3	21.6	18.5	3.3	6.8	2.6
Zanesville	0.0	4.1	0.0	0.0	0.5	33.4	21.8	3.8	0.0	1.7
OKLAHOMA	X	X	X	X	X	X	X	X	X	X
Bartlesville	0.0	10.7	0.0	0.0	0.0	13.5	22.6	9.2	3.6	1.3
Broken Arrow	0.0	16.8	0.0	0.0	2.9	19.9	8.5	11.4	0.0	7.8
Edmond	2.4	11.6	0.0	0.0	0.0	19.2	10.6	15.2	0.0	1.2
Enid	0.0	18.6	0.0	0.0	4.4	17.6	8.6	1.3	3.3	0.5
Lawton	0.0	6.5	0.8	0.0	0.2	22.4	11.9	7.0	4.9	0.8
Midwest City	0.0	6.4	0.0	0.0	4.2	20.2	10.4	8.9	1.3	2.5
Moore	0.0	8.8	0.0	0.0	0.0	17.2	6.7	3.3	1.0	5.3
Muskogee	NA	NA	NA	NA	NA	NA	NA	NA	NA	NA
Norman	0.0	6.4	0.0	0.0	66.6	6.1	6.3	2.2	0.2	2.3
Oklahoma City	0.0	11.5	0.9	0.0	0.0	14.6	14.6	15.5	2.7	5.3
Ponca City	0.0	7.9	0.0	0.0	2.1	14.6	16.6	6.2	2.7	0.8
Shawnee	NA	NA	NA	NA	NA	NA	NA	NA	NA	NA
Stillwater	0.0	4.4	0.0	0.0	5.6	17.8	29.2	10.1	0.0	2.3
Tulsa	4.7	3.5	0.3	0.0	4.1	15.3	18.6	5.1	1.1	12.1
OREGON	X	X	X	X	X	X	X	X	X	X
Albany	0.0	11.9	0.0	0.0	2.9	13.4	16.6	7.6	1.0	3.0
Beaverton	1.6	10.3	0.0	0.0	0.0	22.1	15.9	0.3	4.3	2.4
Bend	0.0	27.1	0.3	0.0	0.0	22.8	15.3	0.0	3.1	3.2
Corvallis	0.0	5.7	0.5	0.0	0.0	10.0	8.5	4.4	4.3	1.3
Eugene	0.0	4.6	1.1	0.0	0.0	13.3	11.3	6.7	4.7	2.2
Gresham	1.3	8.6	0.0	0.0	0.0	23.6	15.1	3.3	1.5	3.8
Hillsboro	0.0	12.4	0.1	0.0	0.0	21.1	21.8	14.6	0.0	0.1
Keizer	NA	NA	NA	NA	NA	NA	NA	NA	NA	NA

Table D. Cities — City Government Finances, City Government Employment, and Climate

City	City government finances, 2002 (cont'd) Debt outstanding — Total (mil dol)	Per capita[1] (dollars)	Percent utility	City government employment, 2002	Climate[2] Average daily temperature (degrees Fahrenheit) Mean — January	Mean July	Limits January[3]	Limits July[4]	Annual precipitation (inches)	Heating degree days	Cooling degree days
	137	138	139	140	141	142	143	144	145	146	147
OHIO—Cont'd											
Delaware	11.9	450	0.0	259	NA	NA	NA	NA	NA	NA	NA
Dublin	102.0	3 110	5.5	426	NA	NA	NA	NA	NA	NA	NA
East Cleveland	NA	NA	NA	264	24.8	71.9	17.6	82.4	36.63	6 201	621
Elyria	31.1	552	8.2	619	26.2	73.3	17.9	85.0	35.95	5 818	779
Euclid	55.6	1 071	0.0	581	24.8	71.9	17.6	82.4	36.63	6 201	621
Fairborn	5.6	173	5.5	246	26.0	74.2	17.9	84.9	36.64	5 708	886
Fairfield	31.2	741	18.0	311	26.1	73.9	15.8	86.2	41.79	5 791	830
Findlay	39.6	1 003	45.8	381	23.6	72.8	16.5	82.7	34.26	6 302	720
Gahanna	9.8	293	14.9	148	26.4	73.2	18.5	83.7	38.09	5 708	797
Garfield Heights	28.2	933	0.0	238	24.8	71.9	17.6	82.4	36.63	6 201	621
Grove City	23.1	798	3.7	138	NA	NA	NA	NA	NA	NA	NA
Hamilton	339.0	5 642	76.1	732	26.1	73.9	15.8	86.2	41.79	NA	NA
Huber Heights	39.2	1 029	31.5	179	26.0	74.2	17.9	84.9	36.64	5 791	830
Kent	20.3	731	0.0	237	24.8	74.2	17.9	84.9	36.64	5 708	886
Kettering	8.7	154	0.0	928	26.0	74.2	16.9	82.3	36.82	5 708	625
Lakewood	75.9	1 372	7.7	625	24.8	71.9	17.6	82.4	36.63	6 201	621
Lancaster	7.9	220	0.0	449	25.4	72.8	16.0	84.7	36.32	5 988	724
Lima	14.0	343	39.8	426	23.6	73.6	15.2	84.4	35.94	6 253	810
Lorain	34.3	507	29.9	580	26.2	73.3	17.9	85.0	35.95	5 818	779
Mansfield	19.3	381	20.2	639	24.5	72.1	16.8	82.1	39.66	6 258	666
Maple Heights	9.5	370	0.0	278	24.8	71.9	17.6	82.4	36.63	6 201	621
Marion	11.1	298	0.0	342	23.4	72.6	14.3	84.5	36.91	6 407	692
Massillon	30.5	966	0.0	596	24.8	71.9	16.9	82.3	36.82	6 160	625
Medina	22.4	859	16.3	189	NA	NA	NA	NA	NA	NA	NA
Mentor	40.5	808	0.0	422	26.6	71.9	19.3	81.2	35.93	5 929	636
Middletown	35.0	684	13.1	581	26.6	74.3	17.5	85.5	39.26	5 694	897
Newark	20.2	436	70.8	479	26.7	73.2	18.2	85.0	41.48	5 657	767
North Olmsted	71.0	2 102	0.0	372	24.8	71.9	17.6	82.4	36.63	6 201	621
North Royalton	4.8	155	0.0	198	NA	NA	NA	NA	NA	NA	NA
Parma	68.0	805	0.0	593	24.8	71.9	17.6	82.4	36.63	6 201	621
Reynoldsburg	24.0	731	7.1	141	26.4	73.2	18.5	83.7	38.09	5 708	797
Sandusky	28.4	1 037	6.7	309	24.8	73.6	17.5	82.4	34.05	6 131	752
Shaker Heights	8.1	282	0.0	453	24.8	71.9	17.6	82.4	36.63	6 201	621
Springfield	41.7	650	13.0	662	24.3	72.2	15.3	83.7	38.31	6 254	649
Stow	8.5	250	0.0	223	24.8	71.9	16.9	82.3	36.82	6 160	625
Strongsville	35.1	789	0.0	384	24.8	71.9	17.6	82.4	36.63	6 201	621
Toledo	328.8	1 064	17.8	2 999	22.5	72.1	14.9	83.4	32.97	6 579	610
Trotwood city	3.6	134	0.0	148	NA	NA	NA	NA	NA	NA	NA
Upper Arlington	19.9	604	0.0	292	26.4	73.2	18.5	83.7	38.09	5 708	797
Warren	39.6	839	27.7	447	24.4	70.5	15.3	83.2	36.11	6 402	491
Westerville	39.2	1 102	20.0	391	25.9	73.2	16.5	85.5	39.32	5 719	786
Westlake	64.9	2 018	0.0	295	24.8	71.9	17.6	82.4	36.63	6 201	621
Youngstown	32.7	409	3.8	929	23.6	70.3	16.4	81.3	37.32	6 544	497
Zanesville	6.5	257	22.9	374	26.8	72.7	18.3	83.5	39.42	5 714	716
OKLAHOMA	X	X	X	X	X	X	X	X	X	X	X
Bartlesville	15.9	458	20.4	349	34.7	82.1	22.5	94.7	35.91	3 777	1 868
Broken Arrow	85.8	1 032	2.2	482	35.2	83.3	24.9	93.7	40.59	3 691	2 017
Edmond	81.7	1 158	57.9	571	35.9	82.0	25.2	93.4	33.36	3 659	1 859
Enid	44.3	953	95.1	480	35.1	83.3	24.7	95.2	32.35	3 788	2 008
Lawton	69.3	758	50.2	822	36.8	83.5	23.7	95.8	29.27	3 457	2 069
Midwest City	39.3	721	0.0	483	35.9	82.0	25.2	93.4	33.36	3 659	1 859
Moore	30.9	706	0.0	230	35.9	82.0	25.2	93.4	33.36	3 659	1 859
Muskogee	NA	NA	NA	470	37.3	82.2	26.6	93.8	41.74	3 413	1 937
Norman	90.9	929	2.6	2 229	37.8	82.2	25.6	94.8	35.41	3 295	1 967
Oklahoma City	937.1	1 806	24.3	4 706	35.9	82.0	25.2	93.4	33.36	3 659	1 859
Ponca City	38.0	1 474	95.0	418	32.4	82.5	22.1	93.8	34.24	4 226	1 865
Shawnee	NA	NA	NA	276	38.3	82.0	25.9	94.9	38.27	3 222	1 954
Stillwater	45.7	1 127	53.4	1 130	33.6	81.6	21.4	93.1	33.85	4 028	1 755
Tulsa	1 448.4	3 696	6.8	4 441	35.2	83.3	24.9	93.7	40.59	3 691	2 017
OREGON	X	X	X	X	X	X	X	X	X	X	X
Albany	44.8	1 061	26.0	335	38.3	64.3	31.6	78.4	66.42	5 287	172
Beaverton	43.3	543	48.3	439	38.9	65.8	32.5	79.7	37.57	5 011	232
Bend	46.1	808	10.4	337	NA	NA	NA	NA	NA	NA	NA
Corvallis	88.9	1 785	39.0	425	39.3	65.6	33.0	80.2	42.70	4 923	203
Eugene	284.6	2 027	52.8	1 978	40.8	67.3	35.2	81.7	49.37	4 546	300
Gresham	85.3	901	19.1	547	39.6	68.2	33.7	79.9	36.30	4 522	371
Hillsboro	14.2	187	92.9	568	38.9	65.8	32.5	79.7	37.57	5 011	232
Keizer	NA	NA	NA	171	NA	NA	NA	NA	NA	NA	NA

1. Based on the population estimated as of July 1 of the year shown. 2. Represents normal values based on the 30-year period, 1961–1990. 3. Average daily minimum. 4. Average daily maximum.

STATE Place code	City	Land area,[1] 2000 (sq km)	Population, 2003			Population characteristics, 2000 Percent Race (alone or in combination)					Hispanic or Latino[2]	Non-Hispanic White
			Total persons	Rank	Per square kilometer	White	Black	Am. Indian, Alaska Native	Asian and Pacific Islander	Other race		
		1	2	3	4	5	6	7	8	9	10	11
	OREGON—Cont'd											
41 40550	Lake Oswego	26.8	36 085	890	1 346.5	93.4	0.9	0.8	6.2	1.3	2.3	89.7
41 45000	McMinnville	25.6	28 514	1 110	1 113.8	89.0	1.0	2.4	2.4	8.3	14.6	80.4
41 47000	Medford	56.2	66 638	431	1 185.7	93.0	0.8	2.2	2.1	5.1	9.2	86.0
41 55200	Oregon City	21.1	28 407	1 115	1 346.3	94.8	1.1	2.1	2.1	2.7	5.0	90.1
41 59000	Portland	347.9	538 544	28	1 548.0	81.3	7.9	2.3	8.2	4.9	6.8	75.5
41 64900	Salem	118.4	142 914	156	1 207.0	86.1	1.8	2.7	3.8	9.1	14.6	77.7
41 69600	Springfield	37.3	54 773	571	1 468.4	93.1	1.3	3.2	2.5	3.9	6.9	86.7
41 73650	Tigard	28.1	45 538	711	1 620.6	88.0	1.7	1.3	7.6	4.6	8.9	80.8
42 00000	PENNSYLVANIA	116 074.5	12 365 455	X	106.5	86.3	10.5	0.4	2.1	1.9	3.2	84.1
42 02000	Allentown	45.9	105 958	221	2 308.5	75.5	9.3	0.7	2.8	15.5	24.4	64.4
42 02184	Altoona	25.3	47 980	666	1 896.4	96.8	3.0	0.3	0.5	0.4	0.7	95.6
42 06064	Bethel Park Borough	30.3	32 915	980	1 086.3	97.6	1.2	0.2	1.5	0.2	0.5	96.7
42 06088	Bethlehem	49.9	72 570	385	1 454.3	83.9	4.5	0.6	2.6	11.0	18.2	74.9
42 13208	Chester	12.6	37 017	871	2 937.9	19.7	76.9	0.6	0.9	3.6	5.4	17.9
42 21648	Easton	11.0	26 189	1 197	2 380.8	81.0	14.4	0.9	2.2	4.8	9.8	73.5
42 24000	Erie	56.9	101 373	240	1 781.6	82.6	15.5	0.7	1.1	2.6	4.4	78.7
42 32800	Harrisburg	21.0	48 322	661	2 301.0	34.3	57.5	1.1	3.4	7.8	11.7	28.6
42 41216	Lancaster	19.2	55 351	556	2 882.9	64.5	16.3	1.0	3.0	19.4	30.8	51.8
42 52330	Monroeville Borough	51.3	28 707	1 106	559.6	86.5	9.0	0.4	4.9	0.5	0.8	85.1
42 53368	New Castle	22.1	25 338	1 218	1 146.5	88.5	12.0	0.5	0.3	0.6	0.8	86.4
42 54656	Norristown	9.1	31 069	1 029	3 414.2	56.7	36.7	0.9	3.4	5.7	10.5	49.4
42 60000	Philadelphia	349.9	1 479 339	5	4 227.9	46.4	44.3	0.7	5.1	6.0	8.5	42.5
42 61000	Pittsburgh	144.0	325 337	54	2 259.3	68.8	28.1	0.7	3.2	1.1	1.3	66.9
42 61536	Plum Borough	74.1	26 797	1 178	361.6	96.0	3.0	0.2	1.0	0.2	0.6	95.1
42 63624	Reading	25.4	80 305	337	3 161.6	62.4	14.1	1.0	2.1	24.8	37.3	48.1
42 69000	Scranton	65.3	74 320	379	1 138.1	94.5	3.6	0.3	1.3	1.5	2.6	92.3
42 73808	State College Borough	11.8	39 728	811	3 366.8	85.4	4.1	0.4	9.9	1.9	3.0	82.9
42 85152	Wilkes-Barre	17.7	41 630	773	2 352.0	93.3	5.8	0.4	1.1	0.8	1.6	91.4
42 85312	Williamsport	23.0	29 871	1 068	1 298.7	85.7	13.9	0.7	0.7	0.7	1.1	83.6
42 87048	York	13.5	40 081	796	2 969.0	62.8	27.6	1.0	2.0	10.7	17.2	54.2
44 00000	RHODE ISLAND	2 706.3	1 076 164	X	397.7	86.9	5.5	1.0	2.9	6.6	8.7	81.9
44 19180	Cranston	74.0	81 679	326	1 103.8	90.4	4.2	0.6	3.8	2.7	4.6	87.2
44 22960	East Providence	34.7	49 906	635	1 438.2	89.2	6.9	1.3	1.6	5.3	1.9	85.5
44 49960	Newport	20.6	26 136	1 199	1 268.7	86.6	9.7	1.8	2.2	3.5	5.5	81.7
44 54640	Pawtucket	22.6	74 330	378	3 288.9	78.6	9.7	0.8	1.5	15.0	13.9	69.1
44 59000	Providence	47.8	176 365	120	3 689.6	58.1	17.1	2.2	7.4	21.7	30.0	45.8
44 74300	Warwick	91.9	87 365	304	950.7	96.3	1.6	0.7	1.8	1.0	1.6	94.3
44 80780	Woonsocket	20.0	44 654	723	2 232.7	85.5	5.7	0.8	5.0	6.4	9.3	79.8
45 00000	SOUTH CAROLINA	77 983.2	4 147 152	X	53.2	68.0	29.9	0.7	1.2	1.3	2.4	66.1
45 00550	Aiken	41.9	26 456	1 192	631.4	67.5	30.8	0.7	1.7	0.7	1.5	65.9
45 01360	Anderson	35.8	25 563	1 215	714.1	64.0	34.6	0.6	1.1	1.0	1.5	62.5
45 13330	Charleston	251.2	101 024	242	402.2	63.8	34.4	0.4	1.6	0.8	1.5	62.3
45 16000	Columbia	324.3	117 357	197	361.9	50.1	46.7	0.6	2.3	1.8	3.0	48.2
45 25810	Florence	45.8	30 267	1 056	660.9	53.5	45.0	0.4	1.3	0.4	0.8	52.7
45 29815	Goose Creek	82.1	30 574	1 044	372.4	80.5	15.0	1.2	3.9	2.0	4.0	76.6
45 30850	Greenville	67.5	55 926	548	828.5	63.0	34.4	0.4	1.6	1.8	3.4	60.6
45 34045	Hilton Head Island	108.9	34 407	939	316.0	86.4	8.5	0.3	0.7	5.3	11.5	79.0
45 48535	Mount Pleasant	108.5	54 788	569	505.0	90.9	7.4	0.4	1.5	0.7	1.3	89.3
45 50875	North Charleston	151.6	81 577	328	538.1	46.2	50.3	1.0	2.3	3.2	4.0	43.2
45 61405	Rock Hill	80.4	56 114	545	697.9	59.5	37.7	0.8	1.7	1.3	2.5	57.6
45 68290	Spartanburg	49.6	38 718	830	780.6	47.8	50.1	0.4	1.7	1.1	1.8	46.5
45 70270	Summerville	39.8	31 734	1 011	797.3	78.2	19.9	0.9	1.4	1.0	2.0	76.1
45 70405	Sumter	68.9	39 790	809	577.5	50.5	46.9	0.6	2.0	1.6	2.4	48.7
46 00000	SOUTH DAKOTA	196 540.3	764 309	X	3.9	89.9	0.9	9.0	0.9	0.7	1.4	88.0
46 52980	Rapid City	115.5	60 876	483	527.1	86.8	1.5	12.0	1.5	1.1	2.8	83.2
46 59020	Sioux Falls	145.9	133 834	168	917.3	93.4	2.4	2.6	1.6	1.8	2.5	90.9
47 00000	TENNESSEE	106 751.8	5 841 748	X	54.7	81.2	16.8	0.7	1.3	1.3	2.2	79.2
47 03440	Bartlett	49.4	42 245	759	855.2	93.1	5.0	0.5	1.6	0.5	1.1	91.7
47 14000	Chattanooga	350.2	154 887	136	442.3	60.7	36.7	0.7	2.0	1.4	2.1	58.9
47 15160	Clarksville	245.7	107 953	219	439.4	70.5	24.7	1.3	3.7	3.5	6.0	65.3
47 15400	Cleveland	64.6	37 368	861	578.5	90.3	7.5	0.8	1.3	1.7	2.9	87.7
47 16420	Collierville	63.6	35 445	909	557.3	90.6	7.5	0.4	1.8	0.6	1.5	88.9
47 16540	Columbia	76.7	33 305	966	434.2	75.9	21.9	0.6	0.6	2.6	4.7	72.8
47 27740	Franklin	77.8	46 528	690	598.0	85.5	10.6	0.5	2.0	2.6	4.8	82.2
47 28960	Germantown	45.5	37 520	857	824.6	93.7	2.5	0.4	3.8	0.5	1.1	92.1

1. Dry land or land partially or temporarily covered by water. 2. Hispanic or Latino persons may be of any race.

Table D. Cities — **Population and Households**

City	Age of population (percent)									Percent female	Population Census counts		Percent change	
	Under 5 years	5 to 17 years	18 to 24 years	25 to 34 years	35 to 44 years	45 to 54 years	55 to 64 years	65 to 74 years	75 years and over	Percent female	1990	2000	1990–2000	2000–2003
	12	13	14	15	16	17	18	19	20	21	22	23	24	25
OREGON—Cont'd														
Lake Oswego	4.9	19.8	6.1	9.9	16.9	20.6	10.4	5.7	5.7	51.9	30 576	35 278	15.4	2.3
McMinnville	7.6	18.7	14.7	13.6	13.3	11.2	6.7	6.2	8.0	51.6	17 894	26 499	48.1	7.6
Medford	7.0	18.8	8.6	12.8	14.5	13.5	8.3	7.2	9.4	52.1	47 021	63 154	34.3	5.5
Oregon City	8.4	18.6	10.3	16.5	16.1	13.3	7.1	4.5	5.3	50.8	14 698	25 754	75.2	10.3
Portland	6.1	15.0	10.3	18.3	16.4	14.8	7.6	5.3	6.2	50.6	485 975	529 121	14.1	1.8
Salem	7.4	18.0	11.4	15.1	15.0	13.3	7.3	5.5	6.9	49.8	107 793	136 924	27.0	4.4
Springfield	8.2	19.0	11.1	15.9	15.5	12.7	7.2	4.9	5.4	51.1	44 664	52 864	18.4	3.6
Tigard	7.7	17.8	9.0	16.3	17.7	14.2	7.2	4.5	5.6	51.0	29 435	41 223	40.0	10.5
PENNSYLVANIA	5.9	17.9	8.9	12.7	15.9	13.9	9.2	7.9	7.7	51.7	11 882 842	12 281 054	3.4	0.7
Allentown	7.1	17.6	11.2	14.8	15.0	11.6	7.5	7.1	8.0	52.1	105 301	106 632	1.3	-0.6
Altoona	6.3	16.6	10.9	12.7	14.6	13.1	8.9	8.2	8.6	53.1	51 881	49 523	-4.5	-3.1
Bethel Park Borough	5.3	18.4	5.0	9.9	16.8	15.6	10.9	9.6	8.5	52.1	33 823	33 556	-0.8	-1.9
Bethlehem	5.4	15.5	14.4	12.9	13.7	12.0	8.1	8.1	9.8	52.2	71 427	71 329	-0.1	-0.3
Chester	8.4	21.4	13.0	12.9	14.0	11.3	7.3	6.0	5.8	52.9	41 856	36 854	-12.0	0.4
Easton	6.2	17.1	16.3	15.0	14.9	11.6	7.0	5.8	6.2	50.7	26 276	26 263	0.0	-0.3
Erie	7.2	18.2	11.6	14.3	14.2	11.7	7.5	7.1	8.2	52.4	108 718	103 717	-4.6	-2.3
Harrisburg	8.1	20.1	9.2	15.5	15.4	13.2	7.6	5.7	5.1	53.0	52 376	48 950	-6.5	-1.3
Lancaster	7.9	19.6	13.9	15.6	14.8	11.0	6.7	5.3	5.2	51.2	55 551	56 348	1.4	-1.8
Monroeville Borough	4.9	15.4	6.2	12.1	15.3	15.4	10.5	10.0	10.3	53.0	29 169	29 349	0.6	-2.2
New Castle	6.7	17.1	8.1	12.5	13.6	12.4	8.9	9.2	11.5	52.4	28 334	26 309	-7.1	-3.7
Norristown	6.9	18.2	10.5	16.5	16.1	12.0	8.1	6.2	5.6	51.3	30 754	31 282	1.7	-0.7
Philadelphia	6.5	18.8	11.1	14.8	14.5	12.0	8.3	7.1	7.0	53.5	1 585 577	1 517 550	-4.3	-2.5
Pittsburgh	5.3	14.6	14.8	14.6	14.0	12.3	8.0	7.9	8.5	52.4	369 879	334 563	-9.5	-2.8
Plum Borough	6.3	18.5	6.1	13.4	17.6	14.4	10.4	7.1	6.0	51.2	25 609	26 940	5.2	-0.5
Reading	8.7	21.3	11.7	15.1	13.9	10.3	6.8	6.1	6.3	51.7	78 380	81 207	3.6	-1.1
Scranton	5.3	15.5	12.3	11.8	13.8	12.5	8.7	9.0	11.1	53.5	81 805	76 415	-6.6	-2.7
State College Borough	1.8	3.9	65.5	11.3	4.9	4.1	2.6	2.5	3.3	47.9	38 981	38 420	-1.4	3.4
Wilkes-Barre	4.9	15.0	12.6	12.3	13.8	12.1	8.7	9.5	11.1	51.8	47 523	43 123	-9.3	-3.5
Williamsport	6.0	16.5	18.0	12.7	13.9	11.9	7.4	6.4	7.0	50.6	31 933	30 706	-3.8	-2.7
York	8.0	20.4	11.4	15.5	14.6	11.6	7.5	5.5	5.4	51.8	42 192	40 862	-3.2	-1.9
RHODE ISLAND	6.1	17.5	10.2	13.4	16.2	13.5	8.5	7.0	7.5	52.0	1 003 464	1 048 319	4.5	2.7
Cranston	5.3	16.3	7.7	14.0	17.4	13.7	8.3	8.0	9.3	51.1	76 060	79 269	4.2	3.0
East Providence	5.4	16.3	7.4	13.4	16.0	13.2	9.4	8.8	10.1	53.5	50 380	48 688	-3.4	2.5
Newport	5.8	13.9	14.6	16.0	15.6	13.1	8.2	6.2	6.7	51.8	28 227	26 475	-6.2	-1.3
Pawtucket	6.7	18.1	9.1	15.3	16.0	12.0	7.9	7.2	7.7	52.6	72 644	72 958	0.4	1.9
Providence	7.3	18.8	18.9	15.6	13.0	10.0	6.0	4.9	5.6	52.2	160 728	173 618	8.0	1.6
Warwick	5.4	16.5	6.7	12.8	17.3	14.8	9.5	8.3	8.7	52.4	85 427	85 808	0.4	1.8
Woonsocket	7.6	18.2	9.2	15.3	14.7	12.0	7.7	7.0	8.2	52.3	43 877	43 224	-1.5	3.3
SOUTH CAROLINA	6.6	18.6	10.2	14.0	15.6	13.7	9.3	6.7	5.4	51.4	3 486 310	4 012 012	15.1	3.4
Aiken	5.8	17.4	9.4	11.3	14.2	14.2	9.8	8.7	9.2	53.4	20 386	25 337	24.3	4.4
Anderson	6.7	15.5	10.7	13.2	13.1	12.1	8.3	8.8	11.7	54.8	26 385	25 514	-3.3	0.2
Charleston	5.4	14.6	17.2	15.2	13.6	12.4	8.1	6.7	6.8	52.7	88 256	96 650	20.9	4.5
Columbia	5.6	14.5	22.9	16.8	13.3	10.6	6.0	5.0	5.3	51.0	110 734	116 278	5.0	0.9
Florence	6.4	18.6	8.7	13.6	14.6	14.2	8.9	7.4	7.7	54.7	29 913	30 248	1.1	0.1
Goose Creek	8.6	21.0	18.2	16.2	16.2	9.8	5.6	2.8	1.4	46.4	24 692	29 208	18.3	4.7
Greenville	5.6	14.3	13.8	16.8	14.5	12.5	7.9	6.4	8.0	52.7	58 256	56 002	-3.9	-0.1
Hilton Head Island	4.4	12.9	6.9	11.8	12.8	13.4	13.9	14.0	10.1	50.0	23 694	33 862	42.9	1.6
Mount Pleasant	7.5	17.6	6.5	16.7	18.6	14.8	8.0	5.3	5.0	52.1	30 108	47 609	58.1	15.1
North Charleston	8.0	19.8	13.4	16.8	15.2	10.9	6.8	5.0	4.0	50.5	70 304	79 641	13.3	2.4
Rock Hill	7.0	18.0	14.8	16.2	14.2	11.5	6.9	5.1	6.2	54.2	42 112	49 765	19.6	12.8
Spartanburg	6.5	18.7	12.2	13.0	13.6	12.5	8.0	7.1	8.4	55.7	43 479	39 673	-8.8	-2.4
Summerville	7.0	21.8	7.8	14.6	16.6	14.2	7.5	5.4	5.2	52.6	22 519	27 752	23.2	14.3
Sumter	8.1	19.7	12.5	13.9	14.3	10.8	7.1	6.4	7.2	52.8	40 977	39 643	-3.3	0.4
SOUTH DAKOTA	6.8	20.1	10.3	12.1	15.3	12.9	8.3	7.0	7.3	50.4	696 004	754 844	8.5	1.3
Rapid City	7.0	18.3	11.8	13.2	15.5	13.0	7.9	6.7	6.5	51.0	54 523	59 607	9.3	2.1
Sioux Falls	7.3	17.9	11.8	16.0	16.3	12.5	7.1	5.6	5.5	50.7	100 836	123 975	22.9	8.0
TENNESSEE	6.6	18.0	9.6	14.3	15.9	13.8	9.4	6.7	5.6	51.3	4 877 203	5 689 283	16.7	2.7
Bartlett	6.6	22.4	6.8	11.1	18.9	16.9	8.6	5.2	3.4	51.2	27 038	40 543	50.2	4.2
Chattanooga	6.1	16.3	10.8	14.3	14.5	13.6	9.1	7.8	7.4	52.8	152 393	155 554	2.1	-0.4
Clarksville	9.0	19.8	13.6	19.0	15.7	9.8	5.8	4.2	3.1	49.8	75 542	103 455	37.0	4.3
Cleveland	6.5	15.5	15.4	13.9	13.6	11.9	9.3	7.2	6.7	52.8	32 236	37 192	15.4	0.5
Collierville	7.6	25.8	5.8	10.4	22.0	15.7	6.6	3.7	2.3	50.6	14 501	31 872	119.8	11.2
Columbia	7.5	18.3	9.8	13.3	15.3	12.8	8.2	7.4	7.4	52.6	28 583	33 055	15.6	0.8
Franklin	8.5	19.4	7.5	18.7	19.4	13.1	6.1	3.7	3.7	51.7	20 098	41 842	108.2	11.2
Germantown	5.2	22.8	5.8	6.6	16.9	21.7	11.7	5.7	3.5	51.3	33 159	37 348	13.1	0.5

Table D. Cities — Group Quarters, Crime, and Education

City	Households, 2000					Persons in group quarters, 2000				Serious crimes known to police,[2] 2002				Education, 2000			
				Percent			Institutional			Total		Rate[2]		School enrollment[4]		Attainment[5] (percent)	
	Number	Percent change, 1990–2000	Persons per house-hold	Female family house-holder[1]	One-person	Total	Total	Persons in nursing homes	Non-institu-tional	Number	Rate[3]	Violent	Property	Public	Private	High school grad-uate or less	Bach-elor's degree or more
	26	27	28	29	30	31	32	33	34	35	36	37	38	39	40	41	42
OREGON—Cont'd																	
Lake Oswego	14 769	18.3	2.38	6.9	27.9	163	76	0	87	824	2 269	91	2 178	7 981	1 890	10.4	62.0
McMinnville	9 367	41.8	2.66	10.8	23.9	1 602	572	327	1 030	1 164	4 268	194	4 073	5 254	2 125	49.1	20.8
Medford	25 093	33.0	2.47	11.7	27.7	1 285	670	432	615	4 434	6 821	391	6 431	13 187	1 785	46.4	21.1
Oregon City	9 471	72.9	2.62	12.3	22.4	903	823	322	80	1 246	4 700	196	4 504	5 502	885	41.5	18.4
Portland	223 737	19.5	2.30	10.8	34.6	14 992	5 454	2 569	9 538	43 327	7 956	828	7 127	102 372	26 495	36.6	32.6
Salem	50 676	23.8	2.53	11.6	28.3	8 884	6 360	1 063	2 524	12 389	8 791	244	8 547	28 119	6 390	42.4	24.1
Springfield	20 514	17.6	2.55	14.3	25.4	635	93	93	542	4 063	7 467	217	7 250	12 340	1 128	50.3	13.8
Tigard	16 507	36.9	2.48	9.2	25.4	221	107	107	114	2 442	5 755	257	5 499	8 529	1 772	27.4	36.5
PENNSYLVANIA	4 777 003	6.3	2.48	11.6	27.7	433 301	213 790	114 113	219 511	350 446	2 841	402	2 439	2 398 189	737 745	56.2	22.4
Allentown	42 032	-1.7	2.42	15.1	33.1	4 996	2 260	880	2 736	5 944	5 550	574	4 976	20 874	6 499	63.8	15.4
Altoona	20 059	-3.0	2.37	13.8	31.6	1 930	439	390	1 491	2 058	4 137	356	3 782	10 647	1 618	67.9	12.1
Bethel Park Borough	13 362	5.3	2.48	7.2	26.1	382	271	263	111	388	1 151	71	1 080	6 458	1 779	36.4	37.8
Bethlehem	28 116	3.1	2.34	12.8	32.3	5 652	1 275	1 003	4 377	2 418	3 375	342	3 033	11 717	8 925	54.8	23.8
Chester	12 814	-11.9	2.64	32.1	31.2	2 977	1 364	387	1 613	1 874	5 063	1 829	3 234	9 072	2 322	71.2	8.5
Easton	9 544	1.6	2.46	16.6	31.6	2 760	927	306	1 833	1 193	4 523	823	3 700	5 220	2 741	64.8	14.9
Erie	40 938	-2.8	2.39	16.8	33.4	5 854	2 356	1 160	3 498	3 560	3 417	432	2 985	17 318	10 766	61.7	17.4
Harrisburg	20 561	-4.5	2.32	24.4	39.3	1 252	565	351	687	2 928	5 955	1 363	4 593	10 583	1 972	63.4	14.3
Lancaster	20 933	-1.2	2.52	19.0	33.1	3 690	1 666	596	2 024	3 725	6 582	843	5 739	12 446	3 228	69.5	14.0
Monroeville Borough	12 376	4.6	2.30	9.7	30.8	940	474	382	466	951	3 226	319	2 907	5 042	1 365	38.8	35.6
New Castle	10 727	-5.7	2.36	16.9	33.5	999	725	472	274	1 398	5 290	806	4 484	5 264	1 504	67.9	12.0
Norristown	12 028	-1.3	2.52	19.8	32.7	995	848	231	147	1 851	5 891	1 194	4 698	5 936	1 504	64.6	13.3
Philadelphia	590 071	-2.2	2.48	22.3	33.8	54 731	20 411	10 164	34 320	83 392	5 471	1 316	4 155	294 382	145 925	62.1	17.9
Pittsburgh	143 739	-6.3	2.17	16.5	39.4	22 814	8 191	2 580	14 623	19 737	5 762	1 108	4 654	67 057	31 821	51.5	26.2
Plum Borough	10 270	13.3	2.60	8.5	21.5	233	44	44	189	NA	NA	NA	NA	5 614	1 263	45.0	28.0
Reading	30 113	-4.1	2.63	20.2	31.7	2 125	261	222	1 864	6 218	7 623	1 333	6 291	18 789	3 821	75.0	8.6
Scranton	31 303	-4.1	2.29	13.8	36.7	4 876	1 560	883	3 316	2 549	3 321	289	3 032	12 194	7 916	63.5	15.6
State College Borough	12 024	9.9	2.30	3.4	33.5	10 725	198	198	10 527	925	1 786	87	1 699	27 827	1 129	14.1	69.2
Wilkes-Barre	17 961	-7.6	2.20	14.0	39.0	3 674	2 212	721	1 462	2 329	5 377	582	4 795	7 303	2 464	64.5	12.8
Williamsport	12 219	-2.9	2.30	15.5	35.1	2 597	514	150	2 083	1 473	4 776	415	4 361	6 737	1 920	59.9	16.3
York	16 137	-4.4	2.48	20.6	33.1	887	167	119	720	NA	NA	NA	NA	8 805	1 920	71.7	10.6
RHODE ISLAND	408 424	8.1	2.47	12.9	28.6	38 816	13 801	9 222	25 015	38 393	3 589	285	3 304	219 700	70 905	49.8	25.6
Cranston	30 954	5.5	2.41	12.5	29.4	4 659	4 051	242	608	2 632	3 254	182	3 072	15 326	2 456	49.9	24.6
East Providence	20 530	2.9	2.33	12.7	32.4	755	659	639	96	1 025	2 063	171	1 892	8 838	2 729	58.3	18.0
Newport	11 566	3.3	2.11	13.6	39.4	2 082	245	245	1 837	1 576	5 834	526	5 309	4 496	2 729	34.3	41.5
Pawtucket	30 047	1.1	2.41	16.8	32.3	657	422	422	235	3 209	4 310	349	3 961	15 022	3 776	63.8	14.3
Providence	62 389	5.9	2.56	20.5	32.3	13 648	1 491	1 375	12 157	13 864	7 826	735	7 091	39 644	23 940	57.3	24.4
Warwick	35 517	6.2	2.39	10.2	29.8	991	650	634	341	2 931	3 347	147	3 200	16 600	4 186	47.2	24.5
Woonsocket	17 750	1.0	2.37	16.2	32.7	1 075	742	742	333	1 551	3 516	469	3 047	9 095	1 450	68.0	10.1
SOUTH CAROLINA	1 533 854	21.9	2.53	14.8	25.0	135 037	60 533	20 867	74 504	217 569	5 297	822	4 475	905 055	148 097	53.6	20.4
Aiken	10 287	32.8	2.34	13.7	29.6	1 263	754	534	509	1 335	5 147	386	4 761	5 518	1 036	37.0	38.1
Anderson	10 641	1.3	2.22	18.7	36.0	1 890	1 007	716	883	1 831	7 010	946	6 064	4 683	1 283	57.3	20.0
Charleston	40 791	32.6	2.23	15.2	30.7	5 510	455	438	5 055	7 038	7 113	873	6 240	32 977	6 086	37.9	35.7
Columbia	42 245	24.5	2.21	17.6	37.0	22 990	6 053	578	16 937	10 460	8 787	1 323	7 464	23 779	6 497	36.0	37.5
Florence	11 925	7.7	2.44	20.7	29.5	1 155	779	362	376	3 653	11 797	1 259	10 537	6 403	1 335	39.8	20.6
Goose Creek	8 947	21.0	2.94	10.6	12.9	2 893	28	28	2 865	855	2 859	268	2 592	7 017	1 335	48.4	26.4
Greenville	24 382	1.2	2.11	15.5	40.8	4 495	1 121	244	3 374	4 640	8 093	1 172	6 921	9 492	5 110	41.4	34.2
Hilton Head Island	14 408	39.3	2.32	6.2	23.8	442	234	200	208	NA	NA	NA	NA	4 163	1 568	25.7	45.9
Mount Pleasant	19 025	61.4	2.47	8.3	24.1	665	569	496	96	1 942	3 984	213	3 771	8 686	3 417	20.1	52.6
North Charleston	29 783	26.7	2.51	22.8	28.6	4 958	2 282	457	2 676	8 913	10 932	1 672	9 260	18 886	3 625	55.9	13.8
Rock Hill	18 750	27.8	2.49	18.3	27.5	3 118	721	670	2 397	3 647	7 159	1 076	6 083	13 647	1 549	49.1	24.3
Spartanburg	15 989	-4.3	2.33	23.0	34.0	2 428	409	295	2 019	4 772	11 749	1 989	9 760	6 823	1 284	51.4	26.0
Summerville	10 391	28.2	2.61	14.0	23.0	608	266	266	342	1 515	5 332	707	4 625	9 785	2 150	41.1	26.7
Sumter	14 564	14.3	2.57	19.3	27.3	2 221	322	322	1 899	3 632	8 950	1 343	7 607	9 785	2 150	47.6	22.5
SOUTH DAKOTA	290 245	12.0	2.50	9.0	27.6	28 418	14 387	7 791	14 031	17 342	2 279	177	2 101	184 458	23 771	48.3	21.5
Rapid City	23 969	13.3	2.39	12.6	29.4	2 233	841	511	1 392	2 930	4 875	356	4 519	14 178	1 923	40.1	26.7
Sioux Falls	49 731	25.0	2.40	10.0	29.8	4 802	2 746	952	2 056	4 189	3 351	317	3 034	24 834	7 207	40.5	27.8
TENNESSEE	2 232 905	20.5	2.48	12.9	25.8	147 946	83 397	36 994	64 549	290 961	5 019	717	4 302	1 203 685	211 420	55.7	19.6
Bartlett	13 773	62.9	2.92	8.7	12.1	327	313	150	14	918	2 222	126	2 096	9 467	2 435	34.4	28.2
Chattanooga	65 499	5.3	2.29	17.3	33.5	5 826	2 763	1 225	3 063	15 911	10 038	1 517	8 521	31 885	6 793	49.5	21.5
Clarksville	36 969	45.3	2.69	13.1	21.1	4 080	897	534	3 183	6 069	5 757	613	5 144	27 313	2 923	43.4	19.8
Cleveland	15 037	25.4	2.33	13.0	30.4	2 151	646	478	1 505	2 382	6 285	715	5 570	7 221	3 205	49.1	22.3
Collierville	10 368	134.1	3.06	8.0	11.8	107	107	107	0	652	2 008	176	1 832	8 720	1 877	25.7	41.2
Columbia	13 059	15.9	2.46	16.3	27.8	928	863	653	65	2 408	7 149	1 036	6 113	6 519	1 329	58.4	15.1
Franklin	16 128	106.0	2.55	10.8	25.0	717	526	189	191	1 144	2 683	183	2 500	8 645	2 153	29.5	42.3
Germantown	13 220	23.4	2.82	6.1	14.6	34	29	29	5	865	2 273	87	2 186	7 729	3 708	13.0	60.0

1. No spouse present.   2. Data for serious crimes have not been adjusted for underreporting. This may affect comparability between geographic areas and over time.   3. Per 100,000 population estimated by the FBI.   4. All persons 3 years old and over enrolled in nursery school through college.   5. Persons 25 years old and over.

Table D. Cities — Income, Poverty, and Housing

City	Money income, 1999							Housing units, 2000					
	Households				Percent below poverty					Vacant units			
	Median income				Persons		Families						
	Per capita income[1] (dollars)	Dollars	Percent change, 1989–1999 (constant 1999 dollars)	Percent with income of $100,000 or more	Total	Percent change in rate, 1989–1999	Total	Total	Percent change, 1990–2000	Vacant units for sale or rent[2]	For seasonal use (percent)	Home owner vacancy rate	Renter vacancy rate
	43	44	45	46	47	48	49	50	51	52	53	54	55
OREGON—Cont'd													
Lake Oswego	42 166	71 597	3.5	35.2	3.4	-8.1	2.3	15 741	20.1	972	0.8	3.0	7.8
McMinnville	17 085	38 953	12.0	6.4	12.9	0.0	8.2	9 834	45.1	467	0.2	1.8	6.0
Medford	20 170	36 481	5.7	8.2	13.9	-3.5	10.3	26 297	33.6	1 204	0.3	1.8	4.9
Oregon City	19 870	45 531	18.1	7.8	8.9	-3.3	6.5	10 110	78.1	639	0.2	3.4	7.7
Portland	22 643	40 146	16.8	10.2	13.1	-9.7	8.5	237 307	19.6	13 570	0.4	2.3	6.2
Salem	19 141	38 881	14.7	8.0	15.0	3.4	10.5	53 817	26.3	3 141	0.3	2.5	7.0
Springfield	15 616	33 031	12.1	4.0	17.9	8.5	14.8	21 500	18.6	986	0.3	2.1	4.3
Tigard	25 110	51 581	7.6	15.8	6.6	37.5	5.0	17 369	37.9	862	0.3	1.9	6.9
PENNSYLVANIA	20 880	40 106	2.7	10.3	11.0	-0.9	7.8	5 249 750	6.3	472 747	2.8	1.6	7.2
Allentown	16 282	32 016	-8.3	4.9	18.5	43.4	14.6	45 960	0.7	3 928	0.3	2.6	8.4
Altoona	15 213	28 248	1.6	3.4	17.7	-1.7	12.9	21 681	-4.5	1 622	0.1	1.4	9.7
Bethel Park Borough	25 867	53 791	-2.7	15.8	3.7	-2.6	2.5	13 871	6.7	509	0.4	1.4	6.0
Bethlehem	18 987	35 815	-6.1	7.4	15.0	15.4	11.1	29 631	4.0	1 515	0.3	1.7	6.0
Chester	13 052	25 703	-8.3	4.2	27.2	7.9	22.8	14 976	-9.3	2 162	0.2	3.2	5.2
Easton	15 949	33 162	-6.4	4.3	16.0	16.8	12.3	10 545	2.3	1 001	0.2	4.6	7.4
Erie	14 972	28 387	-4.1	3.1	18.8	-2.6	13.8	44 971	-1.0	4 033	0.3	2.1	9.6
Harrisburg	15 787	26 920	-1.4	4.3	24.6	-8.9	23.4	24 314	-1.1	3 753	0.8	5.4	12.0
Lancaster	13 955	29 770	-0.2	3.2	21.2	1.4	17.9	23 024	2.5	2 091	0.2	4.3	8.5
Monroeville Borough	24 031	44 653	-8.7	12.4	6.6	53.5	4.9	13 159	4.1	783	0.5	0.9	11.2
New Castle	13 730	25 598	11.4	3.1	20.8	5.6	17.1	11 709	-6.0	982	0.2	2.5	9.3
Norristown	17 977	35 714	-7.2	6.0	17.2	81.1	13.5	13 531	3.4	1 503	0.2	4.6	10.1
Philadelphia	16 509	30 746	-7.0	6.3	22.9	12.8	18.4	661 958	-1.9	71 887	0.3	1.9	7.0
Pittsburgh	18 816	28 588	2.6	7.0	20.4	-4.7	15.0	163 366	-4.0	19 627	0.5	2.8	8.8
Plum Borough	20 863	48 386	-2.1	9.9	5.3	23.3	4.0	10 624	14.4	354	0.2	0.8	5.9
Reading	13 086	26 698	-10.1	3.4	26.1	34.5	22.3	34 314	0.1	4 201	0.2	4.9	9.1
Scranton	16 174	28 805	1.8	4.1	15.0	-1.3	10.7	35 336	0.1	4 033	0.3	2.8	10.1
State College Borough	12 155	21 186	-13.6	6.7	46.9	3.3	9.7	12 488	7.4	464	0.7	0.8	2.9
Wilkes-Barre	15 050	26 711	1.8	3.3	17.8	15.6	12.1	20 294	-2.1	2 333	0.3	2.8	11.9
Williamsport	14 707	25 946	-4.8	4.5	21.5	1.9	13.7	13 524	1.5	1 305	0.2	2.9	8.7
York	13 439	26 475	-9.7	2.0	23.8	17.2	20.0	18 534	0.7	2 397	0.1	4.1	12.8
RHODE ISLAND	21 688	42 090	-2.7	11.5	11.9	24.0	8.9	439 837	6.1	31 413	3.0	1.0	5.0
Cranston	21 978	44 108	-4.9	11.2	7.3	12.3	5.6	32 068	5.1	1 114	0.3	0.9	4.1
East Providence	19 527	39 108	-6.1	6.3	8.6	26.5	6.3	21 309	2.4	779	0.3	0.7	3.5
Newport	25 441	40 669	-0.9	12.5	14.4	15.2	12.9	13 226	1.0	1 660	6.5	1.5	6.7
Pawtucket	17 008	31 775	-10.9	5.1	16.8	58.5	14.9	31 819	0.6	1 772	0.2	1.1	5.5
Providence	15 525	26 867	-9.7	7.0	29.1	26.5	23.9	67 915	1.7	5 526	0.5	2.3	6.1
Warwick	23 410	46 483	-3.3	10.3	5.9	22.9	4.2	37 085	5.5	1 568	1.3	1.1	3.9
Woonsocket	16 223	30 819	-9.6	4.4	19.4	39.6	16.7	18 757	0.1	1 007	0.2	0.9	5.1
SOUTH CAROLINA	18 795	37 082	5.1	8.1	14.1	-8.4	10.7	1 753 670	23.1	219 816	4.0	1.9	12.0
Aiken	23 172	44 172	-1.2	14.3	14.4	-8.3	10.1	11 373	33.1	1 086	1.0	3.1	10.6
Anderson	18 577	27 716	6.2	6.4	20.8	4.5	15.4	12 068	4.9	1 427	0.3	3.4	13.5
Charleston	22 414	35 295	4.4	11.3	19.1	-11.6	13.3	44 563	29.8	3 772	1.1	1.8	6.5
Columbia	18 853	31 141	-0.2	9.5	22.1	4.2	17.0	46 142	25.0	3 897	0.5	2.2	7.7
Florence	20 336	35 388	5.8	9.9	19.3	-11.5	15.3	13 090	11.0	1 165	0.4	2.1	9.4
Goose Creek	16 905	45 919	13.9	7.5	6.8	-24.4	5.8	9 482	23.4	535	0.1	1.5	3.2
Greenville	23 242	33 144	2.9	11.6	16.1	-9.0	12.2	27 295	3.2	2 913	0.7	2.4	10.9
Hilton Head Island	36 621	60 438	4.6	25.3	7.3	4.3	4.7	24 647	14.6	10 239	29.9	1.5	40.6
Mount Pleasant	30 823	61 054	17.7	21.8	5.0	-13.8	3.2	20 197	62.3	1 172	0.8	1.5	8.7
North Charleston	14 361	29 307	0.0	3.3	23.2	6.9	19.9	33 631	26.4	3 848	0.3	2.1	10.6
Rock Hill	18 929	37 336	4.4	8.2	14.0	-14.6	9.7	20 287	29.4	1 537	0.3	3.1	7.8
Spartanburg	18 136	28 735	-4.6	7.0	23.3	6.9	19.4	17 696	-1.4	1 707	0.3	3.0	9.6
Summerville	20 103	43 635	3.3	9.9	9.2	-6.1	6.1	11 087	25.5	696	0.4	1.7	6.8
Sumter	16 949	31 590	10.8	7.5	16.6	-19.8	13.0	16 032	17.5	1 468	0.4	2.2	8.2
SOUTH DAKOTA	17 562	35 282	16.7	5.9	13.2	-17.0	9.3	323 208	10.5	32 963	3.0	1.8	8.0
Rapid City	19 445	35 978	4.0	7.1	12.7	-6.6	9.4	25 096	11.4	1 127	0.4	0.9	5.7
Sioux Falls	21 374	41 221	12.4	9.1	8.4	-1.2	5.6	51 680	24.3	1 949	0.2	1.0	5.2
TENNESSEE	19 393	36 360	9.1	8.3	13.5	-14.0	10.3	2 439 443	20.4	206 538	1.5	2.0	8.8
Bartlett	24 616	66 369	4.3	17.3	2.7	17.4	2.1	14 021	59.2	248	0.1	1.0	4.2
Chattanooga	19 689	32 006	7.3	7.6	17.9	-1.6	14.0	72 108	3.6	6 609	0.4	2.5	8.9
Clarksville	16 686	37 548	10.3	5.7	10.6	-20.3	8.4	40 041	44.9	3 072	0.2	3.0	7.3
Cleveland	18 316	30 098	-2.1	6.7	16.1	-7.5	11.3	16 431	25.9	1 394	0.3	2.2	9.8
Collierville	30 252	80 575	26.2	35.5	2.4	-63.6	1.9	10 770	133.5	402	0.2	2.1	4.7
Columbia	18 004	35 879	5.8	7.4	13.9	-2.8	10.9	14 322	18.0	1 263	0.6	2.6	11.5
Franklin	27 276	56 431	29.8	20.7	6.7	-6.9	5.1	17 296	97.7	1 168	0.3	3.7	6.2
Germantown	44 021	94 609	2.0	46.8	2.1	90.9	1.6	13 676	22.9	456	0.4	1.2	10.3

1. Based on population enumerated as of April 1, 2000. 2. Includes units rented or sold but not occupied.

Table D. Cities — Housing, Labor Force, Employment, and Disability

City	Housing units, 2000 (cont'd) — Occupied units					Civilian labor force, 2003		Unemployment		Civilian employment,[2] 2000	Percent		Disability, 2000
	Total	Percent owner occupied	Percent renter occupied	Average size owner occupied	Average size renter occupied	Total	Percent change, 2002–2003	Total	Rate[1]	Total	Management, professional, and related occupations	Production, transportation, and material moving occupations	Employment disabled persons[3] (percent)
	56	57	58	59	60	61	62	63	64	65	66	67	68
OREGON—Cont'd													
Lake Oswego	14 769	70.6	29.4	2.58	1.89	22 202	-0.1	1 173	5.3	18 305	57.3	4.3	5.1
McMinnville	9 367	60.4	39.6	2.71	2.58	11 820	0.4	968	8.2	11 437	25.3	19.0	10.9
Medford	25 093	57.3	42.7	2.52	2.39	32 361	3.4	2 246	6.9	28 067	29.2	13.8	11.2
Oregon City	9 471	59.8	40.2	2.74	2.45	9 864	0.0	592	6.0	12 830	28.3	14.4	10.2
Portland	223 737	55.8	44.2	2.47	2.08	283 480	-0.1	26 909	9.5	276 081	37.2	14.0	11.0
Salem	50 676	57.1	42.9	2.59	2.44	69 402	2.0	5 535	8.0	60 661	32.6	13.2	11.7
Springfield	20 514	53.6	46.4	2.57	2.52	27 068	1.4	2 366	8.7	24 855	21.5	20.7	11.5
Tigard	16 507	58.3	41.7	2.66	2.24	26 255	0.0	1 868	7.1	21 893	38.3	11.1	7.9
PENNSYLVANIA	4 777 003	71.3	28.7	2.62	2.12	6 170 013	-1.8	343 884	5.6	5 653 500	32.6	16.3	10.6
Allentown	42 032	53.0	47.0	2.55	2.26	57 719	5.3	3 628	6.3	46 100	24.8	21.3	14.1
Altoona	20 059	65.9	34.1	2.51	2.11	23 848	-1.7	1 241	5.2	21 218	24.3	16.8	13.9
Bethel Park Borough	13 362	79.9	20.1	2.69	1.66	18 739	-2.2	762	4.1	16 319	45.5	7.1	7.8
Bethlehem	28 116	58.1	41.9	2.44	2.19	34 800	0.7	1 896	5.4	31 580	33.0	15.7	10.5
Chester	12 814	47.7	52.3	2.69	2.60	15 347	-1.2	1 399	9.1	13 238	21.9	16.7	14.3
Easton	9 544	48.5	51.5	2.67	2.27	12 118	-1.5	580	4.8	11 599	24.5	23.3	10.2
Erie	40 938	56.2	43.8	2.51	2.24	48 808	-3.1	3 687	7.6	44 729	25.1	20.5	12.3
Harrisburg	20 561	42.3	57.7	2.44	2.23	24 263	-1.7	1 542	6.4	20 991	25.0	18.1	15.7
Lancaster	20 933	46.6	53.4	2.58	2.46	27 066	-1.7	1 716	6.3	24 654	21.4	27.2	15.1
Monroeville Borough	12 376	69.7	30.3	2.52	1.78	18 127	-2.5	652	3.6	14 273	42.7	8.0	7.9
New Castle	10 727	64.6	35.4	2.47	2.15	10 009	-1.6	942	9.4	9 925	24.6	18.2	13.7
Norristown	12 028	48.1	51.9	2.70	2.35	16 751	-1.8	1 025	6.1	14 892	23.8	15.5	12.9
Philadelphia	590 071	59.3	40.7	2.65	2.23	666 933	-1.4	50 903	7.6	584 957	31.5	12.5	15.8
Pittsburgh	143 739	52.1	47.9	2.37	1.95	158 080	-2.3	8 627	5.5	144 768	36.9	9.3	11.4
Plum Borough	10 270	79.8	20.2	2.74	2.03	16 317	-2.0	703	4.3	13 323	36.9	10.7	7.5
Reading	30 113	51.0	49.0	2.74	2.51	35 215	-3.8	3 177	9.0	31 299	17.7	29.7	16.0
Scranton	31 303	54.5	45.5	2.49	2.04	35 363	-1.7	1 969	5.6	32 782	25.0	18.2	13.5
State College Borough	12 024	22.8	77.2	2.32	2.30	15 817	-2.9	234	1.5	16 504	48.1	4.1	2.1
Wilkes-Barre	17 961	53.5	46.5	2.41	1.95	20 423	-1.4	1 319	6.5	17 810	24.1	18.2	14.5
Williamsport	12 219	44.8	55.2	2.47	2.16	13 388	-2.2	986	7.4	13 094	23.7	21.2	14.0
York	16 137	46.8	53.2	2.51	2.45	18 156	-2.4	1 480	8.2	17 747	19.0	29.1	16.3
RHODE ISLAND	408 424	60.0	40.0	2.66	2.19	572 956	3.6	30 158	5.3	500 731	33.9	15.2	12.7
Cranston	30 954	66.9	33.1	2.64	1.96	42 259	3.7	2 170	5.1	37 148	35.0	13.4	13.2
East Providence	20 530	58.9	41.1	2.63	1.92	27 077	3.0	1 503	5.6	23 117	28.4	17.7	14.5
Newport	11 566	41.9	58.1	2.22	2.03	14 638	4.4	648	4.4	12 648	39.0	8.2	9.2
Pawtucket	30 047	44.4	55.6	2.59	2.26	40 818	3.6	2 618	6.4	33 192	23.2	26.0	18.3
Providence	62 389	34.6	65.4	2.71	2.49	83 395	3.6	5 313	6.4	69 570	32.9	20.2	14.2
Warwick	35 517	72.7	27.3	2.58	1.87	48 289	3.5	2 311	4.8	44 058	33.6	13.1	11.3
Woonsocket	17 750	35.0	65.0	2.66	2.22	22 035	3.4	1 535	7.0	19 315	20.4	24.7	17.5
SOUTH CAROLINA	1 533 854	72.2	27.8	2.59	2.37	2 002 520	3.0	136 297	6.8	1 824 700	29.1	19.0	14.3
Aiken	10 287	66.1	33.9	2.42	2.19	10 238	4.3	545	5.3	11 083	45.9	13.8	10.1
Anderson	10 641	53.4	46.6	2.27	2.16	14 260	3.4	1 429	10.0	10 109	29.1	19.7	17.8
Charleston	40 791	51.1	48.9	2.43	2.03	47 143	3.5	2 205	4.7	45 266	40.5	7.3	10.4
Columbia	42 245	45.6	54.4	2.29	2.14	49 786	2.4	3 134	6.3	48 133	41.0	8.8	11.5
Florence	11 925	61.4	38.6	2.52	2.32	16 219	3.0	1 569	9.7	13 273	37.4	13.4	14.8
Goose Creek	8 947	63.5	36.5	2.89	3.03	10 029	3.8	373	3.7	11 220	31.7	13.2	13.2
Greenville	24 382	47.0	53.0	2.21	2.03	35 903	2.9	2 094	5.8	28 379	37.8	12.6	10.8
Hilton Head Island	14 408	77.7	22.3	2.21	2.70	19 998	6.6	340	1.7	15 245	34.3	5.1	11.2
Mount Pleasant	19 025	74.0	26.0	2.61	2.05	20 483	3.2	360	1.8	24 704	50.9	5.5	8.6
North Charleston	29 783	46.4	53.6	2.52	2.50	33 178	3.7	2 021	6.1	31 788	21.1	16.0	18.2
Rock Hill	18 750	53.4	46.6	2.57	2.39	28 616	4.4	3 239	11.3	23 764	30.1	18.7	15.1
Spartanburg	15 989	49.8	50.2	2.40	2.26	23 337	3.1	2 294	9.8	16 400	32.3	19.2	16.1
Summerville	10 391	65.7	34.3	2.81	2.23	14 081	3.7	579	4.1	13 217	36.3	13.9	12.5
Sumter	14 564	53.1	46.9	2.58	2.55	15 605	4.1	1 313	8.4	14 281	31.5	19.2	14.6
SOUTH DAKOTA	290 245	68.2	31.8	2.64	2.22	424 876	1.4	15 270	3.6	374 373	32.6	14.2	9.4
Rapid City	23 969	59.3	40.7	2.53	2.20	34 786	1.6	1 138	3.3	29 586	32.8	11.5	9.9
Sioux Falls	49 731	61.1	38.9	2.65	2.00	80 027	1.8	2 541	3.2	69 520	31.1	14.4	9.8
TENNESSEE	2 232 905	69.9	30.1	2.57	2.29	2 909 445	-0.6	168 954	5.8	2 651 638	29.5	19.9	13.2
Bartlett	13 773	92.2	7.8	2.93	2.81	16 406	-1.4	350	2.1	21 313	39.4	8.5	8.7
Chattanooga	65 499	54.9	45.1	2.40	2.15	79 176	-1.9	3 890	4.9	70 505	31.4	18.1	14.4
Clarksville	36 969	57.5	42.5	2.79	2.55	45 000	-0.8	2 376	5.3	40 450	27.3	19.3	12.4
Cleveland	15 037	51.8	48.2	2.48	2.17	16 793	-0.8	1 023	6.1	17 308	30.5	22.6	12.3
Collierville	10 368	86.4	13.6	3.15	2.51	8 113	-1.3	189	2.3	15 824	43.8	10.2	5.0
Columbia	13 059	63.5	36.5	2.50	2.38	19 500	-1.2	1 322	6.8	15 673	23.7	24.8	11.3
Franklin	16 128	63.5	36.5	2.78	2.15	19 153	-1.1	657	3.4	22 335	44.8	8.9	7.4
Germantown	13 220	89.0	11.0	2.89	2.25	19 225	-1.4	385	2.0	18 954	52.8	6.0	5.2

1. Percent of civilian labor force.   2. Persons 16 years old and over.   3. Persons 16 to 64 years old.

Table D. Cities — Construction, Wholesale Trade, and Retail Trade

City	Value of residential construction authorized by building permits, 2003			Wholesale trade, 1997				Retail trade,[1] 1997			
	New construction ($1,000)	Number of housing units	Percent single family	Number of establishments	Number of employees	Sales (mil dol)	Annual payroll (mil dol)	Number of establishments	Number of employees	Sales (mil dol)	Annual payroll (mil dol)
	69	70	71	72	73	74	75	76	77	78	79
OREGON—Cont'd											
Lake Oswego	27 027	76	100.0	166	1 448	2 076.1	70.5	151	1 357	251.4	28.3
McMinnville	37 232	289	91.7	22	169	99.2	4.9	137	1 938	379.5	34.4
Medford	95 040	930	70.6	149	1 216	462.5	38.3	499	6 687	1 306.9	121.6
Oregon City	61 965	283	91.5	19	244	183.7	9.4	108	1 661	238.5	24.4
Portland	371 898	3 566	30.7	1 700	26 464	23 728.9	948.6	2 621	34 060	6 190.4	683.9
Salem	93 790	714	93.6	171	2 083	694.8	60.3	665	10 054	1 826.2	181.9
Springfield	43 322	324	71.6	53	642	242.0	15.7	248	3 141	504.6	47.6
Tigard	81 903	380	100.0	246	3 515	3 212.5	157.4	335	7 330	1 429.4	139.7
PENNSYLVANIA	6 051 793	47 356	81.4	17 138	237 567	159 354.2	8 588.2	50 208	650 144	109 948.5	10 561.9
Allentown	8 823	51	100.0	203	2 749	1 531.9	92.2	452	5 234	1 037.1	99.6
Altoona	868	13	61.5	85	2 011	1 090.2	61.7	326	5 126	814.4	71.5
Bethel Park Borough	18 955	81	100.0	56	483	157.2	15.7	122	2 087	335.8	31.4
Bethlehem	2 954	21	100.0	111	1 344	858.8	55.4	228	2 856	486.2	49.9
Chester	0	0	0.0	30	311	96.2	10.3	79	657	156.2	16.0
Easton	2 293	29	93.1	46	1 235	624.2	52.6	129	1 071	167.2	19.3
Erie	5 792	101	41.6	128	1 861	487.4	57.8	494	5 859	772.3	83.3
Harrisburg	2 602	38	100.0	91	3 726	2 544.3	110.2	229	2 977	591.3	57.6
Lancaster	1 503	21	100.0	97	953	420.9	29.4	311	4 582	750.2	82.5
Monroeville Borough	16 958	81	88.9	81	824	331.7	31.8	335	7 123	1 173.7	108.9
New Castle	942	14	100.0	51	515	231.5	14.3	176	2 650	379.3	38.8
Norristown	0	0	0.0	77	1 416	549.7	50.9	106	1 337	225.5	25.8
Philadelphia	133 705	1 754	7.3	1 403	22 298	12 004.0	848.4	4 782	51 398	8 118.2	887.1
Pittsburgh	34 256	209	50.7	742	12 740	12 543.4	517.2	1 544	19 790	2 734.1	311.3
Plum Borough	15 556	90	71.1	46	515	257.2	20.7	60	673	103.4	10.6
Reading	784	17	17.6	95	1 851	583.5	61.0	310	2 919	502.8	55.7
Scranton	6 019	54	100.0	130	1 835	464.3	44.8	473	6 503	902.8	91.5
State College Borough	2 385	22	54.5	29	384	69.0	10.0	271	3 665	424.5	43.2
Wilkes-Barre	216	4	100.0	77	1 379	417.8	35.9	319	5 659	894.0	80.8
Williamsport	2 794	11	100.0	58	1 181	238.7	28.8	175	2 081	321.0	34.4
York	135	3	100.0	98	1 612	549.1	48.1	190	1 861	338.4	38.8
RHODE ISLAND	338 012	2 286	85.2	1 590	18 762	7 602.7	635.2	4 169	45 747	7 505.8	752.1
Cranston	20 441	134	100.0	153	2 776	961.9	97.3	305	4 031	689.4	61.3
East Providence	3 354	44	72.7	128	1 981	966.3	75.6	189	2 134	393.1	39.2
Newport	4 341	16	100.0	31	119	89.5	4.3	247	1 442	200.5	21.3
Pawtucket	8 788	129	20.9	92	953	231.7	27.8	233	2 489	434.7	49.7
Providence	2 684	61	57.4	295	3 589	1 462.4	125.9	611	5 155	772.6	92.2
Warwick	10 828	118	68.6	206	1 924	782.6	66.6	519	8 920	1 446.6	137.5
Woonsocket	3 030	36	100.0	45	683	161.6	19.6	152	1 806	245.0	24.1
SOUTH CAROLINA	4 616 026	38 191	82.6	5 035	58 910	34 179.8	1 866.8	18 481	209 256	33 634.3	3 107.2
Aiken	30 479	274	99.3	42	261	82.4	6.3	259	3 137	424.3	41.1
Anderson	10 997	106	98.1	57	685	241.9	17.0	378	5 272	718.7	69.6
Charleston	136 857	1 724	58.2	111	1 064	455.5	34.9	793	9 394	1 351.2	137.8
Columbia	61 397	500	74.4	276	3 637	1 584.9	136.6	827	11 608	1 917.3	190.5
Florence	NA	NA	NA	93	D	D	D	415	5 954	926.9	89.6
Goose Creek	40 465	248	100.0	10	D	D	D	60	768	121.0	10.7
Greenville	25 506	230	76.5	288	3 975	6 613.6	162.4	812	12 028	2 011.1	186.8
Hilton Head Island	119 953	362	80.7	67	208	64.4	6.8	333	3 386	540.9	61.4
Mount Pleasant	157 406	938	99.1	52	178	161.2	7.5	234	2 625	357.2	38.0
North Charleston	109 222	1 425	60.6	203	3 211	2 237.3	107.6	507	7 214	1 341.4	125.7
Rock Hill	110 996	845	100.0	100	1 137	415.4	41.5	330	4 249	699.1	64.1
Spartanburg	1 022	7	100.0	105	D	D	D	440	6 349	1 017.1	96.4
Summerville	111 976	1 060	66.8	35	372	115.5	7.7	182	2 976	440.0	38.3
Sumter	NA	NA	NA	56	D	D	D	340	4 355	654.1	62.8
SOUTH DAKOTA	540 686	4 986	81.4	1 402	15 509	7 874.2	389.8	4 311	45 867	11 707.1	689.6
Rapid City	55 750	424	81.8	144	1 897	633.9	54.2	486	6 368	1 040.6	102.1
Sioux Falls	167 917	1 755	73.8	313	5 146	2 073.5	157.5	696	11 676	1 913.6	184.8
TENNESSEE	4 478 748	37 530	85.8	8 234	120 228	82 626.4	3 975.4	24 808	304 452	50 813.2	4 810.3
Bartlett	63 293	372	100.0	50	D	D	D	144	3 110	466.7	44.4
Chattanooga	90 652	753	80.5	602	8 378	3 688.8	255.1	1 150	16 191	2 707.0	268.0
Clarksville	91 166	1 576	62.6	86	D	D	D	485	6 674	1 143.3	105.4
Cleveland	24 123	238	58.8	73	2 213	1 616.1	47.1	355	3 937	721.6	63.9
Collierville	148 646	489	100.0	42	542	369.3	19.9	101	1 759	265.6	22.8
Columbia	20 129	231	57.6	43	556	205.2	16.1	247	3 119	528.0	51.7
Franklin	156 826	726	100.0	65	596	693.4	30.1	369	5 762	1 092.5	108.0
Germantown	NA	NA	NA	66	472	1 417.2	28.3	186	3 200	368.0	37.7

1. Establishments with payroll.

Table D. Cities — Real Estate, Professional Services, and Manufacturing

City	Real estate and rental and leasing, 1997				Professional, scientific, and technical services,[1] 1997				Manufacturing, 1997			
	Number of establishments	Number of employees	Receipts (mil dol)	Annual payroll (mil dol)	Number of establishments	Number of employees	Receipts (mil dol)	Annual payroll (mil dol)	Number of establishments	Number of employees	Receipts (mil dol)	Annual payroll (mil dol)
	80	81	82	83	84	85	86	87	88	89	90	91
OREGON—Cont'd												
Lake Oswego	105	880	100.6	22.4	253	1 559	185.0	74.1	54	1 083	127.8	36.3
McMinnville	40	167	20.2	2.8	54	242	18.9	7.0	51	2 318	491.4	66.9
Medford	117	640	60.7	10.3	212	1 377	76.5	26.4	74	2 007	344.8	61.9
Oregon City	38	107	9.9	1.6	79	250	23.0	8.1	31	964	200.2	36.8
Portland	945	7 255	926.8	189.9	2 478	22 439	2 245.3	931.2	1 144	39 059	7 385.1	1 310.6
Salem	225	1 232	136.8	29.0	395	2 357	178.2	70.4	224	7 085	1 226.0	211.4
Springfield	65	282	28.2	4.5	44	347	13.7	6.1	87	3 334	915.3	123.3
Tigard	110	667	117.5	19.8	247	2 528	234.0	108.3	110	3 706	566.4	125.5
PENNSYLVANIA	8 684	57 519	7 668.6	1 360.5	23 184	235 025	26 240.3	10 448.3	17 128	826 521	172 193.2	27 641.3
Allentown	115	645	80.2	12.0	258	1 624	136.1	54.9	238	8 310	4 060.0	325.0
Altoona	48	244	20.4	4.8	100	1 149	104.9	35.6	68	2 622	424.7	62.7
Bethel Park Borough	25	116	17.4	2.6	71	275	33.4	9.6	49	527	71.3	15.7
Bethlehem	52	320	43.4	7.7	177	1 388	175.9	55.3	109	6 650	1 063.1	237.3
Chester	10	47	5.5	1.0	9	52	4.2	1.8	34	2 372	782.6	101.3
Easton	16	41	7.2	1.1	92	290	43.6	8.8	53	3 748	639.5	112.4
Erie	74	386	34.7	8.1	207	1 486	121.7	43.3	203	10 286	1 789.0	357.2
Harrisburg	52	348	52.5	8.4	265	2 426	290.6	99.4	58	2 299	478.9	69.9
Lancaster	60	586	39.4	13.5	179	1 502	145.2	59.6	108	9 758	2 038.5	382.2
Monroeville Borough	55	435	50.9	8.8	104	2 796	416.0	124.2	26	687	82.2	19.6
New Castle	26	167	17.3	3.7	57	358	23.9	9.6	89	2 483	436.9	76.0
Norristown	27	155	25.4	3.5	117	834	89.6	33.3	63	1 517	196.6	48.8
Philadelphia	964	9 550	1 158.1	253.5	2 444	49 894	6 317.4	2 690.5	1 342	47 928	11 098.1	1 582.4
Pittsburgh	492	3 974	786.2	107.1	1 488	21 926	2 700.8	1 091.7	479	13 924	2 395.0	471.6
Plum Borough	18	55	6.5	1.4	36	297	49.0	15.6	36	1 523	194.2	48.1
Reading	50	298	36.9	7.8	132	925	88.6	46.2	160	16 969	3 654.2	737.4
Scranton	55	339	31.0	5.4	188	1 235	118.7	42.9	124	4 567	591.2	114.1
State College Borough	65	442	54.3	8.7	100	1 160	84.6	38.6	38	2 140	251.8	66.0
Wilkes-Barre	54	330	36.5	8.4	148	982	93.1	39.5	69	3 390	422.4	81.3
Williamsport	28	D	D	D	76	593	41.9	17.5	72	6 023	1 284.3	182.7
York	36	238	27.0	4.8	177	1 390	122.6	50.4	123	9 253	1 924.0	332.3
RHODE ISLAND	922	4 649	573.4	105.4	2 349	14 866	1 418.1	541.5	2 535	75 599	10 482.0	2 288.6
Cranston	70	301	29.3	5.7	185	1 072	107.0	34.3	252	7 160	949.0	213.3
East Providence	49	251	36.0	5.4	123	1 161	113.6	42.5	133	4 397	555.5	129.2
Newport	40	184	21.1	4.7	91	432	46.1	15.1	NA	NA	NA	NA
Pawtucket	57	275	31.0	5.0	94	355	30.2	11.4	205	9 766	1 535.2	294.3
Providence	175	1 374	125.8	29.5	689	4 672	517.3	206.2	570	12 465	1 294.1	337.1
Warwick	100	1 030	152.0	27.2	277	1 266	121.0	43.4	260	6 751	1 154.8	206.0
Woonsocket	30	94	13.4	1.5	43	199	15.0	5.8	84	2 700	317.3	80.5
SOUTH CAROLINA	3 541	18 760	2 012.6	377.1	6 576	47 679	6 820.9	1 850.5	4 450	346 142	70 797.0	10 369.4
Aiken	48	139	14.2	2.9	112	D	D	D	38	4 692	1 009.2	139.6
Anderson	59	204	22.1	3.1	125	501	36.8	10.3	73	9 005	2 141.4	285.6
Charleston	195	D	D	D	482	4 132	412.8	185.0	84	1 985	602.9	65.7
Columbia	240	1 132	162.2	35.3	699	6 453	771.7	256.8	105	7 137	1 648.3	253.4
Florence	74	244	29.9	5.0	129	1 006	70.5	28.6	52	4 653	701.2	148.6
Goose Creek	20	407	54.4	7.4	18	63	3.3	1.4	12	2 621	1 205.2	107.2
Greenville	202	1 047	137.6	24.2	617	8 440	3 116.3	437.3	159	14 641	4 021.7	504.2
Hilton Head Island	155	1 071	150.4	27.0	204	1 259	132.0	62.1	NA	NA	NA	NA
Mount Pleasant	66	280	28.5	5.3	153	607	52.1	19.5	NA	NA	NA	NA
North Charleston	93	724	71.9	14.6	190	2 160	203.1	65.0	108	5 292	1 237.0	188.6
Rock Hill	68	267	25.8	5.7	144	721	50.6	20.6	75	4 658	901.1	151.9
Spartanburg	102	435	47.7	9.9	197	1 296	121.5	43.6	93	8 867	2 339.5	311.4
Summerville	40	151	25.1	3.0	53	390	21.7	8.7	40	1 654	284.1	45.2
Sumter	60	233	22.1	3.6	101	423	26.6	8.3	59	10 009	1 522.3	234.4
SOUTH DAKOTA	719	2 951	245.7	45.1	1 282	6 228	450.4	161.7	888	46 539	12 305.5	1 162.6
Rapid City	108	487	50.3	8.6	195	1 104	88.7	30.2	109	3 513	756.2	77.3
Sioux Falls	176	919	95.3	17.2	343	2 341	181.1	72.6	133	11 605	2 995.2	301.9
TENNESSEE	4 999	29 626	3 732.0	667.3	8 812	72 225	6 911.8	2 686.6	7 407	483 823	98 503.1	14 351.9
Bartlett	24	136	15.6	3.2	66	320	25.1	10.8	31	1 327	242.8	29.5
Chattanooga	264	1 740	209.6	52.7	529	4 252	370.0	151.8	389	23 272	4 091.4	739.9
Clarksville	100	370	49.6	5.9	113	736	39.7	11.7	70	6 047	1 190.7	169.5
Cleveland	65	248	25.4	3.8	108	678	47.0	17.5	122	11 978	2 618.5	322.0
Collierville	23	64	9.7	1.2	49	199	24.3	9.9	40	3 281	809.9	89.9
Columbia	63	248	27.5	4.3	74	350	27.9	9.8	42	D	D	D
Franklin	73	804	90.4	18.2	118	706	59.9	25.8	71	3 760	704.2	107.3
Germantown	55	205	32.6	4.2	97	509	62.6	25.0	NA	NA	NA	NA

1. Firms subject to federal tax.

Accommodation and Foodservices, Entertainment, and Health Care

City	Accommodation and foodservices, 1997				Arts, entertainment, and recreation,[1] 1997				Health care and social assistance,[1] 1997			
	Number of establishments	Number of employees	Sales (mil dol)	Annual payroll (mil dol)	Number of establishments	Number of employees	Receipts (mil dol)	Annual payroll (mil dol)	Number of establishments	Number of employees	Receipts (mil dol)	Annual payroll (mil dol)
	92	93	94	95	96	97	98	99	100	101	102	103
OREGON—Cont'd												
Lake Oswego	88	1 404	47.0	12.8	16	89	6.3	1.9	138	1 006	58.0	22.4
McMinnville	63	947	28.3	8.2	6	90	2.9	1.0	78	1 018	69.0	25.4
Medford	213	3 634	119.0	35.3	17	207	12.6	3.3	219	2 920	196.6	92.9
Oregon City	56	862	27.6	7.5	6	16	1.3	0.2	80	632	46.5	19.5
Portland	1 679	28 839	1 134.9	322.8	167	2 453	179.1	72.9	1 430	15 676	1 098.2	489.0
Salem	335	5 642	186.1	52.4	43	646	37.6	8.3	442	4 213	269.5	120.0
Springfield	136	2 369	82.0	22.2	18	197	4.6	1.4	124	1 280	77.1	36.0
Tigard	130	2 541	88.4	25.5	12	129	5.9	1.7	139	1 413	112.6	40.2
PENNSYLVANIA	24 465	365 158	12 227.2	3 364.1	2 883	40 892	2 439.3	810.6	24 888	262 603	17 633.5	7 994.9
Allentown	230	3 665	132.1	36.5	25	225	10.5	3.1	268	2 036	145.4	66.5
Altoona	152	2 419	65.8	17.6	20	245	6.2	1.9	182	2 033	160.9	67.5
Bethel Park Borough	64	D	D	D	8	155	6.3	1.1	67	781	42.9	17.2
Bethlehem	182	2 120	81.1	21.7	8	84	2.8	0.8	196	1 642	133.8	53.5
Chester	51	335	12.7	3.1	NA	NA	NA	NA	43	568	36.1	15.6
Easton	89	884	33.8	9.6	8	87	4.1	1.3	51	639	31.1	15.3
Erie	238	2 926	81.0	21.5	25	225	13.4	3.5	301	3 261	286.6	138.2
Harrisburg	174	1 958	71.1	18.5	17	86	6.2	1.7	117	970	74.6	37.0
Lancaster	129	1 932	68.4	19.2	17	276	14.6	4.2	138	1 711	156.0	88.1
Monroeville Borough	109	3 260	98.5	28.3	15	265	9.2	3.0	168	2 369	186.6	78.0
New Castle	86	1 333	34.3	9.2	12	152	6.8	1.6	84	893	52.9	24.2
Norristown	68	D	D	D	5	31	3.2	1.1	90	2 402	243.1	102.2
Philadelphia	2 989	38 521	1 691.6	461.1	160	4 595	413.7	224.1	2 574	27 295	1 931.1	899.0
Pittsburgh	1 065	19 012	677.3	188.2	84	2 331	237.3	128.5	1 070	15 743	1 402.7	622.3
Plum Borough	29	470	13.0	3.8	6	64	2.3	0.6	26	144	8.2	3.5
Reading	164	D	D	D	13	180	32.0	6.8	120	1 168	65.7	30.9
Scranton	201	2 913	86.6	22.4	21	135	6.6	1.5	249	2 599	202.0	93.8
State College Borough	139	2 908	84.1	22.2	13	228	5.5	1.4	120	1 214	82.8	37.5
Wilkes-Barre	143	2 487	73.7	20.2	5	0	0.0	0.0	140	1 709	125.5	57.7
Williamsport	98	854	24.7	6.4	2	0	0.0	0.0	108	1 042	76.1	36.3
York	111	D	D	D	10	0	0.0	0.0	65	667	46.6	25.6
RHODE ISLAND	2 617	34 162	1 220.9	340.6	307	3 877	234.8	58.1	2 074	25 368	1 459.3	647.4
Cranston	162	D	D	D	23	219	16.5	3.7	198	1 735	113.4	49.0
East Providence	108	D	D	D	18	509	13.7	4.1	102	1 611	96.8	43.0
Newport	182	2 938	144.4	43.1	18	441	20.2	6.3	57	499	32.6	13.5
Pawtucket	122	D	D	D	13	90	7.2	2.3	112	1 167	72.3	32.1
Providence	443	6 216	237.6	63.7	29	274	25.8	5.5	401	4 950	336.8	160.2
Warwick	232	4 899	155.0	43.7	31	202	14.8	3.4	271	3 314	223.8	86.0
Woonsocket	89	D	D	D	5	76	2.1	0.7	68	1 287	60.5	28.2
SOUTH CAROLINA	7 775	150 621	4 835.8	1 313.8	1 325	18 499	1 107.1	251.9	6 261	78 888	5 318.5	2 361.3
Aiken	116	2 090	63.1	16.4	23	280	10.3	3.6	118	2 411	187.0	72.2
Anderson	130	2 792	87.3	23.4	14	108	4.2	0.8	169	2 358	154.2	81.7
Charleston	388	9 484	346.4	97.6	50	614	30.0	6.2	356	2 858	222.6	101.5
Columbia	387	7 826	242.4	69.7	44	662	33.7	7.8	490	7 599	621.7	288.1
Florence	162	3 838	113.0	31.5	20	379	13.9	2.4	206	4 637	360.9	175.9
Goose Creek	43	D	D	D	5	185	7.2	3.0	23	180	8.5	3.4
Greenville	342	7 560	238.0	68.3	43	601	31.5	8.3	297	2 931	237.8	113.5
Hilton Head Island	185	4 759	228.0	63.8	50	961	49.7	13.3	82	939	82.9	28.3
Mount Pleasant	103	2 181	72.8	19.8	18	244	14.2	3.5	139	1 710	94.6	41.7
North Charleston	211	4 297	135.1	35.1	29	262	27.4	3.9	233	4 631	321.2	122.9
Rock Hill	134	3 179	92.2	24.4	27	243	8.5	2.5	144	3 527	222.1	97.3
Spartanburg	194	4 282	109.8	31.9	18	155	8.0	2.4	166	2 617	209.1	94.3
Summerville	96	2 077	55.4	16.2	13	81	3.5	1.1	82	1 175	78.1	27.2
Sumter	107	2 148	65.3	17.7	16	136	6.0	1.6	115	1 165	75.4	37.4
SOUTH DAKOTA	2 258	30 131	888.0	234.4	432	4 647	299.2	60.2	1 314	14 080	881.6	414.3
Rapid City	234	4 643	135.5	37.6	63	485	23.9	5.1	217	2 295	162.4	65.3
Sioux Falls	352	7 691	215.0	61.8	67	746	48.1	10.0	269	4 275	351.5	194.4
TENNESSEE	9 604	197 881	6 790.2	1 880.3	1 755	18 263	1 228.7	394.3	10 113	155 667	10 753.0	4 659.9
Bartlett	53	D	D	D	4	84	3.2	1.0	74	646	45.7	17.2
Chattanooga	528	10 682	366.7	103.6	55	648	27.3	9.3	611	9 114	727.1	332.2
Clarksville	221	D	D	D	28	0	0.0	0.0	143	1 979	115.0	48.0
Cleveland	130	2 476	80.2	21.3	18	0	0.0	0.0	195	10 316	437.6	199.4
Collierville	42	D	D	D	2	0	0.0	0.0	38	383	19.8	7.4
Columbia	81	1 836	48.3	13.1	16	90	4.6	1.6	117	1 411	102.5	36.3
Franklin	120	2 748	93.2	27.2	44	319	20.2	8.1	125	1 617	106.6	48.8
Germantown	61	D	D	D	5	96	4.5	2.0	101	1 056	84.1	36.3

1. Firms subject to federal tax.

Table D. Cities — Other Services and Federal Funds

City	Other services,[1] 1997				Selected federal funds, 2002–2003 (mil dol)								
					Procurement contracts		Grants						
	Number of establishments	Number of employees	Receipts (mil dol)	Annual payroll (mil dol)	Defense	Other	Total[2]	Medicaid and other health related	Nutrition and family welfare	Energy and environment	Education	Housing and community development	Direct payments for individuals for educational assistance
	104	105	106	107	108	109	110	111	112	113	114	115	116
OREGON—Cont'd													
Lake Oswego	76	387	33.9	8.8	3.2	1.4	1.1	0.0	0.0	0.8	0.0	0.2	0.8
McMinnville	32	185	12.6	3.7	5.1	7.2	5.7	0.0	1.5	0.0	3.2	0.7	2.0
Medford	118	798	52.8	14.8	0.5	7.7	17.5	2.4	0.3	0.0	1.1	7.4	0.2
Oregon City	34	187	13.5	4.2	6.1	1.7	8.2	1.4	2.0	0.0	1.5	1.5	3.9
Portland	1 094	8 597	621.8	189.4	131.6	243.8	408.4	211.7	1.1	34.5	22.5	57.5	49.8
Salem	230	1 433	81.6	26.9	2.4	10.2	612.1	28.3	144.1	21.8	141.3	57.5	12.3
Springfield	85	604	34.2	10.4	0.2	7.9	8.4	0.0	5.0	0.4	0.7	2.2	0.1
Tigard	91	607	48.5	15.8	0.1	1.1	0.7	0.3	0.0	0.0	0.3	0.0	0.1
PENNSYLVANIA	19 754	107 502	7 085.7	2 049.0	5 606.6	2 530.1	18 623.5	9 647.4	2 512.6	148.5	1 272.3	1 425.3	725.7
Allentown	216	1 528	97.0	31.0	212.4	2.8	-58.4	3.3	0.9	-86.7	0.2	15.7	6.3
Altoona	138	719	37.7	10.5	0.5	2.6	20.6	0.2	2.8	0.0	0.2	12.2	1.3
Bethel Park Borough	84	428	21.9	7.1	1.3	0.0	0.9	0.0	0.0	0.0	0.0	0.8	0.0
Bethlehem	108	947	51.8	20.1	0.6	1.4	42.4	4.1	7.7	1.9	3.3	15.5	8.2
Chester	29	110	6.6	2.2	3.0	0.3	25.6	1.6	0.0	0.0	1.6	19.3	3.3
Easton	69	440	31.7	11.0	3.3	0.2	6.2	0.5	0.0	0.0	0.0	2.6	0.0
Erie	193	936	64.8	17.6	24.4	8.8	36.4	2.2	5.9	0.2	2.0	20.1	11.0
Harrisburg	104	638	48.6	14.0	17.0	22.5	2 128.8	229.6	592.0	133.9	357.4	102.7	43.5
Lancaster	97	697	40.1	14.9	55.9	4.1	51.7	2.0	9.1	1.0	4.0	23.8	2.9
Monroeville Borough	87	594	29.9	10.0	0.0	0.0	0.0	0.0	0.0	0.0	0.0	0.0	0.0
New Castle	77	347	18.6	4.9	0.3	0.2	11.1	0.0	2.7	0.0	0.0	7.8	0.3
Norristown	41	258	20.4	6.4	7.8	0.5	9.0	0.8	0.0	0.0	0.0	8.2	0.0
Philadelphia	1 913	10 971	737.4	199.6	1 783.1	334.5	1 530.5	900.2	61.3	14.2	58.2	316.4	114.4
Pittsburgh	722	4 725	317.6	91.7	125.0	232.2	976.0	479.3	27.0	40.4	17.2	199.1	88.8
Plum Borough	35	176	9.4	2.7	0.0	0.0	0.4	0.0	0.0	0.0	0.0	0.3	0.0
Reading	106	943	52.6	16.0	26.6	2.2	25.3	0.4	4.3	0.0	2.2	15.9	9.5
Scranton	151	998	57.0	16.7	14.9	3.6	35.2	3.6	5.1	0.9	0.9	23.7	9.1
State College Borough	53	533	25.7	8.2	34.3	0.8	193.5	52.3	0.4	20.3	8.1	2.8	51.6
Wilkes-Barre	95	441	25.1	6.9	7.8	14.8	43.6	4.2	6.1	0.2	1.8	18.6	9.8
Williamsport	63	324	27.9	6.3	25.5	5.6	14.5	0.0	3.3	0.0	0.6	9.8	7.9
York	63	414	27.5	8.1	394.5	5.4	22.2	3.1	3.3	0.3	0.8	12.0	5.5
RHODE ISLAND	1 949	8 602	546.2	167.8	498.8	160.3	2 234.4	1 119.4	249.0	38.1	147.4	248.8	71.1
Cranston	177	838	51.5	17.3	0.7	0.2	64.5	3.5	25.6	0.0	0.5	12.8	0.0
East Providence	115	466	36.2	10.6	0.2	1.0	16.2	0.1	1.1	0.0	0.0	14.2	0.6
Newport	52	210	12.8	4.5	68.8	8.7	16.7	0.0	3.7	0.0	3.5	9.2	1.2
Pawtucket	132	822	51.2	16.2	0.6	10.2	25.9	6.5	0.0	0.5	1.8	16.4	2.8
Providence	284	1 466	107.9	32.3	29.1	25.4	508.3	170.1	34.5	35.6	59.3	100.2	33.9
Warwick	199	918	58.2	17.5	2.0	2.5	18.6	0.4	4.4	0.2	2.7	8.3	16.7
Woonsocket	81	275	14.0	4.2	8.9	1.6	30.5	2.9	1.3	0.1	0.5	24.9	0.0
SOUTH CAROLINA	5 672	32 166	1 901.0	563.8	1 486.5	2 127.9	5 969.0	3 127.8	661.9	62.6	564.4	305.7	229.9
Aiken	66	410	16.4	4.9	12.0	1 591.8	6.4	0.0	2.5	0.3	0.2	2.4	7.2
Anderson	83	563	29.4	10.2	1.0	10.3	17.9	0.7	0.0	0.0	2.6	11.6	2.5
Charleston	174	1 409	51.5	19.6	211.4	60.2	194.0	110.3	0.5	2.7	7.3	24.1	10.5
Columbia	235	2 020	103.6	34.8	110.9	75.6	758.0	135.8	143.9	40.0	187.6	64.5	64.4
Florence	84	746	37.7	11.8	2.0	4.9	17.9	1.1	5.5	0.2	3.9	4.3	11.5
Goose Creek	33	146	7.5	1.8	6.6	0.0	0.4	0.0	0.0	0.0	0.0	0.4	0.0
Greenville	233	2 135	123.3	37.8	190.4	118.9	42.6	3.4	12.0	1.9	3.3	17.4	10.6
Hilton Head Island	76	295	19.3	5.8	1.2	0.0	0.0	0.0	0.0	0.0	0.0	0.6	0.0
Mount Pleasant	90	537	35.2	10.6	1.5	0.8	1.7	0.1	0.0	1.0	0.0	0.3	0.0
North Charleston	211	1 976	139.8	45.0	199.0	8.0	29.7	1.0	0.0	1.0	0.0	14.7	1.3
Rock Hill	121	700	42.8	13.9	0.1	0.1	16.2	1.6	5.1	0.2	2.4	4.8	9.6
Spartanburg	119	772	44.4	13.2	0.9	2.9	23.4	2.3	4.7	0.0	1.3	11.3	12.7
Summerville	85	385	21.4	6.5	38.6	0.3	3.9	0.0	7.0	0.0	0.1	3.7	0.0
Sumter	87	676	38.3	11.4	3.2	3.5	21.1	0.6	7.0	0.0	5.2	6.4	9.3
SOUTH DAKOTA	1 356	5 828	344.7	90.7	196.3	184.7	1 697.6	468.6	176.3	29.3	181.9	93.7	114.1
Rapid City	170	940	49.1	15.7	11.8	14.8	42.9	7.1	5.3	0.2	1.6	11.3	8.0
Sioux Falls	246	1 786	95.6	30.4	13.3	41.8	38.0	4.4	2.3	0.4	1.0	14.3	60.2
TENNESSEE	7 767	49 204	2 996.7	918.7	2 161.0	5 361.0	9 057.0	5 306.6	994.5	86.2	659.1	457.7	298.1
Bartlett	65	345	17.6	6.3	2.0	0.1	0.3	0.0	0.0	0.0	0.0	0.0	0.0
Chattanooga	385	2 809	167.9	53.5	12.5	476.2	62.0	7.8	8.1	0.6	5.5	22.9	14.9
Clarksville	157	755	39.7	10.8	4.3	0.1	12.0	0.0	1.4	0.0	3.7	4.2	12.9
Cleveland	91	1 239	63.5	24.1	0.0	0.4	6.2	0.0	3.2	0.0	0.1	2.6	7.0
Collierville	33	183	8.9	3.0	0.6	0.4	0.3	0.0	0.0	0.0	0.0	0.0	0.0
Columbia	80	500	26.8	8.6	0.0	3.3	2.0	0.0	0.0	0.0	0.2	1.6	3.8
Franklin	103	640	58.9	14.7	0.7	1.7	0.6	0.3	0.0	0.0	0.0	0.2	0.2
Germantown	45	428	17.1	7.5	0.0	0.0	0.1	0.0	0.0	0.0	0.0	0.1	0.0

1. Firms subject to federal tax.   2. Includes program categories not shown separately. State totals include additional categories not allocated by city.

Table D. Cities — City Government Finances

City	City government finances, 2002									
	General revenue							General expenditure		
		Intergovernmental		Taxes					Per capita[1] (dollars)	
					Per capita[1] (dollars)					
	Total (mil dol)	Total (mil dol)	Percent from state government	Total (mil dol)	Total	Property	Sales and gross receipts	Total (mil dol)	Total	Capital outlays
	117	118	119	120	121	122	123	124	125	126
OREGON—Cont'd										
Lake Oswego	43.5	4.5	100.0	26.8	747	592	47	41.2	1 149	403
McMinnville	31.4	4.1	48.1	12.6	450	285	70	24.9	888	153
Medford	51.9	8.3	48.0	33.9	525	294	80	49.7	769	183
Oregon City	29.7	3.0	75.6	12.9	463	314	74	26.4	950	169
Portland	723.9	117.1	32.6	322.9	599	370	99	875.6	1 623	291
Salem	138.9	22.1	84.1	65.1	462	356	81	152.5	1 082	177
Springfield	58.8	7.8	99.4	16.0	296	229	35	51.0	944	75
Tigard	25.3	4.2	58.1	15.8	351	194	67	23.1	512	78
PENNSYLVANIA	X	X	X	X	X	X	X	X	X	X
Allentown	82.9	14.6	67.5	38.2	360	203	0	82.7	779	34
Altoona	NA	NA	NA	NA	NA	NA	NA	NA	NA	NA
Bethel Park Borough	16.6	1.7	64.9	9.2	279	89	2	19.7	593	19
Bethlehem	58.2	13.2	29.9	23.7	330	195	0	64.4	897	217
Chester	23.5	3.7	96.2	16.6	448	223	0	27.5	741	1
Easton	22.1	4.1	41.6	7.2	274	158	0	31.8	1 215	217
Erie	82.2	15.5	56.5	31.2	306	228	0	69.9	685	47
Harrisburg	77.3	18.9	91.5	19.7	405	255	0	86.0	1 771	270
Lancaster	43.0	8.7	73.7	18.5	332	260	0	41.1	738	30
Monroeville Borough	26.8	1.9	49.0	18.0	621	146	0	28.3	976	129
New Castle	NA	NA	NA	NA	NA	NA	NA	NA	NA	NA
Norristown	17.0	3.2	33.5	12.1	388	183	0	19.2	613	51
Philadelphia	4 756.5	2 032.9	70.5	2 042.7	1 369	250	127	4 826.5	3 234	340
Pittsburgh	508.1	144.0	48.5	275.9	841	377	124	480.5	1 465	132
Plum Borough	7.7	1.2	63.4	5.2	193	76	0	9.2	340	68
Reading	65.0	15.8	93.3	24.1	299	181	3	78.9	981	3
Scranton	66.2	22.3	57.3	36.3	486	168	0	85.8	1 149	278
State College Borough	19.4	2.5	55.6	6.3	165	53	0	32.3	848	279
Wilkes-Barre	NA	NA	NA	NA	NA	NA	NA	NA	NA	NA
Williamsport	18.9	9.1	36.0	8.2	271	152	NA	17.6	585	NA
York	NA	NA	NA	NA	NA	NA	NA	NA	NA	54
RHODE ISLAND	X	X	X	X	X	X	X	X	X	X
Cranston	177.5	42.3	95.5	110.3	1 359	1 338	0	180.9	2 230	31
East Providence	105.5	35.9	95.1	59.8	1 205	1 191	0	110.5	2 225	62
Newport	85.2	21.1	93.8	50.9	1 933	1 792	12	91.0	3 459	468
Pawtucket	152.2	80.5	92.3	66.1	892	880	0	146.2	1 975	88
Providence	530.7	264.2	86.7	220.5	1 253	1 232	3	492.3	2 799	112
Warwick	228.4	51.2	98.0	152.8	1 756	1 703	12	235.4	2 705	70
Woonsocket	NA	NA	NA	NA	NA	NA	NA	NA	NA	NA
SOUTH CAROLINA	X	X	X	X	X	X	X	X	X	X
Aiken	25.7	2.8	69.4	12.8	490	248	59	31.0	1 191	329
Anderson	27.4	4.3	42.6	13.9	541	327	58	25.4	987	95
Charleston	152.5	26.7	30.8	71.7	726	402	37	101.1	1 023	37
Columbia	148.5	25.2	31.5	55.8	475	270	61	132.7	1 131	251
Florence	26.1	8.0	30.1	9.5	318	76	68	33.0	1 100	238
Goose Creek	9.1	3.1	30.9	4.3	142	24	29	8.4	278	24
Greenville	90.2	8.8	68.1	53.7	955	496	162	88.4	1 573	237
Hilton Head Island	27.2	4.7	99.9	19.7	570	246	111	31.1	900	150
Mount Pleasant	41.2	7.6	31.9	20.9	394	172	68	38.1	718	113
North Charleston	59.0	13.5	16.6	34.0	421	238	76	61.4	761	109
Rock Hill	33.6	3.5	50.6	19.3	354	243	7	34.9	639	22
Spartanburg	33.9	6.0	52.1	19.6	501	218	98	29.6	757	28
Summerville	17.9	1.9	74.7	9.0	300	146	34	14.7	491	28
Sumter	25.1	7.3	24.8	10.9	276	96	84	19.3	491	43
SOUTH DAKOTA	X	X	X	X	X	X	X	X	X	X
Rapid City	69.9	5.1	16.5	39.8	661	136	499	67.0	1 112	128
Sioux Falls	135.7	9.8	36.6	93.9	720	454	239	116.2	890	128
TENNESSEE	X	X	X	X	X	X	X	X	X	X
Bartlett	33.8	13.2	42.4	11.9	284	219	51	31.3	747	84
Chattanooga	291.3	81.9	35.1	113.3	729	533	178	256.5	1 650	175
Clarksville	66.3	22.7	52.8	24.8	234	182	35	76.0	718	220
Cleveland	63.5	36.3	57.3	13.2	354	292	51	56.8	1 520	48
Collierville	33.6	8.7	45.9	15.4	451	339	60	33.2	971	225
Columbia	28.7	11.0	33.9	6.3	191	116	64	31.3	945	214
Franklin	NA	NA	NA	NA	NA	NA	NA	NA	NA	NA
Germantown	38.6	11.3	53.1	15.8	419	358	47	39.1	1 037	173

1. Based on population estimated as of July 1 of the year shown.

Table D. Cities — City Government Finances (cont'd)

	City government finances, 2002 (cont'd)									
	General expenditure									
	Percent of total for—									
City	Public welfare	Highways	Parking facilities	Education	Health and hospitals	Police protection	Sewerage and sanitation	Parks and recreation	Housing and community development	Interest on debt
	127	128	129	130	131	132	133	134	135	136
OREGON—Cont'd										
Lake Oswego	0.0	1.3	0.0	0.0	0.0	11.6	12.7	12.3	0.0	4.6
McMinnville	0.0	5.7	0.0	0.0	9.1	15.8	11.7	12.5	0.2	8.7
Medford	0.0	18.0	0.4	0.0	0.0	23.8	14.8	6.2	2.3	3.8
Oregon City	0.0	11.2	0.8	0.0	0.0	13.5	18.3	7.2	6.8	1.7
Portland	0.0	12.5	0.6	0.0	0.0	14.4	20.7	7.9	4.7	10.5
Salem	0.0	10.3	0.9	0.0	0.0	14.4	27.3	5.5	4.5	2.2
Springfield	0.0	9.6	0.0	0.0	7.8	17.5	28.5	0.1	6.8	1.2
Tigard	0.6	10.8	0.0	0.0	0.0	27.4	6.1	9.5	0.0	0.5
PENNSYLVANIA	X	X	X	X	X	X	X	X	X	X
Allentown	0.0	6.1	0.0	0.0	5.0	21.0	19.2	4.1	7.2	6.8
Altoona	NA	NA	NA	NA	NA	NA	NA	NA	NA	NA
Bethel Park Borough	0.0	15.6	0.0	0.0	0.0	17.9	18.9	8.8	0.4	0.7
Bethlehem	0.0	16.5	0.0	0.0	1.9	11.8	11.9	5.2	13.3	3.9
Chester	0.0	9.4	0.0	0.0	3.8	35.8	7.1	2.9	0.1	0.0
Easton	0.0	3.3	1.6	0.0	0.2	13.3	18.3	2.6	4.1	6.1
Erie	0.0	8.8	0.0	0.0	0.0	18.4	20.2	6.2	8.6	6.7
Harrisburg	0.0	8.5	2.6	0.0	0.2	15.7	16.7	13.2	15.1	8.0
Lancaster	0.0	5.4	0.0	0.0	0.0	21.9	14.8	3.4	9.0	5.7
Monroeville Borough	0.0	16.3	0.0	0.0	0.3	23.2	15.6	6.0	2.9	2.4
New Castle	NA	NA	NA	NA	NA	NA	NA	NA	NA	NA
Norristown	0.0	10.9	0.0	0.0	0.9	26.0	2.9	2.0	7.9	3.9
Philadelphia	9.0	2.0	0.0	0.5	20.8	10.3	5.6	2.0	3.7	3.7
Pittsburgh	0.0	7.1	0.0	0.0	3.0	14.8	4.2	1.9	15.0	13.6
Plum Borough	0.0	40.8	0.0	0.0	0.1	25.5	9.5	1.0	2.6	1.7
Reading	0.0	5.9	0.0	0.0	2.4	20.7	14.5	2.7	15.1	5.3
Scranton	0.0	14.1	1.0	0.0	2.3	13.8	2.2	0.7	10.4	1.2
State College Borough	0.0	1.9	2.8	0.0	0.7	13.8	18.4	1.2	3.3	3.1
Wilkes-Barre	NA	NA	NA	NA	NA	NA	NA	NA	NA	NA
Williamsport	0.0	8.8	0.0	0.0	0.0	24.8	0.1	2.2	15.1	0.3
York	NA	NA	NA	NA	NA	NA	NA	NA	NA	NA
RHODE ISLAND	X	X	X	X	X	X	X	X	X	X
Cranston	0.1	2.5	0.0	52.6	0.0	10.4	9.1	1.0	0.6	2.0
East Providence	0.1	5.1	0.0	57.6	0.2	7.5	5.8	2.2	1.9	1.1
Newport	0.0	2.3	0.5	53.4	0.0	8.6	6.0	2.4	0.9	0.6
Pawtucket	0.1	1.7	0.0	58.6	0.0	8.9	2.5	1.9	5.4	2.5
Providence	0.1	0.8	0.2	51.8	0.1	7.4	1.7	2.2	4.3	4.3
Warwick	0.8	2.5	0.0	58.6	0.0	6.7	2.6	1.0	0.6	3.2
Woonsocket	NA	NA	NA	NA	NA	NA	NA	NA	NA	NA
SOUTH CAROLINA	X	X	X	X	X	X	X	X	X	X
Aiken	0.0	4.8	0.5	0.0	0.0	13.3	20.3	24.4	3.3	0.8
Anderson	0.0	5.4	0.0	0.0	0.3	22.4	20.5	4.8	5.7	4.9
Charleston	0.6	2.6	6.8	0.0	0.6	23.5	18.3	7.0	4.2	4.0
Columbia	0.0	2.7	1.7	0.0	0.7	19.1	18.6	6.7	1.4	1.0
Florence	0.0	5.7	0.0	0.0	0.2	16.6	33.2	5.9	0.0	4.8
Goose Creek	0.0	5.7	0.0	0.0	6.9	33.8	9.2	8.0	0.0	4.2
Greenville	0.0	9.2	1.7	0.0	0.2	14.5	6.6	22.7	1.5	4.1
Hilton Head Island	0.0	0.0	0.0	0.0	0.5	6.8	0.0	7.9	0.0	15.5
Mount Pleasant	0.0	6.2	0.0	0.0	0.0	17.8	22.8	8.8	0.0	2.3
North Charleston	1.1	8.2	0.0	0.0	0.3	25.6	7.1	11.5	2.4	3.3
Rock Hill	0.0	3.5	0.0	0.0	0.0	20.4	11.0	9.2	0.0	7.3
Spartanburg	0.0	6.7	0.7	0.0	0.5	28.1	13.1	0.8	5.3	2.1
Summerville	0.0	9.4	0.0	0.0	0.0	19.7	22.3	7.7	0.0	0.7
Sumter	0.0	4.6	0.0	0.0	0.0	33.9	16.9	6.1	0.0	1.1
SOUTH DAKOTA	X	X	X	X	X	X	X	X	X	X
Rapid City	0.0	19.6	0.6	0.0	0.6	11.6	7.1	24.5	2.5	5.2
Sioux Falls	0.0	20.4	1.5	0.0	4.0	13.8	10.5	12.7	3.0	5.8
TENNESSEE	X	X	X	X	X	X	X	X	X	X
Bartlett	0.0	15.9	0.0	0.0	3.5	25.6	12.1	14.7	0.0	3.3
Chattanooga	4.5	7.2	0.2	3.5	0.6	13.9	12.6	8.5	4.0	8.9
Clarksville	0.0	11.3	0.0	0.0	0.0	17.3	9.2	4.0	1.8	5.9
Cleveland	0.0	4.9	0.0	50.3	0.7	10.0	10.8	2.3	0.0	4.2
Collierville	0.0	9.5	0.0	0.0	0.7	18.2	14.6	10.6	0.0	3.2
Columbia	0.0	7.4	0.0	0.0	0.1	16.3	34.6	3.7	0.0	3.3
Franklin	NA	NA	NA	NA	NA	NA	NA	NA	NA	NA
Germantown	0.0	5.0	0.0	0.0	0.0	17.1	12.3	24.6	4.6	4.7

Table D. Cities — City Government Finances, City Government Employment, and Climate

City	City government finances, 2002 (cont'd) Debt outstanding — Total (mil dol)	Per capita[1] (dollars)	Percent utility	City government employment, 2002	Climate[2] — Average daily temperature (degrees Fahrenheit) Mean — January	July	Limits — January[3]	July[4]	Annual precipitation (inches)	Heating degree days	Cooling degree days
	137	138	139	140	141	142	143	144	145	146	147
OREGON—Cont'd											
Lake Oswego	61.2	1 708	11.0	324	39.6	68.2	33.7	79.9	36.30	4 522	371
McMinnville	46.4	1 659	0.0	238	NA	NA	NA	NA	NA	NA	NA
Medford	39.4	609	0.0	489	38.1	72.9	30.4	90.5	18.86	4 611	725
Oregon City	15.7	567	21.4	183	NA	NA	NA	NA	NA	NA	NA
Portland	1 991.3	3 692	7.9	5 535	39.6	68.2	33.7	79.9	36.30	4 522	371
Salem	151.0	1 071	71.1	1 279	39.6	66.3	32.7	81.6	39.16	4 927	247
Springfield	24.9	462	46.3	510	40.8	67.3	35.2	81.7	49.37	4 546	300
Tigard	7.2	159	0.0	250	38.9	65.8	32.5	79.7	37.57	5 011	232
PENNSYLVANIA	X	X	X	X	X	X	X	X	X	X	X
Allentown	159.8	1 506	25.4	967	26.6	74.1	18.8	84.5	43.52	5 785	773
Altoona	NA	NA	NA	286	26.0	71.3	19.1	81.5	36.81	6 140	582
Bethel Park Borough	3.7	112	0.0	119	26.1	72.1	18.5	82.6	36.85	5 968	654
Bethlehem	174.2	2 428	84.6	699	26.6	74.1	18.8	84.5	43.52	5 785	773
Chester	0.0	0	0.0	332	32.4	78.3	26.4	87.3	42.45	4 586	1 291
Easton	79.1	3 026	0.0	255	26.6	74.1	18.8	84.5	43.52	5 785	773
Erie	94.7	927	0.0	844	25.4	71.3	18.2	79.9	41.53	6 279	550
Harrisburg	120.3	2 478	0.0	734	28.6	75.7	21.2	85.8	40.50	5 347	962
Lancaster	72.3	1 299	36.9	547	27.9	74.1	19.2	84.9	41.22	5 584	780
Monroeville Borough	14.9	515	0.0	143	26.1	72.1	18.5	82.6	36.85	5 968	654
New Castle	NA	NA	NA	145	24.1	70.6	15.0	83.2	37.38	6 542	489
Norristown	22.2	708	0.0	156	29.8	75.9	21.4	86.5	44.38	5 114	1 022
Philadelphia	5 157.7	3 456	48.0	30 195	30.4	76.7	22.8	86.1	41.41	4 954	1 101
Pittsburgh	1 130.0	3 446	0.0	4 235	26.1	72.1	18.5	82.6	36.85	5 968	654
Plum Borough	3.7	137	0.0	72	26.1	72.1	18.5	82.6	36.85	5 968	654
Reading	110.5	1 373	0.0	705	26.6	74.0	17.0	85.1	44.71	5 796	759
Scranton	26.8	358	0.0	602	24.7	71.7	17.5	81.8	36.18	6 291	539
State College Borough	15.7	413	0.0	214	24.7	71.3	16.7	82.0	37.48	6 364	529
Wilkes-Barre	NA	NA	NA	304	24.7	71.7	17.5	81.8	36.18	6 291	539
Williamsport	0.8	26	0.0	199	25.2	72.3	17.1	83.1	40.72	6 087	622
York	NA	NA	NA	395	29.0	74.5	19.4	86.9	40.40	5 256	860
RHODE ISLAND	X	X	X	X	X	X	X	X	X	X	X
Cranston	84.9	1 046	3.5	2 344	27.9	72.7	19.1	82.1	45.53	5 884	606
East Providence	24.3	490	0.0	1 617	27.9	72.7	19.1	82.1	45.53	5 884	606
Newport	44.8	1 702	21.5	886	30.3	70.7	22.6	78.3	44.81	5 659	464
Pawtucket	56.7	766	3.9	2 426	27.9	72.7	19.1	82.1	45.53	5 884	606
Providence	457.7	2 602	5.5	5 471	27.9	72.7	19.1	82.1	45.53	5 884	606
Warwick	150.6	1 730	1.8	2 614	27.9	72.7	19.1	82.1	45.53	5 884	606
Woonsocket	NA	NA	NA	1 278	27.9	72.7	19.1	82.1	45.53	5 884	606
SOUTH CAROLINA	X	X	X	X	X	X	X	X	X	X	X
Aiken	13.2	508	51.9	316	NA	NA	NA	NA	NA	NA	NA
Anderson	21.0	817	0.0	357	42.1	79.8	32.2	89.9	46.38	2 891	1 807
Charleston	356.3	3 607	81.7	1 939	47.8	81.5	37.7	90.2	51.53	2 013	2 266
Columbia	193.8	1 651	75.6	1 978	43.8	80.8	32.1	91.6	49.91	2 649	1 966
Florence	63.1	2 101	53.0	414	43.8	80.6	33.4	90.4	43.84	2 585	1 993
Goose Creek	6.4	212	12.3	143	NA	NA	NA	NA	NA	NA	NA
Greenville	177.3	3 156	58.5	1 003	40.1	78.2	30.0	88.2	51.27	3 272	1 473
Hilton Head Island	77.8	2 249	0.0	237	NA	NA	NA	NA	NA	NA	NA
Mount Pleasant	49.1	925	48.6	452	47.8	81.5	37.7	90.2	51.53	2 013	2 266
North Charleston	36.1	447	0.0	851	47.8	81.5	37.7	90.2	51.53	2 013	2 266
Rock Hill	85.6	1 567	52.7	651	40.9	79.1	30.9	89.2	48.65	3 054	1 624
Spartanburg	140.0	3 583	77.6	644	41.9	79.4	31.5	90.6	49.87	2 887	1 688
Summerville	5.7	191	74.9	266	NA	NA	NA	NA	NA	NA	NA
Sumter	27.0	686	81.4	485	44.0	80.0	32.4	91.1	48.14	2 609	1 888
SOUTH DAKOTA	X	X	X	X	X	X	X	X	X	X	X
Rapid City	69.8	1 159	6.5	954	22.3	72.2	10.7	86.2	16.64	7 301	611
Sioux Falls	131.1	1 004	14.5	984	13.8	74.3	3.3	86.3	23.86	7 809	744
TENNESSEE	X	X	X	X	X	X	X	X	X	X	X
Bartlett	33.0	789	35.7	400	39.7	82.6	30.9	92.3	52.10	3 082	2 118
Chattanooga	454.1	2 922	8.5	3 177	37.4	78.7	28.0	89.0	53.46	3 587	1 544
Clarksville	176.4	1 666	43.5	1 047	34.0	78.1	23.3	90.0	50.75	4 159	1 417
Cleveland	81.8	2 188	52.2	1 411	36.5	76.6	25.8	88.0	54.65	3 884	1 236
Collierville	38.1	1 116	45.0	403	NA	NA	NA	NA	NA	NA	NA
Columbia	46.1	1 393	31.1	472	34.4	77.1	23.2	88.8	54.26	4 206	1 281
Franklin	NA	NA	NA	457	NA	NA	NA	NA	NA	NA	NA
Germantown	36.0	955	18.3	404	39.7	82.6	30.9	92.3	52.10	3 082	2 118

1. Based on the population estimated as of July 1 of the year shown.   2. Represents normal values based on the 30-year period, 1961–1990.   3. Average daily minimum.   4. Average daily maximum.

Table D. Cities — Land Area and Population

STATE Place code	City	Land area,[1] 2000 (sq km)	Population, 2003 Total persons	Rank	Per square kilometer	White	Black	Am. Indian, Alaska Native	Asian and Pacific Islander	Other race	Hispanic or Latino[2]	Non-Hispanic White
		1	2	3	4	5	6	7	8	9	10	11
	TENNESSEE—Cont'd											
47 33280	Hendersonville	70.8	43 027	746	607.7	93.8	4.3	0.6	1.4	0.9	1.7	92.0
47 37640	Jackson	128.2	61 110	478	476.7	55.9	42.5	0.5	1.1	1.1	2.2	54.2
47 38320	Johnson City	101.7	57 394	527	564.3	91.3	7.0	0.7	1.4	1.0	1.9	89.0
47 39560	Kingsport	114.1	44 231	726	387.7	94.3	4.6	0.7	1.1	0.6	1.0	92.7
47 40000	Knoxville	240.0	173 278	122	722.0	81.1	16.8	0.9	1.8	1.1	1.6	79.0
47 48000	Memphis	723.4	645 978	17	893.0	35.2	61.9	0.5	1.8	1.8	3.0	33.3
47 51560	Murfreesboro	101.0	78 074	355	773.0	80.9	14.4	0.7	3.2	2.3	3.5	78.4
47 52004	Nashville-Davidson	1 300.9	569 842	24	438.0	68.5	26.6	0.7	2.9	3.3	4.6	65.1
47 55120	Oak Ridge	221.6	27 338	1 150	123.4	88.5	8.9	0.9	2.5	0.9	1.9	85.9
47 69420	Smyrna	59.1	30 172	1 059	510.5	88.7	8.4	0.7	1.6	2.4	4.3	85.1
48 00000	TEXAS	678 051.4	22 118 509	X	32.6	73.1	12.0	1.0	3.2	13.3	32.0	52.4
48 01000	Abilene	272.3	114 889	203	421.9	80.1	9.5	1.1	2.0	9.8	19.4	68.8
48 01924	Allen	68.2	62 400	466	915.0	88.7	4.8	1.0	4.3	3.1	7.0	83.2
48 03000	Amarillo	232.7	178 612	119	767.6	79.5	6.4	1.4	2.4	12.6	21.9	68.4
48 04000	Arlington	248.2	355 007	49	1 430.3	70.1	14.5	1.2	6.8	10.4	18.3	59.6
48 05000	Austin	651.4	672 011	16	1 031.6	67.8	10.7	1.1	5.6	18.0	30.5	52.9
48 06128	Baytown	84.6	67 251	424	794.9	70.2	14.0	0.9	1.4	16.3	34.2	50.2
48 07000	Beaumont	220.2	112 434	207	510.6	47.5	46.4	0.6	2.9	4.2	7.9	42.7
48 07132	Bedford	25.9	48 572	655	1 875.4	89.3	4.0	1.1	4.5	3.1	7.2	83.4
48 08236	Big Spring	49.5	24 556	1 227	496.1	78.8	5.7	1.2	1.0	16.0	44.6	48.4
48 10768	Brownsville	208.2	156 178	135	750.1	83.8	0.5	0.6	0.8	16.7	91.3	7.7
48 10912	Bryan	112.2	67 774	421	604.0	66.5	18.2	0.8	2.0	14.7	27.8	51.7
48 13024	Carrollton	94.5	116 714	200	1 235.1	74.1	6.7	0.9	11.9	9.2	19.5	61.2
48 13492	Cedar Hill	91.0	39 260	820	431.4	58.4	34.4	1.0	2.5	6.0	11.9	50.8
48 13552	Cedar Park	44.0	41 482	774	942.8	88.4	3.6	0.9	3.3	6.0	13.5	79.0
48 15364	Cleburne	72.0	27 928	1 141	387.9	87.9	4.8	1.0	0.8	7.3	19.9	73.9
48 15976	College Station	104.3	73 536	380	705.0	82.2	5.7	0.7	8.1	5.4	10.0	75.7
48 16432	Conroe	97.9	39 896	802	407.5	73.8	11.5	0.8	1.4	15.6	32.6	54.5
48 16612	Coppell	38.5	38 938	827	1 011.4	84.7	3.6	0.7	10.4	2.7	6.9	78.7
48 16624	Copperas Cove	36.1	29 988	1 063	830.7	69.4	22.3	1.8	5.3	6.8	11.7	60.6
48 17000	Corpus Christi	400.5	279 208	63	697.1	74.4	5.1	1.1	1.9	20.9	54.3	38.5
48 19000	Dallas	887.2	1 208 318	9	1 361.9	53.0	26.5	1.0	3.2	19.2	35.6	34.6
48 19624	Deer Park	26.8	28 844	1 102	1 076.3	91.6	1.4	0.9	1.7	6.1	15.2	80.8
48 19792	Del Rio	40.0	35 136	923	878.4	79.5	1.4	1.1	0.8	20.0	81.0	16.7
48 19972	Denton	159.3	93 435	273	586.5	77.7	9.6	1.2	4.0	10.0	16.4	69.0
48 20092	DeSoto	55.9	41 703	772	746.0	49.9	46.1	0.7	1.6	3.2	7.3	44.7
48 21628	Duncanville	29.2	35 670	901	1 221.6	65.6	25.4	0.8	2.5	7.9	15.3	56.5
48 22660	Edinburg	96.8	55 302	558	571.3	75.4	0.7	0.7	0.9	24.7	88.7	9.8
48 24000	El Paso	645.1	584 113	22	905.5	76.3	3.5	1.2	1.7	20.8	76.6	18.3
48 24768	Euless	42.1	50 118	632	1 190.5	77.7	7.1	1.2	10.2	6.9	13.3	68.4
48 25452	Farmers Branch	31.1	27 025	1 168	869.0	80.8	2.7	1.0	3.4	14.8	37.2	55.8
48 26232	Flower Mound	105.9	60 621	489	572.4	91.7	3.2	0.9	3.7	2.3	5.6	86.9
48 27000	Fort Worth	757.7	585 122	20	772.2	62.0	20.8	1.1	3.2	15.7	29.8	45.8
48 27648	Friendswood	54.4	32 460	993	596.7	91.5	3.0	0.8	2.9	3.4	8.8	84.5
48 27684	Frisco	181.0	55 126	563	304.6	89.0	4.1	0.8	3.0	5.1	11.0	81.4
48 28068	Galveston	119.5	56 667	536	474.2	60.7	26.0	0.9	3.8	11.3	25.8	44.2
48 29000	Garland	147.9	218 027	82	1 474.2	67.7	12.4	1.1	8.0	13.7	25.6	53.3
48 29336	Georgetown	59.1	34 815	929	589.1	87.0	3.7	0.7	1.1	9.4	18.1	76.8
48 30464	Grand Prairie	184.9	136 671	165	739.2	64.8	14.1	1.3	5.1	18.1	33.0	47.2
48 30644	Grapevine	83.6	46 891	684	560.9	89.6	2.6	1.1	3.2	5.3	11.6	81.8
48 31928	Haltom City	32.1	40 475	791	1 260.9	78.9	3.1	1.3	8.6	10.7	19.9	67.4
48 32372	Harlingen	88.2	60 769	484	689.0	81.1	1.1	0.8	1.1	18.6	72.8	25.0
48 35000	Houston	1 500.7	2 009 690	4	1 339.2	51.8	25.9	0.8	5.9	18.8	37.4	30.8
48 35528	Huntsville	80.0	35 567	905	444.6	67.1	26.6	0.7	1.5	5.8	16.2	55.3
48 35576	Hurst	25.6	37 141	868	1 450.8	87.7	4.5	1.3	2.6	6.0	11.0	80.8
48 37000	Irving	174.1	194 455	107	1 116.9	66.8	10.8	1.2	9.1	15.4	31.2	48.2
48 38632	Keller	47.8	33 951	952	710.3	95.0	1.7	0.9	2.3	1.7	4.5	90.7
48 39148	Killeen	91.5	96 159	261	1 050.9	49.7	36.1	1.7	7.5	11.2	17.8	39.8
48 39352	Kingsville	35.8	25 270	1 221	705.9	74.1	4.7	1.1	2.2	21.4	67.1	26.1
48 40588	Lake Jackson	49.3	26 950	1 175	546.7	87.9	4.2	0.8	2.8	6.1	14.7	77.6
48 41212	Lancaster	75.9	27 814	1 142	366.5	39.1	53.8	1.0	0.7	7.5	11.6	33.6
48 41440	La Porte	49.1	33 263	967	677.5	83.2	6.6	1.0	1.5	9.9	20.5	70.7
48 41464	Laredo	203.2	197 488	99	971.9	84.6	0.5	0.6	0.6	16.2	94.1	5.0
48 41980	League City	132.7	54 775	570	412.8	85.7	5.5	0.8	3.8	6.3	13.5	76.6
48 42508	Lewisville	95.3	87 127	307	914.2	79.3	7.9	1.3	4.5	9.6	17.8	69.1
48 43888	Longview	141.6	74 902	373	529.0	71.4	22.5	1.0	1.1	5.6	10.3	65.5
48 45000	Lubbock	297.4	206 481	90	694.3	74.6	9.1	1.0	1.9	15.6	27.5	61.3
48 45072	Lufkin	69.2	33 162	971	479.2	61.2	27.1	0.6	1.6	11.2	17.6	53.7
48 45384	McAllen	119.1	116 501	201	978.2	81.0	0.7	0.6	2.3	18.2	80.3	16.8

1. Dry land or land partially or temporarily covered by water.   2. Hispanic or Latino persons may be of any race.

Table D. Cities — **Population and Households**

City	Population characteristics, 2000 (cont'd)										Population			
	Age of population (percent)										Census counts		Percent change	
	Under 5 years	5 to 17 years	18 to 24 years	25 to 34 years	35 to 44 years	45 to 54 years	55 to 64 years	65 to 74 years	75 years and over	Percent female	1990	2000	1990–2000	2000–2003
	12	13	14	15	16	17	18	19	20	21	22	23	24	25
TENNESSEE—Cont'd														
Hendersonville	6.6	19.2	7.8	14.2	17.2	14.8	10.0	5.7	4.4	51.3	32 188	40 620	26.2	5.9
Jackson	7.2	18.6	12.8	14.3	14.4	12.0	7.5	6.4	6.8	53.4	49 145	59 643	21.4	2.5
Johnson City	5.5	14.3	13.7	13.9	14.2	13.2	9.3	7.9	8.0	52.3	50 354	55 469	10.2	3.5
Kingsport	5.7	16.0	6.5	12.1	14.1	14.1	11.2	9.5	10.8	54.3	40 457	44 905	11.0	-1.5
Knoxville	5.9	13.7	16.8	15.7	13.8	11.9	7.7	6.9	7.5	52.6	169 761	173 890	2.4	-0.4
Memphis	7.8	20.1	10.8	15.8	14.9	12.4	7.2	5.6	5.3	52.7	618 652	650 100	5.1	-0.6
Murfreesboro	6.5	16.2	20.5	16.4	14.4	11.0	6.3	4.6	4.2	50.3	44 922	68 816	53.2	13.5
Nashville-Davidson	6.6	15.6	11.6	17.6	16.4	13.2	7.9	5.9	5.3	51.6	488 188	569 891	11.6	0.0
Oak Ridge	4.8	17.7	6.6	9.5	14.1	15.7	10.6	9.7	11.4	53.2	27 310	27 387	0.3	-0.2
Smyrna	8.6	19.0	10.5	17.3	17.8	12.4	7.5	3.9	2.9	51.1	14 720	25 569	73.7	18.0
TEXAS	7.8	20.4	10.5	15.2	15.9	12.5	7.7	5.5	4.5	50.4	16 986 335	20 851 820	22.8	6.1
Abilene	7.1	18.5	15.3	14.1	14.7	10.9	7.3	6.3	5.7	49.5	106 707	115 930	8.6	-0.9
Allen	10.7	24.3	5.4	17.4	23.2	11.7	4.5	1.7	1.1	50.1	19 315	43 554	125.5	43.3
Amarillo	8.0	19.9	10.2	13.9	14.9	12.5	8.0	6.7	5.9	52.0	157 571	173 627	10.2	2.9
Arlington	8.3	20.0	11.0	18.5	17.2	12.3	6.5	3.6	2.5	50.0	261 717	332 969	27.2	6.6
Austin	7.1	15.4	16.6	21.1	16.0	11.6	5.6	3.5	3.2	48.6	472 020	656 562	39.1	2.4
Baytown	8.7	21.3	11.2	15.2	14.2	12.4	7.0	4.9	5.0	51.5	63 843	66 430	4.1	1.2
Beaumont	7.1	20.0	10.4	13.2	14.8	13.0	8.2	6.8	6.6	52.5	114 323	113 866	-0.4	-1.3
Bedford	5.9	16.6	9.7	15.9	17.1	16.7	9.5	4.8	3.9	51.8	43 762	47 152	7.7	3.0
Big Spring	6.1	17.5	9.9	16.3	16.4	12.2	7.6	7.2	6.9	44.4	23 093	25 233	9.3	-2.7
Brownsville	9.9	24.8	11.2	14.6	12.9	10.6	6.6	5.4	4.1	52.9	107 027	139 722	30.5	11.8
Bryan	8.0	19.0	18.1	16.6	13.2	9.7	6.1	4.5	4.8	50.2	55 002	65 660	19.4	3.2
Carrollton	7.9	20.3	8.0	17.3	19.8	14.3	7.1	3.2	2.1	50.5	82 169	109 576	33.4	6.5
Cedar Hill	8.5	24.1	7.7	15.9	19.9	13.7	5.6	2.6	2.1	52.3	19 988	32 093	60.6	22.3
Cedar Park	11.0	22.6	6.0	19.2	21.1	11.0	4.8	2.4	1.9	50.6	5 161	26 049	404.7	59.2
Cleburne	8.2	19.7	9.7	14.7	13.9	12.3	7.8	6.5	7.3	51.5	22 205	26 005	17.1	7.4
College Station	4.5	10.0	51.2	13.0	8.3	6.0	3.4	1.9	1.7	48.9	52 443	67 890	29.5	8.3
Conroe	8.7	19.4	13.4	17.5	14.1	10.6	6.7	4.9	4.8	49.7	27 675	36 811	33.0	8.4
Coppell	9.5	25.2	4.5	13.7	25.3	14.5	4.7	1.6	1.0	50.7	16 881	35 958	113.0	8.3
Copperas Cove	10.2	21.8	14.2	17.8	15.5	9.2	6.1	3.3	1.7	50.5	24 079	29 592	22.9	1.3
Corpus Christi	7.8	20.4	10.6	13.6	15.6	13.2	7.8	6.1	5.0	51.1	257 428	277 454	7.8	0.6
Dallas	8.3	18.2	11.8	19.8	15.5	11.1	6.5	4.5	4.1	49.6	1 007 618	1 188 580	18.0	1.7
Deer Park	6.3	22.7	9.4	12.1	18.2	15.9	8.0	4.6	2.8	50.3	27 424	28 520	4.0	1.1
Del Rio	8.6	23.1	8.8	14.2	13.4	11.4	8.8	6.5	5.2	51.5	30 705	33 867	10.3	3.7
Denton	6.2	14.5	25.0	17.9	12.9	9.9	5.8	3.8	4.1	50.8	66 270	80 537	21.5	16.0
DeSoto	7.0	21.1	7.6	12.5	17.7	16.0	8.8	4.9	4.4	53.0	30 544	37 646	23.3	10.8
Duncanville	6.5	21.6	8.5	12.3	15.4	16.1	10.0	5.7	3.9	52.6	35 008	36 081	3.1	-1.1
Edinburg	9.8	23.2	13.1	16.3	13.5	9.9	6.0	4.8	3.5	51.2	31 091	48 465	55.9	14.1
El Paso	8.5	22.6	10.0	14.3	14.8	11.7	7.5	6.2	4.4	52.5	515 342	563 662	9.4	3.6
Euless	7.4	17.5	9.8	20.5	19.2	12.5	7.3	3.8	2.0	50.4	38 149	46 005	20.6	8.9
Farmers Branch	7.3	18.4	9.5	15.4	16.0	12.0	9.3	7.5	4.6	49.7	24 250	27 508	13.4	-1.8
Flower Mound	10.7	24.1	4.2	14.8	24.7	13.9	4.9	1.6	1.1	50.2	15 527	50 702	226.5	19.6
Fort Worth	8.5	19.8	11.3	17.0	15.7	11.5	6.7	5.0	4.6	50.7	447 619	534 694	19.5	9.4
Friendswood	6.6	23.5	6.2	10.4	19.0	16.5	9.2	4.8	3.8	51.6	22 814	29 037	27.3	11.8
Frisco	12.8	18.0	5.3	25.6	20.3	9.5	5.0	2.2	1.4	50.5	6 138	33 714	449.3	63.5
Galveston	6.6	16.7	11.3	14.5	15.3	13.1	8.7	7.5	6.2	51.7	59 067	57 247	-3.1	-1.0
Garland	8.2	21.6	9.6	16.0	17.0	13.1	7.4	4.2	2.9	50.4	180 635	215 768	19.4	1.0
Georgetown	6.4	17.0	11.4	12.6	13.7	11.4	9.8	9.6	8.0	51.3	14 840	28 339	90.9	22.9
Grand Prairie	8.9	21.7	10.1	17.2	16.9	12.1	6.7	3.7	2.6	50.5	99 606	127 427	27.9	7.3
Grapevine	7.4	21.9	7.5	14.5	22.1	15.7	6.2	2.5	2.2	49.9	29 407	42 059	44.0	11.5
Haltom City	8.2	18.9	10.2	17.1	15.8	11.9	7.5	5.8	4.6	49.8	32 856	39 018	18.8	3.7
Harlingen	9.1	21.7	9.6	13.9	12.7	11.0	7.0	7.5	7.6	52.4	48 746	57 564	18.1	5.6
Houston	8.2	19.2	11.2	18.1	15.6	12.0	7.1	4.8	3.6	50.1	1 654 348	1 953 631	19.3	2.9
Huntsville	4.6	10.5	29.3	15.0	15.7	10.5	5.9	4.4	4.1	39.5	30 628	35 078	25.6	1.4
Hurst	7.2	18.2	8.3	13.6	16.7	13.3	10.3	7.4	5.0	51.4	33 574	36 273	8.0	2.4
Irving	8.1	17.0	11.9	22.8	16.7	10.8	6.5	3.7	2.4	49.0	155 037	191 615	23.6	1.5
Keller	8.6	25.1	4.7	11.6	23.1	15.6	7.0	2.8	1.6	50.3	13 683	27 345	99.8	24.2
Killeen	10.1	19.8	16.0	20.7	15.0	8.9	4.6	3.2	1.7	49.8	63 535	86 911	36.8	10.6
Kingsville	8.0	18.9	17.3	15.3	11.8	10.6	7.7	5.6	4.9	50.1	25 276	25 575	1.2	-1.2
Lake Jackson	7.4	23.2	7.6	12.5	17.8	14.3	7.4	5.5	4.4	51.2	22 771	26 386	15.9	2.1
Lancaster	8.2	22.2	8.6	15.2	17.1	12.8	6.8	4.5	4.5	53.9	22 117	25 894	17.1	7.4
La Porte	7.9	21.8	8.9	15.1	17.6	14.7	7.1	3.9	3.0	50.4	27 923	31 880	14.2	4.3
Laredo	10.5	25.0	11.4	16.1	13.4	9.7	6.1	4.4	3.4	52.0	122 893	176 576	43.7	11.8
League City	8.1	21.3	6.6	15.1	20.7	14.8	7.4	3.4	2.5	50.2	30 159	45 444	50.7	20.5
Lewisville	9.1	17.5	11.8	23.4	17.8	10.6	5.5	2.5	1.8	50.0	46 521	77 737	67.1	12.1
Longview	7.4	19.4	10.8	13.7	15.0	12.4	8.1	6.9	6.4	51.8	70 311	73 344	4.3	2.1
Lubbock	7.2	17.8	17.9	14.2	13.5	11.3	7.1	5.9	5.2	51.4	186 206	199 564	7.2	3.5
Lufkin	8.0	19.0	10.6	13.6	13.7	11.8	8.3	7.1	8.1	52.9	30 210	32 709	8.3	1.4
McAllen	8.7	22.1	10.5	15.3	14.0	11.8	7.1	5.6	4.9	52.6	84 021	106 414	26.7	9.5

Table D. Cities — Group Quarters, Crime, and Education

City	Households, 2000					Persons in group quarters, 2000				Serious crimes known to police,[2] 2002				Education, 2000			
				Percent			Institutional			Total		Rate[2]		School enrollment[4]		Attainment[5] (percent)	
	Number	Percent change, 1990–2000	Persons per household	Female family householder[1]	One-person	Total	Total	Persons in nursing homes	Non-institutional	Number	Rate[3]	Violent	Property	Public	Private	High school graduate or less	Bachelor's degree or more
	26	27	28	29	30	31	32	33	34	35	36	37	38	39	40	41	42
TENNESSEE—Cont'd																	
Hendersonville	15 823	38.3	2.55	10.7	22.3	229	224	219	5	1 087	2 626	312	2 315	8 698	1 514	38.5	26.4
Jackson	23 503	22.4	2.40	19.4	30.3	3 150	1 185	882	1 965	4 664	7 674	1 127	6 547	11 941	4 765	51.0	22.7
Johnson City	23 720	20.6	2.20	11.6	33.9	3 373	1 176	708	2 197	3 909	6 916	649	6 267	14 325	1 251	44.4	29.4
Kingsport	19 662	25.8	2.22	12.7	32.5	1 167	923	900	244	3 258	7 120	806	6 314	8 551	767	52.6	23.6
Knoxville	76 650	9.5	2.12	13.7	38.3	11 034	2 738	1 922	8 296	12 047	6 799	1 116	5 683	45 471	5 155	49.9	24.6
Memphis	250 721	9.1	2.52	23.8	30.5	17 226	11 067	3 709	6 159	65 894	9 947	1 572	8 375	159 350	26 370	51.6	20.9
Murfreesboro	26 511	54.9	2.42	11.9	28.3	4 648	1 280	647	3 368	3 703	5 281	679	4 602	22 061	1 741	41.7	30.8
Nashville-Davidson	237 405	14.4	2.30	14.3	33.4	24 165	10 298	2 335	13 867	46 022	8 209	1 549	6 660	99 953	41 247	43.1	30.5
Oak Ridge	12 062	2.5	2.24	11.1	32.7	423	282	271	141	1 877	6 726	584	6 142	6 085	465	34.4	37.9
Smyrna	9 608	98.7	2.62	14.2	21.1	367	342	185	25	1 131	4 341	372	3 969	5 546	854	52.8	19.8
TEXAS	7 393 354	21.8	2.74	12.7	23.7	561 109	374 704	105 052	186 405	1 130 292	5 190	579	4 611	5 268 790	679 470	49.2	23.2
Abilene	41 570	8.3	2.53	11.9	26.6	10 932	5 832	754	5 100	5 394	4 455	367	4 088	25 527	9 398	48.3	22.0
Allen	14 205	140.9	3.07	7.4	11.9	13	1	1	12	NA	NA	NA	NA	12 194	1 925	19.0	47.5
Amarillo	67 699	10.7	2.53	12.8	27.7	2 309	1 625	1 459	684	13 476	7 431	815	6 616	43 524	4 591	46.3	20.5
Arlington	124 686	23.9	2.65	11.8	24.7	2 448	954	832	1 494	23 594	6 784	633	6 151	82 761	14 465	36.0	30.4
Austin	265 649	38.3	2.40	10.8	32.8	20 130	6 799	1 892	13 331	42 979	6 267	467	5 800	170 678	21 503	33.6	40.4
Baytown	23 483	4.7	2.80	14.2	23.0	631	443	417	188	3 303	4 760	353	4 407	18 231	1 287	53.2	13.6
Beaumont	44 361	2.3	2.50	18.1	29.5	3 069	2 045	771	1 024	10 443	8 781	967	7 814	28 110	4 239	49.2	21.5
Bedford	20 251	15.2	2.30	8.8	31.6	533	519	491	14	1 913	3 884	177	3 708	9 485	1 779	27.0	35.2
Big Spring	8 155	-1.2	2.51	14.1	29.2	4 786	4 392	147	394	1 105	4 193	258	3 935	6 038	458	62.6	11.1
Brownsville	38 174	45.0	3.62	20.9	13.7	1 691	1 454	688	237	12 759	8 743	552	8 190	45 082	3 099	65.5	13.4
Bryan	23 759	14.8	2.65	14.0	26.1	2 622	2 241	387	381	4 447	6 484	714	5 770	21 531	1 635	50.4	26.0
Carrollton	39 136	28.5	2.78	9.9	20.1	589	375	370	214	4 289	3 747	225	3 523	24 854	5 015	31.0	37.0
Cedar Hill	10 748	63.6	2.96	14.4	15.0	272	138	129	134	1 401	4 179	459	3 720	8 470	2 191	33.9	28.3
Cedar Park	8 621	417.5	3.00	9.6	12.5	168	144	133	24	NA	NA	NA	NA	6 484	966	25.3	36.6
Cleburne	9 335	14.5	2.71	11.9	24.0	700	644	341	56	1 793	6 601	479	6 123	6 056	634	59.2	14.0
College Station	24 691	38.1	2.32	6.8	27.1	10 703	217	217	10 486	2 972	4 191	199	3 992	42 273	1 866	18.4	58.1
Conroe	13 145	31.2	2.73	13.5	27.2	862	774	187	88	3 048	7 927	918	7 009	8 060	983	58.2	18.3
Coppell	12 211	103.6	2.94	8.1	16.1	4	1	0	3	923	2 458	77	2 380	9 757	2 093	13.0	62.6
Copperas Cove	10 273	27.2	2.85	12.7	16.7	284	180	180	104	1 275	4 125	440	3 685	8 028	651	38.4	17.1
Corpus Christi	98 791	10.4	2.75	15.4	23.2	5 332	2 536	1 329	2 796	21 237	7 328	712	6 616	73 301	7 397	48.9	19.6
Dallas	451 833	12.4	2.58	14.9	32.9	21 164	15 899	5 399	5 265	112 040	9 025	1 371	7 654	249 576	46 046	49.3	27.7
Deer Park	9 615	9.0	2.93	11.5	14.0	303	89	89	214	596	2 001	111	1 890	8 318	614	44.2	16.5
Del Rio	10 778	13.9	3.09	15.8	18.7	528	433	185	95	1 254	3 545	192	3 353	9 040	752	67.5	13.6
Denton	30 895	20.1	2.35	9.5	31.5	7 842	2 463	667	5 379	3 908	4 646	442	4 203	29 147	2 293	36.9	35.5
DeSoto	13 709	27.5	2.71	14.1	20.6	434	423	423	11	1 901	4 835	356	4 479	9 012	2 223	33.7	30.2
Duncanville	12 896	3.1	2.79	16.1	17.6	90	63	57	27	1 928	5 116	475	4 641	8 359	1 769	39.1	27.5
Edinburg	14 183	67.4	3.29	19.0	15.4	1 779	1 525	82	254	5 189	10 250	561	9 689	15 779	726	59.4	19.4
El Paso	182 063	13.4	3.07	18.5	19.2	5 129	3 248	1 329	1 881	26 998	4 586	661	3 925	168 426	16 449	53.9	18.3
Euless	19 218	24.3	2.38	10.9	31.0	213	166	165	47	1 714	3 567	223	3 344	9 737	1 791	35.5	29.5
Farmers Branch	9 766	11.3	2.80	9.8	22.9	156	6	0	150	1 382	4 810	251	4 559	5 549	1 389	45.8	27.2
Flower Mound	16 179	222.4	3.12	5.4	9.1	212	142	93	70	770	1 454	96	1 358	13 423	2 788	14.5	53.1
Fort Worth	195 078	15.9	2.67	14.7	28.6	14 754	9 513	3 392	5 241	44 797	8 021	760	7 261	119 116	25 500	51.3	22.3
Friendswood	10 107	30.3	2.85	8.7	17.0	242	232	232	10	474	1 563	148	1 414	7 703	1 274	25.7	38.6
Frisco	12 065	482.9	2.78	6.3	15.6	115	77	77	38	NA	NA	NA	NA	6 667	1 689	18.8	49.8
Galveston	23 842	-1.3	2.30	16.9	35.6	2 364	1 250	330	1 114	NA	NA	NA	NA	14 278	1 467	50.3	23.7
Garland	73 241	15.9	2.93	13.7	19.8	1 037	557	517	480	9 734	4 319	279	4 040	53 888	7 353	47.5	21.8
Georgetown	10 393	100.7	2.52	9.5	21.5	2 119	1 062	468	1 057	599	2 024	142	1 882	5 555	1 945	34.8	36.6
Grand Prairie	43 791	25.3	2.90	13.7	20.7	420	377	377	43	7 924	5 953	393	5 561	32 421	4 456	51.1	19.3
Grapevine	15 712	43.2	2.66	9.4	22.2	212	211	211	1	1 897	4 318	223	4 095	10 463	1 774	24.5	43.2
Haltom City	14 922	17.0	2.61	12.0	27.1	126	126	125	0	2 007	4 925	361	4 564	8 427	1 112	58.9	12.4
Harlingen	19 021	23.5	2.94	16.2	20.9	1 590	1 174	732	416	4 041	6 721	481	6 240	15 747	1 436	57.6	16.8
Houston	717 945	16.4	2.67	15.3	29.6	33 256	18 819	5 774	14 437	149 247	7 314	1 223	6 091	469 560	67 272	50.0	27.0
Huntsville	10 266	30.7	2.31	12.5	30.8	11 377	8 904	249	2 473	1 138	3 106	459	2 647	12 296	1 002	55.6	22.4
Hurst	14 076	10.1	2.56	11.6	22.4	231	217	216	14	2 649	6 992	396	6 596	7 829	1 140	38.4	24.5
Irving	76 241	20.6	2.50	11.2	31.3	1 073	468	410	605	10 812	5 402	401	5 001	40 980	6 914	42.7	30.0
Keller	8 827	96.7	3.09	5.6	8.9	28	28	28	0	615	2 153	298	1 856	7 302	1 446	20.1	44.6
Killeen	32 447	39.6	2.67	13.4	22.3	310	255	230	55	6 505	7 166	783	6 383	22 147	2 016	38.8	15.7
Kingsville	8 943	4.9	2.73	14.9	23.5	1 180	279	143	901	1 712	6 409	887	5 521	9 000	718	54.6	20.5
Lake Jackson	9 588	17.8	2.74	8.5	20.0	106	106	106	0	1 005	3 647	138	3 509	7 137	1 104	28.2	35.3
Lancaster	9 182	19.2	2.77	20.8	21.3	497	497	247	0	1 756	6 492	839	5 653	6 672	1 287	46.5	18.9
La Porte	10 928	19.5	2.90	11.4	17.4	235	38	38	197	762	2 288	237	2 051	8 686	932	49.7	13.2
Laredo	46 852	46.3	3.70	18.7	12.7	3 044	1 929	388	1 115	12 952	7 023	600	6 422	56 284	4 428	63.5	14.7
League City	16 189	52.9	2.78	8.2	18.4	390	357	261	33	1 249	2 631	70	2 562	11 266	2 048	29.1	35.5
Lewisville	30 043	69.9	2.58	9.6	25.2	361	127	115	234	4 218	5 195	260	4 935	16 882	2 586	34.4	32.4
Longview	28 363	4.3	2.50	14.5	27.9	2 496	1 601	790	895	5 771	7 533	751	6 783	16 575	2 734	47.7	20.6
Lubbock	77 527	12.1	2.47	12.9	28.3	8 456	2 653	1 054	5 803	14 371	6 894	1 206	5 688	62 134	6 420	44.3	26.6
Lufkin	12 247	9.1	2.58	14.7	27.9	1 122	824	633	298	2 013	5 892	503	5 389	7 849	741	51.6	20.6
McAllen	33 151	33.1	3.18	16.0	17.9	986	811	752	175	8 982	8 081	480	7 601	31 858	2 556	53.7	23.6

1. No spouse present.   2. Data for serious crimes have not been adjusted for underreporting. This may affect comparability between geographic areas and over time.   3. Per 100,000 population estimated by the FBI.   4. All persons 3 years old and over enrolled in nursery school through college.   5. Persons 25 years old and over.

Table D. Cities — Income, Poverty, and Housing

City	Money income, 1999							Housing units, 2000					
	Per capita income[1] (dollars)	Households			Percent below poverty					Vacant units			
		Median income			Persons		Families						
		Dollars	Percent change, 1989–1999 (constant 1999 dollars)	Percent with income of $100,000 or more	Total	Percent change in rate, 1989–1999	Total	Total	Percent change, 1990–2000	Vacant units for sale or rent[2]	For seasonal use (percent)	Home owner vacancy rate	Renter vacancy rate
	43	44	45	46	47	48	49	50	51	52	53	54	55
TENNESSEE—Cont'd													
Hendersonville	24 165	50 108	-2.0	14.7	6.2	37.8	5.2	16 507	32.4	684	0.3	1.9	6.2
Jackson	18 495	33 194	17.3	7.8	17.1	-18.6	14.0	25 501	23.0	1 998	0.4	2.2	9.1
Johnson City	20 364	30 835	-0.4	8.3	15.9	-8.1	11.4	25 730	21.1	2 010	0.4	2.9	8.5
Kingsport	20 549	30 524	-0.1	8.9	17.1	-5.5	14.2	21 796	30.2	2 134	0.4	3.5	12.8
Knoxville	18 171	27 492	2.7	5.7	20.8	0.0	14.4	84 981	11.2	8 331	0.3	2.9	10.5
Memphis	17 838	32 285	6.0	7.3	20.6	-10.4	17.2	271 552	9.2	20 831	0.3	2.0	8.4
Murfreesboro	20 219	39 705	12.0	9.7	14.1	-11.9	8.2	28 815	54.0	2 304	0.4	3.1	9.8
Nashville-Davidson	23 069	39 797	4.4	10.6	13.0	0.0	10.0	252 977	10.4	15 572	0.4	2.0	6.5
Oak Ridge	24 793	41 950	-4.3	13.3	10.9	14.7	8.0	13 417	5.7	1 355	0.4	2.3	18.3
Smyrna	19 704	44 405	6.1	7.6	8.8	-20.0	6.7	10 016	88.6	408	0.1	1.8	5.3
TEXAS	19 617	39 927	10.0	11.5	15.4	-14.9	12.0	8 157 575	16.4	764 221	2.1	1.8	8.5
Abilene	16 577	33 007	-0.6	5.9	15.4	0.7	10.9	45 618	2.7	4 048	0.4	2.3	10.4
Allen	28 575	78 924	22.7	31.6	3.0	-3.2	2.0	15 227	146.7	1 022	0.1	1.6	26.3
Amarillo	18 621	34 940	4.4	7.3	14.5	-13.7	11.1	72 408	5.6	4 709	0.3	1.7	8.1
Arlington	22 445	47 622	1.1	13.0	9.9	20.7	7.3	130 628	15.8	5 942	0.3	1.4	6.1
Austin	24 163	42 689	25.0	13.6	14.4	-19.6	9.1	276 842	27.5	11 193	0.5	1.0	3.5
Baytown	17 641	40 559	0.1	9.8	15.5	-3.7	13.0	26 203	4.7	2 720	0.6	1.4	14.3
Beaumont	18 632	32 559	-1.1	8.9	19.6	-7.1	16.4	48 815	-0.4	4 454	0.4	1.7	9.9
Bedford	29 466	54 436	-4.6	19.4	3.7	2.8	2.4	21 113	12.0	862	0.2	0.7	6.7
Big Spring	14 119	28 257	-1.3	4.9	22.2	-5.1	17.1	9 865	0.1	1 710	0.4	4.9	23.7
Brownsville	9 762	24 468	14.6	4.1	36.0	-18.0	32.4	42 323	46.0	4 149	3.0	1.1	8.0
Bryan	15 770	31 672	4.4	6.2	22.3	1.4	15.5	25 703	11.7	1 944	0.6	2.0	7.7
Carrollton	26 746	62 406	1.4	23.2	5.6	24.4	4.1	40 458	22.6	1 322	0.4	1.0	5.0
Cedar Hill	23 389	60 136	8.0	16.3	5.5	48.6	4.2	11 075	57.3	327	0.1	1.3	2.8
Cedar Park	24 767	67 527	NA	18.9	4.1	NA	3.0	8 914	385.2	293	0.1	1.5	4.6
Cleburne	16 762	35 481	1.4	6.5	13.5	-9.4	10.0	9 910	7.3	575	0.3	1.9	4.6
College Station	15 170	21 180	8.9	9.1	37.4	-1.6	15.4	26 054	31.3	1 363	0.4	1.4	5.0
Conroe	16 841	34 123	7.5	7.2	19.3	2.7	15.0	14 378	25.0	1 233	0.3	1.5	10.0
Coppell	40 219	96 935	22.7	48.2	1.9	-24.0	1.4	12 587	96.5	376	0.3	1.2	5.5
Copperas Cove	15 995	37 869	14.6	4.9	9.6	-20.0	8.1	11 120	19.5	847	0.2	2.6	9.9
Corpus Christi	17 419	36 414	5.2	8.0	17.6	-12.0	14.1	107 831	7.6	9 040	1.0	2.0	9.5
Dallas	22 183	37 628	1.9	12.4	17.8	-1.1	14.9	484 117	4.0	32 284	0.3	1.4	7.0
Deer Park	24 440	61 334	-1.2	21.2	5.6	7.7	4.0	9 921	8.7	306	0.2	0.4	8.3
Del Rio	12 199	27 387	17.2	5.2	27.0	-29.5	22.9	11 895	11.3	1 117	0.7	1.9	8.4
Denton	19 365	35 422	13.9	9.6	16.2	-21.7	8.7	32 716	13.6	1 821	0.2	2.0	5.5
DeSoto	25 650	57 699	-5.7	19.0	5.5	37.5	4.1	14 069	20.8	360	0.2	1.2	2.6
Duncanville	22 924	51 654	-6.3	15.0	6.1	60.5	3.9	13 290	-0.5	394	0.1	1.0	4.6
Edinburg	11 854	28 938	13.6	5.4	29.2	-13.6	25.2	16 031	74.1	1 848	2.5	1.7	8.2
El Paso	14 388	32 124	1.9	6.9	22.2	-12.3	19.0	193 663	14.8	11 600	0.4	1.6	7.9
Euless	23 764	49 582	5.6	10.7	7.0	29.6	5.7	20 136	17.6	918	0.3	1.0	5.9
Farmers Branch	24 921	54 734	7.1	19.7	6.3	-6.0	4.0	10 115	9.8	349	0.3	1.1	4.8
Flower Mound	34 699	95 416	32.3	46.2	2.5	127.3	2.2	16 833	213.7	654	0.1	1.6	17.2
Fort Worth	18 800	37 074	3.9	8.9	15.9	-8.6	12.7	211 035	8.5	15 957	0.3	1.9	9.1
Friendswood	28 615	69 384	2.3	26.8	3.3	13.8	2.3	10 405	29.3	298	0.2	1.1	6.1
Frisco	34 089	79 149	NA	30.8	3.4	NA	2.2	13 683	504.6	1 618	0.2	2.0	34.9
Galveston	18 275	28 895	3.3	7.6	22.3	-7.9	17.8	30 017	-2.9	6 175	7.5	3.2	15.9
Garland	20 000	49 156	-1.8	12.3	8.9	14.1	6.8	75 300	8.2	2 059	0.1	1.1	3.5
Georgetown	24 287	54 098	55.1	17.7	7.2	-59.8	4.4	10 902	89.0	509	0.6	2.2	3.6
Grand Prairie	18 978	46 816	1.0	10.4	11.1	11.0	8.7	46 425	19.9	2 634	0.4	1.2	7.8
Grapevine	31 549	71 680	9.1	30.8	4.8	14.3	3.1	16 486	38.5	774	0.3	0.6	9.2
Haltom City	17 740	38 818	13.8	6.4	10.0	-17.4	7.6	15 716	12.0	794	0.4	1.1	5.4
Harlingen	13 886	30 296	8.1	6.3	24.9	-16.7	19.3	23 008	29.3	3 987	8.9	2.3	13.1
Houston	20 101	36 616	3.8	11.8	19.2	-7.2	16.0	782 009	7.7	64 064	0.5	1.6	8.7
Huntsville	13 576	27 075	12.7	7.4	23.9	-20.3	13.1	11 508	26.0	1 242	0.5	2.3	11.5
Hurst	23 247	50 369	0.0	13.8	6.6	-15.4	4.5	14 729	6.7	653	0.2	0.7	9.1
Irving	23 419	44 956	5.3	11.9	10.6	1.0	8.0	80 293	13.0	4 052	0.6	1.1	5.2
Keller	31 986	86 232	16.6	38.1	1.4	-44.0	1.0	9 216	92.3	389	0.1	2.9	6.9
Killeen	15 323	34 461	14.2	3.4	12.9	-11.0	11.2	35 343	33.7	2 896	0.2	3.0	9.1
Kingsville	13 003	27 624	-6.8	4.9	28.3	3.7	22.6	10 427	3.2	1 484	0.4	2.3	17.1
Lake Jackson	25 877	60 901	-1.5	22.2	6.4	88.2	5.4	10 475	16.9	887	0.8	1.6	16.7
Lancaster	18 731	43 773	3.5	8.4	8.1	-19.8	6.1	9 590	13.5	408	0.2	1.6	5.2
La Porte	21 178	55 810	-0.5	12.0	7.5	-14.8	6.2	11 720	17.6	792	0.4	1.9	11.4
Laredo	11 084	29 108	17.8	6.4	29.6	-20.6	25.2	50 319	48.0	3 467	0.9	1.3	5.8
League City	27 170	67 838	12.1	22.2	4.8	-2.0	3.6	17 280	51.8	1 091	0.6	2.3	11.5
Lewisville	24 703	54 771	13.2	15.1	6.0	0.0	3.9	31 764	61.0	1 721	0.2	1.5	7.7
Longview	18 768	33 858	-0.7	7.8	16.0	-5.9	13.0	30 726	1.4	2 363	0.4	2.0	10.1
Lubbock	17 511	31 844	-1.8	7.0	18.4	-6.1	12.0	84 066	8.0	6 539	0.2	1.7	10.1
Lufkin	17 613	32 989	9.8	8.4	18.8	-10.0	15.0	13 402	7.3	1 155	0.5	2.2	8.3
McAllen	14 939	33 641	13.5	9.4	23.8	-27.2	20.9	37 922	32.6	4 771	4.5	2.2	10.7

1. Based on population enumerated as of April 1, 2000.   2. Includes units rented or sold but not occupied.

Table D. Cities — **Housing, Labor Force, Employment, and Disability**

City	Housing units, 2000 (cont'd) Occupied units					Civilian labor force, 2003		Unemployment		Civilian employment,[2] 2000	Percent		Disability, 2000
	Total	Percent owner occupied	Percent renter occupied	Average size owner occupied	Average size renter occupied	Total	Percent change, 2002–2003	Total	Rate[1]	Total	Management, professional, and related occupations	Production, transportation, and material moving occupations	Employment disabled persons[3] (percent)
	56	57	58	59	60	61	62	63	64	65	66	67	68
TENNESSEE—Cont'd													
Hendersonville	15 823	71.4	28.6	2.72	2.13	24 297	-1.1	853	3.5	21 572	36.6	9.7	9.7
Jackson	23 503	56.7	43.3	2.50	2.28	31 419	-2.4	2 072	6.6	26 751	31.7	20.7	13.3
Johnson City	23 720	57.2	42.8	2.36	1.98	28 305	-1.9	1 491	5.3	26 476	35.1	13.1	12.5
Kingsport	19 662	64.8	35.2	2.31	2.08	17 173	-0.8	1 059	6.2	17 638	34.0	13.9	13.7
Knoxville	76 650	51.2	48.8	2.29	1.95	99 365	-0.1	4 003	4.0	80 496	32.6	12.4	11.7
Memphis	250 721	55.8	44.2	2.62	2.40	327 056	-0.4	25 312	7.7	280 121	29.5	16.6	16.1
Murfreesboro	26 511	52.1	47.9	2.63	2.19	41 105	-0.7	2 286	5.6	36 001	34.1	15.4	8.2
Nashville-Davidson	237 405	55.3	44.7	2.43	2.13	314 434	-0.9	14 050	4.5	291 283	37.2	11.9	11.6
Oak Ridge	12 062	68.4	31.6	2.33	2.03	15 049	-0.1	539	3.6	12 058	46.6	8.8	8.7
Smyrna	9 608	64.5	35.5	2.76	2.38	12 056	-0.8	564	4.7	13 785	29.4	20.2	10.1
TEXAS	7 393 354	63.8	36.2	2.87	2.53	10 910 344	2.1	737 516	6.8	9 234 372	33.3	13.2	12.5
Abilene	41 570	58.6	41.4	2.61	2.40	54 390	3.6	2 419	4.4	47 818	32.5	10.6	10.6
Allen	14 205	85.7	14.3	3.13	2.69	22 203	0.5	1 273	5.7	22 748	54.4	4.8	5.4
Amarillo	67 699	63.3	36.7	2.64	2.34	99 384	4.0	4 228	4.3	81 080	29.0	14.1	11.3
Arlington	124 686	54.7	45.3	2.87	2.38	201 415	1.3	11 391	5.7	175 452	36.1	12.3	11.0
Austin	265 649	44.8	55.2	2.65	2.19	406 989	1.1	25 354	6.2	359 804	43.1	8.6	9.8
Baytown	23 483	59.6	40.4	2.91	2.64	38 057	2.5	3 048	8.0	27 492	26.8	17.2	12.8
Beaumont	44 361	59.9	40.1	2.58	2.37	58 611	2.9	5 120	8.7	47 715	32.4	12.6	13.6
Bedford	20 251	55.0	45.0	2.64	1.89	35 718	1.2	1 424	4.0	28 276	42.2	8.5	7.3
Big Spring	8 155	63.6	36.4	2.53	2.47	9 744	-0.1	537	5.5	8 339	31.8	13.2	14.9
Brownsville	38 174	61.2	38.8	3.74	3.42	54 363	3.5	6 902	12.7	43 989	27.6	16.9	15.7
Bryan	23 759	50.8	49.2	2.80	2.51	39 335	3.5	914	2.3	30 603	32.4	13.0	10.1
Carrollton	39 136	65.7	34.3	2.90	2.56	75 020	0.7	3 364	4.5	61 483	42.3	10.0	8.2
Cedar Hill	10 748	81.0	19.0	3.03	2.67	12 948	0.6	590	4.6	16 963	39.4	11.8	11.0
Cedar Park	8 621	84.4	15.6	3.04	2.80	6 030	1.2	417	6.9	13 756	47.6	8.7	7.2
Cleburne	9 335	66.8	33.2	2.71	2.70	14 071	1.8	1 261	9.0	11 474	24.9	22.0	18.1
College Station	24 691	30.6	69.4	2.78	2.11	33 005	3.5	795	2.4	31 807	46.1	5.7	3.0
Conroe	13 145	47.3	52.7	3.00	2.50	24 220	2.2	1 369	5.7	16 652	24.7	13.8	18.1
Coppell	12 211	77.2	22.8	3.15	2.23	12 153	0.6	348	2.9	18 858	59.2	4.4	5.8
Copperas Cove	10 273	54.2	45.8	2.94	2.76	10 712	1.8	706	6.6	10 844	29.3	10.2	10.7
Corpus Christi	98 791	59.6	40.4	2.89	2.56	137 653	3.1	9 045	6.6	118 307	30.7	11.4	12.5
Dallas	451 833	43.2	56.8	2.78	2.44	695 388	0.5	63 226	9.1	549 191	33.0	13.1	15.9
Deer Park	9 615	79.3	20.7	2.97	2.79	18 423	2.1	989	5.4	14 332	31.5	17.7	10.2
Del Rio	10 778	64.6	35.4	3.17	2.96	16 744	4.3	1 402	8.4	11 860	26.5	14.0	13.3
Denton	30 895	41.9	58.1	2.67	2.12	63 491	1.1	4 568	7.2	43 026	35.2	9.8	8.5
DeSoto	13 709	72.2	27.8	2.88	2.30	21 443	0.6	1 106	5.2	19 685	41.2	10.8	8.5
Duncanville	12 896	71.7	28.3	2.84	2.66	24 045	0.6	1 379	5.7	18 035	37.6	12.1	10.9
Edinburg	14 183	61.7	38.3	3.45	3.03	19 998	6.3	2 410	12.1	17 598	36.6	10.8	13.6
El Paso	182 063	61.4	38.6	3.20	2.86	267 748	2.7	24 818	9.3	207 408	31.3	14.9	12.7
Euless	19 218	43.8	56.2	2.66	2.17	31 500	1.2	1 472	4.7	26 520	38.0	10.8	9.8
Farmers Branch	9 766	68.0	32.0	2.70	3.02	16 977	0.5	1 145	6.7	14 390	32.3	15.2	10.4
Flower Mound	16 179	92.9	7.1	3.15	2.74	15 025	0.9	633	4.2	26 506	54.5	5.3	3.7
Fort Worth	195 078	55.9	44.1	2.84	2.44	293 626	1.4	24 854	8.5	240 119	30.2	16.1	15.0
Friendswood	10 107	80.1	19.9	3.00	2.25	15 247	2.6	640	4.2	14 319	48.2	7.9	6.5
Frisco	12 065	81.3	18.7	2.86	2.44	7 211	0.4	530	7.3	18 292	54.5	5.0	5.5
Galveston	23 842	43.6	56.4	2.43	2.20	33 681	3.8	3 569	10.6	24 243	35.2	8.0	13.1
Garland	73 241	65.6	34.4	2.98	2.84	124 862	0.6	7 652	6.1	106 449	31.9	14.4	13.2
Georgetown	10 393	68.7	31.3	2.54	2.48	15 832	1.2	965	6.1	12 802	39.6	9.5	10.6
Grand Prairie	43 791	61.2	38.8	3.06	2.65	66 521	0.7	4 847	7.3	61 275	30.1	16.8	13.7
Grapevine	15 712	65.0	35.0	2.88	2.26	22 478	1.2	786	3.5	23 708	45.3	8.6	6.7
Haltom City	14 922	59.5	40.5	2.77	2.37	22 471	1.3	1 416	6.3	19 415	22.3	18.6	15.5
Harlingen	19 021	61.1	38.9	2.94	2.94	29 613	3.1	2 347	7.9	19 783	33.8	11.3	12.9
Houston	717 945	45.8	54.2	2.84	2.54	1 101 970	2.5	91 847	8.3	859 961	33.9	12.9	14.6
Huntsville	10 266	43.5	56.5	2.54	2.13	12 955	4.0	511	3.9	12 515	32.9	8.1	8.2
Hurst	14 076	66.1	33.9	2.60	2.48	25 333	1.3	1 558	6.2	18 837	35.9	11.3	9.9
Irving	76 241	37.2	62.8	2.76	2.35	116 628	0.5	7 634	6.5	104 617	35.6	12.1	12.9
Keller	8 827	92.7	7.3	3.12	2.74	9 846	1.2	323	3.3	13 849	48.2	7.6	6.2
Killeen	32 447	46.4	53.6	2.92	2.45	30 389	2.4	2 693	8.9	29 754	25.7	13.1	12.0
Kingsville	8 943	55.0	45.0	2.85	2.58	11 835	8.9	727	6.1	9 970	31.7	11.5	10.8
Lake Jackson	9 588	71.1	28.9	2.87	2.41	14 713	2.0	855	5.8	12 246	44.9	11.4	9.9
Lancaster	9 182	65.6	34.4	2.88	2.55	14 286	0.5	966	6.8	11 913	31.6	14.5	12.9
La Porte	10 928	77.2	22.8	2.98	2.61	18 386	2.1	974	5.3	15 746	27.3	18.5	11.1
Laredo	46 852	64.4	35.6	3.87	3.40	78 734	4.7	5 620	7.1	58 602	27.5	14.3	13.8
League City	16 189	77.0	23.0	2.92	2.32	19 510	3.0	719	3.7	23 437	47.9	9.6	7.9
Lewisville	30 043	53.9	46.1	2.92	2.18	49 837	0.9	2 216	4.4	45 574	38.5	9.7	7.7
Longview	28 363	58.3	41.7	2.61	2.34	40 989	2.5	2 917	7.1	31 660	30.3	16.7	13.1
Lubbock	77 527	55.8	44.2	2.64	2.25	110 370	2.0	3 973	3.6	95 035	34.2	10.1	11.2
Lufkin	12 247	60.0	40.0	2.64	2.49	16 571	2.6	1 051	6.3	13 760	32.0	19.3	13.2
McAllen	33 151	63.3	36.7	3.33	2.92	57 597	6.2	5 600	9.7	40 618	37.4	9.2	12.1

1. Percent of civilian labor force.   2. Persons 16 years old and over.   3. Persons 16 to 64 years old.

City	Value of residential construction authorized by building permits, 2003			Wholesale trade, 1997				Retail trade,[1] 1997			
	New construction ($1,000)	Number of housing units	Percent single family	Number of establish-ments	Number of employees	Sales (mil dol)	Annual payroll (mil dol)	Number of establish-ments	Number of employees	Sales (mil dol)	Annual payroll (mil dol)
	69	70	71	72	73	74	75	76	77	78	79
TENNESSEE—Cont'd											
Hendersonville	52 938	445	98.7	71	437	218.2	16.4	139	1 552	238.5	23.6
Jackson	51 888	591	76.0	143	1 975	702.1	55.1	547	7 771	1 152.3	110.0
Johnson City	58 695	432	69.4	126	1 843	1 086.4	47.4	435	6 118	1 012.9	91.9
Kingsport	14 929	142	100.0	102	1 167	464.7	31.1	415	5 841	996.0	92.4
Knoxville	30 559	440	99.5	671	8 791	4 595.8	309.0	1 431	22 302	4 031.1	386.5
Memphis	NA	NA	NA	1 470	27 381	24 961.4	948.4	2 535	37 267	6 358.3	635.4
Murfreesboro	187 003	1 723	93.0	92	935	477.6	28.3	433	6 874	1 187.9	113.8
Nashville-Davidson	529 150	3 879	79.4	1 445	26 012	17 005.2	962.7	3 017	44 452	7 737.6	782.7
Oak Ridge	9 684	71	66.2	30	180	52.7	6.1	192	2 625	455.4	41.1
Smyrna	42 945	543	91.0	26	388	155.6	12.7	84	1 366	225.5	20.9
TEXAS	19 551 763	177 194	75.7	33 346	425 744	323 111.7	15 504.9	74 105	950 848	182 516.1	16 197.1
Abilene	30 409	211	89.6	200	1 861	653.2	50.5	586	6 820	1 223.1	112.4
Allen	215 886	1 326	92.8	29	171	77.2	5.9	57	615	100.1	11.0
Amarillo	130 629	1 007	73.2	307	3 565	1 466.5	115.7	910	11 528	2 196.0	195.4
Arlington	291 139	2 724	63.2	519	6 347	4 614.2	226.9	1 152	18 925	3 806.7	368.2
Austin	488 740	5 298	58.8	1 065	16 673	8 086.0	661.5	2 604	40 259	7 561.4	749.7
Baytown	50 525	396	100.0	46	D	D	D	268	4 289	755.0	69.2
Beaumont	55 066	583	44.4	271	3 246	1 379.4	107.6	656	9 662	1 674.4	150.7
Bedford	14 529	104	100.0	84	332	335.6	17.8	141	2 039	448.9	36.3
Big Spring	361	3	100.0	36	448	166.4	18.9	136	1 474	244.0	20.7
Brownsville	138 234	1 737	94.9	220	1 952	585.7	37.3	518	6 661	985.0	91.5
Bryan	42 478	710	36.6	90	1 097	278.4	28.8	281	3 555	657.5	58.5
Carrollton	68 225	547	45.5	431	7 788	14 382.2	312.8	320	5 405	1 230.5	124.8
Cedar Hill	70 085	473	96.2	17	D	D	D	47	726	93.5	10.5
Cedar Park	139 906	1 316	81.5	NA	NA	NA	NA	NA	NA	NA	NA
Cleburne	14 726	141	100.0	32	444	156.0	9.8	168	2 139	399.5	34.0
College Station	131 856	1 138	75.6	22	368	79.5	7.8	268	4 342	653.5	62.1
Conroe	60 894	819	50.4	103	D	D	D	360	5 170	1 146.7	92.0
Coppell	19 462	55	100.0	32	304	159.9	10.1	45	692	174.7	12.9
Copperas Cove	19 595	282	28.4	5	4	0.6	0.1	80	1 115	157.5	14.3
Corpus Christi	131 316	1 454	82.7	453	4 708	1 656.2	144.5	1 183	16 289	2 666.6	255.7
Dallas	706 168	6 960	37.3	3 470	49 621	35 859.7	2 128.0	4 365	60 881	12 436.0	1 266.1
Deer Park	16 411	115	100.0	31	529	157.0	24.1	73	768	112.0	11.4
Del Rio	8 012	142	79.6	30	291	54.5	5.1	166	1 777	275.5	25.0
Denton	267 765	1 946	54.7	101	1 152	796.3	32.0	374	5 476	966.8	87.2
DeSoto	125 968	656	99.7	42	194	68.0	6.3	88	1 287	256.3	22.3
Duncanville	1 773	13	100.0	51	309	132.6	9.9	126	2 015	365.8	34.9
Edinburg	71 245	1 154	74.2	45	1 145	204.9	15.9	99	1 699	254.1	22.2
El Paso	293 859	5 024	91.2	950	10 705	5 954.5	300.9	2 006	28 171	4 588.9	420.2
Euless	67 726	377	100.0	69	606	294.5	25.1	83	1 076	191.3	16.6
Farmers Branch	2 595	7	100.0	398	10 070	8 354.8	444.9	197	3 417	636.2	78.0
Flower Mound	138 492	455	100.0	34	117	283.2	6.5	42	792	136.5	13.7
Fort Worth	893 645	8 858	82.3	843	14 840	9 968.1	524.9	1 856	23 572	4 703.3	449.2
Friendswood	65 180	244	100.0	26	252	78.5	8.2	192	2 648	375.3	39.8
Frisco	656 779	2 809	99.5	NA	NA	NA	NA	NA	NA	NA	NA
Galveston	37 826	408	35.3	55	606	212.3	16.5	252	2 777	362.0	37.8
Garland	98 862	543	100.0	283	4 671	2 727.3	170.5	543	7 133	1 426.8	135.5
Georgetown	101 496	632	91.8	31	D	D	D	126	1 310	289.1	26.2
Grand Prairie	231 820	1 777	81.4	326	6 538	5 025.1	236.1	305	4 760	920.0	92.9
Grapevine	45 120	285	54.4	60	411	425.5	21.7	206	2 205	573.7	48.2
Haltom City	2 764	27	100.0	116	1 305	431.6	42.4	149	1 527	291.9	28.2
Harlingen	36 221	429	77.4	96	1 170	359.9	27.4	326	4 106	611.4	59.0
Houston	1 221 031	13 800	40.2	5 750	82 917	99 680.2	3 389.1	7 871	112 989	21 778.4	2 078.3
Huntsville	6 946	63	71.4	25	D	D	D	157	2 122	371.1	30.7
Hurst	45 360	456	40.4	63	416	183.4	14.6	282	4 233	685.2	69.8
Irving	73 990	755	53.8	522	16 189	22 890.4	741.9	651	13 102	3 255.9	277.4
Keller	116 068	411	100.0	11	39	21.6	1.0	33	335	48.7	5.0
Killeen	115 804	1 333	72.2	25	206	54.3	3.9	329	3 879	660.3	61.2
Kingsville	737	9	100.0	9	D	D	D	105	1 385	209.2	19.7
Lake Jackson	14 023	54	100.0	12	48	17.9	1.6	126	2 549	361.3	32.6
Lancaster	89 240	1 110	47.9	11	D	D	D	65	1 092	196.0	19.2
La Porte	21 072	169	100.0	38	378	144.4	16.5	72	977	212.0	18.3
Laredo	136 485	1 671	94.6	335	D	D	D	723	9 027	1 520.8	138.5
League City	215 206	1 494	100.0	31	161	49.9	4.5	116	1 339	279.8	25.5
Lewisville	46 961	773	20.3	95	1 348	773.7	43.6	402	6 554	1 412.4	125.0
Longview	28 227	199	99.0	245	2 772	847.9	87.5	583	7 436	1 252.4	121.7
Lubbock	271 219	2 908	45.3	446	6 118	3 705.7	170.6	992	13 893	2 519.8	226.6
Lufkin	15 880	154	90.3	59	919	193.3	22.6	291	3 824	626.6	57.9
McAllen	106 668	1 554	56.3	295	2 443	966.8	54.6	757	10 916	1 665.7	165.9

1. Establishments with payroll.

Table D. Cities — Real Estate, Professional Services, and Manufacturing

City	Real estate and rental and leasing, 1997				Professional, scientific, and technical services,[1] 1997				Manufacturing, 1997			
	Number of establish-ments	Number of employees	Receipts (mil dol)	Annual payroll (mil dol)	Number of establish-ments	Number of employees	Receipts (mil dol)	Annual payroll (mil dol)	Number of establish-ments	Number of employees	Receipts (mil dol)	Annual payroll (mil dol)
	80	81	82	83	84	85	86	87	88	89	90	91
TENNESSEE—Cont'd												
Hendersonville	49	183	29.9	3.2	87	621	24.9	9.5	62	1 917	307.2	52.7
Jackson	78	394	38.0	6.8	136	974	76.9	36.6	123	D	D	D
Johnson City	103	459	45.5	8.1	166	1 231	66.9	24.2	101	8 801	1 074.1	211.5
Kingsport	71	320	32.2	5.1	123	734	70.2	39.8	61	D	D	D
Knoxville	332	2 227	243.7	51.7	650	6 376	551.0	209.5	318	14 827	2 429.9	394.5
Memphis	609	5 875	691.5	144.7	1 300	13 282	1 328.0	496.3	688	32 938	8 888.5	1 104.8
Murfreesboro	102	358	44.0	5.5	150	622	48.1	17.7	87	5 660	1 415.5	170.8
Nashville-Davidson	866	6 603	1 119.8	173.2	1 694	15 055	1 636.8	605.8	752	31 716	6 721.8	1 100.0
Oak Ridge	54	277	36.0	5.7	142	7 814	926.4	382.3	59	5 669	897.3	247.3
Smyrna	27	D	D	D	28	116	12.1	3.3	21	D	D	D
TEXAS	20 753	128 915	15 957.4	3 119.2	42 492	351 422	42 044.1	15 906.7	21 808	959 665	297 657.0	32 760.8
Abilene	165	867	88.2	16.6	223	1 116	92.7	30.2	106	2 798	977.5	74.0
Allen	20	55	6.0	0.8	70	182	20.0	8.2	16	509	81.3	19.1
Amarillo	232	1 113	125.1	20.5	344	2 794	194.5	83.6	176	D	D	D
Arlington	322	1 787	217.8	43.8	649	3 950	342.5	130.0	323	13 408	2 909.8	481.6
Austin	1 022	5 751	725.1	140.4	2 699	25 127	2 897.0	1 179.9	596	46 780	13 235.1	1 892.1
Baytown	67	474	46.1	7.3	83	652	53.3	28.0	44	D	D	D
Beaumont	182	1 113	139.3	24.2	336	3 370	432.1	181.8	131	5 882	5 041.5	250.9
Bedford	52	293	33.7	7.3	148	731	59.7	23.3	24	D	D	D
Big Spring	36	D	D	D	37	121	9.0	3.0	22	D	D	D
Brownsville	131	525	39.3	6.3	185	940	72.4	24.5	110	6 511	963.3	123.6
Bryan	77	582	33.6	9.5	157	814	52.8	21.9	73	2 527	309.3	63.4
Carrollton	129	1 198	128.7	29.4	278	1 963	195.8	79.7	227	13 714	2 502.0	532.5
Cedar Hill	8	33	3.3	0.5	27	66	6.1	2.5	NA	NA	NA	NA
Cedar Park	NA	NA	NA	NA	NA	NA	NA	NA	NA	NA	NA	NA
Cleburne	35	91	12.2	1.5	46	250	25.4	7.3	35	2 429	426.8	59.4
College Station	93	471	42.1	6.7	102	1 229	144.8	51.9	NA	NA	NA	NA
Conroe	59	273	36.5	5.3	127	478	39.2	15.0	91	2 544	806.8	86.4
Coppell	30	76	13.5	1.6	66	97	18.8	5.4	NA	NA	NA	NA
Copperas Cove	36	106	6.2	1.3	17	64	3.2	1.3	NA	NA	NA	NA
Corpus Christi	358	2 379	327.1	61.4	678	4 376	413.8	149.6	205	D	D	D
Dallas	2 139	19 869	2 751.0	670.4	5 564	68 907	8 686.8	3 694.5	1 762	77 920	15 722.9	2 884.1
Deer Park	21	163	21.2	4.8	35	440	37.0	14.8	31	4 364	7 583.0	260.7
Del Rio	31	105	8.5	1.4	34	111	7.0	1.8	NA	NA	NA	NA
Denton	110	543	51.0	10.0	163	1 115	62.7	25.0	73	4 187	1 350.0	143.7
DeSoto	37	291	22.7	6.0	54	207	12.0	4.8	NA	NA	NA	NA
Duncanville	38	161	20.7	3.0	59	151	18.1	4.8	40	2 452	237.3	50.3
Edinburg	39	144	13.8	2.3	66	469	32.3	12.5	26	2 134	471.5	32.5
El Paso	533	2 400	282.0	46.9	909	5 633	389.3	158.9	599	33 212	7 602.1	716.2
Euless	32	159	21.0	2.8	63	269	25.1	9.3	41	1 060	107.1	31.0
Farmers Branch	96	1 176	202.5	31.0	310	4 592	446.0	216.4	134	7 477	1 299.6	251.2
Flower Mound	23	61	11.2	1.3	75	193	22.0	6.3	NA	NA	NA	NA
Fort Worth	535	3 489	445.1	92.6	1 297	9 539	1 064.3	404.8	821	56 215	11 198.3	2 337.9
Friendswood	31	173	21.9	4.2	61	241	29.3	13.0	NA	NA	NA	NA
Frisco	NA	NA	NA	NA	NA	NA	NA	NA	NA	NA	NA	NA
Galveston	73	282	34.8	7.3	104	438	48.0	17.3	32	592	56.3	15.8
Garland	168	883	110.7	19.3	256	1 439	222.5	59.6	377	16 285	2 944.6	556.5
Georgetown	49	182	22.7	4.0	84	283	24.6	9.1	54	D	D	D
Grand Prairie	93	1 052	165.9	22.6	130	768	59.1	22.8	232	12 709	2 014.2	464.0
Grapevine	34	169	35.4	4.2	106	307	45.9	14.0	36	1 539	310.4	47.6
Haltom City	44	203	30.9	4.9	35	136	9.2	3.1	138	3 292	361.3	89.7
Harlingen	74	349	39.4	7.3	105	731	43.4	14.7	65	4 480	562.4	86.1
Houston	2 912	27 355	3 223.5	680.8	7 763	91 030	14 150.3	4 922.5	2 969	104 218	32 595.8	3 599.3
Huntsville	43	207	38.5	4.0	48	D	D	D	NA	NA	NA	NA
Hurst	52	215	26.2	3.9	150	1 666	102.3	52.0	43	716	104.7	17.5
Irving	276	3 529	532.3	87.7	542	9 262	1 086.1	415.1	240	11 146	2 590.9	435.9
Keller	17	43	4.8	0.8	29	50	7.2	2.9	NA	NA	NA	NA
Killeen	123	614	50.6	8.2	64	929	87.6	16.6	NA	NA	NA	NA
Kingsville	22	D	D	D	22	D	D	D	NA	NA	NA	NA
Lake Jackson	32	139	18.0	3.0	29	110	8.7	3.3	NA	NA	NA	NA
Lancaster	20	116	14.0	2.0	11	26	1.9	0.6	30	1 275	191.0	35.9
La Porte	30	230	20.4	5.2	43	553	63.7	21.7	35	2 442	1 819.1	132.5
Laredo	155	574	64.3	10.0	206	973	64.8	21.3	86	D	D	D
League City	34	202	17.5	3.6	58	176	15.9	5.6	NA	NA	NA	NA
Lewisville	72	300	35.8	5.6	106	640	62.7	20.9	85	5 347	930.8	219.5
Longview	107	452	56.1	10.5	246	1 416	110.8	43.0	135	10 208	3 074.3	374.8
Lubbock	285	1 883	132.4	30.5	474	2 495	197.1	67.2	210	6 357	1 465.0	182.3
Lufkin	65	229	18.5	4.0	99	487	43.0	14.2	52	5 006	763.2	120.1
McAllen	168	577	62.4	8.9	302	1 677	124.3	38.6	100	3 709	511.4	69.5

1. Firms subject to federal tax.

Accommodation and Foodservices, Entertainment, and Health Care

City	Accommodation and foodservices, 1997				Arts, entertainment, and recreation,[1] 1997				Health care and social assistance,[1] 1997			
	Number of establish-ments	Number of employees	Sales (mil dol)	Annual payroll (mil dol)	Number of establish-ments	Number of employees	Receipts (mil dol)	Annual payroll (mil dol)	Number of establish-ments	Number of employees	Receipts (mil dol)	Annual payroll (mil dol)
	92	93	94	95	96	97	98	99	100	101	102	103
TENNESSEE—Cont'd												
Hendersonville	61	1 135	34.8	10.4	22	241	16.6	5.8	108	1 526	101.1	40.2
Jackson	177	4 079	137.1	36.9	20	162	5.2	1.5	198	3 728	290.1	147.4
Johnson City	160	4 131	125.2	36.0	13	116	2.9	1.0	211	3 117	247.7	115.2
Kingsport	155	3 545	115.0	33.0	15	147	6.1	2.1	213	3 881	288.1	132.9
Knoxville	586	12 873	405.9	117.2	71	869	31.0	10.1	700	8 146	798.6	378.2
Memphis	1 071	25 344	920.6	254.9	99	2 062	90.7	24.4	1 364	17 644	1 635.3	695.0
Murfreesboro	171	4 785	151.0	44.6	18	158	6.4	1.8	189	3 057	166.6	83.2
Nashville-Davidson	1 407	37 523	1 511.7	426.3	545	6 077	560.4	211.3	1 462	27 389	2 174.0	925.5
Oak Ridge	79	1 504	48.1	13.3	6	53	1.8	0.5	113	1 243	93.1	51.2
Smyrna	43	914	27.7	7.7	5	92	2.8	0.7	40	505	27.8	8.8
TEXAS	34 160	638 333	22 698.8	6 175.4	3 894	65 218	3 743.8	1 143.4	37 974	557 007	35 620.9	14 725.4
Abilene	246	5 225	143.9	39.5	41	312	19.2	4.2	305	5 117	306.6	121.2
Allen	28	372	12.3	2.9	7	160	4.5	1.4	63	558	30.6	12.4
Amarillo	442	7 732	247.9	67.1	40	403	15.3	4.3	476	6 338	506.8	215.0
Arlington	548	13 989	521.9	139.3	65	4 831	246.8	107.3	702	8 890	618.9	257.8
Austin	1 491	33 899	1 215.7	348.8	171	2 810	126.8	45.5	1 550	27 475	1 894.7	770.0
Baytown	124	1 960	72.3	18.8	14	135	5.5	1.5	178	1 905	124.8	53.0
Beaumont	265	5 794	182.0	49.1	28	232	10.4	2.4	450	7 396	426.4	193.3
Bedford	82	1 850	67.6	18.5	14	250	6.6	2.5	176	2 119	161.4	62.2
Big Spring	66	945	23.3	6.5	5	0	0.0	0.0	60	1 000	63.6	24.7
Brownsville	221	3 035	105.3	26.4	21	235	8.9	2.6	230	4 623	272.4	109.4
Bryan	115	1 743	53.1	14.4	10	0	0.0	0.0	166	1 402	102.8	46.5
Carrollton	164	2 974	106.0	28.8	29	306	11.6	2.9	203	2 265	156.4	65.5
Cedar Hill	35	D	D	D	3	0	0.0	0.0	34	345	17.2	6.0
Cedar Park	NA	NA	NA	NA	NA	NA	NA	NA	NA	NA	NA	NA
Cleburne	62	D	D	D	6	24	1.1	0.3	76	971	48.0	21.4
College Station	156	3 909	117.4	33.7	17	300	8.9	3.4	94	1 432	109.2	38.4
Conroe	98	1 963	73.7	19.6	15	122	6.1	1.7	152	2 793	219.6	83.0
Coppell	38	461	18.3	5.3	9	98	4.6	1.4	43	301	21.2	9.6
Copperas Cove	32	D	D	D	4	0	0.0	0.0	22	270	8.4	3.5
Corpus Christi	647	11 822	382.5	102.0	56	579	30.5	7.6	831	14 413	768.8	343.7
Dallas	2 374	58 031	2 354.8	663.2	313	4 772	393.1	123.6	3 009	40 422	3 923.9	1 567.6
Deer Park	30	485	17.1	4.3	4	31	0.5	0.2	36	216	13.8	4.2
Del Rio	80	1 010	31.8	8.2	8	0	0.0	0.0	53	0	0.0	0.0
Denton	171	3 395	110.9	30.6	18	211	5.3	1.7	216	3 437	247.9	99.7
DeSoto	47	1 109	40.2	11.6	6	100	3.4	1.0	138	1 837	97.5	42.4
Duncanville	57	1 231	40.8	11.5	8	107	3.0	0.9	124	1 399	68.5	30.5
Edinburg	78	1 034	34.4	8.3	4	69	1.4	0.3	97	3 396	320.8	95.0
El Paso	1 040	18 828	687.2	189.6	73	1 710	94.0	23.4	970	16 345	1 159.2	453.7
Euless	54	871	35.0	9.1	4	0	0.0	0.0	74	674	51.4	22.1
Farmers Branch	82	1 884	75.4	21.0	14	559	31.0	10.3	126	2 247	212.1	76.2
Flower Mound	27	D	D	D	7	0	0.0	0.0	37	457	25.9	11.9
Fort Worth	881	17 152	614.7	172.6	81	1 342	70.0	19.7	1 159	14 987	1 053.0	487.1
Friendswood	51	771	28.0	7.0	7	88	1.0	0.3	54	450	25.2	11.9
Frisco	NA	NA	NA	NA	NA	NA	NA	NA	NA	NA	NA	NA
Galveston	190	4 240	141.4	41.2	34	280	15.5	5.8	104	1 048	49.4	17.2
Garland	301	4 471	165.6	42.4	37	632	30.3	7.5	342	5 525	261.5	111.7
Georgetown	55	869	27.0	7.5	6	135	4.6	1.5	68	647	29.7	12.1
Grand Prairie	151	2 236	88.0	21.6	20	311	76.3	5.9	157	1 633	85.4	34.8
Grapevine	92	3 629	180.8	51.8	14	295	3.9	1.4	112	1 036	74.3	33.4
Haltom City	52	664	26.5	6.4	8	0	0.0	0.0	34	804	22.8	12.2
Harlingen	126	2 269	77.1	21.0	7	48	2.4	0.5	207	5 611	184.3	90.6
Houston	3 902	83 796	3 398.9	903.4	361	8 000	654.1	203.5	4 768	66 288	5 075.2	2 087.9
Huntsville	73	1 477	44.0	12.2	4	0	0.0	0.0	70	0	0.0	0.0
Hurst	84	1 262	39.4	10.6	8	128	5.4	1.1	98	856	55.2	23.0
Irving	397	11 448	575.3	140.2	36	1 182	271.6	102.8	382	4 602	347.3	148.3
Keller	20	218	8.1	2.1	4	6	0.7	0.0	34	296	14.7	6.4
Killeen	174	3 022	90.5	23.9	16	162	5.9	1.3	101	866	46.3	15.1
Kingsville	66	923	28.0	7.6	3	0	0.0	0.0	51	0	0.0	0.0
Lake Jackson	53	1 487	40.8	12.9	7	65	2.4	0.6	121	801	58.8	25.7
Lancaster	26	434	12.7	3.7	2	0	0.0	0.0	45	1 040	51.7	22.3
La Porte	46	660	19.5	5.2	3	0	0.0	0.0	24	323	14.0	6.6
Laredo	249	4 341	144.2	37.3	17	0	0.0	0.0	226	0	0.0	0.0
League City	46	966	34.2	9.4	16	188	10.9	2.6	69	843	42.4	19.1
Lewisville	134	3 713	122.2	35.0	14	163	8.0	2.6	142	2 024	151.4	57.4
Longview	213	3 927	128.0	37.0	22	266	8.8	2.8	288	4 662	285.4	120.5
Lubbock	488	10 760	321.1	84.3	56	503	29.8	6.6	586	8 074	556.8	235.6
Lufkin	102	1 781	56.8	16.4	9	0	0.0	0.0	170	2 914	162.7	69.7
McAllen	253	6 005	188.6	50.0	16	282	13.7	2.5	436	8 354	663.1	251.5

1. Firms subject to federal tax.

City	Other services,[1] 1997				Selected federal funds, 2002–2003 (mil dol)								
					Procurement contracts		Grants						Direct payments for individuals for educational assistance
	Number of establishments	Number of employees	Receipts (mil dol)	Annual payroll (mil dol)	Defense	Other	Total[2]	Medicaid and other health related	Nutrition and family welfare	Energy and environment	Education	Housing and community development	
	104	105	106	107	108	109	110	111	112	113	114	115	116
TENNESSEE—Cont'd													
Hendersonville	83	451	22.7	6.6	1.9	20.4	1.1	0.0	0.0	0.0	0.0	1.1	0.0
Jackson	151	995	51.1	16.7	0.5	3.2	16.5	0.0	0.0	0.0	3.5	9.5	11.8
Johnson City	133	965	44.4	17.1	1.0	425.8	10.5	0.0	0.0	0.0	2.2	7.2	10.5
Kingsport	127	1 014	48.7	18.1	41.5	1.7	17.0	0.0	7.4	0.5	0.1	8.6	0.0
Knoxville	497	3 653	188.1	60.9	116.2	323.3	143.5	20.4	7.6	9.1	8.7	39.9	59.0
Memphis	1 039	8 210	534.1	166.8	57.7	368.8	304.9	136.5	23.3	0.8	8.7	89.8	44.3
Murfreesboro	132	701	41.4	12.2	7.0	31.5	16.2	0.6	0.0	0.1	1.0	6.8	18.0
Nashville-Davidson	1 092	8 627	530.2	163.9	62.5	276.8	1 366.5	431.5	203.9	72.5	227.9	119.8	42.2
Oak Ridge	63	337	16.6	6.1	19.2	2 300.3	10.3	2.3	0.0	0.1	0.1	3.3	0.1
Smyrna	31	147	7.9	2.6	0.5	0.1	2.4	0.0	0.0	0.0	0.0	2.4	0.0
TEXAS	29 162	197 113	12 477.7	3 785.0	20 821.0	9 002.4	28 422.5	12 679.1	3 982.0	371.7	3 108.6	1 625.5	1 096.8
Abilene	208	1 767	98.3	32.3	24.4	10.6	19.5	0.6	5.1	0.0	2.0	7.8	9.0
Allen	32	207	11.2	3.9	0.0	0.0	2.0	0.0	0.0	0.0	1.9	0.0	0.0
Amarillo	336	2 310	133.7	39.8	104.2	374.8	18.5	0.1	9.6	0.1	0.6	5.9	0.8
Arlington	438	3 628	216.4	70.4	159.1	8.8	30.0	1.3	0.1	1.9	2.2	15.4	33.7
Austin	1 210	8 761	558.0	183.2	354.6	158.1	3 515.6	456.2	739.3	197.1	1 060.4	171.7	62.2
Baytown	115	1 151	59.8	21.8	0.0	0.0	12.3	0.0	0.0	0.0	0.9	11.1	4.2
Beaumont	286	2 024	123.7	34.7	23.7	73.7	24.4	0.0	0.0	1.0	2.1	17.5	7.6
Bedford	68	395	19.4	6.2	10.0	0.4	0.0	0.0	0.0	0.0	0.0	0.0	0.0
Big Spring	50	231	10.2	3.0	20.0	4.3	7.5	0.0	0.0	0.0	0.2	6.7	3.0
Brownsville	144	1 217	50.0	15.9	11.6	5.9	36.6	6.1	0.0	2.1	5.0	19.0	18.3
Bryan	126	782	45.3	12.5	3.5	2.7	15.2	0.9	4.0	0.2	0.2	5.0	12.6
Carrollton	201	1 592	101.3	34.6	3.5	16.9	1.7	0.0	0.0	0.0	0.1	1.6	0.1
Cedar Hill	26	96	7.5	1.7	0.6	0.0	1.1	0.0	0.0	0.2	0.1	0.7	0.0
Cedar Park	NA	NA	NA	NA	1.6	0.3	0.2	0.0	0.0	0.0	0.0	0.0	0.0
Cleburne	66	321	18.7	5.3	0.0	0.1	2.4	0.0	0.0	0.0	0.0	2.0	0.0
College Station	56	408	15.8	4.9	16.3	16.9	1 279.2	57.3	1.3	10.8	6.2	7.3	20.5
Conroe	113	822	41.6	12.1	2.1	2.6	9.7	0.2	0.5	0.0	0.3	8.3	0.0
Coppell	32	199	10.2	3.3	0.3	0.0	0.0	0.0	0.0	0.0	0.0	0.0	0.0
Copperas Cove	38	158	7.7	2.2	0.1	0.0	9.9	0.0	0.0	0.0	9.6	0.3	0.0
Corpus Christi	510	3 465	205.2	63.8	77.8	17.3	57.3	2.6	9.1	0.8	5.0	33.2	16.8
Dallas	1 973	16 667	1 070.5	341.7	356.4	159.7	484.8	231.9	36.1	3.5	17.3	128.2	26.1
Deer Park	55	516	30.4	11.7	345.0	0.3	0.0	0.0	0.0	0.0	0.0	0.0	0.0
Del Rio	47	0	0.0	0.0	0.9	3.5	5.0	0.0	1.9	0.0	0.0	2.7	0.0
Denton	137	806	83.9	15.5	0.5	2.2	21.4	1.2	1.2	0.3	7.9	6.5	22.8
DeSoto	49	317	19.3	5.2	2.8	2.2	1.0	0.0	0.0	0.0	0.1	0.5	0.5
Duncanville	85	489	38.4	10.7	0.2	0.1	1.2	0.0	0.0	0.0	0.0	1.1	0.1
Edinburg	56	182	11.7	2.1	0.5	1.2	45.4	1.7	22.7	0.0	9.7	8.7	29.0
El Paso	791	5 613	258.7	85.7	493.5	106.2	154.0	22.7	25.5	11.6	17.5	51.5	95.0
Euless	49	330	23.8	6.6	8.7	0.3	0.2	0.0	0.0	0.0	0.0	0.2	0.0
Farmers Branch	97	2 145	214.6	78.4	0.3	0.1	0.0	0.0	0.0	0.0	0.0	0.0	0.0
Flower Mound	24	147	5.5	2.1	0.8	0.0	0.0	0.0	0.0	0.0	0.0	0.0	0.0
Fort Worth	783	5 483	355.5	111.6	9 711.3	132.0	124.2	24.7	20.0	0.0	13.2	50.9	27.9
Friendswood	41	246	14.3	4.4	-0.1	1.4	0.1	0.0	0.0	0.0	0.0	0.0	0.0
Frisco	NA	NA	NA	NA	0.1	0.0	0.4	0.0	0.0	0.0	0.0	0.0	0.0
Galveston	97	472	23.8	6.7	7.4	58.6	238.5	216.6	2.8	0.5	1.3	13.6	2.0
Garland	316	1 901	118.2	34.9	72.5	20.6	7.6	0.0	0.0	0.2	0.0	7.4	-19.9
Georgetown	42	151	10.2	2.9	2.7	0.0	6.9	0.1	4.1	0.0	0.2	1.2	0.7
Grand Prairie	154	1 133	88.5	28.4	962.7	67.6	10.7	0.0	0.0	0.0	1.2	8.2	3.9
Grapevine	74	388	28.7	8.2	0.3	0.3	0.2	0.0	0.0	0.0	0.0	0.2	0.0
Haltom City	83	455	30.7	9.3	0.4	0.5	0.4	0.0	0.0	0.0	0.0	0.3	0.0
Harlingen	116	719	33.0	10.3	0.2	1.2	19.3	5.7	0.0	0.0	2.7	6.1	6.1
Houston	3 429	32 465	2 289.5	694.0	1 007.5	4 213.2	1 270.1	601.8	42.5	19.7	80.7	243.0	122.9
Huntsville	42	245	10.1	3.3	0.0	0.2	10.3	0.0	0.0	0.0	2.9	2.2	8.7
Hurst	102	549	29.0	10.0	22.7	0.0	1.4	0.0	0.0	0.0	0.0	0.0	2.2
Irving	306	2 356	146.5	50.5	7.7	9.1	41.3	1.2	0.0	0.3	0.6	7.0	3.9
Keller	24	120	5.5	1.8	0.2	11.7	0.1	0.0	0.0	0.0	0.0	0.0	0.0
Killeen	151	731	35.6	11.1	8.5	0.7	53.0	0.0	0.0	0.0	39.5	1.3	8.2
Kingsville	46	0	0.0	0.0	15.3	0.0	11.2	2.3	0.0	0.0	2.5	5.0	10.2
Lake Jackson	38	333	10.5	3.6	0.0	0.0	0.5	0.0	0.0	0.0	0.4	0.0	1.5
Lancaster	38	258	22.7	7.4	0.0	0.8	1.4	0.0	0.0	0.0	0.0	1.3	31.6
La Porte	46	913	109.6	36.8	0.4	0.1	2.0	0.0	0.0	0.0	0.0	1.9	0.0
Laredo	189	0	0.0	0.0	9.9	26.5	100.1	4.1	68.8	0.0	6.2	14.4	18.3
League City	77	697	40.7	13.9	0.5	0.2	1.6	0.9	0.0	0.0	0.5	0.0	0.0
Lewisville	122	816	57.9	16.8	80.1	2.4	3.2	0.0	0.0	0.0	0.8	2.3	0.0
Longview	176	1 336	85.5	23.5	0.6	0.2	10.5	1.2	0.2	0.0	0.0	8.9	2.8
Lubbock	354	2 842	163.8	48.8	10.9	3.0	67.6	14.7	4.0	2.8	3.4	26.1	19.8
Lufkin	115	594	40.5	11.1	0.1	0.6	2.9	0.0	0.0	0.0	0.0	2.0	7.1
McAllen	179	1 169	52.9	15.7	218.7	5.4	22.1	2.6	0.0	0.0	1.3	10.6	31.4

1. Firms subject to federal tax.   2. Includes program categories not shown separately. State totals include additional categories not allocated by city.

Table D. Cities — **City Government Finances**

City	City government finances, 2002									
	General revenue							General expenditure		
		Intergovernmental		Taxes					Per capita[1] (dollars)	
					Per capita[1] (dollars)					
	Total (mil dol)	Total (mil dol)	Percent from state government	Total (mil dol)	Total	Property	Sales and gross receipts	Total (mil dol)	Total	Capital outlays
	117	118	119	120	121	122	123	124	125	126
TENNESSEE—Cont'd										
Hendersonville	21.1	10.1	42.8	6.8	161	113	24	22.5	534	59
Jackson	83.1	29.6	19.6	25.6	422	335	43	72.1	1 188	183
Johnson City	124.8	59.6	52.1	33.4	589	490	65	115.4	2 033	191
Kingsport	113.1	49.7	53.3	38.4	866	793	63	104.2	2 348	299
Knoxville	256.7	53.4	55.8	123.5	711	451	251	226.5	1 304	231
Memphis	1 601.8	1 030.8	49.1	364.4	562	468	91	1 520.3	2 343	134
Murfreesboro	99.9	54.0	51.7	28.0	374	317	43	129.4	1 728	500
Nashville-Davidson	1 711.4	598.4	57.8	682.9	1 196	1 032	73	1 642.0	2 877	260
Oak Ridge	71.8	40.7	56.8	17.2	632	571	53	70.0	2 572	229
Smyrna	NA	NA	NA	NA	NA	NA	NA	NA	NA	NA
TEXAS	X	X	X	X	X	X	X	X	X	X
Abilene	84.1	8.0	32.3	51.7	449	215	223	85.3	741	104
Allen	54.5	0.5	100.0	33.3	582	285	264	59.7	1 044	468
Amarillo	187.2	19.3	49.6	77.8	439	100	333	156.9	886	171
Arlington	291.0	32.7	67.4	159.6	457	230	216	276.4	790	116
Austin	970.8	81.5	40.3	407.0	606	290	274	1 028.2	1 530	414
Baytown	63.8	7.0	79.9	40.2	596	383	209	60.9	904	159
Beaumont	104.4	12.5	26.0	64.1	568	213	344	110.3	978	130
Bedford	29.8	0.7	16.3	21.6	446	165	266	27.5	568	0
Big Spring	56.7	0.6	57.9	8.4	338	106	217	57.3	2 309	103
Brownsville	103.5	14.5	25.7	44.5	296	119	166	110.7	736	188
Bryan	63.5	2.8	76.3	26.5	398	189	204	68.2	1 024	277
Carrollton	105.8	0.3	6.7	70.2	610	359	240	99.9	868	261
Cedar Hill	24.7	0.5	4.7	14.8	398	235	149	23.4	629	50
Cedar Park	NA	NA	NA	NA	NA	NA	NA	NA	NA	NA
Cleburne	26.4	1.7	4.2	12.5	453	240	196	23.7	860	67
College Station	55.2	3.5	46.4	27.7	393	152	230	71.5	1 013	305
Conroe	38.4	1.3	16.0	29.1	745	162	567	39.5	1 011	277
Coppell	44.2	0.3	44.6	31.4	795	490	244	45.4	1 151	447
Copperas Cove	14.5	0.0	NA	6.6	224	130	91	14.6	494	147
Corpus Christi	237.0	15.9	47.2	111.1	399	193	200	223.6	803	119
Dallas	1 744.1	83.4	37.3	798.4	659	350	295	2 013.2	1 662	555
Deer Park	22.6	0.0	NA	16.2	557	431	126	19.6	675	32
Del Rio	25.4	4.4	72.5	9.0	259	85	163	24.4	705	199
Denton	90.1	6.7	91.1	40.0	443	182	259	103.4	1 145	282
DeSoto	34.7	0.3	0.0	20.9	529	292	228	39.0	988	223
Duncanville	29.5	1.5	100.0	18.3	504	274	206	29.3	809	77
Edinburg	36.1	2.6	100.0	18.8	357	189	162	37.3	708	161
El Paso	444.1	69.9	16.5	208.3	361	188	162	438.2	759	198
Euless	39.7	0.9	100.0	20.1	415	158	247	56.8	1 173	378
Farmers Branch	54.3	1.2	12.8	38.4	1 397	590	765	48.6	1 771	252
Flower Mound	27.2	0.2	100.0	20.1	343	189	114	33.3	568	30
Fort Worth	624.2	39.5	100.0	346.9	611	305	223	566.2	998	192
Friendswood	18.4	0.6	88.9	12.5	396	255	108	15.0	475	76
Frisco	NA	NA	NA	NA	NA	NA	NA	NA	1 215	40
Galveston	88.0	7.7	22.0	35.1	620	206	401	68.9	884	207
Garland	166.7	14.0	65.6	78.5	358	228	121	194.3	1 153	232
Georgetown	23.0	0.2	100.0	10.8	324	153	150	38.3	993	199
Grand Prairie	136.5	14.7	100.0	76.5	566	279	277	134.3	NA	NA
Grapevine	NA	NA	NA	NA	NA	NA	NA	NA	587	85
Haltom City	22.7	0.3	67.6	16.0	402	139	247	23.4	1 129	131
Harlingen	61.7	5.5	9.6	27.6	464	137	319	67.1	1 294	389
Houston	2 290.3	212.3	19.4	1 212.3	603	306	279	2 600.9	994	393
Huntsville	23.1	0.8	71.0	9.8	274	82	185	35.5	915	175
Hurst	39.3	0.4	54.4	28.4	771	206	549	33.7	1 083	157
Irving	206.1	2.8	23.1	142.1	725	331	367	212.5	NA	NA
Keller	NA	NA	NA	NA	NA	NA	NA	NA	562	97
Killeen	55.7	1.3	0.0	31.2	337	147	180	52.1	545	40
Kingsville	14.6	0.7	16.7	8.2	326	145	172	13.7	717	127
Lake Jackson	21.4	0.1	100.0	13.2	489	216	269	19.3	1 101	293
Lancaster	26.2	4.0	59.5	14.9	550	119	406	29.8	870	104
La Porte	34.0	0.7	100.0	16.4	493	334	151	28.9	951	203
Laredo	188.5	23.3	37.8	65.1	340	144	169	182.2	609	59
League City	38.1	0.3	100.0	23.5	457	271	148	31.3	583	6
Lewisville	76.7	0.8	67.5	43.3	515	225	274	49.0	1 002	244
Longview	72.0	5.9	37.2	42.7	575	278	286	74.5	844	161
Lubbock	164.1	16.3	36.5	78.0	383	187	190	171.9	1 129	162
Lufkin	35.1	0.9	83.3	18.2	556	189	360	37.0	1 069	147
McAllen	144.7	9.4	55.0	63.9	561	149	405	121.8		

1. Based on population estimated as of July 1 of the year shown.

City	City government finances, 2002 (cont'd)									
	General expenditure									
	Percent of total for—									
	Public welfare	Highways	Parking facilities	Education	Health and hospitals	Police protection	Sewerage and sanitation	Parks and recreation	Housing and community development	Interest on debt
	127	128	129	130	131	132	133	134	135	136
TENNESSEE—Cont'd										
Hendersonville	0.7	25.2	0.0	0.0	0.0	20.6	11.9	8.3	0.0	1.7
Jackson	0.0	10.9	0.0	0.0	0.1	14.0	27.1	10.8	1.4	7.4
Johnson City	0.0	6.3	0.0	39.1	0.0	8.8	13.1	5.0	0.9	6.5
Kingsport	0.0	3.6	0.0	44.9	0.0	6.7	12.4	4.0	0.5	6.1
Knoxville	3.7	2.9	0.1	0.1	0.0	16.6	12.2	2.9	0.8	4.8
Memphis	0.0	1.6	0.0	56.7	0.8	10.2	4.7	5.3	1.7	2.8
Murfreesboro	0.3	2.7	0.1	31.7	2.7	7.2	16.8	4.9	0.3	3.7
Nashville-Davidson	1.3	1.9	0.0	34.4	9.0	7.1	5.7	3.9	0.0	9.4
Oak Ridge	0.2	3.3	0.0	55.6	0.0	6.2	11.8	4.6	0.3	3.3
Smyrna	NA	NA	NA	NA	NA	NA	NA	NA	NA	NA
TEXAS	X	X	X	X	X	X	X	X	X	X
Abilene	1.1	11.2	0.0	0.0	3.9	16.2	14.7	5.5	9.0	2.1
Allen	0.0	5.6	0.0	0.0	0.0	13.5	7.7	20.6	2.1	6.9
Amarillo	0.0	9.1	0.0	0.0	9.8	12.7	13.5	5.7	5.9	5.8
Arlington	1.3	12.7	0.0	0.0	0.7	19.2	13.4	8.7	8.1	6.9
Austin	0.8	2.3	0.0	0.0	8.0	12.0	14.6	12.2	1.3	6.9
Baytown	0.0	10.6	0.0	0.0	1.0	31.6	16.1	5.3	1.9	6.7
Beaumont	0.0	14.2	0.0	0.0	5.0	19.2	9.2	3.8	6.5	5.8
Bedford	0.0	7.7	0.0	0.0	0.0	26.1	9.2	8.9	0.0	12.4
Big Spring	0.0	2.7	0.0	0.0	2.3	5.1	5.9	1.6	0.0	0.2
Brownsville	0.4	7.0	0.5	0.0	3.1	17.3	10.7	8.9	2.0	3.9
Bryan	0.0	15.1	0.0	0.0	2.5	13.7	19.2	7.4	2.7	2.6
Carrollton	0.0	8.8	0.0	0.0	1.8	14.9	6.3	31.8	0.0	5.4
Cedar Hill	0.0	11.2	0.0	0.0	0.0	20.2	12.7	7.1	0.0	5.7
Cedar Park	NA	NA	NA	NA	NA	NA	NA	NA	NA	NA
Cleburne	0.0	7.9	0.1	0.0	0.0	14.8	28.4	3.9	5.8	3.3
College Station	0.0	13.5	6.8	0.0	0.0	10.0	19.7	8.8	2.1	6.2
Conroe	0.0	5.7	0.0	0.0	0.0	17.3	8.2	14.8	1.6	5.5
Coppell	0.0	19.9	0.0	0.0	0.7	11.3	3.0	25.2	0.0	7.8
Copperas Cove	0.0	7.8	0.0	0.0	0.0	27.4	19.1	8.0	0.0	2.6
Corpus Christi	0.0	8.0	0.1	0.0	3.7	18.1	19.2	7.4	0.6	11.6
Dallas	0.1	5.3	0.1	0.0	1.2	11.6	9.6	8.0	2.1	12.4
Deer Park	0.0	3.5	0.0	0.0	0.0	19.6	27.3	13.4	0.0	6.3
Del Rio	6.3	6.7	0.0	0.0	0.0	16.6	24.4	3.9	0.0	5.6
Denton	0.0	4.0	0.0	0.0	0.8	11.4	25.1	6.0	1.9	4.4
DeSoto	0.0	24.0	0.0	0.0	0.0	14.8	9.8	4.5	0.0	15.2
Duncanville	0.0	10.3	0.0	0.0	0.0	19.4	22.4	4.9	0.5	8.1
Edinburg	0.0	7.1	0.0	0.0	2.8	14.4	19.1	23.8	2.4	5.3
El Paso	0.0	3.5	0.0	0.0	3.7	18.8	11.1	5.1	5.4	6.3
Euless	0.0	9.1	0.0	0.0	0.3	25.0	8.2	12.7	0.0	8.0
Farmers Branch	0.0	10.8	0.0	0.0	1.2	17.2	13.5	17.2	0.0	2.8
Flower Mound	0.4	5.2	0.0	0.0	1.2	13.3	13.2	4.5	0.0	10.4
Fort Worth	0.0	11.9	0.0	0.0	1.8	21.4	14.9	11.2	2.1	5.5
Friendswood	0.0	5.7	0.0	0.0	0.0	26.1	16.9	10.7	0.0	1.3
Frisco	NA	NA	NA	NA	NA	NA	NA	NA	NA	NA
Galveston	0.0	6.8	0.0	0.0	0.0	17.5	9.9	16.5	1.5	17.4
Garland	2.9	13.0	0.0	0.0	1.1	15.0	11.0	7.8	6.4	9.3
Georgetown	0.3	3.8	0.0	0.0	0.8	10.3	11.3	6.5	0.5	5.1
Grand Prairie	0.0	8.0	0.0	0.0	1.1	16.6	15.1	12.3	8.9	6.4
Grapevine	NA	NA	NA	NA	NA	NA	NA	NA	NA	NA
Haltom City	0.0	14.6	0.0	0.0	2.2	23.9	17.3	7.0	0.0	3.2
Harlingen	0.7	5.6	0.0	0.0	4.6	12.3	20.0	8.5	2.1	2.2
Houston	0.0	7.3	0.0	0.0	3.6	16.9	13.8	5.7	2.2	9.0
Huntsville	0.0	25.9	0.0	0.0	0.3	9.1	33.2	3.2	0.6	4.7
Hurst	0.0	10.6	0.0	0.0	2.6	26.4	12.8	15.1	0.0	4.5
Irving	0.0	13.6	0.0	0.0	4.4	16.2	12.9	9.9	2.6	3.3
Keller	NA	NA	NA	NA	NA	NA	NA	NA	NA	NA
Killeen	0.0	6.9	0.0	0.0	1.1	21.6	19.1	6.2	2.1	3.0
Kingsville	0.0	13.4	0.0	0.0	1.5	30.1	18.8	2.0	0.0	2.0
Lake Jackson	0.0	12.2	0.0	0.0	0.0	17.3	17.0	15.7	0.0	9.1
Lancaster	0.0	3.4	0.0	0.0	8.4	9.5	17.4	8.5	4.5	3.5
La Porte	0.0	8.6	0.0	6.3	4.3	22.2	14.4	15.7	0.0	2.5
Laredo	0.0	20.0	0.4	0.0	6.7	16.4	9.9	6.9	4.1	5.7
League City	0.0	10.3	0.0	0.0	2.4	19.6	12.7	6.9	0.0	7.4
Lewisville	0.4	8.4	0.0	0.0	3.1	22.7	5.4	11.9	2.1	6.5
Longview	0.2	8.8	0.0	0.0	2.2	16.6	22.3	5.9	5.5	4.3
Lubbock	0.0	8.2	0.0	0.0	2.8	17.5	17.4	8.0	3.5	4.8
Lufkin	0.0	19.4	0.0	0.0	0.0	17.1	16.8	10.7	0.3	2.9
McAllen	3.8	8.1	0.0	0.0	0.4	21.6	12.0	8.1	2.5	11.2

Table D. Cities — City Government Finances, City Government Employment, and Climate

City	City government finances, 2002 (cont'd) Debt outstanding — Total (mil dol)	Per capita[1] (dollars)	Percent utility	City government employment, 2002	Climate[2] Average daily temperature (degrees Fahrenheit) Mean — January	July	Limits January[3]	July[4]	Annual precipitation (inches)	Heating degree days	Cooling degree days
	137	138	139	140	141	142	143	144	145	146	147
TENNESSEE—Cont'd											
Hendersonville	7.4	175	0.0	224	36.2	79.3	26.5	89.5	47.30	3 729	1 616
Jackson	152.2	2 509	34.3	976	37.0	80.1	27.3	90.9	52.88	3 540	1 744
Johnson City	266.1	4 688	28.3	1 912	34.0	74.4	24.3	84.6	40.72	4 406	972
Kingsport	116.8	2 633	14.9	1 708	36.1	75.8	26.4	87.1	43.79	3 901	1 167
Knoxville	494.0	2 844	40.0	2 720	36.0	76.6	26.0	87.1	47.14	3 937	1 266
Memphis	1 088.4	1 677	13.2	25 723	39.7	82.6	30.9	92.3	52.10	3 082	2 118
Murfreesboro	153.9	2 055	41.6	1 628	35.2	77.9	24.5	89.3	53.17	3 992	1 406
Nashville-Davidson	3 515.9	6 160	27.5	19 780	NA	NA	NA	NA	NA	NA	NA
Oak Ridge	81.2	2 981	55.5	1 022	35.0	75.8	25.1	86.7	53.77	4 183	1 156
Smyrna	NA	NA	NA	283	NA	NA	NA	NA	NA	NA	NA
TEXAS	X	X	X	X	X	X	X	X	X	X	X
Abilene	107.3	931	67.3	1 120	42.8	84.0	30.8	95.2	24.40	2 584	2 451
Allen	96.1	1 679	17.1	423	NA	NA	NA	NA	NA	NA	NA
Amarillo	162.6	919	21.7	1 848	35.1	78.6	21.2	91.7	19.56	4 258	1 354
Arlington	413.7	1 182	22.0	2 537	43.4	85.3	32.7	96.5	33.70	2 407	2 603
Austin	4 391.3	6 536	67.8	11 040	48.8	84.5	38.6	95.0	31.88	1 688	3 016
Baytown	94.6	1 405	32.2	660	50.5	83.1	40.6	91.4	51.85	1 550	2 809
Beaumont	156.6	1 388	32.4	1 402	49.6	82.3	39.5	91.9	55.58	1 677	2 581
Bedford	65.1	1 345	0.0	356	43.4	85.3	32.7	96.5	33.70	2 407	2 603
Big Spring	7.2	292	75.1	283	NA	NA	NA	NA	NA	NA	NA
Brownsville	362.9	2 413	70.0	1 281	59.4	84.5	49.9	93.3	26.61	635	3 888
Bryan	89.6	1 343	36.9	873	48.5	83.6	38.7	93.8	39.08	1 788	2 776
Carrollton	146.0	1 268	12.8	904	43.4	85.3	32.7	96.5	33.70	2 407	2 603
Cedar Hill	28.3	759	22.2	225	NA	NA	NA	NA	NA	NA	NA
Cedar Park	NA	NA	NA	266	NA	NA	NA	NA	NA	NA	NA
Cleburne	85.1	3 097	67.7	294	NA	NA	NA	NA	NA	NA	NA
College Station	123.2	1 746	26.5	736	48.5	83.6	38.7	93.8	39.08	1 788	2 776
Conroe	46.3	1 184	8.3	417	48.8	83.1	37.9	94.0	47.33	1 774	2 676
Coppell	83.9	2 125	21.5	311	NA	NA	NA	NA	NA	NA	NA
Copperas Cove	23.5	793	24.0	218	NA	NA	NA	NA	NA	NA	NA
Corpus Christi	619.7	2 225	20.5	2 933	55.1	84.1	45.3	93.3	30.13	1 016	3 439
Dallas	5 108.1	4 216	10.6	15 058	44.6	85.9	34.5	95.7	36.08	2 259	2 763
Deer Park	37.3	1 285	25.8	275	52.2	83.5	42.9	92.3	50.83	1 371	3 012
Del Rio	53.8	1 555	43.4	365	50.2	85.2	38.5	96.2	18.24	1 506	3 142
Denton	302.9	3 352	70.1	1 102	41.9	83.2	30.3	94.0	37.27	2 665	2 225
DeSoto	102.9	2 609	3.7	285	44.6	85.9	34.5	95.7	36.08	2 259	2 763
Duncanville	33.5	926	0.0	255	44.6	85.9	34.5	95.7	36.08	2 259	2 763
Edinburg	45.7	866	18.0	973	58.5	85.4	48.5	95.8	22.83	693	4 076
El Paso	807.1	1 398	35.8	5 406	42.8	82.3	29.4	96.1	8.81	2 708	2 094
Euless	81.7	1 687	7.0	380	43.4	85.3	32.7	96.5	33.70	2 407	2 603
Farmers Branch	28.8	1 047	20.1	456	NA	NA	NA	NA	NA	NA	NA
Flower Mound	94.7	1 615	41.1	387	NA	NA	NA	NA	NA	NA	NA
Fort Worth	1 120.2	1 974	52.4	5 895	43.4	85.3	32.7	96.5	33.70	2 407	2 603
Friendswood	23.5	746	87.6	171	NA	NA	NA	NA	NA	NA	NA
Frisco	NA	NA	NA	293	NA	NA	NA	NA	NA	NA	NA
Galveston	266.4	4 700	19.4	835	52.7	83.3	47.1	87.3	42.28	1 263	2 994
Garland	394.3	1 795	26.8	1 924	44.6	85.9	34.5	95.7	36.08	2 259	2 763
Georgetown	58.2	1 750	36.9	335	NA	NA	NA	NA	NA	NA	NA
Grand Prairie	199.7	1 476	10.8	1 155	43.4	85.3	32.7	96.5	33.70	2 407	2 603
Grapevine	NA	NA	NA	564	41.6	83.7	30.0	94.9	33.68	2 683	2 328
Haltom City	29.2	732	42.0	305	43.4	85.3	32.7	96.5	33.70	2 407	2 603
Harlingen	57.2	963	42.5	752	57.3	83.9	46.7	94.4	27.53	813	3 662
Houston	8 205.1	4 082	16.5	25 662	52.2	83.5	42.9	92.3	50.83	1 371	3 012
Huntsville	54.0	1 511	37.6	252	47.6	83.3	37.6	94.4	44.96	1 862	2 654
Hurst	37.1	1 009	34.9	353	43.4	85.3	32.7	96.5	33.70	2 407	2 603
Irving	259.7	1 324	39.6	2 010	44.6	85.9	34.5	95.7	36.08	2 259	2 763
Keller	NA	NA	NA	230	NA	NA	NA	NA	NA	NA	NA
Killeen	82.1	886	52.3	744	45.4	84.0	34.5	95.2	34.87	2 153	2 623
Kingsville	9.8	391	16.2	257	56.4	84.3	44.7	95.0	27.60	911	3 590
Lake Jackson	41.0	1 522	0.0	227	NA	NA	NA	NA	NA	NA	NA
Lancaster	28.4	1 048	37.2	228	NA	NA	NA	NA	NA	NA	NA
La Porte	26.8	808	41.4	384	52.2	83.5	42.9	92.3	50.83	1 371	3 012
Laredo	281.9	1 472	7.5	2 053	54.4	86.9	42.9	98.8	21.42	1 025	3 915
League City	75.7	1 474	15.3	340	52.2	83.5	42.9	92.3	50.83	1 371	3 012
Lewisville	113.0	1 346	51.2	663	41.9	83.2	30.3	94.0	37.27	2 665	2 225
Longview	140.1	1 885	55.2	782	44.0	82.6	32.7	93.2	47.27	2 433	2 249
Lubbock	324.3	1 592	44.0	1 890	38.8	80.0	24.6	91.9	18.65	3 431	1 689
Lufkin	29.5	901	44.0	478	47.6	82.8	36.9	93.2	42.40	1 951	2 551
McAllen	227.5	1 998	18.2	1 321	58.5	85.4	48.5	95.8	22.83	693	4 076

1. Based on the population estimated as of July 1 of the year shown.   2. Represents normal values based on the 30-year period, 1961–1990.   3. Average daily minimum.   4. Average daily maximum.

Table D. Cities — Land Area and Population

STATE Place code	City	Land area,[1] 2000 (sq km)	Population, 2003 Total persons	Rank	Per square kilometer	White	Black	Am. Indian, Alaska Native	Asian and Pacific Islander	Other race	Hispanic or Latino[2]	Non-Hispanic White
		1	2	3	4	5	6	7	8	9	10	11
	TEXAS—Cont'd											
48 45744	McKinney	150.3	79 958	342	532.0	80.3	7.7	1.1	1.9	11.3	18.2	71.5
48 46452	Mansfield	94.5	33 123	972	350.5	87.9	4.8	1.0	1.6	6.6	12.8	80.3
48 47892	Mesquite	112.4	129 270	171	1 150.1	75.6	13.8	1.2	4.2	7.6	15.7	65.4
48 48072	Midland	172.5	96 573	260	559.8	77.2	8.7	1.0	1.3	13.7	29.0	60.6
48 48768	Mission	62.5	54 619	575	873.9	79.8	0.5	0.6	0.8	20.7	81.0	17.7
48 48804	Missouri City	76.9	62 570	464	813.7	45.7	39.1	0.5	11.3	5.5	10.9	38.6
48 50256	Nacogdoches	65.3	30 441	1 049	466.2	67.3	25.4	0.7	1.6	6.6	10.8	61.9
48 50820	New Braunfels	75.8	42 693	751	563.2	86.3	1.6	1.0	0.9	12.5	34.5	62.5
48 52356	North Richland Hills	47.2	60 238	493	1 276.2	90.3	2.9	1.2	3.3	4.3	9.5	83.1
48 53388	Odessa	95.3	91 113	286	956.1	76.1	6.2	1.3	1.2	18.2	41.4	50.8
48 55080	Paris	110.7	26 523	1 189	239.6	74.3	22.9	1.7	0.9	1.9	4.1	70.8
48 56000	Pasadena	114.4	144 413	153	1 262.4	74.2	1.9	1.1	2.2	23.8	48.2	47.2
48 56348	Pearland	101.9	47 903	670	470.1	84.3	5.6	0.8	4.2	7.0	16.2	73.4
48 57200	Pharr	53.9	54 452	578	1 010.2	81.4	0.3	0.8	0.3	19.2	90.6	8.9
48 58016	Plano	185.4	241 991	71	1 305.2	80.2	5.4	0.8	11.1	4.9	10.1	72.8
48 58820	Port Arthur	214.8	57 042	534	265.6	40.6	44.3	0.8	6.3	10.2	17.5	31.8
48 61796	Richardson	74.0	99 536	248	1 345.1	77.5	6.6	1.0	12.8	4.8	10.3	69.6
48 63500	Round Rock	67.7	77 946	357	1 151.3	78.9	8.4	0.9	3.8	10.7	22.1	65.6
48 63572	Rowlett	52.4	51 102	612	975.2	83.4	9.4	0.8	3.9	4.4	8.8	77.3
48 64472	San Angelo	144.8	87 922	298	607.2	79.2	5.2	1.2	1.5	15.5	33.2	59.9
48 65000	San Antonio	1 055.6	1 214 725	8	1 150.7	70.8	7.4	1.3	2.3	22.0	58.7	31.8
48 65516	San Juan	28.5	28 894	1 097	1 013.8	82.9	0.5	0.8	0.2	17.6	95.1	4.4
48 65600	San Marcos	47.2	43 007	747	911.2	75.0	6.0	1.2	1.9	18.8	36.5	55.2
48 67496	Sherman	99.8	36 261	884	363.3	80.8	11.9	2.4	1.6	6.1	12.1	72.6
48 68636	Socorro	45.3	28 140	1 126	621.2	76.1	0.5	1.5	0.1	24.6	96.4	2.7
48 70808	Sugar Land	62.4	70 815	399	1 134.9	67.8	5.5	0.5	25.2	3.5	8.0	60.8
48 72176	Temple	169.3	54 975	566	324.7	71.8	17.3	1.0	2.2	10.4	17.8	62.7
48 72368	Texarkana	66.4	35 199	918	530.1	60.1	37.6	0.8	1.1	1.7	2.9	58.1
48 72392	Texas City	161.5	43 233	741	267.7	62.5	28.0	0.8	1.2	9.6	20.5	50.1
48 72530	The Colony	35.4	35 189	919	994.0	86.9	5.7	1.3	2.3	6.5	13.3	77.5
48 74144	Tyler	127.7	88 316	295	691.6	63.3	27.0	0.7	1.3	9.4	15.8	55.6
48 75428	Victoria	85.4	61 410	473	719.1	73.2	8.0	0.8	1.3	19.1	42.9	47.7
48 76000	Waco	218.1	116 887	199	535.9	62.6	23.3	1.0	1.8	13.7	23.6	51.1
48 77272	Weslaco	32.9	30 416	1 050	924.5	76.9	0.4	0.7	1.3	22.9	83.8	14.7
48 79000	Wichita Falls	183.1	102 340	233	558.9	77.6	13.2	1.7	3.0	7.7	14.0	68.9
49 00000	**UTAH**	212 751.1	2 351 467	X	11.1	91.1	1.1	1.8	3.2	5.1	9.0	85.3
49 07690	Bountiful	34.9	41 401	776	1 186.3	96.8	0.4	0.5	2.3	1.5	2.9	94.1
49 13850	Clearfield	20.1	27 146	1 161	1 350.5	86.2	4.5	2.4	4.8	6.1	10.6	79.0
49 20120	Draper	78.6	31 020	1 032	394.7	93.0	1.8	1.3	2.6	3.5	5.8	88.9
49 43660	Layton	53.6	60 769	484	1 133.8	92.1	2.1	1.1	3.6	3.9	7.0	86.9
49 45860	Logan	42.8	43 675	735	1 020.4	90.3	0.9	1.1	4.5	4.8	8.2	85.4
49 49710	Midvale	15.1	27 166	1 159	1 799.1	84.8	1.6	1.7	3.2	11.5	20.8	73.4
49 53230	Murray	24.9	43 617	736	1 751.7	93.3	1.4	0.9	2.9	3.5	7.5	87.6
49 55980	Ogden	69.0	78 293	353	1 134.7	81.5	2.9	1.9	2.3	14.4	23.6	70.2
49 57300	Orem	47.8	87 599	301	1 832.6	92.7	0.6	1.2	3.3	4.5	8.6	86.7
49 62470	Provo	102.7	105 410	224	1 026.4	90.7	0.7	1.3	4.0	6.0	10.5	84.0
49 64340	Riverton	32.6	29 244	1 088	897.1	97.5	0.4	0.5	1.4	1.5	3.2	94.7
49 65110	Roy	19.7	35 249	916	1 789.3	92.6	1.5	0.9	2.6	4.4	7.7	87.5
49 65330	St. George	166.8	56 382	541	338.0	93.9	0.5	2.2	1.9	3.5	6.7	89.0
49 67000	Salt Lake City	282.5	179 894	117	636.8	82.2	2.5	1.9	6.6	10.6	18.8	70.6
49 67440	Sandy	57.8	89 319	289	1 545.3	95.0	0.7	0.6	3.4	2.1	4.4	91.1
49 70850	South Jordan	54.0	33 589	961	622.0	96.7	0.4	0.4	2.3	1.7	3.3	93.8
49 75360	Taylorsville	27.7	58 701	515	2 119.2	87.7	1.3	1.4	5.6	6.6	12.2	79.9
49 82950	West Jordan	80.0	84 701	315	1 058.8	90.8	0.9	1.0	3.9	5.8	10.1	84.4
49 83470	West Valley City	91.7	111 687	210	1 218.0	81.1	1.6	1.7	8.5	10.7	18.5	70.3
50 00000	**VERMONT**	23 956.2	619 107	X	25.8	97.9	0.7	1.1	1.2	0.4	0.9	96.2
50 10675	Burlington	27.4	39 148	823	1 428.8	94.2	2.4	1.3	3.3	1.2	1.4	91.5
51 00000	**VIRGINIA**	102 548.2	7 386 330	X	72.0	73.9	20.4	0.7	4.4	2.7	4.7	70.2
51 01000	Alexandria	39.3	128 923	172	3 280.5	62.7	24.0	0.7	6.9	10.1	14.7	53.7
51 07784	Blacksburg	50.1	40 066	797	799.7	86.2	4.9	0.5	9.0	1.9	2.3	83.1
51 14968	Charlottesville	26.6	39 162	822	1 472.3	71.2	23.2	0.5	5.9	1.5	2.4	68.4
51 16000	Chesapeake	882.5	210 834	88	238.9	68.1	29.2	0.9	2.5	1.0	2.0	65.9
51 21344	Danville	111.5	46 988	679	421.4	54.5	44.5	0.4	0.8	0.7	1.3	53.3
51 35000	Hampton	134.1	146 878	149	1 095.3	51.1	46.1	1.1	2.7	1.6	2.8	48.5
51 35624	Harrisonburg	45.5	41 170	781	904.8	87.1	6.7	0.5	4.2	4.3	8.8	80.1
51 44984	Leesburg	30.0	33 319	965	1 110.6	85.2	10.0	0.5	3.3	3.3	5.9	80.4

1. Dry land or land partially or temporarily covered by water.   2. Hispanic or Latino persons may be of any race.

Table D. Cities — **Population and Households**

City	Population characteristics, 2000 (cont'd)										Population			
	Age of population (percent)										Census counts		Percent change	
	Under 5 years	5 to 17 years	18 to 24 years	25 to 34 years	35 to 44 years	45 to 54 years	55 to 64 years	65 to 74 years	75 years and over	Percent female	1990	2000	1990–2000	2000–2003
	12	13	14	15	16	17	18	19	20	21	22	23	24	25
TEXAS—Cont'd														
McKinney	10.1	20.9	9.3	18.1	18.3	10.7	5.8	3.5	3.3	49.4	21 283	54 369	155.5	47.1
Mansfield	8.4	23.4	7.8	14.9	19.7	13.2	6.9	3.4	2.3	49.3	15 615	28 031	79.5	18.2
Mesquite	7.7	22.8	9.2	15.2	18.7	12.4	6.9	4.3	2.8	51.8	101 484	124 523	22.7	3.8
Midland	7.5	22.4	9.0	12.2	16.0	13.1	7.4	6.9	5.4	52.0	89 343	94 996	6.2	1.7
Mission	9.2	22.9	9.8	13.8	13.0	10.1	6.9	7.4	6.8	52.3	28 653	45 408	58.5	20.3
Missouri City	7.3	23.5	7.0	11.3	19.7	17.8	7.9	3.5	1.9	51.6	36 143	52 913	46.3	18.3
Nacogdoches	5.8	14.4	30.9	12.1	10.2	9.5	6.0	5.2	5.9	53.3	30 872	29 914	-3.1	1.8
New Braunfels	7.1	18.6	8.5	14.2	14.2	12.6	8.0	7.6	9.3	52.1	27 334	36 494	33.5	17.0
North Richland Hills	7.1	20.2	9.0	14.3	18.3	14.4	7.9	5.0	3.9	50.8	45 895	55 635	21.2	8.3
Odessa	8.0	21.8	10.6	12.9	14.9	12.3	7.7	6.5	5.2	51.8	89 699	90 943	1.4	0.2
Paris	7.4	17.9	10.0	12.7	13.1	11.6	9.2	7.7	10.3	53.7	24 799	25 898	4.4	2.4
Pasadena	9.3	22.3	11.4	15.8	15.4	11.4	6.5	4.5	3.4	50.0	119 604	141 674	18.5	1.9
Pearland	8.0	20.9	7.3	15.1	19.1	13.7	7.5	5.0	3.4	50.9	18 927	37 640	98.9	27.3
Pharr	10.6	24.2	11.3	14.6	11.7	9.2	6.7	6.8	5.1	52.4	32 921	46 660	41.7	16.7
Plano	8.3	20.4	7.0	16.0	20.5	15.4	7.5	2.9	2.1	50.2	127 885	222 030	73.6	9.0
Port Arthur	7.8	20.8	9.7	12.1	14.1	12.0	7.9	7.7	7.8	52.3	58 551	57 755	-1.4	-1.2
Richardson	6.7	18.1	8.7	15.2	17.5	14.5	9.4	5.9	4.1	50.6	74 840	91 802	22.7	8.4
Round Rock	9.7	22.2	8.5	19.6	19.2	11.6	4.7	2.3	2.2	50.2	30 923	61 136	97.7	27.5
Rowlett	8.7	24.8	5.6	15.1	21.9	13.2	5.6	3.1	2.1	50.6	23 260	44 503	91.3	14.8
San Angelo	7.1	18.8	13.8	13.0	13.9	11.7	7.9	6.9	6.9	52.1	84 462	88 439	4.7	-0.6
San Antonio	8.1	20.5	10.8	15.5	15.3	12.1	7.3	5.6	4.8	51.7	976 514	1 144 646	19.3	6.1
San Juan	10.5	26.9	11.9	15.1	12.3	10.0	5.5	4.4	3.3	51.7	12 561	26 229	108.8	10.2
San Marcos	4.9	10.4	41.9	16.0	8.8	6.5	4.2	3.3	3.9	50.8	28 743	34 733	20.9	23.8
Sherman	7.2	17.3	13.1	13.6	14.2	11.6	7.7	6.9	8.3	52.1	31 584	35 082	11.1	3.4
Socorro	9.2	26.9	11.5	13.6	14.3	11.5	6.7	4.2	2.1	51.6	22 995	27 152	18.1	3.6
Sugar Land	6.1	25.0	6.2	9.0	19.7	19.7	7.5	3.8	3.0	51.1	33 712	63 328	87.9	11.8
Temple	7.8	18.5	9.2	14.2	14.4	12.3	7.8	7.1	8.7	52.2	46 150	54 514	18.1	0.8
Texarkana	7.1	18.9	10.0	13.1	14.5	12.6	8.1	7.3	8.5	52.9	32 294	34 782	7.7	1.2
Texas City	6.8	19.9	9.6	12.9	14.9	14.1	8.3	7.3	6.1	52.8	40 822	41 521	1.7	4.1
The Colony	8.4	25.6	7.4	16.4	21.5	12.9	4.9	1.9	1.0	50.3	22 113	26 531	20.0	32.6
Tyler	7.4	18.7	11.7	13.3	13.6	12.0	8.0	7.3	7.9	53.2	75 450	83 650	10.9	5.6
Victoria	7.9	20.9	9.7	13.1	14.9	13.0	8.0	6.6	6.0	51.9	55 076	60 603	10.0	1.3
Waco	7.6	17.8	20.3	12.9	12.0	9.7	6.3	6.2	7.2	52.3	103 590	113 726	9.8	2.8
Weslaco	9.5	22.3	9.9	14.2	11.7	10.1	7.1	7.5	7.6	53.2	22 739	26 935	18.5	12.9
Wichita Falls	7.1	17.5	15.2	14.3	15.0	11.3	7.3	6.5	5.8	48.5	96 259	104 197	8.2	-1.8
UTAH	9.4	22.8	14.2	14.6	13.4	10.6	6.4	4.5	4.0	49.9	1 722 850	2 233 169	29.6	5.3
Bountiful	8.0	21.7	11.6	11.3	12.6	11.2	9.4	7.8	6.5	51.4	37 544	41 301	10.0	0.2
Clearfield	12.2	24.0	16.0	18.0	12.6	7.6	3.8	2.8	2.9	49.3	21 435	25 974	21.2	4.5
Draper	10.5	21.5	11.2	20.5	17.8	10.0	4.8	2.2	1.5	43.5	7 143	25 220	253.1	23.0
Layton	10.3	24.7	12.1	15.3	14.9	11.2	5.6	3.5	2.2	49.6	41 784	58 474	39.9	3.9
Logan	9.5	13.9	34.3	17.6	7.9	6.1	3.6	3.1	4.0	52.1	32 771	42 670	30.2	2.4
Midvale	9.5	16.3	16.7	19.2	12.7	9.4	7.2	4.8	4.2	49.3	11 886	27 029	127.4	0.5
Murray	7.5	19.8	13.3	14.2	14.4	12.3	7.3	6.0	5.4	51.1	31 274	34 024	8.8	28.2
Ogden	9.8	18.9	14.6	15.9	13.2	10.1	6.2	5.3	6.0	49.4	63 943	77 226	20.8	1.4
Orem	10.6	24.8	17.4	14.8	11.0	9.2	5.3	3.6	3.3	50.3	67 561	84 324	24.8	3.9
Provo	8.7	13.6	40.2	16.5	6.7	5.1	3.5	2.8	2.9	51.9	86 835	105 166	21.1	0.2
Riverton	12.4	30.2	8.9	15.8	16.3	9.2	3.9	2.0	1.3	49.7	11 261	25 011	122.1	16.9
Roy	10.1	23.4	11.6	16.2	14.4	10.1	5.9	4.8	3.6	50.5	24 560	32 885	33.7	7.2
St. George	8.6	19.7	13.7	11.5	10.4	8.9	7.8	9.8	9.5	51.4	28 572	49 663	73.8	13.5
Salt Lake City	7.9	15.7	15.2	19.7	13.8	10.8	5.9	4.9	6.1	49.4	159 928	181 743	13.6	-1.0
Sandy	7.9	26.5	11.1	11.4	16.0	14.9	6.9	2.8	2.4	49.8	75 240	88 418	17.5	1.0
South Jordan	8.4	30.8	10.5	10.6	16.5	12.5	6.0	2.7	2.0	49.8	12 215	29 437	141.0	14.1
Taylorsville	8.4	22.3	14.7	15.0	13.9	12.7	6.8	3.8	2.5	50.0	51 426	57 439	11.6	2.2
West Jordan	11.3	26.5	12.2	17.0	15.1	10.4	4.4	1.9	1.3	49.8	42 915	68 336	59.2	23.9
West Valley City	10.6	23.1	12.9	16.9	13.8	10.8	6.6	3.4	2.0	49.4	86 969	108 896	25.2	2.6
VERMONT	5.6	18.6	9.3	12.2	16.7	15.4	9.3	6.7	6.0	51.0	562 758	608 827	8.2	1.7
Burlington	4.6	11.7	25.4	17.5	13.5	10.5	6.3	5.0	5.5	51.7	39 127	38 889	-0.6	0.7
VIRGINIA	6.5	18.0	9.6	14.6	17.0	14.1	8.9	6.1	5.1	51.0	6 189 197	7 078 515	14.4	4.3
Alexandria	6.2	10.6	9.2	25.4	18.1	13.8	7.8	4.4	4.6	51.7	111 182	128 283	15.4	0.5
Blacksburg	2.9	6.7	57.4	12.3	6.6	5.7	3.5	2.6	2.4	44.1	34 590	39 573	14.4	1.2
Charlottesville	4.4	10.8	33.8	14.6	11.2	9.3	5.9	5.1	5.0	53.3	40 475	45 049	11.3	-13.1
Chesapeake	7.2	21.6	8.2	13.5	18.9	13.8	7.9	5.1	3.8	51.4	151 982	199 184	31.1	5.8
Danville	6.0	17.3	8.0	11.5	14.0	13.8	9.8	9.7	9.9	54.5	53 056	48 411	-8.8	-2.9
Hampton	6.3	17.9	12.6	14.8	17.7	12.4	8.0	5.8	4.5	50.4	133 811	146 437	9.4	0.3
Harrisonburg	4.7	10.7	40.9	11.3	9.9	8.0	5.2	4.3	5.0	52.6	30 707	40 468	31.8	1.7
Leesburg	9.8	19.6	6.4	18.3	20.6	12.6	6.7	3.1	3.0	50.9	16 202	28 311	74.7	17.7

Table D. Cities — Group Quarters, Crime, and Education

City	Households, 2000 Number	Percent change, 1990–2000	Persons per house-hold	Percent Female family house-holder[1]	Percent One-person	Persons in group quarters, 2000 Total	Institutional Total	Persons in nursing homes	Non-institutional	Serious crimes known to police,[2] 2002 Total Number	Rate[3]	Violent	Property	Education, 2000 School enrollment[4] Public	Private	Attainment[5] (percent) High school graduate or less	Bachelor's degree or more
	26	27	28	29	30	31	32	33	34	35	36	37	38	39	40	41	42
TEXAS—Cont'd																	
McKinney	18 186	139.4	2.89	9.5	19.0	1 827	1 093	397	734	NA	NA	NA	NA	12 993	2 064	32.6	39.1
Mansfield	8 881	73.1	3.08	8.3	10.9	648	574	68	74	1 067	3 644	202	3 443	7 434	1 297	35.3	32.8
Mesquite	43 926	22.5	2.82	14.0	20.6	700	643	615	57	6 480	4 982	344	4 638	31 979	4 396	46.5	18.5
Midland	35 674	7.6	2.62	11.9	25.8	1 422	1 042	718	380	4 143	4 175	565	3 610	24 293	3 957	41.3	27.2
Mission	13 766	65.6	3.29	14.5	15.3	110	105	105	5	2 849	6 007	169	5 838	13 489	692	62.8	17.9
Missouri City	17 069	47.9	3.09	12.5	11.9	141	14	14	127	1 460	2 642	275	2 367	14 313	2 775	23.2	44.5
Nacogdoches	11 220	-0.8	2.30	13.7	33.5	4 133	486	295	3 647	1 229	3 933	688	3 245	12 797	746	44.9	30.4
New Braunfels	13 558	35.6	2.60	11.5	24.8	1 178	819	558	359	2 726	7 151	766	6 385	7 872	1 140	52.0	24.6
North Richland Hills	20 793	23.0	2.66	10.3	20.4	269	202	194	67	2 957	5 089	272	4 817	12 816	2 135	33.9	26.1
Odessa	33 661	2.5	2.65	14.5	25.7	1 837	1 563	627	274	5 747	6 050	567	5 483	25 397	1 640	55.2	14.7
Paris	10 570	7.8	2.35	17.0	32.5	1 050	732	502	318	3 272	12 096	1 545	10 550	5 760	550	57.9	15.2
Pasadena	47 031	11.9	2.99	13.1	20.4	1 050	865	747	185	7 184	4 855	418	4 436	37 504	3 431	60.8	12.7
Pearland	13 192	100.2	2.84	9.7	15.8	182	165	165	17	1 393	3 543	247	3 296	9 224	1 509	34.8	29.1
Pharr	12 798	47.8	3.64	16.9	13.3	21	0	0	21	3 086	6 332	624	5 708	14 345	487	73.2	11.2
Plano	80 875	82.3	2.73	7.5	20.2	1 124	531	496	593	9 020	3 889	288	3 601	51 533	11 385	18.3	53.3
Port Arthur	21 839	-2.2	2.61	19.7	29.4	734	497	471	237	2 883	4 779	610	4 169	14 735	947	64.9	9.3
Richardson	35 191	29.3	2.59	8.9	22.9	809	548	509	261	3 825	3 989	294	3 695	21 490	4 440	22.8	47.7
Round Rock	21 076	99.4	2.87	11.0	18.1	550	438	438	112	1 813	2 839	182	2 658	15 291	2 329	32.1	32.9
Rowlett	14 266	88.7	3.09	8.0	10.6	356	295	283	61	1 074	2 310	103	2 207	11 845	2 041	30.8	32.5
San Angelo	34 006	10.9	2.48	12.5	28.8	3 955	1 123	787	2 832	5 723	6 195	427	5 769	23 863	1 536	51.7	20.1
San Antonio	405 474	24.1	2.77	16.4	25.1	23 180	11 682	5 641	11 498	94 132	7 873	817	7 056	289 226	46 762	49.1	21.6
San Juan	6 606	137.3	3.95	17.1	8.6	135	124	119	11	1 286	4 694	288	4 406	9 110	145	75.0	8.3
San Marcos	12 660	28.5	2.31	10.1	31.0	5 528	793	337	4 735	1 595	4 396	405	3 991	16 545	699	44.4	29.0
Sherman	13 739	10.3	2.42	13.4	30.4	1 770	940	552	830	2 378	6 490	491	5 998	7 133	1 880	48.1	20.1
Socorro	6 756	29.0	4.02	17.0	7.1	1	0	0	1	425	1 499	173	1 326	9 749	275	77.7	4.3
Sugar Land	20 515	153.3	3.06	8.4	12.6	491	270	270	221	1 937	2 928	274	2 655	17 407	4 114	20.0	53.7
Temple	21 543	18.7	2.44	13.6	29.9	1 994	1 578	1 083	416	3 133	5 502	407	5 095	12 097	1 665	46.5	22.9
Texarkana	13 569	8.8	2.42	19.3	29.9	1 911	1 597	656	314	2 983	8 211	994	7 217	8 442	688	49.9	20.4
Texas City	15 479	2.4	2.62	17.3	24.8	922	871	473	51	3 915	9 027	1 317	7 711	10 873	786	56.0	11.5
The Colony	8 462	25.0	3.14	10.4	11.4	0	0	0	0	1 040	3 753	177	3 576	7 661	887	33.9	24.0
Tyler	32 525	10.7	2.48	14.5	30.2	3 053	1 811	967	1 242	6 614	7 570	737	6 833	19 475	2 740	41.8	27.5
Victoria	22 129	11.9	2.68	14.3	24.5	1 222	951	478	271	3 889	6 144	755	5 389	15 096	2 156	51.0	18.5
Waco	42 279	7.1	2.49	16.2	31.1	8 443	3 430	1 599	5 013	11 001	9 261	796	8 466	27 101	13 266	54.5	18.6
Weslaco	8 295	25.9	3.21	17.0	18.4	341	339	323	2	2 216	7 877	526	7 351	7 446	312	66.3	13.5
Wichita Falls	37 970	7.0	2.46	12.3	28.7	10 951	5 273	765	5 678	8 532	7 839	917	6 922	25 425	2 997	48.2	21.5
UTAH	701 281	30.5	3.13	9.4	17.8	40 480	19 467	6 853	21 013	103 129	4 452	237	4 216	645 683	95 841	36.9	26.1
Bountiful	13 341	19.6	3.05	8.9	16.7	564	429	427	135	1 069	2 496	75	2 421	11 507	1 176	25.4	35.6
Clearfield	7 921	28.4	3.12	13.9	16.3	1 271	111	93	1 160	985	3 656	193	3 463	7 616	740	45.0	14.8
Draper	6 305	359.2	3.40	5.6	10.6	3 802	3 787	86	15	NA	NA	NA	NA	6 858	1 296	26.7	33.5
Layton	18 282	43.6	3.19	9.7	15.2	99	6	4	93	2 583	4 259	200	4 059	17 671	1 637	32.8	27.1
Logan	13 902	26.0	2.92	7.7	17.9	2 138	372	306	1 766	1 202	2 716	111	2 605	19 148	767	29.3	34.5
Midvale	10 089	117.9	2.66	12.7	25.3	201	0	0	201	1 716	6 121	439	5 682	5 595	783	45.8	20.7
Murray	12 673	8.2	2.68	11.3	24.6	90	84	67	6	3 710	10 513	459	10 054	8 612	953	34.4	25.5
Ogden	27 384	13.0	2.73	13.1	26.2	2 356	1 011	367	1 345	5 332	6 657	591	6 066	19 672	1 529	51.6	16.9
Orem	23 382	33.0	3.57	9.5	12.4	751	624	301	127	3 649	4 172	75	4 097	26 242	5 725	23.9	35.3
Provo	29 192	22.6	3.34	7.8	11.8	7 572	879	231	6 693	3 686	3 379	151	3 228	21 773	31 281	25.3	35.7
Riverton	6 348	131.3	3.93	5.7	5.8	55	7	7	48	NA	NA	NA	NA	8 644	848	35.3	23.3
Roy	10 689	39.6	3.06	10.3	15.8	172	170	126	2	961	2 817	229	2 589	9 305	657	40.5	16.3
St. George	17 367	83.8	2.81	8.6	19.4	859	399	372	460	1 668	3 238	278	2 961	12 982	1 159	38.5	22.0
Salt Lake City	71 461	7.2	2.48	10.2	33.2	4 573	1 134	735	3 439	19 118	10 142	657	9 485	45 370	6 796	36.3	34.9
Sandy	25 737	32.5	3.42	8.6	11.6	524	322	304	202	3 647	3 977	198	3 778	27 389	4 298	26.8	34.7
South Jordan	7 507	165.4	3.92	5.0	7.9	12	7	7	5	875	2 866	115	2 751	10 581	927	26.6	30.9
Taylorsville	18 530	NA	3.09	11.9	17.6	184	77	77	107	NA	NA	NA	NA	16 112	1 530	40.8	17.8
West Jordan	18 897	69.6	3.60	10.0	10.2	396	237	129	159	3 529	4 979	267	4 712	20 663	2 370	38.6	20.2
West Valley City	32 253	24.4	3.36	13.2	14.7	495	200	86	295	7 009	6 206	392	5 813	29 843	2 468	53.0	11.4
VERMONT	240 634	14.2	2.44	9.3	26.2	20 760	5 663	4 037	15 097	15 600	2 530	107	2 423	134 366	29 790	45.9	29.4
Burlington	15 885	8.2	2.19	10.0	35.6	4 022	485	477	3 537	1 813	4 603	289	4 314	11 966	2 587	35.1	42.0
VIRGINIA	2 699 173	17.8	2.54	11.9	25.1	231 398	111 484	38 865	119 914	229 039	3 140	291	2 849	1 566 180	301 921	44.5	29.5
Alexandria	61 889	16.2	2.04	9.2	43.4	1 901	1 439	948	462	5 233	3 959	317	3 642	19 122	7 387	25.8	54.3
Blacksburg	13 162	17.8	2.37	5.3	26.6	8 444	188	188	8 256	757	1 857	181	1 675	26 066	722	17.8	64.2
Charlottesville	16 851	5.3	2.27	13.1	34.9	6 832	374	374	6 458	1 745	3 759	754	3 005	19 629	1 340	40.6	40.8
Chesapeake	69 900	34.5	2.79	14.0	18.0	4 114	3 205	716	909	8 773	4 275	665	3 610	49 452	8 933	42.6	24.7
Danville	20 607	-5.1	2.27	19.6	33.9	1 679	1 078	609	601	2 266	4 543	603	3 939	9 878	1 263	62.2	13.9
Hampton	53 887	8.5	2.49	16.4	26.6	12 468	9 341	720	3 127	6 235	4 132	404	3 729	32 810	9 495	42.5	21.8
Harrisonburg	13 133	27.4	2.53	9.3	28.3	7 194	898	591	6 296	1 242	2 979	309	2 669	17 686	1 818	46.7	31.2
Leesburg	10 325	62.8	2.69	9.7	22.9	518	495	324	23	916	3 140	285	2 856	5 969	1 429	29.5	41.3

1. No spouse present.   2. Data for serious crimes have not been adjusted for underreporting. This may affect comparability between geographic areas and over time.   3. Per 100,000 population. estimated by the FBI.   4. All persons 3 years old and over enrolled in nursery school through college.   5. Persons 25 years old and over.

Table D. Cities — Income, Poverty, and Housing

City	Money income, 1999							Housing units, 2000					
	Per capita income[1] (dollars)	Households			Percent below poverty					Vacant units			
		Median income			Persons		Families						
		Dollars	Percent change, 1989–1999 (constant 1999 dollars)	Percent with income of $100,000 or more	Total	Percent change in rate, 1989–1999	Total	Total	Percent change, 1990–2000	Vacant units for sale or rent[2]	For seasonal use (percent)	Home owner vacancy rate	Renter vacancy rate
	43	44	45	46	47	48	49	50	51	52	53	54	55
TEXAS—Cont'd													
McKinney	28 185	63 366	73.2	25.4	8.5	-51.4	4.9	19 462	127.9	1 276	0.2	2.7	10.4
Mansfield	26 446	66 764	30.4	24.9	4.0	-45.2	2.7	9 172	66.2	291	0.2	1.4	5.0
Mesquite	20 890	50 424	4.4	11.1	6.8	-11.7	5.0	46 245	17.8	2 319	0.2	1.4	8.5
Midland	20 884	39 320	-7.2	12.4	12.9	-10.4	10.1	39 855	3.6	4 181	0.3	2.3	17.7
Mission	12 796	30 647	30.4	7.2	26.8	-28.2	22.6	17 723	66.3	3 957	15.0	1.7	7.9
Missouri City	27 210	72 434	3.7	28.7	3.3	-2.9	2.4	17 481	41.6	412	0.1	1.3	3.5
Nacogdoches	14 546	22 700	6.1	7.0	32.3	2.5	20.9	12 329	0.6	1 109	0.6	1.7	8.9
New Braunfels	18 548	40 078	13.0	7.6	10.9	-26.8	9.0	14 896	34.6	1 338	1.7	1.4	11.2
North Richland Hills	25 516	56 150	9.0	16.4	4.7	-7.8	3.1	21 600	19.2	807	0.2	0.8	7.0
Odessa	16 096	31 209	-4.6	6.2	18.6	-4.1	16.0	37 966	0.6	4 305	0.4	2.0	17.3
Paris	17 137	27 438	9.0	5.4	20.6	-18.9	16.5	11 777	5.2	1 207	0.6	2.3	9.2
Pasadena	16 301	38 522	-0.2	8.7	16.0	13.5	13.2	50 367	5.9	3 336	0.2	1.3	9.5
Pearland	26 306	64 156	12.2	22.6	4.7	0.0	3.4	13 922	103.9	730	0.1	1.9	10.8
Pharr	9 462	24 333	16.1	3.3	35.5	-20.2	30.8	16 537	49.9	3 739	11.9	1.5	16.6
Plano	36 514	78 722	8.7	36.8	4.3	30.3	3.0	86 078	81.7	5 203	0.3	1.4	12.6
Port Arthur	14 183	26 455	6.2	4.7	25.2	-10.3	22.9	24 713	-4.0	2 874	0.6	1.8	8.4
Richardson	29 551	62 392	-7.6	24.0	6.3	43.2	3.3	36 530	27.1	1 339	0.2	1.0	5.5
Round Rock	24 911	60 354	35.2	17.4	4.0	-55.6	2.8	21 766	86.1	690	0.3	1.0	3.5
Rowlett	26 144	70 947	9.7	22.7	3.0	20.0	2.2	14 580	78.8	314	0.1	1.1	4.9
San Angelo	17 289	32 232	1.9	5.6	15.7	-15.1	11.6	37 699	8.9	3 693	0.7	2.2	11.2
San Antonio	17 487	36 214	14.3	8.6	17.3	-23.5	14.0	433 122	18.5	27 648	0.5	1.4	6.9
San Juan	7 945	22 706	18.2	3.3	34.4	-11.6	32.7	7 719	144.4	1 113	7.0	1.2	6.9
San Marcos	13 468	25 809	29.7	3.6	28.5	-23.2	13.8	13 340	22.1	680	0.3	1.3	4.5
Sherman	18 717	34 211	2.8	6.1	13.3	-14.7	9.6	14 926	4.7	1 187	0.3	2.0	8.9
Socorro	7 287	24 087	13.1	1.5	32.6	-21.8	30.9	7 140	31.0	384	0.4	0.6	6.3
Sugar Land	33 506	81 767	7.6	38.6	3.8	52.0	3.2	21 090	145.8	575	0.3	1.1	5.1
Temple	19 360	35 135	12.7	7.8	13.9	-27.6	10.8	23 511	13.5	1 968	0.3	2.5	8.4
Texarkana	17 815	29 727	1.8	8.0	24.0	10.1	19.4	15 105	5.5	1 536	0.4	2.2	11.5
Texas City	17 057	35 963	2.4	6.4	14.9	-11.3	12.0	16 715	0.2	1 236	0.3	1.6	9.5
The Colony	22 903	64 080	11.6	19.9	2.8	-3.4	1.6	8 812	23.2	350	0.0	2.3	7.2
Tyler	20 184	34 163	7.5	10.4	16.8	-13.8	13.0	35 337	7.5	2 812	0.4	1.9	9.4
Victoria	19 009	36 829	7.2	9.2	14.7	-22.2	12.2	24 192	11.0	2 063	0.5	1.4	11.3
Waco	14 584	26 264	9.5	5.4	26.3	-8.4	19.3	45 819	1.6	3 540	0.3	1.9	6.6
Weslaco	11 235	26 573	12.1	4.6	30.9	-13.0	26.5	10 230	15.6	1 935	10.2	1.5	9.2
Wichita Falls	16 761	32 554	2.8	5.7	13.9	-16.3	10.8	41 916	3.8	3 946	0.4	2.6	11.2
UTAH	18 185	45 726	15.5	11.2	9.4	-17.5	6.5	768 594	28.4	67 313	3.9	2.1	6.5
Bountiful	23 967	55 993	8.7	18.9	4.0	-18.4	3.0	13 819	20.3	478	0.3	1.5	4.8
Clearfield	13 945	38 946	7.9	4.3	12.2	-30.3	8.7	8 374	28.5	453	0.2	3.3	5.8
Draper	22 747	72 341	NA	27.0	2.7	NA	1.8	6 588	348.8	283	0.4	2.2	4.9
Layton	19 604	52 128	12.6	13.2	5.6	-21.1	5.0	19 145	42.2	863	0.3	2.4	6.5
Logan	13 765	30 778	7.5	5.5	22.7	5.1	12.6	14 692	28.4	790	0.6	2.3	4.6
Midvale	17 609	40 130	41.0	5.8	13.1	-36.7	9.4	10 730	115.8	641	0.6	1.4	6.9
Murray	21 094	45 569	17.2	10.4	6.3	-21.3	5.5	13 327	7.9	654	0.2	2.1	6.9
Ogden	16 632	34 047	7.9	6.0	16.5	-1.8	12.6	29 763	9.4	2 379	0.3	3.2	9.9
Orem	16 590	47 529	13.2	13.3	8.4	-6.7	5.8	24 166	34.5	784	0.3	1.2	3.4
Provo	13 207	34 313	20.7	7.3	26.8	-9.5	12.5	30 374	23.6	1 182	0.4	2.2	2.4
Riverton	17 643	63 980	31.4	15.3	2.6	-42.2	2.4	6 555	131.5	207	0.2	1.3	5.0
Roy	17 794	49 611	5.4	8.0	5.5	25.0	4.2	11 053	39.3	364	0.2	2.0	5.6
St. George	17 022	36 505	4.7	7.5	11.6	-8.7	7.4	21 083	79.2	3 716	11.9	3.7	6.6
Salt Lake City	20 752	36 944	21.1	10.2	15.3	-6.7	10.4	77 054	4.5	5 593	0.8	2.1	6.8
Sandy	22 928	66 458	12.5	23.2	3.8	-9.5	2.8	26 579	32.2	842	0.3	1.3	6.7
South Jordan	20 938	75 433	28.2	25.4	1.7	-46.9	0.9	7 721	167.6	214	0.1	1.0	8.8
Taylorsville	17 812	47 236	NA	9.3	5.9	NA	4.5	19 159	NA	629	0.3	1.3	4.8
West Jordan	17 221	55 794	24.8	11.0	5.2	-25.7	4.1	19 597	68.4	700	0.1	1.7	6.4
West Valley City	15 031	45 773	15.4	5.9	8.7	-24.3	6.7	33 488	22.4	1 235	0.1	1.7	5.1
VERMONT	20 625	40 856	2.1	8.7	9.4	-5.1	6.3	294 382	8.5	53 748	14.6	1.4	4.2
Burlington	19 011	33 070	-3.6	6.8	20.0	3.6	10.4	16 395	5.9	510	1.1	0.6	1.6
VIRGINIA	23 975	46 677	4.2	15.1	9.6	-5.9	7.0	2 904 192	16.3	205 019	1.9	1.5	5.2
Alexandria	37 645	56 054	0.6	22.0	8.9	25.4	6.8	64 251	10.3	2 362	0.8	1.0	2.4
Blacksburg	13 946	22 513	-9.9	7.7	43.2	15.5	15.9	13 732	15.8	570	0.4	1.6	3.2
Charlottesville	16 973	31 007	-4.6	7.6	25.9	9.3	12.0	17 591	4.8	740	0.4	1.1	2.4
Chesapeake	20 949	50 743	5.7	11.9	7.3	-18.9	6.1	72 672	30.4	2 772	0.3	1.4	3.6
Danville	17 151	26 900	-1.9	5.2	20.0	5.3	15.9	23 108	-0.8	2 501	0.4	2.8	11.6
Hampton	19 774	39 532	-2.4	6.9	11.3	4.6	8.8	57 311	6.9	3 424	0.5	2.0	5.6
Harrisonburg	14 898	29 949	-11.9	7.0	30.1	40.0	11.5	13 689	25.6	556	0.3	1.7	3.3
Leesburg	30 116	68 861	28.5	27.2	3.6	-41.0	2.4	10 671	52.6	346	0.4	0.6	3.4

1. Based on population enumerated as of April 1, 2000.   2. Includes units rented or sold but not occupied.

Table D. Cities — Housing, Labor Force, Employment, and Disability

City	Housing units, 2000 (cont'd) Occupied units					Civilian labor force, 2003		Unemployment		Civilian employment,[2] 2000	Percent		Disability, 2000
	Total	Percent owner occupied	Percent renter occupied	Average size owner occupied	Average size renter occupied	Total	Percent change, 2002–2003	Total	Rate[1]	Total	Management, professional, and related occupations	Production, transportation, and material moving occupations	Employment disabled persons[3] (percent)
	56	57	58	59	60	61	62	63	64	65	66	67	68
TEXAS—Cont'd													
McKinney	18 186	70.2	29.8	3.00	2.62	22 564	0.4	2 392	10.6	26 456	43.7	9.3	7.5
Mansfield	8 881	86.6	13.4	3.08	3.08	10 535	1.3	620	5.9	14 456	41.2	11.8	6.2
Mesquite	43 926	65.5	34.5	2.99	2.50	68 963	0.6	4 093	5.9	64 561	30.9	12.6	10.9
Midland	35 674	66.1	33.9	2.81	2.25	54 264	3.9	2 407	4.4	42 552	36.9	9.3	9.6
Mission	13 766	74.9	25.1	3.27	3.36	16 457	6.3	1 894	11.5	14 849	30.5	12.5	12.7
Missouri City	17 069	90.8	9.2	3.08	3.18	35 359	2.2	1 361	3.8	26 854	49.2	8.2	9.2
Nacogdoches	11 220	43.5	56.5	2.49	2.15	15 145	2.9	832	5.5	13 169	30.9	12.3	9.0
New Braunfels	13 558	64.4	35.6	2.69	2.45	22 558	1.8	1 072	4.8	16 959	32.8	15.9	11.1
North Richland Hills	20 793	67.1	32.9	2.81	2.36	34 850	1.2	1 726	5.0	30 101	36.9	10.1	11.2
Odessa	33 661	64.1	35.9	2.80	2.38	48 695	3.8	3 384	6.9	37 715	25.9	14.8	10.7
Paris	10 570	54.3	45.7	2.34	2.36	11 995	3.0	1 009	8.4	10 265	26.4	18.2	19.2
Pasadena	47 031	56.1	43.9	3.10	2.85	74 860	2.4	5 614	7.5	58 608	23.5	16.9	14.2
Pearland	13 192	79.4	20.6	2.95	2.41	12 748	1.9	698	5.5	19 466	40.9	10.5	9.0
Pharr	12 798	73.2	26.8	3.68	3.55	18 492	6.4	2 987	16.2	14 509	23.2	15.2	14.6
Plano	80 875	68.8	31.2	2.97	2.21	157 896	0.5	8 445	5.3	120 230	55.5	4.5	7.3
Port Arthur	21 839	62.2	37.8	2.69	2.48	26 383	3.6	3 742	14.2	19 790	20.8	18.8	14.7
Richardson	35 191	64.4	35.6	2.70	2.37	57 363	0.5	3 181	5.5	49 592	51.9	6.2	9.7
Round Rock	21 076	65.3	34.7	3.03	2.58	37 458	1.2	1 747	4.7	32 046	41.9	10.2	7.4
Rowlett	14 266	92.2	7.8	3.09	3.16	17 084	0.6	659	3.9	23 060	45.2	7.9	6.6
San Angelo	34 006	60.8	39.2	2.62	2.27	43 824	1.8	1 800	4.1	38 241	27.8	13.1	12.3
San Antonio	405 474	58.1	41.9	2.95	2.51	564 572	2.4	34 876	6.2	488 747	32.1	10.7	14.1
San Juan	6 606	76.7	23.3	4.03	3.69	6 567	6.3	829	12.6	8 035	18.7	17.1	15.5
San Marcos	12 660	30.2	69.8	2.75	2.12	24 661	1.8	1 997	8.1	18 621	30.4	8.6	6.6
Sherman	13 739	56.4	43.6	2.53	2.29	17 724	2.4	1 428	8.1	15 528	30.3	17.9	13.1
Socorro	6 756	81.1	18.9	4.11	3.64	10 963	3.4	1 687	15.4	8 491	13.9	28.9	15.0
Sugar Land	20 515	84.1	15.9	3.15	2.61	23 362	2.6	1 142	4.9	30 809	56.8	5.0	7.0
Temple	21 543	55.9	44.1	2.59	2.25	29 573	2.0	1 211	4.1	23 819	33.7	16.4	11.6
Texarkana	13 569	58.7	41.3	2.44	2.40	15 057	1.8	1 036	6.9	13 540	31.5	15.5	13.1
Texas City	15 479	63.3	36.7	2.72	2.45	22 668	3.7	2 177	9.6	17 218	26.5	15.2	13.3
The Colony	8 462	82.5	17.5	3.14	3.12	21 236	1.0	1 134	5.3	14 394	37.2	9.4	10.0
Tyler	32 525	56.2	43.8	2.63	2.28	48 640	2.9	2 830	5.8	37 289	32.4	15.5	15.8
Victoria	22 129	60.8	39.2	2.76	2.57	33 628	0.2	1 858	5.5	27 758	30.1	14.4	12.1
Waco	42 279	46.4	53.6	2.60	2.40	53 769	2.4	3 587	6.7	45 672	28.6	15.7	12.9
Weslaco	8 295	65.4	34.6	3.29	3.06	13 582	6.5	2 278	16.8	8 658	29.4	12.9	14.0
Wichita Falls	37 970	57.8	42.2	2.54	2.34	47 152	1.0	2 446	5.2	41 075	30.1	14.5	11.2
UTAH	701 281	71.5	28.5	3.28	2.75	1 184 385	1.7	66 653	5.6	1 044 362	32.5	13.5	8.9
Bountiful	13 341	77.7	22.3	3.19	2.59	25 860	1.7	1 083	4.2	19 512	39.0	9.3	8.5
Clearfield	7 921	55.1	44.9	3.19	3.04	12 036	1.7	1 032	8.6	10 739	21.1	19.0	9.0
Draper	6 305	83.8	16.2	3.54	2.63	3 194	1.2	125	3.9	10 888	43.6	6.2	7.0
Layton	18 282	74.5	25.5	3.42	2.52	29 144	1.7	1 604	5.5	28 107	33.8	12.2	7.7
Logan	13 902	44.0	56.0	3.05	2.81	24 587	3.6	1 114	4.5	22 149	32.7	18.0	4.7
Midvale	10 089	48.1	51.9	2.66	2.66	8 863	0.7	751	8.5	14 410	27.5	12.0	14.1
Murray	12 673	66.7	33.3	2.81	2.40	23 340	1.2	915	3.9	17 705	32.7	9.6	8.3
Ogden	27 384	61.2	38.8	2.84	2.57	43 859	2.2	4 228	9.6	34 280	25.0	19.9	12.9
Orem	23 382	67.1	32.9	3.82	3.06	44 892	1.8	1 727	3.8	38 223	37.9	11.0	7.5
Provo	29 192	42.6	57.4	3.45	3.27	65 811	1.4	3 414	5.2	52 101	38.3	9.4	4.8
Riverton	6 348	94.0	6.0	3.96	3.50	6 939	1.2	293	4.2	11 381	30.8	10.8	5.2
Roy	10 689	84.3	15.7	3.11	2.81	17 605	1.9	860	4.9	16 002	28.5	17.2	9.1
St. George	17 367	67.9	32.1	2.78	2.88	29 960	6.4	1 436	4.8	20 118	27.3	12.0	8.5
Salt Lake City	71 461	51.2	48.8	2.69	2.26	117 580	0.9	7 827	6.7	92 074	38.3	12.0	12.4
Sandy	25 737	84.3	15.7	3.53	2.82	49 393	1.2	2 107	4.3	44 710	37.7	8.7	7.7
South Jordan	7 507	89.7	10.3	4.09	2.44	7 494	1.2	288	3.8	13 717	37.5	10.2	6.2
Taylorsville	18 530	71.2	28.8	3.25	2.70	37 484	1.1	1 872	5.0	30 555	27.3	15.0	10.5
West Jordan	18 897	81.9	18.1	3.72	3.05	27 872	1.1	1 225	4.4	34 250	28.9	14.0	9.0
West Valley City	32 253	72.6	27.4	3.48	3.05	62 341	0.8	4 674	7.5	51 842	20.1	22.2	13.5
VERMONT	240 634	70.6	29.4	2.58	2.11	350 684	0.6	16 013	4.6	317 134	36.3	14.0	9.7
Burlington	15 885	41.5	58.5	2.39	2.06	24 260	0.2	970	4.0	21 335	39.2	10.4	9.1
VIRGINIA	2 699 173	68.1	31.9	2.62	2.36	3 773 263	1.1	153 522	4.1	3 412 647	38.2	12.5	10.9
Alexandria	61 889	40.0	60.0	2.03	2.05	82 877	1.2	2 252	2.7	76 584	56.2	5.2	9.1
Blacksburg	13 162	30.4	69.6	2.45	2.33	17 043	6.2	506	3.0	16 732	52.2	4.8	3.6
Charlottesville	16 851	40.8	59.2	2.27	2.26	20 676	0.9	685	3.3	20 943	44.0	7.4	7.4
Chesapeake	69 900	74.9	25.1	2.87	2.56	112 832	2.2	4 112	3.6	92 376	35.6	11.5	11.5
Danville	20 607	58.1	41.9	2.28	2.25	24 089	1.5	2 710	11.2	19 668	23.9	26.0	15.6
Hampton	53 887	58.6	41.4	2.55	2.40	73 879	2.0	3 766	5.1	60 810	32.1	13.7	11.3
Harrisonburg	13 133	39.0	61.0	2.52	2.54	21 587	1.4	527	2.4	18 834	31.2	16.4	6.3
Leesburg	10 325	67.9	32.1	2.88	2.30	22 668	1.1	642	2.8	15 535	48.4	6.6	7.6

1. Percent of civilian labor force.   2. Persons 16 years old and over.   3. Persons 16 to 64 years old.

City	Value of residential construction authorized by building permits, 2003			Wholesale trade, 1997				Retail trade,[1] 1997			
	New construction ($1,000)	Number of housing units	Percent single family	Number of establishments	Number of employees	Sales (mil dol)	Annual payroll (mil dol)	Number of establishments	Number of employees	Sales (mil dol)	Annual payroll (mil dol)
	69	70	71	72	73	74	75	76	77	78	79
TEXAS—Cont'd											
McKinney	388 797	3 075	90.9	70	690	344.4	22.1	144	1 893	414.7	40.1
Mansfield	84 434	604	97.8	44	600	214.3	17.6	49	795	106.6	11.3
Mesquite	56 278	621	67.8	88	1 505	1 384.1	48.8	476	8 899	1 572.8	147.3
Midland	30 268	260	100.0	223	1 921	1 304.9	67.5	516	6 500	1 199.4	105.6
Mission	98 661	1 263	92.3	36	264	96.7	6.0	136	1 963	314.9	28.8
Missouri City	146 829	892	86.1	33	117	35.8	4.2	85	1 163	145.3	15.0
Nacogdoches	5 286	62	100.0	37	355	118.3	10.0	230	2 749	431.0	40.4
New Braunfels	86 831	883	78.7	65	506	301.5	16.8	262	2 979	584.0	51.9
North Richland Hills	48 843	298	100.0	57	270	218.4	11.0	236	4 647	993.9	87.3
Odessa	25 924	173	100.0	234	2 279	738.8	73.7	489	5 614	1 063.4	98.2
Paris	7 094	136	41.2	54	418	107.2	10.2	205	2 394	448.4	36.6
Pasadena	60 356	894	40.2	110	1 583	589.6	56.5	422	5 739	878.2	88.1
Pearland	319 311	1 841	91.4	47	767	178.2	29.0	89	1 663	276.1	24.8
Pharr	39 036	830	76.3	55	713	201.6	14.0	160	1 587	208.8	21.9
Plano	171 823	1 114	76.8	443	4 766	5 038.9	194.4	804	14 928	3 167.2	290.9
Port Arthur	17 303	263	67.7	33	1 053	355.0	34.5	215	2 585	399.6	39.0
Richardson	58 231	175	100.0	478	10 306	8 145.8	565.8	417	6 096	1 597.7	141.5
Round Rock	163 893	1 453	100.0	70	767	433.2	27.9	162	D	D	D
Rowlett	120 349	670	100.0	37	135	66.1	5.7	53	511	108.2	10.1
San Angelo	30 985	265	100.0	141	1 282	346.5	29.6	446	5 246	874.8	82.8
San Antonio	914 945	8 146	74.9	1 650	23 198	12 097.5	756.4	3 848	55 174	9 723.6	947.0
San Juan	13 463	259	100.0	17	143	39.5	3.2	43	241	44.5	3.3
San Marcos	42 980	499	35.5	35	D	D	D	285	3 449	599.1	50.5
Sherman	16 856	178	93.3	67	569	206.6	15.7	250	4 231	749.1	67.8
Socorro	4 512	75	100.0	9	D	D	D	37	196	30.6	2.4
Sugar Land	58 862	459	63.6	92	924	1 726.2	44.6	271	4 472	743.8	68.9
Temple	41 557	312	98.7	76	2 081	1 271.7	69.5	305	4 196	730.0	71.3
Texarkana	28 127	331	36.9	102	1 411	879.6	44.5	331	4 263	768.3	69.6
Texas City	30 082	408	52.9	40	223	109.0	9.0	184	3 127	460.0	42.5
The Colony	43 273	356	57.0	4	8	7.5	0.2	37	618	95.1	8.5
Tyler	71 261	465	82.2	186	2 189	990.8	71.3	643	8 822	1 692.9	154.3
Victoria	12 827	117	100.0	125	D	D	D	379	4 913	846.3	77.9
Waco	59 170	560	55.5	210	2 956	1 481.1	82.1	601	8 053	1 393.7	128.1
Weslaco	17 907	266	91.7	21	D	D	D	130	2 194	398.3	35.0
Wichita Falls	44 810	464	55.6	176	1 771	391.2	41.0	514	6 450	1 070.1	96.4
UTAH	3 081 981	22 525	81.8	3 278	44 319	21 115.5	1 420.5	7 656	114 474	19 964.6	1 856.9
Bountiful	35 924	131	70.2	51	221	95.9	6.7	142	2 425	510.2	45.7
Clearfield	19 410	187	97.9	32	815	306.1	23.0	49	517	76.3	6.8
Draper	90 353	734	77.2	NA	NA	NA	NA	NA	NA	NA	NA
Layton	54 811	438	81.7	41	401	121.1	8.3	208	3 631	676.9	58.0
Logan	28 973	276	56.2	53	409	74.9	8.1	248	3 895	500.8	53.8
Midvale	9 039	63	93.7	63	490	220.0	15.4	96	1 815	444.0	32.3
Murray	21 196	99	100.0	186	2 103	967.7	64.1	343	6 445	1 418.9	128.5
Ogden	37 944	292	85.6	127	1 654	504.5	45.5	408	6 090	922.8	94.7
Orem	41 066	339	44.0	103	1 047	481.7	31.4	420	7 352	1 170.3	116.2
Provo	71 303	446	56.1	91	3 704	1 748.9	114.1	252	3 782	638.1	60.9
Riverton	42 184	313	93.3	13	49	21.7	1.1	29	466	56.2	6.3
Roy	13 453	124	100.0	7	D	D	D	54	886	120.0	13.2
St. George	206 859	1 699	77.0	66	559	216.8	16.4	332	4 151	784.5	68.4
Salt Lake City	24 950	215	51.6	714	13 524	7 479.4	471.0	1 039	15 539	3 041.0	278.5
Sandy	49 382	544	42.1	NA	NA	NA	NA	NA	NA	NA	NA
South Jordan	100 193	680	95.7	13	D	D	D	25	215	44.8	4.1
Taylorsville	34 686	289	49.5	NA	NA	NA	NA	NA	NA	NA	NA
West Jordan	207 090	1 721	64.3	53	626	262.3	17.7	97	2 173	330.7	32.8
West Valley City	84 277	937	52.7	NA	NA	NA	NA	NA	NA	NA	NA
VERMONT	405 980	2 843	85.5	941	10 987	4 731.4	330.6	4 093	36 306	5 898.6	603.3
Burlington	6 483	19	100.0	58	678	331.5	24.6	261	3 041	354.9	42.6
VIRGINIA	6 876 972	55 936	82.7	7 868	106 365	61 046.7	3 784.4	29 032	379 039	62 569.9	6 202.6
Alexandria	13 811	72	27.8	137	1 830	899.6	75.1	593	7 746	1 507.6	160.0
Blacksburg	15 411	142	84.5	8	D	D	D	127	1 773	191.3	21.2
Charlottesville	18 708	356	16.0	81	954	265.9	29.7	360	4 345	730.3	73.2
Chesapeake	212 408	1 660	65.5	246	3 833	1 768.2	115.7	779	12 554	1 993.3	184.5
Danville	9 466	82	78.0	55	964	211.8	22.6	334	3 787	585.5	56.9
Hampton	36 499	630	31.4	94	1 073	370.7	31.3	514	9 930	1 638.9	150.5
Harrisonburg	22 384	281	77.6	62	971	749.2	25.5	308	4 161	690.8	64.0
Leesburg	NA	NA	NA	22	D	D	D	143	1 807	326.2	32.4

1. Establishments with payroll.

City	Real estate and rental and leasing, 1997				Professional, scientific, and technical services,[1] 1997				Manufacturing, 1997			
	Number of establishments	Number of employees	Receipts (mil dol)	Annual payroll (mil dol)	Number of establishments	Number of employees	Receipts (mil dol)	Annual payroll (mil dol)	Number of establishments	Number of employees	Receipts (mil dol)	Annual payroll (mil dol)
	80	81	82	83	84	85	86	87	88	89	90	91
TEXAS—Cont'd												
McKinney	55	200	23.1	4.9	93	412	42.8	14.7	48	4 537	1 327.9	204.0
Mansfield	15	25	2.9	0.7	39	152	16.1	4.2	70	2 715	434.5	77.9
Mesquite	99	670	55.5	11.4	121	514	36.2	13.0	72	3 338	1 147.3	111.1
Midland	171	821	77.5	14.5	323	1 898	228.7	70.7	73	901	119.1	32.4
Mission	28	161	8.5	1.6	16	52	3.9	1.3	27	1 176	177.9	22.1
Missouri City	29	168	18.6	3.0	54	D	D	D	18	675	163.4	28.3
Nacogdoches	51	163	17.3	2.6	46	174	12.7	3.1	36	3 101	719.6	92.5
New Braunfels	62	285	20.3	4.2	89	302	23.5	7.3	59	3 525	449.9	86.2
North Richland Hills	41	165	26.3	3.3	81	573	38.1	18.0	33	1 980	405.3	59.4
Odessa	120	697	64.3	12.4	181	949	65.4	25.1	120	1 886	758.9	62.1
Paris	42	122	14.6	1.8	49	243	13.5	4.2	44	4 585	2 032.3	157.0
Pasadena	120	811	99.9	19.9	137	1 410	176.9	69.1	100	5 905	4 893.4	270.7
Pearland	34	280	45.1	8.4	69	188	20.5	5.4	57	793	76.5	21.8
Pharr	17	76	6.7	0.9	30	112	8.5	2.2	NA	NA	NA	NA
Plano	224	1 332	261.6	41.9	683	3 535	535.3	179.3	124	8 614	2 547.5	448.6
Port Arthur	22	205	22.1	4.5	50	355	27.5	10.2	33	3 915	6 712.2	234.9
Richardson	159	667	101.7	21.2	521	4 020	459.1	191.2	179	11 246	3 350.5	444.5
Round Rock	54	171	17.7	2.6	83	870	152.9	40.6	69	D	D	D
Rowlett	18	46	4.4	0.6	37	123	10.7	4.5	44	771	62.6	20.3
San Angelo	128	535	50.6	8.0	149	735	58.1	16.2	85	4 323	803.4	101.8
San Antonio	1 170	8 005	974.7	187.0	2 507	19 099	1 831.9	729.7	953	32 870	5 199.7	911.6
San Juan	6	16	1.2	0.2	2	D	D	D	NA	NA	NA	NA
San Marcos	55	208	28.3	3.5	61	251	20.5	6.1	42	1 972	245.7	54.0
Sherman	63	250	23.0	4.0	108	484	34.6	12.9	58	6 992	2 672.0	274.4
Socorro	3	D	D	D	2	D	D	D	NA	NA	NA	NA
Sugar Land	63	174	22.8	3.1	168	D	D	D	40	2 703	983.4	105.3
Temple	69	325	28.1	5.6	77	602	49.1	20.6	59	5 515	1 164.7	183.0
Texarkana	65	351	42.0	6.1	108	503	50.5	15.1	49	2 717	608.3	90.3
Texas City	37	318	26.0	6.2	53	304	20.9	9.3	27	5 408	8 922.0	327.2
The Colony	12	53	11.4	0.5	17	19	2.1	0.8	NA	NA	NA	NA
Tyler	142	690	73.5	15.5	325	2 173	256.0	83.9	115	9 228	2 068.8	339.0
Victoria	89	D	D	D	135	705	58.4	21.0	60	2 765	1 195.5	111.0
Waco	170	938	120.8	19.1	241	1 910	125.0	54.7	177	14 884	3 608.3	444.3
Weslaco	29	122	7.6	1.4	36	234	14.7	5.1	18	1 414	77.8	24.9
Wichita Falls	129	467	48.3	7.5	200	1 037	83.4	30.6	121	6 090	1 069.6	206.0
UTAH	2 169	12 318	1 342.6	236.0	4 282	36 468	3 306.1	1 303.1	2 860	119 140	24 014.4	3 726.1
Bountiful	46	153	18.5	3.2	115	516	31.3	12.1	37	504	54.1	12.3
Clearfield	15	99	26.8	2.2	17	208	14.8	8.0	49	3 745	603.2	103.6
Draper	NA	NA	NA	NA	NA	NA	NA	NA	NA	NA	NA	NA
Layton	56	322	28.3	4.6	56	340	21.4	10.5	NA	NA	NA	NA
Logan	55	401	22.3	6.4	101	777	42.4	16.9	79	5 455	909.8	124.5
Midvale	32	188	33.1	4.0	48	256	31.5	9.6	NA	NA	NA	NA
Murray	103	632	71.0	12.6	198	2 165	255.9	93.1	148	2 680	247.3	61.9
Ogden	96	479	44.9	8.9	200	1 932	123.4	53.2	130	13 226	2 696.5	410.9
Orem	77	349	36.9	5.7	188	2 031	112.8	46.3	99	2 359	272.6	61.3
Provo	99	489	49.9	7.6	199	2 966	268.1	114.6	93	3 367	346.7	79.8
Riverton	12	19	1.4	0.3	13	24	2.2	0.5	NA	NA	NA	NA
Roy	22	79	5.0	0.9	14	51	2.3	0.7	11	D	D	D
St. George	86	277	28.9	4.0	105	552	33.7	14.0	60	1 377	191.3	35.5
Salt Lake City	362	3 606	380.2	80.9	1 123	12 408	1 400.3	558.4	512	25 306	4 894.8	813.8
Sandy	NA	NA	NA	NA	NA	NA	NA	NA	92	2 662	309.5	82.1
South Jordan	18	31	4.5	0.7	34	181	12.2	3.7	12	D	D	D
Taylorsville	NA	NA	NA	NA	NA	NA	NA	NA	NA	NA	NA	NA
West Jordan	33	127	14.5	1.5	31	74	5.1	1.5	76	2 567	433.5	91.1
West Valley City	NA	NA	NA	NA	NA	NA	NA	NA	170	6 627	1 199.4	230.8
VERMONT	701	2 362	240.6	42.2	1 622	7 792	719.1	279.0	1 226	42 533	7 803.0	1 459.6
Burlington	62	323	42.0	7.7	203	1 597	147.9	62.4	55	D	D	D
VIRGINIA	6 717	43 976	5 749.2	1 028.4	17 539	212 632	24 151.7	9 729.8	5 986	370 595	83 814.0	11 557.8
Alexandria	202	2 023	354.1	57.9	894	12 710	1 456.2	634.2	114	1 907	328.1	59.4
Blacksburg	37	345	39.7	7.9	99	1 046	105.0	38.0	23	1 910	225.3	57.8
Charlottesville	97	458	50.1	9.8	206	1 448	118.7	49.7	67	D	D	D
Chesapeake	144	704	98.0	15.9	263	2 653	198.1	84.5	132	4 558	1 085.0	147.0
Danville	59	242	18.1	3.5	76	577	27.3	11.6	47	D	D	D
Hampton	113	1 241	89.2	20.6	211	3 190	270.9	120.4	80	4 636	971.0	123.4
Harrisonburg	48	263	30.8	5.5	95	618	50.9	19.6	38	3 687	725.8	102.6
Leesburg	48	241	41.0	6.8	154	768	77.1	29.8	NA	NA	NA	NA

1. Firms subject to federal tax.

— # Accommodation and Foodservices, Entertainment, and Health Care

City	Accommodation and foodservices, 1997				Arts, entertainment, and recreation,[1] 1997				Health care and social assistance,[1] 1997			
	Number of establishments	Number of employees	Sales (mil dol)	Annual payroll (mil dol)	Number of establishments	Number of employees	Receipts (mil dol)	Annual payroll (mil dol)	Number of establishments	Number of employees	Receipts (mil dol)	Annual payroll (mil dol)
	92	93	94	95	96	97	98	99	100	101	102	103
TEXAS—Cont'd												
McKinney	61	1 156	36.7	10.9	9	250	10.2	3.1	110	1 876	120.8	47.6
Mansfield	26	426	13.0	3.3	2	0	0.0	0.0	29	518	26.2	10.7
Mesquite	168	4 278	148.4	40.5	25	514	17.3	4.9	235	3 408	238.2	90.9
Midland	225	D	D	D	28	0	0.0	0.0	238	2 931	248.9	101.2
Mission	70	923	30.8	8.0	5	172	5.5	1.5	83	1 148	54.6	26.5
Missouri City	39	531	17.9	4.4	3	0	0.0	0.0	80	1 196	76.1	29.2
Nacogdoches	78	1 789	54.0	14.9	10	0	0.0	0.0	148	2 224	127.6	48.3
New Braunfels	128	2 162	72.7	20.7	20	111	3.5	1.0	128	1 220	63.5	26.3
North Richland Hills	91	2 570	76.8	21.3	13	277	7.1	2.5	91	1 616	109.9	44.2
Odessa	217	3 704	117.9	32.4	32	231	8.1	1.6	220	3 646	164.0	69.1
Paris	84	1 352	42.5	12.2	9	0	0.0	0.0	139	2 668	98.5	45.4
Pasadena	174	3 081	108.6	28.8	18	195	6.9	2.2	308	4 293	298.3	116.7
Pearland	48	843	28.4	7.8	8	93	4.1	1.1	49	438	17.3	6.7
Pharr	48	678	25.1	5.9	4	21	1.1	0.2	54	1 030	32.1	12.0
Plano	347	8 108	298.8	83.9	57	979	49.6	13.2	582	6 465	591.2	227.3
Port Arthur	86	1 265	44.5	12.2	7	79	2.8	0.9	126	1 934	153.4	59.0
Richardson	205	3 633	149.7	39.4	24	433	19.8	6.0	330	3 203	195.2	80.3
Round Rock	102	2 130	77.2	21.5	12	111	4.1	1.6	103	1 208	87.1	34.6
Rowlett	20	310	9.4	2.5	4	50	0.9	0.5	52	1 014	62.8	20.5
San Angelo	184	3 706	108.6	32.0	16	0	0.0	0.0	180	3 316	207.7	91.1
San Antonio	2 237	50 503	1 844.1	509.4	233	8 152	343.9	104.2	2 525	47 329	2 859.8	1 165.6
San Juan	14	149	5.2	1.0	NA	NA	NA	NA	12	90	3.8	2.0
San Marcos	131	2 444	74.6	20.6	10	72	2.9	0.8	101	1 129	66.8	29.2
Sherman	95	1 921	63.6	17.6	10	60	1.8	0.5	160	2 632	147.5	68.3
Socorro	7	D	D	D	NA	NA	NA	NA	2	0	0.0	0.0
Sugar Land	104	2 200	78.7	21.2	9	234	11.6	3.9	152	1 257	78.9	32.6
Temple	130	2 497	77.5	20.8	19	256	7.4	2.4	139	4 347	333.1	111.0
Texarkana	102	2 081	70.2	17.1	12	0	0.0	0.0	194	3 204	208.9	101.9
Texas City	82	1 471	42.8	11.5	9	53	2.0	0.5	82	1 712	77.9	40.7
The Colony	24	435	13.8	4.1	3	0	0.3	0.0	18	168	6.5	3.1
Tyler	228	5 027	152.5	41.6	23	386	33.3	6.2	374	4 539	375.6	176.6
Victoria	147	2 680	78.5	21.5	15	0	0.0	0.0	228	0	0.0	0.0
Waco	276	5 511	177.4	48.3	29	431	18.9	6.7	293	4 296	238.5	115.2
Weslaco	59	1 063	34.0	8.6	5	12	0.4	0.1	89	1 217	67.8	32.0
Wichita Falls	234	D	D	D	23	319	14.4	3.7	235	3 396	193.7	77.9
UTAH	3 780	74 390	2 309.0	648.8	480	9 444	412.4	137.7	3 851	46 989	2 988.8	1 226.7
Bountiful	57	1 026	26.6	7.6	10	98	2.7	0.9	157	1 892	108.3	46.9
Clearfield	34	454	12.9	3.2	4	0	0.0	0.0	20	503	28.7	12.8
Draper	NA	NA	NA	NA	NA	NA	NA	NA	NA	NA	NA	NA
Layton	94	2 520	66.1	18.6	7	79	2.8	0.9	68	1 164	103.1	43.3
Logan	85	1 561	41.9	10.5	13	190	4.3	1.8	139	1 207	77.1	26.6
Midvale	49	1 074	33.5	9.1	6	120	4.3	1.0	26	135	9.9	4.7
Murray	95	2 186	62.1	18.2	15	64	3.0	0.8	185	2 209	149.7	71.9
Ogden	183	3 153	84.0	24.2	24	471	9.5	3.2	216	2 855	197.0	76.6
Orem	103	2 253	59.3	15.8	24	258	7.9	2.3	143	2 013	97.0	39.2
Provo	142	3 759	105.8	31.6	21	609	11.8	4.4	233	2 874	177.7	82.2
Riverton	18	164	6.7	1.5	NA	NA	NA	NA	15	103	3.7	1.1
Roy	40	690	20.6	5.1	5	81	1.4	0.4	40	445	17.7	9.0
St. George	133	2 961	83.9	24.4	18	0	0.0	0.0	166	1 501	104.0	37.7
Salt Lake City	638	15 653	572.6	157.4	71	1 709	150.4	60.6	567	8 700	668.8	265.0
Sandy	NA	NA	NA	NA	NA	NA	NA	NA	NA	NA	NA	NA
South Jordan	13	D	D	D	3	47	2.4	0.6	23	202	12.7	5.3
Taylorsville	NA	NA	NA	NA	NA	NA	NA	NA	NA	NA	NA	NA
West Jordan	61	1 054	30.7	8.3	5	88	2.9	0.7	78	971	60.9	25.2
West Valley City	NA	NA	NA	NA	NA	NA	NA	NA	NA	NA	NA	NA
VERMONT	1 932	27 088	910.2	277.2	293	5 450	226.9	61.4	1 262	11 481	631.6	273.9
Burlington	136	1 862	66.4	19.1	15	96	21.3	4.3	112	1 937	120.0	55.7
VIRGINIA	12 343	233 639	8 281.2	2 320.7	1 613	26 624	1 397.9	392.9	12 014	150 797	9 859.6	4 417.9
Alexandria	310	6 616	308.3	92.3	35	357	32.1	13.4	323	2 788	216.5	105.2
Blacksburg	72	1 689	42.9	11.6	6	0	0.0	0.0	60	1 216	84.7	31.6
Charlottesville	179	3 521	121.5	34.7	21	292	27.9	9.6	162	2 092	138.9	54.6
Chesapeake	305	6 321	187.4	51.6	29	482	17.6	4.4	338	3 228	195.7	87.9
Danville	114	2 159	65.7	18.8	12	61	2.0	0.6	126	1 459	89.6	42.0
Hampton	229	5 002	149.9	41.1	29	251	10.6	2.6	192	1 976	106.4	51.9
Harrisonburg	109	2 318	70.2	19.0	12	147	3.5	1.3	116	1 538	90.7	41.6
Leesburg	55	1 071	43.9	13.6	11	147	8.3	2.1	85	927	64.0	25.2

1. Firms subject to federal tax.

City	Other services,[1] 1997				Selected federal funds, 2002–2003 (mil dol)								
					Procurement contracts		Grants						
	Number of establishments	Number of employees	Receipts (mil dol)	Annual payroll (mil dol)	Defense	Other	Total[2]	Medicaid and other health related	Nutrition and family welfare	Energy and environment	Education	Housing and community development	Direct payments for individuals for educational assistance
	104	105	106	107	108	109	110	111	112	113	114	115	116
TEXAS—Cont'd													
McKinney	50	375	13.7	4.4	373.0	10.0	4.3	0.0	0.0	0.1	0.0	3.9	0.0
Mansfield	25	342	38.3	8.5	16.2	1.6	0.0	0.0	0.0	0.0	0.0	0.0	0.0
Mesquite	167	1 020	65.0	19.6	0.2	0.2	9.8	0.0	0.0	0.0	3.5	5.9	0.3
Midland	186	1 226	84.8	21.7	1.5	0.5	10.8	0.0	1.9	-0.1	3.5	2.3	4.0
Mission	62	320	13.9	3.9	0.1	0.9	8.4	0.0	0.0	0.0	2.0	5.9	0.0
Missouri City	44	228	11.6	3.6	0.3	0.2	0.5	0.0	0.0	0.0	0.0	0.4	0.0
Nacogdoches	63	397	15.9	5.4	0.2	0.3	18.9	1.3	3.7	0.2	1.2	8.2	10.2
New Braunfels	88	455	25.2	7.2	0.7	0.3	3.8	0.0	0.3	0.0	0.7	2.7	0.0
North Richland Hills	95	525	30.1	9.7	0.0	0.2	0.3	0.0	0.0	0.0	0.0	0.2	0.0
Odessa	175	1 168	128.6	24.1	0.1	0.2	21.5	0.0	5.8	0.0	3.3	11.8	7.4
Paris	75	367	16.9	4.7	0.0	0.4	5.1	0.0	1.4	0.0	1.0	2.3	4.4
Pasadena	184	1 502	87.4	33.6	390.8	0.7	15.5	0.0	0.0	0.0	0.0	14.6	13.7
Pearland	64	255	18.4	4.7	0.2	0.0	0.0	0.0	0.0	0.0	0.0	0.0	0.0
Pharr	53	314	11.6	3.5	0.0	0.9	12.3	6.3	0.0	0.0	0.9	4.6	0.0
Plano	280	1 758	108.0	34.1	62.4	27.8	5.1	0.8	1.1	0.0	0.3	2.9	4.2
Port Arthur	63	396	21.3	6.0	1.5	1.1	35.4	1.8	2.0	0.0	0.2	30.6	5.7
Richardson	183	1 408	99.3	33.6	49.1	801.4	17.9	3.3	5.9	0.4	1.7	0.2	5.3
Round Rock	81	670	39.7	12.5	434.1	267.0	5.2	0.0	0.0	0.0	3.6	1.4	0.5
Rowlett	31	214	13.3	3.2	0.1	0.0	0.0	0.0	0.0	0.0	0.0	0.0	0.0
San Angelo	167	912	53.8	15.3	2.2	1.4	18.6	4.7	1.4	0.0	0.7	8.9	6.8
San Antonio	1 821	13 038	723.0	233.0	1 503.2	1 007.9	580.7	207.9	54.0	106.7	43.7	121.6	111.2
San Juan	15	41	1.9	0.5	0.3	0.0	2.6	0.0	0.0	0.0	0.0	2.6	0.0
San Marcos	64	343	14.0	4.2	3.1	82.9	19.1	1.9	4.5	0.0	7.9	2.5	16.3
Sherman	66	317	15.0	4.4	0.3	1.9	1.8	0.0	0.1	0.0	0.0	1.3	1.3
Socorro	11	22	1.1	0.3	0.0	0.0	0.2	0.0	0.0	0.0	0.0	0.0	0.0
Sugar Land	78	649	33.1	11.2	0.2	1.1	1.8	0.6	0.0	0.4	0.3	0.2	0.0
Temple	112	613	28.8	9.5	-0.6	18.8	21.1	1.9	0.7	5.5	1.6	8.0	3.2
Texarkana	92	616	34.9	10.3	2.3	4.0	8.9	0.0	0.4	0.0	0.9	7.0	4.1
Texas City	56	248	13.3	3.6	247.6	0.7	7.5	0.0	0.0	0.0	1.1	3.1	2.6
The Colony	21	88	4.8	1.6	0.0	0.0	0.0	0.0	0.0	0.0	0.0	0.0	0.0
Tyler	194	1 722	90.1	28.7	46.0	1.7	23.6	3.6	2.8	0.0	3.0	12.2	14.5
Victoria	132	900	53.7	15.8	0.7	0.7	13.4	0.0	4.5	0.0	3.0	4.2	4.5
Waco	210	1 389	73.9	24.1	67.5	4.2	43.2	3.3	5.9	0.4	4.1	26.1	65.5
Weslaco	40	207	7.1	2.1	0.1	0.2	5.1	0.0	0.0	0.0	1.5	2.3	2.2
Wichita Falls	182	1 296	70.8	22.9	33.1	46.0	27.3	1.0	4.2	0.0	3.0	15.3	4.4
UTAH	2 728	17 612	1 090.5	312.6	1 871.1	793.8	2 844.9	1 130.0	392.9	58.5	293.2	117.5	180.8
Bountiful	67	372	17.5	5.2	0.1	1.3	0.4	0.0	0.0	0.0	0.0	0.3	0.1
Clearfield	20	113	7.9	2.4	877.6	29.8	3.0	0.0	0.0	0.0	0.0	3.0	0.0
Draper	NA	NA	NA	NA	1.6	0.4	18.2	0.0	0.0	0.0	0.0	0.0	0.0
Layton	44	341	16.0	4.5	4.6	1.1	4.2	0.0	0.0	0.0	0.0	3.9	0.2
Logan	83	425	23.4	6.3	4.2	27.7	47.8	10.8	4.6	1.9	8.0	1.2	22.4
Midvale	44	314	25.1	6.1	1.2	0.3	0.9	0.0	0.0	0.0	0.0	0.8	0.0
Murray	135	901	55.4	16.3	0.2	2.5	1.4	0.9	0.0	0.0	0.0	0.3	0.0
Ogden	156	1 097	58.0	17.8	39.5	21.7	42.7	1.9	4.9	0.0	3.0	20.1	20.0
Orem	107	849	37.3	10.7	0.8	4.4	5.9	0.2	0.8	0.0	1.1	0.7	20.7
Provo	121	863	36.7	11.0	5.9	7.9	31.0	4.5	5.2	2.6	5.5	7.5	31.2
Riverton	19	64	3.9	1.0	2.3	0.0	0.1	0.0	0.0	0.0	0.0	0.1	0.0
Roy	33	158	6.7	1.8	0.3	0.3	0.9	0.0	0.0	0.0	0.0	0.8	0.0
St. George	75	356	27.3	7.2	1.0	1.9	7.4	0.8	0.5	0.0	2.1	2.1	5.4
Salt Lake City	445	3 886	262.3	80.8	456.2	92.8	734.9	214.1	93.2	46.1	106.1	41.1	65.2
Sandy	NA	NA	NA	NA	4.8	1.9	4.2	0.2	0.0	1.4	1.6	0.0	0.1
South Jordan	7	35	2.5	0.8	0.4	0.1	0.4	0.0	0.0	0.0	0.0	0.0	0.0
Taylorsville	NA	NA	NA	NA	0.2	0.1	0.4	0.0	0.0	0.0	0.0	0.4	0.0
West Jordan	52	255	15.2	4.1	1.4	0.1	2.3	0.0	0.0	0.7	0.0	1.5	1.0
West Valley City	NA	NA	NA	NA	0.2	1.0	1.7	0.0	0.0	0.0	0.0	0.0	0.0
VERMONT	1 171	4 490	304.7	76.4	454.9	111.1	1 331.3	615.3	161.6	32.4	115.8	86.3	46.6
Burlington	74	469	34.4	11.3	365.2	8.2	130.8	77.5	4.0	3.8	5.0	14.2	9.2
VIRGINIA	11 301	68 807	4 397.2	1 360.3	19 493.0	11 345.7	7 886.0	3 056.7	983.9	143.4	813.0	565.0	493.7
Alexandria	267	1 919	122.4	42.9	1 297.8	491.4	173.5	14.5	2.9	25.7	32.3	22.6	0.5
Blacksburg	42	246	9.4	3.6	22.3	10.2	76.9	8.9	0.0	6.2	1.6	3.5	9.4
Charlottesville	133	827	41.6	14.5	61.6	13.8	284.9	165.1	1.9	3.5	5.5	4.7	5.9
Chesapeake	305	2 846	241.4	53.0	201.5	14.8	23.9	0.0	0.0	0.0	2.4	14.2	0.0
Danville	123	735	36.0	10.2	0.0	3.0	22.0	0.4	1.8	0.0	4.8	11.0	4.7
Hampton	178	1 129	64.8	20.9	81.7	262.3	59.9	5.5	0.0	0.8	8.6	19.9	12.2
Harrisonburg	84	434	28.1	7.5	2.7	1.6	7.0	0.2	0.0	0.0	0.8	3.2	2.6
Leesburg	45	235	17.6	5.7	13.7	12.3	6.3	0.4	0.8	0.0	0.2	2.7	0.0

1. Firms subject to federal tax.   2. Includes program categories not shown separately. State totals include additional categories not allocated by city.

City	General revenue Total (mil dol)	Intergovernmental Total (mil dol)	Intergovernmental Percent from state government	Taxes Total (mil dol)	Taxes Per capita[1] (dollars) Total	Taxes Per capita[1] (dollars) Property	Taxes Per capita[1] (dollars) Sales and gross receipts	General expenditure Total (mil dol)	General expenditure Per capita[1] (dollars) Total	General expenditure Per capita[1] (dollars) Capital outlays
	117	118	119	120	121	122	123	124	125	126
TEXAS—Cont'd										
McKinney	61.8	0.5	18.6	38.6	529	293	163	58.7	803	290
Mansfield	34.7	0.4	100.0	21.9	693	316	215	31.4	991	276
Mesquite	95.0	6.7	2.1	59.8	465	191	262	98.7	766	76
Midland	83.6	4.6	14.1	44.8	468	222	238	96.0	1 002	259
Mission	26.8	2.8	12.2	14.2	276	134	132	28.5	554	126
Missouri City	27.0	2.7	8.7	21.1	356	219	108	28.8	487	140
Nacogdoches	24.5	1.8	0.7	12.3	405	176	217	24.2	798	163
New Braunfels	NA	NA	NA	NA	NA	NA	NA	NA	NA	NA
North Richland Hills	59.6	1.0	57.6	36.1	611	224	364	55.8	943	165
Odessa	61.7	4.1	34.2	28.3	311	118	189	64.1	705	59
Paris	26.8	2.8	54.1	13.8	526	228	284	28.9	1 101	193
Pasadena	101.8	9.0	6.8	68.0	469	135	324	91.5	631	85
Pearland	31.8	0.2	7.0	22.5	504	247	214	29.5	663	33
Pharr	NA	NA	NA	NA	NA	NA	NA	NA	NA	NA
Plano	245.0	6.0	0.0	155.4	653	327	296	242.0	1 016	137
Port Arthur	48.2	5.3	69.0	15.6	273	128	139	51.7	909	38
Richardson	119.2	0.9	54.0	63.6	656	368	271	164.7	1 699	589
Round Rock	75.5	1.5	59.3	52.4	710	83	617	81.9	1 109	480
Rowlett	NA	NA	NA	NA	NA	NA	NA	NA	NA	NA
San Angelo	64.7	6.7	8.1	38.9	445	229	209	56.6	648	58
San Antonio	1 079.2	175.8	72.0	444.8	372	176	183	1 121.5	939	174
San Juan	7.9	1.2	11.3	3.7	133	87	46	9.9	350	129
San Marcos	37.2	2.3	43.0	21.0	504	54	437	38.9	934	186
Sherman	31.3	1.0	26.4	18.4	514	152	355	35.1	980	164
Socorro	3.5	0.6	100.0	2.0	71	52	12	2.7	98	0
Sugar Land	64.5	0.7	87.1	46.0	671	243	415	47.1	687	65
Temple	52.9	2.2	96.9	29.9	549	234	311	55.5	1 020	211
Texarkana	34.5	1.8	50.1	19.0	540	187	347	30.9	879	82
Texas City	NA	NA	NA	NA	NA	NA	NA	NA	NA	NA
The Colony	17.3	0.0	NA	11.8	367	214	104	15.5	479	NA
Tyler	72.6	8.9	12.6	33.6	386	103	276	65.8	756	8
Victoria	57.4	3.4	67.3	34.5	566	306	251	54.4	891	38
Waco	125.8	11.7	60.2	62.0	535	223	305	117.2	1 012	205
Weslaco	23.5	1.6	92.4	13.7	472	205	256	22.2	762	140
Wichita Falls	85.0	9.3	35.5	47.9	466	177	270	82.0	797	114
UTAH	X	X	X	X	X	X	X	X	X	56
Bountiful	24.3	1.7	96.7	10.4	252	67	173	33.1	802	404
Clearfield	16.4	0.7	100.0	8.9	338	137	179	14.6	555	104
Draper	20.0	1.0	91.7	10.9	372	134	190	16.2	555	182
Layton	30.9	3.3	55.8	17.8	296	85	198	30.2	503	112
Logan	38.0	4.5	38.1	11.8	275	76	183	36.1	840	104
Midvale	15.4	2.0	54.5	9.6	353	71	266	16.0	587	100
Murray	NA	NA	NA	NA	NA	NA	NA	NA	NA	NA
Ogden	66.2	6.5	46.0	34.2	435	186	229	69.5	884	13
Orem	53.8	4.6	54.7	28.5	340	78	250	62.7	749	211
Provo	74.3	11.8	46.8	34.4	327	120	198	73.0	694	157
Riverton	11.3	1.1	93.1	5.4	191	53	117	11.9	421	125
Roy	15.1	1.1	96.8	8.2	235	76	149	14.4	410	82
St. George	52.4	1.9	100.0	23.1	428	112	289	41.7	771	88
Salt Lake City	348.6	21.6	30.1	147.7	815	441	335	389.7	2 150	696
Sandy	49.3	6.0	58.9	29.8	334	86	231	54.1	607	189
South Jordan	19.3	1.2	100.0	9.6	301	134	137	24.4	765	340
Taylorsville	17.8	3.8	48.3	11.7	198	67	120	17.1	289	94
West Jordan	36.4	4.1	72.8	20.6	281	88	173	55.0	750	339
West Valley City	83.1	14.0	32.7	37.3	335	106	207	112.8	1 014	280
VERMONT	X	X	X	X	X	X	X	X	X	X
Burlington	60.1	8.3	10.0	21.1	534	423	68	63.9	1 619	292
VIRGINIA	X	X	X	X	X	X	X	X	X	X
Alexandria	479.5	118.3	83.0	293.3	2 242	1 568	454	468.4	3 581	406
Blacksburg	21.8	6.7	56.0	8.4	210	65	98	20.1	501	81
Charlottesville	135.0	59.0	80.8	59.2	1 351	761	479	137.7	3 142	419
Chesapeake	595.7	264.3	96.0	264.1	1 278	859	300	596.2	2 885	254
Danville	142.0	67.6	84.5	40.0	841	472	282	147.6	3 101	320
Hampton	374.2	162.0	82.2	158.4	1 086	722	271	427.0	2 926	174
Harrisonburg	88.0	19.9	87.1	40.4	988	438	416	91.9	2 247	246
Leesburg	32.3	6.4	55.4	15.8	500	233	197	25.6	812	28

1. Based on population estimated as of July 1 of the year shown.

City	City government finances, 2002 (cont'd)									
	General expenditure									
	Percent of total for—									
	Public welfare	Highways	Parking facilities	Education	Health and hospitals	Police protection	Sewerage and sanitation	Parks and recreation	Housing and community development	Interest on debt
	127	128	129	130	131	132	133	134	135	136
TEXAS—Cont'd										
McKinney	0.0	14.8	0.0	0.0	0.9	12.8	10.7	10.0	0.1	4.1
Mansfield	1.1	18.1	0.0	0.0	0.5	11.3	9.1	7.2	0.0	11.4
Mesquite	0.3	11.3	0.0	0.0	0.9	21.6	9.3	5.4	6.2	5.5
Midland	0.0	5.6	0.0	0.0	3.0	15.0	11.4	22.3	1.7	4.2
Mission	0.4	16.5	0.0	0.0	0.0	20.9	17.6	9.8	1.4	2.5
Missouri City	0.0	20.7	0.0	0.0	0.5	18.5	2.5	8.6	0.0	5.2
Nacogdoches	0.2	4.1	0.8	0.0	0.6	13.1	21.2	4.9	0.0	4.3
New Braunfels	NA	NA	NA	NA	NA	NA	NA	NA	NA	NA
North Richland Hills	0.0	12.1	0.0	0.0	0.0	21.0	11.8	18.1	0.0	7.5
Odessa	0.0	7.1	0.0	0.0	0.0	21.4	12.8	4.2	2.8	4.6
Paris	0.0	17.9	0.0	0.0	8.6	18.2	13.2	4.4	2.4	2.8
Pasadena	0.0	7.4	0.0	0.0	1.6	31.0	19.0	7.6	7.1	3.0
Pearland	0.0	6.4	0.0	0.0	0.7	18.3	15.1	6.5	0.0	6.3
Pharr	NA	NA	NA	NA	NA	NA	NA	NA	NA	NA
Plano	0.0	2.0	0.0	0.0	0.8	14.5	17.1	10.4	0.5	7.3
Port Arthur	2.4	11.0	0.0	0.0	2.7	18.9	13.5	3.3	2.1	9.1
Richardson	0.0	13.7	0.0	0.0	0.6	10.8	10.3	30.2	0.0	5.3
Round Rock	0.0	36.9	0.0	0.0	0.0	12.2	7.0	10.5	0.7	7.5
Rowlett	NA	NA	NA	NA	NA	NA	NA	NA	NA	NA
San Angelo	0.0	11.5	0.0	0.0	6.9	21.2	12.8	8.0	2.3	5.7
San Antonio	5.6	8.3	1.1	3.4	3.6	16.5	12.8	13.3	1.6	5.7
San Juan	0.0	0.0	0.0	0.0	0.0	16.4	46.8	5.5	0.0	6.6
San Marcos	4.9	15.9	0.0	0.0	1.4	17.4	14.0	5.5	1.7	4.7
Sherman	0.0	10.5	0.0	0.0	1.2	13.2	22.9	6.4	1.3	0.4
Socorro	0.0	0.0	0.0	0.0	4.0	28.5	0.0	3.5	0.0	2.6
Sugar Land	0.0	8.1	0.0	0.0	0.8	17.3	12.7	3.5	0.0	14.7
Temple	0.0	4.9	0.0	0.0	2.2	13.7	14.5	5.1	4.7	3.4
Texarkana	0.9	8.8	0.0	0.0	3.4	18.3	19.7	6.0	1.2	5.4
Texas City	NA	NA	NA	NA	NA	NA	NA	NA	NA	NA
The Colony	0.0	6.4	0.0	0.0	0.0	20.5	12.6	8.6	0.0	11.2
Tyler	5.2	5.1	0.0	0.0	0.0	21.3	18.0	5.7	7.6	12.9
Victoria	0.0	13.2	0.0	0.0	0.5	15.7	21.6	4.9	1.2	5.7
Waco	0.0	5.8	0.0	0.0	4.2	17.6	19.5	9.1	4.3	11.3
Weslaco	0.0	7.4	0.0	0.0	0.3	17.2	16.2	9.7	0.0	3.6
Wichita Falls	0.0	7.3	0.0	0.0	4.6	17.2	17.0	4.8	6.4	1.0
UTAH	X	X	X	X	X	X	X	X	X	X
Bountiful	0.0	10.2	0.0	0.0	0.0	12.8	48.5	11.6	0.2	0.8
Clearfield	0.0	5.8	0.0	0.0	1.5	18.1	17.9	9.1	1.1	7.7
Draper	0.0	16.0	0.0	0.0	2.3	20.5	7.7	6.9	9.8	0.0
Layton	0.0	16.6	0.0	0.0	0.0	19.9	21.0	16.5	1.2	1.2
Logan	0.0	10.4	0.0	0.0	0.0	15.3	20.6	16.7	1.4	4.7
Midvale	0.0	16.6	0.0	0.0	2.3	25.4	6.3	2.3	7.6	2.0
Murray	NA	NA	NA	NA	NA	NA	NA	NA	NA	NA
Ogden	0.0	8.2	0.0	0.0	0.0	16.4	17.4	9.6	17.6	4.2
Orem	0.0	13.5	0.0	0.0	0.0	13.6	15.3	10.3	3.0	2.3
Provo	0.0	10.3	0.0	0.0	0.0	16.4	10.3	7.2	6.3	6.4
Riverton	0.0	16.6	0.0	0.0	0.0	9.4	7.6	5.8	27.2	3.8
Roy	0.0	13.0	0.0	0.0	0.0	20.3	19.8	14.0	0.9	0.2
St. George	0.0	16.5	0.0	0.0	0.0	14.7	21.9	24.6	0.0	7.8
Salt Lake City	0.0	6.7	0.0	0.0	0.0	11.2	8.2	3.9	6.8	4.5
Sandy	0.0	17.4	0.0	0.0	0.0	18.3	6.1	23.7	2.8	5.6
South Jordan	0.0	41.6	0.0	0.0	0.0	9.7	8.9	5.6	4.0	1.4
Taylorsville	0.0	20.1	0.0	0.0	0.0	18.2	2.3	17.9	1.7	2.0
West Jordan	0.0	22.4	0.0	0.0	0.3	11.0	20.1	9.6	4.2	2.3
West Valley City	0.0	7.4	0.0	0.0	0.0	13.8	2.4	15.9	12.0	9.1
VERMONT	X	X	X	X	X	X	X	X	X	X
Burlington	0.0	6.1	7.4	0.0	0.0	11.6	8.0	5.3	6.4	7.8
VIRGINIA	X	X	X	X	X	X	X	X	X	X
Alexandria	8.5	4.1	0.4	34.6	5.9	7.4	4.5	3.5	2.7	3.6
Blacksburg	0.0	9.1	0.0	0.0	1.7	20.5	17.3	9.3	0.0	2.4
Charlottesville	7.4	2.7	0.1	35.0	5.0	7.3	4.4	4.6	3.0	1.8
Chesapeake	3.6	6.3	0.0	49.1	2.9	6.6	6.2	3.7	5.4	6.9
Danville	5.0	5.0	0.0	38.5	0.5	5.7	2.6	5.5	5.2	2.4
Hampton	4.9	0.5	0.3	51.3	0.8	5.6	2.6	5.5	5.2	2.4
Harrisonburg	1.2	6.4	0.0	39.8	0.7	5.3	7.7	2.5	0.0	18.1
Leesburg	0.0	10.5	0.5	0.0	0.0	16.2	19.1	13.5	0.0	9.8

City	City government finances, 2002 (cont'd) Debt outstanding Total (mil dol)	Per capita[1] (dollars)	Percent utility	City government employment, 2002	Climate[2] Average daily temperature (degrees Fahrenheit) Mean January	July	Limits January[3]	July[4]	Annual precipitation (inches)	Heating degree days	Cooling degree days
	137	138	139	140	141	142	143	144	145	146	147
TEXAS—Cont'd											
McKinney	76.0	1 040	29.5	473	NA	NA	NA	NA	NA	NA	NA
Mansfield	93.2	2 945	31.3	213	NA	NA	NA	NA	NA	NA	NA
Mesquite	103.9	807	30.5	980	44.6	85.9	34.5	95.7	36.08	2 259	2 763
Midland	114.9	1 200	28.6	893	43.6	81.4	28.5	94.6	15.21	2 570	2 132
Mission	27.7	539	47.1	365	57.1	85.5	45.8	96.7	22.82	829	3 985
Missouri City	30.2	510	0.0	235	52.2	83.5	42.9	92.3	50.83	1 371	3 012
Nacogdoches	33.9	1 119	25.0	310	47.6	82.8	36.9	93.2	42.40	1 951	2 551
New Braunfels	NA	NA	NA	464	48.2	83.7	36.5	95.3	34.27	1 790	2 791
North Richland Hills	77.5	1 310	5.8	552	43.4	85.3	32.7	96.5	33.70	2 407	2 603
Odessa	107.8	1 185	58.3	801	42.5	82.0	28.5	95.4	14.96	2 751	2 163
Paris	47.3	1 803	79.1	158	NA	NA	NA	NA	NA	NA	NA
Pasadena	106.9	737	52.5	964	52.2	83.5	42.9	92.3	50.83	1 371	3 012
Pearland	68.3	1 533	48.5	285	NA	NA	NA	NA	NA	NA	NA
Pharr	NA	NA	NA	349	58.5	85.4	48.5	95.8	22.83	693	4 076
Plano	316.8	1 331	8.5	2 077	43.4	85.3	32.7	96.5	33.70	2 407	2 603
Port Arthur	77.6	1 364	0.0	638	50.9	82.8	41.5	91.9	57.18	1 499	2 764
Richardson	187.1	1 930	10.2	1 044	44.6	85.9	34.5	95.7	36.08	2 259	2 763
Round Rock	121.4	1 644	0.0	544	48.8	84.5	38.6	95.0	31.88	1 688	3 016
Rowlett	NA	NA	NA	292	NA	NA	NA	NA	NA	NA	NA
San Angelo	73.2	837	6.3	880	43.7	82.7	30.6	96.2	20.45	2 414	2 400
San Antonio	4 812.7	4 030	68.9	16 447	49.3	85.0	37.9	95.0	30.98	1 644	2 996
San Juan	10.2	360	0.0	145	NA	NA	NA	NA	NA	NA	NA
San Marcos	100.8	2 423	64.4	447	48.1	83.2	36.2	94.7	34.55	1 818	2 712
Sherman	5.0	141	66.2	421	40.5	83.3	29.8	94.6	40.39	2 890	2 209
Socorro	1.6	58	0.0	68	NA	NA	NA	NA	NA	NA	NA
Sugar Land	137.6	2 005	12.1	431	NA	NA	NA	NA	NA	NA	NA
Temple	63.7	1 171	36.6	596	45.4	84.0	34.5	95.2	34.87	2 153	2 623
Texarkana	41.2	1 170	32.2	570	44.5	82.8	35.0	93.0	46.89	2 295	2 380
Texas City	NA	NA	NA	465	52.7	83.3	47.1	87.3	42.28	1 263	2 994
The Colony	48.5	1 502	21.2	239	NA	NA	NA	NA	NA	NA	NA
Tyler	154.3	1 773	23.7	723	46.4	83.2	35.0	95.2	39.74	2 105	2 490
Victoria	141.6	2 321	52.0	594	52.7	84.1	42.5	93.5	37.41	1 296	3 118
Waco	257.7	2 226	17.3	1 359	45.2	85.6	34.2	96.8	31.96	2 179	2 816
Weslaco	24.2	831	27.1	306	NA	NA	NA	NA	NA	NA	NA
Wichita Falls	197.7	1 921	89.8	1 154	39.8	85.0	27.6	97.2	28.90	3 042	2 340
UTAH	X	X	X	X	X	X	X	X	X	X	X
Bountiful	3.1	74	0.0	347	27.9	77.9	19.3	92.2	16.18	5 765	1 047
Clearfield	18.8	713	3.0	141	NA	NA	NA	NA	NA	NA	NA
Draper	0.4	13	100.0	90	NA	NA	NA	NA	NA	NA	NA
Layton	6.5	108	2.3	295	NA	NA	NA	NA	NA	NA	NA
Logan	53.1	1 237	51.5	433	28.6	76.2	19.6	92.0	22.09	5 799	927
Midvale	5.2	191	3.5	150	23.6	73.0	15.5	86.7	19.52	6 854	623
Murray	NA	NA	NA	410	27.9	77.9	19.3	92.2	16.18	5 765	1 047
Ogden	53.7	683	9.4	723	28.9	77.8	19.8	92.3	22.59	5 557	1 096
Orem	41.4	495	0.0	491	28.0	74.5	18.3	90.2	17.04	5 907	745
Provo	103.1	980	42.9	694	28.0	74.5	18.3	90.2	17.04	5 907	745
Riverton	15.0	530	100.0	54	NA	NA	NA	NA	NA	NA	NA
Roy	0.9	25	0.0	171	NA	NA	NA	NA	NA	NA	NA
St. George	75.1	1 389	34.0	504	32.2	73.5	19.8	88.8	18.23	5 452	687
Salt Lake City	391.2	2 158	8.1	3 037	27.9	77.9	19.3	92.2	16.18	5 765	1 047
Sandy	68.0	762	10.8	615	27.9	77.9	19.3	92.2	16.18	5 765	1 047
South Jordan	27.3	858	0.0	168	NA	NA	NA	NA	NA	NA	NA
Taylorsville	4.6	78	0.0	25	NA	NA	NA	NA	NA	NA	NA
West Jordan	36.2	493	1.8	378	27.9	77.9	19.3	92.2	16.18	5 765	1 047
West Valley City	173.8	1 562	0.0	622	27.9	77.9	19.3	92.2	16.18	5 765	1 047
VERMONT	X	X	X	X	X	X	X	X	X	X	X
Burlington	165.0	4 181	53.7	693	16.3	70.5	7.5	81.2	34.47	7 771	388
VIRGINIA	X	X	X	X	X	X	X	X	X	X	X
Alexandria	286.8	2 192	0.0	4 697	34.6	80.0	26.8	88.5	38.63	4 047	1 549
Blacksburg	13.2	329	32.6	323	29.6	70.6	19.0	82.3	40.91	5 574	514
Charlottesville	59.8	1 364	26.8	1 719	34.5	76.4	25.5	86.7	47.29	4 224	1 156
Chesapeake	718.3	3 476	13.2	8 740	39.1	78.2	30.9	86.4	44.64	3 495	1 422
Danville	192.9	4 053	14.6	2 510	36.1	78.0	25.4	89.6	43.18	3 944	1 381
Hampton	212.9	1 459	0.0	6 172	39.1	78.2	30.9	86.4	44.64	3 495	1 422
Harrisonburg	310.8	7 598	3.4	1 187	31.3	74.3	20.5	86.7	35.24	4 908	876
Leesburg	82.7	2 619	46.9	237	NA	NA	NA	NA	NA	NA	NA

1. Based on the population estimated as of July 1 of the year shown. 2. Represents normal values based on the 30-year period, 1961–1990. 3. Average daily minimum. 4. Average daily maximum.

Table D. Cities — Land Area and Population

STATE Place code	City	Land area,[1] 2000 (sq km)	Population, 2003			Population characteristics, 2000						
			Total persons	Rank	Per square kilometer	Percent						
						Race (alone or in combination)					Hispanic or Latino[2]	Non-Hispanic White
						White	Black	Am. Indian, Alaska Native	Asian and Pacific Islander	Other race		
		1	2	3	4	5	6	7	8	9	10	11
	VIRGINIA—Cont'd											
51 47672	Lynchburg	127.9	65 113	442	509.1	67.8	30.6	0.7	1.6	0.9	1.3	66.0
51 48952	Manassas	25.7	37 166	866	1 446.1	74.8	13.9	0.8	4.2	9.7	15.1	66.3
51 56000	Newport News	176.9	181 647	115	1 026.8	55.4	40.6	1.1	3.4	2.6	4.2	52.0
51 57000	Norfolk	139.2	241 727	72	1 736.5	50.1	45.3	1.1	3.9	2.4	3.8	47.0
51 61832	Petersburg	59.3	33 091	975	558.0	19.1	79.6	0.5	1.0	0.8	1.4	18.2
51 64000	Portsmouth	85.9	99 617	247	1 159.7	47.0	51.5	1.1	1.3	0.9	1.7	45.1
51 67000	Richmond	155.6	194 729	106	1 251.5	39.2	58.1	0.7	1.7	2.0	2.6	37.7
51 68000	Roanoke	111.1	92 863	276	835.9	70.8	27.7	0.7	1.5	1.3	1.5	68.8
51 76432	Suffolk	1 036.0	73 515	381	71.0	54.7	44.1	0.8	1.2	0.6	1.3	53.3
51 82000	Virginia Beach	643.1	439 467	39	683.4	73.6	20.0	1.0	6.3	2.2	4.2	69.5
53 00000	WASHINGTON	172 348.3	6 131 445	X	35.6	84.9	4.0	2.7	7.4	4.9	7.5	78.9
53 03180	Auburn	55.1	44 655	722	810.4	86.8	3.5	4.0	5.9	4.9	7.5	79.9
53 05210	Bellevue	79.6	112 344	208	1 411.4	77.0	2.6	0.8	19.5	3.5	5.3	71.8
53 05280	Bellingham	66.4	71 289	397	1 073.6	90.6	1.6	2.5	5.8	2.9	4.6	85.9
53 07380	Bothell	31.2	30 568	1 046	979.7	89.9	1.7	1.2	8.0	2.4	4.4	84.8
53 07695	Bremerton	58.7	39 597	814	674.6	80.4	9.4	4.1	9.5	3.8	6.6	72.3
53 17635	Des Moines	16.4	29 039	1 093	1 770.7	78.0	8.7	2.1	11.9	4.6	6.6	71.7
53 20750	Edmonds	23.1	39 882	803	1 726.5	90.4	1.9	1.7	7.4	1.9	3.3	86.1
53 22640	Everett	84.2	96 643	258	1 147.8	84.7	4.3	2.8	8.3	4.4	7.1	77.9
53 35275	Kennewick	59.4	59 334	507	998.9	86.1	1.7	1.7	3.0	11.0	15.5	78.1
53 35415	Kent	72.6	81 567	329	1 123.5	75.0	9.9	2.2	12.7	6.3	8.1	67.9
53 35940	Kirkland	27.6	45 573	710	1 651.2	87.8	2.1	1.1	9.6	2.4	4.1	83.1
53 36745	Lacey	41.3	32 781	987	793.7	82.2	6.0	2.5	11.2	3.2	5.9	75.4
53 40245	Longview	35.5	35 741	899	1 006.8	92.0	1.2	3.1	3.2	3.6	5.8	87.2
53 40840	Lynnwood	19.8	33 704	958	1 702.2	78.0	4.2	2.0	16.2	4.3	7.0	70.9
53 43955	Marysville	24.8	28 260	1 121	1 139.5	90.9	1.5	2.3	5.8	2.7	4.8	86.0
53 47560	Mount Vernon	28.8	27 935	1 140	970.0	78.1	1.1	1.7	3.6	18.7	25.1	68.4
53 51300	Olympia	43.3	43 963	731	1 015.3	88.6	2.7	2.5	7.8	2.5	4.4	83.1
53 53545	Pasco	72.7	38 233	836	525.9	56.2	3.7	1.4	2.6	40.3	56.3	37.0
53 56695	Puyallup	31.4	35 641	902	1 135.1	91.5	2.3	2.1	5.7	2.9	4.7	85.8
53 57535	Redmond	41.1	46 391	694	1 128.7	81.8	2.1	1.1	15.1	3.4	5.6	76.4
53 57745	Renton	44.1	54 028	586	1 225.1	71.7	10.0	1.8	15.9	5.6	7.6	65.4
53 58235	Richland	90.2	42 537	756	471.6	91.6	1.8	1.5	5.0	2.6	4.7	87.2
53 61115	Sammamish	46.8	33 916	954	724.7	90.1	1.2	0.7	9.5	1.0	2.5	86.1
53 63000	Seattle	217.2	569 101	25	2 620.2	73.4	9.9	2.1	15.9	3.7	5.3	67.9
53 63960	Shoreline	30.2	52 380	604	1 734.4	80.5	3.6	2.0	15.9	2.6	3.9	75.2
53 67000	Spokane	149.6	196 624	102	1 314.3	92.6	3.0	3.0	3.4	1.7	3.0	87.9
53 70000	Tacoma	129.7	196 790	101	1 517.3	74.1	13.7	3.6	11.2	4.4	6.9	66.5
53 74060	Vancouver	110.8	151 654	143	1 368.7	88.2	3.3	2.1	6.5	4.0	6.3	82.2
53 75775	Walla Walla	28.0	30 134	1 060	1 076.2	86.3	3.0	2.0	2.3	9.5	17.4	75.7
53 77105	Wenatchee	17.8	28 636	1 108	1 608.8	83.2	0.6	1.9	1.7	15.2	21.5	74.7
53 80010	Yakima	52.1	80 223	339	1 539.8	72.2	2.7	3.1	2.0	24.2	33.7	59.8
54 00000	WEST VIRGINIA	62 361.0	1 810 354	X	29.0	95.9	3.5	0.6	0.7	0.3	0.7	94.6
54 14600	Charleston	81.9	51 394	610	627.5	82.3	16.2	0.9	2.2	0.6	0.8	80.1
54 39460	Huntington	41.2	49 533	638	1 202.3	91.0	8.2	0.8	1.2	0.5	0.8	89.1
54 55756	Morgantown	25.4	27 969	1 137	1 101.1	90.8	4.7	0.5	4.9	0.8	1.5	88.6
54 62140	Parkersburg	30.6	32 100	999	1 049.0	97.3	2.2	0.6	0.6	0.3	0.8	95.8
54 86452	Wheeling	36.0	30 096	1 061	836.0	93.7	5.6	0.3	1.2	0.3	0.6	92.3
55 00000	WISCONSIN	140 662.5	5 472 299	X	38.9	90.0	6.1	1.3	2.0	2.0	3.6	87.3
55 02375	Appleton	54.1	70 354	402	1 300.4	92.5	1.3	1.0	5.3	1.4	2.5	90.2
55 06500	Beloit	42.6	35 505	907	833.5	78.1	16.8	0.9	1.6	5.5	9.1	71.9
55 10025	Brookfield	70.4	39 637	812	563.0	94.9	1.0	0.2	4.4	0.4	1.2	93.3
55 22300	Eau Claire	78.4	62 496	465	797.1	94.5	1.0	1.0	4.3	0.6	1.0	92.9
55 26275	Fond du Lac	43.7	42 095	763	963.3	94.7	2.2	1.0	1.8	1.6	2.9	92.2
55 27300	Franklin	89.7	31 994	1 003	356.7	91.6	5.4	0.6	2.4	1.0	2.6	89.1
55 31000	Green Bay	113.6	101 467	239	893.2	87.5	1.9	4.1	4.2	4.3	7.1	83.2
55 31175	Greenfield	29.9	36 101	889	1 207.4	94.9	1.3	0.7	2.6	1.9	3.9	91.6
55 37825	Janesville	71.3	61 145	477	857.6	96.4	1.7	0.6	1.3	1.3	2.6	93.9
55 39225	Kenosha	61.7	92 871	275	1 505.2	85.7	8.6	1.0	1.4	5.7	10.0	79.3
55 40775	La Crosse	52.2	51 001	616	977.0	92.6	2.0	0.9	5.3	0.6	1.1	91.0
55 48000	Madison	177.9	218 432	81	1 227.8	86.0	6.8	0.9	6.6	2.2	4.1	82.0
55 48500	Manitowoc	43.7	34 080	947	779.9	94.0	0.8	0.9	4.2	1.2	2.5	91.8
55 51000	Menomonee Falls	86.2	33 727	957	391.3	97.2	1.7	0.4	1.0	0.3	1.2	95.6
55 53000	Milwaukee	248.8	586 941	19	2 359.1	52.1	38.6	1.5	3.5	7.2	12.0	45.4
55 56375	New Berlin	95.4	38 627	833	404.9	96.5	0.6	0.4	2.5	0.6	1.6	94.9
55 58800	Oak Creek	74.1	31 983	1 004	431.6	93.3	2.2	1.0	2.8	2.4	4.5	89.7
55 60500	Oshkosh	61.2	63 237	460	1 033.3	93.6	2.4	0.8	3.5	0.7	1.7	91.8

1. Dry land or land partially or temporarily covered by water. 2. Hispanic or Latino persons may be of any race.

Table D. Cities — Population and Households

City	Age of population (percent)									Percent female	Census counts		Percent change	
	Under 5 years	5 to 17 years	18 to 24 years	25 to 34 years	35 to 44 years	45 to 54 years	55 to 64 years	65 to 74 years	75 years and over		1990	2000	1990–2000	2000–2003
	12	13	14	15	16	17	18	19	20	21	22	23	24	25
VIRGINIA—Cont'd														
Lynchburg	5.8	16.3	15.5	12.2	13.1	12.4	8.4	7.5	8.8	54.3	66 049	65 269	-1.2	-0.2
Manassas	8.6	21.0	9.8	17.4	18.4	13.1	6.3	3.1	2.3	49.1	27 957	35 135	25.7	5.8
Newport News	7.9	19.6	11.5	15.8	16.4	11.5	7.3	5.4	4.7	51.6	171 439	180 150	5.1	0.8
Norfolk	7.1	17.0	18.2	15.6	14.3	10.7	6.2	5.5	5.4	48.9	261 250	234 403	-10.3	3.1
Petersburg	6.4	18.7	8.9	13.0	14.5	13.2	9.7	8.0	7.6	54.3	37 027	33 740	-8.9	-1.9
Portsmouth	7.1	18.6	11.1	14.0	15.1	12.3	8.0	6.8	6.9	51.7	103 910	100 565	-3.2	-0.9
Richmond	6.3	15.6	13.1	16.6	15.1	12.6	7.5	6.5	6.7	53.5	202 798	197 790	-2.5	-1.5
Roanoke	6.5	16.1	8.2	15.2	15.3	13.8	8.5	7.8	8.6	53.1	96 509	94 911	-1.7	-2.2
Suffolk	7.3	20.6	7.1	13.4	17.8	13.4	9.2	6.3	5.2	52.2	52 143	63 677	22.1	15.4
Virginia Beach	7.2	20.3	10.0	16.4	17.8	12.7	7.1	4.9	3.6	50.5	393 089	425 257	8.2	3.3
WASHINGTON	6.7	19.0	9.5	14.3	16.5	14.4	8.4	5.7	5.5	50.2	4 866 669	5 894 121	21.1	4.0
Auburn	7.7	18.9	9.5	15.1	16.5	12.5	8.2	5.7	5.9	50.4	33 650	40 314	19.8	10.8
Bellevue	5.6	15.5	7.8	16.0	16.6	14.8	10.2	7.1	6.4	50.4	95 213	109 569	26.1	2.5
Bellingham	5.2	12.5	23.8	14.3	12.2	12.9	6.6	5.3	7.2	51.9	52 179	67 171	28.7	6.1
Bothell	6.0	19.2	8.1	14.8	18.4	15.8	8.1	4.6	5.0	51.0	12 575	30 150	144.2	1.4
Bremerton	8.1	16.4	15.5	16.1	14.3	10.8	6.4	5.1	7.4	49.1	38 142	37 259	-2.3	6.3
Des Moines	6.6	17.2	8.3	14.5	16.6	13.5	8.5	6.0	8.9	51.8	20 830	29 267	69.3	-0.8
Edmonds	5.0	15.6	7.0	11.5	15.9	16.8	11.5	8.8	7.8	52.7	30 743	39 515	28.5	0.9
Everett	7.8	17.3	12.3	17.0	16.3	12.3	6.7	4.7	5.6	49.1	70 937	91 488	29.0	5.6
Kennewick	8.4	21.2	10.3	13.8	15.5	13.3	7.3	5.2	5.0	50.4	42 148	54 693	29.8	8.5
Kent	8.4	19.3	10.3	17.4	17.5	12.7	7.0	4.0	3.3	50.4	37 960	79 524	109.5	2.6
Kirkland	5.5	13.0	9.3	19.9	18.2	15.3	8.6	5.0	5.2	51.3	40 059	45 054	12.5	1.2
Lacey	7.7	18.6	9.7	15.0	15.6	13.0	7.0	5.3	8.0	52.2	19 279	31 226	62.0	5.0
Longview	7.1	18.8	8.9	13.1	14.0	13.8	8.8	6.8	8.6	51.8	31 499	34 660	10.0	3.1
Lynnwood	7.1	17.3	10.4	15.4	16.7	13.1	8.1	6.0	5.8	51.3	28 637	33 847	18.2	-0.4
Marysville	8.2	21.9	7.9	15.5	17.4	11.3	6.4	4.9	6.4	51.2	12 248	25 315	106.7	11.6
Mount Vernon	8.4	20.6	11.9	14.9	14.1	11.4	6.2	5.3	7.2	51.0	17 647	26 232	48.6	6.5
Olympia	5.4	16.0	11.9	15.2	15.1	15.1	7.8	5.8	7.6	52.2	33 729	42 514	26.0	3.4
Pasco	11.1	24.4	11.8	15.6	12.9	9.8	5.8	4.6	4.1	48.4	20 337	32 066	57.7	19.2
Puyallup	6.9	20.3	10.2	13.9	17.0	13.6	7.2	4.8	6.1	51.7	23 878	33 011	38.2	8.0
Redmond	6.4	15.1	9.5	20.8	17.1	14.1	7.8	3.9	5.4	49.9	35 800	45 256	26.4	2.5
Renton	7.0	14.8	10.2	19.8	17.1	12.9	7.9	4.9	5.4	50.3	41 688	50 052	20.1	7.9
Richland	6.6	20.6	7.5	11.5	15.6	15.4	10.0	6.7	6.1	51.0	32 315	38 708	19.8	9.9
Sammamish	8.4	25.0	4.8	11.2	22.0	18.0	6.7	2.4	1.6	49.6	NA	34 104	NA	-0.6
Seattle	4.7	10.9	11.9	21.7	16.9	14.5	7.5	5.2	6.8	50.1	516 259	563 374	9.1	1.0
Shoreline	5.2	17.3	7.7	12.8	17.6	16.3	8.5	6.8	7.8	51.8	49 229	53 025	7.7	-1.2
Spokane	7.0	17.8	11.1	14.5	15.1	13.1	7.4	6.2	7.8	51.8	177 165	195 629	10.4	0.5
Tacoma	7.0	18.8	10.4	15.4	16.2	12.9	7.4	5.4	6.5	51.2	176 664	193 556	9.6	1.7
Vancouver	8.0	18.7	9.8	16.3	15.8	13.1	7.5	5.2	5.5	50.8	62 065	143 560	162.7	5.6
Walla Walla	6.0	16.8	15.2	13.5	14.0	12.3	7.2	6.2	8.9	48.0	26 482	29 686	12.1	1.5
Wenatchee	8.0	19.4	10.0	14.0	14.3	12.2	7.1	6.8	8.2	51.1	21 746	27 856	28.1	2.8
Yakima	8.9	20.5	10.8	14.5	13.1	11.0	7.2	5.9	8.2	51.1	58 427	71 845	23.0	11.7
WEST VIRGINIA	5.6	16.6	9.5	12.7	15.1	15.0	10.2	8.2	7.1	51.4	1 793 477	1 808 344	0.8	0.1
Charleston	5.5	15.1	8.4	12.6	15.4	15.6	9.7	8.5	9.1	53.4	57 287	53 421	-6.7	-3.8
Huntington	4.9	12.9	17.5	12.7	12.2	12.8	9.0	8.7	9.3	53.0	54 844	51 475	-6.1	-3.8
Morgantown	3.0	8.1	44.7	11.9	8.5	8.4	5.0	4.8	5.6	48.9	25 879	26 809	3.6	4.3
Parkersburg	5.6	15.6	9.1	12.9	14.2	13.7	10.0	9.1	9.7	53.3	33 862	33 099	-2.3	-3.0
Wheeling	4.9	15.7	9.1	10.5	13.8	14.6	9.8	10.1	11.5	54.3	34 882	31 419	-9.9	-4.2
WISCONSIN	6.4	19.1	9.7	13.2	16.3	13.7	8.5	6.6	6.5	50.6	4 891 769	5 363 675	9.6	2.0
Appleton	6.9	20.5	9.7	14.7	17.1	12.9	6.9	5.5	5.8	50.8	65 695	70 087	6.7	0.4
Beloit	7.7	20.0	11.5	14.1	14.5	11.9	7.5	6.3	6.6	52.1	35 571	35 775	0.6	-0.8
Brookfield	5.4	21.4	4.6	6.8	16.4	16.9	10.9	9.6	8.0	51.6	35 184	38 649	9.8	2.6
Eau Claire	5.8	15.9	22.1	13.2	12.8	12.0	6.2	5.5	6.4	52.4	56 806	61 704	8.6	1.3
Fond du Lac	6.5	17.6	10.7	14.1	15.3	13.1	7.4	6.5	8.8	53.0	37 755	42 203	11.8	-0.3
Franklin	5.6	17.8	8.4	13.1	19.7	16.9	8.7	6.0	3.9	47.8	21 855	29 494	35.0	8.5
Green Bay	7.2	18.3	11.6	15.7	16.0	12.5	7.0	5.7	6.1	50.7	96 466	102 313	6.1	-0.8
Greenfield	4.5	14.4	8.1	13.1	15.2	14.4	9.9	9.3	11.1	53.1	33 403	35 476	6.2	1.8
Janesville	7.0	19.2	8.3	15.1	16.2	12.7	8.7	6.8	6.1	51.1	52 210	59 498	14.0	2.8
Kenosha	7.5	19.7	10.1	15.0	16.5	11.8	7.2	5.9	6.3	50.8	80 426	90 352	12.3	2.8
La Crosse	4.8	14.0	24.4	12.6	12.4	10.3	6.7	6.6	8.3	52.9	51 140	51 818	1.3	-1.6
Madison	5.2	12.7	21.4	17.8	14.4	12.8	6.5	4.6	4.7	50.9	190 766	208 054	9.1	5.0
Manitowoc	6.2	18.0	8.2	12.2	15.7	12.9	8.5	8.2	10.2	51.6	32 521	34 053	4.7	0.1
Menomonee Falls	6.6	18.4	5.4	11.9	18.6	13.6	9.8	8.9	6.8	51.6	26 840	32 647	21.6	3.3
Milwaukee	8.0	20.7	12.2	15.8	14.4	11.4	6.6	5.5	5.4	52.2	628 088	596 974	-5.0	-1.7
New Berlin	6.0	18.8	6.4	10.8	18.2	16.7	10.4	7.6	5.1	50.8	33 592	38 220	13.8	1.1
Oak Creek	6.7	18.3	9.3	16.7	18.7	13.7	7.8	5.3	3.5	50.2	19 513	28 456	45.8	12.4
Oshkosh	5.4	15.3	18.1	14.8	14.9	11.5	6.8	6.0	7.1	50.0	55 006	62 916	14.4	0.5

Table D. Cities — **Group Quarters, Crime, and Education**

City	Households, 2000 Number	Percent change, 1990–2000	Persons per household	Percent Female family householder[1]	Percent One-person	Persons in group quarters, 2000 Total	Institutional Total	Persons in nursing homes	Non-institutional	Serious crimes known to police,[2] 2002 Total Number	Total Rate[3]	Rate[2] Violent	Rate[2] Property	School enrollment[4] Public	Private	Attainment[5] (percent) High school graduate or less	Bachelor's degree or more
	26	27	28	29	30	31	32	33	34	35	36	37	38	39	40	41	42
VIRGINIA—Cont'd																	
Lynchburg	25 477	1.3	2.30	16.0	32.7	6 551	1 703	1 085	4 848	2 648	3 937	458	3 480	12 090	7 488	49.7	25.2
Manassas	11 757	24.0	2.92	11.3	21.1	861	747	228	114	1 261	3 483	287	3 196	8 163	1 778	42.7	28.1
Newport News	69 686	9.0	2.50	17.9	27.0	5 833	2 064	1 122	3 769	9 971	5 372	730	4 642	43 803	6 412	45.6	19.9
Norfolk	86 210	-3.7	2.45	18.8	30.2	23 289	3 000	1 095	20 289	15 501	6 418	559	5 859	54 611	9 256	51.2	19.6
Petersburg	13 799	-6.3	2.38	26.1	32.2	906	589	330	317	2 574	7 404	765	6 639	7 446	745	61.7	14.8
Portsmouth	38 170	-1.5	2.51	20.9	27.5	4 814	1 798	356	3 016	7 029	6 783	967	5 816	22 551	3 584	54.2	13.8
Richmond	84 549	-0.9	2.21	20.4	37.6	11 236	3 179	1 365	8 057	18 234	8 947	1 304	7 643	43 669	10 379	48.4	29.5
Roanoke	42 003	2.4	2.20	16.5	35.9	2 538	1 698	1 055	840	4 361	4 459	523	3 937	18 279	2 321	54.4	18.7
Suffolk	23 283	25.7	2.69	16.8	20.2	979	874	417	105	3 379	5 150	655	4 495	14 916	2 781	52.8	17.3
Virginia Beach	154 455	13.9	2.70	12.4	20.4	7 683	2 794	1 753	4 889	16 087	3 671	219	3 452	102 553	18 862	35.5	28.1
WASHINGTON	2 271 398	21.3	2.53	9.9	26.2	136 382	57 218	23 275	79 164	309 931	5 107	345	4 761	1 368 232	216 469	37.8	27.7
Auburn	16 108	20.6	2.47	13.4	29.1	593	218	177	375	3 955	9 528	658	8 870	8 579	1 053	49.1	15.6
Bellevue	45 836	28.2	2.37	7.5	28.4	791	209	209	582	4 640	4 113	124	3 989	20 801	4 997	18.4	54.1
Bellingham	27 999	32.1	2.24	9.2	33.0	4 593	1 071	696	3 522	5 108	7 385	237	7 148	21 411	1 935	34.5	33.0
Bothell	11 923	142.4	2.51	8.9	25.7	216	175	175	41	878	2 828	139	2 690	6 726	1 163	27.0	38.6
Bremerton	15 096	2.6	2.30	13.3	35.4	2 586	401	348	2 185	2 917	7 603	1 061	6 542	8 113	799	44.0	14.8
Des Moines	11 337	60.7	2.47	12.2	27.8	1 262	1 240	1 220	22	1 030	3 418	262	3 156	6 251	900	38.3	22.9
Edmonds	16 904	33.9	2.32	8.7	29.0	352	174	169	178	1 160	2 851	74	2 777	7 288	2 017	26.9	36.4
Everett	36 325	26.7	2.40	12.5	31.7	4 203	882	211	3 321	6 745	7 160	538	6 622	19 370	1 981	42.9	18.5
Kennewick	20 786	29.3	2.60	12.2	26.1	594	490	162	104	2 851	5 063	316	4 746	13 691	1 298	41.6	22.1
Kent	31 113	91.5	2.53	12.8	28.5	698	165	46	533	5 861	7 158	342	6 816	17 827	2 518	39.8	24.0
Kirkland	20 736	20.5	2.13	8.1	35.6	848	279	266	569	1 614	3 479	138	3 341	7 456	2 099	20.5	47.4
Lacey	12 459	61.3	2.47	11.4	28.2	470	297	297	173	1 529	4 755	280	4 475	6 829	1 326	33.8	26.9
Longview	14 066	9.3	2.40	12.3	30.1	861	549	401	312	3 157	8 846	518	8 327	7 735	789	49.8	14.6
Lynnwood	13 328	17.6	2.50	11.5	29.3	522	47	15	475	2 613	7 498	284	7 214	7 507	1 290	38.6	22.4
Marysville	9 400	119.2	2.66	11.3	23.5	280	117	98	163	1 189	4 561	207	4 354	6 242	722	41.7	19.0
Mount Vernon	9 276	34.7	2.75	11.4	26.1	764	505	334	259	2 171	8 038	255	7 782	6 702	825	45.9	18.6
Olympia	18 670	24.9	2.21	10.4	35.2	1 312	893	487	419	2 791	6 376	329	6 047	9 952	1 552	29.2	40.3
Pasco	9 619	40.6	3.30	14.3	20.1	352	256	116	96	1 696	5 137	457	4 679	9 041	405	65.7	10.6
Puyallup	12 870	43.9	2.53	11.7	26.9	496	276	264	220	2 776	8 167	241	7 926	7 604	1 266	42.3	22.8
Redmond	19 102	35.0	2.33	7.6	30.4	833	347	251	486	1 972	4 232	170	4 062	9 011	1 672	17.0	52.9
Renton	21 708	19.2	2.29	10.8	34.0	401	312	265	89	4 584	8 895	468	8 427	9 576	1 893	38.5	27.8
Richland	15 549	18.1	2.48	9.3	27.2	135	80	62	55	1 363	3 420	156	3 264	9 562	1 437	27.1	38.9
Sammamish	11 131	NA	3.06	5.3	9.4	0	0	0	0	488	1 390	85	1 304	9 173	1 926	11.4	61.5
Seattle	258 499	9.2	2.08	8.1	40.8	26 655	6 860	2 951	19 795	46 432	8 004	705	7 299	104 391	32 472	25.8	47.2
Shoreline	20 716	NA	2.50	10.0	26.4	1 302	538	352	764	1 918	3 513	223	3 289	11 497	2 250	29.7	37.3
Spokane	81 512	8.5	2.32	12.4	33.0	6 152	2 693	1 522	3 459	15 895	7 891	646	7 245	44 055	9 312	38.2	25.4
Tacoma	76 152	8.9	2.45	13.9	31.7	6 731	3 033	1 195	3 698	20 182	10 126	1 095	9 032	43 511	8 770	45.5	20.0
Vancouver	56 628	181.2	2.50	12.1	27.6	2 082	1 345	597	737	7 773	5 258	360	4 899	31 550	4 075	40.5	21.7
Walla Walla	10 596	6.9	2.44	11.0	31.9	3 829	2 825	373	1 004	1 691	5 532	415	5 117	6 628	2 375	46.1	21.6
Wenatchee	10 741	19.5	2.53	10.2	30.1	677	477	197	200	2 074	7 231	425	6 806	6 759	1 129	45.6	23.4
Yakima	26 498	22.7	2.63	14.2	30.3	2 139	1 669	732	470	6 845	9 253	477	8 776	16 992	1 936	57.2	16.0
WEST VIRGINIA	736 481	7.0	2.40	10.7	27.1	43 147	24 009	11 601	19 138	45 320	2 515	234	2 281	380 827	37 726	64.2	14.8
Charleston	24 505	-3.2	2.11	13.5	38.9	1 670	833	432	837	4 514	8 480	1 054	7 426	9 330	2 230	43.6	32.6
Huntington	22 955	-2.0	2.12	13.1	37.6	2 866	977	470	1 889	3 216	6 270	487	5 783	13 607	1 197	52.3	22.4
Morgantown	10 782	12.5	2.08	7.0	37.3	4 329	181	93	4 148	1 100	4 118	442	3 676	14 263	640	30.9	47.8
Parkersburg	14 467	0.0	2.23	13.5	34.0	870	516	377	354	1 123	3 405	194	3 211	6 157	754	61.1	12.9
Wheeling	13 719	-8.8	2.17	12.2	38.3	1 622	584	476	1 038	NA	NA	NA	NA	5 579	2 215	54.1	23.2
WISCONSIN	2 084 544	14.4	2.50	9.6	26.8	155 958	79 073	41 370	76 885	176 987	3 253	225	3 028	1 209 333	253 705	49.5	22.4
Appleton	26 864	8.2	2.52	8.7	27.6	2 405	1 035	504	1 370	1 967	2 767	179	2 588	15 754	4 223	42.2	29.7
Beloit	13 370	0.5	2.57	16.6	27.5	1 410	349	349	1 061	2 144	5 908	383	5 525	7 827	1 910	62.5	13.5
Brookfield	13 891	16.3	2.74	5.5	16.7	652	481	481	171	1 108	2 826	43	2 783	7 129	3 368	25.0	49.0
Eau Claire	24 016	13.7	2.38	9.3	30.0	4 641	862	391	3 779	2 792	4 460	248	4 213	20 029	1 908	40.1	28.8
Fond du Lac	16 638	13.7	2.38	9.8	30.9	2 686	1 974	846	712	1 669	3 898	142	3 756	8 364	2 357	53.1	19.0
Franklin	10 602	42.6	2.58	6.6	22.5	2 103	1 879	0	224	555	1 855	127	1 728	5 850	1 610	38.0	29.1
Green Bay	41 591	8.4	2.40	10.8	31.6	2 695	1 164	825	1 531	3 762	3 625	375	3 250	22 022	4 680	52.7	19.3
Greenfield	15 697	13.9	2.20	8.0	34.6	922	606	606	316	1 259	3 498	83	3 415	5 808	1 896	48.5	20.2
Janesville	23 894	17.2	2.45	10.5	27.4	921	512	370	409	3 499	5 797	244	5 554	12 896	2 048	51.7	18.9
Kenosha	34 411	15.0	2.54	13.9	28.4	2 980	1 457	781	1 523	2 785	3 038	226	2 813	20 998	4 744	50.9	18.2
La Crosse	21 110	5.7	2.23	9.3	37.0	4 806	998	633	3 808	1 798	3 420	217	3 204	15 436	2 909	43.9	24.1
Madison	89 019	15.1	2.19	7.8	35.3	12 833	2 456	978	10 377	8 847	4 192	358	3 834	65 729	7 356	25.7	48.2
Manitowoc	14 235	8.3	2.32	9.1	32.5	960	788	580	172	1 317	3 812	116	3 697	6 292	1 927	57.0	17.1
Menomonee Falls	12 844	30.8	2.52	6.5	23.7	243	211	211	32	545	1 646	54	1 591	6 008	1 968	41.2	30.4
Milwaukee	232 188	-3.5	2.50	21.1	33.5	16 403	6 464	3 645	9 939	46 315	7 648	955	6 693	141 645	43 423	55.3	18.3
New Berlin	14 495	23.9	2.62	5.7	19.0	219	130	130	89	619	1 597	39	1 558	6 736	3 106	34.7	36.8
Oak Creek	11 239	58.7	2.52	7.1	25.3	99	19	19	80	947	3 281	114	3 166	5 861	1 704	43.7	24.4
Oshkosh	24 082	14.9	2.31	9.1	32.4	7 342	3 516	599	3 826	2 440	3 823	224	3 599	17 372	2 081	51.8	23.1

1. No spouse present.   2. Data for serious crimes have not been adjusted for underreporting. This may affect comparability between geographic areas and over time.   3. Per 100,000 population estimated by the FBI.   4. All persons 3 years old and over enrolled in nursery school through college.   5. Persons 25 years old and over.

Table D. Cities — Income, Poverty, and Housing

City	Money income, 1999							Housing units, 2000					
	Households				Percent below poverty						Vacant units		
	Median income				Persons		Families						
	Per capita income[1] (dollars)	Dollars	Percent change, 1989–1999 (constant 1999 dollars)	Percent with income of $100,000 or more	Total	Percent change in rate, 1989–1999	Total	Total	Percent change, 1990–2000	Vacant units for sale or rent[2]	For seasonal use (percent)	Home owner vacancy rate	Renter vacancy rate
	43	44	45	46	47	48	49	50	51	52	53	54	55
VIRGINIA—Cont'd													
Lynchburg	18 263	32 234	1.1	7.3	15.9	-3.0	12.3	27 640	1.5	2 163	0.5	2.2	7.1
Manassas	24 453	60 409	-3.7	19.5	6.3	65.8	3.7	12 114	18.4	357	0.2	1.0	3.6
Newport News	17 843	36 597	-0.8	5.9	13.8	-1.4	11.3	74 117	6.3	4 431	0.3	1.9	6.2
Norfolk	17 372	31 815	0.5	6.3	19.4	0.5	15.5	94 416	-4.4	8 206	0.3	3.2	6.9
Petersburg	15 989	28 851	0.8	4.4	19.6	-3.4	16.7	15 955	-1.5	2 156	0.1	3.4	12.4
Portsmouth	16 507	33 742	2.1	4.8	16.2	-8.5	13.3	41 605	-1.6	3 435	0.3	2.6	6.9
Richmond	20 337	31 121	-1.6	8.3	21.4	2.4	17.1	92 282	-2.0	7 733	0.3	2.4	6.4
Roanoke	18 468	30 719	1.2	5.0	15.9	-1.2	12.9	45 257	2.0	3 254	0.4	2.0	6.4
Suffolk	18 836	41 115	17.1	9.0	13.2	-23.7	10.8	24 704	23.5	1 421	0.3	1.7	6.2
Virginia Beach	22 365	48 705	-0.1	12.1	6.5	10.2	5.1	162 277	10.4	7 822	1.4	1.5	4.0
WASHINGTON	22 973	45 776	9.3	12.6	10.6	-2.8	7.3	2 451 075	20.6	179 677	2.5	1.8	5.9
Auburn	19 630	39 208	-2.7	7.0	12.8	18.5	10.2	16 767	20.0	659	0.1	1.7	4.0
Bellevue	36 905	62 338	5.9	26.4	5.7	1.8	3.8	48 396	29.3	2 560	1.1	1.6	5.3
Bellingham	19 483	32 530	-2.0	8.0	20.6	23.4	9.4	29 474	33.3	1 475	0.5	2.3	4.6
Bothell	26 483	59 264	18.7	17.4	5.1	41.7	3.6	12 303	139.1	380	0.2	1.0	4.6
Bremerton	16 724	30 950	1.9	4.3	19.4	7.2	16.0	16 631	6.0	1 535	0.4	4.3	7.8
Des Moines	24 127	48 971	13.4	11.5	7.6	2.7	5.6	11 777	58.3	440	0.5	1.2	4.4
Edmonds	30 076	53 522	-1.7	18.5	4.6	-2.1	2.6	17 508	35.2	604	0.5	1.3	3.3
Everett	20 577	40 100	5.0	7.7	12.9	7.5	10.1	38 512	25.1	2 187	0.2	1.9	6.2
Kennewick	20 152	41 213	8.5	9.2	12.9	-7.2	9.7	22 043	28.1	1 257	0.3	1.3	8.1
Kent	21 390	46 046	6.0	10.5	11.6	31.8	8.7	32 488	85.8	1 375	0.3	1.1	4.9
Kirkland	38 903	60 332	16.8	22.2	5.3	-7.0	3.9	21 831	20.9	1 095	0.7	1.7	5.2
Lacey	20 224	43 848	10.9	7.5	9.2	16.5	7.4	13 160	62.9	701	0.3	2.5	6.0
Longview	18 559	35 171	2.5	7.4	16.7	4.4	12.3	15 225	13.3	1 159	0.3	2.5	10.6
Lynnwood	19 971	42 814	4.4	8.9	9.5	2.2	6.2	13 808	16.3	480	0.2	1.3	3.8
Marysville	20 414	47 088	34.2	10.5	5.6	-20.0	3.7	9 730	113.1	330	0.4	1.2	3.8
Mount Vernon	17 041	37 999	4.7	6.9	15.9	20.5	10.8	9 686	35.1	410	0.3	2.1	4.3
Olympia	22 590	40 846	9.4	9.6	12.1	-6.9	6.9	19 738	23.9	1 068	0.4	1.6	6.4
Pasco	13 404	34 540	43.6	6.5	23.3	-29.4	19.5	10 341	34.3	722	0.3	2.5	7.4
Puyallup	22 401	47 269	7.1	11.6	6.7	-4.3	4.7	13 467	43.6	597	0.2	0.9	6.1
Redmond	36 233	66 735	17.4	26.6	5.3	47.2	3.3	20 248	35.2	1 146	1.1	1.5	5.7
Renton	24 346	45 820	5.3	11.5	9.7	38.6	7.0	22 676	17.8	968	0.4	1.2	4.7
Richland	25 494	53 092	7.9	16.3	8.2	5.1	5.7	16 458	18.6	909	0.3	1.5	7.1
Sammamish	42 971	101 592	NA	51.3	2.0	NA	1.6	11 599	NA	468	0.6	2.1	6.5
Seattle	30 306	45 736	16.0	15.9	11.8	-4.8	6.9	270 524	8.6	12 025	0.7	1.2	3.5
Shoreline	24 959	51 658	NA	14.0	6.9	NA	4.4	21 338	NA	622	0.3	1.1	3.2
Spokane	18 451	32 273	8.2	6.5	15.9	-8.1	11.1	87 941	10.1	6 429	0.3	2.4	9.4
Tacoma	19 130	37 879	11.3	7.5	15.9	-5.4	11.4	81 102	7.9	4 950	0.3	1.9	6.4
Vancouver	20 192	41 618	43.7	8.4	12.2	-28.7	9.4	60 039	185.6	3 411	0.4	2.3	6.4
Walla Walla	15 792	31 855	11.3	5.8	18.0	-6.7	13.1	11 400	7.1	804	0.4	2.2	7.6
Wenatchee	19 498	34 897	13.9	8.5	15.3	-19.0	10.6	11 486	21.5	745	0.2	3.4	6.9
Yakima	15 920	29 475	-1.1	6.0	22.4	10.9	17.1	28 643	24.7	2 145	0.4	2.0	8.7
WEST VIRGINIA	16 477	29 696	6.3	5.0	17.9	-9.1	13.9	844 623	8.1	108 142	3.9	2.2	9.1
Charleston	26 017	34 009	7.3	13.1	16.7	-11.2	12.7	27 131	-3.5	2 626	0.6	2.7	9.3
Huntington	16 717	23 234	-5.4	4.6	24.7	6.5	17.5	25 888	-2.9	2 933	0.3	3.0	8.7
Morgantown	14 459	20 649	-14.7	6.0	38.4	25.1	15.0	11 721	12.5	939	0.4	3.1	6.6
Parkersburg	16 106	26 990	-1.8	3.5	19.8	4.2	16.1	16 100	-1.5	1 633	0.8	2.4	10.0
Wheeling	17 923	27 388	-3.2	5.4	18.0	6.5	13.1	15 706	-8.3	1 987	0.3	2.5	14.7
WISCONSIN	21 271	43 791	10.7	9.4	8.7	-18.7	5.6	2 321 144	12.9	236 600	6.1	1.2	5.6
Appleton	22 478	47 285	6.6	10.3	5.5	-19.1	3.3	27 736	8.6	872	0.3	1.1	4.4
Beloit	16 912	36 414	4.8	5.6	12.5	-28.6	9.6	14 262	1.6	892	0.1	1.9	8.2
Brookfield	37 292	76 225	-0.7	33.5	2.2	100.0	1.4	14 208	15.9	317	0.6	0.6	3.8
Eau Claire	18 230	36 399	9.5	5.8	13.6	-26.9	5.5	24 895	13.8	879	0.3	1.0	3.5
Fond du Lac	18 996	41 113	14.1	5.6	7.5	-21.9	4.6	17 519	15.4	881	0.2	1.4	7.5
Franklin	27 474	64 315	9.6	20.8	2.7	28.6	1.4	10 936	41.1	334	0.2	0.8	6.0
Green Bay	19 269	38 820	7.9	6.5	10.5	-21.6	7.4	43 123	8.6	1 532	0.3	0.9	4.1
Greenfield	23 755	44 230	-6.2	9.2	4.7	38.2	3.4	16 203	13.3	506	0.3	0.9	3.4
Janesville	22 224	45 961	8.3	9.8	6.5	-21.7	4.3	25 083	18.6	1 189	0.3	1.3	7.4
Kenosha	19 578	41 902	12.3	8.0	9.5	-25.2	7.0	36 004	15.4	1 593	0.3	1.3	4.9
La Crosse	17 650	31 103	5.5	5.2	17.2	-18.1	7.8	22 233	6.4	1 123	0.5	1.0	5.1
Madison	23 498	41 941	6.1	10.7	15.0	-6.8	5.8	92 394	15.4	3 375	0.3	0.8	3.9
Manitowoc	19 954	38 203	17.5	5.2	7.9	-26.2	5.0	15 007	9.3	772	0.4	1.1	7.7
Menomonee Falls	27 454	57 952	1.9	17.0	2.2	-21.4	1.1	13 140	30.8	296	0.3	0.8	2.8
Milwaukee	16 181	32 216	1.5	4.7	21.3	-4.1	17.4	249 225	-2.0	17 037	0.2	1.3	6.0
New Berlin	29 789	67 576	1.8	24.8	2.0	17.6	1.3	14 921	23.3	426	0.2	1.1	4.8
Oak Creek	23 586	53 779	0.1	11.3	3.1	40.9	1.2	11 897	63.8	658	0.1	1.2	8.7
Oshkosh	18 964	37 636	11.3	5.5	10.2	-19.0	5.2	25 420	16.5	1 338	0.4	1.3	6.5

1. Based on population enumerated as of April 1, 2000. 2. Includes units rented or sold but not occupied.

Table D. Cities — Housing, Labor Force, Employment, and Disability

City	Housing units, 2000 (cont'd) — Occupied units — Total	Percent owner occupied	Percent renter occupied	Average size owner occupied	Average size renter occupied	Civilian labor force, 2003 — Total	Percent change, 2002–2003	Unemployment Total	Rate[1]	Civilian employment,[2] 2000 — Total	Percent — Management, professional, and related occupations	Percent — Production, transportation, and material moving occupations	Disability, 2000 — Employment disabled persons[3] (percent)
	56	57	58	59	60	61	62	63	64	65	66	67	68
VIRGINIA—Cont'd													
Lynchburg	25 477	58.5	41.5	2.44	2.12	29 302	-1.2	1 790	6.1	29 160	33.3	16.1	14.3
Manassas	11 757	69.8	30.2	2.98	2.78	21 081	0.5	624	3.0	18 238	38.5	8.3	9.8
Newport News	69 686	52.4	47.6	2.61	2.39	88 753	2.3	4 775	5.4	78 194	30.5	13.6	11.6
Norfolk	86 210	45.5	54.5	2.51	2.40	93 714	2.2	6 138	6.5	87 490	29.1	13.2	14.2
Petersburg	13 799	51.5	48.5	2.40	2.36	15 384	2.1	1 580	10.3	13 170	24.9	24.4	19.3
Portsmouth	38 170	58.6	41.4	2.52	2.49	46 807	2.2	2 855	6.1	40 353	27.7	14.7	15.1
Richmond	84 549	46.1	53.9	2.30	2.12	97 888	0.1	6 397	6.5	90 745	35.5	12.5	15.1
Roanoke	42 003	56.3	43.7	2.30	2.07	48 439	-1.7	2 518	5.2	44 455	26.7	17.2	14.8
Suffolk	23 283	72.2	27.8	2.71	2.64	34 577	2.1	1 547	4.5	27 519	30.9	18.5	16.2
Virginia Beach	154 455	65.6	34.4	2.79	2.54	220 878	2.1	8 229	3.7	194 923	35.9	9.0	9.7
WASHINGTON	2 271 398	64.6	35.4	2.65	2.32	3 139 877	1.0	236 965	7.5	2 793 722	35.6	12.7	10.6
Auburn	16 108	54.2	45.8	2.55	2.37	21 134	-0.4	1 688	8.0	19 296	26.0	17.4	11.0
Bellevue	45 836	61.5	38.5	2.54	2.10	60 921	-0.6	3 034	5.0	57 415	53.1	6.2	9.2
Bellingham	27 999	48.2	51.8	2.36	2.12	38 430	3.4	2 306	6.0	33 704	30.3	11.7	7.2
Bothell	11 923	68.0	32.0	2.69	2.14	8 219	-0.5	443	5.4	16 382	43.2	11.7	8.3
Bremerton	15 096	41.4	58.6	2.34	2.27	17 333	2.0	1 728	10.0	13 463	25.5	12.1	13.1
Des Moines	11 337	61.0	39.0	2.56	2.33	11 157	-0.5	769	6.9	14 110	32.2	14.4	9.7
Edmonds	16 904	68.1	31.9	2.46	2.01	24 235	-0.4	1 550	6.4	20 079	41.3	8.8	10.4
Everett	36 325	46.0	54.0	2.51	2.32	50 231	-0.2	6 064	12.1	42 252	27.2	17.0	12.5
Kennewick	20 786	59.7	40.3	2.75	2.38	29 567	4.1	2 457	8.3	25 783	32.4	12.9	10.5
Kent	31 113	48.8	51.2	2.70	2.38	27 233	-0.5	1 917	7.0	40 322	30.5	15.2	10.3
Kirkland	20 736	57.0	43.0	2.30	1.91	29 647	-0.5	1 675	5.6	27 454	49.2	6.2	10.3
Lacey	12 459	55.5	44.5	2.59	2.31	12 271	5.1	669	5.5	13 939	33.5	9.7	7.4
Longview	14 066	57.8	42.2	2.45	2.34	15 815	-0.6	1 685	10.7	14 628	23.9	20.5	10.6
Lynnwood	13 328	53.0	47.0	2.63	2.35	22 786	-0.3	1 999	8.8	17 026	31.3	12.8	13.3
Marysville	9 400	63.4	36.6	2.83	2.37	6 665	-0.4	454	6.8	11 808	29.0	15.5	12.3
Mount Vernon	9 276	57.3	42.7	2.74	2.75	12 731	2.4	1 011	7.9	11 593	25.4	17.3	10.7
Olympia	18 670	50.3	49.7	2.43	1.98	24 268	5.1	1 365	5.6	21 744	42.4	7.9	10.6
Pasco	9 619	60.0	40.0	3.26	3.35	13 107	4.0	1 727	13.2	12 085	20.1	19.5	9.5
Puyallup	12 870	54.9	45.1	2.83	2.15	15 187	2.4	1 043	6.9	15 872	32.6	15.1	17.5
Redmond	19 102	55.1	44.9	2.53	2.07	25 692	-0.6	1 206	4.7	26 112	56.7	6.9	10.3
Renton	21 708	50.0	50.0	2.47	2.11	28 998	-0.5	2 164	7.5	27 552	34.3	11.8	7.4
Richland	15 549	66.3	33.7	2.61	2.23	23 814	3.7	1 433	6.0	18 343	50.8	8.4	13.0
Sammamish	11 131	90.1	9.9	3.12	2.52	7 612	-0.5	488	6.4	17 438	58.9	5.2	7.9
Seattle	258 499	48.4	51.6	2.32	1.84	358 253	-0.4	28 476	7.9	321 524	48.4	8.2	4.7
Shoreline	20 716	68.0	32.0	2.60	2.27	31 824	-0.5	1 894	6.0	26 798	40.2	10.2	9.3
Spokane	81 512	58.8	41.2	2.47	2.11	105 127	1.4	8 105	7.7	89 043	32.4	12.2	10.7
Tacoma	76 152	54.7	45.3	2.60	2.27	107 044	2.5	9 574	8.9	86 787	29.2	15.6	12.3
Vancouver	56 628	52.9	47.1	2.57	2.42	78 987	0.2	10 090	12.8	67 720	29.1	17.7	13.6
Walla Walla	10 596	59.1	40.9	2.56	2.27	14 053	2.2	1 098	7.8	11 479	35.4	9.7	11.5
Wenatchee	10 741	57.7	42.3	2.64	2.37	14 796	1.4	1 555	10.5	11 498	31.6	11.8	13.9
Yakima	26 498	53.2	46.8	2.67	2.58	32 119	2.2	3 443	10.7	27 018	28.0	16.5	15.3
WEST VIRGINIA	736 481	75.2	24.8	2.47	2.17	787 286	-2.0	48 210	6.1	732 673	27.9	16.4	13.2
Charleston	24 505	58.1	41.9	2.27	1.90	28 192	-3.4	1 442	5.1	24 398	43.6	8.0	11.3
Huntington	22 955	54.6	45.4	2.27	1.94	22 353	-1.7	1 313	5.9	21 128	31.1	9.9	12.5
Morgantown	10 782	41.7	58.3	2.26	1.96	13 424	-0.5	464	3.5	12 312	42.6	5.6	5.9
Parkersburg	14 467	62.0	38.0	2.28	2.13	16 215	-2.6	1 256	7.7	13 708	25.2	16.5	13.2
Wheeling	13 719	62.7	37.3	2.36	1.85	15 856	-2.6	646	4.1	13 029	34.7	11.4	11.8
WISCONSIN	2 084 544	68.4	31.6	2.66	2.15	3 078 254	1.8	173 533	5.6	2 734 925	31.3	19.8	9.1
Appleton	26 864	68.7	31.3	2.72	2.08	46 571	0.9	3 148	6.8	36 997	34.3	18.6	7.4
Beloit	13 370	61.9	38.1	2.60	2.53	17 356	0.3	1 683	9.7	15 840	21.7	31.4	12.3
Brookfield	13 891	89.9	10.1	2.81	2.06	21 357	0.6	781	3.7	18 807	51.3	9.0	4.9
Eau Claire	24 016	57.3	42.7	2.57	2.12	36 674	2.8	1 939	5.3	33 423	30.2	14.7	7.6
Fond du Lac	16 638	61.7	38.3	2.59	2.03	24 025	1.4	1 713	7.1	21 414	25.6	24.9	8.1
Franklin	10 602	78.4	21.6	2.75	1.97	14 780	0.7	773	5.2	15 784	40.0	14.8	8.6
Green Bay	41 591	56.0	44.0	2.56	2.19	63 908	3.2	5 165	8.1	52 778	26.6	20.9	10.7
Greenfield	15 697	59.5	40.5	2.49	1.78	19 570	1.5	918	4.7	19 081	32.0	16.3	8.8
Janesville	23 894	68.2	31.8	2.60	2.14	32 259	1.5	2 274	7.0	30 438	26.6	25.8	9.0
Kenosha	34 411	62.2	37.8	2.69	2.29	49 388	2.9	3 496	7.1	43 023	28.4	21.3	11.7
La Crosse	21 110	50.9	49.1	2.39	2.06	28 821	1.4	1 518	5.3	26 761	27.9	15.9	8.1
Madison	89 019	47.7	52.3	2.40	2.00	139 375	2.5	4 063	2.9	121 828	46.9	8.7	6.6
Manitowoc	14 235	67.6	32.4	2.51	1.93	17 609	0.8	1 700	9.7	16 702	24.0	27.8	8.8
Menomonee Falls	12 844	77.4	22.6	2.75	1.75	19 853	0.9	814	4.1	17 354	39.6	13.7	6.0
Milwaukee	232 188	45.3	54.7	2.60	2.42	276 455	0.8	26 785	9.7	256 244	28.0	21.1	14.2
New Berlin	14 495	81.3	18.7	2.79	1.91	23 827	0.6	980	4.1	21 039	43.4	11.4	5.6
Oak Creek	11 239	60.9	39.1	2.89	1.95	15 511	1.0	931	6.0	16 418	33.3	17.0	6.6
Oshkosh	24 082	57.5	42.5	2.49	2.06	40 247	1.3	2 318	5.8	32 131	28.3	20.6	8.3

1. Percent of civilian labor force.   2. Persons 16 years old and over.   3. Persons 16 to 64 years old.

Table D. Cities — **Construction, Wholesale Trade, and Retail Trade**

City	Value of residential construction authorized by building permits, 2003			Wholesale trade, 1997				Retail trade,[1] 1997			
	New construction ($1,000)	Number of housing units	Percent single family	Number of establish-ments	Number of employees	Sales (mil dol)	Annual payroll (mil dol)	Number of establish-ments	Number of employees	Sales (mil dol)	Annual payroll (mil dol)
	69	70	71	72	73	74	75	76	77	78	79
VIRGINIA—Cont'd											
Lynchburg	49 558	395	99.5	100	1 292	504.6	43.8	446	7 209	1 228.5	115.8
Manassas	14 215	132	100.0	59	1 008	626.3	41.0	230	3 355	647.5	64.9
Newport News	35 175	472	54.4	132	1 634	604.2	50.3	681	9 284	1 488.6	143.6
Norfolk	81 768	771	56.7	324	5 845	2 914.6	183.9	918	12 628	1 900.4	207.3
Petersburg	481	10	100.0	35	538	139.2	16.8	189	1 764	290.0	29.5
Portsmouth	32 129	378	34.9	63	712	167.3	23.6	295	3 291	468.4	51.2
Richmond	44 671	495	56.4	464	7 572	5 979.5	283.5	1 013	11 579	1 738.1	193.5
Roanoke	20 774	247	88.7	299	3 768	1 292.7	121.0	792	12 425	1 843.7	191.3
Suffolk	131 824	1 404	78.9	61	1 305	822.5	43.7	212	2 697	380.0	38.0
Virginia Beach	238 877	1 941	90.6	479	5 642	1 922.8	159.4	1 621	21 987	3 342.7	337.2
WASHINGTON	6 346 021	42 825	77.3	10 039	118 810	75 397.8	4 376.0	22 841	283 653	52 472.9	5 385.9
Auburn	77 763	299	81.3	135	2 935	1 409.5	90.0	297	4 494	931.4	92.9
Bellevue	46 809	121	100.0	579	6 532	11 707.9	316.2	789	13 580	2 745.9	266.2
Bellingham	101 356	1 005	26.5	154	1 264	570.4	38.9	502	6 902	1 126.8	115.3
Bothell	34 965	211	57.3	90	1 232	869.2	59.1	115	1 596	667.0	51.6
Bremerton	5 314	56	75.0	24	289	86.9	10.0	182	2 149	463.6	48.3
Des Moines	8 672	31	100.0	18	76	67.1	3.6	57	518	86.6	10.2
Edmonds	32 642	180	50.6	70	316	325.1	11.4	160	1 788	361.2	38.5
Everett	45 582	345	57.7	144	1 570	592.6	56.1	473	6 518	1 340.0	133.5
Kennewick	55 050	336	97.6	59	419	193.2	11.3	378	5 236	890.7	83.8
Kent	53 221	301	100.0	454	9 062	5 480.1	346.8	315	4 399	929.9	94.4
Kirkland	57 744	190	90.5	206	2 341	2 421.9	135.7	250	3 984	1 012.9	86.1
Lacey	31 037	214	93.5	25	155	28.6	4.7	135	2 180	352.1	37.7
Longview	9 661	80	72.5	46	488	108.0	12.9	224	3 019	554.5	56.4
Lynnwood	12 560	108	67.6	87	835	726.1	29.7	404	7 637	1 374.9	139.4
Marysville	53 425	396	90.2	21	207	96.9	6.9	123	1 788	313.7	32.3
Mount Vernon	38 157	382	56.3	27	274	79.4	8.7	161	1 716	291.0	32.3
Olympia	21 705	158	83.5	74	647	204.8	23.7	371	4 670	853.5	86.5
Pasco	124 248	1 075	81.0	70	862	345.4	25.5	158	1 959	438.2	41.6
Puyallup	14 944	67	76.1	29	145	74.5	4.8	262	4 512	955.6	90.0
Redmond	86 387	449	59.7	344	4 489	4 405.2	202.9	271	3 061	543.6	65.2
Renton	126 311	669	82.5	126	3 117	1 709.3	121.8	228	4 662	1 417.5	121.1
Richland	77 024	414	77.5	22	D	D	D	131	1 338	203.0	21.8
Sammamish	NA	NA	NA	NA	NA	NA	NA	NA	NA	NA	NA
Seattle	313 968	2 705	33.8	1 860	23 635	16 085.6	978.1	2 698	34 886	6 146.2	717.7
Shoreline	14 044	68	100.0	NA	NA	NA	NA	NA	NA	NA	NA
Spokane	98 849	905	54.8	521	7 028	2 709.8	214.1	1 054	13 757	2 389.8	263.0
Tacoma	56 493	456	60.7	318	4 790	2 819.6	181.7	832	11 432	2 180.3	226.6
Vancouver	101 346	1 145	39.5	248	2 277	1 237.4	86.5	440	6 900	1 298.4	137.9
Walla Walla	7 726	64	76.6	56	D	D	D	190	2 233	348.4	38.9
Wenatchee	17 597	138	61.6	77	821	519.8	31.6	211	2 634	475.4	50.7
Yakima	13 361	117	64.1	152	2 984	1 047.5	87.5	443	6 123	1 053.7	107.1
WEST VIRGINIA	645 988	5 133	90.9	1 956	23 805	10 290.4	681.1	8 082	90 087	14 057.9	1 309.3
Charleston	9 195	47	87.2	179	2 738	1 386.6	84.0	466	7 135	961.8	102.2
Huntington	1 665	18	77.8	136	1 803	551.4	50.0	313	4 091	637.5	65.4
Morgantown	7 911	78	23.1	36	D	D	D	267	3 650	505.5	54.9
Parkersburg	1 752	23	91.3	78	917	350.0	23.9	291	3 667	617.1	58.5
Wheeling	2 085	15	100.0	89	1 694	1 361.1	47.1	223	2 342	354.3	39.2
WISCONSIN	5 504 609	40 884	70.3	8 025	110 309	57 192.9	3 764.9	21 717	305 255	50 520.5	4 826.2
Appleton	47 692	300	71.0	94	1 631	583.2	56.7	329	4 683	691.0	73.9
Beloit	10 079	180	28.9	17	288	185.9	13.7	141	1 994	385.6	32.3
Brookfield	34 023	258	29.5	226	3 092	1 541.1	141.5	349	6 557	939.4	94.0
Eau Claire	42 644	348	70.7	100	1 629	754.4	52.3	372	6 849	1 007.5	95.3
Fond du Lac	20 929	173	65.3	66	848	361.7	27.2	270	4 084	635.9	61.5
Franklin	51 085	367	46.6	41	357	192.4	12.1	61	1 347	258.5	21.4
Green Bay	53 550	399	63.4	201	2 733	1 316.0	88.9	515	8 419	1 395.5	135.8
Greenfield	15 444	153	26.1	36	D	D	D	184	4 012	707.8	65.8
Janesville	40 265	330	76.4	68	1 829	1 270.6	60.4	310	5 461	992.1	98.4
Kenosha	69 798	677	32.8	66	853	208.6	27.3	313	4 549	699.7	66.4
La Crosse	10 213	101	46.5	92	2 701	1 746.4	88.7	336	5 685	905.3	90.9
Madison	309 097	2 660	36.1	324	4 530	1 621.6	149.1	1 078	18 263	2 761.0	282.4
Manitowoc	7 040	80	42.5	34	370	192.3	15.3	162	2 411	357.3	34.4
Menomonee Falls	39 379	207	72.9	151	1 762	1 051.2	74.2	152	3 142	535.1	56.1
Milwaukee	119 134	906	28.0	753	14 029	8 379.2	531.4	1 700	22 655	3 381.2	360.6
New Berlin	26 130	193	37.3	166	2 918	1 064.5	107.1	92	1 481	213.6	24.3
Oak Creek	33 145	247	70.9	38	755	473.2	27.1	57	1 695	291.6	29.7
Oshkosh	33 880	497	32.0	72	1 078	323.1	32.7	332	4 744	841.5	83.3

1. Establishments with payroll.

Table D. Cities — **Real Estate, Professional Services, and Manufacturing**

City	Real estate and rental and leasing, 1997				Professional, scientific, and technical services,[1] 1997				Manufacturing, 1997			
	Number of establish-ments	Number of employees	Receipts (mil dol)	Annual payroll (mil dol)	Number of establish-ments	Number of employees	Receipts (mil dol)	Annual payroll (mil dol)	Number of establish-ments	Number of employees	Receipts (mil dol)	Annual payroll (mil dol)
	80	81	82	83	84	85	86	87	88	89	90	91
VIRGINIA—Cont'd												
Lynchburg	95	390	37.4	8.2	182	2 715	260.3	107.1	117	12 535	3 096.4	481.1
Manassas	51	302	41.1	5.5	153	1 058	126.9	44.8	34	2 822	791.6	188.5
Newport News	226	1 720	169.9	35.8	286	3 023	218.8	88.6	131	24 707	3 300.5	898.4
Norfolk	273	2 128	203.8	44.2	439	6 582	468.7	207.0	199	10 996	5 737.3	402.2
Petersburg	28	131	11.1	2.2	45	1 122	79.8	42.1	43	2 553	409.6	72.4
Portsmouth	84	457	37.8	7.4	105	1 023	82.1	31.5	71	1 812	368.7	52.0
Richmond	265	2 166	213.5	54.8	732	8 113	853.7	356.0	325	21 879	11 748.3	941.2
Roanoke	158	1 861	114.5	31.8	331	2 632	211.6	88.7	152	8 489	2 156.3	242.9
Suffolk	43	210	24.1	3.4	59	273	21.4	9.2	52	2 257	1 103.5	63.8
Virginia Beach	472	3 101	333.0	66.8	895	8 910	726.1	302.6	236	5 806	967.2	139.2
WASHINGTON	7 544	41 899	5 352.8	935.3	13 411	101 848	10 564.8	4 247.3	7 801	328 511	78 852.5	13 004.1
Auburn	57	264	32.7	6.1	73	310	18.9	8.3	167	13 946	1 875.8	605.2
Bellevue	458	4 723	685.5	151.0	1 073	12 563	1 645.8	651.9	163	2 740	681.8	93.3
Bellingham	134	529	60.7	8.1	254	1 909	187.7	80.7	130	3 457	583.9	91.5
Bothell	48	220	47.2	4.4	104	1 054	167.2	52.1	50	4 260	707.0	217.1
Bremerton	48	288	25.6	4.1	71	976	65.6	27.1	NA	NA	NA	NA
Des Moines	16	57	6.8	0.9	27	127	6.9	3.4	NA	NA	NA	NA
Edmonds	70	175	27.9	5.8	146	555	53.5	20.5	NA	NA	NA	NA
Everett	138	787	108.4	14.5	221	1 390	119.7	51.0	130	D	D	D
Kennewick	86	678	82.9	16.1	118	D	D	D	46	D	D	D
Kent	95	677	120.6	17.9	162	1 387	140.7	51.6	295	26 894	3 997.4	1 274.8
Kirkland	129	800	102.8	18.3	302	4 454	330.1	148.9	93	1 941	315.8	63.2
Lacey	34	110	13.6	1.7	44	1 035	84.1	36.7	NA	NA	NA	NA
Longview	66	315	35.9	5.7	79	466	29.1	12.8	46	2 556	824.3	115.2
Lynnwood	94	519	56.3	10.4	120	618	58.5	28.2	61	1 526	145.9	40.8
Marysville	33	81	11.7	1.6	29	98	5.9	2.2	53	1 374	199.8	47.4
Mount Vernon	44	175	18.0	2.6	86	355	25.1	8.6	27	527	75.8	13.2
Olympia	108	465	50.1	7.7	253	1 248	90.1	39.2	47	1 368	387.0	47.3
Pasco	33	195	20.3	3.9	35	112	11.7	4.3	34	D	D	D
Puyallup	63	712	38.8	8.3	66	296	15.4	5.8	38	2 482	320.5	83.1
Redmond	73	441	82.7	12.3	278	3 426	269.9	125.3	227	11 807	2 183.7	448.5
Renton	76	801	176.5	22.7	122	627	67.1	26.1	70	D	D	D
Richland	41	143	13.4	2.0	127	3 310	278.2	166.8	28	1 449	294.2	65.6
Sammamish	NA	NA	NA	NA	NA	NA	NA	NA	NA	NA	NA	NA
Seattle	1 391	8 567	1 302.0	228.0	3 235	31 669	3 703.6	1 489.6	1 213	33 935	5 021.1	1 132.7
Shoreline	NA	NA	NA	NA	NA	NA	NA	NA	NA	NA	NA	NA
Spokane	291	1 800	202.8	33.8	635	4 413	357.4	151.9	315	6 862	927.5	210.0
Tacoma	237	1 695	152.4	36.9	434	2 722	278.6	108.7	276	10 894	2 625.6	363.5
Vancouver	206	1 376	154.5	30.6	333	2 070	158.3	68.3	193	13 073	2 515.9	494.0
Walla Walla	40	170	14.9	2.4	59	265	17.5	6.8	43	1 137	154.7	31.2
Wenatchee	63	265	26.4	5.3	78	467	36.6	15.4	32	621	71.6	13.5
Yakima	115	659	72.8	11.9	158	1 038	102.6	37.0	102	4 624	747.7	124.0
WEST VIRGINIA	1 449	5 812	665.0	100.8	2 517	15 714	1 166.9	395.2	1 505	72 813	18 293.3	2 460.7
Charleston	172	907	118.7	17.5	371	3 413	326.8	103.7	44	2 152	278.2	85.5
Huntington	101	464	39.6	7.1	140	992	67.8	24.1	72	5 111	1 034.8	176.3
Morgantown	60	246	20.8	2.8	98	647	52.5	17.4	20	D	D	D
Parkersburg	61	363	36.6	7.3	97	668	44.0	15.0	30	1 103	113.6	31.6
Wheeling	58	D	D	D	107	836	74.4	20.9	53	D	D	D
WISCONSIN	4 598	23 924	2 637.5	464.1	9 281	70 689	6 398.9	2 542.3	9 936	562 479	117 383.0	18 766.4
Appleton	61	345	30.6	5.9	165	1 457	130.3	52.9	120	8 235	2 168.1	314.7
Beloit	24	82	17.9	1.3	41	185	9.4	3.5	52	4 896	1 257.5	198.9
Brookfield	118	796	92.6	22.0	314	3 071	321.0	139.2	90	2 873	456.6	102.5
Eau Claire	86	391	42.2	6.2	136	1 328	100.5	43.3	93	4 353	623.5	115.6
Fond du Lac	49	222	22.2	3.3	91	468	36.3	14.8	93	7 301	1 609.5	297.4
Franklin	14	49	6.6	0.7	31	195	38.2	6.5	37	2 479	367.2	95.8
Green Bay	107	618	61.0	10.5	209	1 763	140.9	66.2	200	16 692	4 634.5	695.3
Greenfield	35	160	39.1	3.1	65	676	38.4	18.0	NA	NA	NA	NA
Janesville	52	217	29.1	3.6	99	564	39.6	15.2	104	12 380	8 390.6	504.2
Kenosha	80	336	34.3	5.0	126	544	36.7	16.2	126	5 949	1 287.7	280.6
La Crosse	80	683	47.5	11.8	139	1 403	105.9	49.4	91	7 001	1 110.3	246.2
Madison	328	2 523	277.3	51.3	702	8 705	759.2	341.9	228	11 464	2 573.9	370.4
Manitowoc	27	114	8.1	1.5	53	441	35.9	9.5	88	9 202	1 478.9	280.1
Menomonee Falls	30	191	21.2	6.5	89	585	45.3	21.3	211	9 784	1 476.3	354.1
Milwaukee	484	3 899	462.3	90.6	1 092	14 871	1 570.3	628.8	848	46 467	8 392.4	1 643.5
New Berlin	25	123	40.9	4.4	91	1 062	215.1	45.7	150	6 647	1 299.8	259.0
Oak Creek	14	80	11.5	0.9	16	101	9.7	4.5	65	7 192	2 537.0	300.2
Oshkosh	87	485	41.6	7.5	94	774	85.7	20.9	114	8 692	1 860.5	291.8

1. Firms subject to federal tax.

Table D. Cities — **Accommodation and Foodservices, Entertainment, and Health Care**

City	Accommodation and foodservices, 1997				Arts, entertainment, and recreation,[1] 1997				Health care and social assistance,[1] 1997			
	Number of establishments	Number of employees	Sales (mil dol)	Annual payroll (mil dol)	Number of establishments	Number of employees	Receipts (mil dol)	Annual payroll (mil dol)	Number of establishments	Number of employees	Receipts (mil dol)	Annual payroll (mil dol)
	92	93	94	95	96	97	98	99	100	101	102	103
VIRGINIA—Cont'd												
Lynchburg	173	3 808	110.8	30.9	22	212	5.6	1.5	177	2 893	171.0	86.8
Manassas	74	D	D	D	10	174	5.7	1.7	106	1 161	67.1	34.9
Newport News	312	5 464	170.1	47.7	31	516	17.2	4.3	324	3 878	217.6	122.3
Norfolk	539	9 980	299.4	85.1	49	707	27.3	7.4	400	6 583	451.7	219.1
Petersburg	83	1 194	34.2	10.1	9	79	5.1	0.9	89	1 438	64.1	32.6
Portsmouth	137	2 040	58.7	15.8	17	108	7.1	1.3	170	2 393	134.8	71.8
Richmond	551	9 087	304.2	91.4	45	840	25.1	10.0	540	14 788	1 111.6	414.8
Roanoke	325	6 380	203.4	58.7	34	674	17.4	5.4	274	3 623	274.3	127.4
Suffolk	62	1 027	32.8	8.9	4	0	0.0	0.0	89	1 334	69.9	34.9
Virginia Beach	888	18 145	576.3	163.3	131	1 656	89.3	18.7	809	8 315	473.4	223.9
WASHINGTON	13 105	194 955	6 995.1	1 962.9	1 680	27 971	1 620.1	544.6	12 310	122 813	7 797.7	3 390.2
Auburn	112	1 894	55.3	15.5	19	1 406	106.7	32.1	126	2 433	125.2	60.5
Bellevue	332	6 369	272.5	73.9	59	1 186	62.5	18.1	560	4 476	340.0	147.2
Bellingham	264	3 793	112.0	31.9	32	225	11.1	3.7	305	3 076	176.5	72.4
Bothell	79	1 153	38.5	11.3	7	0	0.0	0.0	69	533	34.6	13.3
Bremerton	108	1 613	49.4	13.6	15	129	4.4	1.0	148	2 235	115.0	56.8
Des Moines	48	915	30.7	7.6	2	0	0.0	0.0	29	140	8.4	3.7
Edmonds	92	1 167	41.6	11.4	9	238	10.5	2.6	151	1 271	96.3	43.4
Everett	263	4 184	143.5	37.7	25	352	17.8	4.5	253	3 407	216.0	117.4
Kennewick	141	2 339	77.2	20.2	19	327	12.3	2.9	149	1 329	88.3	34.1
Kent	181	2 744	96.2	25.7	13	183	8.5	2.2	133	1 620	110.3	44.2
Kirkland	168	3 838	150.1	45.2	20	356	82.1	58.2	225	2 116	132.9	57.7
Lacey	77	1 253	41.5	11.3	6	66	1.5	0.7	55	454	20.5	9.6
Longview	94	1 642	45.7	13.3	11	79	2.3	0.6	131	1 564	93.8	41.6
Lynnwood	150	3 142	106.4	29.1	12	152	5.7	1.9	125	1 069	66.0	24.9
Marysville	65	D	D	D	6	43	1.4	0.3	65	525	30.4	14.3
Mount Vernon	78	1 419	43.3	11.5	8	166	6.1	2.1	89	1 222	84.6	42.9
Olympia	202	3 426	106.9	32.9	22	314	14.3	3.0	288	3 199	258.6	111.4
Pasco	70	931	30.9	8.2	3	0	0.0	0.0	71	623	38.0	15.0
Puyallup	119	2 251	71.9	20.4	14	176	10.2	2.4	155	1 862	116.3	49.9
Redmond	134	2 062	79.7	22.3	21	310	16.5	5.1	126	1 491	95.3	36.5
Renton	165	2 468	84.4	24.0	16	231	27.6	2.4	174	1 763	115.1	50.8
Richland	79	1 483	47.2	13.4	9	133	5.1	1.5	148	1 108	79.9	32.9
Sammamish	NA	NA	NA	NA	NA	NA	NA	NA	NA	NA	NA	NA
Seattle	2 105	34 197	1 550.6	445.9	263	3 786	308.8	151.4	1 643	17 217	1 318.7	574.4
Shoreline	NA	NA	NA	NA	NA	NA	NA	NA	NA	NA	NA	NA
Spokane	568	9 847	306.0	88.5	59	863	47.1	8.8	622	8 079	505.9	234.3
Tacoma	425	6 735	220.6	61.9	44	1 260	116.1	30.2	598	7 046	461.2	215.1
Vancouver	254	4 169	137.0	39.9	36	537	21.1	4.7	293	4 380	286.1	135.3
Walla Walla	96	1 287	38.2	10.7	8	0	0.0	0.0	81	958	59.7	26.3
Wenatchee	96	1 721	49.4	13.4	4	84	2.0	0.6	95	1 623	147.3	58.8
Yakima	219	3 445	115.8	31.9	24	419	18.9	5.3	243	3 102	209.0	96.9
WEST VIRGINIA	3 290	51 506	1 633.2	462.3	408	4 996	273.3	56.6	3 266	40 085	2 575.0	1 056.9
Charleston	210	3 967	147.6	38.9	24	252	11.6	3.0	314	3 898	365.3	151.4
Huntington	187	3 573	102.1	28.6	20	118	4.4	1.2	199	3 237	254.2	121.2
Morgantown	150	2 726	72.4	21.0	15	122	4.6	1.3	74	1 887	133.2	68.6
Parkersburg	129	2 367	69.1	19.6	10	113	3.8	1.3	145	1 819	118.3	51.8
Wheeling	130	1 837	51.6	15.0	17	328	34.7	4.3	175	1 572	105.7	44.6
WISCONSIN	13 252	190 411	5 641.0	1 548.5	1 730	22 339	1 327.5	384.3	9 315	114 562	6 917.4	3 447.3
Appleton	168	3 336	94.0	28.1	18	195	8.7	2.0	185	2 058	164.6	85.6
Beloit	91	1 360	37.8	10.9	4	57	2.6	0.7	54	1 153	55.7	30.6
Brookfield	99	2 519	93.9	24.5	17	429	10.7	3.6	162	1 696	115.7	53.9
Eau Claire	200	4 659	108.4	32.9	20	230	14.9	3.8	148	2 706	179.9	105.4
Fond du Lac	134	2 525	69.3	19.4	19	180	5.3	1.9	106	1 325	162.2	45.2
Franklin	36	D	D	D	7	100	2.1	0.6	33	225	15.6	7.7
Green Bay	286	5 153	137.9	40.1	31	0	0.0	0.0	223	3 256	240.5	131.0
Greenfield	74	2 176	58.4	17.3	13	163	6.1	1.7	94	2 414	103.1	55.5
Janesville	154	3 107	88.3	24.2	16	242	7.9	2.2	104	1 618	116.7	55.0
Kenosha	207	2 787	78.6	21.8	25	703	37.8	9.0	217	2 182	120.3	58.6
La Crosse	208	3 799	98.3	29.2	23	465	9.5	3.9	90	629	40.3	18.5
Madison	602	12 763	390.8	110.9	75	1 475	49.2	14.2	431	6 355	549.7	235.5
Manitowoc	92	1 480	38.2	10.6	10	86	3.8	0.7	91	1 058	61.7	32.4
Menomonee Falls	56	868	24.5	7.4	9	105	8.0	1.8	62	1 647	108.1	57.0
Milwaukee	1 143	17 743	606.5	170.4	90	1 781	368.8	90.7	915	11 854	781.1	426.7
New Berlin	54	D	D	D	10	184	4.3	1.5	70	674	39.8	18.2
Oak Creek	42	777	23.6	6.1	9	52	2.1	0.5	24	169	10.5	4.4
Oshkosh	177	3 591	93.5	27.3	22	212	8.6	1.9	143	1 518	99.6	47.1

1. Firms subject to federal tax.

Table D. Cities — Other Services and Federal Funds

City	Other services,[1] 1997				Selected federal funds, 2002–2003 (mil dol)								
					Procurement contracts		Grants						Direct payments for individuals for educational assistance
	Number of establishments	Number of employees	Receipts (mil dol)	Annual payroll (mil dol)	Defense	Other	Total[2]	Medicaid and other health related	Nutrition and family welfare	Energy and environment	Education	Housing and community development	
	104	105	106	107	108	109	110	111	112	113	114	115	116
VIRGINIA—Cont'd													
Lynchburg	152	933	51.6	15.6	19.1	617.0	21.0	0.1	2.9	0.4	0.0	14.1	12.8
Manassas	108	832	60.2	22.2	417.7	99.1	32.0	18.1	2.0	0.8	1.3	3.7	0.1
Newport News	306	2 234	116.3	41.1	297.7	117.9	60.4	7.3	4.5	0.0	5.0	31.3	5.8
Norfolk	388	2 569	147.8	49.7	1 840.7	110.1	104.9	12.3	10.8	1.2	13.8	40.9	23.5
Petersburg	76	620	32.6	12.0	3.5	4.9	20.8	0.0	0.0	0.0	4.3	10.2	12.5
Portsmouth	163	1 364	74.6	27.2	325.6	42.6	16.3	1.0	0.0	0.1	2.5	11.4	15.3
Richmond	504	3 887	256.6	82.0	98.3	78.5	1 204.6	224.4	243.1	69.7	241.5	128.9	20.9
Roanoke	337	2 403	123.8	43.2	145.0	10.4	52.8	1.2	9.8	0.0	1.0	19.4	7.1
Suffolk	85	453	22.2	6.7	125.7	5.5	6.9	0.0	0.0	0.0	0.1	6.3	0.1
Virginia Beach	716	4 870	254.7	89.2	428.6	41.8	45.6	0.3	0.8	0.0	17.4	20.4	17.4
WASHINGTON	8 771	49 756	3 492.0	1 033.0	3 196.0	3 432.5	8 880.8	4 200.4	1 257.9	159.4	715.4	574.3	243.3
Auburn	115	653	50.4	15.8	5.5	15.0	11.5	4.1	1.4	0.0	1.3	4.2	3.0
Bellevue	320	2 011	173.5	48.4	12.8	17.3	17.8	0.2	0.0	3.9	0.5	10.4	3.6
Bellingham	133	770	49.7	13.4	5.6	3.3	49.6	9.5	4.0	0.4	3.6	7.8	13.0
Bothell	34	221	10.4	3.4	17.7	14.7	7.3	2.1	0.0	0.9	0.2	0.4	0.8
Bremerton	65	376	22.8	6.9	204.8	13.3	21.5	1.2	0.0	4.5	0.5	0.0	3.7
Des Moines	26	111	5.6	1.7	0.0	0.0	0.5	0.0	0.0	0.0	0.0	2.5	0.0
Edmonds	83	343	21.8	6.8	0.9	0.1	4.3	0.7	0.9	0.0	0.0	2.5	0.2
Everett	197	1 591	105.4	36.7	35.3	25.5	38.5	5.4	0.1	0.0	0.7	29.1	9.0
Kennewick	113	642	32.0	10.4	2.8	2.1	13.2	0.0	0.0	0.7	0.0	9.1	0.0
Kent	179	1 507	120.9	38.4	23.8	7.2	7.9	1.9	0.0	0.3	0.2	4.9	0.0
Kirkland	154	914	65.0	21.1	10.4	-13.3	4.3	0.0	0.0	0.9	0.4	3.0	2.3
Lacey	60	395	19.4	6.2	7.3	1.0	3.0	0.0	0.0	0.0	0.0	2.8	0.0
Longview	76	402	24.4	7.6	1.5	1.9	11.5	0.8	2.3	0.1	3.3	4.8	3.5
Lynnwood	113	560	42.3	13.7	11.5	3.4	5.7	0.0	2.9	0.0	1.1	1.6	3.2
Marysville	57	358	20.3	6.3	0.2	0.0	4.7	0.0	0.4	0.3	1.8	1.8	0.0
Mount Vernon	39	221	16.2	4.8	6.3	0.5	6.8	0.0	3.5	0.0	2.1	0.9	3.8
Olympia	111	505	32.7	10.3	0.4	3.6	1 098.5	116.4	229.4	100.6	201.4	32.5	9.5
Pasco	55	321	26.8	7.3	2.6	0.2	17.4	2.0	3.6	1.5	5.7	3.5	4.0
Puyallup	64	344	24.6	8.0	0.3	0.3	3.7	0.0	0.0	0.0	2.0	1.2	0.0
Redmond	116	879	75.2	23.6	65.0	13.0	4.0	1.8	0.3	0.4	0.0	1.3	0.0
Renton	118	786	54.5	17.7	14.0	10.5	15.3	0.0	0.0	0.0	0.8	11.7	1.5
Richland	45	313	20.9	6.2	4.9	2 386.4	13.0	6.2	0.0	0.6	0.1	3.6	0.0
Sammamish	NA	NA	NA	NA	0.1	0.3	0.1	0.0	0.0	0.1	0.0	0.0	0.0
Seattle	1 266	9 352	756.9	207.1	1 624.0	266.3	1 326.4	809.4	33.6	27.7	41.6	122.3	64.8
Shoreline	NA	NA	NA	NA	0.0	0.0	0.2	0.0	0.0	0.0	0.0	0.0	26.0
Spokane	444	2 938	180.0	54.2	19.0	41.5	95.4	6.6	8.5	0.4	9.5	45.2	18.0
Tacoma	318	2 360	154.4	52.2	108.1	17.5	175.6	4.7	7.0	0.4	16.6	42.9	6.7
Vancouver	224	1 319	84.7	26.0	7.3	29.3	36.6	2.0	5.4	0.7	4.1	11.9	4.6
Walla Walla	49	240	16.5	4.6	3.8	3.2	6.4	0.0	0.9	0.0	0.7	3.5	3.9
Wenatchee	65	291	19.4	5.8	0.0	2.4	9.7	2.1	2.5	0.0	1.2	2.6	7.0
Yakima	153	918	59.3	18.5	4.1	8.4	29.5	0.0	10.8	0.0	4.7	9.3	
WEST VIRGINIA	2 512	14 805	867.4	255.9	184.8	480.1	3 561.9	1 664.8	424.7	72.3	283.1	176.3	104.1
Charleston	141	1 196	64.5	20.1	11.7	18.3	488.2	55.2	92.0	36.6	96.5	52.2	6.1
Huntington	113	808	44.3	14.6	7.2	15.8	57.4	21.2	7.3	0.0	2.8	18.3	15.2
Morgantown	83	590	37.8	11.1	2.2	58.8	81.2	25.4	1.5	14.5	1.9	2.8	16.4
Parkersburg	109	1 365	106.1	24.6	6.8	48.8	15.1	0.0	3.7	0.0	0.0	9.7	5.9
Wheeling	96	755	39.7	13.8	0.7	1.2	46.2	0.0	4.5	2.6	3.9	9.5	5.6
WISCONSIN	8 648	49 101	2 991.3	886.4	1 243.7	763.9	7 543.7	3 725.1	1 099.4	128.8	635.7	438.4	202.6
Appleton	158	1 218	72.0	20.5	35.6	10.8	18.1	0.0	0.6	0.1	0.7	3.8	4.5
Beloit	55	222	11.2	2.9	2.6	0.0	6.8	0.8	0.2	0.2	1.0	4.4	1.0
Brookfield	110	1 153	86.9	29.4	4.8	0.7	0.7	0.5	0.0	0.0	0.0	0.0	1.6
Eau Claire	150	1 026	51.0	15.8	2.5	1.2	11.1	0.9	0.0	0.0	2.2	5.1	11.2
Fond du Lac	98	709	31.2	10.4	1.1	0.3	9.3	0.0	2.5	0.0	0.3	5.2	3.2
Franklin	43	271	14.4	4.3	0.5	0.0	1.3	0.0	0.0	0.0	0.0	1.3	0.0
Green Bay	191	1 332	76.5	24.8	14.5	46.4	31.3	1.3	5.1	1.9	2.3	7.3	7.7
Greenfield	78	537	26.1	9.0	0.0	0.0	2.9	0.0	0.0	0.0	0.0	2.9	0.0
Janesville	107	542	32.7	8.8	33.5	2.8	7.7	0.0	3.4	0.0	1.0	3.0	2.3
Kenosha	159	931	46.9	14.0	14.8	9.2	19.6	1.1	2.9	0.0	0.3	13.2	9.2
La Crosse	123	882	47.4	15.9	63.0	14.7	15.2	0.3	2.4	0.0	3.4	4.0	12.3
Madison	343	2 911	162.8	57.6	27.0	47.2	1 530.8	381.7	215.7	110.0	215.1	77.3	32.2
Manitowoc	55	257	14.1	4.3	0.1	1.8	2.7	0.0	0.0	0.0	0.0	2.4	0.9
Menomonee Falls	70	964	113.6	28.4	5.0	0.3	0.9	0.1	0.0	0.0	0.0	0.6	0.0
Milwaukee	755	5 080	307.4	97.3	93.0	134.0	386.5	136.9	31.6	3.5	28.1	137.0	46.6
New Berlin	61	741	71.0	19.9	2.8	0.3	0.5	0.2	0.0	0.0	0.0	0.3	0.0
Oak Creek	36	200	11.3	3.5	15.5	0.5	6.1	0.0	0.0	0.0	0.0	5.9	0.0
Oshkosh	101	711	31.6	9.4	601.2	12.5	12.2	0.3	4.0	0.4	2.5	3.9	7.0

1. Firms subject to federal tax. 2. Includes program categories not shown separately. State totals include additional categories not allocated by city.

City	City government finances, 2002									
	General revenue							General expenditure		
		Intergovernmental		Taxes					Per capita[1] (dollars)	
					Per capita[1] (dollars)					
	Total (mil dol)	Total (mil dol)	Percent from state government	Total (mil dol)	Total	Property	Sales and gross receipts	Total (mil dol)	Total	Capital outlays
	117	118	119	120	121	122	123	124	125	126
VIRGINIA—Cont'd										
Lynchburg	202.5	80.2	90.0	80.7	1 249	759	478	198.1	3 066	311
Manassas	115.5	38.6	93.9	57.1	1 532	1 162	249	109.7	2 942	218
Newport News	604.1	294.2	79.4	216.9	1 203	807	307	585.7	3 249	373
Norfolk	886.7	419.4	78.4	288.2	1 206	673	430	899.0	3 761	384
Petersburg	NA	NA	NA	NA	NA	NA	NA	NA	NA	NA
Portsmouth	316.9	176.5	88.7	94.1	943	600	285	317.6	3 182	239
Richmond	886.1	378.8	77.6	332.3	1 683	1 157	370	864.8	4 380	372
Roanoke	337.7	157.9	77.5	131.0	1 395	757	498	328.8	3 503	547
Suffolk	181.4	84.3	93.8	77.1	1 103	773	239	185.8	2 656	335
Virginia Beach	1 342.1	649.4	58.0	582.7	1 343	905	328	1 272.8	2 933	144
WASHINGTON	X	X	X	X	X	X	X	X	X	X
Auburn	87.3	19.8	76.5	37.0	838	250	501	69.3	1 569	478
Bellevue	194.1	20.1	38.2	121.5	1 076	236	609	177.2	1 570	388
Bellingham	87.7	11.4	56.7	45.9	651	168	357	73.6	1 044	200
Bothell	39.3	3.8	53.3	23.5	766	201	532	32.0	1 044	237
Bremerton	45.5	8.8	87.2	18.8	519	160	277	49.6	1 367	481
Des Moines	20.7	5.0	65.6	9.5	323	103	191	18.0	614	125
Edmonds	36.0	3.3	67.1	18.9	472	238	213	33.4	835	215
Everett	151.0	19.3	57.2	82.9	854	266	413	155.5	1 601	512
Kennewick	47.0	5.6	81.4	27.0	465	117	318	42.9	741	226
Kent	125.8	28.1	58.6	58.3	714	258	433	132.5	1 621	635
Kirkland	66.5	7.9	54.9	34.0	747	212	495	69.8	1 532	349
Lacey	34.1	3.5	89.1	16.5	509	167	278	31.0	957	193
Longview	37.9	5.3	43.3	18.4	520	180	276	36.6	1 032	108
Lynnwood	51.5	10.6	87.8	25.3	745	211	487	42.7	1 259	329
Marysville	27.2	1.7	67.3	12.5	450	184	235	29.9	1 077	175
Mount Vernon	41.7	13.9	88.8	13.1	482	168	291	40.9	1 502	713
Olympia	75.1	9.4	77.0	33.1	760	196	457	64.7	1 488	242
Pasco	30.5	2.8	60.9	15.1	428	102	291	25.3	714	169
Puyallup	44.7	2.1	83.5	27.7	781	268	486	42.4	1 198	281
Redmond	86.9	8.0	46.6	49.6	1 080	273	685	68.4	1 490	397
Renton	91.8	5.5	70.3	52.0	977	324	572	88.7	1 669	280
Richland	52.1	4.2	60.6	24.7	595	192	365	46.3	1 115	348
Sammamish	28.7	5.1	53.7	20.1	593	394	164	29.9	883	413
Seattle	1 297.5	135.5	69.0	688.5	1 207	444	483	1 299.8	2 279	384
Shoreline	31.8	6.0	72.0	21.2	402	120	221	25.4	482	92
Spokane	238.8	21.1	82.1	94.7	482	197	258	214.3	1 091	184
Tacoma	293.3	24.8	64.8	124.4	629	214	277	255.3	1 292	319
Vancouver	140.4	25.4	50.5	64.1	428	195	201	148.5	991	301
Walla Walla	31.7	6.5	64.8	9.9	332	85	230	30.4	1 018	294
Wenatchee	24.7	4.3	91.7	13.1	463	130	315	22.1	782	129
Yakima	68.5	11.9	45.6	35.2	481	147	315	59.0	805	132
WEST VIRGINIA	X	X	X	X	X	X	X	X	X	X
Charleston	90.1	6.5	28.7	43.1	833	154	91	83.6	1 617	146
Huntington	48.4	8.2	32.4	20.2	405	101	52	47.6	953	10
Morgantown	26.9	3.5	13.4	11.1	407	69	38	26.9	984	184
Parkersburg	NA	NA	NA	NA	NA	NA	NA	NA	NA	NA
Wheeling	27.3	2.6	13.8	13.9	458	113	335	28.8	948	104
WISCONSIN	X	X	X	X	X	X	X	X	X	X
Appleton	84.4	28.3	76.9	29.0	411	380	4	84.1	1 191	264
Beloit	53.2	25.8	89.0	9.7	272	250	8	53.4	1 496	189
Brookfield	48.3	8.1	78.2	26.4	667	588	48	48.8	1 235	191
Eau Claire	65.4	23.9	69.7	22.2	356	306	17	65.6	1 051	207
Fond du Lac	45.7	14.9	83.4	16.2	384	349	11	48.8	1 153	284
Franklin	28.7	4.8	72.6	17.1	541	457	2	40.7	1 289	560
Green Bay	220.4	42.2	84.8	36.7	361	337	2	226.0	2 226	1 306
Greenfield	29.8	6.6	88.9	16.2	451	424	1	27.1	754	112
Janesville	55.5	17.7	75.7	20.6	339	314	10	64.2	1 054	310
Kenosha	97.7	37.2	76.6	39.5	427	401	5	93.0	1 005	116
La Crosse	71.4	27.3	81.9	23.9	466	431	12	86.7	1 693	239
Madison	308.7	112.9	73.7	121.6	565	503	28	270.5	1 257	148
Manitowoc	41.5	12.7	88.9	10.1	297	259	10	52.7	1 541	396
Menomonee Falls	44.2	6.9	100.0	20.0	599	536	0	49.1	1 474	398
Milwaukee	883.8	439.5	72.2	207.8	352	333	0	862.2	1 459	196
New Berlin	38.7	5.9	91.2	18.7	484	451	2	36.7	950	103
Oak Creek	29.5	6.7	94.8	16.4	536	476	13	33.1	1 082	323
Oshkosh	65.7	27.3	86.5	21.6	340	302	11	67.6	1 065	178

1. Based on population estimated as of July 1 of the year shown.

City	Public welfare	Highways	Parking facilities	Education	Health and hospitals	Police protection	Sewerage and sanitation	Parks and recreation	Housing and community development	Interest on debt
					City government finances, 2002 (cont'd)					
					General expenditure					
					Percent of total for—					
	127	128	129	130	131	132	133	134	135	136
VIRGINIA—Cont'd										
Lynchburg	1.6	6.8	0.0	40.6	6.1	5.6	4.7	0.8	2.7	5.7
Manassas	2.7	7.4	0.0	49.5	3.3	8.2	8.0	2.4	0.5	3.2
Newport News	7.1	3.5	0.3	41.1	5.6	5.6	3.2	3.5	5.9	5.3
Norfolk	6.4	4.0	1.6	32.2	3.1	5.1	3.5	4.4	11.3	6.3
Petersburg	NA	NA	NA	NA	NA	NA	NA	NA	NA	NA
Portsmouth	6.9	1.5	0.4	37.9	3.5	5.9	5.5	2.1	5.3	4.3
Richmond	8.1	3.1	0.0	30.9	5.8	6.8	7.7	2.6	10.9	2.7
Roanoke	8.0	3.6	1.3	34.4	0.6	4.6	4.3	1.9	9.8	6.4
Suffolk	6.1	2.4	0.0	45.3	0.7	4.8	5.7	1.5	2.9	4.9
Virginia Beach	2.3	1.8	0.1	62.7	2.9	4.8	4.0	3.5	0.9	3.7
WASHINGTON	X	X	X	X	X	X	X	X	X	X
Auburn	0.0	25.7	0.0	0.0	0.7	13.0	23.6	6.5	0.8	0.8
Bellevue	0.1	18.3	0.0	0.0	4.8	10.6	13.2	13.3	4.2	1.6
Bellingham	0.0	9.5	0.7	0.0	0.9	13.4	9.6	14.4	3.8	3.1
Bothell	0.0	13.2	0.0	0.7	3.3	24.9	11.7	4.2	2.0	2.4
Bremerton	0.0	14.9	0.5	0.0	3.5	13.3	20.5	11.9	1.5	4.1
Des Moines	0.0	21.0	0.0	0.0	0.3	28.0	3.2	17.4	0.9	2.5
Edmonds	0.0	6.1	0.0	0.0	4.7	17.5	4.3	6.7	0.0	4.3
Everett	0.2	15.4	0.2	0.0	2.8	12.8	9.3	14.5	1.3	1.4
Kennewick	0.0	18.2	0.0	0.0	4.7	14.7	8.5	17.1	0.9	2.4
Kent	0.2	16.2	0.0	0.0	1.6	11.1	18.0	7.3	0.5	4.3
Kirkland	0.5	12.9	0.1	0.0	0.0	10.7	19.3	9.7	0.3	2.3
Lacey	0.0	23.3	0.0	0.0	0.4	15.4	19.1	10.0	0.0	1.8
Longview	0.4	9.8	0.1	0.0	1.6	16.6	24.3	10.7	3.7	2.2
Lynnwood	0.0	20.9	0.0	0.0	1.6	16.2	6.0	12.7	1.2	4.3
Marysville	0.0	10.9	0.0	0.0	2.6	11.1	19.2	9.5	0.0	6.8
Mount Vernon	0.0	35.7	0.0	0.0	0.1	9.7	24.8	3.0	0.0	1.6
Olympia	0.0	15.0	0.3	0.0	2.1	11.3	24.3	7.2	1.1	1.8
Pasco	0.0	4.3	0.0	0.0	4.1	17.5	21.3	8.8	1.1	10.2
Puyallup	0.0	11.8	0.0	0.0	3.0	14.7	11.8	4.6	0.8	5.6
Redmond	0.0	25.5	0.0	0.0	3.5	9.3	15.7	7.7	0.9	1.4
Renton	0.0	15.6	0.0	0.0	0.2	11.4	18.9	10.0	1.9	3.9
Richland	0.1	10.6	0.0	0.0	2.1	10.2	11.4	5.8	3.9	5.1
Sammamish	0.1	47.7	0.0	0.0	0.0	10.5	2.4	1.3	2.9	0.1
Seattle	0.3	8.0	0.2	0.0	1.3	12.1	19.9	14.0	3.5	3.1
Shoreline	0.0	11.3	0.0	0.0	0.0	24.8	1.7	9.2	4.0	0.0
Spokane	0.0	8.0	0.3	0.0	0.1	14.7	25.9	9.9	1.4	7.2
Tacoma	0.3	10.3	0.3	0.0	2.8	13.7	26.0	12.0	1.3	5.7
Vancouver	0.0	15.0	3.1	0.7	0.0	11.3	13.2	14.7	3.1	8.9
Walla Walla	0.0	13.1	8.6	0.0	3.8	11.6	15.5	10.7	0.0	8.8
Wenatchee	0.0	21.2	0.0	0.0	0.6	15.4	12.1	11.1	1.8	4.9
Yakima	0.0	9.0	0.3	0.0	2.4	18.1	15.3	8.2	3.5	2.5
WEST VIRGINIA	X	X	X	X	X	X	X	X	X	X
Charleston	1.0	6.0	2.9	0.0	0.3	16.9	14.4	14.4	3.8	10.0
Huntington	0.1	3.6	1.4	0.0	0.2	17.7	16.0	6.0	11.0	5.7
Morgantown	0.0	8.6	9.0	0.0	0.1	14.0	9.8	8.3	0.0	5.0
Parkersburg	NA	NA	NA	NA	NA	NA	NA	NA	NA	NA
Wheeling	0.2	11.5	1.9	0.0	0.0	16.2	17.3	3.2	8.2	0.2
WISCONSIN	X	X	X	X	X	X	X	X	X	X
Appleton	0.0	20.5	2.2	0.0	1.2	15.0	15.4	8.3	5.6	5.9
Beloit	0.0	10.2	7.2	0.0	5.1	16.5	18.1	6.0	2.9	5.4
Brookfield	0.0	19.9	0.0	0.0	4.5	13.6	24.9	6.8	0.0	7.5
Eau Claire	0.0	25.3	0.6	0.0	6.3	15.6	7.9	10.4	2.8	5.0
Fond du Lac	0.0	19.3	0.8	0.0	4.0	19.6	13.7	8.2	2.0	7.4
Franklin	0.0	13.3	0.0	0.0	3.2	29.9	10.5	1.1	0.2	7.5
Green Bay	0.0	9.2	3.3	0.0	0.1	9.2	8.3	49.4	0.6	3.8
Greenfield	0.0	22.0	0.0	0.0	6.3	25.9	10.3	3.8	0.0	1.5
Janesville	3.1	15.5	0.8	0.0	3.2	15.0	20.8	9.0	2.9	4.8
Kenosha	0.0	11.1	0.0	0.0	6.3	18.4	13.0	8.5	1.7	8.7
La Crosse	0.0	15.6	1.0	0.1	0.3	13.4	9.2	11.3	2.1	6.6
Madison	0.0	9.7	2.5	0.0	4.2	16.0	15.2	10.3	5.3	5.5
Manitowoc	0.0	20.1	0.1	0.0	0.5	10.2	18.9	5.7	0.5	6.9
Menomonee Falls	0.0	18.2	0.0	0.0	0.1	16.7	20.4	2.3	0.1	11.0
Milwaukee	0.0	12.1	2.1	0.0	3.1	23.0	12.2	0.7	10.1	4.4
New Berlin	0.0	16.2	0.0	0.0	0.6	22.5	25.0	4.8	0.0	7.0
Oak Creek	0.0	29.9	0.0	0.0	10.3	20.1	11.6	3.2	0.0	1.0
Oshkosh	0.0	19.2	0.3	0.0	2.4	13.8	14.2	8.1	1.7	11.1

City	City government finances, 2002 (cont'd) Debt outstanding — Total (mil dol)	Per capita[1] (dollars)	Percent utility	City government employment, 2002	Climate[2] — Average daily temperature (degrees Fahrenheit) — Mean January	Mean July	Limits January[3]	Limits July[4]	Annual precipitation (inches)	Heating degree days	Cooling degree days
	137	138	139	140	141	142	143	144	145	146	147
VIRGINIA—Cont'd											
Lynchburg	265.9	4 116	7.6	2 982	34.2	75.6	24.7	86.0	40.88	4 340	1 048
Manassas	73.7	1 976	25.5	1 338	33.0	77.2	22.9	88.7	36.13	4 447	1 198
Newport News	745.9	4 138	23.9	8 506	39.1	78.2	30.9	86.4	44.64	3 495	1 422
Norfolk	1 201.3	5 026	27.0	11 502	39.1	78.2	30.9	86.4	44.64	3 495	1 422
Petersburg	NA	NA	NA	1 671	38.6	78.9	27.8	90.3	43.53	3 408	1 533
Portsmouth	229.5	2 300	0.0	5 015	39.1	78.2	30.9	86.4	44.64	3 495	1 422
Richmond	974.8	4 937	38.2	8 723	35.7	78.0	25.7	88.4	43.16	3 963	1 348
Roanoke	429.0	4 570	5.7	4 438	34.5	75.6	25.0	86.4	41.13	4 360	1 052
Suffolk	259.4	3 708	21.1	2 952	39.1	78.2	30.9	86.4	44.64	3 495	1 422
Virginia Beach	961.3	2 215	10.4	18 108	39.1	78.2	30.9	86.4	44.64	3 495	1 422
WASHINGTON	X	X	X	X	X	X	X	X	X	X	X
Auburn	26.9	610	53.3	431	39.7	64.7	33.1	78.0	39.39	4 996	139
Bellevue	79.8	707	0.5	1 607	40.1	65.2	35.2	75.2	37.19	4 908	190
Bellingham	41.6	590	27.4	829	37.6	62.2	31.8	70.9	36.17	5 609	51
Bothell	14.2	462	2.7	268	NA	NA	NA	NA	NA	NA	NA
Bremerton	50.7	1 396	7.3	367	39.1	64.1	33.7	75.0	51.65	5 119	134
Des Moines	7.8	267	0.0	147	NA	NA	NA	NA	NA	NA	NA
Edmonds	30.7	766	0.0	22	40.1	65.2	35.2	75.2	37.19	4 908	190
Everett	111.4	1 147	38.4	1 102	39.1	62.9	33.3	72.2	36.51	5 311	80
Kennewick	39.8	688	14.7	374	33.1	74.7	26.1	90.3	7.49	4 895	830
Kent	110.4	1 351	2.0	856	39.7	64.7	33.1	78.0	39.39	4 996	139
Kirkland	34.3	752	0.0	405	40.1	65.2	35.2	75.2	37.19	4 908	190
Lacey	16.1	497	0.0	221	NA	NA	NA	NA	NA	NA	NA
Longview	27.4	773	37.2	376	39.0	63.8	32.7	76.4	46.54	5 094	132
Lynnwood	32.3	951	0.0	349	40.1	65.2	35.2	75.2	37.19	4 908	190
Marysville	31.3	1 129	0.0	213	NA	NA	NA	NA	NA	NA	NA
Mount Vernon	19.7	726	0.0	224	NA	NA	NA	NA	NA	NA	NA
Olympia	21.6	497	35.8	599	38.0	62.9	31.6	76.5	50.59	5 655	101
Pasco	54.9	1 549	17.8	173	NA	NA	NA	NA	NA	NA	NA
Puyallup	58.4	1 649	16.1	323	NA	NA	NA	NA	NA	NA	NA
Redmond	19.0	413	17.2	565	40.1	65.2	35.2	75.2	37.19	4 908	190
Renton	77.3	1 453	22.0	625	40.1	65.2	35.2	75.2	37.19	4 908	190
Richland	122.7	2 956	68.4	487	33.4	74.4	25.9	89.4	6.99	4 882	822
Sammamish	9.5	280	0.0	51	NA	NA	NA	NA	NA	NA	NA
Seattle	3 109.2	5 451	66.8	11 129	40.1	65.2	35.2	75.2	37.19	4 908	190
Shoreline	1.3	25	0.0	117	NA	NA	NA	NA	NA	NA	NA
Spokane	231.9	1 181	0.0	2 232	27.1	68.8	20.8	83.1	16.49	6 842	398
Tacoma	896.8	4 539	62.4	3 491	40.1	65.2	35.2	75.2	37.19	4 908	190
Vancouver	240.2	1 603	27.5	1 076	38.1	64.6	31.2	77.1	41.30	5 196	183
Walla Walla	74.8	2 510	47.4	264	34.1	75.1	28.4	89.4	19.49	4 958	889
Wenatchee	29.6	1 046	8.5	226	NA	NA	NA	NA	NA	NA	NA
Yakima	38.0	518	8.9	652	29.7	69.9	21.8	86.7	7.97	5 967	458
WEST VIRGINIA	X	X	X	X	X	X	X	X	X	X	X
Charleston	117.6	2 274	0.0	782	32.1	75.1	23.0	85.7	42.53	4 646	1 031
Huntington	36.4	730	0.0	454	32.0	74.7	23.2	84.3	41.49	4 665	1 005
Morgantown	24.1	880	13.2	353	29.0	72.9	20.8	83.2	41.21	5 363	785
Parkersburg	0.0	0	0.0	367	29.9	74.4	21.7	84.2	41.51	5 063	953
Wheeling	18.4	605	95.9	835	27.7	73.3	17.6	85.4	40.81	5 598	788
WISCONSIN	X	X	X	X	X	X	X	X	X	X	X
Appleton	150.0	2 124	45.8	733	15.5	71.9	7.2	81.9	30.75	7 693	539
Beloit	55.1	1 545	0.7	493	17.6	72.7	8.8	83.7	33.05	7 161	636
Brookfield	107.4	2 719	14.1	349	19.9	73.6	12.3	84.3	31.11	6 804	725
Eau Claire	65.3	1 047	15.8	581	10.7	71.5	0.8	83.2	31.61	8 330	507
Fond du Lac	64.5	1 525	22.6	374	16.1	72.0	7.9	82.0	29.39	7 541	562
Franklin	59.2	1 874	4.9	202	NA	NA	NA	NA	NA	NA	NA
Green Bay	164.9	1 624	15.2	1 051	14.3	69.7	5.8	80.5	28.83	8 089	381
Greenfield	7.2	199	0.0	238	18.9	70.9	11.6	79.9	32.93	7 324	479
Janesville	62.2	1 022	13.6	483	17.6	72.7	8.8	83.7	33.05	7 161	636
Kenosha	178.9	1 934	17.0	850	20.0	69.7	11.7	78.7	33.21	7 195	410
La Crosse	91.6	1 789	4.9	665	14.4	73.5	5.3	84.5	30.55	7 491	692
Madison	225.2	1 046	11.6	2 577	16.0	71.0	7.2	82.4	30.88	7 673	485
Manitowoc	76.6	2 239	32.3	439	17.9	69.8	9.7	80.1	29.11	7 597	374
Menomonee Falls	114.1	3 426	15.3	262	18.9	70.9	11.6	79.9	32.93	7 324	479
Milwaukee	738.8	1 250	0.0	7 880	19.9	73.6	12.3	84.3	31.11	6 804	725
New Berlin	52.5	1 359	11.4	273	19.8	73.6	12.3	83.0	32.33	6 795	708
Oak Creek	26.8	877	66.6	256	NA	NA	NA	NA	NA	NA	NA
Oshkosh	153.1	2 413	34.5	642	14.8	71.8	5.4	82.5	31.15	7 852	522

1. Based on the population estimated as of July 1 of the year shown. 2. Represents normal values based on the 30-year period, 1961–1990. 3. Average daily minimum. 4. Average daily maximum.

Table D. Cities — **Land Area and Population**

STATE Place code	City	Land area,[1] 2000 (sq km)	Population, 2003			Population characteristics, 2000 Percent							
						Race (alone or in combination)							
			Total persons	Rank	Per square kilometer	White	Black	Am. Indian, Alaska Native	Asian and Pacific Islander	Other race	Hispanic or Latino[2]	Non-Hispanic White
		1	2	3	4	5	6	7	8	9	10	11
	WISCONSIN—Cont'd											
55 66000	Racine	40.2	80 266	338	1 996.7	71.1	21.6	0.9	0.9	8.2	14.0	63.5
55 72975	Sheboygan	36.0	49 263	642	1 368.4	88.8	1.1	0.9	7.3	3.5	6.0	85.0
55 78650	Superior	95.7	27 206	1 156	284.3	95.8	1.1	3.2	1.2	0.5	0.8	93.8
55 84250	Waukesha	56.0	66 840	429	1 193.6	92.7	1.7	0.8	2.6	4.0	8.6	86.7
55 84475	Wausau	42.7	37 430	860	876.6	86.8	0.8	1.1	12.2	0.5	1.0	85.4
55 84675	Wauwatosa	34.3	46 260	699	1 348.7	95.0	2.5	0.5	2.4	0.8	1.7	92.9
55 85300	West Allis	29.4	60 192	494	2 047.3	95.3	1.8	1.2	1.7	1.6	3.5	92.1
55 85350	West Bend	32.9	28 932	1 095	879.4	98.0	0.5	0.8	0.7	0.8	1.8	96.2
56 00000	**WYOMING**	251 488.9	501 242	X	2.0	93.7	1.0	3.0	0.9	3.2	6.4	88.9
56 13150	Casper	62.0	50 632	625	816.6	95.5	1.2	1.6	0.8	2.6	5.4	91.3
56 13900	Cheyenne	54.7	54 374	580	994.0	90.4	3.4	1.6	1.9	5.5	12.5	81.4
56 45050	Laramie	28.8	26 956	1 174	936.0	92.9	1.5	1.7	2.5	3.7	7.9	86.8

1. Dry land or land partially or temporarily covered by water.   2. Hispanic or Latino persons may be of any race.

City	Population characteristics, 2000 (cont'd)										Population			
	Age of population (percent)											Census counts		Percent change	
	Under 5 years	5 to 17 years	18 to 24 years	25 to 34 years	35 to 44 years	45 to 54 years	55 to 64 years	65 to 74 years	75 years and over	Percent female	1990	2000	1990–2000	2000–2003
	12	13	14	15	16	17	18	19	20	21	22	23	24	25
WISCONSIN—Cont'd														
Racine	8.0	20.7	9.9	14.3	15.7	12.0	7.2	6.0	6.3	51.3	84 298	81 855	-2.9	-1.9
Sheboygan	7.0	18.6	9.2	14.6	15.4	11.8	7.7	6.9	8.9	51.0	49 587	50 792	2.4	-3.0
Superior	6.0	16.7	12.9	13.1	14.8	13.7	7.9	6.4	8.6	52.0	27 134	27 368	0.9	-0.6
Waukesha	7.4	17.3	10.8	17.2	16.4	13.0	7.2	5.0	5.6	51.1	56 894	64 825	13.9	3.1
Wausau	6.2	19.2	9.6	13.0	14.5	12.5	7.9	7.3	9.8	52.0	37 060	38 426	3.7	-2.6
Wauwatosa	6.5	16.8	5.5	14.5	16.7	14.2	7.6	7.4	10.8	53.7	49 366	47 271	-4.2	-2.1
West Allis	5.8	15.7	8.4	15.3	16.9	12.9	7.7	7.5	9.8	51.8	63 221	61 254	-3.1	-1.7
West Bend	7.2	18.3	8.6	15.4	15.7	12.6	7.7	6.4	8.0	51.8	24 470	28 152	15.0	2.8
WYOMING	6.3	19.8	10.1	12.1	16.0	15.0	9.0	6.3	5.3	49.7	453 589	493 782	8.9	1.5
Casper......................	6.6	19.3	10.5	12.3	15.4	14.1	8.2	7.3	6.3	51.3	46 765	49 644	6.2	2.0
Cheyenne..................	6.5	18.5	8.8	13.9	15.8	14.0	8.8	7.0	6.8	51.2	50 008	53 011	6.0	2.6
Laramie	5.1	12.4	31.8	15.0	10.9	11.1	5.7	4.0	4.1	48.3	26 687	27 204	1.9	-0.9

Table D. Cities — **Group Quarters, Crime, and Education**

City	Households, 2000					Persons in group quarters, 2000				Serious crimes known to police,[2] 2002				Education, 2000			
				Percent			Institutional			Total		Rate[2]		School enrollment[4]		Attainment[5] (percent)	
	Number	Percent change, 1990–2000	Persons per household	Female family householder[1]	One-person	Total	Total	Persons in nursing homes	Non-institutional	Number	Rate[3]	Violent	Property	Public	Private	High school graduate or less	Bachelor's degree or more
	26	27	28	29	30	31	32	33	34	35	36	37	38	39	40	41	42
WISCONSIN—Cont'd																	
Racine	31 449	-1.0	2.54	17.9	29.4	1 872	1 541	463	331	4 758	5 730	489	5 241	18 919	4 102	55.3	15.6
Sheboygan	20 779	5.5	2.39	9.4	32.2	1 207	937	724	270	2 460	4 774	173	4 602	10 285	2 503	58.7	15.9
Superior	11 609	5.5	2.26	12.3	34.2	1 125	419	298	706	1 803	6 494	259	6 235	6 478	837	48.7	19.2
Waukesha	25 663	20.9	2.43	9.8	29.0	2 445	1 213	510	1 232	1 609	2 447	84	2 363	12 635	4 463	40.3	30.6
Wausau	15 678	6.5	2.37	9.5	33.6	1 290	847	598	443	1 532	3 930	228	3 702	8 297	1 349	51.6	21.5
Wauwatosa	20 388	2.7	2.27	7.9	33.9	983	833	495	150	2 386	4 975	181	4 794	8 022	3 971	26.1	47.6
West Allis	27 604	3.0	2.19	10.6	37.3	922	596	529	326	2 689	4 327	249	4 078	10 820	3 172	53.4	16.4
West Bend	11 375	31.0	2.44	9.4	27.5	405	324	216	81	698	2 444	49	2 395	5 413	1 625	47.6	22.0
WYOMING	193 608	14.7	2.48	8.7	26.3	14 083	7 861	2 869	6 222	17 858	3 581	274	3 307	126 439	9 700	43.1	21.9
Casper	20 343	9.9	2.38	11.1	29.1	1 226	554	470	672	2 725	5 435	295	5 140	12 931	772	40.1	22.1
Cheyenne	22 324	10.3	2.33	10.6	31.3	991	651	472	340	2 476	4 625	202	4 423	11 881	1 348	37.5	24.5
Laramie	11 336	9.0	2.19	8.0	33.2	2 362	133	101	2 229	1 018	3 705	531	3 174	12 192	1 207	26.5	46.7

1. No spouse present.　2. Data for serious crimes have not been adjusted for underreporting. This may affect comparability between geographic areas and over time.　3. Per 100,000 population estimated by the FBI.　4. All persons 3 years old and over enrolled in nursery school through college.　5. Persons 25 years old and over.

City	Money income, 1999							Housing units, 2000					
	Households				Percent below poverty					Vacant units			
	Median income				Persons		Families						
	Per capita income[1] (dollars)	Dollars	Percent change, 1989–1999 (constant 1999 dollars)	Percent with income of $100,000 or more	Total	Percent change in rate, 1989–1999	Total	Total	Percent change, 1990–2000	Vacant units for sale or rent[2]	For seasonal use (percent)	Home owner vacancy rate	Renter vacancy rate
	43	44	45	46	47	48	49	50	51	52	53	54	55
WISCONSIN—Cont'd													
Racine	17 705	37 164	4.2	5.2	13.9	-12.6	10.8	33 414	0.8	1 965	0.2	1.0	7.2
Sheboygan	19 270	40 066	7.9	4.4	8.3	-10.8	6.2	21 762	5.7	983	0.4	1.2	5.1
Superior	17 253	31 921	13.7	3.9	13.4	-21.6	9.6	12 196	4.4	587	0.3	0.6	6.2
Waukesha	23 242	50 084	3.0	10.6	5.4	-11.5	3.0	26 856	21.7	1 193	0.2	0.7	6.3
Wausau	20 227	36 831	7.5	7.9	11.4	-2.6	7.2	16 668	8.8	990	0.4	1.6	7.7
Wauwatosa	28 834	54 519	1.3	15.3	3.8	15.2	2.3	20 917	3.1	529	0.2	0.5	3.5
West Allis	20 914	39 394	-1.0	5.0	6.5	22.6	4.6	28 708	4.4	1 104	0.1	1.1	4.5
West Bend	22 116	48 315	4.7	9.0	5.0	13.6	3.4	11 926	34.2	551	0.3	2.0	6.1
WYOMING	19 134	37 892	4.1	6.7	11.4	-4.2	8.0	223 854	10.1	30 246	5.5	2.1	9.7
Casper...........................	19 409	36 567	-1.7	6.4	11.4	0.0	8.5	21 872	0.8	1 529	0.5	1.5	8.1
Cheyenne........................	19 809	38 856	2.9	5.8	8.8	-14.6	6.3	23 782	8.8	1 458	0.4	1.3	7.9
Laramie	16 036	27 319	3.5	4.7	22.6	7.6	11.1	11 994	8.3	658	0.5	1.9	4.9

1. Based on population enumerated as of April 1, 2000. 2. Includes units rented or sold but not occupied.

Table D. Cities — Housing, Labor Force, Employment, and Disability

City	Housing units, 2000 (cont'd)					Civilian labor force, 2003				Civilian employment,[2] 2000			Disability, 2000
	Occupied units							Unemployment			Percent		
	Total	Percent owner occupied	Percent renter occupied	Average size owner occupied	Average size renter occupied	Total	Percent change, 2002–2003	Total	Rate[1]	Total	Management, professional, and related occupations	Production, transportation, and material moving occupations	Employment disabled persons[3] (percent)
	56	57	58	59	60	61	62	63	64	65	66	67	68
WISCONSIN—Cont'd													
Racine	31 449	60.3	39.7	2.61	2.44	38 644	2.2	5 017	13.0	35 975	25.2	25.9	12.4
Sheboygan	20 779	61.1	38.9	2.55	2.13	28 068	1.5	1 812	6.5	25 840	22.6	34.0	10.6
Superior	11 609	61.7	38.3	2.47	1.93	14 660	1.7	866	5.9	13 152	25.8	15.1	11.3
Waukesha	25 663	56.5	43.5	2.71	2.06	40 400	0.8	2 531	6.3	35 802	36.0	15.3	8.8
Wausau	15 678	61.7	38.3	2.54	2.10	21 891	2.4	1 321	6.0	18 489	30.6	19.3	10.1
Wauwatosa	20 388	67.8	32.2	2.55	1.68	23 570	0.4	976	4.1	24 593	50.5	8.0	6.5
West Allis	27 604	58.1	41.9	2.47	1.80	32 138	1.0	2 017	6.3	31 855	26.9	18.8	9.3
West Bend	11 375	62.2	37.8	2.65	2.08	16 079	1.5	1 328	8.3	14 732	29.4	23.5	8.1
WYOMING	193 608	70.0	30.0	2.58	2.25	278 367	3.1	12 204	4.4	241 055	30.0	12.8	9.8
Casper	20 343	66.9	33.1	2.50	2.13	27 907	4.0	1 246	4.5	25 003	29.7	10.7	11.2
Cheyenne	22 324	66.0	34.0	2.47	2.06	30 991	4.0	1 260	4.1	24 541	33.0	12.4	9.4
Laramie	11 336	47.5	52.5	2.41	1.99	16 960	3.9	319	1.9	14 616	40.5	8.4	5.6

1. Percent of civilian labor force.   2. Persons 16 years old and over.   3. Persons 16 to 64 years old.

City	Value of residential construction authorized by building permits, 2003			Wholesale trade, 1997				Retail trade,[1] 1997			
	New construction ($1,000)	Number of housing units	Percent single family	Number of establish-ments	Number of employees	Sales (mil dol)	Annual payroll (mil dol)	Number of establish-ments	Number of employees	Sales (mil dol)	Annual payroll (mil dol)
	69	70	71	72	73	74	75	76	77	78	79
WISCONSIN—Cont'd											
Racine..........................	7 214	72	44.4	101	1 974	2 300.4	67.7	362	5 297	710.0	70.1
Sheboygan....................	7 765	52	92.3	57	1 173	712.8	38.1	210	3 565	523.9	54.7
Superior........................	3 772	43	76.7	48	D	D	D	128	1 884	309.2	28.6
Waukesha.....................	51 152	337	95.3	203	2 738	3 554.5	114.7	242	4 556	970.8	82.6
Wausau........................	24 189	232	48.3	71	873	306.1	27.8	251	5 060	745.9	77.5
Wauwatosa...................	597	4	100.0	140	2 622	1 773.5	89.9	289	6 903	942.9	121.4
West Allis.....................	1 114	14	42.9	128	1 797	578.4	66.2	311	5 485	1 013.5	93.2
West Bend....................	25 622	205	60.0	37	339	101.5	10.6	149	2 341	661.9	34.3
WYOMING	389 272	2 814	80.5	800	5 761	2 547.1	161.9	2 939	26 934	4 530.5	426.7
Casper..........................	24 762	139	100.0	122	921	687.1	25.6	346	3 702	595.2	59.6
Cheyenne......................	61 970	592	73.5	56	457	178.2	13.4	308	4 496	761.4	71.9
Laramie........................	16 956	197	60.4	19	101	81.5	2.3	158	1 607	332.6	26.9

1. Establishments with payroll.

Table D. Cities — Real Estate, Professional Services, and Manufacturing

City	Real estate and rental and leasing, 1997				Professional, scientific, and technical services,[1] 1997				Manufacturing, 1997			
	Number of establishments	Number of employees	Receipts (mil dol)	Annual payroll (mil dol)	Number of establishments	Number of employees	Receipts (mil dol)	Annual payroll (mil dol)	Number of establishments	Number of employees	Receipts (mil dol)	Annual payroll (mil dol)
	80	81	82	83	84	85	86	87	88	89	90	91
WISCONSIN—Cont'd												
Racine	68	388	31.0	6.8	139	898	59.3	24.8	219	9 065	1 845.0	322.3
Sheboygan	47	212	24.0	3.4	83	786	57.8	24.6	99	7 887	1 415.6	260.6
Superior	34	113	8.5	1.5	45	300	19.7	7.4	45	D	D	D
Waukesha	83	620	72.7	12.5	186	1 971	199.1	75.7	195	9 902	2 578.4	394.2
Wausau	33	174	14.2	2.9	103	727	64.5	27.9	83	8 190	1 192.1	228.8
Wauwatosa	76	510	65.9	11.6	281	1 880	196.1	70.9	81	7 766	1 388.8	342.8
West Allis	66	1 011	113.6	21.4	135	843	73.8	29.5	145	7 537	864.7	226.4
West Bend	24	101	14.5	1.4	59	321	22.8	9.7	65	4 972	586.5	150.9
WYOMING	717	2 463	220.8	39.5	1 264	5 274	388.8	146.9	503	8 448	2 955.1	256.4
Casper	91	329	29.3	5.6	182	798	66.6	23.9	NA	NA	NA	NA
Cheyenne	77	300	26.1	5.0	186	807	61.9	23.7	35	D	D	D
Laramie	44	125	9.0	1.4	98	527	39.2	16.8	NA	NA	NA	NA

1. Firms subject to federal tax.

City	Accommodation and foodservices, 1997				Arts, entertainment, and recreation,[1] 1997				Health care and social assistance,[1] 1997			
	Number of establishments	Number of employees	Sales (mil dol)	Annual payroll (mil dol)	Number of establishments	Number of employees	Receipts (mil dol)	Annual payroll (mil dol)	Number of establishments	Number of employees	Receipts (mil dol)	Annual payroll (mil dol)
	92	93	94	95	96	97	98	99	100	101	102	103
WISCONSIN—Cont'd												
Racine	166	2 653	78.4	21.8	14	150	6.1	1.4	123	1 629	150.1	69.4
Sheboygan	136	1 809	49.3	13.3	9	99	2.4	0.6	117	1 904	110.6	62.9
Superior	111	1 447	37.6	10.5	10	90	5.1	0.9	47	583	29.3	14.0
Waukesha	127	2 688	79.9	23.3	21	236	7.8	2.4	185	2 249	134.2	73.3
Wausau	101	1 496	39.7	11.5	14	289	6.4	1.5	118	1 795	147.9	85.2
Wauwatosa	114	2 559	82.0	23.1	12	184	5.6	1.6	436	4 766	378.0	216.5
West Allis	159	D	D	D	15	284	16.3	2.9	170	2 274	139.8	74.1
West Bend	65	1 285	32.0	8.8	7	31	1.5	0.3	68	516	24.6	10.3
WYOMING	1 751	24 950	808.9	219.0	262	2 108	93.3	23.3	1 006	7 875	493.6	210.3
Casper	138	2 644	69.9	19.7	23	123	7.3	1.6	165	0	0.0	0.0
Cheyenne	156	3 423	90.4	26.9	18	0	0.0	0.0	142	1 524	103.7	50.3
Laramie	92	1 866	42.5	12.0	14	0	0.0	0.0	70	0	0.0	0.0

1. Firms subject to federal tax.

Table D. Cities — Other Services and Federal Funds

City	Other services,[1] 1997				Selected federal funds, 2002–2003 (mil dol)								
					Procurement contracts		Grants						
	Number of establishments	Number of employees	Receipts (mil dol)	Annual payroll (mil dol)	Defense	Other	Total[2]	Medicaid and other health related	Nutrition and family welfare	Energy and environment	Education	Housing and community development	Direct payments for individuals for educational assistance
	104	105	106	107	108	109	110	111	112	113	114	115	116
WISCONSIN—Cont'd													
Racine	141	979	52.7	18.5	13.7	0.3	19.3	0.0	4.0	1.8	2.0	10.7	0.3
Sheboygan	97	685	41.0	10.5	0.7	7.6	6.0	0.2	1.0	0.0	0.0	4.8	0.0
Superior	61	357	20.9	5.5	1.1	0.8	15.0	0.0	3.7	1.2	1.3	6.8	2.8
Waukesha	126	774	41.2	13.3	11.8	2.1	14.0	0.3	2.6	3.0	0.7	7.1	1.7
Wausau	84	477	19.9	5.9	0.2	2.3	7.9	0.5	1.4	0.0	1.1	4.5	2.5
Wauwatosa	89	822	43.9	14.1	0.0	0.0	4.6	0.9	0.0	0.0	0.0	3.3	0.0
West Allis	164	1 167	77.2	25.1	0.0	0.0	6.5	0.0	0.0	0.0	0.0	6.5	0.0
West Bend	66	418	23.1	6.6	0.9	0.0	2.7	0.0	1.0	0.0	0.0	1.6	0.0
WYOMING	980	4 866	422.8	94.8	71.8	274.2	1 616.2	279.0	119.8	30.7	118.8	34.4	27.4
Casper	117	627	37.1	11.2	0.8	11.9	17.3	2.8	0.0	0.3	0.9	10.6	2.8
Cheyenne	103	1 046	159.5	22.7	3.9	17.2	243.1	19.2	22.4	23.3	46.8	5.4	5.9
Laramie	56	338	15.5	4.9	1.1	4.0	44.6	9.4	1.6	5.8	6.5	0.6	11.3

1. Firms subject to federal tax.   2. Includes program categories not shown separately. State totals include additional categories not allocated by city.

City	City government finances, 2002									
	General revenue							General expenditure		
		Intergovernmental		Taxes					Per capita[1] (dollars)	
					Per capita[1] (dollars)					
	Total (mil dol)	Total (mil dol)	Percent from state government	Total (mil dol)	Total	Property	Sales and gross receipts	Total (mil dol)	Total	Capital outlays
	117	118	119	120	121	122	123	124	125	126
WISCONSIN—Cont'd										
Racine..................................	114.9	54.1	78.4	35.0	434	415	2	110.0	1 363	226
Sheboygan...........................	56.7	23.2	90.3	19.9	402	365	13	57.1	1 156	184
Superior...............................	40.6	16.7	85.0	10.9	399	333	15	36.4	1 338	126
Waukesha............................	63.1	15.1	90.6	32.0	484	446	9	71.5	1 080	274
Wausau	45.6	16.8	81.0	17.1	454	423	14	44.8	1 186	259
Wauwatosa	53.8	14.4	58.4	27.5	588	546	16	57.2	1 224	202
West Allis	70.5	24.3	73.3	28.6	471	442	1	65.8	1 084	85
West Bend	29.7	8.0	83.5	14.2	496	461	5	35.5	1 238	413
WYOMING	X	X	X	X	X	X	X	X	X	X
Casper..................................	58.9	34.0	67.0	5.2	104	49	40	70.1	1 400	397
Cheyenne.............................	62.4	34.0	68.5	7.3	137	56	56	58.8	1 096	351
Laramie	26.4	16.5	70.6	2.2	81	45	22	26.0	965	163

1. Based on population estimated as of July 1 of the year shown.

Table D. Cities — City Government Finances (cont'd)

City	City government finances, 2002 (cont'd)									
	General expenditure									
	Percent of total for—									
	Public welfare	Highways	Parking facilities	Education	Health and hospitals	Police protection	Sewerage and sanitation	Parks and recreation	Housing and community development	Interest on debt
	127	128	129	130	131	132	133	134	135	136
WISCONSIN—Cont'd										
Racine	0.0	16.0	1.0	0.0	3.4	22.2	12.4	9.8	2.6	5.5
Sheboygan	0.0	19.3	0.6	0.0	0.1	15.8	15.3	7.4	5.3	6.0
Superior	0.0	15.4	0.0	0.0	0.2	15.3	13.3	8.0	6.5	12.6
Waukesha	0.0	10.9	0.7	0.0	1.4	16.5	21.2	6.2	0.3	6.0
Wausau	0.0	22.5	1.5	0.0	3.5	12.8	10.9	5.3	10.1	6.5
Wauwatosa	0.0	20.8	0.0	0.0	7.0	20.0	14.3	1.4	2.1	3.5
West Allis	3.0	15.0	0.1	0.0	5.7	23.1	13.0	0.7	5.3	3.5
West Bend	0.0	22.0	0.2	0.0	1.3	16.0	13.3	9.4	0.7	9.1
WYOMING	X	X	X	X	X	X	X	X	X	X
Casper	2.5	17.3	0.1	0.0	1.7	13.6	15.1	14.3	0.8	0.3
Cheyenne	3.1	28.2	0.4	0.0	3.1	12.2	12.3	8.6	1.2	2.3
Laramie	0.0	9.0	0.0	0.0	2.2	18.0	19.2	7.0	0.0	5.9

City	City government finances, 2002 (cont'd)			City government employment, 2002	Climate[2]						
	Debt outstanding				Average daily temperature (degrees Fahrenheit)						
					Mean		Limits				
	Total (mil dol)	Per capita[1] (dollars)	Percent utility		January	July	January[3]	July[4]	Annual precipitation (inches)	Heating degree days	Cooling degree days
	137	138	139	140	141	142	143	144	145	146	147
WISCONSIN—Cont'd											
Racine	111.1	1 376	29.1	1 001	19.4	71.0	11.2	79.7	34.37	7 167	509
Sheboygan	93.6	1 892	0.0	554	20.3	70.9	12.8	80.4	31.19	7 087	472
Superior	64.3	2 364	11.0	290	10.0	65.9	0.1	77.5	28.91	9 483	206
Waukesha	98.6	1 490	7.7	576	18.6	72.3	10.8	82.8	32.55	7 117	600
Wausau	49.0	1 298	15.0	332	12.0	70.0	2.8	80.8	32.82	8 427	402
Wauwatosa	63.3	1 355	11.8	461	19.9	73.6	12.3	84.3	31.11	6 804	725
West Allis	56.1	925	3.6	630	19.8	73.6	12.3	83.0	32.33	6 795	708
West Bend	73.5	2 564	12.5	281	NA	NA	NA	NA	NA	NA	NA
WYOMING	X	X	X	X	X	X	X	X	X	X	X
Casper	2.9	57	9.9	478	22.4	70.8	12.0	87.6	12.52	7 682	445
Cheyenne	86.7	1 616	75.2	603	26.5	68.4	15.2	82.2	14.40	7 326	285
Laramie	33.4	1 242	23.1	248	20.0	64.1	8.0	80.4	10.88	9 008	74

1. Based on the population estimated as of July 1 of the year shown.   2. Represents normal values based on the 30-year period, 1961–1990.   3. Average daily minimum.   4. Average daily maximum.

PART E:

Congressional Districts of the 109th Congress

(For explanation of symbols, see page xii)

TABLE E Highlights and Rankings

Every 10 years, the Census Bureau conducts a count to reapportion the seats in the U.S. House of Representatives. The 435 seats in the House of Representatives are divided among the 50 states. (The District of Columbia has no representative in Congress, though it has a nonvoting delegate.) The seats are reapportioned using the population measured on April 1 of the census year to account for population changes among the states over the previous decade. The average congressional district in 2000 held about 645,000 people, up from about 572,000 in 1990.

As the state with the largest population, California has the most representatives with 53. Texas (32) and New York (29) are second and third, respectively. There are six states with just one representative. These states' representatives are considered 'At Large' because they represent the entire state rather than a specific congressional district within the state.

As the number of representatives is limited to 435, states with larger population growth add seats, while states with low, or no, growth lose seats. After the 2000 census, eight states gained seats. Arizona, Florida, Georgia, and Texas all gained two seats. Ten states lost one or more seats, with New York and Pennsylvania each losing two seats. These reapportioned seats reflect the population changes that are occurring in the United States. The population growth in states in the South and West has resulted in an increasing number of representatives.

The South and West regions each experienced a net gain of five seats, while the Northeast and the Midwest regions both lost five seats.

While most of the congressional districts have about the same population size, they vary widely in other demographic characteristics. Alaska's At Large seat represents the entire state, more than 1.4 million square kilometers, while New York's 15th district is just 27 square kilometers in size. In Colorado's 6th district, 95.6 percent of the residents are high school graduates, compared with just 46.3 percent in California's 34th district. California's 3rd district has 6.3 percent of its residents holding bachelor's degrees, and in New York's 14th district, 56.9 percent of residents are college graduates.

In California's 14th district, which includes part of the Bay Area and Silicon Valley, 38.4 percent of households have an annual income exceeding $100,000. Not surprising, this district also has the highest median value for owner-occupied homes, at $626,500. The 28th district of Texas has the lowest median home value at $49,800. Virginia's 11th district has a median household income of $80,397 compared with $19,311 in New York's 16th district. This New York district is one of the poorest congressional districts in the nation. It has the highest unemployment rate (20.3 percent), lowest median household income ($19,311), highest proportion of female-headed family households (38.2 percent) and highest rate of families living in poverty (39.9 percent).

Congressional Districts of the 109th Congress of the United States
Selected Rankings

Population, 2000			Total land area, 2000			Population density, 2000		
Population rank	State/congressional district	Population [col 2]	Land area rank	State/congressional district	Land area (square kilometers) [col 1]	Density rank	State/congressional district	Population density (per square kilometer) [col 3]
1	MT At Large	902 195	1	AK At Large	1 481 347	1	NY District 15	24 562.6
2	DE At Large	783 600	2	MT At Large	376 979	2	NY District 16	21 366.3
3	SD At Large	754 844	3	NV District 2	272 153	3	NY District 11	20 967.0
4	UT District 2	744 390	4	WY At Large	251 489	4	NY District 14	20 100.3
4	UT District 3	744 390	5	SD At Large	196 540	5	NY District 8	16 981.6
6	UT District 1	744 389	6	NM District 2	179 986	6	NY District 10	14 131.3
7	MS District 4	711 219	7	OR District 2	179 982	7	NY District 12	13 488.1
8	MS District 2	711 164	8	ND At Large	178 647	8	NY District 7	9 581.9
9	MS District 1	711 160	9	NE District 3	167 083	9	CA District 8	6 974.2
10	MS District 3	711 115	10	AZ District 1	151 795	10	NY District 9	6 823.7
11	OK District 1	690 131	11	KS District 1	148 596	11	IL District 4	6 448.6
11	OK District 3	690 131	12	TX District 23	143 524	12	NY District 6	6 388.7
11	OK District 4	690 131	13	CO District 3	139 765	13	CA District 31	6 267.3
11	OK District 5	690 131	14	NM District 3	122 108	14	MA District 8	6 019.6
15	OK District 2	690 130	15	UT District 2	118 166	15	CA District 33	5 125.2
16	OR District 1	684 280	16	ID District 2	111 946	16	CA District 47	4 511.2
16	OR District 2	684 280	17	ID District 1	102 369	17	IL District 7	4 478.8
16	OR District 4	684 280	18	TX District 13	102 206	18	CA District	4 453.0
16	OR District 5	684 280	19	OK District 3	88 289	19	IL District 5	4 428.6
20	OR District 3	684 279	20	TX District 17	86 931	20	NJ District 13	4 404.7
21	CT District 1	681 113	21	MN District 7	82 353	21	PA District 1	4 243.4
21	CT District 2	681 113	22	CO District 4	80 025	22	PA District 2	4 242.6
21	CT District 3	681 113	23	MN District 8	71 439	23	CA District 34	4 232.8
21	CT District 4	681 113	24	ME District 2	70 563	24	NY District 13	3 903.4
21	CT District 5	681 113	25	MI District 1	64 458	25	NY District 5	3 812.7
26	IN District 2	675 766	26	AZ District 7	59 240	26	CA District 39	3 807.4
27	IN District 7	675 674	27	WA District 5	59 217	27	NJ District 10	3 786.7
28	IN District 6	675 669	28	CA District 2	56 353	28	DC Delegate	3 597.1
29	IN District 4	675 617	29	CA District 25	55 644	29	IL District 9	3 350.2
30	IN District 9	675 599	30	UT District 1	53 790	30	CA District 37	3 308.7
31	IN District 5	675 577	31	OK District 4	53 258	31	CA District 36	3 295.9
32	IN District 8	675 564	32	AR District 4	53 107	32	CA District 28	3 197.0
33	IN District 1	675 562	33	AZ District 2	52 369	33	NY District 4	2 812.5
34	IN District 3	675 457	34	WA District 4	49 343	34	CA District 32	2 686.7
35	KY District 3	674 032	35	WI District 7	48 657	35	NJ District 9	2 682.9
36	KY District 5	673 670	36	MO District 8	48 384	36	CA District 53	2 599.1
37	KY District 1	673 629	37	IA District 5	47 520	37	IL District 1	2 579.3
38	KY District 6	673 626	38	TX District 19	45 347	38	FL District 17	2 557.2
39	KY District 4	673 588	39	OR District 4	44 498	39	CA District 40	2 466.2
40	KY District 2	673 224	40	AR District 1	44 422	40	CA District 29	2 433.3
41	AR District 3	672 756	41	CA District 4	42 614	41	CA District 38	2 375.1
42	KS District 3	672 124	42	IA District 4	40 818	42	MI District 13	2 366.6
43	KS District 2	672 102	43	UT District 3	40 795	43	NJ District 8	2 340.1
44	KS District 4	672 101	44	MO District 4	37 669	44	WI District 4	2 313.4
45	KS District 1	672 091	45	TX District 14	37 447	45	CA District 12	2 110.0
46	WI District 8	670 480	46	KS District 2	36 606	46	MI District 14	2 085.1
47	WI District 3	670 462	47	MO District 9	36 067	47	IL District 3	2 027.2
47	WI District 7	670 462	48	LA District 5	35 677	48	VA District 8	2 017.8
49	WI District 1	670 458	49	TX District 2	35 509	49	NY District 17	1 995.1
49	WI District 4	670 458	50	MS District 2	35 288	50	MN District 5	1 916.2
49	WI District 5	670 458	51	WI District 3	35 134	51	CA District 9	1 865.3
52	WI District 2	670 457	52	MN District 1	34 503	52	FL District 21	1 829.4
53	WI District 6	670 440	53	CA District 31	34 484	53	OH District 11	1 810.2
54	SC District 6	668 670	54	NY District 23	34 278	54	WA District 7	1 789.3
55	SC District 3	668 669	55	MS District 3	34 106	55	CA District 5	1 678.4
55	SC District 4	668 669	56	MO District 6	33 753	56	CA District 27	1 636.9
57	SC District 1	668 668	57	TX District 1	32 486	57	MI District 12	1 595.8
57	SC District 2	668 668	58	NE District 1	30 952	58	PA District 14	1 554.7
57	SC District 5	668 668	59	TX District 28	30 575	59	FL District 20	1 538.4
60	AR District 1	668 360	60	KY District 1	30 259	60	TX District 32	1 527.6
61	ME District 1	666 936	61	IL District 19	29 833	61	NV District 1	1 450.6
62	AR District 4	666 226	62	MS District 1	29 559	62	MA District 7	1 438.2
63	NV District 1	666 088	63	GA District 1	29 092	63	FL District 10	1 414.1
64	NV District 2	666 087	64	CA District 1	28 505	64	CO District 1	1 384.7
65	NV District 3	666 082	65	PA District 5	28 470	65	NY District 3	1 377.6
66	AR District 2	666 058	66	TX District 21	28 435	66	IL District 2	1 366.9
67	MI District 1	662 563	67	GA District 3	28 269	67	TX District	1 352.5
67	MI District 2	662 563	68	LA District 4	27 881	68	TX District 7	1 297.8
67	MI District 3	662 563	69	KY District 5	27 652	69	CA District 43	1 292.7
67	MI District 4	662 563	70	AL District 2	27 199	70	NJ District 6	1 272.8
67	MI District 5	662 563	71	CA District 22	26 980	71	OH District 10	1 245.9
67	MI District 6	662 563	72	OK District 4	26 449	72	AZ District 4	1 241.8
67	MI District 7	662 563	73	IL District 15	26 088	73	HI District 1	1 227.3
67	MI District 8	662 563	74	TN District 4	25 999	74	IL District 6	1 182.4
67	MI District 9	662 563	75	WI District 8	25 228	75	MN District 4	1 176.2
67	MI District 11	662 563						
67	MI District 12	662 563						
67	MI District 13	662 563						
67	MI District 14	662 563						
67	MI District 15	662 563						

Congressional Districts of the 109th Congress of the United States
Selected Rankings

	Percent White, not Hispanic or Latino, 2000			Percent Black, 2000			Percent American Indian, Alaska Native, 2000	
White rank	State/congressional district	Percent White [col 10]	Black rank	State/congressional district	Percent Black [col 5]	American Indian, Alaska Native rank	State/congressional district	Percent American Indian, Alaska Native [col 6]
1	KY District 5	97.1	1	IL District 1	66.2	1	AZ District 1	23.5
2	ME District 2	96.7	2	NY District 10	65.3	2	OK District 2	23.0
3	PA District 9	96.4	3	LA District 2	64.8	3	NM District 3	20.7
4	ME District 1	96.3	4	MS District 2	63.9	4	AK At Large	19.0
5	VT At Large	96.2	5	NY District 11	63.6	5	OK District 1	9.4
6	PA District 5	96.1	6	IL District 2	63.4	6	NC District 7	9.1
6	WI District 3	96.1	7	IL District 7	62.8	7	SD At Large	9.0
8	OH District 18	95.9	8	PA District 2	62.6	8	OK District 3	8.8
9	WV District 1	95.8	9	AL District 7	62.4	9	OK District 4	8.4
10	PA District 10	95.5	10	MI District 14	62.3	10	MT At Large	7.4
11	PA District 18	95.4	11	MI District 13	61.8	11	AZ District 7	7.2
12	OH District 6	95.2	12	DC Delegate	61.3	12	OK District 5	7.1
13	KY District 4	95.1	13	TN District 9	60.2	13	NM District 2	6.3
13	NH District 1	95.1	14	FL District 17	60.0	14	ND At Large	5.5
13	NH District 2	95.1	14	MD District 7	60.0	15	CA District 1	4.5
13	WI District 7	95.1	16	NJ District 10	59.9	15	NM District 1	4.5
17	TN District 1	95.0	17	MD District 4	58.8	17	AZ District 4	4.0
18	MN District 6	94.9	18	NY District 6	57.8	17	CA District 2	4.0
18	PA District 12	94.9	19	VA District 3	57.5	17	WA District 6	4.0
20	IA District 4	94.7	20	SC District 6	57.4	20	MI District 1	3.6
21	MN District 8	94.6	21	GA District 5	56.9	21	WA District 5	3.5
22	PA District 4	94.3	21	OH District 11	56.9	22	NV District 2	3.4
23	WI District 6	94.1	23	FL District 23	55.5	23	MN District 8	3.3
24	IL District 19	94.0	24	GA District 4	54.7	23	OR District 2	3.3
24	IN District 9	94.0	25	FL District 3	51.4	23	WI District 8	3.3
24	OH District 14	94.0	26	NC District 1	51.2	26	MN District 7	3.1
24	WI District 5	94.0	27	MO District 1	50.7	26	WA District 2	3.1
28	WV District 2	93.9	28	PA District 1	47.1	26	WA District 4	3.1
28	WV District 3	93.9	29	NC District 12	45.8	29	WY At Large	3.0
30	MI District 1	93.8	30	GA District 2	45.2	30	CO District 3	2.9
31	IA District 5	93.7	31	GA District 12	43.2	30	OR District 4	2.9
31	IN District 8	93.7	32	TX District 18	43.0	32	AZ District 2	2.8
31	OH District 5	93.7	33	GA District 13	42.0	32	CA District 5	2.8
31	PA District 3	93.7	34	TX District 30	41.4	32	UT District 2	2.8
35	IN District 4	93.6	35	GA District 3	40.3	35	AZ District 5	2.7
35	MI District 10	93.6	36	NY District 16	39.1	35	CA District 19	2.7
37	IN District 6	93.4	37	NY District 15	37.3	35	CA District 4	2.7
37	NY District 20	93.4	38	CA District 35	35.8	35	CA District 41	2.7
39	PA District 11	93.3	39	WI District 4	34.6	39	CA District 18	2.6
39	VA District 9	93.3	40	NY District 17	34.4	39	CA District 20	2.6
41	IN District 5	93.2	41	LA District 5	34.1	39	CA District 21	2.6
41	MN District 1	93.2	42	LA District 4	33.9	39	HI District 2	2.6
41	MO District 2	93.2	42	VA District 4	33.9	39	WA District 9	2.6
44	MN District 7	93.1	44	LA District 6	33.6	44	CA District 22	2.5
45	MO District 7	92.9	45	MS District 3	33.5	44	MN District 5	2.5
45	NY District 23	92.9	46	AL District 3	32.7	46	AR District 3	2.4
47	MI District 4	92.8	46	SC District 5	32.7	46	KS District 4	2.4
48	MO District 9	92.6	48	CA District 33	32.1	48	CA District 25	2.3
48	TN District 4	92.6	49	MD District 5	31.4	48	CA District 3	2.3
50	MO District 8	92.5	50	NC District 2	31.1	48	CA District 49	2.3
50	NY District 29	92.5	51	IN District 7	30.5	48	NC District 8	2.3
52	IA District 2	92.4	52	NY District 28	30.4	48	OR District 5	2.3
52	MO District 4	92.4	53	AL District 2	30.0	48	WA District 3	2.3
52	MO District 6	92.4	54	FL District 11	29.3	54	CA District 43	2.2
52	OH District 16	92.4	55	GA District 11	29.1	54	CO District 1	2.2
56	NY District 26	92.3	56	AL District 1	28.4	54	ID District 1	2.2
57	MA District 10	92.2	57	OH District 1	28.3	54	KS District 2	2.2
57	NY District 24	92.2	58	CA District 9	28.2	54	OR District 3	2.2
57	PA District 19	92.2	58	MD District 2	28.2	54	WA District 7	2.2
57	WI District 8	92.2	60	NC District 13	27.7	60	CA District 23	2.1
61	IA District 1	92.1	61	NC District 8	27.6	60	CO District 5	2.1
62	NE District 3	91.9	62	SC District 2	26.9	60	LA District 3	2.1
63	MN District 2	91.8	63	MS District 1	26.5	60	MO District 7	2.1
63	OH District 8	91.8	64	CA District 37	26.4	60	NC District 11	2.1
65	ND At Large	91.7	65	MA District 8	25.5	60	NY District 6	2.1
65	OH District 2	91.7	66	LA District 7	25.3	66	CA District 17	2.0
65	OH District 4	91.7	66	MO District 5	25.3	66	ID District 2	2.0
68	MD District 6	91.5	68	LA District 3	25.0	66	NY District 16	2.0
69	PA District 8	90.8	69	AR District 4	24.9	66	WI District 7	2.0
70	KY District 2	90.6	70	VA District 5	24.5	70	AL District 5	1.9
71	NE District 1	90.5	71	TN District 5	24.2	70	AZ District 3	1.9
72	AL District 4	90.4	72	TX District 25	23.7	70	CA District 44	1.9
73	IA District 3	90.1	73	NC District 7	23.6	70	CA District 6	1.9
73	TN District 2	90.1	73	PA District 14	23.6	70	CA District 7	1.9
75	IL District 18	90.0	75	GA District 1	23.2	70	CO District 7	1.9
			75	OH District 12	23.2			

Congressional Districts of the 109th Congress of the United States
Selected Rankings

Percent Asian and Pacific Islander, 2000

Asian rank	State/congressional district	Percent Asian [col 7]
1	HI District 1	84.8
2	HI District 2	78.0
3	CA District 13	33.0
4	CA District 12	32.7
5	CA District 15	32.2
6	CA District 8	31.5
7	CA District 16	26.3
8	NY District 5	26.0
9	CA District 29	25.7
10	CA District 32	20.0
11	CA District 5	19.0
12	CA District 14	18.8
13	CA District 9	18.1
14	CA District 42	18.0
15	CA District 40	17.9
16	CA District 46	17.6
17	NY District 12	17.3
18	CA District 26	17.2
19	CA District 7	16.8
20	CA District 36	16.2
20	WA District 7	16.2
22	NY District 9	16.0
23	CA District 51	15.5
24	CA District 47	15.4
25	CA District 31	15.2
26	CA District 48	14.8
27	CA District 37	14.5
28	NY District 7	14.4
29	IL District 9	13.6
30	CA District 33	13.5
31	NY District 14	12.9
32	CA District 50	12.5
32	VA District 11	12.5
34	CA District 10	12.3
34	CA District 27	12.3
36	NY District 8	12.2
37	MD District 8	12.1
37	TX District 7	12.1
39	NY District 6	12.0
40	CA District 18	11.7
40	CA District 38	11.7
40	NJ District 9	11.7
43	CA District 11	11.5
44	CA District 39	11.2
45	VA District 8	11.1
46	CA District 53	10.8
47	CA District 30	10.6
47	WA District 9	10.6
49	WA District 1	10.2
50	NY District 13	10.0
51	NJ District 12	9.8
51	WA District 8	9.8
53	MA District 8	9.2
54	NJ District 6	9.1
54	TX District 22	9.1
56	NJ District 7	8.9
57	IL District 6	8.8
58	MN District 4	8.6
59	CA District 3	8.2
59	NV District 3	8.2
59	TX District 3	8.2
62	CA District 52	7.8
63	VA District 10	7.7
64	IL District 5	7.5
65	IL District 13	7.3
66	CA District 17	7.2
66	OR District 3	7.2
66	WA District 6	7.2
69	CA District 28	7.1
69	CA District 35	7.1
69	NJ District 5	7.1
69	TX District 32	7.1
73	NJ District 11	7.0
74	CA District 20	6.9
74	NV District 1	6.9

Percent Hispanic or Latino,[1] 2000

Hispanic rank	State/congressional district	Percent Hispanic [col 9]
1	TX District 15	78.3
2	TX District 16	77.7
3	CA District 34	77.2
4	IL District 4	74.5
5	TX District 27	71.6
6	CA District 38	70.6
7	CA District 31	70.2
8	FL District 21	69.7
9	TX District 28	69.6
10	TX District 20	68.2
11	TX District 23	66.8
12	CA District 47	65.3
13	CA District 20	63.1
14	NY District 16	62.8
15	FL District 18	62.7
16	FL District 25	62.4
17	CA District 32	62.3
18	TX District 29	62.2
19	CA District 39	61.2
20	CA District 43	58.3
21	AZ District 4	58.0
22	CA District 28	55.6
23	CA District 51	53.3
24	AZ District 7	50.6
25	NY District 12	48.5
26	NY District 15	47.9
27	NJ District 13	47.6
28	CA District 35	47.4
29	NM District 2	47.3
30	CA District 21	43.4
31	CA District 37	43.2
32	CA District 17	42.9
33	NM District 1	42.6
34	CA District 18	41.9
35	CA District 23	41.7
36	NY District 7	39.5
37	CA District 45	38.0
37	TX District 24	38.0
39	CA District 16	37.6
40	CA District 27	36.5
41	NM District 3	36.3
42	CA District 44	35.0
43	CA District 33	34.6
44	TX District 25	34.3
45	TX District 19	34.1
46	TX District 10	33.0
47	TX District 18	32.6
48	TX District 14	32.0
49	TX District 30	31.1
50	CA District 36	30.3
51	CO District 1	30.0
52	CA District 40	29.6
53	CA District 49	29.5
54	CA District 53	29.4
55	CA District 19	28.2
55	NV District 1	28.2
57	TX District 32	27.4
58	CA District 25	27.1
59	WA District 4	26.4
60	CA District 29	26.1
61	TX District 7	25.9
62	NJ District 8	25.8
63	CA District 26	24.4
64	CA District 42	23.8
65	NY District 5	23.5
66	CA District 41	23.4
67	IL District 5	23.0
68	CA District 24	22.3
69	TX District 13	21.6
70	CO District 3	21.5
71	CA District 7	21.4
72	IL District 3	21.3
73	FL District 17	21.2
74	CA District 13	21.1
75	CA District 22	21.0

Percent under 18 years old, 2000

Under 18 years old rank	State/congressional district	Percent under 18 years old [col 12 and 13]
1	CA District 43	36.6
2	CA District 20	34.9
3	NY District 16	34.5
3	UT District 3	34.5
5	CA District 18	33.5
6	CA District 47	33.2
6	TX District 29	33.2
8	AZ District 4	33.0
8	CA District 37	33.0
10	CA District 35	32.8
10	TX District 15	32.8
12	CA District 39	32.5
12	TX District 28	32.5
14	CA District 21	32.4
14	CA District 34	32.4
16	UT District 1	32.3
17	CA District 25	32.2
17	TX District 23	32.2
19	IL District 4	31.8
20	CA District 38	31.7
21	TX District 16	31.6
22	TX District 27	31.2
23	CA District 32	31.0
24	CA District 44	30.7
24	CA District 51	30.7
26	AK At Large	30.4
26	WA District 4	30.4
28	NY District 10	30.2
29	TX District 22	30.1
30	CA District 31	30.0
30	MI District 13	30.0
32	TX District 24	29.9
33	MN District 2	29.8
34	AZ District 7	29.7
35	UT District 2	29.6
36	CO District 6	29.5
37	GA District 7	29.4
37	IL District 2	29.4
37	MS District 2	29.4
37	TX District 30	29.4
37	TX District 8	29.4
42	FL District 17	29.3
42	TX District 6	29.3
44	MN District 6	29.2
44	NM District 3	29.2
46	CA District 45	29.1
46	CA District 49	29.1
48	MI District 14	29.0
48	TX District 3	29.0
50	ID District 2	28.9
50	NM District 2	28.9
52	LA District 3	28.8
52	TX District 20	28.8
54	CA District 11	28.7
54	IL District 14	28.7
54	TX District 25	28.7
57	CA District 22	28.6
57	CA District 28	28.6
57	FL District 25	28.6
60	CA District 19	28.4
60	CA District 41	28.4
60	GA District 13	28.4
60	IL District 1	28.4
60	MD District 4	28.4
60	PA District 1	28.4
60	TX District 19	28.4
67	CA District 42	28.3
67	CA District 5	28.3
67	FL District 3	28.3
67	IL District 13	28.3
67	LA District 2	28.3
72	AZ District 1	28.2
72	FL District 23	28.2
72	IL District 8	28.2
72	IN District 3	28.2
72	VA District 10	28.2

1. Hispanic or Latino persons may be of any race.

Congressional Districts of the 109th Congress of the United States
Selected Rankings

Percent 65 years old and over, 2000			Percent female-headed family households, 2000			Percent of households composed of one person, 2000		
65 years old and over rank	State/congressional district	Percent 65 years old and over [col 19 and 20]	Female-headed family households rank	State/congressional district	Percent female households, [col 24]	One person household rank	State/congressional district	Percent one person households [col 25]
1	FL District 19	29.7	1	NY District 16	38.2	1	NY District 14	49.6
2	FL District 13	28.5	2	NY District 10	29.7	2	NY District 8	45.8
3	FL District 14	27.3	3	NY District 11	26.6	3	DC Delegate	43.8
4	FL District 5	25.6	4	MI District 13	26.5	4	CA District 8	40.9
5	FL District 16	25.5	5	IL District 1	26.3	5	CO District 1	39.2
6	FL District 10	23.3	6	PA District 1	26.0	6	CA District 30	39.0
7	FL District 22	20.8	7	NY District 15	25.6	7	WA District 7	38.9
8	FL District 9	20.5	8	LA District 2	25.1	8	GA District 5	37.6
9	AZ District 2	20.4	8	MI District 14	25.1	8	MN District 5	37.6
10	FL District 15	20.2	10	MS District 2	24.9	10	PA District 14	37.3
11	PA District 12	19.0	11	NJ District 10	24.7	11	IL District 7	37.2
12	FL District 7	18.2	12	IL District 2	24.2	12	PA District 2	37.1
13	PA District 11	18.0	13	FL District 17	24.0	13	MA District 8	36.9
13	PA District 14	18.0	14	NY District 6	23.9	14	NY District 15	36.3
15	FL District 18	17.8	15	CA District 35	23.5	15	VA District 8	36.0
15	NC District 11	17.8	16	PA District 2	23.3	16	IL District 9	35.8
17	PA District 18	17.7	17	AL District 7	22.9	17	CA District 53	35.6
18	FL District 20	17.4	18	TN District 9	22.7	17	TX District 32	35.6
19	NE District 3	17.3	19	IL District 7	22.6	19	FL District 10	35.1
19	PA District 13	17.3	20	MD District 7	22.5	20	OH District 11	35.0
21	PA District 4	17.2	21	FL District 3	22.4	21	IL District 5	34.8
22	FL District 12	17.1	22	OH District 11	21.7	22	CA District 33	34.5
22	IA District 5	17.1	22	VA District 3	21.7	23	NY District 28	33.9
24	MI District 1	17.0	24	SC District 6	21.4	24	WI District 4	33.7
24	NJ District 3	17.0	25	NY District 12	21.3	25	IN District 7	33.0
26	AZ District 8	16.8	26	MO District 1	20.9	26	OH District 10	32.8
26	MA District 10	16.8	27	CA District 37	20.8	27	FL District 22	32.5
26	MN District 7	16.8	28	TX District 30	20.6	28	FL District 20	32.3
26	NY District 9	16.8	29	FL District 23	20.5	28	OH District 1	32.3
30	PA District 10	16.6	30	GA District 2	20.2	30	CA District 9	32.1
31	IA District 4	16.4	31	MD District 4	19.9	30	TX District 10	32.1
31	KS District 1	16.4	31	WI District 4	19.9	32	MO District 1	32.0
33	NJ District 4	16.3	33	NY District 7	19.6	32	MO District 5	32.0
34	IL District 17	16.2	33	TX District 18	19.6	34	NY District 21	31.6
35	OH District 10	16.1	35	NC District 1	19.4	35	TN District 5	31.5
36	PA District 17	16.0	36	NY District 17	19.3	36	FL District 11	31.4
37	PA District 9	15.9	37	DC Delegate	18.9	36	MI District 12	31.4
38	MN District 8	15.8	37	NC District 12	18.9	38	FL District 18	31.3
38	MO District 8	15.8	39	NY District 28	18.8	39	CA District 36	31.2
38	NY District 27	15.8	40	CA District 20	18.7	40	MI District 13	31.1
38	WV District 1	15.8	41	GA District 12	18.3	40	MN District 4	31.1
42	CA District 45	15.7	41	GA District 3	18.3	40	MO District 3	31.1
43	AR District 4	15.6	41	GA District 5	18.3	43	PA District 1	31.0
43	MA District 7	15.6	44	CA District 43	18.2	44	KY District 3	30.8
43	MI District 12	15.6	44	GA District 13	18.2	44	OH District 15	30.8
43	WV District 3	15.6	44	TX District 16	18.2	46	FL District 19	30.6
47	IL District 9	15.5	47	CA District 34	17.8	47	TN District 9	30.5
47	NY District 21	15.5	48	CA District 31	17.7	48	RI District 1	30.2
47	OH District 11	15.5	48	CA District 51	17.7	48	TX District 7	30.2
47	OH District 6	15.5	48	TX District 20	17.7	50	CA District 5	29.9
47	PA District 15	15.5	51	GA District 4	17.6	50	MA District 7	29.9
52	FL District 6	15.4	52	NJ District 13	17.5	50	NY District 9	29.9
52	PA District 3	15.4	53	CA District 32	17.3	50	OK District 5	29.9
52	PA District 5	15.4	53	CA District 33	17.3	54	MD District 7	29.8
52	PA District 7	15.4	53	TX District 28	17.3	54	NY District 27	29.8
52	RI District 1	15.4	56	FL District 11	17.1	56	TX District 18	29.7
57	IL District 19	15.3	57	CA District 38	17.0	57	AL District 7	29.6
58	OK District 2	15.2	57	LA District 5	17.0	57	VA District 3	29.6
58	OR District 2	15.2	59	AZ District 4	16.9	59	IL District 17	29.3
58	OR District 4	15.2	60	IN District 7	16.8	59	ND At Large	29.3
58	WI District 7	15.2	61	LA District 4	16.6	59	NY District 22	29.3
62	AR District 1	15.1	62	SC District 5	16.4	62	PA District 11	29.2
62	HI District 1	15.1	62	TX District 27	16.4	62	PA District 12	29.2
62	MN District 1	15.1	62	TX District 29	16.4	64	FL District 13	29.1
62	NY District 24	15.1	65	CA District 39	16.3	64	MD District 3	29.1
62	TX District 17	15.1	65	CA District 5	16.3	66	LA District 2	29.0
67	IL District 18	15.0	67	MD District 2	16.2	67	NC District 13	28.9
67	VA District 6	15.0	68	MI District 5	16.1	68	CT District 3	28.8
69	TX District 1	14.9	69	FL District 25	16.0	68	OH District 3	28.8
70	CT District 1	14.8	69	OH District 1	16.0	70	OH District 9	28.7
70	ME District 2	14.8	69	PA District 14	16.0	71	AZ District 8	28.6
70	NJ District 9	14.8	72	CA District 18	15.9	72	IL District 15	28.5
70	NY District 5	14.8	72	TX District 24	15.9	72	NJ District 9	28.5
70	OH District 17	14.8	74	GA District 11	15.7	74	CT District 1	28.4
70	VA District 5	14.8	74	IL District 4	15.7	74	IL District 1	28.4
75	NY District 29	14.8	74	GA District 3	15.5	74	MI District 14	28.4
75	OH District 10	14.8	74	NY District 30	15.5			

Congressional Districts of the 109th Congress of the United States
Selected Rankings

Percent college graduates (bachelor's degree or higher), 2000			Median household income, 1999			Percent of persons below the poverty level, 1999		
Percent college graduate rank	State/congressional district	Percent college graduates [col 32]	House-hold income rank	State/congressional district	Median income (dollars) [col 34]	Poverty rate rank	State/congressional district	Poverty rate [col 36]
1	NY District 14	56.9	1	VA District 11	80 397	1	NY District 16	42.2
2	VA District 8	53.8	2	NJ District 11	79 009	2	CA District 20	32.2
3	MD District 8	53.7	3	CA District 14	77 985	3	NY District 15	30.5
4	CA District 30	53.5	4	GA District 6	75 611	3	TX District 15	30.5
5	CA District 14	52.2	5	CA District 15	74 947	5	CA District 31	30.1
6	GA District 6	50.7	6	NJ District 7	74 823	6	NY District 10	29.0
7	VA District 11	48.9	7	CO District 6	73 393	7	NY District 12	28.3
8	NC District 4	48.0	8	NJ District 5	72 781	8	KY District 5	28.1
9	NY District 8	47.8	9	IL District 13	71 686	9	MS District 2	27.3
10	IL District 10	47.5	10	IL District 10	71 663	10	PA District 1	26.9
11	CO District 6	46.8	11	VA District 10	71 560	11	LA District 2	26.8
12	CA District 48	46.5	12	NY District 2	71 147	12	TX District 28	26.7
13	NJ District 11	45.2	13	NY District 3	70 561	13	TX District 27	26.5
14	WA District 7	44.1	14	CA District 42	70 463	14	CA District 35	26.4
15	CA District 8	44.0	15	CA District 12	70 307	15	CA District 34	26.0
16	NY District 18	43.8	16	NJ District 12	69 668	16	AZ District 4	25.6
17	MI District 9	43.5	17	CA District 48	69 663	17	CA District 37	25.2
18	TX District 32	43.2	18	NY District 18	68 887	18	AL District 7	24.7
19	VA District 10	43.1	19	MD District 8	68 306	19	MI District 13	24.4
20	IL District 13	42.4	20	CA District 16	67 689	20	IL District 7	24.0
21	NJ District 12	42.3	21	NY District 4	66 799	21	PA District 2	23.8
22	CT District 4	42.2	22	CT District 4	66 598	22	TX District 18	23.7
23	CA District 15	41.6	23	TX District 3	65 546	23	LA District 5	23.6
23	TX District 3	41.6	24	MI District 9	65 358	23	TX District 16	23.6
25	NJ District 7	41.5	25	CA District 10	65 245	25	CA District 33	23.5
26	CA District 12	40.7	26	NY District 19	64 337	26	FL District 17	23.3
27	MN District 3	40.1	27	WA District 8	63 854	27	NY District 11	23.2
28	CA District 50	40.0	28	MN District 2	63 816	28	CA District 18	22.7
29	MA District 8	39.8	29	GA District 7	63 455	29	GA District 2	22.5
29	TX District 7	39.8	30	VA District 8	63 430	30	NM District 2	22.4
31	AZ District 5	39.6	31	IL District 8	62 762	30	SC District 6	22.4
31	IL District 9	39.6	32	TX District 22	62 678	32	TX District 23	22.1
33	MA District 7	39.5	33	MD District 5	62 661	33	FL District 23	21.9
34	CO District 2	39.3	34	IL District 6	62 640	33	WV District 3	21.9
35	DC Delegate	39.1	35	CA District 13	62 415	35	AZ District 7	21.8
35	KS District 3	39.1	36	CA District 11	61 996	36	GA District 12	21.7
37	TX District 32	38.9	37	NY District 1	61 884	37	FL District 3	21.5
37	TX District 26	38.9	38	CA District 46	61 567	37	TX District 29	21.5
39	NJ District 5	38.6	39	CA District 24	61 453	39	NC District 1	21.1
40	MO District 2	38.3	40	MO District 2	61 416	40	CA District 32	20.7
41	CA District 6	37.9	41	MN District 2	61 344	40	CA District 43	20.7
42	CA District 9	37.4	42	TX District 26	61 287	42	AZ District 1	20.3
42	WA District 8	37.4	43	CA District 30	60 713	42	TX District 20	20.3
44	GA District 5	37.3	44	TX District 8	60 198	44	CA District 53	20.2
45	CA District 36	36.9	45	CA District 50	59 813	44	DC Delegate	20.2
45	MA District 4	36.9	46	PA District 8	59 184	44	IL District 4	20.2
47	MD District 3	36.5	47	MI District 11	59 177	47	LA District 4	20.0
48	CA District 46	36.4	48	CA District 6	59 115	48	GA District 3	19.9
48	WA District 1	36.4	49	CA District 26	58 968	48	LA District 7	19.9
50	CA District 10	36.2	50	WI District 5	58 594	48	MA District 8	19.9
51	PA District 7	36.1	51	WA District 1	58 565	51	WI District 4	19.8
52	GA District 4	35.9	52	MA District 6	57 826	52	CA District 5	19.7
52	NC District 9	35.9	53	MD District 4	57 727	52	GA District 5	19.7
54	MA District 6	35.1	54	NY District 14	57 152	52	IL District 1	19.7
54	TX District 10	35.1	55	MN District 6	56 862	52	MI District 14	19.7
56	WI District 5	35.0	56	IL District 14	56 314	56	OH District 11	19.5
57	MN District 5	34.9	57	MA District 5	56 217	57	TN District 9	19.4
58	CA District 42	34.8	58	PA District 7	56 154	58	FL District 18	19.3
59	IL District 6	34.6	59	MA District 7	56 110	59	MS District 3	19.2
60	CO District 1	34.3	60	NJ District 6	55 681	60	CA District 28	19.1
61	FL District 22	34.1	61	PA District 6	55 615	60	CA District 47	19.1
62	IL District 5	33.9	62	MA District 9	55 407	60	TX District 30	19.1
62	PA District 6	33.9	63	NJ District 3	55 282	63	NM District 3	19.0
64	MA District 9	33.8	64	CO District 2	55 204	64	VA District 3	18.9
65	MA District 5	33.6	65	NC District 9	55 059	65	AL District 3	18.8
65	NY District 5	33.6	66	CT District 2	54 498	66	NY District 28	18.7
67	MA District 10	33.5	67	CA District 40	54 356	66	NY District 8	18.7
68	CA District 29	33.4	68	NJ District 4	54 073	68	LA District 3	18.6
69	OR District 1	33.3	69	NC District 4	53 847	69	AR District 1	18.5
70	TX District 22	33.2	70	MA District 4	53 169	69	AR District 4	18.5
70	VA District 7	33.2	71	CT District 5	53 118	69	OK District 2	18.5
72	MN District 4	33.0	72	CA District 52	52 940	72	MO District 8	18.2
73	TX District 8	32.9	73	MD District 3	52 906	73	CA District 32	18.0
74	MD District 4	32.7	74	IN District 5	52 800	73	NJ District 13	18.0
75	CA District 26	32.4	75	CA District 7	52 778	75	NY District 7	17.7

COLUMN HEADINGS FOR CONGRESSIONAL DISTRICTS

Table E. Congressional Districts 109th Congress — **Land Area and Population**

STATE District	Representative	Land area,[1] 2000 (sq km)	Total persons	Per square kilometer	White	Black	Am. Indian, Alaska Native	Asian and Pacific Islander	Other race	Hispanic or Latino[2]	Non-Hispanic White	Two or more races	Under 5 years	5 to 17 years	18 to 24 years
			Population and population characteristics, 2000												
										Percent				**Age**	
					Race alone or in combination										
			1	2	3	4	5	6	7	8	9	10	11	12	13	14

1. Dry land or land partially or temporarily covered by water.   2. Hispanic or Latino persons may be of any race.   Note: Data were tabulated for the 108th Congress and some boundary changes have occurred.

Table E. Congressional Districts 109th Congress — **Population, Households, Group Quarters, and Education**

STATE District	25 to 34 years	35 to 44 years	45 to 54 years	55 to 64 years	65 to 74 years	75 years and over	Percent female	Number	Persons per household	Female family householder[1]	One person	Persons in correctional institutions, 2000	Persons in nursing homes, 2000	Persons in military quarters, 2000	Public	Private
	Population and population characteristics, 2000 (cont'd)							**Households, 2000**								**Education, 2000**	
	Percent (cont'd)									**Percent**						**School enrollment[2]**	
	Age (cont'd)																
	15	16	17	18	19	20	21	22	23	24	25	26	27	28	29	30

1. No spouse present.   2. All persons 3 years old and over enrolled in nursery school through college.   Note: Data were tabulated for the 108th Congress and some boundary changes have occurred.

Table E. Congressional Districts 109th Congress — **Education, Money Income, Poverty, and Housing**

STATE District	High school graduate or more	Bachelor's degree or more	Per capita income[2]	Median income	Percent with income of $100,000 or more	Total	Total	Total	Total	Percent	Median value[3] (dollars)	With a mortgage	Without a mortgage[4]
	Education, 2000 (cont'd)		**Money income, 1999**			**Percent below poverty level, 1999**		**Housing units, 2000**					
	Attainment[1] (percent)			**Households**		Persons	Families		**Occupied units**				
										Owner-occupied			
												Owner cost as a percent of income	
	31	32	33	34	35	36	37	38	39	40	41	42	43

1. Persons 25 years old and over.   2. Based on the population enumerated as of April 1, 2000.   3. Specified owner-occupied units.   4. Median monthly owner costs is often in the minimum category—9.9 percent or less, which is indicated as 9.9 percent.   Note: Data were tabulated for the 108th Congress and some boundary changes have occurred.

Table E. Congressional Districts 109th Congress — **Housing, Labor Force, and Employment**

STATE District	Median rent[1] (dollars)	Rent as a percent of income	Substandard units[2] (percent)	Total	Total	Rate[3]	Total	Management, professional, and related occupations	Production, transportation, and material moving occupations	Employment disabled persons[5] (percent)
	Housing units, 2000 (cont'd)			**Civilian labor force, 2000**			**Civilian employment,[4] 2000**			**Disability, 2000**
	Occupied units (cont'd)				**Unemployment**			**Percent**		
	Renter-occupied									
	44	45	46	47	48	49	50	51	52	53

1. Specified renter-occupied units.   2. Overcrowded or lacking complete plumbing facilities.   3. Percent of total civilian labor force.   4. Persons 16 years old and over.   5. Persons 16 to 64 years old.   Note: Data were tabulated for the 108th Congress and some boundary changes have occurred.

STATE District	Representative	Land area,[1] 2000 (sq km)	Population and population characteristics, 2000 Total persons	Per square kilometer	Race alone or in combination White	Black	Am. Indian, Alaska Native	Asian and Pacific Islander	Other race	Percent Hispanic or Latino[2]	Non-Hispanic White	Two or more races	Age Under 5 years	5 to 17 years	18 to 24 years
		1	2	3	4	5	6	7	8	9	10	11	12	13	14
ALABAMA		131 426	4 447 100	33.8	72.0	26.3	1.0	1.0	0.9	1.7	70.3	1.0	6.7	18.6	9.9
District 1	Jo Bonner (R)	16 361	635 300	38.8	69.3	28.4	1.5	1.3	0.6	1.3	67.8	1.0	7.0	19.7	9.3
District 2	Terry Everett (R)	27 199	635 300	23.4	68.6	30.0	0.9	0.9	0.7	1.5	67.0	1.0	6.6	18.9	9.7
District 3	Mike Rogers (R)	20 290	635 300	31.3	66.2	32.7	0.6	0.9	0.5	1.2	64.9	0.8	6.4	18.2	12.1
District 4	Robert B. Aderholt (R)	21 684	635 300	29.3	92.6	5.3	1.0	0.4	1.7	3.0	90.4	1.0	6.5	17.8	8.6
District 5	Bud Cramer (D)	11 618	635 300	54.7	80.2	17.4	1.9	1.3	0.9	2.0	77.7	1.6	6.5	18.4	9.1
District 6	Spencer Bachus (R)	11 821	635 300	53.7	90.4	7.9	0.6	1.1	0.8	1.6	88.8	0.8	6.5	18.0	8.5
District 7	Artur Davis (D)	22 453	635 300	28.3	36.5	62.4	0.5	0.8	0.7	1.3	35.5	0.7	7.0	19.3	11.9
ALASKA		1 481 347	626 932	0.4	74.0	4.3	19.0	6.1	2.4	4.1	67.6	5.4	7.6	22.8	9.1
At Large	Don Young (R)	1 481 347	626 932	0.4	74.0	4.3	19.0	6.1	2.4	4.1	67.6	5.4	7.6	22.8	9.1
ARIZONA		294 312	5 130 632	17.4	77.9	3.6	5.7	2.6	13.2	25.3	63.8	2.9	7.5	19.2	10.0
District 1	Rick Renzi (R)	151 795	641 329	4.2	67.7	1.5	23.5	0.9	8.6	16.4	58.4	2.2	7.0	21.2	9.6
District 2	Trent Franks (R)	52 369	641 329	12.2	87.5	2.6	2.8	2.5	7.0	14.2	78.4	2.3	6.4	17.6	7.2
District 3	John Shadegg (R)	1 550	641 329	413.8	87.9	2.9	1.9	2.9	7.0	14.1	78.5	2.5	7.1	17.9	9.2
District 4	Ed Pastor (D)	516	641 329	1 241.8	57.6	8.7	4.0	2.1	32.0	58.0	29.3	4.2	10.4	22.6	13.0
District 5	J. D. Hayworth (R)	3 641	641 329	176.1	85.2	3.3	2.7	4.4	7.2	13.3	76.8	2.7	6.3	16.3	12.0
District 6	Jeff Flake (R)	1 874	641 329	342.2	86.4	2.5	1.6	2.7	9.5	17.2	76.6	2.5	8.4	19.5	8.4
District 7	Raul Grijalva (D)	59 240	641 329	10.8	64.9	3.5	7.2	2.0	26.0	50.6	38.6	3.5	8.2	21.5	12.0
District 8	Jim Kolbe (R)	23 327	641 329	27.5	86.3	3.8	1.8	3.1	8.2	18.2	73.9	3.0	5.9	18.7	8.7
ARKANSAS		134 856	2 673 400	19.8	81.2	16.0	1.4	1.1	1.8	3.2	78.6	1.3	6.8	18.7	9.8
District 1	Marion Berry (D)	44 422	668 360	15.0	81.9	17.0	1.0	0.5	0.7	1.6	80.2	1.0	6.7	19.0	9.2
District 2	Vic Snyder (D)	15 338	666 058	43.4	77.8	19.9	1.0	1.2	1.4	2.4	75.6	1.3	6.8	18.3	10.2
District 3	John Boozman (R)	21 989	672 756	30.6	91.9	2.3	2.4	1.9	3.5	6.3	87.3	1.9	7.1	18.6	10.4
District 4	Mike Ross (D)	53 107	666 226	12.5	73.1	24.9	1.1	0.6	1.6	2.7	71.0	1.1	6.5	18.7	9.4
CALIFORNIA		403 933	33 871 648	83.9	63.4	7.4	1.9	13.0	19.4	32.4	46.7	4.7	7.3	20.0	9.9
District 1	Mike Thompson (D)	28 505	639 087	22.4	82.5	1.9	4.5	5.4	10.3	17.9	71.2	4.2	6.0	18.5	11.4
District 2	Wally Herger (R)	56 353	639 087	11.3	85.1	1.7	4.0	4.8	8.7	14.0	76.2	4.0	6.3	20.1	10.2
District 3	Dan Lungren (R)	8 739	639 088	73.1	83.2	5.3	2.3	8.2	6.1	10.7	74.4	4.7	6.7	19.5	7.9
District 4	John Doolittle (R)	42 614	639 088	15.0	91.5	1.5	2.7	3.6	4.1	8.9	83.8	3.2	5.9	19.8	7.0
District 5	Robert T. Matsui (D)	381	639 087	1 678.4	56.6	16.7	2.8	19.0	13.2	20.8	43.4	6.7	7.6	20.7	10.7
District 6	Lynn Woolsey (D)	4 208	639 087	151.9	85.9	2.7	1.9	5.4	8.3	14.5	76.1	3.9	5.8	17.0	7.7
District 7	George Miller (D)	904	639 088	707.0	56.3	18.6	1.9	16.8	12.8	21.4	43.2	5.9	7.2	20.2	9.0
District 8	Nancy Pelosi (D)	92	639 088	6 974.2	52.7	9.7	1.2	31.5	9.5	15.7	42.9	4.4	4.1	10.2	9.1
District 9	Barbara Lee (D)	343	639 088	1 865.3	46.1	28.2	1.7	18.1	11.8	18.7	35.2	5.2	6.5	16.7	11.2
District 10	Ellen Tauscher (D)	2 624	639 088	243.5	76.7	6.8	1.6	12.3	8.5	15.0	65.4	5.4	6.9	19.6	7.8
District 11	Richard Pombo (R)	5 897	639 088	108.4	76.3	4.1	1.7	11.5	11.7	19.7	64.1	5.0	7.3	21.4	8.2
District 12	Tom Lantos (D)	303	639 088	2 110.0	59.6	3.2	1.0	32.7	9.1	15.7	48.2	5.1	5.7	15.1	7.9
District 13	Pete Stark (D)	573	639 088	1 115.1	52.4	7.5	1.6	33.0	12.5	21.1	38.4	6.4	7.1	18.3	8.7
District 14	Anna Eshoo (D)	2 138	639 088	298.9	70.6	3.6	1.1	18.8	10.0	17.5	59.6	3.8	6.4	16.1	8.5
District 15	Michael Honda (D)	741	639 088	862.1	58.5	3.1	1.3	32.2	9.9	17.2	47.1	4.6	7.0	17.2	8.5
District 16	Zoe Lofgren (D)	595	639 088	1 073.4	49.9	4.2	1.6	26.3	23.5	37.6	31.9	5.2	7.8	19.5	10.6
District 17	Sam Farr (D)	12 484	639 087	51.2	65.0	3.4	2.0	7.2	27.6	42.9	46.3	4.9	7.4	19.9	11.3
District 18	Dennis Cardoza (D)	7 906	639 088	80.8	57.9	6.8	2.6	11.7	27.4	41.9	39.1	6.1	8.7	24.8	10.4
District 19	George Radanovich (R)	17 333	639 088	36.9	74.7	4.1	2.7	5.9	17.5	28.2	59.9	4.7	7.3	21.1	9.6
District 20	Jim Costa (D)	12 904	639 088	49.5	43.7	8.1	2.6	6.9	43.5	63.1	21.4	4.6	9.5	25.4	12.0
District 21	Devin Nunes (R)	20 787	639 088	30.7	64.6	2.7	2.6	6.2	28.7	43.4	46.4	4.6	8.5	23.9	10.7
District 22	Bill Thomas (R)	26 980	639 088	23.7	78.7	6.5	2.5	4.2	12.3	21.0	66.8	4.0	7.1	21.5	9.5
District 23	Lois Capps (D)	2 698	639 088	236.9	69.0	2.7	2.1	6.6	24.2	41.7	48.7	4.3	6.8	18.4	14.4
District 24	Elton Gallegly (R)	10 057	639 088	63.5	82.4	2.2	1.7	6.1	11.6	22.3	68.6	3.7	6.9	20.7	7.8
District 25	Buck McKeon (R)	55 644	639 087	11.5	72.7	9.1	2.3	5.4	15.5	27.1	57.2	4.7	8.1	24.1	8.7
District 26	David Dreier (R)	1 947	639 088	328.2	67.8	5.2	1.4	17.2	13.1	24.4	52.7	4.4	6.3	20.7	9.2
District 27	Brad Sherman (D)	390	639 087	1 636.9	65.3	5.4	1.4	12.3	21.3	36.5	44.9	5.4	7.2	18.3	9.8
District 28	Howard L. Berman (D)	200	639 087	3 197.0	58.0	5.0	1.4	7.1	34.1	55.6	31.4	5.4	8.4	20.2	10.5
District 29	Adam Schiff (D)	263	639 088	2 433.3	56.3	6.8	1.1	25.7	16.4	26.1	39.1	6.5	6.1	16.9	8.6
District 30	Henry Waxman (D)	740	639 088	864.2	84.6	3.3	0.8	10.6	4.9	8.3	76.4	3.9	4.5	12.4	9.0
District 31	Xavier Becerra (D)	102	639 088	6 267.3	38.9	5.2	1.8	15.2	44.9	70.2	9.8	5.8	9.1	20.9	12.1
District 32	Hilda Solis (D)	238	639 087	2 686.7	44.9	3.2	1.8	20.0	34.9	62.3	14.8	4.5	8.6	22.4	11.2
District 33	Diane E. Watson (D)	125	639 088	5 125.2	35.3	32.1	1.4	13.5	23.2	34.6	19.9	5.1	6.9	17.5	11.2
District 34	Lucille Roybal-Allard (D)	151	639 088	4 232.8	45.6	5.2	1.7	6.4	46.0	77.2	11.4	4.8	9.5	22.9	12.1
District 35	Maxine Waters (D)	144	639 088	4 453.0	29.3	35.8	1.3	7.1	31.2	47.4	10.4	4.5	9.4	22.0	10.9
District 36	Jane Harman (D)	194	639 087	3 295.9	65.5	4.9	1.4	16.2	17.4	30.3	48.4	5.0	6.7	16.5	8.5
District 37	Juanita Millender-McDonald (D)	193	639 088	3 308.7	33.7	26.4	1.6	14.5	29.2	43.2	16.6	5.0	9.1	23.9	11.1
District 38	Grace Napolitano (D)	269	639 088	2 375.1	47.6	4.3	1.8	11.7	39.6	70.6	13.6	4.9	8.5	23.2	11.3
District 39	Linda Sanchez (D)	168	639 088	3 807.4	48.9	6.8	1.6	11.2	36.4	61.2	21.0	4.7	8.8	23.7	11.0
District 40	Edward R. Royce (R)	259	639 088	2 466.2	66.5	2.9	1.4	17.9	15.9	29.6	49.3	4.3	7.3	19.6	9.7
District 41	Jerry Lewis (R)	34 484	639 087	18.5	77.6	6.3	2.7	5.2	13.1	23.4	63.5	4.5	7.0	21.4	9.7

1. Dry land or land partially or temporarily covered by water.   2. Hispanic or Latino persons may be of any race.   Note: Data were tabulated for the 108th Congress and some boundary changes have occurred.

STATE District	25 to 34 years	35 to 44 years	45 to 54 years	55 to 64 years	65 to 74 years	75 years and over	Percent female	Number	Persons per household	Female family householder[1]	One person	Persons in correctional institutions, 2000	Persons in nursing homes, 2000	Persons in military quarters, 2000	Public	Private
	15	16	17	18	19	20	21	22	23	24	25	26	27	28	29	30
ALABAMA	13.6	15.4	13.5	9.3	7.1	5.9	51.7	1 737 080	2.49	14.2	26.1	33 542	26 697	5 370	994 978	160 526
District 1	13.0	15.3	13.3	9.4	7.1	5.8	51.7	241 376	2.57	15.5	24.5	3 825	3 113	61	134 546	31 235
District 2	13.7	15.3	13.2	9.3	7.1	6.2	51.5	246 607	2.48	15.0	26.5	11 533	3 833	4 715	139 694	23 795
District 3	13.3	14.6	13.2	9.2	7.1	5.8	51.9	248 618	2.47	15.2	27.0	4 965	4 446	4	157 300	21 391
District 4	13.4	15.0	13.7	10.5	8.0	6.5	51.2	251 477	2.49	10.3	24.4	2 019	4 856	0	130 650	11 491
District 5	13.8	16.6	13.6	9.7	7.0	5.3	51.3	252 819	2.46	11.6	26.3	4 268	2 892	587	142 029	21 923
District 6	14.6	16.6	14.5	9.2	6.7	5.6	51.2	249 318	2.50	9.0	24.6	4 223	3 220	0	130 201	28 798
District 7	13.3	14.5	12.8	8.1	6.8	6.2	53.5	246 865	2.49	22.9	29.6	2 709	4 337	3	160 558	21 893
ALASKA	14.3	18.2	15.1	7.1	3.6	2.1	48.3	221 600	2.74	10.8	23.5	3 331	803	3 970	166 991	18 769
At Large	14.3	18.2	15.1	7.1	3.6	2.1	48.3	221 600	2.74	10.8	23.5	3 331	803	3 970	166 991	18 769
ARIZONA	14.5	15.0	12.2	8.6	7.1	5.9	50.1	1 901 327	2.64	11.1	24.8	45 783	13 607	5 256	1 253 669	148 171
District 1	11.8	14.1	12.8	9.7	7.9	5.8	49.2	223 831	2.74	12.2	23.3	19 019	2 410	0	175 286	13 636
District 2	11.9	14.0	11.9	10.5	10.5	9.9	51.1	249 882	2.52	8.5	23.3	4 316	3 160	681	134 625	17 906
District 3	15.8	16.9	14.1	8.7	5.5	4.8	50.2	254 358	2.50	10.5	27.0	1 229	408	0	138 815	28 443
District 4	18.0	14.1	9.6	5.7	3.8	2.9	48.0	196 214	3.18	16.9	24.1	8 656	1 421	0	166 830	12 618
District 5	16.8	16.4	13.4	8.4	5.7	4.5	50.2	261 912	2.42	9.2	27.4	60	1 169	0	158 737	23 865
District 6	15.0	15.2	11.0	8.0	7.6	6.9	50.7	233 971	2.72	9.0	21.1	0	2 073	0	153 836	17 895
District 7	14.0	14.0	11.2	7.8	6.6	4.7	50.3	216 299	2.88	14.7	22.4	4 758	875	1 677	182 080	12 548
District 8	12.5	15.1	13.9	10.1	8.9	7.9	51.0	264 860	2.36	9.6	28.6	7 745	2 091	2 898	143 460	21 260
ARKANSAS	13.2	14.9	13.1	9.6	7.4	6.6	51.2	1 042 696	2.49	12.1	25.6	20 565	21 379	1 290	602 713	72 396
District 1	12.3	14.5	13.0	10.2	8.1	7.0	51.5	260 695	2.50	12.8	25.1	7 787	6 049	0	152 187	12 780
District 2	14.4	15.6	13.5	8.9	6.5	5.7	51.5	263 453	2.46	12.8	26.7	2 763	4 460	1 246	144 462	31 091
District 3	13.8	15.0	12.7	9.2	7.0	6.0	50.6	259 465	2.54	9.5	24.2	1 416	4 407	27	153 695	16 217
District 4	12.2	14.4	13.1	10.0	8.1	7.5	51.2	259 083	2.48	13.5	26.3	8 599	6 463	17	152 369	12 308
CALIFORNIA	15.4	16.2	12.8	7.7	5.6	5.0	50.2	11 502 870	2.87	12.6	23.5	248 516	120 724	58 810	8 703 390	1 426 600
District 1	12.5	14.9	14.6	8.9	6.6	6.6	50.4	240 438	2.56	11.0	26.4	5 410	2 903	1	173 606	19 617
District 2	11.3	14.5	13.7	9.4	7.5	7.1	50.7	241 216	2.59	11.2	24.8	2 366	2 760	512	173 877	15 331
District 3	13.2	17.2	14.3	8.9	6.6	5.6	50.3	237 600	2.61	11.2	23.2	8 143	2 934	235	154 567	25 194
District 4	10.9	16.8	16.0	9.8	7.4	6.4	49.8	240 821	2.59	9.5	22.1	10 152	2 551	0	156 515	18 803
District 5	15.6	15.1	12.3	7.2	5.5	5.3	51.4	237 330	2.64	16.3	29.9	2 104	2 649	104	177 822	20 229
District 6	13.0	17.1	17.0	9.7	6.2	6.6	50.6	248 221	2.49	9.8	27.5	7 730	2 994	331	135 840	28 866
District 7	14.5	17.0	14.3	8.0	5.2	4.6	50.4	218 697	2.85	15.3	22.5	10 352	2 143	25	159 666	27 220
District 8	24.4	17.4	13.6	8.2	6.7	6.3	48.6	276 619	2.25	8.7	40.9	1 369	1 582	36	108 543	37 938
District 9	17.3	15.8	14.0	7.7	5.3	5.6	51.5	247 822	2.52	15.1	32.1	979	2 595	0	159 469	32 944
District 10	13.2	17.4	14.6	8.7	6.0	5.9	51.0	232 855	2.70	10.0	22.3	1 109	2 967	2 019	152 487	29 212
District 11	13.0	17.5	14.3	8.4	5.2	4.6	50.5	219 211	2.84	10.2	19.5	7 216	2 622	15	159 708	30 278
District 12	16.0	17.2	15.0	9.3	7.0	6.9	51.2	235 831	2.67	10.0	25.0	20	2 670	0	126 264	40 564
District 13	16.5	17.7	13.5	7.8	5.5	4.9	50.5	217 121	2.91	11.7	20.8	40	2 327	224	147 480	30 747
District 14	16.9	17.5	14.3	8.8	5.9	5.7	49.4	240 550	2.59	7.9	26.0	2 019	2 684	281	123 435	47 314
District 15	18.0	18.6	13.2	8.0	5.2	4.3	49.6	222 685	2.82	10.3	21.4	3 112	2 810	0	142 153	35 632
District 16	17.6	16.7	12.3	7.4	4.5	3.5	48.9	186 226	3.38	12.1	17.5	1 255	1 102	0	165 509	25 132
District 17	15.7	15.6	12.9	7.1	5.1	4.8	49.0	202 490	3.02	11.4	22.5	12 888	2 009	2 478	168 208	20 777
District 18	14.0	14.8	11.0	6.7	5.1	4.5	49.9	193 379	3.22	15.9	19.2	6 821	2 373	3	190 670	14 788
District 19	13.2	15.2	13.3	8.4	6.4	5.5	51.1	220 020	2.82	12.3	21.4	11 476	1 649	0	173 681	17 949
District 20	15.8	14.7	9.6	5.6	4.0	3.5	46.2	163 634	3.61	18.7	16.1	39 151	2 157	1 085	197 981	10 133
District 21	13.3	14.4	11.7	7.2	5.4	4.9	50.4	200 404	3.14	13.8	18.5	1 222	3 039	0	191 635	15 878
District 22	13.0	16.6	13.3	8.1	6.0	5.0	49.0	221 297	2.73	12.4	22.7	22 515	2 213	742	172 164	21 600
District 23	14.6	14.5	12.1	7.4	6.0	5.8	49.8	213 124	2.91	10.8	24.3	959	2 098	892	180 804	22 299
District 24	12.7	17.5	14.4	8.7	5.8	5.5	50.3	218 748	2.86	10.0	19.4	5 466	1 896	1 029	159 696	30 243
District 25	13.4	18.1	12.6	6.9	4.6	3.4	49.6	206 878	3.01	12.5	18.7	9 342	1 288	1 632	180 773	25 660
District 26	12.6	16.7	15.0	8.6	5.7	5.2	51.4	215 713	2.89	12.1	19.7	1 971	2 861	0	161 834	42 411
District 27	16.5	16.7	12.9	7.9	5.5	5.1	50.5	221 666	2.83	12.4	24.5	24	4 155	0	147 272	37 300
District 28	18.5	16.0	11.3	6.4	4.5	4.1	49.7	207 748	3.06	13.0	25.9	144	1 088	0	157 864	27 501
District 29	16.2	16.9	13.6	8.6	6.6	6.6	52.1	233 307	2.69	13.2	26.8	42	5 296	0	144 779	40 449
District 30	17.5	17.3	14.9	9.6	7.1	7.5	51.2	291 562	2.12	7.0	39.0	107	3 205	0	111 237	50 007
District 31	19.1	15.0	10.4	5.9	4.1	3.3	49.2	191 693	3.29	17.7	22.3	367	2 359	0	177 542	21 474
District 32	16.2	14.7	11.0	6.9	5.1	3.9	50.6	170 640	3.70	17.3	14.2	102	2 023	0	182 946	24 710
District 33	18.5	16.3	11.9	7.5	5.4	4.9	51.5	246 077	2.55	17.3	34.5	190	1 919	0	150 618	42 911
District 34	18.1	14.2	9.8	5.6	4.0	3.6	48.9	172 589	3.55	17.8	19.8	11 903	1 817	0	188 072	16 982
District 35	16.6	15.0	10.4	6.5	4.4	3.4	51.7	198 116	3.19	23.5	22.8	185	1 279	0	185 434	27 973
District 36	18.9	17.9	13.2	8.0	5.6	4.7	50.1	255 157	2.49	10.8	31.2	8	1 894	44	142 602	29 469
District 37	16.3	14.8	10.5	6.3	4.3	3.7	51.2	193 764	3.25	20.8	23.3	52	2 604	0	196 498	20 442
District 38	15.7	14.4	10.9	6.9	5.2	3.8	50.4	166 175	3.79	17.0	13.5	45	2 300	0	190 326	21 334
District 39	15.7	14.9	11.1	6.7	4.4	3.7	50.6	173 625	3.64	16.3	14.3	1 205	1 955	0	188 519	26 120
District 40	15.7	16.3	12.4	8.3	5.9	4.7	50.4	205 968	3.04	12.4	18.8	2 446	2 872	0	162 946	29 701
District 41	12.1	15.1	12.7	8.4	7.1	6.4	50.6	226 250	2.74	13.1	23.3	2 019	2 290	5 583	164 932	26 251

1. No spouse present. 2. All persons 3 years old and over enrolled in nursery school through college. Note: Data were tabulated for the 108th Congress and some boundary changes have occurred.

STATE District	Education, 2000 (cont'd) Attainment[1] (percent) High school graduate or more	Bachelor's degree or more	Money income, 1999 Per capita income[2]	Median income	Percent with income of $100,000 or more	Percent below poverty level, 1999 Persons Total	Families Total	Housing units, 2000 Total	Occupied units Total	Owner-occupied Percent	Median value[3] (dollars)	Owner cost as a percent of income With a mortgage	Without a mortgage[4]
	31	32	33	34	35	36	37	38	39	40	41	42	43
ALABAMA	75.3	19.0	18 189	34 135	7.6	16.1	12.5	1 963 711	1 737 080	72.5	85 100	19.8	9.9
District 1	77.0	18.5	17 622	34 739	7.0	16.9	13.7	281 691	241 434	73.1	85 300	20.1	9.9
District 2	74.3	18.0	17 139	32 460	6.6	17.2	13.6	281 290	246 539	71.6	79 100	19.3	9.9
District 3	71.9	16.7	16 363	30 806	5.8	18.8	13.8	286 010	248 689	71.0	76 400	20.0	9.9
District 4	68.9	11.3	16 456	31 344	5.3	14.7	11.4	282 766	251 545	78.0	75 000	20.1	9.9
District 5	78.5	23.5	20 060	38 054	9.5	12.5	9.7	278 684	252 745	72.5	90 500	19.0	9.9
District 6	82.9	29.6	25 007	46 946	14.8	8.1	5.9	271 212	249 160	78.0	129 100	19.5	9.9
District 7	73.2	15.1	14 684	26 672	4.2	24.7	20.4	282 058	246 968	62.8	68 100	21.4	11.0
ALASKA	88.3	24.7	22 660	51 571	16.1	9.4	6.7	260 978	221 600	62.5	144 200	22.3	9.9
At Large	88.3	24.7	22 660	51 571	16.1	9.4	6.7	260 978	221 600	62.5	144 200	22.3	9.9
ARIZONA	81.0	23.5	20 275	40 558	10.8	13.9	9.9	2 189 189	1 901 327	68.0	121 300	22.1	9.9
District 1	77.3	17.5	15 357	32 979	6.1	20.3	15.0	293 918	223 930	71.5	103 500	22.4	9.9
District 2	84.1	19.3	20 896	42 432	9.7	8.9	5.9	287 665	249 789	79.3	118 000	22.3	9.9
District 3	87.8	30.3	26 923	48 108	16.1	8.7	5.7	271 149	254 432	66.4	140 400	21.7	9.9
District 4	59.1	10.2	12 205	30 624	4.2	25.6	21.1	210 309	196 221	50.8	80 300	23.0	11.6
District 5	91.7	39.6	29 141	51 780	19.2	8.4	4.8	289 147	261 936	62.9	160 500	21.1	9.9
District 6	85.4	23.6	21 312	47 976	12.2	7.7	5.4	283 059	233 942	77.5	135 200	22.4	9.9
District 7	68.0	13.3	13 756	30 828	4.9	21.8	17.2	258 949	216 094	66.1	85 800	22.7	9.9
District 8	88.5	30.6	22 614	40 656	10.8	10.5	7.3	294 993	264 983	67.1	124 600	22.1	9.9
ARKANSAS	75.3	16.7	16 904	32 182	6.0	15.8	12.0	1 173 043	1 042 696	69.4	72 800	19.4	9.9
District 1	70.4	12.3	15 170	28 940	4.4	18.5	14.4	297 612	260 695	69.6	63 600	19.7	10.6
District 2	81.3	23.2	19 615	37 221	8.3	12.7	9.5	289 170	263 453	67.1	83 800	19.3	9.9
District 3	76.8	17.9	17 269	33 915	6.5	13.7	9.9	286 029	259 465	68.7	82 200	19.4	9.9
District 4	72.7	13.3	15 564	29 675	4.7	18.5	14.2	300 232	259 083	72.2	59 300	19.0	10.5
CALIFORNIA	76.8	26.6	22 711	47 493	17.3	14.2	10.6	12 214 549	11 502 870	56.9	211 500	25.3	9.9
District 1	81.0	25.0	20 615	38 918	11.7	15.3	9.7	265 264	240 381	60.7	182 600	24.8	10.0
District 2	79.4	17.4	17 185	33 559	6.9	17.0	12.0	264 073	241 200	63.1	120 600	24.2	10.5
District 3	88.3	27.0	24 426	51 313	16.1	8.5	5.8	254 967	237 926	68.6	162 500	23.6	9.9
District 4	88.1	25.2	24 527	49 387	16.0	8.7	6.1	285 170	240 815	73.1	191 500	24.8	10.4
District 5	77.8	21.4	17 871	36 719	8.3	19.7	15.3	250 552	237 038	49.6	120 300	24.0	9.9
District 6	87.7	37.9	33 036	59 115	24.7	7.7	4.4	261 714	248 258	63.3	352 800	25.6	9.9
District 7	81.4	22.4	22 016	52 778	16.4	10.0	7.5	225 446	218 711	64.0	190 100	24.6	9.9
District 8	79.8	44.0	34 552	52 322	23.5	12.2	8.8	291 770	276 659	30.2	367 300	25.4	9.9
District 9	79.6	37.4	25 201	44 314	17.6	16.9	12.3	257 833	247 798	45.6	286 300	25.3	9.9
District 10	89.3	36.2	31 093	65 245	26.5	6.3	4.3	239 481	232 728	69.8	274 300	24.8	9.9
District 11	83.8	29.1	28 420	61 996	26.5	8.8	6.2	227 298	219 367	69.0	254 500	24.6	9.9
District 12	87.3	40.7	34 448	70 307	31.3	5.4	3.2	241 928	235 780	62.3	443 400	25.6	9.9
District 13	82.9	31.8	26 076	62 415	23.8	7.1	5.0	222 171	217 139	60.7	295 000	24.9	9.9
District 14	88.5	52.2	43 063	77 985	38.4	6.4	3.8	249 007	240 537	58.5	626 500	24.2	9.9
District 15	86.8	41.6	32 617	74 947	34.2	6.6	4.4	227 528	222 721	57.9	432 400	24.0	9.9
District 16	73.8	26.9	25 064	67 689	29.6	9.8	6.7	190 099	186 227	64.1	376 700	25.0	9.9
District 17	72.3	24.9	21 244	49 234	16.4	13.3	9.0	219 266	202 486	55.5	298 100	26.8	9.9
District 18	62.4	9.7	13 564	34 211	6.0	22.7	18.1	203 907	193 333	56.8	108 100	25.0	10.2
District 19	76.8	20.3	19 280	41 225	11.1	14.8	11.0	240 531	219 833	64.5	131 900	24.0	10.1
District 20	50.2	6.3	10 968	26 800	4.1	32.2	27.4	176 246	163 772	50.1	79 600	25.8	11.5
District 21	67.8	15.0	15 175	36 047	8.4	20.7	15.8	217 443	200 508	61.6	105 400	24.2	10.1
District 22	79.9	18.3	19 263	41 801	10.7	13.7	10.8	244 916	221 335	65.2	115 100	23.3	9.9
District 23	74.9	26.2	20 747	44 874	14.1	15.7	9.4	227 219	213 117	53.7	248 600	26.7	9.9
District 24	85.9	30.0	26 998	61 453	24.3	7.2	5.0	225 932	218 728	71.0	256 400	25.1	9.9
District 25	80.8	18.8	20 175	49 002	15.1	12.6	9.9	231 086	206 818	70.0	147 600	24.7	10.3
District 26	85.8	32.4	26 699	58 968	23.1	8.4	6.2	223 524	215 830	68.7	238 300	25.3	9.9
District 27	76.3	25.8	21 578	46 781	15.4	13.4	10.1	228 414	221 730	54.1	211 300	26.8	10.8
District 28	63.0	23.7	20 611	40 439	14.6	19.1	16.0	215 489	207 603	43.8	195 400	28.2	10.5
District 29	78.4	33.4	22 880	43 895	15.7	14.5	11.6	240 952	233 376	44.0	270 000	26.6	9.9
District 30	92.5	53.5	47 498	60 713	30.1	9.0	4.8	306 415	291 693	47.7	490 000	26.7	9.9
District 31	47.5	13.7	11 702	26 093	5.3	30.1	27.5	202 367	191 535	23.0	173 300	27.9	10.8
District 32	59.1	13.6	14 150	41 394	9.9	18.0	14.6	175 474	170 594	55.9	169 500	26.3	9.9
District 33	71.5	26.9	19 250	31 655	10.1	23.5	19.9	258 985	246 339	30.4	228 200	28.6	10.3
District 34	46.3	8.7	11 816	29 863	6.0	26.0	22.1	180 892	172 533	30.6	178 300	29.1	9.9
District 35	60.7	13.3	14 041	32 156	7.6	26.4	23.2	210 148	198 170	39.5	169 800	29.1	9.9
District 36	81.9	36.9	28 962	51 633	21.1	12.7	9.7	265 718	255 228	44.8	320 200	25.6	9.9
District 37	63.5	15.2	14 286	34 006	8.2	25.2	22.1	204 200	193 734	44.1	163 200	27.4	9.9
District 38	58.4	12.5	14 021	42 488	10.2	16.3	13.3	171 136	166 057	62.5	162 500	26.5	9.9
District 39	62.9	14.7	15 250	45 307	11.7	15.7	12.5	178 949	173 624	59.5	184 600	26.5	9.9
District 40	79.9	26.4	22 434	54 356	18.9	10.2	7.1	210 868	205 982	60.0	238 700	24.6	9.9
District 41	80.2	18.1	18 201	38 721	9.5	15.2	11.8	279 807	226 258	66.9	119 100	23.7	10.9

1. Persons 25 years old and over.   2. Based on the population enumerated as of April 1, 2000.   3. Specified owner-occupied units.   4. Median monthly owner costs is often in the minimum category—9.9 percent or less, which is indicated as 9.9 percent.   Note: Data were tabulated for the 108th Congress and some boundary changes have occurred.

STATE District	Housing units, 2000 (cont'd)			Civilian labor force, 2000			Civilian employment,[4] 2000			Disability, 2000
	Occupied units (cont'd)				Unemployment			Percent		
	Renter-occupied									
	Median rent[1] (dollars)	Rent as a percent of income	Substandard units[2] (percent)	Total	Total	Rate[3]	Total	Management, professional, and related occupations	Production, transportation, and material moving occupations	Employment disabled persons[5] (percent)
	44	45	46	47	48	49	50	51	52	53
ALABAMA	447	24.8	3.5	2 047 100	126 911	6.2	1 920 189	29.5	19.0	13.7
District 1	474	26.0	4.4	283 003	19 249	6.8	263 754	28.2	17.0	14.4
District 2	437	24.2	3.8	282 546	18 140	6.4	264 406	28.9	18.1	14.1
District 3	412	26.7	3.7	285 817	19 177	6.7	266 640	26.9	22.0	14.6
District 4	380	22.7	2.9	290 954	16 368	5.6	274 586	23.2	27.0	14.7
District 5	449	23.9	2.6	311 310	17 169	5.5	294 141	33.3	19.3	12.2
District 6	593	22.6	2.1	320 823	10 906	3.4	309 917	38.5	11.6	10.0
District 7	432	26.9	5.2	272 647	25 902	9.5	246 745	25.4	19.0	15.9
ALASKA	720	24.8	13.0	309 485	27 953	9.0	281 532	34.4	10.8	8.3
At Large	720	24.8	13.0	309 485	27 953	9.0	281 532	34.4	10.8	8.3
ARIZONA	619	26.6	9.3	2 366 372	133 368	5.6	2 233 004	32.7	10.9	12.2
District 1	537	25.2	13.9	256 697	22 875	8.9	233 822	28.5	11.9	12.9
District 2	661	26.8	5.2	275 469	13 789	5.0	261 680	30.0	11.1	12.8
District 3	675	26.2	6.1	349 589	14 073	4.0	335 516	37.4	8.3	10.2
District 4	546	27.3	23.9	265 410	22 244	8.4	243 166	18.3	18.3	18.1
District 5	760	26.4	4.7	360 594	13 550	3.8	347 044	42.4	7.9	9.1
District 6	686	26.2	6.3	300 849	11 470	3.8	289 379	33.8	11.4	10.5
District 7	483	27.4	14.9	260 671	21 793	8.4	238 878	25.1	13.5	14.2
District 8	577	26.8	4.3	297 093	13 574	4.6	283 519	38.8	7.7	10.2
ARKANSAS	453	24.4	4.4	1 249 546	76 147	6.1	1 173 399	27.7	21.0	13.8
District 1	410	25.1	3.9	295 920	18 884	6.4	277 036	24.9	24.1	15.4
District 2	517	24.7	3.8	332 428	19 860	6.0	312 568	32.3	14.9	12.7
District 3	460	23.7	5.4	328 381	18 168	5.5	310 213	27.9	22.1	13.0
District 4	411	24.4	4.4	292 817	19 235	6.6	273 582	25.1	23.5	14.4
CALIFORNIA.....................	747	27.7	15.6	15 829 202	1 110 274	7.0	14 718 928	36.0	12.7	12.8
District 1	653	29.4	8.7	303 818	21 112	6.9	282 706	34.5	11.6	12.0
District 2	537	28.7	7.8	281 395	26 830	9.5	254 565	29.6	13.4	12.5
District 3	705	25.6	5.4	316 253	16 878	5.3	299 375	38.4	9.2	10.6
District 4	704	27.3	4.9	303 767	16 568	5.5	287 199	36.5	9.0	11.3
District 5	626	27.7	12.1	289 249	23 577	8.2	265 672	33.1	11.5	14.6
District 6	956	27.9	6.3	337 888	12 840	3.8	325 048	41.9	8.7	11.0
District 7	810	27.0	11.2	307 841	18 804	6.1	289 037	31.8	12.0	13.1
District 8	902	24.5	14.9	372 676	17 831	4.8	354 845	47.4	7.7	12.7
District 9	734	27.9	13.4	320 654	21 919	6.8	298 735	44.4	10.4	12.8
District 10	923	26.8	5.8	317 796	14 449	4.5	303 347	41.7	8.7	9.7
District 11	771	26.3	7.7	311 562	18 560	6.0	293 002	39.7	10.7	10.5
District 12	1 160	26.1	11.1	343 505	10 656	3.1	332 849	44.2	8.0	10.7
District 13	992	25.6	14.0	323 905	15 679	4.8	308 226	39.2	14.3	12.5
District 14	1 189	24.9	10.4	343 485	12 323	3.6	331 162	57.2	6.5	8.4
District 15	1 218	25.4	12.8	342 084	11 947	3.5	330 137	50.0	10.7	10.5
District 16	1 059	27.9	21.6	316 431	15 059	4.8	301 372	36.3	15.8	14.8
District 17	812	27.6	18.0	302 767	23 707	7.8	279 060	31.9	10.8	13.2
District 18	554	28.5	20.3	259 784	37 096	14.3	222 688	21.9	19.5	15.4
District 19	609	27.5	10.4	288 191	25 900	9.0	262 291	32.3	12.8	13.2
District 20	478	29.4	30.0	224 015	43 225	19.3	180 790	17.7	18.1	17.3
District 21	526	27.8	16.6	276 915	31 566	11.4	245 349	28.1	13.2	14.2
District 22	587	27.6	7.9	274 850	21 088	7.7	253 762	32.0	11.7	12.6
District 23	806	30.3	16.3	310 505	21 040	6.8	289 465	31.9	12.0	12.5
District 24	917	27.1	7.9	313 594	14 839	4.7	298 755	40.1	9.2	10.9
District 25	697	27.9	10.4	281 740	22 100	7.8	259 640	33.3	12.2	10.8
District 26	794	26.8	9.4	314 001	16 751	5.3	297 250	42.0	10.0	10.3
District 27	735	28.1	18.2	316 511	23 208	7.3	293 303	35.8	11.7	13.9
District 28	703	28.2	28.9	292 738	25 604	8.7	267 134	32.3	16.5	16.1
District 29	752	28.1	19.9	308 152	20 336	6.6	287 816	42.1	10.2	13.2
District 30	961	27.3	5.4	361 708	20 287	5.6	341 421	58.2	3.8	9.2
District 31	567	29.3	46.7	262 801	29 380	11.2	233 421	20.1	24.1	18.7
District 32	713	28.5	32.6	266 931	21 933	8.2	244 998	23.2	23.1	16.3
District 33	658	29.8	23.8	297 523	30 816	10.4	266 707	35.3	11.4	15.8
District 34	604	28.7	44.1	241 969	27 549	11.4	214 420	17.6	30.2	16.9
District 35	643	30.1	30.6	255 704	28 574	11.2	227 130	24.1	20.1	16.9
District 36	851	25.8	13.8	337 513	18 790	5.6	318 723	44.3	9.8	10.6
District 37	615	29.3	29.6	260 489	29 199	11.2	231 290	25.9	20.4	15.8
District 38	698	28.7	31.9	258 529	22 286	8.6	236 243	22.5	24.5	16.2
District 39	709	27.8	30.4	267 612	22 185	8.3	245 427	25.4	22.0	14.3
District 40	851	27.5	16.2	313 482	16 991	5.4	296 491	34.9	13.8	11.8
District 41	609	27.7	9.3	268 848	21 411	8.0	247 437	31.4	12.9	13.9

1. Specified renter-occupied units.   2. Overcrowded or lacking complete plumbing facilities.   3. Percent of total civilian labor force.   4. Persons 16 years old and over.   5. Persons 16 to 64 years old.   Note: Data were tabulated for the 108th Congress and some boundary changes have occurred.

Table E. Congressional Districts 109th Congress — **Land Area and Population**

STATE District	Representative	Land area,[1] 2000 (sq km)	Population and population characteristics, 2000											
					Race alone or in combination					Percent			Age		
			Total persons	Per square kilometer	White	Black	Am. Indian, Alaska Native	Asian and Pacific Islander	Other race	Hispanic or Latino[2]	Non-Hispanic White	Two or more races	Under 5 years	5 to 17 years	18 to 24 years
		1	2	3	4	5	6	7	8	9	10	11	12	13	14
CALIFORNIA—Cont'd															
District 42	Gary Miller (R)	813	639 088	786.4	69.5	3.4	1.1	18.0	12.3	23.8	54.4	4.1	7.2	21.1	8.3
District 43	Joe Baca (D)	494	639 087	1 292.7	48.1	13.9	2.2	4.6	36.8	58.3	23.4	5.3	10.0	26.6	10.9
District 44	Ken Calvert (R)	1 352	639 088	472.6	69.1	6.5	1.9	6.5	20.9	35.0	51.3	4.6	8.2	22.5	10.3
District 45	Mary Bono (R)	15 488	639 088	41.3	68.9	7.3	1.8	4.2	22.0	38.0	50.1	3.9	7.5	21.6	8.6
District 46	Dana Rohrabacher (R)	683	639 088	935.9	74.1	1.9	1.3	17.6	9.1	16.9	62.8	3.9	6.0	15.9	8.3
District 47	Loretta Sanchez (D)	142	639 087	4 511.2	47.3	2.2	1.7	15.4	38.3	65.3	17.3	4.7	10.0	23.2	11.9
District 48	Christopher Cox (R)	550	639 087	1 162.6	78.6	1.9	0.9	14.8	7.9	14.7	68.0	3.8	6.5	16.9	8.5
District 49	Darrell Issa (R)	4 378	639 087	146.0	73.7	6.1	2.3	5.8	16.9	29.5	57.9	4.4	7.9	21.2	11.4
District 50	Randy "Duke" Cunningham (R)	778	639 087	821.8	77.6	2.5	1.3	12.5	10.4	18.8	65.8	4.0	6.9	18.4	8.4
District 51	Bob Filner (D)	11 868	639 087	53.9	47.4	10.8	1.7	15.5	30.2	53.3	21.3	5.2	7.8	22.9	10.5
District 52	Duncan Hunter (R)	5 473	639 087	116.8	83.6	4.6	1.7	7.8	7.2	13.7	72.9	4.5	7.0	19.6	8.5
District 53	Susan A. Davis (D)	246	639 087	2 599.1	67.1	8.6	1.6	10.8	17.3	29.4	51.0	5.0	6.2	14.6	16.1
COLORADO		268 627	4 301 261	16.0	85.2	4.4	1.9	3.0	8.5	17.1	74.5	2.8	6.9	18.7	10.0
District 1	Diana DeGette (D)	444	614 465	1 384.7	70.1	11.4	2.2	3.7	16.7	30.0	54.3	3.7	6.7	15.1	10.7
District 2	Mark Udall (D)	14 542	614 465	42.3	88.5	1.4	1.4	4.1	7.3	14.7	78.9	2.5	6.8	17.9	11.8
District 3	John T. Salazar (D)	139 765	614 467	4.4	88.6	1.0	2.9	0.9	9.2	21.5	74.6	2.5	6.3	18.8	9.4
District 4	Marilyn Musgrave (R)	80 025	614 466	7.7	89.0	1.0	1.5	1.7	9.1	17.0	79.4	2.3	6.9	19.2	12.2
District 5	Joel Hefley (R)	19 963	614 467	30.8	85.7	7.0	2.1	3.6	5.6	11.1	77.4	3.6	7.2	19.5	10.0
District 6	Thomas Tancredo (R)	10 629	614 466	57.8	93.0	2.4	1.0	3.5	2.3	5.8	87.7	2.0	7.4	22.1	5.9
District 7	Bob Beauprez (R)	3 259	614 465	188.6	81.7	6.9	1.9	3.8	9.2	19.6	68.9	3.3	7.2	18.0	10.0
CONNECTICUT		12 548	3 405 565	271.4	83.3	10.0	0.7	2.9	5.5	9.4	77.5	2.2	6.6	18.2	8.0
District 1	John Larson (D)	1 691	681 113	402.7	76.8	14.2	0.7	3.0	7.9	11.4	71.6	2.4	6.4	18.0	7.7
District 2	Rob Simmons (R)	5 253	681 113	129.7	92.1	4.2	1.2	2.2	2.4	4.3	88.6	1.9	6.2	18.1	9.1
District 3	Rosa DeLauro (D)	1 189	681 113	572.7	81.4	12.7	0.7	3.0	4.4	8.0	76.1	2.0	6.2	17.4	8.9
District 4	Christopher Shays (R)	1 183	681 113	575.5	79.4	12.3	0.5	3.8	6.7	12.8	70.9	2.5	7.4	18.6	6.9
District 5	Nancy Johnson (R)	3 231	681 113	210.8	86.8	6.3	0.6	2.6	6.0	10.5	80.2	2.2	6.6	18.7	7.3
DELAWARE		5 060	783 600	154.9	75.9	20.1	0.8	2.5	2.6	4.8	72.5	1.7	6.6	18.3	9.6
At Large	Michael N. Castle (R)	5 060	783 600	154.9	75.9	20.1	0.8	2.5	2.6	4.8	72.5	1.7	6.6	18.3	9.6
DISTRICT OF COLUMBIA		159	572 059	3 597.9	32.2	61.3	0.8	3.2	5.0	7.9	27.8	2.4	5.7	14.4	12.7
Delegate	Eleanor Holmes Norton (D)	159	572 059	3 597.1	32.2	61.3	0.8	3.3	5.0	7.9	27.8	2.4	5.7	14.4	12.7
FLORIDA		139 670	15 982 378	114.4	79.7	15.5	0.7	2.3	4.4	16.8	65.4	2.4	5.9	16.9	8.3
District 1	Jeff Miller (R)	12 022	639 295	53.2	81.7	14.7	1.8	2.9	1.4	3.0	78.0	2.3	6.2	18.1	10.3
District 2	Allen Boyd (D)	24 410	639 295	26.2	74.7	22.8	1.1	1.7	1.3	3.3	71.5	1.5	5.8	18.0	13.4
District 3	Corrine Brown (D)	4 652	639 295	137.4	43.9	51.4	0.8	2.3	4.5	8.0	38.4	2.7	7.5	20.8	10.7
District 4	Ander Crenshaw (R)	10 665	639 295	59.9	81.9	14.2	0.9	3.1	1.8	4.2	77.8	1.8	6.6	17.7	9.2
District 5	Virginia Brown-Waite (R)	10 474	639 295	61.0	92.5	4.9	0.9	1.1	1.9	5.6	87.7	1.3	5.0	15.3	5.7
District 6	Cliff Stearns (R)	7 541	639 295	84.8	83.6	12.5	0.9	2.9	2.0	5.2	78.9	1.8	5.7	17.2	12.2
District 7	John Mica (R)	4 654	639 295	137.4	87.1	9.4	0.7	1.9	2.5	6.9	81.3	1.5	5.4	16.7	7.9
District 8	Ric Keller (R)	2 556	639 295	250.2	82.8	8.5	0.8	3.8	7.0	17.6	69.9	2.8	6.2	17.2	9.0
District 9	Mike Bilirakis (R)	1 642	639 296	389.4	91.9	4.0	0.7	2.3	2.8	7.9	85.2	1.6	5.7	16.2	6.5
District 10	C.W. Bill Young (R)	452	639 295	1 414.1	92.3	4.1	0.8	2.8	1.7	4.4	88.0	1.6	4.6	13.4	6.2
District 11	Jim Davis (D)	632	639 295	1 012.1	63.8	29.3	0.9	2.8	6.4	20.0	48.3	2.9	6.9	18.3	10.3
District 12	Adam Putnam (R)	5 066	639 296	126.2	80.1	13.9	0.9	1.5	5.6	12.0	72.1	1.9	6.7	18.6	8.5
District 13	Katherine Harris (R)	6 732	639 295	95.0	91.5	4.9	0.6	1.1	3.1	7.7	86.0	1.2	4.6	13.4	5.9
District 14	Connie Mack (R)	2 736	639 295	233.6	90.7	5.8	0.5	1.1	3.5	9.0	83.8	1.5	4.8	13.5	5.7
District 15	Dave Weldon (R)	6 591	639 295	97.0	86.5	8.3	0.8	2.3	4.4	11.3	77.8	2.1	5.4	16.7	7.1
District 16	Mark Foley (R)	11 755	639 295	54.4	89.1	6.4	0.7	1.4	4.1	10.1	81.8	1.5	5.1	16.0	6.0
District 17	Kendrick Meek (D)	250	639 295	2 557.2	34.8	60.0	0.6	2.4	7.1	21.2	18.4	4.7	7.4	21.9	10.1
District 18	Ileana Ros-Lehtinen (R)	919	639 295	695.4	86.7	7.8	0.5	1.4	7.0	62.7	29.7	3.2	5.2	14.2	8.2
District 19	Robert Wexler (D)	598	639 295	1 068.4	88.1	7.0	0.4	2.5	4.2	12.7	77.5	2.1	5.1	13.8	5.8
District 20	Debbie Wasserman Schultz (D)	416	639 295	1 538.4	85.5	9.2	0.5	3.0	4.6	20.6	66.9	2.7	5.8	15.5	6.6
District 21	Lincoln Diaz-Balart (R)	349	639 295	1 829.4	85.0	8.3	0.3	2.4	7.6	69.7	21.0	3.5	6.5	17.9	8.5
District 22	E. Clay Shaw Jr. (R)	694	639 295	921.7	91.7	4.5	0.4	2.2	3.1	10.7	82.3	1.8	4.9	13.9	5.7
District 23	Alcee L. Hastings (D)	8 708	639 295	73.4	39.1	55.5	0.7	2.0	7.8	13.7	29.4	4.9	7.5	20.7	9.9
District 24	Tom Feeney (R)	4 101	639 295	155.9	87.9	7.1	0.8	2.7	3.6	9.8	80.0	2.0	5.7	17.4	9.4
District 25	Mario Diaz-Balart (R)	11 054	639 295	57.8	79.2	12.0	0.5	2.3	10.1	62.4	24.3	3.9	7.6	21.0	9.5
GEORGIA		149 976	8 186 453	54.6	66.1	29.2	0.6	2.5	2.9	5.3	62.6	1.4	7.3	19.2	10.2
District 1	Jack Kingston (R)	29 092	629 761	21.6	73.7	23.2	0.7	1.4	2.4	4.1	71.0	1.3	7.5	20.1	10.4
District 2	Sanford D. Bishop Jr. (D)	25 185	629 735	25.0	52.2	45.2	0.7	0.9	2.1	3.5	50.3	1.0	7.5	20.2	11.6
District 3	Jim Marshall (D)	28 269	629 748	22.3	57.7	40.3	0.5	0.8	1.6	2.6	56.2	0.8	6.8	19.5	10.2
District 4	Cynthia Ann McKinney (D)	650	629 690	968.7	37.1	54.7	0.7	4.9	5.1	8.5	32.0	2.2	7.3	17.7	11.0
District 5	John Lewis (D)	652	629 727	965.5	38.0	56.9	0.6	2.7	3.5	6.1	34.4	1.5	6.4	15.4	13.1
District 6	Thomas Edmunds Price (R)	1 127	629 725	559.0	86.9	7.4	0.5	4.6	2.3	4.5	83.0	1.5	7.3	20.3	6.8

1. Dry land or land partially or temporarily covered by water. 2. Hispanic or Latino persons may be of any race. Note: Data were tabulated for the 108th Congress and some boundary changes have occurred.

Table E. Congressional Districts 109th Congress — Population, Households, Group Quarters, and Education

STATE District	Population and population characteristics, 2000 (cont'd)							Households, 2000				Persons in correctional institutions, 2000	Persons in nursing homes, 2000	Persons in military quarters, 2000	Education, 2000	
	Percent (cont'd)									Percent					School enrollment[2]	
	Age (cont'd)															
	25 to 34 years	35 to 44 years	45 to 54 years	55 to 64 years	65 to 74 years	75 years and over	Percent female	Number	Persons per household	Female family householder[1]	One person				Public	Private
	15	16	17	18	19	20	21	22	23	24	25	26	27	28	29	30
CALIFORNIA—Cont'd																
District 42	13.7	18.5	14.8	8.1	4.6	3.7	50.4	205 634	3.04	10.0	15.8	9 726	569	0	166 860	36 806
District 43	15.6	15.2	10.1	5.3	3.5	2.8	50.3	174 806	3.61	18.2	15.4	2 257	1 703	0	201 258	16 025
District 44	14.6	16.7	12.4	7.0	4.5	3.9	50.0	200 177	3.12	12.1	18.2	5 968	2 049	1	177 293	27 518
District 45	12.3	14.9	11.2	8.2	8.2	7.5	49.9	218 502	2.85	11.4	23.1	9 748	1 971	0	162 474	17 140
District 46	16.1	16.8	14.0	9.9	6.9	6.0	50.3	241 993	2.60	9.1	26.3	1 375	1 618	154	144 105	30 223
District 47	18.9	14.9	9.2	5.3	3.6	2.8	48.6	150 284	4.20	13.8	13.8	2 473	1 653	0	185 943	14 857
District 48	15.6	17.7	14.4	8.6	5.6	6.2	51.4	247 176	2.54	8.8	26.4	944	1 850	0	151 703	32 394
District 49	13.6	15.6	11.0	6.8	6.4	6.2	49.3	209 018	2.95	10.4	19.2	1 141	1 026	15 770	161 177	21 277
District 50	14.3	17.3	14.3	8.1	6.1	6.2	50.3	231 839	2.72	9.3	22.4	148	2 512	4 114	149 416	28 869
District 51	14.7	15.6	11.5	7.1	5.7	4.2	49.9	184 751	3.33	17.7	15.9	17 028	942	2 700	193 636	17 650
District 52	14.0	17.6	14.1	8.1	5.9	5.2	51.0	232 804	2.71	11.2	21.0	1 280	3 288	0	160 389	26 772
District 53	20.8	15.3	10.9	6.1	4.7	5.2	48.1	252 619	2.35	11.2	35.6	2 402	2 611	18 800	163 162	27 686
COLORADO	15.4	17.1	14.3	7.9	5.3	4.4	49.6	1 658 238	2.53	9.6	26.3	30 136	18 495	8 512	1 003 508	162 496
District 1	20.4	15.7	12.9	7.2	5.5	5.8	49.5	266 388	2.26	10.8	39.2	3 059	3 257	0	116 233	28 477
District 2	17.6	17.9	14.3	7.0	4.0	2.7	48.9	233 172	2.59	8.5	23.5	782	1 579	0	149 615	22 921
District 3	12.4	15.6	14.9	9.3	7.2	6.2	50.0	240 903	2.48	9.9	25.9	3 787	3 290	0	143 752	14 767
District 4	14.0	16.1	13.4	7.8	5.4	5.0	49.6	227 615	2.61	8.6	23.4	6 726	3 667	0	166 081	17 938
District 5	14.7	17.7	13.8	7.7	5.3	4.0	49.1	228 136	2.58	9.8	24.1	11 375	2 477	8 321	142 277	26 608
District 6	13.3	20.2	16.9	7.8	3.9	2.7	50.3	221 373	2.76	7.2	17.7	1 260	1 357	0	151 091	29 660
District 7	15.8	16.7	13.8	8.4	5.6	4.5	50.1	240 651	2.51	11.8	27.8	3 147	2 868	191	134 459	22 125
CONNECTICUT	13.3	17.1	14.1	9.1	6.8	7.0	51.6	1 301 670	2.53	12.1	26.4	20 023	32 223	2 097	731 418	179 451
District 1	13.3	16.5	14.1	9.2	7.1	7.7	52.3	269 019	2.46	14.0	28.4	1 055	9 159	0	149 877	27 218
District 2	12.9	17.9	14.5	9.1	6.4	5.9	50.2	255 449	2.53	9.7	24.4	11 896	4 781	2 081	158 447	28 479
District 3	14.0	16.4	13.6	8.8	7.0	7.7	52.1	267 124	2.47	13.2	28.8	1 365	6 254	16	139 264	46 966
District 4	13.2	17.4	13.9	9.2	6.8	6.5	51.8	250 190	2.67	12.0	24.1	880	4 982	0	136 317	46 114
District 5	12.9	17.2	14.5	9.1	6.6	7.2	51.4	259 888	2.55	11.3	26.2	4 827	7 047	0	147 513	30 674
DELAWARE	13.9	16.3	13.3	9.1	7.2	5.8	51.4	298 736	2.54	13.1	25.0	5 965	4 852	381	164 193	45 786
At Large	13.9	16.3	13.3	9.1	7.2	5.8	51.4	298 736	2.54	13.1	25.0	5 965	4 852	381	164 193	45 786
DISTRICT OF COLUMBIA	17.8	15.3	13.2	8.7	6.3	5.9	52.9	248 338	2.16	18.9	43.8	2 838	3 759	927	105 998	51 477
Delegate	17.8	15.3	13.2	8.7	6.3	5.9	52.9	248 338	2.16	18.9	43.8	2 838	3 759	927	105 998	51 477
FLORIDA	13.0	15.5	12.9	9.8	9.1	8.5	51.2	6 337 929	2.46	12.0	26.6	139 148	88 828	13 457	3 257 226	676 053
District 1	13.6	16.3	13.2	9.5	7.3	5.4	49.8	242 609	2.49	12.7	24.7	15 657	4 065	7 702	142 370	23 571
District 2	13.7	15.4	13.6	9.2	6.8	5.2	50.3	248 654	2.42	12.9	26.9	19 044	3 904	527	170 884	18 564
District 3	14.7	15.4	12.1	7.9	6.0	4.8	51.5	236 230	2.63	22.4	26.7	8 532	2 292	0	165 629	20 284
District 4	15.6	17.2	14.1	8.5	6.0	5.1	50.1	246 192	2.49	11.2	25.2	14 104	3 651	4 036	130 604	30 773
District 5	10.0	13.4	12.3	12.8	14.3	11.3	51.1	263 158	2.37	8.4	23.1	8 846	3 476	0	108 408	16 602
District 6	12.5	14.8	12.7	9.4	8.6	6.8	51.0	247 842	2.48	10.9	23.4	8 762	3 756	4	162 669	22 598
District 7	11.3	15.5	14.3	10.6	9.6	8.6	51.5	259 206	2.41	10.7	25.9	1 636	4 702	0	121 149	33 012
District 8	15.4	16.9	13.0	8.6	7.3	6.5	51.0	254 707	2.48	11.0	25.9	879	3 301	0	128 221	30 451
District 9	11.8	15.7	13.7	9.9	9.8	10.7	52.0	267 147	2.36	9.0	27.5	81	5 265	0	118 002	26 627
District 10	11.8	15.7	14.2	10.7	10.8	12.5	52.1	294 543	2.12	9.4	35.1	3 269	5 370	56	96 176	28 403
District 11	15.8	15.9	12.6	8.2	6.3	5.7	51.5	257 416	2.42	17.1	31.4	3 076	3 095	412	145 529	28 211
District 12	12.8	14.7	12.3	9.5	9.0	8.1	50.9	243 066	2.56	12.3	23.7	5 835	3 901	0	132 778	24 155
District 13	10.0	13.0	12.5	12.1	14.2	14.3	51.6	281 888	2.21	7.9	29.1	4 010	5 854	13	96 375	18 497
District 14	10.0	13.0	12.4	13.2	15.0	12.3	51.3	279 349	2.26	7.8	26.1	1 709	4 190	16	93 605	17 944
District 15	11.4	15.6	12.9	10.6	10.8	9.4	51.2	262 084	2.40	10.3	25.9	1 621	3 084	215	120 917	25 992
District 16	9.7	14.0	12.4	11.3	13.4	12.1	50.8	262 499	2.39	8.3	24.5	4 212	3 995	7	114 240	19 682
District 17	14.0	15.5	12.4	7.9	5.7	5.1	52.3	213 262	2.93	24.0	24.3	4 154	3 635	262	181 892	28 392
District 18	15.0	16.0	13.2	10.5	9.2	8.6	50.6	254 897	2.45	12.9	31.3	2 509	2 504	179	113 955	35 304
District 19	11.4	13.8	11.3	9.1	12.7	17.0	53.1	283 779	2.23	8.3	30.6	382	2 370	0	102 259	26 631
District 20	14.5	17.5	13.8	9.0	7.8	9.6	51.7	275 076	2.30	10.3	32.3	91	2 130	0	112 060	40 711
District 21	15.2	16.7	12.6	9.7	7.4	5.5	52.1	211 124	2.99	15.6	17.0	1 148	2 602	11	142 986	35 479
District 22	12.0	16.8	14.8	11.0	10.0	10.8	51.2	285 462	2.21	7.5	32.5	0	3 667	11	94 283	38 953
District 23	14.8	15.9	11.6	7.4	5.8	6.3	50.6	224 179	2.75	20.5	27.2	13 767	3 442	0	163 803	20 256
District 24	13.2	16.8	13.4	9.4	8.2	6.5	50.5	249 141	2.51	10.1	23.3	7 132	2 691	5	139 918	29 237
District 25	15.8	17.3	12.3	7.8	5.1	3.5	50.5	194 419	3.21	16.0	13.7	8 692	1 886	1	158 514	35 724
GEORGIA	15.9	16.5	13.2	8.1	5.3	4.3	50.8	3 006 369	2.65	14.5	23.6	81 773	34 812	25 461	1 892 188	319 500
District 1	14.6	15.8	12.7	8.5	6.0	4.6	49.9	228 671	2.64	12.9	22.3	10 727	3 625	8 840	148 035	18 173
District 2	13.9	14.3	12.3	8.2	6.4	5.6	51.6	228 845	2.62	20.2	25.3	7 617	4 275	9 816	160 701	16 661
District 3	13.7	15.6	13.1	9.0	6.5	5.6	50.9	229 679	2.58	18.3	25.8	23 414	6 075	0	148 511	20 862
District 4	19.5	17.2	12.8	6.9	4.2	3.5	51.4	234 065	2.63	17.6	26.3	3 181	1 881	0	135 039	38 076
District 5	21.6	15.7	12.0	6.9	4.5	4.3	50.7	261 651	2.29	18.3	37.6	7 705	1 683	88	126 564	37 689
District 6	14.8	19.7	16.3	8.0	3.9	2.9	50.6	229 908	2.73	7.6	19.3	34	1 063	0	137 490	38 019

1. No spouse present.   2. All persons 3 years old and over enrolled in nursery school through college.   Note: Data were tabulated for the 108th Congress and some boundary changes have occurred.

Table E. Congressional Districts 109th Congress — Education, Money Income, Poverty, and Housing

STATE District	Education, 2000 (cont'd) Attainment (percent) High school graduate or more	Bachelor's degree or more	Money income, 1999 Households Per capita income[2]	Median income	Percent with income of $100,000 or more	Percent below poverty level, 1999 Persons Total	Families Total	Housing units, 2000 Total	Occupied units Total	Owner-occupied Percent	Median value[3] (dollars)	Owner cost as a percent of income With a mortgage	Without a mortgage[4]
	31	32	33	34	35	36	37	38	39	40	41	42	43
CALIFORNIA—Cont'd													
District 42	87.5	34.8	27 572	70 463	29.6	6.0	4.2	210 045	205 667	76.4	262 500	25.4	9.9
District 43	61.7	8.8	12 861	37 390	6.8	20.7	17.4	188 239	174 721	59.9	118 200	26.3	9.9
District 44	77.2	21.1	21 335	51 578	17.5	12.1	8.7	209 663	200 212	65.8	175 300	25.2	9.9
District 45	74.3	17.4	19 423	40 468	11.9	15.0	11.3	278 037	218 350	69.2	138 400	25.5	11.4
District 46	86.7	36.4	30 942	61 567	25.5	7.8	5.0	251 008	241 898	61.6	305 000	24.6	9.9
District 47	50.4	10.0	12 541	41 618	8.8	19.1	15.4	153 695	150 209	47.4	183 600	26.8	9.9
District 48	91.8	46.5	37 242	69 663	31.6	6.3	3.7	263 177	247 151	65.1	338 100	25.3	9.9
District 49	80.1	20.7	19 659	46 445	13.1	11.9	8.7	222 495	209 193	66.8	187 600	26.6	9.9
District 50	87.1	40.0	29 877	59 813	24.5	8.1	5.0	241 791	231 948	65.9	282 000	25.0	9.9
District 51	69.0	15.2	14 923	39 243	8.9	16.3	13.8	193 519	184 647	56.7	158 500	26.0	9.9
District 52	88.5	28.6	24 544	52 940	17.7	8.1	5.7	241 211	232 585	63.9	232 300	25.3	9.9
District 53	80.1	32.2	21 715	36 637	10.6	20.2	15.4	267 484	252 788	34.4	218 700	26.3	9.9
COLORADO	86.9	32.7	24 049	47 203	14.2	9.3	6.2	1 808 037	1 658 238	67.3	166 600	22.6	9.9
District 1	79.6	34.3	24 622	39 658	11.5	13.7	10.1	279 664	266 247	52.2	164 800	23.2	9.9
District 2	89.7	39.3	26 544	55 204	18.0	7.4	4.0	270 633	233 172	69.2	196 500	22.9	9.9
District 3	83.8	23.8	19 148	35 970	7.6	12.8	9.2	284 931	240 911	70.4	116 000	22.9	9.9
District 4	85.3	28.7	20 836	43 389	11.2	10.9	6.7	245 293	227 695	68.0	151 800	22.8	9.9
District 5	90.2	29.8	21 605	45 454	11.5	8.3	5.9	249 295	228 166	66.5	145 100	22.7	9.9
District 6	95.6	46.8	33 175	73 393	30.1	2.7	1.9	229 881	221 355	84.9	214 200	21.9	9.9
District 7	84.6	26.0	22 412	46 149	11.3	8.9	6.4	248 340	240 692	63.2	161 200	22.5	9.9
CONNECTICUT	84.0	31.4	28 766	53 935	20.2	7.9	5.6	1 385 975	1 301 670	66.8	166 900	22.4	13.1
District 1	82.2	28.2	25 084	50 227	16.0	9.6	7.3	284 112	268 880	63.6	145 100	22.0	12.8
District 2	86.7	28.8	25 548	54 498	17.2	5.8	3.7	277 468	255 470	72.0	147 000	21.7	11.9
District 3	83.6	28.0	24 655	49 752	15.6	8.8	6.4	283 365	267 105	63.6	155 000	23.1	14.1
District 4	84.6	42.2	41 147	66 598	33.2	7.4	5.4	262 015	250 230	67.8	347 200	23.1	13.7
District 5	82.9	29.9	27 396	53 118	19.5	7.7	5.5	279 015	259 985	67.5	167 000	22.3	13.2
DELAWARE	82.6	25.0	23 305	47 381	14.0	9.2	6.5	343 072	298 736	72.3	130 400	20.8	9.9
At Large	82.6	25.0	23 305	47 381	14.0	9.2	6.5	343 072	298 736	72.3	130 400	20.8	9.9
DISTRICT OF COLUMBIA	77.8	39.1	28 659	40 127	16.4	20.2	16.7	274 845	248 338	40.8	157 200	22.2	9.9
Delegate	77.8	39.1	28 659	40 127	16.4	20.2	16.7	274 845	248 338	40.8	157 200	22.2	9.9
FLORIDA	79.9	22.3	21 557	38 819	10.4	12.5	9.0	7 302 947	6 337 929	70.1	105 500	22.8	10.5
District 1	82.5	20.2	18 814	36 738	7.3	13.1	10.3	275 740	242 696	70.6	91 200	21.2	9.9
District 2	80.1	24.1	18 462	34 718	7.8	16.5	11.1	309 196	248 547	68.4	95 600	21.1	9.9
District 3	71.3	12.9	14 473	29 785	4.2	21.5	17.4	265 456	236 276	55.6	69 300	22.8	10.2
District 4	84.7	24.4	22 332	43 947	11.6	9.1	6.6	267 645	246 246	69.4	104 200	20.4	9.9
District 5	78.8	14.3	18 631	34 815	6.0	10.6	7.6	306 780	263 218	85.2	94 800	22.0	9.9
District 6	82.8	21.4	18 983	36 846	8.0	13.4	8.3	272 294	247 789	72.9	93 300	21.0	9.9
District 7	84.5	24.5	23 153	40 525	12.0	10.1	7.0	290 206	259 281	74.1	106 400	22.2	9.9
District 8	83.7	25.9	22 292	41 568	10.9	9.4	6.9	280 007	254 858	66.4	107 900	22.5	10.2
District 9	83.6	24.6	23 837	40 742	12.5	8.6	6.0	301 672	266 733	76.3	107 000	22.1	10.8
District 10	84.3	22.6	24 045	37 168	9.3	8.9	5.8	344 300	294 533	71.7	94 400	22.3	11.4
District 11	76.5	21.2	19 149	33 559	7.8	17.5	13.4	282 666	257 770	55.4	81 000	22.3	11.6
District 12	76.3	16.6	18 544	37 769	7.2	12.4	9.0	283 392	243 267	72.7	87 600	21.1	9.9
District 13	83.8	23.7	25 055	40 187	10.9	9.4	6.1	347 572	281 788	77.5	119 400	23.2	10.6
District 14	84.2	24.4	28 159	42 541	13.4	8.8	5.9	375 780	279 398	77.3	128 000	23.4	10.5
District 15	83.8	22.3	21 721	39 397	9.2	9.8	7.1	305 220	261 939	73.2	99 200	22.3	9.9
District 16	81.0	20.0	22 996	39 408	11.0	10.0	6.7	316 721	262 341	81.7	103 500	22.7	10.3
District 17	66.5	13.5	13 676	30 426	5.3	23.3	20.0	236 236	213 285	57.4	89 600	27.0	13.5
District 18	67.1	25.6	22 786	32 298	12.5	19.3	14.5	300 463	255 055	47.9	161 500	27.3	14.1
District 19	85.7	25.7	26 810	42 237	13.4	7.7	5.2	326 763	283 625	79.1	134 300	23.4	11.3
District 20	85.3	29.6	26 845	44 034	15.2	9.6	6.8	318 204	275 276	69.9	138 600	24.0	12.9
District 21	68.8	22.9	18 829	41 426	12.4	13.0	10.6	220 665	211 014	61.9	139 800	25.7	13.1
District 22	88.6	34.1	35 484	51 200	21.0	7.1	4.6	343 404	285 359	74.3	165 200	23.7	12.2
District 23	66.5	12.8	14 715	31 309	5.0	21.9	18.3	250 353	224 530	56.5	85 400	24.8	12.7
District 24	86.4	25.5	22 114	43 954	11.4	8.7	5.5	273 931	248 930	74.3	105 800	21.9	9.9
District 25	72.4	20.3	17 030	44 489	11.4	13.7	11.0	208 281	194 175	72.7	126 200	25.7	12.3
GEORGIA	78.6	24.3	21 154	42 433	12.3	13.0	9.9	3 281 737	3 006 369	67.5	111 200	20.8	9.9
District 1	77.2	17.9	18 080	36 158	8.3	14.8	11.7	262 566	228 520	71.4	89 400	20.5	10.3
District 2	70.3	13.9	15 128	29 354	5.6	22.5	18.3	260 092	228 773	62.5	71 200	20.4	10.6
District 3	70.6	12.8	15 532	31 433	5.6	19.9	15.9	262 533	229 691	69.0	71 000	20.0	9.9
District 4	85.4	35.9	23 851	49 307	15.6	10.5	7.6	244 662	234 301	57.7	135 000	21.3	9.9
District 5	80.8	37.3	26 024	39 725	14.6	19.7	16.5	287 484	261 795	42.1	132 700	22.6	10.8
District 6	93.9	50.7	35 781	75 611	33.9	3.7	2.4	239 049	229 887	79.2	185 100	20.1	9.9

1. Persons 25 years old and over.   2. Based on the population enumerated as of April 1, 2000.   3. Specified owner-occupied units.   4. Median monthly owner costs is often in the minimum category—9.9 percent or less, which is indicated as 9.9 percent.   Note: Data were tabulated for the 108th Congress and some boundary changes have occurred.

STATE District	Median rent[1] (dollars)	Rent as a percent of income	Substandard units[2] (percent)	Total	Unemployment Total	Rate[3]	Total	Management, professional, and related occupations	Production, transportation, and material moving occupations	Employment disabled persons[5] (percent)
	44	45	46	47	48	49	50	51	52	53
CALIFORNIA—Cont'd										
District 42	956	27.6	8.9	321 090	13 938	4.3	307 152	43.5	9.1	9.3
District 43	625	30.1	25.3	251 321	26 054	10.4	225 267	19.2	24.0	16.1
District 44	727	28.2	13.3	294 136	19 434	6.6	274 702	31.9	15.1	11.5
District 45	644	28.6	12.7	258 909	19 777	7.6	239 132	26.5	11.5	15.0
District 46	963	25.5	9.1	338 212	14 022	4.1	324 190	44.1	9.0	10.1
District 47	787	29.0	44.6	266 300	20 797	7.8	245 503	17.2	26.4	18.3
District 48	1 151	27.0	7.4	341 555	13 621	4.0	327 934	50.1	5.9	8.3
District 49	774	28.8	12.2	264 780	17 020	6.4	247 760	30.9	13.5	12.3
District 50	907	27.4	8.5	318 693	13 853	4.3	304 840	45.2	8.6	9.5
District 51	638	28.5	22.4	251 072	21 965	8.7	229 107	26.4	13.4	14.1
District 52	785	27.1	6.7	317 273	15 442	4.9	301 831	38.8	8.5	9.7
District 53	709	28.7	14.5	316 680	23 458	7.4	293 222	38.6	8.9	11.7
COLORADO	671	26.4	4.9	2 304 454	99 260	4.3	2 205 194	37.4	10.5	9.9
District 1	634	26.1	7.9	335 614	18 454	5.5	317 160	37.7	10.3	13.5
District 2	817	26.9	4.4	361 893	14 225	3.9	347 668	39.9	10.1	8.3
District 3	529	27.0	4.6	305 359	16 902	5.5	288 457	30.2	11.1	11.3
District 4	619	26.8	4.7	323 987	14 066	4.3	309 921	35.2	13.3	9.3
District 5	648	26.2	3.9	300 659	13 848	4.6	286 811	36.2	10.6	9.1
District 6	931	25.2	1.8	344 973	7 625	2.2	337 348	48.0	6.1	6.0
District 7	698	26.4	6.5	331 969	14 140	4.3	317 829	32.6	12.1	11.8
CONNECTICUT	681	25.4	3.2	1 757 108	92 668	5.3	1 664 440	39.1	12.0	11.0
District 1	651	25.0	3.7	351 736	22 373	6.4	329 363	38.0	12.5	11.9
District 2	645	24.0	1.8	358 658	15 678	4.4	342 980	37.4	12.0	9.9
District 3	695	26.3	2.9	354 342	20 702	5.8	333 640	37.5	12.9	11.2
District 4	844	26.5	4.4	340 503	17 539	5.2	322 964	45.3	8.6	10.9
District 5	637	25.0	3.2	351 869	16 376	4.7	335 493	37.7	13.7	10.9
DELAWARE	639	24.3	3.1	397 360	20 549	5.2	376 811	35.3	12.5	11.2
At Large	639	24.3	3.1	397 360	20 549	5.2	376 811	35.3	12.5	11.2
DISTRICT OF COLUMBIA...	618	24.8	9.5	294 952	31 844	10.8	263 108	51.1	5.2	13.5
Delegate	618	24.8	9.5	294 952	31 844	10.8	263 108	51.1	5.2	13.5
FLORIDA	641	27.5	6.8	7 407 458	412 411	5.6	6 995 047	31.5	10.8	14.2
District 1	540	25.7	3.5	279 915	16 334	5.8	263 581	29.8	11.6	12.8
District 2	550	28.6	4.2	305 536	20 586	6.7	284 950	34.8	9.5	11.7
District 3	546	27.5	9.3	289 439	22 454	7.8	266 985	22.6	15.8	18.5
District 4	648	24.3	3.7	320 152	13 143	4.1	307 009	34.5	10.6	12.3
District 5	512	25.2	2.7	250 766	12 323	4.9	238 443	26.8	12.8	15.5
District 6	571	27.9	3.4	295 340	15 720	5.3	279 620	33.1	11.2	12.0
District 7	643	27.3	3.2	307 532	15 453	5.0	292 079	33.4	10.3	12.7
District 8	710	26.1	5.5	330 246	14 205	4.3	316 041	34.1	10.3	12.9
District 9	653	26.2	3.1	298 490	11 536	3.9	286 954	36.7	9.3	13.7
District 10	611	26.3	2.6	313 336	12 402	4.0	300 934	33.9	11.5	15.0
District 11	588	27.0	8.4	316 564	23 135	7.3	293 429	30.0	12.3	15.9
District 12	540	24.1	5.5	292 604	16 122	5.5	276 482	27.3	14.9	15.6
District 13	666	26.9	3.4	275 829	10 573	3.8	265 256	30.2	10.4	13.8
District 14	690	26.2	3.6	276 619	9 522	3.4	267 097	29.6	8.5	13.5
District 15	639	27.1	4.0	293 120	14 023	4.8	279 097	30.7	10.6	13.9
District 16	630	26.5	4.0	268 557	11 056	4.1	257 501	29.5	10.0	14.5
District 17	587	30.0	21.2	274 068	30 476	11.1	243 592	23.3	13.7	17.9
District 18	617	30.7	18.9	292 745	22 905	7.8	269 840	32.3	10.3	16.0
District 19	828	28.0	4.2	273 756	13 022	4.8	260 734	34.3	7.8	13.2
District 20	807	28.7	6.4	325 891	15 662	4.8	310 229	38.2	7.9	11.5
District 21	711	29.8	20.4	297 583	21 490	7.2	276 093	31.2	13.4	13.9
District 22	798	27.6	3.2	321 652	11 924	3.7	309 728	39.6	7.1	11.8
District 23	627	29.5	15.6	288 291	23 996	8.3	264 295	21.6	13.5	19.5
District 24	694	26.5	3.3	322 757	13 635	4.2	309 122	35.5	9.4	11.2
District 25	726	29.1	18.4	296 670	20 714	7.0	275 956	29.5	10.1	14.9
GEORGIA	613	24.9	5.3	4 062 808	223 052	5.5	3 839 756	32.7	15.7	12.6
District 1	476	23.7	4.5	274 508	14 289	5.2	260 219	28.4	17.8	12.9
District 2	418	25.0	6.7	270 954	20 632	7.6	250 322	25.9	20.4	15.1
District 3	418	24.9	5.2	271 328	18 533	6.8	252 795	25.2	19.6	15.0
District 4	769	25.6	7.9	348 009	18 985	5.5	329 024	38.8	11.1	11.9
District 5	705	26.0	7.4	343 563	36 463	10.6	307 100	41.2	10.4	12.8
District 6	903	24.3	2.1	347 255	9 336	2.7	337 919	50.1	5.3	7.2

1. Specified renter-occupied units.   2. Overcrowded or lacking complete plumbing facilities.   3. Percent of total civilian labor force.   4. Persons 16 years old and over.   5. Persons 16 to 64 years old.   Note: Data were tabulated for the 108th Congress and some boundary changes have occurred.

STATE District	Representative	Land area,[1] 2000 (sq km)	Population and population characteristics, 2000												
					Percent										
					Race alone or in combination								Age		
			Total persons	Per square kilometer	White	Black	Am. Indian, Alaska Native	Asian and Pacific Islander	Other race	Hispanic or Latino[2]	Non-Hispanic White	Two or more races	Under 5 years	5 to 17 years	18 to 24 years
		1	2	3	4	5	6	7	8	9	10	11	12	13	14
GEORGIA—Cont'd															
District 7	John Linder (R)	3 095	629 706	203.5	86.4	7.4	0.6	4.3	2.8	5.4	82.4	1.4	8.4	21.0	7.2
District 8	Lynn A. Westmoreland (R)	9 097	629 700	69.2	84.9	12.9	0.6	1.6	1.0	2.1	82.8	1.0	6.9	20.4	8.3
District 9	Charlie Norwood (R)	17 992	629 762	35.0	83.5	14.1	0.7	1.6	1.3	2.6	81.2	1.1	6.8	19.0	8.8
District 10	Nathan Deal (R)	9 690	629 702	65.0	90.8	3.6	0.7	1.0	5.1	9.4	85.4	1.2	7.5	18.8	9.0
District 11	Phil Gingrey (R)	9 585	629 730	65.7	66.0	29.1	0.7	1.7	4.2	7.2	61.7	1.6	7.3	18.8	10.2
District 12	John Jenkins Barrow (D)	13 530	629 735	46.5	54.1	43.2	0.6	2.0	1.6	2.9	51.9	1.3	6.7	18.6	15.8
District 13	David Scott (D)	2 014	629 732	312.7	48.4	42.0	0.8	5.8	5.3	10.2	42.1	2.1	8.1	20.3	10.5
HAWAII		16 635	1 211 537	72.8	39.3	2.8	2.1	81.3	3.9	7.2	22.9	21.4	6.5	18.0	9.5
District 1	Neil Abercrombie (D)	494	606 718	1 227.3	30.5	2.9	1.5	84.8	3.0	5.4	17.7	16.9	5.8	15.9	9.2
District 2	Ed Case (D)	16 140	604 819	37.5	48.2	2.6	2.6	78.0	4.9	9.0	28.0	26.0	7.1	20.0	9.8
IDAHO		214 314	1 293 953	6.0	92.8	0.6	2.1	1.5	5.0	7.9	88.0	2.0	7.5	21.0	10.7
District 1	C. L. Otter (R)	102 369	648 774	6.3	93.5	0.5	2.2	1.6	4.4	6.8	89.0	2.0	7.4	20.7	9.3
District 2	Mike Simpson (R)	111 946	645 179	5.8	92.2	0.8	2.0	1.5	5.6	8.9	87.1	2.0	7.7	21.2	12.1
ILLINOIS		143 961	12 419 293	86.3	75.1	15.6	0.6	3.9	6.8	12.3	67.8	1.9	7.1	19.1	9.8
District 1	Bobby L. Rush (D)	253	653 647	2 579.3	30.4	66.2	0.5	1.8	2.6	4.8	27.3	1.4	7.4	21.0	9.9
District 2	Jesse L. Jackson Jr. (D)	478	653 647	1 366.9	30.9	63.4	0.7	0.9	6.1	10.4	25.6	1.8	7.6	21.8	9.0
District 3	Daniel Lipinski (D)	322	653 647	2 027.2	80.4	6.1	0.6	3.3	12.4	21.3	68.2	2.7	7.1	18.6	8.9
District 4	Luis V. Gutierrez (D)	101	653 647	6 448.6	50.4	4.9	1.1	2.4	46.0	74.5	18.4	4.5	9.7	22.1	13.2
District 5	Rahm Emanuel (D)	148	653 647	4 428.6	80.5	2.7	0.7	7.5	12.2	23.0	65.9	3.5	6.1	13.7	10.6
District 6	Henry Hyde (R)	553	653 647	1 182.4	84.0	3.1	0.5	8.8	5.7	12.5	75.3	2.0	7.2	18.9	8.8
District 7	Danny K. Davis (D)	146	653 647	4 478.8	30.9	62.8	0.5	4.3	3.3	5.8	27.3	1.5	7.3	19.5	10.8
District 8	Melissa Bean (D)	1 600	653 647	408.5	86.0	3.7	0.6	6.3	5.3	10.8	78.8	1.8	7.8	20.4	7.7
District 9	Jan Schakowsky (D)	195	653 647	3 350.2	71.0	11.7	0.7	13.6	6.5	11.5	62.5	3.3	5.8	14.8	9.7
District 10	Mark Steven Kirk (R)	646	653 647	1 011.3	82.7	5.8	0.4	6.6	6.3	12.3	75.2	1.7	7.1	20.0	8.3
District 11	Jerry Weller (R)	10 984	653 647	59.5	88.2	8.3	0.5	1.1	3.3	6.7	83.7	1.3	7.1	19.7	10.7
District 12	Jerry Costello (D)	11 460	653 647	57.0	81.7	16.8	0.7	1.2	0.9	1.8	79.7	1.2	6.3	18.8	10.3
District 13	Judy Biggert (R)	918	653 647	711.8	86.2	5.4	0.4	7.3	2.4	5.5	81.6	1.5	7.7	20.6	7.4
District 14	Dennis J. Hastert (R)	7 386	653 647	88.5	85.1	5.2	0.6	2.2	9.0	18.5	74.0	1.9	8.1	20.6	10.6
District 15	Timothy Johnson (R)	26 088	653 647	25.1	90.6	6.2	0.5	2.7	1.3	2.2	88.5	1.2	6.1	17.4	13.5
District 16	Don Manzullo (R)	10 614	653 647	61.6	90.2	5.8	0.6	1.7	3.3	6.5	85.7	1.4	7.3	20.3	7.6
District 17	Lane Evans (D)	21 031	653 647	31.1	90.2	7.8	0.6	0.8	3.0	3.7	87.3	1.3	6.1	17.9	10.4
District 18	Ray LaHood (R)	21 202	653 647	30.8	91.8	6.9	0.5	1.1	0.8	1.5	90.0	1.0	6.2	18.1	8.9
District 19	John Shimkus (R)	29 833	653 647	21.9	95.3	3.8	0.6	0.7	0.5	1.1	94.0	0.8	6.0	18.3	8.8
INDIANA		92 895	6 080 485	65.5	88.6	8.8	0.6	1.3	2.0	3.5	85.8	1.2	7.0	18.9	10.1
District 1	Pete Visclosky (D)	5 722	675 562	118.1	76.4	18.8	0.7	1.1	4.8	10.0	69.8	1.7	7.0	19.6	9.4
District 2	Chris Chocola (R)	9 529	675 766	70.9	87.9	8.8	0.8	1.2	3.1	5.0	84.4	1.7	7.1	19.1	9.9
District 3	Mark E. Souder (R)	8 391	675 457	80.5	90.6	6.1	0.7	1.2	2.8	4.5	87.6	1.4	7.7	20.5	9.3
District 4	Steve Buyer (R)	10 403	675 617	64.9	95.7	1.6	0.6	1.8	1.4	2.6	93.6	0.9	6.9	18.9	11.6
District 5	Dan Burton (R)	8 459	675 577	79.9	95.0	2.9	0.6	1.7	0.8	1.6	93.2	1.0	7.2	19.6	7.9
District 6	Mike Pence (R)	14 375	675 669	47.0	94.9	4.1	0.5	0.7	0.7	1.3	93.4	0.9	6.6	18.6	9.9
District 7	Julia Carson (D)	677	675 674	997.6	66.2	30.5	0.7	1.7	2.7	4.4	63.0	1.8	7.6	18.2	10.6
District 8	John Hostettler (R)	18 238	675 564	37.0	95.0	4.1	0.6	0.8	0.5	0.9	93.7	0.9	6.3	18.1	10.4
District 9	Michael Sodrel (R)	17 101	675 599	39.5	95.7	2.6	0.6	1.2	0.9	1.5	94.0	1.0	6.4	17.8	12.0
IOWA		144 701	2 926 324	20.2	94.9	2.5	0.6	1.6	1.6	2.8	92.6	1.1	6.4	18.6	10.2
District 1	Jim Nussle (R)	18 691	585 302	31.3	94.2	4.3	0.5	1.1	1.1	2.0	92.1	1.2	6.4	18.9	10.4
District 2	Jim Leach (R)	19 595	585 241	29.9	94.9	2.5	0.6	1.9	1.5	2.7	92.4	1.2	6.4	17.8	11.7
District 3	Leonard Boswell (D)	18 076	585 305	32.4	92.7	3.7	0.8	2.3	2.0	3.2	90.1	1.3	7.0	18.6	9.0
District 4	Tom Latham (R)	40 818	585 305	14.3	96.5	1.0	0.4	1.4	1.5	2.5	94.7	0.8	6.0	18.4	11.1
District 5	Steve King (R)	47 520	585 171	12.3	96.3	0.9	0.8	1.1	1.9	3.6	93.7	0.9	6.3	19.4	8.7
KANSAS		211 900	2 688 418	12.7	87.9	6.3	1.8	2.2	4.0	7.0	83.1	2.1	7.0	19.5	10.3
District 1	Jerry Moran (R)	148 596	672 091	4.5	90.5	2.6	1.1	1.3	6.3	10.9	84.5	1.7	6.7	19.7	9.5
District 2	Jim Ryun (R)	36 606	672 102	18.4	90.9	5.7	2.2	1.4	2.0	3.8	87.3	2.1	6.5	18.8	11.9
District 3	Dennis Moore (D)	2 014	672 124	333.7	84.4	9.5	1.3	3.1	3.7	6.8	79.6	2.0	7.4	19.2	10.5
District 4	Todd Tiahrt (R)	24 684	672 101	27.2	85.8	7.6	2.4	3.0	4.0	6.6	81.0	2.6	7.4	20.3	9.1
KENTUCKY		102 896	4 041 769	39.3	91.0	7.7	0.6	1.0	0.8	1.5	89.3	1.1	6.6	18.0	9.9
District 1	Ed Whitfield (R)	30 259	673 629	22.3	91.4	7.7	0.6	0.6	0.8	1.5	89.7	1.0	6.5	17.6	9.8
District 2	Ron Lewis (R)	19 598	673 224	34.4	92.5	6.1	0.7	1.0	1.0	1.7	90.6	1.2	6.8	18.9	10.1
District 3	Anne Northup (R)	950	674 032	709.7	78.2	19.9	0.6	1.8	1.1	1.8	76.0	1.4	6.7	17.5	8.9
District 4	Geoffrey C. Davis (R)	14 707	673 588	45.8	96.5	2.5	0.5	0.7	0.6	1.1	95.1	0.8	6.9	19.1	8.8
District 5	Hal Rogers (R)	27 652	673 670	24.4	98.2	1.3	0.6	0.4	0.2	0.7	97.1	0.7	6.2	18.4	9.7
District 6	Ben Chandler (D)	9 729	673 626	69.2	89.4	8.8	0.6	1.5	1.1	2.1	87.1	1.2	6.4	16.7	12.4

1. Dry land or land partially or temporarily covered by water.   2. Hispanic or Latino persons may be of any race.   Note: Data were tabulated for the 108th Congress and some boundary changes have occurred.

Table E. Congressional Districts 109th Congress — Population, Households, Group Quarters, and Education

STATE District	25 to 34 years	35 to 44 years	45 to 54 years	55 to 64 years	65 to 74 years	75 years and over	Percent female	Number	Persons per household	Female family householder[1]	One person	Persons in correctional institutions, 2000	Persons in nursing homes, 2000	Persons in military quarters, 2000	Public	Private
	15	16	17	18	19	20	21	22	23	24	25	26	27	28	29	30
GEORGIA—Cont'd																
District 7	16.0	20.0	14.2	7.1	3.6	2.4	50.0	213 686	2.92	8.6	14.8	2 167	900	0	147 768	24 878
District 8	13.8	17.4	14.8	9.0	5.5	3.9	50.8	225 113	2.75	10.1	17.9	4 105	1 473	0	144 846	26 082
District 9	13.7	15.8	13.8	9.9	6.9	5.3	50.9	235 853	2.62	11.3	21.4	3 361	2 586	1 084	136 231	21 106
District 10	15.3	16.3	13.3	9.2	6.2	4.3	50.0	228 012	2.73	10.1	19.7	3 271	2 393	0	132 916	15 143
District 11	16.5	16.0	12.2	8.1	6.0	5.0	50.9	233 574	2.62	15.7	24.5	7 428	3 903	159	141 697	20 461
District 12	14.3	14.3	11.9	7.6	5.6	5.0	51.7	235 441	2.55	18.3	26.9	6 328	2 226	4 657	180 710	21 582
District 13	18.5	16.8	12.1	6.7	3.9	3.0	50.9	221 871	2.80	18.2	22.6	2 435	2 729	817	151 680	20 768
HAWAII	14.1	15.8	14.1	8.8	7.0	6.2	49.8	403 240	2.92	12.4	21.9	3 233	2 949	13 992	255 215	65 627
District 1	15.0	15.9	13.9	9.2	7.8	7.3	50.1	209 875	2.80	11.9	24.7	2 302	1 799	5 063	118 992	36 574
District 2	13.3	15.7	14.4	8.5	6.2	5.2	49.4	193 365	3.04	12.9	18.7	931	1 150	8 929	136 223	29 053
IDAHO	13.1	14.9	13.2	8.3	5.9	5.4	49.9	469 645	2.69	8.7	22.4	7 401	5 735	673	323 683	44 896
District 1	13.0	15.3	13.8	8.9	6.1	5.5	49.9	237 250	2.67	8.6	21.2	4 341	3 233	0	154 730	21 377
District 2	13.2	14.5	12.5	7.8	5.6	5.4	49.8	232 395	2.71	8.8	23.6	3 060	2 502	673	168 953	23 519
ILLINOIS	14.6	16.0	13.1	8.4	6.2	5.9	51.0	4 591 779	2.63	12.3	26.8	67 820	91 887	10 865	2 787 463	663 141
District 1	13.4	14.8	12.3	8.5	6.9	5.8	53.8	233 410	2.75	26.3	28.4	0	3 128	0	158 357	42 717
District 2	13.1	15.0	12.7	9.1	6.5	5.1	53.5	228 212	2.84	24.2	24.8	81	3 092	0	165 960	35 717
District 3	14.1	15.5	12.9	8.4	7.1	7.4	51.5	236 988	2.73	12.6	26.5	0	3 828	0	120 554	48 674
District 4	20.2	14.1	9.2	5.3	3.4	2.7	48.3	192 910	3.37	15.7	21.1	0	831	0	161 776	29 064
District 5	22.0	15.8	12.2	7.8	5.8	6.0	50.7	266 778	2.42	9.5	34.8	0	3 551	0	96 279	56 358
District 6	15.4	17.4	13.7	8.3	5.5	4.9	50.4	232 594	2.76	8.5	22.9	718	4 828	0	139 389	38 691
District 7	17.5	15.4	12.2	7.8	5.4	4.3	52.7	250 404	2.50	22.6	37.2	11 587	3 450	0	152 579	41 131
District 8	15.4	18.6	14.1	7.9	4.5	3.6	50.2	234 791	2.77	8.8	21.9	307	2 385	0	150 233	31 203
District 9	16.0	15.8	13.5	8.9	7.4	8.1	51.4	268 439	2.35	9.7	35.8	35	8 800	0	113 374	58 798
District 10	11.9	16.5	14.8	9.1	6.6	5.7	50.5	229 497	2.75	7.9	22.3	846	4 643	10 432	142 666	37 846
District 11	13.3	16.2	12.9	8.2	6.0	5.9	50.7	236 451	2.66	10.3	23.8	3 972	5 718	0	158 151	29 070
District 12	13.0	15.5	12.9	8.7	7.4	7.1	51.3	255 607	2.47	13.7	28.1	7 433	6 193	427	161 424	21 885
District 13	14.3	18.5	14.7	7.9	4.6	4.3	50.7	230 971	2.78	7.6	21.0	2 691	4 007	0	148 844	40 767
District 14	14.5	16.6	13.1	7.5	4.7	4.3	49.8	220 852	2.88	9.2	20.4	3 274	4 110	0	164 054	29 395
District 15	12.8	14.8	12.9	8.6	7.0	7.0	50.8	257 370	2.41	8.9	28.5	6 999	6 814	0	180 828	16 300
District 16	13.3	17.0	13.7	8.8	6.3	5.8	50.6	244 763	2.64	9.6	23.4	1 104	4 659	0	147 034	29 443
District 17	12.0	14.6	13.4	9.4	7.9	8.3	51.4	260 837	2.40	11.2	29.3	5 788	8 296	0	144 964	24 426
District 18	12.6	15.4	14.2	9.5	7.5	7.5	51.2	257 277	2.44	9.8	27.5	9 157	6 874	6	134 871	31 038
District 19	12.4	15.9	13.6	9.6	7.7	7.6	50.4	253 628	2.47	9.0	26.1	13 828	6 680	0	146 126	20 618
INDIANA	13.7	15.8	13.4	8.7	6.5	5.9	51.0	2 336 306	2.53	11.1	25.9	34 676	48 745	7	1 337 569	265 985
District 1	12.7	15.7	14.0	9.0	6.8	5.9	51.6	252 318	2.64	14.5	24.8	1 124	4 161	0	152 617	29 589
District 2	13.4	15.3	13.4	8.6	6.8	6.5	50.7	256 547	2.54	11.4	26.3	6 561	4 992	4	139 474	37 119
District 3	13.8	15.6	13.4	8.2	6.0	5.5	50.4	252 897	2.63	10.0	24.6	1 952	5 022	0	141 191	35 029
District 4	13.8	16.0	13.3	8.5	5.8	5.2	50.3	252 434	2.57	8.6	22.9	3 643	6 127	0	168 145	22 506
District 5	13.7	17.2	14.2	8.8	6.1	5.3	51.0	258 353	2.56	8.3	23.5	2 248	4 907	0	140 332	35 883
District 6	12.7	15.0	13.5	9.7	7.4	6.7	51.1	262 404	2.50	10.0	25.3	4 086	5 861	0	150 726	21 088
District 7	16.8	16.2	12.1	7.4	5.8	5.3	51.7	277 370	2.37	16.8	33.0	4 361	4 955	0	135 407	35 907
District 8	12.5	15.6	13.6	9.3	7.3	7.0	50.9	263 004	2.46	10.0	26.9	8 089	7 194	3	147 802	26 962
District 9	13.6	15.6	13.5	9.0	6.5	5.6	50.7	260 979	2.49	9.9	25.4	2 612	5 526	0	161 875	21 902
IOWA	12.4	15.2	13.4	8.8	7.2	7.7	50.9	1 149 276	2.46	8.6	27.2	11 771	33 428	4	669 809	122 248
District 1	12.1	15.0	13.7	9.0	7.1	7.3	51.2	227 405	2.48	9.5	26.6	2 158	5 532	1	132 760	31 341
District 2	13.4	15.2	13.7	8.5	6.5	6.8	50.8	232 880	2.42	8.5	27.8	3 579	5 256	3	143 323	22 092
District 3	14.2	16.0	13.3	8.5	6.6	6.7	51.2	231 632	2.46	9.1	27.4	2 260	5 534	0	123 395	26 479
District 4	11.2	14.8	13.1	8.9	7.7	8.7	50.6	229 320	2.43	7.4	27.4	2 182	9 081	0	144 643	18 617
District 5	11.2	15.0	13.3	9.0	8.3	8.8	51.0	228 039	2.48	8.2	26.9	1 592	8 025	0	125 688	23 719
KANSAS	13.0	15.6	13.2	8.2	6.5	6.7	50.6	1 037 891	2.51	9.3	27.0	16 703	25 248	4 580	654 604	102 356
District 1	11.4	14.9	12.7	8.7	7.8	8.6	50.4	260 490	2.49	7.7	27.6	4 964	9 184	0	163 192	15 858
District 2	12.3	15.2	13.1	8.6	6.7	6.9	50.2	257 856	2.49	9.2	26.7	7 674	6 723	4 067	171 476	22 213
District 3	15.0	16.6	13.7	7.5	5.2	4.9	51.1	258 439	2.55	10.3	26.1	544	4 101	0	161 511	34 170
District 4	13.1	15.9	13.2	8.0	6.5	6.5	50.7	261 106	2.52	10.1	27.6	3 521	5 240	513	158 425	30 115
KENTUCKY	14.1	15.9	13.8	9.2	6.8	5.7	51.1	1 590 647	2.47	11.8	26.0	28 388	29 266	7 277	859 020	148 432
District 1	13.2	14.8	13.4	10.1	7.7	7.0	51.1	267 254	2.44	10.7	26.0	4 931	6 788	4 648	142 717	14 871
District 2	13.7	16.2	13.5	9.2	6.5	5.1	50.7	255 503	2.56	11.0	23.3	4 027	4 667	2 629	148 745	21 348
District 3	14.1	16.3	14.2	8.7	7.3	6.5	52.3	280 037	2.36	14.7	30.8	1 169	5 182	0	127 624	42 579
District 4	14.2	16.7	13.9	9.0	6.4	5.2	50.7	257 362	2.56	10.9	24.2	6 197	4 284	0	138 117	30 323
District 5	13.7	15.5	14.2	9.8	6.9	5.5	50.9	262 131	2.50	12.0	24.2	6 288	4 609	0	147 377	11 893
District 6	15.5	15.9	13.6	8.5	5.9	5.1	51.2	268 360	2.41	11.4	27.2	5 776	3 736	0	154 440	27 418

1. No spouse present.   2. All persons 3 years old and over enrolled in nursery school through college.   Note: Data were tabulated for the 108th Congress and some boundary changes have occurred.

Items 15—30

STATE District	Education, 2000 (cont'd) Attainment[1] (percent)		Money income, 1999			Percent below poverty level, 1999		Housing units, 2000					
				Households		Persons	Families		Occupied units				
										Owner-occupied			
												Owner cost as a percent of income	
	High school graduate or more	Bach-elor's degree or more	Per capita income[2]	Median income	Percent with income of $100,000 or more	Total	Total	Total	Total	Percent	Median value[3] (dollars)	With a mortgage	Without a mortgage[4]
	31	32	33	34	35	36	37	38	39	40	41	42	43
GEORGIA—Cont'd													
District 7	86.8	31.9	25 773	63 455	21.9	4.5	3.2	221 733	213 675	85.0	143 600	20.7	9.9
District 8	83.0	23.4	23 202	52 406	15.0	6.3	4.6	238 674	224 673	80.6	120 300	20.6	9.9
District 9	75.4	18.5	19 475	39 987	9.0	11.2	8.6	271 003	235 801	77.0	103 200	21.2	9.9
District 10	71.4	15.9	19 331	42 037	9.4	10.3	7.5	249 631	227 841	76.3	108 200	20.5	9.9
District 11	72.6	16.9	17 953	37 582	7.1	13.8	10.7	250 471	233 726	64.1	89 300	20.9	9.9
District 12	74.9	19.3	16 295	31 108	6.2	21.7	15.9	260 247	235 515	58.3	80 900	21.3	10.2
District 13	77.8	19.4	18 590	43 429	8.7	11.2	8.8	233 592	222 171	59.3	99 800	21.7	9.9
HAWAII	84.6	26.2	21 525	49 820	16.6	10.7	7.6	460 542	403 240	56.5	272 700	26.3	9.9
District 1	84.1	28.9	23 028	50 798	18.0	9.7	6.6	232 131	209 847	53.1	328 900	26.3	9.9
District 2	85.1	23.1	20 018	48 686	15.0	11.7	8.7	228 411	193 393	60.2	227 600	26.3	9.9
IDAHO	84.7	21.7	17 841	37 572	7.3	11.8	8.3	527 824	469 645	72.4	106 300	21.5	9.9
District 1	84.3	20.3	17 861	38 364	7.2	11.0	7.9	268 098	237 288	75.7	113 500	22.2	9.9
District 2	85.2	23.1	17 820	36 934	7.5	12.6	8.7	259 726	232 357	69.0	97 700	20.6	9.9
ILLINOIS	81.4	26.1	23 104	46 590	14.4	10.7	7.8	4 885 615	4 591 779	67.3	130 800	21.7	11.1
District 1	77.5	18.7	17 352	37 222	9.0	19.7	15.9	254 874	233 426	54.4	118 900	23.3	12.1
District 2	79.3	18.1	18 280	41 330	9.7	15.2	12.3	243 889	228 365	66.2	96 700	22.8	11.6
District 3	77.3	20.5	21 785	48 048	13.5	8.3	6.4	246 643	236 791	72.6	145 600	23.0	12.2
District 4	51.7	13.6	13 833	35 935	7.3	20.2	17.8	208 851	193 008	39.2	124 000	25.4	13.0
District 5	79.3	33.9	26 689	48 531	15.8	8.5	6.2	238 484	232 718	75.8	181 700	24.0	13.0
District 6	86.7	34.6	27 669	62 640	22.6	4.3	3.0	280 304	250 442	41.9	144 900	23.1	12.1
District 7	76.1	32.1	25 329	40 361	16.6	24.0	20.5	280 304	250 442	41.9	144 900	23.1	12.1
District 8	88.0	32.1	28 215	62 762	22.5	4.4	3.2	244 538	234 592	77.6	170 400	23.2	11.6
District 9	84.0	39.6	26 344	46 531	16.2	11.0	7.7	279 283	268 430	54.7	222 100	23.8	11.8
District 10	88.7	47.5	38 722	71 663	34.6	4.8	3.1	237 175	229 591	78.7	268 100	22.3	11.6
District 11	84.0	18.5	20 906	47 800	11.7	8.4	5.7	250 349	236 533	74.6	117 600	21.5	11.0
District 12	79.5	16.8	17 821	35 198	6.4	15.0	11.4	278 780	255 599	69.4	67 300	19.4	11.0
District 13	91.9	42.4	32 321	71 686	30.1	2.9	1.9	239 926	230 918	80.7	203 000	22.2	10.8
District 14	82.1	26.3	23 406	56 314	17.8	7.0	4.6	229 912	220 953	74.8	150 000	22.8	11.5
District 15	84.8	23.2	19 524	38 583	8.1	11.7	6.6	277 193	257 248	68.8	79 200	18.9	9.9
District 16	84.2	21.1	22 606	48 960	13.0	7.3	5.2	261 384	244 751	75.5	112 900	21.5	11.3
District 17	81.3	14.7	17 894	35 066	5.5	12.5	9.0	284 299	260 924	71.0	66 100	18.6	10.4
District 18	84.5	20.7	20 936	41 934	8.9	8.9	6.2	276 737	257 236	73.6	85 000	19.0	9.9
District 19	81.5	17.1	19 356	38 955	7.5	9.1	6.6	275 894	253 590	78.1	76 100	19.2	10.4
INDIANA	82.1	19.4	20 397	41 567	9.2	9.5	6.7	2 532 319	2 336 306	71.4	94 300	19.3	9.9
District 1	82.3	17.1	20 374	44 087	9.8	10.5	8.1	269 523	252 348	71.0	102 800	19.8	10.6
District 2	80.3	17.2	19 231	40 381	7.8	9.5	6.9	279 083	256 650	72.8	85 700	19.0	9.9
District 3	82.1	18.4	20 606	44 013	9.2	7.8	5.5	278 814	252 847	75.0	93 600	18.7	9.9
District 4	85.6	22.1	21 198	45 947	10.9	8.0	4.9	268 893	252 284	73.5	112 600	19.6	9.9
District 5	88.4	30.6	26 186	52 800	16.9	5.2	3.5	275 056	258 319	76.0	122 000	19.1	9.9
District 6	80.6	14.7	19 160	39 002	7.3	9.7	6.7	281 053	262 371	74.3	83 200	18.8	9.9
District 7	78.5	21.2	19 559	36 522	7.2	13.5	10.6	307 838	277 502	55.8	87 600	20.4	9.9
District 8	81.3	15.9	18 467	36 732	6.6	10.7	7.7	288 649	263 037	73.9	77 900	18.8	9.9
District 9	80.1	17.3	18 796	39 011	7.1	10.5	6.7	283 410	260 948	71.7	92 600	19.4	9.9
IOWA	86.1	21.2	19 674	39 469	7.3	9.1	6.0	1 232 511	1 149 276	72.3	82 500	19.1	9.9
District 1	85.6	20.0	19 236	38 727	6.9	10.1	6.9	241 991	227 405	72.6	82 500	18.9	9.9
District 2	87.5	25.0	20 515	40 121	8.1	9.9	6.0	248 194	232 880	70.8	89 500	19.2	9.9
District 3	87.2	24.6	21 777	43 176	9.4	8.0	5.4	245 617	231 632	71.5	93 100	19.7	10.5
District 4	86.7	20.4	18 869	38 242	6.4	8.9	5.5	247 124	229 320	73.3	75 200	18.8	9.9
District 5	83.6	16.1	17 976	36 773	5.6	8.9	6.3	249 585	228 039	73.6	71 900	18.9	10.1
KANSAS	86.0	25.8	20 506	40 624	9.3	9.9	6.7	1 131 200	1 037 891	69.2	83 500	19.3	9.9
District 1	82.3	18.0	17 255	34 869	5.2	11.0	7.8	292 436	260 475	71.4	63 100	19.0	9.9
District 2	86.9	23.2	18 595	37 855	6.7	11.2	7.1	280 213	257 846	69.0	74 900	19.0	10.0
District 3	89.9	39.1	26 133	51 118	17.1	7.8	4.9	272 721	258 464	67.7	131 600	19.7	9.9
District 4	85.0	23.0	20 041	40 917	8.1	9.6	7.0	285 830	261 106	68.9	76 800	19.2	9.9
KENTUCKY	74.1	17.1	18 093	33 672	7.2	15.8	12.7	1 750 927	1 590 647	70.8	86 700	19.6	9.9
District 1	71.3	11.8	16 269	30 360	4.7	16.5	12.7	302 480	267 297	74.0	66 900	19.2	9.9
District 2	75.5	13.9	17 413	35 724	6.0	13.3	10.3	282 766	255 468	73.5	85 900	19.5	9.9
District 3	82.1	25.3	22 514	39 468	10.9	12.4	9.5	298 522	280 034	64.7	104 500	19.7	9.9
District 4	77.4	17.5	19 722	40 150	9.3	11.4	9.1	280 766	257 417	73.4	96 100	19.6	9.9
District 5	59.2	9.6	12 513	21 915	3.0	28.1	24.0	297 361	262 110	76.3	58 300	21.3	9.9
District 6	79.1	24.6	20 124	37 544	8.9	13.2	9.6	289 032	268 321	63.2	97 200	19.2	9.9

1. Persons 25 years old and over. 2. Based on the population enumerated as of April 1, 2000. 3. Specified owner-occupied units. 4. Median monthly owner costs is often in the minimum category—9.9 percent or less, which is indicated as 9.9 percent. Note: Data were tabulated for the 108th Congress and some boundary changes have occurred.

STATE District	Housing units, 2000 (cont'd) Occupied units (cont'd) Renter-occupied			Civilian labor force, 2000	Unemployment		Civilian employment,[4] 2000 Percent			Disability, 2000
	Median rent[1] (dollars)	Rent as a percent of income	Substandard units[2] (percent)	Total	Total	Rate[3]	Total	Management, professional, and related occupations	Production, transportation, and material moving occupations	Employment disabled persons[5] (percent)
	44	45	46	47	48	49	50	51	52	53
GEORGIA—Cont'd										
District 7	775	24.0	3.2	338 850	9 092	2.7	329 758	39.5	10.1	9.1
District 8	631	23.4	2.7	321 890	11 332	3.5	310 558	33.1	15.1	10.7
District 9	497	23.4	3.6	305 969	12 747	4.2	293 222	28.6	19.3	12.9
District 10	523	22.8	5.3	316 568	10 830	3.4	305 738	25.9	24.2	13.8
District 11	600	24.7	6.1	309 823	18 005	5.8	291 818	26.1	20.3	14.7
District 12	508	28.2	5.7	291 280	25 441	8.7	265 839	28.6	17.5	13.9
District 13	720	24.9	8.4	322 811	17 367	5.4	305 444	26.6	16.7	14.1
HAWAII	779	27.2	16.1	573 795	35 886	6.3	537 909	32.2	8.9	11.4
District 1	787	27.3	16.2	291 195	16 765	5.8	274 430	34.0	8.5	11.2
District 2	768	26.9	16.1	282 600	19 121	6.8	263 479	30.4	9.3	11.6
IDAHO	515	25.3	5.4	636 237	36 784	5.8	599 453	31.4	14.2	9.4
District 1	524	25.9	4.9	317 934	19 640	6.2	298 294	30.5	14.7	10.0
District 2	507	24.8	5.9	318 303	17 144	5.4	301 159	32.3	13.7	8.9
ILLINOIS	605	24.4	5.3	6 208 597	375 412	6.0	5 833 185	34.2	15.7	10.8
District 1	570	27.2	7.1	288 919	37 143	12.9	251 776	30.3	14.0	14.1
District 2	598	27.1	6.7	296 330	30 819	10.4	265 511	29.6	16.3	12.8
District 3	632	23.4	6.3	314 037	17 796	5.7	296 241	28.6	17.6	11.3
District 4	576	24.2	21.5	278 214	25 883	9.3	252 331	19.7	29.5	19.1
District 5	705	23.0	7.2	367 505	17 490	4.8	350 015	38.2	14.1	12.5
District 6	817	23.8	5.4	357 017	13 009	3.6	344 008	38.2	12.9	8.8
District 7	640	26.2	8.3	303 554	37 018	12.2	266 536	42.2	11.9	12.8
District 8	830	24.5	4.1	355 245	12 152	3.4	343 093	37.8	12.9	8.7
District 9	693	26.2	8.2	339 586	18 159	5.3	321 427	42.6	10.9	12.1
District 10	805	24.5	4.5	326 047	12 254	3.8	313 793	47.3	9.4	8.5
District 11	534	23.2	2.8	334 528	19 130	5.7	315 398	28.4	17.8	9.4
District 12	451	25.3	2.8	306 474	21 439	7.0	285 035	28.4	16.7	11.7
District 13	840	23.6	2.2	347 465	11 102	3.2	336 363	45.6	8.8	6.5
District 14	651	24.3	5.8	338 820	15 807	4.7	323 013	32.5	17.6	9.9
District 15	488	25.0	2.3	336 264	16 825	5.0	319 439	33.0	17.7	8.4
District 16	522	23.1	2.8	338 929	16 732	4.9	322 197	31.0	20.2	9.5
District 17	423	23.5	2.1	324 396	22 143	6.8	302 253	26.4	20.2	10.4
District 18	472	22.1	1.7	330 607	15 282	4.6	315 325	32.6	15.9	9.1
District 19	434	22.2	1.8	324 660	15 229	4.7	309 431	30.5	18.0	9.6
INDIANA	521	23.9	2.7	3 117 897	152 723	4.9	2 965 174	28.7	21.4	11.3
District 1	558	24.3	3.9	329 270	21 566	6.5	307 704	26.8	19.2	11.1
District 2	510	23.3	3.2	339 374	16 950	5.0	322 424	26.6	25.2	11.4
District 3	505	22.1	2.9	355 352	13 987	3.9	341 365	27.3	26.6	10.4
District 4	557	24.7	2.3	357 594	14 987	4.2	342 607	31.1	19.2	11.5
District 5	592	22.5	1.4	359 982	11 796	3.3	348 186	37.0	16.5	9.6
District 6	459	23.5	2.1	338 364	17 603	5.2	320 761	25.7	24.8	11.0
District 7	549	24.6	4.0	350 697	22 003	6.3	328 694	29.5	16.8	13.8
District 8	435	23.8	2.2	336 951	18 758	5.6	318 193	26.6	20.7	12.2
District 9	507	25.1	2.4	350 313	15 073	4.3	335 240	26.9	23.9	11.1
IOWA	470	23.2	2.3	1 554 722	64 906	4.2	1 489 816	31.3	18.1	9.3
District 1	447	23.5	2.1	306 491	14 426	4.7	292 065	29.7	19.6	9.5
District 2	488	24.4	2.3	317 969	13 139	4.1	304 830	32.8	17.9	8.9
District 3	535	23.4	2.9	319 004	13 902	4.4	305 102	33.4	15.3	9.9
District 4	437	22.7	1.8	308 531	12 018	3.9	296 513	32.0	18.0	8.2
District 5	427	21.9	2.6	302 727	11 421	3.8	291 306	28.3	19.7	10.1
KANSAS	498	23.4	3.4	1 374 698	58 415	4.2	1 316 283	33.9	15.0	10.2
District 1	413	22.1	4.0	336 551	13 804	4.1	322 747	29.4	17.8	10.7
District 2	472	24.2	2.7	337 216	14 531	4.3	322 685	32.3	15.3	10.2
District 3	624	24.0	3.2	364 189	13 988	3.8	350 201	41.5	10.2	9.0
District 4	489	23.0	3.7	336 742	16 092	4.8	320 650	31.5	17.0	11.0
KENTUCKY	445	24.0	2.9	1 907 614	109 350	5.7	1 798 264	28.7	19.7	13.9
District 1	387	23.6	2.8	305 242	19 375	6.3	285 867	24.2	24.8	14.7
District 2	432	23.0	3.0	327 050	17 267	5.3	309 783	25.2	23.5	13.2
District 3	492	23.9	2.6	343 087	17 366	5.1	325 721	33.4	15.4	11.9
District 4	477	23.5	2.5	331 098	15 536	4.7	315 562	29.1	18.4	12.7
District 5	331	26.4	4.0	247 286	22 129	8.9	225 157	24.5	20.3	19.1
District 6	487	24.3	2.6	353 851	17 677	5.0	336 174	33.4	16.7	12.0

1. Specified renter-occupied units.   2. Overcrowded or lacking complete plumbing facilities.   3. Percent of total civilian labor force.   4. Persons 16 years old and over.   5. Persons 16 to 64 years old.   Note: Data were tabulated for the 108th Congress and some boundary changes have occurred.

STATE District	Representative	Land area,[1] 2000 (sq km)	Population and population characteristics, 2000												
							Percent								
					Race alone or in combination								Age		
			Total persons	Per square kilometer	White	Black	Am. Indian, Alaska Native	Asian and Pacific Islander	Other race	Hispanic or Latino[2]	Non-Hispanic White	Two or more races	Under 5 years	5 to 17 years	18 to 24 years
		1	2	3	4	5	6	7	8	9	10	11	12	13	14
LOUISIANA		112 825	4 468 976	39.6	64.8	32.9	1.0	1.5	1.1	2.4	62.5	1.1	7.1	20.2	10.6
District 1	Bobby Jindal (R)	6 221	638 355	102.6	83.8	13.2	0.7	1.9	1.8	4.7	79.6	1.3	6.5	18.4	8.8
District 2	William J. Jefferson (D)	689	638 562	927.0	31.2	64.8	0.7	3.0	1.8	3.8	28.3	1.4	7.3	21.0	11.2
District 3	Charles Melacon (D)	18 157	638 322	35.2	71.9	25.0	2.1	1.3	1.0	2.1	69.7	1.1	7.3	21.5	9.7
District 4	Jim McCrery (R)	27 881	638 466	22.9	64.0	33.9	1.4	1.1	1.0	2.0	62.0	1.3	7.2	20.0	10.4
District 5	Rodney Alexander (D)	35 677	638 517	17.9	64.7	34.1	0.7	0.7	0.5	1.3	63.4	0.7	7.0	20.1	11.2
District 6	Richard Baker (R)	7 966	638 324	80.1	64.4	33.6	0.5	1.7	0.7	1.6	62.7	0.8	7.1	19.7	12.6
District 7	Charles Boustany (R)	16 234	638 430	39.3	73.5	25.3	0.6	0.9	0.6	1.4	72.0	0.8	7.4	20.7	10.3
MAINE		79 931	1 274 923	16.0	97.9	0.7	1.0	1.0	0.4	0.7	96.5	1.0	5.5	18.1	8.1
District 1	Tom Allen (D)	9 368	666 936	71.2	97.7	0.9	0.7	1.2	0.4	0.8	96.3	1.0	5.7	18.1	7.7
District 2	Michael Michaud (D)	70 563	607 987	8.6	98.0	0.6	1.4	0.7	0.4	0.7	96.7	1.0	5.4	18.1	8.7
MARYLAND		25 314	5 296 486	209.2	65.4	28.8	0.7	4.6	2.5	4.3	62.1	2.0	6.7	18.9	8.5
District 1	Wayne Gilchrest (R)	9 461	662 062	70.0	86.4	11.6	0.6	1.7	0.8	1.6	84.7	1.1	6.0	19.1	7.5
District 2	Dutch Ruppersberger (D)	919	662 060	720.2	68.6	28.2	0.8	3.0	1.3	2.2	66.3	1.8	6.9	18.8	8.9
District 3	Ben Cardin (D)	758	662 062	873.2	78.7	17.1	0.7	3.8	1.7	2.9	75.7	1.8	6.4	16.6	9.1
District 4	Albert R. Wynn (D)	816	662 062	811.0	31.9	58.8	0.9	6.5	5.0	7.5	27.6	2.7	7.6	20.8	8.4
District 5	Steny Hoyer (D)	3 896	662 060	169.9	63.5	31.4	1.0	4.4	2.0	3.5	60.4	2.2	6.8	19.5	9.5
District 6	Roscoe Bartlett (R)	7 931	662 060	83.5	93.3	5.3	0.5	1.4	0.7	1.4	91.5	1.0	6.5	19.5	7.7
District 7	Elijah E. Cummings (D)	762	662 060	868.8	35.9	60.0	0.7	4.1	1.0	1.7	34.2	1.5	6.5	19.6	9.8
District 8	Chris Van Hollen (D)	769	662 060	860.5	65.1	18.0	0.8	12.1	7.8	13.7	56.1	3.6	6.7	17.7	7.2
MASSACHUSETTS		20 306	6 349 097	312.7	86.2	6.3	0.6	4.3	5.1	6.8	81.9	2.3	6.3	17.4	9.1
District 1	John Olver (D)	8 032	634 479	79.0	92.8	2.4	0.7	2.1	3.8	6.3	88.8	1.7	5.8	18.4	10.5
District 2	Richard E. Neal (D)	2 387	634 444	265.8	87.1	6.6	0.6	1.8	6.0	9.2	82.5	1.9	6.5	19.1	8.6
District 3	Jim McGovern (D)	1 505	634 585	421.7	90.6	3.4	0.6	3.7	3.8	6.0	86.2	2.0	6.9	18.6	8.3
District 4	Barney Frank (D)	1 895	634 624	334.8	91.1	3.0	0.6	3.7	3.9	3.3	87.9	2.2	6.3	17.7	8.8
District 5	Martin T. Meehan (D)	1 465	635 326	433.6	85.4	2.9	0.5	5.9	7.6	11.6	79.7	2.3	7.3	20.0	7.6
District 6	John Tierney (D)	1 244	636 554	511.7	92.6	2.7	0.4	3.0	2.9	4.4	89.8	1.5	6.5	17.7	6.9
District 7	Edward Markey (D)	441	634 287	1 438.2	87.9	4.2	0.4	6.4	3.6	4.8	83.5	2.3	5.9	14.7	8.2
District 8	Mike Capuano (D)	105	634 835	6 019.6	57.7	25.5	0.9	9.2	11.9	15.9	48.9	4.9	5.1	13.3	18.7
District 9	Stephen F. Lynch (D)	811	634 062	781.9	82.7	10.0	0.6	4.2	5.4	4.6	79.3	2.8	6.4	17.4	7.9
District 10	Bill Delahunt (D)	2 420	635 901	262.8	94.2	2.1	0.7	3.1	1.5	1.3	92.2	1.4	5.9	16.8	6.0
MICHIGAN		147 121	9 938 444	67.6	81.8	14.8	1.3	2.2	2.0	3.3	78.6	1.9	6.8	19.4	9.4
District 1	Bart Stupak (D)	64 458	662 563	10.3	95.8	1.2	3.6	0.6	0.4	0.9	93.8	1.5	5.4	17.7	8.4
District 2	Peter Hoekstra (R)	13 895	662 563	47.7	91.2	5.0	1.3	1.3	2.8	5.2	87.5	1.6	7.0	20.6	9.6
District 3	Vernon J. Ehlers (R)	4 803	662 563	138.0	86.5	8.9	1.1	2.0	3.7	6.2	82.2	2.0	7.6	20.5	10.2
District 4	Dave Camp (R)	19 299	662 563	34.3	95.4	2.4	1.5	1.0	1.1	2.4	92.8	1.3	6.0	18.6	11.1
District 5	Dale E. Kildee (D)	4 543	662 563	145.9	78.5	19.5	1.4	0.9	1.9	3.6	75.0	2.1	7.1	20.2	8.8
District 6	Fred Upton (R)	8 628	662 563	76.8	87.6	9.7	1.3	1.4	2.1	3.6	84.3	1.9	6.6	19.3	10.7
District 7	John "Joe" Schwarz (R)	11 125	662 563	59.6	91.6	6.3	1.1	1.1	1.7	3.2	88.5	1.7	6.5	19.6	8.5
District 8	Mike Rogers (R)	5 837	662 563	113.5	91.2	5.6	1.1	2.3	1.8	3.5	87.7	1.9	6.9	19.5	11.8
District 9	Joe Knollenberg (R)	806	662 563	821.7	84.7	8.6	0.7	6.2	1.8	3.0	81.4	1.8	6.6	17.9	7.0
District 10	Candice Miller (R)	9 193	662 562	72.1	96.2	1.8	0.8	1.5	1.1	2.1	93.6	1.4	6.8	19.8	7.9
District 11	Thaddeus McCotter (R)	1 032	662 563	641.8	92.3	4.0	0.8	3.5	0.9	2.0	89.5	1.5	7.0	18.5	7.4
District 12	Sander Levin (D)	415	662 563	1 595.8	84.6	12.7	1.0	2.9	1.2	1.5	81.7	2.2	6.1	16.6	7.9
District 13	Carolyn Kilpatrick (D)	280	662 563	2 366.6	33.5	61.8	1.0	1.6	4.6	7.2	28.9	2.3	7.8	22.2	9.4
District 14	John Conyers Jr. (D)	318	662 563	2 085.1	35.9	62.3	0.9	1.8	2.7	1.8	32.1	3.5	7.5	21.5	9.2
District 15	John D. Dingell (D)	2 490	662 563	266.1	82.8	12.6	1.1	4.3	1.6	2.8	79.2	2.3	6.7	17.9	12.9
MINNESOTA		206 189	4 919 479	23.9	90.8	4.1	1.6	3.4	1.8	2.9	88.2	1.7	6.7	19.5	9.6
District 1	Gil Gutknecht (R)	34 503	614 935	17.8	95.3	1.3	0.5	2.1	1.8	3.0	93.2	1.0	6.2	19.3	10.4
District 2	John Kline (R)	7 861	614 934	78.2	94.4	2.1	0.8	2.8	1.4	2.6	91.8	1.4	7.9	21.9	8.1
District 3	Jim Ramstad (R)	1 211	614 935	507.7	90.8	4.5	0.7	4.6	1.1	1.8	88.6	1.6	6.8	19.8	7.3
District 4	Betty McCollum (D)	523	614 935	1 176.2	81.9	7.8	1.4	8.6	3.3	5.2	77.7	2.7	6.9	18.9	10.8
District 5	Martin Olav Sabo (D)	321	614 935	1 916.2	75.9	14.8	2.5	6.1	4.4	6.0	71.2	3.6	6.4	15.1	12.2
District 6	Mark Kennedy (R)	7 979	614 935	77.1	96.7	1.3	0.8	1.8	0.6	1.3	94.9	1.1	7.6	21.6	9.7
District 7	Collin C. Peterson (D)	82 353	614 935	7.5	95.2	0.5	3.1	0.8	1.5	2.6	93.1	1.0	6.1	20.0	9.3
District 8	James L. Oberstar (D)	71 439	614 935	8.6	96.1	0.8	3.3	0.7	0.3	0.8	94.6	1.1	5.7	19.1	8.6
MISSISSIPPI		121 488	2 844 658	23.4	61.9	36.6	0.7	0.9	0.7	1.4	60.7	0.7	7.2	20.1	10.9
District 1	Roger Wicker (R)	29 559	711 160	24.1	72.4	26.5	0.4	0.6	0.7	1.4	71.3	0.6	7.1	19.6	9.6
District 2	Bennie G. Thompson (D)	35 288	711 164	20.2	35.3	63.9	0.4	0.6	0.5	1.2	34.5	0.6	7.6	21.8	11.8
District 3	Charles W. "Chip" Pickering	34 106	711 115	20.9	64.7	33.5	1.2	0.8	0.5	1.2	63.7	0.6	7.0	19.4	10.6
District 4	Gene Taylor (D)	22 535	711 219	31.6	75.3	22.6	0.8	1.6	0.9	1.8	73.5	1.0	7.1	19.5	10.9

1. Dry land or land partially or temporarily covered by water.   2. Hispanic or Latino persons may be of any race.   Note: Data were tabulated for the 108th Congress and some boundary changes have occurred.

STATE District	Percent (cont'd) — Age (cont'd) 25 to 34 years	35 to 44 years	45 to 54 years	55 to 64 years	65 to 74 years	75 years and over	Percent female	Households, 2000 Number	Persons per household	Percent Female family householder[1]	One person	Persons in correctional institutions, 2000	Persons in nursing homes, 2000	Persons in military quarters, 2000	Education, 2000 — School enrollment[2] Public	Private
	15	16	17	18	19	20	21	22	23	24	25	26	27	28	29	30
LOUISIANA	13.5	15.5	13.1	8.5	6.3	5.2	51.6	1 656 053	2.62	16.6	25.3	49 854	31 521	3 877	1 030 634	240 665
District 1	13.4	16.4	14.7	9.1	6.8	5.9	51.6	251 124	2.50	12.1	27.0	3 084	3 563	0	114 676	55 156
District 2	14.3	15.1	13.0	7.9	5.6	4.7	52.9	235 765	2.63	25.1	29.0	6 160	3 214	284	149 580	48 961
District 3	13.3	16.2	12.9	8.4	6.1	4.6	51.3	223 828	2.81	15.3	20.2	3 168	3 435	30	145 546	32 082
District 4	13.2	14.7	12.7	8.9	6.9	6.0	51.5	241 334	2.56	16.6	26.3	6 708	5 441	3 563	157 460	16 642
District 5	12.7	14.6	12.5	8.8	7.0	6.1	51.5	233 462	2.59	17.0	25.4	15 020	7 007	0	157 398	20 261
District 6	14.3	15.7	13.3	7.9	5.3	4.3	51.0	232 972	2.62	15.6	24.5	11 998	3 924	0	155 796	39 126
District 7	13.1	15.8	12.7	8.3	6.5	5.1	51.5	237 568	2.63	14.8	24.4	3 716	4 937	0	150 178	28 437
MAINE	12.4	16.7	15.1	9.7	7.5	6.8	51.3	518 200	2.39	9.5	27.0	2 864	9 339	688	275 158	45 883
District 1	12.8	17.1	15.2	9.4	7.2	6.8	51.5	270 935	2.40	9.5	27.2	1 957	4 244	547	140 099	27 646
District 2	11.9	16.2	15.0	9.9	7.9	6.9	51.2	247 265	2.39	9.5	26.8	907	5 095	141	135 059	18 237
MARYLAND	14.1	17.3	14.3	8.9	6.1	5.2	51.7	1 980 859	2.61	14.1	25.0	35 698	26 716	7 412	1 174 026	301 458
District 1	11.5	17.0	15.1	10.4	7.5	5.9	51.1	248 464	2.60	10.4	21.6	4 635	3 870	263	142 945	32 374
District 2	14.8	16.9	13.3	8.2	6.4	5.9	52.5	260 345	2.51	16.2	27.1	1 179	2 908	1 570	146 111	31 482
District 3	16.0	16.8	13.9	8.7	6.4	6.2	51.4	262 561	2.42	11.9	29.1	7 924	3 034	3 427	126 399	49 346
District 4	15.5	17.7	14.4	8.3	4.3	2.9	52.6	236 346	2.78	19.9	22.7	1 283	1 196	892	163 739	38 080
District 5	14.3	18.2	14.2	8.8	5.0	3.7	51.0	234 254	2.75	12.5	20.9	846	3 012	612	160 274	39 963
District 6	12.8	17.8	14.6	9.1	6.4	5.7	50.3	240 846	2.65	9.2	21.7	11 658	4 591	254	145 541	27 553
District 7	13.4	16.7	13.7	8.6	6.3	5.4	52.7	247 804	2.56	22.5	29.8	7 523	3 934	0	159 077	36 487
District 8	14.8	17.2	14.9	9.1	6.2	6.3	52.0	250 239	2.61	10.6	26.5	650	4 171	394	129 940	46 173
MASSACHUSETTS	14.6	16.7	13.8	8.6	6.7	6.8	51.8	2 443 580	2.51	11.9	28.0	23 513	55 837	472	1 276 945	449 166
District 1	12.1	16.3	14.5	8.5	6.8	7.2	51.5	245 033	2.47	11.5	27.8	1 441	6 041	0	154 478	28 608
District 2	13.1	16.7	13.8	8.4	6.6	7.1	52.2	242 706	2.53	13.6	26.8	2 133	5 649	0	137 807	35 230
District 3	14.0	17.5	13.6	8.2	6.4	6.6	51.5	240 487	2.56	11.4	26.3	1 220	5 999	0	133 149	39 532
District 4	13.8	16.6	14.3	8.9	6.6	7.1	52.4	241 809	2.53	11.2	26.5	2 824	6 020	55	125 355	46 339
District 5	13.8	18.0	13.9	8.4	5.7	5.4	51.0	227 369	2.72	12.5	23.1	5 521	4 844	0	143 930	32 990
District 6	12.6	17.7	15.0	9.3	7.3	7.1	51.9	243 310	2.55	10.5	26.4	1 340	6 165	21	128 869	36 893
District 7	16.4	16.8	13.6	8.9	7.7	7.9	52.4	255 231	2.41	10.3	29.9	812	5 748	163	103 883	48 721
District 8	22.7	14.2	10.2	6.5	4.8	4.5	51.4	254 393	2.31	15.3	36.9	2 088	3 652	79	108 106	104 678
District 9	14.8	16.9	13.7	8.8	7.0	7.2	51.9	238 795	2.57	12.7	27.6	4 330	6 207	97	121 970	46 350
District 10	12.6	16.8	14.9	10.1	8.6	8.2	52.0	254 447	2.45	9.7	27.9	1 804	5 512	57	119 398	29 825
MICHIGAN	13.7	16.1	13.8	8.7	6.5	5.8	51.0	3 785 661	2.56	12.5	26.2	65 330	50 113	112	2 397 577	382 801
District 1	10.8	15.3	14.3	11.1	9.1	7.9	49.6	266 138	2.39	8.5	27.4	11 355	5 196	63	149 681	13 402
District 2	12.7	15.9	13.2	8.6	6.5	5.9	50.4	241 996	2.65	9.8	22.7	5 672	3 948	7	156 168	28 525
District 3	14.7	16.3	12.9	7.3	5.4	5.1	50.4	243 190	2.65	11.1	24.9	6 740	4 455	0	150 575	37 470
District 4	11.9	15.4	13.7	9.8	7.3	6.3	50.6	252 123	2.52	9.2	24.1	7 806	3 769	0	165 753	21 584
District 5	13.3	15.8	13.7	8.8	6.7	5.6	51.9	257 344	2.54	16.1	26.7	1 699	2 695	0	160 802	21 049
District 6	12.7	15.5	13.8	8.9	6.6	5.9	51.1	253 972	2.53	11.3	25.5	1 645	3 305	4	162 977	25 427
District 7	12.8	16.3	14.7	9.2	6.6	5.9	50.3	248 443	2.56	10.8	24.4	13 350	4 017	0	151 371	24 734
District 8	13.5	17.0	14.4	8.1	4.8	4.0	50.6	245 198	2.62	9.6	23.4	1 037	2 127	0	188 217	23 619
District 9	14.5	17.1	15.3	9.3	6.4	6.0	51.1	263 960	2.47	8.7	28.1	1 813	2 729	0	144 608	33 792
District 10	13.5	17.3	14.4	9.2	6.0	5.1	50.2	244 586	2.67	8.7	22.0	2 717	2 451	34	157 631	21 038
District 11	14.8	18.2	14.3	8.3	6.2	5.4	51.0	257 798	2.54	9.4	25.8	1 953	2 931	0	150 122	27 279
District 12	15.4	16.1	13.3	8.9	7.8	7.8	51.9	274 665	2.39	12.2	31.4	1 316	3 695	0	137 583	25 994
District 13	14.9	15.0	12.3	6.9	5.8	5.7	51.9	239 673	2.70	26.5	31.1	4 151	2 891	4	171 810	24 593
District 14	14.6	14.5	12.7	8.0	6.5	5.8	52.9	243 508	2.69	25.1	28.4	884	3 648	0	169 630	27 968
District 15	15.5	15.7	13.5	7.9	5.5	4.5	50.8	253 067	2.52	11.9	26.9	3 192	2 256	0	180 649	26 327
MINNESOTA	13.7	16.8	13.5	8.2	6.0	6.1	50.5	1 895 127	2.52	8.9	26.9	16 999	40 506	12	1 146 595	215 912
District 1	11.8	15.5	13.1	8.6	7.1	8.0	50.6	237 884	2.49	7.4	26.8	2 467	6 343	0	144 359	26 119
District 2	14.6	19.2	13.4	7.3	4.2	3.4	50.1	217 579	2.77	8.2	19.5	1 894	2 405	0	148 006	32 210
District 3	13.6	18.3	15.4	8.7	5.6	4.6	51.1	237 636	2.56	8.5	24.2	792	2 219	0	136 977	28 868
District 4	14.7	16.1	13.3	7.7	5.7	6.0	51.8	242 053	2.46	11.7	31.1	590	4 701	0	132 764	43 616
District 5	19.2	16.0	12.4	7.0	5.3	6.4	50.5	263 538	2.25	11.4	37.6	804	7 481	0	132 535	28 174
District 6	14.2	18.4	13.4	7.3	4.2	3.5	49.4	214 096	2.80	7.9	18.8	4 633	2 713	0	157 176	26 846
District 7	10.6	14.9	13.0	9.3	7.9	8.9	50.3	238 482	2.49	7.3	27.2	2 092	8 798	0	149 637	16 121
District 8	10.8	15.7	14.3	10.1	8.1	7.7	50.1	243 859	2.45	8.5	27.1	3 727	5 846	12	145 141	13 958
MISSISSIPPI	13.4	15.0	12.7	8.6	6.5	5.5	51.7	1 046 434	2.63	17.3	24.6	25 778	18 382	5 722	688 942	100 961
District 1	13.7	15.0	12.7	9.1	6.7	5.7	51.7	267 660	2.59	14.7	23.9	2 631	4 876	247	168 199	20 127
District 2	13.0	14.4	12.2	7.7	5.9	5.5	52.4	245 889	2.76	24.9	25.1	12 515	4 798	4	188 818	29 675
District 3	13.4	15.0	13.1	8.7	6.9	6.0	51.9	268 942	2.56	15.6	25.6	5 653	5 092	628	163 508	30 405
District 4	13.6	15.4	12.9	9.0	6.7	5.0	50.9	263 943	2.61	14.6	23.9	4 979	3 616	4 843	168 417	20 754

1. No spouse present.　　2. All persons 3 years old and over enrolled in nursery school through college.　　Note: Data were tabulated for the 108th Congress and some boundary changes have occurred.

Table E. Congressional Districts 109th Congress — Education, Money Income, Poverty, and Housing

STATE District	Education, 2000 (cont'd) Attainment[1] (percent) High school graduate or more	Bachelor's degree or more	Money income, 1999 Per capita income[2]	Households Median income	Percent with income of $100,000 or more	Percent below poverty level, 1999 Persons Total	Families Total	Housing units, 2000 Total	Occupied units Total	Owner-occupied Percent	Median value[3] (dollars)	Owner cost as a percent of income With a mortgage	Without a mortgage[4]
	31	32	33	34	35	36	37	38	39	40	41	42	43
LOUISIANA	74.8	18.7	16 912	32 566	7.4	19.6	15.8	1 847 181	1 656 053	67.9	85 000	19.6	9.9
District 1	82.4	27.4	22 255	40 948	12.2	12.1	9.1	271 732	250 838	70.3	123 800	20.2	9.9
District 2	72.1	19.4	15 183	27 514	5.9	26.8	22.8	265 337	236 008	50.4	80 100	22.5	11.0
District 3	68.9	10.8	15 336	34 463	5.8	18.6	15.6	248 774	223 921	77.5	81 700	19.0	9.9
District 4	76.5	16.7	16 284	31 085	6.2	20.0	16.0	277 450	241 288	68.5	71 400	19.2	9.9
District 5	70.5	15.5	14 462	27 453	5.3	23.6	18.7	264 734	233 533	70.3	65 500	19.7	10.1
District 6	80.3	24.1	18 650	37 931	9.7	16.6	12.5	255 967	232 902	68.7	98 100	19.2	9.9
District 7	72.3	16.6	16 228	31 453	6.7	19.9	16.2	263 187	237 563	70.3	78 100	18.5	9.9
MAINE	85.4	22.9	19 533	37 240	7.1	10.9	7.8	651 901	518 200	71.6	98 700	21.4	12.1
District 1	87.9	27.5	21 736	41 585	9.3	8.8	6.2	326 739	270 935	70.4	119 000	21.8	12.2
District 2	82.5	17.7	17 116	32 678	4.8	13.2	9.5	325 162	247 265	72.8	80 800	20.9	12.1
MARYLAND	83.8	31.4	25 614	52 868	18.1	8.5	6.1	2 145 283	1 980 859	67.7	146 000	22.2	9.9
District 1	84.2	27.3	25 197	51 918	17.0	7.3	5.2	294 381	248 619	78.5	148 900	21.9	9.9
District 2	79.8	20.3	21 211	44 309	9.6	9.8	7.5	277 397	260 455	62.4	110 500	22.0	10.8
District 3	84.1	36.5	27 694	52 906	18.2	7.7	5.2	278 853	262 186	67.5	134 600	21.7	10.4
District 4	86.3	32.7	25 134	57 727	20.2	7.3	5.5	247 830	236 464	62.8	154 500	23.3	9.9
District 5	87.7	28.7	25 744	62 661	21.0	5.6	3.4	248 441	234 188	74.8	158 100	22.8	9.9
District 6	83.8	23.7	23 014	50 957	14.7	6.4	4.6	258 628	240 769	75.7	144 900	22.2	9.9
District 7	76.2	27.5	20 676	38 885	13.4	17.6	13.6	280 497	247 981	55.5	104 300	22.4	10.9
District 8	88.4	53.7	36 245	68 306	31.3	6.2	4.2	259 256	250 197	65.3	229 000	21.5	9.9
MASSACHUSETTS	84.8	33.2	25 952	50 502	17.7	9.3	6.7	2 621 989	2 443 580	61.7	185 700	21.9	12.4
District 1	84.4	25.4	20 758	42 570	10.0	10.5	7.3	267 100	245 029	65.5	127 200	21.4	12.0
District 2	81.9	23.1	21 312	44 386	11.7	10.8	8.2	255 284	242 706	65.8	132 900	21.5	12.7
District 3	82.4	30.8	24 429	50 223	17.1	9.0	6.6	250 039	240 491	62.9	168 800	21.3	11.8
District 4	82.1	36.9	29 388	53 169	21.2	8.4	6.2	256 748	241 784	65.1	187 900	21.4	12.1
District 5	83.6	33.6	27 215	56 217	22.6	8.9	6.7	234 513	227 344	67.2	206 900	21.6	12.2
District 6	88.4	35.1	28 560	57 826	22.3	6.3	4.3	253 272	243 310	68.9	239 800	22.2	12.3
District 7	87.5	39.5	30 381	56 110	21.8	6.7	4.6	262 033	255 260	57.1	251 600	22.3	12.7
District 8	78.4	39.8	23 274	39 300	13.1	19.9	15.6	266 754	254 471	28.4	200 900	22.7	12.6
District 9	86.9	33.8	27 287	55 407	20.3	7.5	5.4	246 476	238 738	64.4	200 600	22.0	12.2
District 10	90.8	33.5	26 907	51 928	17.3	5.9	4.1	329 770	254 447	73.6	194 600	22.9	12.8
MICHIGAN	83.4	21.8	22 168	44 667	12.7	10.5	7.4	4 234 279	3 785 661	73.8	115 600	19.6	9.9
District 1	83.0	15.6	17 700	34 076	5.3	11.2	7.8	390 670	266 115	80.1	79 600	19.6	9.9
District 2	83.6	18.3	19 325	42 589	8.5	8.9	6.3	290 170	242 071	80.0	107 900	19.6	9.9
District 3	84.7	23.9	21 265	45 936	11.1	8.6	6.2	257 995	243 184	72.5	112 800	19.5	9.9
District 4	84.5	18.6	19 347	39 020	8.6	10.5	6.6	311 749	252 141	77.8	95 900	19.3	9.9
District 5	82.0	15.1	19 823	39 675	9.5	13.7	10.6	278 055	257 373	73.8	87 200	18.8	9.9
District 6	83.5	21.1	20 031	40 943	9.0	11.4	7.5	286 509	253 892	72.9	98 100	19.3	9.9
District 7	85.3	19.1	21 216	45 181	10.8	7.9	5.4	271 488	248 411	76.7	103 400	19.3	9.9
District 8	89.5	29.0	24 409	52 510	17.4	8.4	4.9	259 014	245 099	75.2	144 600	19.7	9.9
District 9	90.1	43.5	36 072	65 358	28.5	5.4	3.5	275 727	264 060	74.3	198 000	19.9	9.9
District 10	84.6	16.9	23 597	52 690	16.2	6.0	4.3	266 867	244 523	82.1	152 000	19.8	9.9
District 11	88.0	28.5	27 921	59 177	20.5	4.3	3.0	266 956	257 783	78.5	153 700	19.6	10.0
District 12	81.4	19.5	23 560	46 784	11.8	7.3	5.4	284 031	274 732	73.0	121 400	19.9	10.9
District 13	69.4	14.1	17 078	31 165	8.5	24.4	19.8	268 629	239 745	55.7	71 600	20.5	11.8
District 14	75.6	14.2	17 546	36 099	8.9	19.7	15.9	261 530	243 452	64.9	84 500	20.4	11.4
District 15	84.7	27.5	23 628	48 963	14.9	10.3	6.3	264 889	253 080	68.4	130 500	19.6	9.9
MINNESOTA	87.9	27.4	23 198	47 111	12.6	7.9	5.1	2 065 946	1 895 127	74.6	122 400	20.0	9.9
District 1	85.1	21.6	19 889	40 941	7.7	8.5	5.3	251 376	237 886	76.9	89 300	18.9	9.9
District 2	91.6	31.2	25 718	61 344	19.1	3.9	2.5	224 445	217 641	82.2	149 900	20.7	9.9
District 3	94.0	40.1	32 594	63 816	24.4	3.5	2.3	242 995	237 651	77.4	159 000	20.0	9.9
District 4	88.1	33.0	23 853	46 811	13.4	9.6	6.6	248 075	242 046	65.3	127 800	19.9	9.9
District 5	87.0	34.9	23 798	41 569	10.7	12.7	8.2	271 495	263 486	57.2	121 300	20.2	9.9
District 6	90.6	24.5	23 533	56 862	15.5	4.7	2.8	223 743	214 072	82.8	137 500	20.7	9.9
District 7	82.1	16.4	17 603	36 453	5.3	10.3	6.8	283 841	238 530	77.8	77 100	19.2	9.9
District 8	85.2	17.7	18 596	37 911	6.1	10.4	6.9	319 976	243 815	80.1	87 100	19.9	9.9
MISSISSIPPI	72.9	16.9	15 853	31 330	6.0	19.9	16.0	1 161 953	1 046 434	72.3	71 400	20.4	9.9
District 1	70.4	13.9	16 156	32 535	5.5	16.4	12.9	294 894	267 649	75.1	74 000	20.2	9.9
District 2	68.6	16.8	13 616	26 894	5.0	27.3	22.7	271 865	245 770	65.7	58 700	21.3	11.0
District 3	74.8	20.2	17 218	31 907	7.5	19.2	15.4	299 676	269 154	75.7	74 900	19.9	9.9
District 4	77.4	16.7	16 422	33 023	6.0	16.9	13.4	295 518	263 861	72.4	78 000	20.2	9.9

1. Persons 25 years old and over.   2. Based on the population enumerated as of April 1, 2000.   3. Specified owner-occupied units.   4. Median monthly owner costs is often in the minimum category—9.9 percent or less, which is indicated as 9.9 percent.   Note: Data were tabulated for the 108th Congress and some boundary changes have occurred.

Table E. Congressional Districts 109th Congress — Housing, Labor Force, and Employment

STATE District	Housing units, 2000 (cont'd) Occupied units (cont'd) Renter-occupied Median rent[1] (dollars)	Rent as a percent of income	Substandard units[2] (percent)	Civilian labor force, 2000 Total	Unemployment Total	Rate[3]	Civilian employment,[4] 2000 Total	Percent Management, professional, and related occupations	Production, transportation, and material moving occupations	Disability, 2000 Employment disabled persons[5] (percent)
	44	45	46	47	48	49	50	51	52	53
LOUISIANA	466	25.8	5.8	1 997 995	146 218	7.3	1 851 777	29.9	14.1	12.9
District 1	558	24.4	3.6	312 697	14 881	4.8	297 816	37.2	9.7	11.9
District 2	481	28.6	9.0	277 929	26 580	9.6	251 349	29.2	12.7	14.4
District 3	431	23.2	6.5	275 775	19 525	7.1	256 250	23.8	18.9	13.0
District 4	435	24.9	5.2	274 658	22 872	8.3	251 786	27.2	16.2	13.3
District 5	396	26.7	5.3	268 061	22 970	8.6	245 091	28.0	15.1	13.9
District 6	498	25.7	5.3	305 823	18 429	6.0	287 394	33.3	12.5	11.8
District 7	420	24.8	5.8	283 052	20 961	7.4	262 091	28.7	14.8	12.3
MAINE	497	25.3	2.1	655 176	31 165	4.8	624 011	31.5	15.3	11.7
District 1	558	25.4	1.7	351 663	13 291	3.8	338 372	34.6	13.4	10.6
District 2	436	25.3	2.5	303 513	17 874	5.9	285 639	28.0	17.6	12.8
MARYLAND	689	24.7	4.0	2 737 359	128 902	4.7	2 608 457	41.3	9.5	10.8
District 1	598	24.6	2.0	344 194	13 505	3.9	330 689	37.0	11.5	10.2
District 2	617	24.6	3.1	335 143	16 657	5.0	318 486	31.8	13.2	12.8
District 3	713	24.3	2.7	349 405	14 060	4.0	335 345	44.8	8.5	9.9
District 4	753	25.0	7.7	349 641	18 452	5.3	331 189	42.6	8.1	11.6
District 5	804	24.3	3.8	357 211	14 580	4.1	342 631	41.4	8.1	10.1
District 6	559	23.5	1.5	339 226	12 219	3.6	327 007	35.5	12.1	9.2
District 7	545	26.6	4.7	309 164	26 645	8.6	282 519	40.4	10.2	14.1
District 8	888	24.5	6.7	353 375	12 784	3.6	340 591	55.6	4.8	8.9
MASSACHUSETTS	684	25.5	3.4	3 312 039	150 952	4.6	3 161 087	41.1	11.3	11.8
District 1	545	25.4	2.7	330 011	16 564	5.0	313 447	34.8	15.1	10.4
District 2	559	25.2	2.7	322 084	15 004	4.7	307 080	34.2	15.5	13.0
District 3	584	23.8	2.9	326 531	14 238	4.4	312 293	39.6	13.2	12.0
District 4	603	24.7	2.1	332 139	16 341	4.9	315 798	43.5	11.9	10.7
District 5	656	25.3	4.1	320 718	12 504	3.9	308 214	42.5	13.4	12.1
District 6	704	25.2	2.5	335 384	13 491	4.0	321 893	42.4	9.9	10.3
District 7	842	24.8	3.1	344 427	11 937	3.5	332 490	46.8	8.1	11.9
District 8	829	27.5	8.7	342 061	24 301	7.1	317 760	46.9	8.3	13.2
District 9	759	25.5	3.1	329 389	13 712	4.2	315 677	41.3	9.8	12.4
District 10	768	25.9	1.9	329 295	12 860	3.9	316 435	38.3	7.9	12.0
MICHIGAN	546	24.4	3.4	4 922 453	284 992	5.8	4 637 461	31.5	18.5	10.7
District 1	405	24.4	2.5	303 731	24 237	8.0	279 494	26.3	17.2	10.6
District 2	511	23.3	3.1	332 577	16 546	5.0	316 031	27.3	23.6	10.4
District 3	544	23.4	3.5	342 955	15 258	4.4	327 697	30.4	21.3	10.0
District 4	495	25.0	2.6	323 137	20 049	6.2	303 088	28.4	18.2	9.9
District 5	488	25.9	3.3	312 205	23 261	7.5	288 944	26.3	21.0	11.8
District 6	497	24.5	3.1	341 751	19 970	5.8	321 781	29.0	22.0	10.7
District 7	516	23.4	2.3	332 697	16 145	4.9	316 552	29.2	22.0	10.7
District 8	568	25.6	2.4	355 162	15 499	4.4	339 663	36.4	13.7	8.4
District 9	714	23.2	2.7	350 327	12 581	3.6	337 746	48.7	9.0	7.8
District 10	579	23.2	2.4	339 023	15 124	4.5	323 899	30.3	20.4	9.6
District 11	656	22.4	2.4	352 653	11 858	3.4	340 795	37.5	14.5	8.0
District 12	629	24.0	3.3	339 775	15 837	4.7	323 938	31.2	17.6	10.4
District 13	474	26.1	7.4	272 991	35 350	12.9	237 641	24.8	21.2	16.8
District 14	525	26.5	6.8	281 728	27 739	9.8	253 989	25.2	20.6	16.6
District 15	630	25.3	3.7	341 741	15 538	4.5	326 203	34.9	17.1	9.7
MINNESOTA	566	24.7	3.3	2 689 115	109 069	4.1	2 580 046	35.8	14.9	8.6
District 1	439	23.1	2.5	333 528	13 247	4.0	320 281	32.9	18.3	8.3
District 2	672	24.1	2.3	350 641	10 498	3.0	340 143	37.2	13.5	7.6
District 3	773	24.5	2.7	352 017	9 737	2.8	342 280	43.2	10.4	6.6
District 4	611	25.5	4.9	334 376	13 904	4.2	320 472	39.1	12.7	8.8
District 5	605	25.5	5.8	354 730	17 078	4.8	337 652	39.7	12.3	9.7
District 6	544	23.7	2.2	345 494	10 489	3.0	335 005	33.4	16.7	7.5
District 7	401	24.4	2.6	313 071	15 728	5.0	297 343	30.4	19.2	9.9
District 8	417	25.4	3.3	305 258	18 388	6.0	286 870	28.6	16.8	10.3
MISSISSIPPI	439	25.0	5.7	1 267 092	93 778	7.4	1 173 314	27.4	20.4	14.4
District 1	417	24.0	4.3	329 209	19 955	6.1	309 254	24.0	27.4	14.3
District 2	409	26.4	8.5	297 585	30 984	10.4	266 601	27.2	19.2	15.4
District 3	451	24.7	5.2	321 173	21 409	6.7	299 764	31.3	18.1	13.4
District 4	485	25.0	4.9	319 125	21 430	6.7	297 695	27.0	16.4	14.7

1. Specified renter-occupied units.   2. Overcrowded or lacking complete plumbing facilities.   3. Percent of total civilian labor force.   4. Persons 16 years old and over.   5. Persons 16 to 64 years old.   Note: Data were tabulated for the 108th Congress and some boundary changes have occurred.

STATE District	Representative	Land area,[1] 2000 (sq km)	Population and population characteristics, 2000											
					Percent									
					Race alone or in combination								Age	
			Total persons	Per square kilometer	White	Black	Am. Indian, Alaska Native	Asian and Pacific Islander	Other race	Hispanic or Latino[2]	Non-Hispanic White	Two or more races	Under 5 years	5 to 17 years	18 to 24 years
		1	2	3	4	5	6	7	8	9	10	11	12	13	14
MISSOURI		178 414	5 595 211	31.4	86.1	11.7	1.1	1.5	1.2	2.1	83.8	1.5	6.6	18.9	9.6
District 1	William "Lacy" Clay Jr. (D)	562	621 690	1 105.5	47.5	50.7	0.6	1.9	0.8	1.3	45.8	1.4	6.5	19.9	9.5
District 2	Todd Akin (R)	3 232	621 690	192.4	95.1	2.5	0.5	2.4	0.6	1.4	93.2	1.0	7.0	20.3	7.4
District 3	Russ Carnahan (D)	3 230	621 690	192.5	88.0	9.7	0.7	2.1	1.1	1.8	85.7	1.5	6.5	18.2	9.3
District 4	Ike Skelton (D)	37 669	621 690	16.5	94.7	3.6	1.3	1.0	1.1	1.9	92.4	1.5	6.5	19.0	9.6
District 5	Emanuel Cleaver (D)	1 325	621 691	469.3	70.7	25.3	1.3	1.9	3.3	5.6	66.3	2.3	7.0	18.6	9.1
District 6	Sam Graves (R)	33 753	621 690	18.4	95.0	3.2	1.0	1.2	1.1	2.4	92.4	1.4	6.6	18.8	9.3
District 7	Roy Blunt (R)	14 192	621 690	43.8	95.8	1.6	2.1	1.0	1.4	2.6	92.9	1.7	6.7	17.8	11.1
District 8	Jo Ann Emerson (R)	48 384	621 690	12.8	94.2	4.6	1.4	0.6	0.5	1.0	92.5	1.2	6.3	18.8	9.2
District 9	Kenny Hulshof (R)	36 067	621 690	17.2	94.3	4.3	0.9	1.2	0.5	1.1	92.6	1.2	6.4	18.7	11.6
MONTANA		376 979	902 195	2.4	92.2	0.5	7.4	0.9	0.9	2.0	89.5	1.7	6.1	19.4	9.5
At Large	Dennis Rehberg (R)	376 979	902 195	2.4	92.2	0.5	7.4	0.9	0.9	2.0	89.5	1.7	6.1	19.4	9.5
NEBRASKA		199 099	1 711 263	8.6	90.8	4.4	1.3	1.7	3.3	5.5	87.3	1.4	6.8	19.5	10.2
District 1	Jeff Fortenberry (R)	30 952	570 325	18.4	93.4	1.8	1.7	1.9	2.7	4.2	90.5	1.4	6.6	18.7	11.9
District 2	Lee Terry (R)	1 063	570 421	536.5	83.8	11.0	1.1	2.4	3.7	6.3	79.6	1.9	7.6	19.8	10.2
District 3	Tom Osborne (R)	167 083	570 517	3.4	95.3	0.4	1.1	0.7	3.5	6.0	91.9	1.0	6.3	19.9	8.5
NEVADA		284 448	1 998 257	7.0	78.4	7.5	2.1	6.4	9.7	19.7	65.2	3.8	7.3	18.3	9.0
District 1	Shelley Berkley (D)	459	666 088	1 450.6	69.5	13.2	1.6	6.9	13.6	28.2	51.5	4.5	8.2	18.5	9.8
District 2	Jim Gibbons (R)	272 153	666 087	2.4	84.6	2.9	3.4	4.2	8.2	15.3	74.8	3.1	7.0	18.9	8.8
District 3	Jon Porter (R)	11 836	666 082	56.3	80.9	6.4	1.4	8.2	7.3	15.6	69.3	3.9	6.7	17.6	8.4
NEW HAMPSHIRE		23 227	1 235 786	53.2	97.0	1.0	0.6	1.7	0.9	1.7	95.1	1.1	6.1	18.9	8.4
District 1	Jeb Bradley (R)	6 342	617 575	97.4	97.1	1.1	0.6	1.6	0.8	1.6	95.1	1.1	6.2	18.8	8.4
District 2	Charlie Bass (R)	16 885	618 211	36.6	96.9	0.9	0.7	1.7	0.9	1.7	95.1	1.1	6.0	19.1	8.3
NEW JERSEY		19 211	8 414 350	438.0	74.4	14.4	0.6	6.3	6.9	13.3	66.0	2.5	6.7	18.1	8.0
District 1	Robert E. Andrews (D)	867	647 258	746.5	75.3	17.9	0.6	3.2	5.0	8.2	71.2	1.8	6.7	19.8	8.8
District 2	Frank A. LoBiondo (R)	5 133	647 258	126.1	77.2	15.3	0.9	2.9	5.9	10.3	71.7	2.1	6.3	19.0	7.8
District 3	Jim Saxton (R)	2 397	647 257	270.0	86.9	9.4	0.5	3.3	1.6	3.8	83.4	1.6	5.9	18.1	6.6
District 4	Chris Smith (R)	1 862	647 258	347.7	86.6	8.4	0.5	2.7	3.6	7.6	81.3	1.7	7.1	18.0	7.3
District 5	Scott Garrett (R)	2 846	647 258	227.4	90.3	1.8	0.4	7.1	1.6	4.5	86.3	1.3	6.8	19.3	5.8
District 6	Frank Pallone Jr. (D)	509	647 257	1 272.8	69.3	17.8	0.6	9.1	5.9	11.7	61.7	2.6	6.7	17.1	10.4
District 7	Mike Ferguson (R)	1 541	647 257	420.0	84.7	4.9	0.4	8.9	2.9	6.9	79.0	1.6	6.9	18.0	5.9
District 8	Bill Pascrell Jr. (D)	277	647 258	2 340.1	66.3	14.4	0.6	6.1	16.5	25.8	53.7	3.8	7.1	18.0	8.8
District 9	Steve Rothman (D)	241	647 257	2 682.9	74.2	7.9	0.6	11.7	9.4	18.8	61.3	3.5	5.9	15.3	7.9
District 10	Donald M. Payne (D)	171	647 258	3 786.7	30.2	59.9	0.8	4.4	8.9	15.0	21.4	3.9	7.4	19.7	10.2
District 11	Rodney Frelinghuysen (R)	1 580	647 258	409.6	88.7	3.1	0.3	7.0	2.4	6.8	82.9	1.5	7.1	18.0	6.1
District 12	Rush Holt (D)	1 640	647 258	394.6	76.7	12.3	0.4	9.8	2.7	5.5	72.4	1.8	6.5	18.4	7.9
District 13	Robert Menendez (D)	147	647 258	4 404.7	60.7	14.1	0.9	6.5	23.9	47.6	32.3	5.8	6.7	16.7	11.1
NEW MEXICO		314 309	1 819 046	5.8	69.9	2.3	10.5	1.7	19.4	42.1	44.7	3.6	7.2	20.8	9.8
District 1	Heather Wilson (R)	12 216	606 400	49.6	74.7	3.3	4.5	2.6	19.4	42.6	48.5	4.2	6.9	18.8	10.1
District 2	Steve Pearce (R)	179 986	606 406	3.4	71.8	2.2	6.3	1.0	22.1	47.3	44.3	3.3	7.3	21.6	10.2
District 3	Tom Udall (D)	122 108	606 240	5.0	63.3	1.5	20.7	1.3	16.7	36.3	41.4	3.4	7.3	21.9	9.0
NEW YORK		122 283	18 976 457	155.2	70.0	17.0	0.9	6.4	9.1	15.1	62.0	3.1	6.5	18.2	9.3
District 1	Timothy Bishop (D)	1 674	654 360	390.8	90.6	4.9	0.7	2.9	2.8	7.5	84.5	1.7	6.9	18.8	8.1
District 2	Steve Israel (D)	620	654 360	1 055.5	80.1	11.3	0.6	3.6	7.0	13.9	71.5	2.4	7.3	19.4	7.3
District 3	Peter King (R)	475	654 361	1 377.6	92.4	2.6	0.3	3.5	2.7	6.9	86.9	1.5	6.6	17.8	6.4
District 4	Carolyn McCarthy (D)	233	654 360	2 812.5	70.6	19.3	0.6	5.2	7.3	13.6	62.3	2.8	6.6	18.6	8.3
District 5	Gary Ackerman (D)	172	654 361	3 812.7	58.4	6.5	0.7	26.0	12.4	23.5	44.2	3.9	6.0	15.7	8.8
District 6	Gregory W. Meeks (D)	102	654 361	6 388.7	20.9	57.8	2.1	12.0	15.4	16.9	12.8	7.7	7.1	19.9	10.0
District 7	Joseph Crowley (D)	68	654 360	9 581.9	48.8	20.3	1.2	14.4	21.3	39.5	27.6	5.6	6.6	17.0	9.5
District 8	Jerrold Nadler (D)	39	654 360	16 981.6	77.2	6.8	0.6	12.2	6.9	11.7	68.7	3.3	5.5	12.4	9.6
District 9	Anthony D. Weiner (D)	96	654 360	6 823.7	73.7	5.2	0.6	16.0	8.6	13.6	64.0	3.9	5.9	15.3	8.2
District 10	Edolphus Towns (D)	46	654 361	14 131.3	22.7	65.3	0.9	3.6	11.7	17.2	16.2	4.0	8.0	22.2	10.6
District 11	Major Owens (D)	31	654 360	20 967.0	26.5	63.6	0.8	5.3	8.1	12.1	21.4	4.1	7.4	19.7	10.4
District 12	Nydia M. Velázquez (D)	49	654 361	13 488.1	43.7	12.4	1.3	17.3	31.5	48.5	23.3	5.9	7.2	18.5	11.5
District 13	Vito Fossella (R)	168	654 361	3 903.4	79.3	7.5	0.5	10.0	5.9	11.0	70.9	3.1	6.4	17.3	8.4
District 14	Carolyn Maloney (D)	33	654 361	20 100.3	76.4	6.0	0.6	12.9	8.6	14.0	65.9	4.3	4.5	8.8	9.4
District 15	Charles B. Rangel (D)	27	654 361	24 562.6	31.8	37.3	1.7	3.8	31.8	47.9	16.4	5.9	6.4	17.6	11.7
District 16	José E. Serrano (D)	31	654 360	21 366.3	24.0	39.1	2.0	2.6	39.2	62.8	2.9	6.6	9.6	24.9	11.7
District 17	Eliot L. Engel (D)	328	654 360	1 995.1	51.2	34.4	0.9	5.5	12.4	20.4	41.3	4.2	7.4	19.2	8.9
District 18	Nita M. Lowey (D)	575	654 360	1 137.3	77.1	10.8	0.5	6.0	8.7	16.2	67.1	2.9	6.8	17.9	7.2
District 19	Sue Kelly (R)	3 629	654 361	180.3	89.5	6.0	0.6	2.7	3.1	7.7	83.5	1.7	7.1	19.9	7.7
District 20	John Sweeney (R)	18 176	654 360	36.0	95.6	2.8	0.6	1.1	1.0	2.2	93.4	1.1	5.8	18.7	7.7

1. Dry land or land partially or temporarily covered by water.   2. Hispanic or Latino persons may be of any race.   Note: Data were tabulated for the 108th Congress and some boundary changes have occurred.

STATE District	Population and population characteristics, 2000 (cont'd)							Households, 2000				Persons in correctional institutions, 2000	Persons in nursing homes, 2000	Persons in military quarters, 2000	Education, 2000	
	Percent (cont'd)									Percent					School enrollment[2]	
	Age (cont'd)															
	25 to 34 years	35 to 44 years	45 to 54 years	55 to 64 years	65 to 74 years	75 years and over	Percent female	Number	Persons per house-hold	Female family house-holder[1]	One person				Public	Private
	15	16	17	18	19	20	21	22	23	24	25	26	27	28	29	30
MISSOURI	13.2	15.9	13.3	9.1	7.0	6.5	51.4	2 194 594	2.48	11.6	27.3	35 206	48 708	5 435	1 205 378	274 195
District 1	13.4	15.4	12.8	8.5	7.2	6.6	53.5	249 047	2.44	20.9	32.0	1 113	4 782	0	139 258	39 987
District 2	12.5	17.7	14.8	9.0	6.2	5.2	51.2	230 645	2.65	8.2	21.7	1 441	4 897	0	123 821	51 235
District 3	14.7	16.8	13.3	8.1	6.4	6.6	51.7	251 971	2.42	11.8	31.1	1 386	4 780	6	113 062	51 249
District 4	12.4	15.3	12.9	10.0	7.8	6.7	50.1	238 395	2.50	8.8	24.8	7 065	5 827	5 429	135 471	19 548
District 5	14.8	16.2	12.9	8.4	6.7	6.3	51.9	254 600	2.40	15.0	32.0	1 602	4 319	0	131 792	29 142
District 6	13.3	16.2	13.6	9.0	6.7	6.6	50.8	241 518	2.49	9.3	25.8	7 902	5 672	0	139 330	21 503
District 7	13.1	14.9	13.0	9.4	7.3	6.6	51.3	246 019	2.44	9.6	26.0	1 910	5 090	0	136 492	23 827
District 8	11.9	14.6	13.1	10.3	8.3	7.5	51.2	245 479	2.46	10.6	26.2	4 486	7 332	0	138 289	13 318
District 9	12.7	15.7	13.0	8.9	6.7	6.3	50.8	236 920	2.50	9.1	25.6	8 301	6 009	0	147 863	24 386
MONTANA	11.4	15.7	15.0	9.4	6.9	6.5	50.2	358 667	2.45	8.9	27.4	4 124	6 470	404	217 183	24 571
At Large	11.4	15.7	15.0	9.4	6.9	6.5	50.2	358 667	2.45	8.9	27.4	4 124	6 470	404	217 183	24 571
NEBRASKA	13.0	15.4	13.2	8.3	6.8	6.8	50.7	666 184	2.49	9.1	27.6	6 060	16 195	590	398 031	82 674
District 1	12.9	15.3	13.1	8.1	6.6	6.8	50.4	220 837	2.48	8.3	27.1	3 142	5 242	0	137 120	27 009
District 2	15.4	16.3	13.1	7.5	5.4	4.7	50.9	219 997	2.53	11.7	27.9	1 847	3 430	590	128 681	37 989
District 3	10.8	14.7	13.4	9.2	8.3	9.0	50.8	225 350	2.46	7.2	27.6	1 071	7 523	0	132 230	17 676
NEVADA	15.3	16.1	13.5	9.5	6.6	4.4	49.1	751 165	2.62	11.1	24.9	15 940	4 895	1 312	448 044	44 841
District 1	17.1	15.9	12.0	8.6	6.0	4.0	48.5	244 497	2.68	13.0	27.2	4 811	1 918	0	146 221	13 985
District 2	13.6	16.3	14.4	9.7	6.6	4.7	48.7	253 325	2.56	9.8	25.4	9 188	2 039	945	159 032	14 759
District 3	15.3	16.1	14.0	10.3	7.2	4.4	50.0	253 343	2.61	10.6	22.1	1 941	938	367	142 791	16 097
NEW HAMPSHIRE	13.0	17.9	14.9	8.9	6.3	5.6	50.8	474 606	2.53	9.1	24.4	3 468	9 316	95	264 403	68 485
District 1	13.5	18.2	14.7	8.6	6.2	5.5	50.9	238 422	2.53	9.2	24.6	1 422	4 224	89	133 348	32 440
District 2	12.5	17.6	15.1	9.1	6.5	5.8	50.7	236 184	2.53	8.9	24.3	2 046	5 092	6	131 055	36 045
NEW JERSEY	14.1	17.1	13.8	9.0	6.8	6.4	51.5	3 064 645	2.68	12.6	24.5	47 941	51 493	3 291	1 735 248	482 584
District 1	14.1	16.9	13.5	8.2	6.3	5.7	51.7	236 866	2.68	15.0	25.1	3 610	3 678	0	149 773	32 224
District 2	13.0	16.3	13.8	9.3	7.3	6.8	51.0	238 555	2.61	13.9	25.5	10 556	4 555	355	141 894	24 853
District 3	11.8	16.6	14.1	9.9	9.0	8.0	51.5	243 882	2.60	9.9	23.3	5 637	4 410	1 229	133 018	28 056
District 4	12.8	16.7	13.1	8.8	7.8	8.5	51.7	241 143	2.63	10.2	25.5	4 396	5 554	1 409	122 774	39 957
District 5	11.2	18.3	15.4	9.8	6.9	6.4	51.4	229 151	2.78	8.1	19.5	267	6 190	0	136 077	36 953
District 6	15.5	16.9	13.4	8.4	6.1	5.6	51.3	234 153	2.69	12.6	25.6	19	3 879	23	143 880	35 234
District 7	13.2	18.6	15.1	9.2	6.8	6.3	51.2	233 323	2.72	8.5	21.1	5 226	2 852	0	128 324	35 677
District 8	14.8	16.2	13.2	8.6	6.6	6.8	52.0	225 635	2.81	14.8	24.1	1 921	3 653	0	129 617	40 084
District 9	16.1	16.8	13.8	9.4	7.5	7.3	51.8	251 137	2.55	11.8	28.5	980	1 609	0	111 061	44 091
District 10	15.4	15.8	12.3	8.4	5.8	5.1	53.0	228 446	2.76	24.7	27.7	4 594	3 038	0	147 289	41 996
District 11	13.2	18.5	15.2	9.9	6.4	5.5	51.1	233 288	2.72	7.7	21.3	1 669	4 444	10	126 603	41 863
District 12	13.1	17.8	14.8	8.8	6.6	6.0	51.3	232 923	2.67	9.8	23.0	5 240	3 810	255	134 303	44 733
District 13	19.5	15.9	11.5	7.8	5.7	5.0	50.2	236 143	2.68	17.5	28.2	3 826	3 821	10	130 635	36 863
NEW MEXICO	12.9	15.5	13.5	8.7	6.5	5.2	50.8	677 971	2.63	13.2	25.4	10 940	6 810	1 827	476 022	57 764
District 1	14.0	16.2	14.1	8.5	6.1	5.3	51.0	238 282	2.50	12.7	27.8	2 444	1 835	431	145 845	24 287
District 2	11.9	14.5	12.5	9.0	7.4	5.6	50.6	218 601	2.70	13.4	23.5	6 324	2 729	834	168 380	13 396
District 3	12.7	15.8	13.9	8.8	6.0	4.7	50.9	221 088	2.70	13.6	24.7	2 172	2 246	562	161 797	20 081
NEW YORK	14.5	16.2	13.5	8.9	6.7	6.2	51.8	7 056 860	2.61	14.7	28.1	108 088	123 852	8 598	3 987 395	1 229 635
District 1	13.3	17.4	14.3	9.3	6.3	5.9	50.9	223 857	2.84	9.9	20.1	1 471	4 450	21	151 000	28 355
District 2	13.4	17.7	13.8	9.6	6.7	4.8	51.1	206 786	3.12	11.5	15.7	0	3 867	18	147 062	32 952
District 3	12.6	18.0	14.6	9.4	8.0	6.6	51.5	225 363	2.87	9.9	18.7	0	3 039	4	126 603	41 204
District 4	12.8	16.3	14.1	9.0	7.4	7.0	52.1	212 500	3.03	13.0	19.4	1 423	3 214	0	133 768	47 163
District 5	15.2	16.2	13.9	9.4	7.5	7.3	51.4	228 353	2.82	11.8	23.6	0	4 694	0	124 307	42 197
District 6	14.9	16.1	12.6	8.8	5.9	4.7	53.3	204 544	3.14	23.9	20.7	0	4 814	0	154 071	43 372
District 7	16.8	15.9	12.5	8.9	6.7	6.1	52.3	239 163	2.69	19.6	27.8	0	5 561	0	124 509	50 116
District 8	20.1	16.2	13.7	8.7	6.9	6.9	50.7	303 231	2.08	8.0	45.8	2 517	2 669	0	77 585	75 030
District 9	14.9	15.4	14.1	9.5	8.2	8.6	52.4	256 229	2.53	11.5	29.9	467	2 869	0	106 560	54 482
District 10	14.9	14.8	11.9	8.0	5.4	4.2	54.4	225 520	2.83	29.7	27.2	695	2 710	0	162 700	52 555
District 11	16.5	15.8	12.7	8.1	5.2	4.0	54.5	238 136	2.71	26.6	28.2	141	2 198	0	155 014	49 339
District 12	18.6	15.5	11.7	7.6	5.4	4.1	50.9	225 095	2.87	21.3	26.4	1 421	1 306	0	149 632	31 545
District 13	15.1	16.3	14.0	9.2	7.0	6.4	51.8	240 922	2.67	13.0	26.3	944	4 108	230	118 999	51 261
District 14	24.2	16.7	13.3	9.8	6.9	6.4	52.9	340 071	1.88	6.8	49.6	620	2 532	0	64 413	59 717
District 15	17.5	15.9	12.1	8.1	5.7	5.0	52.2	247 307	2.49	25.6	36.3	13 642	3 176	0	142 337	52 438
District 16	15.6	14.6	10.2	6.7	4.0	2.8	53.5	211 326	3.01	38.2	24.2	955	2 669	0	194 810	31 948
District 17	14.7	15.4	12.7	9.0	6.5	6.2	53.3	235 573	2.71	19.3	27.7	9	6 659	0	126 423	64 076
District 18	13.1	16.3	14.2	9.6	7.5	6.8	51.9	235 481	2.70	10.9	24.6	3 735	5 336	0	122 625	51 069
District 19	12.2	18.5	14.8	9.0	5.9	5.0	50.1	223 760	2.79	8.9	21.0	8 686	3 946	3 695	140 351	43 790
District 20	12.2	16.9	15.0	10.0	7.3	6.4	50.1	250 202	2.50	9.4	25.1	11 583	4 962	0	139 575	25 873

1. No spouse present.   2. All persons 3 years old and over enrolled in nursery school through college.   Note: Data were tabulated for the 108th Congress and some boundary changes have occurred.

Table E. Congressional Districts 109th Congress — Education, Money Income, Poverty, and Housing

STATE District	High school graduate or more	Bachelor's degree or more	Per capita income[2]	Median income	Percent with income of $100,000 or more	Persons Total	Families Total	Housing units Total	Occupied units Total	Owner-occupied Percent	Median value[3] (dollars)	Owner cost with a mortgage	Owner cost without a mortgage[4]
	31	32	33	34	35	36	37	38	39	40	41	42	43
MISSOURI	81.3	21.6	19 936	37 934	8.8	11.7	8.6	2 442 017	2 194 594	70.3	89 900	19.5	9.9
District 1	80.0	22.4	19 888	36 314	8.4	15.8	12.4	277 297	249 256	62.1	73 200	19.9	9.9
District 2	90.8	38.3	29 668	61 416	22.6	3.6	2.5	239 987	230 452	81.6	147 900	19.2	9.9
District 3	80.4	23.2	21 338	41 091	9.2	10.1	7.4	273 573	251 895	68.9	97 500	19.2	9.9
District 4	79.6	15.6	17 127	34 541	5.4	12.1	8.9	289 412	238 497	73.5	80 200	19.6	9.9
District 5	82.8	22.9	20 465	38 311	8.3	12.4	9.4	276 362	254 560	62.3	83 100	19.8	10.6
District 6	85.7	21.2	20 307	41 225	8.9	8.7	6.2	263 791	241 504	72.0	92 100	19.3	9.9
District 7	81.7	18.8	17 508	32 929	5.7	13.0	9.0	272 623	246 008	68.9	83 200	20.0	9.9
District 8	70.4	11.9	14 862	27 865	3.8	18.2	13.7	279 981	245 519	72.0	64 100	19.1	9.9
District 9	80.5	19.9	18 262	36 693	7.2	11.8	7.7	268 991	236 903	72.6	87 800	19.2	9.9
MONTANA	87.2	24.4	17 151	33 024	5.6	14.6	10.5	412 633	358 667	69.1	99 500	22.2	10.4
At Large	87.2	24.4	17 151	33 024	5.6	14.6	10.5	412 633	358 667	69.1	99 500	22.2	10.4
NEBRASKA	86.6	23.7	19 613	39 250	8.1	9.7	6.7	722 668	666 184	67.4	88 000	19.7	10.5
District 1	86.8	23.9	19 268	40 021	7.5	9.2	5.9	236 749	220 835	67.4	92 100	19.9	10.0
District 2	88.4	30.5	22 610	45 235	11.9	8.8	6.0	231 702	219 999	63.8	103 300	19.8	10.4
District 3	84.7	17.1	16 962	33 866	5.0	11.1	8.1	254 217	225 350	71.0	66 700	19.2	11.0
NEVADA	80.7	18.2	21 989	44 581	11.3	10.5	7.5	827 457	751 165	60.9	142 000	23.8	9.9
District 1	74.3	14.6	19 240	39 480	8.8	13.9	10.3	266 632	244 538	51.8	126 000	24.0	9.9
District 2	82.8	19.3	21 988	43 879	10.5	10.1	7.1	284 474	253 503	63.6	147 300	23.5	9.9
District 3	84.6	20.4	24 743	50 749	14.5	7.5	5.4	276 351	253 124	66.9	150 500	23.8	9.9
NEW HAMPSHIRE	87.4	28.7	23 844	49 467	13.8	6.5	4.3	547 024	474 606	69.7	133 300	22.3	13.6
District 1	87.5	28.5	23 943	50 135	13.7	6.7	4.4	276 597	238 422	68.6	139 000	22.6	13.8
District 2	87.3	28.9	23 744	48 762	13.9	6.4	4.2	270 427	236 184	70.9	127 000	22.0	13.5
NEW JERSEY	82.1	29.8	27 006	55 146	21.3	8.5	6.3	3 310 275	3 064 645	65.6	170 800	23.7	15.3
District 1	80.2	20.7	21 419	47 473	12.8	9.9	7.6	253 865	236 875	70.0	108 600	23.4	15.6
District 2	77.6	17.9	20 964	44 173	11.3	10.3	7.6	313 388	238 517	71.1	116 000	23.9	14.9
District 3	86.3	27.2	26 248	55 282	18.8	5.1	3.5	287 981	243 939	82.4	137 300	23.7	15.3
District 4	83.8	25.4	25 475	54 073	18.8	6.6	4.5	259 359	241 042	77.7	145 800	23.8	16.1
District 5	90.1	38.6	34 617	72 781	32.5	3.6	2.3	239 808	229 150	81.6	238 400	24.3	14.8
District 6	83.4	29.7	25 410	55 681	20.0	9.1	6.2	249 016	234 071	61.3	164 000	23.9	15.0
District 7	89.1	41.5	35 692	74 823	34.2	3.4	2.2	239 070	233 383	78.7	224 300	22.9	14.7
District 8	76.8	28.0	25 253	51 954	20.9	10.7	8.1	232 828	225 542	56.7	200 700	24.4	16.8
District 9	80.6	29.5	26 887	52 437	18.9	7.6	5.6	259 435	251 055	52.8	198 100	25.2	16.9
District 10	72.7	18.3	18 804	38 177	11.0	17.5	14.9	244 902	228 419	38.6	144 000	25.6	17.3
District 11	90.9	45.2	38 244	79 009	36.9	3.5	2.2	240 141	233 258	77.9	256 900	22.9	13.8
District 12	88.8	42.3	33 047	69 668	31.0	5.2	3.4	242 791	233 010	75.1	206 000	22.7	14.5
District 13	64.6	20.5	19 019	37 129	11.2	18.0	15.6	247 691	236 384	28.9	140 100	26.2	17.1
NEW MEXICO	78.9	23.5	17 261	34 133	7.6	18.4	14.5	780 579	677 971	70.0	108 100	22.2	9.9
District 1	83.9	29.5	20 348	38 413	10.0	14.0	10.4	258 465	238 379	65.4	127 100	23.0	9.9
District 2	73.1	16.9	14 239	29 269	4.5	22.4	17.9	261 112	218 546	72.0	76 900	20.6	9.9
District 3	79.3	23.7	17 193	35 058	8.2	19.0	15.2	261 002	221 046	72.9	114 100	22.3	9.9
NEW YORK	79.1	27.4	23 389	43 393	15.3	14.6	11.5	7 679 307	7 056 860	53.0	148 700	23.2	13.6
District 1	87.2	27.2	26 080	61 884	23.3	6.0	4.0	267 495	223 885	79.4	176 700	25.0	15.9
District 2	85.6	30.6	28 129	71 147	30.1	5.9	3.9	214 733	206 854	81.7	204 200	25.3	15.8
District 3	88.5	31.3	30 955	70 561	29.9	4.3	2.8	231 217	225 221	81.7	224 500	24.8	16.1
District 4	83.3	31.0	27 633	66 799	28.1	6.4	4.4	217 342	212 562	77.3	224 700	25.6	16.5
District 5	77.9	33.6	26 526	51 156	21.3	12.1	9.4	236 264	228 362	53.3	341 000	25.3	13.6
District 6	73.0	18.0	17 048	43 546	12.1	14.5	12.1	216 188	204 235	52.7	180 000	28.5	12.9
District 7	71.6	19.8	17 305	36 990	8.4	17.7	14.9	250 324	238 573	32.3	204 900	28.3	13.9
District 8	81.8	47.8	39 901	47 061	23.8	18.7	15.5	322 592	303 343	26.1	260 000	29.1	13.4
District 9	80.7	31.0	22 680	45 426	14.4	12.2	9.9	268 397	255 970	46.2	246 000	25.6	12.2
District 10	67.6	17.5	14 771	30 212	8.1	29.0	25.8	244 308	226 363	28.6	193 900	28.4	12.7
District 11	72.2	25.0	18 119	34 082	10.2	23.2	21.1	249 902	238 213	21.6	214 800	26.0	12.2
District 12	56.4	17.1	14 812	29 195	6.9	28.3	25.5	237 811	224 653	18.8	189 700	29.4	13.6
District 13	79.4	24.0	23 208	50 092	17.0	11.9	9.6	251 733	240 389	54.0	217 800	23.6	12.0
District 14	86.6	56.9	53 752	57 152	27.9	12.4	9.4	367 087	340 543	25.8	252 500	29.2	14.0
District 15	63.1	25.0	18 094	27 934	9.3	30.5	27.6	265 132	247 218	10.0	314 700	30.1	10.9
District 16	50.5	7.8	9 803	19 311	2.8	42.2	39.9	225 444	211 904	7.1	155 600	30.8	15.0
District 17	77.7	28.5	22 364	44 868	16.8	16.0	13.4	245 682	235 347	41.2	230 600	25.4	14.6
District 18	84.3	43.8	39 446	68 887	34.0	7.8	5.5	242 577	235 623	63.7	346 500	23.9	15.2
District 19	86.4	32.3	28 488	64 337	26.2	6.4	4.2	236 151	223 647	75.2	188 800	23.6	13.6
District 20	84.4	24.7	21 891	44 239	11.2	7.9	5.5	303 978	250 312	73.8	110 600	22.1	12.5

1. Persons 25 years old and over. 2. Based on the population enumerated as of April 1, 2000. 3. Specified owner-occupied units. 4. Median monthly owner costs is often in the minimum category—9.9 percent or less, which is indicated as 9.9 percent. Note: Data were tabulated for the 108th Congress and some boundary changes have occurred.

Table E. Congressional Districts 109th Congress — Housing, Labor Force, and Employment

STATE District	Median rent[1] (dollars)	Rent as a percent of income	Substandard units[2] (percent)	Civilian labor force, 2000 Total	Unemployment Total	Rate[3]	Civilian employment[4], 2000 Total	Percent Management, professional, and related occupations	Percent Production, transportation, and material moving occupations	Employment disabled persons[5] (percent)
	44	45	46	47	48	49	50	51	52	53
MISSOURI	484	24.0	2.9	2 806 718	148 794	5.3	2 657 924	31.5	16.3	10.8
District 1	522	25.8	3.8	301 078	25 018	8.3	276 060	32.7	13.9	12.5
District 2	662	22.7	1.4	332 595	10 385	3.1	322 210	42.2	9.6	6.4
District 3	492	23.4	3.0	327 327	18 419	5.6	308 908	32.6	14.6	10.5
District 4	425	22.5	2.9	292 747	13 481	4.6	279 266	26.9	19.7	11.5
District 5	532	24.5	3.8	315 116	18 479	5.9	296 637	32.7	13.6	12.6
District 6	502	22.3	2.1	322 893	12 240	3.8	310 653	31.7	15.7	9.8
District 7	450	24.6	3.0	317 094	17 855	5.6	299 239	27.6	18.8	10.7
District 8	366	24.7	3.3	280 264	18 269	6.5	261 995	24.7	23.1	13.2
District 9	448	24.1	2.7	317 604	14 648	4.6	302 956	30.1	18.8	9.8
MONTANA	447	25.3	3.8	454 687	28 710	6.3	425 977	33.1	11.2	9.3
At Large	447	25.3	3.8	454 687	28 710	6.3	425 977	33.1	11.2	9.3
NEBRASKA	491	23.0	3.0	909 524	32 287	3.5	877 237	33.0	15.1	9.4
District 1	486	23.3	2.9	312 761	11 167	3.6	301 594	32.1	16.6	8.9
District 2	551	23.5	3.4	303 619	11 474	3.8	292 145	36.5	11.6	9.5
District 3	416	22.0	2.8	293 144	9 646	3.3	283 498	30.2	17.3	9.8
NEVADA	699	26.5	8.9	995 200	61 920	6.2	933 280	25.7	10.4	14.5
District 1	655	27.6	13.1	319 873	25 015	7.8	294 858	21.3	10.3	17.7
District 2	650	25.4	7.9	331 001	18 435	5.6	312 566	27.8	12.3	12.8
District 3	806	26.2	5.9	344 326	18 470	5.4	325 856	27.6	8.6	12.8
NEW HAMPSHIRE	646	24.2	2.1	676 371	25 500	3.8	650 871	35.8	14.8	10.1
District 1	658	24.2	2.1	340 399	11 524	3.4	328 875	35.2	14.3	10.2
District 2	630	24.2	2.0	335 972	13 976	4.2	321 996	36.4	15.3	9.9
NEW JERSEY	751	25.5	5.4	4 193 145	243 116	5.8	3 950 029	38.0	12.0	11.6
District 1	640	26.2	4.2	324 364	20 137	6.2	304 227	32.8	13.6	11.5
District 2	649	27.3	4.4	313 837	24 255	7.7	289 582	27.9	12.9	13.3
District 3	790	26.7	1.8	312 554	13 753	4.4	298 801	38.1	9.9	10.1
District 4	781	27.0	3.3	308 687	13 845	4.5	294 842	36.4	11.1	10.5
District 5	855	25.8	1.9	331 568	11 018	3.3	320 550	44.0	8.4	7.6
District 6	785	25.2	6.2	339 656	19 637	5.8	320 019	37.4	12.5	11.0
District 7	906	23.5	3.0	338 393	10 908	3.2	327 485	47.5	8.9	7.8
District 8	759	25.8	8.1	312 967	20 487	6.5	292 480	35.5	15.5	14.8
District 9	825	24.8	7.2	334 581	17 983	5.4	316 598	36.0	12.7	13.1
District 10	664	26.4	11.1	296 420	32 443	10.9	263 977	27.7	16.8	16.3
District 11	891	23.8	2.6	343 993	11 666	3.4	332 327	48.6	7.6	8.1
District 12	825	23.9	3.2	332 225	18 141	5.5	314 084	48.8	7.7	8.0
District 13	685	25.4	13.9	303 900	28 843	9.5	275 057	28.2	20.4	18.1
NEW MEXICO	503	26.6	8.7	823 440	60 324	7.3	763 116	34.0	10.7	12.3
District 1	557	27.7	6.1	300 737	17 578	5.8	283 159	37.3	9.6	12.1
District 2	417	26.0	9.0	248 877	21 767	8.7	227 110	28.9	13.1	12.9
District 3	521	25.4	11.1	273 826	20 979	7.7	252 847	34.9	9.9	12.0
NEW YORK	672	26.8	8.4	9 023 096	640 108	7.1	8 382 988	36.7	11.7	13.2
District 1	925	28.9	3.0	329 050	13 638	4.1	315 412	36.0	9.3	9.9
District 2	991	27.8	4.2	325 702	12 272	3.8	313 430	37.3	11.4	11.4
District 3	989	26.6	2.3	328 676	11 058	3.4	317 618	38.6	8.4	10.4
District 4	905	27.3	6.1	317 441	12 831	4.0	304 610	37.6	9.2	12.3
District 5	838	27.3	16.9	309 459	18 428	6.0	291 031	36.9	11.6	15.3
District 6	730	26.7	15.5	296 869	28 139	9.5	268 730	27.2	12.6	18.1
District 7	705	25.9	18.1	286 792	25 160	8.8	261 632	27.9	13.1	17.6
District 8	817	25.6	11.5	341 751	22 980	6.7	318 771	55.0	6.5	12.6
District 9	770	25.7	11.3	299 639	17 728	5.9	281 911	39.0	10.3	15.5
District 10	606	27.9	15.1	260 646	35 297	13.5	225 349	31.0	10.9	18.4
District 11	689	27.2	17.5	302 527	35 141	11.6	267 386	35.1	9.2	18.5
District 12	645	27.7	21.2	281 025	30 782	11.0	250 243	25.9	19.3	18.1
District 13	745	25.6	7.4	301 859	18 446	6.1	283 413	34.9	10.0	14.2
District 14	993	24.4	8.3	390 942	20 278	5.2	370 664	57.7	4.9	11.2
District 15	586	26.2	18.7	273 272	39 498	14.5	233 774	38.1	10.8	16.5
District 16	564	30.0	28.7	215 754	43 819	20.3	171 935	18.2	15.7	19.6
District 17	737	26.8	12.2	302 608	22 939	7.6	279 669	37.8	8.7	15.5
District 18	881	26.1	6.3	321 066	12 441	3.9	308 625	47.5	6.3	11.2
District 19	796	25.8	2.8	323 292	13 673	4.2	309 619	40.6	8.5	9.8
District 20	582	24.9	1.8	328 986	15 412	4.7	313 574	35.7	12.8	10.2

1. Specified renter-occupied units.   2. Overcrowded or lacking complete plumbing facilities.   3. Percent of total civilian labor force.   4. Persons 16 years old and over.   5. Persons 16 to 64 years old.   Note: Data were tabulated for the 108th Congress and some boundary changes have occurred.

STATE District	Representative	Land area,[1] 2000 (sq km)	Population and population characteristics, 2000											
			Total persons	Per square kilometer	Percent									
					Race alone or in combination							Age		
					White	Black	Am. Indian, Alaska Native	Asian and Pacific Islander	Other race	Hispanic or Latino[2]	Non-Hispanic White	Two or more races	Under 5 years	5 to 17 years	18 to 24 years
		1	2	3	4	5	6	7	8	9	10	11	12	13	14
NEW YORK—Cont'd															
District 21	Michael McNulty (D)	5 012	654 361	130.6	88.4	8.6	0.6	2.5	1.7	3.2	85.5	1.7	5.9	17.5	10.2
District 22	Maurice Hinchey (D)	8 407	654 361	77.8	85.5	9.2	0.8	3.1	3.9	7.8	79.9	2.3	6.0	17.8	12.0
District 23	John M. McHugh (R)	34 278	654 361	19.1	94.7	3.0	1.4	0.8	1.2	2.1	92.9	1.0	5.9	19.2	11.1
District 24	Sherwood Boehlert (R)	15 964	654 361	41.0	94.5	3.9	0.6	1.2	1.2	2.3	92.2	1.3	5.7	18.7	9.5
District 25	James T. Walsh (R)	4 195	654 361	156.0	89.2	8.1	1.2	2.1	1.2	2.3	86.6	1.7	6.4	19.5	8.5
District 26	Thomas M. Reynold (R)	7 073	654 361	92.5	94.2	3.5	0.6	1.8	0.9	1.9	92.3	1.0	5.8	18.8	9.2
District 27	Brian Higgins (D)	4 740	654 361	138.0	92.0	4.7	1.2	0.9	2.6	4.6	88.8	1.4	6.0	18.0	8.6
District 28	Louise M. Slaughter (D)	1 383	654 360	473.0	65.5	30.4	1.1	1.9	3.5	5.5	62.0	2.2	6.7	19.3	9.8
District 29	Randy Kuhl (R)	14 660	654 361	44.6	94.3	3.1	0.9	2.1	0.7	1.4	92.5	1.1	6.0	19.1	9.4
NORTH CAROLINA		126 161	8 049 313	63.8	73.1	22.1	1.6	1.8	2.8	4.7	70.2	1.3	6.7	17.7	10.0
District 1	G.K. Butterfield (D)	18 645	619 178	33.2	46.1	51.2	1.1	0.7	2.0	3.1	44.4	1.0	6.7	19.3	9.6
District 2	Bob Etheridge (D)	10 246	619 178	60.4	63.0	31.1	1.1	1.5	5.1	7.9	59.1	1.7	7.4	18.1	12.8
District 3	Walter B. Jones (R)	16 037	619 178	38.6	79.1	17.3	0.9	1.5	2.8	4.4	76.3	1.5	6.6	17.2	13.3
District 4	David Price (D)	3 246	619 178	190.8	72.2	21.3	0.8	4.5	3.0	5.0	68.8	1.6	6.9	17.7	11.4
District 5	Virginia Ann Foxx (R)	11 401	619 178	54.3	90.3	7.1	0.5	1.0	2.1	3.6	87.9	0.9	6.3	16.9	8.7
District 6	Howard Coble (R)	7 624	619 178	81.2	88.0	9.0	0.7	1.2	2.1	3.9	85.3	0.9	6.3	17.5	7.9
District 7	Mike McIntyre (D)	15 766	619 178	39.3	65.3	23.6	9.1	0.8	2.4	3.9	63.0	1.1	6.6	17.9	9.6
District 8	Robin Hayes (R)	8 502	619 178	72.8	66.0	27.6	2.3	2.3	3.7	6.6	61.8	1.8	7.4	18.7	10.6
District 9	Sue Wilkins Myrick (R)	2 566	619 178	241.3	85.7	10.8	0.6	2.4	1.7	3.5	82.9	1.1	7.2	18.1	7.1
District 10	Patrick T. McHenry (R)	8 552	619 178	72.4	87.3	9.5	0.5	1.8	1.8	3.5	84.9	0.9	6.4	17.8	8.3
District 11	Charles H. Taylor (R)	15 605	619 177	39.7	92.1	4.9	2.1	0.7	1.3	2.6	89.8	1.0	5.5	15.8	8.1
District 12	Melvin L. Watt (D)	2 127	619 178	291.0	48.3	45.8	0.8	2.5	4.4	7.1	44.6	1.6	7.1	18.5	11.6
District 13	Brad Miller (D)	5 842	619 178	106.0	67.1	27.7	0.8	2.5	3.7	6.0	63.3	1.6	6.6	16.5	11.2
NORTH DAKOTA		178 647	642 200	3.6	93.4	0.8	5.5	0.9	0.6	1.2	91.7	1.2	6.1	18.9	11.4
At Large	Earl Pomeroy (D)	178 647	642 200	3.6	93.4	0.8	5.5	0.8	0.6	1.2	91.7	1.2	6.1	18.9	11.4
OHIO		106 056	11 353 140	107.0	86.1	12.1	0.7	1.5	1.1	1.9	84.0	1.4	6.6	18.8	9.3
District 1	Steve Chabot (R)	1 078	630 730	585.0	70.2	28.3	0.6	1.6	0.8	1.1	68.6	1.4	6.8	19.5	10.5
District 2	Rob Portman (R)	6 764	630 730	93.3	93.3	5.1	0.7	1.6	0.5	1.0	91.7	1.0	6.9	19.3	7.8
District 3	Michael Turner (R)	4 132	630 730	152.6	81.1	17.6	0.7	1.4	0.7	1.1	79.5	1.3	6.7	18.3	9.2
District 4	Michael G. Oxley (R)	11 966	630 730	52.7	93.4	5.7	0.6	0.8	0.7	1.2	91.7	1.1	6.6	19.3	9.0
District 5	Paul E. Gillmor (R)	15 872	630 730	39.7	96.5	1.4	0.5	0.6	2.1	3.8	93.7	1.1	6.6	19.8	10.1
District 6	Ted Strickland (D)	13 461	630 730	46.9	96.6	2.8	0.6	0.6	0.3	0.8	95.2	0.9	5.5	17.4	10.2
District 7	Dave Hobson (R)	7 377	630 730	85.5	90.6	8.2	0.9	1.3	0.7	1.1	88.7	1.5	6.6	18.8	9.9
District 8	John Boehner (R)	5 216	630 730	120.9	93.5	4.9	0.6	1.5	0.7	1.3	91.8	1.2	7.0	19.3	10.3
District 9	Marcy Kaptur (D)	2 853	630 730	221.1	83.2	14.6	0.8	1.3	2.2	4.0	79.6	2.0	6.5	19.1	9.5
District 10	Dennis J. Kucinich (D)	506	630 730	1 245.9	91.1	4.9	0.6	2.1	3.2	5.0	87.2	1.9	6.3	17.1	7.7
District 11	Stephanie Tubbs Jones (D)	348	630 730	1 810.2	40.8	56.9	0.7	2.0	1.5	2.3	38.8	1.6	6.9	19.3	8.7
District 12	Pat Tiberi (R)	2 632	630 730	239.7	74.3	23.2	0.8	2.6	1.4	1.7	72.1	2.0	7.5	19.7	9.2
District 13	Sherrod Brown (D)	1 374	630 730	459.0	84.7	13.1	0.7	1.4	1.9	3.5	81.5	1.7	6.8	19.0	7.7
District 14	Steven C. LaTourette (R)	4 654	630 730	135.5	95.7	2.8	0.4	1.4	0.7	1.3	94.0	0.9	6.4	19.6	6.9
District 15	Deborah Pryce (R)	3 052	630 730	206.7	87.8	8.1	0.8	3.8	1.6	2.3	85.2	1.9	6.9	16.6	13.0
District 16	Ralph Regula (R)	4 486	630 730	140.6	94.0	5.4	0.6	0.8	0.4	0.9	92.4	1.2	6.6	19.1	8.5
District 17	Timothy Ryan (D)	2 604	630 730	242.2	86.5	12.4	0.7	1.0	0.9	1.6	84.5	1.4	6.2	17.7	10.3
District 18	Bob Ney (R)	17 680	630 730	35.7	97.3	2.4	0.8	0.4	0.3	0.6	95.9	1.0	6.7	19.3	9.0
OKLAHOMA		177 847	3 450 654	19.4	80.3	8.3	11.4	1.8	3.0	5.2	74.1	4.5	6.8	19.0	10.3
District 1	John Sullivan (R)	4 498	690 131	153.4	80.3	10.2	9.4	1.9	3.0	5.3	73.8	4.6	7.2	19.2	9.6
District 2	Daniel David Boren (D)	53 258	690 130	13.0	77.2	4.6	23.0	0.5	1.3	2.4	70.2	6.5	6.6	19.4	9.0
District 3	Frank Lucas (R)	88 289	690 131	7.8	86.2	4.3	8.8	1.2	3.1	5.2	81.0	3.5	6.4	19.1	10.9
District 4	Tom Cole (R)	26 449	690 131	26.1	83.4	7.5	8.4	2.4	2.5	4.8	77.6	4.1	6.8	19.0	11.4
District 5	Ernest J. Istook (R)	5 353	690 131	128.9	74.3	14.7	7.1	3.2	4.9	8.3	67.7	4.0	7.3	18.3	10.9
OREGON		248 631	3 421 399	13.8	89.3	2.1	2.5	4.2	5.2	8.0	83.5	3.1	6.5	18.2	9.6
District 1	David Wu (D)	7 618	684 280	89.8	87.6	1.6	1.7	6.6	5.7	9.4	81.1	3.0	7.1	18.2	9.6
District 2	Gregory Walden (R)	179 980	684 280	3.8	91.5	0.7	3.3	1.5	5.7	8.8	86.1	2.5	6.4	19.2	8.3
District 3	Earl Blumenauer (D)	2 644	684 279	258.8	83.2	6.3	2.2	7.2	5.4	7.6	77.2	4.0	6.8	17.2	9.8
District 4	Pete DeFazio (D)	44 498	684 280	15.4	94.6	0.9	2.9	2.5	2.3	4.2	89.7	3.0	5.7	17.6	10.0
District 5	Darlene Hooley (D)	13 889	684 280	49.3	89.8	1.1	2.3	3.1	6.8	10.3	83.6	2.9	6.6	19.0	10.2
PENNSYLVANIA		116 074	12 281 054	105.8	86.3	10.5	0.4	2.1	1.9	3.2	84.1	1.2	5.9	17.9	8.9
District 1	Robert A. Brady (D)	152	646 331	4 243.4	38.9	47.1	0.8	5.5	10.6	15.0	33.1	2.7	7.2	21.2	10.8
District 2	Chaka Fattah (D)	152	646 361	4 242.6	31.8	62.6	0.8	5.0	2.1	3.0	29.8	2.0	6.1	18.1	12.4
District 3	Phil English (R)	10 241	646 364	63.1	95.3	3.9	0.4	0.7	0.7	1.3	93.7	0.9	5.9	18.3	9.9
District 4	Melissa Hart (R)	3 428	646 476	188.6	95.4	3.7	0.3	1.1	0.3	0.6	94.3	0.7	5.8	18.0	6.5
District 5	John E. Peterson (R)	28 470	646 371	22.7	97.1	1.5	0.4	1.3	0.4	0.8	96.1	0.6	5.4	16.9	12.5
District 6	Jim Gerlach (R)	2 174	646 483	297.4	89.2	7.4	0.4	2.3	2.0	3.5	86.6	1.3	6.4	18.2	8.1

1. Dry land or land partially or temporarily covered by water.   2. Hispanic or Latino persons may be of any race.   Note: Data were tabulated for the 108th Congress and some boundary changes have occurred.

Table E. Congressional Districts 109th Congress — Population, Households, Group Quarters, and Education

STATE District	Population and population characteristics, 2000 (cont'd) — Percent (cont'd) — Age (cont'd)							Households, 2000				Persons in correctional institutions, 2000	Persons in nursing homes, 2000	Persons in military quarters, 2000	Education, 2000 — School enrollment[2]	
	25 to 34 years	35 to 44 years	45 to 54 years	55 to 64 years	65 to 74 years	75 years and over	Percent female	Number	Persons per house-hold	Female family house-holder[1]	One person				Public	Private
	15	16	17	18	19	20	21	22	23	24	25	26	27	28	29	30
NEW YORK—Cont'd																
District 21	12.9	15.5	14.0	8.6	7.4	8.1	51.9	265 363	2.35	12.3	31.6	2 318	7 427	0	139 587	37 827
District 22	12.5	15.7	13.5	6.9	6.7	6.7	51.0	248 889	2.47	11.9	29.3	5 924	4 959	1	151 455	40 743
District 23	13.0	16.3	13.3	8.8	6.7	5.7	49.2	240 469	2.54	10.1	25.2	15 753	4 102	4 616	157 625	21 504
District 24	12.0	15.7	13.9	9.3	7.4	7.7	50.7	251 338	2.46	10.9	27.7	11 480	5 614	13	153 660	23 141
District 25	12.5	16.5	14.1	8.7	7.1	6.8	51.8	255 854	2.49	11.9	27.5	1 418	4 167	0	144 471	39 465
District 26	12.0	16.8	14.4	8.9	7.0	7.0	51.0	243 470	2.56	9.5	25.1	11 383	6 652	0	150 070	32 038
District 27	12.8	15.9	13.7	9.3	8.0	7.8	51.6	261 667	2.42	12.3	29.8	6 647	4 623	0	138 615	29 571
District 28	13.7	15.3	12.7	8.1	6.9	7.3	52.7	268 208	2.37	18.8	33.9	939	6 330	0	148 304	37 558
District 29	11.5	15.8	14.5	9.6	7.3	6.8	50.8	248 381	2.52	9.8	25.4	3 917	5 199	0	141 264	39 306
NORTH CAROLINA	15.1	16.0	13.5	9.0	6.6	5.4	51.0	3 132 013	2.49	12.5	25.4	46 614	50 892	37 022	1 762 124	281 101
District 1	12.8	15.1	13.3	9.2	7.6	6.5	52.4	236 609	2.52	19.4	26.9	6 678	5 476	4 016	146 886	15 287
District 2	16.5	15.5	12.1	7.8	5.5	4.3	49.7	223 225	2.60	14.1	23.9	6 490	3 414	13 857	145 416	20 412
District 3	13.8	15.3	13.0	9.2	6.9	4.7	49.4	234 242	2.50	10.7	23.2	3 660	2 148	18 531	139 481	17 580
District 4	17.2	17.8	13.8	7.1	4.3	3.8	51.3	240 138	2.49	10.2	25.7	958	3 566	0	147 471	37 238
District 5	13.9	16.1	14.5	10.3	7.4	6.0	51.1	249 380	2.43	9.3	25.0	731	4 931	0	127 634	18 514
District 6	14.0	16.4	14.3	9.9	7.5	6.2	51.0	246 125	2.48	9.4	23.5	1 576	3 267	0	121 984	23 176
District 7	13.9	15.3	13.9	10.1	7.4	5.3	51.2	243 125	2.49	14.0	25.3	5 092	2 654	244	141 922	14 249
District 8	16.7	15.9	12.3	7.9	5.8	4.8	50.9	233 428	2.58	14.2	24.9	5 094	4 180	374	146 372	18 557
District 9	16.7	18.1	14.4	8.4	5.5	4.4	51.2	243 745	2.51	9.1	24.2	556	2 751	0	118 781	34 525
District 10	14.4	15.9	14.1	10.1	7.3	5.8	50.7	241 093	2.51	11.0	23.6	3 898	4 254	0	127 199	15 148
District 11	12.5	14.6	14.4	11.3	9.4	8.4	51.7	257 353	2.33	9.8	27.1	2 927	5 871	0	119 793	16 426
District 12	16.2	15.7	12.3	7.8	5.8	5.1	51.6	235 544	2.52	18.9	27.8	4 210	4 922	0	142 495	26 505
District 13	17.4	16.4	13.0	8.0	5.9	4.9	50.9	248 006	2.42	12.6	28.9	4 744	3 458	0	136 690	23 484
NORTH DAKOTA	12.0	15.3	13.3	8.3	7.1	7.6	50.1	257 152	2.41	7.8	29.3	1 518	7 254	1 244	163 677	15 990
At Large	12.0	15.3	13.3	8.3	7.1	7.6	50.1	257 152	2.41	7.8	29.3	1 518	7 254	1 244	163 677	15 990
OHIO	13.4	15.9	13.8	8.9	7.0	6.3	51.4	4 445 773	2.49	12.1	27.3	68 873	93 157	369	2 475 221	539 239
District 1	13.7	15.6	12.7	8.1	6.8	6.2	52.2	254 959	2.42	16.0	32.3	1 251	5 363	0	134 625	44 791
District 2	14.1	16.8	14.1	8.7	6.4	5.8	51.5	247 211	2.51	9.9	26.6	3 152	5 563	0	127 648	32 863
District 3	13.4	15.8	13.8	9.2	7.2	6.4	51.6	252 366	2.42	12.6	28.8	5 432	5 814	0	133 689	34 735
District 4	12.8	15.7	13.8	9.2	7.1	6.5	50.2	238 947	2.54	10.2	25.0	12 856	5 856	0	135 706	24 623
District 5	12.2	15.6	13.8	8.9	6.8	6.3	51.0	237 931	2.58	9.1	23.8	1 141	5 073	0	151 298	22 806
District 6	11.9	15.1	14.4	9.9	8.1	7.4	51.3	246 785	2.46	10.2	26.1	6 504	5 373	0	144 325	18 334
District 7	13.4	16.0	14.0	9.3	6.6	5.4	50.3	236 211	2.56	11.1	23.5	12 404	4 694	341	141 780	27 411
District 8	13.3	16.0	13.6	8.7	6.5	5.3	51.1	238 796	2.58	10.7	23.5	878	4 323	0	147 930	22 872
District 9	13.1	15.4	13.9	8.8	7.0	6.6	51.2	251 012	2.46	13.4	28.7	679	5 772	17	139 391	34 537
District 10	14.4	16.2	13.3	8.8	7.8	8.3	52.0	262 996	2.36	11.5	32.8	58	5 422	0	109 689	41 193
District 11	13.5	14.9	12.7	8.4	7.7	7.8	53.8	258 872	2.36	21.7	35.0	3 075	6 048	5	139 432	38 478
District 12	14.9	16.9	14.0	8.1	5.4	4.4	51.9	248 553	2.49	13.7	27.2	276	4 265	0	140 539	37 377
District 13	12.9	16.5	14.6	9.0	7.1	6.5	51.6	244 603	2.53	12.9	26.1	5 007	4 800	1	133 517	29 021
District 14	11.8	16.9	15.3	9.8	7.2	6.2	51.2	238 693	2.61	9.1	23.0	481	4 607	5	130 858	32 040
District 15	17.9	16.2	12.4	7.1	5.3	4.7	50.5	256 769	2.37	10.2	30.8	6 635	3 183	0	154 172	27 265
District 16	12.2	15.9	14.4	9.3	7.2	6.8	51.5	240 988	2.55	10.3	24.6	844	6 369	0	131 704	29 616
District 17	12.9	15.2	13.9	9.0	7.8	7.0	51.6	249 485	2.45	13.5	28.0	4 629	4 526	0	145 470	20 851
District 18	12.5	15.5	13.6	9.6	7.4	6.3	51.0	240 596	2.56	10.2	24.5	3 571	6 106	0	133 448	20 426
OKLAHOMA	13.1	15.2	13.1	9.2	7.0	6.2	50.9	1 342 293	2.49	11.4	26.7	33 919	28 021	7 616	832 166	98 699
District 1	14.1	15.7	13.6	8.6	6.4	5.6	51.4	275 234	2.46	11.6	28.2	1 303	4 163	0	151 619	34 791
District 2	11.9	14.3	13.1	10.5	8.2	7.0	50.8	264 439	2.52	11.3	25.2	9 036	6 779	4	165 416	8 481
District 3	11.9	15.1	13.0	9.4	7.3	6.9	50.2	263 375	2.51	9.6	25.6	11 514	6 585	510	178 021	12 304
District 4	13.3	15.5	13.0	8.9	6.6	5.5	50.3	262 122	2.53	10.9	24.4	5 969	5 677	7 102	180 322	14 682
District 5	14.4	15.2	13.0	8.5	6.6	5.9	51.5	277 123	2.42	13.3	29.9	6 097	4 817	0	156 788	28 441
OREGON	13.8	15.4	14.8	8.9	6.4	6.4	50.4	1 333 723	2.51	9.8	26.1	19 523	14 677	95	753 762	122 730
District 1	16.3	15.6	14.4	7.8	5.0	5.1	49.9	268 476	2.49	8.5	28.1	3 805	2 305	45	144 551	31 980
District 2	11.6	14.6	14.8	10.0	7.8	7.4	50.3	264 607	2.52	9.7	24.3	6 665	3 438	0	151 787	16 856
District 3	16.3	16.4	14.7	7.8	5.2	5.7	50.7	268 508	2.50	11.6	27.9	1 953	3 000	0	139 148	29 645
District 4	11.8	14.4	15.3	10.0	7.8	7.4	50.7	275 617	2.44	9.7	25.7	1 732	2 524	33	161 815	17 536
District 5	12.6	15.0	14.9	8.9	6.3	6.4	50.4	256 515	2.58	9.5	24.3	5 368	3 410	17	156 461	26 713
PENNSYLVANIA	12.7	15.9	13.9	9.2	7.9	7.7	51.7	4 777 003	2.48	11.6	27.7	76 553	114 113	758	2 398 189	737 745
District 1	14.7	14.7	11.7	7.7	6.2	5.7	53.3	238 686	2.63	26.0	31.0	1 222	2 710	531	146 049	47 216
District 2	14.9	14.2	12.2	8.3	6.9	6.9	54.5	259 939	2.37	23.3	37.1	369	5 347	0	132 177	70 354
District 3	12.1	15.2	13.9	9.3	7.7	7.7	51.2	247 416	2.49	10.4	26.7	4 627	7 321	0	133 730	34 322
District 4	11.1	16.7	14.9	9.7	8.8	8.4	52.1	254 007	2.49	9.5	25.6	534	6 089	0	127 709	28 449
District 5	12.3	14.8	13.2	9.6	8.1	7.3	50.5	250 179	2.45	8.5	26.4	8 054	5 483	0	158 781	17 695
District 6	13.3	17.0	14.3	8.9	7.1	6.8	51.3	244 904	2.54	9.2	25.3	4 165	5 758	0	119 837	49 414

1. No spouse present. 2. All persons 3 years old and over enrolled in nursery school through college. Note: Data were tabulated for the 108th Congress and some boundary changes have occurred.

STATE District	Education, 2000 (cont'd) Attainment[1] (percent) High school graduate or more	Bachelor's degree or more	Money income, 1999 Per capita income[2]	Median income	Percent with income of $100,000 or more	Percent below poverty level, 1999 Persons Total	Families Total	Housing units, 2000 Total	Occupied units Total	Owner-occupied Percent	Median value[3] (dollars)	Owner cost as a percent of income With a mortgage	Without a mortgage[4]
	31	32	33	34	35	36	37	38	39	40	41	42	43
NEW YORK—Cont'd													
District 21	84.1	27.0	21 493	40 254	10.4	11.2	7.8	292 439	265 380	60.8	100 500	21.4	12.3
District 22	81.4	23.9	19 490	38 586	9.6	14.3	9.3	290 893	248 893	61.2	98 500	21.9	12.8
District 23	79.6	16.0	16 862	35 434	5.7	13.5	9.5	306 304	240 431	71.0	71 900	20.1	12.3
District 24	80.9	19.3	17 979	36 082	6.5	12.6	8.8	286 350	251 360	69.8	75 300	20.9	12.8
District 25	85.8	27.8	21 692	43 188	11.5	10.4	7.2	277 474	255 813	69.1	89 000	21.2	13.1
District 26	85.7	25.5	21 731	46 653	11.6	6.9	4.7	257 303	243 482	75.0	97 600	21.7	13.0
District 27	81.3	19.9	18 916	36 884	7.3	12.0	8.8	289 475	261 614	66.2	84 500	21.7	13.7
District 28	79.2	21.2	17 872	31 751	6.4	18.7	15.3	301 358	268 193	55.4	76 900	21.6	13.5
District 29	85.6	26.1	21 255	41 875	11.2	9.9	6.8	283 354	248 477	74.0	87 700	20.8	12.0
NORTH CAROLINA	78.1	22.5	20 307	39 184	9.4	12.3	9.0	3 523 944	3 132 013	69.4	108 300	21.3	9.9
District 1	69.2	12.0	14 864	28 410	4.2	21.1	17.1	271 800	236 646	63.4	73 500	22.0	12.3
District 2	76.3	15.9	17 046	36 510	6.2	14.3	10.9	246 226	223 122	66.5	96 400	21.8	10.8
District 3	81.4	20.1	18 799	37 510	7.4	12.4	8.8	292 103	234 158	70.9	100 700	21.6	9.9
District 4	88.4	48.0	27 508	53 847	20.7	9.2	5.7	257 496	240 099	64.1	167 300	21.0	9.9
District 5	76.4	20.1	21 041	39 710	9.0	9.5	6.5	278 177	249 357	76.8	109 800	20.3	9.9
District 6	79.1	22.7	22 551	43 503	10.9	8.2	5.8	265 995	246 278	76.7	117 200	20.7	9.9
District 7	75.6	17.8	17 874	33 998	7.1	16.7	12.7	295 203	243 322	73.1	98 900	22.6	11.1
District 8	77.5	18.2	18 201	38 390	7.1	12.4	9.7	256 713	233 377	66.2	93 200	21.9	10.9
District 9	86.3	35.9	29 290	55 059	19.6	6.2	4.3	259 245	243 854	72.8	146 200	20.9	9.9
District 10	71.9	14.1	18 640	37 649	6.8	10.6	7.8	269 419	241 060	75.1	93 500	20.8	9.9
District 11	78.5	20.5	19 005	34 720	6.4	12.0	8.4	310 382	257 331	75.4	107 700	21.5	9.9
District 12	74.7	19.2	17 901	35 775	6.9	15.9	12.4	254 282	235 533	56.8	93 000	22.1	9.9
District 13	80.4	27.3	21 244	41 060	9.7	11.6	8.1	266 903	247 876	62.4	117 500	21.4	9.9
NORTH DAKOTA	83.9	22.0	17 769	34 604	5.7	11.9	8.3	289 677	257 152	66.6	74 400	19.4	10.2
At Large	83.9	22.0	17 769	34 604	5.7	11.9	8.3	289 677	257 152	66.6	74 400	19.4	10.2
OHIO	83.0	21.1	21 003	40 956	9.8	10.6	7.8	4 783 051	4 445 773	69.1	103 700	20.6	10.6
District 1	80.1	22.3	20 427	37 414	9.2	13.9	10.5	276 519	254 914	57.6	100 000	20.8	11.1
District 2	83.3	29.0	25 560	46 813	15.4	8.4	6.3	263 424	247 290	71.5	124 000	20.6	10.5
District 3	83.8	22.7	22 147	41 591	10.8	10.2	7.4	273 309	252 297	67.4	102 800	20.8	11.0
District 4	82.4	13.1	18 732	40 100	6.9	9.4	7.1	258 218	238 920	73.9	88 300	19.3	9.9
District 5	84.2	14.6	19 031	41 701	6.9	7.6	5.2	251 978	237 945	76.5	92 800	19.3	9.9
District 6	81.2	14.2	17 039	32 888	5.5	14.0	10.2	270 657	246 659	75.1	78 400	19.8	10.1
District 7	83.5	18.7	20 194	43 248	9.4	8.8	6.4	251 533	236 171	71.1	103 600	20.6	9.9
District 8	82.5	18.7	20 725	43 753	10.0	8.8	6.0	253 280	238 870	71.2	105 500	20.3	10.1
District 9	83.3	19.8	20 885	40 265	9.4	12.0	8.9	278 489	250 985	68.4	97 900	20.1	11.2
District 10	82.7	23.3	22 455	41 841	9.6	9.1	6.6	277 697	262 940	68.0	116 000	21.8	12.3
District 11	78.2	23.4	19 510	31 998	8.3	19.5	16.0	287 490	258 965	54.2	92 300	22.7	12.8
District 12	87.5	32.1	24 958	47 289	15.4	10.0	7.8	268 166	248 615	62.5	131 800	20.9	10.3
District 13	84.6	22.3	22 631	44 524	12.1	9.4	7.2	258 456	244 563	72.7	117 700	21.2	11.1
District 14	87.2	27.1	25 423	51 304	16.2	5.7	4.0	251 507	238 653	79.6	142 300	21.3	11.0
District 15	85.5	32.1	22 680	43 885	10.9	10.8	6.7	272 859	256 778	59.1	119 500	21.2	11.0
District 16	83.9	19.2	20 529	41 801	9.2	8.3	6.1	254 317	241 013	73.6	108 600	20.4	9.9
District 17	82.2	15.8	18 531	36 705	6.4	12.3	9.2	268 809	249 550	70.1	85 800	20.0	10.8
District 18	77.5	11.3	16 603	34 462	4.9	12.6	9.7	266 343	240 645	74.3	83 800	20.0	9.9
OKLAHOMA	80.6	20.3	17 646	33 400	6.6	14.7	11.2	1 514 400	1 342 293	68.4	70 700	19.2	9.9
District 1	84.7	25.6	20 780	38 610	9.6	11.3	8.5	296 941	275 329	64.8	85 800	19.0	9.9
District 2	73.8	13.2	14 491	27 885	3.9	18.5	14.6	314 110	264 390	74.3	56 400	19.3	10.2
District 3	80.5	18.1	16 350	32 098	5.4	15.0	10.9	301 501	263 332	72.5	60 800	18.8	9.9
District 4	82.5	20.2	17 507	35 510	6.5	13.1	9.7	294 070	262 143	69.7	73 200	19.2	9.9
District 5	81.5	24.5	19 100	33 893	7.7	15.8	12.2	307 778	277 099	61.3	73 600	19.8	9.9
OREGON	85.1	25.1	20 940	40 916	10.0	11.6	7.9	1 452 709	1 333 723	64.3	152 100	23.2	10.5
District 1	88.4	33.3	24 667	48 464	14.6	8.7	5.4	288 871	268 505	59.6	180 800	22.7	10.0
District 2	82.7	19.0	18 218	35 600	6.9	13.0	9.4	296 961	264 616	68.2	121 900	22.6	10.3
District 3	84.5	24.8	20 835	42 063	9.3	11.7	8.1	285 413	268 551	61.3	156 300	24.1	11.8
District 4	84.9	21.4	18 674	35 796	6.9	13.7	9.4	297 841	275 607	65.7	132 200	22.9	10.2
District 5	85.1	27.0	22 307	44 409	12.5	10.9	7.2	283 623	256 444	66.5	163 800	23.2	10.1
PENNSYLVANIA	81.9	22.4	20 880	40 106	10.3	11.0	7.8	5 249 750	4 777 003	71.3	97 000	21.6	12.2
District 1	66.8	13.8	14 430	28 295	4.9	26.9	22.8	271 614	238 801	60.4	51 400	22.7	13.8
District 2	74.3	24.2	18 111	30 626	7.9	23.8	18.5	296 488	259 831	53.4	58 300	21.6	13.2
District 3	83.7	18.0	17 649	35 876	5.9	11.6	8.1	273 414	247 453	73.5	83 100	20.3	11.5
District 4	87.1	27.2	23 469	43 628	12.8	7.5	5.6	268 903	253 991	78.5	99 400	21.1	12.5
District 5	82.1	17.0	16 692	33 320	5.1	13.5	8.3	305 133	250 158	72.9	73 900	20.6	11.1
District 6	85.8	33.9	29 377	55 615	20.8	5.9	3.7	256 599	244 878	74.2	142 400	21.6	12.2

1. Persons 25 years old and over. 2. Based on the population enumerated as of April 1, 2000. 3. Specified owner-occupied units. 4. Median monthly owner costs is often in the minimum category—9.9 percent or less, which is indicated as 9.9 percent. Note: Data were tabulated for the 108th Congress and some boundary changes have occurred.

Table E. Congressional Districts 109th Congress — Housing, Labor Force, and Employment

| STATE District | Housing units, 2000 (cont'd) — Occupied units (cont'd) — Renter-occupied | | | Civilian labor force, 2000 | Unemployment | | Civilian employment,[4] 2000 | Percent | | Disability, 2000 |
	Median rent[1] (dollars)	Rent as a percent of income	Substandard units[2] (percent)	Total	Total	Rate[3]	Total	Management, professional, and related occupations	Production, transportation, and material moving occupations	Employment disabled persons[5] (percent)
	44	45	46	47	48	49	50	51	52	53
NEW YORK—Cont'd										
District 21	567	25.7	2.0	331 000	21 354	6.5	309 646	37.8	11.6	11.0
District 22	572	28.2	3.5	317 043	20 451	6.5	296 592	35.0	12.9	11.4
District 23	470	26.3	2.4	300 553	24 688	8.2	275 865	28.4	16.8	11.4
District 24	477	26.6	1.8	317 059	20 585	6.5	296 474	32.5	15.9	11.5
District 25	557	27.1	2.0	328 395	16 577	5.0	311 818	37.7	13.8	9.3
District 26	569	26.3	1.6	333 782	19 081	5.7	314 701	35.6	15.5	8.4
District 27	496	27.1	2.2	319 934	20 108	6.3	299 826	30.8	17.4	11.1
District 28	528	30.3	3.0	308 311	26 719	8.7	281 592	31.9	16.6	13.0
District 29	543	25.8	1.9	329 663	20 585	6.2	309 078	36.8	15.2	9.4
NORTH CAROLINA	548	24.3	4.0	4 039 732	214 991	5.3	3 824 741	31.2	18.7	13.3
District 1	428	26.4	5.7	265 000	22 468	8.5	242 532	23.3	23.0	17.1
District 2	521	24.8	5.3	288 777	21 420	7.4	267 357	27.5	19.5	14.2
District 3	502	23.6	3.2	284 966	14 831	5.2	270 135	30.5	13.9	12.6
District 4	717	25.8	3.9	341 867	12 514	3.7	329 353	51.1	7.1	8.0
District 5	493	22.6	2.6	323 785	12 693	3.9	311 092	30.0	22.1	12.4
District 6	563	22.2	2.9	327 799	11 928	3.6	315 871	30.4	21.1	12.6
District 7	508	26.7	4.1	291 882	19 513	6.7	272 369	26.9	18.4	15.8
District 8	579	24.0	5.0	303 822	18 335	6.0	285 487	27.8	20.0	15.2
District 9	703	23.3	2.6	341 928	12 758	3.7	329 170	40.4	12.1	10.0
District 10	474	21.8	3.3	320 051	13 167	4.1	306 884	23.0	30.9	15.1
District 11	486	24.4	2.7	299 108	15 534	5.2	283 574	28.3	19.2	13.4
District 12	533	24.7	6.1	314 800	24 272	7.7	290 528	25.7	22.0	14.9
District 13	620	24.8	4.5	335 947	15 558	4.6	320 389	34.7	15.7	11.8
NORTH DAKOTA	412	22.3	2.5	331 889	15 257	4.6	316 632	33.3	12.4	9.3
At Large	412	22.3	2.5	331 889	15 257	4.6	316 632	33.3	12.4	9.3
OHIO	515	24.2	2.1	5 684 790	282 615	5.0	5 402 175	31.0	19.0	10.3
District 1	459	24.6	3.0	313 585	17 766	5.7	295 819	31.8	14.7	10.7
District 2	544	23.2	1.8	318 645	13 205	4.1	305 440	37.4	14.3	10.0
District 3	522	24.3	1.9	311 924	15 182	4.9	296 742	33.5	17.9	10.8
District 4	463	22.6	1.8	311 153	13 123	4.2	298 030	24.5	28.0	10.7
District 5	465	21.6	1.8	327 661	14 927	4.6	312 734	24.6	29.8	9.7
District 6	420	25.3	2.0	287 781	19 869	6.9	267 912	26.2	20.4	11.1
District 7	540	23.9	1.8	314 800	14 545	4.6	300 255	29.9	18.5	10.2
District 8	537	23.6	1.7	321 752	13 643	4.2	308 109	30.0	20.8	9.9
District 9	489	24.4	2.0	314 321	17 789	5.7	296 532	29.2	20.2	10.9
District 10	550	23.9	1.9	319 123	14 524	4.6	304 599	32.6	15.3	9.8
District 11	523	27.3	2.9	286 988	25 127	8.8	261 861	34.2	15.9	13.5
District 12	590	24.0	2.5	335 819	14 903	4.4	320 916	38.9	11.6	9.5
District 13	538	24.7	1.7	317 370	15 568	4.9	301 802	31.6	17.6	10.4
District 14	613	23.5	1.5	329 023	11 469	3.5	317 554	35.4	16.4	8.6
District 15	596	24.4	2.4	348 605	12 910	3.7	335 695	37.7	12.7	9.1
District 16	498	23.2	1.7	320 035	13 091	4.1	306 944	29.0	21.5	9.3
District 17	482	24.9	1.9	308 423	18 369	6.0	290 054	25.2	22.6	10.4
District 18	421	23.1	2.6	297 782	16 605	5.6	281 177	23.4	26.0	12.0
OKLAHOMA	456	24.3	4.2	1 632 128	86 832	5.3	1 545 296	30.3	15.4	12.5
District 1	511	24.0	4.2	350 799	16 359	4.7	334 440	33.5	12.8	11.7
District 2	370	23.9	4.6	297 761	19 426	6.5	278 335	25.5	20.7	14.8
District 3	414	24.0	3.6	325 743	16 530	5.1	309 213	29.3	16.0	11.1
District 4	466	24.5	3.6	323 272	16 467	5.1	306 805	30.6	15.0	11.2
District 5	477	24.6	5.0	334 553	18 050	5.4	316 503	31.8	13.3	13.5
OREGON	620	26.9	5.3	1 740 298	112 529	6.5	1 627 769	33.1	14.7	10.6
District 1	678	25.9	5.2	370 323	19 393	5.2	350 930	39.1	12.8	9.5
District 2	543	26.7	5.3	323 084	25 160	7.8	297 924	29.2	15.7	10.9
District 3	643	27.0	6.1	370 033	23 570	6.4	346 463	31.6	15.7	11.4
District 4	575	28.7	4.3	333 311	23 091	6.9	310 220	30.5	16.6	11.1
District 5	625	26.5	5.5	343 547	21 315	6.2	322 232	34.1	13.1	10.0
PENNSYLVANIA	531	25.0	2.4	5 992 886	339 386	5.7	5 653 500	32.6	16.3	10.6
District 1	546	28.8	8.0	266 534	33 954	12.7	232 580	27.2	14.7	16.9
District 2	585	28.5	5.4	288 415	33 808	11.7	254 607	37.8	10.0	14.9
District 3	437	24.5	2.0	310 396	17 860	5.8	292 536	27.7	21.7	9.7
District 4	510	23.7	1.2	315 925	13 795	4.4	302 130	36.2	13.6	8.4
District 5	442	26.2	2.2	306 912	17 857	5.8	289 055	28.0	22.9	9.6
District 6	692	23.9	1.8	341 122	16 690	4.9	324 432	40.9	12.8	8.6

1. Specified renter-occupied units.   2. Overcrowded or lacking complete plumbing facilities.   3. Percent of total civilian labor force.   4. Persons 16 years old and over.   5. Persons 16 to 64 years old.   Note: Data were tabulated for the 108th Congress and some boundary changes have occurred.

STATE District	Representative	Land area,[1] 2000 (sq km)	Population and population characteristics, 2000											
					Percent									
					Race alone or in combination								Age	
			Total persons	Per square kilometer	White	Black	Am. Indian, Alaska Native	Asian and Pacific Islander	Other race	Hispanic or Latino[2]	Non-Hispanic White	Two or more races	Under 5 years	5 to 17 years	18 to 24 years
		1	2	3	4	5	6	7	8	9	10	11	12	13	14
PENNSYLVANIA—Cont'd															
District 7	Curt Weldon (R)	751	646 530	861.0	90.0	5.9	0.3	4.1	0.7	1.3	88.4	1.0	6.1	17.8	8.1
District 8	Mike Fitzpatrick (R)	1 604	646 340	403.0	93.0	3.9	0.4	2.8	1.2	2.3	90.8	1.0	6.4	19.1	7.0
District 9	Bill Shuster (R)	18 765	645 612	34.4	97.5	1.9	0.3	0.5	0.5	0.9	96.4	0.6	5.9	17.7	8.4
District 10	Don Sherwood (R)	17 053	646 537	37.9	97.0	2.2	0.4	0.7	0.5	1.4	95.5	0.7	5.4	18.1	8.0
District 11	Paul E. Kanjorski (D)	5 744	646 209	112.5	95.4	3.0	0.4	0.9	1.3	2.5	93.3	1.0	5.2	17.0	9.2
District 12	John Murtha (D)	7 132	646 079	90.6	96.0	3.7	0.3	0.4	0.3	0.6	94.9	0.8	5.2	16.1	9.0
District 13	Allyson Y. Schwartz (D)	643	646 167	1 005.2	88.1	6.5	0.4	4.5	1.9	3.1	85.6	1.2	6.1	17.4	7.2
District 14	Mike Doyle (D)	416	646 196	1 554.7	74.6	23.6	0.6	2.0	0.8	1.1	72.9	1.5	5.5	15.5	11.2
District 15	Charlie Wieder Dent (R)	2 100	646 495	307.8	90.9	3.7	0.4	2.0	4.6	7.9	86.4	1.6	5.9	18.1	8.4
District 16	Joe Pitts (R)	3 351	646 156	192.8	88.9	5.0	0.5	1.7	5.5	9.2	84.3	1.5	7.1	19.9	9.9
District 17	Tim Holden (D)	5 933	646 465	109.0	89.7	8.1	0.4	1.4	1.8	3.2	87.3	1.1	5.7	17.5	7.5
District 18	Tim Murphy (R)	3 696	646 817	175.0	96.4	2.3	0.2	1.5	0.3	0.6	95.4	0.7	5.5	16.9	6.4
District 19	Todd Platts (R)	4 270	647 065	151.6	94.4	3.5	0.4	1.4	1.5	2.7	92.2	1.1	5.8	17.9	8.8
RHODE ISLAND		2 706	1 048 319	387.4	86.9	5.5	1.0	2.9	6.6	8.7	81.9	2.7	6.1	17.5	10.2
District 1	Patrick J. Kennedy (D)	841	524 157	623.3	87.8	5.6	0.8	2.5	6.4	7.5	82.6	2.9	5.9	16.8	10.8
District 2	Jim Langevin (D)	1 865	524 162	281.0	86.0	5.5	1.2	3.2	6.8	9.8	81.2	2.5	6.3	18.3	9.5
SOUTH CAROLINA		77 983	4 012 012	51.4	68.0	29.9	0.7	1.2	1.3	2.4	66.1	1.0	6.6	18.6	10.2
District 1	Henry Brown (R)	6 849	668 668	97.6	75.9	21.5	0.8	1.8	1.4	2.5	73.7	1.3	6.4	17.7	10.5
District 2	Joe Wilson (R)	12 347	668 668	54.2	70.4	26.9	0.7	1.6	1.8	3.3	68.0	1.2	6.7	18.6	10.1
District 3	J. Gresham Barrett (R)	13 966	668 669	47.9	77.6	20.9	0.6	0.8	1.0	1.9	76.0	0.8	6.4	17.9	10.3
District 4	Bob Inglis (R)	5 570	668 669	120.1	77.1	20.2	0.5	1.6	1.7	3.2	74.6	1.1	6.7	18.0	9.4
District 5	John Spratt (D)	18 221	668 668	36.7	65.5	32.7	1.0	0.8	1.0	1.8	64.1	0.8	6.8	19.5	9.1
District 6	James E. Clyburn (D)	21 030	668 670	31.8	41.3	57.4	0.6	0.8	0.8	1.5	40.3	0.8	6.5	19.8	11.6
SOUTH DAKOTA		196 540	754 844	3.8	89.9	0.9	9.0	0.9	0.7	1.4	88.0	1.3	6.8	20.1	10.3
At Large	Stephanie M. Herseth (D)	196 540	754 844	3.8	89.9	0.9	9.0	0.9	0.7	1.4	88.0	1.3	6.8	20.1	10.3
TENNESSEE		106 752	5 689 283	53.3	81.2	16.8	0.7	1.3	1.3	2.2	79.2	1.1	6.6	18.0	9.6
District 1	Bill Jenkins (R)	10 601	632 143	59.6	96.5	2.4	0.6	0.6	0.8	1.5	95.0	0.8	5.8	16.2	8.5
District 2	John J. Duncan Jr. (R)	6 285	632 144	100.6	91.8	6.6	0.8	1.2	0.8	1.3	90.1	1.1	6.1	16.6	10.3
District 3	Zach Wamp (R)	8 834	632 143	71.6	86.9	11.5	0.8	1.1	0.9	1.6	85.2	1.1	6.1	17.3	9.5
District 4	Lincoln Davis (D)	25 999	632 143	24.3	94.2	4.7	0.8	0.4	0.9	1.6	92.6	0.9	6.3	17.9	8.5
District 5	Jim Cooper (D)	2 315	632 143	273.1	71.4	24.2	0.7	2.6	3.0	4.2	68.2	1.8	6.7	16.2	11.3
District 6	Bart Gordon (D)	14 194	632 143	44.5	91.2	6.7	0.7	1.1	1.4	2.6	89.0	1.0	6.9	18.6	10.4
District 7	Marsha Blackburn (R)	16 296	632 139	38.8	85.7	11.9	0.7	2.0	1.2	2.2	83.5	1.2	7.0	20.2	8.1
District 8	John Tanner (D)	21 398	632 142	29.5	76.0	22.8	0.7	0.7	0.9	1.6	74.4	0.9	6.8	19.1	9.6
District 9	Harold Ford Jr. (D)	830	632 143	761.5	36.8	60.2	0.5	1.9	1.8	3.0	34.9	1.0	7.7	19.8	10.7
TEXAS		678 051	20 851 820	30.8	73.1	12.0	1.0	3.2	13.3	32.0	52.4	2.5	7.8	20.4	10.5
District 1	Louie B. Gohmert (R)	32 486	651 619	20.1	78.9	16.6	1.1	0.6	4.1	7.4	74.7	1.3	6.5	19.0	9.9
District 2	Ted Poe (R)	35 509	651 619	18.4	80.1	14.2	1.0	0.6	4.6	8.8	75.6	1.3	6.6	19.1	9.9
District 3	Sam Johnson (R)	1 198	651 620	544.1	78.7	7.1	1.0	8.2	7.4	14.4	69.6	2.3	8.4	20.6	7.9
District 4	Ralph Hall (R)	15 905	651 620	41.0	82.3	12.1	1.3	0.8	5.2	9.4	76.6	1.6	6.9	19.9	9.0
District 5	Jeb Hensarling (R)	18 899	651 620	34.5	72.7	16.4	1.1	2.2	9.8	17.7	63.0	2.1	7.4	19.5	9.2
District 6	Joe Barton (R)	9 937	651 620	65.6	80.3	10.8	1.1	3.1	6.8	13.5	71.8	2.1	7.7	21.6	8.7
District 7	John Culberson (R)	502	651 620	1 297.8	66.0	12.1	0.8	12.1	12.7	25.9	49.6	3.6	7.7	18.6	9.5
District 8	Kevin Brady (R)	2 968	651 619	219.5	86.3	5.6	0.8	3.6	5.7	13.0	77.2	1.9	7.5	21.9	8.0
District 9	Al Green (D)	5 333	651 619	122.2	69.2	21.8	0.9	3.2	6.9	14.4	60.1	1.9	7.0	19.5	9.5
District 10	Michael McCaul (R)	1 424	651 619	457.5	65.7	11.8	1.2	5.2	19.4	33.0	49.7	3.1	7.3	15.7	16.9
District 11	Mike Conaway (R)	23 293	651 620	28.0	73.0	16.7	1.2	2.6	9.4	16.4	64.2	2.7	7.7	19.6	13.3
District 12	Kay Granger (R)	3 449	651 619	188.9	83.2	4.9	1.2	2.9	10.1	19.9	71.4	2.3	7.6	19.7	9.8
District 13	Mac Thornberry (R)	102 206	651 619	6.4	81.2	6.1	1.5	1.5	12.0	21.6	70.0	2.2	7.2	19.9	10.4
District 14	Ron Paul (R)	37 447	651 620	17.4	77.3	8.3	1.0	1.2	14.7	32.0	58.2	2.3	7.0	20.3	10.6
District 15	Rubén Hinojosa (D)	16 462	651 619	39.6	79.9	1.6	0.7	0.9	19.3	78.3	19.2	2.3	9.2	23.6	11.3
District 16	Silvestre Reyes (D)	1 504	651 619	433.2	76.8	3.6	1.1	1.6	20.3	77.7	17.4	3.2	8.6	23.0	10.6
District 17	Chet Edwards (D)	86 931	651 619	7.5	86.3	4.2	1.1	0.9	9.4	19.6	74.7	1.9	6.4	19.2	10.5
District 18	Sheila Jackson Lee (D)	482	651 620	1 352.5	39.2	43.0	0.8	3.3	16.4	32.6	21.2	2.5	7.6	19.6	11.1
District 19	Randy Neugebauer (R)	45 347	651 619	14.4	77.1	6.1	1.1	1.1	16.8	34.1	58.2	2.2	7.4	21.0	12.0
District 20	Charlie A. Gonzalez (D)	785	651 619	829.8	69.8	6.2	1.5	2.1	24.8	68.2	23.7	4.2	8.4	20.4	12.6
District 21	Lamar Smith (R)	28 435	651 619	22.9	90.0	2.4	1.0	2.6	6.1	17.2	77.2	2.0	6.4	18.6	6.9
District 22	Tom DeLay (R)	4 326	651 619	150.6	72.6	10.6	0.8	9.1	9.4	19.7	60.1	2.4	7.5	22.6	7.7
District 23	Henry Bonilla (R)	143 524	651 619	4.5	82.1	1.8	0.9	1.5	16.5	66.8	29.8	2.6	8.6	23.6	9.8
District 24	Kenny Marchant (R)	644	651 619	1 012.2	54.2	22.7	1.2	3.7	21.5	38.0	35.3	3.1	9.0	20.9	11.9
District 25	Lloyd Doggett (D)	671	651 619	971.1	55.5	23.7	0.8	5.5	17.8	34.3	36.6	3.1	8.9	19.8	11.1
District 26	Michael Burgess (R)	2 783	651 619	234.1	85.2	5.5	1.1	4.8	5.6	11.0	77.8	2.1	7.9	20.0	10.0
District 27	Solomon P. Ortiz (D)	10 199	651 619	63.9	78.4	2.6	0.9	1.1	19.8	71.6	24.6	2.7	8.7	22.5	10.6
District 28	Henry Roberto Cuellar (D)	30 575	651 620	21.3	69.8	8.2	1.1	1.2	22.9	69.6	21.2	3.0	8.8	23.7	9.9

1. Dry land or land partially or temporarily covered by water.   2. Hispanic or Latino persons may be of any race.   Note: Data were tabulated for the 108th Congress and some boundary changes have occurred.

STATE District	Population and population characteristics, 2000 (cont'd) — Percent (cont'd) — Age (cont'd)						Percent female	Households, 2000				Persons in correctional institutions, 2000	Persons in nursing homes, 2000	Persons in military quarters, 2000	Education, 2000 — School enrollment[2]	
	25 to 34 years	35 to 44 years	45 to 54 years	55 to 64 years	65 to 74 years	75 years and over		Number	Persons per household	Female family householder[1]	One person				Public	Private
	15	16	17	18	19	20	21	22	23	24	25	26	27	28	29	30
PENNSYLVANIA—Cont'd																
District 7	13.1	16.7	13.9	8.9	7.8	7.6	51.8	246 528	2.53	9.8	27.0	2 820	5 374	0	107 654	66 192
District 8	12.7	17.9	15.0	9.3	6.8	5.8	51.0	236 744	2.69	9.0	21.6	917	4 713	0	120 145	49 338
District 9	12.6	15.4	14.1	10.0	8.3	7.6	50.7	249 573	2.50	8.8	24.6	7 081	6 706	32	125 015	19 846
District 10	11.7	15.4	14.3	10.2	8.5	8.1	50.7	250 596	2.47	9.1	26.4	9 206	6 216	0	124 405	30 679
District 11	11.9	15.4	13.7	9.7	8.9	9.1	51.8	256 256	2.42	11.1	29.2	4 921	6 679	3	125 965	33 648
District 12	11.7	14.9	14.3	9.7	9.3	9.7	52.0	262 232	2.38	11.1	29.2	4 379	4 280	0	129 059	19 634
District 13	13.0	16.2	13.7	9.2	8.2	9.1	52.1	250 285	2.51	10.8	27.8	6 359	7 644	159	99 071	61 157
District 14	13.6	14.6	13.1	8.6	8.7	9.3	53.0	280 325	2.21	16.0	37.3	4 713	4 657	0	124 171	45 063
District 15	12.5	16.6	14.1	9.0	7.7	7.8	51.5	248 092	2.52	10.0	25.4	1 989	6 881	0	123 731	41 876
District 16	12.6	15.8	13.1	8.4	6.6	6.7	51.1	233 433	2.67	9.6	23.3	1 029	6 839	0	131 373	36 948
District 17	13.0	16.2	14.6	9.4	8.2	7.8	51.1	256 370	2.43	10.6	27.5	7 633	7 733	0	120 835	24 444
District 18	11.8	16.6	15.3	10.1	8.9	8.8	52.0	261 165	2.42	8.6	27.3	1 252	6 735	3	121 173	29 598
District 19	12.9	16.7	14.5	9.3	7.3	6.8	51.0	250 273	2.49	8.8	24.5	5 283	6 948	30	127 309	31 872
RHODE ISLAND	13.4	16.2	13.5	8.5	7.0	7.5	52.0	408 424	2.47	12.9	28.6	3 576	9 222	870	219 700	70 905
District 1	13.6	15.8	13.2	8.5	7.3	8.1	52.3	208 431	2.41	12.7	30.2	324	5 800	867	100 168	44 329
District 2	13.2	16.6	13.9	8.5	6.8	6.9	51.6	199 993	2.54	13.1	26.8	3 252	3 422	3	119 532	26 576
SOUTH CAROLINA	14.0	15.6	13.7	9.3	6.7	5.4	51.4	1 533 854	2.53	14.8	25.0	34 909	20 867	17 102	905 055	148 097
District 1	14.7	15.8	13.6	9.5	7.0	4.8	51.1	263 903	2.48	12.6	24.7	1 488	2 952	3 350	144 325	28 952
District 2	14.8	16.2	13.7	8.8	6.3	4.9	50.7	254 612	2.52	12.7	24.6	8 651	2 923	12 829	149 785	24 567
District 3	13.3	15.1	13.6	9.9	7.4	6.0	51.3	258 762	2.50	13.0	24.6	5 285	4 060	0	151 317	20 850
District 4	14.7	16.0	13.9	9.3	6.5	5.6	51.4	261 279	2.49	13.1	26.0	4 309	2 994	0	134 941	32 145
District 5	13.7	15.7	14.0	9.2	6.5	5.4	51.7	251 331	2.59	16.4	23.9	5 802	4 501	830	151 513	19 192
District 6	12.8	14.7	13.6	9.0	6.6	5.4	52.4	243 967	2.60	21.4	26.1	9 374	3 437	93	173 174	22 391
SOUTH DAKOTA	12.1	15.3	12.9	8.3	7.0	7.3	50.4	290 245	2.50	9.0	27.6	4 479	7 791	566	184 458	23 771
At Large	12.1	15.3	12.9	8.3	7.0	7.3	50.4	290 245	2.50	9.0	27.6	4 479	7 791	566	184 458	23 771
TENNESSEE	14.3	15.9	13.8	9.4	6.7	5.6	51.3	2 232 905	2.48	12.9	25.8	38 481	36 994	2 593	1 203 685	211 420
District 1	13.8	15.3	14.5	11.2	8.0	6.5	51.2	259 346	2.38	10.6	25.9	3 381	4 982	0	123 907	12 335
District 2	14.0	15.8	14.2	9.8	7.2	6.1	51.6	258 081	2.38	10.5	27.2	1 241	3 855	1	136 801	20 767
District 3	13.5	15.4	14.4	10.2	7.4	6.2	51.7	253 062	2.44	12.0	25.9	1 599	4 293	10	125 685	27 188
District 4	13.0	15.2	13.9	10.7	8.1	6.4	51.0	248 333	2.49	11.2	23.9	4 242	5 132	45	126 886	13 931
District 5	17.1	16.7	13.3	8.0	5.7	5.0	51.4	258 297	2.35	14.0	31.5	5 947	2 507	0	114 497	43 099
District 6	14.5	16.3	13.4	9.0	6.0	4.9	50.6	238 955	2.59	10.8	22.1	1 695	3 978	0	146 196	15 961
District 7	13.7	17.5	15.0	8.8	5.6	4.2	50.4	229 626	2.68	9.5	19.6	6 801	3 398	2 287	134 750	33 508
District 8	13.3	15.4	13.2	9.3	7.0	6.2	51.5	242 532	2.53	14.7	24.8	7 198	5 826	250	141 723	18 150
District 9	16.0	15.2	12.6	7.2	5.5	5.2	52.5	244 673	2.52	22.7	30.5	6 377	3 023	0	153 240	26 481
TEXAS	15.2	15.9	12.5	7.7	5.5	4.5	50.4	7 393 354	2.74	12.7	23.7	244 363	105 052	34 056	5 268 790	679 470
District 1	12.1	14.6	13.1	9.9	7.8	7.1	51.0	246 990	2.54	12.1	25.1	9 600	6 285	0	156 388	13 968
District 2	13.0	15.3	13.0	9.7	7.6	5.9	49.1	232 117	2.63	11.6	23.0	32 390	4 602	0	153 109	13 208
District 3	17.2	19.5	13.6	7.0	3.4	2.4	50.2	235 091	2.75	8.9	21.4	768	1 778	0	153 302	29 367
District 4	12.5	15.4	13.2	9.4	7.2	6.5	51.1	242 255	2.61	11.4	23.3	4 978	6 354	0	149 879	19 435
District 5	15.5	16.5	12.4	8.0	6.2	5.3	49.8	236 267	2.63	13.5	25.0	22 252	4 622	0	144 882	19 699
District 6	14.2	17.3	13.5	8.0	5.1	3.9	50.7	228 245	2.82	11.0	18.7	2 272	3 096	0	159 491	26 679
District 7	18.6	17.5	13.4	7.2	4.3	3.2	50.7	254 811	2.54	10.6	30.2	13	2 222	0	147 038	29 313
District 8	13.8	17.9	15.3	8.3	4.4	2.9	50.6	230 984	2.81	9.4	18.5	617	2 026	0	163 095	25 736
District 9	14.1	16.7	13.7	8.3	6.2	5.0	50.2	243 728	2.58	13.6	25.8	16 032	3 304	26	160 134	18 954
District 10	21.3	15.7	11.0	5.5	3.5	3.1	48.5	258 830	2.44	11.5	32.1	3 544	1 828	0	172 486	19 162
District 11	14.7	14.7	11.2	7.5	5.9	5.4	50.3	230 337	2.65	11.9	23.1	12 111	5 905	12 262	155 646	29 618
District 12	15.3	16.9	12.8	7.8	5.5	4.7	50.4	240 202	2.65	10.8	24.8	7 844	3 813	271	142 952	28 439
District 13	12.8	15.0	12.3	8.7	7.3	6.4	50.0	241 219	2.57	10.7	25.8	16 905	5 254	4 696	162 980	14 438
District 14	12.5	15.1	12.8	8.6	6.9	6.1	50.2	232 198	2.70	11.4	22.9	9 412	5 801	10	165 584	16 993
District 15	14.5	13.4	10.6	6.9	5.9	4.6	50.6	190 813	3.32	15.2	15.9	12 371	2 224	839	198 131	9 688
District 16	14.5	14.8	11.4	7.2	5.9	4.1	51.8	203 028	3.15	18.2	18.2	6 220	1 329	2 833	197 987	17 943
District 17	12.0	14.7	12.6	9.4	7.9	7.2	50.2	243 675	2.53	10.1	25.5	16 732	6 051	2 313	155 590	18 569
District 18	16.7	15.6	12.2	7.6	5.5	4.1	50.0	231 392	2.72	19.6	29.7	9 600	2 138	0	163 776	17 307
District 19	12.8	14.9	12.2	7.9	6.5	5.3	50.9	238 568	2.64	12.1	24.8	8 332	3 732	0	183 892	16 452
District 20	16.5	14.7	10.8	6.8	5.4	4.6	50.9	222 232	2.82	17.7	25.6	6 243	3 262	9 451	166 665	23 652
District 21	12.3	17.1	15.5	9.6	7.2	6.5	51.2	256 244	2.50	8.1	24.4	1 012	4 564	12	137 746	28 358
District 22	13.5	19.3	15.2	7.5	4.1	2.6	49.5	213 430	2.98	9.7	15.5	12 482	1 517	0	171 590	27 769
District 23	14.0	14.9	12.3	7.6	5.3	3.9	51.0	203 807	3.14	12.8	17.1	6 575	1 829	271	188 457	19 470
District 24	17.6	15.3	11.3	6.5	4.2	3.4	49.8	224 016	2.87	15.9	24.7	1 768	2 792	0	161 392	21 861
District 25	18.0	15.7	12.2	6.5	4.2	3.7	50.9	241 176	2.68	15.0	27.8	3	2 226	0	159 805	28 801
District 26	17.1	19.5	13.7	6.6	3.0	2.2	50.3	242 126	2.65	8.3	22.7	857	2 398	0	165 904	26 491
District 27	13.7	14.1	11.8	7.5	6.3	4.9	51.5	207 550	3.09	16.4	19.3	3 330	2 801	468	187 453	14 382
District 28	14.0	14.2	11.3	7.6	6.0	4.6	51.2	204 225	3.14	17.3	18.2	3 714	2 463	604	184 597	13 728

1. No spouse present.   2. All persons 3 years old and over enrolled in nursery school through college.   Note: Data were tabulated for the 108th Congress and some boundary changes have occurred.

Table E. Congressional Districts 109th Congress — Education, Money Income, Poverty, and Housing

STATE District	Education, 2000 (cont'd) Attainment[1] (percent) High school graduate or more	Bachelor's degree or more	Money income, 1999 Per capita income[2]	Households Median income	Percent with income of $100,000 or more	Percent below poverty level, 1999 Persons Total	Families Total	Housing units, 2000 Total	Occupied units Total	Owner-occupied Percent	Median value[3] (dollars)	Owner cost as a percent of income With a mortgage	Without a mortgage[4]
	31	32	33	34	35	36	37	38	39	40	41	42	43
PENNSYLVANIA—Cont'd													
District 7	89.0	36.1	28 392	56 154	20.7	5.4	3.6	256 304	246 536	74.2	148 300	22.0	13.2
District 8	88.3	30.6	27 209	59 184	21.1	4.5	3.2	243 907	236 562	77.5	158 300	22.8	12.9
District 9	78.9	12.9	16 805	34 850	4.8	11.1	8.0	279 094	249 778	76.6	83 000	20.9	10.7
District 10	81.6	17.1	18 188	35 984	6.7	10.3	7.2	311 850	250 685	75.7	91 400	21.8	11.9
District 11	80.4	15.9	17 920	34 979	6.3	11.3	7.8	300 865	256 175	70.2	90 100	22.3	13.2
District 12	80.1	13.6	16 403	30 614	4.5	13.6	9.9	287 537	262 145	73.4	68 400	20.6	11.9
District 13	83.3	28.7	25 057	49 311	16.3	7.1	5.1	260 378	250 492	72.3	122 400	21.5	13.0
District 14	82.3	21.3	18 240	30 140	5.7	17.1	12.7	313 843	280 219	57.9	61 300	20.8	13.4
District 15	81.2	22.3	21 842	45 419	11.8	8.2	5.9	261 024	248 085	71.6	119 600	22.1	12.4
District 16	77.6	23.0	21 226	45 941	12.0	9.5	6.5	245 278	233 425	69.5	124 000	22.1	10.4
District 17	80.0	17.3	20 370	40 334	8.0	8.4	6.1	277 381	256 371	72.6	94 100	21.1	11.7
District 18	88.5	29.3	23 711	44 864	12.4	6.3	4.4	275 928	261 211	77.2	101 800	20.8	11.8
District 19	82.4	21.3	21 632	45 363	9.7	6.8	4.4	264 210	250 207	74.9	113 600	21.9	10.2
RHODE ISLAND	78.0	25.6	21 688	42 090	11.5	11.9	8.9	439 837	408 424	60.0	133 000	22.7	13.4
District 1	76.3	26.0	21 885	40 616	11.4	11.9	8.9	221 472	208 498	55.7	136 500	22.5	13.5
District 2	79.6	25.2	21 491	44 129	11.6	11.9	8.8	218 365	199 926	64.6	129 700	23.0	13.3
SOUTH CAROLINA	76.3	20.4	18 795	37 082	8.1	14.1	10.7	1 753 670	1 533 854	72.2	94 900	20.5	9.9
District 1	83.8	25.4	21 130	40 713	9.7	11.5	8.2	328 140	263 896	69.4	120 800	21.4	9.9
District 2	83.6	28.5	21 892	42 915	11.4	11.0	8.1	289 168	254 578	73.4	113 900	20.5	9.9
District 3	73.2	17.1	17 710	36 092	6.6	13.3	9.6	292 329	258 800	75.5	86 900	19.6	9.9
District 4	76.4	22.3	20 487	39 417	9.7	11.4	8.6	285 176	261 236	70.1	99 500	20.3	9.9
District 5	71.0	14.8	17 101	35 416	6.4	15.2	11.9	279 434	251 219	74.7	83 200	19.9	9.9
District 6	69.6	14.1	14 453	28 967	4.6	22.4	18.4	279 423	244 125	70.2	73 000	20.8	10.8
SOUTH DAKOTA	84.6	21.5	17 562	35 282	5.9	13.2	9.3	323 208	290 245	68.2	79 600	19.7	10.5
At Large	84.6	21.5	17 562	35 282	5.9	13.2	9.3	323 208	290 245	68.2	79 600	19.7	10.5
TENNESSEE	75.9	19.6	19 393	36 360	8.3	13.5	10.3	2 439 443	2 232 905	69.9	93 000	21.1	9.9
District 1	71.8	15.0	17 231	31 228	5.2	14.8	11.3	290 120	259 389	74.2	86 900	20.6	9.9
District 2	79.2	23.3	20 502	36 796	8.8	12.2	8.5	281 817	258 049	70.9	97 300	20.7	9.9
District 3	75.2	18.9	19 205	35 434	7.8	13.4	10.4	277 848	253 042	70.5	90 300	20.2	9.9
District 4	69.0	11.3	16 592	31 645	5.3	15.2	11.9	276 371	248 234	76.7	78 400	21.0	9.9
District 5	80.9	27.9	22 303	40 419	10.0	12.2	9.3	275 069	258 235	58.1	115 600	21.7	9.9
District 6	74.7	16.3	18 698	39 721	7.5	11.1	7.9	257 944	238 975	73.3	102 900	21.2	9.9
District 7	83.7	29.2	24 839	50 090	17.6	8.0	6.2	248 373	229 831	79.3	137 900	21.1	9.9
District 8	71.8	12.5	16 475	33 001	5.3	15.0	11.9	267 354	242 466	70.3	74 100	20.4	9.9
District 9	77.3	22.1	18 687	33 806	8.0	19.4	16.1	264 547	244 684	56.9	77 600	22.2	11.3
TEXAS	75.7	23.2	19 617	39 927	11.5	15.4	12.0	8 157 575	7 393 354	63.8	82 500	20.1	10.9
District 1	74.8	14.8	16 544	31 894	5.8	16.8	12.8	284 165	247 017	73.9	62 000	19.2	11.0
District 2	72.5	11.4	15 755	32 986	5.8	15.9	12.3	279 072	231 958	77.7	62 700	19.1	10.6
District 3	88.7	41.6	29 906	65 546	26.2	5.7	3.9	248 340	234 849	68.9	134 600	20.4	10.9
District 4	78.6	18.7	19 185	38 677	9.2	12.5	9.5	267 376	242 326	72.2	79 400	19.7	10.9
District 5	75.5	18.2	19 112	39 227	9.4	12.3	9.7	264 001	236 230	65.7	81 700	19.9	11.2
District 6	82.6	23.0	20 996	49 763	12.8	8.2	6.3	242 096	228 292	74.4	90 700	19.9	11.2
District 7	84.1	39.8	28 112	48 561	19.0	10.6	8.3	274 645	255 047	49.6	109 400	19.9	9.9
District 8	87.1	32.9	27 182	60 198	23.1	6.7	4.9	247 008	231 136	74.5	118 400	19.4	9.9
District 9	80.9	20.9	20 237	41 416	11.3	13.6	10.9	274 673	243 665	65.8	77 900	19.4	11.0
District 10	81.5	35.1	21 835	41 374	10.8	14.8	9.5	269 227	258 776	45.8	112 400	21.3	9.9
District 11	80.4	19.0	17 295	36 378	7.4	13.6	10.1	253 342	230 351	61.4	75 100	20.1	10.7
District 12	79.6	22.7	21 677	44 624	11.9	9.8	7.1	256 389	240 157	65.3	85 600	20.1	11.4
District 13	75.8	17.4	16 778	33 361	6.2	14.4	11.2	273 337	241 230	68.4	58 800	19.0	10.5
District 14	72.9	15.0	16 756	35 966	7.1	15.0	11.3	271 115	232 098	71.0	70 200	19.0	10.2
District 15	58.1	14.1	11 514	27 530	5.4	30.5	25.8	229 435	190 740	70.8	55 400	21.7	11.9
District 16	66.4	17.0	13 624	31 245	6.5	23.6	20.2	216 744	203 161	62.8	70 000	21.8	10.0
District 17	75.4	16.8	16 640	32 413	6.0	15.1	11.3	289 106	243 664	70.7	55 900	19.3	11.3
District 18	65.6	18.2	16 255	31 725	7.9	23.7	20.1	254 069	231 443	51.1	63 400	20.8	12.0
District 19	73.1	18.7	16 710	32 409	7.1	17.5	13.5	268 155	238 564	66.7	57 800	19.2	10.4
District 20	70.3	15.6	14 208	31 801	4.5	20.3	17.0	237 619	222 272	52.7	59 400	20.7	10.1
District 21	89.5	38.9	29 069	52 751	20.1	7.0	4.9	287 995	256 321	73.3	135 200	20.6	9.9
District 22	85.5	33.2	25 177	62 678	23.9	6.6	5.0	225 131	213 552	79.1	111 200	19.5	9.9
District 23	67.2	23.2	16 680	36 158	12.0	22.1	17.9	230 463	203 679	72.2	84 700	20.8	11.5
District 24	68.0	18.2	16 906	36 962	8.3	17.2	14.1	239 108	223 821	52.9	69 600	20.8	11.5
District 25	74.3	28.0	21 448	38 048	12.2	16.3	13.7	260 337	241 020	46.5	82 600	19.7	10.1
District 26	90.7	38.9	29 202	61 287	24.5	5.7	3.6	255 072	242 156	64.6	140 100	20.6	10.6
District 27	64.1	15.8	13 611	30 431	6.1	26.5	22.1	243 311	207 532	64.1	60 800	22.0	12.2
District 28	61.1	9.8	12 199	29 127	4.4	26.7	22.8	233 165	204 249	71.8	49 800	21.0	11.2

1. Persons 25 years old and over.   2. Based on the population enumerated as of April 1, 2000.   3. Specified owner-occupied units.   4. Median monthly owner costs is often in the minimum category—9.9 percent or less, which is indicated as 9.9 percent.   Note: Data were tabulated for the 108th Congress and some boundary changes have occurred.

Table E. Congressional Districts 109th Congress — Housing, Labor Force, and Employment

	Housing units, 2000 (cont'd)			Civilian labor force, 2000			Civilian employment,[4] 2000			Disability, 2000
	Occupied units (cont'd)				Unemployment			Percent		
	Renter-occupied									
STATE District	Median rent[1] (dollars)	Rent as a percent of income	Substandard units[2] (percent)	Total	Total	Rate[3]	Total	Management, professional, and related occupations	Production, transportation, and material moving occupations	Employment disabled persons[5] (percent)
	44	45	46	47	48	49	50	51	52	53
PENNSYLVANIA—Cont'd										
District 7	727	24.6	1.7	332 203	11 970	3.6	320 233	43.3	8.4	8.6
District 8	737	24.2	1.9	344 468	12 077	3.5	332 391	38.2	12.0	10.0
District 9	417	23.1	2.0	306 444	16 231	5.3	290 213	25.0	22.3	11.1
District 10	448	24.2	1.6	305 393	16 048	5.3	289 345	28.1	20.7	11.5
District 11	453	24.9	1.4	309 003	18 917	6.1	290 086	26.4	19.8	12.4
District 12	386	24.8	1.5	289 532	21 236	7.3	268 296	25.7	19.0	11.5
District 13	652	25.3	2.6	320 385	14 726	4.6	305 659	38.1	11.2	11.2
District 14	479	26.6	2.0	309 111	25 847	8.4	283 264	32.7	11.1	11.9
District 15	586	25.1	2.1	328 062	14 456	4.4	313 606	32.5	17.5	9.2
District 16	569	24.3	3.4	329 550	12 562	3.8	316 988	30.0	20.2	9.9
District 17	502	22.9	2.0	324 533	14 925	4.6	309 608	29.1	20.4	9.6
District 18	544	23.7	1.0	323 871	14 051	4.3	309 820	38.0	11.6	8.2
District 19	542	23.1	1.6	341 027	12 376	3.6	328 651	30.1	20.0	9.1
RHODE ISLAND	553	25.7	3.3	530 590	29 859	5.6	500 731	33.9	15.2	12.7
District 1	544	25.2	3.0	265 772	14 685	5.5	251 087	34.5	15.6	13.2
District 2	567	26.2	3.6	264 818	15 174	5.7	249 644	33.4	14.8	12.2
SOUTH CAROLINA	510	24.4	3.8	1 938 195	113 495	5.9	1 824 700	29.1	19.0	14.3
District 1	616	25.1	3.3	337 031	15 643	4.6	321 388	32.0	11.4	13.8
District 2	583	24.1	3.5	324 336	13 804	4.3	310 532	35.9	12.0	12.1
District 3	449	24.2	3.1	322 296	17 345	5.4	304 951	26.6	24.4	14.5
District 4	519	23.6	3.2	340 960	17 262	5.1	323 698	30.1	20.6	12.8
District 5	442	23.4	4.2	319 317	21 953	6.9	297 364	24.4	25.3	15.9
District 6	430	26.1	5.6	294 255	27 488	9.3	266 767	24.2	21.2	16.6
SOUTH DAKOTA	426	22.9	3.6	391 594	17 221	4.4	374 373	32.6	14.2	9.4
At Large	426	22.9	3.6	391 594	17 221	4.4	374 373	32.6	14.2	9.4
TENNESSEE	505	24.8	3.3	2 805 234	153 596	5.5	2 651 638	29.5	19.9	13.2
District 1	418	24.1	2.5	303 462	16 675	5.5	286 787	25.4	23.0	14.3
District 2	475	25.1	2.0	317 938	15 617	4.9	302 321	32.4	16.5	11.7
District 3	472	24.2	2.7	311 075	16 946	5.4	294 129	29.1	21.3	13.5
District 4	413	23.7	3.0	292 189	16 460	5.6	275 729	23.0	27.7	14.7
District 5	611	25.2	4.0	340 143	17 078	5.0	323 065	35.6	12.9	11.8
District 6	520	25.4	3.1	329 537	15 172	4.6	314 365	26.9	22.6	12.3
District 7	607	23.4	2.6	310 785	11 719	3.8	299 066	37.2	15.3	9.9
District 8	443	24.2	3.6	296 911	19 265	6.5	277 646	23.8	25.2	14.6
District 9	553	26.3	6.4	303 194	24 664	8.1	278 530	30.5	16.3	15.7
TEXAS	574	24.4	10.0	9 830 559	596 187	6.1	9 234 372	33.3	13.2	12.5
District 1	435	24.6	5.8	289 608	19 303	6.7	270 305	26.0	19.2	13.7
District 2	450	24.2	6.8	272 049	18 760	6.9	253 289	24.3	18.2	13.8
District 3	781	23.1	6.0	358 023	11 891	3.3	346 132	47.8	7.7	8.9
District 4	502	23.9	5.6	309 464	16 779	5.4	292 685	29.7	16.7	13.4
District 5	595	24.3	8.7	306 834	16 423	5.4	290 411	29.4	13.7	13.5
District 6	610	23.9	6.4	333 940	14 870	4.5	319 070	33.6	15.0	11.1
District 7	667	23.2	11.1	348 447	17 338	5.0	331 109	42.6	8.2	11.1
District 8	691	23.3	5.2	339 050	13 036	3.8	326 014	40.3	9.7	9.6
District 9	555	24.2	6.3	307 789	20 700	6.7	287 089	34.2	12.9	11.4
District 10	707	27.3	10.0	371 493	16 766	4.5	354 727	39.7	9.6	10.3
District 11	521	24.3	6.5	277 603	17 989	6.5	259 614	30.5	14.4	11.8
District 12	593	23.6	7.0	328 030	14 387	4.4	313 643	32.0	14.0	12.8
District 13	446	23.4	6.0	297 671	16 339	5.5	281 332	28.7	15.8	11.7
District 14	477	23.4	8.3	301 448	18 171	6.0	283 277	27.3	16.3	12.7
District 15	424	25.2	19.8	242 357	25 643	10.6	216 714	28.0	13.7	14.0
District 16	469	27.2	14.5	256 006	24 126	9.4	231 880	29.7	16.3	13.0
District 17	440	23.9	5.3	295 406	19 460	6.6	275 946	28.9	15.0	12.4
District 18	524	24.7	15.1	293 244	27 865	9.5	265 379	28.3	15.9	16.3
District 19	461	25.4	7.3	301 060	19 115	6.3	281 945	30.6	13.0	11.6
District 20	525	25.1	13.4	281 539	19 443	6.9	262 096	26.8	11.9	15.5
District 21	695	24.0	3.7	330 313	10 232	3.1	320 081	45.5	7.2	9.5
District 22	660	22.5	6.5	325 447	14 613	4.5	310 834	42.6	10.7	10.1
District 23	481	24.5	14.5	270 887	20 234	7.5	250 653	35.0	11.8	12.2
District 24	573	24.2	15.3	310 916	20 208	6.5	290 708	26.5	17.7	16.2
District 25	570	24.4	16.1	317 635	21 758	6.9	295 877	34.6	12.6	13.8
District 26	719	24.1	4.5	371 932	12 294	3.3	359 638	43.0	8.8	7.1
District 27	488	25.9	16.5	264 557	25 340	9.6	239 217	28.7	13.6	13.6
District 28	449	25.5	16.1	254 951	23 057	9.0	231 894	22.1	15.7	16.9

1. Specified renter-occupied units.   2. Overcrowded or lacking complete plumbing facilities.   3. Percent of total civilian labor force.   4. Persons 16 years old and over.   5. Persons 16 to 64 years old.   Note: Data were tabulated for the 108th Congress and some boundary changes have occurred.

Table E. Congressional Districts 109th Congress — Land Area and Population

STATE District	Representative	Land area,[1] 2000 (sq km)	Total persons	Per square kilometer	White	Black	Am. Indian, Alaska Native	Asian and Pacific Islander	Other race	Hispanic or Latino[2]	Non-Hispanic White	Two or more races	Under 5 years	5 to 17 years	18 to 24 years
		1	2	3	4	5	6	7	8	9	10	11	12	13	14
TEXAS—Cont'd															
District 29	Gene Green (D)	618	651 620	1 054.6	54.1	15.3	1.0	2.6	30.6	62.2	20.0	3.6	9.9	23.3	12.5
District 30	Eddie Bernice Johnson (D)	748	651 620	871.5	40.8	41.4	0.9	2.7	16.6	31.1	24.7	2.4	8.4	21.0	11.5
District 31	John Carter (R)	13 038	651 620	50.0	79.8	9.6	0.9	3.7	8.3	16.9	69.4	2.1	7.7	20.4	13.9
District 32	Pete Sessions (R)	427	651 619	1 527.6	71.6	9.7	0.9	7.1	13.5	27.4	55.2	2.8	7.5	15.8	11.1
UTAH		212 751	2 233 169	10.5	91.1	1.1	1.8	3.2	5.1	9.0	85.3	2.1	9.4	22.8	14.2
District 1	Rob Bishop (R)	53 790	744 389	13.8	89.9	1.6	1.4	3.0	6.4	11.1	83.3	2.3	9.4	22.9	13.5
District 2	Jim Matheson (D)	118 166	744 390	6.3	92.6	0.9	2.8	2.6	3.2	5.9	88.0	1.9	8.3	21.3	12.6
District 3	Chris Cannon (R)	40 795	744 390	18.2	90.8	0.8	1.2	3.8	5.7	10.0	84.5	2.2	10.4	24.1	16.6
VERMONT		23 956	608 827	25.4	97.9	0.7	1.1	1.2	0.4	0.9	96.2	1.2	5.6	18.6	9.3
At Large	Bernie Sanders (I)	23 956	608 827	25.4	97.9	0.7	1.1	1.1	0.4	0.9	96.2	1.2	5.6	18.6	9.3
VIRGINIA		102 548	7 078 515	69.0	73.9	20.4	0.7	4.4	2.7	4.7	70.2	2.0	6.5	18.0	9.6
District 1	Jo Ann Davis (R)	9 771	643 514	65.9	77.7	19.5	1.0	2.4	1.5	3.0	74.7	2.0	6.8	19.7	9.1
District 2	Thelma Sawyers Drake (R)	2 489	643 510	258.5	71.3	22.8	1.1	5.3	2.4	4.4	67.4	2.6	6.9	18.8	12.3
District 3	Robert C. "Bobby" Scott (D)	2 895	643 476	222.2	39.8	57.5	1.1	2.0	1.7	2.6	37.7	1.9	7.0	18.9	11.9
District 4	J. Randy Forbes (R)	11 626	643 477	55.3	63.9	33.9	0.7	1.8	1.1	2.0	62.0	1.3	6.7	20.0	8.4
District 5	Virgil H. Goode Jr. (I)	23 108	643 497	27.8	74.0	24.5	0.5	1.2	0.8	1.6	72.4	1.0	5.7	16.9	9.7
District 6	Bob Goodlatte (R)	14 625	643 504	44.0	86.9	11.5	0.6	1.3	1.1	2.0	84.8	1.2	5.7	16.6	11.0
District 7	Eric Cantor (R)	9 102	643 499	70.7	80.1	16.7	0.6	2.7	1.2	2.0	78.2	1.2	6.4	18.6	7.6
District 8	Jim Moran (D)	319	643 503	2 017.8	67.9	14.8	0.8	11.1	10.0	16.4	57.1	4.4	6.4	13.3	8.9
District 9	Rick Boucher (D)	22 801	643 514	28.2	94.7	4.1	0.5	1.0	0.6	1.1	93.3	0.8	5.3	15.5	11.9
District 10	Frank Wolf (R)	4 808	643 512	133.9	82.8	7.5	0.6	7.7	4.1	7.1	77.2	2.5	8.0	20.2	7.1
District 11	Tom Davis (R)	1 004	643 509	640.8	74.2	11.1	0.7	12.5	5.0	9.1	66.8	3.4	7.0	20.0	7.6
WASHINGTON		172 348	5 894 121	34.2	84.9	4.0	2.7	7.4	4.9	7.5	78.9	3.6	6.7	19.0	9.5
District 1	Jay Inslee (D)	1 138	654 904	575.7	86.8	2.5	1.8	10.2	2.5	4.3	81.6	3.5	6.5	19.0	8.2
District 2	Rick Larsen (D)	17 002	654 903	38.5	90.6	1.6	3.1	4.3	3.6	5.8	85.6	2.9	6.8	19.7	9.9
District 3	Brian Baird (D)	19 465	654 898	33.6	92.5	1.7	2.3	4.0	2.7	4.6	87.7	2.9	7.0	20.2	8.6
District 4	Doc Hastings (R)	49 343	654 901	13.3	78.4	1.3	3.1	2.0	18.4	26.4	67.8	3.0	8.1	22.3	9.9
District 5	Cathy Anne McMorris (R)	59 217	654 900	11.1	92.2	1.8	3.5	2.7	2.7	4.5	87.7	2.7	6.3	19.1	11.4
District 6	Norm Dicks (D)	17 564	654 902	37.3	83.8	7.0	4.0	7.2	3.1	5.1	77.7	4.8	6.4	18.6	9.4
District 7	Jim McDermott (D)	366	654 902	1 789.3	72.6	9.9	2.2	16.2	4.1	5.8	66.9	4.6	4.9	12.1	11.3
District 8	David G. Reichert (R)	6 680	654 905	98.0	86.9	2.7	1.7	9.8	2.4	4.0	82.1	3.2	6.9	20.8	7.0
District 9	Adam Smith (D)	1 574	654 902	416.1	80.1	7.9	2.6	10.6	4.3	6.7	73.3	5.0	7.2	19.1	9.7
WEST VIRGINIA		62 361	1 808 344	29.0	95.9	3.5	0.6	0.7	0.3	0.7	94.6	0.9	5.6	16.6	9.5
District 1	Alan B. Mollohan (D)	16 281	602 545	37.0	97.1	2.0	0.5	0.9	0.3	0.7	95.8	0.8	5.4	16.4	10.6
District 2	Shelley Moore Capito (R)	21 909	602 243	27.5	95.3	4.0	0.6	0.7	0.4	0.8	93.9	1.0	5.9	17.2	8.4
District 3	Nick Rahall (D)	24 170	603 556	25.0	95.1	4.4	0.6	0.5	0.2	0.6	93.9	0.8	5.6	16.3	9.6
WISCONSIN		140 663	5 363 675	38.1	90.0	6.1	1.3	2.0	2.0	3.6	87.3	1.2	6.4	19.1	9.7
District 1	Paul Ryan (R)	4 351	670 458	154.1	91.4	5.2	0.7	1.3	3.0	5.7	87.4	1.4	6.6	19.5	8.2
District 2	Tammy Baldwin (D)	9 095	670 457	73.7	92.0	4.2	0.8	2.8	1.8	3.4	89.0	1.6	6.1	17.3	12.8
District 3	Ron Kind (D)	35 134	670 462	19.1	97.3	0.7	0.9	1.5	0.5	0.9	96.1	0.8	6.1	19.2	11.9
District 4	Gwendolynn Moore (D)	290	670 458	2 313.4	56.8	34.6	1.5	3.3	6.7	11.2	50.4	2.6	7.8	20.2	11.8
District 5	James Sensenbrenner (R)	3 298	670 458	203.3	96.1	1.6	0.5	1.8	1.0	2.2	94.0	0.9	6.3	19.1	6.8
District 6	Tom Petri (R)	14 611	670 440	45.9	96.1	1.2	0.7	1.8	1.1	2.3	94.1	0.8	6.0	18.8	9.0
District 7	Dave Obey (D)	48 657	670 462	13.8	96.3	0.4	2.0	1.8	0.4	0.9	95.1	0.8	5.9	19.4	8.5
District 8	Mark Green (R)	25 228	670 480	26.6	94.1	0.9	3.3	1.7	1.2	2.2	92.2	1.0	6.3	19.5	8.5
WYOMING		251 489	493 782	2.0	93.7	1.0	3.0	0.9	3.2	6.4	88.9	1.8	6.3	19.8	10.1
At Large	Barbara Cubin (R)	251 489	493 782	2.0	93.7	1.0	3.0	1.0	3.2	6.4	88.9	1.8	6.3	19.8	10.1

1. Dry land or land partially or temporarily covered by water. have occurred.   2. Hispanic or Latino persons may be of any race.   Note: Data were tabulated for the 108th Congress and some boundary changes

STATE District	25 to 34 years	35 to 44 years	45 to 54 years	55 to 64 years	65 to 74 years	75 years and over	Percent female	Number	Persons per house-hold	Female family house-holder[1]	One person	Persons in correctional institutions, 2000	Persons in nursing homes, 2000	Persons in military quarters, 2000	Public	Private
	15	16	17	18	19	20	21	22	23	24	25	26	27	28	29	30
TEXAS—Cont'd																
District 29	17.1	14.7	10.5	5.9	3.7	2.5	49.2	195 942	3.30	16.4	18.7	1 454	889	0	180 980	11 424
District 30	17.4	15.4	11.3	7.0	4.6	3.5	50.6	221 920	2.85	20.6	25.2	10 696	2 639	0	159 925	19 334
District 31	15.0	16.9	12.4	6.4	3.9	3.3	50.1	227 470	2.76	9.9	19.9	4 223	2 922	0	197 559	21 714
District 32	21.0	16.9	12.2	7.1	4.5	3.9	49.0	272 466	2.37	9.0	35.6	13	2 386	0	120 375	37 518
UTAH	14.6	13.4	10.6	6.4	4.5	4.0	49.9	701 281	3.13	9.4	17.8	9 921	6 853	1 760	645 683	95 841
District 1	14.7	13.9	10.7	6.3	4.6	4.0	49.7	238 393	3.07	9.5	19.0	1 483	2 417	1 760	222 739	17 214
District 2	14.0	13.7	11.8	7.4	5.6	5.2	50.0	252 582	2.89	9.2	20.9	6 732	3 113	0	206 225	25 703
District 3	15.3	12.6	9.5	5.4	3.4	2.7	50.0	210 306	3.48	9.5	12.6	1 706	1 323	0	216 719	52 924
VERMONT	12.2	16.7	15.4	9.3	6.7	6.0	51.0	240 634	2.44	9.3	26.2	1 219	4 037	22	134 366	29 790
At Large	12.2	16.7	15.4	9.3	6.7	6.0	51.0	240 634	2.44	9.3	26.2	1 219	4 037	22	134 366	29 790
VIRGINIA	14.6	17.0	14.1	8.9	6.1	5.1	51.0	2 699 173	2.54	11.9	25.1	64 036	38 865	33 752	1 566 180	301 921
District 1	13.2	17.3	13.6	9.0	6.2	5.0	51.0	237 802	2.63	10.7	21.6	2 627	3 397	2 927	152 979	25 224
District 2	16.0	17.2	12.2	7.3	5.3	4.1	49.2	231 695	2.62	12.8	22.7	9 271	2 664	20 694	147 310	27 570
District 3	14.9	15.6	12.5	7.8	6.1	5.5	52.3	250 285	2.46	21.7	29.6	7 809	3 562	5 185	156 845	23 205
District 4	13.5	17.8	14.0	8.9	6.0	4.7	50.8	231 868	2.66	14.8	20.9	14 067	3 133	3 008	150 300	23 228
District 5	12.7	15.6	14.3	10.4	8.1	6.7	51.5	253 987	2.42	12.5	26.5	10 311	4 415	0	141 252	20 110
District 6	12.5	15.3	14.1	9.8	7.8	7.2	51.9	254 318	2.40	11.2	27.4	4 458	6 376	0	132 731	31 676
District 7	13.8	17.4	15.1	9.0	6.5	5.6	51.8	252 155	2.50	10.5	25.1	3 854	4 265	0	134 185	30 232
District 8	22.0	18.0	14.3	8.2	4.6	4.3	50.6	277 891	2.29	8.8	36.0	926	2 774	1 795	109 080	38 856
District 9	13.1	14.7	14.3	10.7	8.0	6.6	50.8	259 819	2.38	10.0	26.0	5 731	3 874	2	149 387	11 468
District 10	15.4	19.3	14.6	8.0	4.2	3.2	50.3	228 147	2.80	8.6	19.3	1 222	2 381	77	140 401	35 406
District 11	14.1	18.4	16.3	9.1	4.5	3.1	50.4	221 206	2.87	8.9	17.2	3 760	2 024	64	151 710	34 946
WASHINGTON	14.3	16.5	14.4	8.4	5.7	5.5	50.2	2 271 398	2.53	9.9	26.2	28 871	23 275	13 868	1 368 232	216 469
District 1	14.6	18.1	15.7	8.3	4.9	4.6	50.3	250 896	2.57	8.7	23.7	3 679	1 858	879	148 527	26 913
District 2	13.3	16.3	14.1	8.3	5.9	5.7	50.1	247 485	2.59	9.4	23.7	1 119	2 115	3 365	158 437	19 155
District 3	13.0	16.1	14.8	9.0	6.0	5.5	50.4	249 440	2.59	10.2	23.6	2 290	2 405	13	153 377	19 443
District 4	12.8	14.7	12.9	8.1	5.8	5.4	49.8	228 850	2.82	10.6	22.3	2 498	2 657	9	172 943	15 545
District 5	12.3	15.2	14.1	8.7	6.4	6.5	50.6	253 206	2.48	10.3	27.4	6 122	3 706	698	164 605	27 026
District 6	12.7	15.5	14.2	9.3	7.1	6.8	50.7	259 477	2.45	11.7	27.7	6 116	3 235	2 049	144 753	23 212
District 7	20.6	17.0	14.6	7.6	5.3	6.5	50.1	292 364	2.15	8.7	38.9	3 394	3 074	232	124 602	35 784
District 8	13.7	19.1	15.2	8.4	4.8	4.0	50.0	240 770	2.70	8.3	20.0	36	1 158	0	153 370	27 219
District 9	15.3	17.0	13.6	8.1	5.3	4.7	49.9	248 910	2.56	11.3	25.5	3 617	3 067	6 623	147 618	22 172
WEST VIRGINIA	12.7	15.1	15.0	10.2	8.2	7.1	51.4	736 481	2.40	10.7	27.1	10 505	11 601	59	380 827	37 726
District 1	12.4	14.7	14.5	10.2	8.2	7.6	51.5	245 352	2.38	10.2	27.7	2 416	4 578	0	135 371	14 451
District 2	12.8	15.8	15.0	10.3	8.0	6.6	51.2	244 587	2.42	10.6	26.5	2 212	3 380	59	120 399	13 844
District 3	12.7	14.7	15.3	10.2	8.5	7.1	51.5	246 542	2.39	11.5	27.1	5 877	3 643	0	125 057	9 431
WISCONSIN	13.2	16.3	13.7	8.5	6.6	6.5	50.6	2 084 544	2.50	9.6	26.8	31 068	41 370	82	1 209 333	253 705
District 1	13.2	17.3	14.1	8.7	6.4	5.9	50.5	254 833	2.57	10.0	24.6	5 713	4 116	5	144 956	33 764
District 2	14.8	16.3	13.9	7.7	5.5	5.4	50.6	267 178	2.42	8.3	28.1	3 069	3 941	0	175 523	22 211
District 3	12.1	15.4	13.4	8.4	6.7	6.8	50.3	254 507	2.53	7.8	25.6	2 696	6 088	52	168 635	23 061
District 4	15.7	14.7	11.6	6.7	5.7	5.7	52.1	264 201	2.47	19.9	33.7	2 152	4 151	13	155 651	46 756
District 5	12.2	17.5	15.2	9.3	7.0	6.7	51.2	261 618	2.52	7.2	24.6	1 053	5 384	0	131 661	44 848
District 6	12.8	16.6	13.6	8.9	7.2	7.1	49.9	258 247	2.49	7.6	25.8	11 286	5 797	3	138 927	32 289
District 7	11.6	16.0	13.9	9.5	7.6	7.6	50.3	263 671	2.49	8.0	26.0	1 484	5 985	2	150 432	21 256
District 8	13.0	16.7	13.5	9.0	6.9	6.6	50.2	260 289	2.51	8.0	25.5	3 615	5 908	7	143 548	29 520
WYOMING	12.1	16.0	15.0	9.0	6.3	5.3	49.7	193 608	2.48	8.7	26.3	4 176	2 869	545	126 439	9 700
At Large	12.1	16.0	15.0	9.0	6.3	5.3	49.7	193 608	2.48	8.7	26.3	4 176	2 869	545	126 439	9 700

1. No spouse present. 2. All persons 3 years old and over enrolled in nursery school through college. Note: Data were tabulated for the 108th Congress and some boundary changes have occurred.

STATE District	Education, 2000 (cont'd) Attainment[1] (percent) High school graduate or more	Bachelor's degree or more	Money income, 1999 Per capita income[2]	Households Median income	Percent with income of $100,000 or more	Percent below poverty level, 1999 Persons Total	Families Total	Housing units, 2000 Total	Occupied units Total	Owner-occupied Percent	Median value[3] (dollars)	Owner cost as a percent of income With a mortgage	Without a mortgage[4]
	31	32	33	34	35	36	37	38	39	40	41	42	43
TEXAS—Cont'd													
District 29	52.3	8.1	12 493	32 128	4.6	21.5	18.8	211 731	195 953	53.0	56 400	20.5	11.2
District 30	66.9	16.3	16 321	35 612	7.2	19.1	15.9	236 861	222 064	49.5	71 400	21.3	12.1
District 31	84.5	31.6	21 619	50 252	15.7	11.3	6.8	244 828	227 320	69.1	111 300	19.9	10.3
District 32	82.1	43.2	32 700	48 848	20.7	11.3	8.3	289 659	272 711	42.9	166 400	20.3	10.9
UTAH	87.7	26.1	18 185	45 726	11.2	9.4	6.5	768 594	701 281	71.5	146 100	22.9	9.9
District 1	86.7	24.7	18 151	45 058	10.4	9.5	6.6	261 937	238 384	70.8	137 800	22.6	9.9
District 2	89.4	30.9	20 725	45 583	13.5	9.0	6.6	285 074	252 500	70.6	164 500	22.5	9.9
District 3	86.9	22.1	15 679	46 568	9.2	9.7	6.2	221 583	210 397	73.5	140 700	23.5	9.9
VERMONT	86.4	29.4	20 625	40 856	8.7	9.4	6.3	294 382	240 634	70.6	111 500	22.4	13.9
At Large	86.4	29.4	20 625	40 856	8.7	9.4	6.3	294 382	240 634	70.6	111 500	22.4	13.9
VIRGINIA	81.5	29.5	23 975	46 677	15.1	9.6	7.0	2 904 192	2 699 173	68.1	125 400	21.4	9.9
District 1	84.6	26.8	22 918	50 257	13.7	6.7	4.8	261 616	237 490	72.7	131 400	21.9	9.9
District 2	87.5	25.5	21 371	44 193	10.5	8.7	6.6	249 962	231 653	63.5	113 900	23.6	10.7
District 3	75.1	17.2	16 870	32 238	5.5	18.9	15.3	272 317	250 417	52.1	83 600	23.1	11.9
District 4	78.5	19.6	20 085	45 249	10.2	9.5	7.6	246 716	231 889	73.5	105 700	22.1	9.9
District 5	72.4	19.0	18 919	35 739	7.2	13.2	9.2	287 779	253 996	72.4	92 900	20.3	9.9
District 6	77.6	20.8	19 544	37 773	7.7	11.0	7.3	275 234	254 321	69.2	99 500	20.5	9.9
District 7	84.9	33.2	25 861	50 990	15.9	6.1	4.4	267 394	252 282	72.9	128 800	20.8	9.9
District 8	87.1	53.8	35 613	63 430	26.1	7.5	5.2	288 494	277 916	50.1	227 500	20.6	9.9
District 9	68.7	14.0	16 336	29 783	4.5	16.2	11.2	290 839	259 829	74.2	75 700	19.7	9.9
District 10	88.2	43.1	32 933	71 560	31.0	4.4	2.8	237 654	228 202	75.4	189 900	21.3	9.9
District 11	91.7	48.9	33 268	80 397	36.3	3.8	2.5	226 187	221 178	76.6	210 300	20.9	9.9
WASHINGTON	87.1	27.7	22 973	45 776	12.6	10.6	7.3	2 451 075	2 271 398	64.6	168 300	23.8	10.4
District 1	92.8	36.4	28 011	58 565	19.3	5.6	3.8	261 949	250 775	67.9	229 300	24.2	10.6
District 2	87.3	22.4	21 331	45 441	10.3	10.0	6.6	275 632	247 566	67.2	170 900	24.9	10.9
District 3	86.4	21.4	20 718	44 426	10.1	10.5	7.7	271 188	249 432	67.9	147 400	23.7	9.9
District 4	75.2	18.7	17 355	37 764	8.1	16.2	12.0	253 517	228 819	66.0	119 200	21.9	9.9
District 5	87.1	23.8	18 086	35 720	7.0	14.4	9.6	279 931	253 204	66.0	110 800	22.7	9.9
District 6	85.8	20.1	19 740	39 205	7.9	13.2	9.5	290 042	259 518	63.3	133 300	23.8	11.0
District 7	88.5	44.1	29 099	45 864	15.3	11.5	7.0	306 241	292 385	50.5	242 800	24.2	11.3
District 8	92.1	37.4	30 536	63 854	24.0	5.1	3.5	251 807	240 810	75.6	237 700	24.0	10.2
District 9	87.4	22.3	21 879	46 495	10.8	9.2	6.7	260 768	248 889	59.6	160 500	23.7	10.5
WEST VIRGINIA	75.2	14.8	16 477	29 696	5.0	17.9	13.9	844 623	736 481	75.2	72 800	19.5	9.9
District 1	79.4	16.3	16 511	30 303	5.0	17.0	12.3	277 962	245 352	74.0	71 000	19.3	9.9
District 2	76.9	16.2	17 872	33 198	6.2	14.8	11.6	280 581	244 587	75.5	83 900	19.2	9.9
District 3	69.4	12.0	15 053	25 630	3.9	21.9	17.7	286 080	246 542	76.0	63 300	20.0	9.9
WISCONSIN	85.1	22.4	21 271	43 791	9.4	8.7	5.6	2 321 144	2 084 544	68.4	112 200	20.9	11.2
District 1	85.4	21.5	22 730	50 372	11.8	6.3	4.3	275 814	254 793	70.8	127 100	21.3	11.8
District 2	89.1	32.1	23 246	46 979	11.2	8.7	4.2	281 854	267 211	62.3	134 600	22.1	11.0
District 3	85.5	19.5	18 786	40 006	7.0	9.8	6.5	276 405	254 520	72.1	91 400	20.3	10.9
District 4	75.8	17.8	16 607	33 121	4.8	19.8	15.9	282 806	264 190	46.6	84 200	21.0	12.5
District 5	90.9	35.0	29 064	58 594	19.3	3.4	2.2	271 491	261 626	73.4	161 700	21.4	11.6
District 6	84.0	17.1	20 506	44 242	7.1	6.1	3.8	287 232	258 274	73.4	99 100	20.4	11.1
District 7	83.8	16.6	18 749	39 026	6.1	8.6	5.7	323 333	263 682	76.1	86 100	19.5	10.5
District 8	85.3	19.1	20 480	43 274	8.1	6.8	4.6	322 209	260 248	73.4	103 600	20.4	11.0
WYOMING	87.9	21.9	19 134	37 892	6.7	11.4	8.0	223 854	193 608	70.0	96 600	19.7	9.9
At Large	87.9	21.9	19 134	37 892	6.7	11.4	8.0	223 854	193 608	70.0	96 600	19.7	9.9

1. Persons 25 years old and over.   2. Based on the population enumerated as of April 1, 2000.   3. Specified owner-occupied units.   4. Median monthly owner costs is often in the minimum category—9.9 percent or less, which is indicated as 9.9 percent.   Note: Data were tabulated for the 108th Congress and some boundary changes have occurred.

Table E. Congressional Districts 109th Congress — **Housing, Labor Force, and Employment**

STATE District	Housing units, 2000 (cont'd) Occupied units (cont'd) Renter-occupied — Median rent[1] (dollars)	Rent as a percent of income	Substandard units[2] (percent)	Civilian labor force, 2000 — Total	Unemployment Total	Rate[3]	Civilian employment,[4] 2000 Total	Percent — Management, professional, and related occupations	Production, transportation, and material moving occupations	Disability, 2000 — Employment disabled persons[5] (percent)
	44	45	46	47	48	49	50	51	52	53
TEXAS—Cont'd										
District 29	511	24.1	24.4	267 614	23 651	8.8	243 963	16.7	20.6	17.8
District 30	605	24.8	16.8	301 409	24 012	8.0	277 397	25.6	16.8	17.4
District 31	635	28.0	5.9	338 040	16 927	5.0	321 113	40.1	10.5	8.5
District 32	693	23.4	11.5	365 797	15 457	4.2	350 340	43.4	8.8	11.6
UTAH	597	24.9	6.3	1 098 923	54 561	5.0	1 044 362	32.5	13.5	8.9
District 1	563	25.2	6.2	367 461	19 934	5.4	347 527	31.3	15.6	9.3
District 2	621	24.4	5.2	368 080	16 879	4.6	351 201	36.0	10.3	8.7
District 3	613	25.5	7.7	363 382	17 748	4.9	345 634	30.1	14.8	8.6
VERMONT	553	26.2	2.0	331 131	13 997	4.2	317 134	36.3	14.0	9.7
At Large	553	26.2	2.0	331 131	13 997	4.2	317 134	36.3	14.0	9.7
VIRGINIA	650	24.5	3.9	3 563 772	151 125	4.2	3 412 647	38.2	12.5	10.9
District 1	671	24.4	2.9	316 021	14 531	4.6	301 490	36.7	11.0	9.6
District 2	677	26.1	3.8	293 350	14 711	5.0	278 639	34.0	10.6	10.6
District 3	535	27.4	4.9	295 625	23 330	7.9	272 295	27.8	15.5	14.3
District 4	568	24.9	3.2	305 287	13 428	4.4	291 859	31.4	15.7	12.7
District 5	469	24.0	3.4	308 990	15 727	5.1	293 263	29.3	20.4	13.0
District 6	478	23.4	2.5	325 347	14 280	4.4	311 067	29.3	18.5	11.6
District 7	667	23.9	2.4	342 769	9 501	2.8	333 268	39.8	10.1	9.4
District 8	899	23.4	8.5	381 816	11 499	3.0	370 317	55.9	4.7	9.6
District 9	403	24.7	2.6	291 961	16 508	5.7	275 453	26.2	23.1	14.4
District 10	883	23.8	3.4	354 174	8 374	2.4	345 800	48.2	7.6	8.1
District 11	988	23.5	4.4	348 432	9 236	2.7	339 196	52.1	5.2	6.9
WASHINGTON	663	26.5	5.5	2 979 824	186 102	6.2	2 793 722	35.6	12.7	10.6
District 1	841	25.4	3.9	351 321	13 377	3.8	337 944	42.5	9.3	8.7
District 2	675	27.5	5.2	324 602	20 927	6.4	303 675	30.0	14.9	10.0
District 3	634	26.6	4.6	322 188	20 812	6.5	301 376	30.9	15.9	11.1
District 4	527	26.3	11.1	304 106	29 402	9.7	274 704	30.1	14.5	12.5
District 5	509	27.7	4.4	316 391	26 851	8.5	289 540	33.5	12.3	10.9
District 6	589	27.3	5.1	300 480	22 484	7.5	277 996	29.5	13.9	12.5
District 7	718	26.6	6.0	385 486	19 970	5.2	365 516	46.3	9.2	9.9
District 8	848	25.2	3.7	347 381	13 906	4.0	333 475	41.7	11.1	8.7
District 9	690	25.8	6.2	327 869	18 373	5.6	309 496	30.6	14.5	11.3
WEST VIRGINIA	401	25.8	2.3	790 694	58 021	7.3	732 673	27.9	16.4	13.2
District 1	402	26.8	1.9	274 428	20 115	7.3	254 313	28.4	16.8	10.8
District 2	430	23.9	2.4	279 072	16 512	5.9	262 560	29.1	17.0	12.8
District 3	374	27.1	2.6	237 194	21 394	9.0	215 800	25.9	15.2	16.0
WISCONSIN	540	23.4	2.8	2 869 236	134 311	4.7	2 734 925	31.3	19.8	9.1
District 1	602	23.4	2.6	358 046	16 558	4.6	341 488	31.0	20.0	9.0
District 2	614	24.9	2.8	389 553	16 797	4.3	372 756	37.9	14.5	7.6
District 3	464	22.7	2.6	364 522	16 358	4.5	348 164	29.6	20.1	8.9
District 4	529	25.3	6.2	322 788	28 492	8.8	294 296	27.5	21.2	13.7
District 5	674	22.7	1.5	368 809	9 976	2.7	358 833	40.9	14.1	6.7
District 6	490	21.0	2.0	359 115	13 403	3.7	345 712	26.4	26.3	8.1
District 7	439	22.7	2.6	350 415	18 474	5.3	331 941	27.3	22.0	9.8
District 8	498	21.8	2.4	355 988	14 253	4.0	341 735	28.6	21.0	8.9
WYOMING	437	22.5	3.2	254 508	13 453	5.3	241 055	30.0	12.8	9.8
At Large	437	22.5	3.2	254 508	13 453	5.3	241 055	30.0	12.8	9.8

1. Specified renter-occupied units.   2. Overcrowded or lacking complete plumbing facilities.   3. Percent of total civilian labor force.   4. Persons 16 years old and over.   5. Persons 16 to 64 years old.   Note: Data were tabulated for the 108th Congress and some boundary changes have occurred.

Appendices

APPENDIX A
GEOGRAPHIC CONCEPTS AND CODES

AREAS FOR WHICH DATA ARE PRESENTED

County and City Extra presents data for States (Table A), States and Counties (Table B), Metropolitan Areas (Table C), Cities (Table D), and Congressional Districts (Table E).

STATES AND COUNTIES

Data are presented for each of the 50 states, the District of Columbia, and the United States as a whole. The states are arranged alphabetically, and in Table B counties are arranged alphabetically within each state.

Data are presented for 3,141 counties and county equivalents. Maps of each state, showing their counties and county equivalents are contained in Appendix D.

County equivalents

In Louisiana, the primary divisions of the state are known as parishes rather than counties. In Alaska, the county equivalents are the organized boroughs, together with the census areas that were developed for general statistical purposes by the State of Alaska and the U.S. Bureau of the Census. Four states—Maryland, Missouri, Nevada, and Virginia—have one or more incorporated places that are legally independent of any county and thus constitute primary divisions of their states. Within each state, independent cities are listed alphabetically following the list of counties. A list of independent cities is given at the end of this appendix. The District of Columbia is not divided into counties or county equivalents—data for the entire District are presented as a county equivalent. New York City contains five counties—Bronx, Kings, New York, Queens, and Richmond.

County changes since the 1990 Census

- Dade County in Florida officially became Miami-Dade County.
- Denali Borough in Alaska was formed primarily from the Yukon-Koyukuk census area and a small part of the Southeast Fairbanks census area.
- The Skagway-Yakutat-Angoon census area in Alaska was dissolved and replaced by Yakutat Borough and the Skagway-Hoonah-Angoon census area.
- South Boston City in Virginia, formerly an independent city, became a town within Halifax County.
- Yellowstone Park in Montana, which had not been part of any county, was dissolved as a county equivalent and became part of Park and Gallatin Counties.
- The city of Takoma Park, Maryland, formerly split between Montgomery and Prince George's Counties, moved its boundary, and now lies completely within Montgomery County.

County changes since the 2000 Census

Broomfield County, CO was created from parts of Adams, Boulder, Jefferson, and Weld Counties, effective November 15, 2001. The boundaries of Broomfield County reflect the boundaries of Broomfield city legally in effect on that date. In this volume, we have included as much data as possible. The 2003 population estimates and the 2003 Labor Force data both recognized Broomfield County. Because the 2000 census includes place parts within counties, we were able to subtract Broomfield city from the four counties that included parts of Broomfield city in 2000, resulting in unduplicated 2000 census data. For some other sources, such as the FBI crime data, there is duplication because it was possible to include Broomfield County by using the city data, but we could not subtract Broomfield city from the other four counties.

Clifton Forge City, VA, formerly an independent city, became a town within Alleghany County, effective July 1, 2001. Clifton Forge has been dropped from this volume. New data reflect the new designations. Where possible, we have included Clifton Forge data in the Alleghany County numbers on older data sources.

METROPOLITAN AREAS

Table C presents data for 361 Metropolitan Statistical Areas and 29 Metropolitan Divisions within the 11 largest Metropolitan Statistical Areas. These are newly defined areas and are not the same as the Metropolitan Areas included in previous editions of *County and City Extra* prior to 2003. The Metropolitan Statistical Areas are listed alphabetically, and the Metropolitan Divisions are listed alphabetically under the Metropolitan Statistical Area of which they are components.

The United States Office of Management and Budget (OMB) defines metropolitan and micropolitan statistical areas according to published standards. The major purpose of defining these areas is to enable all U.S. government agencies to use the same geographic definitions in tabulating and publishing data. The general concept of a metropolitan or micropolitan statistical area is that of a core area containing a substantial population nucleus, together with adjacent communities having a high degree of economic and social integration with that core. Currently defined metropolitan and micropolitan statistical areas are based on application of the new 2000 standards to 2000 decennial census data. Current metropolitan and micropolitan statistical area definitions were announced by OMB effective June 6, 2003, and revised December 2003.

Standard definitions of metropolitan areas were first issued in 1949 by the then Bureau of the Budget (predecessor of OMB), under the designation "standard metropolitan area" (SMA). The term was changed to "standard metropolitan statistical area" (SMSA) in 1959, and to "metropolitan statistical area" (MSA) in 1983. The term "metropolitan area" (MA) was adopted in 1990 and referred collectively to metropolitan statistical areas

(MSAs), consolidated metropolitan statistical areas (CMSAs), and primary metropolitan statistical areas (PMSAs). The term "core based statistical area" (CBSA) became effective in 2000 and refers collectively to metropolitan and micropolitan statistical areas.

The 2000 standards provide that each CBSA must contain at least one urban area of 10,000 or more population. Each metropolitan statistical area must have at least one urbanized area of 50,000 or more inhabitants. Each micropolitan statistical area must have at least one urban cluster of at least 10,000 but less than 50,000 population.

Under the standards, the county (or counties) in which at least 50 percent of the population resides within urban areas of 10,000 or more population, or that contain at least 5,000 people residing within a single urban area of 10,000 or more population, is identified as a "central county" (counties). Additional "outlying counties" are included in the CBSA if they meet specified requirements of commuting to or from the central counties. Counties or equivalent entities form the geographic "building blocks" for metropolitan and micropolitan statistical areas throughout the United States.

If specified criteria are met, a metropolitan statistical area containing a single core with a population of 2.5 million or more may be subdivided to form smaller groupings of counties referred to as "metropolitan divisions."

As of December 2003, there are 361 metropolitan statistical areas and 573 micropolitan statistical areas in the United States. Table C includes the 361 Metropolitan Statistical Areas and 29 Metropolitan Divisions. The original 362 Metropolitan Statistical Areas and 560 Micropolitan Statistical Areas, as of June 2003, are listed in Appendix C with their 2000 census populations.

The largest city in each metropolitan or micropolitan statistical area is designated a "principal city." Additional cities qualify if specified requirements are met concerning population size and employment. The title of each metropolitan or micropolitan statistical area consists of the names of up to three of its principal cities and the name of each state into which the metropolitan or micropolitan statistical area extends. Titles of metropolitan divisions also typically are based on principal city names but in certain cases consist of county names. The principal city need not be an incorporated place if it meets the requirements of population size and employment. Usually such a principal city is a Census Designated Place in decennial census data, but it is not included in most data sources and is not in Table D (cities) in this volume.

In view of the importance of cities and towns in New England, the 2000 standards also provide for a set of geographic areas that are defined using cities and towns in the six New England states. These New England city and town areas (NECTAs) are not included in this volume.

CITIES

Table D presents data for 1,237 cities with 2000 census populations of 25,000 or more. Corresponding data for states are also provided. The states are arranged alphabetically, and the cities are arranged alphabetically within each state.

As used in this volume, the term *city* refers to places that have been incorporated as cities, boroughs, towns, or villages under the laws of their respective states. Towns in the New England

states and New York are treated as minor civil divisions (MCDs) and are not included in the cities database. For Hawaii, data for census designated places (CDPs) are included in the cities table, since the U.S. Bureau of the Census does not recognize any incorporated places in Hawaii. CDPs are delineated by the U.S. Bureau of the Census, in cooperation with states and localities, as statistical counterparts of incorporated places for purposes of the decennial census. CDPs comprise densely settled concentrations of population that are identifiable by name but are not legally incorporated places.

A consolidated city is an incorporated place that has combined its governmental functions with a county or subcounty entity but contains one or more other semi-independent incorporated places that continue to function as local governments within the consolidated government. Consolidated cities included in this volume are Milford, CT; Athens-Clarke County, GA; Augusta-Richmond County, GA; Columbus, GA; Indianapolis, IN; Butte-Silver Bow, MT; and Nashville-Davidson, TN.

CONGRESSIONAL DISTRICTS

The congressional districts shown in this volume are the districts used for the election of the 109th Congress, which convened in January 2005. These are the districts that were established following the 2000 census and are based on population data from that census. Data are shown for the 435 regular districts, plus the District of Columbia, which has no representative. Corresponding data for each state are also included. States are listed alphabetically and districts numerically within each state. Table E includes the name and party affiliation of each representative in early 2005. A map showing congressional districts can be found in Appendix D. Some boundary changes have occurred since the 108th Congress but they are not reflected in this volume.

GEOGRAPHIC CODES

Tables A, B, C, and D provide, in one or more columns at the beginning of the table, a geographic code or codes for each area.

In Table B (States and Counties), a five-digit state and county code is given for each state and county. The first two digits indicate the state; the remaining three represent the county. Within each state the counties are numbered in alphabetical order, beginning with 001, with even numbers usually omitted. Independent cities follow the counties and begin with the number 510. In the second column of Table B, a five-digit Core Based Statistical Area (CBSA) code is given for those counties that are within metropolitan or micropolitan areas. In Table A, a two-digit state code is provided. The state code is a sequential numbering, with some gaps, of the states and the District of Columbia in alphabetical order from Alabama (01) to Wyoming (56).

These codes have been established by the U.S. government as Federal Information Processing Standards and are often referred to as *FIPS codes*. They are used by U.S. government agencies and many other organizations for data presentation. The codes are provided in this volume for use in matching the data given here with other data sources in which counties may be identified by FIPS code. The metro area codes will also enable the user to identify the metro area of which a county is a component. Table C

(Metropolitan Areas) provides the same metro area codes for each metropolitan area, as well as Metropolitan Division codes where appropriate.

Table D (Cities) provides, in the first column, a seven-digit state and place code. The first two digits identify the state and are the same as the state FIPS codes described above. The remaining five digits are the place FIPS codes established by the U.S. government.

INDEPENDENT CITIES

Independent cities are not included in any county; data are presented separately in this volume.

MARYLAND:
　　Baltimore:　(Separate from Baltimore County)

MISSOURI:
　　St. Louis:　(Separate from St. Louis County)

NEVADA:
　　Carson City

VIRGINIA:

Alexandria	Manassas
Bedford	Manassas Park
Bristol	Martinsville
Buena Vista	Newport News
Charlottesville	Norfolk
Chesapeake	Norton
Colonial Heights	Petersburg
Covington	Poquoson
Danville	Portsmouth
Emporia	Radford
Fairfax	Richmond
Falls Church	Roanoke
Franklin	Salem
Fredericksburg	Staunton
Galax	Suffolk
Hampton	Virginia Beach
Harrisonburg	Waynesboro
Hopewell	Williamsburg
Lexington	Winchester
Lynchburg	

COUNTY TYPE

Table B (States and Counties) provides, in the third column, a *county type* code that identifies each county by its metropolitan/nonmetropolitan status and its size. These are the "rural-urban continuum codes" developed by the Economic Research Service of the U.S. Department of Agriculture.

The 2003 Rural-Urban Continuum Codes form a classification scheme that distinguishes metropolitan counties by size and nonmetropolitan counties by degree of urbanization and proximity to metro areas. The standard Office of Management and Budget (OMB) metro and nonmetro categories have been subdivided into three metro and six nonmetro categories, resulting in a nine-part county codification. This scheme was originally developed in 1974. The codes were updated in 1983 and 1993, and slightly revised in 1988. The 1988 revision was first published in 1990. This scheme allows researchers to break county data into finer residential groups, beyond metro and nonmetro, particularly for the analysis of trends in nonmetro areas that are related to population density and metro influence. The 2003 Rural-Urban Continuum Codes are not directly comparable with the codes from previous years because of the new methodology used in developing the 2003 Metropolitan areas.

Metropolitan counties:
1. Counties in metro areas of 1 million population or more.
2. Counties in metro areas of 250,000 to 1 million population.
3. Counties in metro areas of fewer than 250,000 population.

Nonmetropolitan counties:
4. Urban population of 20,000 or more, adjacent to a metro area.
5. Urban population of 20,000 or more, not adjacent to a metro area.
6. Urban population of 2,500 to 19,999, adjacent to a metro area.
7. Urban population of 2,500 to 19,999, not adjacent to a metro area.
8. Completely rural or less than 2,500 urban population, adjacent to a metro area.
9. Completely rural or less than 2,500 urban population, not adjacent to a metro area.

APPENDIX B
METROPOLITAN STATISTICAL AREAS, METROPOLITAN DIVISIONS, AND COMPONENTS
(As of December 2003)

Core Based Statistical Area	State/County FIPS Code	Title and Geographic Components	2000 Census Population	Core Based Statistical Area	State/County FIPS Code	Title and Geographic Components	2000 Census Population
10180		Abilene, TX MSA	160 245	11500		Anniston-Oxford, AL MSA	112 249
	48 059	Callahan County, TX	12 905		01 015	Calhoun County, AL	112 249
	48 253	Jones County, TX	20 785	11540		Appleton, WI MSA	201 602
	48 441	Taylor County, TX	126 555		55 015	Calumet County, WI	40 631
10420		Akron, OH MSA	694 960		55 087	Outagamie County, WI	160 971
	39 133	Portage County, OH	152 061	11700		Asheville, NC MSA	369 171
	39 153	Summit County, OH	542 899		37 021	Buncombe County, NC	206 330
10500		Albany, GA MSA	157 833		37 087	Haywood County, NC	54 033
	13 007	Baker County, GA	4 074		37 089	Henderson County, NC	89 173
	13 095	Dougherty County, GA	96 065		37 115	Madison County, NC	19 635
	13 177	Lee County, GA	24 757	12020		Athens-Clarke County, GA MSA	166 079
	13 273	Terrell County, GA	10 970		13 059	Clarke County, GA	101 489
	13 321	Worth County, GA	21 967		13 195	Madison County, GA	25 730
10580		Albany-Schenectady-Troy, NY MSA	825 875		13 219	Oconee County, GA	26 225
	36 001	Albany County, NY	294 565		13 221	Oglethorpe County, GA	12 635
	36 083	Rensselaer County, NY	152 538	12060		Atlanta-Sandy Springs-Marietta, GA MSA	4 247 981
	36 091	Saratoga County, NY	200 635		13 013	Barrow County, GA	46 144
	36 093	Schenectady County, NY	146 555		13 015	Bartow County, GA	76 019
	36 095	Schoharie County, NY	31 582		13 035	Butts County, GA	19 522
10740		Albuquerque, NM MSA	729 649		13 045	Carroll County, GA	87 268
	35 001	Bernalillo County, NM	556 678		13 057	Cherokee County, GA	141 903
	35 043	Sandoval County, NM	89 908		13 063	Clayton County, GA	236 517
	35 057	Torrance County, NM	16 911		13 067	Cobb County, GA	607 751
	35 061	Valencia County, NM	66 152		13 077	Coweta County, GA	89 215
10780		Alexandria, LA MSA	145 035		13 085	Dawson County, GA	15 999
	22 043	Grant Parish, LA	18 698		13 089	DeKalb County, GA	665 865
	22 079	Rapides Parish, LA	126 337		13 097	Douglas County, GA	92 174
10900		Allentown-Bethlehem-Easton, PA-NJ MSA	740 395		13 113	Fayette County, GA	91 263
	34 041	Warren County, NJ	102 437		13 117	Forsyth County, GA	98 407
	42 025	Carbon County, PA	58 802		13 121	Fulton County, GA	816 006
	42 077	Lehigh County, PA	312 090		13 135	Gwinnett County, GA	588 448
	42 095	Northampton County, PA	267 066		13 143	Haralson County, GA	25 690
11020		Altoona, PA MSA	129 144		13 149	Heard County, GA	11 012
	42 013	Blair County, PA	129 144		13 151	Henry County, GA	119 341
11100		Amarillo, TX MSA	226 522		13 159	Jasper County, GA	11 426
	48 011	Armstrong County, TX	2 148		13 171	Lamar County, GA	15 912
	48 065	Carson County, TX	6 516		13 199	Meriwether County, GA	22 534
	48 375	Potter County, TX	113 546		13 217	Newton County, GA	62 001
	48 381	Randall County, TX	104 312		13 223	Paulding County, GA	81 678
11180		Ames, IA MSA	79 981		13 227	Pickens County, GA	22 983
	19 169	Story County, IA	79 981		13 231	Pike County, GA	13 688
11260		Anchorage, AK MSA	319 605		13 247	Rockdale County, GA	70 111
	02 020	Anchorage Municipality, AK	260 283		13 255	Spalding County, GA	58 417
	02 170	Matanuska-Susitna Borough, AK	59 322		13 297	Walton County, GA	60 687
11300		Anderson, IN MSA	133 358	12100		Atlantic City, NJ MSA	252 552
	18 095	Madison County, IN	133 358		34 001	Atlantic County, NJ	252 552
11340		Anderson, SC MSA	165 740	12220		Auburn-Opelika, AL MSA	115 092
	45 007	Anderson County, SC	165 740		01 081	Lee County, AL	115 092
11460		Ann Arbor, MI MSA	322 895	12260		Augusta-Richmond County, GA-SC MSA	499 684
	26 161	Washtenaw County, MI	322 895		13 033	Burke County, GA	22 243
					13 073	Columbia County, GA	89 288
					13 189	McDuffie County, GA	21 231
					13 245	Richmond County, GA	199 775
					45 003	Aiken County, SC	142 552
					45 037	Edgefield County, SC	24 595

Metropolitan Statistical Areas, Metropolitan Divisions, and Components (As of December 2003) – Continued

Core Based Statistical Area	State/County FIPS Code	Title and Geographic Components	2000 Census Population	Core Based Statistical Area	State/County FIPS Code	Title and Geographic Components	2000 Census Population
12420		Austin-Round Rock, TX MSA...............	1 249 763	13820		Birmingham-Hoover, AL MSA..........	1 052 238
	48 021	Bastrop County, TX	57 733		01 007	Bibb County, AL..........................	20 826
	48 055	Caldwell County, TX	32 194		01 009	Blount County, AL.......................	51 024
	48 209	Hays County, TX	97 589		01 021	Chilton County, AL......................	39 593
	48 453	Travis County, TX	812 280		01 073	Jefferson County, AL..................	662 047
	48 491	Williamson County, TX	249 967		01 115	St. Clair County, AL....................	64 742
12540		Bakersfield, CA MSA.......................	661 645		01 117	Shelby County, AL......................	143 293
	06 029	Kern County, CA............................	661 645		01 127	Walker County, AL......................	70 713
12580		Baltimore-Towson, MD MSA.............	2 552 994	13900		Bismarck, ND MSA	94 719
	24 003	Anne Arundel County, MD..............	489 656		38 015	Burleigh County, ND...................	69 416
	24 005	Baltimore County, MD....................	754 292		38 059	Morton County, ND.....................	25 303
	24 013	Carroll County, MD........................	150 897	13980		Blacksburg-Christiansburg-Radford, VA MSA .	151 272
	24 025	Harford County, MD.......................	218 590		51 071	Giles County, VA........................	16 657
	24 027	Howard County, MD.......................	247 842		51 121	Montgomery County, VA	83 629
	24 035	Queen Anne's County, MD.............	40 563		51 155	Pulaski County, VA......................	35 127
	24 510	Baltimore city, MD.........................	651 154		51 750	Radford city, VA.........................	15 859
12620		Bangor, ME MSA	144 919	14020		Bloomington, IN MSA...................	175 506
	23 019	Penobscot County, ME...................	144 919		18 055	Greene County, IN......................	33 157
12700		Barnstable Town, MA MSA..............	222 230		18 105	Monroe County, IN......................	120 563
	25 001	Barnstable County, MA...................	222 230		18 119	Owen County, IN........................	21 786
12940		Baton Rouge, LA MSA....................	705 973	14060		Bloomington-Normal, IL MSA.........	150 433
	22 005	Ascension Parish, LA	76 627		17 113	McLean County, IL......................	150 433
	22 033	East Baton Rouge Parish, LA	412 852	14260		Boise City-Nampa, ID MSA...........	464 840
	22 037	East Feliciana Parish, LA	21 360		16 001	Ada County, ID...........................	300 904
	22 047	Iberville Parish, LA........................	33 320		16 015	Boise County, ID........................	6 670
	22 063	Livingston Parish, LA.....................	91 814		16 027	Canyon County, ID......................	131 441
	22 077	Pointe Coupee Parish, LA	22 763		16 045	Gem County, ID..........................	15 181
	22 091	St. Helena Parish, LA....................	10 525		16 073	Owyhee County, ID.....................	10 644
	22 121	West Baton Rouge Parish, LA	21 601	14460		Boston-Cambridge-Quincy, MA-NH MSA	4 391 344
	22 125	West Feliciana Parish, LA	15 111			Essex County, MA Metro Div. 21604..............	723 419
12980		Battle Creek, MI MSA	137 985		25 009	Essex County, MA	723 419
	26 025	Calhoun County, MI.......................	137 985			Cambridge-Newton-Framingham, MA Metro Div. 15764	1 465 396
13020		Bay City, MI MSA...........................	110 157		25 017	Middlesex County, MA.................	1 465 396
	26 017	Bay County, MI.............................	110 157			Boston-Quincy, MA Metro Div. 14484..............	1 812 937
13140		Beaumont-Port Arthur, TX MSA.......	385 090		25 021	Norfolk County, MA	650 308
	48 199	Hardin County, TX	48 073		25 023	Plymouth County, MA..................	472 822
	48 245	Jefferson County, TX.....................	252 051		25 025	Suffolk County, MA.....................	689 807
	48 361	Orange County, TX........................	84 966			Rockingham County-Strafford County, NH Metro Div. 40484	389 592
13380		Bellingham, WA MSA......................	166 814		33 015	Rockingham County, NH...............	277 359
	53 073	Whatcom County, WA	166 814		33 017	Strafford County, NH	112 233
13460		Bend, OR MSA...............................	115 367	14500		Boulder, CO MSA........................	269 814
	41 017	Deschutes County, OR...................	115 367		08 013	Boulder County, CO	269 814
13740		Billings, MT MSA............................	138 904	14540		Bowling Green, KY MSA..............	104 166
	30 009	Carbon County, MT........................	9 552		21 061	Edmonson County, KY................	11 644
	30 111	Yellowstone County, MT.................	129 352		21 227	Warren County, KY......................	92 522
13780		Binghamton, NY MSA.....................	252 320	14740		Bremerton-Silverdale, WA MSA.....	231 969
	36 007	Broome County, NY........................	200 536		53 035	Kitsap County, WA	231 969
	36 107	Tioga County, NY..........................	51 784	14860		Bridgeport-Stamford-Norwalk, CT MSA..........	882 567
					09 001	Fairfield County, CT....................	882 567
				15180		Brownsville-Harlingen, TX MSA......	335 227
					48 061	Cameron County, TX...................	335 227

Core Based Statistical Area	State/ County FIPS Code	Title and Geographic Components	2000 Census Population	Core Based Statistical Area	State/ County FIPS Code	Title and Geographic Components	2000 Census Population
15260		Brunswick, GA MSA................................	93 044	16820		Charlottesville, VA MSA........................	174 021
	13 025	Brantley County, GA........................	14 629		51 003	Albemarle County, VA....................	79 236
	13 127	Glynn County, GA............................	67 568		51 065	Fluvanna County, VA......................	20 047
	13 191	McIntosh County, GA	10 847		51 079	Greene County, VA.........................	15 244
					51 125	Nelson County, VA..........................	14 445
15380		Buffalo-Niagara Falls, NY MSA.............	1 170 111		51 540	Charlottesville city, VA..................	45 049
	36 029	Erie County, NY...............................	950 265				
	36 063	Niagara County, NY.........................	219 846	16860		Chattanooga, TN-GA MSA......................	476 531
					13 047	Catoosa County, GA.......................	53 282
15500		Burlington, NC MSA..............................	130 800		13 083	Dade County, GA	15 154
	37 001	Alamance County, NC......................	130 800		13 295	Walker County, GA.........................	61 053
					47 065	Hamilton County, TN.......................	307 896
15540		Burlington-South Burlington, VT MSA.............	198 889		47 115	Marion County, TN..........................	27 776
	50 007	Chittenden County, VT	146 571		47 153	Sequatchie County, TN	11 370
	50 011	Franklin County, VT.........................	45 417				
	50 013	Grand Isle County, VT.....................	6 901	16940		Cheyenne, WY MSA	81 607
					56 021	Laramie County, WY	81 607
15940		Canton-Massillon, OH MSA	406 934				
	39 019	Carroll County, OH..........................	28 836	16980		Chicago-Naperville-Joliet, IL-IN-WI MSA........	9 098 316
	39 151	Stark County, OH............................	378 098			Chicago-Naperville-Joliet, IL Metro Div. 16974	7 628 412
15980		Cape Coral-Fort Myers, FL MSA	440 888		17 031	Cook County, IL...........................	5 376 741
	12 071	Lee County, FL...............................	440 888		17 037	DeKalb County, IL........................	88 969
					17 043	DuPage County, IL.......................	904 161
16180		Carson City, NV MSA	52 457		17 063	Grundy County, IL........................	37 535
	32 510	Carson City, NV..............................	52 457		17 089	Kane County, IL...........................	404 119
					17 093	Kendall County, IL........................	54 544
16220		Casper, WY MSA.................................	66 533		17 111	McHenry County, IL......................	260 077
	56 025	Natrona County, WY.........................	66 533		17 197	Will County, IL	502 266
						Lake County-Kenosha County, IL-WI Metro Div. 29404	793 933
16300		Cedar Rapids, IA MSA...........................	237 230		17 097	Lake County, IL............................	644 356
	19 011	Benton County, IA...........................	25 308		55 059	Kenosha County, WI......................	149 577
	19 105	Jones County, IA............................	20 221			Gary, IN Metro Div. 23844	675 971
	19 113	Linn County, IA..............................	191 701		18 073	Jasper County, IN.........................	30 043
					18 089	Lake County, IN...........................	484 564
16580		Champaign-Urbana, IL MSA	210 275		18 111	Newton County, IN........................	14 566
	17 019	Champaign County, IL......................	179 669		18 127	Porter County, IN.........................	146 798
	17 053	Ford County, IL..............................	14 241				
	17 147	Piatt County, IL..............................	16 365	17020		Chico, CA MSA...................................	203 171
					06 007	Butte County, CA..........................	203 171
16620		Charleston, WV MSA	309 635				
	54 005	Boone County, WV.........................	25 535	17140		Cincinnati-Middletown, OH-KY-IN MSA..........	2 009 632
	54 015	Clay County, WV............................	10 330		18 029	Dearborn County, IN.......................	46 109
	54 039	Kanawha County, WV	200 073		18 047	Franklin County, IN........................	22 151
	54 043	Lincoln County, WV........................	22 108		18 115	Ohio County, IN............................	5 623
	54 079	Putnam County, WV........................	51 589		21 015	Boone County, KY.........................	85 991
					21 023	Bracken County, KY	8 279
16700		Charleston-North Charleston, SC MSA	549 033		21 037	Campbell County, KY.....................	88 616
	45 015	Berkeley County, SC	142 651		21 077	Gallatin County, KY.......................	7 870
	45 019	Charleston County, SC....................	309 969		21 081	Grant County, KY..........................	22 384
	45 035	Dorchester County, SC....................	96 413		21 117	Kenton County, KY........................	151 464
					21 191	Pendleton County, KY....................	14 390
16740		Charlotte-Gastonia-Concord, NC-SC MSA......	1 330 448		39 015	Brown County, OH.........................	42 285
	37 007	Anson County, NC..........................	25 275		39 017	Butler County, OH.........................	332 807
	37 025	Cabarrus County, NC	131 063		39 025	Clermont County, OH.....................	177 977
	37 071	Gaston County, NC.........................	190 365		39 061	Hamilton County, OH......................	845 303
	37 119	Mecklenburg County, NC	695 454		39 165	Warren County, OH........................	158 383
	37 179	Union County, NC..........................	123 677				
	45 091	York County, SC............................	164 614	17300		Clarksville, TN-KY MSA.........................	232 000
					21 047	Christian County, KY	72 265
					21 221	Trigg County, KY	12 597
					47 125	Montgomery County, TN..................	134 768
					47 161	Stewart County, TN	12 370

Core Based Statistical Area	State/County FIPS Code	Title and Geographic Components	2000 Census Population
17420		Cleveland, TN MSA	104 015
	47 011	Bradley County, TN	87 965
	47 139	Polk County, TN	16 050
17460		Cleveland-Elyria-Mentor, OH MSA	2 148 143
	39 035	Cuyahoga County, OH	1 393 978
	39 055	Geauga County, OH	90 895
	39 085	Lake County, OH	227 511
	39 093	Lorain County, OH	284 664
	39 103	Medina County, OH	151 095
17660		Coeur d'Alene, ID MSA	108 685
	16 055	Kootenai County, ID	108 685
17780		College Station-Bryan, TX MSA	184 885
	48 041	Brazos County, TX	152 415
	48 051	Burleson County, TX	16 470
	48 395	Robertson County, TX	16 000
17820		Colorado Springs, CO MSA	537 484
	08 041	El Paso County, CO	516 929
	08 119	Teller County, CO	20 555
17860		Columbia, MO MSA	145 666
	29 019	Boone County, MO	135 454
	29 089	Howard County, MO	10 212
17900		Columbia, SC MSA	647 158
	45 017	Calhoun County, SC	15 185
	45 039	Fairfield County, SC	23 454
	45 055	Kershaw County, SC	52 647
	45 063	Lexington County, SC	216 014
	45 079	Richland County, SC	320 677
	45 081	Saluda County, SC	19 181
17980		Columbus, GA-AL MSA	281 768
	01 113	Russell County, AL	49 756
	13 053	Chattahoochee County, GA	14 882
	13 145	Harris County, GA	23 695
	13 197	Marion County, GA	7 144
	13 215	Muscogee County, GA	186 291
18020		Columbus, IN MSA	71 435
	18 005	Bartholomew County, IN	71 435
18140		Columbus, OH MSA	1 612 694
	39 041	Delaware County, OH	109 989
	39 045	Fairfield County, OH	122 759
	39 049	Franklin County, OH	1 068 978
	39 089	Licking County, OH	145 491
	39 097	Madison County, OH	40 213
	39 117	Morrow County, OH	31 628
	39 129	Pickaway County, OH	52 727
	39 159	Union County, OH	40 909
18580		Corpus Christi, TX MSA	403 280
	48 007	Aransas County, TX	22 497
	48 355	Nueces County, TX	313 645
	48 409	San Patricio County, TX	67 138
18700		Corvallis, OR MSA	78 153
	41 003	Benton County, OR	78 153
19060		Cumberland, MD-WV MSA	102 008
	24 001	Allegany County, MD	74 930
	54 057	Mineral County, WV	27 078
19100		Dallas-Fort Worth-Arlington, TX MSA	5 161 544
		Dallas-Plano-Irving, TX Metro Div. 19124	3 451 226
	48 085	Collin County, TX	491 675
	48 113	Dallas County, TX	2 218 899
	48 119	Delta County, TX	5 327
	48 121	Denton County, TX	432 976
	48 139	Ellis County, TX	111 360
	48 231	Hunt County, TX	76 596
	48 257	Kaufman County, TX	71 313
	48 397	Rockwall County, TX	43 080
		Fort Worth-Arlington, TX Metro Div. 23104	1 710 318
	48 251	Johnson County, TX	126 811
	48 367	Parker County, TX	88 495
	48 439	Tarrant County, TX	1 446 219
	48 497	Wise County, TX	48 793
19140		Dalton, GA MSA	120 031
	13 213	Murray County, GA	36 506
	13 313	Whitfield County, GA	83 525
19180		Danville, IL MSA	83 919
	17 183	Vermilion County, IL	83 919
19260		Danville, VA MSA	110 156
	51 143	Pittsylvania County, VA	61 745
	51 590	Danville city, VA	48 411
19340		Davenport-Moline-Rock Island, IA-IL MSA	376 019
	17 073	Henry County, IL	51 020
	17 131	Mercer County, IL	16 957
	17 161	Rock Island County, IL	149 374
	19 163	Scott County, IA	158 668
19380		Dayton, OH MSA	848 153
	39 057	Greene County, OH	147 886
	39 109	Miami County, OH	98 868
	39 113	Montgomery County, OH	559 062
	39 135	Preble County, OH	42 337
19460		Decatur, AL MSA	145 867
	01 079	Lawrence County, AL	34 803
	01 103	Morgan County, AL	111 064
19500		Decatur, IL MSA	114 706
	17 115	Macon County, IL	114 706
19660		Deltona-Daytona Beach-Ormond Beach, FL MSA	443 343
	12 127	Volusia County, FL	443 343

Core Based Statistical Area	State/ County FIPS Code	Title and Geographic Components	2000 Census Population	Core Based Statistical Area	State/ County FIPS Code	Title and Geographic Components	2000 Census Population
19740		Denver-Aurora, CO MSA	2 179 240	21140		Elkhart-Goshen, IN MSA	182 791
	08 001	Adams County, CO........................	348 618		18 039	Elkhart County, IN	182 791
	08 005	Arapahoe County, CO........................	487 967				
	08 014	Broomfield County, CO........................	38 272	21300		Elmira, NY MSA........................	91 070
	08 019	Clear Creek County, CO	9 322		36 015	Chemung County, NY........................	91 070
	08 031	Denver County, CO........................	554 636				
	08 035	Douglas County, CO........................	175 766	21340		El Paso, TX MSA........................	679 622
	08 039	Elbert County, CO	19 872		48 141	El Paso County, TX........................	679 622
	08 047	Gilpin County, CO........................	4 757				
	08 059	Jefferson County, CO........................	525 507	21500		Erie, PA MSA........................	280 843
	08 093	Park County, CO	14 523		42 049	Erie County, PA........................	280 843
19780		Des Moines, IA MSA........................	481 394	21660		Eugene-Springfield, OR MSA	322 959
	19 049	Dallas County, IA........................	40 750		41 039	Lane County, OR........................	322 959
	19 077	Guthrie County, IA........................	11 353				
	19 121	Madison County, IA........................	14 019	21780		Evansville, IN-KY MSA........................	342 815
	19 153	Polk County, IA........................	374 601		18 051	Gibson County, IN........................	32 500
	19 181	Warren County, IA........................	40 671		18 129	Posey County, IN........................	27 061
					18 163	Vanderburgh County, IN........................	171 922
19820		Detroit-Warren-Livonia, MI MSA	4 452 557		18 173	Warrick County, IN........................	52 383
		Warren-Farmington Hills-Troy, MI Metro Div. 47644	2 391 395		21 101	Henderson County, KY........................	44 829
	26 087	Lapeer County, MI	87 904		21 233	Webster County, KY	14 120
	26 093	Livingston County, MI	156 951	21820		Fairbanks, AK MSA........................	82 840
	26 099	Macomb County, MI	788 149		02 090	Fairbanks North Star Borough, AK........................	82 840
	26 125	Oakland County, MI	1 194 156				
	26 147	St. Clair County, MI	164 235	22020		Fargo, ND-MN MSA........................	174 367
		Detroit-Livonia-Dearborn, MI Metro Div. 19804	2 061 162		27 027	Clay County, MN........................	51 229
	26 163	Wayne County, MI	2 061 162		38 017	Cass County, ND........................	123 138
				22140		Farmington, NM MSA........................	113 801
20020		Dothan, AL MSA	130 861		35 045	San Juan County, NM	113 801
	01 061	Geneva County, AL	25 764				
	01 067	Henry County, AL	16 310	22180		Fayetteville, NC MSA........................	336 609
	01 069	Houston County, AL	88 787		37 051	Cumberland County, NC	302 963
					37 093	Hoke County, NC........................	33 646
20100		Dover, DE MSA........................	126 697				
	10 001	Kent County, DE........................	126 697	22220		Fayetteville-Springdale-Rogers, AR-MO MSA .	347 045
					05 007	Benton County, AR........................	153 406
20220		Dubuque, IA MSA........................	89 143		05 087	Madison County, AR........................	14 243
	19 061	Dubuque County, IA........................	89 143		05 143	Washington County, AR	157 715
					29 119	McDonald County, MO	21 681
20260		Duluth, MN-WI MSA........................	275 486				
	27 017	Carlton County, MN	31 671	22380		Flagstaff, AZ MSA........................	116 320
	27 137	St. Louis County, MN	200 528		04 005	Coconino County, AZ........................	116 320
	55 031	Douglas County, WI........................	43 287				
				22420		Flint, MI MSA........................	436 141
20500		Durham, NC MSA	426 493		26 049	Genesee County, MI........................	436 141
	37 037	Chatham County, NC	49 329				
	37 063	Durham County, NC........................	223 314	22500		Florence, SC MSA........................	193 155
	37 135	Orange County, NC........................	118 227		45 031	Darlington County, SC........................	67 394
	37 145	Person County, NC........................	35 623		45 041	Florence County, SC........................	125 761
20740		Eau Claire, WI MSA........................	148 337	22520		Florence-Muscle Shoals, AL MSA	142 950
	55 017	Chippewa County, WI........................	55 195		01 033	Colbert County, AL	54 984
	55 035	Eau Claire County, WI........................	93 142		01 077	Lauderdale County, AL........................	87 966
20940		El Centro, CA MSA	142 361	22540		Fond du Lac, WI MSA........................	97 296
	06 025	Imperial County, CA	142 361		55 039	Fond du Lac County, WI	97 296
21060		Elizabethtown, KY MSA	107 547	22660		Fort Collins-Loveland, CO MSA........................	251 494
	21 093	Hardin County, KY........................	94 174		08 069	Larimer County, CO........................	251 494
	21 123	Larue County, KY	13 373				

Metropolitan Statistical Areas, Metropolitan Divisions, and Components (As of December 2003) – Continued

Core Based Statistical Area	State/County FIPS Code	Title and Geographic Components	2000 Census Population	Core Based Statistical Area	State/County FIPS Code	Title and Geographic Components	2000 Census Population
22900		Fort Smith, AR-OK MSA	273 170	24780		Greenville, NC MSA	152 772
	05 033	Crawford County, AR	53 247		37 079	Greene County, NC	18 974
	05 047	Franklin County, AR	17 771		37 147	Pitt County, NC	133 798
	05 131	Sebastian County, AR	115 071	24860		Greenville, SC MSA	559 940
	40 079	Le Flore County, OK	48 109		45 045	Greenville County, SC	379 616
	40 135	Sequoyah County, OK	38 972		45 059	Laurens County, SC	69 567
23020		Fort Walton Beach-Crestview-Destin, FL MSA	170 498		45 077	Pickens County, SC	110 757
	12 091	Okaloosa County, FL	170 498	25060		Gulfport-Biloxi, MS MSA	246 190
23060		Fort Wayne, IN MSA	390 156		28 045	Hancock County, MS	42 967
	18 003	Allen County, IN	331 849		28 047	Harrison County, MS	189 601
	18 179	Wells County, IN	27 600		28 131	Stone County, MS	13 622
	18 183	Whitley County, IN	30 707	25180		Hagerstown-Martinsburg, MD-WV MSA	222 771
23420		Fresno, CA MSA	799 407		24 043	Washington County, MD	131 923
	06 019	Fresno County, CA	799 407		54 003	Berkeley County, WV	75 905
23460		Gadsden, AL MSA	103 459		54 065	Morgan County, WV	14 943
	01 055	Etowah County, AL	103 459	25260		Hanford-Corcoran, CA MSA	129 461
23540		Gainesville, FL MSA	232 392		06 031	Kings County, CA	129 461
	12 001	Alachua County, FL	217 955	25420		Harrisburg-Carlisle, PA MSA	509 074
	12 041	Gilchrist County, FL	14 437		42 041	Cumberland County, PA	213 674
23580		Gainesville, GA MSA	139 277		42 043	Dauphin County, PA	251 798
	13 139	Hall County, GA	139 277		42 099	Perry County, PA	43 602
24020		Glens Falls, NY MSA	124 345	25500		Harrisonburg, VA MSA	108 193
	36 113	Warren County, NY	63 303		51 165	Rockingham County, VA	67 725
	36 115	Washington County, NY	61 042		51 660	Harrisonburg city, VA	40 468
24140		Goldsboro, NC MSA	113 329	25540		Hartford-West Hartford-East Hartford, CT MSA	1 148 618
	37 191	Wayne County, NC	113 329		09 003	Hartford County, CT	857 183
24220		Grand Forks, ND-MN MSA	97 478		09 007	Middlesex County, CT	155 071
	27 119	Polk County, MN	31 369		09 013	Tolland County, CT	136 364
	38 035	Grand Forks County, ND	66 109	25620		Hattiesburg, MS MSA	123 812
24300		Grand Junction, CO MSA	116 255		28 035	Forrest County, MS	72 604
	08 077	Mesa County, CO	116 255		28 073	Lamar County, MS	39 070
24340		Grand Rapids-Wyoming, MI MSA	740 482		28 111	Perry County, MS	12 138
	26 015	Barry County, MI	56 755	25860		Hickory-Lenoir-Morganton, NC MSA	341 851
	26 067	Ionia County, MI	61 518		37 003	Alexander County, NC	33 603
	26 081	Kent County, MI	574 335		37 023	Burke County, NC	89 148
	26 123	Newaygo County, MI	47 874		37 027	Caldwell County, NC	77 415
24500		Great Falls, MT MSA	80 357		37 035	Catawba County, NC	141 685
	30 013	Cascade County, MT	80 357	25980		Hinesville-Fort Stewart, GA MSA	71 914
24540		Greeley, CO MSA	180 926		13 179	Liberty County, GA	61 610
	08 123	Weld County, CO	180 926		13 183	Long County, GA	10 304
24580		Green Bay, WI MSA	282 599	26100		Holland-Grand Haven, MI MSA	238 314
	55 009	Brown County, WI	226 778		26 139	Ottawa County, MI	238 314
	55 061	Kewaunee County, WI	20 187	26180		Honolulu, HI MSA	876 156
	55 083	Oconto County, WI	35 634		15 003	Honolulu County, HI	876 156
24660		Greensboro-High Point, NC MSA	643 430	26300		Hot Springs, AR MSA	88 068
	37 081	Guilford County, NC	421 048		05 051	Garland County, AR	88 068
	37 151	Randolph County, NC	130 454	26380		Houma-Bayou Cane-Thibodaux, LA MSA	194 477
	37 157	Rockingham County, NC	91 928		22 057	Lafourche Parish, LA	89 974
					22 109	Terrebonne Parish, LA	104 503

Core Based Statistical Area	State/County FIPS Code	Title and Geographic Components	2000 Census Population	Core Based Statistical Area	State/County FIPS Code	Title and Geographic Components	2000 Census Population
26420		Houston-Baytown-Sugar Land, TX MSA	4 715 407	27260		Jacksonville, FL MSA..............................	1 122 750
	48 015	Austin County, TX................................	23 590		12 003	Baker County, FL..............................	22 259
	48 039	Brazoria County, TX.............................	241 767		12 019	Clay County, FL...............................	140 814
	48 071	Chambers County, TX	26 031		12 031	Duval County, FL..............................	778 879
	48 157	Fort Bend County, TX	354 452		12 089	Nassau County, FL............................	57 663
	48 167	Galveston County, TX	250 158		12 109	St. Johns County, FL..........................	123 135
	48 201	Harris County, TX	3 400 578				
	48 291	Liberty County, TX...............................	70 154	27340		Jacksonville, NC MSA	150 355
	48 339	Montgomery County, TX	293 768		37 133	Onslow County, NC	150 355
	48 407	San Jacinto County, TX	22 246				
	48 473	Waller County, TX................................	32 663	27500		Janesville, WI MSA	152 307
					55 105	Rock County, WI..............................	152 307
26580		Huntington-Ashland, WV-KY-OH MSA	288 649				
	21 019	Boyd County, KY	49 752	27620		Jefferson City, MO MSA	140 052
	21 089	Greenup County, KY	36 891		29 027	Callaway County, MO..........................	40 766
	39 087	Lawrence County, OH	62 319		29 051	Cole County, MO	71 397
	54 011	Cabell County, WV	96 784		29 135	Moniteau County, MO	14 827
	54 099	Wayne County, WV	42 903		29 151	Osage County, MO	13 062
26620		Huntsville, AL MSA	342 376	27740		Johnson City, TN MSA	181 607
	01 083	Limestone County, AL	65 676		47 019	Carter County, TN	56 742
	01 089	Madison County, AL	276 700		47 171	Unicoi County, TN	17 667
					47 179	Washington County, TN	107 198
26820		Idaho Falls, ID MSA	101 677				
	16 019	Bonneville County, ID	82 522	27780		Johnstown, PA MSA	152 598
	16 051	Jefferson County, ID	19 155		42 021	Cambria County, PA	152 598
26900		Indianapolis, IN MSA	1 525 104	27860		Jonesboro, AR MSA	107 762
	18 011	Boone County, IN	46 107		05 031	Craighead County, AR..........................	82 148
	18 013	Brown County, IN	14 957		05 111	Poinsett County, AR	25 614
	18 057	Hamilton County, IN	182 740				
	18 059	Hancock County, IN	55 391	27900		Joplin, MO MSA	157 322
	18 063	Hendricks County, IN............................	104 093		29 097	Jasper County, MO	104 686
	18 081	Johnson County, IN	115 209		29 145	Newton County, MO	52 636
	18 097	Marion County, IN	860 454				
	18 109	Morgan County, IN	66 689	28020		Kalamazoo-Portage, MI MSA	314 866
	18 133	Putnam County, IN	36 019		26 077	Kalamazoo County, MI	238 603
	18 145	Shelby County, IN................................	43 445		26 159	Van Buren County, MI	76 263
26980		Iowa City, IA MSA	131 676	28100		Kankakee-Bradley, IL MSA	103 833
	19 103	Johnson County, IA	111 006		17 091	Kankakee County, IL	103 833
	19 183	Washington County, IA..........................	20 670				
				28140		Kansas City, MO-KS MSA	1 836 038
27060		Ithaca, NY MSA..................................	96 501		20 059	Franklin County, KS............................	24 784
	36 109	Tompkins County, NY	96 501		20 091	Johnson County, KS	451 086
					20 103	Leavenworth County, KS	68 691
27100		Jackson, MI MSA	158 422		20 107	Linn County, KS................................	9 570
	26 075	Jackson County, MI	158 422		20 121	Miami County, KS	28 351
					20 209	Wyandotte County, KS	157 882
27140		Jackson, MS MSA	497 197		29 013	Bates County, MO	16 653
	28 029	Copiah County, MS	28 757		29 025	Caldwell County, MO	8 969
	28 049	Hinds County, MS...............................	250 800		29 037	Cass County, MO	82 092
	28 089	Madison County, MS	74 674		29 047	Clay County, MO	184 006
	28 121	Rankin County, MS	115 327		29 049	Clinton County, MO	18 979
	28 127	Simpson County, MS	27 639		29 095	Jackson County, MO	654 880
					29 107	Lafayette County, MO	32 960
27180		Jackson, TN MSA	107 377		29 165	Platte County, MO	73 781
	47 023	Chester County, TN	15 540		29 177	Ray County, MO	23 354
	47 113	Madison County, TN	91 837				
				28420		Kennewick-Richland-Pasco, WA MSA	191 822
					53 005	Benton County, WA............................	142 475
					53 021	Franklin County, WA...........................	49 347

Metropolitan Statistical Areas,
Metropolitan Divisions,
and Components
(As of December 2003) – Continued

Core Based Statistical Area	State/ County FIPS Code	Title and Geographic Components	2000 Census Population	Core Based Statistical Area	State/ County FIPS Code	Title and Geographic Components	2000 Census Population
28660		Killeen-Temple-Fort Hood, TX MSA	330 714	29940		Lawrence, KS MSA............................	99 962
	48 027	Bell County, TX............................	237 974		20 045	Douglas County, KS	99 962
	48 099	Coryell County, TX	74 978	30020		Lawton, OK MSA............................	114 996
	48 281	Lampasas County, TX	17 762		40 031	Comanche County, OK...............	114 996
28700		Kingsport-Bristol-Bristol, TN-VA MSA	230 014	30140		Lebanon, PA MSA............................	120 327
	47 073	Hawkins County, TN........................	53 563		42 075	Lebanon County, PA..................	120 327
	47 163	Sullivan County, TN........................	153 048	30300		Lewiston, ID-WA MSA........................	57 961
	51 191	Washington County, VA	51 103		16 069	Nez Perce County, ID.................	37 410
	51 520	Bristol City, VA...............................	17 367		53 003	Asotin County, WA	20 551
	51 169	Scott County, VA............................	23 403	30340		Lewiston-Auburn, ME MSA...................	103 793
28740		Kingston, NY MSA............................	177 749		23 001	Androscoggin County, ME................	103 793
	36 111	Ulster County, NY...........................	177 749	30460		Lexington-Fayette, KY MSA..................	408 326
28940		Knoxville, TN MSA...........................	616 079		21 017	Bourbon County, KY...................	19 360
	47 001	Anderson County, TN......................	71 330		21 049	Clark County, KY.......................	33 144
	47 009	Blount County, TN.........................	105 823		21 067	Fayette County, KY...................	260 512
	47 093	Knox County, TN...........................	382 032		21 113	Jessamine County, KY.................	39 041
	47 105	Loudon County, TN........................	39 086		21 209	Scott County, KY.......................	33 061
	47 173	Union County, TN..........................	17 808		21 239	Woodford County, KY.................	23 208
29020		Kokomo, IN MSA.............................	101 541	30620		Lima, OH MSA...............................	108 473
	18 067	Howard County, IN........................	84 964		39 003	Allen County, OH......................	108 473
	18 159	Tipton County, IN..........................	16 577	30700		Lincoln, NE MSA............................	266 787
29100		La Crosse, WI-MN MSA....................	126 838		31 109	Lancaster County, NE.................	250 291
	27 055	Houston County, MN......................	19 718		31 159	Seward County, NE....................	16 496
	55 063	La Crosse County, WI	107 120	30780		Little Rock-North Little Rock, AR MSA	610 518
29140		Lafayette, IN MSA..........................	178 541		05 045	Faulkner County, AR..................	86 014
	18 007	Benton County, IN........................	9 421		05 053	Grant County, AR......................	16 464
	18 015	Carroll County, IN........................	20 165		05 085	Lonoke County, AR....................	52 828
	18 157	Tippecanoe County, IN...................	148 955		05 105	Perry County, AR......................	10 209
29180		Lafayette, LA MSA..........................	239 086		05 119	Pulaski County, AR....................	361 474
	22 055	Lafayette Parish, LA	190 503		05 125	Saline County, AR.....................	83 529
	22 099	St. Martin Parish, LA	48 583	30860		Logan, UT-ID MSA...........................	102 720
29340		Lake Charles, LA MSA......................	193 568		16 041	Franklin County, ID...................	11 329
	22 019	Calcasieu Parish, LA	183 577		49 005	Cache County, UT	91 391
	22 023	Cameron Parish, LA	9 991	30980		Longview, TX MSA...........................	194 042
29460		Lakeland, FL MSA...........................	483 924		48 183	Gregg County, TX......................	111 379
	12 105	Polk County, FL............................	483 924		48 401	Rusk County, TX.......................	47 372
29540		Lancaster, PA MSA..........................	470 658		48 459	Upshur County, TX.....................	35 291
	42 071	Lancaster County, PA.....................	470 658	31020		Longview, WA MSA...........................	92 948
29620		Lansing-East Lansing, MI MSA.............	447 728		53 015	Cowlitz County, WA....................	92 948
	26 037	Clinton County, MI........................	64 753	31100		Los Angeles-Long Beach-Santa Ana, CA MSA........................	12 365 627
	26 045	Eaton County, MI.........................	103 655			Los Angeles-Long Beach-Glendale, CA Metro Div. 31804..................	9 519 338
	26 065	Ingham County, MI........................	279 320		06 037	Los Angeles County, CA	9 519 338
29700		Laredo, TX MSA.............................	193 117			Santa Ana-Anaheim-Irvine, CA Metro Div. 42044..................	2 846 289
	48 479	Webb County, TX..........................	193 117		06 059	Orange County, CA	2 846 289
29740		Las Cruces, NM MSA	174 682				
	35 013	Dona Ana County, NM	174 682				
29820		Las Vegas-Paradise, NV MSA...............	1 375 765				
	32 003	Clark County, NV...........................	1 375 765				

Metropolitan Statistical Areas,
Metropolitan Divisions,
and Components
(As of December 2003) – Continued

Core Based Statistical Area	State/County FIPS Code	Title and Geographic Components	2000 Census Population	Core Based Statistical Area	State/County FIPS Code	Title and Geographic Components	2000 Census Population
31140		Louisville, KY-IN MSA	1 161 975	32900		Merced, CA MSA	210 554
	18 019	Clark County, IN	96 472		06 047	Merced County, CA	210 554
	18 043	Floyd County, IN	70 823	33100		Miami-Fort Lauderdale-Miami Beach, FL MSA	5 007 564
	18 061	Harrison County, IN	34 325			Fort Lauderdale-Pompano Beach-Deerfield	
	18 175	Washington County, IN	27 223			Beach, FL Metro Div. 22744	1 623 018
	21 029	Bullitt County, KY	61 236		12 011	Broward County, FL	1 623 018
	21 103	Henry County, KY	15 060			Miami-Miami Beach-Kendall, FL	
	21 111	Jefferson County, KY	693 604			Metro Div. 33124	2 253 362
	21 163	Meade County, KY	26 349		12 086	Miami-Dade County, FL	2 253 362
	21 179	Nelson County, KY	37 477			West Palm Beach-Boca Raton-Boynton	
	21 185	Oldham County, KY	46 178			Beach, FL Metro Div. 48424	1 131 184
	21 211	Shelby County, KY	33 337		12 099	Palm Beach County, FL	1 131 184
	21 215	Spencer County, KY	11 766				
	21 223	Trimble County, KY	8 125	33140		Michigan City-La Porte, IN MSA	110 106
31180		Lubbock, TX MSA	249 700		18 091	LaPorte County, IN	110 106
	48 107	Crosby County, TX	7 072	33260		Midland, TX MSA	116 009
	48 303	Lubbock County, TX	242 628		48 329	Midland County, TX	116 009
31340		Lynchburg, VA MSA	228 616	33340		Milwaukee-Waukesha-West Allis, WI MSA	1 500 741
	51 009	Amherst County, VA	31 894		55 079	Milwaukee County, WI	940 164
	51 011	Appomattox County, VA	13 705		55 089	Ozaukee County, WI	82 317
	51 019	Bedford County, VA	60 371		55 131	Washington County, WI	117 493
	51 031	Campbell County, VA	51 078		55 133	Waukesha County, WI	360 767
	51 515	Bedford city, VA	6 299	33460		Minneapolis-St. Paul-Bloomington, MN-WI	
	51 680	Lynchburg city, VA	65 269			MSA	2 968 806
31420		Macon, GA MSA	222 368		27 003	Anoka County, MN	298 084
	13 021	Bibb County, GA	153 887		27 019	Carver County, MN	70 205
	13 079	Crawford County, GA	12 495		27 025	Chisago County, MN	41 101
	13 169	Jones County, GA	23 639		27 037	Dakota County, MN	355 904
	13 207	Monroe County, GA	21 757		27 053	Hennepin County, MN	1 116 200
	13 289	Twiggs County, GA	10 590		27 059	Isanti County, MN	31 287
31460		Madera, CA MSA	123 109		27 123	Ramsey County, MN	511 035
	06 039	Madera County, CA	123 109		27 139	Scott County, MN	89 498
31540		Madison, WI MSA	501 774		27 141	Sherburne County, MN	64 417
	55 021	Columbia County, WI	52 468		27 163	Washington County, MN	201 130
	55 025	Dane County, WI	426 526		27 171	Wright County, MN	89 986
	55 049	Iowa County, WI	22 780		55 093	Pierce County, WI	36 804
31700		Manchester-Nashua, NH MSA	380 841		55 109	St. Croix County, WI	63 155
	33 011	Hillsborough County, NH	380 841	33540		Missoula, MT MSA	95 802
31900		Mansfield, OH MSA	128 852		30 063	Missoula County, MT	95 802
	39 139	Richland County, OH	128 852	33660		Mobile, AL MSA	399 843
32580		McAllen-Edinburg-Pharr, TX MSA	569 463		01 097	Mobile County, AL	399 843
	48 215	Hidalgo County, TX	569 463	33700		Modesto, CA MSA	446 997
32780		Medford, OR MSA	181 269		06 099	Stanislaus County, CA	446 997
	41 029	Jackson County, OR	181 269	33740		Monroe, LA MSA	170 053
32820		Memphis, TN-MS-AR MSA	1 205 204		22 073	Ouachita Parish, LA	147 250
	05 035	Crittenden County, AR	50 866		22 111	Union Parish, LA	22 803
	28 033	DeSoto County, MS	107 199	33780		Monroe, MI MSA	145 945
	28 093	Marshall County, MS	34 993		26 115	Monroe County, MI	145 945
	28 137	Tate County, MS	25 370	33860		Montgomery, AL MSA	346 528
	28 143	Tunica County, MS	9 227		01 001	Autauga County, AL	43 671
	47 047	Fayette County, TN	28 806		01 051	Elmore County, AL	65 874
	47 157	Shelby County, TN	897 472		01 085	Lowndes County, AL	13 473
	47 167	Tipton County, TN	51 271		01 101	Montgomery County, AL	223 510

Core Based Statistical Area	State/ County FIPS Code	Title and Geographic Components	2000 Census Population	Core Based Statistical Area	State/ County FIPS Code	Title and Geographic Components	2000 Census Population
34060		Morgantown, WV MSA............................	111 200	35620		New York-Northern New Jersey-Long Island, NY-NJ-PA MSA	18 323 002
	54 061	Monongalia County, WV.......................	81 866			Edison, NJ Metro Div. 20764	2 173 869
	54 077	Preston County, WV............................	29 334		34 023	Middlesex County, NJ.....................	750 162
34100		Morristown, TN MSA.............................	123 081		34 025	Monmouth County, NJ....................	615 301
	47 057	Grainger County, TN	20 659		34 029	Ocean County, NJ	510 916
	47 063	Hamblen County, TN..........................	58 128		34 035	Somerset County, NJ	297 490
	47 089	Jefferson County, TN.........................	44 294			Nassau-Suffolk, NY Metro Div. 35004	2 753 913
34580		Mount Vernon-Anacortes, WA MSA	102 979		36 059	Nassau County, NY........................	1 134 544
	53 057	Skagit County, WA	102 979		36 103	Suffolk County, NY	1 419 369
34620		Muncie, IN MSA	118 769			Newark-Union, NJ-PA Metro Div. 35084	2 098 843
	18 035	Delaware County, IN	118 769		34 013	Essex County, NJ.........................	793 633
34740		Muskegon-Norton Shores, MI MSA	170 200		34 019	Hunterdon County, NJ....................	121 989
	26 121	Muskegon County, MI.........................	170 200		34 027	Morris County, NJ........................	470 212
34820		Myrtle Beach-Conway-North Myrtle Beach, SC MSA,	196 629		34 037	Sussex County, NJ	144 166
	45 051	Horry County, SC	196 629		34 039	Union County, NJ.........................	522 541
34900		Napa, CA MSA	124 279		42 103	Pike County, PA	46 302
	06 055	Napa County, CA.............................	124 279			New York-Wayne-White Plains, NY-NJ Metro Div. 35644	11 296 377
34940		Naples-Marco Island, FL MSA	251 377		34 003	Bergen County, NJ	884 118
	12 021	Collier County, FL	251 377		34 017	Hudson County, NJ	608 975
34980		Nashville-Davidson-Murfreesboro, TN MSA	1 311 789		34 031	Passaic County, NJ	489 049
	47 015	Cannon County, TN	12 826		36 005	Bronx County, NY	1 332 650
	47 021	Cheatham County, TN	35 912		36 047	Kings County, NY	2 465 326
	47 037	Davidson County, TN	569 891		36 061	New York County, NY	1 537 195
	47 043	Dickson County, TN	43 156		36 079	Putnam County, NY.......................	95 745
	47 081	Hickman County, TN	22 295		36 081	Queens County, NY	2 229 379
	47 111	Macon County, TN...........................	20 386		36 085	Richmond County, NY	443 728
	47 147	Robertson County, TN	54 433		36 087	Rockland County, NY	286 753
	47 149	Rutherford County, TN	182 023		36 119	Westchester County, NY	923 459
	47 159	Smith County, TN	17 712				
	47 165	Sumner County, TN..........................	130 449	35660		Niles-Benton Harbor, MI MSA................	162 453
	47 169	Trousdale County, TN	7 259		26 021	Berrien County, MI.........................	162 453
	47 187	Williamson County, TN	126 638				
	47 189	Wilson County, TN	88 809	35980		Norwich-New London, CT MSA	259 088
					09 011	New London County, CT	259 088
35300		New Haven-Milford, CT MSA...................	824 008				
	09 009	New Haven County, CT......................	824 008	36100		Ocala, FL MSA...............................	258 916
					12 083	Marion County, FL	258 916
35380		New Orleans-Metairie-Kenner, LA MSA	1 316 510				
	22 051	Jefferson Parish, LA	455 466	36140		Ocean City, NJ MSA	102 326
	22 071	Orleans Parish, LA	484 674		34 009	Cape May County, NJ	102 326
	22 075	Plaquemines Parish, LA	26 757				
	22 087	St. Bernard Parish, LA	67 229	36220		Odessa, TX MSA	121 123
	22 089	St. Charles Parish, LA.......................	48 072		48 135	Ector County, TX	121 123
	22 095	St. John the Baptist Parish, LA	43 044				
	22 103	St. Tammany Parish, LA	191 268	36260		Ogden-Clearfield, UT MSA	442 656
					49 011	Davis County, UT	238 994
					49 029	Morgan County, UT	7 129
					49 057	Weber County, UT	196 533
				36420		Oklahoma City, OK MSA	1 095 421
					40 017	Canadian County, OK	87 697
					40 027	Cleveland County, OK	208 016
					40 051	Grady County, OK	45 516
					40 081	Lincoln County, OK........................	32 080
					40 083	Logan County, OK	33 924
					40 087	McClain County, OK	27 740
					40 109	Oklahoma County, OK.....................	660 448
				36500		Olympia, WA MSA	207 355
					53 067	Thurston County, WA	207 355

Core Based Statistical Area	State/ County FIPS Code	Title and Geographic Components	2000 Census Population	Core Based Statistical Area	State/ County FIPS Code	Title and Geographic Components	2000 Census Population
36540		Omaha-Council Bluffs, NE-IA MSA..................	767 041	37980		Philadelphia-Camden-Wilmington, PA-NJ-DE-MD MSA..................	5 687 147
	19 085	Harrison County, IA	15 666			Wilmington, DE-MD-NJ Metro Div. 48864	650 501
	19 129	Mills County, IA..................	14 547		10 003	New Castle County, DE..................	500 265
	19 155	Pottawattamie County, IA	87 704		24 015	Cecil County, MD..................	85 951
	31 025	Cass County, NE..................	24 334		34 033	Salem County, NJ..................	64 285
	31 055	Douglas County, NE..................	463 585			Camden, NJ Metro Div. 15804..................	1 186 999
	31 153	Sarpy County, NE..................	122 595		34 005	Burlington County, NJ..................	423 394
	31 155	Saunders County, NE..................	19 830		34 007	Camden County, NJ	508 932
	31 177	Washington County, NE	18 780		34 015	Gloucester County, NJ	254 673
36740		Orlando, FL MSA	1 644 561			Philadelphia, PA Metro Div. 37964	3 849 647
	12 069	Lake County, FL..................	210 528		42 017	Bucks County, PA..................	597 635
	12 095	Orange County, FL..................	896 344		42 029	Chester County, PA..................	433 501
	12 097	Osceola County, FL..................	172 493		42 045	Delaware County, PA..................	550 864
	12 117	Seminole County, FL..................	365 196		42 091	Montgomery County, PA	750 097
36780		Oshkosh-Neenah, WI MSA	156 763		42 101	Philadelphia County, PA..................	1 517 550
	55 139	Winnebago County, WI..................	156 763	38060		Phoenix-Mesa-Scottsdale, AZ MSA..................	3 251 876
36980		Owensboro, KY MSA	109 875		04 013	Maricopa County, AZ..................	3 072 149
	21 059	Daviess County, KY..................	91 545		04 021	Pinal County, AZ..................	179 727
	21 091	Hancock County, KY..................	8 392	38220		Pine Bluff, AR MSA..................	107 341
	21 149	McLean County, KY..................	9 938		05 025	Cleveland County, AR	8 571
37100		Oxnard-Thousand Oaks-Ventura, CA MSA	753 197		05 069	Jefferson County, AR	84 278
	06 111	Ventura County, CA..................	753 197		05 079	Lincoln County, AR..................	14 492
37340		Palm Bay-Melbourne-Titusville, FL MSA	476 230	38300		Pittsburgh, PA MSA	2 431 087
	12 009	Brevard County, FL..................	476 230		42 003	Allegheny County, PA..................	1 281 666
37460		Panama City-Lynn Haven, FL MSA..................	148 217		42 005	Armstrong County, PA..................	72 392
	12 005	Bay County, FL..................	148 217		42 007	Beaver County, PA..................	181 412
37620		Parkersburg-Marietta, WV-OH MSA	164 624		42 019	Butler County, PA..................	174 083
	39 167	Washington County, OH..................	63 251		42 051	Fayette County, PA..................	148 644
	54 073	Pleasants County, WV..................	7 514		42 125	Washington County, PA..................	202 897
	54 105	Wirt County, WV..................	5 873		42 129	Westmoreland County, PA..................	369 993
	54 107	Wood County, WV	87 986	38340		Pittsfield, MA MSA	134 953
37700		Pascagoula, MS MSA	150 564		25 003	Berkshire County, MA..................	134 953
	28 039	George County, MS	19 144	38540		Pocatello, ID MSA	83 103
	28 059	Jackson County, MS..................	131 420		16 005	Bannock County, ID..................	75 565
37860		Pensacola-Ferry Pass-Brent, FL MSA.............	412 153		16 077	Power County, ID	7 538
	12 033	Escambia County, FL..................	294 410	38860		Portland-South Portland-Biddeford, ME MSA	487 568
	12 113	Santa Rosa County, FL..................	117 743		23 005	Cumberland County, ME..................	265 612
37900		Peoria, IL MSA	366 899		23 023	Sagadahoc County, ME..................	35 214
	17 123	Marshall County, IL..................	13 180		23 031	York County, ME	186 742
	17 143	Peoria County, IL..................	183 433	38900		Portland-Vancouver-Beaverton, OR-WA MSA.....	1 927 881
	17 175	Stark County, IL..................	6 332		41 005	Clackamas County, OR..................	338 391
	17 179	Tazewell County, IL..................	128 485		41 009	Columbia County, OR..................	43 560
	17 203	Woodford County, IL..................	35 469		41 051	Multnomah County, OR..................	660 486
					41 067	Washington County, OR..................	445 342
					41 071	Yamhill County, OR..................	84 992
					53 011	Clark County, WA..................	345 238
					53 059	Skamania County, WA	9 872
				38940		Port St. Lucie-Fort Pierce, FL MSA	319 426
					12 085	Martin County, FL..................	126 731
					12 111	St. Lucie County, FL..................	192 695
				39100		Poughkeepsie-Newburgh-Middletown, NY MSA..................	621 517
					36 027	Dutchess County, NY	280 150
					36 071	Orange County, NY	341 367

Metropolitan Statistical Areas, Metropolitan Divisions, and Components (As of December 2003) – Continued

Core Based Statistical Area	State/ County FIPS Code	Title and Geographic Components	2000 Census Population	Core Based Statistical Area	State/ County FIPS Code	Title and Geographic Components	2000 Census Population
39140		Prescott, AZ MSA....................................	167 517	40140		Riverside-San Bernardino-Ontario, CA MSA ...	3 254 821
	04 025	Yavapai County, AZ.............................	167 517		06 065	Riverside County, CA	1 545 387
39300		Providence-New Bedford-Fall River, RI-MA			06 071	San Bernardino County, CA......................	1 709 434
		MSA...	1 582 997	40220		Roanoke, VA MSA	288 309
	25 005	Bristol County, MA.............................	534 678		51 023	Botetourt County, VA...........................	30 496
	44 001	Bristol County, RI.............................	50 648		51 045	Craig County, VA..............................	5 091
	44 003	Kent County, RI...............................	167 090		51 067	Franklin County, VA...........................	47 286
	44 005	Newport County, RI............................	85 433		51 161	Roanoke County, VA...........................	85 778
	44 007	Providence County, RI.........................	621 602		51 770	Roanoke city, VA.............................	94 911
	44 009	Washington County, RI.........................	123 546		51 775	Salem city, VA...............................	24 747
39340		Provo-Orem, UT MSA.............................	376 774	40340		Rochester, MN MSA	163 618
	49 023	Juab County, UT...............................	8 238		27 039	Dodge County, MN..............................	17 731
	49 049	Utah County, UT...............................	368 536		27 109	Olmsted County, MN	124 277
39380		Pueblo, CO MSA.................................	141 472		27 157	Wabasha County, MN	21 610
	08 101	Pueblo County, CO.............................	141 472	40380		Rochester, NY MSA	1 037 831
39460		Punta Gorda, FL MSA............................	141 627		36 051	Livingston County, NY.........................	64 328
	12 015	Charlotte County, FL..........................	141 627		36 055	Monroe County, NY.............................	735 343
39540		Racine, WI MSA.................................	188 831		36 069	Ontario County, NY............................	100 224
	55 101	Racine County, WI.............................	188 831		36 073	Orleans County, NY............................	44 171
39580		Raleigh-Cary, NC MSA	797 071		36 117	Wayne County, NY..............................	93 765
	37 069	Franklin County, NC...........................	47 260	40420		Rockford, IL MSA	320 204
	37 101	Johnston County, NC...........................	121 965		17 007	Boone County, IL..............................	41 786
	37 183	Wake County, NC...............................	627 846		17 201	Winnebago County, IL..........................	278 418
39660		Rapid City, SD MSA.............................	112 818	40580		Rocky Mount, NC MSA	143 026
	46 093	Meade County, SD..............................	24 253		37 065	Edgecombe County, NC..........................	55 606
	46 103	Pennington County, SD.........................	88 565		37 127	Nash County, NC...............................	87 420
39740		Reading, PA MSA................................	373 638	40660		Rome, GA MSA..................................	90 565
	42 011	Berks County, PA..............................	373 638		13 115	Floyd County, GA..............................	90 565
39820		Redding, CA MSA................................	163 256	40900		Sacramento-Arden-Arcade-Roseville, CA	
	06 089	Shasta County, CA.............................	163 256			MSA...	1 796 857
39900		Reno-Sparks, NV MSA............................	342 885		06 017	El Dorado County, CA..........................	156 299
	32 029	Storey County, NV.............................	3 399		06 061	Placer County, CA.............................	248 399
	32 031	Washoe County, NV.............................	339 486		06 067	Sacramento County, CA.........................	1 223 499
40060		Richmond, VA MSA	1 096 957		06 113	Yolo County, CA...............................	168 660
	51 007	Amelia County, VA	11 400	40980		Saginaw-Saginaw Township North, MI MSA ...	210 039
	51 033	Caroline County, VA...........................	22 121		26 145	Saginaw County, MI	210 039
	51 036	Charles City County, VA.......................	6 926	41060		St. Cloud, MN MSA	167 392
	51 041	Chesterfield County, VA.......................	259 903		27 009	Benton County, MN.............................	34 226
	51 049	Cumberland County, VA.........................	9 017		27 145	Stearns County, MN............................	133 166
	51 053	Dinwiddie County, VA..........................	24 533	41100		St. George, UT MSA	90 354
	51 075	Goochland County, VA..........................	16 863		49 053	Washington County, UT	90 354
	51 085	Hanover County, VA............................	86 320	41140		St. Joseph, MO-KS MSA	122 336
	51 087	Henrico County, VA............................	262 300		20 043	Doniphan County, KS...........................	8 249
	51 097	King and Queen County, VA.....................	6 630		29 003	Andrew County, MO.............................	16 492
	51 101	King William County, VA.......................	13 146		29 021	Buchanan County, MO	85 998
	51 109	Louisa County, VA.............................	25 627		29 063	DeKalb County, MO.............................	11 597
	51 127	New Kent County, VA...........................	13 462				
	51 145	Powhatan County, VA...........................	22 377				
	51 149	Prince George County, VA......................	33 047				
	51 183	Sussex County, VA.............................	12 504				
	51 570	Colonial Heights city, VA.....................	16 897				
	51 670	Hopewell city, VA.............................	22 354				
	51 730	Petersburg city, VA...........................	33 740				
	51 760	Richmond city, VA.............................	197 790				

Metropolitan Statistical Areas, Metropolitan Divisions, and Components (As of December 2003) – Continued

Core Based Statistical Area	State/ County FIPS Code	Title and Geographic Components	2000 Census Population	Core Based Statistical Area	State/ County FIPS Code	Title and Geographic Components	2000 Census Population
41180		St. Louis, MO-IL MSA	2 698 687	41940		San Jose-Sunnyvale-Santa Clara, CA MSA....	1 735 819
	17 005	Bond County, IL...............................	17 633		06 069	San Benito County, CA	53 234
	17 013	Calhoun County, IL	5 084		06 085	Santa Clara County, CA	1 682 585
	17 027	Clinton County, IL.............................	35 535				
	17 083	Jersey County, IL..............................	21 668	42020		San Luis Obispo-Paso Robles, CA MSA........	246 681
	17 117	Macoupin County, IL..........................	49 019		06 079	San Luis Obispo County, CA	246 681
	17 119	Madison County, IL...........................	258 941				
	17 133	Monroe County, IL............................	27 619	42060		Santa Barbara-Santa Maria-Goleta, CA MSA......	399 347
	17 163	St. Clair County, IL...........................	256 082		06 083	Santa Barbara County, CA......................	399 347
	29 071	Franklin County, MO..........................	93 807				
	29 099	Jefferson County, MO........................	198 099	42100		Santa Cruz-Watsonville, CA MSA...............	255 602
	29 113	Lincoln County, MO	38 944		06 087	Santa Cruz County, CA	255 602
	29 183	St. Charles County, MO......................	283 883				
	29 189	St. Louis County, MO.........................	1 016 315	42140		Santa Fe, NM MSA	129 292
	29 219	Warren County, MO	24 525		35 049	Santa Fe County, NM	129 292
	29 221	Washington County, MO	23 344				
	29 510	St. Louis city, MO.............................	348 189	42220		Santa Rosa-Petaluma, CA MSA.................	458 614
41420		Salem, OR MSA	347 214		06 097	Sonoma County, CA	458 614
	41 047	Marion County, OR............................	284 834	42260		Sarasota-Bradenton-Venice, FL MSA...........	589 959
	41 053	Polk County, OR...............................	62 380		12 081	Manatee County, FL............................	264 002
41500		Salinas, CA MSA..................................	401 762		12 115	Sarasota County, FL	325 957
	06 053	Monterey County, CA	401 762	42340		Savannah, GA MSA	293 000
41540		Salisbury, MD MSA	109 391		13 029	Bryan County, GA	23 417
	24 039	Somerset County, MD	24 747		13 051	Chatham County, GA	232 048
	24 045	Wicomico County, MD	84 644		13 103	Effingham County, GA	37 535
41620		Salt Lake City, UT MSA	968 858	42540		Scranton-Wilkes-Barre, PA MSA	560 625
	49 035	Salt Lake County, UT	898 387		42 069	Lackawanna County, PA	213 295
	49 043	Summit County, UT	29 736		42 079	Luzerne County, PA	319 250
	49 045	Tooele County, UT	40 735		42 131	Wyoming County, PA	28 080
41660		San Angelo, TX MSA	105 781	42660		Seattle-Tacoma-Bellevue, WA MSA	3 043 878
	48 235	Irion County, TX...............................	1 771			Seattle-Bellevue-Everett, WA	
	48 451	Tom Green County, TX	104 010			Metro Div. 42644	2 343 058
41700		San Antonio, TX MSA	1 711 703		53 033	King County, WA	1 737 034
	48 013	Atascosa County, TX..........................	38 628		53 061	Snohomish County, WA	606 024
	48 019	Bandera County, TX...........................	17 645			Tacoma, WA Metro Div. 45104	700 820
	48 029	Bexar County, TX	1 392 931		53 053	Pierce County, WA	700 820
	48 091	Comal County, TX.............................	78 021				
	48 187	Guadalupe County, TX........................	89 023	43100		Sheboygan, WI MSA	112 646
	48 259	Kendall County, TX............................	23 743		55 117	Sheboygan County, WI.........................	112 646
	48 325	Medina County, TX	39 304				
	48 493	Wilson County, TX.............................	32 408	43300		Sherman-Denison, TX MSA	110 595
					48 181	Grayson County, TX	110 595
41740		San Diego-Carlsbad-San Marcos, CA MSA	2 813 833	43340		Shreveport-Bossier City, LA MSA..................	375 965
	06 073	San Diego County, CA	2 813 833		22 015	Bossier Parish, LA	98 310
					22 017	Caddo Parish, LA	252 161
41780		Sandusky, OH MSA	79 551		22 031	De Soto Parish, LA	25 494
	39 043	Erie County, OH	79 551	43580		Sioux City, IA-NE-SD MSA	143 053
41860		San Francisco-Oakland-Fremont, CA MSA.....	4 123 740		19 193	Woodbury County, IA	103 877
		Oakland-Fremont-Hayward, CA			31 043	Dakota County, NE	20 253
		Metro Div. 36084	2 392 557		31 051	Dixon County, NE	6 339
	06 001	Alameda County, CA	1 443 741		46 127	Union County, SD	12 584
	06 013	Contra Costa County, CA	948 816	43620		Sioux Falls, SD MSA.............................	187 093
		San Francisco-San Mateo-Redwood City, CA			46 083	Lincoln County, SD	24 131
		Metro Div. 41884	1 731 183		46 087	McCook County, SD	5 832
	06 041	Marin County, CA	247 289		46 099	Minnehaha County, SD	148 281
	06 075	San Francisco County, CA	776 733		46 125	Turner County, SD.............................	8 849
	06 081	San Mateo County, CA..........................	707 161				

Metropolitan Statistical Areas, Metropolitan Divisions, and Components (As of December 2003) – Continued

Core Based Statistical Area	State/ County FIPS Code	Title and Geographic Components	2000 Census Population	Core Based Statistical Area	State/ County FIPS Code	Title and Geographic Components	2000 Census Population
43780		South Bend-Mishawaka, IN-MI MSA	316 663	45780		Toledo, OH MSA................................	659 188
	18 141	St. Joseph County, IN	265 559		39 051	Fulton County, OH	42 084
	26 027	Cass County, MI	51 104		39 095	Lucas County, OH	455 054
43900		Spartanburg, SC MSA...............................	253 791		39 123	Ottawa County, OH	40 985
	45 083	Spartanburg County, SC	253 791		39 173	Wood County, OH	121 065
44060		Spokane, WA MSA	417 939	45820		Topeka, KS MSA................................	224 551
	53 063	Spokane County, WA	417 939		20 085	Jackson County, KS	12 657
44100		Springfield, IL MSA	201 437		20 087	Jefferson County, KS.................................	18 426
	17 129	Menard County, IL	12 486		20 139	Osage County, KS	16 712
	17 167	Sangamon County, IL.................................	188 951		20 177	Shawnee County, KS	169 871
44140		Springfield, MA MSA	680 014		20 197	Wabaunsee County, KS	6 885
	25 011	Franklin County, MA	71 535	45940		Trenton-Ewing, NJ MSA.........................	350 761
	25 013	Hampden County, MA	456 228		34 021	Mercer County, NJ....................................	350 761
	25 015	Hampshire County, MA	152 251	46060		Tucson, AZ MSA................................	843 746
44180		Springfield, MO MSA.................................	368 374		04 019	Pima County, AZ	843 746
	29 043	Christian County, MO	54 285	46140		Tulsa, OK MSA................................	859 532
	29 059	Dallas County, MO	15 661		40 037	Creek County, OK	67 367
	29 077	Greene County, MO	240 391		40 111	Okmulgee County, OK.	39 685
	29 167	Polk County, MO	26 992		40 113	Osage County, OK	44 437
	29 225	Webster County, MO	31 045		40 117	Pawnee County, OK	16 612
44220		Springfield, OH MSA	144 742		40 131	Rogers County, OK	70 641
	39 023	Clark County, OH	144 742		40 143	Tulsa County, OK	563 299
44300		State College, PA MSA.................................	135 758		40 145	Wagoner County, OK	57 491
	42 027	Centre County, PA.................................	135 758	46220		Tuscaloosa, AL MSA................................	192 034
44700		Stockton, CA MSA	563 598		01 063	Greene County, AL	9 974
	06 077	San Joaquin County, CA	563 598		01 065	Hale County, AL	17 185
44940		Sumter, SC MSA.................................	104 646		01 125	Tuscaloosa County, AL	164 875
	45 085	Sumter County, SC	104 646	46340		Tyler, TX MSA................................	174 706
45060		Syracuse, NY MSA	650 154		48 423	Smith County, TX	174 706
	36 053	Madison County, NY.................................	69 441	46540		Utica-Rome, NY MSA	299 896
	36 067	Onondaga County, NY	458 336		36 043	Herkimer County, NY.................................	64 427
	36 075	Oswego County, NY	122 377		36 065	Oneida County, NY.................................	235 469
45220		Tallahassee, FL MSA.................................	320 304	46660		Valdosta, GA MSA	119 560
	12 039	Gadsden County, FL	45 087		13 027	Brooks County, GA	16 450
	12 065	Jefferson County, FL	12 902		13 101	Echols County, GA	3 754
	12 073	Leon County, FL	239 452		13 173	Lanier County, GA	7 241
	12 129	Wakulla County, FL	22 863		13 185	Lowndes County, GA.................................	92 115
45300		Tampa-St. Petersburg-Clearwater, FL MSA	2 395 997	46700		Vallejo-Fairfield, CA MSA.........................	394 542
	12 053	Hernando County, FL	130 802		06 095	Solano County, CA	394 542
	12 057	Hillsborough County, FL	998 948	46940		Vero Beach, FL MSA	112 947
	12 101	Pasco County, FL	344 765		12 061	Indian River County, FL.........................	112 947
	12 103	Pinellas County, FL	921 482	47020		Victoria, TX MSA	111 663
45460		Terre Haute, IN MSA	170 943		48 057	Calhoun County, TX	20 647
	18 021	Clay County, IN	26 556		48 175	Goliad County, TX	6 928
	18 153	Sullivan County, IN	21 751		48 469	Victoria County, TX.................................	84 088
	18 165	Vermillion County, IN	16 788	47220		Vineland-Millville-Bridgeton, NJ MSA..............	146 438
	18 167	Vigo County, IN	105 848		34 011	Cumberland County, NJ	146 438
45500		Texarkana, TX-Texarkana, AR MSA	129 749				
	05 091	Miller County, AR.................................	40 443				
	48 037	Bowie County, TX.................................	89 306				

Metropolitan Statistical Areas, Metropolitan Divisions, and Components (As of December 2003) – Continued

Core Based Statistical Area	State/County FIPS Code	Title and Geographic Components	2000 Census Population	Core Based Statistical Area	State/County FIPS Code	Title and Geographic Components	2000 Census Population
47260		Virginia Beach-Norfolk-Newport News, VA-NC MSA	1 576 370	48260		Weirton-Steubenville, WV-OH MSA	132 008
	37 053	Currituck County, NC	18 190		39 081	Jefferson County, OH	73 894
	51 073	Gloucester County, VA	34 780		54 009	Brooke County, WV	25 447
	51 093	Isle of Wight County, VA	29 728		54 029	Hancock County, WV	32 667
	51 095	James City County, VA	48 102	48300		Wenatchee, WA MSA	99 219
	51 115	Mathews County, VA	9 207		53 007	Chelan County, WA	66 616
	51 181	Surry County, VA	6 829		53 017	Douglas County, WA	32 603
	51 199	York County, VA	56 297				
	51 550	Chesapeake city, VA	199 184	48540		Wheeling, WV-OH MSA	153 172
	51 650	Hampton city, VA	146 437		39 013	Belmont County, OH	70 226
	51 700	Newport News city, VA	180 150		54 051	Marshall County, WV	35 519
	51 710	Norfolk city, VA	234 403		54 069	Ohio County, WV	47 427
	51 735	Poquoson city , VA	11 566				
	51 740	Portsmouth city, VA	100 565	48620		Wichita, KS MSA	571 166
	51 800	Suffolk city, VA	63 677		20 015	Butler County, KS	59 482
	51 810	Virginia Beach city, VA	425 257		20 079	Harvey County, KS	32 869
	51 830	Williamsburg city, VA	11 998		20 173	Sedgwick County, KS	452 869
					20 191	Sumner County, KS	25 946
47300		Visalia-Porterville, CA MSA	368 021				
	06 107	Tulare County, CA	368 021	48660		Wichita Falls, TX MSA	151 524
47380		Waco, TX MSA	213 517		48 009	Archer County, TX	8 854
	48 309	McLennan County, TX	213 517		48 077	Clay County, TX	11 006
					48 485	Wichita County, TX	131 664
47580		Warner Robins, GA MSA	110 765	48700		Williamsport, PA MSA	120 044
	13 153	Houston County, GA	110 765		42 081	Lycoming County, PA	120 044
47900		Washington-Arlington-Alexandria, DC-VA-MD-WV MSA	4 796 183	48900		Wilmington, NC MSA	274 532
		Washington-Arlington-Alexandria, DC-VA-MD-WV Metro Div. 47894	3 727 565		37 019	Brunswick County, NC	73 143
	11 001	District of Columbia, DC	572 059		37 129	New Hanover County, NC	160 307
	24 009	Calvert County, MD	74 563		37 141	Pender County, NC	41 082
	24 017	Charles County, MD	120 546	49020		Winchester, VA-WV MSA	102 997
	24 033	Prince George's County, MD	801 515		51 069	Frederick County, VA	59 209
	51 013	Arlington County, VA	189 453		51 840	Winchester city , VA	23 585
	51 043	Clarke County, VA	12 652		54 027	Hampshire County, WV	20 203
	51 059	Fairfax County, VA	969 749	49180		Winston-Salem, NC MSA	421 961
	51 061	Fauquier County, VA	55 139		37 059	Davie County, NC	34 835
	51 107	Loudoun County, VA	169 599		37 067	Forsyth County, NC	306 067
	51 153	Prince William County, VA	280 813		37 169	Stokes County, NC	44 711
	51 177	Spotsylvania County, VA	90 395		37 197	Yadkin County, NC	36 348
	51 179	Stafford County, VA	92 446				
	51 187	Warren County, VA	31 584	49340		Worcester, MA MSA	750 963
	51 510	Alexandria city, VA	128 283		25 027	Worcester County, MA	750 963
	51 600	Fairfax city, VA	21 498				
	51 610	Falls Church city, VA	10 377	49420		Yakima, WA MSA	222 581
	51 630	Fredericksburg city, VA	19 279		53 077	Yakima County, WA	222 581
	51 683	Manassas city, VA	35 135	49620		York-Hanover, PA MSA	381 751
	51 685	Manassas Park city, VA	10 290		42 133	York County, PA	381 751
	54 037	Jefferson County, WV	42 190				
		Bethesda-Frederick-Gaithersburg, MD Metro Div. 13644	1 068 618	49660		Youngstown-Warren-Boardman, OH-PA MSA	602 964
	24 021	Frederick County, MD	195 277		39 099	Mahoning County, OH	257 555
	24 031	Montgomery County, MD	873 341		39 155	Trumbull County, OH	225 116
					42 085	Mercer County, PA	120 293
47940		Waterloo-Cedar Falls, IA MSA	163 706	49700		Yuba City, CA MSA	139 149
	19 013	Black Hawk County, IA	128 012		06 101	Sutter County, CA	78 930
	19 017	Bremer County, IA	23 325		06 115	Yuba County, CA	60 219
	19 075	Grundy County, IA	12 369				
				49740		Yuma, AZ MSA	160 026
48140		Wausau, WI MSA	125 834		04 027	Yuma County, AZ	160 026
	55 073	Marathon County, WI	125 834				

APPENDIX C
CORE BASED STATISTICAL AREAS
(Metropolitan and Micropolitan),
AND METROPOLITAN DIVISIONS
WITH 2000 CENSUS POPULATION AND
PERCENT OF THE POPULATION THAT IS RURAL
(As of June 2003)

Core Based Statistical Area Code	State/County FIPS Code	Statistical Area Name	2000 Census Population	Percent Rural	Core Based Statistical Area Code	State/County FIPS Code	Statistical Area Name	2000 Census Population	Percent Rural
10020		Abbeville, LA Micro SA........	53 807	56.8		34 041	Warren County, NJ	102 437	42.9
	22 113	Vermilion Parish, LA	53 807	56.8		42 025	Carbon County, PA...........	58 802	50.5
10100		Aberdeen, SD Micro SA........	39 827	37.9		42 077	Lehigh County, PA............	312 090	9.7
	46 013	Brown County, SD	35 460	30.3		42 095	Northampton County, PA..............	267 066	15.3
	46 045	Edmunds County, SD	4 367	100.0	10940		Alma, MI Micro SA	42 285	54.4
10140		Aberdeen, WA Micro SA........	67 194	39.4		26 057	Gratiot County, MI............	42 285	54.4
	53 027	Grays Harbor County, WA..........	67 194	39.4	10980		Alpena, MI Micro SA	31 314	51.4
10180		Abilene, TX Metro SA..........	160 245	24.5		26 007	Alpena County, MI............	31 314	51.4
	48 059	Callahan County, TX	12 905	73.7	11020		Altoona, PA Metro SA..........	129 144	26.0
	48 253	Jones County, TX	20 785	60.7		42 013	Blair County, PA	129 144	26.0
	48 441	Taylor County, TX..........	126 555	13.6	11060		Altus, OK Micro SA............	28 439	25.7
10220		Ada, OK Micro SA..........	35 143	53.3		40 065	Jackson County, OK..........	28 439	25.7
	40 123	Pontotoc County, OK	35 143	53.3	11100		Amarillo, TX Metro SA..........	226 522	14.4
10300		Adrian, MI Micro SA..........	98 890	54.2		48 011	Armstrong County, TX	2 148	100.0
	26 091	Lenawee County, MI..........	98 890	54.2		48 065	Carson County, TX...........	6 516	96.4
10420		Akron, OH Metro SA	694 960	12.4		48 375	Potter County, TX	113 546	9.0
	39 133	Portage County, OH	152 061	41.4		48 381	Randall County, TX	104 312	13.5
	39 153	Summit County, OH..........	542 899	4.3	11140		Americus, GA Micro SA	36 966	49.3
10460		Alamogordo, NM Micro SA........	62 298	29.8		13 249	Schley County, GA	3 766	100.0
	35 035	Otero County, NM..........	62 298	29.8		13 261	Sumter County, GA...........	33 200	43.5
10500		Albany, GA Metro SA..........	157 833	32.0	11180		Ames, IA Metro SA..........	79 981	25.1
	13 007	Baker County, GA..........	4 074	100.0		19 169	Story County, IA............	79 981	25.1
	13 095	Dougherty County, GA..........	96 065	13.5	11220		Amsterdam, NY Micro SA	49 708	40.9
	13 177	Lee County, GA	24 757	49.6		36 057	Montgomery County, NY	49 708	40.9
	13 273	Terrell County, GA..........	10 970	53.7	11260		Anchorage, AK Metro SA..........	319 605	15.0
	13 321	Worth County, GA..........	21 967	70.0		02 020	Anchorage Municipality, AK..........	260 283	3.9
10540		Albany-Lebanon, OR Micro SA..........	103 069	36.5		02 170	Matanuska-Susitna Borough, AK ...	59 322	64.0
	41 043	Linn County, OR	103 069	36.5	11300		Anderson, IN Metro SA	133 358	23.5
10580		Albany-Schenectady-Troy, NY Metro SA..........	825 875	21.8	11340	18 095	Madison County, IN..........	133 358	23.5
	36 001	Albany County, NY	294 565	9.8			Anderson, SC Metro SA	165 740	41.7
	36 083	Rensselaer County, NY	152 538	32.1	11340	45 007	Anderson County, SC.........	165 740	41.7
	36 091	Saratoga County, NY..........	200 635	31.6	11380		Andrews, TX Micro SA..........	13 004	19.1
	36 093	Schenectady County, NY	146 555	9.0		48 003	Andrews County, TX..........	13 004	19.1
	36 095	Schoharie County, NY	31 582	83.2	11420		Angola, IN Micro SA	33 214	68.5
10620		Albemarle, NC Micro SA..........	58 100	67.7		18 151	Steuben County, IN	33 214	68.5
	37 167	Stanly County, NC	58 100	67.7	11460		Ann Arbor, MI Metro SA..........	322 895	17.5
10660		Albert Lea, MN Micro SA	32 584	44.1		26 161	Washtenaw County, MI..........	322 895	17.5
	27 047	Freeborn County, MN	32 584	44.1	11500		Anniston-Oxford, AL Metro SA...........	112 249	30.9
10700		Albertville, AL Micro SA..........	82 231	57.4		01 015	Calhoun County, AL	112 249	30.9
	01 095	Marshall County, AL	82 231	57.4	11540		Appleton, WI Metro SA..........	201 602	28.6
10740		Albuquerque, NM Metro SA	729 649	10.2		55 015	Calumet County, WI..........	40 631	39.6
	35 001	Bernalillo County, NM	556 678	4.3		55 087	Outagamie County, WI	160 971	25.9
	35 043	Sandoval County, NM..........	89 908	23.4	11580		Arcadia, FL Micro SA..........	32 209	54.2
	35 057	Torrance County, NM..........	16 911	95.2		12 027	DeSoto County, FL..........	32 209	54.2
	35 061	Valencia County, NM..........	66 152	19.8	11620		Ardmore, OK Micro SA..........	54 452	62.5
10780		Alexandria, LA Metro SA..........	145 035	45.9		40 019	Carter County, OK	45 621	55.2
	22 043	Grant Parish, LA	18 698	100.0		40 085	Love County, OK	8 831	100.0
	22 079	Rapides Parish, LA	126 337	37.8	11660		Arkadelphia, AR Micro SA..........	23 546	55.8
10820		Alexandria, MN Micro SA..........	32 821	57.6		05 019	Clark County, AR..........	23 546	55.8
	27 041	Douglas County, MN	32 821	57.6	11700		Asheville, NC Metro SA..........	369 171	39.9
10860		Alice, TX Micro SA..........	39 326	36.7		37 021	Buncombe County, NC..........	206 330	29.0
	48 249	Jim Wells County, TX	39 326	36.7		37 087	Haywood County, NC..........	54 033	47.9
10880		Allegan, MI Micro SA..........	105 665	70.3		37 089	Henderson County, NC.........	89 173	47.2
	26 005	Allegan County, MI	105 665	70.3		37 115	Madison County, NC	19 635	100.0
10900		Allentown-Bethlehem-Easton, PA-NJ Metro SA..........	740 395	19.6	11740	39 005	Ashland, OH Micro SA..........	52 523	54.1
							Ashland County, OH	52 523	54.1
					11780		Ashtabula, OH Micro SA..........	102 728	45.8

Core Based Statistical Areas (Metropolitan and Micropolitan), and Metropolitan Divisions with 2000 Census Population and Percent of the Population That is Rural (As of June 2003) – Continued

Core Based Statistical Area Code	State/County FIPS Code	Statistical Area Name	2000 Census Population	Percent Rural	Core Based Statistical Area Code	State/County FIPS Code	Statistical Area Name	2000 Census Population	Percent Rural
	39 007	Ashtabula County, OH	102 728	45.8		27 099	Mower County, MN	38 603	38.8
11820		Astoria, OR Micro SA	35 630	41.1	12420		Austin-Round Rock, TX Metro SA	1 249 763	15.4
	41 007	Clatsop County, OR	35 630	41.1		48 021	Bastrop County, TX	57 733	67.1
11860		Atchison, KS Micro SA	16 774	37.5		48 055	Caldwell County, TX	32 194	45.8
	20 005	Atchison County, KS	16 774	37.5		48 209	Hays County, TX	97 589	42.2
11900		Athens, OH Micro SA	62 223	41.2		48 453	Travis County, TX	812 280	7.0
	39 009	Athens County, OH	62 223	41.2		48 491	Williamson County, TX	249 967	16.5
11940		Athens, TN Micro SA	49 015	58.5	12460		Bainbridge, GA Micro SA	28 240	58.0
	47 107	McMinn County, TN	49 015	58.5		13 087	Decatur County, GA	28 240	58.0
11980		Athens, TX Micro SA	73 277	54.6	12540		Bakersfield, CA Metro SA	661 645	11.7
	48 213	Henderson County, TX	73 277	54.6		06 029	Kern County, CA	661 645	11.7
12020		Athens-Clarke County, GA Metro SA	166 079	35.8	12580		Baltimore-Towson, MD Metro SA	2 552 994	9.6
	13 059	Clarke County, GA	101 489	8.7		24 003	Anne Arundel County, MD	489 656	5.6
	13 195	Madison County, GA	25 730	96.0		24 005	Baltimore County, MD	754 292	6.2
	13 219	Oconee County, GA	26 225	50.3		24 013	Carroll County, MD	150 897	43.1
	13 221	Oglethorpe County, GA	12 635	99.9		24 025	Harford County, MD	218 590	22.2
12060		Atlanta-Sandy Springs-Marietta, GA Metro SA	4 247 981	13.8		24 027	Howard County, MD	247 842	12.6
	13 013	Barrow County, GA	46 144	53.1		24 035	Queen Anne's County, MD	40 563	60.7
	13 015	Bartow County, GA	76 019	41.2		24 510	Baltimore city, MD	651 154	0.0
	13 035	Butts County, GA	19 522	77.4	12620		Bangor, ME Metro SA	144 919	55.9
	13 045	Carroll County, GA	87 268	52.8		23 019	Penobscot County, ME	144 919	55.9
	13 057	Cherokee County, GA	141 903	25.2	12660		Baraboo, WI Micro SA	55 225	49.9
	13 063	Clayton County, GA	236 517	1.2		55 111	Sauk County, WI	55 225	49.9
	13 067	Cobb County, GA	607 751	0.5	12700		Barnstable Town, MA Metro SA	222 230	8.8
	13 077	Coweta County, GA	89 215	45.6		25 001	Barnstable County, MA	222 230	8.8
	13 085	Dawson County, GA	15 999	100.0	12740		Barre, VT Micro SA	58 039	51.3
	13 089	DeKalb County, GA	665 865	0.4		50 023	Washington County, VT	58 039	51.3
	13 097	Douglas County, GA	92 174	20.1	12780		Bartlesville, OK Micro SA	48 996	21.7
	13 113	Fayette County, GA	91 263	21.9		40 147	Washington County, OK	48 996	21.7
	13 117	Forsyth County, GA	98 407	34.1	12820		Bastrop, LA Micro SA	31 021	47.9
	13 121	Fulton County, GA	816 006	2.1		22 067	Morehouse Parish, LA	31 021	47.9
	13 135	Gwinnett County, GA	588 448	2.5	12860		Batavia, NY Micro SA	60 370	59.5
	13 143	Haralson County, GA	25 690	83.0		36 037	Genesee County, NY	60 370	59.5
	13 149	Heard County, GA	11 012	100.0	12900		Batesville, AR Micro SA	34 233	68.6
	13 151	Henry County, GA	119 341	27.9		05 063	Independence County, AR	34 233	68.6
	13 159	Jasper County, GA	11 426	100.0	12940		Baton Rouge, LA Metro SA	705 973	25.5
	13 171	Lamar County, GA	15 912	57.1		22 005	Ascension Parish, LA	76 627	24.6
	13 199	Meriwether County, GA	22 534	82.9		22 033	East Baton Rouge Parish, LA	412 852	7.1
	13 217	Newton County, GA	62 001	44.3		22 037	East Feliciana Parish, LA	21 360	83.5
	13 223	Paulding County, GA	81 678	39.9		22 047	Iberville Parish, LA	33 320	49.2
	13 227	Pickens County, GA	22 983	78.2		22 063	Livingston Parish, LA	91 814	54.5
	13 231	Pike County, GA	13 688	100.0		22 077	Pointe Coupee Parish, LA	22 763	58.6
	13 247	Rockdale County, GA	70 111	15.1		22 091	St. Helena Parish, LA	10 525	100.0
	13 255	Spalding County, GA	58 417	40.1		22 121	West Baton Rouge Parish, LA	21 601	40.0
	13 297	Walton County, GA	60 687	57.8		22 125	West Feliciana Parish, LA	15 111	100.0
12100		Atlantic City, NJ Metro SA	252 552	14.3	12980		Battle Creek, MI Metro SA	137 985	30.3
	34 001	Atlantic County, NJ	252 552	14.3		26 025	Calhoun County, MI	137 985	30.3
12140		Auburn, IN Micro SA	40 285	41.9	13020		Bay City, MI Metro SA	110 157	29.1
	18 033	DeKalb County, IN	40 285	41.9		26 017	Bay County, MI	110 157	29.1
12180		Auburn, NY Micro SA	81 963	52.6	13060		Bay City, TX Micro SA	37 957	34.0
	36 011	Cayuga County, NY	81 963	52.6		48 321	Matagorda County, TX	37 957	34.0
12220		Auburn-Opelika, AL Metro SA	115 092	33.1	13100		Beatrice, NE Micro SA	22 993	43.9
	01 081	Lee County, AL	115 092	33.1		31 067	Gage County, NE	22 993	43.9
12260		Augusta-Richmond County, GA-SC Metro SA	499 684	28.8	13140		Beaumont-Port Arthur, TX Metro SA	385 090	20.4
	13 033	Burke County, GA	22 243	75.3		48 199	Hardin County, TX	48 073	57.4
	13 073	Columbia County, GA	89 288	26.2		48 245	Jefferson County, TX	252 051	8.3
	13 189	McDuffie County, GA	21 231	62.1		48 361	Orange County, TX	84 966	35.2
	13 245	Richmond County, GA	199 775	7.8	13180		Beaver Dam, WI Micro SA	85 897	52.2
	45 003	Aiken County, SC	142 552	39.1		55 027	Dodge County, WI	85 897	52.2
	45 037	Edgefield County, SC	24 595	78.8	13220		Beckley, WV Micro SA	79 220	40.4
12300		Augusta-Waterville, ME Micro SA	117 114	61.2		54 081	Raleigh County, WV	79 220	40.4
	23 011	Kennebec County, ME	117 114	61.2	13260		Bedford, IN Micro SA	45 922	55.8
12380		Austin, MN Micro SA	38 603	38.8		18 093	Lawrence County, IN	45 922	55.8
					13300		Beeville, TX Micro SA	32 359	30.6

Core Based Statistical Areas (Metropolitan and Micropolitan), and Metropolitan Divisions with 2000 Census Population and Percent of the Population That is Rural (As of June 2003) – Continued

Core Based Statistical Area Code	State/ County FIPS Code	Statistical Area Name	2000 Census Population	Percent Rural	Core Based Statistical Area Code	State/ County FIPS Code	Statistical Area Name	2000 Census Population	Percent Rural
	48 025	Bee County, TX	32 359	30.6		16 015	Boise County, ID..........................	6 670	100.0
13340		Bellefontaine, OH Micro SA	46 005	55.6		16 027	Canyon County, ID	131 441	26.7
	39 091	Logan County, OH	46 005	55.6		16 045	Gem County, ID	15 181	46.0
13380		Bellingham, WA Metro SA..............	166 814	32.3		16 073	Owyhee County, ID.....................	10 644	74.2
	53 073	Whatcom County, WA	166 814	32.3	14340		Boone, IA Micro SA......................	26 224	51.8
13420		Bemidji, MN Micro SA	39 650	68.5		19 015	Boone County, IA	26 224	51.8
	27 007	Beltrami County, MN....................	39 650	68.5	14380		Boone, NC Micro SA	42 695	60.0
13460		Bend, OR Metro SA	115 367	37.1		37 189	Watauga County, NC	42 695	60.0
	41 017	Deschutes County, OR.................	115 367	37.1	14420		Borger, TX Micro SA	23 857	23.4
13500		Bennettsville, SC Micro SA	28 818	47.2		48 233	Hutchinson County, TX................	23 857	23.4
	45 069	Marlboro County, SC	28 818	47.2	14460		Boston-Cambridge-Quincy, MA-NH Metro SA........................	4 391 344	6.2
13540		Bennington, VT Micro SA	36 994	61.8			Essex County, MA Metro Div. 21604............................	723 419	4.7
	50 003	Bennington County, VT	36 994	61.8		25 009	Essex County, MA	723 419	4.7
13620		Berlin, NH-VT Micro SA	39 570	71.2			Cambridge-Newton-Framingham, MA Metro Div. 15764.................	1 465 396	3.3
	33 007	Coos County, NH........................	33 111	65.6		25 017	Middlesex County, MA.................	1 465 396	3.3
	50 009	Essex County, VT	6 459	100.0			Boston-Quincy, MA Metro Div. 14484............................	1 812 937	3.8
13660		Big Rapids, MI Micro SA	40 553	71.0		25 021	Norfolk County, MA.....................	650 308	3.3
	26 107	Mecosta County, MI....................	40 553	71.0		25 023	Plymouth County, MA...................	472 822	10.0
13700		Big Spring, TX Micro SA	33 627	21.6		25 025	Suffolk County, MA.....................	689 807	0.0
	48 227	Howard County, TX.....................	33 627	21.6			Rockingham County-Strafford County, NH Metro Div. 40484	389 592	31.0
13740		Billings, MT Metro SA...................	138 904	22.4		33 015	Rockingham County, NH	277 359	29.5
	30 009	Carbon County, MT	9 552	100.0		33 017	Strafford County, NH...................	112 233	34.7
	30 111	Yellowstone County, MT..............	129 352	16.7	14500		Boulder, CO Metro SA	269 814	9.9
13780		Binghamton, NY Metro SA............	252 320	34.2		08 013	Boulder County, CO	269 814	9.9
	36 007	Broome County, NY.....................	200 536	26.2	14540		Bowling Green, KY Metro SA........	104 166	44.1
	36 107	Tioga County, NY........................	51 784	65.1		21 061	Edmonson County, KY	11 644	100.0
13820		Birmingham-Hoover, AL Metro SA.....	1 052 238	31.5		21 227	Warren County, KY.....................	92 522	37.0
	01 007	Bibb County, AL........................	20 826	81.8	14580		Bozeman, MT Micro SA	67 831	43.3
	01 009	Blount County, AL.......................	51 024	90.8		30 031	Gallatin County, MT....................	67 831	43.3
	01 021	Chilton County, AL......................	39 593	87.9	14620		Bradford, PA Micro SA	45 936	63.4
	01 073	Jefferson County, AL...................	662 047	10.7		42 083	McKean County, PA	45 936	63.4
	01 115	St. Clair County, AL....................	64 742	87.7	14660		Brainerd, MN Micro SA	82 249	74.9
	01 117	Shelby County, AL......................	143 293	35.7		27 021	Cass County, MN........................	27 150	100.0
	01 127	Walker County, AL......................	70 713	77.3		27 035	Crow Wing County, MN................	55 099	62.5
13860		Bishop, CA Micro SA...................	17 945	42.0	14700		Branson, MO Micro SA	68 361	70.8
	06 027	Inyo County, CA........................	17 945	42.0		29 209	Stone County, MO	28 658	100.0
13900		Bismarck, ND Metro SA	94 719	21.4		29 213	Taney County, MO......................	39 703	49.7
	38 015	Burleigh County, ND	69 416	16.6	14740		Bremerton-Silverdale, WA Metro SA................................	231 969	19.6
	38 059	Morton County, ND.....................	25 303	34.6		53 035	Kitsap County, WA......................	231 969	19.6
13940		Blackfoot, ID Micro SA	41 735	58.0	14780		Brenham, TX Micro SA	30 373	54.2
	16 011	Bingham County, ID	41 735	58.0		48 477	Washington County, TX................	30 373	54.2
13980		Blacksburg-Christiansburg-Radford, VA Metro SA............................	151 272	38.2	14820		Brevard, NC Micro SA	29 334	62.9
	51 071	Giles County, VA	16 657	83.0		37 175	Transylvania County, NC..............	29 334	62.9
	51 121	Montgomery County, VA	83 629	30.8	14860		Bridgeport-Stamford-Norwalk, CT Metro SA................................	882 567	4.2
	51 155	Pulaski County, VA	35 127	50.8		09 001	Fairfield County, CT....................	882 567	4.2
	51 750	Radford city, VA	15 859	2.6	14940		Brigham City, UT Micro SA	42 745	34.4
14020		Bloomington, IN Metro SA............	175 506	40.7		49 003	Box Elder County, UT.................	42 745	34.4
	18 055	Greene County, IN......................	33 157	64.9	14980		Bristol, VA Metro SA	68 470	52.2
	18 105	Monroe County, IN......................	120 563	23.3		51 191	Washington County, VA	51 103	69.7
	18 119	Owen County, IN........................	21 786	100.0		51 520	Briston city, VA	17 367	0.8
14060		Bloomington-Normal, IL Metro SA	150 433	22.9	15020		Brookhaven, MS Micro SA...........	33 166	64.0
	17 113	McLean County, IL	150 433	22.9		28 085	Lincoln County, MS	33 166	64.0
14100		Bloomsburg-Berwick, PA Micro SA....	82 387	46.5	15060		Brookings, OR Micro SA..............	21 137	53.1
	42 037	Columbia County, PA	64 151	44.3		41 015	Curry County, OR.......................	21 137	53.1
	42 093	Montour County, PA	18 236	54.3	15100		Brookings, SD Micro SA..............	28 220	34.2
14140		Bluefield, WV-VA Micro SA	107 578	51.6		46 011	Brookings County, SD	28 220	34.2
	51 185	Tazewell County, VA	44 598	58.3	15140		Brownsville, TN Micro SA............	19 797	47.9
	54 055	Mercer County, WV.....................	62 980	46.8		47 075	Haywood County, TN	19 797	47.9
14180		Blytheville, AR Micro SA	51 979	34.5					
	05 093	Mississippi County, AR................	51 979	34.5					
14220		Bogalusa, LA Micro SA	43 926	62.1					
	22 117	Washington Parish, LA................	43 926	62.1					
14260		Boise City-Nampa, ID Metro SA	464 840	16.6					
	16 001	Ada County, ID	300 904	6.8					

Core Based Statistical Area Code	State/ County FIPS Code	Statistical Area Name	2000 Census Population	Percent Rural	Core Based Statistical Area Code	State/ County FIPS Code	Statistical Area Name	2000 Census Population	Percent Rural
15180		Brownsville-Harlingen, TX Metro SA..	335 227	12.7	16260		Cedar City, UT Micro SA..............	33 779	34.1
	48 061	Cameron County, TX.....................	335 227	12.7		49 021	Iron County, UT	33 779	34.1
15220		Brownwood, TX Micro SA................	37 674	41.7	16300		Cedar Rapids, IA Metro SA..............	237 230	25.5
	48 049	Brown County, TX......................	37 674	41.7		19 011	Benton County, IA	25 308	70.4
15260		Brunswick, GA Metro SA................	93 044	41.0		19 105	Jones County, IA	20 221	55.9
	13 025	Brantley County, GA..................	14 629	98.9		19 113	Linn County, IA	191 701	16.3
	13 127	Glynn County, GA.....................	67 568	23.3	16340		Cedartown, GA Micro SA	38 127	51.7
	13 191	McIntosh County, GA.................	10 847	73.5		13 233	Polk County, GA	38 127	51.7
15340		Bucyrus, OH Micro SA.................	46 966	33.6	16380		Celina, OH Micro SA...................	40 924	60.1
	39 033	Crawford County, OH	46 966	33.6		39 107	Mercer County, OH	40 924	60.1
15380		Buffalo-Cheektowaga-Tonawanda, NY Metro SA............................	1 170 111	12.0	16420		Central City, KY Micro SA..............	31 839	68.0
						21 177	Muhlenberg County, KY	31 839	68.0
	36 029	Erie County, NY........................	950 265	9.0	16460		Centralia, IL Micro SA.................	41 691	41.7
	36 063	Niagara County, NY..................	219 846	25.0		17 121	Marion County, IL	41 691	41.7
15420		Burley, ID Micro SA.....................	41 590	56.0	16500		Centralia, WA Micro SA................	68 600	64.1
	16 031	Cassia County, ID.....................	21 416	56.1		53 041	Lewis County, WA	68 600	64.1
	16 067	Minidoka County, ID..................	20 174	55.9	16540		Chambersburg, PA Micro SA............	129 313	47.2
15460		Burlington, IA-IL Micro SA..............	50 564	39.9		42 055	Franklin County, PA....................	129 313	47.2
	17 071	Henderson County, IL..................	8 213	98.5	16580		Champaign-Urbana, IL Metro SA.......	210 275	21.6
	19 057	Des Moines County, IA...............	42 351	28.5		17 019	Champaign County, IL	179 669	15.7
15500		Burlington, NC Metro SA...............	130 800	30.7		17 053	Ford County, IL	14 241	42.9
	37 001	Alamance County, NC...............	130 800	30.7		17 147	Piatt County, IL	16 365	68.8
15540		Burlington-South Burlington, VT Metro SA...............................	198 889	40.4	16620		Charleston, WV Metro SA................	309 635	40.4
						54 005	Boone County, WV	25 535	88.0
	50 007	Chittenden County, VT	146 571	28.0		54 015	Clay County, WV	10 330	100.0
	50 011	Franklin County, VT...................	45 417	71.3		54 039	Kanawha County, WV	200 073	24.6
	50 013	Grand Isle County, VT...............	6 901	100.0		54 043	Lincoln County, WV	22 108	100.0
15580		Butte-Silver Bow, MT Micro SA........	34 606	11.8		54 079	Putnam County, WV	51 589	40.4
	30 093	Silver Bow County, MT..............	34 606	11.8	16660		Charleston-Mattoon, IL Micro SA......	64 449	37.2
15620		Cadillac, MI Micro SA...................	44 962	75.2		17 029	Coles County, IL	53 196	24.0
	26 113	Missaukee County, MI	14 478	100.0		17 035	Cumberland County, IL................	11 253	100.0
	26 165	Wexford County, MI..................	30 484	63.4	16700		Charleston-North Charleston, SC Metro SA...............................	549 033	21.3
15660		Calhoun, GA Micro SA.................	44 104	65.8					
	13 129	Gordon County, GA	44 104	65.8		45 015	Berkeley County, SC	142 651	34.0
15700		Cambridge, MD Micro SA	30 674	59.5		45 019	Charleston County, SC	309 969	13.7
	24 019	Dorchester County, MD	30 674	59.5		45 035	Dorchester County, SC...............	96 413	27.0
15740		Cambridge, OH Micro SA..............	40 792	59.4	16740		Charlotte-Gastonia-Concord, NC-SC Metro SA...............................	1 330 448	18.3
	39 059	Guernsey County, OH...............	40 792	59.4					
15780		Camden, AR Micro SA.................	34 534	64.3		37 007	Anson County, NC	25 275	73.6
	05 013	Calhoun County, AR..................	5 744	100.0		37 025	Cabarrus County, NC..................	131 063	27.6
	05 103	Ouachita County, AR.................	28 790	57.1		37 071	Gaston County, NC....................	190 365	22.5
15820		Campbellsville, KY Micro SA............	22 927	49.2		37 119	Mecklenburg County, NC	695 454	3.8
	21 217	Taylor County, KY	22 927	49.2		37 179	Union County, NC......................	123 677	49.8
15860		Canon City, CO Micro SA..............	46 145	26.6		45 091	York County, SC	164 614	35.7
	08 043	Fremont County, CO..................	46 145	26.6	16820		Charlottesville, VA Metro SA..........	174 021	47.2
15900		Canton, IL Micro SA....................	38 250	54.1		51 003	Albemarle County, VA	79 236	48.3
	17 057	Fulton County, IL	38 250	54.1		51 065	Fluvanna County, VA	20 047	70.3
15940		Canton-Massillon, OH Metro SA.......	406 934	17.7		51 079	Greene County, VA	15 244	100.0
	39 019	Carroll County, OH	28 836	68.8		51 125	Nelson County, VA	14 445	100.0
	39 151	Stark County, OH.....................	378 098	13.8		51 540	Charlottesville city, VA	45 049	0.0
15980		Cape Coral-Fort Myers, FL Metro SA	440 888	11.5	16860		Chattanooga, TN-GA Metro SA	476 531	24.7
	12 071	Lee County, FL........................	440 888	11.5		13 047	Catoosa County, GA...................	53 282	29.0
16020		Cape Girardeau-Jackson, MO-IL Micro SA................................	90 312	44.3		13 083	Dade County, GA......................	15 154	79.8
						13 295	Walker County, GA	61 053	43.5
	17 003	Alexander County, IL..................	9 590	58.6		47 065	Hamilton County, TN	307 896	9.7
	29 017	Bollinger County, MO	12 029	100.0		47 115	Marion County, TN.....................	27 776	79.3
	29 031	Cape Girardeau County, MO........	68 693	32.5		47 153	Sequatchie County, TN	11 370	100.0
16060		Carbondale, IL Micro SA...............	59 612	37.2	16900		Chester, SC Micro SA.................	34 068	67.3
	17 077	Jackson County, IL	59 612	37.2		45 023	Chester County, SC	34 068	67.3
16100		Carlsbad-Artesia, NM Micro SA	51 658	24.5	16940		Cheyenne, WY Metro SA..............	81 607	16.5
	35 015	Eddy County, NM......................	51 658	24.5		56 021	Laramie County, WY...................	81 607	16.5
16180		Carson City, NV Metro SA	52 457	6.0	16980		Chicago-Naperville-Joliet, IL-IN-WI Metro SA...............................	9 098 316	2.8
	32 510	Carson City, NV.......................	52 457	6.0					
16220		Casper, WY Metro SA.................	66 533	13.4			Chicago-Naperville-Joliet, IL Metro Div. 16974............................	7 628 412	1.9
	56 025	Natrona County, WY..................	66 533	13.4					

Core Based Statistical Areas (Metropolitan and Micropolitan), and Metropolitan Divisions with 2000 Census Population and Percent of the Population That is Rural (As of June 2003) – Continued

Core Based Statistical Area Code	State/County FIPS Code	Statistical Area Name	2000 Census Population	Percent Rural	Core Based Statistical Area Code	State/County FIPS Code	Statistical Area Name	2000 Census Population	Percent Rural
	17 031	Cook County, IL	5 376 741	0.1	17500		Clewiston, FL Micro SA	36 210	36.3
	17 037	DeKalb County, IL	88 969	22.7		12 051	Hendry County, FL	36 210	36.3
	17 043	DuPage County, IL	904 161	0.1	17540		Clinton, IA Micro SA	50 149	31.9
	17 063	Grundy County, IL	37 535	38.6		19 045	Clinton County, IA	50 149	31.9
	17 089	Kane County, IL	404 119	6.2	17580		Clovis, NM Micro SA	45 044	14.7
	17 093	Kendall County, IL	54 544	26.3		35 009	Curry County, NM	45 044	14.7
	17 111	McHenry County, IL	260 077	12.0	17660		Coeur d'Alene, ID Metro SA	108 685	26.5
	17 197	Will County, IL	502 266	6.6		16 055	Kootenai County, ID	108 685	26.5
		Lake County-Kenosha County, IL-WI Metro Div. 29404	793 933	3.5	17700		Coffeyville, KS Micro SA	36 252	42.3
	17 097	Lake County, IL	644 356	1.7		20 125	Montgomery County, KS	36 252	42.3
	55 059	Kenosha County, WI	149 577	11.0	17740		Coldwater, MI Micro SA	45 787	68.5
		Gary, IN Metro Div. 23844	675 971	12.9		26 023	Branch County, MI	45 787	68.5
	18 073	Jasper County, IN	30 043	61.3	17780		College Station-Bryan, TX Metro SA	184 885	24.3
	18 089	Lake County, IN	484 564	4.6		48 041	Brazos County, TX	152 415	12.8
	18 111	Newton County, IN	14 566	97.4		48 051	Burleson County, TX	16 470	83.8
	18 127	Porter County, IN	146 798	21.8		48 395	Robertson County, TX	16 000	72.6
17020		Chico, CA Metro SA	203 171	17.9	17820		Colorado Springs, CO Metro SA	537 484	11.3
	06 007	Butte County, CA	203 171	17.9		08 041	El Paso County, CO	516 929	9.5
17060		Chillicothe, OH Micro SA	73 345	58.2		08 119	Teller County, CO	20 555	58.4
	39 141	Ross County, OH	73 345	58.2	17860		Columbia, MO Metro SA	145 666	27.0
17140		Cincinnati-Middletown, OH-KY-IN Metro SA	2 009 632	16.2		29 019	Boone County, MO	135 454	24.4
	18 029	Dearborn County, IN	46 109	62.9		29 089	Howard County, MO	10 212	62.1
	18 047	Franklin County, IN	22 151	79.6	17900		Columbia, SC Metro SA	647 158	30.1
	18 115	Ohio County, IN	5 623	100.0		45 017	Calhoun County, SC	15 185	100.0
	21 015	Boone County, KY	85 991	24.7		45 039	Fairfield County, SC	23 454	74.6
	21 023	Bracken County, KY	8 279	100.0		45 055	Kershaw County, SC	52 647	62.1
	21 037	Campbell County, KY	88 616	15.7		45 063	Lexington County, SC	216 014	33.7
	21 077	Gallatin County, KY	7 870	100.0		45 079	Richland County, SC	320 677	12.8
	21 081	Grant County, KY	22 384	77.8		45 081	Saluda County, SC	19 181	81.3
	21 117	Kenton County, KY	151 464	7.4	17940		Columbia, TN Micro SA	69 498	43.6
	21 191	Pendleton County, KY	14 390	100.0		47 119	Maury County, TN	69 498	43.6
	39 015	Brown County, OH	42 285	80.6	17980		Columbus, GA-AL Metro SA	281 768	19.9
	39 017	Butler County, OH	332 807	11.4		01 113	Russell County, AL	49 756	36.3
	39 025	Clermont County, OH	177 977	28.8		13 053	Chattahoochee County, GA	14 882	21.4
	39 061	Hamilton County, OH	845 303	2.5		13 145	Harris County, GA	23 695	97.1
	39 165	Warren County, OH	158 383	22.5		13 197	Marion County, GA	7 144	100.0
17180		City of The Dalles, OR Micro SA	23 791	33.8		13 215	Muscogee County, GA	186 291	2.5
	41 065	Wasco County, OR	23 791	33.8	18020		Columbus, IN Metro SA	71 435	31.7
17220		Clarksburg, WV Micro SA	92 144	50.8		18 005	Bartholomew County, IN	71 435	31.7
	54 017	Doddridge County, WV	7 403	100.0	18060		Columbus, MS Micro SA	61 586	39.7
	54 033	Harrison County, WV	68 652	43.2		28 087	Lowndes County, MS	61 586	39.7
	54 091	Taylor County, WV	16 089	60.9	18100		Columbus, NE Micro SA	31 662	33.5
17260		Clarksdale, MS Micro SA	30 622	32.1		31 141	Platte County, NE	31 662	33.5
	28 027	Coahoma County, MS	30 622	32.1	18140		Columbus, OH Metro SA	1 612 694	15.9
17300		Clarksville, TN-KY Metro SA	232 000	33.0		39 041	Delaware County, OH	109 989	32.1
	21 047	Christian County, KY	72 265	27.4		39 045	Fairfield County, OH	122 759	39.0
	21 221	Trigg County, KY	12 597	78.9		39 049	Franklin County, OH	1 068 978	1.8
	47 125	Montgomery County, TN	134 768	25.6		39 089	Licking County, OH	145 491	39.4
	47 161	Stewart County, TN	12 370	100.0		39 097	Madison County, OH	40 213	48.5
17340		Clearlake, CA Micro SA	58 309	44.4		39 117	Morrow County, OH	31 628	88.9
	06 033	Lake County, CA	58 309	44.4		39 129	Pickaway County, OH	52 727	45.1
17380		Cleveland, MS Micro SA	40 633	42.2		39 159	Union County, OH	40 909	60.4
	28 011	Bolivar County, MS	40 633	42.2	18180		Concord, NH Metro SA	136 225	53.9
17420		Cleveland, TN Metro SA	104 015	43.8		33 013	Merrimack County, NH	136 225	53.9
	47 011	Bradley County, TN	87 965	33.6	18220		Connersville, IN Micro SA	25 588	34.3
	47 139	Polk County, TN	16 050	100.0		18 041	Fayette County, IN	25 588	34.3
17460		Cleveland-Elyria-Mentor, OH Metro SA	2 148 143	8.5	18260		Cookeville, TN Micro SA	93 417	56.1
	39 035	Cuyahoga County, OH	1 393 978	0.8		47 087	Jackson County, TN	10 984	100.0
	39 055	Geauga County, OH	90 895	63.1		47 133	Overton County, TN	20 118	84.3
	39 085	Lake County, OH	227 511	7.9		47 141	Putnam County, TN	62 315	39.3
	39 093	Lorain County, OH	284 664	16.3	18300		Coos Bay, OR Micro SA	62 779	37.4
	39 103	Medina County, OH	151 095	33.9		41 011	Coos County, OR	62 779	37.4
					18340		Corbin, KY Micro SA	35 865	62.5
						21 235	Whitley County, KY	35 865	62.5

Core Based Statistical Areas (Metropolitan and Micropolitan), and Metropolitan Divisions with 2000 Census Population and Percent of the Population That is Rural (As of June 2003) – Continued

Core Based Statistical Area Code	State/ County FIPS Code	Statistical Area Name	2000 Census Population	Percent Rural	Core Based Statistical Area Code	State/ County FIPS Code	Statistical Area Name	2000 Census Population	Percent Rural
18380		Cordele, GA Micro SA	21 996	41.3	19340		Davenport-Moline-Rock Island, IA-IL Metro SA	376 019	20.3
	13 081	Crisp County, GA	21 996	41.3		17 073	Henry County, IL	51 020	44.4
18420		Corinth, MS Micro SA	34 558	65.9		17 131	Mercer County, IL	16 957	79.4
	28 003	Alcorn County, MS	34 558	65.9		17 161	Rock Island County, IL	149 374	11.1
18460		Cornelia, GA Micro SA	35 902	64.9		19 163	Scott County, IA	158 668	14.8
	13 137	Habersham County, GA	35 902	64.9	19380		Dayton, OH Metro SA	848 153	13.7
18500		Corning, NY Micro SA	98 726	62.4		39 057	Greene County, OH	147 886	16.5
	36 101	Steuben County, NY	98 726	62.4		39 109	Miami County, OH	98 868	31.8
18580		Corpus Christi, TX Metro SA	403 280	9.7		39 113	Montgomery County, OH	559 062	4.6
	48 007	Aransas County, TX	22 497	33.8		39 135	Preble County, OH	42 337	81.4
	48 355	Nueces County, TX	313 645	5.6	19460		Decatur, AL Metro SA	145 867	55.3
	48 409	San Patricio County, TX	67 138	21.0		01 079	Lawrence County, AL	34 803	92.5
18620		Corsicana, TX Micro SA	45 124	48.7		01 103	Morgan County, AL	111 064	43.6
	48 349	Navarro County, TX	45 124	48.7	19500		Decatur, IL Metro SA	114 706	15.8
18660		Cortland, NY Micro SA	48 599	45.1		17 115	Macon County, IL	114 706	15.8
	36 023	Cortland County, NY	48 599	45.1	19540		Decatur, IN Micro SA	33 625	56.5
18700		Corvallis, OR Metro SA	78 153	19.1		18 001	Adams County, IN	33 625	56.5
	41 003	Benton County, OR	78 153	19.1	19580		Defiance, OH Micro SA	39 500	47.5
18740		Coshocton, OH Micro SA	36 655	59.2		39 039	Defiance County, OH	39 500	47.5
	39 031	Coshocton County, OH	36 655	59.2	19620		Del Rio, TX Micro SA	44 856	9.5
18820		Crawfordsville, IN Micro SA	37 629	55.6		48 465	Val Verde County, TX	44 856	9.5
	18 107	Montgomery County, IN	37 629	55.6	19660		Deltona-Daytona Beach-Ormond Beach, FL Metro SA	443 343	9.3
18860		Crescent City North, CA Micro SA	27 507	32.1		12 127	Volusia County, FL	443 343	9.3
	06 015	Del Norte County, CA	27 507	32.1	19700		Deming, NM Micro SA	25 016	40.2
18900		Crossville, TN Micro SA	46 802	68.9		35 029	Luna County, NM	25 016	40.2
	47 035	Cumberland County, TN	46 802	68.9	19740		Denver-Aurora, CO Metro SA	2 179 240	6.2
18940		Crowley, LA Micro SA	58 861	49.5		08 001	Adams County, CO	348 618	4.1
	22 001	Acadia Parish, LA	58 861	49.5		08 005	Arapahoe County, CO	487 967	2.0
18980		Cullman, AL Micro SA	77 483	75.7		08 014	Broomfield County, CO	38 272	0.2
	01 043	Cullman County, AL	77 483	75.7		08 019	Clear Creek County, CO	9 322	97.8
19060		Cumberland, MD-WV Metro SA	102 008	35.6		08 031	Denver County, CO	554 636	0.0
	24 001	Allegany County, MD	74 930	25.7		08 035	Douglas County, CO	175 766	14.3
	54 057	Mineral County, WV	27 078	62.9		08 039	Elbert County, CO	19 872	100.0
19100		Dallas-Fort Worth-Arlington, TX Metro SA	5 161 544	8.7		08 047	Gilpin County, CO	4 757	100.0
		Dallas-Plano-Irving, TX Metro Div. 19124	3 451 226	7.8		08 059	Jefferson County, CO	525 507	6.8
	48 085	Collin County, TX	491 675	10.1		08 093	Park County, CO	14 523	100.0
	48 113	Dallas County, TX	2 218 899	0.9	19760		De Ridder, LA Micro SA	32 986	70.5
	48 119	Delta County, TX	5 327	100.0		22 011	Beauregard Parish, LA	32 986	70.5
	48 121	Denton County, TX	432 976	11.5	19780		Des Moines, IA Metro SA	481 394	16.3
	48 139	Ellis County, TX	111 360	41.1		19 049	Dallas County, IA	40 750	47.3
	48 231	Hunt County, TX	76 596	55.3		19 077	Guthrie County, IA	11 353	100.0
	48 257	Kaufman County, TX	71 313	66.2		19 121	Madison County, IA	14 019	65.3
	48 397	Rockwall County, TX	43 080	20.4		19 153	Polk County, IA	374 601	5.8
		Fort Worth-Arlington, TX Metro Div. 23104	1 710 318	10.5		19 181	Warren County, IA	40 671	41.4
	48 251	Johnson County, TX	126 811	45.0	19820		Detroit-Warren-Livonia, MI Metro SA	4 452 557	6.5
	48 367	Parker County, TX	88 495	65.6			Warren-Farmington Hills-Troy, MI Metro Div. 47644	2 391 395	11.6
	48 439	Tarrant County, TX	1 446 219	1.8		26 087	Lapeer County, MI	87 904	76.1
	48 497	Wise County, TX	48 793	81.3		26 093	Livingston County, MI	156 951	38.8
19140		Dalton, GA Metro SA	120 031	44.4		26 099	Macomb County, MI	788 149	3.2
	13 213	Murray County, GA	36 506	73.6		26 125	Oakland County, MI	1 194 156	5.1
	13 313	Whitfield County, GA	83 525	31.6		26 147	St. Clair County, MI	164 235	37.8
19180		Danville, IL Metro SA	83 919	29.7			Detroit-Livonia-Dearborn, MI Metro Div. 19804	2 061 162	0.7
	17 183	Vermilion County, IL	83 919	29.7		26 163	Wayne County, MI	2 061 162	0.7
19220		Danville, KY Micro SA	51 058	56.8	19860		Dickinson, ND Micro SA	23 524	33.1
	21 021	Boyle County, KY	27 697	36.8		38 007	Billings County, ND	888	100.0
	21 137	Lincoln County, KY	23 361	80.4		38 089	Stark County, ND	22 636	30.5
19260		Danville, VA Metro SA	110 156	53.0	19900		Dillon, SC Micro SA	30 722	65.7
	51 143	Pittsylvania County, VA	61 745	89.6		45 033	Dillon County, SC	30 722	65.7
	51 590	Danville city, VA	48 411	6.3	19940		Dixon, IL Micro SA	36 062	44.2
19300		Daphne-Fairhope, AL Micro SA	140 415	54.6		17 103	Lee County, IL	36 062	44.2
	01 003	Baldwin County, AL	140 415	54.6					

Core Based Statistical Area Code	State/ County FIPS Code	Statistical Area Name	2000 Census Population	Percent Rural	Core Based Statistical Area Code	State/ County FIPS Code	Statistical Area Name	2000 Census Population	Percent Rural
19980		Dodge City, KS Micro SA..............	32 458	20.0		37 143	Perquimans County, NC..............	11 368	100.0
	20 057	Ford County, KS......................	32 458	20.0	21060		Elizabethtown, KY Metro SA..............	107 547	41.3
20020		Dothan, AL Metro SA..............	130 861	53.2		21 093	Hardin County, KY......................	94 174	36.3
	01 061	Geneva County, AL..............	25 764	86.8		21 123	Larue County, KY......................	13 373	76.7
	01 067	Henry County, AL..............	16 310	100.0	21140		Elkhart-Goshen, IN Metro SA..............	182 791	21.8
	01 069	Houston County, AL..............	88 787	34.9		18 039	Elkhart County, IN......................	182 791	21.8
20060		Douglas, GA Micro SA..............	45 022	72.5	21220		Elko, NV Micro SA..............	46 942	49.1
	13 003	Atkinson County, GA..............	7 609	100.0		32 007	Elko County, NV......................	45 291	47.2
	13 069	Coffee County, GA..............	37 413	66.9		32 011	Eureka County, NV......................	1 651	100.0
20100		Dover, DE Metro SA..............	126 697	35.5	21260		Ellensburg, WA Micro SA..............	33 362	40.5
	10 001	Kent County, DE......................	126 697	35.5		53 037	Kittitas County, WA......................	33 362	40.5
20140		Dublin, GA Micro SA..............	53 434	64.0	21300		Elmira, NY Metro SA..............	91 070	26.2
	13 167	Johnson County, GA..............	8 560	100.0		36 015	Chemung County, NY......................	91 070	26.2
	13 175	Laurens County, GA..............	44 874	57.1	21340		El Paso, TX Metro SA..............	679 622	3.0
20180		DuBois, PA Micro SA..............	83 382	54.1		48 141	El Paso County, TX......................	679 622	3.0
	42 033	Clearfield County, PA..............	83 382	54.1	21380		Emporia, KS Micro SA..............	38 965	31.2
20220		Dubuque, IA Metro SA..............	89 143	25.7		20 017	Chase County, KS......................	3 030	100.0
	19 061	Dubuque County, IA..............	89 143	25.7		20 111	Lyon County, KS......................	35 935	25.4
20260		Duluth, MN-WI Metro SA..............	275 486	40.0	21420		Enid, OK Micro SA..............	57 813	21.1
	27 017	Carlton County, MN..............	31 671	63.3		40 047	Garfield County, OK......................	57 813	21.1
	27 137	St. Louis County, MN..............	200 528	36.6	21460		Enterprise-Ozark, AL Micro SA..............	92 744	55.1
	55 031	Douglas County, WI..............	43 287	38.7		01 031	Coffee County, AL......................	43 615	55.4
20300		Dumas, TX Micro SA..............	20 121	17.1		01 045	Dale County, AL......................	49 129	54.8
	48 341	Moore County, TX..............	20 121	17.1	21500		Erie, PA Metro SA..............	280 843	19.6
20340		Duncan, OK Micro SA..............	43 182	43.3		42 049	Erie County, PA......................	280 843	19.6
	40 137	Stephens County, OK..............	43 182	43.3	21540		Escanaba, MI Micro SA..............	38 520	45.2
20380		Dunn, NC Micro SA..............	91 025	66.2		26 041	Delta County, MI......................	38 520	45.2
	37 085	Harnett County, NC..............	91 025	66.2	21580		Espanola, NM Micro SA..............	41 190	57.1
20420		Durango, CO Micro SA..............	43 941	64.7		35 039	Rio Arriba County, NM......................	41 190	57.1
	08 067	La Plata County, CO..............	43 941	64.7	21660		Eugene-Springfield, OR Metro SA.....	322 959	19.4
20460		Durant, OK Micro SA..............	36 534	63.5		41 039	Lane County, OR......................	322 959	19.4
	40 013	Bryan County, OK..............	36 534	63.5	21700		Eureka-Arcata-Fortuna, CA Micro SA	126 518	30.5
20500		Durham, NC Metro SA..............	426 493	28.3		06 023	Humboldt County, CA......................	126 518	30.5
	37 037	Chatham County, NC..............	49 329	80.7	21740		Evanston, WY Micro SA..............	19 742	41.4
	37 063	Durham County, NC..............	223 314	7.5		56 041	Uinta County, WY......................	19 742	41.4
	37 135	Orange County, NC..............	118 227	32.0	21780		Evansville, IN-KY Metro SA..............	342 815	28.6
	37 145	Person County, NC..............	35 623	73.4		18 051	Gibson County, IN......................	32 500	53.6
20540		Dyersburg, TN Micro SA..............	37 279	44.5		18 129	Posey County, IN......................	27 061	69.1
	47 045	Dyer County, TN..............	37 279	44.5		18 163	Vanderburgh County, IN..............	171 922	10.1
20580		Eagle Pass, TX Micro SA..............	47 297	10.8		18 173	Warrick County, IN......................	52 383	28.6
	48 323	Maverick County, TX..............	47 297	10.8		21 101	Henderson County, KY..............	44 829	40.8
20620		East Liverpool-Salem, OH				21 233	Webster County, KY..............	14 120	78.7
		Micro SA..............	112 075	43.2	21820		Fairbanks, AK Metro SA..............	82 840	29.6
	39 029	Columbiana County, OH..............	112 075	43.2		02 090	Fairbanks North Star Borough, AK.	82 840	29.6
20660		Easton, MD Micro SA..............	33 812	63.3	21860		Fairmont, MN Micro SA..............	21 802	53.0
	24 041	Talbot County, MD..............	33 812	63.3		27 091	Martin County, MN......................	21 802	53.0
20700		East Stroudsburg, PA Micro SA........	138 687	49.6	21900		Fairmont, WV Micro SA..............	56 598	41.5
	42 089	Monroe County, PA..............	138 687	49.6		54 049	Marion County, WV......................	56 598	41.5
20740		Eau Claire, WI Metro SA..............	148 337	33.8	21980		Fallon, NV Micro SA..............	23 982	35.0
	55 017	Chippewa County, WI..............	55 195	52.4		32 001	Churchill County, NV..............	23 982	35.0
	55 035	Eau Claire County, WI..............	93 142	22.7	22020		Fargo, ND-MN Metro SA..............	174 367	18.3
20780		Edwards, CO Micro SA..............	49 471	29.8		27 027	Clay County, MN......................	51 229	30.0
	08 037	Eagle County, CO..............	41 659	31.3		38 017	Cass County, ND......................	123 138	13.5
	08 065	Lake County, CO..............	7 812	21.9	22060		Faribault-Northfield, MN Micro SA.....	56 665	31.1
20820		Effingham, IL Micro SA..............	34 264	59.3		27 131	Rice County, MN......................	56 665	31.1
	17 049	Effingham County, IL..............	34 264	59.3	22100		Farmington, MO Micro SA..............	55 641	41.2
20900		El Campo, TX Micro SA..............	41 188	49.7		29 187	St. Francois County, MO..............	55 641	41.2
	48 481	Wharton County, TX..............	41 188	49.7	22140		Farmington, NM Metro SA..............	113 801	40.8
20940		El Centro, CA Metro SA..............	142 361	14.8		35 045	San Juan County, NM..............	113 801	40.8
	06 025	Imperial County, CA..............	142 361	14.8	22180		Fayetteville, NC Metro SA..............	336 609	17.0
20980		El Dorado, AR Micro SA..............	45 629	51.8		37 051	Cumberland County, NC..............	302 963	12.7
	05 139	Union County, AR..............	45 629	51.8		37 093	Hoke County, NC......................	33 646	56.5
21020		Elizabeth City, NC Micro SA	53 150	63.9	22220		Fayetteville-Springdale-Rogers, AR-MO Metro SA	347 045	42.4
	37 029	Camden County, NC	6 885	100.0		05 007	Benton County, AR..............	153 406	41.3
	37 139	Pasquotank County, NC..............	34 897	45.1					

Core Based Statistical Areas (Metropolitan and Micropolitan), and Metropolitan Divisions with 2000 Census Population and Percent of the Population That is Rural (As of June 2003) – Continued

Core Based Statistical Area Code	State/County FIPS Code	Statistical Area Name	2000 Census Population	Percent Rural	Core Based Statistical Area Code	State/County FIPS Code	Statistical Area Name	2000 Census Population	Percent Rural
	05 087	Madison County, AR	14 243	100.0		01 055	Etowah County, AL	103 459	39.9
	05 143	Washington County, AR	157 715	30.4	23500		Gaffney, SC Micro SA	52 537	61.3
	29 119	McDonald County, MO	21 681	100.0		45 021	Cherokee County, SC	52 537	61.3
22260		Fergus Falls, MN Micro SA	57 159	77.2	23540		Gainesville, FL Metro SA	232 392	30.3
	27 111	Otter Tail County, MN	57 159	77.2		12 001	Alachua County, FL	217 955	25.6
22300		Findlay, OH Micro SA	71 295	32.0		12 041	Gilchrist County, FL	14 437	100.0
	39 063	Hancock County, OH	71 295	32.0	23580		Gainesville, GA Metro SA	139 277	33.0
22340		Fitzgerald, GA Micro SA	27 415	46.9		13 139	Hall County, GA	139 277	33.0
	13 017	Ben Hill County, GA	17 484	34.8	23620		Gainesville, TX Micro SA	36 363	57.6
	13 155	Irwin County, GA	9 931	68.4		48 097	Cooke County, TX	36 363	57.6
22380		Flagstaff, AZ Metro SA	116 320	36.0	23660		Galesburg, IL Micro SA	74 571	30.1
	04 005	Coconino County, AZ	116 320	36.0		17 095	Knox County, IL	55 836	24.8
22420		Flint, MI Metro SA	436 141	16.2		17 187	Warren County, IL	18 735	46.0
	26 049	Genesee County, MI	436 141	16.2	23700		Gallup, NM Micro SA	74 798	60.7
22460		Florence, AL Metro SA	142 950	50.0		35 031	McKinley County, NM	74 798	60.7
	01 033	Colbert County, AL	54 984	47.1	23780		Garden City, KS Micro SA	40 523	19.1
	01 077	Lauderdale County, AL	87 966	51.8		20 055	Finney County, KS	40 523	19.1
22500		Florence, SC Metro SA	193 155	46.4	23820		Gardnerville Ranchos, NV Micro SA	41 259	31.1
	45 031	Darlington County, SC	67 394	54.6		32 005	Douglas County, NV	41 259	31.1
	45 041	Florence County, SC	125 761	42.0	23860		Georgetown, SC Micro SA	55 797	45.3
22540		Fond du Lac, WI Metro SA	97 296	38.1		45 043	Georgetown County, SC	55 797	45.3
	55 039	Fond du Lac County, WI	97 296	38.1	23900		Gettysburg, PA Micro SA	91 292	59.8
22580		Forest City, NC Micro SA	62 899	63.0		42 001	Adams County, PA	91 292	59.8
	37 161	Rutherford County, NC	62 899	63.0	23940		Gillette, WY Micro SA	33 698	38.5
22620		Forrest City, AR Micro SA	29 329	51.1		56 005	Campbell County, WY	33 698	38.5
	05 123	St. Francis County, AR	29 329	51.1	23980		Glasgow, KY Micro SA	48 070	71.6
22660		Fort Collins-Loveland, CO Metro SA	251 494	13.5		21 009	Barren County, KY	38 033	64.1
	08 069	Larimer County, CO	251 494	13.5		21 169	Metcalfe County, KY	10 037	100.0
22700		Fort Dodge, IA Micro SA	40 235	36.1	24020		Glens Falls, NY Metro SA	124 345	54.7
	19 187	Webster County, IA	40 235	36.1		36 113	Warren County, NY	63 303	39.5
22780		Fort Leonard Wood, MO Micro SA	41 165	49.2		36 115	Washington County, NY	61 042	70.4
	29 169	Pulaski County, MO	41 165	49.2	24100		Gloversville, NY Micro SA	55 073	50.0
22820		Fort Morgan, CO Micro SA	27 171	31.6		36 035	Fulton County, NY	55 073	50.0
	08 087	Morgan County, CO	27 171	31.6	24140		Goldsboro, NC Metro SA	113 329	44.8
22860		Fort Polk South, LA Micro SA	52 531	47.0		37 191	Wayne County, NC	113 329	44.8
	22 115	Vernon Parish, LA	52 531	47.0	24180		Granbury, TX Micro SA	47 909	46.7
22900		Fort Smith, AR-OK Metro SA	273 170	46.8		48 221	Hood County, TX	41 100	37.9
	05 033	Crawford County, AR	53 247	54.9		48 425	Somervell County, TX	6 809	100.0
	05 047	Franklin County, AR	17 771	84.1	24220		Grand Forks, ND-MN Metro SA	97 478	28.3
	05 131	Sebastian County, AR	115 071	21.0		27 119	Polk County, MN	31 369	51.0
	40 079	Le Flore County, OK	48 109	69.3		38 035	Grand Forks County, ND	66 109	17.6
	40 135	Sequoyah County, OK	38 972	67.4	24260		Grand Island, NE Micro SA	68 305	29.2
22980		Fort Valley, GA Micro SA	23 668	36.4		31 079	Hall County, NE	53 534	15.8
	13 225	Peach County, GA	23 668	36.4		31 093	Howard County, NE	6 567	100.0
23020		Fort Walton Beach-Crestview-Destin, FL Metro SA	170 498	12.0		31 121	Merrick County, NE	8 204	59.9
	12 091	Okaloosa County, FL	170 498	12.0	24300		Grand Junction, CO Metro SA	116 255	15.2
23060		Fort Wayne, IN Metro SA	390 156	21.0		08 077	Mesa County, CO	116 255	15.2
	18 003	Allen County, IN	331 849	13.4	24340		Grand Rapids-Wyoming, MI Metro SA	740 482	27.7
	18 179	Wells County, IN	27 600	51.4		26 015	Barry County, MI	56 755	80.7
	18 183	Whitley County, IN	30 707	75.8		26 067	Ionia County, MI	61 518	57.2
23140		Frankfort, IN Micro SA	33 866	50.2		26 081	Kent County, MI	574 335	14.8
	18 023	Clinton County, IN	33 866	50.2		26 123	Newaygo County, MI	47 874	82.8
23180		Frankfort, KY Micro SA	66 798	32.9	24380		Grants, NM Micro SA	25 595	59.8
	21 005	Anderson County, KY	19 111	49.1		35 006	Cibola County, NM	25 595	59.8
	21 073	Franklin County, KY	47 687	26.4	24420		Grants Pass, OR Micro SA	75 726	48.1
23300		Freeport, IL Micro SA	48 979	38.9		41 033	Josephine County, OR	75 726	48.1
	17 177	Stephenson County, IL	48 979	38.9	24460		Great Bend, KS Micro SA	28 205	33.3
23340		Fremont, NE Micro SA	36 160	28.7		20 009	Barton County, KS	28 205	33.3
	31 053	Dodge County, NE	36 160	28.7	24500		Great Falls, MT Metro SA	80 357	19.8
23380		Fremont, OH Micro SA	61 792	41.6		30 013	Cascade County, MT	80 357	19.8
	39 143	Sandusky County, OH	61 792	41.6	24540		Greeley, CO Metro SA	180 926	28.1
23420		Fresno, CA Metro SA	799 407	12.6		08 123	Weld County, CO	180 926	28.1
	06 019	Fresno County, CA	799 407	12.6	24580		Green Bay, WI Metro SA	282 599	28.9
23460		Gadsden, AL Metro SA	103 459	39.9		55 009	Brown County, WI	226 778	16.1

Core Based Statistical Area Code	State/County FIPS Code	Statistical Area Name	2000 Census Population	Percent Rural	Core Based Statistical Area Code	State/County FIPS Code	Statistical Area Name	2000 Census Population	Percent Rural
	55 061	Kewaunee County, WI	20 187	82.3		09 013	Tolland County, CT	136 364	38.2
	55 083	Oconto County, WI	35 634	80.3	25580		Hastings, NE Micro SA	38 190	36.8
24620		Greeneville, TN Micro SA	62 909	69.1		31 001	Adams County, NE	31 151	22.5
	47 059	Greene County, TN	62 909	69.1		31 035	Clay County, NE	7 039	100.0
24660		Greensboro-High Point, NC Metro SA	643 430	31.3	25620		Hattiesburg, MS Metro SA	123 812	50.6
	37 081	Guilford County, NC	421 048	16.2		28 035	Forrest County, MS	72 604	33.3
	37 151	Randolph County, NC	130 454	60.3		28 073	Lamar County, MS	39 070	67.6
	37 157	Rockingham County, NC	91 928	59.3		28 111	Perry County, MS	12 138	100.0
24700		Greensburg, IN Micro SA	24 555	57.7	25660		Havre, MT Micro SA	16 673	38.0
	18 031	Decatur County, IN	24 555	57.7		30 041	Hill County, MT	16 673	38.0
24740		Greenville, MS Micro SA	62 977	17.1	25700		Hays, KS Micro SA	27 507	25.1
	28 151	Washington County, MS	62 977	17.1		20 051	Ellis County, KS	27 507	25.1
24780		Greenville, NC Metro SA	152 772	42.7	25740		Helena, MT Micro SA	65 765	41.4
	37 079	Greene County, NC	18 974	100.0		30 043	Jefferson County, MT	10 049	100.0
	37 147	Pitt County, NC	133 798	34.6		30 049	Lewis and Clark County, MT	55 716	30.8
24820		Greenville, OH Micro SA	53 309	65.8	25780		Henderson, NC Micro SA	42 954	50.8
	39 037	Darke County, OH	53 309	65.8		37 181	Vance County, NC	42 954	50.8
24860		Greenville, SC Metro SA	559 940	27.9	25820		Hereford, TX Micro SA	18 561	17.6
	45 045	Greenville County, SC	379 616	17.0		48 117	Deaf Smith County, TX	18 561	17.6
	45 059	Laurens County, SC	69 567	65.7	25860		Hickory-Morganton-Lenoir, NC Metro SA	341 851	43.2
	45 077	Pickens County, SC	110 757	41.7		37 003	Alexander County, NC	33 603	82.8
24900		Greenwood, MS Micro SA	48 716	38.7		37 023	Burke County, NC	89 148	45.6
	28 015	Carroll County, MS	10 769	100.0		37 027	Caldwell County, NC	77 415	38.3
	28 083	Leflore County, MS	37 947	21.3		37 035	Catawba County, NC	141 685	35.1
24940		Greenwood, SC Micro SA	66 271	43.2	25900		Hilo, HI Micro SA	148 677	41.5
	45 047	Greenwood County, SC	66 271	43.2		15 001	Hawaii County, HI	148 677	41.5
24980		Grenada, MS Micro SA	23 263	44.3	25940		Hilton Head Island-Beaufort, SC Micro SA	141 615	36.4
	28 043	Grenada County, MS	23 263	44.3		45 013	Beaufort County, SC	120 937	28.6
25060		Gulfport-Biloxi, MS Metro SA	246 190	27.7		45 053	Jasper County, SC	20 678	82.5
	28 045	Hancock County, MS	42 967	38.5	25980		Hinesville-Fort Stewart, GA Metro SA	71 914	29.9
	28 047	Harrison County, MS	189 601	21.6		13 179	Liberty County, GA	61 610	19.9
	28 131	Stone County, MS	13 622	78.8		13 183	Long County, GA	10 304	89.8
25100		Guymon, OK Micro SA	20 107	47.7	26020		Hobbs, NM Micro SA	55 511	21.3
	40 139	Texas County, OK	20 107	47.7		35 025	Lea County, NM	55 511	21.3
25180		Hagerstown-Martinsburg, MD-WV Metro SA	222 771	41.4	26100		Holland-Grand Haven, MI Metro SA	238 314	23.8
	24 043	Washington County, MD	131 923	32.2		26 139	Ottawa County, MI	238 314	23.8
	54 003	Berkeley County, WV	75 905	45.7	26140		Homosassa Springs, FL Micro SA	118 085	42.1
	54 065	Morgan County, WV	14 943	100.0		12 017	Citrus County, FL	118 085	42.1
25220		Hammond, LA Micro SA	100 588	53.6	26180		Honolulu, HI Metro SA	876 156	1.6
	22 105	Tangipahoa Parish, LA	100 588	53.6		15 003	Honolulu County, HI	876 156	1.6
25260		Hanford-Corcoran, CA Metro SA	129 461	13.1	26220		Hood River, OR Micro SA	20 411	57.4
	06 031	Kings County, CA	129 461	13.1		41 027	Hood River County, OR	20 411	57.4
25300		Hannibal, MO Micro SA	37 915	43.4	26260		Hope, AR Micro SA	33 542	60.0
	29 127	Marion County, MO	28 289	25.1		05 057	Hempstead County, AR	23 587	55.9
	29 173	Ralls County, MO	9 626	97.3		05 099	Nevada County, AR	9 955	69.6
25340		Harriman, TN Micro SA	51 910	49.7	26300		Hot Springs, AR Metro SA	88 068	36.7
	47 145	Roane County, TN	51 910	49.7		05 051	Garland County, AR	88 068	36.7
25380		Harrisburg, IL Micro SA	26 733	36.7	26340		Houghton, MI Micro SA	38 317	47.6
	17 165	Saline County, IL	26 733	36.7		26 061	Houghton County, MI	36 016	44.2
25420		Harrisburg-Carlisle, PA Metro SA	509 074	25.2		26 083	Keweenaw County, MI	2 301	100.0
	42 041	Cumberland County, PA	213 674	25.1	26380		Houma-Bayou Cane-Thibodaux, LA Metro SA	194 477	26.3
	42 043	Dauphin County, PA	251 798	14.7		22 057	Lafourche Parish, LA	89 974	27.8
	42 099	Perry County, PA	43 602	86.3		22 109	Terrebonne Parish, LA	104 503	25.0
25460		Harrison, AR Micro SA	42 556	69.3	26420		Houston-Baytown-Sugar Land, TX Metro SA	4 715 407	8.7
	05 009	Boone County, AR	33 948	61.5		48 015	Austin County, TX	23 590	62.8
	05 101	Newton County, AR	8 608	100.0		48 039	Brazoria County, TX	241 767	28.4
25500		Harrisonburg, VA Metro SA	108 193	42.1		48 071	Chambers County, TX	26 031	64.2
	51 165	Rockingham County, VA	67 725	67.2		48 157	Fort Bend County, TX	354 452	10.1
	51 660	Harrisonburg city, VA	40 468	0.2		48 167	Galveston County, TX	250 158	8.4
25540		Hartford-West Hartford-East Hartford, CT Metro SA	1 148 618	12.4		48 201	Harris County, TX	3 400 578	1.8
	09 003	Hartford County, CT	857 183	5.5		48 291	Liberty County, TX	70 154	64.1
	09 007	Middlesex County, CT	155 071	28.0					

Core Based Statistical Area Code	State/ County FIPS Code	Statistical Area Name	2000 Census Population	Percent Rural	Core Based Statistical Area Code	State/ County FIPS Code	Statistical Area Name	2000 Census Population	Percent Rural
	48 339	Montgomery County, TX...............	293 768	36.0		16 081	Teton County, ID............................	5 999	100.0
	48 407	San Jacinto County, TX...............	22 246	100.0		56 039	Teton County, WY...........................	18 251	43.9
	48 473	Waller County, TX........................	32 663	63.4	27260		Jacksonville, FL Metro SA..................	1 122 750	12.1
26460		Hudson, NY Micro SA	63 094	70.6		12 003	Baker County, FL............................	22 259	62.3
	36 021	Columbia County, NY	63 094	70.6		12 019	Clay County, FL..............................	140 814	24.9
26500		Huntingdon, PA Micro SA	45 586	69.3		12 031	Duval County, FL............................	778 879	3.8
	42 061	Huntingdon County, PA	45 586	69.3		12 089	Nassau County, FL..........................	57 663	50.5
26540		Huntington, IN Micro SA	38 075	51.7		12 109	St. Johns County, FL......................	123 135	23.2
	18 069	Huntington County, IN	38 075	51.7	27300		Jacksonville, IL Micro SA	42 153	44.0
26580		Huntington-Ashland, WV-KY-OH Metro SA	288 649	36.6		17 137	Morgan County, IL..........................	36 616	35.5
	21 019	Boyd County, KY	49 752	25.7		17 171	Scott County, IL.............................	5 537	100.0
	21 089	Greenup County, KY	36 891	38.7	27340		Jacksonville, NC Metro SA................	150 355	28.8
	39 087	Lawrence County, OH	62 319	47.9		37 133	Onslow County, NC	150 355	28.8
	54 011	Cabell County, WV	96 784	23.1	27380		Jacksonville, TX Micro SA................	46 659	61.0
	54 099	Wayne County, WV	42 903	61.7		48 073	Cherokee County, TX......................	46 659	61.0
26620		Huntsville, AL Metro SA................	342 376	31.3	27420		Jamestown, ND Micro SA.................	21 908	28.7
	01 083	Limestone County, AL	65 676	66.7		38 093	Stutsman County, ND.......................	21 908	28.7
	01 089	Madison County, AL	276 700	22.9	27460		Jamestown-Dunkirk-Fredonia, NY Micro SA	139 750	41.2
26660		Huntsville, TX Micro SA	61 758	36.3		36 013	Chautauqua County, NY..................	139 750	41.2
	48 471	Walker County, TX........................	61 758	36.3	27500		Janesville, WI Metro SA...................	152 307	22.1
26700		Huron, SD Micro SA	17 023	29.7		55 105	Rock County, WI..............................	152 307	22.1
	46 005	Beadle County, SD	17 023	29.7	27540		Jasper, IN Micro SA	52 511	59.4
26740		Hutchinson, KS Micro SA	64 790	31.6		18 037	Dubois County, IN..........................	39 674	52.8
	20 155	Reno County, KS	64 790	31.6		18 125	Pike County, IN..............................	12 837	79.6
26780		Hutchinson, MN Micro SA	34 898	46.9	27620		Jefferson City, MO Metro SA...........	140 052	48.5
	27 085	McLeod County, MN	34 898	46.9		29 027	Callaway County, MO......................	40 766	62.1
26820		Idaho Falls, ID Metro SA................	101 677	30.5		29 051	Cole County, MO............................	71 397	30.6
	16 019	Bonneville County, ID	82 522	18.8		29 135	Moniteau County, MO......................	14 827	51.4
	16 051	Jefferson County, ID	19 155	81.2		29 151	Osage County, MO.........................	13 062	100.0
26860		Indiana, PA Micro SA.....................	89 605	62.1	27660		Jennings, LA Micro SA.....................	31 435	48.1
	42 063	Indiana County, PA	89 605	62.1		22 053	Jefferson Davis Parish, LA	31 435	48.1
26900		Indianapolis, IN Metro SA	1 525 104	14.6	27700		Jesup, GA Micro SA........................	26 565	51.8
	18 011	Boone County, IN	46 107	45.8		13 305	Wayne County, GA..........................	26 565	51.8
	18 013	Brown County, IN	14 957	100.0	27740		Johnson City, TN Metro SA	181 607	36.2
	18 057	Hamilton County, IN.......................	182 740	11.6		47 019	Carter County, TN..........................	56 742	39.9
	18 059	Hancock County, IN	55 391	37.4		47 171	Unicoi County, TN..........................	17 667	45.8
	18 063	Hendricks County, IN	104 093	29.6		47 179	Washington County, TN	107 198	32.6
	18 081	Johnson County, IN	115 209	16.9	27780		Johnstown, PA Metro SA.................	152 598	32.4
	18 097	Marion County, IN	860 454	1.0		42 021	Cambria County, PA.......................	152 598	32.4
	18 109	Morgan County, IN	66 689	53.3	27860		Jonesboro, AR Metro SA	107 762	41.8
	18 133	Putnam County, IN	36 019	73.2		05 031	Craighead County, AR.....................	82 148	35.1
	18 145	Shelby County, IN	43 445	56.4		05 111	Poinsett County, AR........................	25 614	63.3
26940		Indianola, MS Micro SA	34 369	36.6	27900		Joplin, MO Metro SA........................	157 322	38.5
	28 133	Sunflower County, MS	34 369	36.6		29 097	Jasper County, MO.........................	104 686	25.4
26980		Iowa City, IA Metro SA...................	131 676	30.2		29 145	Newton County, MO........................	52 636	64.7
	19 103	Johnson County, IA	111 006	23.3	27940		Juneau, AK Micro SA.......................	30 711	18.4
	19 183	Washington County, IA	20 670	67.2		02 110	Juneau City and Borough, AK........	30 711	18.4
27020		Iron Mountain, MI-WI Micro SA..........	32 560	39.0	27980		Kahului-Wailuku, HI Micro SA...........	128 094	12.4
	26 043	Dickinson County, MI	27 472	27.7		15 009	Maui County, HI..............................	128 094	12.4
	55 037	Florence County, WI	5 088	100.0	28020		Kalamazoo-Portage, MI Metro SA	314 866	32.8
27060		Ithaca, NY Metro SA......................	96 501	42.1		26 077	Kalamazoo County, MI....................	238 603	19.9
	36 109	Tompkins County, NY	96 501	42.1		26 159	Van Buren County, MI	76 263	72.9
27100		Jackson, MI Metro SA....................	158 422	41.4	28060		Kalispell, MT Micro SA....................	74 471	52.6
	26 075	Jackson County, MI	158 422	41.4		30 029	Flathead County, MT.......................	74 471	52.6
27140		Jackson, MS Metro SA..................	497 197	30.0	28100		Kankakee-Bradley, IL Metro SA.......	103 833	27.0
	28 029	Copiah County, MS	28 757	58.9		17 091	Kankakee County, IL......................	103 833	27.0
	28 049	Hinds County, MS	250 800	15.2	28140		Kansas City, MO-KS Metro SA..........	1 836 038	13.9
	28 089	Madison County, MS	74 674	33.3		20 059	Franklin County, KS........................	24 784	52.4
	28 121	Rankin County, MS	115 327	40.0		20 091	Johnson County, KS........................	451 086	5.0
	28 127	Simpson County, MS	27 639	84.0		20 103	Leavenworth County, KS..................	68 691	31.8
27180		Jackson, TN Metro SA...................	107 377	34.1		20 107	Linn County, KS.............................	9 570	100.0
	47 023	Chester County, TN	15 540	66.3		20 121	Miami County, KS...........................	28 351	55.5
	47 113	Madison County, TN	91 837	28.6		20 209	Wyandotte County, KS....................	157 882	5.3
27220		Jackson, WY-ID Micro SA................	24 250	57.8					

Core Based Statistical Areas (Metropolitan and Micropolitan), and Metropolitan Divisions with 2000 Census Population and Percent of the Population That is Rural (As of June 2003) – Continued

Core Based Statistical Area Code	State/ County FIPS Code	Statistical Area Name	2000 Census Population	Percent Rural	Core Based Statistical Area Code	State/ County FIPS Code	Statistical Area Name	2000 Census Population	Percent Rural
	29 013	Bates County, MO	16 653	77.5	29020		Kokomo, IN Metro SA	101 541	28.8
	29 025	Caldwell County, MO	8 969	100.0		18 067	Howard County, IN	84 964	21.9
	29 037	Cass County, MO	82 092	37.4		18 159	Tipton County, IN	16 577	64.5
	29 047	Clay County, MO	184 006	10.6	29060		Laconia, NH Micro SA	56 325	60.1
	29 049	Clinton County, MO	18 979	77.3		33 001	Belknap County, NH	56 325	60.1
	29 095	Jackson County, MO	654 880	4.0	29100		La Crosse, WI-MN Metro SA	126 838	23.0
	29 107	Lafayette County, MO	32 960	58.8		27 055	Houston County, MN	19 718	56.3
	29 165	Platte County, MO	73 781	20.0		55 063	La Crosse County, WI	107 120	16.9
	29 177	Ray County, MO	23 354	71.1	29140		Lafayette, IN Metro SA	178 541	27.3
28180		Kapaa, HI Micro SA	58 463	18.7		18 007	Benton County, IN	9 421	100.0
	15 007	Kauai County, HI	58 463	18.7		18 015	Carroll County, IN	20 165	80.3
28260		Kearney, NE Micro SA	49 141	39.0		18 157	Tippecanoe County, IN	148 955	15.5
	31 019	Buffalo County, NE	42 259	35.8	29180		Lafayette, LA Metro SA	239 086	23.3
	31 099	Kearney County, NE	6 882	58.1		22 055	Lafayette Parish, LA	190 503	12.0
28300		Keene, NH Micro SA	73 825	66.2		22 099	St. Martin Parish, LA	48 583	67.6
	33 005	Cheshire County, NH	73 825	66.2	29220		La Follette, TN Micro SA	39 854	56.1
28340		Kendallville, IN Micro SA	46 275	66.4		47 013	Campbell County, TN	39 854	56.1
	18 113	Noble County, IN	46 275	66.4	29260		La Grande, OR Micro SA	24 530	42.2
28380		Kennett, MO Micro SA	33 155	49.6		41 061	Union County, OR	24 530	42.2
	29 069	Dunklin County, MO	33 155	49.6	29300		LaGrange, GA Micro SA	58 779	42.7
28420		Kennewick-Richland-Pasco, WA Metro SA	191 822	14.2		13 285	Troup County, GA	58 779	42.7
	53 005	Benton County, WA	142 475	12.3	29340		Lake Charles, LA Metro SA	193 568	26.4
	53 021	Franklin County, WA	49 347	19.8		22 019	Calcasieu Parish, LA	183 577	22.4
28460		Keokuk-Fort Madison, IA-MO Micro SA	45 468	50.1		22 023	Cameron Parish, LA	9 991	100.0
	19 111	Lee County, IA	38 052	40.4	29380		Lake City, FL Micro SA	56 513	67.8
	29 045	Clark County, MO	7 416	100.0		12 023	Columbia County, FL	56 513	67.8
28500		Kerrville, TX Micro SA	43 653	39.2	29420		Lake Havasu City-Kingman, AZ Micro SA	155 032	24.4
	48 265	Kerr County, TX	43 653	39.2		04 015	Mohave County, AZ	155 032	24.4
28540		Ketchikan, AK Micro SA	14 070	23.5	29460		Lakeland-Winter Haven, FL Metro SA	483 924	20.2
	02 130	Ketchikan Gateway Borough, AK	14 070	23.5		12 105	Polk County, FL	483 924	20.2
28580		Key West-Marathon, FL Micro SA	79 589	6.7	29500		Lamesa, TX Micro SA	14 985	18.0
	12 087	Monroe County, FL	79 589	6.7		48 115	Dawson County, TX	14 985	18.0
28620		Kill Devil Hills, NC Micro SA	29 967	30.4	29540		Lancaster, PA Metro SA	470 658	24.7
	37 055	Dare County, NC	29 967	30.4		42 071	Lancaster County, PA	470 658	24.7
28660		Killeen-Temple-Fort Hood, TX Metro SA	330 714	20.5	29580		Lancaster, SC Micro SA	61 351	61.4
	48 027	Bell County, TX	237 974	18.4		45 057	Lancaster County, SC	61 351	61.4
	48 099	Coryell County, TX	74 978	17.5	29620		Lansing-East Lansing, MI Metro SA	447 728	26.2
	48 281	Lampasas County, TX	17 762	60.6		26 037	Clinton County, MI	64 753	60.5
28700		Kingsport-Bristol, TN-VA Metro SA	230 014	40.2		26 045	Eaton County, MI	103 655	39.5
	47 073	Hawkins County, TN	53 563	61.4		26 065	Ingham County, MI	279 320	13.3
	47 163	Sullivan County, TN	153 048	26.5	29660		Laramie, WY Micro SA	32 014	11.8
	51 169	Scott County, VA	23 403	81.2		56 001	Albany County, WY	32 014	11.8
28740		Kingston, NY Metro SA	177 749	49.0	29700		Laredo, TX Metro SA	193 117	4.2
	36 111	Ulster County, NY	177 749	49.0		48 479	Webb County, TX	193 117	4.2
28780		Kingsville, TX Micro SA	31 963	19.8	29740		Las Cruces, NM Metro SA	174 682	19.9
	48 261	Kenedy County, TX	414	100.0		35 013	Dona Ana County, NM	174 682	19.9
	48 273	Kleberg County, TX	31 549	18.7	29780		Las Vegas, NM Micro SA	30 126	40.3
28820		Kinston, NC Micro SA	59 648	44.7		35 047	San Miguel County, NM	30 126	40.3
	37 107	Lenoir County, NC	59 648	44.7	29820		Las Vegas-Paradise, NV Metro SA	1 375 765	2.3
28860		Kirksville, MO Micro SA	29 147	43.4		32 003	Clark County, NV	1 375 765	2.3
	29 001	Adair County, MO	24 977	33.9	29860		Laurel, MS Micro SA	83 107	68.5
	29 197	Schuyler County, MO	4 170	100.0		28 061	Jasper County, MS	18 149	100.0
28900		Klamath Falls, OR Micro SA	63 775	35.5		28 067	Jones County, MS	64 958	59.7
	41 035	Klamath County, OR	63 775	35.5	29900		Laurinburg, NC Micro SA	35 998	52.8
28940		Knoxville, TN Metro SA	616 079	25.2		37 165	Scotland County, NC	35 998	52.8
	47 001	Anderson County, TN	71 330	41.0	29940		Lawrence, KS Metro SA	99 962	12.8
	47 009	Blount County, TN	105 823	36.6		20 045	Douglas County, KS	99 962	12.8
	47 093	Knox County, TN	382 032	13.1	29980		Lawrenceburg, TN Micro SA	39 926	75.0
	47 105	Loudon County, TN	39 086	49.9		47 099	Lawrence County, TN	39 926	75.0
	47 173	Union County, TN	17 808	100.0	30020		Lawton, OK Metro SA	114 996	21.9
28980		Kodiak, AK Micro SA	13 913	24.0		40 031	Comanche County, OK	114 996	21.9
	02 150	Kodiak Island Borough, AK	13 913	24.0	30060		Lebanon, MO Micro SA	32 513	64.1
						29 105	Laclede County, MO	32 513	64.1

Appendix C

C-11

Core Based Statistical Areas (Metropolitan and Micropolitan), and Metropolitan Divisions with 2000 Census Population and Percent of the Population That is Rural (As of June 2003) – Continued

Core Based Statistical Area Code	State/ County FIPS Code	Statistical Area Name	2000 Census Population	Percent Rural	Core Based Statistical Area Code	State/ County FIPS Code	Statistical Area Name	2000 Census Population	Percent Rural
30100		Lebanon, NH-VT Micro SA................	167 387	73.8	31060		Los Alamos, NM Micro SA................	18 343	11.6
	33 009	Grafton County, NH	81 743	64.8		35 028	Los Alamos County, NM.................	18 343	11.6
	50 017	Orange County, VT	28 226	97.7	31100		Los Angeles-Long Beach-Santa Ana,		
	50 027	Windsor County, VT	57 418	74.9			CA Metro SA	12 365 627	0.6
30140		Lebanon, PA Metro SA.....................	120 327	31.1			Los Angeles-Long Beach-Glendale, CA Metro Div. 31084......	9 519 338	0.7
	42 075	Lebanon County, PA	120 327	31.1		06 037	Los Angeles County, CA	9 519 338	0.7
30220		Levelland, TX Micro SA....................	22 716	40.6			Santa Ana-Anaheim-Irvine, CA Metro Div. 42044	2 846 289	0.2
	48 219	Hockley County, TX	22 716	40.6		06 059	Orange County, CA	2 846 289	0.2
30260		Lewisburg, PA Micro SA	41 624	45.0	31140		Louisville, KY-IN Metro SA..............	1 161 975	20.5
	42 119	Union County, PA	41 624	45.0		18 019	Clark County, IN	96 472	23.5
30300		Lewiston, ID-WA Metro SA	57 961	13.0		18 043	Floyd County, IN	70 823	20.7
	16 069	Nez Perce County, ID	37 410	16.9		18 061	Harrison County, IN	34 325	87.3
	53 003	Asotin County, WA	20 551	5.8		18 175	Washington County, IN.................	27 223	77.0
30340		Lewiston-Auburn, ME Metro SA.........	103 793	42.7		21 029	Bullitt County, KY	61 236	35.4
	23 001	Androscoggin County, ME.............	103 793	42.7		21 103	Henry County, KY	15 060	100.0
30380		Lewistown, PA Micro SA.................	46 486	55.8		21 111	Jefferson County, KY....................	693 604	1.8
	42 087	Mifflin County, PA	46 486	55.8		21 163	Meade County, KY	26 349	83.2
30420		Lexington, NE Micro SA	26 508	32.8		21 179	Nelson County, KY	37 477	62.6
	31 047	Dawson County, NE	24 365	26.9		21 185	Oldham County, KY	46 178	34.8
	31 073	Gosper County, NE	2 143	100.0		21 211	Shelby County, KY	33 337	60.1
30460		Lexington-Fayette, KY Metro SA.......	408 326	16.3		21 215	Spencer County, KY	11 766	100.0
	21 017	Bourbon County, KY	19 360	45.1		21 223	Trimble County, KY	8 125	94.1
	21 049	Clark County, KY	33 144	33.4	31180		Lubbock, TX Metro SA.....................	249 700	15.0
	21 067	Fayette County, KY	260 512	4.3		48 107	Crosby County, TX	7 072	100.0
	21 113	Jessamine County, KY	39 041	30.6		48 303	Lubbock County, TX	242 628	12.5
	21 209	Scott County, KY	33 061	42.4	31260		Lufkin, TX Micro SA	80 130	44.7
	21 239	Woodford County, KY	23 208	41.2		48 005	Angelina County, TX.....................	80 130	44.7
30500		Lexington Park, MD Micro SA............	86 211	61.8	31300		Lumberton, NC Micro SA	123 339	65.5
	24 037	St. Mary's County, MD.................	86 211	61.8		37 155	Robeson County, NC	123 339	65.5
30540		Lexington-Thomasville, NC Micro SA	147 246	56.9	31340		Lynchburg, VA Metro SA..................	228 616	51.8
	37 057	Davidson County, NC	147 246	56.9		51 009	Amherst County, VA	31 894	63.1
30580		Liberal, KS Micro SA......................	22 510	14.2		51 011	Appomattox County, VA................	13 705	100.0
	20 175	Seward County, KS	22 510	14.2		51 019	Bedford County, VA......................	60 371	84.7
30620		Lima, OH Metro SA.........................	108 473	26.6		51 031	Campbell County, VA....................	51 078	61.7
	39 003	Allen County, OH	108 473	26.6		51 515	Bedford city, VA...........................	6 299	0.0
30660		Lincoln, IL Micro SA.......................	31 183	41.4		51 680	Lynchburg city, VA.......................	65 269	3.0
	17 107	Logan County, IL	31 183	41.4	31380		Macomb, IL Micro SA......................	32 913	31.6
30700		Lincoln, NE Metro SA......................	266 787	12.7		17 109	McDonough County, IL.................	32 913	31.6
	31 109	Lancaster County, NE	250 291	9.5	31420		Macon, GA Metro SA.......................	222 368	36.6
	31 159	Seward County, NE	16 496	61.6		13 021	Bibb County, GA	153 887	14.8
30740		Lincolnton, NC Micro SA..................	63 780	62.1		13 079	Crawford County, GA....................	12 495	100.0
	37 109	Lincoln County, NC......................	63 780	62.1		13 169	Jones County, GA	23 639	81.6
30780		Little Rock-North Little Rock, AR Metro SA......................................	610 518	29.7		13 207	Monroe County, GA	21 757	74.9
	05 045	Faulkner County, AR	86 014	48.9		13 289	Twiggs County, GA	10 590	100.0
	05 053	Grant County, AR	16 464	77.4	31460		Madera, CA Metro SA......................	123 109	34.0
	05 085	Lonoke County, AR	52 828	54.8		06 039	Madera County, CA	123 109	34.0
	05 105	Perry County, AR.........................	10 209	100.0	31500		Madison, IN Micro SA	31 705	44.9
	05 119	Pulaski County, AR.......................	361 474	12.7		18 077	Jefferson County, IN.....................	31 705	44.9
	05 125	Saline County, AR	83 529	49.7	31540		Madison, WI Metro SA.....................	501 774	23.5
30820		Lock Haven, PA Micro SA.................	37 914	50.8		55 021	Columbia County, WI....................	52 468	63.2
	42 035	Clinton County, PA	37 914	50.8		55 025	Dane County, WI	426 526	15.5
30860		Logan, UT-ID Metro SA....................	102 720	22.5		55 049	Iowa County, WI	22 780	82.8
	16 041	Franklin County, ID......................	11 329	69.7	31580		Madisonville, KY Micro SA	46 519	45.8
	49 005	Cache County, UT	91 391	16.7		21 107	Hopkins County, KY......................	46 519	45.8
30900		Logansport, IN Micro SA	40 930	46.4	31620		Magnolia, AR Micro SA....................	25 603	59.2
	18 017	Cass County, IN...........................	40 930	46.4		05 027	Columbia County, AR....................	25 603	59.2
30940		London, KY Micro SA......................	52 715	67.5	31660		Malone, NY Micro SA.......................	51 134	60.8
	21 125	Laurel County, KY........................	52 715	67.5		36 033	Franklin County, NY......................	51 134	60.8
30980		Longview, TX Metro SA....................	194 042	42.6	31700		Manchester-Nashua, NH Metro SA....	380 841	22.0
	48 183	Gregg County, TX.........................	111 379	20.0		33 011	Hillsborough County, NH...............	380 841	22.0
	48 401	Rusk County, TX...........................	47 372	67.3	31740		Manhattan, KS Micro SA..................	108 999	24.9
	48 459	Upshur County, TX........................	35 291	80.5		20 061	Geary County, KS.........................	27 947	14.1
31020		Longview-Kelso, WA Metro SA..........	92 948	32.6		20 149	Pottawatomie County, KS..............	18 209	76.7
	53 015	Cowlitz County, WA......................	92 948	32.6					

Core Based Statistical Area Code	State/ County FIPS Code	Statistical Area Name	2000 Census Population	Percent Rural	Core Based Statistical Area Code	State/ County FIPS Code	Statistical Area Name	2000 Census Population	Percent Rural
	20 161	Riley County, KS	62 843	14.7		47 167	Tipton County, TN	51 271	66.3
31820		Manitowoc, WI Micro SA	82 887	39.0	32860		Menomonie, WI Micro SA	39 858	58.5
	55 071	Manitowoc County, WI	82 887	39.0		55 033	Dunn County, WI	39 858	58.5
31860		Mankato-North Mankato, MN Micro SA	85 712	33.8	32900		Merced, CA Metro SA	210 554	16.9
	27 013	Blue Earth County, MN	55 941	36.9		06 047	Merced County, CA	210 554	16.9
	27 103	Nicollet County, MN	29 771	28.0	32940		Meridian, MS Micro SA	106 569	61.8
31900		Mansfield, OH Metro SA	128 852	29.6		28 023	Clarke County, MS	17 955	100.0
	39 139	Richland County, OH	128 852	29.6		28 069	Kemper County, MS	10 453	100.0
31940		Marinette, WI-MI Micro SA	68 710	61.3		28 075	Lauderdale County, MS	78 161	47.9
	26 109	Menominee County, MI	25 326	63.5	32980		Merrill, WI Micro SA	29 641	55.4
	55 075	Marinette County, WI	43 384	60.0		55 069	Lincoln County, WI	29 641	55.4
31980		Marion, IN Micro SA	73 403	28.8	33020		Mexico, MO Micro SA	25 853	42.4
	18 053	Grant County, IN	73 403	28.8		29 007	Audrain County, MO	25 853	42.4
32020		Marion, OH Micro SA	66 217	31.0	33060		Miami, OK Micro SA	33 194	49.4
	39 101	Marion County, OH	66 217	31.0		40 115	Ottawa County, OK	33 194	49.4
32060		Marion-Herrin, IL Micro SA	61 296	36.0	33100		Miami-Fort Lauderdale-Miami Beach, FL Metro SA	5 007 564	0.7
	17 199	Williamson County, IL	61 296	36.0			Fort Lauderdale-Pompano Beach-Deerfield Beach, FL Metro Div. 22744	1 623 018	0.1
32100		Marquette, MI Micro SA	64 634	41.9		12 011	Broward County, FL	1 623 018	0.1
	26 103	Marquette County, MI	64 634	41.9			Miami-Miami Beach-Kendall, FL Metro Div. 33124	2 253 362	0.7
32140		Marshall, MN Micro SA	25 425	50.4		12 086	Miami-Dade County, FL	2 253 362	0.7
	27 083	Lyon County, MN	25 425	50.4			West Palm Beach-Boca Raton-Boynton Beach, FL Metro Div. 48424	1 131 184	1.7
32180		Marshall, MO Micro SA	23 756	46.5		12 099	Palm Beach County, FL	1 131 184	1.7
	29 195	Saline County, MO	23 756	46.5	33140		Michigan City-La Porte, IN Metro SA	110 106	35.4
32220		Marshall, TX Micro SA	62 110	59.3		18 091	LaPorte County, IN	110 106	35.4
	48 203	Harrison County, TX	62 110	59.3	33180		Middlesborough, KY Micro SA	30 060	63.0
32260		Marshalltown, IA Micro SA	39 311	33.6		21 013	Bell County, KY	30 060	63.0
	19 127	Marshall County, IA	39 311	33.6	33220		Midland, MI Micro SA	82 874	45.3
32300		Martinsville, VA Micro SA	73 346	51.0		26 111	Midland County, MI	82 874	45.3
	51 089	Henry County, VA	57 930	64.5	33260		Midland, TX Metro SA	116 009	12.9
	51 690	Martinsville city, VA	15 416	0.0		48 329	Midland County, TX	116 009	12.9
32340		Maryville, MO Micro SA	21 912	47.1	33300		Milledgeville, GA Micro SA	54 776	38.9
	29 147	Nodaway County, MO	21 912	47.1		13 009	Baldwin County, GA	44 700	34.0
32380		Mason City, IA Micro SA	54 356	32.7		13 141	Hancock County, GA	10 076	60.6
	19 033	Cerro Gordo County, IA	46 447	21.3	33340		Milwaukee-Waukesha-West Allis, WI Metro SA	1 500 741	7.2
	19 195	Worth County, IA	7 909	100.0		55 079	Milwaukee County, WI	940 164	0.3
32460		Mayfield, KY Micro SA	37 028	69.8		55 089	Ozaukee County, WI	82 317	25.2
	21 083	Graves County, KY	37 028	69.8		55 131	Washington County, WI	117 493	34.7
32500		Maysville, KY Micro SA	30 892	73.1		55 133	Waukesha County, WI	360 767	12.0
	21 135	Lewis County, KY	14 092	100.0	33380		Minden, LA Micro SA	41 831	53.4
	21 161	Mason County, KY	16 800	50.5		22 119	Webster Parish, LA	41 831	53.4
32540		McAlester, OK Micro SA	43 953	49.6	33420		Mineral Wells, TX Micro SA	27 026	47.6
	40 121	Pittsburg County, OK	43 953	49.6		48 363	Palo Pinto County, TX	27 026	47.6
32580		McAllen-Edinburg-Pharr, TX Metro SA	569 463	6.6	33460		Minneapolis-St. Paul-Bloomington, MN-WI Metro SA	2 968 806	12.1
	48 215	Hidalgo County, TX	569 463	6.6		27 003	Anoka County, MN	298 084	14.3
32620		McComb, MS Micro SA	52 539	64.8		27 019	Carver County, MN	70 205	22.7
	28 005	Amite County, MS	13 599	100.0		27 025	Chisago County, MN	41 101	64.5
	28 113	Pike County, MS	38 940	52.4		27 037	Dakota County, MN	355 904	6.1
32660		McMinnville, TN Micro SA	38 276	62.3		27 053	Hennepin County, MN	1 116 200	2.3
	47 177	Warren County, TN	38 276	62.3		27 059	Isanti County, MN	31 287	73.4
32700		McPherson, KS Micro SA	29 554	42.7		27 123	Ramsey County, MN	511 035	0.1
	20 113	McPherson County, KS	29 554	42.7		27 139	Scott County, MN	89 498	27.3
32740		Meadville, PA Micro SA	90 366	65.4		27 141	Sherburne County, MN	64 417	56.4
	42 039	Crawford County, PA	90 366	65.4		27 163	Washington County, MN	201 130	18.0
32780		Medford, OR Metro SA	181 269	22.5		27 171	Wright County, MN	89 986	53.4
	41 029	Jackson County, OR	181 269	22.5		55 093	Pierce County, WI	36 804	61.5
32820		Memphis, TN-MS-AR Metro SA	1 205 204	15.7		55 109	St. Croix County, WI	63 155	57.3
	05 035	Crittenden County, AR	50 866	20.3	33500		Minot, ND Micro SA	67 392	32.8
	28 033	DeSoto County, MS	107 199	32.4					
	28 093	Marshall County, MS	34 993	80.8					
	28 137	Tate County, MS	25 370	68.8					
	28 143	Tunica County, MS	9 227	59.0					
	47 047	Fayette County, TN	28 806	100.0					
	47 157	Shelby County, TN	897 472	3.3					

Core Based Statistical Areas (Metropolitan and Micropolitan), and Metropolitan Divisions with 2000 Census Population and Percent of the Population That is Rural (As of June 2003) – Continued

Core Based Statistical Area Code	State/ County FIPS Code	Statistical Area Name	2000 Census Population	Percent Rural	Core Based Statistical Area Code	State/ County FIPS Code	Statistical Area Name	2000 Census Population	Percent Rural
	38 049	McHenry County, ND	5 987	100.0	34580		Mount Vernon-Anacortes, WA Metro SA	102 979	32.9
	38 075	Renville County, ND	2 610	100.0		53 057	Skagit County, WA	102 979	32.9
	38 101	Ward County, ND	58 795	23.0	34620		Muncie, IN Metro SA	118 769	23.4
33540		Missoula, MT Metro SA	95 802	27.5		18 035	Delaware County, IN	118 769	23.4
	30 063	Missoula County, MT	95 802	27.5	34660		Murray, KY Micro SA	34 177	52.4
33580		Mitchell, SD Micro SA	21 880	33.6		21 035	Calloway County, KY	34 177	52.4
	46 035	Davison County, SD	18 741	22.4	34700		Muscatine, IA Micro SA	53 905	45.2
	46 061	Hanson County, SD	3 139	100.0		19 115	Louisa County, IA	12 183	100.0
33620		Moberly, MO Micro SA	24 663	51.6		19 139	Muscatine County, IA	41 722	29.2
	29 175	Randolph County, MO	24 663	51.6	34740		Muskegon-Norton Shores, MI Metro SA	170 200	26.1
33660		Mobile, AL Metro SA	399 843	19.7		26 121	Muskegon County, MI	170 200	26.1
	01 097	Mobile County, AL	399 843	19.7	34780		Muskogee, OK Micro SA	69 451	39.3
33700		Modesto, CA Metro SA	446 997	9.0		40 101	Muskogee County, OK	69 451	39.3
	06 099	Stanislaus County, CA	446 997	9.0	34820		Myrtle Beach-Conway-North Myrtle Beach, SC Metro SA	196 629	39.6
33740		Monroe, LA Metro SA	170 053	31.1		45 051	Horry County, SC	196 629	39.6
	22 073	Ouachita Parish, LA	147 250	22.6	34860		Nacogdoches, TX Micro SA	59 203	47.6
	22 111	Union Parish, LA	22 803	85.8		48 347	Nacogdoches County, TX	59 203	47.6
33780		Monroe, MI Metro SA	145 945	37.1	34900		Napa, CA Metro SA	124 279	15.9
	26 115	Monroe County, MI	145 945	37.1		06 055	Napa County, CA	124 279	15.9
33820		Monroe, WI Micro SA	33 647	57.2	34940		Naples-Marco Island, FL Metro SA	251 377	10.3
	55 045	Green County, WI	33 647	57.2		12 021	Collier County, FL	251 377	10.3
33860		Montgomery, AL Metro SA	346 528	29.0	34980		Nashville-Davidson—Murfreesboro, TN Metro SA	1 311 789	27.2
	01 001	Autauga County, AL	43 671	44.6		47 015	Cannon County, TN	12 826	100.0
	01 051	Elmore County, AL	65 874	62.5		47 021	Cheatham County, TN	35 912	93.2
	01 085	Lowndes County, AL	13 473	100.0		47 037	Davidson County, TN	569 891	4.6
	01 101	Montgomery County, AL	223 510	11.9		47 043	Dickson County, TN	43 156	68.8
33940		Montrose, CO Micro SA	33 432	53.1		47 081	Hickman County, TN	22 295	100.0
	08 085	Montrose County, CO	33 432	53.1		47 111	Macon County, TN	20 386	81.5
33980		Morehead City, NC Micro SA	59 383	38.0		47 147	Robertson County, TN	54 433	57.8
	37 031	Carteret County, NC	59 383	38.0		47 149	Rutherford County, TN	182 023	24.7
34020		Morgan City, LA Micro SA	53 500	17.0		47 159	Smith County, TN	17 712	79.5
	22 101	St. Mary Parish, LA	53 500	17.0		47 165	Sumner County, TN	130 449	30.6
34060		Morgantown, WV Metro SA	111 200	46.5		47 169	Trousdale County, TN	7 259	100.0
	54 061	Monongalia County, WV	81 866	31.7		47 187	Williamson County, TN	126 638	29.3
	54 077	Preston County, WV	29 334	88.0		47 189	Wilson County, TN	88 809	46.1
34100		Morristown, TN Metro SA	123 081	56.1	35020		Natchez, MS-LA Micro SA	54 587	33.9
	47 057	Grainger County, TN	20 659	100.0		22 029	Concordia Parish, LA	20 247	38.3
	47 063	Hamblen County, TN	58 128	25.8		28 001	Adams County, MS	34 340	31.4
	47 089	Jefferson County, TN	44 294	75.3	35060		Natchitoches, LA Micro SA	39 080	50.7
34140		Moscow, ID Micro SA	34 935	37.7		22 069	Natchitoches Parish, LA	39 080	50.7
	16 057	Latah County, ID	34 935	37.7	35100		New Bern, NC Micro SA	114 751	46.0
34180		Moses Lake, WA Micro SA	74 698	47.2		37 049	Craven County, NC	91 436	32.2
	53 025	Grant County, WA	74 698	47.2		37 103	Jones County, NC	10 381	100.0
34220		Moultrie, GA Micro SA	42 053	63.5		37 137	Pamlico County, NC	12 934	100.0
	13 071	Colquitt County, GA	42 053	63.5	35140		Newberry, SC Micro SA	36 108	66.9
34260		Mountain Home, AR Micro SA	38 386	67.4		45 071	Newberry County, SC	36 108	66.9
	05 005	Baxter County, AR	38 386	67.4	35220		New Castle, IN Micro SA	48 508	44.5
34300		Mountain Home, ID Micro SA	29 130	23.4		18 065	Henry County, IN	48 508	44.5
	16 039	Elmore County, ID	29 130	23.4	35260		New Castle, PA Micro SA	94 643	41.1
34340		Mount Airy, NC Micro SA	71 219	69.8		42 073	Lawrence County, PA	94 643	41.1
	37 171	Surry County, NC	71 219	69.8	35300		New Haven-Milford, CT Metro SA	824 008	4.2
34380		Mount Pleasant, MI Micro SA	63 351	50.3		09 009	New Haven County, CT	824 008	4.2
	26 073	Isabella County, MI	63 351	50.3	35340		New Iberia, LA Micro SA	73 266	32.4
34420		Mount Pleasant, TX Micro SA	28 118	52.2		22 045	Iberia Parish, LA	73 266	32.4
	48 449	Titus County, TX	28 118	52.2	35380		New Orleans-Metairie-Kenner, LA Metro SA	1 316 510	6.1
34460		Mount Sterling, KY Micro SA	40 195	74.7		22 051	Jefferson Parish, LA	455 466	1.0
	21 011	Bath County, KY	11 085	100.0		22 071	Orleans Parish, LA	484 674	0.7
	21 165	Menifee County, KY	6 556	100.0		22 075	Plaquemines Parish, LA	26 757	31.5
	21 173	Montgomery County, KY	22 554	55.0		22 087	St. Bernard Parish, LA	67 229	4.0
34500		Mount Vernon, IL Micro SA	48 666	58.2		22 089	St. Charles Parish, LA	48 072	14.0
	17 065	Hamilton County, IL	8 621	66.8					
	17 081	Jefferson County, IL	40 045	56.3					
34540		Mount Vernon, OH Micro SA	54 500	58.5					
	39 083	Knox County, OH	54 500	58.5					

Core Based Statistical Areas (Metropolitan and Micropolitan), and Metropolitan Divisions with 2000 Census Population and Percent of the Population That is Rural (As of June 2003) – Continued

Core Based Statistical Area Code	State/County FIPS Code	Statistical Area Name	2000 Census Population	Percent Rural
	22 095	St. John the Baptist Parish, LA	43 044	14.5
	22 103	St. Tammany Parish, LA.	191 268	25.2
35420		New Philadelphia-Dover, OH Micro SA	90 914	41.7
	39 157	Tuscarawas County, OH	90 914	41.7
35460		Newport, TN Micro SA	33 565	67.5
	47 029	Cocke County, TN	33 565	67.5
35500		Newton, IA Micro SA	37 213	56.2
	19 099	Jasper County, IA	37 213	56.2
35580		New Ulm, MN Micro SA	26 911	37.4
	27 015	Brown County, MN	26 911	37.4
35620		New York-Newark-Edison, NY-NJ-PA Metro SA	18 323 002	2.1
		Edison, NJ Metro Div. 20764	2 173 869	3.3
	34 023	Middlesex County, NJ	750 162	1.0
	34 025	Monmouth County, NJ	615 301	4.6
	34 029	Ocean County, NJ	510 916	2.9
	34 035	Somerset County, NJ	297 490	6.9
		Newark-Union, NJ-PA Metro Div. 35084	2 098 843	9.6
	34 013	Essex County, NJ	793 633	0.0
	34 019	Hunterdon County, NJ	121 989	53.1
	34 027	Morris County, NJ	470 212	7.9
	34 037	Sussex County, NJ	144 166	39.9
	34 039	Union County, NJ	522 541	0.0
	42 103	Pike County, PA	46 302	89.4
		New York-Wayne-White Plains, NY-NJ Metro Div. 35644	11 296 377	0.6
	34 003	Bergen County, NJ	884 118	0.2
	34 017	Hudson County, NJ	608 975	0.0
	34 031	Passaic County, NJ	489 049	2.4
	36 005	Bronx County, NY	1 332 650	0.0
	36 047	Kings County, NY	2 465 326	0.0
	36 061	New York County, NY	1 537 195	0.0
	36 079	Putnam County, NY	95 745	24.2
	36 081	Queens County, NY	2 229 379	0.0
	36 085	Richmond County, NY	443 728	0.0
	36 087	Rockland County, NY	286 753	1.0
	36 119	Westchester County, NY	923 459	3.5
		Suffolk County-Nassau County, NY Metro Div. 44844	2 753 913	1.6
	36 059	Nassau County, NY	1 334 544	0.2
	36 103	Suffolk County, NY	1 419 369	3.0
35660		Niles-Benton Harbor, MI Metro SA	162 453	30.4
	26 021	Berrien County, MI	162 453	30.4
35700		Nogales, AZ Micro SA	38 381	32.4
	04 023	Santa Cruz County, AZ	38 381	32.4
35740		Norfolk, NE Micro SA	49 538	47.3
	31 119	Madison County, NE	35 226	30.3
	31 139	Pierce County, NE	7 857	100.0
	31 167	Stanton County, NE	6 455	75.6
35820		North Platte, NE Micro SA	35 939	33.0
	31 111	Lincoln County, NE	34 632	30.5
	31 113	Logan County, NE	774	100.0
	31 117	McPherson County, NE	533	100.0
35860		North Vernon, IN Micro SA	27 554	58.7
	18 079	Jennings County, IN	27 554	58.7
35900		North Wilkesboro, NC Micro SA	65 632	73.7
	37 193	Wilkes County, NC	65 632	73.7
35940		Norwalk, OH Micro SA	59 487	46.2
	39 077	Huron County, OH	59 487	46.2
35980		Norwich-New London, CT Metro SA	259 088	27.6
	09 011	New London County, CT	259 088	27.6
36020		Oak Harbor, WA Micro SA	71 558	48.1
	53 029	Island County, WA	71 558	48.1
36060		Oak Hill, WV Micro SA	47 579	60.7
	54 019	Fayette County, WV	47 579	60.7
36100		Ocala, FL Metro SA	258 916	38.9
	12 083	Marion County, FL	258 916	38.9
36140		Ocean City, NJ Metro SA	102 326	16.8
	34 009	Cape May County, NJ	102 326	16.8
36180		Ocean Pines, MD Micro SA	46 543	36.4
	24 047	Worcester County, MD	46 543	36.4
36220		Odessa, TX Metro SA	121 123	9.2
	48 135	Ector County, TX	121 123	9.2
36260		Ogden-Clearfield, UT Metro SA	442 656	5.6
	49 011	Davis County, UT	238 994	1.9
	49 029	Morgan County, UT	7 129	100.0
	49 057	Weber County, UT	196 533	6.7
36300		Ogdensburg-Massena, NY Micro SA	111 931	60.8
	36 089	St. Lawrence County, NY	111 931	60.8
36340		Oil City, PA Micro SA	57 565	54.0
	42 121	Venango County, PA	57 565	54.0
36380		Okeechobee, FL Micro SA	35 910	42.5
	12 093	Okeechobee County, FL	35 910	42.5
36420		Oklahoma City, OK Metro SA	1 095 421	19.2
	40 017	Canadian County, OK	87 697	23.4
	40 027	Cleveland County, OK	208 016	20.3
	40 051	Grady County, OK	45 516	65.9
	40 081	Lincoln County, OK	32 080	92.3
	40 083	Logan County, OK	33 924	67.9
	40 087	McClain County, OK	27 740	81.5
	40 109	Oklahoma County, OK	660 448	6.4
36460		Olean, NY Micro SA	83 955	58.5
	36 009	Cattaraugus County, NY	83 955	58.5
36500		Olympia, WA Metro SA	207 355	24.7
	53 067	Thurston County, WA	207 355	24.7
36540		Omaha-Council Bluffs, NE-IA Metro SA	767 041	14.3
	19 085	Harrison County, IA	15 666	79.8
	19 129	Mills County, IA	14 547	61.7
	19 155	Pottawattamie County, IA	87 704	27.1
	31 025	Cass County, NE	24 334	70.6
	31 055	Douglas County, NE	463 585	2.4
	31 153	Sarpy County, NE	122 595	7.3
	31 155	Saunders County, NE	19 830	80.1
	31 177	Washington County, NE	18 780	60.8
36580		Oneonta, NY Micro SA	61 676	74.0
	36 077	Otsego County, NY	61 676	74.0
36620		Ontario, OR-ID Micro SA	52 193	41.8
	16 075	Payette County, ID	20 578	43.8
	41 045	Malheur County, OR	31 615	40.5
36660		Opelousas-Eunice, LA Micro SA	87 700	44.7
	22 097	St. Landry Parish, LA	87 700	44.7
36700		Orangeburg, SC Micro SA	91 582	66.9
	45 075	Orangeburg County, SC	91 582	66.9
36740		Orlando, FL Metro SA	1 644 561	9.1
	12 069	Lake County, FL	210 528	30.4
	12 095	Orange County, FL	896 344	3.4
	12 097	Osceola County, FL	172 493	23.4
	12 117	Seminole County, FL	365 196	4.0
36780		Oshkosh-Neenah, WI Metro SA	156 763	15.8
	55 139	Winnebago County, WI	156 763	15.8
36820		Oskaloosa, IA Micro SA	22 335	45.8
	19 123	Mahaska County, IA	22 335	45.8
36860		Ottawa-Streator, IL Micro SA	153 098	40.4
	17 011	Bureau County, IL	35 503	61.7
	17 099	La Salle County, IL	111 509	30.4
	17 155	Putnam County, IL	6 086	100.0

Core Based Statistical Areas (Metropolitan and Micropolitan), and Metropolitan Divisions with 2000 Census Population and Percent of the Population That is Rural (As of June 2003) – Continued

Core Based Statistical Area Code	State/County FIPS Code	Statistical Area Name	2000 Census Population	Percent Rural	Core Based Statistical Area Code	State/County FIPS Code	Statistical Area Name	2000 Census Population	Percent Rural
36900		Ottumwa, IA Micro SA	36 051	30.2	37900		Peoria, IL Metro SA	366 899	24.3
	19 179	Wapello County, IA	36 051	30.2		17 123	Marshall County, IL	13 180	80.7
36940		Owatonna, MN Micro SA	33 680	33.8		17 143	Peoria County, IL	183 433	14.9
	27 147	Steele County, MN	33 680	33.8		17 175	Stark County, IL	6 332	100.0
36980		Owensboro, KY Metro SA	109 875	37.7		17 179	Tazewell County, IL	128 485	18.6
	21 059	Daviess County, KY	91 545	26.2		17 203	Woodford County, IL	35 469	58.8
	21 091	Hancock County, KY	8 392	89.0	37940		Peru, IN Micro SA	36 082	49.4
	21 149	McLean County, KY	9 938	100.0		18 103	Miami County, IN	36 082	49.4
37020		Owosso, MI Micro SA	71 687	54.5	37980		Philadelphia-Camden-Wilmington, PA-NJ-DE-MD Metro SA	5 687 147	5.9
	26 155	Shiawassee County, MI	71 687	54.5			Wilmington, DE-MD-NJ Metro Div. 48864	650 501	15.2
37060		Oxford, MS Micro SA	38 744	49.2		10 003	New Castle County, DE	500 265	5.6
	28 071	Lafayette County, MS	38 744	49.2		24 015	Cecil County, MD	85 951	52.1
37100		Oxnard-Thousand Oaks-Ventura, CA Metro SA	753 197	3.2		34 033	Salem County, NJ	64 285	41.1
	06 111	Ventura County, CA	753 197	3.2			Camden, NJ Metro Div. 15804	1 186 999	5.4
37140		Paducah, KY-IL Micro SA	98 765	45.0		34 005	Burlington County, NJ	423 394	7.5
	17 127	Massac County, IL	15 161	50.2		34 007	Camden County, NJ	508 932	0.7
	21 007	Ballard County, KY	8 286	100.0		34 015	Gloucester County, NJ	254 673	11.1
	21 139	Livingston County, KY	9 804	100.0			Philadelphia, PA Metro Div. 37964	3 849 647	4.5
	21 145	McCracken County, KY	65 514	28.6		42 017	Bucks County, PA	597 635	9.9
37220		Pahrump, NV Micro SA	32 485	55.0		42 029	Chester County, PA	433 501	19.0
	32 023	Nye County, NV	32 485	55.0		42 045	Delaware County, PA	550 864	1.1
37260		Palatka, FL Micro SA	70 423	54.4		42 091	Montgomery County, PA	750 097	3.5
	12 107	Putnam County, FL	70 423	54.4		42 101	Philadelphia County, PA	1 517 550	0.0
37300		Palestine, TX Micro SA	55 109	41.3	38020		Phoenix Lake-Cedar Ridge, CA Micro SA	54 501	46.6
	48 001	Anderson County, TX	55 109	41.3		06 109	Tuolumne County, CA	54 501	46.6
37340		Palm Bay-Melbourne-Titusville, FL Metro SA	476 230	4.5	38060		Phoenix-Mesa-Scottsdale, AZ Metro SA	3 251 876	4.7
	12 009	Brevard County, FL	476 230	4.5		04 013	Maricopa County, AZ	3 072 149	2.9
37380		Palm Coast, FL Micro SA	49 832	32.6		04 021	Pinal County, AZ	179 727	35.4
	12 035	Flagler County, FL	49 832	32.6	38100		Picayune, MS Micro SA	48 621	69.7
37420		Pampa, TX Micro SA	23 631	23.9		28 109	Pearl River County, MS	48 621	69.7
	48 179	Gray County, TX	22 744	20.9	38180		Pierre, SD Micro SA	19 253	26.2
	48 393	Roberts County, TX	887	100.0		46 065	Hughes County, SD	16 481	24.5
37460		Panama City-Lynn Haven, FL Metro SA	148 217	10.6		46 117	Stanley County, SD	2 772	36.3
	12 005	Bay County, FL	148 217	10.6	38200		Pierre Part, LA Micro SA	23 388	43.7
37500		Paragould, AR Micro SA	37 331	48.9		22 007	Assumption Parish, LA	23 388	43.7
	05 055	Greene County, AR	37 331	48.9	38220		Pine Bluff, AR Metro SA	107 341	45.6
37540		Paris, TN Micro SA	31 115	67.2		05 025	Cleveland County, AR	8 571	100.0
	47 079	Henry County, TN	31 115	67.2		05 069	Jefferson County, AR	84 278	30.7
37580		Paris, TX Micro SA	48 499	45.8		05 079	Lincoln County, AR	14 492	100.0
	48 277	Lamar County, TX	48 499	45.8	38260		Pittsburg, KS Micro SA	38 242	36.5
37620		Parkersburg-Marietta, WV-OH Metro SA	164 624	45.4		20 037	Crawford County, KS	38 242	36.5
	39 167	Washington County, OH	63 251	64.8	38300		Pittsburgh, PA Metro SA	2 431 087	18.5
	54 073	Pleasants County, WV	7 514	57.4		42 003	Allegheny County, PA	1 281 666	2.7
	54 105	Wirt County, WV	5 873	100.0		42 005	Armstrong County, PA	72 392	63.1
	54 107	Wood County, WV	87 986	26.8		42 007	Beaver County, PA	181 412	26.8
37660		Parsons, KS Micro SA	22 835	51.2		42 019	Butler County, PA	174 083	46.7
	20 099	Labette County, KS	22 835	51.2		42 051	Fayette County, PA	148 644	46.8
37700		Pascagoula, MS Metro SA	150 564	40.9		42 125	Washington County, PA	202 897	36.9
	28 039	George County, MS	19 144	100.0		42 129	Westmoreland County, PA	369 993	25.7
	28 059	Jackson County, MS	131 420	32.3	38340		Pittsfield, MA Metro SA	134 953	30.2
37740		Payson, AZ Micro SA	51 335	44.0		25 003	Berkshire County, MA	134 953	30.2
	04 007	Gila County, AZ	51 335	44.0	38380		Plainview, TX Micro SA	36 602	24.0
37780		Pecos, TX Micro SA	13 137	17.5		48 189	Hale County, TX	36 602	24.0
	48 389	Reeves County, TX	13 137	17.5	38420		Platteville, WI Micro SA	49 597	65.5
37820		Pendleton-Hermiston, OR Micro SA	81 543	32.8		55 043	Grant County, WI	49 597	65.5
	41 049	Morrow County, OR	10 995	47.2	38460		Plattsburgh, NY Micro SA	79 894	61.1
	41 059	Umatilla County, OR	70 548	30.5		36 019	Clinton County, NY	79 894	61.1
37860		Pensacola-Ferry Pass-Brent, FL Metro SA	412 153	16.2	38500		Plymouth, IN Micro SA	45 128	63.1
	12 033	Escambia County, FL	294 410	11.0		18 099	Marshall County, IN	45 128	63.1
	12 113	Santa Rosa County, FL	117 743	29.4	38540		Pocatello, ID Metro SA	83 103	19.8
						16 005	Bannock County, ID	75 565	17.3

Core Based Statistical Areas (Metropolitan and Micropolitan), and Metropolitan Divisions with 2000 Census Population and Percent of the Population That is Rural (As of June 2003) – Continued

Core Based Statistical Area Code	State/ County FIPS Code	Statistical Area Name	2000 Census Population	Percent Rural	Core Based Statistical Area Code	State/ County FIPS Code	Statistical Area Name	2000 Census Population	Percent Rural
	16 077	Power County, ID......................	7 538	45.2		29 111	Lewis County, MO	10 494	100.0
38580		Point Pleasant, WV-OH Micro SA......	57 026	74.3	39540		Racine, WI Metro SA......................	188 831	12.7
	39 053	Gallia County, OH......................	31 069	77.1		55 101	Racine County, WI......................	188 831	12.7
	54 053	Mason County, WV......................	25 957	70.9	39580		Raleigh-Cary, NC Metro SA..............	797 071	25.2
38620		Ponca City, OK Micro SA................	48 080	25.3		37 069	Franklin County, NC	47 260	91.3
	40 071	Kay County, OK......................	48 080	25.3		37 101	Johnston County, NC	121 965	68.4
38700		Pontiac, IL Micro SA......................	39 678	41.2		37 183	Wake County, NC......................	627 846	11.9
	17 105	Livingston County, IL....................	39 678	41.2	39660		Rapid City, SD Metro SA	112 818	28.1
38740		Poplar Bluff, MO Micro SA................	40 867	53.0		46 093	Meade County, SD......................	24 253	45.5
	29 023	Butler County, MO......................	40 867	53.0		46 103	Pennington County, SD	88 565	23.3
38780		Portales, NM Micro SA....................	18 018	36.0	39700		Raymondville, TX Micro SA	20 082	49.0
	35 041	Roosevelt County, NM................	18 018	36.0		48 489	Willacy County, TX......................	20 082	49.0
38820		Port Angeles, WA Micro SA..............	64 525	47.8	39740		Reading, PA Metro SA....................	373 638	27.2
	53 009	Clallam County, WA......................	64 525	47.8		42 011	Berks County, PA	373 638	27.2
38860		Portland-South Portland, ME Metro SA.	487 568	43.4	39780		Red Bluff, CA Micro SA..................	56 039	49.1
	23 005	Cumberland County, ME..............	265 612	34.3		06 103	Tehama County, CA	56 039	49.1
	23 023	Sagadahoc County, ME..............	35 214	59.0	39820		Redding, CA Metro SA....................	163 256	31.1
	23 031	York County, ME......................	186 742	53.5		06 089	Shasta County, CA	163 256	31.1
38900		Portland-Vancouver-Beaverton, OR-WA Metro SA.	1 927 881	11.9	39860		Red Wing, MN Micro SA................	44 127	51.0
	41 005	Clackamas County, OR	338 391	21.2		27 049	Goodhue County, MN	44 127	51.0
	41 009	Columbia County, OR..................	43 560	47.4	39900		Reno-Sparks, NV Metro SA............	342 885	8.0
	41 051	Multnomah County, OR................	660 486	1.8		32 029	Storey County, NV......................	3 399	94.4
	41 067	Washington County, OR..............	445 342	6.9		32 031	Washoe County, NV......................	339 486	7.1
	41 071	Yamhill County, OR	84 992	29.5	39940		Rexburg, ID Micro SA....................	39 286	42.9
	53 011	Clark County, WA	345 238	17.6		16 043	Fremont County, ID	11 819	72.2
	53 059	Skamania County, WA................	9 872	100.0		16 065	Madison County, ID	27 467	30.3
38940		Port St. Lucie-Fort Pierce, FL Metro SA.	319 426	8.0	39980		Richmond, IN Micro SA..................	71 097	31.1
	12 085	Martin County, FL......................	126 731	11.0		18 177	Wayne County, IN......................	71 097	31.1
	12 111	St. Lucie County, FL....................	192 695	6.1	40020		Richmond, KY Micro SA..................	87 454	49.3
39020		Portsmouth, OH Micro SA..............	79 195	50.6		21 151	Madison County, KY................	70 872	41.4
	39 145	Scioto County, OH......................	79 195	50.6		21 203	Rockcastle County, KY	16 582	83.0
39060		Pottsville, PA Micro SA..................	150 336	36.5	40060		Richmond, VA Metro SA	1 096 957	24.8
	42 107	Schuylkill County, PA	150 336	36.5		51 007	Amelia County, VA......................	11 400	100.0
39100		Poughkeepsie-Newburgh-Middletown, NY Metro SA.	621 517	26.5		51 033	Caroline County, VA......................	22 121	100.0
	36 027	Dutchess County, NY................	280 150	29.2		51 036	Charles City County, VA..............	6 926	100.0
	36 071	Orange County, NY	341 367	24.3		51 041	Chesterfield County, VA..............	259 903	10.5
39140		Prescott, AZ Metro SA	167 517	37.4		51 049	Cumberland County, VA..............	9 017	96.1
	04 025	Yavapai County, AZ	167 517	37.4		51 053	Dinwiddie County, VA..................	24 533	73.1
39220		Price, UT Micro SA	20 422	39.1		51 075	Goochland County, VA................	16 863	94.7
	49 007	Carbon County, UT......................	20 422	39.1		51 085	Hanover County, VA....................	86 320	43.4
39260		Prineville, OR Micro SA	19 182	46.6		51 087	Henrico County, VA....................	262 300	5.6
	41 013	Crook County, OR	19 182	46.6		51 097	King and Queen County, VA	6 630	100.0
39300		Providence-New Bedford-Fall River, RI-MA Metro SA.	1 582 997	9.4		51 101	King William County, VA..............	13 146	80.6
	25 005	Bristol County, MA	534 678	10.1		51 109	Louisa County, VA	25 627	100.0
	44 001	Bristol County, RI......................	50 648	0.4		51 127	New Kent County, VA..................	13 462	100.0
	44 003	Kent County, RI	167 090	6.8		51 145	Powhatan County, VA..................	22 377	89.8
	44 005	Newport County, RI	85 433	11.0		51 149	Prince George County, VA	33 047	59.7
	44 007	Providence County, RI	621 602	6.0		51 183	Sussex County, VA	12 504	100.0
	44 009	Washington County, RI................	123 546	29.8		51 570	Colonial Heights city, VA..............	16 897	0.0
39340		Provo-Orem, UT Metro SA................	376 774	6.8		51 670	Hopewell city, VA......................	22 354	0.0
	49 023	Juab County, UT......................	8 238	44.5		51 730	Petersburg city, VA	33 740	2.6
	49 049	Utah County, UT......................	368 536	6.0		51 760	Richmond city, VA	197 790	0.0
39380		Pueblo, CO Metro SA....................	141 472	12.8	40100		Rio Grande City, TX Micro SA..........	53 597	20.7
	08 101	Pueblo County, CO......................	141 472	12.8		48 427	Starr County, TX......................	53 597	20.7
39420		Pullman, WA Micro SA....................	40 740	32.6	40140		Riverside-San Bernardino-Ontario, CA Metro SA.	3 254 821	6.2
	53 075	Whitman County, WA................	40 740	32.6		06 065	Riverside County, CA	1 545 387	6.8
39460		Punta Gorda, FL Metro SA..............	141 627	9.4		06 071	San Bernardino County, CA	1 709 434	5.6
	12 015	Charlotte County, FL....................	141 627	9.4	40180		Riverton, WY Micro SA................	35 804	52.4
39500		Quincy, IL-MOMicro SA..................	78 771	42.6		56 013	Fremont County, WY	35 804	52.4
	17 001	Adams County, IL......................	68 277	33.7	40220		Roanoke, VA Metro SA..................	288 309	30.3
						51 023	Botetourt County, VA..................	30 496	67.1
						51 045	Craig County, VA......................	5 091	100.0
						51 067	Franklin County, VA....................	47 286	91.0
						51 161	Roanoke County, VA....................	85 778	22.0

Core Based Statistical Areas (Metropolitan and Micropolitan), and Metropolitan Divisions with 2000 Census Population and Percent of the Population That is Rural (As of June 2003) – Continued

Core Based Statistical Area Code	State/ County FIPS Code	Statistical Area Name	2000 Census Population	Percent Rural	Core Based Statistical Area Code	State/ County FIPS Code	Statistical Area Name	2000 Census Population	Percent Rural
	51 770	Roanoke city, VA	94 911	0.0		29 021	Buchanan County, MO	85 998	13.4
	51 775	Salem city, VA	24 747	0.0		29 063	DeKalb County, MO	11 597	66.5
40260		Roanoke Rapids, NC Micro SA	79 456	66.5	41180		St. Louis, MO-IL Metro SA	2 698 687	14.0
	37 083	Halifax County, NC	57 370	57.4		17 005	Bond County, IL	17 633	60.0
	37 131	Northampton County, NC	22 086	90.2		17 013	Calhoun County, IL	5 084	100.0
40300		Rochelle, IL Micro SA	51 032	48.2		17 027	Clinton County, IL	35 535	41.4
	17 141	Ogle County, IL	51 032	48.2		17 083	Jersey County, IL	21 668	61.8
40340		Rochester, MN Metro SA	163 618	30.8		17 117	Macoupin County, IL	49 019	58.5
	27 039	Dodge County, MN	17 731	68.9		17 119	Madison County, IL	258 941	14.6
	27 109	Olmsted County, MN	124 277	19.4		17 133	Monroe County, IL	27 619	44.4
	27 157	Wabasha County, MN	21 610	65.4		17 163	St. Clair County, IL	256 082	10.5
40380		Rochester, NY Metro SA	1 037 831	21.4		29 071	Franklin County, MO	93 807	58.0
	36 051	Livingston County, NY	64 328	54.8		29 099	Jefferson County, MO	198 099	34.8
	36 055	Monroe County, NY	735 343	7.0		29 113	Lincoln County, MO	38 944	79.0
	36 069	Ontario County, NY	100 224	50.8		29 183	St. Charles County, MO	283 883	8.0
	36 073	Orleans County, NY	44 171	56.9		29 189	St. Louis County, MO	1 016 315	1.4
	36 117	Wayne County, NY	93 765	63.4		29 219	Warren County, MO	24 525	78.6
40420		Rockford, IL Metro SA	320 204	11.1		29 221	Washington County, MO	23 344	79.8
	17 007	Boone County, IL	41 786	30.4		29 510	St. Louis city, MO	348 189	0.0
	17 201	Winnebago County, IL	278 418	8.2	41220		St. Marys, GA Micro SA	43 664	35.8
40460		Rockingham, NC Micro SA	46 564	45.8		13 039	Camden County, GA	43 664	35.8
	37 153	Richmond County, NC	46 564	45.8	41260		St. Marys, PA Micro SA	35 112	47.8
40500		Rockland, ME Micro SA	39 618	61.6		42 047	Elk County, PA	35 112	47.8
	23 013	Knox County, ME	39 618	61.6	41420		Salem, OR Metro SA	347 214	16.7
40540		Rock Springs, WY Micro SA	37 613	10.9		41 047	Marion County, OR	284 834	15.2
	56 037	Sweetwater County, WY	37 613	10.9		41 053	Polk County, OR	62 380	23.6
40580		Rocky Mount, NC Metro SA	143 026	47.2	41460		Salina, KS Micro SA	59 760	23.8
	37 065	Edgecombe County, NC	55 606	45.1		20 143	Ottawa County, KS	6 163	100.0
	37 127	Nash County, NC	87 420	48.5		20 169	Saline County, KS	53 597	15.0
40620		Rolla, MO Micro SA	39 825	47.7	41500		Salinas, CA Metro SA	401 762	10.8
	29 161	Phelps County, MO	39 825	47.7		06 053	Monterey County, CA	401 762	10.8
40660		Rome, GA Metro SA	90 565	34.8	41540		Salisbury, MD Metro SA	109 391	36.2
	13 115	Floyd County, GA	90 565	34.8		24 039	Somerset County, MD	24 747	51.7
40700		Roseburg, OR Micro SA	100 399	41.9		24 045	Wicomico County, MD	84 644	31.6
	41 019	Douglas County, OR	100 399	41.9	41580		Salisbury, NC Micro SA	130 340	41.2
40740		Roswell, NM Micro SA	61 382	23.2		37 159	Rowan County, NC	130 340	41.2
	35 005	Chaves County, NM	61 382	23.2	41620		Salt Lake City, UT Metro SA	968 858	3.7
40780		Russellville, AR Micro SA	75 608	64.6		49 035	Salt Lake County, UT	898 387	1.2
	05 115	Pope County, AR	54 469	58.1		49 043	Summit County, UT	29 736	52.9
	05 149	Yell County, AR	21 139	81.3		49 045	Tooele County, UT	40 735	24.2
40820		Ruston, LA Micro SA	57 906	44.8	41660		San Angelo, TX Metro SA	105 781	16.7
	22 049	Jackson Parish, LA	15 397	67.9		48 235	Irion County, TX	1 771	100.0
	22 061	Lincoln Parish, LA	42 509	36.5		48 451	Tom Green County, TX	104 010	15.3
40860		Rutland, VT Micro SA	63 400	61.4	41700		San Antonio, TX Metro SA	1 711 703	15.1
	50 021	Rutland County, VT	63 400	61.4		48 013	Atascosa County, TX	38 628	60.4
40900		Sacramento-Arden-Arcade-Roseville, CA Metro SA	1 796 857	8.6		48 019	Bandera County, TX	17 645	100.0
	06 017	El Dorado County, CA	156 299	37.0		48 029	Bexar County, TX	1 392 931	6.0
	06 061	Placer County, CA	248 399	21.2		48 091	Comal County, TX	78 021	43.0
	06 067	Sacramento County, CA	1 223 499	2.4		48 187	Guadalupe County, TX	89 023	41.8
	06 113	Yolo County, CA	168 660	9.3		48 259	Kendall County, TX	23 743	62.7
40940		Safford, AZ Micro SA	42 036	54.4		48 325	Medina County, TX	39 304	55.7
	04 009	Graham County, AZ	33 489	55.7		48 493	Wilson County, TX	32 408	82.6
	04 011	Greenlee County, AZ	8 547	49.4	41740		San Diego-Carlsbad-San Marcos, CA Metro SA	2 813 833	3.9
40980		Saginaw-Saginaw Township North, MI Metro SA	210 039	30.5		06 073	San Diego County, CA	2 813 833	3.9
	26 145	Saginaw County, MI	210 039	30.5	41780		Sandusky, OH Metro SA	79 551	26.5
41060		St. Cloud, MN Metro SA	167 392	43.1		39 043	Erie County, OH	79 551	26.5
	27 009	Benton County, MN	34 226	40.9	41820		Sanford, NC Micro SA	49 040	48.1
	27 145	Stearns County, MN	133 166	43.6		37 105	Lee County, NC	49 040	48.1
41100		St. George, UT Metro SA	90 354	19.7	41860		San Francisco-Oakland-Fremont, CA Metro SA	4 123 740	1.3
	49 053	Washington County, UT	90 354	19.7			Oakland-Fremont-Hayward, CA Metro Div. 36084	2 392 557	1.2
41140		St. Joseph, MO-KS Metro SA	122 336	29.8		06 001	Alameda County, CA	1 443 741	0.6
	20 043	Doniphan County, KS	8 249	87.9		06 013	Contra Costa County, CA	948 816	2.1
	29 003	Andrew County, MO	16 492	60.3					

Core Based Statistical Area Code	State/County FIPS Code	Statistical Area Name	2000 Census Population	Percent Rural
		San Francisco-San Mateo-Redwood City, CA Metro Div. 41884	1 731 183	1.4
	06 041	Marin County, CA	247 289	5.8
	06 075	San Francisco County, CA	776 733	0.0
	06 081	San Mateo County, CA	707 161	1.4
41940		San Jose-Sunnyvale-Santa Clara, CA Metro SA	1 735 819	1.9
	06 069	San Benito County, CA	53 234	22.4
	06 085	Santa Clara County, CA	1 682 585	1.2
42020		San Luis Obispo-Paso Robles, CA Metro SA	246 681	18.8
	06 079	San Luis Obispo County, CA	246 681	18.8
42060		Santa Barbara-Santa Maria-Goleta, CA Metro SA	399 347	4.8
	06 083	Santa Barbara County, CA	399 347	4.8
42100		Santa Cruz-Watsonville, CA Metro SA	255 602	14.7
	06 087	Santa Cruz County, CA	255 602	14.7
42140		Santa Fe, NM Metro SA	129 292	24.6
	35 049	Santa Fe County, NM	129 292	24.6
42220		Santa Rosa-Petaluma, CA Metro SA	458 614	14.3
	06 097	Sonoma County, CA	458 614	14.3
42260		Sarasota-Bradenton-Venice, FL Metro SA	589 959	6.3
	12 081	Manatee County, FL	264 002	8.1
	12 115	Sarasota County, FL	325 957	4.9
42300		Sault Ste. Marie, MI Micro SA	38 543	44.7
	26 033	Chippewa County, MI	38 543	44.7
42340		Savannah, GA Metro SA	293 000	19.1
	13 029	Bryan County, GA	23 417	60.5
	13 051	Chatham County, GA	232 048	5.5
	13 103	Effingham County, GA	37 535	77.2
42380		Sayre, PA Micro SA	62 761	72.2
	42 015	Bradford County, PA	62 761	72.2
42420		Scottsbluff, NE Micro SA	37 770	34.9
	31 007	Banner County, NE	819	100.0
	31 157	Scotts Bluff County, NE	36 951	33.4
42460		Scottsboro, AL Micro SA	53 926	76.3
	01 071	Jackson County, AL	53 926	76.3
42500		Scottsburg, IN Micro SA	22 960	50.7
	18 143	Scott County, IN	22 960	50.7
42540		Scranton—Wilkes-Barre, PA Metro SA	560 625	22.5
	42 069	Lackawanna County, PA	213 295	17.5
	42 079	Luzerne County, PA	319 250	20.4
	42 131	Wyoming County, PA	28 080	85.0
42580		Seaford, DE Micro SA	156 638	53.5
	10 005	Sussex County, DE	156 638	53.5
42620		Searcy, AR Micro SA	67 165	55.5
	05 145	White County, AR	67 165	55.5
42660		Seattle-Tacoma-Bellevue, WA Metro SA	3 043 878	6.1
		Seattle-Bellevue-Everett, WA Metro Div. 42644	2 343 058	5.6
	53 033	King County, WA	1 737 034	3.7
	53 061	Snohomish County, WA	606 024	11.0
		Tacoma, WA Metro Div. 45104	700 820	7.9
	53 053	Pierce County, WA	700 820	7.9
42700		Sebring, FL Micro SA	87 366	33.4
	12 055	Highlands County, FL	87 366	33.4
42740		Sedalia, MO Micro SA	39 403	37.8
	29 159	Pettis County, MO	39 403	37.8
42780		Selinsgrove, PA Micro SA	37 546	71.3
	42 109	Snyder County, PA	37 546	71.3
42820		Selma, AL Micro SA	46 365	47.3
	01 047	Dallas County, AL	46 365	47.3
42860		Seneca, SC Micro SA	66 215	70.6
	45 073	Oconee County, SC	66 215	70.6
42900		Seneca Falls, NY Micro SA	33 342	57.4
	36 099	Seneca County, NY	33 342	57.4
42940		Sevierville, TN Micro SA	71 170	65.0
	47 155	Sevier County, TN	71 170	65.0
42980		Seymour, IN Micro SA	41 335	43.8
	18 071	Jackson County, IN	41 335	43.8
43060		Shawnee, OK Micro SA	65 521	51.5
	40 125	Pottawatomie County, OK	65 521	51.5
43100		Sheboygan, WI Metro SA	112 646	29.2
	55 117	Sheboygan County, WI	112 646	29.2
43140		Shelby, NC Micro SA	96 287	55.5
	37 045	Cleveland County, NC	96 287	55.5
43180		Shelbyville, TN Micro SA	37 586	59.3
	47 003	Bedford County, TN	37 586	59.3
43220		Shelton, WA Micro SA	49 405	74.7
	53 045	Mason County, WA	49 405	74.7
43260		Sheridan, WY Micro SA	26 560	35.8
	56 033	Sheridan County, WY	26 560	35.8
43300		Sherman-Denison, TX Metro SA	110 595	46.3
	48 181	Grayson County, TX	110 595	46.3
43340		Shreveport-Bossier City, LA Metro SA	375 965	22.9
	22 015	Bossier Parish, LA	98 310	27.9
	22 017	Caddo Parish, LA	252 161	15.9
	22 031	De Soto Parish, LA	25 494	73.6
43380		Sidney, OH Micro SA	47 910	57.3
	39 149	Shelby County, OH	47 910	57.3
43420		Sierra Vista-Douglas, AZ Micro SA	117 755	33.6
	04 003	Cochise County, AZ	117 755	33.6
43460		Sikeston, MO Micro SA	40 422	38.0
	29 201	Scott County, MO	40 422	38.0
43500		Silver City, NM Micro SA	31 002	42.4
	35 017	Grant County, NM	31 002	42.4
43540		Silverthorne, CO Micro SA	23 548	26.8
	08 117	Summit County, CO	23 548	26.8
43580		Sioux City, IA-NE-SD Metro SA	143 053	25.9
	19 193	Woodbury County, IA	103 877	16.5
	31 043	Dakota County, NE	20 253	21.6
	31 051	Dixon County, NE	6 339	100.0
	46 127	Union County, SD	12 584	73.4
43620		Sioux Falls, SD Metro SA	187 093	27.9
	46 083	Lincoln County, SD	24 131	60.8
	46 087	McCook County, SD	5 832	100.0
	46 099	Minnehaha County, SD	148 281	15.4
	46 125	Turner County, SD	8 849	100.0
43660		Snyder, TX Micro SA	16 361	33.0
	48 415	Scurry County, TX	16 361	33.0
43700		Somerset, KY Micro SA	56 217	60.5
	21 199	Pulaski County, KY	56 217	60.5
43740		Somerset, PA Micro SA	80 023	74.5
	42 111	Somerset County, PA	80 023	74.5
43780		South Bend-Mishawaka, IN-MI Metro SA	316 663	19.6
	18 141	St. Joseph County, IN	265 559	8.5
	26 027	Cass County, MI	51 104	77.3
43860		Southern Pines, NC Micro SA	74 769	58.7
	37 125	Moore County, NC	74 769	58.7
43900		Spartanburg, SC Metro SA	253 791	35.2
	45 083	Spartanburg County, SC	253 791	35.2
43940		Spearfish, SD Micro SA	21 802	34.4

Core Based Statistical Area Code	State/County FIPS Code	Statistical Area Name	2000 Census Population	Percent Rural	Core Based Statistical Area Code	State/County FIPS Code	Statistical Area Name	2000 Census Population	Percent Rural
	46 081	Lawrence County, SD	21 802	34.4		40 021	Cherokee County, OK	42 521	59.9
43980		Spencer, IA Micro SA	17 372	36.7	45180		Talladega-Sylacauga, AL Micro SA	80 321	55.3
	19 041	Clay County, IA	17 372	36.7		01 121	Talladega County, AL	80 321	55.3
44020		Spirit Lake, IA Micro SA	16 424	30.2	45220		Tallahassee, FL Metro SA	320 304	31.3
	19 059	Dickinson County, IA	16 424	30.2		12 039	Gadsden County, FL	45 087	66.2
44060		Spokane, WA Metro SA	417 939	13.9		12 065	Jefferson County, FL	12 902	100.0
	53 063	Spokane County, WA	417 939	13.9		12 073	Leon County, FL	239 452	14.4
44100		Springfield, IL Metro SA	201 437	18.4		12 129	Wakulla County, FL	22 863	100.0
	17 129	Menard County, IL	12 486	75.3	45260		Tallulah, LA Micro SA	13 728	22.8
	17 167	Sangamon County, IL	188 951	14.6		22 065	Madison Parish, LA	13 728	22.8
44140		Springfield, MA Metro SA	680 014	18.4	45300		Tampa-St. Petersburg-Clearwater, FL Metro SA	2 395 997	5.8
	25 011	Franklin County, MA	71 535	54.6		12 053	Hernando County, FL	130 802	23.9
	25 013	Hampden County, MA	456 228	9.7		12 057	Hillsborough County, FL	998 948	5.6
	25 015	Hampshire County, MA	152 251	27.5		12 101	Pasco County, FL	344 765	14.8
44180		Springfield, MO Metro SA	368 374	34.6		12 103	Pinellas County, FL	921 482	0.1
	29 043	Christian County, MO	54 285	50.7	45340		Taos, NM Micro SA	29 979	59.4
	29 059	Dallas County, MO	15 661	83.1		35 055	Taos County, NM	29 979	59.4
	29 077	Greene County, MO	240 391	18.1	45380		Taylorville, IL Micro SA	35 372	43.3
	29 167	Polk County, MO	26 992	68.8		17 021	Christian County, IL	35 372	43.3
	29 225	Webster County, MO	31 045	80.3	45460		Terre Haute, IN Metro SA	170 943	39.3
44220		Springfield, OH Metro SA	144 742	23.8		18 021	Clay County, IN	26 556	62.1
	39 023	Clark County, OH	144 742	23.8		18 153	Sullivan County, IN	21 751	66.5
44260		Starkville, MS Micro SA	42 902	39.2		18 165	Vermillion County, IN	16 788	58.6
	28 105	Oktibbeha County, MS	42 902	39.2		18 167	Vigo County, IN	105 848	24.9
44300		State College, PA Metro SA	135 758	35.7	45500		Texarkana, TX-Texarkana, AR Metro SA	129 749	35.9
	42 027	Centre County, PA	135 758	35.7		05 091	Miller County, AR	40 443	41.6
44340		Statesboro, GA Micro SA	55 983	51.5		48 037	Bowie County, TX	89 306	33.2
	13 031	Bulloch County, GA	55 983	51.5	45540		The Villages, FL Micro SA	53 345	50.6
44380		Statesville-Mooresville, NC Micro SA	122 660	49.6		12 119	Sumter County, FL	53 345	50.6
	37 097	Iredell County, NC	122 660	49.6	45580		Thomaston, GA Micro SA	27 597	45.8
44420		Staunton-Waynesboro, VA Micro SA	108 988	47.5		13 293	Upson County, GA	27 597	45.8
	51 015	Augusta County, VA	65 615	78.0	45620		Thomasville, GA Micro SA	42 737	51.0
	51 790	Staunton city, VA	23 853	0.9		13 275	Thomas County, GA	42 737	51.0
	51 820	Waynesboro city, VA	19 520	2.3	45660		Tiffin-Fostoria, OH Micro SA	58 683	45.8
44500		Stephenville, TX Micro SA	33 001	43.2		39 147	Seneca County, OH	58 683	45.8
	48 143	Erath County, TX	33 001	43.2	45700		Tifton, GA Micro SA	38 407	44.0
44540		Sterling, CO Micro SA	20 504	40.5		13 277	Tift County, GA	38 407	44.0
	08 075	Logan County, CO	20 504	40.5	45740		Toccoa, GA Micro SA	25 435	60.0
44580		Sterling, IL Micro SA	60 653	35.3		13 257	Stephens County, GA	25 435	60.0
	17 195	Whiteside County, IL	60 653	35.3	45780		Toledo, OH Metro SA	659 188	16.7
44620		Stevens Point, WI Micro SA	67 182	38.5		39 051	Fulton County, OH	42 084	57.0
	55 097	Portage County, WI	67 182	38.5		39 095	Lucas County, OH	455 054	5.5
44660		Stillwater, OK Micro SA	68 190	32.1		39 123	Ottawa County, OH	40 985	53.0
	40 119	Payne County, OK	68 190	32.1		39 173	Wood County, OH	121 065	32.6
44700		Stockton, CA Metro SA	563 598	9.9	45820		Topeka, KS Metro SA	224 551	35.1
	06 077	San Joaquin County, CA	563 598	9.9		20 085	Jackson County, KS	12 657	74.1
44740		Storm Lake, IA Micro SA	20 411	47.7		20 087	Jefferson County, KS	18 426	100.0
	19 021	Buena Vista County, IA	20 411	47.7		20 139	Osage County, KS	16 712	100.0
44780		Sturgis, MI Micro SA	62 422	56.0		20 177	Shawnee County, KS	169 871	16.1
	26 149	St. Joseph County, MI	62 422	56.0		20 197	Wabaunsee County, KS	6 885	100.0
44860		Sulphur Springs, TX Micro SA	31 960	59.1	45860		Torrington, CT Micro SA	182 193	43.9
	48 223	Hopkins County, TX	31 960	59.1		09 005	Litchfield County, CT	182 193	43.9
44900		Summerville, GA Micro SA	25 470	56.3	45900		Traverse City, MI Micro SA	131 342	67.9
	13 055	Chattooga County, GA	25 470	56.3		26 019	Benzie County, MI	15 998	100.0
44940		Sumter, SC Metro SA	104 646	37.9		26 055	Grand Traverse County, MI	77 654	50.6
	45 085	Sumter County, SC	104 646	37.9		26 079	Kalkaska County, MI	16 571	83.1
44980		Sunbury, PA Micro SA	94 556	37.0		26 089	Leelanau County, MI	21 119	95.0
	42 097	Northumberland County, PA	94 556	37.0			Trenton-Ewing, NJ Metro SA	350 761	4.2
45020		Sweetwater, TX Micro SA	15 802	29.0	45940				
	48 353	Nolan County, TX	15 802	29.0		34 021	Mercer County, NJ	350 761	4.2
45060		Syracuse, NY Metro SA	650 154	27.8	45980		Troy, AL Micro SA	29 605	60.2
	36 053	Madison County, NY	69 441	58.2		01 109	Pike County, AL	29 605	60.2
	36 067	Onondaga County, NY	458 336	13.4	46020		Truckee-Grass Valley, CA Micro SA	92 033	43.3
	36 075	Oswego County, NY	122 377	64.5		06 057	Nevada County, CA	92 033	43.3
45140		Tahlequah, OK Micro SA	42 521	59.9					

Core Based Statistical Areas (Metropolitan and Micropolitan), and Metropolitan Divisions with 2000 Census Population and Percent of the Population That is Rural (As of June 2003) – Continued

Core Based Statistical Area Code	State/County FIPS Code	Statistical Area Name	2000 Census Population	Percent Rural	Core Based Statistical Area Code	State/County FIPS Code	Statistical Area Name	2000 Census Population	Percent Rural
46060		Tucson, AZ Metro SA	843 746	8.5		48 057	Calhoun County, TX	20 647	41.8
	04 019	Pima County, AZ	843 746	8.5		48 175	Goliad County, TX	6 928	100.0
46100		Tullahoma, TN Micro SA	93 024	60.3		48 469	Victoria County, TX	84 088	27.2
	47 031	Coffee County, TN	48 014	47.6	47180		Vincennes, IN Micro SA	39 256	36.0
	47 051	Franklin County, TN	39 270	70.1		18 083	Knox County, IN	39 256	36.0
	47 127	Moore County, TN	5 740	100.0	47220		Vineland-Millville-Bridgeton, NJ Metro SA	146 438	19.9
46140		Tulsa, OK Metro SA	859 532	21.8		34 011	Cumberland County, NJ	146 438	19.9
	40 037	Creek County, OK	67 367	53.9	47260		Virginia Beach-Norfolk-Newport News, VA-NC Metro SA	1 576 370	9.0
	40 111	Okmulgee County, OK	39 685	48.8		37 053	Currituck County, NC	18 190	100.0
	40 113	Osage County, OK	44 437	58.9		51 073	Gloucester County, VA	34 780	72.0
	40 117	Pawnee County, OK	16 612	80.9		51 093	Isle of Wight County, VA	29 728	66.0
	40 131	Rogers County, OK	70 641	56.9		51 095	James City County, VA	48 102	29.2
	40 143	Tulsa County, OK	563 299	4.7		51 115	Mathews County, VA	9 207	100.0
	40 145	Wagoner County, OK	57 491	44.4		51 181	Surry County, VA	6 829	100.0
46180		Tupelo, MS Micro SA	125 251	61.8		51 199	York County, VA	56 297	9.5
	28 057	Itawamba County, MS	22 770	87.9		51 550	Chesapeake city, VA	199 184	10.0
	28 081	Lee County, MS	75 755	46.2		51 650	Hampton city, VA	146 437	0.2
	28 115	Pontotoc County, MS	26 726	84.0		51 700	Newport News city, VA	180 150	0.0
46220		Tuscaloosa, AL Metro SA	192 034	38.0		51 710	Norfolk city, VA	234 403	0.0
	01 063	Greene County, AL	9 974	100.0		51 735	Poquoson city , VA	11 566	4.2
	01 065	Hale County, AL	17 185	84.8		51 740	Portsmouth city, VA	100 565	0.0
	01 125	Tuscaloosa County, AL	164 875	29.3		51 800	Suffolk city, VA	63 677	27.5
46260		Tuskegee, AL Micro SA	24 105	49.3		51 810	Virginia Beach city, VA	425 257	1.4
	01 087	Macon County, AL	24 105	49.3		51 830	Williamsburg city, VA	11 998	0.0
46300		Twin Falls, ID Micro SA	82 626	38.1	47300		Visalia-Porterville, CA Metro SA	368 021	18.9
	16 053	Jerome County, ID	18 342	57.1		06 107	Tulare County, CA	368 021	18.9
	16 083	Twin Falls County, ID	64 284	32.6	47340		Wabash, IN Micro SA	34 960	48.1
46340		Tyler, TX Metro SA	174 706	38.2		18 169	Wabash County, IN	34 960	48.1
	48 423	Smith County, TX	174 706	38.2	47380		Waco, TX Metro SA	213 517	25.1
46380		Ukiah, CA Micro SA	86 265	46.0		48 309	McLennan County, TX	213 517	25.1
	06 045	Mendocino County, CA	86 265	46.0	47420		Wahpeton, ND-MN Micro SA	25 136	51.4
46420		Union, SC Micro SA	29 881	64.3		27 167	Wilkin County, MN	7 138	50.4
	45 087	Union County, SC	29 881	64.3		38 077	Richland County, ND	17 998	51.8
46460		Union City, TN-KY Micro SA	40 202	60.1	47460		Walla Walla, WA Micro SA	55 180	19.0
	21 075	Fulton County, KY	7 752	63.8		53 071	Walla Walla County, WA	55 180	19.0
	47 131	Obion County, TN	32 450	59.2	47500		Walterboro, SC Micro SA	38 264	73.8
46500		Urbana, OH Micro SA	38 890	70.2		45 029	Colleton County, SC	38 264	73.8
	39 021	Champaign County, OH	38 890	70.2	47540		Wapakoneta, OH Micro SA	46 611	40.8
46540		Utica-Rome, NY Metro SA	299 896	38.9		39 011	Auglaize County, OH	46 611	40.8
	36 043	Herkimer County, NY	64 427	51.6	47580		Warner Robins, GA Metro SA	110 765	15.1
	36 065	Oneida County, NY	235 469	35.4		13 153	Houston County, GA	110 765	15.1
46620		Uvalde, TX Micro SA	25 926	32.1	47620		Warren, PA Micro SA	43 863	54.6
	48 463	Uvalde County, TX	25 926	32.1		42 123	Warren County, PA	43 863	54.6
46660		Valdosta, GA Metro SA	119 560	43.2	47660		Warrensburg, MO Micro SA	48 258	49.0
	13 027	Brooks County, GA	16 450	70.3		29 101	Johnson County, MO	48 258	49.0
	13 101	Echols County, GA	3 754	100.0	47700		Warsaw, IN Micro SA	74 057	53.4
	13 173	Lanier County, GA	7 241	94.0		18 085	Kosciusko County, IN	74 057	53.4
	13 185	Lowndes County, GA	92 115	32.1	47780		Washington, IN Micro SA	29 820	58.9
46700		Vallejo-Fairfield, CA Metro SA	394 542	4.1		18 027	Daviess County, IN	29 820	58.9
	06 095	Solano County, CA	394 542	4.1	47820		Washington, NC Micro SA	44 958	68.7
46740		Valley, AL Micro SA	36 583	49.7		37 013	Beaufort County, NC	44 958	68.7
	01 017	Chambers County, AL	36 583	49.7	47860		Washington, OH Micro SA	28 433	48.3
46780		Van Wert, OH Micro SA	29 659	51.4		39 047	Fayette County, OH	28 433	48.3
	39 161	Van Wert County, OH	29 659	51.4	47900		Washington-Arlington-Alexandria, DC-VA-MD-WV Metro SA	4 796 183	8.2
46820		Vermillion, SD Micro SA	13 537	24.9			Washington-Arlington-Alexandria, DC-VA-MD-WV Metro Div. 47894 ..	3 727 565	8.4
	46 027	Clay County, SD	13 537	24.9		11 001	District of Columbia, DC	572 059	0.0
46860		Vernal, UT Micro SA	25 224	54.3		24 009	Calvert County, MD	74 563	45.9
	49 047	Uintah County, UT	25 224	54.3		24 017	Charles County, MD	120 546	33.7
46900		Vernon, TX Micro SA	14 676	23.2		24 033	Prince George's County, MD	801 515	2.6
	48 487	Wilbarger County, TX	14 676	23.2		51 013	Arlington County, VA	189 453	0.0
46940		Vero Beach, FL Metro SA	112 947	8.2		51 043	Clarke County, VA	12 652	76.4
	12 061	Indian River County, FL	112 947	8.2					
46980		Vicksburg, MS Micro SA	49 644	36.8					
	28 149	Warren County, MS	49 644	36.8					
47020		Victoria, TX Metro SA	111 663	34.4					

Core Based Statistical Area Code	State/County FIPS Code	Statistical Area Name	2000 Census Population	Percent Rural
	51 059	Fairfax County, VA	969 749	1.4
	51 061	Fauquier County, VA	55 139	72.3
	51 107	Loudoun County, VA	169 599	15.7
	51 153	Prince William County, VA	280 813	9.2
	51 177	Spotsylvania County, VA	90 395	34.8
	51 179	Stafford County, VA	92 446	26.6
	51 187	Warren County, VA	31 584	56.0
	51 510	Alexandria city, VA	128 283	0.0
	51 600	Fairfax city, VA	21 498	0.0
	51 610	Falls Church city, VA	10 377	0.0
	51 630	Fredericksburg city, VA	19 279	0.4
	51 683	Manassas city, VA	35 135	0.1
	51 685	Manassas Park city, VA	10 290	0.0
	54 037	Jefferson County, WV	42 190	68.5
		Bethesda-Frederick-Gaithersburg, MD Metro Div. 13644	1 068 618	7.5
	24 021	Frederick County, MD	195 277	28.2
	24 031	Montgomery County, MD	873 341	2.8
47940		Waterloo-Cedar Falls, IA Metro SA	163 706	29.3
	19 013	Black Hawk County, IA	128 012	15.5
	19 017	Bremer County, IA	23 325	67.8
	19 075	Grundy County, IA	12 369	100.0
47980		Watertown, SD Micro SA	31 437	37.6
	46 029	Codington County, SD	25 897	24.2
	46 057	Hamlin County, SD	5 540	100.0
48020		Watertown-Fort Atkinson, WI Micro SA	74 021	42.2
	55 055	Jefferson County, WI	74 021	42.2
48060		Watertown-Fort Drum, NY Micro SA	111 738	52.8
	36 045	Jefferson County, NY	111 738	52.8
48100		Wauchula, FL Micro SA	26 938	47.4
	12 049	Hardee County, FL	26 938	47.4
48140		Wausau, WI Metro SA	125 834	44.8
	55 073	Marathon County, WI	125 834	44.8
48180		Waycross, GA Micro SA	51 119	43.4
	13 229	Pierce County, GA	15 636	77.5
	13 299	Ware County, GA	35 483	28.4
48260		Weirton-Steubenville, WV-OH Metro SA	132 008	38.8
	39 081	Jefferson County, OH	73 894	39.7
	54 009	Brooke County, WV	25 447	42.6
	54 029	Hancock County, WV	32 667	33.6
48300		Wenatchee, WA Metro SA	99 219	35.5
	53 007	Chelan County, WA	66 616	38.0
	53 017	Douglas County, WA	32 603	30.4
48340		West Helena, AR Micro SA	26 445	47.6
	05 107	Phillips County, AR	26 445	47.6
48460		West Plains, MO Micro SA	37 238	73.1
	29 091	Howell County, MO	37 238	73.1
48540		Wheeling, WV-OH Metro SA	153 172	39.8
	39 013	Belmont County, OH	70 226	47.8
	54 051	Marshall County, WV	35 519	49.7
	54 069	Ohio County, WV	47 427	20.4
48580		Whitewater, WI Micro SA	93 759	35.9
	55 127	Walworth County, WI	93 759	35.9
48620		Wichita, KS Metro SA	571 166	16.2
	20 015	Butler County, KS	59 482	44.1
	20 079	Harvey County, KS	32 869	31.2
	20 173	Sedgwick County, KS	452 869	8.8
	20 191	Sumner County, KS	25 946	62.4
48660		Wichita Falls, TX Metro SA	151 524	17.0
	48 009	Archer County, TX	8 854	88.8
	48 077	Clay County, TX	11 006	73.1
	48 485	Wichita County, TX	131 664	7.5
48700		Williamsport, PA Metro SA	120 044	36.0
	42 081	Lycoming County, PA	120 044	36.0
48740		Willimantic, CT Micro SA	109 091	49.0
	09 015	Windham County, CT	109 091	49.0
48780		Williston, ND Micro SA	19 761	34.0
	38 105	Williams County, ND	19 761	34.0
48820		Willmar, MN Micro SA	41 203	46.0
	27 067	Kandiyohi County, MN	41 203	46.0
48900		Wilmington, NC Metro SA	274 532	34.1
	37 019	Brunswick County, NC	73 143	66.2
	37 129	New Hanover County, NC	160 307	4.6
	37 141	Pender County, NC	41 082	92.1
48940		Wilmington, OH Micro SA	40 543	55.2
	39 027	Clinton County, OH	40 543	55.2
48980		Wilson, NC Micro SA	73 814	36.9
	37 195	Wilson County, NC	73 814	36.9
49020		Winchester, VA-WV Metro SA	102 997	47.9
	51 069	Frederick County, VA	59 209	49.3
	51 840	Winchester city , VA	23 585	0.0
	54 027	Hampshire County, WV	20 203	100.0
49060		Winfield, KS Micro SA	36 291	34.4
	20 035	Cowley County, KS	36 291	34.4
49100		Winona, MN Micro SA	49 985	35.4
	27 169	Winona County, MN	49 985	35.4
49180		Winston-Salem, NC Metro SA	421 961	28.8
	37 059	Davie County, NC	34 835	77.2
	37 067	Forsyth County, NC	306 067	9.1
	37 169	Stokes County, NC	44 711	79.9
	37 197	Yadkin County, NC	36 348	86.1
49220		Wisconsin Rapids-Marshfield, WI Micro SA	75 555	36.9
	55 141	Wood County, WI	75 555	36.9
49260		Woodward, OK Micro SA	18 486	41.1
	40 153	Woodward County, OK	18 486	41.1
49300		Wooster, OH Micro SA	111 564	51.9
	39 169	Wayne County, OH	111 564	51.9
49340		Worcester, MA Metro SA	750 963	19.2
	25 027	Worcester County, MA	750 963	19.2
49380		Worthington, MN Micro SA	20 832	46.5
	27 105	Nobles County, MN	20 832	46.5
49420		Yakima, WA Metro SA	222 581	28.8
	53 077	Yakima County, WA	222 581	28.8
49460		Yankton, SD Micro SA	21 652	39.4
	46 135	Yankton County, SD	21 652	39.4
49540		Yazoo City, MS Micro SA	28 149	47.2
	28 163	Yazoo County, MS	28 149	47.2
49620		York-Hanover, PA Metro SA	381 751	28.5
	42 133	York County, PA	381 751	28.5
49660		Youngstown-Warren-Boardman, OH-PA Metro SA	602 964	25.6
	39 099	Mahoning County, OH	257 555	14.4
	39 155	Trumbull County, OH	225 116	26.5
	42 085	Mercer County, PA	120 293	48.1
49700		Yuba City-Marysville, CA Metro SA	139 149	21.3
	06 101	Sutter County, CA	78 930	14.5
	06 115	Yuba County, CA	60 219	30.1
49740		Yuma, AZ Metro SA	160 026	13.1
	04 027	Yuma County, AZ	160 026	13.1
49780		Zanesville, OH Micro SA	84 585	46.2
	39 119	Muskingum County, OH	84 585	46.2

Maps of Congressional Districts and States

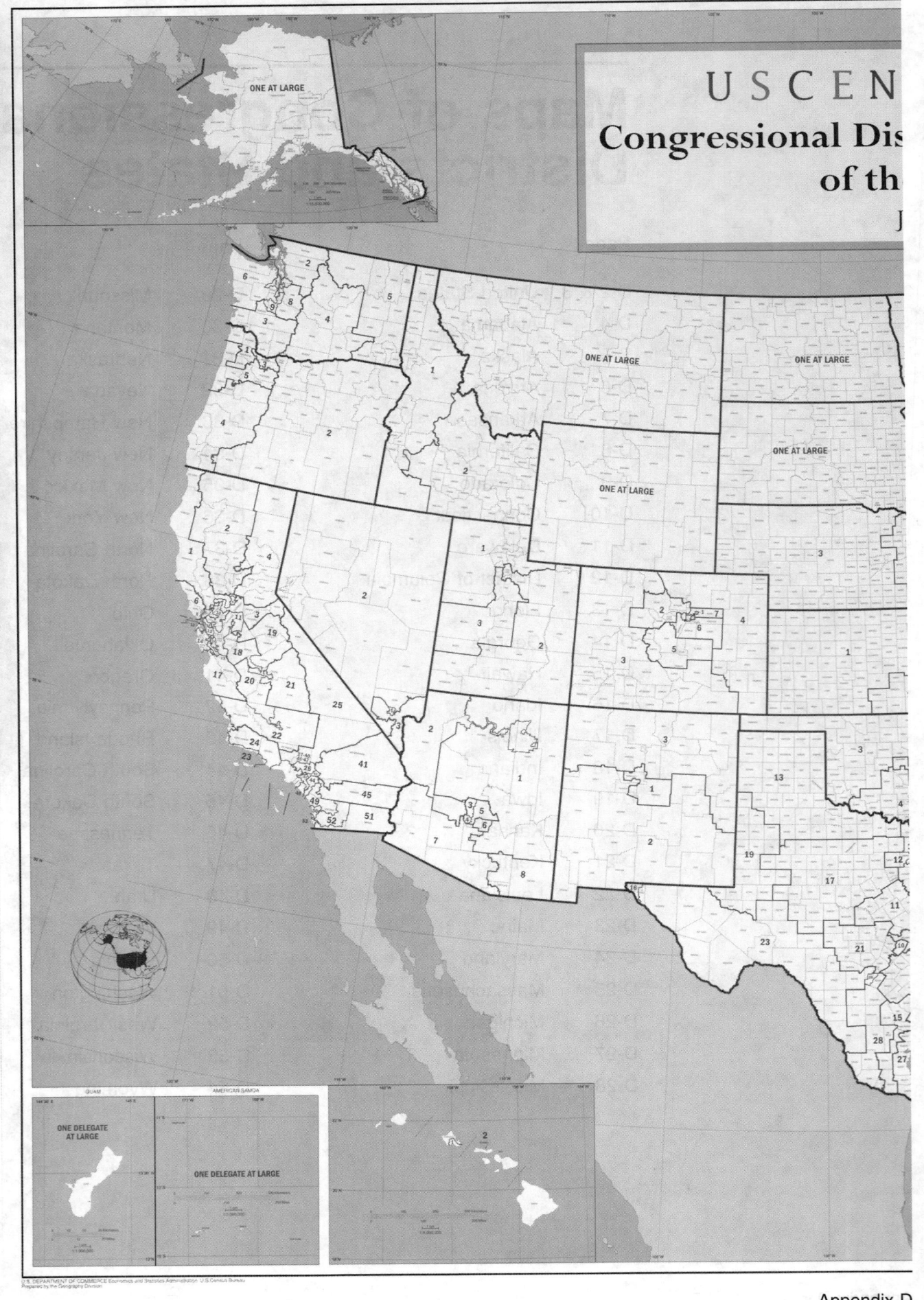

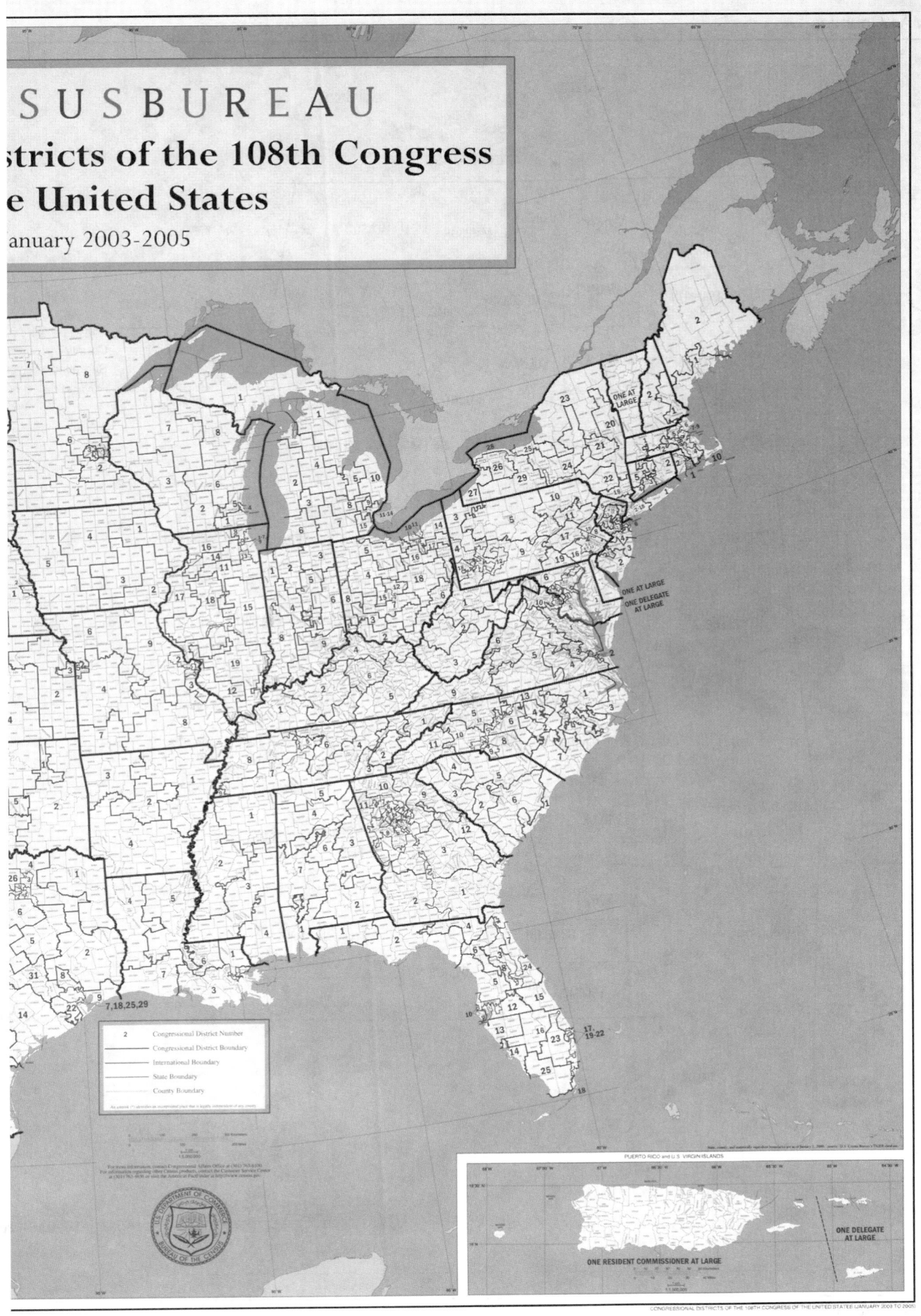

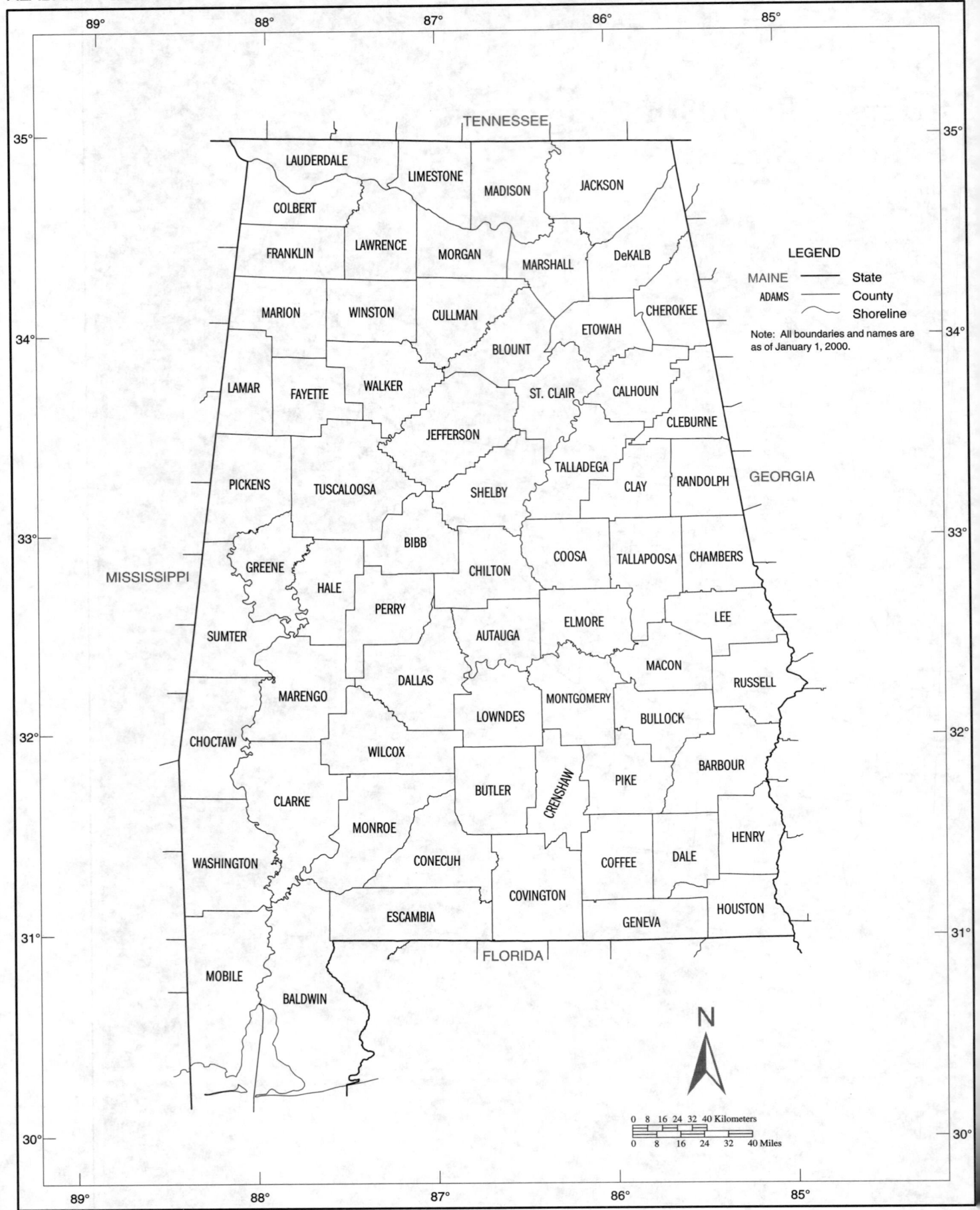

ALASKA - Boroughs and Census Areas

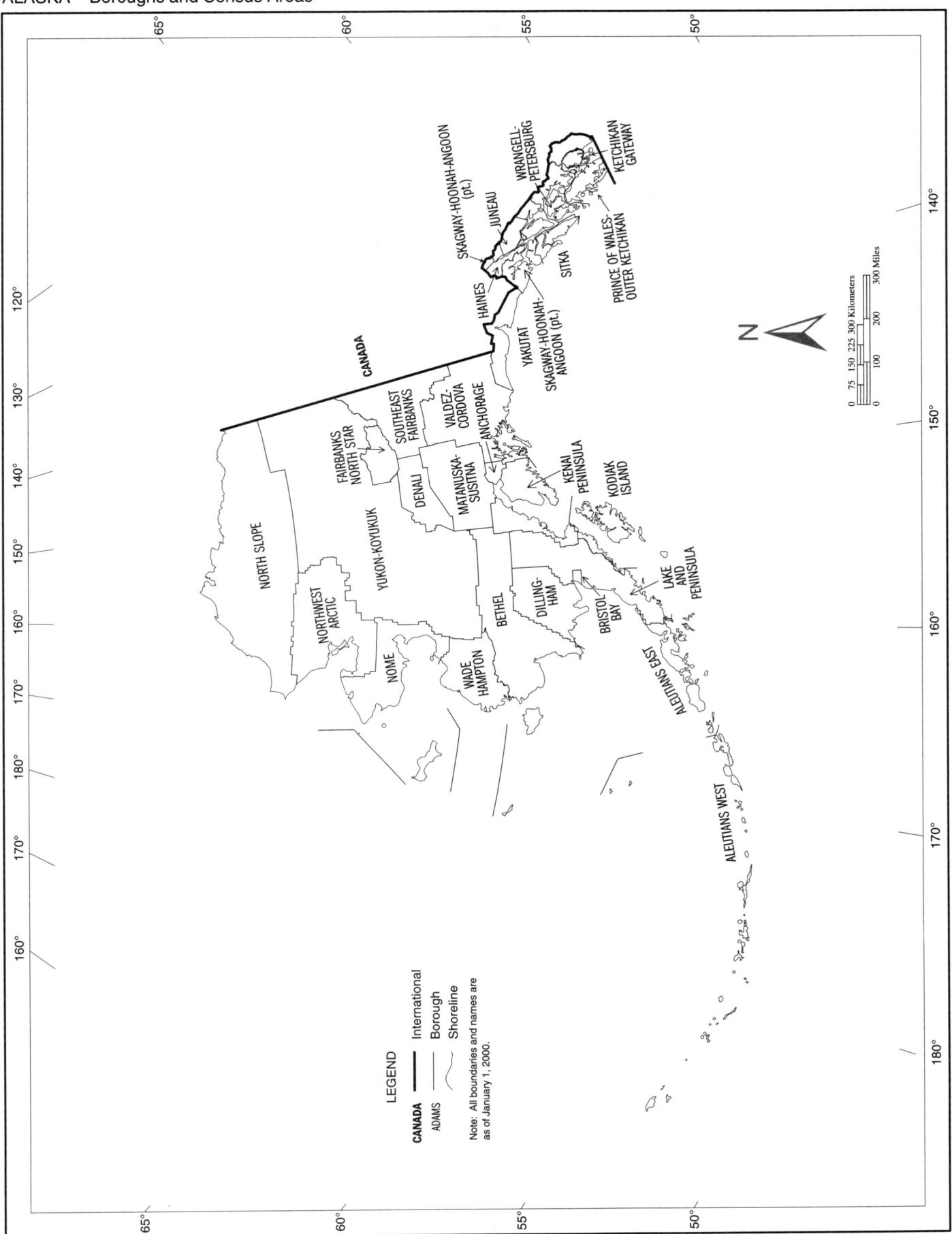

LEGEND

CANADA International

ADAMS Borough

Shoreline

Note: All boundaries and names are
as of January 1, 2000.

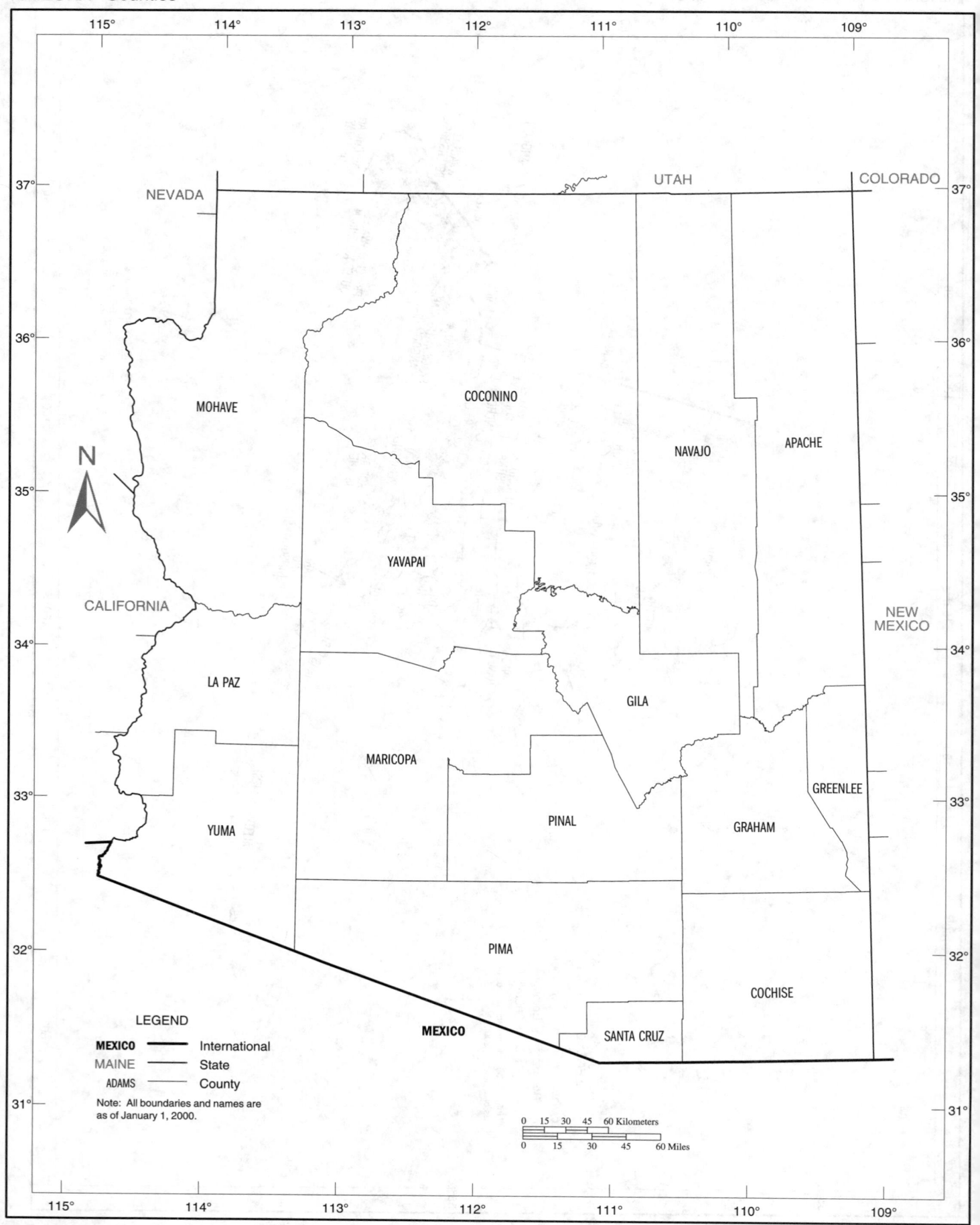

LEGEND

MEXICO ——————— International
MAINE ——————— State
ADAMS ——————— County

Note: All boundaries and names are
as of January 1, 2000.

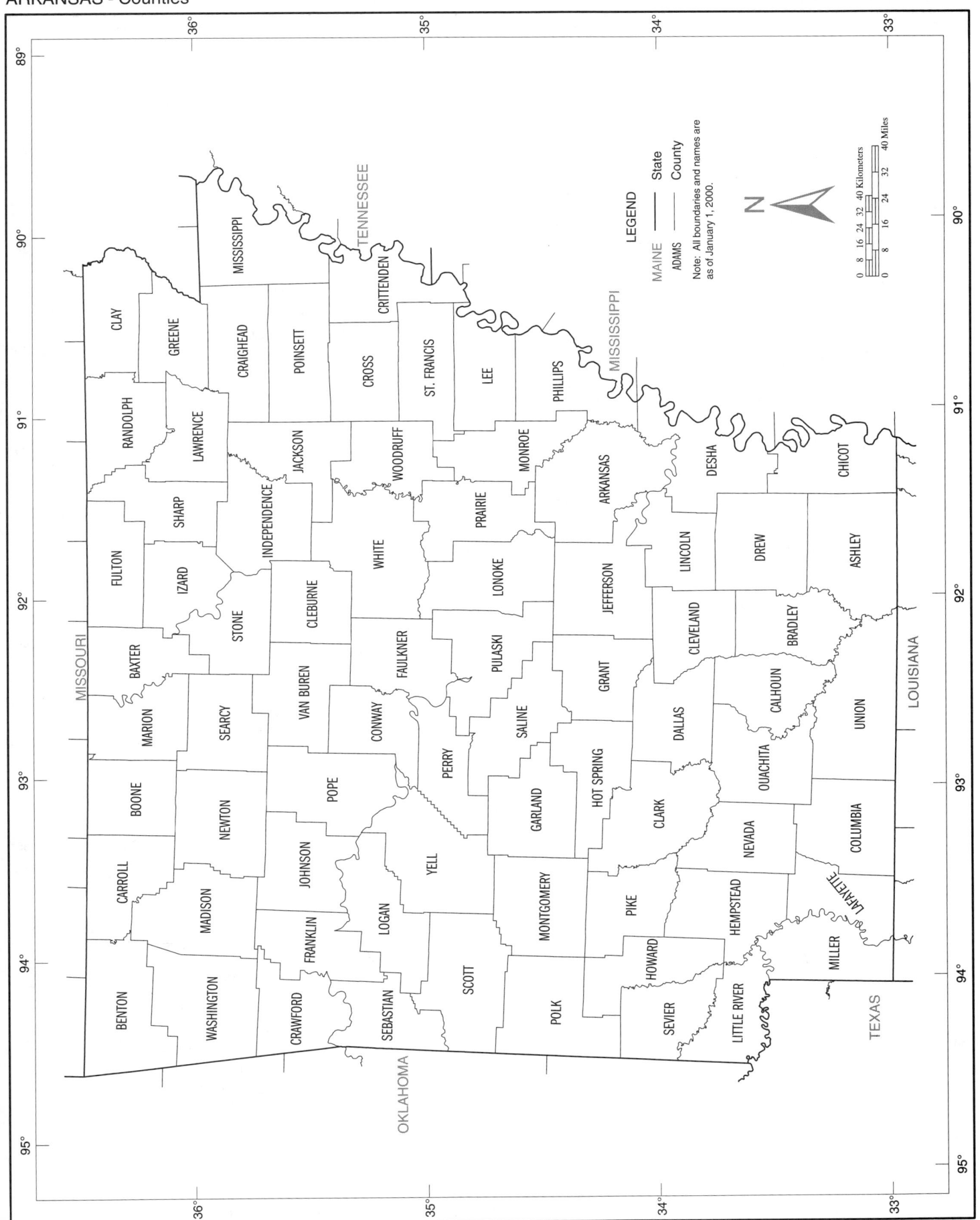

LEGEND

MEXICO — International
MAINE — State
ADAMS — County
⌒ Shoreline

Note: All boundaries and names are as of January 1, 2000.

COLORADO - Counties

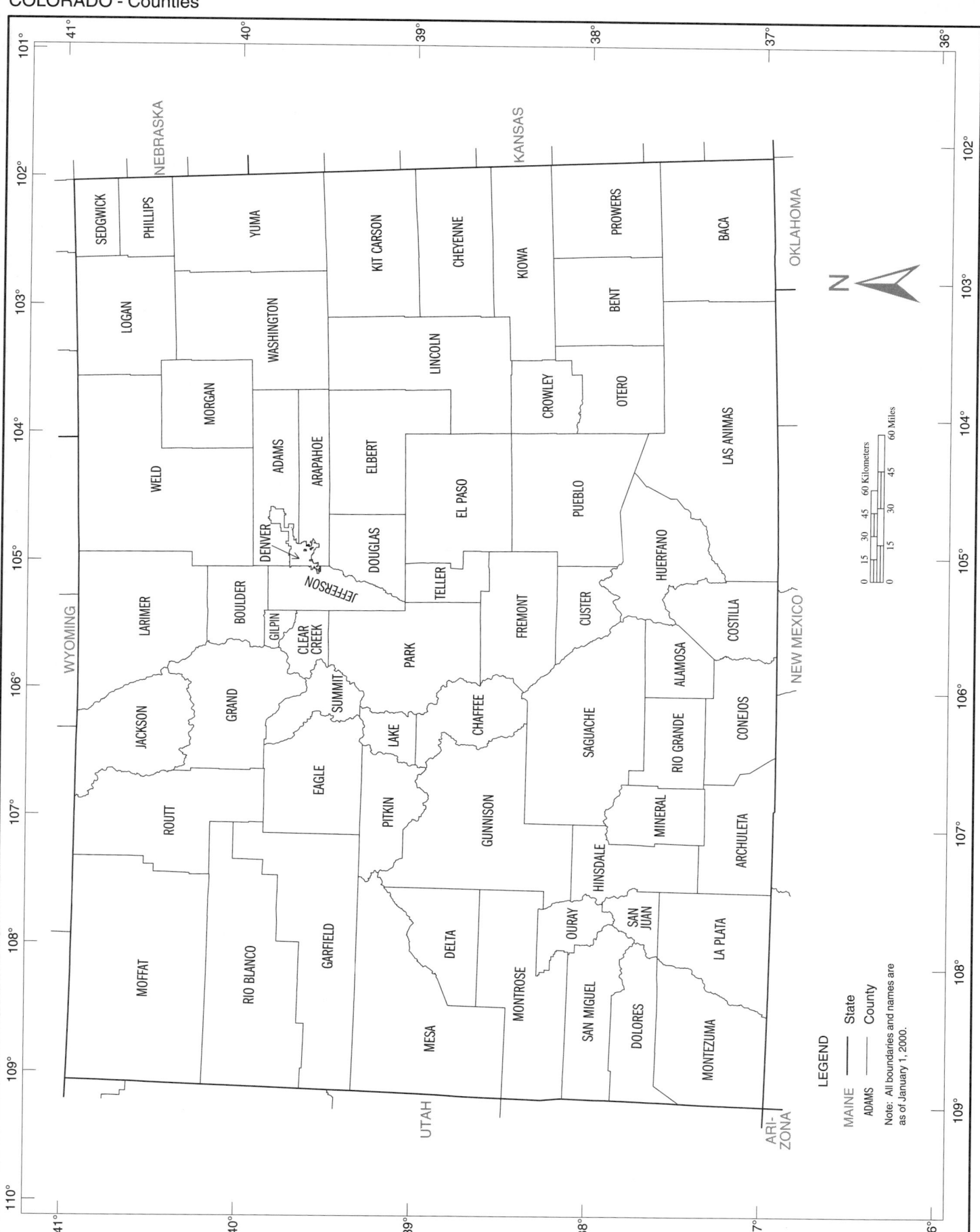

LEGEND

MAINE ——— State
ADAMS ——— County

Note: All boundaries and names are
as of January 1, 2000.

U.S. Census Bureau, Census 2000

Appendix D

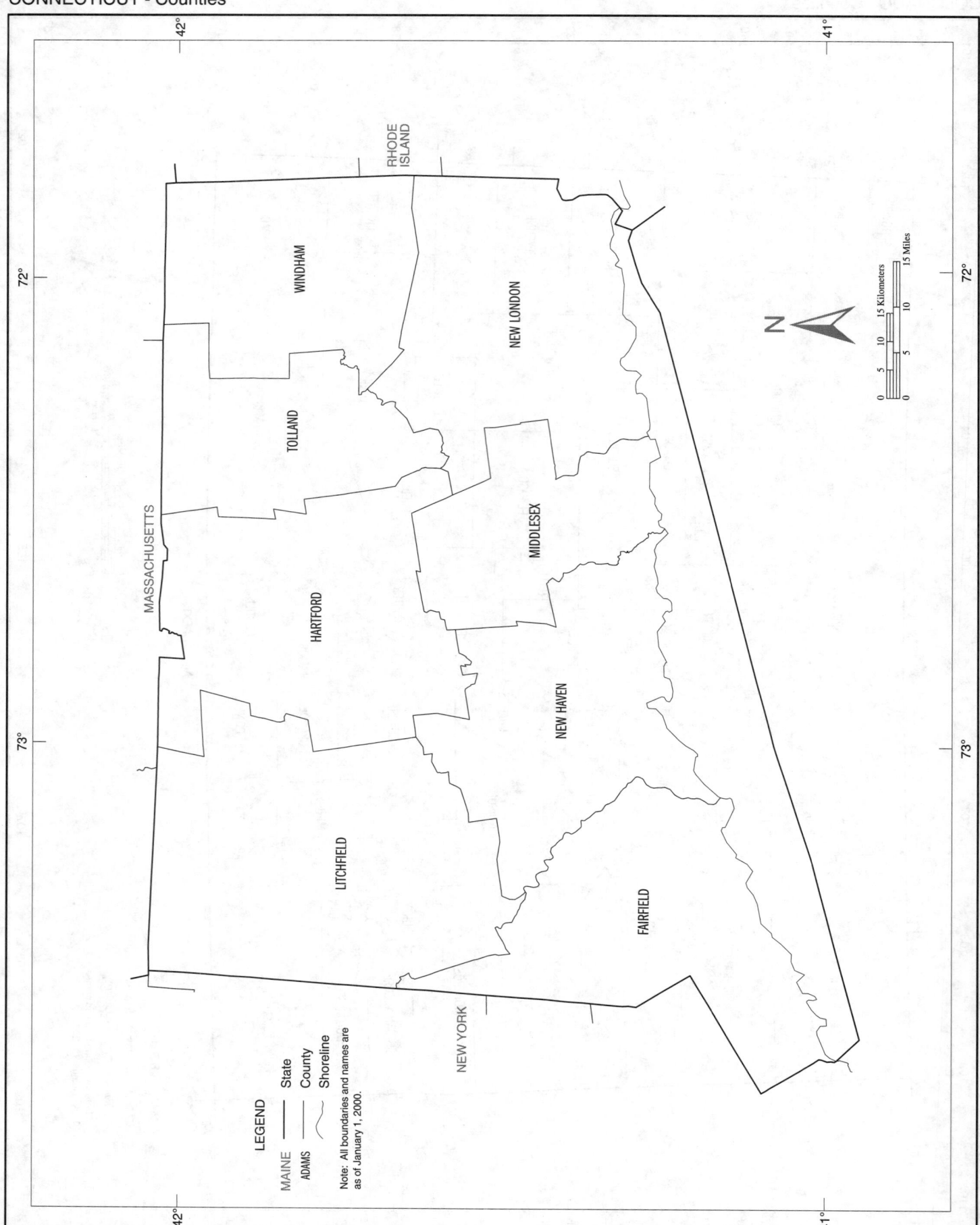

LEGEND

MAINE — State

ADAMS — County

Shoreline

Note: All boundaries and names are
as of January 1, 2000.

WINDHAM

NEW LONDON

TOLLAND

MASSACHUSETTS

MIDDLESEX

HARTFORD

NEW HAVEN

LITCHFIELD

FAIRFIELD

RHODE ISLAND

NEW YORK

DELAWARE - Counties

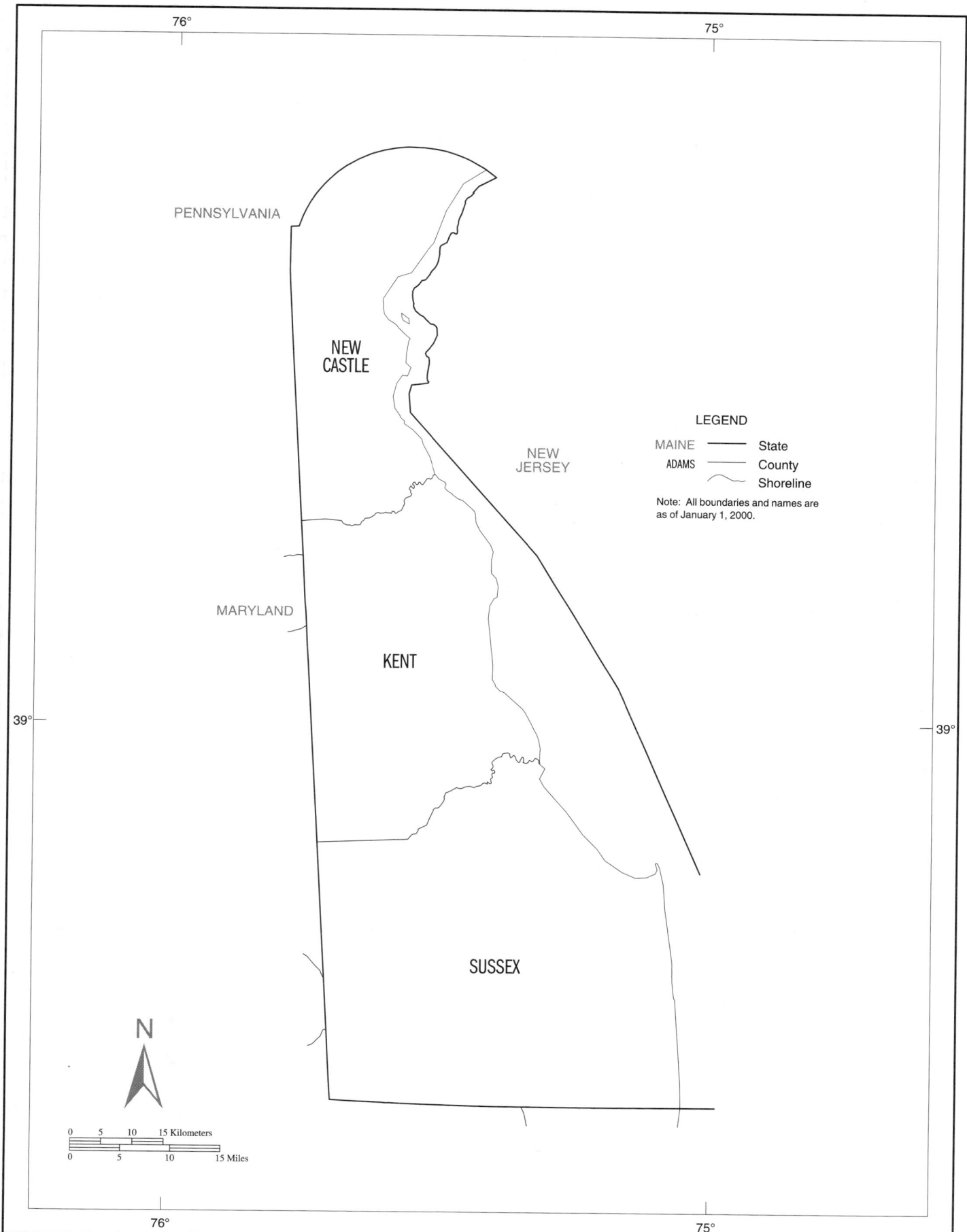

LEGEND

MAINE ——— State
ADAMS ——— County
~~~ Shoreline

Note: All boundaries and names are
as of January 1, 2000.

PENNSYLVANIA

NEW
CASTLE

NEW
JERSEY

MARYLAND

KENT

SUSSEX

76° 75°

39° 39°

76° 75°

N

0   5   10   15 Kilometers
0   5   10   15 Miles

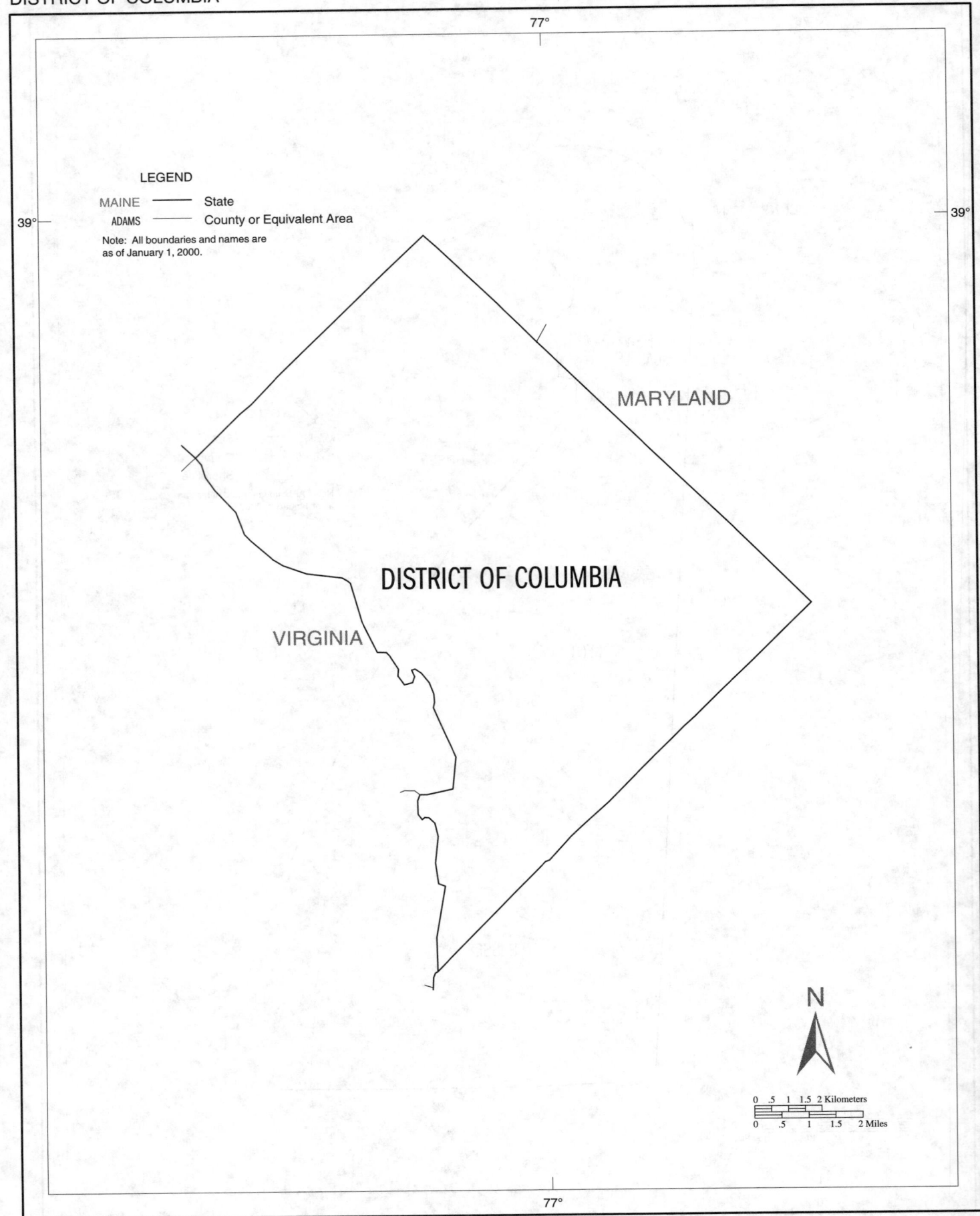

77°

39°

LEGEND

MAINE ——— State

ADAMS ——— County or Equivalent Area

Note: All boundaries and names are
as of January 1, 2000.

39°

MARYLAND

DISTRICT OF COLUMBIA

VIRGINIA

N

```
0   .5   1   1.5   2 Kilometers
|===|===|===|===|
0   .5   1   1.5   2 Miles
```

77°

FLORIDA - Counties

NASSAU

DUVAL

ST. JOHNS

FLAGLER

CLAY

PUTNAM

VOLUSIA

MARION

BAKER

UNION

BRADFORD

ALACHUA

COLUMBIA

GILCHRIST

LEVY

CITRUS

SUMTER

LAKE

SEMINOLE

ORANGE

BREVARD

INDIAN RIVER

ST. LUCIE

MARTIN

PALM BEACH

BROWARD

MIAMI-DADE

OKEECHOBEE

OSCEOLA

POLK

HIGH-LANDS

GLADES

HENDRY

COLLIER

MONROE

HARDEE

DeSOTO

CHAR-LOTTE

LEE

HILLS-BOROUGH

PASCO

HER-NANDO

MANATEE

SARASOTA

PINELLAS

HAMILTON

SUWAN-NEE

LAFAY-ETTE

DIXIE

MADISON

TAYLOR

JEFFERSON

LEON

WAKULLA

GADSDEN

LIBERTY

FRANKLIN

GULF

CALHOUN

JACKSON

WASH-INGTON

BAY

HOLMES

WALTON

OKALOOSA

SANTA ROSA

ESCAMBIA

GEORGIA

ALABAMA

LEGEND

MAINE — State

ADAMS — County

— Shoreline

Note: All boundaries and names are as of January 1, 2000.

N

0 15 30 45 60 Kilometers

0 15 30 45 60 Miles

U.S. Census Bureau, Census 2000

Appendix D

D-13

GEORGIA - Counties

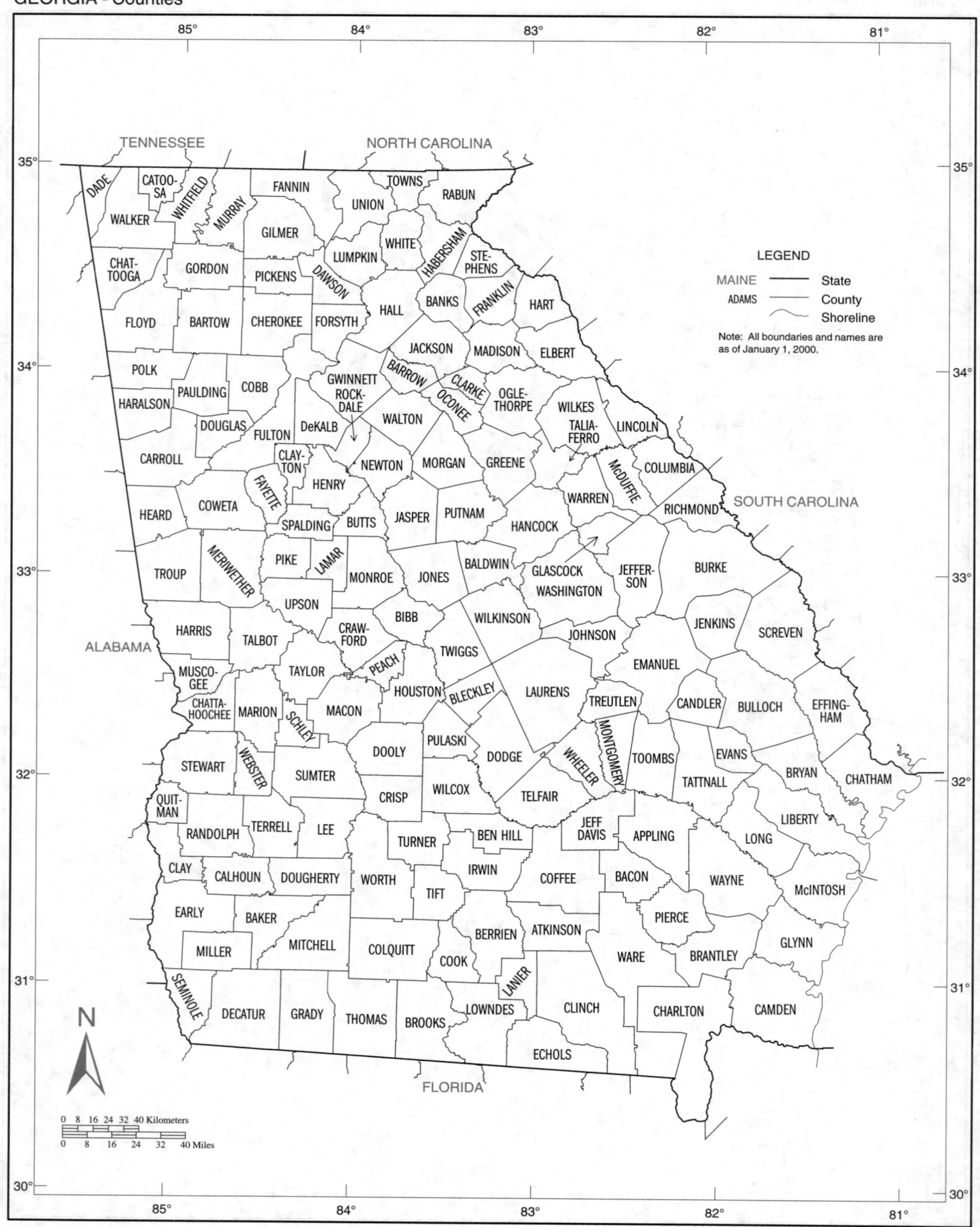

LEGEND

MAINE ——— State
ADAMS ——— County
~~~ Shoreline

Note: All boundaries and names are as of January 1, 2000.

HAWAII - Counties

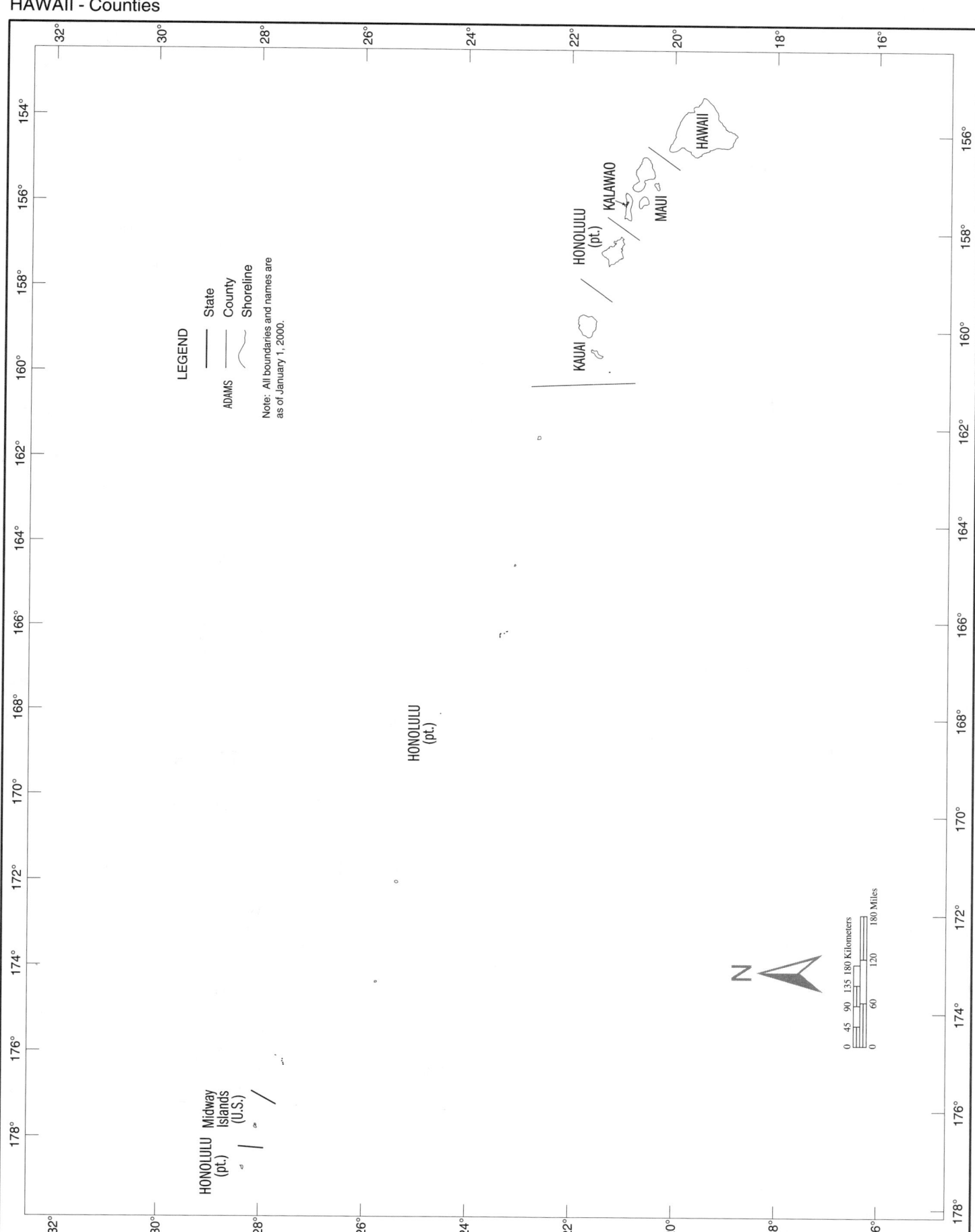

LEGEND

ADAMS

State
County
Shoreline

Note: All boundaries and names are
as of January 1, 2000.

KAUAI

HONOLULU
(pt.)

KALAWAO

MAUI

HAWAII

HONOLULU
(pt.)

HONOLULU
(pt.)

Midway
Islands
(U.S.)

N

0 45 90 135 180 Kilometers
0   60   120   180 Miles

IDAHO - Counties

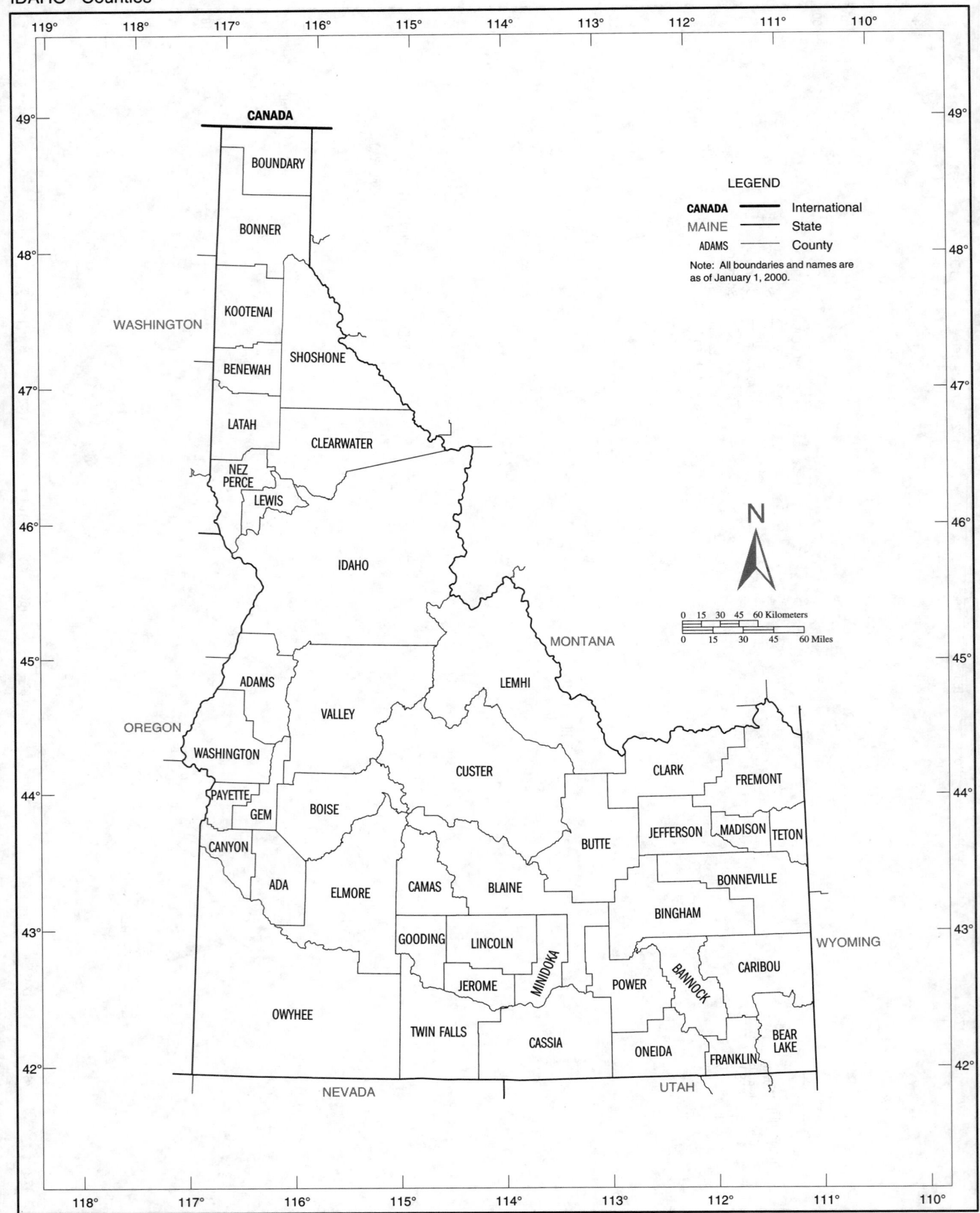

LEGEND

CANADA ▬▬▬ International
MAINE ▬▬▬ State
ADAMS ─── County

Note: All boundaries and names are as of January 1, 2000.

ILLINOIS - Counties

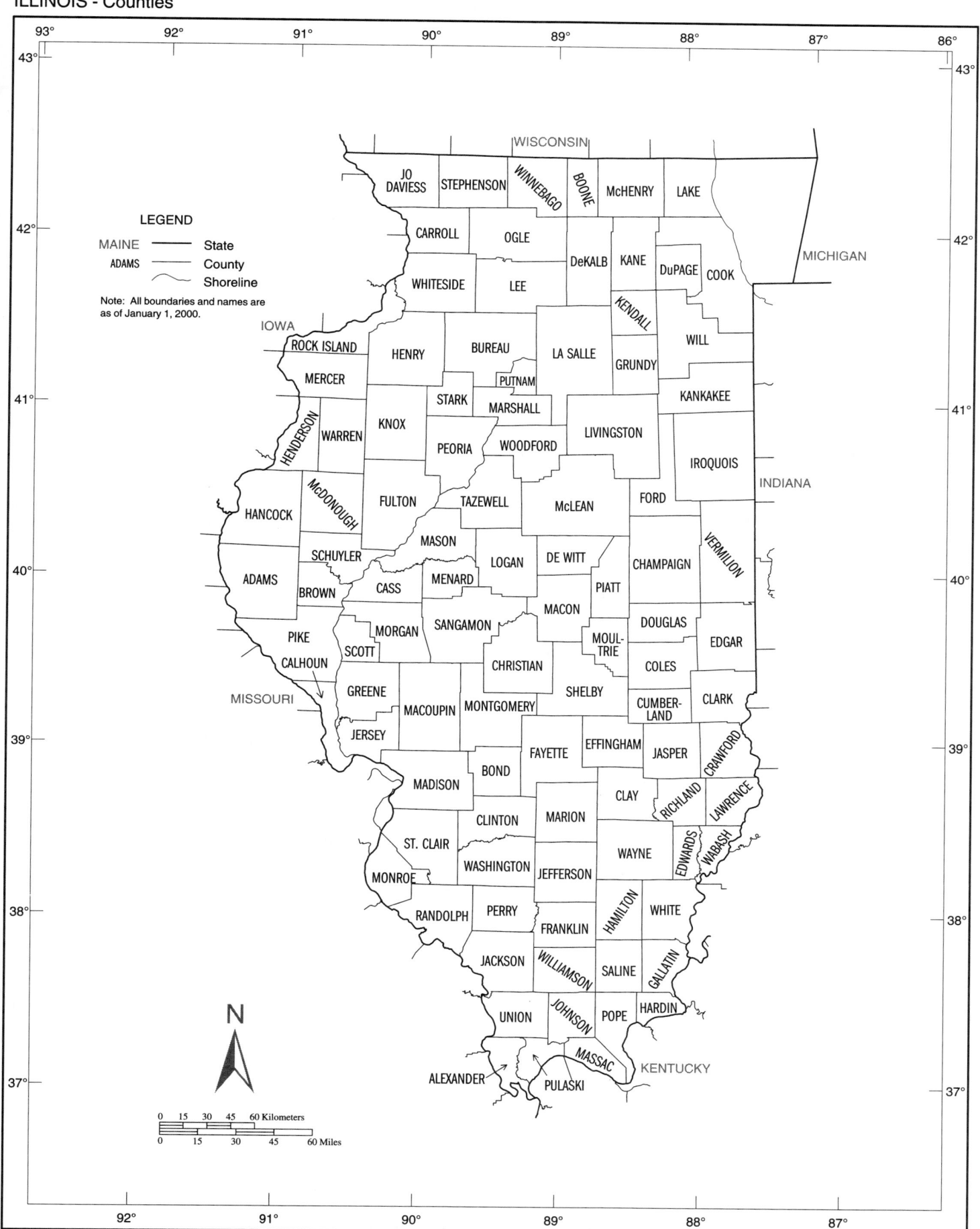

LEGEND

MAINE —— State
ADAMS —— County
　　 ～～～ Shoreline

Note: All boundaries and names are
as of January 1, 2000.

N

| 0 | 15 | 30 | 45 | 60 Kilometers |
| 0 | 15 | 30 | 45 | 60 Miles |

U.S. Census Bureau, Census 2000

Appendix D

D-17

INDIANA - Counties

IOWA - Counties

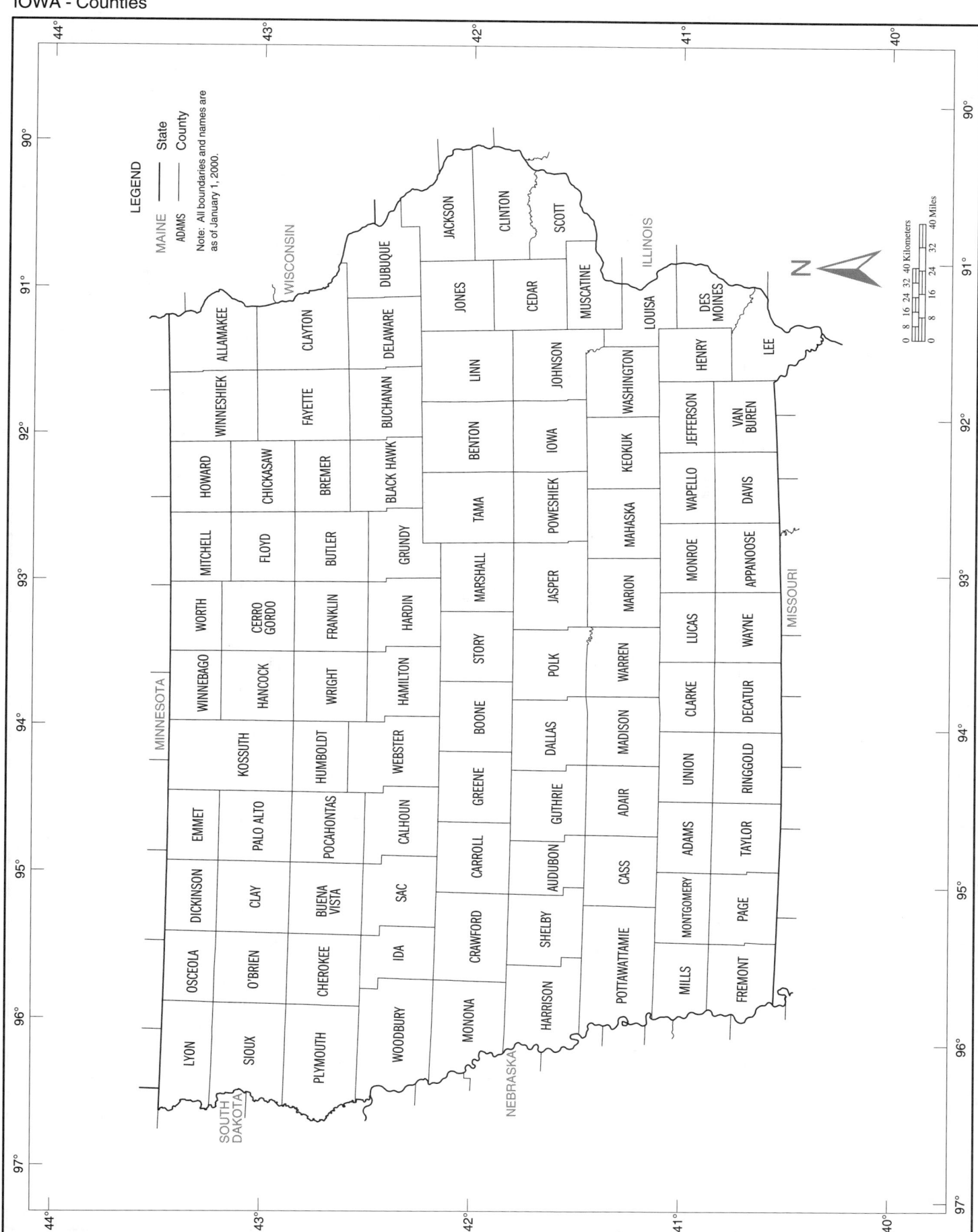

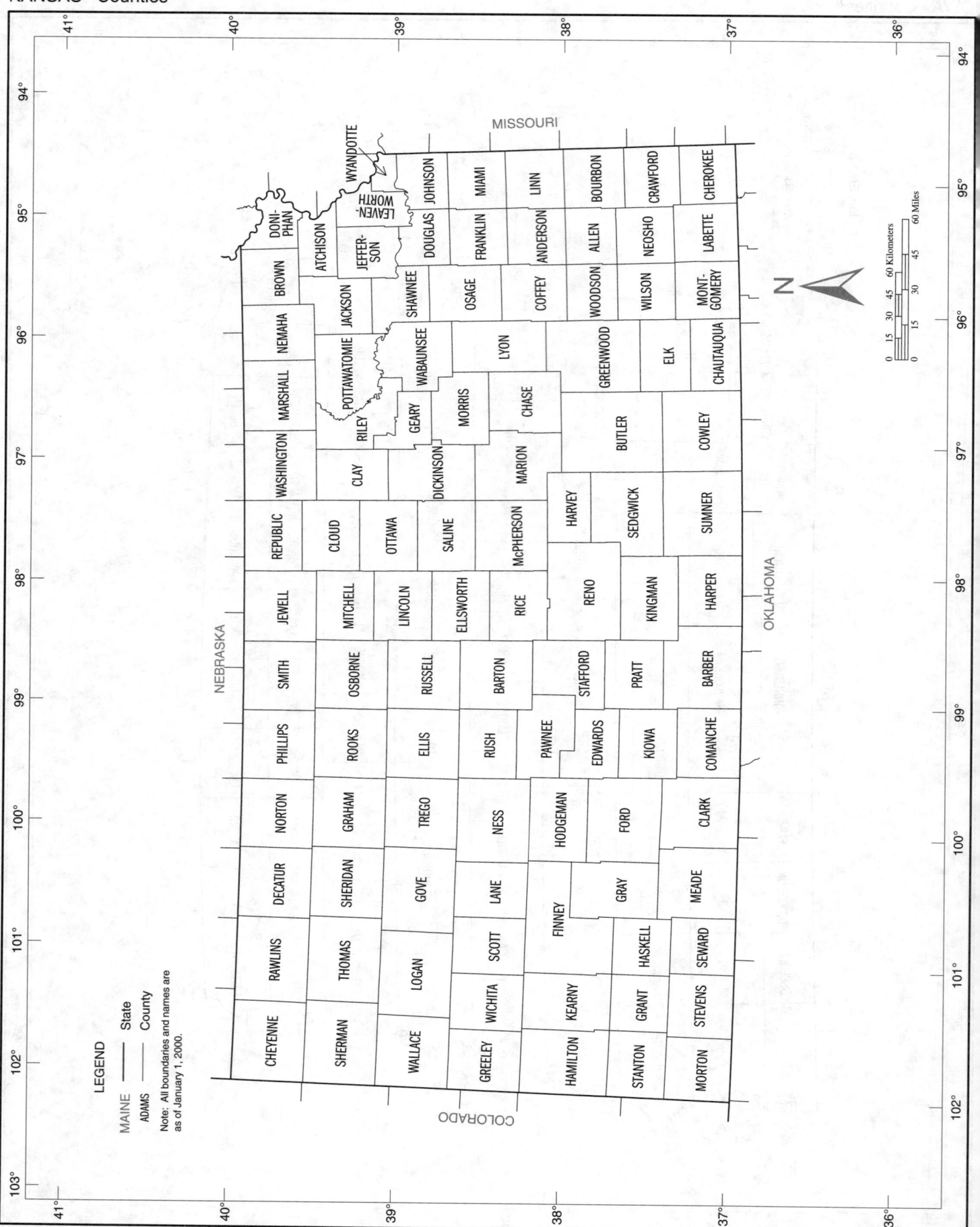

LEGEND

MAINE ———— State

ADAMS ———— County

Note: All boundaries and names are
as of January 1, 2000.

KENTUCKY - Counties

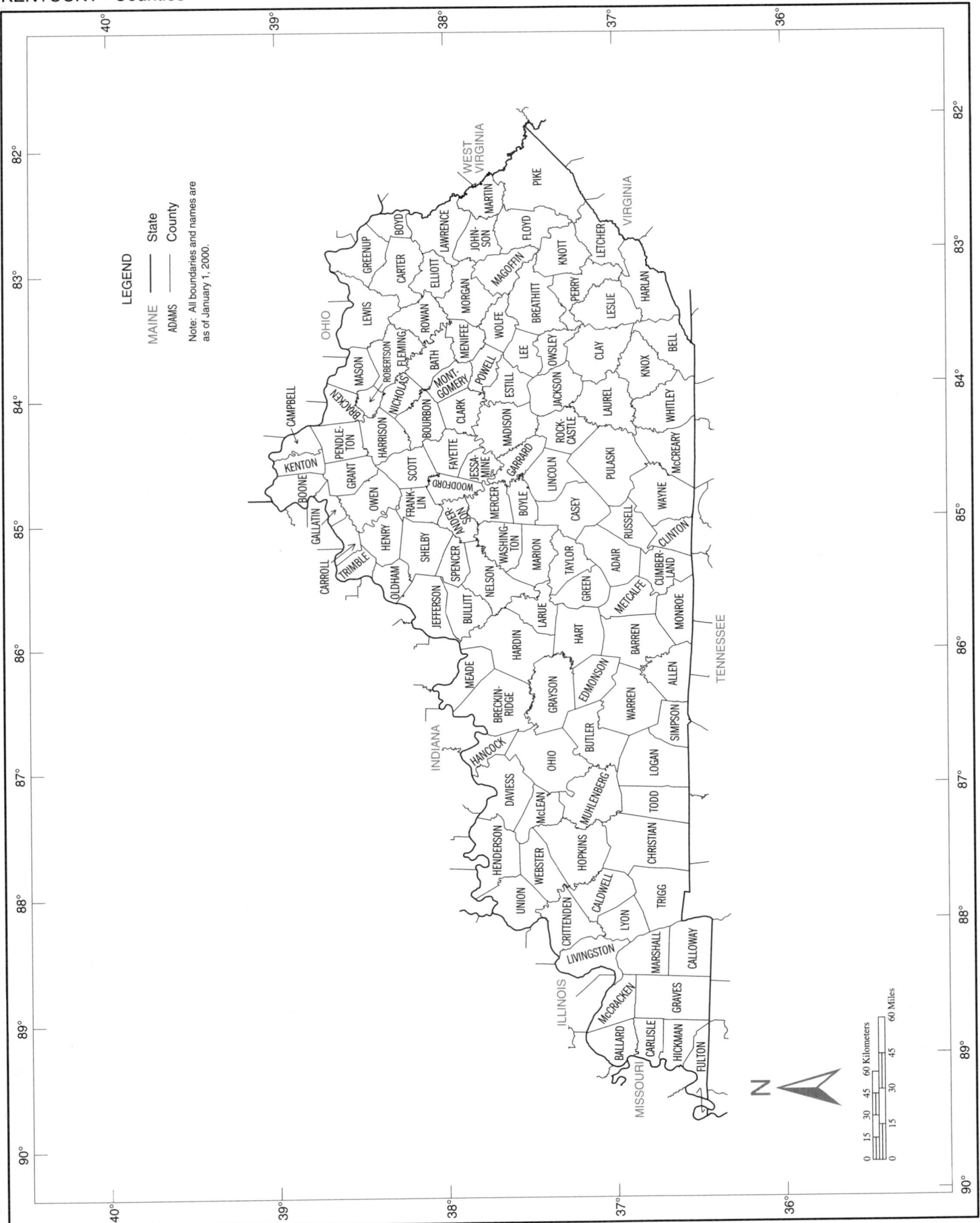

LEGEND

MAINE —— State

ADAMS —— County

Note: All boundaries and names are
as of January 1, 2000.

N

0 15 30 45 60 Kilometers
0   15   30   45   60 Miles

LOUISIANA - Parishes

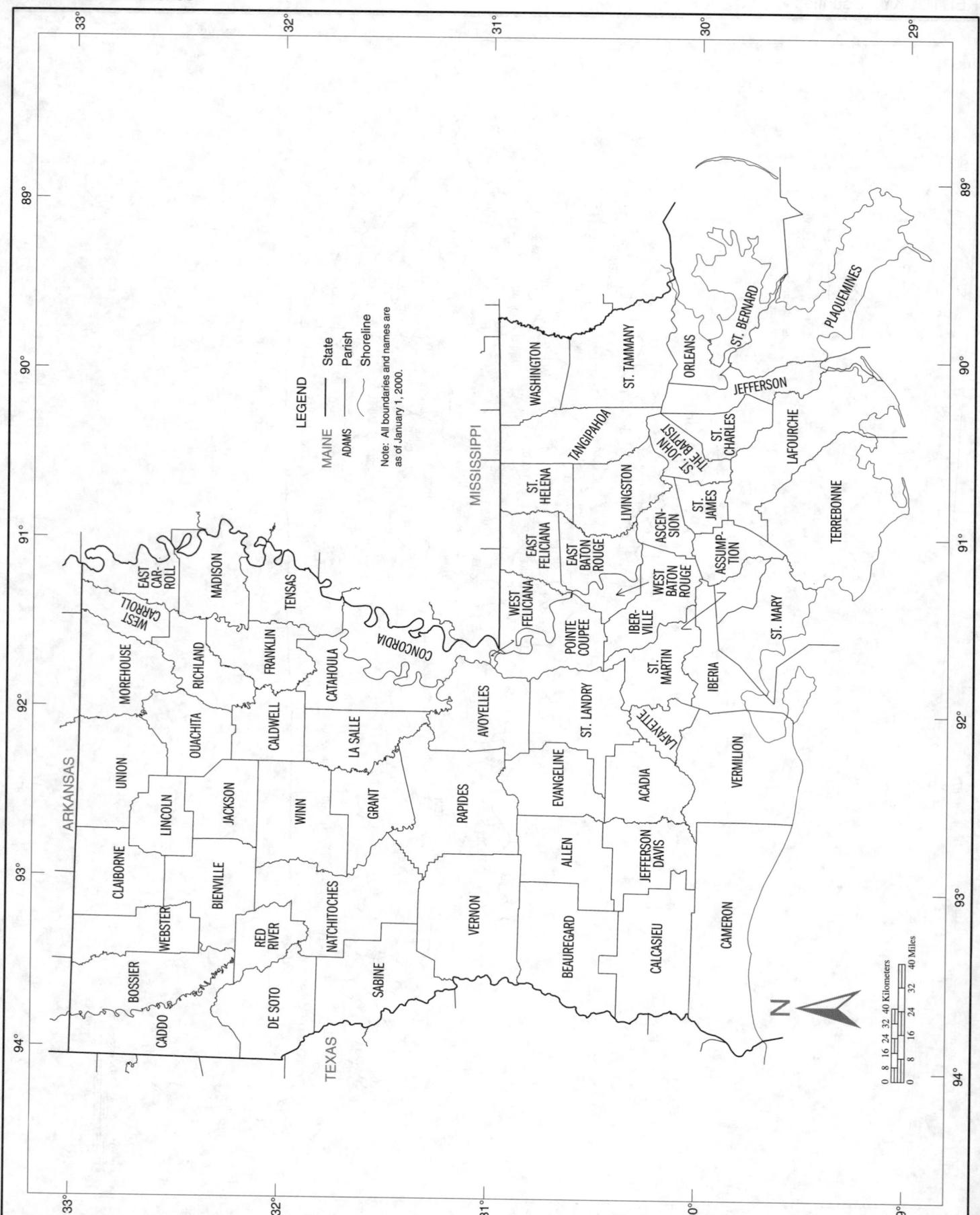

LEGEND

MAINE —— State

ADAMS —— Parish

—— Shoreline

Note: All boundaries and names are
as of January 1, 2000.

MAINE - Counties

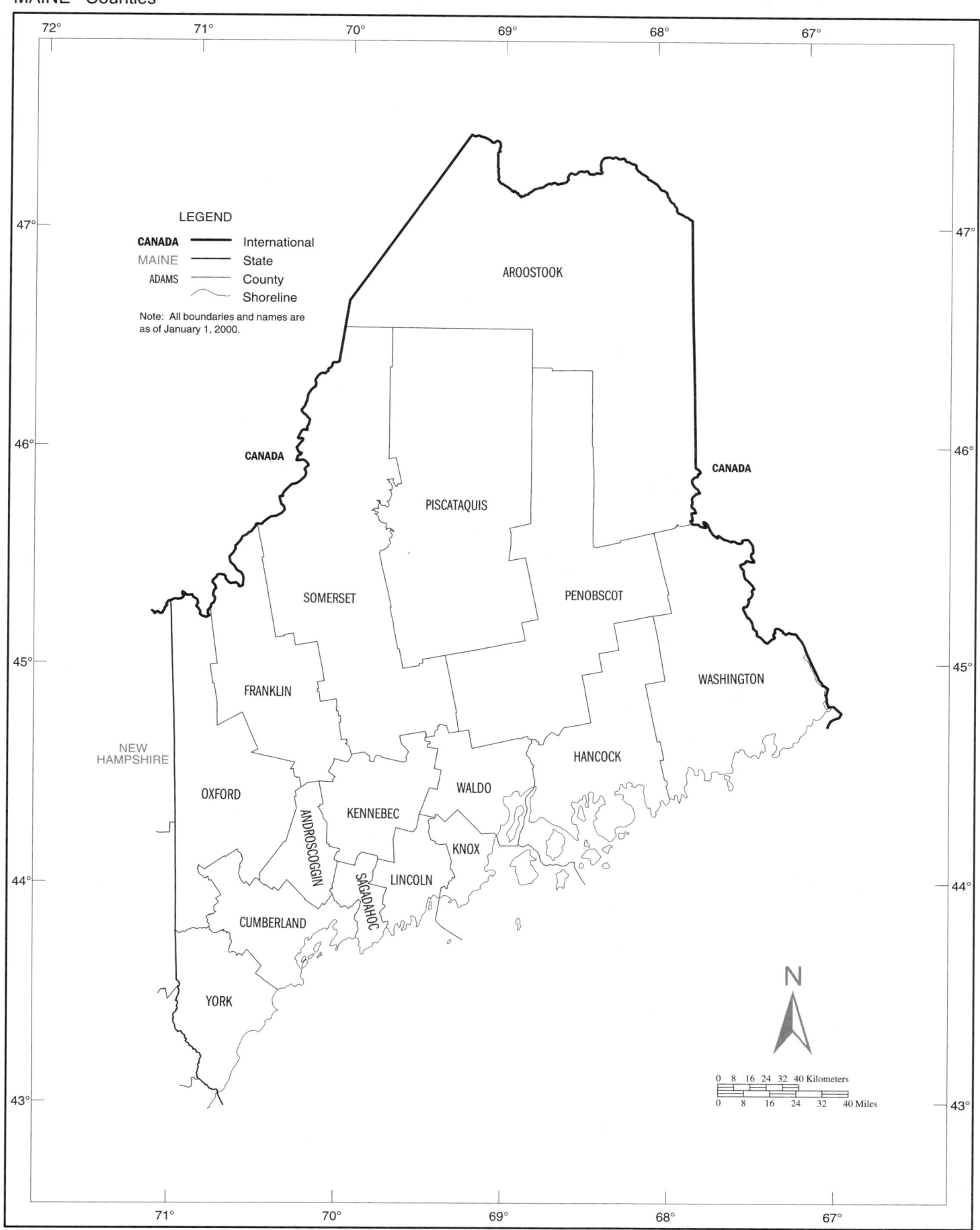

LEGEND

CANADA ━━━ International
MAINE ━━━ State
ADAMS ─── County
〰 Shoreline

Note: All boundaries and names are
as of January 1, 2000.

CANADA

CANADA

AROOSTOOK

PISCATAQUIS

SOMERSET

PENOBSCOT

FRANKLIN

WASHINGTON

NEW
HAMPSHIRE

OXFORD

HANCOCK

WALDO

KENNEBEC

ANDROSCOGGIN

KNOX

SAGADAHOC

LINCOLN

CUMBERLAND

YORK

N

0 8 16 24 32 40 Kilometers
0 8 16 24 32 40 Miles

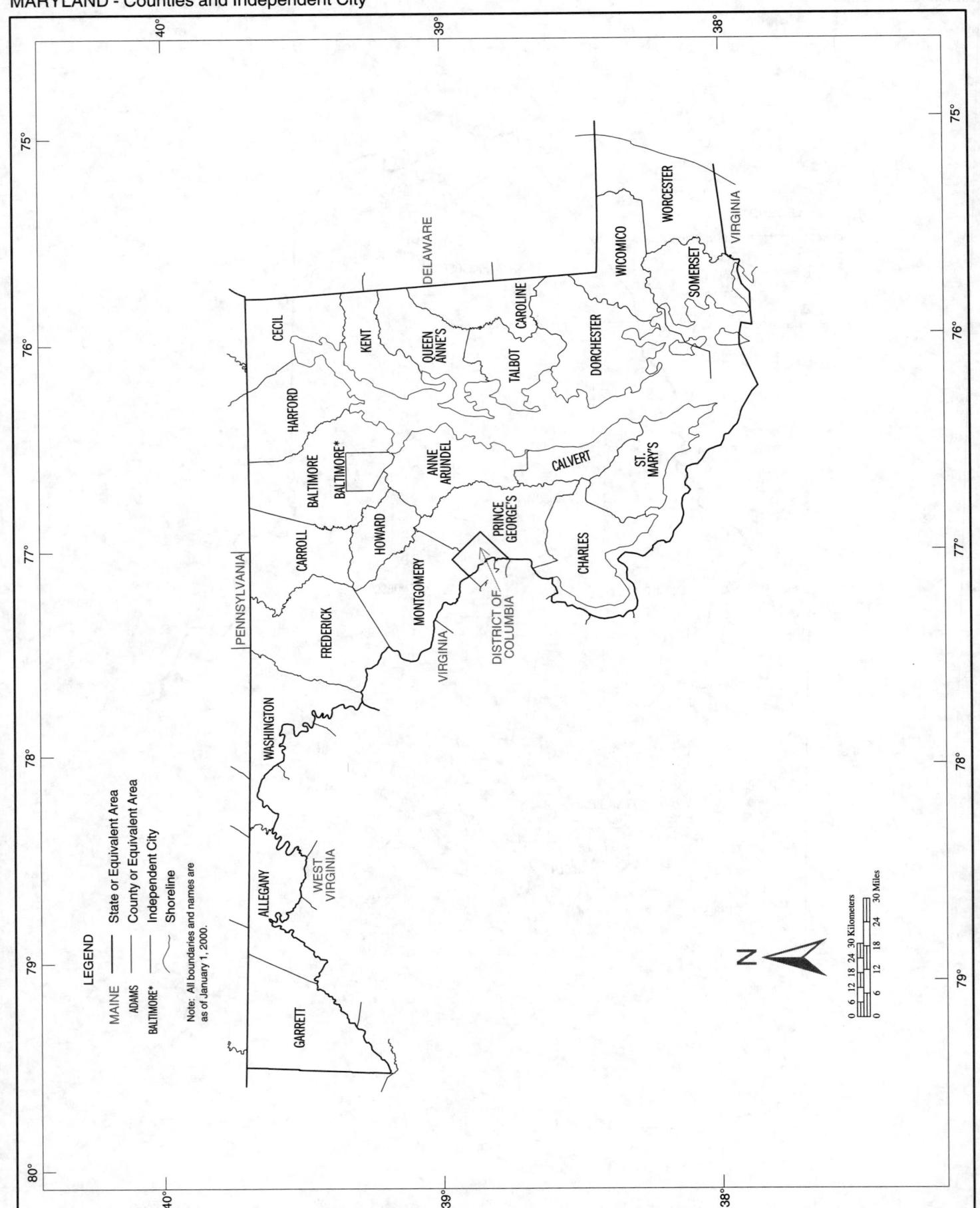

LEGEND

MAINE — State or Equivalent Area

ADAMS — County or Equivalent Area

BALTIMORE* — Independent City

— Shoreline

Note: All boundaries and names are as of January 1, 2000.

MASSACHUSETTS - Counties

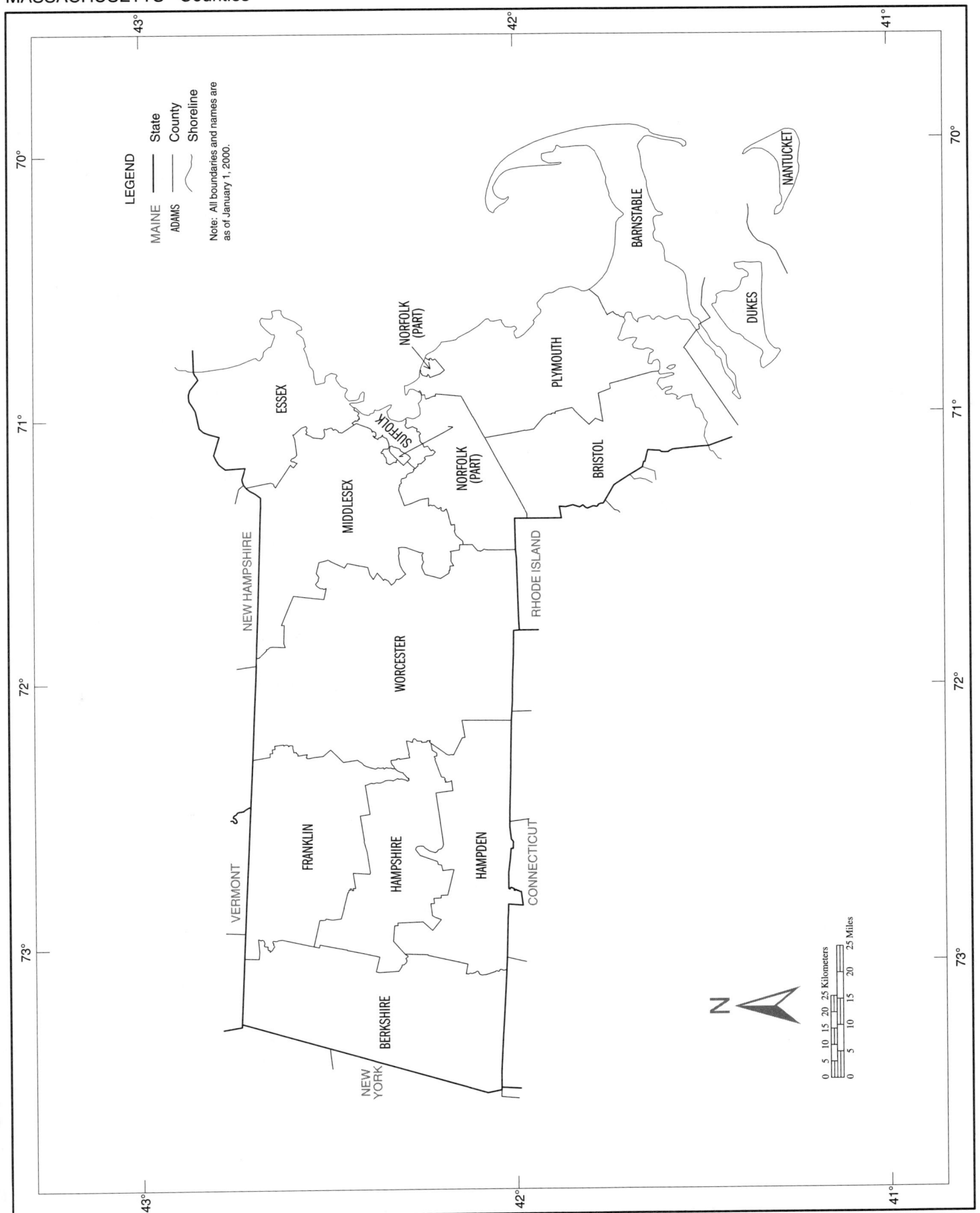

LEGEND

MAINE — State

ADAMS — County

Shoreline

Note: All boundaries and names are as of January 1, 2000.

NANTUCKET

BARNSTABLE

DUKES

NORFOLK (PART)

ESSEX

SUFFOLK

MIDDLESEX

NORFOLK (PART)

PLYMOUTH

BRISTOL

NEW HAMPSHIRE

RHODE ISLAND

WORCESTER

VERMONT

FRANKLIN

HAMPSHIRE

HAMPDEN

CONNECTICUT

BERKSHIRE

NEW YORK

N

0 5 10 15 20 25 Kilometers
0 5 10 15 20 25 Miles

MICHIGAN - Counties

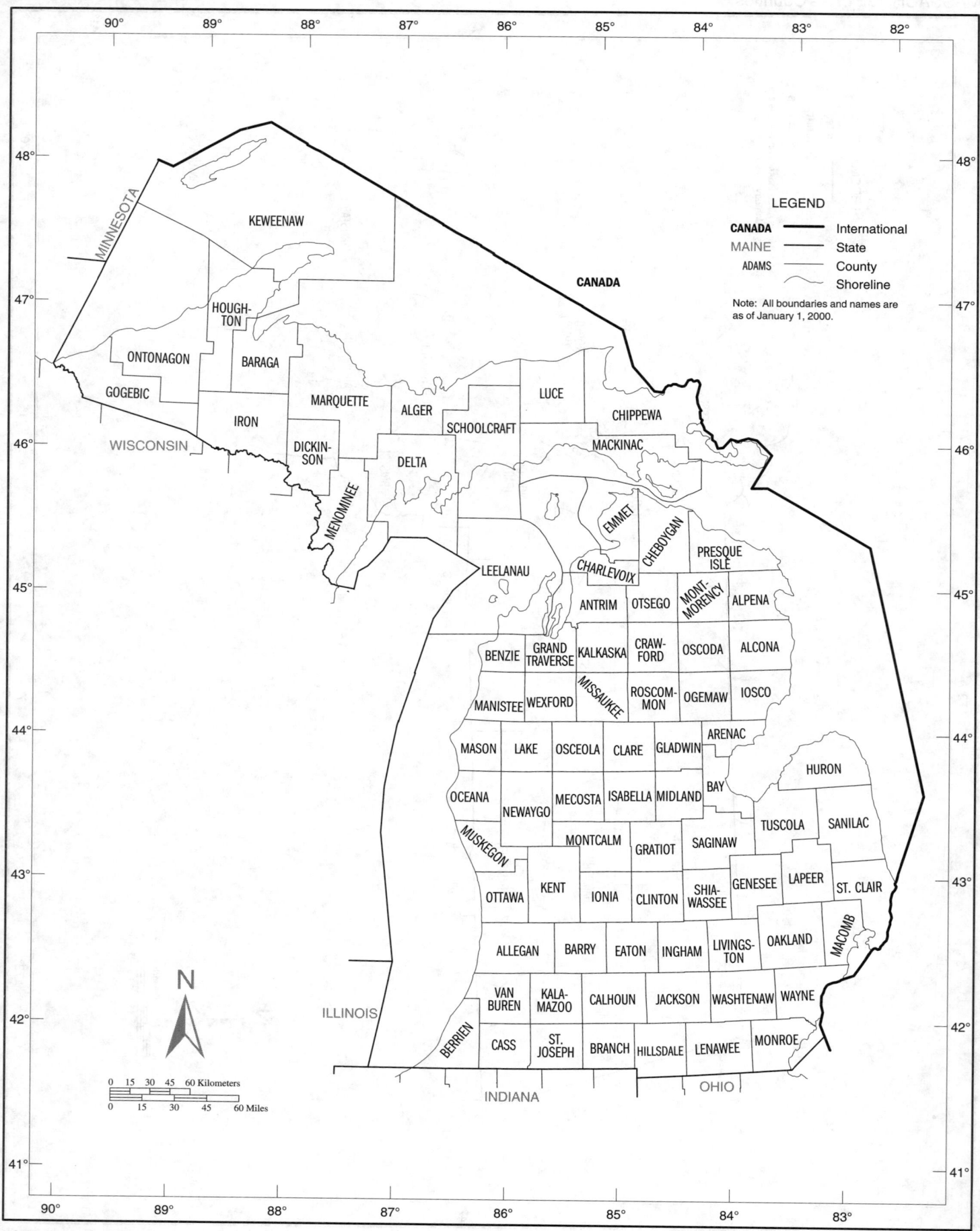

LEGEND

CANADA	International
MAINE	State
ADAMS	County
	Shoreline

Note: All boundaries and names are as of January 1, 2000.

CANADA

MINNESOTA

KEWEENAW

HOUGH-TON

ONTONAGON

BARAGA

GOGEBIC

IRON

MARQUETTE

ALGER

LUCE

CHIPPEWA

WISCONSIN

DICKIN-SON

SCHOOLCRAFT

MACKINAC

MENOMINEE

DELTA

EMMET

CHEBOYGAN

PRESQUE ISLE

LEELANAU

CHARLEVOIX

ANTRIM

OTSEGO

MONT-MORENCY

ALPENA

BENZIE

GRAND TRAVERSE

KALKASKA

CRAW-FORD

OSCODA

ALCONA

MANISTEE

WEXFORD

MISSAUKEE

ROSCOM-MON

OGEMAW

IOSCO

MASON

LAKE

OSCEOLA

CLARE

GLADWIN

ARENAC

HURON

OCEANA

NEWAYGO

MECOSTA

ISABELLA

MIDLAND

BAY

TUSCOLA

SANILAC

MUSKEGON

MONTCALM

GRATIOT

SAGINAW

OTTAWA

KENT

IONIA

CLINTON

SHIA-WASSEE

GENESEE

LAPEER

ST. CLAIR

MACOMB

ALLEGAN

BARRY

EATON

INGHAM

LIVINGS-TON

OAKLAND

ILLINOIS

VAN BUREN

KALA-MAZOO

CALHOUN

JACKSON

WASHTENAW

WAYNE

BERRIEN

CASS

ST. JOSEPH

BRANCH

HILLSDALE

LENAWEE

MONROE

INDIANA

OHIO

N

0 15 30 45 60 Kilometers
0 15 30 45 60 Miles

U.S. Census Bureau, Census 2000

D-26

Appendix D

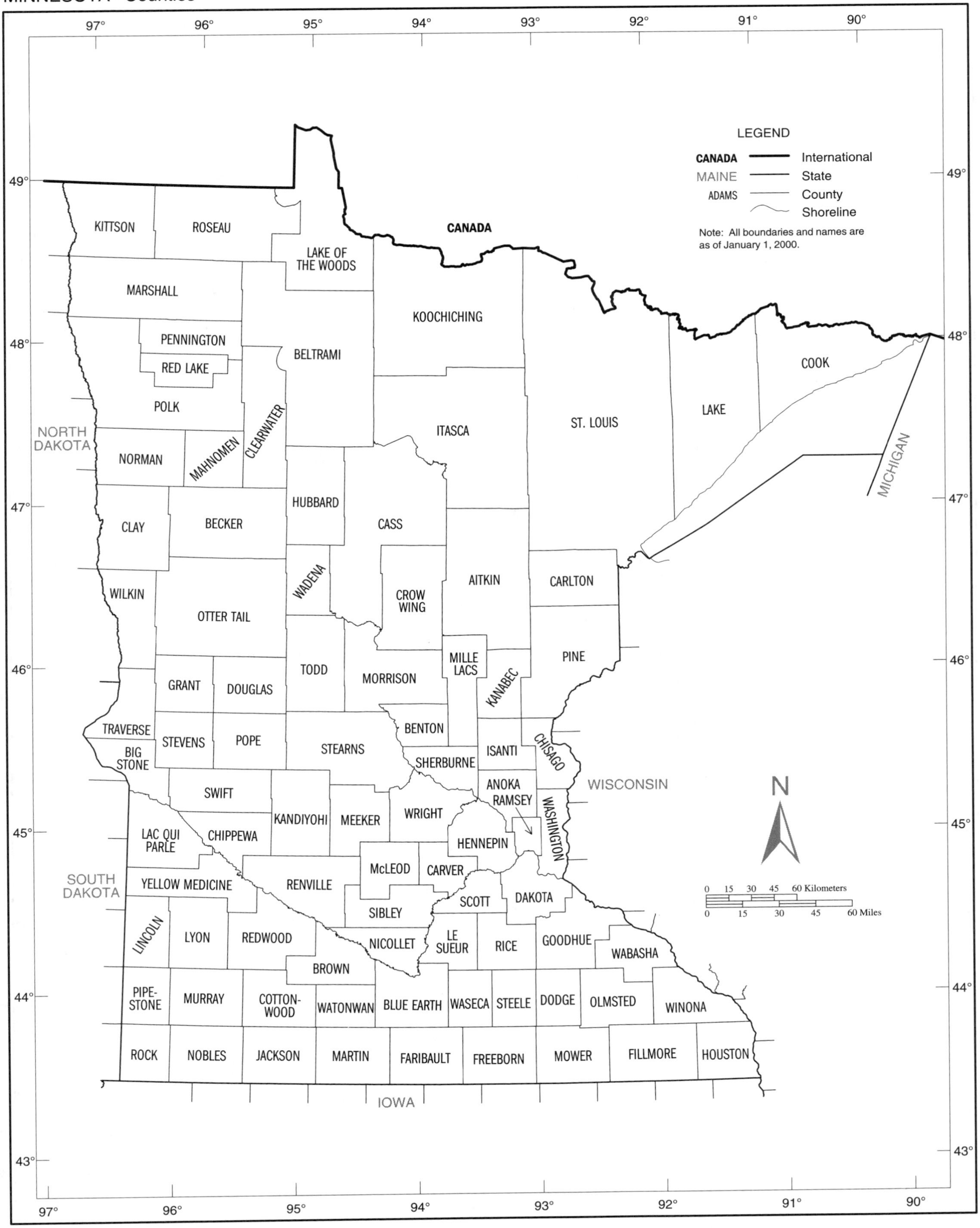

MINNESOTA - Counties

LEGEND

CANADA	International
MAINE	State
ADAMS	County
	Shoreline

Note: All boundaries and names are as of January 1, 2000.

KITTSON

ROSEAU

LAKE OF THE WOODS

CANADA

MARSHALL

KOOCHICHING

PENNINGTON

RED LAKE

BELTRAMI

POLK

NORTH DAKOTA

NORMAN

MAHNOMEN

CLEARWATER

ITASCA

ST. LOUIS

LAKE

COOK

CLAY

BECKER

HUBBARD

CASS

MICHIGAN

WILKIN

OTTER TAIL

WADENA

CROW WING

AITKIN

CARLTON

GRANT

DOUGLAS

TODD

MORRISON

MILLE LACS

KANABEC

PINE

TRAVERSE

BIG STONE

STEVENS

POPE

STEARNS

BENTON

SHERBURNE

ISANTI

CHISAGO

SWIFT

KANDIYOHI

MEEKER

WRIGHT

ANOKA

RAMSEY

WASHINGTON

WISCONSIN

LAC QUI PARLE

CHIPPEWA

HENNEPIN

SOUTH DAKOTA

YELLOW MEDICINE

RENVILLE

McLEOD

CARVER

SCOTT

DAKOTA

LINCOLN

LYON

REDWOOD

SIBLEY

NICOLLET

LE SUEUR

RICE

GOODHUE

WABASHA

BROWN

PIPE-STONE

MURRAY

COTTON-WOOD

WATONWAN

BLUE EARTH

WASECA

STEELE

DODGE

OLMSTED

WINONA

ROCK

NOBLES

JACKSON

MARTIN

FARIBAULT

FREEBORN

MOWER

FILLMORE

HOUSTON

IOWA

N

| 0 | 15 | 30 | 45 | 60 Kilometers |
| 0 | 15 | 30 | 45 | 60 Miles |

MISSISSIPPI - Counties

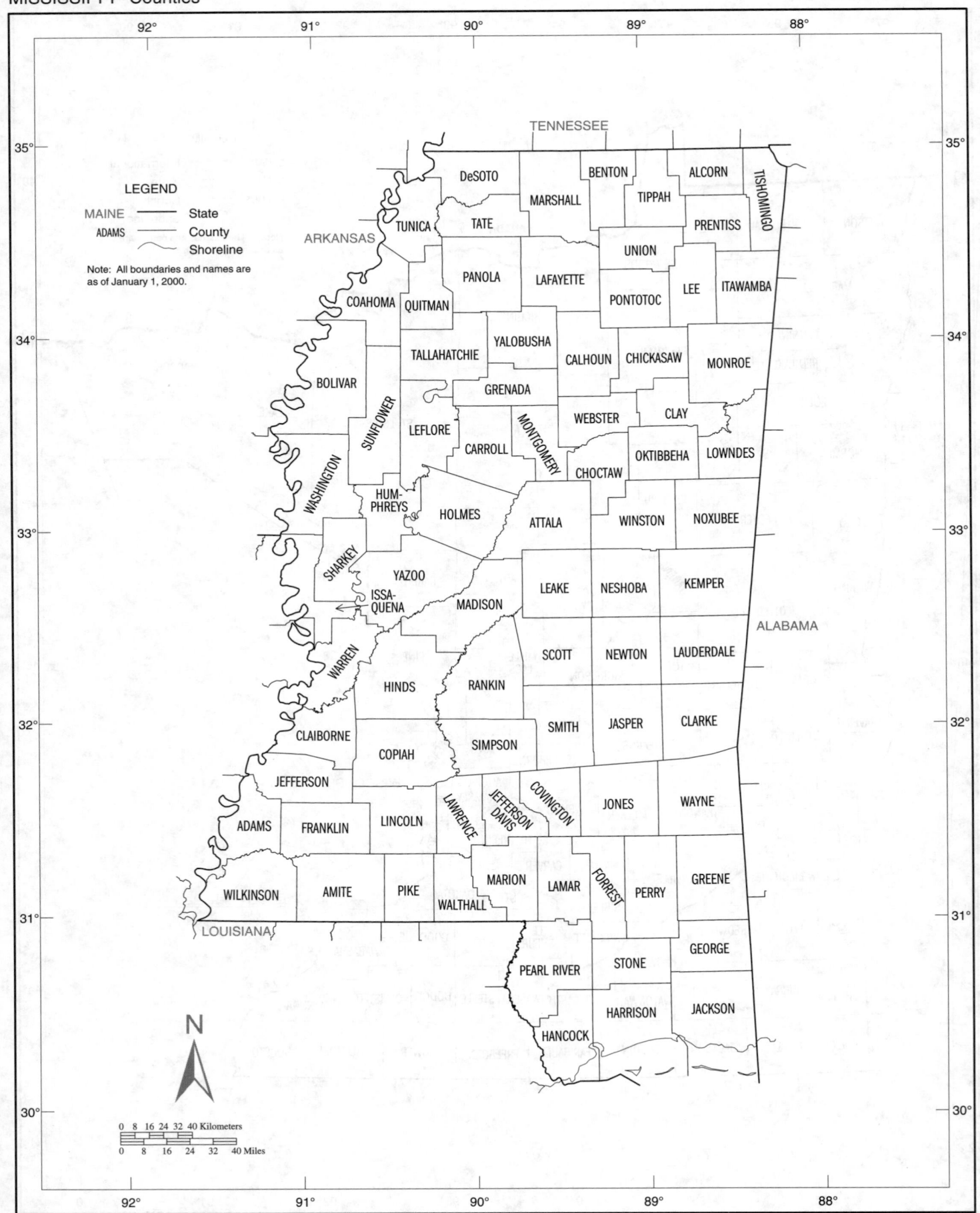

LEGEND

MAINE ———— State
ADAMS ———— County
～～～～ Shoreline

Note: All boundaries and names are
as of January 1, 2000.

TENNESSEE

ARKANSAS

ALABAMA

LOUISIANA

N

0 8 16 24 32 40 Kilometers
0 8   16   24   32   40 Miles

U.S. Census Bureau, Census 2000

D-28

Appendix D

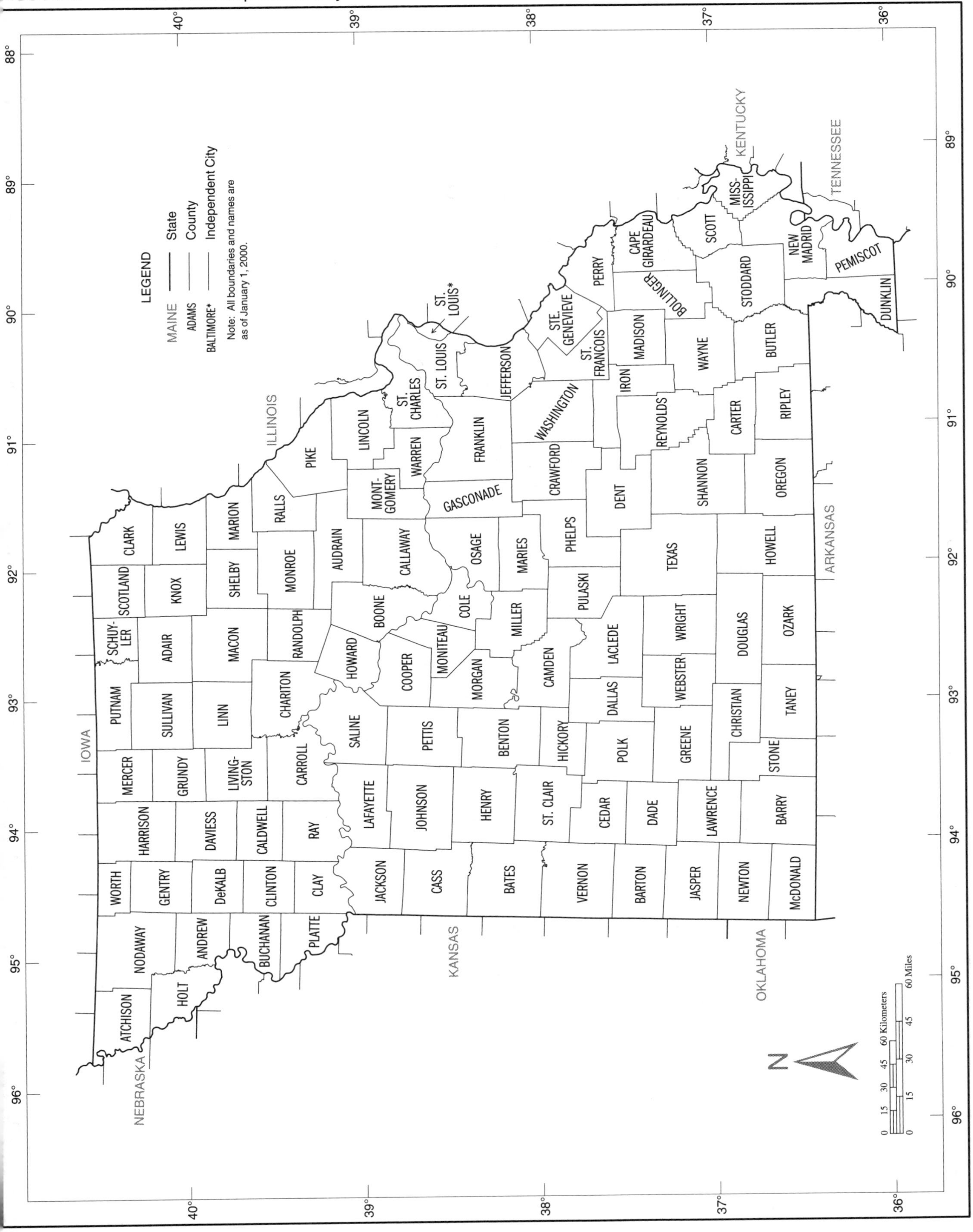

LEGEND

MAINE — State
ADAMS — County
BALTIMORE* — Independent City

Note: All boundaries and names are as of January 1, 2000.

88°
89°
90°
91°
92°
93°
94°
95°
96°

40°
39°
38°
37°
36°

KENTUCKY
TENNESSEE
ILLINOIS
IOWA
NEBRASKA
KANSAS
OKLAHOMA
ARKANSAS

MISS-ISSIPPI
NEW MADRID
PEMISCOT
DUNKLIN
SCOTT
STODDARD
BUTLER
RIPLEY
CAPE GIRARDEAU
BOLLINGER
WAYNE
CARTER
OREGON
PERRY
STE. GENEVIEVE
ST. FRANCOIS
MADISON
IRON
REYNOLDS
SHANNON
HOWELL
ST. LOUIS*
JEFFERSON
WASHINGTON
CRAWFORD
DENT
TEXAS
ST. CHARLES
FRANKLIN
GASCONADE
PHELPS
OZARK
LINCOLN
WARREN
MONT-GOMERY
OSAGE
MARIES
PULASKI
LACLEDE
WRIGHT
DOUGLAS
PIKE
RALLS
AUDRAIN
CALLAWAY
COLE
MILLER
CAMDEN
DALLAS
WEBSTER
CHRISTIAN
TANEY
MARION
MONROE
BOONE
MONITEAU
MORGAN
POLK
GREENE
STONE
CLARK
LEWIS
SHELBY
RANDOLPH
HOWARD
COOPER
BENTON
HICKORY
ST. CLAIR
CEDAR
DADE
LAWRENCE
BARRY
SCOTLAND
KNOX
MACON
CHARITON
SALINE
PETTIS
SCHUY-LER
ADAIR
SULLIVAN
LINN
LIVING-STON
CARROLL
LAFAYETTE
JOHNSON
HENRY
VERNON
BARTON
JASPER
NEWTON
McDONALD
PUTNAM
MERCER
GRUNDY
RAY
JACKSON
CASS
BATES
HARRISON
DAVIESS
CALDWELL
CLAY
WORTH
GENTRY
DeKALB
CLINTON
NODAWAY
ANDREW
BUCHANAN
PLATTE
ATCHISON
HOLT

N

0 15 30 45 60 Miles
0 15 30 45 60 Kilometers

LEGEND

CANADA International
MAINE State
ADAMS County

Note: All boundaries and names are
as of January 1, 2000.

NEBRASKA - Counties

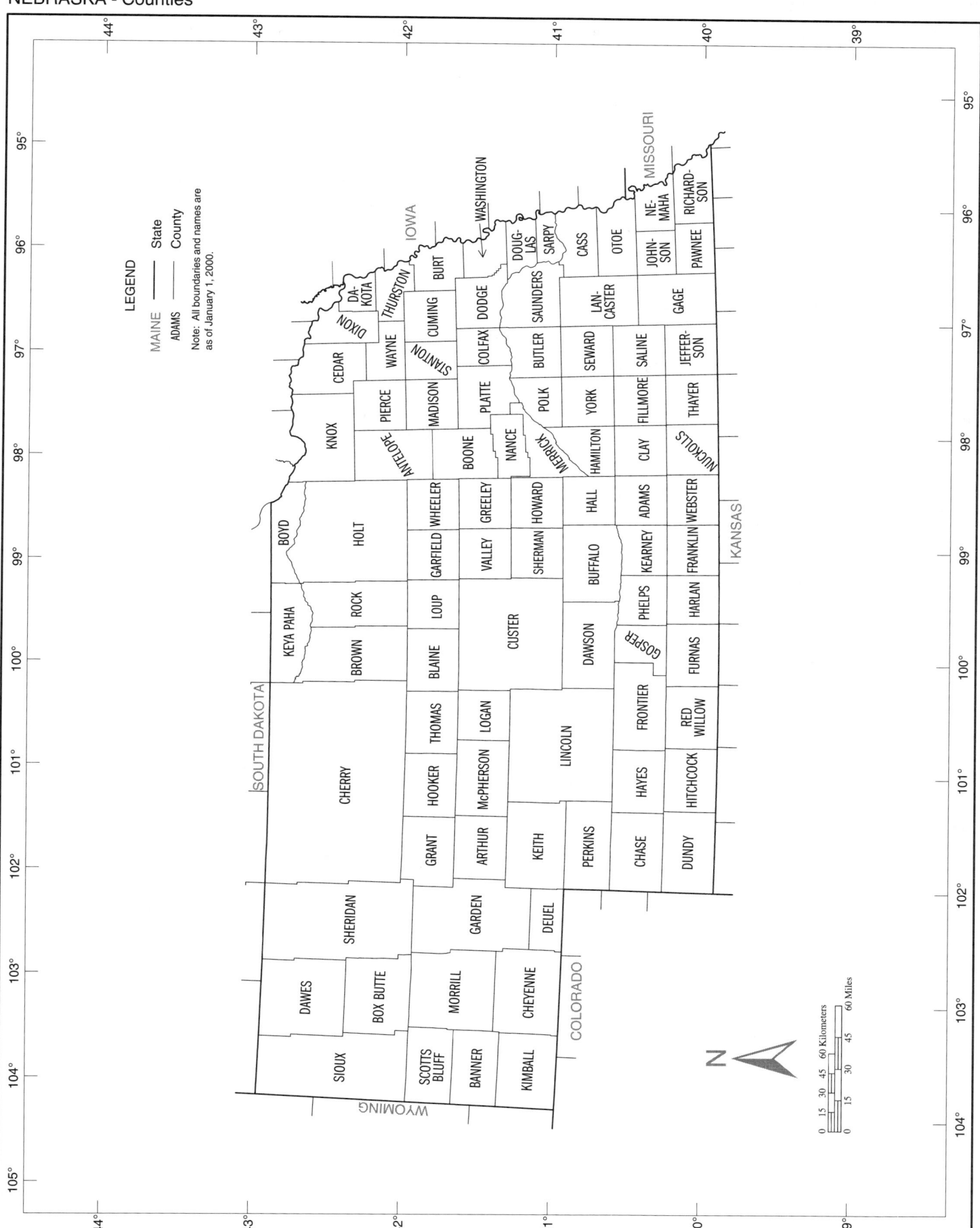

LEGEND

MAINE — State
ADAMS — County

Note: All boundaries and names are as of January 1, 2000.

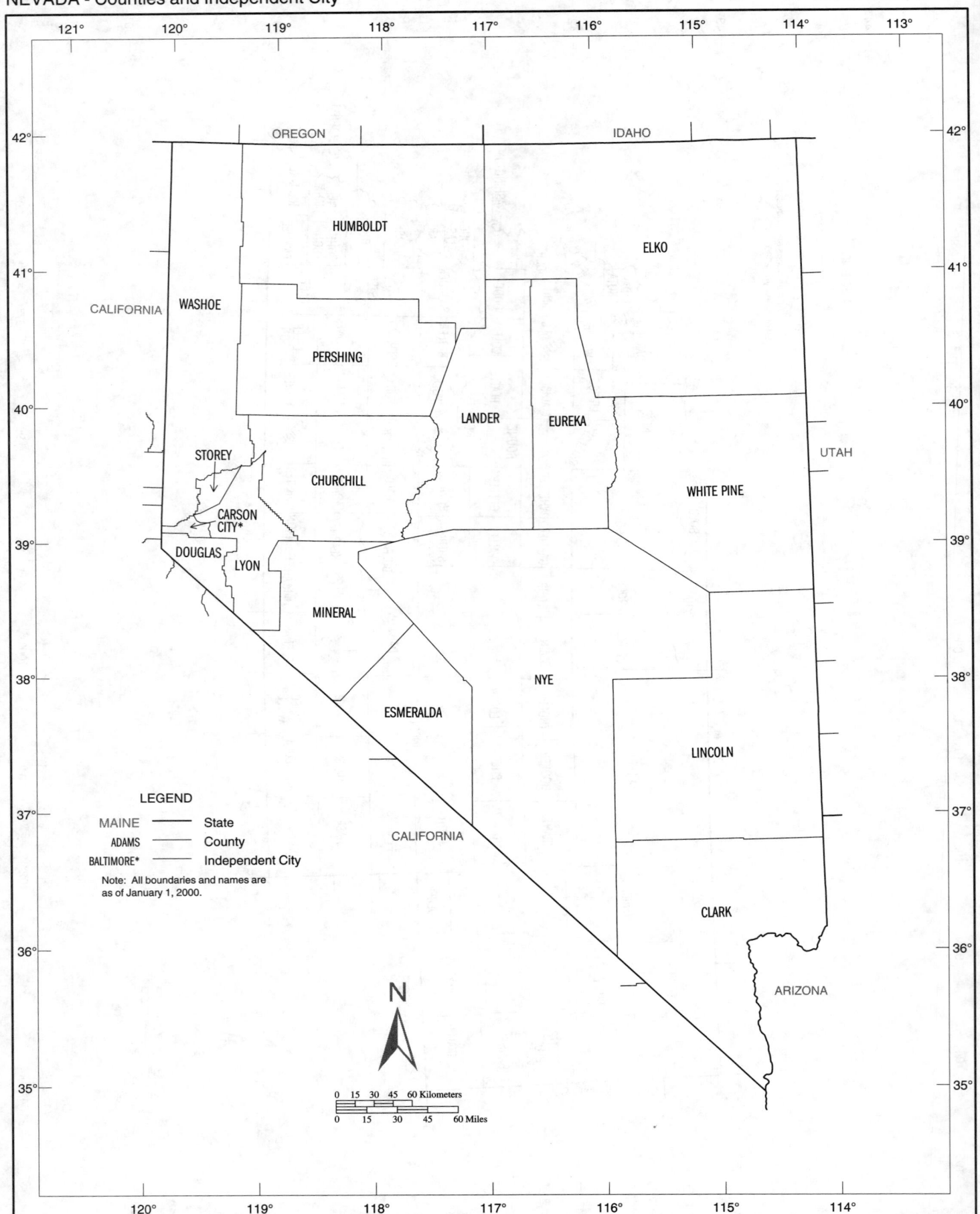

NEVADA - Counties and Independent City

OREGON

IDAHO

HUMBOLDT

ELKO

CALIFORNIA

WASHOE

PERSHING

LANDER

EUREKA

UTAH

STOREY

CHURCHILL

WHITE PINE

CARSON
CITY*

DOUGLAS

LYON

MINERAL

NYE

LINCOLN

ESMERALDA

CALIFORNIA

CLARK

ARIZONA

LEGEND

MAINE		State
ADAMS		County
BALTIMORE*		Independent City

Note: All boundaries and names are
as of January 1, 2000.

N

0 15 30 45   60 Kilometers

0   15   30   45   60 Miles

NEW HAMPSHIRE - Counties

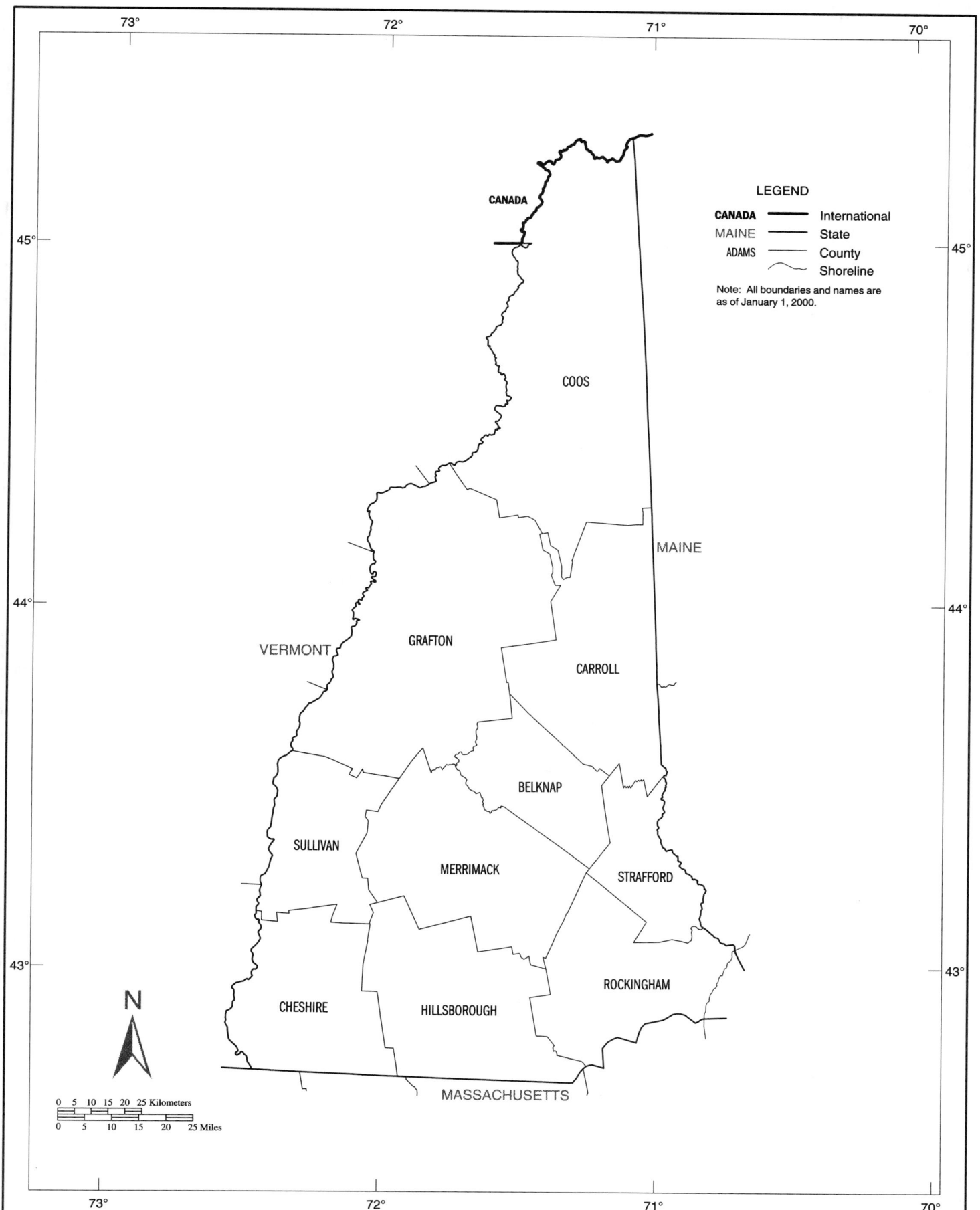

LEGEND

CANADA —— International
MAINE —— State
ADAMS —— County
〜〜 Shoreline

Note: All boundaries and names are
as of January 1, 2000.

CANADA

COOS

MAINE

VERMONT

GRAFTON

CARROLL

BELKNAP

SULLIVAN

MERRIMACK

STRAFFORD

ROCKINGHAM

CHESHIRE

HILLSBOROUGH

MASSACHUSETTS

N

0 5 10 15 20 25 Kilometers

0 5 10 15 20 25 Miles

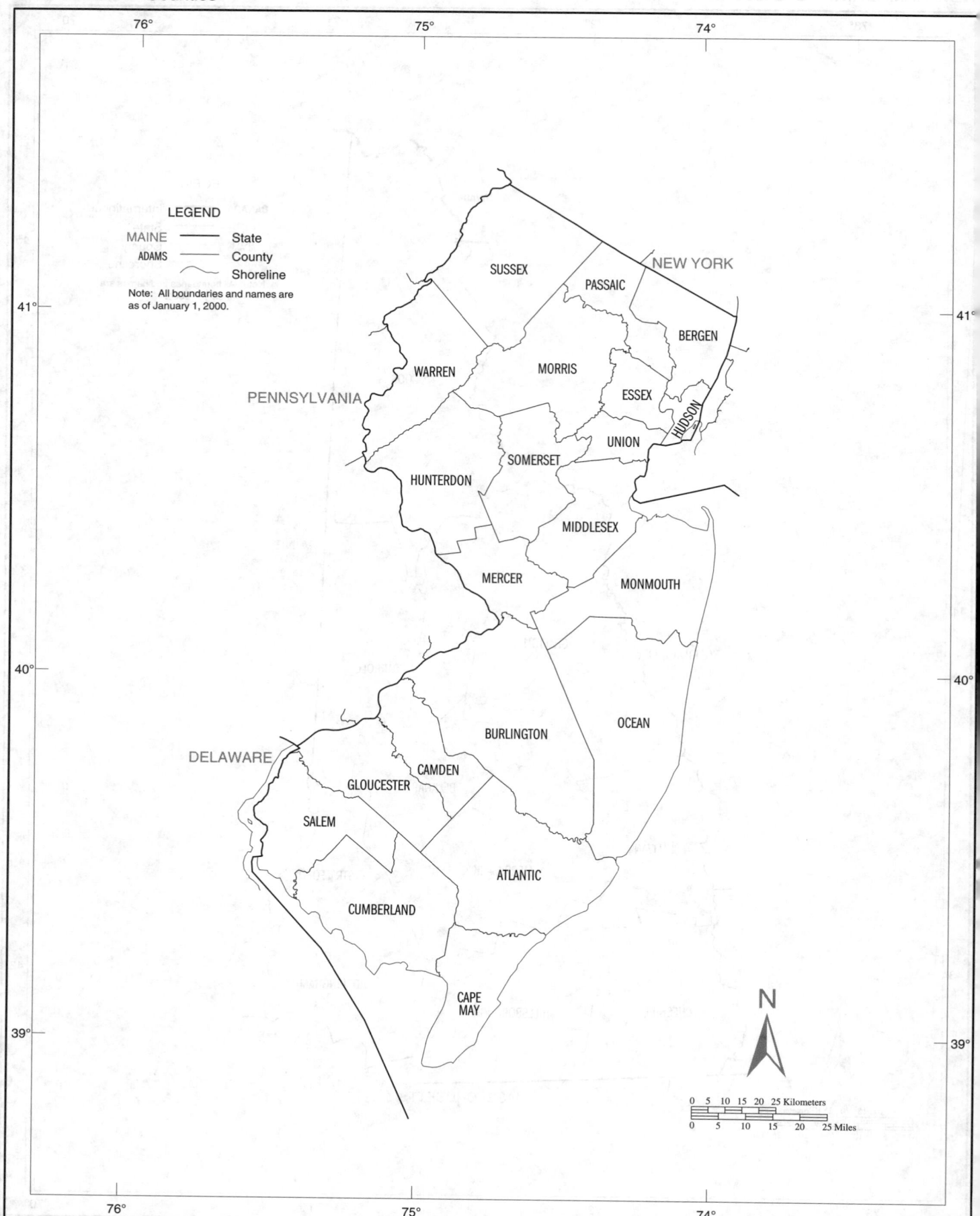

LEGEND

MAINE ——— State

ADAMS ——— County

~~~ Shoreline

Note: All boundaries and names are
as of January 1, 2000.

76°

75°

74°

41°

40°

39°

NEW YORK

PENNSYLVANIA

DELAWARE

SUSSEX

PASSAIC

BERGEN

WARREN

MORRIS

ESSEX

HUDSON

UNION

SOMERSET

HUNTERDON

MIDDLESEX

MERCER

MONMOUTH

OCEAN

BURLINGTON

CAMDEN

GLOUCESTER

SALEM

ATLANTIC

CUMBERLAND

CAPE
MAY

N

0 5 10 15 20 25 Kilometers

0 5   10   15   20   25 Miles

NEW MEXICO - Counties

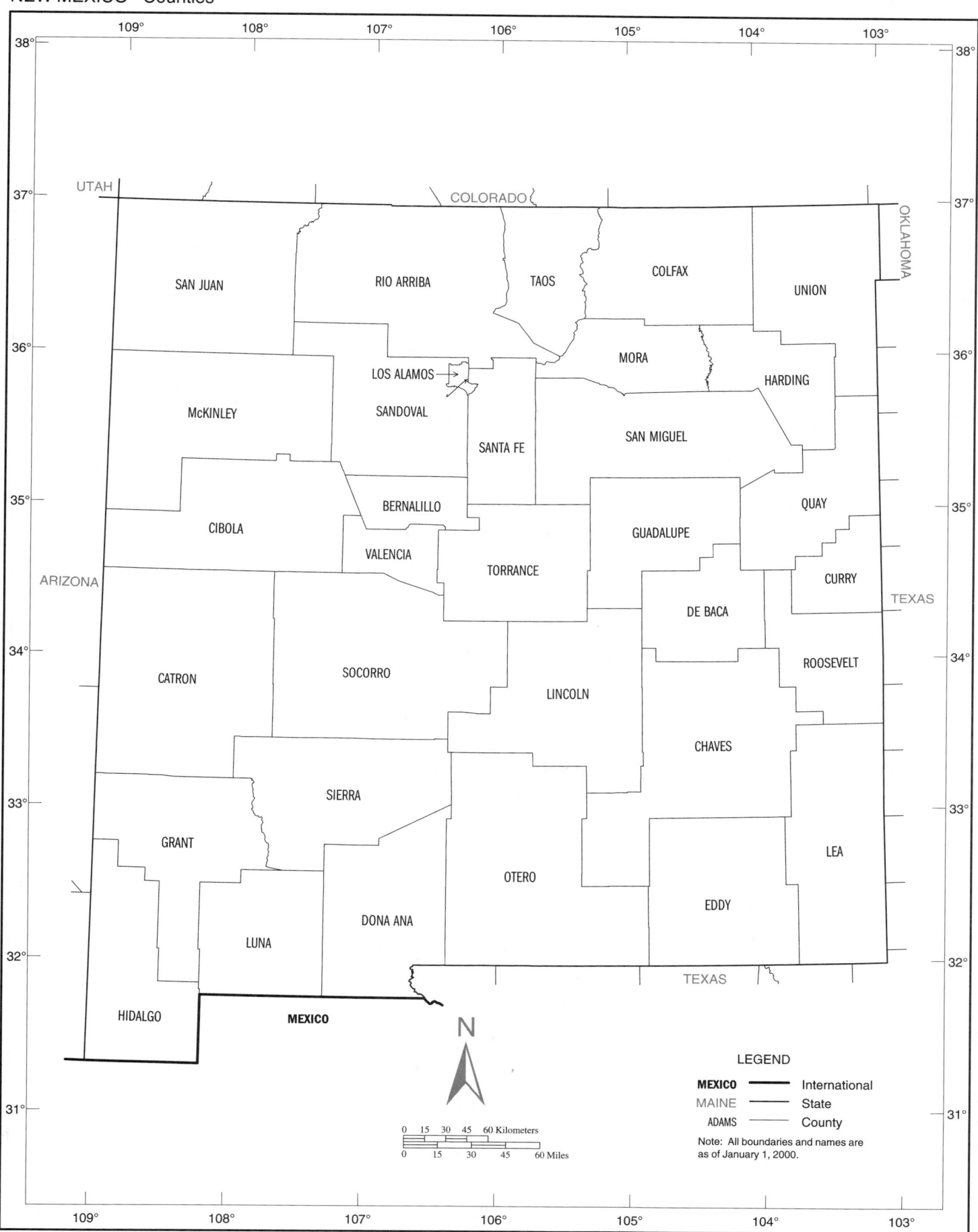

Appendix D

D-35

LEGEND

CANADA International
MAINE State
ADAMS County
Shoreline

Note: All boundaries and names are
as of January 1, 2000.

CLINTON
ESSEX
FRANKLIN
ST. LAWRENCE
CANADA
WASHINGTON
WARREN
SARATOGA
SCHENEC-TADY
HAMILTON
JEFFERSON
LEWIS
FULTON
MONTGOMERY
HERKIMER
ONEIDA
OSWEGO
MADISON
ONONDAGA
CAYUGA
CORTLAND
SENECA
WAYNE
YATES
ONTARIO
SCHUYLER
TOMPKINS
CHEMUNG
TIOGA
MONROE
LIVINGSTON
STEUBEN
ORLEANS
GENESEE
WYOMING
ALLEGANY
NIAGARA
ERIE
CATTARAUGUS
CHAUTAUQUA

RENSSELAER
COLUMBIA
ALBANY
SCHOHARIE
GREENE
OTSEGO
DELAWARE
CHENANGO
BROOME
DUTCHESS
PUTNAM
WEST-CHESTER
ULSTER
ORANGE
ROCKLAND
SULLIVAN
NASSAU
SUFFOLK
QUEENS
KINGS
RICHMOND
BRONX
NEW YORK

VERMONT
MASSACHUSETTS
CONNECTICUT
NEW JERSEY
PENNSYLVANIA

60 Kilometers
60 Miles
0 15 30 45
N

NORTH CAROLINA - Counties

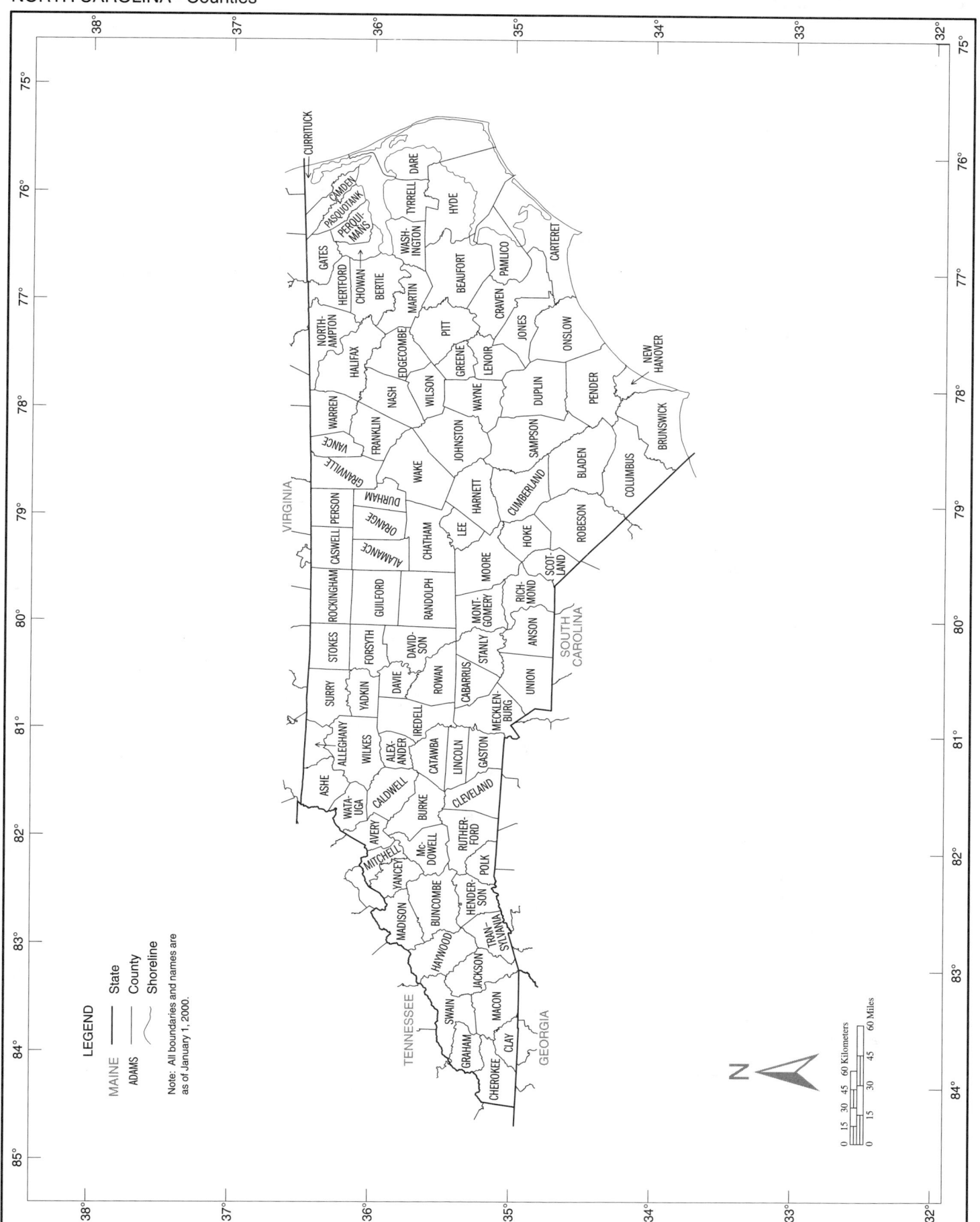

LEGEND

MAINE — State

ADAMS ～ County

Shoreline

Note: All boundaries and names are as of January 1, 2000.

CURRITUCK

CAMDEN
PASQUOTANK
PERQUI-MANS
GATES
HERTFORD
CHOWAN
BERTIE
WASH-INGTON
MARTIN
DARE
TYRRELL
HYDE
BEAUFORT
PAMLICO
CARTERET
CRAVEN
NORTH-AMPTON
HALIFAX
EDGECOMBE
PITT
GREENE
LENOIR
JONES
ONSLOW
NASH
WILSON
WAYNE
DUPLIN
PENDER
NEW HANOVER
WARREN
VANCE
FRANKLIN
JOHNSTON
SAMPSON
BRUNSWICK
GRANVILLE
WAKE
HARNETT
CUMBERLAND
BLADEN
COLUMBUS
DURHAM
PERSON
ORANGE
ALAMANCE
CHATHAM
LEE
HOKE
ROBESON
CASWELL
SCOT-LAND
ROCKINGHAM
GUILFORD
RANDOLPH
MOORE
RICH-MOND
ANSON
MONT-GOMERY
STOKES
FORSYTH
DAVID-SON
STANLY
UNION
SURRY
YADKIN
DAVIE
ROWAN
CABARRUS
MECKLEN-BURG
ALLEGHANY
WILKES
ALEX-ANDER
IREDELL
LINCOLN
GASTON
CATAWBA
ASHE
WATA-UGA
CALDWELL
BURKE
CLEVELAND
AVERY
MITCHELL
Mc-DOWELL
RUTHER-FORD
YANCEY
POLK
MADISON
BUNCOMBE
HENDER-SON
TRAN-SYLVANIA
HAYWOOD
JACKSON
SWAIN
MACON
GRAHAM
CHEROKEE
CLAY

VIRGINIA
SOUTH CAROLINA
TENNESSEE
GEORGIA

N

60 Miles
0 15 30 45 60 Kilometers
0 15 30 45

U.S. Census Bureau, Census 2000

NORTH DAKOTA - Counties

CANADA

MINNESOTA

SOUTH DAKOTA

MONTANA

N

60 Miles
60 Kilometers

PEMBINA
WALSH
GRAND FORKS
TRAILL
CASS
RICHLAND
SARGENT
RANSOM
CAVALIER
NELSON
STEELE
GRIGGS
BARNES
LaMOURE
DICKEY
RAMSEY
EDDY
FOSTER
STUTSMAN
TOWNER
BENSON
WELLS
LOGAN
McINTOSH
ROLETTE
PIERCE
SHERIDAN
KIDDER
BOTTINEAU
McHENRY
BURLEIGH
EMMONS
WARD
McLEAN
OLIVER
MORTON
SIOUX
RENVILLE
MERCER
GRANT
BURKE
MOUNTRAIL
DUNN
STARK
HETTINGER
ADAMS
DIVIDE
WILLIAMS
McKENZIE
BILLINGS
SLOPE
BOWMAN
GOLDEN VALLEY

LEGEND

CANADA International
MAINE State
ADAMS County

Note: All boundaries and names are as of January 1, 2000.

OHIO - Counties

OKLAHOMA - Counties

MISSOURI
ARKANSAS
KANSAS
TEXAS
COLORADO

OTTAWA
DELAWARE
ADAIR
SEQUOYAH
LE FLORE
McCURTAIN
CRAIG
MAYES
CHEROKEE
HASKELL
LATIMER
PUSHMATAHA
CHOCTAW
NOWATA
ROGERS
WAGONER
MUSKOGEE
McINTOSH
PITTSBURG
ATOKA
BRYAN
TULSA
OKMUL-GEE
COAL
WASHING-TON
OSAGE
CREEK
OKFUSKEE
HUGHES
PONTOTOC
JOHNSTON
MARSH-ALL
PAWNEE
PAYNE
LINCOLN
SEMINOLE
MURRAY
CARTER
LOVE
KAY
NOBLE
LOGAN
OKLAHOMA
POTTA-WATOMIE
CLEVE-LAND
McCLAIN
GARVIN
TEXAS
GRANT
GARFIELD
KING-FISHER
CANADIAN
GRADY
STEPHENS
JEFFERSON
ALFALFA
BLAINE
CADDO
COMANCHE
COTTON
WOODS
MAJOR
DEWEY
CUSTER
WASHITA
KIOWA
TILLMAN
WOODWARD
GREER
JACKSON
HARPER
ELLIS
ROGER MILLS
BECKHAM
HARMON
BEAVER
TEXAS
CIMARRON

LEGEND
MAINE ———— State
ADAMS ———— County
Note: All boundaries and names are as of January 1, 2000.

N

0 15 30 45 60 Kilometers
0 15 30 45 60 Miles

OREGON - Counties

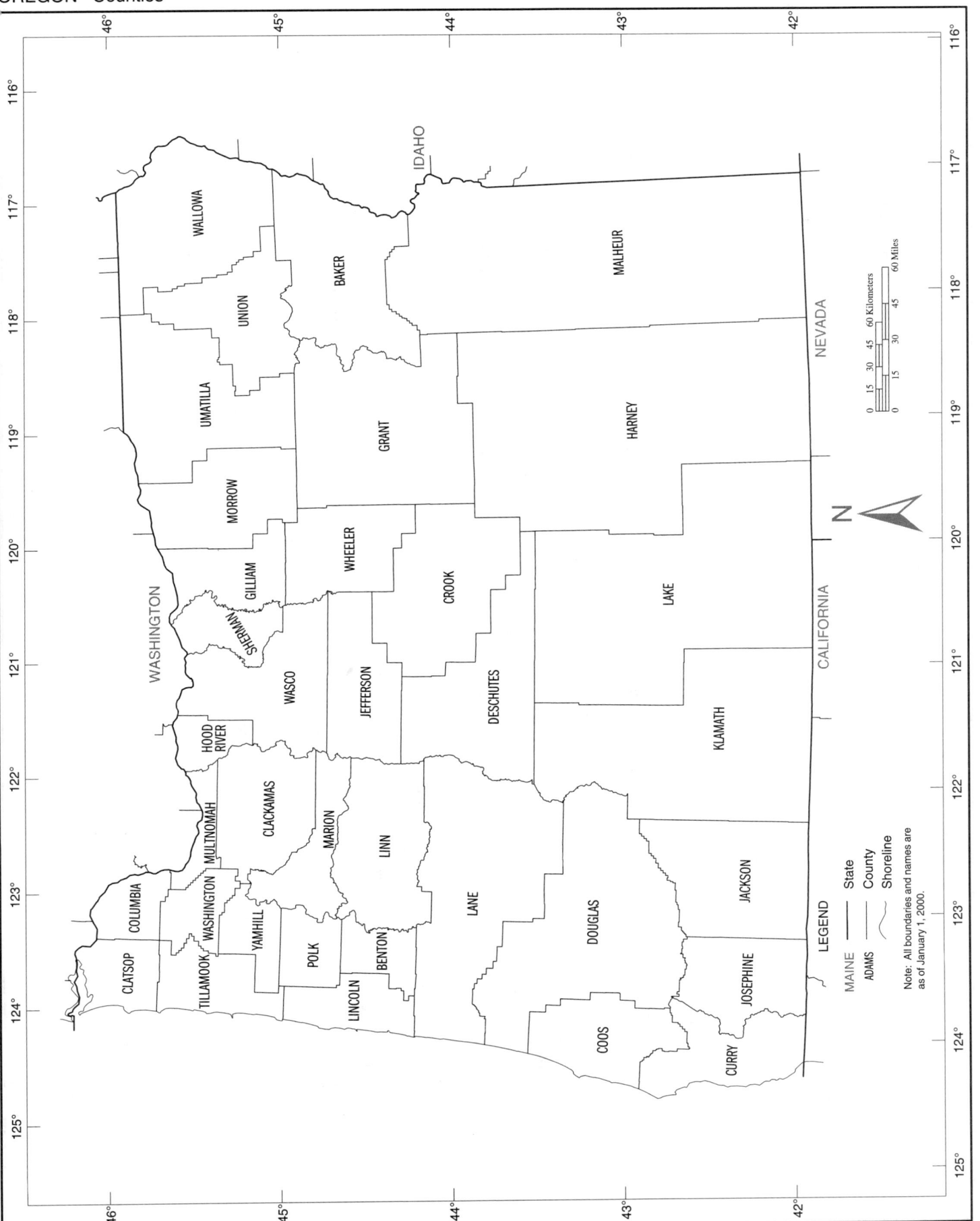

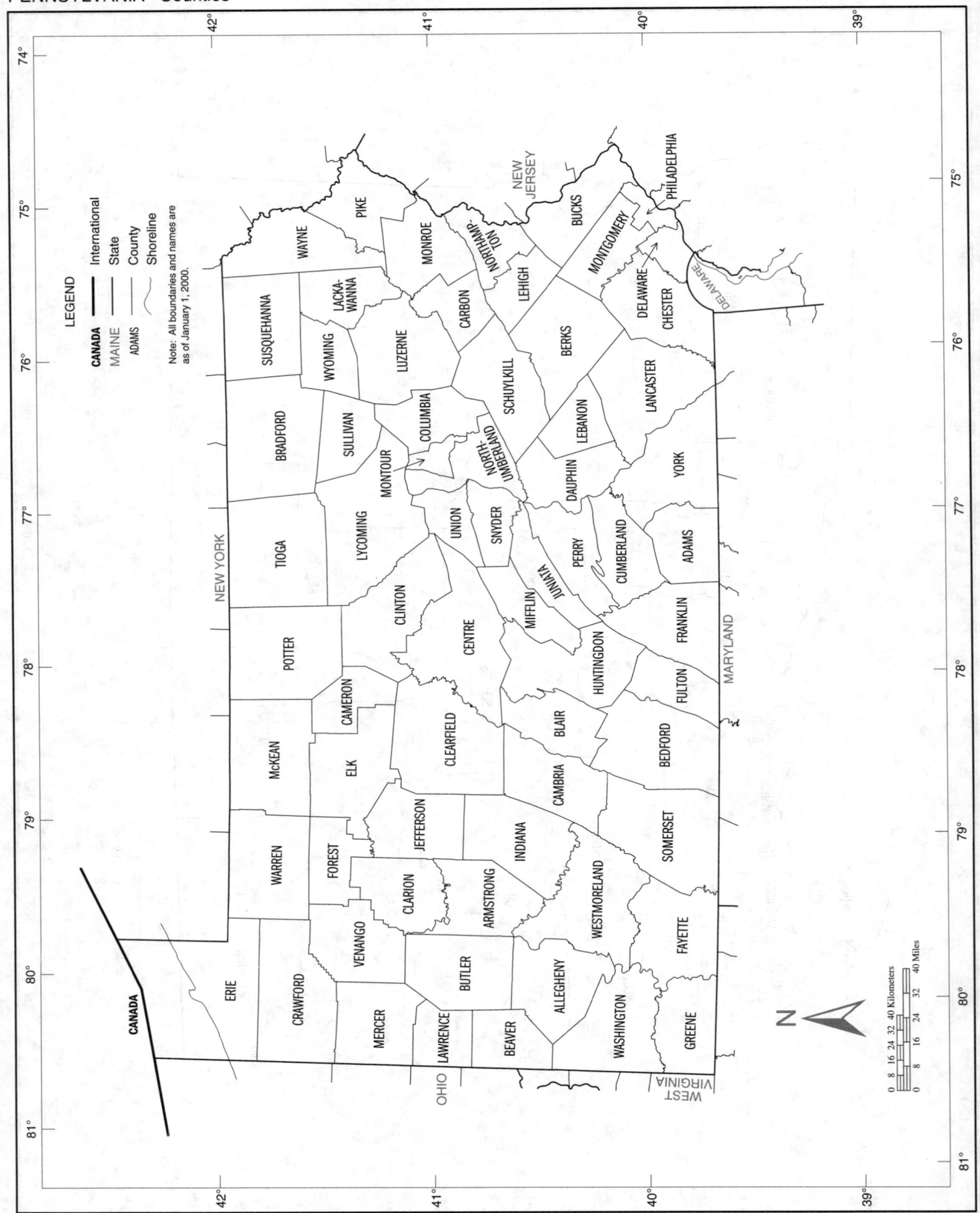

LEGEND

CANADA International
MAINE State
ADAMS County
⌇ Shoreline

Note: All boundaries and names are
as of January 1, 2000.

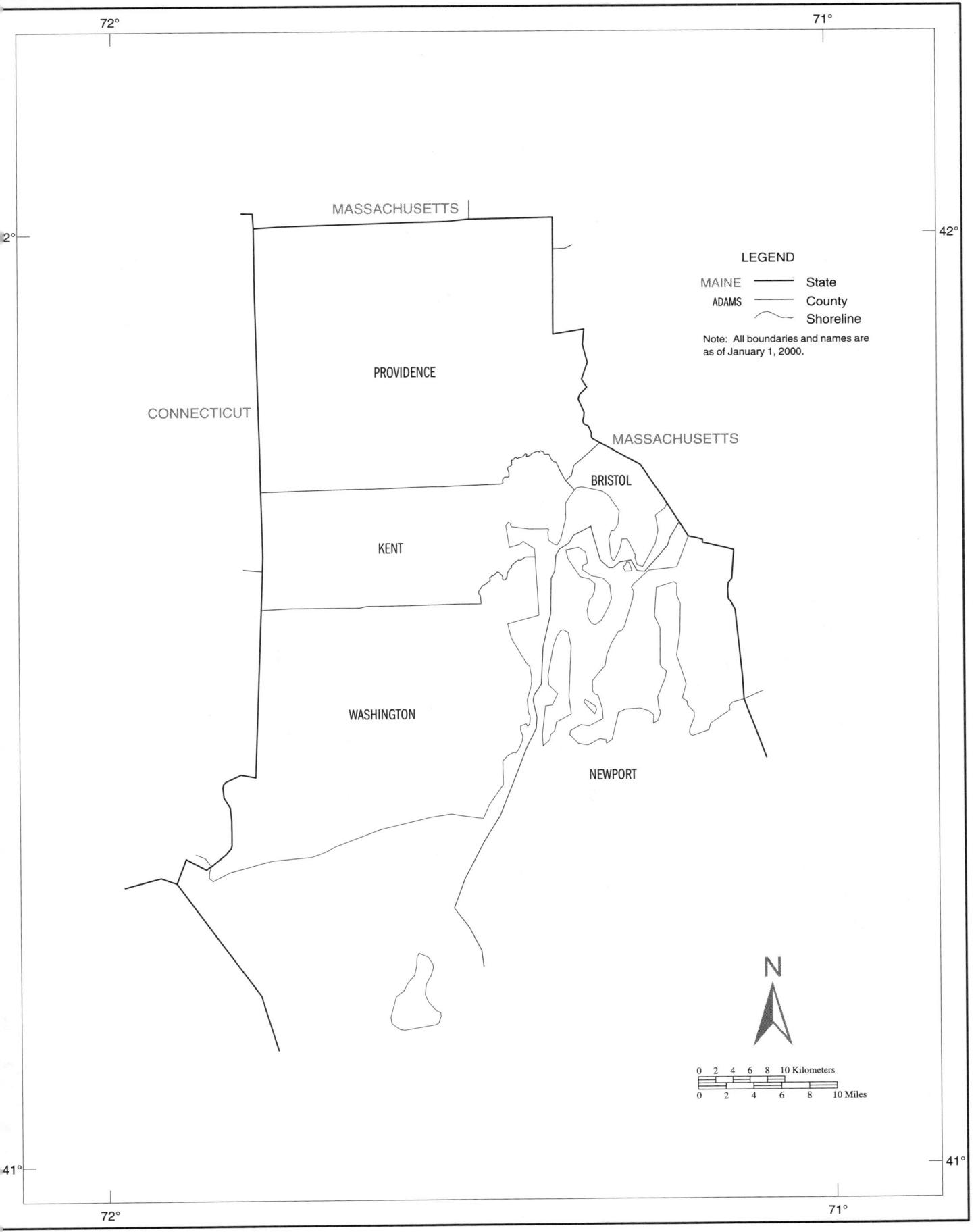

MASSACHUSETTS

MAINE

CONNECTICUT

PROVIDENCE

MASSACHUSETTS

BRISTOL

KENT

WASHINGTON

NEWPORT

LEGEND

MAINE ——— State

ADAMS ——— County

—⌒— Shoreline

Note: All boundaries and names are
as of January 1, 2000.

72°   71°   42°

41°

72°   71°

N

0 2 4 6 8 10 Kilometers
0 2 4 6 8 10 Miles

SOUTH CAROLINA - Counties

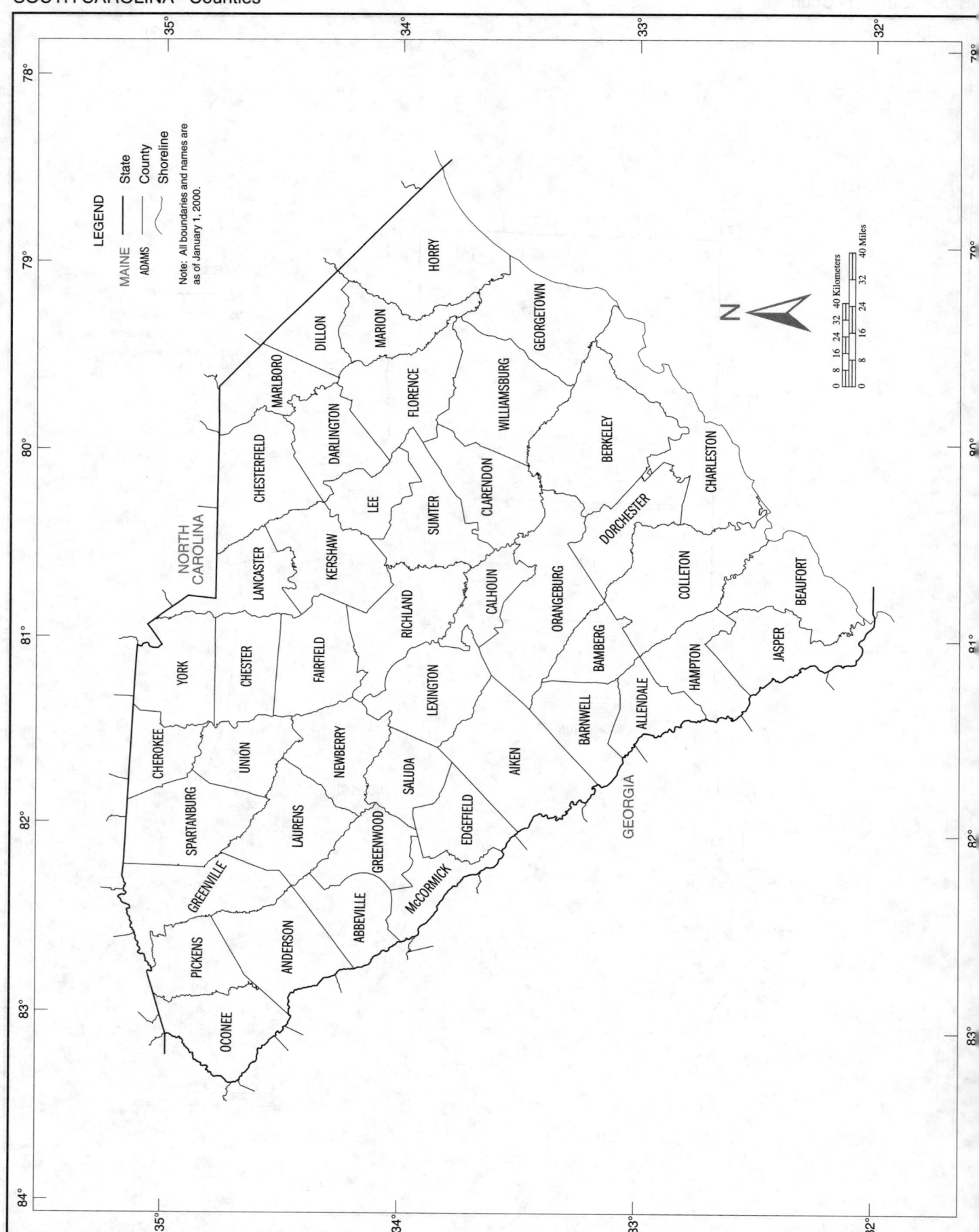

LEGEND

MAINE — State
ADAMS — County
Shoreline

Note: All boundaries and names are as of January 1, 2000.

0 8 16 24 32 40 Kilometers
0 8 16 24 32 40 Miles

NORTH CAROLINA

HORRY
DILLON
MARION
GEORGETOWN
MARLBORO
FLORENCE
WILLIAMSBURG
CHESTERFIELD
DARLINGTON
BERKELEY
LEE
SUMTER
CLARENDON
CHARLESTON
LANCASTER
KERSHAW
DORCHESTER
RICHLAND
CALHOUN
COLLETON
YORK
CHESTER
FAIRFIELD
ORANGEBURG
BEAUFORT
LEXINGTON
BAMBERG
HAMPTON
JASPER
CHEROKEE
UNION
NEWBERRY
AIKEN
BARNWELL
ALLENDALE
SPARTANBURG
LAURENS
SALUDA
EDGEFIELD
GEORGIA
GREENVILLE
GREENWOOD
McCORMICK
PICKENS
ANDERSON
ABBEVILLE
OCONEE

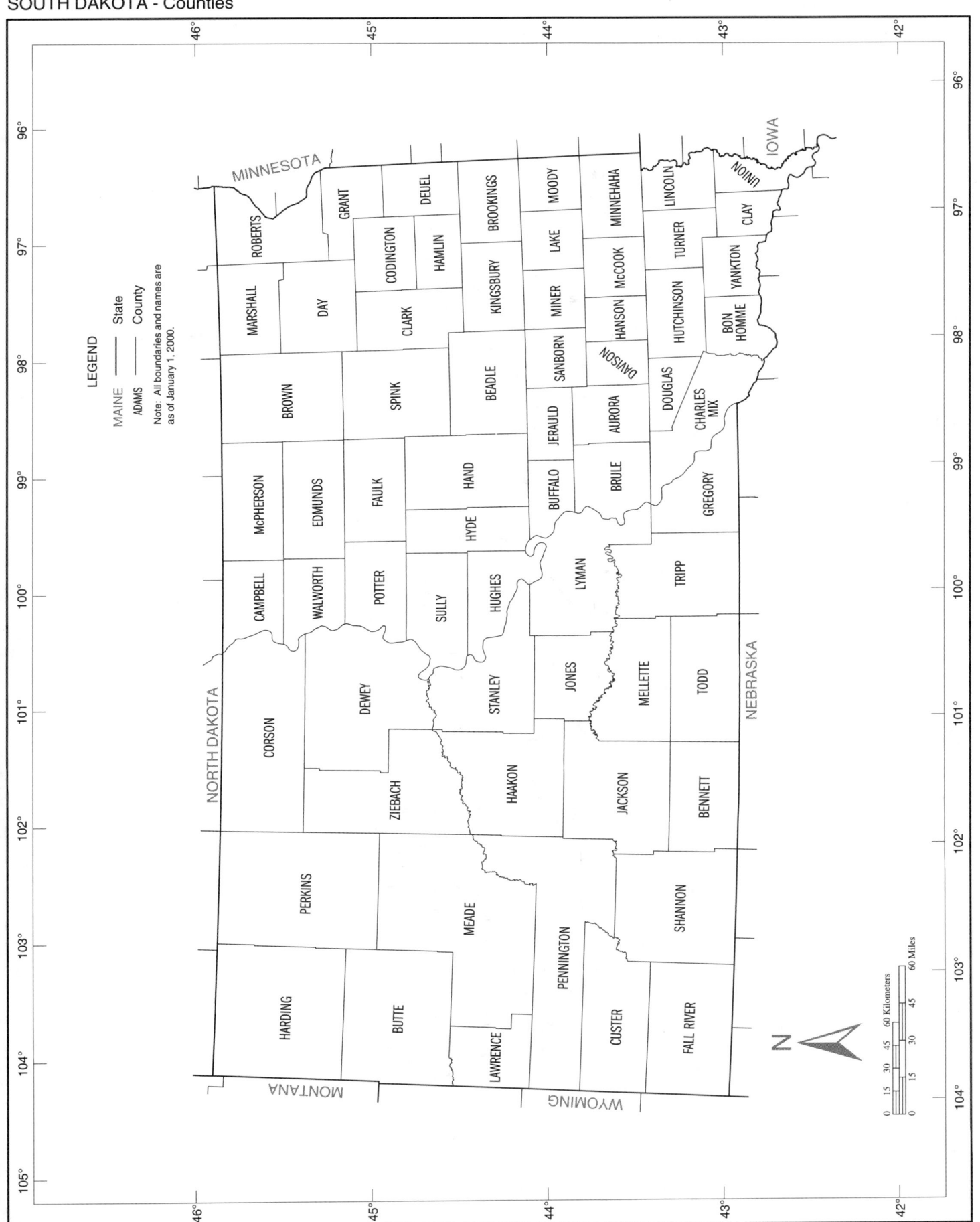

LEGEND

MAINE ———— State

ADAMS ———— County

Note: All boundaries and names are as of January 1, 2000.

TENNESSEE - Counties

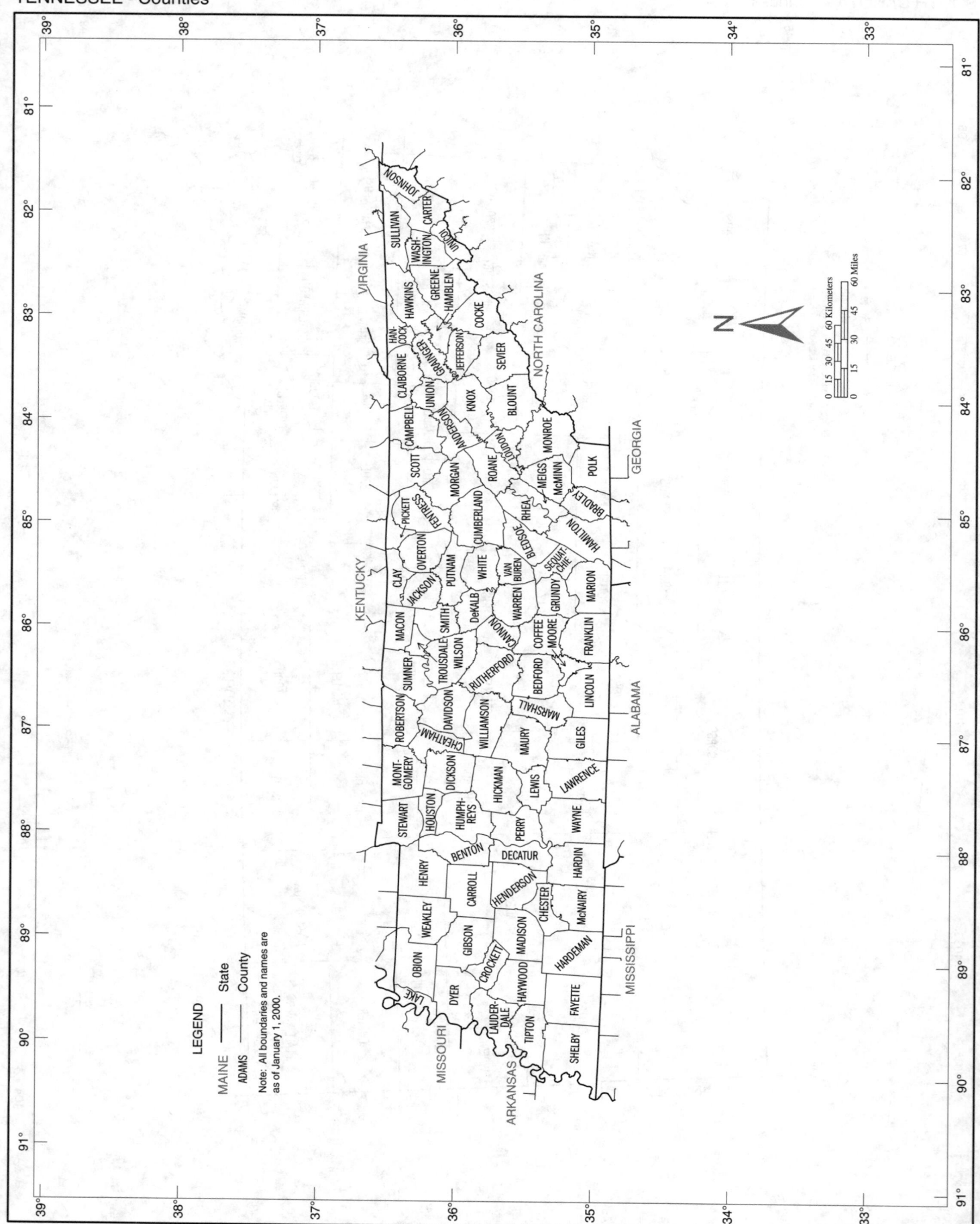

LEGEND

MAINE —— State

ADAMS —— County

Note: All boundaries and names are as of January 1, 2000.

TEXAS - Counties

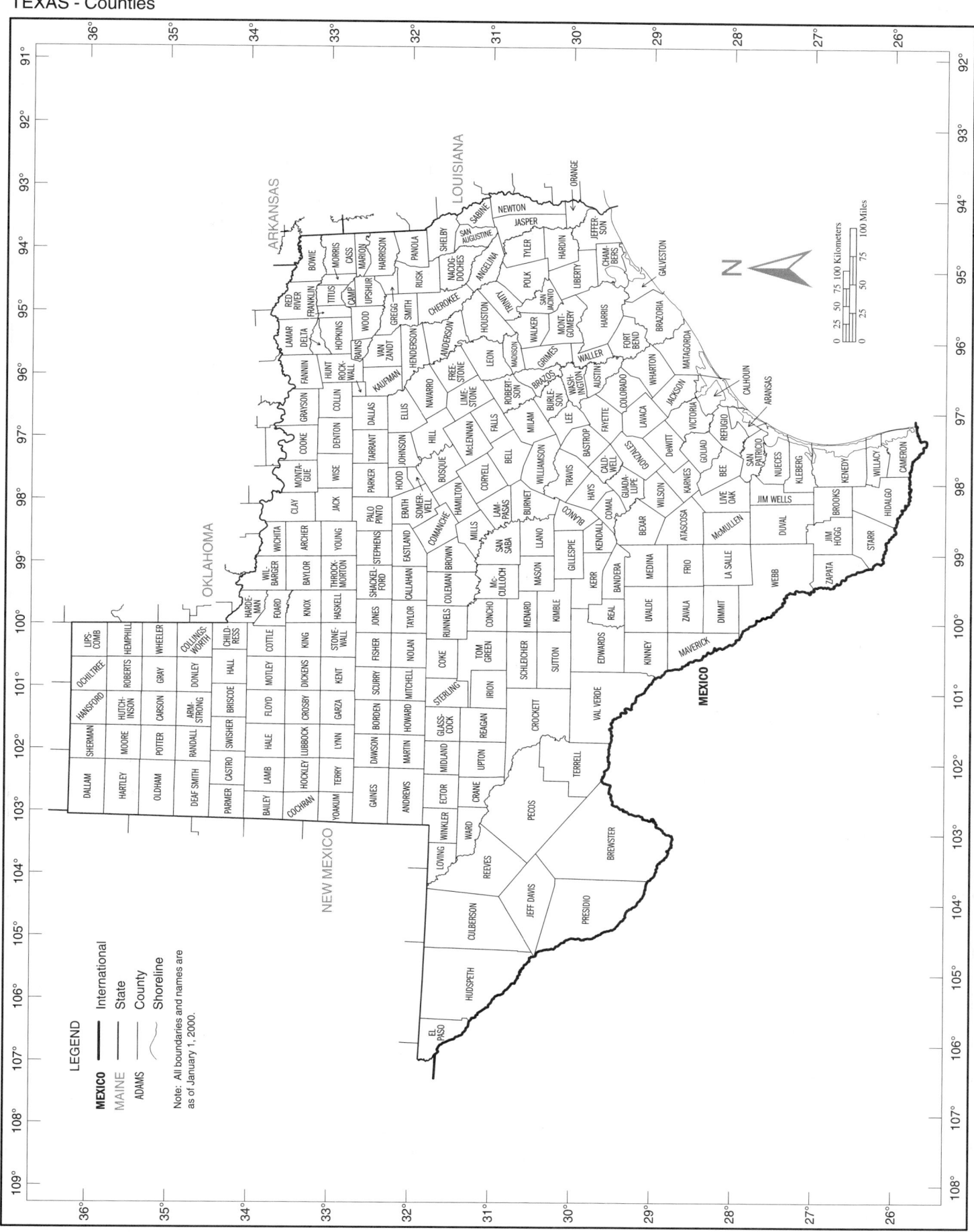

UTAH - Counties

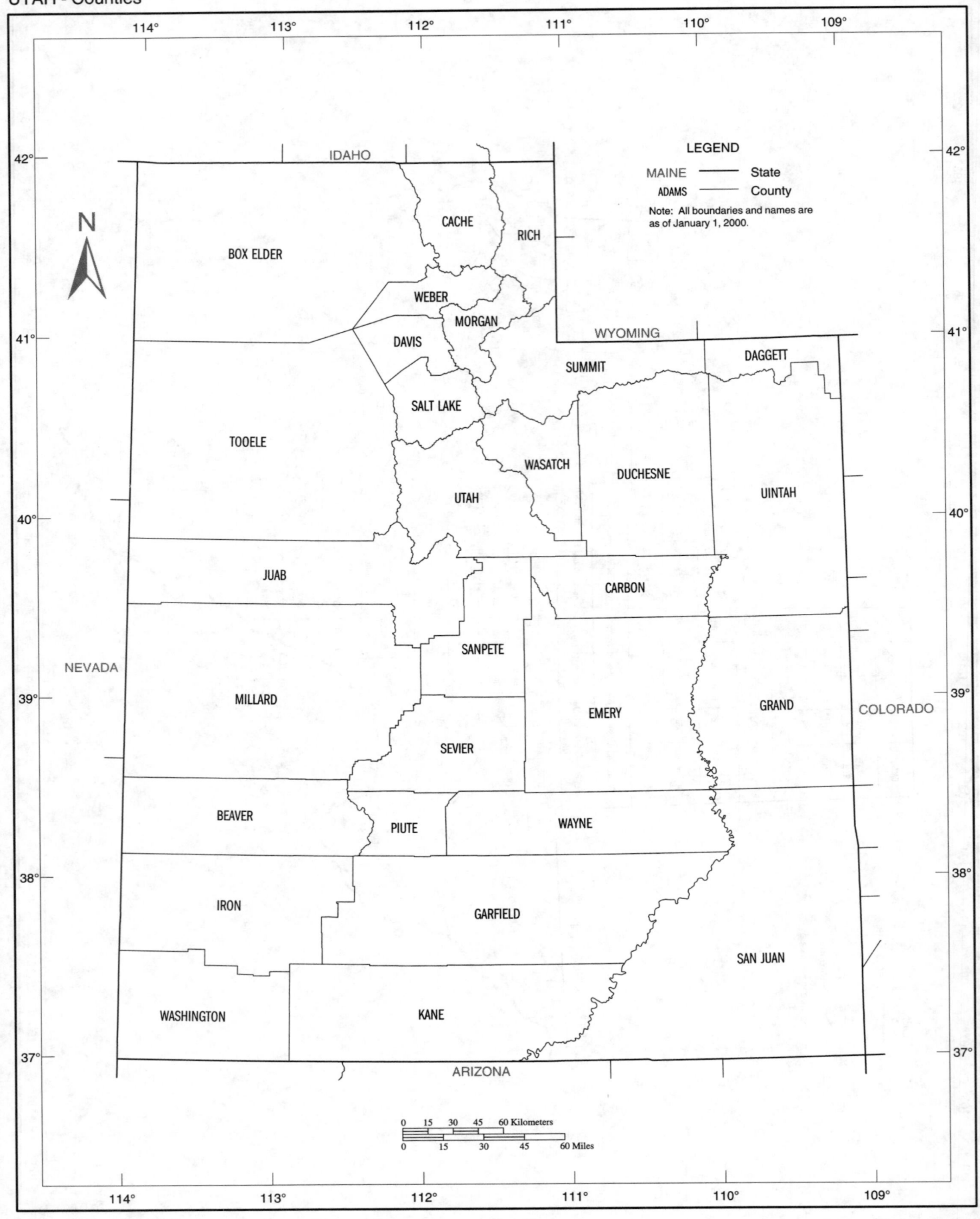

Appendix D

VERMONT - Counties

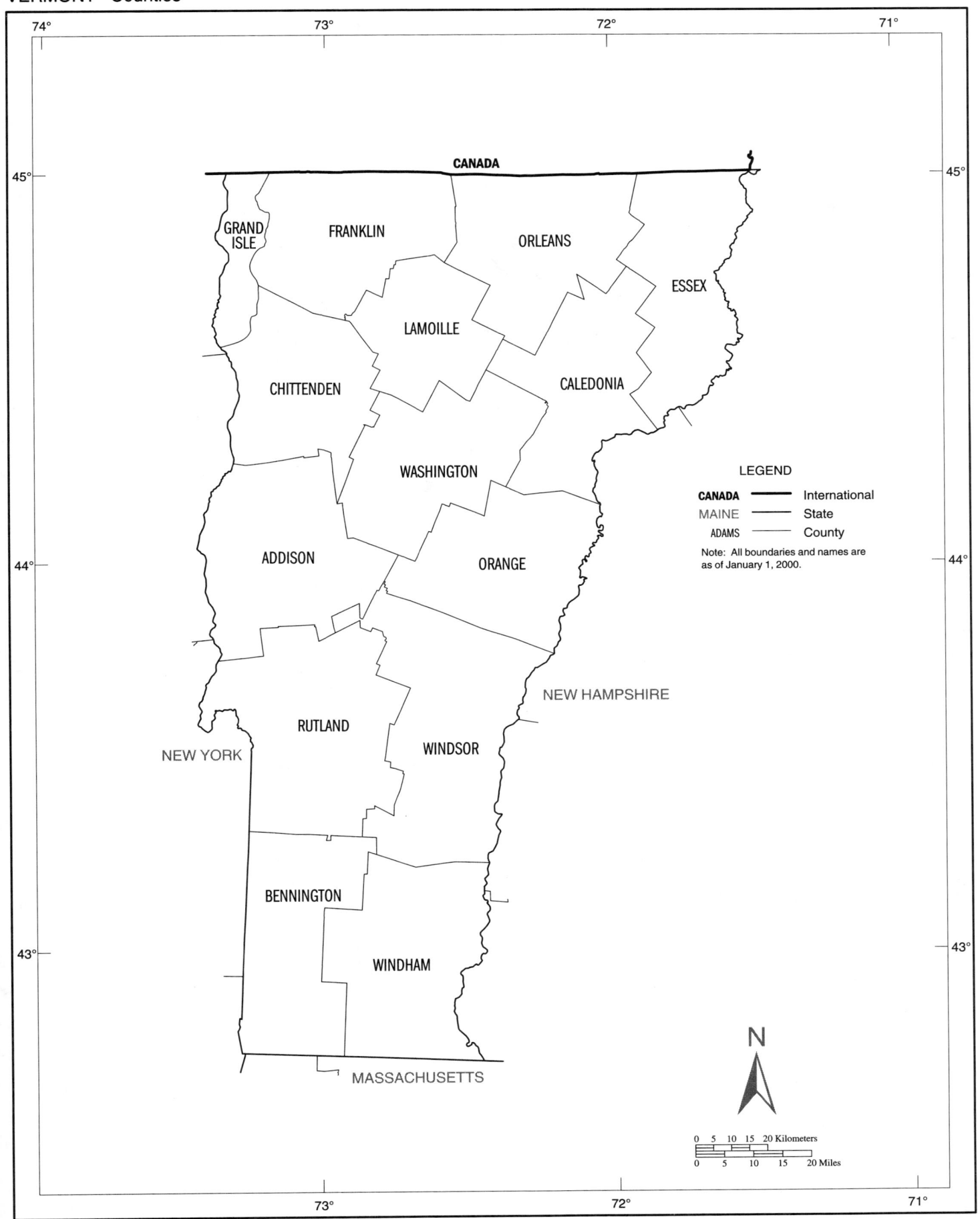

LEGEND

CANADA ———	International
MAINE ———	State
ADAMS ———	County

Note: All boundaries and names are as of January 1, 2000.

CANADA

GRAND ISLE

FRANKLIN

ORLEANS

ESSEX

LAMOILLE

CHITTENDEN

CALEDONIA

WASHINGTON

ADDISON

ORANGE

NEW HAMPSHIRE

RUTLAND

WINDSOR

NEW YORK

BENNINGTON

WINDHAM

MASSACHUSETTS

N

0 5 10 15 20 Kilometers

0 5 10 15 20 Miles

VIRGINIA - Counties and Independent Cities

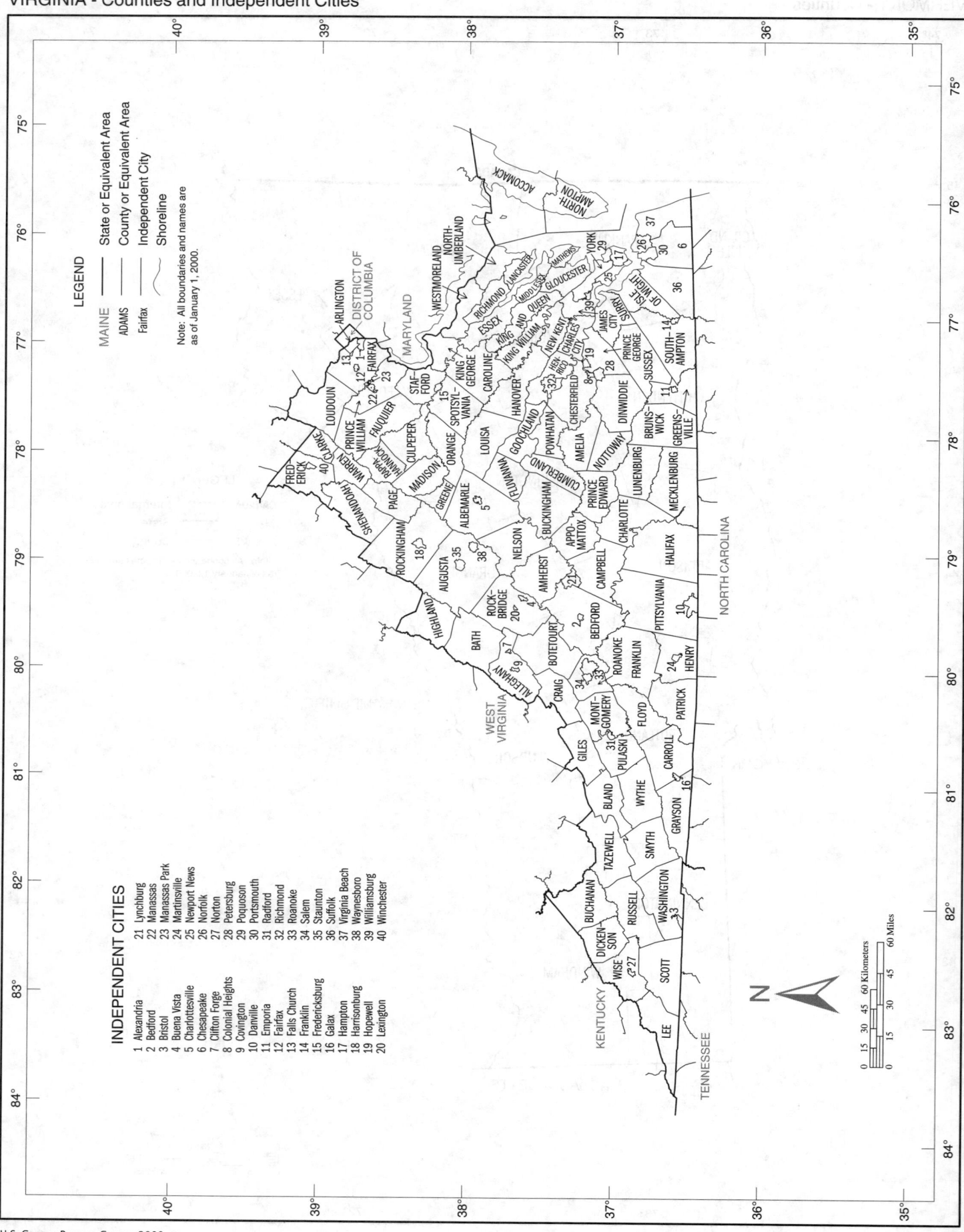

LEGEND

MAINE ———	State or Equivalent Area
ADAMS ———	County or Equivalent Area
Fairfax ———	Independent City
⌇⌇⌇	Shoreline

Note: All boundaries and names are
as of January 1, 2000.

INDEPENDENT CITIES

1	Alexandria	21	Lynchburg
2	Bedford	22	Manassas
3	Bristol	23	Manassas Park
4	Buena Vista	24	Martinsville
5	Charlottesville	25	Newport News
6	Chesapeake	26	Norfolk
7	Clifton Forge	27	Norton
8	Colonial Heights	28	Petersburg
9	Covington	29	Poquoson
10	Danville	30	Portsmouth
11	Emporia	31	Radford
12	Fairfax	32	Richmond
13	Falls Church	33	Roanoke
14	Franklin	34	Salem
15	Fredericksburg	35	Staunton
16	Galax	36	Suffolk
17	Hampton	37	Virginia Beach
18	Harrisonburg	38	Waynesboro
19	Hopewell	39	Williamsburg
20	Lexington	40	Winchester

WASHINGTON - Counties

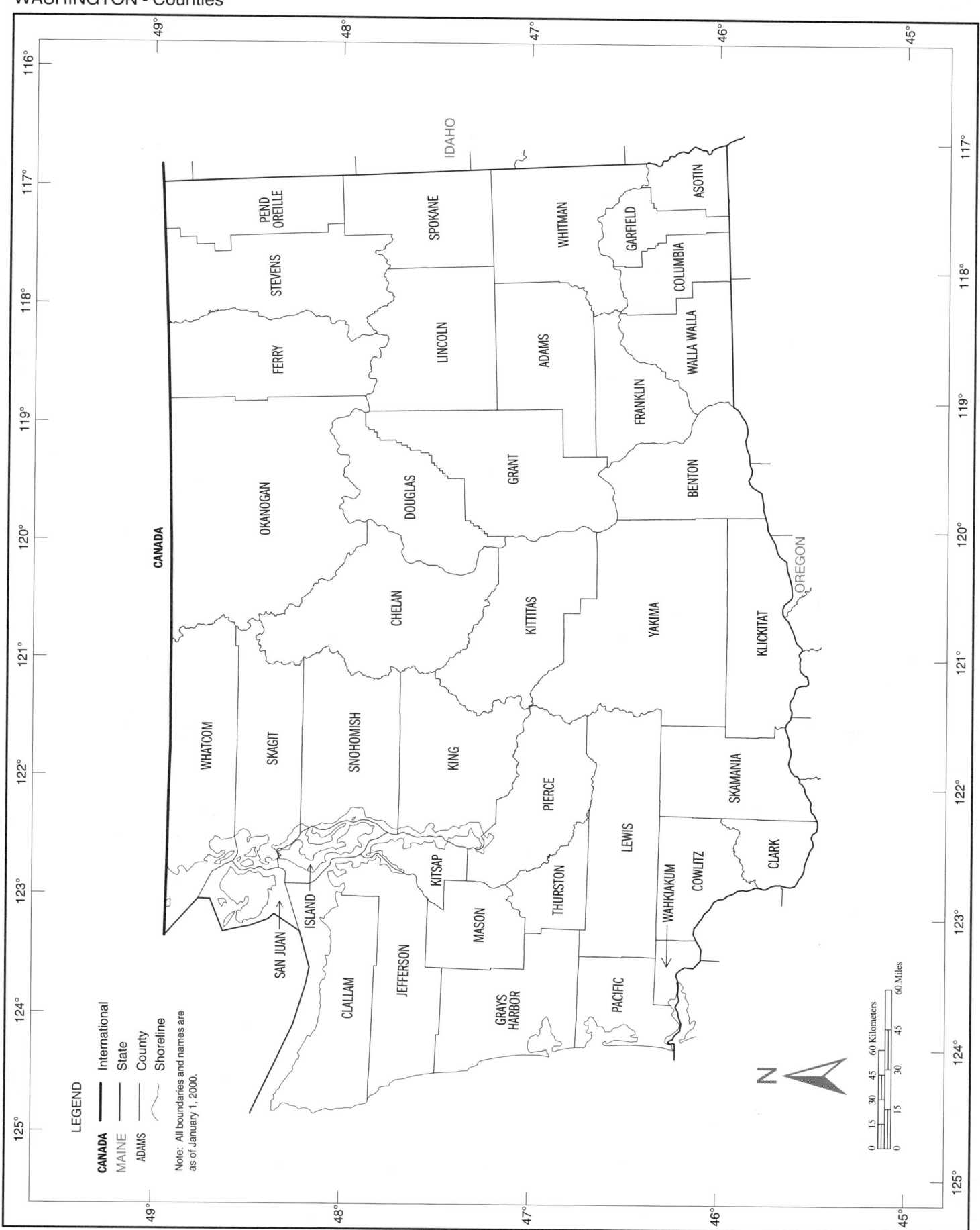

U.S. Census Bureau, Census 2000

Appendix D

D-51

WEST VIRGINIA - Counties

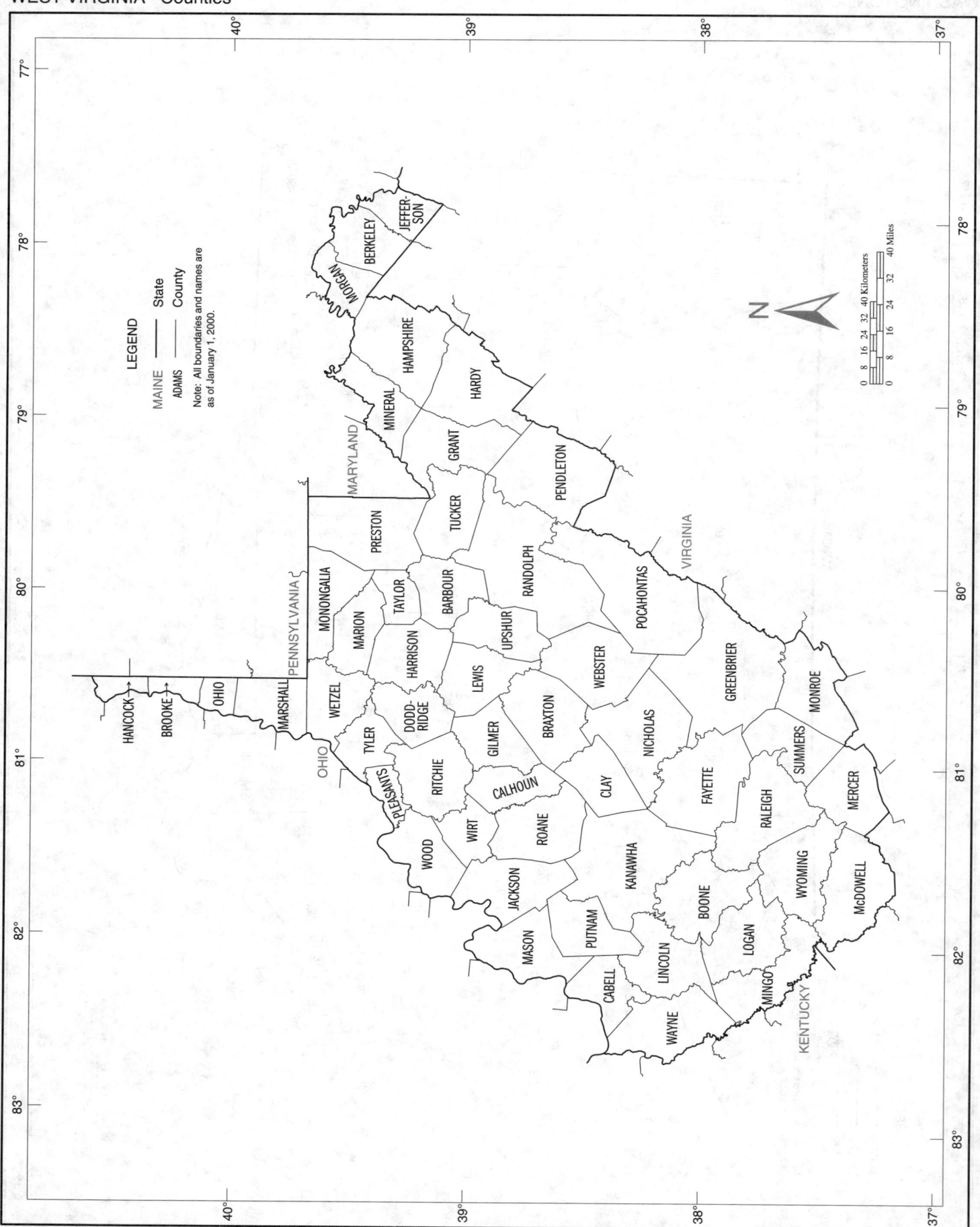

LEGEND

MAINE — State
ADAMS — County

Note: All boundaries and names are as of January 1, 2000.

N

0 8 16 24 32 40 Kilometers
0 8 16 24 32 40 Miles

WISCONSIN - Counties

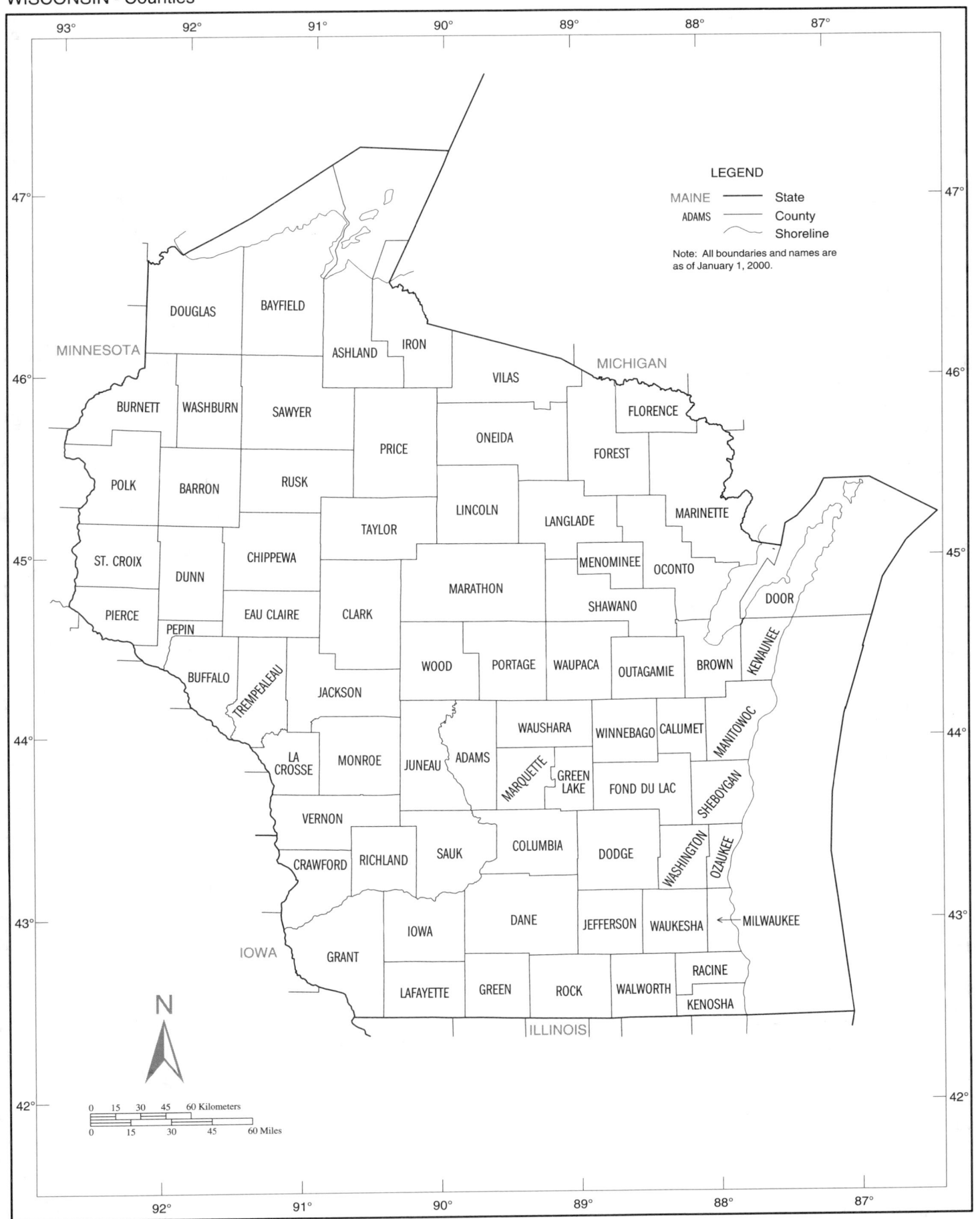

LEGEND

MAINE ——— State

ADAMS ——— County

~~~ Shoreline

Note: All boundaries and names are
as of January 1, 2000.

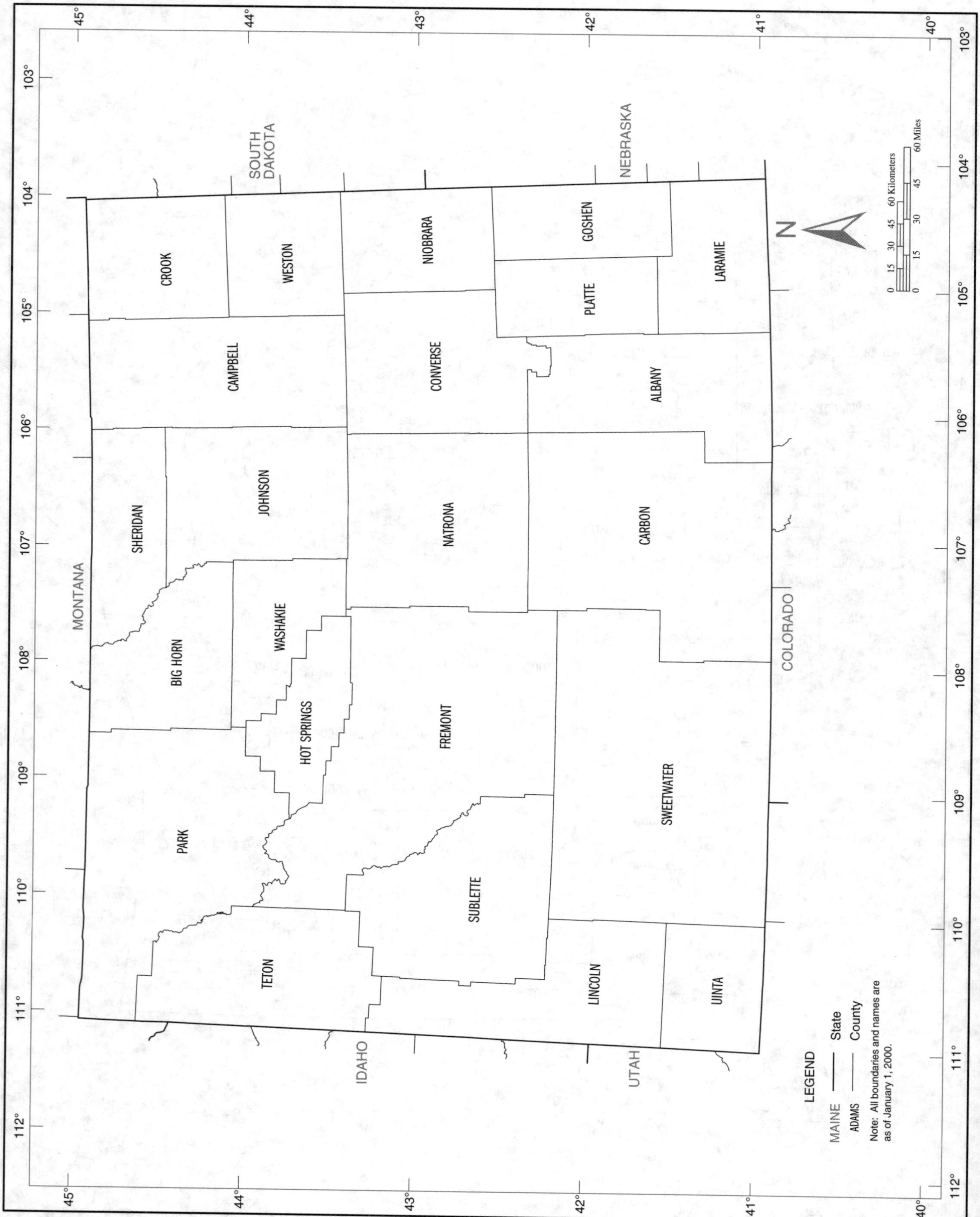

WYOMING - Counties

MONTANA

SOUTH DAKOTA

NEBRASKA

CROOK

WESTON

NIOBRARA

GOSHEN

LARAMIE

CAMPBELL

CONVERSE

PLATTE

ALBANY

SHERIDAN

JOHNSON

NATRONA

CARBON

BIG HORN

WASHAKIE

COLORADO

PARK

HOT SPRINGS

FREMONT

SWEETWATER

TETON

SUBLETTE

LINCOLN

UINTA

IDAHO

UTAH

N

60 Miles
60 Kilometers

LEGEND

MAINE ——— State
ADAMS ——— County

Note: All boundaries and names are
as of January 1, 2000.

APPENDIX E
CITIES BY COUNTY

The following table is arranged alphabetically by state. Under each state heading are listed all cities with a 2000 census population over 25,000 along with their component counties and the population in each component.

State Code	Place Code	County Code	Geographic Area Name	2000 Census Population	State Code	Place Code	County Code	Geographic Area Name	2000 Census Population
01			**ALABAMA**	4 447 100	04			**ARIZONA**	5 130 632
01	03076		Auburn city	42 987	04	02830		Apache Junction city	31 814
01	03076	081	Lee County	42 987	04	02830	013	Maricopa County	273
					04	02830	021	Pinal County	31 541
01	05980		Bessemer city	29 672					
01	05980	073	Jefferson County	29 672	04	04720		Avondale city	35 883
					04	04720	013	Maricopa County	35 883
01	07000		Birmingham city	242 820					
01	07000	073	Jefferson County	242 307	04	08220		Bullhead City city	33 769
01	07000	117	Shelby County	513	04	08220	015	Mohave County	33 769
01	20104		Decatur city	53 929	04	10530		Casa Grande city	25 224
01	20104	083	Limestone County	83	04	10530	021	Pinal County	25 224
01	20104	103	Morgan County	53 846					
					04	12000		Chandler city	176 581
01	21184		Dothan city	57 737	04	12000	013	Maricopa County	176 581
01	21184	045	Dale County	650					
01	21184	067	Henry County	5	04	23620		Flagstaff city	52 894
01	21184	069	Houston County	57 082	04	23620	005	Coconino County	52 894
01	26896		Florence city	36 264	04	27400		Gilbert town	109 697
01	26896	077	Lauderdale County	36 264	04	27400	013	Maricopa County	109 697
01	28696		Gadsden city	38 978	04	27820		Glendale city	218 812
01	28696	055	Etowah County	38 978	04	27820	013	Maricopa County	218 812
01	35800		Homewood city	25 043	04	39370		Lake Havasu City city	41 938
01	35800	073	Jefferson County	25 043	04	39370	015	Mohave County	41 938
01	35896		Hoover city	62 742	04	46000		Mesa city	396 375
01	35896	073	Jefferson County	46 868	04	46000	013	Maricopa County	396 375
01	35896	117	Shelby County	15 874					
					04	51600		Oro Valley town	29 700
01	37000		Huntsville city	158 216	04	51600	019	Pima County	29 700
01	37000	083	Limestone County	264					
01	37000	089	Madison County	157 952	04	54050		Peoria city	108 364
					04	54050	013	Maricopa County	108 363
01	45784		Madison city	29 329	04	54050	025	Yavapai County	1
01	45784	083	Limestone County	139					
01	45784	089	Madison County	29 190	04	55000		Phoenix city	1 321 045
					04	55000	013	Maricopa County	1 321 045
01	50000		Mobile city	198 915					
01	50000	097	Mobile County	198 915	04	57380		Prescott city	33 938
					04	57380	025	Yavapai County	33 938
01	51000		Montgomery city	201 568					
01	51000	101	Montgomery County	201 568	04	65000		Scottsdale city	202 705
					04	65000	013	Maricopa County	202 705
01	59472		Phenix City city	28 265					
01	59472	081	Lee County	1 980	04	66820		Sierra Vista city	37 775
01	59472	113	Russell County	26 285	04	66820	003	Cochise County	37 775
01	62496		Prichard city	28 633	04	71510		Surprise city	30 848
01	62496	097	Mobile County	28 633	04	71510	013	Maricopa County	30 848
01	77256		Tuscaloosa city	77 906	04	73000		Tempe city	158 625
01	77256	125	Tuscaloosa County	77 906	04	73000	013	Maricopa County	158 625
02			**ALASKA**	626 932	04	77000		Tucson city	486 699
02	03000		Anchorage municipality	260 283	04	77000	019	Pima County	486 699
02	03000	020	Anchorage Municipality	260 283					
					04	85540		Yuma city	77 515
02	24230		Fairbanks city	30 224	04	85540	027	Yuma County	77 515
02	24230	090	Fairbanks North Star Borough	30 224					
					05			**ARKANSAS**	2 673 400
02	36400		Juneau city and borough	30 711	05	15190		Conway city	43 167
02	36400	110	Juneau City and Borough	30 711	05	15190	045	Faulkner County	43 167

Cities by County – Continued

State Code	Place Code	County Code	Geographic Area Name	2000 Census Population	State Code	Place Code	County Code	Geographic Area Name	2000 Census Population
05	23290		Fayetteville city	58 047	06	04982		Bellflower city	72 878
05	23290	143	Washington County	58 047	06	04982	037	Los Angeles County	72 878
05	24550		Fort Smith city	80 268	06	04996		Bell Gardens city	44 054
05	24550	131	Sebastian County	80 268	06	04996	037	Los Angeles County	44 054
05	33400		Hot Springs city	35 750	06	05108		Belmont city	25 123
05	33400	051	Garland County	35 750	06	05108	081	San Mateo County	25 123
05	34750		Jacksonville city	29 916	06	05290		Benicia city	26 865
05	34750	119	Pulaski County	29 916	06	05290	095	Solano County	26 865
05	35710		Jonesboro city	55 515	06	06000		Berkeley city	102 743
05	35710	031	Craighead County	55 515	06	06000	001	Alameda County	102 743
05	41000		Little Rock city	183 133	06	06308		Beverly Hills city	33 784
05	41000	119	Pulaski County	183 133	06	06308	037	Los Angeles County	33 784
05	50450		North Little Rock city	60 433	06	08100		Brea city	35 410
05	50450	119	Pulaski County	60 433	06	08100	059	Orange County	35 410
05	55310		Pine Bluff city	55 085	06	08786		Buena Park city	78 282
05	55310	069	Jefferson County	55 085	06	08786	059	Orange County	78 282
05	60410		Rogers city	38 829	06	08954		Burbank city	100 316
05	60410	007	Benton County	38 829	06	08954	037	Los Angeles County	100 316
05	66080		Springdale city	45 798	06	09066		Burlingame city	28 158
05	66080	007	Benton County	2 011	06	09066	081	San Mateo County	28 158
05	66080	143	Washington County	43 787	06	09710		Calexico city	27 109
05	68810		Texarkana city	26 448	06	09710	025	Imperial County	27 109
05	68810	091	Miller County	26 448	06	10046		Camarillo city	57 077
05	74540		West Memphis city	27 666	06	10046	111	Ventura County	57 077
05	74540	035	Crittenden County	27 666	06	10345		Campbell city	38 138
06			**CALIFORNIA**	33 871 648	06	10345	085	Santa Clara County	38 138
06	00562		Alameda city	72 259	06	11194		Carlsbad city	78 247
06	00562	001	Alameda County	72 259	06	11194	073	San Diego County	78 247
06	00884		Alhambra city	85 804	06	11530		Carson city	89 730
06	00884	037	Los Angeles County	85 804	06	11530	037	Los Angeles County	89 730
06	02000		Anaheim city	328 014	06	12048		Cathedral City city	42 647
06	02000	059	Orange County	328 014	06	12048	065	Riverside County	42 647
06	02252		Antioch city	90 532	06	12524		Ceres city	34 609
06	02252	013	Contra Costa County	90 532	06	12524	099	Stanislaus County	34 609
06	02364		Apple Valley town	54 239	06	12552		Cerritos city	51 488
06	02364	071	San Bernardino County	54 239	06	12552	037	Los Angeles County	51 488
06	02462		Arcadia city	53 054	06	13014		Chico city	59 954
06	02462	037	Los Angeles County	53 054	06	13014	007	Butte County	59 954
06	03064		Atascadero city	26 411	06	13210		Chino city	67 168
06	03064	079	San Luis Obispo County	26 411	06	13210	071	San Bernardino County	67 168
06	03386		Azusa city	44 712	06	13392		Chula Vista city	173 556
06	03386	037	Los Angeles County	44 712	06	13392	073	San Diego County	173 556
06	03526		Bakersfield city	247 057	06	13756		Claremont city	33 998
06	03526	029	Kern County	247 057	06	13756	037	Los Angeles County	33 998
06	03666		Baldwin Park city	75 837	06	14218		Clovis city	68 468
06	03666	037	Los Angeles County	75 837	06	14218	019	Fresno County	68 468
06	04870		Bell city	36 664	06	14890		Colton city	47 662
06	04870	037	Los Angeles County	36 664	06	14890	071	San Bernardino County	47 662

Cities by County – Continued

State Code	Place Code	County Code	Geographic Area Name	2000 Census Population	State Code	Place Code	County Code	Geographic Area Name	2000 Census Population
06	15044		Compton city	93 493	06	24638		Folsom city	51 884
06	15044	037	Los Angeles County	93 493	06	24638	067	Sacramento County	51 884
06	16000		Concord city	121 780	06	24680		Fontana city	128 929
06	16000	013	Contra Costa County	121 780	06	24680	071	San Bernardino County	128 929
06	16350		Corona city	124 966	06	25338		Foster City city	28 803
06	16350	065	Riverside County	124 966	06	25338	081	San Mateo County	28 803
06	16532		Costa Mesa city	108 724	06	25380		Fountain Valley city	54 978
06	16532	059	Orange County	108 724	06	25380	059	Orange County	54 978
06	16742		Covina city	46 837	06	26000		Fremont city	203 413
06	16742	037	Los Angeles County	46 837	06	26000	001	Alameda County	203 413
06	17568		Culver City city	38 816	06	27000		Fresno city	427 652
06	17568	037	Los Angeles County	38 816	06	27000	019	Fresno County	427 652
06	17610		Cupertino city	50 546	06	28000		Fullerton city	126 003
06	17610	085	Santa Clara County	50 546	06	28000	059	Orange County	126 003
06	17750		Cypress city	46 229	06	28168		Gardena city	57 746
06	17750	059	Orange County	46 229	06	28168	037	Los Angeles County	57 746
06	17918		Daly City city	103 621	06	29000		Garden Grove city	165 196
06	17918	081	San Mateo County	103 621	06	29000	059	Orange County	165 196
06	17946		Dana Point city	35 110	06	29504		Gilroy city	41 464
06	17946	059	Orange County	35 110	06	29504	085	Santa Clara County	41 464
06	17988		Danville town	41 715	06	30000		Glendale city	194 973
06	17988	013	Contra Costa County	41 715	06	30000	037	Los Angeles County	194 973
06	18100		Davis city	60 308	06	30014		Glendora city	49 415
06	18100	113	Yolo County	60 308	06	30014	037	Los Angeles County	49 415
06	18394		Delano city	38 824	06	31960		Hanford city	41 686
06	18394	029	Kern County	38 824	06	31960	031	Kings County	41 686
06	19192		Diamond Bar city	56 287	06	32548		Hawthorne city	84 112
06	19192	037	Los Angeles County	56 287	06	32548	037	Los Angeles County	84 112
06	19766		Downey city	107 323	06	33000		Hayward city	140 030
06	19766	037	Los Angeles County	107 323	06	33000	001	Alameda County	140 030
06	20018		Dublin city	29 973	06	33182		Hemet city	58 812
06	20018	001	Alameda County	29 973	06	33182	065	Riverside County	58 812
06	20956		East Palo Alto city	29 506	06	33434		Hesperia city	62 582
06	20956	081	San Mateo County	29 506	06	33434	071	San Bernardino County	62 582
06	21712		El Cajon city	94 869	06	33588		Highland city	44 605
06	21712	073	San Diego County	94 869	06	33588	071	San Bernardino County	44 605
06	21782		El Centro city	37 835	06	34120		Hollister city	34 413
06	21782	025	Imperial County	37 835	06	34120	069	San Benito County	34 413
06	22230		El Monte city	115 965	06	36000		Huntington Beach city	189 594
06	22230	037	Los Angeles County	115 965	06	36000	059	Orange County	189 594
06	22678		Encinitas city	58 014	06	36056		Huntington Park city	61 348
06	22678	073	San Diego County	58 014	06	36056	037	Los Angeles County	61 348
06	22804		Escondido city	133 559	06	36294		Imperial Beach city	26 992
06	22804	073	San Diego County	133 559	06	36294	073	San Diego County	26 992
06	23042		Eureka city	26 128	06	36448		Indio city	49 116
06	23042	023	Humboldt County	26 128	06	36448	065	Riverside County	49 116
06	23182		Fairfield city	96 178	06	36546		Inglewood city	112 580
06	23182	095	Solano County	96 178	06	36546	037	Los Angeles County	112 580

Cities by County – Continued

State Code	Place Code	County Code	Geographic Area Name	2000 Census Population	State Code	Place Code	County Code	Geographic Area Name	2000 Census Population
06	36770		Irvine city	143 072	06	45778		Marina city	25 101
06	36770	059	Orange County	143 072	06	45778	053	Monterey County	25 101
06	39248		Laguna Niguel city	61 891	06	46114		Martinez city	35 866
06	39248	059	Orange County	61 891	06	46114	013	Contra Costa County	35 866
06	39290		La Habra city	58 974	06	46492		Maywood city	28 083
06	39290	059	Orange County	58 974	06	46492	037	Los Angeles County	28 083
06	39486		Lake Elsinore city	28 928	06	46870		Menlo Park city	30 785
06	39486	065	Riverside County	28 928	06	46870	081	San Mateo County	30 785
06	39496		Lake Forest city	58 707	06	46898		Merced city	63 893
06	39496	059	Orange County	58 707	06	46898	047	Merced County	63 893
06	39892		Lakewood city	79 345	06	47766		Milpitas city	62 698
06	39892	037	Los Angeles County	79 345	06	47766	085	Santa Clara County	62 698
06	40004		La Mesa city	54 749	06	48256		Mission Viejo city	93 102
06	40004	073	San Diego County	54 749	06	48256	059	Orange County	93 102
06	40032		La Mirada city	46 783	06	48354		Modesto city	188 856
06	40032	037	Los Angeles County	46 783	06	48354	099	Stanislaus County	188 856
06	40130		Lancaster city	118 718	06	48648		Monrovia city	36 929
06	40130	037	Los Angeles County	118 718	06	48648	037	Los Angeles County	36 929
06	40340		La Puente city	41 063	06	48788		Montclair city	33 049
06	40340	037	Los Angeles County	41 063	06	48788	071	San Bernardino County	33 049
06	40830		La Verne city	31 638	06	48816		Montebello city	62 150
06	40830	037	Los Angeles County	31 638	06	48816	037	Los Angeles County	62 150
06	40886		Lawndale city	31 711	06	48872		Monterey city	29 674
06	40886	037	Los Angeles County	31 711	06	48872	053	Monterey County	29 674
06	41992		Livermore city	73 345	06	48914		Monterey Park city	60 051
06	41992	001	Alameda County	73 345	06	48914	037	Los Angeles County	60 051
06	42202		Lodi city	56 999	06	49138		Moorpark city	31 415
06	42202	077	San Joaquin County	56 999	06	49138	111	Ventura County	31 415
06	42524		Lompoc city	41 103	06	49270		Moreno Valley city	142 381
06	42524	083	Santa Barbara County	41 103	06	49270	065	Riverside County	142 381
06	43000		Long Beach city	461 522	06	49278		Morgan Hill city	33 556
06	43000	037	Los Angeles County	461 522	06	49278	085	Santa Clara County	33 556
06	43280		Los Altos city	27 693	06	49670		Mountain View city	70 708
06	43280	085	Santa Clara County	27 693	06	49670	085	Santa Clara County	70 708
06	44000		Los Angeles city	3 694 820	06	50076		Murrieta city	44 282
06	44000	037	Los Angeles County	3 694 820	06	50076	065	Riverside County	44 282
06	44028		Los Banos city	25 869	06	50258		Napa city	72 585
06	44028	047	Merced County	25 869	06	50258	055	Napa County	72 585
06	44112		Los Gatos town	28 592	06	50398		National City city	54 260
06	44112	085	Santa Clara County	28 592	06	50398	073	San Diego County	54 260
06	44574		Lynwood city	69 845	06	50916		Newark city	42 471
06	44574	037	Los Angeles County	69 845	06	50916	001	Alameda County	42 471
06	45022		Madera city	43 207	06	51182		Newport Beach city	70 032
06	45022	039	Madera County	43 207	06	51182	059	Orange County	70 032
06	45400		Manhattan Beach city	33 852	06	52526		Norwalk city	103 298
06	45400	037	Los Angeles County	33 852	06	52526	037	Los Angeles County	103 298
06	45484		Manteca city	49 258	06	52582		Novato city	47 630
06	45484	077	San Joaquin County	49 258	06	52582	041	Marin County	47 630

Cities by County – Continued

State Code	Place Code	County Code	Geographic Area Name	2000 Census Population	State Code	Place Code	County Code	Geographic Area Name	2000 Census Population
06	53000		Oakland city..................................	399 484	06	59514		Rancho Palos Verdes city.............	41 145
06	53000	001	Alameda County	399 484	06	59514	037	Los Angeles County	41 145
06	53322		Oceanside city..............................	161 029	06	59920		Redding city.................................	80 865
06	53322	073	San Diego County	161 029	06	59920	089	Shasta County	80 865
06	53896		Ontario city	158 007	06	59962		Redlands city...............................	63 591
06	53896	071	San Bernardino County	158 007	06	59962	071	San Bernardino County	63 591
06	53980		Orange city...................................	128 821	06	60018		Redondo Beach city	63 261
06	53980	059	Orange County	128 821	06	60018	037	Los Angeles County	63 261
06	54652		Oxnard city...................................	170 358	06	60102		Redwood City city	75 402
06	54652	111	Ventura County.......................	170 358	06	60102	081	San Mateo County....................	75 402
06	54806		Pacifica city.................................	38 390	06	60466		Rialto city....................................	91 873
06	54806	081	San Mateo County....................	38 390	06	60466	071	San Bernardino County	91 873
06	55156		Palmdale city	116 670	06	60620		Richmond city..............................	99 216
06	55156	037	Los Angeles County	116 670	06	60620	013	Contra Costa County	99 216
06	55184		Palm Desert city	41 155	06	62000		Riverside city...............................	255 166
06	55184	065	Riverside County	41 155	06	62000	065	Riverside County	255 166
06	55254		Palm Springs city	42 807	06	62364		Rocklin city	36 330
06	55254	065	Riverside County	42 807	06	62364	061	Placer County	36 330
06	55282		Palo Alto city	58 598	06	62546		Rohnert Park city.........................	42 236
06	55282	085	Santa Clara County	58 598	06	62546	097	Sonoma County	42 236
06	55520		Paradise town..............................	26 408	06	62896		Rosemead city.............................	53 505
06	55520	007	Butte County	26 408	06	62896	037	Los Angeles County	53 505
06	55618		Paramount city	55 266	06	62938		Roseville city...............................	79 921
06	55618	037	Los Angeles County	55 266	06	62938	061	Placer County	79 921
06	56000		Pasadena city..............................	133 936	06	64000		Sacramento city...........................	407 018
06	56000	037	Los Angeles County	133 936	06	64000	067	Sacramento County	407 018
06	56700		Perris city....................................	36 189	06	64224		Salinas city	151 060
06	56700	065	Riverside County	36 189	06	64224	053	Monterey County	151 060
06	56784		Petaluma city...............................	54 548	06	65000		San Bernardino city......................	185 401
06	56784	097	Sonoma County	54 548	06	65000	071	San Bernardino County	185 401
06	56924		Pico Rivera city	63 428	06	65028		San Bruno city.............................	40 165
06	56924	037	Los Angeles County	63 428	06	65028	081	San Mateo County....................	40 165
06	57456		Pittsburg city................................	56 769	06	65042		San Buenaventura (Ventura) city....	100 916
06	57456	013	Contra Costa County	56 769	06	65042	111	Ventura County.......................	100 916
06	57526		Placentia city...............................	46 488	06	65070		San Carlos city	27 718
06	57526	059	Orange County	46 488	06	65070	081	San Mateo County....................	27 718
06	57764		Pleasant Hill city..........................	32 837	06	65084		San Clemente city	49 936
06	57764	013	Contra Costa County	32 837	06	65084	059	Orange County	49 936
06	57792		Pleasanton city............................	63 654	06	66000		San Diego city.............................	1 223 400
06	57792	001	Alameda County	63 654	06	66000	073	San Diego County	1 223 400
06	58072		Pomona city.................................	149 473	06	66070		San Dimas city	34 980
06	58072	037	Los Angeles County	149 473	06	66070	037	Los Angeles County	34 980
06	58240		Porterville city..............................	39 615	06	67000		San Francisco city........................	776 733
06	58240	107	Tulare County	39 615	06	67000	075	San Francisco County	776 733
06	58520		Poway city...................................	48 044	06	67042		San Gabriel city...........................	39 804
06	58520	073	San Diego County	48 044	06	67042	037	Los Angeles County	39 804
06	59451		Rancho Cucamonga city..............	127 743	06	68000		San Jose city...............................	894 943
06	59451	071	San Bernardino County	127 743	06	68000	085	Santa Clara County	894 943

State Code	Place Code	County Code	Geographic Area Name	2000 Census Population	State Code	Place Code	County Code	Geographic Area Name	2000 Census Population
06	68028		San Juan Capistrano city	33 826	06	75000		Stockton city	243 771
06	68028	059	Orange County	33 826	06	75000	077	San Joaquin County	243 771
06	68084		San Leandro city	79 452	06	75630		Suisun City city	26 118
06	68084	001	Alameda County	79 452	06	75630	095	Solano County	26 118
06	68154		San Luis Obispo city	44 174	06	77000		Sunnyvale city	131 760
06	68154	079	San Luis Obispo County	44 174	06	77000	085	Santa Clara County	131 760
06	68196		San Marcos city	54 977	06	78120		Temecula city	57 716
06	68196	073	San Diego County	54 977	06	78120	065	Riverside County	57 716
06	68252		San Mateo city	92 482	06	78148		Temple City city	33 377
06	68252	081	San Mateo County	92 482	06	78148	037	Los Angeles County	33 377
06	68294		San Pablo city	30 215	06	78582		Thousand Oaks city	117 005
06	68294	013	Contra Costa County	30 215	06	78582	111	Ventura County	117 005
06	68364		San Rafael city	56 063	06	80000		Torrance city	137 946
06	68364	041	Marin County	56 063	06	80000	037	Los Angeles County	137 946
06	68378		San Ramon city	44 722	06	80238		Tracy city	56 929
06	68378	013	Contra Costa County	44 722	06	80238	077	San Joaquin County	56 929
06	69000		Santa Ana city	337 977	06	80644		Tulare city	43 994
06	69000	059	Orange County	337 977	06	80644	107	Tulare County	43 994
06	69070		Santa Barbara city	92 325	06	80812		Turlock city	55 810
06	69070	083	Santa Barbara County	92 325	06	80812	099	Stanislaus County	55 810
06	69084		Santa Clara city	102 361	06	80854		Tustin city	67 504
06	69084	085	Santa Clara County	102 361	06	80854	059	Orange County	67 504
06	69088		Santa Clarita city	151 088	06	81204		Union City city	66 869
06	69088	037	Los Angeles County	151 088	06	81204	001	Alameda County	66 869
06	69112		Santa Cruz city	54 593	06	81344		Upland city	68 393
06	69112	087	Santa Cruz County	54 593	06	81344	071	San Bernardino County	68 393
06	69196		Santa Maria city	77 423	06	81554		Vacaville city	88 625
06	69196	083	Santa Barbara County	77 423	06	81554	095	Solano County	88 625
06	70000		Santa Monica city	84 084	06	81666		Vallejo city	116 760
06	70000	037	Los Angeles County	84 084	06	81666	095	Solano County	116 760
06	70042		Santa Paula city	28 598	06	82590		Victorville city	64 029
06	70042	111	Ventura County	28 598	06	82590	071	San Bernardino County	64 029
06	70098		Santa Rosa city	147 595	06	82954		Visalia city	91 565
06	70098	097	Sonoma County	147 595	06	82954	107	Tulare County	91 565
06	70224		Santee city	52 975	06	82996		Vista city	89 857
06	70224	073	San Diego County	52 975	06	82996	073	San Diego County	89 857
06	70280		Saratoga city	29 843	06	83332		Walnut city	30 004
06	70280	085	Santa Clara County	29 843	06	83332	037	Los Angeles County	30 004
06	70742		Seaside city	31 696	06	83346		Walnut Creek city	64 296
06	70742	053	Monterey County	31 696	06	83346	013	Contra Costa County	64 296
06	72016		Simi Valley city	111 351	06	83668		Watsonville city	44 265
06	72016	111	Ventura County	111 351	06	83668	087	Santa Cruz County	44 265
06	73080		South Gate city	96 375	06	84200		West Covina city	105 080
06	73080	037	Los Angeles County	96 375	06	84200	037	Los Angeles County	105 080
06	73262		South San Francisco city	60 552	06	84410		West Hollywood city	35 716
06	73262	081	San Mateo County	60 552	06	84410	037	Los Angeles County	35 716
06	73962		Stanton city	37 403	06	84550		Westminster city	88 207
06	73962	059	Orange County	37 403	06	84550	059	Orange County	88 207

State Code	Place Code	County Code	Geographic Area Name	2000 Census Population	State Code	Place Code	County Code	Geographic Area Name	2000 Census Population
06	84816		West Sacramento city	31 615	08	54330		Northglenn city	31 575
06	84816	113	Yolo County	31 615	08	54330	001	Adams County	31 563
					08	54330	123	Weld County	12
06	85292		Whittier city..................................	83 680					
06	85292	037	Los Angeles County	83 680	08	62000		Pueblo city.................................	102 121
					08	62000	101	Pueblo County	102 121
06	86328		Woodland city..............................	49 151					
06	86328	113	Yolo County..........................	49 151	08	77290		Thornton city..............................	82 384
					08	77290	001	Adams County	82 384
06	86832		Yorba Linda city	58 918	08	77290	123	Weld County	0
06	86832	059	Orange County	58 918					
					08	83835		Westminster city	100 940
06	86972		Yuba City city	36 758	08	83835	001	Adams County	57 419
06	86972	101	Sutter County	36 758	08	83835	059	Jefferson County	43 521
06	87042		Yucaipa city	41 207	08	84440		Wheat Ridge city	32 913
06	87042	071	San Bernardino County	41 207	08	84440	059	Jefferson County	32 913
08			**COLORADO**	4 301 261	09			**CONNECTICUT**	3 405 565
08	03455		Arvada city..................................	102 153	09	08000		Bridgeport city	139 529
08	03455	001	Adams County	2 847	09	08000	001	Fairfield County	139 529
08	03455	059	Jefferson County.....................	99 306					
					09	08420		Bristol city..................................	60 062
08	04000		Aurora city..................................	276 393	09	08420	003	Hartford County	60 062
08	04000	001	Adams County	40 249					
08	04000	005	Arapahoe County	236 144	09	18430		Danbury city	74 848
08	04000	035	Douglas County	0	09	18430	001	Fairfield County........................	74 848
08	07850		Boulder city.................................	94 673	09	37000		Hartford city	121 578
08	07850	013	Boulder County	94 673	09	37000	003	Hartford County	121 578
08	09280		Broomfield city............................	38 272	09	46450		Meriden city	58 244
08	09280	001	Adams County	15 239	09	46450	009	New Haven County.....................	58 244
08	09280	013	Boulder County	21 474					
08	09280	059	Jefferson County......................	1 549	09	47290		Middletown city...........................	43 167
08	09280	123	Weld County	10	09	47290	007	Middlesex County	43 167
08	16000		Colorado Springs city	360 890	09	47500		Milford city	52 305
08	16000	041	El Paso County	360 890					
					09	49880		Naugatuck borough.....................	30 989
08	20000		Denver city	554 636	09	49880	009	New Haven County.....................	30 989
08	20000	031	Denver County	554 636					
					09	50370		New Britain city	71 538
08	24785		Englewood city	31 727	09	50370	003	Hartford County	71 538
08	24785	005	Arapahoe County.......................	31 727					
					09	52000		New Haven city	123 626
08	27425		Fort Collins city...........................	118 652	09	52000	009	New Haven County.....................	123 626
08	27425	069	Larimer County	118 652					
					09	52280		New London city..........................	25 671
08	31660		Grand Junction city	41 986	09	52280	011	New London County	25 671
08	31660	077	Mesa County............................	41 986					
					09	55990		Norwalk city................................	82 951
08	32155		Greeley city	76 930	09	55990	001	Fairfield County........................	82 951
08	32155	123	Weld County	76 930					
					09	56200		Norwich city	36 117
08	43000		Lakewood city.............................	144 126	09	56200	011	New London County	36 117
08	43000	059	Jefferson County.......................	144 126					
					09	68100		Shelton city.................................	38 101
08	45255		Littleton city	40 340	09	68100	001	Fairfield County........................	38 101
08	45255	005	Arapahoe County......................	40 168					
08	45255	035	Douglas County	63	09	73000		Stamford city	117 083
08	45255	059	Jefferson County.......................	109	09	73000	001	Fairfield County........................	117 083
08	45970		Longmont city.............................	71 093	09	76500		Torrington city.............................	35 202
08	45970	013	Boulder County	71 069	09	76500	005	Litchfield County	35 202
08	45970	123	Weld County	24					
					09	80000		Waterbury city	107 271
08	46465		Loveland city	50 608	09	80000	009	New Haven County....................	107 271
08	46465	069	Larimer County	50 608					
					09	82800		West Haven city	52 360
					09	82800	009	New Haven County....................	52 360

Cities by County – Continued

State Code	Place Code	County Code	Geographic Area Name	2000 Census Population	State Code	Place Code	County Code	Geographic Area Name	2000 Census Population
10			**DELAWARE**	783 600	12	25175		Gainesville city	95 447
10	21200		Dover city	32 135	12	25175	001	Alachua County	95 447
10	21200	001	Kent County	32 135					
					12	27322		Greenacres city	27 569
10	50670		Newark city	28 547	12	27322	099	Palm Beach County	27 569
10	50670	003	New Castle County	28 547					
					12	28450		Hallandale city	34 282
10	77580		Wilmington city	72 664	12	28450	011	Broward County	34 282
10	77580	003	New Castle County	72 664					
					12	30000		Hialeah city	226 419
11			**DISTRICT OF COLUMBIA**	572 059	12	30000	086	Miami-Dade County	226 419
11	50000		Washington city	572 059					
11	50000	001	District of Columbia	572 059	12	32000		Hollywood city	139 357
					12	32000	011	Broward County	139 357
12			**FLORIDA**	15 982 378					
12	00950		Altamonte Springs city	41 200	12	32275		Homestead city	31 909
12	00950	117	Seminole County	41 200	12	32275	086	Miami-Dade County	31 909
12	01700		Apopka city	26 642	12	35000		Jacksonville city	735 617
12	01700	095	Orange County	26 642	12	35000	031	Duval County	735 617
12	07300		Boca Raton city	74 764	12	35875		Jupiter town	39 328
12	07300	099	Palm Beach County	74 764	12	35875	099	Palm Beach County	39 328
12	07875		Boynton Beach city	60 389	12	36550		Key West city	25 478
12	07875	099	Palm Beach County	60 389	12	36550	087	Monroe County	25 478
12	07950		Bradenton city	49 504	12	36950		Kissimmee city	47 814
12	07950	081	Manatee County	49 504	12	36950	097	Osceola County	47 814
12	10275		Cape Coral city	102 286	12	38250		Lakeland city	78 452
12	10275	071	Lee County	102 286	12	38250	105	Polk County	78 452
12	12875		Clearwater city	108 787	12	39075		Lake Worth city	35 133
12	12875	103	Pinellas County	108 787	12	39075	099	Palm Beach County	35 133
12	13275		Coconut Creek city	43 566	12	39425		Largo city	69 371
12	13275	011	Broward County	43 566	12	39425	103	Pinellas County	69 371
12	14125		Cooper City city	27 939	12	39525		Lauderdale Lakes city	31 705
12	14125	011	Broward County	27 939	12	39525	011	Broward County	31 705
12	14250		Coral Gables city	42 249	12	39550		Lauderhill city	57 585
12	14250	086	Miami-Dade County	42 249	12	39550	011	Broward County	57 585
12	14400		Coral Springs city	117 549	12	43125		Margate city	53 909
12	14400	011	Broward County	117 549	12	43125	011	Broward County	53 909
12	16475		Davie town	75 720	12	43975		Melbourne city	71 382
12	16475	011	Broward County	75 720	12	43975	009	Brevard County	71 382
12	16525		Daytona Beach city	64 112	12	45000		Miami city	362 470
12	16525	127	Volusia County	64 112	12	45000	086	Miami-Dade County	362 470
12	16725		Deerfield Beach city	64 583	12	45025		Miami Beach city	87 933
12	16725	011	Broward County	64 583	12	45025	086	Miami-Dade County	87 933
12	17100		Delray Beach city	60 020	12	45975		Miramar city	72 739
12	17100	099	Palm Beach County	60 020	12	45975	011	Broward County	72 739
12	18575		Dunedin city	35 691	12	49425		North Lauderdale city	32 264
12	18575	103	Pinellas County	35 691	12	49425	011	Broward County	32 264
12	24000		Fort Lauderdale city	152 397	12	49450		North Miami city	59 880
12	24000	011	Broward County	152 397	12	49450	086	Miami-Dade County	59 880
12	24125		Fort Myers city	48 208	12	49475		North Miami Beach city	40 786
12	24125	071	Lee County	48 208	12	49475	086	Miami-Dade County	40 786
12	24300		Fort Pierce city	37 516	12	50575		Oakland Park city	30 966
12	24300	111	St. Lucie County	37 516	12	50575	011	Broward County	30 966

Cities by County – Continued

State Code	Place Code	County Code	Geographic Area Name	2000 Census Population	State Code	Place Code	County Code	Geographic Area Name	2000 Census Population
12	50750		Ocala city	45 943	12	76582		Weston city	49 286
12	50750	083	Marion County	45 943	12	76582	011	Broward County	49 286
12	53000		Orlando city	185 951	12	76600		West Palm Beach city	82 103
12	53000	095	Orange County	185 951	12	76600	099	Palm Beach County	82 103
12	53150		Ormond Beach city	36 301	12	78275		Winter Haven city	26 487
12	53150	127	Volusia County	36 301	12	78275	105	Polk County	26 487
12	53575		Oviedo city	26 316	12	78325		Winter Springs city	31 666
12	53575	117	Seminole County	26 316	12	78325	117	Seminole County	31 666
12	54000		Palm Bay city	79 413	13			**GEORGIA**	8 186 453
12	54000	009	Brevard County	79 413	13	01052		Albany city	76 939
					13	01052	095	Dougherty County	76 939
12	54075		Palm Beach Gardens city	35 058					
12	54075	099	Palm Beach County	35 058	13	01696		Alpharetta city	34 854
					13	01696	121	Fulton County	34 854
12	54700		Panama City city	36 417					
12	54700	005	Bay County	36 417	13	03436		Athens-Clarke County	101 489
12	55775		Pembroke Pines city	137 427	13	04000		Atlanta city	416 474
12	55775	011	Broward County	137 427	13	04000	089	DeKalb County	29 775
					13	04000	121	Fulton County	386 699
12	55925		Pensacola city	56 255					
12	55925	033	Escambia County	56 255	13	04200		Augusta-Richmond County	199 775
12	56975		Pinellas Park city	45 658	13	19000		Columbus city	186 291
12	56975	103	Pinellas County	45 658					
					13	21380		Dalton city	27 912
12	57425		Plantation city	82 934	13	21380	313	Whitfield County	27 912
12	57425	011	Broward County	82 934	13	25720		East Point city	39 595
12	57550		Plant City city	29 915	13	25720	121	Fulton County	39 595
12	57550	057	Hillsborough County	29 915					
					13	31908		Gainesville city	25 578
12	58050		Pompano Beach city	78 191	13	31908	139	Hall County	25 578
12	58050	011	Broward County	78 191					
					13	38964		Hinesville city	30 392
12	58575		Port Orange city	45 823	13	38964	179	Liberty County	30 392
12	58575	127	Volusia County	45 823					
					13	44340		LaGrange city	25 998
12	58715		Port St. Lucie city	88 769	13	44340	285	Troup County	25 998
12	58715	111	St. Lucie County	88 769					
					13	49000		Macon city	97 255
12	60975		Riviera Beach city	29 884	13	49000	021	Bibb County	96 777
12	60975	099	Palm Beach County	29 884	13	49000	169	Jones County	478
12	63000		St. Petersburg city	248 232	13	49756		Marietta city	58 748
12	63000	103	Pinellas County	248 232	13	49756	067	Cobb County	58 748
12	63650		Sanford city	38 291	13	59724		Peachtree City city	31 580
12	63650	117	Seminole County	38 291	13	59724	113	Fayette County	31 580
12	64175		Sarasota city	52 715	13	66668		Rome city	34 980
12	64175	115	Sarasota County	52 715	13	66668	115	Floyd County	34 980
12	69700		Sunrise city	85 779	13	67284		Roswell city	79 334
12	69700	011	Broward County	85 779	13	67284	121	Fulton County	79 334
12	70600		Tallahassee city	150 624	13	69000		Savannah city	131 510
12	70600	073	Leon County	150 624	13	69000	051	Chatham County	131 510
12	70675		Tamarac city	55 588	13	71492		Smyrna city	40 999
12	70675	011	Broward County	55 588	13	71492	067	Cobb County	40 999
12	71000		Tampa city	303 447	13	78800		Valdosta city	43 724
12	71000	057	Hillsborough County	303 447	13	78800	185	Lowndes County	43 724
12	71900		Titusville city	40 670					
12	71900	009	Brevard County	40 670					

Appendix E

E-9

Cities by County – Continued

State Code	Place Code	County Code	Geographic Area Name	2000 Census Population	State Code	Place Code	County Code	Geographic Area Name	2000 Census Population
13	80508		Warner Robins city	48 804	17	03012		Aurora city	142 990
13	80508	153	Houston County	48 787	17	03012	043	DuPage County	38 905
13	80508	225	Peach County	17	17	03012	089	Kane County	100 290
					17	03012	093	Kendall County	840
15			HAWAII	1 211 537	17	03012	197	Will County	2 955
15	14650		Hilo CDP	40 759					
15	14650	001	Hawaii County	40 759	17	04013		Bartlett village	36 706
					17	04013	031	Cook County	12 196
15	17000		Honolulu CDP	371 657	17	04013	043	DuPage County	24 508
15	17000	003	Honolulu County	371 657	17	04013	089	Kane County	2
15	23150		Kailua CDP	36 513	17	04845		Belleville city	41 410
15	23150	003	Honolulu County	36 513	17	04845	163	St. Clair County	41 410
15	28250		Kaneohe CDP	34 970	17	05573		Berwyn city	54 016
15	28250	003	Honolulu County	34 970	17	05573	031	Cook County	54 016
15	51050		Mililani Town CDP	28 608	17	06613		Bloomington city	64 808
15	51050	003	Honolulu County	28 608	17	06613	113	McLean County	64 808
15	62600		Pearl City CDP	30 976	17	07133		Bolingbrook village	56 321
15	62600	003	Honolulu County	30 976	17	07133	043	DuPage County	1 748
15	77750		Waimalu CDP	29 371	17	07133	197	Will County	54 573
15	77750	003	Honolulu County	29 371	17	09447		Buffalo Grove village	42 909
15	79700		Waipahu CDP	33 108	17	09447	031	Cook County	14 418
15	79700	003	Honolulu County	33 108	17	09447	097	Lake County	28 491
16			IDAHO	1 293 953	17	09642		Burbank city	27 902
16	08830		Boise City city	185 787	17	09642	031	Cook County	27 902
16	08830	001	Ada County	185 787	17	10487		Calumet City city	39 071
16	12250		Caldwell city	25 967	17	10487	031	Cook County	39 071
16	12250	027	Canyon County	25 967	17	11332		Carol Stream village	40 438
16	16750		Coeur d'Alene city	34 514	17	11332	043	DuPage County	40 438
16	16750	055	Kootenai County	34 514	17	11358		Carpentersville village	30 586
16	39700		Idaho Falls city	50 730	17	11358	089	Kane County	30 586
16	39700	019	Bonneville County	50 730	17	12385		Champaign city	67 518
16	46540		Lewiston city	30 904	17	12385	019	Champaign County	67 518
16	46540	069	Nez Perce County	30 904	17	14000		Chicago city	2 896 016
16	52120		Meridian city	34 919	17	14000	031	Cook County	2 896 014
16	52120	001	Ada County	34 919	17	14000	043	DuPage County	2
16	56260		Nampa city	51 867	17	14026		Chicago Heights city	32 776
16	56260	027	Canyon County	51 867	17	14026	031	Cook County	32 776
16	64090		Pocatello city	51 466	17	14351		Cicero town	85 616
16	64090	005	Bannock County	51 442	17	14351	031	Cook County	85 616
16	64090	077	Power County	24	17	17887		Crystal Lake city	38 000
16	82810		Twin Falls city	34 469	17	17887	111	McHenry County	38 000
16	82810	083	Twin Falls County	34 469	17	18563		Danville city	33 904
17			ILLINOIS	12 419 293	17	18563	183	Vermilion County	33 904
17	00243		Addison village	35 914	17	18823		Decatur city	81 860
17	00243	043	DuPage County	35 914	17	18823	115	Macon County	81 860
17	01114		Alton city	30 496	17	19161		DeKalb city	39 018
17	01114	119	Madison County	30 496	17	19161	037	DeKalb County	39 018
17	02154		Arlington Heights village	76 031	17	19642		Des Plaines city	58 720
17	02154	031	Cook County	76 031	17	19642	031	Cook County	58 720
17	02154	097	Lake County	0	17	20292		Dolton village	25 614
					17	20292	031	Cook County	25 614

Cities by County – Continued

State Code	Place Code	County Code	Geographic Area Name	2000 Census Population	State Code	Place Code	County Code	Geographic Area Name	2000 Census Population
17	20591		Downers Grove village	48 724	17	47774		Maywood village....................	26 987
17	20591	043	DuPage County	48 724	17	47774	031	Cook County	26 987
17	22255		East St. Louis city	31 542	17	49867		Moline city	43 768
17	22255	163	St. Clair County	31 542	17	49867	161	Rock Island County	43 768
17	23074		Elgin city	94 487	17	51089		Mount Prospect village...........	56 265
17	23074	031	Cook County	20 474	17	51089	031	Cook County	56 265
17	23074	089	Kane County	74 013	17	51349		Mundelein village..............	30 935
17	23256		Elk Grove Village village	34 727	17	51349	097	Lake County	30 935
17	23256	031	Cook County	34 727	17	51622		Naperville city	128 358
17	23256	043	DuPage County	0	17	51622	043	DuPage County	90 984
17	23620		Elmhurst city	42 762	17	51622	197	Will County	37 374
17	23620	031	Cook County	0	17	53000		Niles village	30 068
17	23620	043	DuPage County	42 762	17	53000	031	Cook County	30 068
17	23724		Elmwood Park village..............	25 405	17	53234		Normal town	45 386
17	23724	031	Cook County	25 405	17	53234	113	McLean County....................	45 386
17	24582		Evanston city	74 239	17	53481		Northbrook village.............	33 435
17	24582	031	Cook County	74 239	17	53481	031	Cook County	33 435
17	27884		Freeport city	26 443	17	53559		North Chicago city.............	35 918
17	27884	177	Stephenson County	26 443	17	53559	097	Lake County	35 918
17	28326		Galesburg city	33 706	17	54638		Oak Forest city	28 051
17	28326	095	Knox County	33 706	17	54638	031	Cook County	28 051
17	29730		Glendale Heights village	31 765	17	54820		Oak Lawn village................	55 245
17	29730	043	DuPage County	31 765	17	54820	031	Cook County	55 245
17	29756		Glen Ellyn village..............	26 999	17	54885		Oak Park village................	52 524
17	29756	043	DuPage County	26 999	17	54885	031	Cook County	52 524
17	29938		Glenview village	41 847	17	56640		Orland Park village................	51 077
17	29938	031	Cook County	41 847	17	56640	031	Cook County	51 071
17	30926		Granite City city	31 301	17	56640	197	Will County	6
17	30926	119	Madison County	31 301	17	57225		Palatine village	65 479
17	32018		Gurnee village	28 834	17	57225	031	Cook County	65 479
17	32018	097	Lake County	28 834	17	57875		Park Ridge city	37 775
17	32746		Hanover Park village....................	38 278	17	57875	031	Cook County	37 775
17	32746	031	Cook County	20 755	17	58447		Pekin city....................	33 857
17	32746	043	DuPage County	17 523	17	58447	143	Peoria County	0
17	33383		Harvey city....................	30 000	17	58447	179	Tazewell County	33 857
17	33383	031	Cook County	30 000	17	59000		Peoria city....................	112 936
17	34722		Highland Park city	31 365	17	59000	143	Peoria County	112 936
17	34722	097	Lake County	31 365	17	62367		Quincy city....................	40 366
17	35411		Hoffman Estates village	49 495	17	62367	001	Adams County	40 366
17	35411	031	Cook County	49 495	17	65000		Rockford city....................	150 115
17	35411	089	Kane County	0	17	65000	201	Winnebago County	150 115
17	38570		Joliet city....................	106 221	17	65078		Rock Island city....................	39 684
17	38570	093	Kendall County	624	17	65078	161	Rock Island County	39 684
17	38570	197	Will County	105 597	17	66040		Round Lake Beach village	25 859
17	38934		Kankakee city....................	27 491	17	66040	097	Lake County	25 859
17	38934	091	Kankakee County	27 491	17	66703		St. Charles city....................	27 896
17	42028		Lansing village....................	28 332	17	66703	043	DuPage County	169
17	42028	031	Cook County	28 332	17	66703	089	Kane County	27 727
17	44407		Lombard village....................	42 322					
17	44407	043	DuPage County	42 322					

Cities by County – Continued

State Code	Place Code	County Code	Geographic Area Name	2000 Census Population	State Code	Place Code	County Code	Geographic Area Name	2000 Census Population
17	68003		Schaumburg village	75 386	18	29898		Greenwood city	36 037
17	68003	031	Cook County	75 386	18	29898	081	Johnson County	36 037
17	68003	043	DuPage County	0	18	31000		Hammond city	83 048
17	70122		Skokie village	63 348	18	31000	089	Lake County	83 048
17	70122	031	Cook County	63 348	18	34114		Hobart city	25 363
17	72000		Springfield city	111 454	18	34114	089	Lake County	25 363
17	72000	167	Sangamon County	111 454	18	36000		Indianapolis city	791 926
17	73157		Streamwood village	36 407	18	38358		Jeffersonville city	27 362
17	73157	031	Cook County	36 407	18	38358	019	Clark County	27 362
17	75484		Tinley Park village	48 401	18	40392		Kokomo city	46 113
17	75484	031	Cook County	45 887	18	40392	067	Howard County	46 113
17	75484	197	Will County	2 514	18	40788		Lafayette city	56 397
17	77005		Urbana city	36 395	18	40788	157	Tippecanoe County	56 397
17	77005	019	Champaign County	36 395	18	42426		Lawrence city	38 915
17	79293		Waukegan city	87 901	18	42426	097	Marion County	38 915
17	79293	097	Lake County	87 901	18	46908		Marion city	31 320
17	81048		Wheaton city	55 416	18	46908	053	Grant County	31 320
17	81048	043	DuPage County	55 416	18	48528		Merrillville town	30 560
17	81087		Wheeling village	34 496	18	48528	089	Lake County	30 560
17	81087	031	Cook County	34 496	18	48798		Michigan City city	32 900
17	81087	097	Lake County	0	18	48798	091	LaPorte County	32 900
17	82075		Wilmette village	27 651	18	49932		Mishawaka city	46 557
17	82075	031	Cook County	27 651	18	49932	141	St. Joseph County	46 557
17	83245		Woodridge village	30 934	18	51876		Muncie city	67 430
17	83245	031	Cook County	0	18	51876	035	Delaware County	67 430
17	83245	043	DuPage County	30 934	18	52326		New Albany city	37 603
17	83245	197	Will County	0	18	52326	043	Floyd County	37 603
18			INDIANA	6 080 485	18	54180		Noblesville city	28 590
18	01468		Anderson city	59 734	18	54180	057	Hamilton County	28 590
18	01468	095	Madison County	59 734	18	61092		Portage city	33 496
18	05860		Bloomington city	69 291	18	61092	127	Porter County	33 496
18	05860	105	Monroe County	69 291	18	64260		Richmond city	39 124
18	10342		Carmel city	37 733	18	64260	177	Wayne County	39 124
18	10342	057	Hamilton County	37 733	18	71000		South Bend city	107 789
18	14734		Columbus city	39 059	18	71000	141	St. Joseph County	107 789
18	14734	005	Bartholomew County	39 059	18	75428		Terre Haute city	59 614
18	19486		East Chicago city	32 414	18	75428	167	Vigo County	59 614
18	19486	089	Lake County	32 414	18	78326		Valparaiso city	27 428
18	20728		Elkhart city	51 874	18	78326	127	Porter County	27 428
18	20728	039	Elkhart County	51 874	18	82862		West Lafayette city	28 778
18	22000		Evansville city	121 582	18	82862	157	Tippecanoe County	28 778
18	22000	163	Vanderburgh County	121 582	19			IOWA	2 926 324
18	23278		Fishers town	37 835	19	01855		Ames city	50 731
18	23278	057	Hamilton County	37 835	19	01855	169	Story County	50 731
18	25000		Fort Wayne city	205 727	19	02305		Ankeny city	27 117
18	25000	003	Allen County	205 727	19	02305	153	Polk County	27 117
18	27000		Gary city	102 746	19	06355		Bettendorf city	31 275
18	27000	089	Lake County	102 746	19	06355	163	Scott County	31 275
18	28386		Goshen city	29 383					
18	28386	039	Elkhart County	29 383					

Cities by County – Continued

State Code	Place Code	County Code	Geographic Area Name	2000 Census Population	State Code	Place Code	County Code	Geographic Area Name	2000 Census Population
19	09550		Burlington city.............................	26 839	20	38900		Lawrence city	80 098
19	09550	057	Des Moines County	26 839	20	38900	045	Douglas County	80 098
19	11755		Cedar Falls city............................	36 145	20	39000		Leavenworth city..........................	35 420
19	11755	013	Black Hawk County	36 145	20	39000	103	Leavenworth County.................	35 420
19	12000		Cedar Rapids city	120 758	20	39075		Leawood city	27 656
19	12000	113	Linn County.................................	120 758	20	39075	091	Johnson County........................	27 656
19	14430		Clinton city..................................	27 772	20	39350		Lenexa city	40 238
19	14430	045	Clinton County	27 772	20	39350	091	Johnson County........................	40 238
19	16860		Council Bluffs city........................	58 268	20	44250		Manhattan city	44 831
19	16860	155	Pottawattamie County...............	58 268	20	44250	149	Pottawatomie County................	3
19	19000		Davenport city	98 359	20	44250	161	Riley County	44 828
19	19000	163	Scott County	98 359	20	52575		Olathe city	92 962
19	21000		Des Moines city	198 682	20	52575	091	Johnson County........................	92 962
19	21000	153	Polk County	198 682	20	53775		Overland Park city	149 080
19	22395		Dubuque city	57 686	20	53775	091	Johnson County........................	149 080
19	22395	061	Dubuque County	57 686	20	62700		Salina city	45 679
19	28515		Fort Dodge city............................	25 136	20	62700	169	Saline County	45 679
19	28515	187	Webster County	25 136	20	64500		Shawnee city	47 996
19	38595		Iowa City city...............................	62 220	20	64500	091	Johnson County........................	47 996
19	38595	103	Johnson County	62 220	20	71000		Topeka city	122 377
19	49485		Marion city	26 294	20	71000	177	Shawnee County	122 377
19	49485	113	Linn County.................................	26 294	20	79000		Wichita city	344 284
19	49755		Marshalltown city	26 009	20	79000	173	Sedgwick County	344 284
19	49755	127	Marshall County..........................	26 009	21			**KENTUCKY**	4 041 769
19	50160		Mason City city............................	29 172	21	08902		Bowling Green city	49 296
19	50160	033	Cerro Gordo County	29 172	21	08902	227	Warren County	49 296
19	73335		Sioux City city..............................	85 013	21	17848		Covington city	43 370
19	73335	149	Plymouth County	0	21	17848	117	Kenton County	43 370
19	73335	193	Woodbury County	85 013	21	28900		Frankfort city................................	27 741
19	79950		Urbandale city	29 072	21	28900	073	Franklin County........................	27 741
19	79950	049	Dallas County	327	21	35866		Henderson city	27 373
19	79950	153	Polk County	28 745	21	35866	101	Henderson County....................	27 373
19	82425		Waterloo city................................	68 747	21	37918		Hopkinsville city...........................	30 089
19	82425	013	Black Hawk County	68 747	21	37918	047	Christian County	30 089
19	83910		West Des Moines city	46 403	21	40222		Jeffersontown city.........................	26 633
19	83910	049	Dallas County	3 878	21	40222	111	Jefferson County......................	26 633
19	83910	153	Polk County	42 525	21	46027		Lexington-Fayette.........................	260 512
20			**KANSAS**	2 688 418	21	46027	067	Fayette County	260 512
20	18250		Dodge City city	25 176	21	48000		Louisville city	256 231
20	18250	057	Ford County	25 176	21	48000	111	Jefferson County......................	256 231
20	21275		Emporia city	26 760	21	58620		Owensboro city.............................	54 067
20	21275	111	Lyon County...............................	26 760	21	58620	059	Daviess County........................	54 067
20	25325		Garden City city	28 451	21	58836		Paducah city................................	26 307
20	25325	055	Finney County............................	28 451	21	58836	145	McCracken County	26 307
20	33625		Hutchinson city	40 787	21	65226		Richmond city	27 152
20	33625	155	Reno County	40 787	21	65226	151	Madison County	27 152
20	36000		Kansas City city...........................	146 866	22			**LOUISIANA**	4 468 976
20	36000	209	Wyandotte County	146 866	22	00975		Alexandria city	46 342
					22	00975	079	Rapides Parish	46 342

State Code	Place Code	County Code	Geographic Area Name	2000 Census Population
22	05000		Baton Rouge city	227 818
22	05000	033	East Baton Rouge Parish	227 818
22	08920		Bossier City city	56 461
22	08920	015	Bossier Parish	56 461
22	36255		Houma city	32 393
22	36255	109	Terrebonne Parish	32 393
22	39475		Kenner city	70 517
22	39475	051	Jefferson Parish	70 517
22	40735		Lafayette city	110 257
22	40735	055	Lafayette Parish	110 257
22	41155		Lake Charles city	71 757
22	41155	019	Calcasieu Parish	71 757
22	51410		Monroe city	53 107
22	51410	073	Ouachita Parish	53 107
22	54035		New Iberia city	32 623
22	54035	045	Iberia Parish	32 623
22	55000		New Orleans city	484 674
22	55000	071	Orleans Parish	484 674
22	70000		Shreveport city	200 145
22	70000	015	Bossier Parish	734
22	70000	017	Caddo Parish	199 411
22	70805		Slidell city	25 695
22	70805	103	St. Tammany Parish	25 695
23			**MAINE**	1 274 923
23	02795		Bangor city	31 473
23	02795	019	Penobscot County	31 473
23	38740		Lewiston city	35 690
23	38740	001	Androscoggin County	35 690
23	60545		Portland city	64 249
23	60545	005	Cumberland County	64 249
24			**MARYLAND**	5 296 486
24	01600		Annapolis city	35 838
24	01600	003	Anne Arundel County	35 838
24	04000		Baltimore city	651 154
24	04000	510	Baltimore city	651 154
24	08775		Bowie city	50 269
24	08775	033	Prince George's County	50 269
24	30325		Frederick city	52 767
24	30325	021	Frederick County	52 767
24	31175		Gaithersburg city	52 613
24	31175	031	Montgomery County	52 613
24	36075		Hagerstown city	36 687
24	36075	043	Washington County	36 687
24	67675		Rockville city	47 388
24	67675	031	Montgomery County	47 388
25			**MASSACHUSETTS**	6 349 097
25	00765		Agawam city	28 144
25	00765	013	Hampden County	28 144

State Code	Place Code	County Code	Geographic Area Name	2000 Census Population
25	02690		Attleboro city	42 068
25	02690	005	Bristol County	42 068
25	03600		Barnstable Town city	47 821
25	03600	001	Barnstable County	47 821
25	05595		Beverly city	39 862
25	05595	009	Essex County	39 862
25	07000		Boston city	589 141
25	07000	025	Suffolk County	589 141
25	09000		Brockton city	94 304
25	09000	023	Plymouth County	94 304
25	11000		Cambridge city	101 355
25	11000	017	Middlesex County	101 355
25	13205		Chelsea city	35 080
25	13205	025	Suffolk County	35 080
25	13660		Chicopee city	54 653
25	13660	013	Hampden County	54 653
25	21990		Everett city	38 037
25	21990	017	Middlesex County	38 037
25	23000		Fall River city	91 938
25	23000	005	Bristol County	91 938
25	23875		Fitchburg city	39 102
25	23875	027	Worcester County	39 102
25	25100		Franklin city	29 560
25	25100	021	Norfolk County	29 560
25	26150		Gloucester city	30 273
25	26150	009	Essex County	30 273
25	29405		Haverhill city	58 969
25	29405	009	Essex County	58 969
25	30840		Holyoke city	39 838
25	30840	013	Hampden County	39 838
25	34550		Lawrence city	72 043
25	34550	009	Essex County	72 043
25	35075		Leominster city	41 303
25	35075	027	Worcester County	41 303
25	37000		Lowell city	105 167
25	37000	017	Middlesex County	105 167
25	37490		Lynn city	89 050
25	37490	009	Essex County	89 050
25	37875		Malden city	56 340
25	37875	017	Middlesex County	56 340
25	38715		Marlborough city	36 255
25	38715	017	Middlesex County	36 255
25	39835		Medford city	55 765
25	39835	017	Middlesex County	55 765
25	40115		Melrose city	27 134
25	40115	017	Middlesex County	27 134
25	40710		Methuen city	43 789
25	40710	009	Essex County	43 789

State Code	Place Code	County Code	Geographic Area Name	2000 Census Population	State Code	Place Code	County Code	Geographic Area Name	2000 Census Population
25	45000		New Bedford city	93 768	26	24120		East Lansing city	46 525
25	45000	005	Bristol County	93 768	26	24120	037	Clinton County	34
					26	24120	065	Ingham County	46 491
25	45560		Newton city	83 829					
25	45560	017	Middlesex County	83 829	26	24290		Eastpointe city	34 077
					26	24290	099	Macomb County	34 077
25	46330		Northampton city	28 978					
25	46330	015	Hampshire County	28 978	26	27440		Farmington Hills city	82 111
					26	27440	125	Oakland County	82 111
25	52490		Peabody city	48 129					
25	52490	009	Essex County	48 129	26	29000		Flint city	124 943
					26	29000	049	Genesee County	124 943
25	53960		Pittsfield city	45 793					
25	53960	003	Berkshire County	45 793	26	31420		Garden City city	30 047
					26	31420	163	Wayne County	30 047
25	55745		Quincy city	88 025					
25	55745	021	Norfolk County	88 025	26	34000		Grand Rapids city	197 800
					26	34000	081	Kent County	197 800
25	56585		Revere city	47 283					
25	56585	025	Suffolk County	47 283	26	38640		Holland city	35 048
					26	38640	005	Allegan County	7 202
25	59105		Salem city	40 407	26	38640	139	Ottawa County	27 846
25	59105	009	Essex County	40 407					
					26	40680		Inkster city	30 115
25	62535		Somerville city	77 478	26	40680	163	Wayne County	30 115
25	62535	017	Middlesex County	77 478					
					26	41420		Jackson city	36 316
25	67000		Springfield city	152 082	26	41420	075	Jackson County	36 316
25	67000	013	Hampden County	152 082					
					26	42160		Kalamazoo city	77 145
25	69170		Taunton city	55 976	26	42160	077	Kalamazoo County	77 145
25	69170	005	Bristol County	55 976					
					26	42820		Kentwood city	45 255
25	72600		Waltham city	59 226	26	42820	081	Kent County	45 255
25	72600	017	Middlesex County	59 226					
					26	46000		Lansing city	119 128
25	76030		Westfield city	40 072	26	46000	045	Eaton County	4 807
25	76030	013	Hampden County	40 072	26	46000	065	Ingham County	114 321
25	81035		Woburn city	37 258	26	47800		Lincoln Park city	40 008
25	81035	017	Middlesex County	37 258	26	47800	163	Wayne County	40 008
25	82000		Worcester city	172 648	26	49000		Livonia city	100 545
25	82000	027	Worcester County	172 648	26	49000	163	Wayne County	100 545
26			**MICHIGAN**	9 938 444	26	50560		Madison Heights city	31 101
26	01380		Allen Park city	29 376	26	50560	125	Oakland County	31 101
26	01380	163	Wayne County	29 376					
					26	53780		Midland city	41 685
26	03000		Ann Arbor city	114 024	26	53780	017	Bay County	222
26	03000	161	Washtenaw County	114 024	26	53780	111	Midland County	41 463
26	05920		Battle Creek city	53 364	26	56020		Mount Pleasant city	25 946
26	05920	025	Calhoun County	53 364	26	56020	073	Isabella County	25 946
26	06020		Bay City city	36 817	26	56320		Muskegon city	40 105
26	06020	017	Bay County	36 817	26	56320	121	Muskegon County	40 105
26	12060		Burton city	30 308	26	59440		Novi city	47 386
26	12060	049	Genesee County	30 308	26	59440	125	Oakland County	47 386
26	21000		Dearborn city	97 775	26	59920		Oak Park city	29 793
26	21000	163	Wayne County	97 775	26	59920	125	Oakland County	29 793
26	21020		Dearborn Heights city	58 264	26	65440		Pontiac city	66 337
26	21020	163	Wayne County	58 264	26	65440	125	Oakland County	66 337
26	22000		Detroit city	951 270	26	65560		Portage city	44 897
26	22000	163	Wayne County	951 270	26	65560	077	Kalamazoo County	44 897

Cities by County – Continued

State Code	Place Code	County Code	Geographic Area Name	2000 Census Population	State Code	Place Code	County Code	Geographic Area Name	2000 Census Population
26	65820		Port Huron city	32 338	27	13456		Cottage Grove city	30 582
26	65820	147	St. Clair County	32 338	27	13456	163	Washington County	30 582
26	69035		Rochester Hills city	68 825	27	17000		Duluth city	86 918
26	69035	125	Oakland County	68 825	27	17000	137	St. Louis County	86 918
26	69800		Roseville city	48 129	27	17288		Eagan city	63 557
26	69800	099	Macomb County	48 129	27	17288	037	Dakota County	63 557
26	70040		Royal Oak city	60 062	27	18116		Eden Prairie city	54 901
26	70040	125	Oakland County	60 062	27	18116	053	Hennepin County	54 901
26	70520		Saginaw city	61 799	27	18188		Edina city	47 425
26	70520	145	Saginaw County	61 799	27	18188	053	Hennepin County	47 425
26	70760		St. Clair Shores city	63 096	27	22814		Fridley city	27 449
26	70760	099	Macomb County	63 096	27	22814	003	Anoka County	27 449
26	74900		Southfield city	78 296	27	31076		Inver Grove Heights city	29 751
26	74900	125	Oakland County	78 296	27	31076	037	Dakota County	29 751
26	74960		Southgate city	30 136	27	35180		Lakeville city	43 128
26	74960	163	Wayne County	30 136	27	35180	037	Dakota County	43 128
26	76460		Sterling Heights city	124 471	27	39878		Mankato city	32 427
26	76460	099	Macomb County	124 471	27	39878	013	Blue Earth County	32 427
					27	39878	079	Le Sueur County	0
26	79000		Taylor city	65 868	27	39878	103	Nicollet County	0
26	79000	163	Wayne County	65 868	27	40166		Maple Grove city	50 365
26	80700		Troy city	80 959	27	40166	053	Hennepin County	50 365
26	80700	125	Oakland County	80 959	27	40382		Maplewood city	34 947
26	84000		Warren city	138 247	27	40382	123	Ramsey County	34 947
26	84000	099	Macomb County	138 247	27	43000		Minneapolis city	382 618
26	86000		Westland city	86 602	27	43000	053	Hennepin County	382 618
26	86000	163	Wayne County	86 602	27	43252		Minnetonka city	51 301
26	88900		Wyandotte city	28 006	27	43252	053	Hennepin County	51 301
26	88900	163	Wayne County	28 006	27	43864		Moorhead city	32 177
26	88940		Wyoming city	69 368	27	43864	027	Clay County	32 177
26	88940	081	Kent County	69 368	27	47680		Oakdale city	26 653
27			**MINNESOTA**	4 919 479	27	47680	163	Washington County	26 653
27	01486		Andover city	26 588	27	51730		Plymouth city	65 894
27	01486	003	Anoka County	26 588	27	51730	053	Hennepin County	65 894
27	01900		Apple Valley city	45 527	27	54214		Richfield city	34 439
27	01900	037	Dakota County	45 527	27	54214	053	Hennepin County	34 439
27	06382		Blaine city	44 942	27	54880		Rochester city	85 806
27	06382	003	Anoka County	44 942	27	54880	109	Olmsted County	85 806
27	06382	123	Ramsey County	0	27	55852		Roseville city	33 690
27	06616		Bloomington city	85 172	27	55852	123	Ramsey County	33 690
27	06616	053	Hennepin County	85 172	27	56896		St. Cloud city	59 107
27	07948		Brooklyn Center city	29 172	27	56896	009	Benton County	6 391
27	07948	053	Hennepin County	29 172	27	56896	141	Sherburne County	5 982
27	07966		Brooklyn Park city	67 388	27	56896	145	Stearns County	46 734
27	07966	053	Hennepin County	67 388	27	57220		St. Louis Park city	44 126
27	08794		Burnsville city	60 220	27	57220	053	Hennepin County	44 126
27	08794	037	Dakota County	60 220	27	58000		St. Paul city	287 151
27	13114		Coon Rapids city	61 607	27	58000	123	Ramsey County	287 151
27	13114	003	Anoka County	61 607					

Cities by County – Continued

State Code	Place Code	County Code	Geographic Area Name	2000 Census Population	State Code	Place Code	County Code	Geographic Area Name	2000 Census Population
27	59998		Shoreview city	25 924	29	35000		Independence city	113 288
27	59998	123	Ramsey County	25 924	29	35000	047	Clay County	0
					29	35000	095	Jackson County	113 288
27	71032		Winona city................................	27 069					
27	71032	169	Winona County	27 069	29	37000		Jefferson City city	39 636
					29	37000	027	Callaway County	25
27	71428		Woodbury city.............................	46 463	29	37000	051	Cole County	39 611
27	71428	163	Washington County	46 463					
					29	37592		Joplin city	45 504
28			**MISSISSIPPI**............................	2 844 658	29	37592	097	Jasper County	40 433
28	06220		Biloxi city	50 644	29	37592	145	Newton County	5 071
28	06220	047	Harrison County	50 644					
					29	38000		Kansas City city	441 545
28	15380		Columbus city............................	25 944	29	38000	037	Cass County	104
28	15380	087	Lowndes County	25 944	29	38000	047	Clay County	84 009
					29	38000	095	Jackson County	322 806
28	29180		Greenville city............................	41 633	29	38000	165	Platte County	34 626
28	29180	151	Washington County	41 633					
					29	39044		Kirkwood city	27 324
28	29700		Gulfport city	71 127	29	39044	189	St. Louis County	27 324
28	29700	047	Harrison County	71 127					
					29	41348		Lee's Summit city	70 700
28	31020		Hattiesburg city............................	44 779	29	41348	037	Cass County	1 180
28	31020	035	Forrest County	42 475	29	41348	095	Jackson County	69 520
28	31020	073	Lamar County	2 304					
					29	42032		Liberty city	26 232
28	36000		Jackson city............................	184 256	29	42032	047	Clay County	26 232
28	36000	049	Hinds County	183 723					
28	36000	089	Madison County	533	29	46586		Maryland Heights city	25 756
28	36000	121	Rankin County	0	29	46586	189	St. Louis County	25 756
28	46640		Meridian city	39 968	29	54074		O'Fallon city........................	46 169
28	46640	075	Lauderdale County	39 968	29	54074	183	St. Charles County	46 169
28	55360		Pascagoula city..........................	26 200	29	60788		Raytown city	30 388
28	55360	059	Jackson County	26 200	29	60788	095	Jackson County	30 388
28	69280		Southaven city............................	28 977	29	64082		St. Charles city	60 321
28	69280	033	DeSoto County	28 977	29	64082	183	St. Charles County	60 321
28	74840		Tupelo city............................	34 211	29	64550		St. Joseph city	73 990
28	74840	081	Lee County	34 211	29	64550	021	Buchanan County	73 990
28	76720		Vicksburg city............................	26 407	29	65000		St. Louis city	348 189
28	76720	149	Warren County	26 407	29	65000	510	St. Louis city	348 189
29			**MISSOURI**	5 595 211	29	65126		St. Peters city	51 381
29	03160		Ballwin city............................	31 283	29	65126	183	St. Charles County	51 381
29	03160	189	St. Louis County	31 283					
					29	70000		Springfield city	151 580
29	06652		Blue Springs city	48 080	29	70000	043	Christian County	4
29	06652	095	Jackson County	48 080	29	70000	077	Greene County	151 576
29	11242		Cape Girardeau city	35 349	29	75220		University City city	37 428
29	11242	031	Cape Girardeau County.............	35 349	29	75220	189	St. Louis County	37 428
29	11242	201	Scott County	0					
					29	79820		Wildwood city	32 884
29	13600		Chesterfield city............................	46 802	29	79820	189	St. Louis County	32 884
29	13600	189	St. Louis County	46 802					
					30			**MONTANA**	902 195
29	15670		Columbia city............................	84 531	30	06550		Billings city	89 847
29	15670	019	Boone County	84 531	30	06550	111	Yellowstone County	89 847
29	24778		Florissant city	50 497	30	08950		Bozeman city	27 509
29	24778	189	St. Louis County	50 497	30	08950	031	Gallatin County	27 509
29	27190		Gladstone city............................	26 365	30	11390		Butte-Silver Bow	34 606
29	27190	047	Clay County	26 365					
					30	32800		Great Falls city	56 690
29	31276		Hazelwood city	26 206	30	32800	013	Cascade County	56 690
29	31276	189	St. Louis County	26 206					

State Code	Place Code	County Code	Geographic Area Name	2000 Census Population
30	35600		Helena city	25 780
30	35600	049	Lewis and Clark County	25 780
30	50200		Missoula city	57 053
30	50200	063	Missoula County	57 053
31			NEBRASKA	1 711 263
31	03950		Bellevue city	44 382
31	03950	153	Sarpy County	44 382
31	17670		Fremont city	25 174
31	17670	053	Dodge County	25 174
31	19595		Grand Island city	42 940
31	19595	079	Hall County	42 940
31	25055		Kearney city	27 431
31	25055	019	Buffalo County	27 431
31	28000		Lincoln city	225 581
31	28000	109	Lancaster County	225 581
31	37000		Omaha city	390 007
31	37000	055	Douglas County	390 007
32			NEVADA	1 998 257
32	09700		Carson City	52 457
32	09700	510	Carson City	52 457
32	31900		Henderson city	175 381
32	31900	003	Clark County	175 381
32	40000		Las Vegas city	478 434
32	40000	003	Clark County	478 434
32	51800		North Las Vegas city	115 488
32	51800	003	Clark County	115 488
32	60600		Reno city	180 480
32	60600	031	Washoe County	180 480
32	68400		Sparks city	66 346
32	68400	031	Washoe County	66 346
33			NEW HAMPSHIRE	1 235 786
33	14200		Concord city	40 687
33	14200	013	Merrimack County	40 687
33	18820		Dover city	26 884
33	18820	017	Strafford County	26 884
33	45140		Manchester city	107 006
33	45140	011	Hillsborough County	107 006
33	50260		Nashua city	86 605
33	50260	011	Hillsborough County	86 605
33	65140		Rochester city	28 461
33	65140	017	Strafford County	28 461
34			NEW JERSEY	8 414 350
34	02080		Atlantic City city	40 517
34	02080	001	Atlantic County	40 517
34	03580		Bayonne city	61 842
34	03580	017	Hudson County	61 842
34	05170		Bergenfield borough	26 247
34	05170	003	Bergen County	26 247
34	10000		Camden city	79 904
34	10000	007	Camden County	79 904
34	13690		Clifton city	78 672
34	13690	031	Passaic County	78 672
34	19390		East Orange city	69 824
34	19390	013	Essex County	69 824
34	21000		Elizabeth city	120 568
34	21000	039	Union County	120 568
34	21480		Englewood city	26 203
34	21480	003	Bergen County	26 203
34	22470		Fair Lawn borough	31 637
34	22470	003	Bergen County	31 637
34	24420		Fort Lee borough	35 461
34	24420	003	Bergen County	35 461
34	25770		Garfield city	29 786
34	25770	003	Bergen County	29 786
34	28680		Hackensack city	42 677
34	28680	003	Bergen County	42 677
34	32250		Hoboken city	38 577
34	32250	017	Hudson County	38 577
34	36000		Jersey City city	240 055
34	36000	017	Hudson County	240 055
34	36510		Kearny town	40 513
34	36510	017	Hudson County	40 513
34	40350		Linden city	39 394
34	40350	039	Union County	39 394
34	41310		Long Branch city	31 340
34	41310	025	Monmouth County	31 340
34	46680		Millville city	26 847
34	46680	011	Cumberland County	26 847
34	51000		Newark city	273 546
34	51000	013	Essex County	273 546
34	51210		New Brunswick city	48 573
34	51210	023	Middlesex County	48 573
34	55950		Paramus borough	25 737
34	55950	003	Bergen County	25 737
34	56550		Passaic city	67 861
34	56550	031	Passaic County	67 861
34	57000		Paterson city	149 222
34	57000	031	Passaic County	149 222
34	58200		Perth Amboy city	47 303
34	58200	023	Middlesex County	47 303
34	59190		Plainfield city	47 829
34	59190	039	Union County	47 829
34	61530		Rahway city	26 500
34	61530	039	Union County	26 500
34	65790		Sayreville borough	40 377
34	65790	023	Middlesex County	40 377

Cities by County – Continued

State Code	Place Code	County Code	Geographic Area Name	2000 Census Population	State Code	Place Code	County Code	Geographic Area Name	2000 Census Population
34	74000		Trenton city	85 403	36	38077		Ithaca city	29 287
34	74000	021	Mercer County	85 403	36	38077	109	Tompkins County	29 287
34	74630		Union City city	67 088	36	38264		Jamestown city	31 730
34	74630	017	Hudson County	67 088	36	38264	013	Chautauqua County	31 730
34	76070		Vineland city	56 271	36	42554		Lindenhurst village	27 819
34	76070	011	Cumberland County	56 271	36	42554	103	Suffolk County	27 819
34	79040		Westfield town	29 644	36	43335		Long Beach city	35 462
34	79040	039	Union County	29 644	36	43335	059	Nassau County	35 462
34	79610		West New York town	45 768	36	47042		Middletown city	25 388
34	79610	017	Hudson County	45 768	36	47042	071	Orange County	25 388
35			**NEW MEXICO**	1 819 046	36	49121		Mount Vernon city	68 381
35	01780		Alamogordo city	35 582	36	49121	119	Westchester County	68 381
35	01780	035	Otero County	35 582					
					36	50034		Newburgh city	28 259
35	02000		Albuquerque city	448 607	36	50034	071	Orange County	28 259
35	02000	001	Bernalillo County	448 607					
					36	50617		New Rochelle city	72 182
35	12150		Carlsbad city	25 625	36	50617	119	Westchester County	72 182
35	12150	015	Eddy County	25 625					
					36	51000		New York city	8 008 278
35	16420		Clovis city	32 667	36	51000	005	Bronx County	1 332 650
35	16420	009	Curry County	32 667	36	51000	047	Kings County	2 465 326
					36	51000	061	New York County	1 537 195
35	25800		Farmington city	37 844	36	51000	081	Queens County	2 229 379
35	25800	045	San Juan County	37 844	36	51000	085	Richmond County	443 728
35	32520		Hobbs city	28 657	36	51055		Niagara Falls city	55 593
35	32520	025	Lea County	28 657	36	51055	063	Niagara County	55 593
35	39380		Las Cruces city	74 267	36	53682		North Tonawanda city	33 262
35	39380	013	Dona Ana County	74 267	36	53682	063	Niagara County	33 262
35	63460		Rio Rancho city	51 765	36	59223		Port Chester village	27 867
35	63460	001	Bernalillo County	0	36	59223	119	Westchester County	27 867
35	63460	043	Sandoval County	51 765					
					36	59641		Poughkeepsie city	29 871
35	64930		Roswell city	45 293	36	59641	027	Dutchess County	29 871
35	64930	005	Chaves County	45 293					
					36	63000		Rochester city	219 773
35	70500		Santa Fe city	62 203	36	63000	055	Monroe County	219 773
35	70500	049	Santa Fe County	62 203					
					36	63418		Rome city	34 950
36			**NEW YORK**	18 976 457	36	63418	065	Oneida County	34 950
36	01000		Albany city	95 658					
36	01000	001	Albany County	95 658	36	65255		Saratoga Springs city	26 186
					36	65255	091	Saratoga County	26 186
36	03078		Auburn city	28 574					
36	03078	011	Cayuga County	28 574	36	65508		Schenectady city	61 821
					36	65508	093	Schenectady County	61 821
36	06607		Binghamton city	47 380					
36	06607	007	Broome County	47 380	36	70420		Spring Valley village	25 464
					36	70420	087	Rockland County	25 464
36	11000		Buffalo city	292 648					
36	11000	029	Erie County	292 648	36	73000		Syracuse city	147 306
					36	73000	067	Onondaga County	147 306
36	24229		Elmira city	30 940					
36	24229	015	Chemung County	30 940	36	75484		Troy city	49 170
					36	75484	083	Rensselaer County	49 170
36	27485		Freeport village	43 783					
36	27485	059	Nassau County	43 783	36	76540		Utica city	60 651
					36	76540	065	Oneida County	60 651
36	29113		Glen Cove city	26 622					
36	29113	059	Nassau County	26 622	36	76705		Valley Stream village	36 368
					36	76705	059	Nassau County	36 368
36	33139		Hempstead village	56 554					
36	33139	059	Nassau County	56 554					

Cities by County – Continued

State Code	Place Code	County Code	Geographic Area Name	2000 Census Population	State Code	Place Code	County Code	Geographic Area Name	2000 Census Population
36	78608		Watertown city	26 705	37	55000		Raleigh city	276 093
36	78608	045	Jefferson County	26 705	37	55000	063	Durham County	0
					37	55000	183	Wake County	276 093
36	81677		White Plains city	53 077					
36	81677	119	Westchester County	53 077	37	57500		Rocky Mount city	55 893
					37	57500	065	Edgecombe County	17 297
36	84000		Yonkers city	196 086	37	57500	127	Nash County	38 596
36	84000	119	Westchester County	196 086					
					37	58860		Salisbury city	26 462
37			**NORTH CAROLINA**	8 049 313	37	58860	159	Rowan County	26 462
37	02140		Asheville city	68 889					
37	02140	021	Buncombe County	68 889	37	74440		Wilmington city	75 838
					37	74440	129	New Hanover County	75 838
37	09060		Burlington city	44 917					
37	09060	001	Alamance County	44 917	37	74540		Wilson city	44 405
					37	74540	195	Wilson County	44 405
37	10740		Cary town	94 536					
37	10740	037	Chatham County	19	37	75000		Winston-Salem city	185 776
37	10740	183	Wake County	94 517	37	75000	067	Forsyth County	185 776
37	11800		Chapel Hill town	48 715	38			**NORTH DAKOTA**	642 200
37	11800	063	Durham County	1 917	38	07200		Bismarck city	55 532
37	11800	135	Orange County	46 798	38	07200	015	Burleigh County	55 532
37	12000		Charlotte city	540 828	38	25700		Fargo city	90 599
37	12000	119	Mecklenburg County	540 828	38	25700	017	Cass County	90 599
37	14100		Concord city	55 977	38	32060		Grand Forks city	49 321
37	14100	025	Cabarrus County	55 977	38	32060	035	Grand Forks County	49 321
37	19000		Durham city	187 035	38	53380		Minot city	36 567
37	19000	063	Durham County	186 996	38	53380	101	Ward County	36 567
37	19000	135	Orange County	39					
37	19000	183	Wake County	0	39			**OHIO**	11 353 140
					39	01000		Akron city	217 074
37	22920		Fayetteville city	121 015	39	01000	153	Summit County	217 074
37	22920	051	Cumberland County	121 015					
					39	03828		Barberton city	27 899
37	25580		Gastonia city	66 277	39	03828	153	Summit County	27 899
37	25580	071	Gaston County	66 277					
					39	04720		Beavercreek city	37 984
37	26880		Goldsboro city	39 043	39	04720	057	Greene County	37 984
37	26880	191	Wayne County	39 043					
					39	07972		Bowling Green city	29 636
37	28000		Greensboro city	223 891	39	07972	173	Wood County	29 636
37	28000	081	Guilford County	223 891					
					39	09680		Brunswick city	33 388
37	28080		Greenville city	60 476	39	09680	103	Medina County	33 388
37	28080	147	Pitt County	60 476					
					39	12000		Canton city	80 806
37	31060		Hickory city	37 222	39	12000	151	Stark County	80 806
37	31060	023	Burke County	63					
37	31060	027	Caldwell County	14	39	15000		Cincinnati city	331 285
37	31060	035	Catawba County	37 145	39	15000	061	Hamilton County	331 285
37	31400		High Point city	85 839	39	16000		Cleveland city	478 403
37	31400	057	Davidson County	1 163	39	16000	035	Cuyahoga County	478 403
37	31400	067	Forsyth County	6					
37	31400	081	Guilford County	84 656	39	16014		Cleveland Heights city	49 958
37	31400	151	Randolph County	14	39	16014	035	Cuyahoga County	49 958
37	34200		Jacksonville city	66 715	39	18000		Columbus city	711 470
37	34200	133	Onslow County	66 715	39	18000	041	Delaware County	1 891
					39	18000	045	Fairfield County	7 447
37	35200		Kannapolis city	36 910	39	18000	049	Franklin County	702 132
37	35200	025	Cabarrus County	27 890					
37	35200	159	Rowan County	9 020	39	19778		Cuyahoga Falls city	49 374
					39	19778	153	Summit County	49 374
37	43920		Monroe city	26 228					
37	43920	179	Union County	26 228	39	21000		Dayton city	166 179
					39	21000	113	Montgomery County	166 179

Appendix E

State Code	Place Code	County Code	Geographic Area Name	2000 Census Population	State Code	Place Code	County Code	Geographic Area Name	2000 Census Population
39	21434		Delaware city	25 243	39	48244		Massillon city	31 325
39	21434	041	Delaware County	25 243	39	48244	151	Stark County	31 325
39	22694		Dublin city	31 392	39	48790		Medina city	25 139
39	22694	041	Delaware County	4 283	39	48790	103	Medina County	25 139
39	22694	049	Franklin County	27 087					
39	22694	159	Union County	22	39	49056		Mentor city	50 278
					39	49056	085	Lake County	50 278
39	23380		East Cleveland city	27 217					
39	23380	035	Cuyahoga County	27 217	39	49840		Middletown city	51 605
					39	49840	017	Butler County	49 574
39	25256		Elyria city	55 953	39	49840	165	Warren County	2 031
39	25256	093	Lorain County	55 953					
					39	54040		Newark city	46 279
39	25704		Euclid city	52 717	39	54040	089	Licking County	46 279
39	25704	035	Cuyahoga County	52 717					
					39	56882		North Olmsted city	34 113
39	25914		Fairborn city	32 052	39	56882	035	Cuyahoga County	34 113
39	25914	057	Greene County	32 052					
					39	57008		North Royalton city	28 648
39	25970		Fairfield city	42 097	39	57008	035	Cuyahoga County	28 648
39	25970	017	Butler County	42 097					
39	25970	061	Hamilton County	0	39	61000		Parma city	85 655
					39	61000	035	Cuyahoga County	85 655
39	27048		Findlay city	38 967					
39	27048	063	Hancock County	38 967	39	66390		Reynoldsburg city	32 069
					39	66390	045	Fairfield County	0
39	29106		Gahanna city	32 636	39	66390	049	Franklin County	26 388
39	29106	049	Franklin County	32 636	39	66390	089	Licking County	5 681
39	29428		Garfield Heights city	30 734	39	70380		Sandusky city	27 844
39	29428	035	Cuyahoga County	30 734	39	70380	043	Erie County	27 844
39	32592		Grove City city	27 075	39	71682		Shaker Heights city	29 405
39	32592	049	Franklin County	27 075	39	71682	035	Cuyahoga County	29 405
39	33012		Hamilton city	60 690	39	74118		Springfield city	65 358
39	33012	017	Butler County	60 690	39	74118	023	Clark County	65 358
39	36610		Huber Heights city	38 212	39	74944		Stow city	32 139
39	36610	109	Miami County	35	39	74944	153	Summit County	32 139
39	36610	113	Montgomery County	38 177					
					39	75098		Strongsville city	43 858
39	39872		Kent city	27 906	39	75098	035	Cuyahoga County	43 858
39	39872	133	Portage County	27 906					
					39	77000		Toledo city	313 619
39	40040		Kettering city	57 502	39	77000	095	Lucas County	313 619
39	40040	057	Greene County	0					
39	40040	113	Montgomery County	57 502	39	77504		Trotwood city	27 420
					39	77504	113	Montgomery County	27 420
39	41664		Lakewood city	56 646					
39	41664	035	Cuyahoga County	56 646	39	79002		Upper Arlington city	33 686
					39	79002	049	Franklin County	33 686
39	41720		Lancaster city	35 335					
39	41720	045	Fairfield County	35 335	39	80892		Warren city	46 832
					39	80892	155	Trumbull County	46 832
39	43554		Lima city	40 081					
39	43554	003	Allen County	40 081	39	83342		Westerville city	35 318
					39	83342	041	Delaware County	5 900
39	44856		Lorain city	68 652	39	83342	049	Franklin County	29 418
39	44856	093	Lorain County	68 652					
					39	83622		Westlake city	31 719
39	47138		Mansfield city	49 346	39	83622	035	Cuyahoga County	31 719
39	47138	139	Richland County	49 346					
					39	88000		Youngstown city	82 026
39	47306		Maple Heights city	26 156	39	88000	099	Mahoning County	82 026
39	47306	035	Cuyahoga County	26 156	39	88000	155	Trumbull County	0
39	47754		Marion city	35 318	39	88084		Zanesville city	25 586
39	47754	101	Marion County	35 318	39	88084	119	Muskingum County	25 586

Cities by County – Continued

State Code	Place Code	County Code	Geographic Area Name	2000 Census Population	State Code	Place Code	County Code	Geographic Area Name	2000 Census Population
40			**OKLAHOMA**	3 450 654	41	34100		Hillsboro city	70 186
40	04450		Bartlesville city	34 748	41	34100	067	Washington County	70 186
40	04450	113	Osage County	2					
40	04450	147	Washington County	34 746	41	38500		Keizer city	32 203
					41	38500	047	Marion County	32 203
40	09050		Broken Arrow city	74 859					
40	09050	143	Tulsa County	67 791	41	40550		Lake Oswego city	35 278
40	09050	145	Wagoner County	7 068	41	40550	005	Clackamas County	32 989
					41	40550	051	Multnomah County	2 274
40	23200		Edmond city	68 315	41	40550	067	Washington County	15
40	23200	109	Oklahoma County	68 315					
					41	45000		McMinnville city	26 499
40	23950		Enid city	47 045	41	45000	071	Yamhill County	26 499
40	23950	047	Garfield County	47 045					
					41	47000		Medford city	63 154
40	41850		Lawton city	92 757	41	47000	029	Jackson County	63 154
40	41850	031	Comanche County	92 757					
					41	55200		Oregon City city	25 754
40	48350		Midwest City city	54 088	41	55200	005	Clackamas County	25 754
40	48350	109	Oklahoma County	54 088					
					41	59000		Portland city	529 121
40	49200		Moore city	41 138	41	59000	005	Clackamas County	747
40	49200	027	Cleveland County	41 138	41	59000	051	Multnomah County	526 986
					41	59000	067	Washington County	1 388
40	50050		Muskogee city	38 310					
40	50050	101	Muskogee County	38 310	41	64900		Salem city	136 924
					41	64900	047	Marion County	119 040
40	52500		Norman city	95 694	41	64900	053	Polk County	17 884
40	52500	027	Cleveland County	95 694					
					41	69600		Springfield city	52 864
40	55000		Oklahoma City city	506 132	41	69600	039	Lane County	52 864
40	55000	017	Canadian County	26 311					
40	55000	027	Cleveland County	47 271	41	73650		Tigard city	41 223
40	55000	109	Oklahoma County	432 498	41	73650	067	Washington County	41 223
40	55000	125	Pottawatomie County	52					
					42			**PENNSYLVANIA**	12 281 054
40	59850		Ponca City city	25 919	42	02000		Allentown city	106 632
40	59850	071	Kay County	25 919	42	02000	077	Lehigh County	106 632
40	59850	113	Osage County	0					
					42	02184		Altoona city	49 523
40	66800		Shawnee city	28 692	42	02184	013	Blair County	49 523
40	66800	125	Pottawatomie County	28 692					
					42	06064		Bethel Park borough	33 556
40	70300		Stillwater city	39 065	42	06064	003	Allegheny County	33 556
40	70300	119	Payne County	39 065					
					42	06088		Bethlehem city	71 329
40	75000		Tulsa city	393 049	42	06088	077	Lehigh County	19 029
40	75000	113	Osage County	5 630	42	06088	095	Northampton County	52 300
40	75000	131	Rogers County	0					
40	75000	143	Tulsa County	387 419	42	13208		Chester city	36 854
					42	13208	045	Delaware County	36 854
41			**OREGON**	3 421 399					
41	01000		Albany city	40 852	42	21648		Easton city	26 263
41	01000	003	Benton County	5 104	42	21648	095	Northampton County	26 263
41	01000	043	Linn County	35 748					
					42	24000		Erie city	103 717
41	05350		Beaverton city	76 129	42	24000	049	Erie County	103 717
41	05350	067	Washington County	76 129					
					42	32800		Harrisburg city	48 950
41	05800		Bend city	52 029	42	32800	043	Dauphin County	48 950
41	05800	017	Deschutes County	52 029					
					42	41216		Lancaster city	56 348
41	15800		Corvallis city	49 322	42	41216	071	Lancaster County	56 348
41	15800	003	Benton County	49 322					
					42	52330		Municipality of Monroeville borough	29 349
41	23850		Eugene city	137 893					
41	23850	039	Lane County	137 893	42	52330	003	Allegheny County	29 349
41	31250		Gresham city	90 205	42	53368		New Castle city	26 309
41	31250	051	Multnomah County	90 205	42	53368	073	Lawrence County	26 309

Cities by County – Continued

State Code	Place Code	County Code	Geographic Area Name	2000 Census Population	State Code	Place Code	County Code	Geographic Area Name	2000 Census Population
42	54656		Norristown borough	31 282	45	29815		Goose Creek city	29 208
42	54656	091	Montgomery County	31 282	45	29815	015	Berkeley County	29 208
					45	29815	019	Charleston County	0
42	60000		Philadelphia city	1 517 550					
42	60000	101	Philadelphia County	1 517 550	45	30850		Greenville city	56 002
					45	30850	045	Greenville County	56 002
42	61000		Pittsburgh city	334 563					
42	61000	003	Allegheny County	334 563	45	34045		Hilton Head Island town	33 862
					45	34045	013	Beaufort County	33 862
42	61536		Plum borough	26 940					
42	61536	003	Allegheny County	26 940	45	48535		Mount Pleasant town	47 609
					45	48535	019	Charleston County	47 609
42	63624		Reading city	81 207					
42	63624	011	Berks County	81 207	45	50875		North Charleston city	79 641
					45	50875	019	Charleston County	76 244
42	69000		Scranton city	76 415	45	50875	035	Dorchester County	3 397
42	69000	069	Lackawanna County	76 415					
					45	61405		Rock Hill city	49 765
42	73808		State College borough	38 420	45	61405	091	York County	49 765
42	73808	027	Centre County	38 420					
					45	68290		Spartanburg city	39 673
42	85152		Wilkes-Barre city	43 123	45	68290	083	Spartanburg County	39 673
42	85152	079	Luzerne County	43 123					
					45	70270		Summerville town	27 752
42	85312		Williamsport city	30 706	45	70270	015	Berkeley County	945
42	85312	081	Lycoming County	30 706	45	70270	019	Charleston County	20
					45	70270	035	Dorchester County	26 787
42	87048		York city	40 862					
42	87048	133	York County	40 862	45	70405		Sumter city	39 643
					45	70405	085	Sumter County	39 643
44			**RHODE ISLAND**	1 048 319					
44	19180		Cranston city	79 269	46			**SOUTH DAKOTA**	754 844
44	19180	007	Providence County	79 269	46	52980		Rapid City city	59 607
					46	52980	103	Pennington County	59 607
44	22960		East Providence city	48 688					
44	22960	007	Providence County	48 688	46	59020		Sioux Falls city	123 975
					46	59020	083	Lincoln County	6 620
44	49960		Newport city	26 475	46	59020	099	Minnehaha County	117 355
44	49960	005	Newport County	26 475					
					47			**TENNESSEE**	5 689 283
44	54640		Pawtucket city	72 958	47	03440		Bartlett city	40 543
44	54640	007	Providence County	72 958	47	03440	157	Shelby County	40 543
44	59000		Providence city	173 618	47	14000		Chattanooga city	155 554
44	59000	007	Providence County	173 618	47	14000	065	Hamilton County	155 554
					47	14000	115	Marion County	0
44	74300		Warwick city	85 808					
44	74300	003	Kent County	85 808	47	15160		Clarksville city	103 455
					47	15160	125	Montgomery County	103 455
44	80780		Woonsocket city	43 224					
44	80780	007	Providence County	43 224	47	15400		Cleveland city	37 192
					47	15400	011	Bradley County	37 192
45			**SOUTH CAROLINA**	4 012 012					
45	00550		Aiken city	25 337	47	16420		Collierville town	31 872
45	00550	003	Aiken County	25 337	47	16420	157	Shelby County	31 872
45	01360		Anderson city	25 514	47	16540		Columbia city	33 055
45	01360	007	Anderson County	25 514	47	16540	119	Maury County	33 055
45	13330		Charleston city	96 650	47	27740		Franklin city	41 842
45	13330	015	Berkeley County	1 122	47	27740	187	Williamson County	41 842
45	13330	019	Charleston County	95 528					
					47	28960		Germantown city	37 348
45	16000		Columbia city	116 278	47	28960	157	Shelby County	37 348
45	16000	063	Lexington County	402					
45	16000	079	Richland County	115 876	47	33280		Hendersonville city	40 620
					47	33280	165	Sumner County	40 620
45	25810		Florence city	30 248					
45	25810	041	Florence County	30 248	47	37640		Jackson city	59 643
					47	37640	113	Madison County	59 643

Cities by County – Continued

State Code	Place Code	County Code	Geographic Area Name	2000 Census Population	State Code	Place Code	County Code	Geographic Area Name	2000 Census Population
47	38320		Johnson City city	55 469	48	13492		Cedar Hill city	32 093
47	38320	019	Carter County	1 138	48	13492	113	Dallas County	32 044
47	38320	163	Sullivan County	240	48	13492	139	Ellis County	49
47	38320	179	Washington County	54 091					
					48	13552		Cedar Park city	26 049
47	39560		Kingsport city	44 905	48	13552	453	Travis County	541
47	39560	073	Hawkins County	2 907	48	13552	491	Williamson County	25 508
47	39560	163	Sullivan County	41 998					
					48	15364		Cleburne city	26 005
47	40000		Knoxville city	173 890	48	15364	251	Johnson County	26 005
47	40000	093	Knox County	173 890					
					48	15976		College Station city	67 890
47	48000		Memphis city	650 100	48	15976	041	Brazos County	67 890
47	48000	157	Shelby County	650 100					
					48	16432		Conroe city	36 811
47	51560		Murfreesboro city	68 816	48	16432	339	Montgomery County	36 811
47	51560	149	Rutherford County	68 816					
					48	16612		Coppell city	35 958
47	52004		Nashville-Davidson	569 891	48	16612	113	Dallas County	35 734
					48	16612	121	Denton County	224
47	55120		Oak Ridge city	27 387					
47	55120	001	Anderson County	24 610	48	16624		Copperas Cove city	29 592
47	55120	145	Roane County	2 777	48	16624	027	Bell County	0
					48	16624	099	Coryell County	29 455
47	69420		Smyrna town	25 569	48	16624	281	Lampasas County	137
47	69420	149	Rutherford County	25 569					
					48	17000		Corpus Christi city	277 454
48			**TEXAS**	20 851 820	48	17000	273	Kleberg County	0
48	01000		Abilene city	115 930	48	17000	355	Nueces County	277 450
48	01000	253	Jones County	5 488	48	17000	409	San Patricio County	4
48	01000	441	Taylor County	110 442					
					48	19000		Dallas city	1 188 580
48	01924		Allen city	43 554	48	19000	085	Collin County	45 155
48	01924	085	Collin County	43 554	48	19000	113	Dallas County	1 121 131
					48	19000	121	Denton County	22 273
48	03000		Amarillo city	173 627	48	19000	257	Kaufman County	0
48	03000	375	Potter County	99 833	48	19000	397	Rockwall County	21
48	03000	381	Randall County	73 794					
					48	19624		Deer Park city	28 520
48	04000		Arlington city	332 969	48	19624	201	Harris County	28 520
48	04000	439	Tarrant County	332 969					
					48	19792		Del Rio city	33 867
48	05000		Austin city	656 562	48	19792	465	Val Verde County	33 867
48	05000	453	Travis County	644 752					
48	05000	491	Williamson County	11 810	48	19972		Denton city	80 537
					48	19972	121	Denton County	80 537
48	06128		Baytown city	66 430					
48	06128	071	Chambers County	3 081	48	20092		DeSoto city	37 646
48	06128	201	Harris County	63 349	48	20092	113	Dallas County	37 646
48	07000		Beaumont city	113 866	48	21628		Duncanville city	36 081
48	07000	245	Jefferson County	113 866	48	21628	113	Dallas County	36 081
48	07132		Bedford city	47 152	48	22660		Edinburg city	48 465
48	07132	439	Tarrant County	47 152	48	22660	215	Hidalgo County	48 465
48	08236		Big Spring city	25 233	48	24000		El Paso city	563 662
48	08236	227	Howard County	25 233	48	24000	141	El Paso County	563 662
48	10768		Brownsville city	139 722	48	24768		Euless city	46 005
48	10768	061	Cameron County	139 722	48	24768	439	Tarrant County	46 005
48	10912		Bryan city	65 660	48	25452		Farmers Branch city	27 508
48	10912	041	Brazos County	65 660	48	25452	113	Dallas County	27 508
48	13024		Carrollton city	109 576	48	26232		Flower Mound town	50 702
48	13024	085	Collin County	0	48	26232	121	Denton County	50 702
48	13024	113	Dallas County	49 822	48	26232	439	Tarrant County	0
48	13024	121	Denton County	59 754					

Cities by County – Continued

State Code	Place Code	County Code	Geographic Area Name	2000 Census Population	State Code	Place Code	County Code	Geographic Area Name	2000 Census Population
48	27000		Fort Worth city	534 694	48	41464		Laredo city	176 576
48	27000	121	Denton County	44	48	41464	479	Webb County	176 576
48	27000	439	Tarrant County	534 650					
					48	41980		League City city	45 444
48	27648		Friendswood city	29 037	48	41980	167	Galveston County	45 306
48	27648	167	Galveston County	21 237	48	41980	201	Harris County	138
48	27648	201	Harris County	7 800					
					48	42508		Lewisville city	77 737
48	27684		Frisco city	33 714	48	42508	113	Dallas County	2
48	27684	085	Collin County	30 312	48	42508	121	Denton County	77 735
48	27684	121	Denton County	3 402					
					48	43888		Longview city	73 344
48	28068		Galveston city	57 247	48	43888	183	Gregg County	71 746
48	28068	167	Galveston County	57 247	48	43888	203	Harrison County	1 598
48	29000		Garland city	215 768	48	45000		Lubbock city	199 564
48	29000	085	Collin County	0	48	45000	303	Lubbock County	199 564
48	29000	113	Dallas County	215 768					
48	29000	397	Rockwall County	0	48	45072		Lufkin city	32 709
					48	45072	005	Angelina County	32 709
48	29336		Georgetown city	28 339					
48	29336	491	Williamson County	28 339	48	45384		McAllen city	106 414
					48	45384	215	Hidalgo County	106 414
48	30464		Grand Prairie city	127 427					
48	30464	113	Dallas County	99 760	48	45744		McKinney city	54 369
48	30464	139	Ellis County	46	48	45744	085	Collin County	54 369
48	30464	439	Tarrant County	27 621					
					48	46452		Mansfield city	28 031
48	30644		Grapevine city	42 059	48	46452	139	Ellis County	129
48	30644	113	Dallas County	0	48	46452	251	Johnson County	622
48	30644	121	Denton County	2	48	46452	439	Tarrant County	27 280
48	30644	439	Tarrant County	42 057					
					48	47892		Mesquite city	124 523
48	31928		Haltom City city	39 018	48	47892	113	Dallas County	124 522
48	31928	439	Tarrant County	39 018	48	47892	257	Kaufman County	1
48	32372		Harlingen city	57 564	48	48072		Midland city	94 996
48	32372	061	Cameron County	57 564	48	48072	317	Martin County	0
					48	48072	329	Midland County	94 996
48	35000		Houston city	1 953 631					
48	35000	157	Fort Bend County	33 384	48	48768		Mission city	45 408
48	35000	201	Harris County	1 919 789	48	48768	215	Hidalgo County	45 408
48	35000	339	Montgomery County	458					
					48	48804		Missouri City city	52 913
48	35528		Huntsville city	35 078	48	48804	157	Fort Bend County	47 419
48	35528	471	Walker County	35 078	48	48804	201	Harris County	5 494
48	35576		Hurst city	36 273	48	50256		Nacogdoches city	29 914
48	35576	439	Tarrant County	36 273	48	50256	347	Nacogdoches County	29 914
48	37000		Irving city	191 615	48	50820		New Braunfels city	36 494
48	37000	113	Dallas County	191 615	48	50820	091	Comal County	35 328
					48	50820	187	Guadalupe County	1 166
48	38632		Keller city	27 345					
48	38632	439	Tarrant County	27 345	48	52356		North Richland Hills city	55 635
					48	52356	439	Tarrant County	55 635
48	39148		Killeen city	86 911					
48	39148	027	Bell County	86 911	48	53388		Odessa city	90 943
					48	53388	135	Ector County	89 901
48	39352		Kingsville city	25 575	48	53388	329	Midland County	1 042
48	39352	273	Kleberg County	25 575					
					48	55080		Paris city	25 898
48	40588		Lake Jackson city	26 386	48	55080	277	Lamar County	25 898
48	40588	039	Brazoria County	26 386					
					48	56000		Pasadena city	141 674
48	41212		Lancaster city	25 894	48	56000	201	Harris County	141 674
48	41212	113	Dallas County	25 894					
					48	56348		Pearland city	37 640
48	41440		La Porte city	31 880	48	56348	039	Brazoria County	35 696
48	41440	201	Harris County	31 880	48	56348	157	Fort Bend County	0
					48	56348	201	Harris County	1 944

State Code	Place Code	County Code	Geographic Area Name	2000 Census Population	State Code	Place Code	County Code	Geographic Area Name	2000 Census Population
48	57200		Pharr city	46 660	48	79000		Wichita Falls city	104 197
48	57200	215	Hidalgo County	46 660	48	79000	485	Wichita County	104 197
48	58016		Plano city	222 030	49			**UTAH**	2 233 169
48	58016	085	Collin County	219 890	49	07690		Bountiful city	41 301
48	58016	121	Denton County	2 140	49	07690	011	Davis County	41 301
48	58820		Port Arthur city	57 755	49	13850		Clearfield city	25 974
48	58820	245	Jefferson County	57 755	49	13850	011	Davis County	25 974
48	58820	361	Orange County	0	49	20120		Draper city	25 220
48	61796		Richardson city	91 802	49	20120	035	Salt Lake County	25 220
48	61796	085	Collin County	20 873	49	20120	049	Utah County	0
48	61796	113	Dallas County	70 929					
					49	43660		Layton city	58 474
48	63500		Round Rock city	61 136	49	43660	011	Davis County	58 474
48	63500	453	Travis County	1 076					
48	63500	491	Williamson County	60 060	49	45860		Logan city	42 670
					49	45860	005	Cache County	42 670
48	63572		Rowlett city	44 503					
48	63572	113	Dallas County	37 462	49	49710		Midvale city	27 029
48	63572	397	Rockwall County	7 041	49	49710	035	Salt Lake County	27 029
48	64472		San Angelo city	88 439	49	53230		Murray city	34 024
48	64472	451	Tom Green County	88 439	49	53230	035	Salt Lake County	34 024
48	65000		San Antonio city	1 144 646	49	55980		Ogden city	77 226
48	65000	029	Bexar County	1 144 646	49	55980	057	Weber County	77 226
48	65000	091	Comal County	0					
					49	57300		Orem city	84 324
48	65516		San Juan city	26 229	49	57300	049	Utah County	84 324
48	65516	215	Hidalgo County	26 229					
					49	62470		Provo city	105 166
48	65600		San Marcos city	34 733	49	62470	049	Utah County	105 166
48	65600	055	Caldwell County	0					
48	65600	209	Hays County	34 733	49	64340		Riverton city	25 011
					49	64340	035	Salt Lake County	25 011
48	67496		Sherman city	35 082					
48	67496	181	Grayson County	35 082	49	65110		Roy city	32 885
					49	65110	057	Weber County	32 885
48	68636		Socorro city	27 152					
48	68636	141	El Paso County	27 152	49	65330		St. George city	49 663
					49	65330	053	Washington County	49 663
48	70808		Sugar Land city	63 328					
48	70808	157	Fort Bend County	63 328	49	67000		Salt Lake City city	181 743
					49	67000	035	Salt Lake County	181 743
48	72176		Temple city	54 514					
48	72176	027	Bell County	54 514	49	67440		Sandy city	88 418
					49	67440	035	Salt Lake County	88 418
48	72368		Texarkana city	34 782					
48	72368	037	Bowie County	34 782	49	70850		South Jordan city	29 437
					49	70850	035	Salt Lake County	29 437
48	72392		Texas City city	41 521					
48	72392	071	Chambers County	0	49	75360		Taylorsville city	57 439
48	72392	167	Galveston County	41 521	49	75360	035	Salt Lake County	57 439
48	72530		The Colony city	26 531	49	82950		West Jordan city	68 336
48	72530	121	Denton County	26 531	49	82950	035	Salt Lake County	68 336
48	74144		Tyler city	83 650	49	83470		West Valley City city	108 896
48	74144	423	Smith County	83 650	49	83470	035	Salt Lake County	108 896
48	75428		Victoria city	60 603	50			**VERMONT**	608 827
48	75428	469	Victoria County	60 603	50	10675		Burlington city	38 889
					50	10675	007	Chittenden County	38 889
48	76000		Waco city	113 726					
48	76000	309	McLennan County	113 726	51			**VIRGINIA**	7 078 515
					51	01000		Alexandria city	128 283
48	77272		Weslaco city	26 935	51	01000	510	Alexandria city	128 283
48	77272	215	Hidalgo County	26 935					

State Code	Place Code	County Code	Geographic Area Name	2000 Census Population	State Code	Place Code	County Code	Geographic Area Name	2000 Census Population
51	07784		Blacksburg town	39 573	53	20750		Edmonds city	39 515
51	07784	121	Montgomery County	39 573	53	20750	061	Snohomish County	39 515
51	14968		Charlottesville city	45 049	53	22640		Everett city	91 488
51	14968	540	Charlottesville city	45 049	53	22640	061	Snohomish County	91 488
51	16000		Chesapeake city	199 184	53	35275		Kennewick city	54 693
51	16000	550	Chesapeake city	199 184	53	35275	005	Benton County	54 693
51	21344		Danville city	48 411	53	35415		Kent city	79 524
51	21344	590	Danville city	48 411	53	35415	033	King County	79 524
51	35000		Hampton city	146 437	53	35940		Kirkland city	45 054
51	35000	650	Hampton city	146 437	53	35940	033	King County	45 054
51	35624		Harrisonburg city	40 468	53	36745		Lacey city	31 226
51	35624	660	Harrisonburg city	40 468	53	36745	067	Thurston County	31 226
51	44984		Leesburg town	28 311	53	40245		Longview city	34 660
51	44984	107	Loudoun County	28 311	53	40245	015	Cowlitz County	34 660
51	47672		Lynchburg city	65 269	53	40840		Lynnwood city	33 847
51	47672	680	Lynchburg city	65 269	53	40840	061	Snohomish County	33 847
51	48952		Manassas city	35 135	53	43955		Marysville city	25 315
51	48952	683	Manassas city	35 135	53	43955	061	Snohomish County	25 315
51	56000		Newport News city	180 150	53	47560		Mount Vernon city	26 232
51	56000	700	Newport News city	180 150	53	47560	057	Skagit County	26 232
51	57000		Norfolk city	234 403	53	51300		Olympia city	42 514
51	57000	710	Norfolk city	234 403	53	51300	067	Thurston County	42 514
51	61832		Petersburg city	33 740	53	53545		Pasco city	32 066
51	61832	730	Petersburg city	33 740	53	53545	021	Franklin County	32 066
51	64000		Portsmouth city	100 565	53	56695		Puyallup city	33 011
51	64000	740	Portsmouth city	100 565	53	56695	053	Pierce County	33 011
51	67000		Richmond city	197 790	53	57535		Redmond city	45 256
51	67000	760	Richmond city	197 790	53	57535	033	King County	45 256
51	68000		Roanoke city	94 911	53	57745		Renton city	50 052
51	68000	770	Roanoke city	94 911	53	57745	033	King County	50 052
51	76432		Suffolk city	63 677	53	58235		Richland city	38 708
51	76432	800	Suffolk city	63 677	53	58235	005	Benton County	38 708
51	82000		Virginia Beach city	425 257	53	61115		Sammamish city	34 104
51	82000	810	Virginia Beach city	425 257	53	61115	033	King County	34 104
53			**WASHINGTON**	5 894 121	53	63000		Seattle city	563 374
53	03180		Auburn city	40 314	53	63000	033	King County	563 374
53	03180	033	King County	40 168					
53	03180	053	Pierce County	146	53	63960		Shoreline city	53 025
					53	63960	033	King County	53 025
53	05210		Bellevue city	109 569					
53	05210	033	King County	109 569	53	67000		Spokane city	195 629
					53	67000	063	Spokane County	195 629
53	05280		Bellingham city	67 171					
53	05280	073	Whatcom County	67 171	53	70000		Tacoma city	193 556
					53	70000	053	Pierce County	193 556
53	07380		Bothell city	30 150					
53	07380	033	King County	16 185	53	74060		Vancouver city	143 560
53	07380	061	Snohomish County	13 965	53	74060	011	Clark County	143 560
53	07695		Bremerton city	37 259	53	75775		Walla Walla city	29 686
53	07695	035	Kitsap County	37 259	53	75775	071	Walla Walla County	29 686
53	17635		Des Moines city	29 267	53	77105		Wenatchee city	27 856
53	17635	033	King County	29 267	53	77105	007	Chelan County	27 856

Cities by County – Continued

State Code	Place Code	County Code	Geographic Area Name	2000 Census Population	State Code	Place Code	County Code	Geographic Area Name	2000 Census Population
53	80010		Yakima city	71 845	55	56375		New Berlin city	38 220
53	80010	077	Yakima County	71 845	55	56375	133	Waukesha County	38 220
54			WEST VIRGINIA	1 808 344	55	58800		Oak Creek city	28 456
54	14600		Charleston city	53 421	55	58800	079	Milwaukee County	28 456
54	14600	039	Kanawha County	53 421					
					55	60500		Oshkosh city	62 916
54	39460		Huntington city	51 475	55	60500	139	Winnebago County	62 916
54	39460	011	Cabell County	47 341					
54	39460	099	Wayne County	4 134	55	66000		Racine city	81 855
					55	66000	101	Racine County	81 855
54	55756		Morgantown city	26 809					
54	55756	061	Monongalia County	26 809	55	72975		Sheboygan city	50 792
					55	72975	117	Sheboygan County	50 792
54	62140		Parkersburg city	33 099					
54	62140	107	Wood County	33 099	55	78650		Superior city	27 368
					55	78650	031	Douglas County	27 368
54	86452		Wheeling city	31 419					
54	86452	051	Marshall County	360	55	84250		Waukesha city	64 825
54	86452	069	Ohio County	31 059	55	84250	133	Waukesha County	64 825
55			WISCONSIN	5 363 675	55	84475		Wausau city	38 426
55	02375		Appleton city	70 087	55	84475	073	Marathon County	38 426
55	02375	015	Calumet County	10 974					
55	02375	087	Outagamie County	58 301	55	84675		Wauwatosa city	47 271
55	02375	139	Winnebago County	812	55	84675	079	Milwaukee County	47 271
55	06500		Beloit city	35 775	55	85300		West Allis city	61 254
55	06500	105	Rock County	35 775	55	85300	079	Milwaukee County	61 254
55	10025		Brookfield city	38 649	55	85350		West Bend city	28 152
55	10025	133	Waukesha County	38 649	55	85350	131	Washington County	28 152
55	22300		Eau Claire city	61 704	56			WYOMING	493 782
55	22300	017	Chippewa County	1 910	56	13150		Casper city	49 644
55	22300	035	Eau Claire County	59 794	56	13150	025	Natrona County	49 644
55	26275		Fond du Lac city	42 203	56	13900		Cheyenne city	53 011
55	26275	039	Fond du Lac County	42 203	56	13900	021	Laramie County	53 011
55	27300		Franklin city	29 494	56	45050		Laramie city	27 204
55	27300	079	Milwaukee County	29 494	56	45050	001	Albany County	27 204
55	31000		Green Bay city	102 313					
55	31000	009	Brown County	102 313					
55	31175		Greenfield city	35 476					
55	31175	079	Milwaukee County	35 476					
55	37825		Janesville city	59 498					
55	37825	105	Rock County	59 498					
55	39225		Kenosha city	90 352					
55	39225	059	Kenosha County	90 352					
55	40775		La Crosse city	51 818					
55	40775	063	La Crosse County	51 818					
55	48000		Madison city	208 054					
55	48000	025	Dane County	208 054					
55	48500		Manitowoc city	34 053					
55	48500	071	Manitowoc County	34 053					
55	51000		Menomonee Falls village	32 647					
55	51000	133	Waukesha County	32 647					
55	53000		Milwaukee city	596 974					
55	53000	079	Milwaukee County	596 974					
55	53000	131	Washington County	0					
55	53000	133	Waukesha County	0					

APPENDIX F
SOURCE NOTES AND EXPLANATIONS

TABLE A—STATES

Table A presents 332 items for the United States as a whole, each state, and the District of Columbia. The states are presented in alphabetical order.

The following documentation is provided in the order in which the items appear in the databases.

LAND AREA, Items 1 and 4
Source: U.S. Bureau of the Census

Land area measurements are shown to the nearest square kilometer. Land area includes dry land and land temporarily or partially covered by water, such as marshlands, swamps, and river floodplains.

POPULATION AND POPULATION CHANGE, Items 2–4; 29–31; and 32–39
Source: U.S. Bureau of the Census

The population data for 2003 are U.S. Bureau of the Census estimates of the resident population as of July 1 of that year.

The population data for 1980, 1990, and 2000 are from the decennial censuses and represent the resident population as of April 1, 1980, 1990, and 2000 respectively. The change in population between 2000 and 2003 is composed of (a) natural increase—the excess of births over deaths, and (b) net migration—the difference between the number of persons moving into a particular state and the number of persons moving out. Net migration is composed of internal and international migration.

POPULATION AND POPULATION CHARACTERISTICS, Items 2–20 and 40–56
Source: U.S. Bureau of the Census—2000 Census of Population and Housing for 2000 data and Census Bureau Estimates for 2003 data

The data on **race** were derived from answers to the 2000 census question on race that was asked of all people. The concept of race, as used by the Census Bureau, reflects self-identification by people according to the race or races with which they most closely identify. These categories are socio-political constructs and should not be interpreted as being scientific or anthropological in nature. Furthermore, the race categories include both racial and national-origin groups.

In the 2000 census, respondents were offered the option of selecting one or more races. Items five through eight identify persons who specified each race group alone or in combination with other races, and who specified that they were not Hispanic or Latino. Items 40 through 43 identify persons who specified

"one race only" with those who claimed "some other race" combined with "two or more races" in item 44.

The **White** population is defined as persons who indicated their race as white, as well as persons who did not classify themselves in one of the specific race categories listed on the questionnaire but entered a nationality such as Irish, German, Italian, Lebanese, Near Easterner, Arab, or Polish.

The **Black** population includes persons who indicated their race as "Black, African American, or Negro," as well as persons who did not classify themselves in one of the specific race categories but reported entries such as African American, Afro American, Kenyan, Nigerian, or Haitian.

The **American Indian or Alaska Native** population includes persons who indicated their race as American Indian or Alaska Native, as well as persons who did not classify themselves in one of the specific race categories but reported entries such as Canadian Indian, French American Indian, Spanish-American Indian, Eskimo, Aleut, Alaska Indian, or any of the American Indian or Alaska Native tribes.

The **Asian** population includes persons who indicated their race as Asian Indian, Chinese, Filipino, Japanese, Korean, Vietnamese, or "Other Asian," as well as persons who provided write-in entries of such Asian groups as Cambodian, Laotian, Hmong, Pakistani, or Taiwanese. Also, persons who wrote in an entry indicating one of the specific categories were classified accordingly. The **Native Hawaiian or Other Pacific Islander** population includes persons who indicated their race as "Native Hawaiian," "Guamanian or Chamorro," "Samoan" or "Other Pacific Islander," as well as persons who reported entries such as Part Hawaiian, American Samoan, Fijian, Melanesian, or Tahitian. Also, persons who wrote in an entry indicating one of the specific categories were classified accordingly. In 1990, the **Asian** and **Native Hawaiian or Other Pacific Islander** categories were combined as **Asian and Pacific Islander**. This volume continues to use the 1990 combination.

The population of **other race** includes all persons who indicated "Some other race" as well as persons who wrote in a category not included in the race categories described above, including entries such as multiracial, mixed, interracial, or a Hispanic/Latino group such as Mexican, Puerto Rican, or Cuban in the "Some other race" write-in space. In item 41, "other" also include persons of "two or more races."

Changes in specific listing of racial categories, the new practice of allowing more than one selection in 2000, and the order in which questions appeared on the questionnaire, could all affect comparability between the 2000 and 1990 censuses.

The Hispanic or Latino population is based on a complete-count question that asked respondents "Is this person Spanish/Hispanic/Latino?" Persons marking any one of the four Hispanic or Latino categories (Mexican, Puerto Rican, Cuban, or other Spanish) are collectively referred to as Hispanic or Latino.

In the 2000 census, the Hispanic or Latino Origin question was placed before the race question and specific instructions indicated that both questions should be answered. These changes were designed to improve accuracy, and may affect comparability with 1990 data.

The **foreign-born population** is based on birthplace and citizenship questions asked of a sample of persons in the 2000 census. **Foreign-born** includes persons not born in the United States, Puerto Rico, or an outlying area of the United States. Persons who were born in a foreign country but who have at least one American parent are not included.

Age is defined as age at last birthday (number of completed years from birth to April 1, 2000 for the 2000 census).

The 2000 census also asked for the specific date of birth of the respondent, and 2000 census procedures used the birth date for deriving age data. For this reason, it is likely that the 2000 data have fewer problems than prior censuses, such as a tendency to round ages or report the person's age on the date the questionnaire was filled out rather than on April 1.

HOUSEHOLDS, Items 21–27 and 57–61
Source: U.S. Bureau of the Census—2003 American Community Survey and 2000 Census of Population and Housing

A household consists of persons occupying a single housing unit. A housing unit is a house, an apartment, a group of rooms, or a single room occupied as separate living quarters. The occupants may be a single family, one person living alone, two or more families living together, or any other group of related or unrelated persons who share a housing unit. The number of households is the same as the number of year-round occupied housing units.

A family household consists of two or more persons, including the householder, who are related by birth, marriage, or adoption and who live together as one household; all such persons are considered as members of one family. A married-couple family is one in which the householder and spouse are enumerated as members of the same household.

The measure of persons per household is obtained by dividing the number of persons in households by the number of households or householders. The category **Female family householder** includes only female-headed family households with no spouse present. One person in each household is designated as the householder. In most cases, this is the person, or one of the persons, in whose name the home is owned, being bought, or rented. If there is no such person in the household, any adult household member 15 years old and over could be designated as the householder.

IMMIGRANTS, Item 28
Source: Department of Homeland Security, U.S. Citizenship and Immigration Services

The number of immigrants by their state of intended residence is summarized from the administrative records of the Immigration and Naturalization Service. This information is compiled from immigrant visas and forms granting legal permanent resident status.

An **immigrant** is an alien admitted to the United States as a lawful permanent resident. Immigrants are those persons lawfully accorded the privilege of residing permanently in the United States. They may be newly arrived individuals who were issued immigrant visas by the Department of State overseas or they may be U.S. residents who were admitted to permanent resident status in 2003 by the Immigration and Naturalization Service in the United States.

BIRTHS AND DEATHS, Items 62–68
Source: U.S. Centers for Disease Control

The registration of births, deaths, and other vital events in the United States is primarily a state and local function. The civil laws of every state provide for a continuous and permanent birth and death registration system. Through the National Vital Statistics System, the National Center for Health Statistics (NCHS) obtains data on births and deaths from the registration offices of each state, New York City, and the District of Columbia.

Birth and death statistics are limited to events occurring during the year. The data are by place of residence and exclude events occurring to nonresidents of the United States. Births or deaths that occur outside the United States are excluded.

Birth and death rates represent the number of births and deaths per 1,000 resident population enumerated as of April 1 for decennial census years and estimated as of July 1 for other years.

Figures for infant deaths include deaths of children under 1 year of age—they exclude fetal deaths. The infant death rate is per 1,000 live births.

The rates of almost all causes of disease, injury, and death vary by age. Age adjustment is a technique for "removing" the effects of age from crude rates, so as to allow meaningful comparisons across populations with different underlying age structures. For example, comparing the crude death rate in Florida to that of California is misleading, since the relatively older population in Florida will lead to a higher crude death rate. For such a comparison, age-adjusted rates would be preferable.

The population estimates were developed by the Census Bureau's Population Division using a traditional cohort component method. Starting with a basic population from the 2000 census, each component of population change—births, deaths, domestic mirgration, and international migration—is estimated separately for each birth cohort by sex, race, and Hispanic or Latino origin.

Age-adjusted rates are calculated by applying the age-specific rates of various populations to a single standard population. In this volume, the standard population is 2000. After many years of using 1940 as the standard population for age-adjusted death rates, the CDC has recently switched to 2000. For this reason, the 2002 age-adjusted rates are almost identical to the actual death rates.

PHYSICIANS, Items 69–70

Source: Health Market Science, Inc., as published in Bernan's *Health and Healthcare in the United States*, copyright 1999 NationsHealth Corporation, LLC. Reprinted with permission.

Physicians are health practitioners having the degree of M.D. (Doctor of Medicine) or D.O. (Doctor of Osteopathy) primarily engaged in the practice of general or specialized medicine or surgery. The rate of physicians per 100,000 resident population is an indicator of the supply of physicians within a geographic area.

HOSPITALS, Items 71–73

Source: Health Market Science, Inc., as published in Bernan's *Health and Healthcare in the United States*, copyright 2001 NationsHealth Corporation, LLC. Reprinted with permission.

Hospitals are licensed institutions with at least six beds whose primary function is to provide diagnostic and therapeutic patient services for medical conditions by an organized physician staff, and have continuous nursing services under the supervision of registered nurses. Only short term general hospitals are included in these figures.

A hospital bed is any bed that is licensed for use by inpatients. The count of beds in a facility typically represents the count of beds at the end of the reporting period (a year) regardless of whether it is operational or not. The number of hospital beds per 100,000 population is a measure of the supply of hospital beds within a geographic area.

MEDICARE ENROLLEES, Item 74

Source: Centers for Medicare and Medicaid Services (CMS)

The Centers for Medicare and Medicaid Services (CMS) administers Medicare, which provides health insurance to people aged 65 and over and those who have permanent kidney failure and certain people with disabilities. Medicare has two parts: Hospital Insurance and Supplemental Medical Insurance. The numbers in this volume include persons enrolled in either or both parts of the program as of July 1, 2003, by their state of residence.

CRIME, Items 75–78

Source: U.S. Federal Bureau of Investigation— Uniform Crime Reports

Crime data are as reported to the FBI by law enforcement agencies and have not been adjusted for under-reporting. This may affect comparability between geographic areas or over time.

For some states, reporting by jurisdictions within the state is not sufficiently complete to be representative of the state as a whole, and state totals for these states have been estimated by the FBI.

Through the voluntary contribution of crime statistics by law enforcement agencies across the United States, the Uniform Crime Reporting (UCR) Program provides periodic assessments of crime in the nation as measured by offenses coming to the attention of the law enforcement community. The Committee on Uniform Crime Records of the International Association of Chiefs of Police initiated this voluntary national data-collection effort in 1930. UCR Program contributors compile and submit their crime data by one of two means: either directly to the FBI or through the state UCR Programs.

Seven offenses, because of their seriousness, frequency of occurrence, and likelihood of being reported to police, were initially selected to serve as an index for evaluating fluctuations in the volume of crime. These serious crimes were murder and nonnegligent manslaughter, forcible rape, robbery, aggravated assault, burglary, larceny/theft, and motor vehicle theft. By congressional mandate, arson was added as the eighth index offense in 1979. Arson is not included in the totals given in this volume.

Violent offenses include four crime categories: (1) Murder and nonnegligent manslaughter, as defined in the UCR Program, is the willful (nonnegligent) killing of one human being by another. This offense excludes deaths caused by negligence, suicide or accident; justifiable homicides; and attempts to murder or assaults to murder. (2) Forcible rape is the carnal knowledge of a female forcibly and against her will. Assaults or attempts to commit rape by force or threat of force are also included; however, statutory rape (without force) and other sex offenses are excluded. (3) Robbery is the taking or attempting to take anything of value from the care, custody, or control of a person or persons by force or threat of force or violence and/or by putting the victim in fear. (4) Aggravated assault is an unlawful attack by one person upon another for the purpose of inflicting severe or aggravated bodily injury. This type of assault is usually accompanied by the use of a weapon or by means likely to produce death or great bodily harm. Attempts are included since an injury does not necessarily have to result when a gun, knife, or other weapon is used, which could and probably would result in a serious personal injury if the crime were successfully completed.

Property crimes include three categories: (1) Burglary, or breaking and entering, is the unlawful entry of a structure to commit a felony or theft, even though no force was used to gain entrance. (2) Larceny/theft is the unauthorized taking of the personal property of another, without the use of force. (3) Motor vehicle theft is the unauthorized taking of any motor vehicle.

ELEMENTARY AND SECONDARY SCHOOL ENROLLMENT, Items 79–80

Source: U.S. Department of Education, National Center for Education Statistics; Common Core of Data for public schools, and Private School Survey for private schools.

Data on public school enrollment is from the *Common Core of Data* 2001–2002 survey while that for private elementary and secondary enrollment is from the *Private School Survey* of 2001–2002. The private school figures include grades kindergarten through grade 12, including special education, vocational/technical education, and alternative schools. Excluded from private enrollment is prekindergarten enrollment or enrollment in schools that do not offer first grade or above. Public school enrollment includes prekindergarten through grade 12 and ungraded students.

EDUCATIONAL ATTAINMENT, Items 81–84
Source: U.S. Bureau of the Census—Current Population Survey

Statistics for educational attainment are for persons 25 years old and over. The data were derived from a question on the Current Population Survey that asked respondents for the highest level of school they had completed or the highest degree they had received. Persons who passed a high school equivalency examination were considered high school graduates. Schooling received in foreign schools was to be reported as the equivalent grade or years in the regular American school system.

LOCAL GOVERNMENT EDUCATION EXPENDITURES, Items 85–86
Source: U.S. Department of Education, National Center for Education Statistics, Common Core of Data

These data pertain to expenditures for public elementary and secondary education. Current expenditures includes expenditures for instruction, school administration, operation and maintenance, student transportation, food services, support services, adult education, and community services. Total expenditures also includes capital outlay and interest on debt. Current expenditures per student is the current expenditures divided by the number of students in membership as reported in the Common Core of Data Nonfiscal Survey for school year 2001–2002. Student membership is the count of students enrolled on or about October 1.

MONEY INCOME AND POVERTY, Items 87–98
Source: U.S. Bureau of the Census—2000 Census of Population and Housing for 1999 data and the Current Population Survey for 1998–2000 and 2000 data

The data on income and poverty are derived from the responses of a sample of persons 15 years old and over. The data for 1999 are from the 2000 census "long form" sample—a sample large enough to permit publication of data for small geographic areas. The 2001–2003 and 2002 data were gathered each March from a national sample of about 60,000 households. These data are available for states but not for counties or cities.

Total money income is defined by the Bureau of the Census for statistical purposes as the sum of the following: wage or salary income; nonfarm self-employment income; net farm self-employment income; Social Security and railroad retirement income; public assistance income; and all other regularly received income such as interest, dividends, veterans payments, pensions, unemployment compensation, and alimony. Receipts not counted as income include various "lump sum" payments such as capital gains or inheritances.

The total represents the amount of income received before deductions for personal income taxes, Social Security, bond purchases, union dues, Medicare deductions, etc.

Per capita income for 1999 is based on resident population enumerated as of April 1, 2000.

Household income includes the income of the householder and all other persons 15 years old and over in the household. Median household income is usually less than median family income because many households consist of only one person. The median divides the income distribution into two equal parts, one having incomes above the median, the other with incomes below.

The constant-dollar figures are based on an annual average Consumer Price Index from the Bureau of Labor Statistics. Constant-dollar figures are estimates representing an effort to remove the effects of price changes from statistical series reported in dollar terms. However, the estimates do not reflect the price and cost-of-living differences that may exist between areas.

Money income differs in definition from personal income (item 101). For example, money income does not include the pension rights, employer provided health insurance, food stamps, or Medicare payments that are included in personal income.

Poverty status is based on the definition prescribed by the U.S. Office of Management and Budget as the standard to be used by federal agencies for statistical purposes. Families and persons are classified as below the poverty level if their total family income or unrelated individual income was less than the poverty threshold specified for the applicable family size, age of householder, and number of related children under 18 years old present. The average poverty threshold for a four-person family was $17,603 in 2000 and $18,660 in 2003.

In the 2000 census, poverty status was determined for all families (and by implication all family members). For persons not in families, poverty status is determined by their income in relation to the appropriate poverty threshold. Inmates of institutions, persons in military group quarters or college dormitories, and unrelated individuals under 15 years old are excluded.

PERSONS LACKING HEALTH INSURANCE, Items 99–100
Source: U.S. Bureau of the Census—Current Population Survey

The data on which these estimates are based were gathered in March 2003 from a national sample of about 60,000 households—the same sample from which the 2000 data on income and poverty were obtained. Data are available for states but not for counties or cities.

Those lacking coverage are the percentage of the population of each state who were covered neither by private health plans nor by Medicaid, Medicare, or military health care.

PERSONAL INCOME AND EARNINGS, Items 101–125
Source: U.S. Bureau of Economic Analysis, Regional Economic Information System

Total personal income is the current income received by residents of an area from all sources. It is measured before deductions of income and other personal taxes but after deduction of personal contributions for Social Security, government retirement, and other social insurance programs. It consists of wage and salary disbursements (covering all employee earnings, including executive salaries, bonuses, commissions, payments-in-kind, incentive payments, and tips), various types of supplementary earnings, such as employers' contributions to pension funds (termed "other labor income"); proprietors' income; rental income of persons; dividends; personal interest income; and government and business transfer payments.

Proprietors' income is the monetary income and income in-kind of proprietorships and partnerships, including the independent professions, and of tax-exempt cooperatives. **Dividends** are cash payments by corporations to stockholders who are U.S. residents. **Interest** is the monetary and imputed interest income of persons from all sources. **Rent** is the monetary income of persons from the rental of real property, except the income of persons primarily engaged in the real estate business, the imputed net rental income of owner-occupants of nonfarm dwellings, and the royalties received by persons.

Transfer payments are income for which services are not currently rendered. They consist of both government and business transfer payments. Government transfer payments include payments under the following programs: Federal Old Age, Survivors, and Disability Insurance ("Social Security"); Medicare and medical vendor payments; unemployment insurance, railroad and government retirement; federal and state government-insured workers' compensation; veterans benefits, including veterans life insurance; food stamps; black lung; Supplemental Security Income; and Aid to Families with Dependent Children. Government payments to nonprofit institutions, other than for work under research and development contracts, are also included. The principal business transfers are corporate gifts to nonprofit institutions and consumer bad debts.

Per capita personal income is based on resident population estimated as of July 1 of the year shown.

Personal tax payments includes taxes paid by individuals to federal, state, and local governments. Personal taxes include individual income taxes, estate and gift taxes, motor vehicle license taxes, and personal property taxes. Personal contributions to social insurance ("Social Security taxes") are not included, nor are sales taxes.

Disposable personal income equals personal income less personal tax payments. It is a measure of the income available to persons for spending or saving.

Earnings cover wage and salary disbursements, other labor income, and proprietors' income.

Data for earnings obtained from the Bureau of Economic Analysis (BEA) are based on place of work. In computing personal income, BEA makes an "adjustment for residence" to earnings, based on commuting patterns, so that personal income is presented on a place of residence basis.

Farm earnings include the income of farm workers (wages and salaries and other labor income) and farm proprietors. Farm proprietors' income includes only the income of sole proprietorships and partnerships.

Farm earning estimates are benchmarked to data collected in the Census of Agriculture and the revised U.S. Department of Agriculture state totals of income and expense items.

Goods related industries include mining, construction, and manufacturing. Service-related and other include private sector earnings in agricultural services, forestry and fisheries; transportation and public utilities; wholesale trade; retail trade; finance, insurance, and real estate; and services. Government earnings include all levels of government.

GROSS STATE PRODUCT, Item 126
Source: Bureau of Economic Analysis, Regional Economic Information System

GSP for a state is derived as the sum of gross state product originating in all industries in the state. In concept, an industry's GSP, referred to as its "value added," is equivalent to its gross output (sales or receipts and other operating income, commodity taxes, and inventory change) minus its intermediate inputs (consumption of goods and services purchased from other industries or imported). As such, it is often referred to as the state counterpart of the nation's gross domestic product (GDP). In practice, GSP estimates are measured as the sum of distributions by industry of the components of gross domestic income—that is, the sum of the costs incurred (such as compensation of employees, net interest, and indirect business taxes) and the profits earned in production.

HOUSING, Items 127–141
Source: U.S. Bureau of the Census—2000 Census of Population and Housing and 2003 American Community Survey

Housing data for 2003 are from the American Community Survey, a nationwide continuous survey designed to eventually replace the long form in the 2010 census. A sample of households is surveyed to provide estimates. The survey is limited to the household population and excludes the population living in institutions, college dormitories, and other group quarters. Housing data for 2000 are from the 2000 census.

A **housing unit** is a house, apartment, mobile home or trailer, group of rooms, or single room occupied or, if vacant, intended for occupancy as separate living quarters. Separate living quarters are those in which the occupants do not live and eat with any other persons in the structure and which have direct access from the outside of the building through a common hall.

The occupants of a housing unit may be a single family, one person living alone, or two or more families living together, or any other group of related or unrelated persons who share living arrangements. Both occupied and vacant housing units are included in the housing inventory, with the exception that recreational vehicles, tents, caves, boats, railroad cars, and the like are included only if they are occupied as a person's usual place of residence.

A housing unit is classified as occupied if it is the usual place of residence of the person or group of persons living in it at the time of enumeration or if the occupants are only temporarily absent (away on vacation). A household consists of all persons who occupy a housing unit as their usual place of residence.

Median value is the dollar amount that divides the distribution of owner occupied housing units into two equal parts, one half of the units falling below this value and the other half exceeding it. Value is defined as the respondent's estimate of what the house would sell for if for sale. Data are presented for one-family units on less than 10 acres and with no business or medical office on the property.

Median rent divides the distribution of renter-occupied housing units into two equal parts. The rent concept used in this volume is gross rent, which includes the amount of cash rent a renter pays (contract rent) plus the estimated average cost of utilities and fuels if paid by the renter. The rent is the amount of rent only for living quarters, not for any business or other space occupied. Single family houses on lots of 10 or more acres are excluded.

Housing cost as a percent of income is shown separately for owners with mortgages, owners without mortgages, and renters. Rent as a percent of income is a computed ratio of gross rent and monthly household income (total household income in 1999 divided by 12). Selected owner costs include utilities and fuels, as well as mortgage payments, insurance, taxes, etc. In each case, the ratio of housing cost to income is computed separately for each housing unit. The ratios for one-half of the units are above the median shown in this book, and one-half are below.

Substandard units are occupied units which are overcrowded or lack complete plumbing facilities. For the purposes of this item, "overcrowded" is defined as having 1.01 persons or more per room. Complete plumbing facilities include hot and cold piped water, a flush toilet, and a bathtub or shower. These facilities must be located inside the housing unit but not necessarily in the same room.

SOCIAL SECURITY AND SUPPLEMENTAL SECURITY INCOME, Items 142–144
Source: U.S. Social Security Administration

Social Security beneficiaries is the number of persons receiving benefits under the Old Age, Survivors, and Disability Insurance Program. These include retired or disabled workers covered by the program, their spouses and dependent children, and the surviving spouses and dependent children of deceased workers.

Supplemental Security Income (SSI) recipients is the number of persons receiving SSI payments. Data are as of December of the year shown.

CIVILIAN EMPLOYMENT, Items 145–147
Source: U.S. Bureau of the Census— Current Population Survey, March 2000

Total employment includes all civilians 16 years old and older who were either (1) "at work"—those who did any work at all during the reference week as paid employees, worked in their own business or profession, worked on their own farm, or worked 15 hours or more as unpaid workers in a family farm or business; or were (2) "with a job, but not at work"—those who had a job but were not at work that week due to illness, weather, industrial dispute, vacation, or other personal reasons. The "reference week" for these employment questions was during March.

The **occupational categories** shown are consistent with the 1980 edition of the *Standard Occupational Classification Manual* (SOC), published by the Office of Federal Statistical Policy and Standards, U.S. Department of Commerce. Professional, managerial, and technical occupations include the following categories:

executive, administrative, and managerial occupations (000–042); professional specialty occupations (043–202); and technicians and related support occupations (203–42). Precision production, craft, and repair include SOC codes 503–702.

CIVILIAN LABOR FORCE AND UNEMPLOYMENT, Items 148–152
Source: U.S. Bureau of Labor Statistics

Data for the civilian labor force are the product of a federal-state cooperative program in which state employment security agencies prepare labor force and unemployment estimates under concepts, definitions, and technical procedures established by the Bureau of Labor Statistics. The civilian labor force consists of all civilians 16 years and over who are either employed or unemployed.

Unemployment includes all persons who did not work during the survey week, made specific efforts to find a job in the prior 4 weeks, and were available for work during the survey week (except for temporary illness). Persons waiting to be called back to a job from which they had been laid off and those waiting to report to a new job within the next 30 days are included in unemployment figures.

PRIVATE NONFARM EMPLOYMENT AND EARNINGS, Items 153–163
Source: U.S. Bureau of Labor Statistics, Current Employment Survey

Data for private nonfarm employment and earnings are compiled from payroll information reported monthly on a voluntary basis to the BLS and its cooperating state agencies. More than 350,000 establishments represent all industries except agriculture.

Employment is the annual average of monthly totals of persons who received pay for any part of the pay period including the 12th day of the month. Included are all full-time and part-time workers in nonfarm establishments. Not covered are government employees, proprietors, the self-employed, unpaid volunteers or family workers, farm workers, and domestic workers in households. The data by industry conform to the new definitions used in the North American Industry Classification System (NAICS).

Earnings of production workers in manufacturing industries are derived from reports of gross payrolls and corresponding paid hours. Payroll is reported before deductions of any kind. Total hours during the pay period include all hours worked (including overtime hours) and hours paid for holidays, vacations, and sick leave.

AGRICULTURE, Items 164–181
Source: U.S. Department of Agriculture, National Agricultural Statistics Service 2002 Census of Agriculture

Data for the 2002 Census of Agriculture were collected in 2003 and pertain to the year 2002.

The Bureau of the Census took a census of agriculture every 10 years from 1840 to 1920 and roughly every 5 years from 1925 to the present. The 1997 Census of Agriculture was transferred to the National Agricultural Statistics Service of the U.S. Department of Agriculture. Over time, the definition of a farm has varied. For recent censuses, including the 2002 census, a farm has been defined as any place from which $1,000 or more of agricultural products were sold or normally would have been sold during the census year.

The term **operator** refers to a person who operates a farm, either doing the work or making day-to-day decisions about such things as planting, harvesting, feeding, marketing, etc. The operator may be the owner, a member of the owner's household, a salaried manager, a tenant, a renter, or a sharecropper. For partnerships, only one partner is counted as an operator. For census purposes, the number of operators is the same as the number of farms.

The acreage designated as **land in farms** consists primarily of agricultural land used for crops, pasture, or grazing. It also includes woodland and wasteland not actually under cultivation or used for pasture or grazing, provided it was part of the farm operator's total operation.

Land in farms is an operating-unit concept and includes land owned and operated, as well as land rented from others. Land used rent free is classified as land rented from others. All land in Indian reservations used for growing crops or grazing livestock is classified as land in farms.

Irrigated land covers any land in farms to which water was artificially applied in the census year. Land irrigated prior to but not in the census year is not included. Irrigation may have been used for producing a harvested crop, for pasture or grazing lands, for cultivated summer fallow, or for land planted with a crop intended for future harvest. Land flooded during high-water periods was included as irrigated only if water was diverted to agricultural lands by dams, canals, or other works.

Cropland consists of land from which crops were harvested and land that could have been used for crops without additional improvements. This includes land in nonbearing orchards and vineyards, land from which any hay was cut, land on which crops failed, idle or fallow land, and land used for grazing purposes.

Respondents were asked to report their estimate of the current market **value of land and buildings** owned, rented, or leased from others, and rented and leased to others. Market value refers to the respondent's estimate of what the land and buildings would sell for under current market conditions.

The **value of machinery and equipment** was estimated by the respondent as the current market value of all cars, trucks, tractors, combines, balers, irrigation equipment, etc., used on the farm. This value is an estimate of what the machinery and equipment would sell for in its present condition and not the replacement or depreciated value. Share interests are reported at full value at the farm where the equipment and machinery are usually kept. Only equipment that was actually used in 2001 and 2002, or newly purchased but not yet used, and physically located at the farm on December 31, 2002 is included.

The **value of farm products sold** by farms represents the gross market value before taxes and production expenses of all agricultural products sold or removed from the place in 2002 regardless of who received the payment. It includes sales by the operator as well as the value of any share received by partners, landlords, contractors, and others associated with the operation. It represents the sum of all crops, including nursery products, sold and livestock and poultry and their products sold.

The value of crops sold in 2002 does not necessarily represent the sales from crops harvested that year. The data include sales from crops produced in earlier years and exclude some crops produced in 2002 but held in storage and not sold in the census year. For crops sold through a co-op that made payments in several installments, only the total value received in the census year was to be reported.

LAND USE, Items 182–183
Source: U.S. Department of Agriculture, Natural Resources Conservation Service, 1997 National Resources Inventory

The National Resources Inventory has been conducted every 5 years since 1982. The 1997 NRI is based on a sample of about 800,000 locations throughout the United States (excluding Alaska and the District of Columbia). Federally owned lands include military bases, national forests, wildlife refuges, parks, grassland game preserves, scenic waterways, wilderness areas, monuments, lakeshore, parkways, battlefields, Bureau of Land Management lands, and other federal lands. Developed land includes any built-up area greater than one-fourth acre. Built-up areas include residential, industrial, commercial, and institutional land; construction sites; public administrative sites; railroad yards; cemeteries; airports; golf courses; sanitary landfills; sewage treatment plants; water control structures and spillways; other land used for such purposes; small parks (less than 10 acres) within urban and built-up areas; and highways, railroads, and other transportation facilities if they are surrounded by urban areas. Also included are tracts of less than 10 acres that do not meet the above definition but are completely surrounded by urban and built-up land and all highways, roads, railroads, and associated rights-of-way outside urban and built-up areas (including private roads to farmsteads or ranch headquarters, logging roads, and other private roads).

WATER CONSUMPTION, Item 184
Source: U.S. Geological Survey, National Water Use Information Program, 2000 Water Use Data

Every 5 years the U.S. Geological Survey compiles national water-use estimates. This volume includes the total freshwater withdrawals expressed as million gallons per day. Estimates of withdrawals of ground and surface water are given for the following categories of use: public water supplies, domestic, commercial, irrigation, livestock, industrial, mining, and thermoelectric power.

MANUFACTURES, Items 185–194
Source: U.S. Bureau of the Census— 2001 Annual Survey of Manufacturers

The Annual Survey of Manufacturers has been conducted every year since 1949.

The **all employees** number is the average number of production workers for the payroll periods including the 12th of March, May,

August, and November plus the number of other employees in mid-March. Included are all persons on paid sick leave, paid holidays, and paid vacations during the pay period. Officers of corporations are included as employees—proprietors and partners of unincorporated firms are excluded.

Payroll figures include the gross annual earnings of all employees on the payroll of operating manufacturing establishments. The definition, which is the same as the one used for calculating the federal withholding tax, includes all forms of compensation, such as salaries, wages, commissions, dismissal pay, all bonuses, vacation and sick leave pay, and compensation-in-kind, prior to such deductions as employees' Social Security contributions, withholding taxes, group insurance, union dues, and savings bonds. The total includes salaries of officers of corporations but excludes payments to proprietors or partners of unincorporated concerns. Also excluded are payments to members of the Armed Forces and to pensioners carried on the active payroll of manufacturing establishments.

Production workers include workers (up through the line-supervisor level) engaged in fabricating; processing; assembling; inspecting; receiving; storing; handling; packing; warehousing; shipping (but not delivering); maintenance; repair; janitorial and guard services; product development; auxiliary production for plant's own use (for example, power plant); record-keeping; and other services closely associated with these production operations. Employees above the working supervisor level are excluded.

The number of production workers is the average for the payroll periods including the 12th of March, May, August, and November. Not included in this classification are all other employees, defined as non-production employees, including those engaged in factory supervision above the line-supervisor level.

Production worker hours cover hours worked or paid for at the plant, including actual overtime hours (not straight-time-equivalent hours). The data exclude hours paid for vacations, holidays, or sick leave. Production wages represent all compensation paid to production workers.

Value added by manufacture is derived by subtracting the cost of materials, supplies, containers, fuel, purchased electricity, and contract work from the value of shipments (products manufactured plus receipts for services rendered). The result of this calculation is adjusted by the addition of value added by merchandising operations (the difference between the sales value and cost of merchandise sold without further manufacture, processing, or assembly) plus the net change in finished goods and work in process between the beginning- and end-of-year inventories.

Value of shipments covers the received or receivable net selling values; free on board plant (exclusive freight charges and taxes) of all products shipped, both primary and secondary; as well as miscellaneous receipts, such as receipts for contract work performed for others, installation and repair, sales of scrap, and sales of products bought and resold without further processing. Included are all items made by or for the establishment from materials owned by it, whether sold, transferred to other plants of the same company, or shipped on consignment. The net selling value of products made in one plant on a contract basis from materials owned by another was reported by the plant providing the materials.

In the case of multi-unit companies, the manufacturer was requested to report the value of products transferred to other establishments of the same company at full economic or commercial value, including not only the direct costs of production but also a reasonable proportion of "all other costs" (including company overhead) and profit.

The aggregate of the value of shipments figure for industry groups and for all manufacturing industries includes large amounts of duplication since the products of some industries are used as materials by others. Estimates as to the overall extent of this duplication indicate that the value of manufactured products exclusive of such duplication (the value of finished manufactures) tend to approximate two-thirds of the total value of products reported in the census of manufactures.

Total capital expenditures (new and used). For establishments in operation and any known plants under construction, manufacturers were asked to report their new and used expenditures for (1) permanent additions and major alterations to manufacturing establishments and (2) machinery and equipment used for replacement and additions to plant capacity if they were of the type for which depreciation accounts were ordinarily maintained.

Totals for expenditures include the costs of assets leased from nonmanufacturing concerns through capital leases. New facilities owned by the federal government but operated under contract by private companies and plant and equipment furnished to the manufacturer by communities and nonprofit organizations are excluded. Also excluded are expenditures for land and cost of maintenance and repairs charged as current operating expenses.

For any equipment or structure transferred for the use of the reporting establishment by the parent company or one of its subsidiaries, the value at which it was transferred to the establishment was to be reported.

If an establishment changed ownership during the year, the cost of the fixed assets (building and equipment) was to be reported.

1997 ECONOMIC CENSUS: OVERVIEW
Items 195–282
Source: U.S. Bureau of the Census

The Economic Census provides a detailed portrait of the nation's economy once every 5 years, from the national to the local level. The 1997 Economic Census covers nearly all of the U.S. economy in its basic collection of establishment statistics. It is the first major data source to use the new North American Industry Classification System (NAICS) and is therefore not comparable to economic data from prior years, which were based on the Standard Industrial Classification (SIC) system.

NAICS, developed in cooperation with Canada and Mexico, classifies North America's economic activities at two-, three-, four-, and five-digit levels of detail, and the U.S. version of NAICS further defines industries to a sixth digit. The Economic Census takes advantage of this hierarchy to publish data at these successive levels of detail: sector (two-digit); subsector (three-digit); industry group (four-digit); industry (five-digit); and U.S. industry (six-digit.) Information in Table A is at the two-digit level, with a few three- and four-digit items.

Several key statistics are tabulated for all industries included in this volume: number of establishments (or companies); number of employees; payroll; and a measure of output (sales, receipts, revenue, value of shipments, or value of construction work done).

Number of Establishments. An establishment is a single physical location at which business is conducted. It is not necessarily identical with a company or enterprise, which may consist of one establishment or more. Economic Census figures represent a summary of reports for individual establishments rather than companies. For cases where a census report was received, separate information was obtained for each location where business was conducted. When administrative records of other federal agencies were used instead of a census report, no information was available on the number of locations operated. Each Economic Census establishment was tabulated according to the physical location at which the business was conducted. The count of establishments represents those in business at any time during 1997.

When two activities or more were carried on at a single location under a single ownership, all activities generally were grouped together as a single establishment. The entire establishment was classified on the basis of its major activity and all data for it were included in that classification. However, when distinct and separate economic activities (for which different industry classification codes were appropriate) were conducted at a single location under a single ownership, separate establishment reports for each of the different activities were obtained in the census.

Number of Employees. Paid employees consist of the full-time and part-time employees, including salaried officers and executives of corporations. Included are employees on paid sick leave, paid holidays, and paid vacations; not included are proprietors and partners of unincorporated businesses. The definition of paid employees is the same as that used on IRS form 941.

Payroll. Payroll includes all forms of compensation such as salaries, wages, commissions, dismissal pay, bonuses, vacation allowances, sick-leave pay, and employee contributions to qualified pension plans paid during the year to all employees. For corporations, payroll includes amounts paid to officers and executives; for unincorporated businesses, it does not include profit or other compensation of proprietors or partners. Payroll is reported before deductions for social security, income tax, insurance, union dues, etc. This definition of payroll is the same as that used by the IRS on form 941.

Sales, Shipments, Receipts, Revenue, or Business Done. This measure includes the total sales, shipments, receipts, revenue, or business done by establishments within the scope of the Economic Census. The definition of each of these items is specific to the economic sector measured.

CONSTRUCTION (Items 195–198)
Source: U.S. Bureau of the Census,
1997 Economic Census
(See Overview of 1997 Economic Census prior to Item 195)

The Construction sector (sector 23) comprises establishments primarily engaged in the construction of buildings and other structures, heavy construction (except buildings), additions, alterations, reconstruction, installation, and maintenance and repairs. Establishments engaged in demolition or wrecking of buildings

and other structures, clearing of building sites, and sale of materials from demolished structures are also included. This sector also includes those establishments engaged in blasting, test drilling, landfill, leveling, earthmoving, excavating, land drainage, and other land preparation. The industries within this sector have been defined on the basis of their unique production processes. As with all industries, the production processes are distinguished by their use of specialized human resources and specialized physical capital. Construction activities are generally administered or managed at a relatively fixed place of business, but the actual construction work is performed at one or more different project sites. This sector is divided into three subsectors of construction activities: (1) building construction and land subdivision and land development; (2) heavy construction (except buildings), such as highways, power plants, and pipelines; and (3) construction activity by special trade contractors.

WHOLESALE TRADE, Items 199–202
Source: U.S. Bureau of the Census,
1997 Economic Census
(See Overview of 1997 Economic Census prior to Item 195)

The Wholesale Trade sector (sector 42) comprises establishments engaged in wholesaling merchandise, generally without transformation, and rendering services incidental to the sale of merchandise. The wholesaling process is an intermediate step in the distribution of merchandise. Wholesalers are organized to sell or arrange the purchase or sale of (a) goods for resale (goods sold to other wholesalers or retailers), (b) capital or durable nonconsumer goods, and (c) raw and intermediate materials and supplies used in production.

Wholesalers sell merchandise to other businesses and normally operate from a warehouse or office. These warehouses and offices are characterized by having little or no display of merchandise. In addition, neither the design nor the location of the premises is intended to solicit walk-in traffic. Wholesalers do not normally use advertising directed to the general public. Customers are generally reached initially via telephone, in-person marketing, or by specialized advertising that may include Internet and other electronic means. Follow-up orders are either vendor-initiated or client-initiated, generally based on previous sales, and typically exhibit strong ties between sellers and buyers. In fact, transactions are often conducted between wholesalers and clients that have long-standing business relationships.

This sector comprises two main types of wholesalers: those that sell goods on their own account and those that arrange sales and purchases for others for a commission or fee.

(1) Establishments that sell goods on their own account are known as wholesale merchants, distributors, jobbers, drop shippers, import/export merchants, and sales branches. These establishments typically maintain their own warehouse, where they receive and handle goods for their customers. Goods are generally sold without transformation, but may include integral functions, such as sorting, packaging, labeling, and other marketing services.

(2) Establishments arranging for the purchase or sale of goods owned by others or purchasing goods on a commission basis are known as agents and brokers, commission merchants, import/

export agents and brokers, auction companies, and manufacturers' representatives. These establishments operate from offices and generally do not own or handle the goods they sell.

Some wholesale establishments may be connected with a single manufacturer and promote and sell the particular manufacturer's products to a wide range of other wholesalers or retailers. Other wholesalers may be connected to a retail chain or a limited number of retail chains and only provide a variety of products needed by that particular retail operation(s). These wholesalers may obtain the products from a wide range of manufacturers. Still other wholesalers may not take title to the goods, but act as agents and brokers for a commission.

Although, in general, wholesaling normally denotes sales in large volumes, durable nonconsumer goods may be sold in single units. Sales of capital or durable nonconsumer goods used in the production of goods and services, such as farm machinery, medium and heavy duty trucks, and industrial machinery, are always included in wholesale trade.

RETAIL TRADE, Items 203–210
Source: U.S. Bureau of the Census, 1997 Economic Census (See Overview of 1997 Economic Census prior to Item 195)

The Retail Trade sector (44-45) comprises establishments engaged in retailing merchandise, generally without transformation, and rendering services incidental to the sale of merchandise.

The retailing process is the final step in the distribution of merchandise; retailers are, therefore, organized to sell merchandise in small quantities to the general public. This sector comprises two main types of retailers: store and nonstore retailers.

Store retailers operate fixed point-of-sale locations, located and designed to attract a high volume of walk-in customers. In general, retail stores have extensive displays of merchandise and use mass-media advertising to attract customers. They typically sell merchandise to the general public for personal or household consumption, but some also serve business and institutional clients. These include establishments, such as office supply stores, computer and software stores, building materials dealers, plumbing supply stores, and electrical supply stores. Catalog showrooms, gasoline service stations, automotive dealers, and mobile home dealers are treated as store retailers.

In addition to retailing merchandise, some types of store retailers are also engaged in the provision of after-sales services, such as repair and installation. For example, new automobile dealers, electronic and appliance stores, and musical instrument and supply stores often provide repair services. As a general rule, establishments engaged in retailing merchandise and providing after-sales services are classified in this sector.

Nonstore retailers, like store retailers, are organized to serve the general public, but their retailing methods differ. The establishments of this subsector reach customers and market merchandise with methods, such as the broadcasting of "infomercials," the broadcasting and publishing of direct-response advertising, the publishing of paper and electronic catalogs, door-to-door solicitation, in-home demonstration, selling from portable stalls (street vendors, except food), and distribution through vending machines. Establishments engaged in the direct sale (nonstore) of products, such as home heating oil dealers and home delivery newspaper routes.

The buying of goods for resale is a characteristic of retail trade establishments that particularly distinguishes them from establishments in the agriculture, manufacturing, and construction industries. For example, farms that sell their products at or from the point of production are not classified in retail, but rather in agriculture. Similarly, establishments that both manufacture and sell their products to the general public are not classified in retail, but rather in manufacturing. However, establishments that engage in processing activities incidental to retailing are classified in retail.

Industries in the **Motor Vehicle and Parts Dealers** subsector (441) retail motor vehicle and parts merchandise from fixed point-of-sale locations. Establishments in this subsector typically operate from a showroom and/or an open lot where the vehicles are on display. The display of vehicles and the related parts require little by way of display equipment. The personnel generally include both the sales and sales support staff familiar with the requirements for registering and financing a vehicle as well as a staff of parts experts and mechanics trained to provide repair and maintenance services for the vehicles. Specific industries have been included in this subsector to identify the type of vehicle being retailed. Sales of capital or durable nonconsumer goods, such as medium and heavy-duty trucks, are always included in wholesale trade. These goods are virtually never sold through retail methods.

Industries in the **Food and Beverage Stores** subsector (445) usually retail food and beverage merchandise from fixed point-of-sale locations. Establishments in this subsector have special equipment (freezers, refrigerated display cases, refrigerators) for displaying food and beverage goods. They have staff trained in the processing of food products to guarantee the proper storage and sanitary conditions required by regulatory authority.

Industries in the **Clothing and Clothing Accessories Stores** subsector (448) retail new clothing and clothing accessories merchandise from fixed point-of-sale locations. Establishments in this subsector have similar display equipment and staff that is knowledgeable regarding fashion trends and the proper match of styles, colors, and combinations of clothing and accessories to the characteristics and tastes of the customer.

Industries in the **General Merchandise Stores** subsector (452) retail new general merchandise from fixed point-of-sale locations. Establishments in this subsector are unique in that they have the equipment and staff capable of retailing a large variety of goods from a single location. This includes a variety of display equipment and staff trained to provide information on many lines of products.

TRANSPORTATION AND WAREHOUSING, Items 211–214
Source: U.S. Bureau of the Census, 1997 Economic Census (See Overview of 1997 Economic Census prior to Item 195)

The Transportation and Warehousing sector (48-49) includes industries providing transportation of passengers and cargo, warehousing and storage for goods, scenic and sightseeing transportation, and support activities related to modes of transportation.

Establishments in these industries use transportation equipment or transportation related facilities as a productive asset. The type of equipment depends on the mode of transportation. The modes of transportation are air, rail, water, road, and pipeline.

The Transportation and Warehousing sector distinguishes three basic types of activities: subsectors for each mode of transportation, a subsector for warehousing and storage, and a subsector for establishments providing support activities for transportation. In addition, there are subsectors for establishments that provide passenger transportation for scenic and sightseeing purposes, postal services, and courier services.

FINANCE AND INSURANCE, Items 215–218
Source: U.S. Bureau of the Census, 1997 Economic Census
(See Overview of 1997 Economic Census prior to Item 195)

The Finance and Insurance sector (52) comprises establishments primarily engaged in financial transactions (transactions involving the creation, liquidation, or change in ownership of financial assets) and/or in facilitating financial transactions. Three principal types of activities are identified:

(1) Raising funds by taking deposits and/or issuing securities and, in the process, incurring liabilities. Establishments engaged in this activity use raised funds to acquire financial assets by making loans and/or purchasing securities. Putting themselves at risk, they channel funds from lenders to borrowers and transform or repackage the funds with respect to maturity, scale and risk. This activity is known as financial intermediation.

(2) Pooling of risk by underwriting insurance and annuities. Establishments engaged in this activity collect fees, insurance premiums, or annuity considerations; build up reserves; invest those reserves; and make contractual payments. Fees are based on the expected incidence of the insured risk and the expected return on investment.

(3) Providing specialized services facilitating or supporting financial intermediation, insurance, and employee benefit programs.

In addition, monetary authorities charged with monetary control are included in this sector.

REAL ESTATE AND RENTAL AND LEASING, Items 219–222
Source: U.S. Bureau of the Census, 1997 Economic Census
(See Overview of 1997 Economic Census prior to Item 195)

The Real Estate and Rental and Leasing sector (53) comprises establishments primarily engaged in renting, leasing, or otherwise allowing the use of tangible or intangible assets, and establishments providing related services. The major portion of this sector comprises establishments that rent, lease, or otherwise allow the use of their own assets by others. The assets may be tangible, as is the case of real estate and equipment, or intangible, as is the case with patents and trademarks.

This sector also includes establishments primarily engaged in managing real estate for others, selling, renting and/or buying real estate for others, and appraising real estate. These activities are closely related to this sector's main activity, and it was felt that from a production basis they would best be included here. In addition, a substantial proportion of property management is self-performed by lessors.

The main components of this sector are the real estate lessors industries; equipment lessors industries (including motor vehicles, computers, and consumer goods); and lessors of nonfinancial intangible assets (except copyrighted works).

INFORMATION, Items 223–230
Source: U.S. Bureau of the Census, 1997 Economic Census
(See Overview of 1997 Economic Census prior to Item 195)

The Information sector (51) comprises establishments engaged in the following processes: (a) producing and distributing information and cultural products, (b) providing the means to transmit or distribute these products as well as data or communications, and (c) processing data.

The main components of this sector are the publishing industries, including software publishing, the motion picture and sound recording industries, the broadcasting and telecommunications industries, and the information services and data processing industries.

For the purpose of NAICS, it is the transformation of information into a commodity that is produced and distributed by a number of growing industries that is at issue. The Information sector groups three types of establishments: (1) those engaged in producing and distributing information and cultural products; (2) those that provide the means to transmit or distribute these products as well as data or communications; and (3) those that process data. Cultural products are those that directly express attitudes, opinions, ideas, values, and artistic creativity; provide entertainment; or offer information and analysis concerning the past and present. Included in this definition are popular, mass-produced, products as well as cultural products that normally have a more limited audience, such as poetry books, literary magazines, or classical records. These activities were formerly classified throughout the existing national classifications. Traditional publishing was in manufacturing; broadcasting in communications; software production in business services; film production in amusement services; and so forth.

Industries in the **Publishing Industries** subsector (511) group establishments engaged in the publishing of newspapers, magazines, other periodicals, and books, as well as database and software publishing. In general, these establishments, which are known as publishers, issue copies of works for which they usually possess copyright. Works may be in one or more formats including traditional print form, CD-ROM, or on-line. Publishers may publish works originally created by others for which they have obtained the rights and/or works that they have created in-house. Software publishing is included here because the activity, creation of a copyrighted product and bringing it to market, is equivalent to the creation process for other types of intellectual products.

In NAICS, publishing—the reporting, writing, editing, and other processes that are required to create an edition of a book or a newspaper—is treated as a major economic activity in its own right, rather than as a subsidiary activity to a manufacturing activity, printing. Thus, publishing is classified in the Information sector; whereas, printing remains in the NAICS Manufacturing sector. In part, the NAICS classification reflects the fact that publishing increasingly takes place in establishments that are physically separate from the associated printing establishments. More crucially, the NAICS classification of book and newspaper publishing is intended to portray their roles in a modern economy, in which they do not resemble manufacturing activities.

Music publishers are not included in the Publishing Industries subsector, but are included in the Motion Picture and Sound Recording Industries subsector. Reproduction of prepackaged software is treated in NAICS as a manufacturing activity; on-line distribution of software products is in the Information sector, and custom design of software to client specifications is included in the Professional, Scientific, and Technical Services sector. These distinctions arise because of the different ways that software is created, reproduced, and distributed.

The Information sector does not include products, such as manifold business forms. Information is not the essential component of these items. Establishments producing these items are included in Subsector 323, Printing and Related Support Activities.

Industries in the **Motion Picture and Sound Recording Industries** subsector (512) group establishments involved in the production and distribution of motion pictures and sound recordings. While producers and distributors of motion pictures and sound recordings issue works for sale as traditional publishers do, the processes are sufficiently different to warrant placing establishments engaged in these activities in a separate subsector. Production is typically a complex process that involves several distinct types of establishments that are engaged in activities, such as contracting with performers, creating the film or sound content, and providing technical postproduction services. Film distribution is often to exhibitors, such as theaters and broadcasters, rather than through the wholesale and retail distribution chain. When the product is in a mass-produced form, NAICS treats production and distribution as the major economic activity as it does in the Publishing Industries subsector, rather than as a subsidiary activity to the manufacture of such products.

This subsector does not include establishments primarily engaged in the wholesale distribution of video cassettes and sound recordings, such as compact discs and audio tapes; these establishments are included in the Wholesale Trade sector. Reproduction of video cassettes and sound recordings that is carried out separately from establishments engaged in production and distribution is treated in NAICS as a manufacturing activity.

Industries in the **Broadcasting and Telecommunications** subsector (513) include establishments providing point-to-point communications and the services related to that activity. The industry groups (Radio and Television Broadcasting, Cable Networks and Program Distribution, and Telecommunications) are based on differences in the methods of communication and in the nature of services provided. The Radio and Television Broadcasting industry group includes establishments that operate broadcasting studios and facilities for over the air or satellite delivery of radio and television programs of entertainment, news, talk, and the like. These establishments are often engaged in the production and purchase of programs and generating revenues from the sale of air time to advertisers and from donations, subsidies, and/or the sale of programs. The Cable Networks and Program Distribution industry group includes two types of establishments. Those in the Cable Networks industry operate studios and facilities for the broadcasting of programs that are typically narrowcast in nature (limited format, such as news, sports, education, and youth-oriented programming). The services of these establishments are typically sold on a subscription or fee basis. Delivery of the programs to customers is handled by other establishments, in the Cable and Other Program Distribution industry, that operate cable systems, direct-to-home satellite systems, or other similar systems. The Telecommunications industry group is primarily engaged in operating, maintaining, and/or providing access to facilities for the transmission of voice, data, text, sound, and full motion picture video between network termination points. A transmission facility may be based on a single technology or a combination of technologies. Establishments primarily engaged as independent contractors in the maintenance and installation of broadcasting and telecommunications systems are classified in sector 23, Construction.

Industries in the **Information Services and Data Processing Services** subsector (514) group establishments providing information, storing information, providing access to information, and processing information. The main components of the subsector are news syndicates, libraries, archives, on-line information service providers, and data processors.

UTILITIES, Items 231–234
Source: U.S. Bureau of the Census, 1997 Economic Census
(See Overview of 1997 Economic Census prior to Item 195)

The Utilities sector (22) comprises establishments engaged in the provision of the following utility services: electric power, natural gas, steam supply, water supply, and sewage removal. Within this sector, the specific activities associated with the utility services provided vary by utility: electric power includes generation, transmission, and distribution; natural gas includes distribution; steam supply includes provision and/or distribution; water supply includes treatment and distribution; and sewage removal includes collection, treatment, and disposal of waste through sewer systems and sewage treatment facilities.

Excluded from this sector are establishments primarily engaged in waste management services classified in subsector 562, Waste Management and Remediation Services, which also collect, treat, and dispose of waste materials; however, they do not use sewer systems or sewage treatment facilities.

PROFESSIONAL, SCIENTIFIC, AND TECHNICAL SERVICES, Items 235–242

Source: U.S. Bureau of the Census,
1997 Economic Census
(See Overview of 1997 Economic Census
prior to Item 195)

The Professional, Scientific, and Technical Services sector (54) comprises establishments that specialize in performing professional, scientific, and technical activities for others. These activities require a high degree of expertise and training. The establishments in this sector specialize according to expertise and provide these services to clients in a variety of industries and, in some cases, to households. Activities performed include: legal advice and representation; accounting, bookkeeping, and payroll services; architectural, engineering, and specialized design services; computer services; consulting services; research services; advertising services; photographic services; translation and interpretation services; veterinary services; and other professional, scientific, and technical services.

This volume includes only those establishments subject to federal income tax.

This sector excludes establishments primarily engaged in providing a range of day-to-day office administrative services, such as financial planning, billing and recordkeeping, personnel, and physical distribution and logistics. These establishments are classified in Sector 56, Administrative and Support and Waste Management and Remediation Services.

Legal Services is a NAICS industry group (5411) that includes establishments classified in the following NAICS industries: 54111, Offices of Lawyers; and 54119, Other Legal Services.

Accounting, Tax Preparation, Bookkeeping, and Payroll Services is a NAICS industry group (5412) that comprises establishments primarily engaged in providing services, such as auditing of accounting records, designing accounting systems, preparing financial statements, developing budgets, preparing tax returns, processing payrolls, bookkeeping, and billing.

Architectural, Engineering, and Related Services is a NAICS industry group (5413) that includes establishments classified in the following NAICS industries: 54131, Architectural Services; 54133, Engineering Services; 54134, Drafting Services; 54135, Building Inspection Services; 54136, Geophysical Surveying and Mapping Services; 54137, Surveying and Mapping (Except Geophysical) Services; and 54138, Testing Laboratories.

Computer Systems Design and Related Services is a NAICS industry that comprises establishments primarily engaged in providing expertise in the field of information technologies through one or more of the following activities: (1) writing, modifying, testing, and supporting software to meet the needs of a particular customer; (2) planning and designing computer systems that integrate computer hardware, software, and communication technologies; (3) on-site management and operation of clients' computer systems and/or data processing facilities; and (4) other professional and technical computer-related advice and services.

ARTS, ENTERTAINMENT, AND RECREATION, Items 243–246

Source: U.S. Bureau of the Census,
1997 Economic Census
(See Overview of 1997 Economic Census
prior to Item 195)

The Arts, Entertainment, and Recreation sector (71) includes a wide range of establishments that operate facilities or provide services to meet varied cultural, entertainment, and recreational interests of their patrons. This sector comprises (1) establishments that are involved in producing, promoting, or participating in live performances, events, or exhibits intended for public viewing; (2) establishments that preserve and exhibit objects and sites of historical, cultural, or educational interest; and (3) establishments that operate facilities or provide services that enable patrons to participate in recreational activities or pursue amusement, hobby, and leisure time interests.

Some establishments that provide cultural, entertainment, or recreational facilities and services are classified in other sectors. Excluded from this sector are: (1) establishments that provide both accommodations and recreational facilities, such as hunting and fishing camps and resort and casino hotels are classified in subsector 721, Accommodation; (2) restaurants and night clubs that provide live entertainment in addition to the sale of food and beverages are classified in subsector 722, Food Services and Drinking Places; (3) motion picture theaters, libraries and archives, and publishers of newspapers, magazines, books, periodicals, and computer software are classified in sector 51, Information; and (4) establishments using transportation equipment to provide recreational and entertainment services, such as those operating sightseeing buses, dinner cruises, or helicopter rides are classified in subsector 487, Scenic and Sightseeing Transportation.

HEALTH CARE AND SOCIAL ASSISTANCE, Items 247–258

Source: U.S. Bureau of the Census,
1997 Economic Census
(See Overview of 1997 Economic Census

prior to Item 195)

The Health Care and Social Assistance sector (62) comprises establishments providing health care and social assistance for individuals. The sector includes both health care and social assistance because it is sometimes difficult to distinguish between the boundaries of these two activities. The industries in this sector are arranged on a continuum starting with those establishments providing medical care exclusively, continuing with those providing health care and social assistance, and finally finishing with those providing only social assistance. The services provided by establishments in this sector are delivered by trained professionals. All industries in the sector share this commonality of process, namely, labor inputs of health practitioners or social workers with the requisite expertise. Many of the industries in the sector are defined based on the educational degree held by the practitioners included in the industry.

In this volume, taxable and tax-exempt establishments are presented separately.

Excluded from this sector are aerobic classes in subsector 713, Amusement, Gambling and Recreation Industries and nonmedical diet and weight reducing centers in subsector 812, Personal and Laundry Services. Although these can be viewed as health services, these services are not typically delivered by health practitioners.

Industries in the **Ambulatory Health Care Services** subsector (621) provide health care services directly or indirectly to ambulatory patients and do not usually provide inpatient services. Health practitioners in this subsector provide outpatient services, with the facilities and equipment not usually being the most significant part of the production process.

Industries in the **Hospitals** subsector (622) provide medical, diagnostic, and treatment services that include physician, nursing, and other health services to inpatients and the specialized accommodation services required by inpatients. Hospitals may also provide outpatient services as a secondary activity. Establishments in the Hospitals subsector provide inpatient health services, many of which can only be provided using the specialized facilities and equipment that form a significant and integral part of the production process.

ACCOMMODATION AND FOOD SERVICES, Items 259–270
Source: U.S. Bureau of the Census,
1997 Economic Census
(See Overview of 1997 Economic Censu
prior to Item 195)

The Accommodation and Food Services sector (72) comprises establishments providing customers with lodging and/or preparing meals, snacks, and beverages for immediate consumption. The sector includes both accommodation and food services establishments because the two activities are often combined at the same establishment.

Excluded from this sector are civic and social organizations; amusement and recreation parks; theaters; and other recreation or entertainment facilities providing food and beverage services.

Industries in the **Food Services and Drinking Places** subsector (722) prepare meals, snacks, and beverages to customer order for immediate on-premises and off-premises consumption. There is a wide range of establishments in these industries. Some provide food and drink only; while others provide various combinations of seating space, waiter/waitress services and incidental amenities, such as limited entertainment. The industries in the subsector are grouped based on the type and level of services provided. The industry groups are full-service restaurants; limited-service eating places; special food services, such as food service contractors, caterers, and mobile food services, and drinking places.

Food services and drink activities at hotels and motels; amusement parks, theaters, casinos, country clubs, and similar recreational facilities; and civic and social organizations are included in this subsector only if these services are provided by a separate establishment primarily engaged in providing food and beverage services.

Excluded from this subsector are establishments operating dinner cruises. These establishments are classified in subsector 487, Scenic and Sightseeing Transportation because those establishments utilize transportation equipment to provide scenic recreational entertainment.

OTHER SERVICES, Items 264–270
Source: U.S. Bureau of the Census,
1997 Economic Census
(See Overview of 1997 Economic Census
prior to Item 195)

The Other Services (except Public Administration) sector (81) comprises establishments engaged in providing services not specifically provided for elsewhere in the classification system. Establishments in this sector are primarily engaged in activities, such as equipment and machinery repairing, promoting or administering religious activities, grantmaking, advocacy, and providing drycleaning and laundry services, personal care services, death care services, pet care services, photofinishing services, temporary parking services, and dating services.

Private households that engage in employing workers on or about the premises in activities primarily concerned with the operation of the household are included in this sector.

In this volume, only firms subject to federal tax are included in the categories that include the full "other services" sector, as well as the number of employees in the "Repair and Maintenance" and "Personal and Laundry Services" subsectors. However, the number of employees in the "Religious, Civic, and Similar Services" subsector include only non-taxable establishments.

Excluded from this sector are establishments primarily engaged in retailing new equipment and also performing repairs and general maintenance on equipment. These establishments are classified in sector 44-45, Retail Trade.

Industries in the **Repair and Maintenance** subsector (811) restore machinery, equipment, and other products to working order. These establishments also typically provide general or routine maintenance (that is servicing) on such products to ensure they work efficiently and to prevent breakdown and unnecessary repairs.

The NAICS structure for this subsector brings together most types of repair and maintenance establishments and categorizes them based on production processes (that is on the type of repair and maintenance activity performed, and the necessary skills, expertise, and processes that are found in different repair and maintenance establishments). This NAICS classification does not delineate between repair services provided to businesses versus those that serve households. Although some industries primarily serve either businesses or households, separation by class of customer is limited by the fact that many establishments serve both. Establishments repairing computers and consumer electronics products are two examples of such overlap.

The Repair and Maintenance subsector does not include all establishments that do repair and maintenance. For example, a substantial amount of repair is done by establishments that also manufacture machinery, equipment, and other goods. These establishments are included in the Manufacturing sector in NAICS. In addition, repair of transportation equipment is often provided by or based at transportation facilities, such as airports, seaports, and these activities are included in the Transportation and Warehousing sector. A particularly unique situation exists with repair of buildings. Plumbing, electrical installation and repair, painting and decorating, and other construction-related establishments are often involved in performing installation or other work on new construction as well as providing repair services on existing structures. While some specialize in repair, it is difficult to distinguish between the two types and all have been included in the Construction sector.

Excluded from this subsector are establishments primarily engaged in rebuilding or remanufacturing machinery and equipment. These are classified in sector 31-33, Manufacturing. Also excluded are retail establishments that provide after-sale services and repair. These are classified in sector 44-45, Retail Trade.

Industries in the **Personal and Laundry Services** subsector (812) group establishments that provide personal and laundry services to individuals, households, and businesses. Services performed include: personal care services; death care services; laundry and drycleaning services; and a wide range of other personal services, such as pet care (except veterinary) services, photofinishing services, temporary parking services, and dating services.

The Personal and Laundry Services subsector is by no means all-inclusive of the services that could be termed personal services (those provided to individuals rather than businesses). There are many other subsectors, as well as sectors, that provide services to persons. Establishments providing legal, accounting, tax preparation, architectural, portrait photography, and similar professional services are classified in sector 54, Professional, Scientific, and Technical Services; those providing job placement, travel arrangement, home security, interior and exterior house cleaning, exterminating, lawn and garden care, and similar support services are classified in sector 56, Administrative and Support, Waste Management and Remediation Services; those providing health and social services are classified in sector 62, Health Care and Social Assistance; those providing amusement and recreation services are classified in sector 71, Arts, Entertainment and Recreation; those providing educational instruction are classified in sector 61, Educational Services; those providing repair services are classified in subsector 811, Repair and Maintenance; and those providing spiritual, civic, and advocacy services are classified in subsector 813, Religious, Grantmaking, Civic, Professional, and Similar Organizations.

Industries in the **Religious, Grantmaking, Civic, Professional, and Similar Organizations** subsector (813) group establishments that organize and promote religious activities; support various causes through grantmaking; advocate various social and political causes; and promote and defend the interests of their members. This category includes only tax-exempt establishments.

The industry groups within the subsector are defined in terms of their activities, such as establishments that provide funding for specific causes or for a variety of charitable causes; establishments that advocate and actively promote causes and beliefs for the public good; and establishments that have an active membership structure to promote causes and represent the interests of their members. Establishments in this subsector may publish newsletters, books, and periodicals, for distribution to their membership.

ECONOMIC CENSUS BY SIC CODE
(Items 271–282)
Source: U.S. Bureau of the Census, 1997 Economic Census
(See Overview of 1997 Economic Census prior to Item 195)

Because the 1997 Economic Census used the new North American Industry Classification System (NAICS), it is not directly comparable with Economic Census data from previous years. Because 1997 Economic Census records were assigned both SIC and NAICS codes, the Census Bureau was able to compile comparative statistics in which the 1997 data are compared with 1992 data using the Standard Industrial Classification (SIC) system. This volume includes the number of employees and the percent change from 1992 for six SIC sectors.

While many of the individual SIC industries correspond directly to industries as defined under the NAICS system, most of the higher level groupings do not. Particular care should be taken in comparing data for retail trade, wholesale trade, and manufacturing, which are sector titles used in both NAICS and SIC, but cover somewhat different groups of industries. The industry definitions discuss the relationships between NAICS and SIC industries. Where changes are significant, it will not be possible to construct time series that include data for points both before and after 1997.

For the SIC-based tables from the 1997 Economic Census, all auxiliaries are included in the category titled ''Auxiliaries'' and are not included in this volume. Note that in published reports from previous censuses for manufacturing and mining, auxiliary establishments were included in, or along with, data for the industries served; for other SIC divisions, auxiliary establishments were excluded from the detailed tables.

Construction. While some changes affecting construction were within the sector, this sector now includes industries that were previously classified in other sectors. Prominent among these industries are construction management and land subdividers and developers. In addition, although the construction sector is enumerated on an establishment basis, statistical information was obtained in the census by a survey which included all large employers and a sample of the smaller ones.

Manufacturing. While most of the changes affecting the manufacturing sector were within the sector, this sector now excludes industries which were previously within the scope of manufacturing and includes others that were not in manufacturing. Prominent among the industries that are excluded from manufacturing are logging and portions of publishing. Prominent among the industries that are now included in manufacturing are bakeries, candy stores where candy is made on the premises, custom tailors, makers of custom draperies, and tire retreading. The Information sector (new) includes publishing establishments that were classified in Manufacturing under the SIC.

Wholesale Trade. This sector includes most of what was classified in Wholesale Trade under the SIC system. Excluded from this sector, however, are establishments with retail selling characteristics; these establishments are now clasified in the Retail Trade sector. Prominent examples of these are auto parts, farm supplies, and building products dealers and lumber yards.

In addition, this sector now includes prerecorded video tape wholesalers; this industry was previously classified in Services Industries under the SIC system.

Retail Trade. This sector includes much of what was classified in Retail Trade under the SIC system. Excluded from this sector, however, are eating and drinking places and mobile foodservices (which are now in the Accommodation and Foodservices sector); pawn shops (which are now in the Finance and Insurance sector); and bakeries (which are now in the Manufacturing sector).

In addition, this sector now includes industries previously classified in Wholesale Trade that sold merchandise using facilities open to the general public. Prominent examples of these are automotive supplies dealers, computer and peripheral equipment merchants, office supplies dealers, farm supplies dealers, and building materials dealers.

Finance, Insurance, and Real Estate. The Finance and Insurance sector and the Real Estate Rental and Leasing sector were created from the SIC Finance, Insurance, and Real Estate sector. While most of the changes affecting finance and insurance were minor at the sector level, some industries left the finance part of this sector and other industries came into this sector. Prominent among those leaving are holding companies and patent owners and lessors. Prominent among the industries coming into the sector are pawnshops. Also, there are conceptual differences in what defines an establishment in this sector, since distinct activities have a less physical/geographical basis than industries in most other sectors. Note that funds, trusts, and other financial vehicles (except for REITs), although part of this sector, are not in scope of the 1997 Economic Census.

While most of the changes affecting real estate were minor at the sector level, some industries left the real estate part of this sector and other industries came into this sector. Prominent among those leaving are title abstract offices and land subdividers and developers. Prominent among the industries coming into the sector are patent owners and lessors, miniwarehouses, and most of the rental industries previously classified in the Services Division of the SIC, including video tape, motor vehicle, computer, and equipment rental and leasing. Rental of equipment with operators is classified elsewhere, depending on the services provided.

Service Industries. The Professional, Scientific, and Technical Services sector primarily includes professional and other highly specialized technical service establishments that were classified Services under the SIC. The Educational Services sector, the Health Care and Social Assistance sector, the Arts, Entertainment, and Recreation sector, and the Other Services Sector primarily include establishments that were classified as Services under the SIC.

BUILDING PERMITS, Items 283–285
Source: U.S. Bureau of the Census— Building Permits Survey

Figures represent private residential construction authorized by building permits in approximately 19,000 places in the United States. Valuation represents the expected cost of construction as recorded on the building permit. This figure usually excludes the cost of on-site and off-site development and improvements and the cost of heating, plumbing, electrical, and elevator installations.

County, state, and U.S. totals were obtained by adding the data for permit issuing places within each jurisdiction. These totals thus are limited to permits issued in the 19,000 place universe covered by the Census Bureau and may not include all permits issued within the state.

Residential building permits include buildings with any number of housing units. Apartment hotels, hotels, dormitories, fraternity houses, and other non-housekeeping residential buildings are not included.

MANUFACTURED HOUSING UNITS, Item 286
Source: U.S. Bureau of the Census, Survey of New Mobile Home Placements

The Survey of New Mobile Home Placements involves a monthly sample of new mobile homes shipped by manufacturers. The dealer to whom the sampled unit was shipped is contacted by telephone and asked about the status of the unit. This is done each month until that unit is reported as placed.

A mobile home, often referred to as a manufactured housing unit, is defined as a movable dwelling, 8 feet or more wide and 40 feet or more long, designed to be towed on its own chassis, with transportation gear integral to the unit when it leaves the factory, and without need of a permanent foundation. These mobile homes include multiwides, which are counted as single units, and expandable mobile homes. Excluded are travel trailers, motor homes, and modular housing.

EXPORTS, Items 287–289
Source: U.S. Bureau of the Census

The data on exports of goods by state of origin are based on the location of the exporter, that is, the principal party responsible for effecting export from the United States. Exporters often are intermediaries, so the data do not necessarily represent the states where the goods were actually produced. The total includes reexports of foreign goods.

FEDERAL FUNDS, Items 290–307
Source: U.S. Bureau of the Census— Consolidated Federal Funds Report

Data on federal expenditures and obligations are obtained from a report prepared by the Bureau of the Census in accordance with the Consolidated Federal Funds Report (CFFR) Act of 1982 (P.L. 97-326). The data are for federal fiscal years beginning on October 1 and ending the following September 30.

Direct payments for individuals include social security benefits, federal government retirement, medicare, supplemental security income, food stamps, educational and housing assistance, and other categories not shown separately. All data represent actual expenditures during the fiscal year.

Direct payments for educational assistance consist primarily of higher education grants and insured loans. Direct housing assistance includes primarily the Low Income Housing Assistance Program.

Grants data represent the federal obligations incurred at the time the grant is awarded. The amounts reported do not represent actual expenditures since obligations in one time period may not result in outlays during the same time period. Moreover, initial amounts obligated may be adjusted at a later date, either through enhancements or de-obligations.

Medicaid and other health-related grants include a variety of grants from the Department of Health and Human Services for health services and research.

Nutrition and family welfare grants include a variety of grants by the Department of Health and Human Services for child welfare, special programs for the aging, and related areas. The school lunch program and other nutritional assistance programs administered by the Department of Agriculture are also included.

Energy and environment grants include grants from the Department of Energy for energy development, energy conservation, and nuclear waste disposal, as well as from the Environmental Protection Agency for a variety of pollution control and waste management activities.

Education grants include a variety of grant programs relating to elementary, secondary, and post-secondary education; adult education; vocational education; faculty training; and related areas.

Housing and community development grants include Community Development Block Grants, housing demonstration programs, rental housing rehabilitation, and other housing programs.

Salaries and wages represent actual federal expenditures during the fiscal year; the geographic distribution of these amounts by state and county was estimated based upon place of employment.

Procurement contract awards cover awards by the United States Postal Service (USPS) as well as all other federal agencies. Amounts provided by the USPS represent actual outlays for contractual commitments, while amounts for other agencies represent the value of obligations for contract actions and do not reflect actual federal government expenditures. In general, only current-year contract actions are included—however, multiple-year obligations may be reported for contract actions of less than 3 years duration.

STATE GOVERNMENT FINANCES, Items 308–326
Source: U.S. Bureau of the Census

Data are from an annual survey conducted by the Bureau of the Census and pertain to state government fiscal years ending between July 1, 2001 and June 30, 2002.

Total general revenue includes all revenue except utility, liquor stores, and insurance trust revenue. All tax revenue and intergovernmental revenue, even if designated for employee-retirement or local utility purpose, are classified as general revenue.

Intergovernmental revenue covers amounts received from the federal government as fiscal aid, reimbursements for performance of general government functions and specific services for the paying government, or in lieu of taxes. It excludes any amounts received from other governments for sale of property, commodities, and utility services.

Taxes consist of compulsory contributions exacted by governments for public purposes. However, this category excludes employer and employee payments for retirement and social insurance purposes, which are classified as insurance trust revenue, and special assessments, which are classified as non-tax general revenue. Sales and gross receipts taxes, including "licenses" at more than normal rates, are based on volume or value of transfers of goods or services, on gross receipts, or on gross income, and related taxes based on use, storage, production, importation, or consumption of goods. Sales and gross receipts taxes exclude dealer discounts or "commissions" allowed to merchants for collection of taxes from consumers. General sales taxes and selected taxes on sales of motor fuels, tobacco products, and other particular commodities and services are included.

General government expenditure includes capital outlay, of which a major portion is commonly financed by borrowing, while governmental revenue does not include receipts from borrowing. Among other things, this distorts the relationship between totals of revenue and expenditure figures that are presented and renders it useless as a direct measure of the degree of budgetary "balance," as that term is generally applied.

Direct general expenditure comprises all expenditures of the state governments, excluding utility, liquor stores, insurance trust expenditures, and any intergovernmental payments.

State government expenditures for **education** are mainly for provision and support of schools and other educational facilities and services, including those for educational institutions beyond high school. They cover such related services as pupil transportation; school lunch and other cafeteria operations; school health, recreation, and library services; and dormitories, dining halls, and bookstores operated by public institutions of higher education.

Health and hospital expenditures include health research; clinics; nursing; immunization; and other categorical, environmental, and general health services provided by health agencies; establishment and operation of hospital facilities; provision of hospital care; and support of other public and private hospitals.

Highway expenditure is for provision and maintenance of highway facilities, including toll turnpikes, bridges, tunnels, and ferries, as well as regular roads, highways, and streets. Also included are expenditures for street lighting and for snow and ice removal.

Public safety expenditure includes police and correctional institution expenditure.

Public welfare expenditure covers support of and assistance to needy persons contingent upon their needs. Included are cash assistance paid directly to needy persons under categorical (Old Age Assistance, Aid to Families with Dependent Children, Aid to the Blind, and Aid to the Disabled) and other welfare programs; vendor payments made directly to private purveyors for medical care, burials, and other commodities and services provided under welfare programs; welfare institutions; and any intergovernmental or other direct expenditure for welfare purposes. Pensions to former employees and other benefits not contingent on need are excluded.

Debt outstanding includes all long-term debt obligations of the government and its agencies (exclusive of utility debt) and all interest-bearing short-term (repayable within 1 year) debt obligations remaining unpaid at the close of the fiscal year. It includes judgments, mortgages, and revenue bonds, as well as general obligation bonds, notes, and interest-bearing warrants. It includes non-interest-bearing short-term obligations; inter-fund obligations; amounts owed in a trust or agency capacity; advances and contingent loans from other governments; and rights of individuals to benefits from government-administered employee retirement funds.

GOVERNMENT EMPLOYMENT, Items 327–329
Source: U.S. Bureau of Economic Analysis

Employment is measured as the average annual number of jobs, full-time plus part-time. The estimates are on a place-of-work basis. The data for federal civilian employment include civilian employees of the Department of Defense. Military employment includes all person on active duty status.

ELECTION STATISTICS, Items 330–332
Source: Unofficial preliminary numbers

Election results show the percentage of the total vote cast for the Democratic and Republican candidates, as well as the combined percentage for all other candidates in the 2004 presidential election.

TABLES B AND C—STATES/ COUNTIES and METRO AREAS

Table B presents 197 items for the United States as a whole; each state and the District of Columbia; and each county, county equivalent, or independent city. The counties are presented in alphabetical order within states, which are also in alphabetical order. Independent cities, which are found in Maryland, Missouri, Nevada, and Virginia, are placed in alphabetical order at the end of the list of counties for those states. The District of Columbia is included in Table B as both a county and a state (it is also included as a city in Table D).

Table C presents the same data for each of the 361 metropolitan statistical areas and 29 Metropolitan Divisions.

LAND AREA, Items 1 and 4
Source: U.S. Bureau of the Census

Land area measurements are shown to the nearest square kilometer. Land area includes dry land and land temporarily or partially covered by water, such as marshland, swamps, and river floodplains.

POPULATION, Items 2–4
Source: U.S. Bureau of the Census

The population data are based on the population estimated as of July 1, 2003. The ranks are shown for counties (including independent cities and the District of Columbia) and separately for metropolitan statistical areas but excluding Metropolitan Divisions.

POPULATION BY AGE, RACE, SEX AND HISPANIC OR LATINO ORIGIN, Items 5–19
Source: U.S. Bureau of the Census

County estimates of population characteristics are developed in a two-step procedure. First, a set of state estimates is developed using a cohort-component technique. Then, county estimates are derived by applying ratios to an independent estimate of the county population. The concept of race, as used by the Census Bureau, reflects self-identification by people according to the race or races with which they most closely identify. These categories are socio-political constructs and should not be interpreted as being scientific or anthropological in nature. Furthermore, the race categories include both racial and national-origin groups.

Beginning with the 2000 census, respondents were offered the option of selecting one or more races. This was not the case in prior censuses, so comparisons should be made with caution. In Table B and C, items five through eight refer to individuals who identified with each racial category, either alone or in combination with other races. The estimates exclude persons of Hispanic or Latino origin from all race groups.

The **White** population is defined as persons who indicated their race as white, as well as persons who did not classify themselves in one of the specific race categories listed on the questionnaire but entered a nationality such as Irish, German, Italian, Lebanese, Near Easterner, Arab, or Polish.

The **Black** population includes persons who indicated their race as "Black, African Am., or Negro," as well as persons who did not classify themselves in one of the specific race categories but reported entries such as African American, Afro American, Kenyan, Nigerian, or Haitian.

The **American Indian or Alaska Native** population includes persons who indicated their race as American Indian or Alaska Native, as well as persons who did not classify themselves in one of the specific race categories but reported entries such as Canadian Indian, French American Indian, Spanish-American Indian, Eskimo, Aleut, Alaska Indian, or any of the American Indian or Alaska Native tribes.

The **Asian** population includes persons who indicated their race as Asian Indian, Chinese, Filipino, Japanese, Korean, Vietnamese, or "Other Asian," as well as persons who provided write-in entries of such Asian groups as Cambodian, Laotian, Hmong, Pakistani, or Taiwanese. Also, persons who wrote in an entry indicating one of the specific categories were classified accordingly. The **Native Hawaiian or Other Pacific Islander** population includes persons who indicated their race as "Native Hawaiian," "Guamanian or Chamorro," "Samoan" or "Other Pacific Islander," as well as persons who reported entries such as Part Hawaiian, American Samoan, Fijian, Melanesian, or Tahitian. Also, persons who wrote in an entry indicating one of the specific categories were classified accordingly. In 1990, the **Asian** and **Native Hawaiian or Other Pacific Islander** categories were combined as **Asian and Pacific Islander**. This volume uses the 1990 combination.

Changes in specific listing of racial categories, the new practice of allowing more than one selection in 2000, and the order in which questions appeared on the questionnaire, could all affect comparability between the 2000 and 1990 censuses.

The Hispanic or Latino population is based on a complete-count question that asked respondents "Is this person Spanish/ Hispanic/Latino?" Persons marking any one of the four Hispanic categories (Mexican, Puerto Rican, Cuban, or other Spanish) are collectively referred to as Hispanic or Latino.

In the 2000 census, the Hispanic or Latino Origin question was placed before the race question and specific instructions indicated that both questions should be answered. These changes were designed to improve accuracy, and may affect comparability with 1990 data.

Age derived from the census (2000) is classified as age at last birthday (number of completed years from birth to April 1). The percent figures are derived by dividing the number of persons in a specified age group by the total population of a given geographic area. Data on age are based on complete counts of resident population.

The 2000 census also asked for the specific date of birth of the respondent, and 2000 census procedures used the birth date for deriving age data. For this reason, it is likely that the 2000 data have fewer problems than prior censuses, such as a tendency to round ages or report the person's age on the date the questionnaire was filled out rather than on April 1.

The female population of a geographic area is shown as a percent of the total population of the area.

POPULATION—COMPONENTS OF CHANGE, Items 20–26
Source: U.S. Bureau of the Census

Data on components of change cover an area's population for a specified number of years. Net change is the difference between the count of persons in the 1990 and 2000 census and the Census Bureau's estimate of the population on July 1, 2003. It is equal to natural change (the number of births minus the number of deaths) plus net migration. Natural change shows the total number of births and deaths in a particular area during the decade. Net migration represents the difference between the number of persons moving into a particular area and the number of persons moving away from the area. A positive figure indicates net immigration to the area; a negative figure indicates net out-migration from the area.

Because the 2003 population estimates are based on a model that begins with a national population estimate, the county components of change do not always exactly add up to the difference between the 2000 census population and the 2003 estimates.

HOUSEHOLDS, Items 27–31
Source: U.S. Bureau of the Census— 2000 Census of Population and Housing

A household consists of persons occupying a single housing unit. A housing unit is a house, an apartment, a group of rooms, or a single room occupied as separate living quarters. The occupants may be a single family, one person living alone, two or more families living together, or any other group of related or unrelated persons sharing a housing unit. The number of households is the same as the number of year-round occupied housing units.

A family household consists of two or more persons, including the householder, who are related by birth, marriage, or adoption and who live together as one household; all such persons are considered as members of one family.

The measure of persons per household is obtained by dividing the number of persons in households by the number of households or householders. The category **female family householder** includes only female-headed family households with no spouse present.

BIRTHS AND DEATHS, Items 32–37
Source: U.S. Centers for Disease Control (CDC)

The registration of births, deaths, and other vital events in the United States is primarily a state and local function. The civil laws of every state provide for a continuous and permanent birth and death registration system. Through the National Vital Statistics System, the National Center for Health Statistics (NCHS) obtains data on births and deaths from the registration offices of each state, New York City, and the District of Columbia.

Birth and death statistics are limited to events occurring during the year. The data are by place of residence and exclude events occurring to nonresidents of the United States. Births or deaths that occur outside the United States are excluded.

Birth and death rates represent the number of births and deaths per 1,000 resident population enumerated as of April 1 for decennial census years and estimated as of July 1 for other years.

Figures for infant deaths include deaths of children under 1 year of age; they exclude fetal deaths. The infant death rate is per 1,000 live births.

In order to protect the privacy of individuals, the Centers for Disease Control does not make county-level data available where the number of individual events falls below a threshold figure. Since a 3-year time span allows time for more events to occur, cumulative data covering 3 years tend to be more complete than data for a single year. Also, an average for a 3-year period may more accurately represent the trend level when the number of events each year is small. For these reasons, the county data in this volume are presented as an average computed from data covering a 3-year time span. State data in this table are presented on the same basis in order to maintain comparability. Even with the 3-year average, death rates based on fewer than 20 deaths should be considered unreliable.

PHYSICIANS, Items 38–39
Source: Health Market Science, Inc., as published in Bernan's *Health and Healthcare in the United States*, copyright 2001 NationsHealth Corporation, LLC. Reprinted with permission.

Physicians are health practitioners having the degree of M.D. (Doctor of Medicine) or D.O. (Doctor of Osteopathy) primarily engaged in the practice of general or specialized medicine or surgery. The rate of physicians per 100,000 resident population is an indicator of the supply of physicians within a geographic area.

HOSPITALS, Items 40–42
Source: Health Market Science, Inc., as published in Bernan's *Health and Healthcare in the United States*, copyright 1999 NationsHealth Corporation, LLC. Reprinted with permission.

Hospitals are licensed institutions with at least six beds whose primary function is to provide diagnostic and therapeutic patient services for medical conditions by an organized physician staff, and have continuous nursing services under the supervision of registered nurses. Only short term general hospitals are included in these figures.

A hospital bed is any bed that is licensed for use by inpatients. The count of beds in a facility typically represents the count of beds at the end of the reporting period (a year) regardless of whether it is operational or not. The number of hospital beds per 100,000 population is a measure of the supply of hospital beds within a geographic area.

MEDICARE ENROLLEES, Item 43
Source: Centers for Medicare and Medicaid Services (CMS)

The Centers for Medicare and Medicaid Services (CMS) administers Medicare which provides health insurance to people aged 65 and over and those who have permanent kidney failure and certain people with disabilities. Medicare has two parts: Hospital Insurance and Supplemental Medical Insurance. The numbers in this volume include persons enrolled in either or both parts of the program as of July 1, 2003, by their state of residence.

CRIME, Items 44–47
Source: U.S. Federal Bureau of Investigation— Uniform Crime Reports

Crime data are as reported to the FBI by law enforcement agencies and have not been adjusted for under-reporting. This may affect comparability between geographic areas or over time.

Through the voluntary contribution of crime statistics by law enforcement agencies across the United States, the Uniform Crime Reporting (UCR) Program provides periodic assessments of crime in the nation as measured by those offenses which come to the attention of the law enforcement community. The Committee on Uniform Crime Records of the International Association of Chiefs of Police initiated this voluntary national data-collection effort in 1930. UCR Program contributors compile and submit their crime data in one of two manners: either directly to the FBI or through the state UCR Programs.

Seven offenses, because of their seriousness, frequency of occurrence, and likelihood of being reported to police, were initially selected to serve as an index for evaluating fluctuations in the volume of crime. These serious crimes were murder and nonnegligent manslaughter, forcible rape, robbery, aggravated assault, burglary, larceny-theft, and motor vehicle theft. By congressional mandate, arson was added as the eighth index offense in 1979. The totals shown in this volume do not include arson.

Violent offenses include four crime categories: (1) Murder and nonnegligent manslaughter, as defined in the UCR Program, is the willful (nonnegligent) killing of one human being by another. This offense excludes deaths caused by negligence, suicide, or accident; justifiable homicides; and attempts to murder or assaults to murder. (2) Forcible rape is the carnal knowledge of a female forcibly and against her will. Assaults or attempts to commit rape by force or threat of force are also included; however, statutory rape (without force) and other sex offenses are excluded. (3) Robbery is the taking or attempting to take anything of value from the care, custody, or control of a person or persons by force or threat of force or violence and/or by putting the victim in fear. (4) Aggravated assault is an unlawful attack by one person upon another for the purpose of inflicting severe or aggravated bodily injury. This type of assault is usually accompanied by the use of a weapon or by means likely to produce death or great bodily harm. Attempts are included since an injury does not necessarily have to result when a gun, knife, or other weapon is used, which could and probably would result in a serious personal injury if the crime were successfully completed.

Property crimes include three categories: (1) Burglary, or breaking and entering, is the unlawful entry of a structure to commit a felony or theft, even though no force was used to gain entrance. (2) Larceny/theft is the unauthorized taking of the personal property of another, without the use of force. (3) Motor vehicle theft is the unauthorized taking of any motor vehicle.

Rates are based on population estimates provided by the FBI. The county totals published in this volume were obtained by aggregating individual reporting units within each county and MSA. If the population total for the units aggregated was less than 75 percent of the county's population (as estimated by the Bureau of the Census), the total was not considered representative of the county as a whole and is not published. State and U.S. totals include FBI estimates for those areas.

EDUCATION—SCHOOL ENROLLMENT AND EDUCATIONAL ATTAINMENT, Items 48–51
Source: U.S. Bureau of the Census— 2000 Census of Population and Housing

Data on school enrollment and educational attainment were derived from a sample of the population. Persons were classified as enrolled in school if they reported attending a "regular" public or private school (or college) at any time between February 1, 2000 and the time of enumeration. The instructions were to "include only nursery school, kindergarten, elementary school, and schooling which would lead to a high school diploma or a college degree" as regular school. Public school is defined as "any school or college controlled and supported by a local, county, state, or federal government." Schools supported and controlled primarily by religious organizations or other private groups are defined as private.

Statistics for levels of school completed are for persons 25 years old and over. The data were derived from a question on the 2000 census questionnaire that asked respondents for the highest level of school they had completed or the highest degree they had received. Persons who passed a high school equivalency examination were considered high school graduates. Schooling received in foreign schools was to be reported as the equivalent grade or years in the regular American school system.

LOCAL GOVERNMENT EDUCATION EXPENDITURES, Items 52–53
Source: U.S. National Center for Educational Statistics

Total expenditure for education includes provision or support of schools and facilities for elementary and secondary education. It encompasses instructional, support, and auxiliary services (school lunch, student activities, and community services) offered by public school systems. Retirement benefits paid to former education employees and interest payments are not included. Current expenditure includes all components of total expenditure except capital outlay. Expenditure data are obtained by the U.S. Bureau of the Census through its annual surveys of government finances and are supplied by the Bureau of the Census to the National Center for Education Statistics. Current expenditures per pupil is current expenditures divided by the number of students enrolled. The number of students enrolled is based on an annual ''membership'' count of students on or about October 1.

NCES uses the Common Core of Data (CCD) Survey to acquire and maintain statistical data from each of the 50 states, the District of Columbia, and the outlying areas. The state education agencies compile and submit data for approximately 85,000 schools and 15,000 local school districts. Typically this results in varying interpretation of NCES definitions and different record-keeping systems, leading to large amounts of missing data for several states in this volume. Schools and school districts are included in the county where the school district offices (the Local Education Agency) are located.

INCOME AND POVERTY, Items 54–61
Source: U.S. Bureau of the Census—
2000 Census of Population and Housing

The data on income are derived from the responses of a sample of persons 15 years old and over. **Total money income** is defined by the Bureau of the Census for statistical purposes as the sum of the following: wage or salary income; nonfarm self-employment income; net farm self-employment income; Social Security and railroad retirement income; public assistance income; and all other regularly received income such as interest, dividends, veterans' payments, pensions, unemployment compensation, and alimony. Receipts not counted as income include various ''lump sum'' payments such as capital gains or inheritances.

The total represents the amount of income received before deductions for personal income taxes, Social Security, bond purchases, union dues, Medicare deductions, etc.

Per capita income is based on resident population enumerated as of April 1, 2000.

Income of households includes the income of the householder and all other persons 15 years old and over in the household. Median household income is usually less than median family income because many households consist of only one person. The median divides the income distribution into two equal parts, one having incomes above the median, the other with incomes below. For metropolitan areas, mean income is provided (aggregate income divided by the number of households).

The constant-dollar figures are based on an annual average Consumer Price Index from the Bureau of Labor Statistics. Constant-dollar figures are estimates representing an effort to remove the effects of price changes from statistical series reported in dollar terms. However, the estimates do not reflect the price and cost-of-living differences that may exist between areas.

Money income differs in definition from personal income (item 62). For example, money income does not include the pension rights, employer provided health insurance, food stamps, or Medicare payments that are included in personal income.

Poverty status is based on the definition prescribed by the Federal Office of Management and Budget as the standard to be used by federal agencies for statistical purposes. Families and persons are classified as being below the poverty level if their total family income or unrelated individual income was less than the poverty threshold specified for the applicable family size, age of householder, and number of related children present under 18.

Poverty status is determined for all families (and by implication all family members). For persons not in families, poverty status is determined by their income in relation to the appropriate poverty threshold. Inmates of institutions, persons in military group quarters or college dormitories, and unrelated individuals under 15 are excluded.

The 1999 poverty thresholds are shown in Figure 1.

Figure 1.
Poverty Thresholds in 1999 by Size of Family

Size of Family Unit	Weighted average thresholds
One person (unrelated individual)	$8,501
Under 65 years old	8,667
65 years old and over	7,990
Two persons	10,869
Householder under 65 years old	11,214
Householder 65 years old and over	10,075
Three persons	13,290
Four persons	17,029
Five persons	20,127
Six persons	22,727
Seven persons	25,912
Eight persons	28,967
Nine or more persons	34,417

PERSONAL INCOME AND EARNINGS, Items 62–83
Source: U.S. Bureau of Economic Analysis

Total personal income is the current income received by residents of an area from all sources. It is measured before deductions of income and other personal taxes but after deduction of personal contributions for Social Security, government retirement, and other social insurance programs. It consists of **wage and salary disbursements** (covering all employee earnings, including executive salaries, bonuses, commissions, payments-in-kind, incentive payments, and tips), **other labor income** (primarily employer contributions to private pension funds), proprietors' income, rental income of persons, dividends, personal interest income, and government and business transfer payments.

Proprietors' income is the monetary income and income in-kind of proprietorships and partnerships, including the independent professions, and of tax-exempt cooperatives. **Dividends** are cash payments by for-profit corporations to stockholders who are U.S. residents. **Interest** is the monetary and imputed interest income of persons from all sources. **Rent** is the monetary income of persons from the rental of real property except the income of persons primarily engaged in the real estate business, the imputed net rental income of owner-occupants of nonfarm dwellings, and the royalties received by persons.

Transfer payments are income for which services are not currently rendered. They consist of both government and business transfer payments. Government transfer payments include payments under the following programs: Federal Old-Age, Survivors, and Disability Insurance (''Social Security''); Medicare and medical vendor payments; unemployment insurance, railroad and government retirement; federal and state government-insured workers' compensation; veterans benefits, including veterans life insurance; food stamps; black lung; Supplemental Security Income; and Aid to Families with Dependent Children. Government payments to nonprofit institutions, other than for work under research and development contracts, are also included. The principal business transfers are corporate gifts to nonprofit institutions and consumer bad debts.

Per capita personal income is based on resident population estimated as of July 1 of the year shown.

Personal income differs in definition from money income (items 54–57). For example, personal income includes pension rights, employer provided health insurance, food stamps, and Medicare. These are not included in the definition of money income.

Earnings cover wage and salary disbursements, other labor income, and proprietors' income.

Data for earnings obtained from the Bureau of Economic Analysis (BEA) are based on place of work. In computing personal income, BEA makes an ''adjustment for residence'' to earnings based on commuting patterns, so that personal income is presented on a place of residence basis.

Farm earnings include the income of farm workers (wages and salaries and other labor income) and farm proprietors. Farm proprietors' income includes only the income of sole proprietorships and partnerships.

Farm earning estimates are benchmarked to data collected in the Census of Agriculture and the revised U.S. Department of Agriculture State totals of income and expense items.

''Goods-related'' industries include mining, construction, and manufacturing. ''Service-related and other'' includes private sector earnings in agricultural services, forestry and fisheries; transportation and public utilities; wholesale trade; retail trade; finance, insurance, and real estate; and services. Government earnings include all levels of government. Industries are categorized under the North American Industry Classification System, and are not comparable to prior years.

SOCIAL SECURITY AND SUPPLEMENTAL SECURITY INCOME, Items 84–86
Source: U.S. Social Security Administration

Social Security beneficiaries is the number of persons receiving benefits under the Old-Age, Survivors, and Disability Insurance Program. These include retired or disabled workers covered by the program, their spouses and dependent children, and the surviving spouses and dependent children of deceased workers.

Supplemental Security Income (SSI) recipients are the number of persons receiving SSI payments. Data are as of December of the year shown.

HOUSING, Items 87–96
Source: U.S. Bureau of the Census—
2000 Census of Population and Housing and 2003 American Community Survey

Housing data for 2003 are from the American Community Survey, a nationwide continuous survey designed to eventually replace the long form in the 2010 census. A sample of households is surveyed to provide estimates. The survey is limited to the household population and excludes the population living in institutins, college dormitories, and other group quarters. Housing data for 2000 are from the 2000 census.

A **housing unit** is a house, apartment, mobile home or trailer, group of rooms, or single room occupied or, if vacant, intended for occupancy as separate living quarters. Separate living quarters are those in which the occupants do not live and eat with any other persons in the structure and which have direct access from the outside of the building through a common hall.

The occupants of a housing unit may be a single family, one person living alone, two or more families living together, or a group of related or unrelated persons who share living arrangements. For vacant units, the criteria of separateness and direct access are applied to the intended occupants whenever possible. If that information cannot be obtained, the criteria are applied to the previous occupants. Both occupied and vacant housing units are included in the housing inventory, except that recreational vehicles, tents, caves, boats, railroad cars, and the like are included only if they are occupied as someone's usual place of residence.

A housing unit is classified as occupied if it is the usual place of residence of the person or group of persons living in it at the time of enumeration, or if the occupants are only temporarily absent (away on vacation). A household consists of all persons who occupy a housing unit as their usual place of residence.

Median value is the dollar amount that divides the distribution of owner-occupied housing units into two equal parts, with one half of the units falling below this value and the other half exceeding it. Value is defined as the respondent's estimate of what the house would sell for, if it were for sale. Data are presented for one-family units on less than 10 acres and with no business or medical office on the property.

Mean value is the aggregate value divided by the number of owned housing units.

Median rent divides the distribution of renter-occupied housing units into two equal parts. Median rent represents the amount of cash rent a renter pays (contract rent) plus the estimated average cost of utilities and fuels if paid by the renter (gross rent). Rent is to be reported only for living quarters, not for any business or other space occupied. Single family houses on lots of 10 or more acres are excluded.

Mean rent is the aggregate rent divided by the number of rented housing units.

Housing cost as a percent of income is shown separately for owners with mortgages, owners without mortgages, and renters. Rent as a percentage of income is a computed ratio of gross rent and monthly household income (total household income in 1999 divided by 12). Selected owner costs include utilities and fuels, as well as mortgage payments, insurance, taxes, etc. In each case, the ratio of housing cost to income is computed separately for each housing unit. The ratios for one-half of the units are above the median shown in this book, and one-half are below. For metropolitan areas, the measure is the percentage of owners or renters who pay 35 percent of their income or more for the specified costs or for rent.

Substandard units are occupied units which are overcrowded or lack complete plumbing facilities. For the purposes of this item "overcrowded" is defined as having 1.01 persons or more per room. Complete plumbing facilities include hot and cold piped water, a flush toilet, and a bathtub or shower. These facilities must be located inside the housing unit but not necessarily in the same room.

CIVILIAN LABOR FORCE AND UNEMPLOYMENT, Items 97–100
Source: U.S. Bureau of Labor Statistics

Data for the civilian labor force are the product of a federal-state cooperative program in which state employment security agencies prepare labor force and unemployment estimates under concepts, definitions, and technical procedures established by the Bureau of Labor Statistics. The civilian labor force consists of all civilians 16 years old and over who are either employed in a civilian job or unemployed.

Unemployment includes all persons who did not work during the survey week, made specific efforts to find a job in the prior four weeks, and were available for work during the survey week (except for temporary illness). Persons waiting to be called back to a job from which they had been laid off and those waiting to report to a new job within the next 30 days are included in unemployment figures.

CIVILIAN EMPLOYMENT, 2000
Items 101–103
Source: U.S. Bureau of the Census— 2000 Census of Population and Housing

Total employment includes all civilians 16 years old or over who were either (1) "at work"—those who did any work at all during the reference week as paid employees, worked in their own business or profession, worked on their own farm, or worked 15 hours or more as unpaid workers in a family farm or business; or were (2) "with a job, but not at work"—those who had a job but were not at work that week due to illness, weather, industrial dispute, vacation, or other personal reasons.

The **occupation categories** shown are consistent with the 2000 edition of the *Standard Occupational Classification Manual (SOC)*, published by the Office of Federal Statistical Policy and Standards, U.S. Department of Commerce.

PRIVATE NONFARM ESTABLISHMENTS AND EMPLOYMENT, Items 104–112
Source: U.S. Bureau of the Census— County Business Patterns

Data for private nonfarm establishments, employment, and payroll are reported in the U.S. Bureau of the Census publication

County Business Patterns. The estimates are based on surveys conducted by the Bureau of the Census and administrative records from the Internal Revenue Service (IRS).

The following types of employment are excluded from the tables: government employment; self employed persons; farm workers; and domestic service workers. Railroad employment jointly covered by social security and railroad retirement programs, employment on oceanborne vessels, and employment in foreign countries are also excluded.

Annual payroll is the combined amount of wages paid, tips reported, and other compensation (including salaries, vacation allowances, bonuses, commissions, sick leave pay, and the value of payments-in-kind such as free meals and lodging) paid to employees before deductions for Social Security, income tax, insurance, union dues, etc. All forms of compensation are included, whether or not subject to income tax or Federal Insurance Contributions Act tax, with the exception of annuities, third-party sick pay, and supplemental unemployment compensation benefits (even if income tax was withheld). For corporations, total annual payroll includes compensation paid to officers and executives; for unincorporated businesses, it does not include profit or other compensation of proprietors or partners.

AGRICULTURE, Items 113–132
Source: U.S. Department of Agriculture, National Agricultural Statistics Service— 2002 Census of Agriculture

Data for the 2002 Census of Agriculture were collected in 2003 and pertain to the year 2002.

The Bureau of the Census took a census of agriculture every 10 years from 1840 to 1920 and roughly every 5 years from 1925 to 2003. The 2002 Census of Agriculture was transfered to the National Agricultural Statistics Service of the U.S. Department of Agriculture. Over time, the definition of a farm has varied. For recent censuses, including the 2002 census, a farm has been defined as any place from which $1,000 or more of agricultural products were sold or normally would have been sold during the census year.

The term **operator** refers to a person who operates a farm, either doing the work or making day-to-day decisions about such things as planting, harvesting, feeding, marketing, etc. The operator may be the owner, a member of the owner's household, a salaried manager, a tenant, a renter, or a sharecropper. For partnerships, only one partner is counted as an operator. For census purposes, the number of operators is the same as the number of farms.

The acreage designated as **land in farms** consists primarily of agricultural land used for crops, pasture, or grazing. It also includes woodland and wasteland not actually under cultivation or used for pasture or grazing, if it was part of the operator's total operation.

Land in farms is an operating-unit concept and includes land owned and operated, as well as land rented from others. Land used rent free was to be reported as land rented from others. All land in Indian reservations used for growing crops or grazing livestock was to be included as land in farms.

With few exceptions, the land in each farm was tabulated as being in the operator's principal county. The principal county was defined as the one where the largest value of agricultural products were raised or produced; it was usually the county containing all or the largest proportion of the land in the farm. For a limited number of Western states, this procedure resulted in the allocation of more land in farms to a county than the total land area of the county.

Irrigated land covers any land in farms to which water was artificially applied in the census year. Land irrigated prior to, but not in the census year, is not included. Irrigation may have been used for producing a harvested crop, for pasture or grazing lands, for cultivated summer fallow, or for land planted to a crop intended for future harvest. Land flooded during high-water periods was included as irrigated only if water was diverted to agricultural lands by dams, canals, or other works.

Cropland consists of land from which crops were harvested and land that could have been used for crops without additional improvements. This includes land in nonbearing orchards and vineyards, land from which any hay was cut, land on which crops failed, idle or fallow land, and land used for grazing purposes.

Respondents were asked to report their estimate of the current market value of land and buildings owned, rented, or leased from others, and rented and leased to others. Market value refers to the respondent's estimate of what the land and buildings would sell for under current market conditions. If the value of land and buildings was not reported, it was estimated during processing by using the average value of land and buildings from similar farms in the same geographic area.

The **value of machinery and equipment** was estimated by the respondent as the current market value of all cars, trucks, tractors, combines, balers, and irrigation equipment, used on the farm. This value is an estimate of what the machinery and equipment would sell for in its present condition and not the replacement or depreciated value. Share interests are reported at full value at the farm where the equipment and machinery are usually kept. Only equipment that was actually used in 2001 and 2002, or newly purchased but not yet used, and physically located at the farm on December 31, 2002 is included.

The **value of farm products sold** by farms represents the gross market value before taxes and production expenses of all agricultural products sold or removed from the place in 2002 regardless of who received the payment. It includes sales by the operator as well as the value of any share received by partners, landlords, contractors, and others associated with the operation. It represents the sum of all crops, including nursery products sold and livestock and poultry and their products sold.

The value of crops sold in 2002 does not necessarily represent the sales from crops harvested that year. The data include sales from crops produced in earlier years and exclude some crops produced in 2002 but held in storage and not sold in the census year. For crops sold through a co-op that made payments in several installments, only the total value received in the census year was to be reported.

Government Payments consist of Government Payments Received from the Conservation Reserve Program (CRP) and Wetlands Reserve Program (WRP) plus Government Payments Received from Federal Programs Other than the Conservation

Reserve Program, Wetlands Reserve Program, and Commodity Credit Corporation (CCC).

CONSTRUCTION—BUILDING PERMITS, Items 133–134
Source: U.S. Bureau of the Census— Building Permits Survey

Figures represent private residential construction authorized by building permits in approximately 19,000 places in the United States. Valuation represents the cost of construction as recorded on the building permit. This figure usually excludes the cost of on-site and off-site development and improvements and the cost of heating, plumbing, electrical, and elevator installations.

County, state, metropolitan, and U.S. totals were obtained by summing the data for permit-issuing places within each jurisdiction. Thus, these totals are limited to permits issued in the 19,000 place universe covered by the Census Bureau and may not include all permits issued within the county. If a county does not contain permit-issuing places covered by the Census Bureau, an "NA" is shown. Counties with permit-issuing places that issued no permits during the period are represented by a "0."

Residential building permits include buildings with any number of housing units. Hotels, apartment hotels, dormitories, fraternity houses, and other non-housekeeping residential buildings are not included.

1997 ECONOMIC CENSUS: OVERVIEW Items 135–166
Source: U.S. Bureau of the Census

The Economic Census provides a detailed portrait of the nation's economy once every 5 years, from the national to the local level. The 1997 Economic Census covers nearly all of the U.S. economy in its basic collection of establishment statistics. It is the first major data source to use the new North American Industry Classification System (NAICS) and is therefore not comparable to economic data from prior years which were based on the Standard Industrial Classification (SIC) system.

NAICS, developed in cooperation with Canada and Mexico, classifies North America's economic activities at two-, three-, four-, and five-digit levels of detail, and the U.S. version of NAICS further defines industries to a sixth digit. The Economic Census takes advantage of this hierarchy to publish data at these successive levels of detail: sector (two-digit); subsector (three-digit); industry group (four-digit); industry(five-digit); and U.S. industry(six-digit.)

This volume was published during the initial release of the 1997 Economic Census and therefore includes those sectors that were available at the time of publication. The information in Tables B and C is at the two-digit level.

Several key statistics are tabulated for all industries included in this volume: number of establishments (or companies); number of employees; payroll; and a measure of output (sales, receipts, revenue, value of shipments, or value of construction work done.)

Number of Establishments. An establishment is a single physical location at which business is conducted. It is not necessarily identical with a company or enterprise, which may consist of one establishment or more. Economic Census figures represent a summary of reports for individual establishments rather than companies. For cases where a census report was received, separate information was obtained for each location where business was conducted. When administrative records of other federal agencies were used instead of a census report, no information was available on the number of locations operated. Each Economic Census establishment was tabulated according to the physical location at which the business was conducted. The count of establishments represents those in business at any time during 1997.

When two activities or more were carried on at a single location under a single ownership, all activities generally were grouped together as a single establishment. The entire establishment was classified on the basis of its major activity and all data for it were included in that classification. However, when distinct and separate economic activities (for which different industry classification codes were appropriate) were conducted at a single location under a single ownership, separate establishment reports for each of the different activities were obtained in the census.

Number of Employees. Paid employees consist of the full-time and part-time employees, including salaried officers and executives of corporations. Included are employees on paid sick leave, paid holidays, and paid vacations; not included are proprietors and partners of unincorporated businesses. The definition of paid employees is the same as that used on IRS form 941.

Payroll. Payroll includes all forms of compensation such as salaries, wages, commissions, dismissal pay, bonuses, vacation allowances, sick-leave pay, and employee contributions to qualified pension plans paid during the year to all employees. For corporations, payroll includes amounts paid to officers and executives; for unincorporated businesses, it does not include profit or other compensation of proprietors or partners. Payroll is reported before deductions for social security, income tax, insurance, union dues, etc. This definition of payroll is the same as that used by the IRS on form 941.

Sales, Shipments, Receipts, Revenue, or Business Done. This measure includes the total sales, shipments, receipts, revenue, or business done by establishments within the scope of the Economic Census. The definition of each of these items is specific to the economic sector measured.

WHOLESALE TRADE, Items 135–138
Source: U.S. Bureau of the Census,
1997 Economic Census
(See Overview of 1997 Economic Census
prior to Item 135)

The Wholesale Trade sector (sector 42) comprises establishments engaged in wholesaling merchandise, generally without transformation, and rendering services incidental to the sale of merchandise. The wholesaling process is an intermediate step in the distribution of merchandise.

Wholesalers are organized to sell or arrange the purchase or sale of (a) goods for resale (goods sold to other wholesalers or

retailers), (b) capital or durable nonconsumer goods, and (c) raw and intermediate materials and supplies used in production.

Wholesalers sell merchandise to other businesses and normally operate from a warehouse or office. These warehouses and offices are characterized by having little or no display of merchandise. In addition, neither the design nor the location of the premises is intended to solicit walk-in traffic. Wholesalers do not normally use advertising directed to the general public. Customers are generally reached initially via telephone, in-person marketing, or by specialized advertising that may include Internet and other electronic means. Follow-up orders are either vendor-initiated or client-initiated, generally based on previous sales, and typically exhibit strong ties between sellers and buyers. In fact, transactions are often conducted between wholesalers and clients that have long-standing business relationships.

This sector comprises two main types of wholesalers: those that sell goods on their own account and those that arrange sales and purchases for others for a commission or fee.

(1) Establishments that sell goods on their own account are known as wholesale merchants, distributors, jobbers, drop shippers, import/export merchants, and sales branches. These establishments typically maintain their own warehouse, where they receive and handle goods for their customers. Goods are generally sold without transformation, but may include integral functions, such as sorting, packaging, labeling, and other marketing services.

(2) Establishments arranging for the purchase or sale of goods owned by others or purchasing goods on a commission basis are known as agents and brokers, commission merchants, import/export agents and brokers, auction companies, and manufacturers' representatives. These establishments operate from offices and generally do not own or handle the goods they sell.

Some wholesale establishments may be connected with a single manufacturer and promote and sell the particular manufacturer's products to a wide range of other wholesalers or retailers. Other wholesalers may be connected to a retail chain or a limited number of retail chains and only provide a variety of products needed by that particular retail operation(s). These wholesalers may obtain the products from a wide range of manufacturers. Still other wholesalers may not take title to the goods, but act as agents and brokers for a commission.

Although, in general, wholesaling normally denotes sales in large volumes, durable nonconsumer goods may be sold in single units. Sales of capital or durable nonconsumer goods used in the production of goods and services, such as farm machinery, medium and heavy duty trucks, and industrial machinery, are always included in wholesale trade.

RETAIL TRADE, Items 139–142
Source: U.S. Bureau of the Census,
1997 Economic Census
(See Overview of 1997 Economic Census
prior to Item 135)

The Retail Trade sector (44-45) comprises establishments engaged in retailing merchandise, generally without transformation, and rendering services incidental to the sale of merchandise.

The retailing process is the final step in the distribution of merchandise; retailers are, therefore, organized to sell merchandise in small quantities to the general public. This sector comprises two main types of retailers: store and nonstore retailers.

Store retailers operate fixed point-of-sale locations, located and designed to attract a high volume of walk-in customers. In general, retail stores have extensive displays of merchandise and use mass-media advertising to attract customers. They typically sell merchandise to the general public for personal or household consumption, but some also serve business and institutional clients. These include establishments, such as office supply stores, computer and software stores, building materials dealers, plumbing supply stores, and electrical supply stores. Catalog showrooms, gasoline service stations, automotive dealers, and mobile home dealers are treated as store retailers.

In addition to retailing merchandise, some types of store retailers are also engaged in the provision of after-sales services, such as repair and installation. For example, new automobile dealers, electronic and appliance stores, and musical instrument and supply stores often provide repair services. As a general rule, establishments engaged in retailing merchandise and providing after-sales services are classified in this sector.

Nonstore retailers, like store retailers, are organized to serve the general public, but their retailing methods differ. The establishments of this subsector reach customers and market merchandise with methods, such as the broadcasting of "infomercials," the broadcasting and publishing of direct-response advertising, the publishing of paper and electronic catalogs, door-to-door solicitation, in-home demonstration, selling from portable stalls (street vendors, except food), and distribution through vending machines. Establishments engaged in the direct sale (nonstore) of products, such as home heating oil dealers and home delivery newspaper routes.

The buying of goods for resale is a characteristic of retail trade establishments that particularly distinguishes them from establishments in the agriculture, manufacturing, and construction industries. For example, farms that sell their products at or from the point of production are not classified in retail, but rather in agriculture. Similarly, establishments that both manufacture and sell their products to the general public are not classified in retail, but rather in manufacturing. However, establishments that engage in processing activities incidental to retailing are classified in retail.

REAL ESTATE AND RENTAL AND LEASING, Items 143–146
Source: U.S. Bureau of the Census, 1997 Economic Census
(See Overview of 1997 Economic Census prior to Item 135)

The Real Estate and Rental and Leasing sector (53) comprises establishments primarily engaged in renting, leasing, or otherwise allowing the use of tangible or intangible assets, and establishments providing related services. The major portion of this sector comprises establishments that rent, lease, or otherwise allow the use of their own assets by others. The assets may be tangible, as

is the case of real estate and equipment, or intangible, as is the case with patents and trademarks.

This sector also includes establishments primarily engaged in managing real estate for others, selling, renting and/or buying real estate for others, and appraising real estate. These activities are closely related to this sector's main activity, and it was felt that from a production basis they would best be included here. In addition, a substantial proportion of property management is self-performed by lessors.

The main components of this sector are the real estate lessors industries; equipment lessors industries (including motor vehicles, computers, and consumer goods); and lessors of nonfinancial intangible assets (except copyrighted works).

PROFESSIONAL, SCIENTIFIC, AND TECHNICAL SERVICES, Items 147–150
Source: U.S. Bureau of the Census, 1997 Economic Census
(See Overview of 1997 Economic Census prior to Item 135)

The Professional, Scientific, and Technical Services sector (54) comprises establishments that specialize in performing professional, scientific, and technical activities for others. These activities require a high degree of expertise and training. The establishments in this sector specialize according to expertise and provide these services to clients in a variety of industries and, in some cases, to households. Activities performed include: legal advice and representation; accounting, bookkeeping, and payroll services; architectural, engineering, and specialized design services; computer services; consulting services; research services; advertising services; photographic services; translation and interpretation services; veterinary services; and other professional, scientific, and technical services.

This volume includes only those establishments subject to federal income tax.

This sector excludes establishments primarily engaged in providing a range of day-to-day office administrative services, such as financial planning, billing and recordkeeping, personnel, and physical distribution and logistics. These establishments are classified in sector 56, Administrative and Support and Waste Management and Remediation Services.

MANUFACTURING, Items 151–154
Source: U.S. Bureau of the Census, 1997 Economic Census
(See Overview of 1997 Economic Census prior to Item 135)

The Manufacturing sector comprises establishments engaged in the mechanical, physical, or chemical transformation of materials, substances, or components into new products. The assembling of component parts of manufactured products is considered manufacturing, except in cases where the activity is appropriately classified as Construction. Establishments in the Manufacturing sector are often described as plants, factories, or mills and characteristically use power-driven machines and materials-handling equipment. However, establishments that transform materials or substances into new products by hand or in the worker's home and those engaged in selling to the general public products made on the same premises from which they are sold, such as bakeries, candy stores, and custom tailors, may also be included in this sector. Manufacturing establishments may process materials or may contract with other establishments to process their materials for them. Both types of establishments are included in manufacturing. The materials, substances, or components transformed by manufacturing establishments are raw materials that are products of agriculture, forestry, fishing, mining, or quarrying as well as products of other manufacturing establishments. The materials used may be purchased directly from producers, obtained through customary trade channels, or secured without recourse to the market by transferring the product from one establishment to another, under the same ownership. The new product of a manufacturing establishment may be finished in the sense that it is ready for utilization or consumption, or it may be semifinished to become an input for an establishment engaged in further manufacturing. For example, the product of the alumina refinery is the input used in the primary production of aluminum; primary aluminum is the input to an aluminum wire drawing plant; and aluminum wire is the input for a fabricated wire product manufacturing establishment.

Data are included for counties with 500 or more employees in the manufacturing sector.

ACCOMMODATION AND FOOD SERVICES, Items 155–158
Source: U.S. Bureau of the Census,
1997 Economic Census
(See Overview of 1997 Economic Census
prior to Item 135)

The Accommodation and Food Services sector (72) comprises establishments providing customers with lodging and/or preparing meals, snacks, and beverages for immediate consumption. The sector includes both accommodation and food services establishments because the two activities are often combined at the same establishment.

Excluded from this sector are civic and social organizations; amusement and recreation parks; theaters; and other recreation or entertainment facilities providing food and beverage services.

HEALTH CARE AND SOCIAL ASSISTANCE, Items 159–162
Source: U.S. Bureau of the Census,
1997 Economic Census
(See Overview of 1997 Economic Census
prior to Item 135)

The Health Care and Social Assistance sector (62) comprises establishments providing health care and social assistance for individuals. The sector includes both health care and social assistance because it is sometimes difficult to distinguish between the boundaries of these two activities. The industries in this sector are arranged on a continuum starting with those establishments providing medical care exclusively, continuing with those providing health care and social assistance, and finally finishing with those providing only social assistance. The services provided by establishments in this sector are delivered by trained professionals. All industries in the sector share this commonality of process, namely, labor inputs of health practitioners or social workers with the requisite expertise. Many of the industries in the sector are defined based on the educational degree held by the practitioners included in the industry.

In this volume, only taxable establishments are included in Table B and Table C.

Excluded from this sector are aerobic classes in Subsector 713, Amusement, Gambling and Recreation Industries and nonmedical diet and weight reducing centers in Subsector 812, Personal and Laundry Services. Although these can be viewed as health services, these services are not typically delivered by health practitioners.

OTHER SERVICES, Items 163–166
Source: U.S. Bureau of the Census,
1997 Economic Census
(See Overview of 1997 Economic Census
prior to Item 135)

The Other Services (except Public Administration) sector (81) comprises establishments engaged in providing services not specifically provided for elsewhere in the classification system. Establishments in this sector are primarily engaged in activities, such as equipment and machinery repairing, promoting or administering religious activities, grantmaking, advocacy, and providing drycleaning and laundry services, personal care services, death care services, pet care services, photofinishing services, temporary parking services, and dating services.

Private households that engage in employing workers on or about the premises in activities primarily concerned with the operation of the household are included in this sector.

In this volume, only firms subject to federal tax are included.

Excluded from this sector are establishments primarily engaged in retailing new equipment and also performing repairs and general maintenance on equipment. These establishments are classified in sector 44-45, Retail Trade.

FEDERAL FUNDS, Items 167–177
Source: U.S. Bureau of the Census—
Consolidated Federal Funds Report

Data on federal expenditures and obligations are obtained from a report prepared by the Bureau of the Census in accordance with the Consolidated Federal Funds Report (CFFR) Act of 1982 (P.L. 97-326). The data are for federal fiscal years beginning on October 1 and ending the following September 30. Dollar amounts reported can reflect expenditures or obligations. In some cases dollar amounts are negative representing de-obligations of financial assistance that had been previously awarded. Such amounts generally appear in the grant categories.

Direct payments for individuals include social security benefits, federal government retirement, medicare, supplemental security income, food stamps, and certain other payments, including educational and housing assistance, not shown separately. All data represent actual expenditures during the fiscal year.

Salaries and wages represent actual federal expenditures during the fiscal year; the geographic distribution of these amounts by state and county was estimated based upon place of employment.

Procurement contract awards cover awards by the United States Postal Service (USPS) as well as all other federal agencies. Amounts provided by the USPS represent actual outlays for contractual commitments, while amounts for other agencies represent the value of obligations for contract actions and do not reflect actual federal government expenditures. In general, only current-year contract actions are included—however, multiple-year obligations may be reported for contract actions of less than 3 years duration.

Grants data represent the federal obligations incurred at the time the grant is awarded. The amounts reported do not represent actual expenditures since obligations in one time period may not result in outlays during the same time period. Moreover, initial amounts obligated may be adjusted at a later date, either through enhancements or de-obligations. All grant awards were reported by state, county, and city of the initial recipient. For many grants, this recipient is the state government even though the grant monies are subsequently distributed to county, municipal, or township governments.

Medicaid and other health-related grants include a variety of grants from the Department of Health and Human Services for health services and research.

Nutrition and family welfare grants include a variety of grants by the Department of Health and Human Services for child welfare, special programs for the aging, and related areas. The school lunch program and other nutritional assistance programs administered by the Department of Agriculture are also included.

Education grants include a variety of grant programs relating to elementary, secondary, and post-secondary education; adult education; vocational education; faculty training; and related areas.

LOCAL GOVERNMENT FINANCES, Items 178–191
Source: U.S. Bureau of the Census

Data on local government finances are based on results of the 2002 Census of Governments. For each county area, the financial data comprise amounts for all local governments—not only the county government but also any municipalities, townships, school districts, and special districts within the county. Statistics from governmental units located in two or more county areas are assigned to the county area containing the administrative office.

Revenue and expenditure items include all amounts of money received and paid out, respectively, by a government and its agencies (net of correcting transactions such as recoveries of refunds), with the exception of amounts for debt issuance and retirement and for loan and investment, agency, and private transactions.

Payments among the various funds and agencies of a particular government are excluded from revenue and expenditure items as representing internal transfers. Therefore, a government's contribution to a retirement fund that it administers is not counted as expenditure, nor is the receipt of this contribution by the retirement fund counted as revenue.

Total **general revenue** includes all revenue except utility, liquor stores, and insurance trust revenue. All tax revenue and intergovernmental revenue, even if designated for employee-retirement or local utility purpose, are classified as general revenue. However, to avoid duplication, revenue figures are net of reported transactions between local governments.

Intergovernmental revenue covers amounts received from the federal or state government as fiscal aid, reimbursements for performance of general government functions and specific services for the paying government, or amounts received in lieu of taxes. It excludes amounts received from other governments for sale of property, commodities, and utility services.

Taxes consist of compulsory contributions exacted by governments for public purposes. However, this category excludes employer and employee payments for retirement and social insurance purposes, which are classified as insurance trust revenue, and special assessments, which are classified as non-tax general revenue. Property taxes are taxes conditioned on ownership of property and assessed by its value.

Government expenditure includes all capital outlay, of which a major portion is commonly financed by borrowing, while governmental revenue does not include receipts from borrowing. Among other things, this distorts the relationship between totals of revenue and expenditure figures that are presented, and renders this relationship useless as a direct measure of the degree of budgetary "balance," as that term is generally applied.

Direct general expenditure comprises all expenditures of the local governments, excluding utility, liquor stores, insurance trust expenditures, and any intergovernmental payments.

Local government expenditures for **education** are mainly for provision and support of schools and other educational facilities and services, including those for educational institutions beyond the high school level operated by local governments. They cover such related services as pupil transportation; school lunch and other cafeteria operations; school health, recreation, and library services administered by local school systems; and dormitories, dining halls, and bookstores operated by public institutions of higher education.

Health and hospital expenditures include health research, clinics, nursing, immunization, and other categorical, environmental, and general health services provided by health agencies. It also includes establishment and operation of hospital facilities, provision of hospital care, and support of other public and private hospitals.

Police protection expenditure includes police activities such as patrols, communications, custody of persons awaiting trial, and vehicular inspection.

Public welfare expenditure covers support of and assistance to needy persons contingent upon their needs. Included are cash assistance paid directly to needy persons under categorical (Old Age Assistance, Aid to Families with Dependent Children, Aid to the Blind, and Aid to the Disabled) and other welfare programs;

vendor payments made directly to private purveyors for medical care, burials, and other commodities and services provided under welfare programs; welfare institutions; and any intergovernmental or other direct expenditure for welfare purposes. Pensions to former employees and other benefits not contingent upon need are excluded.

Highway expenditure is for provision and maintenance of highway facilities, including toll turnpikes, bridges, tunnels, and ferries, as well as regular roads, highways, and streets. Also included are expenditures for street lighting and for snow and ice removal.

Debt outstanding includes all long-term debt obligations of the government and its agencies (exclusive of utility debt) and all interest-bearing short-term (repayable within one year) debt obligations remaining unpaid at the close of the fiscal year. It includes judgments, mortgages, and revenue bonds, as well as general obligation bonds, notes, and interest-bearing warrants. It includes non-interest-bearing short-term obligations, inter-fund obligations, amounts owed in a trust or agency capacity, advances and contingent loans from other governments, and rights of individuals to benefits from government-administered employee retirement funds.

GOVERNMENT EMPLOYMENT, Items 192–194
Source: U.S. Bureau of Economic Analysis

Employment is measured as the average annual number of jobs, full-time plus part-time. The estimates are on a place-of-work basis. State and local government employment includes employment in all state and local government agencies and enterprises.

Federal civilian employment includes all civilian employees of the federal government, including civilian employees of the Department of Defense. Military employment includes all person on active duty status.

ELECTION STATISTICS, Items 195–197
Source: Unofficial preliminary numbers

Election results show the percentage of the total vote cast for each of the Democratic and Republican candidates, as well as the combined percentage for all other candidates in the 2004 presidential election.

TABLE D—CITIES

Table D presents 147 items of data for cities that had a population of 25,000 or more at the time of the 2000 census.

LAND AREA, Items 1 and 4
Source: U.S. Bureau of the Census

Land area measurements are shown to the nearest square kilometer. Land area includes dry land and land temporarily or partially covered by water, such as marshland, swamps, and river floodplains.

POPULATION, Items 2–4
Source: U.S. Bureau of the Census

The population data are U.S. Bureau of the Census estimates of the resident population as of July 1 of the year shown.

POPULATION BY RACE AND HISPANIC OR LATINO ORIGIN, Items 5–11
Source: U.S. Bureau of the Census—
2000 Census of Population and Housing

The data on **race** were derived from answers to the question on race that was asked of all people. The concept of race, as used by the Census Bureau, reflects self-identification by people according to the race or races with which they most closely identify. These categories are socio-political constructs and should not be interpreted as being scientific or anthropological in nature. Furthermore, the race categories include both racial and national-origin groups.

In the 2000 census, respondents were offered the option of selecting one or more races. This was not the case in prior censuses, so comparisons should be made with caution. In Table D, columns 9 through 13 refer to individuals who identified with each racial category, either alone or in combination with other races.

The **White** population is defined as persons who indicated their race as white, as well as persons who did not classify themselves in one of the specific race categories listed on the questionnaire, but entered a nationality such as Irish, German, Italian, Lebanese, Near Easterner, Arab, or Polish.

The **Black** population includes persons who indicated their race as "Black, African Am., or Negro," as well as persons who did not classify themselves in one of the specific race categories, but reported entries such as African American, Afro American, Kenyan, Nigerian, or Haitian.

The **American Indian or Alaska Native** population includes persons who indicated their race as American Indian or Alaska Native, as well as persons who did not classify themselves in one of the specific race categories but reported entries such as Canadian Indian, French American Indian, Spanish-American Indian, Eskimo, Aleut, Alaska Indian, or any of the American Indian or Alaska Native tribes.

The **Asian** population includes persons who indicated their race as Asian Indian, Chinese, Filipino, Japanese, Korean, Vietnamese, or "Other Asian," as well as persons who provided write-in entries of such Asian groups as Cambodian, Laotian,

Hmong, Pakistani, or Taiwanese. Also, persons who wrote in an entry indicating one of the specific categories were classified accordingly. The **Native Hawaiian or Other Pacific Islander** population includes persons who indicated their race as "Native Hawaiian," "Guamanian or Chamorro," "Samoan" or "Other Pacific Islander," as well as persons who reported entries such as Part Hawaiian, American Samoan, Fijian, Melanesian, or Tahitian. Also, persons who wrote in an entry indicating one of the specific categories were classified accordingly. In 1990, the **Asian** and **Native Hawaiian or Other Pacific Islander** categories were combined as **Asian and Pacific Islander**. This volume uses the 1990 combination.

The population of **Some other race** includes all persons who indicated "Some other race" as well as persons who wrote in a category not included in the race categories described above, including entries such as multiracial, mixed, interracial, or a Hispanic/Latino group such as Mexican, Puerto Rican, or Cuban in the "Some other race" write-in space.

Changes in specific listing of racial categories, the new practice of allowing more than one selection in 2000, and the order in which questions appeared on the questionnaire, could all affect comparability between the 2000 and 1990 censuses.

The Hispanic or Latino population is based on a complete-count question that asked respondents "Is this person Spanish/Hispanic/Latino?" Persons marking any one of the four Hispanic or Latino categories (Mexican, Puerto Rican, Cuban, or other Spanish) are collectively referred to as Hispanic or Latino.

In the 2000 census, the Hispanic or Latino origin question was placed before the race question and specific instructions indicated that both questions should be answered. These changes were designed to improve accuracy, and may affect comparability with 1990 data.

POPULATION—AGE, Items 12–20
Source: U.S. Bureau of the Census—
2000 Census of Population and Housing

Age derived from the census (2000) is classified as age at last birthday (number of completed years from birth to April 1). The percent figures are derived by dividing the number of persons in a specified age group by the total population of a given geographic area. Data on age are based on complete counts of resident population.

The 2000 census also asked for the specific date of birth of the respondent, and 2000 census procedures used the birth date for deriving age data. For this reason, it is likely that the 2000 data have fewer problems than prior censuses, such as a tendency to round ages or report the person's age on the date the questionnaire was filled out rather than on April 1.

POPULATION—PERCENT FEMALE, Item 21
Source: U.S. Bureau of the Census—
2000 Census of Population and Housing

The female population of a geographic area is shown as a percent of the total population of the area.

POPULATION AND POPULATION CHANGE, Items 22–25
Source: U.S. Bureau of the Census

These population counts are from the decennial census and represent resident population as of April 1, 1990 and 2000 respectively, and estimates of the population as of July 1, 2003.

Population change 1990–2000 is calculated from census data based on city boundaries as they existed in 1990 and 2000 respectively. No attempt was made to adjust the data to reflect boundary changes.

HOUSEHOLDS, 2000, Items 26–30
Source: U.S. Bureau of the Census— 2000 Census of Population and Housing

A household consists of persons occupying a single housing unit. A housing unit is a house, an apartment, a group of rooms, or a single room occupied as separate living quarters. The occupants may be a single family, one person living alone, two or more families living together, or any other group of related or unrelated persons who share a housing unit. The number of households is the same as the number of year-round occupied housing units.

A family household consists of two or more persons, including the householder, who are related by birth, marriage, or adoption and who live together as one household; all such persons are considered as members of one family.

The measure of persons per household is obtained by dividing the number of persons in households by the number of households or householders. The category **female family householder** includes only female-headed family households with no spouse present.

GROUP QUARTERS, Items 31–34
Source: U.S. Bureau of the Census— 2000 Census of Population and Housing

All persons not living in households are classified by the Census Bureau as living in group quarters. This volume includes the total number of persons in group quarters and in selected types of group quarters.

Institutionalized population includes people under formally authorized, supervised care or custody in institutions at the time of enumeration. These include correctional institutions, nursing homes, mental (psychiatric) hospitals, hospitals or wards for the chronically ill, schools, hospitals, or wards for the mentally retarded, the physically handicapped, or for drug/alcohol abuse, wards in general or military hospitals for patients who have no usual home elsewhere, and juvenile institutions.

Nursing homes comprise a heterogeneous group of places. The majority of patients are elderly, although persons who require nursing care because of chronic physical conditions may be found in these homes regardless of their age. Included in this category are skilled-nursing facilities, intermediate-care facilities, long-term care rooms in wards or buildings on the grounds of hospitals, or long-term care rooms/nursing wings in congregate housing facilities. Also included are nursing, convalescent, and rest homes, such as soldiers', sailors', veterans', and fraternal or religious homes for the aged, with or without nursing care.

The Noninstitutionalized population includes people who live in group quarters other than institutions, such as college dormitories and military quarters.

CRIME, Items 35–38
Source: U.S. Federal Bureau of Investigation— Uniform Crime Reports

Crime data are as reported to the FBI by law enforcement agencies and have not been adjusted for under-reporting. This may affect comparability between geographic areas or over time.

Through the voluntary contribution of crime statistics by law enforcement agencies across the United States, the Uniform Crime Reporting (UCR) Program provides periodic assessments of crime in the nation as measured by those offenses which come to the attention of the law enforcement community. The Committee on Uniform Crime Records of the International Association of Chiefs of Police initiated this voluntary national data-collection effort in 1930. UCR Program contributors compile and submit their crime data in one of two manners: either directly to the FBI or through the State UCR Programs.

Seven offenses, because of their seriousness, frequency of occurrence, and likelihood of being reported to police, were initially selected to serve as an index for evaluating fluctuations in the volume of crime. These serious crimes were murder and nonnegligent manslaughter, forcible rape, robbery, aggravated assault, burglary, larceny-theft, and motor vehicle theft. By congressional mandate, arson was added as the eighth index offense in 1979. The totals shown in this volume do not include arson.

Violent offenses include four crime categories: (1) Murder and nonnegligent manslaughter, as defined in the UCR Program, is the willful (nonnegligent) killing of one human being by another. This offense excludes deaths caused by negligence, suicide or accident; justifiable homicides; and attempts to murder or assaults to murder. (2) Forcible rape is the carnal knowledge of a female forcibly and against her will. Assaults or attempts to commit rape by force or threat of force are also included; however, statutory rape (without force) and other sex offenses are excluded. (3) Robbery is the taking or attempting to take anything of value from the care, custody, or control of a person or persons by force or threat of force or violence and/or by putting the victim in fear. (4) Aggravated assault is an unlawful attack by one person upon another for the purpose of inflicting severe or aggravated bodily injury. This type of assault is usually accompanied by the use of a weapon or by means likely to produce death or great bodily harm. Attempts are included since an injury does not necessarily have to result when a gun, knife, or other weapon is used, which could and probably would result in a serious personal injury if the crime were successfully completed.

Property crimes include three categories: (1) Burglary, or breaking and entering, is the unlawful entry of a structure to commit a felony or theft, even though no force was used to gain entrance. (2) Larceny/theft is the unauthorized taking of the personal property of another, without the use of force. (3) Motor vehicle theft is the unauthorized taking of any motor vehicle.

Rates are based on population estimates provided by the FBI.

EDUCATION—SCHOOL ENROLLMENT AND EDUCATIONAL ATTAINMENT, Items 39–42
Source: U.S. Bureau of the Census—
2000 Census of Population and Housing

Data on school enrollment and educational attainment were derived from a sample of the population. Persons were classified as enrolled in school if they reported attending a "regular" public or private school (or college) at any time between February 1, 2000 and the time of enumeration. The instructions were to "include only nursery school, kindergarten, elementary school, and schooling which would lead to a high school diploma or a college degree" as regular school. Public school is defined as "any school or college controlled and supported by a local, county, state, or federal government." Schools supported and controlled primarily by religious organizations or other private groups are defined as private.

Statistics for levels of school completed are for persons 25 years old and over. The data were derived from a question on the 2000 census questionnaire that asked respondents for the highest level of school they had completed or the highest degree they had received. Persons who passed a high school equivalency examination were considered high school graduates. Schooling received in foreign schools was to be reported as the equivalent grade or years in the regular American school system.

MONEY INCOME, Items 43–46
Source: U.S. Bureau of the Census—
2000 Census of Population and Housing

The data on income are derived from the responses of a sample of persons 15 years old and over. **Total money income** is defined by the Bureau of the Census for statistical purposes as the sum of the following: wage or salary income; nonfarm self-employment income; net farm self-employment income; Social Security and railroad retirement income; public assistance income; and all other regularly received income such as interest, dividends, veterans' payments, pensions, unemployment compensation, and alimony. Receipts not counted as income include various "lump sum" payments such as capital gains or inheritances.

The total represents the amount of income received before deductions for personal income taxes, Social Security, bond purchases, union dues, Medicare deductions, etc.

Per capita income is based on resident population enumerated as of April 1, 2000.

Income of households includes the income of the householder and all other persons 15 years old and over in the household. Household income is usually less than family income because many households consist of only one person. The median divides the income distribution into two equal parts, one having incomes above the median, the other with incomes below. The constant-dollar figures are based on an annual average Consumer Price Index from the Bureau of Labor Statistics. Constant-dollar figures are estimates representing an effort to remove the effects of price changes from statistical series reported in dollar terms. However, the estimates do not reflect the price and cost-of-living differences that may exist between areas.

POVERTY, Items 47–49
Source: U.S. Bureau of the Census—
2000 Census of Population and Housing

The data on poverty are derived from the same questions as the data on money income. Poverty status is based on the definition prescribed by the Federal Office of Management and Budget as the standard to be used by federal agencies for statistical purposes. Families and persons are classified as below the poverty level if their total family income or unrelated individual income was less than the poverty threshold specified for the applicable family size, age of householder, and number of related children present under 18 years old. Poverty status is determined for all families (and by implication all family members). For persons not in families, poverty status is determined by their income in relation to the appropriate poverty threshold. Inmates of institutions, persons in military group quarters or college dormitories, and unrelated individuals under 15 years old are excluded.

The 1999 poverty thresholds are shown in Figure 1.

Figure 1.
Poverty Thresholds in 1999 by Size of Family

Size of Family Unit	Weighted average thresholds
One person (unrelated individual)	$8,501
Under 65 years old	8,667
65 years old and over	7,990
Two persons	10,869
Householder under 65 years old	11,214
Householder 65 years old and over	10,075
Three persons	13,290
Four persons	17,029
Five persons	20,127
Six persons	22,727
Seven persons	25,912
Eight persons	28,967
Nine or more persons	34,417

HOUSING, Items 50–60
Source: U.S. Bureau of the Census—
2000 Census of Population and Housing

A **housing unit** is a house, apartment, mobile home or trailer, group of rooms, or single room occupied or, if vacant, intended for occupancy as separate living quarters. Separate living quarters are those in which the occupants do not live and eat with any other persons in the structure and which have direct access from the outside of the building through a common hall.

The occupants of a housing unit may be a single family, one person living alone, two or more families living together, or a group of related or unrelated persons who share living arrangements. For vacant units, the criteria of separateness and direct access are applied to the intended occupants whenever possible. If that information cannot be obtained, the criteria are applied to the previous occupants. Both occupied and vacant housing units are included in the housing inventory, except that recreational vehicles, tents, caves, boats, railroad cars, and the like are included only if they are occupied as someone's usual place of residence.

A housing unit is classified as occupied if it is the usual place of residence of the person or group of persons living in it at the time of enumeration or if the occupants are only temporarily absent (away on vacation). A household consists of all persons who occupy a housing unit as their usual place of residence. Vacant units for sale or rent include units rented or sold but not occupied and any other units held off the market.

The percent change represents the difference in the number of total housing units in a specified area over the decade 1980–1990.

Vacant housing units are considered for **seasonal, recreational, or occasional use** if they are used or intended for use only in certain seasons, for weekends, or other occasional use throughout the year. Seasonal units include those used for summer or winter sports or recreation, such as beach cottages and hunting cabins. Seasonal units also may include quarters for such workers as herders and loggers. Interval ownership units, sometimes called shared-ownership or time-sharing condominiums, also are included in this category.

The **homeowner vacancy rate** is the proportion of the homeowner housing inventory that is vacant for sale. It is computed by dividing the number of vacant units for sale only by the sum of the owner-occupied units and vacant units that are for sale only.

The **rental vacancy rate** is the proportion of the rental inventory that is vacant for rent. It is computed by dividing the number of vacant units for rent by the sum of the renter-occupied units and the number of vacant units for rent.

A housing unit is **owner occupied** if the owner or co-owner lives in the unit even if it is mortgaged or not fully paid for. The owner or co-owner must live in the unit and usually is Person one on the census questionnaire.

All occupied housing units that are not owner occupied, whether they are rented for cash rent or occupied without payment of cash rent, are classified as **renter occupied**.

Average Household Size of Owner-Occupied Units is a measure obtained by dividing the number of people living in owner-occupied housing units by the number of owner-occupied housing units.

Average Household Size of Renter-Occupied Units is a measure obtained by dividing the number of people living in renter-occupied housing units by the number of renter-occupied housing units.

CIVILIAN LABOR FORCE AND UNEMPLOYMENT, Items 61–64
Source: U.S. Bureau of Labor Statistics

Data for the civilian labor force are the product of a federal-state cooperative program in which state employment security agencies prepare labor force and unemployment estimates under concepts, definitions, and technical procedures established by the Bureau of Labor Statistics. The civilian labor force consists of all persons 16 years and over who are either employed in a civilian job or unemployed.

Unemployment includes all persons who did not work during the survey week, made specific efforts to find a job in the prior 4 weeks, and were available for work during the survey week (except for temporary illness). Persons waiting to be called back

to a job from which they had been laid off and those waiting to report to a new job within the next 30 days are included in unemployment figures.

CIVILIAN EMPLOYMENT, 2000, Items 65–67
Source: U.S. Bureau of the Census— 2000 Census of Population and Housing

Total employment includes all civilians 16 years old or over who were either (1) ''at work''—those who did any work at all during the reference week as paid employees, worked in their own business or profession, worked on their own farm, or worked 15 hours or more as unpaid workers in a family farm or business; or were (2) ''with a job, but not at work''—those who had a job but were not at work that week due to illness, weather, industrial dispute, vacation, or other personal reasons.

The **occupation categories** shown are consistent with the 2000 edition of the *Standard Occupational Classification Manual (SOC)* published by the Office of Federal Statistical Policy and Standards, U.S. Department of Commerce.

EMPLOYMENT DISABILITY, Item 68
Source: U.S. Bureau of the Census— 2000 Census of Population and Housing

Data are shown for persons 16 to 64 years old in 2000. Persons were identified as having an employment disability if they reported a health condition that had lasted 6 months or more and which limited the kind or amount of work they could do at a job or business.

CONSTRUCTION—BUILDING PERMITS, Items 69–71
Source: U.S. Bureau of the Census— Building Permits Survey

Figures represent private residential construction authorized by building permits in approximately 19,000 places in the United States. Valuation represents the cost of construction as recorded on the building permit. This figure usually excludes the cost of on-site and off-site development and improvements and the cost of heating, plumbing, electrical, and elevator installations.

If a city is not a permit-issuing place covered by the Census Bureau, an ''NA'' is shown. Cities that are permit-issuing places but that issued no permits during the period are represented by a ''0.'' State and U.S. totals were obtained by summing the data for permit issuing places within each jurisdiction.

Residential building permits include buildings with any number of housing units. Hotels, apartment hotels, dormitories, fraternity houses, and other non-housekeeping residential buildings are not included.

1997 ECONOMIC CENSUS: OVERVIEW
Items 72–107
Source: U.S. Bureau of the Census

The Economic Census provides a detailed portrait of the nation's economy once every 5 years, from the national to the local level. The 1997 Economic Census covers nearly all of the U.S. economy in its basic collection of establishment statistics. It is the first major data source to use the new North American Industry Classification System (NAICS) and is therefore not comparable to economic data from prior years which were based on the Standard Industrial Classification (SIC) system.

NAICS, developed in cooperation with Canada and Mexico, classifies North America's economic activities at two-, three-, four-, and five-digit levels of detail, and the U.S. version of NAICS further defines industries to a sixth digit. The Economic Census takes advantage of this hierarchy to publish data at these successive levels of detail: sector (two-digit); subsector (three-digit); industry group (four-digit); industry(five-digit); and U.S. industry(six-digit.)

This volume was published during the initial release of the 1997 Economic Census and therefore includes those sectors that were available at the time of publication. The information in Table D is at the two-digit level.

Several key statistics are tabulated for all industries included in this volume: number of establishments (or companies); number of employees; payroll; and a measure of output (sales, receipts, revenue, value of shipments, or value of construction work done.)

Number of Establishments. An establishment is a single physical location at which business is conducted. It is not necessarily identical with a company or enterprise, which may consist of one establishment or more. Economic Census figures represent a summary of reports for individual establishments rather than companies. For cases where a census report was received, separate information was obtained for each location where business was conducted. When administrative records of other Federal agencies were used instead of a census report, no information was available on the number of locations operated. Each Economic Census establishment was tabulated according to the physical location at which the business was conducted. The count of establishments represents those in business at any time during 1997.

When two activities or more were carried on at a single location under a single ownership, all activities generally were grouped together as a single establishment. The entire establishment was classified on the basis of its major activity and all data for it were included in that classification. However, when distinct and separate economic activities (for which different industry classification codes were appropriate) were conducted at a single location under a single ownership, separate establishment reports for each of the different activities were obtained in the census.

Number of Employees. Paid employees consist of the full-time and part-time employees, including salaried officers and executives of corporations. Included are employees on paid sick leave, paid holidays, and paid vacations; not included are proprietors and partners of unincorporated businesses. The definition of paid employees is the same as that used on IRS form 941.

Payroll. Payroll includes all forms of compensation such as salaries, wages, commissions, dismissal pay, bonuses, vacation allowances, sick-leave pay, and employee contributions to qualified pension plans paid during the year to all employees. For corporations, payroll includes amounts paid to officers and executives; for unincorporated businesses, it does not include profit or other compensation of proprietors or partners. Payroll is reported before deductions for social security, income tax, insurance, union dues, etc. This definition of payroll is the same as that used by the IRS on form 941.

Sales, Shipments, Receipts, Revenue, or Business Done. This measure includes the total sales, shipments, receipts, revenue, or business done by establishments within the scope of the Economic Census. The definition of each of these items is specific to the economic sector measured.

WHOLESALE TRADE, Items 72–75
Source: U.S. Bureau of the Census,
1997 Economic Census
(See Overview of 1997 Economic Census
prior to Item 72)

The Wholesale Trade sector (sector 42) comprises establishments engaged in wholesaling merchandise, generally without transformation, and rendering services incidental to the sale of merchandise. The wholesaling process is an intermediate step in the distribution of merchandise.

Wholesalers are organized to sell or arrange the purchase or sale of (a) goods for resale (goods sold to other wholesalers or retailers), (b) capital or durable nonconsumer goods, and (c) raw and intermediate materials and supplies used in production.

Wholesalers sell merchandise to other businesses and normally operate from a warehouse or office. These warehouses and offices are characterized by having little or no display of merchandise. In addition, neither the design nor the location of the premises is intended to solicit walk-in traffic. Wholesalers do not normally use advertising directed to the general public. Customers are generally reached initially via telephone, in-person marketing, or by specialized advertising that may include Internet and other electronic means. Follow-up orders are either vendor-initiated or client-initiated, generally based on previous sales, and typically exhibit strong ties between sellers and buyers. In fact, transactions are often conducted between wholesalers and clients that have long-standing business relationships.

This sector comprises two main types of wholesalers: those that sell goods on their own account and those that arrange sales and purchases for others for a commission or fee.

(1) Establishments that sell goods on their own account are known as wholesale merchants, distributors, jobbers, drop shippers, import/export merchants, and sales branches. These establishments typically maintain their own warehouse, where they receive and handle goods for their customers. Goods are generally sold without transformation, but may include integral functions, such as sorting, packaging, labeling, and other marketing services.

(2) Establishments arranging for the purchase or sale of goods owned by others or purchasing goods on a commission basis are known as agents and brokers, commission merchants, import/export agents and brokers, auction companies, and manufacturers' representatives. These establishments operate from offices and generally do not own or handle the goods they sell.

Some wholesale establishments may be connected with a single manufacturer and promote and sell the particular manufacturer's products to a wide range of other wholesalers or retailers. Other wholesalers may be connected to a retail chain or a limited number of retail chains and only provide a variety of products needed by that particular retail operation(s). These wholesalers may obtain the products from a wide range of manufacturers. Still other wholesalers may not take title to the goods, but act as agents and brokers for a commission.

Although, in general, wholesaling normally denotes sales in large volumes, durable nonconsumer goods may be sold in single units. Sales of capital or durable nonconsumer goods used in the production of goods and services, such as farm machinery, medium and heavy duty trucks, and industrial machinery, are always included in wholesale trade.

RETAIL TRADE, Items 76–79
Source: U.S. Bureau of the Census,
1997 Economic Census
(See Overview of 1997 Economic Census
prior to Item 72)

The Retail Trade sector (44-45) comprises establishments engaged in retailing merchandise, generally without transformation, and rendering services incidental to the sale of merchandise.

The retailing process is the final step in the distribution of merchandise; retailers are, therefore, organized to sell merchandise in small quantities to the general public. This sector comprises two main types of retailers: store and nonstore retailers.

Store retailers operate fixed point-of-sale locations, located and designed to attract a high volume of walk-in customers. In general, retail stores have extensive displays of merchandise and use mass-media advertising to attract customers. They typically sell merchandise to the general public for personal or household consumption, but some also serve business and institutional clients. These include establishments, such as office supply stores, computer and software stores, building materials dealers, plumbing supply stores, and electrical supply stores. Catalog showrooms, gasoline service stations, automotive dealers, and mobile home dealers are treated as store retailers.

In addition to retailing merchandise, some types of store retailers are also engaged in the provision of after-sales services, such as repair and installation. For example, new automobile dealers, electronic and appliance stores, and musical instrument and supply stores often provide repair services. As a general rule, establishments engaged in retailing merchandise and providing after-sales services are classified in this sector.

Nonstore retailers, like store retailers, are organized to serve the general public, but their retailing methods differ. The establishments of this subsector reach customers and market merchandise with methods, such as the broadcasting of ''infomercials,'' the broadcasting and publishing of direct-response advertising, the publishing of paper and electronic catalogs, door-to-door solicitation, in-home demonstration, selling from portable stalls (street vendors, except food), and distribution through vending machines. Establishments engaged in the direct sale (nonstore) of products, such as home heating oil dealers and home delivery newspaper routes.

The buying of goods for resale is a characteristic of retail trade establishments that particularly distinguishes them from establishments in the agriculture, manufacturing, and construction industries. For example, farms that sell their products at or from the point of production are not classified in retail, but rather in agriculture. Similarly, establishments that both manufacture and sell their products to the general public are not classified in retail, but rather in manufacturing. However, establishments that engage in processing activities incidental to retailing are classified in retail.

REAL ESTATE AND RENTAL AND LEASING, Items 80–83
Source: U.S. Bureau of the Census,
1997 Economic Census
(See Overview of 1997 Economic Census
prior to Item 72)

The Real Estate and Rental and Leasing sector (53) comprises establishments primarily engaged in renting, leasing, or otherwise allowing the use of tangible or intangible assets, and establishments providing related services. The major portion of this sector comprises establishments that rent, lease, or otherwise allow the use of their own assets by others. The assets may be tangible, as is the case of real estate and equipment, or intangible, as is the case with patents and trademarks.

This sector also includes establishments primarily engaged in managing real estate for others, selling, renting and/or buying real estate for others, and appraising real estate. These activities are closely related to this sector's main activity, and it was felt that from a production basis they would best be included here. In addition, a substantial proportion of property management is self-performed by lessors.

The main components of this sector are the real estate lessors industries; equipment lessors industries (including motor vehicles, computers, and consumer goods); and lessors of nonfinancial intangible assets (except copyrighted works).

PROFESSIONAL, SCIENTIFIC, AND TECHNICAL SERVICES, Items 84–87
Source: U.S. Bureau of the Census,
1997 Economic Census
(See Overview of 1997 Economic Census
prior to Item 72)

The Professional, Scientific, and Technical Services sector (54) comprises establishments that specialize in performing professional, scientific, and technical activities for others. These activities require a high degree of expertise and training. The establishments in this sector specialize according to expertise and provide these services to clients in a variety of industries and, in some cases, to households. Activities performed include: legal advice and representation; accounting, bookkeeping, and payroll services; architectural, engineering, and specialized design services; computer services; consulting services; research services;

advertising services; photographic services; translation and interpretation services; veterinary services; and other professional, scientific, and technical services.

This volume includes only those establishments subject to federal income tax.

This sector excludes establishments primarily engaged in providing a range of day-to-day office administrative services, such as financial planning, billing and recordkeeping, personnel, and physical distribution and logistics. These establishments are classified in sector 56, Administrative and Support and Waste Management and Remediation Services.

MANUFACTURING, Items 88–91
Source: U.S. Bureau of the Census, 1997 Economic Census
(See Overview of 1997 Economic Census prior to Item 72)

The Manufacturing sector comprises establishments engaged in the mechanical, physical, or chemical transformation of materials, substances, or components into new products. The assembling of component parts of manufactured products is considered manufacturing, except in cases where the activity is appropriately classified as Construction. Establishments in the Manufacturing sector are often described as plants, factories, or mills and characteristically use power-driven machines and materials-handling equipment. However, establishments that transform materials or substances into new products by hand or in the worker's home and those engaged in selling to the general public products made on the same premises from which they are sold, such as bakeries, candy stores, and custom tailors, may also be included in this sector. Manufacturing establishments may process materials or may contract with other establishments to process their materials for them. Both types of establishments are included in manufacturing. The materials, substances, or components transformed by manufacturing establishments are raw materials that are products of agriculture, forestry, fishing, mining, or quarrying as well as products of other manufacturing establishments. The materials used may be purchased directly from producers, obtained through customary trade channels, or secured without recourse to the market by transferring the product from one establishment to another, under the same ownership. The new product of a manufacturing establishment may be finished in the sense that it is ready for utilization or consumption, or it may be semifinished to become an input for an establishment engaged in further manufacturing. For example, the product of the alumina refinery is the input used in the primary production of aluminum; primary aluminum is the input to an aluminum wire drawing plant; and aluminum wire is the input for a fabricated wire product manufacturing establishment.

Data are included for cities with 500 or more employees in the manufacturing sector.

ACCOMMODATION AND FOOD SERVICES, Items 92–95
Source: U.S. Bureau of the Census, 1997 Economic Census
(See Overview of 1997 Economic Census prior to Item 72)

The Accommodation and Food Services sector (72) comprises establishments providing customers with lodging and/or preparing meals, snacks, and beverages for immediate consumption. The sector includes both accommodation and food services establishments because the two activities are often combined at the same establishment.

Excluded from this sector are civic and social organizations; amusement and recreation parks; theaters; and other recreation or entertainment facilities providing food and beverage services.

ARTS, ENTERTAINMENT, AND RECREATION, Items 96–99
Source: U.S. Bureau of the Census, 1997 Economic Census
(See Overview of 1997 Economic Census prior to Item 72)

The Arts, Entertainment, and Recreation sector (71) includes a wide range of establishments that operate facilities or provide services to meet varied cultural, entertainment, and recreational interests of their patrons. This sector comprises (1) establishments that are involved in producing, promoting, or participating in live performances, events, or exhibits intended for public viewing; (2) establishments that preserve and exhibit objects and sites of historical, cultural, or educational interest; and (3) establishments that operate facilities or provide services that enable patrons to participate in recreational activities or pursue amusement, hobby, and leisure time interests.

Some establishments that provide cultural, entertainment, or recreational facilities and services are classified in other sectors. Excluded from this sector are: (1) establishments that provide both accommodations and recreational facilities, such as hunting and fishing camps and resort and casino hotels are classified in Subsector 721, Accommodation; (2) restaurants and night clubs that provide live entertainment in addition to the sale of food and beverages are classified in Subsector 722, Food Services and Drinking Places; (3) motion picture theaters, libraries and archives, and publishers of newspapers, magazines, books, periodicals, and computer software are classified in Sector 51, Information; and (4) establishments using transportation equipment to provide recreational and entertainment services, such as those operating sightseeing buses, dinner cruises, or helicopter rides are classified in Subsector 487, Scenic and Sightseeing Transportation.

HEALTH CARE AND SOCIAL ASSISTANCE, Items 100–103
Source: U.S. Bureau of the Census, 1997 Economic Census
(See Overview of 1997 Economic Census prior to Item 72)

The Health Care and Social Assistance sector (62) comprises establishments providing health care and social assistance for individuals. The sector includes both health care and social assistance because it is sometimes difficult to distinguish between the boundaries of these two activities. The industries in this sector are arranged on a continuum starting with those establishments providing medical care exclusively, continuing with those providing health care and social assistance, and finally finishing with those providing only social assistance. The services provided by establishments in this sector are delivered by trained professionals. All industries in the sector share this commonality of process, namely, labor inputs of health practitioners or social workers with the requisite expertise. Many of the industries in the sector are defined based on the educational degree held by the practitioners included in the industry.

In this volume, only taxable establishments are included in Table D.

Excluded from this sector are aerobic classes in Subsector 713, Amusement, Gambling and Recreation Industries and nonmedical diet and weight reducing centers in Subsector 812, Personal and Laundry Services. Although these can be viewed as health services, these services are not typically delivered by health practitioners.

OTHER SERVICES, Items 104–107
Source: U.S. Bureau of the Census, 1997 Economic Census
(See Overview of 1997 Economic Census prior to Item 72)

The Other Services (except Public Administration) sector (81) comprises establishments engaged in providing services not specifically provided for elsewhere in the classification system. Establishments in this sector are primarily engaged in activities, such as equipment and machinery repairing, promoting or administering religious activities, grantmaking, advocacy, and providing drycleaning and laundry services, personal care services, death care services, pet care services, photofinishing services, temporary parking services, and dating services.

Private households that engage in employing workers on or about the premises in activities primarily concerned with the operation of the household are included in this sector.

In this volume, only firms subject to federal tax are included.

Excluded from this sector are establishments primarily engaged in retailing new equipment and also performing repairs and general maintenance on equipment. These establishments are classified in Sector 44–45, Retail Trade.

FEDERAL FUNDS, Items 108–116
Source: U.S. Bureau of the Census— Consolidated Federal Funds Report

Data on federal expenditures and obligations are obtained from a report prepared by the Bureau of the Census in accordance with the Consolidated Federal Funds Report (CFFR) Act of 1982 (P.L. 97-326). The data are for federal fiscal years beginning on October 1 and ending the following September 30.

Only selected categories of data from the CFFR can be allocated to the city level. The city items shown in this book are "selected" federal funds and do not represent all federal funds received by individuals and entities within the city.

Dollar amounts reported can reflect expenditure or obligations. In some cases, dollar amounts are negative, representing de-obligations of financial assistance that had been previously awarded. Such amounts generally appear in the grant categories. Many categories are assigned only to state and county levels and never assigned to cities.

Direct payments for individuals represent actual expenditures during the fiscal year. Direct payments data at the city level are limited largely to educational and housing assistance payments. Direct payments for educational assistance consist primarily of higher education grants and insured loans. Data on other types of direct payments, including food stamps, social security, and federal retirement, and data on federal wages and salaries are available for counties but not for cities.

Procurement contract awards cover awards by the United States Postal Service (USPS) as well as all other federal agencies. Amounts provided by the USPS represent actual outlays for contractual commitments, while amounts for other agencies represent the value of obligations for contract actions and do not reflect actual federal government expenditures. In general, only current-year contract actions are included—however, multiple-year obligations may be reported for contract actions of less than 3 years duration. The procurement contract data for cities are relatively complete.

Salaries and wages represent actual federal expenditures during the fiscal year; the geographic distribution of these amounts by state and county was estimated based upon place of employment.

Grants data represent the federal obligations incurred at the time the grant is awarded. The amounts reported do not represent actual expenditures since obligations in one time period may not result in outlays during the same time period. Moreover, initial amounts obligated may be adjusted at a later date, either through enhancements or de-obligations. All grant awards were reported by state, county, and city of the initial recipient. For many grants, this recipient is the state government even though the grant monies are subsequently distributed to county, municipal, or township governments.

Medicaid and other health-related grants include a variety of grants from the Department of Health and Human Services for health services and research.

Nutrition and family welfare grants include a variety of grants by the Department of Health and Human Services for child welfare, special programs for the aging, and related areas. The school lunch program and other nutritional assistance programs administered by the Department of Agriculture are also included.

Energy and environment grants include grants from the U.S. Department of Energy for energy development, energy conservation, and nuclear waste disposal, as well as from the Environmental Protection Agency for a variety of pollution control and waste management activities.

Education grants include a variety of grant programs relating to elementary, secondary, and post-secondary education; adult education; vocational education; faculty training; and related areas.

Housing and community development grants include Community Development Block Grants, housing demonstration programs, rental housing rehabilitation, and other housing programs.

CITY GOVERNMENT FINANCES, Items 117–139
Source: U.S. Bureau of the Census— Survey of Governments, 2002: Finance Statistics

Revenue and expenditure data for the city government only are included in this table. The numbers do not include funds of any special district governments located in the city.

Total **general revenue** includes all government revenue except utility, liquor store, and employee-retirement or other insurance trust revenue. It includes all tax collections and intergovernmental revenue, even if designated for employee-retirement or local utility purposes.

Intergovernmental revenue consists of amounts received from other governments as fiscal aid in the form of shared revenues and grants-in-aid, as reimbursements for performance of general expenditure functions and specific services for the paying government (for example care of prisoners or contractual research), or amounts in lieu of taxes. It excludes amounts received from other governments for sale of property, commodities, and utility services. All intergovernmental revenue is classified as general revenue. Intergovernmental revenue from the state government includes amounts originally from the federal government, but channeled through the state.

Taxes are compulsory contributions exacted by a government for public purposes, and exclude employee and employer assessments for retirement and social insurance purposes, which are classified as insurance trust revenue. All tax revenue is classified as general revenue and comprises amounts received (including interest and penalties but excluding protested amounts and refunds) from all taxes imposed by a government. Note that local government tax revenue excludes any amounts from shares of state-imposed and collected taxes, which are classified as intergovernmental revenue.

Property taxes are based on ownership of property and measured by its value. They include general property taxes related to property as a whole—real and personal, tangible or intangible—whether taxed at a single rate or at classified rates. Also included are taxes on selected types of property, such as motor vehicles or certain or all intangibles.

Sales and gross receipts taxes include: "licenses" at more than nominal rates, based on volume or value of transfers of goods or services; taxes upon gross receipts, or upon gross income; and related taxes based upon use, storage, production (other than severance of natural resources), importation, or consumption of goods. Dealer discounts of "commissions" allowed to merchants for collection of taxes from consumers are excluded.

Total **general expenditure** includes all city expenditure other than the specifically enumerated kinds of expenditure classified as utility, liquor store, and employee retirement and other insurance trust expenditures.

Capital outlays are direct expenditures for contract or force account construction of buildings, roads, and other improvements, and for purchases of equipment, land, and existing structures. They include amounts for additions, replacements, and major alterations to fixed works and structures. Expenditure for repair to such works and structures, however, is classified as current operation expenditure.

A major portion of capital outlay is commonly financed by borrowing, while governmental revenue does not include receipts from borrowing. Among other things, this distorts the relationship between the totals presented for revenue and expenditure and renders this relationship useless as a direct measure of the degree of budgetary "balance," as that term is generally applied.

Public welfare is defined as support of and assistance to needy persons contingent upon their need. This excludes pensions to former employees and other benefits not contingent upon need. Health and hospital services provided directly by the government through its own hospitals and health agencies, as well as any payments to other governments for such purposes, are classified under those functional headings rather than being included as part of public welfare.

Highways includes construction, maintenance, and operation of highways, streets, and related structures, including toll highways, bridges, tunnels, ferries, street lighting, and snow and ice removal. Not included are highway policing and traffic control, which are considered as part of police protection.

Parking facilities include the construction, purchase, maintenance, and operation of public-use parking lots, garages, parking meters, and other distinctive parking facilities on a commercial basis.

Education includes provision or support of schools and facilities for elementary and secondary, higher, and other education. Elementary and secondary education includes the provision of public kindergarten through high school education by local governments. It encompasses instructional, support, and auxiliary services (school lunch, student activities, and community services) offered by public school systems. Higher education consists of all local institutions of higher education.

Health expenditures include outpatient health services other than hospital care, such as public health administration; research and education; categorical health programs; treatment and immunization clinics; nursing; environmental health activities such as air and water pollution control; ambulance service if provided separately from fire protection services; and other general public health activities such as mosquito abatement. School health services provided by health agencies (rather than school agencies) are included here. Not included are sewage treatment operations, which are classified as part of sewerage and sanitation. Hospital expenditures include financing, construction, acquisition, maintenance and operation of hospital facilities, provision of hospital care, and support of public or private hospitals.

Police protection encompasses expenditures for the preservation of law and order, as well as for traffic safety. It includes police patrols and communications, crime prevention activities, detention and custody of persons awaiting trial, traffic safety, and vehicular inspection.

Sewerage and sanitation includes sanitary and storm sewers, sewage disposal facilities and services, and other government activities for such purposes. Street cleaning and the collection and disposal of garbage and other waste are also included.

Parks and recreation includes cultural and scientific activities such as museums and art galleries; organized recreation, including playgrounds and playing fields, swimming pools, and bathing beaches; and municipal parks and special recreation facilities, such as auditoriums, stadiums, auto camps, recreation piers, and boat harbors.

Housing and community development includes city housing and redevelopment projects and the regulation, promotion, and support of private housing and redevelopment activities. Data from Arizona, Kentucky, Michigan, New Mexico, New York, and Virginia generally include municipal housing authorities. Housing authorities for other cities are usually classified as independent governments, and data for them are not included.

Interest on debt are the amounts paid for the use of borrowed money.

Total **debt** outstanding is the total of all debt obligations remaining unpaid on the date specified.

Utility debt is that portion of outstanding debt originally issued specifically to finance government owned and operated water, electric, gas, or transit utility facilities.

CITY GOVERNMENT EMPLOYMENT, Item 140
Source: U.S. Bureau of the Census— Survey of Governments, 2003: Employment Statistics

The data are from an annual survey conducted by the Bureau of the Census and represent paid employment by city governments during October 2003. Full-time equivalent employment is a computed statistic representing the number of full-time employees that would have been employed if the hours worked by the part-time employees were converted to full-time equivalents.

CLIMATE, Items 141–147
Source: National Oceanic and Atmospheric Administration

All climate data are average values for the 30-year period from 1961 to 1990.

Mean temperatures for January and July were determined by adding the average daily maximum temperatures and the average daily minimum temperatures and dividing by two.

Temperature limits represent average daily minimum for January and average daily maximum for July.

Annual precipitation values are the average annual water equivalent of all precipitation for the 30-year period.

Heating and cooling degree days are used as relative measures of the energy required for heating and cooling buildings. One heating degree day is accumulated for each whole degree that the mean daily temperature is below 65 degrees Fahrenheit (a mean daily temperature of 62 degrees Fahrenheit will produce three heating degree days). Cooling degree days are accumulated in similar fashion for deviations of the mean daily temperature above 65 degrees Fahrenheit.

TABLE E—CONGRESSIONAL DISTRICTS OF THE 109TH CONGRESS

LAND AREA, Items 1–3
Source: U.S. Bureau of the Census

Land area measurements are shown to the nearest square kilometer. Land area includes dry land and land temporarily or partially covered by water, such as marshland, swamps, and river floodplains. Data were tabulated for the 108th Congress and some boundary changes have occurred.

POPULATION, Items 2–3
Source: U.S. Bureau of the Census— 2000 Census of Population and Housing

The population data are based on the 100 percent count from the 2000 census. Data were tabulated for the 108th Congress and some boundary changes have occurred.

POPULATION BY RACE AND HISPANIC OR LATINO ORIGIN, Items 4–11
Source: U.S. Bureau of the Census— 2000 Census of Population and Housing

The data on **race** were derived from answers to the question on race that was asked of all people. The concept of race, as used by the Census Bureau, reflects self-identification by people according to the race or races with which they most closely identify. These categories are socio-political constructs and should not be interpreted as being scientific or anthropological in nature. Furthermore, the race categories include both racial and national-origin groups.

In the 2000 census, respondents were offered the option of selecting one or more races. This was not the case in prior censuses, so comparisons should be made with caution. In Table E, columns 4 through 11 refer to individuals who identified with each racial category, either alone or in combination with other races.

The **White** population is defined as persons who indicated their race as white, as well as persons who did not classify themselves in one of the specific race categories listed on the questionnaire but entered a nationality such as Irish, German, Italian, Lebanese, Near Easterner, Arab, or Polish.

The **Black** population includes persons who indicated their race as "Black, African Am., or Negro," as well as persons who did not classify themselves in one of the specific race categories but reported entries such as African American, Afro American, Kenyan, Nigerian, or Haitian.

The **American Indian or Alaska Native** population includes persons who indicated their race as American Indian or Alaska Native, as well as persons who did not classify themselves in one of the specific race categories but reported entries such as Canadian Indian, French American Indian, Spanish-American Indian, Eskimo, Aleut, Alaska Indian, or any of the American Indian or Alaska Native tribes.

The **Asian** population includes persons who indicated their race as Asian Indian, Chinese, Filipino, Japanese, Korean, Vietnamese, or "Other Asian," as well as persons who provided write-in entries of such Asian groups as Cambodian, Laotian, Hmong, Pakistani, or Taiwanese. Also, persons who wrote in an entry indicating one of the specific categories were classified accordingly. The **Native Hawaiian or Other Pacific Islander** population includes persons who indicated their race as "Native Hawaiian," "Guamanian or Chamorro," "Samoan" or "Other Pacific Islander," as well as persons who reported entries such as Part Hawaiian, American Samoan, Fijian, Melanesian, or Tahitian. Also, persons who wrote in an entry indicating one of the specific categories were classified accordingly. In 1990, the **Asian** and **Native Hawaiian or Other Pacific Islander** categories were combined as **Asian and Pacific Islander**. This volume uses the 1990 combination.

The population of **Some other race** includes all persons who indicated "Some other race" as well as persons who wrote in a category not included in the race categories described above, including entries such as multiracial, mixed, interracial, or a Hispanic/Latino group such as Mexican, Puerto Rican, or Cuban in the "Some other race" write-in space.

Changes in specific listing of racial categories, the new practice of allowing more than one selection in 2000, and the order in which questions appeared on the questionnaire, could all affect comparability between the 2000 and 1990 censuses.

The Hispanic or Latino population is based on a complete-count question that asked respondents "Is this person Spanish/Hispanic/Latino?" Persons marking any one of the four Hispanic or Latino categories (Mexican, Puerto Rican, Cuban, or other Spanish) are collectively referred to as Hispanic or Latino.

In the 2000 census, the Hispanic or Latino Origin question was placed before the race question and specific instructions indicated that both questions should be answered. These changes were designed to improve accuracy, and may affect comparability with 1990 data.

POPULATION—AGE, Items 12–20
Source: U.S. Bureau of the Census— 2000 Census of Population and Housing

Age derived from the census (2000) is classified as age at last birthday (number of completed years from birth to April 1). The percent figures are derived by dividing the number of persons in a specified age group by the total population of a given geographic area.

The 2000 census also asked for the specific date of birth of the respondent, and 2000 census procedures used the birth date for deriving age data. For this reason, it is likely that the 2000 data have fewer problems than prior censuses, such as a tendency to round ages or report the person's age on the date the questionnaire was filled out rather than on April 1.

POPULATION—PERCENT FEMALE, Item 21
**Source: U.S. Bureau of the Census—
2000 Census of Population and Housing**

The female population of a geographic area is shown as a percent of the total population of the area.

HOUSEHOLDS, Items 22–25
**Source: U.S. Bureau of the Census—
2000 Census of Population and Housing**

A household consists of persons occupying a single housing unit. A housing unit is a house, an apartment, a group of rooms, or a single room occupied as separate living quarters. The occupants may be a single family, one person living alone, two or more families living together, or any other group of related or unrelated persons sharing a housing unit. The number of households is the same as the number of year-round occupied housing units.

A family household consists of two or more persons, including the householder, who are related by birth, marriage, or adoption and who live together as one household; all such persons are considered as members of one family.

The measure of persons per household is obtained by dividing the number of persons in households by the number of households or householders. The category **female family householder** includes only female-headed family households with no spouse present.

PERSONS IN CORRECTIONAL INSTITUTIONS, Item 26
**Source: U.S. Bureau of the Census—
2000 Census of Population and Housing**

Correctional institutions includes prisons, federal detention centers, military disciplinary barracks and jails, police lockups, halfway houses used for correctional purposes, local jails, and other confinement facilities, including work farms.

PERSONS IN NURSING HOMES, Item 27
**Source: U.S. Bureau of the Census—
2000 Census of Population and Housing**

Nursing homes comprise a heterogeneous group of places. The majority of patients are elderly, although persons who require nursing care because of chronic physical conditions may be found in these homes regardless of their age. Included in this category are skilled-nursing facilities, intermediate-care facilities, long-term care rooms in wards or buildings on the grounds of hospitals, or long-term care rooms/nursing wings in congregate housing facilities. Also included are nursing, convalescent, and rest homes, such as soldiers', sailors', veterans', and fraternal or religious homes for the aged, with or without nursing care.

PERSONS IN MILITARY QUARTERS, Item 28
**Source: U.S. Bureau of the Census—
2000 Census of Population and Housing**

Military quarters includes military personnel living in barracks and dormitories on base, transient quarters on base for temporary residents (both civilian and military), and military ships. However, patients in military hospitals receiving treatment for chronic diseases or who had no usual home elsewhere, and people being held in military disciplinary barracks were included as part of the institutionalized population.

EDUCATION—SCHOOL ENROLLMENT AND EDUCATIONAL ATTAINMENT, Items 29–32
**Source: U.S. Bureau of the Census—
2000 Census of Population and Housing**

Data on school enrollment and educational attainment were derived from a sample of the population. Persons were classified as enrolled in school if they reported attending a "regular" public or private school (or college) at any time between February 1, 2000 and the time of enumeration. The instructions were to "include only nursery school, kindergarten, elementary school, and schooling which would lead to a high school diploma or a college degree" as regular school. Public school is defined as "any school or college controlled and supported by a local, county, state, or federal government." Schools supported and controlled primarily by religious organizations or other private groups are defined as private. Statistics for years of school completed are for persons 25 years old and over. The data were derived from a question on the 2000 census questionnaire that asked respondents for the highest level of school they had completed or the highest degree they had received. Persons who passed a high school equivalency examination were considered high school graduates. Schooling received in foreign schools was to be reported as the equivalent grade or years in the regular American school system.

MONEY INCOME, Items 33–35
**Source: U.S. Bureau of the Census—
2000 Census of Population and Housing**

The data on income are derived from the responses of a sample of persons 15 years old and over. **Total money income** is defined by the Bureau of the Census for statistical purposes as the sum of the following: wage or salary income; nonfarm self-employment income; net farm self-employment income; Social Security and railroad retirement income; public assistance income; and all other regularly received income such as interest, dividends, veterans' payments, pensions, unemployment compensation, and alimony. Receipts not counted as income include various "lump sum" payments such as capital gains or inheritances.

The total represents the amount of income received before deductions for personal income taxes, Social Security, bond purchases, union dues, Medicare deductions, etc.

Per capita income is based on resident population enumerated as of April 1, 2000.

Income of households includes the income of the householder and all other persons 15 years old and over in the household. Median household income is usually less than median family income because many households consist of only one person. The median divides the income distribution into two equal parts, one having incomes above the median, the other with incomes below.

POVERTY, Items 36–37
Source: U.S. Bureau of the Census— 2000 Census of Population and Housing

The data on poverty are derived from the same questions as the data on money income. Poverty status is based on the definition prescribed by the Federal Office of Management and Budget as the standard to be used by federal agencies for statistical purposes. Families and persons are classified as being below the poverty level if their total family income or unrelated individual income was less than the poverty threshold specified for the applicable family size, age of householder, and number of related children present under 18 years old. Poverty status is determined for all families (and by implication all family members). For persons not in families, poverty status is determined by their income in relation to the appropriate poverty threshold. Inmates of institutions, persons in military group quarters or college dormitories, and unrelated individuals under 15 years old are excluded.

The 1999 poverty thresholds are shown in Figure 1.

Figure 1.
Poverty Thresholds in 1999 by Size of Family

Size of Family Unit	Weighted average thresholds
One person (unrelated individual)	$8,501
Under 65 years old	8,667
65 years old and over	7,990
Two persons	10,869
Householder under 65 years old	11,214
Householder 65 years old and over	10,075
Three persons	13,290
Four persons	17,029
Five persons	20,127
Six persons	22,727
Seven persons	25,912
Eight persons	28,967
Nine or more persons	34,417

HOUSING, Items 38–46
Source: U.S. Bureau of the Census— 2000 Census of Population and Housing

A **housing unit** is a house, apartment, mobile home or trailer, group of rooms, or single room occupied or, if vacant, intended for occupancy as separate living quarters. Separate living quarters are those in which the occupants do not live and eat with any other persons in the structure and which have direct access from the outside of the building through a common hall.

The occupants of a housing unit may be a single family, one person living alone, two or more families living together, or any other group of related or unrelated persons who share living arrangements (except as described in the definition for persons ''living in group quarters''). For vacant units, the criteria of separateness and direct access are applied to the intended occupants whenever possible. If that information cannot be obtained, the criteria are applied to the previous occupants. Both occupied and vacant housing units are included in the housing inventory, except that recreational vehicles, tents, caves, boats, railroad cars, and the like are included only if they are occupied as someone's usual place of residence.

A housing unit is classified as occupied if it is the usual place of residence of the person or group of persons living in it at the time of enumeration, or if the occupants are only temporarily absent (away on vacation). A household consists of all persons who occupy a housing unit as their usual place of residence.

The percent change represents the difference in the number of total housing units in a specified area over the decade 1980–1990.

Median value is the dollar amount that divides the distribution of owner occupied housing units into two equal parts, with one half of the units falling below this value and the other half exceeding it. Value is defined as the respondent's estimate of what the house would sell for if it were for sale. Data are presented for one-family units on less than 10 acres and with no business or medical office on the property.

Median rent divides the distribution of renter-occupied housing units into two equal parts. Median rent represents the amount of cash rent a renter pays (contract rent) plus the estimated average cost of utilities and fuels if paid by the renter (gross rent). Rent is to be reported only for living quarters, not for any business or other space occupied. Single family houses on lots of 10 or more acres are excluded.

Housing cost as a percent of income is shown separately for owners with mortgages, owners without mortgages, and renters. Rent as a percentage of income is a computed ratio of gross rent and monthly household income (total household income in 1999 divided by 12). Selected owner costs include utilities and fuels, as well as mortgage payments, insurance, taxes, etc. In each case, the ratio of housing cost to income is computed separately for each housing unit. The ratio for one-half of the units is above the median shown in this book, and one-half is below.

Substandard units are occupied units which are overcrowded or lack complete plumbing facilities. For the purposes of this item ''overcrowded'' is defined as having 1.01 persons or more per room. Complete plumbing facilities include hot and cold piped water, a flush toilet, and a bathtub or shower. These facilities must be located inside the housing unit but not necessarily in the same room.

CIVILIAN LABOR FORCE, UNEMPLOYMENT, EMPLOYMENT, Items 47–52
Source: U.S. Bureau of the Census— 2000 Census of Population and Housing

All data pertain to persons 16 years old and over. The civilian labor force consists of persons classified as either employed or unemployed in accordance with the criteria described below.

Unemployment data include all persons who did not work during the survey week, made specific efforts to find a job in the prior 4 weeks, and were available for work during the survey week (except for temporary illness). Persons waiting to be called back to a job from which they had been laid off and those waiting to report to a new job within the next 30 days are included in unemployment figures.

Total employment includes all civilians who were either (1) "at work" —those who did any work at all during the reference week as paid employees, worked in their own business or profession, worked on their own farm, or worked 15 hours or more as unpaid workers in a family farm or business; or were (2) "with a job but not at work"—those who had a job but were not at work that week due to illness, weather, industrial dispute, vacation, or other personal reasons.

The occupation categories shown are consistent with the 2000 edition of the *Standard Occupational Classification Manual (SOC)*, published by the Office of Federal Statistical Policy and Standards, U.S. Department of Commerce.

EMPLOYMENT DISABILITY, Item 53
Source: U.S. Bureau of the Census— 2000 Census of Population and Housing

Data are shown for persons 16 to 64 years old in 2000. Persons were identified as having an employment disability if they reported a health condition that had lasted 6 months or more and which limited the kind or amount of work they could do at a job or business.